D1601915

PRESENTED TO

BY

ON

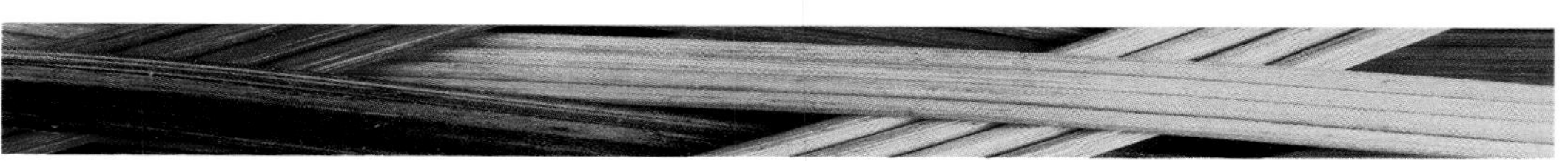

All Scripture is God-breathed
and is useful for teaching,
rebuking, correcting
and training in righteousness,
so that the man of God
may be thoroughly equipped
for every good work.

2 Timothy 3:16-17

Dedication

TO MARGARET

my love, my soulmate, my sancho
who gave me the courage
to start on this Bible
twenty years ago and believed
it could be done in the dark and lonely times.

"Many waters cannot quench love;
rivers cannot wash it away.
If one were to give
all the wealth of his house for love,
it would be utterly scorned."

Song of Songs 8:7

MY GROUP MEMBERS

NAME **PHONE Number**

SERENDIPITY'S

Interactive

STUDY BIBLE

SERENDIPITY'S

Interactive

STUDY BIBLE

Lyman Coleman, Editor

James F. Couch, Jr.
Bible Editor

Sharon Penington
Production

Deborah Shepherd
Copy Editor

Erika Tiepel
Graphics Designer

NEW INTERNATIONAL VERSION
SERENDIPITY HOUSE
LITTLETON

Interactive Study Bible

Serendipity is a publishing house specializing in equipping pastors and church leaders for small group ministry. A list of training events and catalog of resources can be obtained by writing to: SERENDIPITY HOUSE, P.O. Box 1012, Littleton, CO 80160 or call: 1-800-525-9563. Please visit our Web site at www.serendipityhouse.com.

Printed in the United States of America.

01 02 03 04 05 8 7 6 5 4 3 2 1

SERENDIPITY HOUSE / Box 1012 / Littleton, CO 80160 / 1-800-525-9563
www.serendipityhouse.com

CONTRIBUTORS

WRITERS AND EDITORS

John T. Anderson; Ken Anderson; Mari R. Anderson; Verne Becker; Greg Arthur; Gregoire Benoit; Sharon Blackmon; Gary Christopherson; Karen Couch; John Crosby; Steve and Betsy Crowe; William F. Cutler; Steve Decker; Carol Detoni; Mark Dubis; James E. Erwin; Mark Fackler; Heidi Flock; Rob Frost; Alicia Glendenning; Edward C. Grube; Katy Harris; Doug Haugen; Gary Hofmeyer; David G. Horn; Mark Horton; Judy Johnson; Doug LaBudde; Matthew Lockhart; Keith Madsen; John Mallison; Richard C. Meyer; Michael R. Mitchell; David and Ruth Montzingo; Larry A. Moody; Mary H. Naegeli; Phil Nelson; Peter Pagan; Doug L. Perkins; Elsa Petersen; Lance Pierson; Brenda Quinn; Steven Saint; Deborah Schneider; Mark Shepard; James M. Singleton, Jr.; Andrew Sloan; Daryl Smith; Joe Snider; Melissa Strong; Cathy Tardiff; Bonnie Taylor; Luther H. Thoreson; Jeanie Thorndike; Bill Tucker; Sue Tyler; Christopher J. Weinhold; Christopher Werner; Charles E. White; Gus White; John and Fay Winson; Graham Young.

Sally Graves, Brad Folsom, Julie Bergland and Larry Pfander at Art Forms, Englewood, CO; Billie Herwig, Doug LaBudde, Fay and John Winson at Frontline Marketing; James Steffen at Serendipity House.

TYPESETTING

THE LIVINGSTONE COMPANY
Greg Asimakoupoulos; Bruce Barton; Paige Drygas; Donald Dumbacher; Mark Fackler; Christopher Hudson; Barbara Kois; MaryAnn Lackland; Carol Smith; Roddy Smith; Randy Southern; Ed Strauss; Ashley Taylor; Nancy Taylor; Peter Wallace; Linda Washington.

BOOKS OF THE BIBLE

TABLE OF CONTENTS

THE STORY BEHIND THIS BIBLE

This Bible began with a dream and a shoestring. The dream began in 1973 with the struggle to find a way to make it possible to have lay people who did not know a lot about group process techniques to still be able to lead a small group. At the time Lyman Coleman was leading training events around the country called Serendipity Workshops. People would come up after the meeting and say, "I would love to go back to my church and start a small group, but I don't know enough to start one."

There was a lot of personal Bible study around in those days for individuals, but there was very little for group sharing Bible study—and there is a difference. Personal Bible study is left brain. Group Bible study is right brain. Personal Bible study is analytical. Group Bible study is relational. Personal Bible study asks you to (1) observe the facts, (2) interpret the facts, and (3) apply the facts. Group Bible study asks you to share with a small group what God is saying to you in the story of Scripture and ask the group to hold you accountable for what you are going to do about it. There is a need for both approaches, and this is what we have in this Bible.

THE INTERACTIVE STUDY BIBLE

This exciting new resource from Serendipity House takes you to a new level in Small Groups. In almost every place that we offer small group training, we discover that people are longing to be "real" and "safe" with someone. They long to live in relationships of trust within environments of grace. They also want their lives to be better. We have found that when we combine community building techniques within life-changing Bible study lessons, people can be empowered to:

- **Encounter God Personally**: Telling our stories through the stories of the Bible
- **Engage in Authentic Community**: The three-part agenda to connect your group members
- **Experience Transformed Lives:** Choose from one of five methods to study the Bible

To help you understand this journey, let us take you through a hypothetical group and explain the Serendipity process for authentic community.

Our Hypothetical Group

In writing the questions and the resource notes for this Bible, we have tried to imagine six people sitting in a small group together. Our goal is that this group will: encounter God personally, engage in authentic community and experience transformed lives.

Our group members:

- Bob is a space engineer. Bright, but ignorant about the Bible. He comes because his wife makes him. He is very shy.
- Mary, Bob's wife, is a graduate of a Bible college. She grew up in a strict religious home and has some bad feelings about the way women were treated in her church.
- Bill is an All Pro Linebacker. He makes a million dollars a year, but has never read a book in his life.
- Sally is a single parent, who grew up Catholic and is an agnostic. She lives in a condo with her teenage children and struggles to pay the bills.
- Phil is a post-modern church drop out. He drives a BMW and has plenty of everything except happiness. He doesn't know where he stands with God, but he's open.
- Kevin arrives at the meeting on a motorcycle in his new "leathers." He is socially outgoing but feels a little insecure around religious people.

ENCOUNTER GOD PERSONALLY

The trick is to find a way to welcome all six of these people into the same small group and to help them to become a caring community. The way we have done this is to ask questions that allows a person to share where the Scripture story intersects with their own story. Our questions are right brain, open-ended and no right or wrong answers; such as in the lesson about the Prodigal Son (Luke 15:11–32):

❐ Who do you identify with in this story—the younger brother or the older brother?

❐ Who do you feel will make a better parent: The older brother or the younger brother?

❐ If you had been in the audience when Jesus told this story, how would you be feeling?

❐ Where are you in the birth order of your family—youngest, oldest, in the middle?

❐ How old were you when you left home? Where did you go?

If you were any of the six people in our hypothetical group, would you be able to answer these questions? Would you be able to answer these questions if you had never heard this story? Could you come up with your answers in three seconds. This is the first step to encountering God personally.

ENGAGE IN AUTHENTIC COMMUNITY

Our questions are designed to help each member begin to connect with one another and establish those relationships of trust within environments of grace. We have deliberately arranged the questions into a three-part agenda with: (1) The coffee cup—to start off a meeting; (2) The book—to move into the Scripture and (3) The heart—to enable you to "take your shirt off" and "put it on the table."

OPEN: These questions are designed to warm up a group and "level the playing field." Before the group gets into the story in Scripture, the questions allow the group to share something from their own story that helps them to start the process of feeling the situation in the Scripture story. For instance, if the story in Scripture is about a younger son who left home, good questions would be: "When did you leave home for the first time? Were you ready? What happened?" The questions are often mischievous to allow the group to tell something about the human side of their life. Usually these questions contain humor and "break the ice" for the group.

STUDY: These questions are designed to move across a pendulum from low risk to high risk, and from "first impressions" to "guiding principles on overriding truth" in the Scripture story. For instance, in the Prodigal Son story, we ask the questions, "What caused the younger brother to want to leave home? How do you think the older son felt when he heard about the party?" Right away, you have all two of the principal characters in this story identified and the questions allow each person in the group to project themselves into the story. The questions are open-ended that each person can answer the questions without the fear of being right or wrong. The next question may go into more detail into the Scripture story. By the last question, the group is beginning to establish a trust level with one another to the place where they can "get honest."

APPLY: Now comes the million dollar question—the heart question. The small group started out by sharing something revealing and human to break the ice. Then, the group shared how their story intersects with the story of Scripture. Now, they are ready to "put it on the table" and move into prayer. This is what the heart questions are designed to do. This will set the groundwork for a group to be able to move into issues in their own life where God is at work or he needs to be invited in to do a little clean-up work.

EXPERIENCE TRANSFORMED LIVES

At the core of the *Interactive Study Bible* is the desire to create a safe place where people can do "soul work" and receive "soul care" in their life. Worship and celebration are important in the larger church family. We need to gather as the "body of Christ" and share life together, but we can't do "soul work" or "soul care" in a large meeting. This is where this Bible is helpful.

The "apply questions" are designed to allow a person to share their insight, personal struggles and victories at whatever level they feel comfortable. As in the lesson of the Prodigal Son, we ask:

❒ Of the two brothers, which reminds you of your own personal story?

❒ In your spiritual pilgrimage, what do you identify as your "far country time"?

❒ Where are you right now in your spiritual pilgrimage?

Once again there is no right or wrong answer to these questions. Hopefully by the time one member has answered the question, other members are realizing there is love and acceptance and will open up as the group meets together.

This *Interactive Study Bible* is designed to enable lay people with no professional training to meet together in small groups and "let their fingers do the walking" or better yet, let their fingers do the leading. Here is how we would recommend you start a group.

❒ Start with yourself. You will be the hard person to convince. Invite a few friends, preferably with the same felt need. "I need a safe place where I can belong and share my life. Do you have this same need?"

❒ Choose a course or book of the Bible to study. There are 100 courses in the next few pages to choose from—with appropriate Scripture passages to go to for study.

❒ Agree on four absolutes: (1) Absolute love; (2) Absolute honesty; (3) Absolute confidentiality and (4) Absolute truth. The last one is the most important. Absolute truth means that I am willing to submit my life every week before God and this group and do what God tells me to do through Scripture.

❒ Keep an empty chair. The mission is to reach out to others who are hurting and draw them into the group. When the group gets to ten to twelve, the group multiplies and keeps growing. New people can enter the group at any time as long as they agree to the Four Absolutes.

On the following pages you will find 5 Interactive Methods for Bible Study.

5 INTERACTIVE METHODS for Bible Study

To help you get started in a group study, we have organized this Bible to be used in a variety of interactive ways:

- Book Study
- Life-Need Study
- Lectionary Study
- Build Your Own Study
- Key Bible Stories

1. Book Study

If your pastor or spiritual leader is teaching through a particular book in the Bible, like Romans or the Gospel of John, you can study along with the teaching as a small group by studying the same passage before or after the teaching.

In the Introduction to each book in the Bible is a reading plan to follow. There is a longer passage to read before the small group meeting and a shorter passage to focus on at the meeting.

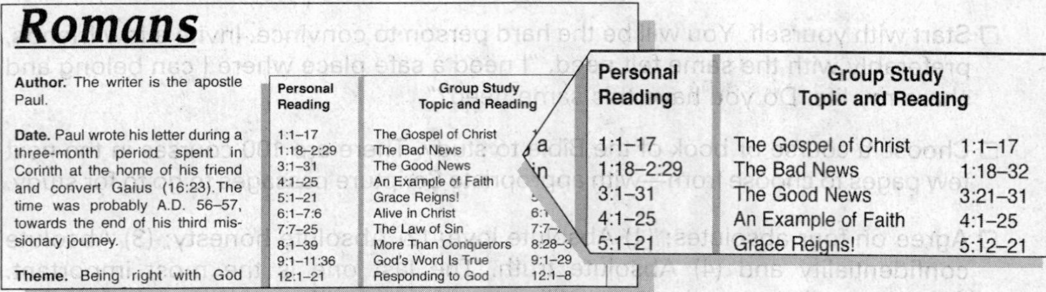

Romans

Author. The writer is the apostle Paul.

Date. Paul wrote his letter during a three-month period spent in Corinth at the home of his friend and convert Gaius (16:23). The time was probably A.D. 56–57, towards the end of his third missionary journey.

Theme. Being right with God

Personal Reading	Group Study Topic and Reading	
1:1–17	The Gospel of Christ	
1:18–2:29	The Bad News	
3:1–31	The Good News	
4:1–25	An Example of Faith	
5:1–21	Grace Reigns!	
6:1–7:6	Alive in Christ	6:1
7:7–25	The Law of Sin	7:7–
8:1–39	More Than Conquerors	8:28–
9:1–11:36	God's Word Is True	9:1–29
12:1–21	Responding to God	12:1–8

Personal Reading	Group Study Topic and Reading	
1:1–17	The Gospel of Christ	1:1–17
1:18–2:29	The Bad News	1:18–32
3:1–31	The Good News	3:21–31
4:1–25	An Example of Faith	4:1–25
5:1–21	Grace Reigns!	5:12–21

All you need to do is look up the Scripture passage and follow the questions in the margin. The Resource Notes at the bottom of each page will help you understand that passage more clearly.

Churches often *choose this model for* church-wide groups in which all of the *groups study* the same Scripture passage with the pastor or spiritual leader leading the way.

2. Life-Need Study

For groups that are based on affinity (Men, Women, Parents, etc.) or groups that are formed around a life-need (stress, spiritual dryness, etc.) there are 100 courses with 624 lessons to choose from beginning on page 18. These courses are organized in five categories:

- Group Life
- Community Life
- Spiritual Life
- Personal Life
- Biblical Subjects

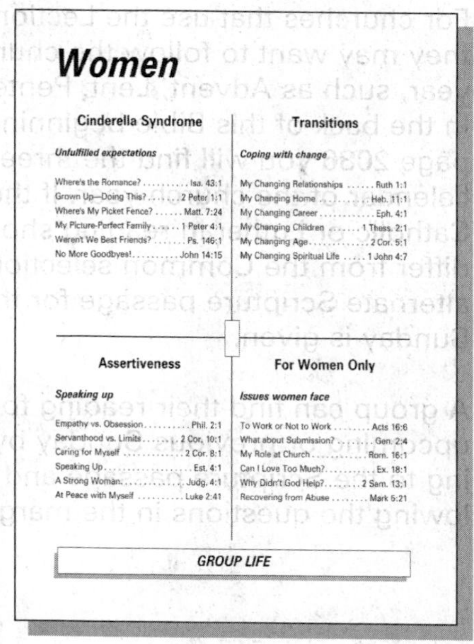

Women

Cinderella Syndrome

Unfulfilled expectations

Where's the Romance?	Isa. 43:1
Grown Up—Doing This?	2 Peter 1:1
Where's My Picket Fence?	Matt. 7:24
My Picture-Perfect Family	1 Peter 4:1
Weren't We Best Friends?	Ps. 146:1
No More Goodbyes!	John 14:15

Transitions

Coping with change

My Changing Relationships	Ruth 1:1
My Changing Home	Heb. 11:1
My Changing Career	Eph. 4:1
My Changing Children	1 Thess. 2:1
My Changing Age	2 Cor. 5:1
My Changing Spiritual Life	1 John 4:7

Assertiveness

Speaking up

Empathy vs. Obsession	Phil. 2:1
Servanthood vs. Limits	2 Cor. 10:1
Caring for Myself	2 Cor. 8:1
Speaking Up	Est. 4:1
A Strong Woman	Judg. 4:1
At Peace with Myself	Luke 2:41

For Women Only

Issues women face

To Work or Not to Work	Acts 16:6
What about Submission?	Gen. 2:4
My Role at Church	Rom. 16:1
Can I Love Too Much?	Ex. 18:1
Why Didn't God Help?	2 Sam. 13:1
Recovering from Abuse	Mark 5:21

GROUP LIFE

You can publish the target group or life-need in your small group brochure and let people sign-up for the group of their choice based on affinity or life-need. Or you can ask groups that are already underway to look over the list and choose a course for the next leg of their journey together.

2 The king of Jericho was told, "Look! Some of the Israelites have
come here tonight to spy out the land." 3 So the king of Jericho sent
this message to Rahab: "Bring out the men who came to you and entered your house, because they have come to spy out the whole land."
4 But the woman had taken the two men and hidden them. She said,
"Yes, the men came to me, but I did not know where they had come
from. 5 At dusk, when it was time to close the city gate, the men left. I
don't know which way they went. Go after them quickly. You may
catch up with them." 6 (But she had taken them up to the roof and
hidden them under the stalks of flax she had laid out on the roof.) 7 So
the men set out in pursuit of the spies on the road that leads to the fords of the Jordan, and as soon as the pursuers had gone out, the gate was shut.
8 Before the spies lay down for the night, she went up on the roof
9 and said to them, "I know that the LORD has given this land to you and that a great fear of you has fallen on us, so that all who live in
this country are melting in fear because of you. 10 We have heard how
the LORD dried up the water of the Red Sea[b] for you when you came out of Egypt, and what you did to Sihon and Og, the two kings of the Amorites east of the Jordan, whom you completely destroyed.[c]
11 When we heard of it, our hearts melted and everyone's courage failed because of you, for the LORD your God is God in heaven above
and on the earth below. 12 Now then, please swear to me by the LORD

[a] 1 Or possibly *an innkeeper* [b] 10 Hebrew *Yam Suph;* that is, Sea of Reeds [c] 10 The Hebrew term refers to the irrevocable giving over of things or persons to the LORD, often by totally destroying them.

... an identity would you assume?

STUDY The Israelites sit across the Jordan River from Jericho, poised to invade the Promised Land. At great risk, two spies are sent to scout out the situation. 1. Why would Rahab risk her own safety to provide safety for the spies? 2. Why do you think the spies trusted Rahab, a woman of "questionable reputation"? 3. What kind of relationship do you think Rahab had with God at this point: She knew him by reputation only? She feared God but didn't really know him? She was a "closet" believer? With the Israelites ready to attack, she saw the light? Other? 4. Why were Rahab and her family spared? 5. What report did the spies make to Joshua, and how did he respond (vv. 23–24)? How would you have responded? 6. Given her disreputable occupation and her obvious lie, what in this story builds Rahab's reputation as a woman of faith (Heb. 11:31; James 2:25)?

APPLY 1. What is the "scarlet cord" you hold on to in times of trial, stress or pain: My faith in Jesus Christ? God's mercy despite my failings? The support of family and

1:18 will be put to death. Success was the only option for the Israelites. Any distractions from their goal would be eliminated.

2:1–24 The theme of this story is risk. Rahab, the prostitute, risked her own life by harboring Joshua's spies. And the spies themselves took great risk by trusting her instructions and her vow of silence. As a result of their combined risk, Joshua received the go-ahead from the spies' report and prepared to conquer the city of Jericho.

2:6 But she had taken them. The grain she was drying on her flat roof made a perfect hiding spot for her fugitives.

2:8–11 the LORD your God is God. No one ever taught Rahab as a child not to talk to strangers. In fact, she put a strange amount of faith in two people she hardly knew. And why was she so convinced of their God? After all, she was a prostitute, not a parishioner. Even so, she is represented in the New Testament as a woman of great faith (Heb. 11:31) and is part of Jesus' lineage.

2:12 Give me a sure sign. Realizing she had spared their lives, Rahab knew to negotiate a tremendous favor from the two spies. Perhaps strengthened by her own confession, she wanted their assurance that the physical and also spiritual health of her family would be protected.

The questions in the margin have been carefully selected to address the issues for this target audience or life-need. When you turn to the Scripture passage, simply follow the questions in the margin.

The Resource Notes are there for everyone to use. This helps level the playing field for those who feel intimidated because of a perceived lack of Bible knowledge.

3. Lectionary Study

For churches that use the Lectionary, they may want to follow the church year, such as Advent, Lent, Pentecost. In the back of this Bible beginning on page 2086 you will find the three-year calendar of the church year. If the Catholic or Lutheran reading should differ from the Common selection, the alternate Scripture passage for that Sunday is given.

A group can find their reading for the upcoming or previous Sunday by turning to the Scripture passage and following the questions in the margin.

LECTIONARY YEAR A*

C = Common R = Roman L = Lutheran

Absence of letter is same for all

Alternative Readings and Psalms are not included

	READING 1	READING 2	GOSPEL
ADVENT SEASON			
Advent 1	Isa. 2:1–5	Rom. 13:11–14	Matt. 24:36–44 (C,L) Matt. 24:37–44 (R)
Advent 2	Isa. 11:1–10	Rom. 15:4–13 (C,L) Rom. 15:4–9 (R)	Matt. 3:1–12
Advent 3	Isa. 35:1–10 (C,L) Isa. 35:1–6a,10 (R)	James 5:7–10	Matt. 11:2–11
Advent 4	Isa. 7:10–16 (C,L) Isa. 7:10–14 (R)	Rom. 1:1–7	Matt. 1:18–25 (C,L) Matt. 1:18–24 (R)
CHRISTMAS DAY	**Nativity of Our Lord** (Primary Service)		
	Isa. 9:1–6 (R)[1] Isa. 9:2–7 (C,L)	Titus 2:11–14	Luke 2:1–14 (15–20) (C,L) Luke 2:1–14 (R)
CHRISTMAS SEASON			

4. Build Your Own Study

In the back of the Bible on page 2115 we have provided an Index to the Lesson Subjects. This contains over 4600 subjects that appear in the lessons in the *Interactive Study Bible*. You can custom design your own group study using this Lesson Index. Each entry will take you to a group study in the side-bar material of the Bible. These have been linked together in the 100 Life-Need Courses.

Index to the Lesson Subjects

5. Key Bible Stories

For years Serendipity has said that the greatest gift we have to give each other is our own personal stories. As you have learned in previous pages, Serendipity has developed a method where you can tell your story to your group through the stories of the Bible. God has gifted us with stories of real people who we can identify with and learn from. It is a wonderful way to get to know the members of your group and learn from the stories of the Bible. To use this method of study, turn to page 2108 and look through the list of key Bible stories.

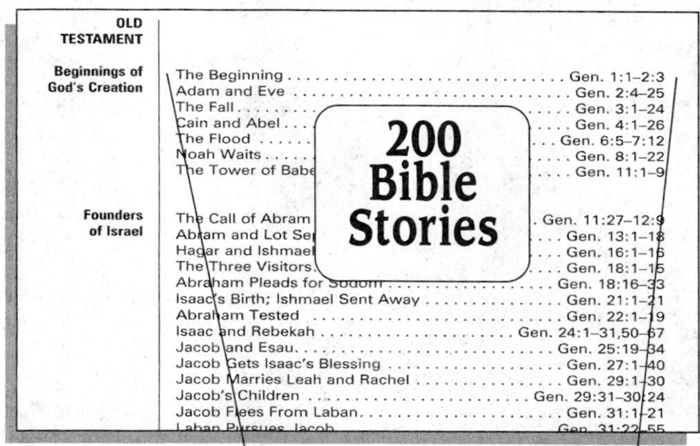

OLD TESTAMENT

200 Bible Stories

Beginnings of God's Creation	The Beginning	Gen. 1:1–2:3
	Adam and Eve	Gen. 2:4–25
	The Fall	Gen. 3:1–24
	Cain and Abel	Gen. 4:1–26
	The Flood	Gen. 6:5–7:12
	Noah Waits	Gen. 8:1–22
	The Tower of Babe	Gen. 11:1–9
Founders of Israel	The Call of Abram	Gen. 11:27–12:9
	Abram and Lot Se	Gen. 13:1–18
	Hagar and Ishmael	Gen. 16:1–16
	The Three Visitors	Gen. 18:1–15
	Abraham Pleads for Sodom	Gen. 18:16–33
	Isaac's Birth; Ishmael Sent Away	Gen. 21:1–21
	Abraham Tested	Gen. 22:1–19
	Isaac and Rebekah	Gen. 24:1–31,50–67
	Jacob and Esau	Gen. 25:19–34
	Jacob Gets Isaac's Blessing	Gen. 27:1–40
	Jacob Marries Leah and Rachel	Gen. 29:1–30
	Jacob's Children	Gen. 29:31–30:24
	Jacob Flees From Laban	Gen. 31:1–21
	Laban Pursues Jacob	Gen. 31:22–55

- Choose from a list of over 200 stories
- Identify the one your group wants to study
- Develop your own study using the stories

OPEN 1. Where do you go when you want to get away from it all and be close to God in his creation? 2. What time of day are you the most creative?

STUDY This passage is a summary account of God's creation of the world. The Bible always assumes rather than argues the existence of God. As Psalm 90:2 states, creation had a beginning but God has always been. 1. As you read this story of creation, what comes to mind: Your childhood home, listening to one of your parents read this story? A camping trip in the mountains, looking up at the stars and being overwhelmed by it all? Seeing the movie "Star Wars" and remembering the sound track for the opening scene? 2. How would you describe the kind of literature in this passage: A hymn of praise? A historical narrative? A theology textbook? A science paper? A Bible story book? 3. If you were teaching this story to children, what would you want them to learn? 4. What does it mean to be created in God's image? What does this do to your own self-image? How about your body? Your relationship with God? With other people? 5. How does this story effect the way you treat the land, water, plants and animals in God's world? 6. If you were asked to share your faith story, how would you relate your life to this story? 7. How does Jesus Christ fit into the story of creation (Col. 1:15–20)? 8. How

The Beginning

1 In the beginning God created the heavens and the earth. [2]Now
the earth was[a] formless and empty, darkness was over the
surface of the deep, and the Spirit of God was hovering over
the waters.
[3]And God said, "Let there be light," and there was light. [4]God saw
that the light was good, and he separated the light from the
darkness. [5]God called the light "day," and the darkness he
called "night." And there was evening, and there was morning—the first day.
[6]And God said, "Let there be an expanse between the waters to separate water from water." [7]So God made the expanse and separated the water under the expanse from the water above it.
And it was so. [8]God called the expanse "sky." And there was
evening, and there was morning—the second day.
[9]And God said, "Let the water under the sky be gathered to one
place, and let dry ground appear." And it was so. [10]God called
the dry ground "land," and the gathered waters he called
"seas." And God saw that it was good.
[11]Then God said, "Let the land produce vegetation: seed-bearing plants and trees on the land that bear fruit with seed
in it, according to their various kinds." And it was so. [12]The
land produced vegetation: plants bearing seed according to
their kinds and trees bearing fruit with seed in it according to
their kinds. And God saw that it was good. [13]And there was
evening, and there was morning—the third day.
[14]And God said, "Let there be lights in the expanse of the sky to separate the day from the night, and let them serve as signs to
mark seasons and days and years, [15]and let them be lights in

[a]2 Or possibly *became*

1:1 God created. This is the first and greatest assumption of the Word of God. The basic understanding that God is, that he created all things, and that he brought us to be, provides the deepest foundation for our understanding of

1:4 the light was good. As God created the world, it worked in harmony. Everything he created was "good" (vv. 10,12,18,21,25). It included no chaos, evil, or anything in rebellion with the Creator.

was done. It is a picture for us of the peace our world could have if it were completely aligned with God's will.

1:9 one place. When God gathered the water into one place, he was form-

100 LIFE-NEED COURSES

LIFE-NEED COURSES

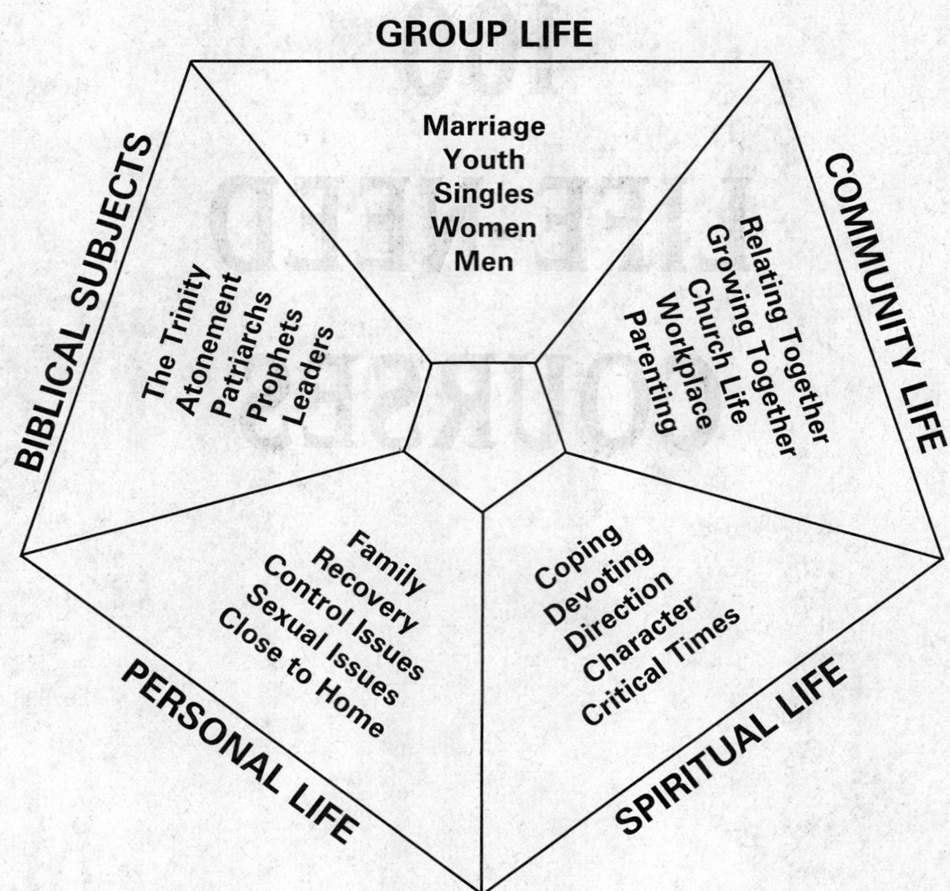

A complete curriculum using the entire Bible that is designed to help you ...

- Encounter God Personally
- Engage in Authentic Community
- Experience Transformed Lives

Men

Accountability

Getting real and keeping our word

Our Need for Others . . . . 1 Cor. 12:12
Our Need for Accountability. . . . . . Gal. 2:11
Our Need for Support . . . . Heb. 10:19
Our Need for Counsel. . . . . Matt. 18:15
Our Need for Correction . . . . James 5:7
Our Need for Mentoring . . . . 1 Cor. 4:1

Attitude Adjustment

What to do when pressure builds

Pressures . . . . 2 Cor. 1:11
Demands. . . . . 2 Cor. 11:16
Chaos . . . . 2 Cor. 4:1
Blowing It . . . . 1 John 1:1
Family Stress. . . . . Heb. 12:1
Fourth and Goal . . . . James 1:1

Men At Work

Winning over worry and anxiety

Who Is the Boss? . . . . .Col. 3:1
My Responsibility . . . . .2 Thess. 3:1
God's Responsibility . . . . .James 4:13
Working for Tyrants . . . . .1 Peter 2:13
Worry Warts . . . . .Matt. 6:19
Being Content . . . . .Phil. 4:10

For Men Only

Issues men face

Opening Up . . . . .1 Cor. 10:1
Fatal Attraction . . . . .Matt. 5:27
My Dark Side . . . . .Rom. 7:7
My Doubts . . . . .1 John 5:13
Authority Figures . . . . .1 Sam. 13:1
Spiritual Responsibility . . . . . . .1 Sam. 2:12

Women

Cinderella Syndrome

Unfulfilled expectations

Where's the Romance? . . . . Isa. 43:1
Grown Up—Doing This? . . . . 2 Peter 1:1
Where's My Picket Fence? . . . . . . Matt. 7:24
My Picture-Perfect Family . . . . 1 Peter 4:1
Weren't We Best Friends? . . . . Ps. 146:1
No More Goodbyes! . . . . John 14:15

Transitions

Coping with change

My Changing Relationships . . . . . Ruth 1:1
My Changing Home . . . . Heb. 11:1
My Changing Career . . . . Eph. 4:1
My Changing Children . . . . 1 Thess. 2:1
My Changing Age . . . . 2 Cor. 5:1
My Changing Spiritual Life . . . . . 1 John 4:7

Assertiveness

Speaking up

Empathy vs. Obsession . . . . Phil. 2:1
Servanthood vs. Limits . . . . 2 Cor. 10:1
Caring for Myself . . . . 2 Cor. 8:1
Speaking Up . . . . Est. 4:1
A Strong Woman. . . . . Judg. 4:1
At Peace with Myself . . . . Luke 2:41

For Women Only

Issues women face

To Work or Not to Work . . . . Acts 16:6
What about Submission? . . . . Gen. 2:4
My Role at Church . . . . Rom. 16:1
Can I Love Too Much? . . . . Ex. 18:1
Why Didn't God Help? . . . . 2 Sam. 13:1
Recovering from Abuse . . . . Mark 5:21

Singles

Love and Loneliness

Understanding and handling personal needs

I Don't Fit Anywhere . . . . Phil. 3:1
My Need for a Loving Touch. . . 1 John 3:11
My Need for Communication . . . . Acts 2:42
My Need for Companionship . . . . Gen. 24:1
Busyness vs. Loneliness . . . . Phil. 4:2
Making the Most of My Life . . . . 1 Cor. 7:25

Pressures

Keeping it together when it's falling apart

Making My Own Living . . . . 2 Kin. 4:1
Coping With Crisis . . . . Gen. 39:1
Dealing With My Health . . . . 2 Cor. 12:1
Managing My Finances. . . . . Matt. 25:14
Dealing With Family Issues . . . . . . Eph. 2:11
Handling My Emotions. . . . . Col. 3:1

The Single Jesus

Serving the Lord as a single

Did Jesus Ever Feel Lonely?. . . . . Matt. 3:13
The Gift of Singleness . . . . Acts 9:1
Am I Called to Be Single? . . . . . . 1 Sam. 3:1
How Can I Best Serve?. . . . . 2 Tim. 2:14
How Should I Pray? . . . . Mark 14:32
A Whole in One . . . . Mark 9:1

Choices

Issues singles face

Whom to Pick for Friends? . . . . . 1 Sam. 20:1
When to Risk With Others? . . . . . 1 Peter 3:8
Where to Live?. . . . . Num. 10:11
How to Spend My Life? . . . . Mic. 6:1
Where to Use My Talents? . . . 1 Sam. 16:14
What About the Future? . . . . Gen. 7:11

Youth

Up Close

Discovering your real identity

Being Real .Luke 18:1
My Uniqueness . . . . .Luke 19:1
My Personality . . . . .Luke 10:38
My Abilities . . . . .2 Chr. 1:1
Strengths and Weaknesses . . . . .Ex. 4:1
God's Call . . . . .Luke 5:1

Belonging

Finding friends and fitting in

Acceptance . . . . .Acts 9:19
Fitting In . . . . .Matt. 7:1
Being Myself . . . . .1 Sam. 17:1
Feeling Secure . . . . .Prov. 27:1
Getting Close . . . . .Acts 4:32
True Friends . . . . .Mark 2:1

Hassles

Getting along with my parents

Parental Requests. . . . . John 2:1
Parental Expectations . . . . Gen. 21:8
Family Tension. . . . . Prov. 20:1
Dealing With Frustrations. . . . . . . Mark 3:20
Arguing Over Relationships . . . . . Gen. 13:1
Making Things Right. . . . . Matt. 5:38

Hot Issues

Facing the big issues

Life in the Jungle . . . . Luke 4:1
Loose Morals. . . . . 2 Sam. 11:1
Hidden Secrets . . . . 2 Sam. 24:1
Don't Get Used . . . . Mark 6:14
Just Say No. Dan. 1:1
Take a Stand . . . . Dan. 6:1

Marriage

Balancing Act

Demands of work and family needs

Teammates . . . . 1 Cor. 11:2
Roommates. . . . . 1 Cor. 12:31
Work and Stress . . . . Heb. 4:1
Stress Management . . . . Mark 1:29
Serving Each Other . . . . James 2:14
Faithful and Fulfilled . . . . Acts 18:18

Communication / Conflict

How to relate to grow closer

Power of Commitment . . . . Matt. 1:18
Power of Words . . . . 2 Sam. 6:1
Acting on Impulse . . . . James 3:1
Dealing With Conflict. . . . . Eph. 4:17
Pulling Apart . . . . Gen. 3:1
Pulling Together . . . . John 4:27

Intimacy

Romance based on love rather than sex

God's Gift. . . . . Song 1:1
Sharing Yourself . . . . Song 1:15
The Rhythm of Romance . . . . Song 2:16
Only You . . . . Prov. 5:1
Sensitive Sex . . . . Song 5:2
Committed Love. . . . . Song 7:9

Miscarriage

Why our child?

When Life Falls Apart . . . . Job 16:1
Shattered Dreams . . . . 2 Kin. 4:8
Marital Stress . . . . Gen. 29:31
Releasing the Pain . . . . Ps. 6:1
God Cares. . . . . John 11:17
Life Goes On . . . . 2 Sam. 12:1

Parenting

Family Time

Building a rewarding childhood for your children

Proper Priorities . . . . Ex. 16:1
Time Together . . . . Phil. 2:19
Family Traditions . . . . Ex. 12:1
Family Vacations . . . . Mark 6:30
Worshiping Together . . . . Deut. 31:1
Lasting Values . . . . 2 Tim. 3:10

Parenting Adolescents

Making it through your child's adolescence

Stressful Times . . . . Luke 15:11
Confusing Times . . . . James 1:19
Angry Times . . . . Ex. 32:1
Decisions, Decisions . . . . Gen. 37:12
A Parent's Responsibility . . . . Prov. 1:8
Getting Along . . . . Gen. 37:1

Strong-Willed Children

Raising a strong-willed child

Where Are My Instructions? . . . . . Prov. 3:1
Born to Be Wild . . . . Prov. 22:1
Necessary Discipline . . . . Prov. 18:1
Dealing with Anger . . . . Num. 11:1
When Kids Drive You Crazy . . . . Gen. 25:19
Happy Endings . . . . 2 Tim. 1:1

Challenging Issues

Special kids with special needs

Adopted Children . . . . Eph. 1:1
Children of Divorce . . . . Rom. 12:9
Single-Parent Children . . . . 1 Kin. 17:1
Children With Disabilities . . . . Ps. 139:1
Gifted Children . . . . 1 Cor. 12:1
Substitute Parents . . . . Est. 2:1

COMMUNITY LIFE

Workplace

Relationships At Work

Getting along with the people you work with

Entrepreneurs

Working for yourself, making your dream come true

Employment

Being contented in the workplace

Stressed Out

Finding relief to personal pressures

Church Life

Church Life

What makes a church alive?

Living Churches Reproduce. . . . . Acts 14:21
Living Churches Heal . . . . Acts 15:22
Living Churches in Society . . . . . . 1 Tim. 2:1
Service in the Church . . . . 1 Cor. 4:1
Teaching in the Church . . . . James 3:1
Leadership of the Church . . . . 1 Tim. 3:1

Missions

Following the Spirit to reach the world

Together in Mission . . . . Mark 6:6
Called to a Wider Mission . . . . Acts 13:1
Sharing Our Triumphs . . . . Acts 14:21
Divide and Conquer . . . . Acts 15:36
A Spirit-Led Mission . . . . Acts 16:6

Sheep and Shepherds

Being a true shepherd of God's flock

Humble Shepherds. . . . . Matt. 18:1
Caring Shepherds. . . . . Jer. 23:1
Shepherds of Truth . . . . Zech. 10:1
Committed Shepherds . . . . Ezek. 34:1
Judgment of Shepherds . . . . Zech. 13:7
The Good Shepherd . . . . John 10:1

Worship

Worship that blesses God

Worshiping With Our Hearts . . . . . . Isa. 29:1
Worship the Creator. . . . . Deut. 16:21
Worshiping the True God . . . . Isa. 44:6
Orderly Worship . . . . 1 Cor. 14:26
Worshiping With Gifts. . . . . 2 Chr. 31:2
Worshiping in Spirit and Truth . . . . John 4:1

COMMUNITY LIFE

Growing Together

Praising God

Praise is a way of life

False Teachers

Discernment in a deceptive world

Restoration

Mending broken people

Women

Who is a Godly woman?

Relating Together

Human Relationships

Relating with integrity

Working With Integrity . . . . Col. 3:18
From Status to Brotherhood . . . . . Philem. 1
Respecting Authority at Work. . . . . Titus 2:1
Honoring Commitments. . . . . . . Deut. 21:10
Witnessing in Marriage . . . . 1 Peter 3:1
Being a Spiritual Mentor. . . . . 2 Tim. 1:1

Authority

Relating to those who are responsible

Respecting Authority . . . . Acts 24:1
Being Good Citizens . . . . 1 Peter 2:13
God and Government . . . . Dan. 3:1
Chain of Command . . . . Num. 12:1
Who's in Charge at Home? . . . . Est. 2:1
Insurrection in the Church . . . . . . 1 Cor. 9:1

Believers

Bonded together in belief

Imperfect Believers . . . . Gen. 18:1
Believers in a Promise . . . . John 14:1
Believers in the Future Joy . . . . John 16:17
Believers United by Love. . . . . 1 John 4:7
Fruitful Believers . . . . Luke 6:43
Believers Who are Doers . . . . . . Matt. 25:31

Leaders

What it means to be a worthy leader

Leaders Learn by Following. . . . . . . Ex. 24:1
The Burden of Leadership . . . . . James 3:1
A Humble Leader . . . . Matt. 18:1
An Exemplary Leader . . . . Titus 1:1
A Faithful Leader . . . . 1 Tim. 4:1
A Righteous Leader . . . . 1 Tim. 6:11

COMMUNITY LIFE

Coping

Pain and Suffering

Understanding how God can allow terrible things to happen

Harsh Realities . . . . Job 1:1
When Will It End? . . . . Job 2:1
Hard Questions. . . . . John 9:1
Finding God. . . . . 1 Sam. 23:7
Comforted by Others . . . . Mark 2:1
Things Can Change . . . . Job 42:1

Spirituality

A believer's spiritual orientation

Spiritually Accountable . . . . Ezek. 3:16
Maintaining Spiritual Purity . . . . . . Ezra 10:1
Spirituality and Leadership . . . . . 2 Chr. 19:4
Victory in Spiritual Warfare . . . . . . Rev. 12:1
Maintaining Spiritual Focus. . . . . . . Heb. 2:1
Inward Spirituality . . . . Mark 7:1
A Spiritual Lifestyle . . . . Gal. 5:16

Coming Home

Restoration of a believer

The Call of Love . . . . Luke 15:11
Hide and Seek. . . . . Gen. 3:1
Straying from God . . . . Jonah 1:1
Returning to God . . . . Jonah 3:1
Obstacles in the Road . . . . Ex. 13:18
A Clean Slate. . . . . Luke 7:36

Wisdom

Wisdom from God

Passionately Seeking Wisdom . . . . Prov. 2:1
Wisdom vs. Materialism . . . . Eccl. 2:1
Wisdom in Conflict . . . . 1 Sam. 25:1
Priority of Wisdom . . . . 1 Kin. 3:1
Wisdom for All Occasions . . . . . Prov. 22:17
Eternal Wisdom . . . . Prov. 8:1

Devotion

Obedience

Obedience—a way of life

Obedience and Prosperity . . . . Lev. 26:1
Blessings of Obedience . . . . Deut. 28:1
Obedience to Civil Authority . . . . . . Eccl. 8:1
Obedience to Our Deliverer . . . . . Deut. 11:1
Freedom in Obedience . . . . John 8:31
Love Through Obedience . . . . . . 1 John 2:3
God's Promise in Obedience . . . . Gen. 12:1

Righteousness

The impossibility of righteousness

National Righteousness . . . . Ps. 99:1
Human Righteousness . . . . Job 25:1
Righteous Giving . . . . Mal. 3:6
Example of Righteousness . . . . Gen. 6:9
Righteous Living. . . . . Prov. 29:1
None Righteous . . . . Rom. 3:1
Righteousness by Faith . . . . Rom. 4:1

Wholeness

Becoming a well-rounded believer

Spiritual Life . . . . Matt. 13:1
Physical Life . . . . Dan. 1:1
Vocational Life . . . . 2 Cor. 6:3
Emotional Life . . . . 1 Kin. 19:1
Relational Life . . . . Num. 12:1
Volitional Life . . . . Num. 22:21

Prayer

Effective prayer of the righteous

Prayer of Penitence . . . . Neh. 1:1
Prayer and Fasting . . . . Joel 1:13
A Prayer of Protection . . . . 2 Chr. 20:1
An Exemplary Prayer . . . . Luke 11:1
Faith to Ask . . . . Matt. 7:1
Effectiveness of Prayer . . . . James 5:7

SPIRITUAL LIFE

Direction

Gifts

What is God's will for my life?

Calling

Understanding God's direction

Discipleship

The price of a life of service

Following Christ

Follow by watching the leader

SPIRITUAL LIFE

Character

Character

Developing a Godly character

Learning Loyalty . . . . Matt. 26:69
Proper Priorities . . . . 2 Chr. 1:1
Courage in the Court . . . . Est. 7:1
Ever Encouraging . . . . Acts 11:19
Showing Selflessness . . . . Phil. 2:19
Bearers of Blessing . . . . Luke 6:17

Deception

Telling the truth

Not-So-White Lie . . . . Gen. 12:10
When Lying is Habitual . . . . Gen. 20:1
It Runs in the Family . . . . Gen. 26:1
Family Deception . . . . Gen. 27:1
Tell the Truth or Run From it. . . . Gen. 31:22
Deceit in God's Name . . . . 1 Kin. 13:1

Responsibility

The believer's responsibility

Each Carrying His Load . . . . Num. 4:21
Being Responsible to God . . . . . . Rom. 3:21
Taking Responsibility for Sin . . . . . Lam. 5:1
Our Responsibility to Grow. . . . . . 1 Cor. 3:1
Responsible for Ourselves . . . . . . Ezek. 18:1
Our Responsibility to Others . . . . Ezek. 33:1

Trust

God deserves our complete trust

Trust Not Shaken . . . . Ps. 125:1
Trust in the Face of Enemies . . . . . . Ps. 21:1
Who Can We Trust? . . . . Matt. 2:13
Trust in the Face of Death . . . . . John 11:17
Trusting When Jesus Delays . . . . John 11:1
Trusting God's Commands . . . . . . Prov. 3:1

SPIRITUAL LIFE

Critical Times

Suffering

The refining grace of suffering

Salvation

Saved—why? what? how?

Pride

It is a long way to fall

Disobedience

Paying the price of disobedience

Family

Empty Nesters

Now the kids are gone

Tough Times . . . . Ruth 1:1
New Perspective . . . . Ruth 4:13
Looking Ahead . . . . Luke 12:13
Hearing God . . . . Heb. 11:1
Investing Yourself . . . . Ex. 3:1
Taking Risks . . . . Matt. 14:22

Growing Old

Celebrate and pass-on the mantle

Faith Journey . . . . Gen. 12:1
Never too Old . . . . Gen. 6:9
The Power of Blessing . . . . Luke 2:21
Leaving a Legacy . . . . Num. 27:1
Looking Back . . . . Josh. 23:1
Looking Ahead . . . . 1 Cor. 15:35

Adultery

The deception of sexual desire

A Test for Adultery . . . . Num. 5:11
The Trap of Unfaithfulness . . . . Prov. 7:1
The Lure of Adultery . . . . Prov. 5:1
Forgiveness After Falling . . . . Ps. 51:1
The Pain of Adultery . . . . Hos. 2:2
Before Adultery Starts . . . . Matt. 5:27

Purity

Developing a pure life

A Pure Heart . . . . Ps. 24:1
A Pure Sacrifice . . . . Num. 19:1
Purity in Lifestyle . . . . Prov. 20:1
Maintaining Purity . . . . Ps. 101:1
Purity in Marriage . . . . Heb. 13:1
Called to a Pure Life . . . . 1 Thess. 4:1

PERSONAL LIFE

Recovery

Healthy Habits

Being in control of your body

Frustrations. . . . . Mark 14:32
Healthy Habits. . . . . Dan. 1:1
Living in Balance . . . . Ex. 16:1
A Matter of Control . . . . Num. 11:4
Don't Give Up . . . . Num. 14:1
Consistent and Persistent . . . . . . Josh. 5:13

Mending Fences

Healing significant relationships

I Have a Dream . . . . Luke 15:11
Heart's Desire . . . . 2 Sam. 14:1
Called to Reconcile. . . . . Matt. 18:21
Taking the Initiative. . . . . Gen. 45:1
Anxious Anticipation. . . . . Gen. 32:1
Homecoming . . . . Gen. 33:1

Grief and Loss

Working through the stages of grief

Denial . . . . 2 Kin. 4:8
Anger . . . . Ruth 1:1
Bargaining . . . . 2 Sam. 12:1
Depression . . . . Gen. 37:12
Acceptance . . . . Phil. 4:10
Hope. . . . . John 11:17

Hope

God: the source of real hope

Hope for Deliverance. . . . . Ps. 59:1
A Secure Hope . . . . Ps. 16:1
Hope for the Lord's Coming . . . . Zeph. 1:14
A Comforting Hope. . . . . Isa. 40:1
Hope for a Remnant . . . . Mic. 2:6
Hope for the Lame. . . . . Mic. 4:6

PERSONAL LIFE

Control Issues

Knowledge

The source of real knowledge

Knowing God's Power . . . . Ps. 46:1
God's Knowledge of Us . . . . Ps. 139:1
Responsibility of Knowledge. . . . . Amos 3:1
Knowing the Mystery of Christ. . . . Col. 1:24
Knowing the Gift of God. . . . . John 4:1
Knowledge From Above. . . . . John 7:14
Beyond Human Knowledge . . . . . . Gal. 1:11

Faith

Having faith that endures

An Intuitive Faith . . . . Josh. 2:1
A Call to National Faith . . . . Isa. 26:1
Justified by Faith . . . . Rom. 4:1
Faith in Rough Times . . . . Matt. 14:22
Faith Shown by Action. . . . . James 2:14
Humble Faith . . . . Phil. 2:1
Faith Through the Centuries . . . . . Heb. 11:1

Power

God is the super power

Tenuous Political Power . . . . Isa. 23:1
Superiority of God's Power . . . . . . Acts 4:23
Pompous Power . . . . Acts 25:23
Power of the Universe . . . . Ps. 97:1
Overcoming Spiritual Powers. . . . . Mark 5:1
Power of Life and Death. . . . . Mark 5:21

Anger

It will eat you alive

Turning Away Anger . . . . Prov. 29:1
Anger's Venom . . . . Ps. 58:1
When Anger Turns Violent . . . . 1 Sam. 20:1
Arousing God's Anger . . . . Num. 11:1
Consumed by God's Anger . . . . Ps. 90:1
Righteous Anger . . . . Luke 19:28

Sexual Issues

Temptation

Learning not to give in

Sin

Winning over sin

Love

What is real love?

Sexual Control

The rewards of purity

Close to Home

Self

Getting real with yourself

Self-Examination . . . . 1 Cor. 11:17
Principles for Self-Discipline. . . . . Prov. 13:1
Encouraging Self-Control . . . . Titus 2:1
Losing Self to Find Life. . . . . Matt. 16:13
Self-Control in Sexuality. . . . . Song 2:16
Seeing Self Clearly . . . . Job 27:1

Poverty and Riches

Making your resources count for God

The Wisdom of Compassion . . . . Prov. 14:1
Justice as an Act of Worship . . . . . Isa. 58:1
Opening Ears to the Poor. . . . . . . Prov. 21:1
A Covetous Society . . . . Mic. 2:1
Keeping Integrity at Work. . . . . . . Prov. 13:1
Opting for the Simple Life . . . . . . Prov. 30:1

Divorce

God's view of divorce

A Provision for Divorce . . . . Deut. 24:1
Keeping Faith in Each Other . . . . . Mal. 2:10
An Adulterous Act . . . . Matt. 5:27
What God has Joined . . . . Mark 10:1
God's Intent for Marriage . . . . Matt. 19:1

Death

Getting through death

Viewing the Promised Land . . . . . Deut. 34:1
What We Gain in Death . . . . Phil. 1:12
A Temporary Sleep . . . . Matt. 9:18
The Great Leveler . . . . Luke 16:19
No More Sting. . . . . 1 Cor. 15:35
A Source of Comfort . . . . 1 Thess. 4:13

PERSONAL LIFE

Leaders

David

Highlights of David's life

The Pick of the Litter . . . . .1 Sam. 16:1
A Narrow Escape . . . . .1 Sam. 23:7
Remembering an Old Friend . . . .2 Sam. 9:1
A Royal Scandal . . . . .2 Sam. 11:1
The Scandal Revealed . . . . .2 Sam. 12:1
Paying the Cost . . . . .2 Sam. 24:18
Holy Preparations . . . . .1 Chr. 22:2

Solomon

Highlights of Solomon's life

In His Father's Footsteps . . . . . . .1 Kin. 1:28
An Appeal for Wisdom . . . . .1 Kin. 3:1
Building a Dream . . . . .1 Kin. 5:1
Living Up to a Reputation . . . . . . .2 Chr. 9:1
A Life of Splendor . . . . .1 Kin. 10:14
Led Astray . . . . .1 Kin. 11:1
The Seeds of Dissension . . . . . .1 Kin. 11:26

Paul

Highlights of Paul's life

A Dramatic Turn-Around . . . . .Acts 9:1
A Message of Fulfillment . . . . . . .Acts 13:13
A Witness in Prison . . . . .Phil. 1:12
Encouraging the Faithful . . . . .1 Thess. 2:17
Evidencing Mighty Works . . . . . . .Acts 20:1
On Trial for the Gospel . . . . .Acts 25:1
A Stormy Journey . . . . .Acts 27:1

Peter

Highlights of Peter's life

A Fisher of Men . . . . .Luke 5:1
A Flash of Insight . . . . .Luke 9:18
A Predicted Failure . . . . .Matt. 26:31
Failing a Friend . . . . .Mark 14:66
Back in Good Graces . . . . .John 21:15
Preaching at Pentecost . . . . .Acts 2:14
An Agent in Resurrection . . . . . . .Acts 9:32

Prophets

Elijah

Highlights of Elijah's life

Isaiah

Highlights of Isaiah's life

Elisha

Highlights of Elisha's life

Daniel

Highlights of Daniel's life

Patriarchs

Abraham

Highlights of Abraham's life

Father to a Nation . . . . .Gen. 12:1
Blessed With Prosperity . . . . .Gen. 13:1
Blessing from Melchizedek . . . . . .Gen. 14:1
Promise of an Heir . . . . .Gen. 15:1
Promise Confirmed . . . . .Gen. 17:1
Test of Nerve . . . . .Gen. 22:1
Called Righteousness. . . . . Rom. 4:1

Jacob

Highlights of Jacob's life

Born for Conflict . . . . .Gen. 25:19
Family Feud . . . . .Gen. 27:1
Love at First Sight . . . . .Gen. 29:1
Prosperity—By Hook or Crook . .Gen. 30:25
Seeing the Face of God . . . . .Gen. 33:1
A Big Family Move . . . . .Gen. 46:1
Saying Good-Bye . . . . .Gen. 49:1

Joseph

Highlights of Joseph's life

God-given Dream . . . . .Gen. 37:1
Sold Out! .Gen. 37:12
Using His Talent . . . . .Gen. 40:1
His Talent Discovered . . . . .Gen. 41:1
Tense Reunion . . . . .Gen. 43:1
Toying With His Brothers . . . . . . .Gen. 44:1
His Secret Unveiled . . . . .Gen. 45:1

Moses

Highlights of Moses' life

From Rags to Riches . . . . .Ex. 2:1
Reluctant Prophet . . . . .Ex. 3:1
Mountaintop Experience . . . . .Ex. 19:1
Face-to-Face Encounter . . . . .Ex. 34:29
Fatal Misstep . . . . .Num. 20:1
Transition of Power . . . . .Deut. 31:14
Viewing the Promised Land . . . . .Deut. 34:1

Atonement

The Gospel

Ministering the good news

The Gospel of Salvation . . . . . . .1 Cor. 15:1
Good News to the Poor . . . . .Luke 4:14
Proclaimed by Prophets . . . . .Rom. 1:1
Light for the Gentiles . . . . .Acts 13:13
On Trial for the Gospel . . . . .Acts 25:23
Proclaimed With Power . . . . . . .1 Thess. 1:1

The Cross

Separated from the Father

Taking on the Curse . . . . .Deut. 21:22
The Power of God . . . . .1 Cor. 1:18
Feeling Forsaken . . . . .Ps. 22:1
A Crucified King . . . . .John 19:1
An Earth-Shattering Death . . . . .Matt. 27:45
A Bringer of Peace . . . . .Eph. 2:11

Forgiveness

True forgiveness: its rewards

When to Forgive . . . . .Philem. 1
How Much Forgiveness? . . . . . . .Matt. 18:21
Forgetting Youthful Rebellion . . . . .Ps. 25:1
Wiping the Slate Clean . . . . .Ps. 130:1
Dealing With Our Separation . . . . .Isa. 59:1
Authority to Forgive . . . . .Mark 2:1
Forgiven and Sent . . . . .John 21:15

Messiah

Hope for all creation

Salvation to All Nations . . . . .Ps. 67:1
Light for Those in Darkness . . . . . . .Isa. 9:1
A Righteous Judge . . . . .Isa. 11:1
One Who is Mourned . . . . .Zech. 12:10
More Than David's Son . . . . . . .Mark 12:35
Source of Love . . . . .Matt. 22:34
Source of Eternal Life . . . . .1 John 5:1

The Trinity

God

Who is God?

Creator of the Heavens . . . . .Isa. 45:14
Hope of the Earth . . . . .Ps. 65:1
Judge With a Mighty Hand . . . . .Ezek. 20:30
One Who Leads Us Forward . . . . .Ex. 13:17
God of Wonders . . . . .Job 9:1
One Who Sees All . . . . .Rom. 8:28
A Faithful God . . . . .Deut. 31:30

Christ

Who is Christ?

Cross: the Stumbling Block . . . . 1 Cor. 1:18
One With the Father . . . . .John 10:22
He Brings Eternal Life . . . . .John 17:1
Nature of a Servant . . . . .Phil. 2:1
Heir of All Things . . . . .Heb. 1:1
Bringer of Life . . . . .Rom. 5:12
The Coming King . . . . .Rev. 20:1

Holy Spirit

Who is the Holy Spirit?

Our Heavenly Counselor . . . . . . .John 14:15
Our Guide to Truth . . . . .John 16:5
Leading Us in Ministry . . . . .Acts 18:18
Unifier of Our Fellowship . . . . .Acts 4:32
Our Intercessor . . . . .Rom. 8:18
Preparing for the Spirit . . . . .Acts 1:12
An Unforgivable Sin . . . . .Luke 12:1

Creation

The work of God the Creator

In the Beginning . . . . .Gen. 1:1
Garden of God . . . . .Gen. 2:4
Fallen Creation . . . . .Gen. 3:1
Stretching Out the Heavens . . . . . .Ps. 104:1
The Praise of the Universe . . . . . . .Ps. 148:1
New Heavens and New Earth . . . .Isa. 65:17
Remembering Our Creator . . . . . .Eccl. 11:7

BIBLICAL SUBJECTS

PREFACE

THE NEW INTERNATIONAL VERSION is a completely new translation of the Holy Bible made by over a hundred scholars working directly from the best available Hebrew, Aramaic and Greek texts. It had its beginning in 1965 when, after several years of exploratory study by committees from the Christian Reformed Church and the National Association of Evangelicals, a group of scholars met at Palos Heights, Illinois, and concurred in the need for a new translation of the Bible in contemporary English. This group, though not made up of official church representatives, was transdenominational. Its conclusion was endorsed by a large number of leaders from many denominations who met in Chicago in 1966.

Responsibility for the new version was delegated by the Palos Heights group to a self-governing body of fifteen, the Committee on Bible Translation, composed for the most part of biblical scholars from colleges, universities and seminaries. In 1967 the New York Bible Society (now the International Bible Society) generously undertook the financial sponsorship of the project—a sponsorship that made it possible to enlist the help of many distinguished scholars. The fact that participants from the United States, Great Britain, Canada, Australia and New Zealand worked together gave the project its international scope. That they were from many denominations—including Anglican, Assemblies of God, Baptist, Brethren, Christian Reformed, Church of Christ, Evangelical Free, Lutheran, Mennonite, Methodist, Nazarene, Presbyterian, Wesleyan and other churches—helped to safeguard the translation from sectarian bias.

How it was made helps to give the New International Version its distinctiveness. The translation of each book was assigned to a team of scholars. Next, one of the Intermediate Editorial Committees revised the initial translation, with constant reference to the Hebrew, Aramaic or Greek. Their work then went to one of the General Editorial Committees, which checked it in detail and made another thorough revision. This revision in turn was carefully reviewed by the Committee on Bible Translation, which made further changes and then released the final version for publication. In this way the entire Bible underwent three revisions, during each of which the translation was examined for its faithfulness to the original languages and for its English style.

All this involved many thousands of hours of research and discussion regarding the meaning of the texts and the precise way of putting them into English. It may well be that no other translation has been made by a more thorough process of review and revision from committee to committee than this one.

From the beginning of the project, the Committee on Bible Translation held to certain goals for the New International Version: that it would be an accurate translation and one that would have clarity and literary quality and so prove suitable for public and private reading, teaching, preaching, memorizing and liturgical use. The Committee also sought to preserve some measure of continuity with the long tradition of translating the Scriptures into English.

In working toward these goals, the translators were united in their commitment to the authority and infallibility of the Bible as God's Word in written form. They believe that it contains the divine answer to the deepest needs of humanity, that it sheds unique light on our path in a dark world, and that it sets forth the way to our eternal well-being.

The first concern of the translators has been the accuracy of the translation and its fidelity to the thought of the biblical writers. They have weighed the significance of the lexical and grammatical details of the Hebrew, Aramaic and Greek texts. At the same time, they have striven for more than a word-for-word translation. Because thought patterns and syntax differ from language to language, faithful communication of the meaning of the writers of the Bible demands frequent modifications in sentence structure and constant regard for the contextual meanings of words.

A sensitive feeling for style does not always accompany scholarship. Accordingly, the Committee on Bible Translation submitted the developing version to a number of stylistic consultants. Two of them read every book of both Old and New Testaments twice—once before and once after the last major revision—and made invaluable suggestions. Samples of the translation were tested for clarity and ease of reading by various kinds of people—young and old, highly educated and less well educated, ministers and laymen.

Concern for clear and natural English—that the New International Version should be idiomatic but not idiosyncratic, contemporary but not dated—motivated the translators and consultants. At the same time, they tried to reflect the differing styles of the biblical writers. In view of the international use of English, the translators sought to avoid obvious Americanisms on the one hand and obvious Anglicisms on the other. A British edition reflects the comparatively few differences of significant idiom and of spelling.

As for the traditional pronouns "thou," "thee" and "thine" in reference to the Deity, the translators judged that to use these archaisms (along with the old verb forms such as "doest," "wouldest" and "hadst") would violate accuracy in translation. Neither Hebrew, Aramaic nor Greek uses special pronouns for the persons of the Godhead. A present-day translation is not enhanced by forms that in the time of the King James Version were used in everyday speech, whether referring to God or man.

For the Old Testament the standard Hebrew text, the Masoretic Text as published in the latest edition of *Biblia Hebraica*, was used throughout. The Dead Sea Scrolls contain material bearing on an earlier stage of the Hebrew text. They were consulted, as were the Samaritan Pentateuch and the ancient scribal traditions relating to textual changes. Sometimes a variant Hebrew reading in the margin of the Masoretic Text was followed instead of the text itself. Such instances, being variants within the Masoretic tradition, are not specified by footnotes. In rare cases, words in the consonantal text were divided differently from the way they appear in the Masoretic Text. Footnotes indicate this. The translators also consulted the more important early versions—the Septuagint; Aquila, Symmachus and Theodotion; the Vulgate; the Syriac Peshitta; the Targums; and for the Psalms the *Juxta Hebraica* of Jerome. Readings from these versions were occasionally followed where the Masoretic Text seemed doubtful and where accepted principles of textual criticism showed that one or more of these textual witnesses appeared to provide the correct reading. Such instances are footnoted. Sometimes vowel letters and vowel signs did not, in the judgment of the translators, represent the correct vowels for the original consonantal text. Accordingly some words were read with a different set of vowels. These instances are usually not indicated by footnotes.

The Greek text used in translating the New Testament was an eclectic one. No other piece of ancient literature has such an abundance of manuscript witnesses as does the New Testament. Where existing manuscripts differ, the translators made their choice of readings according to accepted principles of New Testament textual criticism. Footnotes call attention to places where there was uncertainty about what the original text was. The best current printed texts of the Greek New Testament were used.

There is a sense in which the work of translation is never wholly finished. This applies to all great literature and uniquely so to the Bible. In 1973 the New Testament in the New International Version was published. Since then, suggestions for corrections and revisions have been received from various sources. The Committee on Bible Translation carefully considered the suggestions and adopted a number of them. These were incorporated in the first printing of the entire Bible in 1978. Additional revisions were made by the Committee on Bible Translation in 1983 and appear in printings after that date.

As in other ancient documents, the precise meaning of the biblical texts is sometimes uncertain. This is more often the case with the Hebrew and Aramaic texts than with the Greek text. Although archaeological and linguistic discoveries in this century aid in understanding difficult passages, some uncertainties remain. The more significant of these have been called to the reader's attention in the footnotes.

In regard to the divine name *YHWH*, commonly referred to as the *Tetragrammaton*, the translators adopted the device used in most English versions of rendering that name as "LORD" in capital letters to distinguish it from *Adonai*, another Hebrew word rendered "Lord," for which small letters are used. Wherever the two names stand together in the Old Testament as a compound name of God, they are rendered "Sovereign LORD."

Because for most readers today the phrases "the LORD of hosts" and "God of hosts" have little meaning, this version renders them "the LORD Almighty" and "God Almighty." These renderings convey the sense of the Hebrew, namely, "he who is sovereign over all the 'hosts' (powers) in heaven and on earth, especially over the 'hosts' (armies) of Israel." For readers unacquainted with Hebrew this does not make clear the distinction between *Sabaoth* ("hosts" or "Almighty") and *Shaddai* (which can also be translated "Almighty"), but the latter occurs infre-

quently and is always footnoted. When *Adonai* and *YHWH Sabaoth* occur together, they are rendered "the Lord, the LORD Almighty."

As for other proper nouns, the familiar spellings of the King James Version are generally retained. Names traditionally spelled with "ch," except where it is final, are usually spelled in this translation with "k" or "c," since the biblical languages do not have the sound that "ch" frequently indicates in English—for example, in *chant*. For well-known names such as Zechariah, however, the traditional spelling has been retained. Variation in the spelling of names in the original languages has usually not been indicated. Where a person or place has two or more different names in the Hebrew, Aramaic or Greek texts, the more familiar one has generally been used, with footnotes where needed.

To achieve clarity the translators sometimes supplied words not in the original texts but required by the context. If there was uncertainty about such material, it is enclosed in brackets. Also for the sake of clarity or style, nouns, including some proper nouns, are sometimes substituted for pronouns, and vice versa. And though the Hebrew writers often shifted back and forth between first, second and third personal pronouns without change of antecedent, this translation often makes them uniform, in accordance with English style and without the use of footnotes.

Poetical passages are printed as poetry, that is, with indentation of lines and with separate stanzas. These are generally designed to reflect the structure of Hebrew poetry. This poetry is normally characterized by parallelism in balanced lines. Most of the poetry in the Bible is in the Old Testament, and scholars differ regarding the scansion of Hebrew lines. The translators determined the stanza divisions for the most part by analysis of the subject matter. The stanzas therefore serve as poetic paragraphs.

As an aid to the reader, italicized sectional headings are inserted in most of the books. They are not to be regarded as part of the NIV text, are not for oral reading, and are not intended to dictate the interpretation of the sections they head.

The footnotes in this version are of several kinds, most of which need no explanation. Those giving alternative translations begin with "Or" and generally introduce the alternative with the last word preceding it in the text, except when it is a single-word alternative; in poetry quoted in a footnote a slant mark indicates a line division. Footnotes introduced by "Or" do not have uniform significance. In some cases two possible translations were considered to have about equal validity. In other cases, though the translators were convinced that the translation in the text was correct, they judged that another interpretation was possible and of sufficient importance to be represented in a footnote.

In the New Testament, footnotes that refer to uncertainty regarding the original text are introduced by "Some manuscripts" or similar expressions. In the Old Testament, evidence for the reading chosen is given first and evidence for the alternative is added after a semicolon (for example: Septuagint; Hebrew *father*). In such notes the term "Hebrew" refers to the Masoretic Text.

It should be noted that minerals, flora and fauna, architectural details, articles of clothing and jewelry, musical instruments and other articles cannot always be identified with precision. Also measures of capacity in the biblical period are particularly uncertain (see the table of weights and measures following the text).

Like all translations of the Bible, made as they are by imperfect man, this one undoubtedly falls short of its goals. Yet we are grateful to God for the extent to which he has enabled us to realize these goals and for the strength he has given us and our colleagues to complete our task. We offer this version of the Bible to him in whose name and for whose glory it has been made. We pray that it will lead many into a better understanding of the Holy Scriptures and a fuller knowledge of Jesus Christ the incarnate Word, of whom the Scriptures so faithfully testify.

The Committee on Bible Translation

June 1978
(Revised August 1983)

Names of the translators and editors may be secured
from the International Bible Society,
translation sponsors of the New International Version,
1820 Jet Stream Drive, Colorado Springs, Colorado 80921-3696 U.S.A

THE OLD TESTAMENT

Genesis

Author. Traditionally, Moses has been considered the author of the first five books of the Bible, Genesis through Deuteronomy. Christ himself referred to Moses as the author (John 7:19). Although much biblical and historical evidence points to Mosaic authorship, many modern scholars have suggested a compilation of various sources identified by the various names for God in these books and by the unique phraseology.

Personal Reading	Group Study Topic and Reading	
1:1–2:25	The Creation	1:1–2:3
3:1–4:26	The Fall	3:1–24
5:1–10:32	The Flood	6:5–7:12
11:1–26	Tower of Babel	11:1–9
11:27–14:24	Abram's Call	11:27–12:9
15:1–19:38	The Three Visitors	18:1–15
20:1–23:20	Abraham Tested	22:1–19
24:1–27:40	Isaac's Blessing	27:1–40
27:41–31:55	Jacob Marries	29:1–30
32:1–36:43	Jacob Wrestles	32:22–32
37:1–40:23	Joseph Sold	37:12–36
41:1–44:34	Pharaoh's Dreams	41:1–40
45:1–50:26	Joseph Reveals Self	45:1–28

Date. Genesis was probably written during the early part of the Hebrews' travels after they left Egypt, sometime around 1450 B.C.

Purpose. Genesis provides a historical context for pre-history. It also provides a foundation for God's work in the world through Abraham's descendants, the Hebrews. Genesis gives us a sense of roots, both in this world and in God's heart. Genesis begins with, "In the beginning," and the book provides the story of the beginnings of earth, the human race, the Hebrew nation, etc.

Historical Background. Genesis is not only the book at the beginning of the Bible, it is the description of the beginning of history, when God spoke the universe into existence. From the creation of the universe, this historical narrative moves to the development of human civilization and finally to the ancestry of the Hebrew people. The narrative of Genesis stretches over vast amounts of time.

Archeological evidence in Palestine and documentary evidence from Mesopotamia and Egypt provide a clear picture of the patriarchal period which was the beginning of Israel's founding fathers described in 11:27–50:26. The patriarchs (Abraham, Isaac and Jacob) founded the Hebrew nation and faith. Evidence from Mesopotamia supports the theory that the historical roots of the patriarchs lie in that region. The tower of Babel was built in Mesopotamia. Abram was born there. The region shaped the lives of Isaac and Jacob. Although Palestine became the homeland for the Hebrews, Mesopotamia was their original home.

Rule by Age. God started the Hebrew nation at a time in history when society was ruled by tribes or clans. That, in itself, explains the importance of genealogies in the ancient manuscripts. In this phase of society, the leadership of the clan was passed down to the oldest son. This leadership right was called a "birthright" and also carried with it a greater share of the inheritance. Throughout the beginnings of the Hebrew nation, the leadership of the family was in contest. Esau and Jacob fought over it. Joseph and his brothers came to blows over it. The decisions made in these early family matters affected the events of the remainder of the Old Testament and even current events today.

The great themes of Scripture and literature have their roots in Genesis. The origin and mission of humanity, the understanding of good and evil, the definition of sin and the fall of Adam, human responsibility and the sovereignty of God, divine justice and grace, tradition and civil government all have their beginnings in Genesis.

OPEN 1. Where do you go when you want to get away from it all and be close to God in his creation? **2.** What time of day are you the most creative?

STUDY This passage is a summary account of God's creation of the world. The Bible always assumes rather than argues the existence of God. As Psalm 90:2 states, creation had a beginning but God has always been. **1.** As you read this story of creation, what comes to mind: Your childhood home, listening to one of your parents read this story? A camping trip in the mountains, looking up at the stars and being overwhelmed by it all? Seeing the movie "Star Wars" and remembering the sound track for the opening scene? **2.** How would you describe the kind of literature in this passage: A hymn of praise? A historical narrative? A theology textbook? A science paper? A Bible story book? **3.** If you were teaching this story to children, what would you want them to learn? **4.** What does it mean to be created in God's image? What does this do to your own self-image? How about your body? Your relationship with God? With other people? **5.** How does this story effect the way you treat the land, water, plants and animals in God's world? **6.** If you were asked to share your faith story, how would you relate your life to this story? **7.** How does Jesus Christ fit into the story of creation (Col. 1:15–20)? **8.** How

The Beginning

1 In the beginning God created the heavens and the earth. 2Now
the earth was[a] formless and empty, darkness was over the
surface of the deep, and the Spirit of God was hovering over
the waters.
3And God said, "Let there be light," and there was light. 4God saw
that the light was good, and he separated the light from the
darkness. 5God called the light "day," and the darkness he
called "night." And there was evening, and there was morning—the first day.
6And God said, "Let there be an expanse between the waters to separate water from water." 7So God made the expanse and separated the water under the expanse from the water above it.
And it was so. 8God called the expanse "sky." And there was
evening, and there was morning—the second day.
9And God said, "Let the water under the sky be gathered to one
place, and let dry ground appear." And it was so. 10God called
the dry ground "land," and the gathered waters he called
"seas." And God saw that it was good.
11Then God said, "Let the land produce vegetation: seed-bearing plants and trees on the land that bear fruit with seed
in it, according to their various kinds." And it was so. 12The
land produced vegetation: plants bearing seed according to
their kinds and trees bearing fruit with seed in it according to
their kinds. And God saw that it was good. 13And there was
evening, and there was morning—the third day.
14And God said, "Let there be lights in the expanse of the sky to separate the day from the night, and let them serve as signs to
mark seasons and days and years, 15and let them be lights in

[a]2 Or possibly *became*

1:1 God created. This is the first and greatest assumption of the Word of God. The basic understanding that God is, that he created all things, and that he brought us to be, provides the deepest foundation for our understanding of ourselves and the world around us.

1:2 Spirit of God was hovering over the waters. Once we have read the Bible entirely, we will see God as he exists within the Trinity. First, as Jehovah creator; next, as the Holy Spirit; and last as Jesus—our Savior. The creation account reveals that the creative power of God was at work in all three dimensions of his character.

1:3 Let there be light. These are the first recorded words that God spoke in creation. They exposed his work and ultimate purpose—to give life. It's interesting to note that the revelation through Jesus Christ, the light of the world (John 8:12), served that same purpose: To expose the work that God was doing in the world and to give eternal life.

1:4 the light was good. As God created the world, it worked in harmony. Everything he created was "good" (vv. 10,12,18,21,25). It included no chaos, evil, or anything in rebellion with the Creator.

1:5 the first day. There are a variety of views on creation. God certainly had the power to create the world within literal twenty-four hour days; he also could have done these acts over a length of time. In either case, God did indeed create the world. And all that he created was good.

1:6 expanse. Today we would understand this word as "atmosphere." God separated the water (which at that time covered the whole earth) and the clouds (the moisture that topped the atmosphere). He separated earth and sky.

1:7 it was so. The world, as God created it, was completely obedient to him. He spoke, "Let there be ..." and his will was done. It is a picture for us of the peace our world could have if it were completely aligned with God's will.

1:9 one place. When God gathered the water into one place, he was forming the oceans. This pictures God gathering the water into seas around the lands.

1:11 kinds. God did not just create, he expressed his creativity. He created many kinds of vegetation, not just one fruit and one vegetable. God also created these many living organisms with the ability to bear seeds "according to their kinds." The plants would not need to be recreated; they would bear seeds and grow more of their own kind.

1:14 signs. This kind of "sign" does not refer to zodiac signs; instead, it refers to the created order in the expanse of the stars across the night sky that guides sailors home at night and that changes with the seasons.

the expanse of the sky to give light on the earth." And it was
so. 16God made two great lights—the greater light to govern
the day and the lesser light to govern the night. He also made
the stars. 17God set them in the expanse of the sky to give
light on the earth, 18to govern the day and the night, and
to separate light from darkness. And God saw that it was
good. 19And there was evening, and there was morning—the
fourth day.
20And God said, "Let the water teem with living creatures, and let
birds fly above the earth across the expanse of the sky." 21So
God created the great creatures of the sea and every living
and moving thing with which the water teems, according to
their kinds, and every winged bird according to its kind. And
God saw that it was good. 22God blessed them and said, "Be
fruitful and increase in number and fill the water in the seas,
and let the birds increase on the earth." 23And there was evening, and there was morning—the fifth day.
24And God said, "Let the land produce living creatures according to
their kinds: livestock, creatures that move along the ground,
and wild animals, each according to its kind." And it was so.
25God made the wild animals according to their kinds, the
livestock according to their kinds, and all the creatures that
move along the ground according to their kinds. And God
saw that it was good.
26Then God said, "Let us make man in our image, in our
likeness, and let them rule over the fish of the sea and the
birds of the air, over the livestock, over all the earth,[a] and
over all the creatures that move along the ground."
27So God created man in his own image,
in the image of God he created him;
male and female he created them.

28God blessed them and said to them, "Be fruitful and increase in number; fill the earth and subdue it. Rule over the
fish of the sea and the birds of the air and over every living
creature that moves on the ground."
29Then God said, "I give you every seed-bearing plant on
the face of the whole earth and every tree that has fruit with
seed in it. They will be yours for food. 30And to all the beasts
of the earth and all the birds of the air and all the creatures
that move on the ground—everything that has the breath of
life in it—I give every green plant for food." And it was so.

[a]26 Hebrew; Syriac *all the wild animals*

does Hebrews 11:3 answer the person who cannot believe in a God behind the harmony and beauty in the universe?

APPLY 1. When did you come to the place in your life where you realized there must be a God behind the beauty and harmony in the universe? **2.** As you raise your children and grandchildren, what do you want them to realize about creation?

1:26 image ... likeness. God created people to be like him. Adam and Eve became unlike God only when they tried to be "like" him in terms of authority (3:5). Romans 8:29 reminds us that it is still God's intention to make us into his likeness, the likeness as revealed in Jesus Christ.

1:27 male and female. Who of us is not aware of the differences between men and women? And yet, both were created in the image of God and given the responsibility to take care of the earth. In how men and women relate to each other, we are different; in how we relate to God, we are the same.

1:28 Rule over. God gave people the responsibility to rule over the world. Ruling over and subduing does not mean merely "being the boss" nor is it an invitation to exploit. Instead, people's "rule" over the world means nurturing it with creativity and care.

31 God saw all that he had made, and it was very good. And
there was evening, and there was morning—the sixth day.

2

Thus the heavens and the earth were completed in all their
vast array.

2 By the seventh day God had finished the work he had been doing;
so on the seventh day he rested[a] from all his work. 3 And God
blessed the seventh day and made it holy, because on it he
rested from all the work of creating that he had done.

Adam and Eve

4 This is the account of the heavens and the earth when they were
created.

When the LORD God made the earth and the heavens— 5 and no
shrub of the field had yet appeared on the earth[b] and no plant of the
field had yet sprung up, for the LORD God had not sent rain on
the earth[b] and there was no man to work the ground, 6 but streams[c]
came up from the earth and watered the whole surface of the
ground— 7 the LORD God formed the man[d] from the dust of the ground
and breathed into his nostrils the breath of life, and the man became
a living being.

8 Now the LORD God had planted a garden in the east, in Eden; and
there he put the man he had formed. 9 And the LORD God made all
kinds of trees grow out of the ground—trees that were pleasing to the
eye and good for food. In the middle of the garden were the tree of
life and the tree of the knowledge of good and evil.

10 A river watering the garden flowed from Eden; from there it was
separated into four headwaters. 11 The name of the first is the Pishon; it
winds through the entire land of Havilah, where there is gold. 12 (The
gold of that land is good; aromatic resin[e] and onyx are also there.)
13 The name of the second river is the Gihon; it winds through the entire land of Cush.[f] 14 The name of the third river is the Tigris; it runs
along the east side of Asshur. And the fourth river is the Euphrates.

15 The LORD God took the man and put him in the Garden of Eden to

[a]2 Or *ceased*; also in verse 3 [b]5 Or *land*; also in verse 6 [c]6 Or *mist* [d]7 The Hebrew for *man (adam)* sounds like and may be related to the Hebrew for *ground (adamah)*; it is also the name *Adam* (see Gen. 2:20). [e]12 Or *good; pearls* [f]13 Possibly southeast Mesopotamia

OPEN 1. Who is the green thumb in your family? If you had to make a living by gardening, how would you do? **2.** Who was your first heart-throb? How did it turn out?

STUDY Many scholars suggest that verse 4a summarizes the creation account in 1:1–2:3. The creation account in 2:4–25 is focused on the creation of humanity. **1.** Why do you think the Bible singles out people from now on? **2.** How would you describe the creation of Adam in verse 7? What makes Adam different from the animals (1:26–27)? What does this say about the original purpose for creating humanity? **3.** Where did God put Adam? Why did God put Adam in a paradise on earth and then turn around and put a tree in the garden that he could not eat from (2:9,17; 3:6)? **4.** Why does God intervene after he has created Adam (v. 18)? What is the need in Adam that only a woman can fill? How would you illustrate this from your own experience? **5.** How would you describe the story of God creating woman (vv. 21–23)? What does this say about their relationship? **6.** Is it possible for a man and a woman to have a beautiful, transparent (naked) relationship with each other without each having a

1:31 very good ... sixth day. This last day of creation was not just described as "good" but as "very good." It was the culmination of God's work in creating our world. It was an apt description of the world God intended for us to live in and wanted us to have.

2:3 he rested. "Sabbath" comes from the Hebrew word "to rest." Though his energy is unlimited, God rested from his creative work. When God gave the Ten Commandments he referred back to this: "Remember the Sabbath day by keeping it holy" (Ex. 20:8).

2:4 account. Genesis tells us the stories of the main players in the history of the nation of Israel. Most of those stories begin with, "This is the account of ..." This first "account" is the story of the first family, Adam and Eve.

2:7 formed. God made humankind. The complexity and the miracle of the human person is God's handiwork. The word "formed" pictures a potter working with clay. We owe to God the wonder of our bodies, minds, and souls.

2:9 tree of the knowledge of good and evil. This is the tree whose fruit God told Adam and Eve not to eat (v. 17). Adam and Eve already had a conscience. They obviously knew that they had a choice to obey God or not. By giving them the opportunity to disobey, God showed his love for them. He wanted their complete trust and unquestioning obedience. Unfortunately, they chose to disobey (3:6,7).

2:15 work it and take care of it. In God's plan, he gave to human beings the role of working and guarding creation as they functioned in the role of stewards. This is as true today as when the responsibility was first announced and understood. That is why, no matter what our task, we should say, "What does God require of me here, in this place, now?"

work it and take care of it. [16]And the LORD God commanded the man,
"You are free to eat from any tree in the garden; [17]but you must not
eat from the tree of the knowledge of good and evil, for when you eat
of it you will surely die."
[18]The LORD God said, "It is not good for the man to be alone. I will
make a helper suitable for him."
[19]Now the LORD God had formed out of the ground all the beasts of
the field and all the birds of the air. He brought them to the man to
see what he would name them; and whatever the man called each living creature, that was its name. [20]So the man gave names to all the
livestock, the birds of the air and all the beasts of the field.

But for Adam[a] no suitable helper was found. [21]So the LORD God
caused the man to fall into a deep sleep; and while he was sleeping,
he took one of the man's ribs[b] and closed up the place with flesh.
[22]Then the LORD God made a woman from the rib[c] he had taken out of
the man, and he brought her to the man.
[23]The man said,

"This is now bone of my bones
and flesh of my flesh;
she shall be called 'woman,[d]'
for she was taken out of man."

[24]For this reason a man will leave his father and mother and be united
to his wife, and they will become one flesh.
[25]The man and his wife were both naked, and they felt no shame.

The Fall of Man

3 Now the serpent was more crafty than any of the wild animals
the LORD God had made. He said to the woman, "Did God really
say, 'You must not eat from any tree in the garden'?"
[2]The woman said to the serpent, "We may eat fruit from the trees
in the garden, [3]but God did say, 'You must not eat fruit from the tree
that is in the middle of the garden, and you must not touch it, or you
will die.' "

[a]20 Or *the man* [b]21 Or *took part of the man's side* [c]22 Or *part* [d]23 The Hebrew for *woman* sounds like the Hebrew for *man.*

transparent relationship with God, their creator?

APPLY 1. As you think back, what is the closest you have come to feeling all alone? How did God intervene in your life to satisfy your need? **2.** In what relationship today are you free to be totally transparent and feel safe and protected? Is this person also transparent with you about the deepest needs in their life? **3.** How transparent can you be with this group?

OPEN 1. When you were growing up, what room in the house or spot in town was "off limits"? Did you ever get into big trouble for being there? **2.** What creature scares you: Spider? Mouse? Snake? Other?

STUDY In the previous chapters, God has created a perfect universe and turned over the care of his creation to humanity—namely Adam and Eve. They are given the

2:18 not good for the man to be alone. God made people to need each other. One of the reasons is the practical matter of procreation. God is a creative God. He created the plants with seeds to procreate. He created a man and then a woman to bring children into the world.

2:20 the man gave names to all the livestock. This was Adam's first act of stewardship over the earth—naming the animals. First, God had named the elements: the sun, the moon, the sky and the land. Then God allowed Adam to name the living creatures.

2:24 leave ... and be united. From the beginning of creation God established the order of the family. Just as Eve was made from Adam's own body, so when a couple is married, the two become one. A man leaves his home, the roots from which he came, and establishes a new life with his new family. Even though polygamy is practiced in the Old Testament, it is clear from this verse that God's plan was for a man and a woman to become one in lifelong service and union.

2:25 no shame. It is difficult to imagine a world with no shame, a completely innocent world. Yet this is the world that God provided for Adam and Eve. This gives a wonderful picture of God's plan for people; a plan that was soon to be ruined by the arrival of sin.

3:1 Did God really say, "You must not eat ... " God did not say this (2:16). Evil was ushered into the world because trust was broken. With one question, the serpent tempted Eve to distrust both God and her understanding of God's world.

3:3 you must not touch it. God had not said anything about touching the fruit; they were not to eat it (2:17). Eve did understand, however, that God had set a boundary that she was not to cross.

Garden of Eden to enjoy with one exception. They cannot eat of the "tree of the knowledge of good and evil." **1.** As you read this story of the fall, what does it remind you of: Modern soap opera? Two-bit, late night movie? A couple in divorce court? You, when you are caught speeding? **2.** How would you describe the serpent in this story? Which statements of the serpent are true and not true (vv. 1,4–5)? Why do you think the serpent mixes the truth with lies? How does Eve misquote God (compare Eve's responses with what God actually said and did in 2:9,16–17)? How does Eve hedge, fixate and amplify God's commandments? **3.** How might someone today fall prey to the same tempting question, "Did God really say ...?" **4.** How can something "good"—the beauty, nourishment or wisdom conveyed by the fruit—be "wrong" when it feels so good? What does this imply for our "if-it-feels-good-do-it" generation? **5.** Why do you think Adam eats the fruit? Could he have resisted? What should he have done? Do you think Adam is more, or less, responsible than Eve? Why? **6.** What has become of the beautiful, transparent (naked) relationship in chapter 2 between the man and the woman? What about the relationship of both with God? **7.** Who takes the initiative to restore fellowship? What does Adam try to do? What about Eve? What

4"You will not surely die," the serpent said to the woman. 5"For God
knows that when you eat of it your eyes will be opened, and you will
be like God, knowing good and evil."

6When the woman saw that the fruit of the tree was good for food
and pleasing to the eye, and also desirable for gaining wisdom, she
took some and ate it. She also gave some to her husband, who was
with her, and he ate it. 7Then the eyes of both of them were opened,
and they realized they were naked; so they sewed fig leaves together
and made coverings for themselves.

8Then the man and his wife heard the sound of the LORD God as he
was walking in the garden in the cool of the day, and they hid from
the LORD God among the trees of the garden. 9But the LORD God
called to the man, "Where are you?"

10He answered, "I heard you in the garden, and I was afraid because I was naked; so I hid."

11And he said, "Who told you that you were naked? Have you eaten
from the tree that I commanded you not to eat from?"

12The man said, "The woman you put here with me—she gave me
some fruit from the tree, and I ate it."

13Then the LORD God said to the woman, "What is this you have done?"

The woman said, "The serpent deceived me, and I ate."

14So the LORD God said to the serpent, "Because you have done
this,

"Cursed are you above all the livestock
 and all the wild animals!
You will crawl on your belly
 and you will eat dust
 all the days of your life.

3:4 You will not surely die. Jesus said that lies were Satan's native tongue (John 8:44). In Eve's case, Satan's lie was in saying that God did not really mean what he said. Satan still uses that device today, trying to get people to water down, distrust or discount God's words entirely.

3:5 you will be like God. Satan made it sound to Eve like God was trying to hold onto a position and did not want anyone to become like him. God was pictured as selfish. Satan still tries to twist God's words to make us believe things that are not true about him.

3:6 good ... pleasing ... desirable. Temptation has not changed over thousands of years. The New Testament describes the basic components of temptation as "the cravings of sinful man, the lust of his eyes and the boasting of what he has and does" (1 John 2:16). Basically, Satan told Eve that the fruit would taste good (satisfy a craving), that it looked good (temptation comes with the first look) and that it would make her more wise (giving her something new). Satan uses the same tactics today to tempt people away from God. None of these outcomes, even if they seem realistic, are worth disregarding God's presence and power in our lives.

3:7 made coverings for themselves. Adam and Eve had not gained great wisdom from the fruit; they had only succeeded in disobeying God and realizing the shame and guilt of that disobedience. With the advent of sin, everything looked different. Adam and Eve saw their own nakedness and looked for their own solution to the problem: covering themselves. But that was not a solution at all; covering themselves could not hide their disobedience or remove their guilt.

3:8 they hid. Adam and Eve foolishly tried to hide from the God who knew everything about them. The One who was the source of everything they needed was the One from whom they were hiding. Sin had disrupted their relationship with God. People still think that they can hide from God, but their efforts to do so are just as futile.

3:9 Where are you? God's goal is always to connect with us. He could have gone to where Adam and Eve were hiding, for he obviously knew where they were. However, he invited them to respond to him. God immediately began to seek those who were lost.

3:12 The woman you put here. Adam did what is natural for most people. He not only passed the blame, but ultimately blamed God for his own disobedience. Adam refused to take responsibility for his actions.

3:13 serpent deceived me. Eve, when given the blame by Adam then passed the blame on to the serpent. While it was true that the serpent had told her a lie, she was at fault for being willing to take the serpent's word over God's. This is more accurately called a "choice" than a "deception."

[15]And I will put enmity
between you and the woman,
and between your offspring[a] and hers;
he will crush[b] your head,
and you will strike his heel."

[16]To the woman he said,

"I will greatly increase your pains in childbearing;
with pain you will give birth to children.
Your desire will be for your husband,
and he will rule over you."

[17]To Adam he said, "Because you listened to your wife and ate from
the tree about which I commanded you, 'You must not eat of it,'

"Cursed is the ground because of you;
through painful toil you will eat of it
all the days of your life.
[18]It will produce thorns and thistles for you,
and you will eat the plants of the field.
[19]By the sweat of your brow
you will eat your food
until you return to the ground,
since from it you were taken;
for dust you are
and to dust you will return."

[20]Adam[c] named his wife Eve,[d] because she would become the
mother of all the living.
[21]The LORD God made garments of skin for Adam and his wife and
clothed them. [22]And the LORD God said, "The man has now become
like one of us, knowing good and evil. He must not be allowed to
reach out his hand and take also from the tree of life and eat, and live
forever." [23]So the LORD God banished him from the Garden of Eden to

[a]15 Or *seed* [b]15 Or *strike* [c]20 Or *The man* [d]20 *Eve* probably means *living.*

does this remind you of? **8.** What is different about each of the three punishments? **9.** Who do you feel sorry for in this story: Adam? Eve? God? Serpent?

APPLY 1. In your spiritual pilgrimage, what is the closest you have come to "blowing it" like Adam and Eve in this story? What enticed you? **2.** How would you describe your relationship with God right now in one or two words?

3:15 crush your head ... strike his heel. This is the first prophecy of Christ's work. In Adam's sin and in Christ's death, Satan dealt a blow (he would "strike his heel," a harmful, but not ultimately deadly wound). However, in the resurrection, Christ crushed Satan's "head," for he completely destroyed the work of Satan.

3:16 pains in childbearing ... desire will be for your husband. Eve did not lose the good things in life with her innocence. She still would bear children and love her husband. But with the knowledge of good and evil came the price that is paid for these realizations. Children would bring pain as well as joy. Sexual relations would be a power over her, not just love and intimacy. Life became two sided, with each good thing bearing its price of burden.

3:17–18 through painful toil you will eat. Again, there would be a price to be paid for the good things in life. Adam was still able to grow food and feed himself and his family. But now that task meant painful and difficult labor. His dominion over the earth would be a struggle that would end in death.

3:19 dust. Referring to death. Adam's life and sustenance came from the ground. In his death, he would return to that same state.

3:21 made garments of skin. God meets us in our disobedience (v. 7). He does not merely stand back and say, "So, what are you going to do *now*?" He covered Adam and Eve; however, to do so, he killed an animal. This foreshadowed the blood sacrifices that would be required to atone for sin; and the eventual sacrifice of Christ that would take away the punishment for sin. In his grace, God met us in our sinful state and provided what we needed in order to have a relationship with him.

3:22 good and evil. Before eating from the forbidden tree, Adam and Eve knew good. They knew God. How amazing it would be to live in a world where good was the only reality. After the fall into sin, however, Adam and Eve discovered evil and its deadly consequences (Rom. 5:12; 6:23).

3:23 banished. This was the deciding moment. The man and woman were ejected from the garden, from the tree of life and from the delightful, comfortable walks with God. They were not robbed of life immediately, but were banished to an eventual death. God had to send them from the garden because they could not, in their sinful state, eat from the tree of life and live forever.

work the ground from which he had been taken. 24After he drove the
man out, he placed on the east side[a] of the Garden of Eden cherubim
and a flaming sword flashing back and forth to guard the way to the
tree of life.

Cain and Abel

4 Adam[b] lay with his wife Eve, and she became pregnant and gave
birth to Cain.[c] She said, "With the help of the LORD I have
brought forth[d] a man." 2Later she gave birth to his brother Abel.
Now Abel kept flocks, and Cain worked the soil. 3In the course of
time Cain brought some of the fruits of the soil as an offering to the
LORD. 4But Abel brought fat portions from some of the firstborn of his
flock. The LORD looked with favor on Abel and his offering, 5but on
Cain and his offering he did not look with favor. So Cain was very angry, and his face was downcast.
6Then the LORD said to Cain, "Why are you angry? Why is your face
downcast? 7If you do what is right, will you not be accepted? But if
you do not do what is right, sin is crouching at your door; it desires to
have you, but you must master it."
8Now Cain said to his brother Abel, "Let's go out to the field."[e] And
while they were in the field, Cain attacked his brother Abel and killed
him.
9Then the LORD said to Cain, "Where is your brother Abel?"
"I don't know," he replied. "Am I my brother's keeper?"
10The LORD said, "What have you done? Listen! Your brother's
blood cries out to me from the ground. 11Now you are under a curse
and driven from the ground, which opened its mouth to receive your
brother's blood from your hand. 12When you work the ground, it will

[a]24 Or *placed in front* [b]1 Or *The man* [c]1 *Cain* sounds like the Hebrew for *brought forth* or *acquired.*
[d]1 Or *have acquired* [e]8 Samaritan Pentateuch, Septuagint, Vulgate and Syriac; Masoretic Text does not have *"Let's go out to the field."*

OPEN 1. How many brothers/sisters do you have? What caused you to get into squabbles? **2.** How did your parents deal with fights between you and your brothers/sisters?

STUDY The story of the "fall" in the previous chapter is immediately followed by this story of the first case of domestic violence. **1.** Reading between the lines in verse 7, what do you learn about why Cain's offering was not accepted? If you were a successful agri-businessman and decided to give back to God some of the fruits of your hard labor, how would you feel if God told you that your offering was not acceptable (Heb. 11:4)? **2.** Why do you think Cain decided to take out his anger toward God on his brother? What does this tell you about a lot of domestic violence? **3.** How would you describe the murder of Cain in criminology terms (v. 8)? Could a good lawyer make a case for "temporary insanity"? **4.** How does Cain respond when confronted by God? If a psychiatrist were to interview Cain at this point, what would he say about Cain? **5.** What is the punishment God places on Cain? In practical terms,

---

3:24 cherubim. Cherubim are winged angels. Ezekiel described his vision that included cherubim in Ezekiel 10. **tree of life.** Sin destroyed people's access to the tree of life and the eternal life for which God created us, but that access will be restored in the new heaven and earth (Rev. 2:7; 22:2,14,19).

4:4 fat portions ... firstborn. The conflict between the offerings of Cain and Abel was not a conflict regarding vegetables or animals. It was a conflict between the attitude of the giver who simply brings God something and the giver who brings God the best. Offerings to God were to be the first fruits, the best. That is why Abel brought the fat portions of the firstborn of his flock. The best always belongs to the Lord. When we give God the best, we are making a statement that we trust him enough to offer a gift to him first, knowing that he will care for our needs. The writer of Hebrews said that Abel's example still speaks about the kind of commitment God desires (Heb. 11:4).

4:5 Cain was very angry. We learn a lot about Cain's character from his reaction to God's disapproval. He basically got mad and pouted. Cain brought an offering, but not because he wanted to honor God.

4:7 crouching. What a visual image of sin: crouching just waiting to overtake us. God knew Cain's heart, and knew that he was dangerously close to being overtaken by sin.

4:8 Cain attacked his brother Abel and killed him. With malicious intent Cain set about to rid himself of someone more favored than he. This is a sad picture of fallen humanity. Cain's concern was not for his own relationship with God but for retribution, pride, and jealous revenge. What a long way humanity fell in the time between Genesis 1 and Genesis 4. (Matt. 23:35; Heb. 11:4).

4:9 Am I my brother's keeper? Cain made some choices that brought severe consequences. He first lied to God, saying he did not know where Abel was. Then he questioned God's authority like a rebellious teenager. He had no pricks of conscience regarding his brother's death.

4:10 Your brother's blood cries out to me. The first murder. The first human blood shed. The horror of this first murder, the taking of someone's life without remorse, reveals the depths of evil to which people can sink. Cain may have thought he got away with it, but God knew exactly what had happened—and why.

4:12 the ground ... will no longer yield its crops for you. Cain's punishment was severe. He had farmed the land, but now the land would not produce for him. He would be driven from his home and from the Lord's presence (vv. 14,16). **restless wanderer.** It would be one thing to choose the life of a nomad, to love the open road. But Cain would be a restless wanderer—always moving on because he did not belong, never able to go home again. For Cain, the worst part was knowing that the gate had been shut by God himself.

no longer yield its crops for you. You will be a restless wanderer on
the earth."
13Cain said to the LORD, "My punishment is more than I can bear.
14Today you are driving me from the land, and I will be hidden from
your presence; I will be a restless wanderer on the earth, and whoever finds me will kill me."
15But the LORD said to him, "Not so[a]; if anyone kills Cain, he will
suffer vengeance seven times over." Then the LORD put a mark on
Cain so that no one who found him would kill him. 16So Cain went
out from the LORD's presence and lived in the land of Nod,[b] east of
Eden.
17Cain lay with his wife, and she became pregnant and gave birth to
Enoch. Cain was then building a city, and he named it after his son
Enoch. 18To Enoch was born Irad, and Irad was the father of Mehujael, and Mehujael was the father of Methushael, and Methushael
was the father of Lamech.
19Lamech married two women, one named Adah and the other Zillah. 20Adah gave birth to Jabal; he was the father of those who live in
tents and raise livestock. 21His brother's name was Jubal; he was the
father of all who play the harp and flute. 22Zillah also had a son, Tubal-
Cain, who forged all kinds of tools out of[c] bronze and iron. Tubal-
Cain's sister was Naamah.
23Lamech said to his wives,

"Adah and Zillah, listen to me;
 wives of Lamech, hear my words.
I have killed[d] a man for wounding me,
 a young man for injuring me.
24If Cain is avenged seven times,
 then Lamech seventy-seven times."

25Adam lay with his wife again, and she gave birth to a son and
named him Seth,[e] saying, "God has granted me another child in place
of Abel, since Cain killed him." 26Seth also had a son, and he named
him Enosh.
At that time men began to call on[f] the name of the LORD.

From Adam to Noah

5 This is the written account of Adam's line.

When God created man, he made him in the likeness of God. 2He
created them male and female and blessed them. And when they were
created, he called them "man.[g]"

[a]15 Septuagint, Vulgate and Syriac; Hebrew *Very well* [b]16 *Nod* means *wandering* (see verses 12 and 14). [c]22 Or *who instructed all who work in* [d]23 Or *I will kill* [e]25 *Seth* probably means *granted.* [f]26 Or *to proclaim* [g]2 Hebrew *adam*

what will this mean to his future? Does Cain show remorse or self-pity? What is Cain afraid of? **6.** What is the sad ending to this story (v. 16)? Do you feel sorry for Cain? What is the difference between this story and the story of the Prodigal Son? **7.** Why do you think this story is in the Bible? What is this story all about?

APPLY 1. By temperament, are you more likely to lash out when you feel rejected and discounted or crawl into a hole and sulk? **2.** What is the thing you have found helpful when you get angry? **3.** What relationship in your life right now is a little frayed?

OPEN 1. How far back can you track your ancestors? **2.** Are there any "colorful characters" in your family tree?

STUDY The story of Cain and Abel in the previous chapter ends with the recitation of the descendants of Cain and the birth of a new son to Adam and Eve to carry on the lineage. **1.** What do you think the Bible

4:13 more than I can bear. Cain did not cry for his brother or repent before God. His reaction was based on fear for himself.

4:15 the LORD put a mark on Cain. The mark put on Cain was some kind of identifiable sign that he was under divine protection. God did not leave Cain defenseless. Instead, he gave him a lifetime to live with the consequences of his violence.

4:25 another child. In the mess that people had created came a fresh beginning: a baby. Seth's birth reminds us that God's grace always provides another opportunity. This baby would carry on the line that would eventually result in the world's Savior (Luke 3:37).

5:1–3 in his own likeness. God had created Adam "in the likeness of God" (1:27). Then Adam and Eve had a child. The exciting truth is that even with the advent of sin, Adam still retained the

means when it says that Adam "had a son in his own likeness and in his own image" (v. 3)? What does humanity retain of the likeness and image of God after the "fall"? How would you explain your opinion, using your own story as a case in point? **2.** What stands out in your mind as you read through the lineage of Seth? What is the one exception in this family tree (v. 24)? What was it about this person that made him so special (Heb. 11:5)? **3.** In Biblical times (and even today in the Near East) genealogies are very important. Why do you think this record has been put in the Bible?

APPLY 1. As you think back over your spiritual heritage, who comes to mind in your family tree as a person of great faith and spiritual power? **2.** What are you doing to pass on your spiritual heritage?

[3]When Adam had lived 130 years, he had a son in his own likeness,
in his own image; and he named him Seth. [4]After Seth was born,
Adam lived 800 years and had other sons and daughters. [5]Altogether,
Adam lived 930 years, and then he died.
[6]When Seth had lived 105 years, he became the father[a] of Enosh.
[7]And after he became the father of Enosh, Seth lived 807 years and
had other sons and daughters. [8]Altogether, Seth lived 912 years, and
then he died.
[9]When Enosh had lived 90 years, he became the father of Kenan.
[10]And after he became the father of Kenan, Enosh lived 815 years and
had other sons and daughters. [11]Altogether, Enosh lived 905 years,
and then he died.
[12]When Kenan had lived 70 years, he became the father of Mahalalel. [13]And after he became the father of Mahalalel, Kenan lived 840
years and had other sons and daughters. [14]Altogether, Kenan lived
910 years, and then he died.
[15]When Mahalalel had lived 65 years, he became the father of Jared. [16]And after he became the father of Jared, Mahalalel lived 830
years and had other sons and daughters. [17]Altogether, Mahalalel
lived 895 years, and then he died.
[18]When Jared had lived 162 years, he became the father of Enoch.
[19]And after he became the father of Enoch, Jared lived 800 years and
had other sons and daughters. [20]Altogether, Jared lived 962 years,
and then he died.
[21]When Enoch had lived 65 years, he became the father of Methuselah. [22]And after he became the father of Methuselah, Enoch walked
with God 300 years and had other sons and daughters. [23]Altogether,
Enoch lived 365 years. [24]Enoch walked with God; then he was no
more, because God took him away.
[25]When Methuselah had lived 187 years, he became the father of
Lamech. [26]And after he became the father of Lamech, Methuselah
lived 782 years and had other sons and daughters. [27]Altogether, Methuselah lived 969 years, and then he died.
[28]When Lamech had lived 182 years, he had a son. [29]He named him
Noah[b] and said, "He will comfort us in the labor and painful toil of
our hands caused by the ground the LORD has cursed." [30]After Noah
was born, Lamech lived 595 years and had other sons and daughters.
[31]Altogether, Lamech lived 777 years, and then he died.
[32]After Noah was 500 years old, he became the father of Shem,
Ham and Japheth.

[a]6 *Father* may mean *ancestor*; also in verses 7-26. [b]29 *Noah* sounds like the Hebrew for *comfort*.

image of God and passed it down to Seth. The sad truth is that Adam passed down his fallen human nature as well. The need for redemption is passed down through the generations in the offspring of Adam.

5:5 Adam lived 930 years, and then he died. There are several viewpoints about how long Adam lived. Some take the verse literally. Others look at general cultural records (parallel to biblical records) which include even longer life spans in their tallies. These records span the time between main characters, as in a dynasty. Others say the large numbers are symbolic and portray a long and full life.

5:22 walked with God. Enoch's life is a wonderful contrast to Genesis 3:8, when God walked through the garden while Adam and Eve hid from him. Enoch really walked *with* God. The Bible records his life as one that we should model.

5:24 then he was no more. Enoch is the only person listed in the Genesis account who did not die. Every other person's life account ends with "and then he died." But for Enoch, who walked with God in a special way, God simply took him away (Heb. 11:5). Elijah is the only other Old Testament person who escaped death (2 Kin. 2:10–12).

The Flood

6 When men began to increase in number on the earth and
daughters were born to them, 2the sons of God saw that the
daughters of men were beautiful, and they married any of them they
chose. 3Then the LORD said, "My Spirit will not contend with[a] man forever, for he is mortal[b]; his days will be a hundred and twenty years."
4The Nephilim were on the earth in those days—and also afterward—when the sons of God went to the daughters of men and had
children by them. They were the heroes of old, men of renown.
5The LORD saw how great man's wickedness on the earth had become, and that every inclination of the thoughts of his heart was only
evil all the time. 6The LORD was grieved that he had made man on the
earth, and his heart was filled with pain. 7So the LORD said, "I will
wipe mankind, whom I have created, from the face of the earth—men
and animals, and creatures that move along the ground, and birds of
the air—for I am grieved that I have made them." 8But Noah found
favor in the eyes of the LORD.
9This is the account of Noah.

Noah was a righteous man, blameless among the people of his
time, and he walked with God. 10Noah had three sons: Shem, Ham
and Japheth.
11Now the earth was corrupt in God's sight and was full of violence.
12God saw how corrupt the earth had become, for all the people on
earth had corrupted their ways. 13So God said to Noah, "I am going to
put an end to all people, for the earth is filled with violence because
of them. I am surely going to destroy both them and the earth. 14So
make yourself an ark of cypress[c] wood; make rooms in it and coat it
with pitch inside and out. 15This is how you are to build it: The ark is
to be 450 feet long, 75 feet wide and 45 feet high.[d] 16Make a roof for it
and finish[e] the ark to within 18 inches[f] of the top. Put a door in the

[a]3 Or *My spirit will not remain in* [b]3 Or *corrupt* [c]14 The meaning of the Hebrew for this word is uncertain. [d]15 Hebrew *300 cubits long, 50 cubits wide and 30 cubits high* (about 140 meters long, 23 meters wide and 13.5 meters high) [e]16 Or *Make an opening for light by finishing* [f]16 Hebrew *a cubit* (about 0.5 meter)

OPEN What recent movie or TV program has done more to corrupt the morals of children than any other in your estimation?

STUDY If you asked the average person, "What is your favorite story in the Bible?" they would probably say Noah. But the story does not start out this nice. **1.** What happened when the "sons of God" (probably the descendants of Seth) intermarried with the "daughters of men" (probably the descendants of violent Cain)? **2.** How did God look upon the condition of the world he had created? What did he decide to do?

APPLY As you look upon the world today, how would you compare it to the world of Noah's day?

OPEN 1. Have you ever made a boat? **2.** How long did it take you to build it?

STUDY In this second installment of the story of the flood, God asks Noah to build an ark. **1.** What does God say about the character of Noah? How does Noah stand in contrast to all of the rest of the people? Was it raining when Noah started to build the ark? **2.** What does God determine to do? Do you think Noah was the only person that God warned or the only person that would listen (v. 13; Heb. 11:7)? **3.** How would you describe the boat that God told Noah to make? Do you think Noah made it in his backyard or some place out of sight? **4.** What does God promise Noah if he will build this boat (v. 18)?

6:2 sons of God ... daughters of men. Some have interpreted this to mean angels who became involved with earthly women. Others interpret this to mean godly men, maybe even descendants of Seth, who became involved with "daughters of men," meaning ungodly women (descendants of Cain).

6:4 Nephilim. The name for large, strong people—"giants." In Numbers the Israelites got to the border of the Promised Land, saw the Nephilim and said they felt like grasshoppers compared to them (Num. 13:33).

6:5 every inclination ... was only evil all the time. This description of humanity is only a few generations after the Fall.

6:6 The LORD was grieved. God did not think he had made a mistake. He had given humanity the choice to obey him or not, to love him or not; however, their choice to turn from him and his love grieved him deeply.

6:7 wipe mankind ... from the face of the earth. What would it be like to give your creation a perfect world and watch them turn it into an evil place? God was not only going to destroy mankind, who had spearheaded the destruction, but even the creatures of the world he had placed under their control.

6:8–9 blameless among the people of his time. The Bible describes Noah as righteous, finding favor in God's eyes, and walking with God. Noah was the one person in all the world at that time who understood the relationship God originally intended to have with people. The flood was God's reset button for human history.

6:14 make yourself an ark ... coat it with pitch. The other place where the Hebrew word for "ark" is used is for the basket that held baby Moses. Like Noah, Moses' mother coated her little "ark" with pitch to keep the water out (Ex. 2:3).

6:16 Make a roof. God was concerned with the practical. Noah was building a boat that had to last for forty days of rain and 150 days of floating. Because of that, air circulation had to be a concern. They could not have open areas for windows or the rain would come into the boat. This roof may have had an overhang and some open windows directly underneath it for light and air.

Who is included in this contract? **5.** If you were building this boat, what would be the most difficult problem you would face?

APPLY 1. If God called you on the phone today and asked you to build a boat the size of a football field, what would you say? **2.** If God didn't ask you to build a boat, what else might he ask you to do today? Are you willing to do it?

OPEN 1. What is the closest you have come to experiencing a flood? **2.** If your house was about to be washed away, what three things would you quickly grab, not including pets or children?

side of the ark and make lower, middle and upper decks. 17I am going
to bring floodwaters on the earth to destroy all life under the heavens, every creature that has the breath of life in it. Everything on
earth will perish. 18But I will establish my covenant with you, and you
will enter the ark—you and your sons and your wife and your sons'
wives with you. 19You are to bring into the ark two of all living creatures, male and female, to keep them alive with you. 20Two of every
kind of bird, of every kind of animal and of every kind of creature that
moves along the ground will come to you to be kept alive. 21You are to
take every kind of food that is to be eaten and store it away as food
for you and for them."

22Noah did everything just as God commanded him.

7 The LORD then said to Noah, "Go into the ark, you and your
whole family, because I have found you righteous in this generation. 2Take with you seven[a] of every kind of clean animal, a male and
its mate, and two of every kind of unclean animal, a male and its
mate, 3and also seven of every kind of bird, male and female, to keep
their various kinds alive throughout the earth. 4Seven days from now
I will send rain on the earth for forty days and forty nights, and I will
wipe from the face of the earth every living creature I have made."

5And Noah did all that the LORD commanded him.

6Noah was six hundred years old when the floodwaters came on
the earth. 7And Noah and his sons and his wife and his sons' wives
entered the ark to escape the waters of the flood. 8Pairs of clean and
unclean animals, of birds and of all creatures that move along the
ground, 9male and female, came to Noah and entered the ark, as God
had commanded Noah. 10And after the seven days the floodwaters
came on the earth.

11In the six hundredth year of Noah's life, on the seventeenth day
of the second month—on that day all the springs of the great deep
burst forth, and the floodgates of the heavens were opened. 12And
rain fell on the earth forty days and forty nights.

13On that very day Noah and his sons, Shem, Ham and Japheth, to-

[a]2 Or *seven pairs*; also in verse 3

6:17 destroy all life under the heavens. The Bible is quite clear in saying that *all life* was destroyed on earth. This has been understood to refer to a universal, worldwide flood. Some have suggested that the flood did not have to be worldwide to destroy all life because the earth was so much newer and less populated. Still others say that Moses was writing about the world as he knew it, the ancient Near East. Nevertheless, there was a flood and only Noah, his family and the animals in the ark survived.

6:18 establish my covenant. A covenant is an agreement, almost like a contract. It is a promise made between two parties. God made a covenant with Noah to save his family if Noah built the ark and entered into it by faith in God. After the flood, Noah built an altar and God gave the rainbow as a sign that he would not destroy the earth again with a flood.

6:19 two of all living creatures. God gave Noah two instructions about the animals to take in the ark. A pair of each animal—male and female—was needed to replenish the earth after the flood. In addition, he was to take seven pairs of the kinds of animals that could be used for eating and for sacrifice (7:2).

6:22 just as God commanded him. Noah was completely obedient. He did not cut corners, but did *exactly* what God said.

7:1 Go into the ark. After months were spent constructing the vessel according to God's instructions, it was time for Noah and his family to enter the boat that would save them. **righteous.** Noah lived according to God's ways, and this set him apart from his peers. Second Peter 2:5 suggests that Noah had warned the people around him that God was angry, but no one had listened.

7:4 forty days and forty nights. Rain lasting for this long is impossible today because of the conditions of our atmosphere. Some speculate that there was a thermal water layer covering the earth that was condensed and then dumped on the entire world to cause the flood (v. 10). In this case, God demonstrated his power through a natural phenomenon.

7:7 entered the ark to escape. Noah and his family were untouched by God's judgment. They were safely tucked away in the ark when the first raindrops fell.

7:13 When the floods covered the earth, God's judgment was complete.

gether with his wife and the wives of his three sons, entered the ark.
14They had with them every wild animal according to its kind, all livestock according to their kinds, every creature that moves along the
ground according to its kind and every bird according to its kind,
everything with wings. 15Pairs of all creatures that have the breath of
life in them came to Noah and entered the ark. 16The animals going in
were male and female of every living thing, as God had commanded
Noah. Then the LORD shut him in.
17For forty days the flood kept coming on the earth, and as the waters increased they lifted the ark high above the earth. 18The waters
rose and increased greatly on the earth, and the ark floated on the
surface of the water. 19They rose greatly on the earth, and all the high
mountains under the entire heavens were covered. 20The waters rose
and covered the mountains to a depth of more than twenty feet.[a,b]
21Every living thing that moved on the earth perished—birds, livestock, wild animals, all the creatures that swarm over the earth, and
all mankind. 22Everything on dry land that had the breath of life in its
nostrils died. 23Every living thing on the face of the earth was wiped
out; men and animals and the creatures that move along the ground
and the birds of the air were wiped from the earth. Only Noah was
left, and those with him in the ark.
24The waters flooded the earth for a hundred and fifty days.

8 But God remembered Noah and all the wild animals and the livestock that were with him in the ark, and he sent a wind over the
earth, and the waters receded. 2Now the springs of the deep and the
floodgates of the heavens had been closed, and the rain had stopped
falling from the sky. 3The water receded steadily from the earth. At the
end of the hundred and fifty days the water had gone down, 4and on
the seventeenth day of the seventh month the ark came to rest on the
mountains of Ararat. 5The waters continued to recede until the tenth
month, and on the first day of the tenth month the tops of the mountains became visible.
6After forty days Noah opened the window he had made in the ark
7and sent out a raven, and it kept flying back and forth until the water
had dried up from the earth. 8Then he sent out a dove to see if the
water had receded from the surface of the ground. 9But the dove
could find no place to set its feet because there was water over all the
surface of the earth; so it returned to Noah in the ark. He reached out
his hand and took the dove and brought it back to himself in the ark.
10He waited seven more days and again sent out the dove from the

[a]20 Hebrew *fifteen cubits* (about 6.9 meters) [b]20 Or *rose more than twenty feet, and the mountains were covered*

STUDY In the midst of a wicked and corrupt world, God asks one person to build a boat the size of a football field and fill it with animals. **1.** Do you think Noah knew what he was getting into when he said, "yes" to God? **2.** How do you think Noah's wife has been feeling all of the years that Noah has been working on the ark? Do you think it took faith on her part to pack all her stuff and move into the boat (remember she only had seven days warning)? **3.** What do you think the ark smelled like with all of the animals? Who cleaned up the elephant droppings? What did Mrs. Noah say to her husband over supper? **4.** How do you think the people inside the boat felt when it started raining? When the water started to rise? When the water covered the earth? **5.** In the 40 days of rain and another 150 days of waiting for the water to subside, how would you have felt? **6.** What is the lesson for you in the dove and the olive branch? **7.** What is the first thing Noah did when his feet were on dry ground? What do you think he said to God?

APPLY 1. If you had to compare your situation today to a flood, where are you right now: (a) Feeling a few raindrops? (b) It's starting to pour? (c) It's getting over my head? (d) It's starting to subside? (e) I'm seeing the dove and olive branch? **2.** How good are you at waiting on God for the water to subside? **3.** Where do you feel right now that you are waiting or "on hold"?

Only eight people survived to replenish God's creation.

7:14 wild animal ... livestock ... creature ... bird. God preserved all of his creation. A selection of *every* animal, livestock, creature of the ground, and bird had a place on the ark with Noah and his family.

7:16 the LORD shut him in. Before he sent his holy judgment on the world, God demonstrated his loving concern and protection for the man who had remained faithful to him by closing the door of the ark that would save his life and the lives of all those with him.

7:20 mountains ... more than twenty feet. The ark was able to float freely because the water covered the mountains by at least twenty feet. Even the highest mountains in the area, the mountains of Ararat (8:4), which are about 17,000 feet high, were covered by the waters.

7:22 breath of life. The creatures that God called "very good" (1:31) now were dead because of sin.

8:1 God remembered Noah. With floodwaters covering all the territory under judgment, the Lord kept Noah and his family safe and prepared to return them to dry land.

ark. [11]When the dove returned to him in the evening, there in its beak
was a freshly plucked olive leaf! Then Noah knew that the water had
receded from the earth. [12]He waited seven more days and sent the
dove out again, but this time it did not return to him.

[13]By the first day of the first month of Noah's six hundred and first
year, the water had dried up from the earth. Noah then removed the
covering from the ark and saw that the surface of the ground was dry.
[14]By the twenty-seventh day of the second month the earth was completely dry.

[15]Then God said to Noah, [16]"Come out of the ark, you and your wife
and your sons and their wives. [17]Bring out every kind of living creature that is with you—the birds, the animals, and all the creatures
that move along the ground—so they can multiply on the earth and
be fruitful and increase in number upon it."

[18]So Noah came out, together with his sons and his wife and his
sons' wives. [19]All the animals and all the creatures that move along
the ground and all the birds—everything that moves on the earth—
came out of the ark, one kind after another.

[20]Then Noah built an altar to the LORD and, taking some of all the
clean animals and clean birds, he sacrificed burnt offerings on it.
[21]The LORD smelled the pleasing aroma and said in his heart: "Never
again will I curse the ground because of man, even though[a] every inclination of his heart is evil from childhood. And never again will I destroy all living creatures, as I have done.

[22]"As long as the earth endures,
seedtime and harvest,
cold and heat,
summer and winter,
day and night
will never cease."

God's Covenant With Noah

9 Then God blessed Noah and his sons, saying to them, "Be fruitful and increase in number and fill the earth. [2]The fear and dread
of you will fall upon all the beasts of the earth and all the birds of the
air, upon every creature that moves along the ground, and upon all
the fish of the sea; they are given into your hands. [3]Everything that

[a]21 Or *man, for*

OPEN 1. What is the most spectacular rainbow you have ever seen? **2.** In school, what did you give your "special one" to seal your relationship?

STUDY In this last episode of the story of the flood, God promises Noah a new covenant and

8:11 the dove returned. Imagine the joy on the ark when Noah's winged scout finally brought back evidence of plant life on the earth. The dove's choice of food indicated that new life had begun to grow and therefore Noah's family could survive outside the ark. God had fulfilled his promise and saved Noah and his family from the flood!

8:17 multiply. As he did at Creation (1:22), God gave his blessing to the creatures that would populate the planet.

8:20 burnt offerings. Noah had preserved and cared for the clean animals and birds on the ark for this very purpose. God's faithful servant left no doubt as to where his priorities lay. As soon as his feet hit dry ground, he was busy building a structure for sacrifice and worship of the Lord.

8:21 smelled the pleasing aroma. The Lord accepted Noah's sacrifice and took pleasure in his worship. **Never ... curse ... never destroy.** God promised that he would never again destroy the earth again by flood. See 2 Peter 3:3–10 for how God will destroy the earth in the future. **every ... is evil.** We are all born sinful and our natural tendency is to go astray and forget God. Only by God's grace are we able to resist temptation and live for him.

8:22 As long as the earth endures. God reestablished the seasons after the destruction that the flood caused and promised not to disrupt them again until the end of time.

9:1 God blessed Noah. The image here is of God expressing his extreme pleasure with his faithful servant.

9:2–3 given into your hands ... Everything that lives and moves will be food. What seems to have changed in the post-deluge world is the

lives and moves will be food for you. Just as I gave you the green
plants, I now give you everything.
4"But you must not eat meat that has its lifeblood still in it. 5And for
your lifeblood I will surely demand an accounting. I will demand an
accounting from every animal. And from each man, too, I will demand an accounting for the life of his fellow man.

6"Whoever sheds the blood of man,
by man shall his blood be shed;
for in the image of God
has God made man.

7As for you, be fruitful and increase in number; multiply on the earth
and increase upon it."
8Then God said to Noah and to his sons with him: 9"I now establish
my covenant with you and with your descendants after you 10and
with every living creature that was with you—the birds, the livestock
and all the wild animals, all those that came out of the ark with you—
every living creature on earth. 11I establish my covenant with you:
Never again will all life be cut off by the waters of a flood; never again
will there be a flood to destroy the earth."
12And God said, "This is the sign of the covenant I am making between me and you and every living creature with you, a covenant for
all generations to come: 13I have set my rainbow in the clouds, and it
will be the sign of the covenant between me and the earth. 14When-
ever I bring clouds over the earth and the rainbow appears in the
clouds, 15I will remember my covenant between me and you and all
living creatures of every kind. Never again will the waters become a
flood to destroy all life. 16Whenever the rainbow appears in the
clouds, I will see it and remember the everlasting covenant between
God and all living creatures of every kind on the earth."
17So God said to Noah, "This is the sign of the covenant I have established between me and all life on the earth."

The Sons of Noah

18The sons of Noah who came out of the ark were Shem, Ham and
Japheth. (Ham was the father of Canaan.) 19These were the three sons
of Noah, and from them came the people who were scattered over the
earth.
20Noah, a man of the soil, proceeded[a] to plant a vineyard. 21When

[a]20 *Or soil, was the first*

seals it with a rainbow. **1.** If you had just gone through the most frightening and devastating time in your life in which everything in your world had been destroyed except for your family and the animals, how would you feel? What would you want to hear from God? **2.** In Biblical times, human sacrifice was practiced by many of the cultures in the world. What does God say about human sacrifice? What does God allow Noah to eat for the first time (v. 3)? What is the condition? Why? **3.** What is the promise (covenant) that God makes with Noah? What is the sign? What causes this sign to appear? Why would God use this natural phenomena to remind Noah of their covenant?

APPLY **1.** What is the closest you have come to a time when your world came to an end and like Noah you felt absolutely desolate? **2.** What did God give you at that time as a sign that gave you hope and encouragement? **3.** Where do you need a sign today to give you new hope?

OPEN **1.** What fruits or vegetables have you grown? **2.** What is your favorite recipe?

STUDY In a world that was full of wickedness, one man stood out as righteous and blameless. After the flood God gave a new covenant to Noah that he would never

animals' attitude toward humans. After the flood, animals and birds developed an innate fear of humans. People were *now free to eat the animals for nourishment.*

9:4 meat ... lifeblood. Blood represented the source of the animal's life. Since all life comes from God, the blood could be used only in sacrifice to him. You can read more about this restriction in Leviticus 17:11,12.

9:6 Whoever sheds the blood ... his blood be shed. God gave humans the responsibility of carrying out justice for those found guilty of murder. He expected Noah and his descendants to treat murder as seriously as he did. **image of God ... God made man.** Because God identifies humans so closely with himself, he views the taking of a human life as an act of contempt toward him.

9:9 establish my covenant. Noah, the only person judged to be righteous by God during the time of the Flood, was rewarded for his faithfulness with a personal promise from the Lord. Abraham (15:9–21; 17:1–27) and David (2 Sam. 7:5–16) received similar promises or covenants from the Lord.

9:11–13 Never again. This was not simply a promise to Noah and his descendants. It was an eternal covenant, an oath that God would never again wipe out his creation again by a flood. God made the rainbow as a sign, a reminder, of his covenant promise.

again destroy the earth. **1.** Is it hard for you to believe that a man like Noah who "walked with God" could disgrace himself by getting drunk right after he had been used of God in such a mighty way? How would you describe your feelings about Noah for acting this way? **2.** How did Noah's children react when they heard what Noah had done? **3.** What is the lesson in this story for you?

APPLY Have you ever experienced the disappointment of seeing someone you admired fall into disgrace? How did you deal with your disappointment? Were you able to forgive them as God did Noah?

OPEN 1. How good are you at remembering names? **2.** In your family, who likes to read about ancient history and anthropology?

STUDY Scientists now believe that all people can be traced to a few sources. **1.** Why do you think this list of the descendants of Noah is in the Bible? Why would it be important to God's people to understand the ties between themselves and the various groups around them? **2.** Archeology has uncovered the remains of many of these places and

he drank some of its wine, he became drunk and lay uncovered inside
his tent. 22Ham, the father of Canaan, saw his father's nakedness and
told his two brothers outside. 23But Shem and Japheth took a garment and laid it across their shoulders; then they walked in backward
and covered their father's nakedness. Their faces were turned the
other way so that they would not see their father's nakedness.
24When Noah awoke from his wine and found out what his youngest son had done to him, 25he said,

"Cursed be Canaan!
The lowest of slaves
will he be to his brothers."

26He also said,

"Blessed be the LORD, the God of Shem!
May Canaan be the slave of Shem.[a]
27May God extend the territory of Japheth[b];
may Japheth live in the tents of Shem,
and may Canaan be his[c] slave."

28After the flood Noah lived 350 years. 29Altogether, Noah lived 950
years, and then he died.

The Table of Nations

10 This is the account of Shem, Ham and Japheth, Noah's sons, who themselves had sons after the flood.

The Japhethites

2The sons[d] of Japheth:
Gomer, Magog, Madai, Javan, Tubal, Meshech and Tiras.
3The sons of Gomer:
Ashkenaz, Riphath and Togarmah.

[a]26 Or *be his slave* [b]27 *Japheth* sounds like the Hebrew for *extend.* [c]27 Or *their* [d]2 *Sons* may mean *descendants* or *successors* or *nations*; also in verses 3, 4, 6, 7, 20-23, 29 and 31.

9:21 he became drunk and lay uncovered inside his tent. Immodesty and lowered inhibitions are common results of drunkenness. Noah, the apple of God's eye in chapters 6–8, proved to be all too human when he overindulged in the fruits of his vineyard.

9:22 Ham The reference is not simply to Ham's son, whose name was Canaan (10:6), but to the nation of Canaanites that would be their descendants (and would be Israel's enemies). **told his two brothers.** This seems to have been more than just a simple sharing of information. Ham may have made fun of his father or showed some kind of disrespect in his report to his brothers.

9:23 faces were turned. Shem and Japheth went out of their way to spare their father any further humiliation or disgrace. They did not want even to glance at his nakedness.

9:24 Noah awoke from his wine. When the effects of the alcohol wore off, Noah was given the news of Ham's disgraceful actions.

9:25 Cursed be Canaan. The descendants of Ham received a sentence of judgment. God already knew the type of people the Canaanites would be and already was preparing them for their future defeat by the Israelites. Their sinfulness would be the basis for God's *judgment against* them.

10:1 Chapter 10 reports the daunting task of Noah's family members to repopulate the earth. Naturally, several biblical nations find their origin in Noah's family members, including the Egyptians, Greeks and Hebrews.

10:2 Japheth. Japheth, Noah's oldest son, represents many of the biblical nations in what is now known as Europe and Asia Minor. From Japheth, the Greeks became a small, but important nation. **Magog** was the father of the Scythian people. **Madai.** The Medes, who teamed with the Babylonians to put an end to Assyria, are descendants of Japheth's son, Madai. **Javan.** The father of the Greek people. **Magog, Tubal, Meshech.** All are mentioned in Assyrian inscriptions discovered by archaeologists. Japheth may have been mentioned least in the story of Noah, but his influence in history is great.

[4]The sons of Javan:
Elishah, Tarshish, the Kittim and the Rodanim.[a] [5](From these
the maritime peoples spread out into their territories by their
clans within their nations, each with its own language.)

The Hamites

[6]The sons of Ham:
Cush, Mizraim,[b] Put and Canaan.
[7]The sons of Cush:
Seba, Havilah, Sabtah, Raamah and Sabteca.
The sons of Raamah:
Sheba and Dedan.

[8]Cush was the father[c] of Nimrod, who grew to be a mighty warrior
on the earth. [9]He was a mighty hunter before the LORD; that is why it
is said, "Like Nimrod, a mighty hunter before the LORD." [10]The first
centers of his kingdom were Babylon, Erech, Akkad and Calneh, in[d]
Shinar.[e] [11]From that land he went to Assyria, where he built Nineveh,
Rehoboth Ir,[f] Calah [12]and Resen, which is between Nineveh and Calah; that is the great city.

[13]Mizraim was the father of
the Ludites, Anamites, Lehabites, Naphtuhites, [14]Pathrusites,
Casluhites (from whom the Philistines came) and Caphtorites.
[15]Canaan was the father of
Sidon his firstborn,[g] and of the Hittites, [16]Jebusites, Amorites,
Girgashites, [17]Hivites, Arkites, Sinites, [18]Arvadites, Zemarites
and Hamathites.

Later the Canaanite clans scattered [19]and the borders of Canaan
reached from Sidon toward Gerar as far as Gaza, and then toward
Sodom, Gomorrah, Admah and Zeboiim, as far as Lasha.

[a]4 Some manuscripts of the Masoretic Text and Samaritan Pentateuch (see also Septuagint and 1 Chron. 1:7); most manuscripts of the Masoretic Text *Dodanim* [b]6 That is, Egypt; also in verse 13 [c]8 *Father* may mean *ancestor* or *predecessor* or *founder*; also in verses 13, 15, 24 and 26. [d]10 Or *Erech and Akkad—all of them in* [e]10 That is, Babylonia [f]11 Or *Nineveh with its city squares* [g]15 Or *of the Sidonians, the foremost*

people groups, such as Nineveh, Babylon, Cush (lower Egypt) etc. What does this tell you about the Bible? How important is it to your faith that these names and places actually existed? **3.** If you could ask God one question about this list of descendants, what would it be?

APPLY 1. If you had to track on a map where your descendants came from, what would it be? **2.** As you get older, are you more or less interested in your roots?

10:6 Ham. The descendants of Ham are the origin of several biblical nations. **Cush** lived in the upper region of the Nile River. **Mizraim,** reference to the upper and lower regions of Egypt. **Put** could be the father of what is commonly referred to today as Somalia. The recipient of Noah's curse, Ham, heralded a number of descendants who became future *enemies of* God's people, including the Egyptians, the Canaanites, the Amorites and the Hittites. The Philistines, of the giant Goliath's fame, are also descendants of Ham.

10:12 great city. Nimrod was the great-great-grandson of Noah and the founder of the "great city" of Nineveh. Later, history records Jonah's assignment to preach repentance to Nineveh—a great city gone bad.

10:14 Noah's family continued to form pieces of a people-group puzzle. The Pathrusites covered the upper half of Egypt. The Philistines are the direct descendants of the Casluhites. The Philistines temporarily called tiny Crete home—an unlikely spot to raise a giant like Goliath (1 Sam. 17:4)! The Caphtorites also claimed the tiny island of Crete as their homeland.

10:15 Canaan. Behind the familiar name of the fertile stretch of land between the Mediterranean Sea and barren desert is a person. Canaan, one of Ham's many sons, became the namesake of this central stage where much of the Old Testament story takes place. His son, Sidon, became the namesake of a powerful Canaanite city.

10:16 When the children of Israel sought to enter the land of Canaan, they came across several people groups who already called Canaan "home." Although the people of Canaan were generally referred to as Canaanites, the Jebusites, in fact, were residents of Jerusalem (2 Sam. 5:6). The Amorites were also nestled in the hills of Canaan when the Israelites arrived (Josh. 3:10).

10:19 Sodom, Gomorrah. The people of Sodom and Gomorrah were so evil that God would erase them and their cities from existence (19:24,25).

[20]These are the sons of Ham by their clans and languages, in their territories and nations.

The Semites

[21]Sons were also born to Shem, whose older brother was[a] Japheth; Shem was the ancestor of all the sons of Eber.

[22]The sons of Shem:
Elam, Asshur, Arphaxad, Lud and Aram.
[23]The sons of Aram:
Uz, Hul, Gether and Meshech.[b]
[24]Arphaxad was the father of[c] Shelah,
and Shelah the father of Eber.
[25]Two sons were born to Eber:
One was named Peleg,[d] because in his time the earth was divided; his brother was named Joktan.
[26]Joktan was the father of
Almodad, Sheleph, Hazarmaveth, Jerah, [27]Hadoram, Uzal,
Diklah, [28]Obal, Abimael, Sheba, [29]Ophir, Havilah and Jobab. All
these were sons of Joktan.

[30]The region where they lived stretched from Mesha toward Sephar, in the eastern hill country.

[31]These are the sons of Shem by their clans and languages, in their territories and nations.

[32]These are the clans of Noah's sons, according to their lines of descent, within their nations. From these the nations spread out over the earth after the flood.

The Tower of Babel

11 Now the whole world had one language and a common speech. [2]As men moved eastward,[e] they found a plain in Shinar[f] and settled there.

[3]They said to each other, "Come, let's make bricks and bake them

[a]*21 Or Shem, the older brother of* [b]*23* See Septuagint and 1 Chron. 1:17; Hebrew *Mash* [c]*24* Hebrew; Septuagint *father of Cainan, and Cainan was the father of* [d]*25 Peleg* means *division.* [e]*2* Or *from the east;* or *in the east* [f]*2* That is, Babylonia

OPEN Did you like to play with mud as a kid?

STUDY In Biblical times, the people groups that migrated east to the mouth of the Tigris and Euphrates Rivers (Persian Gulf) developed into an early civilization with a king, priests and cultic practices with a common language. **1.** Why do you

10:21 Shem is referred to as the "chosen line" because the Hebrews descended from him. In Hebrew language, the name Eber (a descendant of Shem) is the origin of the word "Hebrew." All of the Hebrew nation descended from Shem and Eber.

10:25 The earth was divided. This refers to the results of the next event in chapter 11—the Tower of Babel. Here, God dispersed the people all across the earth as a result of their prideful behavior.

10:26 Joktan. Joktan's name means "smaller," perhaps indicating a shorter stature for this father of many Arabian kingdoms.

10:28 Sheba. Solomon's hospitality toward the Queen of Sheba highlights the legacy of this son of Shem. Although she took her place much later in the line of descent, she inherited a prosperous region.

10:29 Ophir. Only a sailor could navigate the region of Ophir, accessible only by watercraft. Once there, one would find mountains of gold, the source for much of Solomon's wealth. Solomon imported loads of Ophir's precious metal, making him the richest man who has ever lived (1 Kin. 9:28).

11:1–9 This story explains why there are hundreds of dialects and languages representing thousands of people groups throughout the entire world. The people who remained after the flood began building a great city for their own reputation. The culprit of their demise was pride; the symbol of their pride was a tower reaching toward the skies. After God scattered the people abroad and confused their languages as punishment, the tower became appropriately known as the Tower of Babel.

11:1 the whole world. The world was a relatively new one. The flood had destroyed all of the earth except for Noah's family, from whom God repopulated the earth. However, it was not long until human pride resurfaced. The story of Babel is further tribute to the persistence of sinful human nature and emphasizes the need for an ultimate Savior.

thoroughly." They used brick instead of stone, and tar for mortar.
4Then they said, "Come, let us build ourselves a city, with a tower that
reaches to the heavens, so that we may make a name for ourselves
and not be scattered over the face of the whole earth."
5But the LORD came down to see the city and the tower that the
men were building. 6The LORD said, "If as one people speaking the
same language they have begun to do this, then nothing they plan to
do will be impossible for them. 7Come, let us go down and confuse
their language so they will not understand each other."
8So the LORD scattered them from there over all the earth, and they
stopped building the city. 9That is why it was called Babel[a]—because
there the LORD confused the language of the whole world. From there
the LORD scattered them over the face of the whole earth.

From Shem to Abram

10This is the account of Shem.

Two years after the flood, when Shem was 100 years old, he
became the father[b] of Arphaxad. 11And after he became the father of
Arphaxad, Shem lived 500 years and had other sons and daughters.
12When Arphaxad had lived 35 years, he became the father of Shelah. 13And after he became the father of Shelah, Arphaxad lived 403
years and had other sons and daughters.[c]
14When Shelah had lived 30 years, he became the father of Eber.
15And after he became the father of Eber, Shelah lived 403 years and
had other sons and daughters.
16When Eber had lived 34 years, he became the father of Peleg.
17And after he became the father of Peleg, Eber lived 430 years and
had other sons and daughters.
18When Peleg had lived 30 years, he became the father of Reu.
19And after he became the father of Reu, Peleg lived 209 years and
had other sons and daughters.
20When Reu had lived 32 years, he became the father of Serug.

[a]9 That is, Babylon; *Babel* sounds like the Hebrew for *confused*. [b]10 *Father* may mean *ancestor*; also in verses 11-25. [c]12,13 Hebrew; Septuagint (see also Luke 3:35, 36 and note at Gen. 10:24) *35 years, he became the father of Cainan. 13And after he became the father of Cainan, Arphaxad lived 430 years and had other sons and daughters, and then he died. When Cainan had lived 130 years, he became the father of Shelah. And after he became the father of Shelah, Cainan lived 330 years and had other sons and daughters*

think this early civilization wanted to build a tower? **2.** How did God throw a monkey wrench into the building project? Can you imagine what happened?

APPLY 1. What are you putting all of your energy into right now? **2.** Is this going to be a monument to yourself or God?

OPEN 1. In your family tree, who lived the longest? **2.** Where are you in the birth order with your brothers and sisters? Do you think this has made a difference in your personality?

STUDY In the Old Testament, genealogies are important and especially this genealogy because it leads up to Abram, (later named Abraham), the father of the special covenant people in the Bible. **1.** What do you learn about Abram from this passage? Where was he living when he was born? Who was his father? His brothers? What happened to one of his brothers and his brother's son? **2.** Do you think Abram's father deserves some of the credit for leaving the comfort of home and going to a new place far from home? Do you think Abram's father had "wander-lust" or some feeling of God's calling? **3.** What have you learned in the first eleven chapters of Genesis about God's story of salvation?

11:3 brick. Archaeologists have discovered remnants of mud brick and tar as the choice building material of that day. The Tower of Babel was no easy architectural feat. It was most likely in the form of a ziggurat—a pyramid with giant steps or ramps leading up the sides. Ziggurats as high as 300 feet have been documented.

11:4 us ... ourselves ... we. Me. Myself. I. If ever a common language of humankind were developed, it would have these three words at its core. An inordinate concern for self is the hallmark of the human race, and the architects of the tower were no exception. At a height of nearly 300 feet, this monstrosity of human pride was offensive in its feeble attempt to reach God's level.

11:6 Imagine what the human race would have become if it were allowed to pursue world-wide united domination! God's intent in destroying the city was not his own ego versus human ego. Rather, as a loving Father sensing strong rebellion, he sought to put an end to their plans. The tower was not destroyed for his sake. Instead, he provided for their own good. Its destruction encouraged response, not rebellion.

11:7 confuse their language. Without a common language, the builders would not be able to communicate. Thus, the temple would have to be abandoned and left incomplete.

11:8 scattered. Imagine bricklayers and masonry workers throwing down their tools in frustration over the sudden end to their plans. The city's inhabitants filled the roads in masses, leaving the city in confusion on their way to multiple destinations. Perhaps, in their own new language, they taught succeeding generations about the day they learned the futility of human achievement apart from God.

11:10–26 As the chosen line, the family tree of Shem is a key piece of biblical history. In ten generations, the line of Shem is traced to the outset of Abram's story and the beginning of family blessing. Noah's blessing on his son Shem begins with the birth of the entire Jewish nation through Abram.

APPLY **1.** As you look back, what did your grandparents start that is still being carried on in your family? **2.** How has this effected the person you are today?

[21]And after he became the father of Serug, Reu lived 207 years and
had other sons and daughters.
[22]When Serug had lived 30 years, he became the father of Nahor.
[23]And after he became the father of Nahor, Serug lived 200 years and
had other sons and daughters.
[24]When Nahor had lived 29 years, he became the father of Terah.
[25]And after he became the father of Terah, Nahor lived 119 years and
had other sons and daughters.
[26]After Terah had lived 70 years, he became the father of Abram,
Nahor and Haran.

[27]This is the account of Terah.

Terah became the father of Abram, Nahor and Haran. And Haran
became the father of Lot. [28]While his father Terah was still alive, Haran died in Ur of the Chaldeans, in the land of his birth. [29]Abram and
Nahor both married. The name of Abram's wife was Sarai, and the
name of Nahor's wife was Milcah; she was the daughter of Haran, the
father of both Milcah and Iscah. [30]Now Sarai was barren; she had no
children.
[31]Terah took his son Abram, his grandson Lot son of Haran, and his
daughter-in-law Sarai, the wife of his son Abram, and together they
set out from Ur of the Chaldeans to go to Canaan. But when they
came to Haran, they settled there.
[32]Terah lived 205 years, and he died in Haran.

OPEN **1.** Where is "home" for you? When did you first leave home? **2.** What did you take with you? Leave behind?

STUDY The story of Abram begins with the death of his father in Haran and moving with his family four hundred miles to the south into a semi-nomadic land called Canaan? **1.** What was the main reason Abram was willing to pick up and take off into the unknown? How would you react if God called you on the phone today and asked you what he asked Abram? **2.** What did God promise

The Call of Abram

12 The LORD had said to Abram, "Leave your country, your people and your father's household and go to the land I will
show you.

[2]"I will make you into a great nation
and I will bless you;
I will make your name great,
and you will be a blessing.
[3]I will bless those who bless you,
and whoever curses you I will curse;
and all peoples on earth
will be blessed through you."

11:26 Abram, Nahor and Haran. Haran was the father of Lot, one of the main characters in the story of Sodom and Gomorrah's destruction. However, tracing his family history reveals it did not have to be that way. The Bible records the fact that Haran, Lot's father, died. According to custom, Abram became responsible for his nephew. How tragic that with a predominantly God-fearing family history, Lot did not have more of a godly future.

11:28 Ur of the Chaldeans. Abram was raised in a wealthy and influential area known for its vast trade relations and an ever-increasing library. Most likely, Abram was a well-educated man—an important foundation for the crucial decisions he would face during his life.

11:30 barren. Sarai was unable to have children. This foreshadows God's provision. God would soon promise to make Abram the father of many nations by miraculously giving his barren wife a child.

11:31 Haran. This city played an important role in Abram's family. It became Abram's first home on his way to Canaan. Generations later, his descendants Isaac and Jacob would find their wives in Haran.

12:1 Leave your country. Before there was a promising future, Abram needed to renounce his past. He had to leave the familiar in order to find his future. Following an indirect route via the rivers, Abram left Ur to head to Haran. And from Haran, he eventually settled in Canaan.

12:2–3 God did not predict Abram's future. He promised it. His promise to Abram assured him of blessing, reputation, influence and legacy. At seventy-five years of age, who would not long to receive such a promise? However, at that time, Abram could not have imagined the extent of God's promise. Out of his descendants the entire Jewish nation and, eventually, the Savior himself would arise.

4So Abram left, as the LORD had told him; and Lot went with him.
Abram was seventy-five years old when he set out from Haran. 5He
took his wife Sarai, his nephew Lot, all the possessions they had accumulated and the people they had acquired in Haran, and they set
out for the land of Canaan, and they arrived there.
6Abram traveled through the land as far as the site of the great tree
of Moreh at Shechem. At that time the Canaanites were in the land.
7The LORD appeared to Abram and said, "To your offspring[a] I will give
this land." So he built an altar there to the LORD, who had appeared
to him.
8From there he went on toward the hills east of Bethel and pitched
his tent, with Bethel on the west and Ai on the east. There he built an
altar to the LORD and called on the name of the LORD. 9Then Abram
set out and continued toward the Negev.

Abram in Egypt

10Now there was a famine in the land, and Abram went down to
Egypt to live there for a while because the famine was severe. 11As he
was about to enter Egypt, he said to his wife Sarai, "I know what a
beautiful woman you are. 12When the Egyptians see you, they will
say, 'This is his wife.' Then they will kill me but will let you live. 13Say
you are my sister, so that I will be treated well for your sake and my life
will be spared because of you."
14When Abram came to Egypt, the Egyptians saw that she was a very
beautiful woman. 15And when Pharaoh's officials saw her, they praised
her to Pharaoh, and she was taken into his palace. 16He treated Abram
well for her sake, and Abram acquired sheep and cattle, male and female donkeys, menservants and maidservants, and camels.
17But the LORD inflicted serious diseases on Pharaoh and his
household because of Abram's wife Sarai. 18So Pharaoh summoned
Abram. "What have you done to me?" he said. "Why didn't you tell me

[a]7 Or *seed*

Abram if he obeyed? Do you think Sarai (Abram's wife) deserves any credit for going along with Abram? Who has traveled with you in your faith journey? **3.** Do you think Abram realized what he was getting into when he started on his journey?

APPLY 1. How many bathroom stops would it take for you to travel 400 miles on foot with your family? **2.** Would you be willing to pick up and move your entire family when you were 75 if God asked you to do this?

OPEN What did your parents do if they caught you telling a lie or a half truth?

STUDY Famine was common in biblical times when there was not enough rainfall. Soon after Abram and his family arrived in Canaan, Abram had to deal with famine. **1.** Do you think Abram made a good decision to go to Egypt? What about God's promise in verse 2? How would you have felt? **2.** Is it hard for you to believe that a man like Abram could ask his wife to tell a lie to save his own skin (vv. 11–13)? **3.** Why do you think Abram got out of this predicament the way he did? What does this tell you about God's grace?

12:4 Abram left. Delay was not in Abram's vocabulary. Although he was short on specific instructions, Abram packed up his belongings, got his nephew Lot and got going. Abram's life is a model of faith in action.

12:5 people they had acquired. Abram's response to God's promise affected several people in the immediate picture. Of course, his family members were along for the ride. But his extended "family" of servants and workers who tended his wealth of flocks and herds were also affected by the news.

12:7 The LORD appeared. While the Lord's appearance would be an unusual event to most modern readers, it was not an uncommon experience for Abram. The altar became a special symbol between God and Abram. When God appeared to Abram and affirmed his promise to him, Abram often built an altar to remember the experience. The stone and earthen altar would remain as a visible reminder of his journey of faith.

12:8 Bethel. About 12 miles north of Jerusalem is Bethel, a landmark in Jewish history. The site of another of Abram's altars, the city of Bethel also marked the future place of Jacob's dream with God and housed the Ark of the Covenant for some time as well.

12:9 Negev. Abram's route took him through the Negev, literally "dry land"—referring to the southern desert wasteland. At the end of this desert trip, Abram would be eager for the resources found in the lush landscape of nearby Egypt.

12:10 went down to Egypt. How easy it would have been for Abram to give up on God's promises at the point of the famine? Was this land of shortage the outcome of God's promise? Instead of giving up, Abram was going on to Egypt, where the Nile River provided year-round resources.

12:11 beautiful. Sarai was admired by many for her beauty. Abram feared her beauty would impede their safe travel among potentially desirous male suitors.

12:13 Say you are my sister. Abram tried to rationalize his lie since Sarai was, in fact, his half-sister. However, his lie was a losing proposition for all involved. If Pharaoh had believed this lie, Sarai could have been permanently added to his harem. If Pharaoh knew the truth that Sarai was married to Abram, he would have had to kill Abram to receive her.

12:16 He treated Abram well for her sake. As a gesture of kindness, Pharaoh rewarded Abram with the hospitality of the day: livestock, camels and other farm animals. Abram added these to his already large array of animals.

APPLY **1.** Do you think that God has a plan for your life—even when you blow it? **2.** What is a recent case in point?

OPEN **1.** Who is your favorite aunt or uncle? Your kissin' cousin? Your spoiled nephew? **2.** Where do you like to go for walks?

STUDY The land of Canaan (modern day Israel) is made up of hilly country in the middle and level farmland on both sides. On the west is the Mediterranean Sea. On the east is the Jordan Valley and the Dead Sea. When Abram returns from Egypt, he is faced with another decision. **1.** How would you describe the conflict between Abram and Lot? **2.** What would you have done if you had been in Abram's shoes? **3.** Who do you think got the best of the bargain? Do you think Lot knew about the reputation of the "cities of the plain" when he made his choice? What would this do to his children? **4.** Why do you think this story is in the Bible? What is the lesson here for resolving conflicts? What about squabbles in business? in the church? **5.** What happened in the relationship between Abram and God as soon as the conflict with Lot was resolved? What was God saying to Abram?

APPLY **1.** In your own life, when did you have to make a critical choice in a conflict with another person over property rights? **2.** When the conflict you described was resolved, how has this effected the rest of your life?

she was your wife? [19]Why did you say, 'She is my sister,' so that I took
her to be my wife? Now then, here is your wife. Take her and go!"
[20]Then Pharaoh gave orders about Abram to his men, and they sent
him on his way, with his wife and everything he had.

Abram and Lot Separate

13 So Abram went up from Egypt to the Negev, with his wife and
everything he had, and Lot went with him. [2]Abram had become very wealthy in livestock and in silver and gold.
[3]From the Negev he went from place to place until he came to
Bethel, to the place between Bethel and Ai where his tent had been
earlier [4]and where he had first built an altar. There Abram called on
the name of the LORD.
[5]Now Lot, who was moving about with Abram, also had flocks and
herds and tents. [6]But the land could not support them while they
stayed together, for their possessions were so great that they were
not able to stay together. [7]And quarreling arose between Abram's
herdsmen and the herdsmen of Lot. The Canaanites and Perizzites
were also living in the land at that time.
[8]So Abram said to Lot, "Let's not have any quarreling between you
and me, or between your herdsmen and mine, for we are brothers. [9]Is
not the whole land before you? Let's part company. If you go to the
left, I'll go to the right; if you go to the right, I'll go to the left."
[10]Lot looked up and saw that the whole plain of the Jordan was
well watered, like the garden of the LORD, like the land of Egypt, toward Zoar. (This was before the LORD destroyed Sodom and Gomorrah.) [11]So Lot chose for himself the whole plain of the Jordan and set
out toward the east. The two men parted company: [12]Abram lived in
the land of Canaan, while Lot lived among the cities of the plain and
pitched his tents near Sodom. [13]Now the men of Sodom were wicked
and were sinning greatly against the LORD.
[14]The LORD said to Abram after Lot had parted from him, "Lift up
your eyes from where you are and look north and south, east and
west. [15]All the land that you see I will give to you and your offspring[a]
forever. [16]I will make your offspring like the dust of the earth, so that

[a]*15 Or* seed; *also in verse 16*

12:19 Caught in a lie, Abram faced the Pharaoh's caustic anger and quickly excused himself from the Pharaoh's presence. Even in light of God's infinite resources, Abram's reliance upon himself and his cleverness was a lesson he would too soon repeat.

13:4 Abram called on ... the LORD. Perhaps as an attempt to rekindle the faith and trust he had known in that place before his disastrous trip to Egypt, Abram worshiped God.

13:6 the land could not support them. God was leading Abram on through necessity. He could not rest his flocks and herds of his nephew, Lot, in a region that lacked ample water. God used necessity as a key circumstance to bring Lot and Abram to a crucial choice.

13:9 Abram was older and had the right to choose first. Abram's confidence in God's previous promise to him must have encouraged him to be generous with his nephew. Regardless of the outcome, God would bless Abram.

13:10 plain. Imagine a fertile stretch of land with well-watered fields and plentiful foliage. This depiction of the Jordan valley prior to its fiery destruction has been supported by recent archaeological findings. **Sodom and Gomorrah.** The beautiful valley was shadowed by two cities of wickedness: Sodom and Gomorrah. The sin that existed in these cities later destroyed the beauty of the Jordan valley making it a desolate land.

13:12 pitched his tents near Sodom. Lot's choice was self-centered and foreshadowed his eventual self-destruction. By living so close to the vile people of the cities, Lot soon came under God's judgment.

13:14 look north and south, east and west. The Lord unfolded his promise to Abram in the picture of land stretching out as far as each direction would go. The span of Abram's view was a vivid reminder of the Lord's infinite promise and assurance.

13:16 like the dust of the earth. It would be impossible to number the dust particles on all of the earth. Abram's descendants would also be infinite as attested by history.

if anyone could count the dust, then your offspring could be counted.
17Go, walk through the length and breadth of the land, for I am giving
it to you."
18So Abram moved his tents and went to live near the great trees of
Mamre at Hebron, where he built an altar to the LORD.

Abram Rescues Lot

14 At this time Amraphel king of Shinar,[a] Arioch king of Ellasar,
Kedorlaomer king of Elam and Tidal king of Goiim 2went to
war against Bera king of Sodom, Birsha king of Gomorrah, Shinab
king of Admah, Shemeber king of Zeboiim, and the king of Bela (that
is, Zoar). 3All these latter kings joined forces in the Valley of Siddim
(the Salt Sea[b]). 4For twelve years they had been subject to Kedorlaomer, but in the thirteenth year they rebelled.
5In the fourteenth year, Kedorlaomer and the kings allied with him
went out and defeated the Rephaites in Ashteroth Karnaim, the Zu-
zites in Ham, the Emites in Shaveh Kiriathaim 6and the Horites in the
hill country of Seir, as far as El Paran near the desert. 7Then they
turned back and went to En Mishpat (that is, Kadesh), and they conquered the whole territory of the Amalekites, as well as the Amorites
who were living in Hazazon Tamar.
8Then the king of Sodom, the king of Gomorrah, the king of Admah, the king of Zeboiim and the king of Bela (that is, Zoar) marched
out and drew up their battle lines in the Valley of Siddim 9against
Kedorlaomer king of Elam, Tidal king of Goiim, Amraphel king of Shinar and Arioch king of Ellasar—four kings against five. 10Now the
Valley of Siddim was full of tar pits, and when the kings of Sodom and
Gomorrah fled, some of the men fell into them and the rest fled to the
hills. 11The four kings seized all the goods of Sodom and Gomorrah
and all their food; then they went away. 12They also carried off Abram's
nephew Lot and his possessions, since he was living in Sodom.
13One who had escaped came and reported this to Abram the Hebrew. Now Abram was living near the great trees of Mamre the Amorite, a brother[c] of Eshcol and Aner, all of whom were allied with
Abram. 14When Abram heard that his relative had been taken captive,
he called out the 318 trained men born in his household and went in
pursuit as far as Dan. 15During the night Abram divided his men to

[a] *1* That is, Babylonia; also in verse 9 [b] *3* That is, the Dead Sea [c] *13* Or *a relative*; or *an ally*

OPEN 1. Who is the history buff in your family, particularly war history? **2.** Who started you on the habit of giving a portion of your income to God?

STUDY In the first recorded war in the Bible, all of the kings in the northern part of Canaan invaded the rich cities of the south. Abram is not involved in this skirmish but his nephew Lot is captured and taken north with the spoils. **1.** If you had been Abram and you heard that your nephew Lot had moved into the wicked city of Sodom (v. 12) and had been captured by an invading army and taken north, what would you do? **2.** How would you describe Abram's attack on the northern army (v. 15)? How could 318 men chase a whole army? **3.** How do you think Abram felt about the mayor of Salem coming out to greet him (vv. 17; 21–24)? **4.** What does Abram give to Melchizedek that becomes the precedent for all future giving in the Bible? Does this precedent still hold today?

APPLY 1. Do you find it difficult to give a tithe of 10% of your income to God? **2.** What have you found helpful in starting the giving habit? **3.** What are you teaching your children/grandchildren about giving?

13:17 walk through the ... land. As a demonstration of his ownership and a picture of his confidence in the promise, Abram covered the territory before him.

13:18 Hebron. Abram made his home near a grove of massive trees named for an Amorite resident, Mamre. Hebron was well watered and enjoyed a fertile, crop-producing altitude. Hebron played an important role in Jewish history as the home of Abram and later as the site where David was crowned king.

14:1 Amraphel king of Shinar. He invaded the Jordan valley and seized the goods of Sodom and Gomorrah along with Lot himself. **Goiim.** The Hebrew word for Gentile nations who went to war against the cities of Sodom and Gomorrah.

14:3 Salt Sea. Another name for the Dead Sea, a modern phenomenon consisting of such a combination and high percentage of sea salts that no living creature can inhabit its waters.

14:12 Lot ... was living in Sodom. Note the progression from having settled near the town (13:12) to actually living within its walls. Predictably, Lot succumbed to the temptations of the evil city. Thus, he became part of the loot carried away by the conquering tribes.

14:13 Hebrew. Abram is the first character in Genesis with this title. The Hebrew people were God's chosen people—confounding numerous people groups throughout the history of the Jews who considered them an inferior race. The reference here to Abram, as the father of the Hebrews, is in contrast to the vile behavior of his nephew, Lot.

14:14 trained men. Abram was a nomad as well as a wealthy and well-educated man. Therefore, he had a small army of male servants at his disposal to attack the evil conquering king. Utilizing their skillful training, they restored the goods and returned his nephew Lot safety.

attack them and he routed them, pursuing them as far as Hobah, north of Damascus. 16He recovered all the goods and brought back his relative Lot and his possessions, together with the women and the other people.

17After Abram returned from defeating Kedorlaomer and the kings allied with him, the king of Sodom came out to meet him in the Valley of Shaveh (that is, the King's Valley).

18Then Melchizedek king of Salem[a] brought out bread and wine. He was priest of God Most High, 19and he blessed Abram, saying,

"Blessed be Abram by God Most High,
Creator[b] of heaven and earth.
20And blessed be[c] God Most High,
who delivered your enemies into your hand."

Then Abram gave him a tenth of everything.

21The king of Sodom said to Abram, "Give me the people and keep the goods for yourself."

22But Abram said to the king of Sodom, "I have raised my hand to the LORD, God Most High, Creator of heaven and earth, and have taken an oath 23that I will accept nothing belonging to you, not even a thread or the thong of a sandal, so that you will never be able to say, 'I made Abram rich.' 24I will accept nothing but what my men have eaten and the share that belongs to the men who went with me—to Aner, Eshcol and Mamre. Let them have their share."

God's Covenant With Abram

15 After this, the word of the LORD came to Abram in a vision:

"Do not be afraid, Abram.
I am your shield,[d]
your very great reward.[e]"

2But Abram said, "O Sovereign LORD, what can you give me since I remain childless and the one who will inherit[f] my estate is Eliezer of Damascus?" 3And Abram said, "You have given me no children; so a servant in my household will be my heir."

4Then the word of the LORD came to him: "This man will not be your heir, but a son coming from your own body will be your heir."

[a]18 That is, Jerusalem [b]19 Or *Possessor*; also in verse 22 [c]20 Or *And praise be to* [d]1 Or *sovereign*
[e]1 Or *shield; / your reward will be very great* [f]2 The meaning of the Hebrew for this phrase is uncertain.

OPEN 1. Can you point out the "milky way" in the stars? How many stars make up the milky way? **2.** How long did you try before you gave birth to your first child?

STUDY It has been several years since God made a promise to Abram—that he would reward Abram's faith by making him the father of many nations. But a father needs a son and Abram didn't have one. **1.** If you had been Abram and you had tried for years to have a son to be your heir, how would you be feeling? **2.** What does God do to assure Abram that he will do what he promised (v. 5)? **3.** If you were 80 plus years old, how much faith would it take for

14:18 Melchizedek king of Salem. Melchizedek is as much of a mystery as he is a known biblical character. The name means "king of righteousness," and in Hebrews 7:3 is said to have had no geneology. He served as both a king and a priest in the city of Salem (Jerusalem). His appearance in the story further exalts Abram as God's chosen recipient of an incredible blessing and promise. Melchizedek is discussed at length in Hebrews 7.

14:23 accept nothing. As the recipient of God's infinite resources, Abram saw no need to incorporate additional human wealth into his fold. In this way, the king of Sodom could have no future claim on Abram. Although the human reward may have been tempting, Abram remained resolute due to his confidence in God's provision alone.

15:1 I am your shield. In the context of his recent encounters with tribal kings and even Melchizedek the priest-king, Abram was reminded by God of his ultimate allegiance. The imagery of a shining shield emphasizes Abram's loyalty to his King, the Lord.

15:2 Eliezer. As Sarai was barren, Abram had made arrangements for the wealth of his estate to transfer to one of his most esteemed servants, Eliezer.

15:3–4 a son coming from your own body. The transfer of the estate to Eliezer was practical, but hardly satisfying. Abram loved the Lord, but still did not understand how God's promise to him could be fulfilled if he had no children. God promised that Abram would indeed have a son of his own who would be his heir.

[5]He took him outside and said, "Look up at the heavens and count
the stars—if indeed you can count them." Then he said to him, "So shall
your off-spring be."
[6]Abram believed the LORD, and he credited it to him as righteousness.
[7]He also said to him, "I am the LORD, who brought you out of Ur of
the Chaldeans to give you this land to take possession of it."
[8]But Abram said, "O Sovereign LORD, how can I know that I will
gain possession of it?"
[9]So the LORD said to him, "Bring me a heifer, a goat and a ram, each
three years old, along with a dove and a young pigeon."
[10]Abram brought all these to him, cut them in two and arranged the
halves opposite each other; the birds, however, he did not cut in half.
[11]Then birds of prey came down on the carcasses, but Abram drove
them away.
[12]As the sun was setting, Abram fell into a deep sleep, and a thick
and dreadful darkness came over him. [13]Then the LORD said to him,
"Know for certain that your descendants will be strangers in a country not their own, and they will be enslaved and mistreated four hundred years. [14]But I will punish the nation they serve as slaves, and
afterward they will come out with great possessions. [15]You, however,
will go to your fathers in peace and be buried at a good old age. [16]In
the fourth generation your descendants will come back here, for the
sin of the Amorites has not yet reached its full measure."
[17]When the sun had set and darkness had fallen, a smoking firepot
with a blazing torch appeared and passed between the pieces. [18]On
that day the LORD made a covenant with Abram and said, "To your descendants I give this land, from the river[a] of Egypt to the great river,

[a]18 Or *Wadi*

you to believe that you could have a "son from your own body"? **4.** In addition to promising Abram he would have a son, what else does God promise (v. 7)? How does Abram respond? Do you think Abram is being a little pushy? **5.** What does God ask Abram to do? How would you describe the dream? What is God showing Abram in this dream? If you had been in this situation, how would you have felt at the end? **6.** Do you think Abram realized at this time how significant his faith would be in God's whole plan of salvation for the world (v. 6)?

APPLY 1. When is the last time you and God counted the stars and dreamed about your future? **2.** Do you think God is still making promises to men and women of faith who are crazy enough to believe him? How about you?

15:5 count the stars. Add this image to the mental picture book God gave to Abram. The promise was as limitless as the dust particles on the earth (13:16). His land stretched as far as his eyes could gaze. And now Abram must count the thousands upon thousands of stars in the sky to grasp the infinite results of the promise.

15:6 Abram believed the LORD. With this affirmation, Abram stands as the first so far in the biblical story to profess a faith relationship with the Lord. Abram's story is one of progression. God initiated a promise. Abram responded in belief. God then credited Abram with the blessing of righteousness. Faith is a necessary demonstration and a prerequisite for God's blessing (Rom. 4).

15:7 I am the LORD, who brought you out. It was not that Abram forgot all he had been through. He simply needed to be reminded who brought him through all of it. Abram would have recognized this review of the past as a preamble to God's next move.

15:8 how can I know ... I will gain possession of it? Picture one man, standing alone, in the midst of thousands of square miles of land wondering how he is going to possess all of it. In very human terms, Abram wanted to have a guarantee of God's promise to him.

15:9 Bring me a heifer. God requested a series of animal sacrifices from Abram. Each heifer, goat and ram was the prime age for eating or selling for a profit, making for a more valuable sacrifice. Abram asked God for a sign, but God requested a sacrifice first.

15:10 Abram cut the animals in half, as was tradition for sacrifice. He may have chosen to keep the birds whole because they were so small.

15:16 In the fourth generation. Although Abram could not have understood it then, God's dream-like message to Abram focused on the Israelites' future enslavement in Egypt. In Abram's case, four generations later would total four hundred years. This was the amount of time the Israelites would spend in hard labor under the cruel hand of the pharaoh in Egypt. It also signaled the beginning of their long return journey from Egypt to the Promised Land. However, Abram would only dream of these events, never experience them.

15:17 a smoking firepot with a blazing torch. Symbolizing God's presence (much like the account of the children of Israel being guided by a flame at night). **passed between the pieces.** This refers to the halves of the slaughtered animals. The torch passed between the pieces as was customary for a person making an oath. This strange custom symbolized a person's good faith and guaranteed a person's word. In the same way, God used a familiar picture for Abram to guarantee his promise.

15:18 made a covenant. The animal sacrifice was a picture of God's promise to Abram. Through this act, God declared Abram's ownership of the land before him. With Joshua leading the charge, the children of Israel would one day see this promise come to fruition.

OPEN **1.** How long did you (or would you) wait before having kids? **2.** Growing up, who "wore the pants" in your family: Mom? Dad? Kids? Or was decision-making mutual?

STUDY Though God had promised Abram a son, Abram and Sarai were now around 85 and 75 years old respectively. In this story, they decide to practice a common custom of their time in order to have a son. **1.** If you had been trying for ten years to have a child, how would you feel? **2.** What do you think drove Sarai, Abram's wife, to this course of action? **3.** Why did the plan backfire? If it was Sarai's idea in the first place, why did she take out her feelings on her husband? **4.** How would you describe the communication between Sarai and Abram? What would you have done (or should have done) if you were Abram? **5.** If you had been in Hagar's shoes, would you have run away from Sarai? How do you think she got along with Sarai when she returned home? **6.** Of the three main characters in this story, who do you like the most? The least? Why? **7.** Do you think this whole, sad story could have been avoided if Abram had stood up to his wife?

APPLY **1.** What have you been praying about for a long time? How are you coping with the delay? **2.** How can this group help you this week in prayer?

the Euphrates— 19the land of the Kenites, Kenizzites, Kadmonites,
20Hittites, Perizzites, Rephaites, 21Amorites, Canaanites, Girgashites
and Jebusites."

Hagar and Ishmael

16 Now Sarai, Abram's wife, had borne him no children. But she
had an Egyptian maidservant named Hagar; 2so she said to
Abram, "The LORD has kept me from having children. Go, sleep with
my maidservant; perhaps I can build a family through her."
Abram agreed to what Sarai said. 3So after Abram had been living
in Canaan ten years, Sarai his wife took her Egyptian maidservant
Hagar and gave her to her husband to be his wife. 4He slept with Hagar, and she conceived.

When she knew she was pregnant, she began to despise her mistress. 5Then Sarai said to Abram, "You are responsible for the wrong I
am suffering. I put my servant in your arms, and now that she knows
she is pregnant, she despises me. May the LORD judge between you
and me."

6"Your servant is in your hands," Abram said. "Do with her whatever
you think best." Then Sarai mistreated Hagar; so she fled from her.

7The angel of the LORD found Hagar near a spring in the desert; it
was the spring that is beside the road to Shur. 8And he said, "Hagar,
servant of Sarai, where have you come from, and where are you going?"

"I'm running away from my mistress Sarai," she answered.

9Then the angel of the LORD told her, "Go back to your mistress and
submit to her." 10The angel added, "I will so increase your descendants that they will be too numerous to count."

11The angel of the LORD also said to her:

"You are now with child
  and you will have a son.
You shall name him Ishmael,[a]
  for the LORD has heard of your misery.
12He will be a wild donkey of a man;
  his hand will be against everyone
  and everyone's hand against him,
and he will live in hostility
  toward[b] all his brothers."

[a] 11 Ishmael means *God hears.* [b] 12 Or *live to the east / of*

16:1 Egyptian maidservant. More than likely, Abram and Sarai obtained Hagar during their move from Canaan to Egypt with Abram's nephew Lot. Hagar's name means "flight" or "run away."

16:2 kept me from having children. God had not fulfilled his promise (15:4), and Sarai began to doubt. **sleep with my maidservant.** Sarai knew of the Sumerian custom of using a concubine to obtain a male heir in the case of a wife's barrenness. A concubine did not have the same rights as the wife.

16:4 despise her mistress. Dissension between Sarai and Hagar was the fruit of Sarai taking matters into her own hands. Childlessness was a great burden to women, for it was seen as a lack of blessing from the Lord. Hagar's pregnancy placed her in a more favored position.

16:5 May the LORD judge. A common statement of doubt or suspicion.

16:7 The angel of the LORD. Some think this refers to an appearance of Christ; others say this was a special messenger of God. When God spoke to Abraham he was identified the second time as the angel of the Lord (22:1, 15).

16:8 running away ... mistress. Hagar's answer shows her aimlessness. The *Code of Hammurabi* and laws of Mesopotamia prescribed punishments for runaway slaves, some of which were very severe.

16:12 wild donkey. A promise of Ishmael's eventual nomadic lifestyle. **hostility toward all his brothers.** Points to the hostility between the descendants of Isaac (the Israelites) and Ishmael (the Ishmaelites).

13She gave this name to the LORD who spoke to her: "You are the
God who sees me," for she said, "I have now seen[a] the One who sees
me." 14That is why the well was called Beer Lahai Roi[b]; it is still there,
between Kadesh and Bered.
15So Hagar bore Abram a son, and Abram gave the name Ishmael to
the son she had borne. 16Abram was eighty-six years old when Hagar
bore him Ishmael.

The Covenant of Circumcision

17 When Abram was ninety-nine years old, the LORD appeared
to him and said, "I am God Almighty[c]; walk before me and be
blameless. 2I will confirm my covenant between me and you and will
greatly increase your numbers."
3Abram fell facedown, and God said to him, 4"As for me, this is my
covenant with you: You will be the father of many nations. 5No longer
will you be called Abram[d]; your name will be Abraham,[e] for I have
made you a father of many nations. 6I will make you very fruitful; I will
make nations of you, and kings will come from you. 7I will establish my
covenant as an everlasting covenant between me and you and your
descendants after you for the generations to come, to be your God and
the God of your descendants after you. 8The whole land of Canaan,
where you are now an alien, I will give as an everlasting possession to
you and your descendants after you; and I will be their God."
9Then God said to Abraham, "As for you, you must keep my covenant, you and your descendants after you for the generations to
come. 10This is my covenant with you and your descendants after
you, the covenant you are to keep: Every male among you shall be
circumcised. 11You are to undergo circumcision, and it will be the
sign of the covenant between me and you. 12For the generations to
come every male among you who is eight days old must be circumcised, including those born in your household or bought with money
from a foreigner—those who are not your offspring. 13Whether born
in your household or bought with your money, they must be circumcised. My covenant in your flesh is to be an everlasting covenant.

[a]13 Or *seen the back of* [b]14 *Beer Lahai Roi* means *well of the Living One who sees me.* [c]1 Hebrew *El-Shaddai* [d]5 *Abram* means *exalted father.* [e]5 *Abraham* means *father of many.*

OPEN **1.** If you could change your name, what name would you choose? **2.** What is the most serious contract you ever signed?

STUDY It has been 24 years since God promised Abram a son and a place to call home. Now, God is about to make good on his promises? **1.** If you were God and you wanted to demonstrate to Abram that you were "God Almighty" and that you could do anything, how long would you wait until you made good on your promise to give Abram a son? **2.** What promise does God want out of Abram in return (v. 1)? How would you describe this contract between God and Abram? Are there strings attached to God's covenant? **3.** What is the significance of God changing Abram's and Sarai's names from the singular to the plural—Abraham and Sarah? **4.** Up to now, Abram has been living in Canaan as a Hebrew (meaning "without ownership of the land") or an alien (v. 8). What does God promise Abraham now? If you had been homeless for 25 years like Abraham, how would you feel? **5.** Circumcision was an ancient practice to signify ownership and loyalty to a king or lord. In asking Abraham to circumcise himself and all his household, what was God asking of Abraham? What would be a modern-day practice like this? **6.** Why

17:1 God Almighty. A translation of the Hebrew *El-Shaddai* (also "God of the Mountains"). **walk before me and be blameless.** God called Abram to a life or "walk" of faith. The sign of his faith was his obedience. Abram had to be patient and wait for God to fulfill his promise of a son and an heir. Trying to fulfill that promise in his own way (through Hagar and Ishmael) had only resulted in pain and disaster.

17:2 I will confirm my covenant. What God promised, he would do. God also made covenants with Noah (9:8–17) and with David (2 Sam. 7:5–16).

17:5 Abram ... Abraham. The name Abram means "father is exalted" or "high father," while Abraham means "father of many" or "father of nations." This name was a sign of special favor with God and showed God's covenant promise.

17:6 I will make nations of you. God's promise of increase of offspring, as mentioned in verse two.

17:7 an everlasting covenant. God would always keep his end of the bargain. **your God.** God would stand by his people as their leader and provider. God later repeats this promise to Moses as part of his message to the Israelites.

17:8 everlasting possession. Canaan would belong to Abraham's descendants permanently, as long as they continued in obedience.

17:9 you must keep my covenant. God assigned a condition for Abraham and his descendants: obedience.

17:10–11 circumcised ... sign of the covenant. God chose the circumcision of males as the sign of this covenant. This act was symbolic of God's rule over his people. Although circumcision was widely practiced at this time, other nations were not included in this covenant.

17:12 eight days old. The time allotted before circumcision could take place.

[14]Any uncircumcised male, who has not been circumcised in the
flesh, will be cut off from his people; he has broken my covenant."
[15]God also said to Abraham, "As for Sarai your wife, you are no
longer to call her Sarai; her name will be Sarah. [16]I will bless her and
will surely give you a son by her. I will bless her so that she will be the
mother of nations; kings of peoples will come from her."
[17]Abraham fell facedown; he laughed and said to himself, "Will a
son be born to a man a hundred years old? Will Sarah bear a child at
the age of ninety?" [18]And Abraham said to God, "If only Ishmael
might live under your blessing!"
[19]Then God said, "Yes, but your wife Sarah will bear you a son, and
you will call him Isaac.[a] I will establish my covenant with him as an
everlasting covenant for his descendants after him. [20]And as for Ishmael, I have heard you: I will surely bless him; I will make him fruitful
and will greatly increase his numbers. He will be the father of twelve
rulers, and I will make him into a great nation. [21]But my covenant I
will establish with Isaac, whom Sarah will bear to you by this time
next year." [22]When he had finished speaking with Abraham, God went
up from him.
[23]On that very day Abraham took his son Ishmael and all those
born in his household or bought with his money, every male in his
household, and circumcised them, as God told him. [24]Abraham was
ninety-nine years old when he was circumcised, [25]and his son Ishmael was thirteen; [26]Abraham and his son Ishmael were both circumcised on that same day. [27]And every male in Abraham's household,
including those born in his household or bought from a foreigner,
was circumcised with him.

The Three Visitors

18 The LORD appeared to Abraham near the great trees of Mamre
while he was sitting at the entrance to his tent in the heat of
the day. [2]Abraham looked up and saw three men standing nearby.
When he saw them, he hurried from the entrance of his tent to meet
them and bowed low to the ground.
[3]He said, "If I have found favor in your eyes, my lord,[b] do not pass
your servant by. [4]Let a little water be brought, and then you may all
wash your feet and rest under this tree. [5]Let me get you something to
eat, so you can be refreshed and then go on your way—now that you
have come to your servant."
"Very well," they answered, "do as you say."

[a]19 *Isaac* means *he laughs.* [b]3 Or *O Lord*

did Abraham go ahead and circumcise himself and his household if he believed he was too old to have a son (vv. 9–14)? **7.** Do you have a problem with God choosing Abraham's future son with Sarah (Isaac) and not choosing Abraham's son with her handmaiden (Ishmael) to be the heir to the covenant (v. 21)? **8.** In this story who comes out the winner: Abraham? Ishmael? God? How will this covenant effect the rest of the Bible story?

APPLY 1. In your own spiritual development, when did this covenant between God and Abraham start making sense to you? **2.** How would you describe your relationship with God right now? **3.** How can this group help you this week in prayer?

OPEN What visitor would motivate you to clean your house: Mother? Mother-in-law? Pastor? Dignitary? Rock star?

STUDY In the Near East, hospitality for a traveler was very important, almost obligatory. **1.** What do you learn about the culture by the way Abraham treats these three strangers? What is the closest you have come to being treated this way? **2.** Do you think the three are messengers for God, or could one of the messengers be a pre-incarnation appearance of Jesus himself? **3.** How

17:14 cut off from his people. Since circumcision was the mark of the covenant, a person's refusal to be circumcised meant that he was cut off from God's people and God's promises.

17:15 Sarai ... Sarah. Sarai and Sarah both mean "princess," but as with Abraham, the name change was a sign of God's favor and God's promise that she would be the mother of many.

17:16 a son by her. Not through Hagar or any other person, but through Sarah this son would be born. Isaac was this promised son (21:1–7).

17:17 Abraham ... laughed. This was his reaction to the seeming impossibility of the promise. God then names him Isaac (v. 19) which means "he laughs."

17:21 But my covenant I will establish with Isaac. God reminded Abraham that his covenant would be with the son Abraham and Sarah would have and not with Ishmael, the son born to Abraham but not to Sarah.

17:22 God went up from him. The Lord concluded their meeting as he did during a later visit to Abraham (18:33) and after a confrontation with Aaron and Miriam (Num. 12:9).

18:2 three men. It's obvious these were not ordinary visitors. The context would suggest that two of them were angels and the third was the Lord. The hospitality Abraham showed the three men was customary for the day. He immediately took care of his guests.

6So Abraham hurried into the tent to Sarah. "Quick," he said, "get
three seahs[a] of fine flour and knead it and bake some bread."
7Then he ran to the herd and selected a choice, tender calf and
gave it to a servant, who hurried to prepare it. 8He then brought some
curds and milk and the calf that had been prepared, and set these before them. While they ate, he stood near them under a tree.
9"Where is your wife Sarah?" they asked him.
"There, in the tent," he said.
10Then the LORD[b] said, "I will surely return to you about this time
next year, and Sarah your wife will have a son."
Now Sarah was listening at the entrance to the tent, which was
behind him. 11Abraham and Sarah were already old and well advanced in years, and Sarah was past the age of childbearing. 12So Sarah laughed to herself as she thought, "After I am worn out and my
master[c] is old, will I now have this pleasure?"
13Then the LORD said to Abraham, "Why did Sarah laugh and say,
'Will I really have a child, now that I am old?' 14Is anything too hard
for the LORD? I will return to you at the appointed time next year and
Sarah will have a son."
15Sarah was afraid, so she lied and said, "I did not laugh."
But he said, "Yes, you did laugh."

Abraham Pleads for Sodom

16When the men got up to leave, they looked down toward Sodom,
and Abraham walked along with them to see them on their way.
17Then the LORD said, "Shall I hide from Abraham what I am about to
do? 18Abraham will surely become a great and powerful nation, and
all nations on earth will be blessed through him. 19For I have chosen
him, so that he will direct his children and his household after him to
keep the way of the LORD by doing what is right and just, so that the
LORD will bring about for Abraham what he has promised him."
20Then the LORD said, "The outcry against Sodom and Gomorrah is
so great and their sin so grievous 21that I will go down and see if what
they have done is as bad as the outcry that has reached me. If not, I
will know."
22The men turned away and went toward Sodom, but Abraham remained standing before the LORD.[d] 23Then Abraham approached him
and said: "Will you sweep away the righteous with the wicked? 24What

[a]6 That is, probably about 20 quarts (about 22 liters) [b]10 Hebrew *Then he* [c]12 Or *husband* [d]22 Masoretic Text; an ancient Hebrew scribal tradition *but the LORD remained standing before Abraham*

do you take Sarah's response to the announcement that she would bear a child within a year? Was she laughing at God or at herself? What is the Lord's reply (v. 13)? **4.** If you were told you would have a child by this time next year, what would you say?

APPLY 1. If God had told you ten years ago that you would be where you are today, what would you have said? **2.** Is it hard for you to look at the difficulties in your life today and say, "Is there anything too hard for the Lord"?

OPEN 1. When you were a kid and wanted something from your parents, how did you try to persuade them? **2.** How much haggling over price will you do when you buy a new car?

STUDY Abraham and his wife had just been visited by three "men." One of these men may have been the Lord himself in a pre-incarnate appearance. Now as the visitors are about to go, the Lord chooses to reveal to Abraham his plans to check out Sodom and Gomorrah. **1.** If you knew that someone you loved was living in a city known for sin and that the judgment of God was about to fall on this city, what would you do? **2.** What does this story tell you about the relationship that Abraham had with the Lord? **3.** Why would Abraham be concerned about the people in

---

18:6 bread. This is not a loaf of bread as we would imagine it. The Hebrew word suggests more than one loaf. What Sarah baked for the guests was a *basketful* of flat unleavened bread common to that area. Our pita bread is similar to what was served.

18:12 laughed. Unable to contain her disbelief, Sarah quietly chuckled to herself. The thought of conceiving a child at her advanced age was a joke.

18:14 Is anything too hard for the LORD? It is clear that this is a rhetorical question. Then and now, whatever God wants to do, he will do. What a wonderful truth for God's people to ponder when we face tasks that seem impossible.

18:18 all nations on earth will be blessed through him. Through Abraham, the entire world would be invited to be part of God's covenant family, for Jesus Christ would be his descendant.

18:19 chosen. God intimately knows who he desires to fulfill his will and chooses them to be part of his plan, just as he knew and chose Abraham.

18:20 outcry. Those who wanted to please God were fed up with the moral decadence of Sodom and Gomorrah.

18:21 I will go down. God visited the earth for the purpose of judgment. His holiness would not tolerate the sin in Sodom and Gomorrah.

18:22 Abraham remained standing. Even though Abraham knew he was in the presence of God, he knew that it was permissible to confidently approach God with his concerns and not be afraid.

Sodom and Gomorrah? Do you think Abraham was being audacious by his questions to God in verses 23–35? If you had been God, how would you have replied? **4.** How would you describe Abraham as a negotiator? Would you like to have Abraham to negotiate for you the next time you buy a car? **5.** What is the lesson for you in this story? What quality in Abraham do you admire?

APPLY 1. In your early spiritual pilgrimage, who interceded for you like Abraham interceded for his family members in Sodom and Gomorrah? **2.** Do you believe that your intercession with God for the life of another person would be effective in God working in this person's life? **3.** For whom is God calling you to intercede as Abraham did? **4.** If you could ask God one question, what would you ask?

OPEN 1. What is the closest you have come to being in a natural disaster? **2.** If you had to get out of your house in a hurry, what would you grab first?

STUDY The word "sodomy" comes from this story in the Bible. The practice of men having sex with other men was known to occur in cultures in the Near East at that time, but Sodom and Gomorrah were notorious for this sin. Lot was the nephew of Abraham. They had a quarrel over grazing rights. Abraham and Lot separated and Lot moved to the rich "cities of the plain near Sodom" (13:12–13). **1.** Do you suppose Lot knew what he was getting into when he moved into the city and became one

if there are fifty righteous people in the city? Will you really sweep it away and not spare[a] the place for the sake of the fifty righteous people in it? 25Far be it from you to do such a thing—to kill the righteous with the wicked, treating the righteous and the wicked alike. Far be it from you! Will not the Judge[b] of all the earth do right?"

26The LORD said, "If I find fifty righteous people in the city of Sodom, I will spare the whole place for their sake."

27Then Abraham spoke up again: "Now that I have been so bold as to speak to the Lord, though I am nothing but dust and ashes, 28what if the number of the righteous is five less than fifty? Will you destroy the whole city because of five people?"

"If I find forty-five there," he said, "I will not destroy it."

29Once again he spoke to him, "What if only forty are found there?"

He said, "For the sake of forty, I will not do it."

30Then he said, "May the Lord not be angry, but let me speak. What if only thirty can be found there?"

He answered, "I will not do it if I find thirty there."

31Abraham said, "Now that I have been so bold as to speak to the Lord, what if only twenty can be found there?"

He said, "For the sake of twenty, I will not destroy it."

32Then he said, "May the Lord not be angry, but let me speak just once more. What if only ten can be found there?"

He answered, "For the sake of ten, I will not destroy it."

33When the LORD had finished speaking with Abraham, he left, and Abraham returned home.

Sodom and Gomorrah Destroyed

19 The two angels arrived at Sodom in the evening, and Lot was sitting in the gateway of the city. When he saw them, he got up to meet them and bowed down with his face to the ground. 2"My lords," he said, "please turn aside to your servant's house. You can wash your feet and spend the night and then go on your way early in the morning."

"No," they answered, "we will spend the night in the square."

3But he insisted so strongly that they did go with him and entered his house. He prepared a meal for them, baking bread without yeast, and they ate. 4Before they had gone to bed, all the men from every part of the city of Sodom—both young and old—surrounded the house. 5They called to Lot, "Where are the men who came to you tonight? Bring them out to us so that we can have sex with them."

[a]24 Or *forgive*; also in verse 26 [b]25 Or *Ruler*

18:25 Will not the Judge of all the earth do right? Abraham understood the power and authority of God. No wonder his requests are grounded in uncanny confidence. The Lord of the universe knows all, sees all, and always does what is right.

18:27 dust and ashes. *The image* here is one that is far removed from the elevated holiness of God.

18:32 just once more. Like the widow in Jesus' parable who kept bringing her case before the judge (Luke 18:1–8), Abraham's repetition demonstrated his sincere desire to save his relatives.

18:33 home. Abraham went back to his tree-lined campsite in Mamre (v. 1) *to spend the night*. The next day he returned to the place where he carried on his conversation with the Lord.

19:1 gateway of the city. Lot apparently had great influence. Those who sat at the city gates were the recognized leaders of the community. It was at the gateway where business was debated and civil cases tried. Lot apparently had become a member of Sodom's city council.

19:3 bread without yeast. If the dough does not have yeast, it does not need to rise. Thus, it can be made in a hurry.

[6]Lot went outside to meet them and shut the door behind him [7]and said, "No, my friends. Don't do this wicked thing. [8]Look, I have two daughters who have never slept with a man. Let me bring them out to you, and you can do what you like with them. But don't do anything to these men, for they have come under the protection of my roof."

[9]"Get out of our way," they replied. And they said, "This fellow came here as an alien, and now he wants to play the judge! We'll treat you worse than them." They kept bringing pressure on Lot and moved forward to break down the door.

[10]But the men inside reached out and pulled Lot back into the house and shut the door. [11]Then they struck the men who were at the door of the house, young and old, with blindness so that they could not find the door.

[12]The two men said to Lot, "Do you have anyone else here—sons-in-law, sons or daughters, or anyone else in the city who belongs to you? Get them out of here, [13]because we are going to destroy this place. The outcry to the LORD against its people is so great that he has sent us to destroy it."

[14]So Lot went out and spoke to his sons-in-law, who were pledged to marry[a] his daughters. He said, "Hurry and get out of this place, because the LORD is about to destroy the city!" But his sons-in-law thought he was joking.

[15]With the coming of dawn, the angels urged Lot, saying, "Hurry! Take your wife and your two daughters who are here, or you will be swept away when the city is punished."

[16]When he hesitated, the men grasped his hand and the hands of his wife and of his two daughters and led them safely out of the city, for the LORD was merciful to them. [17]As soon as they had brought them out, one of them said, "Flee for your lives! Don't look back, and don't stop anywhere in the plain! Flee to the mountains or you will be swept away!"

[18]But Lot said to them, "No, my lords,[b] please! [19]Your[c] servant has found favor in your[c] eyes, and you[c] have shown great kindness to me in sparing my life. But I can't flee to the mountains; this disaster will overtake me, and I'll die. [20]Look, here is a town near enough to run to, and it is small. Let me flee to it—it is very small, isn't it? Then my life will be spared."

[21]He said to him, "Very well, I will grant this request too; I will not overthrow the town you speak of. [22]But flee there quickly, because I cannot do anything until you reach it." (That is why the town was called Zoar.[d])

[a]*14 Or were married to* [b]*18* Or *No, Lord;* or *No, my lord* [c]*19* The Hebrew is singular. [d]*22 Zoar* means *small.*

of the prominent citizens that sat "in the gateway of the city" (v. 1)? **2.** When the men of the city showed up at Lot's house to have sex with the visitors, do you think Lot was surprised? How would you describe what went on between Lot and the men of the city? **3.** What do you think kept God from zapping the city right on the spot (18:32)? **4.** When Lot had a few hours to get his family and leave before God destroyed the city, what happened? Do you think Lot really wanted to leave (v. 16)? **5.** What is the lesson with Lot's wife? What do you think caused Lot's wife to do this?

APPLY 1. Have you ever lived in a town like Sodom and Gomorrah? What kept you from falling prey to the sex culture? **2.** When you can't flee to the mountains, what do you do to keep pornography from coming into your home via the internet and the media? With the peer pressure our children face, how do we guide them to do what is modest and appropriate?

19:8 under the protection of my roof. Responsibility for his guests' safety caused Lot to extend such protection.

19:9 an alien. Lot had arrived in Sodom as an outsider, but had moved into a position of influence. Yet it seems no one had forgotten that he really was not one of their own.

19:13 destroy this place. Judgment is inevitable. Because of the casual attitude with which Sodom looked at sin, they would not escape. Because ten righteous individuals could not be found (18:32), the city would be destroyed. However, God graciously spared Lot and his daughters.

19:14 thought he was joking. Coming to terms with God's holiness and inevitable judgment of sin is difficult in a permissive society. Even though Lot told the truth to his daughters' husbands, they were not convinced that they should believe him.

19:16 he hesitated. Perhaps Lot was having second thoughts about leaving behind his home, his possessions, and his sons-in-law; or perhaps he was not sure he really believed anything was going to happen. **grasped his hand.** It's comforting to know that even when we are slow to obey, God provides the necessary push to get us going.

23By the time Lot reached Zoar, the sun had risen over the land.
24Then the LORD rained down burning sulfur on Sodom and Gomorrah—from the LORD out of the heavens. 25Thus he overthrew those
cities and the entire plain, including all those living in the cities—and
also the vegetation in the land. 26But Lot's wife looked back, and she
became a pillar of salt.

27Early the next morning Abraham got up and returned to the place
where he had stood before the LORD. 28He looked down toward Sodom and Gomorrah, toward all the land of the plain, and he saw dense
smoke rising from the land, like smoke from a furnace.

29So when God destroyed the cities of the plain, he remembered
Abraham, and he brought Lot out of the catastrophe that overthrew
the cities where Lot had lived.

Lot and His Daughters

30Lot and his two daughters left Zoar and settled in the mountains,
for he was afraid to stay in Zoar. He and his two daughters lived in a
cave. 31One day the older daughter said to the younger, "Our father is
old, and there is no man around here to lie with us, as is the custom
all over the earth. 32Let's get our father to drink wine and then lie
with him and preserve our family line through our father."

33That night they got their father to drink wine, and the older
daughter went in and lay with him. He was not aware of it when she
lay down or when she got up.

34The next day the older daughter said to the younger, "Last night I
lay with my father. Let's get him to drink wine again tonight, and you
go in and lie with him so we can preserve our family line through our
father." 35So they got their father to drink wine that night also, and
the younger daughter went and lay with him. Again he was not aware
of it when she lay down or when she got up.

36So both of Lot's daughters became pregnant by their father. 37The
older daughter had a son, and she named him Moab[a]; he is the father
of the Moabites of today. 38The younger daughter also had a son, and
she named him Ben-Ammi[b]; he is the father of the Ammonites of today.

Abraham and Abimelech

20 Now Abraham moved on from there into the region of the
Negev and lived between Kadesh and Shur. For a while he
stayed in Gerar, 2and there Abraham said of his wife Sarah, "She is

[a]37 *Moab* sounds like the Hebrew for *from father.* [b]38 *Ben-Ammi* means *son of my people.*

OPEN What is the most disgusting movie you have seen in years?

STUDY Lot chose to live in Sodom and barely escaped with his life and two daughters. **1.** How would you describe Lot in this story: Weakling? Pathetic? Wasted? Broken? **2.** For a man who was one of the prominent citizens in Sodom, how do you think he felt living in a cave? **3.** How would you describe Lot's family? Was this caused by alcoholism—or something deeper than that? How many generations in this story are effected by Lot's alcoholism?

APPLY What is the closest you have come to seeing the results of alcoholism in a family?

OPEN Have you played the game "Three Facts, One Lie"? Let one person finish these four sentences and make one of the four a lie and see if the others can guess which one is the lie? **1.** My favorite game as a child was ... **2.** At 12, my

---

19:24 rained down burning sulfur. Because subterranean asphalt is located in this part of the world, it is possible that God caused an eruption that rained down black molten tar.

19:26 Lot's wife looked back. When we insist on resisting God's direction and prompting to do what is right, there are dire consequences. Lot's wife not only never made it to safety, her disobedience became a warning for the faint hearts on the journey of faith.

19:29 God ... remembered Abraham. Although Abraham had interceded for the righteous inhabitants of Sodom, his heart of compassion beat most strongly for his nephew and his family. Here is an unforgettable reminder of the power of intercessory prayer (18:32).

19:33 they got their father to drink wine ... and lay with him. Lot's daughters, apparently not having gained much moral training from their father and having taken in far too much of the morals of Sodom, fell upon this plan in order to preserve their family line. Not only did his daughters sin, but Lot's indulgence led to this consequence.

19:36–38 The roots of wrong choices do not lie dormant. They grow into prickly bushes that snag us on the road of life. Curiously, the sons that resulted from Lot's incest were the ancestors of the Moabites and Ammonites who plagued Abraham's descendants, the Hebrews, for centuries.

my sister." Then Abimelech king of Gerar sent for Sarah and took her.
3But God came to Abimelech in a dream one night and said to him,
"You are as good as dead because of the woman you have taken; she
is a married woman."

4Now Abimelech had not gone near her, so he said, "Lord, will you
destroy an innocent nation? 5Did he not say to me, 'She is my sister,'
and didn't she also say, 'He is my brother'? I have done this with a
clear conscience and clean hands."

6Then God said to him in the dream, "Yes, I know you did this with a
clear conscience, and so I have kept you from sinning against me. That
is why I did not let you touch her. 7Now return the man's wife, for he
is a prophet, and he will pray for you and you will live. But if you do
not return her, you may be sure that you and all yours will die."

8Early the next morning Abimelech summoned all his officials, and
when he told them all that had happened, they were very much
afraid. 9Then Abimelech called Abraham in and said, "What have you
done to us? How have I wronged you that you have brought such
great guilt upon me and my kingdom? You have done things to me
that should not be done." 10And Abimelech asked Abraham, "What
was your reason for doing this?"

11Abraham replied, "I said to myself, 'There is surely no fear of God
in this place, and they will kill me because of my wife.' 12Besides, she
really is my sister, the daughter of my father though not of my mother; and she became my wife. 13And when God had me wander from
my father's household, I said to her, 'This is how you can show your
love to me: Everywhere we go, say of me, "He is my brother." ' "

14Then Abimelech brought sheep and cattle and male and female
slaves and gave them to Abraham, and he returned Sarah his wife to
him. 15And Abimelech said, "My land is before you; live wherever you
like."

16To Sarah he said, "I am giving your brother a thousand shekels[a]
of silver. This is to cover the offense against you before all who are
with you; you are completely vindicated."

17Then Abraham prayed to God, and God healed Abimelech, his
wife and his slave girls so they could have children again, 18for the
LORD had closed up every womb in Abimelech's household because
of Abraham's wife Sarah.

The Birth of Isaac

21 Now the LORD was gracious to Sarah as he had said, and the
LORD did for Sarah what he had promised. 2Sarah became

[a]16 That is, about 25 pounds (about 11.5 kilograms)

hero was ... **3.** At 15, my favorite music was ... **4.** Right now my favorite pastime is ...

STUDY Abraham was a man of faith and God rewarded his faith by promising him that he was to have a homeland to call his own and a son to inherit the land. But Abraham was also a man of fear. In this story fear gets the best of him—again! **1.** Are you shocked to find Abraham committing the same mistake that he committed before (12:10–20)? **2.** Why do you think God intervenes and warns Abimelech, "you are as good as dead" (vv. 3,6)? **3.** How do you feel about the way Abraham tries to get out of the mess he has caused (vv. 10–13)? How do you think Sarah, his wife, felt when she was told, "this is the way you can show your love for me: Everywhere we go, say of me 'He is my brother' " (v. 13)? **4.** Would you have given Abraham 1000 shekels if you had been Abimelech? **5.** What is the redeeming lesson for you in his story?

APPLY 1. As you look back, what is the most recent experience you have had in which God stepped in and saved you from yourself when you had made a bad decision? **2.** Do you learn from your mistakes or make the same mistake over and over again?

OPEN How did you get your name? What does it mean?

STUDY 1. Why do you think God waited 25 years to give Abraham a son? How would you feel

20:2 Abimelech. As with many Old Testament names, this king had a son or grandson by the same name in (26:1).

20:3 dream. Dreams were one of the more common ways God got the attention of people in these days. He used this nocturnal opportunity to offer caution or provide guidance. In this case, God uses a dream to orchestrate circumstances so that Sarah will be able to bear the child he promised Abraham.

20:11 fear of God. What Abraham means is that this community had no indicators that God was known or revered. When the phrase "fear of God" is used in Scripture, it does not suggest fright or fearful apprehension but worshipful respect and allegiance.

20:12 she really is my sister. Even though Abraham was half right, his deception was all wrong as far as God was concerned. Attempting to shade the truth to save our skin is an affront to God's promise to save us even when there's no obvious escape.

20:16 shekels. The king felt obligated to compensate Abraham for the inconvenience he had caused. The shekel referred not to a coin, but to a measure of weight. Shekels were the most common currency in this period.

21:1 did ... what he had promised. Finally, the impossible promise came true (15:4; 17:15–19).

if you were in Abraham's shoes? **2.** Are the parents being funny or serious when they named him Isaac which means he laughs?

APPLY What dream of yours has God fulfilled?

OPEN How did your oldest child react when a new member joined your family?

STUDY When Sarah, Abraham's wife, did not get pregnant, Sarah offered her maidservant to her husband to produce an heir. Then ten years later, God fulfilled his promise to Abraham for a son (Isaac) with his wife Sarah. **1.** How would you like to live in a tent with two women? Or be one of those women? **2.** How do you suppose Hagar (Sarah's maidservant) and Ishmael (her son with Abraham) felt when Isaac was born? **3.** What do you think provoked Sarah to tell Abraham, "Get rid of that slave woman and her son" (v. 10)? **4.** How would you describe Abraham's response? How would you have felt if you had been in Abraham's shoes? **5.** God intervened and provided for Hagar's and Ishmael's immediate needs. What is the lesson here for you?

APPLY 1. What relationship in your extended family causes you the most stress? **2.** How can this group pray for you about this relationship?

pregnant and bore a son to Abraham in his old age, at the very time
God had promised him. 3Abraham gave the name Isaac[a] to the son
Sarah bore him. 4When his son Isaac was eight days old, Abraham
circumcised him, as God commanded him. 5Abraham was a hundred
years old when his son Isaac was born to him.
6Sarah said, "God has brought me laughter, and everyone who
hears about this will laugh with me." 7And she added, "Who would
have said to Abraham that Sarah would nurse children? Yet I have
borne him a son in his old age."

Hagar and Ishmael Sent Away

8The child grew and was weaned, and on the day Isaac was weaned
Abraham held a great feast. 9But Sarah saw that the son whom Hagar
the Egyptian had borne to Abraham was mocking, 10and she said to
Abraham, "Get rid of that slave woman and her son, for that slave
woman's son will never share in the inheritance with my son Isaac."
11The matter distressed Abraham greatly because it concerned his
son. 12But God said to him, "Do not be so distressed about the boy
and your maidservant. Listen to whatever Sarah tells you, because it
is through Isaac that your offspring[b] will be reckoned. 13I will make
the son of the maidservant into a nation also, because he is your offspring."
14Early the next morning Abraham took some food and a skin of
water and gave them to Hagar. He set them on her shoulders and
then sent her off with the boy. She went on her way and wandered in
the desert of Beersheba.
15When the water in the skin was gone, she put the boy under one
of the bushes. 16Then she went off and sat down nearby, about a bow-
shot away, for she thought, "I cannot watch the boy die." And as she
sat there nearby, she[c] began to sob.
17God heard the boy crying, and the angel of God called to Hagar
from heaven and said to her, "What is the matter, Hagar? Do not be
afraid; God has heard the boy crying as he lies there. 18Lift the boy up
and take him by the hand, for I will make him into a great nation."
19Then God opened her eyes and she saw a well of water. So she
went and filled the skin with water and gave the boy a drink.
20God was with the boy as he grew up. He lived in the desert and

[a]3 *Isaac* means *he laughs.* [b]12 Or *seed* [c]16 Hebrew; Septuagint *the child*

21:3 Isaac. The name means "he laughs." Abraham once laughed, scoffing at the idea of fathering a son at his age (17:17). Sarah had laughed, too (18:12). This time, the laughter was happier.

21:5 God promised Abraham, now 100 years old, that he would be the father of a son by Sarah (17:16–17).

21:9 the son whom Hagar ... had borne. This refers to Ishmael.

21:10 slave woman and her son. Sarah didn't want her son to share his inheritance. This act was considered wrong in their culture.

21:11 distressed Abraham. Abraham clearly cared for his son Ishmael. He was greatly concerned that Ishmael would have a very difficult life being the estranged son of a servant woman.

21:12 Listen to whatever Sarah tells you. Once again God set Abraham straight, promising that both sons, Isaac and Ishmael, would father great nations. Even so, God's plan for Abraham's descendants would unfold through Isaac's line, regardless of the pain his disobedient servants were causing themselves in the process.

21:14 next morning. Despite certain anxiety, Abraham obeyed God's command immediately, even though it meant being away from Ishmael.

21:17 God heard ... God has heard. The name Ishmael means "God hears."

21:19 God opened her eyes. Hagar's grief was so deep that God had to open her eyes so she could see the much-needed water. The Old Testament often uses a spring or water well to symbolize both spiritual and physical salvation.

became an archer. [21]While he was living in the Desert of Paran, his
mother got a wife for him from Egypt.

The Treaty at Beersheba

[22]At that time Abimelech and Phicol the commander of his forces
said to Abraham, "God is with you in everything you do. [23]Now swear
to me here before God that you will not deal falsely with me or my
children or my descendants. Show to me and the country where you
are living as an alien the same kindness I have shown to you."

[24]Abraham said, "I swear it."

[25]Then Abraham complained to Abimelech about a well of water
that Abimelech's servants had seized. [26]But Abimelech said, "I don't
know who has done this. You did not tell me, and I heard about it
only today."

[27]So Abraham brought sheep and cattle and gave them to Abimelech, and the two men made a treaty. [28]Abraham set apart seven ewe
lambs from the flock, [29]and Abimelech asked Abraham, "What is the
meaning of these seven ewe lambs you have set apart by themselves?"

[30]He replied, "Accept these seven lambs from my hand as a witness
that I dug this well."

[31]So that place was called Beersheba,[a] because the two men swore
an oath there.

[32]After the treaty had been made at Beersheba, Abimelech and Phicol the commander of his forces returned to the land of the Philistines. [33]Abraham planted a tamarisk tree in Beersheba, and there he
called upon the name of the LORD, the Eternal God. [34]And Abraham
stayed in the land of the Philistines for a long time.

Abraham Tested

22 Some time later God tested Abraham. He said to him, "Abraham!"

"Here I am," he replied.

[2]Then God said, "Take your son, your only son, Isaac, whom you
love, and go to the region of Moriah. Sacrifice him there as a burnt
offering on one of the mountains I will tell you about."

[3]Early the next morning Abraham got up and saddled his donkey.
He took with him two of his servants and his son Isaac. When he had
cut enough wood for the burnt offering, he set out for the place God

[a]31 *Beersheba* can mean *well of seven* or *well of the oath.*

OPEN 1. How did your parents settle disputes between you and your brother/sister? 2. Have you ever planted a tree as a memorial?

STUDY The land along the coast and to the south was inhabited by the Philistines. They were ranchers like Abraham and wells were very important for watering their flocks and herds. **1.** How would you describe Abimelech and Phicol, the commander of his forces? Wouldn't it be nice if two leaders could be this way today? **2.** When a dispute came up over the well of water, how did the two leaders settle the problem? **3.** What did Abraham do to remind the two leaders of the oath they made? **4.** What are some principles you see in this story for settling conflicts?

APPLY 1. By nature, are you more like "Peace at any price," or "Let's have it out"? 2. What have you found helpful in settling disputes in your own relationships?

OPEN 1. In school, how did you feel before a big test? 2. If you were to take a treadmill test today, how would you do?

STUDY After years of waiting Abraham (age 100) and Sarah (age 90) have the son God promised. In this story, God puts Abraham's faith to the test. **1.** If you had been promised a son, what would you have said to God when he asked you to sacrifice your son as a burnt offering? **2.** When Abraham got to his destination, what was he expecting God to do

21:21 his mother got a wife for him from Egypt. Hagar made sure Ishmael married one of her kind.

21:22 Abimelech. This is not the same Abimelech who was king of Gerar (20:2).

21:27 sheep and cattle. These animals were most likely used to seal the deal in making the covenant or treaty.

21:31 Beersheba, because the two men swore an oath there. Beersheba means "well of the oath," so the place was named after the event that took place there.

21:33 tamarisk. Not many large plants grow in the desert, but the tamarisk, a shrub or small tree, is an exception. **Eternal God.** This title for God, *El Olam* in Hebrew, is found only here.

22:1 Some time later. By this time, Isaac was a teenager or young man. **tested.** As a way to confirm Abraham's faith and commitment to him (Ex. 20:20; Deut. 8:2).

22:2 Isaac, whom you love. Isaac was the only son of God's promise (21:12). God knew how much Abraham loved his son, but God wanted Abraham's complete allegiance to remain in him. God desires his people's complete obedience. **Sacrifice him.** This test looked ahead to the coming sacrifice of God's own Son—Jesus Christ—who would consecrate Abraham's spiritual descendants to God and fulfill the covenant promises.

22:3 Early the next morning. Again Abraham obeyed God immediately and without question.

when he said to his servants to wait until "we came back to you" (v. 5)? See also Hebrews 11:15. **3.** In the dramatic turn of events that followed, how did the simple question of Isaac (v. 7) get answered by God (v. 13)? How does this story illustrate the gospel and God's answer for the problem of sin in providing a substitute to take our place? **4.** Do you think he realized how significant this experience would be in the years ahead? **5.** What do you think this story teaches about giving your children to God—and God giving your children back to you?

APPLY 1. What is God saying to you in this story about your own obedience? Are you willing to put it all on the line for God? **2.** What is the test right now in your own life that could well effect the rest of your life?

had told him about. [4]On the third day Abraham looked up and saw
the place in the distance. [5]He said to his servants, "Stay here with the
donkey while I and the boy go over there. We will worship and then
we will come back to you."

[6]Abraham took the wood for the burnt offering and placed it on his
son Isaac, and he himself carried the fire and the knife. As the two of
them went on together, [7]Isaac spoke up and said to his father Abraham,
"Father?"

"Yes, my son?" Abraham replied.

"The fire and wood are here," Isaac said, "but where is the lamb for
the burnt offering?"

[8]Abraham answered, "God himself will provide the lamb for the
burnt offering, my son." And the two of them went on together.

[9]When they reached the place God had told him about, Abraham
built an altar there and arranged the wood on it. He bound his son
Isaac and laid him on the altar, on top of the wood. [10]Then he reached
out his hand and took the knife to slay his son. [11]But the angel of the
LORD called out to him from heaven, "Abraham! Abraham!"

"Here I am," he replied.

[12]"Do not lay a hand on the boy," he said. "Do not do anything to
him. Now I know that you fear God, because you have not withheld
from me your son, your only son."

[13]Abraham looked up and there in a thicket he saw a ram[a] caught
by its horns. He went over and took the ram and sacrificed it as a
burnt offering instead of his son. [14]So Abraham called that place The
LORD Will Provide. And to this day it is said, "On the mountain of the
LORD it will be provided."

[15]The angel of the LORD called to Abraham from heaven a second
time [16]and said, "I swear by myself, declares the LORD, that because
you have done this and have not withheld your son, your only son, [17]I
will surely bless you and make your descendants as numerous as the
stars in the sky and as the sand on the seashore. Your descendants
will take possession of the cities of their enemies, [18]and through your
offspring[b] all nations on earth will be blessed, because you have
obeyed me."

[a] *13* Many manuscripts of the Masoretic Text, Samaritan Pentateuch, Septuagint and Syriac; most manuscripts of the Masoretic Text *a ram behind him* [b] *18* Or *seed*

22:4 third day. It took three days to journey from Beersheba to the region of Moriah. Surely these were an agonizing three days of travel for Abraham as he contemplated what God had asked him to do.

22:5 we will come back to you. Abraham left his servants behind so he could obey God without hindrance. Notice Abraham said "we will come back." The author of Hebrews tells us Abraham knew he could trust God to fulfill his promise of descendants through Isaac, even raising him from the dead if it came to that (Heb. 11:19).

22:8 God himself will provide the lamb. Abraham continued to trust God. In verse 13, God did provide a substitute sacrifice. This passage looks forward to the sacrifice of Christ (1 Peter 2:24).

22:11 Abraham! Abraham! Abraham was just about to carry out the sacrifice, doing what he had been told by God to do. The angel called out to stop him.

22:12 Now I know. God certainly already knew how Abraham would respond, but by saying this God is in effect applauding Abraham for his complete trust. **fear God.** This means to *trust God reverently* and with sober commitment, to hold him in awe.

22:13 burnt offering. This is the first time in the Bible that the concept of substituting a sacrifice is mentioned. The ram took Isaac's place on the altar, just as Christ who "died as a ransom to set them free" (Heb. 9:15).

22:14 mountain of the LORD. As God had provided a ram to replace Abraham's son, he would provide his own Son as a sacrifice near this very spot. The mountain of the Lord refers to Jerusalem and the place where his temple would be built.

22:16 I swear by myself. Oaths are made by calling upon someone greater to witness the oath; God swore by his own name. **your only son.** Abraham had shown his great love for God by being willing to give up his son at God's command.

19 Then Abraham returned to his servants, and they set off together
for Beersheba. And Abraham stayed in Beersheba.

Nahor's Sons

20 Some time later Abraham was told, "Milcah is also a mother; she
has borne sons to your brother Nahor: 21 Uz the firstborn, Buz his
brother, Kemuel (the father of Aram), 22 Kesed, Hazo, Pildash, Jidlaph
and Bethuel." 23 Bethuel became the father of Rebekah. Milcah bore
these eight sons to Abraham's brother Nahor. 24 His concubine,
whose name was Reumah, also had sons: Tebah, Gaham, Tahash and
Maacah.

The Death of Sarah

23 Sarah lived to be a hundred and twenty-seven years old.
2 She died at Kiriath Arba (that is, Hebron) in the land of Canaan, and Abraham went to mourn for Sarah and to weep over her.
3 Then Abraham rose from beside his dead wife and spoke to the
Hittites.[a] He said, 4 "I am an alien and a stranger among you. Sell me
some property for a burial site here so I can bury my dead."
5 The Hittites replied to Abraham, 6 "Sir, listen to us. You are a
mighty prince among us. Bury your dead in the choicest of our
tombs. None of us will refuse you his tomb for burying your dead."
7 Then Abraham rose and bowed down before the people of the
land, the Hittites. 8 He said to them, "If you are willing to let me bury
my dead, then listen to me and intercede with Ephron son of Zohar
on my behalf 9 so he will sell me the cave of Machpelah, which belongs to him and is at the end of his field. Ask him to sell it to me for
the full price as a burial site among you."
10 Ephron the Hittite was sitting among his people and he replied to
Abraham in the hearing of all the Hittites who had come to the gate of
his city. 11 "No, my lord," he said. "Listen to me; I give[b] you the field,
and I give[b] you the cave that is in it. I give[b] it to you in the presence of
my people. Bury your dead."
12 Again Abraham bowed down before the people of the land 13 and
he said to Ephron in their hearing, "Listen to me, if you will. I will pay
the price of the field. Accept it from me so I can bury my dead there."
14 Ephron answered Abraham, 15 "Listen to me, my lord; the land is
worth four hundred shekels[c] of silver, but what is that between me
and you? Bury your dead."

[a]3 Or *the sons of Heth*; also in verses 5, 7, 10, 16, 18 and 20 [b]11 Or *sell* [c]15 That is, about 10 pounds (about 4.5 kilograms)

OPEN 1. What big wheeler-dealer have you been warned about in town? **2.** What do you do when someone starts haggling over the price?

STUDY Abraham has the promise from God that one day his descendants will own the land, but right now he is still considered an alien. So, when his wife Sarah dies, he must buy a burial plot. This chapter reflects many Hittite laws and customs, plus one wheeler dealer who seems generous but expects a hefty price. **1.** Why do you think Abraham decided to bury his wife in Canaan rather than take her back to the family burial ground? **2.** Do you think Ephron, the Hittite, really wanted to give the burial ground to Abraham for nothing or was he just following the custom for negotiating? How did Ephron get around to mentioning 400 shekels (which was an exorbitant price)? **3.** Before there were written contracts, what did they do to make sure the agreement would be honored? Would that be a good idea today? **4.** How would you like to negotiate with Ephron? If he started to haggle, what would you do?

APPLY 1. Where do you want to be buried? What kind of a funeral do you want to have?

22:20–24 Abraham's brother Nahor's children would become the ancestors of the 12 Aramean tribes.

23:1 Sarah lived long enough to see her son, Isaac, reach adulthood.

23:3 Hittites. This tribe lived in the area of Hebron during this time. This would be one of the tribes driven out by the Hebrews (Josh. 3:10).

23:4 an alien and a stranger. Abraham was living in a land he knew, would one day belong to his descendants. He never possessed the land; instead, he lived as a nomad and bought land in order to bury his beloved wife. Abraham was using this expression to bargain.

23:6 You are a mighty prince. The Hittites probably knew of Abraham's great wealth. Despite his nomadic lifestyle, he did own much lifestock and other forms of wealth.

23:9 cave of Machpelah. Although no one knows the exact location of this cave, according to tradition, it is beneath a Muslim shrine in Hebron.

23:10 sitting among his people. A city's primary gateway was the traditional place where important matters were settled. The exchange between Ephron and Abraham was traditional bargaining and took place in the hearing of many witnesses (v. 16).

23:15 the land is worth. Ephron was acting as though his offer was generous, but 400 shekels was an extremely

2. What do you want on your tombstone?

____

OPEN **1.** Do you have any memories of going on a "blind date"? **2.** As a teenager, where did you go to "hang out" with the opposite sex? **3.** If you could pick a mate for your son or daughter, what would you look for?

STUDY God promised Abraham that he would be the "father of many nations." Now, after his wife's death, Abraham has to find a wife for his son, Isaac, to carry on the family. This is possibly the greatest love story in the Bible outside of the cross. **1.** If you were to make this love story into a movie, who would you choose to play the part of: Abraham? Abraham's servant? Rebekah? Rebekah's mother? Laban, Rebekah's brother? **2.** What do you think about arranged marriages? Why would Abraham want to pick a wife for his son from his ancestral homeland? **3.** If you were Abraham's servant, how would you feel about being the "matchmaker"? **4.** When Abraham's servant reached his destination, what sign did he ask for to show him the right one? What sign did you look for in your courting days? **5.** How do you think Abraham's servant felt when Rebekah

16 Abraham agreed to Ephron's terms and weighed out for him the
price he had named in the hearing of the Hittites: four hundred shekels of silver, according to the weight current among the merchants.
17 So Ephron's field in Machpelah near Mamre—both the field and
the cave in it, and all the trees within the borders of the field—was
deeded 18 to Abraham as his property in the presence of all the Hittites
who had come to the gate of the city. 19 Afterward Abraham buried his
wife Sarah in the cave in the field of Machpelah near Mamre (which is
at Hebron) in the land of Canaan. 20 So the field and the cave in it were
deeded to Abraham by the Hittites as a burial site.

Isaac and Rebekah

24 Abraham was now old and well advanced in years, and the
LORD had blessed him in every way. 2 He said to the chief[a] servant in his household, the one in charge of all that he had, "Put your
hand under my thigh. 3 I want you to swear by the LORD, the God of
heaven and the God of earth, that you will not get a wife for my son
from the daughters of the Canaanites, among whom I am living, 4 but
will go to my country and my own relatives and get a wife for my son
Isaac."
5 The servant asked him, "What if the woman is unwilling to come
back with me to this land? Shall I then take your son back to the
country you came from?"
6 "Make sure that you do not take my son back there," Abraham
said. 7 "The LORD, the God of heaven, who brought me out of my
father's household and my native land and who spoke to me and
promised me on oath, saying, 'To your offspring[b] I will give this
land'—he will send his angel before you so that you can get a wife for
my son from there. 8 If the woman is unwilling to come back with you,
then you will be released from this oath of mine. Only do not take my
son back there." 9 So the servant put his hand under the thigh of his
master Abraham and swore an oath to him concerning this matter.
10 Then the servant took ten of his master's camels and left, taking
with him all kinds of good things from his master. He set out for Aram
Naharaim[c] and made his way to the town of Nahor. 11 He had the cam-

[a]2 Or *oldest* [b]7 Or *seed* [c]*10* That is, Northwest Mesopotamia

high price for such a property. Ephron seems to have been taking advantage of Abraham.

23:16 according to the weight. Abraham paid the current correct amount, even though standards changed at various times.

23:17 field ... cave ... trees. Ephron managed to free himself of all his legal and financial obligations relating to the property by negotiating the sale not only of the cave of Machpelah (which is all Abraham really wanted) but the entire field and its contents. *This is the only land Abraham ever really owned.*

23:19 buried his wife. By establishing this "family plot" in Canaan, Abraham was expressing his deep faith in God's promise to give his descendants the land. Canaan was his home now and would be for a long time. Years later he would be buried here as well (25:10).

24:2 chief servant. Most likely Eliezer (15:2–3). **Put your hand.** Abraham wanted his chief servant to make an oath, an oath so important that it was to be sworn on the Lord.

24:4 my country. Abraham sent his most trusted servant to find a wife for *his son, Isaac. Abraham did not want* Isaac to intermarry with the Canaanites, so he sent Eliezer back to where Abraham had come from, to find his relatives and to bring a suitable wife for Isaac.

24:7 To your offspring. Abraham never forgot God's promise to give the land of Canaan to his descendants. **angel.** This is grammatically equivalent to the phrase "the angel of the LORD," a way of referring to the presence of God himself that would guide Eliezer to successfully complete this task (16:7; 22:11; 48:16).

24:10 Aram Naharaim. The area between the Tigris and Euphrates Rivers, later known as "Mesopotamia." **Nahor.** This may have been named for Abraham's brother Nahor (11:26; 22:20–23).

24:11 toward evening. The women of the town would go to the well in the late afternoon, before dark but after the heat of the day.

els kneel down near the well outside the town; it was toward evening, the time the women go out to draw water.
[12]Then he prayed, "O LORD, God of my master Abraham, give me success today, and show kindness to my master Abraham. [13]See, I am standing beside this spring, and the daughters of the townspeople are coming out to draw water. [14]May it be that when I say to a girl, 'Please let down your jar that I may have a drink,' and she says, 'Drink, and I'll water your camels too'—let her be the one you have chosen for your servant Isaac. By this I will know that you have shown kindness to my master."
[15]Before he had finished praying, Rebekah came out with her jar on her shoulder. She was the daughter of Bethuel son of Milcah, who was the wife of Abraham's brother Nahor. [16]The girl was very beautiful, a virgin; no man had ever lain with her. She went down to the spring, filled her jar and came up again.
[17]The servant hurried to meet her and said, "Please give me a little water from your jar."
[18]"Drink, my lord," she said, and quickly lowered the jar to her hands and gave him a drink.
[19]After she had given him a drink, she said, "I'll draw water for your camels too, until they have finished drinking." [20]So she quickly emptied her jar into the trough, ran back to the well to draw more water, and drew enough for all his camels. [21]Without saying a word, the man watched her closely to learn whether or not the LORD had made his journey successful.
[22]When the camels had finished drinking, the man took out a gold nose ring weighing a beka[a] and two gold bracelets weighing ten shekels.[b] [23]Then he asked, "Whose daughter are you? Please tell me, is there room in your father's house for us to spend the night?"
[24]She answered him, "I am the daughter of Bethuel, the son that Milcah bore to Nahor." [25]And she added, "We have plenty of straw and fodder, as well as room for you to spend the night."
[26]Then the man bowed down and worshiped the LORD, [27]saying, "Praise be to the LORD, the God of my master Abraham, who has not abandoned his kindness and faithfulness to my master. As for me, the LORD has led me on the journey to the house of my master's relatives."
[28]The girl ran and told her mother's household about these things.
[29]Now Rebekah had a brother named Laban, and he hurried out to

[a]22 That is, about 1/5 ounce (about 5.5 grams) [b]22 That is, about 4 ounces (about 110 grams)

showed up and did everything he asked for and more? **6.** Why do you think Rebekah's mother and brother were impressed with the servant's proposal? How did your spouse's mother respond to your engagement announcement? **7.** What do you think Abraham's servant told Rebekah about Isaac on their way back home? **8.** How does this love story compare to your love story?

APPLY **1.** As a parent or grandparent, what are you praying for in a spouse for your children/grandchildren? **2.** How do you see the work of the Holy Spirit in your own life?

24:12 O LORD, God of my master Abraham. Abraham's servant was making his appeal on the basis of God's covenant relationship with his master.

24:14 I will know. Eliezer prayed, asking God for a sign to discern the woman God had chosen for Isaac. This sign was unusual and would cause this woman to stand out from any others. Any woman might offer a drink to a weary traveler at the well, but for a woman to offer water for his camel, she would have to be a woman with a strong servant's spirit.

24:15 Isaac would be marrying within Abraham's extended family–Abraham's grandniece–just as Abraham had requested (v. 4).

24:22 beka. A measure of weight. As the shekel was not a coin, but a weight (20:16), so a beka was a measure of weight, amounting to half a shekel. The value of the nose ring and the bracelets are here recorded by their weight and were very valuable. This would show the woman and her father that the family into which she could marry had great wealth.

24:26 bowed down and worshiped the LORD. The servant was overwhelmed by God's gracious work and prostrated himself on the ground to thank him.

the man at the spring. 30As soon as he had seen the nose ring, and the
bracelets on his sister's arms, and had heard Rebekah tell what the
man said to her, he went out to the man and found him standing by
the camels near the spring. 31"Come, you who are blessed by the
LORD," he said. "Why are you standing out here? I have prepared the
house and a place for the camels."

32So the man went to the house, and the camels were unloaded.
Straw and fodder were brought for the camels, and water for him and
his men to wash their feet. 33Then food was set before him, but he
said, "I will not eat until I have told you what I have to say."

"Then tell us," ⌊Laban⌋ said.

34So he said, "I am Abraham's servant. 35The LORD has blessed my
master abundantly, and he has become wealthy. He has given him
sheep and cattle, silver and gold, menservants and maidservants, and
camels and donkeys. 36My master's wife Sarah has borne him a son
in her[a] old age, and he has given him everything he owns. 37And my
master made me swear an oath, and said, 'You must not get a wife for
my son from the daughters of the Canaanites, in whose land I live,
38but go to my father's family and to my own clan, and get a wife
for my son.'

39"Then I asked my master, 'What if the woman will not come
back with me?'

40"He replied, 'The LORD, before whom I have walked, will send his
angel with you and make your journey a success, so that you can get
a wife for my son from my own clan and from my father's family.
41Then, when you go to my clan, you will be released from my oath
even if they refuse to give her to you—you will be released from my
oath.'

42"When I came to the spring today, I said, 'O LORD, God of my master Abraham, if you will, please grant success to the journey on which
I have come. 43See, I am standing beside this spring; if a maiden
comes out to draw water and I say to her, "Please let me drink a little
water from your jar," 44and if she says to me, "Drink, and I'll draw
water for your camels too," let her be the one the LORD has chosen
for my master's son.'

45"Before I finished praying in my heart, Rebekah came out, with
her jar on her shoulder. She went down to the spring and drew water,
and I said to her, 'Please give me a drink.'

46"She quickly lowered her jar from her shoulder and said, 'Drink,
and I'll water your camels too.' So I drank, and she watered the camels also.

47"I asked her, 'Whose daughter are you?'

"She said, 'The daughter of Bethuel son of Nahor, whom Milcah
bore to him.'

"Then I put the ring in her nose and the bracelets on her arms,
48and I bowed down and worshiped the LORD. I praised the LORD, the
God of my master Abraham, who had led me on the right road to get

[a]36 Or *his*

the granddaughter of my master's brother for his son. 49 Now if you
will show kindness and faithfulness to my master, tell me; and if not,
tell me, so I may know which way to turn."
50 Laban and Bethuel answered, "This is from the LORD; we can say
nothing to you one way or the other. 51 Here is Rebekah; take her and
go, and let her become the wife of your master's son, as the LORD has
directed."
52 When Abraham's servant heard what they said, he bowed down
to the ground before the LORD. 53 Then the servant brought out gold
and silver jewelry and articles of clothing and gave them to Rebekah;
he also gave costly gifts to her brother and to her mother. 54 Then he
and the men who were with him ate and drank and spent the night
there.

When they got up the next morning, he said, "Send me on my way
to my master."
55 But her brother and her mother replied, "Let the girl remain with
us ten days or so; then you[a] may go."
56 But he said to them, "Do not detain me, now that the LORD has
granted success to my journey. Send me on my way so I may go to my
master."
57 Then they said, "Let's call the girl and ask her about it." 58 So they
called Rebekah and asked her, "Will you go with this man?"

"I will go," she said.
59 So they sent their sister Rebekah on her way, along with her
nurse and Abraham's servant and his men. 60 And they blessed Rebekah and said to her,

"Our sister, may you increase
to thousands upon thousands;
may your offspring possess
the gates of their enemies."

61 Then Rebekah and her maids got ready and mounted their camels and went back with the man. So the servant took Rebekah and
left.
62 Now Isaac had come from Beer Lahai Roi, for he was living in the
Negev. 63 He went out to the field one evening to meditate,[b] and as he
looked up, he saw camels approaching. 64 Rebekah also looked up
and saw Isaac. She got down from her camel 65 and asked the servant,
"Who is that man in the field coming to meet us?"

"He is my master," the servant answered. So she took her veil and
covered herself.
66 Then the servant told Isaac all he had done. 67 Isaac brought her
into the tent of his mother Sarah, and he married Rebekah. So she

[a]55 Or *she* [b]63 The meaning of the Hebrew for this word is uncertain.

24:52 bowed down to the ground. Once again the servant stopped to offer a public acknowledgment of God's provision.

24:53 Rebekah was being asked to leave all that she loved. But the jewelry and clothing given to her and her family, revealing the wealth of her new household, most likely softened the blow.

24:58 I will go. After all the discussion with the family, the next morning Rebekah is finally asked her opinion—indeed, she is willing to go.

24:65 covered herself. Rebekah properly covered her face as was the custom for an unmarried woman.

24:67 tent. Rebekah entered the "tent" symbolically by entering the family through marriage, and literally by intimacy with Isaac in one of the tents which would be their home.

OPEN If you had to divide up everything you owned to give to your family and friends upon your death, who would you give your inheritance? Your books? Your Bible? Your souvenirs?

STUDY Abraham, the founder of a special tribe of people that God chose to bless, is dead. All that remains of his story is the burial and the designation of his heir. **1.** How would you like to have as many concubines as Abraham had? How would you like to be one of the concubines? **2.** Why were all of Abraham's possessions given to Isaac and not split with Ishmael? Do you think this will cause problems later on? **3.** When you think back over Abraham's life, what stands out in your mind as his "greatest hour" (Heb. 11:8–10; 17–19)? **4.** With only a few days in Abraham's life recorded in the Bible, would you call the story of Abraham a biography or a chapter in God's story of salvation?

APPLY 1. If you had to choose three or four days in your life as the turning points in your life, what would you choose? **2.** What would you like to pass on to your children?

became his wife, and he loved her; and Isaac was comforted after his
mother's death.

The Death of Abraham

25 Abraham took[a] another wife, whose name was Keturah. 2She
bore him Zimran, Jokshan, Medan, Midian, Ishbak and Shuah. 3Jokshan was the father of Sheba and Dedan; the descendants of
Dedan were the Asshurites, the Letushites and the Leummites. 4The
sons of Midian were Ephah, Epher, Hanoch, Abida and Eldaah. All
these were descendants of Keturah.
5Abraham left everything he owned to Isaac. 6But while he was still
living, he gave gifts to the sons of his concubines and sent them away
from his son Isaac to the land of the east.
7Altogether, Abraham lived a hundred and seventy-five years. 8Then
Abraham breathed his last and died at a good old age, an old man and
full of years; and he was gathered to his people. 9His sons Isaac and
Ishmael buried him in the cave of Machpelah near Mamre, in the field
of Ephron son of Zohar the Hittite, 10the field Abraham had bought
from the Hittites.[b] There Abraham was buried with his wife Sarah.
11After Abraham's death, God blessed his son Isaac, who then lived
near Beer Lahai Roi.

Ishmael's Sons

12This is the account of Abraham's son Ishmael, whom Sarah's
maidservant, Hagar the Egyptian, bore to Abraham.

13These are the names of the sons of Ishmael, listed in the order of
their birth: Nebaioth the firstborn of Ishmael, Kedar, Adbeel, Mibsam,
14Mishma, Dumah, Massa, 15Hadad, Tema, Jetur, Naphish and Kedemah. 16These were the sons of Ishmael, and these are the names of
the twelve tribal rulers according to their settlements and camps.
17Altogether, Ishmael lived a hundred and thirty-seven years. He
breathed his last and died, and he was gathered to his people. 18His
descendants settled in the area from Havilah to Shur, near the border
of Egypt, as you go toward Asshur. And they lived in hostility toward[c]
all their brothers.

[a]1 Or *had taken* [b]10 Or *the sons of Heth* [c]18 Or *lived to the east of*

25:1 another wife. Abraham had been married to Sarah, but apparently had many concubines, as noted in verse 6. Keturah may have been another concubine. Her descendants figure into Israel's later history and thus were given special mention here.

25:5 left everything. In this culture, the inheritance was divided among a man's sons, with the firstborn son receiving a double portion. Even though Ishmael was born first, Abraham counted Isaac as his firstborn son *according to law and according to God's plan.* Isaac was the son of God's promise, so Abraham left everything to Isaac so that all of God's promises and blessings would be kept within Isaac's line. **concubines.** God does not speak against polygamy, but generally many children caused problems in these families. Abraham had been forced to send Ishmael away (21:8–14), and here also had to send his many other sons far away.

25:7 a hundred and seventy-five years. Abraham left Haran at age 75 (12:4). God had kept his promise concerning a long life, allowing him to die at *a good old age* (12:2; 15:15). **gathered to his people.** A poetic way of saying Abraham had died and was buried among his relatives. Two of his sons, Isaac and Ishmael, buried him in the cave of Machpelah where Sarah had been buried (23:19).

25:12–19 Ishmael's genealogy (the line of the secondary promise) is followed by Isaac's (the line of the primary promise). Ishmael's line includes many names that are Arabian, showing that Ishmael was the ancestor of that line of people.

25:16 twelve ... rulers. There were 12 major tribes that descended from Ishmael; twelve major tribes also descended from Isaac's son Jacob, which became the twelve tribes of Israel (49:28).

Jacob and Esau

[19]This is the account of Abraham's son Isaac.

Abraham became the father of Isaac, [20]and Isaac was forty years
old when he married Rebekah daughter of Bethuel the Aramean from
Paddan Aram[a] and sister of Laban the Aramean.
[21]Isaac prayed to the LORD on behalf of his wife, because she was
barren. The LORD answered his prayer, and his wife Rebekah became
pregnant. [22]The babies jostled each other within her, and she said,
"Why is this happening to me?" So she went to inquire of the LORD.
[23]The LORD said to her,

"Two nations are in your womb,
 and two peoples from within you will be separated;
one people will be stronger than the other,
 and the older will serve the younger."

[24]When the time came for her to give birth, there were twin boys in
her womb. [25]The first to come out was red, and his whole body was
like a hairy garment; so they named him Esau.[b] [26]After this, his
brother came out, with his hand grasping Esau's heel; so he was
named Jacob.[c] Isaac was sixty years old when Rebekah gave birth to
them.
[27]The boys grew up, and Esau became a skillful hunter, a man of
the open country, while Jacob was a quiet man, staying among the
tents. [28]Isaac, who had a taste for wild game, loved Esau, but Rebekah loved Jacob.
[29]Once when Jacob was cooking some stew, Esau came in from the
open country, famished. [30]He said to Jacob, "Quick, let me have some
of that red stew! I'm famished!" (That is why he was also called
Edom.[d])
[31]Jacob replied, "First sell me your birthright."
[32]"Look, I am about to die," Esau said. "What good is the birthright to me?"
[33]But Jacob said, "Swear to me first." So he swore an oath to him,
selling his birthright to Jacob.

[a]20 That is, Northwest Mesopotamia [b]25 *Esau* may mean *hairy*; he was also called Edom, which means *red*. [c]26 *Jacob* means *he grasps the heel* (figuratively, *he deceives*). [d]30 *Edom* means *red*.

OPEN **1.** What have you been told about the particulars of your birth? **2.** Growing up, were you Mom's favorite or Dad's? How did that feel? **3.** Growing up, what was the "worst swap" you ever made with a brother or sister? Why did you do it?

STUDY The plot thickens. Or rather the pot thickens. Two sons are born to Isaac and Rebekah and the older brother sells his birthright to his younger brother for a pot of stew. This is no ordinary birthright. This is the right to all of the promises made to Abraham in the covenant. **1.** Putting the implications in this story aside, which one of these two brothers do you like? Why? **2.** What happened when the twins were born that will characterize their relationship from now on? **3.** How would you describe Esau: Temperament? Personality? Values? **4.** How would you describe Jacob: Temperament? Values? Personality? **5.** Do you think Jacob took advantage of his brother in a weak moment? How does their action fulfill the prophecy in verse 23? **6.** How do you think the parents felt when they heard about this? Do you think they could have done anything? **7.** What do you learn from this story about the ways of God?

APPLY **1.** By temperament, who do you identify with in this story? **2.** What is the decision you are facing that could have far-reaching consequences?

25:21 prayed. The Hebrew verb has the idea of pleading, so Isaac prays passionately for his wife.

25:23 older ... younger. Traditionally in this culture, the older son, received the double portion of the inheritance as well as special rights. The eldest son was given a position of prominence. In this case, the older son would be only a few minutes older, but God's plan was to bless the younger son and continue the line of promise through him. God chooses whom he will, and works as he desires (Rom. 9:10–12).

25:24–26 The birth of the twins provides two more examples of the way names were given descriptively—and often prophetically. Twins were considered a special blessing.

25:26 grasping Esau's heel. This is an early picture of the ultimate hostility that would become the rule between Jacob's descendants (the Israelites) and Esau's descendants (the Edomites). (Num. 20:14–21; 1 Sam. 14:47).

25:31 birthright. The birthright in ancient times involved the firstborn's rights of inheritance. Jacob, a schemer and deceiver right from the womb, tried any means possible to gain a personal advantage. God had already said that Jacob would be considered as the firstborn, but apparently neither Jacob nor his parents were willing to let God work in his way. Instead, Jacob tried to fulfill his own destiny his own way. The results were the same, but he could have saved himself much pain and heartache had he entrusted himself to God.

25:33 Swear. The transaction that would change lives forever was made fully legal and binding by a simple verbal oath.

OPEN **1.** What was the weather like in your area when you were growing up? **2.** Have you ever lived in an area where there was not enough rain for crops?

STUDY In Canaan where this story takes place, water was like oil today. It was the stuff that made the economy thrive or collapse. As the scene opens in this story, Canaan is having another of its periodic famines. **1.** Knowing that Isaac was given land from the covenant between God and Abraham, do you think he would be justified leaving it during a famine? **2.** How do you feel about Isaac telling the men of the area that his wife was his sister? How did it turn out? **3.** How does the Bible in the Old Testament look at prosperity (vv. 12–13)? What did Jesus revise in the Sermon on the Mount (Matt. 6:25–34)? **4.** How would you describe the reaction of the local herdsmen? Do you blame Abimelech for what he does (v. 16)? How do you think Isaac felt when he was asked to leave? How did God turn this into a blessing? **5.** Why did Abimelech and Phicol, his commander, reverse themselves and want to sign a peace treaty? How did they go about it? **6.** What lessons do you see in all of this about the working of God in the affairs of his covenant people?

APPLY **1.** As you look back at your own life, has prosper-

34Then Jacob gave Esau some bread and some lentil stew. He ate
and drank, and then got up and left.
So Esau despised his birthright.

Isaac and Abimelech

26 Now there was a famine in the land—besides the earlier
famine of Abraham's time—and Isaac went to Abimelech
king of the Philistines in Gerar. 2The LORD appeared to Isaac and said,
"Do not go down to Egypt; live in the land where I tell you to live.
3Stay in this land for a while, and I will be with you and will bless you.
For to you and your descendants I will give all these lands and will
confirm the oath I swore to your father Abraham. 4I will make your
descendants as numerous as the stars in the sky and will give them
all these lands, and through your offspring[a] all nations on earth will
be blessed, 5because Abraham obeyed me and kept my requirements,
my commands, my decrees and my laws." 6So Isaac stayed in Gerar.
7When the men of that place asked him about his wife, he said,
"She is my sister," because he was afraid to say, "She is my wife." He
thought, "The men of this place might kill me on account of Rebekah,
because she is beautiful."
8When Isaac had been there a long time, Abimelech king of the Philistines looked down from a window and saw Isaac caressing his wife
Rebekah. 9So Abimelech summoned Isaac and said, "She is really
your wife! Why did you say, 'She is my sister'?"
Isaac answered him, "Because I thought I might lose my life on account of her."
10Then Abimelech said, "What is this you have done to us? One of
the men might well have slept with your wife, and you would have
brought guilt upon us."
11So Abimelech gave orders to all the people: "Anyone who molests
this man or his wife shall surely be put to death."
12Isaac planted crops in that land and the same year reaped a hun-
dredfold, because the LORD blessed him. 13The man became rich, and

[a]4 Or *seed*

25:34 lentil stew. Lentils grow well even in harsh conditions, so they were an important source of nourishment in this arid land. **Esau despised his birthright.** Jacob was scheming to obtain what Esau did not care to have. Esau, the older son and the one destined to receive the inheritance and the promises of God, apparently did not appreciate all that this entailed. The New Testament calls him "godless" (Heb. 12:16), for he showed how unimportant he considered God's covenant promises.

26:1–6,23–25 The events in this chapter *may not be chronological to the* Genesis account. They serve to remind the reader of the covenant promise that had been passed from Abraham, to Isaac, and then on to Jacob.

26:1 Abimelech. He is likely the descendant of an earlier king who had the same name, with whom Abraham had a similar encounter (20:1–18). **Philistines.** They were a seafaring people who had migrated to southwest Canaan along the shores of the Mediterranean Sea. They would later become great enemies to the Israelites (Judg. 10:6–7; 13:1,5; 16:30; 1 Sam. 17).

26:2 The LORD appeared. God's first recorded appearance to Isaac. God repeated to Isaac the covenant he had made with his father Abraham (15:4–5).

26:3 with you. Precious words to Isaac. The God of the universe promised to be with his chosen servant. The promise is repeated throughout the Bible, for God continues to be with those who love him (28:15; 31:3; Ex. 3:12; Josh. 1:5; Matt. 28:20; John 15:5).

26:4 numerous as the stars in the sky. God had made this same promise to Abraham, and so here echoed it to his son, Isaac, through whom the promised line would continue (15:5). **through your offspring.** Isaac's descendants would influence the entire world. This echoes God's promise to Abraham recorded in 12:2–3.

26:5 Abraham obeyed me. Abraham was blessed by God because he obeyed God. **my requirements.** All the bases are covered in this legal language describing God's laws and regulations. Israel is reminded that their father Abraham obeyed God's will as revealed in his time.

his wealth continued to grow until he became very wealthy. 14He had so many flocks and herds and servants that the Philistines envied him. 15So all the wells that his father's servants had dug in the time of his father Abraham, the Philistines stopped up, filling them with earth.

16Then Abimelech said to Isaac, "Move away from us; you have become too powerful for us."

17So Isaac moved away from there and encamped in the Valley of Gerar and settled there. 18Isaac reopened the wells that had been dug in the time of his father Abraham, which the Philistines had stopped up after Abraham died, and he gave them the same names his father had given them.

19Isaac's servants dug in the valley and discovered a well of fresh water there. 20But the herdsmen of Gerar quarreled with Isaac's herdsmen and said, "The water is ours!" So he named the well Esek,[a] because they disputed with him. 21Then they dug another well, but they quarreled over that one also; so he named it Sitnah.[b] 22He moved on from there and dug another well, and no one quarreled over it. He named it Rehoboth,[c] saying, "Now the LORD has given us room and we will flourish in the land."

23From there he went up to Beersheba. 24That night the LORD appeared to him and said, "I am the God of your father Abraham. Do not be afraid, for I am with you; I will bless you and will increase the number of your descendants for the sake of my servant Abraham."

25Isaac built an altar there and called on the name of the LORD. There he pitched his tent, and there his servants dug a well.

26Meanwhile, Abimelech had come to him from Gerar, with Ahuzzath his personal adviser and Phicol the commander of his forces. 27Isaac asked them, "Why have you come to me, since you were hostile to me and sent me away?"

28They answered, "We saw clearly that the LORD was with you; so we said, 'There ought to be a sworn agreement between us'—between us and you. Let us make a treaty with you 29that you will do us no harm, just as we did not molest you but always treated you well and sent you away in peace. And now you are blessed by the LORD."

30Isaac then made a feast for them, and they ate and drank. 31Early the next morning the men swore an oath to each other. Then Isaac sent them on their way, and they left him in peace.

32That day Isaac's servants came and told him about the well they had dug. They said, "We've found water!" 33He called it Shibah,[d] and to this day the name of the town has been Beersheba.[e]

[a]20 *Esek* means *dispute.* [b]21 *Sitnah* means *opposition.* [c]22 *Rehoboth* means *room.*
[d]33 *Shibah* can mean *oath* or *seven.* [e]33 *Beersheba* can mean *well of the oath* or *well of seven.*

ity brought you closer to God or come between you and God? **2.** What is the closest you have come to being asked to "move on"? In retrospect, how did God use this to give you a blessing?

26:16 too powerful for us. The presence of God's people in the land, worshiping their unseen God who blessed them greatly, was seen as a threat by the inhabitants even at this early time.

26:20 The water is ours! It was hard work in this arid land to find and dig a well. So wells were greatly valued and protected. Disagreements such as this over the fresh water in a well were the norm.

26:21 Sitnah. The word, which means "opposition," is related to the Hebrew name "Satan."

26:25 built an altar. Isaac followed his father's practice of building an altar to worship God in a place where God appeared to him (12:7–8; 13:18). By doing this, Isaac was affirming the presence of the one true God with him.

26:30 feast. Often a feast would be held after a treaty was made. To sit down and eat with someone signified friendship and peace. This bound the two parties to the oath they had sworn.

34When Esau was forty years old, he married Judith daughter of
Beeri the Hittite, and also Basemath daughter of Elon the Hittite.
35They were a source of grief to Isaac and Rebekah.

Jacob Gets Isaac's Blessing

27 When Isaac was old and his eyes were so weak that he could
no longer see, he called for Esau his older son and said to
him, "My son."

"Here I am," he answered.

2Isaac said, "I am now an old man and don't know the day of my
death. 3Now then, get your weapons—your quiver and bow—and go
out to the open country to hunt some wild game for me. 4Prepare me
the kind of tasty food I like and bring it to me to eat, so that I may give
you my blessing before I die."

5Now Rebekah was listening as Isaac spoke to his son Esau. When
Esau left for the open country to hunt game and bring it back, 6Re-
bekah said to her son Jacob, "Look, I overheard your father say to
your brother Esau, 7'Bring me some game and prepare me some tasty
food to eat, so that I may give you my blessing in the presence of the
LORD before I die.' 8Now, my son, listen carefully and do what I tell
you: 9Go out to the flock and bring me two choice young goats, so I
can prepare some tasty food for your father, just the way he likes it.
10Then take it to your father to eat, so that he may give you his blessing before he dies."

11Jacob said to Rebekah his mother, "But my brother Esau is a hairy
man, and I'm a man with smooth skin. 12What if my father touches
me? I would appear to be tricking him and would bring down a curse
on myself rather than a blessing."

13His mother said to him, "My son, let the curse fall on me. Just do
what I say; go and get them for me."

14So he went and got them and brought them to his mother, and
she prepared some tasty food, just the way his father liked it. 15Then
Rebekah took the best clothes of Esau her older son, which she had
in the house, and put them on her younger son Jacob. 16She also covered his hands and the smooth part of his neck with the goatskins.
17Then she handed to her son Jacob the tasty food and the bread she
had made.

OPEN 1. When you were a child, who "blessed you" and made you feel special? **2.** Did you ever play a practical joke on someone by changing your identity or pretending to be somebody else?

STUDY The two sons of Isaac are at it again. Esau has already sold his birthright to his brother Jacob for a pot of stew. Now he loses the customary blessing for the eldest son. Oral statements given as blessings and curses were considered very powerful in ancient times and had legal force. **1.** Who do you feel sorry for in this story: Isaac? Rebekah? Jacob? Esau? Why? **2.** Why was the "blessing" so important in Biblical times? What would the "blessing" be in families today? **3.** How would you describe Rebekah in this story? If you were a judge in a court of justice today, what would you say about Rebekah's activity? **4.** How would you describe Jacob in this story? Was he a partner in crime or just being a mama's boy? **5.** How did Esau react when he found out that his younger brother had stolen his blessing? How would you have reacted? **6.** What disturbs you the most about this story? How do you feel about Jacob getting the "blessing" of Isaac and all of the promises of the covenant of God by dishonest means?. **7.** What does this story say about the mystery of God's ways?

APPLY 1. Whose "blessing" and approval have you sought

26:34 he married. Esau married not one, but two women, and they were not Israelites, but Hittites who believed in many pagan gods (26:34, 35; Judg. 3:5).

27:1 Isaac was old. Actually, he would not die for many more years (35:27–29)—he was just taking precautions. But he was becoming aged and was losing his eyesight.

27:4 food I like. Isaac loved the wild game that Esau would bring back from his hunting (25:28). *He was asking Esau* to prepare a special meal so that he could pronounce his blessing upon his eldest son. This was an important ceremony. Esau was supposed to have received both the birthright and the blessing, but he had already given away his birthright (25:34). Apparently, he had not understood the importance of that act, and he still fully expected to receive his father's blessing.

27:5 Rebekah was listening. God had told Rebekah when she was pregnant that the inheritance would go to the younger son (25:23). She did not allow God to work his plan, but instead schemed to make it happen. The transfer of the birthright had already occurred through Esau's own lack of concern for it. God would have shaped the events as he saw fit and accomplished his will without Rebekah's "help"; Rebekah, however, stepped in and resorted to deceiving her husband. She had eavesdropped and learned that the time of blessing was about to occur.

27:8 do what I tell you. Jacob's name means "deceit" (27:36), but Rebekah proves to be just as tricky and shrewd. She worked on Jacob's behalf; Isaac sought to bless Esau. Their favoritism (25:28) would hurt their sons.

27:13 let the curse fall on me. Jacob seems to have feared consequences for this deceitful plan, but his mother did not. She offered to accept the "curse," perhaps thinking that there would be no curse as all of this would fulfill God's plan anyway (25:23).

[18]He went to his father and said, "My father."

"Yes, my son," he answered. "Who is it?"

[19]Jacob said to his father, "I am Esau your firstborn. I have done as
you told me. Please sit up and eat some of my game so that you may
give me your blessing."

[20]Isaac asked his son, "How did you find it so quickly, my son?"

"The LORD your God gave me success," he replied.

[21]Then Isaac said to Jacob, "Come near so I can touch you, my son,
to know whether you really are my son Esau or not."

[22]Jacob went close to his father Isaac, who touched him and said,
"The voice is the voice of Jacob, but the hands are the hands of Esau."
[23]He did not recognize him, for his hands were hairy like those of his
brother Esau; so he blessed him. [24]"Are you really my son Esau?" he
asked.

"I am," he replied.

[25]Then he said, "My son, bring me some of your game to eat, so
that I may give you my blessing."

Jacob brought it to him and he ate; and he brought some wine and
he drank. [26]Then his father Isaac said to him, "Come here, my son,
and kiss me."

[27]So he went to him and kissed him. When Isaac caught the smell
of his clothes, he blessed him and said,

"Ah, the smell of my son
is like the smell of a field
that the LORD has blessed.
[28]May God give you of heaven's dew
and of earth's richness—
an abundance of grain and new wine.
[29]May nations serve you
and peoples bow down to you.
Be lord over your brothers,
and may the sons of your mother bow down to you.
May those who curse you be cursed
and those who bless you be blessed."

[30]After Isaac finished blessing him and Jacob had scarcely left his
father's presence, his brother Esau came in from hunting. [31]He too
prepared some tasty food and brought it to his father. Then he said to
him, "My father, sit up and eat some of my game, so that you may give
me your blessing."

[32]His father Isaac asked him, "Who are you?"

"I am your son," he answered, "your firstborn, Esau."

[33]Isaac trembled violently and said, "Who was it, then, that hunted

to obtain all of your life? Did you get it? **2.** How has the "blessing" and approval or lack of it shaped the person you are today? **3.** What are you doing right now to pass on the "blessing" to your children and grandchildren? **4.** In your spiritual family, who has affirmed you and made you feel special? How has this effected your spiritual life?

27:18–27 Jacob layered lie upon lie to convince his father he was Esau.

27:20 the LORD your God. Jacob referred to his father's God as "your God" until later in life when he began to build his own faith and trust in God (28:20–22; 33:18–20).

27:27 kissed him. In his sneaky attempts to obtain the covenant blessing, Jacob betrayed his father with a kiss. He was surely hardened with deceit to be able to do such a thing to the father whom he should have loved and respected. (Mark 14:44.)

27:29 over your brothers. The customary blessing included the fact that the elder son would be "lord over" his brothers. As Isaac spoke these words to his younger son, Jacob, he fulfilled what God had promised (25:23). So significant were the words of the blessing that once they were spoken, they could not be taken back. However, the deceit with which this was accomplished had its own sad repercussions.

27:33 will be blessed. There was nothing that Isaac could do. The words of the blessing were like a binding and legal oath that could not be broken.

game and brought it to me? I ate it just before you came and I blessed
him—and indeed he will be blessed!"
34When Esau heard his father's words, he burst out with a loud and
bitter cry and said to his father, "Bless me—me too, my father!"
35But he said, "Your brother came deceitfully and took your
blessing."
36Esau said, "Isn't he rightly named Jacob[a]? He has deceived me
these two times: He took my birthright, and now he's taken my blessing!" Then he asked, "Haven't you reserved any blessing for me?"
37Isaac answered Esau, "I have made him lord over you and have
made all his relatives his servants, and I have sustained him with
grain and new wine. So what can I possibly do for you, my son?"
38Esau said to his father, "Do you have only one blessing, my father? Bless me too, my father!" Then Esau wept aloud.
39His father Isaac answered him,

"Your dwelling will be
 away from the earth's richness,
 away from the dew of heaven above.
40You will live by the sword
 and you will serve your brother.
But when you grow restless,
 you will throw his yoke
 from off your neck."

Jacob Flees to Laban

41Esau held a grudge against Jacob because of the blessing his father had given him. He said to himself, "The days of mourning for my
father are near; then I will kill my brother Jacob."
42When Rebekah was told what her older son Esau had said, she
sent for her younger son Jacob and said to him, "Your brother Esau is
consoling himself with the thought of killing you. 43Now then, my
son, do what I say: Flee at once to my brother Laban in Haran. 44Stay
with him for a while until your brother's fury subsides. 45When your
brother is no longer angry with you and forgets what you did to him,
I'll send word for you to come back from there. Why should I lose
both of you in one day?"
46Then Rebekah said to Isaac, "I'm disgusted with living because of

OPEN **1.** When you get together with your brothers/sisters at family reunions, what is the atmosphere like when you play board games or touch football? **2.** Did your parents ever have to "bail you out" of a jam at school or traffic court?

STUDY Jacob has just stolen the "blessing" from his brother Esau, with a lot of help from his mother. Now, it's payback time. **1.** If you had been Esau and your brother stole the "blessing" that belonged to you, what would you feel like doing? **2.** How would you describe the reaction of Rebekah when she heard what Esau was planning to do? How would you have felt? **3.** How did

[a]*36 Jacob* means *he grasps the heel* (figuratively, *he deceives*).

Isaac had passed along the covenant blessing to Jacob and his words could not be withdrawn.

27:34 loud and bitter cry. The gravity of the situation overwhelmed Esau. He should have known that with losing his birthright he had also tossed away his blessing—whether he considered them taken deceitfully or not. God's will had been accomplished and could not be undone (Heb. 12:17). This did not make Jacob's actions right, but God worked through his people's imperfect actions to accomplish what he had planned from the beginning.

27:36 named Jacob? His name means "he grasps the heel," which figuratively means "he deceives." **He has deceived me these two times.** Esau wrongly blamed Jacob for deceiving him over the birthright. Jacob had not taken it by deceit; Esau had despised it and given it away (25:34). The birthright and blessing always went to the same son, and there was no point in trying to distinguish between them. Esau was not taking responsibility for his actions.

27:39 No blessing could be given to Esau except that he would one day be free from the yoke of his brother.

27:43 I say. Apparently Jacob often had to do as his mother said (v. 8). Because of their deceit, Jacob was forced to flee from home. Rebekah had planned to bring him back one day, but, she would never see him again.

27:45 should I lose both of you. Rebekah had "lost" one son through her obvious deceit against him; she could lose Jacob if Esau carried out his plan to kill him (v. 41).

these Hittite women. If Jacob takes a wife from among the women
of this land, from Hittite women like these, my life will not be worth
living."

28 So Isaac called for Jacob and blessed[a] him and commanded
him: "Do not marry a Canaanite woman. 2Go at once to Paddan Aram,[b] to the house of your mother's father Bethuel. Take a wife
for yourself there, from among the daughters of Laban, your
mother's brother. 3May God Almighty[c] bless you and make you fruitful and increase your numbers until you become a community of
peoples. 4May he give you and your descendants the blessing given to
Abraham, so that you may take possession of the land where you now
live as an alien, the land God gave to Abraham." 5Then Isaac sent Jacob on his way, and he went to Paddan Aram, to Laban son of Bethuel
the Aramean, the brother of Rebekah, who was the mother of Jacob
and Esau.

6Now Esau learned that Isaac had blessed Jacob and had sent him
to Paddan Aram to take a wife from there, and that when he blessed
him he commanded him, "Do not marry a Canaanite woman," 7and
that Jacob had obeyed his father and mother and had gone to Paddan
Aram. 8Esau then realized how displeasing the Canaanite women
were to his father Isaac; 9so he went to Ishmael and married Mahalath, the sister of Nebaioth and daughter of Ishmael son of Abraham,
in addition to the wives he already had.

Jacob's Dream at Bethel

10Jacob left Beersheba and set out for Haran. 11When he reached a
certain place, he stopped for the night because the sun had set. Taking one of the stones there, he put it under his head and lay down to
sleep. 12He had a dream in which he saw a stairway[d] resting on the
earth, with its top reaching to heaven, and the angels of God were ascending and descending on it. 13There above it[e] stood the LORD, and
he said: "I am the LORD, the God of your father Abraham and the God
of Isaac. I will give you and your descendants the land on which you
are lying. 14Your descendants will be like the dust of the earth, and
you will spread out to the west and to the east, to the north and to the

[a]1 Or *greeted* [b]2 That is, Northwest Mesopotamia; also in verses 5, 6 and 7 [c]3 Hebrew *El-Shaddai* [d]12 Or *ladder* [e]13 Or *There beside him*

Rebekah get her husband to go along with her plan (v. 46)? **4.** Knowing Jacob was his "mama's boy," how do you think he felt being sent away from home? Do you feel sorry for him? **5.** How did Esau react when he learned that his brother had left home? What did Esau do when he heard that his father had insisted that Jacob not marry a Canaan woman? What does that tell you about Esau? **6.** Looking back at these two sons, do you think it was a good idea for God to choose Jacob rather than Esau to carry on the covenant?

APPLY 1. When did you cut the "apron-strings" and leave home emotionally? Was it easy or hard? What motivated you? **2.** As you look back on your past at home, how do you feel? What is your relationship right now with your parents?

OPEN 1. What is the longest walk you have taken? How long did it take you? **2.** When you were a young kid, what did you dream about?

STUDY Jacob had to leave his home and his family in a big hurry. His brother, Esau, was going to kill him for stealing the "blessing" of his father. Jacob stops to sleep on his trip north. **1.** If you had been in Jacob's shoes, how would you be feeling as he leaves home? **2.** Up to now, the Bible does not record a single time when Jacob was interested in being with God. What do you think motivated

---

28:1 Canaanite. Rebekah concocted another deceitful plan by saying that she was sending Jacob away to keep him from marrying a Canaanite woman, as Esau had done (26:34–35; 27:46). The Hittities were a tribe that descended from Canaan (10:15).

28:3 God Almighty. This Hebrew name for God, "El Shaddai," was the name God would later use when identifying himself to Moses (Ex. 6:3).

28:4 the blessing given to Abraham. Paul later extended this blessing to Christians: "[Christ] redeemed us in order that the blessing given to Abraham might come to the Gentiles through Christ Jesus, so that by faith we might receive the promise of the Spirit" (Gal. 3:14).

28:9 in addition ... wives. Realizing that his current wives were a problem (26:34–35), Esau attempted to please his father by marrying a relative. So he went to his Uncle Ishmael's family (his father, Isaac's, older brother, 16:1–4; 21:1–21) and took a wife from there.

28:11 Taking one of the stones there, he put it under his head. As strange as it sounds, this made a more comfortable bed for Jacob. People traveled only with a cloak and some food, using the hard ground for a bed.

28:12 stairway. We may sing about "Jacob's ladder," but he probably saw a stairway. **angels of God ... on it.** In this dream, God demonstrated that he wanted a relationship with Jacob, that he wanted to be not only the God of his grandfather Abraham and of his father Isaac, but of Jacob as well.

28:13 above it. At the top of this stairway stood the Lord. The Lord was showing himself to be above all gods, and he was inviting Jacob into a relationship with him.

28:14 All peoples on earth. God had said these words to Jacob's grandfather, Abraham (12:3), repeated them to his father Isaac (26:4), and continued his covenant by repeating them to Jacob.

Jacob? **3.** What did God say to Jacob and what would this mean to Jacob at this time? **4.** How did Jacob respond? Would you call Jacob's experience: A conversion? A recommitment of his life to God? An existential encounter? A "fox hole" religious experience? **5.** Why did Jacob take the stone he had used for a pillow and turn it into a monument? What does Jacob promise God?

APPLY 1. Where is the "Bethel" in your spiritual pilgrimage? **2.** What is your dream right now?

OPEN 1. What do you remember about your "first kiss"? **2.** If you are married, where did you meet your spouse? What were your first impressions?

STUDY Jacob arrives at his mother's homeland where he has gone to find a wife. **1.** After a walk of many days, possibly weeks, how do you think Jacob was feeling when he got to his mother's homeland? **2.** What grade would you give Jacob for "opening lines"? Could you have done better? **3.** If you had been Rachel and a stranger rolled away a huge stone (that took three local herdsmen to move) and gave you a kiss, how would you feel? What do you think made Jacob break down and cry? **4.** What do you think impressed Rachel's father about Jacob? What first impression did you make upon your future in-laws?

APPLY 1. How would you compare this love story to your love story? **2.** When you met your

south. All peoples on earth will be blessed through you and your offspring. 15I am with you and will watch over you wherever you go, and
I will bring you back to this land. I will not leave you until I have done
what I have promised you."
16When Jacob awoke from his sleep, he thought, "Surely the LORD
is in this place, and I was not aware of it." 17He was afraid and said,
"How awesome is this place! This is none other than the house of
God; this is the gate of heaven."
18Early the next morning Jacob took the stone he had placed under
his head and set it up as a pillar and poured oil on top of it. 19He
called that place Bethel,[a] though the city used to be called Luz.
20Then Jacob made a vow, saying, "If God will be with me and will
watch over me on this journey I am taking and will give me food to eat
and clothes to wear 21so that I return safely to my father's house, then
the LORD[b] will be my God 22and[c] this stone that I have set up as a pillar
will be God's house, and of all that you give me I will give you a tenth."

Jacob Arrives in Paddan Aram

29 Then Jacob continued on his journey and came to the land of
the eastern peoples. 2There he saw a well in the field, with
three flocks of sheep lying near it because the flocks were watered
from that well. The stone over the mouth of the well was large. 3When
all the flocks were gathered there, the shepherds would roll the stone
away from the well's mouth and water the sheep. Then they would
return the stone to its place over the mouth of the well.
4Jacob asked the shepherds, "My brothers, where are you from?"
"We're from Haran," they replied.
5He said to them, "Do you know Laban, Nahor's grandson?"
"Yes, we know him," they answered.
6Then Jacob asked them, "Is he well?"
"Yes, he is," they said, "and here comes his daughter Rachel with
the sheep."
7"Look," he said, "the sun is still high; it is not time for the flocks to
be gathered. Water the sheep and take them back to pasture."
8"We can't," they replied, "until all the flocks are gathered and the
stone has been rolled away from the mouth of the well. Then we will
water the sheep."
9While he was still talking with them, Rachel came with her

[a]*19 Bethel* means *house of God.* [b]*20,21* Or *Since God . . . father's house, the* LORD [c]*21,22* Or *house, and the* LORD *will be my God,* [22]*then*

28:15 I am with you. God had made this promise to Isaac (26:3). Again God promises to protect and sustain with his presence. **I will not leave you.** It did not matter where Jacob went, the one true God would be with him. Jacob was running away from all that he knew, but he could not run from what God had planned for him.

28:17 house of God. Jacob had experienced the God that *his father had* known (27:20). God himself and his heaven had come down to the place where Jacob slept. Jacob was rightly in awe.

28:18 pillar. At this location, Jacob's grandfather, Abraham, had built an altar and called on the name of the Lord (12:8). Jacob took the stone on which he had slept and consecrated it with oil to remember what had occurred at this spot.

28:20 vow. Jacob's promise of faithfulness to God was conditional. He desired to be cared for on his lonely journey and to one day return safely. He knew nothing more about this God who had revealed himself, but he was open to following him. God did bring Jacob safely back to Bethel, where Jacob built an altar to him (35:1–15).

28:22 this stone. The stone would be a reminder of Jacob's meeting with God at Bethel, and Jacob never forgot the power of this meeting (35:3,6). **of all that you give me ... tenth.** This was a tangible way for Jacob to acknowledge the Lord as his God. The tenth, or tithe, was seen in Abraham's gift to Melchizedek the priest (14:20) and later was required by the Mosaic Law (Deut. 14:22).

29:9 shepherdess. Women often undertook the difficult job of caring for sheep and goats in the Middle East.

father's sheep, for she was a shepherdess. [10]When Jacob saw Rachel
daughter of Laban, his mother's brother, and Laban's sheep, he went
over and rolled the stone away from the mouth of the well and watered his uncle's sheep. [11]Then Jacob kissed Rachel and began to
weep aloud. [12]He had told Rachel that he was a relative of her father
and a son of Rebekah. So she ran and told her father.
[13]As soon as Laban heard the news about Jacob, his sister's son, he
hurried to meet him. He embraced him and kissed him and brought
him to his home, and there Jacob told him all these things. [14]Then
Laban said to him, "You are my own flesh and blood."

Jacob Marries Leah and Rachel

After Jacob had stayed with him for a whole month, [15]Laban said to
him, "Just because you are a relative of mine, should you work for me
for nothing? Tell me what your wages should be."
[16]Now Laban had two daughters; the name of the older was Leah,
and the name of the younger was Rachel. [17]Leah had weak[a] eyes, but
Rachel was lovely in form, and beautiful. [18]Jacob was in love with
Rachel and said, "I'll work for you seven years in return for your
younger daughter Rachel."
[19]Laban said, "It's better that I give her to you than to some other
man. Stay here with me." [20]So Jacob served seven years to get Rachel,
but they seemed like only a few days to him because of his love for her.
[21]Then Jacob said to Laban, "Give me my wife. My time is completed, and I want to lie with her."
[22]So Laban brought together all the people of the place and gave a
feast. [23]But when evening came, he took his daughter Leah and gave
her to Jacob, and Jacob lay with her. [24]And Laban gave his servant girl
Zilpah to his daughter as her maidservant.
[25]When morning came, there was Leah! So Jacob said to Laban,
"What is this you have done to me? I served you for Rachel, didn't I?
Why have you deceived me?"
[26]Laban replied, "It is not our custom here to give the younger
daughter in marriage before the older one. [27]Finish this daughter's
bridal week; then we will give you the younger one also, in return for
another seven years of work."
[28]And Jacob did so. He finished the week with Leah, and then Laban gave him his daughter Rachel to be his wife. [29]Laban gave his
servant girl Bilhah to his daughter Rachel as her maidservant. [30]Jacob

[a]17 Or *delicate*

future mate, was God very much in this first encounter?

OPEN 1. If you are married, what was the funniest thing that happened on your honeymoon? **2.** What was the worst practical joke you ever had played on you?

STUDY Jacob goes back to his mother's homeland to find a wife. He meets Rachel and immediately falls for her. Rachel's father makes a deal with Jacob for Rachel. **1.** How would you feel if you woke up after your wedding night and found out you married your sweetheart's sister? **2.** How do you like the deal that Laban struck with Jacob—seven years for his daughter Rachel? How does this compare with the deal your parents made for you? **3.** What do you think was the real reason Laban tricked Jacob and gave him Leah instead of Rachel? How do you think Laban was able to pull this off? **4.** Do you feel sorry for Jacob? If you had been in Jacob's shoes, would you have worked another seven years for your sweetheart? **5.** What is the lesson here for someone thinking about getting married?

APPLY 1. Did you have to wait a long time to get married? **2.** Could you say about your romance that waiting "seemed like only a few days because of your love"?

29:11 weep aloud. This was the kind of weeping done when overwhelmed with relief and joy. Jacob was overjoyed to find his relatives after his long, lonely journey.

29:16–17 two daughters ... Leah ... Rachel. The scene is set for the upcoming cruel contest engaged in by Leah and Rachel for Jacob's love.

29:17 lovely in form, and beautiful. Rachel's description is similar to Sarai's (12:11) and Rebekah's (24:16).

29:21 my wife. Jacob did not specify Rachel's name (apparently Jacob did not feel that he needed to; it was surely apparent who Jacob loved and wanted to marry). But by not making it specific, Laban took advantage of him. Jacob, who had deceived his brother out of his blessing, would be getting a taste of his own medicine.

29:22 feast. A wedding feast normally lasted a week (vv. 27–28; Judg. 14:10, 12).

29:23 Jacob lay with her. Jacob did not realize he had been tricked because of the darkness.

29:25 you deceived me. The tables are turned on the one who had acted as a deceiver. Jacob had deceived Esau in order to gain the birthright and blessing that should have gone to the firstborn son. In an ironic twist, the rights of the firstborn were turned on Jacob and he received the firstborn daughter as his wife.

29:28 Laban gave ... Rachel. At least Jacob did not have to wait another seven years before gaining Rachel as a wife. But he honored his commitment to Laban for seven more years of labor (v. 30).

OPEN **1.** What size family did you grow up in? **2.** Growing up, how much competition was there between you and your brothers/sisters? Over what?

STUDY Jacob traveled to his mother's homeland to find a wife and meet his mother's brother, Laban. Laban offered to give his daughter, Rachel, to Jacob in exchange for seven years of work. On his wedding night Laban switched his oldest daughter, Leah, for Rachel and Jacob had to work another seven years for Rachel. **1.** If you were Leah and you knew that your father had tricked Jacob into marrying you, how would you feel? **2.** How does God comfort Leah for not being loved by her husband? **3.** What effect do you think Rachel's childlessness had on her marriage to Jacob? On her own self-esteem? **4.** How do you think Jacob felt about all of this? How would you like to live in a tent with two wives and their maidservants and eleven children? **5.** Do you think Jacob realized in all of this that he was giving birth to his destiny—to be the father of the twelve tribes?

APPLY **1.** If you had it to do all over again, what would you do different (if anything) in planning for a family? **2.** What have you found helpful in dealing with family disagreements and struggles?

lay with Rachel also, and he loved Rachel more than Leah. And he worked for Laban another seven years.

Jacob's Children

31 When the LORD saw that Leah was not loved, he opened her womb, but Rachel was barren. 32 Leah became pregnant and gave birth to a son. She named him Reuben,[a] for she said, "It is because the LORD has seen my misery. Surely my husband will love me now."

33 She conceived again, and when she gave birth to a son she said, "Because the LORD heard that I am not loved, he gave me this one too." So she named him Simeon.[b]

34 Again she conceived, and when she gave birth to a son she said, "Now at last my husband will become attached to me, because I have borne him three sons." So he was named Levi.[c]

35 She conceived again, and when she gave birth to a son she said, "This time I will praise the LORD." So she named him Judah.[d] Then she stopped having children.

30 When Rachel saw that she was not bearing Jacob any children, she became jealous of her sister. So she said to Jacob, "Give me children, or I'll die!"

2 Jacob became angry with her and said, "Am I in the place of God, who has kept you from having children?"

3 Then she said, "Here is Bilhah, my maidservant. Sleep with her so that she can bear children for me and that through her I too can build a family."

4 So she gave him her servant Bilhah as a wife. Jacob slept with her, 5 and she became pregnant and bore him a son. 6 Then Rachel said, "God has vindicated me; he has listened to my plea and given me a son." Because of this she named him Dan.[e]

7 Rachel's servant Bilhah conceived again and bore Jacob a second son. 8 Then Rachel said, "I have had a great struggle with my sister, and I have won." So she named him Naphtali.[f]

9 When Leah saw that she had stopped having children, she took her maidservant Zilpah and gave her to Jacob as a wife. 10 Leah's servant Zilpah bore Jacob a son. 11 Then Leah said, "What good fortune!"[g] So she named him Gad.[h]

12 Leah's servant Zilpah bore Jacob a second son. 13 Then Leah said,

[a] 32 *Reuben* sounds like the Hebrew for *he has seen my misery;* the name means *see, a son.* [b] 33 *Simeon* probably means *one who hears.* [c] 34 *Levi* sounds like and may be derived from the Hebrew for *attached.* [d] 35 *Judah* sounds like and may be derived from the Hebrew for *praise.* [e] 6 *Dan* here means *he has vindicated.* [f] 8 *Naphtali* means *my struggle.* [g] 11 Or *"A troop is coming!"* [h] 11 *Gad* can mean *good fortune* or *a troop.*

29:31–35 God saw that Leah was not the wife Jacob loved, so he gave her Jacob's first four sons. Judah was the ancestor of Jesus (Matt. 1:2).

29:32 Reuben ... misery. Children were often named due to the circumstances into which they were born. Leah was unloved by Jacob and so lived a very difficult life. Reuben's name reflected that.

30:1 jealous of her sister. The word used for jealousy describes a strong inner rage. **I'll die!** Despite having Jacob's favor, Rachel got wrapped up in jealousy. She felt that she needed to have children or her life would not be worth living.

30:2 in the place of God. No matter how many schemes or tricks he might have played throughout his life, Jacob could do nothing to bring about the blessing of children. That gift was in God's hands.

30:3 so that she can bear children for me. If a man's wife could not conceive, it was an ancient custom for men to sleep with their maidservants to ensure the birth of a male heir. The child would then be considered the child of the wife and raised as an heir (16:1–2).

30:4 as a wife. Jacob did not actually marry Bilhah; she was a concubine through whom Rachel could bear children.

30:5–20 Jacob had twelve sons in all: six through Leah, two through Rachel, two through the maidservant Bilhah, and two through the maidservant Zilpah. He also had one daughter who was born to Leah.

"How happy I am! The women will call me happy." So she named him
Asher.[a]
14During wheat harvest, Reuben went out into the fields and found
some mandrake plants, which he brought to his mother Leah. Rachel
said to Leah, "Please give me some of your son's mandrakes."
15But she said to her, "Wasn't it enough that you took away my husband? Will you take my son's mandrakes too?"
"Very well," Rachel said, "he can sleep with you tonight in return
for your son's mandrakes."
16So when Jacob came in from the fields that evening, Leah went
out to meet him. "You must sleep with me," she said. "I have hired
you with my son's mandrakes." So he slept with her that night.
17God listened to Leah, and she became pregnant and bore Jacob a
fifth son. 18Then Leah said, "God has rewarded me for giving my
maidservant to my husband." So she named him Issachar.[b]
19Leah conceived again and bore Jacob a sixth son. 20Then Leah
said, "God has presented me with a precious gift. This time my husband will treat me with honor, because I have borne him six sons." So
she named him Zebulun.[c]
21Some time later she gave birth to a daughter and named her Dinah.
22Then God remembered Rachel; he listened to her and opened her
womb. 23She became pregnant and gave birth to a son and said, "God
has taken away my disgrace." 24She named him Joseph,[d] and said,
"May the LORD add to me another son."

Jacob's Flocks Increase

25After Rachel gave birth to Joseph, Jacob said to Laban, "Send me
on my way so I can go back to my own homeland. 26Give me my wives
and children, for whom I have served you, and I will be on my way.
You know how much work I've done for you."
27But Laban said to him, "If I have found favor in your eyes, please
stay. I have learned by divination that[e] the LORD has blessed me because of you." 28He added, "Name your wages, and I will pay them."
29Jacob said to him, "You know how I have worked for you and how

[a]13 *Asher* means *happy.* [b]18 *Issachar* sounds like the Hebrew for *reward.* [c]20 *Zebulun* probably means *honor.* [d]24 *Joseph* means *may he add.* [e]27 Or possibly *have become rich and*

OPEN 1. What do you know about raising sheep or goats? **2.** Did you ever try breeding any animals?

STUDY Jacob is still in the north country living and working for his father-in-law Laban and raising eleven children. But Jacob wants to return home. **1.** If you were Laban, how would you feel if Jacob told you that he wanted to take his wives, and children and go home? **2.** What does Jacob ask to take with him (vv. 31–33)?

30:14 mandrakes. Eating the roots of the mandrake plant, a Mediterranean herb, were thought to help a woman conceive. Their aroma was also associated with lovemaking (Song 7:13).

30:22 God remembered Rachel. When the Bible uses the word "remember" in this way, it means more than simple recollection. It is to act lovingly, with concern and care toward another (8:1).

30:23 disgrace. In ancient times, children were a sign of God's favor; so much so that a woman who could not have children was disgraced, shamed by God. For her to finally conceive was a time of rejoicing indeed.

30:24 another son. Rachel experienced the great joy of having a son all her own. She rejoiced and hoped that she would be able to have another son. Unfortunately, the birth of her next son would result in her death (35:16–19).

30:26 I will be on my way. Laban probably did not have a son at the time of Jacob's visit, since the text speaks only of his daughters (29:16). Jacob was likely adopted as his son and primary heir, a common practice. As such, Jacob and his family were considered part of Laban's household. However, in the intervening years Laban had fathered sons who could threaten Jacob's status (31:1). Jacob may have asked to leave, and it seemed like an appropriate time. Jacob desired to return to his homeland and his father's house, from which he had fled from many years ago (28:21; 31:13).

30:27 divination. Divination, the reading of signs in various places by various means, was forbidden to Israel because it did not place God as the sovereign ruler of the universe (Deut. 18:10). It was fairly commonplace, however, for finding out answers to one's questions. **blessed me because of you.** Surely Jacob's hard work, marriage to Laban's daughters, and many offspring had been a source of great blessing to Laban. This may also refer to the prophecy of 12:3.

How does Laban react (vv. 34–36)? **3.** How does Jacob get the best of his uncle? Is this a case of chemical manipulation, selective breeding or the intervention of God? **4.** How would you describe the character of Jacob? If you could put in one good word for Jacob so far in the story of his life, what would you say? **5.** Do you have a problem in believing that God could pick a person like Jacob to accomplish his purposes? **6.** Why do you think this story is in the Bible?

APPLY 1. How would you compare your personality to Jacob's personality? **2.** Do you think God has used or overruled the flaws in your character to accomplish his will for your life? **3.** What gives you hope today as you look at your life?

---

your livestock has fared under my care. [30]The little you had before I came has increased greatly, and the LORD has blessed you wherever I have been. But now, when may I do something for my own household?"

[31]"What shall I give you?" he asked.

"Don't give me anything," Jacob replied. "But if you will do this one thing for me, I will go on tending your flocks and watching over them: [32]Let me go through all your flocks today and remove from them every speckled or spotted sheep, every dark-colored lamb and every spotted or speckled goat. They will be my wages. [33]And my honesty will testify for me in the future, whenever you check on the wages you have paid me. Any goat in my possession that is not speckled or spotted, or any lamb that is not dark-colored, will be considered stolen."

[34]"Agreed," said Laban. "Let it be as you have said." [35]That same day he removed all the male goats that were streaked or spotted, and all the speckled or spotted female goats (all that had white on them) and all the dark-colored lambs, and he placed them in the care of his sons. [36]Then he put a three-day journey between himself and Jacob, while Jacob continued to tend the rest of Laban's flocks.

[37]Jacob, however, took fresh-cut branches from poplar, almond and plane trees and made white stripes on them by peeling the bark and exposing the white inner wood of the branches. [38]Then he placed the peeled branches in all the watering troughs, so that they would be directly in front of the flocks when they came to drink. When the flocks were in heat and came to drink, [39]they mated in front of the branches. And they bore young that were streaked or speckled or spotted. [40]Jacob set apart the young of the flock by themselves, but made the rest face the streaked and dark-colored animals that belonged to Laban. Thus he made separate flocks for himself and did not put them with Laban's animals. [41]Whenever the stronger females were in heat, Jacob would place the branches in the troughs in front of the animals so they would mate near the branches, [42]but if the animals were weak, he would not place them there. So the weak animals went to Laban and the strong ones to Jacob. [43]In this way the man grew exceedingly prosperous and came to own large flocks, and maidservants and menservants, and camels and donkeys.

OPEN 1. Did you ever sneak out of the house when you were a kid? Where did you go? **2.** If you could sneak off for a weekend now, where would you go?

Jacob Flees From Laban

31 Jacob heard that Laban's sons were saying, "Jacob has taken everything our father owned and has gained all this wealth from what belonged to our father." [2]And Jacob noticed that Laban's attitude toward him was not what it had been.

30:35 he removed. Laban did not seem to mind pulling tricks on his son-in-law. He had done it with his daughters (29:23), and would do it with these sheep and goats. By hiding them from Jacob, he would keep those sheep for himself. He always hoped to gain an advantage over Jacob, even though he knew he had been blessed by Jacob's presence (v. 27).

30:37–42 This strange custom must have been a belief among herdsmen regarding selective breeding of sheep and goats. Although Laban had done his best to trick Jacob, God was watching and cared for Jacob so that he would not be hurt by Laban's deception.

30:39 Jacob worked at selectively breeding the sheep and goats so that the odds were in his favor. He did realize, however, that God had been at work blessing him (31:7–9). This all occurred over a period of six years (31:41).

30:43 exceedingly prosperous. While Jacob lived in Haran, he gained wives, children, and wealth in the form of livestock.

3Then the LORD said to Jacob, "Go back to the land of your fathers
and to your relatives, and I will be with you."
4So Jacob sent word to Rachel and Leah to come out to the fields
where his flocks were. 5He said to them, "I see that your father's attitude toward me is not what it was before, but the God of my father
has been with me. 6You know that I've worked for your father with all
my strength, 7yet your father has cheated me by changing my wages
ten times. However, God has not allowed him to harm me. 8If he said,
'The speckled ones will be your wages,' then all the flocks gave birth
to speckled young; and if he said, 'The streaked ones will be your
wages,' then all the flocks bore streaked young. 9So God has taken
away your father's livestock and has given them to me.
10"In breeding season I once had a dream in which I looked up and
saw that the male goats mating with the flock were streaked, speckled or spotted. 11The angel of God said to me in the dream, 'Jacob.' I
answered, 'Here I am.' 12And he said, 'Look up and see that all the
male goats mating with the flock are streaked, speckled or spotted,
for I have seen all that Laban has been doing to you. 13I am the God of
Bethel, where you anointed a pillar and where you made a vow to me.
Now leave this land at once and go back to your native land.' "
14Then Rachel and Leah replied, "Do we still have any share in the
inheritance of our father's estate? 15Does he not regard us as foreigners? Not only has he sold us, but he has used up what was paid for us.
16Surely all the wealth that God took away from our father belongs to
us and our children. So do whatever God has told you."
17Then Jacob put his children and his wives on camels, 18and he
drove all his livestock ahead of him, along with all the goods he had
accumulated in Paddan Aram,[a] to go to his father Isaac in the land of
Canaan.
19When Laban had gone to shear his sheep, Rachel stole her
father's household gods. 20Moreover, Jacob deceived Laban the Aramean by not telling him he was running away. 21So he fled with all he
had, and crossing the River,[b] he headed for the hill country of Gilead.

Laban Pursues Jacob

22On the third day Laban was told that Jacob had fled. 23Taking his
relatives with him, he pursued Jacob for seven days and caught up
with him in the hill country of Gilead. 24Then God came to Laban the
Aramean in a dream at night and said to him, "Be careful not to say
anything to Jacob, either good or bad."

[a]*18* That is, Northwest Mesopotamia [b]*21* That is, the Euphrates

STUDY It has been 20 years since Jacob came to his father-in-law, Laban. In the exchange for marrying Laban's two daughters, Jacob worked for Laban 14 years. The next six years found Jacob and Laban trying to outsmart each other in the growth of their individual herds of livestock. **1.** If you could gather up your family and all of your possessions and return to the land where you grew up, would you do it? **2.** Why do you think Jacob wanted to go back to his homeland? **3.** How did Jacob's two wives, Rachel and Leah, react when he told them he wanted to go home? What was their reason for going along with the plan? **4.** If you had been in Jacob's shoes, would you have told your father-in-law that you were leaving or sneaked off like Jacob did? **5.** Why do you think Rachel stole the household gods from her father, Laban? **6.** Jacob seems to have a history of running away—first from his brother Esau and now from his father-in-law Laban. Is this a flaw in his personality or a coping mechanism?

APPLY 1. When you are faced with a tough situation that you do not know how to deal with, what do you do? **2.** What are you facing now that you would like to run away from? **3.** How can this group help you to make the right decision?

OPEN 1. Where did you hide your secret "treasures" when you were a child? **2.** What happened when you got caught "with your hand in the cookie jar"?

STUDY After years of conflict with his father-in-law, Laban, Jacob was called by God to

31:3 Go back. Good news for Jacob. He had desired to leave six years earlier, but had waited at the request of his father-in-law (30:25–27). At last God told him that it was time to go. He had been away from home for twenty years (31:41).

31:4 Rachel and Leah. In the Bible, often the order in which names are listed is significant. Rachel, the younger, is mentioned before her older sister. She was Jacob's first and true love.

31:18 Paddan Aram. This area was just east of Haran. Jacob had been sent here twenty years earlier to find a wife (28:1–7). He had done that—marrying two wives and becoming very prosperous (30:43).

31:19 stole her father's household gods. As with discovering answers to questions by divination (30:27), it was common for people in this part of the world to keep small wooden or metal idols in different rooms of their home. These "gods" were treated as heirlooms and were thought to be a source of protection or guidance. Rachel was unfortunately influenced by her pagan culture. Like a rabbit's foot, the gods she packed were the objects of trust for the journey ahead.

31:20–21 deceived ... So he fled. Jacob's track record is marked by his incriminating footprints. Because of his tendency to shade the truth, he could not afford to stand still. He had to run once again from someone he had deceived (27:42–43).

return to his homeland with his wives, Rachel and Leah. Jacob flees with his family and possessions. Something Jacob did not know was that Rachel had stolen her father's "household gods"—small portable idols. **1.** How would you feel if you were Laban and woke up one morning to find that your son-in-law had taken your two daughters, eleven grandchildren and all of their possessions and left town without saying good-bye? **2.** Why didn't Laban harm his son-in-law? What did God's warning to Laban mean: Don't chew him out? Don't mess with Jacob? Work out your differences peacefully? **3.** What was the final straw for Laban (v. 30)? Why do you think Rachel stole the household gods of her father? What does Jacob promise (v. 32)? How does Rachel get by with it? **4.** Who does Jacob sound like in the defense of his actions (vv. 36–41)? What kept Laban from sending his son-in-law away empty handed after 20 years of work (v. 42)? **5.** How did Laban and Jacob finally resolve their differences? What was the purpose of the "heap" of stones? **6.** How would you describe the relationship between Jacob and his in-laws? **7.** Do you believe that the tendency to deceive, cheat, lie and defraud one another was a character flaw that was inherited or a learned behavior? Would you say that abusive behavior today—like child and spouse abuse, drug and alcohol addiction, gambling and theft, lust and adultery, cheating, lying, stealing, etc.—are likewise inherited or learned behaviors in a dysfunctional family?

APPLY 1. How are you at resolving conflicts in your family or among your in-laws? **2.** When you cannot reach an amicable solution, what have you found helpful in getting on with life?

25Jacob had pitched his tent in the hill country of Gilead when Laban overtook him, and Laban and his relatives camped there too.
26Then Laban said to Jacob, "What have you done? You've deceived
me, and you've carried off my daughters like captives in war. 27Why
did you run off secretly and deceive me? Why didn't you tell me, so I
could send you away with joy and singing to the music of tambourines and harps? 28You didn't even let me kiss my grandchildren and
my daughters good-by. You have done a foolish thing. 29I have the
power to harm you; but last night the God of your father said to me,
'Be careful not to say anything to Jacob, either good or bad.' 30Now
you have gone off because you longed to return to your father's
house. But why did you steal my gods?"

31Jacob answered Laban, "I was afraid, because I thought you
would take your daughters away from me by force. 32But if you find
anyone who has your gods, he shall not live. In the presence of our
relatives, see for yourself whether there is anything of yours here
with me; and if so, take it." Now Jacob did not know that Rachel had
stolen the gods.

33So Laban went into Jacob's tent and into Leah's tent and into the
tent of the two maidservants, but he found nothing. After he came out
of Leah's tent, he entered Rachel's tent. 34Now Rachel had taken the
household gods and put them inside her camel's saddle and was sitting on them. Laban searched through everything in the tent but
found nothing.

35Rachel said to her father, "Don't be angry, my lord, that I cannot
stand up in your presence; I'm having my period." So he searched but
could not find the household gods.

36Jacob was angry and took Laban to task. "What is my crime?" he
asked Laban. "What sin have I committed that you hunt me down?
37Now that you have searched through all my goods, what have you
found that belongs to your household? Put it here in front of your
relatives and mine, and let them judge between the two of us.

38"I have been with you for twenty years now. Your sheep and goats
have not miscarried, nor have I eaten rams from your flocks. 39I did
not bring you animals torn by wild beasts; I bore the loss myself. And
you demanded payment from me for whatever was stolen by day or
night. 40This was my situation: The heat consumed me in the daytime
and the cold at night, and sleep fled from my eyes. 41It was like this
for the twenty years I was in your household. I worked for you fourteen years for your two daughters and six years for your flocks, and
you changed my wages ten times. 42If the God of my father, the God of

---

31:26–27 You've deceived me. The deceiver was being reprimanded for having deceived the one who deceived him! **Why didn't you tell me?** Surely Jacob knew the answer to Laban's question—he had tried to leave six years earlier and had been talked out of it (30:27–28). God had told Jacob to leave (31:3), but instead of leaving the *details to God, Jacob followed his old* pattern of deceiving and then running.

31:32 he shall not live. Obviously Jacob did not know the whole story. His wife was as deceptive as he was. His rash statement almost backfired in his face. Fortunately, Rachel was spared.

31:34 inside her camel's saddle. These "gods" were mere trinkets. How small is the faith of one who must trust for protection in gods that fit into her *saddle!*

31:35 I cannot stand up in your presence. Rachel used the excuse of menstruation (considered unclean) as a way of keeping her father from looking through the saddle on which she was sitting. Here is another example of Rachel's tendency to bend the truth. Although she appears to get away with lying, God despises it for he is a God of truth (Ps. 31:5; Isa. 65:16). Consequences are not always immediate, but a pattern of deception is always found out.

31:42 God of Abraham and the Fear of Isaac. This is another way of referring to God. It does imply fear as

Abraham and the Fear of Isaac, had not been with me, you would
surely have sent me away empty-handed. But God has seen my hardship and the toil of my hands, and last night he rebuked you."
43Laban answered Jacob, "The women are my daughters, the children are my children, and the flocks are my flocks. All you see is
mine. Yet what can I do today about these daughters of mine, or
about the children they have borne? 44Come now, let's make a covenant, you and I, and let it serve as a witness between us."
45So Jacob took a stone and set it up as a pillar. 46He said to his relatives, "Gather some stones." So they took stones and piled them in a
heap, and they ate there by the heap. 47Laban called it Jegar Sahadutha,[a] and Jacob called it Galeed.[b]
48Laban said, "This heap is a witness between you and me today."
That is why it was called Galeed. 49It was also called Mizpah,[c] because he said, "May the LORD keep watch between you and me when
we are away from each other. 50If you mistreat my daughters or if you
take any wives besides my daughters, even though no one is with us,
remember that God is a witness between you and me."
51Laban also said to Jacob, "Here is this heap, and here is this pillar
I have set up between you and me. 52This heap is a witness, and this
pillar is a witness, that I will not go past this heap to your side to
harm you and that you will not go past this heap and pillar to my side
to harm me. 53May the God of Abraham and the God of Nahor, the
God of their father, judge between us."
So Jacob took an oath in the name of the Fear of his father Isaac.
54He offered a sacrifice there in the hill country and invited his relatives to a meal. After they had eaten, they spent the night there.
55Early the next morning Laban kissed his grandchildren and his
daughters and blessed them. Then he left and returned home.

Jacob Prepares to Meet Esau

32 Jacob also went on his way, and the angels of God met him.
2When Jacob saw them, he said, "This is the camp of God!"
So he named that place Mahanaim.[d]

[a]47 The Aramaic *Jegar Sahadutha* means *witness heap.* [b]47 The Hebrew *Galeed* means *witness heap.*
[c]49 *Mizpah* means *watchtower.* [d]2 *Mahanaim* means *two camps.*

OPEN 1. When you pack for a trip, do you pack light or take all but the kitchen sink? **2.** For the same amount of money, would you choose two nights in a fancy hotel or seven nights camping in the boonies?

much as it suggests paying reverence and honor. Jacob knew about his father's relationship with God.

31:48 This heap is a witness ... That is why it was called ... It was customary to build an altar (in this case, no more than a heap of stones) to stand as a "witness" to an agreement between two parties, and then to symbolically name the witness (Josh. 22:10–12,34).

31:51–52 heap ... pillar. Jacob and Laban made a pile of stones to symbolize the significance of their agreement and to serve as a boundary marker. Laban appears to have wanted Jacob to agree to protect his daughters, but also never to come back to harm him. Laban, knowing himself to be untrustworthy, apparently would not even trust Jacob without this oath.

31:53 God of their father. The reference to the god of Nahor (Abraham's brother) and to the god of Abraham and Nahor's father suggests the culture of the day embraced many gods. Abraham's belief in a single deity went against the grain.

31:54 sacrifice ... meal. Covenants (or agreements) in Old Testament days were sealed with a sacrifice of some sort and a shared meal to celebrate the benefits of the agreement (Ex. 24:5–8, 11).

31:55 blessed. More than expressed affection or a token good-bye, Laban's gesture of blessing was considered a tangible promise of divine protection and success.

32:1 angels ... met him. These visitors were not your ordinary houseguests. Whereas some messengers from God appeared as humans, these were obviously different looking since Jacob recognized them immediately.

32:2 Mahanaim. The name Jacob gave this place means "two camps." In addition to his family camping here, there was another group of campers he had not counted on. The angel camp was a welcome surprise. He had left Laban, but knew that he would be again meeting his brother, Esau, who had wanted to kill him many years earlier (27:41-45).

STUDY Twenty years earlier Jacob had tricked his father into giving him the "blessing" intended for his brother Esau. Hearing of Esau's threats to kill him, Jacob fled to the north country where his mother had come from. Now, Jacob is on his way back home with his eleven children, two wives and possessions. But he has one problem. His brother Esau. **1.** If your brother had threatened to kill you 20 years before, how would you be feeling at the thought of meeting your brother again? **2.** What precaution does Jacob make before meeting his brother? What would you call his strategy? **3.** It has been 20 years since Jacob prayed. What do you think motivated him? How would you describe his prayer (vv. 9–12)? What do you think about people that "get religion" when they are in a jam? **4.** What does Jacob do in addition to prayer (vv. 13–21)? Do you think this was to impress his brother or to make a peace offering? How do you think Esau felt when he saw all of these animals coming toward him? **5.** Why do you think Jacob "spent the night in the camp" rather than going to meet his brother (v. 21)?

APPLY 1. What is the closest you have come to going through the experience that Jacob went through? **2.** How do you deal with a "showdown" with someone you have been estranged from? **3.** What is a relationship you would like this group to remember in prayer?

[3]Jacob sent messengers ahead of him to his brother Esau in the land of Seir, the country of Edom. [4]He instructed them: "This is what you are to say to my master Esau: 'Your servant Jacob says, I have been staying with Laban and have remained there till now. [5]I have cattle and donkeys, sheep and goats, menservants and maidservants. Now I am sending this message to my lord, that I may find favor in your eyes.' "

[6]When the messengers returned to Jacob, they said, "We went to your brother Esau, and now he is coming to meet you, and four hundred men are with him."

[7]In great fear and distress Jacob divided the people who were with him into two groups,[a] and the flocks and herds and camels as well. [8]He thought, "If Esau comes and attacks one group,[b] the group[b] that is left may escape."

[9]Then Jacob prayed, "O God of my father Abraham, God of my father Isaac, O LORD, who said to me, 'Go back to your country and your relatives, and I will make you prosper,' [10]I am unworthy of all the kindness and faithfulness you have shown your servant. I had only my staff when I crossed this Jordan, but now I have become two groups. [11]Save me, I pray, from the hand of my brother Esau, for I am afraid he will come and attack me, and also the mothers with their children. [12]But you have said, 'I will surely make you prosper and will make your descendants like the sand of the sea, which cannot be counted.' "

[13]He spent the night there, and from what he had with him he selected a gift for his brother Esau: [14]two hundred female goats and twenty male goats, two hundred ewes and twenty rams, [15]thirty female camels with their young, forty cows and ten bulls, and twenty female donkeys and ten male donkeys. [16]He put them in the care of his servants, each herd by itself, and said to his servants, "Go ahead of me, and keep some space between the herds."

[17]He instructed the one in the lead: "When my brother Esau meets you and asks, 'To whom do you belong, and where are you going, and who owns all these animals in front of you?' [18]then you are to say, 'They belong to your servant Jacob. They are a gift sent to my lord Esau, and he is coming behind us.' "

[19]He also instructed the second, the third and all the others who followed the herds: "You are to say the same thing to Esau when you meet him. [20]And be sure to say, 'Your servant Jacob is coming behind us.' " For he thought, "I will pacify him with these gifts I am sending

[a]7 *Or camps;* also in verse 10 [b]8 *Or camp*

32:3 land of Seir. Seir (modern-day Petra) in the land of Edom was a long way from where Jacob was headed. Jacob was concerned about catching his brother by surprise. Jacob went out of his way to let his brother Esau know he was headed home.

32:4 Your servant. This was Jacob's *way of saying he was sorry for his big*-shot attitude and big-time deception years before.

32:6 coming to meet you. Like the advance of dark clouds on the horizon, what is headed our way can be either welcome rain or a destructive storm. The word that Esau was headed his way with four hundred men must have been a source of anxiety to Jacob.

32:9 Jacob prayed. Even though the beast that approached was only a potentially vicious brother, Jacob climbed into a foxhole to seek God's help. Curiously, this is the first time we have seen Jacob in a posture of prayer since he left Bethel (28:20–22).

32:12 like the sand of the sea. God promised Abraham, Isaac and Jacob they would have descendants too numerous to count (22:17; 26:4). Jacob was remembering God's words to him (28:14).

32:13 gift. Not sure if God will answer his prayer, Jacob hedges his bets. Perhaps he can butter up his brother with a herd of milk-producing goats.

on ahead; later, when I see him, perhaps he will receive me." [21]So Jacob's gifts went on ahead of him, but he himself spent the night in the camp.

Jacob Wrestles With God

[22]That night Jacob got up and took his two wives, his two maidservants and his eleven sons and crossed the ford of the Jabbok. [23]After he had sent them across the stream, he sent over all his possessions. [24]So Jacob was left alone, and a man wrestled with him till daybreak. [25]When the man saw that he could not overpower him, he touched the socket of Jacob's hip so that his hip was wrenched as he wrestled with the man. [26]Then the man said, "Let me go, for it is daybreak."

But Jacob replied, "I will not let you go unless you bless me."

[27]The man asked him, "What is your name?"

"Jacob," he answered.

[28]Then the man said, "Your name will no longer be Jacob, but Israel,[a] because you have struggled with God and with men and have overcome."

[29]Jacob said, "Please tell me your name."

But he replied, "Why do you ask my name?" Then he blessed him there.

[30]So Jacob called the place Peniel,[b] saying, "It is because I saw God face to face, and yet my life was spared."

[31]The sun rose above him as he passed Peniel,[c] and he was limping because of his hip. [32]Therefore to this day the Israelites do not eat the tendon attached to the socket of the hip, because the socket of Jacob's hip was touched near the tendon.

Jacob Meets Esau

33 Jacob looked up and there was Esau, coming with his four hundred men; so he divided the children among Leah, Rachel and the two maidservants. [2]He put the maid-servants and their children in front, Leah and her children next, and Rachel and Joseph in the rear. [3]He himself went on ahead and bowed down to the ground seven times as he approached his brother.

[a]28 *Israel* means *he struggles with God.* [b]30 *Peniel* means *face of God.* [c]31 Hebrew *Penuel,* a variant of *Peniel*

OPEN 1. Who is the person in your family who will not give up until they get what they want? **2.** What was your nickname in school?

STUDY 1. If you had spent your life cheating, deceiving and stealing and you were going to meet someone you had wronged the next day and this guy said he was going to kill you, how would you spend the night? **2.** How would you describe the wrestling match between Jacob and this man/angel? Who won? What does this mean? **3.** What do you think Jacob was after when he said, "I will not let you go unless you bless me"? **4.** When the angel changed Jacob's name to Israel, what was he saying?

APPLY Where is the Peniel in your life—the place where you and God meet face to face and your life will never be the same?

OPEN How did you feel before a big test in school? How did you prepare for it?

STUDY Jacob has not seen his brother for 20 years. Jacob used cunning and trickery to steal his brother's birthright and "blessing" as the older brother. Now they are going to meet again. **1.** When Jacob looked up and saw his brother coming, how

32:24 left alone. When we are concerned about the future, there is no more vulnerable place to be than alone with our God. **wrestled.** Jacob was known as a "heel grabber." He attempted to pin Esau to the mat early in his life. He wrestled Laban to gain an advantage, and now he attempted to twist God's arm. He would learn who held ultimate control over his life.

32:25 his hip was wrenched as he wrestled. Jacob could wrestle with God. Yet God, with one touch, revealed that he had the ultimate power.

32:26 not ... unless you bless me. Jacob was not penalized for holding. Rather, his unwavering persistence is a positive example. Hanging on to God for dear life is a key to blessing. Jacob realized that if he was going to be blessed, God would have to do it.

32:28 Israel. Not only was Jacob given a new walk (his limp is to remind him of God's controlling power, v. 31), he was given a new name. As a way of underscoring the significance of Jacob's change in character, his name was changed to Israel and would become a point of reference for an entire nation.

32:29 Why do you ask my name? Speaking of names, Jacob wondered about the name of him who had given him a new name. God cannot be reduced to a name. He is God.

32:30 Peniel. The name means "face of God." In a never-to-be-forgotten encounter with the Almighty, Jacob knew that in wrestling all night with God, he had been graced with God's almighty presence and had been blessed.

33:1–2 Leah ... children ... Rachel and Joseph in the rear. As Jacob neared his meeting with Esau, he divided up his family. In this procession of progeny, his favorite wife and favorite son brought up the rear. He protected those he loved the most from possible danger.

33:3 bowed. Bending face first seven times was an honor reserved for a king. Jacob's show of honor was to cool his brother's anger.

4But Esau ran to meet Jacob and embraced him; he threw his arms
around his neck and kissed him. And they wept. 5Then Esau looked
up and saw the women and children. "Who are these with you?" he
asked.

Jacob answered, "They are the children God has graciously given
your servant."

6Then the maidservants and their children approached and bowed
down. 7Next, Leah and her children came and bowed down. Last of
all came Joseph and Rachel, and they too bowed down.

8Esau asked, "What do you mean by all these droves I met?"

"To find favor in your eyes, my lord," he said.

9But Esau said, "I already have plenty, my brother. Keep what you
have for yourself."

10"No, please!" said Jacob. "If I have found favor in your eyes, accept this gift from me. For to see your face is like seeing the face of
God, now that you have received me favorably. 11Please accept the
present that was brought to you, for God has been gracious to me
and I have all I need." And because Jacob insisted, Esau accepted it.

12Then Esau said, "Let us be on our way; I'll accompany you."

13But Jacob said to him, "My lord knows that the children are tender and that I must care for the ewes and cows that are nursing their
young. If they are driven hard just one day, all the animals will die.
14So let my lord go on ahead of his servant, while I move along slowly
at the pace of the droves before me and that of the children, until I
come to my lord in Seir."

15Esau said, "Then let me leave some of my men with you."

"But why do that?" Jacob asked. "Just let me find favor in the eyes
of my lord."

16So that day Esau started on his way back to Seir. 17Jacob, however, went to Succoth, where he built a place for himself and made shelters for his livestock. That is why the place is called Succoth.[a]

18After Jacob came from Paddan Aram,[b] he arrived safely at the[c] city
of Shechem in Canaan and camped within sight of the city. 19For a
hundred pieces of silver,[d] he bought from the sons of Hamor, the father of Shechem, the plot of ground where he pitched his tent.
20There he set up an altar and called it El Elohe Israel.[e]

Dinah and the Shechemites

34 Now Dinah, the daughter Leah had borne to Jacob, went out
to visit the women of the land. 2When Shechem son of Hamor the Hivite, the ruler of that area, saw her, he took her and violated her. 3His heart was drawn to Dinah daughter of Jacob, and he

[a]17 *Succoth* means *shelters.* [b]18 That is, Northwest Mesopotamia [c]18 Or *arrived at Shalem, a* [d]19 Hebrew *hundred kesitahs;* a kesitah was a unit of money of unknown weight and value. [e]20 *El Elohe Israel* can mean *God, the God of Israel* or *mighty is the God of Israel.*

do you think he felt? **2.** How would you describe the meeting of Jacob and Esau? Do you think Esau has forgiven his brother for stealing his birthright or just forgotten about it? **3.** Do you think Jacob is truly sorry or just protecting his own hide in offering these gifts? **4.** Why do you think Jacob settled down in Shechem and didn't go with his brother to Seir to the south? What does the altar that Jacob built tell you about Jacob? **5.** As you look back over the story of these two brothers, who would you like to have as a buddy? As a business partner? **6.** Do you look upon the 20 years that Jacob spent away from home and away from God as "wasted years"?

APPLY 1. As you look back over your life, what are the years you spent in the north country away from God? **2.** Were these wasted years or learning years?

OPEN 1. What is the most recent story you have read in the newspaper of rape? **2.** Can you remember a movie about "revenge" killing?

STUDY Two things are important to remember to put this story in context. First, Jacob and his family are the descendants of the

---

33:4 Esau ran to meet Jacob. All Jacob's actions proved to be unnecessary obstacles to a forgiving brother bent on embracing the one he had not seen in years. *Esau ran and threw his arms around* the one who had so wronged him. God's grace toward Jacob and family solidarity cannot be missed in this moving scene.

33:9 my brother. Whereas, Jacob felt the need to try and impress Esau with hyperbolic expressions of servitude, Esau said it like it was. No game playing necessary. In spite of past mistakes, they were still brothers. Commitment covers a multitude of imperfections.

34:1–31 This chapter tells a story of violence, perversion and revenge.

34:2 Shechem. Shechem was the name of both a Canaanite town and the son of one of its powerful men. Abraham had built an altar there (12:6–7); likewise, Jacob had purchased land near the city of Shechem and built an altar there (33:18–20).

loved the girl and spoke tenderly to her. 4And Shechem said to his father Hamor, "Get me this girl as my wife."
5When Jacob heard that his daughter Dinah had been defiled, his
sons were in the fields with his livestock; so he kept quiet about it
until they came home.
6Then Shechem's father Hamor went out to talk with Jacob. 7Now
Jacob's sons had come in from the fields as soon as they heard what
had happened. They were filled with grief and fury, because Shechem
had done a disgraceful thing in[a] Israel by lying with Jacob's daughter—a thing that should not be done.
8But Hamor said to them, "My son Shechem has his heart set on
your daughter. Please give her to him as his wife. 9Intermarry with us;
give us your daughters and take our daughters for yourselves. 10You
can settle among us; the land is open to you. Live in it, trade[b] in it,
and acquire property in it."
11Then Shechem said to Dinah's father and brothers, "Let me find
favor in your eyes, and I will give you whatever you ask. 12Make the
price for the bride and the gift I am to bring as great as you like, and
I'll pay whatever you ask me. Only give me the girl as my wife."
13Because their sister Dinah had been defiled, Jacob's sons replied
deceitfully as they spoke to Shechem and his father Hamor. 14They
said to them, "We can't do such a thing; we can't give our sister to a
man who is not circumcised. That would be a disgrace to us. 15We will
give our consent to you on one condition only: that you become like
us by circumcising all your males. 16Then we will give you our daughters and take your daughters for ourselves. We'll settle among you
and become one people with you. 17But if you will not agree to be circumcised, we'll take our sister[c] and go."
18Their proposal seemed good to Hamor and his son Shechem.
19The young man, who was the most honored of all his father's
household, lost no time in doing what they said, because he was delighted with Jacob's daughter. 20So Hamor and his son Shechem went
to the gate of their city to speak to their fellow townsmen. 21"These
men are friendly toward us," they said. "Let them live in our land and

[a]7 Or *against* [b]10 Or *move about freely*; also in verse 21 [c]17 Hebrew *daughter*

covenant given to Abraham. As the "chosen" people of the covenant, they were not supposed to intermarry with the native population. Second, the sign of their distinctive relationship with God was circumcision which was performed soon after birth. **1.** If this story happened today, where would it appear in the newspaper: Local news? Crime section? Front page feature? Special supplement? Editorial? **2.** What would you do if your daughter was raped by a guy of another religion and your sons wanted to kill every male of this religion in your town? **3.** Do you think the guy who committed the rape and his father acted honorably in inviting Jacob and his family to settle down and intermarry with their people? **4.** How would you describe the behavior of Jacob's sons (vv. 13–17)? Where did they get their deceit? **5.** Do you think the sons of Jacob committed this atrocity: Out of revenge? Offended moral conviction? Desire to keep their family pure for the covenant with God? Or greed? **6.** What is Jacob concerned about? If you had been in his shoes, how would you be feeling? **7.** Why do you think this story is in the Bible? What is the lesson in this story for today?

APPLY **1.** How do you feel about intermarriage of a believer with a non-believer? **2.** How are you going to deal with this issue when it comes up with your children or grandchildren?

34:7 grief and fury. Dinah's brothers responded in this way not just because the offense was against their sister. Their whole family had suffered loss and violation by Shechem's actions.

34:9 Intermarry. Rather than fight with the clan of Israel, Hamor proposed a diplomatic solution. He desired Jacob's family, goods and wealth. However, Jacob himself had been commanded by his father not to marry a Canaanite woman, and he did not want his sons to do so (28:1).

34:10 acquire property. Little did Hamor know that the entire land already belonged to the family to whom he was speaking (28:13).

34:12 I'll pay whatever you ask me. Shechem's offer was an ironic parallel to Jacob's dealings with his father-in-law. Jacob paid with years of work, not money (29:18). In this culture, fathers would receive gifts in exchange for giving a daughter away in marriage.

34:13 Jacob's sons replied deceitfully. No doubt they had learned this practice at their father's knee, hearing how Jacob had tricked his own father and brother, Esau. They were also responding to Hamor's deception.

34:15 circumcising all your males. Like Hamor's proposal (vv. 8–10), the demands of Dinah's brothers seemed reasonable on the surface. Circumcision was a sacred ceremony (17:10), but these brothers' intentions were dishonorable and brought terrible consequences.

trade in it; the land has plenty of room for them. We can marry their
daughters and they can marry ours. 22But the men will consent to live
with us as one people only on the condition that our males be circumcised, as they themselves are. 23Won't their livestock, their property and all their other animals become ours? So let us give our
consent to them, and they will settle among us."

24All the men who went out of the city gate agreed with Hamor and
his son Shechem, and every male in the city was circumcised.

25Three days later, while all of them were still in pain, two of
Jacob's sons, Simeon and Levi, Dinah's brothers, took their swords
and attacked the unsuspecting city, killing every male. 26They put
Hamor and his son Shechem to the sword and took Dinah from
Shechem's house and left. 27The sons of Jacob came upon the dead
bodies and looted the city where[a] their sister had been defiled. 28They
seized their flocks and herds and donkeys and everything else of
theirs in the city and out in the fields. 29They carried off all their
wealth and all their women and children, taking as plunder everything in the houses.

30Then Jacob said to Simeon and Levi, "You have brought trouble
on me by making me a stench to the Canaanites and Perizzites, the
people living in this land. We are few in number, and if they join
forces against me and attack me, I and my household will be destroyed."

31But they replied, "Should he have treated our sister like a prostitute?"

Jacob Returns to Bethel

35 Then God said to Jacob, "Go up to Bethel and settle there,
and build an altar there to God, who appeared to you when
you were fleeing from your brother Esau."

2So Jacob said to his household and to all who were with him, "Get
rid of the foreign gods you have with you, and purify yourselves and
change your clothes. 3Then come, let us go up to Bethel, where I will
build an altar to God, who answered me in the day of my distress and
who has been with me wherever I have gone." 4So they gave Jacob all
the foreign gods they had and the rings in their ears, and Jacob buried them under the oak at Shechem. 5Then they set out, and the terror
of God fell upon the towns all around them so that no one pursued
them.

[a]27 Or *because*

OPEN 1. If you could go back to the first place where God became real to you, where would it be? **2.** What family heirloom do you have that was given to you from the family?

STUDY As a youth, Jacob camped out at a place called Bethel. In a dream, God promised that he would one day return to this campsite safely. Jacob has been away from his God a long time but God has not forgotten him. **1.** Why do you think Jacob asks all of his family to get rid of the foreign gods? What does that tell you about his lifestyle for the last 20 years? **2.** Do you think a family can bury their past simply by digging a hole

34:23 let us give our consent. For the Canaanites, their circumcision was simply a way to close a lucrative business deal. The act of marriage was just part of the transaction. But this sacred rite had far greater implications—as the Canaanites soon learned.

34:24 every male in the city was circumcised. Not just a few of the Canaanites were greedy. All of the *men of the city were willing* to undergo this painful ritual for the chance to get their hands on more property and animals.

34:25 attacked the unsuspecting. When Simeon and Levi slaughtered the males of Shechem, they were avenging the violation of their whole family, not just of their sister. Nevertheless, it was a terrible act of revenge. Again, violence begets violence. Simeon and Levi paid for this in the end when their father cursed their descendants because of this horrible act (49:5–7).

35:1 Bethel. This had been the site of Jacob's dream, his covenant with God and his commitment to tithe (28:10–22). God sent him back to complete the process. It was the land of God's promise to him and the place of Jacob's promise to God.

35:3 God, who answered me. After the terrible events at Shechem, God gave Jacob the opportunity to remember God's constant love and presence. It was also a time of renewal and recommitment.

35:5 terror of God. For those who do not know him (and for some who do), God can be frightening. Here, God used this fear to protect his servant.

6Jacob and all the people with him came to Luz (that is, Bethel) in
the land of Canaan. 7There he built an altar, and he called the place El
Bethel,[a] because it was there that God revealed himself to him when
he was fleeing from his brother.

8Now Deborah, Rebekah's nurse, died and was buried under the
oak below Bethel. So it was named Allon Bacuth.[b]

9After Jacob returned from Paddan Aram,[c] God appeared to him
again and blessed him. 10God said to him, "Your name is Jacob,[d] but
you will no longer be called Jacob; your name will be Israel.[e]" So he
named him Israel.

11And God said to him, "I am God Almighty[f]; be fruitful and increase in number. A nation and a community of nations will come
from you, and kings will come from your body. 12The land I gave to
Abraham and Isaac I also give to you, and I will give this land to your
descendants after you." 13Then God went up from him at the place
where he had talked with him.

14Jacob set up a stone pillar at the place where God had talked with
him, and he poured out a drink offering on it; he also poured oil on it.
15Jacob called the place where God had talked with him Bethel.[g]

The Deaths of Rachel and Isaac

16Then they moved on from Bethel. While they were still some distance from Ephrath, Rachel began to give birth and had great difficulty. 17And as she was having great difficulty in childbirth, the
midwife said to her, "Don't be afraid, for you have another son." 18As
she breathed her last—for she was dying—she named her son Ben-
Oni.[h] But his father named him Benjamin.[i]

19So Rachel died and was buried on the way to Ephrath (that is,
Bethlehem). 20Over her tomb Jacob set up a pillar, and to this day that
pillar marks Rachel's tomb.

21Israel moved on again and pitched his tent beyond Migdal Eder.
22While Israel was living in that region, Reuben went in and slept with
his father's concubine Bilhah, and Israel heard of it.

Jacob had twelve sons:
23The sons of Leah:
Reuben the firstborn of Jacob,

[a]7 *El Bethel* means *God of Bethel.* [b]8 *Allon Bacuth* means *oak of weeping.* [c]9 That is, Northwest Mesopotamia; also in verse 26 [d]10 *Jacob* means *he grasps the heel* (figuratively, *he deceives*). [e]10 *Israel* means *he struggles with God.* [f]11 Hebrew *El-Shaddai* [g]15 *Bethel* means *house of God.* [h]18 *Ben-Oni* means *son of my trouble.* [i]18 *Benjamin* means *son of my right hand.*

and putting their past into it? Is this a good idea? **3.** When Jacob set up a stone and poured out a "thanks" offering, what was he thanking God for?

APPLY 1. What is the closest you have come to a time when you had to dig a hole and bury something in order to get on with your life? **2.** Where did you set up a stone as a "thanks" offering for God bringing you through a rough situation safely?

OPEN Do you like to watch the biography channel on TV?

STUDY This is the story of the end of two important people in the Bible—the death of Rachel, Jacob's wife, and the death of Isaac, Jacob's father. **1.** When it was all said and done, what does the Bible record of Rachel's contribution to God's story? **2.** In all of his 180 years, only a few days are mentioned in the life of Isaac—his birth, his father's offer to sacrifice him on Mt. Moriah, his marriage, the birth of his two sons, his son Jacob tricking him for his brother's "blessing" and his death. What does this tell you about the way the Bible records history? How would you describe this kind of literature?

APPLY 1. If someone were to boil down your life to the most important five or six days, what would they be? **2.** What has been your

35:10 your name will be Israel. When Jacob was at Bethel earlier (28:13–15), God had made promises to him. Now that Jacob had returned, God sealed those promises by changing Jacob's name, much as he had done with Abram (17:5). The new name had been promised in 32:28 and changed here.

35:11–13 God proclaimed a blessing on Jacob and his descendants and confirmed his promises to them. These were the covenant promises made to Abraham and passed through Isaac to the chosen son, Jacob.

35:17 you have another son. At Joseph's birth, Rachel had asked for another son (30:24). Though she got what she asked for, it came at a high price—her own life.

35:18 Ben-Oni ... Benjamin. Rachel's name for her son means "son of my trouble," a logical name for a son born with such difficulty. The name Benjamin means "son of my right hand."

35:19 Rachel died. Rachel died in childbirth on the way to Ephrath, the old name for Bethlehem. This is perhaps a foreshadowing of Mary and Joseph's successful trip to the same city under similar stages of pregnancy. In ancient times, death in childbirth because of complications was not uncommon (1 Sam. 4:20).

35:22 slept with his father's concubine. By this action, Reuben prematurely claimed the rights to his inheritance as the firstborn, specifically the right to inherit his father's concubine. Jacob, of course, had some experience in matters of birthright (25:30–34). While the text merely says that Jacob (Israel) "heard of it," he did not forget it. Reuben was cursed for this act (49:2–4).

contribution to God's story so far in your life?

Simeon, Levi, Judah, Issachar and Zebulun.
24 The sons of Rachel:
Joseph and Benjamin.
25 The sons of Rachel's maidservant Bilhah:
Dan and Naphtali.
26 The sons of Leah's maidservant Zilpah:
Gad and Asher.
These were the sons of Jacob, who were born to him in Paddan Aram.

27 Jacob came home to his father Isaac in Mamre, near Kiriath Arba
(that is, Hebron), where Abraham and Isaac had stayed. 28 Isaac lived
a hundred and eighty years. 29 Then he breathed his last and died and
was gathered to his people, old and full of years. And his sons Esau
and Jacob buried him.

OPEN **1.** Who in your family likes to track the family tree down to cousins and "shirt tail" cousins? **2.** What area of the country did your grandparents come from?

STUDY Esau was the son of Isaac who gave up his birthright to be the carrier of the covenant to the next generation. He settled in the mountainous country to the south between Canaan and the Sinai desert. He intermarried with the native population and adopted the religion of the locals. This is the record of his descendants. **1.** What do you remember about the birth of Esau and his brother Jacob (25:19–34)? **2.** What do you remember about the time when Esau exchanged his "birthright" for a pot of stew? When Esau found out that his brother had gotten his father's "blessing," what did Esau do to get even with his father (28:8–9)? **3.** Why did Esau take all of his wives and possessions and move into the hill country of Seir? **4.** What is significant in the shift from "sons" in verses 10–14 to "chiefs" in verses 15–19 to "kings" in verses 31–39? How does this fulfill the prophecy (27:39–40) given to Esau by his fa-

Esau's Descendants

36 This is the account of Esau (that is, Edom).

2 Esau took his wives from the women of Canaan: Adah daughter of Elon the Hittite, and Oholibamah daughter of Anah and
granddaughter of Zibeon the Hivite— 3 also Basemath daughter
of Ishmael and sister of Nebaioth.
4 Adah bore Eliphaz to Esau, Basemath bore Reuel, 5 and Oholibamah bore Jeush, Jalam and Korah. These were the sons of
Esau, who were born to him in Canaan.
6 Esau took his wives and sons and daughters and all the members of his household, as well as his livestock and all his other
animals and all the goods he had acquired in Canaan, and
moved to a land some distance from his brother Jacob. 7 Their
possessions were too great for them to remain together; the land
where they were staying could not support them both because of
their livestock. 8 So Esau (that is, Edom) settled in the hill country of Seir.

9 This is the account of Esau the father of the Edomites in the hill
country of Seir.

10 These are the names of Esau's sons:
Eliphaz, the son of Esau's wife Adah, and Reuel, the son of Esau's wife Basemath.
11 The sons of Eliphaz:

35:29 Esau and Jacob buried him. According to custom, this was the time the older brother, Esau, would have inherited his birthright. It was ironic then that the two brothers put the past aside and buried their father peacefully.

36:1 Esau (that is, Edom). Esau was called Edom (meaning "red") because of the red lentil *stew he had traded for his birthright* (25:30). His descendants were called the Edomites not only because they were the offspring of Edom, but also because the land they inhabited had reddish rock formations. The nation of Edom no longer exists (Obad. 18; Mal. 1:4), but these red formations are still visible in the area south of the Dead Sea.

36:8 Seir. Though this is the name of a Horite living in the region before Esau arrived (v. 20), it has also become an*other* name for the region of the Edomites.

36:10–14 According to these verses and 1 Chronicles 1, these are the tribal chiefs of the Edomites. They were certainly not all friendly to their cousins, the descendants of Jacob—the people of Israel. Although it seems Jacob and Esau were able to put aside their differences, their descendants would constantly be at odds (Num. 20:14–21; 1 Sam. 14:47; 2 Sam. 8:13–14; Obad. 1–21).

36:11 Eliphaz: Teman. The appearance of this Edomite name helps clarify some of Job's story. Eliphaz the Temanite was a friend of Job (Job 2:11).

Teman, Omar, Zepho, Gatam and Kenaz.
[12]Esau's son Eliphaz also had a concubine named Timna, who bore him Amalek. These were grandsons of Esau's wife Adah.
[13]The sons of Reuel:
Nahath, Zerah, Shammah and Mizzah. These were grandsons of Esau's wife Basemath.
[14]The sons of Esau's wife Oholibamah daughter of Anah and granddaughter of Zibeon, whom she bore to Esau:
Jeush, Jalam and Korah.

[15]These were the chiefs among Esau's descendants:
The sons of Eliphaz the firstborn of Esau:
Chiefs Teman, Omar, Zepho, Kenaz, [16]Korah,[a] Gatam and Amalek. These were the chiefs descended from Eliphaz in Edom; they were grandsons of Adah.
[17]The sons of Esau's son Reuel:
Chiefs Nahath, Zerah, Shammah and Mizzah. These were the chiefs descended from Reuel in Edom; they were grandsons of Esau's wife Basemath.
[18]The sons of Esau's wife Oholibamah:
Chiefs Jeush, Jalam and Korah. These were the chiefs descended from Esau's wife Oholibamah daughter of Anah.
[19]These were the sons of Esau (that is, Edom), and these were their chiefs.

[20]These were the sons of Seir the Horite, who were living in the region:
Lotan, Shobal, Zibeon, Anah, [21]Dishon, Ezer and Dishan. These sons of Seir in Edom were Horite chiefs.
[22]The sons of Lotan:
Hori and Homam.[b] Timna was Lotan's sister.
[23]The sons of Shobal:
Alvan, Manahath, Ebal, Shepho and Onam.
[24]The sons of Zibeon:
Aiah and Anah. This is the Anah who discovered the hot springs[c] in the desert while he was grazing the donkeys of his father Zibeon.
[25]The children of Anah:
Dishon and Oholibamah daughter of Anah.
[26]The sons of Dishon[d]:
Hemdan, Eshban, Ithran and Keran.
[27]The sons of Ezer:
Bilhan, Zaavan and Akan.
[28]The sons of Dishan:
Uz and Aran.
[29]These were the Horite chiefs:
Lotan, Shobal, Zibeon, Anah, [30]Dishon, Ezer and Dishan. These were the Horite chiefs, according to their divisions, in the land of Seir.

[a]16 Masoretic Text; Samaritan Pentateuch (see also Gen. 36:11 and 1 Chron. 1:36) does not have *Korah.* [b]22 Hebrew *Hemam,* a variant of *Homam* (see 1 Chron. 1:39) [c]24 Vulgate; Syriac *discovered water;* the meaning of the Hebrew for this word is uncertain. [d]26 Hebrew *Dishan,* a variant of *Dishon*

ther? **5.** Who are the descendants of these people today? How does this explain a lot of what is going on in the world today?

APPLY 1. Do you look at history from the ground or from a balloon high in the sky? **2.** From where you are today, what are you doing of eternal significance?

The Rulers of Edom

31 These were the kings who reigned in Edom before any Israelite
king reigned[a]:

32 Bela son of Beor became king of Edom. His city was named
Dinhabah.
33 When Bela died, Jobab son of Zerah from Bozrah succeeded him
as king.
34 When Jobab died, Husham from the land of the Temanites succeeded him as king.
35 When Husham died, Hadad son of Bedad, who defeated Midian
in the country of Moab, succeeded him as king. His city was
named Avith.
36 When Hadad died, Samlah from Masrekah succeeded him as king.
37 When Samlah died, Shaul from Rehoboth on the river[b] succeeded him as king.
38 When Shaul died, Baal-Hanan son of Acbor succeeded him as
king.
39 When Baal-Hanan son of Acbor died, Hadad[c] succeeded him as
king. His city was named Pau, and his wife's name was Mehetabel daughter of Matred, the daughter of Me-Zahab.

40 These were the chiefs descended from Esau, by name, according
to their clans and regions:
Timna, Alvah, Jetheth, 41 Oholibamah, Elah, Pinon, 42 Kenaz, Teman, Mibzar, 43 Magdiel and Iram. These were the chiefs of
Edom, according to their settlements in the land they occupied.

This was Esau the father of the Edomites.

OPEN 1. How well did you get along with your brothers/sisters while growing up? **2.** As a child, what did you want to be when you grew up?

STUDY This begins the epic story of Joseph, the eleventh son of Jacob. His mother was Rachel, the favorite wife of Jacob. **1.** Can you think of a "perfect" family in the Bible? **2.** How do you think the older brothers felt when Jacob made a "richly ornamented robe" for Joseph? **3.** How would you describe Joseph's behavior? How would you feel if you were the brothers? Or the father? **4.** What would a family therapist say about this family?

Joseph's Dreams

37 Jacob lived in the land where his father had stayed, the land
of Canaan.

2 This is the account of Jacob.

Joseph, a young man of seventeen, was tending the flocks with his
brothers, the sons of Bilhah and the sons of Zilpah, his father's
wives, and he brought their father a bad report about them.
3 Now Israel loved Joseph more than any of his other sons, because
he had been born to him in his old age; and he made a richly
ornamented[d] robe for him. 4 When his brothers saw that their father

[a] 31 Or *before an Israelite king reigned over them* [b] 37 Possibly the Euphrates [c] 39 Many manuscripts of the Masoretic Text, Samaritan Pentateuch and Syriac (see also 1 Chron. 1:50); most manuscripts of the Masoretic Text *Hadar* [d] 3 The meaning of the Hebrew for *richly ornamented* is uncertain; also in verses 23 and 32.

36:31 Israelite king reigned. This verse implies that the reader knows about the Israelite monarchy established hundreds of years after the events here. This notation was probably *added many years later.*

36:43 Esau the father of the Edomites. Though Esau had lost his birthright, he produced his own nation. Because of its later treatment of their brothers, the Israelites, the nation would be destroyed (Obad. 1–21).

37:1 the land of Canaan. After much *wandering,* Jacob had returned to his father's land, the Promised Land. He too would live as a nomad, but one day his descendants would occupy this land.

37:2 account of Jacob. While introduced as the account of Jacob, the story that follows actually centers on Joseph. It is through Joseph's story that we see God's covenant family become a nation.

37:3 robe. This robe was not only a gift of love but of favoritism as well. It was more appropriate for courtly life than for tending a flock.

loved him more than any of them, they hated him and could not speak a kind word to him.
[5]Joseph had a dream, and when he told it to his brothers, they
hated him all the more. [6]He said to them, "Listen to this dream I had:
[7]We were binding sheaves of grain out in the field when suddenly my sheaf rose and stood upright, while your sheaves gathered around mine and bowed down to it."
[8]His brothers said to him, "Do you intend to reign over us? Will you actually rule us?" And they hated him all the more because of his dream and what he had said.
[9]Then he had another dream, and he told it to his brothers. "Listen," he said, "I had another dream, and this time the sun and moon and eleven stars were bowing down to me."
[10]When he told his father as well as his brothers, his father rebuked him and said, "What is this dream you had? Will your mother and I and your brothers actually come and bow down to the ground before
you?" [11]His brothers were jealous of him, but his father kept the matter in mind.

Joseph Sold by His Brothers

[12]Now his brothers had gone to graze their father's flocks near
Shechem, [13]and Israel said to Joseph, "As you know, your brothers are grazing the flocks near Shechem. Come, I am going to send you to them."

"Very well," he replied.
[14]So he said to him, "Go and see if all is well with your brothers and with the flocks, and bring word back to me." Then he sent him off from the Valley of Hebron.
When Joseph arrived at Shechem, [15]a man found him wandering around in the fields and asked him, "What are you looking for?"
[16]He replied, "I'm looking for my brothers. Can you tell me where they are grazing their flocks?"
[17]"They have moved on from here," the man answered. "I heard them say, 'Let's go to Dothan.' "
So Joseph went after his brothers and found them near Dothan.
[18]But they saw him in the distance, and before he reached them, they plotted to kill him.
[19]"Here comes that dreamer!" they said to each other. [20]"Come

APPLY **1.** What is the number one cause for conflict in your family right now? **2.** What do you do when you have dreams for personal success? What are you dreaming about now?

OPEN **1.** As a child, who was the "baby" in your family? **2.** Who acts like the "oldest" and tries to be the responsible person for everyone?

STUDY When Joseph shared his dreams with his older brothers—that he would one day rule over them—they were furious. Now, they have a chance to get even. **1.** If you were a novelist and you wanted to write a novel about a lowly shepherd boy becoming the second in command to the greatest power in the world, how would you go about it? **2.** Who do you feel sorry for in this story: Joseph? Israel (Jacob)? Reuben? The other brothers? **3.** How would you describe the plan the brothers came up with to do away with Joseph? Why would Reuben be concerned about his brother (35:23)? **4.** Do you think Judah realized that he was fitting into the plan and purpose of God for Joseph when he proposed that Joseph be sold

---

37:5 Joseph had a dream. Dreams were a common means of revelation in the Old Testament. Jacob, his father, had dreamed of a stairway leading up to *heaven and* of God's promise and blessing (28:10–15). Joseph's dreams were more symbolic in nature.

37:7 bowed down. Joseph's brothers actually do bow to him later (42:6; 43:26; 44:14). Joseph's dream was thus prophetic in a different way than his father's. While God used dreams to reveal his promises and blessings to Jacob, he revealed specific parts of his plan for Joseph's life through dreams.

37:8 Do you intend to reign over us? There is no indication that Joseph did intend to rule over his brothers, but the interpretation of these dreams was unmistakable. Joseph's mistake was in telling his brothers these dreams in the first place. However, through the working out of God's promises to Abraham and Jacob, Joseph came to serve the role of a good ruler to them. He provided for them and protected them from famine and hunger.

37:10 father rebuked him. Joseph's dream really irked Jacob. He was bothered not only because it was presumptuous, but perhaps it also reminded him of the blessing he had stolen from his brother Esau (27:27–29).

37:11 his father kept the matter in mind. Jacob did not forget Joseph's dream as time passed. Certainly the events that were to take place made him reflect on it many times.

37:19 dreamer. In Hebrew the word means, "master of dreams." The brothers have had about enough of their little brother, and their sarcasm showed just how much their resentment had grown.

to the Ishmaelites? **5.** How do you think Joseph felt when he was being carried off to Egypt to be sold as a slave? **6.** How would you describe the chain of events that occurred to bring Joseph to the household of Potiphar, the chief of staff to the king of the greatest power at that time?

APPLY 1. In your wildest dreams, would you ever have imagined that you would be where you are today—living where you are, married to the person you are married to and having the children you have? **2.** When is the last time you took off for a day to seriously think about why God has put you where you are today and what he has in mind for your life?

---

now, let's kill him and throw him into one of these cisterns and say that a ferocious animal devoured him. Then we'll see what comes of his dreams."

21When Reuben heard this, he tried to rescue him from their hands. "Let's not take his life," he said. 22"Don't shed any blood. Throw him into this cistern here in the desert, but don't lay a hand on him." Reuben said this to rescue him from them and take him back to his father.

23So when Joseph came to his brothers, they stripped him of his robe—the richly ornamented robe he was wearing— 24and they took him and threw him into the cistern. Now the cistern was empty; there was no water in it.

25As they sat down to eat their meal, they looked up and saw a caravan of Ishmaelites coming from Gilead. Their camels were loaded with spices, balm and myrrh, and they were on their way to take them down to Egypt.

26Judah said to his brothers, "What will we gain if we kill our brother and cover up his blood? 27Come, let's sell him to the Ishmaelites and not lay our hands on him; after all, he is our brother, our own flesh and blood." His brothers agreed.

28So when the Midianite merchants came by, his brothers pulled Joseph up out of the cistern and sold him for twenty shekels[a] of silver to the Ishmaelites, who took him to Egypt.

29When Reuben returned to the cistern and saw that Joseph was not there, he tore his clothes. 30He went back to his brothers and said, "The boy isn't there! Where can I turn now?"

31Then they got Joseph's robe, slaughtered a goat and dipped the robe in the blood. 32They took the ornamented robe back to their father and said, "We found this. Examine it to see whether it is your son's robe."

33He recognized it and said, "It is my son's robe! Some ferocious animal has devoured him. Joseph has surely been torn to pieces."

34Then Jacob tore his clothes, put on sackcloth and mourned for his son many days. 35All his sons and daughters came to comfort him, but he refused to be comforted. "No," he said, "in mourning will I go down to the grave[b] to my son." So his father wept for him.

36Meanwhile, the Midianites[c] sold Joseph in Egypt to Potiphar, one of Pharaoh's officials, the captain of the guard.

[a]28 That is, about 8 ounces (about 0.2 kilogram) [b]35 Hebrew *Sheol* [c]36 Samaritan Pentateuch, Septuagint, Vulgate and Syriac (see also verse 28); Masoretic Text *Medanites*

37:21 Reuben ... tried to rescue him. As the oldest brother, Reuben should have been able to prevent his brothers' actions. He had lost his brothers' respect, and they showed no mercy to Joseph.

37:23 stripped him of his robe. First, the brothers stripped Joseph of his precious robe. For them, it was a symbol of their father's favoritism. Then they threw him in a dry cistern to die.

37:28 twenty shekels of silver. The brothers received what was considered a fair price for Joseph. Though no longer a free man, at least he was alive.

37:34 tore his clothes. Tearing clothes and putting on coarse, uncomfortable sackcloth were signs of tragic loss. Nothing and no one could comfort Jacob.

37:36 the Midianites sold Joseph. The narrative shifts from Canaan to Egypt and back—from the brothers to Joseph and back. These events must have been hectic and frightening for Joseph. He went from a nomadic life to the greatest civilization of his day, and from freedom to slavery.

Judah and Tamar

38 At that time, Judah left his brothers and went down to stay with a man of Adullam named Hirah. 2There Judah met the daughter of a Canaanite man named Shua. He married her and lay with her; 3she became pregnant and gave birth to a son, who was named Er. 4She conceived again and gave birth to a son and named him Onan. 5She gave birth to still another son and named him Shelah. It was at Kezib that she gave birth to him.

6Judah got a wife for Er, his firstborn, and her name was Tamar. 7But Er, Judah's firstborn, was wicked in the LORD's sight; so the LORD put him to death.

8Then Judah said to Onan, "Lie with your brother's wife and fulfill your duty to her as a brother-in-law to produce offspring for your brother." 9But Onan knew that the offspring would not be his; so whenever he lay with his brother's wife, he spilled his semen on the ground to keep from producing offspring for his brother. 10What he did was wicked in the LORD's sight; so he put him to death also.

11Judah then said to his daughter-in-law Tamar, "Live as a widow in your father's house until my son Shelah grows up." For he thought, "He may die too, just like his brothers." So Tamar went to live in her father's house.

12After a long time Judah's wife, the daughter of Shua, died. When Judah had recovered from his grief, he went up to Timnah, to the men who were shearing his sheep, and his friend Hirah the Adullamite went with him.

13When Tamar was told, "Your father-in-law is on his way to Timnah to shear his sheep," 14she took off her widow's clothes, covered herself with a veil to disguise herself, and then sat down at the entrance to Enaim, which is on the road to Timnah. For she saw that, though Shelah had now grown up, she had not been given to him as his wife.

15When Judah saw her, he thought she was a prostitute, for she had covered her face. 16Not realizing that she was his daughter-in-law, he went over to her by the roadside and said, "Come now, let me sleep with you."

"And what will you give me to sleep with you?" she asked.

17"I'll send you a young goat from my flock," he said.

"Will you give me something as a pledge until you send it?" she asked.

OPEN 1. What did your parents do to censure the things you could read or look at on TV? **2.** What is the most disgusting TV show on right now—that makes you sick to look at it?

STUDY To understand this story, you need to know three things about the culture in biblical times. First, women were expected to bear children. If a husband died, the husband's brother was to take the widow and bear a child so that the child could look after her in her old age. If she bore a child, her deceased husband's property would pass through to the child. If she did not bear a child, her husband's property would go to the brother. Part of the pagan Canaanite religion was shrine prostitution for the pleasure of men. In this X-rated story in the Bible, one of the sons of Israel (Jacob) proves to be less than admirable. **1.** Would you like to take this story out of the Bible? If you keep it in, how would you use it? **2.** Judah had three sons. When Judah's first son (Er) died, what did Judah ask his second son to do? What happened? **3.** When Judah's second son died, what did Judah do? **4.** When Judah did not give his third son to Tamar so that she could have a child, what did Tamar decide to do? How did Tamar trap her father-in-law? What happened? **5.** Why do you think this sordid story of family intrigue, contraception, prostitution and incest is inserted into the middle of the beautiful story of Joseph? **6.** If you could find anything good in this story what would it be? **7.** From Judah in this story came David and from David came Jesus. How do you explain God using a guy like Judah in his great plan of salvation for the world?

38:1–30 This chapter contrasts Joseph and his brothers. It shows how God's plan for his people was carried out through the younger son rather than the older, through the son whose life demonstrated integrity and strength rather than the one without either.

38:1 left his brothers. Joseph was forcibly removed from his family, but Judah left to try his own way in the world. He seemed to have no sense of building up his family's position, just his own.

38:8 produce offspring for your brother. Without children, Tamar had no means of support. The custom described here (called "levirate marriage") was meant to give her an heir who could receive her former husband's inheritance and thus take care of her. One of the most famous levirate marriages was that of Ruth and Boaz (Ruth 4:9–13).

38:9 to keep from producing offspring for his brother. This form of birth control was meant to ensure that no heir would be produced who would take part of the family inheritance. Onan was obviously a very selfish man, and God dealt with him harshly. By short-circuiting his levirate duties, Onan was, in effect, condemning Tamar to a desperate life. In other words, he was denying her the provision God intended her to have.

38:11 He may die too. Not wanting to lose another son, Judah himself short-circuits the levirate marriage custom. It is not clear if he suspects the real problem.

38:14 Shelah ... his wife. Tamar had figured that Judah had no intention of honoring his duty. Once again, deception plays a role in Jacob's family. Tamar had been deceived, so, in her desperation, she deceives.

18 He said, "What pledge should I give you?"

"Your seal and its cord, and the staff in your hand," she answered. So he gave them to her and slept with her, and she became pregnant by him. 19 After she left, she took off her veil and put on her widow's clothes again.

20 Meanwhile Judah sent the young goat by his friend the Adullamite in order to get his pledge back from the woman, but he did not find her. 21 He asked the men who lived there, "Where is the shrine prostitute who was beside the road at Enaim?"

"There hasn't been any shrine prostitute here," they said.

22 So he went back to Judah and said, "I didn't find her. Besides, the men who lived there said, 'There hasn't been any shrine prostitute here.' "

23 Then Judah said, "Let her keep what she has, or we will become a laughingstock. After all, I did send her this young goat, but you didn't find her."

24 About three months later Judah was told, "Your daughter-in-law Tamar is guilty of prostitution, and as a result she is now pregnant."

Judah said, "Bring her out and have her burned to death!"

25 As she was being brought out, she sent a message to her father-in-law. "I am pregnant by the man who owns these," she said. And she added, "See if you recognize whose seal and cord and staff these are."

26 Judah recognized them and said, "She is more righteous than I, since I wouldn't give her to my son Shelah." And he did not sleep with her again.

27 When the time came for her to give birth, there were twin boys in her womb. 28 As she was giving birth, one of them put out his hand; so the midwife took a scarlet thread and tied it on his wrist and said, "This one came out first." 29 But when he drew back his hand, his brother came out, and she said, "So this is how you have broken out!" And he was named Perez.[a] 30 Then his brother, who had the scarlet thread on his wrist, came out and he was given the name Zerah.[b]

Joseph and Potiphar's Wife

39 Now Joseph had been taken down to Egypt. Potiphar, an Egyptian who was one of Pharaoh's officials, the captain of the guard, bought him from the Ishmaelites who had taken him there.

[a]29 *Perez* means *breaking out.* [b]30 *Zerah* can mean *scarlet* or *brightness.*

APPLY 1. When you encounter stories like this in the Bible, what do you do? Say to your children? **2.** What are you going to do when your children get out there in the world and encounter this kind of stuff in the culture?

OPEN 1. What was your first real job? **2.** When have you been accused of something you did not do?

STUDY The story of Joseph is looked upon by some scholars as a picture of Jesus. He was

38:18 What pledge. Tamar wants proof of her act with Judah. If she becomes pregnant, she can claim that her child has rights to inheritance.

38:21 shrine prostitute. In Canaan, shrine prostitutes had the religious and social role of ensuring fertility. The Adullamite is being polite to Judah by assuming that the prostitute was not a common "road-sitter." Or perhaps Judah had told him the story in a less-than-truthful manner.

38:24 Bring her out ... burned to death! Though he had been with a "prostitute" himself, Judah was ready to "cast the first stone" or light the first match. For him the issue was not morality. If Tamar had a child from prostitution, she had still not provided an heir, and she had brought dishonor on his family.

38:27–30 Not only do twins seem to run in the family, as with Esau and Jacob, but also unusual births (25:24–26). This time, however, the baby himself is not red like Esau, just the scarlet thread around his wrist.

38:29 Perez. Perez went on to become the head of the most important tribe in Judah, and an ancestor of Jesus (Matt. 1:3).

39:1 Joseph ... down to Egypt. The scene shifts back to Egypt. From the sordid abuse of family customs, the action moves to intrigue at the highest levels of Egyptian culture.

2The LORD was with Joseph and he prospered, and he lived in the house of his Egyptian master. 3When his master saw that the LORD was with him and that the LORD gave him success in everything he did, 4Joseph found favor in his eyes and became his attendant. Potiphar put him in charge of his household, and he entrusted to his care everything he owned. 5From the time he put him in charge of his household and of all that he owned, the LORD blessed the household of the Egyptian because of Joseph. The blessing of the LORD was on everything Potiphar had, both in the house and in the field. 6So he left in Joseph's care everything he had; with Joseph in charge, he did not concern himself with anything except the food he ate.

Now Joseph was well-built and handsome, 7and after a while his master's wife took notice of Joseph and said, "Come to bed with me!"

8But he refused. "With me in charge," he told her, "my master does not concern himself with anything in the house; everything he owns he has entrusted to my care. 9No one is greater in this house than I am. My master has withheld nothing from me except you, because you are his wife. How then could I do such a wicked thing and sin against God?" 10And though she spoke to Joseph day after day, he refused to go to bed with her or even be with her.

11One day he went into the house to attend to his duties, and none of the household servants was inside. 12She caught him by his cloak and said, "Come to bed with me!" But he left his cloak in her hand and ran out of the house.

13When she saw that he had left his cloak in her hand and had run out of the house, 14she called her household servants. "Look," she said to them, "this Hebrew has been brought to us to make sport of us! He came in here to sleep with me, but I screamed. 15When he heard me scream for help, he left his cloak beside me and ran out of the house."

16She kept his cloak beside her until his master came home. 17Then she told him this story: "That Hebrew slave you brought us came to me to make sport of me. 18But as soon as I screamed for help, he left his cloak beside me and ran out of the house."

19When his master heard the story his wife told him, saying, "This is how your slave treated me," he burned with anger. 20Joseph's master took him and put him in prison, the place where the king's prisoners were confined.

betrayed by his brothers. Sold as a slave to traveling merchants for 20 pieces of silver and taken to Egypt. God had a bigger plan. **1.** If you were a movie producer and you wanted to produce a movie around this story, who would you choose to play the role of Joseph? Potiphar? Potiphar's wife? Would this movie be rated G; PG13, R or X? **2.** At the beginning of the story, how would you describe Joseph's career opportunity? How did he get along with his boss? **3.** How would you describe the physical appearance of Joseph in modern terms (v. 6)? How would you describe Potiphar's wife? **4.** If you were in Joseph's shoes, would you be tempted by Potiphar's wife? What are Joseph's reasons for not giving into Potiphar's wife (v. 9)? What does Joseph decide to do? **5.** In desperation, what does Potiphar's wife do and how does Joseph respond? **6.** If you were going to teach this story to teenagers, what are three or four lessons in this story for resisting sexual advances? **7.** What were the immediate consequences to Joseph for saying "no" to Potiphar's wife? What did this do to his career?

APPLY 1. When are you most vulnerable to advances from the opposite sex? **2.** What have you found helpful when you find yourself in tempting situations?

39:2 LORD was with Joseph and he prospered. Though a slave, Joseph was blessed by God. God's provision never depends on location or social standing.

39:5 the LORD blessed ... because of Joseph. When God called Abram (12:2–3), he promised him that the nations of the earth would be blessed through him. Joseph's success was part of the fulfillment of that promise.

39:6 left in Joseph's care. Joseph was the kind of man people trusted with their lives. While he was extremely capable, it was the way God worked through him that made him so effective.

39:7 took notice. The eyes will certainly lead a person astray. More than simply "taking notice" of Joseph, Potiphar's wife lusted after him.

39:9 How then could I do such a wicked thing and sin against God? Joseph would not hurt his master who trusted him, nor would he do something he knew would be considered a sin against God. His response stands in contrast to Adam and Eve. They had only one thing withheld from them, but chose to sin against God (3:1–6).

39:10,12 he refused ... and ran. Joseph knew how to deal with temptation. He knew that problems were all that could come from contact with his boss's wife, so when the problem reached a boiling point, he ran from her. Jesus later prayed, "Lead us not into temptation, but deliver us from the evil one" (Matt. 6:13). Joseph avoided temptation and was given the moral fortitude to be delivered from evil.

39:20 the king's prisoners. Though prison would never have been pleasant, it could have been much worse for Joseph. Potiphar could have had him executed or put into a dungeon. Perhaps Potiphar used some discernment about both his wife and Joseph.

But while Joseph was there in the prison, 21the LORD was with him;
he showed him kindness and granted him favor in the eyes of the
prison warden. 22So the warden put Joseph in charge of all those held
in the prison, and he was made responsible for all that was done
there. 23The warden paid no attention to anything under Joseph's
care, because the LORD was with Joseph and gave him success in
whatever he did.

The Cupbearer and the Baker

40 Some time later, the cupbearer and the baker of the king of
Egypt offended their master, the king of Egypt. 2Pharaoh was
angry with his two officials, the chief cupbearer and the chief baker,
3and put them in custody in the house of the captain of the guard, in
the same prison where Joseph was confined. 4The captain of the
guard assigned them to Joseph, and he attended them.

After they had been in custody for some time, 5each of the two
men—the cupbearer and the baker of the king of Egypt, who were
being held in prison—had a dream the same night, and each dream
had a meaning of its own.

6When Joseph came to them the next morning, he saw that they
were dejected. 7So he asked Pharaoh's officials who were in custody
with him in his master's house, "Why are your faces so sad today?"

8"We both had dreams," they answered, "but there is no one to interpret them."

Then Joseph said to them, "Do not interpretations belong to God?
Tell me your dreams."

9So the chief cupbearer told Joseph his dream. He said to him, "In
my dream I saw a vine in front of me, 10and on the vine were three
branches. As soon as it budded, it blossomed, and its clusters ripened
into grapes. 11Pharaoh's cup was in my hand, and I took the grapes,
squeezed them into Pharaoh's cup and put the cup in his hand."

12"This is what it means," Joseph said to him. "The three branches
are three days. 13Within three days Pharaoh will lift up your head and
restore you to your position, and you will put Pharaoh's cup in his
hand, just as you used to do when you were his cupbearer. 14But
when all goes well with you, remember me and show me kindness;
mention me to Pharaoh and get me out of this prison. 15For I was
forcibly carried off from the land of the Hebrews, and even here I
have done nothing to deserve being put in a dungeon."

16When the chief baker saw that Joseph had given a favorable
interpretation, he said to Joseph, "I too had a dream: On my head

OPEN 1. What is the most vivid dream you have had recently? **2.** What do you do when a movie gets scary?

STUDY Joseph has been thrown into prison because he was accused by his boss's wife of trying to seduce her (which was not true). Joseph had a very unique gift of interpreting dreams. **1.** Sold into slavery. Thrown into prison for something he did not do. How do you think Joseph was feeling about now? **2.** Do you think it was purely coincidental that Joseph was thrown into prison with two officers of the king's court or was this all part of the plan and purpose of God for his life? Do you think Joseph realized this when he was sitting in prison? **3.** What strikes you most about the dreams of the cupbearer and the baker? How do you account for Joseph's ability to interpret these dreams? **4.** Why do you think the cupbearer forgot his promise to remember Joseph when he was restored to his position? **5.** If you were to graph the life of Joseph up to now, how would you show this time in his life?

APPLY 1. If you were to make a graph of your life up to this point, would this time in your life be a high point, a low point, or a big question mark? **2.** As you think back over your life, what low point turned out to be God preparing you for something quite beautiful?

40:2 cupbearer. Though the title sounds comical today, this was an important position within Pharoah's inner circle. The cupbearer presided in Pharaoh's household, acted as a taster of his food, and had easy access to the ruler's ear. This would work to Joseph's favor.

40:5 each ... had a dream. *Dreams had important roles in the Bible.* Jacob dreamed of the stairway into heaven (28:12). Joseph's dreams got him into trouble (37:5–11). Pharaoh's dreams were the beginning of Joseph's rise to power.

40:8 Joseph said ... interpretations belong to God? Joseph was presented with the opportunity to serve as God's mouthpiece. Though he had a gift of dream interpretation, the truth he spoke was God's truth.

40:13 lift up your head. A Hebrew idiom is used here and elsewhere (Ps. 3:3) to describe the act of freeing a prisoner.

40:14 remember me ... to Pharaoh. Joseph had political savvy as well as the ability to interpret dreams. Joseph "positioned" himself with the cupbearer. He "networked" from a jail cell. Though the chief cupbearer forgot about him for two years, in the end, Joseph was remembered and rescued.

40:15 dungeon. The same Hebrew word is translated as "cistern" in 37:24, which may reflect that it was below ground.

were three baskets of bread.[a] 17In the top basket were all kinds of
baked goods for Pharaoh, but the birds were eating them out of the
basket on my head."
18"This is what it means," Joseph said. "The three baskets are three
days. 19Within three days Pharaoh will lift off your head and hang you
on a tree.[b] And the birds will eat away your flesh."
20Now the third day was Pharaoh's birthday, and he gave a feast for
all his officials. He lifted up the heads of the chief cupbearer and the
chief baker in the presence of his officials: 21He restored the chief
cupbearer to his position, so that he once again put the cup into
Pharaoh's hand, 22but he hanged[c] the chief baker, just as Joseph had
said to them in his interpretation.
23The chief cupbearer, however, did not remember Joseph; he forgot him.

Pharaoh's Dreams

41 When two full years had passed, Pharaoh had a dream: He
was standing by the Nile, 2when out of the river there came up
seven cows, sleek and fat, and they grazed among the reeds. 3After
them, seven other cows, ugly and gaunt, came up out of the Nile and
stood beside those on the riverbank. 4And the cows that were ugly
and gaunt ate up the seven sleek, fat cows. Then Pharaoh woke up.
5He fell asleep again and had a second dream: Seven heads of
grain, healthy and good, were growing on a single stalk. 6After them,
seven other heads of grain sprouted—thin and scorched by the east
wind. 7The thin heads of grain swallowed up the seven healthy, full
heads. Then Pharaoh woke up; it had been a dream.
8In the morning his mind was troubled, so he sent for all the magicians and wise men of Egypt. Pharaoh told them his dreams, but no
one could interpret them for him.
9Then the chief cupbearer said to Pharaoh, "Today I am reminded
of my shortcomings. 10Pharaoh was once angry with his servants,
and he imprisoned me and the chief baker in the house of the captain
of the guard. 11Each of us had a dream the same night, and each
dream had a meaning of its own. 12Now a young Hebrew was there
with us, a servant of the captain of the guard. We told him our
dreams, and he interpreted them for us, giving each man the interpretation of his dream. 13And things turned out exactly as he interpreted them to us: I was restored to my position, and the other man
was hanged.[c]"
14So Pharaoh sent for Joseph, and he was quickly brought from the

[a]16 Or *three wicker baskets* [b]19 Or *and impale you on a pole* [c]22; 13 Or *impaled*

OPEN 1. As a kid, what would you do when you had a bad dream? **2.** How did you learn to save your money for a rainy day?

STUDY First, Joseph was sold into slavery by his jealous brothers. He then came to be in charge of his master's household in Egypt until he was falsely accused of assaulting his master's wife—for which he was thrown in prison. While in prison, he accurately interpreted the dream of the king's cupbearer and got a promise from the cupbearer that he would mention Joseph's name to the king when he got out. **1.** As the story begins, how long has Joseph been sitting in jail? **2.** What was the economy like in Egypt when the king had these dreams? If someone had come to the king and said that hard times were coming, what would the advisers to the king say? **3.** What did the two dreams do to the king? What role did the cupbearer play? **4.** How did Joseph look upon his own ability to forecast economic cycles? Why would the king listen to him? **5.** What does the king decide to do? What would the economic plan do to the national economy in the first seven years? If the president tried to get this through congress, what would happen? **6.** What is the lesson in this story for your own

---

41:2 out of the river ... seven cows. Cows often submerge their bodies to stay cool and fend off insects.

41:6 east wind. Given Egypt's location, an east wind, dry and hot, came from the desert, withering plants and drying waterways.

41:8 magicians and wise men. Magicians were originally magi—wise men devoted to the practice of religion. As time passed, the term took on the connotation of the occult of man's attempt to control both nature and destiny. In Joseph's case, the magicians failed to do what God enabled him to do.

41:13 exactly. The strength of the testimony of the cupbearer was that Joseph's interpretation was correct not only in part or by coincidence. It was *exactly* correct. Joseph's ability was a gift from God.

41:14 Pharaoh sent for Joseph. Joseph had appealed, not to Potiphar, but to Pharaoh himself (40:14) and was answered in God's timing. Later, Daniel faced a similar situation in Persia. When the king's magicians were unable to interpret his dream, Daniel, a foreigner who worshiped the one true God, was able to help (Dan. 2:24).

budget? For your church? For your country?

APPLY **1.** What are you doing in the seven fat years of plenty in your life to lay aside for the seven lean years? **2.** What would you have to cut out to lay aside 20% of your income for the future?

---

dungeon. When he had shaved and changed his clothes, he came before Pharaoh.
15 Pharaoh said to Joseph, "I had a dream, and no one can interpret
it. But I have heard it said of you that when you hear a dream you can
interpret it."
16 "I cannot do it," Joseph replied to Pharaoh, "but God will give
Pharaoh the answer he desires."
17 Then Pharaoh said to Joseph, "In my dream I was standing on the
bank of the Nile, 18 when out of the river there came up seven cows,
fat and sleek, and they grazed among the reeds. 19 After them, seven
other cows came up—scrawny and very ugly and lean. I had never
seen such ugly cows in all the land of Egypt. 20 The lean, ugly cows ate
up the seven fat cows that came up first. 21 But even after they ate
them, no one could tell that they had done so; they looked just as
ugly as before. Then I woke up.
22 "In my dreams I also saw seven heads of grain, full and good,
growing on a single stalk. 23 After them, seven other heads sprouted—
withered and thin and scorched by the east wind. 24 The thin heads of
grain swallowed up the seven good heads. I told this to the magicians, but none could explain it to me."
25 Then Joseph said to Pharaoh, "The dreams of Pharaoh are one
and the same. God has revealed to Pharaoh what he is about to do.
26 The seven good cows are seven years, and the seven good heads of
grain are seven years; it is one and the same dream. 27 The seven lean,
ugly cows that came up afterward are seven years, and so are the
seven worthless heads of grain scorched by the east wind: They are
seven years of famine.
28 "It is just as I said to Pharaoh: God has shown Pharaoh what he is
about to do. 29 Seven years of great abundance are coming throughout the land of Egypt, 30 but seven years of famine will follow them.
Then all the abundance in Egypt will be forgotten, and the famine will
ravage the land. 31 The abundance in the land will not be remembered, because the famine that follows it will be so severe. 32 The reason the dream was given to Pharaoh in two forms is that the matter
has been firmly decided by God, and God will do it soon.
33 "And now let Pharaoh look for a discerning and wise man and put
him in charge of the land of Egypt. 34 Let Pharaoh appoint commissioners over the land to take a fifth of the harvest of Egypt during the
seven years of abundance. 35 They should collect all the food of these
good years that are coming and store up the grain under the authority of Pharaoh, to be kept in the cities for food. 36 This food should be
held in reserve for the country, to be used during the seven years of
famine that will come upon Egypt, so that the country may not be
ruined by the famine."
37 The plan seemed good to Pharaoh and to all his officials. 38 So

---

41:16 God will give Pharaoh the answer. Joseph's integrity is clearly demonstrated when he repeatedly reminds the people around him that God's power (rather than his own) makes all the difference (39:9; 40:8; 41:32).

41:27 famine. Abraham left his home to escape famine conditions (12:10), and then Isaac in the next generation (26:1). The famine that Joseph described to Pharaoh would bring Jacob and his whole family to Egypt for survival. Famine caused Naomi to leave Bethlehem for Moab (Ruth 1:1). Elijah dealt with famine in Samaria (1 Kin. 18:2) and then Elisha in Gilgal (2 Kin. 4:38). Since the world at that time was largely agricultural, famine was one of the greatest threats to survival. Seven years of famine would be devastating.

41:38 the spirit of God. What a testimony Joseph wielded among a people who did not even honor the presence of God. Joseph lived with integrity, met people at their point of

Pharaoh asked them, "Can we find anyone like this man, one in
whom is the spirit of God[a]?"
39Then Pharaoh said to Joseph, "Since God has made all this
known to you, there is no one so discerning and wise as you. 40You
shall be in charge of my palace, and all my people are to submit to
your orders. Only with respect to the throne will I be greater than
you."

Joseph in Charge of Egypt

41So Pharaoh said to Joseph, "I hereby put you in charge of the
whole land of Egypt." 42Then Pharaoh took his signet ring from his
finger and put it on Joseph's finger. He dressed him in robes of fine
linen and put a gold chain around his neck. 43He had him ride in a
chariot as his second-in-command,[b] and men shouted before him,
"Make way[c]!" Thus he put him in charge of the whole land of Egypt.
44Then Pharaoh said to Joseph, "I am Pharaoh, but without your
word no one will lift hand or foot in all Egypt." 45Pharaoh gave Joseph
the name Zaphenath-Paneah and gave him Asenath daughter of Potiphera, priest of On,[d] to be his wife. And Joseph went throughout the
land of Egypt.
46Joseph was thirty years old when he entered the service of Pharaoh king of Egypt. And Joseph went out from Pharaoh's presence and
traveled throughout Egypt. 47During the seven years of abundance
the land produced plentifully. 48Joseph collected all the food produced in those seven years of abundance in Egypt and stored it in the
cities. In each city he put the food grown in the fields surrounding it.
49Joseph stored up huge quantities of grain, like the sand of the sea; it
was so much that he stopped keeping records because it was beyond
measure.
50Before the years of famine came, two sons were born to Joseph
by Asenath daughter of Potiphera, priest of On. 51Joseph named his
firstborn Manasseh[e] and said, "It is because God has made me forget

[a]38 Or *of the gods* [b]43 Or *in the chariot of his second-in-command*; or *in his second chariot* [c]43 Or *Bow down* [d]45 That is, Heliopolis; also in verse 50 [e]51 *Manasseh* sounds like and may be derived from the Hebrew for *forget*.

OPEN 1. Would you rather play first string on a losing team or second string on a winning team? **2.** What is the story behind the ring(s) you are wearing?

STUDY When Joseph was in prison for a crime he did not commit, he was able to interpret the dreams of the king. Joseph predicted that there would be seven years of famine. He recommended storing up grain in the good years for the bad years. **1.** How do you think Joseph felt when he was put in charge of the national economy as the second in command to the king? How would you have felt? **2.** If Joseph were appointed the Secretary of Agriculture today, would he be cleared by the FBI: He was a foreigner, a Hebrew, a slave, a convicted felon and spent two years in jail for attempted rape? **3.** Where did Joseph get his training to be the prime minister of the most powerful country at that time? **4.** If you had Joseph's job, which would have been harder for you: The seven years collecting the grain, or the seven years running a welfare program during a famine? **5.** Do you think Joseph could look back and see how God had used all of the unfortunate experiences in his family, with his brothers, in the

need, and gave God the credit. In the end, Joseph's faithfulness made God's presence irrefutable.

41:40 Only ... will I be greater. Pharaoh gave Joseph complete leadership. He only stopped short of making him king. That was a huge destiny for a seventeen-year-old kid who had been dragged into town as a bought servant. Joseph went from the bottom of the pit to the highest office in a foreign land. Why? Because he proved himself faithful to God's purpose no matter what the circumstance. Daniel had a parallel experience in Babylon where he became third in command (Dan. 5:16).

41:42 signet ring. The signet ring was the king's stamp of authority. It worked with clay or wax the way a notary's stamp works with paper today. **robes of fine linen ... gold chain.** Joseph received the symbols of honor because he was first an honorable man. God used and rewarded his faithfulness.

41:43 in charge ... of Egypt. Pharaoh basically did everything to honor Joseph short of playing "Hail to the Chief." No one watching the procession that day could have doubted that Joseph had become Pharaoh's right-hand man, the highest in his cabinet of advisors.

41:45 name ... wife. A new job, new status, new name and new wife—even the daughter of a priest. Four hundred years later Moses, another Israelite, would also be given royal status in Egypt and would continue the work that Joseph's promotion had begun: The realization of God's promise to Abraham.

41:46 thirty years old. It was 13 years since Joseph had been abused by his brothers and the course of his life had changed forever (37:2). During those years he had suffered hardship and rejection as a slave, a falsely accused servant and a prisoner.

41:49 stopped keeping records. In our world of mega-gig hard-drive memories, to stop keeping records would be incredible. Joseph's preparation was so huge that no one could keep track any more.

41:51 Manasseh. Joseph's first son's name meant "forget." Joseph was able to forget the pain of his early life and separation from home and family because God had given him a new home and family.

household of Potiphar and in jail to prepare him for the job he was to do?

APPLY 1. As you look back over your own life, are you able to see the hand of God in all of the experiences in your life as a preparation for the work you are in at the moment? **2.** If you could recall one hardship in particular that God has used, what would this be?

OPEN 1. What is the longest you have gone without food? **2.** What is the longest you have been away from home?

STUDY When Joseph was a young boy, he had a dream that one day he would rule over his older brothers and they were furious. They sold Joseph to merchants going to Egypt and reported to his father that he must have been killed because they found his coat of many colors in the desert. Joseph is sold to Potiphar as a servant, is accused of trying to rape Potiphar's wife and put into prison. While in prison, Joseph interprets a dream for the king about a coming famine and the king puts Joseph in charge of setting aside grain. Now, seven years later, famine is everywhere and Joseph's brothers come to Egypt for grain. **1.** How do you think Joseph felt when he saw his ten brothers standing before him? Could you have sat there and let your brothers bow before you and plead for food?

all my trouble and all my father's household." [52]The second son he named Ephraim[a] and said, "It is because God has made me fruitful in the land of my suffering."

[53]The seven years of abundance in Egypt came to an end, [54]and the seven years of famine began, just as Joseph had said. There was famine in all the other lands, but in the whole land of Egypt there was food. [55]When all Egypt began to feel the famine, the people cried to Pharaoh for food. Then Pharaoh told all the Egyptians, "Go to Joseph and do what he tells you."

[56]When the famine had spread over the whole country, Joseph opened the storehouses and sold grain to the Egyptians, for the famine was severe throughout Egypt. [57]And all the countries came to Egypt to buy grain from Joseph, because the famine was severe in all the world.

Joseph's Brothers Go to Egypt

42 When Jacob learned that there was grain in Egypt, he said to his sons, "Why do you just keep looking at each other?" [2]He continued, "I have heard that there is grain in Egypt. Go down there and buy some for us, so that we may live and not die."

[3]Then ten of Joseph's brothers went down to buy grain from Egypt. [4]But Jacob did not send Benjamin, Joseph's brother, with the others, because he was afraid that harm might come to him. [5]So Israel's sons were among those who went to buy grain, for the famine was in the land of Canaan also.

[6]Now Joseph was the governor of the land, the one who sold grain to all its people. So when Joseph's brothers arrived, they bowed down to him with their faces to the ground. [7]As soon as Joseph saw his brothers, he recognized them, but he pretended to be a stranger and spoke harshly to them. "Where do you come from?" he asked.

"From the land of Canaan," they replied, "to buy food."

[8]Although Joseph recognized his brothers, they did not recognize him. [9]Then he remembered his dreams about them and said to them, "You are spies! You have come to see where our land is unprotected."

[a]52 *Ephraim* sounds like the Hebrew for *twice fruitful.*

41:52 Ephraim. Joseph gave both his sons Hebrew names. Ephraim means "fruitful." Instead of becoming bitter, Joseph brought his heritage into his new world, continuing to honor God's promise to his people.

41:57 all the countries came to Egypt. When a person is faithful to God's wisdom, the benefits ripple like a pebble in water. Pharaoh saw Joseph's character, honored him and believed Joseph's witness concerning God's truth. Thus Egypt survived and *Pharaoh's kingdom multiplied. As Egypt* prospered, surrounding nations sought its help. All this from one faithful young man who had chosen to make the best of bad circumstances.

42:4 Benjamin. Jacob had two wives, one the beloved Rachel, the other her sister Leah. Joseph and Benjamin were Jacob's only sons by Rachel. As far as Jacob knew, he had sent Joseph out on an errand and lost him forever. It seems natural then, that Jacob would be especially protective of Benjamin and not allow him to travel with his brothers to a foreign land.

42:5 those who went to buy grain. The law of supply and demand had made Egypt a wealthy supplier of all the *nations of that region.*

42:6 they bowed down to him. This is the first step in the fulfillment of Joseph's adolescent dreams that his brothers (figuratively, stars and sheaves of wheat, 37:5–8) would bow down to him. The brothers were unaware, because they had yet to recognize Joseph.

42:8 they did not recognize him. There are several reasons why Joseph would recognize his brothers, but they would not recognize him. Joseph had grown into a man. He was dressed in Egyptian garb and barbered according to the more clean-shaven Egyptian style. He spoke a foreign language, using an interpreter. The brothers, on the other hand, were already adults the last time Joseph had seen them. They were living in the same culture, making their living the same way. They would have changed very little.

[10]"No, my lord," they answered. "Your servants have come to buy
food. [11]We are all the sons of one man. Your servants are honest men,
not spies."

[12]"No!" he said to them. "You have come to see where our land is
unprotected."

[13]But they replied, "Your servants were twelve brothers, the sons of one man, who lives in the land of Canaan. The youngest is now with our father, and one is no more."

[14]Joseph said to them, "It is just as I told you: You are spies! [15]And
this is how you will be tested: As surely as Pharaoh lives, you will not
leave this place unless your youngest brother comes here. [16]Send one
of your number to get your brother; the rest of you will be kept in prison, so that your words may be tested to see if you are telling the truth. If you are not, then as surely as Pharaoh lives, you are spies!"
[17]And he put them all in custody for three days.

[18]On the third day, Joseph said to them, "Do this and you will live,
for I fear God: [19]If you are honest men, let one of your brothers stay
here in prison, while the rest of you go and take grain back for your
starving households. [20]But you must bring your youngest brother to
me, so that your words may be verified and that you may not die."
This they proceeded to do.

[21]They said to one another, "Surely we are being punished because of our brother. We saw how distressed he was when he pleaded with us for his life, but we would not listen; that's why this distress has come upon us."

[22]Reuben replied, "Didn't I tell you not to sin against the boy? But
you wouldn't listen! Now we must give an accounting for his blood."
[23]They did not realize that Joseph could understand them, since he
was using an interpreter.

[24]He turned away from them and began to weep, but then turned back and spoke to them again. He had Simeon taken from them and bound before their eyes.

[25]Joseph gave orders to fill their bags with grain, to put each man's silver back in his sack, and to give them provisions for their journey.
After this was done for them, [26]they loaded their grain on their don-
keys and left.

[27]At the place where they stopped for the night one of them opened his sack to get feed for his donkey, and he saw his silver in the mouth
of his sack. [28]"My silver has been returned," he said to his brothers.
"Here it is in my sack."

Their hearts sank and they turned to each other trembling and said, "What is this that God has done to us?"

Why do you think Joseph let his brothers do this? **2.** What is the ruse Joseph uses for testing his brothers? Why would the Hebrews be considered a risk? **3.** When Joseph heard his brothers talking about him in verse 21, how did he react? Why didn't he reveal himself to them at that time? **4.** Why do you think Joseph orders that their money be put back into their grain sacks? How did the brothers take this? **5.** When the brothers got home and told Jacob that they have to bring Benjamin with them, what does Jacob do? Why would Jacob be so careful with Benjamin? **6.** What do you feel about the people in this story: The ten brothers? Simeon, who was kept as a hostage? Jacob the father? Joseph? **7.** Do you think Joseph realized that his dream as a child was being fulfilled before his eyes?

APPLY 1. When growing up, were you the one who loaned your brothers/sisters money or the one who was always asking for a loan? **2.** Where are you right now in your relationship with your brothers/sisters? Where are they right now in their relationship with God?

42:10 Your servants. In that moment when Joseph's worlds collided, was he aware that his dreams were being fulfilled? How ironic that he had envisioned his brothers as sheaves of wheat bowing down to him (37:7). Because of grain, they had come and called themselves his servants.

42:15 As surely as Pharaoh lives. Cultures often swore by their monarch, like people today take an oath in court with a hand on the Bible. **your youngest brother.** Joseph touched them at their most vulnerable place. Their greatest failure, the skeleton in their closet, was their treatment of a younger brother and what their actions did to their father. Joseph could not have made a more difficult request.

42:21 We saw how distressed he was. Even though 17 years had passed since Joseph's brothers betrayed him, the moment was still present with them. They immediately made the connection between their actions and the consequences they were facing. This verse actually gives us more insight into Joseph's experience than does Genesis 37.

42:24 He had Simeon taken from them. It seems unusual that Joseph would have bound Simeon, the second oldest, rather than Reuben, the oldest. Reuben, however, had saved Joseph's life (37:21–22).

29When they came to their father Jacob in the land of Canaan, they
told him all that had happened to them. They said, 30"The man who is
lord over the land spoke harshly to us and treated us as though we
were spying on the land. 31But we said to him, 'We are honest men;
we are not spies. 32We were twelve brothers, sons of one father. One
is no more, and the youngest is now with our father in Canaan.'
33"Then the man who is lord over the land said to us, 'This is how I
will know whether you are honest men: Leave one of your brothers
here with me, and take food for your starving households and go.
34But bring your youngest brother to me so I will know that you are
not spies but honest men. Then I will give your brother back to you,
and you can trade[a] in the land.' "
35As they were emptying their sacks, there in each man's sack was
his pouch of silver! When they and their father saw the money
pouches, they were frightened. 36Their father Jacob said to them,
"You have deprived me of my children. Joseph is no more and Simeon
is no more, and now you want to take Benjamin. Everything is
against me!"
37Then Reuben said to his father, "You may put both of my sons to
death if I do not bring him back to you. Entrust him to my care, and I
will bring him back."
38But Jacob said, "My son will not go down there with you; his
brother is dead and he is the only one left. If harm comes to him on
the journey you are taking, you will bring my gray head down to the
grave[b] in sorrow."

The Second Journey to Egypt

43 Now the famine was still severe in the land. 2So when they
had eaten all the grain they had brought from Egypt, their
father said to them, "Go back and buy us a little more food."
3But Judah said to him, "The man warned us solemnly, 'You will not
see my face again unless your brother is with you.' 4If you will send our
brother along with us, we will go down and buy food for you. 5But if
you will not send him, we will not go down, because the man said to
us, 'You will not see my face again unless your brother is with you.' "
6Israel asked, "Why did you bring this trouble on me by telling the
man you had another brother?"
7They replied, "The man questioned us closely about ourselves and
our family. 'Is your father still living?' he asked us. 'Do you have another brother?' We simply answered his questions. How were we to
know he would say, 'Bring your brother down here'?"
8Then Judah said to Israel his father, "Send the boy along with me
and we will go at once, so that we and you and our children may live
and not die. 9I myself will guarantee his safety; you can hold me personally responsible for him. If I do not bring him back to you and set

a34 Or move about freely b38 Hebrew *Sheol*

OPEN 1. What is the closest you have come to being in a very important person's house? **2.** Have you ever eaten at the official residence of a very important person?

STUDY Many years ago Joseph had a dream that he would one day rule over his brothers. Now he is the prime minister of the greatest power in the world. His brothers came to Egypt to get food which he gave them, but he demanded that they bring Joseph's younger brother Benjamin with them if they came back for more food. Jacob (Israel) their father refused to let Benjamin go. **1.** If your family was out of food and your father asked you to go to the governor of a world power and ask for food, and the governor's steward took you to the governor's mansion and laid before you the largest meal you had ever seen, what would you think? **2.** If you knew that all of the money you had spent to buy food on a previous trip was

42:37 both of my sons. Reuben's offer of laying down the lives of both his sons was meant to secure Benjamin's safety. For Jacob, though, it must have been little relief. God had promised his family a host of descendants, yet he was losing sons one at a time. To be assured that he could lose two more heirs if Benjamin did not return was only another hardship to endure.

43:3 Judah. Even though Judah was actually the fourth born, he took a more outspoken leadership role from this point. He was also the brother who had made the suggestion of selling Joseph years earlier (37:26–27).

43:9 you can hold me personally responsible. Judah spoke to his father as a man who expected to be trusted.

him here before you, I will bear the blame before you all my life. 10As it is, if we had not delayed, we could have gone and returned twice."

11Then their father Israel said to them, "If it must be, then do this: Put some of the best products of the land in your bags and take them down to the man as a gift—a little balm and a little honey, some spices and myrrh, some pistachio nuts and almonds. 12Take double the amount of silver with you, for you must return the silver that was put back into the mouths of your sacks. Perhaps it was a mistake. 13Take your brother also and go back to the man at once. 14And may God Almighty[a] grant you mercy before the man so that he will let your other brother and Benjamin come back with you. As for me, if I am bereaved, I am bereaved."

15So the men took the gifts and double the amount of silver, and Benjamin also. They hurried down to Egypt and presented themselves to Joseph. 16When Joseph saw Benjamin with them, he said to the steward of his house, "Take these men to my house, slaughter an animal and prepare dinner; they are to eat with me at noon."

17The man did as Joseph told him and took the men to Joseph's house. 18Now the men were frightened when they were taken to his house. They thought, "We were brought here because of the silver that was put back into our sacks the first time. He wants to attack us and overpower us and seize us as slaves and take our donkeys."

19So they went up to Joseph's steward and spoke to him at the entrance to the house. 20"Please, sir," they said, "we came down here the first time to buy food. 21But at the place where we stopped for the night we opened our sacks and each of us found his silver—the exact weight—in the mouth of his sack. So we have brought it back with us. 22We have also brought additional silver with us to buy food. We don't know who put our silver in our sacks."

23"It's all right," he said. "Don't be afraid. Your God, the God of your father, has given you treasure in your sacks; I received your silver." Then he brought Simeon out to them.

24The steward took the men into Joseph's house, gave them water to wash their feet and provided fodder for their donkeys. 25They prepared their gifts for Joseph's arrival at noon, because they had heard that they were to eat there.

26When Joseph came home, they presented to him the gifts they had brought into the house, and they bowed down before him to the ground. 27He asked them how they were, and then he said, "How is your aged father you told me about? Is he still living?"

28They replied, "Your servant our father is still alive and well." And they bowed low to pay him honor.

29As he looked about and saw his brother Benjamin, his own

[a]14 Hebrew *El-Shaddai*

left in your grocery sacks, how would you be feeling when you went back to this place to buy more food? **3.** How do you think the nine brothers are dressed for this occasion? How do they look? Smell? Feel? **4.** How do you imagine the atmosphere in the room when Joseph appears? What does he ask about? How would you be feeling if you were Joseph when you saw your little brother Benjamin? **5.** Why did they sit at three separate tables? What does this tell you about the Hebrews? **6.** Who do you think felt the most uncomfortable at this dinner: Joseph, knowing his brothers? The brothers, not knowing it was Joseph? Or the Egyptians, not knowing anything? How would you have felt?

APPLY **1.** What is the closest you have come to needing help from an outside source to get you through hard times in your life? **2.** What did you learn from this experience that has made you a better person today?

While Reuben had offered the lives of his sons (42:37), Judah offered his own life in exchange for Benjamin.

43:11 do this. Jacob started to get organized. In his younger days he had been a wheeler-dealer. Here he settled on a strategy for winning favor in an effort to protect Benjamin's safety.

43:26 they bowed down. Imagine the pressure Joseph's brothers felt to bring Benjamin back home safely. They had come quite a long way from the cruel young men who so easily betrayed Joseph and broke their father's heart.

43:29 his brother Benjamin. In a world where a patriarch had children by several wives and servants over a long life span, one family could function more like several extended families. Benjamin was Joseph's only full brother. They were the youngest of Jacob's sons and were the only sons of Jacob's beloved wife, Rachel. They represented Jacob's last memories of her since she died during Benjamin's birth. The bond

mother's son, he asked, "Is this your youngest brother, the one you
told me about?" And he said, "God be gracious to you, my son."
30 Deeply moved at the sight of his brother, Joseph hurried out and
looked for a place to weep. He went into his private room and wept
there.

31 After he had washed his face, he came out and, controlling himself, said, "Serve the food."

32 They served him by himself, the brothers by themselves, and the
Egyptians who ate with him by themselves, because Egyptians could
not eat with Hebrews, for that is detestable to Egyptians. 33 The men
had been seated before him in the order of their ages, from the firstborn to the youngest; and they looked at each other in astonishment.
34 When portions were served to them from Joseph's table, Benjamin's portion was five times as much as anyone else's. So they
feasted and drank freely with him.

A Silver Cup in a Sack

44 Now Joseph gave these instructions to the steward of his
house: "Fill the men's sacks with as much food as they can
carry, and put each man's silver in the mouth of his sack. 2 Then put
my cup, the silver one, in the mouth of the youngest one's sack,
along with the silver for his grain." And he did as Joseph said.

3 As morning dawned, the men were sent on their way with their
donkeys. 4 They had not gone far from the city when Joseph said to his
steward, "Go after those men at once, and when you catch up with
them, say to them, 'Why have you repaid good with evil? 5 Isn't this
the cup my master drinks from and also uses for divination? This is a
wicked thing you have done.' "

6 When he caught up with them, he repeated these words to them.
7 But they said to him, "Why does my lord say such things? Far be it
from your servants to do anything like that! 8 We even brought back to
you from the land of Canaan the silver we found inside the mouths of
our sacks. So why would we steal silver or gold from your master's
house? 9 If any of your servants is found to have it, he will die; and the
rest of us will become my lord's slaves."

10 "Very well, then," he said, "let it be as you say. Whoever is found
to have it will become my slave; the rest of you will be free from
blame."

11 Each of them quickly lowered his sack to the ground and opened

OPEN 1. When you were growing up, when did your parents bring out the special silverware and china? **2.** Where did your parents keep the expensive silver for safekeeping?

STUDY Joseph's brothers have returned to Egypt for more food. They have brought with them the youngest son, Benjamin. They have eaten a huge feast with Joseph and are ready to return home with their food. They still do not know that the prime minister is none other than Joseph, the brother they sold as a slave many years before. **1.** Where do you think Joseph learned his tricks of deception and false identity? **2.** Why would Joseph ask his steward to put the silver cup in the youngest son's sack (Benjamin)? **3.** If you had been one of the brothers and Joseph's steward met your caravan as you were leaving town and accused you of stealing the silver cup, what would you say? **4.** If you were responsible for Benjamin and the silver cup was found in Benjamin's sack, how would you

---

between Benjamin and Joseph was much different than the bond between Joseph and his other brothers.

43:30 Deeply moved. Joseph was suddenly with people whom he had thought he might never see again. By God's grace, despite the trouble these brothers had brought into his life, Joseph had a tender heart and was moved to tears.

43:32 brothers by themselves. The Hebrews typically kept themselves separate from other nations. In this case though, it was the Egyptians who were separating themselves from the Hebrews.

43:33–34 in the order of their ages ... Benjamin's portion. What questions must have run through the brothers' minds when this unknown ruler seated them in the exact order of their ages and then gave the youngest brother special treatment. However, they were glad to share the bounty.

44:9 he will die. Whoever had stolen the silver would lose his life, and the rest would lose their freedom. In making this promise, the brothers proclaimed their innocence and unknowingly put Benjamin's life on the line.

44:10 will become my slave. Joseph's steward immediately made a more reasonable deal. Instead of putting the guilty to death and enslaving the rest, he described a scenario in which the guilty would be enslaved and the rest go free. This would create an unbearable dilemma for the brothers: returning to their father without his youngest son.

it. 12Then the steward proceeded to search, beginning with the oldest
and ending with the youngest. And the cup was found in Benjamin's
sack. 13At this, they tore their clothes. Then they all loaded their donkeys and returned to the city.
14Joseph was still in the house when Judah and his brothers came
in, and they threw themselves to the ground before him. 15Joseph
said to them, "What is this you have done? Don't you know that a
man like me can find things out by divination?"
16"What can we say to my lord?" Judah replied. "What can we say?
How can we prove our innocence? God has uncovered your servants'
guilt. We are now my lord's slaves—we ourselves and the one who
was found to have the cup."
17But Joseph said, "Far be it from me to do such a thing! Only the
man who was found to have the cup will become my slave. The rest of
you, go back to your father in peace."
18Then Judah went up to him and said: "Please, my lord, let your
servant speak a word to my lord. Do not be angry with your servant,
though you are equal to Pharaoh himself. 19My lord asked his servants, 'Do you have a father or a brother?' 20And we answered, 'We
have an aged father, and there is a young son born to him in his old
age. His brother is dead, and he is the only one of his mother's sons
left, and his father loves him.'
21"Then you said to your servants, 'Bring him down to me so I can
see him for myself.' 22And we said to my lord, 'The boy cannot leave
his father; if he leaves him, his father will die.' 23But you told your
servants, 'Unless your youngest brother comes down with you, you
will not see my face again.' 24When we went back to your servant my
father, we told him what my lord had said.
25"Then our father said, 'Go back and buy a little more food.' 26But
we said, 'We cannot go down. Only if our youngest brother is with us
will we go. We cannot see the man's face unless our youngest brother
is with us.'
27"Your servant my father said to us, 'You know that my wife bore
me two sons. 28One of them went away from me, and I said, "He has
surely been torn to pieces." And I have not seen him since. 29If you
take this one from me too and harm comes to him, you will bring my
gray head down to the grave[a] in misery.'
30"So now, if the boy is not with us when I go back to your servant

[a]29 Hebrew *Sheol*; also in verse 31

feel? **5.** Who is Judah primarily concerned about as he pleads for Benjamin's life: His own? His father's? Benjamin's? **6.** Why do you think Joseph puts his brothers through this cruel treatment? Could you have done this to your brothers? **7.** Why does the Bible devote three chapters to an internal squabble of twelve brothers? What does this have to do with the big picture in God's story?

APPLY 1. How would you compare the relationship of Joseph and his brothers in this story to the relationships in your own family when one brother becomes wealthy and successful? **2.** As you get older, have you found that you are more forgiving of your parents and siblings for the things they did to you or did not do for you?

44:12 oldest ... youngest. This is the second time the brothers were dealt with in birth order. In 43:33 the brothers had been seated for the meal in birth order. This had astonished them. Now the search was conducted in the very order that would create the most drama—leaving the guilty party last.

44:13 tore their clothes. In Jeremiah 36:24, it is a criteria for judging responses. Joel encouraged people to repentance: "Rend your hearts and not your garments" (Joel 2:13).

44:14 threw themselves. This was not the action of men who would carelessly toss their brother and their father's peace of mind to the wind. Joseph was testing his brothers to determine who they had become. Were they still heartless—would they treat Benjamin as they had treated him?

44:16 We are now my lord's slaves. The latest deal was that Benjamin would be Joseph's slave because of the alleged theft of silver. Judah's statement, makes clear that they were all implicated, a sure indication that all of the brothers had matured.

44:18 let your servant speak. Judah begged Joseph for the life of Benjamin and the peace of mind of his father, Jacob.

44:30 closely bound up. Judah described Jacob's relationship to Benjamin as "tied together." In begging for Benjamin's life, Judah was also begging for Jacob's life. There may still have been favoritism, transferred from Joseph to Benjamin, but the brothers seem to have matured past it.

my father and if my father, whose life is closely bound up with the
boy's life, 31sees that the boy isn't there, he will die. Your servants will
bring the gray head of our father down to the grave in sorrow. 32Your
servant guaranteed the boy's safety to my father. I said, 'If I do not
bring him back to you, I will bear the blame before you, my father, all
my life!'

33"Now then, please let your servant remain here as my lord's slave
in place of the boy, and let the boy return with his brothers. 34How
can I go back to my father if the boy is not with me? No! Do not let me
see the misery that would come upon my father."

Joseph Makes Himself Known

45 Then Joseph could no longer control himself before all his at
tendants, and he cried out, "Have everyone leave my presence!" So there was no one with Joseph when he made himself
known to his brothers. 2And he wept so loudly that the Egyptians
heard him, and Pharaoh's household heard about it.

3Joseph said to his brothers, "I am Joseph! Is my father still living?"
But his brothers were not able to answer him, because they were terrified at his presence.

4Then Joseph said to his brothers, "Come close to me." When they
had done so, he said, "I am your brother Joseph, the one you sold
into Egypt! 5And now, do not be distressed and do not be angry with
yourselves for selling me here, because it was to save lives that God
sent me ahead of you. 6For two years now there has been famine in
the land, and for the next five years there will not be plowing and
reaping. 7But God sent me ahead of you to preserve for you a remnant on earth and to save your lives by a great deliverance.[a]

8"So then, it was not you who sent me here, but God. He made me
father to Pharaoh, lord of his entire household and ruler of all Egypt.

[a]7 Or *save you as a great band of survivors*

OPEN Who in your family has trouble showing their emotions? Who shows their emotions easily?

STUDY Joseph went from slave to prisoner to second in command in Egypt. When Joseph's brothers come to buy grain, he recognized them but they didn't recognize him. He refused to let them buy more food unless they returned with Benjamin, Joseph's only full brother. Later, when Joseph sent them on their way, he had his silver cup planted in Benjamin's sack. When Joseph declared Benjamin's punishment would be to become his slave, the others fell down and begged for mercy. **1.** Why did Joseph wait so long to reveal his true identity to his brothers? Could you have waited this long? **2.** How do you think the brothers felt when Joseph ordered his attendants out of the room and revealed who he was? How did

44:33 let your servant remain. In Judah's last plea, he offered himself for his brother. There could be no doubt in Joseph's mind that his brother, who had once sold him away, had changed.

44:34 the misery that would come upon my father. Once before, Judah had seen his father's misery at the loss of a son. He knew what it would be like for his father to go through that again. Judah's compassion touched Joseph deeply.

45:1 could no longer control himself. The climactic moment had come. Joseph had controlled himself as long as he could. He was ready for a moment of authenticity and intimacy, to be known for who he was, to be alone with his brothers and to let go of the façade.

45:3 they were terrified. What other response could we expect? They were in the process of negotiating with a foreign diplomat in a fashion that had brought back memories of their greatest wrongs. They had just gone through a traumatic scenario in which one brother was begging for the life of another. They had bet the farm and were about to lose it all. Now they were face-to-face with their worst nightmare: The person they had wronged had complete power over them.

45:4 your brother Joseph. Not just "I am Joseph," as in the previous verse. Now he attached himself to them and to the violation that had happened between them.

45:5 do not be distressed. Joseph revealed to his brothers immediately that he had it all worked out in his mind. His life was governed by God. The brothers' wickedness was theirs to deal with; Joseph was okay because God had a gracious plan. Despite Joseph's simple honesty, it was years later before the brothers finally accepted his forgiveness.

45:6 two years. Joseph was thirty when he became second in command. Pharaoh's dream had revealed seven years of plenty and seven years of famine. Joseph states they were in their second year of famine. So nine years had passed since Pharaoh's dream. Joseph was thirty-nine when he revealed himself to his brothers.

45:7 a great deliverance. Joseph's acceptance of his brothers was the beginning of the Exodus, still hundreds of years away. The great deliverance of the nation of Israel began with the family of Israel being saved from famine.

9Now hurry back to my father and say to him, 'This is what your son
Joseph says: God has made me lord of all Egypt. Come down to me;
don't delay. 10You shall live in the region of Goshen and be near me—
you, your children and grandchildren, your flocks and herds, and all
you have. 11I will provide for you there, because five years of famine
are still to come. Otherwise you and your household and all who belong to you will become destitute.'
12"You can see for yourselves, and so can my brother Benjamin,
that it is really I who am speaking to you. 13Tell my father about all
the honor accorded me in Egypt and about everything you have seen.
And bring my father down here quickly."
14Then he threw his arms around his brother Benjamin and wept,
and Benjamin embraced him, weeping. 15And he kissed all his brothers and wept over them. Afterward his brothers talked with him.
16When the news reached Pharaoh's palace that Joseph's brothers
had come, Pharaoh and all his officials were pleased. 17Pharaoh said
to Joseph, "Tell your brothers, 'Do this: Load your animals and return
to the land of Canaan, 18and bring your father and your families back
to me. I will give you the best of the land of Egypt and you can enjoy
the fat of the land.'
19"You are also directed to tell them, 'Do this: Take some carts from
Egypt for your children and your wives, and get your father and
come. 20Never mind about your belongings, because the best of all
Egypt will be yours.' "
21So the sons of Israel did this. Joseph gave them carts, as Pharaoh
had commanded, and he also gave them provisions for their journey.
22To each of them he gave new clothing, but to Benjamin he gave
three hundred shekels[a] of silver and five sets of clothes. 23And this is
what he sent to his father: ten donkeys loaded with the best things of
Egypt, and ten female donkeys loaded with grain and bread and other
provisions for his journey. 24Then he sent his brothers away, and as
they were leaving he said to them, "Don't quarrel on the way!"
25So they went up out of Egypt and came to their father Jacob in the
land of Canaan. 26They told him, "Joseph is still alive! In fact, he is
ruler of all Egypt." Jacob was stunned; he did not believe them. 27But
when they told him everything Joseph had said to them, and when he
saw the carts Joseph had sent to carry him back, the spirit of their father Jacob revived. 28And Israel said, "I'm convinced! My son Joseph
is still alive. I will go and see him before I die."

[a]22 That is, about 7 1/2 pounds (about 3.5 kilograms)

the brother's respond? How would you have responded? 3. How could Joseph embrace his brothers after what they did to him? How long do you think it took for Joseph to understand God's purpose in all of this (v. 5)? If you had been Joseph, could you have understood this? 4. Who is Joseph especially concerned for? 5. How would you describe the way the brothers arrived in Egypt to buy food and the way they returned home? If you had been their father Jacob, would you have been skeptical when they shared what happened? 6. Do you think Jacob remembered the dream that Joseph shared with him, that one day he would rule over his brothers? 7. Do you think God caused all of the bad things that happened in Joseph's life or simply used these things to turn them into something good?

APPLY 1. As you look back on your life, what is the most painful period that was inflicted on you because of someone or something else? **2.** How has God used this painful time or experience for his purpose in making you into the person you are today?

45:9 God has made me lord of all Egypt. True to his character, Joseph gives credit where it is due. He does not say, "Pharaoh has made me Lord of all *Egypt," but rather gives God the glory.* Neither did he remind them of his dreams with a subtle "I told you so." Joseph has matured as well. **don't delay.** Joseph wants the brothers to hurry home with the news.

45:12 it is really I. Joseph spoke to them in their native tongue rather than through an interpreter.

45:14 Benjamin embraced him. Joseph's joy is returned by Benjamin.

45:15 his brothers talked with him. The real reunion happened, after the shock, after the convincing. In a matter of moments the eleven brothers had gone from fearing for their lives to being rescued by someone they once had plotted to murder.

45:18 I will give you the best. Joseph is a picture of God's grace and forgiveness. He returned good for evil because he focused on the good he had received from God.

45:22 five sets. Once again Benjamin received five times that of his brothers. In 43:34, Benjamin had received five times the normal portion of food at the meal. Joseph had special love for his only full brother.

45:24 Don't quarrel on the way! Even at this exciting moment, Joseph had the wisdom to know that on the long ride home his brothers could easily turn on each other.

OPEN **1.** How many times have you moved to a different part of the country? **2.** Have you ever lived in a foreign country? **3.** On a long trip, who sat with you in the back seat when you were a child?

STUDY Joseph has revealed to his brothers that he is their long-lost brother that they sold many years before into Egypt where he has become the prime minister. When Joseph finds out that his father is still alive, he requests that the whole family come to live in Egypt. **1.** If you were very old and you had lived in the same place for many years, how would you feel about pulling up your roots and moving to another country? **2.** Jacob (Israel) was named Jacob because he was cunning, deceitful and tricky. He tricked his father into giving him his brother's birthright. How do you see Jacob now? **3.** When Jacob was fleeing from his brother, he had a dream (28:10–22) that he would one day return to his homeland. How would you compare that dream to his vision here (vv. 2–4)? What is the difference between dreams and visions? What does God do for Jacob in this vision? **4.** How many carts do you think it took to transport seventy people and all of their possessions to Egypt? How many would it take for your family? **5.** Why do you think the Bible recorded all of the twelve sons of Jacob and their sons who came into Egypt? **6.** In your imagination, how do you picture the meeting of Joseph and his father? What exactly did Jacob (Israel) mean by saying, "Now I am ready to die, since I have seen for myself that you are still alive" (v. 30)? **7.** Why would

Jacob Goes to Egypt

46 So Israel set out with all that was his, and when he reached Beersheba, he offered sacrifices to the God of his father Isaac.
[2]And God spoke to Israel in a vision at night and said, "Jacob! Jacob!"

"Here I am," he replied.

[3]"I am God, the God of your father," he said. "Do not be afraid to go down to Egypt, for I will make you into a great nation there. [4]I will go down to Egypt with you, and I will surely bring you back again. And Joseph's own hand will close your eyes."

[5]Then Jacob left Beersheba, and Israel's sons took their father Jacob and their children and their wives in the carts that Pharaoh had sent to transport him. [6]They also took with them their livestock and the possessions they had acquired in Canaan, and Jacob and all his offspring went to Egypt. [7]He took with him to Egypt his sons and grandsons and his daughters and granddaughters—all his offspring.

[8]These are the names of the sons of Israel (Jacob and his descendants) who went to Egypt:

Reuben the firstborn of Jacob.
[9]The sons of Reuben:
Hanoch, Pallu, Hezron and Carmi.
[10]The sons of Simeon:
Jemuel, Jamin, Ohad, Jakin, Zohar and Shaul the son of a Canaanite woman.
[11]The sons of Levi:
Gershon, Kohath and Merari.
[12]The sons of Judah:
Er, Onan, Shelah, Perez and Zerah (but Er and Onan had died in the land of Canaan).
The sons of Perez:
Hezron and Hamul.

46:1 with all that was his. There were flocks and herds, wives and servants. This would be a complicated move. **Beersheba.** This was actually Jacob's hometown. **sacrifices to the God of his father.** This is not to imply that Jacob was only honoring God historically. It affirms that God had been honored throughout all the generations in Jacob's family. In fact, grandfather Abraham, as well as father Isaac, had worshiped in this same place.

46:2 God spoke to Israel in a vision. *God spoke to Jacob (Israel) in this* same place where he had also spoken to Isaac, Jacob's father (26:4).

46:3 Do not be afraid to go down. When God spoke to Isaac (Jacob's father) in Beersheba he told Isaac to trust God by staying right where he was. When God spoke to Jacob, he told Jacob to trust God by traveling to Egypt. Both acts required faith. **I will make you into a great nation.** This echoes God's promise to Abraham passed down to Isaac and then to Jacob. God told Abraham that he would make his descendants as numerous as the stars in the sky or the sands of the seashore (22:17).

46:4 I will surely bring you back again. This promise referred to Jacob's descendants. He died in Egypt, but his family returned to Canaan or Israel. **Joseph's own hand will close your eyes.** Imagine the gladness of this promise. Jacob had believed his son Joseph to be dead for years. This promise from God referred to Jacob's death. For the rest of Jacob's life, he would be cared for by his lost son Joseph.

46:8 the sons of Israel. These 12 names are the basis of the tribes of the Old Testament. Their families are the organizational structure for the wilderness journey after the Exodus from Egypt as well as the division of land and responsibilities in Canaan. The rest of the Bible describes God's people in terms of the sons of Israel from whom they descended. (Acts 4:36, Joseph, the Levite; Luke 2:36, Anna of the tribe of Asher). Regions of Israel are given these tribal names (Matt. 4:15).

[13]The sons of Issachar:
Tola, Puah,[a] Jashub[b] and Shimron.
[14]The sons of Zebulun:
Sered, Elon and Jahleel.
[15]These were the sons Leah bore to Jacob in Paddan Aram,[c] besides
his daughter Dinah. These sons and daughters of his were thirty-
three in all.

[16]The sons of Gad:
Zephon,[d] Haggi, Shuni, Ezbon, Eri, Arodi and Areli.
[17]The sons of Asher:
Imnah, Ishvah, Ishvi and Beriah.
Their sister was Serah.
The sons of Beriah:
Heber and Malkiel.
[18]These were the children born to Jacob by Zilpah, whom Laban
had given to his daughter Leah—sixteen in all.

[19]The sons of Jacob's wife Rachel:
Joseph and Benjamin.
[20]In Egypt, Manasseh and Ephraim
were born to Joseph by Asenath daughter of Potiphera, priest
of On.[e]
[21]The sons of Benjamin:
Bela, Beker, Ashbel, Gera, Naaman, Ehi, Rosh, Muppim, Huppim and Ard.
[22]These were the sons of Rachel who were born to Jacob—fourteen
in all.

[23]The son of Dan:
Hushim.
[24]The sons of Naphtali:
Jahziel, Guni, Jezer and Shillem.
[25]These were the sons born to Jacob by Bilhah, whom Laban had
given to his daughter Rachel—seven in all.

[26]All those who went to Egypt with Jacob—those who were his
direct descendants, not counting his sons' wives—numbered sixty-
six persons.
[27]With the two sons[f] who had been born to Joseph in
Egypt, the members of Jacob's family, which went to Egypt, were
seventy[g] in all.

[28]Now Jacob sent Judah ahead of him to Joseph to get directions to
Goshen. When they arrived in the region of Goshen,
[29]Joseph had his
chariot made ready and went to Goshen to meet his father Israel. As

[a]*13* Samaritan Pentateuch and Syriac (see also 1 Chron. 7:1); Masoretic Text *Puvah* [b]*13* Samaritan Pentateuch and some Septuagint manuscripts (see also Num. 26:24 and 1 Chron. 7:1); Masoretic Text *Iob* [c]*15* That is, Northwest Mesopotamia [d]*16* Samaritan Pentateuch and Septuagint (see also Num. 26:15); Masoretic Text *Ziphion* [e]*20* That is, Heliopolis [f]*27* Hebrew; Septuagint *the nine children* [g]*27* Hebrew (see also Exodus 1:5 and footnote); Septuagint (see also Acts 7:14) *seventy-five*

Joseph be concerned that Pharaoh give special permission for Jacob's family to be settled in Egypt? **8.** Do you think Jacob and his sons realized how important their family would be in the overall plan of God?

APPLY **1.** The Bible says that young men "dream dreams" and old men "see visions." Which are you doing? **2.** What are you dreaming about—or seeing in a vision now? **3.** Are you aware that you are part of God's master plan and that God is doing his thing in your life this very day?

46:27 seventy in all. That's quite a convoy. Imagine the difficulty of uprooting extended families and resettling together in a new culture. Joseph had two sons who eventually received blessing and inheritance from Jacob, which is why there is no tribe of Joseph. The organizational structure passed to his sons. Adding in Joseph and his sons, Jacob's family was once again complete. From this small number grew a great nation that would eventually return to Canaan (Ex. 1:5; 12:37).

46:29 Goshen. Joseph's whole family settled in Goshen, some of the most fertile land in Egypt, in the northeastern section of the Nile delta. **threw his arms around his father and wept.** Jacob and Joseph had an enthusiastic reunion. Not just a family reunion, this was the reuniting of God's people with God's promise. Joseph was the God-appointed leader of his family.

soon as Joseph appeared before him, he threw his arms around his
father[a] and wept for a long time.
30 Israel said to Joseph, "Now I am ready to die, since I have seen
for myself that you are still alive."
31 Then Joseph said to his brothers and to his father's household, "I
will go up and speak to Pharaoh and will say to him, 'My brothers and
my father's household, who were living in the land of Canaan, have
come to me. 32 The men are shepherds; they tend livestock, and they
have brought along their flocks and herds and everything they own.'
33 When Pharaoh calls you in and asks, 'What is your occupation?'
34 you should answer, 'Your servants have tended livestock from our
boyhood on, just as our fathers did.' Then you will be allowed to settle in the region of Goshen, for all shepherds are detestable to the
Egyptians."

47

Joseph went and told Pharaoh, "My father and brothers, with
their flocks and herds and everything they own, have come
from the land of Canaan and are now in Goshen." 2 He chose five of
his brothers and presented them before Pharaoh.
3 Pharaoh asked the brothers, "What is your occupation?"
"Your servants are shepherds," they replied to Pharaoh, "just as
our fathers were." 4 They also said to him, "We have come to live here
awhile, because the famine is severe in Canaan and your servants'
flocks have no pasture. So now, please let your servants settle in Goshen."
5 Pharaoh said to Joseph, "Your father and your brothers have come
to you, 6 and the land of Egypt is before you; settle your father and
your brothers in the best part of the land. Let them live in Goshen.
And if you know of any among them with special ability, put them in
charge of my own livestock."
7 Then Joseph brought his father Jacob in and presented him before
Pharaoh. After Jacob blessed[b] Pharaoh, 8 Pharaoh asked him, "How
old are you?"
9 And Jacob said to Pharaoh, "The years of my pilgrimage are a hundred and thirty. My years have been few and difficult, and they do not
equal the years of the pilgrimage of my fathers." 10 Then Jacob
blessed[c] Pharaoh and went out from his presence.
11 So Joseph settled his father and his brothers in Egypt and gave
them property in the best part of the land, the district of Rameses, as
Pharaoh directed. 12 Joseph also provided his father and his brothers
and all his father's household with food, according to the number of
their children.

[a]29 Hebrew *around him* [b]7 Or *greeted* [c]10 Or *said farewell to*

46:34 shepherds. When Joseph's brothers told Pharaoh they were shepherds, he gave them land in the Egyptian *boondocks. Shepherds* were not valued, because the Egyptians had cattle not sheep. This helped Jacob's family to maintain their own identity as a people.

47:9 the years of my pilgrimage. Since the days of grandfather Abraham, Jacob's family had been on a journey. In Jacob's lifetime he had lived as a man on the run for years, leaving home under the threat of violence. Now he was ending his pilgrimage in a strange land.

47:11 Rameses. This refers to a famous Egyptian Pharaoh who lived much later. The land was later called Rameses, but at the time it was called Goshen (46:29). Years later, when the Israelites were put into slavery, they would be forced to build two store cities—Pithom and Rameses (Ex. 1:11).

Joseph and the Famine

13 There was no food, however, in the whole region because the
famine was severe; both Egypt and Canaan wasted away because of
the famine. 14 Joseph collected all the money that was to be found in
Egypt and Canaan in payment for the grain they were buying, and he
brought it to Pharaoh's palace. 15 When the money of the people of
Egypt and Canaan was gone, all Egypt came to Joseph and said, "Give
us food. Why should we die before your eyes? Our money is used up."
16 "Then bring your livestock," said Joseph. "I will sell you food in
exchange for your livestock, since your money is gone." 17 So they
brought their livestock to Joseph, and he gave them food in exchange
for their horses, their sheep and goats, their cattle and donkeys. And
he brought them through that year with food in exchange for all their
livestock.
18 When that year was over, they came to him the following year and
said, "We cannot hide from our lord the fact that since our money is
gone and our livestock belongs to you, there is nothing left for our
lord except our bodies and our land. 19 Why should we perish before
your eyes—we and our land as well? Buy us and our land in exchange
for food, and we with our land will be in bondage to Pharaoh. Give us
seed so that we may live and not die, and that the land may not become desolate."
20 So Joseph bought all the land in Egypt for Pharaoh. The Egyptians, one and all, sold their fields, because the famine was too severe for them. The land became Pharaoh's, 21 and Joseph reduced the
people to servitude,[a] from one end of Egypt to the other. 22 However,
he did not buy the land of the priests, because they received a regular
allotment from Pharaoh and had food enough from the allotment
Pharaoh gave them. That is why they did not sell their land.
23 Joseph said to the people, "Now that I have bought you and your
land today for Pharaoh, here is seed for you so you can plant the
ground. 24 But when the crop comes in, give a fifth of it to Pharaoh.
The other four-fifths you may keep as seed for the fields and as food
for yourselves and your households and your children."
25 "You have saved our lives," they said. "May we find favor in the
eyes of our lord; we will be in bondage to Pharaoh."
26 So Joseph established it as a law concerning land in Egypt—still
in force today—that a fifth of the produce belongs to Pharaoh. It was
only the land of the priests that did not become Pharaoh's.
27 Now the Israelites settled in Egypt in the region of Goshen. They
acquired property there and were fruitful and increased greatly in
number.
28 Jacob lived in Egypt seventeen years, and the years of his life

[a]21 Samaritan Pentateuch and Septuagint (see also Vulgate); Masoretic Text *and he moved the people into the cities*

OPEN 1. Who generally wins in your family when you play Monopoly? **2.** What do you do when all of your money is gone in Monopoly and you still want to stay in the game?

STUDY Jacob has moved with all of his sons and possessions to Egypt where Joseph is second in command to Pharaoh. Joseph set aside grain during the good years and is now selling grain during the famine years. This story explains how the Egyptian people became serfs in their own land. **1.** How would you describe Joseph as a banker? How would you like to do business with him? **2.** If the government tried to do today what Joseph did, what would happen? What is different between giving the government 20% of your crops and giving the government 20% of your income in taxes? **3.** Why do you think Jacob wanted to be buried back in Canaan? How important would that be to you? **4.** If you had to put in a good word for Joseph for doing what he did on behalf of the people of Egypt, what would it be? If you could put in a good word for Joseph for being what he was in the master plan of God, what would it be? **5.** At one time in his life, Jacob would have been considered a wealthy man. What is really important to him now?

APPLY **1.** If you were to live a normal life of 70 or 80 years and you could divide your life into four quarters like a ball game, what quarter would you be in now? **2.** What is going to be important in the next quarter?

47:16 in exchange. Joseph had saved Egypt, but Pharaoh did not release food without a price. By the end of the famine, the people had sold all they owned to the government, including themselves as slaves.

47:21 reduced the people to servitude. In order to stay alive, the people of Egypt became a nation of sharecroppers and slaves. But Joseph was a kind ruler, and the people appreciated what he did to save them (vv. 23–25).

47:26 fifth of the produce. After the famine, none of the people could consider their farmland their own. It belonged to Pharaoh.

47:27 acquired property. Amazingly, while the Egyptian population was selling land and becoming slaves to the government, the Israelites were acquiring property.

were a hundred and forty-seven. 29When the time drew near for Israel
to die, he called for his son Joseph and said to him, "If I have found
favor in your eyes, put your hand under my thigh and promise that
you will show me kindness and faithfulness. Do not bury me in Egypt,
30but when I rest with my fathers, carry me out of Egypt and bury me
where they are buried."
"I will do as you say," he said.
31"Swear to me," he said. Then Joseph swore to him, and Israel
worshiped as he leaned on the top of his staff.[a]

Manasseh and Ephraim

48 Some time later Joseph was told, "Your father is ill." So he
took his two sons Manasseh and Ephraim along with him.
2When Jacob was told, "Your son Joseph has come to you," Israel
rallied his strength and sat up on the bed.
3Jacob said to Joseph, "God Almighty[b] appeared to me at Luz in the
land of Canaan, and there he blessed me 4and said to me, 'I am going
to make you fruitful and will increase your numbers. I will make you
a community of peoples, and I will give this land as an everlasting
possession to your descendants after you.'
5"Now then, your two sons born to you in Egypt before I came to
you here will be reckoned as mine; Ephraim and Manasseh will be
mine, just as Reuben and Simeon are mine. 6Any children born to you
after them will be yours; in the territory they inherit they will be reckoned under the names of their brothers. 7As I was returning from
Paddan,[c] to my sorrow Rachel died in the land of Canaan while we
were still on the way, a little distance from Ephrath. So I buried her
there beside the road to Ephrath" (that is, Bethlehem).
8When Israel saw the sons of Joseph, he asked, "Who are these?"
9"They are the sons God has given me here," Joseph said to his father.
Then Israel said, "Bring them to me so I may bless them."
10Now Israel's eyes were failing because of old age, and he could

[a]31 Or *Israel bowed down at the head of his bed* [b]3 Hebrew *El-Shaddai* [c]7 That is, Northwest Mesopotamia

OPEN **1.** What do you remember about your grandparents? **2.** Where are you in the birth order of your family: Youngest? Oldest? Middle? What "privilege" did you get because of your place in this birth order?

STUDY Jacob is old now. He has brought all of his family to Egypt because Joseph was the second in command to Pharaoh. Joseph has two sons. This story is about Jacob adopting these sons as his own children, and giving them his "blessing." **1.** Does this story remind you of your grandparents or great grandparents? What can grandparents and great grandparents do that parents cannot do? **2.** What is it that makes grandparents rally when their kids show up with the grandkids? Can you forgive Jacob for wanting to reminisce about his youth when God told him he was going to have a big family? **3.** Do you think Jacob has forgotten all the trouble that his kids got into when they were growing up? **4.** When Jacob adopted the two sons of Joseph as his own, what rights did this give to the sons? **5.** How would you describe the moment when Joseph presented his

47:29 hand under my thigh. This sign of oath was used when Abraham's servant promised to find a bride for Isaac (24:2). The action signifies that the one making the promise is under threat of attack from the descendants of the one receiving the promise. **Do not bury me in Egypt.** Jacob's body would find its rest in the manner of Jacob's life, on a journey.

47:30 bury me where they are buried. Jacob was referring to the family burial plot purchased by Abraham to bury Sarah, the cave of Machpelah (23:14–20).

47:31 Israel worshiped. Jacob (Israel) was finished with his funeral and burial arrangements. Now he waited for life to end. In the face of death, he settled his affairs and then worshiped God.

48:5 reckoned as mine. In the ancient world, sons received the blessing of the father and family inheritance according to birth order. When Jacob reckoned Joseph's boys as his, he was including them as equals with his other eleven sons. That meant that Joseph's family would receive twice the normal inheritance. When Jacob's descendants settled in Canaan, territory was apportioned not for Joseph, but for the tribes of Ephraim and Manasseh.

48:6 under the names of their brothers. If Joseph's boys were each considered sons of Israel (in terms of inheritance), then why 12 tribes of Israel rather than thirteen (since Israel had 12 sons)? Once the Israelites arrived in Canaan, the Levites (priests and tabernacle workers) received no land. So the land was divided among ten sons of Israel and two grandsons.

48:7 Rachel died. Jacob had two wives, Leah and Rachel. He loved Rachel but had been coerced to marry Leah, the older daughter. Rachel's two sons, Benjamin and Joseph, were Jacob's favorites. As Jacob passed on his blessing to Joseph's son, he reminisced about Rachel, the love of his life.

48:8 Who are these? Was Jacob being introduced to his grandsons for the first time? Perhaps his eyesight was so dim he did not know who they were. It must have been amazing for a grandfather to meet the children of the son he thought dead.

48:10 he could hardly see. This scene imitates Jacob's history. When

hardly see. So Joseph brought his sons close to him, and his father
kissed them and embraced them.
[11]Israel said to Joseph, "I never expected to see your face again,
and now God has allowed me to see your children too."
[12]Then Joseph removed them from Israel's knees and bowed down
with his face to the ground. [13]And Joseph took both of them, Ephraim
on his right toward Israel's left hand and Manasseh on his left toward
Israel's right hand, and brought them close to him. [14]But Israel
reached out his right hand and put it on Ephraim's head, though he
was the younger, and crossing his arms, he put his left hand on
Manasseh's head, even though Manasseh was the firstborn.
[15]Then he blessed Joseph and said,

"May the God before whom my fathers
Abraham and Isaac walked,
the God who has been my shepherd
all my life to this day,
[16]the Angel who has delivered me from all harm
—may he bless these boys.
May they be called by my name
and the names of my fathers Abraham and Isaac,
and may they increase greatly
upon the earth."

[17]When Joseph saw his father placing his right hand on Ephraim's
head he was displeased; so he took hold of his father's hand to move
it from Ephraim's head to Manasseh's head. [18]Joseph said to him,
"No, my father, this one is the firstborn; put your right hand on his
head."
[19]But his father refused and said, "I know, my son, I know. He too
will become a people, and he too will become great. Nevertheless, his
younger brother will be greater than he, and his descendants will become a group of nations." [20]He blessed them that day and said,

"In your[a] name will Israel pronounce this blessing:
'May God make you like Ephraim and Manasseh.' "

So he put Ephraim ahead of Manasseh.
[21]Then Israel said to Joseph, "I am about to die, but God will be

[a]20 The Hebrew is singular.

two sons to Jacob, his father? How do you think Jacob felt? **6.** Do you think Jacob made a mistake in giving the younger son the older son's blessing—or was he just being prophetic? **7.** How would you describe the blessing Jacob gave to Joseph in verses 15–16?

APPLY 1. What is the "blessing" your grandparents gave to you? Did they do this in words or in ways that could not be put into words? **2.** If you could pass on a "blessing" to your grandchildren, what would it be? **3.** When is the last time you told your grandparents how much you appreciate them?

Jacob had received the blessing from his father, Isaac had such poor eyesight that Jacob could trick him into believing he was Esau.

48:13 Manasseh on his left. The right hand was the favored hand in Joseph's day. He placed his older son next to Jacob's right. Joseph assumed that when Jacob reached out his hands to bless the boys, he would naturally place his right hand on Manasseh's head. Thus Manasseh would receive the greater blessing.

48:15 Joseph. Joseph's name is used here as head of the family. Jacob's hands were actually on the heads of Joseph's sons. As with many tribal groups today, connections among family were honored more than individuals in that family. When Jacob gave his blessing to Joseph's children, he was for all practical purposes blessing Joseph.

48:16 the Angel who has delivered me. This could refer to Jacob's wrestling with God (Hos. 12:4). Jacob received a blessing and a new name from God after wrestling all night (32:24–30).

48:19 I know. Joseph must have assumed that Jacob had switched blessings by accident, giving the younger son the greater blessing. Jacob assured Joseph, though, that God was doing something different, that the switched blessing was no accident. Jacob himself had benefitted from such an arrangement, for God had chosen him over his older brother, Esau (25:23).

48:20 Ephraim and Manasseh. Business owners may haggle over whose name goes first on their shingle. Jacob declared Joseph's sons in the order of their birthright: Ephraim first. But Ephraim was the younger.

48:21 the land of your fathers. God first promised the land of Canaan to Abraham, asking him to pick up and move. Isaac lived in Canaan also, but Jacob moved to Egypt to survive a famine.

with you[a] and take you[a] back to the land of your[a] fathers. [22]And to you, as one who is over your brothers, I give the ridge of land[b] I took from the Amorites with my sword and my bow."

Jacob Blesses His Sons

49 Then Jacob called for his sons and said: "Gather around so I can tell you what will happen to you in days to come.

[2] "Assemble and listen, sons of Jacob;
listen to your father Israel.

[3] "Reuben, you are my firstborn,
my might, the first sign of my strength,
excelling in honor, excelling in power.
[4] Turbulent as the waters, you will no longer excel,
for you went up onto your father's bed,
onto my couch and defiled it.

[5] "Simeon and Levi are brothers—
their swords[c] are weapons of violence.
[6] Let me not enter their council,
let me not join their assembly,
for they have killed men in their anger
and hamstrung oxen as they pleased.
[7] Cursed be their anger, so fierce,
and their fury, so cruel!
I will scatter them in Jacob
and disperse them in Israel.

[8] "Judah,[d] your brothers will praise you;
your hand will be on the neck of your enemies;
your father's sons will bow down to you.
[9] You are a lion's cub, O Judah;
you return from the prey, my son.
Like a lion he crouches and lies down,
like a lioness—who dares to rouse him?
[10] The scepter will not depart from Judah,
nor the ruler's staff from between his feet,

[a]*21* The Hebrew is plural. [b]*22* Or *And to you I give one portion more than to your brothers—the portion* [c]*5* The meaning of the Hebrew for this word is uncertain. [d]*8 Judah* sounds like and may be derived from the Hebrew for *praise.*

OPEN 1. When you write your last will and testament, are you going to write a brief word to each child? What are you going to say? **2.** What was the nickname given to you by your grandparents that has stuck with you?

STUDY Jacob is on his death bed. He has brought his sons to Egypt because of the famine in his homeland. Now, all that remains is to give a "blessing" to each son which is almost a prophecy of their life. **1.** If you had a chance to gather all of your children before you died and give them one parting shot, what would you say? **2.** How do you feel about Jacob bringing up past mistakes of Reuben and Simeon in this time of "blessing" (vv. 3–7)? **3.** Do you think the blessing for Judah was fulfilled in King David (vv. 8–12)? **4.** How would you feel if you were compared to a "rawboned donkey" (Issachar), or a "doe set free" (Naphtali) or a "ravenous wolf" (Benjamin)? If you were passing out "blessings," would you be a little kinder? **5.** How much of these blessings are figurative and how much are prophetic? Do you think the way your parents affirm you has anything to do with the way you end up? **6.** Why do you think this list of blessings is in the Bible?

APPLY 1. Who was the person in your life that affirmed you over and over again—that you were special, important and highly valued? **2.** How much of your own self-image is based on the affirmation that significant people in your life gave you?

49:2 listen to your father. Jacob blessed his sons by naming them and describing them. This blessing, one of the longest in the Bible, is a poem. In most cases the traits Jacob listed for his sons were the same traits that their descendants displayed as history unfolded.

49:4 Turbulent as the waters. Jacob identified Reuben as one who troubled the waters. The tribe of Reuben came to be known for their indecision (Judg. 5:16). **your father's bed.** This refers to Reuben's act of adultery and incest with Jacob's concubine (35:22).

49:5 violence. Jacob identified violence as the trait of Simeon and Levi. They were the brothers who tricked the Shechemites into circumcision and then destroyed them to avenge their sister's rape (34:25–29).

49:7 scatter ... disperse. The tribes of Simeon and Levi eventually did become scattered. Simeon was absorbed into Judah's territory. Levi's descendants served as priests throughout the territories.

49:8 your brothers will praise you. Through Judah, King David descended. Also through Judah's line Jesus was born. Judah was the brother who had begged Joseph for Benjamin's life (44:18–34).

49:9 lion's cub ... lion ... lioness. The tribe of Judah is often compared to a lion. Jesus, a descendant of Judah, is called the lion of the tribe of Judah (Rev. 5:5).

49:10 scepter ... ruler's staff. Most people understand this verse to refer to the coming Messiah, Jesus (thus it is called a messianic prophecy). It speaks of Jesus' power and future reign.

until he comes to whom it belongs[a]
and the obedience of the nations is his.
11 He will tether his donkey to a vine,
his colt to the choicest branch;
he will wash his garments in wine,
his robes in the blood of grapes.
12 His eyes will be darker than wine,
his teeth whiter than milk.[b]

13 "Zebulun will live by the seashore
and become a haven for ships;
his border will extend toward Sidon.

14 "Issachar is a rawboned[c] donkey
lying down between two saddlebags.[d]
15 When he sees how good is his resting place
and how pleasant is his land,
he will bend his shoulder to the burden
and submit to forced labor.

16 "Dan[e] will provide justice for his people
as one of the tribes of Israel.
17 Dan will be a serpent by the roadside,
a viper along the path,
that bites the horse's heels
so that its rider tumbles backward.

18 "I look for your deliverance, O LORD.
19 "Gad[f] will be attacked by a band of raiders,
but he will attack them at their heels.

20 "Asher's food will be rich;
he will provide delicacies fit for a king.
21 "Naphtali is a doe set free
that bears beautiful fawns.[g]

22 "Joseph is a fruitful vine,
a fruitful vine near a spring,

[a]10 Or *until Shiloh comes;* or *until he comes to whom tribute belongs* [b]12 Or *will be dull from wine, / his teeth white from milk* [c]14 Or *strong* [d]14 Or *campfires* [e]16 *Dan* here means *he provides justice.* [f]19 *Gad* can mean *attack* and *band of raiders.* [g]21 Or *free; / he utters beautiful words*

49:11 vine ... wine ... grapes. The land of Judah (territories were named after tribes) was productive wine country, but these phrases also speak to the general abundance found there (Num. 13:23).

49:13 by the seashore. The tribe of Zebulun settled within ten miles of the Mediterranean shore.

49:17 serpent ... viper. Jacob identified treachery in the life of Dan and his tribe (Judg. 18:25–31).

49:18 your deliverance. In the midst of this blessing and prophecy Jacob prayed. Maybe he wanted to point out the family's great need for God. Maybe he was overwhelmed with the plight of his sons.

49:19 Gad will be attacked. Gad means "attack," so this is a play on words. The tribe settled on the east side of the Jordan River (Josh. 1:12–13). Tribes on Jordan's west side lived between the river and the sea, so enemies had more difficulty reaching them. Gad's location, though, placed the people between the river and several strong nations. Gad was in for a tough fight.

49:20 Asher's food will be rich. Jacob's blessing came true for the descendants of Asher. They settled in the fertile section of northern Canaan.

49:21 Naphtali. Naphtali settled in the hill country of Canaan, northwest of the Sea of Galilee.

49:22 fruitful. A play on words for Joseph's family, just as "attack" was a play on words for the tribe of Gad. The name Ephraim (Joseph's younger son who received the greater blessing) means "fruitful."

whose branches climb over a wall.[a]
23 With bitterness archers attacked him;
they shot at him with hostility.
24 But his bow remained steady,
his strong arms stayed[b] limber,
because of the hand of the Mighty One of Jacob,
because of the Shepherd, the Rock of Israel,
25 because of your father's God, who helps you,
because of the Almighty,[c] who blesses you
with blessings of the heavens above,
blessings of the deep that lies below,
blessings of the breast and womb.
26 Your father's blessings are greater
than the blessings of the ancient mountains,
than[d] the bounty of the age-old hills.
Let all these rest on the head of Joseph,
on the brow of the prince among[e] his brothers.

27 "Benjamin is a ravenous wolf;
in the morning he devours the prey,
in the evening he divides the plunder."

28 All these are the twelve tribes of Israel, and this is what their father said to them when he blessed them, giving each the blessing appropriate to him.

OPEN 1. Where would you like to be buried? What kind of service? **2.** What do you want inscribed on your tombstone?

STUDY Jacob is one of the few characters in the Bible whose whole life is recorded—from birth to death. His death occurred in Egypt where embalming had become a highly developed science. This gave them the time to take Jacob back to his homeland for burial? **1.** Why do you think it was so important to Jacob to be buried back in Canaan? Do you think Jacob was motivated by family tradition or the covenant of God to his grandfather Abraham? **2.** Why would the Egyptians give Jacob a

The Death of Jacob

29 Then he gave them these instructions: "I am about to be gathered
to my people. Bury me with my fathers in the cave in the field of
Ephron the Hittite, 30 the cave in the field of Machpelah, near Mamre
in Canaan, which Abraham bought as a burial place from Ephron the
Hittite, along with the field. 31 There Abraham and his wife Sarah were
buried, there Isaac and his wife Rebekah were buried, and there I
buried Leah. 32 The field and the cave in it were bought from the
Hittites.[f]"
33 When Jacob had finished giving instructions to his sons, he drew
his feet up into the bed, breathed his last and was gathered to his
people.

[a]22 *Or Joseph is a wild colt, / a wild colt near a spring, / a wild donkey on a terraced hill* [b]23,24 Or *archers will attack . . . will shoot . . . will remain . . . will stay* [c]25 Hebrew *Shaddai* [d]26 Or *of my progenitors, / as great as* [e]26 Or *the one separated from* [f]32 Or *the sons of Heth*

49:24 his bow remained steady. This blessing points to Ephraim's future victories in battle. It also seems an apt description of Joseph as he suffered from jealous brothers and then false accusations, yet stayed true to God's call and lived with integrity. He was steady as a bow and straight as an arrow.

49:25 blessings. This verse promises blessings to Joseph's sons. Joshua, Deborah and Samuel were from Ephraim. Gideon and Jephthah were from Manasseh. All were victorious for Israel.

49:26 prince among his brothers. This phrase echoes blessings past and future. Joseph dreamed of supremacy over his brothers. His son's tribe, Ephraim, would gain control over the northern tribes of Israel.

49:27 devours the prey. Benjamin's childhood is obscure, yet in this blessing we learn about Benjamin's character. This trait of savagery is borne out in Benjamin's tribe. Ehud, who murdered Eglon, was a Benjamite (Judg. 3:12–30). King Saul, a mighty warrior, was from Benjamin's tribe (1 Sam. 10). In fact, the other tribes together faced a standoff against the tribe of Benjamin because of their brutal actions (Judg. 20).

49:29 gathered to my people. This was Jacob's way of saying he was about to die. **Bury me with my fathers.** This is the modern equivalent of being carried home for burial. Even though Jacob had settled in Goshen, his heritage was based on the promise God made to Abraham about his homeland (47:30).

50 Joseph threw himself upon his father and wept over him and
kissed him. 2Then Joseph directed the physicians in his service to embalm his father Israel. So the physicians embalmed him,
3taking a full forty days, for that was the time required for embalming. And the Egyptians mourned for him seventy days.
4When the days of mourning had passed, Joseph said to Pharaoh's
court, "If I have found favor in your eyes, speak to Pharaoh for me.
Tell him, 5'My father made me swear an oath and said, "I am about to
die; bury me in the tomb I dug for myself in the land of Canaan." Now
let me go up and bury my father; then I will return.' "
6Pharaoh said, "Go up and bury your father, as he made you swear
to do."
7So Joseph went up to bury his father. All Pharaoh's officials accompanied him—the dignitaries of his court and all the dignitaries of
Egypt— 8besides all the members of Joseph's household and his
brothers and those belonging to his father's household. Only their
children and their flocks and herds were left in Goshen. 9Chariots
and horsemen[a] also went up with him. It was a very large company.
10When they reached the threshing floor of Atad, near the Jordan,
they lamented loudly and bitterly; and there Joseph observed a
seven-day period of mourning for his father. 11When the Canaanites
who lived there saw the mourning at the threshing floor of Atad, they
said, "The Egyptians are holding a solemn ceremony of mourning."
That is why that place near the Jordan is called Abel Mizraim.[b]
12So Jacob's sons did as he had commanded them: 13They carried
him to the land of Canaan and buried him in the cave in the field of
Machpelah, near Mamre, which Abraham had bought as a burial
place from Ephron the Hittite, along with the field. 14After burying his
father, Joseph returned to Egypt, together with his brothers and all
the others who had gone with him to bury his father.

Joseph Reassures His Brothers

15When Joseph's brothers saw that their father was dead, they said,
"What if Joseph holds a grudge against us and pays us back for all the
wrongs we did to him?" 16So they sent word to Joseph, saying, "Your
father left these instructions before he died: 17'This is what you are to
say to Joseph: I ask you to forgive your brothers the sins and the

[a]9 Or *charioteers* [b]11 *Abel Mizraim* means *mourning of the Egyptians.*

state funeral with 40 days for embalming and 70 days for mourning? **3.** Why do you think Joseph had to get permission from Pharaoh to go back to Canaan to bury his father? **4.** How do you think the brothers of Joseph felt in the funeral procession along with "Pharaoh's officials—the dignitaries of his court and all the dignitaries of Egypt" (v. 7)? How do you think the neighbors back in Canaan felt when they saw this procession coming? **5.** As you look back over Jacob's life, do you think God used this person because of his character or in spite of his character? **6.** What would be the adjective you would use to describe Jacob: Cunning? Complex? Checkered? Flawed? Colorful? Chameleon? Crazy? Other?

APPLY 1. As you bury your parents and grandparents one at a time, how does this effect your outlook on life? **2.** If you were to describe your life with God up to now with one or two adjectives, what would they be?

OPEN Which memory is harder for you to shake: Rejection or guilt?

STUDY Jacob is dead. Joseph and his brothers are back in Egypt after the funeral. **1.** Why would the brother's fear Joseph?

50:2 embalm. Joseph directed the Egyptian physicians to embalm Jacob. They removed the organs of the body and filled the body with salts and preservatives.

50:3 forty days ... seventy days. Forty days was the typical time span for an Egyptian embalming. In the meantime, Jacob's family and Joseph's nation were grieving for Jacob. Seventy days to mourn was just two days shy of the mourning period for an Egyptian Pharaoh, an indication of how much respect the Egyptians had for Joseph.

50:5 let me go. Joseph was not just asking for a mere day off to attend his father's funeral. Joseph faced the same journey his descendants would make 400 years later. When those descendants made that journey, they would carry Joseph's bones for burial (Ex. 13:19).

50:10 threshing floor. In an ancient community threshing floors (where grain was processed) were located at the edge of town. When the convoy arrived at the threshing floor, they were home. There they had to fully face the reality of burying their father.

50:15 pays us back. Thirty-nine years had passed since Joseph was sold into slavery. Now with their father gone, the brothers were afraid that Joseph would take his revenge. He was certainly in a position to do so. This echoes the vengefulness between Jacob and his twin, Esau. At one point Esau made plans to kill Jacob after his father's death (27:41).

50:17 Joseph wept. This is not the first time Genesis records Joseph's tears. He wept to see his brothers in Egypt (43:30), to see his father after so many years (46:29) and now at the realization that even after so many years, his brothers were still fearful of retribution.

2. What do the brothers do? 3. What does Joseph say to his brothers?

APPLY 1. As you look back over your life, what incident comes to mind where something bad happened to you that God turned into a blessing for you? 2. What is going on now where you cannot see something good coming from it yet?

OPEN Do you read the last chapter of a book first?

STUDY The Book of Genesis—the beginning of God's story—is finished. The special people of the covenant are in Egypt. 1. What does Joseph say to his brothers that sets the stage for the Book of Exodus? 2. How important is the Book of Genesis for your understanding of God's story?

APPLY How important to you are your own spiritual roots?

wrongs they committed in treating you so badly.' Now please forgive
the sins of the servants of the God of your father." When their message came to him, Joseph wept.
[18]His brothers then came and threw themselves down before him.
"We are your slaves," they said.
[19]But Joseph said to them, "Don't be afraid. Am I in the place of
God? [20]You intended to harm me, but God intended it for good to accomplish what is now being done, the saving of many lives. [21]So
then, don't be afraid. I will provide for you and your children." And he
reassured them and spoke kindly to them.

The Death of Joseph

[22]Joseph stayed in Egypt, along with all his father's family. He lived
a hundred and ten years [23]and saw the third generation of Ephraim's
children. Also the children of Makir son of Manasseh were placed at
birth on Joseph's knees.[a]
[24]Then Joseph said to his brothers, "I am about to die. But God will
surely come to your aid and take you up out of this land to the land he
promised on oath to Abraham, Isaac and Jacob." [25]And Joseph made
the sons of Israel swear an oath and said, "God will surely come to
your aid, and then you must carry my bones up from this place."
[26]So Joseph died at the age of a hundred and ten. And after they
embalmed him, he was placed in a coffin in Egypt.

[a]*23* That is, were counted as his

50:18 We are your slaves. The moment described here fulfills the dreams Joseph had as a young man for which his brothers had resented him. He had envisioned his family as both wheat and stars, that bowed down to him (37:7,9). As Joseph's brothers had declared themselves his slaves, when Joseph had accused them of stealing, they were trying to escape unpleasant consequences.

50:20 You intended to harm me. In Joseph's explanation of his ability to forgive, he clarified whose plan he followed. Joseph's ability to forgive was grounded in his belief that God was in charge all the time, no matter what the brothers had intended.

50:23 placed at birth on Joseph's knees. Joseph lived to see great-great-grandchildren. The custom of placing babies on his knees signified that they belonged to him.

50:24 promised on oath to Abraham, Isaac and Jacob. The legacy of God's promise to Abraham was so strong that even on Joseph's deathbed, after relocating his whole family to the farmlands of Goshen, he held on to the promise of another place. Hundreds of years later that legacy began to be fulfilled in the exodus of Israel from Egypt (Ex. 1:5–8).

50:25 carry my bones up. Joseph's desire was the same as his father's. He wanted to be buried in the home God had promised his family. His bones were eventually buried at Shechem (Ex. 13:19; Josh. 24:32).

Exodus

Author. Ancient Jews as well as the Christian church credit Moses with the authorship of Exodus.

Date. Exodus was probably written during the early part of the Hebrews' travels after they left Egypt, possibly around 1450 B.C. The events described in Exodus span about 145 years, from Joseph's death to the giving of the Ten Commandments and tabernacle plans at Mount Sinai.

Purpose. Exodus describes events for posterity. This book was Moses' record of God's rescue and preservation of the twelve tribes of Israel. It functions as a history of God's people as well as a record of God's faithfulness and guidance and ultimately his mercy.

Personal Reading	Group Study Topic and Reading	
1:1–2:25	Moses' Beginnings	1:22–2:25
3:1–4:31	God Calls Moses	3:1–22
5:1–6:27	God's Promise	5:22–6:12
6:28–10:29	Plagues Begin	6:28–7:24
11:1–13:16	The Passover	12:1–30
13:17–15:21	Crossing the Sea	14:5–31
15:22–16:36	Manna and Quail	16:1–36
17:1–18:27	Jethro Visits Moses	18:1–27
19:1–24:18	Ten Commandments	19:10–20:21
25:1–33:6	The Golden Calf	32:1–35
33:7–34:35	Moses Sees God	33:12–23
35:1–39:43	Tabernacle Inspected	39:32–43
40:1–38	Glory of the Lord	40:34–38

Historical Background. The Israelites originally came to Egypt because of a famine in their homeland. Jacob's son, Joseph had risen to power under Pharaoh, and Joseph brought the seventy members of Jacob's family to Egypt for food and safety. After Joseph's death, the family continued to grow into an entire culture of their own rather than just a family living in Egypt. Eventually, an unnamed pharaoh enslaved the Israelites. They became a nation of slaves within the nation of Egypt. God called Moses with the assistance of his brother Aaron to confront Pharaoh and demand his people's freedom, which began the long story of the Israelites' escape from Egypt and their journey home. Whereas they had entered Egypt as stragglers from a famine, they left as a clearly defined nation. Along the journey, they lived as nomads, with an unwieldy collection of families, belongings and livestock.

In the face of oppression and lordship the Hebrews began to pull together into a real community with common goals and squabbles, but they often rebelled against Moses and God. To handle the stress of a huge society living in close community they needed the stability and order provided by a legal system. God gave them the law for civil, governmental and religious order and made a covenant with the nation of Israel at Mount Sinai.

The Tabernacle. At the close of the book of Exodus, God's presence comes to inhabit the tabernacle. This was the spiritual destination of God's people, as the Promised Land was their physical destination. God's presence with them was their strength and salvation. The sacrifices offered at the tabernacle foreshadowed God's ultimate sacrifice for all time—the Messiah, Jesus. Building the tabernacle strengthened the faith of the Hebrews. They followed God's specific plans. They trusted their leader, Moses, to convey and execute those plans. The tabernacle represented the covenant between God and his people: He would lead and care for them, and they would worship and obey him.

OPEN 1. When did your ancestors move to this country? **2.** In your family tree, who had the biggest family? **3.** Do you know of a baby that was born at home, with a midwife delivering the baby?

STUDY The children of Israel are living in Egypt, the greatest power in the world. They were moved here by Joseph many years before during a famine. They were given land in a fertile valley to raise cattle and sheep. **1.** What would you do if you were Pharaoh (the king) and a group of aliens had multiplied from a few hundred to many thousand, had their own religion, language and culture and you were afraid they might side with an invading army? **2.** What do you remember about the twelve sons of Jacob and especially Joseph? How did Jacob and his family get down to Egypt? **3.** When Jacob's family arrived in Egypt, how were they treated? How are they treated now? **4.** How would you describe Pharaoh's plan to limit the Hebrew population growth? How did God frustrate this plan?

APPLY 1. As you look back over your life, what time comes to mind as a time when you felt like you were put down, discounted or mistreated? **2.** How did God work in these circumstances to prepare you for something to further his will for your life?

The Israelites Oppressed

1 These are the names of the sons of Israel who went to Egypt with
Jacob, each with his family: 2Reuben, Simeon, Levi and Judah;
3Issachar, Zebulun and Benjamin; 4Dan and Naphtali;Gad and Asher.
5The descendants of Jacob numbered seventy[a] in all; Joseph was
already in Egypt.
6Now Joseph and all his brothers and all that generation died, 7but
the Israelites were fruitful and multiplied greatly and became exceedingly numerous, so that the land was filled with them.
8Then a new king, who did not know about Joseph, came to power
in Egypt. 9"Look," he said to his people, "the Israelites have become
much too numerous for us. 10Come, we must deal shrewdly with
them or they will become even more numerous and, if war breaks
out, will join our enemies, fight against us and leave the country."
11So they put slave masters over them to oppress them with forced
labor, and they built Pithom and Rameses as store cities for Pharaoh.
12But the more they were oppressed, the more they multiplied and
spread; so the Egyptians came to dread the Israelites 13and worked
them ruthlessly. 14They made their lives bitter with hard labor in brick
and mortar and with all kinds of work in the fields; in all their hard
labor the Egyptians used them ruthlessly.
15The king of Egypt said to the Hebrew midwives, whose names
were Shiphrah and Puah, 16"When you help the Hebrew women in
childbirth and observe them on the delivery stool, if it is a boy, kill
him; but if it is a girl, let her live." 17The midwives, however, feared
God and did not do what the king of Egypt had told them to do; they
let the boys live. 18Then the king of Egypt summoned the midwives
and asked them, "Why have you done this? Why have you let the boys
live?"
19The midwives answered Pharaoh, "Hebrew women are not like
Egyptian women; they are vigorous and give birth before the midwives arrive."
20So God was kind to the midwives and the people increased and

[a]5 Masoretic Text (see also Gen. 46:27); Dead Sea Scrolls and Septuagint (see also Acts 7:14 and note at Gen. 46:27) *seventy-five*

1:1–5 sons of Israel who went to Egypt. Jacob (also called Israel, Gen. 32:28) and his sons had traveled to Egypt at the invitation of his son, Joseph, who had risen to prominence in Egypt (Gen. 46:1–7). The Israelites had settled in the land of Goshen, separate from the Egyptians (Gen. 46:31–34). Seventy of them had come and settled (Gen. 46:27). The book of Exodus picks up the story of Jacob's descendants a couple hundred years later. In all, the Israelites would be in Egypt for 430 years before returning to the Promised Land (Gen. 15:13).

1:7 exceedingly numerous. Only 70 people had arrived in Egypt (Gen. 46:27); when the Israelites left Egypt they numbered about 600,000 men plus women and children (12:37). **the land.** Refers to Goshen, a region in the eastern Nile delta area. It was very fertile, and a good location for these Israelite shepherds to have cared for their herds (Gen. 45:10,18).

1:11 slave masters. God had mercifully allowed the Israelites to live unhindered for most of the 400 years they were in Egypt. But they grew in number quickly in the last period, causing Pharaoh to put these "chiefs of slave gangs" over them. **Pharaoh.** An Egyptian word that means "great house." It's a title, like "king," rather than a person's name.

1:14 made their lives bitter. The Israelites had lived unhindered for many years, and had multiplied and flourished. The fear of Pharaoh was that the many men might rise up against Egypt, which caused him to force the people into slavery. **all kinds of work in the fields.** The Nile River made for fertile fields along the delta in Egypt. The Israelites were forced to go to work in these fields—this probably included harvesting, irrigating, planting, etc. In any case, it was difficult work that made their lives "bitter."

1:16 delivery stool. The place on which a woman would sit as she was giving birth. **boy, kill him.** Pharaoh ordered the male babies killed because he feared the increasing number of male Israelites as a potential military threat.

1:17 feared God. The Hebrew word refers to piety, obedience and true worship of God. The midwives deeply desired to please God even when their own lives were at stake. God honored their obedience (vv. 20–21).

became even more numerous. [21]And because the midwives feared God, he gave them families of their own.

[22]Then Pharaoh gave this order to all his people: "Every boy that is born[a] you must throw into the Nile, but let every girl live."

The Birth of Moses

2 Now a man of the house of Levi married a Levite woman, [2]and she became pregnant and gave birth to a son. When she saw that he was a fine child, she hid him for three months. [3]But when she could hide him no longer, she got a papyrus basket for him and coated it with tar and pitch. Then she placed the child in it and put it among the reeds along the bank of the Nile. [4]His sister stood at a distance to see what would happen to him.

[5]Then Pharaoh's daughter went down to the Nile to bathe, and her attendants were walking along the river bank. She saw the basket among the reeds and sent her slave girl to get it. [6]She opened it and saw the baby. He was crying, and she felt sorry for him. "This is one of the Hebrew babies," she said.

[7]Then his sister asked Pharaoh's daughter, "Shall I go and get one of the Hebrew women to nurse the baby for you?"

[8]"Yes, go," she answered. And the girl went and got the baby's mother. [9]Pharaoh's daughter said to her, "Take this baby and nurse him for me, and I will pay you." So the woman took the baby and nursed him. [10]When the child grew older, she took him to Pharaoh's daughter and he became her son. She named him Moses,[b] saying, "I drew him out of the water."

Moses Flees to Midian

[11]One day, after Moses had grown up, he went out to where his own people were and watched them at their hard labor. He saw an Egyptian beating a Hebrew, one of his own people. [12]Glancing this way and that and seeing no one, he killed the Egyptian and hid him in the sand. [13]The next day he went out and saw two Hebrews fighting.

[a]22 Masoretic Text; Samaritan Pentateuch, Septuagint and Targums *born to the Hebrews* [b]10 *Moses* sounds like the Hebrew for *draw out.*

OPEN **1.** How much do you know about your birth—time, place, weight? **2.** Do you know of anyone who was adopted or gave up a child for adoption?

STUDY Jacob (Israel) and his family moved to Egypt. After a time, the Egyptians became fearful of the rapidly growing Hebrew population. They enslaved them and drowned the newborn males. **1.** What impresses you most about Moses' birth mother? **2.** Do you think she deliberately placed the baby where the daughter of Pharaoh would be bathing? **3.** Do you think Pharaoh's daughter arriving at the Nile and finding this child was merely coincidental or all part of the plan and purpose of God?

APPLY As you look back at your own life, how important were your early formative years?

OPEN **1.** As a youth, what cause did you give your life to? **2.** Did you ever try to break up a fight between friends and got caught in the middle?

STUDY In the eyes of the Hebrew slaves, Moses was an Egyptian because he had been adopted by Pharaoh's daughter and

2:2 a fine child. Moses was an exceptional baby. Acts 7:20 and Hebrews 11:23 note that he was "no ordinary child." God led these parents to go to extraordinary measures to insure the safety of this child whom God had chosen to one day deliver his people. Moses had two older siblings–Miriam (v. 4) and Aaron (4:14; 7:7).

2:3 papyrus basket. The little basket was woven with papyrus reeds, and coated with "tar and pitch" to make it waterproof. The Hebrew word for "basket" is used only here and of Noah's ark, which was also coated with pitch (Gen. 6:14).

2:5 went down to the Nile to bathe. Though Egyptians customarily bathed frequently, bathing in the Nile was a special ritual because they considered the waters to be holy.

2:6–8 This is one of the Hebrew babies. When she unwrapped the baby, Pharaoh's daughter no doubt noticed he had been circumcised, since Israelites performed that rite on the eighth day after birth. Egyptians practiced circumcision but not on infants. She surely understood that some Hebrew mother was attempting to protect her child. This woman's heart went out to the child, and she took him home with her. Ironically, Moses' own mother was then hired to nurse the baby.

2:10 he became her son. Pharaoh had tried to destroy the Israelites, but God would not allow it. The text does not tell us how Pharaoh's daughter was allowed to take this child as her son, except that God, of course, was controlling these events. **Moses ... drew him out.** "Moses" sounds like the Hebrew "draw out."

2:11 Moses had grown up. At this point, Moses is forty years old (Acts 7:23). As the son of Pharaoh's daughter, he would have received the finest education the world offered at the time, with training in the Egyptian, Akkadian and Hebrew languages. At this point, he recognized the cruel treatment of his own people by those who had adopted him. While he had lived in the lap of luxury, his own people had been abused.

2:12 he killed the Egyptian. Moses' immediate solution was rash and violent. He murdered as a way to deal with injustice. Now his own injustice would carry a price.

raised in Pharaoh's house. But Moses never forgot his roots. **1.** Do you think Moses was wrong in taking the law into his own hands when he killed the Egyptian slave-driver? **2.** Why do abused people turn on the very person that is trying to help them? **3.** How do you think Moses felt when he had to flee for his life? How would you describe the change in his lifestyle from Egypt to Midian? **4.** How important do you think the 40 years in the desert were in God's plan for Moses?

APPLY 1. As you look back on your youth, what did you get involved in that God has used to prepare you for what you are doing today? **2.** Are you as passionate about making a difference with your life today as you were in your youth?

He asked the one in the wrong, "Why are you hitting your fellow
Hebrew?"
14 The man said, "Who made you ruler and judge over us? Are you
thinking of killing me as you killed the Egyptian?" Then Moses was
afraid and thought, "What I did must have become known."
15 When Pharaoh heard of this, he tried to kill Moses, but Moses
fled from Pharaoh and went to live in Midian, where he sat down by a
well. 16 Now a priest of Midian had seven daughters, and they came to
draw water and fill the troughs to water their father's flock. 17 Some
shepherds came along and drove them away, but Moses got up and
came to their rescue and watered their flock.
18 When the girls returned to Reuel their father, he asked them,
"Why have you returned so early today?"
19 They answered, "An Egyptian rescued us from the shepherds. He
even drew water for us and watered the flock."
20 "And where is he?" he asked his daughters. "Why did you leave
him? Invite him to have something to eat."
21 Moses agreed to stay with the man, who gave his daughter
Zipporah to Moses in marriage. 22 Zipporah gave birth to a son, and
Moses named him Gershom,[a] saying, "I have become an alien in a
foreign land."
23 During that long period, the king of Egypt died. The Israelites
groaned in their slavery and cried out, and their cry for help because
of their slavery went up to God. 24 God heard their groaning and he
remembered his covenant with Abraham, with Isaac and with Jacob.
25 So God looked on the Israelites and was concerned about them.

OPEN 1. After a hard day, what does it take to get you up in the morning? **2.** What is the place you consider "holy ground"?

STUDY Though a Hebrew by birth, Moses was adopted

Moses and the Burning Bush

3 Now Moses was tending the flock of Jethro his father-in-law, the
priest of Midian, and he led the flock to the far side of the desert
and came to Horeb, the mountain of God. 2 There the angel of the

[a] *22 Gershom* sounds like the Hebrew for *an alien there.*

2:14 Who made you ruler and judge over us? At this point, no one knew that Moses would indeed become their ruler, judge, and deliverer. It would be another forty years, however, before Moses would be ready to do God's will and bring the Israelites out of Egypt (7:7).

2:15 Pharaoh. Here it probably refers to Thutmose III. **Midian.** A dry wilderness that was quite different than Moses' sumptuous home in Egypt. He would remain here for forty years (Acts 7:29–30).

2:16 priest of Midian. His name was Reuel (v. 18), which means "friend of God." He was also called Jethro (3:1). *Like Melchizedek, Reuel* seems to have been a foreigner who had come to worship the one true God and to lead others in worship, as a priest would.

2:17 Moses ... came to their rescue. Again Moses' instinct for justice brings him to the aid of the oppressed—in this case, the daughters of the priest who were drawing water.

2:20 Invite him to have something to eat. By doing so, Reuel was attempting to recruit Moses as a husband for one of his seven daughters.

2:22 Gershom. This name means "a stranger there." Not only were Moses' people aliens in Egypt, but he himself was removed from them—a double estrangement.

2:23–25 groaned ... cried out ... cry ... groaning. Four different Hebrew words are used to describe *Israel's* actions. These feelings went deep. **heard ... remembered ... looked on ... was concerned.** God's gracious response is captured in four more Hebrew words.

2:24 remembered his covenant. God had promised Abraham, Isaac and Jacob, that he would give the Promised Land to their descendants (Gen.15:18–21; 26:2–6; 28:13–15). Abraham had also been told, however, that his descendants would "be strangers in a country not their own, and they will be enslaved and mistreated four hundred years" (Gen. 15:13).

3:1 tending the flock. The call of God came to Moses to lead Israel. Like David he went from the role of shepherd to leader of God's flock (2 Sam. 7:8). **Jethro.** Another name for Reuel (2:18). **Horeb, the mountain of God.** Some suggest that this is another name for Mount Sinai, to which the Israelites would return after being freed (v. 12; 19:1–2).

3:2 angel of the LORD. Here the angel of the Lord appeared, later it is the Lord (v. 4) and finally God (v. 4). It seems that each is describing God himself.

LORD appeared to him in flames of fire from within a bush. Moses saw
that though the bush was on fire it did not burn up. 3So Moses
thought, "I will go over and see this strange sight—why the bush
does not burn up."
4When the LORD saw that he had gone over to look, God called to
him from within the bush, "Moses! Moses!"
And Moses said, "Here I am."
5"Do not come any closer," God said. "Take off your sandals, for the
place where you are standing is holy ground." 6Then he said, "I am
the God of your father, the God of Abraham, the God of Isaac and the
God of Jacob." At this, Moses hid his face, because he was afraid to
look at God.
7The LORD said, "I have indeed seen the misery of my people in
Egypt. I have heard them crying out because of their slave drivers,
and I am concerned about their suffering. 8So I have come down to
rescue them from the hand of the Egyptians and to bring them up out
of that land into a good and spacious land, a land flowing with milk
and honey—the home of the Canaanites, Hittites, Amorites, Perizzites, Hivites and Jebusites. 9And now the cry of the Israelites has
reached me, and I have seen the way the Egyptians are oppressing
them. 10So now, go. I am sending you to Pharaoh to bring my people
the Israelites out of Egypt."
11But Moses said to God, "Who am I, that I should go to Pharaoh
and bring the Israelites out of Egypt?"
12And God said, "I will be with you. And this will be the sign to you
that it is I who have sent you: When you have brought the people out
of Egypt, you[a] will worship God on this mountain."
13Moses said to God, "Suppose I go to the Israelites and say to
them, 'The God of your fathers has sent me to you,' and they ask me,
'What is his name?' Then what shall I tell them?"
14God said to Moses, "I AM WHO I AM.[b] This is what you are to say to
the Israelites: 'I AM has sent me to you.'"
15God also said to Moses, "Say to the Israelites, 'The LORD,[c] the

[a]*12* The Hebrew is plural. [b]*14* Or *I WILL BE WHAT I WILL BE* [c]*15* The Hebrew for *LORD* sounds like and may be derived from the Hebrew for *I AM* in verse 14.

by Pharaoh's daughter. After killing an Egyptian slave-driver who was mistreating a Hebrew slave, Moses fled to the desert where he married and became a shepherd. According to Acts 7:23–30, Moses was 40 years old when he fled from Egypt and 80 years old when this story occurred. **1.** Why do you think God waited 40 years to call Moses to lead the Israelites? **2.** How would you describe the way God got Moses' attention? How does God identify himself? How does Moses react? How would you have reacted? **3.** In the job interview with Moses, what is the position God offers to Moses? What reassurance does God give to Moses? If God asked you to do something like he asked Moses to do, what would be your response? **4.** What did 400 years of servitude do to the self-esteem of the Israelite people? What is God saying about himself when he refers to himself as "I AM THAT I AM"? **5.** What does God ask Moses to start doing? If you were to ask the elders of your church to do this, how far would you get? **6.** Forty years before, Moses wanted to liberate the Hebrew people. In fact he killed an Egyptian who was mistreating a Hebrew slave. What has caused him to be so timid and reserved now?

APPLY 1. As you look back over your life, what has God used to get your attention? **2.** How would you describe the communication between you and God right now: A little static on the line? The line is tied up? The line is wide open? **3.** How can this group help you in prayer this week?

3:5 holy ground. The earth itself wasn't holy; God made it holy by being there.

3:6 afraid to look at God. To see God's face, Israelites believed, was to die (Gen. 16:13; 32:30). In 19:3, Moses would meet with God again on this very mountain. Moses discovered a relationship with God that made him unafraid (33:11), and at that point, Moses would even call on God to "show me your glory" (33:18).

3:8 I have come down to rescue. Picture God coming down out of heaven to work on behalf of his people. This "rescue" had been the source of the nation's prayers for many years (2:23). **land flowing with milk and honey.** This was a common way of describing the beautiful landscape of Canaan.

3:11 Who am I. Moses several times expressed a desire *not* to be the one chosen to speak to Pharaoh (4:1,10,13). He may have wondered why God would send him back to the land where he had so many memories—including having committed murder, and where he had been a wanted man (2:15).

3:12 I will be with you. Moses may have wondered "who" he was to be the deliverer (v. 11), but God's answer had nothing to do with Moses. Instead, God simply promised his presence with his servant. With God, Moses could accomplish anything God desired. **this will be the sign.** God offers proof that he would certainly accomplish his word. When the people came out of Egypt, they did indeed "worship God on this mountain" (v.1; 19:1–2; Sinai is another name for Horeb).

3:13 What is his name? Moses surely had learned about the Hebrew God, but he had been raised in Egypt—a land with many gods all with different names. Moses asked God for his name.

3:14 I AM WHO I AM. This is the astonishing name God used for himself, the name Israel would call him. It's a name that expresses God's character as eternal, dependable and faithful. **I AM.** In John 8:53–58, Jesus used this phrase to describe himself, in effect identifying himself as God. In John 18:6, the power behind the words "I am he," caused his captors to fall to the ground.

3:15 The LORD. In Hebrew this is "Yahweh," which means "He is" or "He will be."

God of your fathers—the God of Abraham, the God of Isaac and the
God of Jacob—has sent me to you.' This is my name forever, the
name by which I am to be remembered from generation to generation.
16"Go, assemble the elders of Israel and say to them, 'The LORD, the
God of your fathers—the God of Abraham, Isaac and Jacob—
appeared to me and said: I have watched over you and have seen
what has been done to you in Egypt. 17And I have promised to bring
you up out of your misery in Egypt into the land of the Canaanites,
Hittites, Amorites, Perizzites, Hivites and Jebusites—a land flowing
with milk and honey.'
18"The elders of Israel will listen to you. Then you and the elders are
to go to the king of Egypt and say to him, 'The LORD, the God of the
Hebrews, has met with us. Let us take a three-day journey into the
desert to offer sacrifices to the LORD our God.' 19But I know that
the king of Egypt will not let you go unless a mighty hand compels
him. 20So I will stretch out my hand and strike the Egyptians with all
the wonders that I will perform among them. After that, he will let
you go.
21"And I will make the Egyptians favorably disposed toward this people, so that when you leave you will not go empty-handed. 22Every
woman is to ask her neighbor and any woman living in her house for
articles of silver and gold and for clothing, which you will put on your
sons and daughters. And so you will plunder the Egyptians."

Signs for Moses

4 Moses answered, "What if they do not believe me or listen to me
and say, 'The LORD did not appear to you'?"
2Then the LORD said to him, "What is that in your hand?"
"A staff," he replied.
3The LORD said, "Throw it on the ground."
Moses threw it on the ground and it became a snake, and he ran
from it. 4Then the LORD said to him, "Reach out your hand and take it
by the tail." So Moses reached out and took hold of the snake and
it turned back into a staff in his hand. 5"This," said the LORD, "is so
that they may believe that the LORD, the God of their fathers—the God
of Abraham, the God of Isaac and the God of Jacob—has appeared
to you."

OPEN **1.** As a kid, what excuse did you use for not doing your chores or homework? **2.** What is your best excuse now for not getting the house chores done?

STUDY Many years before, Moses fled in fear for his life from Egypt to the desert. God has just revealed himself to Moses at the burning bush on Mt. Horeb—asking him to return to Egypt and lead the Hebrews out of their bondage. **1.** What do Moses' objections sound like to you? What would you have said if you were in Moses' shoes? **2.** How would

3:16 elders. These were older men with life experience, wisdom and influence in society—traits necessary for an elder to function properly. These "elders" would have been the esteemed older men of the various families and tribes whom Moses was to meet with upon his arrival in Egypt (4:29–31).

3:18 three-day journey ... sacrifices. Moses' first request of Pharaoh would be that he allow the people to make a short journey into the desert to offer sacrifices. However, God knew Pharaoh's responses ahead of time. In the end, the request for a short respite would become total deliverance.

3:20 all the wonders. This looks forward prophetically to the ten plagues God would send against Egypt to persuade Pharaoh to grant the Israelites their freedom. Each plague would indeed be a wonder, for each plague would reveal the powerlessness of the many gods of Egypt.

3:21 favorably disposed. In Genesis 15:14 God had promised Abraham that Israel would return from Egypt "with great possessions." Indeed, when the Israelites left, the Egyptians gladly gave them whatever they asked for (12:35–36). Later they would give these same treasures to God for use in the tabernacle (ch. 35).

4:1 What if they do not believe me ...? What a comfort to realize that a man as great as Moses began his journey with God lacking self-esteem. Moses had not yet experienced the power of God, so God gave him miraculous signs to help him here. In Egypt, Moses would see miracles beyond his wildest imagination.

4:3 snake. All of the miracles God performed in Egypt were designed to show the powerlessness of Egypt's many gods. Even this miracle of making a staff turn into a snake showed the powerlessness of the Pharaoh, who used a cobra to symbolize his power and authority.

[6]Then the LORD said, "Put your hand inside your cloak." So Moses
put his hand into his cloak, and when he took it out, it was leprous,[a]
like snow.
[7]"Now put it back into your cloak," he said. So Moses put his hand
back into his cloak, and when he took it out, it was restored, like the
rest of his flesh.
[8]Then the LORD said, "If they do not believe you or pay attention to
the first miraculous sign, they may believe the second. [9]But if they do
not believe these two signs or listen to you, take some water from the
Nile and pour it on the dry ground. The water you take from the river
will become blood on the ground."
[10]Moses said to the LORD, "O Lord, I have never been eloquent, neither in the past nor since you have spoken to your servant. I am slow
of speech and tongue."
[11]The LORD said to him, "Who gave man his mouth? Who makes
him deaf or mute? Who gives him sight or makes him blind? Is it not
I, the LORD? [12]Now go; I will help you speak and will teach you what
to say."
[13]But Moses said, "O Lord, please send someone else to do it."
[14]Then the LORD's anger burned against Moses and he said, "What
about your brother, Aaron the Levite? I know he can speak well. He is
already on his way to meet you, and his heart will be glad when he
sees you. [15]You shall speak to him and put words in his mouth; I will
help both of you speak and will teach you what to do. [16]He will speak
to the people for you, and it will be as if he were your mouth and as if
you were God to him. [17]But take this staff in your hand so you can
perform miraculous signs with it."

Moses Returns to Egypt

[18]Then Moses went back to Jethro his father-in-law and said to
him, "Let me go back to my own people in Egypt to see if any of them
are still alive."
Jethro said, "Go, and I wish you well."
[19]Now the LORD had said to Moses in Midian, "Go back to Egypt, for

[a]6 The Hebrew word was used for various diseases affecting the skin—not necessarily leprosy.

you characterize God's response to Moses? **3.** What is the purpose of the miraculous signs? Would these signs have given you the confidence to face Pharaoh if you had been in Moses' shoes? Have you ever felt like God was telling you something? **4.** Can you understand the reservation Moses had about speaking because of his fear of standing before Pharaoh? How is this problem overcome (vv. 14–17)? **5.** At the close of this encounter with God, do you think Moses was convinced that he could carry out this mission? Do you think he realized what he was getting into for the next 40 years of his life?

APPLY 1. When is the last time you took a day off to go into the desert to seriously consider the next few years in your life? **2.** What is the scary mission that God is laying on your heart right now? **3.** How can this group help you this week in prayer to get going?

OPEN 1. Do you have a longing to go back to the town where you grew up to see the people you grew up with? **2.** Who or what would you like to visit?

STUDY After 40 years in the desert, Moses is called by God to return to Egypt and lead the

---

4:6 leprous, like snow. This further demonstration of God's power involved a fearsome disease on Moses' hand. Several skin diseases were called leprosy in the Bible. Severe forms of leprosy killed the nerve endings and caused a person's limbs to turn white like snow (Num. 12:10).

4:8 first miraculous sign. The clear purpose of such a supernatural occurrence was to show that Moses came with the authority of the one true God, who was prepared to do even mightier signs than these to prove his power.

4:10 slow of speech and tongue. Moses probably was not referring to a speech impediment for Stephen described Moses as "powerful in speech" (Acts 7:22). Instead he was expressing his fear that he wasn't articulate enough or able to think quickly enough when he spoke to the Pharaoh.

4:11–12 Who gave man his mouth? God reminded Moses that he has the power to help Moses get the message out properly. As we will see, God enlisted Aaron to help.

4:13 Again, Moses revealed his reluctance to take on this mission (3:11,13; 4:1,10). His behavior may feel painfully familiar to some of us!

4:14 the LORD's anger burned. God had answered each of Moses' concerns—promising to be with him (3:12), telling his name (3:14), giving him miracles to perform (vv. 3–9), and promising him the right words (v. 12). Even after all of these assurances, Moses still pled not to have to serve God. No wonder God was angry. Yet once again, God provided an assurance for Moses. **Levite.** Aaron was from the tribe of Levi, meaning so were Moses and Miriam (6:16–20). Through Aaron would come the priesthood, with the Levites always serving as priests in God's tabernacle and temple (Num. 1:50–51). Somehow Aaron escaped from Egypt and had come looking for his brother.

4:15–17 I will help both of you speak. The prophet is God's mouthpiece. God would allow Moses to transmit God's message through Aaron to the Pharaoh. Moses, however, would still be the one in charge, for he would carry his staff and perform miraculous signs with it.

Hebrew people out of slavery to the Promised Land. **1.** Why do you think Moses kept from his father-in-law his real purpose in going back to Egypt? **2.** What had Moses neglected to do for his son when he was born? Why would this be important before he could accomplish his mission? **3.** How important would it be to you to have a brother along in accomplishing a dangerous mission? **4.** How did the elders respond when they were first presented with the plan of God to liberate his people?

APPLY **1.** Who is the "brother/sister" in your life who came alongside of you when you needed it most? What did (or do) you accomplish together that you could not have done by yourself? **2.** How close are you to your real brother/sister?

all the men who wanted to kill you are dead." 20So Moses took his
wife and sons, put them on a donkey and started back to Egypt. And
he took the staff of God in his hand.
21The LORD said to Moses, "When you return to Egypt, see that you
perform before Pharaoh all the wonders I have given you the power
to do. But I will harden his heart so that he will not let the people go.
22Then say to Pharaoh, 'This is what the LORD says: Israel is my firstborn son, 23and I told you, "Let my son go, so he may worship me."
But you refused to let him go; so I will kill your firstborn son.' "
24At a lodging place on the way, the LORD met ⌞Moses⌟[a] and was
about to kill him. 25But Zipporah took a flint knife, cut off her son's
foreskin and touched ⌞Moses'⌟ feet with it.[b] "Surely you are a bridegroom of blood to me," she said. 26So the LORD let him alone. (At that
time she said "bridegroom of blood," referring to circumcision.)
27The LORD said to Aaron, "Go into the desert to meet Moses." So
he met Moses at the mountain of God and kissed him. 28Then Moses
told Aaron everything the LORD had sent him to say, and also about all
the miraculous signs he had commanded him to perform.
29Moses and Aaron brought together all the elders of the Israelites,
30and Aaron told them everything the LORD had said to Moses. He
also performed the signs before the people, 31and they believed. And
when they heard that the LORD was concerned about them and had
seen their misery, they bowed down and worshiped.

OPEN **1.** Who has been the meanest boss you have ever had? **2.** What is the hardest thing about your work now?

STUDY God has called Moses, with the help of his brother Aaron, to lead the Israelites out of slavery to the Promised Land. Now, Moses and Aaron approach Pharaoh for the first time. They request permission to go into the desert to make sacrifices to their God. **1.** If you were

Bricks Without Straw

5 Afterward Moses and Aaron went to Pharaoh and said, "This is
what the LORD, the God of Israel, says: 'Let my people go, so that
they may hold a festival to me in the desert.' "
2Pharaoh said, "Who is the LORD, that I should obey him and let
Israel go? I do not know the LORD and I will not let Israel go."
3Then they said, "The God of the Hebrews has met with us. Now let
us take a three-day journey into the desert to offer sacrifices to the
LORD our God, or he may strike us with plagues or with the sword."

[a]24 Or ⌞*Moses' son*⌟; Hebrew *him* [b]25 Or *and drew near* ⌞*Moses'*⌟ *feet*

4:21 I will harden his heart so that he will not let the people go. Pharaoh was the cause of the hardening of his heart in each of the first five plagues. Not until the sixth plague did God confirm Pharaoh's act of will and "harden his heart," as he told Moses here.

4:22–23 Israel is my firstborn son. Israel had a special relationship with God, but the pharaohs had treated the people horribly–killing the baby boys, and finally enslaving the people in "cruel bondage" (6:9). Punishment for that would be severe. **I will kill your firstborn son.** This looks forward to the tenth plague, the death of Egypt's first-*born* (11:5; 12:12).

4:24 The LORD ... was about to kill him. Apparently God was angry because Moses had not obeyed him by circumcising his son (Gen. 17:9–14). This shows how serious God is about obedience. Moses may not have circumcised his son in order to please his Midianite family. Even so, Moses' disobedience was a serious offense against God. Moses would need to be in a state of complete obedience to God and his covenant if he was to be able to accomplish the task ahead.

4:25–26 Zipporah ... cut off her son's foreskin. Moses' wife realized that God was displeased with her husband. So she quickly performed the circumcision on their young son. She obviously was not happy about it. **bridegroom of blood.** Zipporah was shocked and angry that God would require circumcision of her son.

4:27 So he met Moses. The reunion of brothers was deeply emotional after forty years of separation. In fact the Hebrew word for "met" indicates greeting with a strong bear hug. **at the mountain of God.** It's fitting they met here, where they would minister together later (19:1–25).

4:29–31 The Israelites welcomed Moses and Aaron and responded worshipfully to God—a stark contrast to much of their behavior after leaving Egypt.

5:1 Let my people go. Moses and Aaron approached Pharaoh boldly, but it was in God's plan that Pharaoh not agree to their initial demands.

5:2 Who is the Lord, that I should obey him ...? Pharaoh, surrounded by opulence, splendor, and wealth, could see no reason to listen to the god of a group of slaves. Obviously, such a god could not be very powerful.

4But the king of Egypt said, "Moses and Aaron, why are you taking
the people away from their labor? Get back to your work!" 5Then
Pharaoh said, "Look, the people of the land are now numerous, and
you are stopping them from working."
6That same day Pharaoh gave this order to the slave drivers and
foremen in charge of the people: 7"You are no longer to supply the
people with straw for making bricks; let them go and gather their
own straw. 8But require them to make the same number of bricks as
before; don't reduce the quota. They are lazy; that is why they are crying out, 'Let us go and sacrifice to our God.' 9Make the work harder
for the men so that they keep working and pay no attention to lies."
10Then the slave drivers and the foremen went out and said to the
people, "This is what Pharaoh says: 'I will not give you any more
straw. 11Go and get your own straw wherever you can find it, but your
work will not be reduced at all.' " 12So the people scattered all over
Egypt to gather stubble to use for straw. 13The slave drivers kept
pressing them, saying, "Complete the work required of you for each
day, just as when you had straw." 14The Israelite foremen appointed
by Pharaoh's slave drivers were beaten and were asked, "Why didn't
you meet your quota of bricks yesterday or today, as before?"
15Then the Israelite foremen went and appealed to Pharaoh: "Why
have you treated your servants this way? 16Your servants are given no
straw, yet we are told, 'Make bricks!' Your servants are being beaten,
but the fault is with your own people."
17Pharaoh said, "Lazy, that's what you are—lazy! That is why you
keep saying, 'Let us go and sacrifice to the LORD.' 18Now get to work.
You will not be given any straw, yet you must produce your full quota
of bricks."
19The Israelite foremen realized they were in trouble when they
were told, "You are not to reduce the number of bricks required of
you for each day." 20When they left Pharaoh, they found Moses and
Aaron waiting to meet them, 21and they said, "May the LORD look
upon you and judge you! You have made us a stench to Pharaoh and
his officials and have put a sword in their hand to kill us."

God Promises Deliverance

22Moses returned to the LORD and said, "O Lord, why have you
brought trouble upon this people? Is this why you sent me? 23Ever
since I went to Pharaoh to speak in your name, he has brought trouble upon this people, and you have not rescued your people at all."
6 Then the LORD said to Moses, "Now you will see what I will do to
Pharaoh: Because of my mighty hand he will let them go; because of my mighty hand he will drive them out of his country."
2God also said to Moses, "I am the LORD. 3I appeared to Abraham,

considered to be a god, as Pharaoh was, how would you react to a religious group that came to you and said their god wanted them to go on a three-day holiday to offer sacrifices to their god? **2.** How do you think Moses felt when he was ushered into the presence of Pharaoh? Do you think Pharaoh remembered him from 40 years before? **3.** How did Pharaoh respond to Moses' request? What would you have done if you had been Pharaoh? **4.** How would you describe the morale in the Israelite camp when they were pressed to find straw to make bricks and their foremen were beaten if they did not produce as many bricks as before? **5.** Who got the blame for getting the Israelites in trouble? **6.** If you had been Moses, how would you have felt when it appeared you were failing? **7.** What do you think Moses' wife and children were saying?

APPLY 1. What is the closest you have come to suffering a temporary setback when you tried to do what you thought God wanted you to do? **2.** How did your family handle the situation? **3.** What did you learn from this experience that has proved valuable?

OPEN 1. As a kid, when you needed to get permission, who did you usually go to—your mom or your dad? **2.** Who is a national spokesperson that you admire today?

STUDY Pharaoh's response to Moses' request to let the Israelites worship their God in the desert is to increase the work load on the Israelites. The Israelite foremen

5:6 Pharaoh instigates harsh measures on the Israelite workers to punish Moses and Aaron for their audacity. **slave drivers.** Those who oversaw the slaves (1:11). **foremen.** Israelite supervisors. Their function is seen in verses 14–19.

5:7–8 gather their own straw. The straw served as an aggregate and binding agent to make the bricks stronger. By no longer supplying the straw, the Egyptians forced the Israelites to gather their own straw—more work and less time off, yet with the same quota.

5:20–21 May the LORD ... judge you! The Hebrew foremen turned their anger against Moses and Aaron with a harsh curse.

5:23 you have not rescued your people. It seems Moses had expected Pharaoh to give up immediately and let the Israelites go, even though God had warned Moses otherwise (3:19; 4:21).

6:1 Now. God is ready—a word of encouragement for Moses that things were going to change.

who are beaten for not meeting their quota of bricks, take out their frustrations on Moses and Aaron, his brother. **1.** How would you describe Moses as he approaches God at the beginning of this story? What would you have said to God if you were in his situation? **2.** How does God respond to Moses? **3.** If you were Moses, how would it feel if God told you to go over the head of the elders and foremen and appeal directly to the people? **4.** Do you feel a little sorry for Moses? Do you think God expected more out of Moses than he could handle?

APPLY 1. What are you facing right now that is almost more than you can handle? **2.** What is the handicap (like Moses' speech impediment) that you use as an excuse for not doing something? **3.** How can this group keep you this week in prayer?

OPEN 1. Who was the ringleader in your high school class? **2.** How far back can you trace your roots?

STUDY The story of Exodus is interrupted for a commercial break to give you the family genealogy of Moses. Some scholars feel that Moses compiled the first five books of the Bible. This may explain why the tribe of Levi is detailed here. **1.** If you were writing the history of the Israelites, how important would it be to list the genealogy of Moses and Aaron? **2.** Do you think Moses was planning ahead when he made his own tribe the priests and worship leaders (Korah) for this nation? What would this mean in the days ahead? **3.** How important is

to Isaac and to Jacob as God Almighty,[a] but by my name the LORD[b] I
did not make myself known to them.[c] 4I also established my covenant
with them to give them the land of Canaan, where they lived as
aliens. 5Moreover, I have heard the groaning of the Israelites, whom
the Egyptians are enslaving, and I have remembered my covenant.
6"Therefore, say to the Israelites: 'I am the LORD, and I will bring
you out from under the yoke of the Egyptians. I will free you from
being slaves to them, and I will redeem you with an outstretched arm
and with mighty acts of judgment. 7I will take you as my own people,
and I will be your God. Then you will know that I am the LORD your
God, who brought you out from under the yoke of the Egyptians. 8And
I will bring you to the land I swore with uplifted hand to give to Abraham, to Isaac and to Jacob. I will give it to you as a possession. I am
the LORD.' "
9Moses reported this to the Israelites, but they did not listen to him
because of their discouragement and cruel bondage.
10Then the LORD said to Moses, 11"Go, tell Pharaoh king of Egypt to
let the Israelites go out of his country."
12But Moses said to the LORD, "If the Israelites will not listen to me,
why would Pharaoh listen to me, since I speak with faltering lips[d]?"

Family Record of Moses and Aaron

13Now the LORD spoke to Moses and Aaron about the Israelites and
Pharaoh king of Egypt, and he commanded them to bring the Israelites out of Egypt.
14These were the heads of their families[e]:

The sons of Reuben the firstborn son of Israel were Hanoch
and Pallu, Hezron and Carmi. These were the clans of Reuben.
15The sons of Simeon were Jemuel, Jamin, Ohad, Jakin, Zohar
and Shaul the son of a Canaanite woman. These were the clans
of Simeon.
16These were the names of the sons of Levi according to their
records: Gershon, Kohath and Merari. Levi lived 137 years.

[a]3 Hebrew *El-Shaddai* [b]3 See note at Exodus 3:15. [c]3 Or *Almighty, and by my name the LORD did I not let myself be known to them?* [d]12 Hebrew *I am uncircumcised of lips*; also in verse 30 [e]14 The Hebrew for *families* here and in verse 25 refers to units larger than clans.

6:4–5 established my covenant ... remembered my covenant. This refers to God's covenant with Abraham, Isaac, and Jacob to one day give the land of Canaan to their descendants (Gen. 15:18–21; 26:2–6; 28:13–15). Because of his promises to them, he would act now on behalf of those descendants.

6:6 I will redeem you. God would redeem his people from the yoke of the Egyptians. He would one day redeem all *people from the burden of sin* (Gal. 3:13).

6:7 my own people ... your God. These words fulfilled the covenant to Abraham, that God would choose his descendants to be a nation special to him (Gen. 17:7).

6:9 discouragement. Moses reported God's word to the Israelites, but they didn't believe him. Their pain and discouragement kept them stuck—until they experience the reality of the living God themselves.

6:12 will not listen to me. Moses was facing exactly what he had feared—he had spoken and no one had listened (4:1). In fact, as far as he could tell, he had made matters worse. In addition, he had not been quick enough with Pharaoh, proving his other previous argument that he could not speak well (4:11). In essence, he was telling God, "I told you I couldn't do this ..." This is repeated in verses 29–30, with God's answer in 7:1–5.

6:13 Moses and Aaron. While this seems like an interruption in the narrative, the family background of Moses and Aaron was included in order to prove their credentials and authority. At this point in the story, the Israelites were doubting that authority (5:21), but this genealogy shows it in no uncertain terms. Only a partial genealogy is given to establish that Moses and Aaron both came from the tribe of Levi (4:14).

[17]The sons of Gershon, by clans, were Libni and Shimei.
[18]The sons of Kohath were Amram, Izhar, Hebron and Uzziel.
Kohath lived 133 years.
[19]The sons of Merari were Mahli and Mushi.
These were the clans of Levi according to their records.
[20]Amram married his father's sister Jochebed, who bore him
Aaron and Moses. Amram lived 137 years.
[21]The sons of Izhar were Korah, Nepheg and Zicri.
[22]The sons of Uzziel were Mishael, Elzaphan and Sithri.
[23]Aaron married Elisheba, daughter of Amminadab and sister
of Nahshon, and she bore him Nadab and Abihu, Eleazar and
Ithamar.
[24]The sons of Korah were Assir, Elkanah and Abiasaph. These
were the Korahite clans.
[25]Eleazar son of Aaron married one of the daughters of Putiel,
and she bore him Phinehas.

These were the heads of the Levite families, clan by clan.

[26]It was this same Aaron and Moses to whom the LORD said, "Bring
the Israelites out of Egypt by their divisions." [27]They were the ones
who spoke to Pharaoh king of Egypt about bringing the Israelites out
of Egypt. It was the same Moses and Aaron.

Aaron to Speak for Moses

[28]Now when the LORD spoke to Moses in Egypt, [29]he said to him, "I
am the LORD. Tell Pharaoh king of Egypt everything I tell you."
[30]But Moses said to the LORD, "Since I speak with faltering lips,
why would Pharaoh listen to me?"
7 Then the LORD said to Moses, "See, I have made you like God to
Pharaoh, and your brother Aaron will be your prophet. [2]You are
to say everything I command you, and your brother Aaron is to tell
Pharaoh to let the Israelites go out of his country. [3]But I will harden
Pharaoh's heart, and though I multiply my miraculous signs and
wonders in Egypt, [4]he will not listen to you. Then I will lay my hand
on Egypt and with mighty acts of judgment I will bring out my divisions, my people the Israelites. [5]And the Egyptians will know that I
am the LORD when I stretch out my hand against Egypt and bring the
Israelites out of it."
[6]Moses and Aaron did just as the LORD commanded them. [7]Moses
was eighty years old and Aaron eighty-three when they spoke to
Pharaoh.

it to you to know about your family's history?

APPLY 1. Who was the spiritual patriarch in your family? **2.** How often does your family pause to remember their spiritual heritage?

OPEN 1. What did you do the last time you saw a snake? **2.** What magic tricks can you do?

STUDY Pharaoh was not at all receptive to Moses' first visit. He not only refused to let the Israelites go to worship their Lord, but he increased their suffering. God is asking Moses to return to Pharaoh again. **1.** Have you ever felt like God wanted you to do something and you were afraid to do it? How do you think Moses felt when God had to take him aside (v. 28)? How did Moses answer God? **2.** What did God mean by saying to Moses, "See, I have made you like God to Pharaoh ..." (v. 1)? **3.** How would you feel making this request of Pharaoh, if his answer was going to be no? Why did God do this? **4.** How would you describe the first test of

6:20 Amram ... Aaron and Moses. *Most likely Amram and Jochebed were not Aaron and Moses' immediate parents but their ancestors.* Since Aaron was the firstborn (7:7), he's listed first in the official genealogy. Daughters were generally not listed in genealogies unless there were special circumstances or they bore special sons, so their sister Miriam's name is absent (2:4).

7:1–2 Aaron will be your prophet. Aaron had been chosen to speak for Moses because of Moses' complaint about his own inability to speak (4:10–16). God would speak to Moses, but Aaron would act as the prophet who would transmit God's message to Pharaoh.

7:3–4 I will harden ... he will not listen. As in 4:21, Pharaoh's heart is hardened by God only after Pharaoh hardened his own heart. Pharaoh's stubbornness was part of God's plan to demonstrate all the more clearly his power to deliver his people. Pharaoh's hardness of heart would give God the opportunity to unleash miraculous signs and wonders upon the land.

7:5 the Egyptians will know that I am the LORD. With the first nine plagues, God used supernatural forces of nature to bring judgment, but in the tenth God would personally bring judgment upon Egypt.

strength between Moses and the Pharaoh's magicians?

APPLY **1.** How do you handle it when you get the door slammed in your face? **2.** What have you found helpful in getting back on your feet?

OPEN **1.** What do you do at the sight of blood? **2.** Where is the place in your town where the big wheels like to go to be seen?

STUDY Moses has tried and failed to convince Pharaoh to let the Israelites go into the desert to offer sacrifices to God. Now the power struggle between the Lord of the Israelites and Pharaoh begins. **1.** How do you think Pharaoh felt when he found Moses and Aaron while on his morning walk by the river? **2.** In God's instructions to Moses, what purpose does God reveal for the calamities that will come upon Egypt? **3.** Why do you think God started off by turning the River Nile to blood? **4.** Do you believe that there is a power struggle going on today between the God of the universe and the forces of evil?

APPLY **1.** Do you sometimes feel that the forces of evil in the world are winning the battle? **2.** What do you do when you feel like giving up?

Aaron's Staff Becomes a Snake

[8]The LORD said to Moses and Aaron, [9]"When Pharaoh says to you,
'Perform a miracle,' then say to Aaron, 'Take your staff and throw it
down before Pharaoh,' and it will become a snake."
[10]So Moses and Aaron went to Pharaoh and did just as the LORD
commanded. Aaron threw his staff down in front of Pharaoh and his
officials, and it became a snake. [11]Pharaoh then summoned wise men
and sorcerers, and the Egyptian magicians also did the same things
by their secret arts: [12]Each one threw down his staff and it became a
snake. But Aaron's staff swallowed up their staffs. [13]Yet Pharaoh's
heart became hard and he would not listen to them, just as the LORD
had said.

The Plague of Blood

[14]Then the LORD said to Moses, "Pharaoh's heart is unyielding; he
refuses to let the people go. [15]Go to Pharaoh in the morning as he
goes out to the water. Wait on the bank of the Nile to meet him, and
take in your hand the staff that was changed into a snake. [16]Then say
to him, 'The LORD, the God of the Hebrews, has sent me to say to you:
Let my people go, so that they may worship me in the desert. But
until now you have not listened. [17]This is what the LORD says: By this
you will know that I am the LORD: With the staff that is in my hand I
will strike the water of the Nile, and it will be changed into blood.
[18]The fish in the Nile will die, and the river will stink; the Egyptians
will not be able to drink its water.' "
[19]The LORD said to Moses, "Tell Aaron, 'Take your staff and stretch
out your hand over the waters of Egypt—over the streams and
canals, over the ponds and all the reservoirs'—and they will turn
to blood. Blood will be everywhere in Egypt, even in the wooden
buckets and stone jars."
[20]Moses and Aaron did just as the LORD had commanded. He raised
his staff in the presence of Pharaoh and his officials and struck the
water of the Nile, and all the water was changed into blood. [21]The fish
in the Nile died, and the river smelled so bad that the Egyptians could
not drink its water. Blood was everywhere in Egypt.
[22]But the Egyptian magicians did the same things by their secret
arts, and Pharaoh's heart became hard; he would not listen to Moses
and Aaron, just as the LORD had said. [23]Instead, he turned and went
into his palace, and did not take even this to heart. [24]And all the Egyp-

---

7:11 secret arts. Pharaoh did everything he could do not to be outdone by the God of Moses. The wise men were learned counselors. Sorcerers practiced divination. Magicians were thought to possess occult knowledge. They were able to duplicate Moses' and Aaron's miracle—something God had not prepared them for. However, occult power is very real. These men used either tricks or demonic power to duplicate this and two other miracles (v. 22; 8:7). Finally, however, even they would have to admit to a power greater than their own (8:18–19).

7:12 Aaron's staff swallowed up their staffs. Head to head, God was able to overcome Pharaoh and the pagan gods he served. His ultimate power and authority are established.

7:17–20 the water of the Nile ... will be changed into blood. This first plague, on the mighty Nile River, giver of life to the entire nation, would have alone been devastating. The Egyptians worshiped Hopi, the god of the Nile, who would kindly rise and irrigate the fields when pleased. But even the great god of the mighty Nile could not keep the water from becoming blood at Moses' command. Not only the Nile, but the water located anywhere inland, even in the wooden buckets and stone jars, was turned to blood.

7:23 he turned and went into his palace. Pharaoh's actions not only show his disdain for the display of God's power, they also reveal his lack of concern for his suffering people.

7:24 dug along the Nile. The fouled water would have been safer for drinking after being flushed through the earth along the river. After this God allowed some time in between the plagues, perhaps so the Egyptians could meditate on the power of their gods versus the power of Israel's God.

tians dug along the Nile to get drinking water, because they could not
drink the water of the river.

The Plague of Frogs

8 25Seven days passed after the LORD struck the Nile. 1Then the
LORD said to Moses, "Go to Pharaoh and say to him, 'This is what
the LORD says: Let my people go, so that they may worship me. 2If you
refuse to let them go, I will plague your whole country with frogs.
3The Nile will teem with frogs. They will come up into your palace and
your bedroom and onto your bed, into the houses of your officials
and on your people, and into your ovens and kneading troughs. 4The
frogs will go up on you and your people and all your officials.' "
5Then the LORD said to Moses, "Tell Aaron, 'Stretch out your hand
with your staff over the streams and canals and ponds, and make
frogs come up on the land of Egypt.' "
6So Aaron stretched out his hand over the waters of Egypt, and the
frogs came up and covered the land. 7But the magicians did the same
things by their secret arts; they also made frogs come up on the land
of Egypt.
8Pharaoh summoned Moses and Aaron and said, "Pray to the LORD
to take the frogs away from me and my people, and I will let your
people go to offer sacrifices to the LORD."
9Moses said to Pharaoh, "I leave to you the honor of setting the
time for me to pray for you and your officials and your people that
you and your houses may be rid of the frogs, except for those that
remain in the Nile."
10"Tomorrow," Pharaoh said.
Moses replied, "It will be as you say, so that you may know there is
no one like the LORD our God. 11The frogs will leave you and your
houses, your officials and your people; they will remain only in the
Nile."
12After Moses and Aaron left Pharaoh, Moses cried out to the LORD
about the frogs he had brought on Pharaoh. 13And the LORD did what
Moses asked. The frogs died in the houses, in the courtyards and in
the fields. 14They were piled into heaps, and the land reeked of them.
15But when Pharaoh saw that there was relief, he hardened his heart
and would not listen to Moses and Aaron, just as the LORD had said.

The Plague of Gnats

16Then the LORD said to Moses, "Tell Aaron, 'Stretch out your staff
and strike the dust of the ground,' and throughout the land of Egypt

OPEN When is the last time you found an unwelcome creature in your food?

STUDY The Egyptians worshiped the River Nile like a god. In the first calamity their river god is discredited when the river turns to blood which killed the fish. In the second calamity, the god of frogs is discredited when the frogs in the river invade the land. **1.** How would you feel if you woke up one morning and found frogs in your bed? **2.** If you were an "official" in Egypt when Moses warned of a frog infestation, what would you say to Pharaoh when you found frogs in your house? **3.** Why would frogs get the attention of Pharaoh when the blood in the River Nile did not? **4.** If you were Pharaoh, what would make you swallow your pride and go to Moses to ask for prayer to his God to remove the frogs? **5.** What do you think it smelled like when they piled up the dead frogs into heaps in the streets? **6.** What would this calamity do to the morale of the people?

APPLY **1.** When is the last time your area was hit by a natural calamity? **2.** How did this calamity affect the people? Did it cause people to think soberly about their relationship with God?

OPEN Have you ever had a chigger attack? Gnat attack?

8:2 plague ... with frogs. This second plague caused frogs to overrun Egypt and revealed the powerlessness of the goddess Heqt, a frog goddess who allegedly helped women deliver babies.

8:7 the magicians did the same things. The magicians were able to use their secret arts (demonic powers) to duplicate the plague, they were only making the problem worse. Apparently, they could duplicate the problem, but could do nothing to make the frogs go away. Pharaoh had to call Moses and Aaron to do that (v. 8).

8:9 setting the time. Moses invited Pharaoh to set the time for him to pray, thus proving that God's work was the active agent, and not mere coincidence.

8:13 what Moses asked. God had promised to be with his servant (3:12). Not only could Moses cause the plagues to descend upon Egypt, but he could also make them go away because God's power was working through him.

8:15 Pharaoh saw that there was relief. A pattern is revealed in Pharaoh's actions. When the deck was stacked against him he would promise anything. He told Moses and Aaron that he would let the people go (v. 8). But as soon as an emergency ended he would harden his heart and not follow through with his promise.

STUDY 1. Which would be worse, frogs in your bed or gnats swarming all over you? **2.** What could the magicians do about the gnats? **3.** Have you ever had something bothersome that you could do nothing about?

APPLY When is the last time God used something tiny like a gnat bite to get your attention?

OPEN What is your sure-fire way for catching flies?

STUDY 1. What is the closest you have come to being targeted by an invasion of flies? **2.** What was unique about this calamity (vv. 22–23)? What would this show to Pharaoh? **3.** What was different about the response of Pharaoh this time? Why didn't Moses take up Pharaoh on his offer? Why do you think the religious sacrifices of the Israelites were so offensive to the Egyptians? **4.** Why did Moses ask only for a three-day holiday when he actually intended to keep on going? Have you ever shaded your request while asking for one thing when you were really expecting to get something else? **5.** Do you think Pharaoh really intended to let the Israelites go this time or was he just pretending? **6.** If Moses knew all along that Pharaoh was not going to give in until Pharaoh's son was taken, why did Moses go through this charade of playing along with Pharaoh?

APPLY 1. If you had to describe your spiritual life right now in terms of a battlefield report, what would it be? **2.** How can your group keep you this week in prayer?

---

the dust will become gnats." 17 They did this, and when Aaron
stretched out his hand with the staff and struck the dust of the
ground, gnats came upon men and animals. All the dust throughout
the land of Egypt became gnats. 18 But when the magicians tried to
produce gnats by their secret arts, they could not. And the gnats were
on men and animals.
19 The magicians said to Pharaoh, "This is the finger of God." But
Pharaoh's heart was hard and he would not listen, just as the LORD
had said.

The Plague of Flies

20 Then the LORD said to Moses, "Get up early in the morning and
confront Pharaoh as he goes to the water and say to him, 'This is
what the LORD says: Let my people go, so that they may worship me.
21 If you do not let my people go, I will send swarms of flies on
you and your officials, on your people and into your houses. The
houses of the Egyptians will be full of flies, and even the ground
where they are.
22 " 'But on that day I will deal differently with the land of Goshen,
where my people live; no swarms of flies will be there, so that you
will know that I, the LORD, am in this land. 23 I will make a distinction[a]
between my people and your people. This miraculous sign will occur
tomorrow.' "
24 And the LORD did this. Dense swarms of flies poured into
Pharaoh's palace and into the houses of his officials, and throughout
Egypt the land was ruined by the flies.
25 Then Pharaoh summoned Moses and Aaron and said, "Go, sacrifice to your God here in the land."
26 But Moses said, "That would not be right. The sacrifices we offer
the LORD our God would be detestable to the Egyptians. And if we
offer sacrifices that are detestable in their eyes, will they not stone
us? 27 We must take a three-day journey into the desert to offer sacrifices to the LORD our God, as he commands us."
28 Pharaoh said, "I will let you go to offer sacrifices to the LORD your
God in the desert, but you must not go very far. Now pray for me."
29 Moses answered, "As soon as I leave you, I will pray to the LORD,
and tomorrow the flies will leave Pharaoh and his officials and his
people. Only be sure that Pharaoh does not act deceitfully again by
not letting the people go to offer sacrifices to the LORD."
30 Then Moses left Pharaoh and prayed to the LORD, 31 and the LORD
did what Moses asked: The flies left Pharaoh and his officials and his
people; not a fly remained. 32 But this time also Pharaoh hardened his
heart and would not let the people go.

[a]23 Septuagint and Vulgate; Hebrew *will put a deliverance*

8:19 finger of God. The magicians had been able to duplicate the previous *miracles (v. 7; 7:11,22). However, at this* point, their powers stopped and they could no longer duplicate Moses' acts. They had to admit that this was being done by a power they did not possess.

8:21 swarms of flies. These pesky flies bit people and animals.

8:23 I will make a distinction. In a further demonstration of his power, God brought this plague upon Egypt, but did not allow it to affect the Israelites (who lived separately in the land of Goshen, 47:4).

8:32 Pharaoh hardened his heart. Again, as soon as God removed the plague of flies, Pharaoh returned to his stubborn ways.

The Plague on Livestock

9 Then the LORD said to Moses, "Go to Pharaoh and say to him,
'This is what the LORD, the God of the Hebrews, says: "Let my
people go, so that they may worship me." 2If you refuse to let them go
and continue to hold them back, 3the hand of the LORD will bring a
terrible plague on your livestock in the field—on your horses and
donkeys and camels and on your cattle and sheep and goats. 4But the
LORD will make a distinction between the livestock of Israel and that
of Egypt, so that no animal belonging to the Israelites will die.'"
5The LORD set a time and said, "Tomorrow the LORD will do this in
the land." 6And the next day the LORD did it: All the livestock of the
Egyptians died, but not one animal belonging to the Israelites died.
7Pharaoh sent men to investigate and found that not even one of the
animals of the Israelites had died. Yet his heart was unyielding and he
would not let the people go.

The Plague of Boils

8Then the LORD said to Moses and Aaron, "Take handfuls of soot
from a furnace and have Moses toss it into the air in the presence of
Pharaoh. 9It will become fine dust over the whole land of Egypt, and
festering boils will break out on men and animals throughout the
land."
10So they took soot from a furnace and stood before Pharaoh. Moses tossed it into the air, and festering boils broke out on men and
animals. 11The magicians could not stand before Moses because of
the boils that were on them and on all the Egyptians. 12But the LORD
hardened Pharaoh's heart and he would not listen to Moses and
Aaron, just as the LORD had said to Moses.

The Plague of Hail

13Then the LORD said to Moses, "Get up early in the morning,
confront Pharaoh and say to him, 'This is what the LORD, the God of
the Hebrews, says: Let my people go, so that they may worship me,
14or this time I will send the full force of my plagues against you
and against your officials and your people, so you may know that
there is no one like me in all the earth. 15For by now I could have
stretched out my hand and struck you and your people with a plague
that would have wiped you off the earth. 16But I have raised you

OPEN Have you ever lived around livestock?

STUDY Up to now, the calamities have been an inconvenience and an annoyance for Egypt. Now, there is economic loss. **1.** What will the loss of all animals in the fields do to the Egyptian economy? **2.** If you were Pharaoh and you found out that none of the Israelites' livestock were affected, what would that tell you?

APPLY What is the closest you have come to having your livelihood wiped out?

OPEN Have you ever had a painful boil?

STUDY The calamities start getting more and more painful: **1.** How is this calamity different from all the previous calamities? **2.** How did this affect the court magicians?

APPLY If your body could talk, what would it say to you right now about your health?

OPEN What is the worst hailstorm you have ever been in? How much damage did it do?

STUDY Some scholars believe the calamities come in groups of three with the last three the most devastating. The economy of Egypt was based on agriculture which would make this calamity particularly devastating. **1.** How do you think Pharaoh felt

---

9:3 plague on your livestock. Many animals were worshiped by the Egyptians, who had a number of animal-headed gods including Apis and Mnevis (bull gods), Hathor (cow god) and Khnum (ram god). This plague revealed that all of these gods had no power to protect the livestock.

9:4 make a distinction. As in the plague of flies (8:22), God begins to separate his people from the Egyptians. The Egyptians' animals were wiped out, but the Israelites' animals were unaffected.

9:6 All the livestock of the Egyptians died. Obviously not all Egyptian livestock died (vv. 19–21). The plague was only aimed at livestock in the field (v. 3).

9:8 handfuls of soot. As Moses had struck the dust to begin the plague of gnats (8:16), he here took soot and tossed it into the air in Pharaoh's presence to make his point about the effects of this coming plague.

9:9 boils. This is the first plague that affects the people's physical bodies, giving them painful, festering boils. Although not specifically mentioned, this plague probably did not affect the Israelites.

9:11 magicians could not stand. In another ironic twist, the complete powerlessness of the Egyptian magicians is revealed in that they were so afflicted by the plague that they could not appear.

9:14 no one like me. God shows that he was beyond comparison to the hapless Egyptian gods, who were now under direct assault.

9:16 I have raised you up for this very purpose. God was speaking through Moses to Pharaoh, demonstrating his power. God is in complete control of all nations and leaders (Ps. 2). Pharaoh only had power because God

meeting Moses after six calamities? **2.** What does Moses remind Pharaoh of about the purpose of these calamities (vv. 16–17)? **3.** What do some of the officials do when they hear the warning about the hailstorm? What does that tell you about the impact Moses is having in Pharaoh's court? **4.** How will this calamity effect the livelihood of the people? What will it do to the national economy? To Pharaoh's prestige? **5.** What admission did Pharaoh make this time? Do you think he really believed it or was he just trying to get the help of Moses? **6.** How would you describe the game that Moses and Pharaoh are playing?

APPLY 1. Where are you trying to strike a bargain with God right now? **2.** What are you promising to do if he comes through for you?

up[a] for this very purpose, that I might show you my power and that
my name might be proclaimed in all the earth. 17 You still set yourself
against my people and will not let them go. 18 Therefore, at this time
tomorrow I will send the worst hailstorm that has ever fallen on
Egypt, from the day it was founded till now. 19 Give an order now to
bring your livestock and everything you have in the field to a place of
shelter, because the hail will fall on every man and animal that has
not been brought in and is still out in the field, and they will die.' "
20 Those officials of Pharaoh who feared the word of the LORD
hurried to bring their slaves and their livestock inside. 21 But those
who ignored the word of the LORD left their slaves and livestock in the
field.
22 Then the LORD said to Moses, "Stretch out your hand toward the
sky so that hail will fall all over Egypt—on men and animals and on
everything growing in the fields of Egypt." 23 When Moses stretched
out his staff toward the sky, the LORD sent thunder and hail, and lightning flashed down to the ground. So the LORD rained hail on the land
of Egypt; 24 hail fell and lightning flashed back and forth. It was the
worst storm in all the land of Egypt since it had become a nation.
25 Throughout Egypt hail struck everything in the fields—both men
and animals; it beat down everything growing in the fields and
stripped every tree. 26 The only place it did not hail was the land of
Goshen, where the Israelites were.
27 Then Pharaoh summoned Moses and Aaron. "This time I have
sinned," he said to them. "The LORD is in the right, and I and my people are in the wrong. 28 Pray to the LORD, for we have had enough
thunder and hail. I will let you go; you don't have to stay any longer."
29 Moses replied, "When I have gone out of the city, I will spread out
my hands in prayer to the LORD. The thunder will stop and there will
be no more hail, so you may know that the earth is the LORD's. 30 But
I know that you and your officials still do not fear the LORD God."
31 (The flax and barley were destroyed, since the barley had headed
and the flax was in bloom. 32 The wheat and spelt, however, were not
destroyed, because they ripen later.)
33 Then Moses left Pharaoh and went out of the city. He spread out
his hands toward the LORD; the thunder and hail stopped, and the
rain no longer poured down on the land. 34 When Pharaoh saw that
the rain and hail and thunder had stopped, he sinned again: He and
his officials hardened their hearts. 35 So Pharaoh's heart was hard
and he would not let the Israelites go, just as the LORD had said
through Moses.

[a]16 Or *have spared you*

had placed him there; and Pharaoh had been placed there in order for God to make his name known throughout the earth. The miracle of the Exodus was spread far and wide. The people of Jericho had heard this story and were frightened of the Israelites because of it (Josh. 2:8–12).

9:18 hailstorm. So severe would be this hailstorm that any person or animal outside and unprotected would be killed.

9:20 Those ... who feared. Clearly God's words and works were having an impact on at least some members of Pharaoh's staff, who acted to protect their servants and livestock from the next coming plague. In the end, it seems that some Egyptians were convinced by God's power and left Egypt with the Israelites (12:38).

9:27 This time I have sinned. The Pharaoh confessed his sinfulness, but Moses knew better (v. 30). Nevertheless, Moses stopped the plague at Pharaoh's request. Unfortunately, he would take these words back in his stubbornness (v. 34).

The Plague of Locusts

10 Then the LORD said to Moses, "Go to Pharaoh, for I have
hardened his heart and the hearts of his officials so that I
may perform these miraculous signs of mine among them 2that you
may tell your children and grandchildren how I dealt harshly with the
Egyptians and how I performed my signs among them, and that you
may know that I am the LORD."
3So Moses and Aaron went to Pharaoh and said to him, "This is
what the LORD, the God of the Hebrews, says: 'How long will you
refuse to humble yourself before me? Let my people go, so that they
may worship me. 4If you refuse to let them go, I will bring locusts into
your country tomorrow. 5They will cover the face of the ground so
that it cannot be seen. They will devour what little you have left after
the hail, including every tree that is growing in your fields. 6They will
fill your houses and those of all your officials and all the Egyptians—
something neither your fathers nor your forefathers have ever seen
from the day they settled in this land till now.' " Then Moses turned
and left Pharaoh.
7Pharaoh's officials said to him, "How long will this man be a snare
to us? Let the people go, so that they may worship the LORD their
God. Do you not yet realize that Egypt is ruined?"
8Then Moses and Aaron were brought back to Pharaoh. "Go, worship the LORD your God," he said. "But just who will be going?"
9Moses answered, "We will go with our young and old, with our
sons and daughters, and with our flocks and herds, because we are
to celebrate a festival to the LORD."
10Pharaoh said, "The LORD be with you—if I let you go, along with
your women and children! Clearly you are bent on evil.[a] 11No! Have
only the men go; and worship the LORD, since that's what you have
been asking for." Then Moses and Aaron were driven out of
Pharaoh's presence.
12And the LORD said to Moses, "Stretch out your hand over Egypt so
that locusts will swarm over the land and devour everything growing
in the fields, everything left by the hail."
13So Moses stretched out his staff over Egypt, and the LORD made
an east wind blow across the land all that day and all that night. By
morning the wind had brought the locusts; 14they invaded all Egypt
and settled down in every area of the country in great numbers.
Never before had there been such a plague of locusts, nor will there
ever be again. 15They covered all the ground until it was black. They
devoured all that was left after the hail—everything growing in the

[a]10 Or *Be careful, trouble is in store for you!*

OPEN When you were a kid, did you play with grasshoppers? What was your method for catching them?

STUDY In Africa, swarms of locust still swarm over the land, eating everything in their path. They are carried by the wind coming over the Red Sea. Within a few days they can devastate an entire country. **1.** If you had just gone through a terrible hailstorm in which all of your spring crops were wiped out, how would you feel if you were told a swarm of locusts were going to invade your land and eat everything that was left? **2.** Why do you think Pharaoh's officials finally relented and recommended to let the Israelites go? **3.** Why would Pharaoh insist on the women and children staying behind while the men go to worship God in the desert? Do you think Pharaoh had a sneaking suspicion that the real plan was to flee Egypt when they got out of the country? **4.** When Moses carries out his warning and the land is devastated by swarms of locust, do you think Pharaoh realized that he was dealing with someone that was more powerful than he was? **5.** Who would you compare Pharaoh to in modern history?

APPLY 1. As you read the newspaper and watch TV, are you able to see beyond the human tragedies and calamities to the hand of God working through history? **2.** What is God laying on your heart right now to pray for?

10:2 tell your children. By recounting the stories of God's acts of deliverance to their descendants, the Israelites would keep their memory alive.

10:3 refuse to humble yourself. Pharaoh's immense pride led to his downfall. He considered himself a god. Perhaps he thought that giving in to the one true God would expose him as a mere human.

10:4–5 I will bring locusts. Locusts would eat everything in sight; a locust plague could devastate a country. The hail had already damaged the crops in the fields (9:25); the locusts would devour what little was left.

10:7 Egypt is ruined. The officials perceived what Pharaoh would not. The devastation of their livestock and fields had already ruined the nation; a locust plague would be completely devastating. But Pharaoh, in his pride, would not be convinced.

10:11 Have only the men go. Pharaoh obviously feared that the Israelites were planning to escape from slavery. To let them all out of his sight would be asking for trouble. So Pharaoh attempted to compromise by sending the men, but keeping the women and children behind to insure that they would return.

fields and the fruit on the trees. Nothing green remained on tree or plant in all the land of Egypt.

[16]Pharaoh quickly summoned Moses and Aaron and said, "I have sinned against the LORD your God and against you. [17]Now forgive my sin once more and pray to the LORD your God to take this deadly plague away from me."

[18]Moses then left Pharaoh and prayed to the LORD. [19]And the LORD changed the wind to a very strong west wind, which caught up the locusts and carried them into the Red Sea.[a] Not a locust was left anywhere in Egypt. [20]But the LORD hardened Pharaoh's heart, and he would not let the Israelites go.

The Plague of Darkness

[21]Then the LORD said to Moses, "Stretch out your hand toward the sky so that darkness will spread over Egypt—darkness that can be felt." [22]So Moses stretched out his hand toward the sky, and total darkness covered all Egypt for three days. [23]No one could see anyone else or leave his place for three days. Yet all the Israelites had light in the places where they lived.

[24]Then Pharaoh summoned Moses and said, "Go, worship the LORD. Even your women and children may go with you; only leave your flocks and herds behind."

[25]But Moses said, "You must allow us to have sacrifices and burnt offerings to present to the LORD our God. [26]Our livestock too must go with us; not a hoof is to be left behind. We have to use some of them in worshiping the LORD our God, and until we get there we will not know what we are to use to worship the LORD."

[27]But the LORD hardened Pharaoh's heart, and he was not willing to let them go. [28]Pharaoh said to Moses, "Get out of my sight! Make sure you do not appear before me again! The day you see my face you will die."

[29]"Just as you say," Moses replied, "I will never appear before you again."

The Plague on the Firstborn

11 Now the LORD had said to Moses, "I will bring one more plague on Pharaoh and on Egypt. After that, he will let you go from here, and when he does, he will drive you out completely. [2]Tell the people that men and women alike are to ask their neighbors for articles of silver and gold." [3](The LORD made the Egyptians favorably disposed toward the people, and Moses himself was highly regarded in Egypt by Pharaoh's officials and by the people.)

[4]So Moses said, "This is what the LORD says: 'About midnight I will go throughout Egypt. [5]Every firstborn son in Egypt will die, from the firstborn son of Pharaoh, who sits on the throne, to the firstborn son of the slave girl, who is at her hand mill, and all the firstborn of the

[a]19 Hebrew *Yam Suph;* that is, Sea of Reeds

OPEN As a child, what did you do when you had a nightmare?

STUDY The Egyptians worshiped the sun god. Darkness was feared and seen as an insult to their god. **1.** What effect would three days of total darkness have upon the people? Upon Pharaoh? **2.** What concession does Pharaoh make this time and what does he refuse to allow? How does Moses answer Pharaoh? **3.** How would you describe the tone in Pharaoh's voice in verse 28? **4.** How would you describe the relationship between Moses and Pharaoh?

APPLY What comes to mind in your own story as you think about the painful and emotional ending of the relationship between Moses and Pharaoh?

OPEN What is the most precious thing in your life right now? What would happen if this was suddenly taken away from you?

STUDY This is the last of ten calamities to fall on Egypt that led to the expulsion of the Israelites. **1.** Up to now, Pharaoh has reneged on every decision to let the Israelites go. What does God tell Moses will happen after this calamity? **2.** What favor are the Israelites to ask of their neighbors? **3.** What does Moses tell Pharaoh will happen at midnight? **4.** Do you struggle with the harshness of this calamity? How do you feel

10:19 the LORD changed the wind. God had brought the locusts in (v. 13), and he could take them away. He is clearly in charge.

10:21 darkness that can be felt. One of Egypt's chief gods was Ra, the sun god. The darkness ridiculed this god, revealing his complete powerlessness to keep darkness from covering Egypt for three full days. God is the only God, and creator of the sun. He alone could have brought this darkness while still giving sunlight to the Israelites.

11:5 firstborn son. All of Egypt's firstborn sons would die. No family was exempt from it.

cattle as well. 6There will be loud wailing throughout Egypt—worse than there has ever been or ever will be again. 7But among the Israelites not a dog will bark at any man or animal.' Then you will know that the LORD makes a distinction between Egypt and Israel. 8All these officials of yours will come to me, bowing down before me and saying, 'Go, you and all the people who follow you!' After that I will leave." Then Moses, hot with anger, left Pharaoh.

9The LORD had said to Moses, "Pharaoh will refuse to listen to you—so that my wonders may be multiplied in Egypt." 10Moses and Aaron performed all these wonders before Pharaoh, but the LORD hardened Pharaoh's heart, and he would not let the Israelites go out of his country.

The Passover

12 The LORD said to Moses and Aaron in Egypt, 2"This month is to be for you the first month, the first month of your year. 3Tell the whole community of Israel that on the tenth day of this month each man is to take a lamb[a] for his family, one for each household. 4If any household is too small for a whole lamb, they must share one with their nearest neighbor, having taken into account the number of people there are. You are to determine the amount of lamb needed in accordance with what each person will eat. 5The animals you choose must be year-old males without defect, and you may take them from the sheep or the goats. 6Take care of them until the fourteenth day of the month, when all the people of the community of Israel must slaughter them at twilight. 7Then they are to take some of the blood and put it on the sides and tops of the doorframes of the houses where they eat the lambs. 8That same night they are to eat the meat roasted over the fire, along with bitter herbs, and bread made without yeast. 9Do not eat the meat raw or cooked in water, but roast it over the fire—head, legs and inner parts. 10Do not leave any of it till morning; if some is left till morning, you must burn it. 11This is how you are to eat it: with your cloak tucked into your belt, your sandals on your feet and your staff in your hand. Eat it in haste; it is the LORD's Passover.

12"On that same night I will pass through Egypt and strike down every firstborn—both men and animals—and I will bring judgment

[a]3 The Hebrew word can mean *lamb* or *kid*; also in verse 4.

about people dying as a result of God's actions?

APPLY 1. What is the warning God is giving you about your country? **2.** Who is bringing God's warning to your country as Moses did?

OPEN 1. Do you remember as a kid ever having to take the blame for somebody else's wrongdoing? **2.** Have you ever gotten off scott free from a speeding ticket because the cop extended you a little "grace"?

STUDY The Passover Feast described in this passage is probably the most important story in the Old Testament because it gives a "show and tell" picture of how God will postpone or "passed-over" sin until the ultimate sacrifice of Jesus Christ is made as a payment for the sin of all humankind. The "lamb" in the sacrifice here is a symbol of the real "lamb of God" who will later "take away" the sin of the world as a substitute—John 1:36. **1.** How would you have taught the consequences of sin, and the Son of God's payment on the cross to the Israelites? **2.** Why did the lamb chosen to be sacrificed for each family have to be "without defect" (v. 5)? How does this portray Jesus Christ? **3.** What were the Israelites to do with the blood of the lamb when it was slaughtered? What was the blood on the door to cause the angel to do

12:2 the first month of your year. God made the time of the nation's Exodus from Egypt the beginning of their year. Every year, the new year celebration would remind the nation of its escape from slavery.

12:3 take a lamb. The message had to get to every slave household in Egypt, for every family would be responsible to get a lamb and place its blood on the doorframes of its home.

12:5 males without defect. The sacrificed lambs or goats had to be chosen from the best of the herd on the tenth day of the month (v. 3). Centuries later, Jesus would be the perfect, sacrificial Lamb chosen by God to pay the price for all sin.

12:6–7 take some of the blood. Four days after choosing the lamb (v. 12), the lamb was to be killed and eaten. The blood of the animal was a visible sign that a sacrifice had taken place on behalf of each household. That sacrifice would be their only means of escaping the coming plague.

12:8 along with bitter herbs. This was indeed a "salad of sorrow." Eating bitter herbs found in Egypt would remind the Israelites of their years of slavery when they sat down to eat this meal every year during what would become their Passover celebration (Num. 9:11).

12:11 Eat it in haste. The phrase "eat and run" could have been coined for this meal. The Israelites were to be dressed to travel, for their deliverance was at hand. **the LORD's Passover.** God's messenger of death would only pass over the homes that had blood on the doorframes.

12:12 the gods of Egypt. With the plagues, God showed the ineffectiveness of the many gods of Egypt. No matter who they were or what power they had been assigned, none of them could stop the plague that God would bring upon the nation.

when the angel came to their home? **4.** How were the Israelites to dress before eating the "Passover" feast in their homes? **5.** How often were the Israelites to celebrate this feast? **6.** Why would yeast be forbidden during this feast for seven days? When the Israelites have to taste the flat bread, what are they going to remember? **7.** When Jesus performed this feast on his Last Supper with his disciples, how did the meaning of the blood and the unleavened bread change?

APPLY 1. When did you come to understand the full meaning of Christ's death for you? **2.** In our culture today, how many people do you think understand the meaning of Christ's sacrifice?

on all the gods of Egypt. I am the LORD. [13]The blood will be a sign for
you on the houses where you are; and when I see the blood, I will
pass over you. No destructive plague will touch you when I strike
Egypt.
[14]"This is a day you are to commemorate; for the generations
to come you shall celebrate it as a festival to the LORD—a lasting
ordinance. [15]For seven days you are to eat bread made without yeast.
On the first day remove the yeast from your houses, for whoever eats
anything with yeast in it from the first day through the seventh must
be cut off from Israel. [16]On the first day hold a sacred assembly, and
another one on the seventh day. Do no work at all on these days,
except to prepare food for everyone to eat—that is all you may do.
[17]"Celebrate the Feast of Unleavened Bread, because it was on this
very day that I brought your divisions out of Egypt. Celebrate this day
as a lasting ordinance for the generations to come. [18]In the first
month you are to eat bread made without yeast, from the evening of
the fourteenth day until the evening of the twenty-first day. [19]For
seven days no yeast is to be found in your houses. And whoever eats
anything with yeast in it must be cut off from the community of Israel,
whether he is an alien or native-born. [20]Eat nothing made with yeast.
Wherever you live, you must eat unleavened bread."
[21]Then Moses summoned all the elders of Israel and said to them,
"Go at once and select the animals for your families and slaughter the
Passover lamb. [22]Take a bunch of hyssop, dip it into the blood in the
basin and put some of the blood on the top and on both sides of the
doorframe. Not one of you shall go out the door of his house until
morning. [23]When the LORD goes through the land to strike down the
Egyptians, he will see the blood on the top and sides of the doorframe and will pass over that doorway, and he will not permit the
destroyer to enter your houses and strike you down.
[24]"Obey these instructions as a lasting ordinance for you and your
descendants. [25]When you enter the land that the LORD will give you as
he promised, observe this ceremony. [26]And when your children ask
you, 'What does this ceremony mean to you?' [27]then tell them, 'It is
the Passover sacrifice to the LORD, who passed over the houses of the
Israelites in Egypt and spared our homes when he struck down the

---

12:13 a sign for you. God would again distinguish between the Israelites and the Egyptians in a plague, but the people would have to submit to his command that they place blood on the doorframes of their homes. This showed their faith in him, and would be a sign of God's mercy on them.

12:14 a lasting ordinance. The Passover was not to be a one-time celebration. God's people were to regularly observe this feast. This tradition was to be passed from generation to generation.

12:15 bread made without yeast. God's people were instructed to only make bread without yeast for the seven days of this celebration. This would be a reminder of this night when they had no time to wait for bread to rise, so the people had made unleavened bread to eat with their hasty meal. Many Jewish families today conduct a "yeast search" as part of their Passover tradition.

12:17 Feast of Unleavened Bread. This seven-day festival began with the Passover meal. The celebration commemorated Israel's deliverance from Egypt (Matt. 26:17; Acts 12:3; 20:6).

12:21 the Passover lamb. The time had come to select the Passover lamb and to put its blood on their doorframes. Jesus later became known as the Passover Lamb (1 Cor. 5:7).

12:22 Take a bunch of hyssop. This strongly scented flowering plant of the mint family could be found in Egypt and in Palestine. Its twigs were used for sprinkling liquids. Some believe *hyssop* to be another name for marjoram. While Jesus hung on the cross, hyssop was used to raise a sponge soaked in wine vinegar to his lips.

12:23 the destroyer. This may refer to an angel or, possibly, to the Angel of the Lord. This grim messenger would carry out God's plan.

12:26 your children. This event was to be celebrated annually by the Israelites as a natural way for parents to pass along to their children the story of God's great deliverance of his people.

Egyptians.' " Then the people bowed down and worshiped. [28]The Israelites did just what the LORD commanded Moses and Aaron.

[29]At midnight the LORD struck down all the firstborn in Egypt, from the firstborn of Pharaoh, who sat on the throne, to the firstborn of the prisoner, who was in the dungeon, and the firstborn of all the livestock as well. [30]Pharaoh and all his officials and all the Egyptians got up during the night, and there was loud wailing in Egypt, for there was not a house without someone dead.

The Exodus

[31]During the night Pharaoh summoned Moses and Aaron and said, "Up! Leave my people, you and the Israelites! Go, worship the LORD as you have requested. [32]Take your flocks and herds, as you have said, and go. And also bless me."

[33]The Egyptians urged the people to hurry and leave the country. "For otherwise," they said, "we will all die!" [34]So the people took their dough before the yeast was added, and carried it on their shoulders in kneading troughs wrapped in clothing. [35]The Israelites did as Moses instructed and asked the Egyptians for articles of silver and gold and for clothing. [36]The LORD had made the Egyptians favorably disposed toward the people, and they gave them what they asked for; so they plundered the Egyptians.

[37]The Israelites journeyed from Rameses to Succoth. There were about six hundred thousand men on foot, besides women and children. [38]Many other people went up with them, as well as large droves of livestock, both flocks and herds. [39]With the dough they had brought from Egypt, they baked cakes of unleavened bread. The dough was without yeast because they had been driven out of Egypt and did not have time to prepare food for themselves.

[40]Now the length of time the Israelite people lived in Egypt[a] was 430 years. [41]At the end of the 430 years, to the very day, all the LORD's divisions left Egypt. [42]Because the LORD kept vigil that night to bring them out of Egypt, on this night all the Israelites are to keep vigil to honor the LORD for the generations to come.

Passover Restrictions

[43]The LORD said to Moses and Aaron, "These are the regulations for the Passover:

"No foreigner is to eat of it. [44]Any slave you have bought may eat of it after you have circumcised him, [45]but a temporary resident and a hired worker may not eat of it.

[46]"It must be eaten inside one house; take none of the meat outside

[a]40 Masoretic Text; Samaritan Pentateuch and Septuagint *Egypt and Canaan*

OPEN If you had to suddenly leave your house in the middle of the night and you could only grab three things (besides the children and pets), what would you grab?

STUDY While the Israelites are still eating the "Passover" feast to celebrate the passing-over of the death angel, Pharaoh suddenly changes his mind and commands the Israelites to get out of the country. **1.** How would you organize a mass exodus of all the men, women and children in your town in the middle of the night? **2.** How do you think Moses is feeling with this responsibility?

APPLY **1.** What is the largest number of people you have been responsible for at one time? **2.** Is it easier for you to do something daring yourself or to convince fearful people to do something daring?

OPEN What was the rule in your family about dating people outside of your faith?

STUDY Rules had to be made for those non-Israelites who left with them. **1.** Does it sound like God is demanding the Israelites to be exclusive? Why? **2.** What does God expect of someone who wants to join

---

12:29 the firstborn of Pharaoh ... firstborn of the prisoner. No one would be exempt from God's judgment, as 11:5 also indicated, except for the Israelites who had obeyed God and placed the blood of a lamb on their doorframes.

12:31 During the night Pharaoh summoned Moses. God's judgment of Egypt drew a swift response from hard-hearted Pharaoh. God had earlier revealed to Moses that "his wonders" (3:20) would force Pharaoh's hand.

12:36 plundered the Egyptians. Their land had been decimated, now the Israelites would take their wealth as well. God had promised that this would be the case (3:21; Gen. 15:14).

12:37 about six hundred thousand. The actual number of people who took part in the Exodus was around two million. The figure reported here counts men only.

12:41 430 years. The number of years of Israel's sojourn in Egypt. God had foretold this to Abraham (Gen. 15:13).

12:46 any of the bones. The Passover lamb was not to have any of its bones

the Israelites? By doing this, what are these people committing to?

APPLY Where do you draw the line on being inclusive of other religions?

OPEN Where are you in the birth order of your family? Were there any expectations (spoken or unspoken) placed on the oldest in your family?

STUDY The Israelites have been roused in the middle of the night and commanded to leave the country. Moses is told to start a tradition to remind the Israelites of their exodus from Egypt by celebrating a "passover" meal each year just like they did on their last night in Egypt. The death angel killed every firstborn male, human or animal except for those of the Israelites who had sprinkled the blood of a lamb over their door. **1.** What does God expect the Israelites to do with their firstborn? **2.** If a family wants to keep their firstborn male, human or animal, what must they do? **3.** How did the parents of Jesus observe this when they didn't have enough money to buy an animal (Luke 2:21–24)? **4.** What are the parents to do when they perform these rituals every year after year in their families?

APPLY What kind of ritual or tradition do you use to teach your children that they belong to God?

the house. Do not break any of the bones. 47The whole community of Israel must celebrate it.

48"An alien living among you who wants to celebrate the LORD's Passover must have all the males in his household circumcised; then he may take part like one born in the land. No uncircumcised male may eat of it. 49The same law applies to the native-born and to the alien living among you."

50All the Israelites did just what the LORD had commanded Moses and Aaron. 51And on that very day the LORD brought the Israelites out of Egypt by their divisions.

Consecration of the Firstborn

13 The LORD said to Moses, 2"Consecrate to me every firstborn male. The first offspring of every womb among the Israelites belongs to me, whether man or animal."

3Then Moses said to the people, "Commemorate this day, the day you came out of Egypt, out of the land of slavery, because the LORD brought you out of it with a mighty hand. Eat nothing containing yeast. 4Today, in the month of Abib, you are leaving. 5When the LORD brings you into the land of the Canaanites, Hittites, Amorites, Hivites and Jebusites—the land he swore to your forefathers to give you, a land flowing with milk and honey—you are to observe this ceremony in this month: 6For seven days eat bread made without yeast and on the seventh day hold a festival to the LORD. 7Eat unleavened bread during those seven days; nothing with yeast in it is to be seen among you, nor shall any yeast be seen anywhere within your borders. 8On that day tell your son, 'I do this because of what the LORD did for me when I came out of Egypt.' 9This observance will be for you like a sign on your hand and a reminder on your forehead that the law of the LORD is to be on your lips. For the LORD brought you out of Egypt with his mighty hand. 10You must keep this ordinance at the appointed time year after year.

11"After the LORD brings you into the land of the Canaanites and gives it to you, as he promised on oath to you and your forefathers, 12you are to give over to the LORD the first offspring of every womb. All the firstborn males of your livestock belong to the LORD. 13Redeem with a lamb every firstborn donkey, but if you do not redeem it, break its neck. Redeem every firstborn among your sons.

14"In days to come, when your son asks you, 'What does this mean?' say to him, 'With a mighty hand the LORD brought us out of Egypt, out of the land of slavery. 15When Pharaoh stubbornly refused to let us go, the LORD killed every firstborn in Egypt, both man and animal. This is why I sacrifice to the LORD the first male offspring of

---

broken. At the crucifixion, a similar decision was made to avoid breaking any of Jesus' bones. The apostle John considered this action a fulfillment of *God's commandment* (Ps. 34:20; John 19:36).

12:48 circumcised. Circumcision was required for eating the Passover meal. God had established circumcision as a mark of his covenant with Abraham (Gen. 17:10-11).

13:2 every firstborn male. All firstborn males, including animals, were to be dedicated to the Lord because he had protected the firstborn males of Israel from the tenth plague.

13:9 a reminder on your forehead. This was an expression meaning that the ceremony would be an annual reminder of God's mighty works on behalf of his people. Some of the religious leaders in Jesus' day had taken this commandment literally by tying little boxes, called phylacteries with parchment inside, across their foreheads. Jesus condemned this act because the people's hearts were far from him (Matt. 23:5).

every womb and redeem each of my firstborn sons.' 16And it will be
like a sign on your hand and a symbol on your forehead that the LORD
brought us out of Egypt with his mighty hand."

Crossing the Sea

17When Pharaoh let the people go, God did not lead them on the
road through the Philistine country, though that was shorter. For God
said, "If they face war, they might change their minds and return to
Egypt." 18So God led the people around by the desert road toward the
Red Sea.[a] The Israelites went up out of Egypt armed for battle.
19Moses took the bones of Joseph with him because Joseph had
made the sons of Israel swear an oath. He had said, "God will surely
come to your aid, and then you must carry my bones up with you
from this place."[b]
20After leaving Succoth they camped at Etham on the edge of the
desert. 21By day the LORD went ahead of them in a pillar of cloud to
guide them on their way and by night in a pillar of fire to give them
light, so that they could travel by day or night. 22Neither the pillar of
cloud by day nor the pillar of fire by night left its place in front of the
people.

14 Then the LORD said to Moses, 2"Tell the Israelites to turn back
and encamp near Pi Hahiroth, between Migdol and the sea.
They are to encamp by the sea, directly opposite Baal Zephon. 3Phar-
aoh will think, 'The Israelites are wandering around the land in
confusion, hemmed in by the desert.' 4And I will harden Pharaoh's
heart, and he will pursue them. But I will gain glory for myself
through Pharaoh and all his army, and the Egyptians will know that I
am the LORD." So the Israelites did this.
5When the king of Egypt was told that the people had fled, Pharaoh
and his officials changed their minds about them and said, "What
have we done? We have let the Israelites go and have lost their
services!" 6So he had his chariot made ready and took his army with
him. 7He took six hundred of the best chariots, along with all the
other chariots of Egypt, with officers over all of them. 8The LORD
hardened the heart of Pharaoh king of Egypt, so that he pursued the
Israelites, who were marching out boldly. 9The Egyptians—all
Pharaoh's horses and chariots, horsemen[c] and troops—pursued the
Israelites and overtook them as they camped by the sea near Pi Hahiroth, opposite Baal Zephon.
10As Pharaoh approached, the Israelites looked up, and there were

[a]18 Hebrew *Yam Suph*; that is, Sea of Reeds [b]19 See Gen. 50:25. [c]9 Or *charioteers*; also in verses 17, 18, 23, 26 and 28

OPEN 1. Who likes to read military books and watch war history in your family? **2.** Are you familiar with tidewater currents that come and go?

STUDY The Israelites have just started on their journey from Egypt to the Promised Land. They could have taken a short cut along the coast into Canaan but this stretch was well fortified with Egyptian forts. The other road was not really a road at all. It crossed the Red Sea into the desert area where Moses had spent 40 years. **1.** Would you have taken the short cut to Canaan or gone the route of Moses? **2.** What do you think the pillar of cloud by day and fire by night looked like? What was the purpose? In your spiritual journey what is the closest you have come to having these kinds of directional guides? **3.** Why do you think Pharaoh changed his mind and came after the Israelites? Was it wounded pride or the thought of losing his free labor force? What would you have done if you had been Pharaoh? **4.** When the Israelites saw the 300 chariots of Pharaoh coming after them, what did they do? Who did they blame? **5.** If you had been in Moses' shoes and God told you to start walking right up to the edge of the waters of the Red Sea, what would you have said? What did God do to keep the Egyptians from attacking until the Israelites were across the Red Sea? **6.** What do you think Moses said to his wife that night?

APPLY 1. If you were to compare your spiritual life right now to the Israelites' journey in this passage, where are you right now: Still in Egypt? Checking the map? Looking for the pillar of fire? Backed up against the Red Sea? Sticking your

13:17 Philistine country. The shorter route through this area apparently was guarded by many fortresses with armies that might try to intercept the escaping slaves. God knew that facing war with well-trained Egyptian soldiers would daunt the Israelites (even though they were prepared, v. 18), so he led them on a longer route south across the Wilderness of Sinai.

13:18 Red Sea. The name means "sea of reeds." This body of water may have included parts of the Gulf of Suez and the Gulf of Aqaba.

13:19 bones of Joseph. Joseph, previous ruler in Egypt before the Hebrews had become slaves, had believed that God would one day return his people to Canaan. He had requested that, when they returned, they take his bones with them (Gen. 50:24–25).

13:21 pillar of cloud ... pillar of fire. God stayed with his people throughout their wanderings.

14:2 turn back. God instructed Moses to turn north in the direction of their escape. The Lord's strategy for his people was not to maneuver a simple flight. Like a commander, God misled the enemy (v. 3) and planned their destruction (v. 4).

toe in the water? Seeing the waters part? **2.** How can this group help you in prayer this week?

the Egyptians, marching after them. They were terrified and cried out to the LORD. [11]They said to Moses, "Was it because there were no graves in Egypt that you brought us to the desert to die? What have you done to us by bringing us out of Egypt? [12]Didn't we say to you in Egypt, 'Leave us alone; let us serve the Egyptians'? It would have been better for us to serve the Egyptians than to die in the desert!"

[13]Moses answered the people, "Do not be afraid. Stand firm and you will see the deliverance the LORD will bring you today. The Egyptians you see today you will never see again. [14]The LORD will fight for you; you need only to be still."

[15]Then the LORD said to Moses, "Why are you crying out to me? Tell the Israelites to move on. [16]Raise your staff and stretch out your hand over the sea to divide the water so that the Israelites can go through the sea on dry ground. [17]I will harden the hearts of the Egyptians so that they will go in after them. And I will gain glory through Pharaoh and all his army, through his chariots and his horsemen. [18]The Egyptians will know that I am the LORD when I gain glory through Pharaoh, his chariots and his horsemen."

[19]Then the angel of God, who had been traveling in front of Israel's army, withdrew and went behind them. The pillar of cloud also moved from in front and stood behind them, [20]coming between the armies of Egypt and Israel. Throughout the night the cloud brought darkness to the one side and light to the other side; so neither went near the other all night long.

[21]Then Moses stretched out his hand over the sea, and all that night the LORD drove the sea back with a strong east wind and turned it into dry land. The waters were divided, [22]and the Israelites went through the sea on dry ground, with a wall of water on their right and on their left.

[23]The Egyptians pursued them, and all Pharaoh's horses and chariots and horsemen followed them into the sea. [24]During the last watch of the night the LORD looked down from the pillar of fire and cloud at the Egyptian army and threw it into confusion. [25]He made the wheels of their chariots come off[a] so that they had difficulty driving. And the Egyptians said, "Let's get away from the Israelites! The LORD is fighting for them against Egypt."

[26]Then the LORD said to Moses, "Stretch out your hand over the sea so that the waters may flow back over the Egyptians and their chariots and horsemen." [27]Moses stretched out his hand over the sea, and at daybreak the sea went back to its place. The Egyptians were fleeing

[a]25 Or *He jammed the wheels of their chariots* (see Samaritan Pentateuch, Septuagint and Syriac)

14:14 The LORD will fight for you. Both the victory and the glory belonged to God. The people were to proceed in faith.

14:20 brought darknes ... and light. The pillar of cloud that guided the Israelites now protected them. God's presence stood between his people and their enemies, putting the Egyptians in darkness and the Israelites in light. Jesus reminded the people of this contrast in John 8:12.

14:21 the LORD drove the sea back. Many differing opinions make the exact location of this sea impossible to determine. Nonetheless, God controlled nature to produce a strong east wind to divide the waters and deliver his people. The Lord had used the east wind previously to bring in the plague of locusts (10:13).

14:22 on dry ground. In this miraculous deliverance, God showed his great love by delivering the people from bondage, then saving them from destruction.

14:25 The LORD is fighting. Even the Egyptian soldiers realized that God was fighting for the Israelites (v. 14). They panicked and fled as God showed his power, just as God predicted they would (v. 4). God made the hunter afraid of the prey.

14:27 into the sea. The Lord rules over nature and everything in it. As the sea had

toward[a] it, and the LORD swept them into the sea. 28The water flowed
back and covered the chariots and horsemen—the entire army of
Pharaoh that had followed the Israelites into the sea. Not one of
them survived.
29But the Israelites went through the sea on dry ground, with a wall
of water on their right and on their left. 30That day the LORD saved
Israel from the hands of the Egyptians, and Israel saw the Egyptians
lying dead on the shore. 31And when the Israelites saw the great
power the LORD displayed against the Egyptians, the people feared
the LORD and put their trust in him and in Moses his servant.

The Song of Moses and Miriam

15 Then Moses and the Israelites sang this song to the LORD:

"I will sing to the LORD,
for he is highly exalted.
The horse and its rider
he has hurled into the sea.
2The LORD is my strength and my song;
he has become my salvation.
He is my God, and I will praise him,
my father's God, and I will exalt him.
3The LORD is a warrior;
the LORD is his name.
4Pharaoh's chariots and his army
he has hurled into the sea.
The best of Pharaoh's officers
are drowned in the Red Sea.[b]
5The deep waters have covered them;
they sank to the depths like a stone.

6"Your right hand, O LORD,
was majestic in power.
Your right hand, O LORD,
shattered the enemy.
7In the greatness of your majesty
you threw down those who opposed you.
You unleashed your burning anger;
it consumed them like stubble.
8By the blast of your nostrils
the waters piled up.
The surging waters stood firm like a wall;
the deep waters congealed in the heart of the sea.

9"The enemy boasted,
'I will pursue, I will overtake them.
I will divide the spoils;

[a]27 Or *from* [b]4 Hebrew *Yam Suph*; that is, Sea of Reeds; also in verse 22

OPEN **1.** What is the closest you have come to writing a poem? **2.** If you read poetry, what poet do you read?

STUDY This may be the oldest poem or psalm recorded in the Bible. It celebrates the victory over the army of Egypt and was intended to be sung and danced to. **1.** How would you describe the tone in this psalm? Have you ever been so happy that you just had to sing or dance? **2.** Who is this psalm directed to? What is the main theme? How is this theme developed in each stanza? Is this poem more like an opera, a rock song, or a country music song? **3.** How does the author of this psalm view God? His power? His character? **4.** In verses 13–18, what does this psalm look forward to for the Israelites?

APPLY **1.** If you were to write a poem about God's victory in your life, what event would you write about? **2.** What would be the main point of this poem? **3.** How important is music and dance in worship to you? **4.** What would it take to get you to actually write this poem? **5.** Do you think you could say in your poem that God in his strength will guide you into the future (v. 13)?

---

opened to allow the Israelites through, so it closed to stop their pursuers.

14:31 trust in him and in Moses. Prior to this miraculous deliverance, the Israelites had a morbid fear of the Egyptians (v. 10) and little respect for Moses (v. 11). Now they enjoyed a healthy fear of God and new trust in Moses' competence.

15:1–18 This song is about God's victory over the Egyptians. The Hebrews' despair and fear (14:12) has turned to joy and confidence in God. His name appears ten times.

I will gorge myself on them.
I will draw my sword
and my hand will destroy them.'
10 But you blew with your breath,
and the sea covered them.
They sank like lead
in the mighty waters.

11 "Who among the gods is like you, O LORD?
Who is like you—
majestic in holiness,
awesome in glory,
working wonders?
12 You stretched out your right hand
and the earth swallowed them.

13 "In your unfailing love you will lead
the people you have redeemed.
In your strength you will guide them
to your holy dwelling.
14 The nations will hear and tremble;
anguish will grip the people of Philistia.
15 The chiefs of Edom will be terrified,
the leaders of Moab will be seized with trembling,
the people[a] of Canaan will melt away;
16 terror and dread will fall upon them.
By the power of your arm
they will be as still as a stone—
until your people pass by, O LORD,
until the people you bought[b] pass by.
17 You will bring them in and plant them
on the mountain of your inheritance—
the place, O LORD, you made for your dwelling,
the sanctuary, O Lord, your hands established.
18 The LORD will reign
for ever and ever."

19 When Pharaoh's horses, chariots and horsemen[c] went into the
sea, the LORD brought the waters of the sea back over them, but the
Israelites walked through the sea on dry ground. 20 Then Miriam
the prophetess, Aaron's sister, took a tambourine in her hand, and all
the women followed her, with tambourines and dancing. 21 Miriam
sang to them:

"Sing to the LORD,
for he is highly exalted.

[a]15 Or *rulers* [b]16 Or *created* [c]19 Or *charioteers*

15:11 Who among the gods is like you. The Lord is above all gods. He defeated not only the Pharaoh (whom the Egyptians considered a man-god) and his soldiers, but their gods as well.

15:14–15 Philistia ... Edom ... Moab ... Canaan. News of the miraculous deliverance at the Red Sea would travel along this route, as would the Israelites after they left Mount Sinai. As God predicted (9:16; 14:4), his glory among the nations would increase as a result of the Israelites' deliverance from Egypt.

15:21 Miriam. The sister of Moses and Aaron (2:4).

The horse and its rider
he has hurled into the sea."

The Waters of Marah and Elim

[22]Then Moses led Israel from the Red Sea and they went into the
Desert of Shur. For three days they traveled in the desert without
finding water. [23]When they came to Marah, they could not drink its
water because it was bitter. (That is why the place is called Marah.[a])
[24]So the people grumbled against Moses, saying, "What are we to
drink?"
[25]Then Moses cried out to the LORD, and the LORD showed him a
piece of wood. He threw it into the water, and the water became
sweet.
There the LORD made a decree and a law for them, and there he
tested them. [26]He said, "If you listen carefully to the voice of the LORD
your God and do what is right in his eyes, if you pay attention to his
commands and keep all his decrees, I will not bring on you any of the
diseases I brought on the Egyptians, for I am the LORD, who heals
you."
[27]Then they came to Elim, where there were twelve springs and
seventy palm trees, and they camped there near the water.

Manna and Quail

16 The whole Israelite community set out from Elim and came
to the Desert of Sin, which is between Elim and Sinai, on the
fifteenth day of the second month after they had come out of Egypt.
[2]In the desert the whole community grumbled against Moses and
Aaron. [3]The Israelites said to them, "If only we had died by the LORD's
hand in Egypt! There we sat around pots of meat and ate all the food
we wanted, but you have brought us out into this desert to starve this
entire assembly to death."
[4]Then the LORD said to Moses, "I will rain down bread from heaven
for you. The people are to go out each day and gather enough for that
day. In this way I will test them and see whether they will follow my
instructions. [5]On the sixth day they are to prepare what they bring in,
and that is to be twice as much as they gather on the other days."
[6]So Moses and Aaron said to all the Israelites, "In the evening you
will know that it was the LORD who brought you out of Egypt, [7]and in
the morning you will see the glory of the LORD, because he has heard
your grumbling against him. Who are we, that you should grumble
against us?" [8]Moses also said, "You will know that it was the LORD

[a]23 *Marah* means *bitter.*

OPEN **1.** What is the longest you have gone without having a drink of water? **2.** Where was the watering hole for the teenagers in your town to hang out?

STUDY The Israelites number many thousands and there are few watering holes. **1.** If you had to describe the atmosphere in the Israelite camp in this passage, what would you say? **2.** What does Moses do about the situation? **3.** What does God promise the Israelites in return for their obedience?

APPLY What spiritual victory have you had that was followed by a time of testing?

OPEN **1.** What do you like to complain about: Traffic? Weather? Etc.? **2.** What food could you eat every day? **3.** When was the last time a new dish was served in your house and someone asked, "What is it?"

STUDY God has just delivered the Israelites from bondage in Egypt and miraculously led them through the Red Sea. Now the Israelites start complaining. In 15:22–27 they complain about the lack of water and here they complain about the lack of food. **1.** If you were Moses and you had thousands of the people complaining about everything, what would you do? **2.** Why do you think the Israelites, having seen so recently God's awesome power, could complain so soon? **3.** When the Israelites complain to Moses, what does Moses say (v. 8)? What happens while Aaron is speaking? **4.** How do you explain the

---

15:24 grumbled against Moses. Only three days into the journey, there was already discontent. The Israelites changed quickly from being joyful and trusting (vv. 1–18) to fearful and questioning. This pattern would continue for many years. Whenever life was rough, they grumbled at Moses and, ultimately, at God.

15:25 he tested them. First, the Lord provided sweet water for the Israelites, then he tested them. He did not give them water because they passed the test. He provided it, then took the opportunity (while his gift was fresh in their minds) to declare a test of their obedience.

16:3 to starve this entire assembly. How little these people understood of God. After all the miracles he had performed on their behalf in order to bring them out of Egypt, surely he had shown his love for them. Yet the people complained that he apparently had brought them out of Egypt in order to starve them in the desert.

16:4 gather enough for that day. The food God provided would keep the Israelites alive. He would provide, but they would have to trust him. The fact that they were to gather only enough for one day meant they were to trust God to provide for them daily.

sudden appearance of quail in the evening and manna in the morning for the Israelites to eat? **5.** What is the lesson for you in the instructions about gathering the manna (vv. 16–19)? What was the purpose for gathering twice as much on the sixth day? **6.** Have you ever tasted something like manna as it is described in verse 31? **7.** Why would Moses want to put a sample of the manna in the chest that the Israelites brought to the Promised Land? **8.** Do you think Moses realized when he volunteered to lead the Israelites to the Promised Land that he would have to listen to their complaints for 40 years?

APPLY 1. How would you describe your spiritual life at the moment in one or two words? **2.** How would you describe your habit of gathering manna for your spiritual life: Good? Sporadic? Bitter? Pretty bad? Awful? **3.** What have you found most helpful in developing a healthy, balanced, spiritual diet?

when he gives you meat to eat in the evening and all the bread you
want in the morning, because he has heard your grumbling against
him. Who are we? You are not grumbling against us, but against the
LORD."
9 Then Moses told Aaron, "Say to the entire Israelite community,
'Come before the LORD, for he has heard your grumbling.' "
10 While Aaron was speaking to the whole Israelite community, they
looked toward the desert, and there was the glory of the LORD
appearing in the cloud.
11 The LORD said to Moses, 12 "I have heard the grumbling of the
Israelites. Tell them, 'At twilight you will eat meat, and in the morning
you will be filled with bread. Then you will know that I am the LORD
your God.' "
13 That evening quail came and covered the camp, and in the morning there was a layer of dew around the camp. 14 When the dew was
gone, thin flakes like frost on the ground appeared on the desert
floor. 15 When the Israelites saw it, they said to each other, "What is
it?" For they did not know what it was.
Moses said to them, "It is the bread the LORD has given you to eat.
16 This is what the LORD has commanded: 'Each one is to gather as
much as he needs. Take an omer[a] for each person you have in your
tent.' "
17 The Israelites did as they were told; some gathered much, some
little. 18 And when they measured it by the omer, he who gathered
much did not have too much, and he who gathered little did not have
too little. Each one gathered as much as he needed.
19 Then Moses said to them, "No one is to keep any of it until
morning."
20 However, some of them paid no attention to Moses; they kept
part of it until morning, but it was full of maggots and began to smell.
So Moses was angry with them.
21 Each morning everyone gathered as much as he needed, and
when the sun grew hot, it melted away. 22 On the sixth day, they gathered twice as much—two omers[b] for each person—and the leaders of
the community came and reported this to Moses. 23 He said to them,
"This is what the LORD commanded: 'Tomorrow is to be a day of rest,
a holy Sabbath to the LORD. So bake what you want to bake and boil
what you want to boil. Save whatever is left and keep it until morning.' "
24 So they saved it until morning, as Moses commanded, and it did
not stink or get maggots in it. 25 "Eat it today," Moses said, "because
today is a Sabbath to the LORD. You will not find any of it on the
ground today. 26 Six days you are to gather it, but on the seventh day,
the Sabbath, there will not be any."

[a]*16* That is, probably about 2 quarts (about 2 liters); also in verses 18, 32, 33 and 36 [b]*22* That is, probably about 4 quarts (about 4.5 liters)

16:13 quail came. The meat that the Lord had promised arrived right on schedule. Later in the journey God provided quail once again, but with less satisfying results (Num. 11:31–34).

16:14 flakes like frost. Like the quail, this food came from God in an unexpected way. It came with the dew, appeared when the dew evaporated and melted in the sun.

16:23 a day of rest. This is the first occurrence of the word "Sabbath" in Scripture. However, the idea of a seventh day of rest and holiness is presented in the creation account (Gen. 2:2). Here, the Lord commanded the Israelites to observe the Sabbath and told them how.

[27]Nevertheless, some of the people went out on the seventh day to
gather it, but they found none. [28]Then the LORD said to Moses, "How
long will you[a] refuse to keep my commands and my instructions?
[29]Bear in mind that the LORD has given you the Sabbath; that is why
on the sixth day he gives you bread for two days. Everyone is to stay
where he is on the seventh day; no one is to go out." [30]So the people
rested on the seventh day.

[31]The people of Israel called the bread manna.[b] It was white like
coriander seed and tasted like wafers made with honey. [32]Moses said,
"This is what the LORD has commanded: 'Take an omer of manna and
keep it for the generations to come, so they can see the bread I gave
you to eat in the desert when I brought you out of Egypt.' "

[33]So Moses said to Aaron, "Take a jar and put an omer of manna in
it. Then place it before the LORD to be kept for the generations to
come."

[34]As the LORD commanded Moses, Aaron put the manna in front of
the Testimony, that it might be kept. [35]The Israelites ate manna forty
years, until they came to a land that was settled; they ate manna until
they reached the border of Canaan.

[36](An omer is one tenth of an ephah.)

Water From the Rock

17 The whole Israelite community set out from the Desert of
Sin, traveling from place to place as the LORD commanded.
They camped at Rephidim, but there was no water for the people to
drink. [2]So they quarreled with Moses and said, "Give us water to
drink."

Moses replied, "Why do you quarrel with me? Why do you put the
LORD to the test?"

[3]But the people were thirsty for water there, and they grumbled
against Moses. They said, "Why did you bring us up out of Egypt to
make us and our children and livestock die of thirst?"

[4]Then Moses cried out to the LORD, "What am I to do with these
people? They are almost ready to stone me."

[a]28 The Hebrew is plural. [b]31 *Manna* means *What is it?* (see verse 15).

OPEN Where is there a natural spring in your area, where you can drink the water?

STUDY The Israelites are back to complaining on their journey through the desert. **1.** Do you sympathize a little with the Israelites for the lack of water in the desert? **2.** Do you feel like Moses is getting a little upset with the Israelites? Are you more like Moses or the Israelites in this story? **3.** What is the lesson in verses 5–7 for dealing with people who are ready to revolt?

APPLY How do you deal with complaints when you are in a

16:31 manna. Many naturalistic, unsatisfying explanations of manna have been suggested. It came in the form of thin flakes (v. 14), looked like resin (Num. 11:7), was white like coriander seed (Num. 11:7) and tasted like honey wafers (16:31) or "something made with olive oil" (Num. 11:8). As Exodus 16:15 indicates, the Israelites did not recognize manna as a naturally occurring food. It was God's unique provision for his people in a time of need.

16:34 in front of the Testimony. Moses was getting a little ahead of himself. After he received the Ten Commandments ("two tablets of the Testimony," 31:18), and they were placed in the Ark of the Covenant, the ark was called the "ark of the Testimony," along with a jar of manna (Heb. 9:4). Though that event was still some time in the future, Moses here referred to the ark by this name.

16:35 ate manna forty years. As in verse 34, Moses was anticipating the future. The manna continued until the Israelites celebrated their first Passover in Canaan. After that, they ate the "produce of the land" (Josh. 5:10–12).

17:1 traveling ... as the LORD commanded. The people followed the pillars of cloud and fire, moving when they moved, stopping when they stopped (13:21; 40:36–38). The Lord was guiding his people along this route, and oddly enough, guided them to a location where there was no water. Clearly God was going to test the people's willingness to trust in his provision. He had already shown them that he would provide both food and water; what would happen this time?

17:2 Why do you put the LORD to the test? The Lord had promised the Israelites he would provide for them, and their response to his provision would be a test for them (16:4). By demanding water from Moses, they failed the test by not trusting the Lord. Not only were they questioning God's ability to provide, but they were certainly also testing his patience.

17:4 Moses cried out to the LORD. Previously, the people had complained that Moses had brought them into the desert to starve (16:3). Here they grumbled that Moses must have brought them into the desert to die of thirst. God had always met their needs, already having provided water for them (15:23–25). When the Israelites grumbled to Moses, he took the issue to God. He was forced into an intermediary role

position of responsibility? Do you tend to panic and scream at God?

OPEN When you were a kid, how often did you hold up your hand in class?

STUDY The Amalekites are the descendants of Esau. **1.** What is different about the attack of the Amalekites from the previous problems Moses has had to face? Would this be more difficult for you to handle? **2.** What is the significance of Moses holding up his hands for the Israelites to see during the battle? **3.** What is the lesson here in having Aaron and Hur to steady Moses' hands when Moses got weary?

APPLY What is the battle you are facing right now where you could use some support?

OPEN 1. Growing up, how were arguments settled in your family? **2.** What is the longest time you have been away from your spouse and children *or* from your family?

STUDY When Moses fled Egypt 40 years before, after killing an Egyptian, he lived with Jethro, his father-in-law, in the desert and married his daughter. Now, 40 years later, Jethro meets up with his son-in-law when Moses returns to the desert

[5]The LORD answered Moses, "Walk on ahead of the people. Take
with you some of the elders of Israel and take in your hand the staff
with which you struck the Nile, and go. [6]I will stand there before you
by the rock at Horeb. Strike the rock, and water will come out of it for
the people to drink." So Moses did this in the sight of the elders of
Israel. [7]And he called the place Massah[a] and Meribah[b] because the
Israelites quarreled and because they tested the LORD saying, "Is the
LORD among us or not?"

The Amalekites Defeated

[8]The Amalekites came and attacked the Israelites at Rephidim.
[9]Moses said to Joshua, "Choose some of our men and go out to fight
the Amalekites. Tomorrow I will stand on top of the hill with the staff
of God in my hands."
[10]So Joshua fought the Amalekites as Moses had ordered, and Moses, Aaron and Hur went to the top of the hill. [11]As long as Moses held
up his hands, the Israelites were winning, but whenever he lowered
his hands, the Amalekites were winning. [12]When Moses' hands grew
tired, they took a stone and put it under him and he sat on it. Aaron
and Hur held his hands up—one on one side, one on the other—so
that his hands remained steady till sunset. [13]So Joshua overcame the
Amalekite army with the sword.
[14]Then the LORD said to Moses, "Write this on a scroll as something
to be remembered and make sure that Joshua hears it, because I will
completely blot out the memory of Amalek from under heaven."
[15]Moses built an altar and called it The LORD is my Banner. [16]He
said, "For hands were lifted up to the throne of the LORD. The[c] LORD
will be at war against the Amalekites from generation to generation."

Jethro Visits Moses

18 Now Jethro, the priest of Midian and father-in-law of Moses,
heard of everything God had done for Moses and for his
people Israel, and how the LORD had brought Israel out of Egypt.
[2]After Moses had sent away his wife Zipporah, his father-in-law
Jethro received her [3]and her two sons. One son was named
Gershom,[d] for Moses said, "I have become an alien in a foreign land";
[4]and the other was named Eliezer,[e] for he said, "My father's God was
my helper; he saved me from the sword of Pharaoh."

[a]7 *Massah* means *testing.* [b]7 *Meribah* means *quarreling.* [c]16 Or *"Because a hand was against the throne of the LORD, the* [d]3 *Gershom* sounds like the Hebrew for *an alien there.* [e]4 *Eliezer* means *my God is helper.*

much like the later prophets of Israel would have. In this instance, he felt alienation, frustration and fear. The nation later had become "these people" instead of "my people," for they were so rebellious they were ready to kill him.

17:6 Strike the rock, and water will come out of it. Again, God's *miraculous power and love for his people* were channeled through Moses.

17:7 Massah and Meribah. Psalm 95:7–8 and Hebrews 3:7–8,15 refer to the events of verses 1–7. These passages define "Massah" as "temptation" and "Meribah" as "rebellion." Both names carry ominous connotations and are reminders of the Israelites' lack of faith and obedience.

17:9 Joshua. Moses chose a man who possessed military prowess. Both this incident and the conquest of Canaan forty years later demonstrated Moses' ability to pick the right man for the job. Joshua's faith in God made him a worthy leader of the Israelites (Deut. 34:9).

17:11 held up his hands. The soldiers fought the battle, but God determined the outcome. Moses held his staff above his head to appeal for God's help and as a symbol of the Israelites' total dependence on God for victory.

18:2 Zipporah. Moses sent his wife to her father with the good news that the Israelites had successfully left Egypt. Domestic and political reasons likely played a role, too. Midianites could become either allies or enemies to the Israelites, and Jethro could be influential. Zipporah is never mentioned

[5]Jethro, Moses' father-in-law, together with Moses' sons and wife,
came to him in the desert, where he was camped near the mountain
of God. [6]Jethro had sent word to him, "I, your father-in-law Jethro,
am coming to you with your wife and her two sons."
[7]So Moses went out to meet his father-in-law and bowed down and
kissed him. They greeted each other and then went into the tent.
[8]Moses told his father-in-law about everything the LORD had done to
Pharaoh and the Egyptians for Israel's sake and about all the hardships they had met along the way and how the LORD had saved them.
[9]Jethro was delighted to hear about all the good things the LORD
had done for Israel in rescuing them from the hand of the Egyptians.
[10]He said, "Praise be to the LORD, who rescued you from the hand of
the Egyptians and of Pharaoh, and who rescued the people from the
hand of the Egyptians. [11]Now I know that the LORD is greater than all
other gods, for he did this to those who had treated Israel arrogantly." [12]Then Jethro, Moses' father-in-law, brought a burnt offering
and other sacrifices to God, and Aaron came with all the elders of
Israel to eat bread with Moses' father-in-law in the presence of God.
[13]The next day Moses took his seat to serve as judge for the people,
and they stood around him from morning till evening. [14]When his
father-in-law saw all that Moses was doing for the people, he said,
"What is this you are doing for the people? Why do you alone sit as
judge, while all these people stand around you from morning till
evening?"
[15]Moses answered him, "Because the people come to me to seek
God's will. [16]Whenever they have a dispute, it is brought to me, and I
decide between the parties and inform them of God's decrees and
laws."
[17]Moses' father-in-law replied, "What you are doing is not good.
[18]You and these people who come to you will only wear yourselves
out. The work is too heavy for you; you cannot handle it alone. [19]Lis-
ten now to me and I will give you some advice, and may God be with
you. You must be the people's representative before God and bring
their disputes to him. [20]Teach them the decrees and laws, and show
them the way to live and the duties they are to perform. [21]But select
capable men from all the people—men who fear God, trustworthy
men who hate dishonest gain—and appoint them as officials over
thousands, hundreds, fifties and tens. [22]Have them serve as judges
for the people at all times, but have them bring every difficult case to
you; the simple cases they can decide themselves. That will make
your load lighter, because they will share it with you. [23]If you do this
and God so commands, you will be able to stand the strain, and all
these people will go home satisfied."
[24]Moses listened to his father-in-law and did everything he said.
[25]He chose capable men from all Israel and made them leaders of the

with thousands of Israelites that he is responsible for. **1.** Why do you think Jethro decided to visit his son-in-law? **2.** How would you describe their meeting? How would you have felt if you had not seen your father-in-law for awhile? **3.** What did Jethro pick up on by observing the way Moses was dealing with disputes among the Israelites? Why hadn't Moses seen this problem himself? **4.** How would you describe the organizational chart that Jethro recommends? Do you think this structure could work in the church today? What would it look like? How would you organize it? **5.** How would you describe the relationship of Moses and his father-in-law Jethro? **6.** How long do you think Jethro stayed for this visit? How long do you recommend for in-laws to stay when they visit?

APPLY **1.** How would you describe your relationship with your in-laws or future in-laws? **2.** If you are the "in-laws" how far do you go in giving advice to your son or daughter-in-law? **3.** What do you do when you see something they are doing that is "not good"? What is one subject you never give your son or daughter-in-law advice on?

again. It is possible that Moses married another woman (Num. 12:1).

18:11 Now I know. God's victory over the Egyptians brought him glory as he predicted (14:4). Whether Jethro was a true convert or simply a well-meaning Midianite priest is not explained. Some Samaritans had a similar response to Jesus (John 4:42).

18:12 eat bread with. Sharing bread or a meal was a sign of friendship, a means of sealing an agreement and sometimes an act of profound religious significance (Jesus' last meal with his disciples).

18:14 you alone sit as judge. Moses was driven to do everything himself. Jethro provides wise counsel.

18:16 God's decrees and laws. Moses led by right of divine calling, so his authority was from God even in practical matters. God's decrees and laws extended into all areas of life, not just the spiritual.

people, officials over thousands, hundreds, fifties and tens. [26]They served as judges for the people at all times. The difficult cases they brought to Moses, but the simple ones they decided themselves.

[27]Then Moses sent his father-in-law on his way, and Jethro returned to his own country.

At Mount Sinai

19 In the third month after the Israelites left Egypt—on the very day—they came to the Desert of Sinai. [2]After they set out from Rephidim, they entered the Desert of Sinai, and Israel camped there in the desert in front of the mountain.

[3]Then Moses went up to God, and the LORD called to him from the mountain and said, "This is what you are to say to the house of Jacob and what you are to tell the people of Israel: [4]'You yourselves have seen what I did to Egypt, and how I carried you on eagles' wings and brought you to myself. [5]Now if you obey me fully and keep my covenant, then out of all nations you will be my treasured possession. Although the whole earth is mine, [6]you[a] will be for me a kingdom of priests and a holy nation.' These are the words you are to speak to the Israelites."

[7]So Moses went back and summoned the elders of the people and set before them all the words the LORD had commanded him to speak. [8]The people all responded together, "We will do everything the LORD has said." So Moses brought their answer back to the LORD.

[9]The LORD said to Moses, "I am going to come to you in a dense cloud, so that the people will hear me speaking with you and will always put their trust in you." Then Moses told the LORD what the people had said.

[10]And the LORD said to Moses, "Go to the people and consecrate them today and tomorrow. Have them wash their clothes [11]and be ready by the third day, because on that day the LORD will come down on Mount Sinai in the sight of all the people. [12]Put limits for the people around the mountain and tell them, 'Be careful that you do not go up the mountain or touch the foot of it. Whoever touches the mountain shall surely be put to death. [13]He shall surely be stoned or shot with arrows; not a hand is to be laid on him. Whether man or animal, he shall not be permitted to live.' Only when the ram's horn sounds a long blast may they go up to the mountain."

[14]After Moses had gone down the mountain to the people, he consecrated them, and they washed their clothes. [15]Then he said to the

[a]5,6 *Or possession, for the whole earth is mine.* [6]*You*

OPEN Have you ever seen how the wind will lift the wings of an eagle and help the eagle to soar?

STUDY It has been three months since God delivered the Israelites from the bondage of the Egyptians. They are homeless without a lot of structure and no laws. Moses has brought them back to the area where he lived for 40 years and pauses in the journey to let the people regroup and receive instructions for the new nation to be created. **1.** If you were Moses and your nerves were already frazzled after three months of trying to lead the Israelites, what would you do? **2.** What basically did the Lord do with Moses when he went on a little spiritual retreat to recharge his batteries (vv. 3–6)? What did God promise the Israelites would become? **3.** When Moses got home from his retreat with God, what did he do? How did the leaders respond? **4.** When Moses went back to talk with God, how would you describe the plan that God laid out for Moses to teach the Israelites the awesome power of God? Why require the people to clean up? Why the boundary limits around the mountain? **5.** If you had been in the audience on the third day when the mountain started to erupt with smoke, how would you have felt? What do you think the Israelites learned in this experience that they could not learn in any other way? **6.** How important do you think this experience at the foot of the mountain was for the people in receiving the Ten Commandments?

19:4 eagles' wings. The strength and majesty of the eagle is used as a recurring image of God in his role as savior. Isaiah 40:31 shows this strength being given to those who "hope in the LORD."

19:5 obey me fully and keep my covenant. God made a covenant with Israel at Mount Sinai based on obedience. This covenant was an extension of the one God had made with Abraham hundreds of years before. According to the covenant, Israel's obedience would result in being favored by God and given a special role in his kingdom.

19:6 holy nation. God's people would be different from all the other peoples and would be given the special task of representing God.

19:9 put their trust in you. God was concerned with Israel's relationship with Moses. To fulfill the covenant, Israel needed strong leadership. By speaking to Moses so all could hear, God strengthened Moses' authority.

19:10 consecrate them. The Israelites had to be purified before entering the presence of God. Ceremonial cleansing involved washing clothes, not a regular desert chore. This outward purification symbolizes the inner consecration God demands from his people.

19:12 Put limits. God set limits to protect his holiness and their future. God could not tolerate the unholy in his presence. Even the mountain where he will descend must be consecrated and kept clean from all corruption.

people, "Prepare yourselves for the third day. Abstain from sexual
relations."
16On the morning of the third day there was thunder and lightning,
with a thick cloud over the mountain, and a very loud trumpet blast.
Everyone in the camp trembled. 17Then Moses led the people out
of the camp to meet with God, and they stood at the foot of the
mountain. 18Mount Sinai was covered with smoke, because the LORD
descended on it in fire. The smoke billowed up from it like smoke
from a furnace, the whole mountain[a] trembled violently, 19and the
sound of the trumpet grew louder and louder. Then Moses spoke and
the voice of God answered him.[b]
20The LORD descended to the top of Mount Sinai and called Moses
to the top of the mountain. So Moses went up 21and the LORD said to
him, "Go down and warn the people so they do not force their way
through to see the LORD and many of them perish. 22Even the priests,
who approach the LORD, must consecrate themselves, or the LORD
will break out against them."
23Moses said to the LORD, "The people cannot come up Mount Sinai, because you yourself warned us, 'Put limits around the mountain
and set it apart as holy.'"
24The LORD replied, "Go down and bring Aaron up with you. But the
priests and the people must not force their way through to come up
to the LORD, or he will break out against them."
25So Moses went down to the people and told them.

APPLY **1.** As you think back on your spiritual pilgrimage, where was the "mountain" where you first experienced God in a personal way? **2.** When is the last time you went away to a mountain to recharge your spiritual batteries? Do you need a good recharge right now?

The Ten Commandments

20 And God spoke all these words:

2"I am the LORD your God, who brought you out of Egypt,
out of the land of slavery.
3"You shall have no other gods before[c] me.
4"You shall not make for yourself an idol in the form of anything
in heaven above or on the earth beneath or in the waters
below. 5You shall not bow down to them or worship them;
for I, the LORD your God, am a jealous God, punishing the
children for the sin of the fathers to the third and fourth
generation of those who hate me, 6but showing love to a
thousand ⌞generations⌟ of those who love me and keep my
commandments.

[a]18 Most Hebrew manuscripts; a few Hebrew manuscripts and Septuagint *all the people* [b]19 Or *and God answered him with thunder* [c]3 Or *besides*

OPEN **1.** Who laid down the law in your family when you were a child? **2.** What was the most important rule in your family? What happened when you broke this rule?

STUDY While the Israelites were camped at the base of Mount Sinai, God appeared to them in a demonstration of his power. Moses went to be with God on the mountain and received what has come to be called the Ten Commandments. **1.** What does God remind the people of before he gives them the Ten Commandments? **2.** For the Israelites who have lived for 400 years in Egypt with a multitude of gods, what does God want to make clear to the Israelites? What will be the consequences if the

19:15 sexual relations. This was a temporary abstinence so that they would be ritually clean.

19:22 priests. This was before the priesthood was established as an institution. That system would change with the founding of the priesthood under Aaron.

20:2 I am the LORD your God. Before God gave the Law to his people, he asserted his authority to do so. Israel had agreed to a covenant relationship with God (19:8). Here, God put that relationship into words and gave it a historical context.

20:3 no other gods before me. This commandment followed directly from the relationship described in verse 2. God asserted his authority over the Israelites and commanded them to live in submission to that authority. They had to make God the single ruler of their lives and hearts.

20:4 idol. Idolatry was common in the days of the exodus. Making an image of God would be limiting, insulting and inaccurate.

20:5–6 punishing ... showing love. Rejecting the covenant with God had terrible consequences for the individual, his family and the community. This punishment was due to the breakdown of the relationship between God and his people. Because of his holiness and love, God would not tolerate being rejected or replaced. Similarly, returning God's love in kind yielded abundant blessings.

Israelites start to worship other gods? What is the message here for our country today? **3.** How far do you take the commandment about misusing the name of the Lord? **4.** Of the first four commandments which one do you feel is most abused today in your society? **5.** What shift do you see in the focus in the last six commandments? **6.** How did Jesus restate the commandments about murder and adultery in the Sermon on the Mount (Matt. 5:2–30)? What was Jesus getting at? **7.** What is the point that Paul makes in Romans 7:7–8 and 14–15 about the purpose of the Law?

APPLY 1. What did you find out when you tried to live a clean, moral, honest and sin-free life? **2.** What are the gods that you have to face on a daily basis that our society worships? **3.** What have you found helpful in keeping your focus on God?

OPEN Where do you put the altar in your church?

7 "You shall not misuse the name of the LORD your God, for the LORD will not hold anyone guiltless who misuses his name.
8 "Remember the Sabbath day by keeping it holy. 9 Six days you shall labor and do all your work, 10 but the seventh day is a Sabbath to the LORD your God. On it you shall not do any work, neither you, nor your son or daughter, nor your manservant or maidservant, nor your animals, nor the alien within your gates. 11 For in six days the LORD made the heavens and the earth, the sea, and all that is in them, but he rested on the seventh day. Therefore the LORD blessed the Sabbath day and made it holy.
12 "Honor your father and your mother, so that you may live long in the land the LORD your God is giving you.
13 "You shall not murder.
14 "You shall not commit adultery.
15 "You shall not steal.
16 "You shall not give false testimony against your neighbor.
17 "You shall not covet your neighbor's house. You shall not covet your neighbor's wife, or his manservant or maidservant, his ox or donkey, or anything that belongs to your neighbor."

18 When the people saw the thunder and lightning and heard the
trumpet and saw the mountain in smoke, they trembled with fear.
They stayed at a distance 19 and said to Moses, "Speak to us yourself
and we will listen. But do not have God speak to us or we will die."
20 Moses said to the people, "Do not be afraid. God has come to
test you, so that the fear of God will be with you to keep you from sinning."
21 The people remained at a distance, while Moses approached the
thick darkness where God was.

Idols and Altars

22 Then the LORD said to Moses, "Tell the Israelites this: 'You have
seen for yourselves that I have spoken to you from heaven: 23 Do not

20:7 name of the LORD. Using God's name in a way that brings disrespect to his character is a misuse of his name. Making an oath using the name of God and then failing to keep that oath (22:10,11; Lev. 19:12) was to question his existence. God's name is holy and should never be used to suit our own needs.

20:8 Remember the Sabbath day. God commanded the Israelites to set aside the Sabbath as a day to remember and cultivate their relationship with God. God had rested on the seventh day of creation. He commanded that all work stop so that everyone, including servants, could participate in a day of rest and renewal.

20:12 Honor your father and your mother. After defining the proper relationship between people (vv. 2–11), the Law sets forth the right relationship between parents and children. Israelites' sons and daughters are to treat their parents with adoration, respect and obedience—exactly what he demanded from them.

20:14 adultery. This commandment helped define the relationship between man and woman. Marriage is a relationship of faithfulness. Adultery is a sin against the marriage relationship itself (Gen. 39:9).

20:17 shall not covet. God commands against unhealthy desire or lust for things that belong to someone else. A stable society based on mutual respect requires such a law. Too much "wanting" is the road to ruin for a person trying to lead a righteous life.

20:18 trembled with fear. Israel responded to God's presence with fear and awe. The intensity of these feelings led to their request for a mediator between themselves and God—a request that was granted in several different forms. Moses suggested that the people's fear could have a positive effect: obedience.

20:20 come to test you. Moses seemed to contradict himself by telling the Israelites not to be afraid, then telling them that fear would help them obey. Actually, he tried to comfort the Israelites by assuring them that they were in no physical danger. He went on to say, however, that their fear was the right reaction to the "Lord your God" because it would help them obey his commands. In this way, Moses defined "fear" of God not as terror but as dread of the consequences of sin.

20:22 I have spoken to you. Though

make any gods to be alongside me; do not make for yourselves gods
of silver or gods of gold.
24“ ‘Make an altar of earth for me and sacrifice on it your burnt offerings and fellowship offerings,[a] your sheep and goats and your cattle. Wherever I cause my name to be honored, I will come to you and
bless you. 25If you make an altar of stones for me, do not build it with
dressed stones, for you will defile it if you use a tool on it. 26And do
not go up to my altar on steps, lest your nakedness be exposed on it.’

21 “These are the laws you are to set before them:

Hebrew Servants

2“If you buy a Hebrew servant, he is to serve you for six years. But
in the seventh year, he shall go free, without paying anything. 3If he
comes alone, he is to go free alone; but if he has a wife when
he comes, she is to go with him. 4If his master gives him a wife and
she bears him sons or daughters, the woman and her children shall
belong to her master, and only the man shall go free.
5“But if the servant declares, ‘I love my master and my wife and
children and do not want to go free,’ 6then his master must take him
before the judges.[b] He shall take him to the door or the doorpost and
pierce his ear with an awl. Then he will be his servant for life.
7“If a man sells his daughter as a servant, she is not to go free as
menservants do. 8If she does not please the master who has selected
her for himself,[c] he must let her be redeemed. He has no right to sell
her to foreigners, because he has broken faith with her. 9If he selects
her for his son, he must grant her the rights of a daughter. 10If he
marries another woman, he must not deprive the first one of her
food, clothing and marital rights. 11If he does not provide her with
these three things, she is to go free, without any payment of money.

Personal Injuries

12“Anyone who strikes a man and kills him shall surely be put to
death. 13However, if he does not do it intentionally, but God lets it
happen, he is to flee to a place I will designate. 14But if a man

[a]24 Traditionally *peace offerings* [b]6 Or *before God* [c]8 Or *master so that he does not choose her*

STUDY What do you see in the rules about making handmade gods and polished altars to worship?

APPLY If God were to speak to the church today, what would he warn the church about?

OPEN If you could be slave for a day to someone, who would you choose?

STUDY The Israelites have just been liberated from Egypt. Now, they will need to develop a set of laws for their society to function. **1.** How does God's law about the Israelites owning another Israelite differ from their days in serving Pharaoh? **2.** What is God protecting here? **3.** How will this affect class barriers? **4.** Do these laws condone slavery? How do these laws differ from the slave laws in America before the Civil War?

APPLY **1.** What is the closest you have come to feeling enslaved by others? **2.** How does your treatment of employees and fellow workers apply to God's rules here?

OPEN How were you punished as a child? Did the punishment vary with the seriousness of the offense?

STUDY As long as the Israelites were in Egypt,

God had “descended to the top of Mount Sinai” (19:20), he was still speaking from his dwelling place in heaven.

20:23–23:19 These verses are an expansion and explanation of the Ten Commandments. Like the Commandments, these explanations focused on relationships between God, the people, *families and society as a whole.* They provided practical instruction on the proper conduct of a righteous life.

20:23 gods of silver or gods of gold. God is everywhere—capable of speaking from heaven while present on Mount Sinai. It is impossible to represent him with an idol (vv. 4–6), and no other god is worthy of being in his presence.

20:24 altar of earth. An altar of earth could be built anywhere. It did not require riches, just commitment. Instead of gold or silver idols, God commanded the Israelites to make offerings of the resources they had—sheep, goats and cattle.

20:25 dressed stones. It is not clear why shaping a stone with a tool defiled it. Perhaps it was because the pagans built that way (just as they built idols). It may also be that “undressed” stones are easy to find in the Middle East, so an altar of stones could be built wherever and whenever Israel desired.

20:26 steps ... nakedness. If a man walked up steps, his body could be exposed before God (and possibly other worshipers). Priests serving at such altars were instructed to wear linen underclothes (28:42).

21:2 Hebrew servant. It was not unlawful to have a Hebrew servant. Since the Hebrews were God's servants as well, servitude was never, like slavery, perpetual, except by the servant's own choice, as noted in verse 6.

21:12–14 lets it happen ... deliberately. Murder was defined precisely. The law distinguished between intentional and accidental killing. Murder (intentional killing) was an evil act, literally “boiling up” against God and humankind (20:13). Accidental manslaughter was terrible, but the punishment was not as severe and

the Israelites basically had no rights. They were the property of Pharaoh. Now they have to develop domestic laws to cover all kinds of situations. **1.** As you read over these laws, do they seem fair and reasonable to you? **2.** What situations require the death penalty? How would these compare to today? **3.** What are the three or four situations where compensation is required? **4.** The Old Testament law on domestic violence has been characterized by the words "an eye for an eye and a tooth for a tooth." Do you think the rules in this passage are that simple? **5.** Could you have ruled on domestic issues within those laws if you were a judge? Were they fair?

APPLY **1.** What do you believe about punishment for situations today involving domestic violence, spouse abuse and crimes against humanity? **2.** Are you for laws that mandate punishment or maximum time in jail for certain crimes?

schemes and kills another man deliberately, take him away from my
altar and put him to death.
15"Anyone who attacks[a] his father or his mother must be put to
death.
16"Anyone who kidnaps another and either sells him or still has
him when he is caught must be put to death.
17"Anyone who curses his father or mother must be put to death.
18"If men quarrel and one hits the other with a stone or with his
fist[b] and he does not die but is confined to bed, 19the one who struck
the blow will not be held responsible if the other gets up and walks
around outside with his staff; however, he must pay the injured man
for the loss of his time and see that he is completely healed.
20"If a man beats his male or female slave with a rod and the slave
dies as a direct result, he must be punished, 21but he is not to be punished if the slave gets up after a day or two, since the slave is his
property.
22"If men who are fighting hit a pregnant woman and she gives
birth prematurely[c] but there is no serious injury, the offender must be
fined whatever the woman's husband demands and the court allows.
23But if there is serious injury, you are to take life for life, 24eye for
eye, tooth for tooth, hand for hand, foot for foot, 25burn for burn,
wound for wound, bruise for bruise.
26"If a man hits a manservant or maidservant in the eye and
destroys it, he must let the servant go free to compensate for the eye.
27And if he knocks out the tooth of a manservant or maidservant, he
must let the servant go free to compensate for the tooth.
28"If a bull gores a man or a woman to death, the bull must be
stoned to death, and its meat must not be eaten. But the owner of the
bull will not be held responsible. 29If, however, the bull has had the
habit of goring and the owner has been warned but has not kept it
penned up and it kills a man or woman, the bull must be stoned and
the owner also must be put to death. 30However, if payment is
demanded of him, he may redeem his life by paying whatever is
demanded. 31This law also applies if the bull gores a son or daughter.
32If the bull gores a male or female slave, the owner must pay thirty

[a]15 Or *kills* [b]18 Or *with a tool* [c]22 Or *she has a miscarriage*

allowed for escape to a city of refuge (Num. 35:9–34).

21:20–21 slave is his property. The law did not prohibit slavery. It did, however, place limitations on the slaveholder. A slave was not mere property. This verse was included in the section of law concerned with criminal acts against people, and the implication of that should not be ignored.

21:23 serious injury. This injury could be to the mother, child or both. This fact weakens the case for rigid application of the law of retaliation; a person killing mother and child would have only one life to give up as punishment.

21:24 life for life, eye for eye. This is often misquoted and misunderstood. The law did not promote retaliation. The focus of the law was that the punishment for an offense should fit the severity of the offense. That legal approach was as much a protection for the offender as it was of the victim.

21:28 bull must be stoned. Even though the bull is not capable of deciding right from wrong, it must take the penalty for its actions. But this also protected the owner, who would come under intense community criticism if the bull repeatedly (and each time with an animal's moral innocence) killed or injured someone.

21:30 redeem his life by paying. A man could save his own life by paying a ransom to the victim or the victim's family. This payment was not compensation for the offense. It was simply a price the offender must pay to stay alive. For the believer, Jesus paid the ransom with his life so that those who believe in him might live.

21:32 thirty shekels of silver. This was the price of a slave, a large sum of money. Judas' payment to betray Jesus (Matt. 26:14).

shekels[a] of silver to the master of the slave, and the bull must be
stoned.
33 "If a man uncovers a pit or digs one and fails to cover it and an ox
or a donkey falls into it, 34 the owner of the pit must pay for the loss;
he must pay its owner, and the dead animal will be his.
35 "If a man's bull injures the bull of another and it dies, they are to
sell the live one and divide both the money and the dead animal
equally. 36 However, if it was known that the bull had the habit of
goring, yet the owner did not keep it penned up, the owner must pay,
animal for animal, and the dead animal will be his.

Protection of Property

22 "If a man steals an ox or a sheep and slaughters it or sells it,
he must pay back five head of cattle for the ox and four
sheep for the sheep.
2 "If a thief is caught breaking in and is struck so that he dies, the
defender is not guilty of bloodshed; 3 but if it happens[b] after sunrise,
he is guilty of bloodshed.
"A thief must certainly make restitution, but if he has nothing, he
must be sold to pay for his theft.
4 "If the stolen animal is found alive in his possession—whether ox
or donkey or sheep—he must pay back double.
5 "If a man grazes his livestock in a field or vineyard and lets them
stray and they graze in another man's field, he must make restitution
from the best of his own field or vineyard.
6 "If a fire breaks out and spreads into thornbushes so that it burns
shocks of grain or standing grain or the whole field, the one who
started the fire must make restitution.
7 "If a man gives his neighbor silver or goods for safekeeping and
they are stolen from the neighbor's house, the thief, if he is caught,
must pay back double. 8 But if the thief is not found, the owner of the
house must appear before the judges[c] to determine whether he has
laid his hands on the other man's property. 9 In all cases of illegal possession of an ox, a donkey, a sheep, a garment, or any other lost
property about which somebody says, 'This is mine,' both parties are
to bring their cases before the judges. The one whom the judges
declare[d] guilty must pay back double to his neighbor.
10 "If a man gives a donkey, an ox, a sheep or any other animal to his
neighbor for safekeeping and it dies or is injured or is taken away
while no one is looking, 11 the issue between them will be settled by
the taking of an oath before the LORD that the neighbor did not lay

[a]32 That is, about 12 ounces (about 0.3 kilogram) [b]3 Or *if he strikes him* [c]8 Or *before God*; also in verse 9 [d]9 Or *whom God declares*

OPEN **1.** What is the most personal thing that you have had stolen? **2.** What was the rule in your family if you broke something that was not yours?

STUDY Moses may be one of the first great lawgivers. His practical rules for protection of property are the foundation for much of the laws that we have now. **1.** Why are laws necessary in a society where everyone is governed and guided by God? **2.** Reading between the lines, what do you think must be happening in the community of the Israelites to make these practical rules necessary? How would you like to be in charge of thousands of nomads with these problems? **3.** Which one of these rules would you have a problem with or disagree with? **4.** What is the guiding principle in these rules for making restitution? **5.** How do these laws limit liability when the damage was unintentional? **6.** How are differences of opinion to be decided? **7.** How would these laws apply today to property theft of music, tapes, videos, computer programs, etc.?

APPLY **1.** What is the closest you have come to having a property dispute? How did you settle this dispute? **2.** What did you learn from this experience that has made you wiser and happier today?

22:1–15 *These property rights laws* focused both on the nature of the offense and the proper restitution. The restitution was in the form of compensation, not punishment. The only exception was one specific instance when a crime against property escalated into a crime against a person.

22:3 after sunrise, he is guilty of bloodshed. It was not permitted to kill a prowler during the day. Because the killer could see the intruder, some level of premeditation would exist. This also may imply that the person is killed later after the sun has risen so that it would be premeditated.

22:5 lets them stray. There could be great temptation to allow one's animals to eat someone else's food. A restitution of identical means and amount would not be punishment at all. However, being forced to give up the "best" of a vineyard or field would serve as a just punishment and deterrent.

22:6 If a fire breaks out. A man was to be held responsible for his actions, the actions of his animals (21:28–36) and for events he set in motion. Preventing arson was not the intent of this provision, but arson would certainly be covered by this law.

hands on the other person's property. The owner is to accept this, and no restitution is required. [12]But if the animal was stolen from the neighbor, he must make restitution to the owner. [13]If it was torn to pieces by a wild animal, he shall bring in the remains as evidence and he will not be required to pay for the torn animal.

[14]"If a man borrows an animal from his neighbor and it is injured or dies while the owner is not present, he must make restitution. [15]But if the owner is with the animal, the borrower will not have to pay. If the animal was hired, the money paid for the hire covers the loss.

Social Responsibility

[16]"If a man seduces a virgin who is not pledged to be married and sleeps with her, he must pay the bride-price, and she shall be his wife. [17]If her father absolutely refuses to give her to him, he must still pay the bride-price for virgins.

[18]"Do not allow a sorceress to live.

[19]"Anyone who has sexual relations with an animal must be put to death.

[20]"Whoever sacrifices to any god other than the LORD must be destroyed.[a]

[21]"Do not mistreat an alien or oppress him, for you were aliens in Egypt.

[22]"Do not take advantage of a widow or an orphan. [23]If you do and they cry out to me, I will certainly hear their cry. [24]My anger will be aroused, and I will kill you with the sword; your wives will become widows and your children fatherless.

[25]"If you lend money to one of my people among you who is needy, do not be like a moneylender; charge him no interest.[b] [26]If you take your neighbor's cloak as a pledge, return it to him by sunset, [27]because his cloak is the only covering he has for his body. What else will he sleep in? When he cries out to me, I will hear, for I am compassionate.

[28]"Do not blaspheme God[c] or curse the ruler of your people.

[29]"Do not hold back offerings from your granaries or your vats.[d]

"You must give me the firstborn of your sons. [30]Do the same with your cattle and your sheep. Let them stay with their mothers for seven days, but give them to me on the eighth day.

[a]20 The Hebrew term refers to the irrevocable giving over of things or persons to the LORD, often by totally destroying them. [b]25 Or *excessive interest* [c]28 Or *Do not revile the judges* [d]29 The meaning of the Hebrew for this phrase is uncertain.

OPEN When you were growing up, who did your parents tell you that you could not play with?

STUDY The Israelites were to be "my holy people" (v. 31) and as such needed rules for living among pagan people with a different set of moral standards. Some of the rules in this passage may sound bizarre, but they must be studied in the context of that day. **1.** What do you think is the basic assumption behind all of these laws? **2.** Of the ten rules in this passage, which one do you have a problem with if you have any? **3.** What is the warning here on taking advantage of aliens, widows, orphans and poor people who come to you for loans? **4.** Do you think the church today could do more to care for the needs of society?

APPLY 1. What is the closest you have come to living in a pagan culture where the moral standards were non-existent? **2.** What group of people in our society is God laying on your heart? What are you doing about it?

22:16 bride-price. In order to get a wife, a man was required to pay his future father-in-law for the privilege. In this case the man who has violated the man's daughter must satisfy the father, a steep price could be expected for that satisfaction.

22:19 sexual relations with an animal. This offense was a violation of God's restrictions against adultery or fornication. It also violated common morality.

22:21–24 These verses focused on the treatment of the unfortunate: aliens, widows and orphans. These people receive God's special attention and care. Those who violate the unfortunate may suffer God's direct sanction.

22:25 do not be like a moneylender. *Lending* money for profit is not prohibited. Taking advantage of the poor is an offense that triggers God's compassion for the victim and anger at the perpetrator.

22:26–27 cloak. A man with only clothes to offer as security would be desperately poor—both in Moses' time and today.

22:29 firstborn of your sons. The firstborn son belonged to God and was dedicated to him at his circumcision.

22:30 give them to me on the eighth day. This sacrifice parallels the circumcision of sons on the eighth day.

31"You are to be my holy people. So do not eat the meat of an animal torn by wild beasts; throw it to the dogs.

Laws of Justice and Mercy

23 "Do not spread false reports. Do not help a wicked man by
being a malicious witness.
2"Do not follow the crowd in doing wrong. When you give testimony in a lawsuit, do not pervert justice by siding with the crowd,
3and do not show favoritism to a poor man in his lawsuit.
4"If you come across your enemy's ox or donkey wandering off, be
sure to take it back to him. 5If you see the donkey of someone who
hates you fallen down under its load, do not leave it there; be sure
you help him with it.
6"Do not deny justice to your poor people in their lawsuits. 7Have
nothing to do with a false charge and do not put an innocent or honest person to death, for I will not acquit the guilty.
8"Do not accept a bribe, for a bribe blinds those who see and twists
the words of the righteous.
9"Do not oppress an alien; you yourselves know how it feels to be
aliens, because you were aliens in Egypt.

Sabbath Laws

10"For six years you are to sow your fields and harvest the crops,
11but during the seventh year let the land lie unplowed and unused.
Then the poor among your people may get food from it, and the wild
animals may eat what they leave. Do the same with your vineyard and
your olive grove.
12"Six days do your work, but on the seventh day do not work, so
that your ox and your donkey may rest and the slave born in your
household, and the alien as well, may be refreshed.
13"Be careful to do everything I have said to you. Do not invoke the
names of other gods; do not let them be heard on your lips.

The Three Annual Festivals

14"Three times a year you are to celebrate a festival to me.
15"Celebrate the Feast of Unleavened Bread; for seven days eat
bread made without yeast, as I commanded you. Do this at the appointed time in the month of Abib, for in that month you came out of
Egypt.
"No one is to appear before me empty-handed.
16"Celebrate the Feast of Harvest with the firstfruits of the crops
you sow in your field.
"Celebrate the Feast of Ingathering at the end of the year, when you
gather in your crops from the field.

OPEN When you were in trouble, did your parents give out justice or mercy?

STUDY When disputes arose among the Israelites, someone had to judge. **1.** Do you think you would make a good judge in a civil court? **2.** What is the warning here about accepting testimony or going along with the crowd? **3.** When it comes to feeling sorry for "poor people" what are two things to guard against? What about people who buy favors?

APPLY If you could be governor for a year, what issue would you work on?

OPEN What do you know about crop rotation?

STUDY Long before there was crop science, the Israelites had discovered the need for Sabbath rest. What is the universal principle that underlies the need for agricultural and human rejuvenation?

APPLY If your body could speak, what would your body say to you today?

OPEN What was the holiday you looked forward to as a kid?

STUDY The festivals were more than holidays. They were times to remember and celebrate what God had done for the Israelites. **1.** What do you remember about how the Festival of Unleavened Bread got started (12:31–36)? Why does God forbid sacrifices with yeast or the boiling of a goat in its mother's milk?

23:4–5 A person's enemies musbe treated with the same regard as friels. He should return hostility with kindns. Here the enemy is a Hebrew.

23:7 I will not acquit the guil Although man might bear false witne and fool the judges, God, who cann be fooled, will not let the guilty go u punished.

23:8 blinds those who see. In modern terms, a bribe makes someone "turn a blind eye" toward an offender. This is a perversion of justice, which seeks faithfully after the truth.

23:15 Feast of Unleavened Bread. This feast was celebrated from around mid-March to mid-April. It was in memory of the Israelites' rapid escape from Egypt (12:17–20).

23:16 Feast of Harvest. This feast was celebrated seven weeks after the Feast of Unleavened Bread during the time of the wheat harvest. At this feast, the Israelites made offerings to God of the firstfruits of the harvest.

2. What would the festivals having to do with crops help the Israelites do?

APPLY 1. What is the lesson on giving for you in this passage? **2.** What have you found helpful in making your offerings to God?

OPEN Have you ever lived in an underdeveloped country that practiced voodoo, witchcraft, sorcery, ritual prostitution, Satan worship or cultic religion?

STUDY The Israelites were headed for a land that had immoral and unhealthy pagan cultures. The warning in the passage deals with the problem of living among the people without adopting their ways. **1.** What do you know about the culture and religions of the primitive people that lived in Canaan before the Israelites arrived? **2.** What does God promise? What is the catch? **3.** Why are the Israelites to demolish the pagan shrines? How does this command relate to staying healthy and avoiding miscarriage and infertility? **4.** What are going to be the borders of the land they will occupy? Why not take possession of the land all at once?

APPLY 1. What is your game plan for the next few years in your life? **2.** What are you doing to stay spiritually healthy?

OPEN 1. What is the most awesome mountain you have ever been on? **2.** As a young child, how did you picture God?

17 “Three times a year all the men are to appear before the Sovereign LORD.
18 “Do not offer the blood of a sacrifice to me along with anything
containing yeast.
“The fat of my festival offerings must not be kept until morning.
19 “Bring the best of the firstfruits of your soil to the house of the
LORD your God.
“Do not cook a young goat in its mother’s milk.

God’s Angel to Prepare the Way

20 “See, I am sending an angel ahead of you to guard you along the
way and to bring you to the place I have prepared. 21 Pay attention to
him and listen to what he says. Do not rebel against him; he will not
forgive your rebellion, since my Name is in him. 22 If you listen carefully to what he says and do all that I say, I will be an enemy to your
enemies and will oppose those who oppose you. 23 My angel will go
ahead of you and bring you into the land of the Amorites, Hittites,
Perizzites, Canaanites, Hivites and Jebusites, and I will wipe them
out. 24 Do not bow down before their gods or worship them or follow
their practices. You must demolish them and break their sacred
stones to pieces. 25 Worship the LORD your God, and his blessing will
be on your food and water. I will take away sickness from among you,
26 and none will miscarry or be barren in your land. I will give you a
full life span.
27 “I will send my terror ahead of you and throw into confusion
every nation you encounter. I will make all your enemies turn their
backs and run. 28 I will send the hornet ahead of you to drive the Hivites, Canaanites and Hittites out of your way. 29 But I will not drive
them out in a single year, because the land would become desolate
and the wild animals too numerous for you. 30 Little by little I will
drive them out before you, until you have increased enough to take
possession of the land.
31 “I will establish your borders from the Red Sea[a] to the Sea of the
Philistines,[b] and from the desert to the River.[c] I will hand over to you
the people who live in the land and you will drive them out before
you. 32 Do not make a covenant with them or with their gods. 33 Do not
let them live in your land, or they will cause you to sin against me,
because the worship of their gods will certainly be a snare to you.”

The Covenant Confirmed

24 Then he said to Moses, “Come up to the LORD, you and
Aaron, Nadab and Abihu, and seventy of the elders of Israel.

[a] *31* Hebrew *Yam Suph*; that is, Sea of Reeds [b] *31* That is, the Mediterranean [c] *31* That is, the Euphrates

---

23:17 all the men. This law required the men to go to the tabernacle and later the temple to make sacrifices. Usually their families accompanied them.

23:18 anything containing yeast. In his instructions for the Passover, God prohibited yeast, a symbol of sin and impurity, from even being in the home during that festival (12:14–16). Jesus refers to this symbol in Matthew 16:5–12.

23:19 firstfruits. Offering the first portion of the harvest to God symbolized that all the harvest belonged to him and that all blessings came from God. The concept of firstfruits is an important New Testament concept as well. In 1 Corinthians 15:20–23, Jesus is described as the firstfruits of those who have eternal life.

23:20 place I have prepared. The words Jesus used to describe our place in heaven echo the language here (John 14:2–4). No one can see the future, but God is already there making provision for his people.

23:31 God outlined the borders of the Promised Land. The area described is a confirmation of God’s covenant promise to Abraham (Gen. 15:18).

You are to worship at a distance, [2]but Moses alone is to approach the
LORD; the others must not come near. And the people may not come
up with him."
[3]When Moses went and told the people all the LORD's words and
laws, they responded with one voice, "Everything the LORD has said
we will do." [4]Moses then wrote down everything the LORD had said.
He got up early the next morning and built an altar at the foot of
the mountain and set up twelve stone pillars representing the twelve
tribes of Israel. [5]Then he sent young Israelite men, and they offered
burnt offerings and sacrificed young bulls as fellowship offerings[a] to
the LORD. [6]Moses took half of the blood and put it in bowls, and the
other half he sprinkled on the altar. [7]Then he took the Book of the
Covenant and read it to the people. They responded, "We will do
everything the LORD has said; we will obey."
[8]Moses then took the blood, sprinkled it on the people and said,
"This is the blood of the covenant that the LORD has made with you in
accordance with all these words."
[9]Moses and Aaron, Nadab and Abihu, and the seventy elders of
Israel went up [10]and saw the God of Israel. Under his feet was something like a pavement made of sapphire,[b] clear as the sky itself. [11]But
God did not raise his hand against these leaders of the Israelites; they
saw God, and they ate and drank.
[12]The LORD said to Moses, "Come up to me on the mountain and
stay here, and I will give you the tablets of stone, with the law and
commands I have written for their instruction."
[13]Then Moses set out with Joshua his aide, and Moses went up on
the mountain of God. [14]He said to the elders, "Wait here for us until
we come back to you. Aaron and Hur are with you, and anyone involved in a dispute can go to them."
[15]When Moses went up on the mountain, the cloud covered it,
[16]and the glory of the LORD settled on Mount Sinai. For six days the
cloud covered the mountain, and on the seventh day the LORD called

[a]5 Traditionally *peace offerings* [b]10 Or *lapis lazuli*

STUDY God now confirms to Moses the contract he made with Abraham 400 years before: (1) his descendants would become a special people and, (2) they would be given a land where they could live. **1.** If you were the leader of a huge number of people, how important would it be to you to develop leaders immediately under you? **2.** As their leader, what does Moses do that would immediately demonstrate the importance of being a holy nation? **3.** If you had been one of the seventy elders who were given a view of God, how would you feel (vv. 9–11)? **4.** What do you think was the purpose for Moses spending 40 days on the mountain? **5.** To the Israelites down below, what did they see? How would you have responded if you were there?

APPLY 1. Have you had an experience like Moses—alone with God? What impact did this have on your life? **2.** When are you going to do this again?

24:2 Moses alone. Though God allowed tribal elders to come nearer than the rest of Israel, only Moses, the mediator between God and Israel, is allowed direct access. Jesus becomes the "mediator of a new covenant" with God (Heb. 12:24), bridging the gulf between human and divine. Jesus is a greater mediator than Moses (v. 8; Heb. 3:3; 9:15).

24:3 words and laws ... we will do. The Ten Commandments and the law of the Covenant were the essential elements of the new covenant between God and Israel. As such, the Israelites had to agree to follow the commandments and the law for the covenant to be binding.

24:5 young Israelite men. Since God had not yet established a priesthood, these young men were designated to cary out the offerings and sacrifices. Perhaps they represented the strongest and best Israel had to offer God.

24:6 half of the blood. This covenant must be sealed with blood. Half of the blood is placed in bowls and reserved for the Israelites. The other half is sprinkled on the altar and offered to God. The blood on the altar is a sign of God's acceptance of the covenant.

24:8 sprinkled it on the people. Blood sprinkled on the people symbolizes their acceptance of the covenant. It is also a reminder of the first Passover in Egypt in which the blood beside and above the door marked the homes of the Israelites and saved them. The sprinkling in this verse marks the Israelites as children of this new covenant. Christ's blood seals the covenant of forgiveness between God and humankind (Matt. 26:28).

24:10 saw the God of Israel. God allowed them to see some portion of his glory, but not all. Even Moses could not do that. It would be too much for humans to handle (33:20).

24:11 ate and drank. The leaders of Israel had a meal in God's presence. After a wedding it is traditional to eat, drink and celebrate. The Lord's Supper is very much the same event (v. 8; Matt. 26:26–29). It celebrates the new covenant of forgiveness established through Christ's death. We still have this tradition today—especially in the marriage covenant.

24:12 instruction. The law and commands are not merely codes of conduct to be posted on a wall. They are divine commands to be taken seriously and to be studied and followed.

to Moses from within the cloud. [17]To the Israelites the glory of the
LORD looked like a consuming fire on top of the mountain. [18]Then
Moses entered the cloud as he went on up the mountain. And he
stayed on the mountain forty days and forty nights.

Offerings for the Tabernacle

25 The LORD said to Moses, [2]"Tell the Israelites to bring me an
offering. You are to receive the offering for me from each
man whose heart prompts him to give. [3]These are the offerings you
are to receive from them: gold, silver and bronze; [4]blue, purple and
scarlet yarn and fine linen; goat hair; [5]ram skins dyed red and hides
of sea cows[a]; acacia wood; [6]olive oil for the light; spices for the
anointing oil and for the fragrant incense; [7]and onyx stones and
other gems to be mounted on the ephod and breastpiece.
[8]"Then have them make a sanctuary for me, and I will dwell among
them. [9]Make this tabernacle and all its furnishings exactly like the
pattern I will show you.

The Ark

[10]"Have them make a chest of acacia wood—two and a half cubits
long, a cubit and a half wide, and a cubit and a half high.[b] [11]Overlay it
with pure gold, both inside and out, and make a gold molding around
it. [12]Cast four gold rings for it and fasten them to its four feet, with
two rings on one side and two rings on the other. [13]Then make poles
of acacia wood and overlay them with gold. [14]Insert the poles into the
rings on the sides of the chest to carry it. [15]The poles are to remain in
the rings of this ark; they are not to be removed. [16]Then put in the ark
the Testimony, which I will give you.
[17]"Make an atonement cover[c] of pure gold—two and a half cubits

[a]5 That is, dugongs [b]10 That is, about 3 3/4 feet (about 1.1 meters) long and 2 1/4 feet (about 0.7 meter) wide and high [c]17 Traditionally *a mercy seat*

OPEN When is the last time you had a scavenger hunt?

STUDY In the desert, the Israelites needed a physical structure for God to be present with them in their journey. **1.** Where are the Israelites going to get all of these articles in the desert? **2.** Why would a tent be important?

APPLY Where do you go when you want to be alone with God?

OPEN What treasure do you still have that you made with your own hands when you were growing up?

STUDY The Israelites needed a safe place to carry their important documents while traveling in the desert. This chest was called the Ark of the Covenant. **1.** From the description of the chest in this passage, could you make a drawing of how you think it looked (a cubit was about 18 inches)? **2.** What do you think this chest did for the Israelites as they carried it from place to place? **3.** What do you think the cherubim that hovered over

---

24:18 forty days and forty nights. An important time frame. The flood brought rain for forty days and nights (Gen. 7:12), and Christ fasted for that same time in the desert (Matt. 4:2).

25:2 heart prompts him to give. This offering was voluntary, not a covenant command. The items to be offered were precious. Most Israelites would not surrender them without some pain.

25:4 blue, purple and scarlet. Furnishing the tabernacle with these royal colors would be appropriate for the new relationship between God and humankind. Under this covenant, Israel was to be a holy nation led by God. The tabernacle furnishings are those of a royal chamber.

25:5 hides of sea cows. *It is hard to* imagine a people in the desert having these. But sea cows were present in the Red Sea, and leather made from their skin would be quite precious.

25:6 spices ... incense. These items would include myrrh, cinnamon, cane, cassia, onycha, galbanum and frankincense (30:22–24,34). The gifts of the Magi to the infant Jesus would have been much the same. Just as the offerings for the tabernacle were acknowledgments of God's kingship, so were the gifts to Jesus.

25:8 I will dwell among them. God would be a ruler of his covenant people in their presence, not from afar. The tabernacle provided a haven for him—a holy place set apart. This portrait of God illustrates how it is his character to be among us and foreshadows the coming of Christ to live among us and yet to become the "King of Kings" (Rev. 19:16).

25:10 chest. The ark was built like and *functioned as* a treasure chest: precious in its construction, in what it contained and what it stood for. It was the resting place of Israel's true king, God himself.

25:11 Overlay it with pure gold, both inside and out. Pure gold never rots like wood. It is worthy material for a king's throne. Symbolically, it is eternal, not tainted by sin.

25:12 rings. Such a chest with gold overlay would be heavy to carry, and the Israelites were still a nation without a homeland. Ring poles were inserted for carrying the weight.

25:16 Testimony. The Testimony was comprised of the two tablets of the Ten Commandments, evidence of the covenant established by the giving and accepting of the Law.

25:17 atonement cover. This has been translated "mercy seat" in other versions and is a reminder of the saving work of God. People are reconciled to God through grace. Atonement is the process whereby God bidges the gulf of alienation caused by human sin and makes people "at one" wth him. Blood

long and a cubit and a half wide.[a] [18]And make two cherubim out of hammered gold at the ends of the cover. [19]Make one cherub on one end and the second cherub on the other; make the cherubim of one piece with the cover, at the two ends. [20]The cherubim are to have their wings spread upward, overshadowing the cover with them. The cherubim are to face each other, looking toward the cover. [21]Place the cover on top of the ark and put in the ark the Testimony, which I will give you. [22]There, above the cover between the two cherubim that are over the ark of the Testimony, I will meet with you and give you all my commands for the Israelites.

The Table

[23]"Make a table of acacia wood—two cubits long, a cubit wide and a cubit and a half high.[b] [24]Overlay it with pure gold and make a gold molding around it. [25]Also make around it a rim a handbreadth[c] wide and put a gold molding on the rim. [26]Make four gold rings for the table and fasten them to the four corners, where the four legs are. [27]The rings are to be close to the rim to hold the poles used in carrying the table. [28]Make the poles of acacia wood, overlay them with gold and carry the table with them. [29]And make its plates and dishes of pure gold, as well as its pitchers and bowls for the pouring out of offerings. [30]Put the bread of the Presence on this table to be before me at all times.

The Lampstand

[31]"Make a lampstand of pure gold and hammer it out, base and shaft; its flowerlike cups, buds and blossoms shall be of one piece with it. [32]Six branches are to extend from the sides of the lampstand—three on one side and three on the other. [33]Three cups shaped like almond flowers with buds and blossoms are to be on one branch, three on the next branch, and the same for all six branches extending from the lampstand. [34]And on the lampstand there are to be four cups shaped like almond flowers with buds and blossoms. [35]One bud shall be under the first pair of branches extending from the lampstand, a second bud under the second pair, and a third bud under the third pair—six branches in all. [36]The buds and branches shall all be of one piece with the lampstand, hammered out of pure gold.

[37]"Then make its seven lamps and set them up on it so that they light the space in front of it. [38]Its wick trimmers and trays are to be of pure gold. [39]A talent[d] of pure gold is to be used for the lampstand

[a] *17* That is, about 3 3/4 feet (about 1.1 meters) long and 2 1/4 feet (about 0.7 meter) wide [b] *23* That is, about 3 feet (about 0.9 meter) long and 1 1/2 feet (about 0.5 meter) wide and 2 1/4 feet (about 0.7 meter) high [c] *25* That is, about 3 inches (about 8 centimeters) [d] *39* That is, about 75 pounds (about 34 kilograms)

the top of the ark symbolized? Can you visualize this? **4.** What does the top of the ark represent? What is to happen there?

APPLY What do you take with you as you journey on your spiritual life?

____

OPEN What was the shape of the dining table in your home?

STUDY The table in the tabernacle was to hold the bread used for offerings. **1.** From the description of the table, what would it look like? **2.** What do you find out from Leviticus 24:5–9 about the bread?

APPLY Where is the communion table placed in your church?

____

OPEN 1. What is the biggest lamp you have in your house? **2.** Have you ever used an oil lamp?

STUDY The lampstand not only provided light but also symbolized the presence of God in the tabernacle. **1.** From the description here, could you draw the lampstand? What would it look like? **2.** If you walked into the tabernacle and saw this huge lamp glistening with gold illuminated by oil lamps on the main stem and seven branches, what would you think? **3.** When Jesus referred to the lampstand in his ministry, do you remember what he said?

APPLY How would you compare the light given off by your life in a dark world to a lampstand: Bright? Dim? Flickering? Low on oil? Gone out?

____

is always involved in atonement. In the Old Testament, the blood of sacrificed animals makes atonement possible. In the New Testament, Jesus' blood makes atonement for sin once and for all.

25:18 cherubim. These two golden statues represented winged angels.

25:23 table. Even the table, which is to hold the items used in ceremonies—plates, cups, bowls—must be made of hard, long-lasting wood and overlaid with gold.

25:30 bread of the Presence. Twelve loaves of bread, one for each tribe of Israel, were kept on this table as a perpetual sacrifice. Further, the bread served as a reminder that all blessings come from God and that God provides bountifully. This has been called the showbread because it is placed before God.

25:37 light the space in front of it. The tabernacle would never be in the dark. Priests later insured that these lamps burned all night (27:20–21). The lighted lamps are the Israelites' response to the light of God's glory (29:43).

and all these accessories. 40See that you make them according to the
pattern shown you on the mountain.

The Tabernacle

26 "Make the tabernacle with ten curtains of finely twisted
linen and blue, purple and scarlet yarn, with cherubim
worked into them by a skilled craftsman. 2All the curtains are to be
the same size—twenty-eight cubits long and four cubits wide.[a] 3Join
five of the curtains together, and do the same with the other five.
4Make loops of blue material along the edge of the end curtain in one
set, and do the same with the end curtain in the other set. 5Make fifty
loops on one curtain and fifty loops on the end curtain of the other
set, with the loops opposite each other. 6Then make fifty gold clasps
and use them to fasten the curtains together so that the tabernacle is
a unit.

7"Make curtains of goat hair for the tent over the tabernacle—elev-
en altogether. 8All eleven curtains are to be the same size—thirty
cubits long and four cubits wide.[b] 9Join five of the curtains together
into one set and the other six into another set. Fold the sixth curtain
double at the front of the tent. 10Make fifty loops along the edge of the
end curtain in one set and also along the edge of the end curtain in
the other set. 11Then make fifty bronze clasps and put them in the
loops to fasten the tent together as a unit. 12As for the additional
length of the tent curtains, the half curtain that is left over is to hang
down at the rear of the tabernacle. 13The tent curtains will be a cubit[c]
longer on both sides; what is left will hang over the sides of the tabernacle so as to cover it. 14Make for the tent a covering of ram skins
dyed red, and over that a covering of hides of sea cows.[d]

15"Make upright frames of acacia wood for the tabernacle. 16Each
frame is to be ten cubits long and a cubit and a half wide,[e] 17with two
projections set parallel to each other. Make all the frames of the
tabernacle in this way. 18Make twenty frames for the south side of the
tabernacle 19and make forty silver bases to go under them—two
bases for each frame, one under each projection. 20For the other side,
the north side of the tabernacle, make twenty frames 21and forty
silver bases—two under each frame. 22Make six frames for the far
end, that is, the west end of the tabernacle, 23and make two frames
for the corners at the far end. 24At these two corners they must be

[a] *2* That is, about 42 feet (about 12.5 meters) long and 6 feet (about 1.8 meters) wide [b] *8* That is, about 45 feet (about 13.5 meters) long and 6 feet (about 1.8 meters) wide [c] *13* That is, about 1 1/2 feet (about 0.5 meter) [d] *14* That is, dugongs [e] *16* That is, about 15 feet (about 4.5 meters) long and 2 1/4 feet (about 0.7 meter) wide

OPEN Have you ever tried to put up a tent on a camping trip? Have you done this in a heavy wind or rainstorm?

STUDY The Israelites are in transition from Egypt to the Promised Land and from a nomadic tribe to a nation. God is teaching them what it means to be the special people of the covenant. This passage tells the story of the special tent they are to build as a worship place. **1.** From the dimensions given here, what would you compare the size of this tent to? **2.** What skill could you contribute to building this tabernacle? Who in your group would you nominate to be the architect? The head seamstress? The master craftsperson? **3.** What impression do you think the tabernacle gave in the setting sun with its blue, purple and scarlet curtains with gold poles and silver bases? **4.** What was the purpose of having an inner curtain (vv. 33–35; Heb. 9:1–5)? What was to go behind the curtain? **5.** What happened to the curtain (veil) when Jesus died on the cross (Mark 15:38)? What does this mean (Heb. 9:11–15; 10:19–24)? **6.** Can you imagine putting up and taking down this tent every time you moved? **7.** What do you think the Israelites learned about God by having this tent? What does the word "tabernacle" mean to you? **8.** In the cathedrals that were built in the 10th to 16th centuries in Europe, what did they do to incorporate the elements of the tabernacle in their architecture? How did the Reformation influence architectural changes? **9.** How does your church compare to the architecture of the tabernacle?

APPLY 1. When did you first understand the meaning behind the curtain in the tabernacle

---

25:40 pattern shown you on the mountain. God had specific designs for items in the tabernacle (27:8). Stephen said that these designs are made by God as he directed Moses (Acts 7:44).

26:1 tabernacle. *The tabernacle* was a rectangular tent, comprised of several layers of covering. The inner layer was made of embroidered linen containing images of cherubim. The three other layers were made of woven goat hair, dyed ram skins and the hides of sea cows. All of its construction material was precious and fit for a royal chamber.

26:2 curtains. The curtains, although *very large,* were arranged in ten sections for ease of movement.

26:16 frames. The frames or boards were engineered for quick erection. This was a house of worship that was constantly being moved.

26:23 two frames for the corners at the far end. God's attention to detail was that of a grand architect. He understood the nature of the structure, had an intimate knowledge of its use, understood the need for strength and portability and had full knowledge of the materials.

double from the bottom all the way to the top, and fitted into a single
ring; both shall be like that. 25So there will be eight frames and sixteen silver bases—two under each frame.
26"Also make crossbars of acacia wood: five for the frames on one
side of the tabernacle, 27five for those on the other side, and five for
the frames on the west, at the far end of the tabernacle. 28The center
crossbar is to extend from end to end at the middle of the frames.
29Overlay the frames with gold and make gold rings to hold the crossbars. Also overlay the crossbars with gold.
30"Set up the tabernacle according to the plan shown you on the
mountain.
31"Make a curtain of blue, purple and scarlet yarn and finely twisted linen, with cherubim worked into it by a skilled craftsman. 32Hang
it with gold hooks on four posts of acacia wood overlaid with gold
and standing on four silver bases. 33Hang the curtain from the clasps
and place the ark of the Testimony behind the curtain. The curtain
will separate the Holy Place from the Most Holy Place. 34Put the
atonement cover on the ark of the Testimony in the Most Holy Place.
35Place the table outside the curtain on the north side of the tabernacle and put the lampstand opposite it on the south side.
36"For the entrance to the tent make a curtain of blue, purple and
scarlet yarn and finely twisted linen—the work of an embroiderer.
37Make gold hooks for this curtain and five posts of acacia wood
overlaid with gold. And cast five bronze bases for them.

The Altar of Burnt Offering

27 "Build an altar of acacia wood, three cubits[a] high; it is to be
square, five cubits long and five cubits wide.[b] 2Make a horn at
each of the four corners, so that the horns and the altar are of one
piece, and overlay the altar with bronze. 3Make all its utensils of
bronze—its pots to remove the ashes, and its shovels, sprinkling
bowls, meat forks and firepans. 4Make a grating for it, a bronze network, and make a bronze ring at each of the four corners of the network. 5Put it under the ledge of the altar so that it is halfway up the
altar. 6Make poles of acacia wood for the altar and overlay them with
bronze. 7The poles are to be inserted into the rings so they will be on
two sides of the altar when it is carried. 8Make the altar hollow, out of
boards. It is to be made just as you were shown on the mountain.

[a]1 That is, about 4 1/2 feet (about 1.3 meters) [b]1 That is, about 7 1/2 feet (about 2.3 meters) long and wide

and how Jesus removed this curtain when he died on the cross? 2. Do you go through priests to approach God or through Jesus Christ directly? 3. How would you describe your relationship with God right now?

OPEN What do you use to do your cooking on a camping trip?

STUDY The Israelites were to offer sacrifices on a daily basis to God on their journey in the desert. **1.** From the description here, how would you describe this altar? **2.** What is different from this altar and the altar in churches today? Why?

APPLY What do you use for an altar in your home?

26:26 acacia wood. The framework, of the supporting crossbars, was made of hard, long-lasting acacia wood found in the Sinai Peninsula.

26:29 Overlay the frames with gold. Sealing the acacia wood in this way would make the tabernacle framework a long-lasting wooden structure.

26:31–35 Make a curtain. These verses gave instructions for dividing the tabernacle interior into the Holy Place and the Most Holy Place with an embroidered curtain.

26:31 curtain. The Holy Place was divided from the Most Holy Place by an embroidered curtain or veil. The Most Holy Place contained only the ark and represented God's throne room. The curtain separated this section from the Holy Place, which contained the table for the bread of the Presence, the lampstand and the altar of incense.

27:1 altar. This altar, outside the Holy Place in the courtyard, is known as the bronze altar or the altar of burnt offering. The altar was about seven and a half feet square.

27:2 horn at each of the four corners. Each of the four corners projected higher than the sides of the altar. These horns came to symbolize safety, refuge and atonement (1 Kin. 1:50). During offerings, they were sprinkled with blood.

27:3 all its utensils. This list of utensils sounds like that of a modern barbecue. While the focus of the burnt offering was spiritual, practical issues, such as handling the fire and the meat, had to be considered.

OPEN When you were growing up, what was the size of the yard? What was special about your yard?

STUDY The tabernacle that God asked the Israelites to build for worship needed a place where sacrifices could be offered to God. **1.** From the dimensions for the courtyard, how would you compare the size to a football field? (A cubit was about 18 inches.) **2.** Why do you think the tabernacle needed to be fenced in? How would you feel when you walked through the outer entrance into the courtyard and saw this huge bronze altar? **3.** Why do you think the Israelites are to keep the lampstand in the tabernacle burning through the night? What is the significance of the pure oil?

APPLY 1. What is the yard like surrounding your church? **2.** Is it inviting to people who are looking for help and a new relationship with God?

OPEN 1. How did your parents want you to dress for church? **2.** Who is the most fashionable in your group?

STUDY The Israelites needed to set apart a special class of people for tabernacle service. The clothing that these priests were to wear while performing tabernacle worship was significant. **1.** Why were the garments for Aaron and his sons important (v. 2)? **2.** From the descrip-

The Courtyard

9"Make a courtyard for the tabernacle. The south side shall be a
hundred cubits[a] long and is to have curtains of finely twisted linen,
10with twenty posts and twenty bronze bases and with silver hooks
and bands on the posts. 11The north side shall also be a hundred cubits long and is to have curtains, with twenty posts and twenty
bronze bases and with silver hooks and bands on the posts.
12"The west end of the courtyard shall be fifty cubits[b] wide and
have curtains, with ten posts and ten bases. 13On the east end, toward the sunrise, the courtyard shall also be fifty cubits wide. 14Cur-
tains fifteen cubits[c] long are to be on one side of the entrance, with
three posts and three bases, 15and curtains fifteen cubits long are to
be on the other side, with three posts and three bases.
16"For the entrance to the courtyard, provide a curtain twenty
cubits[d] long, of blue, purple and scarlet yarn and finely twisted lin-
en—the work of an embroiderer—with four posts and four bases.
17All the posts around the courtyard are to have silver bands and
hooks, and bronze bases. 18The courtyard shall be a hundred cubits
long and fifty cubits wide,[e] with curtains of finely twisted linen five
cubits[f] high, and with bronze bases. 19All the other articles used in
the service of the tabernacle, whatever their function, including all
the tent pegs for it and those for the courtyard, are to be of bronze.

Oil for the Lampstand

20"Command the Israelites to bring you clear oil of pressed olives
for the light so that the lamps may be kept burning. 21In the Tent of
Meeting, outside the curtain that is in front of the Testimony, Aaron
and his sons are to keep the lamps burning before the LORD from evening till morning. This is to be a lasting ordinance among the Israelites for the generations to come.

The Priestly Garments

28 "Have Aaron your brother brought to you from among the
Israelites, along with his sons Nadab and Abihu, Eleazar and
Ithamar, so they may serve me as priests. 2Make sacred garments for
your brother Aaron, to give him dignity and honor. 3Tell all the skilled
men to whom I have given wisdom in such matters that they are to
make garments for Aaron, for his consecration, so he may serve me

[a]9 That is, about 150 feet (about 46 meters); also in verse 11 [b]12 That is, about 75 feet (about 23 meters); also in verse 13 [c]14 That is, about 22 1/2 feet (about 6.9 meters); also in verse 15 [d]16 That is, about 30 feet (about 9 meters) [e]18 That is, about 150 feet (about 46 meters) long and 75 feet (about 23 meters) wide [f]18 That is, about 7 1/2 feet (about 2.3 meters)

27:9–18 courtyard. The entire tabernacle was a rectangle with its long sides aligned east to west. The Holy Place and Most Holy Place were in the western half, and the bronze altar was in the eastern. The entrance lay on the east end opposite from the Most Holy Place. The curtained opening was quite large, around thirty feet wide. The large courtyard measured 150 by 75 feet. The curtain that cordoned off this area was seven and a half feet high. The outer curtain ensured privacy for the worshipers and protection from weather.

27:20 oil of pressed olives. Olive oil was a versatile resource—a staple for cooking and eating, and a fuel that produced almost no smoke.

27:21 Tent of Meeting. This is another name for the tabernacle. The "meeting" was not a town gathering, but a meeting of God with his people, as a king might meet his subjects.

28:1 they may serve me as priests. The priesthood, which God established through Aaron and his sons, served the needs of the Israelites by serving God. They made sacrifices and offerings to God in accordance with the laws.

28:2 sacred garments. The special garments worn by priests gave them a certain status among the people and insured that those directly serving God were dressed in a manner appropriate to their proximity with the divine.

as priest. [4]These are the garments they are to make: a breastpiece, an
ephod, a robe, a woven tunic, a turban and a sash. They are to make
these sacred garments for your brother Aaron and his sons, so they
may serve me as priests. [5]Have them use gold, and blue, purple and
scarlet yarn, and fine linen.

The Ephod

[6]"Make the ephod of gold, and of blue, purple and scarlet yarn, and
of finely twisted linen—the work of a skilled craftsman. [7]It is to have
two shoulder pieces attached to two of its corners, so it can be fastened. [8]Its skillfully woven waistband is to be like it—of one piece
with the ephod and made with gold, and with blue, purple and scarlet
yarn, and with finely twisted linen.
[9]"Take two onyx stones and engrave on them the names of the sons
of Israel [10]in the order of their birth—six names on one stone and the
remaining six on the other. [11]Engrave the names of the sons of Israel
on the two stones the way a gem cutter engraves a seal. Then mount
the stones in gold filigree settings [12]and fasten them on the shoulder
pieces of the ephod as memorial stones for the sons of Israel. Aaron
is to bear the names on his shoulders as a memorial before the LORD.
[13]Make gold filigree settings [14]and two braided chains of pure gold,
like a rope, and attach the chains to the settings.

The Breastpiece

[15]"Fashion a breastpiece for making decisions—the work of a
skilled craftsman. Make it like the ephod: of gold, and of blue, purple
and scarlet yarn, and of finely twisted linen. [16]It is to be square—a
span[a] long and a span wide—and folded double. [17]Then mount four
rows of precious stones on it. In the first row there shall be a ruby, a
topaz and a beryl; [18]in the second row a turquoise, a sapphire[b] and an
emerald; [19]in the third row a jacinth, an agate and an amethyst; [20]in
the fourth row a chrysolite, an onyx and a jasper.[c] Mount them in
gold filigree settings. [21]There are to be twelve stones, one for each of
the names of the sons of Israel, each engraved like a seal with the
name of one of the twelve tribes.
[22]"For the breastpiece make braided chains of pure gold, like a
rope. [23]Make two gold rings for it and fasten them to two corners of
the breastpiece. [24]Fasten the two gold chains to the rings at the corners of the breastpiece, [25]and the other ends of the chains to the two
settings, attaching them to the shoulder pieces of the ephod at the
front. [26]Make two gold rings and attach them to the other two corners of the breastpiece on the inside edge next to the ephod. [27]Make
two more gold rings and attach them to the bottom of the shoulder

[a]16 That is, about 9 inches (about 22 centimeters) [b]18 Or *lapis lazuli* [c]20 The precise identification of some of these precious stones is uncertain.

tion of the ephod in verses 6–13, how do you think it looked? What would you compare this to today? **3.** What is significant about the decoration on the ephod? Why is Aaron to wear this stuff? **4.** How would this ceremonial attire make an Israelite feel? **5.** Do you think there is a place for nationalistic symbols such as flags, banners and memorials in the church?

APPLY If you were to engrave the names of the spiritual forefathers of your life on your garments, who would you choose?

OPEN **1.** As a child, when did you get your first dress or suit of clothes? **2.** Can you still get into the clothes you wore on your wedding day?

STUDY The high priest who officiated at ceremonies in the tabernacle represented God and as such was expected to be the spiritual director for the nation. For this reason the person was to wear a formal and glittering vest. **1.** From the description of the breastplate in this passage, how would you describe it? What would you compare it to today? **2.** If you were the high priest wearing this breastplate over your outer garments when you went before God for the people, how would you feel? **3.** How would this make the common people feel? **4.** What do you think God was teaching the Israelites with the breastplate? **5.** What will wearing the breastplate do for the high priest who is making decisions for the people?

28:6 ephod. The ephod was a sleeveless cape made of fine linen worn by the high priest.

28:12 memorial stones for the sons of Israel. These stones, fastened to the high priest's ephod, reminded the people that they sprung from 12 tribes. The high priest carried the entire nation of Israel before the Lord when he served in the tabernacle.

28:15 breastpiece for making decisions. The fabric breastpiece or pouch was worn by the high priest whenever he entered the Holy Place (v. 29). In addition to its ornamentation, the breastpiece also held the Urim and Thummim, used by the high priest to seek God's will in major decisions. God was thought to use the casting of lots to reveal his will by making either the Urim ("curses") or Thummim ("perfections") more prevalent.

APPLY 1. What spiritual leader in your pilgrimage made good decisions for you and your church? How have those decisions affected the course of your life? **2.** Who do you depend on now in making spiritual decisions?

OPEN 1. Are you color coordinated today? **2.** Do you make any of your clothes? **3.** Who buys your clothes?

STUDY The priest's clothing is designed to illustrate important elements of worship. The ephod and breastplate have already been described. Now, the robe and undergarments are described. **1.** What would you compare the high priest's robe to? **2.** What was to go around the base of the robe? Why? **3.** How would you describe the head covering? What was to hang from it over the forehead? **4.** Why are Aaron's sons to dress up when they assist in the tabernacle?

APPLY If you could design a cassock or ceremonial robe to be worn in a worship service, what would you have on the robe?

pieces on the front of the ephod, close to the seam just above the
waistband of the ephod. 28 The rings of the breastpiece are to be tied
to the rings of the ephod with blue cord, connecting it to the waistband, so that the breastpiece will not swing out from the ephod.
29 "Whenever Aaron enters the Holy Place, he will bear the names of
the sons of Israel over his heart on the breastpiece of decision as a
continuing memorial before the LORD. 30 Also put the Urim and the
Thummim in the breastpiece, so they may be over Aaron's heart
whenever he enters the presence of the LORD. Thus Aaron will always
bear the means of making decisions for the Israelites over his heart
before the LORD.

Other Priestly Garments

31 "Make the robe of the ephod entirely of blue cloth, 32 with an
opening for the head in its center. There shall be a woven edge like a
collar[a] around this opening, so that it will not tear. 33 Make pomegranates of blue, purple and scarlet yarn around the hem of the robe,
with gold bells between them. 34 The gold bells and the pomegranates
are to alternate around the hem of the robe. 35 Aaron must wear it
when he ministers. The sound of the bells will be heard when he enters the Holy Place before the LORD and when he comes out, so that
he will not die.
36 "Make a plate of pure gold and engrave on it as on a seal: HOLY TO
THE LORD. 37 Fasten a blue cord to it to attach it to the turban; it is to be
on the front of the turban. 38 It will be on Aaron's forehead, and he will
bear the guilt involved in the sacred gifts the Israelites consecrate,
whatever their gifts may be. It will be on Aaron's forehead continually
so that they will be acceptable to the LORD.
39 "Weave the tunic of fine linen and make the turban of fine linen.
The sash is to be the work of an embroiderer. 40 Make tunics, sashes
and headbands for Aaron's sons, to give them dignity and honor. 41 After you put these clothes on your brother Aaron and his sons, anoint
and ordain them. Consecrate them so they may serve me as priests.
42 "Make linen undergarments as a covering for the body, reaching
from the waist to the thigh. 43 Aaron and his sons must wear them
whenever they enter the Tent of Meeting or approach the altar to minister in the Holy Place, so that they will not incur guilt and die.
"This is to be a lasting ordinance for Aaron and his descendants.

[a] 32 The meaning of the Hebrew for this word is uncertain.

28:29 bear the names. Unlike the stones on the ephod which each contained the names of six tribes, the memorial stones on the breastpiece each contained the name of one tribe—12 in all. Thus, the people of Israel were presented to God in two different ways.

28:30 the Urim and the Thummim. These were probably sacred lots that were cast to ascertain the will of God. God would reveal his will by making either the Urim ("lights") or Thummim ("perfections") more prevalent when the lots were cast.

28:31 robe. The priest wore a sleeveless blue robe under the ephod. It hung below the knees and was embroidered around the hem and reinforced at the collar.

28:35 sound of the bells will be heard. The bells on the robe acted like the bird which miners would take with them into a mine. If the bird died, the miners knew something was wrong. If the bells stopped tinkling, those in the vicinity would know that either the priest wasn't interceding for them or he had died.

28:38 will bear the guilt. To perform these offerings, the priest must symbolically bring the peoples' sin before the Lord so atonement can be made.

Consecration of the Priests

29 "This is what you are to do to consecrate them, so they may
serve me as priests: Take a young bull and two rams without
defect. 2And from fine wheat flour, without yeast, make bread, and
cakes mixed with oil, and wafers spread with oil. 3Put them in a basket and present them in it—along with the bull and the two rams.
4Then bring Aaron and his sons to the entrance to the Tent of Meeting
and wash them with water. 5Take the garments and dress Aaron with
the tunic, the robe of the ephod, the ephod itself and the breastpiece.
Fasten the ephod on him by its skillfully woven waistband. 6Put the
turban on his head and attach the sacred diadem to the turban. 7Take
the anointing oil and anoint him by pouring it on his head. 8Bring his
sons and dress them in tunics 9and put headbands on them. Then tie
sashes on Aaron and his sons.[a] The priesthood is theirs by a lasting
ordinance. In this way you shall ordain Aaron and his sons.

10"Bring the bull to the front of the Tent of Meeting, and Aaron and
his sons shall lay their hands on its head. 11Slaughter it in the LORD's
presence at the entrance to the Tent of Meeting. 12Take some of the
bull's blood and put it on the horns of the altar with your finger, and
pour out the rest of it at the base of the altar. 13Then take all the fat
around the inner parts, the covering of the liver, and both kidneys
with the fat on them, and burn them on the altar. 14But burn the bull's
flesh and its hide and its offal outside the camp. It is a sin offering.

15"Take one of the rams, and Aaron and his sons shall lay their
hands on its head. 16Slaughter it and take the blood and sprinkle it
against the altar on all sides. 17Cut the ram into pieces and wash the
inner parts and the legs, putting them with the head and the other
pieces. 18Then burn the entire ram on the altar. It is a burnt offering
to the LORD, a pleasing aroma, an offering made to the LORD by fire.

19"Take the other ram, and Aaron and his sons shall lay their hands
on its head. 20Slaughter it, take some of its blood and put it on the
lobes of the right ears of Aaron and his sons, on the thumbs of their
right hands, and on the big toes of their right feet. Then sprinkle
blood against the altar on all sides. 21And take some of the blood on
the altar and some of the anointing oil and sprinkle it on Aaron and
his garments and on his sons and their garments. Then he and his
sons and their garments will be consecrated.

22"Take from this ram the fat, the fat tail, the fat around the inner
parts, the covering of the liver, both kidneys with the fat on them, and
the right thigh. (This is the ram for the ordination.) 23From the basket
of bread made without yeast, which is before the LORD, take a loaf,
and a cake made with oil, and a wafer. 24Put all these in the hands of

[a]9 Hebrew; Septuagint *on them*

OPEN **1.** Have you ever seen the inauguration of a national leader? **2.** Have you ever been to an ordination service?

STUDY The priests for the Israelites played a very important role. They were not only the mediators of the people to God, but they also handled many of the administrative affairs for the nation. The inauguration for these priests was very important. **1.** What would you do to set apart a special class of people to represent you? **2.** As an observer with little knowledge of the ordination, what would be your first impression as you looked at this ceremony? **3.** What do you think the ceremony is teaching about God and the priesthood by the order of the service: (a) washing of Aaron and his sons; (b) clothing them with new garments; (c) anointing them with oil? **4.** Why is the bull's blood smeared on the altar, the organs burned on the altar and the rest of the carcass removed from the camp? What does the word "atonement" mean? **5.** What are the two rams to be used for? What is the symbolism behind having Aaron and his sons laying their hands on the first ram and then slaughtering it and putting its blood on their garments? What do they get to do with the second ram? **6.** How many times was this ceremony to be conducted (v. 37)? How would you have felt if you had been one of the Israelites? **7.** After this inauguration is over, what are the priests to offer on a daily basis (v. 38)? What does God promise to the Israelites (vv. 42–43)? **8.** Do you think the ordinary Israelites understood what was going on with all of this ceremony? What is really important for them to understand?

APPLY **1.** When did you understand the meaning of the "lamb of God" in the New Testament in light of sacrifices of the Old Testament? **2.** What percentage of people in the church today do you think really understand the connection

---

29:4 wash them with water. The priests must be washed to represent a state of spiritual cleanliness. This cleansing was a public act and demonstrated the priests' own desire for holiness. The use of water for washing in the desert was a real luxury.

29:7 anoint him. Aaron was anointed to serve God as Christ would later be anointed (John 12:3).

29:10 Aaron and his sons shall lay their hands on its head. In order for the priests to have atonement, a special sacrifice must be offered. By laying hands on the bull, Aaron and his sons symbolically transfer their sin to the animal.

29:13 fat around the inner parts. The richest part of the bull is offered to God. Its fat and organ meats are burned on the bronze altar.

29:18 a pleasing aroma. It may be hard to understand that God would be pleased by the smell of burning meat, yet this ceremony of sacrifice came to Israel through God's instruction. The aroma of obedience and atonement would have pleased God most of all.

29:24 wave offering. A wave offering involved waving the sacrifice before the Lord as a means of presenting it to

between the Old Testament and New Testament sacrifices?

Aaron and his sons and wave them before the LORD as a wave offering. 25Then take them from their hands and burn them on the altar
along with the burnt offering for a pleasing aroma to the LORD, an
offering made to the LORD by fire. 26After you take the breast of the
ram for Aaron's ordination, wave it before the LORD as a wave offering, and it will be your share.
27"Consecrate those parts of the ordination ram that belong to
Aaron and his sons: the breast that was waved and the thigh that was
presented. 28This is always to be the regular share from the Israelites
for Aaron and his sons. It is the contribution the Israelites are to
make to the LORD from their fellowship offerings.[a]
29"Aaron's sacred garments will belong to his descendants so that
they can be anointed and ordained in them. 30The son who succeeds
him as priest and comes to the Tent of Meeting to minister in the Holy
Place is to wear them seven days.
31"Take the ram for the ordination and cook the meat in a sacred
place. 32At the entrance to the Tent of Meeting, Aaron and his sons are
to eat the meat of the ram and the bread that is in the basket. 33They
are to eat these offerings by which atonement was made for their ordination and consecration. But no one else may eat them, because
they are sacred. 34And if any of the meat of the ordination ram or any
bread is left over till morning, burn it up. It must not be eaten, because it is sacred.
35"Do for Aaron and his sons everything I have commanded you,
taking seven days to ordain them. 36Sacrifice a bull each day as a sin
offering to make atonement. Purify the altar by making atonement for
it, and anoint it to consecrate it. 37For seven days make atonement for
the altar and consecrate it. Then the altar will be most holy, and
whatever touches it will be holy.
38"This is what you are to offer on the altar regularly each day: two
lambs a year old. 39Offer one in the morning and the other at twilight.
40With the first lamb offer a tenth of an ephah[b] of fine flour mixed
with a quarter of a hin[c] of oil from pressed olives, and a quarter of a
hin of wine as a drink offering. 41Sacrifice the other lamb at twilight
with the same grain offering and its drink offering as in the morning—a pleasing aroma, an offering made to the LORD by fire.
42"For the generations to come this burnt offering is to be made
regularly at the entrance to the Tent of Meeting before the LORD.
There I will meet you and speak to you; 43there also I will meet with
the Israelites, and the place will be consecrated by my glory.
44"So I will consecrate the Tent of Meeting and the altar and will

[a]28 Traditionally *peace offerings* [b]40 That is, probably about 2 quarts (about 2 liters) [c]40 That is, probably about 1 quart (about 1 liter)

him. Sometimes the wave offering was followed by a burnt offering (vv. 24–26). A wave offering was also made for that portion of the sacrificial meat that was reserved for the priests to eat (Lev. 7:30–31; 10:14).

29:28 regular share. The priesthood was supported by the other Israelites, and portions of certain sacrifices were kept by them.

29:31 cook the meat in a sacred place. The meat was probably cooked within the tabernacle courtyard, but certainly not on the altar.

29:38 regularly each day. Sacrifice was not a "sometime" event. Although the law commanded certain special ceremonies where offerings were made (23:15–16), God also commanded a daily sacrifice of "two lambs a year old." The sacrifices were made in the morning and the evening each day.

29:43 there also I will meet with the Israelites. The long list of instructions that precedes this verse (25:1–29:42) involved the entire community of Israel. Building the tabernacle required a huge investment of the community's wealth and effort. Supplying the animals and other materials for sacrifice

consecrate Aaron and his sons to serve me as priests. 45Then I will
dwell among the Israelites and be their God. 46They will know that I
am the LORD their God, who brought them out of Egypt so that I
might dwell among them. I am the LORD their God.

The Altar of Incense

30 "Make an altar of acacia wood for burning incense. 2It is to
be square, a cubit long and a cubit wide, and two cubits
high[a]—its horns of one piece with it. 3Overlay the top and all the
sides and the horns with pure gold, and make a gold molding around
it. 4Make two gold rings for the altar below the molding—two on opposite sides—to hold the poles used to carry it. 5Make the poles of
acacia wood and overlay them with gold. 6Put the altar in front of the
curtain that is before the ark of the Testimony—before the atonement
cover that is over the Testimony—where I will meet with you.
7"Aaron must burn fragrant incense on the altar every morning
when he tends the lamps. 8He must burn incense again when he lights
the lamps at twilight so incense will burn regularly before the LORD for
the generations to come. 9Do not offer on this altar any other incense
or any burnt offering or grain offering, and do not pour a drink offering
on it. 10Once a year Aaron shall make atonement on its horns. This
annual atonement must be made with the blood of the atoning sin
offering for the generations to come. It is most holy to the LORD."

Atonement Money

11Then the LORD said to Moses, 12"When you take a census of the
Israelites to count them, each one must pay the LORD a ransom for
his life at the time he is counted. Then no plague will come on them
when you number them. 13Each one who crosses over to those already counted is to give a half shekel,[b] according to the sanctuary
shekel, which weighs twenty gerahs. This half shekel is an offering to
the LORD. 14All who cross over, those twenty years old or more, are to
give an offering to the LORD. 15The rich are not to give more than a
half shekel and the poor are not to give less when you make the offering to the LORD to atone for your lives. 16Receive the atonement
money from the Israelites and use it for the service of the Tent of
Meeting. It will be a memorial for the Israelites before the LORD, making atonement for your lives."

Basin for Washing

17Then the LORD said to Moses, 18"Make a bronze basin, with its
bronze stand, for washing. Place it between the Tent of Meeting and

[a]2 That is, about 1 1/2 feet (about 0.5 meter) long and wide and about 3 feet (about 0.9 meter) high
[b]13 That is, about 1/5 ounce (about 6 grams); also in verse 15

OPEN What kind of perfume or cologne do you use?

STUDY Inside the tabernacle, in front of the curtain were two pieces of furniture: The large lampstand for light and the altar of incense for smell. **1.** If you were the priest, what would be your first impression when you stepped inside of the tabernacle? **2.** What do you think the altar of incense represents? How did the apostle Paul use this symbol in the New Testament?

APPLY What would you compare incense to today for Christians? How are you an incense to the Lord?

OPEN How do you feel about paying sales taxes?

STUDY What is the purpose for slapping everyone with a census tax? What does this tax teach the Israelites about sin?

APPLY Who paid the ultimate ransom tax and how has this affected your life?

OPEN When you were young, what was the rule in your family for washing your hands before eating?

STUDY The Israelites were a nomadic society living in very

---

would sometimes be a hardship. The newly ordained priesthood would have access to the tabernacle each day; however, the tabernacle was for the people of Israel, not just its religious leaders. Here the common Israelite could come participate in God's glory.

29:45 dwell among the Israelites and be their God. Through the tabernacle, the Israelites would have tangible evidence of God's presence with them—even more tangible than the pillars of cloud and fire. This closeness and attention were the fulfillment of the covenant promise between God and his people (19:5–6; 29:43).

30:12 take a census. Since Israel was to be a holy nation (19:6), there was overlap between its civil and religious sectors. This census could be used to select Israelites for particular service—such as the army (Num. 26:2). And it was a form of state revenue. Each man would pay a fee when counted that functioned as a ransom for his life (21:30).

30:18 bronze basin ... for washing. The priests were ceremonially cleansed

the altar, and put water in it. 19Aaron and his sons are to wash their hands and feet with water from it. 20Whenever they enter the Tent of Meeting, they shall wash with water so that they will not die. Also, when they approach the altar to minister by presenting an offering made to the LORD by fire, 21they shall wash their hands and feet so that they will not die. This is to be a lasting ordinance for Aaron and his descendants for the generations to come."

Anointing Oil

22Then the LORD said to Moses, 23"Take the following fine spices: 500 shekels[a] of liquid myrrh, half as much (that is, 250 shekels) of fragrant cinnamon, 250 shekels of fragrant cane, 24500 shekels of cassia—all according to the sanctuary shekel—and a hin[b] of olive oil. 25Make these into a sacred anointing oil, a fragrant blend, the work of a perfumer. It will be the sacred anointing oil. 26Then use it to anoint the Tent of Meeting, the ark of the Testimony, 27the table and all its articles, the lampstand and its accessories, the altar of incense, 28the altar of burnt offering and all its utensils, and the basin with its stand. 29You shall consecrate them so they will be most holy, and whatever touches them will be holy.

30"Anoint Aaron and his sons and consecrate them so they may serve me as priests. 31Say to the Israelites, 'This is to be my sacred anointing oil for the generations to come. 32Do not pour it on men's bodies and do not make any oil with the same formula. It is sacred, and you are to consider it sacred. 33Whoever makes perfume like it and whoever puts it on anyone other than a priest must be cut off from his people.' "

Incense

34Then the LORD said to Moses, "Take fragrant spices—gum resin, onycha and galbanum—and pure frankincense, all in equal amounts, 35and make a fragrant blend of incense, the work of a perfumer. It is to be salted and pure and sacred. 36Grind some of it to powder and place it in front of the Testimony in the Tent of Meeting, where I will meet with you. It shall be most holy to you. 37Do not make any incense with this formula for yourselves; consider it holy to the LORD. 38Whoever makes any like it to enjoy its fragrance must be cut off from his people."

Bezalel and Oholiab

31 Then the LORD said to Moses, 2"See, I have chosen Bezalel son of Uri, the son of Hur, of the tribe of Judah, 3and I have filled

[a]*23* That is, about 12 1/2 pounds (about 6 kilograms) [b]*24* That is, probably about 4 quarts (about 4 liters)

primitive conditions. Cleanliness and hygiene were extremely important for health reasons and teaching the people the meaning of holiness. Many of these practices are ahead of their time by centuries. **1.** What does the water basin in front of the door of the tabernacle say to you about God? What are the consequences if a priest does not observe the practice of washing? **2.** How would you describe the special oil that the priests are to use in the tabernacle? Why would God want to keep the formula a secret? What was the consequence for someone running off with the formula? **3.** How do you think the incense smelled? **4.** Why do you think God uses these sensory experiences in worship at the tabernacle?

APPLY 1. When you want to have a special time with God, what do you do to set the stage: Play some music? Be quiet and listen to God? **2.** When it comes to private worship are you for meat and potatoes or gourmet cooking?

OPEN Who is the one in your family that is gifted in working with their hands?

STUDY 1. If your group was assigned to build the taberna-

---

and washed with water for their ordination. It was necessary, however, for them to clean their hands and feet whenever they entered the Tent of Meeting. To neglect this and bring dirt into God's presence would be an affront to the Holy.

30:33 cut off from his people. This was a most serious punishment, usually meaning execution or banishment.

30:34 fragrant spices—gum resin, onycha and galbanum—and pure frankincense. With the exception of frankincense, these are the same spices used in the anointing oil. The tabernacle must have smelled wonderfully. Coming inside the courtyard, the Israelites would have been met by the sweet smell of incense. When burnt offerings were carried out, either animal or grain, the smell within the tabernacle would have been pungent and powerful.

31:2 Hur. Perhaps this man was with Aaron and Moses at Rephidim when the Israelites defeated the Amalekites (17:10–12).

31:3 with skill, ability and knowledge. God prepared Bezalel for the work of the tabernacle by giving him the

him with the Spirit of God, with skill, ability and knowledge in all
kinds of crafts— 4to make artistic designs for work in gold, silver and
bronze, 5to cut and set stones, to work in wood, and to engage in all
kinds of craftsmanship. 6Moreover, I have appointed Oholiab son of
Ahisamach, of the tribe of Dan, to help him. Also I have given skill to
all the craftsmen to make everything I have commanded you: 7the
Tent of Meeting, the ark of the Testimony with the atonement cover
on it, and all the other furnishings of the tent— 8the table and its articles, the pure gold lampstand and all its accessories, the altar of
incense, 9the altar of burnt offering and all its utensils, the basin with
its stand— 10and also the woven garments, both the sacred garments
for Aaron the priest and the garments for his sons when they serve as
priests, 11and the anointing oil and fragrant incense for the Holy
Place. They are to make them just as I commanded you."

The Sabbath

12Then the LORD said to Moses, 13"Say to the Israelites, 'You must
observe my Sabbaths. This will be a sign between me and you for the
generations to come, so you may know that I am the LORD, who
makes you holy.[a]
14" 'Observe the Sabbath, because it is holy to you. Anyone who
desecrates it must be put to death; whoever does any work on that
day must be cut off from his people. 15For six days, work is to be
done, but the seventh day is a Sabbath of rest, holy to the LORD. Whoever does any work on the Sabbath day must be put to death. 16The
Israelites are to observe the Sabbath, celebrating it for the generations to come as a lasting covenant. 17It will be a sign between me
and the Israelites forever, for in six days the LORD made the heavens
and the earth, and on the seventh day he abstained from work and
rested.' "
18When the LORD finished speaking to Moses on Mount Sinai, he
gave him the two tablets of the Testimony, the tablets of stone inscribed by the finger of God.

The Golden Calf

32 When the people saw that Moses was so long in coming
down from the mountain, they gathered around Aaron and
said, "Come, make us gods[b] who will go before us. As for this fellow
Moses who brought us up out of Egypt, we don't know what has happened to him."

[a]13 Or *who sanctifies you*; or *who sets you apart as holy* [b]1 Or *a god*; also in verses 23 and 31

cle, who would you assign in your group to do the different tasks in building the tabernacle? **2.** How do you think Bezalel and Oholiab felt when God asked them to use their gifts to oversee the building of the tabernacle? **3.** Do you believe these guys were asked because they had natural gifts or were given special anointing for this job?

APPLY Do you feel your gifts lie in working with your hands or working with people?

OPEN Did your grandparents observe the Sabbath?

STUDY 1. How important is the Sabbath in God's instructions to Israel? **2.** What had the Sabbath become by the time of Christ?

APPLY What are you doing to keep the spirit of the Sabbath?

OPEN 1. Did your parents ever catch you having or going to an unapproved party? **2.** What was the most common punishment your parents used when you did something really bad?

STUDY Forty days earlier, Moses had gone up to Mount Sinai to meet with God. It was during

skills and inspiration he needed. God chooses the right person for a job, then gives him or her the talents, experiences and inspiration needed to do it. Moses' entire life is an example of this principle.

31:14 Observe the Sabbath. God is consistent that the Sabbath should be observed—even with the huge task of building and equipping his tabernacle at hand. The message is that even good works should not keep a worker from the Sabbath.

31:16–17 Sabbath ... sign. The observance of the Sabbath was not only a command but also a symbolic act. Since God created the world in six days, then rested (Gen. 1:1–2:3), the observance of the Sabbath put Israel in the same pattern that God created. This pattern was a sign of the covenant relationship between them.

31:18 inscribed by the finger of God. God had initiated the covenant with Israel and had proclaimed its conditions. He was the author of the agreement; therefore, it is fitting that he wrote it.

32:1 Come, make us gods who will go before us. In only a matter of days (less than forty, according to 24:18), the Israelites had forgotten or turned away from God (19:1–7).

this time that God engraved the Ten Commandments onto tablets of stone. However, while Moses was on the mountain, there was trouble brewing down below. **1.** If you could offer a word in defense for the Israelites for what they did while Moses was away with God, what would you say? Are you more disappointed in the people or in Aaron? **2.** What do you think happened when the people started to worship the golden calf? Have you ever been in a situation where things got out of hand (v. 25)? **3.** How would you describe God's tone in verses 7–10? How would you have responded? **4.** What does Moses do to talk God out of destroying the Israelites on the spot? **5.** Why did Moses throw the tablets he had been working on at the foot of the mountain? What would you have done in that situation? **6.** What was the explanation Aaron gave for making the golden calf? How does his explanation square with verse 4? What would you have said to Aaron? **7.** What do you think of the way Moses assessed the situation (vv. 25–26) and took punitive action? **8.** What is Moses asking of God in verses 31–32 as the leader of the people? Have you ever felt this way? How does God reply?

APPLY **1.** What is the closest you have come to seeing everything you gave your life to wiped out in one experience? **2.** How do you usually react when others disappoint you? **3.** What have you found helpful when you need to get on with life after a terrible setback?

2 Aaron answered them, "Take off the gold earrings that your wives,
your sons and your daughters are wearing, and bring them to me."
3 So all the people took off their earrings and brought them to Aaron.
4 He took what they handed him and made it into an idol cast in the
shape of a calf, fashioning it with a tool. Then they said, "These are
your gods,[a] O Israel, who brought you up out of Egypt."

5 When Aaron saw this, he built an altar in front of the calf and
announced, "Tomorrow there will be a festival to the LORD." 6 So the
next day the people rose early and sacrificed burnt offerings and presented fellowship offerings.[b] Afterward they sat down to eat and
drink and got up to indulge in revelry.

7 Then the LORD said to Moses, "Go down, because your people,
whom you brought up out of Egypt, have become corrupt. 8 They have
been quick to turn away from what I commanded them and have
made themselves an idol cast in the shape of a calf. They have bowed
down to it and sacrificed to it and have said, 'These are your gods,
O Israel, who brought you up out of Egypt.'

9 "I have seen these people," the LORD said to Moses, "and they are
a stiff-necked people. 10 Now leave me alone so that my anger may
burn against them and that I may destroy them. Then I will make you
into a great nation."

11 But Moses sought the favor of the LORD his God. "O LORD," he
said, "why should your anger burn against your people, whom you
brought out of Egypt with great power and a mighty hand? 12 Why
should the Egyptians say, 'It was with evil intent that he brought
them out, to kill them in the mountains and to wipe them off the face
of the earth'? Turn from your fierce anger; relent and do not bring disaster on your people. 13 Remember your servants Abraham, Isaac
and Israel, to whom you swore by your own self: 'I will make your descendants as numerous as the stars in the sky and I will give your
descendants all this land I promised them, and it will be their inheritance forever.'" 14 Then the LORD relented and did not bring on his
people the disaster he had threatened.

15 Moses turned and went down the mountain with the two tablets
of the Testimony in his hands. They were inscribed on both sides,

[a] 4 Or *This is your god*; also in verse 8 [b] 6 Traditionally *peace offerings*

32:2 gold earrings. The Israelites had not left Egypt empty-handed. As the instructions for the tabernacle indicate, Israel had brought out gold, silver, fine incense and spices and fine fabrics. This wealth was part of God's plan, however, and was the result of a promise made by God (3:21–22).

32:4 cast in the shape of a calf. Making this idol was a direct violation of the second commandment.

32:5 When Aaron saw this, he built an altar. Aaron had yielded to public pressure just before (vv. 2–4), Aaron now attached the Lord's name to the idolatry. The quick and probably shabby construction of this idol contrasts sharply with the meticulous detail paid to the construction of the tabernacle.

32:6 indulge in revelry. The idol brings out the worst in the Israelites: a wild party. Note the contrast between the serious nature of the tabernacle feasts commanded by God and the wildness provoked by the idol.

32:7 your people. The Israelites' punishment for breaking the commandments would be giving up God's protection and provision. Because of their sin, God was ready to disown them as his covenant children. **you brought up out of Egypt.** The phrase is thick with irony. It was God who brought Israel out of Egypt. Contrast this verse with 15:1–12 and 19:4.

32:10 Then I will make you into a great nation. In God's anger, he was ready to start over with the descendants of Moses.

32:11 whom you brought out of Egypt. Moses turns God's words (in v. 7) back at him. Here, Moses praises God for his deliverance of Israel.

32:14 the LORD relented. It is inherent in God's character to execute justice within the context of mercy. The entire biblical narrative tells of God's efforts to give humankind still another chance for redemption. This mercy extends to nations as well (Jer. 18:7–8).

32:15 tablets of the Testimony. The Ten Commandments were en-

front and back. 16The tablets were the work of God; the writing was the writing of God, engraved on the tablets.

17When Joshua heard the noise of the people shouting, he said to Moses, "There is the sound of war in the camp."

18Moses replied:

"It is not the sound of victory,
 it is not the sound of defeat;
 it is the sound of singing that I hear."

19When Moses approached the camp and saw the calf and the dancing, his anger burned and he threw the tablets out of his hands, breaking them to pieces at the foot of the mountain. 20And he took the calf they had made and burned it in the fire; then he ground it to powder, scattered it on the water and made the Israelites drink it.

21He said to Aaron, "What did these people do to you, that you led them into such great sin?"

22"Do not be angry, my lord," Aaron answered. "You know how prone these people are to evil. 23They said to me, 'Make us gods who will go before us. As for this fellow Moses who brought us up out of Egypt, we don't know what has happened to him.' 24So I told them, 'Whoever has any gold jewelry, take it off.' Then they gave me the gold, and I threw it into the fire, and out came this calf!"

25Moses saw that the people were running wild and that Aaron had let them get out of control and so become a laughingstock to their enemies. 26So he stood at the entrance to the camp and said, "Whoever is for the LORD, come to me." And all the Levites rallied to him.

27Then he said to them, "This is what the LORD, the God of Israel, says: 'Each man strap a sword to his side. Go back and forth through the camp from one end to the other, each killing his brother and friend and neighbor.' " 28The Levites did as Moses commanded, and that day about three thousand of the people died. 29Then Moses said, "You have been set apart to the LORD today, for you were against your own sons and brothers, and he has blessed you this day."

30The next day Moses said to the people, "You have committed a great sin. But now I will go up to the LORD; perhaps I can make atonement for your sin."

31So Moses went back to the LORD and said, "Oh, what a great sin

---

graved on the tablets as the basic conditions of God's covenant with Israel. The word "testimony" is related to a Babylonian word that meant "covenant stipulations."

32:19 breaking them to pieces. Israel's violation broke the covenant. Shattering the tablets dramatically symbolizes the broken covenant.

32:20 burned it ... ground it ... scattered it. The idol had to be utterly destroyed to conform once again to the second commandment. Moses' dramatic destruction of the golden calf also pointed out clearly to Israel that the idol had no power, that all power came from God.

32:22–23 They said to me. Aaron knew that building the idol was wrong. In his panic over Moses' return, he blamed his fellow Israelites. His role in the emerging priesthood made his bad judgment even more serious.

32:24 out came this calf. Aaron's explanation was almost comical. It sounds like a six-year-old child's excuse for bad behavior.

32:25 people were running wild. This phrase captures the nature of existence for those who do not live in harmony with God's commands.

32:26 Whoever is for the LORD. For the Lord or not? That decision determines everything else.

32:27 killing his brother ... neighbor. Sometimes people are faced with a conflict between allegiance to God, to family and to friends. Jesus spoke directly to this issue in Matthew 10:37, making it clear (as these verses do as well) that one's highest allegiance must always be to God.

32:30 atonement for your sin. Moses, his anger spent and "cleansing" done, moves back into his role as mediator between his people and God. He has taken the spiritual welfare of Israel on his shoulders. He knows how close they were to destruction.

these people have committed! They have made themselves gods of
gold. 32But now, please forgive their sin—but if not, then blot me out
of the book you have written."
33The LORD replied to Moses, "Whoever has sinned against me I
will blot out of my book. 34Now go, lead the people to the place I
spoke of, and my angel will go before you. However, when the time
comes for me to punish, I will punish them for their sin."
35And the LORD struck the people with a plague because of what
they did with the calf Aaron had made.

33 Then the LORD said to Moses, "Leave this place, you and the
people you brought up out of Egypt, and go up to the land I
promised on oath to Abraham, Isaac and Jacob, saying, 'I will give it
to your descendants.' 2I will send an angel before you and drive out
the Canaanites, Amorites, Hittites, Perizzites, Hivites and Jebusites.
3Go up to the land flowing with milk and honey. But I will not go with
you, because you are a stiff-necked people and I might destroy you
on the way."
4When the people heard these distressing words, they began to
mourn and no one put on any ornaments. 5For the LORD had said to
Moses, "Tell the Israelites, 'You are a stiff-necked people. If I were to
go with you even for a moment, I might destroy you. Now take off
your ornaments and I will decide what to do with you.' " 6So the Israelites stripped off their ornaments at Mount Horeb.

OPEN When you were a kid, did you build a tree house or a secret hideaway?

STUDY 1. If you had been Moses after the disaster of the "golden calf," what would you do? **2.** Why do you think Moses "pitched" a tent outside of the camp some distance away and went there every day?

The Tent of Meeting

7Now Moses used to take a tent and pitch it outside the camp some
distance away, calling it the "tent of meeting." Anyone inquiring of
the LORD would go to the tent of meeting outside the camp. 8And
whenever Moses went out to the tent, all the people rose and stood at
the entrances to their tents, watching Moses until he entered the
tent. 9As Moses went into the tent, the pillar of cloud would come
down and stay at the entrance, while the LORD spoke with Moses.
10Whenever the people saw the pillar of cloud standing at the entrance to the tent, they all stood and worshiped, each at the entrance

---

32:33 Whoever has sinned against me. Moses is a good mediator, but he cannot make atonement for sin. Only Jesus can make atonement for someone else.

32:34 my angel will go before you. Though he cannot make atonement, Moses is instructed to reassure Israel that God's covenant is intact. Despite the people's disobedience, God will keep his promises to them. He will continue to lead them.

33:3–5 I will not go with you. Because the people were consistently disobedient, God now takes a side-line seat. Throughout the first five books of the Bible, God is portrayed with almost human-like qualities. Here God takes himself out of the game for a while, almost as if to relax from his agitation over the people's evil behavior. **stiff-necked.** To be stiff-necked is to be stubborn and unyielding. The Hebrews had just proved their lack of faith by creating an idol to worship even while Moses was with God at the top of a mountain receiving the Ten Commandments. God had provided for them ever since the departure from Egypt, yet they continued to stubbornly doubt him. **might destroy you.** One other time God had expressed his frustration with humanity much like he did here—just before he sent the flood in the time of Noah (Gen. 6:6–8).

33:6 stripped off their ornaments. In the ancient world (as we sometimes do today) people adjusted their appearance to suit the occasion. If they were distressed, they often put on sackcloth and rubbed ashes on their face. If they were celebrating, they dressed up. This act of removing accessories, anything that dressed them up, was an act of mourning and remorse because of God's disapproval. Ornaments might have included rings, necklaces, bracelets or anklets—the very things they had offered earlier to create the idol that angered God.

33:7 tent. The tent mentioned here was different from the tabernacle. It was probably Moses' own tent. The plans for the tabernacle were given to Moses starting in chapter 25. The construction of the tabernacle is described starting in chapter 35. This tent was a shrine, a place to pray and inquire of God. It sat outside of camp rather than in the center of it.

33:8 the people rose and stood. Now the people looked to God in reverence. They stood off at a distance in awe of God.

to his tent. [11]The LORD would speak to Moses face to face, as a man speaks with his friend. Then Moses would return to the camp, but his young aide Joshua son of Nun did not leave the tent.

Moses and the Glory of the LORD

[12]Moses said to the LORD, "You have been telling me, 'Lead these people,' but you have not let me know whom you will send with me. You have said, 'I know you by name and you have found favor with me.' [13]If you are pleased with me, teach me your ways so I may know you and continue to find favor with you. Remember that this nation is your people."

[14]The LORD replied, "My Presence will go with you, and I will give you rest."

[15]Then Moses said to him, "If your Presence does not go with us, do not send us up from here. [16]How will anyone know that you are pleased with me and with your people unless you go with us? What else will distinguish me and your people from all the other people on the face of the earth?"

[17]And the LORD said to Moses, "I will do the very thing you have asked, because I am pleased with you and I know you by name."

[18]Then Moses said, "Now show me your glory."

[19]And the LORD said, "I will cause all my goodness to pass in front of you, and I will proclaim my name, the LORD, in your presence. I will have mercy on whom I will have mercy, and I will have compassion on whom I will have compassion. [20]But," he said, "you cannot see my face, for no one may see me and live."

[21]Then the LORD said, "There is a place near me where you may stand on a rock. [22]When my glory passes by, I will put you in a cleft in the rock and cover you with my hand until I have passed by. [23]Then I will remove my hand and you will see my back; but my face must not be seen."

APPLY What have you found helpful in restoring your soul when you are nearly overwhelmed?

OPEN What character trait comes to mind when you think of Abraham Lincoln?

STUDY Moses didn't want the job of leading the Israelites, but he is stuck with it. **1.** Reading between the lines in verses 12–13, describe the emotional state of Moses at this time? **2.** How does God reply (v. 14)? What is God trying to do to Moses? **3.** As a psychiatrist, how would you describe the feelings that Moses is showing in verses 15–16? **4.** How does God deal with Moses' feelings (v. 17)? **5.** What, in turn, does Moses request (v. 18)? How does God deal with this request (vv. 19–23)? **6.** How would you describe this whole episode if you were a leadership trainer?

APPLY What is the closest you have come to having burnout in a job where you felt alone, overwhelmed or forsaken?

33:11 as a man speaks with his friend. By this time, Moses had walked a long journey with God by his side. He had seen God in a burning bush, a cloud, a still small voice and a pillar of fire. He had met with God on a mountain, in a desert and in the middle of a miraculously dry riverbed. He was a friend of God, an intimate friend. **Joshua.** Joshua was the soldier who led the people, following Moses, to conquer the Promised Land. Here he stands watch, but soon he will be in the center of the action.

33:12 you have found favor with me. Personal dealings are always bound by the quality of relationships. Moses does not refer back to a contract or an agreement but to the call of God which had changed the course of his life (chapters 3–4).

33:13 If you are pleased. Of all the things Moses could have asked for (and would ask for), he began with the desire to know God more. He established their relationship in the previous verse, then asked for a deeper relationship. **this nation is your people.** Moses broadened his "argument" to God. Not only had God established a relationship with Moses, he had established a relationship with Moses' people. This was the promise that carried generations of Hebrews to their homeland.

33:14 I will give you rest. This is the product of living in the presence of God. When we live like Moses—sure of who we are in God's sight and never alone—we have peace and rest.

33:17 I know you by name. God reaffirms to Moses the nature of their relationship. We often are like children needing to know from our father that we are in good standing, that we have his favor and that he is accessible. Moses asked for those very things. God responded with the comfort and assurance Moses needed.

33:18 show me your glory. Since God spoke to Moses as a friend (v. 11), it would be a natural request for Moses to want to see God. Moses had based his life and taken tremendous risks for a voice of a person he had never seen. Remember that Moses did not have the Bible to teach him about God. Moses stretched his faith in ways that we will never know, given our access to the history of God's dealing with the world. Nevertheless, Moses wants what all people seek, greater knowledge—direct and irrefutable—of the divine.

33:19 goodness. Moses was going to see God's goodness, the wonder of God. **name.** In ancient days names were more meaningful than they are today. Someone's name revealed their character. In proclaiming his name, God proclaimed his character. **I will ... on whom I will.** God revealed to Moses not only his mercy and compassion but the sovereignty of his choice to offer compassion and mercy.

OPEN What is your latest experience of breaking or losing something when it was nearly finished and you had to start all over?

STUDY Moses had spent 40 days on the mountain with God when he learned that his people were holding a wild party down below. He threw the tablets, along with the Ten Commandments away in anger and disgust. Now he has to start all over. **1.** How would you feel if you had to start all over? **2.** What does God remind Moses of (vv. 5–7)? Describe this in your own words? **3.** How does Moses respond (vv. 9–10)? What does Moses acknowledge? **4.** What does God want Moses to realize about the people in the land where the Israelites are headed? What are the Israelites to guard against? Why? **5.** How would you describe the 10 "do's and don'ts" in verses 15–26? What are they designed to do? **6.** How do you think the Israelites acted this time in the 40 days that Moses was away from the camp? **7.** Do you think the church today needs to draw the line and be more specific about things like marrying unbelievers, observing the Sabbath, giving a tithe, etc.? Where do you draw the line between holy living and legalism?

APPLY 1. As you grow in your faith and understanding of God, how has your perspective changed on what God wants you to be? **2.** What is God teaching you now? **3.** How can this group help you this week in prayer?

The New Stone Tablets

34 The LORD said to Moses, "Chisel out two stone tablets like
the first ones, and I will write on them the words that were
on the first tablets, which you broke. [2]Be ready in the morning, and
then come up on Mount Sinai. Present yourself to me there on top of
the mountain. [3]No one is to come with you or be seen anywhere on
the mountain; not even the flocks and herds may graze in front of the
mountain."

[4]So Moses chiseled out two stone tablets like the first ones and
went up Mount Sinai early in the morning, as the LORD had commanded him; and he carried the two stone tablets in his hands. [5]Then
the LORD came down in the cloud and stood there with him and
proclaimed his name, the LORD. [6]And he passed in front of Moses,
proclaiming, "The LORD, the LORD, the compassionate and gracious
God, slow to anger, abounding in love and faithfulness, [7]maintaining
love to thousands, and forgiving wickedness, rebellion and sin. Yet he
does not leave the guilty unpunished; he punishes the children and
their children for the sin of the fathers to the third and fourth generation."

[8]Moses bowed to the ground at once and worshiped. [9]"O Lord, if I
have found favor in your eyes," he said, "then let the Lord go with us.
Although this is a stiff-necked people, forgive our wickedness and
our sin, and take us as your inheritance."

[10]Then the LORD said: "I am making a covenant with you. Before all
your people I will do wonders never before done in any nation in all
the world. The people you live among will see how awesome is the
work that I, the LORD, will do for you. [11]Obey what I command you
today. I will drive out before you the Amorites, Canaanites, Hittites,
Perizzites, Hivites and Jebusites. [12]Be careful not to make a treaty
with those who live in the land where you are going, or they will be a
snare among you. [13]Break down their altars, smash their sacred
stones and cut down their Asherah poles.[a] [14]Do not worship any
other god, for the LORD, whose name is Jealous, is a jealous God.

[15]"Be careful not to make a treaty with those who live in the land;
for when they prostitute themselves to their gods and sacrifice to
them, they will invite you and you will eat their sacrifices. [16]And when

[a]13 That is, symbols of the goddess Asherah

34:1 I will write. God inscribed the tablets with the commandments both times. The first time Moses threw them down in anger and broke them.

34:6–7 The LORD. God's explanation of himself here is cited many other times in Scripture, including Numbers 14:17–18; Nehemiah 9:17; Psalm 86:15; Joel 2:13 and Jonah 4:2. At that time the books of Moses were the bulk of the Scriptures; therefore this powerful passage was quoted often.

34:10 covenant. A covenant can be as simple as a promise or as complex as a fine-print contract. With God, though, a covenant is not like a contract where both parties are bound equally to their obligations. In ancient days, God did make promises to people, sometimes based on how those people chose to respond. God made a covenant with Noah (Gen. 6:18), Abraham (Gen. 17:3–4), the Hebrews (6:3–4) and others.

34:12 snare. If the Hebrews established treaties with these people, they could be tempted to join in their false worship.

34:15 prostitute themselves. A prostitute trades her (or his) body for money. An idol worshiper trades his spirit for the hope of earthly gain—better crops, bigger family. Nevertheless we all bear the image of God and belong to him. It is to him that we should direct our worship, faith and prayers. **you will eat.** Some ancient sacrifices ended in a kind of barbecue. Meat was offered on a fire. Certain portions of the meat were burned up or offered to the priests. In some cases, though, part of the meat was eaten by the worshiper and his friends and family. The Bible mentions even in the New Testament the conflict between a believer being offered meat that was first offered to an idol. Here God warns the Hebrews that if they hang out with people who worship idols, they will eventually be invited to one of those barbecues.

you choose some of their daughters as wives for your sons and those
daughters prostitute themselves to their gods, they will lead your
sons to do the same.
17"Do not make cast idols.
18"Celebrate the Feast of Unleavened Bread. For seven days eat
bread made without yeast, as I commanded you. Do this at the appointed time in the month of Abib, for in that month you came out of
Egypt.
19"The first offspring of every womb belongs to me, including all
the firstborn males of your livestock, whether from herd or flock.
20Redeem the firstborn donkey with a lamb, but if you do not redeem
it, break its neck. Redeem all your firstborn sons.
"No one is to appear before me empty-handed.
21"Six days you shall labor, but on the seventh day you shall rest;
even during the plowing season and harvest you must rest.
22"Celebrate the Feast of Weeks with the firstfruits of the wheat
harvest, and the Feast of Ingathering at the turn of the year.[a] 23Three
times a year all your men are to appear before the Sovereign LORD,
the God of Israel. 24I will drive out nations before you and enlarge
your territory, and no one will covet your land when you go up three
times each year to appear before the LORD your God.
25"Do not offer the blood of a sacrifice to me along with anything
containing yeast, and do not let any of the sacrifice from the Passover
Feast remain until morning.
26"Bring the best of the firstfruits of your soil to the house of the
LORD your God.
"Do not cook a young goat in its mother's milk."
27Then the LORD said to Moses, "Write down these words, for in accordance with these words I have made a covenant with you and with
Israel." 28Moses was there with the LORD forty days and forty nights
without eating bread or drinking water. And he wrote on the tablets
the words of the covenant—the Ten Commandments.

The Radiant Face of Moses

29When Moses came down from Mount Sinai with the two tablets
of the Testimony in his hands, he was not aware that his face was
radiant because he had spoken with the LORD. 30When Aaron and all
the Israelites saw Moses, his face was radiant, and they were afraid
to come near him. 31But Moses called to them; so Aaron and all the
leaders of the community came back to him, and he spoke to them.
32Afterward all the Israelites came near him, and he gave them all the
commands the LORD had given him on Mount Sinai.
33When Moses finished speaking to them, he put a veil over his

[a]22 That is, in the fall

OPEN Do you sunburn easily?

STUDY Moses has just spent 40 days with God on Mount Sinai to receive the Ten Commandments again. **1.** What do you think caused Moses' face to shine? **2.** How did the leaders and the people react when they saw Moses? **3.** Why do you think Moses wore a veil over his face when he spoke to the people after this? **4.** How does Paul use this episode in 2 Corinthians 3?

34:27 I have made a covenant. In giving Israel guidelines for living, God was establishing their covenant relationship. He was letting them know what he expected and how they should live.

34:28 he wrote. "He" probably refers to God, who said that he would write down the words on the stones that Moses chiseled (v. 1).

34:29 his face was radiant. Moses' face glowed. Everyone could see it. Today a glowing face connotes happiness. Often brides are described as radiant. Moses, though, had more than a happy face. He had to cover his face because the strange glow disturbed the people around him.

34:33 veil. This word for "veil" is used only here in the Old Testament. Its only other occurrence is in 2 Corinthians 3:13, which adds that Moses continued to wear the veil even after the glow began to fade.

APPLY Who is a person who radiates God?

OPEN 1. Who in your family is the organizer for big projects? **2.** Who taught you to give generously?

STUDY The Israelites needed a place for worship for their journey to the Promised Land. God gave them the specifications for building a tabernacle, and the furnishings. Now, they need to get organized and build it. **1.** If you were given the task of organizing this huge undertaking, what would you do? **2.** As you read over the list of items they will need to build and furnish the tabernacle, what is your response? **3.** How would you describe the "sales pitch" that Moses makes to the people: High pressure? Low pressure? No pressure? **4.** If you had been one of the Israelites and Moses had laid out the need for the tabernacle the way he did, would you want to participate? **5.** What are three or four principles here to consider the next time you are involved in a big project for God?

APPLY 1. In your spiritual journey, what project that you got involved in gave you the greatest satisfaction? **2.** Where is God nudging you to give some of your time and resources now?

face. [34]But whenever he entered the LORD's presence to speak with him, he removed the veil until he came out. And when he came out and told the Israelites what he had been commanded, [35]they saw that his face was radiant. Then Moses would put the veil back over his face until he went in to speak with the LORD.

Sabbath Regulations

35 Moses assembled the whole Israelite community and said to them, "These are the things the LORD has commanded you to do: [2]For six days, work is to be done, but the seventh day shall be your holy day, a Sabbath of rest to the LORD. Whoever does any work on it must be put to death. [3]Do not light a fire in any of your dwellings on the Sabbath day."

Materials for the Tabernacle

[4]Moses said to the whole Israelite community, "This is what the LORD has commanded: [5]From what you have, take an offering for the LORD. Everyone who is willing is to bring to the LORD an offering of gold, silver and bronze; [6]blue, purple and scarlet yarn and fine linen; goat hair; [7]ram skins dyed red and hides of sea cows[a]; acacia wood; [8]olive oil for the light; spices for the anointing oil and for the fragrant incense; [9]and onyx stones and other gems to be mounted on the ephod and breastpiece.

[10]"All who are skilled among you are to come and make everything the LORD has commanded: [11]the tabernacle with its tent and its covering, clasps, frames, crossbars, posts and bases; [12]the ark with its poles and the atonement cover and the curtain that shields it; [13]the table with its poles and all its articles and the bread of the Presence; [14]the lampstand that is for light with its accessories, lamps and oil for the light; [15]the altar of incense with its poles, the anointing oil and the fragrant incense; the curtain for the doorway at the entrance to the tabernacle; [16]the altar of burnt offering with its bronze grating, its poles and all its utensils; the bronze basin with its stand; [17]the curtains of the courtyard with its posts and bases, and the curtain for the entrance to the courtyard; [18]the tent pegs for the tabernacle and for the courtyard, and their ropes; [19]the woven garments worn for ministering in the sanctuary—both the sacred garments for Aaron the priest and the garments for his sons when they serve as priests."

[20]Then the whole Israelite community withdrew from Moses' presence, [21]and everyone who was willing and whose heart moved him came and brought an offering to the LORD for the work on the Tent of Meeting, for all its service, and for the sacred garments. [22]All who were willing, men and women alike, came and brought gold jewelry of all kinds: brooches, earrings, rings and ornaments. They all presented their gold as a wave offering to the LORD. [23]Everyone who had blue, purple or scarlet yarn or fine linen, or goat hair, ram skins dyed

[a]7 That is, dugongs; also in verse 23

35:2 holy day, a Sabbath of rest. The Sabbath was serious business to God. The Hebrews were not even supposed to cook meals. It was an extremely important custom directly related to God's resting from creation. By Jesus' time, the Sabbath had taken on legalistic rigor, a development the Lord corrected (Matt. 12:1–14).

35:5 willing. While the Sabbath was a mandatory rest, the gathering of materials for the tabernacle was still required. Yet only those who were willing were asked to bring building materials.

red or hides of sea cows brought them. 24Those presenting an offering of silver or bronze brought it as an offering to the LORD, and
everyone who had acacia wood for any part of the work brought it.
25Every skilled woman spun with her hands and brought what she
had spun—blue, purple or scarlet yarn or fine linen. 26And all the
women who were willing and had the skill spun the goat hair. 27The
leaders brought onyx stones and other gems to be mounted on the
ephod and breastpiece. 28They also brought spices and olive oil for
the light and for the anointing oil and for the fragrant incense. 29All
the Israelite men and women who were willing brought to the LORD
freewill offerings for all the work the LORD through Moses had commanded them to do.

Bezalel and Oholiab

30Then Moses said to the Israelites, "See, the LORD has chosen Bezalel son of Uri, the son of Hur, of the tribe of Judah, 31and he has filled
him with the Spirit of God, with skill, ability and knowledge in all
kinds of crafts— 32to make artistic designs for work in gold, silver
and bronze, 33to cut and set stones, to work in wood and to engage in
all kinds of artistic craftsmanship. 34And he has given both him and
Oholiab son of Ahisamach, of the tribe of Dan, the ability to teach
others. 35He has filled them with skill to do all kinds of work as
craftsmen, designers, embroiderers in blue, purple and scarlet yarn
and fine linen, and weavers—all of them master craftsmen and
36 designers. 1So Bezalel,Oholiab and everyskilled person to
whom the LORD has given skill and ability to know how to
carry out all the work of constructing the sanctuary are to do the
work just as the LORD has commanded."

2Then Moses summoned Bezalel and Oholiab and every skilled
person to whom the LORD had given ability and who was willing to
come and do the work. 3They received from Moses all the offerings
the Israelites had brought to carry out the work of constructing the
sanctuary. And the people continued to bring freewill offerings morning after morning. 4So all the skilled craftsmen who were doing all
the work on the sanctuary left their work 5and said to Moses, "The
people are bringing more than enough for doing the work the LORD
commanded to be done."

6Then Moses gave an order and they sent this word throughout the
camp: "No man or woman is to make anything else as an offering for
the sanctuary." And so the people were restrained from bringing
more, 7because what they already had was more than enough to do
all the work.

The Tabernacle

8All the skilled men among the workmen made the tabernacle with
ten curtains of finely twisted linen and blue, purple and scarlet yarn,
with cherubim worked into them by a skilled craftsman. 9All the
curtains were the same size—twenty-eight cubits long and four cubits wide.[a] 10They joined five of the curtains together and did the
same with the other five. 11Then they made loops of blue material
along the edge of the end curtain in one set, and the same was done
with the end curtain in the other set. 12They also made fifty loops on

[a]9 That is, about 42 feet (about 12.5 meters) long and 6 feet (about 1.8 meters) wide

OPEN When is the last time your church had to turn away gifts?

STUDY In this passage special abilities are recognized as people who are "filled ... with the Spirit of God." **1.** Do you think Bezalel and Oholiab were naturally gifted or given special abilities for this job? How many of these abilities do you possess (vv. 32–33, 35)? **2.** What did Moses have the sense to do (vv. 2–3)? **3.** What happened as the people kept bringing gifts? What did Moses have to do? **4.** Have you ever considered craft skills (v. 31) and the ability to teach others (v. 34) how to work with their hands as "spiritual gifts"? What would this do to the labor force in the church today if these gifts were included in the list of spiritual gifts? What would it do to people who have felt they were second class citizens because they did not have the spectacular gifts?

APPLY **1.** What gift or ability that you have gives you the greatest satisfaction? **2.** What would you say if God asked you to use your gift for a special job?

OPEN **1.** What have you built with your own hands that you take great pride in? **2.** What work project that you were a part of gave you the greatest satisfaction?

STUDY The tabernacle was a temporary structure, like a special tent, that the Israelites could carry with them on their journey to the Promised Land. **1.** From the instructions given here, do you think you could have built the tabernacle? **2.** As you read over the list of things that

were made for the tabernacle, what are your first impressions? **3.** How many people do you think it took for this giant undertaking? **4.** How would you have felt if you had been chosen to be one of the workers? If they could have hired someone to come in and build this project, would they have felt the same? **5.** Why do you think God asked the Israelites to go to so much trouble to build a temporary structure out of these expensive materials? **6.** What will building something that is special likely do for the Israelites?

APPLY **1.** What work project or mission trip do you look back on as a spiritual experience? **2.** What was it about this time that made it so special?

one curtain and fifty loops on the end curtain of the other set, with the loops opposite each other. 13 Then they made fifty gold clasps and used them to fasten the two sets of curtains together so that the tabernacle was a unit.

14 They made curtains of goat hair for the tent over the tabernacle—eleven altogether. 15 All eleven curtains were the same size—thirty cubits long and four cubits wide.[a] 16 They joined five of the curtains into one set and the other six into another set. 17 Then they made fifty loops along the edge of the end curtain in one set and also along the edge of the end curtain in the other set. 18 They made fifty bronze clasps to fasten the tent together as a unit. 19 Then they made for the tent a covering of ram skins dyed red, and over that a covering of hides of sea cows.[b]

20 They made upright frames of acacia wood for the tabernacle. 21 Each frame was ten cubits long and a cubit and a half wide,[c] 22 with two projections set parallel to each other. They made all the frames of the tabernacle in this way. 23 They made twenty frames for the south side of the tabernacle 24 and made forty silver bases to go under them—two bases for each frame, one under each projection. 25 For the other side, the north side of the tabernacle, they made twenty frames 26 and forty silver bases—two under each frame. 27 They made six frames for the far end, that is, the west end of the tabernacle, 28 and two frames were made for the corners of the tabernacle at the far end. 29 At these two corners the frames were double from the bottom all the way to the top and fitted into a single ring; both were made alike. 30 So there were eight frames and sixteen silver bases—two under each frame.

31 They also made crossbars of acacia wood: five for the frames on one side of the tabernacle, 32 five for those on the other side, and five for the frames on the west, at the far end of the tabernacle. 33 They made the center crossbar so that it extended from end to end at the middle of the frames. 34 They overlaid the frames with gold and made gold rings to hold the crossbars. They also overlaid the crossbars with gold.

35 They made the curtain of blue, purple and scarlet yarn and finely twisted linen, with cherubim worked into it by a skilled craftsman. 36 They made four posts of acacia wood for it and overlaid them with gold. They made gold hooks for them and cast their four silver bases. 37 For the entrance to the tent they made a curtain of blue, purple and scarlet yarn and finely twisted linen—the work of an embroiderer; 38 and they made five posts with hooks for them. They overlaid the tops of the posts and their bands with gold and made their five bases of bronze.

OPEN What do you remember about the movie "Raiders of the Lost Ark"?

STUDY The Israelites were a nomadic people. They had lived in Egypt for 400 years as slaves. God delivered them from Pharaoh.

The Ark

37 Bezalel made the ark of acacia wood—two and a half cubits long, a cubit and a half wide, and a cubit and a half high.[d] 2 He overlaid it with pure gold, both inside and out, and made a gold

[a] *15* That is, about 45 feet (about 13.5 meters) long and 6 feet (about 1.8 meters) wide [b] *19* That is, dugongs [c] *21* That is, about 15 feet (about 4.5 meters) long and 2 1/4 feet (about 0.7 meter) wide [d] *1* That is, about 3 3/4 feet (about 1.1 meters) long and 2 1/4 feet (about 0.7 meter) wide and high

37:1–29 Each of the tasks in chapter 37 had been described earlier in chapter 35:10–16, which emphasized the future. Chapter 37 described the work as it was completed. Such repetition can make the book of Exodus seem

molding around it. 3He cast four gold rings for it and fastened them to
its four feet, with two rings on one side and two rings on the other.
4Then he made poles of acacia wood and overlaid them with gold.
5And he inserted the poles into the rings on the sides of the ark to
carry it.
6He made the atonement cover of pure gold—two and a half cubits
long and a cubit and a half wide.[a] 7Then he made two cherubim out of
hammered gold at the ends of the cover. 8He made one cherub on one
end and the second cherub on the other; at the two ends he made
them of one piece with the cover. 9The cherubim had their wings
spread upward, overshadowing the cover with them. The cherubim
faced each other, looking toward the cover.

The Table

10They[b] made the table of acacia wood—two cubits long, a cubit
wide, and a cubit and a half high.[c] 11Then they overlaid it with pure
gold and made a gold molding around it. 12They also made around it
a rim a handbreadth[d] wide and put a gold molding on the rim. 13They
cast four gold rings for the table and fastened them to the four corners, where the four legs were. 14The rings were put close to the rim
to hold the poles used in carrying the table. 15The poles for carrying
the table were made of acacia wood and were overlaid with gold.
16And they made from pure gold the articles for the table—its plates
and dishes and bowls and its pitchers for the pouring out of drink
offerings.

The Lampstand

17They made the lampstand of pure gold and hammered it out,
base and shaft; its flowerlike cups, buds and blossoms were of one
piece with it. 18Six branches extended from the sides of the lampstand—three on one side and three on the other. 19Three cups shaped
like almond flowers with buds and blossoms were on one branch,
three on the next branch and the same for all six branches extending
from the lampstand. 20And on the lampstand were four cups shaped
like almond flowers with buds and blossoms. 21One bud was under
the first pair of branches extending from the lampstand, a second bud
under the second pair, and a third bud under the third pair—six
branches in all. 22The buds and the branches were all of one piece
with the lampstand, hammered out of pure gold.
23They made its seven lamps, as well as its wick trimmers and
trays, of pure gold. 24They made the lampstand and all its accessories
from one talent[e] of pure gold.

The Altar of Incense

25They made the altar of incense out of acacia wood. It was square,
a cubit long and a cubit wide, and two cubits high[f]—its horns of one

[a]*6* That is, about 3 3/4 feet (about 1.1 meters) long and 2 1/4 feet (about 0.7 meter) wide [b]*10* Or *He;* also in verses 11-29 [c]*10* That is, about 3 feet (about 0.9 meter) long, 1 1/2 feet (about 0.5 meter) wide, and 2 1/4 feet (about 0.7 meter) high [d]*12* That is, about 3 inches (about 8 centimeters) [e]*24* That is, about 75 pounds (about 34 kilograms) [f]*25* That is, about 1 1/2 feet (about 0.5 meter) long and wide, and about 3 feet (about 0.9 meter) high

They are now on their way to a land they will have as their own. They need to develop their own special rituals to worship the Lord their God. **1.** What do you know about the temples in Egypt where the Israelites lived before they were liberated? How big were these structures? How high? How impressive? What was their purpose? **2.** How would you compare the tabernacle and the articles described here to these temples? **3.** If you wanted to teach the Israelites not to tolerate sin in any way, how would you go about it? **4.** Why do you think all of the articles in the tabernacle had to be made or overlaid with gold? **5.** Why was the ark (chest) so important? Where did it sit in the tabernacle? **6.** In the first room inside of the tabernacle were three articles: The table of showbread, the lampstand and the altar of incense. How do you think this room looked when a priest stepped inside of it? What would it smell like? **7.** Outside of the tabernacle proper was a courtyard where sacrifices would be offered for the people to God. In this courtyard were two articles: the altar of burnt offering, and the basin for washing. What do you think they looked like? **8.** If you could play the part of God and you wanted to teach your people through the sacrifice the way to approach your Son Jesus Christ, how would you go about teaching them this truth?

APPLY When did you first understand the relationship of the sacrifices in the Old Testament to the sacrifice of Jesus Christ in the New Testament?

---

redundant, but ancient writing typically established facts in several different ways.

37:1 the ark. This ark was the Ark of the Covenant (or ark of the Testimony). It was a holy time capsule that held precious reminders of the Hebrews' journey, kept in the most holy part of the tabernacle where God's presence dwelt.

piece with it. 26They overlaid the top and all the sides and the horns
with pure gold, and made a gold molding around it. 27They made two
gold rings below the molding—two on opposite sides—to hold the
poles used to carry it. 28They made the poles of acacia wood and
overlaid them with gold.

29They also made the sacred anointing oil and the pure, fragrant
incense—the work of a perfumer.

The Altar of Burnt Offering

38 They[a] built the altar of burnt offering of acacia wood, three
cubits[b] high; it was square, five cubits long and five cubits
wide.[c] 2They made a horn at each of the four corners, so that the
horns and the altar were of one piece, and they overlaid the altar with
bronze. 3They made all its utensils of bronze—its pots, shovels,
sprinkling bowls, meat forks and firepans. 4They made a grating for
the altar, a bronze network, to be under its ledge, halfway up the altar. 5They cast bronze rings to hold the poles for the four corners of
the bronze grating. 6They made the poles of acacia wood and overlaid
them with bronze. 7They inserted the poles into the rings so they
would be on the sides of the altar for carrying it. They made it hollow,
out of boards.

Basin for Washing

8They made the bronze basin and its bronze stand from the mirrors
of the women who served at the entrance to the Tent of Meeting.

The Courtyard

9Next they made the courtyard. The south side was a hundred
cubits[d] long and had curtains of finely twisted linen, 10with twenty
posts and twenty bronze bases, and with silver hooks and bands on
the posts. 11The north side was also a hundred cubits long and had
twenty posts and twenty bronze bases, with silver hooks and bands
on the posts.

12The west end was fifty cubits[e] wide and had curtains, with ten
posts and ten bases, with silver hooks and bands on the posts. 13The
east end, toward the sunrise, was also fifty cubits wide. 14Curtains fifteen cubits[f] long were on one side of the entrance, with three posts
and three bases, 15and curtains fifteen cubits long were on the other
side of the entrance to the courtyard, with three posts and three
bases. 16All the curtains around the courtyard were of finely twisted
linen. 17The bases for the posts were bronze. The hooks and bands on
the posts were silver, and their tops were overlaid with silver; so all
the posts of the courtyard had silver bands.

18The curtain for the entrance to the courtyard was of blue, purple
and scarlet yarn and finely twisted linen—the work of an embroiderer. It was twenty cubits[g] long and, like the curtains of the courtyard,
five cubits[h] high, 19with four posts and four bronze bases. Their
hooks and bands were silver, and their tops were overlaid with silver.
20All the tent pegs of the tabernacle and of the surrounding courtyard
were bronze.

---

[a]1 Or *He*; also in verses 2-9 [b]1 That is, about 4 1/2 feet (about 1.3 meters) [c]1 That is, about 7 1/2 feet (about 2.3 meters) long and wide [d]9 That is, about 150 feet (about 46 meters) [e]12 That is, about 75 feet (about 23 meters) [f]14 That is, about 22 1/2 feet (about 6.9 meters) [g]18 That is, about 30 feet (about 9 meters) [h]18 That is, about 7 1/2 feet (about 2.3 meters)

The Materials Used

21These are the amounts of the materials used for the tabernacle,
the tabernacle of the Testimony, which were recorded at Moses' command by the Levites under the direction of Ithamar son of Aaron, the
priest. 22(Bezalel son of Uri, the son of Hur, of the tribe of Judah,
made everything the LORD commanded Moses; 23with him was Oholiab son of Ahisamach, of the tribe of Dan—a craftsman and designer,
and an embroiderer in blue, purple and scarlet yarn and fine linen.)
24The total amount of the gold from the wave offering used for all the
work on the sanctuary was 29 talents and 730 shekels,[a] according to
the sanctuary shekel.
25The silver obtained from those of the community who were
counted in the census was 100 talents and 1,775 shekels,[b] according
to the sanctuary shekel— 26one beka per person, that is, half a
shekel,[c] according to the sanctuary shekel, from everyone who had
crossed over to those counted, twenty years old or more, a total of
603,550 men. 27The 100 talents[d] of silver were used to cast the bases
for the sanctuary and for the curtain—100 bases from the 100 talents, one talent for each base. 28They used the 1,775 shekels[e] to make
the hooks for the posts, to overlay the tops of the posts, and to make
their bands.
29The bronze from the wave offering was 70 talents and 2,400
shekels.[f] 30They used it to make the bases for the entrance to the Tent
of Meeting, the bronze altar with its bronze grating and all its utensils, 31the bases for the surrounding courtyard and those for its entrance and all the tent pegs for the tabernacle and those for the
surrounding courtyard.

The Priestly Garments

39 From the blue, purple and scarlet yarn they made woven
garments for ministering in the sanctuary. They also made
sacred garments for Aaron, as the LORD commanded Moses.

The Ephod

2They[g] made the ephod of gold, and of blue, purple and scarlet
yarn, and of finely twisted linen. 3They hammered out thin sheets of
gold and cut strands to be worked into the blue, purple and scarlet
yarn and fine linen—the work of a skilled craftsman. 4They made
shoulder pieces for the ephod, which were attached to two of its corners, so it could be fastened. 5Its skillfully woven waistband was like
it—of one piece with the ephod and made with gold, and with blue,
purple and scarlet yarn, and with finely twisted linen, as the LORD
commanded Moses.

[a]24 The weight of the gold was a little over one ton (about 1 metric ton). [b]25 The weight of the silver was a little over 3 3/4 tons (about 3.4 metric tons). [c]26 That is, about 1/5 ounce (about 5.5 grams) [d]27 That is, about 3 3/4 tons (about 3.4 metric tons) [e]28 That is, about 45 pounds (about 20 kilograms) [f]29 The weight of the bronze was about 2 1/2 tons (about 2.4 metric tons). [g]2 Or *He*; also in verses 7, 8 and 22

OPEN **1.** How did you dress (or will you dress) for your wedding? **2.** Did you have your clothes custom made? Out of what?

STUDY The garments that Aaron and his sons were to wear while officiating in the tabernacle were very important. Everything about these garments had meaning. The garments were a teaching tool—to explain the relationship of God to his people. **1.** Have you ever been to a ceremony where officials were dressed in robes? What was this like? **2.** If you were an ordinary Israelite and you came to the tabernacle to offer your sacrifice and you saw the high priest wearing this outfit, how would you feel? **3.** What does the book of Hebrews say about the tabernacle and the priests since the death of Christ (Heb. 8–10)? What does Paul say

38:25 talents and ... shekels. At this time the value of coinage was set by weight, not fixed value backed by a government treasury. Often the coins were actually weights that would be placed on scales to buy that same weight of flour or grain. A shekel was about 1/5 of an ounce, and a talent was 75 pounds. Each man over 19 was required to pay a half-shekel for the census offering (30:11–16).

38:26 603,550 men. This census figure corresponds exactly to the number of half-shekels required for the census tax and also to the count found in Numbers 1:46.

about a Christian's new garments to approach God with? **4.** What did the garments for the high priest and serving priests in the tabernacle convey about God that could not be conveyed in any other way (28:2–30)?

APPLY What aspects of worship do you like best?

____

6They mounted the onyx stones in gold filigree settings and engraved them like a seal with the names of the sons of Israel. 7Then they fastened them on the shoulder pieces of the ephod as memorial stones for the sons of Israel, as the LORD commanded Moses.

The Breastpiece

8They fashioned the breastpiece—the work of a skilled craftsman. They made it like the ephod: of gold, and of blue, purple and scarlet yarn, and of finely twisted linen. 9It was square—a span[a] long and a span wide—and folded double. 10Then they mounted four rows of precious stones on it. In the first row there was a ruby, a topaz and a beryl; 11in the second row a turquoise, a sapphire[b] and an emerald; 12in the third row a jacinth, an agate and an amethyst; 13in the fourth row a chrysolite, an onyx and a jasper.[c] They were mounted in gold filigree settings. 14There were twelve stones, one for each of the names of the sons of Israel, each engraved like a seal with the name of one of the twelve tribes.

15For the breastpiece they made braided chains of pure gold, like a rope. 16They made two gold filigree settings and two gold rings, and fastened the rings to two of the corners of the breastpiece. 17They fastened the two gold chains to the rings at the corners of the breastpiece, 18and the other ends of the chains to the two settings, attaching them to the shoulder pieces of the ephod at the front. 19They made two gold rings and attached them to the other two corners of the breastpiece on the inside edge next to the ephod. 20Then they made two more gold rings and attached them to the bottom of the shoulder pieces on the front of the ephod, close to the seam just above the waistband of the ephod. 21They tied the rings of the breastpiece to the rings of the ephod with blue cord, connecting it to the waistband so that the breastpiece would not swing out from the ephod—as the LORD commanded Moses.

Other Priestly Garments

22They made the robe of the ephod entirely of blue cloth—the work of a weaver— 23with an opening in the center of the robe like the opening of a collar,[d] and a band around this opening, so that it would not tear. 24They made pomegranates of blue, purple and scarlet yarn and finely twisted linen around the hem of the robe. 25And they made bells of pure gold and attached them around the hem between the pomegranates. 26The bells and pomegranates alternated around the hem of the robe to be worn for ministering, as the LORD commanded Moses.

27For Aaron and his sons, they made tunics of fine linen—the work of a weaver— 28and the turban of fine linen, the linen headbands and the undergarments of finely twisted linen. 29The sash was of finely twisted linen and blue, purple and scarlet yarn—the work of an embroiderer—as the LORD commanded Moses.

30They made the plate, the sacred diadem, out of pure gold and engraved on it, like an inscription on a seal: HOLY TO THE LORD. 31Then

[a] *9* That is, about 9 inches (about 22 centimeters) [b] *11* Or *lapis lazuli* [c] *13* The precise identification of some of these precious stones is uncertain. [d] *23* The meaning of the Hebrew for this word is uncertain.

they fastened a blue cord to it to attach it to the turban, as the LORD
commanded Moses.

Moses Inspects the Tabernacle

32So all the work on the tabernacle, the Tent of Meeting, was completed. The Israelites did everything just as the LORD commanded
Moses. 33Then they brought the tabernacle to Moses: the tent and all
its furnishings, its clasps, frames, crossbars, posts and bases; 34the
covering of ram skins dyed red, the covering of hides of sea cows[a]
and the shielding curtain; 35the ark of the Testimony with its poles
and the atonement cover; 36the table with all its articles and the
bread of the Presence; 37the pure gold lampstand with its row of
lamps and all its accessories, and the oil for the light; 38the gold altar,
the anointing oil, the fragrant incense, and the curtain for the entrance to the tent; 39the bronze altar with its bronze grating, its poles
and all its utensils; the basin with its stand; 40the curtains of the
courtyard with its posts and bases, and the curtain for the entrance to
the courtyard; the ropes and tent pegs for the courtyard; all the
furnishings for the tabernacle, the Tent of Meeting; 41and the woven
garments worn for ministering in the sanctuary, both the sacred
garments for Aaron the priest and the garments for his sons when
serving as priests.

42The Israelites had done all the work just as the LORD had commanded Moses. 43Moses inspected the work and saw that they had
done it just as the LORD had commanded. So Moses blessed them.

Setting Up the Tabernacle

40 Then the LORD said to Moses: 2"Set up the tabernacle, the
Tent of Meeting, on the first day of the first month. 3Place the
ark of the Testimony in it and shield the ark with the curtain. 4Bring in
the table and set out what belongs on it. Then bring in the lampstand
and set up its lamps. 5Place the gold altar of incense in front of the ark
of the Testimony and put the curtain at the entrance to the tabernacle.

6"Place the altar of burnt offering in front of the entrance to the
tabernacle, the Tent of Meeting; 7place the basin between the Tent of
Meeting and the altar and put water in it. 8Set up the courtyard
around it and put the curtain at the entrance to the courtyard.

9"Take the anointing oil and anoint the tabernacle and everything
in it; consecrate it and all its furnishings, and it will be holy. 10Then
anoint the altar of burnt offering and all its utensils; consecrate the
altar, and it will be most holy. 11Anoint the basin and its stand and
consecrate them.

[a]34 That is, dugongs

OPEN How often did your parents inspect your room?

STUDY From beginning to end the tabernacle was designed by God and the instructions were given to Moses to carry out. Moses delegated the actual building of the tabernacle and the articles to others. **1.** How do you think the workers felt when Moses came to inspect their work? Would you have taken pride in your work if you were one of them? **2.** What do you think this work project did for the whole nation?

APPLY Who is the person in your life who verbally "blessed" you for the work you did while growing up?

OPEN 1. Have you ever built a new house or helped refurbish an existing house? **2.** What do you remember about moving day?

STUDY The tabernacle probably took the work of several hundred people and several months. Now comes the task of bringing everything together and setting it in place. **1.** How would you feel if you were in charge of this assembly project? **2.** Could you make a diagram from this description of the two special rooms and place the articles of furniture where they belong? **3.** What separates the two rooms? What is to go behind the curtain in this very special room? **4.** What is to go in the courtyard outside of the tabernacle? **5.** What does the book of Hebrews say about the purpose and function of this

39:32 just as the LORD commanded. Throughout the Bible, people fail God. But here the Israelites obey him to the letter. Noah did the same with plans for the ark (Gen. 6:22). Moses and Aaron did it in their stand-off with Pharaoh (7:10). David did it in battle (2 Sam. 5:25).

39:43 Moses inspected the work. Moses had a difficult role to play in the lives of his people. He had to rally them as well as chastise them, confront them and mitigate their differences. Here is a rare moment when Moses gets to observe their work and offer them congratulations and blessings.

40:3 shield the ark with the curtain. Instructions for handling the ark were always detailed and cumbersome, but then, it held the people's (and God's) most treasured items. The Israelites were told how to carry it, how to move it and how to fill it. Once seventy men died from looking into the ark (1 Sam. 6:19). Once the ark was carried improperly, and a man died because he touched it to prevent its fall (2 Sam. 6:6–7). The ark was one item for which the user's manual was an important read.

tabernacle (Heb. 9:1–10)? **6.** What does the book of Hebrews say about the consecration of this tabernacle when it was set up (Heb. 9:19–22)? **7.** What did the book of Hebrews say about the sacrifices that were performed every day at this tabernacle and how did the blood of Christ change this (Heb. 9:23–28)? **8.** What happened when everything was in place (vv. 34–38)? How important do you think this was to the Israelites? What do you think that experience was like? **9.** What would the cloud at the door of the tabernacle do for the Israelites for the rest of their journey to the Promised Land? **10.** What has the book of Exodus contributed to the larger story of God's plan of salvation?

APPLY 1. Could you use a pillar of cloud by day and of fire by night to help you decide what God wants you to do? **2.** Is the pillar right now settled at the door of your house or has it started to move? Where? **3.** What do you appreciate most about the group you are in?

---

12 "Bring Aaron and his sons to the entrance to the Tent of Meeting and wash them with water. 13 Then dress Aaron in the sacred garments, anoint him and consecrate him so he may serve me as priest. 14 Bring his sons and dress them in tunics. 15 Anoint them just as you anointed their father, so they may serve me as priests. Their anointing will be to a priesthood that will continue for all generations to come." 16 Moses did everything just as the LORD commanded him.

17 So the tabernacle was set up on the first day of the first month in the second year. 18 When Moses set up the tabernacle, he put the bases in place, erected the frames, inserted the crossbars and set up the posts. 19 Then he spread the tent over the tabernacle and put the covering over the tent, as the LORD commanded him.

20 He took the Testimony and placed it in the ark, attached the poles to the ark and put the atonement cover over it. 21 Then he brought the ark into the tabernacle and hung the shielding curtain and shielded the ark of the Testimony, as the LORD commanded him.

22 Moses placed the table in the Tent of Meeting on the north side of the tabernacle outside the curtain 23 and set out the bread on it before the LORD, as the LORD commanded him.

24 He placed the lampstand in the Tent of Meeting opposite the table on the south side of the tabernacle 25 and set up the lamps before the LORD, as the LORD commanded him.

26 Moses placed the gold altar in the Tent of Meeting in front of the curtain 27 and burned fragrant incense on it, as the LORD commanded him. 28 Then he put up the curtain at the entrance to the tabernacle.

29 He set the altar of burnt offering near the entrance to the tabernacle, the Tent of Meeting, and offered on it burnt offerings and grain offerings, as the LORD commanded him.

30 He placed the basin between the Tent of Meeting and the altar and put water in it for washing, 31 and Moses and Aaron and his sons used it to wash their hands and feet. 32 They washed whenever they entered the Tent of Meeting or approached the altar, as the LORD commanded Moses.

33 Then Moses set up the courtyard around the tabernacle and altar and put up the curtain at the entrance to the courtyard. And so Moses finished the work.

The Glory of the Lord

34 Then the cloud covered the Tent of Meeting, and the glory of the LORD filled the tabernacle. 35 Moses could not enter the Tent of Meeting because the cloud had settled upon it, and the glory of the LORD filled the tabernacle.

36 In all the travels of the Israelites, whenever the cloud lifted from above the tabernacle, they would set out; 37 but if the cloud did not lift, they did not set out—until the day it lifted. 38 So the cloud of the LORD was over the tabernacle by day, and fire was in the cloud by night, in the sight of all the house of Israel during all their travels.

40:16 Moses did everything. God credited Moses with faith and obedience. This verse affirms that he took no shortcuts and beat around no bushes. In fact, God called Moses the most humble man on earth in Numbers 12:3.

40:36 whenever the cloud lifted. The tabernacle became the travel gauge for the Hebrews. Just as God led them with a cloud by day and a pillar of fire by night (13:21), now the cloud settled on the tabernacle and lifted when it was time to pack up.

Leviticus

Author. The writer is Moses. Although his name is not listed in the text, Leviticus is a sequel to Exodus, which does cite Moses as the author. Jesus also referred to Moses as the author when he spoke of Moses' laws regarding leprosy (14:2–32; Mark 1:44).

Date. Leviticus was written shortly after the Hebrews' exodus from Egypt. Many assume it occurred during the last half of the 15th century (1450–1500 B.C.).

Personal Reading	Group Study Topic and Reading	
1:1–5:13	Burnt Offerings	1:1–17
5:14–7:38	Fellowship Offerings	7:11–21
8:1–36	Ordination of Aaron	8:1–36
9:1–10:20	Nadab and Abihu	10:1–20
11:1–13:59	Clean and Unclean	11:1–47
14:1–15:33	Skin Diseases	14:1–32
16:1–17:16	Day of Atonement	16:1–34
18:1–20:27	Various Laws	19:1–37
21:1–22:33	Rules for Priests	21:1–22:16
23:1–24:23	Rules for Feasts	23:1–44
25:1–55	Year of Jubilee	25:8–55
26:1–46	Punishments	26:14–46
27:1–34	Redeeming Values	27:1–34

Purpose. Leviticus is actually an instruction manual for the first Hebrew priests. Even though all of the Levites worked in the tabernacle, only the descendants of Aaron served as priests. Leviticus outlines how to take care of the tabernacle, instruction for offering sacrifices of all kinds and directions for dealing with leprosy and a variety of other physical ailments and functions.

Through the book of Leviticus, Moses taught the priests (and thus the people) the difference between *clean* and *unclean*. The purpose of the information in Leviticus was not only to teach the people how to stay clean, but about the very nature of God. It taught them about his holiness and how sinful people can approach a God who is sinless. Leviticus in its entirety is a picture of the sacrifice of Christ. All that the priests would do would point to Jesus as Messiah.

Historical Background. After the Hebrews left Egypt, they camped at Mount Sinai. There, God met with Moses and gave him the instructions for the tabernacle and the Ten Commandments. Also on Mount Sinai, God gave Moses the guidelines for worship and community life that comprise the book of Leviticus.

The Hebrew people were traveling as nomads in an era before highways and rest stops. They had to diagnose and doctor themselves. They packed and unpacked over and over again. Following the guidelines of Leviticus, worship became the focus of daily life. Because God worked through the priests to regulate so much of the Hebrews' community, he maintained his presence among them in a special way.

Characteristics. Leviticus is not a description of historical events like Exodus. This book is full of details. It offers the *why's* and the *what if's*. In fact, Leviticus most often resembles a legal document and reads like a charter for the original Theocracy (rule by God rather than by a human political leader). From that perspective, it makes sense that the tabernacle, a place of worship, would be the center of activity and that the priests would be the administrators of the Law.

Sacrifices. *Sacrifices* were a part of most ancient religions. In most cases, the sacrifices were meant to maintain open communion with whatever god the culture claimed as their object of worship. In this way, the sacrifices described in Leviticus were similar. The sacrifices did function as a bridge between God and his people. But for the Hebrews, neither the ritual of sacrifice nor the life of the animal provided fellowship. Rather, the faith and intent of the worshipper brought him or her closer to God.

OPEN 1. What was the biggest thing your parents ever gave up for you? Why do you think they did it? **2.** What is the biggest thing you ever had to give up for someone else? Why did you do it? What did you learn in the process?

STUDY The word for offering means "to bring near." Leviticus is an instruction book on how to come near to God even though the Israelites were a rebellious people. **1.** Beginning with Cain and Abel (Gen. 4 and in Lev.), why do you think God chose "animal sacrifice" to restore broken relationships? Couldn't God forgive sins without sacrifice? **2.** Regarding the "burnt offering," what do you think these numerous regulations imply: Why a male, and without defect? Why the laying on of hands? Why sprinkle blood? Why complete burning? Why three categories? **3.** How does an "aroma pleasing to the Lord" (vv. 9,13,17) foreshadow Christ and Christian charity (Eph. 5:2; Phil. 4:18)?

APPLY 1. How would you describe your relationship with God now? **2.** How would you describe your understanding of the provision God made for sin through Christ: Amazed? Unclear? Confused?

The Burnt Offering

1 The LORD called to Moses and spoke to him from the Tent of Meeting. He said, 2"Speak to the Israelites and say to them: 'When any of you brings an offering to the LORD, bring as your offering an animal from either the herd or the flock.

3" 'If the offering is a burnt offering from the herd, he is to offer a male without defect. He must present it at the entrance to the Tent of Meeting so that it[a] will be acceptable to the LORD. 4He is to lay his hand on the head of the burnt offering, and it will be accepted on his behalf to make atonement for him. 5He is to slaughter the young bull before the LORD, and then Aaron's sons the priests shall bring the blood and sprinkle it against the altar on all sides at the entrance to the Tent of Meeting. 6He is to skin the burnt offering and cut it into pieces. 7The sons of Aaron the priest are to put fire on the altar and arrange wood on the fire. 8Then Aaron's sons the priests shall arrange the pieces, including the head and the fat, on the burning wood that is on the altar. 9He is to wash the inner parts and the legs with water, and the priest is to burn all of it on the altar. It is a burnt offering, an offering made by fire, an aroma pleasing to the LORD.

10" 'If the offering is a burnt offering from the flock, from either the sheep or the goats, he is to offer a male without defect. 11He is to slaughter it at the north side of the altar before the LORD, and Aaron's sons the priests shall sprinkle its blood against the altar on all sides. 12He is to cut it into pieces, and the priest shall arrange them, including the head and the fat, on the burning wood that is on the altar. 13He is to wash the inner parts and the legs with water, and the priest is to bring all of it and burn it on the altar. It is a burnt offering, an offering made by fire, an aroma pleasing to the LORD.

14" 'If the offering to the LORD is a burnt offering of birds, he is to offer a dove or a young pigeon. 15The priest shall bring it to the altar, wring off the head and burn it on the altar; its blood shall be drained out on the side of the altar. 16He is to remove the crop with its contents[b] and throw it to the east side of the altar, where the ashes are. 17He shall tear it open by the wings, not severing it completely, and then the priest shall burn it on the wood that is on the fire on the altar. It is a burnt offering, an offering made by fire, an aroma pleasing to the LORD.

[a]3 Or *he* [b]16 Or *crop and the feathers*; the meaning of the Hebrew for this word is uncertain.

1:2 an offering. This is the beginning of a section of guidelines about how the Hebrews should offer sacrifices to God. Most, but not all, offerings were animal sacrifices. The normal offerings involved a sheep, goat or cow. Later, for people unable to pay for large animals, provisions were made to bring birds.

1:3 without defect. The people were to bring the best of their herd. The prophet *Malachi* wrote that a man was cursed if he kept the best of the flock for himself and offered God the blemished animals. In this way the sacrifices pointed to Christ, the perfect lamb who died for all (1 Peter 1:19).

1:5 He is to slaughter. If priests had done all the killing, the process might have been easier. But the sin offering required that the person kill his own animal, symbolically taking an innocent life for his own transgressions. One day the Messiah would come and deal with sin once and for all.

1:6 skin. The worshiper had to kill the sacrifice and skin it. Priests kept the skin of some animals, and even the meat. Priests owned no land on which to raise their own food. By this means, then, they received provision.

1:9,13,17 an aroma pleasing. Sacrifices were thought to "go up" to God. That referred to the rising smoke as well as to the fact that most sacrifices were completely burnt up. Ephesians 5:2 refers to Christ as a fragrant offering as well.

1:14 dove or a young pigeon. Destitute worshipers were allowed to bring birds rather than cows, sheep or goats for the offering. When Jesus overturned the merchant tables at the temple in Jerusalem, doves were being sold to people who came to the temple with little money to spend (Mark 11:15).

The Grain Offering

2 " 'When someone brings a grain offering to the LORD, his offering is to be of fine flour. He is to pour oil on it, put incense on it
2and take it to Aaron's sons the priests. The priest shall take a handful
of the fine flour and oil, together with all the incense, and burn this
as a memorial portion on the altar, an offering made by fire, an aroma
pleasing to the LORD. 3The rest of the grain offering belongs to Aaron
and his sons; it is a most holy part of the offerings made to the LORD
by fire.
4" 'If you bring a grain offering baked in an oven, it is to consist of
fine flour: cakes made without yeast and mixed with oil, or[a] wafers
made without yeast and spread with oil. 5If your grain offering is prepared on a griddle, it is to be made of fine flour mixed with oil, and
without yeast. 6Crumble it and pour oil on it; it is a grain offering. 7If
your grain offering is cooked in a pan, it is to be made of fine flour
and oil. 8Bring the grain offering made of these things to the LORD;
present it to the priest, who shall take it to the altar. 9He shall take out
the memorial portion from the grain offering and burn it on the altar
as an offering made by fire, an aroma pleasing to the LORD. 10The rest
of the grain offering belongs to Aaron and his sons; it is a most holy
part of the offerings made to the LORD by fire.
11" 'Every grain offering you bring to the LORD must be made without yeast, for you are not to burn any yeast or honey in an offering
made to the LORD by fire. 12You may bring them to the LORD as an offering of the firstfruits, but they are not to be offered on the altar as a
pleasing aroma. 13Season all your grain offerings with salt. Do not
leave the salt of the covenant of your God out of your grain offerings;
add salt to all your offerings.
14" 'If you bring a grain offering of firstfruits to the LORD, offer
crushed heads of new grain roasted in the fire. 15Put oil and incense
on it; it is a grain offering. 16The priest shall burn the memorial portion of the crushed grain and the oil, together with all the incense, as
an offering made to the LORD by fire.

The Fellowship Offering

3 " 'If someone's offering is a fellowship offering,[b] and he offers an
animal from the herd, whether male or female, he is to present
before the LORD an animal without defect. 2He is to lay his hand on

[a]4 Or *and* [b]1 Traditionally *peace offering;* also in verses 3, 6 and 9

OPEN 1. Describe the best tasting bread or pastry you've ever eaten. What made it so good? **2.** What aromas bring back positive childhood memories?

STUDY A grain offering had to be made of fine flour. This would have to come from the best grain and therefore be free from impurities. **1.** If you were bringing this offering to God, would you really want to give him your best grain? **2.** Regarding the "grain offering," why do you think these regulations were mandatory? What did they imply? Why grill it? Why without yeast or honey? Why the specified amounts? Why so "fine"? Why salt? Why leave some for Aaron and his sons? **3.** How are these laws part of the reconciliation between God and his people?

APPLY 1. Have you offered your life as a "thank offering" to God? **2.** What formula do you use in giving?

OPEN 1. Have you ever been alienated from a close friend? **2.** Did you try to make peace with that person? How many times? What did you send or say?

2:1 grain offering. These offerings were of flour, oil and incense. **fine flour.** This flour was not ground as finely as flour is today. It would have been more like whole wheat flour or corn meal.

2:3 rest ... belongs to Aaron and his sons. While the Levites were the priestly tribe that attended to the tabernacle, the sons of Aaron were the priests. The priests didn't use these grain offerings to feed their families, but they did eat the bread in the tabernacle.

2:4 without yeast. This means unleavened. The phrase "unleavened bread" is used throughout the Scriptures. Jesus described the faults of the Pharisees with an illustration about yeast being small but affecting the whole loaf. In many churches bread without yeast is used for Holy Communion.

2:5 prepared on a griddle. The scene resembles an outdoor campsite breakfast. There were fires for cooking and griddles for frying. Whatever a person could afford to bring or however an offering might be prepared, the equipment was there to do the job right.

2:11–13 yeast or honey ... salt. While yeast and honey were not allowed as part of the grain offering, honey *was* a part of the firstfruits offering. Salt, though, was always a part of the offerings. It symbolized the covenant between God and his people.

3:1–4 fellowship offering. This sacrifice is called a peace offering in some translations. It was similar to a burnt offering in that an unblemished animal was sacrificed. It was dissimilar, though, in that the animal could be male or female. This offering was motivated by gratitude rather than remorse over sin.

STUDY Because God is supremely holy, sin causes a rift in our relationship with him. The offerings were times of enjoying salvation as a gift from God (7:11–21). **1.** Why must God react to evil with wrath? Would you fear God's wrath as an Israelite? **2.** As an Israelite what would motivate you to seek a peaceful relationship with God? **3.** The Hebrew word for "fellowship" used here can also be translated "peace" or "wholeness." How does this help to explain the function of this offering? **4.** How do the various laws fit the idea of reconciliation between God and his people? **5.** Why was eating any of the fat or blood strictly prohibited (v. 17; 17:11; Deut. 12:23–25)?

APPLY 1. Can you describe how you felt when you first realized that the death of Christ provided peace with God? **2.** Do you have peace with God?

the head of his offering and slaughter it at the entrance to the Tent of
Meeting. Then Aaron's sons the priests shall sprinkle the blood
against the altar on all sides. 3From the fellowship offering he is to
bring a sacrifice made to the LORD by fire: all the fat that covers the
inner parts or is connected to them, 4both kidneys with the fat on
them near the loins, and the covering of the liver, which he will remove with the kidneys. 5Then Aaron's sons are to burn it on the altar
on top of the burnt offering that is on the burning wood, as an offering made by fire, an aroma pleasing to the LORD.
6" 'If he offers an animal from the flock as a fellowship offering to
the LORD, he is to offer a male or female without defect. 7If he offers a
lamb, he is to present it before the LORD. 8He is to lay his hand on the
head of his offering and slaughter it in front of the Tent of Meeting.
Then Aaron's sons shall sprinkle its blood against the altar on all
sides. 9From the fellowship offering he is to bring a sacrifice made to
the LORD by fire: its fat, the entire fat tail cut off close to the backbone, all the fat that covers the inner parts or is connected to them,
10both kidneys with the fat on them near the loins, and the covering
of the liver, which he will remove with the kidneys. 11The priest shall
burn them on the altar as food, an offering made to the LORD by fire.
12" 'If his offering is a goat, he is to present it before the LORD. 13He
is to lay his hand on its head and slaughter it in front of the Tent of
Meeting. Then Aaron's sons shall sprinkle its blood against the altar
on all sides. 14From what he offers he is to make this offering to the
LORD by fire: all the fat that covers the inner parts or is connected to
them, 15both kidneys with the fat on them near the loins, and the
covering of the liver, which he will remove with the kidneys. 16The
priest shall burn them on the altar as food, an offering made by fire, a
pleasing aroma. All the fat is the LORD's.
17" 'This is a lasting ordinance for the generations to come, wherever you live: You must not eat any fat or any blood.' "

OPEN 1. When is the last time you heard this phrase, "I didn't mean to do it?" **2.** Can a person do something wrong and not realize it?

STUDY Leviticus 4 and 5 reveal some unintentional sins of the people of Israel. Although sin is unintentional at times, it is still

The Sin Offering

4 The LORD said to Moses, 2"Say to the Israelites: 'When anyone
sins unintentionally and does what is forbidden in any of the
LORD's commands—
3" 'If the anointed priest sins, bringing guilt on the people, he must
bring to the LORD a young bull without defect as a sin offering for the
sin he has committed. 4He is to present the bull at the entrance to the

---

3:5 on top. The burnt offerings were done morning and night. The fellowship offerings were on top of them. This gives us a useful sense of priorities. We first deal with the sin that separates us from God, then we express our gratitude within a repentant, open relationship.

3:11–16 as food. While priests did sometimes eat meat offered as a sacrifice, and worshipers did sometimes share the meat in a fellowship meal, this phrase points to neither act, nor does it imply that the animal offered becomes food for God. It is merely an expression to denote that the sacrifice was for God only.

3:17 fat ... blood. These two prohibitions for the Hebrew diet are still basic to the kosher diet: fat, because it was the bounty and belonged to the Lord, and blood, because it was the life of the creature and should be respected.

4:2 When. Not "if" anyone sins unintentionally, but "when." **unintentionally.** Often this is understood as those sins that are not committed in direct defiance of God. There was not a sacrifice for premeditated, direct rebellion. The sin offering, though, was for sins committed without either awareness or premeditation.

4:3 bringing guilt on the people. Faith was public and communal. When the high priest sinned, it made Israel a sinful nation. Today our notions of accountability are much more individualistic and private. **he must bring.** The sin offering was a required offering while the burnt, grain and fellowship offerings were voluntary.

4:4 lay his hand on its head. The priest was required to slaughter his

Tent of Meeting before the LORD. He is to lay his hand on its head and slaughter it before the LORD. 5Then the anointed priest shall take some of the bull's blood and carry it into the Tent of Meeting. 6He is to dip his finger into the blood and sprinkle some of it seven times before the LORD, in front of the curtain of the sanctuary. 7The priest shall then put some of the blood on the horns of the altar of fragrant incense that is before the LORD in the Tent of Meeting. The rest of the bull's blood he shall pour out at the base of the altar of burnt offering at the entrance to the Tent of Meeting. 8He shall remove all the fat from the bull of the sin offering—the fat that covers the inner parts or is connected to them, 9both kidneys with the fat on them near the loins, and the covering of the liver, which he will remove with the kidneys— 10just as the fat is removed from the ox[a] sacrificed as a fellowship offering.[b] Then the priest shall burn them on the altar of burnt offering. 11But the hide of the bull and all its flesh, as well as the head and legs, the inner parts and offal— 12that is, all the rest of the bull—he must take outside the camp to a place ceremonially clean, where the ashes are thrown, and burn it in a wood fire on the ash heap.

13" 'If the whole Israelite community sins unintentionally and does what is forbidden in any of the LORD's commands, even though the community is unaware of the matter, they are guilty. 14When they become aware of the sin they committed, the assembly must bring a young bull as a sin offering and present it before the Tent of Meeting. 15The elders of the community are to lay their hands on the bull's head before the LORD, and the bull shall be slaughtered before the LORD. 16Then the anointed priest is to take some of the bull's blood into the Tent of Meeting. 17He shall dip his finger into the blood and sprinkle it before the LORD seven times in front of the curtain. 18He is to put some of the blood on the horns of the altar that is before the LORD in the Tent of Meeting. The rest of the blood he shall pour out at the base of the altar of burnt offering at the entrance to the Tent of Meeting. 19He shall remove all the fat from it and burn it on the altar, 20and do with this bull just as he did with the bull for the sin offering. In this way the priest will make atonement for them, and they will be forgiven. 21Then he shall take the bull outside the camp and burn it as he burned the first bull. This is the sin offering for the community.

[a]*10* The Hebrew word can include both male and female. [b]*10* Traditionally *peace offering;* also in verses 26, 31 and 35

sin and offends God's holiness. **1.** How would you define "unintentional sin" (4:1)? How would you respond if you suddenly realized you had sinned unintentionally? **2.** What did the action of laying hands on the head of the animal to be sacrificed emphasize? **3.** Which different individuals and groups are addressed in this passage (4:3,13,22,27; 5:7)? On what basis do these various regulations distinguish the sacrifices required. **4.** Why is the "sin offering" of the priest required in each instance (4:3,20,25,29,34) along with their own respective sin offerings? **5.** Why must the rest of the bull be taken "outside the camp" (v. 12; 16:26–28; Heb 13:11–13)? **6.** Leviticus repeats the idea that such sacrifices are "an aroma pleasing to God" (1:17; 2:9; 3:5; 4:31). Why do you think it pleases him? What does this say about God's desire for intimate fellowship with us? **7.** What other oft-repeated phrases give you clues as to the central concern of this passage? The phrase "will be forgiven (by God)" is repeated nine times. What does that mean?

APPLY 1. What have you found helpful in keeping the lines of communication between you and God open? **2.** How would you describe your relationship with God now?

sacrifice just as anyone else did. This was no impersonal sacrifice where the killing was done at the slaughterhouse and the meat came out shrink-wrapped. No one at the sacrifice could remain unaware that death was the consequence of sin.

4:5 the bull's blood. With sacrifices or offerings, there was always instruction of what to do with the blood, the life force, because that was the essence of what was being offered. When the one bringing the sacrifice put his hand on the animal's head, symbolically his sin was transferred to that innocent animal. Then when the priests distributed the blood on either the altar, the sides of the altar, the horns of the altar or the mercy seat in the Holy of Holies, the sacrifice was nearly complete. Only the distribution of the carcass remained.

4:12 the rest of the bull ... outside the camp. With some offerings, once the fat and certain organs were burned at the altar, the rest could be used as food. In this instance, though, where the bull had been a substitute for the priest, the whole carcass was disposed of outside of the camp. Jesus, the offering for humanity's sin, was sacrificed outside of the city.

4:20 atonement. To atone is to make amends, to reconcile. The sacrifices themselves, dead animals, did not change the sinful state of humanity. But the sacrifice as an act of faith—the Holy God's revulsion at sin—connected them with God's forgiveness. **they will be forgiven.** The purpose of the entire sacrificial process was forgiveness—no little thing, no small price.

22 "'When a leader sins unintentionally and does what is forbidden
in any of the commands of the LORD his God, he is guilty. 23 When he is
made aware of the sin he committed, he must bring as his offering a
male goat without defect. 24 He is to lay his hand on the goat's head
and slaughter it at the place where the burnt offering is slaughtered
before the LORD. It is a sin offering. 25 Then the priest shall take some
of the blood of the sin offering with his finger and put it on the horns
of the altar of burnt offering and pour out the rest of the blood at the
base of the altar. 26 He shall burn all the fat on the altar as he burned
the fat of the fellowship offering. In this way the priest will make
atonement for the man's sin, and he will be forgiven.

27 "'If a member of the community sins unintentionally and does
what is forbidden in any of the LORD's commands, he is guilty.
28 When he is made aware of the sin he committed, he must bring as
his offering for the sin he committed a female goat without defect.
29 He is to lay his hand on the head of the sin offering and slaughter it
at the place of the burnt offering. 30 Then the priest is to take some of
the blood with his finger and put it on the horns of the altar of burnt
offering and pour out the rest of the blood at the base of the altar.
31 He shall remove all the fat, just as the fat is removed from the fellowship offering, and the priest shall burn it on the altar as an aroma
pleasing to the LORD. In this way the priest will make atonement for
him, and he will be forgiven.

32 "'If he brings a lamb as his sin offering, he is to bring a female
without defect. 33 He is to lay his hand on its head and slaughter it for a
sin offering at the place where the burnt offering is slaughtered.
34 Then the priest shall take some of the blood of the sin offering with
his finger and put it on the horns of the altar of burnt offering and pour
out the rest of the blood at the base of the altar. 35 He shall remove all
the fat, just as the fat is removed from the lamb of the fellowship offering, and the priest shall burn it on the altar on top of the offerings
made to the LORD by fire. In this way the priest will make atonement
for him for the sin he has committed, and he will be forgiven.

5 "'If a person sins because he does not speak up when he hears a
public charge to testify regarding something he has seen or
learned about, he will be held responsible.

2 "'Or if a person touches anything ceremonially unclean—whether
the carcasses of unclean wild animals or of unclean livestock or of
unclean creatures that move along the ground—even though he is
unaware of it, he has become unclean and is guilty.

3 "'Or if he touches human uncleanness—anything that would
make him unclean—even though he is unaware of it, when he learns
of it he will be guilty.

4 "'Or if a person thoughtlessly takes an oath to do anything,
whether good or evil—in any matter one might carelessly swear
about—even though he is unaware of it, in any case when he learns
of it he will be guilty.

4:23 goat. Different levels of leadership offered different kinds of animals. A large cow was worth more than a smaller goat. When the priest sinned, he brought a bull. When a leader sinned, he brought a goat. It was not that the sin was any worse but that the person was even more responsible and so a higher price was paid for their sin. This same concept was addressed in the New Testament (Luke 12:47–48; James 3:1).

5" 'When anyone is guilty in any of these ways, he must confess in
what way he has sinned 6and, as a penalty for the sin he has committed, he must bring to the LORD a female lamb or goat from the flock as
a sin offering; and the priest shall make atonement for him for his sin.
7" 'If he cannot afford a lamb, he is to bring two doves or two
young pigeons to the LORD as a penalty for his sin—one for a sin offering and the other for a burnt offering. 8He is to bring them to the
priest, who shall first offer the one for the sin offering. He is to wring
its head from its neck, not severing it completely, 9and is to sprinkle
some of the blood of the sin offering against the side of the altar; the
rest of the blood must be drained out at the base of the altar. It is a sin
offering. 10The priest shall then offer the other as a burnt offering in
the prescribed way and make atonement for him for the sin he has
committed, and he will be forgiven.
11" 'If, however, he cannot afford two doves or two young pigeons,
he is to bring as an offering for his sin a tenth of an ephah[a] of fine
flour for a sin offering. He must not put oil or incense on it, because
it is a sin offering. 12He is to bring it to the priest, who shall take a
handful of it as a memorial portion and burn it on the altar on top of
the offerings made to the LORD by fire. It is a sin offering. 13In this way
the priest will make atonement for him for any of these sins he has
committed, and he will be forgiven. The rest of the offering will belong to the priest, as in the case of the grain offering.' "

The Guilt Offering

14The LORD said to Moses: 15"When a person commits a violation
and sins unintentionally in regard to any of the LORD's holy things, he
is to bring to the LORD as a penalty a ram from the flock, one without
defect and of the proper value in silver, according to the sanctuary
shekel.[b] It is a guilt offering. 16He must make restitution for what he
has failed to do in regard to the holy things, add a fifth of the value to
that and give it all to the priest, who will make atonement for him
with the ram as a guilt offering, and he will be forgiven.
17"If a person sins and does what is forbidden in any of the LORD's
commands, even though he does not know it, he is guilty and will be
held responsible. 18He is to bring to the priest as a guilt offering a ram
from the flock, one without defect and of the proper value. In this way
the priest will make atonement for him for the wrong he has committed unintentionally, and he will be forgiven. 19It is a guilt offering; he
has been guilty of[c] wrongdoing against the LORD."
6 The LORD said to Moses: 2"If anyone sins and is unfaithful to the
LORD by deceiving his neighbor about something entrusted to
him or left in his care or stolen, or if he cheats him, 3or if he finds lost
property and lies about it, or if he swears falsely, or if he commits any
such sin that people may do— 4when he thus sins and becomes

[a] *11* That is, probably about 2 quarts (about 2 liters) [b] *15* That is, about 2/5 ounce (about 11.5 grams)
[c] *19* Or *has made full expiation for his*

OPEN 1. When is the last time you borrowed something and damaged it? **2.** Did you feel responsible to replace it?

STUDY God required a guilt offering when an offense caused damage or loss whether deliberate or unintentional, and either against God or man. **1.** How is a "sin offering" different than a "guilt offering" (chs. 4–5)? **2.** For what kinds of sin is restitution possible and therefore required (5:16; 6:1–5)? **3.** What does this teach you about God's view of sin? God's view of the reconciliation process? His desire for his followers?

APPLY 1. Do you need to make restitution for a wrong you've committed? **2.** What should motivate us to make restitution for wrongs done to others? **3.** What action will you take this week to make restitution?

5:5 he must confess. Merely offering a sacrifice and doing the slaughtering did not affect forgiveness. God wants all sinners to genuinely repent. Even today, merely doing lip service in church is a fool's errand. God wants the heart of the sinner to repent in remorse and determine to follow God fully. Any genuine conversion or growth in faith requires this step.

5:15–17 guilt offering. When someone committed a sin that required restitution, they offered a guilt offering. The guilty party was required to replace whatever loss they had caused plus 20 percent of its worth in silver.

guilty, he must return what he has stolen or taken by extortion, or what was entrusted to him, or the lost property he found, 5or whatever it was he swore falsely about. He must make restitution in full, add a fifth of the value to it and give it all to the owner on the day he presents his guilt offering. 6And as a penalty he must bring to the priest, that is, to the LORD, his guilt offering, a ram from the flock, one without defect and of the proper value. 7In this way the priest will make atonement for him before the LORD, and he will be forgiven for any of these things he did that made him guilty."

The Burnt Offering

8The LORD said to Moses: 9"Give Aaron and his sons this command: 'These are the regulations for the burnt offering: The burnt offering is to remain on the altar hearth throughout the night, till morning, and the fire must be kept burning on the altar. 10The priest shall then put on his linen clothes, with linen undergarments next to his body, and shall remove the ashes of the burnt offering that the fire has consumed on the altar and place them beside the altar. 11Then he is to take off these clothes and put on others, and carry the ashes outside the camp to a place that is ceremonially clean. 12The fire on the altar must be kept burning; it must not go out. Every morning the priest is to add firewood and arrange the burnt offering on the fire and burn the fat of the fellowship offerings[a] on it. 13The fire must be kept burning on the altar continuously; it must not go out.

The Grain Offering

14" 'These are the regulations for the grain offering: Aaron's sons are to bring it before the LORD, in front of the altar. 15The priest is to take a handful of fine flour and oil, together with all the incense on the grain offering, and burn the memorial portion on the altar as an aroma pleasing to the LORD. 16Aaron and his sons shall eat the rest of it, but it is to be eaten without yeast in a holy place; they are to eat it in the courtyard of the Tent of Meeting. 17It must not be baked with yeast; I have given it as their share of the offerings made to me by fire. Like the sin offering and the guilt offering, it is most holy. 18Any male descendant of Aaron may eat it. It is his regular share of the offerings made to the LORD by fire for the generations to come. Whatever touches them will become holy.[b]' "

19The LORD also said to Moses, 20"This is the offering Aaron and his sons are to bring to the LORD on the day he[c] is anointed: a tenth of an ephah[d] of fine flour as a regular grain offering, half of it in the morning and half in the evening. 21Prepare it with oil on a griddle; bring it well-mixed and present the grain offering broken[e] in pieces as an aroma pleasing to the LORD. 22The son who is to succeed him as

[a] *12* Traditionally *peace offerings* [b] *18* Or *Whoever touches them must be holy*; similarly in verse 27
[c] *20* Or *each* [d] *20* That is, probably about 2 quarts (about 2 liters) [e] *21* The meaning of the Hebrew for this word is uncertain.

OPEN 1. As a child, what foods were considered "off limits"? Why? **2.** When you were growing up, who had to do the dishes most often? For what occasions did you bring out the special plates and silverware?

STUDY This section provides the guidelines for sacrificial meals as to which persons, place and portions were acceptable. **1.** Why do you think God wants the fires for the burnt offerings to burn continuously (vv. 8–13)? What might this say about the perpetual need for, and offer of, reconciliation? **2.** Compare verses 14–23 with 2:1–16. Who brings the two grain offerings (2:1; 6:14)? Who could eat whose offering? And where (6:16,22–23)? **3.** What do such differences tell you about the function of the grain offering? About its place in the process of rebuilding a proper relationship with God? **4.** What is "holy" and "most holy" about the "sin offering" (vv. 24–30)? **5.** What do burnt offerings suggest about how to go about keeping a right relationship with God when you are under conviction of sin? **6.** What do burnt, grain and sin offerings teach you about the process of reconciliation, then and now? **7.** Could the death of an animal bring permanent reconciliation with God (Heb. 10:1–4)? According to Hebrews 10:11–18, what does Christ's death accomplish for those who place their faith in him?

APPLY 1. How has the view of Christ's sacrifice for you changed since studying Leviticus? **2.** How has your view of God been altered by this study?

6:6 the priest ... the Lord. In ancient days the worshiper brought his offering to the priest and by that action brought it also to the Lord. So it is today, when we bring our money or gifts to the ministries of our church, we bring them to God.

6:13 it must not go out. Church was a "round-the-clock" thing for the Old Testament priests. The embers were kept alight. The fire on the altar never went out. In this way, their service was continual.

6:14–15 incense. In the tabernacle were many different aromas. Between burning fat and meats, and the flour and incense offered in the grain offerings, a great mix of smells made it a unique environment.

anointed priest shall prepare it. It is the LORD's regular share and is to
be burned completely. 23Every grain offering of a priest shall be
burned completely; it must not be eaten."

The Sin Offering

24The LORD said to Moses, 25"Say to Aaron and his sons: 'These are
the regulations for the sin offering: The sin offering is to be slaughtered before the LORD in the place the burnt offering is slaughtered; it
is most holy. 26The priest who offers it shall eat it; it is to be eaten in
a holy place, in the courtyard of the Tent of Meeting. 27Whatever
touches any of the flesh will become holy, and if any of the blood is
spattered on a garment, you must wash it in a holy place. 28The clay
pot the meat is cooked in must be broken; but if it is cooked in a
bronze pot, the pot is to be scoured and rinsed with water. 29Any male
in a priest's family may eat it; it is most holy. 30But any sin offering
whose blood is brought into the Tent of Meeting to make atonement
in the Holy Place must not be eaten; it must be burned.

The Guilt Offering

7 " 'These are the regulations for the guilt offering, which is most
holy: 2The guilt offering is to be slaughtered in the place where
the burnt offering is slaughtered, and its blood is to be sprinkled
against the altar on all sides. 3All its fat shall be offered: the fat tail
and the fat that covers the inner parts, 4both kidneys with the fat on
them near the loins, and the covering of the liver, which is to be
removed with the kidneys. 5The priest shall burn them on the altar as
an offering made to the LORD by fire. It is a guilt offering. 6Any male in
a priest's family may eat it, but it must be eaten in a holy place; it is
most holy.

7" 'The same law applies to both the sin offering and the guilt offering: They belong to the priest who makes atonement with them. 8The
priest who offers a burnt offering for anyone may keep its hide for
himself. 9Every grain offering baked in an oven or cooked in a pan or
on a griddle belongs to the priest who offers it, 10and every grain
offering, whether mixed with oil or dry, belongs equally to all the
sons of Aaron.

The Fellowship Offering

11" 'These are the regulations for the fellowship offering[a] a person
may present to the LORD:

12" 'If he offers it as an expression of thankfulness, then along with
this thank offering he is to offer cakes of bread made without yeast

[a]11 Traditionally *peace offering;* also in verses 13-37

OPEN 1. Can you recall a gift you received as a child that made you feel especially grateful? 2. Did you express your gratefulness? How?

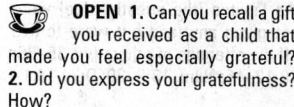

STUDY The fellowship offering was a public proclamation

6:26 a holy place. Some of the remains of the sacrifices could be eaten by priests and their families. In this way these families found provision. The remains of the sin offering could be eaten only at the tabernacle.

7:2 where the burnt offering is slaughtered. Both the burnt offering and the sin offering were to be offered to the north of the altar. The significance of that location is not known.

7:3 fat tail. The tail of a certain kind of sheep could weigh up to 75 pounds, filled with stored fat.

7:11–36 fellowship offering. This is the Bible's original potluck supper. After the sacrifices, a communal meal could include families, priests and the poor. Certain portions of the offering (including bread and meat) were made available to priests and their families. In the case of a fellowship offering for a vow or simply a freewill offering, arrangements were even made to deal with leftovers.

7:12–15 The fellowship offering combined both meat and grain sacrifices. This passage begins to sound like the preparations of a great feast.

of who God is and what he does. It demonstrated the gratefulness of the worshiper toward God for his goodness. **1.** In what ways do fellowship offerings (vv. 11–21) vary from those for sin (6:24–30) and guilt (7:1–10)? **2.** Why do you think animal sacrifice was appropriate for vows, freewill and thanksgiving offerings, as well as for sin offerings? **3.** What is the distinction between "clean" and "unclean" in verse 19? Does this convey ritual purity, physical cleanliness or something else? **4.** What does it mean to be "cut off from his people" (vv. 20–21)? What does this say about the importance of one's fellowship with God?

APPLY 1. When you are particularly thankful to God, how do you show it? In what ways is this like the thanksgiving offering in verses 12–15? **2.** For what are you particularly thankful today? How will you express this to God?

OPEN 1. Have you ever had to turn down some particular food served to you? Why? **2.** When something breaks down and needs replacement, do you buy a new one, borrow a used one or fix the old one?

STUDY Again the Lord gave Moses regulations for Aaron and his sons. Meal, sin and guilt offerings could be eaten only by males of the priestly order, other sacred offerings could be shared by their households. **1.** What links this food law to the laws about animal sacrifice (chs. 3–4)? **2.** Why do you think only the Levites (the priestly tribe) were not given any land but were to live off the offerings of others (vv. 35–36; 10:12–15; Num. 18:8–20; Deut.18:1–

and mixed with oil, wafers made without yeast and spread with oil,
and cakes of fine flour well-kneaded and mixed with oil. [13]Along with
his fellowship offering of thanksgiving he is to present an offering
with cakes of bread made with yeast. [14]He is to bring one of each kind
as an offering, a contribution to the LORD; it belongs to the priest who
sprinkles the blood of the fellowship offerings. [15]The meat of his
fellowship offering of thanksgiving must be eaten on the day it is
offered; he must leave none of it till morning.

[16]" 'If, however, his offering is the result of a vow or is a freewill
offering, the sacrifice shall be eaten on the day he offers it, but
anything left over may be eaten on the next day. [17]Any meat of the
sacrifice left over till the third day must be burned up. [18]If any meat of
the fellowship offering is eaten on the third day, it will not be
accepted. It will not be credited to the one who offered it, for it is
impure; the person who eats any of it will be held responsible.

[19]" 'Meat that touches anything ceremonially unclean must not be
eaten; it must be burned up. As for other meat, anyone ceremonially
clean may eat it. [20]But if anyone who is unclean eats any meat of the
fellowship offering belonging to the LORD, that person must be cut off
from his people. [21]If anyone touches something unclean—whether
human uncleanness or an unclean animal or any unclean, detestable
thing—and then eats any of the meat of the fellowship offering belonging to the LORD, that person must be cut off from his people.' "

Eating Fat and Blood Forbidden

[22]The LORD said to Moses, [23]"Say to the Israelites: 'Do not eat any
of the fat of cattle, sheep or goats. [24]The fat of an animal found dead
or torn by wild animals may be used for any other purpose, but you
must not eat it. [25]Anyone who eats the fat of an animal from which an
offering by fire may be[a] made to the LORD must be cut off from his
people. [26]And wherever you live, you must not eat the blood of any
bird or animal. [27]If anyone eats blood, that person must be cut off
from his people.' "

The Priests' Share

[28]The LORD said to Moses, [29]"Say to the Israelites: 'Anyone who
brings a fellowship offering to the LORD is to bring part of it as his
sacrifice to the LORD. [30]With his own hands he is to bring the offering
made to the LORD by fire; he is to bring the fat, together with the
breast, and wave the breast before the LORD as a wave offering. [31]The

[a]25 Or *fire is*

7:15–18 left over. In the desert heat, meat could not be kept long. For the gratitude offering, no leftovers were allowed, though remains from the other two fellowship offerings were consumed on the second day.

7:16 the result of a vow. This fellowship offering was to thank God for help in some difficult situation where the worshiper had made a vow and the result had been positive.

7:19 unclean. The kind of unclean mentioned here is not *dirty* unclean as much as a *ceremonial* unclean. Sometimes meats were considered unclean simply because of the animal. Other times it had to do with the preparation of the meat, the places it had been or something that it had touched.

7:20 cut off. This was more similar to execution than excommunication.

7:21 cut off from his people. By today's terms these consequences seem severe. But the holiness of God was at stake, and on that point, compromise seems ludicrous.

7:24 fat. The fat of animals was not just prohibited for sacrificial animals. It was a principle that the Hebrews were to live by in every aspect. **any other purpose.** Animal fat could be used for polishing, for lighting, even at times for cleaning, just not for eating.

7:30–34 waved. The breast and thigh were waved back and forth before being offered to the priests. This was

priest shall burn the fat on the altar, but the breast belongs to Aaron
and his sons. 32You are to give the right thigh of your fellowship offerings to the priest as a contribution. 33The son of Aaron who offers the
blood and the fat of the fellowship offering shall have the right thigh
as his share. 34From the fellowship offerings of the Israelites, I have
taken the breast that is waved and the thigh that is presented and
have given them to Aaron the priest and his sons as their regular
share from the Israelites.' "

35This is the portion of the offerings made to the LORD by fire that
were allotted to Aaron and his sons on the day they were presented to
serve the LORD as priests. 36On the day they were anointed, the LORD
commanded that the Israelites give this to them as their regular share
for the generations to come.

37These, then, are the regulations for the burnt offering, the grain
offering, the sin offering, the guilt offering, the ordination offering
and the fellowship offering, 38which the LORD gave Moses on Mount
Sinai on the day he commanded the Israelites to bring their offerings
to the LORD, in the Desert of Sinai.

The Ordination of Aaron and His Sons

8 The LORD said to Moses, 2"Bring Aaron and his sons, their garments, the anointing oil, the bull for the sin offering, the two
rams and the basket containing bread made without yeast, 3and
gather the entire assembly at the entrance to the Tent of Meeting."
4Moses did as the LORD commanded him, and the assembly gathered
at the entrance to the Tent of Meeting.

5Moses said to the assembly, "This is what the LORD has commanded to be done." 6Then Moses brought Aaron and his sons forward and
washed them with water. 7He put the tunic on Aaron, tied the sash
around him, clothed him with the robe and put the ephod on him. He
also tied the ephod to him by its skillfully woven waistband; so it was
fastened on him. 8He placed the breastpiece on him and put the Urim
and Thummim in the breastpiece. 9Then he placed the turban on
Aaron's head and set the gold plate, the sacred diadem, on the front
of it, as the LORD commanded Moses.

10Then Moses took the anointing oil and anointed the tabernacle
and everything in it, and so consecrated them. 11He sprinkled some

5)? Being landless and dependent—would that help, or hinder their performance? How so? **3.** What does this teach you about God's desire for those who are devoted to him?

APPLY 1. How has what you have learned from the first six chapters of Leviticus contributed to your understanding of the life and ministry of Jesus Christ? **2.** Are you thankful that we can look back on this period after the sacrificial death of Jesus?

OPEN 1. Which spiritual leader or Sunday School teacher from your growing up years has left the deepest impression on you? What makes that person so memorable? **2.** When you think of an ordination service, what images come to mind: Wedding? Graduation? Coronation? Other?

STUDY Aaron had presided over Israel's idolatry with the golden calf. Now God gives him a second chance by allowing him to be ordained as God's own high priest. **1.** As an onlooker on the day of Aaron's ordination, what impresses you? As a Levite getting ordained, what impresses you? **2.** What lasting impression do you think God intended this proceeding to make on one and all? What was his purpose in setting aside Aaron and his sons in this public and sacred way? **3.** How does the

---

referred to as a wave offering and a heave offering. Probably the wave offering was waved up and down and the heave offering was waved from side to side.

8:2 anointing oil. Oil has had many uses throughout Scripture. Here the oil is used for anointing men to a special appointment. It was used to anoint Saul (1 Sam. 10:1), David (1 Sam. 16:13) and Solomon (1 Kings 1:39). Jacob anointed a pillar in a sacred place (Gen. 28:18). In verse 10 Moses anointed everything in the tabernacle with oil. In Exodus 30 Moses was even given a recipe for sacred anointing oil.

8:6 washed them. Moses probably washed them at the bronze laver that stood at the entrance of the tent. He was preparing them for service as mediators between God and people. Washing the priests reflected the holiness of the God they served.

8:7 clothed him. With pomp and ceremony, Moses and brother Aaron were organizing the worship of God, and Aaron was being vested with leadership.

8:8 Urim and Thummim. The Urim and Thummim were probably two stones. By some descriptions they function like dice, though determining God's will was no child's game. These stones were used somehow to decide what God wanted his people to do.

8:9 diadem. Some think of this as a crown, but it was actually a gold headband for a turban. It was also called a mitre and symbolized authority. Scripture describes the returning Christ as wearing a diadem (Rev. 19:12).

8:11 seven. The number seven appears often in the Bible. God created the world in seven days (Gen. 2:2). God promised vengeance for Cain's enemies "seven times over" (Gen. 4:15).

elaborate ceremony in this chapter demonstrate the importance of the consecration to God? **4.** What is the purpose of their "sacred garments" (vv. 2, 6–10,30; Ex. 28:2; 39:1)? The breastpiece with the "Urim and Thummim" (v. 8; Ex. 28:15,30)? The "anointing oil" (vv. 10–12,30; Ps. 133)? **5.** Why did Moses apply blood to the high priest on his right ear, thumb and toe (v. 23)? **6.** What do you see as the link between ritual cleanliness and true spiritual cleanliness? Do you think ritual cleanliness was required mainly for God's benefit or for the people's benefit? Why? **7.** Are the rituals in your church full of meaning, or merely humdrum routine?

APPLY **1.** With what (jewelry, clothing, decision-making ritual, offerings) do you symbolize your own faith? **2.** When have the spiritual leaders in your life seemed most real and approachable? Most human and fallible? Most saintly and worldly? **3.** What special demands do spiritual leaders face? Do you think they should be held to a "higher standard"? **4.** What can you do this week to show your spiritual leaders that you support their efforts to lead?

of the oil on the altar seven times, anointing the altar and all its utensils and the basin with its stand, to consecrate them. 12He poured some of the anointing oil on Aaron's head and anointed him to consecrate him. 13Then he brought Aaron's sons forward, put tunics on them, tied sashes around them and put headbands on them, as the LORD commanded Moses.

14He then presented the bull for the sin offering, and Aaron and his sons laid their hands on its head. 15Moses slaughtered the bull and took some of the blood, and with his finger he put it on all the horns of the altar to purify the altar. He poured out the rest of the blood at the base of the altar. So he consecrated it to make atonement for it. 16Moses also took all the fat around the inner parts, the covering of the liver, and both kidneys and their fat, and burned it on the altar. 17But the bull with its hide and its flesh and its offal he burned up outside the camp, as the LORD commanded Moses.

18He then presented the ram for the burnt offering, and Aaron and his sons laid their hands on its head. 19Then Moses slaughtered the ram and sprinkled the blood against the altar on all sides. 20He cut the ram into pieces and burned the head, the pieces and the fat. 21He washed the inner parts and the legs with water and burned the whole ram on the altar as a burnt offering, a pleasing aroma, an offering made to the LORD by fire, as the LORD commanded Moses.

22He then presented the other ram, the ram for the ordination, and Aaron and his sons laid their hands on its head. 23Moses slaughtered the ram and took some of its blood and put it on the lobe of Aaron's right ear, on the thumb of his right hand and on the big toe of his right foot. 24Moses also brought Aaron's sons forward and put some of the blood on the lobes of their right ears, on the thumbs of their right hands and on the big toes of their right feet. Then he sprinkled blood against the altar on all sides. 25He took the fat, the fat tail, all the fat around the inner parts, the covering of the liver, both kidneys and their fat and the right thigh. 26Then from the basket of bread made without yeast, which was before the LORD, he took a cake of bread, and one made with oil, and a wafer; he put these on the fat portions and on the right thigh. 27He put all these in the hands of Aaron and his sons and waved them before the LORD as a wave offering. 28Then Moses took them from their hands and burned them on the altar on top of the burnt offering as an ordination offering, a pleasing aroma, an offering made to the LORD by fire. 29He also took the breast—Moses' share of the ordination ram—and waved it before the LORD as a wave offering, as the LORD commanded Moses.

30Then Moses took some of the anointing oil and some of the blood from the altar and sprinkled them on Aaron and his garments

---

Seven of the clean animals were invited into the ark (Gen. 7:2). Jacob served seven years to marry Leah and then another seven to marry Rachel (Gen. 29). When asked how often we should forgive, Jesus answered "seventy times seven" (Matt. 18:22). Many see the number seven as the number of completion. They would understand Jesus' answer to mean, "as many times as it takes to get the job done."

8:12 anointed him to consecrate him. Anointing someone with oil had to do with setting him apart for something special. Here it was the high priest. At other times it was a king. In Hebrews Jesus is described as being anointed by God with the "oil of joy" (Heb. 1:9). The sick were anointed to set them apart for healing (James 5:14). All Christians have received the anointing of the Holy Spirit (1 John 2:20).

8:14 Aaron and his sons. Since Aaron and his sons were being consecrated, they all placed hands on the bull's head to symbolically transfer their sin to the animal. Priests needed forgiveness as much as anyone else.

8:28 ordination offering. Except for the blood smeared on Aaron and his sons, this offering was a fellowship offering, perhaps because it was a part of a vow.

and on his sons and their garments. So he consecrated Aaron and his
garments and his sons and their garments.
31Moses then said to Aaron and his sons, "Cook the meat at the
entrance to the Tent of Meeting and eat it there with the bread from
the basket of ordination offerings, as I commanded, saying,[a] 'Aaron
and his sons are to eat it.' 32Then burn up the rest of the meat and the
bread. 33Do not leave the entrance to the Tent of Meeting for seven
days, until the days of your ordination are completed, for your
ordination will last seven days. 34What has been done today was
commanded by the LORD to make atonement for you. 35You must stay
at the entrance to the Tent of Meeting day and night for seven days
and do what the LORD requires, so you will not die; for that is what I
have been commanded." 36So Aaron and his sons did everything the
LORD commanded through Moses.

The Priests Begin Their Ministry

9 On the eighth day Moses summoned Aaron and his sons and the
elders of Israel. 2He said to Aaron, "Take a bull calf for your sin
offering and a ram for your burnt offering, both without defect, and
present them before the LORD. 3Then say to the Israelites: 'Take a
male goat for a sin offering, a calf and a lamb—both a year old and
without defect—for a burnt offering, 4and an ox[b] and a ram for a
fellowship offering[c] to sacrifice before the LORD, together with a
grain offering mixed with oil. For today the LORD will appear to you.' "
5They took the things Moses commanded to the front of the Tent of
Meeting, and the entire assembly came near and stood before the
LORD. 6Then Moses said, "This is what the LORD has commanded you
to do, so that the glory of the LORD may appear to you."
7Moses said to Aaron, "Come to the altar and sacrifice your sin
offering and your burnt offering and make atonement for yourself
and the people; sacrifice the offering that is for the people and make
atonement for them, as the LORD has commanded."
8So Aaron came to the altar and slaughtered the calf as a sin offering for himself. 9His sons brought the blood to him, and he dipped his
finger into the blood and put it on the horns of the altar; the rest of
the blood he poured out at the base of the altar. 10On the altar he
burned the fat, the kidneys and the covering of the liver from the sin
offering, as the LORD commanded Moses; 11the flesh and the hide he
burned up outside the camp.
12Then he slaughtered the burnt offering. His sons handed him the
blood, and he sprinkled it against the altar on all sides. 13They handed him the burnt offering piece by piece, including the head, and he
burned them on the altar. 14He washed the inner parts and the legs
and burned them on top of the burnt offering on the altar.

[a]31 Or *I was commanded:* [b]4 The Hebrew word can include both male and female; also in verses 18 and 19. [c]4 *Traditionally peace offering;* also in verses 18 and 22

OPEN 1. Have you ever been served an elaborate "7-course" meal? What was the occasion? How did it feel being treated so special? **2.** What is the most spectacular fireworks display you remember? What made it so spectacular? **3.** What part of the weekly worship service do you relish the most at your church? Why this part?

STUDY The chapter describes the commencement of the public sacrificial system. After the seven days of consecration for Aaron and his sons, they began their ministry. The people were about to meet the ultimate being by his invitation? **1.** What is the significance of this ministry beginning on the "eighth day" (v. 1; 8:33)? **2.** What impressions do the sacrifices leave upon you as an observer? **3.** Why do you think the sacrifice for Aaron's sin (vv. 2,7–11) was made before the one for the people's sin (vv. 15–21)? **4.** What famous three-fold blessing does Aaron give at the end of his service (Num. 6:23–26) to accompany his three-fold offering (v. 22)? **5.** Why do you think God sent the fiery finale? What does this say about Aaron's role in the process of restoring the people to a right relationship with God? **6.** Later Jesus assumes this role. How is Jesus, the High Priest who descended from the tribe of Judah, related to Aaron and his sons, who are descended from the tribe of Levi (Heb. 7:11–28)?

9:1 eighth day. According to Jewish tradition, the ordination of the priest started on the 23rd day of the 12th month and lasted seven days. In this way, the priest began his duties on the first day of the first month. That was also when the tabernacle became functional.

9:2 present them before the Lord. The first official act for the high priest was to admit his own sinfulness.

9:4 today the Lord will appear. Moses' instructions—first a sin offering, then a burnt offering and then a fellowship offering—prepared priests for God's appearance. First repentance, then dedication and then the open hand of fellowship—and God, delighted with each heart, would be in the midst.

APPLY 1. Do you need someone to stand between you and God for reconciliation? Why or why not? 2. Hebrews 7:11–28 tells us that Jesus is now our High Priest. How does that affect your spiritual pilgrimage? 3. How would you explain God's process of reconciliation to someone who did not understand it? With whom will you share it?

15Aaron then brought the offering that was for the people. He took
the goat for the people's sin offering and slaughtered it and offered it
for a sin offering as he did with the first one.
16He brought the burnt offering and offered it in the prescribed
way. 17He also brought the grain offering, took a handful of it and
burned it on the altar in addition to the morning's burnt offering.
18He slaughtered the ox and the ram as the fellowship offering for
the people. His sons handed him the blood, and he sprinkled it
against the altar on all sides. 19But the fat portions of the ox and the
ram—the fat tail, the layer of fat, the kidneys and the covering of the
liver— 20these they laid on the breasts, and then Aaron burned the fat
on the altar. 21Aaron waved the breasts and the right thigh before the
LORD as a wave offering, as Moses commanded.
22Then Aaron lifted his hands toward the people and blessed them.
And having sacrificed the sin offering, the burnt offering and the
fellowship offering, he stepped down.
23Moses and Aaron then went into the Tent of Meeting. When they
came out, they blessed the people; and the glory of the LORD
appeared to all the people. 24Fire came out from the presence of the
LORD and consumed the burnt offering and the fat portions on the
altar. And when all the people saw it, they shouted for joy and fell
facedown.

The Death of Nadab and Abihu

10 Aaron's sons Nadab and Abihu took their censers, put fire in
them and added incense; and they offered unauthorized fire
before the LORD, contrary to his command. 2So fire came out from the
presence of the LORD and consumed them, and they died before the
LORD. 3Moses then said to Aaron, "This is what the LORD spoke of
when he said:

" 'Among those who approach me
I will show myself holy;
in the sight of all the people
I will be honored.' "

Aaron remained silent.
4Moses summoned Mishael and Elzaphan, sons of Aaron's uncle
Uzziel, and said to them, "Come here; carry your cousins outside the
camp, away from the front of the sanctuary." 5So they came and
carried them, still in their tunics, outside the camp, as Moses ordered.

OPEN 1. As a child, what were you told about keeping up your appearance (hair, clothes, eating habits)? If you looked "unkept," what would your parents say? How did you respond? 2. What was your first experience with death: Close friend, aging relative or long-time pet? How old were you then? How did that affect you?

STUDY On the first day of his high priestly ministry, two of Aaron's sons died tragically. 1. Why do you think the death of Aaron's sons is included here? Why were their lives taken (vv. 3,10)? Why do you think repeated mention is made of their death elsewhere (Ex. 28:1; Num. 3:2–4; 26:60–61; 1 Chr. 24:1–2)? 2. At other turning points in redemptive history,

---

9:21 wave. Typically this meant that the meat was waved up and down. When waved right to left it was often called a "heave" offering.

9:22 Aaron ... blessed them. Aaron's blessing ("The LORD bless you and keep you ...") appeared in Numbers 6:23–26.

9:23–24 glory of the LORD. *We don't* know what it looked like, but we know it came from the holiest place and showed itself in a fire-like way because the sacrifices were burned up.

9:24 fell facedown. These people felt joy that God appeared with them, and they showed reverence.

10:1 censers. Saucepans for holding incense while it was being burned, also called firepans. **unauthorized.** What happened here? They might have prepared the incense incorrectly. *They might have prepared themselves* incorrectly. Drunkenness is mentioned in verse 9. Nevertheless, after Moses had been so careful to do everything exactly as God commanded, these two guys stepped outside the plan, and consequences followed.

10:2 they died. Nadab and Abihu were not the last people to die instantly from mishandling God's presence and work. A man named Uzzah died from touching the ark (which was the sacred box kept in the Holy of Holies) as a group of men were moving it (2 Sam. 6:6–7). In the New Testament, Ananias and his wife Sapphira died instantly when confronted with their lies about the church treasury (Acts 5:1–10).

6Then Moses said to Aaron and his sons Eleazar and Ithamar, "Do
not let your hair become unkempt,[a] and do not tear your clothes, or
you will die and the LORD will be angry with the whole community.
But your relatives, all the house of Israel, may mourn for those the
LORD has destroyed by fire. 7Do not leave the entrance to the Tent of
Meeting or you will die, because the LORD's anointing oil is on you."
So they did as Moses said.
8Then the LORD said to Aaron, 9"You and your sons are not to drink
wine or other fermented drink whenever you go into the Tent of Meeting, or you will die. This is a lasting ordinance for the generations to
come. 10You must distinguish between the holy and the common,
between the unclean and the clean, 11and you must teach the Israelites
all the decrees the LORD has given them through Moses."
12Moses said to Aaron and his remaining sons, Eleazar and Ithamar, "Take the grain offering left over from the offerings made to the
LORD by fire and eat it prepared without yeast beside the altar, for it is
most holy. 13Eat it in a holy place, because it is your share and your
sons' share of the offerings made to the LORD by fire; for so I have
been commanded. 14But you and your sons and your daughters may
eat the breast that was waved and the thigh that was presented. Eat
them in a ceremonially clean place; they have been given to you and
your children as your share of the Israelites' fellowship offerings.[b]
15The thigh that was presented and the breast that was waved must
be brought with the fat portions of the offerings made by fire, to be
waved before the LORD as a wave offering. This will be the regular
share for you and your children, as the LORD has commanded."
16When Moses inquired about the goat of the sin offering and
found that it had been burned up, he was angry with Eleazar and Ithamar, Aaron's remaining sons, and asked, 17"Why didn't you eat the
sin offering in the sanctuary area? It is most holy; it was given to you
to take away the guilt of the community by making atonement for
them before the LORD. 18Since its blood was not taken into the Holy
Place, you should have eaten the goat in the sanctuary area, as I
commanded."
19Aaron replied to Moses, "Today they sacrificed their sin offering
and their burnt offering before the LORD, but such things as this have
happened to me. Would the LORD have been pleased if I had eaten the
sin offering today?" 20When Moses heard this, he was satisfied.

Clean and Unclean Food

11 The LORD said to Moses and Aaron, 2"Say to the Israelites: 'Of
all the animals that live on land, these are the ones you may
eat: 3You may eat any animal that has a split hoof completely divided
and that chews the cud.

[a]6 Or *Do not uncover your heads* [b]14 Traditionally *peace offerings*

those who have trifled with holy things have also died suddenly. What do you know about Achan (Josh. 7), Uzzah (2 Sam. 6:1–7), Ananias and Sapphira (Acts 5:1–11)? **3.** In the context of Leviticus, and in the deaths of Nadab and Abihu, what is meant by verse 10? What actions in this chapter could be categorized "holy"? Which are "common"? **4.** It seems Aaron might likewise lose his remaining sons (vv. 16ff). On what basis is Moses "satisfied" with Aaron's intentions?

APPLY 1. How do you know when you have stepped over the line and broken fellowship with God? How do you feel? **2.** Who are you accountable to in your spiritual life to keep you honest?

OPEN 1. On a scale of 1 to 10, how successful are you at regulating what you eat? **2.** Have you ever been forced to go on a specific diet? How well did you do?

STUDY This chapter contains many of the dietary instructions for the children of Israel. God's

10:10 the unclean and the clean. Understanding the difference between clean and unclean was the foundation for understanding the holiness of God.

10:18 If the goat's blood had been taken into the Holy Place, then the whole carcass would have been burnt and no one would have eaten any of it.

10:19–20 he was satisfied. Moses was content with Aaron's explanation; it did not seem to be a matter of open rebellion.

11:2–3 split hoof ... chews the cud. This is the basis for the traditional kosher diet. They could eat beef because cows chewed the cud and had split hooves. Camels were out because they chewed their cud but didn't have split hooves. Horses were out on both counts. Pigs had the right hooves but didn't chew cud.

people could not eat unclean animals because they would make a person spiritually unclean. **1.** Although it is not clear today why certain animals were listed as fit for human consumption and others were not, what reasons might there be back then for such an action by God? **2.** How would the reasons you have listed help the people, both physically and spiritually? **3.** Given the situation the people find themselves in, why would cleanliness be so important? Do we have any parallels today in things that make us unclean? **4.** To this point, Leviticus has been a list of rules for restoring a right relationship with God. How does this chapter develop that theme? What added purpose and incentives to holiness does God give them here (vv. 43–45)?

APPLY 1. If your body could whisper something to you today about your eating habits, what would your body say? **2.** Are there areas in your life where you are spiritually unclean?

4“ ‘There are some that only chew the cud or only have a split hoof,
but you must not eat them. The camel, though it chews the cud, does
not have a split hoof; it is ceremonially unclean for you. 5The coney,[a]
though it chews the cud, does not have a split hoof; it is unclean for
you. 6The rabbit, though it chews the cud, does not have a split hoof;
it is unclean for you. 7And the pig, though it has a split hoof completely divided, does not chew the cud; it is unclean for you. 8You
must not eat their meat or touch their carcasses; they are unclean for
you.

9“ ‘Of all the creatures living in the water of the seas and the
streams, you may eat any that have fins and scales. 10But all creatures
in the seas or streams that do not have fins and scales—whether
among all the swarming things or among all the other living creatures in the water—you are to detest. 11And since you are to detest
them, you must not eat their meat and you must detest their carcasses. 12Anything living in the water that does not have fins and
scales is to be detestable to you.

13“ ‘These are the birds you are to detest and not eat because they
are detestable: the eagle, the vulture, the black vulture, 14the red kite,
any kind of black kite, 15any kind of raven, 16the horned owl, the
screech owl, the gull, any kind of hawk, 17the little owl, the cormorant, the great owl, 18the white owl, the desert owl, the osprey, 19the
stork, any kind of heron, the hoopoe and the bat.[b]

20“ ‘All flying insects that walk on all fours are to be detestable to
you. 21There are, however, some winged creatures that walk on all
fours that you may eat: those that have jointed legs for hopping on
the ground. 22Of these you may eat any kind of locust, katydid, cricket
or grasshopper. 23But all other winged creatures that have four legs
you are to detest.

24“ ‘You will make yourselves unclean by these; whoever touches
their carcasses will be unclean till evening. 25Whoever picks up one of
their carcasses must wash his clothes, and he will be unclean till evening.

26“ ‘Every animal that has a split hoof not completely divided or
that does not chew the cud is unclean for you; whoever touches ⌊the
carcass of⌋ any of them will be unclean. 27Of all the animals that walk
on all fours, those that walk on their paws are unclean for you; whoever touches their carcasses will be unclean till evening. 28Anyone
who picks up their carcasses must wash his clothes, and he will be
unclean till evening. They are unclean for you.

29“ ‘Of the animals that move about on the ground, these are
unclean for you: the weasel, the rat, any kind of great lizard, 30the
gecko, the monitor lizard, the wall lizard, the skink and the chameleon. 31Of all those that move along the ground, these are unclean for
you. Whoever touches them when they are dead will be unclean
till evening. 32When one of them dies and falls on something, that
article, whatever its use, will be unclean, whether it is made of wood,

[a] *5* That is, the hyrax or rock badger [b] *19* The precise identification of some of the birds, insects and animals in this chapter is uncertain.

11:6 rabbit. Rabbits do not actually chew cud, but they appear to, because of repetitive chewing movements.

11:20–21 legs for hopping. Locusts and grasshoppers, not normally in the four food groups, were allowed here as the only flying insects considered kosher. While wandering in the wilderness they would have a source of protein.

cloth, hide or sackcloth. Put it in water; it will be unclean till evening, and then it will be clean. 33If one of them falls into a clay pot, everything in it will be unclean, and you must break the pot. 34Any food that could be eaten but has water on it from such a pot is unclean, and any liquid that could be drunk from it is unclean. 35Anything that one of their carcasses falls on becomes unclean; an oven or cooking pot must be broken up. They are unclean, and you are to regard them as unclean. 36A spring, however, or a cistern for collecting water remains clean, but anyone who touches one of these carcasses is unclean. 37If a carcass falls on any seeds that are to be planted, they remain clean. 38But if water has been put on the seed and a carcass falls on it, it is unclean for you.

39" 'If an animal that you are allowed to eat dies, anyone who touches the carcass will be unclean till evening. 40Anyone who eats some of the carcass must wash his clothes, and he will be unclean till evening. Anyone who picks up the carcass must wash his clothes, and he will be unclean till evening.

41" 'Every creature that moves about on the ground is detestable; it is not to be eaten. 42You are not to eat any creature that moves about on the ground, whether it moves on its belly or walks on all fours or on many feet; it is detestable. 43Do not defile yourselves by any of these creatures. Do not make yourselves unclean by means of them or be made unclean by them. 44I am the LORD your God; consecrate yourselves and be holy, because I am holy. Do not make yourselves unclean by any creature that moves about on the ground. 45I am the LORD who brought you up out of Egypt to be your God; therefore be holy, because I am holy.

46" 'These are the regulations concerning animals, birds, every living thing that moves in the water and every creature that moves about on the ground. 47You must distinguish between the unclean and the clean, between living creatures that may be eaten and those that may not be eaten.' "

Purification After Childbirth

12 The LORD said to Moses, 2"Say to the Israelites: 'A woman who becomes pregnant and gives birth to a son will be ceremonially unclean for seven days, just as she is unclean during her monthly period. 3On the eighth day the boy is to be circumcised. 4Then the woman must wait thirty-three days to be purified from her bleeding. She must not touch anything sacred or go to the sanctuary until the days of her purification are over. 5If she gives birth to a daughter, for two weeks the woman will be unclean, as during her period. Then she must wait sixty-six days to be purified from her bleeding.

OPEN What feelings do you have about babies? Why is that?

STUDY Since childlessness in ancient times was a great misfortune, it may seem strange that childbearing rendered the mother unclean. **1.** If you were a mother having just given birth, how would you view these regulations? **2.** Do you think it really took twice as long to become clean after giving birth to a girl? **3.** What would you have concluded about the

11:36 cistern. When something was found unclean, there were only two options: destroy it or purify it. Here the practical nature of the Law takes over. The practical reality was that people could not destroy or purify their cisterns (holding tanks for water), as cisterns were needed for survival.

11:44 be holy. Leviticus is all about God's holiness and the holiness he desires from his people. Imagine being a people whose every dietary and social custom was born out of an understanding that God and his people were to be special, set apart and utterly spiritually clean.

11:45 out of Egypt. The history of the Hebrews was ever with them. The fact that God miraculously delivered them from Egypt was the starting point for every national policy after that. At a point in time they had been chosen and delivered. Now each day they had to decide how to live.

12:2–5 Why the period of purification was longer after birthing a girl than a boy is not known.

value of all children from the required sacrifices (12:6)? **4.** How did the fact that the mother had to offer the sacrifice for herself demonstrate that women were active participants in Israel's worship (12:6–8)?

APPLY 1. How do these purification regulations make you feel? **2.** How does modern culture affect worship and ritual practices at your church? Is this good or bad?

OPEN 1. What's the worst illness you have ever experienced? **2.** Have you ever procrastinated about going to the doctor?

STUDY Chapters 13–14 pertain to the diagnosis, treatment and ceremonial cleansing of infectious diseases in people, clothing and houses. These conditions would disrupt the wholeness necessary for Levitical worship. **1.** Why would an infectious skin disease make a person unclean (v. 3)? **2.** What action was a person suspecting skin disease to take? **3.** Why was the person with leprosy isolated from the people (v. 46)? **4.** Does this teach us anything about the the nature of sin? What? **5.** What was the task of the priest (vv. 3–8)? Did the priest heal the affected person? Are there any parallels between the priests discerning disease then and spiritual leaders discerning sin today? **6.** How did Jesus treat the sick (Matt. 8:1–4)? Why?

APPLY 1. How important is good health to you? Rank yourself on a scale of 1 (sickly slob) to 10 (health nut). How do you think your lifestyle promotes good health? **2.** In what ways does maintaining good health promote your spiritual vitality? **3.** Do you see ill health as a sign of something wrong "spiritually"? What can you do to make sure that you make the proper response to illness? **4.** What role should Christians take in the care of the sick, especially those who have contagious diseases?

6" 'When the days of her purification for a son or daughter are over,
she is to bring to the priest at the entrance to the Tent of Meeting a
year-old lamb for a burnt offering and a young pigeon or a dove for a
sin offering. 7He shall offer them before the LORD to make atonement
for her, and then she will be ceremonially clean from her flow of
blood.

" 'These are the regulations for the woman who gives birth to a boy
or a girl. 8If she cannot afford a lamb, she is to bring two doves or two
young pigeons, one for a burnt offering and the other for a sin offering. In this way the priest will make atonement for her, and she will
be clean.' "

Regulations About Infectious Skin Diseases

13 The LORD said to Moses and Aaron, 2"When anyone has a
swelling or a rash or a bright spot on his skin that may become an infectious skin disease,[a] he must be brought to Aaron the
priest or to one of his sons[b] who is a priest. 3The priest is to examine
the sore on his skin, and if the hair in the sore has turned white and
the sore appears to be more than skin deep,[c] it is an infectious skin
disease. When the priest examines him, he shall pronounce him
ceremonially unclean. 4If the spot on his skin is white but does not
appear to be more than skin deep and the hair in it has not turned
white, the priest is to put the infected person in isolation for seven
days. 5On the seventh day the priest is to examine him, and if he sees
that the sore is unchanged and has not spread in the skin, he is to
keep him in isolation another seven days. 6On the seventh day the
priest is to examine him again, and if the sore has faded and has not
spread in the skin, the priest shall pronounce him clean; it is only a
rash. The man must wash his clothes, and he will be clean. 7But if the
rash does spread in his skin after he has shown himself to the priest
to be pronounced clean, he must appear before the priest again. 8The
priest is to examine him, and if the rash has spread in the skin, he
shall pronounce him unclean; it is an infectious disease.

9"When anyone has an infectious skin disease, he must be brought
to the priest. 10The priest is to examine him, and if there is a white
swelling in the skin that has turned the hair white and if there is raw
flesh in the swelling, 11it is a chronic skin disease and the priest shall
pronounce him unclean. He is not to put him in isolation, because he
is already unclean.

12"If the disease breaks out all over his skin and, so far as the priest
can see, it covers all the skin of the infected person from head to foot,
13the priest is to examine him, and if the disease has covered his
whole body, he shall pronounce that person clean. Since it has all
turned white, he is clean. 14But whenever raw flesh appears on him,
he will be unclean. 15When the priest sees the raw flesh, he shall pro-

[a]2 Traditionally *leprosy*; the Hebrew word was used for various diseases affecting the skin—not necessarily leprosy; also elsewhere in this chapter. [b]2 Or *descendants* [c]3 Or *be lower than the rest of the skin*; also elsewhere in this chapter

---

13:1–46 *Skin disease* was a concern. Leprosy (Hansen's disease) was the most well-known skin disease and the most severe, resulting in the loss of limbs and a complete excommunication from the community. There were other less severe skin conditions too. This passage is almost pharmaceutical in its description of symptoms and treatments.

13:2 skin. Aaron would decide whether someone's ailment was dangerous to others. A contagious, life-threatening disease would not take long to spread to the entire people.

nounce him unclean. The raw flesh is unclean; he has an infectious
disease. 16 Should the raw flesh change and turn white, he must go to
the priest. 17 The priest is to examine him, and if the sores have turned
white, the priest shall pronounce the infected person clean; then he
will be clean.

18 "When someone has a boil on his skin and it heals, 19 and in the
place where the boil was, a white swelling or reddish-white spot
appears, he must present himself to the priest. 20 The priest is to
examine it, and if it appears to be more than skin deep and the hair in
it has turned white, the priest shall pronounce him unclean. It is an
infectious skin disease that has broken out where the boil was. 21 But
if, when the priest examines it, there is no white hair in it and it is not
more than skin deep and has faded, then the priest is to put him in
isolation for seven days. 22 If it is spreading in the skin, the priest shall
pronounce him unclean; it is infectious. 23 But if the spot is unchanged and has not spread, it is only a scar from the boil, and the
priest shall pronounce him clean.

24 "When someone has a burn on his skin and a reddish-white or
white spot appears in the raw flesh of the burn, 25 the priest is to examine the spot, and if the hair in it has turned white, and it appears to
be more than skin deep, it is an infectious disease that has broken
out in the burn. The priest shall pronounce him unclean; it is an infectious skin disease. 26 But if the priest examines it and there is no
white hair in the spot and if it is not more than skin deep and has faded, then the priest is to put him in isolation for seven days. 27 On the
seventh day the priest is to examine him, and if it is spreading in the
skin, the priest shall pronounce him unclean; it is an infectious skin
disease. 28 If, however, the spot is unchanged and has not spread in
the skin but has faded, it is a swelling from the burn, and the priest
shall pronounce him clean; it is only a scar from the burn.

29 "If a man or woman has a sore on the head or on the chin, 30 the
priest is to examine the sore, and if it appears to be more than skin
deep and the hair in it is yellow and thin, the priest shall pronounce
that person unclean; it is an itch, an infectious disease of the head or
chin. 31 But if, when the priest examines this kind of sore, it does not
seem to be more than skin deep and there is no black hair in it, then
the priest is to put the infected person in isolation for seven days.
32 On the seventh day the priest is to examine the sore, and if the itch
has not spread and there is no yellow hair in it and it does not appear
to be more than skin deep, 33 he must be shaved except for the diseased area, and the priest is to keep him in isolation another seven
days. 34 On the seventh day the priest is to examine the itch, and if it
has not spread in the skin and appears to be no more than skin deep,
the priest shall pronounce him clean. He must wash his clothes, and
he will be clean. 35 But if the itch does spread in the skin after he is
pronounced clean, 36 the priest is to examine him, and if the itch has
spread in the skin, the priest does not need to look for yellow hair;
the person is unclean. 37 If, however, in his judgment it is unchanged
and black hair has grown in it, the itch is healed. He is clean, and the
priest shall pronounce him clean.

38 "When a man or woman has white spots on the skin, 39 the priest
is to examine them, and if the spots are dull white, it is a harmless
rash that has broken out on the skin; that person is clean.

40 "When a man has lost his hair and is bald, he is clean. 41 If he has

lost his hair from the front of his scalp and has a bald forehead, he is clean. [42]But if he has a reddish-white sore on his bald head or forehead, it is an infectious disease breaking out on his head or forehead. [43]The priest is to examine him, and if the swollen sore on his head or forehead is reddish-white like an infectious skin disease, [44]the man is diseased and is unclean. The priest shall pronounce him unclean because of the sore on his head.

[45]"The person with such an infectious disease must wear torn clothes, let his hair be unkempt,[a] cover the lower part of his face and cry out, 'Unclean! Unclean!' [46]As long as he has the infection he remains unclean. He must live alone; he must live outside the camp.

Regulations About Mildew

[47]"If any clothing is contaminated with mildew—any woolen or linen clothing, [48]any woven or knitted material of linen or wool, any leather or anything made of leather— [49]and if the contamination in the clothing, or leather, or woven or knitted material, or any leather article, is greenish or reddish, it is a spreading mildew and must be shown to the priest. [50]The priest is to examine the mildew and isolate the affected article for seven days. [51]On the seventh day he is to examine it, and if the mildew has spread in the clothing, or the woven or knitted material, or the leather, whatever its use, it is a destructive mildew; the article is unclean. [52]He must burn up the clothing, or the woven or knitted material of wool or linen, or any leather article that has the contamination in it, because the mildew is destructive; the article must be burned up.

[53]"But if, when the priest examines it, the mildew has not spread in the clothing, or the woven or knitted material, or the leather article, [54]he shall order that the contaminated article be washed. Then he is to isolate it for another seven days. [55]After the affected article has been washed, the priest is to examine it, and if the mildew has not changed its appearance, even though it has not spread, it is unclean. Burn it with fire, whether the mildew has affected one side or the other. [56]If, when the priest examines it, the mildew has faded after the article has been washed, he is to tear the contaminated part out of the clothing, or the leather, or the woven or knitted material. [57]But if it reappears in the clothing, or in the woven or knitted material, or in the leather article, it is spreading, and whatever has the mildew must be burned with fire. [58]The clothing, or the woven or knitted material, or any leather article that has been washed and is rid of the mildew, must be washed again, and it will be clean."

[59]These are the regulations concerning contamination by mildew in woolen or linen clothing, woven or knitted material, or any leather article, for pronouncing them clean or unclean.

[a]45 Or *clothes, uncover his head*

OPEN 1. Do you regularly cull old clothes from your closet or does your closet look like Cinderella's stepsister's foot in the glass slipper? **2.** How much do you value your clothing on a scale of 1 to 10?

STUDY The closing part of chapter 13 refers to mildew in garments and how to deal with the problem. Cloth, highly valued in the ancient world, was the product of many hours of labor and was not lightly thrown away. **1.** The Hebrew word for mildew is the same word translated "infectious skin diseases." What do the regulations concerning mildew have in common with the regulations concerning infectious diseases? **2.** Why would these rules concerning mildew in clothes have to be written? What attitude toward God would be necessary to give up a valuable piece of clothing? **3.** Do you think that spreading skin disease and mildew have common characteristics with sin in any way? Why or why not?

APPLY 1. What objects have a high value for you? To your spiritual well-being? **2.** What new insights does this passage give you into Jesus' teaching on "treasures that moth and rust destroy" (Matt. 6:19)?

13:45–46 the lower part. Even for an ancient people who had yet to make the connection between germs and disease, still provision was made to cover the *lower* part of the face, much as we do today with colds and *sneezes.* **unclean.** It was up to the infected person to guard the health of others by dress and verbal warning.

13:47 mildew. The mildew mentioned here has some similarities to the mildew of today. It was a pale fungus that grew on almost anything damp. Priests decided how to clean the item or whether to destroy it.

Cleansing From Infectious Skin Diseases

14 The LORD said to Moses, 2"These are the regulations for the
diseased person at the time of his ceremonial cleansing,
when he is brought to the priest: 3The priest is to go outside the camp
and examine him. If the person has been healed of his infectious skin
disease,[a] 4the priest shall order that two live clean birds and some
cedar wood, scarlet yarn and hyssop be brought for the one to be
cleansed. 5Then the priest shall order that one of the birds be killed
over fresh water in a clay pot. 6He is then to take the live bird and dip
it, together with the cedar wood, the scarlet yarn and the hyssop, into
the blood of the bird that was killed over the fresh water. 7Seven
times he shall sprinkle the one to be cleansed of the infectious disease and pronounce him clean. Then he is to release the live bird in
the open fields.

8"The person to be cleansed must wash his clothes, shave off all
his hair and bathe with water; then he will be ceremonially clean. After this he may come into the camp, but he must stay outside his tent
for seven days. 9On the seventh day he must shave off all his hair; he
must shave his head, his beard, his eyebrows and the rest of his hair.
He must wash his clothes and bathe himself with water, and he will
be clean.

10"On the eighth day he must bring two male lambs and one ewe
lamb a year old, each without defect, along with three-tenths of an
ephah[b] of fine flour mixed with oil for a grain offering, and one log[c] of
oil. 11The priest who pronounces him clean shall present both the
one to be cleansed and his offerings before the LORD at the entrance
to the Tent of Meeting.

12"Then the priest is to take one of the male lambs and offer it as a
guilt offering, along with the log of oil; he shall wave them before the
LORD as a wave offering. 13He is to slaughter the lamb in the holy
place where the sin offering and the burnt offering are slaughtered.
Like the sin offering, the guilt offering belongs to the priest; it is most
holy. 14The priest is to take some of the blood of the guilt offering and
put it on the lobe of the right ear of the one to be cleansed, on the
thumb of his right hand and on the big toe of his right foot. 15The
priest shall then take some of the log of oil, pour it in the palm of his
own left hand, 16dip his right forefinger into the oil in his palm, and
with his finger sprinkle some of it before the LORD seven times. 17The
priest is to put some of the oil remaining in his palm on the lobe of
the right ear of the one to be cleansed, on the thumb of his right hand
and on the big toe of his right foot, on top of the blood of the guilt

[a]3 Traditionally *leprosy*; the Hebrew word was used for various diseases affecting the skin—not necessarily leprosy; also elsewhere in this chapter. [b]*10* That is, probably about 6 quarts (about 6.5 liters) [c]*10* That is, probably about 2/3 pint (about 0.3 liter); also in verses 12, 15, 21 and 24

OPEN 1. What was your parents' or grandparents' favorite prescription "for whatever ails ya"? **2.** What did it look, feel, taste or smell like?

STUDY This passage gives explicit instructions for the cleansing of a healed leper so he could be readmitted to fellowship with the holy nation and could again draw near to worship the holy God. **1.** Given such socially ostracizing regulations for infectious skin diseases (13:45–46), how tough do you think it would be for someone healed of a skin disease to then re-enter the social life of the Israelite camp? Who do you think would have the tougher adjustment: The person healed, or the people already in the camp? Why? **2.** Of these rituals listed, which seem to you to have actual "medicinal" value? Which have largely "ceremonial" value? Which may have "relational" value? **3.** In this regard, why kill one bird (v. 5) and release the other (v. 7)? Likewise, why are the offerings for sin or guilt together are with offerings for worship and thanks ("burnt" and "grain" offerings)? **4.** What does all this say about God's concern for the "sick"? The "well"? The "poor"? The "outsiders"? The "insiders"? **5.** What do you think Jesus meant in Matthew 9:12–13, when he described those who needed a physician?

APPLY 1. What people does the Christian community ostracize today? Who are the "lepers" of your society? Who are the "outsiders"? The "poor"? **2.** Whom does your group tend to screen out? How could your group help re-incorporate these people into the church? **3.** How would you or your group go about beginning this process? With whom will you begin such reconciliation during the next "seven days"?

14:1–32 Not all disease in ancient time was lifelong or terminal. Some sick people experienced wellness again. Here are rituals for reincorporating a well person back into the community.

14:4 While the use of the cedar wood, scarlet yarn and hyssop was not explained here, these items were associated with healing in other passages in the Bible (Num. 19:6; Ps. 51:7).

14:5 one of the birds be killed. The bird might have symbolized the death that the well person had escaped.

14:6 live bird. This bird probably symbolized the new life offered in healing from disease.

14:7,16, 51 seven. Throughout the Bible, seven is seen as the number of completion.

14:7 release the live bird. This is a beautiful image of recovery and new life. The well person, like a bird, was set free to live among his own.

offering. [18]The rest of the oil in his palm the priest shall put on the
head of the one to be cleansed and make atonement for him before
the LORD.

[19]"Then the priest is to sacrifice the sin offering and make atonement for the one to be cleansed from his uncleanness. After that, the
priest shall slaughter the burnt offering [20]and offer it on the altar,
together with the grain offering, and make atonement for him, and he
will be clean.

[21]"If, however, he is poor and cannot afford these, he must take one
male lamb as a guilt offering to be waved to make atonement for him,
together with a tenth of an ephah[a] of fine flour mixed with oil for a
grain offering, a log of oil, [22]and two doves or two young pigeons,
which he can afford, one for a sin offering and the other for a burnt
offering.

[23]"On the eighth day he must bring them for his cleansing to the
priest at the entrance to the Tent of Meeting, before the LORD. [24]The
priest is to take the lamb for the guilt offering, together with the log
of oil, and wave them before the LORD as a wave offering. [25]He shall
slaughter the lamb for the guilt offering and take some of its blood
and put it on the lobe of the right ear of the one to be cleansed, on the
thumb of his right hand and on the big toe of his right foot. [26]The
priest is to pour some of the oil into the palm of his own left hand,
[27]and with his right forefinger sprinkle some of the oil from his palm
seven times before the LORD. [28]Some of the oil in his palm he is to put
on the same places he put the blood of the guilt offering—on the lobe
of the right ear of the one to be cleansed, on the thumb of his right
hand and on the big toe of his right foot. [29]The rest of the oil in his
palm the priest shall put on the head of the one to be cleansed, to
make atonement for him before the LORD. [30]Then he shall sacrifice
the doves or the young pigeons, which the person can afford, [31]one[b]
as a sin offering and the other as a burnt offering, together with the
grain offering. In this way the priest will make atonement before the
LORD on behalf of the one to be cleansed."

[32]These are the regulations for anyone who has an infectious skin
disease and who cannot afford the regular offerings for his cleansing.

Cleansing From Mildew

[33]The LORD said to Moses and Aaron, [34]"When you enter the land of
Canaan, which I am giving you as your possession, and I put a
spreading mildew in a house in that land, [35]the owner of the house
must go and tell the priest, 'I have seen something that looks like mildew in my house.' [36]The priest is to order the house to be emptied
before he goes in to examine the mildew, so that nothing in the house
will be pronounced unclean. After this the priest is to go in and inspect the house. [37]He is to examine the mildew on the walls, and if it
has greenish or reddish depressions that appear to be deeper than
the surface of the wall, [38]the priest shall go out the doorway of the
house and close it up for seven days. [39]On the seventh day the priest

[a]*21* That is, probably about 2 quarts (about 2 liters) [b]*31* Septuagint and Syriac; Hebrew *31such as the person can afford, one*

OPEN 1. How would you describe your housekeeping: Comfy? Lived in? Trash collection? Spotless? What does your spouse or your mom have to say about your housekeeping? **2.** What would you prefer to live in: Luxury condo? Older, restored home? Fixer-upper?

STUDY This section is an extension of the law concerning clothing. Since it dealt with houses made of stones it would come into effect after the Israelites entered the land of Canaan. **1.** In addition to health and clothing inspector, what new role is cut out for the priests? Why them? **2.** What similarities do you see here

14:33–53 The ceremonial cleansing from mildew was a lot like the cleansing from skin diseases. The ritual focused on the atonement of the person or the dwelling. The priest would examine the house to determine the outcome.

shall return to inspect the house. If the mildew has spread on the walls, 40he is to order that the contaminated stones be torn out and thrown into an unclean place outside the town. 41He must have all the inside walls of the house scraped and the material that is scraped off dumped into an unclean place outside the town. 42Then they are to take other stones to replace these and take new clay and plaster the house.

43"If the mildew reappears in the house after the stones have been torn out and the house scraped and plastered, 44the priest is to go and examine it and, if the mildew has spread in the house, it is a destructive mildew; the house is unclean. 45It must be torn down—its stones, timbers and all the plaster—and taken out of the town to an unclean place.

46"Anyone who goes into the house while it is closed up will be unclean till evening. 47Anyone who sleeps or eats in the house must wash his clothes.

48"But if the priest comes to examine it and the mildew has not spread after the house has been plastered, he shall pronounce the house clean, because the mildew is gone. 49To purify the house he is to take two birds and some cedar wood, scarlet yarn and hyssop. 50He shall kill one of the birds over fresh water in a clay pot. 51Then he is to take the cedar wood, the hyssop, the scarlet yarn and the live bird, dip them into the blood of the dead bird and the fresh water, and sprinkle the house seven times. 52He shall purify the house with the bird's blood, the fresh water, the live bird, the cedar wood, the hyssop and the scarlet yarn. 53Then he is to release the live bird in the open fields outside the town. In this way he will make atonement for the house, and it will be clean."

54These are the regulations for any infectious skin disease, for an itch, 55for mildew in clothing or in a house, 56and for a swelling, a rash or a bright spot, 57to determine when something is clean or unclean.

These are the regulations for infectious skin diseases and mildew.

Discharges Causing Uncleanness

15 The LORD said to Moses and Aaron, 2"Speak to the Israelites and say to them: 'When any man has a bodily discharge, the discharge is unclean. 3Whether it continues flowing from his body or is blocked, it will make him unclean. This is how his discharge will bring about uncleanness:

4" 'Any bed the man with a discharge lies on will be unclean, and anything he sits on will be unclean. 5Anyone who touches his bed must wash his clothes and bathe with water, and he will be unclean till evening. 6Whoever sits on anything that the man with a discharge sat on must wash his clothes and bathe with water, and he will be unclean till evening.

between cleansing the house and cleansing the leper (14:1–32)? **3.** Since the people still live in tents, why does God give these regulations for controlling mildew in houses? **4.** Of these rituals, which appear to have actual "cleansing" value? Which appear to be largely "ceremonial"? **5.** Are there similar characteristics between spreading mildew and sin? **6.** What does this passage teach us about God's desire to restore fellowship with his people?

APPLY 1. If you could compare your life to a house, where is there a little mildew that needs cleaning: Family room? TV/den? study? Bedroom? Basement/rec room? Upstairs closet? **2.** How would you describe your spiritual life remodel job: Doing well? Work in progress? Sorry you asked?

OPEN 1. Did your mom have any rules to follow before coming to dinner? **2.** What happened if you broke the rules?

STUDY These regulations about uncleanness were given to keep the tabernacle undefiled so that Israel would have a place to atone for sin and meet God. **1.** For what reason are these laws concerning uncleanness given to Israel (v. 31)? Was their uncleanness primarily "physical" and hygienic or "spiritual"?

14:45 torn down. First try cleaning, but if the mildew continues to grow, the structure must be destroyed. In a place without disinfectants, there was no other choice.

15:1–33 This passage falls under the category of "Nobody wants to talk about it, but somebody's got to." For both men and women, discharges caused uncleanness. This uncleanness didn't always have to do with sin or with sickness, but it required some time of separation.

15:2 discharge. Some think that this discharge was related to gonorrhea or a similar sexually transmitted disease. Others say it might have been simply diarrhea. We can safely assume that it had to do with the lower part of the body, not the face, since areas where a man sat or lay were considered unclean.

Why do you think so? **2.** Of the various "discharges" listed here, why do you think each would defile God's dwelling place? **3.** Given this extensive list, how much time do you think the average Israelite spent "unclean"? **4.** Of these various rituals, which do you see that have some real cleansing value? Which ones are largely ceremonial? **5.** What do you see as the function of the sacrifices associated with ceremonial cleansing (vv. 13–15,28–30)? **6.** How do you think these ceremonies would make one feel about: Lengthy discharges (diarrhea, hemorrhaging)? Normal human discharges? Sexual relations? Him or herself as an adolescent coming into puberty? **7.** Now two "Bible trivia" questions: Which rule listed here is the background for David's sin with Bathsheba (2 Sam. 11:4)? Which rule echoes earlier times when Rachel deceived Laban (Gen. 31:35)? **8.** Another not so trivial question: Where would desert people get all the water for the many prescribed baths?

APPLY 1. When do you feel unworthy to approach God: When my self-esteem is low? When I've had a defeating day at work or home? When I know I've sinned? During a bout of lengthy sickness? When I miss church? **2.** What provisions has God made for you to feel better about yourself?

7" 'Whoever touches the man who has a discharge must wash his
clothes and bathe with water, and he will be unclean till evening.
8" 'If the man with the discharge spits on someone who is clean,
that person must wash his clothes and bathe with water, and he will
be unclean till evening.
9" 'Everything the man sits on when riding will be unclean, 10and
whoever touches any of the things that were under him will be unclean till evening; whoever picks up those things must wash his
clothes and bathe with water, and he will be unclean till evening.
11" 'Anyone the man with a discharge touches without rinsing his
hands with water must wash his clothes and bathe with water, and he
will be unclean till evening.
12" 'A clay pot that the man touches must be broken, and any wooden article is to be rinsed with water.
13" 'When a man is cleansed from his discharge, he is to count off
seven days for his ceremonial cleansing; he must wash his clothes
and bathe himself with fresh water, and he will be clean. 14On the
eighth day he must take two doves or two young pigeons and come
before the LORD to the entrance to the Tent of Meeting and give them
to the priest. 15The priest is to sacrifice them, the one for a sin offering and the other for a burnt offering. In this way he will make atonement before the LORD for the man because of his discharge.
16" 'When a man has an emission of semen, he must bathe his
whole body with water, and he will be unclean till evening. 17Any
clothing or leather that has semen on it must be washed with water,
and it will be unclean till evening. 18When a man lies with a woman
and there is an emission of semen, both must bathe with water, and
they will be unclean till evening.
19" 'When a woman has her regular flow of blood, the impurity of
her monthly period will last seven days, and anyone who touches her
will be unclean till evening.
20" 'Anything she lies on during her period will be unclean, and
anything she sits on will be unclean. 21Whoever touches her bed must
wash his clothes and bathe with water, and he will be unclean till
evening. 22Whoever touches anything she sits on must wash his
clothes and bathe with water, and he will be unclean till evening.
23Whether it is the bed or anything she was sitting on, when anyone
touches it, he will be unclean till evening.
24" 'If a man lies with her and her monthly flow touches him, he
will be unclean for seven days; any bed he lies on will be unclean.
25" 'When a woman has a discharge of blood for many days at a
time other than her monthly period or has a discharge that continues
beyond her period, she will be unclean as long as she has the
discharge, just as in the days of her period. 26Any bed she lies on
while her discharge continues will be unclean, as is her bed during

15:13 ceremonial cleansing. It wasn't the temple ritual that cleansed the person. That was just confirmation that the person was healed and could reunite with the community.

15:16 emission. An emission was not necessarily the result of sin. It just meant that the man and his clothing should be washed.

15:19 period. Traditionally a woman was considered untouchable during this time. Earlier in the history of Israel a woman named Rachel stole idols from her father and kept him from finding them because she claimed it was her "time of the month" (Gen. 31:35).

15:24 This probably refers to a woman's period while she is with her husband.

her monthly period, and anything she sits on will be unclean, as
during her period. 27Whoever touches them will be unclean; he must
wash his clothes and bathe with water, and he will be unclean till
evening.

28" 'When she is cleansed from her discharge, she must count off
seven days, and after that she will be ceremonially clean. 29On the
eighth day she must take two doves or two young pigeons and bring
them to the priest at the entrance to the Tent of Meeting. 30The priest
is to sacrifice one for a sin offering and the other for a burnt offering.
In this way he will make atonement for her before the LORD for the
uncleanness of her discharge.

31" 'You must keep the Israelites separate from things that make
them unclean, so they will not die in their uncleanness for defiling my
dwelling place,[a] which is among them.' "

32These are the regulations for a man with a discharge, for anyone
made unclean by an emission of semen, 33for a woman in her monthly period, for a man or a woman with a discharge, and for a man who
lies with a woman who is ceremonially unclean.

The Day of Atonement

16 The LORD spoke to Moses after the death of the two sons of
Aaron who died when they approached the LORD. 2The LORD
said to Moses: "Tell your brother Aaron not to come whenever he
chooses into the Most Holy Place behind the curtain in front of the
atonement cover on the ark, or else he will die, because I appear in
the cloud over the atonement cover.

3"This is how Aaron is to enter the sanctuary area: with a young
bull for a sin offering and a ram for a burnt offering. 4He is to put on
the sacred linen tunic, with linen undergarments next to his body; he
is to tie the linen sash around him and put on the linen turban. These
are sacred garments; so he must bathe himself with water before he
puts them on. 5From the Israelite community he is to take two male
goats for a sin offering and a ram for a burnt offering.

6"Aaron is to offer the bull for his own sin offering to make atonement for himself and his household. 7Then he is to take the two goats
and present them before the LORD at the entrance to the Tent of Meeting. 8He is to cast lots for the two goats—one lot for the LORD and the
other for the scapegoat.[b] 9Aaron shall bring the goat whose lot falls to
the LORD and sacrifice it for a sin offering. 10But the goat chosen by lot
as the scapegoat shall be presented alive before the LORD to be used

[a]31 Or *my tabernacle* [b]8 That is, the goat of removal; Hebrew *azazel*; also in verses 10 and 26

OPEN 1. Did you ever lose your driver's license? What did you have to do to get it back? **2.** Have you ever given blood for someone else?

STUDY God required the Day of Atonement ceremonies to cleanse the sanctuary from the pollution introduced into it by the unclean worshipers (16:16,19). The comprehensiveness of the sins atoned for was staggering. The worshiper simply had to approach God with a heart of penitence and faith. **1.** Based on this chapter, how would you describe the human condition? How do Aaron and his two sons (Nadab and Abihu) typify this basic character flaw (vv. 1–2; 10:1–3)? **2.** What is God's typical response to this basic flaw? How does this affect one's fellowship with God? **3.** Why do you think God chose animal sacrifice to reconcile the differences between sinful people and sinless God? Why is it that "without the shedding of blood there is no forgiveness" (Heb. 9:22)? **4.** What does the fact that

---

15:29 doves or ... pigeons. This is *the first of the last scenarios* where a sacrifice is required. This unusual occurrence, not a natural event, required a seven-day waiting period.

15:31 among them. While we may not understand the customs of a holy God in an ancient world, we know that God's intent was to dwell among his people in holiness. Their understanding of clean and unclean helped them to understand how to live with God.

16:1–34 The day of atonement was a once-a-year event. It was about the sins of the whole nation. It was one more reminder that sin required death and that someone must pay.

16:2 whenever he chooses. God's presence dwelled in the Holy Place. Aaron was not to come and go there at will. Instead there were ceremonial times when he was invited there. **atonement cover.** This was also called the "mercy seat." It was the cover for the Ark of the Covenant.

16:3 When it came time for the day of atonement, Aaron was to come prepared with sacrifices in hand—a burnt offering ready to express devotion and a sin offering to ask for God's forgiveness.

16:5 ram. When Abraham was asked to sacrifice his son, Isaac, God provided a ram in the bushes instead (Gen. 22:13). That was Isaac's day of atonement, long before this formalized version.

this "Day of Atonement" took place *only* "once a year" (v. 34) tell you about its importance? What does the fact that it must be repeated *every* year ("a lasting ordinance") tell you about human nature? And what about the lasting effect of this sacrifice (Heb. 9:9–10)? **5.** As important as this Day was to Israel for restoring a correct relationship with God, how much more important and lasting is Christ's "once for all" sacrifice (Heb. 9:11–10:14)? **6.** How would the elements in the Day of Atonement have helped the Israelites to understand: The *necessity* for having a right relationship with God? The *consequences* to them if they did not make atonement for sin? **7.** What did the release of the scapegoat into the wilderness symbolize for the people? **8.** What is the difference between the Day of Atonement and the atoning work of Christ (Heb. 9:9–10)?

APPLY 1. When did you come to understand the meaning of Christ's death in taking care of your sin? **2.** How many people in the church do you think understand this important truth?

for making atonement by sending it into the desert as a scapegoat.
11"Aaron shall bring the bull for his own sin offering to make atonement for himself and his household, and he is to slaughter the bull
for his own sin offering. 12He is to take a censer full of burning coals
from the altar before the LORD and two handfuls of finely ground
fragrant incense and take them behind the curtain. 13He is to put the
incense on the fire before the LORD, and the smoke of the incense will
conceal the atonement cover above the Testimony, so that he will not
die. 14He is to take some of the bull's blood and with his finger sprinkle it on the front of the atonement cover; then he shall sprinkle
some of it with his finger seven times before the atonement cover.
15"He shall then slaughter the goat for the sin offering for the people and take its blood behind the curtain and do with it as he did with
the bull's blood: He shall sprinkle it on the atonement cover and in
front of it. 16In this way he will make atonement for the Most Holy
Place because of the uncleanness and rebellion of the Israelites,
whatever their sins have been. He is to do the same for the Tent of
Meeting, which is among them in the midst of their uncleanness.
17No one is to be in the Tent of Meeting from the time Aaron goes in to
make atonement in the Most Holy Place until he comes out, having
made atonement for himself, his household and the whole community of Israel.
18"Then he shall come out to the altar that is before the LORD and
make atonement for it. He shall take some of the bull's blood and
some of the goat's blood and put it on all the horns of the altar. 19He
shall sprinkle some of the blood on it with his finger seven times to
cleanse it and to consecrate it from the uncleanness of the Israelites.
20"When Aaron has finished making atonement for the Most Holy
Place, the Tent of Meeting and the altar, he shall bring forward the
live goat. 21He is to lay both hands on the head of the live goat and
confess over it all the wickedness and rebellion of the Israelites—all
their sins—and put them on the goat's head. He shall send the goat
away into the desert in the care of a man appointed for the task. 22The
goat will carry on itself all their sins to a solitary place; and the man
shall release it in the desert.
23"Then Aaron is to go into the Tent of Meeting and take off the lin-
en garments he put on before he entered the Most Holy Place, and he
is to leave them there. 24He shall bathe himself with water in a holy
place and put on his regular garments. Then he shall come out and
sacrifice the burnt offering for himself and the burnt offering for the
people, to make atonement for himself and for the people. 25He shall
also burn the fat of the sin offering on the altar.

16:13 so that he will not die. On several occasions God protected his people from seeing his presence. When Moses was on the mountain, God showed him just his back as he passed by in order to save Moses' life (Ex. 33:20–23). The smoke at the ark functioned the same way for Aaron.

16:14 sprinkle. For many denominations today this picture is recreated through baptism. Here the sprinkling signifies atonement.

16:16 whatever their sins have been. This was not a specific sacrifice for a specific sin. It was a general sacrifice for the whole nation for all the sins committed that year.

16:20–22 goat will carry on itself *all their sins*. Imagine the helpless goat with the priest's hands on its head. This goat journeys to freedom while its sacrificial partner's blood drips down the altar. That is the picture of our freedom as Christ's sacrifice covers our sin.

16:24 burnt offering. Aaron had brought a bull and a ram for himself and two goats and a ram for the people. First Aaron offered the bull as his sin offering. Then he offered one goat and let the scapegoat go free. When all that was done, he still had his ram for a burnt offering and the people's ram for their burnt offering.

[26]"The man who releases the goat as a scapegoat must wash his clothes and bathe himself with water; afterward he may come into the camp. [27]The bull and the goat for the sin offerings, whose blood was brought into the Most Holy Place to make atonement, must be taken outside the camp; their hides, flesh and offal are to be burned up. [28]The man who burns them must wash his clothes and bathe himself with water; afterward he may come into the camp.

[29]"This is to be a lasting ordinance for you: On the tenth day of the seventh month you must deny yourselves[a] and not do any work—whether native-born or an alien living among you— [30]because on this day atonement will be made for you, to cleanse you. Then, before the LORD, you will be clean from all your sins. [31]It is a sabbath of rest, and you must deny yourselves; it is a lasting ordinance. [32]The priest who is anointed and ordained to succeed his father as high priest is to make atonement. He is to put on the sacred linen garments [33]and make atonement for the Most Holy Place, for the Tent of Meeting and the altar, and for the priests and all the people of the community.

[34]"This is to be a lasting ordinance for you: Atonement is to be made once a year for all the sins of the Israelites."

And it was done, as the LORD commanded Moses.

Eating Blood Forbidden

17 The LORD said to Moses, [2]"Speak to Aaron and his sons and to all the Israelites and say to them: 'This is what the LORD has commanded: [3]Any Israelite who sacrifices an ox,[b] a lamb or a goat in the camp or outside of it [4]instead of bringing it to the entrance to the Tent of Meeting to present it as an offering to the LORD in front of the tabernacle of the LORD—that man shall be considered guilty of bloodshed; he has shed blood and must be cut off from his people. [5]This is so the Israelites will bring to the LORD the sacrifices they are now making in the open fields. They must bring them to the priest, that is, to the LORD, at the entrance to the Tent of Meeting and sacrifice them as fellowship offerings.[c] [6]The priest is to sprinkle the blood against the altar of the LORD at the entrance to the Tent of Meeting and burn the fat as an aroma pleasing to the LORD. [7]They must no longer offer any of their sacrifices to the goat idols[d] to whom they prostitute themselves. This is to be a lasting ordinance for them and for the generations to come.'

[8]"Say to them: 'Any Israelite or any alien living among them who

[a]29 Or *must fast;* also in verse 31 [b]3 The Hebrew word can include both male and female. [c]5 Traditionally *peace offerings* [d]7 Or *demons*

OPEN 1. Judging from the number of Christmas letters you send and receive, how many "friends" do you have? **2.** Of those, how many are "close" enough to see regularly?

STUDY This chapter relates not so much to the role of the priests as it does to potential mistakes the common Israelite could make regarding sacrificing and eating. **1.** What problems might arise if sacrifices were offered in an uncontrolled context (vv. 7,10,13–16)? How would limiting sacrifice to the Tent of Meeting help reduce these problems (vv. 3–6)? **2.** What consequences befall those who fail to follow God's command in this regard (vv. 4,9,10,14–16)? **3.** A major theme in Leviticus is that blood covers the people's sins and reconciles them to God. Why do you think God chose blood to do that (vv. 10–14)? **4.** What does this say about the

16:29–31 deny yourselves. This was a day of fasting as well as quiet inactivity. The date was in the month of Tishri, which is our October/November.

16:29 alien. Often in commands and guidelines the Law stipulated whether everyone in the land—visitors (aliens) and natives alike—should take part or whether only the Hebrews should take part.

16:30 you will be clean. The Day of Atonement was like a reset button for the nation of Israel. It was a start-over place, renewing God's forgiveness and their need of it.

16:34 once a year. The Hebrews never got to the place of knowing once and for all they were forgiven. They had this once-a-year ritual to remind them of the atonement to come. Christ made a once-and-for-all-sacrifice, though, so that there was no need for a yearly scapegoat and sacrifice. His sacrifice for us was complete (Heb. 9:11–12, 24–26).

17:1–6 Evidently the Hebrews were offering sacrifices to idols outside of camp, then claiming they were merely slaughtering animals for food. To keep this from happening, all animals were required to be slaughtered at the temple as a fellowship offering if nothing else.

17:7 goat idols. Goats were worshiped in the eastern delta of lower Egypt.

seriousness of sin? The seriousness of reconciliation?

APPLY 1. How important to you is taking time to be a friend with God? How much time do you spend maintaining friendship with God? **2.** What is the most important thing you have learned from chapter 17 about maintaining fellowship with God? How will you begin to incorporate this into your life today?

OPEN 1. When you were growing up, who gave you the "big talk" about sex: Dad? Mom? The kids down the street? **2.** Do you feel uncomfortable with all the attention given to sex in movies and on TV?

STUDY It is hard to believe that any culture could have lower sexual standards than our own. However, the Canaanite culture probably takes the cake. **1.** In chapter 18, Israel is called to be different than other nations (vv. 3,21,24–30). What does this tell you about the sexual practices of these other nations? **2.** How would participation in the fertility religions of these nations have harmed Israel's relationship with God? **3.** Almost all cultures have incest taboos. Judging from the reasons

offers a burnt offering or sacrifice 9and does not bring it to the entrance to the Tent of Meeting to sacrifice it to the LORD—that man must be cut off from his people.

10" 'Any Israelite or any alien living among them who eats any blood—I will set my face against that person who eats blood and will cut him off from his people. 11For the life of a creature is in the blood, and I have given it to you to make atonement for yourselves on the altar; it is the blood that makes atonement for one's life. 12Therefore I say to the Israelites, "None of you may eat blood, nor may an alien living among you eat blood."

13" 'Any Israelite or any alien living among you who hunts any animal or bird that may be eaten must drain out the blood and cover it with earth, 14because the life of every creature is its blood. That is why I have said to the Israelites, "You must not eat the blood of any creature, because the life of every creature is its blood; anyone who eats it must be cut off."

15" 'Anyone, whether native-born or alien, who eats anything found dead or torn by wild animals must wash his clothes and bathe with water, and he will be ceremonially unclean till evening; then he will be clean. 16But if he does not wash his clothes and bathe himself, he will be held responsible.' "

Unlawful Sexual Relations

18 The LORD said to Moses, 2"Speak to the Israelites and say to them: 'I am the LORD your God. 3You must not do as they do in Egypt, where you used to live, and you must not do as they do in the land of Canaan, where I am bringing you. Do not follow their practices. 4You must obey my laws and be careful to follow my decrees. I am the LORD your God. 5Keep my decrees and laws, for the man who obeys them will live by them. I am the LORD.

6" 'No one is to approach any close relative to have sexual relations. I am the LORD.

7" 'Do not dishonor your father by having sexual relations with your mother. She is your mother; do not have relations with her.

8" 'Do not have sexual relations with your father's wife; that would dishonor your father.

9" 'Do not have sexual relations with your sister, either your father's daughter or your mother's daughter, whether she was born in the same home or elsewhere.

17:11 it is the blood. Since the life of a creature was found in its blood, it makes sense that the blood got first attention in every sacrifice, then the fat and then the meat.

17:15 found dead or torn. The possibility that blood remained in these beasts required that they not be eaten.

18:1–20:27 *This section includes* guidelines about moral cleanliness that would prepare the Hebrews to live with integrity among the immoral Canaanites.

18:2 I am the LORD. This phrase is repeated throughout the section as the authority upon which God demanded purity from his people and the reason why the people should give it.

18:3 you must not do as they do. God was calling his people to stand up for him and to live life his way. It would have been much easier for these wanderers to simply acclimate to the culture around them. That was not the promise to Abraham generations ago, though.

18:6 any close relative. We now know the physical and emotional complications that can come from incest. This was a new culture, only 400 years old. God established ground rules for them even in this area.

18:7 your mother. In a world where men had multiple wives of different ages, a command like this would make good sense.

18:8 your father's wife. Because of multiple marriages, this was an important distinction. A son could grow up in the house with one of his father's wives who was close to his own age.

10" 'Do not have sexual relations with your son's daughter or your
daughter's daughter; that would dishonor you.
11" 'Do not have sexual relations with the daughter of your father's
wife, born to your father; she is your sister.
12" 'Do not have sexual relations with your father's sister; she is
your father's close relative.
13" 'Do not have sexual relations with your mother's sister, because she is your mother's close relative.
14" 'Do not dishonor your father's brother by approaching his wife
to have sexual relations; she is your aunt.
15" 'Do not have sexual relations with your daughter-in-law. She is
your son's wife; do not have relations with her.
16" 'Do not have sexual relations with your brother's wife; that
would dishonor your brother.
17" 'Do not have sexual relations with both a woman and her
daughter. Do not have sexual relations with either her son's daughter
or her daughter's daughter; they are her close relatives. That is wickedness.
18" 'Do not take your wife's sister as a rival wife and have sexual
relations with her while your wife is living.
19" 'Do not approach a woman to have sexual relations during the
uncleanness of her monthly period.
20" 'Do not have sexual relations with your neighbor's wife and
defile yourself with her.
21" 'Do not give any of your children to be sacrificed[a] to Molech, for
you must not profane the name of your God. I am the LORD.
22" 'Do not lie with a man as one lies with a woman; that is detestable.
23" 'Do not have sexual relations with an animal and defile yourself
with it. A woman must not present herself to an animal to have sexual
relations with it; that is a perversion.
24" 'Do not defile yourselves in any of these ways, because this is
how the nations that I am going to drive out before you became defiled. 25Even the land was defiled; so I punished it for its sin, and the
land vomited out its inhabitants. 26But you must keep my decrees and
my laws. The native-born and the aliens living among you must not
do any of these detestable things, 27for all these things were done by

[a]21 *Or to be passed through ⌊the fire⌋*

given here (vv. 7–18), why is that? What is most dishonoring or detestable about that? **4.** Which of these laws brings to mind the experience of Judah and Tamar (Gen. 38)? Of Amnon and another Tamar (2 Sam. 13)? Of Jacob with Leah and Rachel (Gen. 29)? **5.** What does it mean that those who keep or obey God's laws "will live by them" (v. 5)? Is law-keeping a way of salvation for the lost (Rom. 10:5; Gal. 3:12)? Or is law-keeping a way of life for the redeemed (Ezek. 20:11,13,21)? **6.** Why do you think you would have seen the importance of living a distinctively different life from that of the surrounding nations? **7.** What else do you learn from this chapter about maintaining a correct relationship with a holy and jealous God, who redeems you and calls you to a different life?

APPLY 1. How does this list of unlawful sexual practices strike you: Makes sense? Out-of-date? Up-to-date? Arbitrary? Confining? Liberating? **2.** What aspects of your culture could be called modern day "fertility religions"? **3.** How can you protect yourself and your family against the casual attitude our modern culture has toward sexual relations? **4.** What are you doing to keep your own family holy?

18:11 sister. Tamar, David's daughter, was perhaps the most well-known sister to deal with this prohibition from every angle (2 Sam. 13:9-14).

18:14 aunt. Even after an uncle died, the marriage was to be honored. If an uncle was living, then the act would be adultery and forbidden. This prohibition transcends the "until death do us part" vows. Instead it honors family relationships beyond the Law.

18:15 daughter-in-law. The most well-known account regarding this prohibition was Tamar's deceit posing as a prostitute so that she could have a child by her father-in-law. Her husband was dead and her brothers-in-law would not impregnate her (Gen. 38).

18:16 your brother's wife. An exception to this law in the Levirate law demanded a man marry his brother's widow so that she would not be destitute.

18:17 wickedness. This verse outlines boundaries of decency. It touches on issues that we know at our core are important even before any detailed explanation. Much wickedness is simply the violation of boundaries of decency.

18:18 your wife's sister. The most well-known scenario of this type is the case of Jacob. His father-in-law tricked him into marrying Leah before he could marry her sister, Rachel, whom he really loved. During their lives Rachel and Leah were divided by their desire for Jacob's love and attention (Gen. 29–33).

18:21 Molech. Molech was the national god of the Ammonites. Children were offered to Molech as temple prostitutes and also as burnt sacrifices.

18:22 Later in Leviticus acts of homosexuality are listed as punishable by death.

the people who lived in the land before you, and the land became
defiled. 28And if you defile the land, it will vomit you out as it vomited
out the nations that were before you.

29" 'Everyone who does any of these detestable things—such
persons must be cut off from their people. 30Keep my requirements
and do not follow any of the detestable customs that were practiced
before you came and do not defile yourselves with them. I am the
LORD your God.' "

Various Laws

19 The LORD said to Moses, 2"Speak to the entire assembly of
Israel and say to them: 'Be holy because I, the LORD your
God, am holy.

3" 'Each of you must respect his mother and father, and you must
observe my Sabbaths. I am the LORD your God.

4" 'Do not turn to idols or make gods of cast metal for yourselves. I
am the LORD your God.

5" 'When you sacrifice a fellowship offering[a] to the LORD, sacrifice
it in such a way that it will be accepted on your behalf. 6It shall be
eaten on the day you sacrifice it or on the next day; anything left over
until the third day must be burned up. 7If any of it is eaten on the
third day, it is impure and will not be accepted. 8Whoever eats it will
be held responsible because he has desecrated what is holy to the
LORD; that person must be cut off from his people.

9" 'When you reap the harvest of your land, do not reap to the very
edges of your field or gather the gleanings of your harvest. 10Do not
go over your vineyard a second time or pick up the grapes that have
fallen. Leave them for the poor and the alien. I am the LORD your God.

11" 'Do not steal.

" 'Do not lie.

" 'Do not deceive one another.

12" 'Do not swear falsely by my name and so profane the name of
your God. I am the LORD.

13" 'Do not defraud your neighbor or rob him.

" 'Do not hold back the wages of a hired man overnight.

14" 'Do not curse the deaf or put a stumbling block in front of the
blind, but fear your God. I am the LORD.

OPEN **1.** In your growing up years, who was the disciplinarian in your family? Why that parent? **2.** In your household now, who sets most of the rules? Who has to enforce them? Why? Which of your parents are you like in this regard? How so?

STUDY This passage illustrates that all aspects of life are subject to God's laws. The holiness of God is the pillar that supports practical holiness in every area of life. **1.** Why are the children of Israel required to be holy (19:1–2)? What would they have thought when God demanded them to be as perfect as he was? **2.** Which law detailed here was quoted by Jesus, Paul and James? In this context, who is one's "brother" and "neighbor" (vv. 13–18)? Which laws show compassion and economic justice for the poor? The handicapped? The alien? **3.** Which laws speak of cultic and occult practices? Of parental respect and family values? Of international relations? **4.** Of all these laws, which seem to you to have their application limited to the ancient Israelites? Which laws seem to apply universally, to all people, for all time? How do you make that distinction? **5.** Would you say that God is restricting the Israelites here or is he protecting the defenseless?

[a]5 Traditionally *peace offering*

18:28–29 vomited. God used strong imagery here to describe the reaction of the very earth to the indecency that had been described in the previous verses. The repulsion God describes here resembles that of his reaction to the Laodicean's lukewarm faith—God will spit them out of his mouth (Rev. 3:15–16).

19:2 holy. To get a clear picture of the holiness God wanted from his people, compare the decadence of the previous chapter to the goodness in the following verses.

19:5 accepted on your behalf. This verse reminds us that making sacrifice was not enough. Sacrifices had to be made with one's attitudes focused on God and one's hand attentive to the details of the proper procedure (Lev. 3).

19:6 left over. This offering allows for a kind of potluck supper. You could have leftovers for up to three days (Lev. 7:16–18).

19:8 desecrated. God drew a line in the sand saying, in effect, "If you understand who I am and what I am about, you'll respect this boundary. Keep the holy things on one side and the unholy things on the other." When the people didn't do that, they desecrated God's holy things.

19:9–10 gleanings. This beautiful practice provided for the less fortunate. For instance, the widow Ruth met her future husband, Boaz, by gleaning in his fields (Ruth 2). A contemporary example is when restaurants send unused food to a homeless shelter.

19:13 defraud. A form of deception and exploitation. It takes advantage of naïve people and destroys public trust.

15" 'Do not pervert justice; do not show partiality to the poor or
favoritism to the great, but judge your neighbor fairly.
16" 'Do not go about spreading slander among your people.
" 'Do not do anything that endangers your neighbor's life. I am the
LORD.
17" 'Do not hate your brother in your heart. Rebuke your neighbor
frankly so you will not share in his guilt.
18" 'Do not seek revenge or bear a grudge against one of your
people, but love your neighbor as yourself. I am the LORD.
19" 'Keep my decrees.
" 'Do not mate different kinds of animals.
" 'Do not plant your field with two kinds of seed.
" 'Do not wear clothing woven of two kinds of material.
20" 'If a man sleeps with a woman who is a slave girl promised to
another man but who has not been ransomed or given her freedom,
there must be due punishment. Yet they are not to be put to death,
because she had not been freed. 21The man, however, must bring a
ram to the entrance to the Tent of Meeting for a guilt offering to the
LORD. 22With the ram of the guilt offering the priest is to make atonement for him before the LORD for the sin he has committed, and his
sin will be forgiven.
23" 'When you enter the land and plant any kind of fruit tree, regard
its fruit as forbidden.[a] For three years you are to consider it
forbidden[a]; it must not be eaten. 24In the fourth year all its fruit will be
holy, an offering of praise to the LORD. 25But in the fifth year you may
eat its fruit. In this way your harvest will be increased. I am the LORD
your God.
26" 'Do not eat any meat with the blood still in it.
" 'Do not practice divination or sorcery.
27" 'Do not cut the hair at the sides of your head or clip off the
edges of your beard.
28" 'Do not cut your bodies for the dead or put tattoo marks on
yourselves. I am the LORD.
29" 'Do not degrade your daughter by making her a prostitute, or
the land will turn to prostitution and be filled with wickedness.
30" 'Observe my Sabbaths and have reverence for my sanctuary. I
am the LORD.
31" 'Do not turn to mediums or seek out spiritists, for you will be
defiled by them. I am the LORD your God.
32" 'Rise in the presence of the aged, show respect for the elderly
and revere your God. I am the LORD.
33" 'When an alien lives with you in your land, do not mistreat him.
34The alien living with you must be treated as one of your native-born.

[b]23 Hebrew *uncircumcised*

APPLY 1. What is your motivation for living a holy life? What is the difference between "holy" and "holier than thou"? **2.** How can you avoid the "holier than thou" tag and still be the holy person God wants you to be?

19:17 Rebuke your neighbor frankly. We share a neighbor's guilt when we stand by instead of stepping in when we should.

19:18 love your neighbor. Jesus corrected a misinterpretation of this passage when he began, "You have heard it was said, 'Love your neighbor and hate your enemy, but I tell you…' " (Matt. 5:43–44).

19:26 blood. Leviticus 17:13–14 explains that the life of a creature is in its blood. That is why God asked the Hebrews not to eat the blood. **divination.** To attempt to see the future by mystical means.

19:28 These commands were to keep the Hebrews separate from the cultures around them. If the Hebrews stayed separate in practice and custom, they had a better chance of staying separate in philosophy and worship.

19:33–34 aliens. The generosity of God was to be reflected in the

Love him as yourself, for you were aliens in Egypt. I am the LORD
your God.
35" 'Do not use dishonest standards when measuring length,
weight or quantity. 36Use honest scales and honest weights, an honest ephah[a] and an honest hin.[b] I am the LORD your God, who brought
you out of Egypt.
37" 'Keep all my decrees and all my laws and follow them. I am the
LORD.' "

OPEN 1. What kind of punishment was handed out in your family? 2. What did your parents consider to be the worst thing you could do?

STUDY Chapter 20 emphasizes the punishments for violating God's laws given in the previous two chapters. The harsh punishments were essential to prevent sin from infecting the community. 1. Do you see the laws and their punishments serving more as deterrents to wrong behavior or exhortations to right behavior? If you had to live under these laws what would be your chances of success? 2. What attitude toward sexual behavior in the people would require these kinds of laws? 3. Would you have thought these penalties were too harsh? 4. How would keeping these laws maintain fellowship with God? How would you have viewed having to obey so many laws? 5. Why did God require them to make a distinction between what was clean and unclean (v. 25)? How would you have viewed the command to be as holy as God (19:2)? 6. Why did God demand capital punishment for a medium or spiritist (v. 27)? Would you have supported capital punishment for this offense?

Punishments for Sin

20 The LORD said to Moses, 2"Say to the Israelites: 'Any Israelite
or any alien living in Israel who gives[c] any of his children to
Molech must be put to death. The people of the community are to
stone him. 3I will set my face against that man and I will cut him off
from his people; for by giving his children to Molech, he has defiled
my sanctuary and profaned my holy name. 4If the people of the community close their eyes when that man gives one of his children to
Molech and they fail to put him to death, 5I will set my face against
that man and his family and will cut off from their people both him
and all who follow him in prostituting themselves to Molech.
6" 'I will set my face against the person who turns to mediums and
spiritists to prostitute himself by following them, and I will cut him
off from his people.
7" 'Consecrate yourselves and be holy, because I am the LORD your
God. 8Keep my decrees and follow them. I am the LORD, who makes
you holy.[d]
9" 'If anyone curses his father or mother, he must be put to death.
He has cursed his father or his mother, and his blood will be on his
own head.
10" 'If a man commits adultery with another man's wife—with the
wife of his neighbor—both the adulterer and the adulteress must be
put to death.
11" 'If a man sleeps with his father's wife, he has dishonored his
father. Both the man and the woman must be put to death; their
blood will be on their own heads.
12" 'If a man sleeps with his daughter-in-law, both of them must be

[a]36 An ephah was a dry measure. [b]36 A hin was a liquid measure. [c]2 Or *sacrifices*; also in verses 3 and 4 [d]8 Or *who sanctifies you*; or *who sets you apart as holy*

---

people's treatment of strangers in their midst.

19:35–36 honest scales. Here is street level holiness at its best. The ancient world had no standardized weights and measures. Cheating was easy but integrity was still measured by the same standard.

20:1–27 This chapter is about stiff penalties for many of the sins already listed in chapter 18.

20:3 profaned my holy name. As seriously as we would take a parent or relative hurting an innocent child in the name of *anything*, God makes it clear here that to offer a child to the false god Molech would be a personal affront to him. **cut off**. Most often this usage of the term refers to death.

20:5 prostituting. Earlier in Scripture God related the worship of false gods to spiritual prostitution (Ex. 34:15).

20:6 mediums and spiritists. To consult a medium or spiritist was to trust someone besides God for *the future*. It was the equivalent of bowing down to an idol.

20:7 consecrate. This means to make holy, to keep oneself separate from something in order to honor something else. Today people live this out when they abstain from a behavior in order to live as they think they should.

20:8 decrees. The decrees listed here were actually capital crimes. For God, holiness is a life-or-death issue.

20:12 perversion. Throughout the book of Leviticus, God painted a picture of how he intended the world to work. He carefully outlined the boundaries of decency. A perversion of any kind (including the scenario here of a father with a daughter-in-law) crossed those boundaries of decency.

put to death. What they have done is a perversion; their blood will be on their own heads.

[13] " 'If a man lies with a man as one lies with a woman, both of them have done what is detestable. They must be put to death; their blood will be on their own heads.

[14] " 'If a man marries both a woman and her mother, it is wicked. Both he and they must be burned in the fire, so that no wickedness will be among you.

[15] " 'If a man has sexual relations with an animal, he must be put to death, and you must kill the animal.

[16] " 'If a woman approaches an animal to have sexual relations with it, kill both the woman and the animal. They must be put to death; their blood will be on their own heads.

[17] " 'If a man marries his sister, the daughter of either his father or his mother, and they have sexual relations, it is a disgrace. They must be cut off before the eyes of their people. He has dishonored his sister and will be held responsible.

[18] " 'If a man lies with a woman during her monthly period and has sexual relations with her, he has exposed the source of her flow, and she has also uncovered it. Both of them must be cut off from their people.

[19] " 'Do not have sexual relations with the sister of either your mother or your father, for that would dishonor a close relative; both of you would be held responsible.

[20] " 'If a man sleeps with his aunt, he has dishonored his uncle. They will be held responsible; they will die childless.

[21] " 'If a man marries his brother's wife, it is an act of impurity; he has dishonored his brother. They will be childless.

[22] " 'Keep all my decrees and laws and follow them, so that the land where I am bringing you to live may not vomit you out. [23]You must not live according to the customs of the nations I am going to drive out before you. Because they did all these things, I abhorred them. [24]But I said to you, "You will possess their land; I will give it to you as an inheritance, a land flowing with milk and honey." I am the LORD your God, who has set you apart from the nations.

[25] " 'You must therefore make a distinction between clean and unclean animals and between unclean and clean birds. Do not defile yourselves by any animal or bird or anything that moves along the ground—those which I have set apart as unclean for you. [26]You are to be holy to me[a] because I, the LORD, am holy, and I have set you apart from the nations to be my own.

[27] " 'A man or woman who is a medium or spiritist among you must be put to death. You are to stone them; their blood will be on their own heads.' "

[a]26 Or *be my holy ones*

APPLY 1. What in your life needs to be made holy? What part of your life looks too much like the people who don't follow God? **2.** How can this group hold you accountable to live a life that is set apart from those who refuse to devote their lives to God?

20:21 childless. In ancient days when the command "be fruitful and multiply" was taken literally and seriously, to be childless was the worst of fates for a man or woman.

20:24 milk and honey. This was a typical description of the Promised Land. Canaan later was called Israel and later still Palestine. The phrase always denoted abundance.

OPEN **1.** Who is your favorite spiritual leader? Why? **2.** Do you think spiritual leaders should be held to a higher standard? Why?

STUDY God told the people to, "Be holy, because I ... am Holy" (19:2). This command should be taken even more seriously by priests who ministered at the altar. **1.** Based on this passage, how important was the sacrificial system to God? **2.** How would these rules make you feel if you were married to one of the priests? How would it make you feel if you were handicapped in any way? **3.** Why did God place such a strong emphasis on physical perfection, ceremonial cleanliness and abstinence for the priests? What kind of pressure did these rules place on the priests? Was this good? Why?

APPLY **1.** Do you criticize or try to encourage those who minister to you? **2.** How could you encourage someone who ministers to you this week?

Rules for Priests

21 The LORD said to Moses, "Speak to the priests, the sons of
Aaron, and say to them: 'A priest must not make himself ceremonially unclean for any of his people who die, 2except for a close
relative, such as his mother or father, his son or daughter, his brother,
3or an unmarried sister who is dependent on him since she has no
husband—for her he may make himself unclean. 4He must not make
himself unclean for people related to him by marriage,[a] and so defile
himself.

5" 'Priests must not shave their heads or shave off the edges of
their beards or cut their bodies. 6They must be holy to their God and
must not profane the name of their God. Because they present the
offerings made to the LORD by fire, the food of their God, they are to
be holy.

7" 'They must not marry women defiled by prostitution or divorced
from their husbands, because priests are holy to their God. 8Regard
them as holy, because they offer up the food of your God. Consider
them holy, because I the LORD am holy—I who make you holy.[b]

9" 'If a priest's daughter defiles herself by becoming a prostitute,
she disgraces her father; she must be burned in the fire.

10" 'The high priest, the one among his brothers who has had the
anointing oil poured on his head and who has been ordained to wear
the priestly garments, must not let his hair become unkempt[c] or tear
his clothes. 11He must not enter a place where there is a dead body.
He must not make himself unclean, even for his father or mother,
12nor leave the sanctuary of his God or desecrate it, because he has
been dedicated by the anointing oil of his God. I am the LORD.

13" 'The woman he marries must be a virgin. 14He must not marry a
widow, a divorced woman, or a woman defiled by prostitution, but
only a virgin from his own people, 15so he will not defile his offspring
among his people. I am the LORD, who makes him holy.[d] ' "

16The LORD said to Moses, 17"Say to Aaron: 'For the generations to
come none of your descendants who has a defect may come near to
offer the food of his God. 18No man who has any defect may come
near: no man who is blind or lame, disfigured or deformed; 19no man
with a crippled foot or hand, 20or who is hunchbacked or dwarfed, or
who has any eye defect, or who has festering or running sores or
damaged testicles. 21No descendant of Aaron the priest who has any
defect is to come near to present the offerings made to the LORD by
fire. He has a defect; he must not come near to offer the food of his
God. 22He may eat the most holy food of his God, as well as the holy

[a]4 *Or unclean as a leader among his people* [b]8 Or *who sanctify you*; or *who set you apart as holy* [c]10 Or *not uncover his head* [d]15 Or *who sanctifies him*; or *who sets him apart as holy*

21:1–22:23 The priests were to lead in the effort to follow God's laws. These passages deal with the role of the priests, men from the tribe of Levi and, specifically, descendants of Aaron.

21:1 any of his people who die. In other words, priests were not to touch a corpse unless it was that of an immediate family member. The high priest was not allowed to do even that.

21:5 shave their heads. How a person wore his or her hair was significant in Bible times. The Nazarite vow (which Samson took) included not *cutting the hair at all*. Leaving hair unkempt implied mourning (Lev. 10:6). In the New Testament, women were told to keep their hair long and men to keep their hair short (1 Cor. 11:14–15).

21:8 who make you holy. God gives us two foundations in this verse: first, that he is holy and second, that he makes us holy. We worship him for the first.

21:16–23 who has a defect. In Aaron's day, handicapped priests received their share of everything but were kept from receiving sacrifices and could not be high priests.

food; 23yet because of his defect, he must not go near the curtain or
approach the altar, and so desecrate my sanctuary. I am the LORD,
who makes them holy.[a]' "
24So Moses told this to Aaron and his sons and to all the Israelites.
22 The LORD said to Moses, 2"Tell Aaron and his sons to treat
with respect the sacred offerings the Israelites consecrate to
me, so they will not profane my holy name. I am the LORD.
3"Say to them: 'For the generations to come, if any of your descendants is ceremonially unclean and yet comes near the sacred offerings
that the Israelites consecrate to the LORD, that person must be cut off
from my presence. I am the LORD.
4" 'If a descendant of Aaron has an infectious skin disease[b] or a
bodily discharge, he may not eat the sacred offerings until he is
cleansed. He will also be unclean if he touches something defiled by a
corpse or by anyone who has an emission of semen, 5or if he touches
any crawling thing that makes him unclean, or any person who
makes him unclean, whatever the uncleanness may be. 6The one who
touches any such thing will be unclean till evening. He must not eat
any of the sacred offerings unless he has bathed himself with water.
7When the sun goes down, he will be clean, and after that he may eat
the sacred offerings, for they are his food. 8He must not eat anything
found dead or torn by wild animals, and so become unclean through
it. I am the LORD.
9" 'The priests are to keep my requirements so that they do not become guilty and die for treating them with contempt. I am the LORD,
who makes them holy.[c]
10" 'No one outside a priest's family may eat the sacred offering,
nor may the guest of a priest or his hired worker eat it. 11But if a priest
buys a slave with money, or if a slave is born in his household, that
slave may eat his food. 12If a priest's daughter marries anyone other
than a priest, she may not eat any of the sacred contributions. 13But if
a priest's daughter becomes a widow or is divorced, yet has no
children, and she returns to live in her father's house as in her youth,
she may eat of her father's food. No unauthorized person, however,
may eat any of it.
14" 'If anyone eats a sacred offering by mistake, he must make
restitution to the priest for the offering and add a fifth of the value to
it. 15The priests must not desecrate the sacred offerings the Israelites
present to the LORD 16by allowing them to eat the sacred offerings
and so bring upon them guilt requiring payment. I am the LORD, who
makes them holy.' "

[a]23 Or *who sanctifies them*; or *who sets them apart as holy* [b]4 Traditionally *leprosy*; the Hebrew word was used for various diseases affecting the skin—not necessarily leprosy. [c]9 Or *who sanctifies them*; or *who sets them apart as holy*; also in verse 16

21:23 the curtain. This curtain separated the Holy of Holies from the rest of the tabernacle.

22:3 cut off from my presence. Earlier in Leviticus God often used the term "cut off from his people" to imply capital punishment. Here, the consequence is that the priest would be cut off from God's presence, which is more like excommunication.

22:9 die. Aaron's sons, Nadab and Abihu, died instantly from handling a temple ceremony in an unauthorized way (10:1,2).

22:14 fifth. This was the same percentage that worshipers were to reimburse each other in the case of a guilt offering.

22:16 who makes them holy. When God was giving instructions to the worshipers, it was enough to say, "I am the LORD." In this part of Leviticus, though, he was addressing the priests. Because of their role, it was equally important that they acknowledge not only God's holiness but also his desire to make his people holy. The priests were to support God's effort in every way.

OPEN 1. Describe a time when you took special care in choosing and wrapping a gift. **2.** Why did giving this gift prompt such attention from you?

STUDY 1. Why did God require sacrifices that had no blemishes? What attitude toward God would you be demonstrating if you offered a diseased animal? What attitude toward God would be evident if you brought God a perfect animal? **2.** What would happen if a person brought an unclean sacrifice? Do people today make spiritual offerings to God that are unacceptable? Name some. Why are these unacceptable? **3.** Why did God keep repeating "I am the LORD?" Does our view of God influence how we worship? Do we sometimes forget that God is Lord? How so?

APPLY 1. Is there some area in your life where God is getting the leftovers? **2.** What can you do today to start giving him your best? Will you do that?

OPEN 1. What is your favorite celebration? **2.** Do you think it's important to reflect on special events in your life?

STUDY This chapter describes the national festivals of Israel. The people were to reserve certain days in their appointment books (as it were) for national public worship? **1.** Why would it be important for the people to remember how

Unacceptable Sacrifices

17 The LORD said to Moses, 18 "Speak to Aaron and his sons and to all the Israelites and say to them: 'If any of you—either an Israelite or an alien living in Israel—presents a gift for a burnt offering to the LORD, either to fulfill a vow or as a freewill offering, 19 you must present a male without defect from the cattle, sheep or goats in order that it may be accepted on your behalf. 20 Do not bring anything with a defect, because it will not be accepted on your behalf. 21 When anyone brings from the herd or flock a fellowship offering[a] to the LORD to fulfill a special vow or as a freewill offering, it must be without defect or blemish to be acceptable. 22 Do not offer to the LORD the blind, the injured or the maimed, or anything with warts or festering or running sores. Do not place any of these on the altar as an offering made to the LORD by fire. 23 You may, however, present as a freewill offering an ox[b] or a sheep that is deformed or stunted, but it will not be accepted in fulfillment of a vow. 24 You must not offer to the LORD an animal whose testicles are bruised, crushed, torn or cut. You must not do this in your own land, 25 and you must not accept such animals from the hand of a foreigner and offer them as the food of your God. They will not be accepted on your behalf, because they are deformed and have defects.' "

26 The LORD said to Moses, 27 "When a calf, a lamb or a goat is born, it is to remain with its mother for seven days. From the eighth day on, it will be acceptable as an offering made to the LORD by fire. 28 Do not slaughter a cow or a sheep and its young on the same day.

29 "When you sacrifice a thank offering to the LORD, sacrifice it in such a way that it will be accepted on your behalf. 30 It must be eaten that same day; leave none of it till morning. I am the LORD.

31 "Keep my commands and follow them. I am the LORD. 32 Do not profane my holy name. I must be acknowledged as holy by the Israelites. I am the LORD, who makes[c] you holy[d] 33 and who brought you out of Egypt to be your God. I am the LORD."

23

The LORD said to Moses, 2 "Speak to the Israelites and say to them: 'These are my appointed feasts, the appointed feasts of the LORD, which you are to proclaim as sacred assemblies.

The Sabbath

3 " 'There are six days when you may work, but the seventh day is a Sabbath of rest, a day of sacred assembly. You are not to do any work; wherever you live, it is a Sabbath to the LORD.

[a]21 Traditionally *peace offering* [b]23 The Hebrew word can include both male and female. [c]32 Or *made*
[d]32 Or *who sanctifies you*; or *who sets you apart as holy*

22:18 alien. Evidently those who were not Hebrews living among the Israelites were allowed to bring sacrifices to the tabernacle, at least, as listed here, a fellowship offering for a vow or freewill offering.

22:21 without defect. While the fellowship offerings (7:11–36) *were not* for sin or guilt, they still required the same standards of holiness.

22:24 cut. Defects included birth defects as well as forms of mutilation such as castration.

22:28 its young. Some say this prohibition is to ensure that the mother can increase the herd, but this guideline does not preclude offering the mother as a sacrifice the next day.

22:30 eaten that same day. The thank offering was one of the three types of fellowship offerings. While the food from this offering had to be eaten on the same day, other types could be stored and eaten later (7:16–18).

23:2 feasts. The feasts of the Hebrews were like holidays. Often they commemorated historical events. Always they celebrated God's provision. The book of Esther actually gives the inauguration of the feast called Purim after Esther spared her people from death (Est. 9).

23:3 Sabbath. The Sabbath was considered a feast even though no one was

The Passover and Unleavened Bread

[4]" 'These are the LORD's appointed feasts, the sacred assemblies
you are to proclaim at their appointed times: [5]The LORD's Passover
begins at twilight on the fourteenth day of the first month. [6]On the
fifteenth day of that month the LORD's Feast of Unleavened Bread begins; for seven days you must eat bread made without yeast. [7]On the
first day hold a sacred assembly and do no regular work. [8]For seven
days present an offering made to the LORD by fire. And on the seventh
day hold a sacred assembly and do no regular work.' "

Firstfruits

[9]The LORD said to Moses, [10]"Speak to the Israelites and say to them:
'When you enter the land I am going to give you and you reap its harvest, bring to the priest a sheaf of the first grain you harvest. [11]He is to
wave the sheaf before the LORD so it will be accepted on your behalf;
the priest is to wave it on the day after the Sabbath. [12]On the day you
wave the sheaf, you must sacrifice as a burnt offering to the LORD a
lamb a year old without defect, [13]together with its grain offering of
two-tenths of an ephah[a] of fine flour mixed with oil—an offering made
to the LORD by fire, a pleasing aroma—and its drink offering of a quarter of a hin[b] of wine. [14]You must not eat any bread, or roasted or new
grain, until the very day you bring this offering to your God. This is to
be a lasting ordinance for the generations to come, wherever you live.

Feast of Weeks

[15]" 'From the day after the Sabbath, the day you brought the sheaf
of the wave offering, count off seven full weeks. [16]Count off fifty days
up to the day after the seventh Sabbath, and then present an offering
of new grain to the LORD. [17]From wherever you live, bring two loaves
made of two-tenths of an ephah of fine flour, baked with yeast, as a
wave offering of firstfruits to the LORD. [18]Present with this bread
seven male lambs, each a year old and without defect, one young bull
and two rams. They will be a burnt offering to the LORD, together with
their grain offerings and drink offerings—an offering made by fire, an
aroma pleasing to the LORD. [19]Then sacrifice one male goat for a sin
offering and two lambs, each a year old, for a fellowship offering.[c]
[20]The priest is to wave the two lambs before the LORD as a wave offering, together with the bread of the firstfruits. They are a sacred
offering to the LORD for the priest. [21]On that same day you are to
proclaim a sacred assembly and do no regular work. This is to be a
lasting ordinance for the generations to come, wherever you live.
[22]" 'When you reap the harvest of your land, do not reap to the very

[a]13 That is, probably about 4 quarts (about 4.5 liters); also in verse 17 [b]13 That is, probably about 1 quart (about 1 liter) [c]19 Traditionally *peace offering*

God delivered them from Egypt? How does this feast illustrate the work of Christ, "our Passover lamb" (1 Cor. 5:7)? **2.** Why have the Feast of Unleavened Bread (Ex. 12:14–20)? Some think eating unleavened bread represents the believer's complete break with the old life. What do you think? Why? **3.** Why was it important for the people to bring the first grain of the harvest to God as an offering? Can we glean any lessons from that practice today? **4.** What do you see as the basic purpose of the Feast of Weeks? Do you gain any insight from this festival for understanding Pentecost (Acts 2:1)? **5.** Why did God prohibit work on feast days (vv. 3,7,28–32,35–36)? How would this prohibition strengthen your appreciation of the meaning of the feasts? **6.** How has the work of Christ fulfilled the original purpose of the Day of Atonement (Heb. 9:7–15; 10:1–10; 13:11–12)? **7.** How would the Feast of Tabernacles remind them of their journeys in the wilderness? How would you have felt about moving into a booth for seven days? Why do we need to be reminded of God's work in our lives?

APPLY 1. In what ways has God taken redemptive action in your life? How does this make you feel toward God? **2.** What does he do to remind you of his work of redemption? What do you do regularly to remind yourself of his work?

---

allowed to cook that day. It was a day of remembering—that God created and God rested, that God is the one true God—and so there were extra burnt offerings that day.

23:5 Passover. The Passover feast commemorated the night of the last plague when the people were in bondage in Egypt. The firstborn of each household died unless blood was put on the doorpost. If the lamb's blood was in place, the angel of death passed over that house (Ex. 12).

23:6 the LORD's Feast of Unleavened Bread. This feast coincided with the barley harvest (March/April) rather than the wheat harvest (June/July).

23:15–22 This passage describes a feast known by several names: Weeks, Harvest, Pentecost. This feast celebrated the end of the harvest and the exodus from Egypt.

23:16 Count off. The dates of this feast depended on the dates of the Passover. It was up to the people to keep track of the fifty days.

edges of your field or gather the gleanings of your harvest. Leave them for the poor and the alien. I am the LORD your God.' "

Feast of Trumpets

23The LORD said to Moses, 24"Say to the Israelites: 'On the first day of the seventh month you are to have a day of rest, a sacred assembly commemorated with trumpet blasts. 25Do no regular work, but present an offering made to the LORD by fire.' "

Day of Atonement

26The LORD said to Moses, 27"The tenth day of this seventh month is the Day of Atonement. Hold a sacred assembly and deny yourselves,[a] and present an offering made to the LORD by fire. 28Do no work on that day, because it is the Day of Atonement, when atonement is made for you before the LORD your God. 29Anyone who does not deny himself on that day must be cut off from his people. 30I will destroy from among his people anyone who does any work on that day. 31You shall do no work at all. This is to be a lasting ordinance for the generations to come, wherever you live. 32It is a sabbath of rest for you, and you must deny yourselves. From the evening of the ninth day of the month until the following evening you are to observe your sabbath."

Feast of Tabernacles

33The LORD said to Moses, 34"Say to the Israelites: 'On the fifteenth day of the seventh month the LORD's Feast of Tabernacles begins, and it lasts for seven days. 35The first day is a sacred assembly; do no regular work. 36For seven days present offerings made to the LORD by fire, and on the eighth day hold a sacred assembly and present an offering made to the LORD by fire. It is the closing assembly; do no regular work.

37(" 'These are the LORD's appointed feasts, which you are to proclaim as sacred assemblies for bringing offerings made to the LORD by fire—the burnt offerings and grain offerings, sacrifices and drink offerings required for each day. 38These offerings are in addition to those for the LORD's Sabbaths and[b] in addition to your gifts and whatever you have vowed and all the freewill offerings you give to the LORD.)

39" 'So beginning with the fifteenth day of the seventh month, after you have gathered the crops of the land, celebrate the festival to the LORD for seven days; the first day is a day of rest, and the eighth day also is a day of rest. 40On the first day you are to take choice fruit from the trees, and palm fronds, leafy branches and poplars, and rejoice before the LORD your God for seven days. 41Celebrate this as a festival

[a]27 Or *and fast;* also in verses 29 and 32 [b]38 Or *These feasts are in addition to the LORD's Sabbaths, and these offerings are*

23:24 first day of the seventh month. This is the Jewish New Year, Rosh Hashanah.

23:27 Day of Atonement. This was the yearly sacrifice made by the high priest for the sins of the people. It included two goats: one sacrificed for sin and one freed as a picture of atonement for sin. Today we know this holiday as Yom Kippur.

23:29 deny himself. This probably involved fasting as well as signs of mourning such as wearing sackcloth and ashes. The penalty for ignoring this requirement was capital punishment.

23:34 The Feast of Tabernacles (or Feast of Booths) commemorated the nomadic journey of the people after they left Egypt and began camping their way across the wilderness.

to the LORD for seven days each year. This is to be a lasting ordinance
for the generations to come; celebrate it in the seventh month. [42]Live
in booths for seven days: All native-born Israelites are to live in
booths [43]so your descendants will know that I had the Israelites live
in booths when I brought them out of Egypt. I am the LORD your
God.' "

[44]So Moses announced to the Israelites the appointed feasts of the
LORD.

Oil and Bread Set Before the LORD

24 The LORD said to Moses, [2]"Command the Israelites to bring
you clear oil of pressed olives for the light so that the lamps
may be kept burning continually. [3]Outside the curtain of the Testimony in the Tent of Meeting, Aaron is to tend the lamps before the
LORD from evening till morning, continually. This is to be a lasting
ordinance for the generations to come. [4]The lamps on the pure gold
lampstand before the LORD must be tended continually.

[5]"Take fine flour and bake twelve loaves of bread, using two-tenths
of an ephah[a] for each loaf. [6]Set them in two rows, six in each row, on
the table of pure gold before the LORD. [7]Along each row put some
pure incense as a memorial portion to represent the bread and to be
an offering made to the LORD by fire. [8]This bread is to be set out
before the LORD regularly, Sabbath after Sabbath, on behalf of the
Israelites, as a lasting covenant. [9]It belongs to Aaron and his sons,
who are to eat it in a holy place, because it is a most holy part of their
regular share of the offerings made to the LORD by fire."

A Blasphemer Stoned

[10]Now the son of an Israelite mother and an Egyptian father went
out among the Israelites, and a fight broke out in the camp between
him and an Israelite. [11]The son of the Israelite woman blasphemed
the Name with a curse; so they brought him to Moses. (His mother's
name was Shelomith, the daughter of Dibri the Danite.) [12]They put
him in custody until the will of the LORD should be made clear to
them.

[13]Then the LORD said to Moses: [14]"Take the blasphemer outside the
camp. All those who heard him are to lay their hands on his head, and
the entire assembly is to stone him. [15]Say to the Israelites: 'If anyone
curses his God, he will be held responsible; [16]anyone who blasphemes the name of the LORD must be put to death. The entire
assembly must stone him. Whether an alien or native-born, when he
blasphemes the Name, he must be put to death.

[17]" 'If anyone takes the life of a human being, he must be put to
death. [18]Anyone who takes the life of someone's animal must make
restitution—life for life. [19]If anyone injures his neighbor, whatever he
has done must be done to him: [20]fracture for fracture, eye for eye,

[a]5 That is, probably about 4 quarts (about 4.5 liters)

OPEN 1. What's one of your best memories from attending youth camp in the summer? **2.** How long did you remain on that spiritual high after getting home from camp?

STUDY The transition from the magnificent Feast of Tabernacles to mundane care of furniture in the Tent of Meeting likely illustrates faithfulness to God in the daily routine of living. Spiritual life is more than a mountain top experience. **1.** Why do you think God included these mundane maintenance rules of the glorious feasts? **2.** Do you think God's presence is limited to special occasions? Why? Why not? How could this be a lesson in Christian living for today?

APPLY 1. What are some of the routine disciplines of Christian living? How well are you doing with these exercises? **2.** How can you become more attuned to God's presence in every detail of life?

23:42 booths. Tents.

24:3 lamps. These lamps were the only lights in the holy place in the middle of the tabernacle. It was closed on all sides by curtains. The oil was the finest, made of pressed olives rather than boiled olives.

24:5 bread. In Exodus these 12 loaves are called the "bread of the presence." Twelve loaves for the 12 tribes.

24:8–9 share. The priests shared in this bread each week. It was part of the groceries provided them by the people.

24:20 eye for eye. Christ quoted this verse in Matthew 5:38, reminding

tooth for tooth. As he has injured the other, so he is to be injured.
21Whoever kills an animal must make restitution, but whoever kills a
man must be put to death. 22You are to have the same law for the
alien and the native-born. I am the LORD your God.' "
23Then Moses spoke to the Israelites, and they took the blasphemer outside the camp and stoned him. The Israelites did as the LORD
commanded Moses.

OPEN **1.** What do you own that is of great value to you? **2.** If because of some financial emergency you had to pawn it, would you try to get it back? How would you respond to a friend who redeemed it for you?

STUDY An Israelite was in desperate straits if he had to sell his family's land. Even in this distressing situation, there was hope. A dispossessed family could be saved by a relative who would buy back the land. **1.** What were the regulations about land and slaves in the 50th year? As a businessman would you view these regulations positively? **2.** How would you have felt if some misfortune forced you to sell your land? What kind of misfortunes would lead to such a desperate move? **3.** If no relative could redeem a man's land how could he reclaim it (vv. 26–29)? **4.** What debt do we owe to God (Rom. 3:23)? How does the law of redemption and the law of the Jubilee year symbolize what Jesus Christ did on the cross? **5.** What do the laws about "right of redemption" (vv. 48–53) say about the value of God's people and his relationship with them?

APPLY **1.** Has God redeemed you for his service (v. 25)? What did it cost God to redeem you? **2.** What can you do to demonstrate your gratefulness to God for his redemption?

The Sabbath Year

25 The LORD said to Moses on Mount Sinai, 2"Speak to the
Israelites and say to them: 'When you enter the land I am
going to give you, the land itself must observe a sabbath to the LORD.
3For six years sow your fields, and for six years prune your vineyards
and gather their crops. 4But in the seventh year the land is to have a
sabbath of rest, a sabbath to the LORD. Do not sow your fields or
prune your vineyards. 5Do not reap what grows of itself or harvest the
grapes of your untended vines. The land is to have a year of rest.
6Whatever the land yields during the sabbath year will be food for
you—for yourself, your manservant and maidservant, and the hired
worker and temporary resident who live among you, 7as well as for
your livestock and the wild animals in your land. Whatever the land
produces may be eaten.

The Year of Jubilee

8" 'Count off seven sabbaths of years—seven times seven years—
so that the seven sabbaths of years amount to a period of forty-nine
years. 9Then have the trumpet sounded everywhere on the tenth day
of the seventh month; on the Day of Atonement sound the trumpet
throughout your land. 10Consecrate the fiftieth year and proclaim liberty throughout the land to all its inhabitants. It shall be a jubilee for
you; each one of you is to return to his family property and each to
his own clan. 11The fiftieth year shall be a jubilee for you; do not sow
and do not reap what grows of itself or harvest the untended vines.
12For it is a jubilee and is to be holy for you; eat only what is taken
directly from the fields.
13" 'In this Year of Jubilee everyone is to return to his own property.
14" 'If you sell land to one of your countrymen or buy any from him,
do not take advantage of each other. 15You are to buy from your countryman on the basis of the number of years since the Jubilee. And he
is to sell to you on the basis of the number of years left for harvesting
crops. 16When the years are many, you are to increase the price, and

---

the people that God called them to grace, not vengeance. The truth is, though, that this verse didn't really mean to take an eye *for* an eye. Rather, it meant "let the punishment fit the crime. Don't take a life for a finger. Be reciprocal in your judgment." A faction of the New Testament Pharisees used the verse to endorse revenge.

25:4 land is to have a sabbath. This custom had the same function as our modern system of crop rotation—to keep the land productive and let it renew itself.

25:9 tenth day of the seventh month. This was the month of Tishri, our September/October. It was the yearly sacrifice for the Day of Atonement.

25:10 *jubilee.* *The year of Jubilee was* a year to reestablish homelands and ownership.

25:13 return to his own property. God was evening things out in terms of accumulation of wealth. Later in this chapter, verse 23, he reminds the people that all the land really belongs to him and they are just tenants. That takes the wind out of the sails of a major landowner.

25:15 on the basis. If the year of Jubilee had been regularly observed, then land sales would all work as leases. When the deal was struck, the buyer and seller would know the number of years the deal was valid.

when the years are few, you are to decrease the price, because what he is really selling you is the number of crops. [17]Do not take advantage of each other, but fear your God. I am the LORD your God.

[18]" 'Follow my decrees and be careful to obey my laws, and you will live safely in the land. [19]Then the land will yield its fruit, and you will eat your fill and live there in safety. [20]You may ask, "What will we eat in the seventh year if we do not plant or harvest our crops?" [21]I will send you such a blessing in the sixth year that the land will yield enough for three years. [22]While you plant during the eighth year, you will eat from the old crop and will continue to eat from it until the harvest of the ninth year comes in.

[23]" 'The land must not be sold permanently, because the land is mine and you are but aliens and my tenants. [24]Throughout the country that you hold as a possession, you must provide for the redemption of the land.

[25]" 'If one of your countrymen becomes poor and sells some of his property, his nearest relative is to come and redeem what his countryman has sold. [26]If, however, a man has no one to redeem it for him but he himself prospers and acquires sufficient means to redeem it, [27]he is to determine the value for the years since he sold it and refund the balance to the man to whom he sold it; he can then go back to his own property. [28]But if he does not acquire the means to repay him, what he sold will remain in the possession of the buyer until the Year of Jubilee. It will be returned in the Jubilee, and he can then go back to his property.

[29]" 'If a man sells a house in a walled city, he retains the right of redemption a full year after its sale. During that time he may redeem it. [30]If it is not redeemed before a full year has passed, the house in the walled city shall belong permanently to the buyer and his descendants. It is not to be returned in the Jubilee. [31]But houses in villages without walls around them are to be considered as open country. They can be redeemed, and they are to be returned in the Jubilee.

[32]" 'The Levites always have the right to redeem their houses in the Levitical towns, which they possess. [33]So the property of the Levites is redeemable—that is, a house sold in any town they hold—and is to be returned in the Jubilee, because the houses in the towns of the Levites are their property among the Israelites. [34]But the pastureland belonging to their towns must not be sold; it is their permanent possession.

[35]" 'If one of your countrymen becomes poor and is unable to support himself among you, help him as you would an alien or a temporary resident, so he can continue to live among you. [36]Do not take interest of any kind[a] from him, but fear your God, so that your

[a]36 Or *take excessive interest*; similarly in verse 37

25:24 as a possession. This refers to the land someone has purchased. The original owners of the land are the tribesmen that the land was allotted to when the people returned home. Originally this referred to God's promise to Abraham and to the future division of the land among the tribes of Israel (Gen. 17:8, Josh. 13:6–7). **redemption of the land.** The families that first received the allotment of the land will have the right to take possession again.

25:25 The land represented God's promise, his inheritance. It was a matter of concern for the whole tribe or extended family. That is why if someone sold the land because of financial difficulty, it was a relative's responsibility to step in and make sure the land remained in the family. The book of Ruth illustrates this. In it Boaz talked with the relative nearer to Ruth about his interest in purchasing the land for Ruth and Naomi (Ruth 4:1–10).

25:35–36 countrymen. As with families, it was easier at times to help a wandering foreigner than a down-and-out fellow citizen. The purpose of

countryman may continue to live among you. 37You must not lend
him money at interest or sell him food at a profit. 38I am the LORD
your God, who brought you out of Egypt to give you the land of
Canaan and to be your God.
39" 'If one of your countrymen becomes poor among you and sells
himself to you, do not make him work as a slave. 40He is to be treated
as a hired worker or a temporary resident among you; he is to work
for you until the Year of Jubilee. 41Then he and his children are to be
released, and he will go back to his own clan and to the property of
his forefathers. 42Because the Israelites are my servants, whom I
brought out of Egypt, they must not be sold as slaves. 43Do not rule
over them ruthlessly, but fear your God.
44" 'Your male and female slaves are to come from the nations
around you; from them you may buy slaves. 45You may also buy some
of the temporary residents living among you and members of their
clans born in your country, and they will become your property. 46You
can will them to your children as inherited property and can make
them slaves for life, but you must not rule over your fellow Israelites
ruthlessly.
47" 'If an alien or a temporary resident among you becomes rich
and one of your countrymen becomes poor and sells himself to the
alien living among you or to a member of the alien's clan, 48he retains
the right of redemption after he has sold himself. One of his relatives
may redeem him: 49An uncle or a cousin or any blood relative in his
clan may redeem him. Or if he prospers, he may redeem himself. 50He
and his buyer are to count the time from the year he sold himself up
to the Year of Jubilee. The price for his release is to be based on the
rate paid to a hired man for that number of years. 51If many years
remain, he must pay for his redemption a larger share of the price
paid for him. 52If only a few years remain until the Year of Jubilee, he
is to compute that and pay for his redemption accordingly. 53He is to
be treated as a man hired from year to year; you must see to it that his
owner does not rule over him ruthlessly.
54" 'Even if he is not redeemed in any of these ways, he and his
children are to be released in the Year of Jubilee, 55for the Israelites
belong to me as servants. They are my servants, whom I brought out
of Egypt. I am the LORD your God.

Reward for Obedience

26 " 'Do not make idols or set up an image or a sacred stone for
yourselves, and do not place a carved stone in your land to
bow down before it. I am the LORD your God.
2" 'Observe my Sabbaths and have reverence for my sanctuary. I am
the LORD.
3" 'If you follow my decrees and are careful to obey my commands,

OPEN 1. What rewards did you receive as a student, athlete, employee or volunteer? **2.** What did you do to earn these rewards?

STUDY This chapter describes the blessings for obedience and the punishments for

---

this passage was not to forbid interest but to remind the people that making money from another's misfortune was improper.

25:55 belong to me. The guidelines in this passage seem foreign to our modern economy. But the bottom line of God's message was, "My ways supercede your ways. These were my people before you had money to deal with." The year of Jubilee was a way that God reclaimed his people and his promise to them.

26:1 to bow down. It was not just the image, statue or idol that was forbidden. It was the attitude of the heart that mattered. If the idol was given any place where God should have been—worship, comfort, service—then the idol was forbidden.

26:3–13 If you follow. This passage outlines the blessing that God promised his people if they obeyed him. This passage did not promise

4I will send you rain in its season, and the ground will yield its crops
and the trees of the field their fruit. 5Your threshing will continue
until grape harvest and the grape harvest will continue until planting,
and you will eat all the food you want and live in safety in your land.
6" 'I will grant peace in the land, and you will lie down and no one
will make you afraid. I will remove savage beasts from the land, and
the sword will not pass through your country. 7You will pursue your
enemies, and they will fall by the sword before you. 8Five of you will
chase a hundred, and a hundred of you will chase ten thousand, and
your enemies will fall by the sword before you.
9" 'I will look on you with favor and make you fruitful and increase
your numbers, and I will keep my covenant with you. 10You will still
be eating last year's harvest when you will have to move it out to
make room for the new. 11I will put my dwelling place[a] among you,
and I will not abhor you. 12I will walk among you and be your God,
and you will be my people. 13I am the LORD your God, who brought
you out of Egypt so that you would no longer be slaves to the Egyptians; I broke the bars of your yoke and enabled you to walk with
heads held high.

Punishment for Disobedience

14" 'But if you will not listen to me and carry out all these commands, 15and if you reject my decrees and abhor my laws and fail to
carry out all my commands and so violate my covenant, 16then I will
do this to you: I will bring upon you sudden terror, wasting diseases
and fever that will destroy your sight and drain away your life. You
will plant seed in vain, because your enemies will eat it. 17I will set my
face against you so that you will be defeated by your enemies; those
who hate you will rule over you, and you will flee even when no one is
pursuing you.
18" 'If after all this you will not listen to me, I will punish you for
your sins seven times over. 19I will break down your stubborn pride
and make the sky above you like iron and the ground beneath you like
bronze. 20Your strength will be spent in vain, because your soil will
not yield its crops, nor will the trees of the land yield their fruit.
21" 'If you remain hostile toward me and refuse to listen to me, I
will multiply your afflictions seven times over, as your sins deserve.
22I will send wild animals against you, and they will rob you of your
children, destroy your cattle and make you so few in number that
your roads will be deserted.
23" 'If in spite of these things you do not accept my correction but
continue to be hostile toward me, 24I myself will be hostile toward you
and will afflict you for your sins seven times over. 25And I will bring the
sword upon you to avenge the breaking of the covenant. When you
withdraw into your cities, I will send a plague among you, and you will
be given into enemy hands. 26When I cut off your supply of bread, ten
women will be able to bake your bread in one oven, and they will dole
out the bread by weight. You will eat, but you will not be satisfied.

[a]11 Or *my tabernacle*

disobedience. **1.** Does this passage on rewards for obedience teach us anything about human nature? Does it teach us anything about God's nature? **2.** Would these rewards motivate you to obey God? Why? Do you believe rewards are a legitimate motivation to serve God? Why? Why not? How does God reward his children today?

APPLY 1. Can you describe a time when you felt God rewarded you? **2.** Is salvation a gift or a reward (Eph. 2:8–9)? **3.** Do you feel God will reward you in heaven? Why? Why not? What changes can you make to assure rewards in heaven?

OPEN 1. Were your parents strict? Did they use the "stick" more than the "carrot"? **2.** What's the most severe punishment your parents gave you?

STUDY This section describes the punishment for disobedience. The phrase, "If you will not listen to me," introduces five paragraphs followed by a proclamation of divine disciplines. **1.** Would these punishments motivate you to comply? Why would God need to reveal these punishments to his people? **2.** Does the fact that the list of punishments is much longer than the list of rewards teach us anything about human nature? **3.** How would you have felt after hearing this list of punishments? What would you think of God? **4.** How would your mood have changed after hearing about repentance and restoration (vv. 40–45)? Does God chasten us today (Heb. 12:6)?

APPLY 1. Do you deserve God's chastening? Why? **2.** When have you experienced the forgiveness and restoration of God? Will you share this with someone this week? Who?

that life would be easy in every way, only that God would reward obedience to his children.

26:14–39 if you will not listen. God really couldn't have spelled it out any clearer. This is not so much a list of curses as it is consequences. Yet, in the face of these, Israel did not obey God wholeheartedly.

27" 'If in spite of this you still do not listen to me but continue to be hostile toward me, 28then in my anger I will be hostile toward you, and I myself will punish you for your sins seven times over. 29You will eat the flesh of your sons and the flesh of your daughters. 30I will destroy your high places, cut down your incense altars and pile your dead bodies on the lifeless forms of your idols, and I will abhor you. 31I will turn your cities into ruins and lay waste your sanctuaries, and I will take no delight in the pleasing aroma of your offerings. 32I will lay waste the land, so that your enemies who live there will be appalled. 33I will scatter you among the nations and will draw out my sword and pursue you. Your land will be laid waste, and your cities will lie in ruins. 34Then the land will enjoy its sabbath years all the time that it lies desolate and you are in the country of your enemies; then the land will rest and enjoy its sabbaths. 35All the time that it lies desolate, the land will have the rest it did not have during the sabbaths you lived in it.

36" 'As for those of you who are left, I will make their hearts so fearful in the lands of their enemies that the sound of a windblown leaf will put them to flight. They will run as though fleeing from the sword, and they will fall, even though no one is pursuing them. 37They will stumble over one another as though fleeing from the sword, even though no one is pursuing them. So you will not be able to stand before your enemies. 38You will perish among the nations; the land of your enemies will devour you. 39Those of you who are left will waste away in the lands of their enemies because of their sins; also because of their fathers' sins they will waste away.

40" 'But if they will confess their sins and the sins of their fathers—their treachery against me and their hostility toward me, 41which made me hostile toward them so that I sent them into the land of their enemies—then when their uncircumcised hearts are humbled and they pay for their sin, 42I will remember my covenant with Jacob and my covenant with Isaac and my covenant with Abraham, and I will remember the land. 43For the land will be deserted by them and will enjoy its sabbaths while it lies desolate without them. They will pay for their sins because they rejected my laws and abhorred my decrees. 44Yet in spite of this, when they are in the land of their enemies, I will not reject them or abhor them so as to destroy them completely, breaking my covenant with them. I am the LORD their God. 45But for their sake I will remember the covenant with their ancestors whom I brought out of Egypt in the sight of the nations to be their God. I am the LORD.' "

46These are the decrees, the laws and the regulations that the LORD established on Mount Sinai between himself and the Israelites through Moses.

OPEN 1. When's the last time you made a promise? Did you keep it? **2.** What is your view about the importance of keeping promises? Why?

Redeeming What Is the LORD's

27 The LORD said to Moses, 2"Speak to the Israelites and say to them: 'If anyone makes a special vow to dedicate persons to

---

26:41 uncircumcised hearts. *Since circumcision for the Israelites* was a ritual that showed God's ownership over them, someone with an uncircumcised heart would be a person who did *not show evidence of belonging to God.*

26:44 as to destroy them completely. God has been true to this promise throughout history. The Hebrews have been subjected to blow after blow, yet have never been destroyed.

27:1–34 Some consider this chapter almost an appendix, like a table in the

the LORD by giving equivalent values, 3set the value of a male between
the ages of twenty and sixty at fifty shekels[a] of silver, according to the
sanctuary shekel[b]; 4and if it is a female, set her value at thirty
shekels.[c] 5If it is a person between the ages of five and twenty, set the
value of a male at twenty shekels[d] and of a female at ten shekels.[e] 6If
it is a person between one month and five years, set the value of a
male at five shekels[f] of silver and that of a female at three shekels[g] of
silver. 7If it is a person sixty years old or more, set the value of a male
at fifteen shekels[h] and of a female at ten shekels. 8If anyone making
the vow is too poor to pay the specified amount, he is to present the
person to the priest, who will set the value for him according to what
the man making the vow can afford.

9" 'If what he vowed is an animal that is acceptable as an offering
to the LORD, such an animal given to the LORD becomes holy. 10He
must not exchange it or substitute a good one for a bad one, or a bad
one for a good one; if he should substitute one animal for another,
both it and the substitute become holy. 11If what he vowed is a ceremonially unclean animal—one that is not acceptable as an offering
to the LORD—the animal must be presented to the priest, 12who will
judge its quality as good or bad. Whatever value the priest then sets,
that is what it will be. 13If the owner wishes to redeem the animal, he
must add a fifth to its value.

14" 'If a man dedicates his house as something holy to the LORD,
the priest will judge its quality as good or bad. Whatever value the
priest then sets, so it will remain. 15If the man who dedicates his
house redeems it, he must add a fifth to its value, and the house will
again become his.

16" 'If a man dedicates to the LORD part of his family land, its value
is to be set according to the amount of seed required for it—fifty
shekels of silver to a homer[i] of barley seed. 17If he dedicates his field
during the Year of Jubilee, the value that has been set remains. 18But
if he dedicates his field after the Jubilee, the priest will determine the
value according to the number of years that remain until the next
Year of Jubilee, and its set value will be reduced. 19If the man who
dedicates the field wishes to redeem it, he must add a fifth to its
value, and the field will again become his. 20If, however, he does not
redeem the field, or if he has sold it to someone else, it can never be
redeemed. 21When the field is released in the Jubilee, it will become
holy, like a field devoted to the LORD; it will become the property of
the priests.[j]

22" 'If a man dedicates to the LORD a field he has bought, which is
not part of his family land, 23the priest will determine its value up to

[a]3 That is, about 1 1/4 pounds (about 0.6 kilogram); also in verse 16 [b]3 That is, about 2/5 ounce (about 11.5 grams); also in verse 25 [c]4 That is, about 12 ounces (about 0.3 kilogram) [d]5 That is, about 8 ounces (about 0.2 kilogram) [e]5 That is, about 4 ounces (about 110 grams); also in verse 7 [f]6 That is, about 2 ounces (about 55 grams) [g]6 That is, about 1 1/4 ounces (about 35 grams) [h]7 That is, about 6 ounces (about 170 grams) [i]16 That is, probably about 6 bushels (about 220 liters) [j]21 Or *priest*

STUDY The subjects of vows, gifts and tithes for the sanctuary are closely related and so are appropriately grouped together in this final chapter. **1.** Why would God include these instructions about vows? Is there some defect in human nature that would require these instructions? **2.** How do you think God viewed anything a man dedicated to him? How would these instructions influence your attitude toward dedicating something to God? **3.** Why would a person want to make these gifts to the Lord beyond their regular tithes? Would you have felt prompted to do this? **4.** God required a tenth of a person's resources. Does the way we give to God say anything about our relationship with God? If so, what? **5.** What stories do you know of Bible characters being "dedicated" or "devoted" to the Lord? How does the story of Hannah dedicating Samuel (1 Sam. 1:11,22,28) illustrate this point? What motivates parents like Hannah to irrevocably give over their children to the Lord? **6.** Looking back, what do you see as the overall theme of Leviticus? More than any other book, Hebrews builds on the rich "typology" (analogous or corresponding truth) of Leviticus, and so points to Christ as the fulfillment of the old covenant? Consider a study of Hebrews next.

APPLY **1.** How would you describe your attitude toward giving? **2.** Do you have a plan to worship God through giving? **3.** What gift does God want most (Rom. 12:1–2)? Have you made this dedication? **4.** To close out your group study of Leviticus on a redemptive note, try this fun auction game. You have only $1000 to spend on "redeeming" all aspects of your life—the good, the bad and the ugly. Using no more than the $1000 as your spending limit, with $200 as a minimum bid, which qualities of these biblical characters would you "buy" for yourself? $_____ for the faith of Abraham; $_____ for the patience of Job; $_____ for the generosity of Joseph; $_____ for the humility of

back of a book to check the value of things.

27:2 special vow. Vows were like a special offering, over and above the tithe. People made vows to God out of gratitude or to please him and so receive his favor. As explained here, parents could not give daughters to God's service, but they could give money dedicating a daughter in a vow.

27:10 substitute. The prophet Malachi cited this abuse (Mal. 1:13–14). The people were dedicating acceptable animals but then switching them for the unacceptable.

Moses; $_____ for the joy of David; $_____ for the service of Paul; $_____ for the wisdom of Solomon; $_____ for the hope of the Prophets. **5.** Thank the Lord that his death was limitless and sufficient to buy back all of you, and the whole world besides!

the Year of Jubilee, and the man must pay its value on that day as
something holy to the LORD. [24]In the Year of Jubilee the field will
revert to the person from whom he bought it, the one whose land it
was. [25]Every value is to be set according to the sanctuary shekel,
twenty gerahs to the shekel.

[26]" 'No one, however, may dedicate the firstborn of an animal,
since the firstborn already belongs to the LORD; whether an ox[a] or a
sheep, it is the LORD's. [27]If it is one of the unclean animals, he may
buy it back at its set value, adding a fifth of the value to it. If he does
not redeem it, it is to be sold at its set value.

[28]" 'But nothing that a man owns and devotes[b] to the LORD—
whether man or animal or family land—may be sold or redeemed;
everything so devoted is most holy to the LORD.

[29]" 'No person devoted to destruction[c] may be ransomed; he must
be put to death.

[30]" 'A tithe of everything from the land, whether grain from the soil
or fruit from the trees, belongs to the LORD; it is holy to the LORD. [31]If
a man redeems any of his tithe, he must add a fifth of the value to it.
[32]The entire tithe of the herd and flock—every tenth animal that
passes under the shepherd's rod—will be holy to the LORD. [33]He must
not pick out the good from the bad or make any substitution. If he
does make a substitution, both the animal and its substitute become
holy and cannot be redeemed.' "

[34]These are the commands the LORD gave Moses on Mount Sinai
for the Israelites.

[a]*26* The Hebrew word can include both male and female. [b]*28* The Hebrew term refers to the irrevocable giving over of things or persons to the LORD. [c]*29* The Hebrew term refers to the irrevocable giving over of things or persons to the LORD, often by totally destroying them.

27:28 devotes. Today we talk about devoting or dedicating our lives to the Lord. The action described here was more public than it would be today. Those devoting themselves were more accountable to the people for the outcome of their vow.

27:29 devoted to destruction. This described prisoners and spoils of war. When the Hebrews conquered Jericho they were instructed to destroy everything. That meant that the people and things in Jericho were devoted to destruction. One man, Achan, disobeyed. Until he was found out, God held the nation accountable (Josh. 7:1–20).

27:30 a tithe of everything. Tithes of animals were actually brought to the tabernacle. Tithes of land were redeemed by giving a monetary gift of 10 percent of the value, plus the 20 percent redemption fee.

27:34 This verse functioned as a kind of sign-off, giving the source (God), the author (Moses) and the place (Mount Sinai).

Numbers

Author. Moses is the author of the book of Numbers. Many think that Moses recorded much of Numbers as a log of the journey.

Date. Numbers was probably written around 1400 B.C. It described the time-span between the events at Mount Sinai and the Hebrews' arrival at the border of Canaan after 38 years of wandering.

Purpose. Numbers recorded a significant period of history and brought lessons from that historical narrative. It described the consequences God's people faced when they rejected his leadership.

Personal Reading	Group Study Topic and Reading	
1:1–6:21	The Nazirite	6:1–21
6:22–8:26	The Levites	8:5–26
9:1–10:36	Cloud of Guidance	9:15–10:36
11:1–11:35	Quail From God	11:4–35
12:1–16	Opposition to Moses	12:1–16
13:1–14:45	God's Plan Rejected	13:26–14:45
15:1–16:50	Korah's Rebellion	16:1–50
17:1–20:13	Water From the Rock	20:1–13
20:14–21:35	Bronze Snake	21:4–9
22:1–24:25	Balaam's Donkey	22:1–35
25:1–26:65	Moab Seduces Israel	25:1–18
27:1–32:42	Joshua Succeeds Moses	27:12–23
33:1–36:13	Stages of Israel's Journey	33:1–56

Historical Background. The journey from Egypt to Sinai had taken the Israelites less than a year. Their daily lives had been defined by the law. They had been empowered by their covenant with God. However, when faced with fighting another nation, their resolve failed, and as a result of their lack of faith, their entrance into Canaan was delayed for forty more years.

The Israelites strained against leadership. Even though they could unite and strive toward a common goal, they could just as easily rebel. This rebellion had a terrible impact on the entire generation that left Egypt. Historically, they were still in transition from a collection of families tied together by a heritage to a nation tied together by a common law and faith.

Grumblers. The Hebrews easily slipped into an ungrateful state of mind. They began to disdain the manna that God miraculously provided to feed them in the desert. "We never see anything but this manna!" (11:6). The leaders whom the Hebrews had once considered champions were now treated with contempt. "Why did you bring us up out of Egypt to this terrible place?" (20:5). The Hebrews had once clung to and thanked the Lord for their freedom, but they lost their faith. "Why is the Lord bringing us to this land only to let us fall by the sword?" (14:3). The Hebrews were in a downward spiral of negativity, fear and ingratitude. Some of them died because of it. Yet, those who remained saw God's faithfulness.

The Israelites were given the opportunity early in the book to enter the Promised Land (13:1–14:38). Numbers records the history of the nation wandering around the wilderness until an entire generation of faithless people die. The two leaders, Joshua and Caleb, who believed God's promise and ability led a new generation into the Promised Land.

OPEN 1. What were the results of the latest census of your country? How many people? What major shifts in population? In demographics? **2.** What is the purpose of a national census? Do the numbers make you proud of your nation? Do they make you feel strong? Why?

STUDY After God delivered the Israelites from Egyptian slavery and gave his Law to them at Mount Sinai, it was time to get organized for the journey and for the important task of functioning as a nation. The beginning of that organization was a census, however, only the male population over twenty years of age was counted. **1.** What part does Numbers play in the story of the Pentateuch (first five books of the Old Testament)? At what point chronologically does Numbers fall within the whole story? **2.** Who is to take the census? How would the task be organized? Do you envision this process as: Chaotic? Orderly? Cumbersome? Tedious? Have you ever been on a tour with a large group? How easy was it to keep track of the people? What do you think is the purpose for taking the census at this point? How would this count aid the Israelites in the journey ahead? **3.** Why do you think only the men were numbered? Why only those twenty and over? What part would this numbering restriction play in Israel's future (32:11)? How many were actually counted? **4.** What did this census have to do with the promises of God made to Abraham (Gen. 12:2; 15:5)? What impresses you most about this part of the story: The size of the nation (about two million)? The organization of the census process? The exclusion of the priestly tribe of Levi from the count? The obedience

The Census

1 The LORD spoke to Moses in the Tent of Meeting in the Desert of
Sinai on the first day of the second month of the second year
after the Israelites came out of Egypt. He said: [2]"Take a census of the
whole Israelite community by their clans and families, listing every
man by name, one by one. [3]You and Aaron are to number by their
divisions all the men in Israel twenty years old or more who are able
to serve in the army. [4]One man from each tribe, each the head of his
family, is to help you. [5]These are the names of the men who are to
assist you:

from Reuben, Elizur son of Shedeur;
[6]from Simeon, Shelumiel son of Zurishaddai;
[7]from Judah, Nahshon son of Amminadab;
[8]from Issachar, Nethanel son of Zuar;
[9]from Zebulun, Eliab son of Helon;
[10]from the sons of Joseph:
  from Ephraim, Elishama son of Ammihud;
  from Manasseh, Gamaliel son of Pedahzur;
[11]from Benjamin, Abidan son of Gideoni;
[12]from Dan, Ahiezer son of Ammishaddai;
[13]from Asher, Pagiel son of Ocran;
[14]from Gad, Eliasaph son of Deuel;
[15]from Naphtali, Ahira son of Enan."

[16]These were the men appointed from the community, the leaders
of their ancestral tribes. They were the heads of the clans of Israel.
[17]Moses and Aaron took these men whose names had been given,
[18]and they called the whole community together on the first day of
the second month. The people indicated their ancestry by their clans
and families, and the men twenty years old or more were listed by
name, one by one, [19]as the LORD commanded Moses. And so he
counted them in the Desert of Sinai:

[20]From the descendants of Reuben the firstborn son of Israel:
All the men twenty years old or more who were able to serve in
the army were listed by name, one by one, according to the
records of their clans and families. [21]The number from the
tribe of Reuben was 46,500.

1:1 second year. Many vacationers today camp for a weekend, even a week. Very few persist for a year. Moses had been trekking with these people for over a year. They had seen miracles and disappointments. Mere survival was a feat in itself.

1:2 census. Several are mentioned in the Bible. The first was here at Sinai (ch. 1). The next was at the end of this forty years of wandering (ch. 26). The third census, taken by David, was considered *to be an act of sin* (2 Sam. 24:1–9). The fourth was the census that required Mary and Joseph to travel to Bethlehem just in time for Jesus' birth (Luke 2).

1:3 army. The purpose of this census was to form an army, so it counted only fit males.

1:4 One man from each tribe. This smart move reduced competition among the tribes, and allowed concerns about discrepancies to be sent to the tribe representative rather than to Moses and Aaron. It encouraged consensus and thus left less room for error.

1:5–16 *Ten of these tribes* represented sons of Jacob (also called Israel) by four different women: Rachel, Leah and their two handmaidens (as was the custom of the day). The other two names were the sons of Joseph. The one son missing was Levi. His was the priestly tribe which neither owned land nor went to war. They were counted separately.

1:18–19 clans and families. In ancient days, tribal membership was inherent to a person's identity. People were identified by families, much like native Americans identify themselves by their parents.

1:20–43 thousand. Whether or not the number means a literal thousand, the size of the group makes their organization an impressive feat.

22From the descendants of Simeon:
All the men twenty years old or more who were able to serve in the army were counted and listed by name, one by one, according to the records of their clans and families. 23The number from the tribe of Simeon was 59,300.

24From the descendants of Gad:
All the men twenty years old or more who were able to serve in the army were listed by name, according to the records of their clans and families. 25The number from the tribe of Gad was 45,650.

26From the descendants of Judah:
All the men twenty years old or more who were able to serve in the army were listed by name, according to the records of their clans and families. 27The number from the tribe of Judah was 74,600.

28From the descendants of Issachar:
All the men twenty years old or more who were able to serve in the army were listed by name, according to the records of their clans and families. 29The number from the tribe of Issachar was 54,400.

30From the descendants of Zebulun:
All the men twenty years old or more who were able to serve in the army were listed by name, according to the records of their clans and families. 31The number from the tribe of Zebulun was 57,400.

32From the sons of Joseph:
From the descendants of Ephraim:
All the men twenty years old or more who were able to serve in the army were listed by name, according to the records of their clans and families. 33The number from the tribe of Ephraim was 40,500.

34From the descendants of Manasseh:
All the men twenty years old or more who were able to serve in the army were listed by name, according to the records of their clans and families. 35The number from the tribe of Manasseh was 32,200.

36From the descendants of Benjamin:
All the men twenty years old or more who were able to serve in the army were listed by name, according to the records of their clans and families. 37The number from the tribe of Benjamin was 35,400.

38From the descendants of Dan:
All the men twenty years old or more who were able to serve in the army were listed by name, according to the records of their clans and families. 39The number from the tribe of Dan was 62,700.

of Moses to God's command to count the people? Why? **5.** Why were the Levites exempt from the census (vv. 47–51)? What duties were they assigned? What privilege did they have that was denied everyone else in Israel (v. 51)? How do you think the rest of Israel viewed the Levites knowing they were not counted in the census? What special affinity do the people of God today share with the Levites (1 Peter 2:5,9)? **6.** What was the purpose of the tabernacle of Testimony (Ex. 29:42–46, 40:34–38)? Why do you think it was so important that no one other than the Levites even go near the tabernacle (v. 51)? **7.** Why do you think the people were so obedient at this point, when at other times they were totally rebellious?

APPLY 1. This was one of several "crossroad" events in the history of Israel. What have been some of yours? Are you at a crossroads now? Describe it. **2.** How would you describe your relationship with God right now in one or two words?

1:32–35 Joseph. It may seem that Joseph was skipped over since his sons were given the land. In Hebrew tradition, though, this meant that Joseph's family got a double portion, so for Joseph, it was an honor.

40 From the descendants of Asher:
All the men twenty years old or more who were able to serve in the army were listed by name, according to the records of their clans and families. 41 The number from the tribe of Asher was 41,500.

42 From the descendants of Naphtali:
All the men twenty years old or more who were able to serve in the army were listed by name, according to the records of their clans and families. 43 The number from the tribe of Naphtali was 53,400.

44 These were the men counted by Moses and Aaron and the twelve leaders of Israel, each one representing his family. 45 All the Israelites twenty years old or more who were able to serve in Israel's army were counted according to their families. 46 The total number was 603,550.

47 The families of the tribe of Levi, however, were not counted along with the others. 48 The LORD had said to Moses: 49 "You must not count the tribe of Levi or include them in the census of the other Israelites. 50 Instead, appoint the Levites to be in charge of the tabernacle of the Testimony—over all its furnishings and everything belonging to it. They are to carry the tabernacle and all its furnishings; they are to take care of it and encamp around it. 51 Whenever the tabernacle is to move, the Levites are to take it down, and whenever the tabernacle is to be set up, the Levites shall do it. Anyone else who goes near it shall be put to death. 52 The Israelites are to set up their tents by divisions, each man in his own camp under his own standard. 53 The Levites, however, are to set up their tents around the tabernacle of the Testimony so that wrath will not fall on the Israelite community. The Levites are to be responsible for the care of the tabernacle of the Testimony."

54 The Israelites did all this just as the LORD commanded Moses.

OPEN 1. When was the last time you went on a trip (camping, cruise, tour) with a large group of people? How were the accommodations organized? Were

The Arrangement of the Tribal Camps

2 The LORD said to Moses and Aaron: 2 "The Israelites are to camp around the Tent of Meeting some distance from it, each man under his standard with the banners of his family."

1:46 total. Considering that the nation of Israel started with seventy people who moved to Egypt, the total of 600,000 was phenomenal.

1:47–49 Levi. The Levites were not counted in the census because they were responsible for every detail regarding the tabernacle. They had to move it and maintain it—no small task.

1:50 Testimony. We call this the Ten Commandments. The original tablets were kept in a sacred box in the innermost room of the tabernacle.

1:51 take it down. You can read Exodus 25–27 for instructions on creating the tabernacle. It was a huge task to dismantle, move and set up again.

1:53 Levites ... around the tabernacle. The Levites were the priestly tribe. Their life's work was to serve in the tabernacle. It made sense then that they would set up their tents in a protective circle around the tabernacle while the other tribes established their own camps.

1:54 as the LORD commanded Moses. The Israelites heard God through Moses. They observed his presence at the temple. The amazing thing about the life and ministry of Jesus is that he gave us access to God. At his death the veil that separated the worshipers from the Holy Place (where God's presence dwelt) was ripped from top to bottom and people never again had to go through anyone else to get to God. From then on access to God came by faith alone.

2:2 distance. The presence of God held fear for the people. After all, Aaron's sons Nadab and Abihu had fallen dead because they dealt with God in an unauthorized way. We know God's presence as loving and compassionate, but these people, meeting God for the first time, felt especially his majesty and power.

[3]On the east, toward the sunrise, the divisions of the camp
of Judah are to encamp under their standard. The leader of the
people of Judah is Nahshon son of Amminadab. [4]His division
numbers 74,600.
[5]The tribe of Issachar will camp next to them. The leader of
the people of Issachar is Nethanel son of Zuar. [6]His division
numbers 54,400.
[7]The tribe of Zebulun will be next. The leader of the people of
Zebulun is Eliab son of Helon. [8]His division numbers 57,400.
[9]All the men assigned to the camp of Judah, according to their
divisions, number 186,400. They will set out first.

[10]On the south will be the divisions of the camp of Reuben
under their standard. The leader of the people of Reuben is
Elizur son of Shedeur. [11]His division numbers 46,500.
[12]The tribe of Simeon will camp next to them. The leader of the
people of Simeon is Shelumiel son of Zurishaddai. [13]His division
numbers 59,300.
[14]The tribe of Gad will be next. The leader of the people of Gad
is Eliasaph son of Deuel.[a] [15]His division numbers 45,650.
[16]All the men assigned to the camp of Reuben, according to
their divisions, number 151,450. They will set out second.

[17]Then the Tent of Meeting and the camp of the Levites will set
out in the middle of the camps. They will set out in the same
order as they encamp, each in his own place under his standard.

[18]On the west will be the divisions of the camp of Ephraim
under their standard. The leader of the people of Ephraim is
Elishama son of Ammihud. [19]His division numbers 40,500.
[20]The tribe of Manasseh will be next to them. The leader of the
people of Manasseh is Gamaliel son of Pedahzur. [21]His division
numbers 32,200.
[22]The tribe of Benjamin will be next. The leader of the people
of Benjamin is Abidan son of Gideoni. [23]His division numbers
35,400.
[24]All the men assigned to the camp of Ephraim, according to
their divisions, number 108,100. They will set out third.

[25]On the north will be the divisions of the camp of Dan, under
their standard. The leader of the people of Dan is Ahiezer son of
Ammishaddai. [26]His division numbers 62,700.

[a]14 Many manuscripts of the Masoretic Text, Samaritan Pentateuch and Vulgate (see also Num. 1:14); most manuscripts of the Masoretic Text *Reuel*

you satisfied with how it went? Why or why not? **2.** When it comes to orderliness in your life, would you describe yourself as: A little messy? A neat freak? Somewhat orderly? A slob?

STUDY Following the numbering of the Israelites, God further organizes them into camps arranged around the central position of the tabernacle. The camp was divided into four groups—east, south, west, and north with each person assigned to his own clan. This served not only as the camping layout, but the marching order as well, when they moved from place to place. **1.** Why do you think the camps were to be set up some distance from the Tent of Meeting (tabernacle)? **2.** How would this camping arrangement make Israel's journey easier? Can you think of a more practical arrangement? **3.** Which quadrant of the camp had the most people? Which quadrant of the camp would lead out when they moved? What symbolism do you see in this order, if any? **4.** Describe what you think it would have been like without this order when the people moved from place to place. What logistical problems can you envision in the movement of this great crowd of people? **5.** In view of Israel's history of disobedience, how significant is it that they readily obeyed these commands? Why do you think they obeyed so easily at this point?

APPLY **1.** Do you think God is concerned with how orderly your life is lived? Explain. **2.** Have you resisted his direction for an orderly life? What are the results? **3.** How can this group encourage obedience?

2:3–4 Judah. Judah was not the firstborn, yet his tribe was the first listed here. Jesus was born in his family line.

2:10 Reuben. Jacob had predicted that Reuben's tribe would be known for indecision.

2:12–13 Simeon. Jacob had predicted that Simeon's tribe would eventually be scattered. Later that tribe was absorbed into the tribe of Judah.

2:14 Gad. Gad was the first son of Jacob and Zilpah, Leah's maidservant. Jacob had predicted that Gad's tribe would have a history of being attacked. Eventually this tribe settled east of the Jordan, a geographically vulnerable position.

2:17 each in his own place. The tribal sections were the basis of organization among the Hebrews. Whenever they organized, whether for battle or encampment, they settled according to tribe.

2:18–22 Ephraim, Manasseh, Benjamin. Ephraim and Manasseh were sons of Joseph. Joseph and Benjamin were Jacob's only two sons by Rachel, his beloved wife. They were his most favored sons.

2:25 Dan. Jacob once described Dan's tribe as a serpent and a viper.

[27]The tribe of Asher will camp next to them. The leader of the people of Asher is Pagiel son of Ocran. [28]His division numbers 41,500.

[29]The tribe of Naphtali will be next. The leader of the people of Naphtali is Ahira son of Enan. [30]His division numbers 53,400.

[31]All the men assigned to the camp of Dan number 157,600. They will set out last, under their standards.

[32]These are the Israelites, counted according to their families. All those in the camps, by their divisions, number 603,550. [33]The Levites, however, were not counted along with the other Israelites, as the LORD commanded Moses.

[34]So the Israelites did everything the LORD commanded Moses; that is the way they encamped under their standards, and that is the way they set out, each with his clan and family.

The Levites

3 This is the account of the family of Aaron and Moses at the time the LORD talked with Moses on Mount Sinai.

[2]The names of the sons of Aaron were Nadab the firstborn and Abihu, Eleazar and Ithamar. [3]Those were the names of Aaron's sons, the anointed priests, who were ordained to serve as priests. [4]Nadab and Abihu, however, fell dead before the LORD when they made an offering with unauthorized fire before him in the Desert of Sinai. They had no sons; so only Eleazar and Ithamar served as priests during the lifetime of their father Aaron.

[5]The LORD said to Moses, [6]"Bring the tribe of Levi and present them to Aaron the priest to assist him. [7]They are to perform duties for him and for the whole community at the Tent of Meeting by doing the work of the tabernacle. [8]They are to take care of all the furnishings of the Tent of Meeting, fulfilling the obligations of the Israelites by doing the work of the tabernacle. [9]Give the Levites to Aaron and his sons; they are the Israelites who are to be given wholly to him.[a] [10]Appoint Aaron and his sons to serve as priests; anyone else who approaches the sanctuary must be put to death."

[a]9 Most manuscripts of the Masoretic Text; some manuscripts of the Masoretic Text, Samaritan Pentateuch and Septuagint (see also Num. 8:16) *to me*

OPEN 1. What large project have you participated in which required specific assignments? What was your particular assignment? How did the project go? **2.** Who is the "firstborn" in your family? Does that distinction carry any special privileges in your family? Explain.

STUDY The family of Levi was not counted in the original census of Israel, but now the Lord commands that they be numbered. They were also assigned specific camping spots around the Tent of Meeting (the tabernacle) and specific duties in the care and operation of the tabernacle. **1.** What do you think was the purpose of appointing the entire family of Levi to serve in the care and operation of the tabernacle? Who were the priests? **2.** Which two sons of Aaron were not faithful to their responsibility and paid for it with their lives (v. 4, Lev. 10:1–3)? Why do you think their punishment was so severe?

2:27 Asher. Jacob foretold wealth for Asher.

2:29 Naphtali. Jacob described Naphtali's tribe as mountain people.

2:32 603,550. Keep in mind that this number includes only men twenty years of age and over who were fit for battle. With women, children and Levites, the actual number of persons would have been much greater.

2:33 Levites. The priestly tribe. They were exempt from battle and from land-owning so that they could care for the Tent of Meeting and the tabernacle.

2:34 everything the LORD commanded Moses. The Hebrews had to trust Moses completely. He was God's mouthpiece for them. When they did everything that Moses told them to do, they were credited with obeying God.

3:4 unauthorized. Nadab and Abihu were struck dead shortly after their ordination (Lev. 22:9).

3:5–10 tribe of Levi ... Aaron. While Aaron was a Levite, there was a distinction between his descendants and the rest of the tribe. Aaron's descendants were priests. Other Levites were tabernacle workers and caretakers, but not priests.

3:9 given wholly to him. This is an administrative phrase. Aaron was the one in charge of the service of the whole tribe.

3:10 put to death. For the Hebrews the tabernacle was the place of God's presence. God had chosen Aaron and his descendants to serve as priests, and Aaron's tribe (the Levites) to serve in the tabernacle. No one else was allowed to work in the tabernacle but Levites; no one else was allowed to offer sacrifices or enter the Holy Place or Most Holy Place but the priests. Anyone who did so would be put to death for arrogant disobedience.

[11]The LORD also said to Moses, [12]"I have taken the Levites from
among the Israelites in place of the first male offspring of every Israelite woman. The Levites are mine, [13]for all the firstborn are mine.
When I struck down all the firstborn in Egypt, I set apart for myself
every firstborn in Israel, whether man or animal. They are to be mine.
I am the LORD."

[14]The LORD said to Moses in the Desert of Sinai, [15]"Count the Levites by their families and clans. Count every male a month old or
more." [16]So Moses counted them, as he was commanded by the word
of the LORD.

[17]These were the names of the sons of Levi:
Gershon, Kohath and Merari.
[18]These were the names of the Gershonite clans:
Libni and Shimei.
[19]The Kohathite clans:
Amram, Izhar, Hebron and Uzziel.
[20]The Merarite clans:
Mahli and Mushi.
These were the Levite clans, according to their families.

[21]To Gershon belonged the clans of the Libnites and Shimeites;
these were the Gershonite clans. [22]The number of all the males a
month old or more who were counted was 7,500. [23]The Gershonite
clans were to camp on the west, behind the tabernacle. [24]The leader of
the families of the Gershonites was Eliasaph son of Lael. [25]At the Tent
of Meeting the Gershonites were responsible for the care of the tabernacle and tent, its coverings, the curtain at the entrance to the Tent of
Meeting, [26]the curtains of the courtyard, the curtain at the entrance to
the courtyard surrounding the tabernacle and altar, and the ropes—
and everything related to their use.

[27]To Kohath belonged the clans of the Amramites, Izharites,
Hebronites and Uzzielites; these were the Kohathite clans. [28]The
number of all the males a month old or more was 8,600.[a] The Kohathites were responsible for the care of the sanctuary. [29]The Kohathite
clans were to camp on the south side of the tabernacle. [30]The leader
of the families of the Kohathite clans was Elizaphan son of Uzziel.
[31]They were responsible for the care of the ark, the table, the lampstand, the altars, the articles of the sanctuary used in ministering, the

[a]28 Hebrew; some Septuagint manuscripts *8,300*

3. What was the "work of the tabernacle" the Levites were to perform (v. 8)? Do you envision that the people considered this work as: Busy work? Very important work? Critical to the life of the community? Explain your answer. **4.** What was the significance of the Levites representing the firstborn of all the Israelites (vv. 11–13)? How is the symbology used of Jesus (Luke 2:7, Col. 1:15,18)? How does this apply to you? **5.** How was the count of the Levites different from the count of the rest of Israel (v. 15)? How many were there? **6.** What specific part of the tabernacle was assigned to the Gershonites (vv. 21–26)? The Kohathites (vv. 27–32)? The Merarites (vv. 33–37)? What was the responsibility of Moses and Aaron and his sons (v. 38)? What does this organization teach you about the orderliness of God? What does this organization teach you about everyone in a community having responsibility for the operation and care of the community?

APPLY 1. How important do you think organization is for a church or group to fulfill its mission? **2.** What responsibility do you have in the community of God's people today? Are you doing your part?

3:12–13 first male offspring. At the time of the Exodus, God had spared the firstborn sons of Israel when he killed all the firstborn sons of Egypt (Ex. 12:12,13). Thus, God had a right to the firstborn sons as his own. Instead, God claimed a whole tribe, the Levites, to be his own and to serve before him and lead the worship.

3:15 Count. The Levites, not counted in the census, were counted here. Since the census counted every male older than thirty days, it was counting the keepers of the tabernacle for many years to come.

3:21–38 Because the Hebrews understood the tabernacle to represent God's presence among them, they needed to be fastidious about caring for it in the midst of frequent moves. These verses describe more than a division of committees to handle tablecloths for potluck suppers. These people were the servants who attended God's presence among the people. It was in their hands to know that God was welcomed, honored and obeyed.

3:25–26 curtain. The tabernacle, like the Hebrews' homes, was a tent made of flexible cloth or animal hide curtains held up by stakes or pillars.

3:28 sanctuary. The sanctuary of the tabernacle or temple did not refer to the auditorium, or public gathering place, as the word often does today. The sanctuary usually meant the Holy Place, the least public place of the structure.

3:31 the ark. This was no small responsibility. Death could result from the misuse of the ark of the Testimony, even if the person intended to be helpful (2 Sam. 6:1–7).

curtain, and everything related to their use. 32The chief leader of the Levites was Eleazar son of Aaron, the priest. He was appointed over those who were responsible for the care of the sanctuary.

33To Merari belonged the clans of the Mahlites and the Mushites; these were the Merarite clans. 34The number of all the males a month old or more who were counted was 6,200. 35The leader of the families of the Merarite clans was Zuriel son of Abihail; they were to camp on the north side of the tabernacle. 36The Merarites were appointed to take care of the frames of the tabernacle, its crossbars, posts, bases, all its equipment, and everything related to their use, 37as well as the posts of the surrounding courtyard with their bases, tent pegs and ropes.

38Moses and Aaron and his sons were to camp to the east of the tabernacle, toward the sunrise, in front of the Tent of Meeting. They were responsible for the care of the sanctuary on behalf of the Israelites. Anyone else who approached the sanctuary was to be put to death.

39The total number of Levites counted at the LORD's command by Moses and Aaron according to their clans, including every male a month old or more, was 22,000.

40The LORD said to Moses, "Count all the firstborn Israelite males who are a month old or more and make a list of their names. 41Take the Levites for me in place of all the firstborn of the Israelites, and the livestock of the Levites in place of all the firstborn of the livestock of the Israelites. I am the LORD."

42So Moses counted all the firstborn of the Israelites, as the LORD commanded him. 43The total number of firstborn males a month old or more, listed by name, was 22,273.

44The LORD also said to Moses, 45"Take the Levites in place of all the firstborn of Israel, and the livestock of the Levites in place of their livestock. The Levites are to be mine. I am the LORD. 46To redeem the 273 firstborn Israelites who exceed the number of the Levites, 47collect five shekels[a] for each one, according to the sanctuary shekel, which weighs twenty gerahs. 48Give the money for the redemption of the additional Israelites to Aaron and his sons."

49So Moses collected the redemption money from those who exceeded the number redeemed by the Levites. 50From the firstborn of the Israelites he collected silver weighing 1,365 shekels,[b] according to the sanctuary shekel. 51Moses gave the redemption money to Aaron and his sons, as he was commanded by the word of the LORD.

[a]47 That is, about 2 ounces (about 55 grams) [b]50 That is, about 35 pounds (about 15.5 kilograms)

3:41 firstborn. Because God had saved the firstborn sons from the tenth plague while they were in Egypt (Ex. 11:4–7), he had rights to them. Instead, he took the tribe of Levi to *be his own and to serve in the tabernacle.*

3:43 22,273. Many people think the number of Levite firstborn is low compared to the other tribes. The Levites may have been less productive. Another thought is that Levites counted only the firstborn since they were established as priests.

The Kohathites

4 The LORD said to Moses and Aaron: 2"Take a census of the
Kohathite branch of the Levites by their clans and families.
3Count all the men from thirty to fifty years of age who come to serve
in the work in the Tent of Meeting.
4"This is the work of the Kohathites in the Tent of Meeting: the care
of the most holy things. 5When the camp is to move, Aaron and his
sons are to go in and take down the shielding curtain and cover the
ark of the Testimony with it. 6Then they are to cover this with hides of
sea cows,[a] spread a cloth of solid blue over that and put the poles in
place.
7"Over the table of the Presence they are to spread a blue cloth and
put on it the plates, dishes and bowls, and the jars for drink offerings;
the bread that is continually there is to remain on it. 8Over these they
are to spread a scarlet cloth, cover that with hides of sea cows and
put its poles in place.
9"They are to take a blue cloth and cover the lampstand that is for
light, together with its lamps, its wick trimmers and trays, and all its
jars for the oil used to supply it. 10Then they are to wrap it and all its
accessories in a covering of hides of sea cows and put it on a carrying
frame.
11"Over the gold altar they are to spread a blue cloth and cover that
with hides of sea cows and put its poles in place.
12"They are to take all the articles used for ministering in the
sanctuary, wrap them in a blue cloth, cover that with hides of sea
cows and put them on a carrying frame.
13"They are to remove the ashes from the bronze altar and spread a
purple cloth over it. 14Then they are to place on it all the utensils used
for ministering at the altar, including the firepans, meat forks, shovels and sprinkling bowls. Over it they are to spread a covering of
hides of sea cows and put its poles in place.
15"After Aaron and his sons have finished covering the holy furnishings and all the holy articles, and when the camp is ready to move,
the Kohathites are to come to do the carrying. But they must not
touch the holy things or they will die. The Kohathites are to carry
those things that are in the Tent of Meeting.
16"Eleazar son of Aaron, the priest, is to have charge of the oil for
the light, the fragrant incense, the regular grain offering and the
anointing oil. He is to be in charge of the entire tabernacle and everything in it, including its holy furnishings and articles."
17The LORD said to Moses and Aaron, 18"See that the Kohathite
tribal clans are not cut off from the Levites. 19So that they may live
and not die when they come near the most holy things, do this for
them: Aaron and his sons are to go into the sanctuary and assign
to each man his work and what he is to carry. 20But the Kohathites
must not go in to look at the holy things, even for a moment, or they
will die."

[a]6 That is, dugongs; also in verses 8, 10, 11, 12, 14 and 25

OPEN Of all your worldly goods, which one is a family heirloom that you want to be sure to pass along to a another member of your family?

STUDY After the Levites had been numbered, God began to give the details of the specific assignments to the clans of the Levites. The responsibilities were sacred and serious enough that the Levites' lives were at stake. Specific materials and routines were to be used each time the tabernacle was moved. **1.** How old did the men have to be to serve in the tabernacle (v. 3)? Why do you think the age range was limited? **2.** Have you ever been told not to touch something? What did you want to do? What was the specific work assigned to the Kohathites (v. 4)? What specific tabernacle items did their work involve (vv. 5–13)? What restriction was placed on their work (v. 15)? What was the penalty for violating this restriction? Do you think any of the Kohathites might have been tempted to look or to touch? Would you have been? What does all this say to you about the importance of holy things? **3.** What do you think God was teaching his people with all these routines and restrictions? **4.** What significance do these restrictions, on being in the presence of the holy things of God, give to the thought that we can be in the presence of God himself (Heb. 9:11–14)?

APPLY **1.** What things are holy to you? **2.** Is your relationship with God such that you can enter into his presence (Heb. 10:19-23)?

4:3 thirty to fifty. These were the prime years of service in the tabernacle. Apprenticeships started earlier, then a Levite's ministry began at thirty. Jesus' public ministry began at that age (Luke 3:23).

4:4 holy things. This included the ark, its contents and accessories.

4:16 Eleazar. Since a mishandling of the holy things could result in death, it was no small job for Eleazar to oversee the whole process.

The Gershonites

21The LORD said to Moses, 22"Take a census also of the Gershonites
by their families and clans. 23Count all the men from thirty to fifty
years of age who come to serve in the work at the Tent of Meeting.
24"This is the service of the Gershonite clans as they work and carry burdens: 25They are to carry the curtains of the tabernacle, the Tent
of Meeting, its covering and the outer covering of hides of sea cows,
the curtains for the entrance to the Tent of Meeting, 26the curtains of
the courtyard surrounding the tabernacle and altar, the curtain for
the entrance, the ropes and all the equipment used in its service. The
Gershonites are to do all that needs to be done with these things.
27All their service, whether carrying or doing other work, is to be
done under the direction of Aaron and his sons. You shall assign to
them as their responsibility all they are to carry. 28This is the service
of the Gershonite clans at the Tent of Meeting. Their duties are to be
under the direction of Ithamar son of Aaron, the priest.

The Merarites

29"Count the Merarites by their clans and families. 30Count all the
men from thirty to fifty years of age who come to serve in the work at
the Tent of Meeting. 31This is their duty as they perform service at the
Tent of Meeting: to carry the frames of the tabernacle, its crossbars,
posts and bases, 32as well as the posts of the surrounding courtyard
with their bases, tent pegs, ropes, all their equipment and everything
related to their use. Assign to each man the specific things he is to
carry. 33This is the service of the Merarite clans as they work at the
Tent of Meeting under the direction of Ithamar son of Aaron, the
priest."

The Numbering of the Levite Clans

34Moses, Aaron and the leaders of the community counted the
Kohathites by their clans and families. 35All the men from thirty to
fifty years of age who came to serve in the work in the Tent of
Meeting, 36counted by clans, were 2,750. 37This was the total of all
those in the Kohathite clans who served in the Tent of Meeting.
Moses and Aaron counted them according to the LORD's command
through Moses.
38The Gershonites were counted by their clans and families. 39All
the men from thirty to fifty years of age who came to serve in the
work at the Tent of Meeting, 40counted by their clans and families,
were 2,630. 41This was the total of those in the Gershonite clans who
served at the Tent of Meeting. Moses and Aaron counted them according to the LORD's command.
42The Merarites were counted by their clans and families. 43All the
men from thirty to fifty years of age who came to serve in the work at
the Tent of Meeting, 44counted by their clans, were 3,200. 45This was
the total of those in the Merarite clans. Moses and Aaron counted
them according to the LORD's command through Moses.
46So Moses, Aaron and the leaders of Israel counted all the Levites
by their clans and families. 47All the men from thirty to fifty years of
age who came to do the work of serving and carrying the Tent of
Meeting 48numbered 8,580. 49At the LORD's command through Moses,
each was assigned his work and told what to carry.
Thus they were counted, as the LORD commanded Moses.

OPEN **1.** Have you ever been assigned "grunt work"? What was it and what did you think about having to do it? **2.** What kind of job do you have? Do you work with your hands, head or both?

STUDY As God continues to give specific assignments to the Levites, he assigns the "outside stuff" to the clans of the Gershonites and Merarites. This work, though it did not concern the items on the inside of the tabernacle, was as important as the work of the Kohathites. **1.** What specific items were the responsibility of the Gershonites (vv. 25–26)? The Merarites (vv. 29–32)? Do you think they considered their work as important as the Kohathites? Would you? Might some jealousy have arisen here? **2.** Why were the Gershonites and Merarites not restricted from touching and seeing the items they worked with? **3.** What parallels do you see with this work and the work of the church today?

APPLY **1.** Are you a servant? Are you willing to do the "grunt work" of the church? **2.** Explain how every part of the work of the church is important.

The Purity of the Camp

5 The LORD said to Moses, 2 "Command the Israelites to send away from the camp anyone who has an infectious skin disease[a] or a discharge of any kind, or who is ceremonially unclean because of a dead body. 3 Send away male and female alike; send them outside the camp so they will not defile their camp, where I dwell among them." 4 The Israelites did this; they sent them outside the camp. They did just as the LORD had instructed Moses.

Restitution for Wrongs

5 The LORD said to Moses, 6 "Say to the Israelites: 'When a man or woman wrongs another in any way[b] and so is unfaithful to the LORD, that person is guilty 7 and must confess the sin he has committed. He must make full restitution for his wrong, add one fifth to it and give it all to the person he has wronged. 8 But if that person has no close relative to whom restitution can be made for the wrong, the restitution belongs to the LORD and must be given to the priest, along with the ram with which atonement is made for him. 9 All the sacred contributions the Israelites bring to a priest will belong to him. 10 Each man's sacred gifts are his own, but what he gives to the priest will belong to the priest.' "

The Test for an Unfaithful Wife

11 Then the LORD said to Moses, 12 "Speak to the Israelites and say to them: 'If a man's wife goes astray and is unfaithful to him 13 by sleeping with another man, and this is hidden from her husband and her impurity is undetected (since there is no witness against her and she has not been caught in the act), 14 and if feelings of jealousy come over her husband and he suspects his wife and she is impure—or if he is jealous and suspects her even though she is not impure— 15 then he is to take his wife to the priest. He must also take an offering of a tenth of an ephah[c] of barley flour on her behalf. He must not pour oil on it or put incense on it, because it is a grain offering for jealousy, a reminder offering to draw attention to guilt.

16 " 'The priest shall bring her and have her stand before the LORD. 17 Then he shall take some holy water in a clay jar and put some dust from the tabernacle floor into the water. 18 After the priest has had the

[a]2 Traditionally *leprosy;* the Hebrew word was used for various diseases affecting the skin—not necessarily leprosy. [b]6 Or *woman commits any wrong common to mankind* [c]15 That is, probably about 2 quarts (about 2 liters)

OPEN 1. Have you ever been quarantined? What was it like? **2.** Did you ever get caught stealing something as a kid?

STUDY As the large community of Israel lived and worked together, disease was bound to be a serious problem, especially deadly infectious diseases. The solution was simple—quarantine. Another problem in such a crowd would be respect for each other's property. Again, the solution was simple—restitution. **1.** Do you think the instructions in verses 1–4 are simply health related, or is there a spiritual lesson here as well (1 Cor. 5)? **2.** What is the significance in the statement that when a person wrongs another person, they have been unfaithful to the Lord (v. 6)?

APPLY 1. What is your attitude toward people with "gross" illnesses? **2.** Do you believe in making restitution for wrongs?

OPEN Ever been teased about being a "kleptomaniac" of anything: Clerks' pens? Library books? Copyrighted material? Food? Souvenirs? Kisses? Other?

STUDY As in any society, one of the issues that would face Israel would be marital unfaithfulness. There were strict laws about adultery, but what about cases of suspicion and jealousy? How would the issue be resolved? God gives the Israelites directions for such situations in this "test for an unfaithful wife." **1.** Is this "test" from God or was it just made up like so many other "trials by nature" in various cultures? What is your initial reaction to this "test"? **2.** Is the heart of the issue in this text: Adultery? Jealousy? Male dominance over females? Justice? Truth? The moral

5:2 disease ... discharge. Strict instructions were given to the people in Leviticus 13–15 about diagnosing, treating and dealing with conditions that God defined as "unclean." While this probably resulted in many saved lives, it was also God's way of teaching them the foundations of holiness.

5:5–10 These verses focus on restitution. Preceding verses address cleanliness of the body and the holiness of God. These verses approach cleanliness in terms of human relationships and holiness of heart.

5:11–31 First, this chapter dealt with cleanliness of the body, then of relationships and now it deals with marital relations. The Bible often uses marriage as a metaphor for our relationship with God. It is not surprising then that marital unfaithfulness carried severe penalties.

5:14 jealousy. A husband was responsible to deal with his marriage even if his concern was not fully substantiated. He was not free to wait and see or to look the other way.

5:15–28 These verses, while uncomfortably archaic in method, speak strongly for the importance of purity within a community. They also point out the importance of the role of women within that community. Even though women did not wield great power, they lived under high expectations and scrutiny.

5:18 bitter water. The practices described here may have been like a prehistoric lie detector. All of this was done in the eyes and presence of God, and it was from him that the judgment was expected to fall like a curse.

purity of Israel? **3.** What effect would it have for a guilty woman to understand she was in the presence of the Lord during the "test"? Why do you think the oath and the ritual were so important? Do you think this was a special magical potion, or were the effects of the "bitter water" the work of God? **4.** Since the woman had to say "Amen," or in essence agree to the curse, do you think she might think twice about telling the truth? How could the woman have avoided this "test"? **5.** Why was it so important for a man's jealousy to be quieted? What might happen if the test revealed her guilt (Lev. 20:10)? To which commandment does this "test" relate (Ex. 20:1–17)? **6.** Why was it so important for Israel to have moral standards and strict enforcement? Do you think it is as important for a nation today?

APPLY 1. Can you tell of a time when you were really jealous? What happened? **2.** Are you jealous now? What can you do to get rid of your jealousy (Rom. 13:13–14)? How can this group help?

OPEN 1. Can you remember any "promise rituals" you practiced as a child? What were they and did they make the promise stronger? **2.** When it comes to keeping a promise, would you say you: Fudge a little? Break the promise? Forget the promise? Keep the promise?

STUDY In the spiritual life of an Israelite there would come times when the need to feel a special dedication to the Lord would arise. In order to give some credence to such times, God gave the Israelites instructions on how to take a vow of separation, called a Nazirite vow.

woman stand before the LORD, he shall loosen her hair and place in her hands the reminder offering, the grain offering for jealousy, while he himself holds the bitter water that brings a curse. 19 Then the priest shall put the woman under oath and say to her, "If no other man has slept with you and you have not gone astray and become impure while married to your husband, may this bitter water that brings a curse not harm you. 20 But if you have gone astray while married to your husband and you have defiled yourself by sleeping with a man other than your husband"— 21 here the priest is to put the woman under this curse of the oath—"may the LORD cause your people to curse and denounce you when he causes your thigh to waste away and your abdomen to swell.[a] 22 May this water that brings a curse enter your body so that your abdomen swells and your thigh wastes away.[b]"

" 'Then the woman is to say, "Amen. So be it."

23 " 'The priest is to write these curses on a scroll and then wash them off into the bitter water. 24 He shall have the woman drink the bitter water that brings a curse, and this water will enter her and cause bitter suffering. 25 The priest is to take from her hands the grain offering for jealousy, wave it before the LORD and bring it to the altar. 26 The priest is then to take a handful of the grain offering as a memorial offering and burn it on the altar; after that, he is to have the woman drink the water. 27 If she has defiled herself and been unfaithful to her husband, then when she is made to drink the water that brings a curse, it will go into her and cause bitter suffering; her abdomen will swell and her thigh waste away,[c] and she will become accursed among her people. 28 If, however, the woman has not defiled herself and is free from impurity, she will be cleared of guilt and will be able to have children.

29 " 'This, then, is the law of jealousy when a woman goes astray and defiles herself while married to her husband, 30 or when feelings of jealousy come over a man because he suspects his wife. The priest is to have her stand before the LORD and is to apply this entire law to her. 31 The husband will be innocent of any wrongdoing, but the woman will bear the consequences of her sin.' "

The Nazirite

6 The LORD said to Moses, 2 "Speak to the Israelites and say to them: 'If a man or woman wants to make a special vow, a vow of separation to the LORD as a Nazirite, 3 he must abstain from wine and other fermented drink and must not drink vinegar made from wine or from other fermented drink. He must not drink grape juice or eat grapes or raisins. 4 As long as he is a Nazirite, he must not eat anything that comes from the grapevine, not even the seeds or skins.

5 " 'During the entire period of his vow of separation no razor may be used on his head. He must be holy until the period of his separation to the LORD is over; he must let the hair of his head grow long. 6 Throughout the period of his separation to the LORD he must not go

[a]21 Or *causes you to have a miscarrying womb and barrenness* [b]22 Or *body and cause you to be barren and have a miscarrying womb* [c]27 Or *suffering; she will have barrenness and a miscarrying womb*

5:21 this curse of the oath. Ultimately this curse was sterility.

6:4 Nazirite. Several well-known people in the Bible were Nazirites: John the Baptist (Luke 1:15), Samuel (1 Sam. 1:11) and probably the most famous, Samson (Judg. 13:1–7; 16:17). The Nazirite's long hair was a statement of dedication.

6:6–7 dead body. Avoiding all dead

near a dead body. 7Even if his own father or mother or brother or sister dies, he must not make himself ceremonially unclean on account
of them, because the symbol of his separation to God is on his head.
8Throughout the period of his separation he is consecrated to the
LORD.
9" 'If someone dies suddenly in his presence, thus defiling the hair
he has dedicated, he must shave his head on the day of his cleansing—the seventh day. 10Then on the eighth day he must bring two
doves or two young pigeons to the priest at the entrance to the Tent
of Meeting. 11The priest is to offer one as a sin offering and the other
as a burnt offering to make atonement for him because he sinned by
being in the presence of the dead body. That same day he is to consecrate his head. 12He must dedicate himself to the LORD for the period
of his separation and must bring a year-old male lamb as a guilt
offering. The previous days do not count, because he became defiled
during his separation.
13" 'Now this is the law for the Nazirite when the period of his separation is over. He is to be brought to the entrance to the Tent of
Meeting. 14There he is to present his offerings to the LORD: a year-old
male lamb without defect for a burnt offering, a year-old ewe lamb
without defect for a sin offering, a ram without defect for a fellowship
offering,[a] 15together with their grain offerings and drink offerings,
and a basket of bread made without yeast—cakes made of fine flour
mixed with oil, and wafers spread with oil.
16" 'The priest is to present them before the LORD and make the sin
offering and the burnt offering. 17He is to present the basket of
unleavened bread and is to sacrifice the ram as a fellowship offering
to the LORD, together with its grain offering and drink offering.
18" 'Then at the entrance to the Tent of Meeting, the Nazirite must
shave off the hair that he dedicated. He is to take the hair and put it in
the fire that is under the sacrifice of the fellowship offering.
19" 'After the Nazirite has shaved off the hair of his dedication, the
priest is to place in his hands a boiled shoulder of the ram, and a cake
and a wafer from the basket, both made without yeast. 20The priest
shall then wave them before the LORD as a wave offering; they are
holy and belong to the priest, together with the breast that was
waved and the thigh that was presented. After that, the Nazirite may
drink wine.
21" 'This is the law of the Nazirite who vows his offering to the LORD
in accordance with his separation, in addition to whatever else he
can afford. He must fulfill the vow he has made, according to the law
of the Nazirite.' "

[a]14 Traditionally *peace offering*; also in verses 17 and 18

1. During a Nazirite vow, what things were prohibited (vv. 3–8)? What do you think is the significance of each of these prohibited things? Why was this ritual so important? **2.** Why would the vow and its restrictions be in force even in the event of the death of a loved one (v. 7)? Do you think you could make it through such a time with this level of dedication? **3.** Why do you think there was such an elaborate ceremony at the end of the vow (vv. 13–21)? What message about God would the people of Israel get from the ceremony? **4.** What is the importance of "separation" in a ceremonial vow? Have you ever experienced such a time in your life? What was it like, and what were the results?

APPLY **1.** Is there anything in your life important enough for the discipline of a Nazirite vow? What is it? **2.** Are you at a time in your life when you feel a real need to get away from the world and get closer to God? What can you do to accomplish that? How can others help?

---

bodies, even of family members, may have been a symbol of laying aside all earthly concerns.

6:9–12 This is one of the cases where the Bible demands perfection but makes practical provision for real life. Even though the Nazirite was forbidden to be around a dead body, there are provisions for resuming his vow if his proximity to death was outside his control.

6:13–20 Only a few Nazirites-for-life are mentioned in the Bible, but many took the vow for a certain period of time. This was much like giving up something for Lent, a special time to show dedication to God.

6:21 vow. Because this was a vow, it was followed by the fellowship offering, which was offered simply for gratitude as a freewill offering or to fulfill a vow.

The Priestly Blessing

[22]The LORD said to Moses, [23]"Tell Aaron and his sons, 'This is how
you are to bless the Israelites. Say to them:

[24]" ' "The LORD bless you
and keep you;
[25]the LORD make his face shine upon you
and be gracious to you;
[26]the LORD turn his face toward you
and give you peace." '

[27]"So they will put my name on the Israelites, and I will bless
them."

Offerings at the Dedication of the Tabernacle

7 When Moses finished setting up the tabernacle, he anointed it
and consecrated it and all its furnishings. He also anointed and
consecrated the altar and all its utensils. [2]Then the leaders of Israel,
the heads of families who were the tribal leaders in charge of those
who were counted, made offerings. [3]They brought as their gifts before the LORD six covered carts and twelve oxen—an ox from each
leader and a cart from every two. These they presented before the
tabernacle.

[4]The LORD said to Moses, [5]"Accept these from them, that they may
be used in the work at the Tent of Meeting. Give them to the Levites
as each man's work requires."

[6]So Moses took the carts and oxen and gave them to the Levites.
[7]He gave two carts and four oxen to the Gershonites, as their work
required, [8]and he gave four carts and eight oxen to the Merarites, as
their work required. They were all under the direction of Ithamar son
of Aaron, the priest. [9]But Moses did not give any to the Kohathites,
because they were to carry on their shoulders the holy things, for
which they were responsible.

[10]When the altar was anointed, the leaders brought their offerings
for its dedication and presented them before the altar. [11]For the LORD
had said to Moses, "Each day one leader is to bring his offering for
the dedication of the altar."

[12]The one who brought his offering on the first day was Nahshon son
of Amminadab of the tribe of Judah.

[13]His offering was one silver plate weighing a hundred and thirty
shekels,[a] and one silver sprinkling bowl weighing seventy
shekels,[b] both according to the sanctuary shekel, each filled with

[a]13 That is, about 3 1/4 pounds (about 1.5 kilograms); also elsewhere in this chapter
[b]13 That is, about 1 3/4 pounds (about 0.8 kilogram); also elsewhere in this chapter

OPEN 1. What is the greatest treasure or the most money you have had in one place at one time? **2.** What gift from your past stands out as the most meaningful to you?

STUDY Once the Israelites had finished construction of the tabernacle according to the specifications given to them by God, there remained the necessary items for its operation. Each of the tribes contributed to this need and so the Levites had all they needed to carry on the work of the tabernacle. **1.** Of what use would the six carts and teams of oxen be to the work of the tabernacle? Which clan of the Levites did not receive any carts and oxen? Why (v. 9)? **2.** How would this act of giving help the Israelites relate to the tabernacle? Where do you think they got all the gold and silver for these offerings (Ex. 3:21–22; 12:35–36)? Would you have been willing to give up what you had plundered from the Egyptians? What could motivate you to do so? **3.** How much did the Israelites bring for an offering (vv. 84–88)? Would you have been willing to give? Have you given sacrificially to something before? **4.** Why do you think each tribe gave an identical offering? How would this help build their sense of unity and community? **5.** What is the significance of Moses' conversation with God after the offerings had been given? What do you think they talked about?

6:24–26 This benediction has journeyed through the history of the church. Many worship services today conclude with it. **turn his face toward you.** When God turns his face toward his *people he gives them his presence and* attention. The nomadic Hebrews would have been greatly comforted to know that God had not forgotten them, but was watchful over them.

6:25 make his face shine. This has the connotation of God's pleasure in his people. Even today we describe parents watching their children as "beaming" with pride.

7:1–89 While the people had already received many instructions about the tabernacle, this passage describes the actual dedication of the tabernacle. The people brought gifts to be used in transporting the tabernacle from Mount Sinai on the journey to the Promised Land.

7:12–83 As with the rest of community life, the people gave their gifts according to tribe, in an orderly fashion.

fine flour mixed with oil as a grain offering; [14]one gold dish weighing ten shekels,[a] filled with incense; [15]one young bull, one ram and one male lamb a year old, for a burnt offering; [16]one male goat for a sin offering; [17]and two oxen, five rams, five male goats and five male lambs a year old, to be sacrificed as a fellowship offering.[b] This was the offering of Nahshon son of Amminadab.

[18]On the second day Nethanel son of Zuar, the leader of Issachar, brought his offering.

[19]The offering he brought was one silver plate weighing a hundred and thirty shekels, and one silver sprinkling bowl weighing seventy shekels, both according to the sanctuary shekel, each filled with fine flour mixed with oil as a grain offering; [20]one gold dish weighing ten shekels, filled with incense; [21]one young bull, one ram and one male lamb a year old, for a burnt offering; [22]one male goat for a sin offering; [23]and two oxen, five rams, five male goats and five male lambs a year old, to be sacrificed as a fellowship offering. This was the offering of Nethanel son of Zuar.

[24]On the third day, Eliab son of Helon, the leader of the people of Zebulun, brought his offering.

[25]His offering was one silver plate weighing a hundred and thirty shekels, and one silver sprinkling bowl weighing seventy shekels, both according to the sanctuary shekel, each filled with fine flour mixed with oil as a grain offering; [26]one gold dish weighing ten shekels, filled with incense; [27]one young bull, one ram and one male lamb a year old, for a burnt offering; [28]one male goat for a sin offering; [29]and two oxen, five rams, five male goats and five male lambs a year old, to be sacrificed as a fellowship offering. This was the offering of Eliab son of Helon.

[30]On the fourth day Elizur son of Shedeur, the leader of the people of Reuben, brought his offering.

[31]His offering was one silver plate weighing a hundred and thirty shekels, and one silver sprinkling bowl weighing seventy shekels, both according to the sanctuary shekel, each filled with fine flour mixed with oil as a grain offering; [32]one gold dish weighing ten shekels, filled with incense; [33]one young bull, one ram and one male lamb a year old, for a burnt offering; [34]one male goat for a sin offering; [35]and two oxen, five rams, five male goats and five male lambs a year old, to be sacrificed as a fellowship offering. This was the offering of Elizur son of Shedeur.

[36]On the fifth day Shelumiel son of Zurishaddai, the leader of the people of Simeon, brought his offering.

[37]His offering was one silver plate weighing a hundred and thirty shekels, and one silver sprinkling bowl weighing seventy shekels, both according to the sanctuary shekel, each filled with fine flour mixed with oil as a grain offering; [38]one gold dish weighing ten shekels, filled with incense; [39]one young bull, one ram and one male lamb a year old, for a burnt offering; [40]one male goat for a sin offering; [41]and two oxen, five rams, five male goats and five male lambs a year old, to be sacrificed as a fellowship offering. This was the offering of Shelumiel son of Zurishaddai.

[a]*14* That is, about 4 ounces (about 110 grams); also elsewhere in this chapter [b]*17* Traditionally *peace offering*; also elsewhere in this chapter

APPLY 1. How do you determine how much you will give (1 Cor. 16:2; 2 Cor. 8:12; 9:7)? **2.** What is your motive in giving? How are you doing in your giving?

[42]On the sixth day Eliasaph son of Deuel, the leader of the people of
Gad, brought his offering.
[43]His offering was one silver plate weighing a hundred and thirty
shekels, and one silver sprinkling bowl weighing seventy shekels, both according to the sanctuary shekel, each filled with fine
flour mixed with oil as a grain offering; [44]one gold dish weighing
ten shekels, filled with incense; [45]one young bull, one ram and
one male lamb a year old, for a burnt offering; [46]one male goat
for a sin offering; [47]and two oxen, five rams, five male goats and
five male lambs a year old, to be sacrificed as a fellowship offering. This was the offering of Eliasaph son of Deuel.

[48]On the seventh day Elishama son of Ammihud, the leader of the
people of Ephraim, brought his offering.
[49]His offering was one silver plate weighing a hundred and thirty
shekels, and one silver sprinkling bowl weighing seventy shekels, both according to the sanctuary shekel, each filled with fine
flour mixed with oil as a grain offering; [50]one gold dish weighing
ten shekels, filled with incense; [51]one young bull, one ram and
one male lamb a year old, for a burnt offering; [52]one male goat
for a sin offering; [53]and two oxen, five rams, five male goats and
five male lambs a year old, to be sacrificed as a fellowship offering. This was the offering of Elishama son of Ammihud.

[54]On the eighth day Gamaliel son of Pedahzur, the leader of the people of Manasseh, brought his offering.
[55]His offering was one silver plate weighing a hundred and thirty
shekels, and one silver sprinkling bowl weighing seventy shekels, both according to the sanctuary shekel, each filled with fine
flour mixed with oil as a grain offering; [56]one gold dish weighing
ten shekels, filled with incense; [57]one young bull, one ram and
one male lamb a year old, for a burnt offering; [58]one male goat
for a sin offering; [59]and two oxen, five rams, five male goats and
five male lambs a year old, to be sacrificed as a fellowship offering. This was the offering of Gamaliel son of Pedahzur.

[60]On the ninth day Abidan son of Gideoni, the leader of the people of
Benjamin, brought his offering.
[61]His offering was one silver plate weighing a hundred and thirty
shekels, and one silver sprinkling bowl weighing seventy shekels, both according to the sanctuary shekel, each filled with fine
flour mixed with oil as a grain offering; [62]one gold dish weighing
ten shekels, filled with incense; [63]one young bull, one ram and
one male lamb a year old, for a burnt offering; [64]one male goat
for a sin offering; [65]and two oxen, five rams, five male goats and
five male lambs a year old, to be sacrificed as a fellowship offering. This was the offering of Abidan son of Gideoni.

[66]On the tenth day Ahiezer son of Ammishaddai, the leader of the
people of Dan, brought his offering.
[67]His offering was one silver plate weighing a hundred and thirty
shekels, and one silver sprinkling bowl weighing seventy shekels, both according to the sanctuary shekel, each filled with fine
flour mixed with oil as a grain offering; [68]one gold dish weighing
ten shekels, filled with incense; [69]one young bull, one ram and
one male lamb a year old, for a burnt offering; [70]one male goat

for a sin offering; [71]and two oxen, five rams, five male goats and
five male lambs a year old, to be sacrificed as a fellowship offering. This was the offering of Ahiezer son of Ammishaddai.

[72]On the eleventh day Pagiel son of Ocran, the leader of the people of
Asher, brought his offering.

[73]His offering was one silver plate weighing a hundred and thirty
shekels, and one silver sprinkling bowl weighing seventy shekels, both according to the sanctuary shekel, each filled with fine
flour mixed with oil as a grain offering; [74]one gold dish weighing
ten shekels, filled with incense; [75]one young bull, one ram and
one male lamb a year old, for a burnt offering; [76]one male goat
for a sin offering; [77]and two oxen, five rams, five male goats and
five male lambs a year old, to be sacrificed as a fellowship offering. This was the offering of Pagiel son of Ocran.

[78]On the twelfth day Ahira son of Enan, the leader of the people of
Naphtali, brought his offering.

[79]His offering was one silver plate weighing a hundred and thirty
shekels, and one silver sprinkling bowl weighing seventy shekels, both according to the sanctuary shekel, each filled with fine
flour mixed with oil as a grain offering; [80]one gold dish weighing
ten shekels, filled with incense; [81]one young bull, one ram and
one male lamb a year old, for a burnt offering; [82]one male goat
for a sin offering; [83]and two oxen, five rams, five male goats and
five male lambs a year old, to be sacrificed as a fellowship offering. This was the offering of Ahira son of Enan.

[84]These were the offerings of the Israelite leaders for the dedication of the altar when it was anointed: twelve silver plates, twelve
silver sprinkling bowls and twelve gold dishes. [85]Each silver plate
weighed a hundred and thirty shekels, and each sprinkling bowl
seventy shekels. Altogether, the silver dishes weighed two thousand
four hundred shekels,[a] according to the sanctuary shekel. [86]The
twelve gold dishes filled with incense weighed ten shekels each, according to the sanctuary shekel. Altogether, the gold dishes weighed
a hundred and twenty shekels.[b] [87]The total number of animals for the
burnt offering came to twelve young bulls, twelve rams and twelve
male lambs a year old, together with their grain offering. Twelve male
goats were used for the sin offering. [88]The total number of animals
for the sacrifice of the fellowship offering came to twenty-four oxen,
sixty rams, sixty male goats and sixty male lambs a year old. These
were the offerings for the dedication of the altar after it was anointed.
[89]When Moses entered the Tent of Meeting to speak with the LORD,
he heard the voice speaking to him from between the two cherubim
above the atonement cover on the ark of the Testimony. And he spoke
with him.

[a]*85* That is, about 60 pounds (about 28 kilograms) [b]*86* That is, about 3 pounds (about 1.4 kilograms)

7:84–88 twelve. For the 12 tribes of Israel.

7:89 he spoke with him. The whole purpose of the tabernacle was to be a visual reminder of God's presence and a place for God to communicate with his people.

OPEN **1.** Have you ever gone through a dedication ceremony? What was it like? **2.** In what ways are you dependent upon representatives to serve for you at church? In government? In other councils and meetings?

STUDY Israelites, other than Levites, could not serve in the tabernacle—they couldn't even go in! The Levites were appointed by God for that service, but they needed to be ceremonially cleansed. **1.** What did the cleansing of the Levites involve (vv. 7–14)? What did each ritual mean? **2.** What did it mean for the Levites to be "set apart" for God (v. 14)? Are you "set apart" for God? Do you feel clean and prepared for service? How? **3.** What do you think might have happened if they had refused to follow God's instructions for the dedication of the Levites for service? Do you see any present-day application? **4.** What parallel might there be between the sin offering for the Levites (vv. 8,12) and our need for being cleansed of sin before we serve the Lord? Who is our sin offering? **5.** What do you make of the retirement age of the Levites?

APPLY **1.** Do you think God has separated you out to serve him? If so, how has he done so, and in what way are you serving him? **2.** How can we be separated, yet not lose touch with the world (John 17:14–19, 1 Peter 2:11–12, 1 John. 2:15–16)?

Setting Up the Lamps

8 The LORD said to Moses, [2]"Speak to Aaron and say to him, 'When you set up the seven lamps, they are to light the area in front of the lampstand.' "

[3]Aaron did so; he set up the lamps so that they faced forward on the lampstand, just as the LORD commanded Moses. [4]This is how the lampstand was made: It was made of hammered gold—from its base to its blossoms. The lampstand was made exactly like the pattern the LORD had shown Moses.

The Setting Apart of the Levites

[5]The LORD said to Moses: [6]"Take the Levites from among the other Israelites and make them ceremonially clean. [7]To purify them, do this: Sprinkle the water of cleansing on them; then have them shave their whole bodies and wash their clothes, and so purify themselves. [8]Have them take a young bull with its grain offering of fine flour mixed with oil; then you are to take a second young bull for a sin offering. [9]Bring the Levites to the front of the Tent of Meeting and assemble the whole Israelite community. [10]You are to bring the Levites before the LORD, and the Israelites are to lay their hands on them. [11]Aaron is to present the Levites before the LORD as a wave offering from the Israelites, so that they may be ready to do the work of the LORD.

[12]"After the Levites lay their hands on the heads of the bulls, use the one for a sin offering to the LORD and the other for a burnt offering, to make atonement for the Levites. [13]Have the Levites stand in front of Aaron and his sons and then present them as a wave offering to the LORD. [14]In this way you are to set the Levites apart from the other Israelites, and the Levites will be mine.

[15]"After you have purified the Levites and presented them as a wave offering, they are to come to do their work at the Tent of Meeting. [16]They are the Israelites who are to be given wholly to me. I have taken them as my own in place of the firstborn, the first male offspring from every Israelite woman. [17]Every firstborn male in Israel, whether man or animal, is mine. When I struck down all the firstborn in Egypt, I set them apart for myself. [18]And I have taken the Levites in place of all the firstborn sons in Israel. [19]Of all the Israelites, I have given the Levites as gifts to Aaron and his sons to do the work at the Tent of Meeting on behalf of the Israelites and to make atonement for them so that no plague will strike the Israelites when they go near the sanctuary."

[20]Moses, Aaron and the whole Israelite community did with the Levites just as the LORD commanded Moses. [21]The Levites purified

---

8:10 lay their hands. Today we still have the tradition of laying our hands on someone when we pray for them or when we set them apart for special service. This action had an extra layer of meaning for the Israelites. It was a symbol that the priests represented the Israelites. It was almost like giving power of attorney in a spiritual sense.

8:16 firstborn. Once again, there is a reference to the Passover, the last plague in Egypt. The firstborn of the Israelites were spared, and now the Levites committed themselves to God in a spiritual sense (in lieu of the gift God spared).

8:19 gifts. There was a definite chain of command among the Hebrews. Aaron and the priests were most responsible. God gave them the rest of the Levites to help accomplish the task of maintaining the tabernacle. **no plague.** The Levites and their work protected the Hebrews.

8:20 just as the LORD commanded. So far so good in terms of the Hebrews' obedience. For all Moses' best efforts, though, the story of Numbers is a story of God's people not honoring God or his commands.

themselves and washed their clothes. Then Aaron presented them as
a wave offering before the LORD and made atonement for them to
purify them. 22After that, the Levites came to do their work at the Tent
of Meeting under the supervision of Aaron and his sons. They did
with the Levites just as the LORD commanded Moses.
23The LORD said to Moses, 24"This applies to the Levites: Men
twenty-five years old or more shall come to take part in the work at
the Tent of Meeting, 25but at the age of fifty, they must retire from
their regular service and work no longer. 26They may assist their
brothers in performing their duties at the Tent of Meeting, but they
themselves must not do the work. This, then, is how you are to assign
the responsibilities of the Levites."

The Passover

9 The LORD spoke to Moses in the Desert of Sinai in the first month
of the second year after they came out of Egypt. He said, 2"Have
the Israelites celebrate the Passover at the appointed time. 3Celebrate
it at the appointed time, at twilight on the fourteenth day of this
month, in accordance with all its rules and regulations."
4So Moses told the Israelites to celebrate the Passover, 5and they
did so in the Desert of Sinai at twilight on the fourteenth day of the
first month. The Israelites did everything just as the LORD commanded Moses.
6But some of them could not celebrate the Passover on that day
because they were ceremonially unclean on account of a dead body.
So they came to Moses and Aaron that same day 7and said to Moses,
"We have become unclean because of a dead body, but why should
we be kept from presenting the LORD's offering with the other Israelites at the appointed time?"
8Moses answered them, "Wait until I find out what the LORD commands concerning you."
9Then the LORD said to Moses, 10"Tell the Israelites: 'When any of
you or your descendants are unclean because of a dead body or are
away on a journey, they may still celebrate the LORD's Passover.
11They are to celebrate it on the fourteenth day of the second month
at twilight. They are to eat the lamb, together with unleavened bread
and bitter herbs. 12They must not leave any of it till morning or break
any of its bones. When they celebrate the Passover, they must follow
all the regulations. 13But if a man who is ceremonially clean and not
on a journey fails to celebrate the Passover, that person must be cut

OPEN 1. Can you remember a time when you were away on a journey and could not celebrate a traditional family time, like Christmas? What were the circumstances? **2.** What is your favorite family celebration?

STUDY All of the Israelites were expected to celebrate the Passover at the appointed time. However, the reality was that some could not. **1.** When did the Israelites first celebrate the Passover (Ex. 12)? When was it to be celebrated this time (v. 3)? **2.** Why was it important for the people to celebrate the Passover according to all the rules and regulations? Do you think God cares whether or not his people follow his rules? Why or why not? **3.** Who felt "left out" of this Passover celebration? What did Moses say he would do about it (v. 8)? Why is it important to find out what the Lord wants? **4.** What is said about the character of God by him allowing "an exception to the rule"? What would happen to a person who tried to falsely take advantage of this exception?

APPLY 1. Do you and your church have a rigid attitude about matters of faith and worship, or

8:24–25 retire. This forced retirement system insured that the Levites gave God their prime years of service and that no holding system kept ineffective workers on the job.

8:26 assist. The older Levites were not kept from the work they had come to love. Indeed, they had opportunity to mentor younger men.

9:1–14 These instructions about the Passover made provision for those who could not keep the Passover on schedule, and for those who chose not to.

9:7 kept from presenting. The Israelites considered the Passover an honor and a joy, not a burden.

9:10 God recognizes practical life problems. God wanted holiness without compromise from his people, but on day-to-day matters, God's mercy and flexibility were evident.

9:12 break any of its bones. When Moses had prepared the people for the Passover, he had instructed them to roast a lamb, but not to break any of its bones (Ex. 12:43–51). This was to be in effect whenever the Israelites celebrated the Passover annually. The instruction was repeated here in Numbers as a reminder to the people. In the New Testament, the Passover lamb was a symbol of Christ. Jesus, the Lamb of God (John 1:29), had died to save people from their sins. Like the Passover lambs, none of Jesus' bones were broken (John 19:36).

9:13 fails to celebrate. If someone did not take part in the Passover, he was, in effect, spitting on God's provision for his people, which was an act of extreme disrespect.

can you be flexible? **2.** How might being too rigid or too flexible hinder your relationship with God? Hinder others in their relationship with God?

OPEN 1. Growing up, how many times did your family move? **2.** When you are lost, are you more likely to stop and ask directions or keep looking until you find your way?

STUDY From the time Israel left Egypt and entered the wilderness, God showed them his presence by a special cloud. One year later, when Israel set up the tabernacle—which housed the Ark of the Covenant—the presence of the Lord settled over the tabernacle in the form of that same cloud. What do you think your reaction would have been to the cloud? What would this cloud do for you?

APPLY 1. What is the "cloud" that God uses in your life today to give you direction? **2.** Where is the cloud directing you today?

OPEN What does the sound of a trumpet remind you of: Revelry? A horse race? Charge? High school band? Other?

STUDY God ordered the sound of the trumpet to signal the various movements of the people. **1.** What are the various signals of the trumpet here? How might the people get confused as to the meaning of a trumpet blast? **2.** What feelings do you think the various signals created in the people? **3.** What does your church use to help coordinate the movement of people?

off from his people because he did not present the LORD's offering at
the appointed time. That man will bear the consequences of his sin.
14" 'An alien living among you who wants to celebrate the LORD's
Passover must do so in accordance with its rules and regulations. You
must have the same regulations for the alien and the native-born.' "

The Cloud Above the Tabernacle

15On the day the tabernacle, the Tent of the Testimony, was set up,
the cloud covered it. From evening till morning the cloud above the
tabernacle looked like fire. 16That is how it continued to be; the cloud
covered it, and at night it looked like fire. 17Whenever the cloud lifted
from above the Tent, the Israelites set out; wherever the cloud settled,
the Israelites encamped. 18At the LORD's command the Israelites set
out, and at his command they encamped. As long as the cloud stayed
over the tabernacle, they remained in camp. 19When the cloud
remained over the tabernacle a long time, the Israelites obeyed the
LORD's order and did not set out. 20Sometimes the cloud was over the
tabernacle only a few days; at the LORD's command they would
encamp, and then at his command they would set out. 21Sometimes
the cloud stayed only from evening till morning, and when it lifted in
the morning, they set out. Whether by day or by night, whenever the
cloud lifted, they set out. 22Whether the cloud stayed over the tabernacle for two days or a month or a year, the Israelites would remain in
camp and not set out; but when it lifted, they would set out. 23At the
LORD's command they encamped, and at the LORD's command they set
out. They obeyed the LORD's order, in accordance with his command
through Moses.

The Silver Trumpets

10 The LORD said to Moses: 2"Make two trumpets of hammered
silver, and use them for calling the community together and
for having the camps set out. 3When both are sounded, the whole
community is to assemble before you at the entrance to the Tent of
Meeting. 4If only one is sounded, the leaders—the heads of the clans
of Israel—are to assemble before you. 5When a trumpet blast is
sounded, the tribes camping on the east are to set out. 6At the sounding of a second blast, the camps on the south are to set out. The blast
will be the signal for setting out. 7To gather the assembly, blow the
trumpets, but not with the same signal.
8"The sons of Aaron, the priests, are to blow the trumpets. This is
to be a lasting ordinance for you and the generations to come. 9When

---

9:14 alien living among you. A foreigner must not only submit to dietary rules and daily rituals but must convert and be circumcised.

9:15 the cloud. The cloud had been God's signal to move camp during the wilderness wanderings. Now at the *completion of the tabernacle*—God's formal house—the cloud moved there.

9:18 at his command. The Hebrews followed a personal God—one who interacted with them and provided daily guidance—not a superstitious, arbitrary apparition.

9:23 in accordance ... through Moses. We may well imagine that the cloud was a pillow-like white puff that everyone could see, but Moses still had to interpret the meaning of the cloud's movement. The people needed to trust that Moses heard and saw God's will; and that his leadership was God's design and purpose.

10:2 trumpets. These trumpets were probably long and straight, without valves to push or tubes doubled back and twisted around.

10:3–7 signal. This was an ancient intercom system. Just as we learn to distinguish between the tones and whistles of our computers, these people learned the different sounds of trumpets. In this way, with no electricity for speakers, Moses could coordinate the movements of the people.

you go into battle in your own land against an enemy who is oppressing you, sound a blast on the trumpets. Then you will be remembered
by the LORD your God and rescued from your enemies. [10]Also at your
times of rejoicing—your appointed feasts and New Moon festivals—
you are to sound the trumpets over your burnt offerings and fellowship offerings,[a] and they will be a memorial for you before your God.
I am the LORD your God."

The Israelites Leave Sinai

[11]On the twentieth day of the second month of the second year, the
cloud lifted from above the tabernacle of the Testimony. [12]Then the
Israelites set out from the Desert of Sinai and traveled from place to
place until the cloud came to rest in the Desert of Paran. [13]They set
out, this first time, at the LORD's command through Moses.

[14]The divisions of the camp of Judah went first, under their standard. Nahshon son of Amminadab was in command. [15]Nethanel son
of Zuar was over the division of the tribe of Issachar, [16]and Eliab son
of Helon was over the division of the tribe of Zebulun. [17]Then the
tabernacle was taken down, and the Gershonites and Merarites, who
carried it, set out.

[18]The divisions of the camp of Reuben went next, under their standard. Elizur son of Shedeur was in command. [19]Shelumiel son of
Zurishaddai was over the division of the tribe of Simeon, [20]and
Eliasaph son of Deuel was over the division of the tribe of Gad.
[21]Then the Kohathites set out, carrying the holy things. The tabernacle was to be set up before they arrived.

[22]The divisions of the camp of Ephraim went next, under their standard. Elishama son of Ammihud was in command. [23]Gamaliel son of
Pedahzur was over the division of the tribe of Manasseh, [24]and
Abidan son of Gideoni was over the division of the tribe of Benjamin.
[25]Finally, as the rear guard for all the units, the divisions of the
camp of Dan set out, under their standard. Ahiezer son of Ammishaddai was in command. [26]Pagiel son of Ocran was over the division of
the tribe of Asher, [27]and Ahira son of Enan was over the division of
the tribe of Naphtali. [28]This was the order of march for the Israelite
divisions as they set out.

[29]Now Moses said to Hobab son of Reuel the Midianite, Moses'
father-in-law, "We are setting out for the place about which the LORD
said, 'I will give it to you.' Come with us and we will treat you well,
for the LORD has promised good things to Israel."

[30]He answered, "No, I will not go; I am going back to my own land
and my own people."

[a]10 Traditionally *peace offerings*

APPLY 1. How does God get your attention? **2.** How do you feel about his direction in your life right now?

OPEN 1. When was the last time you took a trip with a group of people? How organized were you? **2.** Do you like to travel? To hike? To explore? Explain.

STUDY It is time for Israel to set out on their journey. As they went, everyone did their job, fell in line, and followed the cloud. **1.** What impresses you about the organization of this great multitude of people? What do you think were some of the logistical matters they had to consider on such a journey? **2.** What was the significance of the order in which the tribes lined up for the march? Would you rather have been first or last, or perhaps in the middle? Why? **3.** Why did Moses want Hobab to come along on the journey (v. 31)? Who was Hobab (v. 29)? How would his guidance harmonize with the guidance of God by means of the cloud? Not being an Israelite, what opposition do you think he might have encountered from the people, if any? **4.** What is the meaning of Moses' words of praise related to the movement of the ark (vv. 35–36)? **5.** What do you think was the mood of the people as they set out? **6.** Do you think the marching instructions made the people feel more or less confident in Moses' leadership?

APPLY 1. Is it easy for you to trust the Lord to guide you into an unknown future, or do you have to know what's ahead? **2.** What will help you trust God more for guidance in your life?

10:10 sound the trumpets. Even today, we are familiar with musical instruments being used to introduce services and special events. These trumpets were used to invoke and celebrate God's very presence among his people.

10:11–28 This passage is a record of the Hebrews' departure from Sinai.

10:11 second year. The Hebrews had been at Sinai for eleven months. That means it had taken them three months to get there. Upon their departure, described in verse 11 and following, it should have taken them only a few months to get to the border of the Promised Land. So why did they wander in the desert for forty years? That is precisely what the book of Numbers is about.

10:14 standard. This was a banner or flag that represented a family and was used to keep the thousands who were marching in organized groups.

10:29 Hobab. Moses' brother-in-law (his wife, Zipporah's, brother). **Reuel.** Another name for Jethro, Moses' father-in-law, who gave Moses administrative advice (Ex. 18:13–14).

31 But Moses said, "Please do not leave us. You know where we
should camp in the desert, and you can be our eyes. 32 If you come
with us, we will share with you whatever good things the LORD
gives us."

33 So they set out from the mountain of the LORD and traveled for
three days. The ark of the covenant of the LORD went before them
during those three days to find them a place to rest. 34 The cloud of
the LORD was over them by day when they set out from the camp.

35 Whenever the ark set out, Moses said,

"Rise up, O LORD!
May your enemies be scattered;
may your foes flee before you."

36 Whenever it came to rest, he said,

"Return, O LORD,
to the countless thousands of Israel."

Fire From the LORD

11 Now the people complained about their hardships in the
hearing of the LORD, and when he heard them his anger was
aroused. Then fire from the LORD burned among them and consumed
some of the outskirts of the camp. 2 When the people cried out to
Moses, he prayed to the LORD and the fire died down. 3 So that place
was called Taberah,[a] because fire from the LORD had burned among
them.

Quail From the LORD

4 The rabble with them began to crave other food, and again the
Israelites started wailing and said, "If only we had meat to eat! 5 We
remember the fish we ate in Egypt at no cost—also the cucumbers,
melons, leeks, onions and garlic. 6 But now we have lost our appetite;
we never see anything but this manna!"

7 The manna was like coriander seed and looked like resin. 8 The
people went around gathering it, and then ground it in a handmill or
crushed it in a mortar. They cooked it in a pot or made it into cakes.
And it tasted like something made with olive oil. 9 When the dew settled on the camp at night, the manna also came down.

10 Moses heard the people of every family wailing, each at the

[a] *3 Taberah means burning.*

OPEN 1. What was your favorite candy when you were a kid? **2.** What did you do as a kid when you didn't get what you wanted?

STUDY God had cared for the Israelites in the wilderness, including providing manna to eat, but some of the people were not satisfied—they wanted meat. After only a few days in the wilderness the Israelites' unbelief began to show as they complained, even wished they were back in Egypt where they had plenty to eat. **1.** What was the real complaint of the Israelites? If you had been in the group, would you have joined in with the complaining, or would you have tried to get others to see the blessings of the Lord? How do you react to others when they complain? **2.** It wasn't just meat the Israelites craved. What other tasty things did they miss (v. 5)? Do you think they really lost their appetite, or were they just complaining? How would you have prepared a tasty dish of manna?

10:31 You know. Evidently Hobab knew the desert and could help the Hebrews in their crossing. According to Judges 1:16, he did indeed travel with the Hebrews because his descendants were listed among those in the Promised Land.

10:35–36 the ark. Because of the *fanfare* around the ark—the most important symbol of God's presence—the people had a constant reminder of God's leadership and care.

10:35 Psalm 68 opens with this call.

11:1 in the hearing of the LORD. Certainly God could hear any complaining that was going on. This phrase probably meant that the people were complaining openly to each other rather than quietly and privately.

11:4 rabble. The meaning of this word is "mixed company." It probably applies to non-Hebrews who came out of Egypt in the Exodus. Perhaps they were servants or in-laws. **crave other food.** The miraculous manna was tasty, but it could not match the variety of food available in Egypt. To complain about the food, though, was to despise God's provision.

11:5–6 lost our appetite. Obviously they had not lost their appetite. They had sharpened it.

11:7 manna. The name "manna" means "What is it?" **coriander seed.** A herb in the carrot family used for cooking and for medicine. **resin.** If you look "resin" up in a thesaurus you will find the following words: gum, pine tar, tree sap, sticky stuff and crude rubber.

11:10 God was angry, while Moses was troubled. Though Moses was the visible leader, God was most agitated by the Hebrews' betrayal of trust.

entrance to his tent. The LORD became exceedingly angry, and Moses
was troubled. 11He asked the LORD, "Why have you brought this trouble on your servant? What have I done to displease you that you put
the burden of all these people on me? 12Did I conceive all these
people? Did I give them birth? Why do you tell me to carry them in my
arms, as a nurse carries an infant, to the land you promised on oath
to their forefathers? 13Where can I get meat for all these people? They
keep wailing to me, 'Give us meat to eat!' 14I cannot carry all these
people by myself; the burden is too heavy for me. 15If this is how you
are going to treat me, put me to death right now—if I have found
favor in your eyes—and do not let me face my own ruin."

16The LORD said to Moses: "Bring me seventy of Israel's elders who
are known to you as leaders and officials among the people. Have
them come to the Tent of Meeting, that they may stand there with
you. 17I will come down and speak with you there, and I will take of
the Spirit that is on you and put the Spirit on them. They will help you
carry the burden of the people so that you will not have to carry it
alone.

18"Tell the people: 'Consecrate yourselves in preparation for tomorrow, when you will eat meat. The LORD heard you when you wailed,
"If only we had meat to eat! We were better off in Egypt!" Now the
LORD will give you meat, and you will eat it. 19You will not eat it for
just one day, or two days, or five, ten or twenty days, 20but for a whole
month—until it comes out of your nostrils and you loathe it—
because you have rejected the LORD, who is among you, and have
wailed before him, saying, "Why did we ever leave Egypt?" ' "

21But Moses said, "Here I am among six hundred thousand men on
foot, and you say, 'I will give them meat to eat for a whole month!'
22Would they have enough if flocks and herds were slaughtered for
them? Would they have enough if all the fish in the sea were caught
for them?"

23The LORD answered Moses, "Is the LORD's arm too short? You will
now see whether or not what I say will come true for you."

24So Moses went out and told the people what the LORD had said.
He brought together seventy of their elders and had them stand
around the Tent. 25Then the LORD came down in the cloud and spoke
with him, and he took of the Spirit that was on him and put the Spirit
on the seventy elders. When the Spirit rested on them, they prophesied, but they did not do so again.[a]

[a]25 Or *prophesied and continued to do so*

3. Why did God get angry with the people? How did Moses react? What should this teach us about our attitudes? **4.** Who did Moses blame for all this trouble? How did he express his lack of faith? What ultimate effect did this burden have on Moses? Where in Moses' reactions can you identify with him? **5.** How did God respond? What do you learn about God from his response to these complaining people and this whining leader? **6.** Why did God place his Spirit on 70 of the leaders of Israel? How do you think he places his Spirit on his leaders today? **7.** Did Moses react to the announcement about the meat with unquestioning faith or with questions of unbelief? Do you need God to explain everything to you before you are ready to obey? **8.** When God said he would make them eat the quail for a month, do you see: Irony? A sense of humor in God? Anger? A desire to teach the people a valuable lesson? After blessing the people with meat to eat, why did God send them a plague (v. 33)?

APPLY 1. What do you have to complain about to God? Do you think he cares? **2.** What do you need to do to strengthen your trust in God? How can this group help?

11:11–15 Moses was at the end of his rope. He was understandably distraught with his people. So he went to the only one who had any power to help, God himself.

11:12 Did I give them birth? Moses raises the ultimate question of responsibility. In his frustration he wanted to pass the buck, and for Moses, there was only one person to pass to.

11:16–34 God helped Moses organize administratively much like Jethro did earlier. Judges would help Moses settle disputes (Ex. 18:13–27).

11:18 better off in Egypt. This was the heart of the Hebrews' complaint. Yes, they wanted meat, but more than that, they doubted God's provision for them. They were saying, in effect, that they would have been better if Moses had left them alone.

11:20 rejected the LORD. Moses did not soften his words with the people. Their sin had to do with ingratitude and a lack of faith, not just an appetite for meat.

11:21 Moses' response to God was similar to the disciples' response to Jesus when he told them to feed 5,000 hungry people on the hillside (John 6:5–9).

11:23 the LORD's arm. God asked Moses a question that tested his faith, "Do you not think I am able? Do you doubt me like these people do?" Even today, it is still far too easy to lose sight of what a big God we serve.

26 However, two men, whose names were Eldad and Medad, had
remained in the camp. They were listed among the elders, but did not
go out to the Tent. Yet the Spirit also rested on them, and they prophesied in the camp. 27 A young man ran and told Moses, "Eldad and
Medad are prophesying in the camp."
28 Joshua son of Nun, who had been Moses' aide since youth, spoke
up and said, "Moses, my lord, stop them!"
29 But Moses replied, "Are you jealous for my sake? I wish that all the
LORD's people were prophets and that the LORD would put his Spirit on
them!" 30 Then Moses and the elders of Israel returned to the camp.
31 Now a wind went out from the LORD and drove quail in from the
sea. It brought them[a] down all around the camp to about three feet[b]
above the ground, as far as a day's walk in any direction. 32 All that
day and night and all the next day the people went out and gathered
quail. No one gathered less than ten homers.[c] Then they spread them
out all around the camp. 33 But while the meat was still between their
teeth and before it could be consumed, the anger of the LORD burned
against the people, and he struck them with a severe plague. 34 Therefore the place was named Kibroth Hattaavah,[d] because there they
buried the people who had craved other food.
35 From Kibroth Hattaavah the people traveled to Hazeroth and
stayed there.

Miriam and Aaron Oppose Moses

12 Miriam and Aaron began to talk against Moses because of his
Cushite wife, for he had married a Cushite. 2 "Has the LORD
spoken only through Moses?" they asked. "Hasn't he also spoken
through us?" And the LORD heard this.
3 (Now Moses was a very humble man, more humble than anyone
else on the face of the earth.)
4 At once the LORD said to Moses, Aaron and Miriam, "Come out to
the Tent of Meeting, all three of you." So the three of them came out.
5 Then the LORD came down in a pillar of cloud; he stood at the entrance to the Tent and summoned Aaron and Miriam. When both of
them stepped forward, 6 he said, "Listen to my words:

"When a prophet of the LORD is among you,
I reveal myself to him in visions,

[a]31 Or *They flew* [b]31 Hebrew *two cubits* (about 1 meter) [c]32 That is, probably about 60 bushels (about 2.2 kiloliters) [d]34 *Kibroth Hattaavah* means *graves of craving.*

OPEN 1. As a kid, how could you tell you were in big trouble with your dad? **2.** Can you remember a time you had to go to the principal's office? What happened?

STUDY Miriam and Aaron—Moses' sister and brother—think Moses has done wrong and is still being blessed by God, so they become jealous. In their jealousy, they challenge the authority of Moses to be God's spokesman. Bad move! **1.** Do you think Miriam's and Aaron's real problem with Moses' wife was: They just didn't like her? They were offended that she didn't share their beliefs? They were prejudice because she was of another race? It was just a smoke screen for their jealousy of Moses? **2.** What did Miriam and Aaron actually

11:28 Joshua. Joshua was loyal to Moses and protective of him. He later succeeded Moses as leader of the people.

11:31–32 three feet. The wind that God sent forced the quail to fly three feet above the ground—a perfect height to be easily captured by the people.

12:1 Miriam and Aaron. Moses' sister, who hid him as a baby in the river, and his brother, the high priest. **Cushite.** Cush was located in what is now southern Egypt, Sudan and northern Ethiopia. The Cushites were not a people that God had warned the Hebrews to shun, yet this wife seems to have raised some issues for Moses' siblings.

12:2 only through Moses. Miriam and Aaron felt insecure and displaced, perhaps due to the seventy elders that Moses had just ordained, the new wife he had married or simple jealousy. Nevertheless, God penalized this ugly attitude.

12:3 a very humble man. Would a truly humble man write this about himself? Either God inspired Moses to affirm his humility or a later editor added this phrase.

12:4 At once. This clause communicates that the Lord knows and deals with the sin that takes place on earth. God called Miriam, Aaron and Moses into the Tent of Meeting to address the jealous dispute that Moses' brother and sister had with him.

12:5 summoned Aaron and Miriam. This would be the first time that any Hebrew besides Moses would hear from God face-to-face.

12:6–8 God seems to be speaking to Moses in a uniquely direct way. Perhaps

I speak to him in dreams.
[7] But this is not true of my servant Moses;
he is faithful in all my house.
[8] With him I speak face to face,
clearly and not in riddles;
he sees the form of the LORD.
Why then were you not afraid
to speak against my servant Moses?"

[9] The anger of the LORD burned against them, and he left them.
[10] When the cloud lifted from above the Tent, there stood Miriam—
leprous,[a] like snow. Aaron turned toward her and saw that she had
leprosy; [11] and he said to Moses, "Please, my lord, do not hold against
us the sin we have so foolishly committed. [12] Do not let her be like a
stillborn infant coming from its mother's womb with its flesh half
eaten away."
[13] So Moses cried out to the LORD, "O God, please heal her!"
[14] The LORD replied to Moses, "If her father had spit in her face,
would she not have been in disgrace for seven days? Confine her outside the camp for seven days; after that she can be brought back."
[15] So Miriam was confined outside the camp for seven days, and the
people did not move on till she was brought back.
[16] After that, the people left Hazeroth and encamped in the Desert of
Paran.

Exploring Canaan

13 The LORD said to Moses, [2] "Send some men to explore the
land of Canaan, which I am giving to the Israelites. From
each ancestral tribe send one of its leaders."
[3] So at the LORD's command Moses sent them out from the Desert
of Paran. All of them were leaders of the Israelites. [4] These are their
names:

from the tribe of Reuben, Shammua son of Zaccur;
[5] from the tribe of Simeon, Shaphat son of Hori;
[6] from the tribe of Judah, Caleb son of Jephunneh;
[7] from the tribe of Issachar, Igal son of Joseph;
[8] from the tribe of Ephraim, Hoshea son of Nun;
[9] from the tribe of Benjamin, Palti son of Raphu;
[10] from the tribe of Zebulun, Gaddiel son of Sodi;
[11] from the tribe of Manasseh (a tribe of Joseph), Gaddi son of Susi;
[12] from the tribe of Dan, Ammiel son of Gemalli;
[13] from the tribe of Asher, Sethur son of Michael;

[a] *10* The Hebrew word was used for various diseases affecting the skin—not necessarily leprosy.

challenge when they challenged the authority of Moses? How do you think you would have felt if you had been Moses? **3.** In essence, what did God say to Miriam and Aaron? Do you think you would have just stood there dumfounded, or do you think you would have said "Yes, sir!"? **4.** Why do you think God punished Miriam but not Aaron? What do you think kept God from just taking their lives? **5.** What do you learn about Moses when he pleaded for Miriam's healing after she had mistreated him?

APPLY 1. What particular problem of jealousy do you have at the moment? Do you need to repent? **2.** How do you show your respect for God's leaders? How can you improve in that regard?

OPEN 1. What do you like to collect on a road trip to show others when you get home? **2.** As a child, what kind of report cards did you generally bring home from school?

STUDY At the request of the people (Deut. 1:21–23), the Lord instructs Moses to select a representative from each of the twelve tribes to spy out the land of Canaan. The report from ten of the spies was good news and bad news—the land is great, but there's no way we can conquer it. **1.** How do you think the Israelites might have felt at this moment when they were about to realize their dream of a homeland? **2.** Why do you think it was necessary to send spies into the land? Didn't the people trust God? How do you think you would have approached this matter? **3.** In the list of the names of the spies, which are memorable? What kind of

no one since Adam had heard God's voice so clearly articulated.

12:8 Why then were you not afraid? To question Moses is to question God.

12:10 leprous. Miriam's leprosy meant the loss of everything. She would now live outside the community, no longer with prestige or position. She went from "first sister" to a life of shame.

12:11 foolishly committed. Aaron was self-aware enough to realize what a mistake he and Miriam had made. And he admitted it.

12:14–15 confined. God responded to Aaron and Miriam's remorse, but Miriam was still treated as one who needed to be purified. **did not move on.** The whole community had to wait until Miriam's penalty was paid.

13:2 From each ancestral tribe. This effort was organized much as was the census at the beginning of the book of Numbers. Selecting one from each tribe would give credibility and unity to their report.

spy would you have been? **4.** What were the spies looking for in the land (vv. 17–20)? What did they find (vv. 23–25)? How would you have reacted if you were one of the spies? **5.** What report did the majority of the spies give? With all their organization, the size of their army, and the success they had already experienced by the power of the Lord, why do you think most of the spies were pessimistic about their chances for victory? What report did Joshua and Caleb give? Why do you think their report is more optimistic? If you had been a spy, which group would you have stood with? Why? **6.** What do you think the phrase "we seemed like grasshoppers in our own eyes" reveals?

APPLY 1. What giants (challenges bigger than you) are you facing in your life right now? **2.** Do you have trouble trusting God when the odds seem to be against you? What will help you trust in God more?

14 from the tribe of Naphtali, Nahbi son of Vophsi;
15 from the tribe of Gad, Geuel son of Maki.

16 These are the names of the men Moses sent to explore the land.
(Moses gave Hoshea son of Nun the name Joshua.)
17 When Moses sent them to explore Canaan, he said, "Go up
through the Negev and on into the hill country. 18 See what the land is
like and whether the people who live there are strong or weak, few or
many. 19 What kind of land do they live in? Is it good or bad? What
kind of towns do they live in? Are they unwalled or fortified? 20 How is
the soil? Is it fertile or poor? Are there trees on it or not? Do your best
to bring back some of the fruit of the land." (It was the season for the
first ripe grapes.)
21 So they went up and explored the land from the Desert of Zin as
far as Rehob, toward Lebo[a] Hamath. 22 They went up through the
Negev and came to Hebron, where Ahiman, Sheshai and Talmai, the
descendants of Anak, lived. (Hebron had been built seven years
before Zoan in Egypt.) 23 When they reached the Valley of Eshcol,[b] they
cut off a branch bearing a single cluster of grapes. Two of them
carried it on a pole between them, along with some pomegranates
and figs. 24 That place was called the Valley of Eshcol because of the
cluster of grapes the Israelites cut off there. 25 At the end of forty days
they returned from exploring the land.

Report on the Exploration

26 They came back to Moses and Aaron and the whole Israelite community at Kadesh in the Desert of Paran. There they reported to them
and to the whole assembly and showed them the fruit of the land.
27 They gave Moses this account: "We went into the land to which you
sent us, and it does flow with milk and honey! Here is its fruit. 28 But
the people who live there are powerful, and the cities are fortified and
very large. We even saw descendants of Anak there. 29 The Amalekites
live in the Negev; the Hittites, Jebusites and Amorites live in the hill
country; and the Canaanites live near the sea and along the Jordan."
30 Then Caleb silenced the people before Moses and said, "We
should go up and take possession of the land, for we can certainly
do it."
31 But the men who had gone up with him said, "We can't attack
those people; they are stronger than we are." 32 And they spread

[a]21 Or *toward the entrance to* [b]23 *Eshcol* means *cluster*; also in verse 24.

13:17–20 strong or weak, few or many. Moses had very explicit instructions for the group of spies who were being sent to Canaan. The spies were not only to bring back a report of the land itself but also on the type of people who occupied the land.

13:21 This journey involved 250 miles *each way.* It was probably the most likely path for success in battle, rather than merely for exploration.

13:23 cluster of grapes. Two men are normally not needed to carry a cluster of grapes. The fact that these explorers needed a pole to carry the weight of the grapes showed the bounty of the land.

13:26–29 It was right for the spies to give an accurate report of both the prosperity and the dangers ahead. Their sin was not in the accuracy of their report but that they did not trust God to carry them through difficulties.

13:30 Caleb. Only Caleb is mentioned here, but we know that Joshua also felt they should trust God and enter the land of Canaan because ten spies brought a negative report and there were twelve spies in all.

13:32 a bad report. The people had endured hardships (and not happily) to come to this place God had promised them, only to hear that the Canaanites could easily destroy them. Their sense of disappointment reflected a big lack of faith. God had brought them this far only to forsake them, was the word buzzing around camp. From the time of Abraham, God had required that his people live by faith. But this cynical

among the Israelites a bad report about the land they had explored.
They said, "The land we explored devours those living in it. All the
people we saw there are of great size. 33We saw the Nephilim there
(the descendants of Anak come from the Nephilim). We seemed like
grasshoppers in our own eyes, and we looked the same to them."

The People Rebel

14 That night all the people of the community raised their voices
and wept aloud. 2All the Israelites grumbled against Moses
and Aaron, and the whole assembly said to them, "If only we had died
in Egypt! Or in this desert! 3Why is the LORD bringing us to this land
only to let us fall by the sword? Our wives and children will be taken
as plunder. Wouldn't it be better for us to go back to Egypt?" 4And
they said to each other, "We should choose a leader and go back to
Egypt."

5Then Moses and Aaron fell facedown in front of the whole Israelite
assembly gathered there. 6Joshua son of Nun and Caleb son of
Jephunneh, who were among those who had explored the land, tore
their clothes 7and said to the entire Israelite assembly, "The land we
passed through and explored is exceedingly good. 8If the LORD is
pleased with us, he will lead us into that land, a land flowing with
milk and honey, and will give it to us. 9Only do not rebel against the
LORD. And do not be afraid of the people of the land, because we will
swallow them up. Their protection is gone, but the LORD is with us.
Do not be afraid of them."

10But the whole assembly talked about stoning them. Then the
glory of the LORD appeared at the Tent of Meeting to all the Israelites.
11The LORD said to Moses, "How long will these people treat me with
contempt? How long will they refuse to believe in me, in spite of all
the miraculous signs I have performed among them? 12I will strike
them down with a plague and destroy them, but I will make you into
a nation greater and stronger than they."

13Moses said to the LORD, "Then the Egyptians will hear about it! By
your power you brought these people up from among them. 14And
they will tell the inhabitants of this land about it. They have already
heard that you, O LORD, are with these people and that you, O LORD,
have been seen face to face, that your cloud stays over them, and that
you go before them in a pillar of cloud by day and a pillar of fire by
night. 15If you put these people to death all at one time, the nations
who have heard this report about you will say, 16'The LORD was not

OPEN 1. Describe a "rebel" you know. **2.** Can you remember when you joined a group in rebellion against something or someone?

STUDY After the bad report had been given by the spies, the people wept all night, not so much because of the bad report, but because they regretted leaving Egypt in the first place. They were so distressed over the matter that they rose up in rebellion against Moses and Aaron. **1.** What about the report caused the people to not only rebel against the leaders, but begin to wish they could have just died in Egypt? Is this a sign of: Lack of faith? Fear? Discouragement? Just being too tired to go on? **2.** What was the significance of Moses and Aaron falling on their faces before the people (v. 5)? **3.** What is the point of the statement of Joshua and Caleb (vv. 7–9)? If you had been in the crowd, would Joshua and Caleb have encouraged you, or would you have gone along with the majority? Why? **4.** What is God's response to the rebellion of the people (vv. 10–12)? **5.** What is the reasoning behind Moses' plea to save the lives of the Israelites (vv. 13–19)?

APPLY 1. How have the circumstances of your life tempted you to question whether or not God really cares for you? **2.** Who do you know that has great faith (like Joshua and Caleb) that you can follow and be encouraged by?

---

report rattled the people to doubt and dismay.

14:1–2 wept aloud. This response fits the pattern of anguish and doubt that had characterized the people from the start of the journey. They succumbed to fear of the unknown instead of trusting in the grace and power of the God who was directing them. At times, these faithless voyagers longed for even a return to slavery in Egypt.

14:3–4 choose a leader ... go back. To them the obstacles seemed too high to overcome and move forward, so they called for a new leader. People cannot follow God without faith.

14:9 the LORD is with us. Joshua and Caleb affirmed the truth that should have blotted out all objections. God's power would make the difference in the struggle.

14:10 glory of the LORD. God makes himself known to all people. They were fuming and fussing, not about the leadership of Moses and Aaron, but against God himself.

14:11 the miraculous signs. People of all times want signs from God. Yet signs do not create faith but only affirm the faith already there. In this case, God was astonished at the low level of faith, despite all he had done.

14:12 a nation greater and stronger than they. God can start over at any time he chooses. Even after all of the journey in the wilderness, God was willing to take the faithful few and still keep his promise to redeem the world.

14:13 Moses appealed to God's reputation. He seemed to care for God's glory more than for an easy life.

able to bring these people into the land he promised them on oath; so
he slaughtered them in the desert.’
17“Now may the Lord’s strength be displayed, just as you have
declared: 18‘The LORD is slow to anger, abounding in love and forgiving sin and rebellion. Yet he does not leave the guilty unpunished;
he punishes the children for the sin of the fathers to the third and
fourth generation.’ 19In accordance with your great love, forgive the
sin of these people, just as you have pardoned them from the time
they left Egypt until now.”
20The LORD replied, “I have forgiven them, as you asked. 21Neverthe-
less, as surely as I live and as surely as the glory of the LORD fills the
whole earth, 22not one of the men who saw my glory and the miraculous signs I performed in Egypt and in the desert but who disobeyed
me and tested me ten times— 23not one of them will ever see the land
I promised on oath to their forefathers. No one who has treated me
with contempt will ever see it. 24But because my servant Caleb has a
different spirit and follows me wholeheartedly, I will bring him into
the land he went to, and his descendants will inherit it. 25Since the
Amalekites and Canaanites are living in the valleys, turn back tomorrow and set out toward the desert along the route to the Red Sea.[a]”
26The LORD said to Moses and Aaron: 27“How long will this wicked
community grumble against me? I have heard the complaints of
these grumbling Israelites. 28So tell them, ‘As surely as I live, declares
the LORD, I will do to you the very things I heard you say: 29In this
desert your bodies will fall—every one of you twenty years old or
more who was counted in the census and who has grumbled against
me. 30Not one of you will enter the land I swore with uplifted hand to
make your home, except Caleb son of Jephunneh and Joshua son of
Nun. 31As for your children that you said would be taken as plunder, I
will bring them in to enjoy the land you have rejected. 32But you—
your bodies will fall in this desert. 33Your children will be shepherds
here for forty years, suffering for your unfaithfulness, until the last of
your bodies lies in the desert. 34For forty years—one year for each of
the forty days you explored the land—you will suffer for your sins and
know what it is like to have me against you.’ 35I, the LORD, have spoken, and I will surely do these things to this whole wicked community, which has banded together against me. They will meet their end in
this desert; here they will die.”
36So the men Moses had sent to explore the land, who returned
and made the whole community grumble against him by spreading a
bad report about it— 37these men responsible for spreading the bad

[a]25 Hebrew *Yam Suph;* that is, Sea of Reeds

OPEN **1.** What consequences did you suffer when you rebelled against your parents? Against school teachers? **2.** Tell of a time when you rebelled and got off “scott free.”

STUDY After the Israelites showed their lack of faith in their rebellion against Moses and Aaron, God demonstrates that consequences must follow. His patience and mercy are shown in that he repents from his plan to destroy the people, but he still expresses his anger. **1.** Why do you think God relents and does not carry out his plan to destroy the people? Do you think Moses actually changed God’s mind, or did God have “Plan B” in mind all along? How can God forgive and still let his people experience the consequences of their sin? **2.** Who would not be allowed to enter the Promised Land because of their rebellion (vv. 22–23,29–30)? Who among them would enter the Promised Land (vv. 24,30–31)? What happened to the 10 unfaithful spies (vv. 36–37)? Why is this judgment fair? Or is it? **3.** What is your reaction to the plan of some of the people to go ahead with an attack on the Promised Land without the help of God? What reasoning does Moses use to try to talk them out of making the attack (vv. 41–43)? Do you think you would have participated in this attack? Why or why not? What happened to those who made the unauthorized attack (vv. 44–45)?

14:17–19 In accordance with your great love. Moses appealed to God’s character. He knew God and had listened to his voice, so he trusted God to be true to his character.

14:22 ten. To say that the people had tested him ten times was not an exaggeration. Taken literally, the list of ten incidents of the people’s testing of God includes: Exodus 14:10–12; 15:22–24; 16:1–3; 16:19–20; 16:27–30; 17:1–4; 32:1–35; Numbers 11:1–3,4–34; and 14:3. The point is that the people had been unfaithful over and over.

14:24 Caleb. Caleb was known as a man who worshiped the Lord wholeheartedly (Josh. 14:13–14). He was one of two (Joshua was the other) who believed God would keep his promise and give the people the land (v. 9).

14:28 the very things I heard you say. The people wished that they had died in the journey (v. 2). God evidently said, “Okay, if you say so.” Thankfully, God doesn’t always answer our prayers that way. But in this case, these people had such a shortage of faith that others were given the task of conquering the land.

14:37 these men responsible. The ten men who came back with a negative report led a whole generation to die in the wilderness, including themselves.

report about the land were struck down and died of a plague before
the LORD. 38Of the men who went to explore the land, only Joshua son
of Nun and Caleb son of Jephunneh survived.
39When Moses reported this to all the Israelites, they mourned
bitterly. 40Early the next morning they went up toward the high hill
country. "We have sinned," they said. "We will go up to the place the
LORD promised."
41But Moses said, "Why are you disobeying the LORD's command?
This will not succeed! 42Do not go up, because the LORD is not with
you. You will be defeated by your enemies, 43for the Amalekites and
Canaanites will face you there. Because you have turned away from
the LORD, he will not be with you and you will fall by the sword."
44Nevertheless, in their presumption they went up toward the high
hill country, though neither Moses nor the ark of the LORD's covenant
moved from the camp. 45Then the Amalekites and Canaanites who
lived in that hill country came down and attacked them and beat
them down all the way to Hormah.

Supplementary Offerings

15 The LORD said to Moses, 2"Speak to the Israelites and say to
them: 'After you enter the land I am giving you as a home
3and you present to the LORD offerings made by fire, from the herd or
the flock, as an aroma pleasing to the LORD—whether burnt offerings
or sacrifices, for special vows or freewill offerings or festival offerings— 4then the one who brings his offering shall present to the LORD
a grain offering of a tenth of an ephah[a] of fine flour mixed with a
quarter of a hin[b] of oil. 5With each lamb for the burnt offering or the
sacrifice, prepare a quarter of a hin of wine as a drink offering.
6" 'With a ram prepare a grain offering of two-tenths of an ephah[c]
of fine flour mixed with a third of a hin[d] of oil, 7and a third of a hin of
wine as a drink offering. Offer it as an aroma pleasing to the LORD.
8" 'When you prepare a young bull as a burnt offering or sacrifice,
for a special vow or a fellowship offering[e] to the LORD, 9bring with the
bull a grain offering of three-tenths of an ephah[f] of fine flour mixed
with half a hin[g] of oil. 10Also bring half a hin of wine as a drink offering. It will be an offering made by fire, an aroma pleasing to the LORD.
11Each bull or ram, each lamb or young goat, is to be prepared in this
manner. 12Do this for each one, for as many as you prepare.
13" 'Everyone who is native-born must do these things in this way
when he brings an offering made by fire as an aroma pleasing to the
LORD. 14For the generations to come, whenever an alien or anyone

[a]4 That is, probably about 2 quarts (about 2 liters) [b]4 That is, probably about 1 quart (about 1 liter); also in verse 5 [c]6 That is, probably about 4 quarts (about 4.5 liters) [d]6 That is, probably about 1 1/4 quarts (about 1.2 liters); also in verse 7 [e]8 Traditionally *peace offering* [f]9 That is, probably about 6 quarts (about 6.5 liters) [g]9 That is, probably about 2 quarts (about 2 liters); also in verse 10

APPLY **1.** What price (consequences) are you paying now for rebellion against God? What lessons have you learned as a result? **2.** Do you think God would rather bless you or punish you? How can you receive his blessings?

OPEN **1.** If you were establishing a religion and were determining what offerings should be made, what food items would you choose for the offerings and how would they be prepared? **2.** What token of appreciation have you received which was especially meaningful to you?

STUDY Even though God had decided to prohibit the Israelites 20 years and older to enter the Promised Land, he had made a covenant with the people that one day they would enter the land. Thus, he continues to give them instructions as though they are about to enter. **1.** What change do you see from chapter 14 to chapter 15? What does this teach you about the faithfulness of God in spite of the unfaithfulness of his people? **2.** How could an offering actually be "an aroma pleasing to the Lord"? What do you have to offer that might please him in the same manner? **3.** What does it mean that the alien and the native born are the same before the Lord (v. 15)? What does this teach you about the universal nature of God? **4.** Why was it important that the part of the offering made from the ground meal be the "first" of the ground meal (v. 20)? In what way does

14:39–45 he will not be with you. The people gave the appearance of repenting but still did not put faith in the only one who could lead them to victory, and so they were defeated.

15:1–41 Because of God's judgment, the older generation would not be around to settle the Promised Land. It was time to pass down traditions to the younger crowd so they could make offerings to God.

15:2 After you enter. What would it have been like to hear this message from Moses, knowing that you would never live to see that entry? All that was left for the older Hebrew generation was to train and prepare the young.

15:3–12 These offerings were a review of earlier teachings from Leviticus, except for the drink offerings, which Paul used to illustrate his own spiritual journey (Phil. 2:17).

15:14 exactly as you do. Foreigners could worship God at the tabernacle,

God expect that which is "first" from you today?

APPLY 1. What do you give to God today that you would consider to be "an offering"? 2. What do you offer God on a continual basis in the way of worship? Do you need to worship him more?

OPEN 1. What was the last unintentional mistake you made? 2. When you were a child, did it make any difference in your punishment if, after making a mistake, you said, "But I didn't mean to"? Explain.

STUDY It was inevitable, in view of all the laws the Israelites were being given, that someone (or perhaps the whole nation) would break one of the laws unintentionally. God knew that so he instituted a sacrifice for unintentional sin, but his attitude was much different for intentional sin. 1. Why do you think a sacrifice was necessary for an unintentional sin? Why wouldn't it have been sufficient just to ignore the sin, since it was unintentional? What does this teach you about the nature of God and the need for reconciliation? 2. Why do you think this law was applied to both the alien and the native-born? 3. What was the difference in God's attitude toward intentional sin (vv. 30–31)? What difference does it make to you if someone wrongs you intentionally or unintentionally? 4. How does God's attitude toward defiant sin affect your desire to obey? 5. What do you think about the example of defiant sin—the Sabbath-breaker (vv. 32–36)? 6. What was the purpose of the tassels on the garments (vv. 39–40)? What do you have that reminds you to obey God?

APPLY 1. How do you deal with sin in your life? 2. Would you say intentional sin or unintentional sin is more of a problem for you?

---

else living among you presents an offering made by fire as an aroma pleasing to the LORD, he must do exactly as you do. [15]The community is to have the same rules for you and for the alien living among you; this is a lasting ordinance for the generations to come. You and the alien shall be the same before the LORD: [16]The same laws and regulations will apply both to you and to the alien living among you.' "

[17]The LORD said to Moses, [18]"Speak to the Israelites and say to them: 'When you enter the land to which I am taking you [19]and you eat the food of the land, present a portion as an offering to the LORD. [20]Present a cake from the first of your ground meal and present it as an offering from the threshing floor. [21]Throughout the generations to come you are to give this offering to the LORD from the first of your ground meal.

Offerings for Unintentional Sins

[22]" 'Now if you unintentionally fail to keep any of these commands the LORD gave Moses— [23]any of the LORD's commands to you through him, from the day the LORD gave them and continuing through the generations to come— [24]and if this is done unintentionally without the community being aware of it, then the whole community is to offer a young bull for a burnt offering as an aroma pleasing to the LORD, along with its prescribed grain offering and drink offering, and a male goat for a sin offering. [25]The priest is to make atonement for the whole Israelite community, and they will be forgiven, for it was not intentional and they have brought to the LORD for their wrong an offering made by fire and a sin offering. [26]The whole Israelite community and the aliens living among them will be forgiven, because all the people were involved in the unintentional wrong.

[27]" 'But if just one person sins unintentionally, he must bring a year-old female goat for a sin offering. [28]The priest is to make atonement before the LORD for the one who erred by sinning unintentionally, and when atonement has been made for him, he will be forgiven. [29]One and the same law applies to everyone who sins unintentionally, whether he is a native-born Israelite or an alien.

[30]" 'But anyone who sins defiantly, whether native-born or alien, blasphemes the LORD, and that person must be cut off from his people. [31]Because he has despised the LORD's word and broken his commands, that person must surely be cut off; his guilt remains on him.' "

The Sabbath-Breaker Put to Death

[32]While the Israelites were in the desert, a man was found gathering wood on the Sabbath day. [33]Those who found him gathering wood brought him to Moses and Aaron and the whole assembly, [34]and they kept him in custody, because it was not clear what should be done to him. [35]Then the LORD said to Moses, "The man must die. The whole assembly must stone him outside the camp." [36]So the assembly took him outside the camp and stoned him to death, as the LORD commanded Moses.

---

but they faced the same requirements as the Hebrews, including circumcision.

15:24 unintentionally. Usually this meant without premeditation. To sin is human; to plan to sin is also human. Paul addressed this same concept in Romans 7:14–20.

15:30 defiantly. The opposite of unintentional sin (v. 22). To sin defiantly is to set out to disobey God. No sacrifice covered that kind of sin. It was this kind of sin that Lucifer was accused of.

Tassels on Garments

37The LORD said to Moses, 38"Speak to the Israelites and say to
them: 'Throughout the generations to come you are to make tassels
on the corners of your garments, with a blue cord on each tassel.
39You will have these tassels to look at and so you will remember all
the commands of the LORD, that you may obey them and not prostitute yourselves by going after the lusts of your own hearts and eyes.
40Then you will remember to obey all my commands and will be
consecrated to your God. 41I am the LORD your God, who brought you
out of Egypt to be your God. I am the LORD your God.' "

Korah, Dathan and Abiram

16 Korah son of Izhar, the son of Kohath, the son of Levi, and
certain Reubenites—Dathan and Abiram, sons of Eliab, and
On son of Peleth—became insolent[a] 2and rose up against Moses.
With them were 250 Israelite men, well-known community leaders
who had been appointed members of the council. 3They came as a
group to oppose Moses and Aaron and said to them, "You have gone
too far! The whole community is holy, every one of them, and the
LORD is with them. Why then do you set yourselves above the LORD's
assembly?"
4When Moses heard this, he fell facedown. 5Then he said to Korah
and all his followers: "In the morning the LORD will show who
belongs to him and who is holy, and he will have that person come
near him. The man he chooses he will cause to come near him. 6You,
Korah, and all your followers are to do this: Take censers 7and tomorrow put fire and incense in them before the LORD. The man the LORD
chooses will be the one who is holy. You Levites have gone too far!"
8Moses also said to Korah, "Now listen, you Levites! 9Isn't it
enough for you that the God of Israel has separated you from the rest
of the Israelite community and brought you near himself to do the
work at the LORD's tabernacle and to stand before the community
and minister to them? 10He has brought you and all your fellow Levites near himself, but now you are trying to get the priesthood too.
11It is against the LORD that you and all your followers have banded
together. Who is Aaron that you should grumble against him?"
12Then Moses summoned Dathan and Abiram, the sons of Eliab.
But they said, "We will not come! 13Isn't it enough that you have
brought us up out of a land flowing with milk and honey to kill us in
the desert? And now you also want to lord it over us? 14Moreover, you
haven't brought us into a land flowing with milk and honey or given
us an inheritance of fields and vineyards. Will you gouge out the eyes
of[b] these men? No, we will not come!"

[a]1 Or *Peleth—took ⌊men⌋* [b]14 Or *you make slaves of*; or *you deceive*

OPEN 1. What natural disaster have you witnessed? How did the experience affect you? **2.** What is your favorite disaster movie: Earthquake? Hurricane? Armageddon? The River? The Perfect Storm? Tornado? Other?

STUDY In a rebellion similar to that of Aaron and Miriam (ch. 12), some of the Levites challenged Moses' authority. The results were catastrophic for the people of Israel. **1.** Who are the rebels (v. 1)? What is their complaint (vv. 2–4)? What do you think is the real issue here? Who is the rebellion really against (v. 11)? **2.** What fatal mistake in judgment did the rebels make when they asked Moses why he set himself above the Lord's assembly? Have you ever witnessed a rebellion? Did you take part? What was the result? **3.** How does Moses respond to this rebellion (vv. 5–11,16–17)? How does he plead the issue before the Lord (v. 15)? How would you have responded? **4.** Why did Dathan and Abiram refuse to appear before Moses (vv. 12–14)? Do you think they really thought Moses had failed as their leader, or were they just angry at the consequences of Israel's unbelief? **5.** What judgment did God pronounce on the rebels (v. 21)? What was Moses' and Aaron's plea in response (v. 22)? **6.** What test did Moses propose to prove the rebels (vv. 28–30)? How did God punish the people involved in the rebellion (vv. 31–35)? How do you feel about this punishment? Was it too severe? Was it fair? **7.** Why were the rest of the people

---

15:41 I am. God's character and his provision had not changed throughout the journey. The people had wavered and doubted, but God was still the God who had delivered them—whether they believed or not, whether they responded or not, whether they obeyed or not.

16:1–7 Korah's complaint was similar to Aaron and Miriam's complaint in chapter 12. Miriam and Aaron asked, "Aren't we as good as you, Moses?" Now leaders of the tribes of Levi (the priests) and Reuben faced Moses and Aaron with the same question, "Aren't we as holy as you?" In his question, Korah missed an important point. God had appointed Moses and Aaron. They were God's choice. Korah paid the price for not accepting that.

16:12–13 milk and honey. Now this phrase is used to describe Egypt, the place from which they had come, the land in which they had been enslaved. Everything was backward once the people chose to stray away from their faith.

also punished (v. 41)? How were they punished (vv. 46-49)? How many died in the plague (v. 49)? How was the plague stopped (vv. 46-48)? Do you think this was fair? **8.** How do you explain the lack of learning from their mistakes on the part of the Israelites?

APPLY 1. How do you feel about your spiritual leaders? Do you respect them and honor them as God's chosen leaders? **2.** What results have you seen when people rebel against God's leaders? **3.** How can you and this group encourage godly leadership?

15Then Moses became very angry and said to the LORD, "Do not
accept their offering. I have not taken so much as a donkey from
them, nor have I wronged any of them."
16Moses said to Korah, "You and all your followers are to appear
before the LORD tomorrow—you and they and Aaron. 17Each man is
to take his censer and put incense in it—250 censers in all—and
present it before the LORD. You and Aaron are to present your censers
also." 18So each man took his censer, put fire and incense in it, and
stood with Moses and Aaron at the entrance to the Tent of Meeting.
19When Korah had gathered all his followers in opposition to them at
the entrance to the Tent of Meeting, the glory of the LORD appeared to
the entire assembly. 20The LORD said to Moses and Aaron, 21"Separate
yourselves from this assembly so I can put an end to them at once."
22But Moses and Aaron fell facedown and cried out, "O God, God of
the spirits of all mankind, will you be angry with the entire assembly
when only one man sins?"
23Then the LORD said to Moses, 24"Say to the assembly, 'Move away
from the tents of Korah, Dathan and Abiram.' "
25Moses got up and went to Dathan and Abiram, and the elders of
Israel followed him. 26He warned the assembly, "Move back from the
tents of these wicked men! Do not touch anything belonging to them,
or you will be swept away because of all their sins." 27So they moved
away from the tents of Korah, Dathan and Abiram. Dathan and Abiram had come out and were standing with their wives, children and
little ones at the entrances to their tents.
28Then Moses said, "This is how you will know that the LORD has
sent me to do all these things and that it was not my idea: 29If these
men die a natural death and experience only what usually happens to
men, then the LORD has not sent me. 30But if the LORD brings about
something totally new, and the earth opens its mouth and swallows
them, with everything that belongs to them, and they go down alive
into the grave,[a] then you will know that these men have treated the
LORD with contempt."
31As soon as he finished saying all this, the ground under them
split apart 32and the earth opened its mouth and swallowed them,
with their households and all Korah's men and all their possessions.
33They went down alive into the grave, with everything they owned;
the earth closed over them, and they perished and were gone from
the community. 34At their cries, all the Israelites around them fled,
shouting, "The earth is going to swallow us too!"
35And fire came out from the LORD and consumed the 250 men who
were offering the incense.
36The LORD said to Moses, 37"Tell Eleazar son of Aaron, the priest,

[a]30 Hebrew *Sheol*; also in verse 33

16:15 so much as a donkey. The complainers accused Moses of abusing his authority and misleading his people. *Moses' defense is that he had followed* God and sacrificed as much as they had. He had not taken from them; he had delivered them.

16:22 This wasn't the first time that Moses had prayed for God's mercy for the people. As recently as the return of the spies in chapter 14, Moses had begged God to spare them.

16:24 Move away. Sometimes, when God asks his people to keep life separate and at a distance from sinners, the reason is to spare his people's lives.

16:30 the LORD brings about. The question at hand was whether God had given Moses authority, a question only God could answer. Moses was at a point similar to when Elijah stood on the mountain and asked God to send fire to burn up the sacrifice, proving to all that God was in charge (1 Kin. 18).

to take the censers out of the smoldering remains and scatter the coals some distance away, for the censers are holy— [38]the censers of the men who sinned at the cost of their lives. Hammer the censers into sheets to overlay the altar, for they were presented before the LORD and have become holy. Let them be a sign to the Israelites."

[39]So Eleazar the priest collected the bronze censers brought by those who had been burned up, and he had them hammered out to overlay the altar, [40]as the LORD directed him through Moses. This was to remind the Israelites that no one except a descendant of Aaron should come to burn incense before the LORD, or he would become like Korah and his followers.

[41]The next day the whole Israelite community grumbled against Moses and Aaron. "You have killed the LORD's people," they said.

[42]But when the assembly gathered in opposition to Moses and Aaron and turned toward the Tent of Meeting, suddenly the cloud covered it and the glory of the LORD appeared. [43]Then Moses and Aaron went to the front of the Tent of Meeting, [44]and the LORD said to Moses, [45]"Get away from this assembly so I can put an end to them at once." And they fell facedown.

[46]Then Moses said to Aaron, "Take your censer and put incense in it, along with fire from the altar, and hurry to the assembly to make atonement for them. Wrath has come out from the LORD; the plague has started." [47]So Aaron did as Moses said, and ran into the midst of the assembly. The plague had already started among the people, but Aaron offered the incense and made atonement for them. [48]He stood between the living and the dead, and the plague stopped. [49]But 14,700 people died from the plague, in addition to those who had died because of Korah. [50]Then Aaron returned to Moses at the entrance to the Tent of Meeting, for the plague had stopped.

The Budding of Aaron's Staff

17 The LORD said to Moses, [2]"Speak to the Israelites and get twelve staffs from them, one from the leader of each of their ancestral tribes. Write the name of each man on his staff. [3]On the staff of Levi write Aaron's name, for there must be one staff for the head of each ancestral tribe. [4]Place them in the Tent of Meeting in front of the Testimony, where I meet with you. [5]The staff belonging to the man I choose will sprout, and I will rid myself of this constant grumbling against you by the Israelites."

[6]So Moses spoke to the Israelites, and their leaders gave him

OPEN 1. What were some of the things you and your friends did as kids to select the leader of your club? **2.** Tell of a time you ran for office and got out-voted.

STUDY The rebellion of Aaron and Miriam and then the rebellion of Korah, Dathan and Abiram necessitated that God clearly designate who was the leader. As God often does, he designates his chosen leader,

---

16:41 whole Israelite community grumbled against Moses. The burden of leading the Israelites meant dealing with their constant complaints. As mediator between God and Israel, Moses took the heat for God's decisions. Without the intervention of Moses and Aaron, God's anger against sin might have been even more severe (v. 21).

16:49 14,700 people died. This holy plague was a serious catastrophe despite the intervention of Moses and Aaron. Though the Israelites were numerous, this many deaths from disease would be a severe blow.

17:1–13 This chapter tells a story which confirms the Levites' preeminent role in the priesthood. It follows the turmoil and tragedy of the destruction of Korah and the death of 14,700 people in a plague sent by God. The story describes the elevation of the priesthood as a means of controlling dissatisfaction with Moses' leadership.

17:3 one staff for the head of each ancestral tribe. The grumbling against Moses and Aaron was not confined to any one tribe. Korah's rebellion had probably drawn supporters from all of them. Therefore, the demonstration had to show that the Levites' power superseded that of any other tribal head.

17:4 in front of the Testimony. The staffs were placed in front of the ark containing the Ten Commandments. If a staff sprouted, it belonged in the Holy Place. The tribe represented by that staff was God's choice to serve in the tabernacle.

Aaron, in a miraculous way. **1.** What was the significance of the staff of each tribe? How did God use these staffs to designate his appointed leader (v. 5)? **2.** Why was it significant that only Aaron's staff sprouted and produced almonds (v. 8)? What does it take for God to convince you? **3.** Why did the Israelites now develop the fear that they might die?

APPLY Why is it so hard to accept God's way of doing things? How do you see him disciplining you to get you to hear his message?

OPEN **1.** How do you make your living? **2.** Do you think the pay public officials receive for their work is: Deserved? Way too much? Adequate? Way too little?

STUDY After several challenges to the appointed leadership of Israel, God gives instructions that Aaron and his family were to be the ones who would serve as priests in Israel. The priesthood would be from Aaron's family and they would be supported through the offerings of the people. **1.** Why do you think God chose only the family of Aaron to serve as priests? How do you think Aaron might have felt after being given such a lofty responsibility? **2.** Why do you think only the immediate family of Aaron could actually go into the tabernacle? What sense of wonder would it create in you not to be able to see what was going on inside the tabernacle? **3.** How might the Levites have felt about being servants to the priests? Why would their service be considered a gift to the priests (v. 6)? In what ways do you consider the opportunity to serve to be a gift? **4.** Why would it

twelve staffs, one for the leader of each of their ancestral tribes, and
Aaron's staff was among them. 7Moses placed the staffs before the
LORD in the Tent of the Testimony.
8The next day Moses entered the Tent of the Testimony and saw
that Aaron's staff, which represented the house of Levi, had not only
sprouted but had budded, blossomed and produced almonds. 9Then
Moses brought out all the staffs from the LORD's presence to all the
Israelites. They looked at them, and each man took his own staff.
10The LORD said to Moses, "Put back Aaron's staff in front of the
Testimony, to be kept as a sign to the rebellious. This will put an end
to their grumbling against me, so that they will not die." 11Moses did
just as the LORD commanded him.
12The Israelites said to Moses, "We will die! We are lost, we are all
lost! 13Anyone who even comes near the tabernacle of the LORD will
die. Are we all going to die?"

Duties of Priests and Levites

18 The LORD said to Aaron, "You, your sons and your father's
family are to bear the responsibility for offenses against the
sanctuary, and you and your sons alone are to bear the responsibility
for offenses against the priesthood. 2Bring your fellow Levites from
your ancestral tribe to join you and assist you when you and your
sons minister before the Tent of the Testimony. 3They are to be responsible to you and are to perform all the duties of the Tent, but they
must not go near the furnishings of the sanctuary or the altar, or both
they and you will die. 4They are to join you and be responsible for the
care of the Tent of Meeting—all the work at the Tent—and no one
else may come near where you are.
5"You are to be responsible for the care of the sanctuary and the
altar, so that wrath will not fall on the Israelites again. 6I myself have
selected your fellow Levites from among the Israelites as a gift to
you, dedicated to the LORD to do the work at the Tent of Meeting. 7But
only you and your sons may serve as priests in connection with
everything at the altar and inside the curtain. I am giving you the
service of the priesthood as a gift. Anyone else who comes near the
sanctuary must be put to death."

Offerings for Priests and Levites

8Then the LORD said to Aaron, "I myself have put you in charge of
the offerings presented to me; all the holy offerings the Israelites give

---

17:8 sprouted ... budded ... blossomed ... produced. Aaron's staff far exceeded the demands of the test. There was no mistaking which tribe God chose for his service. This verse also demonstrates four effects of God's blessing. What happened to a wooden staff can happen spiritually to a follower of God.

17:10 Put back Aaron's staff in front of the Testimony. The staff would remain near the Law in the Holy Place as a reminder of this test. Anyone questioning the special role of Aaron's family would have to overcome this powerful evidence.

17:12 We will die! We are lost. Israel finally realized the consequence of sin. Certainly, recent events had demonstrated the severity of God's wrath in a personal way. The people were afraid of the power of God.

18:1–7 so that wrath will not fall on the Israelites again. Paul wrote in Romans 6:23, "The wages of sin is death." The Israelites learned this truth through a series of lessons. But God, in grace and love, provided Aaron's priesthood to be responsible for the sanctuary and the altar, and thus, for the spiritual welfare of Israel.

18:7 the service of the priesthood as a gift. The spiritual welfare of Israel was a heavy burden. It came to the priesthood along with a blessing. However, only the Aaronic priesthood would be allowed to approach the Holy Place and minister before the Lord. Only they would hold that special relationship with God.

18:8 portion ... share. The Levites

me I give to you and your sons as your portion and regular share. 9You are to have the part of the most holy offerings that is kept from the fire. From all the gifts they bring me as most holy offerings, whether grain or sin or guilt offerings, that part belongs to you and your sons. 10Eat it as something most holy; every male shall eat it. You must regard it as holy.

11"This also is yours: whatever is set aside from the gifts of all the wave offerings of the Israelites. I give this to you and your sons and daughters as your regular share. Everyone in your household who is ceremonially clean may eat it.

12"I give you all the finest olive oil and all the finest new wine and grain they give the LORD as the firstfruits of their harvest. 13All the land's firstfruits that they bring to the LORD will be yours. Everyone in your household who is ceremonially clean may eat it.

14"Everything in Israel that is devoted[a] to the LORD is yours. 15The first offspring of every womb, both man and animal, that is offered to the LORD is yours. But you must redeem every firstborn son and every firstborn male of unclean animals. 16When they are a month old, you must redeem them at the redemption price set at five shekels[b] of silver, according to the sanctuary shekel, which weighs twenty gerahs.

17"But you must not redeem the firstborn of an ox, a sheep or a goat; they are holy. Sprinkle their blood on the altar and burn their fat as an offering made by fire, an aroma pleasing to the LORD. 18Their meat is to be yours, just as the breast of the wave offering and the right thigh are yours. 19Whatever is set aside from the holy offerings the Israelites present to the LORD I give to you and your sons and daughters as your regular share. It is an everlasting covenant of salt before the LORD for both you and your offspring."

20The LORD said to Aaron, "You will have no inheritance in their land, nor will you have any share among them; I am your share and your inheritance among the Israelites.

21"I give to the Levites all the tithes in Israel as their inheritance in return for the work they do while serving at the Tent of Meeting. 22From now on the Israelites must not go near the Tent of Meeting, or they will bear the consequences of their sin and will die. 23It is the Levites who are to do the work at the Tent of Meeting and bear the responsibility for offenses against it. This is a lasting ordinance for the generations to come. They will receive no inheritance among the Israelites. 24Instead, I give to the Levites as their inheritance the tithes that the Israelites present as an offering to the LORD. That is why I said concerning them: 'They will have no inheritance among the Israelites.' "

25The LORD said to Moses, 26"Speak to the Levites and say to them:

[a]14 The Hebrew term refers to the irrevocable giving over of things or persons to the LORD. [b]16 That is, about 2 ounces (about 55 grams)

be necessary for Aaron and his family to be supported by the offerings of the rest of the people (v. 8)? How do you feel about the "clergy" today being supported by your offerings? What dangers do you see in this? **5.** Why do you think God allowed the priests and the Levites to eat the sacrifices made to him, even the "first" and the "finest" of them (vv. 12–13)? **6.** What made these ordinary food items "holy"? What makes your offering "holy"? **7.** What does God command the priests and Levites concerning their offering (vv. 26–32)? How is the priest's inheritance different from all the others in Israel (vv. 20,24)?

APPLY 1. What improvement needs to be made in your attitude about your offerings? In the amount? **2.** How do you feel about supporting others to work full time in ministry?

were not given any land or property; the other eleven tribes would therefore share the task of supporting them. A portion of the offerings would be set aside for the Levites. This provision extended beyond the years in the wilderness and became part of the basic social structure of Israel.

18:11 Everyone ... who is ceremonially clean. Families of priests were included in the "regular share" of the offerings. However, it was necessary that these family members be ceremonially clean to receive the benefit. Leviticus 22:4–8 outlines these cleanliness requirements.

18:12 olive oil ... wine ... grain. The Law required the offering of the firstfruits and the best of everything to the Lord, the Aaronic priesthood would receive its share from this bounty. Therefore, priests would have the best of everything. That was the trade-off for their responsibility to God and the people of Israel.

'When you receive from the Israelites the tithe I give you as your inheritance, you must present a tenth of that tithe as the LORD's offering. 27Your offering will be reckoned to you as grain from the threshing floor or juice from the winepress. 28In this way you also will present an offering to the LORD from all the tithes you receive from the Israelites. From these tithes you must give the LORD's portion to Aaron the priest. 29You must present as the LORD's portion the best and holiest part of everything given to you.'

30"Say to the Levites: 'When you present the best part, it will be reckoned to you as the product of the threshing floor or the winepress. 31You and your households may eat the rest of it anywhere, for it is your wages for your work at the Tent of Meeting. 32By presenting the best part of it you will not be guilty in this matter; then you will not defile the holy offerings of the Israelites, and you will not die.' "

OPEN **1.** What was the last funeral service you attended like? What traditions were observed? **2.** What is the meaning of the phrase "cleanliness is next to godliness"?

STUDY It was inevitable that the Israelites would have to deal with the death of their own. When they had to handle the bodies of the dead, they became ceremonially unclean. Now, God gives them instructions on how to become clean again. **1.** Putting aside the spiritual significance of the purification laws, what health issues might be involved for the Israelites in the desert when someone died? What do you think was the spiritual significance of becoming unclean after contact with a dead body? What did the sacrifice have to do with becoming clean again? How would you feel about coming into contact with a dead body if you had to go through this ceremony over a seven-day period in order to be clean again? **2.** What was involved in the water cleansing ceremony (v. 9)? Who could handle these elements? Why do you think the ceremony was necessary? **3.** Why would the open containers in a tent where someone died be unclean? **4.** What would happen to a person who would not go through the cleansing ceremony when they became unclean (v. 20)? Do you think this is for health reasons, or is there a spiritual issue here? Explain

The Water of Cleansing

19 The LORD said to Moses and Aaron: 2"This is a requirement of the law that the LORD has commanded: Tell the Israelites to bring you a red heifer without defect or blemish and that has never been under a yoke. 3Give it to Eleazar the priest; it is to be taken outside the camp and slaughtered in his presence. 4Then Eleazar the priest is to take some of its blood on his finger and sprinkle it seven times toward the front of the Tent of Meeting. 5While he watches, the heifer is to be burned—its hide, flesh, blood and offal. 6The priest is to take some cedar wood, hyssop and scarlet wool and throw them onto the burning heifer. 7After that, the priest must wash his clothes and bathe himself with water. He may then come into the camp, but he will be ceremonially unclean till evening. 8The man who burns it must also wash his clothes and bathe with water, and he too will be unclean till evening.

9"A man who is clean shall gather up the ashes of the heifer and put them in a ceremonially clean place outside the camp. They shall be kept by the Israelite community for use in the water of cleansing; it is for purification from sin. 10The man who gathers up the ashes of the heifer must also wash his clothes, and he too will be unclean till evening. This will be a lasting ordinance both for the Israelites and for the aliens living among them.

11"Whoever touches the dead body of anyone will be unclean for seven days. 12He must purify himself with the water on the third day and on the seventh day; then he will be clean. But if he does not purify himself on the third and seventh days, he will not be clean. 13Whoever touches the dead body of anyone and fails to purify himself defiles the LORD's tabernacle. That person must be cut off from Israel. Because the water of cleansing has not been sprinkled on him, he is unclean; his uncleanness remains on him.

19:6 cedar wood, hyssop and scarlet wool. Cedar was evergreen. Hyssop was used to smear the blood of the slaughtered lambs above the doors of the Israelites at the first Passover (Ex. 12:22). Scarlet wool was probably chosen, like the red heifer, for its color—the color of blood.

19:12 purify himself with the water. In a community as large as the traveling nation of Israel, there were always dead bodies that needed handling and disposal. A person who touched a dead body was considered unclean and required a purification ritual. The ashes from the red heifer were used to make one ceremonially clean after touching a dead body.

19:13 the LORD's tabernacle ... cut off. Failure to become ceremonially clean was a serious offense. It was an affront to the Law and to the tabernacle. Anything that soiled the tabernacle or defiled it was an insult to God. The punishment was severe: either banishment or execution.

14"This is the law that applies when a person dies in a tent: Anyone
who enters the tent and anyone who is in it will be unclean for seven
days, 15and every open container without a lid fastened on it will be
unclean.
16"Anyone out in the open who touches someone who has been
killed with a sword or someone who has died a natural death, or
anyone who touches a human bone or a grave, will be unclean for
seven days.
17"For the unclean person, put some ashes from the burned purification offering into a jar and pour fresh water over them. 18Then a
man who is ceremonially clean is to take some hyssop, dip it in the
water and sprinkle the tent and all the furnishings and the people
who were there. He must also sprinkle anyone who has touched a
human bone or a grave or someone who has been killed or someone
who has died a natural death. 19The man who is clean is to sprinkle
the unclean person on the third and seventh days, and on the seventh
day he is to purify him. The person being cleansed must wash his
clothes and bathe with water, and that evening he will be clean. 20But
if a person who is unclean does not purify himself, he must be cut off
from the community, because he has defiled the sanctuary of the
LORD. The water of cleansing has not been sprinkled on him, and he
is unclean. 21This is a lasting ordinance for them.
"The man who sprinkles the water of cleansing must also wash his
clothes, and anyone who touches the water of cleansing will be
unclean till evening. 22Anything that an unclean person touches
becomes unclean, and anyone who touches it becomes unclean till
evening."

Water From the Rock

20 In the first month the whole Israelite community arrived at
the Desert of Zin, and they stayed at Kadesh. There Miriam
died and was buried.
2Now there was no water for the community, and the people gathered in opposition to Moses and Aaron. 3They quarreled with Moses
and said, "If only we had died when our brothers fell dead before the
LORD! 4Why did you bring the LORD's community into this desert, that
we and our livestock should die here? 5Why did you bring us up out of
Egypt to this terrible place? It has no grain or figs, grapevines or
pomegranates. And there is no water to drink!"
6Moses and Aaron went from the assembly to the entrance to the

your answer. **5.** What spiritual overtones about your relationship with God do you see in these rituals?

APPLY 1. What would make you feel spiritually unclean? **2.** What is the "cleansing agent" today (Heb. 9:13–14)?

OPEN 1. As a child, how did you react when you didn't get what you wanted? **2.** How do you react now when someone pushes you too far?

STUDY As the Israelites wander again in the desert, a familiar theme is heard—they are not happy with what they have and begin to complain. Their complaining pushes Moses about as far as he can go. **1.** Why are the people so quick to blame Moses any time they are unhappy? **2.** Why would the people wish they had died

19:14 anyone who is in it ... unclean. Plain and simple, contact with a dead body, either deliberate or not, caused uncleanness. Though the cure for this problem was ceremonial cleansing, the problem itself was a practical one. In a hot climate, death brought on rapid decomposition, and the risk of disease was enormous. God was concerned about this situation, and even declared in his commands that the contents of open containers near a body were unclean (v. 15). God was looking out for the health of his people, along with their spiritual well-being.

19:18 dip it in the water and sprinkle. The ritual of cleansing was not complex. Some of the cleansing water, made with the ashes of the red heifer, was sprinkled on everything that had some contact with the dead body. The sprinkling of the water contrasted with the sprinkling of blood at the altar. A similar sprinkling was made with blood at the consecration of the priests (Ex. 29:15–21) in order to ensure their purification.

20:1–29 Here are the accounts of the deaths of two important people, Miriam and Aaron. The chapter also outlines a problem with Edom and presents the sin that will keep Moses out of the Promised Land.

20:2 no water for the community. History repeated itself. Forty years earlier, at Horeb, God had responded to the Israelites' grumbling by having Moses strike a rock with his staff, and water flowed out (Ex. 17:5–7). Now, forty years later, at Kadesh, where Israel had rebelled terribly against God (chs. 13–14), he, once again, gave Moses instructions for getting water.

with their brothers in the rebellion of Korah (ch. 16)? What does their attitude say about their faith? **3.** What do you learn about the faith of Moses and Aaron when they immediately go to the tabernacle to hear from God in this situation (as they have done on many other occasions)? What instructions does God give them (v. 8)? How do they carry out the instructions (vv. 9–11)? **4.** What do you learn about the limit to Moses' patience in this scene? What did he do that was wrong? **5.** What is God's response to Moses' action (v. 12)?

APPLY Why is it hard to trust God in difficult times?

OPEN **1.** How do you feel about having to take a detour when you're on a trip? **2.** How do you react when someone is mean to you?

STUDY As the Israelites journey, they come to the border of Edom, a country whose people are distant kinfolks to the Israelites. They wish only to pass through the land, and are even willing to pay for the water they or their livestock drink, but the Edomites will not let them pass. Meantime, one of the great leaders, Aaron passes away. **1.** Why do you think the king of Edom would be so hesitant to let Israel pass through his land? How would you have felt toward the Edomites at this point? **2.** How does Moses try to persuade the king of Edom to let them pass through (v. 17)? Can you think of a more reasonable offer Moses might have made? **3.** Why do you think Israel

Tent of Meeting and fell facedown, and the glory of the LORD
appeared to them. [7]The LORD said to Moses, [8]"Take the staff, and you
and your brother Aaron gather the assembly together. Speak to that
rock before their eyes and it will pour out its water. You will bring
water out of the rock for the community so they and their livestock
can drink."

[9]So Moses took the staff from the LORD's presence, just as he
commanded him. [10]He and Aaron gathered the assembly together in
front of the rock and Moses said to them, "Listen, you rebels, must
we bring you water out of this rock?" [11]Then Moses raised his arm
and struck the rock twice with his staff. Water gushed out, and the
community and their livestock drank.

[12]But the LORD said to Moses and Aaron, "Because you did not trust
in me enough to honor me as holy in the sight of the Israelites, you
will not bring this community into the land I give them."

[13]These were the waters of Meribah,[a] where the Israelites quarreled with the LORD and where he showed himself holy among them.

Edom Denies Israel Passage

[14]Moses sent messengers from Kadesh to the king of Edom, saying:

"This is what your brother Israel says: You know about all the
hardships that have come upon us. [15]Our forefathers went down
into Egypt, and we lived there many years. The Egyptians
mistreated us and our fathers, [16]but when we cried out to the
LORD, he heard our cry and sent an angel and brought us out of
Egypt.

"Now we are here at Kadesh, a town on the edge of your territory. [17]Please let us pass through your country. We will not go
through any field or vineyard, or drink water from any well. We
will travel along the king's highway and not turn to the right or
to the left until we have passed through your territory."

[18]But Edom answered:

"You may not pass through here; if you try, we will march out
and attack you with the sword."

[a]13 *Meribah* means *quarreling.*

20:8 Take the staff ... Speak to that rock. Moses had carried the staff with him for forty years and had used it according to God's direction to provide for his people. Thus, it was an instrument of God's will. God's instructions were different this time.

20:10 must we bring you water out of this rock. In anger and frustration, Moses mocked the blessing God had sent him to provide. God's reaction implies that "we" referred to Moses and Aaron—not Moses and God.

20:11 raised his aim and struck the rock ... staff. God's direct command to Moses was to speak to the rock, not strike it. God had enabled Moses' voice as the instrument of a miracle, but Moses had used it mockingly (v. 10). God had used Moses' staff as an instrument of divine deliverance and provision (Ex. 14:16; 17:6–7). Now, Moses used it in anger and in violation of God's commands.

20:12 did not trust ... you will not bring this community into the land. God's punishment was quick and severe. After leading Israel for forty years toward the prize of Canaan, Aaron and Moses would not see the sojourn to its conclusion. The punishment was harsh because Moses and Aaron had not shown trust and honor for God in their action (v. 12).

20:14–21 Please let us pass through your country. Moses tried a diplomatic approach with the Edomites. The Edomites were distant relatives of the Israelites, and Moses genuinely tried to avoid conflict with them.

20:14 your brother Israel. The Edomites were descendants of Esau, and the Israelites were descendants of his brother Jacob.

20:17 along the king's highway. Moses requested safe passage along the primary trade route through Edomite territory. This route, which stretched from Arabia to Damascus, was widely used by caravans and traders. Moses

19 The Israelites replied:

"We will go along the main road, and if we or our livestock
drink any of your water, we will pay for it. We only want to pass
through on foot—nothing else."

20 Again they answered:

"You may not pass through."

Then Edom came out against them with a large and powerful army.
21 Since Edom refused to let them go through their territory, Israel
turned away from them.

The Death of Aaron

22 The whole Israelite community set out from Kadesh and came to
Mount Hor. 23 At Mount Hor, near the border of Edom, the LORD said
to Moses and Aaron, 24 "Aaron will be gathered to his people. He will
not enter the land I give the Israelites, because both of you rebelled
against my command at the waters of Meribah. 25 Get Aaron and his
son Eleazar and take them up Mount Hor. 26 Remove Aaron's garments and put them on his son Eleazar, for Aaron will be gathered to
his people; he will die there."

27 Moses did as the LORD commanded: They went up Mount Hor in
the sight of the whole community. 28 Moses removed Aaron's garments and put them on his son Eleazar. And Aaron died there on top
of the mountain. Then Moses and Eleazar came down from the
mountain, 29 and when the whole community learned that Aaron had
died, the entire house of Israel mourned for him thirty days.

Arad Destroyed

21 When the Canaanite king of Arad, who lived in the Negev,
heard that Israel was coming along the road to Atharim, he
attacked the Israelites and captured some of them. 2 Then Israel made
this vow to the LORD: "If you will deliver these people into our hands,
we will totally destroy[a] their cities." 3 The LORD listened to Israel's

[a]2 The Hebrew term refers to the irrevocable giving over of things or persons to the LORD, often by totally destroying them; also in verse 3.

turned away from the army of Edom rather than fight? What would you have wanted to do? **4.** How do you think Moses felt when God told him to prepare Aaron for death? Who was to succeed Aaron (v. 26)? What problems might Aaron's death create for Israel? **5.** After being so rebellious toward Aaron, why do you think the people mourned for him when he died?

APPLY 1. Describe the most recent detour in your life that you believe to be the guidance of God. What have been the results? **2.** What will help you be calm and trust God when he is leading you in another direction, even when you face enemies along the way? **3.** Who is the most significant leader in your life that has died?

OPEN 1. What is your attitude toward snakes? **2.** How do you feel about going to the dentist?

STUDY After the death of Aaron, the king of Arad decides to capture some of the Israelites. Big mistake! The people plead to God for victory against him, and God gives it to them. **1.** Why do you think the

---

was trying to manage a way across Edom without violating God's commands concerning Esau's descendants. In this case, Israel could not fight the Edomites, take any of their land, eat their food or drink their water without making payment for it (Deut. 2:5–6). Moses' letter to the Edomite king reflected his compliance with these commands.

20:20 large and powerful army. Hard feelings generated sparks between these two nations. Some of these were historical in nature, the natural result of the brother-to-brother conflict between Jacob and Esau. As Deuteronomy 2:4–6 points out, however, the Edomites also feared Israel. Israel had been blessed by God, and the Edomites were probably afraid of this huge migration of Israelites through their land.

20:24 both of you rebelled. In God's eyes, Aaron had rebelled against him just as Moses had, at Kadesh (v. 12). Like Moses, Aaron held such a position of power that a lack of trust, obedience and honor for God made him unfit to lead Israel into Canaan.

20:25–28 Aaron and his son Eleazar ... Mount Hor ... put them on his son. God had designated Aaron's family as the spiritual leaders of Israel (Ex. 28:1–29:46). The mantle of family leadership naturally passed from father to son. The responsibilities of leading the priesthood were passed to Aaron's son in the form of his garments. A priest's garments were important to his spiritual role and were prescribed by law (Ex. 28).

20:29 entire house of Israel mourned for him thirty days. Like Moses, Aaron had been the victim of their grumbling, yet he had persevered in leading the Israelites, serving as their priest and making atonement for them. Now they mourned for him.

21:2 totally destroy. The Hebrew term meant to turn over something entirely to the Lord. The implication was that by destroying something entirely it is put back in its original form so that God can do with it as he pleases. We still maintain a semblance of that idea in such phrases as "ashes to ashes." God started with the raw materials, and by destroying a thing entirely, it is returned to that state.

plea and gave the Canaanites over to them. They completely destroyed them and their towns; so the place was named Hormah.[a]

The Bronze Snake

4They traveled from Mount Hor along the route to the Red Sea,[b] to go around Edom. But the people grew impatient on the way; 5they spoke against God and against Moses, and said, "Why have you brought us up out of Egypt to die in the desert? There is no bread! There is no water! And we detest this miserable food!"

6Then the LORD sent venomous snakes among them; they bit the people and many Israelites died. 7The people came to Moses and said, "We sinned when we spoke against the LORD and against you. Pray that the LORD will take the snakes away from us." So Moses prayed for the people.

8The LORD said to Moses, "Make a snake and put it up on a pole; anyone who is bitten can look at it and live." 9So Moses made a bronze snake and put it up on a pole. Then when anyone was bitten by a snake and looked at the bronze snake, he lived.

The Journey to Moab

10The Israelites moved on and camped at Oboth. 11Then they set out from Oboth and camped in Iye Abarim, in the desert that faces Moab toward the sunrise. 12From there they moved on and camped in the Zered Valley. 13They set out from there and camped alongside the Arnon, which is in the desert extending into Amorite territory. The Arnon is the border of Moab, between Moab and the Amorites. 14That is why the Book of the Wars of the LORD says:

". . . Waheb in Suphah[c] and the ravines,
  the Arnon 15and[d] the slopes of the ravines
that lead to the site of Ar
  and lie along the border of Moab."

16From there they continued on to Beer, the well where the LORD said to Moses, "Gather the people together and I will give them water."

17Then Israel sang this song:

"Spring up, O well!
  Sing about it,
18about the well that the princes dug,

[a]3 Hormah means *destruction*. [b]4 Hebrew *Yam Suph*; that is, Sea of Reeds [c]14 The meaning of the Hebrew for this phrase is uncertain. [d]14,15 Or *"I have been given from Suphah and the ravines / of the Arnon* 15*to*

Canaanite king decided to capture some of the Israelites? How do you think this king felt when the fighting started? **2.** What do the Israelites complain about this time? Does this sound familiar? **3.** Why do you think the Lord sent snakes as a punishment this time? What is the future significance of the snake raised on a pole for the healing of the people (John 3:14–15)?

APPLY When did you come to understand the connection of this story to the death of Christ on the cross?

OPEN 1. Do you like to travel around, or do you prefer to just stay home? **2.** When you travel, do you sing? What do you like to do to occupy yourself when traveling?

STUDY As Israel continues to journey toward the Promised Land, they pass through a number of places and then come into contact with Sihon, king of the Amorites, and Og, king of Bashan. The contact ends in conflict and the two kings are defeated by Israel. **1.** How do you think the war songs of this passage would help the Israelites to remember the events of this trip? What importance do songs have in your culture today? **2.** Why do you think Moses had no fear in going to battle with Sihon and Og? What peaceful offer does Moses make to Sihon before they go to battle (v. 22)? What was the outcome of each of these battles (vv. 24,35)? How do you feel about this conquest by Israel?

21:4 to go around Edom. Moses was trying to avoid conflict with the Edomites. God had prohibited war with Edom (Deut. 2:5–6), and Moses tried to comply, but it got him in trouble with Israel. Despite God's prohibition, they were anxious to take on the Edomites.

21:5 no bread ... no water ... we detest this miserable food. Certainly the Israelites were tired of manna. They had been eating it for forty years. However, rejecting God's provision of food was the same as rejecting his provision of grace. This offense carried serious consequences.

21:8–9 bronze snake. The bronze snake was not an idol but a symbol of God's grace and deliverance. The snake did not save the Israelites from the pain of snakebite, but from the consequences. In John 3:14–15, Jesus uses this event to illustrate his being lifted up on the cross like the snake so that he can save humankind from the consequence of sin: death.

21:10–13 Moses leads the Israelites around Edom. Not only is he avoiding conflict with the Edomites, he is positioning the Israelites to enter Canaan by a different route than was explored forty years earlier.

21:16 Gather the people together and I will give them water. In this rare case, the people did not grumble, and the Lord provided.

21:17–18 Sing about it. The Israelites responded to God's provision by

that the nobles of the people sank—
the nobles with scepters and staffs."

Then they went from the desert to Mattanah, 19from Mattanah to
Nahaliel, from Nahaliel to Bamoth, 20and from Bamoth to the valley
in Moab where the top of Pisgah overlooks the wasteland.

Defeat of Sihon and Og

21Israel sent messengers to say to Sihon king of the Amorites:

22"Let us pass through your country. We will not turn aside
into any field or vineyard, or drink water from any well. We will
travel along the king's highway until we have passed through
your territory."

23But Sihon would not let Israel pass through his territory. He mustered his entire army and marched out into the desert against Israel.
When he reached Jahaz, he fought with Israel. 24Israel, however, put
him to the sword and took over his land from the Arnon to the Jabbok, but only as far as the Ammonites, because their border was fortified. 25Israel captured all the cities of the Amorites and occupied
them, including Heshbon and all its surrounding settlements.
26Heshbon was the city of Sihon king of the Amorites, who had
fought against the former king of Moab and had taken from him all
his land as far as the Arnon.
27That is why the poets say:

"Come to Heshbon and let it be rebuilt;
let Sihon's city be restored.

28"Fire went out from Heshbon,
a blaze from the city of Sihon.
It consumed Ar of Moab,
the citizens of Arnon's heights.
29Woe to you, O Moab!
You are destroyed, O people of Chemosh!
He has given up his sons as fugitives
and his daughters as captives
to Sihon king of the Amorites.

30"But we have overthrown them;
Heshbon is destroyed all the way to Dibon.
We have demolished them as far as Nophah,
which extends to Medeba."

31So Israel settled in the land of the Amorites.
32After Moses had sent spies to Jazer, the Israelites captured its
surrounding settlements and drove out the Amorites who were there.

APPLY 1. What significant spiritual events have occurred in your life this year? **2.** How do you react when you come up against strong spiritual enemies in your life? Does it help to know that you have God on your side?

---

singing. The song itself seems much more a product of growing national pride than spiritual pride. However, the song may have been celebrating God's empowerment of Israel as it prepared to invade Canaan.

21:21–26 Let us pass through your country. Just as they had done with the Edomites, the Israelites requested permission to pass through the territory of another tribe. The Amorites resisted. Perhaps they had heard how Israel had responded to Edomite aggression by skirting their territory. This time, because God had not prohibited them from fighting the Amorites, Israel won a crushing victory, and the land of the Amorites came under their control.

21:27–30 Ironically, this poem celebrates the Amorites' earlier victory over the Moabites. The poem placed Israel's victory over the Amorites in an historical context but also served as a reminder that human victory is short-lived.

33 Then they turned and went up along the road toward Bashan, and
Og king of Bashan and his whole army marched out to meet them in
battle at Edrei.
34 The LORD said to Moses, "Do not be afraid of him, for I have
handed him over to you, with his whole army and his land. Do to him
what you did to Sihon king of the Amorites, who reigned in Heshbon."
35 So they struck him down, together with his sons and his whole
army, leaving them no survivors. And they took possession of his
land.

OPEN 1. What do you think of modern "diviners"—palm readers, fortune-tellers, spiritists, especially those you see on TV? **2.** What do you think of voodoo and witch doctors?

STUDY As the Hebrew multitude approached Moab, the king and his people became frightened. In a strategic move, Balak, king of Moab, sends for a "diviner" named Balaam to pronounce a curse against Israel. **1.** Why were the Moabites afraid (vv. 2–3)? In what way were their fears legitimate? Would you have been afraid? **2.** What does Balak's employing a "diviner" say about his belief in the supernatural? Do you think he was just "hedging his bet" or did he really believe a supernatural power would help him defeat the Israelites? Why? **3.** How do you think Balak knew Balaam's reputation (v. 6)? What does it say about Balaam's reputation that Balak sent for him twice (vv. 5,15)? **4.** What exactly does Balak want Balaam to do for him (vv. 6,11)? Do you think Balaam actually had the power to invoke such a curse on Israel? Why or why not? **5.** Why does Balaam deny the messengers the first time (vv. 12–13)? What do you think of Balaam's relationship with God,

Balak Summons Balaam

22 Then the Israelites traveled to the plains of Moab and
camped along the Jordan across from Jericho.[a]
2 Now Balak son of Zippor saw all that Israel had done to the Amorites, 3 and Moab was terrified because there were so many people.
Indeed, Moab was filled with dread because of the Israelites.
4 The Moabites said to the elders of Midian, "This horde is going to
lick up everything around us, as an ox licks up the grass of the field."
So Balak son of Zippor, who was king of Moab at that time, 5 sent
messengers to summon Balaam son of Beor, who was at Pethor, near
the River,[b] in his native land. Balak said:

> "A people has come out of Egypt; they cover the face of the
> land and have settled next to me. 6 Now come and put a curse on
> these people, because they are too powerful for me. Perhaps
> then I will be able to defeat them and drive them out of the coun-
> try. For I know that those you bless are blessed, and those you
> curse are cursed."

7 The elders of Moab and Midian left, taking with them the fee for
divination. When they came to Balaam, they told him what Balak had
said.
8 "Spend the night here," Balaam said to them, "and I will bring you
back the answer the LORD gives me." So the Moabite princes stayed
with him.
9 God came to Balaam and asked, "Who are these men with you?"
10 Balaam said to God, "Balak son of Zippor, king of Moab, sent me

[a]1 Hebrew *Jordan of Jericho;* possibly an ancient name for the Jordan River [b]5 That is, the Euphrates

21:35 took possession of his land. Israel's victory over Og and his armies gave them possession of the entire Transjordan, from Moab in the south to Mount Hermon in the north. So far, the strategy of entering Canaan from the east rather than the south had worked perfectly.

22:1 camped along the Jordan across from Jericho. With the Transjordan secured as their launching pad, Israel moved into position to invade Canaan. Jericho was the first target. It would provide a great base of operations in Canaan if they could capture it. It would give Israel access to the north-south roads they would use to move the army. It would also give them control of the fords across the Jordan and open an escape route in case of setbacks.

22:3 Moab was terrified ... many people. First Sihon beat up on the nation of Moab (21:23–26); then Israel destroyed that bully and his fellow Amorite king, Og. Balak was right to be nervous.

22:4 elders of Midian. Balak knew that the Moabites would not stand a chance against the "horde" of Israel, and sought help from the Midianites.

22:5 Balaam son of Beor. Sending for Balaam, a famous diviner, was the last resort of a desperate man. Balak felt he had one chance to save his people, and that was pagan divination.

22:8 bring back the answer the LORD gives me. Balaam's statement does not imply that he believed in Yahweh (the "Lord"). He might have intended to take the money and run, and his supposed sincerity was part of the act.

22:9 God came to Balaam ... Who are these men? God came to speak with a pagan. If that is not unusual enough, it was a pagan who pursued other gods, perhaps indiscriminately, for profit.

this message: 11'A people that has come out of Egypt covers the face
of the land. Now come and put a curse on them for me. Perhaps then
I will be able to fight them and drive them away.' "
12But God said to Balaam, "Do not go with them. You must not put
a curse on those people, because they are blessed."
13The next morning Balaam got up and said to Balak's princes, "Go
back to your own country, for the LORD has refused to let me go with
you."
14So the Moabite princes returned to Balak and said, "Balaam
refused to come with us."
15Then Balak sent other princes, more numerous and more distinguished than the first. 16They came to Balaam and said:

> "This is what Balak son of Zippor says: Do not let anything
> keep you from coming to me, 17because I will reward you hand-
> somely and do whatever you say. Come and put a curse on these
> people for me."

18But Balaam answered them, "Even if Balak gave me his palace
filled with silver and gold, I could not do anything great or small to go
beyond the command of the LORD my God. 19Now stay here tonight as
the others did, and I will find out what else the LORD will tell me."
20That night God came to Balaam and said, "Since these men have
come to summon you, go with them, but do only what I tell you."

Balaam's Donkey

21Balaam got up in the morning, saddled his donkey and went with
the princes of Moab. 22But God was very angry when he went, and the
angel of the LORD stood in the road to oppose him. Balaam was riding
on his donkey, and his two servants were with him. 23When the donkey saw the angel of the LORD standing in the road with a drawn
sword in his hand, she turned off the road into a field. Balaam beat
her to get her back on the road.
24Then the angel of the LORD stood in a narrow path between two
vineyards, with walls on both sides. 25When the donkey saw the angel
of the LORD, she pressed close to the wall, crushing Balaam's foot
against it. So he beat her again.
26Then the angel of the LORD moved on ahead and stood in a narrow place where there was no room to turn, either to the right or to
the left. 27When the donkey saw the angel of the LORD, she lay down
under Balaam, and he was angry and beat her with his staff. 28Then
the LORD opened the donkey's mouth, and she said to Balaam, "What
have I done to you to make you beat me these three times?"
29Balaam answered the donkey, "You have made a fool of me! If I
had a sword in my hand, I would kill you right now."

considering he had several conversations with God (vv. 9–12,20)? **6.** Why do you think God allowed Balaam to go with Balak's men the second time but not the first? What do you learn about God's wisdom from this story? **7.** What do you think is Balaam's real agenda (24:1)?

APPLY 1. In what ways do you find yourself trying to strike a deal with God? **2.** What has God taught you about the danger in trying to hinder his plans?

OPEN 1. What phrase best describes your personality: Quiet as a mouse? Stubborn as a mule? Loyal as a dog? Wise as an owl? Sly as a fox? Slow as a turtle? Quick as a rabbit? **2.** Tell of a time when you pretended to have a conversation with your pet?

STUDY Balaam had been summoned by King Balak of Moab to pronounce a curse on Israel, and he was vacillating back and forth as to whether or not he would. As he traveled to meet with Balak, God had a great surprise for him. **1.** Do you think Balaam was: A true prophet? A false prophet? An undecided prophet? A for-profit prophet? **2.** Why do you think God is angry with Balaam at this point? What phenomenal thing does God do to get Balaam's attention? **3.** How does Balaam's donkey react to the presence of the angel (vv. 23, 25,27)? What does Balaam do to his

---

22:12 they are blessed. God prohibited Balaam from putting a curse on Israel because they had his blessing. Yet God would know how powerless Balaam was. This event echoes ancient understandings of the battle between good and evil.

22:20 go with them, but. God reversed the instructions he had given to Balaam earlier (v. 12). He allowed Balaam to go, but only to do God's will. Ironically, in verse eight, Balaam had asked for time to discern God's will. Whether or not Balaam was sincere in this request, he was now subject to God's commands.

22:23 donkey saw the angel of the LORD ... she turned off the road. Although he was internationally famous, Balaam was a lousy diviner. His power to see truths revealed by the gods was less than that of his donkey, an animal not known for intelligence.

22:29 If I had a sword. Balaam's spiritual blindness made him a fool.

donkey each time? What do you think you would have done? **4.** What do you find unusual in Balaam's conversation with his donkey (vv. 28–30)? How do you think you might have reacted if your donkey talked to you? **5.** Which do you think is the most important miracle here—a talking donkey, or the opening of Balaam's eyes? How did Balaam react when he saw the angel (v. 31)? How might you have reacted? **6.** According to the angel, how did the donkey save Balaam (vv. 32–33)? What lessons do you think Balaam learned through this experience? What tough lessons has God taught you through unusual circumstances? **7.** Why was Balak a little put out with Balaam (v. 37)? **8.** What do you make of Balaam's response that he can only speak what God puts in his mouth?

APPLY 1. In what way has God recently taught you an important lesson and changed the direction of your life? **2.** How can you know God's will for your life?

OPEN 1. Have you ever been surprised with God's provision for you? **2.** Can you tell of a time you expected one thing and you actually received just the opposite? **3.** Were you disappointed, enraged, neutral, or did you try again to get what you wanted in the first place?

STUDY In expectation of getting what he wants from Balaam, Balak participates with Balaam in a sacrificial ritual. Balaam then goes off to get a word form the Lord, but it is not what Balak wanted to hear. **1.** What do you think the significance of the sacrifices might be? Why seven? Is this a game for Balaam,

30The donkey said to Balaam, "Am I not your own donkey, which you have always ridden, to this day? Have I been in the habit of doing this to you?"

"No," he said.

31Then the LORD opened Balaam's eyes, and he saw the angel of the LORD standing in the road with his sword drawn. So he bowed low and fell facedown.

32The angel of the LORD asked him, "Why have you beaten your donkey these three times? I have come here to oppose you because your path is a reckless one before me.[a]
33The donkey saw me and turned away from me these three times. If she had not turned away, I would certainly have killed you by now, but I would have spared her."

34Balaam said to the angel of the LORD, "I have sinned. I did not realize you were standing in the road to oppose me. Now if you are displeased, I will go back."

35The angel of the LORD said to Balaam, "Go with the men, but speak only what I tell you." So Balaam went with the princes of Balak.

36When Balak heard that Balaam was coming, he went out to meet him at the Moabite town on the Arnon border, at the edge of his territory.
37Balak said to Balaam, "Did I not send you an urgent summons? Why didn't you come to me? Am I really not able to reward you?"

38"Well, I have come to you now," Balaam replied. "But can I say just anything? I must speak only what God puts in my mouth."

39Then Balaam went with Balak to Kiriath Huzoth.
40Balak sacrificed cattle and sheep, and gave some to Balaam and the princes who were with him.
41The next morning Balak took Balaam up to Bamoth Baal, and from there he saw part of the people.

Balaam's First Oracle

23 Balaam said, "Build me seven altars here, and prepare seven bulls and seven rams for me."
2Balak did as Balaam said, and the two of them offered a bull and a ram on each altar.

3Then Balaam said to Balak, "Stay here beside your offering while I go aside. Perhaps the LORD will come to meet with me. Whatever he reveals to me I will tell you." Then he went off to a barren height.

4God met with him, and Balaam said, "I have prepared seven altars, and on each altar I have offered a bull and a ram."

5The LORD put a message in Balaam's mouth and said, "Go back to Balak and give him this message."

6So he went back to him and found him standing beside his offering, with all the princes of Moab.
7Then Balaam uttered his oracle:

[a]32 The meaning of the Hebrew for this clause is uncertain.

22:31 Then the LORD opened Balaam's eyes ... the angel of the LORD. Two miracles happened in three verses. First, a donkey spoke—and spoke the truth at that. Then, Balaam's eyes were opened and he saw the truth.

22:35 Go with the men, but speak only what I tell you. God amended his command to include the words Balaam could speak. For a prophet, pagan or not, speaking the words of God was the real test. A prophet who speaks words of his own mouth is a false prophet. He is to be feared and avoided (Matt. 7:15).

23:1 seven altars ... bulls ... rams. These preparations were typical of pagan sacrificial and divination ceremonies. The number seven was considered to have special power.

23:2 the two of them offered. Balak did not really want to know God's will in the matter. He just wanted the Israelites cursed so he could drive them out of his land (22:6). His participation in a ceremony to determine God's will was hypocritical.

"Balak brought me from Aram,
the king of Moab from the eastern mountains.
'Come,' he said, 'curse Jacob for me;
come, denounce Israel.'
8 How can I curse
those whom God has not cursed?
How can I denounce
those whom the LORD has not denounced?
9 From the rocky peaks I see them,
from the heights I view them.
I see a people who live apart
and do not consider themselves one of the nations.
10 Who can count the dust of Jacob
or number the fourth part of Israel?
Let me die the death of the righteous,
and may my end be like theirs!"

11 Balak said to Balaam, "What have you done to me? I brought you
to curse my enemies, but you have done nothing but bless them!"
12 He answered, "Must I not speak what the LORD puts in my
mouth?"

Balaam's Second Oracle

13 Then Balak said to him, "Come with me to another place where
you can see them; you will see only a part but not all of them. And
from there, curse them for me." 14 So he took him to the field of Zo-
phim on the top of Pisgah, and there he built seven altars and offered
a bull and a ram on each altar.
15 Balaam said to Balak, "Stay here beside your offering while I
meet with him over there."
16 The LORD met with Balaam and put a message in his mouth and
said, "Go back to Balak and give him this message."
17 So he went to him and found him standing beside his offering,
with the princes of Moab. Balak asked him, "What did the LORD say?"
18 Then he uttered his oracle:

"Arise, Balak, and listen;
hear me, son of Zippor.
19 God is not a man, that he should lie,
nor a son of man, that he should change his mind.
Does he speak and then not act?
Does he promise and not fulfill?
20 I have received a command to bless;
he has blessed, and I cannot change it.

or do you think he's serious? **2.** How do you think Balak felt about Balaam's statement that he could only speak what God told him to speak? Which god do you think Balak thought he meant? What do you think you might have done to insure the outcome if you were Balak? **3.** What was the message (vv. 7–10)? How did Balak take it (v. 11)? How did Balaam explain it (v. 12)? What part of the message impresses you the most? Why?

APPLY 1. Can you tell of a time when God totally changed your mind about something? **2.** How do you respond in situations when it is clearly your will against God's will? **3.** What can you do to be more submissive to God?

OPEN 1. What major test have you flunked on the first try? How many times did you try to pass the test? **2.** Which phrase best describes you: Easy to discourage? Inconsistent? Tenacious as a bulldog? Never say die?

STUDY After failing to get Balaam to pronounce a curse on Israel, Balak moves to a new location where they can see Israel in the hopes of pressuring Balaam to pronounce the curse. But the answer is the same. **1.** Why do you think Balak is trying again to persuade Balaam? What does he know about Balaam that makes him think Balaam can be bought? In what way would this pressure have affected you? **2.** What mistaken presumption had Balak made? What is the Lord's answer given directly to Balak this time (vv. 18–20)? How do you think he might have felt to hear that God was with Israel all the way (vv. 21–24)? **3.** What do you see as the key thought, or the key verse in this second oracle?

23:7–24:24 Balaam uttered seven oracles. In these pronouncements, he was bound by what God told him to say. In the first four, he uttered beautiful poetry. The last three are more obscure.

23:7 oracle. Balaam's pronouncements were not the same as those of the Hebrew prophets, and they did not carry the same social and spiritual significance to Israel. Thus his words are called "oracles," not "prophecies."

23:8 How can I curse ... How can I denounce? If Balaam did the divine will, as his reputation suggested, then he could not curse those whom God did not curse. If he went against God's will, he would be powerless to curse those whom God had blessed.

23:10 may my end be like theirs! Instead of cursing Israel, Baalam said he wanted to share in their fate, but that was not to be (31:8).

23:19 God is not a man, that he should lie. Balaam spoke this truth as an expert liar himself. His occupation was that of a glorified charlatan. Even Balaam recognized the uniqueness of God and his holy character.

Explain. **4.** How does Balak respond to this second rejection of his desire (v. 25)? Have you ever been like Balak and fighting against the Lord? **5.** How does Balaam once again reinforce the word of the Lord (v. 26)? Why do you think Balak is so persistent against a clear message from God?

APPLY 1. In what way has God recently told you "no"? **2.** How do you respond when the will of the Lord is different from your will? What can you do to increase your desire to do the will of God?

OPEN 1. What has someone tried to get you to do over and over that you didn't want to do? **2.** What mistake have you repeated many times? Why did you keep repeating it?

STUDY Balak just will not take "no" for an answer. Once again he imagines if he can get Balaam in another place, perhaps the answer will be different, but to his chagrin, the answer is the same. **1.** Wouldn't you think by now Balak would be tired of offering all those bulls and rams? Why did he continue to go through this routine to try to get the result he wanted? **2.** Based on these three attempts by Balak, how would you describe his view of God? Do you think God is sovereign, or can he be manipulated? Why do you think that? Can you think of anyway that you try to manipulate God? **3.** What does it mean that Balaam did not resort to sorcery this time (24:1)? Since he didn't speak directly with God as he had done before, what moved him to speak another oracle in favor of Israel? What do you think the

21 "No misfortune is seen in Jacob,
no misery observed in Israel.[a]
The LORD their God is with them;
the shout of the King is among them.
22 God brought them out of Egypt;
they have the strength of a wild ox.
23 There is no sorcery against Jacob,
no divination against Israel.
It will now be said of Jacob
and of Israel, 'See what God has done!'
24 The people rise like a lioness;
they rouse themselves like a lion
that does not rest till he devours his prey
and drinks the blood of his victims."

25 Then Balak said to Balaam, "Neither curse them at all nor bless
them at all!"
26 Balaam answered, "Did I not tell you I must do whatever the LORD
says?"

Balaam's Third Oracle

27 Then Balak said to Balaam, "Come, let me take you to another
place. Perhaps it will please God to let you curse them for me from
there." 28 And Balak took Balaam to the top of Peor, overlooking the
wasteland.
29 Balaam said, "Build me seven altars here, and prepare seven
bulls and seven rams for me." 30 Balak did as Balaam had said, and
offered a bull and a ram on each altar.

24 Now when Balaam saw that it pleased the LORD to bless
Israel, he did not resort to sorcery as at other times, but
turned his face toward the desert. 2 When Balaam looked out and saw
Israel encamped tribe by tribe, the Spirit of God came upon him 3 and
he uttered his oracle:

"The oracle of Balaam son of Beor,
the oracle of one whose eye sees clearly,
4 the oracle of one who hears the words of God,
who sees a vision from the Almighty,[b]
who falls prostrate, and whose eyes are opened:

5 "How beautiful are your tents, O Jacob,
your dwelling places, O Israel!

[a]21 *Or He has not looked on Jacob's offenses / or on the wrongs found in Israel.* [b]4 Hebrew *Shaddai*; also in verse 16

23:21 The LORD ... with them; the shout ... is among them. The first declaration of God's kingship was spoken by a pagan.

23:23 no divination against Israel. God's blessing of Israel protected them from sorcery or any other pagan power. (23:8)

23:24 rise like a lioness. The lioness was a poignant image of Israel from an enemy's perspective. The lioness was not a frantic hunter, but methodical and deadly. From the outside, Israel's campaign to capture Canaan had appeared to be like that of a hunting lioness: stalking the enemy, striking suddenly with great force and devouring everything.

24:2 the Spirit of God came upon him ... oracle. Balaam was neither filled nor anointed with the Spirit. Rather, he was overcome by the Spirit of God as this truth came to him. This experience was in sharp contrast with the "sorcery" Balaam usually practiced.

24:3–4 one whose eye sees clearly ... who hears the words of God. Despite Balaam's terrible past, God chose him to reveal the truth. The experience was one of being overwhelmed "falls prostrate" and yet seeing with incredible clarity "eyes are opened."

[6] "Like valleys they spread out,
like gardens beside a river,
like aloes planted by the LORD,
like cedars beside the waters.
[7] Water will flow from their buckets;
their seed will have abundant water.

"Their king will be greater than Agag;
their kingdom will be exalted.

[8] "God brought them out of Egypt;
they have the strength of a wild ox.
They devour hostile nations
and break their bones in pieces;
with their arrows they pierce them.
[9] Like a lion they crouch and lie down,
like a lioness—who dares to rouse them?

"May those who bless you be blessed
and those who curse you be cursed!"

[10] Then Balak's anger burned against Balaam. He struck his hands
together and said to him, "I summoned you to curse my enemies, but
you have blessed them these three times. [11] Now leave at once and go
home! I said I would reward you handsomely, but the LORD has kept
you from being rewarded."

[12] Balaam answered Balak, "Did I not tell the messengers you sent
me, [13] 'Even if Balak gave me his palace filled with silver and gold, I
could not do anything of my own accord, good or bad, to go beyond
the command of the LORD—and I must say only what the LORD says'?
[14] Now I am going back to my people, but come, let me warn you of
what this people will do to your people in days to come."

Balaam's Fourth Oracle

[15] Then he uttered his oracle:

"The oracle of Balaam son of Beor,
the oracle of one whose eye sees clearly,
[16] the oracle of one who hears the words of God,
who has knowledge from the Most High,
who sees a vision from the Almighty,
who falls prostrate, and whose eyes are opened:

[17] "I see him, but not now;
I behold him, but not near.
A star will come out of Jacob;
a scepter will rise out of Israel.
He will crush the foreheads of Moab,

difference is between a word from God and sorcery? Which would you rather trust? Why? **4.** In what ways is this third oracle different from the first two? In what ways is it the same? What is the message of this oracle? What is the punch line (v. 9)? **5.** How could Balak say that God caused Balaam to lose his reward? At this point what do you think it meant to Balaam that he lost his reward? Did he care? What is Balaam's answer (vv. 12–13)? What difference would the money have made to you?

APPLY 1. When is it most difficult for you to believe, as this oracle says of Israel, that God only wants what is good for you (Rom. 8:28)? **2.** How does this story change your view of God and your view of your relationship with him?

OPEN 1. What do you like best about a suspense movie: The plot? The hero? The drama? The mystery? The victorious ending? **2.** If you had the power of seeing into the future, what would you want to see? Why?

STUDY The drama is over, but Balaam has several parting things to say. These final words are oracles about Israel's success against her enemies. **1.** When you read verses 15–16, do you get the feeling Balaam is getting another message from God, or is this his own material? Is he just trying to get in the last word? **2.** What

24:11 I would reward ... but the LORD has kept you from being rewarded. Balak wanted Balaam to pronounce only curses. His sarcasm toward Balaam was meant to punish him where it hurts—right in the wallet.

24:15–16 knowledge from the Most High. The fourth oracle began with the same formula as the third. However, the fourth went beyond the third's claim of "visions" to "knowledge." Clearly, the implication is that the visions Balaam experienced gave him a special understanding of the future.

24:17 star ... scepter. This oracle predicts the rise of David and his consolidation of power over the region. Its imagery strongly suggests the coming of a messiah. (Rev. 2:27–28; 22:16).

is the heart of this fourth oracle? Who do you think the "star" might be (Rev. 22:16)? What about this message is the same as the others? What is the unifying theme? **3.** What is the message of Balaam's final oracles (vv. 20–24)? If you had been in the Israelite camp and these words came back to you, how would they make you feel? **4.** What is said about the nature of God in verse 23? What effect do such words have on your faith?

APPLY 1. Who, or what, has tried again and again to persuade you to turn away from God? How have you handled the temptation? **2.** How can a group of believers encourage one another to remain faithful to God, no matter what?

the skulls[a] of [b] all the sons of Sheth.[c]
18 Edom will be conquered;
Seir, his enemy, will be conquered,
but Israel will grow strong.
19 A ruler will come out of Jacob
and destroy the survivors of the city."

Balaam's Final Oracles

20 Then Balaam saw Amalek and uttered his oracle:

"Amalek was first among the nations,
but he will come to ruin at last."

21 Then he saw the Kenites and uttered his oracle:

"Your dwelling place is secure,
your nest is set in a rock;
22 yet you Kenites will be destroyed
when Asshur takes you captive."

23 Then he uttered his oracle:

"Ah, who can live when God does this?[d]
24 Ships will come from the shores of Kittim;
they will subdue Asshur and Eber,
but they too will come to ruin."

25 Then Balaam got up and returned home and Balak went his own way.

Moab Seduces Israel

25 While Israel was staying in Shittim, the men began to indulge
in sexual immorality with Moabite women, 2 who invited
them to the sacrifices to their gods. The people ate and bowed down
before these gods. 3 So Israel joined in worshiping the Baal of Peor.
And the LORD's anger burned against them.
4 The LORD said to Moses, "Take all the leaders of these people, kill
them and expose them in broad daylight before the LORD, so that the
LORD's fierce anger may turn away from Israel."
5 So Moses said to Israel's judges, "Each of you must put to death
those of your men who have joined in worshiping the Baal of Peor."
6 Then an Israelite man brought to his family a Midianite woman

[a] *17* Samaritan Pentateuch (see also Jer. 48:45); the meaning of the word in the Masoretic Text is uncertain. [b] *17* Or possibly *Moab, / batter* [c] *17* Or *all the noisy boasters* [d] *23* Masoretic Text; with a different word division of the Hebrew *A people will gather from the north.*

OPEN 1. Do you think the state of sexual immorality in society is: Not a problem? A little harmless fun? Somewhat destructive to family life? Devastating to the fabric of society? A cause of the terrible judgment of God on the earth? **2.** What do you believe to be the most significant factor in determining sexual standards today? Explain.

STUDY One of the greatest dangers to Israel's relationship with God was the threat of idolatry. That threat became a reality when the Israelites were seduced into idolatry through sexual immorality by the Moabites. **1.** Why do you think the

25:1–18 God protected the people of Israel from Balaam's curse, but not from their own weaknesses. On the very doorstep of Canaan, Israel turned from God toward the sexual immorality of Baal worship. Israelite men were the victims of sexual seduction (v. 2), a seduction that led to apostasy.

25:1 in Shittim ... indulge in sexual immorality. Sex was the bait, Baal worship was the trap. Thus three Commandments were rapidly violated: the commandments against sexual immorality, idol worship and setting other gods before God.

25:4 Take all the leaders ... kill them and expose them in broad daylight. This punishment was severe in proportion to the offense. Execution and public display of the corpses would not only punish the guilty but humiliate their families and frighten everyone. The corpses would serve as a public reminder.

25:6 an Israelite man brought to his family a Midianite woman. The man who did this, Zimri (v. 14), must have lost any sense of decency. First, the woman's presence was an insult to his family and indicated clear defiance of the laws against fornication. Second, Zimri's action, in light of the punishment already mentioned, was plainly ignorant and insensitive. The women had caused the death of many loved ones (24,000, according to v. 9).

right before the eyes of Moses and the whole assembly of Israel while
they were weeping at the entrance to the Tent of Meeting. 7When
Phinehas son of Eleazar, the son of Aaron, the priest, saw this, he left
the assembly, took a spear in his hand 8and followed the Israelite into
the tent. He drove the spear through both of them—through the
Israelite and into the woman's body. Then the plague against the
Israelites was stopped; 9but those who died in the plague numbered
24,000.

10The LORD said to Moses, 11"Phinehas son of Eleazar, the son of
Aaron, the priest, has turned my anger away from the Israelites; for
he was as zealous as I am for my honor among them, so that in my
zeal I did not put an end to them. 12Therefore tell him I am making my
covenant of peace with him. 13He and his descendants will have a
covenant of a lasting priesthood, because he was zealous for the
honor of his God and made atonement for the Israelites."

14The name of the Israelite who was killed with the Midianite woman was Zimri son of Salu, the leader of a Simeonite family. 15And the
name of the Midianite woman who was put to death was Cozbi
daughter of Zur, a tribal chief of a Midianite family.

16The LORD said to Moses, 17"Treat the Midianites as enemies and
kill them, 18because they treated you as enemies when they deceived
you in the affair of Peor and their sister Cozbi, the daughter of a Midianite leader, the woman who was killed when the plague came as a
result of Peor."

The Second Census

26 After the plague the LORD said to Moses and Eleazar son of
Aaron, the priest, 2"Take a census of the whole Israelite
community by families—all those twenty years old or more who are
able to serve in the army of Israel." 3So on the plains of Moab by the
Jordan across from Jericho,[a] Moses and Eleazar the priest spoke with
them and said, 4"Take a census of the men twenty years old or more,
as the LORD commanded Moses."

These were the Israelites who came out of Egypt:

5The descendants of Reuben, the firstborn son of Israel, were:
through Hanoch, the Hanochite clan;
through Pallu, the Palluite clan;
6through Hezron, the Hezronite clan;
through Carmi, the Carmite clan.
7These were the clans of Reuben; those numbered were 43,730.

8The son of Pallu was Eliab, 9and the sons of Eliab were Nemuel,
Dathan and Abiram. The same Dathan and Abiram were the community officials who rebelled against Moses and Aaron and were
among Korah's followers when they rebelled against the LORD. 10The
earth opened its mouth and swallowed them along with Korah,

[a]3 Hebrew *Jordan of Jericho*; possibly an ancient name for the Jordan River; also in verse 63

Moabite women might have been more attractive to the Israelite men than the women of Israel? How could they be so sexually immoral when God had been so clear in his prohibition of sexual sin? **2.** Which do you think was most offensive to God, the immorality or the idolatry? **3.** Why did the idolatry evoke such a drastic response from God (v. 4)? If you had been in charge, what would you have done in this situation? **4.** Why does God consider Phinehas to be so zealous? How serious was the plague his actions stopped (v. 9)? **5.** What was his reward (vv. 12–13)? Why do you think the "honor" of the Lord is so important?

APPLY How can you resist sexual temptations and other temptations to turn away from God? How can you help your friends when they are tempted?

OPEN 1. Do you come from a large or small family? What are the advantages and disadvantages of the size of your family? **2.** How many people have been added to your family in the last 38 years?

STUDY God had told the people of Israel that none of the original Israelites, except Joshua and Caleb, would enter the Promised Land because of their rebellion and unbelief. Now as they prepare once again to enter the Promised Land, another count is to be done. **1.** What do you think was the purpose of this census (vv. 52–56,63–65)? Who was actually counted (v. 2)? What was the final tally (v. 51)? Do you think that would have been a sizeable army in those days? How would it measure up today? **2.** Since the land was to be divided up according to the size of the tribes, who would get the biggest piece of land (v. 22)? The smallest (v. 14)? Do you think this was a fair way to divide up the land? **3.** As you look at the numbers, which tribe has

25:17 Treat the Midianites as enemies and kill them. God declared war on the Midianites, who had been conspiring with Balak since Israel had assumed the dominant position in the Transjordan (22:1–7). The Midianite women had seduced Israelite men into Baal worship and, thus, played a part in the punishing death of 24,000 Israelites.

26:1–51 Census taking played a crucial role in Israel's preparation for war. The lists of eligible soldiers were taken from the census reports compiled for each tribe. (Ex. 30:12) The first census

lost the most? Which tribe has gained the most? What significance is in these changes? **4.** Who receives special mention in this census, and why (vv. 9,19,33,65)? Why are stories of those who failed and those who succeeded important to remember? **5.** How many Levites were counted (v. 62)? Why is their count different from the rest of Israel? **6.** What does it say about the truthfulness of God's Word and his faithfulness to his Word that not one of the original Israelites 20 years or older who came out of Egypt were in this number, except Joshua and Caleb (vv. 64–65)? Do you think God is as serious today about your faithfulness?

APPLY **1.** What does it mean to you to be counted as one of God's people today? **2.** How does it make you feel to know that some are not counted with God's people today? What are you doing about it?

whose followers died when the fire devoured the 250 men. And
they served as a warning sign. 11 The line of Korah, however, did not
die out.

12 The descendants of Simeon by their clans were:
through Nemuel, the Nemuelite clan;
through Jamin, the Jaminite clan;
through Jakin, the Jakinite clan;
13 through Zerah, the Zerahite clan;
through Shaul, the Shaulite clan.
14 These were the clans of Simeon; there were 22,200 men.

15 The descendants of Gad by their clans were:
through Zephon, the Zephonite clan;
through Haggi, the Haggite clan;
through Shuni, the Shunite clan;
16 through Ozni, the Oznite clan;
through Eri, the Erite clan;
17 through Arodi,[a] the Arodite clan;
through Areli, the Arelite clan.
18 These were the clans of Gad; those numbered were 40,500.

19 Er and Onan were sons of Judah, but they died in Canaan.
20 The descendants of Judah by their clans were:
through Shelah, the Shelanite clan;
through Perez, the Perezite clan;
through Zerah, the Zerahite clan.
21 The descendants of Perez were:
through Hezron, the Hezronite clan;
through Hamul, the Hamulite clan.
22 These were the clans of Judah; those numbered were 76,500.

23 The descendants of Issachar by their clans were:
through Tola, the Tolaite clan;
through Puah, the Puite[b] clan;
24 through Jashub, the Jashubite clan;
through Shimron, the Shimronite clan.
25 These were the clans of Issachar; those numbered were 64,300.

26 The descendants of Zebulun by their clans were:
through Sered, the Seredite clan;
through Elon, the Elonite clan;
through Jahleel, the Jahleelite clan.
27 These were the clans of Zebulun; those numbered were 60,500.

28 The descendants of Joseph by their clans through Manasseh and
Ephraim were:

29 The descendants of Manasseh:
through Makir, the Makirite clan (Makir was the father of Gilead);
through Gilead, the Gileadite clan.

[a]17 Samaritan Pentateuch and Syriac (see also Gen. 46:16); Masoretic Text *Arod* [b]23 Samaritan Pentateuch, Septuagint, Vulgate and Syriac (see also 1 Chron. 7:1); Masoretic Text *through Puvah, the Punite*

had been taken over 38 years before. Nearly all the men twenty years old or older in that census were now dead. The new census would give the tribal leaders and Moses an idea of how many soldiers were ready to fight.

[30]These were the descendants of Gilead:
through Iezer, the Iezerite clan;
through Helek, the Helekite clan;
[31]through Asriel, the Asrielite clan;
through Shechem, the Shechemite clan;
[32]through Shemida, the Shemidaite clan;
through Hepher, the Hepherite clan.
[33](Zelophehad son of Hepher had no sons; he had only daughters, whose names were Mahlah, Noah, Hoglah, Milcah and Tirzah.)
[34]These were the clans of Manasseh; those numbered were 52,700.

[35]These were the descendants of Ephraim by their clans:
through Shuthelah, the Shuthelahite clan;
through Beker, the Bekerite clan;
through Tahan, the Tahanite clan.
[36]These were the descendants of Shuthelah:
through Eran, the Eranite clan.
[37]These were the clans of Ephraim; those numbered were 32,500.

These were the descendants of Joseph by their clans.

[38]The descendants of Benjamin by their clans were:
through Bela, the Belaite clan;
through Ashbel, the Ashbelite clan;
through Ahiram, the Ahiramite clan;
[39]through Shupham,[a] the Shuphamite clan;
through Hupham, the Huphamite clan.
[40]The descendants of Bela through Ard and Naaman were:
through Ard,[b] the Ardite clan;
through Naaman, the Naamite clan.
[41]These were the clans of Benjamin; those numbered were 45,600.

[42]These were the descendants of Dan by their clans:
through Shuham, the Shuhamite clan.
These were the clans of Dan: [43]All of them were Shuhamite clans; and those numbered were 64,400.

[44]The descendants of Asher by their clans were:
through Imnah, the Imnite clan;
through Ishvi, the Ishvite clan;
through Beriah, the Beriite clan;
[45]and through the descendants of Beriah:
through Heber, the Heberite clan;
through Malkiel, the Malkielite clan.
[46](Asher had a daughter named Serah.)
[47]These were the clans of Asher; those numbered were 53,400.

[48]The descendants of Naphtali by their clans were:
through Jahzeel, the Jahzeelite clan;
through Guni, the Gunite clan;
[49]through Jezer, the Jezerite clan;
through Shillem, the Shillemite clan.
[50]These were the clans of Naphtali; those numbered were 45,400.

[a]39 A few manuscripts of the Masoretic Text, Samaritan Pentateuch, Vulgate and Syriac (see also Septuagint); most manuscripts of the Masoretic Text *Shephupham* [b]40 Samaritan Pentateuch and Vulgate (see also Septuagint); Masoretic Text does not have *through Ard*.

[51]The total number of the men of Israel was 601,730.

[52]The LORD said to Moses, [53]"The land is to be allotted to them as
an inheritance based on the number of names. [54]To a larger group
give a larger inheritance, and to a smaller group a smaller one; each
is to receive its inheritance according to the number of those listed.
[55]Be sure that the land is distributed by lot. What each group inherits
will be according to the names for its ancestral tribe. [56]Each inheritance is to be distributed by lot among the larger and smaller groups."

[57]These were the Levites who were counted by their clans:
through Gershon, the Gershonite clan;
through Kohath, the Kohathite clan;
through Merari, the Merarite clan.
[58]These also were Levite clans:
the Libnite clan,
the Hebronite clan,
the Mahlite clan,
the Mushite clan,
the Korahite clan.
(Kohath was the forefather of Amram; [59]the name of Amram's
wife was Jochebed, a descendant of Levi, who was born to the
Levites[a] in Egypt. To Amram she bore Aaron, Moses and their sister Miriam. [60]Aaron was the father of Nadab and Abihu, Eleazar
and Ithamar. [61]But Nadab and Abihu died when they made an offering before the LORD with unauthorized fire.)

[62]All the male Levites a month old or more numbered 23,000. They
were not counted along with the other Israelites because they received no inheritance among them.

[63]These are the ones counted by Moses and Eleazar the priest
when they counted the Israelites on the plains of Moab by the Jordan
across from Jericho. [64]Not one of them was among those counted by
Moses and Aaron the priest when they counted the Israelites in the
Desert of Sinai. [65]For the LORD had told those Israelites they would
surely die in the desert, and not one of them was left except Caleb son
of Jephunneh and Joshua son of Nun.

OPEN 1. For what special situation in your life would you like to receive consideration? How would you plead your case? **2.** What are the various ways which heads of government change? Which way do you think is best? Why?

Zelophehad's Daughters

27 The daughters of Zelophehad son of Hepher, the son of
Gilead, the son of Makir, the son of Manasseh, belonged to
the clans of Manasseh son of Joseph. The names of the daughters
were Mahlah, Noah, Hoglah, Milcah and Tirzah. They approached
[2]the entrance to the Tent of Meeting and stood before Moses, Eleazar

[a]59 Or *Jochebed, a daughter of Levi, who was born to Levi*

26:51 601,730. The total population from the first census, 38 years earlier, had been 603,550. Thus, after all those years of wandering, without a permanent source of water and without food other than manna, God had provided for his people, and their numbers had remained stable. Despite the deaths caused by battles, disease, old age and disobedience, Israel had prospered and was almost ready to enter the Promised Land.

26:53 based on the number of names. The amount of land allotted to each of Israel's tribes was determined by the number of names in that tribe. The location of that land would be determined by lot (v. 55).

27:1–11 The plans for distribution of the land among the tribes inevitably brought questions and exceptions. The case of Zelophehad's daughters was extraordinary in that women brought it. Women had very few rights, so their appeal for an inheritance was an unprecedented act of courage. God's position on inheritance was a change

the priest, the leaders and the whole assembly, and said, [3]"Our father died in the desert. He was not among Korah's followers, who banded together against the LORD, but he died for his own sin and left no sons. [4]Why should our father's name disappear from his clan because he had no son? Give us property among our father's relatives."

[5]So Moses brought their case before the LORD [6]and the LORD said to him, [7]"What Zelophehad's daughters are saying is right. You must certainly give them property as an inheritance among their father's relatives and turn their father's inheritance over to them.

[8]"Say to the Israelites, 'If a man dies and leaves no son, turn his inheritance over to his daughter. [9]If he has no daughter, give his inheritance to his brothers. [10]If he has no brothers, give his inheritance to his father's brothers. [11]If his father had no brothers, give his inheritance to the nearest relative in his clan, that he may possess it. This is to be a legal requirement for the Israelites, as the LORD commanded Moses.'"

Joshua to Succeed Moses

[12]Then the LORD said to Moses, "Go up this mountain in the Abarim range and see the land I have given the Israelites. [13]After you have seen it, you too will be gathered to your people, as your brother Aaron was, [14]for when the community rebelled at the waters in the Desert of Zin, both of you disobeyed my command to honor me as holy before their eyes." (These were the waters of Meribah Kadesh, in the Desert of Zin.)

[15]Moses said to the LORD, [16]"May the LORD, the God of the spirits of all mankind, appoint a man over this community [17]to go out and come in before them, one who will lead them out and bring them in, so the LORD's people will not be like sheep without a shepherd."

[18]So the LORD said to Moses, "Take Joshua son of Nun, a man in whom is the spirit,[a] and lay your hand on him. [19]Have him stand before Eleazar the priest and the entire assembly and commission him in their presence. [20]Give him some of your authority so the whole Israelite community will obey him. [21]He is to stand before Eleazar the

[a]18 Or *Spirit*

STUDY After more than 40 years in the wilderness, the Israelites find themselves just across the Jordan River ready to enter the Promised Land. However, a couple of unresolved issues need to be handled first. **1.** What do you admire about the "gutsy" daughters of Zelophehad? What was their case? Do you think they had a point? Why or why not? What was God's answer (vv. 8–11)? **2.** Why do you think it was so important for the Israelites to pass on their family name? Why is that not as important today? **3.** When God told Moses it was time to die, do you think he was: Relieved? Afraid? Uncertain? Ecstatic and ready to go? How will it be for you when it comes your time? Why? **4.** What was Moses' concern for Israel when he was told he was about to depart (vv. 16–17)? What does this tell you about the heart of Moses? **5.** Why was Moses not allowed to enter the Promised Land with the people (vv. 13–14)? Do you think this was a fair judgment, or a little too harsh? **6.** Why was it important to make a show of the transfer of power to Joshua (vv. 18–20)? How would Joshua get wisdom for his decisions (v. 21)? If you were the leader, how important would it be to get your guidance directly from God? Do you think the leaders of nations today lean on God for wisdom?

APPLY 1. What situations among God's people today might deserve special consideration and treatment? **2.** Who are your spiritual leaders? What is your attitude toward them? How can you improve

from the male-dominated inheritance rules that had governed property until this time.

27:3 he died for his own sin and left no sons. The women's claim was based on the fact that their father had committed no act that would preclude their inheritance. He had simply died during the forty years in the wilderness, along with almost everyone of his generation. The women understood that denying them land would be punishment without cause. They understood the Law and knew they had a just case for fair treatment.

27:4–5 our father's name . . . Moses brought their case before the LORD. This phrase gives a glimpse into how justice was meted out among the Israelites. The Lord had written the Law, and he also sat as the highest judge in its application. The appeal to the judge was simple, and the answer was immediate.

27:12–23 God gave Zelophehad's daughters their justice, and these verses show another side of God's justice. Moses had been a faithful servant of God and leader of Israel, but God would not bend his justice to allow Moses to lead Israel into Canaan. No exception was made for his sin at Kadesh when he struck the rock instead of speaking to it (20:1–13). Moses had seen enough of the consequences of sin to accept God's judgment even though it was strict.

27:16 appoint a man over this community. Moses' first concern was for the people he had led for so long. He knew that they were difficult to lead and would be especially troublesome with a war on the horizon.

27:18 Take Joshua son of Nun. Just as Eleazar had been designated Aaron's successor before he died, so Joshua must be made Moses' successor before he died. Joshua was well qualified for the job. He had been one of the original spies into Canaan (13:8,16). This would help him with the upcoming invasion. He had shown courage and willingness to lead during the uprising following the reports of those spies (13:1–14:38). He would need all his courage and fortitude in the days ahead as the leader of Israel.

27:20 Give him some of your authority. Moses had attained his authority

your respect for them and your support of them?

OPEN **1.** What weekly routine do you have that is very important to you—something you never miss? **2.** What weekly routines or observances does your church have to help you focus on your relationship with God?

STUDY Now that the leadership of Israel was in place, God turns his attention to the matter of regular observances among the people which will enable them to worship him. The focus of the observances is the sacrifice rituals—the offerings. **1.** What do you think would make an offering "an aroma pleasing to the Lord"? For whose benefit were all these offerings made? **2.** What is the significance of the sacrificial animals being "without defect"? How does the sacrificial lamb foreshadow the work of Jesus Christ (1 Peter 1:18–21)? What does it mean to you that Jesus was sacrificed as an offering for you? **3.** Why do you think God designed these offerings to be made on a regular basis—daily, weekly, monthly, yearly? Can you imagine the number of animals required for all these sacrifices? Why do you think all this blood needed to be shed? **4.** What event does the Passover commemorate (Ex. 12:17,24–28)? Why do you think God wants the Israelites to celebrate the Passover year after year? What Christian observance is directly related to the Passover (Matt. 26:17–30)? What connections do you see between the Passover and the Last Supper? **5.** What did the Feast of Weeks celebrate (Ex. 34:22–26)? How do you thank the Lord for his abundant provision in your life?

priest, who will obtain decisions for him by inquiring of the Urim
before the LORD. At his command he and the entire community of the
Israelites will go out, and at his command they will come in."
22Moses did as the LORD commanded him. He took Joshua and had
him stand before Eleazar the priest and the whole assembly. 23Then
he laid his hands on him and commissioned him, as the LORD
instructed through Moses.

Daily Offerings

28 The LORD said to Moses, 2"Give this command to the Israelites and say to them: 'See that you present to me at the
appointed time the food for my offerings made by fire, as an aroma
pleasing to me.' 3Say to them: 'This is the offering made by fire that
you are to present to the LORD: two lambs a year old without defect,
as a regular burnt offering each day. 4Prepare one lamb in the morning and the other at twilight, 5together with a grain offering of a tenth
of an ephah[a] of fine flour mixed with a quarter of a hin[b] of oil from
pressed olives. 6This is the regular burnt offering instituted at Mount
Sinai as a pleasing aroma, an offering made to the LORD by fire. 7The
accompanying drink offering is to be a quarter of a hin of fermented
drink with each lamb. Pour out the drink offering to the LORD at the
sanctuary. 8Prepare the second lamb at twilight, along with the same
kind of grain offering and drink offering that you prepare in the
morning. This is an offering made by fire, an aroma pleasing to the
LORD.

Sabbath Offerings

9" 'On the Sabbath day, make an offering of two lambs a year old
without defect, together with its drink offering and a grain offering of
two-tenths of an ephah[c] of fine flour mixed with oil. 10This is the
burnt offering for every Sabbath, in addition to the regular burnt
offering and its drink offering.

Monthly Offerings

11" 'On the first of every month, present to the LORD a burnt offering of two young bulls, one ram and seven male lambs a year old, all
without defect. 12With each bull there is to be a grain offering of
three-tenths of an ephah[d] of fine flour mixed with oil; with the ram, a
grain offering of two-tenths of an ephah of fine flour mixed with oil;
13and with each lamb, a grain offering of a tenth of an ephah of fine

[a]*5* That is, probably about 2 quarts (about 2 liters); also in verses 13, 21 and 29 [b]*5* That is, probably about 1 quart (about 1 liter); also in verses 7 and 14 [c]*9* That is, probably about 4 quarts (about 4.5 liters); also in verses 12, 20 and 28 [d]*12* That is, probably about 6 quarts (about 6.5 liters); also in verses 20 and 28

over the nation of Israel through God's assistance as well as sheer fortitude. Miracles like the parting of the waters and the miraculous escape from the Egyptians had strengthened Moses' leadership. But ultimately it was the *fact that Moses was the mediator* between God and Israel that gave him his power. That role would be hard for a successor to attain, so God commanded a transition period between Moses' leadership and that of Joshua.

28:1–29:40 These chapters provided a break in the narrative before Joshua leads Israel into the Promised Land. The passages also reminded the Israelites *of the importance* of sacrifice and ritual in their lives. The invasion of Canaan was the culmination of hundreds of years of God's faithfulness to his covenant people. Before it took place, Israel got another reminder of their proper response to their God.

28:1–8 offering each day. These verses restated the Law concerning the required daily sacrifices. (Ex. 29:38–43.)

28:9–10 On the Sabbath day. The Sabbath sacrifice was in addition to the sacrifice made every day, including the Sabbath.

flour mixed with oil. This is for a burnt offering, a pleasing aroma, an
offering made to the LORD by fire. 14With each bull there is to be a
drink offering of half a hin[a] of wine; with the ram, a third of a hin[b];
and with each lamb, a quarter of a hin. This is the monthly burnt
offering to be made at each new moon during the year. 15Besides the
regular burnt offering with its drink offering, one male goat is to be
presented to the LORD as a sin offering.

The Passover

16" 'On the fourteenth day of the first month the LORD's Passover is
to be held. 17On the fifteenth day of this month there is to be a festival; for seven days eat bread made without yeast. 18On the first day
hold a sacred assembly and do no regular work. 19Present to the LORD
an offering made by fire, a burnt offering of two young bulls, one ram
and seven male lambs a year old, all without defect. 20With each bull
prepare a grain offering of three-tenths of an ephah of fine flour
mixed with oil; with the ram, two-tenths; 21and with each of the
seven lambs, one-tenth. 22Include one male goat as a sin offering to
make atonement for you. 23Prepare these in addition to the regular
morning burnt offering. 24In this way prepare the food for the offering made by fire every day for seven days as an aroma pleasing to the
LORD; it is to be prepared in addition to the regular burnt offering and
its drink offering. 25On the seventh day hold a sacred assembly and
do no regular work.

Feast of Weeks

26" 'On the day of firstfruits, when you present to the LORD an offering of new grain during the Feast of Weeks, hold a sacred assembly
and do no regular work. 27Present a burnt offering of two young bulls,
one ram and seven male lambs a year old as an aroma pleasing to the
LORD. 28With each bull there is to be a grain offering of three-tenths of
an ephah of fine flour mixed with oil; with the ram, two-tenths; 29and
with each of the seven lambs, one-tenth. 30Include one male goat to
make atonement for you. 31Prepare these together with their drink offerings, in addition to the regular burnt offering and its grain offering.
Be sure the animals are without defect.

Feast of Trumpets

29 " 'On the first day of the seventh month hold a sacred assembly and do no regular work. It is a day for you to sound the
trumpets. 2As an aroma pleasing to the LORD, prepare a burnt offering
of one young bull, one ram and seven male lambs a year old, all without defect. 3With the bull prepare a grain offering of three-tenths of

[a]14 That is, probably about 2 quarts (about 2 liters) [b]14 That is, probably about 1 1/4 quarts (about 1.2 liters)

APPLY 1. What is your daily reminder of what God has done for you? Weekly? Monthly? Yearly? **2.** What can your church do to encourage its members to not forget all that God has done? How can this group help?

OPEN 1. What is your favorite thing to do on a holiday? **2.** If you could create a new national holiday, what would it be?

STUDY As God continues to give instructions to Israel on offerings and festivals, he tells the people to observe the Feast of Trumpets and the Day of Atonement. **1.** Do

28:16–25 These verses restated the Law concerning the observance of Passover. (Lev. 23:4–8.) Passover was closely associated with the Feast of Unleavened Bread (Ex. 12:15).

28:26–31 Feast of Weeks. The Feast of Weeks was observed fifty days after the Feast of Unleavened Bread. Thus, the name Pentecost (meaning "fifty") became associated with the festival. The underlying reason for the feast was the offering of firstfruits from the grain harvest. For that reason, complex instructions governed the grain sacrifice to be made with each animal offering. (Lev. 23:4–14.)

29:1–6 sound the trumpets. The Feast of Trumpets was celebrated in the seventh month. Later, the Feast of Trumpets would become "Rosh Hashanah," the New Year's celebration.

an ephah[a] of fine flour mixed with oil; with the ram, two-tenths[b];
4and with each of the seven lambs, one-tenth.[c] 5Include one male
goat as a sin offering to make atonement for you. 6These are in addition to the monthly and daily burnt offerings with their grain offerings and drink offerings as specified. They are offerings made to the
LORD by fire—a pleasing aroma.

Day of Atonement

7" 'On the tenth day of this seventh month hold a sacred assembly.
You must deny yourselves[d] and do no work. 8Present as an aroma
pleasing to the LORD a burnt offering of one young bull, one ram and
seven male lambs a year old, all without defect. 9With the bull prepare
a grain offering of three-tenths of an ephah of fine flour mixed with
oil; with the ram, two-tenths; 10and with each of the seven lambs,
one-tenth. 11Include one male goat as a sin offering, in addition to
the sin offering for atonement and the regular burnt offering with its
grain offering, and their drink offerings.

Feast of Tabernacles

12" 'On the fifteenth day of the seventh month, hold a sacred
assembly and do no regular work. Celebrate a festival to the LORD for
seven days. 13Present an offering made by fire as an aroma pleasing
to the LORD, a burnt offering of thirteen young bulls, two rams and
fourteen male lambs a year old, all without defect. 14With each of the
thirteen bulls prepare a grain offering of three-tenths of an ephah of
fine flour mixed with oil; with each of the two rams, two-tenths;
15and with each of the fourteen lambs, one-tenth. 16Include one male
goat as a sin offering, in addition to the regular burnt offering with its
grain offering and drink offering.
17" 'On the second day prepare twelve young bulls, two rams and
fourteen male lambs a year old, all without defect. 18With the bulls,
rams and lambs, prepare their grain offerings and drink offerings
according to the number specified. 19Include one male goat as a sin
offering, in addition to the regular burnt offering with its grain offering, and their drink offerings.
20" 'On the third day prepare eleven bulls, two rams and fourteen
male lambs a year old, all without defect. 21With the bulls, rams and
lambs, prepare their grain offerings and drink offerings according to
the number specified. 22Include one male goat as a sin offering, in

[a]3 That is, probably about 6 quarts (about 6.5 liters); also in verses 9 and 14 [b]3 That is, probably about 4 quarts (about 4.5 liters); also in verses 9 and 14 [c]4 That is, probably about 2 quarts (about 2 liters); also in verses 10 and 15 [d]7 Or *must fast*

you think the significance of blowing the trumpets here is: To make beautiful music? To call the army together? To announce the beginning of the feast? To praise God? **2.** What was the purpose of the Day of Atonement (Lev. 16:29–34; 23:26–32)? What connection does this have with the work of Christ (Rom. 3:25–26; Heb. 2:17–18)?

APPLY What does atonement mean? What does that have to do with your relationship with God?

OPEN 1. See if anyone in your group can remember the gifts in the song, "The Twelve Days of Christmas." **2.** Tell of a long religious meeting you have attended. Did you get tired?

STUDY The Feast of Tabernacles celebrated the end of the yearly harvest and was an expression of thanksgiving to God. The feast was designed to do the same thing a little differently each day until the climax was reached after a week. **1.** Where does this feast get its name (Lev. 23:33,43)? What memory was this feast designed to invoke? **2.** Why do you think God instructed these sacrifices in a decreasing order of amount? What might that remind the Israelites of with reference to their wilderness wandering? What would it mean to you? **3.** What would the enormous amount of blood shed during the week of this festival say to you? What does it say to you about God's view of sin? **4.** Why do you think Jesus chose this feast to do some significant work in the temple at Jerusalem (John 7)?

29:7–11 a sacred assembly. This festival was observed on the tenth day of the seventh month. After the celebration of the Feast of Trumpets ten days earlier, this festival turned Israel's attentions inward. It was a festival, not only of sacrifice, but also of confession and contrition. The high priest was required to enter the Most Holy Place alone. No one was even allowed to be in the Tent of Meeting while the priest was in the Most Holy Place. While there, he had to make "atonement for himself, his household and the whole community of Israel" (Lev. 16:17).

29:12–39 Celebrate a festival. The name of this festival is misleading. The Hebrew word was "Sukkot," which could be translated as "tabernacles" or "booths." As Leviticus 23:42–43 explains, the festival was a remembrance of the time after the Exodus when the Israelites lived in small "booths." The festival also celebrated the end of the yearly harvest. Many sacrifices were required over the festival's seven days, including daily sin offerings. The purpose of the Feast of Tabernacles was like that of American Thanksgiving—a time to celebrate provision and reflect on God's blessings.

addition to the regular burnt offering with its grain offering and drink offering.

[23]" 'On the fourth day prepare ten bulls, two rams and fourteen male lambs a year old, all without defect. [24]With the bulls, rams and lambs, prepare their grain offerings and drink offerings according to the number specified. [25]Include one male goat as a sin offering, in addition to the regular burnt offering with its grain offering and drink offering.

[26]" 'On the fifth day prepare nine bulls, two rams and fourteen male lambs a year old, all without defect. [27]With the bulls, rams and lambs, prepare their grain offerings and drink offerings according to the number specified. [28]Include one male goat as a sin offering, in addition to the regular burnt offering with its grain offering and drink offering.

[29]" 'On the sixth day prepare eight bulls, two rams and fourteen male lambs a year old, all without defect. [30]With the bulls, rams and lambs, prepare their grain offerings and drink offerings according to the number specified. [31]Include one male goat as a sin offering, in addition to the regular burnt offering with its grain offering and drink offering.

[32]" 'On the seventh day prepare seven bulls, two rams and fourteen male lambs a year old, all without defect. [33]With the bulls, rams and lambs, prepare their grain offerings and drink offerings according to the number specified. [34]Include one male goat as a sin offering, in addition to the regular burnt offering with its grain offering and drink offering.

[35]" 'On the eighth day hold an assembly and do no regular work. [36]Present an offering made by fire as an aroma pleasing to the LORD, a burnt offering of one bull, one ram and seven male lambs a year old, all without defect. [37]With the bull, the ram and the lambs, prepare their grain offerings and drink offerings according to the number specified. [38]Include one male goat as a sin offering, in addition to the regular burnt offering with its grain offering and drink offering.

[39]" 'In addition to what you vow and your freewill offerings, prepare these for the LORD at your appointed feasts: your burnt offerings, grain offerings, drink offerings and fellowship offerings.[a] ' "

[40]Moses told the Israelites all that the LORD commanded him.

Vows

30 Moses said to the heads of the tribes of Israel: "This is what the LORD commands: [2]When a man makes a vow to the LORD or takes an oath to obligate himself by a pledge, he must not break his word but must do everything he said.

[a]39 Traditionally *peace offerings*

What significant things did he say and do during this feast?

APPLY 1. Would you say God has taught you more in "wilderness wandering" times or in "festival" times? Explain. **2.** Is there anything in your life that works like this feast to remind you of dedication to God? How can you gain more dedication to God? How can this group help?

OPEN 1. Do you think men and women are equal? Explain. **2.** What promises have you recently made?

STUDY One of the things the people of Israel would want to do is make promises to God. God

29:40 Moses told the Israelites all. Though leadership was being transferred to Joshua, Moses still held the reins. Before Moses was replaced, Israel had to be reminded of its covenant obligations—as if to say, the man at the top may change, but the rules stay the same.

30:1–16 When a man makes a vow. Moses tried to make clear the seriousness of a vow or oath. No vow was to be taken lightly. The only legitimate "out" from a vow occurred when the person making it was not fully responsible for keeping it. Moses pointed out the examples of a young woman still at home, a new wife who had made a vow before marriage, and a wife whose husband may or may not know of a vow she had made. These exceptions were directed to women, who often had no rights and needed legal protection. However, they also protected the husband or father from obligations his

3“When a young woman still living in her father’s house makes a vow to the LORD or obligates herself by a pledge 4and her father hears about her vow or pledge but says nothing to her, then all her vows and every pledge by which she obligated herself will stand. 5But if her father forbids her when he hears about it, none of her vows or the pledges by which she obligated herself will stand; the LORD will release her because her father has forbidden her.

6“If she marries after she makes a vow or after her lips utter a rash promise by which she obligates herself 7and her husband hears about it but says nothing to her, then her vows or the pledges by which she obligated herself will stand. 8But if her husband forbids her when he hears about it, he nullifies the vow that obligates her or the rash promise by which she obligates herself, and the LORD will release her.

9“Any vow or obligation taken by a widow or divorced woman will be binding on her.

10“If a woman living with her husband makes a vow or obligates herself by a pledge under oath 11and her husband hears about it but says nothing to her and does not forbid her, then all her vows or the pledges by which she obligated herself will stand. 12But if her husband nullifies them when he hears about them, then none of the vows or pledges that came from her lips will stand. Her husband has nullified them, and the LORD will release her. 13Her husband may confirm or nullify any vow she makes or any sworn pledge to deny herself. 14But if her husband says nothing to her about it from day to day, then he confirms all her vows or the pledges binding on her. He confirms them by saying nothing to her when he hears about them. 15If, however, he nullifies them some time after he hears about them, then he is responsible for her guilt.”

16These are the regulations the LORD gave Moses concerning relationships between a man and his wife, and between a father and his young daughter still living in his house.

Vengeance on the Midianites

31 The LORD said to Moses, 2“Take vengeance on the Midianites for the Israelites. After that, you will be gathered to your people.”

3So Moses said to the people, “Arm some of your men to go to war against the Midianites and to carry out the LORD’s vengeance on them. 4Send into battle a thousand men from each of the tribes of Israel.” 5So twelve thousand men armed for battle, a thousand from

considered those promises binding, with some exceptions. **1.** How serious do you think God is about promises made (v. 2; Deut. 23:21–23; Eccl. 5:1–7)? Would you say you make promises to God cautiously or rashly? Explain. **2.** Why do you think a vow taken by a woman could be nullified by her father or her husband? What application do you think that has in your culture today? **3.** Can you give an example of a rash promise? What was the last rash promise you made? **4.** Why does God have the right to require the keeping of promises (Ps. 145:13)? **5.** What flaw in the character of the people do you think required these instructions? What evidence can you give that people today still have difficulty in keeping their word?

APPLY 1. What effect does breaking a promise have on those around you? How do you feel when someone breaks a promise to you? **2.** In what areas do you need to improve when it comes to making promises to God? How can you improve? How can this group help?

OPEN 1. What did your mom say when you came in from playing outside in wet conditions? Did you ever get in trouble for breaking her rule? How so? **2.** As a teen, who was the one who might have influenced you for evil? How did you resist his or her advances?

---

daughter or wife had made without his knowledge.

30:3–5 a young woman still living in her father’s house. An unmarried woman could be released from a vow by her father’s actions. If he knew of the vow and did nothing, however, the vow was binding.

30:6–8 If she marries. A husband could nullify a vow made by his wife, even if she had made it before they were married. If he knew of the vow and did nothing, however, the vow stood.

30:9 widow or divorced woman. A widow or divorced woman was on her own, bound by whatever vows she made.

30:10–15 a woman living with her husband. Moses made it clear that a husband had the right to nullify a vow his wife had made. As Israel evolved into a more complex society, legal issues such as these became more important.

31:1–24 Moses was commanded to go to war as one of his last acts as the leader of Israel, but not against the foe he really wanted, Canaan. The target instead was the Midianites, who had seduced many Israelites into Baal worship.

31:4 Send into battle a thousand men from each of the tribes of Israel. The responsibility and privilege of doing the work of God is to be shared by all the people of God. We all have a part to play when it is clear what God wants us to do.

each tribe, were supplied from the clans of Israel. 6Moses sent them
into battle, a thousand from each tribe, along with Phinehas son of
Eleazar, the priest, who took with him articles from the sanctuary and
the trumpets for signaling.
7They fought against Midian, as the LORD commanded Moses, and
killed every man. 8Among their victims were Evi, Rekem, Zur, Hur and
Reba—the five kings of Midian. They also killed Balaam son of Beor
with the sword. 9The Israelites captured the Midianite women and
children and took all the Midianite herds, flocks and goods as plunder. 10They burned all the towns where the Midianites had settled, as
well as all their camps. 11They took all the plunder and spoils, including the people and animals, 12and brought the captives, spoils and
plunder to Moses and Eleazar the priest and the Israelite assembly at
their camp on the plains of Moab, by the Jordan across from Jericho.[a]
13Moses, Eleazar the priest and all the leaders of the community
went to meet them outside the camp. 14Moses was angry with the officers of the army—the commanders of thousands and commanders
of hundreds—who returned from the battle.
15"Have you allowed all the women to live?" he asked them.
16"They were the ones who followed Balaam's advice and were the
means of turning the Israelites away from the LORD in what happened
at Peor, so that a plague struck the LORD's people. 17Now kill all the
boys. And kill every woman who has slept with a man, 18but save for
yourselves every girl who has never slept with a man.
19"All of you who have killed anyone or touched anyone who was
killed must stay outside the camp seven days. On the third and
seventh days you must purify yourselves and your captives. 20Purify
every garment as well as everything made of leather, goat hair or
wood."
21Then Eleazar the priest said to the soldiers who had gone into
battle, "This is the requirement of the law that the LORD gave Moses:
22Gold, silver, bronze, iron, tin, lead 23and anything else that can
withstand fire must be put through the fire, and then it will be clean.
But it must also be purified with the water of cleansing. And whatever
cannot withstand fire must be put through that water. 24On the
seventh day wash your clothes and you will be clean. Then you may
come into the camp."

[a]12 Hebrew *Jordan of Jericho*; possibly an ancient name for the Jordan River

STUDY The men of Israel had previously been seduced by the Midianite women and lured into idolatry. Now it's payback time from the Lord. Israel is armed and goes to battle with their old nemesis. **1.** Why do you think the priest, Phinehas, was sent into battle with the Israelite army? **2.** What happened at Peor to bring about this act of vengeance (v. 16, ch. 25)? Does this shed any light on the true nature of Balaam? Why is it significant that we are told Balaam was killed in this raid (v. 8)? **3.** Why was Moses angry that the army had not killed all the Midianites (vv. 14–16)? How did he remedy the problem (vv. 17–18)? Why do you think he allowed the Israelites to keep the virgin Midianites? **4.** Why did Moses command the army to go through the purification rites? What do you think the captives thought about all this?

APPLY **1.** What enemies do you have that might threaten your relationship with God? How serious is the threat? **2.** What can you do to deal with this threat?

31:7 fought against Midian as the LORD commanded Moses. Choosing to fight against the Midianites was not a rash reaction on the part of the Israelites. The battle was God's idea, and God would determine the outcome.

31:8 killed Balaam son of Beor. Even though he was not an enemy king, Balaam's deception and hypocrisy nearly toppled the Israelites. He is to blame for seducing the Israelite males to worship Baal.

31:9–18 The Israelites captured the Midianite women and children. God had commanded that all but the virgin women be annihilated. All the others would jeopardize Israel's inheritance and moral attitudes. Nonetheless, the Israelites let all the women and children live. Apparently the people of God were enticed by the sinful lifestyle of the Midianites. They winked at what they saw rather than obeying God. When we second-guess God's Word, we are first-class fools.

31:19–24 you must purify yourselves. In the process of wiping out Midian, the Israelites had contaminated themselves. Curiously, obeying God's command was not enough. They also had to obey God's ceremonial laws. When contact was made with a dead human or animal, a quarantine of sorts was required. These ceremonial laws of purification were a way of emphasizing the holiness of God.

OPEN 1. Can you tell of a competition for "all the marbles" that you won? Did you enjoy winning or getting the prize the most? **2.** If others shared in the prize, did you gladly share it, or were you a little selfish about it?

STUDY After the battle was won, God allowed the Israelites to divide the spoils of battle. However, a portion of the spoils would be used as an offering to God and would help to maintain the priests and Levites and the work of the tabernacle. **1.** What needs does God meet with the dividing of the spoils (vv. 28–30)? If you had been an Israelite soldier who had put his life on the line for this victory, would you have been pleased with the division of the spoils? Why or why not? **2.** What might the Israelite army have learned from sharing the spoils with the priests and Levites? What part do you think the priests and Levites played in Israel's victory? **3.** What do you think was the motivation for the offering made by the officers (vv. 48–50)? Why do you think Moses and Eleazar so readily accepted the offering (vv. 51–54)? **4.** When you take a look at the accounting of the spoils of battle, does it seem like a lot to you, or do you think it was mighty little to get from another nation?

APPLY 1. In a spiritual sense, can you tell of any spoils you have been given by God for victories you have won in his name? **2.** In what ways do you need to be more willing to share what God has given you?

Dividing the Spoils

25The LORD said to Moses, **26**"You and Eleazar the priest and the
family heads of the community are to count all the people and animals that were captured. **27**Divide the spoils between the soldiers
who took part in the battle and the rest of the community. **28**From the
soldiers who fought in the battle, set apart as tribute for the LORD one out of every five hundred, whether persons, cattle, donkeys, sheep or
goats. **29**Take this tribute from their half share and give it to Eleazar
the priest as the LORD's part. **30**From the Israelites' half, select one out of every fifty, whether persons, cattle, donkeys, sheep, goats or other animals. Give them to the Levites, who are responsible for the care of
the LORD's tabernacle." **31**So Moses and Eleazar the priest did as the LORD commanded Moses.

32The plunder remaining from the spoils that the soldiers took was
675,000 sheep, **33**72,000 cattle, **34**61,000 donkeys **35**and 32,000 women who had never slept with a man.

36The half share of those who fought in the battle was:

337,500 sheep, **37**of which the tribute for the LORD was 675;
3836,000 cattle, of which the tribute for the LORD was 72;
3930,500 donkeys, of which the tribute for the LORD was 61;
4016,000 people, of which the tribute for the LORD was 32.

41Moses gave the tribute to Eleazar the priest as the LORD's part, as the LORD commanded Moses.

42The half belonging to the Israelites, which Moses set apart from
that of the fighting men— **43**the community's half—was 337,500
sheep, **44**36,000 cattle, **45**30,500 donkeys **46**and 16,000 people. **47**From
the Israelites' half, Moses selected one out of every fifty persons and animals, as the LORD commanded him, and gave them to the Levites, who were responsible for the care of the LORD's tabernacle.

48Then the officers who were over the units of the army—the commanders of thousands and commanders of hundreds—went to
Moses **49**and said to him, "Your servants have counted the soldiers
under our command, and not one is missing. **50**So we have brought as an offering to the LORD the gold articles each of us acquired—armlets, bracelets, signet rings, earrings and necklaces—to make atonement for ourselves before the LORD."

51Moses and Eleazar the priest accepted from them the gold—all
the crafted articles. **52**All the gold from the commanders of thousands and commanders of hundreds that Moses and Eleazar presented as a gift to the LORD weighed 16,750 shekels.[a] **53**Each soldier had taken
plunder for himself. **54**Moses and Eleazar the priest accepted the gold
from the commanders of thousands and commanders of hundreds and brought it into the Tent of Meeting as a memorial for the Israelites before the LORD.

[a]52 That is, about 420 pounds (about 190 kilograms)

31:26–35 Divide the spoils. In these wars of the Old Testament, a portion of the spoils was to be offered to God in recognition that God was the commander-in-chief, and even those who stayed behind guarding the supplies were entitled to a share. This was distributed fairly among the community.

The Transjordan Tribes

32 The Reubenites and Gadites, who had very large herds and
flocks, saw that the lands of Jazer and Gilead were suitable
for livestock. 2So they came to Moses and Eleazar the priest and to
the leaders of the community, and said, 3"Ataroth, Dibon, Jazer, Nimrah, Heshbon, Elealeh, Sebam, Nebo and Beon— 4the land the LORD
subdued before the people of Israel—are suitable for livestock, and
your servants have livestock. 5If we have found favor in your eyes,"
they said, "let this land be given to your servants as our possession.
Do not make us cross the Jordan."

6Moses said to the Gadites and Reubenites, "Shall your countrymen
go to war while you sit here? 7Why do you discourage the Israelites
from going over into the land the LORD has given them? 8This is what
your fathers did when I sent them from Kadesh Barnea to look over the
land. 9After they went up to the Valley of Eshcol and viewed the land,
they discouraged the Israelites from entering the land the LORD had
given them. 10The LORD's anger was aroused that day and he swore
this oath: 11'Because they have not followed me wholeheartedly, not
one of the men twenty years old or more who came up out of Egypt
will see the land I promised on oath to Abraham, Isaac and Jacob—
12not one except Caleb son of Jephunneh the Kenizzite and Joshua
son of Nun, for they followed the LORD wholeheartedly.' 13The LORD's
anger burned against Israel and he made them wander in the desert
forty years, until the whole generation of those who had done evil in
his sight was gone.

14"And here you are, a brood of sinners, standing in the place of
your fathers and making the LORD even more angry with Israel. 15If
you turn away from following him, he will again leave all this people
in the desert, and you will be the cause of their destruction."

16Then they came up to him and said, "We would like to build pens
here for our livestock and cities for our women and children. 17But
we are ready to arm ourselves and go ahead of the Israelites until we
have brought them to their place. Meanwhile our women and children will live in fortified cities, for protection from the inhabitants of
the land. 18We will not return to our homes until every Israelite has
received his inheritance. 19We will not receive any inheritance with
them on the other side of the Jordan, because our inheritance has
come to us on the east side of the Jordan."

20Then Moses said to them, "If you will do this—if you will arm
yourselves before the LORD for battle, 21and if all of you will go armed
over the Jordan before the LORD until he has driven his enemies out
before him— 22then when the land is subdued before the LORD, you
may return and be free from your obligation to the LORD and to Israel.
And this land will be your possession before the LORD.

23"But if you fail to do this, you will be sinning against the LORD;
and you may be sure that your sin will find you out. 24Build cities for

OPEN 1. Which of your family members lives farthest away from you? How far do they live? How does this affect your family relationship? **2.** If you could live anywhere you choose, where would it be? Why?

STUDY After Midian had been secured, the families of the tribes of Reuben and Gad requested to possess that land. The problem was it was east of the Jordan and they still had a country to conquer. The solution was that they would help the rest of Israel conquer the land west of the Jordan before they settled into their new home. **1.** Why was Moses angry with these Israelites for making the request to stay on the east side of Jordan (vv. 6–7)? Why does he compare it with what happened forty years earlier (vv. 8–13)? Do you think the other Israelites might have been jealous, or perhaps a little miffed they didn't think of settling east of Jordan first? **2.** What plan did the Reubenites and Gadites come up with to answer Moses' concern (vv. 16–19)? What was Moses' response to this new plan (vv. 20–24)? What do you think about the fairness of this plan to the other Israelites? **3.** Why did Moses rehearse the details of this plan with Eleazar and Joshua (vv. 28–30)? Can you see any potential religious, governmental, communication, or military problems having the nation divided in this manner? **4.** What dangers were the Reubenites and Gadites willing to accept in order to possess the land east of Jordan? What did they do to protect their families and livestock from harm (vv. 34–38)? **5.** What do you think would be the chances of the fighting men not fulfilling their promise to help the rest of Israel conquer the land? What do you think would be the chances of some of the men deciding not to return back to the east side, but staying on the west side of Jordan after the battles were over? What might have lured them either way?

APPLY 1. How important is unity with your fellow Christians to you? What do you do to

---

32:8 This is what your fathers did when I sent them. Moses was suspicious when the two tribes said they wanted to stay on the east side of the Jordan. It was reminiscent of the time the ten spies talked the Israelites out of conquering Canaan (chs. 13–14).

32:17 we are ready to arm ourselves and go ahead. Moses projected his worries unfairly. The two tribes were not insurrectionists. To prove the purity of their motives, they were quick to offer to fight with their brothers beyond the Jordan. Their wives and children would remain behind to stake out the land they wanted to claim.

enhance and strengthen that unity? **2.** How willing are you to "go to battle" with fellow Christians over "turf" that is not your own? What might some of those battles be?

OPEN 1. What has been the longest trip of your life? What major event happened on this trip which you recorded in your notebook or photo album? **2.** Who in this group has been to the most nations? States?

STUDY In order to have a permanent record of the wilderness wanderings, God commanded Moses to make a record of the journey. In this way future generations could

your women and children, and pens for your flocks, but do what you have promised."

25The Gadites and Reubenites said to Moses, "We your servants will do as our lord commands. 26Our children and wives, our flocks and herds will remain here in the cities of Gilead. 27But your servants, every man armed for battle, will cross over to fight before the LORD, just as our lord says."

28Then Moses gave orders about them to Eleazar the priest and Joshua son of Nun and to the family heads of the Israelite tribes. 29He said to them, "If the Gadites and Reubenites, every man armed for battle, cross over the Jordan with you before the LORD, then when the land is subdued before you, give them the land of Gilead as their possession. 30But if they do not cross over with you armed, they must accept their possession with you in Canaan."

31The Gadites and Reubenites answered, "Your servants will do what the LORD has said. 32We will cross over before the LORD into Canaan armed, but the property we inherit will be on this side of the Jordan."

33Then Moses gave to the Gadites, the Reubenites and the half-tribe of Manasseh son of Joseph the kingdom of Sihon king of the Amorites and the kingdom of Og king of Bashan—the whole land with its cities and the territory around them.

34The Gadites built up Dibon, Ataroth, Aroer, 35Atroth Shophan, Jazer, Jogbehah, 36Beth Nimrah and Beth Haran as fortified cities, and built pens for their flocks. 37And the Reubenites rebuilt Heshbon, Elealeh and Kiriathaim, 38as well as Nebo and Baal Meon (these names were changed) and Sibmah. They gave names to the cities they rebuilt.

39The descendants of Makir son of Manasseh went to Gilead, captured it and drove out the Amorites who were there. 40So Moses gave Gilead to the Makirites, the descendants of Manasseh, and they settled there. 41Jair, a descendant of Manasseh, captured their settlements and called them Havvoth Jair.[a] 42And Nobah captured Kenath and its surrounding settlements and called it Nobah after himself.

Stages in Israel's Journey

33 Here are the stages in the journey of the Israelites when they came out of Egypt by divisions under the leadership of Moses and Aaron. 2At the LORD's command Moses recorded the stages in their journey. This is their journey by stages:

3The Israelites set out from Rameses on the fifteenth day of the first month, the day after the Passover. They marched out boldly in full view of all the Egyptians, 4who were burying all

[a]41 *Or them the settlements of Jair*

32:33 and the half-tribe of Manasseh son of Joseph. After Moses and the tribes of Gad and Reuben came to an agreement about their request to settle east of the Jordan, half of another tribe decided to join the party. The same requirements applied. Their men would have to help the other tribes take possession of Canaan.

33:1–49 Like the route on a road atlas traced with a highlighter, we can follow the progress God's people made en route to the land of promise. The number forty in Hebrew culture conveys completion. When God flooded the earth it rained for forty days. When Jesus was tempted in the wilderness he fasted for forty days. What is recorded here is most likely a general summary of the rest stops (as opposed to an exhaustive one). It was compiled to give the Israelites a sacred history of God's leading.

their firstborn, whom the LORD had struck down among them;
for the LORD had brought judgment on their gods.
5The Israelites left Rameses and camped at Succoth.
6They left Succoth and camped at Etham, on the edge of the
desert.
7They left Etham, turned back to Pi Hahiroth, to the east of
Baal Zephon, and camped near Migdol.
8They left Pi Hahiroth[a] and passed through the sea into the
desert, and when they had traveled for three days in the Desert
of Etham, they camped at Marah.
9They left Marah and went to Elim, where there were twelve
springs and seventy palm trees, and they camped there.
10They left Elim and camped by the Red Sea.[b]
11They left the Red Sea and camped in the Desert of Sin.
12They left the Desert of Sin and camped at Dophkah.
13They left Dophkah and camped at Alush.
14They left Alush and camped at Rephidim, where there was no
water for the people to drink.
15They left Rephidim and camped in the Desert of Sinai.
16They left the Desert of Sinai and camped at Kibroth Hattaavah.
17They left Kibroth Hattaavah and camped at Hazeroth.
18They left Hazeroth and camped at Rithmah.
19They left Rithmah and camped at Rimmon Perez.
20They left Rimmon Perez and camped at Libnah.
21They left Libnah and camped at Rissah.
22They left Rissah and camped at Kehelathah.
23They left Kehelathah and camped at Mount Shepher.
24They left Mount Shepher and camped at Haradah.
25They left Haradah and camped at Makheloth.
26They left Makheloth and camped at Tahath.
27They left Tahath and camped at Terah.
28They left Terah and camped at Mithcah.
29They left Mithcah and camped at Hashmonah.
30They left Hashmonah and camped at Moseroth.
31They left Moseroth and camped at Bene Jaakan.
32They left Bene Jaakan and camped at Hor Haggidgad.
33They left Hor Haggidgad and camped at Jotbathah.
34They left Jotbathah and camped at Abronah.
35They left Abronah and camped at Ezion Geber.
36They left Ezion Geber and camped at Kadesh, in the Desert
of Zin.
37They left Kadesh and camped at Mount Hor, on the border of
Edom. 38At the LORD's command Aaron the priest went up Mount
Hor, where he died on the first day of the fifth month of the
fortieth year after the Israelites came out of Egypt. 39Aaron was a
hundred and twenty-three years old when he died on Mount Hor.
40The Canaanite king of Arad, who lived in the Negev of
Canaan, heard that the Israelites were coming.
41They left Mount Hor and camped at Zalmonah.
42They left Zalmonah and camped at Punon.
43They left Punon and camped at Oboth.

[a]8 Many manuscripts of the Masoretic Text, Samaritan Pentateuch and Vulgate; most manuscripts of the Masoretic Text *left from before Hahiroth* [b]10 Hebrew *Yam Suph*; that is, Sea of Reeds; also in verse 11

revisit the places and the stories important to their faith. **1.** See if you can find a map of this incredible journey. What do you make of this text? Is it a: Slide show? Location map for archeological digs? Travel agency's travel brochure? Moses' diary? Time capsule item? Other? **2.** Of the men now ready to enter the Promised Land, how many had first hand experience with the places on this list (32:11–13)? What interest do you think the children and teens would have in this list? Why? **3.** How might this list impact the faith of the people about to enter the Promised Land? How does this list impact your faith? **4.** What hardships can you identify with as you read about this journey? **5.** Why do you think God was so concerned that the Israelites completely drive out the inhabitants of the Promised Land (vv. 50–56)? What would happen if they didn't? What does this say to you about God's concern for his people?

APPLY **1.** Of what importance is this story to your faith? **2.** If you could tell the story of your journey from unbelief to belief, what would you say?

[44]They left Oboth and camped at Iye Abarim, on the border of Moab.
[45]They left Iyim[a] and camped at Dibon Gad.
[46]They left Dibon Gad and camped at Almon Diblathaim.
[47]They left Almon Diblathaim and camped in the mountains of Abarim, near Nebo.
[48]They left the mountains of Abarim and camped on the plains
of Moab by the Jordan across from Jericho.[b] [49]There on the plains
of Moab they camped along the Jordan from Beth Jeshimoth to Abel Shittim.

[50]On the plains of Moab by the Jordan across from Jericho the LORD
said to Moses, [51]"Speak to the Israelites and say to them: 'When you
cross the Jordan into Canaan, [52]drive out all the inhabitants of the land before you. Destroy all their carved images and their cast idols,
and demolish all their high places. [53]Take possession of the land and
settle in it, for I have given you the land to possess. [54]Distribute the land by lot, according to your clans. To a larger group give a larger inheritance, and to a smaller group a smaller one. Whatever falls to them by lot will be theirs. Distribute it according to your ancestral tribes.

[55]" 'But if you do not drive out the inhabitants of the land, those you allow to remain will become barbs in your eyes and thorns in your sides. They will give you trouble in the land where you will live.
[56]And then I will do to you what I plan to do to them.' "

Boundaries of Canaan

34 The LORD said to Moses, [2]"Command the Israelites and say to them: 'When you enter Canaan, the land that will be allotted to you as an inheritance will have these boundaries:

[3]" 'Your southern side will include some of the Desert of Zin along the border of Edom. On the east, your southern boundary will start
from the end of the Salt Sea,[c] [4]cross south of Scorpion[d] Pass, contin-
ue on to Zin and go south of Kadesh Barnea. Then it will go to Hazar
Addar and over to Azmon, [5]where it will turn, join the Wadi of Egypt and end at the Sea.[e]

[6]" 'Your western boundary will be the coast of the Great Sea. This will be your boundary on the west.

[7]" 'For your northern boundary, run a line from the Great Sea to
Mount Hor [8]and from Mount Hor to Lebo[f] Hamath. Then the bound-
ary will go to Zedad, [9]continue to Ziphron and end at Hazar Enan. This will be your boundary on the north.

[10]" 'For your eastern boundary, run a line from Hazar Enan to Shepham. [11]The boundary will go down from Shepham to Riblah on the east side of Ain and continue along the slopes east of the Sea of

[a]45 That is, Iye Abarim [b]48 Hebrew *Jordan of Jericho*; possibly an ancient name for the Jordan River; also in verse 50 [c]3 That is, the Dead Sea; also in verse 12 [d]4 Hebrew *Akrabbim* [e]5 That is, the Mediterranean; also in verses 6 and 7 [f]8 Or *to the entrance to*

OPEN 1. What were the boundaries of your "turf" when you were a child? How large did this territory seem to you then? **2.** What are the boundaries of your territory now? How far do you have to travel before you feel like a stranger?

STUDY One of the major tasks to be accomplished by the Israelites when they entered the Promised Land would be the definition and division of land. God defines the land and then appoints Eleazar and Joshua, along with a representative from each tribe, to divide up the land. **1.** Why do you think God placed a boundary on the land they could have? What might tempt them to exceed these boundaries? **2.** Why do you think God didn't just let the people sort out the land—why have a representative from each tribe carve out the tribal boundaries? Can you think of a better system of dividing the land? If so, what? **3.** Why do you think God allowed Israel to divide up according

33:51 When you cross the Jordan into Canaan. When you are dealing with a God who makes promises, it is not a question of *if* but *when*. There was no doubt that God would be faithful to bring his people across the Jordan into the Promised Land. Because of disobedience and unbelief, the Israelites arrived in "the Land" forty years late. But at last the time had come.

34:3–12 The tribes did not choose their own territory. Each tribe was given a specific plot of real estate according to God's map. The boundaries listed are actually larger than the land occupied by each of the tribes. This description of how God divided up the land is indicative of his generosity.

Kinnereth.[a] 12Then the boundary will go down along the Jordan and
end at the Salt Sea.
" 'This will be your land, with its boundaries on every side.' "
13Moses commanded the Israelites: "Assign this land by lot as an
inheritance. The LORD has ordered that it be given to the nine and a
half tribes, 14because the families of the tribe of Reuben, the tribe of
Gad and the half-tribe of Manasseh have received their inheritance.
15These two and a half tribes have received their inheritance on the
east side of the Jordan of Jericho,[b] toward the sunrise."
16The LORD said to Moses, 17"These are the names of the men who
are to assign the land for you as an inheritance: Eleazar the priest
and Joshua son of Nun. 18And appoint one leader from each tribe to
help assign the land. 19These are their names:

Caleb son of Jephunneh,
from the tribe of Judah;
20Shemuel son of Ammihud,
from the tribe of Simeon;
21Elidad son of Kislon,
from the tribe of Benjamin;
22Bukki son of Jogli,
the leader from the tribe of Dan;
23Hanniel son of Ephod,
the leader from the tribe of Manasseh son of Joseph;
24Kemuel son of Shiphtan,
the leader from the tribe of Ephraim son of Joseph;
25Elizaphan son of Parnach,
the leader from the tribe of Zebulun;
26Paltiel son of Azzan,
the leader from the tribe of Issachar;
27Ahihud son of Shelomi,
the leader from the tribe of Asher;
28Pedahel son of Ammihud,
the leader from the tribe of Naphtali."

29These are the men the LORD commanded to assign the inheritance to the Israelites in the land of Canaan.

Towns for the Levites

35 On the plains of Moab by the Jordan across from Jericho,[c]
the LORD said to Moses, 2"Command the Israelites to give the
Levites towns to live in from the inheritance the Israelites will possess. And give them pasturelands around the towns. 3Then they will
have towns to live in and pasturelands for their cattle, flocks and all
their other livestock.

[a]*11* That is, Galilee [b]*15 Jordan of Jericho* was possibly an ancient name for the Jordan River. [c]*1* Hebrew *Jordan of Jericho*; possibly an ancient name for the Jordan River

to tribes? Why didn't he just let them mix-n-match? **4.** What lessons of cooperation and organization do you learn from this procedure?

APPLY 1. What parallels can you draw from this part of Israel's history with the operation of your church organization? **2.** In what ways do you have a tendency to challenge the boundaries God has placed on your life?

OPEN 1. When you were a child, did you ever run away from home? Where did you go? Did you feel safe or alone and afraid? **2.** Where is your favorite retreat—the place you like to go to get away from it all?

STUDY As the Israelites prepare to settle in the Promised Land, several important issues needed

34:13–15 Since Gad, Reuben and half the tribe of Manasseh had opted to pitch their permanent tents east of the river, the distribution of the land west of the Jordan was to be made among only nine and a half tribes (not all 12).

34:16–29 Moses first learned the wisdom of delegation from his father-in-law, Jethro (Ex. 18). Now that the land was to be settled, Moses was quick to act on God's instruction to put reliable leaders over the task of land allocation. In these verses is a great formula for getting a job done. First, determine what needs to be done. Then give clear instructions to those specifically selected to oversee each part of the project.

35:1–5 Even the Levites had to have a place to live. Although they were not eligible for large sections of land like the other tribes (1:47–53), God wanted them to have specific locations to call

to be addressed. First, the Levites had to have a place to live, so cities were to be designated for the Levites. Second, God made provision for the safety of those who might kill another human accidentally—they were called "cities of refuge." **1.** Since the Levites were not to inherit any land, where would they live (vv. 2–3)? Where would they pasture their animals (vv. 4–5)? **2.** How many cities (not counting the cities of refuge) did the Levites actually get (v. 6)? How would being scattered throughout the land enable the Levites to perform their duties? **3.** What was a "city of refuge" (vv. 10–12)? How many were there (v. 6)? How were they divided; east and west (v. 14)? Why were the cities so important? **4.** What was Israel's definition of murder (vv. 16–21)? More than the specifics, what was the determining factor in a killing being considered a murder? What was Israel's definition of accidental death (vv. 22–24)? What was the determining factor? What do you think about these distinctions? **5.** Who was the avenger of blood (Lev. 24:17)? Under what circumstances could the avenger of blood legally kill someone who had accidentally killed one of his relatives (vv. 26–27)? **6.** What prevented the cities of refuge from being used to provide an easy escape for murders? Do you think these laws preserved justice? Why or why not? **7.** What, if anything, is there in your culture like this today?

APPLY 1. Who do you go to for refuge? Have you run to him? **2.** What protection does Jesus, your refuge, offer?

4"The pasturelands around the towns that you give the Levites will
extend out fifteen hundred feet[a] from the town wall. 5Outside the
town, measure three thousand feet[b] on the east side, three thousand
on the south side, three thousand on the west and three thousand on
the north, with the town in the center. They will have this area as pastureland for the towns.

Cities of Refuge

6"Six of the towns you give the Levites will be cities of refuge, to
which a person who has killed someone may flee. In addition, give
them forty-two other towns. 7In all you must give the Levites forty-
eight towns, together with their pasturelands. 8The towns you give
the Levites from the land the Israelites possess are to be given in proportion to the inheritance of each tribe: Take many towns from a tribe
that has many, but few from one that has few."

9Then the LORD said to Moses: 10"Speak to the Israelites and say to
them: 'When you cross the Jordan into Canaan, 11select some towns
to be your cities of refuge, to which a person who has killed someone
accidentally may flee. 12They will be places of refuge from the avenger, so that a person accused of murder may not die before he stands
trial before the assembly. 13These six towns you give will be your
cities of refuge. 14Give three on this side of the Jordan and three in
Canaan as cities of refuge. 15These six towns will be a place of refuge
for Israelites, aliens and any other people living among them, so that
anyone who has killed another accidentally can flee there.

16" 'If a man strikes someone with an iron object so that he dies, he
is a murderer; the murderer shall be put to death. 17Or if anyone has
a stone in his hand that could kill, and he strikes someone so that he
dies, he is a murderer; the murderer shall be put to death. 18Or if anyone has a wooden object in his hand that could kill, and he hits
someone so that he dies, he is a murderer; the murderer shall be put
to death. 19The avenger of blood shall put the murderer to death;
when he meets him, he shall put him to death. 20If anyone with malice aforethought shoves another or throws something at him intentionally so that he dies 21or if in hostility he hits him with his fist so
that he dies, that person shall be put to death; he is a murderer. The
avenger of blood shall put the murderer to death when he meets him.

22" 'But if without hostility someone suddenly shoves another or
throws something at him unintentionally 23or, without seeing him,
drops a stone on him that could kill him, and he dies, then since he
was not his enemy and he did not intend to harm him, 24the assembly
must judge between him and the avenger of blood according to these

[a]4 Hebrew *a thousand cubits* (about 450 meters) [b]5 Hebrew *two thousand cubits* (about 900 meters)

home. These "Levite" towns were to be scattered throughout the other tribes' land grants.

35:6–15 Six of the Levite towns were special. They were designated as cities *of refuge. Individuals who unintentionally* caused the death of another could seek protection from those seeking revenge. Three of these amnesty bases were on the west side of the Jordan, and three were on the east.

35:16–21 In contrast to situations of accidental manslaughter, here is a list of what crimes were judged to be murder.

35:22 without hostility. Motive is the key. Crimes that were not premeditated or those that did not result from anger would not be judged on the same scale as those that were.

35:24 according to these regulations. Even when justice is celebrated and innocence is guarded, mercy can be held hostage. In order to maintain the integrity of the cities of refuge, a jury of sorts determined whether a candidate for sanctuary was truly deserving.

regulations. 25 The assembly must protect the one accused of murder
from the avenger of blood and send him back to the city of refuge to
which he fled. He must stay there until the death of the high priest,
who was anointed with the holy oil.
26 " 'But if the accused ever goes outside the limits of the city of refuge to which he has fled 27 and the avenger of blood finds him outside
the city, the avenger of blood may kill the accused without being
guilty of murder. 28 The accused must stay in his city of refuge until
the death of the high priest; only after the death of the high priest
may he return to his own property.
29 " 'These are to be legal requirements for you throughout the
generations to come, wherever you live.
30 " 'Anyone who kills a person is to be put to death as a murderer
only on the testimony of witnesses. But no one is to be put to death
on the testimony of only one witness.
31 " 'Do not accept a ransom for the life of a murderer, who deserves
to die. He must surely be put to death.
32 " 'Do not accept a ransom for anyone who has fled to a city of
refuge and so allow him to go back and live on his own land before
the death of the high priest.
33 " 'Do not pollute the land where you are. Bloodshed pollutes the
land, and atonement cannot be made for the land on which blood has
been shed, except by the blood of the one who shed it. 34 Do not defile
the land where you live and where I dwell, for I, the LORD, dwell
among the Israelites.' "

Inheritance of Zelophehad's Daughters

36 The family heads of the clan of Gilead son of Makir, the son
of Manasseh, who were from the clans of the descendants of
Joseph, came and spoke before Moses and the leaders, the heads of
the Israelite families. 2 They said, "When the LORD commanded my
lord to give the land as an inheritance to the Israelites by lot, he ordered you to give the inheritance of our brother Zelophehad to his
daughters. 3 Now suppose they marry men from other Israelite tribes;
then their inheritance will be taken from our ancestral inheritance
and added to that of the tribe they marry into. And so part of the inheritance allotted to us will be taken away. 4 When the Year of Jubilee
for the Israelites comes, their inheritance will be added to that of the
tribe into which they marry, and their property will be taken from the
tribal inheritance of our forefathers."
5 Then at the LORD's command Moses gave this order to the Israelites: "What the tribe of the descendants of Joseph is saying is right.
6 This is what the LORD commands for Zelophehad's daughters: They
may marry anyone they please as long as they marry within the tribal
clan of their father. 7 No inheritance in Israel is to pass from tribe to
tribe, for every Israelite shall keep the tribal land inherited from his
forefathers. 8 Every daughter who inherits land in any Israelite tribe
must marry someone in her father's tribal clan, so that every Israelite

OPEN Is there an heirloom that gets passed down from generation to generation in your family? What is it and who gets it?

STUDY The case of Zelophehad's daughters came before Moses and it was decided that they could possess the inheritance of their father (27:1–11). Now the question is pressed further by other Israelites who want to make sure they don't lose any of their inheritance. **1.** What is the main concern of the clan of Gilead (vv. 3–4)? Do you think they are just being greedy, or do they have a legitimate question? Why do you think that? **2.** Why do you think it was important to the unity and success of Israel for no land to pass from tribe to tribe? What would have happened if it had? **3.** What is your initial reaction when you read that the daughters of Zelophehad married their cousins? What about the gene pool? **4.** After reading all the rules and regulations given to the Israelites on the east side of Jordan, do you think

---

Amnesty was valid only as long as the one seeking protection remained within the city limits.

36:1-13 This passage dealt with a specific inheritance question: a man with two daughters. Upon his death his land would pass to his daughters. What would happen to the land if the daughters married outside of the tribe? Since the land was each tribe's inheritance from God, this was an important matter. The answer proposed here was that daughters marry only within the tribe. In that way no dispute is created.

they are ready to proceed, or will they go into the land "fumbling and bumbling"?

APPLY 1. What issues tend to divide your church? **2.** What can you do as an individual to help maintain the unity of your church? What can this group do?

will possess the inheritance of his fathers. 9No inheritance may
pass from tribe to tribe, for each Israelite tribe is to keep the land it
inherits."
10So Zelophehad's daughters did as the LORD commanded Moses.
11Zelophehad's daughters—Mahlah, Tirzah, Hoglah, Milcah and
Noah—married their cousins on their father's side. 12They married
within the clans of the descendants of Manasseh son of Joseph, and
their inheritance remained in their father's clan and tribe.
13These are the commands and regulations the LORD gave through
Moses to the Israelites on the plains of Moab by the Jordan across
from Jericho.[a]

[a]13 Hebrew *Jordan of Jericho*; possibly an ancient name for the Jordan River

---

36:10 In today's world, where individual choice is valued above community, this act of obedience seems odd. Keep in mind, though, that the tribe that these women belonged to was a large group of people, not merely an extended family. The men over 20 years old numbered more than 32,000 (1:34–35). Also, remember that at stake was the family land. This property was the promise of God that these people had sacrificed for generation after generation.

Deuteronomy

Author. Biblical scholarship and scientific research both indicate that Moses wrote Deuteronomy.

Personal Reading	Group Study Topic and Reading	
1:1–2:37	Review of Rebellion	1:19–46
3:1–4:43	Obedience Commanded	4:1–14
4:44–5:33	Ten Commandments	5:1–33
6:1–25	Great Commandment	6:1–25
7:1–9:29	Do Not Forget the Lord	8:1–20
10:1–11:32	Love and Obey God	11:1–32
12:1–17:7	Following Other Gods	13:1–18
17:8–21:21	Cities of Refuge	19:1–21
21:22–26:19	Various Laws	23:1–25:19
27:1–28:68	Various Curses	28:15–68
29:1–30:20	Life or Death	30:11–20
31:1–32:43	Song of Moses	31:30–32:43
32:44–34:12	Death of Moses	34:1–12

Date. Deuteronomy was probably written around 1400 B.C., just before the Hebrews entered Canaan, the land later known as Palestine, forty years after the Exodus. The events described in Deuteronomy span from the Exodus until the time when the people were poised at the border to reclaim their land.

Purpose. The book of Deuteronomy records Moses' last words to his people. As he faced his own death, Moses reviewed the whole journey. Deuteronomy testifies to God's provision. Moses encouraged his people to remember what God had done in their lives and to teach their children to obey God's Law. Israel's strength and national identity depended on their obedience. The Hebrews lived in covenant with God himself. The laws given at Mount Sinai functioned as the terms of that covenant. Since God would provide the victories and prevent the defeats, they had to obey and rely on him.

Historical Background. The Hebrews received the words of Moses included in Deuteronomy while they waited in the territory of Moab before their conquest of Canaan. In essence, they were about to go to war. The most important information this generation of Hebrews could receive was not a strategy for conflict but a review of the path they had traveled so far. They needed a strong heart for numerous battles and hardships ahead. Instead of battle plans God gave them a pep talk. Have faith. Remember who you are and who I am.

The Hebrews had escaped from Egypt forty years earlier. In the first two years of those forty, they had received the Ten Commandments, built the tabernacle and arrived at the border of their homeland. It was there that they refused to enter because of their fear and lack of faith. For the next 38 years, they wandered. The generation that had left Egyptian bondage and received the Law at Mount Sinai had all passed away. Now, once again on the verge of their invasion and occupation of Canaan, Moses instructed his people once again concerning the law their parents and grandparents had received.

The Great Shema. The heart of Deuteronomy, and in fact all of Jewish law, is found in Moses' call to faith. He said to his people, "Hear, O Israel: The LORD our God, the LORD is one." He then followed it with a command: "Love the LORD your God with all your heart and with all your soul and with all your strength." When Jesus was asked to name the greatest of all God's commandments, he quoted these words from Moses.

Moses then admonished the people to pass on their faith as a matter of course in daily living: "These commandments that I give you today are to be upon your hearts. Impress them on your children. Talk about them when you sit at home and when you walk along the road, when you lie down and when you get up. Tie them as symbols on your hands and bind them on your foreheads. Write them on the doorframes of your houses and on your gates." These words from Deuteronomy 6 establish the basis for faith, worship, and obedience.

OPEN **1.** Have you ever had to sit through a long speech? Was it hard to stay focused? **2.** If you could "take possession" of any land, where would it be?

STUDY After wandering in the desert for 40 years on a journey that should have taken a couple of weeks, the people of Israel come to Kadesh Barnea. They are about to enter the land God had promised them (Gen. 50:24). Now, as God tells them it's time to move on, his servant Moses reminds them of their recent history. **1.** Can you remember a time you had to go "the long way around" because of a wrong decision in your life? **2.** Why do you think the Israelites wandered around so long in the desert? **3.** What do you think it was like for these people who had been wandering so long to hear God finally say that it was time to go into the land he promised long before? **4.** Have you ever received good news like this that was the end of a long ordeal? **5.** What kind of burden would it be for you to be the leader of so many people? **6.** Can you remember a time you had more than you could bear?

APPLY **1.** If you had to describe your spiritual life in terms of a journey, where would you be in the journey right now? **2.** How would it feel to know you are about to be delivered from the consequences of a terrible mistake you have made?

The Command to Leave Horeb

1 These are the words Moses spoke to all Israel in the desert east of the Jordan—that is, in the Arabah—opposite Suph, between Paran and Tophel, Laban, Hazeroth and Dizahab. 2(It takes eleven days to go from Horeb to Kadesh Barnea by theMount Seir road.)

3In the fortieth year, on the first day of the eleventh month, Moses proclaimed to the Israelites all that the LORD had commanded him concerning them. 4This was after he had defeated Sihon king of the Amorites, who reigned in Heshbon, and at Edrei had defeated Og king of Bashan, who reigned in Ashtaroth.

5East of the Jordan in the territory of Moab, Moses began to expound this law, saying:

6The LORD our God said to us at Horeb, "You have stayed long enough at this mountain. 7Break camp and advance into the hill country of the Amorites; go to all the neighboring peoples in the Arabah, in the mountains, in the western foothills, in the Negev and along the coast, to the land of the Canaanites and to Lebanon, as far as the great river, the Euphrates. 8See, I have given you this land. Go in and take possession of the land that the LORD swore he would give to your fathers—to Abraham, Isaac and Jacob—and to their descendants after them."

The Appointment of Leaders

9At that time I said to you, "You are too heavy a burden for me to carry alone. 10The LORD your God has increased your numbers so that today you are as many as the stars in the sky. 11May the LORD, the God of your fathers, increase you a thousand times and bless you as he has promised! 12But how can I bear your problems and your burdens and your disputes all by myself? 13Choose some wise, understanding and respected men from each of your tribes, and I will set them over you."

14You answered me, "What you propose to do is good."

15So I took the leading men of your tribes, wise and respected men, and appointed them to have authority over you—as commanders of thousands, of hundreds, of fifties and of tens and as tribal officials. 16And I charged your judges at that time: Hear the disputes between

---

1:1–5 Think of Deuteronomy as a play. Before dialogue begins, the scene is described. In this play, Moses has almost all the speaking parts. His monologues, which make up most of the book, remind the wandering nation of their history, their sinful tendencies and God's provision and protection.

1:2 Horeb. Another name for Mount Sinai, where Moses received the Ten Commandments from God (Ex. 19:20; 20:1–21). **Kadesh Barnea.** The site where the Israelites camped while the 12 spies spied out Canaan (Num. 13:26).

1:3 fortieth year. What should have taken only 11 days became a forty-year expedition. It wasn't the condition of the roads that accounts for the delay; it was the condition of the Israelites' hearts. God had intended that they enter Canaan from Kadesh Barnea. When they disobeyed (due to fear and lack of faith), however, God punished them with a long detour (Num. 14:33–34).

1:5 Moab. This is territory directly east of the Dead Sea, where the story of Ruth and Naomi begins. It is the real estate that the tribes of Reuben, Gad and half the tribe of Manasseh in Numbers 32 chose to claim (before the Israelites crossed over the Jordan into the land God had promised all the tribes).

1:7 Moses traces out the land to which his people are about to lay claim. The various mountains, foothills and bodies of water provide landmarks. The description of the land is consistent with the promise God gave to Abraham (Gen. 15:18–21).

1:9–18 As the population increased, Moses knew he could not do an adequate job of governing alone. Remembering his father-in-law's advice (Ex. 18), he acted decisively to recruit reliable, wise and understanding assistants. Moses needed fair and just decision makers and other gifted people to serve alongside him.

1:10 as the stars in the sky. A metaphor for Abraham's innumerable descendants (Gen. 15:5; 22:17; 26:4 Ex. 32:13).

your brothers and judge fairly, whether the case is between brother
Israelites or between one of them and an alien. 17 Do not show
partiality in judging; hear both small and great alike. Do not be afraid
of any man, for judgment belongs to God. Bring me any case too hard
for you, and I will hear it. 18 And at that time I told you everything you
were to do.

Spies Sent Out

19 Then, as the LORD our God commanded us, we set out from
Horeb and went toward the hill country of the Amorites through all
that vast and dreadful desert that you have seen, and so we reached
Kadesh Barnea. 20 Then I said to you, "You have reached the hill country of the Amorites, which the LORD our God is giving us. 21 See, the
LORD your God has given you the land. Go up and take possession of
it as the LORD, the God of your fathers, told you. Do not be afraid; do
not be discouraged."
22 Then all of you came to me and said, "Let us send men ahead to
spy out the land for us and bring back a report about the route we are
to take and the towns we will come to."
23 The idea seemed good to me; so I selected twelve of you, one
man from each tribe. 24 They left and went up into the hill country, and
came to the Valley of Eshcol and explored it. 25 Taking with them some
of the fruit of the land, they brought it down to us and reported, "It is
a good land that the LORD our God is giving us."

Rebellion Against the LORD

26 But you were unwilling to go up; you rebelled against the command of the LORD your God. 27 You grumbled in your tents and said,
"The LORD hates us; so he brought us out of Egypt to deliver us into
the hands of the Amorites to destroy us. 28 Where can we go? Our
brothers have made us lose heart. They say, 'The people are stronger
and taller than we are; the cities are large, with walls up to the sky.
We even saw the Anakites there.' "
29 Then I said to you, "Do not be terrified; do not be afraid of them.
30 The LORD your God, who is going before you, will fight for you, as
he did for you in Egypt, before your very eyes, 31 and in the desert.

OPEN **1.** Do you tend to believe the glass is half empty or half full? **2.** Can you tell of a time you were afraid to begin a journey or a project for fear of failure? Did you quit or proceed in spite of your fear?

STUDY Moses reminds the people of how God wanted to bless them, but they refused to trust him. As a result, they were not able to enter the land God had promised, but wandered in the desert for the next 40 years. When they fought the Amorites without the help of God, they were soundly defeated. **1.** What was the sin of the people that resulted in 40 years of desert wandering? **2.** Why didn't Israel take the land (vv. 26–28)? **3.** Can you describe a circumstance when you thought God was punishing you for your unbelief? **4.** How did God address the fear among the people (vv. 29–31)? **5.** How did God punish Israel's unbelief (vv. 35–40)? **6.** Do you see the 40 years of desert wandering as a punishment from God or as a consequence of Israel's unbelief? **7.** What did Israel still have to learn that could only be learned by wandering in the desert? **8.** Does hearing the stories of the Bible about people of unbelief encourage you to try to do better, or does it make you think you can't do any better than they did? **9.** Did your ancestors live with hardship because

---

1:21 as the LORD ... told you. God's Word is the ultimate point of reference, whether spoken (to Abraham and Moses) or written (to us). God had given his word about "the land" many times before (v. 8). Now the time had come to act on the promise. It is important to note that the Lord calls them to "go for it" confi*dently. The trustworthy God urges that* his people not be afraid or discouraged (31:8; Josh. 1:9; 8:1; 10:25).

1:22 Let us send men ahead to spy. The 12 spies Moses selected to cross into Canaan are named in Numbers 13:4–15. Because ten of the 12 could not overcome their fears, the people would have to eat manna for forty more years instead of the fruit of the land.

1:26 you rebelled. Actually, those who heard Moses speak these words had not rebelled. Their parents and grandparents were the guilty ones. Moses was referring to the nation as a group, past and present.

1:27 You grumbled ... "The LORD hates us." The people were good at complaining (Ex. 15:24). They were not very good at discerning the Lord's will and obeying his direction. Time after time God provided for them and promised good things. God showed his love repeatedly, but the people were blind to it.

1:28 Anakites. Not only was the fruit in Canaan impressive (v. 25), so were the inhabitants. The Anakites were huge. At seven to nine feet tall, they hovered over children like kites (2:10,21; 9:2; Num. 13:32).

1:30 as he did for you in Egypt. The character of the Lord is consistent. God led the Israelites to escape the Egyptian army and would lead them to conquer Canaan.

1:31 all the way. The love of God for his people is not conditional. Like a father who carries an exhausted son, the Lord delights in upholding the people. The love pictured here is not "half way" commitment. Based on God's choice (and not the people's obedience), it is dependable.

of unbelief, or were they blessed because of belief?

APPLY 1. Do you remember a time you doubted God? **2.** What do you think makes it hard to trust God? **3.** What frightens you most? How do you deal with fear?

There you saw how the LORD your God carried you, as a father carries
his son, all the way you went until you reached this place."
32 In spite of this, you did not trust in the LORD your God, 33 who
went ahead of you on your journey, in fire by night and in a cloud by
day, to search out places for you to camp and to show you the way
you should go.
34 When the LORD heard what you said, he was angry and solemnly
swore: 35 "Not a man of this evil generation shall see the good land I
swore to give your forefathers, 36 except Caleb son of Jephunneh. He
will see it, and I will give him and his descendants the land he set his
feet on, because he followed the LORD wholeheartedly."
37 Because of you the LORD became angry with me also and said,
"You shall not enter it, either. 38 But your assistant, Joshua son of Nun,
will enter it. Encourage him, because he will lead Israel to inherit it.
39 And the little ones that you said would be taken captive, your children who do not yet know good from bad—they will enter the land. I
will give it to them and they will take possession of it. 40 But as for
you, turn around and set out toward the desert along the route to the
Red Sea.[a]"
41 Then you replied, "We have sinned against the LORD. We will go up
and fight, as the LORD our God commanded us." So every one of you
put on his weapons, thinking it easy to go up into the hill country.
42 But the LORD said to me, "Tell them, 'Do not go up and fight, because I will not be with you. You will be defeated by your enemies.' "
43 So I told you, but you would not listen. You rebelled against the
LORD's command and in your arrogance you marched up into the hill
country. 44 The Amorites who lived in those hills came out against
you; they chased you like a swarm of bees and beat you down from
Seir all the way to Hormah. 45 You came back and wept before the
LORD, but he paid no attention to your weeping and turned a deaf ear
to you. 46 And so you stayed in Kadesh many days—all the time you
spent there.

OPEN 1. What is the longest trip you have ever made? What was it like? **2.** Describe some of your relatives who have a checkered past. What kind of trouble have you had with them?

Wanderings in the Desert

2 Then we turned back and set out toward the desert along the
route to the Red Sea,[a] as the LORD had directed me. For a long
time we made our way around the hill country of Seir.

[a]40,1 Hebrew *Yam Suph*; that is, Sea of Reeds

1:33 in fire ... in a cloud. Both were reminders that the Lord was with them. (Ex. 13:21). In addition, the fire provided warmth, and the cloud shielded the people from an intense desert sun.

1:36 Caleb. Numbers 13:30–14:38 details the story of the 12 spies. Caleb and Joshua were the hands-down heroes. They alone returned with confidence and faith. The ten others were struck down by God's hand of judgment. *Caleb's obedience was rewarded when* he stepped again on the land God had promised, forty years later.

1:37 the LORD became angry. Moses is quick to point a finger at his rebellious followers. Their disobedience leads to God's decision to delay entrance into Canaan. By pointing a finger at them, however, he was pointing three at himself. Moses' sin of striking the rock in anger disqualified him from entering the land.

1:41 Moses is addressing the people about to cross over to the Promise Land. But he refers here to those who disobeyed and were denied entrance (v. 26).

1:43 I told you, but you would not listen. If ever words described what is wrong with the human race, here they are. God speaks and people disregard what he says. It was true of the wandering nation in the wilderness. It was true of the man and woman in the garden. It is true of us.

2:1 a long time. Forty years, to be specific. **hill country of Seir.** This was the rugged land just south of the Dead Sea. It was the area that Esau, Jacob's twin brother, settled (Gen. 32:3). Jacob (whose name was later changed to Israel) was the father of the Hebrews. It was ironic that Israel entered the Promised Land through the territory of his brother.

2Then the LORD said to me, 3"You have made your way around this
hill country long enough; now turn north. 4Give the people these
orders: 'You are about to pass through the territory of your brothers
the descendants of Esau, who live in Seir. They will be afraid of you,
but be very careful. 5Do not provoke them to war, for I will not give
you any of their land, not even enough to put your foot on. I have
given Esau the hill country of Seir as his own. 6You are to pay them in
silver for the food you eat and the water you drink.' "

7The LORD your God has blessed you in all the work of your hands.
He has watched over your journey through this vast desert. These
forty years the LORD your God has been with you, and you have not
lacked anything.

8So we went on past our brothers the descendants of Esau, who
live in Seir. We turned from the Arabah road, which comes up from
Elath and Ezion Geber, and traveled along the desert road of Moab.

9Then the LORD said to me, "Do not harass the Moabites or provoke
them to war, for I will not give you any part of their land. I have given
Ar to the descendants of Lot as a possession."

10(The Emites used to live there—a people strong and numerous,
and as tall as the Anakites. 11Like the Anakites, they too were considered Rephaites, but the Moabites called them Emites. 12Horites used
to live in Seir, but the descendants of Esau drove them out. They
destroyed the Horites from before them and settled in their place, just
as Israel did in the land the LORD gave them as their possession.)

13And the LORD said, "Now get up and cross the Zered Valley." So
we crossed the valley.

14Thirty-eight years passed from the time we left Kadesh Barnea
until we crossed the Zered Valley. By then, that entire generation of
fighting men had perished from the camp, as the LORD had sworn to
them. 15The LORD's hand was against them until he had completely
eliminated them from the camp.

16Now when the last of these fighting men among the people had
died, 17the LORD said to me, 18"Today you are to pass by the region of
Moab at Ar. 19When you come to the Ammonites, do not harass them
or provoke them to war, for I will not give you possession of any land
belonging to the Ammonites. I have given it as a possession to the
descendants of Lot."

20(That too was considered a land of the Rephaites, who used to
live there; but the Ammonites called them Zamzummites. 21They were
a people strong and numerous, and as tall as the Anakites. The LORD
destroyed them from before the Ammonites, who drove them out and
settled in their place. 22The LORD had done the same for the descendants of Esau, who lived in Seir, when he destroyed the Horites from
before them. They drove them out and have lived in their place to this

STUDY As Moses continues his "sermon on the past" he reminds the people of family connections with the descendants of Esau and Lot, warning them to not make trouble with these folks. **1.** What instruction does God give concerning the descendants of Esau and Lot? **2.** How do you think the people of Israel felt about leaving these old enemies alone (Num. 20:14–21; 25:1–18)? **3.** How hard is it for you to leave someone alone who has offended you? **4.** Do you think God's concern for these people, who were not Israelites, shows his love or his faithfulness, or both? **5.** As the Israelites prepare to enter the land promised to them by God, what fears might they have about the people who lived there? How would God's treatment of the descendants of Esau and Lot help the Israelites face their fears? **6.** Does God sometimes surprise you with his attitude toward those you do not accept? Explain. **7.** Do you think the Israelites willingly accepted this command from God? Why or why not?

APPLY **1.** What is the hardest thing for you about forgiving someone who has hurt you? **2.** In what sense is God concerned about non-believers today? **3.** What is the greatest obstacle you face in accepting God's judgment and his justice? What have you learned from this text about God's character and his care for his people that will give you courage for the challenges of your life?

2:5 any of their land. God had given the land of Edom to Esau's descendants as surely as he had promised the land of Canaan to the descendants of Jacob (Esau's twin brother).

2:8 Moab. This land was inhabited by the descendants of Lot, Abraham's nephew of Sodom and Gomorrah fame (Gen. 13:12–13).

2:10 Anakites. This was the tribe of giants that scared the spies sent by Moses into the land (1:28).

2:11 Rephaites. The Rephaites were mentioned as early as Abraham's day (Gen. 14:5). The people of Moab might have actually referred to the Rephaites as Emites (terrors). The Rephaites were exceptionally tall people.

2:12 Horites. The Horites ruled the area of Edom before Esau settled there. Esau (later named Edom) either defeated the Horites or his tribe absorbed them.

2:20 Zamzummites. Another name for Rephaites.

day. [23]And as for the Avvites who lived in villages as far as Gaza, the
Caphtorites coming out from Caphtor[a] destroyed them and settled in
their place.)

Defeat of Sihon King of Heshbon

[24]"Set out now and cross the Arnon Gorge. See, I have given into
your hand Sihon the Amorite, king of Heshbon, and his country. Begin to take possession of it and engage him in battle. [25]This very day
I will begin to put the terror and fear of you on all the nations under
heaven. They will hear reports of you and will tremble and be in anguish because of you."

[26]From the desert of Kedemoth I sent messengers to Sihon king of
Heshbon offering peace and saying, [27]"Let us pass through your
country. We will stay on the main road; we will not turn aside to the
right or to the left. [28]Sell us food to eat and water to drink for their
price in silver. Only let us pass through on foot— [29]as the descendants of Esau, who live in Seir, and the Moabites, who live in Ar, did
for us—until we cross the Jordan into the land the LORD our God is
giving us." [30]But Sihon king of Heshbon refused to let us pass
through. For the LORD your God had made his spirit stubborn and his
heart obstinate in order to give him into your hands, as he has now
done.

[31]The LORD said to me, "See, I have begun to deliver Sihon and his
country over to you. Now begin to conquer and possess his land."

[32]When Sihon and all his army came out to meet us in battle at Jahaz, [33]the LORD our God delivered him over to us and we struck him
down, together with his sons and his whole army. [34]At that time we
took all his towns and completely destroyed[b] them—men, women
and children. We left no survivors. [35]But the livestock and the plunder
from the towns we had captured we carried off for ourselves. [36]From
Aroer on the rim of the Arnon Gorge, and from the town in the gorge,
even as far as Gilead, not one town was too strong for us. The LORD
our God gave us all of them. [37]But in accordance with the command
of the LORD our God, you did not encroach on any of the land of the
Ammonites, neither the land along the course of the Jabbok nor that
around the towns in the hills.

Defeat of Og King of Bashan

3 Next we turned and went up along the road toward Bashan, and
Og king of Bashan with his whole army marched out to meet us
in battle at Edrei. [2]The LORD said to me, "Do not be afraid of him, for
I have handed him over to you with his whole army and his land. Do

[a]23 That is, Crete [b]34 The Hebrew term refers to the irrevocable giving over of things or persons to the LORD, often by totally destroying them.

OPEN 1. Do you have a stubborn streak? If so, how is it manifested? **2.** What are some tough spots you've been in because of stubbornness?

STUDY Unlike God's commands concerning leaving Israel's neighbors alone, he now commands Israel to negotiate with Sihon, the king of Heshbon, to allow Israel to peacefully pass through his land. Because he would not let them peacefully pass through the land, God commanded his people to totally destroy Sihon and his kingdom. The defeat was complete, and Israel took the plunder for themselves. **1.** What is different about the instructions concerning treatment of Sihon when compared to the instructions about the descendants of Esau and Lot? **2.** What part did God play in Sihon's stubbornness? **3.** How do you feel about God commanding his people to war? **4.** If you were in the army of Israel, how would you have responded to the command to destroy Heshbon?

APPLY 1. How would you respond if God demanded something very costly from you? **2.** What is your attitude toward those commands of God that are hard for you to understand?

OPEN Can you remember a time when your team "stomped" the opponent? What was the score?

STUDY Just as he had commanded King Sihon, God now instructs Israel to annihilate Og and the kingdom of Bashan. And, just as

---

2:23 Avvites. From this verse we know that these people lived in the Gaza region. Even though they were described here as being destroyed, a *remnant survived even into Joshua's old* age (Josh. 13:3). **Caphtorites.** Caphtor was the place from which the Philistines originated. Most people believe it to be the island of Crete.

2:24 Arnon. The Arnon River flowed to the east of the Dead Sea, about halfway between the north and south ends.

2:30 God had made. The language of the Old Testament sometimes subordinates a person's will to God's control. This does not mean that the person had no choice, though. King Saul is also described this way (1 Sam. 18:10–12).

2:34 no survivors. It's hard to accept this reality, yet in these ancient days it was the only way to rid the land of idolatry. In many instances (Nineveh, in Jonah 1), God gave people the opportunity to repent before destroying them.

to him what you did to Sihon king of the Amorites, who reigned in Heshbon."

[3]So the LORD our God also gave into our hands Og king of Bashan and all his army. We struck them down, leaving no survivors. [4]At that time we took all his cities. There was not one of the sixty cities that we did not take from them—the whole region of Argob, Og's kingdom in Bashan. [5]All these cities were fortified with high walls and with gates and bars, and there were also a great many unwalled villages. [6]We completely destroyed[a] them, as we had done with Sihon king of Heshbon, destroying[a] every city—men, women and children. [7]But all the livestock and the plunder from their cities we carried off for ourselves.

[8]So at that time we took from these two kings of the Amorites the territory east of the Jordan, from the Arnon Gorge as far as Mount Hermon. [9](Hermon is called Sirion by the Sidonians; the Amorites call it Senir.) [10]We took all the towns on the plateau, and all Gilead, and all Bashan as far as Salecah and Edrei, towns of Og's kingdom in Bashan. [11](Only Og king of Bashan was left of the remnant of the Rephaites. His bed[b] was made of iron and was more than thirteen feet long and six feet wide.[c] It is still in Rabbah of the Ammonites.)

Division of the Land

[12]Of the land that we took over at that time, I gave the Reubenites and the Gadites the territory north of Aroer by the Arnon Gorge, including half the hill country of Gilead, together with its towns. [13]The rest of Gilead and also all of Bashan, the kingdom of Og, I gave to the half tribe of Manasseh. (The whole region of Argob in Bashan used to be known as a land of the Rephaites. [14]Jair, a descendant of Manasseh, took the whole region of Argob as far as the border of the Geshurites and the Maacathites; it was named after him, so that to this day Bashan is called Havvoth Jair.[d]) [15]And I gave Gilead to Makir. [16]But to the Reubenites and the Gadites I gave the territory extending from Gilead down to the Arnon Gorge (the middle of the gorge being the border) and out to the Jabbok River, which is the border of the Ammonites. [17]Its western border was the Jordan in the Arabah, from Kinnereth to the Sea of the Arabah (the Salt Sea[e]), below the slopes of Pisgah.

[18]I commanded you at that time: "The LORD your God has given you this land to take possession of it. But all your able-bodied men, armed for battle, must cross over ahead of your brother Israelites.

[a]6 The Hebrew term refers to the irrevocable giving over of things or persons to the LORD, often by totally destroying them. [b]11 Or *sarcophagus* [c]11 Hebrew *nine cubits long and four cubits wide* (about 4 meters long and 1.8 meters wide) [d]14 Or *called the settlements of Jair* [e]17 That is, the Dead Sea

before, God gives them the victory through his power. **1.** What difference do you see in this battle from the previous one? **2.** How does the defeat of Bashan begin to fulfill the promise of 2:25? **3.** How would you identify your "enemies" that seem to be protected with high walls? **4.** Why do you think the Israelites kept the plunder from these battles? **5.** What major battle of life have you been in? What plunder do you get to keep after your battles?

APPLY 1. Can you give an example of how God's power enabled you to win a victory you thought was too hard? **2.** How do you feel about God being on your side?

OPEN 1. Are you a team player, or do you go it on your own? **2.** Can you remember a time in your life when you had to divide up something with your brothers or sisters? Were you: More than willing to share? Stingy? Angry? Ambivalent?

STUDY The land God intended to give to the families of Reuben, Gad and Manasseh had been conquered, but there was a catch. Before they could possess their land, they were commanded by God to cross into Canaan and help their brothers secure their inheritance. Sadly, Moses would not be allowed to go with them. **1.** What was God's command to the families of Reuben, Gad and Manasseh? How do you think these families reacted to God's command? **2.** Why do you think God allowed part of Israel to settle on the east side of the Jordan? What problems might that create in the future? **3.** How do you feel about sharing in duties and rewards? **4.** What promise did God make to Joshua

3:3 Og king of Bashan. Og was known for his large stature. Defeating him helped the Hebrews overcome their fear that that the Canaanites were invincible.

3:4 Og's kingdom. This was a developed kingdom of sixty walled cities. Its defeat was a notable one for the Hebrews.

3:12–20 As the country was conquered, it was divided between tribes. In this passage the tribes that were instrumental in the victory claimed some or all of the land.

3:14 Jair. Often today we name city streets or wings of hospitals after someone who has contributed much to their cause. This was the case with Jair. He contributed greatly to the defeat of Og's kingdom, so the kingdom then was often referred to with Jair's name.

3:17 Kinnereth. The Sea of Kinnereth was later called the Sea of Galilee (Josh. 12:2; Mark 1:16). **Pisgah.** Mount Pisgah was near Mount Nebo, located on the northeast side of the Dead Sea. It was from Mount Pisgah (after climbing Nebo) that Moses viewed the Promised Land he would never enter.

(vv. 21–22)? **5.** How do you think Moses felt about having to stay behind? **6.** What do you learn about Moses from his prayer (vv. 24–25)? **7.** What do you learn about God from his decision not to let Moses enter the Promised Land?

APPLY 1. What battles of life do you need God's strength for right now? Why are those battles so difficult for you? **2.** How can this group help? How can you help others in this group with their battles?

OPEN 1. Have you ever been caught in a minor infraction of the law, like speeding? How did you feel? **2.** If you could be in charge of the world, what would be your number one law?

STUDY After Moses gives the Israelites a history lesson, he then begins to focus their attention on the Law God gave them. He reminds them that they are a favored nation because of God's care and God's Law, and charges them to be faithful to God. **1.** What two reasons are given for following God's laws? **2.** Why was it important for the Israelites not to add

19However, your wives, your children and your livestock (I know you
have much livestock) may stay in the towns I have given you, 20until
the LORD gives rest to your brothers as he has to you, and they too
have taken over the land that the LORD your God is giving them,
across the Jordan. After that, each of you may go back to the possession I have given you."

Moses Forbidden to Cross the Jordan

21At that time I commanded Joshua: "You have seen with your own
eyes all that the LORD your God has done to these two kings. The
LORD will do the same to all the kingdoms over there where you are
going. 22Do not be afraid of them; the LORD your God himself will
fight for you."
23At that time I pleaded with the LORD: 24"O Sovereign LORD, you
have begun to show to your servant your greatness and your strong
hand. For what god is there in heaven or on earth who can do the
deeds and mighty works you do? 25Let me go over and see the good
land beyond the Jordan—that fine hill country and Lebanon."
26But because of you the LORD was angry with me and would not
listen to me. "That is enough," the LORD said. "Do not speak to me
anymore about this matter. 27Go up to the top of Pisgah and look
west and north and south and east. Look at the land with your own
eyes, since you are not going to cross this Jordan. 28But commission
Joshua, and encourage and strengthen him, for he will lead this
people across and will cause them to inherit the land that you will
see." 29So we stayed in the valley near Beth Peor.

Obedience Commanded

4 Hear now, O Israel, the decrees and laws I am about to teach
you. Follow them so that you may live and may go in and take
possession of the land that the LORD, the God of your fathers, is giving you. 2Do not add to what I command you and do not subtract
from it, but keep the commands of the LORD your God that I give you.
3You saw with your own eyes what the LORD did at Baal Peor. The
LORD your God destroyed from among you everyone who followed
the Baal of Peor, 4but all of you who held fast to the LORD your God
are still alive today.
5See, I have taught you decrees and laws as the LORD my God commanded me, so that you may follow them in the land you are entering
to take possession of it. 6Observe them carefully, for this will show
your wisdom and understanding to the nations, who will hear about

---

3:20 After that. The tribes of Gad, Reuben and Manasseh were given land just inside Canaan's borders, but they were still required to travel past the Jordan to help their kinsmen conquer the rest of the land before they could settle into their inheritance.

3:22 God himself will fight for *you.* *The Hebrew spies who first* explored the Land of Promise had missed this truth (Num. 13). The people compared their own strength to that of the Canaanites, rather than comparing the strength of the Canaanites to the strength of God.

3:23–25 Moses asked God one last time to let him go into the Promised Land. It was not an act of rebellion but an act of childlike honesty. Christ prayed a similar prayer but submitted to his own death instead of receiving deliverance (Matt. 26:42).

3:27 Go up ... and look. Moses looked over the land much as Abraham had once done (Gen. 13:14–17). Both Abraham and Moses looked at the land from the viewpoint of their descendants inhabiting it.

3:28 commission ... encourage ... strengthen. Joshua was to be Moses' successor. He was prepared and ordained much as was Elisha with Elijah (1 Kin. 19:19–21) and Timothy with Paul (2 Tim. 1:5–7).

4:3 Baal of Peor. This refers to an idol worship incident in which 24,000 Hebrews died (Num. 25:1–9).

all these decrees and say, "Surely this great nation is a wise and
understanding people." 7 What other nation is so great as to have
their gods near them the way the LORD our God is near us whenever
we pray to him? 8 And what other nation is so great as to have such
righteous decrees and laws as this body of laws I am setting before
you today?

9 Only be careful, and watch yourselves closely so that you do not
forget the things your eyes have seen or let them slip from your heart
as long as you live. Teach them to your children and to their children
after them. 10 Remember the day you stood before the LORD your God
at Horeb, when he said to me, "Assemble the people before me to
hear my words so that they may learn to revere me as long as they
live in the land and may teach them to their children." 11 You came
near and stood at the foot of the mountain while it blazed with fire to
the very heavens, with black clouds and deep darkness. 12 Then the
LORD spoke to you out of the fire. You heard the sound of words but
saw no form; there was only a voice. 13 He declared to you his covenant, the Ten Commandments, which he commanded you to follow
and then wrote them on two stone tablets. 14 And the LORD directed
me at that time to teach you the decrees and laws you are to follow in
the land that you are crossing the Jordan to possess.

Idolatry Forbidden

15 You saw no form of any kind the day the LORD spoke to you at
Horeb out of the fire. Therefore watch yourselves very carefully, 16 so
that you do not become corrupt and make for yourselves an idol, an
image of any shape, whether formed like a man or a woman, 17 or like
any animal on earth or any bird that flies in the air, 18 or like any creature that moves along the ground or any fish in the waters below.
19 And when you look up to the sky and see the sun, the moon and the
stars—all the heavenly array—do not be enticed into bowing down to
them and worshiping things the LORD your God has apportioned to
all the nations under heaven. 20 But as for you, the LORD took you and
brought you out of the iron-smelting furnace, out of Egypt, to be the
people of his inheritance, as you now are.

21 The LORD was angry with me because of you, and he solemnly
swore that I would not cross the Jordan and enter the good land the
LORD your God is giving you as your inheritance. 22 I will die in this
land; I will not cross the Jordan; but you are about to cross over and

to the commands God would give them? **3.** What happened at Baal Peor (Num. 25:1–3)? **4.** What do you think the people of Israel understood about the absolute nature of God's Law? **5.** Do you tend to think of God's Law as absolute or relative? **6.** Why would having the Law distinguish Israel from other nations? What greatness did the Law bring to Israel? **7.** Why is it important for one generation to pass its heritage on to the next generation? **8.** What place do you think the Ten Commandments have in a modern society?

APPLY **1.** Do you feel that the laws of God are a hindrance or a blessing in your life? **2.** Do you think God's Law expresses his love and concern for you?

OPEN **1.** What comes to mind when you think of "idol worship"? **2.** Can you remember when something captured all your time and affection?

STUDY At the heart of God's relationship with Israel was the concept of one God, with no room for any other deities. God promised his people that he would bless them if they would honor that foundational concept. **1.** What fundamental difference between God and an idol do you see in this reading? Why do you think the idolaters made their images in the form of natural things, like animals, birds or serpents? **2.** In what sense do you think God actually has a personal relationship with his people? **3.** What does it mean to you that God is a

---

4:7 our God is near us. The Hebrews were fortunate to have many reminders of God's presence, including the cloud that guided them and the tabernacle that held the ark (a symbol of God's *presence and a time capsule of his* provision). **whenever we pray to him.** As with us today, the Hebrews knew God was only a prayer away.

4:10 teach them to their children. So much of the Hebrews' customs and lifestyle were about passing down the history of God's provision. Their feasts were object lessons to remind children of how God had led. Here and elsewhere in Deuteronomy they were encouraged to be sure the next generation knew the path they had taken and the God they served.

4:13 two stone tablets. Two sets of stone tablets were inscribed by God. Moses had destroyed the first set in anger at the rebellious Israelites (Ex. 31:18; 32:15; 32:19; 34:1).

4:15 Horeb. Here God spoke to Moses from the burning bush that never burned up (Ex. 3:1–5).

4:19 In many ways our world is not so much different from the world of Moses. Many cultures today face the same enticement to worship the created world more than the Creator of the world.

4:21 The LORD was angry. Moses lost his privilege of entering the land after God commanded him to speak to a rock in order to receive water. In anger, Moses struck the rock instead. God was angry with Moses for his reaction and angry with the people for the same lack of faith that angered Moses (Num. 20:5–12).

take possession of that good land. 23 Be careful not to forget the covenant of the LORD your God that he made with you; do not make for
yourselves an idol in the form of anything the LORD your God has forbidden. 24 For the LORD your God is a consuming fire, a jealous God.
25 After you have had children and grandchildren and have lived in
the land a long time—if you then become corrupt and make any kind
of idol, doing evil in the eyes of the LORD your God and provoking him
to anger, 26 I call heaven and earth as witnesses against you this day
that you will quickly perish from the land that you are crossing the
Jordan to possess. You will not live there long but will certainly be destroyed. 27 The LORD will scatter you among the peoples, and only a
few of you will survive among the nations to which the LORD will
drive you. 28 There you will worship man-made gods of wood and
stone, which cannot see or hear or eat or smell. 29 But if from there
you seek the LORD your God, you will find him if you look for him with
all your heart and with all your soul. 30 When you are in distress and
all these things have happened to you, then in later days you will return to the LORD your God and obey him. 31 For the LORD your God is a
merciful God; he will not abandon or destroy you or forget the covenant with your forefathers, which he confirmed to them by oath.

The LORD Is God

32 Ask now about the former days, long before your time, from the
day God created man on the earth; ask from one end of the heavens
to the other. Has anything so great as this ever happened, or has anything like it ever been heard of? 33 Has any other people heard the
voice of God[a] speaking out of fire, as you have, and lived? 34 Has any
god ever tried to take for himself one nation out of another nation, by
testings, by miraculous signs and wonders, by war, by a mighty hand
and an outstretched arm, or by great and awesome deeds, like all the
things the LORD your God did for you in Egypt before your very eyes?
35 You were shown these things so that you might know that the
LORD is God; besides him there is no other. 36 From heaven he made
you hear his voice to discipline you. On earth he showed you his great
fire, and you heard his words from out of the fire. 37 Because he loved
your forefathers and chose their descendants after them, he brought
you out of Egypt by his Presence and his great strength, 38 to drive out

[a]33 Or *of a god*

"jealous" God? **4.** What is the "if ... then" logic of verses 25–31? Do you think it is fair for God to say to his people, "you will quickly perish ... your God is a merciful God"? Is it fair to tell them that if they don't follow him, they will be destroyed? **5.** In what ways do you see that God was merciful and faithful to his covenant with Israel? With you?

APPLY 1. In what ways do you think God shows his personal concern for you? **2.** How do you think you can actually "find" God?

OPEN 1. Can you describe a time when you were really proud of your nation? **2.** What did you think about when you first wondered about the existence of God?

STUDY Foundational to Israel's relationship with God is the fact that he is the only God. Moses refers to their recent history to reaffirm his uniqueness and his special care for Israel. **1.** Why do you think the people needed to be reminded of God's recent dealings with them? **2.** How does it help you in your relationship with God to look at what he has done in the past? **3.** Why did God choose Israel (vv. 35–38)? **4.** What was involved in the people "acknowledging" God (vv. 39-40)? **5.** What is your thought about there being only one God?

4:24 fire. God's anger is compared to a consuming fire several times in the Old Testament. In 2 Samuel 22 David pens a song that refers to God as a consuming fire. That same song is in Psalm 18.

4:25 if you then become corrupt. God kept sending the same message, but the Hebrews often didn't get it. He was concerned with their faith, worship and holiness. God wanted them to trust *and to worship only him. In that the* Hebrews were never consistent. Nevertheless, in verses like this, where God reiterates the covenant, he reminds them of their obligation to faithfulness.

4:26 perish. This was God's clear-cut alternative to purity in worship. God's covenant with Abraham promised a large nation of descendants. If these descendants continued to be unfaithful, then their destruction would be the destruction of that covenant.

4:29 you will find him. This is a wonderful promise. If you seek God with your whole being, you will surely find him. The Hebrews would face *many* difficulties, but their God would never be lost to them.

4:31 will not abandon or destroy. We can make choices that carry us far away from the presence of God, but that is our choice, never God's. God will not consume us, rather he is merciful and forgiving when we return to him.

4:35 there is no other. This is the first commandment from Exodus 20:3: "Have no other gods before me."

4:37 Because he loved. Moses clearly gives us God's motivation in covenanting with Abraham and protecting that promise throughout the generations. It is the same motivation given in John 3:16: "For God so loved the world ..."

before you nations greater and stronger than you and to bring you into
their land to give it to you for your inheritance, as it is today.
39Acknowledge and take to heart this day that the LORD is God in
heaven above and on the earth below. There is no other. 40Keep his
decrees and commands, which I am giving you today, so that it may
go well with you and your children after you and that you may live
long in the land the LORD your God gives you for all time.

Cities of Refuge

41Then Moses set aside three cities east of the Jordan, 42to which
anyone who had killed a person could flee if he had unintentionally
killed his neighbor without malice aforethought. He could flee into
one of these cities and save his life. 43The cities were these: Bezer in
the desert plateau, for the Reubenites; Ramoth in Gilead, for the Gadites; and Golan in Bashan, for the Manassites.

Introduction to the Law

44This is the law Moses set before the Israelites. 45These are the
stipulations, decrees and laws Moses gave them when they came out
of Egypt 46and were in the valley near Beth Peor east of the Jordan, in
the land of Sihon king of the Amorites, who reigned in Heshbon and
was defeated by Moses and the Israelites as they came out of Egypt.
47They took possession of his land and the land of Og king of Bashan,
the two Amorite kings east of the Jordan. 48This land extended from
Aroer on the rim of the Arnon Gorge to Mount Siyon[a] (that is, Hermon), 49and included all the Arabah east of the Jordan, as far as the
Sea of the Arabah,[b] below the slopes of Pisgah.

The Ten Commandments

5 Moses summoned all Israel and said:
Hear, O Israel, the decrees and laws I declare in your hearing
today. Learn them and be sure to follow them. 2The LORD our God
made a covenant with us at Horeb. 3It was not with our fathers that
the LORD made this covenant, but with us, with all of us who are alive
here today. 4The LORD spoke to you face to face out of the fire on the
mountain. 5(At that time I stood between the LORD and you to declare
to you the word of the LORD, because you were afraid of the fire and
did not go up the mountain.) And he said:

6"I am the LORD your God, who brought you out of Egypt,
out of the land of slavery.

[a]48 Hebrew; Syriac (see also Deut. 3:9) *Sirion* [b]49 That is, the Dead Sea

APPLY **1.** What do you learn about God from this reading? **2.** What are the implications of acknowledging God in your life?

OPEN When you were growing up, who "laid down the law" in your family?

STUDY The Israelites are poised to enter into the land God promised them, but before they do, Moses takes care of a couple of important items. He designates the "cities of refuge" (Num. 35:6–34) and then sets the stage for the heart of his sermon on the Law, beginning with the Ten Commandments. **1.** Why was it important to have the "cities of refuge"? **2.** Why was their location important?

APPLY Do you feel as though you may be at a transition point in your life, ready to cross over into something new?

OPEN **1.** Can you remember a time when you had to listen to someone explain all the rules? What was it like? Were you on the edge of your seat or bored to death? **2.** What is your least favorite rule in life? What is your most favorite rule in life? Explain.

STUDY Before entering the Promised Land, Moses calls all the people together to remind them once again of the Law God had given to them at Sinai (Horeb), including the Ten Commandments. He presents the Law as a covenant with the people, and in describing the scene of the giving of

4:39 Acknowledge and take to heart. This is what God expects of us. It is the essence of faith. God counted Abraham righteous, not from Abraham's works, but because Abraham believed God (Rom. 4:3). It is our faith that God desires. We show that faith by acknowledging that he is the one true God and by taking to heart our relationship with him.

5:2 Horeb. This is the same mountain as Mount Sinai, where Moses received his commission from God (Ex. 3:1). It is also where he brought water out of the rock (Ex. 17:6) and where the people took off their jewelry in repentance to God after they made the golden calf idol (Ex. 33:6).

5:3 The covenant was a living promise to all the descendants. It was an arrangement that God had made; not with one generation of people, but with all their descendants. This is a parallel truth to our understanding of a relationship with God today. Each of us is responsible to build not only that relationship, assisted by the faith and spiritual guidance of people who lived before us, but our own faith too. We do not follow God in someone else's shadow.

5:6 I am the LORD. The Ten Commandments are the basis of all rules of decency. This verse is the basis of the Ten Commandments: God is God. When we understand who God is, then what he speaks becomes priority.

the Law on Mount Sinai, he pictures a fearful and awesome scene of darkness, fire and smoke. **1.** What is a covenant? **2.** What role do these ten laws play in the whole of God's Law? **3.** What impact do these ten laws have in your life? **4.** What law does God begin with in the Ten Commandments? Why do you think this law is first? **5.** How many of the laws have to do with your relationship with God? How many are about how you treat people? **6.** Do you think these laws are an acknowledgement of human nature or an attempt to change it? Explain. **7.** What do you think is the significance in the way God gave the Law (vv. 4–5,22–31)? **8.** What do the first four laws teach you about the kind of relationship God wants with you? What do the last six laws teach you about your relationship with your fellow humans? **9.** What do you perceive to be the intent of God in giving the Ten Commandments? What effect on the law codes of our modern times do you think these Ten Commandments have?

APPLY **1.** What is your "gut" reaction to these laws? Explain. **2.** Do you think obedience of these laws will hinder your life or enhance your life? Why?

---

7 "You shall have no other gods before[a] me.
8 "You shall not make for yourself an idol in the form of anything
in heaven above or on the earth beneath or in the waters
below. 9 You shall not bow down to them or worship them;
for I, the LORD your God, am a jealous God, punishing the
children for the sin of the fathers to the third and fourth
generation of those who hate me, 10 but showing love to a
thousand ⌞generations⌟ of those who love me and keep my
commandments.
11 "You shall not misuse the name of the LORD your God, for the
LORD will not hold anyone guiltless who misuses his name.
12 "Observe the Sabbath day by keeping it holy, as the LORD your
God has commanded you. 13 Six days you shall labor and do
all your work, 14 but the seventh day is a Sabbath to the
LORD your God. On it you shall not do any work, neither
you, nor your son or daughter, nor your manservant or
maidservant, nor your ox, your donkey or any of your
animals, nor the alien within your gates, so that your manservant and maidservant may rest, as you do. 15 Remember
that you were slaves in Egypt and that the LORD your God
brought you out of there with a mighty hand and an
outstretched arm. Therefore the LORD your God has commanded you to observe the Sabbath day.
16 "Honor your father and your mother, as the LORD your God has
commanded you, so that you may live long and that it may
go well with you in the land the LORD your God is giving you.
17 "You shall not murder.
18 "You shall not commit adultery.
19 "You shall not steal.
20 "You shall not give false testimony against your neighbor.
21 "You shall not covet your neighbor's wife. You shall not set your
desire on your neighbor's house or land, his manservant
or maidservant, his ox or donkey, or anything that belongs
to your neighbor."

22 These are the commandments the LORD proclaimed in a loud
voice to your whole assembly there on the mountain from out of the
fire, the cloud and the deep darkness; and he added nothing more.
Then he wrote them on two stone tablets and gave them to me.
23 When you heard the voice out of the darkness, while the mountain was ablaze with fire, all the leading men of your tribes and your
elders came to me. 24 And you said, "The LORD our God has shown us

[a] *7 Or besides*

5:12 Observe the Sabbath. Observing the Sabbath honored God's process of creating the world and stamped his ownership on the Hebrews as their deliverer from Egypt. Observing the Sabbath *was not* just about rest but about honoring God. That is why everyone was to rest that day, Hebrews, foreigners and animals alike.

5:15 Remember. Most of the customs and traditions of the Hebrews were a passing down of oral history. They were about helping the generations remember the history of God's presence, guidance and holiness. This was a world without the printing press, video recorders or copy machines. History was passed down through customs, feasts and stories.

5:16–21 Jesus and the early church leadership quoted often from this passage. Romans 13:9 tells us that we can sum up all these commands with the command to love our neighbor as we love ourselves.

5:20 false testimony. This applies to testimony in court as well as in social situations (slander, gossip).

5:22 he wrote. God did inscribe the commands (Ex. 31:18).

his glory and his majesty, and we have heard his voice from the fire.
Today we have seen that a man can live even if God speaks with him.
25 But now, why should we die? This great fire will consume us, and
we will die if we hear the voice of the LORD our God any longer. 26 For
what mortal man has ever heard the voice of the living God speaking
out of fire, as we have, and survived? 27 Go near and listen to all that
the LORD our God says. Then tell us whatever the LORD our God tells
you. We will listen and obey."

28 The LORD heard you when you spoke to me and the LORD said to
me, "I have heard what this people said to you. Everything they said
was good. 29 Oh, that their hearts would be inclined to fear me and
keep all my commands always, so that it might go well with them and
their children forever!

30 "Go, tell them to return to their tents. 31 But you stay here with me
so that I may give you all the commands, decrees and laws you are to
teach them to follow in the land I am giving them to possess."

32 So be careful to do what the LORD your God has commanded you;
do not turn aside to the right or to the left. 33 Walk in all the way that
the LORD your God has commanded you, so that you may live and
prosper and prolong your days in the land that you will possess.

Love the LORD Your God

6 These are the commands, decrees and laws the LORD your God
directed me to teach you to observe in the land that you are
crossing the Jordan to possess, 2 so that you, your children and their
children after them may fear the LORD your God as long as you live by
keeping all his decrees and commands that I give you, and so that
you may enjoy long life. 3 Hear, O Israel, and be careful to obey so that
it may go well with you and that you may increase greatly in a land
flowing with milk and honey, just as the LORD, the God of your
fathers, promised you.

4 Hear, O Israel: The LORD our God, the LORD is one.[a] 5 Love the LORD
your God with all your heart and with all your soul and with all your
strength. 6 These commandments that I give you today are to be upon

[a]4 Or *The LORD our God is one LORD*; or *The LORD is our God, the LORD is one*; or *The LORD is our God, the LORD alone*

OPEN 1. What unique traditions, customs or sayings in your family have been passed down from generation to generation? **2.** What specific blessing in your family can you think of that has been present for generations?

STUDY As Moses continues to rehearse the Law of God to the people he focuses on the "heart" of the Law—"love the Lord your God with all your heart and with all your soul and with all your strength" (see the words of Jesus in Matt. 22:34–40). He tells them that the success or failure of their nation will depend on whether or not they pass these laws on to following generations.

5:25 we will die. In our mind's eye this picture can seem exciting and full of special effects. For the people at that time, though, it was terrifying. They really did fear death in the awesome power of God's presence.

5:27 Then tell us .... We will listen. The people were more comfortable with a mediator between them and God rather than with a face-to-face (or face-to-voice) encounter. They wanted God's blessing, but at a safe distance.

6:2 fear the LORD ... by keeping. The essence of fearing God is obeying him. It is akin to the reverential fear that we have for our parents when we are children. It is basically the recognition of immense authority.

6:3 be careful to obey. The covenant between God and Israel was not a contract. Who has the right to a contract with God? Both sides did agree to do something, though. God promised the people a land and a national heritage. The people promised to worship and obey him. **flowing with milk and honey.** This phrase is used repeatedly throughout the Old Testament but only once to mean a country other than Canaan. In that instance, the fearful people were pining for Egypt and called Egypt the land of milk and honey (Num. 16:13).

6:4–9 This is one of the known portions of the Old Testament and is called the "Shema," which means "hear." It is at the heart of the Jewish faith. Jews today repeat these verses often.

6:4 the LORD is one. This knowledge brought a comfort to the Hebrews. Their polytheistic (worshiping many gods) neighbors always had to fear the displeasure of the many gods they worshiped. Not so with the Hebrews. They worshiped the one true God and had only to concern themselves with his expectations on their lives. This is foundational in the Christian understanding of the Trinity.

6:6 upon your hearts. The easiest way to put something on your heart is to memorize it. Meditation also is a way to keep God's truth in your mind. In meditation we contemplate the truth of God unhurriedly and peacefully.

1. What does it mean to "fear the Lord"? **2.** Why was it so important for the children of the Israelites to hear the Law generation after generation? Why is it so important for your children to understand the foundations of your belief? **3.** What physical signs did the Israelites use to remind the children of the laws of God? What are some ways one generation can remind the next generation of the laws of God today? **4.** What does it mean to you to "test" the Lord? **5.** If you asked your parents about what they believe, could they tell you? Could you tell your children if they asked you? **6.** Why was God so intent that the Israelites not give their attention to other gods? If God is the only God, how do you explain his warning against following other gods?

APPLY 1. How do you demonstrate that you love God with all your heart and fear him? **2.** How can the members of this group share their faith in such a way that it would encourage you? How can you encourage them?

OPEN 1. What is your favorite "action" movie in which good triumphs over evil and justice reigns? Give the details. **2.** Can you describe a time in your life when you felt empowered by someone who helped you win a battle? What was it like and how did you feel?

your hearts. [7]Impress them on your children. Talk about them when
you sit at home and when you walk along the road, when you lie
down and when you get up. [8]Tie them as symbols on your hands and
bind them on your foreheads. [9]Write them on the doorframes of your
houses and on your gates.
[10]When the LORD your God brings you into the land he swore to
your fathers, to Abraham, Isaac and Jacob, to give you—a land with
large, flourishing cities you did not build, [11]houses filled with all
kinds of good things you did not provide, wells you did not dig, and
vineyards and olive groves you did not plant—then when you eat and
are satisfied, [12]be careful that you do not forget the LORD, who
brought you out of Egypt, out of the land of slavery.
[13]Fear the LORD your God, serve him only and take your oaths in his
name. [14]Do not follow other gods, the gods of the peoples around
you; [15]for the LORD your God, who is among you, is a jealous God and
his anger will burn against you, and he will destroy you from the face
of the land. [16]Do not test the LORD your God as you did at Massah.
[17]Be sure to keep the commands of the LORD your God and the stipulations and decrees he has given you. [18]Do what is right and good in
the LORD's sight, so that it may go well with you and you may go in
and take over the good land that the LORD promised on oath to your
forefathers, [19]thrusting out all your enemies before you, as the LORD
said.
[20]In the future, when your son asks you, "What is the meaning of
the stipulations, decrees and laws the LORD our God has commanded
you?" [21]tell him: "We were slaves of Pharaoh in Egypt, but the LORD
brought us out of Egypt with a mighty hand. [22]Before our eyes the
LORD sent miraculous signs and wonders—great and terrible—upon
Egypt and Pharaoh and his whole household. [23]But he brought us out
from there to bring us in and give us the land that he promised on
oath to our forefathers. [24]The LORD commanded us to obey all these
decrees and to fear the LORD our God, so that we might always prosper and be kept alive, as is the case today. [25]And if we are careful to
obey all this law before the LORD our God, as he has commanded us,
that will be our righteousness."

Driving Out the Nations

7 When the LORD your God brings you into the land you are entering to possess and drives out before you many nations—the
Hittites, Girgashites, Amorites, Canaanites, Perizzites, Hivites and
Jebusites, seven nations larger and stronger than you— [2]and when
the LORD your God has delivered them over to you and you have

6:12 be careful that you do not forget. This was a good warning to the people. Throughout history people have tended to trust God through bad times and forget him in easy times.

6:20 when your son asks you. *It* was Moses' assumption that God's law would be a topic of conversation in Hebrew homes, that fathers would be able to teach their sons about spiritual things and that sons would be interested in learning.

6:23 The first good news was that God brought the people out of Egypt. The next, even better news was that God brought the people out of bondage so that he could bring them into his promise.

6:25 that will be our righteousness. Faith in God produced the obedience that was the righteousness of the people. Jesus faulted the Pharisees with crediting their righteousness to obedience apart from faith (Matt. 23).

7:1 God listed six of these seven nations when he had called Moses to this task over forty years earlier (Ex. 3:17).

7:2–5 Israel was not setting up a political kingdom but a spiritual one. While the demands for total destruction seem

defeated them, then you must destroy them totally.[a] Make no treaty with them, and show them no mercy. [3]Do not intermarry with them. Do not give your daughters to their sons or take their daughters for your sons, [4]for they will turn your sons away from following me to serve other gods, and the LORD's anger will burn against you and will quickly destroy you. [5]This is what you are to do to them: Break down their altars, smash their sacred stones, cut down their Asherah poles[b] and burn their idols in the fire. [6]For you are a people holy to the LORD your God. The LORD your God has chosen you out of all the peoples on the face of the earth to be his people, his treasured possession.

[7]The LORD did not set his affection on you and choose you because you were more numerous than other peoples, for you were the fewest of all peoples. [8]But it was because the LORD loved you and kept the oath he swore to your forefathers that he brought you out with a mighty hand and redeemed you from the land of slavery, from the power of Pharaoh king of Egypt. [9]Know therefore that the LORD your God is God; he is the faithful God, keeping his covenant of love to a thousand generations of those who love him and keep his commands. [10]But

those who hate him he will repay to their face by destruction;
he will not be slow to repay to their face those who hate him.

[11]Therefore, take care to follow the commands, decrees and laws I give you today.

[12]If you pay attention to these laws and are careful to follow them, then the LORD your God will keep his covenant of love with you, as he swore to your forefathers. [13]He will love you and bless you and increase your numbers. He will bless the fruit of your womb, the crops of your land—your grain, new wine and oil—the calves of your herds and the lambs of your flocks in the land that he swore to your forefathers to give you. [14]You will be blessed more than any other people; none of your men or women will be childless, nor any of your livestock without young. [15]The LORD will keep you free from every disease. He will not inflict on you the horrible diseases you knew in Egypt, but he will inflict them on all who hate you. [16]You must destroy all the peoples the LORD your God gives over to you. Do not look on them with pity and do not serve their gods, for that will be a snare to you.

[17]You may say to yourselves, "These nations are stronger than we are. How can we drive them out?" [18]But do not be afraid of them; remember well what the LORD your God did to Pharaoh and to all Egypt.

[a]2 The Hebrew term refers to the irrevocable giving over of things or persons to the LORD, often by totally destroying them; also in verse 26. [b]5 That is, symbols of the goddess Asherah; here and elsewhere in Deuteronomy

STUDY The first task assigned to the Israelites upon entering the Promised Land was to conquer the land. God's intent was for Israel to totally drive out the inhabitants of the land and take possession of the entire area. **1.** What commands did God give to the Israelites concerning the people they would encounter when they entered the Promised Land (vv. 1–5)? Why were these laws so strict? Do you think these laws counteract the mercy of God? Explain. **2.** Why did God favor Israel over the other nations (vv. 7–9)? **3.** What was God's concern about the Israelites intermarrying with the other nations? **4.** Do you think God was fair in his favor toward Israel and his judgment on the other nations? Have you ever been able to rejoice with someone else when God blesses them? **5.** What do you think about God's faithfulness to a thousand generations? Can you give examples of how God has been faithful to the generations of your family? **6.** Can you give examples of the connection between obeying God and being blessed by God? **7.** What do you think was the attitude of the Israelites about the promises of God to them (vv. 12–15)? **8.** How did God deal with the fears the Israelites had about the people who already possessed the land they were entering (vv. 17–26)?

APPLY 1. Can you name some personal enemies you need God's help to overcome? **2.** What has been the greatest battle of your life? What obstacle are you facing right now? How can this group help?

extreme here, such were the means of restoring the land to the worship of the one true God.

7:3 Do not intermarry. The warning against intermarriage with pagan cultures was solely for the purity of the national faith.

7:7–8 The great truth here is that God did not love the Hebrews because they were valuable to him. Instead they were valuable because he loved them.

7:9 to a thousand generations. This means "endlessly" or "forever."

7:12–15 God promised blessings for obedience. Many of these blessings would pour naturally out of a nation that worshiped God with pure hearts. The Hebrews needed only to obey to find these blessings.

7:13 Many of God's promises had to do with fertility. The land would produce crops. The people would produce children. The herds would produce more herds.

[19]You saw with your own eyes the great trials, the miraculous signs
and wonders, the mighty hand and outstretched arm, with which the
LORD your God brought you out. The LORD your God will do the same
to all the peoples you now fear. [20]Moreover, the LORD your God will
send the hornet among them until even the survivors who hide from
you have perished. [21]Do not be terrified by them, for the LORD your
God, who is among you, is a great and awesome God. [22]The LORD
your God will drive out those nations before you, little by little. You
will not be allowed to eliminate them all at once, or the wild animals
will multiply around you. [23]But the LORD your God will deliver them
over to you, throwing them into great confusion until they are destroyed. [24]He will give their kings into your hand, and you will wipe
out their names from under heaven. No one will be able to stand up
against you; you will destroy them. [25]The images of their gods you are
to burn in the fire. Do not covet the silver and gold on them, and do
not take it for yourselves, or you will be ensnared by it, for it is detestable to the LORD your God. [26]Do not bring a detestable thing into your
house or you, like it, will be set apart for destruction. Utterly abhor
and detest it, for it is set apart for destruction.

Do Not Forget the LORD

8 Be careful to follow every command I am giving you today, so
that you may live and increase and may enter and possess the
land that the LORD promised on oath to your forefathers. [2]Remember
how the LORD your God led you all the way in the desert these forty
years, to humble you and to test you in order to know what was in
your heart, whether or not you would keep his commands. [3]He humbled you, causing you to hunger and then feeding you with manna,
which neither you nor your fathers had known, to teach you that man
does not live on bread alone but on every word that comes from the
mouth of the LORD. [4]Your clothes did not wear out and your feet did
not swell during these forty years. [5]Know then in your heart that as a
man disciplines his son, so the LORD your God disciplines you.

[6]Observe the commands of the LORD your God, walking in his ways
and revering him. [7]For the LORD your God is bringing you into a good
land—a land with streams and pools of water, with springs flowing in
the valleys and hills; [8]a land with wheat and barley, vines and fig
trees, pomegranates, olive oil and honey; [9]a land where bread will
not be scarce and you will lack nothing; a land where the rocks are
iron and you can dig copper out of the hills.

[10]When you have eaten and are satisfied, praise the LORD your God
for the good land he has given you. [11]Be careful that you do not forget

OPEN 1. Do you think your prosperity is a blessing or a curse? Explain. **2.** Can you remember a time in your life when you forgot something very important? What was it, and what happened?

STUDY One of the major concerns God had for the nation of Israel was that when they entered the Promised Land, settled down and became comfortable, they would have a tendency to forget the important lessons they learned in the desert wandering. Moses reminds them to not forget what God has done or his commandments. **1.** Why do you think the Israelites needed to experience the discipline of God before entering the Promised Land? **2.** How could Israel forget such powerful lessons from the past? **3.** How would you describe the spiritual "good land" to which God delivers his people today? **4.** In what way can the prosperity of the present cloud your memory of the lessons you learned in difficult times? **5.** What

---

7:20 hornet. Some believe this to refer to actual hornets. Others see it as symbolic. The same word is used in Exodus 23:28.

7:22 little by little. If the land had been depopulated all at once, then it *would have become wild* again before being resettled by the Hebrews.

7:25–26 The Hebrews first had to be brave enough to enter the battle, then brave enough to destroy the idols even though they were made with valuable metals.

7:26 detestable. The idols were detestable for several reasons. They represented false worship, and they were often made to represent a perversion of some kind.

8:3 manna. For a description of manna see Exodus 16:31. Jesus quoted this verse when tempted by Satan (Matt. 4:4).

8:9 you will lack nothing. After the slavery of Egypt and the deprivation of the desert, this land must have sounded too good to be true. **iron ... copper.** Copper and iron can both still be found south of the Dead Sea. Basically, this information meant that the Hebrews would find whatever they needed to survive within their land. No need for imports; home would have it all. That would have been a welcome feeling after the desert they had just wandered through.

the LORD your God, failing to observe his commands, his laws and his
decrees that I am giving you this day. 12Otherwise, when you eat and
are satisfied, when you build fine houses and settle down, 13and
when your herds and flocks grow large and your silver and gold
increase and all you have is multiplied, 14then your heart will become
proud and you will forget the LORD your God, who brought you out of
Egypt, out of the land of slavery. 15He led you through the vast and
dreadful desert, that thirsty and waterless land, with its venomous
snakes and scorpions. He brought you water out of hard rock. 16He
gave you manna to eat in the desert, something your fathers had
never known, to humble and to test you so that in the end it might go
well with you. 17You may say to yourself, "My power and the strength
of my hands have produced this wealth for me." 18But remember the
LORD your God, for it is he who gives you the ability to produce
wealth, and so confirms his covenant, which he swore to your forefathers, as it is today.

19If you ever forget the LORD your God and follow other gods and
worship and bow down to them, I testify against you today that you
will surely be destroyed. 20Like the nations the LORD destroyed before
you, so you will be destroyed for not obeying the LORD your God.

Not Because of Israel's Righteousness

9 Hear, O Israel. You are now about to cross the Jordan to go in
and dispossess nations greater and stronger than you, with
large cities that have walls up to the sky. 2The people are strong and
tall—Anakites! You know about them and have heard it said: "Who
can stand up against the Anakites?" 3But be assured today that the
LORD your God is the one who goes across ahead of you like a
devouring fire. He will destroy them; he will subdue them before you.
And you will drive them out and annihilate them quickly, as the LORD
has promised you.

4After the LORD your God has driven them out before you, do not
say to yourself, "The LORD has brought me here to take possession of
this land because of my righteousness." No, it is on account of the
wickedness of these nations that the LORD is going to drive them out
before you. 5It is not because of your righteousness or your integrity
that you are going in to take possession of their land; but on account
of the wickedness of these nations, the LORD your God will drive them
out before you, to accomplish what he swore to your fathers, to Abraham, Isaac and Jacob. 6Understand, then, that it is not because of

relationship choices are set before the Israelites as they enter the Promised Land? **6.** Can you relate the danger of physical prosperity with the danger of spiritual prosperity? **7.** How do you think God destroys a nation today that does not obey him?

APPLY **1.** Can you remember a personal desert God has brought you through? What was it like? How did God deliver you? **2.** How can this group help each other not to forget all God has done and said?

OPEN Has there been a time in your life when you benefited from another person's downfall?

STUDY God knew that Israel would have a tendency to believe that they conquered the Promised Land because of their goodness. The truth was that they were given the land because God was keeping a promise he made to their forefathers long ago. **1.** Why do you think Israel might have been tempted to be proud of their own goodness? **2.** In what way is God's justice demonstrated in his statement about driving out the wicked nations?

APPLY **1.** Are you trusting your own goodness for salvation? **2.** Do you think you are good enough to go to heaven?

8:15 The harshness of what God had brought them through was a picture God didn't want the people to forget. If *they did, then they might* forget to be thankful for the bounty he had brought them into (Ex. 17:3–7).

8:16 manna ... to test you. The manna was a test in several ways. It tested the people to see if they would accept God's provision for them every day. It was also a test to see if they would obey him by handling the manna as he asked them to.

9:2 You know about them. The Hebrews knew about these people from the initial report they received when they first arrived at the border. It was this report that scared the Hebrews away. The spies specifically mentioned the "descendants of Anak" (Num. 13:26–31).

9:3 ahead of you. God had promised his presence to go before the people both in protection and in guidance. That is why their fear was a distrust of God's power and love.

9:4 on account of the wickedness. This gives us insight into the existing settlers of the land of Canaan. It was because of their wickedness that God wanted them out. God warns the Hebrews here not to assume they had received this land because of their own righteousness. Their victories would be as much about God judging sin as about rewarding obedience.

9:6,13 stiff-necked. This means stubborn and defiant, inflexible and unwilling to follow where they were

your righteousness that the LORD your God is giving you this good
land to possess, for you are a stiff-necked people.

The Golden Calf

[7]Remember this and never forget how you provoked the LORD your
God to anger in the desert. From the day you left Egypt until you arrived here, you have been rebellious against the LORD. [8]At Horeb you
aroused the LORD's wrath so that he was angry enough to destroy
you. [9]When I went up on the mountain to receive the tablets of stone,
the tablets of the covenant that the LORD had made with you, I stayed
on the mountain forty days and forty nights; I ate no bread and drank
no water. [10]The LORD gave me two stone tablets inscribed by the
finger of God. On them were all the commandments the LORD
proclaimed to you on the mountain out of the fire, on the day of the
assembly.

[11]At the end of the forty days and forty nights, the LORD gave me the
two stone tablets, the tablets of the covenant. [12]Then the LORD told
me, "Go down from here at once, because your people whom you
brought out of Egypt have become corrupt. They have turned away
quickly from what I commanded them and have made a cast idol for
themselves."

[13]And the LORD said to me, "I have seen this people, and they are a
stiff-necked people indeed! [14]Let me alone, so that I may destroy
them and blot out their name from under heaven. And I will make you
into a nation stronger and more numerous than they."

[15]So I turned and went down from the mountain while it was
ablaze with fire. And the two tablets of the covenant were in my
hands.[a] [16]When I looked, I saw that you had sinned against the LORD
your God; you had made for yourselves an idol cast in the shape of a
calf. You had turned aside quickly from the way that the LORD had
commanded you. [17]So I took the two tablets and threw them out of
my hands, breaking them to pieces before your eyes.

[18]Then once again I fell prostrate before the LORD for forty days and
forty nights; I ate no bread and drank no water, because of all the sin
you had committed, doing what was evil in the LORD's sight and so
provoking him to anger. [19]I feared the anger and wrath of the LORD,
for he was angry enough with you to destroy you. But again the LORD
listened to me. [20]And the LORD was angry enough with Aaron to destroy him, but at that time I prayed for Aaron too. [21]Also I took that
sinful thing of yours, the calf you had made, and burned it in the fire.
Then I crushed it and ground it to powder as fine as dust and threw
the dust into a stream that flowed down the mountain.

[22]You also made the LORD angry at Taberah, at Massah and at
Kibroth Hattaavah.

[23]And when the LORD sent you out from Kadesh Barnea, he said,

[a]15 Or *And I had the two tablets of the covenant with me, one in each hand*

OPEN 1. Share a time when you rebelled against your parents. What did you do and what were the results? **2.** Can you remember a time you "went to bat" for someone you loved?

STUDY Lest the Israelites think they are good, Moses reminds them of their continual rebellion against God. He reminds them that the entire time of their 40-year wandering in the desert was marked by rebellion. He even tells them that they have been rebellious since he first knew them. **1.** What was the basis of the rebellion associated with making the golden calf to worship (Ex. 32:1-4)? Why was that rebellion so critical? **2.** How do you explain that God could be so patient with such a rebellious people? **3.** What does this portion of Moses' speech, and especially his prayer for the people (vv. 26–29), tell you about his character? **4.** What does God's initial desire to destroy the Israelites tell you about the character of the people? How do you reconcile God's desire to destroy the people for their rebellion with his attribute of patience? **5.** What does God's decision not to destroy the Israelites tell you about what kind of relationship he wants with humans? **6.** How would you define grace? **7.** How does Moses demonstrate his understanding of the heart and plans of God in verses 25–29? **8.** Why was it important for the Israelites to be reminded of this story before they entered the Promised Land?

APPLY 1. When you are rebellious toward God, what do you think God thinks about your rebellion? What do you think he thinks about you? **2.** What do you learn from reading this portion of Israel's story? How will this change your life?

guided, much like a horse that refuses *to turn according to a rider's* commands.

9:19 On several occasions Moses' role as a mediator took on the function of a defense attorney. He appealed to God for mercy for his people. This is the incident with the golden calf, which coincided with the first inscription of the Ten Commandments.

9:22 Taberah. The people complained aloud, and fire destroyed part of the camp (Num. 11:1–3). **Massah.** Here Moses struck the rock to get water for the discontented people (Ex. 17: 6–7). **Kibroth Hattaavah.** Here the people craved other foods and made themselves sick on quail. Some even died (Num. 11:33–34).

"Go up and take possession of the land I have given you." But you
rebelled against the command of the LORD your God. You did not trust
him or obey him. 24You have been rebellious against the LORD ever
since I have known you.
25I lay prostrate before the LORD those forty days and forty nights
because the LORD had said he would destroy you. 26I prayed to the
LORD and said, "O Sovereign LORD, do not destroy your people, your
own inheritance that you redeemed by your great power and brought
out of Egypt with a mighty hand. 27Remember your servants Abraham, Isaac and Jacob. Overlook the stubbornness of this people,
their wickedness and their sin. 28Otherwise, the country from which
you brought us will say, 'Because the LORD was not able to take them
into the land he had promised them, and because he hated them, he
brought them out to put them to death in the desert.' 29But they are
your people, your inheritance that you brought out by your great
power and your outstretched arm."

Tablets Like the First Ones

10 At that time the LORD said to me, "Chisel out two stone tablets like the first ones and come up to me on the mountain.
Also make a wooden chest.[a] 2I will write on the tablets the words that
were on the first tablets, which you broke. Then you are to put them
in the chest."
3So I made the ark out of acacia wood and chiseled out two stone
tablets like the first ones, and I went up on the mountain with the two
tablets in my hands. 4The LORD wrote on these tablets what he had
written before, the Ten Commandments he had proclaimed to you on
the mountain, out of the fire, on the day of the assembly. And the
LORD gave them to me. 5Then I came back down the mountain and
put the tablets in the ark I had made, as the LORD commanded me,
and they are there now.
6(The Israelites traveled from the wells of the Jaakanites to Moserah.
There Aaron died and was buried, and Eleazar his son succeeded him
as priest. 7From there they traveled to Gudgodah and on to Jotbathah,
a land with streams of water. 8At that time the LORD set apart the tribe
of Levi to carry the ark of the covenant of the LORD, to stand before the
LORD to minister and to pronounce blessings in his name, as they still
do today. 9That is why the Levites have no share or inheritance among

[a]1 That is, an ark

OPEN What is your one rule of life that is so important you would carve it in stone?

STUDY When Moses came down from the mountain with the original tablets of stone containing the Ten Commandments, and he saw the people worshipping the golden calf, he threw the stones to the ground and broke them. Now God has called Moses back to the mountain and told him to bring two new stone tablets with him so the Law can be inscribed once again. **1.** What is the significance of the commandments of God being carved in stone? What is the significance of God doing the writing himself? What does this tell you about the nature of God? **2.** What is the significance of the tablets of stone being placed in a special chest and then kept in the care of the Levites?

APPLY How important are the Ten Commandments to you?

9:27 Abraham, Isaac and Jacob. God had made a promise to these men. Moses was asking God to remember that promise rather than his disappointment with the current descendants.

10:1–3 The ark kept in the tabernacle was actually a chest made of wood, a sacred storage place. The terms "ark" and "chest" are used interchangeably here.

10:1 Chisel. Moses chiseled out the tablets, but God engraved them with the commandments. They had already done this once when God provided the stone tablets (Ex. 24:12), but Moses broke those in anger when he saw the people's disobedience.

10:2 The chest, or ark, functioned here almost like a time capsule. Besides the stone tablets, it held some manna and Aaron's rod.

10:6–9 Eleazar. Eleazar was not Aaron's oldest son. In fact, Aaron had two older sons, who died instantly when they administered their duties inappropriately at the tabernacle (Lev. 10:1–2).

10:8 carry. Specific rules governed how to carry the ark. Only certain people were to be involved, and even these people were not to touch the ark. There were rings on each side of the ark so that poles could be inserted without anyone's hands actually touching the sides (Ex. 25:12–15).

10:9 Levites. The Levites were treated as a distinct class of people. The priests all came from the tribe of Levi, specifically the line of Aaron's descendants. The Levites were not given any land to work because they were to care

their brothers; the LORD is their inheritance, as the LORD your God told
them.)
[10]Now I had stayed on the mountain forty days and nights, as I did
the first time, and the LORD listened to me at this time also. It was not
his will to destroy you. [11]"Go," the LORD said to me, "and lead the
people on their way, so that they may enter and possess the land that
I swore to their fathers to give them."

Fear the LORD

[12]And now, O Israel, what does the LORD your God ask of you but to
fear the LORD your God, to walk in all his ways, to love him, to serve
the LORD your God with all your heart and with all your soul, [13]and to
observe the LORD's commands and decrees that I am giving you today
for your own good?
[14]To the LORD your God belong the heavens, even the highest heavens, the earth and everything in it. [15]Yet the LORD set his affection on
your forefathers and loved them, and he chose you, their descendants, above all the nations, as it is today. [16]Circumcise your hearts,
therefore, and do not be stiff-necked any longer. [17]For the LORD your
God is God of gods and Lord of lords, the great God, mighty and awesome, who shows no partiality and accepts no bribes. [18]He defends
the cause of the fatherless and the widow, and loves the alien, giving
him food and clothing. [19]And you are to love those who are aliens, for
you yourselves were aliens in Egypt. [20]Fear the LORD your God and
serve him. Hold fast to him and take your oaths in his name. [21]He is
your praise; he is your God, who performed for you those great and
awesome wonders you saw with your own eyes. [22]Your forefathers
who went down into Egypt were seventy in all, and now the LORD
your God has made you as numerous as the stars in the sky.

Love and Obey the LORD

11 Love the LORD your God and keep his requirements, his
decrees, his laws and his commands always. [2]Remember
today that your children were not the ones who saw and experienced
the discipline of the LORD your God: his majesty, his mighty hand, his
outstretched arm; [3]the signs he performed and the things he did in
the heart of Egypt, both to Pharaoh king of Egypt and to his whole
country; [4]what he did to the Egyptian army, to its horses and

OPEN Who would you follow, and under what circumstances, just because of who they are, no questions asked?

STUDY Moses gives the Israelites a concise summary of what God expects from them, similar to other summary statements about the Law (Josh. 22:5; Mic. 6:8; Matt. 22:37–39). **1.** What does it mean to fear the Lord? Have you ever had a time when the fear of the Lord was very real to you? **2.** How would you describe the expanse of the universe? **3.** What does it mean to you that the God who owns the universe is interested in you? **4.** Why was it important for the Israelites to love the aliens?

APPLY **1.** How has your view of God changed? Why? **2.** In what way do you consider God to be "your" God?

OPEN **1.** When making an important choice do you: Waffle? Consider all the angles? Decide quickly? Let someone else make the choice for you? **2.** What one very important lesson did your father or mother make sure that you learned?

STUDY The Israelite children had not gone through the hard

---

for the tabernacle (later, the temple). They received their sustenance from the sacrifices of the people. They were not counted in the census for war but were set apart completely to care for God's presence and worship. Since Aaron and Moses were brothers, Moses was a Levite as well.

10:12 And now. Moses had reviewed the history of the Hebrews' disobedience and was ready to answer the question, "Now what?" His answer called for the people to be totally committed to God, fearing him, obeying him, loving him and walking with him. Moses was preparing his people to receive their inheritance and live in a manner worthy of it.

10:13 for your own good. For the Hebrews, serving God was not just exchanging one evil taskmaster (Egypt) for another (Jehovah). God offered them blessings and provisions, not just servitude.

10:16 Circumcise your hearts. When the Hebrew men were circumcised, they were "marked" with God's ownership. To circumcise their hearts would be to mark their hearts as owned by God (Gen. 17:10–12).

10:20 Hold fast. Several times in Deuteronomy Moses encouraged the people to hold fast to God. Throughout the wilderness wanderings they had easily and often turned away from God.

10:22 the stars in the sky. This was the promise that God made to Abraham (Gen. 22:15–18). It was also a reminder of what God had accomplished, since only seventy descendants of Abraham had gone into Egypt, but a whole nation had come out.

11:2-7 Moses made the point here that these people had seen for them-

chariots, how he overwhelmed them with the waters of the Red Sea[a] as they were pursuing you, and how the LORD brought lasting ruin on them. [5]It was not your children who saw what he did for you in the desert until you arrived at this place, [6]and what he did to Dathan and Abiram, sons of Eliab the Reubenite, when the earth opened its mouth right in the middle of all Israel and swallowed them up with their households, their tents and every living thing that belonged to them. [7]But it was your own eyes that saw all these great things the LORD has done.

[8]Observe therefore all the commands I am giving you today, so that you may have the strength to go in and take over the land that you are crossing the Jordan to possess, [9]and so that you may live long in the land that the LORD swore to your forefathers to give to them and their descendants, a land flowing with milk and honey. [10]The land you are entering to take over is not like the land of Egypt, from which you have come, where you planted your seed and irrigated it by foot as in a vegetable garden. [11]But the land you are crossing the Jordan to take possession of is a land of mountains and valleys that drinks rain from heaven. [12]It is a land the LORD your God cares for; the eyes of the LORD your God are continually on it from the beginning of the year to its end.

[13]So if you faithfully obey the commands I am giving you today—to love the LORD your God and to serve him with all your heart and with all your soul— [14]then I will send rain on your land in its season, both autumn and spring rains, so that you may gather in your grain, new wine and oil. [15]I will provide grass in the fields for your cattle, and you will eat and be satisfied.

[16]Be careful, or you will be enticed to turn away and worship other gods and bow down to them. [17]Then the LORD's anger will burn against you, and he will shut the heavens so that it will not rain and the ground will yield no produce, and you will soon perish from the good land the LORD is giving you. [18]Fix these words of mine in your hearts and minds; tie them as symbols on your hands and bind them on your foreheads. [19]Teach them to your children, talking about them when you sit at home and when you walk along the road, when you lie down and when you get up. [20]Write them on the doorframes of your houses and on your gates, [21]so that your days and the days of your children may be many in the land that the LORD swore to give

[a]4 Hebrew *Yam Suph*; that is, Sea of Reeds

times that the national faith was built upon. Thus, Moses reminds the people how important it is to "keep the faith," to remember God's Law and to teach it to their children. **1.** What effect did the experience of the Israelites have upon their faith? **2.** What effect do your life experiences have upon your faith? **3.** How were the Israelites asked to love God (vv. 1–9)? What is the link between remembering, loving and obeying? What are the important experiences of your faith that you need to remember and pass on to your children? **4.** What was better about the Promised Land than where the Israelites had previously lived in Egypt (vv. 10–12)? **5.** Upon what conditions were the promised blessings based (vv. 13–15)? **6.** What might have enticed the Israelites to abandon their faith in God? What could entice you away from God? What could entice your children away from God? **7.** In what ways and in what places were the Israelites to remind their children of the words of the Lord? How can followers of God today remind their children of the word of the Lord? **8.** What choice did God set before the Israelites (vv. 26–32)? What choice does he give you?

APPLY 1. What blessings and curses have you experienced in your life because of decisions you have made about faith? **2.** What have your life experiences taught you about God? **3.** With whom can you pass along these experiences?

selves what God had done. Certainly among his audience were some who had been born after the Exodus, but most had been raised during the years of wandering when God provided every day for their needs.

11:8–12 If this passage were a script in a movie, the violin swells would be dramatic. Moses is announcing the inheritance they have waited for for so long.

11:9 live long. The Hebrews' strength, life and vitality were directly related to their obedience to God's commands.

11:10 irrigated. Egypt was in a desert. The Nile was its source of water, but the people had to force the water into the fields.

11:13 heart ... soul. This refers back to the *Shema*, found in Deuteronomy 6:5.

11:14 rain. The irrigation system in Egypt was man-made (v. 10), but in Israel God would control the rains. The rainy season in the land of Canaan was typically from October until April.

11:16–17 other gods. Moses mentioned other gods in relation to rain because the current inhabitants of Canaan, the people that the Hebrews were to conquer, believed that the false gods they worshiped controlled the rain.

11:18–20 talking about them. Moses expected that the faith of the people would be a daily topic of conversation. He didn't see it as something

your forefathers, as many as the days that the heavens are above the
earth.
22 If you carefully observe all these commands I am giving you to
follow—to love the LORD your God, to walk in all his ways and to hold
fast to him— 23 then the LORD will drive out all these nations before
you, and you will dispossess nations larger and stronger than you.
24 Every place where you set your foot will be yours: Your territory will
extend from the desert to Lebanon, and from the Euphrates River to
the western sea.[a] 25 No man will be able to stand against you. The
LORD your God, as he promised you, will put the terror and fear of you
on the whole land, wherever you go.
26 See, I am setting before you today a blessing and a curse— 27 the
blessing if you obey the commands of the LORD your God that I am
giving you today; 28 the curse if you disobey the commands of the
LORD your God and turn from the way that I command you today by
following other gods, which you have not known. 29 When the LORD
your God has brought you into the land you are entering to possess,
you are to proclaim on Mount Gerizim the blessings, and on Mount
Ebal the curses. 30 As you know, these mountains are across the
Jordan, west of the road,[b] toward the setting sun, near the great trees
of Moreh, in the territory of those Canaanites living in the Arabah in
the vicinity of Gilgal. 31 You are about to cross the Jordan to enter and
take possession of the land the LORD your God is giving you. When
you have taken it over and are living there, 32 be sure that you obey all
the decrees and laws I am setting before you today.

OPEN **1.** What are some traditions and rituals you have adopted from another culture? **2.** What are some unusual places people conduct worship assemblies in your town?

STUDY In order to insure faithfulness, God insisted that the Israelites not adopt any of the religious rituals of the people they were driving out of the land. He did not even want them to worship in the same places as the dispossessed people, but to worship only where he said. This chapter begins a long section of lesser requirements or regulations. **1.** Why do you think God was so intent that the

The One Place of Worship

12 These are the decrees and laws you must be careful to follow
in the land that the LORD, the God of your fathers, has given
you to possess—as long as you live in the land. 2 Destroy completely
all the places on the high mountains and on the hills and under every
spreading tree where the nations you are dispossessing worship their
gods. 3 Break down their altars, smash their sacred stones and burn
their Asherah poles in the fire; cut down the idols of their gods and
wipe out their names from those places.
4 You must not worship the LORD your God in their way. 5 But you are
to seek the place the LORD your God will choose from among all your
tribes to put his Name there for his dwelling. To that place you must
go; 6 there bring your burnt offerings and sacrifices, your tithes and

[a]24 That is, the Mediterranean [b]30 Or *Jordan, westward*

---

separate, only for church. This passage reiterates his encouragement to families in chapter six.

11:22–23 If you carefully observe ... then the LORD will drive out. The people's relationship to God and their success in the land were deeply connected. This was both a promise of God *and a consequence* of their actions.

11:24–25 terror and fear. In their wanderings, God's presence had preceded the people in a cloud. Now his presence would precede them in the fear they would stir up in their enemies. When Joshua sent spies to check out Jericho, Rahab confirmed this. She told them that her people had heard about their journey and were afraid (Josh. 2:8–10).

12:3 Break ... smash ... burn ... cut down ... wipe out. This was not the first time Moses had made it clear that *the Hebrews* were to allow no idol worship in the land. (7:5–6/.

12:4 in their way. Moses was wise. The Hebrews could have settled the land and just switched from God to gods, living merrily among the Canaanites. That wasn't God's plan, however. He had set up holy guidelines for worship that didn't include the perverted practices of that day.

12:5 to put his Name. This simply referred to the place where the tabernacle would reside. Names were more symbolic and meaningful in ancient days. God's name was his presence. When Moses asked what name to give when people asked who sent him, God answered, "I AM" (Ex. 3:14).

special gifts, what you have vowed to give and your freewill offerings,
and the firstborn of your herds and flocks. 7There, in the presence of
the LORD your God, you and your families shall eat and shall rejoice
in everything you have put your hand to, because the LORD your God
has blessed you.
8You are not to do as we do here today, everyone as he sees fit,
9since you have not yet reached the resting place and the inheritance
the LORD your God is giving you. 10But you will cross the Jordan and
settle in the land the LORD your God is giving you as an inheritance,
and he will give you rest from all your enemies around you so that
you will live in safety. 11Then to the place the LORD your God will
choose as a dwelling for his Name—there you are to bring everything
I command you: your burnt offerings and sacrifices, your tithes and
special gifts, and all the choice possessions you have vowed to the
LORD. 12And there rejoice before the LORD your God, you, your sons
and daughters, your menservants and maidservants, and the Levites
from your towns, who have no allotment or inheritance of their own.
13Be careful not to sacrifice your burnt offerings anywhere you
please. 14Offer them only at the place the LORD will choose in one of
your tribes, and there observe everything I command you.
15Nevertheless, you may slaughter your animals in any of your
towns and eat as much of the meat as you want, as if it were gazelle
or deer, according to the blessing the LORD your God gives you. Both
the ceremonially unclean and the clean may eat it. 16But you must not
eat the blood; pour it out on the ground like water. 17You must not eat
in your own towns the tithe of your grain and new wine and oil, or
the firstborn of your herds and flocks, or whatever you have vowed to
give, or your freewill offerings or special gifts. 18Instead, you are to
eat them in the presence of the LORD your God at the place the LORD
your God will choose—you, your sons and daughters, your menservants and maidservants, and the Levites from your towns—and you
are to rejoice before the LORD your God in everything you put your
hand to. 19Be careful not to neglect the Levites as long as you live in
your land.
20When the LORD your God has enlarged your territory as he promised you, and you crave meat and say, "I would like some meat," then
you may eat as much of it as you want. 21If the place where the LORD
your God chooses to put his Name is too far away from you, you may
slaughter animals from the herds and flocks the LORD has given you,
as I have commanded you, and in your own towns you may eat as
much of them as you want. 22Eat them as you would gazelle or deer.
Both the ceremonially unclean and the clean may eat. 23But be sure

people not adopt any of the religious customs and rituals of the people they were driving out? **2.** Why would the place of worship be so important for God's people? What is the importance of the place you worship (John 4:21–24)? **3.** What do you learn here about the practices of pagan worship (vv. 2–3,31)? **4.** Why would the Israelites be attracted to other ways of worship? Why would it matter if they adopted some of the ways of the other nations as long as they worshiped God? **5.** Do you think God's reason for commanding the people not to eat the blood of animals was a health reason or a symbolic reason? Do you think it is wrong to eat the blood of animals today? Why or why not? **6.** What kind of present-day worship rituals do you think have the effect of compromising your faith in God? **7.** Why do you think God was so interested in the specific rituals, places and forms of worship? Do you think he is as concerned about such things in our worship today? Why or why not?

APPLY 1. Where is your "place" of worship? What is your "form" (the traditions and rituals) of worship? **2.** In what ways do you think you honor the sovereignty of God with your worship customs?

12:8 everyone as he sees fit. The Hebrews had been camping out for forty years. Evidently they had understood God's commands about the sacrifices and the tabernacle as the ideal, but in the wilderness, actual practice rarely fit that pattern. Here Moses made it clear that once they were settled in the land, they must take worship more seriously.

12:9 resting place. Throughout the Bible God referred to his "rest" as the place of destination for his people. The book of Hebrews compared the *"rest" of the Hebrews* in the Promised Land with the Sabbath that God declared after Creation. The writer of Hebrews also encouraged his readers to continue toward God's "rest"—not a physical place, but a life of peace and faith.

12:12 rejoice. The church today sometimes treats worship as a solemn event. Certainly in these ancient days there was a solemnity to the sacrifices and yet great joy when God was worshiped.

12:13 anywhere you please. The proper order of worship required that offerings be made at the tabernacle and that distinctions be kept between animals slaughtered for food and those offered to God.

12:16,24 blood. Moses constantly reminded the people that the life of an animal was in the blood, which was to be drained from all meat before it was eaten.

you do not eat the blood, because the blood is the life, and you must
not eat the life with the meat. 24You must not eat the blood; pour it
out on the ground like water. 25Do not eat it, so that it may go well
with you and your children after you, because you will be doing what
is right in the eyes of the LORD.
26But take your consecrated things and whatever you have vowed
to give, and go to the place the LORD will choose. 27Present your burnt
offerings on the altar of the LORD your God, both the meat and the
blood. The blood of your sacrifices must be poured beside the altar of
the LORD your God, but you may eat the meat. 28Be careful to obey all
these regulations I am giving you, so that it may always go well with
you and your children after you, because you will be doing what is
good and right in the eyes of the LORD your God.
29The LORD your God will cut off before you the nations you are
about to invade and dispossess. But when you have driven them out
and settled in their land, 30and after they have been destroyed before
you, be careful not to be ensnared by inquiring about their gods, saying, "How do these nations serve their gods? We will do the same."
31You must not worship the LORD your God in their way, because in
worshiping their gods, they do all kinds of detestable things the LORD
hates. They even burn their sons and daughters in the fire as sacrifices to their gods.
32See that you do all I command you; do not add to it or take away
from it.

Worshiping Other Gods

13 If a prophet, or one who foretells by dreams, appears among
you and announces to you a miraculous sign or wonder, 2and
if the sign or wonder of which he has spoken takes place, and he
says, "Let us follow other gods" (gods you have not known) "and let
us worship them," 3you must not listen to the words of that prophet
or dreamer. The LORD your God is testing you to find out whether you
love him with all your heart and with all your soul. 4It is the LORD your
God you must follow, and him you must revere. Keep his commands
and obey him; serve him and hold fast to him. 5That prophet or
dreamer must be put to death, because he preached rebellion against
the LORD your God, who brought you out of Egypt and redeemed you
from the land of slavery; he has tried to turn you from the way the
LORD your God commanded you to follow. You must purge the evil
from among you.
6If your very own brother, or your son or daughter, or the wife you
love, or your closest friend secretly entices you, saying, "Let us go
and worship other gods" (gods that neither you nor your fathers have
known, 7gods of the peoples around you, whether near or far, from
one end of the land to the other), 8do not yield to him or listen to him.
Show him no pity. Do not spare him or shield him. 9You must certainly put him to death. Your hand must be the first in putting him to

OPEN 1. Can you remember a time when someone tried to get you to believe something that was false? How did you feel when you discovered it was false? **2.** If you were to try to convince people not to believe in God, how would you go about it?

STUDY One of the dangers the Israelites would face in the new land would be those who would try to make them abandon their belief in God in favor of false gods. Moses warns them severely about this danger, teaching them that they must put to death anyone who would try to lead them away from their faith in the true God. **1.** Why might Israel be tempted to follow a prophet or miracle worker who worshiped other gods? What was the one factor that determined whether or not the people should listen to this person (vv. 1–3)? **2.** Why was the death penalty appropriate for those who led the people to false gods? **3.** Do you think it was a little harsh for God to tell the people

---

13:1–5 prophet. *This prophet* was trying to convince the people to worship other gods. Moses made this point crystal clear: no miraculous sign was great enough to suggest any god above the true God.

13:3 testing. To see miracles performed in the name of another god was a test of faith for the people.

13:5 he preached rebellion. The miracles themselves were not sinful. But the prophet's encouragement to worship other gods was totally wrong. That, coupled with his power to astonish the people, made the prophet a dangerous man.

death, and then the hands of all the people. [10]Stone him to death, because he tried to turn you away from the LORD your God, who brought you out of Egypt, out of the land of slavery. [11]Then all Israel will hear and be afraid, and no one among you will do such an evil thing again.

[12]If you hear it said about one of the towns the LORD your God is giving you to live in [13]that wicked men have arisen among you and have led the people of their town astray, saying, "Let us go and worship other gods" (gods you have not known), [14]then you must inquire, probe and investigate it thoroughly. And if it is true and it has been proved that this detestable thing has been done among you, [15]you must certainly put to the sword all who live in that town. Destroy it completely,[a] both its people and its livestock. [16]Gather all the plunder of the town into the middle of the public square and completely burn the town and all its plunder as a whole burnt offering to the LORD your God. It is to remain a ruin forever, never to be rebuilt. [17]None of those condemned things[a] shall be found in your hands, so that the LORD will turn from his fierce anger; he will show you mercy, have compassion on you, and increase your numbers, as he promised on oath to your forefathers, [18]because you obey the LORD your God, keeping all his commands that I am giving you today and doing what is right in his eyes.

Clean and Unclean Food

14 You are the children of the LORD your God. Do not cut yourselves or shave the front of your heads for the dead, [2]for you are a people holy to the LORD your God. Out of all the peoples on the face of the earth, the LORD has chosen you to be his treasured possession.

[3]Do not eat any detestable thing. [4]These are the animals you may eat: the ox, the sheep, the goat, [5]the deer, the gazelle, the roe deer, the wild goat, the ibex, the antelope and the mountain sheep.[b] [6]You may eat any animal that has a split hoof divided in two and that chews the cud. [7]However, of those that chew the cud or that have a split hoof completely divided you may not eat the camel, the rabbit or the coney.[c] Although they chew the cud, they do not have a split hoof; they are ceremonially unclean for you. [8]The pig is also unclean; although it has a split hoof, it does not chew the cud. You are not to eat their meat or touch their carcasses.

[a]*15,17* The Hebrew term refers to the irrevocable giving over of things or persons to the LORD, often by totally destroying them. [b]*5* The precise identification of some of the birds and animals in this chapter is uncertain. [c]*7* That is, the hyrax or rock badger

that they must enforce the death penalty even if this person was a family member? Why or why not? **4.** What were the Israelites to do if they discovered a town harboring someone who enticed the people away from God (vv. 12–17)? **5.** How serious is it today for someone to teach falsehood? **6.** What is the point of these harsh words from God about punishing these prophets or false teachers? What do you learn about the nature of God from these instructions?

APPLY **1.** How can you know if someone is teaching you the truth or a lie? **2.** What difference does it make in your life whether you are taught the truth or a lie?

OPEN **1.** What is your favorite meal? **2.** What foods do you consider to be unhealthy? Why do you think they are unhealthy?

STUDY Since the people were unfamiliar with the animals in the land, God instructs them about what is good to eat and what is not good to eat—see Leviticus 11 for a more detailed list. These very strict dietary laws were to be carried out by all the people. **1.** What does God mean when he says to his people, "You are a people holy to the LORD your God"? **2.** What do these dietary laws have to do with the Israelites being God's chosen people? How would they help the Israelites become a distinctive and holy people? **3.** What health issues can you identify in the dietary laws? **4.** Of the animals, fish, birds and insects prohibited for consumption, which one or two would you miss

---

13:13 wicked. The word for "wicked" here would be translated today as "scoundrel." What a travesty it would have been, what a dishonor to God, to have the people turn their faith elsewhere after God had brought them this far.

13:15 Destroy it completely. When the issue came down to idol worship or spiritual unfaithfulness, God demanded complete obedience and often the annihilation of pagan centers. A man named Achan once tried to fudge on this directive from God, and the whole nation suffered for it (Josh. 7:1).

14:1 cut yourselves. This was an ancient custom of idol worship. When Elijah faced the prophets of Baal and Asherah, the prophets slashed themselves with swords and spears in the hope of triggering a response from their god (1 Kin. 18:28). **shave.** This was a sign of mourning.

14:2 treasured. God wanted the Hebrews to walk among the nations as people loved and cared for by the one true God. That would make a profound difference in both how the neighboring people viewed the Hebrews and how the Hebrews viewed themselves.

14:3–21 The diet of the Hebrews set them apart from other nations. Staying within the kosher diet was an act of faith and obedience, a mark of God's ownership.

most? **5.** Do you think these laws should apply today? Why or why not?

APPLY **1.** How do you tend to react when a person tells you that you can't do something? **2.** How do you feel towards God when he prohibits something in your life that you would really like to have?

OPEN Tell about someone you know who is an extremely generous giver. Describe their giving.

STUDY In order to assist the people in understanding the blessings of the Lord in their lives, God commands that they give a tenth in an offering (a tithe). The "serendipity" in their tithe, however, is that they get to enjoy it in the presence of the Lord and with the blessings of the Lord. **1.** How would tithing teach the Israelites to "revere" the Lord? **2.** What do you learn about God in his command to make provision once every three years for those who have no produce? **3.** Do you think tithing is still in order today?

APPLY Tell of a time when you gave generously to a cause or a person and received a blessing or felt really good about it.

OPEN **1.** Who is the most generous person you know? **2.** How do you feel when dealing with someone who is very poor: Sympathetic? Skeptical? Irritated? Judgmental? Other?

9Of all the creatures living in the water, you may eat any that has
fins and scales. 10But anything that does not have fins and scales you
may not eat; for you it is unclean.
11You may eat any clean bird. 12But these you may not eat: the eagle, the vulture, the black vulture, 13the red kite, the black kite, any
kind of falcon, 14any kind of raven, 15the horned owl, the screech owl,
the gull, any kind of hawk, 16the little owl, the great owl, the white
owl, 17the desert owl, the osprey, the cormorant, 18the stork, any kind
of heron, the hoopoe and the bat.
19All flying insects that swarm are unclean to you; do not eat them.
20But any winged creature that is clean you may eat.
21Do not eat anything you find already dead. You may give it to an
alien living in any of your towns, and he may eat it, or you may sell it
to a foreigner. But you are a people holy to the LORD your God.

Do not cook a young goat in its mother's milk.

Tithes

22Be sure to set aside a tenth of all that your fields produce each
year. 23Eat the tithe of your grain, new wine and oil, and the firstborn
of your herds and flocks in the presence of the LORD your God at the
place he will choose as a dwelling for his Name, so that you may
learn to revere the LORD your God always. 24But if that place is too
distant and you have been blessed by the LORD your God and cannot
carry your tithe (because the place where the LORD will choose to put
his Name is so far away), 25then exchange your tithe for silver, and
take the silver with you and go to the place the LORD your God will
choose. 26Use the silver to buy whatever you like: cattle, sheep, wine
or other fermented drink, or anything you wish. Then you and your
household shall eat there in the presence of the LORD your God and
rejoice. 27And do not neglect the Levites living in your towns, for they
have no allotment or inheritance of their own.
28At the end of every three years, bring all the tithes of that year's
produce and store it in your towns, 29so that the Levites (who have no
allotment or inheritance of their own) and the aliens, the fatherless
and the widows who live in your towns may come and eat and be satisfied, and so that the LORD your God may bless you in all the work of
your hands.

The Year for Canceling Debts

15 At the end of every seven years you must cancel debts. 2This
is how it is to be done: Every creditor shall cancel the loan he
has made to his fellow Israelite. He shall not require payment from
his fellow Israelite or brother, because the LORD's time for canceling

14:21 already dead. At issue here was the prohibition on eating blood. When the animals were prepared properly, their blood was drained. To find an animal that was already dead would mean that blood still contaminated the meat.

14:22–29 tithe. A tithe in the Bible is defined as a one-tenth portion, whether money or goods, or in the case of this passage, money exchanged for goods. The tithe provided for the priests and the community. It was an act of faith on the part of the giver that God was the source of provision.

14:22 tenth. This tenth was to come off the top. It was not the last tenth, or the least tenth, but the first and best tenth.

14:23 dwelling for his Name. The tabernacle and later the temple.

14:25 exchange your tithe for silver. The silver currency of this day was not a coin or bill that represented value or gold in some bank. Rather, silver weights were measured in exchange for goods. Often the worth of money was expressed as a weight rather than an amount. Money was put on a scale to be weighed against an item.

debts has been proclaimed. 3You may require payment from a foreigner, but you must cancel any debt your brother owes you. 4However, there should be no poor among you, for in the land the LORD your God is giving you to possess as your inheritance, he will richly bless you, 5if only you fully obey the LORD your God and are careful to follow all these commands I am giving you today. 6For the LORD your God will bless you as he has promised, and you will lend to many nations but will borrow from none. You will rule over many nations but none will rule over you.

7If there is a poor man among your brothers in any of the towns of the land that the LORD your God is giving you, do not be hardhearted or tightfisted toward your poor brother. 8Rather be openhanded and freely lend him whatever he needs. 9Be careful not to harbor this wicked thought: "The seventh year, the year for canceling debts, is near," so that you do not show ill will toward your needy brother and give him nothing. He may then appeal to the LORD against you, and you will be found guilty of sin. 10Give generously to him and do so without a grudging heart; then because of this the LORD your God will bless you in all your work and in everything you put your hand to. 11There will always be poor people in the land. Therefore I command you to be openhanded toward your brothers and toward the poor and needy in your land.

Freeing Servants

12If a fellow Hebrew, a man or a woman, sells himself to you and serves you six years, in the seventh year you must let him go free. 13And when you release him, do not send him away empty-handed. 14Supply him liberally from your flock, your threshing floor and your winepress. Give to him as the LORD your God has blessed you. 15Remember that you were slaves in Egypt and the LORD your God redeemed you. That is why I give you this command today.

16But if your servant says to you, "I do not want to leave you," because he loves you and your family and is well off with you, 17then take an awl and push it through his ear lobe into the door, and he will become your servant for life. Do the same for your maidservant.

18Do not consider it a hardship to set your servant free, because his service to you these six years has been worth twice as much as that of a hired hand. And the LORD your God will bless you in everything you do.

STUDY As the people of Israel enter the Promised Land, God makes certain they continue to understand their interdependence and their responsibility toward one another. He teaches them an important lesson about compassion, generosity and sharing. **1.** Why would God expect the Israelites to be so generous (v. 4)? **2.** What promises did God give the Israelites if they were generous (vv. 5-6,10,18)? **3.** Why were foreigners exempt from this rule? **4.** What kind of attitude did God expect his people to have in giving to the poor? **5.** Who do you know that could use your help?

APPLY 1. What great debt has God forgiven you? **2.** What needs to change in your attitude about helping others?

OPEN 1. What was your first job? **2.** Describe a boss you have known that was totally unfair to his workers.

STUDY Part of the spirit of generosity God calls for from his people, is to treat servants kindly and fairly. In order to encourage this, God gives the command to not only release the servants after seven years, but to generously supply them as they leave. **1.** Was the Hebrew master and servant relationship described here slavery or an employer-employee relationship? **2.** What was to be the motivation behind the generosity (v. 15)? **3.** Can you think of a reason for a slave to choose to stay with his master? **4.** In what ways would a

---

15:3 foreigner. Since a foreigner would not have been required to let his fields lie fallow, he would more likely be able to pay his debts.

15:4 no poor among you. God was establishing neither a socialist nor a capitalist system but an economy with a lot of start-over opportunities. The Sabbath year and the less frequent Jubilee year were economic start-overs for the people.

15:6 You will rule over many nations. This was part of God's promise to Abraham (Gen. 18:18). The Hebrews looked forward to this time mistakenly and hoped Jesus would lead them to it.

15:11 There will always be poor people. Jesus made this same statement (Matt. 26:11).

15:16 I do not want to leave. Servanthood, in this instance, was different from the forced and cruel slavery of American history. A servant may have sold himself to pay off debt but in the process found a home and a better way to make a living.

15:17 push it through his ear lobe. This was a symbol of a servanthood for life. David used this image in Psalm 40:6–8 to show his own lifelong commitment to God.

15:18 Moses gave both a practical logic (you received two times the work for the price) and a spiritual logic (God will bless your obedience).

servant be more valuable than a hired hand? **5.** How would you feel toward a person who was your servant?

APPLY 1. How have you shown generosity toward people in need? **2.** What is your attitude towards the things you possess?

OPEN 1. Does your family have a special holiday tradition? **2.** Do your family holiday traditions cause you to look forward to being with your family?

STUDY In order to help the Israelites remember their relationship with God and all he had done for them, he directs them to conduct three major feasts per year. Each feast was mandatory and each feast represented a particular blessing from God that needed to be remembered to future generations. **1.** What was the purpose of the Passover celebration (v. 3)? Where and when were they to celebrate the Passover (v. 6)? **2.** What was the purpose of the Feast of Weeks (vv. 9–12)? **3.** What was the purpose of the Feast of Tabernacles (v. 15)? **4.** Do you think yearly observances of these celebrations would tend to become "old hat"? Why or why not? What could they do to keep them from getting routine? **5.** Why do you think God wanted different social classes, age-groups and ethnic-groups to celebrate together? **6.** What was the emotional tone of these celebrations? **7.** What was to determine the size of the gift offered at the feasts (v. 17)? **8.** What warning does God give about the system of justice in verse 19? What would be God's reward to them for maintaining justice (v. 20)? How

The Firstborn Animals

19 Set apart for the LORD your God every firstborn male of your
herds and flocks. Do not put the firstborn of your oxen to work, and
do not shear the firstborn of your sheep. 20 Each year you and your
family are to eat them in the presence of the LORD your God at the
place he will choose. 21 If an animal has a defect, is lame or blind, or
has any serious flaw, you must not sacrifice it to the LORD your God.
22 You are to eat it in your own towns. Both the ceremonially unclean
and the clean may eat it, as if it were gazelle or deer. 23 But you must
not eat the blood; pour it out on the ground like water.

Passover

16 Observe the month of Abib and celebrate the Passover of the
LORD your God, because in the month of Abib he brought you
out of Egypt by night. 2 Sacrifice as the Passover to the LORD your God
an animal from your flock or herd at the place the LORD will choose as
a dwelling for his Name. 3 Do not eat it with bread made with yeast,
but for seven days eat unleavened bread, the bread of affliction, because you left Egypt in haste—so that all the days of your life you may
remember the time of your departure from Egypt. 4 Let no yeast be
found in your possession in all your land for seven days. Do not let
any of the meat you sacrifice on the evening of the first day remain
until morning.

5 You must not sacrifice the Passover in any town the LORD your God
gives you 6 except in the place he will choose as a dwelling for his
Name. There you must sacrifice the Passover in the evening, when
the sun goes down, on the anniversary[a] of your departure from Egypt.
7 Roast it and eat it at the place the LORD your God will choose. Then
in the morning return to your tents. 8 For six days eat unleavened
bread and on the seventh day hold an assembly to the LORD your God
and do no work.

Feast of Weeks

9 Count off seven weeks from the time you begin to put the sickle to
the standing grain. 10 Then celebrate the Feast of Weeks to the LORD
your God by giving a freewill offering in proportion to the blessings
the LORD your God has given you. 11 And rejoice before the LORD your
God at the place he will choose as a dwelling for his Name—you,

[a]6 *Or down, at the time of day*

15:19 firstborn. The first and the best always belonged to God. It was a reminder to Israel that everything ultimately belonged to God.

15:21 defect. Moses mentioned throughout his writings that a defective animal was not to be an offering. While some people promised the firstborn, *they actually offered animals* that were imperfect and unusable on the farm.

16:3 remember the time. The feasts and customs that God had passed down to the people through Moses were reminders of how he had provided for their deliverance.

16:6 anniversary. Every year the Hebrews were to celebrate and remember the Passover, the feast that commemorated the last plague in Egypt (death of the firstborn). Jesus was celebrating this feast when he shared the Last Supper with the disciples.

16:7 tents. At this time the people were still not in the land and so they were still living in temporary quarters. The people no longer lived in tents, but they had to travel to the tabernacle to take part in the feast and so needed temporary quarters.

16:9 seven weeks. This feast was called the Feast of Weeks because of the counting of weeks to begin the celebartion. It was also called the Feast of the Harvest and later Pentecost (*pent* in this case refers to fifty, for the fifty days in the seven weeks). This feast was being celebrated the day the Holy Spirit came to the New Testament Christians after Jesus ascended into heaven.

your sons and daughters, your menservants and maidservants, the
Levites in your towns, and the aliens, the fatherless and the widows
living among you. 12Remember that you were slaves in Egypt, and
follow carefully these decrees.

Feast of Tabernacles

13Celebrate the Feast of Tabernacles for seven days after you have
gathered the produce of your threshing floor and your winepress.
14Be joyful at your Feast—you, your sons and daughters, your menservants and maidservants, and the Levites, the aliens, the fatherless
and the widows who live in your towns. 15For seven days celebrate
the Feast to the LORD your God at the place the LORD will choose. For
the LORD your God will bless you in all your harvest and in all the
work of your hands, and your joy will be complete.

16Three times a year all your men must appear before the LORD
your God at the place he will choose: at the Feast of Unleavened
Bread, the Feast of Weeks and the Feast of Tabernacles. No man
should appear before the LORD empty-handed: 17Each of you must
bring a gift in proportion to the way the LORD your God has blessed
you.

Judges

18Appoint judges and officials for each of your tribes in every town
the LORD your God is giving you, and they shall judge the people fairly. 19Do not pervert justice or show partiality. Do not accept a bribe,
for a bribe blinds the eyes of the wise and twists the words of the
righteous. 20Follow justice and justice alone, so that you may live and
possess the land the LORD your God is giving you.

Worshiping Other Gods

21Do not set up any wooden Asherah pole[a] beside the altar you
build to the LORD your God, 22and do not erect a sacred stone, for
these the LORD your God hates.

17 Do not sacrifice to the LORD your God an ox or a sheep that
has any defect or flaw in it, for that would be detestable
to him.

2If a man or woman living among you in one of the towns the LORD
gives you is found doing evil in the eyes of the LORD your God in violation of his covenant, 3and contrary to my command has worshiped

[a]21 Or *Do not plant any tree dedicated to Asherah*

would you relate these words from God to the justice system where you live?

APPLY 1. What Christian celebration reminds you most of God's deliverance and provision? Why? **2.** How will these celebration instructions given to Israel change the way you worship God?

OPEN 1. Can you remember a time in your life when you tried to fully commit yourself to two things at once? What was the result? **2.** What do you think of the legal system where you live? How would you change it?

STUDY Once again God makes sure that the Israelites know that he is the only God, and that they are not to worship any other deity. So important is the matter that God placed the death penalty on those

16:13–15 Feast of Tabernacles. This feast commemorated the sojourn in the desert. The people camped out for a week to commemorate the journey.

16:16 Three times. Of the three pilgrimage feasts, the Feast of Tabernacles was the most prominent and often called simply "the Feast."

16:17 in proportion. The tithe requires that each person give ten percent of what they have, a fair system that required the same set amount from everyone.

16:19 Do not ... show partiality. This literally means "don't recognize faces."

16:21–22 Moses had warned the people before, but here again, not to compromise their worship with the pagan practices around them (12:4).

17:1 defect or flaw. The sacrifices prefigured Jesus as the sacrificial lamb—the "lamb without blemish or defect" (1 Peter 1:19).

17:3 sun or the moon or the stars. God warned the people time and again about worshiping creation over the Creator (4:19). This Egyptian practice was passed down through generations of Hebrews. After the Hebrew kingdom split into north and south, each time a sinful king took reign, the Hebrews fell back into this pagan worship (2 Kin. 17:16; 21:3–5).

who would violate it. **1.** Why would God not want his people to worship the cult objects (16:21–22) or the objects of nature (17:3)? What cult objects or parts of nature do people worship today? **2.** Do you think the death penalty was fair in cases of idolatry? Why or why not? **3.** What does this passage say about testimony in a capital offense (vv. 6–7)? **4.** How would you feel if you had to testify against someone and then throw the first stone in their execution? **5.** What part did the priests play in legal cases (vv. 8–11)? Do you think courts today pay any attention to God's direction? What examples can you give for your answer? **6.** What is the crime of contempt? Why was it so serious? **7.** What general picture do you get of God's desire for the future king of Israel (vv. 14–20)? What do you know about the time in the future when the Israelites actually wanted a king (1 Sam. 8:4–9)? **8.** What do you learn about God's attitude toward justice from this reading?

APPLY **1.** Do you see yourself as a person who respects God and his Law? **2.** What do you think God wants from you with reference to his Law and why?

other gods, bowing down to them or to the sun or the moon or the stars of the sky, [4]and this has been brought to your attention, then you must investigate it thoroughly. If it is true and it has been proved that this detestable thing has been done in Israel, [5]take the man or woman who has done this evil deed to your city gate and stone that person to death. [6]On the testimony of two or three witnesses a man shall be put to death, but no one shall be put to death on the testimony of only one witness. [7]The hands of the witnesses must be the first in putting him to death, and then the hands of all the people. You must purge the evil from among you.

Law Courts

[8]If cases come before your courts that are too difficult for you to judge—whether bloodshed, lawsuits or assaults—take them to the place the LORD your God will choose. [9]Go to the priests, who are Levites, and to the judge who is in office at that time. Inquire of them and they will give you the verdict. [10]You must act according to the decisions they give you at the place the LORD will choose. Be careful to do everything they direct you to do. [11]Act according to the law they teach you and the decisions they give you. Do not turn aside from what they tell you, to the right or to the left. [12]The man who shows contempt for the judge or for the priest who stands ministering there to the LORD your God must be put to death. You must purge the evil from Israel. [13]All the people will hear and be afraid, and will not be contemptuous again.

The King

[14]When you enter the land the LORD your God is giving you and have taken possession of it and settled in it, and you say, "Let us set a king over us like all the nations around us," [15]be sure to appoint over you the king the LORD your God chooses. He must be from among your own brothers. Do not place a foreigner over you, one who is not a brother Israelite. [16]The king, moreover, must not acquire great numbers of horses for himself or make the people return to Egypt to get more of them, for the LORD has told you, "You are not to go back that way again." [17]He must not take many wives, or his heart will be led astray. He must not accumulate large amounts of silver and gold.

[18]When he takes the throne of his kingdom, he is to write for himself on a scroll a copy of this law, taken from that of the priests, who are Levites. [19]It is to be with him, and he is to read it all the days of his life so that he may learn to revere the LORD his God and follow carefully all the words of this law and these decrees [20]and not consider himself better than his brothers and turn from the law to the right or to the left. Then he and his descendants will reign a long time over his kingdom in Israel.

17:6 only one witness. We still have this practice. The way we say this today is, *"It's my word against yours."*

17:7 hands of the witnesses. Perjury would be a much different experience if a lying witness had to participate in putting the accused to death.

17:14 like all the nations around us. This is exactly what happened. The people settled the land and were ruled by judges rather than kings. Soon, however, the nation decided that it needed to be like the other kingdoms and have a human ruler, not God, as their head (1 Sam. 8:5).

17:16 king ... must not acquire. To assure that his people remained dependent upon God, they were instructed to not upgrade their military.

17:20 turn from the law. The best times for Israel would come when a king would submit to God's Law.

Offerings for Priests and Levites

18 The priests, who are Levites—indeed the whole tribe of Levi—are to have no allotment or inheritance with Israel. They shall live on the offerings made to the LORD by fire, for that is their inheritance. 2They shall have no inheritance among their brothers; the LORD is their inheritance, as he promised them.

3This is the share due the priests from the people who sacrifice a bull or a sheep: the shoulder, the jowls and the inner parts. 4You are to give them the firstfruits of your grain, new wine and oil, and the first wool from the shearing of your sheep, 5for the LORD your God has chosen them and their descendants out of all your tribes to stand and minister in the LORD's name always.

6If a Levite moves from one of your towns anywhere in Israel where he is living, and comes in all earnestness to the place the LORD will choose, 7he may minister in the name of the LORD his God like all his fellow Levites who serve there in the presence of the LORD. 8He is to share equally in their benefits, even though he has received money from the sale of family possessions.

Detestable Practices

9When you enter the land the LORD your God is giving you, do not learn to imitate the detestable ways of the nations there. 10Let no one be found among you who sacrifices his son or daughter in[a] the fire, who practices divination or sorcery, interprets omens, engages in witchcraft, 11or casts spells, or who is a medium or spiritist or who consults the dead. 12Anyone who does these things is detestable to the LORD, and because of these detestable practices the LORD your God will drive out those nations before you. 13You must be blameless before the LORD your God.

The Prophet

14The nations you will dispossess listen to those who practice sorcery or divination. But as for you, the LORD your God has not permitted you to do so. 15The LORD your God will raise up for you a prophet like me from among your own brothers. You must listen to him. 16For this is what you asked of the LORD your God at Horeb on the day of the assembly when you said, "Let us not hear the voice of the LORD our God nor see this great fire anymore, or we will die."

17The LORD said to me: "What they say is good. 18I will raise up for them a prophet like you from among their brothers; I will put my words in his mouth, and he will tell them everything I command him.

[a]10 *Or who makes his son or daughter pass through*

OPEN 1. Who is your favorite spiritual leader? Why? **2.** Can you remember a time when you and your friends experimented with a little witchcraft or astrology? What happened?

STUDY 1. What does it mean that "the LORD is their inheritance" (vv. 1–2)? How were they supported? **2.** Why do you think God gave specific instructions as to what parts of the animal should be given to the Levite priests? How would you feel if God told you exactly what to give to your spiritual leader? **3.** Why do you think God "ordained" the Levites to serve anywhere in Israel (vv. 6–8)? **4.** What were the detestable things God warned the Israelites not to adopt in the new land (vv. 10–11)? What would happen to those who participated in these detestable things (v 12)? Why was this such a serious matter?

APPLY What evil practices are present in today's world that are a danger to the faith of God's people?

OPEN 1. Can you remember someone you trusted who disappointed you greatly because they deceived you? **2.** How did this make you feel?

STUDY When God spoke to the people who were at Mount Sinai, they were convinced that if they listened to him, saw him or came into his presence they would die. **1.** Why did God want the Israelites to listen to him and not to the prophets of the land they were entering? **2.** Why were the people afraid to hear the Lord speak? **3.** What would

---

18:2 the LORD is their inheritance. God created a system in which those who worked for him were to learn that they must depend on him. In turn, the rest of the tribes would learn that by taking care of others, they were giving to God.

18:9 do not ... imitate the detestable ways of the nations. God directs us to right and honorable ways of living, and conversely, away from habits that are wrong and detestable. Following God requires that we choose one way over the other.

18:10 sacrifices his son or daughter. Man-made religion will eventually show its ugly underbelly. All these detestable practices come from wrong loyalties. People who practice these things think that God is hidden and must be found by strange devices. Paul said that God "is not far from each one of us" (Acts 17:27).

18:15 God will raise up for you a prophet like me. God is not silent. He never hides himself. On the contrary, Hebrews 1:1 says that God spoke "through the prophets at many times and in various ways." God used prophets to speak for him as an act of kindness. Jesus Christ is the "exact representation" of God (Heb. 1:3).

happen to a prophet who did not speak for God (v. 20)?

APPLY 1. Who do you think is a prophet today? Why? **2.** Do you think today's prophets are on the same level as those in Scripture?

OPEN 1. What is your favorite place to "get away"? Why do you like to go there? **2.** Have you ever hurt someone unintentionally? How did you feel?

STUDY Knowing how human nature works and knowing that revenge can be a powerful motivation, God gives the Israelites a way to deal with accidental killings. He instructs the Israelites to establish six cities (vv. 2,9; Num. 35:6–28; Josh. 20) to which an innocent person may run for refuge. He also gives them instructions about witnesses in criminal cases. **1.** Why was the location of the "cities of refuge" important? **2.** Under what circumstances could a person flee to one of these cities (vv. 3–4)? Under what circumstances was he not welcome in one of these cities (vv. 11–13)? **3.** What example of accidental killing does he give (v. 5)? Can you think of other examples? **4.** What would the Israelites be protected from by establishing the cities of refuge (vv. 8–10)? **5.** What abuse of these cities does God forbid (vv. 11–13)? How would his instructions discourage the abuse of these cities? Should we have "cities of refuge" today? **6.** Why does God require more than one witness (v. 15)? **7.** Who would determine whether a witness was malicious (v. 18)? What is to happen to someone who serves as a malicious witness (vv. 16–19)? What effect would his punishment have on the rest of the people (v. 20)? **8.** Do you think such punishment today would decrease slander and lying? Why or why not? **9.** What do you think about the law of "eye for eye"?

19 If anyone does not listen to my words that the prophet speaks in my
name, I myself will call him to account. 20 But a prophet who pre-
sumes to speak in my name anything I have not commanded him to
say, or a prophet who speaks in the name of other gods, must be put
to death."
21 You may say to yourselves, "How can we know when a message
has not been spoken by the LORD?" 22 If what a prophet proclaims in
the name of the LORD does not take place or come true, that is a
message the LORD has not spoken. That prophet has spoken pre-
sumptuously. Do not be afraid of him.

Cities of Refuge

19 When the LORD your God has destroyed the nations whose
land he is giving you, and when you have driven them out
and settled in their towns and houses, 2 then set aside for yourselves
three cities centrally located in the land the LORD your God is giving
you to possess. 3 Build roads to them and divide into three parts the
land the LORD your God is giving you as an inheritance, so that anyone who kills a man may flee there.
4 This is the rule concerning the man who kills another and flees
there to save his life—one who kills his neighbor unintentionally,
without malice aforethought. 5 For instance, a man may go into the
forest with his neighbor to cut wood, and as he swings his ax to fell a
tree, the head may fly off and hit his neighbor and kill him. That man
may flee to one of these cities and save his life. 6 Otherwise, the
avenger of blood might pursue him in a rage, overtake him if the distance is too great, and kill him even though he is not deserving of
death, since he did it to his neighbor without malice aforethought.
7 This is why I command you to set aside for yourselves three cities.
8 If the LORD your God enlarges your territory, as he promised on
oath to your forefathers, and gives you the whole land he promised
them, 9 because you carefully follow all these laws I command you today—to love the LORD your God and to walk always in his ways—
then you are to set aside three more cities. 10 Do this so that innocent
blood will not be shed in your land, which the LORD your God is giving you as your inheritance, and so that you will not be guilty of
bloodshed.
11 But if a man hates his neighbor and lies in wait for him, assaults
and kills him, and then flees to one of these cities, 12 the elders of his
town shall send for him, bring him back from the city, and hand him
over to the avenger of blood to die. 13 Show him no pity. You must
purge from Israel the guilt of shedding innocent blood, so that it may
go well with you.
14 Do not move your neighbor's boundary stone set up by your predecessors in the inheritance you receive in the land the LORD your
God is giving you to possess.

18:20 anything I have not commanded. God has chosen to use people to communicate his words to other people. The value of the prophet, however, is not in title or position but whether his or her words reflect God's message truthfully. Today we must search the Bible to see if things spoken about God are true (Acts 17:11).

19:14 boundary stone. These stones were like an orange stake that a surveyor uses to mark a property line. A person could move them secretly and never be caught. But God knows all secrets. Moving these stones would bring a curse (27:17) because a man's land was an inheritance from the Lord himself.

Witnesses

[15]One witness is not enough to convict a man accused of any crime
or offense he may have committed. A matter must be established by
the testimony of two or three witnesses.
[16]If a malicious witness takes the stand to accuse a man of a crime,
[17]the two men involved in the dispute must stand in the presence of
the LORD before the priests and the judges who are in office at the
time. [18]The judges must make a thorough investigation, and if the
witness proves to be a liar, giving false testimony against his brother,
[19]then do to him as he intended to do to his brother. You must purge
the evil from among you. [20]The rest of the people will hear of this and
be afraid, and never again will such an evil thing be done among you.
[21]Show no pity: life for life, eye for eye, tooth for tooth, hand for
hand, foot for foot.

Going to War

20 When you go to war against your enemies and see horses
and chariots and an army greater than yours, do not be
afraid of them, because the LORD your God, who brought you up out
of Egypt, will be with you. [2]When you are about to go into battle, the
priest shall come forward and address the army. [3]He shall say: "Hear,
O Israel, today you are going into battle against your enemies. Do not
be fainthearted or afraid; do not be terrified or give way to panic before them. [4]For the LORD your God is the one who goes with you to
fight for you against your enemies to give you victory."
[5]The officers shall say to the army: "Has anyone built a new house
and not dedicated it? Let him go home, or he may die in battle and
someone else may dedicate it. [6]Has anyone planted a vineyard and not
begun to enjoy it? Let him go home, or he may die in battle and someone else enjoy it. [7]Has anyone become pledged to a woman and not
married her? Let him go home, or he may die in battle and someone
else marry her." [8]Then the officers shall add, "Is any man afraid or
fainthearted? Let him go home so that his brothers will not become
disheartened too." [9]When the officers have finished speaking to the
army, they shall appoint commanders over it.
[10]When you march up to attack a city, make its people an offer of

APPLY **1.** Can you remember a time when you were falsely accused? What did you do? **2.** What do these strict rules from God teach you about what he wants in human society?

OPEN **1.** Have you ever won a victory you thought God empowered you to win? Can you describe it? **2.** Can you remember a time you went to "battle" with your friends? What was the "battle" and what was it like?

STUDY Part of the task of driving the people out of the land was going to war. In order to give his people courage for the battles they would face, God assures them that he is with them and would empower them to be victorious. **1.** In going to war, who were the Israelites to trust? **2.** In preparation for battle, what was the priest to say to the army (vv. 2–4)? Was this speech tactical or inspirational? What were the officers to say to the army (vv. 5–8)? What do you make of letting some of the army go home to take care of personal matters? Does this seem to be good military strategy? Why or why not? **3.** What options were the Israelites to

---

19:15 two or three witnesses. God's love is always seen in God's Law. Lying was forbidden by the Ten Commandments (Ex. 20:16) and was to be punished (19:19). By requiring more than one witness, God protected the accused from a false claim and the plaintiff from the consequences of a rash accusation.

19:18 The judges. More than one judge is needed for the same reasons that require two or more witnesses (19:15). These judges gave the first and final ruling on a case, using all their wisdom to get to the truth.

19:19 You must purge the evil from among you. The very fact that a case has made its way to the judges indicates that evil has occurred. The accused must pay for his crime, or the one who has cluttered the court with lies must pay for his. Either way, someone pays.

19:21 life for life. This law of retaliation ensured justice. It limited vengeance by the offended one and prevented cruel and unusual punishment by the judge. Though it may seem harsh, it reveals the goodness of God in protecting his people. Jesus rebuked the misuse of this law and the lack of mercy in personal relationships (Matt. 5:38–42).

20:2 the priest shall ... address. Whether chariots or jet fighters, if the enemy has them and you do not—who starts the battle with a psychological advantage? The priest, as the army chaplain, spoke this message: "If God is for us, who can be against us?" (Rom. 8:31).

20:5–9 The officers shall say. Privates follow the faith of generals. Before the battle, the general must be confident in the Lord's victory and then press upon the troops the words of the priest about trusting in God, not in numbers of weapons and soldiers.

20:10–15 When you march up to attack. There were two sets of rules of engagement. One for taking the inheritance or Promised Land and another for fighting enemies that would remain as neighbors. This first set is for going to war against cities outside of the Promised Land.

peace. 11 If they accept and open their gates, all the people in it shall
be subject to forced labor and shall work for you. 12 If they refuse to
make peace and they engage you in battle, lay siege to that city.
13 When the LORD your God delivers it into your hand, put to the sword
all the men in it. 14 As for the women, the children, the livestock and
everything else in the city, you may take these as plunder for yourselves. And you may use the plunder the LORD your God gives you
from your enemies. 15 This is how you are to treat all the cities that are
at a distance from you and do not belong to the nations nearby.

16 However, in the cities of the nations the LORD your God is giving
you as an inheritance, do not leave alive anything that breathes.
17 Completely destroy[a] them—the Hittites, Amorites, Canaanites, Perizzites, Hivites and Jebusites—as the LORD your God has commanded
you. 18 Otherwise, they will teach you to follow all the detestable
things they do in worshiping their gods, and you will sin against the
LORD your God.

19 When you lay siege to a city for a long time, fighting against it to
capture it, do not destroy its trees by putting an ax to them, because
you can eat their fruit. Do not cut them down. Are the trees of the
field people, that you should besiege them?[b] 20 However, you may cut
down trees that you know are not fruit trees and use them to build
siege works until the city at war with you falls.

Atonement for an Unsolved Murder

21 If a man is found slain, lying in a field in the land the LORD
your God is giving you to possess, and it is not known who
killed him, 2 your elders and judges shall go out and measure the distance from the body to the neighboring towns. 3 Then the elders of the
town nearest the body shall take a heifer that has never been worked
and has never worn a yoke 4 and lead her down to a valley that has not
been plowed or planted and where there is a flowing stream. There in
the valley they are to break the heifer's neck. 5 The priests, the sons of
Levi, shall step forward, for the LORD your God has chosen them to
minister and to pronounce blessings in the name of the LORD and to
decide all cases of dispute and assault. 6 Then all the elders of the
town nearest the body shall wash their hands over the heifer whose

[a] *17* The Hebrew term refers to the irrevocable giving over of things or persons to the LORD, often by totally destroying them. [b] *19* Or *down to use in the siege, for the fruit trees are for the benefit of man.*

give the inhabitants of independent cities (vv. 10–15)? How were they to deal with the cities belonging to the nations they were driving out (vv. 16–18)? Why the difference? **4.** Why were these people the enemies of Israel? Would they have been your enemies? How do you feel about driving out the occupants of the land? **5.** What bit of tactical advice does God give the Israelites in verses 19–20?

APPLY 1. How do you feel about God commanding his people to fight? **2.** How is the justice of God demonstrated in his commanding his people to go to war?

OPEN 1. What is your favorite TV detective or lawyer show? **2.** Is any case ever left unsolved?

STUDY In God's order of things, every wrong needed to be righted. In cases of unsolved crimes, ceremonial atonement was made to right the wrong. **1.** What is at issue in these instructions (19:6,21)? **2.** Do you think some ceremonial cleansing for unsolved murders would be of benefit to your society? **3.** In Israel, who decided all the cases of dispute and assault (v. 5)? Who decides these cases in your society?

20:11 If they accept. Israel was to offer to these nations mercy in exchange for service. Noah prophesied that Canaan would serve Israel, a descendant of Shem (Gen. 9:25–26). A failure to accept these conditions meant death. When Christ conquered for us, we received his mercy and became his servants (Rom. 6:22; Titus 2:14).

20:17 Hittites ... Jebusites. God had already assured victory over these "greater nations" within Canaan (7:1).

20:19 do not destroy its trees. Israel was to trust God greatly and to enjoy his blessings fully. Other armies would strip the land of trees to use for later sieges. Allowing many trees to stand demonstrated that Israel trusted God, not their supplies, for victory. And as a further bonus, they tasted God's goodness each time they ate fruit from the spared trees.

21:1–9 This passage explains what to do about an unsolved murder, either accidental or intentional. The first issue to be settled was jurisdiction, because the people in the town closest to the body had to perform a rite proclaiming their innocence and atoning for the guilt.

21:5 to minister. God set apart the Levite priests to serve the people in the place of worship, leading the people in relationship to God (10:8; 18:5). **to pronounce blessings.** God tells Moses to have Aaron and his sons bless the Israelites in Numbers 6:22–27.

21:6 wash their hands. This action declares that the elders and townspeople are innocent of the slain person's death. Pilate intended the same message regarding Christ's death when he washed his hands (Matt. 27:24).

neck was broken in the valley, 7and they shall declare: "Our hands did
not shed this blood, nor did our eyes see it done. 8Accept this atonement for your people Israel, whom you have redeemed, O LORD, and
do not hold your people guilty of the blood of an innocent man." And
the bloodshed will be atoned for. 9So you will purge from yourselves
the guilt of shedding innocent blood, since you have done what is
right in the eyes of the LORD.

Marrying a Captive Woman

10When you go to war against your enemies and the LORD your God
delivers them into your hands and you take captives, 11if you notice
among the captives a beautiful woman and are attracted to her, you
may take her as your wife. 12Bring her into your home and have her
shave her head, trim her nails 13and put aside the clothes she was
wearing when captured. After she has lived in your house and
mourned her father and mother for a full month, then you may go to
her and be her husband and she shall be your wife. 14If you are not
pleased with her, let her go wherever she wishes. You must not sell
her or treat her as a slave, since you have dishonored her.

The Right of the Firstborn

15If a man has two wives, and he loves one but not the other, and
both bear him sons but the firstborn is the son of the wife he does not
love, 16when he wills his property to his sons, he must not give the
rights of the firstborn to the son of the wife he loves in preference to
his actual firstborn, the son of the wife he does not love. 17He must
acknowledge the son of his unloved wife as the firstborn by giving
him a double share of all he has. That son is the first sign of his
father's strength. The right of the firstborn belongs to him.

A Rebellious Son

18If a man has a stubborn and rebellious son who does not obey his
father and mother and will not listen to them when they discipline
him, 19his father and mother shall take hold of him and bring him to
the elders at the gate of his town. 20They shall say to the elders, "This
son of ours is stubborn and rebellious. He will not obey us. He is a

APPLY **1.** Have you been the victim of an unsolved crime? **2.** What was the crime, and how do you feel about it today?

OPEN **1.** Were you rebellious as a child? **2.** How were you punished?

STUDY As Israel prepared to possess the land God had promised, many issues of community life need to be addressed. God gives them specific instructions concerning various aspects of family relations **1.** How does God protect the captured women in these instructions? **2.** As a woman, what is your reaction to these instructions? As a man? **3.** What was the significance of the right of the firstborn son (v. 17)? Does your family have such a tradition? **4.** What problem about the right of the firstborn son is addressed in these instructions? **5.** What is the character of the rebellious son in these verses (v. 20)? What was his punishment (v. 21)? Do you think that was too harsh? Why or why not?

APPLY **1.** Do you think strict punishment for breaking God's Law encourages righteousness or more rebellion? **2.** How do you react to these strict rules?

21:10 against your enemies. Since women could be taken as wives (v. 11), the enemies here would be those outside Canaan (20:14–15). God had instructed total destruction of the pagan tribes in the land he was giving Israel.

21:12 shave her head. This act symbolizes a new beginning, leaving an old way of life. A shorn head also meant mourning and humiliation. Cleansing rites are detailed in Leviticus 14:8; and Numbers 8:7.

21:14 dishonored. In other contexts this word in Hebrew is used to indicate rape (22:24,29; Judg. 19:24; 20:5). The message, however, is for the divorcing husband to treat his foreign wife with dignity even if the marriage ends as a result of incompatibility.

21:15 two wives. Though God's original intention was one man and one woman (Gen. 2:23–25), the practice of polygamy began with Lamech (Gen. 4:19), who was in the line of Cain. As Genesis 25:6 indicates, polygamy became a common ancient practice even among God's people. It helped ensure male heirs.

21:16 in preference to. The Law makes it clear that birth order, not favoritism, is to determine inheritance.

21:17 double share. The first son is to receive a double portion of the inheritance, no matter what the father might prefer. Receiving this double share led to a continuation of control. **first sign of his father's strength.** The firstborn son was proof that a man was able to produce heirs.

21:18 stubborn and rebellious ... does not obey. Such a son must clearly disobey the commandment to honor his parents in evil, audacious ways over a long period (5:16; Ex. 20:12).

21:19 his father and mother. In the Israelite community, parents were ultimately responsible for their children, while elders oversaw the entire community.

profligate and a drunkard." [21]Then all the men of his town shall stone
him to death. You must purge the evil from among you. All Israel will
hear of it and be afraid.

Various Laws

[22]If a man guilty of a capital offense is put to death and his body is
hung on a tree, [23]you must not leave his body on the tree overnight.
Be sure to bury him that same day, because anyone who is hung on a
tree is under God's curse. You must not desecrate the land the LORD
your God is giving you as an inheritance.

22 If you see your brother's ox or sheep straying, do not ignore
it but be sure to take it back to him. [2]If the brother does not
live near you or if you do not know who he is, take it home with you
and keep it until he comes looking for it. Then give it back to him. [3]Do
the same if you find your brother's donkey or his cloak or anything
he loses. Do not ignore it.

[4]If you see your brother's donkey or his ox fallen on the road, do
not ignore it. Help him get it to its feet.

[5]A woman must not wear men's clothing, nor a man wear women's
clothing, for the LORD your God detests anyone who does this.

[6]If you come across a bird's nest beside the road, either in a tree or
on the ground, and the mother is sitting on the young or on the eggs,
do not take the mother with the young. [7]You may take the young, but
be sure to let the mother go, so that it may go well with you and you
may have a long life.

[8]When you build a new house, make a parapet around your roof so
that you may not bring the guilt of bloodshed on your house if someone falls from the roof.

[9]Do not plant two kinds of seed in your vineyard; if you do, not only
the crops you plant but also the fruit of the vineyard will be defiled.[a]

[10]Do not plow with an ox and a donkey yoked together.

[11]Do not wear clothes of wool and linen woven together.

[12]Make tassels on the four corners of the cloak you wear.

Marriage Violations

[13]If a man takes a wife and, after lying with her, dislikes her [14]and
slanders her and gives her a bad name, saying, "I married this woman,

[a]9 Or *be forfeited to the sanctuary*

OPEN Can you remember a time when you applied the saying "finders keepers, losers weepers"?

STUDY As God continues to instruct the Israelites, he deals with some everyday, common situations. In each case, principles of honoring God and other humans are behind the laws. **1.** What connection is there between God's curse on anyone hung on a tree and the death of Jesus (Gal. 3:13)? **2.** What is the general intent of the instructions in 22:1-4? **3.** What do you make of the instructions about not cross-dressing (v. 5)? **4.** What practical reason can you give for the instructions about the bird and her young (vv. 6–7)? **5.** What is behind the thought of not mixing things together (vv. 9–11)? **6.** Why were the Israelites to have tassels on their clothes (Num. 15:38–41)? Do you know of any modern parallels?

APPLY Do you feel like you function best with more rules or fewer rules in your life? Why?

OPEN 1. Would you prefer to live in a culture where marriage decisions are made for you, including who you will marry, or in a culture where you can make all your own choices about marriage? **2.** Do

---

21:21 stone him to death. The rebellious son had broken the commandment in 5:16, which was reiterated in a curse in 27:16 (Ex. 21:15,17). **You must purge the evil from among you.** God knew that evil in the midst of the nation would dim the people's resolve. While this punishment may seem harsh, God intended to protect his people from evil. This command is repeated in 17:7; 19:19; 22:21,24; 24:7.

21:22 put to death and ... hung on a tree. A murderer is to be put to death and then his body hung or "impaled on a pole," according to the original Hebrew (Gen. 40:19; Est. 2:23).

21:23 not leave his body on the tree overnight. It's one thing to demonstrate justice and another to draw sensational attention to a murderer's grisly fate. **under God's curse.** Being hung on a tree was a symbol of God's righteous judgment and rejection. By taking the total judgment for the sins of the world, Christ became "a curse for us" (Gal. 3:13). Christ actually became a sin offering for us (Rom. 8:3).

22:1 take it back. The Law of God is not intended solely as a guide to punishing misbehavior but a reminder to diligently seek ways of helping others. Verses 1, 3 and 4 give concrete examples of how the Israelites could show concern for others.

22:5 God had established clear differences between men and women which were to be honored and celebrated (Lev. 18:22; 20:13). This rule most likely is related to prohibitions against abnormal sexual practices.

22:8 parapet ... roof. The Israelites were to erect a wall around the roof of a house, so that people using that space, much like a patio today, would not accidentally fall off.

but when I approached her, I did not find proof of her virginity," 15then
the girl's father and mother shall bring proof that she was a virgin to
the town elders at the gate. 16The girl's father will say to the elders, "I
gave my daughter in marriage to this man, but he dislikes her. 17Now
he has slandered her and said, 'I did not find your daughter to be a virgin.' But here is the proof of my daughter's virginity." Then her parents
shall display the cloth before the elders of the town, 18and the elders
shall take the man and punish him. 19They shall fine him a hundred
shekels of silver[a] and give them to the girl's father, because this man
has given an Israelite virgin a bad name. She shall continue to be his
wife; he must not divorce her as long as he lives.
20If, however, the charge is true and no proof of the girl's virginity
can be found, 21she shall be brought to the door of her father's house
and there the men of her town shall stone her to death. She has done
a disgraceful thing in Israel by being promiscuous while still in her
father's house. You must purge the evil from among you.
22If a man is found sleeping with another man's wife, both the man
who slept with her and the woman must die. You must purge the evil
from Israel.
23If a man happens to meet in a town a virgin pledged to be married
and he sleeps with her, 24you shall take both of them to the gate of
that town and stone them to death—the girl because she was in a
town and did not scream for help, and the man because he violated
another man's wife. You must purge the evil from among you.
25But if out in the country a man happens to meet a girl pledged to
be married and rapes her, only the man who has done this shall die.
26Do nothing to the girl; she has committed no sin deserving death.
This case is like that of someone who attacks and murders his neighbor, 27for the man found the girl out in the country, and though the
betrothed girl screamed, there was no one to rescue her.
28If a man happens to meet a virgin who is not pledged to be married and rapes her and they are discovered, 29he shall pay the girl's
father fifty shekels of silver.[b] He must marry the girl, for he has violated her. He can never divorce her as long as he lives.
30A man is not to marry his father's wife; he must not dishonor his
father's bed.

Exclusion From the Assembly

23 No one who has been emasculated by crushing or cutting
may enter the assembly of the LORD.

[a]19 That is, about 2 1/2 pounds (about 1 kilogram) [b]29 That is, about 1 1/4 pounds (about 0.6 kilogram)

you think there is too much divorce today? Why or why not?

STUDY One of the major areas of community life involves handling marriage violations and disputes. God gives these specific instructions to his people as guidelines for difficult relational circumstances. **1.** What is the core issue in these marriage instructions? What injustices were these instructions meant to prevent? **2.** What was to be Israel's attitude toward sexual promiscuity? What is your culture's attitude? What do you think would happen today if the death penalty was enforced for sexual sins? **3.** What was to be Israel's attitude toward divorce? What is your culture's attitude? **4.** How did Jesus approach this issue (Matt. 5:27–32)? **5.** Why is there a difference in the consequences to the victim of rape based on whether it happened in the city or in the country (vv. 23–27)? What do you think about that distinction?

APPLY **1.** What do you think is at the heart of God's laws concerning sex and marriage? **2.** How can we encourage each other to honor God's rules about sexual conduct and marriage? Is that important?

OPEN **1.** Have you ever been refused membership in an organization you really wanted to join? Did you think the reasons for your refusal were legitimate? **2.** What do

22:15 elders at the gate. Also referred to in 25:7. The gates served as a town square where the wise men gathered to administer justice.

22:19 hundred shekels of silver. This is a steep fine, probably double the average price for a bride. This would have certainly forced a husband to be careful about charges made against his wife and would have curtailed any notion of easy divorce.

22:21 father's house. If charges against the woman were proven true, the parents were to be dishonored in the punishment because they had not kept their daughter from illicit sexual activity.

22:28 man. This is a warning that men would be held accountable for actions against women.

22:29 fifty shekels of silver. This was most likely related to the price paid to a girl's father in order to marry her. The practice of paying the father to marry is still found in some Middle Eastern cultures.

22:30 his father's wife. Not the man's mother (27:20). **dishonor his father's bed.** In Hebrew this literally means "uncover the corner of his father's garment" (Ruth 3:9; Ezek. 16:8). Referring to sexual relations, this phrase symbolizes entering into marriage.

23:1 emasculated. Eunuchs guarded harems since they were unable to have

you think society has learned about handling trash and sewage?

STUDY As God continues to instruct the Israelites, he deals with some very "earthy and human" issues, like how to deal with bodily functions, how to handle refuse and other community matters. These instructions demonstrate the "real life" situation in which God's people were living. **1.** Who could not enter the assembly of the Lord (vv. 1–3)? Why? Why was favor given to the Edomites and the Egyptians (vv. 7–8)? **2.** What is the difference between uncleanness and sin (vv. 9–14)? The similarities? **3.** How can you make your "camp" holy (v. 14) in a spiritual sense? **4.** What instructions does God give the Israelites concerning hospitality (vv. 15–16)? Concerning prostitution (vv. 17–18)? Concerning usury (vv. 19–20)? How do you think those instructions apply to us? **5.** What do you learn about God's attitude toward the promises we make in verses 21–23?

APPLY **1.** How do you feel about God's laws? Do you see his sternness or his love in his laws? **2.** How do you think the laws of God can be misapplied and misused in such a way as to harm the people?

2No one born of a forbidden marriage[a] nor any of his descendants
may enter the assembly of the LORD, even down to the tenth generation.
3No Ammonite or Moabite or any of his descendants may enter the
assembly of the LORD, even down to the tenth generation. 4For they
did not come to meet you with bread and water on your way when
you came out of Egypt, and they hired Balaam son of Beor from
Pethor in Aram Naharaim[b] to pronounce a curse on you. 5However,
the LORD your God would not listen to Balaam but turned the curse
into a blessing for you, because the LORD your God loves you. 6Do not
seek a treaty of friendship with them as long as you live.
7Do not abhor an Edomite, for he is your brother. Do not abhor an
Egyptian, because you lived as an alien in his country. 8The third generation of children born to them may enter the assembly of the LORD.

Uncleanness in the Camp

9When you are encamped against your enemies, keep away from
everything impure. 10If one of your men is unclean because of a nocturnal emission, he is to go outside the camp and stay there. 11But as
evening approaches he is to wash himself, and at sunset he may return to the camp.
12Designate a place outside the camp where you can go to relieve
yourself. 13As part of your equipment have something to dig with, and
when you relieve yourself, dig a hole and cover up your excrement.
14For the LORD your God moves about in your camp to protect you
and to deliver your enemies to you. Your camp must be holy, so that he will not see among you anything indecent and turn away from you.

Miscellaneous Laws

15If a slave has taken refuge with you, do not hand him over to his
master. 16Let him live among you wherever he likes and in whatever town he chooses. Do not oppress him.
17No Israelite man or woman is to become a shrine prostitute.
18You must not bring the earnings of a female prostitute or of a male prostitute[c] into the house of the LORD your God to pay any vow, because the LORD your God detests them both.
19Do not charge your brother interest, whether on money or food
or anything else that may earn interest. 20You may charge a foreigner

[a]2 Or *one of illegitimate birth* [b]4 That is, Northwest Mesopotamia [c]18 Hebrew *of a dog*

---

intercourse. The removal of all or part of the sexual organs was a common pagan practice but was forbidden in Israel. Even then, some eunuchs were blessed in later years of Israel's history (Isa. 56:4–5; Acts 8:26–39).

23:2–3 down to the tenth generation. The number ten symbolizes completeness, so this may mean that such a person may never worship corporately.

23:7 Edomite ... your brother. Jacob and Esau were brothers; Esau is the father of Edom and Jacob of Israel (Gen. 25:21–28).

23:15 slave has taken refuge. This refers to a non-Israelite slave who has come to Israel to seek freedom (v. 16; 24:7).

23:17 shrine prostitute. In Canaanite religion, men had sexual relations with cultic prostitutes—an act they believed would bring fertility and prosperity to their families, fields and herds. Such activities brought God's sternest judgment on the Canaanites, perhaps because prostitution is so closely related to adultery—pursuing a lover other than one's spouse. Ultimately Israel would commit spiritual adultery by pursuing false gods.

23:19 interest. Exodus 22:25–27 outlines God's thinking on charging interest. Normally in the ancient Middle East the rate was quite high, often leading to greater debt and sometimes enslavement. In Israel the poor were not to be unfairly charged interest for profit. (Lev. 25:36.) Jesus would encourage even greater generosity in Luke 6:34–35.

interest, but not a brother Israelite, so that the LORD your God may
bless you in everything you put your hand to in the land you are
entering to possess.
[21]If you make a vow to the LORD your God, do not be slow to pay it,
for the LORD your God will certainly demand it of you and you will be
guilty of sin. [22]But if you refrain from making a vow, you will not be
guilty. [23]Whatever your lips utter you must be sure to do, because you
made your vow freely to the LORD your God with your own mouth.
[24]If you enter your neighbor's vineyard, you may eat all the grapes
you want, but do not put any in your basket. [25]If you enter your
neighbor's grainfield, you may pick kernels with your hands, but you
must not put a sickle to his standing grain.

24 If a man marries a woman who becomes displeasing to him
because he finds something indecent about her, and he
writes her a certificate of divorce, gives it to her and sends her from
his house, [2]and if after she leaves his house she becomes the wife of
another man, [3]and her second husband dislikes her and writes her a
certificate of divorce, gives it to her and sends her from his house, or
if he dies, [4]then her first husband, who divorced her, is not allowed to
marry her again after she has been defiled. That would be detestable
in the eyes of the LORD. Do not bring sin upon the land the LORD your
God is giving you as an inheritance.
[5]If a man has recently married, he must not be sent to war or have
any other duty laid on him. For one year he is to be free to stay at
home and bring happiness to the wife he has married.
[6]Do not take a pair of millstones—not even the upper one—as
security for a debt, because that would be taking a man's livelihood
as security.
[7]If a man is caught kidnapping one of his brother Israelites and
treats him as a slave or sells him, the kidnapper must die. You must
purge the evil from among you.
[8]In cases of leprous[a] diseases be very careful to do exactly as the
priests, who are Levites, instruct you. You must follow carefully what
I have commanded them. [9]Remember what the LORD your God did to
Miriam along the way after you came out of Egypt.
[10]When you make a loan of any kind to your neighbor, do not go
into his house to get what he is offering as a pledge. [11]Stay outside
and let the man to whom you are making the loan bring the pledge
out to you. [12]If the man is poor, do not go to sleep with his pledge in
your possession. [13]Return his cloak to him by sunset so that he may

[a]8 The Hebrew word was used for various diseases affecting the skin—not necessarily leprosy.

OPEN 1. What rules did your family have for dating? **2.** What common sense rules does your society practice that make life easier for you?

STUDY As God continues his instructions to the Israelites he addresses them concerning marriage, divorce, financial transactions, kidnapping, infectious diseases, wage laws, responsibility for sins, fair treatment of others and sharing with the needy. All these laws were necessary for the peaceful functioning of their new society. **1.** What is the rule of divorce and remarriage here (vv. 1–4)? Who did the certificate of divorce protect? Is divorce what God wanted in Israel (Matt. 19:1–9)? What do you think God's attitude is on divorce today? **2.** How long could newlyweds honeymoon in Israel (v. 5)? How would you like a honeymoon that long? **3.** What were the rules for collateral against a loan (vv. 6,10-13)? How is collateral different from interest (23:19–20)? **4.** What attribute is involved in the instructions about returning a pledge to a poor man who has borrowed from you? **5.** What were the wage laws given to Israel (vv. 14–15)? Do you think fair wage laws are practiced where you work? Why or why not? **6.** Why did God have to remind the Israelites that each person is responsible for their own sin (v. 16)?

23:20 charge a foreigner interest. God allows Israelites to charge interest to foreigners who intend to make money in business.

23:24,25 enter your neighbor's vineyard ... grainfield. Travelers commonly were allowed to pick grapes or grain to eat (as Jesus and his disciples did in Mark 2:23–28). But harvesting or stockpiling others' crops for later use was prohibited.

24:1 a certificate of divorce. Here divorce is allowed (Lev. 21:7,14; 22:13; Num. 30:9). Later Jesus added a condition to 24:1 (Matt. 5:31–32), pointing to the precedent set by creation (Matt. 19:3–9).

24:6 millstones. These heavy rocks were used to grind grain to make meal. Since they were necessary for food preparation every day, it was wrong to use them to secure debt.

24:7 purge the evil. This is a frequent refrain in Deuteronomy (13:5; 17:7; 19:19; 21:21; 22:21,24; 24:7; 1 Cor. 5:13). A foolproof way to rid the land of evil was to remove the evildoers.

24:8 leprous diseases. A variety of skin disorders were termed "leprosy" in the Bible (Lev. 13:2). Today leprosy is called Hansen's disease.

24:9 Remember. Another common theme in the book is God's desire that Israel keep in mind his leading and guiding them. They had a bad habit of forgetting.

sleep in it. Then he will thank you, and it will be regarded as a righteous act in the sight of the LORD your God.

[14]Do not take advantage of a hired man who is poor and needy, whether he is a brother Israelite or an alien living in one of your towns. [15]Pay him his wages each day before sunset, because he is poor and is counting on it. Otherwise he may cry to the LORD against you, and you will be guilty of sin.

[16]Fathers shall not be put to death for their children, nor children put to death for their fathers; each is to die for his own sin.

[17]Do not deprive the alien or the fatherless of justice, or take the cloak of the widow as a pledge. [18]Remember that you were slaves in Egypt and the LORD your God redeemed you from there. That is why I command you to do this.

[19]When you are harvesting in your field and you overlook a sheaf, do not go back to get it. Leave it for the alien, the fatherless and the widow, so that the LORD your God may bless you in all the work of your hands. [20]When you beat the olives from your trees, do not go over the branches a second time. Leave what remains for the alien, the fatherless and the widow. [21]When you harvest the grapes in your vineyard, do not go over the vines again. Leave what remains for the alien, the fatherless and the widow. [22]Remember that you were slaves in Egypt. That is why I command you to do this.

25 When men have a dispute, they are to take it to court and the judges will decide the case, acquitting the innocent and condemning the guilty. [2]If the guilty man deserves to be beaten, the judge shall make him lie down and have him flogged in his presence with the number of lashes his crime deserves, [3]but he must not give him more than forty lashes. If he is flogged more than that, your brother will be degraded in your eyes.

[4]Do not muzzle an ox while it is treading out the grain.

[5]If brothers are living together and one of them dies without a son, his widow must not marry outside the family. Her husband's brother shall take her and marry her and fulfill the duty of a brother-in-law to her. [6]The first son she bears shall carry on the name of the dead brother so that his name will not be blotted out from Israel.

[7]However, if a man does not want to marry his brother's wife, she shall go to the elders at the town gate and say, "My husband's brother refuses to carry on his brother's name in Israel. He will not fulfill the duty of a brother-in-law to me." [8]Then the elders of his town shall summon him and talk to him. If he persists in saying, "I do not want to marry her," [9]his brother's widow shall go up to him in the presence of the elders, take off one of his sandals, spit in his face and say, "This is what is done to the man who will not build up his brother's family

7. What is the intent of leaving some of the crop behind when harvesting (vv. 19–22)? Does your society have any such practice today? If not, why not, and if so, what is it? **8.** Why do you think God reminds the Israelites several times in these instructions about when they were slaves in Egypt (vv. 18,22)?

APPLY 1. Are you fair in your treatment of other people? **2.** Do you think of God when you make a business deal? **3.** Do you honor God in your decisions and actions in your relationships?

OPEN 1. What is the worst family argument you ever had? What happened and how did it make you feel? **2.** Have you ever been cheated in a business deal?

STUDY The continuing instructions of God to Israel include the establishment of courts, taking care of those who work, fulfilling family responsibilities, fair fighting, honesty in business and payback to the Amalekites. **1.** What kind of punishment was given to the guilty in Israel? Why was it limited (vv. 1–3)? What kind of punishment do you think those guilty of crimes deserve? **2.** What does "don't muzzle the ox" mean (v. 4)? What applications might that have (1 Cor. 9:9–10)? **3.** Why was it so important in Israel for the family name to be passed on? What other reasons would a woman have to get married again? What do you make of the removal of the sandal and spitting in the face (vv. 8–10)?

24:16 die for his own sin. Each person's sin causes eternal separation from God. In Ezekiel 18:4–24 the prophet addresses this issue, which may have arisen from a faulty understanding of Exodus 20:5; 34:6,7.

25:3 forty lashes. A limit is imposed on beatings, since such punishment could easily be inhumane. (See Paul's situation in 2 Cor. 11:24.) Jewish law later set the number at forty minus one to make sure the limit was observed.

25:4 muzzle an ox. Muzzling prevented the animal from eating while working. Paul applies this verse to those who serve Christ in ministry in 1 Corinthians 9:9–10 and 1 Timothy 5:17–18. **treading out the grain.** The ox walks on the grain that is spread over a flat rock or hard ground.

25:5–6 Survival of the family was essential to the governing of land, so these practices, which became foundational elements of the Israelite economy under Moses, were instituted to provide family heirs.

25:9 take off one of his sandals. This signifies a loss of rights in the Israelite community. **spit in his face.** A blatant act of contempt against the

line." [10]That man's line shall be known in Israel as The Family of the Unsandaled.

[11]If two men are fighting and the wife of one of them comes to rescue her husband from his assailant, and she reaches out and seizes him by his private parts, [12]you shall cut off her hand. Show her no pity.

[13]Do not have two differing weights in your bag—one heavy, one light. [14]Do not have two differing measures in your house—one large, one small. [15]You must have accurate and honest weights and measures, so that you may live long in the land the LORD your God is giving you. [16]For the LORD your God detests anyone who does these things, anyone who deals dishonestly.

[17]Remember what the Amalekites did to you along the way when you came out of Egypt. [18]When you were weary and worn out, they met you on your journey and cut off all who were lagging behind; they had no fear of God. [19]When the LORD your God gives you rest from all the enemies around you in the land he is giving you to possess as an inheritance, you shall blot out the memory of Amalek from under heaven. Do not forget!

What does that signify? Are you concerned that your family name be carried on? **4.** Why do you think God detests dishonesty in business (Mic. 6:10–11; Amos 8:4–6)? Do you know of any dishonest business people? Do your business people make honesty the highest priority? **5.** What was the problem with the Amalekites (Ex. 17:8–16; compare 1 Sam. 30)? Do you think God was fair in ordering their complete annihilation?

APPLY 1. How do you feel about taking care of your family? **2.** Are you honest? How can this group encourage honesty in one another?

Firstfruits and Tithes

26 When you have entered the land the LORD your God is giving you as an inheritance and have taken possession of it and settled in it, [2]take some of the firstfruits of all that you produce from the soil of the land the LORD your God is giving you and put them in a basket. Then go to the place the LORD your God will choose as a dwelling for his Name [3]and say to the priest in office at the time, "I declare today to the LORD your God that I have come to the land the LORD swore to our forefathers to give us." [4]The priest shall take the basket from your hands and set it down in front of the altar of the LORD your God. [5]Then you shall declare before the LORD your God: "My father was a wandering Aramean, and he went down into Egypt with a few people and lived there and became a great nation, powerful and numerous. [6]But the Egyptians mistreated us and made us suffer, putting us to hard labor. [7]Then we cried out to the LORD, the God of our fathers, and the LORD heard our voice and saw our misery, toil and oppression. [8]So the LORD brought us out of Egypt with a mighty hand and an outstretched arm, with great terror and with miraculous signs and wonders. [9]He brought us to this place and gave us this

OPEN 1. How do you feel about charities and religious organizations always asking for money? **2.** Can you remember a time you gave to a cause and felt really good about it? What was the cause and how did you feel?

STUDY From the very beginning, God makes sure the Israelites understand the need to give to support the common cause. The instruction about tithing would be a common thread throughout their existence as a nation. **1.** Why do you think God wanted the "firstfruits"? What was the significance of the ritual in the tithe offering? Do you practice any ritual in your tithing? **2.** Why was it important for the Israelites to recite the history of their slavery and deliverance from Egypt by the hand of the Lord? Is it important for you to tell the story of your spiritual journey? **3.** What

---

brother-in-law, indicating the seriousness of the charge.

25:17 Remember. God frequently exhorts Israel to keep in mind his powerful acts on their behalf (4:10; 24:9,18,22). **Amalekites.** The Amalekites (who were introduced in Gen. 14:7) were defeated at Rephidim after they attacked Israel (Ex. 17:8–16; Num. 14:45).

26:2 firstfruits. This is a one-time offering made upon entering the land. The yearly offering of firstfruits was a separate event (18:4). **the place the LORD ... will choose as a dwelling for his Name.** God will direct the location of his dwelling place, the tabernacle. He will choose a city in Canaan as home base. A central place of worship was important as the people spread out and settled around the Promised Land.

26:4 altar. Priests established an altar for sacrifices long before the temple was built.

26:5 wandering Aramean. Jacob, referred to here (also called Israel and the father of the nation), journeyed from southern Canaan to Haran, then returned (Gen. 27–35). He also moved to Egypt with his family (Gen. 46:3–7). Two of his wives were Aramean (Gen. 28:5; 29:16,28). **became a great nation.** While the Israelites lived in Egypt they grew from seventy people (Jacob and his family) to 600,000 men, plus women and children (Ex. 1:5,7).

26:7 the LORD heard ... and saw. God responded to Israel's cries with grace and mercy (Ex. 2:23–25).

26:8 terror ... signs and wonders. A common description of God's miraculous acts on Israel's behalf during the Exodus (4:34; 34:11,12).

was the tithe to be used for (v. 12)? How did this reflect the character of God (10:18–19)? What good works do you do with your giving? **4.** What temptation would the Israelites have with reference to the things that were to be used for the tithe (vv. 13–14)? What tempts you not to tithe? **5.** How do you follow the Lord with "all your heart and all your soul" in command-keeping (v. 16)? **6.** What mutual declaration did God and the Israelites make (vv. 17–19)? Have you made such a declaration to the Lord (Matt. 10:32)?

APPLY 1. Has God's generosity to you encouraged you to be generous to others? How? **2.** Have you ever promised God that you will follow him? Do you think he has promised to be your God and to bless you?

land, a land flowing with milk and honey; [10]and now I bring the firstfruits of the soil that you, O LORD, have given me." Place the basket
before the LORD your God and bow down before him. [11]And you and
the Levites and the aliens among you shall rejoice in all the good
things the LORD your God has given to you and your household.
[12]When you have finished setting aside a tenth of all your produce
in the third year, the year of the tithe, you shall give it to the Levite,
the alien, the fatherless and the widow, so that they may eat in your
towns and be satisfied. [13]Then say to the LORD your God: "I have removed from my house the sacred portion and have given it to the
Levite, the alien, the fatherless and the widow, according to all you
commanded. I have not turned aside from your commands nor have I
forgotten any of them. [14]I have not eaten any of the sacred portion
while I was in mourning, nor have I removed any of it while I was unclean, nor have I offered any of it to the dead. I have obeyed the LORD
my God; I have done everything you commanded me. [15]Look down
from heaven, your holy dwelling place, and bless your people Israel
and the land you have given us as you promised on oath to our forefathers, a land flowing with milk and honey."

Follow the LORD's Commands

[16]The LORD your God commands you this day to follow these decrees and laws; carefully observe them with all your heart and with
all your soul. [17]You have declared this day that the LORD is your God
and that you will walk in his ways, that you will keep his decrees,
commands and laws, and that you will obey him. [18]And the LORD has
declared this day that you are his people, his treasured possession as
he promised, and that you are to keep all his commands. [19]He has
declared that he will set you in praise, fame and honor high above all
the nations he has made and that you will be a people holy to the
LORD your God, as he promised.

OPEN 1. What is your favorite national monument? Why? **2.** What is inscribed on it?

STUDY God had told the people of Israel to remember the Law when they entered the land. **1.** What was the purpose of the altar? Where was the altar to be erected (v. 4)? **2.** What rituals accompanied

The Altar on Mount Ebal

27 Moses and the elders of Israel commanded the people: "Keep
all these commands that I give you today. [2]When you have
crossed the Jordan into the land the LORD your God is giving you, set
up some large stones and coat them with plaster. [3]Write on them all
the words of this law when you have crossed over to enter the land
the LORD your God is giving you, a land flowing with milk and honey,
just as the LORD, the God of your fathers, promised you. [4]And when

26:12 a tenth. Chapter 14:22–29 sets forth more details. This refers to a tithe (ten percent) gathered every third year for the Levites and those in need.

26:15 holy dwelling place. God is everywhere (Isa. 66:1,2), but heaven is seen as the place from which he reigns and answers prayer.

26:16 with all your heart ... soul. This refers to the whole person, implying total commitment to God's Word (4:29).

26:17 This wording is customarily found in treaties and legal covenants. By using this language the people are renewing their vow to follow the one true God and abide by his covenant.

26:18 treasured possession. In the New Testament the same idea is captured in phrases such as "chosen people" and "people belonging to God" (1 Peter 2:9). God clearly has authority and dominion over his people—and he lovingly treasures them.

27:2 large stones. It was common in the ancient Near East to commemorate important events by setting up stones and carving messages in them for people to see and remember. **coat them with plaster.** By doing this, not only will the stones stand out more boldly, but the message can be read more easily (v. 8).

27:3 all the words of this law. The message on these stones was to include the words of Moses' covenant, to which the people had reaffirmed their commitment.

27:4 Mount Ebal. North of Mount

you have crossed the Jordan, set up these stones on Mount Ebal, as I
command you today, and coat them with plaster. [5]Build there an altar
to the LORD your God, an altar of stones. Do not use any iron tool
upon them. [6]Build the altar of the LORD your God with fieldstones and
offer burnt offerings on it to the LORD your God. [7]Sacrifice fellowship
offerings[a] there, eating them and rejoicing in the presence of the
LORD your God. [8]And you shall write very clearly all the words of this
law on these stones you have set up."

Curses From Mount Ebal

[9]Then Moses and the priests, who are Levites, said to all Israel, "Be
silent, O Israel, and listen! You have now become the people of the
LORD your God. [10]Obey the LORD your God and follow his commands
and decrees that I give you today."
[11]On the same day Moses commanded the people:
[12]When you have crossed the Jordan, these tribes shall stand on
Mount Gerizim to bless the people: Simeon, Levi, Judah, Issachar, Joseph and Benjamin. [13]And these tribes shall stand on Mount Ebal to
pronounce curses: Reuben, Gad, Asher, Zebulun, Dan and Naphtali.
[14]The Levites shall recite to all the people of Israel in a loud voice:

[15]"Cursed is the man who carves an image or casts an idol—a
thing detestable to the LORD, the work of the craftsman's
hands—and sets it up in secret."
Then all the people shall say, "Amen!"
[16]"Cursed is the man who dishonors his father or his mother."
Then all the people shall say, "Amen!"
[17]"Cursed is the man who moves his neighbor's boundary
stone."
Then all the people shall say, "Amen!"
[18]"Cursed is the man who leads the blind astray on the road."
Then all the people shall say, "Amen!"
[19]"Cursed is the man who withholds justice from the alien, the
fatherless or the widow."
Then all the people shall say, "Amen!"
[20]"Cursed is the man who sleeps with his father's wife, for he
dishonors his father's bed."
Then all the people shall say, "Amen!"
[21]"Cursed is the man who has sexual relations with any
animal."
Then all the people shall say, "Amen!"
[22]"Cursed is the man who sleeps with his sister, the daughter
of his father or the daughter of his mother."
Then all the people shall say, "Amen!"

[a]7 Traditionally *peace offerings*

the building of the altar (vv. 6–7)? **3.** Is there a principle here for us?

APPLY 1. How do you remind yourself of your relationship with God? **2.** How can this group remember you in prayer?

OPEN 1. Describe your favorite movie scene when a huge crowd all shouted something together. **2.** What comes to mind when you think of "curses"?

STUDY To drive the point home about the importance of following the laws of God, Moses and the Levites set up a huge "visual aid". They gather half the people on one side of the valley and half on the other side and recite curses and blessings, with the people responding each time. It must have been awesome! **1.** What does Moses mean when he tells the people, "You have now become the people of the LORD your God" (v. 9)? **2.** What tribes gathered on Mount Gerizim, the mount of blessings (v. 12)? What tribes gathered on Mount Ebal, the mount of curses (v. 13)? How would you have felt to be in this scene? Which mountain would you have rather been on? Why? Have you ever been part of a group that publicly committed to live holy lives? Has your group made a covenant to grow as disciples of the Lord? **3.** What did the "Amen!" at the end of each statement mean? Can you say "amen" to these curses? **4.** To what specific commandment in the Ten Commandments does each curse relate to (5:6-21)? **5.** What two specific sexual sins are dealt with in the curses (vv. 20–23)? **6.** Why did this scene start with the curses? Why not begin with the blessings? What general curse does this section end with (v. 26)? **7.** Do you think this was an exciting day for the people of Israel or a frightening day? Why?

APPLY 1. Have you ever thought of your relationship

Gerizim (vv. 12–13). The city of Shechem, roughly the center of Canaan, was between the two mountains.

27:5 an altar of stones. A primitive altar of stones that were not to be treated or cut with tools.

27:7 fellowship offerings. Also called peace offerings, these were joyful celebrations acknowledging that the people belonged to God and thanking him for all he had done.

27:15 carves an image ... casts an idol. This activity would break the first two commandments (Ex. 20). **Amen!** This is more than an approving nod of the head. The people formally declare their acceptance of the covenant, agreeing to the various curses and blessings God has set forth. "So be it!"

27:19 alien, the fatherless or the widow. Such people were defenseless and had no resources to protect themselves.

[23]"Cursed is the man who sleeps with his mother-in-law."
Then all the people shall say, "Amen!"
[24]"Cursed is the man who kills his neighbor secretly."
Then all the people shall say, "Amen!"
[25]"Cursed is the man who accepts a bribe to kill an innocent person."
Then all the people shall say, "Amen!"
[26]"Cursed is the man who does not uphold the words of this law by carrying them out."
Then all the people shall say, "Amen!"

with God being a matter of agreement with his Law? **2.** Which of these curses would give you a hard time? Why?

Blessings for Obedience

28 If you fully obey the LORD your God and carefully follow all
his commands I give you today, the LORD your God will set
you high above all the nations on earth. [2]All these blessings will come
upon you and accompany you if you obey the LORD your God:

[3]You will be blessed in the city and blessed in the country.
[4]The fruit of your womb will be blessed, and the crops of your land and the young of your livestock—the calves of your herds and the lambs of your flocks.
[5]Your basket and your kneading trough will be blessed.
[6]You will be blessed when you come in and blessed when you go out.

[7]The LORD will grant that the enemies who rise up against you will
be defeated before you. They will come at you from one direction but
flee from you in seven.
[8]The LORD will send a blessing on your barns and on everything
you put your hand to. The LORD your God will bless you in the land he
is giving you.
[9]The LORD will establish you as his holy people, as he promised you
on oath, if you keep the commands of the LORD your God and walk in
his ways. [10]Then all the peoples on earth will see that you are called
by the name of the LORD, and they will fear you. [11]The LORD will grant
you abundant prosperity—in the fruit of your womb, the young of
your livestock and the crops of your ground—in the land he swore to
your forefathers to give you.
[12]The LORD will open the heavens, the storehouse of his bounty, to
send rain on your land in season and to bless all the work of your
hands. You will lend to many nations but will borrow from none.
[13]The LORD will make you the head, not the tail. If you pay attention

OPEN If you could have all you want in life, what would it be?

STUDY Of equal importance to the Israelites as the curses for disobedience are the blessings for obedience. In this great scene at Mount Gerizim and Mount Ebal, we now hear the blessings. **1.** Upon what were the blessings contingent (vv. 1–2)? Why is the "if-clause" used so many times in this text (vv. 1-2,9,13–14)? **2.** In what six ways would Israel be blessed for following God (vv. 3–6)? How would God bring these blessings about (vv. 7–8,11–12)? Which blessing would be most important to you? Why? **3.** What does the image of enemies coming against them from one direction but scattering in seven directions mean (v. 7)? Can you tell how God has scattered your enemies? **4.** What status among the nations of the world does God promise the Israelites (vv. 9–13)? What status do you think your nation has among the nations of the world today? Why? **5.** What does it mean for God's people to be "holy"? Are you holy?

APPLY 1. What is your true motive for seeking the blessings of God? **2.** Are you living in such a way so as to receive the blessings of God in your life?

27:26 This comprehensive curse, in contrast to specific curses against idolatry, injustice and sexual immorality, fell on anyone who broke any part of the law. In Galatians 3:10 Paul uses this statement to support the idea that humanity is under a curse, since not a single human willingly or fully obeys God's Law. The Israelites are expected not only to give mental assent to the Law but to live by it completely.

28:1–14 While the terminology of the blessings parallel the terminology of the curses in verses 15–44, they are nearly exact opposites of the curses (compare vv. 3–6 with vv. 16–19 in particular).

28:5 basket . . . blessed. In other words, there will be plenty to eat.

28:10 fear you. When Israel obeys God, the nations will see that the Lord is with them and blesses them. As a result they will respect Israel with great awe.

28:12 the storehouse. Heaven is pictured as a gigantic treasury of all good things which God dispenses to the blessed. The term is used frequently to show that God controls the various types of weather in Psalm 104:3, 135:7. **You will lend.** Israel will be so prosperously blessed by God it will have more than enough. The other side of the coin is found in verse 44. If Israel does not obey God's command, the curse will apply (15:6).

28:13 the head, not the tail. Israel would be preeminent, honored among the nations. The parallel curse for this blessing is found in verse 44.

to the commands of the LORD your God that I give you this day and carefully follow them, you will always be at the top, never at the bottom. [14]Do not turn aside from any of the commands I give you today, to the right or to the left, following other gods and serving them.

Curses for Disobedience

[15]However, if you do not obey the LORD your God and do not carefully follow all his commands and decrees I am giving you today, all these curses will come upon you and overtake you:

> [16]You will be cursed in the city and cursed in the country.
> [17]Your basket and your kneading trough will be cursed.
> [18]The fruit of your womb will be cursed, and the crops of your land, and the calves of your herds and the lambs of your flocks.
> [19]You will be cursed when you come in and cursed when you go out.

[20]The LORD will send on you curses, confusion and rebuke in everything you put your hand to, until you are destroyed and come to sudden ruin because of the evil you have done in forsaking him.[a]
[21]The LORD will plague you with diseases until he has destroyed you from the land you are entering to possess. [22]The LORD will strike you with wasting disease, with fever and inflammation, with scorching heat and drought, with blight and mildew, which will plague you until you perish. [23]The sky over your head will be bronze, the ground beneath you iron. [24]The LORD will turn the rain of your country into dust and powder; it will come down from the skies until you are destroyed.
[25]The LORD will cause you to be defeated before your enemies. You will come at them from one direction but flee from them in seven, and you will become a thing of horror to all the kingdoms on earth. [26]Your carcasses will be food for all the birds of the air and the beasts of the earth, and there will be no one to frighten them away. [27]The LORD will afflict you with the boils of Egypt and with tumors, festering sores and the itch, from which you cannot be cured. [28]The LORD will afflict you with madness, blindness and confusion of mind. [29]At midday you will grope about like a blind man in the dark. You will be unsuccessful in everything you do; day after day you will be oppressed and robbed, with no one to rescue you.
[30]You will be pledged to be married to a woman, but another will take her and ravish her. You will build a house, but you will not live in it. You will plant a vineyard, but you will not even begin to enjoy its fruit. [31]Your ox will be slaughtered before your eyes, but you will eat none of it. Your donkey will be forcibly taken from you and will not be returned. Your sheep will be given to your enemies, and no one will rescue them. [32]Your sons and daughters will be given to another nation, and you will wear out your eyes watching for them day after day, powerless to lift a hand. [33]A people that you do not know will eat what your land and labor produce, and you will have nothing but

[a]20 Hebrew *me*

OPEN 1. Can you tell of a time when someone said to you, "If you don't do exactly as I say, you're going to get it!"? How did it make you feel? **2.** Can you remember a time when you did something wrong and had to pay an awful price? Explain.

STUDY Moses and the Levites issue one of the darkest pictures of being cursed imaginable to emphasize the importance of obedience. The description of the consequences of disobedience is all-inclusive—all of life will be effected if they do not obey. **1.** In what six ways, corresponding to the six blessings (vv. 3–6), will the Israelites be cursed for not obeying God (vv. 16–19)? Paraphrase these six curses in modern terms. **2.** What is the nature of the curses in verses 20–35? What is the scope? Which curse would be the worst to you? Why? **3.** How did Moses know the future (vv. 36,41,49-50)? Did these things come to pass? If so, why did they come to pass? **4.** What, or who, would be the instrument of God's wrath in bringing the curses on the disobedient (vv. 49–57)? **5.** What do you find most repulsive in the descriptions of what would happen when the enemy laid siege to the cities of Israel (vv. 53–57)? Why? Do you think people can actually be so barbaric? Can you give a modern example of such barbarism? **6.** What meaning does this chapter give to the "glorious and awesome name" of the Lord God (v. 58)? How can a God of mercy threaten such things? Do you think the things described here are just natural disasters and consequences, or are they the work of the Lord? Why do you think that? **7.** What do you think is God's purpose with these threats of punishment? Do these threats show his anger or his love?

APPLY 1. Do you see God as one who wants to scare you or as one who wants to spare you? What's the difference? **2.** Do these verses build your confidence and trust

28:15 if you do not obey. Israel must obey God in order to receive the wonderful blessings he promises. Otherwise, he will be forced to punish their disobedience.

28:26 Your carcasses will be food. An especially disgusting end to the Israelites. Not being properly buried showed extreme disrespect for the deceased.

in God or cause you to doubt his love for you? Why? **3.** How can this group encourage each other to be obedient to the will of God?

---

cruel oppression all your days. 34The sights you see will drive you
mad. 35The LORD will afflict your knees and legs with painful boils
that cannot be cured, spreading from the soles of your feet to the top
of your head.
36The LORD will drive you and the king you set over you to a nation
unknown to you or your fathers. There you will worship other gods,
gods of wood and stone. 37You will become a thing of horror and an
object of scorn and ridicule to all the nations where the LORD will
drive you.
38You will sow much seed in the field but you will harvest little, because locusts will devour it. 39You will plant vineyards and cultivate
them but you will not drink the wine or gather the grapes, because
worms will eat them. 40You will have olive trees throughout your
country but you will not use the oil, because the olives will drop off.
41You will have sons and daughters but you will not keep them,
because they will go into captivity. 42Swarms of locusts will take over
all your trees and the crops of your land.
43The alien who lives among you will rise above you higher and
higher, but you will sink lower and lower. 44He will lend to you, but
you will not lend to him. He will be the head, but you will be the tail.
45All these curses will come upon you. They will pursue you and
overtake you until you are destroyed, because you did not obey the
LORD your God and observe the commands and decrees he gave you.
46They will be a sign and a wonder to you and your descendants forever. 47Because you did not serve the LORD your God joyfully and
gladly in the time of prosperity, 48therefore in hunger and thirst, in
nakedness and dire poverty, you will serve the enemies the LORD
sends against you. He will put an iron yoke on your neck until he has
destroyed you.
49The LORD will bring a nation against you from far away, from the
ends of the earth, like an eagle swooping down, a nation whose language you will not understand, 50a fierce-looking nation without respect for the old or pity for the young. 51They will devour the young of
your livestock and the crops of your land until you are destroyed.
They will leave you no grain, new wine or oil, nor any calves of your
herds or lambs of your flocks until you are ruined. 52They will lay
siege to all the cities throughout your land until the high fortified
walls in which you trust fall down. They will besiege all the cities
throughout the land the LORD your God is giving you.
53Because of the suffering that your enemy will inflict on you during the siege, you will eat the fruit of the womb, the flesh of the sons
and daughters the LORD your God has given you. 54Even the most

---

28:35 painful boils. This plague also infested the Egyptians in (Ex. 9:11), causing the magicians' legs to be useless.

28:37–43. The curses for disobedience are mirror opposites of the blessings God had promised for obedience.

28:47 serve ... joyfully and gladly. God expects his people to respond positively and naturally to his gracious provision. If they ignore him or disobey him, his wrath must fall.

28:49 ends of the earth. This is a poetic way of saying "very far away." **eagle swooping down.** This word picture is applied to the foreign nations of Assyria and Babylonia, who attacked swiftly and powerfully (Jer. 48:40; 49:22).

28:53 suffering ... during the siege. This phrase is repeated in verses 55 and 57, emphasizing the utter chaos and pain the Israelites would experience as a consequence of their disobedience to God. **you will eat ... sons and daughters.** The intensity of despair the Israelites faced would lead them to cannibalism, an unthinkable crime. But see how this curse turned out in 2 Kings 6:24–29 and Lamentations 2:20; 4:10.

gentle and sensitive man among you will have no compassion on his
own brother or the wife he loves or his surviving children, 55and he
will not give to one of them any of the flesh of his children that he is
eating. It will be all he has left because of the suffering your enemy
will inflict on you during the siege of all your cities. 56The most gentle
and sensitive woman among you—so sensitive and gentle that she
would not venture to touch the ground with the sole of her foot—will
begrudge the husband she loves and her own son or daughter 57the
afterbirth from her womb and the children she bears. For she intends
to eat them secretly during the siege and in the distress that your
enemy will inflict on you in your cities.

58If you do not carefully follow all the words of this law, which are
written in this book, and do not revere this glorious and awesome
name—the LORD your God— 59the LORD will send fearful plagues on
you and your descendants, harsh and prolonged disasters, and severe and lingering illnesses. 60He will bring upon you all the diseases
of Egypt that you dreaded, and they will cling to you. 61The LORD will
also bring on you every kind of sickness and disaster not recorded in
this Book of the Law, until you are destroyed. 62You who were as
numerous as the stars in the sky will be left but few in number,
because you did not obey the LORD your God. 63Just as it pleased the
LORD to make you prosper and increase in number, so it will please
him to ruin and destroy you. You will be uprooted from the land you
are entering to possess.

64Then the LORD will scatter you among all nations, from one end
of the earth to the other. There you will worship other gods—gods of
wood and stone, which neither you nor your fathers have known.
65Among those nations you will find no repose, no resting place for
the sole of your foot. There the LORD will give you an anxious mind,
eyes weary with longing, and a despairing heart. 66You will live in
constant suspense, filled with dread both night and day, never sure of
your life. 67In the morning you will say, "If only it were evening!" and
in the evening, "If only it were morning!"—because of the terror that
will fill your hearts and the sights that your eyes will see. 68The LORD
will send you back in ships to Egypt on a journey I said you should
never make again. There you will offer yourselves for sale to your
enemies as male and female slaves, but no one will buy you.

Renewal of the Covenant

29 These are the terms of the covenant the LORD commanded
Moses to make with the Israelites in Moab, in addition to the
covenant he had made with them at Horeb.

2Moses summoned all the Israelites and said to them:

Your eyes have seen all that the LORD did in Egypt to Pharaoh, to all
his officials and to all his land. 3With your own eyes you saw those

OPEN 1. Have you ever made a deal with someone and they didn't keep it? What was it and how did you feel when they broke it? **2.** What are your fondest memories of "the good ole days"?

STUDY Moses had made the terms of the covenant very

28:58 words of this law. This refers to the book of Deuteronomy itself.

28:59–68. Another summary of the curses for disobedience, including opposites to the blessings of verses 1–14 and plagues from which God protected them in Egypt.

29:1 These are the terms of the covenant. In the Hebrew this can be read either as a concluding comment to the previous chapters or as a preamble to the following chapters 29–32.

29:2 Your eyes have seen. Rather than specifically referring to the people alive at that point, Moses addresses the people as a national entity with a national experience. Not all the Israelites at this point would have witnessed the miracles of God in Egypt. In fact, only those younger than twenty when Israel elected not to enter Canaan at Kadesh Barnea (Num. 14:29) would have lived in Egypt.

clear to the Israelites, and now he calls them to remember the past and commit themselves to faithfulness for the future. He also makes sure they understand how terrible it would be for them to break their covenant with God. **1.** Why does Moses keep reminding the people of the past (vv. 2–8)? What had the Israelites not yet understood (v. 4)? Do you think people tend to learn from the past or to forget the past? Give some examples for your answer. **2.** What would be the result if they carefully followed this covenant (v. 9)? **3.** Who was present at this covenant ceremony (v. 11)? What were the basic agreements of the covenant (vv. 12–13)? How serious do you consider a covenant to be? **4.** Why would Moses refer to idolatry as "bitter poison" (v. 18)? How could the Israelites ever forget what God had done for them in the exodus and turn to idols? Why do you think people turn from God today? **5.** What attitude is being addressed in verse 19? What is the result of such an attitude? How far-reaching are the effects of that attitude (v. 22)? What will be the answer to future generations when they ask what caused the devastation to the land (vv. 24–28)? How do you think that is seen today? **6.** What are the "secret things" that belong only to God (v. 29)? What are the revealed things? What are we to do with the revealed things?

APPLY 1. Do you find it necessary to have everything explained before you obey God, or can you just take him at his word? **2.** Have you made promises to God in the past? If not, do you plan to make commitments to him in the future? Explain.

great trials, those miraculous signs and great wonders. 4But to this
day the LORD has not given you a mind that understands or eyes that
see or ears that hear. 5During the forty years that I led you through
the desert, your clothes did not wear out, nor did the sandals on your
feet. 6You ate no bread and drank no wine or other fermented drink. I
did this so that you might know that I am the LORD your God.

7When you reached this place, Sihon king of Heshbon and Og king
of Bashan came out to fight against us, but we defeated them. 8We
took their land and gave it as an inheritance to the Reubenites, the
Gadites and the half-tribe of Manasseh.

9Carefully follow the terms of this covenant, so that you may prosper in everything you do. 10All of you are standing today in the
presence of the LORD your God—your leaders and chief men, your
elders and officials, and all the other men of Israel, 11together with
your children and your wives, and the aliens living in your camps
who chop your wood and carry your water. 12You are standing here in
order to enter into a covenant with the LORD your God, a covenant
the LORD is making with you this day and sealing with an oath, 13to
confirm you this day as his people, that he may be your God as he
promised you and as he swore to your fathers, Abraham, Isaac and
Jacob. 14I am making this covenant, with its oath, not only with you
15who are standing here with us today in the presence of the LORD
our God but also with those who are not here today.

16You yourselves know how we lived in Egypt and how we passed
through the countries on the way here. 17You saw among them their
detestable images and idols of wood and stone, of silver and gold.
18Make sure there is no man or woman, clan or tribe among you
today whose heart turns away from the LORD our God to go and worship the gods of those nations; make sure there is no root among you
that produces such bitter poison.

19When such a person hears the words of this oath, he invokes a
blessing on himself and therefore thinks, "I will be safe, even though
I persist in going my own way." This will bring disaster on the watered land as well as the dry.[a] 20The LORD will never be willing to forgive him; his wrath and zeal will burn against that man. All the curses
written in this book will fall upon him, and the LORD will blot out his
name from under heaven. 21The LORD will single him out from all the
tribes of Israel for disaster, according to all the curses of the covenant
written in this Book of the Law.

22Your children who follow you in later generations and foreigners
who come from distant lands will see the calamities that have fallen
on the land and the diseases with which the LORD has afflicted it.

[a]19 Or way, in order to add drunkenness to thirst."

29:4 This verse is used by Paul in describing a stubborn, hardened Israel (Rom. 11:8).

29:13 confirm you . . . as his people. The whole purpose of the covenant *was to legally bind God and his people* together.

29:18 bitter poison. Idolatry—rejecting God to pursue other idols—is a poisonous weed whose roots can grow deep and strong and affect others if not removed and destroyed completely.

29:19 blessing on himself. For one who merely pays lip service to God while doing his own thing, the only blessing to be received is the blessing he gives himself. God desires heartfelt obedience, and his true blessing will follow.

29:20 never ... forgive him. This punishment is like that of "blasphemy against the Holy Spirit" (Matt. 12:3).

29:22 calamities. The people of God will suffer many hard times, plagues, diseases, disasters, warring neighbors and eventually defeat due to their stubbornness and pride. Many generations later the Israelites will still be reaping the consequences.

23The whole land will be a burning waste of salt and sulfur—nothing
planted, nothing sprouting, no vegetation growing on it. It will be like
the destruction of Sodom and Gomorrah, Admah and Zeboiim, which
the LORD overthrew in fierce anger. 24All the nations will ask: "Why
has the LORD done this to this land? Why this fierce, burning anger?"
25And the answer will be: "It is because this people abandoned the
covenant of the LORD, the God of their fathers, the covenant he made
with them when he brought them out of Egypt. 26They went off and
worshiped other gods and bowed down to them, gods they did not
know, gods he had not given them. 27Therefore the LORD's anger
burned against this land, so that he brought on it all the curses
written in this book. 28In furious anger and in great wrath the LORD
uprooted them from their land and thrust them into another land, as
it is now."
29The secret things belong to the LORD our God, but the things revealed belong to us and to our children forever, that we may follow all
the words of this law.

Prosperity After Turning to the LORD

30 When all these blessings and curses I have set before you
come upon you and you take them to heart wherever the
LORD your God disperses you among the nations, 2and when you and
your children return to the LORD your God and obey him with all your
heart and with all your soul according to everything I command you
today, 3then the LORD your God will restore your fortunes[a] and have
compassion on you and gather you again from all the nations where
he scattered you. 4Even if you have been banished to the most distant
land under the heavens, from there the LORD your God will gather you
and bring you back. 5He will bring you to the land that belonged to
your fathers, and you will take possession of it. He will make you
more prosperous and numerous than your fathers. 6The LORD your
God will circumcise your hearts and the hearts of your descendants,
so that you may love him with all your heart and with all your soul,
and live. 7The LORD your God will put all these curses on your enemies who hate and persecute you. 8You will again obey the LORD and
follow all his commands I am giving you today. 9Then the LORD your
God will make you most prosperous in all the work of your hands and
in the fruit of your womb, the young of your livestock and the crops
of your land. The LORD will again delight in you and make you prosperous, just as he delighted in your fathers, 10if you obey the LORD
your God and keep his commands and decrees that are written in this

[a]3 Or *will bring you back from captivity*

OPEN 1. Have you traveled outside your native country? What was your favorite place? Your least favorite? **2.** Would you rather be home?

STUDY God knew there would come a time when his people would desert him and be scattered among other nations. His promise is, however, that if they will just obey him with all their hearts, he will restore them to his favor. **1.** How would it be possible for them to live with the consequences of both the blessings and the curses? **2.** What factors are implied in the phrase "return to the LORD" (vv. 2,4,6,8,10)? If you are away from the Lord, what would it take for you to return to the Lord? **3.** What is God's part in this "return" (v. 3)? The people's part? **4.** How would God prosper the people if they would return to him (v. 9)? How does he prosper people today who return to him?

APPLY 1. How would you describe your faithfulness to God? **2.** Has God changed your heart?

30:1–10 God gave Moses a glimpse of *the future when the blessings and curses* of chapter 28 come upon the nation. This included Israel's gross disobedience, resulting in their being scattered among the nations. Moses not only saw Israel's captivity, but he also saw the promise of their return to the land by God's grace (see book of Ezra).

30:3 restore your fortunes. This could also be translated "bring you back from captivity." God promises to restore the wayward nation if it would only return and obey him fully.

30:6 circumcise your hearts. Circumcision was the sign of God's covenant with Abraham, making Abraham's descendants part of God's covenant people (Gen. 17:20). But circumcision of the body was not the main prerequisite—God desired love and obedience from his people. God wanted his people to have hearts that were committed to him (Jer. 4:4). The Apostle Paul wrote about the concept of a circumcised heart (Rom. 2:25–29; Gal. 5:6–11; 6:15; Phil. 3:3; Col. 2:11).

30:7 curses on your enemies. This would fulfill God's covenant promise to Abraham in Genesis 12:3.

30:10 Book of the Law. Another reference to the book of Deuteronomy itself.

Do you need to return to him? How can this group encourage you?

OPEN 1. What is the best deal you have ever been offered? **2.** Have you ever made a choice that literally saved your life? What was it? What happened?

STUDY After a long, detailed, and sometimes repetitive sermon, the Israelites are called to make their choice—life or death, blessings or curses. God wants them to choose life. **1.** Why would the Israelites tend to think the commands of God were out of reach (vv. 11–14)? Where did God say they could find his word? Do you think God's word is too difficult or too lofty for you to reach? **2.** What clear-cut choice is placed before the Israelites (vv. 15–18)? Which would you choose? **3.** Who does God call as his witness to his promises (v. 19)?

APPLY 1. What do you learn about the heart and desire of God for his people in this reading? What do you think he wants for you? **2.** How can you love God, listen to his voice and hold fast to him?

OPEN If you could choose anyone in all of history to be the leader of your nation, who would it be?

STUDY By this time Moses was 120 years old, and it was time to pass the mantle of leadership on to someone else. As he prepares to do so, he encourages the people to follow their new leader, but especially to trust God for the victories ahead. **1.** Why would God not allow Moses to cross over into the Promised Land (3:25–28; 4:21–22; Num. 20:12)? **2.** Who would be the new leader of

Book of the Law and turn to the LORD your God with all your heart
and with all your soul.

The Offer of Life or Death

11 Now what I am commanding you today is not too difficult for you
or beyond your reach. 12 It is not up in heaven, so that you have to
ask, "Who will ascend into heaven to get it and proclaim it to us so we
may obey it?" 13 Nor is it beyond the sea, so that you have to ask,
"Who will cross the sea to get it and proclaim it to us so we may obey
it?" 14 No, the word is very near you; it is in your mouth and in your
heart so you may obey it.

15 See, I set before you today life and prosperity, death and destruction. 16 For I command you today to love the LORD your God, to walk
in his ways, and to keep his commands, decrees and laws; then you
will live and increase, and the LORD your God will bless you in the
land you are entering to possess.

17 But if your heart turns away and you are not obedient, and if you
are drawn away to bow down to other gods and worship them, 18 I declare to you this day that you will certainly be destroyed. You will not
live long in the land you are crossing the Jordan to enter and possess.

19 This day I call heaven and earth as witnesses against you that I
have set before you life and death, blessings and curses. Now choose
life, so that you and your children may live 20 and that you may love
the LORD your God, listen to his voice, and hold fast to him. For the
LORD is your life, and he will give you many years in the land he swore
to give to your fathers, Abraham, Isaac and Jacob.

Joshua to Succeed Moses

31 Then Moses went out and spoke these words to all Israel: 2 "I
am now a hundred and twenty years old and I am no longer
able to lead you. The LORD has said to me, 'You shall not cross the Jordan.' 3 The LORD your God himself will cross over ahead of you. He
will destroy these nations before you, and you will take possession of
their land. Joshua also will cross over ahead of you, as the LORD said.
4 And the LORD will do to them what he did to Sihon and Og, the kings
of the Amorites, whom he destroyed along with their land. 5 The LORD
will deliver them to you, and you must do to them all that I have commanded you. 6 Be strong and courageous. Do not be afraid or terrified
because of them, for the LORD your God goes with you; he will never
leave you nor forsake you."

30:12 not up in heaven. God's word is within everyone's grasp. All are able to hear it, comprehend it, believe it and obey it. While certainly a challenge, fulfilling the covenant was not beyond anyone's ability. Paul used this passage to describe the "word of faith" available to all (Rom. 10:6–10).

30:15 I set before you today. *Moses clearly sets forth the choice the* people must make: obedience, which brings life, prosperity and blessings; or disobedience, which brings death, destruction and curses.

30:20 hold fast. This is the same idea found in a man cleaving to his wife (Gen. 2:24) and in Ruth's close companionship to Naomi ("clung," Ruth 1:14). **the LORD is your life.** Life here means more than mere existence. It is everything rich, real, fulfilling and meaningful. By choosing the one true God, the Israelites have chosen life (v. 19). The Law itself is also described as their "life" (32:46–47). God's Law and *life are woven together*—all part of a life that is full of substance and joy.

31:2 You shall not cross the Jordan. God wouldn't allow Moses into the Promised Land because of his sin (Num. 20:2–13).

31:4 what he did to Sihon and Og. God defeated these kings and their armies (2:26–3:22).

31:6 Be strong and courageous. No matter what the people faced, God would take care of them—provided they were faithful and obedient to him. **he will never leave you nor forsake you.** No matter where his people lived, God would be with them—unlike the localized pagan deities.

7Then Moses summoned Joshua and said to him in the presence
of all Israel, "Be strong and courageous, for you must go with this
people into the land that the LORD swore to their forefathers to give
them, and you must divide it among them as their inheritance. 8The
LORD himself goes before you and will be with you; he will never leave
you nor forsake you. Do not be afraid; do not be discouraged."

The Reading of the Law

9So Moses wrote down this law and gave it to the priests, the sons
of Levi, who carried the ark of the covenant of the LORD, and to all the
elders of Israel. 10Then Moses commanded them: "At the end of every
seven years, in the year for canceling debts, during the Feast of Tabernacles, 11when all Israel comes to appear before the LORD your God at
the place he will choose, you shall read this law before them in their
hearing. 12Assemble the people—men, women and children, and the
aliens living in your towns—so they can listen and learn to fear the
LORD your God and follow carefully all the words of this law. 13Their
children, who do not know this law, must hear it and learn to fear the
LORD your God as long as you live in the land you are crossing the
Jordan to possess."

Israel's Rebellion Predicted

14The LORD said to Moses, "Now the day of your death is near. Call
Joshua and present yourselves at the Tent of Meeting, where I will
commission him." So Moses and Joshua came and presented themselves at the Tent of Meeting.
15Then the LORD appeared at the Tent in a pillar of cloud, and the
cloud stood over the entrance to the Tent. 16And the LORD said to
Moses: "You are going to rest with your fathers, and these people will
soon prostitute themselves to the foreign gods of the land they are
entering. They will forsake me and break the covenant I made with
them. 17On that day I will become angry with them and forsake them;
I will hide my face from them, and they will be destroyed. Many disasters and difficulties will come upon them, and on that day they will
ask, 'Have not these disasters come upon us because our God is not
with us?' 18And I will certainly hide my face on that day because of all
their wickedness in turning to other gods.
19"Now write down for yourselves this song and teach it to the Israelites and have them sing it, so that it may be a witness for me against
them. 20When I have brought them into the land flowing with milk
and honey, the land I promised on oath to their forefathers, and when
they eat their fill and thrive, they will turn to other gods and worship

Israel (vv. 3, 7)? Who would provide the strength to conquer the land (vv. 3–6,8)? Do you think the people really trusted the Lord at this point? Why or why not? Would you have been afraid? Explain. **3.** What task is assigned to Joshua (v. 7)? Do you think you would have wanted to be the leader of these people? **4.** What did Moses do with the Law (v. 9)? What instructions were given regarding the reading of the Law (vv. 10–12)? Why was this reading critical (v. 13)?

APPLY What do you need to conquer in your life that will require the strength of God? Do you trust him for the strength?

OPEN If you were rebellious at sometime in your life, what brought you out of it?

STUDY It is now near the end of Moses' life and time for final instructions from God, so he summons Moses and Joshua to the "Tent of Meeting." The news is not good. Moses will die, Joshua will lead the people to conquer the Promised Land, but then the Israelites will do the very thing Moses has warned them against—they will forsake God. **1.** Why did God ask Joshua to come along with Moses to the Tent of Meeting (v. 14)? What was the purpose for the Tent of Meeting (Ex. 33:7–11)? Have you ever thought of what it would be like to have a meeting with God? Explain. **2.** What news did God have for Moses (v. 16)? How would you have felt if you were Moses? Explain. **3.** What word of encouragement did God give to Joshua (v. 23)? **4.** What did God say he would do in response to the rebellion of his

---

31:7 Joshua. Moses officially conferred upon Joshua his authority, *encouraging the new leader to trust God.*

31:9 wrote ... this law and gave ... priests. Any ancient covenant was transcribed, with a copy kept in the temple. In Israel's case, the Law was kept in the Holy of Holies beside the Ark of the Covenant (Ex. 16:34; 31:18).

31:11 read this law. The priests are instructed to read the Law publicly and teach the people.

31:12 men, women and children, and the aliens. The Word of God is for all to hear, learn and obey, regardless of age, sex or race.

31:15 pillar of cloud. Throughout the exodus this symbolized God's presence with his people (Ex. 13:21–22).

31:18 turning to other gods. God time and again warned Israel that their continual idolatry would bring judgment.

31:19 write down ... teach it. Moses obeys this command in verse 22. The song itself is recorded in 31:30–32:43. The act reveals a bit of God's creativity as well as his desire that his people know and remember his mighty acts on their behalf. What better way to do that than through a song!

them, rejecting me and breaking my covenant. 21And when many disasters and difficulties come upon them, this song will testify against
them, because it will not be forgotten by their descendants. I know
what they are disposed to do, even before I bring them into the land I
promised them on oath." 22So Moses wrote down this song that day
and taught it to the Israelites.
23The LORD gave this command to Joshua son of Nun: "Be strong
and courageous, for you will bring the Israelites into the land I promised them on oath, and I myself will be with you."
24After Moses finished writing in a book the words of this law from
beginning to end, 25he gave this command to the Levites who carried
the ark of the covenant of the LORD: 26"Take this Book of the Law and
place it beside the ark of the covenant of the LORD your God. There it
will remain as a witness against you. 27For I know how rebellious and
stiff-necked you are. If you have been rebellious against the LORD
while I am still alive and with you, how much more will you rebel after I die! 28Assemble before me all the elders of your tribes and all
your officials, so that I can speak these words in their hearing and
call heaven and earth to testify against them. 29For I know that after
my death you are sure to become utterly corrupt and to turn from the
way I have commanded you. In days to come, disaster will fall upon
you because you will do evil in the sight of the LORD and provoke him
to anger by what your hands have made."

The Song of Moses

30And Moses recited the words of this song from beginning to end
in the hearing of the whole assembly of Israel:

32 Listen, O heavens, and I will speak;
hear, O earth, the words of my mouth.
2Let my teaching fall like rain
and my words descend like dew,
like showers on new grass,
like abundant rain on tender plants.

3I will proclaim the name of the LORD.
Oh, praise the greatness of our God!
4He is the Rock, his works are perfect,
and all his ways are just.
A faithful God who does no wrong,
upright and just is he.

5They have acted corruptly toward him;
to their shame they are no longer his children,
but a warped and crooked generation.[a]

[a]5 Or *Corrupt are they and not his children, / a generation warped and twisted to their shame*

people (vv. 17–18)? How does this relate to all the previous messages about blessings and curses? How did God want Moses to communicate this message (v. 19)? Do you think this song would be "number one" on the charts? **5.** What would be a witness against the actions of the Israelites (v. 26)? What would be the verdict if the law witnessed against you? **6.** When Moses talked about the rebellion of the people, was he prophesying or remembering the past, or both (v. 27)?

APPLY 1. If God revealed your future, what do you think he would say? **2.** Has God taught you some hard lessons? Has he brought you back to him?

OPEN 1. What is your favorite ballad? What story does it tell? **2.** If you could write a song about the history of your nation, what would you entitle it?

STUDY God had Moses write all the laws in a book and place it in the Ark of the Covenant for future generations to remind them of their covenant with God. He also had him write a song that would be sung to the people as a witness against them for their evil ways. The song rehearses the past and calls the Israelites into account for their idolatry. Read the song and imagine you are an Israelite listening to the song. **1.** Is the tone of this song: Moralistic? Theological? Poetic? Praise? Reactionary? Doom and gloom? Other? Explain your answer. **2.** What praises of God are expressed at the beginning of this song? Why do you think the song begins with praise of God? **3.** What does it mean to call God "The Rock"

31:24 from beginning to end. This is a reference to the book of Deuteronomy itself, in obedience to verse 9.

31:26 place it beside the ark. As noted in verse 9, it was standard practice to keep a copy of a covenant in a nation's holiest place.

31:29 For I know. It is unclear whether God specifically revealed Israel's dark future or Moses simply came to this conclusion based on *his own* history with the stubborn nation.

32:1 Listen, O heavens. This is a common way to introduce a song (Isa. 1:2; 34:1; Mic. 1:2; 6:1–2). This song is so important that heaven and earth must hear it.

32:4 He is the Rock. This concept is repeated throughout the song (vv. 15,18,30–31). Since a rock symbolizes strength and stability, it speaks of God's protection and power.

[6]Is this the way you repay the LORD,
O foolish and unwise people?
Is he not your Father, your Creator,[a]
who made you and formed you?

[7]Remember the days of old;
consider the generations long past.
Ask your father and he will tell you,
your elders, and they will explain to you.
[8]When the Most High gave the nations their inheritance,
when he divided all mankind,
he set up boundaries for the peoples
according to the number of the sons of Israel.[b]
[9]For the LORD's portion is his people,
Jacob his allotted inheritance.

[10]In a desert land he found him,
in a barren and howling waste.
He shielded him and cared for him;
he guarded him as the apple of his eye,
[11]like an eagle that stirs up its nest
and hovers over its young,
that spreads its wings to catch them
and carries them on its pinions.
[12]The LORD alone led him;
no foreign god was with him.

[13]He made him ride on the heights of the land
and fed him with the fruit of the fields.
He nourished him with honey from the rock,
and with oil from the flinty crag,
[14]with curds and milk from herd and flock
and with fattened lambs and goats,
with choice rams of Bashan
and the finest kernels of wheat.
You drank the foaming blood of the grape.

[15]Jeshurun[c] grew fat and kicked;
filled with food, he became heavy and sleek.
He abandoned the God who made him
and rejected the Rock his Savior.
[16]They made him jealous with their foreign gods
and angered him with their detestable idols.

[a]6 Or *Father, who bought you* [b]8 Masoretic Text; Dead Sea Scrolls (see also Septuagint) *sons of God*
[c]15 *Jeshurun* means *the upright one*, that is, Israel.

(vv. 4,15,18,30–31)? Do you consider a covenant with God to be a solid foundation for your life? **4.** What question is being addressed when the song says God is "a faithful God who does no wrong" (v. 4)? How would you define the sovereignty of God? **5.** How does the song say the people responded to God's faithfulness (v. 5)? Why is their response so unbelievable (v. 6)? Do you think the Israelites understood the consequences of their rebellion? **6.** What kind of parent is God (vv. 10–14,18)? In contrast, what kind of child is Israel (vv. 15–18)? **7.** What was the extent of Israel's rebellion? What was God's response (vv. 19–25)? What kept God from wiping them out altogether (vv. 26–27)? What do you learn about God from this? **8.** What does God think about Israel (vv. 28–29)? About Israel's enemies (vv. 30–33)? Do you think God was fair in his conclusions? Explain. **9.** What is the sarcasm of verses 37–38? What is the point? What gods do you think people trust that are powerless to help in time of need? **10.** What promise is there for Israel in verses 39–43? **11.** What do you think would be the overall reaction of the Israelites in the future when they heard this song? How would you react? Explain.

APPLY 1. Is this your song? In what sense? **2.** If you have left God for other "gods," what, or who are the gods? Do you think God wants you back with him? What will it take for you to return? How can this group help?

32:6 Father. God's role as a loving father is rarely mentioned in the Old Testament. The prophets used this title for God (Isa. 9:6; 63:16; Jer. 3:4; Mal. 2:10). Jesus described God as a Father (John 6:27), as did Paul (Rom. 1:7; 1 Cor. 8:6; 15:24; Gal. 1:1; Eph. 5:20; 6:23; Phil. 2:11; Col. 1:3; 3:17), Peter (1 Peter 1:2; 2 Peter 1:17) and John (2 John 3).

32:7 Remember. Specifically they are to remember how God miraculously redeemed them out of Egyptian bondage.

32:8 Most High. This title for God is unique to Deuteronomy. Borrowed apparently from the Canaanites, it speaks of God's sovereign power over all the earth.

32:14 Bashan. A verdant area east of the Sea of Galilee that was famous for its cattle and oak trees (Ezek. 39:18).

32:15 Jeshurun. An ironic reference to Israel as the "upright one" (Isa. 44:2). **Savior.** Jeshurun rejects the one who can save him.

17 They sacrificed to demons, which are not God—
gods they had not known,
gods that recently appeared,
gods your fathers did not fear.
18 You deserted the Rock, who fathered you;
you forgot the God who gave you birth.

19 The LORD saw this and rejected them
because he was angered by his sons and daughters.
20 "I will hide my face from them," he said,
"and see what their end will be;
for they are a perverse generation,
children who are unfaithful.
21 They made me jealous by what is no god
and angered me with their worthless idols.
I will make them envious by those who are not a people;
I will make them angry by a nation that has no
understanding.
22 For a fire has been kindled by my wrath,
one that burns to the realm of death[a] below.
It will devour the earth and its harvests
and set afire the foundations of the mountains.

23 "I will heap calamities upon them
and spend my arrows against them.
24 I will send wasting famine against them,
consuming pestilence and deadly plague;
I will send against them the fangs of wild beasts,
the venom of vipers that glide in the dust.
25 In the street the sword will make them childless;
in their homes terror will reign.
Young men and young women will perish,
infants and gray-haired men.
26 I said I would scatter them
and blot out their memory from mankind,
27 but I dreaded the taunt of the enemy,
lest the adversary misunderstand
and say, 'Our hand has triumphed;
the LORD has not done all this.' "

28 They are a nation without sense,
there is no discernment in them.
29 If only they were wise and would understand this
and discern what their end will be!
30 How could one man chase a thousand,

[a]22 Hebrew *to Sheol*

32:17 demons. The fact that pagan gods were actually demonic powers is *not often* acknowledged in the Old Testament, but see Psalm 106:37 *and* Amos 2:1.

32:18 fathered you. The Hebrew for "fathered" means "give birth," a thought echoed in the verse. God is pictured as a caring, loving, life-giving parent.

32:21 Paul uses part of this verse in Romans 10:19 to describe Israel's rejection of Jesus the Messiah.

32:22 realm of death. Sheol, the place of departed souls.

32:30 their Rock. A description of "the LORD," the God of Israel. He will protect his people so completely that only by his permission will enemies ever defeat them.

or two put ten thousand to flight,
unless their Rock had sold them,
unless the LORD had given them up?
31 For their rock is not like our Rock,
as even our enemies concede.
32 Their vine comes from the vine of Sodom
and from the fields of Gomorrah.
Their grapes are filled with poison,
and their clusters with bitterness.
33 Their wine is the venom of serpents,
the deadly poison of cobras.

34 "Have I not kept this in reserve
and sealed it in my vaults?
35 It is mine to avenge; I will repay.
In due time their foot will slip;
their day of disaster is near
and their doom rushes upon them."

36 The LORD will judge his people
and have compassion on his servants
when he sees their strength is gone
and no one is left, slave or free.
37 He will say: "Now where are their gods,
the rock they took refuge in,
38 the gods who ate the fat of their sacrifices
and drank the wine of their drink offerings?
Let them rise up to help you!
Let them give you shelter!

39 "See now that I myself am He!
There is no god besides me.
I put to death and I bring to life,
I have wounded and I will heal,
and no one can deliver out of my hand.
40 I lift my hand to heaven and declare:
As surely as I live forever,
41 when I sharpen my flashing sword
and my hand grasps it in judgment,
I will take vengeance on my adversaries
and repay those who hate me.
42 I will make my arrows drunk with blood,
while my sword devours flesh:
the blood of the slain and the captives,
the heads of the enemy leaders."

32:31 their rock. The stability of the Lord is contrasted with "the rock" the pagans must rely upon.

32:34 sealed it in my vaults. God fully intends to make good on his promise to punish sin. His sovereign will for the future has been established and will surely unfold.

32:35–36 The writer of Hebrews uses part of these verses to warn readers about ignoring the claims of Christ (Heb. 10:30).

32:35 I will repay. God alone has the right to punish evildoers. Paul makes that point by using this phrase in Romans 12:19.

32:40 I lift my hand to heaven. God is, in effect, making an oath to himself. He would protect his people and take vengeance on their behalf.

43 Rejoice, O nations, with his people,[a,b]
for he will avenge the blood of his servants;
he will take vengeance on his enemies
and make atonement for his land and people.

44 Moses came with Joshua[c] son of Nun and spoke all the words of
this song in the hearing of the people. 45 When Moses finished reciting all these words to all Israel, 46 he said to them, "Take to heart all
the words I have solemnly declared to you this day, so that you may
command your children to obey carefully all the words of this law.
47 They are not just idle words for you—they are your life. By them you
will live long in the land you are crossing the Jordan to possess."

Moses to Die on Mount Nebo

48 On that same day the LORD told Moses, 49 "Go up into the Abarim
Range to Mount Nebo in Moab, across from Jericho, and view Canaan, the land I am giving the Israelites as their own possession.
50 There on the mountain that you have climbed you will die and be
gathered to your people, just as your brother Aaron died on Mount
Hor and was gathered to his people. 51 This is because both of you
broke faith with me in the presence of the Israelites at the waters of
Meribah Kadesh in the Desert of Zin and because you did not uphold
my holiness among the Israelites. 52 Therefore, you will see the land
only from a distance; you will not enter the land I am giving to the
people of Israel."

Moses Blesses the Tribes

33 This is the blessing that Moses the man of God pronounced
on the Israelites before his death. 2 He said:

"The LORD came from Sinai
and dawned over them from Seir;
he shone forth from Mount Paran.
He came with[d] myriads of holy ones
from the south, from his mountain slopes.[e]
3 Surely it is you who love the people;
all the holy ones are in your hand.
At your feet they all bow down,
and from you receive instruction,
4 the law that Moses gave us,
the possession of the assembly of Jacob.

[a]43 Or *Make his people rejoice, O nations* [b]43 Masoretic Text; Dead Sea Scrolls (see also Septuagint) *people, / and let all the angels worship him /* [c]44 Hebrew *Hoshea*, a variant of *Joshua* [d]2 Or *from* [e]2 The meaning of the Hebrew for this phrase is uncertain.

OPEN Can you remember some significant words spoken by someone you respected that made a great difference in your life? Explain.

STUDY Moses has now finished the whole sermon, including the closing song. He implores them to take all these words to heart, because they are not idle words. They are words that will bring life. **1.** Can you imagine listening to all these words? **2.** Do you think God was fair in not allowing Moses to enter the land (vv. 51–52)? Do you think Moses was sad or relieved? Why?

APPLY Do you consider these words to be critical to your life? Why or why not?

OPEN 1. What is, or will be, your most prized inheritance? **2.** Why is it of such value to you?

STUDY After all the preaching and singing, it is now time for Moses to end his time with the Israelites with a blessing. He pronounces specific blessings on the tribes of Israel. **1.** What do you think is the power of a blessing? In this text, who is being blessed and who is doing the blessing? Have you ever been present when the long-time leader of a group has passed the torch? Was there the sense that he or she was blessing the group? **2.** What image of God do you gain from verses 2–5? Who are the myriads of holy ones (v. 2)? **3.** Why would Moses refer to the Israelites as "the assembly of Jacob" (v. 4)? Who is Jeshurun (vv. 5,26)? **4.** Do you see

---

32:47 By them you will live long. If the Israelites would follow the Law and trust in God, they would live a full, rich, blessed life.

32:50 gathered to your people. In other words, Moses would join his deceased family members in death (Gen. 25:8). **Aaron died on Mount Hor.** This was referred to earlier in 10:6 and Numbers 20:22–29.

32:51 you broke faith with me. This heartbreaking incident when Moses failed to fully obey God is referred to in 1:37; 3:23–26; 4:21–22; 31:2; and Numbers 20:10–13. **Meribah Kadesh in the Desert of Zin.** The place where Moses failed to fully obey God, bringing on the punishment of never entering the Promised Land (33:8; Ex. 17:7).

33:1 blessing. Note similarities between Moses' blessing of the tribes of Israel (verses 6–25) and Jacob's blessing of his sons (Gen. 49:1–28). **man of God.** This is the first time this description is used of Moses.

[5] He was king over Jeshurun[a]
when the leaders of the people assembled,
along with the tribes of Israel.

[6] "Let Reuben live and not die,
nor[b] his men be few."

[7] And this he said about Judah:

"Hear, O LORD, the cry of Judah;
bring him to his people.
With his own hands he defends his cause.
Oh, be his help against his foes!"

[8] About Levi he said:

"Your Thummim and Urim belong
to the man you favored.
You tested him at Massah;
you contended with him at the waters of Meribah.
[9] He said of his father and mother,
'I have no regard for them.'
He did not recognize his brothers
or acknowledge his own children,
but he watched over your word
and guarded your covenant.
[10] He teaches your precepts to Jacob
and your law to Israel.
He offers incense before you
and whole burnt offerings on your altar.
[11] Bless all his skills, O LORD,
and be pleased with the work of his hands.
Smite the loins of those who rise up against him;
strike his foes till they rise no more."

[12] About Benjamin he said:

"Let the beloved of the LORD rest secure in him,
for he shields him all day long,
and the one the LORD loves rests between his shoulders."

[13] About Joseph he said:

"May the LORD bless his land
with the precious dew from heaven above
and with the deep waters that lie below;

[a] 5 *Jeshurun* means *the upright one,* that is, Israel; also in verse 26. [b] 6 Or *but let*

all the tribes of Israel represented in these blessings (Num. 1:20–42)? Who is missing? Can you summarize each of the blessings? Which one seems to receive the most significant blessing? Why? **5.** Compare these blessings with those of Jacob (Gen. 49). What significant differences do you see? **6.** Do you find the specifics of these blessings difficult to understand? What do you think is the general tone of the blessings? Explain. **7.** What do you learn about God from reading these blessings? Does this text make you trust God more? Does it raise difficult questions for you? Explain.

APPLY 1. How has God blessed you in your life? **2.** Are you looking forward to crossing into another land, a "Promised Land"?

33:5 king. Not a human king. The plan was that God himself was to rule the nation Israel (Judg. 8:23). **Jeshurun.** A reference to Israel (Isa. 44:2).

33:7 With his own hands. Moses asks God's blessing on Judah's military battles by strengthening the tribe.

33:8 Thummim and Urim. The sacred lots used to make decisions under the direction of God (Ex. 28:30). **the man you favored.** A reference to the Levites, who were set apart to serve as priests in the tabernacle. **Massah.** (6:16; 9:22.) The Hebrew name means "testing." **Meribah.** (32:51.) The Hebrew name means "rebellion"—fitting descriptions for the places where Israel stubbornly resisted God's will.

33:10 teaches ... Jacob. The Levites' role as priests was to read and teach the Law to the Israelites (31:11). **He offers incense.** The other primary role of the priests was to lead the people in worship in the tabernacle.

33:13 Joseph. Of course there was no tribe of Joseph—his two sons, Ephraim and Manasseh, led two tribes. But Moses tied together his blessing on those two tribes (v. 17) with Joseph himself. **dew from heaven ... deep waters.** A reference to the land made fertile both by rains and by underground water sources.

[14]with the best the sun brings forth
and the finest the moon can yield;
[15]with the choicest gifts of the ancient mountains
and the fruitfulness of the everlasting hills;
[16]with the best gifts of the earth and its fullness
and the favor of him who dwelt in the burning bush.
Let all these rest on the head of Joseph,
on the brow of the prince among[a] his brothers.
[17]In majesty he is like a firstborn bull;
his horns are the horns of a wild ox.
With them he will gore the nations,
even those at the ends of the earth.
Such are the ten thousands of Ephraim;
such are the thousands of Manasseh."

[18]About Zebulun he said:

"Rejoice, Zebulun, in your going out,
and you, Issachar, in your tents.
[19]They will summon peoples to the mountain
and there offer sacrifices of righteousness;
they will feast on the abundance of the seas,
on the treasures hidden in the sand."

[20]About Gad he said:

"Blessed is he who enlarges Gad's domain!
Gad lives there like a lion,
tearing at arm or head.
[21]He chose the best land for himself;
the leader's portion was kept for him.
When the heads of the people assembled,
he carried out the LORD's righteous will,
and his judgments concerning Israel."

[22]About Dan he said:

"Dan is a lion's cub,
springing out of Bashan."

[23]About Naphtali he said:

"Naphtali is abounding with the favor of the LORD
and is full of his blessing;
he will inherit southward to the lake."

[a]16 Or *of the one separated from*

33:17 bull. Ephraim and Manasseh would be especially blessed in battle thanks to God's majesty and strength exhibited through them.

33:19 abundance of the seas ... treasures hidden in the sand. These tribes would enjoy success and wealth from the sea (Gen. 49:13).

33:21 He chose the best land. Good land was required to maintain livestock properly—and livestock signified wealth.

33:22 springing out of Bashan. This could also be translated "keeping away from the viper," presenting a picture of a baby lion running from a snake. Dan would one day behave like a snake (Gen. 49:17). But here Dan was portrayed as meek, like a weak lion cub. Ultimately the tribe would be forced to abandon their land as a result of Philistine attacks and would move to the area of Bashan, south of Mount Hermon (Judg. 18).

33:23 lake. The Sea of Galilee. The tribe of Naphtali inherited the land from above the Waters of Merom in the north to below the Sea of Galilee in the south.

24 About Asher he said:

"Most blessed of sons is Asher;
let him be favored by his brothers,
and let him bathe his feet in oil.
25 The bolts of your gates will be iron and bronze,
and your strength will equal your days.
26 "There is no one like the God of Jeshurun,
who rides on the heavens to help you
and on the clouds in his majesty.
27 The eternal God is your refuge,
and underneath are the everlasting arms.
He will drive out your enemy before you,
saying, 'Destroy him!'
28 So Israel will live in safety alone;
Jacob's spring is secure
in a land of grain and new wine,
where the heavens drop dew.
29 Blessed are you, O Israel!
Who is like you,
a people saved by the LORD?
He is your shield and helper
and your glorious sword.
Your enemies will cower before you,
and you will trample down their high places.[a]"

The Death of Moses

34 Then Moses climbed Mount Nebo from the plains of Moab to
the top of Pisgah, across from Jericho. There the LORD
showed him the whole land—from Gilead to Dan, 2 all of Naphtali, the
territory of Ephraim and Manasseh, all the land of Judah as far as the
western sea,[b] 3 the Negev and the whole region from the Valley of Jericho, the City of Palms, as far as Zoar. 4 Then the LORD said to him,
"This is the land I promised on oath to Abraham, Isaac and Jacob
when I said, 'I will give it to your descendants.' I have let you see it
with your eyes, but you will not cross over into it."
5 And Moses the servant of the LORD died there in Moab, as the
LORD had said. 6 He buried him[c] in Moab, in the valley opposite Beth
Peor, but to this day no one knows where his grave is. 7 Moses was a

[a] 29 *Or will tread upon their bodies* [b] 2 That is, the Mediterranean [c] 6 *Or He was buried*

OPEN 1. What would you like to do that you haven't done or see than you haven't seen before you die? **2.** What is your overall impression of Moses? Do you think you could be friends with him? Why or why not?

STUDY Now the end has come. Moses had faithfully done the work of God as the leader of the people of Israel, but now it is time for him to die. God let him view the land of promise, even though he would not let Moses enter. **1.** What did God let Moses see before he died (vv. 1–3)? How do you think Moses felt at this point in his life? Why? **2.** What

33:24 bathe his feet in oil. This phrase indicates Asher would enjoy God's abundant blessing.

33:26 on the clouds. This description has been found in Canaanite literature in reference to Baal. Its use here (and in Ps. 68:4) indicates that Yahweh is the true God who dwells in the heavens and is sovereign over creation.

33:28 Israel will live in safety. Balaam, the pagan prophet, actually gave this promise of God first, and Moses echoes it here (Num. 23:9).

33:29 A beautiful summary of the rich relationship Israel enjoyed as the people God had chosen. God would protect them gloriously and empower them to overcome their enemies and their false gods.

34:1 Moses climbed Mount Nebo. God commanded him to do so in 32:48–52. **across from Jericho.** That city will be the first in Canaan to fall to the Israelites.

34:4 land I promised. Moses gets to see the fulfillment of God's promise spread out before him (1:8; Gen. 12:1; 15:18; Ex. 33:1).

34:5 servant of the LORD. Only the patriarchs were given this title. It was reserved for those like Abraham (Gen. 26:24) and David (2 Sam. 7:5). It was also applied to Israel as a nation (Isa. 41:8).

34:6 no one knows where his grave is. God kept Moses' burial plot a secret, no doubt to prevent it from becoming a shrine.

does it tell you about the character of God for him to keep a promise he had made generations earlier (Gen 17:5–8; 26:2–3; 28:10–13)? **3.** How old was Moses when he died (v. 7)? Do you consider that to be very old? Did Moses show the signs of aging? **4.** Who buried Moses? Would you have grieved for Moses if you had been there when he died? Why? **5.** What does it mean that Joshua was "filled with the spirit of wisdom"? Why was he filled with the spirit (v. 9)? What does the people's willingness to follow Joshua say about them? **6.** Do you consider Moses to be the greatest character of the Old Testament? Why or why not?

APPLY **1.** Has God given you an understanding (vision) of the spiritual "Promised Land"? Are you anxious to go there? **2.** How does the story of Moses encourage you in your journey of faith?

hundred and twenty years old when he died, yet his eyes were not
weak nor his strength gone. 8The Israelites grieved for Moses in the
plains of Moab thirty days, until the time of weeping and mourning
was over.
9Now Joshua son of Nun was filled with the spirit[a] of wisdom because Moses had laid his hands on him. So the Israelites listened to
him and did what the LORD had commanded Moses.
10Since then, no prophet has risen in Israel like Moses, whom the
LORD knew face to face, 11who did all those miraculous signs and
wonders the LORD sent him to do in Egypt—to Pharaoh and to all his
officials and to his whole land. 12For no one has ever shown the
mighty power or performed the awesome deeds that Moses did in the
sight of all Israel.

[a]9 Or *Spirit*

34:8 grieved ... thirty days. This was the traditional time period for mourning. Moses had made an inestimable impact on the nation, which now had to say goodbye to its beloved leader.

34:10 no prophet has risen in Israel like Moses. While this seems to contradict Moses' promise to the people in 18:15, Moses was unique in standing face-to-face with the Lord.

34:12 no one has ever. Moses was the supreme example of the Old Testament servant of God. The writer of Hebrews contrasts Moses with Christ, the "servant" and the "son," in Hebrews 3:1–6.

Joshua

Personal Reading	Group Study Topic and Reading	
1:1–18	Call of Joshua	1:1–18
2:1–24	Rahab and Spies	2:1–24
3:1–5:12	Crossing Jordan	3:14–4:24
5:13–6:27	Fall of Jericho	5:13–6:21
7:1–8:35	Achan's Sin	7:1–26
9:1–27	Gibeonite Deception	9:1–27
10:1–13:33	Sun Stands Still	10:1–43
14:1–15:63	Caleb's Land	14:1–15
16:1—19:51	Land Allotted	16:1–17:18
20:1—21:45	Cities of Refuge	20:1–9
22:1–34	Altar of Offense	22:1–34
23:1–16	Joshua's Farewell	23:1–16
24:1–33	Covenant Renewal	24:1–27

Author. Joshua is credited as the author. Some of the facts (such as city names) may have been updated by scribes as they copied the manuscript through the years, but the original manuscript was written by Joshua, an eyewitness to the events.

Date. The book of Joshua covers the period of twenty-five years when Joshua led the people to reinhabit Canaan and organize themselves in their new home. Many agree that the Hebrews resettled their land around 1400 B.C. If so, the book was written around 1375 B.C.

Purpose. Joshua's book is an historical record. It records a significant time in the history of the Jews as well as God's faithfulness in honoring their obedience with military victory, as he promised he would.

Historical Background. The Israelites were at war. The timing of their conquest of Canaan was ideal. None of the Babylonians, the Hittites, nor the Egyptians were strong enough at the time to maintain a dominant military presence in the region. The Israelites had circled Canaan to the east, passing through Moab and defeating the Amorites easily. Under Joshua's leadership, they crossed the Jordan River and began the conquest of Canaan itself.

The war was more than the mere military conquest of another nation. It was the culmination of the promise between God and the Israelites as his people. It was a holy war. The Ark of the Covenant was a focal point as the Israelites crossed the Jordan and conquered Jericho. The war was a bloody one as well, typical of most wars in the Late Bronze Age. The purpose for the war was to obtain the land of Canaan, and accordingly, the book of Joshua goes into some detail as to the allotment of the conquered lands. The allotments were based on the division of the Israelites into tribes by family. Twelve tribes received land. Ten of those tribes were sons of Jacob. Two were sons of Joseph, whom Jacob adopted as his own sons.

In the Shadow of Jericho. One of the most famous battles in the Bible is the battle of Jericho recorded in the book of Joshua. The people walked around the city for seven days, then shouted and the city walls collapsed. This left Jericho shocked and defenseless. In the shadow of that victory, though, lies one of the starkest examples of God's standard for obedience. God had given the people specific instructions regarding the spoils of the victory over Jericho. Achan disregarded those instructions, but this was not discovered until the next battle ended in disaster for the Hebrews. In this way, the book of Joshua is more than a record of battles. It is a record of God training his people during a time when violence was the way of life.

OPEN **1.** Have you ever been singled out to accomplish a special task by a parent, teacher, coach or employer? How did you feel? **2.** Who in your life has inspired you to test your own personal limits.

STUDY The book of Joshua opens with the Israelites at the edge of the Promised Land. With Moses dead, Joshua has been selected by God to lead the people. **1.** God commanded Joshua to complete the task of occupying the Promised Land, which began generations earlier. What emotions do you think Joshua was experiencing? **2.** God assured Joshua that he would never leave him or forsake him, and that he would be with Joshua wherever he went. What blessings were promised the Israelites because of God's presence with them? **3.** Verses 7 and 8 link success to obedience to the Law. What do you think this kind of success is like? **4.** Joshua orders his officers to tell the people to prepare to cross the river and enter Canaan in three days. Imagine what the camp must have been like when they heard the news! What were the sights, smells and conversations?

APPLY **1.** Who was the Joshua in your life? What has your spiritual journey been like in the last few years? **2.** Are you ready to move on? **3.** What help do you need to move on?

The LORD Commands Joshua

1 After the death of Moses the servant of the LORD, the LORD said to
Joshua son of Nun, Moses' aide: 2"Moses my servant is dead.
Now then, you and all these people, get ready to cross the Jordan
River into the land I am about to give to them—to the Israelites. 3I
will give you every place where you set your foot, as I promised
Moses. 4Your territory will extend from the desert to Lebanon, and
from the great river, the Euphrates—all the Hittite country—to the
Great Sea[a] on the west. 5No one will be able to stand up against you
all the days of your life. As I was with Moses, so I will be with you; I
will never leave you nor forsake you.
6"Be strong and courageous, because you will lead these people to
inherit the land I swore to their forefathers to give them. 7Be strong
and very courageous. Be careful to obey all the law my servant Moses
gave you; do not turn from it to the right or to the left, that you may
be successful wherever you go. 8Do not let this Book of the Law depart from your mouth; meditate on it day and night, so that you may
be careful to do everything written in it. Then you will be prosperous
and successful. 9Have I not commanded you? Be strong and courageous. Do not be terrified; do not be discouraged, for the LORD your
God will be with you wherever you go."
10So Joshua ordered the officers of the people: 11"Go through the
camp and tell the people, 'Get your supplies ready. Three days from
now you will cross the Jordan here to go in and take possession of
the land the LORD your God is giving you for your own.' "
12But to the Reubenites, the Gadites and the half-tribe of Manasseh, Joshua said, 13"Remember the command that Moses the servant
of the LORD gave you: 'The LORD your God is giving you rest and has
granted you this land.' 14Your wives, your children and your livestock
may stay in the land that Moses gave you east of the Jordan, but all
your fighting men, fully armed, must cross over ahead of your brothers. You are to help your brothers 15until the LORD gives them rest, as
he has done for you, and until they too have taken possession of the

[a]4 That is, the Mediterranean

1:1–18 In an encounter resembling a scene from a presidential inauguration, God instructs Joshua in his duties as Joshua stands before the people he will lead. The instruction that will surely ring in his ears over and over is to be strong and courageous as he leads the people of Israel into their Promised Land. Now, with the whole nation summoned together, the people affirm God's choice for their leader and eagerly look toward God's blessings they will share under Joshua's command.

1:1 Nun, Moses' aide. Although he did not campaign for this position, Joshua consistently rose through the ranks. He served as one of the more exuberant and experienced spies sent into the land of Canaan as well as Moses' captain of the army (Ex. 17:9–14; 33:11; Deut. 31:23).

1:4 This land was a long time in coming. Generations earlier, God promised it to Abraham (Gen. 13:14–17). Nearly forty years earlier, Joshua spied upon it as a middle-aged man (Num. 13:16). Now in his eighties, Joshua would lead his people to conquer it.

1:5 I will never leave you. Although Joshua was God's chosen leader, he likely experienced some fears at this moment. However, his power came as a result of God's presence. In turn, God's presence guaranteed the promises of blessing.

1:7 that you may be successful. In today's world, success is most often a result of hard work and self-motivation. But God offered success as a gift.

1:10 Joshua ordered. Imagine Joshua's voice bellowing instruction to his officers. The inauguration is over. It is time for Joshua to lead.

1:11 giving you for your own. To these migrant escapees, having a land of their own must have seemed like a dream. Joshua's leadership is forthright as well as inspiring.

1:12–15 Although some of the Israelites were already unpacked and settled in parts of the newly conquered land, it would take the entire army to finish the conquest across the Jordan.

1:14 ahead of your brothers. As a symbol of unity, the fighting men who were already settled in the previously conquered land would march ahead. Strong and courageous, they would lead by example.

land that the LORD your God is giving them. After that, you may go back and occupy your own land, which Moses the servant of the LORD gave you east of the Jordan toward the sunrise."

[16]Then they answered Joshua, "Whatever you have commanded us we will do, and wherever you send us we will go. [17]Just as we fully obeyed Moses, so we will obey you. Only may the LORD your God be with you as he was with Moses. [18]Whoever rebels against your word and does not obey your words, whatever you may command them, will be put to death. Only be strong and courageous!"

Rahab and the Spies

2 Then Joshua son of Nun secretly sent two spies from Shittim. "Go, look over the land," he said, "especially Jericho." So they went and entered the house of a prostitute[a] named Rahab and stayed there.

[2]The king of Jericho was told, "Look! Some of the Israelites have come here tonight to spy out the land." [3]So the king of Jericho sent this message to Rahab: "Bring out the men who came to you and entered your house, because they have come to spy out the whole land."

[4]But the woman had taken the two men and hidden them. She said, "Yes, the men came to me, but I did not know where they had come from. [5]At dusk, when it was time to close the city gate, the men left. I don't know which way they went. Go after them quickly. You may catch up with them." [6](But she had taken them up to the roof and hidden them under the stalks of flax she had laid out on the roof.) [7]So the men set out in pursuit of the spies on the road that leads to the fords of the Jordan, and as soon as the pursuers had gone out, the gate was shut.

[8]Before the spies lay down for the night, she went up on the roof [9]and said to them, "I know that the LORD has given this land to you and that a great fear of you has fallen on us, so that all who live in this country are melting in fear because of you. [10]We have heard how the LORD dried up the water of the Red Sea[b] for you when you came out of Egypt, and what you did to Sihon and Og, the two kings of the Amorites east of the Jordan, whom you completely destroyed.[c] [11]When we heard of it, our hearts melted and everyone's courage failed because of you, for the LORD your God is God in heaven above and on the earth below. [12]Now then, please swear to me by the LORD

[a]*1* Or possibly *an innkeeper* [b]*10* Hebrew *Yam Suph*; that is, Sea of Reeds [c]*10* The Hebrew term refers to the irrevocable giving over of things or persons to the LORD, often by totally destroying them.

OPEN 1. When you were a kid, who did you enjoy spying on most: Parents? Older brothers and sisters with their dates? Neighbors? Teachers? The class bully or cut-up? Other? **2.** If you were asked to go "underground" as a spy, what kind of an identity would you assume?

STUDY The Israelites sit across the Jordan River from Jericho, poised to invade the Promised Land. At great risk, two spies are sent to scout out the situation. **1.** Why would Rahab risk her own safety to provide safety for the spies? **2.** Why do you think the spies trusted Rahab, a woman of "questionable reputation"? **3.** What kind of relationship do you think Rahab had with God at this point: She knew him by reputation only? She feared God but didn't really know him? She was a "closet" believer? With the Israelites ready to attack, she saw the light? Other? **4.** Why were Rahab and her family spared? **5.** What report did the spies make to Joshua, and how did he respond (vv. 23–24)? How would you have responded? **6.** Given her disreputable occupation and her obvious lie, what in this story builds Rahab's reputation as a woman of faith (Heb. 11:31; James 2:25)?

APPLY 1. What is the "scarlet cord" you hold on to in times of trial, stress or pain: My faith in Jesus Christ? God's mercy despite my failings? The support of family and

1:18 will be put to death. Success was the only option for the Israelites. Any distractions from their goal would be eliminated.

2:1–24 The theme of this story is risk. Rahab, the prostitute, risked her own life by harboring Joshua's spies. And the spies themselves took great risk by trusting her instructions and her vow of silence. As a result of their combined risk, Joshua received the go-ahead from the spies' report and prepared to conquer the city of Jericho.

2:6 But she had taken them. The grain she was drying on her flat roof made a perfect hiding spot for her fugitives.

2:8–11 the LORD your God is God. No one ever taught Rahab as a child not to talk to strangers. In fact, she put a strange amount of faith in two people she hardly knew. And why was she so convinced of their God? After all, she was a prostitute, not a parishioner. Even so, she is represented in the New Testament as a woman of great faith (Heb. 11:31) and is part of Jesus' lineage.

2:12 Give me a sure sign. Realizing she had spared their lives, Rahab knew to negotiate a tremendous favor from the two spies. Perhaps strengthened by her own confession, she wanted their assurance that the physical and also spiritual health of her family would be protected.

friends? Prayer and Bible study? Church and related activities? Other? **2.** Has God ever surprised you by providing for your need through an unlikely source? How?

---

that you will show kindness to my family, because I have shown kindness to you. Give me a sure sign 13that you will spare the lives of my
father and mother, my brothers and sisters, and all who belong to
them, and that you will save us from death."
14"Our lives for your lives!" the men assured her. "If you don't tell
what we are doing, we will treat you kindly and faithfully when the
LORD gives us the land."
15So she let them down by a rope through the window, for the
house she lived in was part of the city wall. 16Now she had said to
them, "Go to the hills so the pursuers will not find you. Hide yourselves there three days until they return, and then go on your way."
17The men said to her, "This oath you made us swear will not be
binding on us 18unless, when we enter the land, you have tied this
scarlet cord in the window through which you let us down, and unless you have brought your father and mother, your brothers and all
your family into your house. 19If anyone goes outside your house into
the street, his blood will be on his own head; we will not be responsible. As for anyone who is in the house with you, his blood will be on
our head if a hand is laid on him. 20But if you tell what we are doing,
we will be released from the oath you made us swear."
21"Agreed," she replied. "Let it be as you say." So she sent them
away and they departed. And she tied the scarlet cord in the window.
22When they left, they went into the hills and stayed there three
days, until the pursuers had searched all along the road and returned
without finding them. 23Then the two men started back. They went
down out of the hills, forded the river and came to Joshua son of Nun
and told him everything that had happened to them. 24They said to
Joshua, "The LORD has surely given the whole land into our hands; all
the people are melting in fear because of us."

Crossing the Jordan

3 Early in the morning Joshua and all the Israelites set out from
Shittim and went to the Jordan, where they camped before
crossing over. 2After three days the officers went throughout the camp,
3giving orders to the people: "When you see the ark of the covenant of
the LORD your God, and the priests, who are Levites, carrying it, you
are to move out from your positions and follow it. 4Then you will know

OPEN **1.** What is your most treasured souvenir from your teenage years? **2.** What is a favorite story that either a parent or grandparent has told you about their past?

STUDY After 40 years, the day has finally come for the Israelites to enter the Promised Land.

2:14 Our lives for your lives! A serious transaction had taken place and bonded three total strangers. Rahab rescued them from certain death. And Rahab herself would soon barely escape the destruction of her city.

2:15 part of the city wall. Rahab likely made her home—an original high-rise apartment—on planks supported between the two walls surrounding the city of Jericho.

2:18 scarlet cord. To distinguish *Rahab's house from the dozens of other* houses in Jericho, the Israelites would look for a dyed cord from her window. Rahab eagerly hung the cord, a symbol of her faith, as soon as the men left.

2:19 his blood will be on his own head. The spies took responsibility for the chance of a mistake. If anyone in Rahab's family were harmed during the attack, the spies would take the blame.

2:22 into the hills … three days. Hiding spots by the dozens awaited the spies as they traveled toward this cave-ridden area of Palestine. Since they were reported to have left through the city gate, the king's men looked for them along the road.

3:1–4:24 For a people whose journey began with the crossing of the Red Sea, this event must have been a frightening flashback. While Pharaoh was no longer tailing them, it was flood season and no less terrifying. The memorial following the successful crossing was to commemorate the present miracle. But it also reflected on past provisions. Greater still was the promise of a future blessing—something generations would live to tell.

3:3 When you see the ark. Following God instead of their fears, the people stepped into the river at the first sign of the ark's appearance.

3:4 since you have never been this way before. Although prior generations got their feet wet in the Red Sea, this was a new miracle. They knew they would experience a similar outcome. But even the more experienced would have to rely on faith once more.

which way to go, since you have never been this way before. But keep
a distance of about a thousand yards[a] between you and the ark; do not
go near it."
[5]Joshua told the people, "Consecrate yourselves, for tomorrow the
LORD will do amazing things among you."
[6]Joshua said to the priests, "Take up the ark of the covenant and
pass on ahead of the people." So they took it up and went ahead of
them.
[7]And the LORD said to Joshua, "Today I will begin to exalt you in the
eyes of all Israel, so they may know that I am with you as I was with
Moses. [8]Tell the priests who carry the ark of the covenant: 'When you
reach the edge of the Jordan's waters, go and stand in the river.' "
[9]Joshua said to the Israelites, "Come here and listen to the words
of the LORD your God. [10]This is how you will know that the living God
is among you and that he will certainly drive out before you the Canaanites, Hittites, Hivites, Perizzites, Girgashites, Amorites and Jebusites. [11]See, the ark of the covenant of the Lord of all the earth will go
into the Jordan ahead of you. [12]Now then, choose twelve men from
the tribes of Israel, one from each tribe. [13]And as soon as the priests
who carry the ark of the LORD—the Lord of all the earth—set foot in
the Jordan, its waters flowing downstream will be cut off and stand
up in a heap."
[14]So when the people broke camp to cross the Jordan, the priests
carrying the ark of the covenant went ahead of them. [15]Now the Jordan is at flood stage all during harvest. Yet as soon as the priests who
carried the ark reached the Jordan and their feet touched the water's
edge, [16]the water from upstream stopped flowing. It piled up in a
heap a great distance away, at a town called Adam in the vicinity of
Zarethan, while the water flowing down to the Sea of the Arabah (the
Salt Sea[b]) was completely cut off. So the people crossed over opposite Jericho. [17]The priests who carried the ark of the covenant of the
LORD stood firm on dry ground in the middle of the Jordan, while all
Israel passed by until the whole nation had completed the crossing
on dry ground.

4 When the whole nation had finished crossing the Jordan, the
LORD said to Joshua, [2]"Choose twelve men from among the
people, one from each tribe, [3]and tell them to take up twelve stones
from the middle of the Jordan from right where the priests stood and

[a]4 Hebrew *about two thousand cubits* (about 900 meters) [b]16 That is, the Dead Sea

There is only one problem: They have to cross the Jordan River—during flood season no less! The Lord provides them with a miracle and teaches them the importance of remembering all he has done for them. Joshua tells the people to consecrate themselves, for tomorrow the Lord will do amazing things among them. **1.** If you had been an Israelite, what kind of "amazing things" would you have anticipated from God? **2.** Why did God begin Joshua's career with a miracle similar to the one that he gave Moses (vv. 7–8)? Would this have felt like "deja vu" to you? **3.** What did the ark signify (Ex. 25:10)? Why was it important that the ark go before the people (vv. 3–5,11; Num. 10:33–36)? **4.** If you were an Israelite and could have just one picture of this day for your memory album, what would it be? **5.** Why did Joshua set up a monument of 12 stones (4:4–7)? What "monument" in your life commemorates a time when God provided a way for you? **6.** Why did God repeat, in the Jordan River, the miracle he performed in the Red Sea (vv. 23–24)? What is the message you see for yourself in these two verses?

APPLY What life-changing event along your spiritual journey will you be sure to tell your friends, family and group about?

3:5 Consecrate yourselves ... the LORD ... amazing things. Joshua's command is full of eager expectation in preparation for a great event. No doubt they polished their best utensils and readied their finest dress. The people of Israel would meet with God tomorrow. And they had to be ready.

3:7 I am with you. Moses must have been a hard act to follow. Would Joshua do it right? Would others see the same courage in him that they saw in Moses? God's assuring presence was as much for Joshua as it was for the people of Israel.

3:10 Seven people groups would oppose the Israelites' possession of the land. And those same seven people groups would hear about the front-page miracle at the Jordan River.

3:15 Jordan is at flood stage. That God arranged for the Israelites to cross the Jordan during the spring flood stage is no more surprising than the roundabout way he led them to Canaan in the first place. Sure, there was a direct route, just as the river would have been much less intimidating without the melting snow from nearby Mount Hermon. However, less water may have meant less faith.

3:17 firm on dry ground. The depth of God's miracle did not allow for shallow puddles to remain. The priests took their post on dry ground and directed the Israelites across.

4:3 from the middle of the Jordan. As a symbol of their great faith and God's greater miracle, a select group took stones from the deepest part of the river and set them aside for a memorial.

to carry them over with you and put them down at the place where
you stay tonight."
4So Joshua called together the twelve men he had appointed from
the Israelites, one from each tribe, 5and said to them, "Go over before
the ark of the LORD your God into the middle of the Jordan. Each of
you is to take up a stone on his shoulder, according to the number of
the tribes of the Israelites, 6to serve as a sign among you. In the
future, when your children ask you, 'What do these stones mean?'
7tell them that the flow of the Jordan was cut off before the ark of the
covenant of the LORD. When it crossed the Jordan, the waters of the
Jordan were cut off. These stones are to be a memorial to the people
of Israel forever."
8So the Israelites did as Joshua commanded them. They took
twelve stones from the middle of the Jordan, according to the number
of the tribes of the Israelites, as the LORD had told Joshua; and they
carried them over with them to their camp, where they put them
down. 9Joshua set up the twelve stones that had been[a] in the middle
of the Jordan at the spot where the priests who carried the ark of the
covenant had stood. And they are there to this day.
10Now the priests who carried the ark remained standing in the
middle of the Jordan until everything the LORD had commanded
Joshua was done by the people, just as Moses had directed Joshua.
The people hurried over, 11and as soon as all of them had crossed, the
ark of the LORD and the priests came to the other side while the
people watched. 12The men of Reuben, Gad and the half-tribe of
Manasseh crossed over, armed, in front of the Israelites, as Moses
had directed them. 13About forty thousand armed for battle crossed
over before the LORD to the plains of Jericho for war.
14That day the LORD exalted Joshua in the sight of all Israel; and they
revered him all the days of his life, just as they had revered Moses.
15Then the LORD said to Joshua, 16"Command the priests carrying
the ark of the Testimony to come up out of the Jordan."
17So Joshua commanded the priests, "Come up out of the Jordan."
18And the priests came up out of the river carrying the ark of the
covenant of the LORD. No sooner had they set their feet on the dry
ground than the waters of the Jordan returned to their place and ran
at flood stage as before.
19On the tenth day of the first month the people went up from the
Jordan and camped at Gilgal on the eastern border of Jericho. 20And
Joshua set up at Gilgal the twelve stones they had taken out of the
Jordan. 21He said to the Israelites, "In the future when your descendants ask their fathers, 'What do these stones mean?' 22tell them,
'Israel crossed the Jordan on dry ground.' 23For the LORD your God
dried up the Jordan before you until you had crossed over. The LORD
your God did to the Jordan just what he had done to the Red Sea[b]

[a]9 Or *Joshua also set up twelve stones* [b]23 Hebrew *Yam Suph;* that is, Sea of Reeds

4:6 as a sign among you. Bumper stickers. Patches. Flags. People are drawn to symbols as *expressions* of what is important and valued. To the Israelites, this stone monument would help families remember God's faithfulness for generations to come.

4:9 And they are there to this day. Some scholars think this could mean as many as 800 years later.

4:13 forty thousand. This was the number of fighting men recorded in Numbers for one tribe alone. This figure is likely a total of representatives from the fighting tribes.

4:23 God dried up the Jordan before you. The story the Israelites would tell future generations had one moral: God delivers. It was not about

when he dried it up before us until we had crossed over. 24He did this so that all the peoples of the earth might know that the hand of the LORD is powerful and so that you might always fear the LORD your God."

Circumcision at Gilgal

5 Now when all the Amorite kings west of the Jordan and all the Canaanite kings along the coast heard how the LORD had dried up the Jordan before the Israelites until we had crossed over, their hearts melted and they no longer had the courage to face the Israelites.

2At that time the LORD said to Joshua, "Make flint knives and circumcise the Israelites again." 3So Joshua made flint knives and circumcised the Israelites at Gibeath Haaraloth.[a]

4Now this is why he did so: All those who came out of Egypt—all the men of military age—died in the desert on the way after leaving Egypt. 5All the people that came out had been circumcised, but all the people born in the desert during the journey from Egypt had not. 6The Israelites had moved about in the desert forty years until all the men who were of military age when they left Egypt had died, since they had not obeyed the LORD. For the LORD had sworn to them that they would not see the land that he had solemnly promised their fathers to give us, a land flowing with milk and honey. 7So he raised up their sons in their place, and these were the ones Joshua circumcised. They were still uncircumcised because they had not been circumcised on the way. 8And after the whole nation had been circumcised, they remained where they were in camp until they were healed.

9Then the LORD said to Joshua, "Today I have rolled away the reproach of Egypt from you." So the place has been called Gilgal[b] to this day.

10On the evening of the fourteenth day of the month, while camped at Gilgal on the plains of Jericho, the Israelites celebrated the Passover. 11The day after the Passover, that very day, they ate some of the produce of the land: unleavened bread and roasted grain. 12The manna stopped the day after[c] they ate this food from the land; there was no longer any manna for the Israelites, but that year they ate of the produce of Canaan.

OPEN What "rite of passage" marked your entrance into adulthood: First cigarette or drink? Own car? Driver's license? Confirmation? High school graduation? First job? Marriage?

STUDY The Israelites have crossed the Jordan with God's miraculous intervention. Because of this, the Canaanite and Amorite kings have lost the courage to face them. The Israelites revisit two God honoring traditions from their past, as they taste the fruits of their new home. **1.** Why did Joshua have all the men circumcised? Why had they not been circumcised before (vv. 4–7)? **2.** Why did the men of military age have to die before they entered Canaan (vv. 4–7; Num. 14:38)? **3.** What do you think the "reproach of Egypt" was and how was it taken away? **4.** What is the significance of the people of God sharing the Passover meal together at Gilgal? **5.** Why did the manna stop appearing? How would you have felt if you had been there and no manna appeared?

APPLY Have you felt like God stopped the "manna" in your life? What happened to your relationship with God after that? How can your group pray for you right now?

[a]3 *Gibeath Haaraloth* means *hill of foreskins.* [b]9 *Gilgal* sounds like the Hebrew for *roll.* [c]12 Or *the day*

the amount of people's faith or the size of the river. The story was about God himself.

4:24 all the peoples of the earth. *Although this miracle was specific to* the Israelites at that time, God's fame would be spread throughout the world as a result. The timeless truths the event symbolized would be shared for generations.

5:1–12 Like a family resuming family dinners after a particularly busy period of scattered priorities, the Israelites reintroduced two important traditions. The new family members were circumcised and the entire group celebrated Passover together.

5:6 moved about in the desert forty years. The Lord waited for an entire generation to die off before bringing his people to the Promised Land.

5:10 celebrated the Passover. This was the third time the Israelites would celebrate Passover together. The first time was before their exodus from Egypt. The second time was at Sinai, where they received the Commandments. And now they served Passover at Gilgal.

5:11 produce of the land. For the first time, the Israelites were able to enjoy the bounty of their land.

5:12 manna. When the Israelites crossed the Jordan, they crossed into a new era of God's provision. No longer dependent on manna, they were able to further stake their claim on Canaan by enjoying its fruit.

OPEN **1.** As a teen, what was the craziest thing you ever did? **2.** What were you taught about fighting when you were growing up: Walk away? Always throw the first punch? Blessed are the peacemakers? Choose your own fighting ground? Other?

STUDY The Israelites are in the Promised Land and before them stands the fortified city of Jericho. **1.** As Joshua approaches Jericho, he sees a man standing with his sword drawn. When asked whose side he's on, the man says "neither" (5:13–14). What do you think he meant? **2.** How is Joshua's experience of the messenger (5:13–15) similar to Moses' experience of God at the burning bush (Ex. 3:5)? Why do you believe it's important to the author of Joshua to draw parallels between these two men? **3.** Picture yourself as a soldier in the Israelite army. How do you feel about Joshua's battle plan? **4.** What was the purpose of the trumpet blast and the people's shout: The noise collapsed the wall? It was God's cue? Psychological warfare? To test Israel's obedience? An expression of the people's faith? Other? **5.** In 6:10 Joshua commands the people not to say a word while marching around Jericho until he gives them the signal to shout. Why do you think their silence was important? **6.** If you had been present at Jericho when the walls fell, how would this experience have affected your faith in God? How might it have affected the faith of the average Israelite? **7.** What messages did God send to the Israelites, the Canaanites and ultimately to us when he called for the total destruction of Jericho? **8.** When you read that Rahab

The Fall of Jericho

13 Now when Joshua was near Jericho, he looked up and saw a man
standing in front of him with a drawn sword in his hand. Joshua went
up to him and asked, "Are you for us or for our enemies?"
14 "Neither," he replied, "but as commander of the army of the LORD
I have now come." Then Joshua fell facedown to the ground in
reverence, and asked him, "What message does my Lord[a] have for his
servant?"
15 The commander of the LORD's army replied, "Take off your sandals, for the place where you are standing is holy." And Joshua did so.

6 Now Jericho was tightly shut up because of the Israelites. No
one went out and no one came in.
2 Then the LORD said to Joshua, "See, I have delivered Jericho into
your hands, along with its king and its fighting men. 3 March around
the city once with all the armed men. Do this for six days. 4 Have seven
priests carry trumpets of rams' horns in front of the ark. On the
seventh day, march around the city seven times, with the priests blowing the trumpets. 5 When you hear them sound a long blast on the
trumpets, have all the people give a loud shout; then the wall of the
city will collapse and the people will go up, every man straight in."
6 So Joshua son of Nun called the priests and said to them, "Take up
the ark of the covenant of the LORD and have seven priests carry
trumpets in front of it." 7 And he ordered the people, "Advance! March
around the city, with the armed guard going ahead of the ark of the
LORD."
8 When Joshua had spoken to the people, the seven priests carrying
the seven trumpets before the LORD went forward, blowing their
trumpets, and the ark of the LORD's covenant followed them. 9 The
armed guard marched ahead of the priests who blew the trumpets,
and the rear guard followed the ark. All this time the trumpets were
sounding. 10 But Joshua had commanded the people, "Do not give a
war cry, do not raise your voices, do not say a word until the day I tell
you to shout. Then shout!" 11 So he had the ark of the LORD carried
around the city, circling it once. Then the people returned to camp
and spent the night there.

[a]14 Or *lord*

5:13–6:5 Jericho would be no ordinary battle. The stranger's appearance at its onset is a further reminder that the Israelites were fighting a battle the Lord had already won for them. This spiritual encounter sets the tone for the entire record of the battle of Jericho.

5:13 a man standing in front. Regardless of whether the man was an angel on mission, Christ or God himself in human form, the encounter had to be inspiring for Joshua. A supernatural army's presence, in addition to his faithful men, bolstered his confidence.

5:14 commander of the army of the LORD I have now come. Joshua submits in reverence to this supernaturally superior officer.

5:15 the place where you are standing is holy. Moses received the same command at the burning bush. Now, Joshua realizes his own encounter with the Lord has brought him to a holy place.

6:1 Jericho was tightly shut. The story of their miraculous crossing apparently preceded them and terrified the inhabitants of Jericho. Inside two layers of thick walls, the citizens of Jericho awaited their fate.

6:3 March around the city once. Swords ready? Check! Ladders ready? Check! Shields ready? Check! Joshua's battle checklist surely never included merely marching around the walls of Jericho. However, his response was not a question. It was obedience.

6:4 trumpets. Priests used these "jubilee trumpets" in religious ceremonies to announce the presence of the Lord.

6:5 give a loud shout. The terrified and bewildered inhabitants inside Jericho would be stunned by the voices of tens of thousands of warriors, not to mention the roar of their crumbling walls.

6:8–14 do not say a word. Perhaps this was an additional guard against discouragement or negative comments

12Joshua got up early the next morning and the priests took up the
ark of the LORD. 13The seven priests carrying the seven trumpets went
forward, marching before the ark of the LORD and blowing the trumpets. The armed men went ahead of them and the rear guard followed
the ark of the LORD, while the trumpets kept sounding. 14So on the
second day they marched around the city once and returned to the
camp. They did this for six days.
15On the seventh day, they got up at daybreak and marched around
the city seven times in the same manner, except that on that day they
circled the city seven times. 16The seventh time around, when the
priests sounded the trumpet blast, Joshua commanded the people,
"Shout! For the LORD has given you the city! 17The city and all that is
in it are to be devoted[a] to the LORD. Only Rahab the prostitute[b] and all
who are with her in her house shall be spared, because she hid the
spies we sent. 18But keep away from the devoted things, so that you
will not bring about your own destruction by taking any of them.
Otherwise you will make the camp of Israel liable to destruction and
bring trouble on it. 19All the silver and gold and the articles of bronze
and iron are sacred to the LORD and must go into his treasury."
20When the trumpets sounded, the people shouted, and at the
sound of the trumpet, when the people gave a loud shout, the wall
collapsed; so every man charged straight in, and they took the city.
21They devoted the city to the LORD and destroyed with the sword
every living thing in it—men and women, young and old, cattle,
sheep and donkeys.
22Joshua said to the two men who had spied out the land, "Go into
the prostitute's house and bring her out and all who belong to her, in
accordance with your oath to her." 23So the young men who had done
the spying went in and brought out Rahab, her father and mother and
brothers and all who belonged to her. They brought out her entire
family and put them in a place outside the camp of Israel.
24Then they burned the whole city and everything in it, but they put
the silver and gold and the articles of bronze and iron into the treasury of the LORD's house. 25But Joshua spared Rahab the prostitute,
with her family and all who belonged to her, because she hid the men
Joshua had sent as spies to Jericho—and she lives among the Israelites to this day.
26At that time Joshua pronounced this solemn oath: "Cursed before
the LORD is the man who undertakes to rebuild this city, Jericho:

"At the cost of his firstborn son
  will he lay its foundations;

[a]17 The Hebrew term refers to the irrevocable giving over of things or persons to the LORD, often by totally destroying them; also in verses 18 and 21. [b]17 Or possibly *innkeeper*; also in verses 22 and 25

and her household were not only spared, but also brought near to the camp of Israel after Jericho's defeat, what does this tell you about God?

APPLY 1. Have you ever been in a place where God was so obviously at work that you felt that where you were "standing was holy" (5:15)? Describe the scene and what you sensed God doing. **2.** What "wall" exists in your life that separates you from experiencing God's love completely? How do you think God is calling you to dismantle it?

since it was a particularly strange strategy for war.

6:17 devoted to the LORD. To be "devoted" in this case, when God was speaking of cities under his "ban," meant that these were to be completely destroyed. Much like a burnt offering, the entire city of Jericho was to be set aside as a sacrifice.

6:18 destruction. Whenever the Israelites did not obey God's command to destroy the contents of a city, disastrous consequences followed. The high stakes involved in obedience would make sure Israel stayed pure among a pagan people.

6:25 Rahab ... she lives among the Israelites. Rahab's family and future were redeemed due to her fateful encounter with the spies. Apparently, she converted from her pagan ways and worshiped among the Israelites.

6:26 rebuild this city. As conquered land belonging to God, Jericho would never again be restored to its former glory. This curse eventually came true (1 Kin. 16:34).

OPEN **1.** What toy did you always want as a child, but never got? **2.** When you were a kid, did you take something that didn't belong to you and thought no one would miss, only to be "found out" later? How did it feel to get caught then? How do you feel about the experience now as you look back on it?

STUDY Joshua led God's people to a great victory over Jericho as they watched the city walls crumble with the Israelites' shouts and the trumpeting of rams' horns. God brought them victory as they obeyed his laws and commandments. Now, it's discovered that someone in the camp has disobeyed God's orders. **1.** Why did God's anger burn against Israel (6:17–19; 7:10–11)? **2.** How would you describe Joshua's reaction to the stunning defeat at Ai (vv. 6–9)? **3.** What was Achan's sin (vv. 20–21)? How do you think he felt as he watched the tribes, clans and families file past Joshua? **4.** If you had been Joshua, would you have been tempted to: Let Achan go with a slap on the wrist? Send him packing? Punch him out? Make excuses for him? Other? **5.** What did God require the Israelites to do to restore their relationship with him (vv. 13–15)? Why do you think God insisted on such drastic action? **6.** How would you have felt if you had been Achan's wife or one of his children? What if you had been a parent of one of the 36 killed in the attack on Ai?

APPLY **1.** Can you remember a time when you made a selfish decision or action, and later watched as the consequences hurt someone you love? What happened? Was it resolved? How? **2.** How has the

at the cost of his youngest
will he set up its gates."

27So the LORD was with Joshua, and his fame spread throughout
the land.

Achan's Sin

7 But the Israelites acted unfaithfully in regard to the devoted
things[a]; Achan son of Carmi, the son of Zimri,[b] the son of Zerah,
of the tribe of Judah, took some of them. So the LORD's anger burned
against Israel.
2Now Joshua sent men from Jericho to Ai, which is near Beth Aven
to the east of Bethel, and told them, "Go up and spy out the region."
So the men went up and spied out Ai.
3When they returned to Joshua, they said, "Not all the people will
have to go up against Ai. Send two or three thousand men to take it
and do not weary all the people, for only a few men are there." 4So
about three thousand men went up; but they were routed by the men
of Ai, 5who killed about thirty-six of them. They chased the Israelites
from the city gate as far as the stone quarries[c] and struck them down
on the slopes. At this the hearts of the people melted and became like
water.
6Then Joshua tore his clothes and fell facedown to the ground before the ark of the LORD, remaining there till evening. The elders of
Israel did the same, and sprinkled dust on their heads. 7And Joshua
said, "Ah, Sovereign LORD, why did you ever bring this people across
the Jordan to deliver us into the hands of the Amorites to destroy us?
If only we had been content to stay on the other side of the Jordan!
8O Lord, what can I say, now that Israel has been routed by its enemies? 9The Canaanites and the other people of the country will hear
about this and they will surround us and wipe out our name from the
earth. What then will you do for your own great name?"
10The LORD said to Joshua, "Stand up! What are you doing down on
your face? 11Israel has sinned; they have violated my covenant, which
I commanded them to keep. They have taken some of the devoted
things; they have stolen, they have lied, they have put them with their
own possessions. 12That is why the Israelites cannot stand against
their enemies; they turn their backs and run because they have been
made liable to destruction. I will not be with you anymore unless you
destroy whatever among you is devoted to destruction.
13"Go, consecrate the people. Tell them, 'Consecrate yourselves in
preparation for tomorrow; for this is what the LORD, the God of Israel,

[a]*1* The Hebrew term refers to the irrevocable giving over of things or persons to the LORD, often by totally destroying them; also in verses 11, 12, 13 and 15. [b]*1* See Septuagint and 1 Chron. 2:6; Hebrew *Zabdi*; also in verses 17 and 18. [c]*5* Or *as far as Shebarim*

7:1–26 Out of an entire army of tens of thousands, surely Achan was not the only one who was tempted. Yet only he gave in to temptation and *stole what was to be devoted to the Lord alone.* As a result, their next battle at Ai was a total loss. It had to happen sooner or later, some might say. But the tragedy of Achan's story is that sin, whenever it occurred, had to be punished.

7:6 Joshua tore his clothes and fell. Picture the C.E.O. of a major corporation solemnly tossing papers over her head during a frustrating board meeting. Imagine a football coach spiking his headset on the field. Joshua was in great distress at the news of this defeat. He could not imagine what went wrong.

7:11 some of the devoted things. All living things were to be destroyed and burned in Jericho. Anything of value was to be brought into the Lord's treasury.

says: That which is devoted is among you, O Israel. You cannot stand
against your enemies until you remove it.
14" 'In the morning, present yourselves tribe by tribe. The tribe that
the LORD takes shall come forward clan by clan; the clan that the
LORD takes shall come forward family by family; and the family that
the LORD takes shall come forward man by man. 15He who is caught
with the devoted things shall be destroyed by fire, along with all that
belongs to him. He has violated the covenant of the LORD and has
done a disgraceful thing in Israel!' "
16Early the next morning Joshua had Israel come forward by tribes,
and Judah was taken. 17The clans of Judah came forward, and he took
the Zerahites. He had the clan of the Zerahites come forward by families, and Zimri was taken. 18Joshua had his family come forward man
by man, and Achan son of Carmi, the son of Zimri, the son of Zerah,
of the tribe of Judah, was taken.
19Then Joshua said to Achan, "My son, give glory to the LORD,[a] the
God of Israel, and give him the praise.[b] Tell me what you have done;
do not hide it from me."
20Achan replied, "It is true! I have sinned against the LORD, the God
of Israel. This is what I have done: 21When I saw in the plunder a beautiful robe from Babylonia,[c] two hundred shekels[d] of silver and a wedge
of gold weighing fifty shekels,[e] I coveted them and took them. They are
hidden in the ground inside my tent, with the silver underneath."
22So Joshua sent messengers, and they ran to the tent, and there it
was, hidden in his tent, with the silver underneath. 23They took the
things from the tent, brought them to Joshua and all the Israelites
and spread them out before the LORD.
24Then Joshua, together with all Israel, took Achan son of Zerah,
the silver, the robe, the gold wedge, his sons and daughters, his cattle, donkeys and sheep, his tent and all that he had, to the Valley of
Achor. 25Joshua said, "Why have you brought this trouble on us? The
LORD will bring trouble on you today."
Then all Israel stoned him, and after they had stoned the rest, they
burned them. 26Over Achan they heaped up a large pile of rocks,
which remains to this day. Then the LORD turned from his fierce anger. Therefore that place has been called the Valley of Achor[f] ever
since.

Ai Destroyed

8 Then the LORD said to Joshua, "Do not be afraid; do not be discouraged. Take the whole army with you, and go up and attack

[a]19 A solemn charge to tell the truth [b]19 Or *and confess to him* [c]21 Hebrew *Shinar* [d]21 That is, about 5 pounds (about 2.3 kilograms) [e]21 That is, about 1 1/4 pounds (about 0.6 kilogram) [f]26 *Achor* means *trouble.*

Lord had to "get tough" with you to get you back on track?

OPEN What is one "come-from-behind victory" in your life you still remember fondly?

STUDY Joshua and his army have suffered a humiliating defeat at Ai due to the disobedience of

7:13 You cannot stand against your enemies. Israel's potential for victory was based on obedience. According to God's wartime strategy, a perfectly obedient army of ten could defeat tens of thousands of enemies. But one disobedient man amid tens of thousands of Israelites would bring defeat by even the weakest nation.

7:14 tribe that the LORD takes shall come forward. Achan woke up the next morning to a nightmare. In order to reveal the culprit, everyone had to assemble tribe by tribe, family by family and individual by individual. In this type of supernatural lotto, no one wanted the winning number. But Achan's ticket was already burning a hole underneath his tent.

7:25 they burned them. This was supposed to be the original outcome of every living thing in Jericho (6:18–19,24).

7:26 Then the LORD turned from his fierce anger. Meaning, the Lord would once again walk with them.

8:1 Joshua, Do not be afraid. God addressed Joshua's initial fears of returning to a city where they had just been defeated.

Ai. For I have delivered into your hands the king of Ai, his people, his
city and his land. 2You shall do to Ai and its king as you did to Jericho
and its king, except that you may carry off their plunder and livestock
for yourselves. Set an ambush behind the city."
3So Joshua and the whole army moved out to attack Ai. He chose
thirty thousand of his best fighting men and sent them out at night
4with these orders: "Listen carefully. You are to set an ambush behind
the city. Don't go very far from it. All of you be on the alert. 5I and all
those with me will advance on the city, and when the men come out
against us, as they did before, we will flee from them. 6They will pursue us until we have lured them away from the city, for they will say,
'They are running away from us as they did before.' So when we flee
from them, 7you are to rise up from ambush and take the city. The
LORD your God will give it into your hand. 8When you have taken the
city, set it on fire. Do what the LORD has commanded. See to it; you
have my orders."
9Then Joshua sent them off, and they went to the place of ambush
and lay in wait between Bethel and Ai, to the west of Ai—but Joshua
spent that night with the people.
10Early the next morning Joshua mustered his men, and he and the
leaders of Israel marched before them to Ai. 11The entire force that
was with him marched up and approached the city and arrived in
front of it. They set up camp north of Ai, with the valley between them
and the city. 12Joshua had taken about five thousand men and set
them in ambush between Bethel and Ai, to the west of the city. 13They
had the soldiers take up their positions—all those in the camp to the
north of the city and the ambush to the west of it. That night Joshua
went into the valley.
14When the king of Ai saw this, he and all the men of the city hurried out early in the morning to meet Israel in battle at a certain place
overlooking the Arabah. But he did not know that an ambush had
been set against him behind the city. 15Joshua and all Israel let themselves be driven back before them, and they fled toward the desert.
16All the men of Ai were called to pursue them, and they pursued
Joshua and were lured away from the city. 17Not a man remained in Ai
or Bethel who did not go after Israel. They left the city open and went
in pursuit of Israel.
18Then the LORD said to Joshua, "Hold out toward Ai the javelin that
is in your hand, for into your hand I will deliver the city." So Joshua
held out his javelin toward Ai. 19As soon as he did this, the men in the
ambush rose quickly from their position and rushed forward. They
entered the city and captured it and quickly set it on fire.
20The men of Ai looked back and saw the smoke of the city rising
against the sky, but they had no chance to escape in any direction, for
the Israelites who had been fleeing toward the desert had turned
back against their pursuers. 21For when Joshua and all Israel saw that

one man. God got "tough" and required drastic measures to communicate his high standards for a relationship with his people. Now, he encourages Joshua and reveals his victory plan. **1.** The Israelites are sent back to Ai for another battle, only this time God assures them victory and allows them to keep the plunder and livestock for themselves. Why do you think God changed his strategy? **2.** How might Joshua have felt about this after the recent stoning of Achan and his household? What about the other Israelites? **3.** What attitude was Joshua counting on in the king and soldiers of Ai when he chose an ambush for his attack plan (vv. 4–7)? **4.** Why do you think God told Joshua to hold out his javelin while God delivered the city to him: To keep him busy while God did the work? So no human could take credit for God's victory? To allow Joshua to be a partner with him like Moses was? Other? **5.** If you were an Israelite soldier, how would you feel about killing all the people of Ai? Would the experience of Achan in chapter 7 have made it any easier? **6.** Picture yourself as a Canaanite traveling through the land. What would your impression be of the Israelites who left these two burned and desolate cities behind?

APPLY **1.** Is there an area of your life in which you hear the Lord saying to you, "Do not be afraid; do not be discouraged"? **2.** What great thing might you attempt in your life if God assured your success?

8:2–29 Same city. Different battle. Different outcome. Now, with the Lord's help, the Israelites would destroy the city of Ai.

8:2 you may carry off their plunder and livestock. This time, the soldiers were entitled to the riches of their victory. If only Achan had waited.

8:13 take up their positions. The strategy here was to catch the people of Ai in their over-confidence. With an ambush set for the city, and a plan to lure the fighting men away, their victory was certain.

8:17 Bethel. This secondary unit was strategically placed between Bethel and Ai in order to cut off possible reinforcements.

the ambush had taken the city and that smoke was going up from the city, they turned around and attacked the men of Ai. 22The men of the ambush also came out of the city against them, so that they were caught in the middle, with Israelites on both sides. Israel cut them down, leaving them neither survivors nor fugitives. 23But they took the king of Ai alive and brought him to Joshua.

24When Israel had finished killing all the men of Ai in the fields and in the desert where they had chased them, and when every one of them had been put to the sword, all the Israelites returned to Ai and killed those who were in it. 25Twelve thousand men and women fell that day—all the people of Ai. 26For Joshua did not draw back the hand that held out his javelin until he had destroyed[a] all who lived in Ai. 27But Israel did carry off for themselves the livestock and plunder of this city, as the LORD had instructed Joshua.

28So Joshua burned Ai and made it a permanent heap of ruins, a desolate place to this day. 29He hung the king of Ai on a tree and left him there until evening. At sunset, Joshua ordered them to take his body from the tree and throw it down at the entrance of the city gate. And they raised a large pile of rocks over it, which remains to this day.

The Covenant Renewed at Mount Ebal

30Then Joshua built on Mount Ebal an altar to the LORD, the God of Israel, 31as Moses the servant of the LORD had commanded the Israelites. He built it according to what is written in the Book of the Law of Moses—an altar of uncut stones, on which no iron tool had been used. On it they offered to the LORD burnt offerings and sacrificed fellowship offerings.[b] 32There, in the presence of the Israelites, Joshua copied on stones the law of Moses, which he had written. 33All Israel, aliens and citizens alike, with their elders, officials and judges, were standing on both sides of the ark of the covenant of the LORD, facing those who carried it—the priests, who were Levites. Half of the people stood in front of Mount Gerizim and half of them in front of Mount Ebal, as Moses the servant of the LORD had formerly commanded when he gave instructions to bless the people of Israel.

34Afterward, Joshua read all the words of the law—the blessings and the curses—just as it is written in the Book of the Law. 35There was not a word of all that Moses had commanded that Joshua did not read to the whole assembly of Israel, including the women and children, and the aliens who lived among them.

[a]*26* The Hebrew term refers to the irrevocable giving over of things or persons to the LORD, often by totally destroying them. [b]*31* Traditionally *peace offerings*

OPEN When was the last time your whole family gathered together? Where? What for?

STUDY The mighty army of Israel defeated and laid waste to the city of Ai. The people of God then gathered to worship and remember the Law of Moses. **1.** What was the first thing Joshua did after this great victory at Ai? How does this reveal the kind of man he was? **2.** Picture the vast assembly of all Israel at Mount Ebal. What was the purpose of gathering in this place and in this fashion (Deut. 11:29; 27:1–14)? **3.** Why do you think the children and aliens were included in this ceremony?

APPLY What might it mean for you to "build an altar" to the Lord? What would you offer?

8:26 he had destroyed all. Two *battles. Two leveled cities.* It was important that the army of Israel become known in its initial battles for complete victory.

8:29 a large pile of rocks. Like bookmarks in Israel's history, these memorials began popping up across the landscape of Canaan. Although grisly at points, each one symbolized God's might in its own way.

8:30–35 Usually, a victorious army either celebrates or strategizes its next move. Joshua did both. But neither in the traditional sense. His celebration involved an altar of sacrifice and his strategy was to review the Laws of Moses.

8:30 Mount Ebal an altar. Joshua led them here along thirty miles of uninhabited land so they could prepare for a spiritual event without having to look over their shoulders.

8:32 copied on stones the law of Moses. No one knows for sure how much of Moses' law was meticulously copied onto stones. The Ten Commandments alone would have been quite a feat. Yet, this could refer to as much as the entire Law in Deuteronomy.

8:33 All Israel. Imagine having a family meeting with over two million participants!

OPEN **1.** What was your favorite costume as a child? Why that one? **2.** Have you ever bought something that later turned out to be a lemon? How did you feel?

STUDY News of Israel's crushing victories spread across the Promised Land. As the western Canaanite kings planned for war with Israel, the Gibeonites chose a more cunning strategy. **1.** If you had been a king in Canaan, and heard the reports of how the Israelites crossed the Jordan at flood stage and devastated Jericho and Ai, how would you have reacted? **2.** How did the people of Gibeon trick Joshua and the Israelites? Why do you suppose it worked? **3.** What is the significance of the Israelites sampling the provisions but not inquiring of God (v. 14)? How would you apply this lesson to your own life? **4.** What did the Israelites do when they discovered they had been tricked (vv. 16–21)? **5.** How did Joshua finally deal with the Gibeonites? **6.** As a fearful and cursed Gibeonite, would you have fought for your freedom or submitted to perpetual slavery?

APPLY **1.** Have you ever made a promise that later turned out to be difficult or unpopular to keep? What happened? **2.** The men of Israel "did not inquire of the LORD" the way they should have (v. 14). Can you remember making an important decision without consulting God? What was the outcome?

The Gibeonite Deception

9 Now when all the kings west of the Jordan heard about these
things—those in the hill country, in the western foothills, and
along the entire coast of the Great Sea[a] as far as Lebanon (the kings
of the Hittites, Amorites, Canaanites, Perizzites, Hivites and Jebusites)— [2]they came together to make war against Joshua and Israel.
[3]However, when the people of Gibeon heard what Joshua had done
to Jericho and Ai, [4]they resorted to a ruse: They went as a delegation
whose donkeys were loaded[b] with worn-out sacks and old wineskins,
cracked and mended. [5]The men put worn and patched sandals on
their feet and wore old clothes. All the bread of their food supply was
dry and moldy. [6]Then they went to Joshua in the camp at Gilgal and
said to him and the men of Israel, "We have come from a distant
country; make a treaty with us."
[7]The men of Israel said to the Hivites, "But perhaps you live near
us. How then can we make a treaty with you?"
[8]"We are your servants," they said to Joshua.
But Joshua asked, "Who are you and where do you come from?"
[9]They answered: "Your servants have come from a very distant
country because of the fame of the LORD your God. For we have heard
reports of him: all that he did in Egypt, [10]and all that he did to the two
kings of the Amorites east of the Jordan—Sihon king of Heshbon,
and Og king of Bashan, who reigned in Ashtaroth. [11]And our elders
and all those living in our country said to us, 'Take provisions for your
journey; go and meet them and say to them, "We are your servants;
make a treaty with us." ' [12]This bread of ours was warm when we
packed it at home on the day we left to come to you. But now see how
dry and moldy it is. [13]And these wineskins that we filled were new, but
see how cracked they are. And our clothes and sandals are worn out
by the very long journey."
[14]The men of Israel sampled their provisions but did not inquire of
the LORD. [15]Then Joshua made a treaty of peace with them to let them
live, and the leaders of the assembly ratified it by oath.
[16]Three days after they made the treaty with the Gibeonites, the
Israelites heard that they were neighbors, living near them. [17]So the
Israelites set out and on the third day came to their cities: Gibeon,
Kephirah, Beeroth and Kiriath Jearim. [18]But the Israelites did not

[a]*1* That is, the Mediterranean [b]*4* Most Hebrew manuscripts; some Hebrew manuscripts, Vulgate and Syriac (see also Septuagint) *They prepared provisions and loaded their donkeys*

9:1–27 This chapter records how Israel's fame actually served to work against it in some respects. The Gibeonites, aware of the Israelites' recent victories and mildly familiar with the Law of Moses, used this information for their own good. According to Law, Israel was allowed to make treaties with people outside the land (Ex. 23:31–33; 34:12). However, it was to utterly destroy nearby cities. Neighbors with Ai, the city of Gibeon *knew it had to come up with a plan.*

9:1 heard about these things. Backwoods towns thrived on the information gleaned from the grapevine.

9:3 people of Gibeon. Not willing to remain a sitting duck, the city of Gibeon sought to protect its strategic positioning in Canaan.

9:4 ruse: They went as a delegation. What they may have lacked in courage, they made up for in cunning.

9:6 come from a distant country; make a treaty with us. The Gibeonites hoped to avoid both the truth and consequences. Unfortunately, the truth about their actual homeland would have brought consequences they could not bear—certain destruction. So, they lied to gain a treaty that would save their lives.

9:14 men of Israel ... did not inquire of the LORD. Although it may have seemed an obvious move, the officers who inspected the evidence did so on their own accord. They did not seek God's direction, which might have exposed the Gibeonites' game.

9:18 The whole assembly grumbled against the leaders. The whole assembly may have professed their sneaking suspicions after the gig was up—but it was too late at that point.

attack them, because the leaders of the assembly had sworn an oath
to them by the LORD, the God of Israel.

The whole assembly grumbled against the leaders, [19]but all the
leaders answered, "We have given them our oath by the LORD, the
God of Israel, and we cannot touch them now. [20]This is what we will
do to them: We will let them live, so that wrath will not fall on us for
breaking the oath we swore to them." [21]They continued, "Let them
live, but let them be woodcutters and water carriers for the entire
community." So the leaders' promise to them was kept.

[22]Then Joshua summoned the Gibeonites and said, "Why did you
deceive us by saying, 'We live a long way from you,' while actually
you live near us? [23]You are now under a curse: You will never cease to
serve as woodcutters and water carriers for the house of my God."

[24]They answered Joshua, "Your servants were clearly told how the
LORD your God had commanded his servant Moses to give you the
whole land and to wipe out all its inhabitants from before you. So we
feared for our lives because of you, and that is why we did this. [25]We
are now in your hands. Do to us whatever seems good and right to
you."

[26]So Joshua saved them from the Israelites, and they did not kill
them. [27]That day he made the Gibeonites woodcutters and water carriers for the community and for the altar of the LORD at the place the
LORD would choose. And that is what they are to this day.

The Sun Stands Still

10 Now Adoni-Zedek king of Jerusalem heard that Joshua had
taken Ai and totally destroyed[a] it, doing to Ai and its king as
he had done to Jericho and its king, and that the people of Gibeon
had made a treaty of peace with Israel and were living near them. [2]He
and his people were very much alarmed at this, because Gibeon was
an important city, like one of the royal cities; it was larger than Ai, and
all its men were good fighters. [3]So Adoni-Zedek king of Jerusalem
appealed to Hoham king of Hebron, Piram king of Jarmuth, Japhia
king of Lachish and Debir king of Eglon. [4]"Come up and help me
attack Gibeon," he said, "because it has made peace with Joshua and
the Israelites."

[5]Then the five kings of the Amorites—the kings of Jerusalem,
Hebron, Jarmuth, Lachish and Eglon—joined forces. They moved up
with all their troops and took up positions against Gibeon and
attacked it.

[6]The Gibeonites then sent word to Joshua in the camp at Gilgal:
"Do not abandon your servants. Come up to us quickly and save us!
Help us, because all the Amorite kings from the hill country have
joined forces against us."

[7]So Joshua marched up from Gilgal with his entire army, including
all the best fighting men. [8]The LORD said to Joshua, "Do not be afraid

[a]1 The Hebrew term refers to the irrevocable giving over of things or persons to the LORD, often by totally destroying them; also in verses 28, 35, 37, 39 and 40.

OPEN 1. When you were in high school, did you ever take a stand to defend a friend? What happened? **2.** If you could save one day of your life in a bottle to live over and over again, what day would it be?

STUDY Joshua and the Israelites have been deceived into forming a treaty with the Gibeonites of Canaan. The Gibeonites are under attack and cry for help. What will Israel do? **1.** The Amorite kings planned for war against Israel in chapter 9. How would you feel about the action Gibeon took if you had been one of those kings? What would you do about it? **2.** After the trickery in the previous chapter, would you have helped Gibeon if you had been Joshua? **3.** Imagine that you are a reporter for the *Jerusalem Journal* of Joshua's day. Write the headline and opening sentence for a story about Joshua's defeat of the Amorites. **4.** Who was actually responsible for Israel's victory? Why is this important? **5.** What miracles does God perform in this story? Can you think of possible explanations for them? If you

10:1–43 This chapter describes repeated accounts of victories at various cities and their subsequent destruction.

10:2 Gibeon was an important city. No one overlooked Gibeon's prominence. And no one wanted to give her up either. Like children picking teams, the king of Jerusalem challenged Israel to a contest for ownership of Gibeon.

10:6 Do not abandon your servants. The Gibeonites eagerly exercised their rights as treaty-members with Israel. Even though their treaty was based on deceit, Joshua honored it (9:19–23).

of them; I have given them into your hand. Not one of them will be
able to withstand you."
9After an all-night march from Gilgal, Joshua took them by
surprise. 10The LORD threw them into confusion before Israel, who
defeated them in a great victory at Gibeon. Israel pursued them along
the road going up to Beth Horon and cut them down all the way to
Azekah and Makkedah. 11As they fled before Israel on the road down
from Beth Horon to Azekah, the LORD hurled large hailstones down
on them from the sky, and more of them died from the hailstones
than were killed by the swords of the Israelites.
12On the day the LORD gave the Amorites over to Israel, Joshua said
to the LORD in the presence of Israel:

"O sun, stand still over Gibeon,
  O moon, over the Valley of Aijalon."
13So the sun stood still,
  and the moon stopped,
  till the nation avenged itself on[a] its enemies,

as it is written in the Book of Jashar.
The sun stopped in the middle of the sky and delayed going down
about a full day. 14There has never been a day like it before or since, a
day when the LORD listened to a man. Surely the LORD was fighting
for Israel!
15Then Joshua returned with all Israel to the camp at Gilgal.

Five Amorite Kings Killed

16Now the five kings had fled and hidden in the cave at Makkedah.
17When Joshua was told that the five kings had been found hiding in
the cave at Makkedah, 18he said, "Roll large rocks up to the mouth of
the cave, and post some men there to guard it. 19But don't stop! Pursue your enemies, attack them from the rear and don't let them reach
their cities, for the LORD your God has given them into your hand."
20So Joshua and the Israelites destroyed them completely—almost
to a man—but the few who were left reached their fortified cities.
21The whole army then returned safely to Joshua in the camp at Makkedah, and no one uttered a word against the Israelites.
22Joshua said, "Open the mouth of the cave and bring those five
kings out to me." 23So they brought the five kings out of the cave—
the kings of Jerusalem, Hebron, Jarmuth, Lachish and Eglon. 24When
they had brought these kings to Joshua, he summoned all the men of
Israel and said to the army commanders who had come with him,
"Come here and put your feet on the necks of these kings." So they
came forward and placed their feet on their necks.
25Joshua said to them, "Do not be afraid; do not be discouraged. Be
strong and courageous. This is what the LORD will do to all the enemies you are going to fight." 26Then Joshua struck and killed the

[a]13 *Or nation triumphed over*

could think of an explanation, how would that impact your faith?

APPLY 1. Have you experienced a time of struggle when you felt that the Lord listened to you and responded in such a way that you knew he was fighting for you? What was that like? **2.** Who in your life do you feel you could call on in a tight spot? What is it about this person that elicits your trust?

OPEN 1. When you played "hide and seek" as a kid, where was your favorite hiding place? **2.** Have you ever explored a cave? What do you remember most about your experience?

STUDY Joshua and his men, with God's miraculous intervention, have just routed the five Amorite armies who came to destroy Israel's ally, Gibeon. The enemy kings are trapped at Makkedah and Joshua must now deal with them. **1.** Where did the Israelites find the five Amorite kings? Why do you think they weren't fighting with their troops (v. 11)? **2.** Verse 21 tells us that after the Israelite army completely destroyed the enemy and returned safely to their camp at Makkedah, "no one uttered a word against Israel." How do you think Israel silenced its enemies? **3.** How did Joshua encourage the troops? How might succeeding generations of Israelites feel when they see the mound of rocks marking the mouth of the cave at Makkedah?

10:19 has given them into your hand. What runner could not find his second wind if he discovered he was sure to win? The Israelites rushed after the kings with victory in mind.

10:21 army returned ... no one uttered a word. Word of mouth was a powerful wartime tool then as much as it is a powerful social force today. If one city grumbled against an enemy often enough, others would soon gain a common enemy. Consider the power of rumors as a case in point. Silencing one's foes proved to be a powerful tactic.

kings and hung them on five trees, and they were left hanging on the trees until evening.
[27]At sunset Joshua gave the order and they took them down from the trees and threw them into the cave where they had been hiding. At the mouth of the cave they placed large rocks, which are there to this day.
[28]That day Joshua took Makkedah. He put the city and its king to the sword and totally destroyed everyone in it. He left no survivors. And he did to the king of Makkedah as he had done to the king of Jericho.

Southern Cities Conquered

[29]Then Joshua and all Israel with him moved on from Makkedah to
Libnah and attacked it. [30]The LORD also gave that city and its king into
Israel's hand. The city and everyone in it Joshua put to the sword. He left no survivors there. And he did to its king as he had done to the king of Jericho.
[31]Then Joshua and all Israel with him moved on from Libnah to
Lachish; he took up positions against it and attacked it. [32]The LORD
handed Lachish over to Israel, and Joshua took it on the second day. The city and everyone in it he put to the sword, just as he had done to
Libnah. [33]Meanwhile, Horam king of Gezer had come up to help
Lachish, but Joshua defeated him and his army—until no survivors were left.
[34]Then Joshua and all Israel with him moved on from Lachish to
Eglon; they took up positions against it and attacked it. [35]They cap-
tured it that same day and put it to the sword and totally destroyed everyone in it, just as they had done to Lachish.
[36]Then Joshua and all Israel with him went up from Eglon to Hebron
and attacked it. [37]They took the city and put it to the sword, together with its king, its villages and everyone in it. They left no survivors. Just as at Eglon, they totally destroyed it and everyone in it.
[38]Then Joshua and all Israel with him turned around and attacked
Debir. [39]They took the city, its king and its villages, and put them to the sword. Everyone in it they totally destroyed. They left no survivors. They did to Debir and its king as they had done to Libnah and its king and to Hebron.
[40]So Joshua subdued the whole region, including the hill country, the Negev, the western foothills and the mountain slopes, together with all their kings. He left no survivors. He totally destroyed all who breathed, just as the LORD, the God of Israel, had commanded.
[41]Joshua subdued them from Kadesh Barnea to Gaza and from the
whole region of Goshen to Gibeon. [42]All these kings and their lands
Joshua conquered in one campaign, because the LORD, the God of Israel, fought for Israel.
[43]Then Joshua returned with all Israel to the camp at Gilgal.

APPLY Who or what is the enemy you are facing in your life right now? How can this group encourage you and support you in prayer as you seek God for his battle plan?

OPEN Where did you most feel like you were part of a "team": On the soccer field? Basketball court? Friends? Family? Group at church? Playing with the band?

STUDY Joshua continues to move through Canaan, conquering the whole southern region in one crushing campaign that "takes no prisoners." **1.** What major cities did the Israelites attack? What was the outcome of each battle? Do you see a pattern? **2.** The text repeats the phrase, "Joshua and all Israel with him" six times. What message do you see here and why do you think it is important? **3.** Picture yourself exhausted, in the middle of this bloody campaign. Why do you think God commanded the Israelites to destroy the cities *totally*? Might God command something similar today? If so, what "zero tolerance" program comes to mind?

APPLY 1. Has there been a time in your life when God brought you great victory at someone else's expense? **2.** Where in your life is it evident that the Lord is fighting for you now? Does anyone stand alongside you in the battle? Who?

10:27 At the mouth of the cave they placed large rocks. When others would pass the mouths of the caves, they would remember the victory from that day.

10:28 Joshua ... totally destroyed everyone. If it were televised, Israel's total destruction of its enemies would probably earn a Violence-And-Then-Some rating. However, it dramatically portrays God's intolerance for sin. When God destroyed sin, he also protected his people from impurity.

10:41 Kadesh Barnea to Gaza. Here, the author gives the half-time report on the conquering of Canaan. From the southernmost part to the northernmost, the Israelites' string of victories secured their borders.

Northern Kings Defeated

11 When Jabin king of Hazor heard of this, he sent word to Jobab
king of Madon, to the kings of Shimron and Acshaph, 2and to
the northern kings who were in the mountains, in the Arabah south of
Kinnereth, in the western foothills and in Naphoth Dor[a] on the west;
3to the Canaanites in the east and west; to the Amorites, Hittites, Perizzites and Jebusites in the hill country; and to the Hivites below Hermon in the region of Mizpah. 4They came out with all their troops and
a large number of horses and chariots—a huge army, as numerous as
the sand on the seashore. 5All these kings joined forces and made
camp together at the Waters of Merom, to fight against Israel.

6The LORD said to Joshua, "Do not be afraid of them, because by
this time tomorrow I will hand all of them over to Israel, slain. You
are to hamstring their horses and burn their chariots."

7So Joshua and his whole army came against them suddenly at the
Waters of Merom and attacked them, 8and the LORD gave them into
the hand of Israel. They defeated them and pursued them all the way
to Greater Sidon, to Misrephoth Maim, and to the Valley of Mizpah on
the east, until no survivors were left. 9Joshua did to them as the LORD
had directed: He hamstrung their horses and burned their chariots.

10At that time Joshua turned back and captured Hazor and put its
king to the sword. (Hazor had been the head of all these kingdoms.)
11Everyone in it they put to the sword. They totally destroyed[b] them,
not sparing anything that breathed, and he burned up Hazor itself.

12Joshua took all these royal cities and their kings and put them to
the sword. He totally destroyed them, as Moses the servant of the
LORD had commanded. 13Yet Israel did not burn any of the cities built
on their mounds—except Hazor, which Joshua burned. 14The Israelites carried off for themselves all the plunder and livestock of these
cities, but all the people they put to the sword until they completely
destroyed them, not sparing anyone that breathed. 15As the LORD
commanded his servant Moses, so Moses commanded Joshua, and
Joshua did it; he left nothing undone of all that the LORD commanded
Moses.

16So Joshua took this entire land: the hill country, all the Negev,
the whole region of Goshen, the western foothills, the Arabah and
the mountains of Israel with their foothills, 17from Mount Halak,
which rises toward Seir, to Baal Gad in the Valley of Lebanon below
Mount Hermon. He captured all their kings and struck them down,
putting them to death. 18Joshua waged war against all these kings for
a long time. 19Except for the Hivites living in Gibeon, not one city

[a]2 Or *in the heights of Dor* [b]11 The Hebrew term refers to the irrevocable giving over of things or persons to the LORD, often by totally destroying them; also in verses 12, 20 and 21.

OPEN 1. When was the last time you were scared to death? **2.** Early in life, I learned that the secret to success is ________. How has that knowledge served you over the years?

STUDY Joshua and the army of Israel completed their southern campaign and turned toward the northern kingdoms. God gives Joshua his plan for victory and encouragement to continue against a mighty foe. **1.** How did the northern kings respond when they heard about the Israelite victories in the south (vv. 1–5)? **2.** If you had been Joshua and your reconnaissance told you that the enemy gathered against you was as numerous as the "sand on the seashore," what scenarios would have played in your mind as to the outcome of the coming battle? Do they change after God speaks his words of encouragement and comfort? **3.** Why do you think Joshua went on the offensive and attacked his mighty enemy first? How did hamstringing their horses and burning their chariots contribute to God's victory plan? **4.** In verses 12–15, Joshua has all the people in the royal cities destroyed, but keeps the livestock, plunder and city structures for the Israelites. Only the city of Hazor is burned. How has this strategy changed from earlier victories? Why might this be important to the future of Israel? **5.** Moses' name and his command are mentioned in verse 15. How does this reflect on Joshua in the eyes of the Israelites? **6.** According to this chapter, why were Joshua and the Israelites successful in their conquest of the Promised Land, in spite of overwhelming odds against them? What lesson can you draw from this for your own life?

APPLY 1. Thinking back over the past week, at what point do you identify with Joshua: When all his enemies are coming to attack him? When he is winning despite the odds against him? When he is winning, but

11:1–23 From this vantage point, the Israelites began the final phase of conquest in northern Canaan. However, the battles would not be easy, since their reputation was well known among their enemies and coalitions were quickly forming.

11:1 Jabin king of Hazor. A brilliant strategist, the king convinced several nearby cities to amass their troops for one large offensive against the Israelites.

11:6 by this time tomorrow. Considering the size of the combined armies and their mounted chariots, this 24-hour promise seemed almost too good to be true.

11:10 Hazor. The head of the enemy armed forces.

11:15 Joshua ... left nothing undone. Joshua led the people by example and obedience, as did Moses.

11:18 Joshua waged war ... for a long time. Although he was largely outnumbered, on unfamiliar turf, and ill-equipped for fighting sophisticated warriors, Joshua did not give up at any point.

made a treaty of peace with the Israelites, who took them all in battle.
[20]For it was the LORD himself who hardened their hearts to wage war
against Israel, so that he might destroy them totally, exterminating
them without mercy, as the LORD had commanded Moses.
[21]At that time Joshua went and destroyed the Anakites from the hill
country: from Hebron, Debir and Anab, from all the hill country of Judah, and from all the hill country of Israel. Joshua totally destroyed
them and their towns. [22]No Anakites were left in Israelite territory;
only in Gaza, Gath and Ashdod did any survive. [23]So Joshua took the
entire land, just as the LORD had directed Moses, and he gave it as an
inheritance to Israel according to their tribal divisions.

Then the land had rest from war.

List of Defeated Kings

12 These are the kings of the land whom the Israelites had defeated and whose territory they took over east of the Jordan, from the Arnon Gorge to Mount Hermon, including all the eastern side of the Arabah:

[2]Sihon king of the Amorites,
who reigned in Heshbon. He ruled from Aroer on the rim of the
Arnon Gorge—from the middle of the gorge—to the Jabbok
River, which is the border of the Ammonites. This included half
of Gilead. [3]He also ruled over the eastern Arabah from the Sea of
Kinnereth[a] to the Sea of the Arabah (the Salt Sea[b]), to Beth Jeshimoth, and then southward below the slopes of Pisgah.

[4]And the territory of Og king of Bashan,
one of the last of the Rephaites, who reigned in Ashtaroth and
Edrei. [5]He ruled over Mount Hermon, Salecah, all of Bashan to
the border of the people of Geshur and Maacah, and half of Gilead to the border of Sihon king of Heshbon.

[6]Moses, the servant of the LORD, and the Israelites conquered
them. And Moses the servant of the LORD gave their land to the Reubenites, the Gadites and the half-tribe of Manasseh to be their possession.

[7]These are the kings of the land that Joshua and the Israelites conquered on the west side of the Jordan, from Baal Gad in the Valley of
Lebanon to Mount Halak, which rises toward Seir (their lands Joshua
gave as an inheritance to the tribes of Israel according to their tribal
divisions— [8]the hill country, the western foothills, the Arabah, the
mountain slopes, the desert and the Negev—the lands of the Hittites,
Amorites, Canaanites, Perizzites, Hivites and Jebusites):

[9]the king of Jericho — one
the king of Ai (near Bethel) — one

[a]3 That is, Galilee [b]3 That is, the Dead Sea

the war goes on and on? When the land finally has rest from war? Other? **2.** Do you always expect success when you are obedient to God? Does your personal experience match your expectation?

OPEN **1.** Which grandparent most influenced your life? Were you affected by their words or example? **2.** What one accomplishment in your teen years do you take the most pride in?

STUDY The Israelites have completed a long victorious campaign that conquered all the land the Lord commanded Moses to take. The Promised Land is at rest from war and the Israelites take time to record their victories. **1.** Verses 1–6 describe the kings defeated by the Israelites under Moses' leadership. Where were these kings located and why did Israel end up fighting them (Num. 21:21–35; Deut. 2:24–37)? What happened to their land? **2.** Verses 7–24 list the kings defeated under Joshua's leadership west of the Jordan River. What battle stands out in your mind? Can you think of a major trial or battle that you have experienced where writing down the details might be important? **3.** Why do you think so many cities are listed in this chapter? How might such a list be important to future generations of Israelites? Do you think the Hebrew army was a great fighting force? How do you attribute so many battle successes to them? **4.** Picture the whole military campaign described in the first 11 chapters of Joshua. What do you see as the main theme represented here? How might it apply to your own life situation?

APPLY **1.** As you look back over your life, what enemies has God helped you conquer: A bad

11:20 hardened their hearts. God merely confirmed what was already present in the hearts of the Canaanites: a stubborn resistance to his grace. Rahab is a reminder of God's willingness to allow people the opportunity to repent.

12:1–24 These accomplishments read like resumes for Moses and Joshua. In an area no bigger than fifty miles wide and 150 miles long, thirty-one kings representing small city-states were encountered and defeated. The careful attention to detail gave Israel a good reminder of how far it had come.

12:1 whose territory they took over. This first section represented the lands secured by Moses in the first half of the Canaanite battles.

temper? Shyness? Smoking? Addiction? Illness? Phobia? Marriage difficulties? Weight problem? Poor self image? Other? Can you share your victory experience with this group? **2.** Who, in the past year, has helped lead the way to your own spiritual growth?

---

10 the king of Jerusalem one
the king of Hebron one
11 the king of Jarmuth one
the king of Lachish one
12 the king of Eglon one
the king of Gezer one
13 the king of Debir one
the king of Geder one
14 the king of Hormah one
the king of Arad one
15 the king of Libnah one
the king of Adullam one
16 the king of Makkedah one
the king of Bethel one
17 the king of Tappuah one
the king of Hepher one
18 the king of Aphek one
the king of Lasharon one
19 the king of Madon one
the king of Hazor one
20 the king of Shimron Meron one
the king of Acshaph one
21 the king of Taanach one
the king of Megiddo one
22 the king of Kedesh one
the king of Jokneam in Carmel one
23 the king of Dor (in Naphoth Dor[a]) one
the king of Goyim in Gilgal one
24 the king of Tirzah one
thirty-one kings in all.

Land Still to Be Taken

13 When Joshua was old and well advanced in years, the LORD
said to him, "You are very old, and there are still very large
areas of land to be taken over.

2"This is the land that remains: all the regions of the Philistines
and Geshurites: 3from the Shihor River on the east of Egypt to
the territory of Ekron on the north, all of it counted as Canaanite
(the territory of the five Philistine rulers in Gaza, Ashdod, Ashkelon, Gath and Ekron—that of the Avvites); 4from the south, all
the land of the Canaanites, from Arah of the Sidonians as far as
Aphek, the region of the Amorites, 5the area of the Gebalites[b];
and all Lebanon to the east, from Baal Gad below Mount Hermon to Lebo[c] Hamath.

[a]23 Or *in the heights of Dor* [b]5 That is, the area of Byblos [c]5 Or *to the entrance to*

OPEN 1. As a child, did your parents make you eat everything on your plate? **2.** Are you the same with your children?

STUDY At an age when most of us would be comfortably settled into retirement, God reminds Joshua of unfinished business. **1.** What areas still remain to be taken? Why do you think God wants Joshua to finish the job? **2.** If you were Joshua, how would you feel about coming out of retirement to wage war again?

APPLY 1. What things do you find more difficult to accomplish now than when you were

---

12:12 king of Gezer. Although Joshua defeated all of these kings, the record does not necessarily mean their cities were captured as well. The king of Gezer is one example. With a limited army, Joshua was not able to station troops at each city.

13:1–33 Like reading a will, this chapter deals with splitting the inherited land among the family of tribes. Two and one-half tribes received land from Moses on the east of the Jordan. The remaining tribes, with the exception of the Levites, would receive the spoils from Joshua's victories.

13:1 Joshua was old and advanced. Moses and Joshua both became Israel's leaders at around age 80. At the time of these events, Joshua was about 100 years old.

[6]"As for all the inhabitants of the mountain regions from Lebanon
to Misrephoth Maim, that is, all the Sidonians, I myself will drive
them out before the Israelites. Be sure to allocate this land to Israel
for an inheritance, as I have instructed you, [7]and divide it as an inheritance among the nine tribes and half of the tribe of Manasseh."

Division of the Land East of the Jordan

[8]The other half of Manasseh,[a] the Reubenites and the Gadites had received the inheritance that Moses had given them east of the Jordan,
as he, the servant of the LORD, had assigned it to them.

[9]It extended from Aroer on the rim of the Arnon Gorge, and from
the town in the middle of the gorge, and included the whole plateau of Medeba as far as Dibon, [10]and all the towns of Sihon king
of the Amorites, who ruled in Heshbon, out to the border of the
Ammonites. [11]It also included Gilead, the territory of the people
of Geshur and Maacah, all of Mount Hermon and all Bashan as
far as Salecah— [12]that is, the whole kingdom of Og in Bashan,
who had reigned in Ashtaroth and Edrei and had survived as one
of the last of the Rephaites. Moses had defeated them and taken
over their land. [13]But the Israelites did not drive out the people
of Geshur and Maacah, so they continue to live among the Israelites to this day.

[14]But to the tribe of Levi he gave no inheritance, since the offerings
made by fire to the LORD, the God of Israel, are their inheritance, as
he promised them.

[15]This is what Moses had given to the tribe of Reuben, clan by clan:

[16]The territory from Aroer on the rim of the Arnon Gorge, and
from the town in the middle of the gorge, and the whole plateau
past Medeba [17]to Heshbon and all its towns on the plateau, including Dibon, Bamoth Baal, Beth Baal Meon, [18]Jahaz, Kedemoth, Mephaath, [19]Kiriathaim, Sibmah, Zereth Shahar on the
hill in the valley, [20]Beth Peor, the slopes of Pisgah, and Beth Jeshimoth [21]—all the towns on the plateau and the entire realm of
Sihon king of the Amorites, who ruled at Heshbon. Moses had
defeated him and the Midianite chiefs, Evi, Rekem, Zur, Hur and
Reba—princes allied with Sihon—who lived in that country. [22]In
addition to those slain in battle, the Israelites had put to the
sword Balaam son of Beor, who practiced divination. [23]The
boundary of the Reubenites was the bank of the Jordan. These
towns and their villages were the inheritance of the Reubenites,
clan by clan.

[24]This is what Moses had given to the tribe of Gad, clan by clan:

[25]The territory of Jazer, all the towns of Gilead and half the
Ammonite country as far as Aroer, near Rabbah; [26]and from

[a]8 Hebrew *With it* (that is, with the other half of Manasseh)

younger? **2.** Do you have some "unfinished business" with God?

OPEN 1. Do you have immigrant relatives or friends who tell stories about the "old country"? What do they talk about most? **2.** When was the last time you moved?

STUDY Joshua divides the territory east of the Jordan River as Moses had promised, and gives it as an inheritance to the tribes of Gad, Reuben and half of Manasseh. **1.** Where is this land located? How was their inheritance different from the other tribes of Israel? **2.** What potential problems might the Israelites experience because of where these tribes settled? **3.** Imagine that you're a member of a Gaddite clan. What's the first thing you plan to do when you receive your own personal inheritance? **4.** Verse 13 tells us that the Israelites didn't drive out the people of Geshur and Maacah. How do you think this will affect the future of Israel? **5.** In verse 22, we see Balaam singled out in the record of who the Israelites slayed. Why did he deserve this fate (Num. 25; 31:8)? **6.** What reason does God state for not giving the Levites an inheritance of land (vv. 14,33; Num. 18:20–24)? If you were a Levite, would you have felt slighted or doubly blessed? Explain.

APPLY 1. What type of "inheritance" has your parents given you: Spiritual? Cultural? Intellectual? Emotional? Material? Other? Explain. **2.** Can you identify something you feel you have received as a specific "inheritance" from the Lord? What have you done with it?

13:15 to the tribe of Reuben. These Israelites were cattle herders and anxiously awaited the rich grazing land east of the Jordan River.

13:22 divination. Balaam was a pagan fortune-teller who was hired by the king of Moab in order to curse the Israelites on their initial journey through the land years earlier (Num. 22–24).

13:24 to the tribe of Gad. Gad enjoyed the central region of the area.

Heshbon to Ramath Mizpah and Betonim, and from Mahanaim
to the territory of Debir; [27]and in the valley, Beth Haram, Beth
Nimrah, Succoth and Zaphon with the rest of the realm of Sihon
king of Heshbon (the east side of the Jordan, the territory up to
the end of the Sea of Kinnereth[a]). [28]These towns and their villages were the inheritance of the Gadites, clan by clan.

[29]This is what Moses had given to the half-tribe of Manasseh, that is,
to half the family of the descendants of Manasseh, clan by clan:

[30]The territory extending from Mahanaim and including all of
Bashan, the entire realm of Og king of Bashan—all the settlements of Jair in Bashan, sixty towns, [31]half of Gilead, and Ashtaroth and Edrei (the royal cities of Og in Bashan). This was for the
descendants of Makir son of Manasseh—for half of the sons of
Makir, clan by clan.

[32]This is the inheritance Moses had given when he was in the
plains of Moab across the Jordan east of Jericho. [33]But to the tribe of
Levi, Moses had given no inheritance; the LORD, the God of Israel, is
their inheritance, as he promised them.

Division of the Land West of the Jordan

14 Now these are the areas the Israelites received as an inheritance in the land of Canaan, which Eleazar the priest, Joshua
son of Nun and the heads of the tribal clans of Israel allotted to them.
[2]Their inheritances were assigned by lot to the nine-and-a-half
tribes, as the LORD had commanded through Moses. [3]Moses had
granted the two-and-a-half tribes their inheritance east of the Jordan
but had not granted the Levites an inheritance among the rest, [4]for
the sons of Joseph had become two tribes—Manasseh and Ephraim.
The Levites received no share of the land but only towns to live in,
with pasturelands for their flocks and herds. [5]So the Israelites divided the land, just as the LORD had commanded Moses.

Hebron Given to Caleb

[6]Now the men of Judah approached Joshua at Gilgal, and Caleb son
of Jephunneh the Kenizzite said to him, "You know what the LORD
said to Moses the man of God at Kadesh Barnea about you and me. [7]I
was forty years old when Moses the servant of the LORD sent me from
Kadesh Barnea to explore the land. And I brought him back a report
according to my convictions, [8]but my brothers who went up with me
made the hearts of the people melt with fear. I, however, followed the
LORD my God wholeheartedly. [9]So on that day Moses swore to me,
'The land on which your feet have walked will be your inheritance

[a]27 That is, Galilee

OPEN Who made the big decisions in your childhood home? How much input did you have?

STUDY **1.** How did the tribes west of the Jordan receive their land? **2.** Why treat the tribes east of the river and the Levites differently?

APPLY What is your "lot in life"? Did you choose it, or did someone else choose it for you?

OPEN When you were between the ages of 8 and 10, how did you and your buddies choose sides to play?

STUDY The tribal heads of the Israelite clans are dividing the land west of the Jordan by a game of chance, when an old comrade of Joshua's steps forward to remind him of a promise made 45 years earlier. **1.** Who was Caleb and what was his chief "claim to fame"? **2.** If "actions reveal character," what do Caleb's

---

13:29 to the half-tribe of Manasseh. Although the land was beautiful, *none of the areas on the east of the Jordan* benefited from a natural border of protection.

14:1–15 This chapter details the real estate given to the remaining tribes on the west side of the Jordan River. Caleb, one of the original spies sent into Canaan, also reveals his lifelong plans for inheriting Hebron.

14:1 Eleazar. Using the priestly office to divide the land according to lots reemphasized God's supervisory role in each tribe's inheritance. Eleazar was Aaron's son (Num. 3:32).

14:4 two tribes—Manasseh and Ephraim. These were actually Joseph's children, whom Jacob had adopted to form the twelve tribes. They shared full legal rights of inheritance.

and that of your children forever, because you have followed the
LORD my God wholeheartedly.’[a]
10“Now then, just as the LORD promised, he has kept me alive for
forty-five years since the time he said this to Moses, while Israel
moved about in the desert. So here I am today, eighty-five years old!
11I am still as strong today as the day Moses sent me out; I’m just as
vigorous to go out to battle now as I was then. 12Now give me this hill
country that the LORD promised me that day. You yourself heard then
that the Anakites were there and their cities were large and fortified,
but, the LORD helping me, I will drive them out just as he said.”
13Then Joshua blessed Caleb son of Jephunneh and gave him Hebron as his inheritance. 14So Hebron has belonged to Caleb son of
Jephunneh the Kenizzite ever since, because he followed the LORD,
the God of Israel, wholeheartedly. 15(Hebron used to be called Kiriath
Arba after Arba, who was the greatest man among the Anakites.)
Then the land had rest from war.

Allotment for Judah

15 The allotment for the tribe of Judah, clan by clan, extended
down to the territory of Edom, to the Desert of Zin in the
extreme south.
2Their southern boundary started from the bay at the southern
end of the Salt Sea,[b] 3crossed south of Scorpion[c] Pass, continued
on to Zin and went over to the south of Kadesh Barnea. Then it
ran past Hezron up to Addar and curved around to Karka. 4It then
passed along to Azmon and joined the Wadi of Egypt, ending at
the sea. This is their[d] southern boundary.
5The eastern boundary is the Salt Sea as far as the mouth of
the Jordan.
The northern boundary started from the bay of the sea at the
mouth of the Jordan, 6went up to Beth Hoglah and continued
north of Beth Arabah to the Stone of Bohan son of Reuben. 7The
boundary then went up to Debir from the Valley of Achor and
turned north to Gilgal, which faces the Pass of Adummim south
of the gorge. It continued along to the waters of En Shemesh and
came out at En Rogel. 8Then it ran up the Valley of Ben Hinnom
along the southern slope of the Jebusite city (that is, Jerusalem).
From there it climbed to the top of the hill west of the Hinnom
Valley at the northern end of the Valley of Rephaim. 9From the
hilltop the boundary headed toward the spring of the waters of
Nephtoah, came out at the towns of Mount Ephron and went
down toward Baalah (that is, Kiriath Jearim). 10Then it curved
westward from Baalah to Mount Seir, ran along the northern

[a]9 Deut. 1:36 [b]2 That is, the Dead Sea; also in verse 5 [c]3 Hebrew *Akrabbim* [d]4 Hebrew *your*

actions say about the kind of man he was in the prime of life (vv. 6–9)? **3.** How was Caleb different from the others Moses sent to spy on the Promised Land? **4.** In your opinion, has Caleb changed much over the years (vv. 10–12)?

APPLY Think of a time when you took a “faith stand.” Did you have a friend like Caleb standing with you? Who was it? What would your experience have been like if that friend had not been there?

OPEN 1. What kind of fence would you build around your “dream house”: White picket? Red brick? Split rail? Barbed wire? Stone? Other? **2.** How were disputes with your siblings over toys and other possessions handled in your family?

STUDY Judah steps forward to receive its inheritance, the largest of any tribe. Caleb claims his apportionment, and chooses a creative approach to capture an enemy. **1.** The first allotment of land west of the Jordan was given to Judah. What were its major boundaries? How did it compare to the other tribal allotments? **2.** What do we learn about Caleb from verses 13–19? What does he do with the land allotted to him? How was he able to get the best out of others? **3.** Imagine that you are Acsah, Caleb’s daughter. How do you feel about the way your father went about finding you a husband? **4.** Othniel later became a judge (Judg. 3:7–11). How might his family connections have influenced his career? **5.** Verse 63 tells us that Judah couldn’t dislodge the Jebusites from Jerusalem. Do you think that has any relevance to the border disputes in Israel today? How so?

15:1–63 As the largest tribe, Judah’s real estate deed is the longest and most detailed of a single tribe.

15:1 tribe of Judah. Judah would not disappoint the great expectations set on a grand tribe. It would be the tribe of powerful rulers like David and eventually the Messiah himself.

15:2 Their southern boundary. The great detail provided here (vv. 1–12) reveals the importance of the land inheritance to the people and God.

15:4 Wadi of Egypt. This river in Egypt helped form the lower boundaries of Judah.

15:5 Salt Sea. Another name for the Dead Sea. It is a body of water with such high sodium content that a person would actually float in its waters.

APPLY **1.** Do you feel that your family ties have opened doors or closed them for you? How? **2.** If you're married, share with this group the story of how you met your spouse, and when and how you knew that he or she was the "one." If you are *not* married, share your parents' story if you know it.

slope of Mount Jearim (that is, Kesalon), continued down to Beth Shemesh and crossed to Timnah. 11It went to the northern slope of Ekron, turned toward Shikkeron, passed along to Mount Baalah and reached Jabneel. The boundary ended at the sea.

12The western boundary is the coastline of the Great Sea.[a]

These are the boundaries around the people of Judah by their clans.

13In accordance with the LORD's command to him, Joshua gave to Caleb son of Jephunneh a portion in Judah—Kiriath Arba, that is, Hebron. (Arba was the forefather of Anak.) 14From Hebron Caleb drove out the three Anakites—Sheshai, Ahiman and Talmai—descendants of Anak. 15From there he marched against the people living in Debir (formerly called Kiriath Sepher). 16And Caleb said, "I will give my daughter Acsah in marriage to the man who attacks and captures Kiriath Sepher." 17Othniel son of Kenaz, Caleb's brother, took it; so Caleb gave his daughter Acsah to him in marriage.

18One day when she came to Othniel, she urged him[b] to ask her father for a field. When she got off her donkey, Caleb asked her, "What can I do for you?"

19She replied, "Do me a special favor. Since you have given me land in the Negev, give me also springs of water." So Caleb gave her the upper and lower springs.

20This is the inheritance of the tribe of Judah, clan by clan:

21The southernmost towns of the tribe of Judah in the Negev toward the boundary of Edom were:

Kabzeel, Eder, Jagur, 22Kinah, Dimonah, Adadah, 23Kedesh, Hazor, Ithnan, 24Ziph, Telem, Bealoth, 25Hazor Hadattah, Kerioth Hezron (that is, Hazor), 26Amam, Shema, Moladah, 27Hazar Gaddah, Heshmon, Beth Pelet, 28Hazar Shual, Beersheba, Biziothiah, 29Baalah, Iim, Ezem, 30Eltolad, Kesil, Hormah, 31Ziklag, Madmannah, Sansannah, 32Lebaoth, Shilhim, Ain and Rimmon—a total of twenty-nine towns and their villages.

33In the western foothills:

Eshtaol, Zorah, Ashnah, 34Zanoah, En Gannim, Tappuah, Enam, 35Jarmuth, Adullam, Socoh, Azekah, 36Shaaraim, Adithaim and Gederah (or Gederothaim)[c]—fourteen towns and their villages.

37Zenan, Hadashah, Migdal Gad, 38Dilean, Mizpah, Joktheel, 39Lachish, Bozkath, Eglon, 40Cabbon, Lahmas, Kitlish, 41Gederoth, Beth Dagon, Naamah and Makkedah—sixteen towns and their villages.

42Libnah, Ether, Ashan, 43Iphtah, Ashnah, Nezib, 44Keilah, Aczib and Mareshah—nine towns and their villages.

45Ekron, with its surrounding settlements and villages; 46west of Ekron, all that were in the vicinity of Ashdod, together with their villages; 47Ashdod, its surrounding settlements and villages; and Gaza, its settlements and villages, as far as the Wadi of Egypt and the coastline of the Great Sea.

[a]*12* That is, the Mediterranean; also in verse 47 [b]*18* Hebrew and some Septuagint manuscripts; other Septuagint manuscripts (see also note at Judges 1:14) *Othniel, he urged her* [c]*36* Or *Gederah and Gederothaim*

48In the hill country:
Shamir, Jattir, Socoh, 49Dannah, Kiriath Sannah (that is, Debir),
50Anab, Eshtemoh, Anim, 51Goshen, Holon and Giloh—eleven
towns and their villages.
52Arab, Dumah, Eshan, 53Janim, Beth Tappuah, Aphekah,
54Humtah, Kiriath Arba (that is, Hebron) and Zior—nine towns
and their villages.
55Maon, Carmel, Ziph, Juttah, 56Jezreel, Jokdeam, Zanoah,
57Kain, Gibeah and Timnah—ten towns and their villages.
58Halhul, Beth Zur, Gedor, 59Maarath, Beth Anoth and Eltekon—six towns and their villages.
60Kiriath Baal (that is, Kiriath Jearim) and Rabbah—two towns
and their villages.

61In the desert:
Beth Arabah, Middin, Secacah, 62Nibshan, the City of Salt and
En Gedi—six towns and their villages.
63Judah could not dislodge the Jebusites, who were living in Jerusalem; to this day the Jebusites live there with the people of Judah.

Allotment for Ephraim and Manasseh

16 The allotment for Joseph began at the Jordan of Jericho,[a] east of the waters of Jericho, and went up from there through the desert into the hill country of Bethel. 2It went on
from Bethel (that is, Luz),[b] crossed over to the territory of the Arkites in Ataroth, 3descended westward to the territory of the Japhletites as far as the region of Lower Beth Horon and on to Gezer, ending at the sea.
4So Manasseh and Ephraim, the descendants of Joseph, received their inheritance.

5This was the territory of Ephraim, clan by clan:
The boundary of their inheritance went from Ataroth Addar in the east to Upper Beth Horon 6and continued to the sea. From Micmethath on the north it curved eastward to Taanath Shiloh, passing by it to Janoah on the east. 7Then it went down from Janoah to Ataroth and Naarah, touched Jericho and came out at the Jordan. 8From Tappuah the border went west to the Kanah Ravine and ended at the sea. This was the inheritance of the tribe of the Ephraimites, clan by clan. 9It also included all the towns and their villages that were set aside for the Ephraimites within the inheritance of the Manassites.
10They did not dislodge the Canaanites living in Gezer; to this day the Canaanites live among the people of Ephraim but are required to do forced labor.

[a]1 *Jordan of Jericho* was possibly an ancient name for the Jordan River. [b]2 Septuagint; Hebrew *Bethel to Luz*

OPEN 1. What country is your family's "ancestral home"? Have you visited there? **2.** Do you consider yourself more of an "Easterner" or a "Westerner" in your roots and outlook on life? In what way?

STUDY Joseph's inheritance is apportioned to the tribes of Ephraim and Manasseh. This is the day a "complaint department" officially opened in the house of Israel! **1.** Where in the Promised Land was the allotment assigned to the descendants of Joseph (Ephraim and Manasseh)? How would you compare the size of Joseph's share to Judah's? **2.** How was their allotment a fulfillment of *both* God's promise to Jacob and Jacob's blessing of them (Gen. 28:10–19; 48:19–20)? **3.** Imagine that you are one of the guards standing near Joshua and Eleazar when the daughters of Zelophehad enter the court and approach the leaders of Israel. How do you think the other women of Israel felt about these women getting "special treatment"? **4.** Why did Joshua grant these daughters' request (17:3–6; Num. 27:1–11; 36)? **5.** What was it about Joseph's land allotment that the people were so dissatisfied (17:14–16)? **6.** What problems, both

16:1–17:18 Not only do Joseph's tribes, Manasseh and Ephraim, follow Judah in priority, they are also given the beautiful central corridor of Canaan.

16:1 Joseph. Since Joseph played such a key role in the family's survival during the famine, it seems only fitting that his sons should be given such prominence.

16:5 Ephraim. His territory became well known due to Shiloh's role as the location for Israel's house of worship, the tabernacle.

external and internal, will the people of Joseph have to overcome if they are to possess all the land Joshua has given to them? Which of those problems lie closest to your area of challenge as you seek to be all God intends for you to be?

APPLY 1. What coach or teacher really challenged you in school? What kind of mark did their influence leave on your life?. **2.** How do you react when you don't get your fair share of something? **3.** Is there an area in your life where you feel you need to stand up for your rights? What prevents you from doing so? How could you express your need in a way that honors God and yourself?

---

17 This was the allotment for the tribe of Manasseh as Joseph's
firstborn, that is, for Makir, Manasseh's firstborn. Makir was
the ancestor of the Gileadites, who had received Gilead and Bashan
because the Makirites were great soldiers. 2So this allotment was for
the rest of the people of Manasseh—the clans of Abiezer, Helek, Asriel, Shechem, Hepher and Shemida. These are the other male descendants of Manasseh son of Joseph by their clans.
3Now Zelophehad son of Hepher, the son of Gilead, the son of Makir, the son of Manasseh, had no sons but only daughters, whose
names were Mahlah, Noah, Hoglah, Milcah and Tirzah. 4They went to
Eleazar the priest, Joshua son of Nun, and the leaders and said, "The
LORD commanded Moses to give us an inheritance among our brothers." So Joshua gave them an inheritance along with the brothers of
their father, according to the LORD's command. 5Manasseh's share
consisted of ten tracts of land besides Gilead and Bashan east of the
Jordan, 6because the daughters of the tribe of Manasseh received an
inheritance among the sons. The land of Gilead belonged to the rest
of the descendants of Manasseh.
7The territory of Manasseh extended from Asher to Micmethath east of Shechem. The boundary ran southward from there
to include the people living at En Tappuah. 8(Manasseh had the
land of Tappuah, but Tappuah itself, on the boundary of Manasseh, belonged to the Ephraimites.) 9Then the boundary continued south to the Kanah Ravine. There were towns belonging to
Ephraim lying among the towns of Manasseh, but the boundary
of Manasseh was the northern side of the ravine and ended at
the sea. 10On the south the land belonged to Ephraim, on the
north to Manasseh. The territory of Manasseh reached the sea
and bordered Asher on the north and Issachar on the east.
11Within Issachar and Asher, Manasseh also had Beth Shan,
Ibleam and the people of Dor, Endor, Taanach and Megiddo, together with their surrounding settlements (the third in the list is
Naphoth[a]).
12Yet the Manassites were not able to occupy these towns, for the Canaanites were determined to live in that region. 13However, when the
Israelites grew stronger, they subjected the Canaanites to forced labor but did not drive them out completely.
14The people of Joseph said to Joshua, "Why have you given us only
one allotment and one portion for an inheritance? We are a numerous people and the LORD has blessed us abundantly."
15"If you are so numerous," Joshua answered, "and if the hill coun-

[a]11 That is, Naphoth Dor

17:1 Manasseh. The tribe of the oldest son, Manasseh, would become Ephraim's northern neighbor and receive a territory just smaller than that of Judah.

17:3 Zelophehad. The great-great grandson of Manasseh.

17:5 Manasseh's share. As the law indicated, Joshua made sure the inheritance was an equal opportunity for the five daughters.

17:13 Canaanites. Why were Canaanites still allowed to make the rules? Again, many of these cities were not controlled by the Israelites. The tribes had to establish their dominance.

17:14 one allotment and one portion. The Complaint Department officially opened for business on the day of Joseph's tribal inheritance. One of the larger tribes felt too crowded in their current allotment.

17:15 hill country. Joshua encouraged them to see the glass half-full instead of half-empty. He instructed them to leverage their size to dominate their enemies and work a clearing in the hill country to gain more room.

try of Ephraim is too small for you, go up into the forest and clear
land for yourselves there in the land of the Perizzites and Rephaites."
16The people of Joseph replied, "The hill country is not enough for
us, and all the Canaanites who live in the plain have iron chariots,
both those in Beth Shan and its settlements and those in the Valley of
Jezreel."
17But Joshua said to the house of Joseph—to Ephraim and Manasseh—"You are numerous and very powerful. You will have not only
one allotment 18but the forested hill country as well. Clear it, and its
farthest limits will be yours; though the Canaanites have iron chariots and though they are strong, you can drive them out."

Division of the Rest of the Land

18 The whole assembly of the Israelites gathered at Shiloh and
set up the Tent of Meeting there. The country was brought
under their control, 2but there were still seven Israelite tribes who
had not yet received their inheritance.
3So Joshua said to the Israelites: "How long will you wait before
you begin to take possession of the land that the LORD, the God of
your fathers, has given you? 4Appoint three men from each tribe. I
will send them out to make a survey of the land and to write a description of it, according to the inheritance of each. Then they will
return to me. 5You are to divide the land into seven parts. Judah is to
remain in its territory on the south and the house of Joseph in its territory on the north. 6After you have written descriptions of the seven
parts of the land, bring them here to me and I will cast lots for you in
the presence of the LORD our God. 7The Levites, however, do not get a
portion among you, because the priestly service of the LORD is their
inheritance. And Gad, Reuben and the half-tribe of Manasseh have
already received their inheritance on the east side of the Jordan.
Moses the servant of the LORD gave it to them."
8As the men started on their way to map out the land, Joshua
instructed them, "Go and make a survey of the land and write a description of it. Then return to me, and I will cast lots for you here at
Shiloh in the presence of the LORD." 9So the men left and went
through the land. They wrote its description on a scroll, town by
town, in seven parts, and returned to Joshua in the camp at Shiloh.
10Joshua then cast lots for them in Shiloh in the presence of the LORD,
and there he distributed the land to the Israelites according to their
tribal divisions.

Allotment for Benjamin

11The lot came up for the tribe of Benjamin, clan by clan. Their allotted territory lay between the tribes of Judah and Joseph:
12On the north side their boundary began at the Jordan,

OPEN When stuck behind a slow driver, are you more likely to: Pass even if it's dangerous? Tailgate? Lay on the horn? Relax and enjoy the scenery?

STUDY Israel gathers at Shiloh for the final apportionment of the Promised Land to the remaining seven tribes. There's just one hitch, the land is under Israelite control, but they don't "possess" it. Joshua sends out surveyors to divide what remains of Canaan. **1.** Why was Joshua impatient with seven of the tribes when they all gathered at Shiloh? What action did he take to deal with the problem? **2.** What instructions did Joshua give to the surveyors he sent out? Why do you think these surveyors were appointed from every tribe? Would you have volunteered to be one of them? **3.** Picture the surveyors moving through the land. What do you think they found: Milk and honey? Fierce enemies? Friendly citizens?

APPLY What in your life have you begun but never finished? What will it take to get you going again?

OPEN What were your best and worst subjects in school: English? History? Math? P.E.? How did you like geography then? How do you

18:1–19:51 Five down, seven to go. Joshua gathered the tribes in Shiloh at the tabernacle for the final divisions of the land. Surveyors from each tribe investigated and reported on each section of the remaining land. Lots were cast and the tribes were sent on their way. A special allotment of land was set aside for their weary leader, Joshua.

18:1 Israelites gathered at Shiloh. The tabernacle was located here—a perfect spot for group decisions about what was really important in Israel's priorities.

18:3 take possession of the land. It was one thing to conquer a rival king. It was quite another to move in and take over—as the tribes would soon find out.

18:11 Benjamin. His lot was squeezed between the two dominant tribes, Judah and Ephraim.

feel about the geography lesson you are getting in Joshua now?

STUDY Joshua begins a lottery system to complete the apportionment of Canaan. The tribe of Benjamin receives their allotment first. **1.** Why was Benjamin's territory important? What towns in its area played an important role in Israel's history? **2.** From the description given, would you say that Benjamin's land was larger or smaller than the other tribes around it? **3.** Who were some of the famous biblical people that came from the tribe of Benjamin (1 Sam. 9:1; Est. 2:5; Rom. 11:1)?

APPLY Is "bigger" better in your opinion? In God's opinion? Explain.

OPEN What is your birth order among your siblings? What are the benefits and drawbacks to your birth order?

STUDY The lottery continues as the rest of the Israelite tribes and their weary leader, Joshua, receive their inheritance. **1.** Where was Simeon's allotment in relationship to the other tribes? How was this inheritance a fulfillment of Jacob's blessing (Gen. 49:5–7)? **2.** Is there anything in the description of the other tribal allotments that strikes you as interesting? What curious thing does the text omit? **3.** Which of the other allotments do you see as a fulfillment of Jacob's blessing (Gen. 49)? **4.** What

passed the northern slope of Jericho and headed west into the
hill country, coming out at the desert of Beth Aven. 13From there
it crossed to the south slope of Luz (that is, Bethel) and went
down to Ataroth Addar on the hill south of Lower Beth Horon.
14From the hill facing Beth Horon on the south the boundary
turned south along the western side and came out at Kiriath
Baal (that is, Kiriath Jearim), a town of the people of Judah. This
was the western side.
15The southern side began at the outskirts of Kiriath Jearim on
the west, and the boundary came out at the spring of the waters
of Nephtoah. 16The boundary went down to the foot of the hill
facing the Valley of Ben Hinnom, north of the Valley of Rephaim.
It continued down the Hinnom Valley along the southern slope
of the Jebusite city and so to En Rogel. 17It then curved north,
went to En Shemesh, continued to Geliloth, which faces the Pass
of Adummim, and ran down to the Stone of Bohan son of
Reuben. 18It continued to the northern slope of Beth Arabah[a] and
on down into the Arabah. 19It then went to the northern slope of
Beth Hoglah and came out at the northern bay of the Salt Sea,[b] at
the mouth of the Jordan in the south. This was the southern
boundary.
20The Jordan formed the boundary on the eastern side.
These were the boundaries that marked out the inheritance of the
clans of Benjamin on all sides.

21The tribe of Benjamin, clan by clan, had the following cities:
Jericho, Beth Hoglah, Emek Keziz, 22Beth Arabah, Zemaraim,
Bethel, 23Avvim, Parah, Ophrah, 24Kephar Ammoni, Ophni and
Geba—twelve towns and their villages.
25Gibeon, Ramah, Beeroth, 26Mizpah, Kephirah, Mozah,
27Rekem, Irpeel, Taralah, 28Zelah, Haeleph, the Jebusite city (that
is, Jerusalem), Gibeah and Kiriath—fourteen towns and their
villages.
This was the inheritance of Benjamin for its clans.

Allotment for Simeon

19 The second lot came out for the tribe of Simeon, clan by clan.
Their inheritance lay within the territory of Judah. 2It included:
Beersheba (or Sheba),[c] Moladah, 3Hazar Shual, Balah, Ezem,
4Eltolad, Bethul, Hormah, 5Ziklag, Beth Marcaboth, Hazar
Susah, 6Beth Lebaoth and Sharuhen—thirteen towns and their
villages;
7Ain, Rimmon, Ether and Ashan—four towns and their villages— 8and all the villages around these towns as far as Baalath
Beer (Ramah in the Negev).
This was the inheritance of the tribe of the Simeonites, clan by clan.
9The inheritance of the Simeonites was taken from the share of

[a]18 Septuagint; Hebrew *slope facing the Arabah* [b]19 That is, the Dead Sea [c]2 Or *Beersheba, Sheba;* 1 Chron. 4:28 does not have *Sheba.*

Judah, because Judah's portion was more than they needed. So the Simeonites received their inheritance within the territory of Judah.

Allotment for Zebulun

[10]The third lot came up for Zebulun, clan by clan:
The boundary of their inheritance went as far as Sarid. [11]Going
west it ran to Maralah, touched Dabbesheth, and extended to the
ravine near Jokneam. [12]It turned east from Sarid toward the sunrise to the territory of Kisloth Tabor and went on to Daberath and
up to Japhia. [13]Then it continued eastward to Gath Hepher and
Eth Kazin; it came out at Rimmon and turned toward Neah.
[14]There the boundary went around on the north to Hannathon
and ended at the Valley of Iphtah El. [15]Included were Kattath,
Nahalal, Shimron, Idalah and Bethlehem. There were twelve
towns and their villages.
[16]These towns and their villages were the inheritance of Zebulun,
clan by clan.

Allotment for Issachar

[17]The fourth lot came out for Issachar, clan by clan. [18]Their territory
included:
Jezreel, Kesulloth, Shunem, [19]Hapharaim, Shion, Anaharath,
[20]Rabbith, Kishion, Ebez, [21]Remeth, En Gannim, En Haddah and
Beth Pazzez. [22]The boundary touched Tabor, Shahazumah and
Beth Shemesh, and ended at the Jordan. There were sixteen
towns and their villages.
[23]These towns and their villages were the inheritance of the tribe of
Issachar, clan by clan.

Allotment for Asher

[24]The fifth lot came out for the tribe of Asher, clan by clan. [25]Their
territory included:
Helkath, Hali, Beten, Acshaph, [26]Allammelech, Amad and
Mishal. On the west the boundary touched Carmel and Shihor
Libnath. [27]It then turned east toward Beth Dagon, touched
Zebulun and the Valley of Iphtah El, and went north to Beth
Emek and Neiel, passing Cabul on the left. [28]It went to Abdon,[a]
Rehob, Hammon and Kanah, as far as Greater Sidon. [29]The
boundary then turned back toward Ramah and went to the forti-
fied city of Tyre, turned toward Hosah and came out at the sea in
the region of Aczib, [30]Ummah, Aphek and Rehob. There were
twenty-two towns and their villages.
[31]These towns and their villages were the inheritance of the tribe of
Asher, clan by clan.

Allotment for Naphtali

[32]The sixth lot came out for Naphtali, clan by clan:
[33]Their boundary went from Heleph and the large tree in
Zaanannim, passing Adami Nekeb and Jabneel to Lakkum and

[a]*28* Some Hebrew manuscripts (see also Joshua 21:30); most Hebrew manuscripts *Ebron*

did the tribes have to do to fully realize the blessing that was theirs (v. 47)? What will you have to do to receive your family inheritance? **5.** What inheritance did Joshua receive as a reward for his leadership? What is significant about Joshua getting what he asked for? Does this reveal anything about the character of God and rewards for spiritual leaders?

APPLY 1. What principles for decision making do you see in this chapter? What can we learn about leadership here through the uses of: A lottery? Survey work? Divine prophecy? Circumstances and personal desires? **2.** Which of these factors do you weigh more than others in the decisions facing you? **3.** Where are you experiencing difficulty taking possession of your rightful inheritance from Christ? What is holding you back from claiming the victory that is yours in Jesus?

ending at the Jordan. 34The boundary ran west through Aznoth
Tabor and came out at Hukkok. It touched Zebulun on the south,
Asher on the west and the Jordan[a] on the east. 35The fortified
cities were Ziddim, Zer, Hammath, Rakkath, Kinnereth, 36Adamah,
Ramah, Hazor, 37Kedesh, Edrei, En Hazor, 38Iron, Migdal El,
Horem, Beth Anath and Beth Shemesh. There were nineteen
towns and their villages.
39These towns and their villages were the inheritance of the tribe of
Naphtali, clan by clan.

Allotment for Dan

40The seventh lot came out for the tribe of Dan, clan by clan. 41The
territory of their inheritance included:
Zorah, Eshtaol, Ir Shemesh, 42Shaalabbin, Aijalon, Ithlah,
43Elon, Timnah, Ekron, 44Eltekeh, Gibbethon, Baalath, 45Jehud,
Bene Berak, Gath Rimmon, 46Me Jarkon and Rakkon, with the
area facing Joppa.
47(But the Danites had difficulty taking possession of their territory, so they went up and attacked Leshem, took it, put it to the sword
and occupied it. They settled in Leshem and named it Dan after their
forefather.)
48These towns and their villages were the inheritance of the tribe of
Dan, clan by clan.

Allotment for Joshua

49When they had finished dividing the land into its allotted portions, the Israelites gave Joshua son of Nun an inheritance among
them, 50as the LORD had commanded. They gave him the town he
asked for—Timnath Serah[b] in the hill country of Ephraim. And he
built up the town and settled there.
51These are the territories that Eleazar the priest, Joshua son of
Nun and the heads of the tribal clans of Israel assigned by lot at Shiloh in the presence of the LORD at the entrance to the Tent of Meeting.
And so they finished dividing the land.

Cities of Refuge

20 Then the LORD said to Joshua: 2"Tell the Israelites to designate the cities of refuge, as I instructed you through Moses,
3so that anyone who kills a person accidentally and unintentionally
may flee there and find protection from the avenger of blood.
4"When he flees to one of these cities, he is to stand in the entrance
of the city gate and state his case before the elders of that city. Then
they are to admit him into their city and give him a place to live with

[a]34 Septuagint; Hebrew *west, and Judah, the Jordan,* [b]50 Also known as *Timnath Heres* (see Judges 2:9)

OPEN Think back to your childhood between the ages of five and ten. Who did you tell your troubles to?

STUDY The land has been divided, but that doesn't necessarily establish peace. **1.** What was a "city of refuge" and why were they established (Ex. 21:13; Num. 35:6–15)? In what ways can a church be like a "city of refuge"? How can your

19:49 an inheritance among them. A true leader, Joshua served his people first. At last, he was rewarded with the land he desired.

20:1–9 Like the colonists settling America, the Israelites needed to establish their own system of government. One of the more emotionally charged crimes, accidental manslaughter, would be the first issue addressed. A city of refuge would carry out justice under the care of the Levites. In this way, there would be less family feuding and less chance of taking matters into their own hands.

20:3 protection from the avenger of blood. What may sound like a comic book hero was actually a relative of the dead party. The avenger of blood was responsible for slaying the criminal in murder cases.

20:4 entrance of the city gate. What evolved into modern day "city hall" was once the city gate—a place where trials took place.

them. 5If the avenger of blood pursues him, they must not surrender
the one accused, because he killed his neighbor unintentionally and
without malice aforethought. 6He is to stay in that city until he has
stood trial before the assembly and until the death of the high priest
who is serving at that time. Then he may go back to his own home in
the town from which he fled."
7So they set apart Kedesh in Galilee in the hill country of Naphtali,
Shechem in the hill country of Ephraim, and Kiriath Arba (that is,
Hebron) in the hill country of Judah. 8On the east side of the Jordan of
Jericho[a] they designated Bezer in the desert on the plateau in the
tribe of Reuben, Ramoth in Gilead in the tribe of Gad, and Golan in
Bashan in the tribe of Manasseh. 9Any of the Israelites or any alien
living among them who killed someone accidentally could flee to
these designated cities and not be killed by the avenger of blood prior
to standing trial before the assembly.

Towns for the Levites

21 Now the family heads of the Levites approached Eleazar the
priest, Joshua son of Nun, and the heads of the other tribal
families of Israel 2at Shiloh in Canaan and said to them, "The LORD
commanded through Moses that you give us towns to live in, with
pasturelands for our livestock." 3So, as the LORD had commanded,
the Israelites gave the Levites the following towns and pasturelands
out of their own inheritance:
4The first lot came out for the Kohathites, clan by clan. The Levites
who were descendants of Aaron the priest were allotted thirteen
towns from the tribes of Judah, Simeon and Benjamin. 5The rest of
Kohath's descendants were allotted ten towns from the clans of the
tribes of Ephraim, Dan and half of Manasseh.
6The descendants of Gershon were allotted thirteen towns from the
clans of the tribes of Issachar, Asher, Naphtali and the half-tribe of
Manasseh in Bashan.
7The descendants of Merari, clan by clan, received twelve towns
from the tribes of Reuben, Gad and Zebulun.
8So the Israelites allotted to the Levites these towns and their
pasturelands, as the LORD had commanded through Moses.
9From the tribes of Judah and Simeon they allotted the following
towns by name 10(these towns were assigned to the descendants of
Aaron who were from the Kohathite clans of the Levites, because the
first lot fell to them):
11They gave them Kiriath Arba (that is, Hebron), with its surrounding pastureland, in the hill country of Judah. (Arba was the
forefather of Anak.) 12But the fields and villages around the city
they had given to Caleb son of Jephunneh as his possession.
13So to the descendants of Aaron the priest they gave Hebron

[a]8 *Jordan of Jericho* was possibly an ancient name for the Jordan River.

group be a "city of refuge"? **2.** How did a person find safety in a "city of refuge"? **3.** What modern principles of justice do you see in this? **4.** Where were the "cities of refuge" located? How is their placement significant? Could someone "fall through the cracks"? How?

APPLY 1. Describe a time when you felt threatened in some way. **2.** How can this group help when a member feels threatened?

OPEN 1. Which of the following is the hardest for you to share with others: Your car? Your food? Your free time? Your feelings? Your dreams? Why? **2.** What was the first "big ticket" item you saved your money for to buy as a young adult?

STUDY All of Israel has received their inheritance except the Levites. They not only have a special arrangement with God, they will have a unique inheritance among the people. **1.** Why did the family heads of the Levites approach Eleazar and Joshua at Shiloh? What was the basis for their claim (Num. 35:1–8)? **2.** Who were the Levites? How were they divided up? What was unique about the Kohathites (Num. 3)? **3.** How do you think the other tribes felt about cities from their territories being given to the Levites? **4.** If you had been Caleb, how would you have reacted to have your beloved city of Hebron, the land promised to you by Moses, given to the Levites? **5.** How many "cities of refuge" listed in chapter 20 were given to the Levites? Why do you think this was the case? **6.** List the many things God has done for Israel (vv. 43–45). What aspects of the Lord's nature shine through these gifts? **7.** What sorts of things does God now promise to his people during our time?

APPLY 1. Share with your group some of the gifts God

21:1–45 Last but not least, the Levites are given small towns and pasturelands to call home. All along, their inheritance has been the priestly service to the Lord himself. Additionally, they are responsible for the new system of refuge.

21:4 Judah, Simeon and Benjamin. The Levites were the wildcard tribe, since they served as the religious hub of all the tribes. Therefore, it was natural they would share territory from any number of tribes.

21:11 Hebron. Caleb was free to shepherd the range of fields and outlying villages of his beloved Hebron, the resting place of Sarah and her family (Gen. 23:1–2). However, the priests and Levites called the inner-city home.

has given to you in the past year. **2.** What part of your life do you believe the Lord is calling you to share with someone else right now? What keeps you from taking action? **3.** Can you honestly say from personal experience, "Not one of the Lord's promises to me has failed"? If not, can you share some of your disappointment with this group?

(a city of refuge for one accused of murder), Libnah, [14]Jattir, Eshtemoa, [15]Holon, Debir, [16]Ain, Juttah and Beth Shemesh, together
with their pasturelands—nine towns from these two tribes.

[17]And from the tribe of Benjamin they gave them Gibeon,
Geba, [18]Anathoth and Almon, together with their pasturelands—
four towns.

[19]All the towns for the priests, the descendants of Aaron, were thirteen, together with their pasturelands.

[20]The rest of the Kohathite clans of the Levites were allotted towns
from the tribe of Ephraim:

[21]In the hill country of Ephraim they were given Shechem (a
city of refuge for one accused of murder) and Gezer, [22]Kibzaim
and Beth Horon, together with their pasturelands—four towns.

[23]Also from the tribe of Dan they received Eltekeh, Gibbethon,
[24]Aijalon and Gath Rimmon, together with their pasturelands—
four towns.

[25]From half the tribe of Manasseh they received Taanach and
Gath Rimmon, together with their pasturelands—two towns.

[26]All these ten towns and their pasturelands were given to the rest of
the Kohathite clans.

[27]The Levite clans of the Gershonites were given:
from the half-tribe of Manasseh,
Golan in Bashan (a city of refuge for one accused of murder) and
Be Eshtarah, together with their pasturelands—two towns;
[28]from the tribe of Issachar,
Kishion, Daberath, [29]Jarmuth and En Gannim, together with
their pasturelands—four towns;
[30]from the tribe of Asher,
Mishal, Abdon, [31]Helkath and Rehob, together with their pasturelands—four towns;
[32]from the tribe of Naphtali,
Kedesh in Galilee (a city of refuge for one accused of murder),
Hammoth Dor and Kartan, together with their pasturelands—
three towns.

[33]All the towns of the Gershonite clans were thirteen, together with
their pasturelands.

[34]The Merarite clans (the rest of the Levites) were given:
from the tribe of Zebulun,
Jokneam, Kartah, [35]Dimnah and Nahalal, together with their
pasturelands—four towns;
[36]from the tribe of Reuben,
Bezer, Jahaz, [37]Kedemoth and Mephaath, together with their
pasturelands—four towns;
[38]from the tribe of Gad,
Ramoth in Gilead (a city of refuge for one accused of murder),
Mahanaim, [39]Heshbon and Jazer, together with their pasturelands—four towns in all.

[40]All the towns allotted to the Merarite clans, who were the rest of the
Levites, were twelve.

[41]The towns of the Levites in the territory held by the Israelites
were forty-eight in all, together with their pasturelands. [42]Each of

these towns had pasturelands surrounding it; this was true for all
these towns.

43So the LORD gave Israel all the land he had sworn to give their
forefathers, and they took possession of it and settled there. 44The
LORD gave them rest on every side, just as he had sworn to their forefathers. Not one of their enemies withstood them; the LORD handed
all their enemies over to them. 45Not one of all the LORD's good promises to the house of Israel failed; every one was fulfilled.

Eastern Tribes Return Home

22 Then Joshua summoned the Reubenites, the Gadites and the
half-tribe of Manasseh 2and said to them, "You have done all
that Moses the servant of the LORD commanded, and you have obeyed
me in everything I commanded. 3For a long time now—to this very
day—you have not deserted your brothers but have carried out the
mission the LORD your God gave you. 4Now that the LORD your God has
given your brothers rest as he promised, return to your homes in the
land that Moses the servant of the LORD gave you on the other side of
the Jordan. 5But be very careful to keep the commandment and the
law that Moses the servant of the LORD gave you: to love the LORD
your God, to walk in all his ways, to obey his commands, to hold fast
to him and to serve him with all your heart and all your soul."

6Then Joshua blessed them and sent them away, and they went to
their homes. 7(To the half-tribe of Manasseh Moses had given land in
Bashan, and to the other half of the tribe Joshua gave land on the
west side of the Jordan with their brothers.) When Joshua sent them
home, he blessed them, 8saying, "Return to your homes with your
great wealth—with large herds of livestock, with silver, gold, bronze
and iron, and a great quantity of clothing—and divide with your
brothers the plunder from your enemies."

9So the Reubenites, the Gadites and the half-tribe of Manasseh left
the Israelites at Shiloh in Canaan to return to Gilead, their own land,
which they had acquired in accordance with the command of the
LORD through Moses.

10When they came to Geliloth near the Jordan in the land of Canaan, the Reubenites, the Gadites and the half-tribe of Manasseh
built an imposing altar there by the Jordan. 11And when the Israelites
heard that they had built the altar on the border of Canaan at Geliloth
near the Jordan on the Israelite side, 12the whole assembly of Israel
gathered at Shiloh to go to war against them.

OPEN 1. Have you played "telephone"? How accurately was the information passed from beginning to end? **2.** Who was your best friend as a teen? How often and over what did you "fight"? How did you resolve your disagreements?

STUDY The inheritance has been divided up, the wars are over, and now it's time for the eastern tribes to go home. After seven long years of fighting for their brothers' land, one would think that there would be great trust for them within the extended family. Not so! **1.** What did Joshua say to the Reubenites, Gadites and half-tribe of Manasseh that might have made their "ears burn"? What challenge did he give them? Why are both affirmation and exhortation important for God's people? **2.** In what way were the tribes east of the river different from the rest of Israel? **3.** Imagine that you are one of the Israelite women left behind in Gilead while the men were off in Canaan waging war for their brothers. How do you feel when you hear news of their imminent return after seven years of running the family farm or business alone? **4.** What seemingly innocent action did the eastern tribes do on their way home (v. 10)? Why do you think the rest of the tribes reacted the way they did? Do you feel they overreacted? **5.** What was the "sin of Peor" (v. 17; Num. 25)? In light of that incident, why do you think

---

21:43–45 These journey-worn and battle-weary warriors had earned their rest. But God reminded them it was a gift. Every victory, every conquest and every blade of grass in this shining valley of milk and honey was a gift.

22:1–34 Perception is reality in many cases. However, Israel's perception of the meaning behind the altar built by the Eastern tribes could not have been more wrong. It took a heated discussion and a tribal delegation to conclude the conflict.

22:2 you have obeyed me in everything I commanded. Joshua asked a lot of these warriors. He separated them from their families on the east of the Jordan for seven long years to fight for their brothers' rights.

22:5 But be very careful. Like a father talking to a child, Joshua spoke in a tone that betrayed his concern for the baby nation among such a pagan people.

22:11 when the Israelites heard ... built an altar. Like a message in the childhood game of "Telephone," the original meaning of the altar got passed around from person to person, tribe to tribe, until it no longer resembled the truth at all. What was meant to be a symbol of a common faith was now rumored to be rebellion!

22:12 to go to war against them. What an about-face! With snapshots from the happy, smiling family portraits at Shiloh fresh in their minds, the Israelite family was now considering civil war!

Phinehas was chosen to lead the delegation in verses 13–14? Was this a wise choice in your opinion? Why or why not? **6.** What assumptions did the Israelites make about the new altar that upset them so? What did they fear most? **7.** How was this incident like the "sin of Achan" (v. 20; 7:1,20–26)? How was it different? **8.** When given the opportunity to explain their actions, what reasons did the Reubenites, Gadites and half-tribe of Manasseh give for building the new altar? How was it intended to be a positive influence on them? **9.** How did Phinehas, the leaders of the community, and the rest of Israel each respond to this explanation? What might have happened to Israel had they not taken the time to find out the facts?

APPLY 1. One day the Israelites are united, fighting together against their enemies. The next, they are ready to take up arms against each other after a misunderstanding. How is this like or unlike your extended family? Your church? Who acts as the peacemaker when such misunderstandings occur? **2.** Is there someone close to you from whom you will soon be separated from who needs to hear words of encouragement? What will you say to him or her?

13 So the Israelites sent Phinehas son of Eleazar, the priest, to the
land of Gilead—to Reuben, Gad and the half-tribe of Manasseh.
14 With him they sent ten of the chief men, one for each of the tribes of
Israel, each the head of a family division among the Israelite clans.
15 When they went to Gilead—to Reuben, Gad and the half-tribe of
Manasseh—they said to them: 16 "The whole assembly of the LORD
says: 'How could you break faith with the God of Israel like this? How
could you turn away from the LORD and build yourselves an altar in
rebellion against him now? 17 Was not the sin of Peor enough for us?
Up to this very day we have not cleansed ourselves from that sin, even
though a plague fell on the community of the LORD! 18 And are you
now turning away from the LORD?

" 'If you rebel against the LORD today, tomorrow he will be angry
with the whole community of Israel. 19 If the land you possess is defiled, come over to the LORD's land, where the LORD's tabernacle
stands, and share the land with us. But do not rebel against the LORD
or against us by building an altar for yourselves, other than the altar
of the LORD our God. 20 When Achan son of Zerah acted unfaithfully
regarding the devoted things,[a] did not wrath come upon the whole
community of Israel? He was not the only one who died for his sin.' "

21 Then Reuben, Gad and the half-tribe of Manasseh replied to the
heads of the clans of Israel: 22 "The Mighty One, God, the LORD! The
Mighty One, God, the LORD! He knows! And let Israel know! If this has
been in rebellion or disobedience to the LORD, do not spare us this
day. 23 If we have built our own altar to turn away from the LORD and
to offer burnt offerings and grain offerings, or to sacrifice fellowship
offerings[b] on it, may the LORD himself call us to account.

24 "No! We did it for fear that some day your descendants might say
to ours, 'What do you have to do with the LORD, the God of Israel?
25 The LORD has made the Jordan a boundary between us and you—
you Reubenites and Gadites! You have no share in the LORD.' So your
descendants might cause ours to stop fearing the LORD.

26 "That is why we said, 'Let us get ready and build an altar—but not
for burnt offerings or sacrifices.' 27 On the contrary, it is to be a witness between us and you and the generations that follow, that we will
worship the LORD at his sanctuary with our burnt offerings, sacrifices
and fellowship offerings. Then in the future your descendants will
not be able to say to ours, 'You have no share in the LORD.'

28 "And we said, 'If they ever say this to us, or to our descendants,
we will answer: Look at the replica of the LORD's altar, which our
fathers built, not for burnt offerings and sacrifices, but as a witness
between us and you.'

29 "Far be it from us to rebel against the LORD and turn away from
him today by building an altar for burnt offerings, grain offerings and

[a] 20 The Hebrew term refers to the irrevocable giving over of things or persons to the LORD, often by totally destroying them. [b] 23 Traditionally *peace offerings*; also in verse 27

22:13–14 If only Israel had continued to treat the suspicion of sin with as much concern! With as much diplomacy as the young nation could muster, one delegate from each tribe was summoned to accompany Phinehas in the investigation.

22:22 do not spare us this day. The Eastern tribes knew the serious nature of the accusation. Disobedience meant death and they were eager to explain.

22:27 at his sanctuary. The tabernacle at Shiloh was the one, true altar for worship. In fact, the Law required all the Israelite men to gather there three times a year (Ex. 23:17). The Eastern tribes would never worship at the altar—it was merely symbolic.

sacrifices, other than the altar of the LORD our God that stands before his tabernacle."

30 When Phinehas the priest and the leaders of the community—the heads of the clans of the Israelites—heard what Reuben, Gad and Manasseh had to say, they were pleased. 31 And Phinehas son of Eleazar, the priest, said to Reuben, Gad and Manasseh, "Today we know that the LORD is with us, because you have not acted unfaithfully toward the LORD in this matter. Now you have rescued the Israelites from the LORD's hand."

32 Then Phinehas son of Eleazar, the priest, and the leaders returned to Canaan from their meeting with the Reubenites and Gadites in Gilead and reported to the Israelites. 33 They were glad to hear the report and praised God. And they talked no more about going to war against them to devastate the country where the Reubenites and the Gadites lived.

34 And the Reubenites and the Gadites gave the altar this name: A Witness Between Us that the LORD is God.

Joshua's Farewell to the Leaders

23 After a long time had passed and the LORD had given Israel rest from all their enemies around them, Joshua, by then old and well advanced in years, 2 summoned all Israel—their elders, leaders, judges and officials—and said to them: "I am old and well advanced in years. 3 You yourselves have seen everything the LORD your God has done to all these nations for your sake; it was the LORD your God who fought for you. 4 Remember how I have allotted as an inheritance for your tribes all the land of the nations that remain—the nations I conquered—between the Jordan and the Great Sea[a] in the west. 5 The LORD your God himself will drive them out of your way. He will push them out before you, and you will take possession of their land, as the LORD your God promised you.

6 "Be very strong; be careful to obey all that is written in the Book of the Law of Moses, without turning aside to the right or to the left. 7 Do not associate with these nations that remain among you; do not invoke the names of their gods or swear by them. You must not serve them or bow down to them. 8 But you are to hold fast to the LORD your God, as you have until now.

9 "The LORD has driven out before you great and powerful nations; to this day no one has been able to withstand you. 10 One of you routs a thousand, because the LORD your God fights for you, just as he promised. 11 So be very careful to love the LORD your God.

12 "But if you turn away and ally yourselves with the survivors of these nations that remain among you and if you intermarry with

[a]4 That is, the Mediterranean

OPEN 1. Who did you look up to when you were younger? What was the best advice you received from him or her? **2.** What's the most difficult "good-bye" you've ever had to say?

STUDY In his 110 years, Joshua experienced: Slavery in Egypt, the plagues, the Exodus, serving as Moses' successor, leading the Israelites through the miraculous crossing of the Jordan River and commanding the army of Israel in their conquest of the Promised Land. As his life draws to an end, Joshua gives his farewell address. **1.** Who does Joshua summon? What does he remind them about in verses 3–5? Why is this reminder important? **2.** If you stood in Joshua's shoes, how would you feel about the Israelites' future: Hopeful? Worried? Optimistic because of your faith? Pessimistic because of their past failures? Other? **3.** What advice does Joshua give in verses 6–8? What do you think he wants to communicate to the next generation? **4.** Practically speaking, what does it mean for the leaders "to obey all that is written in the Book of the Law of Moses"? **5.** In verses 9–11, what has been the

---

22:31 you have rescued the Israelites from the LORD's hand. Both punishment and reward were family affairs for Israel. The potential of one tribe's sin meant disaster for the entire nation. Therefore, Phinehas was not exaggerating when he thanked the Eastern tribes for sparing their lives as well.

23:1–6 Sensing the end of his life is near, Joshua summons the leaders of Israel who will be his spokespersons to the rest of the nation. His parting words focus on reviewing past accomplishments and an exhortation to continue to obey the Lord.

23:6 Be very strong. From the lips of a weakened dying man comes the exhortation to be strong. Joshua's last words to his people were the first words God spoke to him at the beginning of his command (1:6).

23:12 if you ... associate with them. The temptation to compromise by entertaining trade, business or social opportunities with the pagan people would be very strong for the fledgling nation. What could it hurt? However,

wonderful result of loving and obeying the Lord?

APPLY 1. Looking back over your own life, what memories do you celebrate most? Can you see God's hand at work to make them possible? How so? **2.** Think of a person who knows you well and has been a mentor to you. If they were to give you a word of advice about your future, what might it be?

OPEN 1. When you were a child, were you ever called to the principal's office? What for? **2.** When presented with a challenge in your life, are you more likely to look before you leap or leap before you look? Give an example.

STUDY In the closing days of Joshua's life, the last action he would take as Israel's leader was to call the people together to renew their covenant with the Lord. **1.** Why do you think Joshua recounts Israel's history? **2.** After all they've been through, why were the Israelites given a choice now about who to serve (v. 15)? **3.** Joshua reminded Israel of God's faithfulness. In what way has God shown his faithfulness to you? **4.** Joshua used a stone to remind the people of their commitment (v. 27). What reminds you of your decision to serve God? **5.** How do the Israelites show that they are serious about serving the Lord? What things do you do to show God that you mean business? **6.** Joshua warns the people against serving other gods. What "gods" other than the Lord are you tempted to serve: People? An ideal or cause? Pleasure? Work or career? Money? Security? A habit or addiction? Other?

APPLY Conclude this study with the following five-step exercise patterned after the covenant renewal in this passage. **1.** Share one

them and associate with them, [13]then you may be sure that the LORD
your God will no longer drive out these nations before you. Instead,
they will become snares and traps for you, whips on your backs and
thorns in your eyes, until you perish from this good land, which the
LORD your God has given you.

[14]"Now I am about to go the way of all the earth. You know with all
your heart and soul that not one of all the good promises the LORD
your God gave you has failed. Every promise has been fulfilled; not
one has failed. [15]But just as every good promise of the LORD your God
has come true, so the LORD will bring on you all the evil he has threatened, until he has destroyed you from this good land he has given
you. [16]If you violate the covenant of the LORD your God, which he
commanded you, and go and serve other gods and bow down to
them, the LORD's anger will burn against you, and you will quickly
perish from the good land he has given you."

The Covenant Renewed at Shechem

24 Then Joshua assembled all the tribes of Israel at Shechem.
He summoned the elders, leaders, judges and officials of Israel, and they presented themselves before God.

[2]Joshua said to all the people, "This is what the LORD, the God of
Israel, says: 'Long ago your forefathers, including Terah the father of
Abraham and Nahor, lived beyond the River[a] and worshiped other
gods. [3]But I took your father Abraham from the land beyond the River
and led him throughout Canaan and gave him many descendants. I
gave him Isaac, [4]and to Isaac I gave Jacob and Esau. I assigned the
hill country of Seir to Esau, but Jacob and his sons went down to
Egypt.

[5]" 'Then I sent Moses and Aaron, and I afflicted the Egyptians by
what I did there, and I brought you out. [6]When I brought your fathers
out of Egypt, you came to the sea, and the Egyptians pursued them
with chariots and horsemen[b] as far as the Red Sea.[c] [7]But they cried to
the LORD for help, and he put darkness between you and the Egyptians; he brought the sea over them and covered them. You saw with
your own eyes what I did to the Egyptians. Then you lived in the
desert for a long time.

[8]" 'I brought you to the land of the Amorites who lived east of the
Jordan. They fought against you, but I gave them into your hands. I
destroyed them from before you, and you took possession of their
land. [9]When Balak son of Zippor, the king of Moab, prepared to fight
against Israel, he sent for Balaam son of Beor to put a curse on you.
[10]But I would not listen to Balaam, so he blessed you again and
again, and I delivered you out of his hand.

[11]" 'Then you crossed the Jordan and came to Jericho. The citizens

[a]2 That is, the Euphrates; also in verses 3, 14 and 15 [b]6 Or *charioteers* [c]6 Hebrew *Yam Suph*; that is, Sea of Reeds

---

Joshua spelled it out for his people just as Moses had before: no way.

24:1–33 The credits rolling at the end of Joshua's life repeat a common theme: God alone has achieved the victory. From Abraham to the present moment, Joshua's review of history centers on God's faithfulness to his people. In the context of the past, Joshua provides them with an ultimatum for the future. Israel responds wholeheartedly to serve the Lord alone.

24:10 Balaam. In ultimate irony, the pagan prophet turned hit-man ended up blessing instead of cursing the Israelites as they passed through foreign territory (Num. 23:11). Four times Balaan was used by God, after God used a donkey to get his attention (Num. 22:31–33).

of Jericho fought against you, as did also the Amorites, Perizzites,
Canaanites, Hittites, Girgashites, Hivites and Jebusites, but I gave
them into your hands. [12]I sent the hornet ahead of you, which drove
them out before you—also the two Amorite kings. You did not do it
with your own sword and bow. [13]So I gave you a land on which you
did not toil and cities you did not build; and you live in them and eat
from vineyards and olive groves that you did not plant.'
[14]"Now fear the LORD and serve him with all faithfulness. Throw
away the gods your forefathers worshiped beyond the River and in
Egypt, and serve the LORD. [15]But if serving the LORD seems undesirable to you, then choose for yourselves this day whom you will serve,
whether the gods your forefathers served beyond the River, or the
gods of the Amorites, in whose land you are living. But as for me and
my household, we will serve the LORD."
[16]Then the people answered, "Far be it from us to forsake the LORD
to serve other gods! [17]It was the LORD our God himself who brought
us and our fathers up out of Egypt, from that land of slavery, and
performed those great signs before our eyes. He protected us on our
entire journey and among all the nations through which we traveled.
[18]And the LORD drove out before us all the nations, including the
Amorites, who lived in the land. We too will serve the LORD, because
he is our God."
[19]Joshua said to the people, "You are not able to serve the LORD. He
is a holy God; he is a jealous God. He will not forgive your rebellion
and your sins. [20]If you forsake the LORD and serve foreign gods, he
will turn and bring disaster on you and make an end of you, after he
has been good to you."
[21]But the people said to Joshua, "No! We will serve the LORD."
[22]Then Joshua said, "You are witnesses against yourselves that you
have chosen to serve the LORD."
"Yes, we are witnesses," they replied.
[23]"Now then," said Joshua, "throw away the foreign gods that are
among you and yield your hearts to the LORD, the God of Israel."
[24]And the people said to Joshua, "We will serve the LORD our God
and obey him."
[25]On that day Joshua made a covenant for the people, and there at
Shechem he drew up for them decrees and laws. [26]And Joshua
recorded these things in the Book of the Law of God. Then he took a
large stone and set it up there under the oak near the holy place of
the LORD.
[27]"See!" he said to all the people. "This stone will be a witness
against us. It has heard all the words the LORD has said to us. It will
be a witness against you if you are untrue to your God."

thing God has done for you or your family (vv. 2–13). **2.** Name one concrete spiritual commitment you want to make (vv. 14–18). **3.** Write down on paper the "god" you wish to forsake (vv. 23–34). **4.** Crumple up the paper and throw it away. **5.** End with prayer.

24:15 as for me ... we will serve. One man registers his vote for the supremacy of God. He knows he cannot speak for them. The choice to serve God must be a personal decision.

24:17–18 In light of history's retelling, what choice could the people make other than to serve the Lord? Of course, their self-assurance would return to haunt them in the future.

24:19 You are not able to serve the LORD. If Joshua could talk them out of their commitment, he would try. If they could not confirm their spirituality with absolute certainty in the presence of the family of faith, there was little hope of sticking to it when they returned home.

24:25 Joshua made a covenant for the people. As a symbol of personal commitment, Joshua signed and dated the terms of their agreement in the Book of the Law. Joshua committed himself on behalf of God (v. 19). The people were the other part of the covenant (v. 24).

24:26 near the holy place of the LORD. The significance of this place was not the decision that was made, but the witness before whom it was made: God himself.

OPEN Can you identify someone who has been a "spiritual father or mother" to you?

STUDY Israel remained faithful to the Lord throughout Joshua's 110-year lifetime. **1.** What distinguishes the last days, death and burial of Joshua? **2.** As a news reporter covering the Canaanite campaign, what obituary would you write upon the death of this great leader?

APPLY When you look ahead to the rest of your life, what do you hope will be your greatest contribution to the kingdom of God?

Buried in the Promised Land

28Then Joshua sent the people away, each to his own inheritance.
29After these things, Joshua son of Nun, the servant of the LORD,
died at the age of a hundred and ten. 30And they buried him in the
land of his inheritance, at Timnath Serah[a] in the hill country of
Ephraim, north of Mount Gaash.
31Israel served the LORD throughout the lifetime of Joshua and of
the elders who outlived him and who had experienced everything the
LORD had done for Israel.
32And Joseph's bones, which the Israelites had brought up from
Egypt, were buried at Shechem in the tract of land that Jacob bought
for a hundred pieces of silver[b] from the sons of Hamor, the father of
Shechem. This became the inheritance of Joseph's descendants.
33And Eleazar son of Aaron died and was buried at Gibeah, which
had been allotted to his son Phinehas in the hill country of Ephraim.

[a]30 Also known as *Timnath Heres* (see Judges 2:9) [b]32 Hebrew *hundred kesitahs*; a kesitah was a unit of money of unknown weight and value.

24:29–33 For the first time, Israel had a home in which to live, to die and to be buried. Joshua was buried in the land he conquered—a fitting tribute to a mighty warrior and leader. He now joined all the other great leaders of God's people, with the exception of Moses. Moses was not buried in the land (Deut. 34:6).

24:31 throughout the lifetime of Joshua. A testament to his leadership, Joshua was able to keep Israel on course throughout his term.

24:32 Joseph's bones ... buried at Shechem. In fulfillment of prophecy, Joseph's bones were brought from a land symbolizing slavery to a land of freedom (Gen. 50:24–25). Centrally located in Shechem, his bones would remain between the land given to his two sons—Ephraim and Manasseh. The people carried Joseph's bones home as he had his father's (Gen. 50:12–14).

Judges

Author. We do not know for certain who wrote the book of Judges. Many traditions agree that the prophet Samuel was likely the author.

Date. From the references to the days when Israel "had no king," most believe that the book of Judges was written sometime after Saul's inauguration as king but before David occupied Jerusalem. If so, Judges was written around 1030 B.C.

Purpose. The book of Judges does offer historical information, but the purpose of the book is broader than mere narrative. It illustrates the waywardness of the human heart and the faithfulness of God. Judges records the rule of twelve judges and the cycles of backsliding that Israel experienced between the reign of those judges.

Personal Reading	Group Study Topic and Reading	
1:1–36	Israel Conquers Canaan	1:1–36
2:1–3:6	Disobedience and Defeat	2:6–3:6
3:7–31	Ehud	3:12–30
4:1–5:31	Deborah Leads Israel	4:1–24
6:1–40	Gideon	6:1–40
7:1–8:35	Gideon Defeats Midian	7:1–25
9:1–57	Abimelech	9:1–57
10:1–12:7	Jephthah	11:1–40
12:8–13:25	Samson's Birth	13:1–25
14:1–16:22	Samson and Delilah	16:1–22
16:23–31	Samson's Death	16:23–31
17:1–18:31	Micah's Idols	17:1–13
19:1–21:25	A Levite	19:1–30

Historical Background. The book of Judges describes the period of Israel's history between Joshua's death and Saul's coronation as king. The judges were individuals who rose to power to deliver their people from destruction. The young nation of Israel was still in the process of securing land and establishing itself. However, the people repeatedly turned away from God and faced punishment in the form of military defeat.

One basic conflict between God and Israel was the struggle over who would rule. God had established Israel as his nation; he reserved the authority to rule and to discipline. God used the armies of foreign nations to carry out that discipline. The book of Judges shows the failure of Israel to function as a nation led by God and sets the stage for another form of civil government—the monarchy. Samuel, though not listed in the book of Judges, is said to have been the last judge and the first prophet before Israel's king. This account can be found in 1 Samuel 7:15–17.

Who Were the Judges? In our day, a judge is an arbitrator or official in a legal proceeding. He makes rulings based on legal arguments. During the period of the Book of Judges, it was a very different arrangement. Judges not only arbitrated and provided legal judgment, but they were the prime ministers for both civil government and the military. Deborah was notorious for holding court under a certain palm tree while Samson was known for combat. Moses funtioned as a judge. He also championed the people and led them to unity. The judges lead in similar fashion.

OPEN 1. Are you more of a "stub-your-toe," "mash-your-finger," or "all-thumbs-and-no-fingers" type? Explain. **2.** Who was the bully when you were a child? What was his or her favorite tactic or trick?

STUDY The book of Judges immediately follows Joshua's death. Israel is a loose confederation of tribes spread throughout the Promised Land. The Israelites can't seem to completely root out the influence of Canaanite culture, religion and pagan people. **1.** What do you recall about Joshua? What did Israel accomplish under his leadership? **2.** How do you suppose the Israelites "asked the LORD" and were given such a definitive answer (vv. 1–2)? How do you ask God for guidance? Do you ever feel certain that you understand God's answer? **3.** Why was Judah singled out and sent to be the first wave of troops into this battle for conquest (v. 2; Gen. 49:8–12)? **4.** What was it about Adoni-Bezek that set him apart from the rest of Israel's enemies in this passage? What made him noteworthy? **5.** The story of Caleb's strategy for the capture of Kiriath Sepher is briefly told in verses 11–15 (Josh. 15:13–19). Imagine that you are Acsah. How do you feel about being the "prize" given for victory? Do you think her asking her father for a favor, and his granting it double has anything to do with the unusual way she was given in marriage? **6.** Why was it important to Israel and to God that the Canaanites be eliminated from the Promised Land? How will their continued presence affect Israel's future? **7.** Verses 22–26 tell of a man and his family who were spared when the Israelites conquered the city of Bethel. How is this similar to the story of Rahab (Josh. 2:1–24)?

Israel Fights the Remaining Canaanites

1 After the death of Joshua, the Israelites asked the LORD, "Who
will be the first to go up and fight for us against the Canaanites?"
2 The LORD answered, "Judah is to go; I have given the land into
their hands."
3 Then the men of Judah said to the Simeonites their brothers,
"Come up with us into the territory allotted to us, to fight against the
Canaanites. We in turn will go with you into yours." So the Simeonites went with them.
4 When Judah attacked, the LORD gave the Canaanites and Perizzites
into their hands and they struck down ten thousand men at Bezek. 5 It
was there that they found Adoni-Bezek and fought against him, putting to rout the Canaanites and Perizzites. 6 Adoni-Bezek fled, but they
chased him and caught him, and cut off his thumbs and big toes.
7 Then Adoni-Bezek said, "Seventy kings with their thumbs and big
toes cut off have picked up scraps under my table. Now God has paid
me back for what I did to them." They brought him to Jerusalem, and
he died there.
8 The men of Judah attacked Jerusalem also and took it. They put
the city to the sword and set it on fire.
9 After that, the men of Judah went down to fight against the Canaanites living in the hill country, the Negev and the western foothills. 10 They advanced against the Canaanites living in Hebron
(formerly called Kiriath Arba) and defeated Sheshai, Ahiman and Talmai.
11 From there they advanced against the people living in Debir (formerly called Kiriath Sepher). 12 And Caleb said, "I will give my daughter Acsah in marriage to the man who attacks and captures Kiriath
Sepher." 13 Othniel son of Kenaz, Caleb's younger brother, took it; so
Caleb gave his daughter Acsah in marriage.
14 One day when she came to Othniel, she urged him[a] to ask her father for a field. When she got off her donkey, Caleb asked her, "What
can I do for you?"
15 She replied, "Do me a special favor. Since you have given me land
in the Negev, give me also springs of water." Then Caleb gave her the
upper and lower springs.

[a] 14 Hebrew; Septuagint and Vulgate *Othniel, he urged her*

1:1–3:6 Conquering Canaan was intended to uphold Israel's convictions. Instead, its convictions turned to compromise. It proved easier to put up with idolatry than to put out the pagans (2:2). As a result, the Israelites began a cycle of disobedience and defeat that provided the perfect context for delivery. The Lord gave Israel leader-heroes like the judges for just such a purpose.

1:1–36 The Israelites received the keys to their new homeland, but ousting the former occupants proved to be a chore. Judah was successful to a point (v.19). And Ephraim experienced success at Bethel (v. 22). However, for the most part, Israel did not finish the job.

1:1 After the death of Joshua. Without their military and spiritual leader, Israel entered a new phase of dwindling confidence. Occupying the land was now up to each individual tribe—a daunting task**. asked the LORD.** Similar to a pair of dice, the Urim and Thummin were pieces the priest often used to decipher God's directions (Ex. 28:30). **fight for us.** The Israelites engaged in a military strategy of "you go first." Used to fighting as a family, each tribe wanted the other's help to drive out its enemies.

1:2 Judah. Judah was a natural choice because of the tribe's size. Simeon was also a natural ally since Simeon shared land with Judah (Josh. 19:1).

1:7 Adoni-Bezek. No stranger to humiliation, this "prince of Bezek" had enslaved up to seventy of his own royal captives. He figures it is payback time with whomever it is he considers "God."

1:8 set it on fire. A symbol of dominance, burning the city was the Israelite's way of ascertaining their victory.

1:12 give my daughter Acsah in marriage. Caleb gained a city and a son-in-law with this deal, while Acsah received a nearby spring. Othniel opted to go into battle rather than give a traditional gift to his bride's family.

16The descendants of Moses' father-in-law, the Kenite, went up
from the City of Palms[a] with the men of Judah to live among the people of the Desert of Judah in the Negev near Arad.
17Then the men of Judah went with the Simeonites their brothers
and attacked the Canaanites living in Zephath, and they totally
destroyed[b] the city. Therefore it was called Hormah.[c] 18The men of
Judah also took[d] Gaza, Ashkelon and Ekron—each city with its territory.
19The LORD was with the men of Judah. They took possession of the
hill country, but they were unable to drive the people from the plains,
because they had iron chariots. 20As Moses had promised, Hebron was
given to Caleb, who drove from it the three sons of Anak. 21The Benjamites, however, failed to dislodge the Jebusites, who were living in
Jerusalem; to this day the Jebusites live there with the Benjamites.
22Now the house of Joseph attacked Bethel, and the LORD was with
them. 23When they sent men to spy out Bethel (formerly called Luz),
24the spies saw a man coming out of the city and they said to him,
"Show us how to get into the city and we will see that you are treated
well." 25So he showed them, and they put the city to the sword but
spared the man and his whole family. 26He then went to the land of
the Hittites, where he built a city and called it Luz, which is its name
to this day.
27But Manasseh did not drive out the people of Beth Shan or Taanach or Dor or Ibleam or Megiddo and their surrounding settlements, for the Canaanites were determined to live in that land.
28When Israel became strong, they pressed the Canaanites into
forced labor but never drove them out completely. 29Nor did Ephraim
drive out the Canaanites living in Gezer, but the Canaanites continued to live there among them. 30Neither did Zebulun drive out the
Canaanites living in Kitron or Nahalol, who remained among them;
but they did subject them to forced labor. 31Nor did Asher drive out
those living in Acco or Sidon or Ahlab or Aczib or Helbah or Aphek or
Rehob, 32and because of this the people of Asher lived among the
Canaanite inhabitants of the land. 33Neither did Naphtali drive out
those living in Beth Shemesh or Beth Anath; but the Naphtalites too
lived among the Canaanite inhabitants of the land, and those living in
Beth Shemesh and Beth Anath became forced laborers for them.
34The Amorites confined the Danites to the hill country, not allowing

[a]16 That is, Jericho [b]17 The Hebrew term refers to the irrevocable giving over of things or persons to the LORD, often by totally destroying them. [c]17 Hormah means *destruction*. [d]18 Hebrew; Septuagint *Judah did not take*

Can you remember a time when you were spared from painful consequences because of your obedience to God? Explain.

APPLY **1.** Is there an area of your life where you feel under attack, driven out or relegated to the hill country? Explain. **2.** Who recently has been a "Caleb" in your life and what special favor has he or she done for you? How might God be calling you to be a "Caleb" for someone else?

1:17 attacked the Canaanites. What may seem brutal was actually God's manner of exercising judgment on the already condemned Canaanites. Some of the idolatrous practices of the pagans were so vile that the brute force of the Israelites pales in comparison.

1:19 iron chariots. Their enemy fought from chariots, but the real reason for the Israelites' defeat was not mere weaponry but disobedience.

1:21 Benjamites. The tribe of Benjamin failed to force the foreigners out of Jerusalem. The city would not be under Israelite control until the reign of David (2 Sam. 5:6–9).

1:22 house of Joseph. Referring to the family unit, Ephraim and Manasseh were Joseph's sons (Gen. 48:13).

1:25 spared the man. Similar to Rahab, a prostitute who protected Joshua's spies (Josh. 2:1–21), the man who was helpful to the Israelites escaped destruction.

1:26 to this day. Some scholars point to Samuel, Israel's last judge, as the author of Judges. However, the author is actually uncertain.

1:33 became forced laborers. Those inhabitants who were not destroyed were enslaved by the Israelites.

1:34 confined the Danites. The Amorites enforced imaginary borders on the land belonging to the people of Dan. A sort of house arrest, the Danites forfeited their own freedom to a pagan people.

them to come down into the plain. [35]And the Amorites were determined also to hold out in Mount Heres, Aijalon and Shaalbim, but
when the power of the house of Joseph increased, they too were
pressed into forced labor. [36]The boundary of the Amorites was from
Scorpion[a] Pass to Sela and beyond.

The Angel of the LORD at Bokim

2 The angel of the LORD went up from Gilgal to Bokim and said, "I
brought you up out of Egypt and led you into the land that I
swore to give to your forefathers. I said, 'I will never break my
covenant with you, [2]and you shall not make a covenant with the
people of this land, but you shall break down their altars.' Yet you
have disobeyed me. Why have you done this? [3]Now therefore I tell
you that I will not drive them out before you; they will be ⌊thorns⌋ in
your sides and their gods will be a snare to you."
[4]When the angel of the LORD had spoken these things to all the
Israelites, the people wept aloud, [5]and they called that place Bokim.[b]
There they offered sacrifices to the LORD.

Disobedience and Defeat

[6]After Joshua had dismissed the Israelites, they went to take possession of the land, each to his own inheritance. [7]The people served
the LORD throughout the lifetime of Joshua and of the elders who
outlived him and who had seen all the great things the LORD had
done for Israel.
[8]Joshua son of Nun, the servant of the LORD, died at the age of a
hundred and ten. [9]And they buried him in the land of his inheritance,
at Timnath Heres[c] in the hill country of Ephraim, north of Mount
Gaash.
[10]After that whole generation had been gathered to their fathers,
another generation grew up, who knew neither the LORD nor what he
had done for Israel. [11]Then the Israelites did evil in the eyes of the
LORD and served the Baals. [12]They forsook the LORD, the God of their
fathers, who had brought them out of Egypt. They followed and worshiped various gods of the peoples around them. They provoked the
LORD to anger [13]because they forsook him and served Baal and the
Ashtoreths. [14]In his anger against Israel the LORD handed them over
to raiders who plundered them. He sold them to their enemies all
around, whom they were no longer able to resist. [15]Whenever Israel

[a]36 Hebrew *Akrabbim* [b]5 *Bokim* means *weepers.* [c]9 Also known as *Timnath Serah* (see Joshua 19:50 and 24:30)

OPEN 1. Who has helped keep you on the "straight and narrow"? **2.** When was the last time you failed to carry out the orders of the boss? What happened?

STUDY This passage introduces the painful cycle of disobedience, defeat and delivery that the Israelites chose to live over and over. The consequences this disobedience brings were at times brutal. **1.** What might the emotional climate have been like in Israel after the death of Joshua and the elders: A thick fog? A constant drizzle? Frosty? A break in the clouds? Thunderheads on the horizon? A deluge? Explain. **2.** Why do you think the Israelites didn't listen to their leaders, the judges? Do you ever have difficulty "hearing" people in authority? **3.** The text states that the people would follow a judge until his or her death, then they would turn to the ways of the culture that surrounded them (vv. 16–19). Who was Israel really loyal to? To whom should it have given its allegiance? How does this

1:35 the Amorites were determined also to hold out. The Israelites' battles for occupation of the land were hard fought. The pagans did not give up easily.

2:1–5 Like a couple flipping through pages of their wedding day photo album, God reviews Israel's commitments. An angel of the Lord pointedly showed them how they had broken their vows. As a result, the Israelites wept in remorse.

2:6–3:6 The story of Israel as a nation reads like a case study of good intentions gone bad. Picking up where the book of Joshua left off, their commitment to principle ends and the cycle of disobedience, defeat and delivery begins.

2:8 *Joshua.* *Joshua's death begins a period of intense spiritual struggle for Israel.*

2:10 another generation grew up. Unlike the generation before, this generation knew nothing about the faith story of their ancestors. No Red Sea. No Jordan River. However, they proceed to do battle against the Canaanites, more for political than spiritual reasons. They did not even realize God was no longer with them because of their disobedience.

2:11 Baals. Appropriately named for the god of storms and wars, these foreign idols were controversy incarnate. God opposed the Baals and kept the Israelites from winning wars whenever they worshiped Baals.

went out to fight, the hand of the LORD was against them to defeat them, just as he had sworn to them. They were in great distress.

16Then the LORD raised up judges,[a] who saved them out of the hands of these raiders. 17Yet they would not listen to their judges but prostituted themselves to other gods and worshiped them. Unlike their fathers, they quickly turned from the way in which their fathers had walked, the way of obedience to the LORD's commands. 18Whenever the LORD raised up a judge for them, he was with the judge and saved them out of the hands of their enemies as long as the judge lived; for the LORD had compassion on them as they groaned under those who oppressed and afflicted them. 19But when the judge died, the people returned to ways even more corrupt than those of their fathers, following other gods and serving and worshiping them. They refused to give up their evil practices and stubborn ways.

20Therefore the LORD was very angry with Israel and said, "Because this nation has violated the covenant that I laid down for their forefathers and has not listened to me, 21I will no longer drive out before them any of the nations Joshua left when he died. 22I will use them to test Israel and see whether they will keep the way of the LORD and walk in it as their forefathers did." 23The LORD had allowed those nations to remain; he did not drive them out at once by giving them into the hands of Joshua.

3 These are the nations the LORD left to test all those Israelites who had not experienced any of the wars in Canaan 2(he did this only to teach warfare to the descendants of the Israelites who had not had previous battle experience): 3the five rulers of the Philistines, all the Canaanites, the Sidonians, and the Hivites living in the Lebanon mountains from Mount Baal Hermon to Lebo[b] Hamath. 4They were left to test the Israelites to see whether they would obey the LORD's commands, which he had given their forefathers through Moses.

5The Israelites lived among the Canaanites, Hittites, Amorites, Perizzites, Hivites and Jebusites. 6They took their daughters in marriage and gave their own daughters to their sons, and served their gods.

Othniel

7The Israelites did evil in the eyes of the LORD; they forgot the LORD their God and served the Baals and the Asherahs. 8The anger of the LORD burned against Israel so that he sold them into the hands of Cushan-Rishathaim king of Aram Naharaim,[c] to whom the Israelites were subject for eight years. 9But when they cried out to the LORD, he

[a]16 Or *leaders;* similarly in verses 17-19 [b]3 Or *to the entrance to* [c]8 That is, Northwest Mesopotamia

pattern relate to your walk with God? **4.** What test does God put to Israel (2:20–3:4)? **5.** How was God's treatment of a disobedient Israel similar to the way he treated the pagan people of the Promised Land? How was it different? Does God's behavior seem fair to you? **6.** In your opinion, what does this text reveal about the justice and mercy of God? **7.** If you could go back in time, what would you find the people of Israel doing that would signify that they were serving other gods? What behaviors in your life act as a "tip off" to others that you are living in disobedience?

APPLY 1. Share an area in your life where you find yourself reliving the same mistake over and over again. How does it feel? Does your faith help or hurt the situation? **2.** Who or what in times past has come to rescue you from your distress? How might this group be a "lifesaver" for you now or in the future?

OPEN As you were growing up, whose shoes were you expected to fill?

STUDY God raises up a judge who has leadership with a capital "L" in his genes. **1.** Who was Othniel (v. 9)? Why are his family ties important (1:11–15)? **2.** What role

2:16–19 *The judges were the leader-heroes of the land.* Whenever a judge appeared on the scene, relative calm would result. However, whenever Israel was between heroes, it seemed to forget its priorities.

2:16 raiders. Canaan was full of warring people who did not take kindly to the new kids on the block. However, in actuality, the Israelites were their own worst enemies.

2:20–23 The Israelites experienced God's wrath by compromising his covenant and befriending the pagan people and their practices (Josh. 24:25–27). As a result, God would now give the pagans the upper hand in battle.

3:1–6 Instead of being light in a dark place, the Israelites settled for dusk. They became like the pagan people in many ways, learning to worship their gods in order to have prosperity and peace. They even intermarried with them and began mixed-faith families.

3:2 warfare. In this sense, warfare meant military preparedness. But it also meant learning to be spiritually prepared to rely on God in battle.

3:7–11 Othniel is the first in a series of judges who serve as leader-heroes for the people of Israel. The need for his arrival is a pattern repeated for each of the

does God's Spirit play in the power of a judge?

APPLY Have you ever felt that God's anger "burned" against you? How did you find forgiveness?

OPEN What is your favorite movie or TV show? What kind of stories do you like: Adventure? Romance? Action? Drama? Comedy?

STUDY This is the first of five major accounts of national deliverers, all of which are meant to sicken the reader as well as celebrate Israel's deliverance. **1.** After reading the story of Ehud, what adjectives would you use to describe his personality and actions? **2.** This passage paints a vivid picture of how Ehud delivered Israel from Eglon, king of Moab. What details might you have left out if you had reported the story? What details would you highlight? **3.** How do you feel about Ehud as you learn of his plan and behavior? **4.** Why do you think it was significant to the author that Ehud was left-handed (vv. 15,21)? **5.** How does Ehud deliver Israel from its oppressors (vv. 28–30)? **6.** If you had been a Benjamite during the days of Ehud, what would you celebrate most about his leadership? **7.** Shamgar is the first of six minor judges: What do you learn about him here? (Note: "Anath," Baal's sister, was a goddess of war.)

APPLY 1. When have you sent God an "SOS" call for help? How did he answer? Where in your life would you like to experience God answering one of your calls today? **2.** If you were to "blow a trumpet" in gratitude for something

raised up for them a deliverer, Othniel son of Kenaz, Caleb's younger
brother, who saved them. 10 The Spirit of the LORD came upon him, so
that he became Israel's judge[a] and went to war. The LORD gave
Cushan-Rishathaim king of Aram into the hands of Othniel, who
overpowered him. 11 So the land had peace for forty years, until
Othniel son of Kenaz died.

Ehud

12 Once again the Israelites did evil in the eyes of the LORD, and because they did this evil the LORD gave Eglon king of Moab power over
Israel. 13 Getting the Ammonites and Amalekites to join him, Eglon
came and attacked Israel, and they took possession of the City of
Palms.[b] 14 The Israelites were subject to Eglon king of Moab for eighteen years.

15 Again the Israelites cried out to the LORD, and he gave them a deliverer—Ehud, a left-handed man, the son of Gera the Benjamite. The
Israelites sent him with tribute to Eglon king of Moab. 16 Now Ehud
had made a double-edged sword about a foot and a half[c] long, which
he strapped to his right thigh under his clothing. 17 He presented the
tribute to Eglon king of Moab, who was a very fat man. 18 After Ehud
had presented the tribute, he sent on their way the men who had carried it. 19 At the idols[d] near Gilgal he himself turned back and said, "I
have a secret message for you, O king."

The king said, "Quiet!" And all his attendants left him.

20 Ehud then approached him while he was sitting alone in the upper room of his summer palace[e] and said, "I have a message from
God for you." As the king rose from his seat, 21 Ehud reached with his
left hand, drew the sword from his right thigh and plunged it into the
king's belly. 22 Even the handle sank in after the blade, which came
out his back. Ehud did not pull the sword out, and the fat closed in
over it. 23 Then Ehud went out to the porch[f]; he shut the doors of the
upper room behind him and locked them.

24 After he had gone, the servants came and found the doors of the
upper room locked. They said, "He must be relieving himself in the
inner room of the house." 25 They waited to the point of embarrassment, but when he did not open the doors of the room, they took a

[a] *10* Or *leader* [b] *13* That is, Jericho [c] *16* Hebrew *a cubit* (about 0.5 meter) [d] *19* Or *the stone quarries*; also in verse 26 [e] *20* The meaning of the Hebrew for this phrase is uncertain. [f] *23* The meaning of the Hebrew for this word is uncertain.

---

judges. The pattern includes disobedience, defeat (and usually enslavement of the people) and deliverance by one of the judges.

3:10 Spirit of the LORD came upon him. God maneuvers the judge into place to symbolize his presence among the people.

3:12–30 In a memorable tale of secrets and swords, Ehud became one of the more dramatic deliverers of Israel. Under the guise of a royal tribute, Ehud lands in the court of the portly king of Moab. A personal audience with the king turns into murder. Ehud steals away back to Israel, which then destroys the Moabite nation.

3:14 Israelites. Ehud was from the tribe of Benjamin and joined Ephraim's resentment of Moabite rule.

***3:15* left-handed.** Ehud's uniqueness allowed him to use a concealed weapon on his right thigh at just the right time.

3:16 double-edged sword. The sword was just long enough (about 18 inches) to nicely fit in a strap under his outer garment.

3:19 he himself turned back. Ehud, with a flair for the dramatic, decides to tackle his mission alone. He sends his men on and proposes a personal audience with the king.

3:22 which came out his back. The grisly image of a knife disappearing into the portly stature of the royal king made a lasting impression on the author.

key and unlocked them. There they saw their lord fallen to the floor,
dead.
[26]While they waited, Ehud got away. He passed by the idols and
escaped to Seirah. [27]When he arrived there, he blew a trumpet in the
hill country of Ephraim, and the Israelites went down with him from
the hills, with him leading them.
[28]"Follow me," he ordered, "for the LORD has given Moab, your
enemy, into your hands." So they followed him down and, taking
possession of the fords of the Jordan that led to Moab, they allowed
no one to cross over. [29]At that time they struck down about ten thousand Moabites, all vigorous and strong; not a man escaped. [30]That
day Moab was made subject to Israel, and the land had peace for
eighty years.

Shamgar

[31]After Ehud came Shamgar son of Anath, who struck down six
hundred Philistines with an oxgoad. He too saved Israel.

Deborah

4 After Ehud died, the Israelites once again did evil in the eyes of
the LORD. [2]So the LORD sold them into the hands of Jabin, a king
of Canaan, who reigned in Hazor. The commander of his army was
Sisera, who lived in Harosheth Haggoyim. [3]Because he had nine hundred iron chariots and had cruelly oppressed the Israelites for twenty
years, they cried to the LORD for help.
[4]Deborah, a prophetess, the wife of Lappidoth, was leading[a] Israel
at that time. [5]She held court under the Palm of Deborah between Ramah and Bethel in the hill country of Ephraim, and the Israelites
came to her to have their disputes decided. [6]She sent for Barak son of
Abinoam from Kedesh in Naphtali and said to him, "The LORD, the
God of Israel, commands you: 'Go, take with you ten thousand men
of Naphtali and Zebulun and lead the way to Mount Tabor. [7]I will lure
Sisera, the commander of Jabin's army, with his chariots and his
troops to the Kishon River and give him into your hands.' "
[8]Barak said to her, "If you go with me, I will go; but if you don't go
with me, I won't go."
[9]"Very well," Deborah said, "I will go with you. But because of the
way you are going about this,[b] the honor will not be yours, for the
LORD will hand Sisera over to a woman." So Deborah went with

[a]4 Traditionally *judging* [b]9 Or *But on the expedition you are undertaking*

God has done for you recently, what would it be?

OPEN 1. Who comes to your rescue when you are in a tight spot? **2.** Apart from members of your family, who is the woman you admire most as a leader? What qualities does she possess that set her apart?

STUDY During the period of the judges, Israel went through cycles of turning away from God, suffering from oppression, crying out to the Lord, and being delivered by God through a human agent. On this occasion God's agent was quite unusual for that time and place—a woman. **1.** How was Deborah's leadership style as a judge different from that of Ehud (3:12–30)? **2.** What role did Deborah being a prophetess play in Israel's victory over the Canaanites? **3.** Imagine that you are a Zebulun warrior who fought for Israel's liberation from Canaanite oppression. How do you feel about the honor of victory going to a woman? **4.** In your opinion, why would Heber the Kenite leave his clan to camp near the enemy? What kind of relationship did he have with

---

3:28 for the LORD has given Moab ... into your hands. Ehud realizes he is a mere tool in the Lord's hand to accomplish his purposes.

3:31 Shamgar. A rugged fighter, Shamgar is identified as a judge because he is credited with "saving" Israel from the cycle of disobedience and defeat.

4:1–24 Once again, the Lord demonstrates his presence among the people in the form of a deliverer. Deborah, the judge at this time, directs a victorious military invasion under Barak against a Canaanite army.

4:1–2 Sisera. The Canaanite king ordered Sisera, his commander, to lead his troops in battle against Israel.

4:4 Deborah. Unique to the male-dominated culture of that time, Deborah reigned as a judge, settling disputes among the Israelites. As a spiritual leader or prophetess, she also predicted the victory for Israel's battle against the Canaanites and encouraged them to fight.

4:6 Barak. He was Deborah's top pick for commanding 10,000 troops to war against the enemy. He affirmed Deborah's role as leader by refusing to enter battle without her (v. 8).

4:7 I will lure Sisera. What seemed an ideal battleground for Sisera would soon turn to a muddy pit of disaster, according to the Lord's plan.

4:9 a woman. Courage was up for grabs in this situation. Although Barak passed on the opportunity, Deborah predicted another female counterpart

Jabin the king of Hazor? How do you think Heber felt about his wife, Jael, murdering a family friend? **5.** What made Deborah a leader in a man's world? **6.** What quality of Deborah's do you most admire and would like to possess for yourself?

APPLY 1. Share a time when a leader has asked you to take a step of faith on what seemed to be a risky path? What happened? Did you go for it or hold back? Why? **2.** If you had Deborah's confidence, what would you attempt to do?

Barak to Kedesh, [10]where he summoned Zebulun and Naphtali. Ten
thousand men followed him, and Deborah also went with him.
[11]Now Heber the Kenite had left the other Kenites, the descendants
of Hobab, Moses' brother-in-law,[a] and pitched his tent by the great
tree in Zaanannim near Kedesh.
[12]When they told Sisera that Barak son of Abinoam had gone up to
Mount Tabor, [13]Sisera gathered together his nine hundred iron chariots and all the men with him, from Harosheth Haggoyim to the Kishon
River.
[14]Then Deborah said to Barak, "Go! This is the day the LORD has
given Sisera into your hands. Has not the LORD gone ahead of you?"
So Barak went down Mount Tabor, followed by ten thousand men.
[15]At Barak's advance, the LORD routed Sisera and all his chariots and
army by the sword, and Sisera abandoned his chariot and fled on
foot. [16]But Barak pursued the chariots and army as far as Harosheth
Haggoyim. All the troops of Sisera fell by the sword; not a man was
left.
[17]Sisera, however, fled on foot to the tent of Jael, the wife of Heber
the Kenite, because there were friendly relations between Jabin king
of Hazor and the clan of Heber the Kenite.
[18]Jael went out to meet Sisera and said to him, "Come, my lord,
come right in. Don't be afraid." So he entered her tent, and she put a
covering over him.
[19]"I'm thirsty," he said. "Please give me some water." She opened a
skin of milk, gave him a drink, and covered him up.
[20]"Stand in the doorway of the tent," he told her. "If someone
comes by and asks you, 'Is anyone here?' say 'No.' "
[21]But Jael, Heber's wife, picked up a tent peg and a hammer and
went quietly to him while he lay fast asleep, exhausted. She drove the
peg through his temple into the ground, and he died.
[22]Barak came by in pursuit of Sisera, and Jael went out to meet
him. "Come," she said, "I will show you the man you're looking for."
So he went in with her, and there lay Sisera with the tent peg through
his temple—dead.
[23]On that day God subdued Jabin, the Canaanite king, before the
Israelites. [24]And the hand of the Israelites grew stronger and stronger
against Jabin, the Canaanite king, until they destroyed him.

[a]11 Or *father-in-law*

---

would respond to God's call to courage and help secure the victory (vv. 18–22).

4:11 Heber the Kenite. This Kenite nomad was related to Moses, but he moved his tent in order to sleep with the enemy (v. 17). He likely informed Sisera of Barak's military operations.

4:14 gone ahead of you. Although Deborah herself would not go into battle, the Lord advanced before Barak and his army.

4:18 he entered her tent. As a family friend, Sisera did not consider Jael's warm behavior suspicious.

4:19 Jael, as was customary in the Middle Eastern rules of hospitality, offered the army captain whatever comforts she could provide.

4:21 drove the peg through his temple. Used to the customary pitching and tearing down of the tent, Jael skillfully handled her murder weapons. A woman of great courage, Jael diverted from her husband's allegiance and murdered the captain as Deborah had predicted (v. 9).

4:22 Barak came by in pursuit of Sisera. The great warrior who was initially reluctant to go to battle came by just in time. To his surprise, he discovered Sisera slain by a courageous woman instead.

The Song of Deborah

5 On that day Deborah and Barak son of Abinoam sang this song:

2 "When the princes in Israel take the lead,
when the people willingly offer themselves—
praise the LORD!

3 "Hear this, you kings! Listen, you rulers!
I will sing to[a] the LORD, I will sing;
I will make music to[b] the LORD, the God of Israel.

4 "O LORD, when you went out from Seir,
when you marched from the land of Edom,
the earth shook, the heavens poured,
the clouds poured down water.
5 The mountains quaked before the LORD, the One of Sinai,
before the LORD, the God of Israel.

6 "In the days of Shamgar son of Anath,
in the days of Jael, the roads were abandoned;
travelers took to winding paths.
7 Village life[c] in Israel ceased,
ceased until I,[d] Deborah, arose,
arose a mother in Israel.
8 When they chose new gods,
war came to the city gates,
and not a shield or spear was seen
among forty thousand in Israel.
9 My heart is with Israel's princes,
with the willing volunteers among the people.
Praise the LORD!

10 "You who ride on white donkeys,
sitting on your saddle blankets,
and you who walk along the road,
consider 11 the voice of the singers[e] at the watering places.
They recite the righteous acts of the LORD,
the righteous acts of his warriors[f] in Israel.

"Then the people of the LORD
went down to the city gates.
12 'Wake up, wake up, Deborah!
Wake up, wake up, break out in song!
Arise, O Barak!
Take captive your captives, O son of Abinoam.'

[a]3 Or *of* [b]3 Or / *with song I will praise* [c]7 Or *Warriors* [d]7 Or *you* [e]11 Or *archers*; the meaning of the Hebrew for this word is uncertain. [f]11 Or *villagers*

OPEN 1. What is your favorite song? **2.** When you experience "victory" in your life, how do you celebrate: Laugh? Cry? Shout? Feast? Sing? Shop? Pamper yourself? Treat your friends to something special?

STUDY The Israelite troops of Naphtali and Zebulun have experienced a great victory over a hated oppressor under the leadership of Deborah. Here we find an emotional song of praise filled with gratitude for Israel's deliverance. **1.** What is the purpose and occasion for this psalm of praise (vv. 1–9)? Who is it for (v. 3)? **2.** As songwriters, what do Deborah and Barak have in common with Moses and Miriam (Ex. 15:1–21); Mary (Luke 1:46–55) and Zechariah (Luke 1:68–79)? **3.** What additional light does this song cast on the events recorded in chapter four? **4.** After reading this song, how do you feel about Deborah and Jael? Do you like them, or do you cringe at the lawlessness of these times when Israel had no king? **5.** Of the tribes that participated in the battle (vv. 13–18), which received high marks and which received low ones? In your life, who is pitching in to give you a hand? How? In what areas are you feeling abandoned? **6.** What is your favorite lyric or major theme in this song? How does it relate to events in your life?

APPLY 1. Deborah was a prophet, a leader, a songwriter. If you had to describe yourself in three words, which three would you choose? What is the story behind those words? **2.** When was the last time you recall "singing someone's praises"? Has anyone ever sung your praises? For what? How did it feel?

5:1–31 Great moments make great songs. Deborah's victory over the Canaanite king is no exception. One of the oldest poems penned in the Bible, the song is full of human emotion. It praises God for his faithfulness. This poem was likely read and sung at a celebration in honor of the victory (Ex. 15:1–18).

5:4–5 Deborah begins her poem by retracing the Lord's movement among his people on their way to Canaan.

5:5 Sinai. Deborah reminds the people of their ancestors' commitment to the covenant. Moses mediated the covenant with them during an earth-shaking encounter with God at Mount Sinai (Ex. 19:17–20).

5:11 voice of the singers. Deborah, a judge turned military commander turned worship leader, inspires the people to praise by getting the singers to express the joy of the victory.

[13]"Then the men who were left
came down to the nobles;
the people of the LORD
came to me with the mighty.
[14]Some came from Ephraim, whose roots were in Amalek;
Benjamin was with the people who followed you.
From Makir captains came down,
from Zebulun those who bear a commander's staff.
[15]The princes of Issachar were with Deborah;
yes, Issachar was with Barak,
rushing after him into the valley.
In the districts of Reuben
there was much searching of heart.
[16]Why did you stay among the campfires[a]
to hear the whistling for the flocks?
In the districts of Reuben
there was much searching of heart.
[17]Gilead stayed beyond the Jordan.
And Dan, why did he linger by the ships?
Asher remained on the coast
and stayed in his coves.
[18]The people of Zebulun risked their very lives;
so did Naphtali on the heights of the field.

[19]"Kings came, they fought;
the kings of Canaan fought
at Taanach by the waters of Megiddo,
but they carried off no silver, no plunder.
[20]From the heavens the stars fought,
from their courses they fought against Sisera.
[21]The river Kishon swept them away,
the age-old river, the river Kishon.
March on, my soul; be strong!
[22]Then thundered the horses' hoofs—
galloping, galloping go his mighty steeds.
[23]'Curse Meroz,' said the angel of the LORD.
'Curse its people bitterly,
because they did not come to help the LORD,
to help the LORD against the mighty.'

[24]"Most blessed of women be Jael,
the wife of Heber the Kenite,
most blessed of tent-dwelling women.
[25]He asked for water, and she gave him milk;
in a bowl fit for nobles she brought him curdled milk.
[26]Her hand reached for the tent peg,
her right hand for the workman's hammer.
She struck Sisera, she crushed his head,
she shattered and pierced his temple.

[a]16 Or *saddlebags*

5:13–18 Deborah goes through the roster of tribes to show who contributed to the family effort. Those tribes who were not part of the united effort are criticized for their indifference.

[27]At her feet he sank,
he fell; there he lay.
At her feet he sank, he fell;
where he sank, there he fell—dead.

[28]"Through the window peered Sisera's mother;
behind the lattice she cried out,
'Why is his chariot so long in coming?
Why is the clatter of his chariots delayed?'
[29]The wisest of her ladies answer her;
indeed, she keeps saying to herself,
[30]'Are they not finding and dividing the spoils:
a girl or two for each man,
colorful garments as plunder for Sisera,
colorful garments embroidered,
highly embroidered garments for my neck—
all this as plunder?'

[31]"So may all your enemies perish, O LORD!
But may they who love you be like the sun
when it rises in its strength."

Then the land had peace forty years.

Gideon

6 Again the Israelites did evil in the eyes of the LORD, and for seven
years he gave them into the hands of the Midianites. [2]Because
the power of Midian was so oppressive, the Israelites prepared shelters for themselves in mountain clefts, caves and strongholds.
[3]Whenever the Israelites planted their crops, the Midianites, Amalekites and other eastern peoples invaded the country. [4]They camped on
the land and ruined the crops all the way to Gaza and did not spare a
living thing for Israel, neither sheep nor cattle nor donkeys. [5]They
came up with their livestock and their tents like swarms of locusts. It
was impossible to count the men and their camels; they invaded the
land to ravage it. [6]Midian so impoverished the Israelites that they
cried out to the LORD for help.
[7]When the Israelites cried to the LORD because of Midian, [8]he sent
them a prophet, who said, "This is what the LORD, the God of Israel,
says: I brought you up out of Egypt, out of the land of slavery. [9]I
snatched you from the power of Egypt and from the hand of all your
oppressors. I drove them from before you and gave you their land. [10]I
said to you, 'I am the LORD your God; do not worship the gods of the
Amorites, in whose land you live.' But you have not listened to me."
[11]The angel of the LORD came and sat down under the oak in
Ophrah that belonged to Joash the Abiezrite, where his son Gideon

OPEN 1. What is your least favorite chore? **2.** Which word best describes you—skeptical or gullible? Explain.

STUDY In this story God calls Gideon to be Israel's next judge—to bring Israel back to spiritual faithfulness and out of oppression by the Midianites. Three times Gideon asks God for a visible sign and each time the Lord complies. **1.** Describe the situation from which the Israelites cry out for God's help (vv. 1–10). What, in your opinion, was the real "oppressor" Israel needed deliverance from? **2.** As you read Gideon's story of his call to be a judge in Israel, does he impress you as being a "man of faith"? What role does the Holy Spirit play in this selection process? **3.** How did fear affect Gideon's response to God's call? How does fear affect your ability to obediently follow God in new directions? **4.** What was the significance of Gideon's assignment to tear one altar

5:31 peace. The period of peace completes the cycle the Israelites experienced. However, the renewal of the cycle was as close as the latest judge's last breath.

6:1–9:57 Despite a series of judges and their heroic efforts, the Israelites continue to deteriorate. The emphasis on Gideon's victory shows that Israel flirted with the opportunity to change its course and return to God. However, even Gideon ultimately succumbed to disobedience himself (8:24–27). The following story centers on Abimelech's political upheaval and self-proclaimed royalty (9:1–57). At the end of his reign, things have moved from bad to worse.

6:7 because of Midian. The Israelites were unaware that the Midianites were not the cause of their problems. In fact, God used Midian to punish the Israelites' unfaithfulness to him.

6:11 threshing wheat in a winepress. Usually Gideon would be threshing wheat in the open air so the

down and build a new one (vv. 25–32)? What would you like to "tear down" in your life? What would you build in its place? **5.** What signs did Gideon ask for in order to be certain that it really was God present with him? Why do you think the Lord was so patient with Gideon's requests? How does God respond to you when you ask him for confirmation of his presence in your life? **6.** When have you used a "fleece" to seek direction from God? How do you feel about asking the Lord for signs? Have you ever asked God for a sign? **7.** In this story we get a glimpse of Gideon's strengths and weaknesses. List them. What do you see as being your greatest strength? What is your greatest weakness?

APPLY 1. In the past five years, what are two "sure" signs of God's presence with you? **2.** What do you find is the hardest thing about doing God's will? **3.** In what area of your life do you most need God's direction?

was threshing wheat in a winepress to keep it from the Midianites.
12 When the angel of the LORD appeared to Gideon, he said, "The LORD
is with you, mighty warrior."
13 "But sir," Gideon replied, "if the LORD is with us, why has all this
happened to us? Where are all his wonders that our fathers told us
about when they said, 'Did not the LORD bring us up out of Egypt?'
But now the LORD has abandoned us and put us into the hand of
Midian."
14 The LORD turned to him and said, "Go in the strength you have
and save Israel out of Midian's hand. Am I not sending you?"
15 "But Lord,[a]" Gideon asked, "how can I save Israel? My clan is the
weakest in Manasseh, and I am the least in my family."
16 The LORD answered, "I will be with you, and you will strike down
all the Midianites together."
17 Gideon replied, "If now I have found favor in your eyes, give me a
sign that it is really you talking to me. 18 Please do not go away until I
come back and bring my offering and set it before you."
And the LORD said, "I will wait until you return."
19 Gideon went in, prepared a young goat, and from an ephah[b] of
flour he made bread without yeast. Putting the meat in a basket and
its broth in a pot, he brought them out and offered them to him under
the oak.
20 The angel of God said to him, "Take the meat and the unleavened
bread, place them on this rock, and pour out the broth." And Gideon
did so. 21 With the tip of the staff that was in his hand, the angel of the
LORD touched the meat and the unleavened bread. Fire flared from
the rock, consuming the meat and the bread. And the angel of the
LORD disappeared. 22 When Gideon realized that it was the angel of
the LORD, he exclaimed, "Ah, Sovereign LORD! I have seen the angel of
the LORD face to face!"
23 But the LORD said to him, "Peace! Do not be afraid. You are not
going to die."
24 So Gideon built an altar to the LORD there and called it The LORD
is Peace. To this day it stands in Ophrah of the Abiezrites.
25 That same night the LORD said to him, "Take the second bull from
your father's herd, the one seven years old.[c] Tear down your father's
altar to Baal and cut down the Asherah pole[d] beside it. 26 Then build a
proper kind of[e] altar to the LORD your God on the top of this height.
Using the wood of the Asherah pole that you cut down, offer the
second[f] bull as a burnt offering."

[a] 15 Or *sir* [b] 19 That is, probably about 3/5 bushel (about 22 liters) [c] 25 Or *Take a full-grown, mature bull from your father's herd* [d] 25 That is, a symbol of the goddess Asherah; here and elsewhere in Judges [e] 26 Or *build with layers of stone an* [f] 26 Or *full-grown;* also in verse 28

wind could take away the chaff. However, with the threat of Midianite attack, he sought safety in the winepress.

6:12 mighty warrior. The angel of the Lord saw the potential for a mighty warrior in this laborer.

6:14 Am I not sending you? Gideon did not know it then, but he was selected to be the next judge in a series of leader-heroes who would deliver Israel from her fate.

6:15 how can I save Israel? Gideon's focus was not on his faith in God but on his family—a small family in a small clan at that. How could he be a hero?

6:17 give me a sign. A brazen request from someone in conversation with God himself! Gideon's small faith needed even more assurance. For Gideon, seeing was believing.

6:25 Tear down your father's altar. Gideon's heritage was not a spiritual one. However, Gideon would sacrifice his father's pagan faith, demonstrating God's superiority and Gideon's new start.

27 So Gideon took ten of his servants and did as the LORD told him.
But because he was afraid of his family and the men of the town, he
did it at night rather than in the daytime.
28 In the morning when the men of the town got up, there was
Baal's altar, demolished, with the Asherah pole beside it cut down
and the second bull sacrificed on the newly built altar!
29 They asked each other, "Who did this?"
When they carefully investigated, they were told, "Gideon son of
Joash did it."
30 The men of the town demanded of Joash, "Bring out your son. He
must die, because he has broken down Baal's altar and cut down the
Asherah pole beside it."
31 But Joash replied to the hostile crowd around him, "Are you going
to plead Baal's cause? Are you trying to save him? Whoever fights for
him shall be put to death by morning! If Baal really is a god, he can
defend himself when someone breaks down his altar." 32 So that day
they called Gideon "Jerub-Baal,[a]" saying, "Let Baal contend with
him," because he broke down Baal's altar.
33 Now all the Midianites, Amalekites and other eastern peoples
joined forces and crossed over the Jordan and camped in the Valley of
Jezreel. 34 Then the Spirit of the LORD came upon Gideon, and he blew
a trumpet, summoning the Abiezrites to follow him. 35 He sent messengers throughout Manasseh, calling them to arms, and also into
Asher, Zebulun and Naphtali, so that they too went up to meet them.
36 Gideon said to God, "If you will save Israel by my hand as you
have promised— 37 look, I will place a wool fleece on the threshing
floor. If there is dew only on the fleece and all the ground is dry, then
I will know that you will save Israel by my hand, as you said." 38 And
that is what happened. Gideon rose early the next day; he squeezed
the fleece and wrung out the dew—a bowlful of water.
39 Then Gideon said to God, "Do not be angry with me. Let me make
just one more request. Allow me one more test with the fleece. This
time make the fleece dry and the ground covered with dew." 40 That
night God did so. Only the fleece was dry; all the ground was covered
with dew.

Gideon Defeats the Midianites

7 Early in the morning, Jerub-Baal (that is, Gideon) and all his men
camped at the spring of Harod. The camp of Midian was north of
them in the valley near the hill of Moreh. 2 The LORD said to Gideon,
"You have too many men for me to deliver Midian into their hands. In
order that Israel may not boast against me that her own strength has
saved her, 3 announce now to the people, 'Anyone who trembles with
fear may turn back and leave Mount Gilead.' " So twenty-two thousand men left, while ten thousand remained.
4 But the LORD said to Gideon, "There are still too many men. Take

[a]32 *Jerub-Baal* means *let Baal contend.*

OPEN 1. What musical instruments have you played? **2.** What dream have you had recently that vividly sticks in your mind? What emotion do you associate with it: Joy? Fear? Encouragement? Risk? Comfort? Love? Other?

STUDY Somewhat reluctantly, Gideon had just accepted God's call to Israel against the Midianites. To prepare for the battle, God actually had Gideon reduce his troops. First, those who were afraid to fight

6:34 Spirit of the LORD. God's Spirit empowered Gideon to do his work. In contrast to his prior protests, Gideon is now confident of God's instructions for his life.

7:1–8 Numbers were not high on God's surprising list of requirements for success. In fact, he shaved thousands of men off Gideon's battle plan and accomplished victory with a much smaller group of warriors—300.

7:3 may turn back. God wanted warriors who were confident in God's ability to make them strong.

the battle were excused. Then, only those who drank while remaining alert for attack were retained. **1.** If you had been Gideon, how would you have felt about God reducing your army from 32,000 to 300? Why did God establish such high odds against Israel (v. 2)? **2.** What do you think of God's "winnowing" process of the Israelite troops (vv. 2–6)? Has God done any "winnowing" in your life? **3.** How does Gideon's response to God's direction in this chapter compare to chapter 6? To what would you attribute the change? **4.** How did God encourage Gideon (vv. 9–15)? What encourages you most in your spiritual life? **5.** Where else in the Bible do you remember God speaking to someone in a dream? Does God ever speak to you in dreams, or do you think God no longer does that? **6.** Besides God, what did Gideon's battle plan have going for it? What would the horn-blowing contribute? Why did the Israelites win?

APPLY **1.** What battle are you currently facing? How do you feel about letting God fight that battle for you? **2.** In your life, when has God used one of your weaknesses or failures to help someone else? Which weakness of yours does Gideon's story prompt you to see in a different light?

them down to the water, and I will sift them for you there. If I say,
'This one shall go with you,' he shall go; but if I say, 'This one shall
not go with you,' he shall not go."
5So Gideon took the men down to the water. There the LORD told
him, "Separate those who lap the water with their tongues like a dog
from those who kneel down to drink." 6Three hundred men lapped
with their hands to their mouths. All the rest got down on their knees
to drink.
7The LORD said to Gideon, "With the three hundred men that
lapped I will save you and give the Midianites into your hands. Let all
the other men go, each to his own place." 8So Gideon sent the rest of
the Israelites to their tents but kept the three hundred, who took over
the provisions and trumpets of the others.
Now the camp of Midian lay below him in the valley. 9During that
night the LORD said to Gideon, "Get up, go down against the camp,
because I am going to give it into your hands. 10If you are afraid to
attack, go down to the camp with your servant Purah 11and listen to
what they are saying. Afterward, you will be encouraged to attack the
camp." So he and Purah his servant went down to the outposts of the
camp. 12The Midianites, the Amalekites and all the other eastern peoples had settled in the valley, thick as locusts. Their camels could no
more be counted than the sand on the seashore.
13Gideon arrived just as a man was telling a friend his dream. "I
had a dream," he was saying. "A round loaf of barley bread came tum-
bling into the Midianite camp. It struck the tent with such force that
the tent overturned and collapsed."
14His friend responded, "This can be nothing other than the sword
of Gideon son of Joash, the Israelite. God has given the Midianites
and the whole camp into his hands."
15When Gideon heard the dream and its interpretation, he worshiped God. He returned to the camp of Israel and called out, "Get up!
The LORD has given the Midianite camp into your hands." 16Dividing
the three hundred men into three companies, he placed trumpets and
empty jars in the hands of all of them, with torches inside.
17"Watch me," he told them. "Follow my lead. When I get to the
edge of the camp, do exactly as I do. 18When I and all who are with me
blow our trumpets, then from all around the camp blow yours and
shout, 'For the LORD and for Gideon.' "
19Gideon and the hundred men with him reached the edge of the
camp at the beginning of the middle watch, just after they had
changed the guard. They blew their trumpets and broke the jars that
were in their hands. 20The three companies blew the trumpets and
smashed the jars. Grasping the torches in their left hands and holding in their right hands the trumpets they were to blow, they shouted,
"A sword for the LORD and for Gideon!" 21While each man held his position around the camp, all the Midianites ran, crying out as they fled.
22When the three hundred trumpets sounded, the LORD caused the
men throughout the camp to turn on each other with their swords.

7:8–14 *Eavesdropping became an important morale-booster and battle strategy for Gideon when an enemy's dream is interpreted to predict the Israelites' victory.*

7:13–14 A loaf of bread. A big hill. A crushed tent. These items collided in a Midianite's dream in order to spell victory for the Israelites. While Gideon's confidence increased, a sleepless night awaited the worried Midianite warriors.

7:19 middle watch. About 10:00 p.m., according to the Jewish custom of dividing the nighttime into three parts.

The army fled to Beth Shittah toward Zererah as far as the border of
Abel Meholah near Tabbath. 23 Israelites from Naphtali, Asher and
all Manasseh were called out, and they pursued the Midianites.
24 Gideon sent messengers throughout the hill country of Ephraim,
saying, "Come down against the Midianites and seize the waters of
the Jordan ahead of them as far as Beth Barah."
So all the men of Ephraim were called out and they took the waters
of the Jordan as far as Beth Barah. 25 They also captured two of the
Midianite leaders, Oreb and Zeeb. They killed Oreb at the rock of
Oreb, and Zeeb at the winepress of Zeeb. They pursued the Midianites and brought the heads of Oreb and Zeeb to Gideon, who was by
the Jordan.

Zebah and Zalmunna

8 Now the Ephraimites asked Gideon, "Why have you treated us
like this? Why didn't you call us when you went to fight Midian?"
And they criticized him sharply.
2 But he answered them, "What have I accomplished compared to
you? Aren't the gleanings of Ephraim's grapes better than the full
grape harvest of Abiezer? 3 God gave Oreb and Zeeb, the Midianite
leaders, into your hands. What was I able to do compared to you?" At
this, their resentment against him subsided.
4 Gideon and his three hundred men, exhausted yet keeping up the
pursuit, came to the Jordan and crossed it. 5 He said to the men of
Succoth, "Give my troops some bread; they are worn out, and I am
still pursuing Zebah and Zalmunna, the kings of Midian."
6 But the officials of Succoth said, "Do you already have the hands
of Zebah and Zalmunna in your possession? Why should we give
bread to your troops?"
7 Then Gideon replied, "Just for that, when the LORD has given
Zebah and Zalmunna into my hand, I will tear your flesh with desert
thorns and briers."
8 From there he went up to Peniel[a] and made the same request of
them, but they answered as the men of Succoth had. 9 So he said to
the men of Peniel, "When I return in triumph, I will tear down this
tower."
10 Now Zebah and Zalmunna were in Karkor with a force of about
fifteen thousand men, all that were left of the armies of the eastern
peoples; a hundred and twenty thousand swordsmen had fallen.
11 Gideon went up by the route of the nomads east of Nobah and Jogbehah and fell upon the unsuspecting army. 12 Zebah and Zalmunna,
the two kings of Midian, fled, but he pursued them and captured
them, routing their entire army.
13 Gideon son of Joash then returned from the battle by the Pass of
Heres. 14 He caught a young man of Succoth and questioned him, and
the young man wrote down for him the names of the seventy-seven

[a] 8 Hebrew *Penuel,* a variant of *Peniel;* also in verses 9 and 17

OPEN 1. What have you found most exhausting in the past week? Is it mental, physical or emotional exhaustion? **2.** Describe a time when you talked yourself out of a tight spot at school, work or with your parents when you were a teenager.

STUDY Gideon with his 300 men pursue and capture the kings of Midian. After God gave him a miraculous victory, Gideon shares the plunder and creates an idol, which he later worshiped and displayed in his hometown. **1.** How did Gideon handle the criticism of the Ephraimites? **2.** What reasons can you think of for Succoth and Peniel refusing to give food to Gideon and his troops? In your opinion, did Gideon overreact or was he justified in his treatment of these two towns? **3.** What gave Gideon the determination and stamina to continue to pursue the Midianite kings in the face of adversity? What one thing would you pursue no matter the cost? **4.** Imagine that you are Jether, Gideon's young son. When you are older, how will you remember the capture and assassination of Zebah and Zalmunna (vv. 18–21)? How do you feel about your dad? **5.** How do you think Gideon was able to resist Israel's offer to have him rule over them instead of God (v. 22)? Have you received an offer that was "too good to be true" and resisted it? Where did you find the strength? **6.** How do you explain Gideon's ability to affirm the Lord's rule over Israel (v. 23), and then create an idol out of a gold ephod, set it up on display in his hometown, and

8:1 Ephraimites. Gideon handles their criticism with grace, averting trouble and even skirting a potential civil war.

8:2 grape harvest. Gideon expresses his view in language familiar to him and to many of his worker-warriors. The gleanings were the leftovers—hardly comparable to a full harvest.

8:3 their resentment ... subsided. Gideon points out the mighty Ephraimites have no right to complain. After all, Ephraim took top honors, killing two of the top Midianite officers (7:25).

worship it instead of the Lord (v. 27)? Can you relate to Gideon's inconsistent faith?

APPLY 1. On a scale of 1 (being with diplomatic grace) to 10 (being with defensive anger), how would you rate yourself in handling criticism? What marks would others give you? What changes would you like to make? **2.** What tends to be an "ephod" in your life: Family? Work? Internet? Prized possession? Hobby? How can this group support you in submitting it to God?.

OPEN Describe the largest family you know. Are their family dynamics anything like yours?

STUDY Upon Gideon's death, however, Israel returns to its old ways. It's not only unfaithful to the Lord, it's unkind to Gideon's family. **1.** Once considered the "weakest in

officials of Succoth, the elders of the town. [15]Then Gideon came and
said to the men of Succoth, "Here are Zebah and Zalmunna, about
whom you taunted me by saying, 'Do you already have the hands of
Zebah and Zalmunna in your possession? Why should we give bread
to your exhausted men?' " [16]He took the elders of the town and
taught the men of Succoth a lesson by punishing them with desert
thorns and briers. [17]He also pulled down the tower of Peniel and
killed the men of the town.

[18]Then he asked Zebah and Zalmunna, "What kind of men did you
kill at Tabor?"

"Men like you," they answered, "each one with the bearing of a prince."

[19]Gideon replied, "Those were my brothers, the sons of my own
mother. As surely as the LORD lives, if you had spared their lives, I
would not kill you." [20]Turning to Jether, his oldest son, he said, "Kill
them!" But Jether did not draw his sword, because he was only a boy
and was afraid.

[21]Zebah and Zalmunna said, "Come, do it yourself. 'As is the man,
so is his strength.' " So Gideon stepped forward and killed them, and
took the ornaments off their camels' necks.

Gideon's Ephod

[22]The Israelites said to Gideon, "Rule over us—you, your son
and your grandson—because you have saved us out of the hand of
Midian."

[23]But Gideon told them, "I will not rule over you, nor will my son
rule over you. The LORD will rule over you." [24]And he said, "I do have
one request, that each of you give me an earring from your share of
the plunder." (It was the custom of the Ishmaelites to wear gold earrings.)

[25]They answered, "We'll be glad to give them." So they spread out a
garment, and each man threw a ring from his plunder onto it. [26]The
weight of the gold rings he asked for came to seventeen hundred
shekels,[a] not counting the ornaments, the pendants and the purple
garments worn by the kings of Midian or the chains that were on
their camels' necks. [27]Gideon made the gold into an ephod, which he
placed in Ophrah, his town. All Israel prostituted themselves by worshiping it there, and it became a snare to Gideon and his family.

Gideon's Death

[28]Thus Midian was subdued before the Israelites and did not raise
its head again. During Gideon's lifetime, the land enjoyed peace forty
years.

[29]Jerub-Baal son of Joash went back home to live. [30]He had seventy
sons of his own, for he had many wives. [31]His concubine, who lived in

[a]26 That is, about 43 pounds (about 19.5 kilograms)

8:23 The LORD will rule. Although *Gideon is quick to be theologically correct,* he will fall into idolatry just as quickly (v. 27).

8:27 ephod. This golden chest piece was usually worn as a symbol of priesthood *(Ex. 28:6–30).* However, Gideon and the people worshiped the golden object as an idol.

8:31 bore him a son. Gideon had several wives who bore him at least seventy children. **Abimelech.** The mother of Abimelech was a slave in his household. But her son would soon become a self-proclaimed king (9:2).

Shechem, also bore him a son, whom he named Abimelech. [32]Gideon son of Joash died at a good old age and was buried in the tomb of his father Joash in Ophrah of the Abiezrites.

[33]No sooner had Gideon died than the Israelites again prostituted themselves to the Baals. They set up Baal-Berith as their god and [34]did not remember the LORD their God, who had rescued them from the hands of all their enemies on every side. [35]They also failed to show kindness to the family of Jerub-Baal (that is, Gideon) for all the good things he had done for them.

Abimelech

9 Abimelech son of Jerub-Baal went to his mother's brothers in Shechem and said to them and to all his mother's clan, [2]"Ask all the citizens of Shechem, 'Which is better for you: to have all seventy of Jerub-Baal's sons rule over you, or just one man?' Remember, I am your flesh and blood."

[3]When the brothers repeated all this to the citizens of Shechem, they were inclined to follow Abimelech, for they said, "He is our brother." [4]They gave him seventy shekels[a] of silver from the temple of Baal-Berith, and Abimelech used it to hire reckless adventurers, who became his followers. [5]He went to his father's home in Ophrah and on one stone murdered his seventy brothers, the sons of Jerub-Baal. But Jotham, the youngest son of Jerub-Baal, escaped by hiding. [6]Then all the citizens of Shechem and Beth Millo gathered beside the great tree at the pillar in Shechem to crown Abimelech king.

[7]When Jotham was told about this, he climbed up on the top of Mount Gerizim and shouted to them, "Listen to me, citizens of Shechem, so that God may listen to you. [8]One day the trees went out to anoint a king for themselves. They said to the olive tree, 'Be our king.'

[9]"But the olive tree answered, 'Should I give up my oil, by which both gods and men are honored, to hold sway over the trees?'

[10]"Next, the trees said to the fig tree, 'Come and be our king.'

[11]"But the fig tree replied, 'Should I give up my fruit, so good and sweet, to hold sway over the trees?'

[12]"Then the trees said to the vine, 'Come and be our king.'

[13]"But the vine answered, 'Should I give up my wine, which cheers both gods and men, to hold sway over the trees?'

[14]"Finally all the trees said to the thornbush, 'Come and be our king.'

[a]4 That is, about 1 3/4 pounds (about 0.8 kilogram)

Manasseh" and "least in my family" (6:15), how have Gideon's circumstances changed by the time of his death? As a result of doing what good things? **2.** What, in your opinion, is the moral of Gideon's story (chs. 6–8)?

APPLY Who is your "spiritual hero" whose guidance helps keep you faithful in your walk with God?

OPEN 1. If you had to liken yourself to a tree, would you be an: Oak, "solid and sturdy"? Almond, "a little nutty"? Palm, "warm and comfortable"? Evergreen, "staying green in the midst of winter's blast"? Date, "thankful for, or in need of, human companionship"? **2.** Describe one experience that you would classify as a "reckless adventure" for you.

STUDY Gideon has died and the Israelites are back into Baal worship again. Abimelech, Gideon's bad seed, rises to the status of king after a murderous scheme against Gideon's other sons. God does not reward treachery, and repays wickedness with justice in the end. **1.** Who was Abimelech's mother (8:31)? What is the difference between a wife and a concubine? How might such an upbringing affect the man Abimelech grew up to be? **2.** The name Abimelech literally means "My father is king." If you were a slave woman's child with a name like that, how do you think it might affect your attitude towards life? **3.** Abimelech wanted to be a king, not a judge. In your mind, what is the difference? How might the fact that he was a Baal worshiper (v. 4) have influenced his choice? **4.** What images does Jotham evoke in his parable of the trees (vv. 7–15)? Which tree corresponds with Abimelech and his evil deed? What was the main point of the para-

8:32 At the time of Gideon's death, his pursuits would be remembered as courageous and godly. *However, he fell* prey to idol worship toward the end of his life.

8:33 No sooner had Gideon died. With the people's leader out of sight, their spiritual sense is out of mind. The cycle of disobedience starts over again with the death of the judge Gideon.

9:1–57 The son of a slave girl, Abimelech proves he cannot handle power. His rise to self-proclaimed power is murder in motion. He kills his own family members (v. 5). Renouncing his father's faith, Abimelech looks toward Baal for assistance in his plot. Overcome with evil, Abimelech is killed (vv. 52–54).

9:1 Jerub-Baal. Another name for Gideon (7:1).

9:5 on one stone. Like sacrificing animals, Abimelech murdered his father's sons on a large stone in an attempt to secure his royal position.

9:9–13 Jotham attempts to communicate in the common language of the people, using images that were familiar and of great cultural importance.

9:14 thornbush. The bramblebush is only good for pricking bare heels in sandals and kindling fires.

ble (vv. 16–20)? **5.** Verse 23 states that God sent an evil spirit between Abimelech and the people of Shechem. Describe the scene you picture as you imagine what effect a bad spirit would have on that community. In your opinion, how can evil proceed *from* God? What was God's reason for sending it (vv. 23–25)? **6.** How did Jotham's parable of the trees become reality (vv. 22–55)? What is the moral of the story? How does it relate to your life experience? What does the story of Abimelech tell you about the justice of the Lord?

APPLY 1. When Abimelech started down his murderous path, it seemed as though he couldn't stop himself. Is there a path away from God you've started down that you can't seem to get turned around? **2.** When has God brought an unexpected deliverance for you as he did with the people of Thebez (vv. 50–53)? What "enemy" would you like God to deliver you from right now? How can this group pray for you?

15"The thornbush said to the trees, 'If you really want to anoint me king over you, come and take refuge in my shade; but if not, then let fire come out of the thornbush and consume the cedars of Lebanon!'

16"Now if you have acted honorably and in good faith when you made Abimelech king, and if you have been fair to Jerub-Baal and his family, and if you have treated him as he deserves— 17and to think that my father fought for you, risked his life to rescue you from the hand of Midian 18(but today you have revolted against my father's family, murdered his seventy sons on a single stone, and made Abimelech, the son of his slave girl, king over the citizens of Shechem because he is your brother)— 19if then you have acted honorably and in good faith toward Jerub-Baal and his family today, may Abimelech be your joy, and may you be his, too! 20But if you have not, let fire come out from Abimelech and consume you, citizens of Shechem and Beth Millo, and let fire come out from you, citizens of Shechem and Beth Millo, and consume Abimelech!"

21Then Jotham fled, escaping to Beer, and he lived there because he was afraid of his brother Abimelech.

22After Abimelech had governed Israel three years, 23God sent an evil spirit between Abimelech and the citizens of Shechem, who acted treacherously against Abimelech. 24God did this in order that the crime against Jerub-Baal's seventy sons, the shedding of their blood, might be avenged on their brother Abimelech and on the citizens of Shechem, who had helped him murder his brothers. 25In opposition to him these citizens of Shechem set men on the hilltops to ambush and rob everyone who passed by, and this was reported to Abimelech.

26Now Gaal son of Ebed moved with his brothers into Shechem, and its citizens put their confidence in him. 27After they had gone out into the fields and gathered the grapes and trodden them, they held a festival in the temple of their god. While they were eating and drinking, they cursed Abimelech. 28Then Gaal son of Ebed said, "Who is Abimelech, and who is Shechem, that we should be subject to him? Isn't he Jerub-Baal's son, and isn't Zebul his deputy? Serve the men of Hamor, Shechem's father! Why should we serve Abimelech? 29If only this people were under my command! Then I would get rid of him. I would say to Abimelech, 'Call out your whole army!' "[a]

30When Zebul the governor of the city heard what Gaal son of Ebed said, he was very angry. 31Under cover he sent messengers to Abimelech, saying, "Gaal son of Ebed and his brothers have come to Shechem and are stirring up the city against you. 32Now then, during the night you and your men should come and lie in wait in the fields. 33In the morning at sunrise, advance against the city. When Gaal and his men come out against you, do whatever your hand finds to do."

[a]*29* Septuagint; Hebrew *him." Then he said to Abimelech, "Call out your whole army!"*

9:15 cedars of Lebanon. The influential men of Shechem saw themselves *in this image. The invaluable thornbush* would summarily destroy the valuable cedars.

9:20 fire. The thought of fire was enough to make Jotham's nomadic audience nervous.

9:23 evil spirit. Unable to escape his deadly deeds, Abimelech is soon haunted by the presence of an evil spirit, which unnerves the people.

9:26 Gaal. With Abimelech fallen from grace, Gaal appears on the scene to further deceive the willing people.

9:32 lie in wait. In a favorite military tactic, the governor recommended an ambush to guarantee Abimelech's success.

34So Abimelech and all his troops set out by night and took up concealed positions near Shechem in four companies. 35Now Gaal son of
Ebed had gone out and was standing at the entrance to the city gate
just as Abimelech and his soldiers came out from their hiding place.
36When Gaal saw them, he said to Zebul, "Look, people are coming
down from the tops of the mountains!"
Zebul replied, "You mistake the shadows of the mountains for
men."
37But Gaal spoke up again: "Look, people are coming down from
the center of the land, and a company is coming from the direction of
the soothsayers' tree."
38Then Zebul said to him, "Where is your big talk now, you who
said, 'Who is Abimelech that we should be subject to him?' Aren't
these the men you ridiculed? Go out and fight them!"
39So Gaal led out[a] the citizens of Shechem and fought Abimelech.
40Abimelech chased him, and many fell wounded in the flight—all the
way to the entrance to the gate. 41Abimelech stayed in Arumah, and
Zebul drove Gaal and his brothers out of Shechem.
42The next day the people of Shechem went out to the fields, and
this was reported to Abimelech. 43So he took his men, divided them
into three companies and set an ambush in the fields. When he saw
the people coming out of the city, he rose to attack them. 44Abimelech
and the companies with him rushed forward to a position at the
entrance to the city gate. Then two companies rushed upon those in
the fields and struck them down. 45All that day Abimelech pressed his
attack against the city until he had captured it and killed its people.
Then he destroyed the city and scattered salt over it.
46On hearing this, the citizens in the tower of Shechem went into
the stronghold of the temple of El-Berith. 47When Abimelech heard
that they had assembled there, 48he and all his men went up Mount
Zalmon. He took an ax and cut off some branches, which he lifted to
his shoulders. He ordered the men with him, "Quick! Do what you
have seen me do!" 49So all the men cut branches and followed Abimelech. They piled them against the stronghold and set it on fire over
the people inside. So all the people in the tower of Shechem, about a
thousand men and women, also died.
50Next Abimelech went to Thebez and besieged it and captured it.
51Inside the city, however, was a strong tower, to which all the men
and women—all the people of the city—fled. They locked themselves
in and climbed up on the tower roof. 52Abimelech went to the tower
and stormed it. But as he approached the entrance to the tower to set
it on fire, 53a woman dropped an upper millstone on his head and
cracked his skull.
54Hurriedly he called to his armor-bearer, "Draw your sword and
kill me, so that they can't say, 'A woman killed him.' " So his servant
ran him through, and he died. 55When the Israelites saw that Abimelech was dead, they went home.

[a]39 Or *Gaal went out in the sight of*

9:34 set out by night. Although they took their places at night, the attack would not come until the morning light.

9:53 woman. For a man whose lifelong goal was to rise to royalty, being killed by a lower-class woman was a fitting tribute.

9:54 armor-bearer. A young man who carried an influential man's shield and sword (which weighed several pounds each).

[56]Thus God repaid the wickedness that Abimelech had done to his
father by murdering his seventy brothers. [57]God also made the men
of Shechem pay for all their wickedness. The curse of Jotham son of
Jerub-Baal came on them.

Tola

10 After the time of Abimelech a man of Issachar, Tola son of
Puah, the son of Dodo, rose to save Israel. He lived in Shamir,
in the hill country of Ephraim. [2]He led[a] Israel twenty-three years;
then he died, and was buried in Shamir.

Jair

[3]He was followed by Jair of Gilead, who led Israel twenty-two
years. [4]He had thirty sons, who rode thirty donkeys. They controlled
thirty towns in Gilead, which to this day are called Havvoth Jair.[b]
[5]When Jair died, he was buried in Kamon.

Jephthah

[6]Again the Israelites did evil in the eyes of the LORD. They served
the Baals and the Ashtoreths, and the gods of Aram, the gods of Sidon, the gods of Moab, the gods of the Ammonites and the gods of
the Philistines. And because the Israelites forsook the LORD and no
longer served him, [7]he became angry with them. He sold them into
the hands of the Philistines and the Ammonites, [8]who that year shattered and crushed them. For eighteen years they oppressed all the
Israelites on the east side of the Jordan in Gilead, the land of the
Amorites. [9]The Ammonites also crossed the Jordan to fight against
Judah, Benjamin and the house of Ephraim; and Israel was in great
distress. [10]Then the Israelites cried out to the LORD, "We have sinned
against you, forsaking our God and serving the Baals."

[11]The LORD replied, "When the Egyptians, the Amorites, the Ammonites, the Philistines, [12]the Sidonians, the Amalekites and the
Maonites[c] oppressed you and you cried to me for help, did I not save
you from their hands? [13]But you have forsaken me and served other
gods, so I will no longer save you. [14]Go and cry out to the gods you
have chosen. Let them save you when you are in trouble!"

[a]2 Traditionally *judged;* also in verse 3 [b]4 Or *called the settlements of Jair* [c]12 Hebrew; some Septuagint manuscripts *Midianites*

OPEN How many cars do you have in your family? Who likes to "hoof it"?

STUDY **1.** What do the stories of minor judges Tola and Jair add to our understanding of the book of Judges? **2.** How does the description of Tola differ from that of Jair?

APPLY What is your definition of real wealth? How does that impact the way you use your resources?

OPEN **1.** If you are in a heap of trouble, who do you call: Superman? Police? Your attorney? Your spiritual leader? Your big brother or sister? **2.** Who was the social outcast of your high school? What caused the rejection of this person?

STUDY After the death of Judge Jair, Israel turns back to idolatry in a big way, serving not only the Baals and Ashtoreths, but also the gods of the peoples of Aram, Sidon, Moab, Amon and Philistia. How could God deliver them from such entrenchment? He finds the answer in the person of Jephthah. **1.** Why did God "sell" Israel to their enemy (vv. 6–7)? What did the Israelites do to change God's mind (vv. 10–16)? What does this tell you about God's compassionate nature? **2.** From reading 11:1–3, how would you describe Jephthah's childhood? How does Jephthah's background compare with that of Abimelech's (ch. 9)? In your

---

9:56 God repaid. A vengeful man himself, Abimelech ultimately succumbed to God's wrath.

10:1 Tola. Without foreign oppression, Tola was free to focus his leadership on Israel's internal structural and spiritual woes.

10:3 Gilead. Number seven in the line of judges, Jair represented the tribe of Manasseh—the homeland of the city of Gilead.

10:4 thirty donkeys. Imagine the children of a modern-day rich man, each with his or her own European sports car. In the same manner, donkeys were a recognizable symbol of influence and prestige.

10:6–12:7 Jephthah's story is a loser-turned-hero tale, six years in the making. Rejected by his own townspeople as a young man (11:3), Jephthah eventually became Israel's judge for six years, the shortest recorded reign in its history. Under him, Gilead and Ephraim got into a civil war that cost the Ephraimites 42,000 lives (12:6).

10:6 *Although many of Israel's temptations came from within the borders of Canaan, many were from foreign tyrants. The grisly extremes of the religious practices of these surrounding nations* ranged from human sacrifice to sexual perversion.

10:7 sold them into the hands. Some of the Israelites were sold into forced labor with their oppressors. However, all suffered under the dominance of foreign enemies.

10:11 Egyptians. God begins at the start of their captivity as slaves in Egypt and continues through centuries of history to their present state of oppression.

10:12 did I not save you. The role of the judge was to save the people from oppressors. A series of people had cycled in and out of this role for

15But the Israelites said to the LORD, "We have sinned. Do with us
whatever you think best, but please rescue us now." 16Then they got
rid of the foreign gods among them and served the LORD. And he
could bear Israel's misery no longer.
17When the Ammonites were called to arms and camped in Gilead,
the Israelites assembled and camped at Mizpah. 18The leaders of the
people of Gilead said to each other, "Whoever will launch the attack
against the Ammonites will be the head of all those living in Gilead."
11 Jephthah the Gileadite was a mighty warrior. His father was
Gilead; his mother was a prostitute. 2Gilead's wife also bore
him sons, and when they were grown up, they drove Jephthah away.
"You are not going to get any inheritance in our family," they said,
"because you are the son of another woman." 3So Jephthah fled from
his brothers and settled in the land of Tob, where a group of adventurers gathered around him and followed him.
4Some time later, when the Ammonites made war on Israel, 5the
elders of Gilead went to get Jephthah from the land of Tob. 6"Come,"
they said, "be our commander, so we can fight the Ammonites."
7Jephthah said to them, "Didn't you hate me and drive me from
my father's house? Why do you come to me now, when you're in
trouble?"
8The elders of Gilead said to him, "Nevertheless, we are turning to
you now; come with us to fight the Ammonites, and you will be our
head over all who live in Gilead."
9Jephthah answered, "Suppose you take me back to fight the Ammonites and the LORD gives them to me—will I really be your head?"
10The elders of Gilead replied, "The LORD is our witness; we will
certainly do as you say." 11So Jephthah went with the elders of Gilead,
and the people made him head and commander over them. And he
repeated all his words before the LORD in Mizpah.
12Then Jephthah sent messengers to the Ammonite king with the
question: "What do you have against us that you have attacked our
country?"
13The king of the Ammonites answered Jephthah's messengers,
"When Israel came up out of Egypt, they took away my land from the
Arnon to the Jabbok, all the way to the Jordan. Now give it back
peaceably."
14Jephthah sent back messengers to the Ammonite king, 15saying:
"This is what Jephthah says: Israel did not take the land of Moab
or the land of the Ammonites. 16But when they came up out of

opinion, what made the difference in the way the two men turned out? **3.** Who seemed to be Jephthah's closest friends and patriots (v. 3)? How does this relate to his social class? Do you think Jephthah was a "Robin Hood" or simply a "hood"? How do you feel the social class you were born into affected the opportunities available to you? **4.** What do you believe was Jephthah's motivation for leading the Israelites into battle? Why do you think the elders sought him out to be their leader? If you had been Jephthah, would you have trusted the elders to keep their promise (10:18; 11:4–11)? **5.** What is the purpose of Jephthah's letter to the Ammonite king (vv. 13–27)? On what three arguments does he base his appeal? Why do you think the arguments fell on deaf ears? **6.** What do you feel is the decisive factor in Israel's victory over the Ammonites (vv. 29–33): God's Spirit upon Jephthah? Jephthah's vow to the Lord? Jephthah's military strategy? Explain. **7.** What is the purpose of the story about Jephthath and his daughter? How would you describe the daughter's character? **8.** In God's plan, is human sacrifice ever acceptable? In your opinion, which takes precedence, Jephthah's vow (Num. 30; Eccl.. 5:4–5) or God's rejection of human sacrifice? Explain.

APPLY 1. Jephthah's story can be summed up in four words—rejection, vindication, victory and heartache. Which of these words most closely describe the stage in life you are in right now? How so? **2.** When have you won a hard fought battle, only to lose a heartfelt love? **3.** What did God see in Jephthah that others found hard to see? What does God see in *you* that others might miss on first meeting you? If you have trouble answering, ask your group what God sees in you!

---

decades, representing God's faithfulness to his task.

10:18 Whoever will launch the attack. A desperate people looked for leadership in military might. Fortunately Jephthah, "a mighty warrior," would soon suit their need (11:1).

11:1 his mother was a prostitute. Jephthah was the illegitimate son of Gilead and a prostitute. More than likely then, he was half-Canaanite. He would have been a social outcast for either of these reasons.

11:3 Tob ... adventurers. Evidently the land of Tob was a lot less strict in its laws and customs than was the land of Israel. It did not take long for a group of mercenaries to gather around a charismatic leader.

11:8 be our head. Jephthah's reputation made him a man in high demand. The elders of Gilead were willing to promise him leadership of their region if he would lead them militarily.

11:13 took away my land. The king was twisting history to make his case. As Jephthah pointed out, the land was actually taken from the Amorites who had taken it from the Moabites.

11:14–27 Jephthah sent a very clever letter back to the Ammonite king. He clarified Israel's claim to the land by reviewing how they attained it: from the Amorites not the Ammonites. He then made it clear that Israel's God had given them the land, and that Israel had possessed the land for a long time. All of these factors were strong arguments in the ancient world for keeping a territory from aggression.

Egypt, Israel went through the desert to the Red Sea[a] and on to
Kadesh. [17]Then Israel sent messengers to the king of Edom, saying, 'Give us permission to go through your country,' but the
king of Edom would not listen. They sent also to the king of
Moab, and he refused. So Israel stayed at Kadesh.

[18]"Next they traveled through the desert, skirted the lands of
Edom and Moab, passed along the eastern side of the country of
Moab, and camped on the other side of the Arnon. They did not
enter the territory of Moab, for the Arnon was its border.

[19]"Then Israel sent messengers to Sihon king of the Amorites,
who ruled in Heshbon, and said to him, 'Let us pass through
your country to our own place.' [20]Sihon, however, did not trust
Israel[b] to pass through his territory. He mustered all his men and
encamped at Jahaz and fought with Israel.

[21]"Then the LORD, the God of Israel, gave Sihon and all his men
into Israel's hands, and they defeated them. Israel took over all
the land of the Amorites who lived in that country, [22]capturing
all of it from the Arnon to the Jabbok and from the desert to the
Jordan.

[23]"Now since the LORD, the God of Israel, has driven the Amorites out before his people Israel, what right have you to take it
over? [24]Will you not take what your god Chemosh gives you?
Likewise, whatever the LORD our God has given us, we will possess. [25]Are you better than Balak son of Zippor, king of Moab?
Did he ever quarrel with Israel or fight with them? [26]For three
hundred years Israel occupied Heshbon, Aroer, the surrounding
settlements and all the towns along the Arnon. Why didn't you
retake them during that time? [27]I have not wronged you, but you
are doing me wrong by waging war against me. Let the LORD, the
Judge,[c] decide the dispute this day between the Israelites and the
Ammonites."

[28]The king of Ammon, however, paid no attention to the message
Jephthah sent him.

[29]Then the Spirit of the LORD came upon Jephthah. He crossed Gilead and Manasseh, passed through Mizpah of Gilead, and from there
he advanced against the Ammonites. [30]And Jephthah made a vow to
the LORD: "If you give the Ammonites into my hands, [31]whatever
comes out of the door of my house to meet me when I return in triumph from the Ammonites will be the LORD's, and I will sacrifice it as
a burnt offering."

[32]Then Jephthah went over to fight the Ammonites, and the LORD
gave them into his hands. [33]He devastated twenty towns from Aroer

[a]16 Hebrew *Yam Suph;* that is, Sea of Reeds [b]20 Or *however, would not make an agreement for Israel*
[c]27 Or *Ruler*

11:27 Judge. In all conflicts between men, or nations, God was the final judge. With full confidence in Yahweh, Jephthah placed the issue of land ownership in God's jurisdiction. It is interesting that this was the only appearance of the singular "Judge" in the book of Judges. While men can serve as leaders, only God can make the final decisions.

11:29 Spirit of the LORD. In the Old Testament, the Spirit of the Lord would sometimes overpower a man and lead him into action. In this case, Jephthah was empowered to lead an army against Israel's enemy. For a contrasting intervention of the Spirit of the Lord, see Numbers 24:2.

11:30 made a vow. Vows were taken seriously in Israel. To modern ears, a vow of this sort rings as an attempt to "make a deal" with God. For God's covenant people, however, their entire existence was the product of an arrangement with God. A vow such as this one would not be unusual or offensive.

to the vicinity of Minnith, as far as Abel Keramim. Thus Israel subdued Ammon.
34When Jephthah returned to his home in Mizpah, who should
come out to meet him but his daughter, dancing to the sound of
tambourines! She was an only child. Except for her he had neither
son nor daughter. 35When he saw her, he tore his clothes and cried,
"Oh! My daughter! You have made me miserable and wretched,
because I have made a vow to the LORD that I cannot break."
36"My father," she replied, "you have given your word to the LORD.
Do to me just as you promised, now that the LORD has avenged you of
your enemies, the Ammonites. 37But grant me this one request," she
said. "Give me two months to roam the hills and weep with my
friends, because I will never marry."
38"You may go," he said. And he let her go for two months. She and
the girls went into the hills and wept because she would never marry.
39After the two months, she returned to her father and he did to her
as he had vowed. And she was a virgin.
From this comes the Israelite custom 40that each year the young
women of Israel go out for four days to commemorate the daughter
of Jephthah the Gileadite.

Jephthah and Ephraim

12 The men of Ephraim called out their forces, crossed over to
Zaphon and said to Jephthah, "Why did you go to fight the
Ammonites without calling us to go with you? We're going to burn
down your house over your head."
2Jephthah answered, "I and my people were engaged in a great
struggle with the Ammonites, and although I called, you didn't save
me out of their hands. 3When I saw that you wouldn't help, I took my
life in my hands and crossed over to fight the Ammonites, and the
LORD gave me the victory over them. Now why have you come up today to fight me?"
4Jephthah then called together the men of Gilead and fought against
Ephraim. The Gileadites struck them down because the Ephraimites
had said, "You Gileadites are renegades from Ephraim and Manasseh."
5The Gileadites captured the fords of the Jordan leading to Ephraim,
and whenever a survivor of Ephraim said, "Let me cross over," the men
of Gilead asked him, "Are you an Ephraimite?" If he replied, "No," 6they
said, "All right, say 'Shibboleth.' " If he said, "Sibboleth," because he
could not pronounce the word correctly, they seized him and killed

OPEN Judging from the accents or unique characteristics of the group members, guess which state or country each member's family came from.

STUDY Jephthah led the army that delivered Israel from their Ammonite oppressors, then defeated Ephraim in a civil war. He led his people for a short six years until his death. **1.** What reasons can you think of for the anger of the Ephraimites at not being called out to war with Jephthah? **2.** Compare 12:1–3 and 8:1–3. How do Jephthah and Gideon differ in their responses? What kind of reply is usually your first response to a threatening situation? **3.** What reason does Jephthah give for going to war with Ephraim (vv. 4–6)? In your opinion, does it warrant a civil war that killed 40,000 Ephraimites? How do you feel about Jephthah's "Shibboleth"

11:34 dancing. The entire community celebrated a military victory. In these brutal times, a defeat could well mean destruction for a tribe. It was common for the young girls to lead the celebration (Ex. 15:20, 1 Sam. 18:6).

11:35 tore his clothes. Tearing one's own clothes was an act of extreme grief.

11:37 roam the hills and weep. Jephthah's daughter showed no defiance to her father or to the terrible consequence of his vow. Instead, she acted obediently. The image of her roaming and weeping is poignant indeed. Her father may have offered her as a human sacrifice, or he may simply have kept her from ever marrying, which would have been devastating for the young girl and for the entire family.

11:39–40 Israelite custom. This custom never spread to Israel as a whole. It was mentioned nowhere else in the Old Testament.

12:2 Jephthah answered. In spite of Jephthah's early life as an outcast and leader of adventurers (11:3), his first reaction to the threat was diplomacy. He had tried diplomacy first with the Ammonites too (11:14–27).

12:6 Shibboleth. The Gileadites used a verbal test to separate enemy from friend. Though the tribes lived in close proximity, there were linguistic differences among them. In this case, the difference between a hard "sh" sound and a soft "s" sound was the determiner. This case illustrated that power was not a simple matter of force, but was also a matter of cleverness as well.

test? **4.** Three minor judges follow Jephthah and lead the Israelites a total of 25 years. What is each one of these men remembered for?

APPLY Do you hold a grudge against a family member or friend who has hurt you? How do you feel God is calling you to resolve it?

him at the fords of the Jordan. Forty-two thousand Ephraimites were
killed at that time.
7Jephthah led[a] Israel six years. Then Jephthah the Gileadite died,
and was buried in a town in Gilead.

Ibzan, Elon and Abdon

8After him, Ibzan of Bethlehem led Israel. 9He had thirty sons and
thirty daughters. He gave his daughters away in marriage to those
outside his clan, and for his sons he brought in thirty young women
as wives from outside his clan. Ibzan led Israel seven years. 10Then
Ibzan died, and was buried in Bethlehem.
11After him, Elon the Zebulunite led Israel ten years. 12Then Elon
died, and was buried in Aijalon in the land of Zebulun.
13After him, Abdon son of Hillel, from Pirathon, led Israel. 14He had
forty sons and thirty grandsons, who rode on seventy donkeys. He led
Israel eight years. 15Then Abdon son of Hillel died, and was buried at
Pirathon in Ephraim, in the hill country of the Amalekites.

OPEN 1. Share the story of your birth with your group. Were there any special circumstances or funny stories associated with it? **2.** Share one thing you feel that sets you apart from other people.

STUDY In this story, God promises a childless couple that they will have a very special son—Israel's next judge. Samson would be a Nazirite, meaning he would be separated and dedicated to God. **1.** Why did God give this childless couple a special son (vv. 1–5)? **2.** Compare Samson's birth with Isaac's (Gen. 17:17–19; 21:1–7), Samuel's (1 Sam. 1:10–20); John the Baptist's (Luke 1:5–25) and Jesus' (Luke 1:26–38; 2:1–20). What simi-

The Birth of Samson

13 Again the Israelites did evil in the eyes of the LORD, so the
LORD delivered them into the hands of the Philistines for
forty years.
2A certain man of Zorah, named Manoah, from the clan of the Danites, had a wife who was sterile and remained childless. 3The angel of
the LORD appeared to her and said, "You are sterile and childless, but
you are going to conceive and have a son. 4Now see to it that you
drink no wine or other fermented drink and that you do not eat anything unclean, 5because you will conceive and give birth to a son. No
razor may be used on his head, because the boy is to be a Nazirite, set
apart to God from birth, and he will begin the deliverance of Israel
from the hands of the Philistines."
6Then the woman went to her husband and told him, "A man of
God came to me. He looked like an angel of God, very awesome. I

[a]7 Traditionally *judged*; also in verses 8-14

12:15 hill country of the Amalekites. This reference is puzzling because the Amalekites were always associated with the desert. As Numbers 13:29 showed, the Amalekites lived in the Negev while the Hittites, Amorites and Jebusites lived in the hill country.

13:1–16:31 The story of Samson was the tale of a tragic hero. The character, Samson, also served as a reflection of Israel itself. Like Israel, Samson was especially blessed by God, was consecrated to him and yet had an attraction to foreign, ungodly things. His story was more than the story of a hero then. It was a morality story that made Israel look into a mirror and confront its own *failures. It does the same for the modern reader.*

13:2 remained childless. For a woman, remaining childless was a terrible fate. Bearing sons made her a productive person. Sometimes in the Old Testament narrative, however, this condition was the precursor to something great in the woman's life. See also the stories of Sarah, mother of Isaac (Gen. 11:30); Rebekah, mother of Jacob (Gen. 25:21); and Hannah, mother of Samuel (1 Sam. 1:2).

13:3 you are going to conceive and have a son. On several occasions, God sent an angel to announce the conception and impending birth of a son. In each case, that son held an important role in God's plan. These announcements include Ishmael (Gen. 16:11), John the Baptist (Luke 1:13) and Jesus (Luke 1:31).

13:5 set apart … from birth. Samson was "set apart" as a Nazirite. Usually, becoming a Nazirite involved taking the Nazirite vow, and the condition was temporary. Being a Nazirite involved not cutting your hair, abstaining from any fermented beverage and avoiding all contact with dead bodies. For a complete description of the vow, see Numbers 6:1–21. In Samson's case, however, he was chosen by God to be a Nazirite, and the vow was a lifetime commitment.

13:6 He looked like an angel. Manoah's wife knew something significant had happened, but her account to her husband was not a great example of clarity. The exception to that was her detailed description of Samson's Nazirite requirements. The appearance of the angel left her a little confused: she had not really determined if he was angel or man, and she had not even inquired into his name or from where he came.

didn't ask him where he came from, and he didn't tell me his name.
[7]But he said to me, 'You will conceive and give birth to a son. Now
then, drink no wine or other fermented drink and do not eat anything
unclean, because the boy will be a Nazirite of God from birth until the
day of his death.' "
[8]Then Manoah prayed to the LORD: "O Lord, I beg you, let the man
of God you sent to us come again to teach us how to bring up the boy
who is to be born."
[9]God heard Manoah, and the angel of God came again to the woman while she was out in the field; but her husband Manoah was not
with her. [10]The woman hurried to tell her husband, "He's here! The
man who appeared to me the other day!"
[11]Manoah got up and followed his wife. When he came to the man,
he said, "Are you the one who talked to my wife?"
"I am," he said.
[12]So Manoah asked him, "When your words are fulfilled, what is to
be the rule for the boy's life and work?"
[13]The angel of the LORD answered, "Your wife must do all that I
have told her. [14]She must not eat anything that comes from the
grapevine, nor drink any wine or other fermented drink nor eat anything unclean. She must do everything I have commanded her."
[15]Manoah said to the angel of the LORD, "We would like you to stay
until we prepare a young goat for you."
[16]The angel of the LORD replied, "Even though you detain me, I will
not eat any of your food. But if you prepare a burnt offering, offer it to
the LORD." (Manoah did not realize that it was the angel of the LORD.)
[17]Then Manoah inquired of the angel of the LORD, "What is your
name, so that we may honor you when your word comes true?"
[18]He replied, "Why do you ask my name? It is beyond understanding.[a]" [19]Then Manoah took a young goat, together with the
grain offering, and sacrificed it on a rock to the LORD. And the LORD
did an amazing thing while Manoah and his wife watched: [20]As the
flame blazed up from the altar toward heaven, the angel of the LORD
ascended in the flame. Seeing this, Manoah and his wife fell with
their faces to the ground. [21]When the angel of the LORD did not show
himself again to Manoah and his wife, Manoah realized that it was
the angel of the LORD.
[22]"We are doomed to die!" he said to his wife. "We have seen God!"
[23]But his wife answered, "If the LORD had meant to kill us, he would
not have accepted a burnt offering and grain offering from our hands,
nor shown us all these things or now told us this."

[a]18 Or *is wonderful*

larities do you see? How are they different? **3.** What is the importance of Samson being raised as a Nazirite (Num. 6:1–21)? What three vows did a Nazirite make? How was Samson's call to be a Nazirite different from others? **4.** How do you feel Manoah's wife perceived that she was speaking with an angel? Do you think Manoah believed his wife when she told him her story? When does he realize that he has been talking with an angel of the Lord? Of the two, who do you believe is more "spiritually aware"? **5.** Imagine that you, like Manoah and his wife, had an encounter with an angel. Who could you trust enough to tell your story to, and how would you tell them? What kind of response do you believe you would get? **6.** In your opinion, how did Samson's special beginning affect the choices he made later in life?

APPLY 1. Manoah asked for wisdom in raising Samson (v. 8). How did your parents show wisdom in raising you? **2.** What ministry or task do you feel God has set you apart to fulfill?

13:8 teach us. Manoah accepted *the word of his wife concerning the* birth of a child. The worry that prompted his prayer was that he and his wife were not prepared to carry out the Lord's will in their child's life. This prayer is a poignant extension of any godly person's prayer for guidance with his or her child.

13:12 When your words are fulfilled. Manoah had no doubt of the angel's prophecy. He did not question *if the prophecy* would come true, only when.

13:15 we prepare a young goat for you. Hospitality was an important virtue in ancient Israel. A young goat would have been a delicacy. Preparing such a meal for the visitor would have shown him great honor. This type of hospitality was given to the three visitors who came to visit Abraham and Sarah to announce the birth of Isaac (Gen. 18:1–15).

13:17 What is your name? The name of the messenger was important because of the issue of credibility. If the message were false, there would be someone to hold accountable. If the message were true, the messenger would receive honor. Manoah is sure that the promise will come true, so he wants to know whom to honor.

[24]The woman gave birth to a boy and named him Samson. He grew
and the LORD blessed him, [25]and the Spirit of the LORD began to stir
him while he was in Mahaneh Dan, between Zorah and Eshtaol.

Samson's Marriage

14 Samson went down to Timnah and saw there a young Philistine woman. [2]When he returned, he said to his father and
mother, "I have seen a Philistine woman in Timnah; now get her for
me as my wife."
[3]His father and mother replied, "Isn't there an acceptable woman
among your relatives or among all our people? Must you go to the
uncircumcised Philistines to get a wife?"
But Samson said to his father, "Get her for me. She's the right one
for me." [4](His parents did not know that this was from the LORD, who
was seeking an occasion to confront the Philistines; for at that time
they were ruling over Israel.) [5]Samson went down to Timnah together
with his father and mother. As they approached the vineyards of Timnah, suddenly a young lion came roaring toward him. [6]The Spirit of
the LORD came upon him in power so that he tore the lion apart with
his bare hands as he might have torn a young goat. But he told neither his father nor his mother what he had done. [7]Then he went down
and talked with the woman, and he liked her.
[8]Some time later, when he went back to marry her, he turned aside
to look at the lion's carcass. In it was a swarm of bees and some honey, [9]which he scooped out with his hands and ate as he went along.
When he rejoined his parents, he gave them some, and they too ate it.
But he did not tell them that he had taken the honey from the lion's
carcass.
[10]Now his father went down to see the woman. And Samson made
a feast there, as was customary for bridegrooms. [11]When he appeared, he was given thirty companions.
[12]"Let me tell you a riddle," Samson said to them. "If you can give
me the answer within the seven days of the feast, I will give you thirty
linen garments and thirty sets of clothes. [13]If you can't tell me the
answer, you must give me thirty linen garments and thirty sets of
clothes."

OPEN **1.** What is your favorite riddle or knock-knock joke? **2.** While you were in Junior or Senior High, what friend did your parents least approve of? Why?

STUDY When Samson saw the Timnah woman, it was lust at first sight! He tells his father to get her for him. In this story, Samson's parents are disappointed for two reasons: (1) In their culture, they normally would choose their son's wife; and (2) Samson wanted to marry a non-Israelite. **1.** What do you think verse 4 means that this relationship was "from the LORD"? **2.** What facts about this woman do you see that make her an unlikely match for a Nazarite husband? **3.** The text tells us that the Spirit of the Lord came upon Samson twice to empower him with the strength to kill (vv. 6,19). Why do you believe God enabled Samson to do something against his vows? How else has Samson broken his Nazirite vows in this chapter? Have you ever used your "gifts" to do something that you knew God wouldn't approve of? Explain. **4.** Where did Samson's bride-to-be's loyalty lie? How did she find out the answer to his riddle? Was Samson justified in killing 30 men of Ashkelon (a Philistine city) to make good on his bet? **5.** Imagine that you are Samson's father or mother. What heartfelt advice would you give your son after this wedding fiasco? Do you think it would make any difference in Samson's future decisions? **6.** As this

14:2 get her for me as my wife. Samson showed a strong will in asking for a Philistine wife. Since his father must make all the marriage arrangements for his son, Samson makes this demand of his parents.

14:3 uncircumcised. Being uncircumcised was more than a designation of cultural difference. To Israel, circumcision was the symbol of its unique relationship with God. Thus, calling someone "uncircumcised" was a powerful term of derision. It implied all the actions that God despised: sexual immorality, idol worship, worship of other gods.

14:4 seeking an occasion. Sometimes the Lord allowed Israel to languish. When he chose to act on their behalf, he often used human failures and weaknesses as part of his plan. Though Samson was forbidden to marry a Philistine, God used his wrong desire to further his work against the enemies of God's people (Gen. 50:20, Acts 2:23, Rom. 8:28).

14:5 vineyards of Timnah. Samson had found his wife among the Philistines who lived in this fertile area of lush vineyards. For a man who was prohibited from drinking alcohol, Samson was living very close to the edge in marrying a Philistine in a wine-producing region.

14:10 feast. As the bridegroom, Samson was required to have a feast. This sort of party often accompanied the sealing of covenants such as marriage. Such a feast would include much eating and drinking, and Samson was either tempted or may have even violated his Nazirite vow.

14:11 thirty companions. These "guests of the bridegroom" were evidently not devout Israelite men (who would have been offended by Samson's actions), but possibly armed guards. It would have been their job to protect the party from being "crashed" and to protect the wedding party from injury.

14:12 riddle. Riddles were seen as a courtly form of entertainment. Samson was seeking to show off his cleverness and his strength for the wedding party.

"Tell us your riddle," they said. "Let's hear it."
[14]He replied,

"Out of the eater, something to eat;
out of the strong, something sweet."

For three days they could not give the answer.
[15]On the fourth[a] day, they said to Samson's wife, "Coax your husband into explaining the riddle for us, or we will burn you and your
father's household to death. Did you invite us here to rob us?"
[16]Then Samson's wife threw herself on him, sobbing, "You hate me!
You don't really love me. You've given my people a riddle, but you
haven't told me the answer."
"I haven't even explained it to my father or mother," he replied, "so
why should I explain it to you?" [17]She cried the whole seven days of
the feast. So on the seventh day he finally told her, because she continued to press him. She in turn explained the riddle to her people.
[18]Before sunset on the seventh day the men of the town said
to him,

"What is sweeter than honey?
What is stronger than a lion?"

Samson said to them,

"If you had not plowed with my heifer,
you would not have solved my riddle."

[19]Then the Spirit of the LORD came upon him in power. He went
down to Ashkelon, struck down thirty of their men, stripped them of
their belongings and gave their clothes to those who had explained
the riddle. Burning with anger, he went up to his father's house.
[20]And Samson's wife was given to the friend who had attended him at
his wedding.

Samson's Vengeance on the Philistines

15 Later on, at the time of wheat harvest, Samson took a young
goat and went to visit his wife. He said, "I'm going to my
wife's room." But her father would not let him go in.
[2]"I was so sure you thoroughly hated her," he said, "that I gave her
to your friend. Isn't her younger sister more attractive? Take her instead."

[a]15 Some Septuagint manuscripts and Syriac; Hebrew *seventh*

chapter ends, do you get the sense that Samson is "A Man of God"? "A Man For All Seasons"? or "A Man Out of Control"? Why?

APPLY 1. Samson had communication problems with his parents and his wife. What could help improve the communication in your family? **2.** Where in your life would you like to experience more self-control? **3.** What one area can you invite your group to hold you accountable?

OPEN 1. When you played "capture the flag" as a kid, who was the person you most wanted to tag and put in "jail"? Why? **2.** When it comes to your temper, is your "fuse" long, short or nonexistent?

STUDY Samson returns to Timnah to see his wife, only to discover she has been given to another man. First, he gets even with

14:16 You don't really love me. This accusation was an attack to which Samson would prove to be extremely vulnerable. Delilah would use it as well.

14:18 my heifer. In an instant Samson realized he had been deceived. His anger first expressed itself verbally. Since a heifer is not used for plowing, Samson was calling his wife "my heifer" to indicate he knew she had betrayed his confidence. However, the brunt of his anger was toward the Philistines who had coaxed his wife into the deception.

14:19 came upon him in power. The Spirit of God came over Samson in his anger. This was the first "occasion" (14:4) in which the Lord used Samson as an instrument against the Philistines. He allowed Samson to be among them and interact with them; then, when things went wrong, as God knew they would, he empowered Samson to do his will.

14:20 friend. In this culture, the "friend" of the bridegroom attended to him and assisted him in his wedding much like the "best man" does today. The friend in this verse was probably one of the thirty companions mentioned in verse 11. For the proper role of the "friend" of the bridegroom, as well as its symbolic implications, see John 3:29.

15:2 younger sister. Since Samson's father-in-law had already received the bride-price (Ex. 22:16), he was obligated to give Samson a bride.

3Samson said to them, "This time I have a right to get even with the
Philistines; I will really harm them." 4So he went out and caught
three hundred foxes and tied them tail to tail in pairs. He then fastened
a torch to every pair of tails, 5lit the torches and let the foxes loose in
the standing grain of the Philistines. He burned up the shocks and
standing grain, together with the vineyards and olive groves.
6When the Philistines asked, "Who did this?" they were told, "Samson, the Timnite's son-in-law, because his wife was given to his
friend."
So the Philistines went up and burned her and her father to death.
7Samson said to them, "Since you've acted like this, I won't stop until
I get my revenge on you." 8He attacked them viciously and slaughtered many of them. Then he went down and stayed in a cave in the
rock of Etam.
9The Philistines went up and camped in Judah, spreading out near
Lehi. 10The men of Judah asked, "Why have you come to fight us?"
"We have come to take Samson prisoner," they answered, "to do to
him as he did to us."
11Then three thousand men from Judah went down to the cave in
the rock of Etam and said to Samson, "Don't you realize that the Philistines are rulers over us? What have you done to us?"
He answered, "I merely did to them what they did to me."
12They said to him, "We've come to tie you up and hand you over to
the Philistines."
Samson said, "Swear to me that you won't kill me yourselves."
13"Agreed," they answered. "We will only tie you up and hand you
over to them. We will not kill you." So they bound him with two new
ropes and led him up from the rock. 14As he approached Lehi, the Philistines came toward him shouting. The Spirit of the LORD came upon
him in power. The ropes on his arms became like charred flax, and
the bindings dropped from his hands. 15Finding a fresh jawbone of a
donkey, he grabbed it and struck down a thousand men.
16Then Samson said,

"With a donkey's jawbone
I have made donkeys of them.[a]
With a donkey's jawbone
I have killed a thousand men."

[a]16 Or *made a heap or two*; the Hebrew for *donkey* sounds like the Hebrew for *heap*.

the Philistines. Then, when they retaliate, he responds with a murderous vengeance. **1.** Whose fault is the miscommunication: Samson or his wife (vv. 1–2; ch. 14)? **2.** In verse 3, Samson says, "This time I have a right to get even." Do you believe this is true or false? What does this imply about his previous action (14:19)? Is revenge ever "right"? Explain. **3.** If you were to write the obituary for Samson's wife, how would you explain her demise? What emotions do you observe in Samson that you would include in the article? Which ones seem to be missing? **4.** Why do you think Judah sends 3,000 men to the cave where Samson is hiding? Isn't this "over-kill"? **5.** Describe the scene when Samson is turned over to the Philistines. Does Samson's 20-year term as judge over Israel have any impact on the actions of Judah? **6.** In your opinion, why does God seem to indulge Samson's impulsive behavior? **7.** Choose three words to describe Samson's character. How do you think they shape his actions? What three words best describe your own character? Explain how they affect your choices and actions.

APPLY **1.** The ancient "cities of refuge" were set up to avert endless cycles of revenge (Josh. 20). Where do you turn for refuge from the "cycle of revenge" in your own life? Explain how that place or person is safe for you. **2.** Where could you use the Spirit of the Lord to empower you, or to receive his thirst-quenching water to revive you? How can your group pray for you this week?

15:5 burned up. Samson knew how to strike back at the Philistines by destroying their food. The wheat harvest came at the end of May or beginning of June, at the end of the dry season. The fields would have been very dry and susceptible to fire.

15:7 revenge. Even though Samson certainly had no great love for his father-in-law or his "promised" wife, he was *inflamed to avenge their deaths. It did* not matter that it was his father-in-law's actions that had provoked his burning the Philistine fields. Revenge was a way of life in the Near East. As in this case, there was usually an escalation of violence as the conflict grew from man against man, to family against family, to tribe against tribe, to nation against nation. The problem was so severe that the Lord designated six cities of refuge for those who killed someone either accidentally or unintentionally (Josh. 20:1–9). Those who fled to these cities were safe from the pursuit of avengers.

15:11 What have you done to us? The tribe of Judah was subject to the Philistines' rule and evidently did not mind it. In modern terms, they saw Samson as a troublemaker, a revolutionary who was about to upset their situation. Though they were under Philistine rule, a condition that was contrary to their covenant promise from God, they preferred that to being the enemy of the Philistines. In other words, they preferred the way things were. Perhaps Samson's role was to begin the overthrow of the Philistines by starting the destruction of the status quo (13:5).

15:15 struck down a thousand men. Similar reports of massive slaughter of soldiers by a single man had been made about Shamgar who killed 600 Philistines with an oxgoad (3:31).

17When he finished speaking, he threw away the jawbone; and the
place was called Ramath Lehi.[a]
18Because he was very thirsty, he cried out to the LORD, "You have
given your servant this great victory. Must I now die of thirst and fall
into the hands of the uncircumcised?" 19Then God opened up the
hollow place in Lehi, and water came out of it. When Samson drank,
his strength returned and he revived. So the spring was called En
Hakkore,[b] and it is still there in Lehi.
20Samson led[c] Israel for twenty years in the days of the Philistines.

Samson and Delilah

16 One day Samson went to Gaza, where he saw a prostitute. He
went in to spend the night with her. 2The people of Gaza were
told, "Samson is here!" So they surrounded the place and lay in wait
for him all night at the city gate. They made no move during the
night, saying, "At dawn we'll kill him."
3But Samson lay there only until the middle of the night. Then he
got up and took hold of the doors of the city gate, together with the
two posts, and tore them loose, bar and all. He lifted them to his
shoulders and carried them to the top of the hill that faces Hebron.
4Some time later, he fell in love with a woman in the Valley of Sorek
whose name was Delilah. 5The rulers of the Philistines went to her
and said, "See if you can lure him into showing you the secret of his
great strength and how we can overpower him so we may tie him up
and subdue him. Each one of us will give you eleven hundred
shekels[d] of silver."
6So Delilah said to Samson, "Tell me the secret of your great
strength and how you can be tied up and subdued."
7Samson answered her, "If anyone ties me with seven fresh
thongs[e] that have not been dried, I'll become as weak as any other
man."
8Then the rulers of the Philistines brought her seven fresh thongs
that had not been dried, and she tied him with them. 9With men hidden in the room, she called to him, "Samson, the Philistines are upon
you!" But he snapped the thongs as easily as a piece of string snaps

[a]17 *Ramath Lehi* means *jawbone hill.* [b]19 *En Hakkore* means *caller's spring.* [c]20 Traditionally *judged*
[d]5 That is, about 28 pounds (about 13 kilograms) [e]7 Or *bowstrings*; also in verses 8 and 9

OPEN 1. Growing up, who was your favorite hero and what was his or her power? **2.** Share an April Fool's joke in which you were completely taken in or caught off guard.

STUDY Samson, while leading the Israelites under the Philistine occupation, incited the enemy by his heroic exploits. In this story Samson falls in love again with a Philistine woman who turns out to be an enemy spy. **1.** Gaza was a Philistine city, so why would Samson venture anywhere near such a place? **2.** In Gaza, Samson only steals the city gates instead of waging war on the Philistines. What's the meaning of this more symbolic and less violent response? **3.** What title would you give to the story of Samson and Delilah: "Sleeping with the Enemy"? "Fatal Attraction"? "Money, Sex and Power"? Other? **4.** How could Samson be taken in by a woman like Delilah and thus forsake the third of his Nazirite vows (Num. 6:1–21)? **5.** What do you think drew Samson into this relationship? What was Delilah's motivation (v. 5)? **6.** What was Samson's downfall? **7.** What do you feel is the saddest part of Samson's story?

15:18 You have given your servant this great victory. Samson gave God the credit for his victory. He was correct to do so because he had been empowered by the "Spirit of the LORD" (v. 14). This power was in sharp contrast with his wholly human need for water here and his inability to resist women in 16:1 *and elsewhere. Whereas the Spirit of* the Lord made him strong, his humanness made him weak.

15:19 water came out of it. Just as God provided water for the wandering Israelites (especially at Massah and Meribah, Ex. 17:1–7), God provided it for Samson.

16:1 prostitute. God gave Samson tremendous physical strength. Samson's desire for pleasure, and perhaps for the exotic (14:3), led him to commit sin and suffer its consequences.

16:2 made no move during the night. Samson was probably protected by his own reputation. The Philistines had no understanding that God empowered Samson, and thus feared him in all circumstances.

16:3 lifted them ... carried them. Samson's act was one of defiance and perhaps sinful pride. He was saying to the Philistines that they couldn't hold him with their gates. He placed the gates where the people of Judah could see them as a reminder that they were, in fact, prisoners.

16:5 tie him up and subdue him. The Philistines were still out for revenge, some twenty years after the first conflict between Samson and his father-in-law. They were not concerned with eliminating Samson unless they could torture and humiliate him.

16:7 seven fresh thongs. Samson, in his pride, tried to deceive the Philistines with "secrets" that rang true. Since he knew the Philistines believed his strength was from a supernatural force, he repeatedly used the number seven, which was widely believed to have magical powers.

APPLY 1. Our greatest strength can also be our greatest weakness and downfall. How was Samson's superior strength both an asset and a downfall? What do you consider your greatest asset? How have you experienced it as both strength and weakness? **2.** When do you feel weakest against temptation? **3.** What is the secret of your spiritual strength?

when it comes close to a flame. So the secret of his strength was not
discovered.
10Then Delilah said to Samson, "You have made a fool of me; you
lied to me. Come now, tell me how you can be tied."
11He said, "If anyone ties me securely with new ropes that have
never been used, I'll become as weak as any other man."
12So Delilah took new ropes and tied him with them. Then, with
men hidden in the room, she called to him, "Samson, the Philistines
are upon you!" But he snapped the ropes off his arms as if they were
threads.
13Delilah then said to Samson, "Until now, you have been making a
fool of me and lying to me. Tell me how you can be tied."
He replied, "If you weave the seven braids of my head into the fabric ⌞on the loom⌟ and tighten it with the pin, I'll become as weak as
any other man." So while he was sleeping, Delilah took the seven
braids of his head, wove them into the fabric 14and[a] tightened it with
the pin.
Again she called to him, "Samson, the Philistines are upon you!"
He awoke from his sleep and pulled up the pin and the loom, with the
fabric.
15Then she said to him, "How can you say, 'I love you,' when you
won't confide in me? This is the third time you have made a fool of
me and haven't told me the secret of your great strength." 16With
such nagging she prodded him day after day until he was tired to
death.
17So he told her everything. "No razor has ever been used on my
head," he said, "because I have been a Nazirite set apart to God since
birth. If my head were shaved, my strength would leave me, and I
would become as weak as any other man."
18When Delilah saw that he had told her everything, she sent word
to the rulers of the Philistines, "Come back once more; he has told me
everything." So the rulers of the Philistines returned with the silver in
their hands. 19Having put him to sleep on her lap, she called a man to
shave off the seven braids of his hair, and so began to subdue him.[b]
And his strength left him.
20Then she called, "Samson, the Philistines are upon you!"
He awoke from his sleep and thought, "I'll go out as before and
shake myself free." But he did not know that the LORD had left him.
21Then the Philistines seized him, gouged out his eyes and took
him down to Gaza. Binding him with bronze shackles, they set him to

[a]13,14 Some Septuagint manuscripts; Hebrew "*I can, if you weave the seven braids of my head into the fabric ⌞on the loom⌟.*" [14]*So she* [b]19 Hebrew; some Septuagint manuscripts *and he began to weaken*

16:11 new ropes. Though the vendetta between Samson and the Philistines had been going on for some time, the Philistines had forgotten some of the details. They had tried new ropes before with terrible results (15:13–14).

16:13 making a fool of me and lying to me. Though it is difficult to feel compassion for Delilah, she was actually correct in her assessment of Samson's actions toward her. Out of his arrogant disdain for the Philistines, Samson had been playing a game with her and her people.

16:19–20 his strength left him ... the LORD had left him. Samson's *strength* was from the Spirit of the Lord. When he betrayed his vow, he nullified that special blessing.

16:20 he did not know. Samson did not know that by betraying his Nazirite vow the Lord would leave him, and he would lose his strength. Importantly, that vow had been made for him before he was ever born.

16:21 gouged out his eyes. The Philistines sought to control and humiliate Samson. His blindness would accomplish both goals. They knew that his pride would make his humiliation their best revenge.

grinding in the prison. 22But the hair on his head began to grow again
after it had been shaved.

The Death of Samson

23Now the rulers of the Philistines assembled to offer a great sacrifice to Dagon their god and to celebrate, saying, "Our god has delivered Samson, our enemy, into our hands."
24When the people saw him, they praised their god, saying,

"Our god has delivered our enemy
  into our hands,
the one who laid waste our land
  and multiplied our slain."

25While they were in high spirits, they shouted, "Bring out Samson
to entertain us." So they called Samson out of the prison, and he performed for them.
When they stood him among the pillars, 26Samson said to the
servant who held his hand, "Put me where I can feel the pillars that
support the temple, so that I may lean against them." 27Now the
temple was crowded with men and women; all the rulers of the
Philistines were there, and on the roof were about three thousand
men and women watching Samson perform. 28Then Samson prayed
to the LORD, "O Sovereign LORD, remember me. O God, please
strengthen me just once more, and let me with one blow get revenge
on the Philistines for my two eyes." 29Then Samson reached toward
the two central pillars on which the temple stood. Bracing himself
against them, his right hand on the one and his left hand on the
other, 30Samson said, "Let me die with the Philistines!" Then he
pushed with all his might, and down came the temple on the rulers
and all the people in it. Thus he killed many more when he died than
while he lived.
31Then his brothers and his father's whole family went down to get
him. They brought him back and buried him between Zorah and Eshtaol in the tomb of Manoah his father. He had led[a] Israel twenty years.

Micah's Idols

17 Now a man named Micah from the hill country of Ephraim
2said to his mother, "The eleven hundred shekels[b] of silver
that were taken from you and about which I heard you utter a curse—
I have that silver with me; I took it."

[a]31 Traditionally *judged* [b]2 That is, about 28 pounds (about 13 kilograms)

OPEN 1. When you played "pin the tail on the donkey" as a kid, did you like being blindfolded? Why or why not? **2.** Who is someone you admire for an act of self-sacrifice?

STUDY Samson—the champion of Israel—had been captured by the Philistines, blinded, shackled and relegated to the lowly task of grinding grain. **1.** Why didn't the Philistines kill Samson when they had the chance? **2.** Who was really responsible for Samson's death? **3.** Why do you think God answered Samson's prayer? Was there a time in your life when God answered your prayer when you felt like you didn't deserve it? **4.** How is it that God would choose to use a man such as Samson? **5.** Imagine that you are one of Samson's parents. What do you remember as the most tragic thing about your son's life? What do you see as his most redeeming quality or action? Explain. **6.** How would you rate Samson's death as compared to his life?

APPLY 1. What weakness of yours is in danger of taking away your spiritual strength? **2.** Like Samson, if you could pray for just one thing to happen, what would it be?

OPEN Were you ever caught with "your hand in the cookie jar" when you were young? Who caught you and what happened?

STUDY The story of Micah shows just how far Israel had drifted from its spiritual moorings

---

16:27 three thousand men and women. The Philistines had set the stage for the perfect, public humiliation of Samson. The large crowd was gathered, significantly, at their pagan temple. However, God had other plans for Samson, despite his failings.

16:30 killed many more. The 3,000 that were killed were significantly more than the 1,000 Samson had killed previously (14:19; 15:8,15).

16:31 went down to get him. The Philistines allowed Samson's family to get his body. Evidently, their thirst for revenge had been satisfied.

17:1–21:25 This section contains two stories that illustrate the state of moral and spiritual decay in Israel during the period of the judges. The episodes were narrated at the time of the monarchy in Israel. They looked back at the time before the monarchy reunited the spiritual affairs of the nation, and reestablished a better observance of the covenant law.

17:1–18:31 This first story illustrated how far the spiritual life of Israel had declined. It is a story of theft, curses, idols, the love of money and abandonment of God's plan. It involved the two tribes Ephraim and Dan, and a corrupt young Levite.

17:2 heard you utter a curse. Uttering a curse irresponsibly, over something like the theft of money, was an immoral act. Certainly, however, the curse was all that motivated Micah to return it. These two people had lost their real faith, if they

during this time when "Israel had no king and everyone did as he saw fit." Idol worship and superstition had wormed their way to the very core of spiritual life. **1.** What did Micah hope to escape by confessing his theft (v. 2)? **2.** How do you feel about his mother's response (vv. 2–4)? **3.** What was the spiritual climate of Israel at this time (v. 6)? How does it compare with the spiritual climate of your culture? **4.** What circumstances might have caused the Levite to look for a new home? What has motivated you to move to a new home in the past? **5.** Why do you think Micah wanted the young Levite to become his priest and live in his house (vv. 10–13)?

APPLY Share one area where the confusion of contemporary society makes it difficult for you to serve the Lord.

OPEN 1. When it comes to job hunting and career changes, are you: Comfortable where you are? Eager for advancement? Selling your services short? Looking for that "big break"? Ready to "bail" at any cost? Other? Explain. **2.** When you think of retirement, where is the place of your dreams? Why that location?

STUDY The Danites are looking for land to occupy, because the Amorites and Philistines

Then his mother said, "The LORD bless you, my son!"
3When he returned the eleven hundred shekels of silver to his
mother, she said, "I solemnly consecrate my silver to the LORD for my
son to make a carved image and a cast idol. I will give it back to you."
4So he returned the silver to his mother, and she took two hundred
shekels[a] of silver and gave them to a silversmith, who made them
into the image and the idol. And they were put in Micah's house.
5Now this man Micah had a shrine, and he made an ephod and
some idols and installed one of his sons as his priest. 6In those days
Israel had no king; everyone did as he saw fit.
7A young Levite from Bethlehem in Judah, who had been living
within the clan of Judah, 8left that town in search of some other place
to stay. On his way[b] he came to Micah's house in the hill country of
Ephraim.
9Micah asked him, "Where are you from?"
"I'm a Levite from Bethlehem in Judah," he said, "and I'm looking
for a place to stay."
10Then Micah said to him, "Live with me and be my father and
priest, and I'll give you ten shekels[c] of silver a year, your clothes and
your food." 11So the Levite agreed to live with him, and the young
man was to him like one of his sons. 12Then Micah installed the Levite, and the young man became his priest and lived in his house.
13And Micah said, "Now I know that the LORD will be good to me,
since this Levite has become my priest."

Danites Settle in Laish

18 In those days Israel had no king.
And in those days the tribe of the Danites was seeking a
place of their own where they might settle, because they had not yet
come into an inheritance among the tribes of Israel. 2So the Danites
sent five warriors from Zorah and Eshtaol to spy out the land and explore it. These men represented all their clans. They told them, "Go,
explore the land."
The men entered the hill country of Ephraim and came to the

[a]*4* That is, about 5 pounds (about 2.3 kilograms) [b]*8* Or *To carry on his profession* [c]*10* That is, about 4 ounces (about 110 grams)

ever had it, and had descended into idol worship and superstition.

17:3 consecrate my silver ... to make a carved image and a cast idol. Her actions were perversions of the right approach to offerings. In one breath she wanted to dedicate her wealth to God, and with the next she disobeyed his commands.

17:6 Israel had no king. One of the themes of the book of Judges was that Israel's monarchy had brought order to chaos and restored Israel to its proper relationship with God. Most scholars interpret that as strong evidence that Judges was written during David's reign. It would have been politically wise to take a pro-monarchy approach during the reign of a strong king. Regardless, the period of the judges was characterized by turmoil. Israel struggled with its political enemies, and repeatedly fell into pagan religious practices.

17:8 in search of some other place to stay. As a Levite, he held no property and had no occupation other than priest. When the people of his town quit worshiping and giving offerings, he had no means of support. In essence, he was out of work and looking for a job.

17:10 ten shekels. If this sum is an attractive offer for a yearly salary, then the amounts of money in verses 2–4 are really significant. The young Levite's main concerns were exactly what Micah offered: money, clothes and food.

17:12 became his priest. Micah had a big ego along with his mother's money. Instead of participating in communal worship, Micah wanted his own priest, idols and all the trappings that would imply piety. As verse 13 states, he felt that he could even impress God, and thus receive special favor.

18:1 where they might settle. Not all of the tribes of Israel had been able to claim their homeland. The Danites were allotted a strip of land between Judah and Ephraim, but had not been able to occupy it because of the Amorites and Philistines.

house of Micah, where they spent the night. 3When they were near
Micah's house, they recognized the voice of the young Levite; so they
turned in there and asked him, "Who brought you here? What are you
doing in this place? Why are you here?"
4He told them what Micah had done for him, and said, "He has
hired me and I am his priest."
5Then they said to him, "Please inquire of God to learn whether our
journey will be successful."
6The priest answered them, "Go in peace. Your journey has the
LORD's approval."
7So the five men left and came to Laish, where they saw that the
people were living in safety, like the Sidonians, unsuspecting and
secure. And since their land lacked nothing, they were prosperous.[a]
Also, they lived a long way from the Sidonians and had no relationship with anyone else.[b]
8When they returned to Zorah and Eshtaol, their brothers asked
them, "How did you find things?"
9They answered, "Come on, let's attack them! We have seen that
the land is very good. Aren't you going to do something? Don't hesitate to go there and take it over. 10When you get there, you will find an
unsuspecting people and a spacious land that God has put into your
hands, a land that lacks nothing whatever."
11Then six hundred men from the clan of the Danites, armed for
battle, set out from Zorah and Eshtaol. 12On their way they set up
camp near Kiriath Jearim in Judah. This is why the place west of Kiriath Jearim is called Mahaneh Dan[c] to this day. 13From there they
went on to the hill country of Ephraim and came to Micah's house.
14Then the five men who had spied out the land of Laish said to
their brothers, "Do you know that one of these houses has an ephod,
other household gods, a carved image and a cast idol? Now you
know what to do." 15So they turned in there and went to the house of
the young Levite at Micah's place and greeted him. 16The six hundred
Danites, armed for battle, stood at the entrance to the gate. 17The five
men who had spied out the land went inside and took the carved
image, the ephod, the other household gods and the cast idol while
the priest and the six hundred armed men stood at the entrance to
the gate.
18When these men went into Micah's house and took the carved
image, the ephod, the other household gods and the cast idol, the
priest said to them, "What are you doing?"
19They answered him, "Be quiet! Don't say a word. Come with us,
and be our father and priest. Isn't it better that you serve a tribe and
clan in Israel as priest rather than just one man's household?" 20Then

[a]7 The meaning of the Hebrew for this clause is uncertain. [b]7 Hebrew; some Septuagint manuscripts *with the Arameans* [c]12 *Mahaneh Dan* means *Dan's camp.*

have successfully kept them off the land apportioned to them by God. Instead of continuing the struggle there, they seek the path of least resistance and Laish seems to fit the bill. **1.** What kept the Danites from receiving their inheritance (v. 1; 1:34 and Josh. 19:40–48)? **2.** How is it that the Danite spies "recognized the voice" of the priest? **3.** Instead of roughing him up or restoring him to his proper place, what immediate and future use do the Danites have for the Levites (vv. 5–6,14)? **4.** Choose three words to describe the character of this Levite priest as you see it in chapters 17 and 18. Would you buy a used car from this guy? **5.** Why would the Danites want Micah's religious paraphernalia? What does this tell you about the spiritual maturity of the Danites? **6.** Describe the battle for Laish (vv. 27–28). Why do the Danites choose this place for their new home (vv. 7–9)? What has made the people of Laish susceptible to attack? What does this tell you about the character of the Danites? **7.** How do the actions of the Danites and the priest relate to the main theme of Judges (21:25)?

APPLY **1.** Think of a time in your own life when you did "whatever you saw fit." Who was the real "king" in your life then? What kind of "fruit" did your choices and actions produce? Did God remain faithful to you even though your devotion was less than perfect? How? **2.** What in your life right now might make you susceptible to the enemy's attack?

18:3 recognized the voice. Although the covenant established Israel as a "holy nation" (Ex. 19:6), at this time it was still a loose confederation of tribes, each with its distinct accent and dialect.

18:5 inquire of God. The Danites were asking for an oracle. They were not asking for God's guidance, but instead for a sign concerning their success or failure.

18:6 LORD's approval. This young Levite priest was not unlike Balaam, who knew how to "prophesy" and get well paid for it (Num. 22–24).

18:19 a tribe and clan in Israel. The Danites appealed to the young Levite's greed and pride. The priest forgot, or never believed, that his job was to serve God. Whether that service was on behalf of one household or a tribe was irrelevant. The role of a priest, or indeed of God's people, was to glorify God, not accumulate wealth and power.

the priest was glad. He took the ephod, the other household gods and
the carved image and went along with the people. 21Putting their little
children, their livestock and their possessions in front of them, they
turned away and left.
22When they had gone some distance from Micah's house, the men
who lived near Micah were called together and overtook the Danites.
23As they shouted after them, the Danites turned and said to Micah,
"What's the matter with you that you called out your men to fight?"
24He replied, "You took the gods I made, and my priest, and went
away. What else do I have? How can you ask, 'What's the matter with
you?' "
25The Danites answered, "Don't argue with us, or some hot-tempered men will attack you, and you and your family will lose your
lives." 26So the Danites went their way, and Micah, seeing that they
were too strong for him, turned around and went back home.
27Then they took what Micah had made, and his priest, and went
on to Laish, against a peaceful and unsuspecting people. They attacked them with the sword and burned down their city. 28There was
no one to rescue them because they lived a long way from Sidon and
had no relationship with anyone else. The city was in a valley near
Beth Rehob.
The Danites rebuilt the city and settled there. 29They named it Dan
after their forefather Dan, who was born to Israel—though the city
used to be called Laish. 30There the Danites set up for themselves the
idols, and Jonathan son of Gershom, the son of Moses,[a] and his sons
were priests for the tribe of Dan until the time of the captivity of the
land. 31They continued to use the idols Micah had made, all the time
the house of God was in Shiloh.

A Levite and His Concubine

19 In those days Israel had no king.
Now a Levite who lived in a remote area in the hill country of
Ephraim took a concubine from Bethlehem in Judah. 2But she was
unfaithful to him. She left him and went back to her father's house in
Bethlehem, Judah. After she had been there four months, 3her husband went to her to persuade her to return. He had with him his servant and two donkeys. She took him into her father's house, and
when her father saw him, he gladly welcomed him. 4His father-in-

[a]30 An ancient Hebrew scribal tradition, some Septuagint manuscripts and Vulgate; Masoretic Text *Manasseh*

OPEN 1. When you travel as a family, do you rough it, go first class, or stay with friends? **2.** Who decides where to spend the night: Mom or Dad?

STUDY "In those days Israel had no king." This chapter begins by restating the theme of Judges. The story told here of the Levite and his concubine demonstrates just how low the lawlessness and immorality of God's people can sink. **1.** What is a concubine and how

18:21 in front of them. The men walked behind, protected by their buffer of children, livestock and possessions. This action was a display of their priorities and their cowardice.

18:24 What else do I have? Micah felt despair because he had lost his two possessions: his gods and his priest. Neither of these had any real value, but Micah could not see that. He had placed *great importance* on these meaningless things, and now they were gone.

18:30 set up for themselves the idols. The Danites continued Micah's foolish behavior. They based their new city around some stolen idols and a Levite priest, who was descended from Moses. The "foundation" of that city was laid on very uncertain ground.

19:1–21:25 The second story is one of moral decadence and tribal foolishness. Although the perversion of the tribe of Benjamin at Gibeah was terrible, in this story, no tribe of Israel showed itself truly worthy of admiration. The Israelites were portrayed as just as wicked as the Canaanites, and perhaps worse because they had God's law to guide them. The Gibeah portion of this story is remarkably similar to the account of Lot's efforts in Sodom and Gomorrah (Gen. 19:1–13). Evidently, the writer of Judges was drawing a parallel between the fate of the Benjamites and the citizens of Sodom.

19:3 gladly welcomed him. The story does not tell why the concubine left the Levite in the first place. Her leaving would have brought disgrace on her family, so her father would have been glad to see his daughter and the Levite reunited.

law, the girl's father, prevailed upon him to stay; so he remained with
him three days, eating and drinking, and sleeping there.
5 On the fourth day they got up early and he prepared to leave, but
the girl's father said to his son-in-law, "Refresh yourself with something to eat; then you can go." 6 So the two of them sat down to eat
and drink together. Afterward the girl's father said, "Please stay
tonight and enjoy yourself." 7 And when the man got up to go, his
father-in-law persuaded him, so he stayed there that night. 8 On the
morning of the fifth day, when he rose to go, the girl's father said,
"Refresh yourself. Wait till afternoon!" So the two of them ate
together.
9 Then when the man, with his concubine and his servant, got up to
leave, his father-in-law, the girl's father, said, "Now look, it's almost
evening. Spend the night here; the day is nearly over. Stay and enjoy
yourself. Early tomorrow morning you can get up and be on your way
home." 10 But, unwilling to stay another night, the man left and went
toward Jebus (that is, Jerusalem), with his two saddled donkeys and
his concubine.
11 When they were near Jebus and the day was almost gone, the servant said to his master, "Come, let's stop at this city of the Jebusites
and spend the night."
12 His master replied, "No. We won't go into an alien city, whose
people are not Israelites. We will go on to Gibeah." 13 He added,
"Come, let's try to reach Gibeah or Ramah and spend the night in one
of those places." 14 So they went on, and the sun set as they neared
Gibeah in Benjamin. 15 There they stopped to spend the night. They
went and sat in the city square, but no one took them into his home
for the night.
16 That evening an old man from the hill country of Ephraim, who
was living in Gibeah (the men of the place were Benjamites), came in
from his work in the fields. 17 When he looked and saw the traveler in
the city square, the old man asked, "Where are you going? Where did
you come from?"
18 He answered, "We are on our way from Bethlehem in Judah to a
remote area in the hill country of Ephraim where I live. I have been to
Bethlehem in Judah and now I am going to the house of the LORD. No
one has taken me into his house. 19 We have both straw and fodder for
our donkeys and bread and wine for ourselves your servants—me,
your maidservant, and the young man with us. We don't need anything."
20 "You are welcome at my house," the old man said. "Let me supply
whatever you need. Only don't spend the night in the square." 21 So
he took him into his house and fed his donkeys. After they had
washed their feet, they had something to eat and drink.
22 While they were enjoying themselves, some of the wicked men of
the city surrounded the house. Pounding on the door, they shouted to

is she different from a wife? **2.** What caused the concubine to return to her father? Why might the Levite want her back? Why do you think it took him four months before he went after her? **3.** In your opinion, why did the father keep asking the Levite to stay longer (vv. 4–10)? **4.** How hospitable were the people of Gibeah? How does this compare with the people of your community? **5.** Compare and contrast what happens here to Genesis 19. What do you make of the frightening parallels? Why would the old man offer two women, even his own virgin daughter, rather than the Levite stranger whom he had only met that night? What reasons can you think of for him sending anyone out at all? **6.** How would you assess the behavior of the Levite in this account? What emotions do you feel he had for his concubine? **7.** What motivated the Levite to send a piece of the concubine's body to each tribe of Israel (v. 29; 1 Sam. 11:7)? **8.** Would a king on the throne of Israel have prevented, or at least punished, this kind of evil?

APPLY **1.** Describe a time when you observed an injustice but no one made a courageous stand to meet the challenge. How did you feel? **2.** What evil or inhumane situation in the world especially upsets you and hits you right in the gut? What one small thing could you do that might begin to affect a change?

19:12 alien city. The Levite was afraid to stay in a Jebusite city. Ironically, he may have been just as safe there. The sins demonstrated later in Gibeah were all associated with the Canaanites, showing that the people of Gibeah had descended to the level of their pagan neighbors.

19:21 took him into his house and fed his donkeys. The man showed the Levite the proper hospitality for a fellow Israelite.

19:22 wicked men. The men of Gibeah were morally depraved. The perversions they exhibited were usually associated with the Canaanites. However, there was also a striking resemblance between the men of Gibeah and the inhabitants of Sodom (Gen. 19:5).

the old man who owned the house, "Bring out the man who came to
your house so we can have sex with him."
23 The owner of the house went outside and said to them, "No, my
friends, don't be so vile. Since this man is my guest, don't do this disgraceful thing. 24 Look, here is my virgin daughter, and his concubine.
I will bring them out to you now, and you can use them and do to
them whatever you wish. But to this man, don't do such a disgraceful
thing."
25 But the men would not listen to him. So the man took his concubine and sent her outside to them, and they raped her and abused her
throughout the night, and at dawn they let her go. 26 At daybreak the
woman went back to the house where her master was staying, fell
down at the door and lay there until daylight.
27 When her master got up in the morning and opened the door of
the house and stepped out to continue on his way, there lay his
concubine, fallen in the doorway of the house, with her hands on the
threshold. 28 He said to her, "Get up; let's go." But there was no
answer. Then the man put her on his donkey and set out for home.
29 When he reached home, he took a knife and cut up his concubine, limb by limb, into twelve parts and sent them into all the areas
of Israel. 30 Everyone who saw it said, "Such a thing has never been
seen or done, not since the day the Israelites came up out of Egypt.
Think about it! Consider it! Tell us what to do!"

Israelites Fight the Benjamites

20 Then all the Israelites from Dan to Beersheba and from the
land of Gilead came out as one man and assembled before
the LORD in Mizpah. 2 The leaders of all the people of the tribes of Israel took their places in the assembly of the people of God, four hundred thousand soldiers armed with swords. 3 (The Benjamites heard
that the Israelites had gone up to Mizpah.) Then the Israelites said,
"Tell us how this awful thing happened."
4 So the Levite, the husband of the murdered woman, said, "I and
my concubine came to Gibeah in Benjamin to spend the night. 5 During the night the men of Gibeah came after me and surrounded the
house, intending to kill me. They raped my concubine, and she died.
6 I took my concubine, cut her into pieces and sent one piece to each
region of Israel's inheritance, because they committed this lewd and

OPEN 1. What large, unified gathering stands out in your memory: Rock concert? Sporting event? Parade? Memorial service? Other? Share how it was significant to you. **2.** Would you describe yourself as a person who would rather "fight than switch," or "switch than fight"? Explain by sharing an example.

STUDY Each tribe received a piece of the abused and murdered concubine and now unites in civil war against Benjamin. Caught up in their thirst for vengeance, Israel almost destroys one of its own tribes. **1.** What does it mean that Israel

---

19:23 don't be so vile. The owner of the house had his own set of moral do's and don'ts. Though he called their homosexual demands vile, he also called them "friends" and went on to demonstrate his own perverse sense of values.

19:24 my virgin daughter, and his concubine. This one verse demonstrated the old man's values. He was more than willing to sacrifice his daughter and his guest's concubine to the "vile" demands of the mob, but he was terribly afraid of violating the code of hospitality against his guest. His moral decadence is no less than the mob's, only different.

19:29 cut up his concubine. The Levite was seemingly outraged at the treatment of his concubine. His action of dismembering her into 12 pieces was meant to send a message to the tribes about their morally degenerate state. What he did not recognize was that he was a part of that degeneracy, and that his inaction in protecting his concubine was tantamount to condoning her assault.

20:1–48 The message of the dismembered concubine got Israel's attention and prompted the people into action. The story of the outrageous behavior at Gibeah led them into an act of retribution, not against their enemies, but against their fellow Israelites. Having asked God for guidance, they marched against the Benjamites.

20:1 Dan to Beersheba. In the time of the monarchy, this phrase would have described all of Israel from north to south. The phrase indicated that all of Israel was involved in this conflict (except Jabesh Gilead, 21:8–9). The fact that the tribes could come together as "one man" indicated that the conflict occurred early in the time of the judges, before Israel's enemies began to dominate certain regions.

disgraceful act in Israel. 7Now, all you Israelites, speak up and give
your verdict."
8All the people rose as one man, saying, "None of us will go home.
No, not one of us will return to his house. 9But now this is what we'll
do to Gibeah: We'll go up against it as the lot directs. 10We'll take ten
men out of every hundred from all the tribes of Israel, and a hundred
from a thousand, and a thousand from ten thousand, to get provisions for the army. Then, when the army arrives at Gibeah[a] in
Benjamin, it can give them what they deserve for all this vileness
done in Israel." 11So all the men of Israel got together and united as
one man against the city.
12The tribes of Israel sent men throughout the tribe of Benjamin,
saying, "What about this awful crime that was committed among
you? 13Now surrender those wicked men of Gibeah so that we may
put them to death and purge the evil from Israel."
But the Benjamites would not listen to their fellow Israelites.
14From their towns they came together at Gibeah to fight against the
Israelites. 15At once the Benjamites mobilized twenty-six thousand
swordsmen from their towns, in addition to seven hundred chosen
men from those living in Gibeah. 16Among all these soldiers there
were seven hundred chosen men who were left-handed, each of
whom could sling a stone at a hair and not miss.
17Israel, apart from Benjamin, mustered four hundred thousand
swordsmen, all of them fighting men.
18The Israelites went up to Bethel[b] and inquired of God. They said,
"Who of us shall go first to fight against the Benjamites?"
The LORD replied, "Judah shall go first."
19The next morning the Israelites got up and pitched camp near
Gibeah. 20The men of Israel went out to fight the Benjamites and took
up battle positions against them at Gibeah. 21The Benjamites came
out of Gibeah and cut down twenty-two thousand Israelites on the
battlefield that day. 22But the men of Israel encouraged one another
and again took up their positions where they had stationed themselves the first day. 23The Israelites went up and wept before the LORD
until evening, and they inquired of the LORD. They said, "Shall we go
up again to battle against the Benjamites, our brothers?"
The LORD answered, "Go up against them."
24Then the Israelites drew near to Benjamin the second day. 25This
time, when the Benjamites came out from Gibeah to oppose them,

[a]10 One Hebrew manuscript; most Hebrew manuscripts *Geba*, a variant of *Gibeah* [b]18 Or *to the house of God*; also in verse 26

"came out" as one man (vv. 1,8,11; 1 Sam. 11:7–8)? Who was missing from all Israel? **2.** What motivated Israel to fight the Benjamites? **3.** How did they select which Israelites were to join this battle against their brothers? **4.** In your opinion, why didn't the Benjamites just hand over the guilty parties and avoid the bloodbath? **5.** When did Israel seek God for direction; before or after they had decided to attack Benjamin? Do you normally seek God before or after making a big decision? **6.** Why do you think God let Israel fail in its first two attacks on Benjamin (vv. 19–25)? How did the Israelites respond? What lesson might God have been trying to teach his people? **7.** How many Benjamites were left to start over again? Did the Israelites go too far in the heat of battle (vv. 46–48)? Do you believe they intended to wipe out their sibling tribe in this civil war? **8.** Read Genesis 49:27, where Jacob blesses Benjamin along with his other sons. In what sense has this blessing come true?

APPLY 1. Describe a battle you've experienced in your life. Whose side were you on? What was the outcome? **2.** When in the past five years have you experienced the power of unity, of being "one" with a group of people? What does this unity enable you to do?

20:9 lot. God's will was often sought by the casting of lots (Ex. 28:30).

20:10 ten men out of every hundred. Gathering an army and supplying it required a huge effort. Though the tribes were all Israelite, each had its social and political situations. This method for provisioning an army seemed equitable and possible in the current political climate.

20:13 surrender those wicked men. Israel made a reasonable demand that the guilty men be turned over to them for execution. Their offense was punishable by death, and the Israelites' demand would have brought a peaceful end to the conflict. As a nation, Israel was responsible for punishing the sins of its people. Without this punishment, the nation itself would be held accountable. As Deuteronomy 13:5 commands, "You must purge the evil from among you."

20:16 sling a stone. As David would demonstrate in future years, the sling was a very effective weapon. These 700 men were the ancient equivalent of sharpshooters.

20:21 twenty-two thousand Israelites. Though Israel was in the right, and had the Lord's guidance, the Benjamites scored a big victory. The Benjamites numbered 25,700, and had, therefore, killed almost one enemy each.

they cut down another eighteen thousand Israelites, all of them armed with swords.

26Then the Israelites, all the people, went up to Bethel, and there they sat weeping before the LORD. They fasted that day until evening and presented burnt offerings and fellowship offerings[a] to the LORD. 27And the Israelites inquired of the LORD. (In those days the ark of the covenant of God was there, 28with Phinehas son of Eleazar, the son of Aaron, ministering before it.) They asked, "Shall we go up again to battle with Benjamin our brother, or not?"

The LORD responded, "Go, for tomorrow I will give them into your hands."

29Then Israel set an ambush around Gibeah. 30They went up against the Benjamites on the third day and took up positions against Gibeah as they had done before. 31The Benjamites came out to meet them and were drawn away from the city. They began to inflict casualties on the Israelites as before, so that about thirty men fell in the open field and on the roads—the one leading to Bethel and the other to Gibeah.

32While the Benjamites were saying, "We are defeating them as before," the Israelites were saying, "Let's retreat and draw them away from the city to the roads."

33All the men of Israel moved from their places and took up positions at Baal Tamar, and the Israelite ambush charged out of its place on the west[b] of Gibeah.[c] 34Then ten thousand of Israel's finest men made a frontal attack on Gibeah. The fighting was so heavy that the Benjamites did not realize how near disaster was. 35The LORD defeated Benjamin before Israel, and on that day the Israelites struck down 25,100 Benjamites, all armed with swords. 36Then the Benjamites saw that they were beaten.

Now the men of Israel had given way before Benjamin, because they relied on the ambush they had set near Gibeah. 37The men who had been in ambush made a sudden dash into Gibeah, spread out and put the whole city to the sword. 38The men of Israel had arranged with the ambush that they should send up a great cloud of smoke from the city, 39and then the men of Israel would turn in the battle.

The Benjamites had begun to inflict casualties on the men of Israel (about thirty), and they said, "We are defeating them as in the first battle." 40But when the column of smoke began to rise from the city, the Benjamites turned and saw the smoke of the whole city going up into the sky. 41Then the men of Israel turned on them, and the men of Benjamin were terrified, because they realized that disaster had come upon them. 42So they fled before the Israelites in the direction of the desert, but they could not escape the battle. And the men of Israel who came out of the towns cut them down there. 43They surrounded the Benjamites, chased them and easily[d] overran them in the vicinity of Gibeah on the east. 44Eighteen thousand Benjamites fell, all of them valiant fighters. 45As they turned and fled toward the desert to the rock of Rimmon, the Israelites cut down five thousand men along the roads. They kept pressing after the Benjamites as far as Gidom and struck down two thousand more.

46On that day twenty-five thousand Benjamite swordsmen fell, all

[a]26 Traditionally *peace offerings* [b]33 Some Septuagint manuscripts and Vulgate; the meaning of the Hebrew for this word is uncertain. [c]33 Hebrew *Geba,* a variant of *Gibeah* [d]43 The meaning of the Hebrew for this word is uncertain.

of them valiant fighters. 47But six hundred men turned and fled into
the desert to the rock of Rimmon, where they stayed four months.
48The men of Israel went back to Benjamin and put all the towns to
the sword, including the animals and everything else they found. All
the towns they came across they set on fire.

Wives for the Benjamites

21 The men of Israel had taken an oath at Mizpah: "Not one of us
will give his daughter in marriage to a Benjamite."
2The people went to Bethel,[a] where they sat before God until evening, raising their voices and weeping bitterly. 3"O LORD, the God of
Israel," they cried, "why has this happened to Israel? Why should one
tribe be missing from Israel today?"
4Early the next day the people built an altar and presented burnt offerings and fellowship offerings.[b]
5Then the Israelites asked, "Who from all the tribes of Israel has
failed to assemble before the LORD?" For they had taken a solemn
oath that anyone who failed to assemble before the LORD at Mizpah
should certainly be put to death.
6Now the Israelites grieved for their brothers, the Benjamites. "Today one tribe is cut off from Israel," they said. 7"How can we provide
wives for those who are left, since we have taken an oath by the LORD
not to give them any of our daughters in marriage?" 8Then they
asked, "Which one of the tribes of Israel failed to assemble before the
LORD at Mizpah?" They discovered that no one from Jabesh Gilead
had come to the camp for the assembly. 9For when they counted the
people, they found that none of the people of Jabesh Gilead were
there.
10So the assembly sent twelve thousand fighting men with instructions to go to Jabesh Gilead and put to the sword those living there,
including the women and children. 11"This is what you are to do,"
they said. "Kill every male and every woman who is not a virgin."
12They found among the people living in Jabesh Gilead four hundred
young women who had never slept with a man, and they took them to
the camp at Shiloh in Canaan.
13Then the whole assembly sent an offer of peace to the Benjamites

[a]2 Or *to the house of God* [b]4 Traditionally *peace offerings*

OPEN 1. Has anyone tried to match you up with someone by arranging for a blind date? What happened? **2.** With 20-20 hindsight, how do you view some of the reckless things you've said or done in the past? Do you have "foot-in-mouth" disease, or do you "shoot-first-ask-questions-later"? Explain.

STUDY The civil war is over and Israel grieves the near loss of one of its tribes. The rest of the book of Judges speaks to the fickleness of human nature, the foolishness of war, the seriousness of vows and the bonds of the covenant. **1.** What was the oath the men of Israel took at Mizpah and how would it affect the future of the tribe of Benjamin? Is Israel to be commended or criticized for making this vow? **2.** What caused the change of heart in Israel? Why were they warring one moment, vowing another and weeping the next? **3.** What was Israel's solution to providing wives for the remaining Benjamite men without technically breaking their vow? **4.** Where was God in all this Israelite scheming? When you make plans to "fix" a relationship that is broken, what place does God hold in your plans? **5.** As you look back over this whole story (chs. 19–21), how would you describe the way women were treated? In your opinion, what in the Israelite culture of this time allowed this to go on? Do you see any contemporary parallels in the world

20:47 six hundred men turned and fled. The Benjamites finally succumbed to superior numbers led by God. If these 600 had not escaped, the tribe of Benjamin would have been wiped out.

21:1–25 Israel had nearly destroyed one of its tribes. Though the cause had been just, and the battles directed by God, the Israelites mourned over the loss of their kinsmen, and realized that some provision had to be made for the survival of the tribe of Benjamin.

21:1 taken an oath. The oath not to allow a daughter to marry a Benjamite was not just a vow, but a vow with a curse attached for anyone who might violate it (v. 18).

21:2 weeping bitterly. Israel had done the right thing, according to the law. But the consequences of that action were still disastrous for one of its tribes. The people wept because they could see the terrible condition of their "holy nation."

21:5 failed to assemble. In the midst of their despair, the Israelites remembered another vow and the responsibilities it created. They had vowed to kill anyone of their own people who had failed to participate in the campaign against the Benjamites. They discovered that no assistance had come from Jabesh Gilead.

21:10 twelve thousand. Each of the 11 tribes supplied 1,000 men, with another 1,000 assembled to represent the Benjamites.

21:11 Kill every male and every woman who is not a virgin. This punishment seems brutal, but it was the proper application of the strict covenant law under which Israel was supposed to live.

21:12 took them to the camp. Israel had found a solution to the need for Benjamite wives. They found it in their solution to the Jabesh Gilead problem. By providing the Benjamites with wives from Jabesh Gilead, Israel could skirt around the demands of both their vows (vv. 1,5).

today? How do you believe God feels about this behavior? **6.** What bottom-line slogan sums up your understanding of the book of Judges?

APPLY 1. Israel felt like one of its members had been "cut off." Where are you feeling "cut off" from: Your past? Future inheritance? Friends? Family? **2.** What light has this sobering account of Israel's darker side shed on you and your group? Where do you feel judged by the object lessons? Where do you feel encouraged because God sent a Judge to deliver his people every time, no matter how far they had strayed from him?

at the rock of Rimmon. [14]So the Benjamites returned at that time and
were given the women of Jabesh Gilead who had been spared. But
there were not enough for all of them.
[15]The people grieved for Benjamin, because the LORD had made a
gap in the tribes of Israel. [16]And the elders of the assembly said, "With
the women of Benjamin destroyed, how shall we provide wives for
the men who are left? [17]The Benjamite survivors must have heirs,"
they said, "so that a tribe of Israel will not be wiped out. [18]We can't
give them our daughters as wives, since we Israelites have taken this
oath: 'Cursed be anyone who gives a wife to a Benjamite.' [19]But look,
there is the annual festival of the LORD in Shiloh, to the north of Bethel, and east of the road that goes from Bethel to Shechem, and to the
south of Lebonah."
[20]So they instructed the Benjamites, saying, "Go and hide in the
vineyards [21]and watch. When the girls of Shiloh come out to join in
the dancing, then rush from the vineyards and each of you seize a
wife from the girls of Shiloh and go to the land of Benjamin. [22]When
their fathers or brothers complain to us, we will say to them, 'Do us a
kindness by helping them, because we did not get wives for them
during the war, and you are innocent, since you did not give your
daughters to them.' "
[23]So that is what the Benjamites did. While the girls were dancing,
each man caught one and carried her off to be his wife. Then they returned to their inheritance and rebuilt the towns and settled in them.
[24]At that time the Israelites left that place and went home to their
tribes and clans, each to his own inheritance.
[25]In those days Israel had no king; everyone did as he saw fit.

21:19 annual festival of the LORD. This event was probably the Feast of the Tabernacles (Num. 29:12–40).

21:21 seize a wife. Since all their scheming around their vows had not provided the Benjamites with enough women, the Israelites decided to just allow the Benjamites to "kidnap" women. Since the women weren't actually given to them, the vow was not formally breached.

21:22 When their fathers or brothers complain. It would be only natural that the kidnapping of a sister or daughter would cause some problems. Israel tried to anticipate this reaction and prepared a standard argument to be used in response.

Ruth

Author. We do not know for certain who wrote the book of Ruth. Most traditions suggest that Samuel was the author.

Date. The events described in Ruth probably occurred during the time of the judges (Ruth 1:1) over a span of fifteen to twenty years. The book itself was probably written during David's or Solomon's reign. If so, the date would fall between 1000–950 B.C.

Personal Reading	Group Study Topic and Reading	
1:1–22	Naomi and Ruth	1:1–22
2:1–23	Ruth Meets Boaz	2:1–23
3:1–18	At the Threshing Floor	3:1–18
4:1–22	Boaz Marries Ruth	4:1–22

Purpose. The book of Ruth reveals much about the Israelite culture during the time of the judges. It also reveals much about the nature of God as he provided for a destitute woman and graciously included a foreigner in the Messianic bloodline, from which both King David and Jesus Christ were born. In a practical way, the book of Ruth also establishes David's rights to the throne by establishing his lineage. Ruth closes with the birth of Obed, David's grandfather.

Historical Background. The book of Ruth is a beam of light in a dark period of Israel's history. In a time of repeated apostasy, punishment, and deliverance, Ruth reveals an intimate portrait of a good life. More information on this dark period can be found in the book of Judges. While war rages through much of the era, the events of Ruth take place during a time of peace between Moab and Israel.

The book of Judges shows how God used Israel's neighbors as tools of punishment. In contrast, the book of Ruth shows how one of those neighbors, by embracing the Law that the Israelites rejected, was an instrument of blessing. Among the disturbing public history of the time of the judges, the private history of Ruth is a story of hope.

Widows and Orphans. God's laws for the Hebrews consistently provided for those who had nothing: the poor, the widows and the orphans. God expected his people to take care of their own, to be good neighbors and to feel the pain of the less fortunate among them. Some of these laws protected slaves from paying off debts. Others protected foreigners who wandered through the land. Still others protected the unjustly accused. The book of Ruth hinges on the law of the kinsman-redeemer. If a woman was widowed, the next of kin was responsible to marry her and provide her with children. This protected not only the woman, but also the legacy of her deceased husband.

OPEN 1. What was the economic climate like for the family in which you were raised? 2. When have you felt alone in the world, or most cared for? Explain.

STUDY 1. What is the climate of the times for Naomi? What are her personal disasters (vv. 1–5)? 2. Without husband or sons, what crisis is Naomi facing (vv. 11–13)? In a male-dominated, pre-welfare age, how important would male relatives be for widows? 3. What ethnic hatred complicates prospects for her daughters-in-law? Why this hatred of the Moabites (Gen. 19:30–38; Num. 25:1–3; Deut. 23:2–4)? 4. Given the social problems facing these widows, why do you think Naomi tells Ruth and Orpah to return to their families? Orpah returns to her family while Ruth remains with Naomi, both out of loyalty. Which action was most surprising? Most expected? Why? 5. Both Ruth (vv. 16–17) and Naomi (vv. 20–21) confess God's sovereign control of events, each in her own way. What truth does each convey of God? Of themselves? Of their success in coping with stress? Which confession do you think would most startle the original readers? Why?

APPLY 1. Like Ruth, have you ever had to crossover to another ethnic or cultural group? Were you able to assimilate or did you remain a stranger? 2. What kinds of groups do you feel a stranger among? On what basis: Social class? Race?

Naomi and Ruth

1 In the days when the judges ruled,[a] there was a famine in the land, and a man from Bethlehem in Judah, together with his wife and two sons, went to live for a while in the country of Moab. 2The man's name was Elimelech, his wife's name Naomi, and the names of his two sons were Mahlon and Kilion. They were Ephrathites from Bethlehem, Judah. And they went to Moab and lived there.

3Now Elimelech, Naomi's husband, died, and she was left with her two sons. 4They married Moabite women, one named Orpah and the other Ruth. After they had lived there about ten years, 5both Mahlon and Kilion also died, and Naomi was left without her two sons and her husband.

6When she heard in Moab that the LORD had come to the aid of his people by providing food for them, Naomi and her daughters-in-law prepared to return home from there. 7With her two daughters-in-law she left the place where she had been living and set out on the road that would take them back to the land of Judah.

8Then Naomi said to her two daughters-in-law, "Go back, each of you, to your mother's home. May the LORD show kindness to you, as you have shown to your dead and to me. 9May the LORD grant that each of you will find rest in the home of another husband."

Then she kissed them and they wept aloud 10and said to her, "We will go back with you to your people."

11But Naomi said, "Return home, my daughters. Why would you come with me? Am I going to have any more sons, who could become your husbands? 12Return home, my daughters; I am too old to have another husband. Even if I thought there was still hope for me—even if I had a husband tonight and then gave birth to sons— 13would you wait until they grew up? Would you remain unmarried for them? No, my daughters. It is more bitter for me than for you, because the LORD's hand has gone out against me!"

[a]1 Traditionally *judged*

1:1 when the judges ruled. These events happened after the Hebrews settled in the Promised Land, but before they received their first king, Saul. **Bethlehem.** The Bethlehem where Jesus was born.

1:3 Naomi's husband died. In these times a widow was destitute since women were often unable to work for a living. Naomi was even more at a disadvantage being a widow in a foreign land.

1:4 Moabite. The Moabites were descendants of Lot's son Moab (Gen. 19:30–36). Lot was Abraham's nephew. God had forbidden the Hebrews to marry the Canaanites, but not the Moabites.

1:5 without her two sons and her husband. Naomi was left alone, but in her culture that wasn't the worst of it. She was left with no one to carry on her family name and bloodline, which was of the utmost importance in that day and time.

1:8 Go back. For several reasons Naomi would have seen the prospects for her daughters-in-law as bleak. Since she was widowed and alone, she could offer them few resources. Also, their prospects for marriage back in Bethlehem would be diminished since they were foreigners. **kindness.** The particular brand of kindness described here speaks of God's grace and his loyalty to his covenant people. These women had been good to Naomi and her family. Now she was blessing them with the gracious kindness of God.

1:11 Am I going to have any more sons ... ? According to the Law, when a woman was widowed, her deceased husband's closest relative (often a brother) would step in and care for her. This kept the family inheritance intact. As it stood, Naomi had no one else to offer these women to care for them. **your husbands.** In these ancient days an unmarried woman had no security. Naomi was doing right for Orpah and Ruth to think first and foremost about their marital status.

1:12 I am too old. Naomi seems to feel her options are completely depleted. In this culture a woman's role was to bear children, particularly sons. At one time Naomi had fulfilled that role, but now it had all been taken from her. A lifetime of effort was gone and she had nothing to show for it. She referred to this emptiness in verse 21.

14At this they wept again. Then Orpah kissed her mother-in-law
good-by, but Ruth clung to her.
15"Look," said Naomi, "your sister-in-law is going back to her
people and her gods. Go back with her."
16But Ruth replied, "Don't urge me to leave you or to turn back
from you. Where you go I will go, and where you stay I will stay. Your
people will be my people and your God my God. 17Where you die I will
die, and there I will be buried. May the LORD deal with me, be it ever
so severely, if anything but death separates you and me." 18When
Naomi realized that Ruth was determined to go with her, she stopped
urging her.
19So the two women went on until they came to Bethlehem. When
they arrived in Bethlehem, the whole town was stirred because of
them, and the women exclaimed, "Can this be Naomi?"
20"Don't call me Naomi,[a]" she told them. "Call me Mara,[b] because
the Almighty[c] has made my life very bitter. 21I went away full, but the
LORD has brought me back empty. Why call me Naomi? The LORD has
afflicted[d] me; the Almighty has brought misfortune upon me."
22So Naomi returned from Moab accompanied by Ruth the Moabitess, her daughter-in-law, arriving in Bethlehem as the barley harvest
was beginning.

Ruth Meets Boaz

2 Now Naomi had a relative on her husband's side, from the clan
of Elimelech, a man of standing, whose name was Boaz.
2And Ruth the Moabitess said to Naomi, "Let me go to the fields and
pick up the leftover grain behind anyone in whose eyes I find favor."
Naomi said to her, "Go ahead, my daughter." 3So she went out and
began to glean in the fields behind the harvesters. As it turned out,
she found herself working in a field belonging to Boaz, who was from
the clan of Elimelech.

[a]20 *Naomi* means *pleasant*; also in verse 21. [b]20 *Mara* means *bitter*. [c]20 Hebrew *Shaddai*; also in verse 21 [d]21 Or *has testified against*

Creed? Politics? Past hurts? **3.** Like Ruth, have you embraced God's people as your own? What would you need to do in order to settle into a church? **4.** What has been stressful for you this year? Did you cope like Naomi, Orpah or Ruth? How so? **5.** Who in your life, like Ruth, is loyal to you in your emptiness? How can you be like Ruth to someone else in their loneliness?

OPEN 1. Have you ever worked on a farm? What was it like? **2.** Have you ever been a part of a harvest? What was it like?

STUDY 1. What signs of hope do you see as this chapter opens (vv. 1–3)? As it is harvest time, how long until Naomi and Ruth can grow their own food? In the meantime, how will they meet their most pressing need? **2.** What initiatives do Naomi, Ruth, Boaz and his men take to meet this need? What does that say

1:14 Ruth clung to her. For all Ruth knew at that moment, she was giving up everything that mattered to a woman at that time in order to be loyal to Naomi. This supreme sacrifice on Ruth's part was rewarded in unexpected ways.

1:15 gods. The chief god of Moab was Chemosh. At this point, it must have seemed to Naomi that there was more hope for her daughters-in-law in a culture of false worship than for three women alone traveling from Moab to Bethlehem.

1:16 Ruth made an amazing commitment and sacrifice. She gave up her national identity, her religion, her home and her own personal journey with no promise for any recompense except to share in Naomi's sorrow.

1:17 the LORD. This amounted to a confession of faith for Ruth. She did not swear her loyalty according to her national gods, but to Naomi's God, Jehovah of Israel.

1:20 Naomi. This name meant "sweetness" or "pleasantness." **Mara.** This name meant "bitterness." During the Exodus, the Hebrews arrived at a place named "Marah," which was known for its bitter water (Ex. 15:23).

1:21 full ... empty. The book of Ruth is a story of Naomi's journey from a full to an empty life and back to a full life again. **the LORD has afflicted me.** Still grieving, Naomi acknowledges that God is in control. Whether good times or bad times come, God is the Almighty One.

1:22 Naomi's return to her hometown is significant in several ways. She left in a famine and returned during a harvest (March/April). She returned with a famine in her spirit, yet she had Ruth with her, the one who would bring her such a great harvest of hope.

2:1 relative. The Law brought hope for a widowed woman, if a brother or other relative stepped in to carry on some of the deceased husband's responsibilities (Deut. 25:5–6).

2:2 Let me go. Not simply tagging along, Ruth was taking responsibility for Naomi. It could have been dangerous for her to wander alone in the fields, yet that was the best way to get food. **leftover grain.** In Leviticus 19:9–10, the Hebrews were instructed to leave grain in their fields and grapes in their vineyards for the poor and widowed to glean.

2:3 As it turned out. A typical expression that often denotes a story twist or coincidence, but in this case reveals the provision and providence of God.

about the character of the mother-daughter bond? The owner-harvester rapport? The Hebrew-Moabite fear? The man-woman chemistry? **3.** What hope is awakened at the close of this chapter (vv. 20–22)? What Law about "gleanings" is Boaz heeding (Lev. 19:9–10)? The law provides support for a widow in several ways: Heir for dead brother (Deut. 25:5–10); redeeming related slaves (Lev. 25:47–49); land sold outside the family (Lev. 25:25–28); and avenging a death (Num. 35:19). How do these situations fit Ruth and Naomi? **4.** Do you think Naomi dares to hope in any of these provisions (v. 20)? Or is she still feeling like "Mara" (1:20–21)? How has this change been brought about? What does this reveal about the power of God's love? About Naomi, Ruth and Boaz? **5.** Given the sad state of Israel-Moab relations (Gen. 19:30–38; Num. 25:1–3), what surprising turn of events would the original readers see in this chapter?

APPLY **1.** What mechanisms does your church or group have for coping with the hungry and the homeless? **2.** If you suddenly had no means of supporting yourself, do you think your reaction would be like Orpah, Ruth or Naomi? Why? **3.** When have you shared Naomi's experience of God using a Ruth to show his kindness to you (vv. 11–12)? How did this unmerited act of kindness change you? **4.** Whom do you know who needs to be reminded that God still loves them? What will you do today to demonstrate such love?

4 Just then Boaz arrived from Bethlehem and greeted the harvesters, "The LORD be with you!"
"The LORD bless you!" they called back.
5 Boaz asked the foreman of his harvesters, "Whose young woman
is that?"
6 The foreman replied, "She is the Moabitess who came back from
Moab with Naomi. 7 She said, 'Please let me glean and gather among
the sheaves behind the harvesters.' She went into the field and has
worked steadily from morning till now, except for a short rest in the
shelter."
8 So Boaz said to Ruth, "My daughter, listen to me. Don't go and
glean in another field and don't go away from here. Stay here with my
servant girls. 9 Watch the field where the men are harvesting, and follow along after the girls. I have told the men not to touch you. And
whenever you are thirsty, go and get a drink from the water jars the
men have filled."
10 At this, she bowed down with her face to the ground. She exclaimed, "Why have I found such favor in your eyes that you notice
me—a foreigner?"
11 Boaz replied, "I've been told all about what you have done for
your mother-in-law since the death of your husband—how you left
your father and mother and your homeland and came to live with a
people you did not know before. 12 May the LORD repay you for what
you have done. May you be richly rewarded by the LORD, the God of
Israel, under whose wings you have come to take refuge."
13 "May I continue to find favor in your eyes, my lord," she said.
"You have given me comfort and have spoken kindly to your servant—though I do not have the standing of one of your servant girls."
14 At mealtime Boaz said to her, "Come over here. Have some bread
and dip it in the wine vinegar."
When she sat down with the harvesters, he offered her some roasted grain. She ate all she wanted and had some left over. 15 As she got
up to glean, Boaz gave orders to his men, "Even if she gathers among
the sheaves, don't embarrass her. 16 Rather, pull out some stalks for
her from the bundles and leave them for her to pick up, and don't
rebuke her."
17 So Ruth gleaned in the field until evening. Then she threshed the
barley she had gathered, and it amounted to about an ephah.[a] 18 She
carried it back to town, and her mother-in-law saw how much she

[a] *17* That is, probably about 3/5 bushel (about 22 liters)

2:9 not to touch you. This was a wonderful level of security for Ruth in a world where women had few rights. With the kindness that Boaz showed her, she went from one lonely woman picking up grain amid strangers, to a woman among a group of women in a protected field. That was an amazing provision from God.

2:11 your mother-in-law. Evidently Naomi's story had spread throughout the town. Ruth's reputation of kindness toward Naomi was a good one. Boaz's description of Ruth's journey is reminiscent of his forefather Abram's journey described in Genesis 12:1.

2:12 under whose wings. Boaz used a beautiful image of protection to describe his hopes for Ruth. This same image is used by the psalmist in Psalm 91:4, and by Jesus himself in Matthew 23:37.

2:13 Ruth's character was revealed when she responded to Boaz with humility. She resists opportunism and responds with genuine gratitude.

2:15 The Law regarding gleaning required that the corners of a field and any dropped grain be left untouched for the gleaners. Some generous landowners left up to a fourth of their fields unharvested for the poor—a way of giving back to the community. Boaz went a step further. He asked his men to intentionally leave grain for Ruth.

2:17 she threshed. She beat the grain out from the stalks. **ephah.** About half a bushel, a large amount for one day of gleaning.

had gathered. Ruth also brought out and gave her what she had left
over after she had eaten enough.
19Her mother-in-law asked her, "Where did you glean today? Where
did you work? Blessed be the man who took notice of you!"
Then Ruth told her mother-in-law about the one at whose place
she had been working. "The name of the man I worked with today is
Boaz," she said.
20"The LORD bless him!" Naomi said to her daughter-in-law. "He
has not stopped showing his kindness to the living and the dead."
She added, "That man is our close relative; he is one of our kinsman-
redeemers."
21Then Ruth the Moabitess said, "He even said to me, 'Stay with my
workers until they finish harvesting all my grain.' "
22Naomi said to Ruth her daughter-in-law, "It will be good for you,
my daughter, to go with his girls, because in someone else's field you
might be harmed."
23So Ruth stayed close to the servant girls of Boaz to glean until the
barley and wheat harvests were finished. And she lived with her
mother-in-law.

Ruth and Boaz at the Threshing Floor

3 One day Naomi her mother-in-law said to her, "My daughter,
should I not try to find a home[a] for you, where you will be well
provided for? 2Is not Boaz, with whose servant girls you have been, a
kinsman of ours? Tonight he will be winnowing barley on the threshing floor. 3Wash and perfume yourself, and put on your best clothes.
Then go down to the threshing floor, but don't let him know you are
there until he has finished eating and drinking. 4When he lies down,
note the place where he is lying. Then go and uncover his feet and lie
down. He will tell you what to do."
5"I will do whatever you say," Ruth answered. 6So she went down
to the threshing floor and did everything her mother-in-law told her
to do.
7When Boaz had finished eating and drinking and was in good
spirits, he went over to lie down at the far end of the grain pile. Ruth
approached quietly, uncovered his feet and lay down. 8In the middle

[a]1 Hebrew *find rest* (see Ruth 1:9)

OPEN 1. Did your parents ever encourage you to date, even marry someone? How did you feel about that? **2.** How did (or would) you "pop the question" (or receive it)?

STUDY 1. What instructions does Naomi give to Ruth (vv. 1–4)? In their male-dominated world, how do you account for such boldness? **2.** What factors could lead readers to believe a sexual indiscretion took place: Boaz's "hung over" condition? The secluded "bed"? Naomi's instructions? Uncovering Boaz? Moabite history (Num. 25:1)? Today's culture? Human nature? **3.** What factors assure you that no sexual encounter took place: Uncovering Boaz's feet was not a sexually forward move, but a way to ensure he'd awake on a cold night? "Spread-

2:20 living and the dead. Boaz showed kindness to the dead husbands of Ruth and Naomi by caring for their widows. **kinsman-redeemers.** According to Mosaic Law, a close relative *had the privilege and responsibility* to step in and provide for widows of his extended family. This could happen in a variety of ways, through marriage or through the purchasing of property.

2:23 until the ... harvests were finished. During these few weeks while Ruth was busy gleaning and caring for Naomi, the question remained how the women would fare after the harvest.

3:1 should I not try. Naomi's strategy toward helping Ruth has changed. Before they left Moab, Naomi urged Ruth to abandon her. By this time, though, Naomi wanted to help Ruth in a more positive way, so she counsels the younger woman and by doing so, returns some of Ruth's care.

3:2 winnowing. Both threshing and winnowing were community events. Threshing was beating the grain from the stalks with either "flails" or having oxen walk over the grain. Winnowing was throwing the grain into the air so that the wind would carry away the lighter chaff (like weeds) that had grown up with the grain. After winnowing, the grain was left in piles. Often a landowner (such as Boaz) would spend the night at the threshing floor to protect his product from theft.

3:3 go down to the threshing floor. This was a risky endeavor for Ruth. Women were not usually a part of the festivities. Some even think Ruth's clothes were meant to disguise her until the men were sleeping. To follow Naomi's instructions in this way showed a lot of trust and courage on Ruth's part.

3:4 uncover his feet. A request for marriage.

ing the corner of one's garment" signified a request for marriage and an offer to protect (Ezek. 16:8)? Ruth's indisputable moral integrity (v. 11)? The proper deference of Boaz to others in accord with the law of the kinsman-redeemer (v. 13)? **4.** If found together, who'd likely get blamed: Naomi, Ruth or Boaz (vv. 5–6,14)? Why does Boaz not take advantage of her? Why bless her and consider her proposal (vv. 10–13)?

APPLY 1. If this love story were remade for TV, what liberty with the script might the director take to appeal to viewers? How might that obscure the main point? For whom is this story most appealing, "as is"? **2.** In your circle of friends, what "do's" and "don'ts" of sexual morality prevail? Which "rules" are the first to be bent or broken? **3.** How would Ruth and Boaz fit into your social circle? How does their example help you say "No"?

OPEN 1. Do you like going barefoot? When? Where? **2.** When have you sealed a promise in an unusual way (like being "blood-brothers")?

STUDY 1. From Leviticus 25:23–43 and Deuteronomy 25:5–10, what are God's views on

of the night something startled the man, and he turned and discovered a woman lying at his feet.

9"Who are you?" he asked.

"I am your servant Ruth," she said. "Spread the corner of your garment over me, since you are a kinsman-redeemer."

10"The LORD bless you, my daughter," he replied. "This kindness is greater than that which you showed earlier: You have not run after the younger men, whether rich or poor.
11And now, my daughter, don't be afraid. I will do for you all you ask. All my fellow townsmen know that you are a woman of noble character.
12Although it is true that I am near of kin, there is a kinsman-redeemer nearer than I.
13Stay here for the night, and in the morning if he wants to redeem, good; let him redeem. But if he is not willing, as surely as the LORD lives I will do it. Lie here until morning."

14So she lay at his feet until morning, but got up before anyone could be recognized; and he said, "Don't let it be known that a woman came to the threshing floor."

15He also said, "Bring me the shawl you are wearing and hold it out." When she did so, he poured into it six measures of barley and put it on her. Then he[a] went back to town.

16When Ruth came to her mother-in-law, Naomi asked, "How did it go, my daughter?"

Then she told her everything Boaz had done for her
17and added, "He gave me these six measures of barley, saying, 'Don't go back to your mother-in-law empty-handed.' "

18Then Naomi said, "Wait, my daughter, until you find out what happens. For the man will not rest until the matter is settled today."

Boaz Marries Ruth

4 Meanwhile Boaz went up to the town gate and sat there. When the kinsman-redeemer he had mentioned came along, Boaz said, "Come over here, my friend, and sit down." So he went over and sat down.

2Boaz took ten of the elders of the town and said, "Sit here," and

[a]*15* Most Hebrew manuscripts; many Hebrew manuscripts, Vulgate and Syriac *she*

3:9 Spread the corner of your garment over me. The word used here for "corner" also means "wings." Boaz's blessing to Ruth earlier had mentioned her being under God's wings. Now Ruth was asking to be under Boaz's wings as well.

3:11 fellow townsmen. Probably the elders of the town who often sat at the city gate dispensing wisdom and making judgments. **noble character.** This comment is similar to the one made about Boaz (2:1).

3:12 nearer than I. Here is an example of sophisticated ancient legal customs that involved inheritance and family structure. Boaz knew about a relative closer in bloodline to Ruth's husband than he was. Boaz had to deal with this legal matter before they could move ahead with any plan.

3:13 Stay here. Boaz protected Ruth by not sending her home in the middle of the night. **as surely as the LORD lives.** Boaz acknowledged faith in God as a part of his day-to-day life.

3:15–17 six measures. Perhaps as much as sixty pounds of barley. **empty-handed.** Another beautiful image of God's provision for Naomi as he took her from her emptiness in Moab to her fullness in Bethlehem (1:21).

3:18 the man will not rest. Naomi estimated Boaz well (4:1). Ruth had done what she could. The outcome fell to Boaz.

4:1 went up to the town gate. The area around Jerusalem was hilly and the threshing floor was probably below the city. Boaz went to the city gate where business transactions took place. The kinsman-redeemer relationship involved something similar to a legal contract.

4:2 ten of the elders of the town. These men would function as witnesses of the transaction between Boaz and the nearer relative. No law stipulated ten witnesses, but centuries later that number was required for a synagogue quorum, so it might have had traditional importance here.

they did so. ³Then he said to the kinsman-redeemer, "Naomi, who
has come back from Moab, is selling the piece of land that belonged
to our brother Elimelech. ⁴I thought I should bring the matter to your
attention and suggest that you buy it in the presence of these seated
here and in the presence of the elders of my people. If you will redeem it, do so. But if you[a] will not, tell me, so I will know. For no one
has the right to do it except you, and I am next in line."
"I will redeem it," he said.
⁵Then Boaz said, "On the day you buy the land from Naomi and
from Ruth the Moabitess, you acquire[b] the dead man's widow, in order to maintain the name of the dead with his property."
⁶At this, the kinsman-redeemer said, "Then I cannot redeem it because I might endanger my own estate. You redeem it yourself. I cannot do it."
⁷(Now in earlier times in Israel, for the redemption and transfer of
property to become final, one party took off his sandal and gave it to
the other. This was the method of legalizing transactions in Israel.)
⁸So the kinsman-redeemer said to Boaz, "Buy it yourself." And he
removed his sandal.
⁹Then Boaz announced to the elders and all the people, "Today you
are witnesses that I have bought from Naomi all the property of
Elimelech, Kilion and Mahlon. ¹⁰I have also acquired Ruth the Moabitess, Mahlon's widow, as my wife, in order to maintain the name of
the dead with his property, so that his name will not disappear from
among his family or from the town records. Today you are witnesses!"
¹¹Then the elders and all those at the gate said, "We are witnesses.
May the LORD make the woman who is coming into your home like
Rachel and Leah, who together built up the house of Israel. May you
have standing in Ephrathah and be famous in Bethlehem. ¹²Through
the offspring the LORD gives you by this young woman, may your
family be like that of Perez, whom Tamar bore to Judah."

The Genealogy of David

¹³So Boaz took Ruth and she became his wife. Then he went to her,
and the LORD enabled her to conceive, and she gave birth to a son.

[a]4 Many Hebrew manuscripts, Septuagint, Vulgate and Syriac; most Hebrew manuscripts *he* [b]5 Hebrew; Vulgate and Syriac *Naomi, you acquire Ruth the Moabitess,*

property, poverty and posterity? Given her tenuous position, how would these laws protect Naomi? **2.** What cost is involved for the kinsman-redeemer who follows each of these laws? If a woman marries the kinsman, how much of her property goes to him? How much to her son? How might this account for the nameless redeemer's reluctance to marry Ruth (v. 6)? **3.** What does it say about Boaz that he is willing to take on all the expenses and duties, when he will get nothing tangible in return? What ancestor of Boaz was born from the same practice of this kinsman-redeemer law (vv. 12,18–21; Gen. 38)? How might that have influenced his choice of wife?

APPLY 1. How large a social problem are "the poor, the hungry and the homeless"? How could the biblical principle of gleaning (salvaging or recycling) be applied to your situation? **2.** When have you faced great physical need? How did God provide for you? How is your story like Naomi's and Ruth's?

OPEN 1. Of which ancestors are you very proud? **2.** What would you like to be known for?

STUDY 1. How is the birth of Obed announced? How is

4:3 the piece of land. Because the Hebrews' inheritance was the land God had promised them, each tribe and each family treasured their land. If Naomi's poverty caused her to sell the land, fellow tribesmen were obliged to buy it to keep it within the family.

4:5 maintain the name of the dead. This was the heart of the Law of the kinsman-redeemer. While the Law provided for the family to maintain their inheritance and for a widow to be cared for, the crux was that a man's legacy not be taken away from him even in death. Ruth was honoring and maintaining Mahlon's (her husband, Naomi's son) legacy.

4:6 endanger my own estate. If Naomi had been the only widow involved, she would not have endangered this man's estate. She was past childbearing years. Ruth, on the other hand, could bear sons who would receive part of Ruth's estate, but also the kinsman-redeemer's estate after his death. Ruth's Moabite heritage may have also been a factor in his hesitation.

4:9 bought from Naomi. While Naomi was neither part of the proceedings nor the woman in question, ultimately her right to the land was being transferred.

4:11 Rachel and Leah. The 12 tribes of Israel descended from these two women, the wives of Jacob (who was also called Israel). The elders were blessing Boaz in mentioning these matriarchs.

4:12 Perez. An ancestor of Boaz, Perez was the product of a Levirate union. Tamar was first widowed by Er, then eventually Judah, Er's father, took her in. She bore him twin sons, Perez and Zerah (Gen. 38).

4:13–17 gave birth to a son. At this point, Naomi had come full circle in her journey. She left Bethlehem with a family, then lost them all, and saved Ruth. But through God's provision, Naomi

Ruth's selfless devotion celebrated? What is the point of this unusual birth announcement? **2.** Why do you think the story of Ruth concludes with a genealogy of David? Why two such genealogies (vv. 17–22)? **3.** For David and his descendants, who faced numerous challenges to their right to rule, how would this "famous" connection help to legitimize their claims to royalty (Gen. 49:8–12)? **4.** How would Moabite history likely affect the Israelites' view of the Moabites (Gen. 19:30–38; Num. 25:1–3)? And hence, their view of Israelites, such as David, who are linked to the Moabites? (vv. 13–17; 1 Sam. 22:3–4)? **5.** Define "providence." In this story, what evidence do you see for divine providence?

APPLY 1. Where have you seen God act providentially and redemptively on your behalf? Where have you seen God concern himself equally for all people who put their trust in him? **2.** Who is the "untouchable Moabite" in your life—the one whom you keep at arm's length? How will you bridge the gap between you? **3.** Two book titles in the Bible are women's names. What lesson can be learned with respect to this story? **4.** How has your thinking changed about cross-cultural marriages?

14 The women said to Naomi: "Praise be to the LORD, who this day has
not left you without a kinsman-redeemer. May he become famous
throughout Israel! 15 He will renew your life and sustain you in your
old age. For your daughter-in-law, who loves you and who is better to
you than seven sons, has given him birth."
16 Then Naomi took the child, laid him in her lap and cared for him.
17 The women living there said, "Naomi has a son." And they named
him Obed. He was the father of Jesse, the father of David.
18 This, then, is the family line of Perez:

Perez was the father of Hezron,
19 Hezron the father of Ram,
Ram the father of Amminadab,
20 Amminadab the father of Nahshon,
Nahshon the father of Salmon,[a]
21 Salmon the father of Boaz,
Boaz the father of Obed,
22 Obed the father of Jesse,
and Jesse the father of David.

[a]20 A few Hebrew manuscripts, some Septuagint manuscripts and Vulgate (see also verse 21 and Septuagint of 1 Chron. 2:11); most Hebrew manuscripts *Salma*

now held, again, the inheritance of her husband and family.

4:14 Naomi. Even though the story of the book of Ruth centers on the romance between Ruth and Boaz, the conclusion focuses once again on God's provision for Naomi.

4:15 better to you than seven sons. The highest of praise from Hebrew women. Sons were considered of highest value. Seven sons symbolized all you could ever want. They compared Ruth to seven sons.

4:16 laid him in her lap. Joseph had done the same thing with his grandchildren as a symbol of ownership (Gen. 50:22–23)—that they were as real to him as actual sons. At times this action even symbolized adoption.

4:17 Naomi has a son. In the sense that Obed was Naomi's sole heir, this was a true statement.

4:18–22 This genealogy stands as a reminder that God's plan reaches beyond generations. From Naomi's sorrow came a grandchild who established the family line of both King David and then Messiah, Jesus.

1 Samuel

Author. Samuel is certainly credited with part of the authorship of 1 Samuel. Since some of the events described in the book occurred after Samuel's death, more than one author contributed to the writing.

Date. We are not certain when 1 Samuel was written, but it can be placed in a time frame based on the events mentioned in the book. For instance, it does not mention the fall of Samaria (around 720 B.C.), so it must have been written before then. It does, however mention events that happened after the kingdom was divided (around 930 B.C.), so it was written after that time.

Personal Reading	Group Study Topic and Reading	
1:1–28	Birth of Samuel	1:1–28
2:1–36	Eli's Wicked Sons	2:12–26
3:1–7:1	God Calls Samuel	3:1–21
7:2–8:22	Israel's Request	8:1–22
9:1–12:25	Saul Anointed	9:1–10:8
13:1–14:52	Samuel Rebukes Saul	13:1–15
15:1–16:13	David Anointed	16:1–13
16:14–23	David Serves Saul	16:14–23
17:1–58	David and Goliath	17:12–58
18:1–19:24	Saul's Jealousy	18:1–30
20:1–23:29	David and Jonathan	20:1–42
24:1–27:12	David Spares Saul	24:1–22
28:1–31:13	Saul and a Witch	28:1–25

Purpose. The events of 1 Samuel span from the end of the rule of judges through the reign of King Saul. While this is an important factual record of Israel's history, the book also records *why* events occurred. First Samuel does not merely reveal that King Saul's reign ended in failure. It reveals that King Saul's failure stemmed from a lack of trust in God.

Historical Background. The young nation of Israel turned away from God repeatedly. As a result, it suffered the consequences of its apostasy and God's punishment for its disobedience. Throughout the period of the judges, the cycle of apostasy, punishment and deliverance was repeated again and again. Samuel was a judge who delivered his people. His sons were judges as well. Upon the failure of his sons to lead wisely, the elders requested a king. First Samuel is the account of the final failure of Israel under the judges and the anointing of the first king.

The establishment of the monarchy in Israel ushered in a new era in the nation's history. Israel's existence as a nation was promised by God to Abraham, sealed as a covenant with God at Mount Sinai and established with God's leadership in the invasion of Canaan. All of this established Israel as a holy nation, led by God. Israel failed to fulfill this role. The establishment of the kingship is both a result of that failure and the first step into a new and greater age. First Samuel traces the development of the monarchy through the death of Saul, the first king.

Who Was Samuel? The book of 1 Samuel opens with Samuel's mother, Hannah, promising her baby to God's service. When God gave Hannah her baby boy, she eventually left him at the temple to be reared by the priests there. God's strong call on Samuel's life came early. Samuel was considered the last of the judges and the first of the prophets of Israel. God led him through miraculous circumstances to anoint the first and second kings of Israel, Saul and David. Samuel played an enormous role in the life of Israel.

OPEN **1.** Which of your grandparents or great grandparents did you find most interesting? What did they tell you about your other ancestors? **2.** What were some of the family rituals, religious or otherwise, that you were raised with? **3.** What does your name mean?

STUDY Hannah was barren, and in her day, the value of women related to their ability to bear male children. Being barren was a great tragedy. Hannah's husband, Elkanah, shows that his love for her is not changed by her being barren. **1.** Why do you think Hannah's rival went to such pains to provoke her: She was angry since Elkanah favored Hannah? She needed to make Hannah feel like a failure so she could feel like a success? Other? **2.** How does Elkanah show his love for Hannah? Had you been Elkanah, what might you have done to reassure Hannah? **3.** Why does Eli think Hannah is drunk? How does she show the earnestness of her prayer? **4.** What do you think was most influential in making Hannah's pregnancy happen: The earnestness of her prayer? Her vow to give Samuel back to the Lord? Eli's blessing? Or just that she was more relaxed since she had brought her burden to God? **5.** Why did God wait so long to give Hannah a son: To teach her patience? To keep her in suspense? To wait for her commitment to him? Other?

APPLY **1.** When have you wanted something to happen so badly that you were willing to give up almost anything to see it happen? **2.** Have you had an immediate affirmative answer to prayer? How did you acknowledge what the Lord has done for you?

The Birth of Samuel

1 There was a certain man from Ramathaim, a Zuphite[a] from the
hill country of Ephraim, whose name was Elkanah son of
Jeroham, the son of Elihu, the son of Tohu, the son of Zuph,an
Ephraimite. 2He had two wives; one was called Hannah and the other
Peninnah. Peninnah had children, but Hannah had none.
3Year after year this man went up from his town to worship and
sacrifice to the LORD Almighty at Shiloh, where Hophni and Phinehas,
the two sons of Eli, were priests of the LORD. 4Whenever the day came
for Elkanah to sacrifice, he would give portions of the meat to his
wife Peninnah and to all her sons and daughters. 5But to Hannah he
gave a double portion because he loved her, and the LORD had closed
her womb. 6And because the LORD had closed her womb, her rival
kept provoking her in order to irritate her. 7This went on year after
year. Whenever Hannah went up to the house of the LORD, her rival
provoked her till she wept and would not eat. 8Elkanah her husband
would say to her, "Hannah, why are you weeping? Why don't you eat?
Why are you downhearted? Don't I mean more to you than ten sons?"
9Once when they had finished eating and drinking in Shiloh, Hannah stood up. Now Eli the priest was sitting on a chair by the doorpost of the LORD's temple.[b] 10In bitterness of soul Hannah wept much
and prayed to the LORD. 11And she made a vow, saying, "O LORD Almighty, if you will only look upon your servant's misery and remember me, and not forget your servant but give her a son, then I will give
him to the LORD for all the days of his life, and no razor will ever be
used on his head."
12As she kept on praying to the LORD, Eli observed her mouth.
13Hannah was praying in her heart, and her lips were moving but her
voice was not heard. Eli thought she was drunk 14and said to her,
"How long will you keep on getting drunk? Get rid of your wine."
15"Not so, my lord," Hannah replied, "I am a woman who is deeply
troubled. I have not been drinking wine or beer; I was pouring out my
soul to the LORD. 16Do not take your servant for a wicked woman; I
have been praying here out of my great anguish and grief."
17Eli answered, "Go in peace, and may the God of Israel grant you
what you have asked of him."
18She said, "May your servant find favor in your eyes." Then she
went her way and ate something, and her face was no longer downcast.
19Early the next morning they arose and worshiped before the LORD

[a]*1* Or *from Ramathaim Zuphim* [b]*9* That is, tabernacle

1:1 Ramathaim. This probably referred to Ramah, about 15 miles north of Jerusalem. Samuel was born and buried here. **Ephraimite.** Elkanah, Samuel's father, was Ephraimite by residence, but his ancestry was through the tribe of Levi. It was appropriate, then, for Samuel to become a priest *even though his family was from* Ephraim.

1:3 Year after year. Three times a year, Hebrews journeyed to a central location of worship, in this case at Shiloh, to celebrate a national feast. The temple had not yet been built. Shiloh was in the territory of Ephraim. Joshua had settled the tabernacle there as a more permanent structure (Josh. 18:1). This remained the central place of worship until the ark was stolen.

1:5 closed her womb. Infertility was considered a curse from God at this time. To be barren was the greatest shame any woman could bear.

1:9 doorpost. The tabernacle, here called a temple, had been made a more semi-permanent structure than a moveable tent. It was moved several more times before David settled it in Jerusalem where Solomon built a more permanent and glorious structure.

1:11 remember. Hannah wanted God's favor, much like the thief crucified beside Jesus who said, "Remember me when you come into your kingdom."

and then went back to their home at Ramah. Elkanah lay with Hannah his wife, and the LORD remembered her. 20So in the course of time Hannah conceived and gave birth to a son. She named him Samuel,[a] saying, "Because I asked the LORD for him."

Hannah Dedicates Samuel

21When the man Elkanah went up with all his family to offer the annual sacrifice to the LORD and to fulfill his vow, 22Hannah did not go. She said to her husband, "After the boy is weaned, I will take him and present him before the LORD, and he will live there always."

23"Do what seems best to you," Elkanah her husband told her. "Stay here until you have weaned him; only may the LORD make good his[b] word." So the woman stayed at home and nursed her son until she had weaned him.

24After he was weaned, she took the boy with her, young as he was, along with a three-year-old bull,[c] an ephah[d] of flour and a skin of wine, and brought him to the house of the LORD at Shiloh. 25When they had slaughtered the bull, they brought the boy to Eli, 26and she said to him, "As surely as you live, my lord, I am the woman who stood here beside you praying to the LORD. 27I prayed for this child, and the LORD has granted me what I asked of him. 28So now I give him to the LORD. For his whole life he will be given over to the LORD." And he worshiped the LORD there.

Hannah's Prayer

2 Then Hannah prayed and said:

"My heart rejoices in the LORD;
in the LORD my horn[e] is lifted high.
My mouth boasts over my enemies,
for I delight in your deliverance.

2"There is no one holy[f] like the LORD;
there is no one besides you;
there is no Rock like our God.

3"Do not keep talking so proudly
or let your mouth speak such arrogance,
for the LORD is a God who knows,
and by him deeds are weighed.

4"The bows of the warriors are broken,
but those who stumbled are armed with strength.

[a]20 *Samuel* sounds like the Hebrew for *heard of God.* [b]23 Masoretic Text; Dead Sea Scrolls, Septuagint and Syriac *your* [c]24 Dead Sea Scrolls, Septuagint and Syriac; Masoretic Text *with three bulls* [d]24 That is, probably about 3/5 bushel (about 22 liters) [e]1 *Horn* here symbolizes strength; also in verse 10. [f]2 Or *no Holy One*

OPEN 1. Where did your family live when you were three years old? **2.** When did you leave your parent's home?

STUDY Hannah promised God that if he gave her a son, she would give him to the Lord for all his days. In this story we see that she was a person of her word. In this culture, children were traditionally weaned at three years of age, and that is when she chose to follow through with her vow. **1.** Why do you think Hannah decided not to go with Elkanah to offer a sacrifice: The burden of taking an infant on a trip? The emotional strain of being reminded of her vow? Other? **2.** How would you describe the marriage of Hannah and Elkanah, based on this story?

APPLY When has keeping your word been an especially hard thing for you to do?

OPEN 1. What would you consider to be your biggest personal victory? **2.** What experience would you consider to be the high point of your high school years—a time when things went so well that you just felt like bursting forth in song?

STUDY This was a song that Hannah sang to celebrate God's goodness in responding to her prayer and giving her a son. Compare it to the song of Mary when God promised she would bear Jesus (Luke 1:46–56). **1.** How would you summarize the theme of this song: God favors the "underdog"? Don't get too proud of your own accomplishments? God is the "Great Leveler"? One person with God is a majority? Other? **2.** Name four qualities of God proclaimed by this song. Why do you think these qualities were important

---

1:21 fulfill his vow. The fellowship offering was offered at the fulfillment of a vow. Elkanah could have been making his fellowship offering for the fulfillment of Hannah's vow regarding Samuel.

2:1 horn is lifted high. When an animal lifts his horn, it is a show of strength. This phrase meant that Hannah had been brought from a place of barren weakness to a place of strength and honor.

2:2 Rock. An image of God's strength–immovable and unchanging. David quotes this prayer in Psalm 18.

2:4–5 seven children. Hannah did not have seven children (she had six), but her desire was made complete and so "seven" stands as a symbol of that. The other images in these verses reinforce the fact that life does not always turn out as expected, but God does, indeed, have the last word.

to Hannah at this time of her life? **3.** What categories of the "lowly" does this song specifically speak of God "lifting up"? Why does Hannah seem to identify with them? **4.** What does this song imply is the most important key to a successful life?

APPLY 1. At what time in your life might you have identified with the lowly ones in this song—the hungry, the poor, the stumbling and the barren? **2.** When has God lifted you up after you were low? What did God do and how did you feel at the time? **3.** To what degree would you say that you are depending on your own strength right now, and to what degree are you depending on the strength of God for your success in life: 10%–90%? 25%–75%? 50%-50%? 75%–25%? 90%–10%? What do you think *should* be the percentages?

OPEN 1. Who were the bullies in the neighborhood where you were raised? What did they do to intimidate kids? **2.** What did adults (teachers, parents) do to try to "reign in" these bullies? What would you have liked them to do?

STUDY Not only are the people of the land wicked, but those who are supposed to be their spiritual leaders, are even worse. The situation calls for action. Here we see that Eli's attempts at action were weak and ineffectual. **1.** Why did Eli's sons try to extort more meat from the

[5]Those who were full hire themselves out for food,
but those who were hungry hunger no more.
She who was barren has borne seven children,
but she who has had many sons pines away.

[6]"The LORD brings death and makes alive;
he brings down to the grave[a] and raises up.
[7]The LORD sends poverty and wealth;
he humbles and he exalts.
[8]He raises the poor from the dust
and lifts the needy from the ash heap;
he seats them with princes
and has them inherit a throne of honor.

"For the foundations of the earth are the LORD'S;
upon them he has set the world.
[9]He will guard the feet of his saints,
but the wicked will be silenced in darkness.

"It is not by strength that one prevails;
[10] those who oppose the LORD will be shattered.
He will thunder against them from heaven;
the LORD will judge the ends of the earth.

"He will give strength to his king
and exalt the horn of his anointed."

[11]Then Elkanah went home to Ramah, but the boy ministered before the LORD under Eli the priest.

Eli's Wicked Sons

[12]Eli's sons were wicked men; they had no regard for the LORD.
[13]Now it was the practice of the priests with the people that whenever
anyone offered a sacrifice and while the meat was being boiled, the
servant of the priest would come with a three-pronged fork in his
hand. [14]He would plunge it into the pan or kettle or caldron or pot,
and the priest would take for himself whatever the fork brought up.
This is how they treated all the Israelites who came to Shiloh. [15]But
even before the fat was burned, the servant of the priest would come
and say to the man who was sacrificing, "Give the priest some meat
to roast; he won't accept boiled meat from you, but only raw."

[a]6 Hebrew *Sheol*

2:6–8 These images reinforce God's sovereignty to grant blessings as he sees fit.

2:9 not by strength. Hannah had suffered much at the words of Elkanah's other wife, who had ridiculed her barrenness. Hannah had been faithful, though, trusting in God's power and sovereignty. *By her own strength she* had not borne a child, but only by God's strength.

2:10 his king. At this point Israel was not a monarchy, but through Samuel's leadership God would anoint the first and second kings, Saul and David.

2:12 wicked. The people of Israel as a whole were going their own way. The priests, the spiritual leaders of the nation, were not much better. Eli's sons disregarded God's presence among them.

2:13–16 The priests lived off *some* of the offerings brought to the sanctuary. The three-pronged fork was a random method of giving the priests some food, while leaving the amount and portion up to God. Eli's sons chose a method that put the choice in their hands rather than God's.

2:15 even before the fat was burned. The fat belonged to God in all the sacrifices, without exception. For the priests to take meat before the fat had been boiled or burned off was to claim for themselves what belonged to God by his own decree. It was the ultimate disregard and disrespect.

16 If the man said to him, "Let the fat be burned up first, and then
take whatever you want," the servant would then answer, "No, hand
it over now; if you don't, I'll take it by force."
17 This sin of the young men was very great in the LORD's sight, for
they[a] were treating the LORD's offering with contempt.
18 But Samuel was ministering before the LORD—a boy wearing a
linen ephod. 19 Each year his mother made him a little robe and took it
to him when she went up with her husband to offer the annual sacrifice. 20 Eli would bless Elkanah and his wife, saying, "May the LORD
give you children by this woman to take the place of the one she
prayed for and gave to the LORD." Then they would go home. 21 And
the LORD was gracious to Hannah; she conceived and gave birth to
three sons and two daughters. Meanwhile, the boy Samuel grew up
in the presence of the LORD.
22 Now Eli, who was very old, heard about everything his sons were
doing to all Israel and how they slept with the women who served at
the entrance to the Tent of Meeting. 23 So he said to them, "Why do
you do such things? I hear from all the people about these wicked
deeds of yours. 24 No, my sons; it is not a good report that I hear
spreading among the LORD's people. 25 If a man sins against another
man, God[b] may mediate for him; but if a man sins against the LORD,
who will intercede for him?" His sons, however, did not listen to their
father's rebuke, for it was the LORD's will to put them to death.
26 And the boy Samuel continued to grow in stature and in favor
with the LORD and with men.

Prophecy Against the House of Eli

27 Now a man of God came to Eli and said to him, "This is what the
LORD says: 'Did I not clearly reveal myself to your father's house
when they were in Egypt under Pharaoh? 28 I chose your father out of
all the tribes of Israel to be my priest, to go up to my altar, to burn
incense, and to wear an ephod in my presence. I also gave your
father's house all the offerings made with fire by the Israelites. 29 Why
do you[c] scorn my sacrifice and offering that I prescribed for my dwelling? Why do you honor your sons more than me by fattening yourselves on the choice parts of every offering made by my people Israel?'

[a]17 Or *men* [b]25 Or *the judges* [c]29 The Hebrew is plural.

people than was due them: To feed their physical hunger? To feed their desire for power? Other? **2.** What was Hannah's motivation for making the robes for Samuel: Guilt for giving him up? To make sure he remembered her? To just express her love? **3.** What does Eli say is a worse sin? Why? **4.** What impressions do you get of Eli from this story? What kind of father would you say he was? **5.** Why was it the Lord's will to put Eli's sons to death? **6.** Compare verse 26 to Luke 2:52. What significance do you find in this comparison?

APPLY 1. With whom do you have the hardest time standing up for what is right—family members, friends or complete strangers? **2.** What has been the most painful experience you have had when one of your children (or young person) has disregarded what you said to them?

OPEN What special blessings did God give your parents: A great job? Power and influence in their community? Great friends?

STUDY Eli was of the tribe of Levi, through the priestly line of Aaron and his son Ithamar. Being a priest was a great privilege, it also carried great responsibilities. Since Eli had not held his sons to those responsibilities, they would all be punished. **1.** Why did the man of God begin by talking to Eli of the honor conferred

---

2:16 I'll take it by force. This was an act of extortion. These priests were turning God's Law upside down. Sacrifices were to be voluntary to have any meaning at all. This coercion turned an "offering" into a "do it or else."

2:18 ephod. The high priest wore a sacred, ornamental ephod, a sleeveless, tunic-like garment. Samuel's was linen. David wore a linen ephod when he danced before God as he brought the ark of the testimony to Jerusalem (2 Sam. 6:14–15).

2:19 little robe. Hannah dedicated her son to the Lord (1:28). Now she dedicated herself to supporting his service to the Lord. She continued in her gratitude to God. Probably a knee-length, sleeveless garment worn as a base under the ephod.

2:22 women who served. These women are mentioned only one other time (Ex. 38:8) without much detail as to their duties or qualifications. Eli's sons had gotten involved with the women in a way similar to the idol-worshipers of Canaan. Often prostitutes offered sexual favors at their temples as an act of worship to fertility gods. Eli's sons were blatantly insulting God in mimicking that behavior.

2:23 Eli had lost control of his sons Hophni and Phinehas. Whether he could have removed them from office or not, he did nothing except give this verbal reprimand.

2:25 Eli's explanation of his sons' sin is an apt description of the state of the nation at that time. Israel lived with a disregard for God's presence among them, a "Who cares?" attitude.

2:28 A priest's tasks are listed here, but more than performance, God wanted purity of heart and motive. Even if Eli's sons had done these three tasks appropriately (which they did not), their lack of regard for holiness, for God's presence, was a corruption of their office and calling.

upon his father and their family? **2.** Why did God not just punish Eli's sons? Why did he also punish Eli's heirs (Ex. 20:5)? **3.** This was a time when people did not yet believe in eternal life. As such, the reward a person was to have for righteousness was longevity of life. In that context, what is the significance of the fact God tells Eli, "there will not be an old man in your family line"? **4.** What is the most severe punishment God gave Eli: Removal of the family role as priests? Lack of longevity of life? That descendants who lived would cause him much grief and tears?

APPLY In what ways has God blessed you? What responsibilities go with those blessings?

OPEN **1.** When are you most likely to develop "hearing problems": When your spouse is calling you with a job to do? When someone tries to talk to you while you are reading the paper? When you are angry with someone and they are trying to talk to you? **2.** What has been your most embarrassing case of "mistaken identity"?

STUDY Even the greatest of prophets and saints had to at one time or another learn how to hear God's voice. The prophet Samuel learned it through the difficult experience of hearing a message he probably didn't want to hear—a message of doom against his mentor, Eli and his family. **1.** Why was the word of the Lord rare in those days: God was tired of speaking to people who weren't listening? People hadn't learned yet how to hear his word? God was saving up all he had for when Samuel grew up? **2.** What made Eli finally suspect that Samuel was hearing the voice of the Lord? **3.** Why was Samuel afraid to tell

30"Therefore the LORD, the God of Israel, declares: 'I promised that your house and your father's house would minister before me forever.' But now the LORD declares: 'Far be it from me! Those who honor me I will honor, but those who despise me will be disdained. 31The time is coming when I will cut short your strength and the strength of your father's house, so that there will not be an old man in your family line 32and you will see distress in my dwelling. Although good will be done to Israel, in your family line there will never be an old man. 33Every one of you that I do not cut off from my altar will be spared only to blind your eyes with tears and to grieve your heart, and all your descendants will die in the prime of life.

34" 'And what happens to your two sons, Hophni and Phinehas, will be a sign to you—they will both die on the same day. 35I will raise up for myself a faithful priest, who will do according to what is in my heart and mind. I will firmly establish his house, and he will minister before my anointed one always. 36Then everyone left in your family line will come and bow down before him for a piece of silver and a crust of bread and plead, "Appoint me to some priestly office so I can have food to eat." ' "

The Lord Calls Samuel

3 The boy Samuel ministered before the LORD under Eli. In those days the word of the LORD was rare; there were not many visions.

2One night Eli, whose eyes were becoming so weak that he could barely see, was lying down in his usual place. 3The lamp of God had not yet gone out, and Samuel was lying down in the temple[a] of the LORD, where the ark of God was. 4Then the LORD called Samuel.

Samuel answered, "Here I am." 5And he ran to Eli and said, "Here I am; you called me."

But Eli said, "I did not call; go back and lie down." So he went and lay down.

6Again the LORD called, "Samuel!" And Samuel got up and went to Eli and said, "Here I am; you called me."

"My son," Eli said, "I did not call; go back and lie down."

7Now Samuel did not yet know the LORD: The word of the LORD had not yet been revealed to him.

8The LORD called Samuel a third time, and Samuel got up and went to Eli and said, "Here I am; you called me."

Then Eli realized that the LORD was calling the boy. 9So Eli told Samuel, "Go and lie down, and if he calls you, say, 'Speak, LORD, for

[a]3 That is, tabernacle

2:30 your father's. Eli was of the tribe of Levi through the priestly line of Aaron and his son Ithamar. Though the priesthood had gone bad, God kept the office and began to raise up more adequate candidates.

2:31 not be an old man in your family line. The penalty of death was in store for Eli's only two sons. His family line and its priestly dynasty would end (1 Kin. 2:27).

2:35 Ultimately this prophecy was fulfilled through Jesus Christ, God's anointed Messiah. It was fulfilled as well in ancient Israel when the priesthood was taken away from the descendants of Ithamar (of whom Eli was one) and given to the descendants of Eleazar (another son of Aaron).

3:1 the word of the LORD was rare. This verse describes a "lame duck" period in the life of Israel. God was not speaking, nor were his people listening, for all the reasons listed in the previous chapter. Samuel was about to usher in a new day.

3:3 lamp ... had not yet gone out. According to God's instruction, this lamp was to never go out. Keeping it lit and filled with oil was one of the duties of the priests.

your servant is listening.' " So Samuel went and lay down in his
place.
[10]The LORD came and stood there, calling as at the other times,
"Samuel! Samuel!"
Then Samuel said, "Speak, for your servant is listening."
[11]And the LORD said to Samuel: "See, I am about to do something in
Israel that will make the ears of everyone who hears of it tingle. [12]At
that time I will carry out against Eli everything I spoke against his
family—from beginning to end. [13]For I told him that I would judge his
family forever because of the sin he knew about; his sons made
themselves contemptible,[a] and he failed to restrain them. [14]There-
fore, I swore to the house of Eli, 'The guilt of Eli's house will never be
atoned for by sacrifice or offering.' "
[15]Samuel lay down until morning and then opened the doors of the
house of the LORD. He was afraid to tell Eli the vision, [16]but Eli called
him and said, "Samuel, my son."
Samuel answered, "Here I am."
[17]"What was it he said to you?" Eli asked. "Do not hide it from me.
May God deal with you, be it ever so severely, if you hide from me
anything he told you." [18]So Samuel told him everything, hiding nothing from him. Then Eli said, "He is the LORD; let him do what is good
in his eyes."
[19]The LORD was with Samuel as he grew up, and he let none of his
words fall to the ground. [20]And all Israel from Dan to Beersheba recognized that Samuel was attested as a prophet of the LORD. [21]The
LORD continued to appear at Shiloh, and there he revealed himself to
Samuel through his word.

4 And Samuel's word came to all Israel.

The Philistines Capture the Ark

Now the Israelites went out to fight against the Philistines. The
Israelites camped at Ebenezer, and the Philistines at Aphek. [2]The
Philistines deployed their forces to meet Israel, and as the battle
spread, Israel was defeated by the Philistines, who killed about four
thousand of them on the battlefield. [3]When the soldiers returned to
camp, the elders of Israel asked, "Why did the LORD bring defeat upon
us today before the Philistines? Let us bring the ark of the LORD's covenant from Shiloh, so that it[b] may go with us and save us from the
hand of our enemies."
[4]So the people sent men to Shiloh, and they brought back the ark
of the covenant of the LORD Almighty, who is enthroned between the

[a]13 Masoretic Text; an ancient Hebrew scribal tradition and Septuagint *sons blasphemed God* [b]3 Or *he*

Eli about his vision: He feared Eli wanted to "shoot the messenger"? He feared hurting his mentor? He thought if he didn't say anything, it wouldn't really happen? **4.** Why was Eli so insistent on Samuel telling him his vision? **5.** How do you take Eli's response to the bad news in verse 18: He was a fatalist? He had the faith to submit to God whatever happened? He was "being good" to see if he could get a reprieve? **6.** Are there prophets like Samuel today? If so, how do we recognize them?

APPLY 1. What was the most difficult message you ever had to pass on to someone else? **2.** What standards do you use to determine if it is God who is really talking to you? **3.** When has it been hardest for you to say, "He is the LORD; let him do what is good in his eyes"?

OPEN 1. What would you say was the focus of your biggest "battle": Your weight? Poor self-image? Parents? Tough school subjects? The heart of that "special someone"? **2.** What was your worst defeat in that battle?

STUDY While God had given the people of Israel their land, maintaining their hold on that land meant constant battles with surrounding countries. Winning those battles required a faith in God. **1.** How would you describe the elders' reaction to their first battle loss (vv. 2–3): Superstition? Naïve faith? Flawed logic?

3:17 be it ever so severely. This was a common Hebrew expression similar to, but stronger than, "May I regret the day if I don't keep my vow." Ruth used this expression when making her vow of loyalty to Naomi (Ruth 1:17). Jonathan used it in committing his loyalty and protection to David (20:12–13). David, Abner, Ben-Hadad and even Jezebel also spoke these same words.

3:18 let him do. Eli accepted God's verdict, but it was typical of him to sit back, just as he did with his evil sons, rather than doing something positively to bring about a different outcome.

3:19 none of his words fall to the ground. All Samuel's prophecies proved reliable.

4:1 to all Israel. Samuel's prophecies were most welcome because, "In those days the word of the LORD was rare" (3:1).

4:3–5 At first look, the Hebrews did a faithful thing. When they experienced defeat, they turned to God's presence in the Ark of the Covenant. Unfortunately, instead of seeking God's leadership, they made their own decisions and treated the ark like a good luck charm that would bring them victory.

cherubim. And Eli's two sons, Hophni and Phinehas, were there with
the ark of the covenant of God.
5When the ark of the LORD's covenant came into the camp, all
Israel raised such a great shout that the ground shook. 6Hearing the
uproar, the Philistines asked, "What's all this shouting in the Hebrew
camp?"
When they learned that the ark of the LORD had come into the
camp, 7the Philistines were afraid. "A god has come into the camp,"
they said. "We're in trouble! Nothing like this has happened before.
8Woe to us! Who will deliver us from the hand of these mighty gods?
They are the gods who struck the Egyptians with all kinds of plagues
in the desert. 9Be strong, Philistines! Be men, or you will be subject to
the Hebrews, as they have been to you. Be men, and fight!"
10So the Philistines fought, and the Israelites were defeated and
every man fled to his tent. The slaughter was very great; Israel lost
thirty thousand foot soldiers. 11The ark of God was captured, and
Eli's two sons, Hophni and Phinehas, died.

Death of Eli

12That same day a Benjamite ran from the battle line and went to
Shiloh, his clothes torn and dust on his head. 13When he arrived,
there was Eli sitting on his chair by the side of the road, watching,
because his heart feared for the ark of God. When the man entered
the town and told what had happened, the whole town sent up a cry.
14Eli heard the outcry and asked, "What is the meaning of this
uproar?"
The man hurried over to Eli, 15who was ninety-eight years old and
whose eyes were set so that he could not see. 16He told Eli, "I have
just come from the battle line; I fled from it this very day."
Eli asked, "What happened, my son?"
17The man who brought the news replied, "Israel fled before the
Philistines, and the army has suffered heavy losses. Also your two
sons, Hophni and Phinehas, are dead, and the ark of God has been
captured."
18When he mentioned the ark of God, Eli fell backward off his chair
by the side of the gate. His neck was broken and he died, for he was
an old man and heavy. He had led[a] Israel forty years.
19His daughter-in-law, the wife of Phinehas, was pregnant and near
the time of delivery. When she heard the news that the ark of God had
been captured and that her father-in-law and her husband were
dead, she went into labor and gave birth, but was overcome by her
labor pains. 20As she was dying, the women attending her said,

[a]18 Traditionally *judged*

Other? **2.** Why wasn't the presence of the ark enough to win the second battle: Misplaced faith? The determination of the enemy to get the ark? Their "locker room pep talk" (v. 9)? Punishment of Eli's family (2:27–33)? **3.** Do people today sometimes put more faith in symbols than in God himself? If so, in what ways? **4.** Had you been assigned to say something to Israel's twice defeated army, what might you have said?

APPLY When have you felt like you did everything right, but things still turned out wrong?

OPEN 1. When do you remember hearing news so bad that it affected you physically? **2.** When you suspect bad news is coming, are you more apt to want to avoid it or hear it and get it over with?

STUDY Predictions of doom against Eli's family continue to be fulfilled in this story, when news of the loss of the Ark of the Covenant comes to Shiloh. **1.** Why did Eli fear all along for the ark of God? **2.** Which part of the bad news do you think hit Eli the hardest: The loss of the battle? The death of his sons? The capturing of the ark of God? **3.** Why do Eli and the townspeople react so strongly to the news of the ark? **4.** Why is Eli's daughter-in-law not consoled by the birth of her son? **5.** What is the significance of her son's name?

APPLY 1. What part of your life would you consider to be your "glory days"? When did you realize those "glory days" were over? **2.** When all around you seems to be falling apart, where do you find consolation?

4:7 A god. The ark (and the exodus from Egypt, according to this passage) was famous even with Israel's enemies as the focal point of God's presence.

4:11 The ark of God was captured. Given the reputation of the Ark of the Covenant, this was a huge blow to the reputation of God's people, the Hebrews. The ark had not saved them—it was not their talisman—and now it was gone, captured by the enemy. **Hophni and Phinehas.** God had prophesied the death of these sons of Eli because they misused their position as priests (2:25).

4:12 clothes torn and dust on his head. These were symbols of grief and mourning.

4:13 his heart feared for the ark. Eli's fear was that the people would not recover the ark nor were they confident that God was helping and protecting them.

4:18 forty years. Eli's death ended the era of the judges. His leadership probably overlapped with several of Israel's judges, including Samson.

"Don't despair; you have given birth to a son." But she did not respond or pay any attention.

21 She named the boy Ichabod,[a] saying, "The glory has departed from Israel"—because of the capture of the ark of God and the deaths of her father-in-law and her husband.
22 She said, "The glory has departed from Israel, for the ark of God has been captured."

The Ark in Ashdod and Ekron

5 After the Philistines had captured the ark of God, they took it from Ebenezer to Ashdod.
2 Then they carried the ark into Dagon's temple and set it beside Dagon.
3 When the people of Ashdod rose early the next day, there was Dagon, fallen on his face on the ground before the ark of the LORD! They took Dagon and put him back in his place.
4 But the following morning when they rose, there was Dagon, fallen on his face on the ground before the ark of the LORD! His head and hands had been broken off and were lying on the threshold; only his body remained.
5 That is why to this day neither the priests of Dagon nor any others who enter Dagon's temple at Ashdod step on the threshold.

6 The LORD's hand was heavy upon the people of Ashdod and its vicinity; he brought devastation upon them and afflicted them with tumors.[b]
7 When the men of Ashdod saw what was happening, they said, "The ark of the god of Israel must not stay here with us, because his hand is heavy upon us and upon Dagon our god."
8 So they called together all the rulers of the Philistines and asked them, "What shall we do with the ark of the god of Israel?"

They answered, "Have the ark of the god of Israel moved to Gath." So they moved the ark of the God of Israel.

9 But after they had moved it, the LORD's hand was against that city, throwing it into a great panic. He afflicted the people of the city, both young and old, with an outbreak of tumors.[c]
10 So they sent the ark of God to Ekron.

As the ark of God was entering Ekron, the people of Ekron cried out, "They have brought the ark of the god of Israel around to us to kill us and our people."
11 So they called together all the rulers of the Philistines and said, "Send the ark of the god of Israel away; let it go back to its own place, or it[d] will kill us and our people." For death had filled the city with panic; God's hand was very heavy upon it.
12 Those who did not die were afflicted with tumors, and the outcry of the city went up to heaven.

[a]21 *Ichabod* means *no glory.* [b]6 Hebrew; Septuagint and Vulgate *tumors. And rats appeared in their land, and death and destruction were throughout the city* [c]9 Or *with tumors in the groin* (see Septuagint) [d]11 Or *he*

OPEN 1. When have you won something you thought was good that turned out to be a curse: A girl/boy friend? A promotion? An argument you should have lost? Other? **2.** When you make a mistake, how hard is it for you to backtrack and undo it?

STUDY God wanted to punish Israel so he had them lose a battle and the Ark of the Covenant. But that didn't mean he wanted the symbol of his presence to take up permanent residence in another country. **1.** Why did the false god Dagon keep falling over? **2.** What might it have symbolized that Dagon lost his head and hands? Does this tell us about the risk in putting other things ahead of God in our lives? **3.** How did people know their calamities were related to the presence of the ark? **4.** Why did they move the ark from Ashdod to the other cities? **5.** Why were the Philistines so slow about returning the ark to Israel once they realized these calamities were due to its presence?

APPLY 1. What are you making into a "god" that God is trying to topple? **2.** What do you find yourself holding onto, even though you see it hurting you? What needs to happen to convince you to "send it away"?

4:21 Ichabod. "The glory has departed." God was never confined to a man-made box, but the ark represented God's presence throughout the Hebrew history. When it was lost in battle, the people assumed that God had left them.

5:2 Dagon's temple. This temple was located fifty miles from Shiloh, the central sanctuary of the Hebrews. The Philistines' god Dagon was the mythical father of Baal.

5:3 before the ark of the LORD! The ark had been placed in Dagon's temple as a prize that had been won for the god. The next morning, though, Dagon was in a position of submission before the symbol of Jehovah's presence.

5:6 devastation. The destruction that came on Ashdod was not just on the altar of Dagon. The people of the city were physically affected.

5:8 Gath. A town 12 miles southeast of Israel. The same fate that settled on Ashdod fell on the people of Gath, who sent the ark to Ekron with the same results.

5:11 it will kill us. These people acknowledged God's presence but did not worship him. Theirs was a fear without reverence to God.

OPEN **1.** When you did something wrong, what did your parents expect you to do to show you were truly sorry: Just apologize? Do extra chores? Pay for damages? Other? **2.** When have you lost something precious only to find it again months later? How did you respond?

STUDY After the Philistines decided to return the ark, they still had to decide *how* to return it. They reasoned that one as powerful as the Israelite God might be pretty particular about such things! **1.** Why was it important to send a guilt offering along with the ark? **2.** Why does this offering consist of imitation rats and tumors made from gold? Why five of each (vv. 4, 17–18)? **3.** What "history lesson" do the Philistine priests call their people to remember (v. 6)? **4.** What do you make of the test by which the Philistines are to see if their tribulations had really been from God: Mumbo-jumbo? An inspired way to decide? As good of a way as any? **5.** What do the people of Beth Shemesh do to show their gratitude to God for the ark's return? **6.** How do you react to God's striking down those who had looked into the ark: Inspired by God's power and holiness? Concerned about God's love? Nostalgic for Indiana Jones?

APPLY **1.** When did you last feel like God was punishing you? **2.** How can you determine when God is punishing you, and when it is just chance misfortune? **3.** What blessing has your group recently experienced that really calls for a thanksgiving service to God, such as the people had when the ark was returned?

The Ark Returned to Israel

6 When the ark of the LORD had been in Philistine territory seven
months, 2the Philistines called for the priests and the diviners
and said, "What shall we do with the ark of the LORD? Tell us how we
should send it back to its place."
3They answered, "If you return the ark of the god of Israel, do not
send it away empty, but by all means send a guilt offering to him.
Then you will be healed, and you will know why his hand has not
been lifted from you."
4The Philistines asked, "What guilt offering should we send
to him?"
They replied, "Five gold tumors and five gold rats, according to the
number of the Philistine rulers, because the same plague has struck
both you and your rulers. 5Make models of the tumors and of the rats
that are destroying the country, and pay honor to Israel's god.
Perhaps he will lift his hand from you and your gods and your land.
6Why do you harden your hearts as the Egyptians and Pharaoh did?
When he[a] treated them harshly, did they not send the Israelites out so
they could go on their way?
7"Now then, get a new cart ready, with two cows that have calved
and have never been yoked. Hitch the cows to the cart, but take their
calves away and pen them up. 8Take the ark of the LORD and put it on
the cart, and in a chest beside it put the gold objects you are sending
back to him as a guilt offering. Send it on its way, 9but keep watching
it. If it goes up to its own territory, toward Beth Shemesh, then the
LORD has brought this great disaster on us. But if it does not, then we
will know that it was not his hand that struck us and that it happened
to us by chance."
10So they did this. They took two such cows and hitched them to
the cart and penned up their calves. 11They placed the ark of the LORD
on the cart and along with it the chest containing the gold rats and
the models of the tumors. 12Then the cows went straight up toward
Beth Shemesh, keeping on the road and lowing all the way; they did
not turn to the right or to the left. The rulers of the Philistines followed them as far as the border of Beth Shemesh.
13Now the people of Beth Shemesh were harvesting their wheat in
the valley, and when they looked up and saw the ark, they rejoiced at
the sight. 14The cart came to the field of Joshua of Beth Shemesh, and
there it stopped beside a large rock. The people chopped up the wood

[a]6 That is, God

6:2 diviners. Divining was an ancient way of knowing what to do. A test was often involved, such as the one Gideon proposed when he laid his fleece before God. The purpose was guidance about a "yes" or "no" choice by observing a physical phenomenon.

6:3 guilt offering. *God had given* specific instruction to Israel about how to offer a guilt offering. Evidently guilt offerings were present in other cultures as well.

6:4 tumors ... rats. The gold was in the form of the plagues the Philistines had suffered: tumors and rats. The rats may have been carriers of the disease that caused the plague of tumors.

6:5 pay honor. By acknowledging God's control and power over their fate, the Philistines were showing God honor.

6:6 Egyptians and Pharaoh. The story of the exodus had spread far and wide. These priests and diviners were basically saying, "Don't make the same mistake the Egyptians did in standing against God."

6:7 In setting up this "test," the Philistines made the task as difficult as possible. Cows new to the yoke would not know how to pull together. Leaving calves behind would force cows to go against their natural instincts to return the ark to Israel.

6:9 Beth Shemesh. An Israelite border town about 15 miles west of Jerusalem.

of the cart and sacrificed the cows as a burnt offering to the LORD.
15The Levites took down the ark of the LORD, together with the chest
containing the gold objects, and placed them on the large rock. On
that day the people of Beth Shemesh offered burnt offerings and
made sacrifices to the LORD. 16The five rulers of the Philistines saw all
this and then returned that same day to Ekron.
17These are the gold tumors the Philistines sent as a guilt offering
to the LORD—one each for Ashdod, Gaza, Ashkelon, Gath and Ekron.
18And the number of the gold rats was according to the number of
Philistine towns belonging to the five rulers—the fortified towns with
their country villages. The large rock, on which[a] they set the ark of
the LORD, is a witness to this day in the field of Joshua of Beth Shemesh.
19But God struck down some of the men of Beth Shemesh, putting
seventy[b] of them to death because they had looked into the ark of the
LORD. The people mourned because of the heavy blow the LORD had
dealt them, 20and the men of Beth Shemesh asked, "Who can stand in
the presence of the LORD, this holy God? To whom will the ark go up
from here?"
21Then they sent messengers to the people of Kiriath Jearim, saying,
"The Philistines have returned the ark of the LORD. Come down and
7 take it up to your place." 1So the men of KiriathJearim came and
took up the ark of the LORD. They took it to Abinadab's house on
the hill and consecrated Eleazar his son to guard the ark of the LORD.

Samuel Subdues the Philistines at Mizpah

2It was a long time, twenty years in all, that the ark remained at
Kiriath Jearim, and all the people of Israel mourned and sought after
the LORD. 3And Samuel said to the whole house of Israel, "If you are
returning to the LORD with all your hearts, then rid yourselves of the
foreign gods and the Ashtoreths and commit yourselves to the LORD
and serve him only, and he will deliver you out of the hand of the Philistines." 4So the Israelites put away their Baals and Ashtoreths, and
served the LORD only.
5Then Samuel said, "Assemble all Israel at Mizpah and I will intercede with the LORD for you." 6When they had assembled at Mizpah,
they drew water and poured it out before the LORD. On that day they
fasted and there they confessed, "We have sinned against the LORD."
And Samuel was leader[c] of Israel at Mizpah.
7When the Philistines heard that Israel had assembled at Mizpah,
the rulers of the Philistines came up to attack them. And when the
Israelites heard of it, they were afraid because of the Philistines.
8They said to Samuel, "Do not stop crying out to the LORD our God for
us, that he may rescue us from the hand of the Philistines." 9Then

[a]*18* A few Hebrew manuscripts (see also Septuagint); most Hebrew manuscripts *villages as far as Greater Abel, where* [b]*19* A few Hebrew manuscripts; most Hebrew manuscripts and Septuagint *50,070*
[c]*6* Traditionally *judge*

OPEN 1. When you were in grade school and got into trouble, who was most likely to intercede for you: A sibling? One of your parents? A grandparent? **2.** What "Philistines" did you feel most threatened by: Bullies? Your parents? A rival gang? Other? **3.** Whose voice held the most "thunder" when you were this age?

STUDY The return of the ark, along with the leadership of Samuel, seemed to usher in a religious revival in Israel. That revival results in a military victory. **1.** What was most responsible for the people returning to the Lord "with all their hearts": The return of the ark? Fear of the Philistines? The evidence of God's power? **2.** What does Samuel call them to get rid of to show their sincerity? **3.** Why do the Philistines attack Israel during their assembly? **4.** What do you think it was that scared the Philistines and sent them into a panic: Actual thunder from a storm? A thundering voice from heaven? God just "psyched them

6:19 looked into the ark. The ark was more than a national treasure. While the people were glad to have it back, they still were required to treat the ark with the reverence and awe of worshipers, rather than the playfulness of kids who have found a prize.

7:1 Abinadab's house. One claim to fame marked Abinadab's life: the ark stayed in his family for about 100 years. David finally brought the ark to Jerusalem (2 Sam. 6:2–3).

7:2 Kiriath Jearim. About ten miles northwest of Jerusalem, this was modern-day Abu Ghosh.

7:5 Mizpah. Mizpah, a commonplace gathering spot for Israel, was seven miles north of Jerusalem. There Saul would later be presented as king (10:17–21).

out"? **5.** Why did Samuel set up the stone which he named Ebenezer? **6.** What impression do you get of Samuel from this story?

APPLY 1. What is the closest you have come to going through a religious revival in your life? What do you believe brought it on? **2.** What do you need to get rid of right now in order to truly serve the Lord? **3.** If you could set up a monument to show how God has helped you in your life, what would you name it, and where would you put it?

Samuel took a suckling lamb and offered it up as a whole burnt offering to the LORD. He cried out to the LORD on Israel's behalf, and the
LORD answered him.
10While Samuel was sacrificing the burnt offering, the Philistines
drew near to engage Israel in battle. But that day the LORD thundered
with loud thunder against the Philistines and threw them into such a
panic that they were routed before the Israelites. 11The men of Israel
rushed out of Mizpah and pursued the Philistines, slaughtering them
along the way to a point below Beth Car.
12Then Samuel took a stone and set it up between Mizpah and
Shen. He named it Ebenezer,[a] saying, "Thus far has the LORD helped
us." 13So the Philistines were subdued and did not invade Israelite
territory again.
Throughout Samuel's lifetime, the hand of the LORD was against
the Philistines. 14The towns from Ekron to Gath that the Philistines
had captured from Israel were restored to her, and Israel delivered
the neighboring territory from the power of the Philistines. And there
was peace between Israel and the Amorites.
15Samuel continued as judge over Israel all the days of his life.
16From year to year he went on a circuit from Bethel to Gilgal to Mizpah, judging Israel in all those places. 17But he always went back to
Ramah, where his home was, and there he also judged Israel. And he
built an altar there to the LORD.

Israel Asks for a King

8 When Samuel grew old, he appointed his sons as judges for
Israel. 2The name of his firstborn was Joel and the name of his
second was Abijah, and they served at Beersheba. 3But his sons did
not walk in his ways. They turned aside after dishonest gain and
accepted bribes and perverted justice.
4So all the elders of Israel gathered together and came to Samuel at
Ramah. 5They said to him, "You are old, and your sons do not walk in
your ways; now appoint a king to lead[b] us, such as all the other nations have."
6But when they said, "Give us a king to lead us," this displeased
Samuel; so he prayed to the LORD. 7And the LORD told him: "Listen to
all that the people are saying to you; it is not you they have rejected,
but they have rejected me as their king. 8As they have done from the
day I brought them up out of Egypt until this day, forsaking me and
serving other gods, so they are doing to you. 9Now listen to them; but
warn them solemnly and let them know what the king who will reign
over them will do."
10Samuel told all the words of the LORD to the people who were

[a]12 *Ebenezer* means *stone of help.* [b]5 Traditionally *judge;* also in verses 6 and 20

OPEN 1. What has been your toughest experience with being replaced: Being replaced by a new boyfriend/girlfriend? Being replaced on a project at work? Seeing someone else take your position on the ball team? Other? **2.** When have you insisted on having something happen that you later found out was not for the best? Had anyone warned you this would happen?

STUDY For years since God led the Israelites out of Egypt and into the Promised Land, Israel had been without a king. Rather, the nation had been led by judges—individuals called by God not only to judicial functions, but also to rally the people in times of spiritual and military crises. Now during the tenure of Samuel, Israel's last judge, things are about to change. **1.** What were the sins of Samuel's sons? In their position, why are such sins especially evil? **2.** Why do righteous people, as Sam-

---

7:10 the Philistines drew near. While the Philistines harassed the people of Israel throughout their history, this battle marked a new phase in relations between the two peoples: the bully would become the beaten because Israel was obeying God.

8:5 such as all the other nations have. Israel's real motive for requesting a monarchy was now public: "Everyone else is doing it." Apparently the people expressed concerns about the wickedness of Samuel's sons, while valid, it was a cover.

8:7 they have rejected me. God directed Samuel to look at the deeper spiritual issue. Samuel's wounds were understandable. His leadership was being rejected. The more important issue, however, was that God's leadership was being rejected.

asking him for a king. 11He said, "This is what the king who will reign
over you will do: He will take your sons and make them serve with his
chariots and horses, and they will run in front of his chariots. 12Some
he will assign to be commanders of thousands and commanders of
fifties, and others to plow his ground and reap his harvest, and still
others to make weapons of war and equipment for his chariots. 13He
will take your daughters to be perfumers and cooks and bakers. 14He
will take the best of your fields and vineyards and olive groves and
give them to his attendants. 15He will take a tenth of your grain and of
your vintage and give it to his officials and attendants. 16Your menservants and maidservants and the best of your cattle[a] and donkeys he
will take for his own use. 17He will take a tenth of your flocks, and you
yourselves will become his slaves. 18When that day comes, you will
cry out for relief from the king you have chosen, and the LORD will not
answer you in that day."

19But the people refused to listen to Samuel. "No!" they said. "We
want a king over us. 20Then we will be like all the other nations, with
a king to lead us and to go out before us and fight our battles."

21When Samuel heard all that the people said, he repeated it before
the LORD. 22The LORD answered, "Listen to them and give them a
king."

Then Samuel said to the men of Israel, "Everyone go back to his
town."

Samuel Anoints Saul

9 There was a Benjamite, a man of standing, whose name was
Kish son of Abiel, the son of Zeror, the son of Becorath, the son
of Aphiah of Benjamin. 2He had a son named Saul, an impressive
young man without equal among the Israelites—a head taller than
any of the others.

3Now the donkeys belonging to Saul's father Kish were lost, and
Kish said to his son Saul, "Take one of the servants with you and go
and look for the donkeys." 4So he passed through the hill country of
Ephraim and through the area around Shalisha, but they did not find
them. They went on into the district of Shaalim, but the donkeys were
not there. Then he passed through the territory of Benjamin, but they
did not find them.

5When they reached the district of Zuph, Saul said to the servant
who was with him, "Come, let's go back, or my father will stop thinking about the donkeys and start worrying about us."

6But the servant replied, "Look, in this town there is a man of God;
he is highly respected, and everything he says comes true. Let's go
there now. Perhaps he will tell us what way to take."

7Saul said to his servant, "If we go, what can we give the man? The
food in our sacks is gone. We have no gift to take to the man of God.
What do we have?"

[a]16 Septuagint; Hebrew *young men*

uel and Eli, (2:12–26) sometimes have such unrighteous children? **3.** Why were the people so insistent on having a king? **4.** Why does God say, "it is not you they have rejected, but they have rejected me as their king" (v. 7)? **5.** What is Samuel to warn the people about that the king will do? Is this list an accurate description of what you know of the behavior of monarchs? **6.** What benefit do people seek when they willingly submit themselves to autocratic rulers?

APPLY 1. When are you inclined to want or do something just to be "like everyone else"? **2.** In what ways do you reject God as king: By failing to consult him in your decision making? By taking human advice over biblical direction?

OPEN 1. What are you most likely to have to search for: Glasses? Checkbook? Escaped pets? Kids? **2.** When searching for something lost, what is generally your most frequently used strategy: Asking your spouse? Getting the whole family to search? Retracing your steps? **3.** How persistent of a searcher are you? Don't give up until you find it, or "easy come, easy go"?

STUDY Once it was determined to give the people the king they wanted, the task was to find the right person. Samuel, always seeking God's direction, was given guidance on this as well. **1.** Why was it significant that Saul was a head taller than his peers? **2.** Why does Saul consider giving up the search? What does that say about him? **3.** Why might it have been important to have something to give to the man of God? **4.** How does God use what seems like chance circumstances to accomplish his ends? Have you ever been chosen by your spiritual leaders for a task? Did it seem like it was directed by God?

8:11 He will take your sons. Samuel's words carried an underlying question: Do you really know what you are asking for? Every king would have an army, and every army would require soldiers. Those soldiers would be the sons of the Israelites. So in asking for a king, and thus a more formal national identity, the people were offering their sons to war.

9:6 highly respected. From the vantage point of history, we regard prophets as great men of God proclaiming truth. They were, however, practical men who helped solve everyday minor problems, like where the lost donkeys went.

5. How would you have reacted to the words of Samuel in verses 19–20: With awe at his knowledge of the donkeys? Feeling weird that he seemed to know me? With humility concerning his exalting of me and my family? **6.** Why is Saul surprised at his being chosen (v. 21)? **7.** What is it that will change Saul "into a different person" (10:6)?

APPLY 1. When has God used what seemed like chance circumstances in your life? **2.** If you could be changed into a "different person," how would you want to be changed? To what degree are you open to the Holy Spirit changing you?

8The servant answered him again. "Look," he said, "I have a quarter of a shekel[a] of silver. I will give it to the man of God so that he will tell us what way to take." 9(Formerly in Israel, if a man went to inquire of God, he would say, "Come, let us go to the seer," because the prophet of today used to be called a seer.)

10"Good," Saul said to his servant. "Come, let's go." So they set out for the town where the man of God was.

11As they were going up the hill to the town, they met some girls coming out to draw water, and they asked them, "Is the seer here?"

12"He is," they answered. "He's ahead of you. Hurry now; he has just come to our town today, for the people have a sacrifice at the high place. 13As soon as you enter the town, you will find him before he goes up to the high place to eat. The people will not begin eating until he comes, because he must bless the sacrifice; afterward, those who are invited will eat. Go up now; you should find him about this time."

14They went up to the town, and as they were entering it, there was Samuel, coming toward them on his way up to the high place.

15Now the day before Saul came, the LORD had revealed this to Samuel: 16"About this time tomorrow I will send you a man from the land of Benjamin. Anoint him leader over my people Israel; he will deliver my people from the hand of the Philistines. I have looked upon my people, for their cry has reached me."

17When Samuel caught sight of Saul, the LORD said to him, "This is the man I spoke to you about; he will govern my people."

18Saul approached Samuel in the gateway and asked, "Would you please tell me where the seer's house is?"

19"I am the seer," Samuel replied. "Go up ahead of me to the high place, for today you are to eat with me, and in the morning I will let you go and will tell you all that is in your heart. 20As for the donkeys you lost three days ago, do not worry about them; they have been found. And to whom is all the desire of Israel turned, if not to you and all your father's family?"

21Saul answered, "But am I not a Benjamite, from the smallest tribe of Israel, and is not my clan the least of all the clans of the tribe of Benjamin? Why do you say such a thing to me?"

22Then Samuel brought Saul and his servant into the hall and seated them at the head of those who were invited—about thirty in number. 23Samuel said to the cook, "Bring the piece of meat I gave you, the one I told you to lay aside."

24So the cook took up the leg with what was on it and set it in front of Saul. Samuel said, "Here is what has been kept for you. Eat, because it was set aside for you for this occasion, from the time I said, 'I have invited guests.' " And Saul dined with Samuel that day.

25After they came down from the high place to the town, Samuel

[a]8 That is, about 1/10 ounce (about 3 grams)

9:16 Anoint. Anointing someone was a sign of special power. The ceremony usually involved oil poured over someone's head or placed on the face. Often anointing was accompanied by laying hands on the person. Even today some churches anoint in prayers for healing and lay hands on new leaders as the people pray for wisdom and success (Ex. 28:41; 2 Tim. 1:6; James 5:14).

9:21 Benjamite. Benjamin was the youngest of Israel's sons. As a clan, his descendants were warlike and had dwindled in size.

9:24 leg. The leg was the part of the sacrifice usually kept for the priests (Ex. 29:27; Lev. 7:32). Saul's receiving it foreshadowed the honor in store for him.

talked with Saul on the roof of his house. 26They rose about daybreak
and Samuel called to Saul on the roof, "Get ready, and I will send you
on your way." When Saul got ready, he and Samuel went outside together. 27As they were going down to the edge of the town, Samuel
said to Saul, "Tell the servant to go on ahead of us"—and the servant
did so—"but you stay here awhile, so that I may give you a message
from God."

10 Then Samuel took a flask of oil and poured it on Saul's head
and kissed him, saying, "Has not the LORD anointed you
leader over his inheritance?[a] 2When you leave me today, you will meet
two men near Rachel's tomb, at Zelzah on the border of Benjamin.
They will say to you, 'The donkeys you set out to look for have been
found. And now your father has stopped thinking about them and is
worried about you. He is asking, "What shall I do about my son?" '
3"Then you will go on from there until you reach the great tree of
Tabor. Three men going up to God at Bethel will meet you there. One
will be carrying three young goats, another three loaves of bread, and
another a skin of wine. 4They will greet you and offer you two loaves
of bread, which you will accept from them.
5"After that you will go to Gibeah of God, where there is a Philistine
outpost. As you approach the town, you will meet a procession of
prophets coming down from the high place with lyres, tambourines,
flutes and harps being played before them, and they will be prophesying. 6The Spirit of the LORD will come upon you in power, and you will
prophesy with them; and you will be changed into a different person.
7Once these signs are fulfilled, do whatever your hand finds to do, for
God is with you.
8"Go down ahead of me to Gilgal. I will surely come down to you to
sacrifice burnt offerings and fellowship offerings,[b] but you must wait
seven days until I come to you and tell you what you are to do."

Saul Made King

9As Saul turned to leave Samuel, God changed Saul's heart, and all
these signs were fulfilled that day. 10When they arrived at Gibeah, a
procession of prophets met him; the Spirit of God came upon him in
power, and he joined in their prophesying. 11When all those who had
formerly known him saw him prophesying with the prophets, they
asked each other, "What is this that has happened to the son of Kish?
Is Saul also among the prophets?"
12A man who lived there answered, "And who is their father?" So it
became a saying: "Is Saul also among the prophets?" 13After Saul
stopped prophesying, he went to the high place.
14Now Saul's uncle asked him and his servant, "Where have you
been?"
"Looking for the donkeys," he said. "But when we saw they were
not to be found, we went to Samuel."

[a]1 Hebrew; Septuagint and Vulgate *over his people Israel? You will reign over the LORD's people and save them from the power of their enemies round about. And this will be a sign to you that the LORD has anointed you leader over his inheritance:* [b]8 Traditionally *peace offerings*

OPEN 1. Which of the following have you had the biggest "change of heart" about: God and faith? Politics? Your own image of yourself? Marriage and family? Other? **2.** When in your life have you accomplished something that took others (and perhaps yourself) by surprise?

STUDY The private promises made to Saul in 9:1–10:8 now result in a public presentation of Saul as God's choice to lead Israel as king. People react with varying degrees of support and skepticism. **1.** What seems to be the biggest change in Saul? **2.** Why do you think Saul is hesitant to tell his uncle about the kingship (v. 16): Afraid it was a dream? Afraid it might sound egotistical? Thinking it would preempt Samuel's dramatic announcement? **3.** Why does

10:5 Gibeah of God. Gibeah was Saul's hometown in the region of Benjamin. Only here is the town referred to in this unusual way.

10:8 Gilgal. Gilgal was the site of the first Israelite camp after the Israelites crossed the Jordan into the Promised Land (Josh. 4:19).

10:11 What is this. Saul's people were shocked at his presumptuous new role. The citizens of Nazareth asked similar questions about Jesus (Matt. 13:54–56).

Samuel choose this dramatic way of presenting Israel with their new king (vv. 17–24)? **4.** Why was Saul hiding: Shyness? Fear? Wanting his last moment of privacy? **5.** Why was it said that there was no one like Saul among all the people (9:2)? **6.** What do you think was the reasoning behind the skepticism of the troublemakers: He seemed like just another rural rancher? They were jealous? They were just negative people? They knew something about Saul's weakness that other's didn't?

APPLY 1. Who have been the biggest non-believers in your abilities and character throughout your life: Your teacher? Your parents? Your siblings? Yourself? **2.** What would it take to turn the attitude of these "nay-sayers" around: For God to touch their heart? For God to touch *your* heart?

15Saul's uncle said, "Tell me what Samuel said to you."
16Saul replied, "He assured us that the donkeys had been found."
But he did not tell his uncle what Samuel had said about the kingship.
17Samuel summoned the people of Israel to the LORD at Mizpah
18and said to them, "This is what the LORD, the God of Israel, says: 'I
brought Israel up out of Egypt, and I delivered you from the power of
Egypt and all the kingdoms that oppressed you.' 19But you have now
rejected your God, who saves you out of all your calamities and
distresses. And you have said, 'No, set a king over us.' So now present yourselves before the LORD by your tribes and clans."
20When Samuel brought all the tribes of Israel near, the tribe of
Benjamin was chosen. 21Then he brought forward the tribe of Benjamin, clan by clan, and Matri's clan was chosen. Finally Saul son of
Kish was chosen. But when they looked for him, he was not to be
found. 22So they inquired further of the LORD, "Has the man come
here yet?"
And the LORD said, "Yes, he has hidden himself among the
baggage."
23They ran and brought him out, and as he stood among the people
he was a head taller than any of the others. 24Samuel said to all the
people, "Do you see the man the LORD has chosen? There is no one
like him among all the people."
Then the people shouted, "Long live the king!"
25Samuel explained to the people the regulations of the kingship.
He wrote them down on a scroll and deposited it before the LORD.
Then Samuel dismissed the people, each to his own home.
26Saul also went to his home in Gibeah, accompanied by valiant
men whose hearts God had touched. 27But some troublemakers said,
"How can this fellow save us?" They despised him and brought him
no gifts. But Saul kept silent.

OPEN 1. What movie or comic book hero would you have most liked to have had around to rescue you when you were a child? **2.** From what threat would this hero have needed to rescue you?

STUDY While Samuel had conveyed God's selection of Saul as king, and the people had seen that he looked impressive, it remained for Saul to prove his superior strength in defending his people. He was about to show them in a remarkable military

Saul Rescues the City of Jabesh

11 Nahash the Ammonite went up and besieged Jabesh Gilead.
And all the men of Jabesh said to him, "Make a treaty with us,
and we will be subject to you."
2But Nahash the Ammonite replied, "I will make a treaty with you
only on the condition that I gouge out the right eye of every one of
you and so bring disgrace on all Israel."
3The elders of Jabesh said to him, "Give us seven days so we can
send messengers throughout Israel; if no one comes to rescue us, we
will surrender to you."
4When the messengers came to Gibeah of Saul and reported these

10:17 summoned the people. God had made his choice for king. Now Samuel walked through that choice step by step with the leaders and the people of Israel. Mizpah, where this meeting took place, was one of the most common *assembly places for the Hebrews.*

10:18 I delivered you. God reminded the people that their deliverance was his work on their behalf, not the credit of any human leader. While the Israelites were about to inaugurate a new leader, God would still be their deliverer.

10:20 chosen. Urim and Thummim were stones used in making decisions (Ex. 28:30). This process could be compared to drawing straws or throwing dice—how they were actually used is not known.

10:25 regulations of the kingship. This was uncharted territory for Israel except for Moses' instructions about the responsibilities of the king (Deut. 17:14–20). Undoubtedly Moses' instructions would have been included in these regulations.

11:4 Gibeah of Saul. Before Saul's inauguration, this town was referred to as Gibeah of God. Just as any

terms to the people, they all wept aloud. 5Just then Saul was returning from the fields, behind his oxen, and he asked, "What is wrong
with the people? Why are they weeping?" Then they repeated to him
what the men of Jabesh had said.
6When Saul heard their words, the Spirit of God came upon him in
power, and he burned with anger. 7He took a pair of oxen, cut them
into pieces, and sent the pieces by messengers throughout Israel,
proclaiming, "This is what will be done to the oxen of anyone who
does not follow Saul and Samuel." Then the terror of the LORD fell on
the people, and they turned out as one man. 8When Saul mustered
them at Bezek, the men of Israel numbered three hundred thousand
and the men of Judah thirty thousand.
9They told the messengers who had come, "Say to the men of
Jabesh Gilead, 'By the time the sun is hot tomorrow, you will be delivered.' " When the messengers went and reported this to the men of
Jabesh, they were elated. 10They said to the Ammonites, "Tomorrow
we will surrender to you, and you can do to us whatever seems good
to you."
11The next day Saul separated his men into three divisions; during
the last watch of the night they broke into the camp of the Ammonites
and slaughtered them until the heat of the day. Those who survived
were scattered, so that no two of them were left together.

Saul Confirmed as King

12The people then said to Samuel, "Who was it that asked, 'Shall
Saul reign over us?' Bring these men to us and we will put them to
death."
13But Saul said, "No one shall be put to death today, for this day the
LORD has rescued Israel."
14Then Samuel said to the people, "Come, let us go to Gilgal and
there reaffirm the kingship." 15So all the people went to Gilgal and
confirmed Saul as king in the presence of the LORD. There they sacrificed fellowship offerings[a] before the LORD, and Saul and all the Israelites held a great celebration.

Samuel's Farewell Speech

12 Samuel said to all Israel, "I have listened to everything you
said to me and have set a king over you. 2Now you have a
king as your leader. As for me, I am old and gray, and my sons are
here with you. I have been your leader from my youth until this day.

[a]15 Traditionally *peace offerings*

operation. **1.** Why did Nahash want to gouge out the right eye of the men of Jabesh: He was a Sadist? He wanted to disable them from rebelling? He just wanted to show he had power to do it? **2.** Why did Nahash allow the people of Jabesh to wait and see if a rescuer came: He didn't think they could find anyone? He wanted the challenge? He didn't want to make a final assault unless he had to? **3.** What is Saul doing when news of the threat to Jabesh comes to him? Why do you think that one designated to become king is so enraged? **4.** Why is Saul's threat a necessary and effective way of mobilizing the people? How would you have called the people to action? **5.** What is most impressive to you about how Saul handles this crisis: His method of securing unanimity of the troops (v. 7)? His confidence in himself (v. 9)? His mercy to those who had opposed him (v. 13)? His humility in attributing the victory to God (v. 13)? **6.** Why does Saul resist the call to put his opponents to death: He needed the men? He was a merciful person? He knew the people needed to be unified? Other?

APPLY 1. How would you identify the "Ammonites" in your life right now—what is bringing the greatest threat to your life: Finances? Relational stress? Inner spiritual turmoil? Career difficulties? To whom are you looking for deliverance? **2.** If you truly felt the Spirit of God come to you in prayer, what would you attempt in order to take charge over these "Ammonites"?

OPEN 1. Have you received parting advice from a parent, grandparent or mentor: When moving out on your own? When getting married? When the person was dying? What was that advice and how did you receive it? **2.** What advice would

---

hometown changes with the fame of its most renowned son, so it was with Gibeah.

11:5 behind his oxen. Saul was selected as king while searching for donkeys. After his inauguration, he went back to tending the fields with oxen. With no kingly business yet on the agenda, Saul had gone back to his normal life.

11:6 Spirit of God. Saul's first official act was prompted by God's power and spirit. Saul's later rule would be characterized by pettiness and indecision, but for now, he begins well.

11:11 during the last watch. Somewhere between 2:00 and 6:00 a.m.

11:13 the LORD. At this early stage of his reign, Saul directed the praise and credit back to God.

11:14 reaffirm the kingship. Perhaps a year had passed since Saul's inauguration. Saul's victory ceremony helps him appear kingly. People of all times and nations respect a leader who acts like one.

11:15 confirmed Saul. Saul had been anointed king by Samuel and recognized as king by the leaders at Mizpah. Now in battle he had proved himself. At this confirmation the people formally honor Saul as their choice, as well as God's choice.

you give now if you were in a similar circumstance?

STUDY The people had asked for a king in part because Samuel was old and ailing. Now, as he has given them that king, he wants to make sure that he has the chance to give some parting advice as well. **1.** Why does Samuel need for the people to acknowledge that he is innocent of wrongdoing: Guilty conscience? Need for affirmation? To establish his moral authority? **2.** What is the purpose of Samuel's history lesson (vv. 6–15)? What is the main lesson he thinks they should learn? **3.** Why was it evil for the people to ask for a king (v. 12)? **4.** What is the "great thing" that God did through Samuel as a sign (v. 17)? **5.** Can you think of anything you have asked for that wasn't good for you? What was God's response? **6.** How are the people to serve the Lord (vv. 20, 24)? **7.** What useless things should the people avoid?

APPLY **1.** Had you asked the people where you work to "testify against you" as Samuel did, what would have been their reaction: A long list of grievances? A testimonial of your virtues? They would wonder why you asked? Other? **2.** What personal stories could you tell of how God has stood by you? **3.** Given what God has done for you, what do you need to do to show that you trust him and serve him "with all your heart"?

---

3 Here I stand. Testify against me in the presence of the LORD and his
anointed. Whose ox have I taken? Whose donkey have I taken? Whom
have I cheated? Whom have I oppressed? From whose hand have I
accepted a bribe to make me shut my eyes? If I have done any of
these, I will make it right."
4 "You have not cheated or oppressed us," they replied. "You have
not taken anything from anyone's hand."
5 Samuel said to them, "The LORD is witness against you, and also
his anointed is witness this day, that you have not found anything in
my hand."
"He is witness," they said.
6 Then Samuel said to the people, "It is the LORD who appointed
Moses and Aaron and brought your forefathers up out of Egypt. 7 Now
then, stand here, because I am going to confront you with evidence
before the LORD as to all the righteous acts performed by the LORD for
you and your fathers.
8 "After Jacob entered Egypt, they cried to the LORD for help, and the
LORD sent Moses and Aaron, who brought your forefathers out of
Egypt and settled them in this place.
9 "But they forgot the LORD their God; so he sold them into the hand
of Sisera, the commander of the army of Hazor, and into the hands of
the Philistines and the king of Moab, who fought against them.
10 They cried out to the LORD and said, 'We have sinned; we have forsaken the LORD and served the Baals and the Ashtoreths. But now
deliver us from the hands of our enemies, and we will serve you.'
11 Then the LORD sent Jerub-Baal,[a] Barak,[b] Jephthah and Samuel,[c] and
he delivered you from the hands of your enemies on every side, so
that you lived securely.
12 "But when you saw that Nahash king of the Ammonites was moving against you, you said to me, 'No, we want a king to rule over us'—
even though the LORD your God was your king. 13 Now here is the king
you have chosen, the one you asked for; see, the LORD has set a king
over you. 14 If you fear the LORD and serve and obey him and do not
rebel against his commands, and if both you and the king who reigns
over you follow the LORD your God—good! 15 But if you do not obey
the LORD, and if you rebel against his commands, his hand will be
against you, as it was against your fathers.

[a] 11 Also called *Gideon* [b] 11 Some Septuagint manuscripts and Syriac; Hebrew *Bedan* [c] 11 Hebrew; some Septuagint manuscripts and Syriac *Samson*

12:3 Here I stand. When the people first came to Samuel to request a king, they cited the failure of his sons to lead them (8:4–7). In the face of this criticism, Samuel defends the integrity of his work.

12:6 It is the LORD who appointed. Samuel confronted the people on their lack of wisdom in requesting a king. He referred to the history of God's leadership. *God had chosen Moses and Aaron* (Ex. 4:14–17), but the people chose a king. They wanted something new.

12:7 confront you with evidence. Samuel switched from defending himself to accusing the people. He seems to be playing the role of God's defense attorney. His key point: God keeps promises. Do the people keep theirs?

12:11 he delivered you. During the time of the judges (the era between Joshua and Samuel), God had cared for Israel in every way, delivering them from *enemies.* The people had developed a repetitive cycle of drawing close to God when they needed help, then falling away after the crisis cooled.

12:12 LORD your God was your king. The heart of Samuel's argument was that God had provided for the people in every way a king would, and more. Their insistence on human leadership rejected God's kingship.

12:14 you and the king ... follow the LORD. Samuel reminded the people that their hankering for a king would not change the original covenant (Deut. 6:1–7) in which God claimed these people as his own and established himself as their provider. The covenant required their wholehearted service, trust and devotion. Establishing a king would not change these terms.

[16]"Now then, stand still and see this great thing the LORD is about
to do before your eyes! [17]Is it not wheat harvest now? I will call upon
the LORD to send thunder and rain. And you will realize what an evil
thing you did in the eyes of the LORD when you asked for a king."
[18]Then Samuel called upon the LORD, and that same day the LORD
sent thunder and rain. So all the people stood in awe of the LORD and
of Samuel.
[19]The people all said to Samuel, "Pray to the LORD your God for
your servants so that we will not die, for we have added to all our
other sins the evil of asking for a king."
[20]"Do not be afraid," Samuel replied. "You have done all this evil;
yet do not turn away from the LORD, but serve the LORD with all your
heart. [21]Do not turn away after useless idols. They can do you no
good, nor can they rescue you, because they are useless. [22]For the
sake of his great name the LORD will not reject his people, because
the LORD was pleased to make you his own. [23]As for me, far be it from
me that I should sin against the LORD by failing to pray for you. And I
will teach you the way that is good and right. [24]But be sure to fear the
LORD and serve him faithfully with all your heart; consider what great
things he has done for you. [25]Yet if you persist in doing evil, both you
and your king will be swept away."

Samuel Rebukes Saul

13 Saul was ⌊thirty⌋[a] years old when he became king, and he
reigned over Israel ⌊forty-⌋[b] two years.
[2]Saul[c] chose three thousand men from Israel; two thousand were
with him at Micmash and in the hill country of Bethel, and a thousand were with Jonathan at Gibeah in Benjamin. The rest of the men
he sent back to their homes.
[3]Jonathan attacked the Philistine outpost at Geba, and the Philistines heard about it. Then Saul had the trumpet blown throughout
the land and said, "Let the Hebrews hear!" [4]So all Israel heard the
news: "Saul has attacked the Philistine outpost, and now Israel has
become a stench to the Philistines." And the people were summoned
to join Saul at Gilgal.
[5]The Philistines assembled to fight Israel, with three thousand[d]

[a]1 A few late manuscripts of the Septuagint; Hebrew does not have *thirty.* [b]1 See the round number in Acts 13:21; Hebrew does not have *forty-.* [c]1,2 *Or and when he had reigned over Israel two years,* [2]*he*
[d]5 Some Septuagint manuscripts and Syriac; Hebrew *thirty thousand*

OPEN 1. How do you generally react when someone is late for an appointment? **2.** What has been your own most embarrassing situation of having been late for something?

STUDY Saul has just been installed as Israel's first king. After leading the people to victory over the Ammonites, Saul now faces another enemy—the Philistines. Although Samuel had distinctly told Saul to wait seven days for him to come and offer sacrifices (10:8) before Israel went to battle, Saul gets impatient and proceeds to offer sacrifices himself. **1.** How do the Hebrews react to Saul's "call to arms"? **2.** What impression do you get of Saul's leadership in this story: Foolhardy or

12:17 wheat harvest ... thunder and rain. These acts of nature were most unusual during the months of the wheat harvest. That's what made this a convincing sign.

12:19 all our other sins. The people are finally clear on the lack of trust that their desire for a king represents.

12:20 yet do not turn away. In their repentance, the people fear God and regret their actions. Samuel's response was simple: king or no king, you can still serve God wholeheartedly. That's what matters.

12:23 I will teach you. The establishment of a monarchy did not supersede the role of the prophets. During Saul's reign (and the reigns of every other king of Israel), prophets prayed for and taught the people, and called kings to examine their spiritual and political leadership.

12:24 consider what great things he has done. Israel is constantly encouraged to remember God's provision. Before Moses died, he reminded the people about the exodus and God's miraculous provisions (Deut. 4:10; 5:15; 7:18). Here, Samuel makes the same case: don't forget what God has done for you.

12:25 both you and your king. This is a graphic reminder that no king could save them from God's discipline or from the consequences of their sin. Israel had to face this lesson many times before finally going into captivity.

13:4 stench. Israel was no longer just a border nation to the Philistines. Saul had laid down the gauntlet, and Israel had become an irritant, an enemy. Relations between the two nations remained strained and belligerent for many years.

13:5 three thousand chariots. Without chariots, the Israelites were outnumbered and under-equipped.

fearless? **3.** What does Saul's rationale for offering sacrifices sound like to you: A valid excuse? A rationalization? A snub of Samuel's authority? Have you ever done something spiritual for the wrong reasons? **4.** How do you feel about Saul's punishment? **5.** How does the number of Saul's men (v. 15) compare to the number of the forces of the Philistines (v. 5)? **6.** Why are Saul's men so poorly armed (vv. 19–21)?

APPLY 1. When have you disregarded a directive from someone in authority? **2.** When you get yourself into difficult circumstances, who are you most likely to blame: Yourself? God? Whoever else is available? **3.** When have you found yourself to be up against overwhelming odds, as Saul was in this story? Who did you rely on at that time?

chariots, six thousand charioteers, and soldiers as numerous as the sand on the seashore. They went up and camped at Micmash, east of Beth Aven. 6When the men of Israel saw that their situation was critical and that their army was hard pressed, they hid in caves and thickets, among the rocks, and in pits and cisterns. 7Some Hebrews even crossed the Jordan to the land of Gad and Gilead.

Saul remained at Gilgal, and all the troops with him were quaking with fear. 8He waited seven days, the time set by Samuel; but Samuel did not come to Gilgal, and Saul's men began to scatter. 9So he said, "Bring me the burnt offering and the fellowship offerings.[a]" And Saul offered up the burnt offering. 10Just as he finished making the offering, Samuel arrived, and Saul went out to greet him.

11"What have you done?" asked Samuel.

Saul replied, "When I saw that the men were scattering, and that you did not come at the set time, and that the Philistines were assembling at Micmash, 12I thought, 'Now the Philistines will come down against me at Gilgal, and I have not sought the LORD's favor.' So I felt compelled to offer the burnt offering."

13"You acted foolishly," Samuel said. "You have not kept the command the LORD your God gave you; if you had, he would have established your kingdom over Israel for all time. 14But now your kingdom will not endure; the LORD has sought out a man after his own heart and appointed him leader of his people, because you have not kept the LORD's command."

15Then Samuel left Gilgal[b] and went up to Gibeah in Benjamin, and Saul counted the men who were with him. They numbered about six hundred.

Israel Without Weapons

16Saul and his son Jonathan and the men with them were staying in Gibeah[c] in Benjamin, while the Philistines camped at Micmash. 17Raiding parties went out from the Philistine camp in three detachments. One turned toward Ophrah in the vicinity of Shual, 18another toward Beth Horon, and the third toward the borderland overlooking the Valley of Zeboim facing the desert.

19Not a blacksmith could be found in the whole land of Israel, because the Philistines had said, "Otherwise the Hebrews will make swords or spears!" 20So all Israel went down to the Philistines to have their plowshares, mattocks, axes and sickles[d] sharpened. 21The price

[a]9 Traditionally *peace offerings* [b]15 Hebrew; Septuagint *Gilgal and went his way; the rest of the people went after Saul to meet the army, and they went out of Gilgal* [c]16 Two Hebrew manuscripts; most Hebrew manuscripts *Geba*, a variant of *Gibeah* [d]20 Septuagint; Hebrew *plowshares*

13:8 men began to scatter. Two years had passed since Samuel and Saul had agreed to meet at Gilgal (10:8). During that time Saul had risen to power, gained his first victory, and begun to gather a more organized army. The loss of these men prompted this fair-weather king to forfeit his relationship with God.

13:9 Saul offered up. Saul was from the tribe of Benjamin, not Levi. Offering sacrifices was not his privilege. His priority was military service, not priestly. This choice was the watershed in Saul's reign. From this point, his decisions fail in wisdom and his influence nosedives.

13:13 You acted foolishly. Saul unknowingly traded his kingdom at this point. He failed to trust ultimately in God for deliverance. Even though his sacrifice was meant to ensure God's blessing, he ignored God's leadership in the way he offered it.

13:14 your kingdom will not endure. Though Saul had three sons, his kingdom never passed through his family line. Because of David's kindness and loyalty, Mephibosheth, Jonathan's son and Saul's grandson, eventually ate at King David's table—the closest any of his descendants came to the monarchy (2 Sam. 9).

13:15 six hundred. Saul had 3,000 soldiers at the start, but he lost 2,400 during the war at Gilgal.

was two thirds of a shekel[a] for sharpening plowshares and mattocks, and a third of a shekel[b] for sharpening forks and axes and for repointing goads.
22So on the day of the battle not a soldier with Saul and Jonathan had a sword or spear in his hand; only Saul and his son Jonathan had them.

Jonathan Attacks the Philistines

23Now a detachment of Philistines had gone out to the pass at Micmash.
14 1One day Jonathan son of Saul said to the young man bearing his armor, "Come, let's go over to the Philistine outpost on the other side." But he did not tell his father.
2Saul was staying on the outskirts of Gibeah under a pomegranate tree in Migron. With him were about six hundred men,
3among whom was Ahijah, who was wearing an ephod. He was a son of Ichabod's brother Ahitub son of Phinehas, the son of Eli, the LORD's priest in Shiloh. No one was aware that Jonathan had left.
4On each side of the pass that Jonathan intended to cross to reach the Philistine outpost was a cliff; one was called Bozez, and the other Seneh.
5One cliff stood to the north toward Micmash, the other to the south toward Geba.
6Jonathan said to his young armor-bearer, "Come, let's go over to the outpost of those uncircumcised fellows. Perhaps the LORD will act in our behalf. Nothing can hinder the LORD from saving, whether by many or by few."
7"Do all that you have in mind," his armor-bearer said. "Go ahead; I am with you heart and soul."
8Jonathan said, "Come, then; we will cross over toward the men and let them see us.
9If they say to us, 'Wait there until we come to you,' we will stay where we are and not go up to them.
10But if they say, 'Come up to us,' we will climb up, because that will be our sign that the LORD has given them into our hands."
11So both of them showed themselves to the Philistine outpost. "Look!" said the Philistines. "The Hebrews are crawling out of the holes they were hiding in."
12The men of the outpost shouted to Jonathan and his armor-bearer, "Come up to us and we'll teach you a lesson."
So Jonathan said to his armor-bearer, "Climb up after me; the LORD has given them into the hand of Israel."
13Jonathan climbed up, using his hands and feet, with his armor-bearer right behind him. The Philistines fell before Jonathan, and his armor-bearer followed and killed behind him.
14In that first attack Jonathan and his armor-bearer killed some twenty men in an area of about half an acre.[c]

[a]21 Hebrew *pim;* that is, about 1/4 ounce (about 8 grams) [b]21 That is, about 1/8 ounce (about 4 grams)
[c]14 Hebrew *half a yoke;* a "yoke" was the land plowed by a yoke of oxen in one day.

OPEN 1. What dangerous activity do you remember doing as an adolescent that you didn't tell your parents about? Did they find out later? **2.** Who was your "partner in crime" in doing mischievous acts when you were a teenager?

STUDY Young men in every era are often eager to test their courage and superior strength, and this was the case in this story of Jonathan, the king's son. **1.** Why did Jonathan decide to not tell his father where they were going? **2.** What did Jonathan mean when he said, "Nothing can hinder the LORD from saving, whether by many or by few"? **3.** What attitude does the Philistine taunt reveal (vv. 11–12)? **4.** Why do you think Jonathan felt so confident of God's blessing?

APPLY 1. What "challenging cliff" might you climb if you could be fully confident of God's blessing? **2.** What is keeping you from attempting that "climb": Fear of taking a risk? Uncertainty about God's direction? Lack of skills? Lack of a supporting friend to go with you?

13:22 sword or spear. The Philistines restricted the Israelites from working with metal to prevent their making weapons. The Israelites went to battle with weapons made only from natural substances—bows, arrows and slingshots. They would be at a disadvantage.

14:1 on the other side. The site of this battle was between two cliffs, Bozez and Seneh (v. 4). The terrain made this a popular battleground.

Israel Routs the Philistines

15 Then panic struck the whole army—those in the camp and field,
and those in the outposts and raiding parties—and the ground
shook. It was a panic sent by God.[a]

16 Saul's lookouts at Gibeah in Benjamin saw the army melting
away in all directions. 17 Then Saul said to the men who were with
him, "Muster the forces and see who has left us." When they did, it
was Jonathan and his armor-bearer who were not there.

18 Saul said to Ahijah, "Bring the ark of God." (At that time it was
with the Israelites.)[b] 19 While Saul was talking to the priest, the tumult
in the Philistine camp increased more and more. So Saul said to the
priest, "Withdraw your hand."

20 Then Saul and all his men assembled and went to the battle. They
found the Philistines in total confusion, striking each other with their
swords. 21 Those Hebrews who had previously been with the Philistines and had gone up with them to their camp went over to the Israelites who were with Saul and Jonathan. 22 When all the Israelites who
had hidden in the hill country of Ephraim heard that the Philistines
were on the run, they joined the battle in hot pursuit. 23 So the LORD
rescued Israel that day, and the battle moved on beyond Beth Aven.

Jonathan Eats Honey

24 Now the men of Israel were in distress that day, because Saul had
bound the people under an oath, saying, "Cursed be any man who
eats food before evening comes, before I have avenged myself on my
enemies!" So none of the troops tasted food.

25 The entire army[c] entered the woods, and there was honey on the
ground. 26 When they went into the woods, they saw the honey oozing
out, yet no one put his hand to his mouth, because they feared the
oath. 27 But Jonathan had not heard that his father had bound the
people with the oath, so he reached out the end of the staff that was
in his hand and dipped it into the honeycomb. He raised his hand to
his mouth, and his eyes brightened.[d] 28 Then one of the soldiers told
him, "Your father bound the army under a strict oath, saying, 'Cursed
be any man who eats food today!' That is why the men are faint."

29 Jonathan said, "My father has made trouble for the country. See
how my eyes brightened[e] when I tasted a little of this honey. 30 How
much better it would have been if the men had eaten today some of

[a] 15 Or a terrible panic [b] 18 Hebrew; Septuagint *"Bring the ephod." (At that time he wore the ephod before the Israelites.)* [c] 25 Or *Now all the people of the land* [d] 27 Or *his strength was renewed* [e] 29 Or *my strength was renewed*

OPEN 1. What is most likely to throw you into a panic: Letter from the IRS? Note from your boss? Call from your child's teacher? **2.** When under stress, are you: Calm and cool? Panic-stricken? Other?

STUDY The Philistines' confidence was broken, and they were thrown into a panic. Saul's army takes advantage of the confusion. **1.** Why does Saul want to know who had left them? **2.** Why is it significant that Saul asks for the ark of God? **3.** Who deserved the most credit for this victory? How is that made evident?

APPLY 1. When has a job or challenge you were afraid of facing been turned into a "piece of cake" through God's help? **2.** What "enemy" are you facing right now that you would like to see God "throw into a panic"?

OPEN 1. What is the hardest food for you to do without? **2.** When it comes to dieting or fasting, how disciplined are you?

STUDY Saul wants to finalize the victory described in verses 15–23 and to show commitment, he vows that none of his army shall eat until his vengeance on the Philistines was complete. In this story we see how that vow almost results in disaster. **1.** What effect did Saul's vow have on the soldiers in his army? **2.** When Jonathan was told about the vow, how would you describe his reaction: Practical? Frank? Disrespectful? Arrogant? **3.** Why was there a problem with eating meat with blood in it (v. 33)? **4.** What does Saul assume when God does not answer his inquiry in verse 37? **5.** What method does Saul use to decide who "sinned"? **6.** What saves Jonathan's life? Why do the men of the army stand by Jon-

---

14:15 panic sent by God. This was not the first time God had sent a panic to the enemies of the Israelites. When the Philistines captured the ark, God sent a panic, but through plagues rather than earthquakes (5:9–10).

14:18 Bring the ark. Some manu*scripts refer to the ephod here rather* than the actual ark of the testimony. The ephod was used for making decisions with the Urim and Thummim.

14:19 Withdraw your hand. The priests made decisions by reaching into the pocket of the ephod and pulling out stones. Saul was telling the priest to go ahead, check the stone and make the decision.

14:23 the LORD rescued. Neither Saul nor Jonathan actually won the battle. God provided the victory.

14:24–46 Saul's lack of wisdom becomes obvious in this passage. He makes rash vows that endanger and overextend his army. Then he threatens to execute his own son for breaking a foolish rule. Saul had changed from a man who humbly missed his own inauguration to a man who put ego and power ahead of life, even his son's life.

14:24 oath. An oath was much more serious and binding than a mere promise or intention. **I have avenged myself.** The conflict with the Philistines had become personal for Saul. He was no longer representing God's interests. Instead, he was using the resources of his nation and army for his own agenda.

the plunder they took from their enemies. Would not the slaughter of
the Philistines have been even greater?"
[31]That day, after the Israelites had struck down the Philistines from
Micmash to Aijalon, they were exhausted. [32]They pounced on the
plunder and, taking sheep, cattle and calves, they butchered them on
the ground and ate them, together with the blood. [33]Then someone
said to Saul, "Look, the men are sinning against the LORD by eating
meat that has blood in it."

"You have broken faith," he said. "Roll a large stone over here at
once." [34]Then he said, "Go out among the men and tell them, 'Each of
you bring me your cattle and sheep, and slaughter them here and eat
them. Do not sin against the LORD by eating meat with blood still
in it.' "

So everyone brought his ox that night and slaughtered it there.
[35]Then Saul built an altar to the LORD; it was the first time he had
done this.

[36]Saul said, "Let us go down after the Philistines by night and plunder them till dawn, and let us not leave one of them alive."

"Do whatever seems best to you," they replied.

But the priest said, "Let us inquire of God here."
[37]So Saul asked God, "Shall I go down after the Philistines? Will you
give them into Israel's hand?" But God did not answer him that day.
[38]Saul therefore said, "Come here, all you who are leaders of the
army, and let us find out what sin has been committed today. [39]As
surely as the LORD who rescues Israel lives, even if it lies with my son
Jonathan, he must die." But not one of the men said a word.
[40]Saul then said to all the Israelites, "You stand over there; I and
Jonathan my son will stand over here."

"Do what seems best to you," the men replied.
[41]Then Saul prayed to the LORD, the God of Israel, "Give me the
right answer."[a] And Jonathan and Saul were taken by lot, and the men
were cleared. [42]Saul said, "Cast the lot between me and Jonathan my
son." And Jonathan was taken.
[43]Then Saul said to Jonathan, "Tell me what you have done."

So Jonathan told him, "I merely tasted a little honey with the end of
my staff. And now must I die?"
[44]Saul said, "May God deal with me, be it ever so severely, if you do
not die, Jonathan."
[45]But the men said to Saul, "Should Jonathan die—he who has
brought about this great deliverance in Israel? Never! As surely as the
LORD lives, not a hair of his head will fall to the ground, for he did this
today with God's help." So the men rescued Jonathan, and he was
not put to death.

[a]41 Hebrew; Septuagint *"Why have you not answered your servant today? If the fault is in me or my son Jonathan, respond with Urim, but if the men of Israel are at fault, respond with Thummim."*

athan? How do you think this incident affected how the men of the army viewed Saul's leadership? **7.** Noting especially verses 48 and 52, what would you say were Saul's greatest weaknesses?

APPLY 1. What enemy have you fought all your life: A poor self-image? Prejudice? Health problems? Sexual temptation? Other? **2.** In what ways have your own rash decisions interfered with winning the battle? **3.** What could you do to bring God more on board in this battle?

14:33 meat that has blood in it. One of the main guidelines for the kosher diet was the "no blood" rule. The blood represented the life of the person or creature (Gen. 9:4; Lev. 17:11; Deut. 12:16). To this day, draining of blood is an important part of making meat kosher.

14:35 it was the first time. Saul is described often as a person who had not shown much spiritual sensitivity before his kingship.

14:37 God did not answer him. Saul's inquiry probably took the form of a priest working with the Urim and Thummim.

14:45 with God's help. Saul's army, and not Saul, took the responsibility of defending Saul's son and acknowledging God's help. Saul should have done both himself.

46 Then Saul stopped pursuing the Philistines, and they withdrew to
their own land.
47 After Saul had assumed rule over Israel, he fought against their
enemies on every side: Moab, the Ammonites, Edom, the kings[a] of
Zobah, and the Philistines. Wherever he turned, he inflicted punishment on them.[b] 48 He fought valiantly and defeated the Amalekites,
delivering Israel from the hands of those who had plundered them.

Saul's Family

49 Saul's sons were Jonathan, Ishvi and Malki-Shua. The name of
his older daughter was Merab, and that of the younger was Michal.
50 His wife's name was Ahinoam daughter of Ahimaaz. The name of
the commander of Saul's army was Abner son of Ner, and Ner was
Saul's uncle. 51 Saul's father Kish and Abner's father Ner were sons of
Abiel.
52 All the days of Saul there was bitter war with the Philistines, and
whenever Saul saw a mighty or brave man, he took him into his
service.

OPEN **1.** What would you say was the biggest regret of your high school years: The boy/girl who got away? A youthful indiscretion? Not preparing better for a good profession? Other? **2.** When you have something that you regret, are you more likely to dwell on it, or simply move on to whatever is next?

STUDY We don't often think of God regretting things he has done, but the Bible does record such a case. There was a time when God regretted creating humankind (Gen. 6:6), and here in this story God regrets making Saul king. **1.** What does God command Saul to do in verse 3? What had the Amalekites done that God wanted to punish them in this way (v. 2; Deut. 25:17–19)? **2.** How do you react to God commanding total destruction of the Amalekites, even their children? Should we just accept such troubling incidents, or is it okay to question them? **3.** What does Saul do that he had been commanded not to do? **4.** How does Samuel react to God's judgment against Saul (vv. 11,

The Lord Rejects Saul as King

15 Samuel said to Saul, "I am the one the LORD sent to anoint
you king over his people Israel; so listen now to the message
from the LORD. 2 This is what the LORD Almighty says: 'I will punish the
Amalekites for what they did to Israel when they waylaid them as
they came up from Egypt. 3 Now go, attack the Amalekites and totally
destroy[c] everything that belongs to them. Do not spare them; put to
death men and women, children and infants, cattle and sheep, camels and donkeys.' "
4 So Saul summoned the men and mustered them at Telaim—two
hundred thousand foot soldiers and ten thousand men from Judah.
5 Saul went to the city of Amalek and set an ambush in the ravine.
6 Then he said to the Kenites, "Go away, leave the Amalekites so that I
do not destroy you along with them; for you showed kindness to all
the Israelites when they came up out of Egypt." So the Kenites moved
away from the Amalekites.
7 Then Saul attacked the Amalekites all the way from Havilah to Shur,
to the east of Egypt. 8 He took Agag king of the Amalekites alive, and all
his people he totally destroyed with the sword. 9 But Saul and the army
spared Agag and the best of the sheep and cattle, the fat calves[d] and

[a]47 Masoretic Text; Dead Sea Scrolls and Septuagint *king* [b]47 Hebrew; Septuagint *he was victorious* [c]3 The Hebrew term refers to the irrevocable giving over of things or persons to the LORD, often by totally destroying them; also in verses 8, 9, 15, 18, 20 and 21. [d]9 Or *the grown bulls*; the meaning of the Hebrew for this phrase is uncertain.

14:52 Philistines. The Philistines occupied the land between Israel and the Mediterranean Sea. No natural boundaries—like rivers or valleys—separated the two nations, so the dividing line was always in dispute.

15:1–35 Saul proves that his highest ambition is to build his own kingdom, rather than building the nation under God's leadership.

15:3 destroy everything. This was holy war—God's judgment of a people working against him by opposing the Israelites.

15:6 Kenites. Jethro, Moses' father-in-law, was of the Kenite tribe. Once, he gave Moses administrative advice (Ex. 18:20–23). He also traveled with Moses to help as a guide (Num. 10:29–32).

15:9 they were unwilling to destroy completely. God had commanded the destruction of everything, but Saul seems to be saving the best for himself. He was acting like worshipers who promised God the best sacrifices, but brought blemished animals instead, keeping the best for themselves. This was blatant disobedience. God was grieved, because of the disobedience and lack of respect.

lambs—everything that was good. These they were unwilling to
destroy completely, but everything that was despised and weak they
totally destroyed.
10Then the word of the LORD came to Samuel: 11"I am grieved that I
have made Saul king, because he has turned away from me and has
not carried out my instructions." Samuel was troubled, and he cried
out to the LORD all that night.
12Early in the morning Samuel got up and went to meet Saul, but
he was told, "Saul has gone to Carmel. There he has set up a monument in his own honor and has turned and gone on down to Gilgal."
13When Samuel reached him, Saul said, "The LORD bless you! I have
carried out the LORD's instructions."
14But Samuel said, "What then is this bleating of sheep in my ears?
What is this lowing of cattle that I hear?"
15Saul answered, "The soldiers brought them from the Amalekites;
they spared the best of the sheep and cattle to sacrifice to the LORD
your God, but we totally destroyed the rest."
16"Stop!" Samuel said to Saul. "Let me tell you what the LORD said
to me last night."
"Tell me," Saul replied.
17Samuel said, "Although you were once small in your own
eyes, did you not become the head of the tribes of Israel? The LORD
anointed you king over Israel. 18And he sent you on a mission, saying,
'Go and completely destroy those wicked people, the Amalekites;
make war on them until you have wiped them out.' 19Why did you not
obey the LORD? Why did you pounce on the plunder and do evil in the
eyes of the LORD?"
20"But I did obey the LORD," Saul said. "I went on the mission the
LORD assigned me. I completely destroyed the Amalekites and
brought back Agag their king. 21The soldiers took sheep and cattle
from the plunder, the best of what was devoted to God, in order to
sacrifice them to the LORD your God at Gilgal."
22But Samuel replied:

"Does the LORD delight in burnt offerings and sacrifices
as much as in obeying the voice of the LORD?
To obey is better than sacrifice,
and to heed is better than the fat of rams.
23For rebellion is like the sin of divination,
and arrogance like the evil of idolatry.
Because you have rejected the word of the LORD,
he has rejected you as king."

24Then Saul said to Samuel, "I have sinned. I violated the LORD's
command and your instructions. I was afraid of the people and so I

35)? 5. What is Saul doing when Samuel goes searching for him (v. 12)? What is the implication of verse 17 concerning how Saul now sees himself? **6.** What do verses 19–23 say is the main thing God desires from us? **7.** What symbolism does Samuel see in the torn hem of his robe? **8.** Why is Saul not forgiven: Insincerity? He had missed his chance? Too much damage had been done? Spiritually he was forgiven—he just didn't get his job back? Other?

APPLY 1. Have you felt sorry for something you had done, either because of the damage that had been done, or because it was "too little, too late"? **2.** What do you see as the most important thing you must do to assure you will be forgiven for wrongs against God: Sincere repentance? Be more obedient? Rely on God's grace in Jesus Christ?

15:13 *Saul was already making foolish* decisions. Here he lied, intentionally stealing from God and deceiving God's representative.

15:15 The soldiers. Without much subtlety, Saul passed the blame. He blamed his soldiers and took no responsibility himself. Saul was like Adam when he said, "The woman you put here" and "The serpent deceived me" (Gen. 3:12–13). Saul should have known better. **the LORD your God.** Saul's choice of pronouns, from "my God" to "your God," is an indication of his shift in loyalty.

15:22 Samuel drew a distinction between an attitude of worship and the outward appearance of worship. Saul was banking on rote obedience (when it was also convenient), rather than genuine obedience with wholehearted respect for God's will.

15:23 arrogance ... idolatry. Saul put his own interests before God's kingdom. In that way he rejected God's leadership. In return, God rejected Saul's leadership.

15:24 afraid of the people. First Saul lied to Samuel (v. 13). Then he tried to lay the blame on his soldiers (v. 15). In this weak confession, he blamed the people. In each case Saul refused to take responsibility.

gave in to them. 25Now I beg you, forgive my sin and come back with
me, so that I may worship the LORD."
26But Samuel said to him, "I will not go back with you. You have
rejected the word of the LORD, and the LORD has rejected you as king
over Israel!"
27As Samuel turned to leave, Saul caught hold of the hem of his
robe, and it tore. 28Samuel said to him, "The LORD has torn the
kingdom of Israel from you today and has given it to one of your
neighbors—to one better than you. 29He who is the Glory of Israel
does not lie or change his mind; for he is not a man, that he should
change his mind."
30Saul replied, "I have sinned. But please honor me before the
elders of my people and before Israel; come back with me, so that I
may worship the LORD your God." 31So Samuel went back with Saul,
and Saul worshiped the LORD.
32Then Samuel said, "Bring me Agag king of the Amalekites."
Agag came to him confidently,[a] thinking, "Surely the bitterness of
death is past."
33But Samuel said,

"As your sword has made women childless,
so will your mother be childless among women."

And Samuel put Agag to death before the LORD at Gilgal.
34Then Samuel left for Ramah, but Saul went up to his home in
Gibeah of Saul. 35Until the day Samuel died, he did not go to see Saul
again, though Samuel mourned for him. And the LORD was grieved
that he had made Saul king over Israel.

Samuel Anoints David

16 The LORD said to Samuel, "How long will you mourn for Saul,
since I have rejected him as king over Israel? Fill your horn
with oil and be on your way; I am sending you to Jesse of Bethlehem.
I have chosen one of his sons to be king."
2But Samuel said, "How can I go? Saul will hear about it and
kill me."
The LORD said, "Take a heifer with you and say, 'I have come to sacrifice to the LORD.' 3Invite Jesse to the sacrifice, and I will show you
what to do. You are to anoint for me the one I indicate."
4Samuel did what the LORD said. When he arrived at Bethlehem, the
elders of the town trembled when they met him. They asked, "Do you
come in peace?"
5Samuel replied, "Yes, in peace; I have come to sacrifice to the
LORD. Consecrate yourselves and come to the sacrifice with me."
Then he consecrated Jesse and his sons and invited them to the
sacrifice.

[a]32 Or *him trembling, yet*

OPEN 1. What is the attitude you generally have toward shopping: "I shop, therefore I am" or "Just leave me home!"? **2.** When you shop, are you more likely to pick the first thing that meets your eye, or check out a variety of options and several different stores?

STUDY God had led the prophet Samuel to anoint Saul as Israel's king. Samuel has just told Saul that, because of his disobedience, the kingdom will be torn from him and given to another. So, with God's guidance, Samuel goes shopping for a new king. **1.** What town does Samuel go to in order to search for the new king? Whose sons does he examine? **2.** What does Samuel do to avoid the suspicions of the violent Saul? **3.** In determining who God has chosen to be king, what standard of

15:25 come back with me. Saul still missed the point. He tried to make *things right with Samuel, at least in* appearance, but it was God he had offended.

15:31 Samuel returned with Saul in order to carry out God's request (v. 33).

15:35 the LORD was grieved. This was not the first time God was grieved. Before Noah and the flood, God was grieved that he had even created humankind (Gen. 6:6–8).

16:2 Samuel's fears were real. In order to go where God had commanded, he had to pass through Saul's town. Samuel had already told Saul that his kingdom would be replaced (15:28), so Saul could have been paranoid and on watch for Samuel.

6When they arrived, Samuel saw Eliab and thought, "Surely the
LORD's anointed stands here before the LORD."
7But the LORD said to Samuel, "Do not consider his appearance or
his height, for I have rejected him. The LORD does not look at the
things man looks at. Man looks at the outward appearance, but the
LORD looks at the heart."
8Then Jesse called Abinadab and had him pass in front of Samuel.
But Samuel said, "The LORD has not chosen this one either." 9Jesse
then had Shammah pass by, but Samuel said, "Nor has the LORD
chosen this one." 10Jesse had seven of his sons pass before Samuel,
but Samuel said to him, "The LORD has not chosen these." 11So he
asked Jesse, "Are these all the sons you have?"
"There is still the youngest," Jesse answered, "but he is tending the
sheep."
Samuel said, "Send for him; we will not sit down[a] until he arrives."
12So he sent and had him brought in. He was ruddy, with a fine appearance and handsome features.
Then the LORD said, "Rise and anoint him; he is the one."
13So Samuel took the horn of oil and anointed him in the presence
of his brothers, and from that day on the Spirit of the LORD came
upon David in power. Samuel then went to Ramah.

David in Saul's Service

14Now the Spirit of the LORD had departed from Saul, and an evil[b]
spirit from the LORD tormented him.
15Saul's attendants said to him, "See, an evil spirit from God is tor-
menting you. 16Let our lord command his servants here to search for
someone who can play the harp. He will play when the evil spirit from
God comes upon you, and you will feel better."
17So Saul said to his attendants, "Find someone who plays well and
bring him to me."
18One of the servants answered, "I have seen a son of Jesse of
Bethlehem who knows how to play the harp. He is a brave man and a
warrior. He speaks well and is a fine-looking man. And the LORD is
with him."
19Then Saul sent messengers to Jesse and said, "Send me your son
David, who is with the sheep." 20So Jesse took a donkey loaded with
bread, a skin of wine and a young goat and sent them with his son
David to Saul.

[a]11 Some Septuagint manuscripts; Hebrew *not gather around* [b]14 Or *injurious;* also in verses 15, 16 and 23

selection is Samuel specifically told to avoid using? **4.** If you had been one of David's brothers, how would you have felt watching your younger brother get chosen? **5.** What does Samuel do to indicate that David is the one God has chosen to be king (v. 13)? **6.** Who in this story is most like you: Saul, because you have to make some hard choices? One of the brothers, because you feel passed over? David, because there are high expectations of you?

APPLY 1. How do you feel about God looking at the heart instead of outward appearance? **2.** What do you need to do to make your heart more ready to be examined?

OPEN 1. When you are down, what kind of music is most likely to put you in better spirits? **2.** Who would you choose as a personal musician?

STUDY Saul, unaware that Samuel has chosen David to succeed him, opens the door for the transition by inviting David into the king's home to be his personal musician. **1.** How is the Holy Spirit active in David's life and Saul's (vv. 13–14)? **2.** What instrument is suggested to help heal the spirit of the troubled Saul? **3.** What qualities does the servant of Saul ascribe to David? **4.** What gifts does Jesse send along with David to the king? Why might he have thought it important to send gifts? **5.** What other position of responsibility is David given by Saul?

16:7 appearance ... height. The choice of Saul had been based on distinctive physical attributes. He was an "impressive young man ... a head taller than any of the others" (9:2). Now Samuel is instructed to ignore those criteria.

16:13 This anointing mirrored Saul's anointing (10:1) in several ways. It was private. It was an anointing from God, rather than a formal election. Yet God's Spirit came in a new way.

16:14–17:58 Saul ruled Israel for 15 years after Samuel first proclaimed that the kingdom would be taken from him. These verses describe the beginning of the transition to King David.

16:14 evil spirit from the LORD. Evil spirits, like everything else in creation, are ultimately under God's control and cannot move where they are not allowed. **tormented.** Saul was tormented with depression and jealousy. Since he had been told his kingdom was gone, he had grounds for distress, which now overwhelmed him.

16:16 He will play. David, the future king, calmed Saul's spirit with music. God's Spirit had left Saul and rested on David. And the Spirit, expressed through the music, was the reason Saul felt relief.

16:18–19 David. David was a warrior-musician. Music brought him to the palace, and his fighting skills won the victory against Goliath (17:46–58) and fame among the Israelites. But faith would make him God's choice as king (13:14).

APPLY **1.** Which of the following would an "evil spirit" most likely use on you: Guilt? Fear? Insecurity? Self-doubt? Depression? **2.** What weapon have you found most effective in combating these feelings?

OPEN **1.** When you were a child, who was the most intimidating "giant" in your life: Your father? A teacher? A grumpy neighbor? An older child? **2.** When was a time when you felt the need to stand up to this "giant"?

STUDY The armies of Israel had drawn up a battle line with the Philistines. Day after day, Goliath—the nine-foot Philistine champion—came forward to defy the Israelites and challenge them to send a representative to fight him. **1.** What kind of armor did Goliath wear? Why does the Bible describe it in such detail? **2.** What challenge does Goliath issue the Israelites? **3.** Who would you volunteer from your group to accept Goliath's proposal? **4.** Why does David's brother Eliab get angry with him? **5.** What experiences gave David confidence that he could defeat Goliath? **6.** If you were ringside for this fight, what odds would you have given David? **7.** What is most impressive to you about how David went about this battle: That he was just a boy? That he went without armor? That he used such a simple weapon? That he relied on and gave credit to God's strength? That he had so much confidence?

APPLY **1.** What "giants" are you up against in your life right now? **2.** What weapons, however small, are in your "arsenal"? **3.** What would it take for you to go up against those giants with the confidence that David showed?

21 David came to Saul and entered his service. Saul liked him very
much, and David became one of his armor-bearers. 22 Then Saul sent
word to Jesse, saying, "Allow David to remain in my service, for I am
pleased with him."
23 Whenever the spirit from God came upon Saul, David would take
his harp and play. Then relief would come to Saul; he would feel better, and the evil spirit would leave him.

David and Goliath

17 Now the Philistines gathered their forces for war and assembled at Socoh in Judah. They pitched camp at Ephes
Dammim, between Socoh and Azekah. 2 Saul and the Israelites
assembled and camped in the Valley of Elah and drew up their battle
line to meet the Philistines. 3 The Philistines occupied one hill and the
Israelites another, with the valley between them.
4 A champion named Goliath, who was from Gath, came out of the
Philistine camp. He was over nine feet[a] tall. 5 He had a bronze helmet
on his head and wore a coat of scale armor of bronze weighing five
thousand shekels[b]; 6 on his legs he wore bronze greaves, and a bronze
javelin was slung on his back. 7 His spear shaft was like a weaver's
rod, and its iron point weighed six hundred shekels.[c] His shield
bearer went ahead of him.
8 Goliath stood and shouted to the ranks of Israel, "Why do you
come out and line up for battle? Am I not a Philistine, and are you not
the servants of Saul? Choose a man and have him come down to me.
9 If he is able to fight and kill me, we will become your subjects; but if
I overcome him and kill him, you will become our subjects and serve
us." 10 Then the Philistine said, "This day I defy the ranks of Israel!
Give me a man and let us fight each other." 11 On hearing the
Philistine's words, Saul and all the Israelites were dismayed and terrified.
12 Now David was the son of an Ephrathite named Jesse, who was
from Bethlehem in Judah. Jesse had eight sons, and in Saul's time he
was old and well advanced in years. 13 Jesse's three oldest sons had
followed Saul to the war: The firstborn was Eliab; the second, Abinadab; and the third, Shammah. 14 David was the youngest. The three
oldest followed Saul, 15 but David went back and forth from Saul to
tend his father's sheep at Bethlehem.
16 For forty days the Philistine came forward every morning and
evening and took his stand.
17 Now Jesse said to his son David, "Take this ephah[d] of roasted
grain and these ten loaves of bread for your brothers and hurry to
their camp. 18 Take along these ten cheeses to the commander of their
unit.[e] See how your brothers are and bring back some assurance[f]
from them. 19 They are with Saul and all the men of Israel in the Valley
of Elah, fighting against the Philistines."

[a] 4 Hebrew *was six cubits and a span* (about 3 meters) [b] 5 That is, about 125 pounds (about 57 kilograms) [c] 7 That is, about 15 pounds (about 7 kilograms) [d] 17 That is, probably about 3/5 bushel (about 22 liters) [e] 18 Hebrew *thousand* [f] 18 Or *some token*; or *some pledge of spoils*

17:11 In an age before surveillance equipment and automatic weapons, this battle was proposed as a contest of champions. But Israel's army had no champion willing to face a loud-mouthed nine-foot-plus opponent.

17:15 back and forth. David's services were part-time at best and possibly just on an "as needed" basis.

[20]Early in the morning David left the flock with a shepherd, loaded
up and set out, as Jesse had directed. He reached the camp as the
army was going out to its battle positions, shouting the war cry.
[21]Israel and the Philistines were drawing up their lines facing each
other. [22]David left his things with the keeper of supplies, ran to the
battle lines and greeted his brothers. [23]As he was talking with them,
Goliath, the Philistine champion from Gath, stepped out from his
lines and shouted his usual defiance, and David heard it. [24]When the
Israelites saw the man, they all ran from him in great fear.

[25]Now the Israelites had been saying, "Do you see how this man
keeps coming out? He comes out to defy Israel. The king will give
great wealth to the man who kills him. He will also give him his
daughter in marriage and will exempt his father's family from taxes in
Israel."

[26]David asked the men standing near him, "What will be done for
the man who kills this Philistine and removes this disgrace from
Israel? Who is this uncircumcised Philistine that he should defy the
armies of the living God?"

[27]They repeated to him what they had been saying and told him,
"This is what will be done for the man who kills him."

[28]When Eliab, David's oldest brother, heard him speaking with the
men, he burned with anger at him and asked, "Why have you come
down here? And with whom did you leave those few sheep in the
desert? I know how conceited you are and how wicked your heart is;
you came down only to watch the battle."

[29]"Now what have I done?" said David. "Can't I even speak?" [30]He
then turned away to someone else and brought up the same matter,
and the men answered him as before. [31]What David said was overheard and reported to Saul, and Saul sent for him.

[32]David said to Saul, "Let no one lose heart on account of this Philistine; your servant will go and fight him."

[33]Saul replied, "You are not able to go out against this Philistine
and fight him; you are only a boy, and he has been a fighting man
from his youth."

[34]But David said to Saul, "Your servant has been keeping his
father's sheep. When a lion or a bear came and carried off a sheep
from the flock, [35]I went after it, struck it and rescued the sheep from
its mouth. When it turned on me, I seized it by its hair, struck it and
killed it. [36]Your servant has killed both the lion and the bear; this uncircumcised Philistine will be like one of them, because he has defied
the armies of the living God. [37]The LORD who delivered me from the
paw of the lion and the paw of the bear will deliver me from the hand
of this Philistine."

Saul said to David, "Go, and the LORD be with you."

17:28 how conceited you are. The words of Eliab, David's oldest brother, give insight into David's character. While a brother may perceive conceit, it was David's confidence in himself and God that saved Israel that day.

17:32 lose heart. Goliath was bringing fear into the hearts of the whole Israelite army. Their confidence in God melted at the sound of Goliath's boisterous bragging.

17:33 you are only a boy. By this point, Saul saw only the physical dimensions of the battle. His eyes were blind to the more crucial spiritual battle underway.

17:34 lion. David wasn't the only hero of the Bible to face lions. Samson fought a young lion (Judg.14:5–6). Benaiah, one of David's mighty men, was known for killing a lion (2 Sam. 23:20). And Daniel faced lions—neither killing them nor being killed—as punishment for his crime of praying (Dan. 6:22).

17:37 Go. Saul placed faith in the young David when he could not seem to find faith in God.

38Then Saul dressed David in his own tunic. He put a coat of armor
on him and a bronze helmet on his head. 39David fastened on his
sword over the tunic and tried walking around, because he was not
used to them.
"I cannot go in these," he said to Saul, "because I am not used to
them." So he took them off. 40Then he took his staff in his hand,
chose five smooth stones from the stream, put them in the pouch of
his shepherd's bag and, with his sling in his hand, approached the
Philistine.
41Meanwhile, the Philistine, with his shield bearer in front of him,
kept coming closer to David. 42He looked David over and saw that he
was only a boy, ruddy and handsome, and he despised him. 43He said
to David, "Am I a dog, that you come at me with sticks?" And the Philistine cursed David by his gods. 44"Come here," he said, "and I'll give
your flesh to the birds of the air and the beasts of the field!"
45David said to the Philistine, "You come against me with sword
and spear and javelin, but I come against you in the name of the LORD
Almighty, the God of the armies of Israel, whom you have defied.
46This day the LORD will hand you over to me, and I'll strike you down
and cut off your head. Today I will give the carcasses of the Philistine
army to the birds of the air and the beasts of the earth, and the whole
world will know that there is a God in Israel. 47All those gathered here
will know that it is not by sword or spear that the LORD saves; for the
battle is the LORD's, and he will give all of you into our hands."
48As the Philistine moved closer to attack him, David ran quickly
toward the battle line to meet him. 49Reaching into his bag and taking
out a stone, he slung it and struck the Philistine on the forehead. The
stone sank into his forehead, and he fell facedown on the ground.
50So David triumphed over the Philistine with a sling and a stone;
without a sword in his hand he struck down the Philistine and killed
him.
51David ran and stood over him. He took hold of the Philistine's
sword and drew it from the scabbard. After he killed him, he cut off
his head with the sword.
When the Philistines saw that their hero was dead, they turned and
ran. 52Then the men of Israel and Judah surged forward with a shout
and pursued the Philistines to the entrance of Gath[a] and to the gates
of Ekron. Their dead were strewn along the Shaaraim road to Gath
and Ekron. 53When the Israelites returned from chasing the Philistines, they plundered their camp. 54David took the Philistine's head
and brought it to Jerusalem, and he put the Philistine's weapons in
his own tent.
55As Saul watched David going out to meet the Philistine, he said to

[a]*52* Some Septuagint manuscripts; Hebrew *a valley*

17:40 five smooth stones. The stones used were often the size of a golf ball. A slingshot was a common weapon in battle (Judg. 20:16).

17:45 in the name of the LORD. This was David's center of strength, and the central difference between his reign and Saul's.

17:46 the whole world will know. David's motivation for victory is completely different than Saul's. David's ambitions are directed toward glorifying God.

17:47 not by sword or spear. David's promise of God's victory was later echoed by Zechariah, " 'Not by might nor by power, but by my Spirit,' says the LORD Almighty" (Zech. 4:6).

17:54 the Philistine's weapons. Later, when hiding from Saul, David was given Goliath's sword for protection. At the time it was in the tabernacle, so David must have dedicated the sword, if not the rest of the weapons, to the Lord.

Abner, commander of the army, "Abner, whose son is that young
man?"
Abner replied, "As surely as you live, O king, I don't know."
56 The king said, "Find out whose son this young man is."
57 As soon as David returned from killing the Philistine, Abner took
him and brought him before Saul, with David still holding the
Philistine's head.
58 "Whose son are you, young man?" Saul asked him.
David said, "I am the son of your servant Jesse of Bethlehem."

Saul's Jealousy of David

18 After David had finished talking with Saul, Jonathan became
one in spirit with David, and he loved him as himself. 2 From
that day Saul kept David with him and did not let him return to his
father's house. 3 And Jonathan made a covenant with David because
he loved him as himself. 4 Jonathan took off the robe he was wearing
and gave it to David, along with his tunic, and even his sword, his
bow and his belt.
5 Whatever Saul sent him to do, David did it so successfully[a] that
Saul gave him a high rank in the army. This pleased all the people,
and Saul's officers as well.
6 When the men were returning home after David had killed the Philistine, the women came out from all the towns of Israel to meet King
Saul with singing and dancing, with joyful songs and with tambourines and lutes. 7 As they danced, they sang:

"Saul has slain his thousands,
and David his tens of thousands."

8 Saul was very angry; this refrain galled him. "They have credited
David with tens of thousands," he thought, "but me with only thousands. What more can he get but the kingdom?" 9 And from that time
on Saul kept a jealous eye on David.
10 The next day an evil[b] spirit from God came forcefully upon Saul.
He was prophesying in his house, while David was playing the harp,
as he usually did. Saul had a spear in his hand 11 and he hurled it, saying to himself, "I'll pin David to the wall." But David eluded him
twice.
12 Saul was afraid of David, because the LORD was with David but
had left Saul. 13 So he sent David away from him and gave him command over a thousand men, and David led the troops in their campaigns. 14 In everything he did he had great success,[c] because the
LORD was with him. 15 When Saul saw how successful[d] he was, he was
afraid of him. 16 But all Israel and Judah loved David, because he led
them in their campaigns.

[a]5 Or *wisely* [b]10 Or *injurious* [c]14 Or *he was very wise* [d]15 Or *wise*

OPEN 1. Who was your best friend when you were in high school? **2.** What did you and this friend give or lend to each other as an expression of your friendship: Items of clothing? Jewelry? Record albums? Sports equipment?

STUDY While David had great bravery and physical prowess, these were not his only admirable attributes. He also knew how to be a good friend, as Saul's son Jonathan was to discover. David's positive attributes, however, only served to make Saul more and more jealous of him. **1.** Why do you suppose David and Jonathan hit it off so well? **2.** What does Jonathan give to David to express his friendship? What meaning do you suppose was behind these gifts? **3.** What especially galls Saul about the refrain in verse 7? **4.** Why was Saul afraid of David (vv. 12,15)? Have you ever known someone that made you feel afraid or small, because they were so much better at everything? **5.** Why does David keep refusing to become the king's son-in-law: Humility? Suspicion of the king's motives? Saul's daughters weren't attractive and David wanted to be polite? **6.** What strange dowry does the king ask and David delivers? Why did having to do this make David feel better about becoming Saul's son-in-law?

APPLY 1. Which of the characters in this story are you most like when it comes to making deep, intimate friendships: David (because you know how to reach out and give of yourself)? Saul (because

18:1 Jonathan. David and Jonathan became best friends. Eventually David would be crowned in Jonathan's place as Saul's successor. Their friendship survived even this test.

18:3 a covenant. Jonathan already proved himself practical and wise as he dealt with Saul's armies (14:45). Here he recognized an alliance that meant more to him than the kingship, so he initiated it.

18:7 The real offense of this refrain was that the names of Saul and David were used as equals.

18:13 sent David away. In other words, Saul sent David to war. Saul hoped David would be killed in battle and thus be out of the way. Years later, David would use this same tactic with Uriah, Bathsheba's husband (2 Sam. 11:14–15).

jealousy and competitiveness seem to get in the way of friendships)? **2.** In the spirit of Jonathan, what "armor" do you need to shed in order to open yourself up to more intimate friendships?

---

[17]Saul said to David, "Here is my older daughter Merab. I will give
her to you in marriage; only serve me bravely and fight the battles of
the LORD." For Saul said to himself, "I will not raise a hand against
him. Let the Philistines do that!"
[18]But David said to Saul, "Who am I, and what is my family or my
father's clan in Israel, that I should become the king's son-in-law?"
[19]So[a] when the time came for Merab, Saul's daughter, to be given to
David, she was given in marriage to Adriel of Meholah.
[20]Now Saul's daughter Michal was in love with David, and when
they told Saul about it, he was pleased. [21]"I will give her to him," he
thought, "so that she may be a snare to him and so that the hand of
the Philistines may be against him." So Saul said to David, "Now you
have a second opportunity to become my son-in-law."
[22]Then Saul ordered his attendants: "Speak to David privately and
say, 'Look, the king is pleased with you, and his attendants all like
you; now become his son-in-law.' "
[23]They repeated these words to David. But David said, "Do you
think it is a small matter to become the king's son-in-law? I'm only a
poor man and little known."
[24]When Saul's servants told him what David had said, [25]Saul replied, "Say to David, 'The king wants no other price for the bride than
a hundred Philistine foreskins, to take revenge on his enemies.' "
Saul's plan was to have David fall by the hands of the Philistines.
[26]When the attendants told David these things, he was pleased to
become the king's son-in-law. So before the allotted time elapsed,
[27]David and his men went out and killed two hundred Philistines. He
brought their foreskins and presented the full number to the king so
that he might become the king's son-in-law. Then Saul gave him his
daughter Michal in marriage.
[28]When Saul realized that the LORD was with David and that his
daughter Michal loved David, [29]Saul became still more afraid of him,
and he remained his enemy the rest of his days.
[30]The Philistine commanders continued to go out to battle, and as
often as they did, David met with more success[b] than the rest of
Saul's officers, and his name became well known.

Saul Tries to Kill David

19 Saul told his son Jonathan and all the attendants to kill
David. But Jonathan was very fond of David [2]and warned
him, "My father Saul is looking for a chance to kill you. Be on your
guard tomorrow morning; go into hiding and stay there. [3]I will go out

[a]19 Or *However,* [b]30 Or *David acted more wisely*

OPEN 1. When have you taken a stand for a friend at some risk to your own welfare? What happened? **2.** If you had to pick two friends with whom to entrust your life, who would they be?

18:17 Let the Philistines do that! Saul's motivation was clear. He had become so jealous of David that he wanted him dead. Saul was so desperate that he thought that he could foil God's plan by murdering God's chosen leader.

18:25 price for the bride. A future husband brought some wealth to the father of the bride. This practice is still followed in many parts of the world.

18:28 Michal loved David. No matter how Saul tried to get rid of David, God used that very scheme to bring David closer. Rather than falling in battle, David became a national hero, best friend of the king's son and then husband to the king's daughter. Could Saul be getting a message?

18:29 remained his enemy. Saul never trusted David, who nonetheless showed Saul due respect as king throughout the rest of their time together.

19:1 kill David. In essence, Saul put out a contract on David's life. He was so unaware of the dynamics in his family and court that he shared that news with his son, David's best friend. Saul was running wide open, out of control.

and stand with my father in the field where you are. I'll speak to him
about you and will tell you what I find out."
4 Jonathan spoke well of David to Saul his father and said to him,
"Let not the king do wrong to his servant David; he has not wronged
you, and what he has done has benefited you greatly. 5 He took his life
in his hands when he killed the Philistine. The LORD won a great
victory for all Israel, and you saw it and were glad. Why then would
you do wrong to an innocent man like David by killing him for no
reason?"
6 Saul listened to Jonathan and took this oath: "As surely as the
LORD lives, David will not be put to death."
7 So Jonathan called David and told him the whole conversation. He
brought him to Saul, and David was with Saul as before.
8 Once more war broke out, and David went out and fought the
Philistines. He struck them with such force that they fled before him.
9 But an evil[a] spirit from the LORD came upon Saul as he was sitting
in his house with his spear in his hand. While David was playing the
harp, 10 Saul tried to pin him to the wall with his spear, but David
eluded him as Saul drove the spear into the wall. That night David
made good his escape.
11 Saul sent men to David's house to watch it and to kill him in the
morning. But Michal, David's wife, warned him, "If you don't run for
your life tonight, tomorrow you'll be killed." 12 So Michal let David
down through a window, and he fled and escaped. 13 Then Michal
took an idol[b] and laid it on the bed, covering it with a garment and
putting some goats' hair at the head.
14 When Saul sent the men to capture David, Michal said, "He is ill."
15 Then Saul sent the men back to see David and told them, "Bring
him up to me in his bed so that I may kill him." 16 But when the men
entered, there was the idol in the bed, and at the head was some
goats' hair.
17 Saul said to Michal, "Why did you deceive me like this and send
my enemy away so that he escaped?"
Michal told him, "He said to me, 'Let me get away. Why should I kill
you?' "
18 When David had fled and made his escape, he went to Samuel at
Ramah and told him all that Saul had done to him. Then he and Samuel went to Naioth and stayed there. 19 Word came to Saul: "David is in
Naioth at Ramah"; 20 so he sent men to capture him. But when they
saw a group of prophets prophesying, with Samuel standing there as
their leader, the Spirit of God came upon Saul's men and they also
prophesied. 21 Saul was told about it, and he sent more men, and they
prophesied too. Saul sent men a third time, and they also prophesied.
22 Finally, he himself left for Ramah and went to the great cistern at
Secu. And he asked, "Where are Samuel and David?"
"Over in Naioth at Ramah," they said.
23 So Saul went to Naioth at Ramah. But the Spirit of God came even
upon him, and he walked along prophesying until he came to Naioth.

[a]9 Or *injurious* [b]13 Hebrew *teraphim;* also in verse 16

STUDY Saul's jealousy of David continues, and he makes several attempts to have David killed. All his efforts are thwarted however, as two of his children, Jonathan and Michal, take David's side, and the prophets shelter him. **1.** Why is Saul so eager to kill David? **2.** Why do you think Jonathan and Michal seem to be more loyal to David than to their own father? Is this right or wrong? **3.** Would you trust Saul's vow at this point (vv. 6–7)? Why does David seem to? **4.** Why does Michal feel she has to lie about having protected her husband? **5.** What would you do if there were this kind of hostility between a parent and your spouse? **6.** The "prophesying" here was probably singing and praising the Lord. Why does prophesying seem to keep Saul's men from capturing David (vv. 20–24)?

APPLY **1.** When have you felt like someone you had been close to tried to "nail you to the wall"? **2.** Looking back, in what ways did God intervene to help you in this situation?

19:4 Jonathan spoke. Jonathan's strong character is revealed as he rehearses all the benefits David has brought Saul. Rather than feeling defensive or jealous, Jonathan submits to God and works toward his friend's eventual reign. Beneath Jonathan's reasonable and diplomatic response, he was pleading for David's life.

OPEN 1. When you were in high school, what was most likely to put a strain on your closest friendship: Rivalry over the opposite sex? Disapproval of your friend by your parents? Competitiveness in school or sports? Other? **2.** What "life-saving" favor has a friend done for you?

STUDY King Saul is jealous of David and has attempted to kill him. David turns to his best friend Jonathan—Saul's son—for help and advice. **1.** What thoughts and feelings do you think Jonathan was experiencing upon hearing David's anguish-filled complaint against Saul (vv. 1–3)? **2.** Why is Jonathan so skeptical about Saul's plans when Saul has shown this hostility before? **3.** Is trusting Jonathan easy or hard for David in this situation? What can you point to in support of your answer? **4.** Which do you think angers Saul more and why: David's absence from the table, or his own son's collusion with David? By what "higher principle" does Saul justify his anger (vv. 30–31)? Can you ever remember giving a right sounding reason for a really bad motive? **5.** How does Saul say Jonathan is working against his own best interest (vv. 30–31)? What do you think Jonathan felt about this appeal? **6.** What feelings do you think the two friends were experiencing after the truth of the situation was revealed (vv. 41–42)? Why do you think David "wept the most"?

APPLY 1. Whose circumstances and emotions do you most readily identify with: Saul, feeling you have to fight to preserve your world? David, feeling threatened and not knowing who to trust? Jonathan, feeling torn between competing relationships? **2.** When was the last time

24 He stripped off his robes and also prophesied in Samuel's presence.
He lay that way all that day and night. This is why people say, "Is Saul
also among the prophets?"

David and Jonathan

20 Then David fled from Naioth at Ramah and went to Jonathan
and asked, "What have I done? What is my crime? How have
I wronged your father, that he is trying to take my life?"
2 "Never!" Jonathan replied. "You are not going to die! Look, my
father doesn't do anything, great or small, without confiding in me.
Why would he hide this from me? It's not so!"
3 But David took an oath and said, "Your father knows very well that
I have found favor in your eyes, and he has said to himself, 'Jonathan
must not know this or he will be grieved.' Yet as surely as the LORD
lives and as you live, there is only a step between me and death."
4 Jonathan said to David, "Whatever you want me to do, I'll do
for you."
5 So David said, "Look, tomorrow is the New Moon festival, and I
am supposed to dine with the king; but let me go and hide in the field
until the evening of the day after tomorrow. 6 If your father misses me
at all, tell him, 'David earnestly asked my permission to hurry to
Bethlehem, his hometown, because an annual sacrifice is being
made there for his whole clan.' 7 If he says, 'Very well,' then your
servant is safe. But if he loses his temper, you can be sure that he is
determined to harm me. 8 As for you, show kindness to your servant,
for you have brought him into a covenant with you before the LORD. If
I am guilty, then kill me yourself! Why hand me over to your father?"
9 "Never!" Jonathan said. "If I had the least inkling that my father
was determined to harm you, wouldn't I tell you?"
10 David asked, "Who will tell me if your father answers you
harshly?"
11 "Come," Jonathan said, "let's go out into the field." So they went
there together.
12 Then Jonathan said to David: "By the LORD, the God of Israel, I
will surely sound out my father by this time the day after tomorrow! If
he is favorably disposed toward you, will I not send you word and let
you know? 13 But if my father is inclined to harm you, may the LORD
deal with me, be it ever so severely, if I do not let you know and send
you away safely. May the LORD be with you as he has been with my
father. 14 But show me unfailing kindness like that of the LORD as long
as I live, so that I may not be killed, 15 and do not ever cut off your
kindness from my family—not even when the LORD has cut off every
one of David's enemies from the face of the earth."

19:24 also prophesied. Saul was up against the very Spirit of God. God's Spirit had taken over the men Saul had sent. Still, Saul ignored the futility of his efforts and went himself. God's Spirit overwhelmed him too. Self-deception and paranoia will lead people into destructive behavior.

20:11 Jonathan's words to David were the same as Cain's to Abel (Gen. 4:8). Yet, Jonathan's motivation was to save the life of his friend.

20:13 as he has been with my father. Jonathan understood David's destiny as future king. Here he compared God's presence in David's life to that of Saul's, once again recognizing David's future.

20:14 show me unfailing kindness. In Jonathan's mind, as long as descendants of Saul existed, David might fear a rebellion. In fact, it was common for a new monarch to kill any heirs from the previous royal line. Here, Jonathan spoke to the survival of his family amid the change of kings.

20:15 my family. David honored this request to show kindness to Jonathan's family. Many years later, he invited Jonathan's son, Mephibosheth, to eat at the royal table (2 Sam. 9:6–10).

16So Jonathan made a covenant with the house of David, saying,
"May the LORD call David's enemies to account." 17And Jonathan had
David reaffirm his oath out of love for him, because he loved him as
he loved himself.
18Then Jonathan said to David: "Tomorrow is the New Moon festival. You will be missed, because your seat will be empty. 19The day
after tomorrow, toward evening, go to the place where you hid when
this trouble began, and wait by the stone Ezel. 20I will shoot three
arrows to the side of it, as though I were shooting at a target. 21Then
I will send a boy and say, 'Go, find the arrows.' If I say to him, 'Look,
the arrows are on this side of you; bring them here,' then come,
because, as surely as the LORD lives, you are safe; there is no danger.
22But if I say to the boy, 'Look, the arrows are beyond you,' then you
must go, because the LORD has sent you away. 23And about the matter
you and I discussed—remember, the LORD is witness between you
and me forever."
24So David hid in the field, and when the New Moon festival came,
the king sat down to eat. 25He sat in his customary place by the wall,
opposite Jonathan,[a] and Abner sat next to Saul, but David's place was
empty. 26Saul said nothing that day, for he thought, "Something must
have happened to David to make him ceremonially unclean—surely
he is unclean." 27But the next day, the second day of the month,
David's place was empty again. Then Saul said to his son Jonathan,
"Why hasn't the son of Jesse come to the meal, either yesterday or
today?"
28Jonathan answered, "David earnestly asked me for permission to
go to Bethlehem. 29He said, 'Let me go, because our family is observing a sacrifice in the town and my brother has ordered me to be there.
If I have found favor in your eyes, let me get away to see my brothers.'
That is why he has not come to the king's table."
30Saul's anger flared up at Jonathan and he said to him, "You son of
a perverse and rebellious woman! Don't I know that you have sided
with the son of Jesse to your own shame and to the shame of the
mother who bore you? 31As long as the son of Jesse lives on this
earth, neither you nor your kingdom will be established. Now send
and bring him to me, for he must die!"
32"Why should he be put to death? What has he done?" Jonathan
asked his father. 33But Saul hurled his spear at him to kill him. Then
Jonathan knew that his father intended to kill David.
34Jonathan got up from the table in fierce anger; on that second day
of the month he did not eat, because he was grieved at his father's
shameful treatment of David.
35In the morning Jonathan went out to the field for his meeting
with David. He had a small boy with him, 36and he said to the boy,
"Run and find the arrows I shoot." As the boy ran, he shot an arrow
beyond him. 37When the boy came to the place where Jonathan's

you really wept with a friend? What was at issue?

____

[a]25 Septuagint; Hebrew *wall. Jonathan arose*

20:16 David's enemies. At this point, Saul was David's enemy. Jonathan declared his loyalty to David even at his father's expense.

20:23 the LORD is witness. In other words, nothing could break this covenant—no change in power, no change in heart.

20:31 neither you nor your kingdom. This interaction highlights the difference between Saul's character and Jonathan's. Saul saw the end of their legacy and tried to kill the culprit. Jonathan saw the end of their legacy and wanted to be a part of what God was doing.

arrow had fallen, Jonathan called out after him, "Isn't the arrow beyond you?" 38Then he shouted, "Hurry! Go quickly! Don't stop!" The boy picked up the arrow and returned to his master. 39(The boy knew nothing of all this; only Jonathan and David knew.) 40Then Jonathan gave his weapons to the boy and said, "Go, carry them back to town."

41After the boy had gone, David got up from the south side ⌊of the stone⌋ and bowed down before Jonathan three times, with his face to the ground. Then they kissed each other and wept together—but David wept the most.

42Jonathan said to David, "Go in peace, for we have sworn friendship with each other in the name of the LORD, saying, 'The LORD is witness between you and me, and between your descendants and my descendants forever.'" Then David left, and Jonathan went back to the town.

David at Nob

21 David went to Nob, to Ahimelech the priest. Ahimelech trembled when he met him, and asked, "Why are you alone? Why is no one with you?"

2David answered Ahimelech the priest, "The king charged me with a certain matter and said to me, 'No one is to know anything about your mission and your instructions.' As for my men, I have told them to meet me at a certain place. 3Now then, what do you have on hand? Give me five loaves of bread, or whatever you can find."

4But the priest answered David, "I don't have any ordinary bread on hand; however, there is some consecrated bread here—provided the men have kept themselves from women."

5David replied, "Indeed women have been kept from us, as usual whenever[a] I set out. The men's things[b] are holy even on missions that are not holy. How much more so today!" 6So the priest gave him the consecrated bread, since there was no bread there except the bread of the Presence that had been removed from before the LORD and replaced by hot bread on the day it was taken away.

7Now one of Saul's servants was there that day, detained before the LORD; he was Doeg the Edomite, Saul's head shepherd.

8David asked Ahimelech, "Don't you have a spear or a sword here? I haven't brought my sword or any other weapon, because the king's business was urgent."

9The priest replied, "The sword of Goliath the Philistine, whom you killed in the Valley of Elah, is here; it is wrapped in a cloth behind the ephod. If you want it, take it; there is no sword here but that one."

David said, "There is none like it; give it to me."

[a]5 Or *from us in the past few days since* [b]5 Or *bodies*

OPEN When you "raid the pantry," what kind of food do you most often look for?

STUDY 1. What does Ahimelech fear (v. 1)? Why? How does David seek to calm his fears? **2.** What's the possible sin involved in consuming the consecrated bread (Lev. 24:9)? Why does Ahimelech give it to David? **3.** Why is David wanting to carry Goliath's sword? **4.** If you could give a color to the mood of this passage, what would it be: Black—dark and foreboding? Red—Harsh and deadly? Yellow—cautious? Other?

APPLY What "weapon" are you searching for to vanquish what is threatening you the most right now: Confidence—to overcome your challenges? Faith—to overcome your doubts? Love—to overcome the hostility you feel in others? Power—to influence your world? Other?

21:1 Nob. The Philistines took the ruined *tabernacle from Shiloh to Nob. The ark* still rested at the home of Abinadab (7:1). David went to secure other items in the tabernacle such as the ephod, Goliath's sword and the Urim and Thummim.

21:2 David was less than forthcoming with Ahimelech the priest. David's "the-less-you-know-the-better" tactic unraveled when the priest was killed (22:16–18).

21:4 bread. Bread was always kept at the tabernacle. When a fresh supply was made, the old was given to the priests. David's request broke custom, but not laws, regarding worship. Jesus referred to this incident in Matthew 12:3–4.

David at Gath

10 That day David fled from Saul and went to Achish king of Gath.
11 But the servants of Achish said to him, "Isn't this David, the king of
the land? Isn't he the one they sing about in their dances:

" 'Saul has slain his thousands,
and David his tens of thousands'?"

12 David took these words to heart and was very much afraid of
Achish king of Gath. 13 So he pretended to be insane in their presence;
and while he was in their hands he acted like a madman, making
marks on the doors of the gate and letting saliva run down his beard.
14 Achish said to his servants, "Look at the man! He is insane! Why
bring him to me? 15 Am I so short of madmen that you have to bring
this fellow here to carry on like this in front of me? Must this man
come into my house?"

David at Adullam and Mizpah

22 David left Gath and escaped to the cave of Adullam. When his
brothers and his father's household heard about it, they went
down to him there. 2 All those who were in distress or in debt or discontented gathered around him, and he became their leader. About
four hundred men were with him.
3 From there David went to Mizpah in Moab and said to the king of
Moab, "Would you let my father and mother come and stay with you
until I learn what God will do for me?" 4 So he left them with the king
of Moab, and they stayed with him as long as David was in the
stronghold.
5 But the prophet Gad said to David, "Do not stay in the stronghold.
Go into the land of Judah." So David left and went to the forest of
Hereth.

Saul Kills the Priests of Nob

6 Now Saul heard that David and his men had been discovered. And
Saul, spear in hand, was seated under the tamarisk tree on the hill at
Gibeah, with all his officials standing around him. 7 Saul said to them,
"Listen, men of Benjamin! Will the son of Jesse give all of you fields
and vineyards? Will he make all of you commanders of thousands and
commanders of hundreds? 8 Is that why you have all conspired
against me? No one tells me when my son makes a covenant with the
son of Jesse. None of you is concerned about me or tells me that my
son has incited my servant to lie in wait for me, as he does today."
9 But Doeg the Edomite, who was standing with Saul's officials,
said, "I saw the son of Jesse come to Ahimelech son of Ahitub at Nob.
10 Ahimelech inquired of the LORD for him; he also gave him provisions and the sword of Goliath the Philistine."
11 Then the king sent for the priest Ahimelech son of Ahitub and his

OPEN Have people ever thought you were crazy: When you did strange things in college? When you did something out of character? Other?

STUDY **1.** Gath is a Philistine stronghold. Why then does David go there? **2.** Why does David feel it necessary to act like a madman? **3.** What sort of marks does he make? Where? **4.** If five stars is an Academy Award performance, how many stars would you give David?

APPLY Have you ever given an Academy Award performance to get yourself out of trouble?

OPEN Where was your favorite hiding place when you were in grade school? Who else knew about this spot?

STUDY **1.** Why do men join David's band of fugitives? **2.** Are these types of men likely to be reliable? **3.** Why does David entrust his family to a Moabite king (Ruth 1:1–5; 4:17)?

APPLY Has your family been disrupted because you were going through a tough time? Who helped you during that time?

OPEN **1.** When in your life have you had the hardest time deciding whose "side" to be on in a dispute: When your parents fought or got divorced? When friends got divorced? When there was a labor-management dispute at work? In the last election? Other? **2.** How has taking sides hurt you?

STUDY The dispute between David and Saul is causing great tension in the land. People are feeling they have to take sides, and in this incident Saul makes people pay for being on the "wrong" side. **1.** What is Saul's mental and emotional state? **2.** What motivates Doeg the Edomite to testify against Ahimelech? **3.** What

---

22:2 in distress or in debt or discontented. David's men were the disenfranchised. David himself was a fugitive. Together, they were the beginnings of a royal army.

22:4 Moab. David's great-grandmother, Ruth, came from Moab, so he had extended family there. **the stronghold.** This implies a safe place or hideout, but not an actual fort.

22:5 Gad. The prophet became a regular among David's entourage. In their history together, Gad confronted David's sin (2 Sam. 24:11–14) and served as a biographer (1 Chr. 29:29) and music arranger for some of David's psalms (2 Chr. 29:25).

22:7 Benjamin. Saul's strongest political support was from his own tribe, Benjamin. David was from the tribe of Judah.

defense does Ahimelech offer? **4.** Why do the guards refuse the king's edict to kill Ahimelech and his whole family? **5.** As the sole survivor of the massacre of Ahimelech's family, what kind of ally for David do you think Abiathar will be? **6.** What does David's confession in verse 22 say about his character? Would that confession be likely to make Abiathar more loyal or less so?

APPLY 1. When have you felt like a mistake you made caused another person great pain and heartache? **2.** When you make a mistake that hurts someone else, what are you most likely to do: Cover it up? Confess? Feel guilty about it for months? Ignore it and figure they will forget about it?

OPEN When you were in grade school, where were the places in the neighborhood you were most afraid to go: A grumpy neighbor's? A house said to be haunted? The dark woods?

STUDY 1. By what means does David inquire of God? **2.** Why are David's men afraid to go to Keilah (vv. 3, 7)? **3.** What reassures David that going to Keilah is the right idea?

APPLY When have you felt God was leading you to do something that others thought was dangerous? How did you go about deciding what to do?

father's whole family, who were the priests at Nob, and they all came
to the king. 12Saul said, "Listen now, son of Ahitub."
"Yes, my lord," he answered.
13Saul said to him, "Why have you conspired against me, you and
the son of Jesse, giving him bread and a sword and inquiring of God
for him, so that he has rebelled against me and lies in wait for me, as
he does today?"
14Ahimelech answered the king, "Who of all your servants is as
loyal as David, the king's son-in-law, captain of your bodyguard and
highly respected in your household? 15Was that day the first time I
inquired of God for him? Of course not! Let not the king accuse your
servant or any of his father's family, for your servant knows nothing
at all about this whole affair."
16But the king said, "You will surely die, Ahimelech, you and your
father's whole family."
17Then the king ordered the guards at his side: "Turn and kill the
priests of the LORD, because they too have sided with David. They
knew he was fleeing, yet they did not tell me."
But the king's officials were not willing to raise a hand to strike the
priests of the LORD.
18The king then ordered Doeg, "You turn and strike down the
priests." So Doeg the Edomite turned and struck them down. That
day he killed eighty-five men who wore the linen ephod. 19He also put
to the sword Nob, the town of the priests, with its men and women,
its children and infants, and its cattle, donkeys and sheep.
20But Abiathar, a son of Ahimelech son of Ahitub, escaped and fled
to join David. 21He told David that Saul had killed the priests of the
LORD. 22Then David said to Abiathar: "That day, when Doeg the
Edomite was there, I knew he would be sure to tell Saul. I am responsible for the death of your father's whole family. 23Stay with me; don't
be afraid; the man who is seeking your life is seeking mine also. You
will be safe with me."

David Saves Keilah

23 When David was told, "Look, the Philistines are fighting
against Keilah and are looting the threshing floors," 2he inquired of the LORD, saying, "Shall I go and attack these Philistines?"
The LORD answered him, "Go, attack the Philistines and save
Keilah."
3But David's men said to him, "Here in Judah we are afraid. How
much more, then, if we go to Keilah against the Philistine forces!"
4Once again David inquired of the LORD, and the LORD answered
him, "Go down to Keilah, for I am going to give the Philistines into
your hand." 5So David and his men went to Keilah, fought the Philistines and carried off their livestock. He inflicted heavy losses on the
Philistines and saved the people of Keilah. 6(Now Abiathar son of
Ahimelech had brought the ephod down with him when he fled to
David at Keilah.)

22:17 They knew. *It is unlikely that* the priests knew David's plans, since David was cautious and guarded with Ahimelech. Saul's paranoia is talking louder than his reason.

22:20 Abiathar. Once the priest Abiathar joined the group, David's board of advisors was complete, though he had yet to receive the crown.

23:2 inquired of the LORD. When Abiathar joined David, he brought the ephod with the Urim and Thummim. This gave David access to God's wisdom and direction.

Saul Pursues David

7 Saul was told that David had gone to Keilah, and he said, "God has
handed him over to me, for David has imprisoned himself by entering
a town with gates and bars." 8 And Saul called up all his forces for
battle, to go down to Keilah to besiege David and his men.
9 When David learned that Saul was plotting against him, he said to
Abiathar the priest, "Bring the ephod." 10 David said, "O LORD, God of
Israel, your servant has heard definitely that Saul plans to come to
Keilah and destroy the town on account of me. 11 Will the citizens of
Keilah surrender me to him? Will Saul come down, as your servant
has heard? O LORD, God of Israel, tell your servant."
And the LORD said, "He will."
12 Again David asked, "Will the citizens of Keilah surrender me and
my men to Saul?"
And the LORD said, "They will."
13 So David and his men, about six hundred in number, left Keilah
and kept moving from place to place. When Saul was told that David
had escaped from Keilah, he did not go there.
14 David stayed in the desert strongholds and in the hills of the
Desert of Ziph. Day after day Saul searched for him, but God did not
give David into his hands.
15 While David was at Horesh in the Desert of Ziph, he learned that
Saul had come out to take his life. 16 And Saul's son Jonathan went to
David at Horesh and helped him find strength in God. 17 "Don't be
afraid," he said. "My father Saul will not lay a hand on you. You will
be king over Israel, and I will be second to you. Even my father Saul
knows this." 18 The two of them made a covenant before the LORD.
Then Jonathan went home, but David remained at Horesh.
19 The Ziphites went up to Saul at Gibeah and said, "Is not David
hiding among us in the strongholds at Horesh, on the hill of Hakilah,
south of Jeshimon? 20 Now, O king, come down whenever it pleases
you to do so, and we will be responsible for handing him over to the
king."
21 Saul replied, "The LORD bless you for your concern for me. 22 Go
and make further preparation. Find out where David usually goes and
who has seen him there. They tell me he is very crafty. 23 Find out
about all the hiding places he uses and come back to me with definite
information.[a] Then I will go with you; if he is in the area, I will track
him down among all the clans of Judah."
24 So they set out and went to Ziph ahead of Saul. Now David and
his men were in the Desert of Maon, in the Arabah south of Jeshimon.
25 Saul and his men began the search, and when David was told about
it, he went down to the rock and stayed in the Desert of Maon. When
Saul heard this, he went into the Desert of Maon in pursuit of David.
26 Saul was going along one side of the mountain, and David and
his men were on the other side, hurrying to get away from Saul. As
Saul and his forces were closing in on David and his men to capture

[a]23 Or *me at Nacon*

OPEN **1.** Which of the following places would you least like to be trapped: A Karaoke bar? A rock concert? A professional wrestling arena? A political debate? A place showing foreign art films? **2.** When you get trapped in an unpleasant place, where do you dream of escaping to?

STUDY Because of his jealousy, King Saul has been looking for an opportunity to kill David for some time. Saul thinks he has found his opportunity. **1.** Why is Saul pleased to hear that David is in Keilah (vv. 7–8)? **2.** Why do you think the citizens of Keilah were willing to turn against the man who saved their town from the Philistines (vv. 5, 12)? **3.** Who helps David find strength when he is in the Desert of Ziph? **4.** What are some important things a person can do to help someone else find strength in God? **5.** What benefits do you think the Ziphites were seeking in return for turning David over to Saul? **6.** How would you describe the timing of the message of the Philistine raid (v. 27): Fortuitous? Coincidental? The hand of God? **7.** When has something happened at just the right time to save you from disaster? Do you believe it was coincidental or an action of God?

APPLY **1.** What is seeking to "trap" you right now: Finances? Rivals at work? An ex-spouse? Some inner struggle? **2.** When you have felt "pursued" who has helped you find strength in God?

23:18 Jonathan. This was the last meeting of Jonathan and David. Jonathan had been faithful to David as Saul's successor even though it meant forfeiting his own chance at the top. Jonathan died in battle before David came to the throne, so he never served in David's kingdom (31:2). Jonathan was a unique friend to David.

them, 27a messenger came to Saul, saying, "Come quickly! The Philistines are raiding the land." 28Then Saul broke off his pursuit of David
and went to meet the Philistines. That is why they call this place Sela
Hammahlekoth.[a] 29And David went up from there and lived in the
strongholds of En Gedi.

David Spares Saul's Life

24 After Saul returned from pursuing the Philistines, he was
told, "David is in the Desert of En Gedi." 2So Saul took three
thousand chosen men from all Israel and set out to look for David
and his men near the Crags of the Wild Goats.

3He came to the sheep pens along the way; a cave was there, and
Saul went in to relieve himself. David and his men were far back in
the cave. 4The men said, "This is the day the LORD spoke of when he
said[b] to you, 'I will give your enemy into your hands for you to deal
with as you wish.' " Then David crept up unnoticed and cut off a
corner of Saul's robe.

5Afterward, David was conscience-stricken for having cut off a
corner of his robe. 6He said to his men, "The LORD forbid that I should
do such a thing to my master, the LORD's anointed, or lift my hand
against him; for he is the anointed of the LORD." 7With these words
David rebuked his men and did not allow them to attack Saul. And
Saul left the cave and went his way.

8Then David went out of the cave and called out to Saul, "My lord
the king!" When Saul looked behind him, David bowed down and
prostrated himself with his face to the ground. 9He said to Saul, "Why
do you listen when men say, 'David is bent on harming you'? 10This
day you have seen with your own eyes how the LORD delivered you
into my hands in the cave. Some urged me to kill you, but I spared
you; I said, 'I will not lift my hand against my master, because he is
the LORD's anointed.' 11See, my father, look at this piece of your robe
in my hand! I cut off the corner of your robe but did not kill you. Now
understand and recognize that I am not guilty of wrongdoing or
rebellion. I have not wronged you, but you are hunting me down to
take my life. 12May the LORD judge between you and me. And may the
LORD avenge the wrongs you have done to me, but my hand will not
touch you. 13As the old saying goes, 'From evildoers come evil deeds,'
so my hand will not touch you.

14"Against whom has the king of Israel come out? Whom are you
pursuing? A dead dog? A flea? 15May the LORD be our judge and
decide between us. May he consider my cause and uphold it; may he
vindicate me by delivering me from your hand."

16When David finished saying this, Saul asked, "Is that your voice,
David my son?" And he wept aloud. 17"You are more righteous than

[a]28 *Sela Hammahlekoth* means *rock of parting.* [b]4 Or *"Today the LORD is saying*

OPEN **1.** When you were a child or adolescent, what was your family's favorite "get-away"? **2.** What were the names of some of the local landmarks in that place?

STUDY To keep his hold on the throne, Saul has been seeking to kill David. David demonstrates amazing restraint when he has the opportunity to kill Saul but doesn't. **1.** Near what landmark does Saul search for David? **2.** A king's robe was a symbol of his office. Why does David cut off part of Saul's robe: As part of a "mind game"? Just to prove what he *could* have done? To insult him? To show he was after the kingship? **3.** Why does David feel guilty about this act later? **4.** What impression do you get of David in this story: A humble man who respected authority? A man of peace? A wimp? Other? **5.** What would you have done had you been David? **6.** How do you regard Saul's penitence: Sincere? Manipulative? **7.** Would you trust Saul's "change of heart" at this point in the story?

APPLY **1.** Like David, are you tempted to have revenge against someone? **2.** What can you do to follow David's example of returning good for evil to the "Saul" in your life?

24:4 the LORD spoke. The Bible contains no record of God giving this word to David or his men. It may have been a prophecy not recorded, or an inference on the part of his men based on other statements about David.

24:6 the LORD's anointed. David was consistently loyal to God. Building God's kingdom was his priority. Saul had allowed his reign to degenerate into the normal political games of survival, intrigue and greed. Even so, David would not sink to that level by killing God's anointed king.

24:11 my father. Since David had married Michal, Saul was his father-in-law as well as his king.

24:16 wept aloud. Saul operated at both extremes. While he grieved here, he quickly resumed his posse and forced David into flight again.

I," he said. "You have treated me well, but I have treated you badly.
[18]You have just now told me of the good you did to me; the LORD
delivered me into your hands, but you did not kill me. [19]When a man
finds his enemy, does he let him get away unharmed? May the LORD
reward you well for the way you treated me today. [20]I know that you
will surely be king and that the kingdom of Israel will be established
in your hands. [21]Now swear to me by the LORD that you will not cut
off my descendants or wipe out my name from my father's family."
[22]So David gave his oath to Saul. Then Saul returned home, but
David and his men went up to the stronghold.

David, Nabal and Abigail

25 Now Samuel died, and all Israel assembled and mourned for
him; and they buried him at his home in Ramah.
Then David moved down into the Desert of Maon.[a] [2]A certain man
in Maon, who had property there at Carmel, was very wealthy. He had
a thousand goats and three thousand sheep, which he was shearing
in Carmel. [3]His name was Nabal and his wife's name was Abigail. She
was an intelligent and beautiful woman, but her husband, a Calebite,
was surly and mean in his dealings.
[4]While David was in the desert, he heard that Nabal was shearing
sheep. [5]So he sent ten young men and said to them, "Go up to Nabal
at Carmel and greet him in my name. [6]Say to him: 'Long life to you!
Good health to you and your household! And good health to all that
is yours!
[7]" 'Now I hear that it is sheep-shearing time. When your shepherds
were with us, we did not mistreat them, and the whole time they were
at Carmel nothing of theirs was missing. [8]Ask your own servants and
they will tell you. Therefore be favorable toward my young men, since
we come at a festive time. Please give your servants and your son
David whatever you can find for them.' "
[9]When David's men arrived, they gave Nabal this message in
David's name. Then they waited.
[10]Nabal answered David's servants, "Who is this David? Who is this
son of Jesse? Many servants are breaking away from their masters
these days. [11]Why should I take my bread and water, and the meat I
have slaughtered for my shearers, and give it to men coming from
who knows where?"
[12]David's men turned around and went back. When they arrived,
they reported every word. [13]David said to his men, "Put on your
swords!" So they put on their swords, and David put on his. About
four hundred men went up with David, while two hundred stayed
with the supplies.
[14]One of the servants told Nabal's wife Abigail: "David sent

[a]*1* Some Septuagint manuscripts; Hebrew *Paran*

OPEN 1. What person has died who was an important part of your life as a child or adolescent? **2.** What do you remember of how people honored that person's memory?

STUDY After Samuel's death, David's army goes on the move. He needs provisions for his army, but securing them results in a conflict with a local rancher. **1.** Since Samuel was such an important figure during this time, why is his death and the reaction to it passed over with so little detail? **2.** Had you been asked to say something at Samuel's Memorial Service, what might you have said? **3.** What do Nabal and Saul have in common? **4.** Hospitality was a central value in this culture. Why does Nabal refuse to provide such hospitality: Macho pride? Greed? Ingratitude? Disregard for tradition? **5.** What were David's motives in guarding Nabal's possessions? Does he have a right to be repaid? **6.** What motivates Abigail's actions—fear of reprisal or disdain for her husband? **7.** If you were recently widowed, like Abigail, how would you respond to a sudden proposal like David's? **8.** What role do you think was played by Saul's giving of David's wife (Saul's daughter, Michal) to another man?

APPLY 1. With which person in this story do you most identify: David—people don't appreciate what I've done for them? Abigail—my spouse made mistakes I have to fix? Nabal—people are always wanting what I have? Michal—I'm always

24:22 stronghold. Saul had just proclaimed David's righteousness, but David knew better than to trust Saul's goodwill. He scampered to a cave or similar hideout.

25:1 Samuel died. Samuel bridged the era of the judges and the kings. His impact on Israel's spiritual life was great, though his sons failed to carry on his work.

25:2–44 Nabal. His name meant "fool." He certainly dealt with David foolishly. This passage describes a husband who was as foolish as his wife was wise. Abigail saved the situation, but Nabal didn't survive it.

25:8 Please give. Nabal insulted David by refusing his request. David's men could have plundered Nabal's flocks easily. Nabal's smarter choice would have been to help the renegade leader.

caught in the middle of these conflicts? 2. What "Abigail" has stepped into a conflict you were involved in to keep it from escalating? How did you thank this person?

---

messengers from the desert to give our master his greetings, but he
hurled insults at them. 15Yet these men were very good to us. They did
not mistreat us, and the whole time we were out in the fields near
them nothing was missing. 16Night and day they were a wall around
us all the time we were herding our sheep near them. 17Now think it
over and see what you can do, because disaster is hanging over our
master and his whole household. He is such a wicked man that no
one can talk to him."

18Abigail lost no time. She took two hundred loaves of bread, two
skins of wine, five dressed sheep, five seahs[a] of roasted grain, a hundred cakes of raisins and two hundred cakes of pressed figs, and
loaded them on donkeys. 19Then she told her servants, "Go on ahead;
I'll follow you." But she did not tell her husband Nabal.

20As she came riding her donkey into a mountain ravine, there were
David and his men descending toward her, and she met them. 21David
had just said, "It's been useless—all my watching over this fellow's
property in the desert so that nothing of his was missing. He has paid
me back evil for good. 22May God deal with David,[b] be it ever so severely, if by morning I leave alive one male of all who belong to him!"

23When Abigail saw David, she quickly got off her donkey and
bowed down before David with her face to the ground. 24She fell at
his feet and said: "My lord, let the blame be on me alone. Please let
your servant speak to you; hear what your servant has to say. 25May
my lord pay no attention to that wicked man Nabal. He is just like his
name—his name is Fool, and folly goes with him. But as for me, your
servant, I did not see the men my master sent.

26"Now since the LORD has kept you, my master, from bloodshed
and from avenging yourself with your own hands, as surely as the
LORD lives and as you live, may your enemies and all who intend to
harm my master be like Nabal. 27And let this gift, which your servant
has brought to my master, be given to the men who follow you.
28Please forgive your servant's offense, for the LORD will certainly
make a lasting dynasty for my master, because he fights the LORD's
battles. Let no wrongdoing be found in you as long as you live. 29Even
though someone is pursuing you to take your life, the life of my master will be bound securely in the bundle of the living by the LORD your
God. But the lives of your enemies he will hurl away as from the
pocket of a sling. 30When the LORD has done for my master every
good thing he promised concerning him and has appointed him
leader over Israel, 31my master will not have on his conscience the
staggering burden of needless bloodshed or of having avenged him-

[a]*18* That is, probably about a bushel (about 37 liters) [b]*22* Some Septuagint manuscripts; Hebrew *with David's enemies*

25:22 be it ever so severely. This is a severe Hebrew curse. David's oath of revenge reveals the other side of his leadership: quick, sure, confident and violent.

25:25 his name is Fool. Names often reflect the character of a person, and especially during this era. That's why God often changed a person's name after he or she passed a pivotal point. Even in the New Testament, names are significant. In the book of Philemon, Paul makes a request based on the meaning of a name. He asks that Onesimus (whose name means "useful" or "profitable") be made useful again (Philem. 1:10–11).

25:28 Let no wrongdoing be found. Abigail was a clever diplomat. She appealed to David's legacy, integrity and reputation. David's passion was not indifferent to all this cleverness, and eventually Abigail became his wife (v. 42).

25:29 in the bundle of the living. In other words, God will keep you safe and alive. **from the pocket of a sling.** An apt image given David's victory over Goliath.

self. And when the LORD has brought my master success, remember your servant."

32David said to Abigail, "Praise be to the LORD, the God of Israel, who has sent you today to meet me. 33May you be blessed for your good judgment and for keeping me from bloodshed this day and from avenging myself with my own hands. 34Otherwise, as surely as the LORD, the God of Israel, lives, who has kept me from harming you, if you had not come quickly to meet me, not one male belonging to Nabal would have been left alive by daybreak."

35Then David accepted from her hand what she had brought him and said, "Go home in peace. I have heard your words and granted your request."

36When Abigail went to Nabal, he was in the house holding a banquet like that of a king. He was in high spirits and very drunk. So she told him nothing until daybreak. 37Then in the morning, when Nabal was sober, his wife told him all these things, and his heart failed him and he became like a stone. 38About ten days later, the LORD struck Nabal and he died.

39When David heard that Nabal was dead, he said, "Praise be to the LORD, who has upheld my cause against Nabal for treating me with contempt. He has kept his servant from doing wrong and has brought Nabal's wrongdoing down on his own head."

Then David sent word to Abigail, asking her to become his wife. 40His servants went to Carmel and said to Abigail, "David has sent us to you to take you to become his wife."

41She bowed down with her face to the ground and said, "Here is your maidservant, ready to serve you and wash the feet of my master's servants." 42Abigail quickly got on a donkey and, attended by her five maids, went with David's messengers and became his wife. 43David had also married Ahinoam of Jezreel, and they both were his wives. 44But Saul had given his daughter Michal, David's wife, to Paltiel[a] son of Laish, who was from Gallim.

David Again Spares Saul's Life

26 The Ziphites went to Saul at Gibeah and said, "Is not David hiding on the hill of Hakilah, which faces Jeshimon?"

2So Saul went down to the Desert of Ziph, with his three thousand chosen men of Israel, to search there for David. 3Saul made his camp beside the road on the hill of Hakilah facing Jeshimon, but David stayed in the desert. When he saw that Saul had followed him there, 4he sent out scouts and learned that Saul had definitely arrived.[b]

5Then David set out and went to the place where Saul had camped.

[a]44 Hebrew *Palti,* a variant of *Paltiel* [b]4 Or *had come to Nacon*

OPEN **1.** What kind of sleeper are you: Light—I awaken when a cat walks in the room? Moderate—I can be roused when needed? Heavy—I'd sleep through a hurricane? **2.** What is the most embarrassing or damaging thing you have managed to sleep through?

STUDY In an incident that is very similar to the one in chapter 24, David manages to come within striking distance of Saul, but

25:32 Praise be to the LORD. David could see with spiritual eyes. Abigail had provided supplies for his men and kept him from an error in judgment and needless bloodshed.

25:36 in high spirits and very drunk. Nabal was all that his name implied. Even while his wife was saving the farm, he was partying.

25:37 became like a stone. Perhaps a heart attack or stroke.

25:43 Ahinoam. Ahinoam gave David his first son, Amnon. She and Abigail were at one time captured by the Amalekites and rescued by David (30:5).

26:2 three thousand chosen men. The size of Saul's posse reveals his priorities. Rather than fighting enemies or governing the country, Saul was bent on settling personal vendettas and protecting his ego.

26:5 Abner. Abner and Saul were cousins. Abner was the commander of Saul's army who first brought David to Saul after Goliath was defeated (17:55–58).

chooses again to spare his life. **1.** Compare this passage and David's encounter with Saul in the cave (ch. 24). What are the similarities and differences? **2.** Why does David not let Abishai do what he proposes (vv. 8–11)? **3.** What evidence do we have that the Lord is with David? **4.** How can you tell if the Lord is with someone today? **5.** Why does David encourage Saul to consider whether God or people are inciting him to pursue David? How can a person tell whether they are doing something to please God or to please people? **6.** When David and Saul confer this time (compare with 24:9–22), what is David most concerned to protect (v. 19)? **7.** How does David show he is wiser and less trusting of Saul this time around?

APPLY 1. If you knew the Lord was with you, what "enemy camp" would you dare to walk into? **2.** What kind of person would you want to walk into that "camp" with you to give you support?

He saw where Saul and Abner son of Ner, the commander of the army,
had lain down. Saul was lying inside the camp, with the army
encamped around him.
6 David then asked Ahimelech the Hittite and Abishai son of Zeruiah,
Joab's brother, "Who will go down into the camp with me to Saul?"
"I'll go with you," said Abishai.
7 So David and Abishai went to the army by night, and there was
Saul, lying asleep inside the camp with his spear stuck in the ground
near his head. Abner and the soldiers were lying around him.
8 Abishai said to David, "Today God has delivered your enemy into
your hands. Now let me pin him to the ground with one thrust of my
spear; I won't strike him twice."
9 But David said to Abishai, "Don't destroy him! Who can lay a hand
on the LORD's anointed and be guiltless? 10 As surely as the LORD
lives," he said, "the LORD himself will strike him; either his time will
come and he will die, or he will go into battle and perish. 11 But the
LORD forbid that I should lay a hand on the LORD's anointed. Now get
the spear and water jug that are near his head, and let's go."
12 So David took the spear and water jug near Saul's head, and they
left. No one saw or knew about it, nor did anyone wake up. They were
all sleeping, because the LORD had put them into a deep sleep.
13 Then David crossed over to the other side and stood on top of the
hill some distance away; there was a wide space between them. 14 He
called out to the army and to Abner son of Ner, "Aren't you going to
answer me, Abner?"
Abner replied, "Who are you who calls to the king?"
15 David said, "You're a man, aren't you? And who is like you in
Israel? Why didn't you guard your lord the king? Someone came to destroy your lord the king. 16 What you have done is not good. As surely
as the LORD lives, you and your men deserve to die, because you did
not guard your master, the LORD's anointed. Look around you. Where
are the king's spear and water jug that were near his head?"
17 Saul recognized David's voice and said, "Is that your voice, David
my son?"
David replied, "Yes it is, my lord the king." 18 And he added, "Why is
my lord pursuing his servant? What have I done, and what wrong am
I guilty of? 19 Now let my lord the king listen to his servant's words. If
the LORD has incited you against me, then may he accept an offering.
If, however, men have done it, may they be cursed before the LORD!
They have now driven me from my share in the LORD's inheritance
and have said, 'Go, serve other gods.' 20 Now do not let my blood fall
to the ground far from the presence of the LORD. The king of Israel
has come out to look for a flea—as one hunts a partridge in the
mountains."
21 Then Saul said, "I have sinned. Come back, David my son. Be-

---

26:12 near Saul's head. Saul was sleeping among his men (v. 7). David and Abishai crept into a most dangerous spot, surrounded by adversaries just as David *later described in* Psalm 23. Again, David proved to Saul that he intended Saul no harm.

26:19 If the LORD has incited. In other words, David claimed that there was no reason for conflict between him and Saul. If David had an issue with God, Saul should let David deal with God. Either way, Saul should back off his constant pursuit.

26:20 look for a flea. Once again David reveals the paranoid nature of Saul's pursuit (24:14). Saul was chasing David as if he were a criminal fugitive. And if Saul would catch him and kill him, would Saul recover his reign or reputation? Saul is committed to a no-win campaign of struggling against God.

26:21 you considered my life precious. Sparing Saul's life when he had

cause you considered my life precious today, I will not try to harm
you again. Surely I have acted like a fool and have erred greatly."
22"Here is the king's spear," David answered. "Let one of your
young men come over and get it. 23The LORD rewards every man for
his righteousness and faithfulness. The LORD delivered you into my
hands today, but I would not lay a hand on the LORD'S anointed. 24As
surely as I valued your life today, so may the LORD value my life and
deliver me from all trouble."
25Then Saul said to David, "May you be blessed, my son David; you
will do great things and surely triumph."
So David went on his way, and Saul returned home.

David Among the Philistines

27 But David thought to himself, "One of these days I will be destroyed by the hand of Saul. The best thing I can do is to
escape to the land of the Philistines. Then Saul will give up searching
for me anywhere in Israel, and I will slip out of his hand."
2So David and the six hundred men with him left and went over to
Achish son of Maoch king of Gath. 3David and his men settled in Gath
with Achish. Each man had his family with him, and David had his
two wives: Ahinoam of Jezreel and Abigail of Carmel, the widow of
Nabal. 4When Saul was told that David had fled to Gath, he no longer
searched for him.
5Then David said to Achish, "If I have found favor in your eyes, let a
place be assigned to me in one of the country towns, that I may live
there. Why should your servant live in the royal city with you?"
6So on that day Achish gave him Ziklag, and it has belonged to the
kings of Judah ever since. 7David lived in Philistine territory a year
and four months.
8Now David and his men went up and raided the Geshurites, the
Girzites and the Amalekites. (From ancient times these peoples had
lived in the land extending to Shur and Egypt.) 9Whenever David attacked an area, he did not leave a man or woman alive, but took
sheep and cattle, donkeys and camels, and clothes. Then he returned
to Achish.
10When Achish asked, "Where did you go raiding today?" David
would say, "Against the Negev of Judah" or "Against the Negev of
Jerahmeel" or "Against the Negev of the Kenites." 11He did not leave a

OPEN What is the longest period of time that you have spent in a foreign land? What did you especially like about being there? What did you not like so much?

STUDY Because David did not trust Saul's word that he was truly reformed, he felt the need to escape to the land of the Philistines. From there he conducts a series of raids against Israel's enemies. **1.** Given King Achish's last encounter with David (21:10–15), how do you think Achish felt about David's arrival and settlement in Gath? **2.** Why does David desire to move to a country town (v. 5)? **3.** What was David's motive for totally annihilating those whom he raided (v. 9)? Do you think that was adequate motivation? **4.** Why does David lie to Achish about who he had attacked? Does Achish swallow his story?

APPLY 1. David escapes Saul only to land in Achish's lap. When have you had a similar "out-of-the-frying-pan-into-the-fire" escapade? **2.** Are you involved in anything now that could cause trouble?

---

the chance to kill him, David proved his own intentions and revealed the foolishness of Saul's paranoia.

26:25 surely triumph. This may refer to David's succession as king.

27:1 to the land of the Philistines. *David had fled to Philistia before* (21:10–15). On that occasion he had feigned insanity to escape from the home of King Achish, the very king with whom he was about to establish an alliance.

27:2 Achish. The first time David faced Achish, David was afraid he'd be seen as Goliath's killer. This time his position was much safer. If he were seen as Saul's enemy, Achish would easily accept him. Achish was Saul's enemy too.

27:4 he no longer searched. David's plan succeeded. Saul had no interest in *taking his search* into Philistia. David posed no serious political threat from that far away.

27:5 Since David was seeking sanctuary, he placed himself under obligation to Achish. If David were living in an outlying town, perhaps Achish would call on him less often.

27:7 Philistine territory. David lived in Ziklag (in Philistia) until Saul's death. Ziklag was thereafter a Judean city.

27:8 Geshurites. Two tribes had this name. The tribe David attacked was south of Philistia on the way to Egypt. They were among the settlers Joshua had failed to conquer when the Israelites entered Canaan (Josh. 13:2).

27:9 did not leave a man or woman alive. David's complete destruction of the townspeople accomplished two things. It fulfilled God's original direction to Joshua and it covered David's lie to Achish. David had led the king to believe that his fight was against Judah. Survivors could become informers.

man or woman alive to be brought to Gath, for he thought, "They
might inform on us and say, 'This is what David did.' " And such was
his practice as long as he lived in Philistine territory. 12Achish trusted
David and said to himself, "He has become so odious to his people,
the Israelites, that he will be my servant forever."

Saul and the Witch of Endor

28 In those days the Philistines gathered their forces to fight
against Israel. Achish said to David, "You must understand
that you and your men will accompany me in the army."
2David said, "Then you will see for yourself what your servant
can do."
Achish replied, "Very well, I will make you my bodyguard for life."
3Now Samuel was dead, and all Israel had mourned for him and
buried him in his own town of Ramah. Saul had expelled the mediums and spiritists from the land.
4The Philistines assembled and came and set up camp at Shunem,
while Saul gathered all the Israelites and set up camp at Gilboa.
5When Saul saw the Philistine army, he was afraid; terror filled his
heart. 6He inquired of the LORD, but the LORD did not answer him by
dreams or Urim or prophets. 7Saul then said to his attendants, "Find
me a woman who is a medium, so I may go and inquire of her."
"There is one in Endor," they said.
8So Saul disguised himself, putting on other clothes, and at night
he and two men went to the woman. "Consult a spirit for me," he
said, "and bring up for me the one I name."
9But the woman said to him, "Surely you know what Saul has
done. He has cut off the mediums and spiritists from the land. Why
have you set a trap for my life to bring about my death?"
10Saul swore to her by the LORD, "As surely as the LORD lives, you
will not be punished for this."
11Then the woman asked, "Whom shall I bring up for you?"
"Bring up Samuel," he said.
12When the woman saw Samuel, she cried out at the top of her
voice and said to Saul, "Why have you deceived me? You are Saul!"
13The king said to her, "Don't be afraid. What do you see?"
The woman said, "I see a spirit[a] coming up out of the ground."

[a] 13 Or *see spirits*; or *see gods*

OPEN 1. If you could talk to a person now dead, who would you want to talk to? Would it be someone famous or someone you know personally? **2.** What would you most want to know from him or her?

STUDY Since Samuel was dead and Saul was no longer in favor with God, he felt the need to get some direction in fighting against the Philistines. In this story, the direction he gets is not what he probably had in mind. **1.** Why did Saul expel spiritists and mediums from Israel (Lev. 19:31; 20:6; Deut. 18:10–13)? **2.** Why then does he consult one anyway? Have you ever had a moment where you wanted to know if an opposing religion was true? **3.** Why does the woman fear she might die (Lev. 20:27)? **4.** Why does Saul think Samuel will help him when God won't? **5.** What does Samuel predict for Saul and his sons? **6.** If you were Saul at this time, what would you have done: A lot of praying? Made peace? Disregarded the whole thing as a bad dream? Other?

APPLY 1. When have you earnestly sought God's direction on a matter without getting a clear response? What do you think you should do next in such a situation: Continue to pray? Consult a spiritual leader? Just decide on your own? **2.** If you knew you had but one day to live, how would you live it?

27:12 Achish trusted David. Achish trusted David so much that he made David his bodyguard (28:2).

28:1 you and your men will accompany me. David's collaboration in battle, even against his homeland, was the payoff for sanctuary in Philistia and for getting Ziklag as his own.

28:2 David and Achish were still jockeying for position with each other. David's statement *sounds like* a boast, yet he does not actually promise any loyalty. Achish's promise of the position of bodyguard was probably based on David's performance in battle.

28:3 mediums and spiritists. According to Moses' law, these people were to be put to death (Lev. 20:27). This is likely what Saul did when he "expelled" them.

28:6 the LORD did not answer. Saul's sources for spiritual direction were bleak. Samuel was dead (v. 3). The prophet Abiathar had aligned himself with David and taken the official ephod (the garment that held the Urim and Thummim for decision making). The prophet Gad had aligned himself with David as well. Saul's connections to God as the source of wisdom and strength were dwindling.

28:7 Find me … a medium. Saul's weak spirit gave in to witchcraft rather than waiting on God for an answer. Ironically, Saul had just outlawed witchcraft (v. 3), and now he was seeking it.

28:9 cut off. This phrase often means capital punishment, rather than excommunication.

28:12 she cried out. The image of Samuel surprised and scared the woman. She may have feared for her life because of Saul's murdering of the other spiritists. She also may have been shocked to realize that God was in control of her visions.

14"What does he look like?" he asked.

"An old man wearing a robe is coming up," she said.

Then Saul knew it was Samuel, and he bowed down and prostrated himself with his face to the ground.

15Samuel said to Saul, "Why have you disturbed me by bringing me up?"

"I am in great distress," Saul said. "The Philistines are fighting against me, and God has turned away from me. He no longer answers me, either by prophets or by dreams. So I have called on you to tell me what to do."

16Samuel said, "Why do you consult me, now that the LORD has turned away from you and become your enemy? 17The LORD has done what he predicted through me. The LORD has torn the kingdom out of your hands and given it to one of your neighbors—to David. 18Because you did not obey the LORD or carry out his fierce wrath against the Amalekites, the LORD has done this to you today. 19The LORD will hand over both Israel and you to the Philistines, and tomorrow you and your sons will be with me. The LORD will also hand over the army of Israel to the Philistines."

20Immediately Saul fell full length on the ground, filled with fear because of Samuel's words. His strength was gone, for he had eaten nothing all that day and night.

21When the woman came to Saul and saw that he was greatly shaken, she said, "Look, your maidservant has obeyed you. I took my life in my hands and did what you told me to do. 22Now please listen to your servant and let me give you some food so you may eat and have the strength to go on your way."

23He refused and said, "I will not eat."

But his men joined the woman in urging him, and he listened to them. He got up from the ground and sat on the couch.

24The woman had a fattened calf at the house, which she butchered at once. She took some flour, kneaded it and baked bread without yeast. 25Then she set it before Saul and his men, and they ate. That same night they got up and left.

Achish Sends David Back to Ziklag

29 The Philistines gathered all their forces at Aphek, and Israel camped by the spring in Jezreel. 2As the Philistine rulers marched with their units of hundreds and thousands, David and his men were marching at the rear with Achish. 3The commanders of the Philistines asked, "What about these Hebrews?"

Achish replied, "Is this not David, who was an officer of Saul king of Israel? He has already been with me for over a year, and from the day he left Saul until now, I have found no fault in him."

4But the Philistine commanders were angry with him and said, "Send the man back, that he may return to the place you assigned him. He must not go with us into battle, or he will turn against us during the fighting. How better could he regain his master's favor

OPEN **1.** When have you found people distrusting you because of some affiliation you had? **2.** What were you able to do to build trust when in that situation?

STUDY Saul's hostile treatment of David had driven him to associate with Israel's arch-enemy, the Philistines. A lack of trust, similar to that between David and Saul, arose when David was with the Philistines. **1.** What were the Philistines concerned about in relation to David and his army? **2.** Had you been one of the Philistine soldiers, which of the follow-

---

29:2 Philistine rulers. When the Philistine army captured the ark, bringing plagues on three towns, the leaders asked this same group when assembled for them to find a solution (5:8–6:16).

29:3 I have found no fault. Achish remained oblivious to David's deception. David spent his free time leveling Philistine cities, while Achish was led to believe he was creating mayhem in Judah.

29:4 he will turn. The Hebrews had allied with the Philistines before (14:20–22), and their memories of it were not pleasant. In the heat of battle they left the Philistines to join with Saul and Jonathan.

than by taking the heads of our own men? [5]Isn't this the David they
sang about in their dances:

" 'Saul has slain his thousands,
and David his tens of thousands'?"

[6]So Achish called David and said to him, "As surely as the LORD
lives, you have been reliable, and I would be pleased to have you
serve with me in the army. From the day you came to me until now, I
have found no fault in you, but the rulers don't approve of you. [7]Turn
back and go in peace; do nothing to displease the Philistine rulers."
[8]"But what have I done?" asked David. "What have you found
against your servant from the day I came to you until now? Why can't
I go and fight against the enemies of my lord the king?"
[9]Achish answered, "I know that you have been as pleasing in my
eyes as an angel of God; nevertheless, the Philistine commanders
have said, 'He must not go up with us into battle.' [10]Now get up early,
along with your master's servants who have come with you, and
leave in the morning as soon as it is light."
[11]So David and his men got up early in the morning to go back to
the land of the Philistines, and the Philistines went up to Jezreel.

David Destroys the Amalekites

30 David and his men reached Ziklag on the third day. Now the
Amalekites had raided the Negev and Ziklag. They had
attacked Ziklag and burned it, [2]and had taken captive the women and
all who were in it, both young and old. They killed none of them, but
carried them off as they went on their way.
[3]When David and his men came to Ziklag, they found it destroyed
by fire and their wives and sons and daughters taken captive. [4]So
David and his men wept aloud until they had no strength left to weep.
[5]David's two wives had been captured—Ahinoam of Jezreel and
Abigail, the widow of Nabal of Carmel. [6]David was greatly distressed
because the men were talking of stoning him; each one was bitter in
spirit because of his sons and daughters. But David found strength in
the LORD his God.
[7]Then David said to Abiathar the priest, the son of Ahimelech, "Bring
me the ephod." Abiathar brought it to him, [8]and David inquired of the
LORD, "Shall I pursue this raiding party? Will I overtake them?"
"Pursue them," he answered. "You will certainly overtake them and
succeed in the rescue."
[9]David and the six hundred men with him came to the Besor Ravine, where some stayed behind, [10]for two hundred men were too
exhausted to cross the ravine. But David and four hundred men continued the pursuit.
[11]They found an Egyptian in a field and brought him to David. They
gave him water to drink and food to eat— [12]part of a cake of pressed

ing would have reflected your attitude about this situation: Why can't we all get along? Keep them out front where I can see them? Let's trust our leader's judgment? I can't tell the good guys from the bad guys without a program? **3.** How would you have felt had you been David and Achish asked you to leave: Like a person without a country? Angry my honor had been questioned? Secretly glad I wouldn't be fighting my own people?

APPLY 1. In what way are you caught between conflicting loyalties right now? **2.** How does a primary loyalty to God help you sort out other loyalties?

OPEN 1. If you could recover something you lost earlier in your life, what would you like it to be: A lost boyfriend or girlfriend? A lost job? A lost opportunity? Your lost innocence? A lost loved one? **2.** What would you do to celebrate that recovery?

STUDY 1. How do David and his men react initially to their losses from the attack of the Amalekites? **2.** Why do the men want to stone David? **3.** Where did David find strength for his losses and the rebellion of his men? What do you think was most helpful to David in finding this strength: Prayer? Remembering God's mighty works from the past? Talking to a priest? Other? **4.** How does the ephod relate to David's inquiry and God's will (vv. 7–8; 23:9-12)? **5.** What does David's decision to share the plunder with those who stayed behind, say about his character? **6.** How would you have felt sharing the plunder of a battle with those who you thought should have fought, but didn't? **7.** Why does David send some of the plunder to the elders of Judah: To get in their good graces? Out of love for his peo-

29:6 As surely as the LORD lives. Whether Achish believed in the Lord or not, he was *speaking a language David* understood. God was not the Lord of Philistia, but of Israel, David's nation.

29:8 what have I done? David played along, but this turn of events was fortunate. Saul was still king; David's time had not yet come. Had he fought in this battle, David would have put his sword against his own countrymen.

30:1–31:13 In this episode David defended his own camp while Saul lost his kingdom.

30:1 Amalekites. These were people south of Philistia that David had raided while he claimed to be fighting his own tribe of Judah (27:8).

figs and two cakes of raisins. He ate and was revived, for he had not
eaten any food or drunk any water for three days and three nights.
[13]David asked him, "To whom do you belong, and where do you
come from?"
He said, "I am an Egyptian, the slave of an Amalekite. My master
abandoned me when I became ill three days ago. [14]We raided the
Negev of the Kerethites and the territory belonging to Judah and the
Negev of Caleb. And we burned Ziklag."
[15]David asked him, "Can you lead me down to this raiding party?"
He answered, "Swear to me before God that you will not kill me or
hand me over to my master, and I will take you down to them."
[16]He led David down, and there they were, scattered over the countryside, eating, drinking and reveling because of the great amount of
plunder they had taken from the land of the Philistines and from
Judah. [17]David fought them from dusk until the evening of the next
day, and none of them got away, except four hundred young men who
rode off on camels and fled. [18]David recovered everything the Amalekites had taken, including his two wives. [19]Nothing was missing:
young or old, boy or girl, plunder or anything else they had taken.
David brought everything back. [20]He took all the flocks and herds,
and his men drove them ahead of the other livestock, saying, "This is
David's plunder."
[21]Then David came to the two hundred men who had been too exhausted to follow him and who were left behind at the Besor Ravine.
They came out to meet David and the people with him. As David and
his men approached, he greeted them. [22]But all the evil men and
troublemakers among David's followers said, "Because they did not
go out with us, we will not share with them the plunder we recovered.
However, each man may take his wife and children and go."
[23]David replied, "No, my brothers, you must not do that with what
the LORD has given us. He has protected us and handed over to us the
forces that came against us. [24]Who will listen to what you say? The
share of the man who stayed with the supplies is to be the same as
that of him who went down to the battle. All will share alike." [25]David
made this a statute and ordinance for Israel from that day to this.
[26]When David arrived in Ziklag, he sent some of the plunder to the
elders of Judah, who were his friends, saying, "Here is a present for
you from the plunder of the LORD's enemies."
[27]He sent it to those who were in Bethel, Ramoth Negev and Jattir;
[28]to those in Aroer, Siphmoth, Eshtemoa [29]and Racal; to those in the
towns of the Jerahmeelites and the Kenites; [30]to those in Hormah,
Bor Ashan, Athach [31]and Hebron; and to those in all the other places
where David and his men had roamed.

Saul Takes His Life

31 Now the Philistines fought against Israel; the Israelites fled
before them, and many fell slain on Mount Gilboa. [2]The
Philistines pressed hard after Saul and his sons, and they killed his

ple? Because he believed it was what God wanted?

APPLY 1. When it comes to sharing your bounty with others, which of the following attitudes are you most likely to have: I earned it and I'll keep it? If a person is without, it's because they are lazy!? If I have anything left over, I'll share it? God has blessed me that I might share? Whatever I have is God's? **2.** What would it mean for you to take on David's attitude about sharing with others?

OPEN 1. What fall has hurt you the worst: When you fell for a person who rejected you? When you fell from grace in the eyes of someone you respected? When you

30:23 what the LORD has given us. Crediting God with the victory gave David reason to spread the spoils evenly. In doing so, he prevented quarreling among his troops.

30:26 sent some of the plunder. The Amalekites had plundered Judah, and David was recovering lost goods. He was also winning his people's allegiance and goodwill for the conflict that was soon to come.

31:2 killed his sons. Saul had a fourth son, Ish-Bosheth (2 Sam. 2:8), who was not killed in this battle.

fell out of power in your company? When you had a physical fall? **2.** How confident were you at the time that you would ever recover?

STUDY What Samuel predicted from the grave (28:7–19) was now to come true. Saul's death sealed his demise and marked the final transition to David's kingship. **1.** Why does Saul ask his armor-bearer to kill him? What does Saul hope to preserve by this act? **2.** Why does the armor-bearer refuse Saul's request? **3.** What light does this story throw on the issue of mercy-killing? **4.** Why do the Philistines cut off Saul's head and put his armor in their temple (v. 9)? **5.** Why do the people of Jabesh Gilead retrieve the bodies of Saul and his sons? **6.** If you could summarize Saul's life, which of the following phrases would you choose: Wasted potential? Died of jealousy? Born to be wild? Lost power when he lost God?

APPLY 1. What circumstances are there in which you would no longer want to live? **2.** If you were in the deepest imaginable pit of despair, what would you want your friends to do: End it for you? Get you professional help? Pray for you? Stay by your side?

sons Jonathan, Abinadab and Malki-Shua. [3]The fighting grew fierce
around Saul, and when the archers overtook him, they wounded him
critically.
[4]Saul said to his armor-bearer, "Draw your sword and run me
through, or these uncircumcised fellows will come and run me
through and abuse me."
But his armor-bearer was terrified and would not do it; so Saul
took his own sword and fell on it. [5]When the armor-bearer saw that
Saul was dead, he too fell on his sword and died with him. [6]So Saul
and his three sons and his armor-bearer and all his men died together that same day.
[7]When the Israelites along the valley and those across the Jordan
saw that the Israelite army had fled and that Saul and his sons had
died, they abandoned their towns and fled. And the Philistines came
and occupied them.
[8]The next day, when the Philistines came to strip the dead, they
found Saul and his three sons fallen on Mount Gilboa. [9]They cut off
his head and stripped off his armor, and they sent messengers
throughout the land of the Philistines to proclaim the news in the
temple of their idols and among their people. [10]They put his armor in
the temple of the Ashtoreths and fastened his body to the wall of Beth
Shan.
[11]When the people of Jabesh Gilead heard of what the Philistines
had done to Saul, [12]all their valiant men journeyed through the night
to Beth Shan. They took down the bodies of Saul and his sons from
the wall of Beth Shan and went to Jabesh, where they burned them.
[13]Then they took their bones and buried them under a tamarisk tree
at Jabesh, and they fasted seven days.

31:9 cut off his head. Goliath received the same treatment at the hand of David. Decapitation was proof that the adversary had perished. Anyone still loyal to that adversary should take cover.

31:10 Ashtoreths. Idols representing the Philistine and Canaanite goddess, counterpart to Baal. Placing Saul's armor in the temple credited his defeat to the power of a false god.

31:11–12 Jabesh Gilead. Saul had defended these people in his first act as king. **burned them.** Cremation was not the typical burial for an Israelite. Later David exhumed the bones and reburied them in the territory of Benjamin, Saul's tribe.

2 Samuel

Personal Reading	Group Study Topic and Reading	
1:1–3:5	War Divides	2:8–3:5
3:6–6:23	David and the Ark	6:1–23
7:1–9:13	God Promises David	7:1–17
10:1–11:27	David and Bathsheba	11:1–27
12:1–14	David Rebuked	12:1–14
12:15–31	David Grieves	12:15–25
13:1–22	Amnon and Tamar	13:1–22
13:23–39	Absalom Kills Amnon	13:23–39
14:1–15:37	Absalom Returns	14:1–33
16:1–19:8a	David Mourns	18:19–19:8a
19:8b–21:22	Saul's Sons Destroyed	21:1–14
22:1–23:7	David's Song	22:1–51
23:8–24:25	David's Mighty Men	23:8–23

Author. While this book is named for the prophet Samuel, the events described occurred after Samuel's death. Some believe that other prophets pulled some of the manuscript together from Samuel's notes for 1 Samuel and then completed the historical record. If so, Samuel, Nathan and Gad most likely contributed to the book.

Date. The events recorded in 2 Samuel cover the reign of King David. The time of writing probably occurred between the divided kingdom (930 B.C.) and the fall of Samaria (720 B.C.).

Purpose. Both books of Samuel were originally used as one book. The purpose of the second book is the same as the first—to reveal the events of history (in this case the reign of David) and to explain why, from a spiritual viewpoint, the events occurred as they did.

Historical Background. The monarchy established in 1 Samuel did not solve Israel's problems. Israel was still plagued with war and internal strife. The Philistines troubled the Hebrews constantly. The second book of Samuel depicts the events of David's reign. He was able to unite his country, capture Jerusalem and temporarily defeat the Philistines. At its best, David's rule exemplified the theocratic principle that God is the ultimate ruler and that even an earthly king should concern himself with God's will before his own.

David was not the theocratic ideal, however. His reign was filled with conflict. His own personal sin and its consequences illustrated the dangers of having an earthly king instead of a heavenly one. His reign exhibited all the symptoms of corrupt earthly governing. While David could win battles, he could not bring lasting peace. Political intrigues erupted all around him, even within his own family. Nevertheless, David's reign, as described in 2 Samuel, was later praised as exemplary. That may be more of an indictment of the other Hebrew kings than an endorsement of David's rule.

King David. David was referred to as a man after God's heart. He certainly manifested his devotion to God. He brought the ark, a symbol of God's presence, back to the tabernacle. He made plans for the grand temple that Solomon later built. David was used of God. Yet, he fell many times. He committed adultery and murder. He watched some of his own children self-destruct. David is an example to us all of God's ability to use us where we are with all of our humanity very much intact.

OPEN What death of a famous person do you remember most vividly (JFK, Martin Luther King, Jr., Princess Diana, Kurt Cobain, John Lennon, Yitzhak Rabin, etc.)? Where were you and how did you react?

STUDY Even though Saul sought to kill David for years, it didn't result in David hating him. Rather, when Saul died, David mourned. **1.** How does the Amalekite's account of Saul's death vary from the one told in 1 Samuel 31? How do you think this difference is best explained? **2.** What does the Amalekite young man bring to David? **3.** How do you think the Amalekite young man is expecting to be treated by David, since he is bringing news of the death of David's rival? **4.** Why does David have the Amalekite executed? **5.** What do you think David expected of the Amalekite? **6.** What would *you* have done had Saul asked you to end it for him? **7.** If you could summarize the moral of this story, what would it be: Mercy-killing is wrong? Always respect your leaders, no matter how they act? Each person's death diminishes me? Kill the messenger? Other?

APPLY 1. When was the last time someone brought you a message that gave you deep grief? **2.** How did you react toward the messenger?

David Hears of Saul's Death

1 After the death of Saul, David returned from defeating the Amalekites and stayed in Ziklag two days. 2On the third day a man arrived from Saul's camp, with his clothes torn andwith dust on his head. When he came to David, he fell to the ground to pay him honor.

3"Where have you come from?" David asked him.

He answered, "I have escaped from the Israelite camp."

4"What happened?" David asked. "Tell me."

He said, "The men fled from the battle. Many of them fell and died. And Saul and his son Jonathan are dead."

5Then David said to the young man who brought him the report, "How do you know that Saul and his son Jonathan are dead?"

6"I happened to be on Mount Gilboa," the young man said, "and there was Saul, leaning on his spear, with the chariots and riders almost upon him. 7When he turned around and saw me, he called out to me, and I said, 'What can I do?'

8"He asked me, 'Who are you?'

"'An Amalekite,' I answered.

9"Then he said to me, 'Stand over me and kill me! I am in the throes of death, but I'm still alive.'

10"So I stood over him and killed him, because I knew that after he had fallen he could not survive. And I took the crown that was on his head and the band on his arm and have brought them here to my lord."

11Then David and all the men with him took hold of their clothes and tore them. 12They mourned and wept and fasted till evening for Saul and his son Jonathan, and for the army of the LORD and the house of Israel, because they had fallen by the sword.

13David said to the young man who brought him the report, "Where are you from?"

"I am the son of an alien, an Amalekite," he answered.

14David asked him, "Why were you not afraid to lift your hand to destroy the LORD's anointed?"

15Then David called one of his men and said, "Go, strike him down!" So he struck him down, and he died. 16For David had said to him, "Your blood be on your own head. Your own mouth testified against you when you said, 'I killed the LORD's anointed.'"

1:1 First and Second Samuel are actually one manuscript, so 2 Samuel picks up where 1 Samuel left off. King Saul had died in a battle against the Philistines. David had just rescued his wives in a battle with the Amalekites.

1:8 Amalekite. The Amalekite's story was contrary to the report recorded in 1 Samuel 31:4–6. Either he is providing additional information to the previous account or he *is altering the story* to protect himself.

1:11 David and all the men with him. While alive, King Saul had forced David and his men into hiding. Yet here they wept for their nation's loss.

1:13 Amalekite. David had just rescued his wives from Amalekite kidnappers. He would not kindly welcome an Amalekite deserter into his camp.

1:14 the LORD's anointed. If anyone had good reason to want Saul dead, it was David. On two occasions, David could have killed Saul but did not (1 Sam. 24:3–7; 26:9–12). He understood that the leadership and kingdoms were under God's control. It was not David's right to kill a leader God had selected, nor anyone else's right, either.

1:15 Years before, Saul was told he had lost his kingdom because he failed to destroy the Amalekites (1 Sam. 15:3–9) as God had commanded. It's a strange twist, then, that an alleged Amalekite lost his life because he claimed to have destroyed Saul.

1:16 Your blood ... own head. So deep was David's conviction that the life of Saul was God's to control that he felt no mercy in sentencing Saul's executioner.

David's Lament for Saul and Jonathan

17David took up this lament concerning Saul and his son Jonathan,
18and ordered that the men of Judah be taught this lament of the bow
(it is written in the Book of Jashar):

19"Your glory, O Israel, lies slain on your heights.
  How the mighty have fallen!
20"Tell it not in Gath,
  proclaim it not in the streets of Ashkelon,
 lest the daughters of the Philistines be glad,
  lest the daughters of the uncircumcised rejoice.

21"O mountains of Gilboa,
  may you have neither dew nor rain,
  nor fields that yield offerings ⌊of grain⌋.
 For there the shield of the mighty was defiled,
  the shield of Saul—no longer rubbed with oil.
22From the blood of the slain,
  from the flesh of the mighty,
 the bow of Jonathan did not turn back,
  the sword of Saul did not return unsatisfied.

23"Saul and Jonathan—
  in life they were loved and gracious,
  and in death they were not parted.
 They were swifter than eagles,
  they were stronger than lions.

24"O daughters of Israel,
  weep for Saul,
 who clothed you in scarlet and finery,
  who adorned your garments with ornaments of gold.

25"How the mighty have fallen in battle!
  Jonathan lies slain on your heights.
26I grieve for you, Jonathan my brother;
  you were very dear to me.
 Your love for me was wonderful,
  more wonderful than that of women.

27"How the mighty have fallen!
  The weapons of war have perished!"

OPEN **1.** When you were young, did you have a friend your own age die? How did it affect you? **2.** What was most helpful in helping you to put that death into perspective?

STUDY After Saul and Jonathan died, David wrote a poetic song of lament for their loss. He had men throughout the land sing it. **1.** What motivated David to so publicly mourn for Saul and Jonathan? **2.** Why does David call for censorship in Gath and Ashkelon (v. 20; 1 Sam. 31:8–10)? **3.** How does the way David eulogizes Saul differ from the way he actually was in life (vv. 23–24)? **4.** Is it appropriate to make a person who has died look better than they actually were? **5.** What does verse 26 reveal about the David-Jonathan friendship? **6.** Does this story provide any principles for lasting friendships?

APPLY **1.** If your best friend was to die, what would you want to make sure you said about him or her? **2.** What prevents you from saying it now?

1:18 the bow. The bow was Israel's most common weapon since the nation had little expertise in metalworking. **Book of Jashar.** This lost manuscript is also mentioned in the book of Joshua (Josh. 10:13).

1:19 Your glory ... the mighty. David might have celebrated the death of his longtime adversary, Saul. Instead he honored Saul in death as much as he did in life.

1:21 Gilboa. David's curse was not specifically on the place of Saul's death. The curse was David's way of expressing his grief over his loss.

1:23 Saul and Jonathan. Jonathan walked a tightrope most of his life, torn between his father Saul and his best friend David. He had been son and friend, loyal to both.

1:26 Your love ... more wonderful than that of women. David's comparison noted Jonathan's selflessness in keeping a friendship with the man who would eventually take his kingdom away.

OPEN How often has your family moved? Which move was the hardest?

STUDY After Saul died, David was anointed king over the southern kingdom of Judah. **1.** How might David have felt when he returned home from exile? **2.** Why did he move to Hebron? **3.** How might the people of Jabesh Gilead, Saul's political power base, feel about David becoming king of Judah? **4.** Why would Israel follow David?

APPLY About what future "moves" are you inquiring of the Lord? What is he telling you to do?

OPEN **1.** What is the closest you have come to being involved in a "civil war"? A long-standing dispute with a sibling? A long-standing dispute with parents or adult children? A major difference between you and other family members? **2.** How do you deal with this dispute? Ignore it? Have fun with it? Gloss over the differences? Get angry and bitter? "Wage war" with gusto?

STUDY The division between Saul and David ended with Saul's death. But the division between David and Saul's house continued on as Saul's son Ish-Bosheth became king of Israel. **1.** How do you think Ish-Bosheth felt about David now reigning over part of his father's kingdom, the land of Judah? **2.** Why was representative combat proposed by Abner and accepted by Joab (1 Sam. 17:8–9)? **3.** Why does the combat escalate beyond representative combat to full combat? **4.** With Abner's battle

David Anointed King Over Judah

2 In the course of time, David inquired of the LORD. "Shall I go up
to one of the towns of Judah?" he asked.
The LORD said, "Go up."
David asked, "Where shall I go?"
"To Hebron," the LORD answered.
2 So David went up there with his two wives, Ahinoam of Jezreel
and Abigail, the widow of Nabal of Carmel. 3 David also took the men
who were with him, each with his family, and they settled in Hebron
and its towns. 4 Then the men of Judah came to Hebron and there they
anointed David king over the house of Judah.
When David was told that it was the men of Jabesh Gilead who had
buried Saul, 5 he sent messengers to the men of Jabesh Gilead to say
to them, "The LORD bless you for showing this kindness to Saul your
master by burying him. 6 May the LORD now show you kindness and
faithfulness, and I too will show you the same favor because you
have done this. 7 Now then, be strong and brave, for Saul your master
is dead, and the house of Judah has anointed me king over them."

War Between the Houses of David and Saul

8 Meanwhile, Abner son of Ner, the commander of Saul's army, had
taken Ish-Bosheth son of Saul and brought him over to Mahanaim.
9 He made him king over Gilead, Ashuri[a] and Jezreel, and also over
Ephraim, Benjamin and all Israel.
10 Ish-Bosheth son of Saul was forty years old when he became
king over Israel, and he reigned two years. The house of Judah, however, followed David. 11 The length of time David was king in Hebron
over the house of Judah was seven years and six months.
12 Abner son of Ner, together with the men of Ish-Bosheth son of
Saul, left Mahanaim and went to Gibeon. 13 Joab son of Zeruiah and
David's men went out and met them at the pool of Gibeon. One group
sat down on one side of the pool and one group on the other side.
14 Then Abner said to Joab, "Let's have some of the young men get
up and fight hand to hand in front of us."
"All right, let them do it," Joab said.
15 So they stood up and were counted off—twelve men for Benjamin and Ish-Bosheth son of Saul, and twelve for David. 16 Then each
man grabbed his opponent by the head and thrust his dagger into his

[a]9 Or *Asher*

2:1 inquired of the LORD. David continued to submit to God's timing even though the kingdom was ripe for taking.

2:4 they anointed David. Like Saul, David had been anointed privately by Samuel (1 Sam. 16:13). The anointing before his people was public and official. It announced the next regime and alerted the people concerning their next leader.

2:5 he sent messengers. David's first official act was diplomatic. It had as much to do with honoring Saul's burial as laying the groundwork for an alliance with Jabesh Gilead. It was also an excellent opportunity to cement his claim as king.

2:8 Abner. Abner and David both knew the kingdom was up for grabs. Abner (Saul's cousin and the commander of his army) knew his best play for power was through Saul's one surviving son, Ish-Bosheth.

2:12 Gibeon. Abner and David had the same instinct. David went first to Judah, his own tribe, to establish his sovereignty. Abner took Ish-Bosheth to Gibeon, a town in the region of Benjamin, the tribe of Saul's heritage.

2:13 Joab. Joab was a distant nephew of David. He was commander of David's army and had a reputation for ruthlessness that even David eventually criticized (3:39).

2:16 Helkath Hazzurim. This name means "field of daggers" probably

opponent's side, and they fell down together. So that place in Gibeon
was called Helkath Hazzurim.[a]
17The battle that day was very fierce, and Abner and the men of
Israel were defeated by David's men.
18The three sons of Zeruiah were there: Joab, Abishai and Asahel.
Now Asahel was as fleet-footed as a wild gazelle. 19He chased Abner,
turning neither to the right nor to the left as he pursued him. 20Abner
looked behind him and asked, "Is that you, Asahel?"

"It is," he answered.

21Then Abner said to him, "Turn aside to the right or to the left; take
on one of the young men and strip him of his weapons." But Asahel
would not stop chasing him.
22Again Abner warned Asahel, "Stop chasing me! Why should I
strike you down? How could I look your brother Joab in the face?"
23But Asahel refused to give up the pursuit; so Abner thrust the butt
of his spear into Asahel's stomach, and the spear came out through
his back. He fell there and died on the spot. And every man stopped
when he came to the place where Asahel had fallen and died.
24But Joab and Abishai pursued Abner, and as the sun was setting,
they came to the hill of Ammah, near Giah on the way to the wasteland
of Gibeon. 25Then the men of Benjamin rallied behind Abner. They
formed themselves into a group and took their stand on top of a hill.
26Abner called out to Joab, "Must the sword devour forever? Don't
you realize that this will end in bitterness? How long before you order
your men to stop pursuing their brothers?"
27Joab answered, "As surely as God lives, if you had not spoken, the
men would have continued the pursuit of their brothers until
morning.[b]"
28So Joab blew the trumpet, and all the men came to a halt; they no
longer pursued Israel, nor did they fight anymore.
29All that night Abner and his men marched through the Arabah.
They crossed the Jordan, continued through the whole Bithron[c] and
came to Mahanaim.
30Then Joab returned from pursuing Abner and assembled all his
men. Besides Asahel, nineteen of David's men were found missing.
31But David's men had killed three hundred and sixty Benjamites who
were with Abner. 32They took Asahel and buried him in his father's
tomb at Bethlehem. Then Joab and his men marched all night and arrived at Hebron by daybreak.

3 The war between the house of Saul and the house of David
lasted a long time. David grew stronger and stronger, while the
house of Saul grew weaker and weaker.

[a]*16 Helkath Hazzurim* means *field of daggers* or *field of hostilities.* [b]*27* Or *spoken this morning, the men would not have taken up the pursuit of their brothers;* or *spoken, the men would have given up the pursuit of their brothers by morning* [c]*29* Or *morning;* or *ravine;* the meaning of the Hebrew for this word is uncertain.

strength, why was he running from Asahel? **5.** What is there about Abner's plea for peace that makes it so successful (vv. 26–28): Abner's eloquence? Joab's receptivity to the truth? Everyone was tired of fighting? They realized that they truly were brothers? **6.** What kind of plea do you feel has the best chance of bringing peace between warring parties: Enlightened self-interest? Reminders that we are all brothers and sisters? Only pleas from someone who can blow you off the map?

APPLY 1. What "enemy" seems to be doggedly pursuing you right now: Financial stress? Health problems? A personal enemy? **2.** What strategy do you feel has the best chance of victory over this enemy: Running away? Standing and fighting? Going for reinforcements? Looking to divine intervention?

because of the unusual use of daggers in the contest.

2:21 Asahel. Asahel was the brother of Joab and one of David's mighty men. He was known as a fast runner.

2:22 your brother Joab. Abner knew more was at stake than the life of Asahel. Joab could swear blood revenge on Abner, adding to the problems that were already frustrating his quest for power.

2:26 How long before you order your men to stop. Even though Abner was able to call a truce, the skirmishes continued (3:1).

2:28 all the men came to a halt. Even though the truce failed, each army had time to retreat to its home base. David had lost twenty men. Abner had lost 360.

3:1 The war ... lasted a long time. The battle recounted in chapter 2 wasn't the only conflict between David and

2 Sons were born to David in Hebron:
His firstborn was Amnon the son of Ahinoam of Jezreel;
3 his second, Kileab the son of Abigail the widow of Nabal of Carmel;
the third, Absalom the son of Maacah daughter of Talmai king of Geshur;
4 the fourth, Adonijah the son of Haggith;
the fifth, Shephatiah the son of Abital;
5 and the sixth, Ithream the son of David's wife Eglah.
These were born to David in Hebron.

Abner Goes Over to David

6 During the war between the house of Saul and the house of David,
Abner had been strengthening his own position in the house of Saul.
7 Now Saul had had a concubine named Rizpah daughter of Aiah. And
Ish-Bosheth said to Abner, "Why did you sleep with my father's concubine?"
8 Abner was very angry because of what Ish-Bosheth said and he
answered, "Am I a dog's head—on Judah's side? This very day I am
loyal to the house of your father Saul and to his family and friends. I
haven't handed you over to David. Yet now you accuse me of an
offense involving this woman! 9 May God deal with Abner, be it ever so
severely, if I do not do for David what the LORD promised him on oath
10 and transfer the kingdom from the house of Saul and establish
David's throne over Israel and Judah from Dan to Beersheba." 11 Ish-
Bosheth did not dare to say another word to Abner, because he was
afraid of him.
12 Then Abner sent messengers on his behalf to say to David,
"Whose land is it? Make an agreement with me, and I will help you
bring all Israel over to you."
13 "Good," said David. "I will make an agreement with you. But I demand one thing of you: Do not come into my presence unless you
bring Michal daughter of Saul when you come to see me." 14 Then
David sent messengers to Ish-Bosheth son of Saul, demanding, "Give
me my wife Michal, whom I betrothed to myself for the price of a
hundred Philistine foreskins."
15 So Ish-Bosheth gave orders and had her taken away from her
husband Paltiel son of Laish. 16 Her husband, however, went with her,
weeping behind her all the way to Bahurim. Then Abner said to him,
"Go back home!" So he went back.

OPEN 1. In which of the following "battles" are you *least* likely to "go over to the other side": Republican vs. Democrat? American autos vs. Imports? Ford vs. GM? Coke vs. Pepsi? Your favorite team vs. the competition? **2.** In order to go over to "the other side" in the area you chose, what deal would you require?

STUDY Like an off-season blockbuster trade, Abner, who had just led the forces of Ish-Bosheth against David's forces, decides to come over to David's side. His motivation is an accusation of sexual impropriety by Ish-Bosheth against him. **1.** From the way Abner responds to the Ish-Bosheth's accusation, do you think he was guilty? **2.** If Abner has known all along that God promised to make David king (vv. 9,18), why has he opposed him up until now? **3.** With whom do you have the greatest amount of empathy in relation to Michal's status: Michal, she never did have a choice? David, he was without her for so long? Paltiel, he lost her through no fault of his own? **4.** How extensive is Abner's control over Israel (vv. 17–21)? **5.** If you were David, would you trust Abner at this point? Why or why not?

APPLY 1. Do you remember being falsely accused? How

Saul's loyalists. After several face-offs, David finally came out on top.

3:6 Abner. He gradually overshadows Ish-Bosheth and assumes more power in Saul's regime.

3:7 Rizpah ... my father's concubine? In the ancient Middle East, taking a former king's concubine was often a political statement. That's why Ish-Bosheth asked Abner this question—he worried that it indicated a conspiracy to take the throne from Saul (v. 6; 12:8; 16:21; 1 Kin. 2:22).

3:9 May God deal with Abner ... severely. This is a form of a curse or a warning used often in Scripture (3:35; 19:13; Ruth 1:17; 1 Sam. 3:17; 14:44; 20:13; 25:22; 1 Kin. 2:23; 2 Kin. 6:31). **LORD promised him on oath.** It was already well known throughout the kingdom that God had chosen David to succeed Saul (2:4; 1 Sam. 16:13; 25:28).

3:13 Michal. Michal, whom Saul had given to David earlier (1 Sam. 18:27), had been given to another man, named Paltiel, after David's hasty departure from the court (1 Sam. 25:44). David figured that if he and Michal were reunited, it would aid his claim as heir to the throne because he would truly be Saul's son-in-law.

3:16 weeping behind her. Obviously, Michal's second husband (to whom Saul had given her after David fled) was grieved about her forced return to David. Though nothing is said of her response to the action, she later is said to despise David (6:16). She also never had children, which may have also contributed to her disgust.

[17]Abner conferred with the elders of Israel and said, "For some time
you have wanted to make David your king. [18]Now do it! For the LORD
promised David, 'By my servant David I will rescue my people Israel
from the hand of the Philistines and from the hand of all their
enemies.' "
[19]Abner also spoke to the Benjamites in person. Then he went to
Hebron to tell David everything that Israel and the whole house of
Benjamin wanted to do. [20]When Abner, who had twenty men with
him, came to David at Hebron, David prepared a feast for him and his
men. [21]Then Abner said to David, "Let me go at once and assemble all
Israel for my lord the king, so that they may make a compact with
you, and that you may rule over all that your heart desires." So David
sent Abner away, and he went in peace.

Joab Murders Abner

[22]Just then David's men and Joab returned from a raid and brought
with them a great deal of plunder. But Abner was no longer with David in Hebron, because David had sent him away, and he had gone in
peace. [23]When Joab and all the soldiers with him arrived, he was told
that Abner son of Ner had come to the king and that the king had sent
him away and that he had gone in peace.
[24]So Joab went to the king and said, "What have you done? Look,
Abner came to you. Why did you let him go? Now he is gone! [25]You
know Abner son of Ner; he came to deceive you and observe your
movements and find out everything you are doing."
[26]Joab then left David and sent messengers after Abner, and they
brought him back from the well of Sirah. But David did not know it.
[27]Now when Abner returned to Hebron, Joab took him aside into the
gateway, as though to speak with him privately. And there, to avenge
the blood of his brother Asahel, Joab stabbed him in the stomach,
and he died.
[28]Later, when David heard about this, he said, "I and my kingdom
are forever innocent before the LORD concerning the blood of Abner
son of Ner. [29]May his blood fall upon the head of Joab and upon all
his father's house! May Joab's house never be without someone who
has a running sore or leprosy[a] or who leans on a crutch or who falls
by the sword or who lacks food."

[a]29 The Hebrew word was used for various diseases affecting the skin—not necessarily leprosy.

did you react to the accusation? **2.** What attitude would you like to have toward false accusations: Hey, it happens? We are like Christ, who also was falsely accused? The truly innocent have nothing to fear? God will vindicate the righteous?

OPEN 1. When as an adolescent did someone in the gang you ran with do something that almost got (or did get) you into trouble? **2.** What did this incident do to your friendship?

STUDY Abner has switched sides from Ish-Bosheth's army to David's forces. But his action comes to a violent end, as David's general, Joab, kills Abner in revenge for the death of his brother. **1.** Why do you think Abner wasn't more suspicious of Joab's recall of him (v. 22)? **2.** Why does David feel the need to declare his innocence (vv. 28,37)? **3.** How do you react to David's tribute to Abner (vv. 31–35): Overdone? The act of a sensitive conscience? A political maneuver? **4.** Why were the people pleased with David's actions (vv. 36–37)? **5.** Overall what do you think disturbed David most about this murder: It made him look like he went back on his word? He thought Abner a truly great man? He thought it politically unwise? He needed Abner's support?

3:17 David your king. Support for David was broad among most of the tribes, although Benjamin and Gilead in the Transjordan seemed to provide most of Ish-Bosheth's support (2:8; 2:15; 1 Sam. 11:9–11; 31:11–13).

3:18 the LORD promised David. The promise had come with the anointing of David by the prophet Samuel—an event well known in the land by this time (5:2).

3:19 Abner. Abner wanted to make sure the home tribe of Saul and his family knew what was going on concerning the change in leadership to the tribe of Judah. Whether Abner explained the situation fully and honestly is not known. Nevertheless, the tribe's elders must have given their approval.

3:25 to deceive you. Joab had good reason not to trust Abner, who was a strong leader of the northern tribes. For one thing, Abner had killed Joab's brother (v. 27; 2:18,23). Joab probably also worried about his own job security if Abner became more involved in David's royal affairs. Clearly no love is lost between Joab and Abner, so Joab attempted to discredit the rival as someone trying to take advantage of David's good nature.

3:27 Joab. Joab considered Abner an enemy of war and, more personally, sought to avenge his brother's death. But the murder was unjustified. No state of war existed at this point, and blood revenge (Num. 35:12; Deut. 19:11–13) did not apply because Joab's brother Asahel had been killed in battle (v. 30; 2:21,23). Furthermore, the act occured in Hebron, a city of refuge (Josh. 20:7) where a blood avenger was not permitted to deal with a murderer without a trial (Num. 35:22–24).

3:29 blood fall upon the head of Joab. David first proclaimed his own innocence in the matter of Abner's murder (v. 28), then spoke a curse on Joab and his line.

30(Joab and his brother Abishai murdered Abner because he had
killed their brother Asahel in the battle at Gibeon.)
31Then David said to Joab and all the people with him, "Tear your
clothes and put on sackcloth and walk in mourning in front of Abner." King David himself walked behind the bier. 32They buried Abner
in Hebron, and the king wept aloud at Abner's tomb. All the people
wept also.
33The king sang this lament for Abner:

"Should Abner have died as the lawless die?
34 Your hands were not bound,
your feet were not fettered.
You fell as one falls before wicked men."

And all the people wept over him again.
35Then they all came and urged David to eat something while it was
still day; but David took an oath, saying, "May God deal with me, be it
ever so severely, if I taste bread or anything else before the sun sets!"
36All the people took note and were pleased; indeed, everything the
king did pleased them. 37So on that day all the people and all Israel
knew that the king had no part in the murder of Abner son of Ner.
38Then the king said to his men, "Do you not realize that a prince
and a great man has fallen in Israel this day? 39And today, though I
am the anointed king, I am weak, and these sons of Zeruiah are too
strong for me. May the LORD repay the evildoer according to his evil
deeds!"

Ish-Bosheth Murdered

4 When Ish-Bosheth son of Saul heard that Abner had died in Hebron, he lost courage, and all Israel became alarmed. 2Now
Saul's son had two men who were leaders of raiding bands. One was
named Baanah and the other Recab; they were sons of Rimmon the
Beerothite from the tribe of Benjamin—Beeroth is considered part of
Benjamin, 3because the people of Beeroth fled to Gittaim and have
lived there as aliens to this day.
4(Jonathan son of Saul had a son who was lame in both feet. He
was five years old when the news about Saul and Jonathan came
from Jezreel. His nurse picked him up and fled, but as she hurried to
leave, he fell and became crippled. His name was Mephibosheth.)
5Now Recab and Baanah, the sons of Rimmon the Beerothite, set
out for the house of Ish-Bosheth, and they arrived there in the heat of
the day while he was taking his noonday rest. 6They went into the
inner part of the house as if to get some wheat, and they stabbed him
in the stomach. Then Recab and his brother Baanah slipped away.
7They had gone into the house while he was lying on the bed in his

APPLY **1.** When it comes to trusting others, are you more like Joab or David? Why? **2.** What adversary of yours, that you should be sympathetic to, has had misfortune? What could you do now to show empathy?

OPEN **1.** What would you consider the worst act of treachery you have experienced by a friend? **2.** What did you do in response to that treachery?

STUDY The followers of Ish-Bosheth sense his weakness and two of them kill him in his sleep. When they brag of the act to David, David has them executed for killing an innocent man. **1.** Why would Abner's death cause Ish-Bosheth to lose courage? **2.** What do you think motivated Baanah and Recab to kill Ish-Bosheth: A secret loyalty to David? Desire to "go with a winner"? Concern over Ish-Bosheth's weak leadership? Other? **3.** Why do Baanah and Recab think David will reward them for their act? **4.** Why does David have the two men killed instead? **5.** What does this story say about David's attitude toward

---

3:32 the king wept. It was vital that David rise above the situation and show his own innocence in the matter. Abner was so highly regarded by the northern tribes that *the situation was a powder* keg that could easily lead to the destruction of David's tribal coalition. Verses 36 and 37 indicate that David succeeded in his efforts.

3:35 David took an oath. A meal was customarily served to mourners after the deceased was buried. Had David eaten it, he may have been charged with false remorse. He certainly seemed serious: *He asked God to punish him in the worst* way if he ate before sunset.

4:1 lost courage. The news of Abner's death was a major blow to Ish-Bosheth, who had gained his own position by Abner's efforts (2:8). **all Israel became alarmed.** The northern tribes had lost their leader; the southern tribes feared that the political chaos would cause civil war.

4:4 Jonathan son of Saul. The house of Saul had no other heir to the throne after Ish-Bosheth died (v. 6).

bedroom. After they stabbed and killed him, they cut off his head. Taking it with them, they traveled all night by way of the Arabah. [8]They brought the head of Ish-Bosheth to David at Hebron and said to the king, "Here is the head of Ish-Bosheth son of Saul, your enemy, who tried to take your life. This day the LORD has avenged my lord the king against Saul and his offspring."

[9]David answered Recab and his brother Baanah, the sons of Rimmon the Beerothite, "As surely as the LORD lives, who has delivered me out of all trouble, [10]when a man told me, 'Saul is dead,' and thought he was bringing good news, I seized him and put him to death in Ziklag. That was the reward I gave him for his news! [11]How much more—when wicked men have killed an innocent man in his own house and on his own bed—should I not now demand his blood from your hand and rid the earth of you!"

[12]So David gave an order to his men, and they killed them. They cut off their hands and feet and hung the bodies by the pool in Hebron. But they took the head of Ish-Bosheth and buried it in Abner's tomb at Hebron.

David Becomes King Over Israel

5 All the tribes of Israel came to David at Hebron and said, "We are your own flesh and blood. [2]In the past, while Saul was king over us, you were the one who led Israel on their military campaigns. And the LORD said to you, 'You will shepherd my people Israel, and you will become their ruler.' "

[3]When all the elders of Israel had come to King David at Hebron, the king made a compact with them at Hebron before the LORD, and they anointed David king over Israel.

[4]David was thirty years old when he became king, and he reigned forty years. [5]In Hebron he reigned over Judah seven years and six months, and in Jerusalem he reigned over all Israel and Judah thirty-three years.

David Conquers Jerusalem

[6]The king and his men marched to Jerusalem to attack the Jebusites, who lived there. The Jebusites said to David, "You will not get in here; even the blind and the lame can ward you off." They thought, "David cannot get in here." [7]Nevertheless, David captured the fortress of Zion, the City of David.

politics and authority? **6.** Famed theologian Dietrich Bonhoeffer was in a plot to kill Hitler, and there have been discussions of assassinating leaders like Castro and Khoumeni. Is such an action ever morally acceptable?

APPLY 1. Which of the following is closest to your present attitude toward revenge: "Vengeance is mine says the Lord" or "I don't get mad, I get even"? **2.** Has an effort you made to get revenge ever backfired on you? What did you learn from that experience?

OPEN Which of the following groups would you most like to be king or queen over: My own house!—just reigning supreme there would be sufficient? All my friends—I'm a control freak? Maybe a little country in the Alps, with my own castle! The whole world—give me POWER!?

STUDY The promise which God gave through Samuel finally comes to pass, and David becomes king of Israel. He then conquers Jerusalem and moves the seat of his government there. **1.** What three different things do the elders of Israel affirm about David when they come to ask him to be king (vv. 1–2)? **2.** What do the Jebusites say to David to taunt him? **3.** Why does David choose Jerusalem as his capital (vv. 6–7)? **4.** What does verse 10 say was the source of David's power? Does David acknowledge this fact (v. 12)?

4:8 the LORD has avenged. Recab and Baanah thought they were doing David a favor by killing Ish-Bosheth, and presented their murderous deed to David as an act of righteous vengeance. Clearly they didn't anticipate David's response (vv. 9–12).

4:11 an innocent man. David considered Ish-Bosheth innocent of evil. After all, when Ish-Bosheth's father, Saul, had died, he simply did what an heir was expected to do—such actions in no way warranted murder. **demand his blood from your hand.** David was speaking of executing Recab and Baanah. Unlike his earlier cover-up of Joab (3:29), David acted swiftly to bring these two to justice.

5:3 the king made a compact. David was already king of Judah because the tribe had placed him in that role. Later he conquered and became king over Jerusalem (vv. 6–10). Now in this act of covenant, his reign was extended over the northern tribes; they agreed to submit to his authority. **they anointed David.** David's third anointing as king. First he was privately anointed by Samuel with his family (1 Sam. 16:13), then the tribe of Judah anointed him publicly to acknowledge his leadership over them (2:4).

5:6 Jebusites. These Canaanite people lived there (Gen. 10:15,16; Num. 13:29). The Jebusites could boast because Jerusalem was easy to defend from attack. It was located on a rise surrounded on three sides by deep valleys—a natural fortress.

5:7 City of David. Under David's reign, Jerusalem became the royal city, the nation's capital, and a symbol of the kingdom. The city's location on the border between the two parts of his kingdom was strategic for David, since it favored neither part and made both sides of the united kingdom happy.

8On that day, David said, "Anyone who conquers the Jebusites will
have to use the water shaft[a] to reach those 'lame and blind' who are
David's enemies.[b]" That is why they say, "The 'blind and lame' will
not enter the palace."
9David then took up residence in the fortress and called it the City
of David. He built up the area around it, from the supporting terraces[c]
inward. 10And he became more and more powerful, because the LORD
God Almighty was with him.
11Now Hiram king of Tyre sent messengers to David, along with cedar logs and carpenters and stonemasons, and they built a palace for
David. 12And David knew that the LORD had established him as king
over Israel and had exalted his kingdom for the sake of his people
Israel.
13After he left Hebron, David took more concubines and wives in
Jerusalem, and more sons and daughters were born to him. 14These
are the names of the children born to him there: Shammua, Shobab,
Nathan, Solomon, 15Ibhar, Elishua, Nepheg, Japhia, 16Elishama, Eliada and Eliphelet.

David Defeats the Philistines

17When the Philistines heard that David had been anointed king
over Israel, they went up in full force to search for him, but David
heard about it and went down to the stronghold. 18Now the Philistines had come and spread out in the Valley of Rephaim; 19so David
inquired of the LORD, "Shall I go and attack the Philistines? Will you
hand them over to me?"
The LORD answered him, "Go, for I will surely hand the Philistines
over to you."
20So David went to Baal Perazim, and there he defeated them. He
said, "As waters break out, the LORD has broken out against my enemies before me." So that place was called Baal Perazim.[d] 21The Philistines abandoned their idols there, and David and his men carried
them off.
22Once more the Philistines came up and spread out in the Valley of
Rephaim; 23so David inquired of the LORD, and he answered, "Do not
go straight up, but circle around behind them and attack them in
front of the balsam trees. 24As soon as you hear the sound of marching in the tops of the balsam trees, move quickly, because that will

[a]8 Or *use scaling hooks* [b]8 Or *are hated by David* [c]9 Or *the Millo* [d]20 *Baal Perazim* means *the lord who breaks out.*

5. What famous son of David is listed as one of those born in Jerusalem?

APPLY 1. If you had absolute assurance that "the Lord was with you," how would your behavior in the coming week be affected? What fears would dissipate? What new mission would you take on? **2.** What keeps you from having this faith: Guilt? Uncertainty of God's direction? Lack of submission to God?

OPEN When you were in high school and something good happened, who was generally the first to "rain on your parade": Your mom or dad? A sibling? A rival from school? Yourself?

STUDY After David is anointed as king, his "inauguration festivities" are cut short by a Philistine attack. David, however, is able to repulse this attack, as well as a follow-up one. **1.** Why do the Philistines attack so promptly upon hearing David had become king: They just didn't like the guy? Weakness from confusion in the new administration? They wanted a good challenge? They felt threatened? **2.** Why was David so careful to consult God before each campaign?

APPLY How often do you consult God before making a major decision: Always? Most of the time? Sometime?

5:8 lame and blind. David chided the Jebusites, whose boast in verse 6 proved false.

5:9 City of David. Luke used this phrase of Bethlehem (Luke 2:11), where David was born. Here it refers to Zion, seat of his throne.

5:12 for the sake of his people Israel. David understood why God had made him king over Israel: It was all for the sake of the nation, in order to exalt them as God had promised.

5:13 concubines and wives. These marriages were the result of treaties and alliances with other nations. Concubines were basically wives who did not enjoy the full rights of marriage, but were simply part of a king's harem. A harem's size determined a king's status, though God had warned Israel against the practice (Deut. 17:17).

5:17 When the Philistines heard. This occurred most likely following David's anointing as king (v. 3) and before the conquest of Jerusalem (vv. 6–14). David's reign over Judah had not concerned the Philistines until his kingdom started growing and threatening their own lands in the north, where they dominated after Saul's death (1 Sam. 31).

5:19 David inquired. David habitually sought God's will before engaging in battle (2:1; 1 Sam. 23:2; 30:8).

5:24 sound of marching in the tops of the balsam trees. God's angelic soldiers rustled the leaves as they moved in front of David's forces to do battle (2 Kin. 6:17).

mean the LORD has gone out in front of you to strike the Philistine
army." 25So David did as the LORD commanded him, and he struck
down the Philistines all the way from Gibeon[a] to Gezer.

The Ark Brought to Jerusalem

6 David again brought together out of Israel chosen men, thirty
thousand in all. 2He and all his men set out from Baalah of
Judah[b] to bring up from there the ark of God, which is called by the
Name,[c] the name of the LORD Almighty, who is enthroned between the
cherubim that are on the ark. 3They set the ark of God on a new cart
and brought it from the house of Abinadab, which was on the hill.
Uzzah and Ahio, sons of Abinadab, were guiding the new cart 4with
the ark of God on it,[d] and Ahio was walking in front of it. 5David
and the whole house of Israel were celebrating with all their might
before the LORD, with songs[e] and with harps, lyres, tambourines, sis-
trums and cymbals.
6When they came to the threshing floor of Nacon, Uzzah reached out
and took hold of the ark of God, because the oxen stumbled. 7The
LORD's anger burned against Uzzah because of his irreverent act; therefore God struck him down and he died there beside the ark of God.
8Then David was angry because the LORD's wrath had broken out
against Uzzah, and to this day that place is called Perez Uzzah.[f]
9David was afraid of the LORD that day and said, "How can the ark
of the LORD ever come to me?" 10He was not willing to take the ark of
the LORD to be with him in the City of David. Instead, he took it aside
to the house of Obed-Edom the Gittite. 11The ark of the LORD remained in the house of Obed-Edom the Gittite for three months, and
the LORD blessed him and his entire household.
12Now King David was told, "The LORD has blessed the household
of Obed-Edom and everything he has, because of the ark of God." So
David went down and brought up the ark of God from the house of
Obed-Edom to the City of David with rejoicing. 13When those who
were carrying the ark of the LORD had taken six steps, he sacrificed a

[a]25 Septuagint (see also 1 Chron. 14:16); Hebrew *Geba* [b]2 That is, Kiriath Jearim; Hebrew *Baale Judah*, a variant of *Baalah of Judah* [c]2 Hebrew; Septuagint and Vulgate do not have *the Name*. [d]3,4 Dead Sea Scrolls and some Septuagint manuscripts; Masoretic Text *cart* [4]*and they brought it with the ark of God from the house of Abinadab, which was on the hill* [e]5 See Dead Sea Scrolls, Septuagint and 1 Chronicles 13:8; Masoretic Text *celebrating before the LORD with all kinds of instruments made of pine.* [f]8 Perez Uzzah means *outbreak against Uzzah.*

OPEN 1. What does it take for you to feel like dancing: Any little thing will do? The right music? Maybe at the Second Coming, but not before then? **2.** What was the "in" dance when you were in high school? Can you still do it? Care to show your group?

STUDY David has just been made king of Israel, brought Jerusalem into Israel's control, and made it the nation's capital. God had told the Israelites that his presence would dwell above the ark, a wooden chest covered with gold. To honor the Lord as the true King over both himself and Israel, David decides to bring the ark to Jerusalem. **1.** What are your first impressions of this story: God is touchy, touchy, touchy!? Sounds like superstition? God's holiness must be taken seriously? **2.** Where does this story say God is "enthroned"? How does this relate to your understanding of God's presence everywhere? **3.** Why is David wanting to move the ark? **4.** What do you feel about Uzzah's punishment for his "irreverent act"? **5.** What special reverence does David show the second time he attempts to move the ark (v. 13)? **6.** Why does David dance while so scantily dressed: To show how "buff" he was? So nothing would impede the flow of movement? To show he was God's joyous servant (servants wore little)? He was overcome with emotion? Have you ever been so excited that you wanted to dance? **7.** Why did Michal get upset: She thought he was coming on to the servant girls? She

6:2 enthroned between the cherubim that are on the ark. David set out to recover the Ark of the Covenant. Golden cherubim sat on each end of the ark, their wings spread upward over the top, creating a space in which God's presence was especially evident (Ex. 37:1–9; 1 Chr. 28:2). David knew the ark *was deeply significant because it* served as God's throne on earth.

6:3 new cart ... brought it. Exodus 25:12–14 and Numbers 4:5,6,15 stipulated that the ark should be carried only on the Levites' shoulders. But David followed the Philistines' manner of using a cart (1 Sam. 6:7).

6:7 Uzzah's ... irreverent act. Uzzah had good intentions, but he broke God's clear command for handling the holy ark (Ex. 25:12–14; Num. 4:5,6,15; 1 Chr. 15:13–15;). In the midst of the joy and excitement of the early days of the new kingdom, this situation serves as a bold reminder to Israel and her king *that God has high standards for those* who serve him.

6:8–9 David was angry ... David was afraid. David was at first frustrated. His well-meaning efforts for a joyful celebration of the return of the ark had resulted in the death of a man. His initial anger, however, led to fear—a result of his own anxiety and guilt over the situation rather than the appropriate sense of reverent awe, honor and respect toward God.

6:12 blessed the household of Obed-Edom. God blessed the home where the ark rested while David researched his mistake. The blessing experienced by that home showed David that God would, in the future, also bless the correct transporting of the ark.

6:13 carrying the ark ... six steps. This time David arranged to move the ark properly (Ex. 37:5; 1 Chr. 15:13–15). That was far enough to demonstrate that God was blessing the Levites as they carried the ark (1 Chr. 15:26). This sacrifice would consecrate the whole journey. But some scholars believe the

thought such a dance was below his station? She believed in more emotionally-controlled worship?

APPLY **1.** What do you have to celebrate about right now? **2.** What is most likely to keep you from making worship truly a celebration for you: Emotional inhibition? Fear of what others (like Michal) might think? Music that doesn't speak to you? Distractions in your mind? You are not sure you have anything to be thankful for? **3.** What can you do to keep these factors from hindering worship?

OPEN **1.** Describe the house you lived in as a 10-year-old. How did it compare to your neighbors'? **2.** In what kind of "wandering home" did you spend the most time in during your youth: A tent? A mobile home? An RV? Motels? You didn't wander?

STUDY When things settle down after a series of battles, David starts to feel guilty because he

bull and a fattened calf. 14David, wearing a linen ephod, danced
before the LORD with all his might, 15while he and the entire house of
Israel brought up the ark of the LORD with shouts and the sound of
trumpets.
16As the ark of the LORD was entering the City of David, Michal
daughter of Saul watched from a window. And when she saw King
David leaping and dancing before the LORD, she despised him in her
heart.
17They brought the ark of the LORD and set it in its place inside the
tent that David had pitched for it, and David sacrificed burnt offerings
and fellowship offerings[a] before the LORD. 18After he had finished
sacrificing the burnt offerings and fellowship offerings, he blessed
the people in the name of the LORD Almighty. 19Then he gave a loaf of
bread, a cake of dates and a cake of raisins to each person in the
whole crowd of Israelites, both men and women. And all the people
went to their homes.
20When David returned home to bless his household, Michal
daughter of Saul came out to meet him and said, "How the king of
Israel has distinguished himself today, disrobing in the sight of the
slave girls of his servants as any vulgar fellow would!"
21David said to Michal, "It was before the LORD, who chose me
rather than your father or anyone from his house when he appointed
me ruler over the LORD's people Israel—I will celebrate before the
LORD. 22I will become even more undignified than this, and I will be
humiliated in my own eyes. But by these slave girls you spoke of, I
will be held in honor."
23And Michal daughter of Saul had no children to the day of her
death.

God's Promise to David

7 After the king was settled in his palace and the LORD had given
him rest from all his enemies around him, 2he said to Nathan the
prophet, "Here I am, living in a palace of cedar, while the ark of God
remains in a tent."
3Nathan replied to the king, "Whatever you have in mind, go ahead
and do it, for the LORD is with you."
4That night the word of the LORD came to Nathan, saying:

[a]17 Traditionally *peace offerings*; also in verse 18

Levites stopped every six steps to offer sacrifices—which would have made a very long trip indeed.

6:16 Michal ... despised him. Michal considered David's ebullient leaping and dancing undignified for a king (vv. 20–23). She did not understand or appreciate how deeply significant the return of the ark was to the life of the nation—and why David's joy was so unrestrained.

6:20 king of Israel ... disrobing. David wore a linen ephod (v. 14) but had removed his kingly robe. Ephods were short garments normally worn by priests (1 Sam. 2:18). Though not a Levite, David was performing priestly duties in bringing the ark back, and wore the ephod to honor the Lord. But Michal scoffed at what she considered David's lowering of himself.

6:23 had no children. This emphasis indicated that Michal may have been punished for her haughtiness and judgment of David. It may also have been another of God's judgments against the line of Saul, or simply a result of her estrangement from David.

7:1–29 Though not called a covenant here, this section records God's wonderful promise to David regarding his line. Other references do call this a covenant between God and David (23:5; Ps. 89:3,28,34,39), and David's response indicated that he assumed he had entered into a covenant with God.

7:2 Nathan the prophet. David's royal adviser and God's prophet is introduced here (12:1–14; 1 Kin. 1). **tent**. David felt that since he had a palace which represented his established reign, surely God deserved more than a mere tent (Ps. 132:2–5; Acts 7:46). His desire to build a "palace" for the heavenly King in the nation's capital would be realized by Solomon.

7:3 David had consulted Nathan in order to determine God's will. Nathan

5"Go and tell my servant David, 'This is what the LORD says: Are
you the one to build me a house to dwell in? 6I have not dwelt in a
house from the day I brought the Israelites up out of Egypt to this
day. I have been moving from place to place with a tent as my
dwelling. 7Wherever I have moved with all the Israelites, did I ever
say to any of their rulers whom I commanded to shepherd my
people Israel, "Why have you not built me a house of cedar?" '
8"Now then, tell my servant David, 'This is what the LORD
Almighty says: I took you from the pasture and from following
the flock to be ruler over my people Israel. 9I have been with you
wherever you have gone, and I have cut off all your enemies from
before you. Now I will make your name great, like the names of
the greatest men of the earth. 10And I will provide a place for my
people Israel and will plant them so that they can have a home of
their own and no longer be disturbed. Wicked people will not
oppress them anymore, as they did at the beginning 11and have
done ever since the time I appointed leaders[a] over my people
Israel. I will also give you rest from all your enemies.
" 'The LORD declares to you that the LORD himself will establish a house for you: 12When your days are over and you rest with
your fathers, I will raise up your offspring to succeed you, who
will come from your own body, and I will establish his kingdom.
13He is the one who will build a house for my Name, and I will
establish the throne of his kingdom forever. 14I will be his father,
and he will be my son. When he does wrong, I will punish him
with the rod of men, with floggings inflicted by men. 15But my
love will never be taken away from him, as I took it away from
Saul, whom I removed from before you. 16Your house and your
kingdom will endure forever before me[b]; your throne will be established forever.' "

17Nathan reported to David all the words of this entire revelation.

David's Prayer

18Then King David went in and sat before the LORD, and he said:
"Who am I, O Sovereign LORD, and what is my family, that you
have brought me this far? 19And as if this were not enough in

[a]*11* Traditionally *judges* [b]*16* Some Hebrew manuscripts and Septuagint; most Hebrew manuscripts *you*

lives in a nice home while the ark of God is in a tent. So, he wants to build a temple for the ark. God essentially tells him that such doesn't suit his style, but, lest David feel rejected, God assures him that he is planning great things for David and his offspring. **1.** Why does David feel the ark of God should have a better home than it does? **2.** How would you describe the tone of God's response to David's proposal: Thanks, but no thanks? Irritated—who asked for your help? Offended—are you trying to tie me down? Other? **3.** Why do you think God didn't want his ark in such a house at this time (v. 13)? **4.** Why does God change the topic to what he was planning for David: To show he was thankful for the thought (the proposed temple)? To distract David from a bad idea? To remind David who is in control? To get David to see his future was about more than trivial things like buildings? Other?

APPLY What percentage of your time is going toward things that are temporary, and what percentage of your time is going to things that will be "established forever"?

OPEN When have you been blessed in a way that you were not sure that you deserved?

STUDY God has promised David that he would establish his house and his throne forever. Now he overflows with praise for God

---

approved what he assumed would be God's will because it made sense to him. That night, however, God would tell him otherwise.

7:5 Are you the one to build me a *house?* *God made clear his will* to Nathan that night. While David had a good idea (1 Kin. 8:18,19), God had a different purpose for him: to lead Israel in battle against his enemies until the land was securely held.

7:11 establish a house for you. God will build David a "house"—a royal dynasty—that will ultimately lead to the Messiah and endure forever (v. 16). God's promise to David is grounded in his promise to Abraham at the very beginning of the nation (Gen. 15:18–21).

7:13 He is the one. David's son, Solomon, would ultimately build the temple of God in Jerusalem (1 Kin. 5:3–5).

7:14 his father. God promises David that he will be with David's son, continuing the kind of relationship that David had with God.

7:15 my love will never be taken away. Solomon would certainly be chastened for his sins, but God promised not to remove his merciful love—as he had done with Saul (1 Sam. 13:13,14; 15:22,23).

7:16 established forever. David's throne would ultimately be established forever because his descendant, Jesus the Messiah, will indeed reign forever.

7:18 went in and sat before the LORD. David entered where the Ark of the Covenant was being kept, the place of the Lord's presence with his people (6:17).

7:19 Your way ... O Sovereign LORD? David may have been expressing

because of this wonderful promise. **1.** If you could choose one word to summarize the attitude that David shows in this prayer, what word would you choose? **2.** How many times does David refer to himself as "your servant" in this prayer? What does that say about him? **3.** What would you say is the motivation behind this prayer: To gain more favors? To ensure God won't go back on his word? To just say thanks and praise God? Other? **4.** What gives David courage to offer this prayer, and why does he need such courage? **5.** What are two central qualities that David ascribes to God in this prayer (vv. 22,28)?

APPLY 1. When did you last find God's promises to be trustworthy? Were you confident all along of that trustworthiness, or did you waver? **2.** If you fully believed in God's trustworthiness for the coming week, how would it affect the way you feel and behave?

OPEN 1. Have you ever had a time in your life when it felt like you had "the Midas touch," that everything you did was successful? When? **2.** If you have not had such a time, how do you think you would react in that situation: Become a major egotist? Start taking good things for granted and stop working so hard? Just praise the Lord? Other?

STUDY God's presence with David becomes more and more evident as he has one military victory after another. He consolidates

your sight, O Sovereign LORD, you have also spoken about the
future of the house of your servant. Is this your usual way of
dealing with man, O Sovereign LORD?
20"What more can David say to you? For you know your
servant, O Sovereign LORD. 21For the sake of your word and according to your will, you have done this great thing and made it
known to your servant.
22"How great you are, O Sovereign LORD! There is no one like
you, and there is no God but you, as we have heard with our own
ears. 23And who is like your people Israel—the one nation on
earth that God went out to redeem as a people for himself, and to
make a name for himself, and to perform great and awesome
wonders by driving out nations and their gods from before your
people, whom you redeemed from Egypt?[a] 24You have established your people Israel as your very own forever, and you,
O LORD, have become their God.
25"And now, LORD God, keep forever the promise you have
made concerning your servant and his house. Do as you promised, 26so that your name will be great forever. Then men will say,
'The LORD Almighty is God over Israel!' And the house of your
servant David will be established before you.
27"O LORD Almighty, God of Israel, you have revealed this to
your servant, saying, 'I will build a house for you.' So your servant has found courage to offer you this prayer. 28O Sovereign
LORD, you are God! Your words are trustworthy, and you have
promised these good things to your servant. 29Now be pleased to
bless the house of your servant, that it may continue forever in
your sight; for you, O Sovereign LORD, have spoken, and with
your blessing the house of your servant will be blessed forever."

David's Victories

8 In the course of time, David defeated the Philistines and subdued them, and he took Metheg Ammah from the control of the
Philistines.
2David also defeated the Moabites. He made them lie down on the
ground and measured them off with a length of cord. Every two
lengths of them were put to death, and the third length was allowed
to live. So the Moabites became subject to David and brought tribute.
3Moreover, David fought Hadadezer son of Rehob, king of Zobah,
when he went to restore his control along the Euphrates River. 4David

[a]23 See Septuagint and 1 Chron. 17:21; Hebrew *wonders for your land and before your people, whom you redeemed from Egypt, from the nations and their gods.*

amazement with the way God had blessed him.

7:21 For the sake of your word. The "word" probably refers to God's covenant with Abraham regarding the nation and the land he would give it.

7:23 the one nation on earth. Israel was special not because of anything the nation had accomplished, but simply because God had chosen the people when he had made the promise to their ancestor, Abraham (Gen. 12:2,3; Deut. 7:6–8; 33:26–29). **to make a name … perform great wonders.** God chose Israel as the recipient of his loving care solely for his own purposes, in order to spread his own glory throughout the world (Deut. 9:4,5; Isa. 63:12; Jer. 32:20,21; Ezek. 36:22–38).

7:24 have become their God. David recognized that God's promise to him was made because of God's promise to Israel.

8:3 restore … Euphrates River. Saul had defeated Zobah, enlarging the kingdom to near the Euphrates Valley; but Israelite control of the land had been short-lived. God had originally promised the land from Egypt to the Euphrates to Abraham (Gen. 15:18). So here God's promise is at least partially fulfilled.

8:4 the chariot horses. God earlier told Joshua to cut the tendons of the enemy's horses to prevent them from walking (Josh. 11:6).

captured a thousand of his chariots, seven thousand charioteers[a] and twenty thousand foot soldiers. He hamstrung all but a hundred of the chariot horses.

[5]When the Arameans of Damascus came to help Hadadezer king of Zobah, David struck down twenty-two thousand of them. [6]He put garrisons in the Aramean kingdom of Damascus, and the Arameans became subject to him and brought tribute. The LORD gave David victory wherever he went.

[7]David took the gold shields that belonged to the officers of Hadadezer and brought them to Jerusalem. [8]From Tebah[b] and Berothai, towns that belonged to Hadadezer, King David took a great quantity of bronze.

[9]When Tou[c] king of Hamath heard that David had defeated the entire army of Hadadezer, [10]he sent his son Joram[d] to King David to greet him and congratulate him on his victory in battle over Hadadezer, who had been at war with Tou. Joram brought with him articles of silver and gold and bronze.

[11]King David dedicated these articles to the LORD, as he had done with the silver and gold from all the nations he had subdued: [12]Edom[e] and Moab, the Ammonites and the Philistines, and Amalek. He also dedicated the plunder taken from Hadadezer son of Rehob, king of Zobah.

[13]And David became famous after he returned from striking down eighteen thousand Edomites[f] in the Valley of Salt.

[14]He put garrisons throughout Edom, and all the Edomites became subject to David. The LORD gave David victory wherever he went.

David's Officials

[15]David reigned over all Israel, doing what was just and right for all his people. [16]Joab son of Zeruiah was over the army; Jehoshaphat son of Ahilud was recorder; [17]Zadok son of Ahitub and Ahimelech son of Abiathar were priests; Seraiah was secretary; [18]Benaiah son of Jehoiada was over the Kerethites and Pelethites; and David's sons were royal advisers.[g]

David and Mephibosheth

9 David asked, "Is there anyone still left of the house of Saul to whom I can show kindness for Jonathan's sake?"

[a]*4* Septuagint (see also Dead Sea Scrolls and 1 Chron. 18:4); Masoretic Text *captured seventeen hundred of his charioteers* [b]*8* See some Septuagint manuscripts (see also 1 Chron. 18:8); Hebrew *Betah.* [c]*9* Hebrew *Toi,* a variant of *Tou;* also in verse 10 [d]*10* A variant of *Hadoram* [e]*12* Some Hebrew manuscripts, Septuagint and Syriac (see also 1 Chron. 18:11); most Hebrew manuscripts *Aram* [f]*13* A few Hebrew manuscripts, Septuagint and Syriac (see also 1 Chron. 18:12); most Hebrew manuscripts *Aram* (that is, Arameans) [g]*18* Or *were priests*

his power by building a bureaucracy. **1.** What impression do you get of David from how he handles these victories: Blood thirsty and sadistic? Disciplined and focused on total victory? Dedicated to the Lord's direction? Other? **2.** Why would David hamstring the horses (v. 4)? Why should this act be noted by the writer (Deut. 17:16)? **3.** What was the significance of David dedicating to the Lord all that he had won in battle? **4.** What is the importance for establishing a strong kingdom of doing "what is just and right for all the people" (v. 15)? **5.** Is God implicated, exonerated, exhilarated or glorified by the events in this story? Why do you think so?

APPLY 1. How would your behavior change if you dedicated all that you have earned or been given in this past year to the Lord? **2.** What possession that you have would be the hardest for you to dedicate to God? Why?

OPEN 1. What person close to you has a disability? How well is he or she managing that disability? **2.** If you could wish one thing for this person (other than a healing), what would it be?

STUDY David's power is becoming established, but he still misses the friend of his youth,

8:7 gold shields. The shields may have been adorned with pieces of gold, rather than solid gold.

8:10 articles of silver and gold and bronze. King Tou of Hamath apparently wanted to establish good relations with Israel, in view of the nation's growing power. These gifts may have indicated that Tou would serve as a vassal king under David.

8:15 all Israel. By this point David's kingdom stretched from the Gulf of Aqaba to the River of Egypt to the Euphrates—the area God had promised Abraham (Gen. 15:18). **just and right.** David was a true theocratic king—subject to the authority of God and representing God to the people.

8:18 Kerethites and Pelethites. They served as professional soldiers in David's army (15:18), an elite royal guard (23:22,23). Benaiah was the commander.

9:1–20:26 This lengthy passage is full of detail and insider information, thus it apparently was written by someone in David's court.

9:1–13 These events apparently occurred several years after the conquest of Jerusalem by David.

9:1 can show kindness. David had

Jonathan. In this story he seeks a way to honor that friendship. **1.** What does it show about David that he was wanting to find someone of the house of Saul: He felt guilty? He missed Jonathan? He wanted to honor Jonathan's memory? He wanted to keep Saul's family members where he could watch them? Other? **2.** Why does the story emphasize (vv. 3,13) that Mephibosheth was crippled in both feet? **3.** What might Mephibosheth have felt as he was escorted back to Jerusalem? **4.** Why does Mephibosheth refer to himself as a "dead dog": He's afraid this will be his fate in David's hands? He is putting down his value because of his disability? He doesn't want David to think he is important enough to kill? **5.** What does David's treatment of Mephibosheth say about David's character?

APPLY 1. When have you felt like "a dead dog"? What caused you to feel that way? **2.** When has someone come to you in a loving and merciful way, when you expected much rougher treatment of them? What did you learn from this of God's mercy?

2 Now there was a servant of Saul's household named Ziba. They
called him to appear before David, and the king said to him, "Are you
Ziba?"
"Your servant," he replied.
3 The king asked, "Is there no one still left of the house of Saul to
whom I can show God's kindness?"
Ziba answered the king, "There is still a son of Jonathan; he is crippled in both feet."
4 "Where is he?" the king asked.
Ziba answered, "He is at the house of Makir son of Ammiel in Lo
Debar."
5 So King David had him brought from Lo Debar, from the house of
Makir son of Ammiel.
6 When Mephibosheth son of Jonathan, the son of Saul, came to
David, he bowed down to pay him honor.
David said, "Mephibosheth!"
"Your servant," he replied.
7 "Don't be afraid," David said to him, "for I will surely show you
kindness for the sake of your father Jonathan. I will restore to you all
the land that belonged to your grandfather Saul, and you will always
eat at my table."
8 Mephibosheth bowed down and said, "What is your servant, that
you should notice a dead dog like me?"
9 Then the king summoned Ziba, Saul's servant, and said to him, "I
have given your master's grandson everything that belonged to Saul
and his family. 10 You and your sons and your servants are to farm the
land for him and bring in the crops, so that your master's grandson
may be provided for. And Mephibosheth, grandson of your master,
will always eat at my table." (Now Ziba had fifteen sons and twenty
servants.)
11 Then Ziba said to the king, "Your servant will do whatever my lord
the king commands his servant to do." So Mephibosheth ate at
David's[a] table like one of the king's sons.
12 Mephibosheth had a young son named Mica, and all the members of Ziba's household were servants of Mephibosheth. 13 And Mephibosheth lived in Jerusalem, because he always ate at the king's
table, and he was crippled in both feet.

[a] *11* Septuagint; Hebrew *my*

made a promise to his dear friend Jonathan (1 Sam. 20:15,42) and was determined to keep it with Jonathan's heirs.

9:4 Makir. The crippled Mephibosheth has been cared for by Makir, apparently a man of some wealth. Later Makir would assist David (17:27).

9:10 Ziba had fifteen sons and twenty servants. This indicates the extent of Saul's estate—35 men were required to oversee it.

9:2 Ziba. David summoned Ziba because he was handling Saul's estate as chief steward. The estate had been inherited by Mephibosheth, Saul's grandson.

9:3 a son of Jonathan. Mephibosheth was the primary heir as son of Jonathan, who would have thus been in line for the throne under Saul. Saul did have other descendants, but Mephibosheth would be the most important to David (21:8).

9:7 Don't be afraid. Mephibosheth had every reason to fear David, since typically in the ancient Middle East heirs of previous dynasties were put to death in order to protect the new king. **restore to you.** Saul's land, apparently taken from his family, would be fully restored to Mephibosheth. **eat at my table.** Mephibosheth may not need financial help or free meals; he would be well cared for through the estate of Saul. David's offer rather involved honor and prestige.

9:11 like one of the king's sons. David demonstrated godly grace. Mephibosheth had done nothing to deserve such treatment, yet David was faithful to his promise—a beautiful snapshot of the believer's relationship to a gracious God.

9:13 crippled. Mephibosheth had been injured when his nurse fell with him while they fled from Gibeah after hearing that Saul and Jonathan had been killed (4:4).

David Defeats the Ammonites

10 In the course of time, the king of the Ammonites died, and
his son Hanun succeeded him as king. [2]David thought, "I will
show kindness to Hanun son of Nahash, just as his father showed
kindness to me." So David sent a delegation to express his sympathy
to Hanun concerning his father.
When David's men came to the land of the Ammonites, [3]the
Ammonite nobles said to Hanun their lord, "Do you think David is
honoring your father by sending men to you to express sympathy?
Hasn't David sent them to you to explore the city and spy it out and
overthrow it?" [4]So Hanun seized David's men, shaved off half of each
man's beard, cut off their garments in the middle at the buttocks, and
sent them away.
[5]When David was told about this, he sent messengers to meet the
men, for they were greatly humiliated. The king said, "Stay at Jericho
till your beards have grown, and then come back."
[6]When the Ammonites realized that they had become a stench in
David's nostrils, they hired twenty thousand Aramean foot soldiers
from Beth Rehob and Zobah, as well as the king of Maacah with a
thousand men, and also twelve thousand men from Tob.
[7]On hearing this, David sent Joab out with the entire army of fighting men. [8]The Ammonites came out and drew up in battle formation
at the entrance to their city gate, while the Arameans of Zobah and
Rehob and the men of Tob and Maacah were by themselves in the
open country.
[9]Joab saw that there were battle lines in front of him and behind
him; so he selected some of the best troops in Israel and deployed
them against the Arameans. [10]He put the rest of the men under the
command of Abishai his brother and deployed them against the
Ammonites. [11]Joab said, "If the Arameans are too strong for me, then
you are to come to my rescue; but if the Ammonites are too strong
for you, then I will come to rescue you. [12]Be strong and let us fight
bravely for our people and the cities of our God. The LORD will do
what is good in his sight."
[13]Then Joab and the troops with him advanced to fight the Arameans, and they fled before him. [14]When the Ammonites saw that the
Arameans were fleeing, they fled before Abishai and went inside the
city. So Joab returned from fighting the Ammonites and came to Jerusalem.
[15]After the Arameans saw that they had been routed by Israel,
they regrouped. [16]Hadadezer had Arameans brought from beyond
the River[a]; they went to Helam, with Shobach the commander of
Hadadezer's army leading them.
[17]When David was told of this, he gathered all Israel, crossed the

[a]16 That is, the Euphrates

OPEN **1.** What was your most embarrassing experience in high school? How long did it take you to "get over it"? **2.** If someone wanted to embarrass you now, what would be the best way to do it: Get out your baby pictures? Record your singing in the shower? Talk to your kids about the stupid things you did as a teen? Have you model your wardrobe from the 70's?

STUDY When the king of the Ammonites dies, David sends a delegation to convey his sympathy. But thinking they are spies, the Ammonites humiliate the delegation and the result is war. **1.** While David remembered some kindness on Nahash's part, with what less-than-kind act did Nahash threaten the people of Jabesh Gilead? **2.** Why do the Ammonites suspect David's motives in sending his delegation: It's what they would have done? David had shown himself a crafty warrior? Ammonite troublemakers just wanted to start a fight? **3.** What is done to humiliate David's men? Why was the beard-shaving particularly humiliating? **4.** How do Joab and Abishai reinforce each other? **5.** What does Joab mean by "The LORD will do what is good in his sight" (v. 12)? **6.** What two results came from these victories (v. 19)? **7.** Can God's goodness be reconciled with all of this gore? If so, how?

APPLY **1.** In what area of your life are you feeling the need for "reinforcements"? **2.** What role can your group play in providing these "reinforcements"?

10:3 Hasn't David sent them to ... overthrow it? David's efforts at showing kindness were received with great suspicion. The Ammonite nobles figured he was simply spying out the land in advance of a raid.

10:4 shaved off half of each man's beard ... cut off their garments. Both of these acts were deeply degrading and humiliating.

10:8 city gate. A primary part of a city's defense. Such gates normally had towers where soldiers could defend the city against advancing troops.

10:12 Be strong and let us fight bravely. Joab exhorted his soldiers much as God had encouraged Joshua just before entering Canaan (Josh. 1:6,7).

Jordan and went to Helam. The Arameans formed their battle lines to meet David and fought against him. [18]But they fled before Israel, and David killed seven hundred of their charioteers and forty thousand of their foot soldiers.[a] He also struck down Shobach the commander of their army, and he died there. [19]When all the kings who were vassals of Hadadezer saw that they had been defeated by Israel, they made peace with the Israelites and became subject to them.

So the Arameans were afraid to help the Ammonites anymore.

David and Bathsheba

11 In the spring, at the time when kings go off to war, David sent Joab out with the king's men and the whole Israelite army. They destroyed the Ammonites and besieged Rabbah. But David remained in Jerusalem.

[2]One evening David got up from his bed and walked around on the roof of the palace. From the roof he saw a woman bathing. The woman was very beautiful, [3]and David sent someone to find out about her. The man said, "Isn't this Bathsheba, the daughter of Eliam and the wife of Uriah the Hittite?" [4]Then David sent messengers to get her. She came to him, and he slept with her. (She had purified herself from her uncleanness.) Then[b] she went back home. [5]The woman conceived and sent word to David, saying, "I am pregnant."

[6]So David sent this word to Joab: "Send me Uriah the Hittite." And Joab sent him to David. [7]When Uriah came to him, David asked him how Joab was, how the soldiers were and how the war was going. [8]Then David said to Uriah, "Go down to your house and wash your feet." So Uriah left the palace, and a gift from the king was sent after him. [9]But Uriah slept at the entrance to the palace with all his master's servants and did not go down to his house.

[10]When David was told, "Uriah did not go home," he asked him, "Haven't you just come from a distance? Why didn't you go home?"

[11]Uriah said to David, "The ark and Israel and Judah are staying in tents, and my master Joab and my lord's men are camped in the open

[a]18 Some Septuagint manuscripts (see also 1 Chron. 19:18); Hebrew *horsemen* [b]4 Or *with her. When she purified herself from her uncleanness,*

OPEN 1. What tempting thing do you have the hardest time turning down once you see it: The decadent dessert? An attractive person of the opposite sex? A new car you really can't afford? The latest fashion in the store window? **2.** When you are tempted are you more likely to: Grit your teeth? Look the other way? Yield and think about it later? Get angry at whoever put the temptation in front of you? Say a quick prayer?

STUDY Everything has been going King David's way, and he has had some great victories. But perhaps his most famous defeat did not come at the hands of a foreign army, but rather in relation to a beautiful woman—Bathsheba. **1.** Why do you think David opted to stay in Jerusalem? **2.** What would have been David's best chance of short-circuiting this temptation, and keeping from yielding to it: Looking the other way immediately? "Admiring the view," but not pursuing it further? Inviting her over—but making sure they prayed together? Other? **3.** Given that David was king and essentially an absolute monarch, could Bathsheba have prevented this seduction? **4.** How do you imagine Bathsheba felt about

10:18 seven hundred of their charioteers. The parallel account in 1 Chronicles 19:18 has "seven thousand." One of these texts probably reflects a copyist's mistake.

11:1 In the spring. This is the year after the events recorded in chapter 10—and about ten years after David established his throne in Jerusalem. Normally kings of this period went to war in the spring when the weather was cooperative and food plentiful. Note that David remained in Jerusalem.

11:2 David ... walked around on the roof. Roofs were flat and commonly used as living areas. Bathsheba was probably bathing in her enclosed but roofless courtyard.

11:3 Uriah. A member of David's royal guard (23:39).

11:4 She came to him. Bathsheba did not seem to protest David's adulterous advances. She may have been afraid to protest, however, for she had been summoned by the king. **purified herself.** Bathsheba had just become ceremonially clean (following the seven-day period of uncleanness due to menstruation; Lev. 15:19–30); therefore, she clearly could not have been pregnant by her husband Uriah when David slept with her. Therefore, *her child* could not be Uriah's, but David's.

11:5 The woman conceived. Both were guilty of adultery, a fact that now could not be hidden. The penalty, according to God's law, was death for them both. Thus David acted to deal with the situation swiftly (Lev. 20:10; Deut. 22:22).

11:6 Send me Uriah the Hittite. David called Uriah home, assuming that he would sleep with his wife and thus appear to have made her pregnant.

11:11 ark. It seems that the ark was being kept in a field tent with Israel's army—to provide the soldiers blessing and guidance. David's soldiers were off fighting and God was symbolically in the field with them, while David was safe at home in Jerusalem with too much free time on his hands.

fields. How could I go to my house to eat and drink and lie with my
wife? As surely as you live, I will not do such a thing!"
[12]Then David said to him, "Stay here one more day, and tomorrow
I will send you back." So Uriah remained in Jerusalem that day and
the next. [13]At David's invitation, he ate and drank with him, and David
made him drunk. But in the evening Uriah went out to sleep on his
mat among his master's servants; he did not go home.
[14]In the morning David wrote a letter to Joab and sent it with Uriah.
[15]In it he wrote, "Put Uriah in the front line where the fighting is fierc-
est. Then withdraw from him so he will be struck down and die."
[16]So while Joab had the city under siege, he put Uriah at a place
where he knew the strongest defenders were. [17]When the men of the
city came out and fought against Joab, some of the men in David's
army fell; moreover, Uriah the Hittite died.
[18]Joab sent David a full account of the battle. [19]He instructed the
messenger: "When you have finished giving the king this account of
the battle, [20]the king's anger may flare up, and he may ask you, 'Why
did you get so close to the city to fight? Didn't you know they would
shoot arrows from the wall? [21]Who killed Abimelech son of Jerub-
Besheth[a]? Didn't a woman throw an upper millstone on him from the
wall, so that he died in Thebez? Why did you get so close to the wall?'
If he asks you this, then say to him, 'Also, your servant Uriah the Hittite is dead.' "
[22]The messenger set out, and when he arrived he told David everything Joab had sent him to say. [23]The messenger said to David, "The
men overpowered us and came out against us in the open, but we
drove them back to the entrance to the city gate. [24]Then the archers
shot arrows at your servants from the wall, and some of the king's
men died. Moreover, your servant Uriah the Hittite is dead."
[25]David told the messenger, "Say this to Joab: 'Don't let this upset
you; the sword devours one as well as another. Press the attack
against the city and destroy it.' Say this to encourage Joab."
[26]When Uriah's wife heard that her husband was dead, she
mourned for him. [27]After the time of mourning was over, David had
her brought to his house, and she became his wife and bore him a
son. But the thing David had done displeased the LORD.

Nathan Rebukes David

12 The LORD sent Nathan to David. When he came to him, he
said, "There were two men in a certain town, one rich and

[a]*21* Also known as *Jerub-Baal* (that is, Gideon)

this whole affair: Used? Flattered? Guilty? Swept off her feet? **5.** What superior character qualities does Uriah exhibit in refusing David's overture (vv. 11,13)? Does this surprise you, given that Uriah was a Hittite, a foreigner? **6.** David was one of the most revered persons of the Old Testament (1 Kin. 11:4–6). Should his behavior been different? Why or why not? **7.** With whom do you identify most in this story: David—getting into trouble and making it worse by covering it up? Bathsheba—being taken advantage of? Joab—caught between and not knowing how to act? Uriah—"rewarded" for exemplary behavior with betrayal?

APPLY 1. What do you need to do most to strengthen your own stand against temptation: Learn to "nip it in the bud"? Stay away from situations where you know temptation is likely to come? Pray more? Own up to it and ask for help from supportive friends? Other? **2.** Where is your support to face moral failures—God's grace or your own ability to "cover it up"? If a change is needed, what can you do to make that change?

OPEN 1. What special pet do you remember having when you were a child? What do you remember doing to care for and pamper this pet? **2.** Do you remember any time when someone abused this pet? How did you feel and what did you do?

11:13 he ate and drank. David tried one more time, hoping that if Uriah *were drunk enough*, he might go home and sleep with Bathsheba. But once again, Uriah refused to take things easy when his comrades were at war.

11:15 Put Uriah in the front line. Since all his schemes for a simple cover-up had failed, David took drastic action. He knew full well what would happen to Uriah.

11:21 your servant Uriah ... is dead. Joab knew that David would want to know this immediately (vv. 14,15).

11:23,24 According to the messenger's report, Joab pursued a different plan than David had ordered—namely, to have soldiers removed from around Uriah, leaving him alone against the enemy. Perhaps concerned that such a tactic might raise too many questions, Joab had Uriah's platoon engage the enemy near the city wall, drawing archers' arrows and resulting in several fatalities, including Uriah.

11:27 time of mourning. This was probably seven days in length (Gen. 50:10; 1 Sam. 31:13).

12:1 The LORD sent Nathan. Nathan, in his role as prophet, is God's messenger. In this case, God the true King commissions his ambassador to rebuke the king he had chosen, and to declare judgment upon him.

STUDY The previous chapter records David's sin: His adultery with Bathsheba, his attempts to cover up the fact he got her pregnant—ending with ordering her husband's murder, and then taking Bathsheba as his wife. Now God confronts David, through the prophet Nathan, by using one of the Old Testament's most striking parables. **1.** Why does Nathan speak to David through a parable? How does this parable relate to the events of the previous chapter? **2.** Why is David so angry about the taking of the poor man's ewe in the parable: He was more sensitive to social sin than sexual sin? He could see the sin more clearly when he thought it wasn't his? He may have been redirecting his self-hatred for his act? **3.** Do you think David's confession was sincere? If so, why didn't he do it sooner? **4.** What three sons of David will meet violent deaths in fulfillment of what is said in verse 10 (13:28–29; 18:14–15; 1 Kin. 2:25)? **5.** Who will "lie with David's wives in broad daylight" (vv. 11–12; 16:21–22)? **6.** How do you feel about David's punishment: Too severe? Too lenient? Unfairly included David's family members? **7.** Who can you relate to the most in this story: David—I've suffered for my sins? Nathan—I've had to confront someone else about a wrong they did? David's servants—I've been confused about how to console one in grief? The child—I've sometimes felt like an innocent victim? **8.** What lesson about grief stands out the most to you from this story: Not everyone grieves the same (vv. 21–22)? You cannot bargain away painful realities (vv. 15–17)? You can't bring back the past; you can only move forward (vv. 22–23)? Other?

the other poor. 2 The rich man had a very large number of sheep and cattle, 3 but the poor man had nothing except one little ewe lamb he had bought. He raised it, and it grew up with him and his children. It shared his food, drank from his cup and even slept in his arms. It was like a daughter to him.

4 "Now a traveler came to the rich man, but the rich man refrained from taking one of his own sheep or cattle to prepare a meal for the traveler who had come to him. Instead, he took the ewe lamb that belonged to the poor man and prepared it for the one who had come to him."

5 David burned with anger against the man and said to Nathan, "As surely as the LORD lives, the man who did this deserves to die! 6 He must pay for that lamb four times over, because he did such a thing and had no pity."

7 Then Nathan said to David, "You are the man! This is what the LORD, the God of Israel, says: 'I anointed you king over Israel, and I delivered you from the hand of Saul. 8 I gave your master's house to you, and your master's wives into your arms. I gave you the house of Israel and Judah. And if all this had been too little, I would have given you even more. 9 Why did you despise the word of the LORD by doing what is evil in his eyes? You struck down Uriah the Hittite with the sword and took his wife to be your own. You killed him with the sword of the Ammonites. 10 Now, therefore, the sword will never depart from your house, because you despised me and took the wife of Uriah the Hittite to be your own.'

11 "This is what the LORD says: 'Out of your own household I am going to bring calamity upon you. Before your very eyes I will take your wives and give them to one who is close to you, and he will lie with your wives in broad daylight. 12 You did it in secret, but I will do this thing in broad daylight before all Israel.' "

13 Then David said to Nathan, "I have sinned against the LORD."

Nathan replied, "The LORD has taken away your sin. You are not going to die. 14 But because by doing this you have made the enemies of the LORD show utter contempt,[a] the son born to you will die."

15 After Nathan had gone home, the LORD struck the child that

[a] 14 Masoretic Text; an ancient Hebrew scribal tradition *this you have shown utter contempt for the LORD*

12:5 David burned with anger. Nathan has built his case well: David was furious over the injustice committed. He called for the man's death, though the crime normally would not draw the death penalty. Ironically, by committing adultery and murder, David had become that very man.

12:6 pay for that lamb four times over. Ironically, David knew God's law, despite that fact that he had broken it himself. The penalty he recommended fit the requirements of Exodus 22:1.

12:8 your master's wives into your arms. This may simply mean that God had given David Saul's throne and all it entailed (usually new kings kept the harem of the prior king).

12:10 the sword will never depart. This is fulfilled specifically in the violent deaths of three of David's sons: Amnon (13:23–31), Absalom (18:1–18) and Adonijah (1 Kin. 2:13–25).

12:11 I am going to bring calamity upon you. This is fulfilled when Absalom, conspiring to take the throne from his own father, forced David to flee Jerusalem (15:1–24).

12:13 I have sinned. David's lying, deception and cover-up came to an end as he confronted his own guilt and confessed his sin against God as a result of Nathan's strong rebuke (David's thoughts about the depth of his guilt and sin are captured in Ps. 51). **The LORD has taken away your sin.** The sin was horrible, but God could forgive if David sincerely repented. This must have been welcome news to David (Ps. 32:1,5; 51:8,12).

12:14 the enemies of the LORD. The consequences for David's sin include the death of his son and David's subsequent public suffering in order to demonstrate God's authority. Some manuscripts do not include the prophecy of the son's death.

12:15 the child. No name is given the child, so apparently he did not live long enough to be circumcised on the eighth day, when a son was normally named.

Uriah's wife had borne to David, and he became ill. [16]David pleaded
with God for the child. He fasted and went into his house and spent
the nights lying on the ground. [17]The elders of his household stood
beside him to get him up from the ground, but he refused, and he
would not eat any food with them.
[18]On the seventh day the child died. David's servants were afraid to
tell him that the child was dead, for they thought, "While the child
was still living, we spoke to David but he would not listen to us. How
can we tell him the child is dead? He may do something desperate."
[19]David noticed that his servants were whispering among themselves and he realized the child was dead. "Is the child dead?" he
asked.

"Yes," they replied, "he is dead."

[20]Then David got up from the ground. After he had washed, put on
lotions and changed his clothes, he went into the house of the LORD
and worshiped. Then he went to his own house, and at his request
they served him food, and he ate.
[21]His servants asked him, "Why are you acting this way? While the
child was alive, you fasted and wept, but now that the child is dead,
you get up and eat!"
[22]He answered, "While the child was still alive, I fasted and wept. I
thought, 'Who knows? The LORD may be gracious to me and let the
child live.' [23]But now that he is dead, why should I fast? Can I bring
him back again? I will go to him, but he will not return to me."
[24]Then David comforted his wife Bathsheba, and he went to her
and lay with her. She gave birth to a son, and they named him
Solomon. The LORD loved him; [25]and because the LORD loved him, he
sent word through Nathan the prophet to name him Jedidiah.[a]
[26]Meanwhile Joab fought against Rabbah of the Ammonites and
captured the royal citadel. [27]Joab then sent messengers to David,
saying, "I have fought against Rabbah and taken its water supply.
[28]Now muster the rest of the troops and besiege the city and capture
it. Otherwise I will take the city, and it will be named after me."
[29]So David mustered the entire army and went to Rabbah, and
attacked and captured it. [30]He took the crown from the head of their
king[b]—its weight was a talent[c] of gold, and it was set with precious
stones—and it was placed on David's head. He took a great quantity
of plunder from the city [31]and brought out the people who were there,
consigning them to labor with saws and with iron picks and axes, and
he made them work at brickmaking.[d] He did this to all the Ammonite
towns. Then David and his entire army returned to Jerusalem.

[a]*25 Jedidiah* means *loved by the LORD.* [b]*30* Or *of Milcom* (that is, Molech) [c]*30* That is, about 75 pounds (about 34 kilograms) [d]*31* The meaning of the Hebrew for this clause is uncertain.

APPLY 1. When do you remember having to confront a painful truth about yourself and your own behavior? Who helped you do so? How do you feel about that person now? **2.** In what ways are you presently mourning past mistakes?

12:18 afraid to tell him that the child was dead. The servants had seen how grief-stricken David was before the child died, and assumed that he would rage uncontrollably on hearing the news.

12:20 he went into the house of the LORD. David humbly accepted both the forgiveness of God and the penalty God had imposed, demonstrating his chastened heart by going to worship God personally.

12:25 Jedidiah. This nickname of Solomon, Bathsheba's second son by David, means "loved by the Lord." Surely this was great comfort to David after the death of his and Bathsheba's first son.

12:28,29 capture it. Joab had been working to conquer the Ammonites for years, but he wanted David to take the credit. The city of Rabbah would be renamed in honor of the conqueror.

OPEN 1. Who did you consult regarding your "love life"? What was some of the worst advice? Best advice? **2.** Who was your biggest secret "crush" while in high school?

STUDY As a result of King David's sins, the Lord said through the prophet Nathan that David would reap great calamity in his own household. Now the trouble begins, as David's son Amnon rapes his half-sister Tamar. **1.** What do you think fueled Amnon's initial passion: The "forbidden fruit" effect? Out-of-control adolescent hormones? Simple perversity? Other? **2.** Had Amnon's friend Jonadab been a better, wiser friend, what might he have told Amnon: Get help? Take a cold shower? Get out of the palace and meet someone outside the family? Talk to your father the king (as Tamar advised)? Let me stick around and keep you accountable? **3.** How do you explain Amnon's reversal from "love" to "hate": Typical macho behavior? Projected guilt? She had fallen off the pedestal he had put her on? The experience did not meet up to his fantasies? He was just a sick, sick man? **4.** What emotion do you think Tamar was experiencing when she refused to be sent out of Amnon's room: Shame? Anger? The righteous indignation of one who doesn't want a coverup? **5.** How did David respond (v. 21)? Why didn't David act with more expediency and resolve, once he heard what happened: Lost moral resolve because of the Bathsheba incident? The shame of a father who just wanted it to all go away? The double-standard of a father who winks at his son's indiscretions? **6.** What have you found to be most helpful in moving beyond a traumatic experience?

APPLY 1. Have you ever ended up hating someone you started out loving? What brought about the change? **2.** In what areas of your life do you need to work on healing old hurts?

Amnon and Tamar

13 In the course of time, Amnon son of David fell in love with
Tamar, the beautiful sister of Absalom son of David.
2 Amnon became frustrated to the point of illness on account of his
sister Tamar, for she was a virgin, and it seemed impossible for him to
do anything to her.
3 Now Amnon had a friend named Jonadab son of Shimeah, David's
brother. Jonadab was a very shrewd man. 4 He asked Amnon, "Why do
you, the king's son, look so haggard morning after morning? Won't
you tell me?"
Amnon said to him, "I'm in love with Tamar, my brother Absalom's
sister."
5 "Go to bed and pretend to be ill," Jonadab said. "When your father
comes to see you, say to him, 'I would like my sister Tamar to come
and give me something to eat. Let her prepare the food in my sight so
I may watch her and then eat it from her hand.' "
6 So Amnon lay down and pretended to be ill. When the king came
to see him, Amnon said to him, "I would like my sister Tamar to come
and make some special bread in my sight, so I may eat from her
hand."
7 David sent word to Tamar at the palace: "Go to the house of your
brother Amnon and prepare some food for him." 8 So Tamar went to
the house of her brother Amnon, who was lying down. She took some
dough, kneaded it, made the bread in his sight and baked it. 9 Then
she took the pan and served him the bread, but he refused to eat.
"Send everyone out of here," Amnon said. So everyone left him.
10 Then Amnon said to Tamar, "Bring the food here into my bedroom
so I may eat from your hand." And Tamar took the bread she had prepared and brought it to her brother Amnon in his bedroom. 11 But
when she took it to him to eat, he grabbed her and said, "Come to bed
with me, my sister."
12 "Don't, my brother!" she said to him. "Don't force me. Such a
thing should not be done in Israel! Don't do this wicked thing. 13 What
about me? Where could I get rid of my disgrace? And what about you?
You would be like one of the wicked fools in Israel. Please speak to
the king; he will not keep me from being married to you." 14 But he refused to listen to her, and since he was stronger than she, he raped
her.
15 Then Amnon hated her with intense hatred. In fact, he hated her
more than he had loved her. Amnon said to her, "Get up and get out!"
16 "No!" she said to him. "Sending me away would be a greater
wrong than what you have already done to me."
But he refused to listen to her. 17 He called his personal servant and

---

13:1 Amnon. Amnon was David's oldest son (3:2). Tamar was Amnon's half-sister and Absalom's full sister.

13:13 What about me? According to Hebrew Law, what Amnon suggested was wicked and disgraceful (Lev. 18:9; 20:17, Deut. 27:22). Tamar begged him to consider that rape would cause her to be cursed by the people and unfit for marriage. Raping his half-sister would jeopardize Amnon's right to the throne. **he will not keep me from being married to you.** Tamar may have said this as a way of escaping her immediate danger, since such a marriage was forbidden in Israel. Or perhaps this regulation was not strictly observed.

13:15 Amnon hated. Amnon's lust, now gratified, turned into hatred. His hatred may have been fueled by feelings of guilt over his sin.

13:16 Sending me away. The law demanded that Amnon marry Tamar (Deut. 22:29), but in sending her away, he rejected her as a bride. Now that she was no longer a virgin, Tamar was disgraced and ineligible for marriage (Deut. 22:13–21).

said, "Get this woman out of here and bolt the door after her." 18So
his servant put her out and bolted the door after her. She was wearing
a richly ornamented[a] robe, for this was the kind of garment the virgin
daughters of the king wore. 19Tamar put ashes on her head and tore
the ornamented[b] robe she was wearing. She put her hand on her
head and went away, weeping aloud as she went.
20Her brother Absalom said to her, "Has that Amnon, your brother,
been with you? Be quiet now, my sister; he is your brother. Don't take
this thing to heart." And Tamar lived in her brother Absalom's house,
a desolate woman.
21When King David heard all this, he was furious. 22Absalom never
said a word to Amnon, either good or bad; he hated Amnon because
he had disgraced his sister Tamar.

Absalom Kills Amnon

23Two years later, when Absalom's sheepshearers were at Baal
Hazor near the border of Ephraim, he invited all the king's sons to
come there. 24Absalom went to the king and said, "Your servant has
had shearers come. Will the king and his officials please join me?"
25"No, my son," the king replied. "All of us should not go; we would
only be a burden to you." Although Absalom urged him, he still refused to go, but gave him his blessing.
26Then Absalom said, "If not, please let my brother Amnon come
with us."
The king asked him, "Why should he go with you?" 27But Absalom
urged him, so he sent with him Amnon and the rest of the king's sons.
28Absalom ordered his men, "Listen! When Amnon is in high spirits
from drinking wine and I say to you, 'Strike Amnon down,' then kill
him. Don't be afraid. Have not I given you this order? Be strong and
brave." 29So Absalom's men did to Amnon what Absalom had ordered. Then all the king's sons got up, mounted their mules and fled.
30While they were on their way, the report came to David: "Absalom
has struck down all the king's sons; not one of them is left." 31The
king stood up, tore his clothes and lay down on the ground; and all
his servants stood by with their clothes torn.

[a] *18* The meaning of the Hebrew for this phrase is uncertain. [b] *19* The meaning of the Hebrew for this word is uncertain.

OPEN What was the biggest conflict you remember having with a sibling when you were younger? Are there still hard feelings?

STUDY The Lord pronounced that King David would experience tragedy within his family because of his sins of adultery and murder. That prophecy began to be fulfilled when David's oldest son Amnon raped David's daughter Tamar. Although the king did nothing about Amnon's offense, David's second oldest son Absalom hated Amnon for what he did and now acts on his wrath. **1.** What do you suppose David was thinking when Absalom insisted Amnon come: He was seeking reconciliation? He just wanted family representation? He was up to no good? **2.** If you were David or Amnon, would you have suspected Absalom's invitation to the sheepshearing party? Why or why not? **3.** Why does David finally let Amnon go? **4.** What false rumor was initially spread? How do you think it got started? **5.** Who do you most identify with in this account:

13:19 Tamar put ashes on her head. This action was a sign of great mourning. Tamar showed intense sorrow over the loss of her purity. Not only had she been raped by her own brother, but her dreams of having a family could never be realized.

13:20 Be quiet now, my sister. Absalom wanted Tamar to keep quiet and avoid public scandal. He was planning to take revenge, but wanted to bide his time.

13:21 he was furious. David was extremely angry over Amnon's rape of Tamar, but he did not punish his son as the law prescribed (Lev. 20:17). His failure to discipline his children caused him much grief later on.

13:22 Absalom. Absalom was waiting until an opportune time to take revenge. Absalom waited two full years, ensuring that Amnon would be caught off guard.

13:23 invited all the king's sons. It was customary in Israel to host an annual sheepshearing festival (1 Sam. 25:2,8).

13:26 let my brother Amnon come. David declined Absalom's invitation to the sheepshearing party, so Absalom requested that he send Amnon in his place. After all, Amnon was heir to the throne. **Why should he go?** David showed suspicion about Absalom's motive for asking him to send Amnon. He was well aware of the feud between the brothers (v. 22). Nevertheless, he ignored his doubts and granted permission for Amnon to attend the festival.

13:28 Strike Amnon down. Absalom arranged his brother's murder when Amnon least expected it—two long years after his sin and in the midst of a party Amnon had been invited to attend. Absalom's strategy is clear; his cunning and hard-hearted tactics would both avenge the rape of his sister and secure his position as successor to the throne.

32 But Jonadab son of Shimeah, David's brother, said, "My lord
should not think that they killed all the princes; only Amnon is dead.
This has been Absalom's expressed intention ever since the day
Amnon raped his sister Tamar. 33 My lord the king should not be
concerned about the report that all the king's sons are dead. Only
Amnon is dead."
34 Meanwhile, Absalom had fled.
Now the man standing watch looked up and saw many people on
the road west of him, coming down the side of the hill. The watchman
went and told the king, "I see men in the direction of Horonaim, on
the side of the hill."[a]
35 Jonadab said to the king, "See, the king's sons are here; it has
happened just as your servant said."
36 As he finished speaking, the king's sons came in, wailing loudly.
The king, too, and all his servants wept very bitterly.
37 Absalom fled and went to Talmai son of Ammihud, the king of
Geshur. But King David mourned for his son every day.
38 After Absalom fled and went to Geshur, he stayed there three
years. 39 And the spirit of the king[b] longed to go to Absalom, for he
was consoled concerning Amnon's death.

Absalom Returns to Jerusalem

14 Joab son of Zeruiah knew that the king's heart longed for
Absalom. 2 So Joab sent someone to Tekoa and had a wise
woman brought from there. He said to her, "Pretend you are in
mourning. Dress in mourning clothes, and don't use any cosmetic
lotions. Act like a woman who has spent many days grieving for the
dead. 3 Then go to the king and speak these words to him." And Joab
put the words in her mouth.
4 When the woman from Tekoa went[c] to the king, she fell with her
face to the ground to pay him honor, and she said, "Help me, O king!"
5 The king asked her, "What is troubling you?"
She said, "I am indeed a widow; my husband is dead. 6 I your
servant had two sons. They got into a fight with each other in the
field, and no one was there to separate them. One struck the other
and killed him. 7 Now the whole clan has risen up against your servant; they say, 'Hand over the one who struck his brother down, so
that we may put him to death for the life of his brother whom he
killed; then we will get rid of the heir as well.' They would put out the
only burning coal I have left, leaving my husband neither name nor
descendant on the face of the earth."

[a]34 Septuagint; Hebrew does not have this sentence. [b]39 Dead Sea Scrolls and some Septuagint manuscripts; Masoretic Text *But* ⌞*the spirit of*⌟ *David the king* [c]4 Many Hebrew manuscripts, Septuagint, Vulgate and Syriac; most Hebrew manuscripts *spoke*

David—wishing my family could just get along? Absalom—knowing how it feels to want revenge? Amnon—feeling guilty and having to watch my back? **6.** If David longed to go to Absalom, why didn't he do it (v. 39)?

APPLY 1. With whom does your spirit long for reconciliation? **2.** What is keeping you from having that reconciliation: Your own stubbornness? The other person's lack of receptivity? The need for a mediator? Other?

OPEN 1. If you could choose a person from your past with whom to have a reunion, whom would you choose: A school teacher? A childhood chum? An "old flame" from high school? A family member you haven't seen for a while? **2.** What would you want to talk to this person about?

STUDY David's son Absalom has killed his other son Amnon in revenge for Amnon having raped their sister Tamar. Absalom fled to another country after this action. In spite of the fact that he missed him greatly, David took no action toward a reunion. In this story, David's general, Joab, takes the initiative to bring the two back together. **1.** What motivates Joab to take this action: Love for David? Anxiety over the disruption this is causing in the kingdom? Concern that this might cause a struggle over who would be David's successor? Other? **2.** What acting role does Joab ask this "wise woman" to assume (vv. 2–3)? How well does she play the part (vv. 4–8)? **3.** How does the woman's story relate to David and

---

13:39 he was consoled. David's grief over Amnon's death eventually subsided to the point where he longed to see Absalom. *Apparently he felt it would be* inappropriate to go to Absalom.

14:2 Joab sent. Joab could see that David missed his exiled son and was also concerned about the political ramifications of David's estrangement from the heir to the throne. So he sent a woman from Tekoa to tell David a story designed to convince him to pardon Absalom for the murder of Amnon.

14:7 that we may put him to death. The Israelite punishment for murder was death, a sentence usually carried out by a relative of the victim.
put out the only burning coal I have left. The death of the woman's remaining son would mean the elimination of her only source of financial support and the end of her dead husband's family name. In Israelite culture, to carry on a family line was of great importance.

[8]The king said to the woman, "Go home, and I will issue an order in
your behalf."
[9]But the woman from Tekoa said to him, "My lord the king, let the
blame rest on me and on my father's family, and let the king and his
throne be without guilt."
[10]The king replied, "If anyone says anything to you, bring him to
me, and he will not bother you again."
[11]She said, "Then let the king invoke the LORD his God to prevent
the avenger of blood from adding to the destruction, so that my son
will not be destroyed."

"As surely as the LORD lives," he said, "not one hair of your son's head will fall to the ground."

[12]Then the woman said, "Let your servant speak a word to my lord
the king."

"Speak," he replied.

[13]The woman said, "Why then have you devised a thing like this
against the people of God? When the king says this, does he not convict himself, for the king has not brought back his banished son?
[14]Like water spilled on the ground, which cannot be recovered, so we
must die. But God does not take away life; instead, he devises ways so that a banished person may not remain estranged from him.
[15]"And now I have come to say this to my lord the king because the
people have made me afraid. Your servant thought, 'I will speak to the
king; perhaps he will do what his servant asks. [16]Perhaps the king will
agree to deliver his servant from the hand of the man who is trying to cut off both me and my son from the inheritance God gave us.'
[17]"And now your servant says, 'May the word of my lord the king
bring me rest, for my lord the king is like an angel of God in discerning good and evil. May the LORD your God be with you.' "
[18]Then the king said to the woman, "Do not keep from me the an-
swer to what I am going to ask you."

"Let my lord the king speak," the woman said.

[19]The king asked, "Isn't the hand of Joab with you in all this?"

The woman answered, "As surely as you live, my lord the king, no one can turn to the right or to the left from anything my lord the king says. Yes, it was your servant Joab who instructed me to do this and
who put all these words into the mouth of your servant. [20]Your
servant Joab did this to change the present situation. My lord has wisdom like that of an angel of God—he knows everything that happens in the land."

[21]The king said to Joab, "Very well, I will do it. Go, bring back the
young man Absalom."
[22]Joab fell with his face to the ground to pay him honor, and he
blessed the king. Joab said, "Today your servant knows that he has

Absalom? **4.** Why hadn't David done anything about Absalom's banishment: He was torn between love and anger? He was too proud to reach out? He believed Absalom deserved to be punished? Other? **5.** What does verse 14 say about the nature of God? How does this compare to the New Testament revelation about God's grace? **6.** Why does David refuse to see Absalom once he does return? **7.** What is the significance of Absalom naming his daughter Tamar (v. 27; 13:1)? **8.** What would you have done had you been David in this situation: Forgiven Absalom more quickly? Punished him more severely for this terrible act? Made him "sweat for it" like David did?

APPLY 1. When in your life have you felt like "a banished person"? **2.** Who at this time helped bring you back "home"?

14:11 As surely as the LORD lives. The woman continued to pressure David until he made a formal oath that her son would not be harmed. David's oath was binding—just the type of promise Joab was hoping for.

14:13 a thing like this ... does he not convict himself? The woman accused David of treating Absalom in the same way her family members were treating her murderous son. He was taking away from Israel the heir to the throne, just as they were trying to take away her son. In pardoning a fictitious murderer, David was required to do the same for his own son.

14:14 God does not take away life; instead, he devises ways. The woman suggested that blood revenge was contrary to God's will. In this way she emphasized God's mercy and ignored his justice.

found favor in your eyes, my lord the king, because the king has
granted his servant's request."
23Then Joab went to Geshur and brought Absalom back to Jerusalem. 24But the king said, "He must go to his own house; he must not
see my face." So Absalom went to his own house and did not see the
face of the king.
25In all Israel there was not a man so highly praised for his handsome appearance as Absalom. From the top of his head to the sole of
his foot there was no blemish in him. 26Whenever he cut the hair of
his head—he used to cut his hair from time to time when it became
too heavy for him—he would weigh it, and its weight was two hundred shekels[a] by the royal standard.
27Three sons and a daughter were born to Absalom. The daughter's
name was Tamar, and she became a beautiful woman.
28Absalom lived two years in Jerusalem without seeing the king's
face. 29Then Absalom sent for Joab in order to send him to the king,
but Joab refused to come to him. So he sent a second time, but he
refused to come. 30Then he said to his servants, "Look, Joab's field is
next to mine, and he has barley there. Go and set it on fire." So
Absalom's servants set the field on fire.
31Then Joab did go to Absalom's house and he said to him, "Why
have your servants set my field on fire?"
32Absalom said to Joab, "Look, I sent word to you and said, 'Come
here so I can send you to the king to ask, "Why have I come from
Geshur? It would be better for me if I were still there!" ' Now then, I
want to see the king's face, and if I am guilty of anything, let him put
me to death."
33So Joab went to the king and told him this. Then the king summoned Absalom, and he came in and bowed down with his face to the
ground before the king. And the king kissed Absalom.

Absalom's Conspiracy

15 In the course of time, Absalom provided himself with a
chariot and horses and with fifty men to run ahead of him.
2He would get up early and stand by the side of the road leading to
the city gate. Whenever anyone came with a complaint to be placed
before the king for a decision, Absalom would call out to him, "What
town are you from?" He would answer, "Your servant is from one of

[a]*26* That is, about 5 pounds (about 2.3 kilograms)

OPEN If someone wanted to bribe you with something in order to manipulate you, what should they offer you: Money? Compliments on your appearance? Tickets to your favorite sports team? An introduction to a supermodel? A great job? Other?

STUDY The tension between Absalom and his father has been growing ever since David did

14:24 He must go ... he must not see my face. David refused to grant Absalom access to the palace. Perhaps he was unsure whether it was right to offer forgiveness and reconciliation, or perhaps he wanted to make sure he would not be accused of too much leniency toward his son. In the end, David's coldness toward Absalom drove a wedge between them and contributed to Absalom's later rebellion.

14:26 cut the hair of his head. Hair was a sign of vigor and honor in those days. The mention of Absalom's hair is particularly notable because it eventually played a role in his death (18:9).

14:32 see the king's face. Absalom demanded to either be granted full pardon and restoration or be punished by death. He expressed anger toward the way his father was treating him but gave no sign of repentance for killing Amnon.

14:33 the king kissed Absalom. The kiss was a symbol of David's forgiveness and Absalom's restoration to the royal family. David did not ask for Absalom to repent, thereby further failing to deal with the situation justly. Absalom remained bitter at David's delay in forgiving him.

15:1–2 chariot and horses ... fifty men to run ahead of him. Absalom gave himself the royal treatment to attract the people's attention. He was the first Israelite leader known to have a chariot. The fifty men served as bodyguards and announced his coming. **stand by the side of the road.** Absalom gained popularity by making himself available to hear the complaints of the masses. He was insinuating that the king was too busy to hear them.

the tribes of Israel." [3]Then Absalom would say to him, "Look, your
claims are valid and proper, but there is no representative of the king
to hear you." [4]And Absalom would add, "If only I were appointed
judge in the land! Then everyone who has a complaint or case could
come to me and I would see that he gets justice."
[5]Also, whenever anyone approached him to bow down before him,
Absalom would reach out his hand, take hold of him and kiss him.
[6]Absalom behaved in this way toward all the Israelites who came to
the king asking for justice, and so he stole the hearts of the men of
Israel.
[7]At the end of four[a] years, Absalom said to the king, "Let me go to
Hebron and fulfill a vow I made to the LORD. [8]While your servant was
living at Geshur in Aram, I made this vow: 'If the LORD takes me back
to Jerusalem, I will worship the LORD in Hebron.[b]' "
[9]The king said to him, "Go in peace." So he went to Hebron.
[10]Then Absalom sent secret messengers throughout the tribes of
Israel to say, "As soon as you hear the sound of the trumpets, then
say, 'Absalom is king in Hebron.' " [11]Two hundred men from Jerusalem had accompanied Absalom. They had been invited as guests
and went quite innocently, knowing nothing about the matter.
[12]While Absalom was offering sacrifices, he also sent for Ahithophel
the Gilonite, David's counselor, to come from Giloh, his hometown.
And so the conspiracy gained strength, and Absalom's following kept
on increasing.

David Flees

[13]A messenger came and told David, "The hearts of the men of Israel are with Absalom."
[14]Then David said to all his officials who were with him in Jerusalem, "Come! We must flee, or none of us will escape from Absalom.
We must leave immediately, or he will move quickly to overtake us
and bring ruin upon us and put the city to the sword."
[15]The king's officials answered him, "Your servants are ready to do
whatever our lord the king chooses."
[16]The king set out, with his entire household following him; but he
left ten concubines to take care of the palace. [17]So the king set out,
with all the people following him, and they halted at a place some
distance away. [18]All his men marched past him, along with all the
Kerethites and Pelethites; and all the six hundred Gittites who had accompanied him from Gath marched before the king.
[19]The king said to Ittai the Gittite, "Why should you come along
with us? Go back and stay with King Absalom. You are a foreigner, an
exile from your homeland. [20]You came only yesterday. And today shall

[a]7 Some Septuagint manuscripts, Syriac and Josephus; Hebrew *forty* [b]8 Some Septuagint manuscripts; Hebrew does not have *in Hebron.*

nothing in response to the rape of Absalom's sister Tamar. Now it builds to a new level as Absalom starts building his own power base by ingratiating himself to the people of Israel. **1.** What do "chariots, horses and 50 men" signal of Absalom's ambitions (v. 1; 1 Sam. 8:11)? **2.** After looking at his actions in verses 2–6, which of the following theme phrases would you choose if you were Absalom's PR director: "I'm listening"? "Friend of the common person"? "I'll fight for you in 'City Hall'!"? "It's time for a new generation of leadership!"? Other? **3.** Considering all you know of Absalom, how would you summarize his character?

APPLY When have you felt yourself to be a victim of someone else's power games? What did you do?

OPEN 1. When you were in school, which of the following were you most likely to flee in terror: School work? Dances? Any kind of religious activity? Parties chaperoned by your parents? The neighborhood of a rival gang? **2.** What is most likely to cause you to "flee in terror" today: A solicitor at the door? Teenagers carrying "boom boxes"? The chair of the nominating committee heading your way? The season for political ads on TV? Other?

STUDY When David hears that his son Absalom is plotting a rebellion and that the hearts of the people are with him, he decides to flee the palace. However, he sends back spies to infiltrate Absalom's forces. **1.** What causes David to so readily flee when he hears of Absalom's growing popularity: Fear of his son's military strength? Lack of willingness to engage one he loved in

15:3 no representative of the king to hear you. Using several tactics, Absalom ingratiated himself to the people. Not only did he listen to their complaints, but supported their complaints without investigating them. Then he told them that the king would not help them, an ancient version of dirty politics.

15:7 go to Hebron. This important city was twenty miles south of Jerusalem. Absalom hoped that he could successfully start a rebellion there.

15:18 Kerethites and Pelethites. These were elite units of David's army, trusted men who had been loyal warriors for years, although they were mercenaries from other countries (8:18).

15:19 Go back and stay. David gave his foreign mercenaries the opportunity to leave him. As foreigners, they had no obligation to fight for him and would be safer with Absalom.

battle? Guilt over past behavior and a feeling that God was going to judge him? Other? **2.** Why do you think so many of the people deserted David for Absalom? **3.** Why did "the whole countryside weep aloud" when David's forces passed through? **4.** Why did David send the ark of God back to Jerusalem: He didn't want to endanger it in battle? He felt that was where it belonged? He wanted to see if God would be with him even if the ark wasn't? Other? **5.** Why did David send back Zadok, Abiathar and their sons to Jerusalem? What was he anticipating that they would do for him? **6.** Why did David weep on his way up the Mount of Olives: Out of fear? Out of sadness over his relationship with Absalom? Out of sadness for the state of the country?

APPLY **1.** How easily do you cry? **2.** When was the last time something hit you so hard that you just couldn't stop crying? Who cried with you? **3.** What helped most to dry your tears: An awareness of God's presence with you? Friends who just stood by your side? An improvement in the situation? The passage of time?

I make you wander about with us, when I do not know where I am going? Go back, and take your countrymen. May kindness and faithfulness be with you."

[21]But Ittai replied to the king, "As surely as the LORD lives, and as my lord the king lives, wherever my lord the king may be, whether it means life or death, there will your servant be."

[22]David said to Ittai, "Go ahead, march on." So Ittai the Gittite marched on with all his men and the families that were with him.

[23]The whole countryside wept aloud as all the people passed by. The king also crossed the Kidron Valley, and all the people moved on toward the desert.

[24]Zadok was there, too, and all the Levites who were with him were carrying the ark of the covenant of God. They set down the ark of God, and Abiathar offered sacrifices[a] until all the people had finished leaving the city.

[25]Then the king said to Zadok, "Take the ark of God back into the city. If I find favor in the LORD's eyes, he will bring me back and let me see it and his dwelling place again. [26]But if he says, 'I am not pleased with you,' then I am ready; let him do to me whatever seems good to him."

[27]The king also said to Zadok the priest, "Aren't you a seer? Go back to the city in peace, with your son Ahimaaz and Jonathan son of Abiathar. You and Abiathar take your two sons with you. [28]I will wait at
the fords in the desert until word comes from you to inform me." [29]So
Zadok and Abiathar took the ark of God back to Jerusalem and stayed there.

[30]But David continued up the Mount of Olives, weeping as he went; his head was covered and he was barefoot. All the people with him covered their heads too and were weeping as they went up. [31]Now
David had been told, "Ahithophel is among the conspirators with Absalom." So David prayed, "O LORD, turn Ahithophel's counsel into foolishness."

[32]When David arrived at the summit, where people used to worship God, Hushai the Arkite was there to meet him, his robe torn and dust on his head. [33]David said to him, "If you go with me, you will be a
burden to me. [34]But if you return to the city and say to Absalom, 'I will be your servant, O king; I was your father's servant in the past, but now I will be your servant,' then you can help me by frustrating Ahithophel's advice. [35]Won't the priests Zadok and Abiathar be there
with you? Tell them anything you hear in the king's palace. [36]Their
two sons, Ahimaaz son of Zadok and Jonathan son of Abiathar, are there with them. Send them to me with anything you hear."
[37]So David's friend Hushai arrived at Jerusalem as Absalom was entering the city.

[a]24 Or *Abiathar went up*

15:21 As surely as the LORD lives and as my lord the king lives. Ittai took a binding oath of loyalty to the God of Israel and promised to remain with David even if it meant death.

15:25 Take the ark of God. David understood that the Ark of the Covenant was the symbol of God's presence with his people and therefore belonged in the capital city regardless of where the king was. **he will bring me back.** David trusted himself to God's care, knowing that if it was God's will, he would return as king.

15:27 Aren't you a seer? Go back to the city. David wanted the priests to remain in Jerusalem, ministering in the tabernacle. He wanted them to be available to receive any messages the Lord might give them and then be able to deliver them to David.

David and Ziba

16 When David had gone a short distance beyond the summit, there was Ziba, the steward of Mephibosheth, waiting to meet him. He had a string of donkeys saddled and loaded with two hundred loaves of bread, a hundred cakes of raisins, a hundred cakes of figs and a skin of wine.

2The king asked Ziba, "Why have you brought these?"

Ziba answered, "The donkeys are for the king's household to ride on, the bread and fruit are for the men to eat, and the wine is to refresh those who become exhausted in the desert."

3The king then asked, "Where is your master's grandson?"

Ziba said to him, "He is staying in Jerusalem, because he thinks, 'Today the house of Israel will give me back my grandfather's kingdom.' "

4Then the king said to Ziba, "All that belonged to Mephibosheth is now yours."

"I humbly bow," Ziba said. "May I find favor in your eyes, my lord the king."

Shimei Curses David

5As King David approached Bahurim, a man from the same clan as
Saul's family came out from there. His name was Shimei son of Gera,
and he cursed as he came out. 6He pelted David and all the king's officials with stones, though all the troops and the special guard were
on David's right and left. 7As he cursed, Shimei said, "Get out, get out,
you man of blood, you scoundrel! 8The LORD has repaid you for all the
blood you shed in the household of Saul, in whose place you have reigned. The LORD has handed the kingdom over to your son Absalom. You have come to ruin because you are a man of blood!"

9Then Abishai son of Zeruiah said to the king, "Why should this dead dog curse my lord the king? Let me go over and cut off his head."

10But the king said, "What do you and I have in common, you sons of Zeruiah? If he is cursing because the LORD said to him, 'Curse David,' who can ask, 'Why do you do this?' "

11David then said to Abishai and all his officials, "My son, who is of
my own flesh, is trying to take my life. How much more, then, this
Benjamite! Leave him alone; let him curse, for the LORD has told him
to. 12It may be that the LORD will see my distress and repay me with
good for the cursing I am receiving today."

13So David and his men continued along the road while Shimei was
going along the hillside opposite him, cursing as he went and throwing stones at him and showering him with dirt. 14The king and all the

OPEN **1.** As you look ahead to your "journey" of the coming week, what "provisions" could you most use: An extra measure of humor? A dozen or so of hugs? A reservoir of peace? A full storage container of courage? **2.** What experience do you fear might drain your reserves?

STUDY Every leader has their supporters and their detractors. In this section David meets one of each as he prepares to face Absalom. **1.** What is Ziba's motive in coming to David bearing such gifts: An act of gratitude for past favors (9:1–13)? Investing in one he saw as a winner? A manipulation for special favors? **2.** Compare verse 3 with 19:24–30. Who would you trust? **3.** Is Shimei right in calling David "a man of blood"? How would you defend him against such a charge if you were his defense attorney? What evidence would you point to if you were the prosecutor? **4.** Why does David allow the defiant behavior of Shimei: He believes in free speech? He is afraid Shimei might be right? He sees Shimei as the voice of God? He's afraid that shedding Shimei's blood would just prove him right? **5.** What does this story say about David's mental state at this point?

APPLY **1.** How do you feel about the balance of affirmation and criticism that you are receiving at this point in your life? **2.** Which of the following best states the attitude you are seeking in relation to the opinions of others: "Sticks and stones may break my bones ..."? "What really matters is what I think about myself"? "We must obey God rather than people" (Acts 5:29)? "You can't please all the people all the time"? Other?

16:3 master's grandson. Mephibosheth, Jonathan's son, was crippled. David treated him kindly in honor of his friendship with Jonathan (9:10). **Today the house of Israel will give me back my grandfather's kingdom.** Ziba claimed that Mephibosheth had turned against the king. According to Ziba, Mephibosheth remained in Jerusalem hoping to regain his grandfather Saul's throne.

16:4 All that belonged to Mephibosheth. David believed Ziba's story, assuming the worst of Mephibosheth. Later he ran into Mephibosheth (19:24–30), who claimed that Ziba had been lying to David.

16:8 The LORD has repaid you. Shimei blamed David for the downfall of Saul's family. His accusations were untrue because David did not even strike Saul. In fact, David had made every effort to be kind to his surviving family. **In whose place you have reigned.** Shimei's real complaint was that David sat on the throne of Saul.

16:10 because the LORD said to him. David declined Abishai's offer to decapitate Shimei. He thought it possible that the insults were a message from God—perhaps his reign really was over.

people with him arrived at their destination exhausted. And there he
refreshed himself.

The Advice of Hushai and Ahithophel

15Meanwhile, Absalom and all the men of Israel came to Jerusalem,
and Ahithophel was with him. 16Then Hushai the Arkite, David's
friend, went to Absalom and said to him, "Long live the king! Long
live the king!"

17Absalom asked Hushai, "Is this the love you show your friend?
Why didn't you go with your friend?"

18Hushai said to Absalom, "No, the one chosen by the LORD, by
these people, and by all the men of Israel—his I will be, and I will
remain with him. 19Furthermore, whom should I serve? Should I not
serve the son? Just as I served your father, so I will serve you."

20Absalom said to Ahithophel, "Give us your advice. What should
we do?"

21Ahithophel answered, "Lie with your father's concubines whom
he left to take care of the palace. Then all Israel will hear that you
have made yourself a stench in your father's nostrils, and the hands
of everyone with you will be strengthened." 22So they pitched a tent
for Absalom on the roof, and he lay with his father's concubines in
the sight of all Israel.

23Now in those days the advice Ahithophel gave was like that of one
who inquires of God. That was how both David and Absalom regarded all of Ahithophel's advice.

17 Ahithophel said to Absalom, "I would[a] choose twelve thousand men and set out tonight in pursuit of David. 2I would[b]
attack him while he is weary and weak. I would[b] strike him with terror, and then all the people with him will flee. I would[b] strike down
only the king 3and bring all the people back to you. The death of the
man you seek will mean the return of all; all the people will be unharmed." 4This plan seemed good to Absalom and to all the elders of
Israel.

5But Absalom said, "Summon also Hushai the Arkite, so we can
hear what he has to say." 6When Hushai came to him, Absalom said,
"Ahithophel has given this advice. Should we do what he says? If not,
give us your opinion."

7Hushai replied to Absalom, "The advice Ahithophel has given is
not good this time. 8You know your father and his men; they are fighters, and as fierce as a wild bear robbed of her cubs. Besides, your

[a]1 Or *Let me* [b]2 Or *will*

OPEN 1. When you need advice, who are you more likely to turn to: Your parents? Your spouse? A mentor? A friend? An advice columnist like Ann Landers? **2.** When you get conflicting advice what are you most likely to do: Go with your gut? Go with the majority? Stew, fret and be indecisive? Go with your most experienced advisor? Other?

STUDY David's son Absalom has mounted a powerful revolt against him, and has secured the loyalty of David's trusted advisor Ahithophel. However, in this story David's friend Hushai, who has gone over to Absalom's side specifically to frustrate Ahithophel's advice, does just that. **1.** What does "lying with the king's concubines ... in the sight of all Israel" symbolize (12:8–12)? **2.** What causes Absalom to choose the advice of Hushai over that of Ahithophel: God has clouded his mind? Absalom figured Hushai knew David better? He wasn't psychologically ready to attack, as Ahithophel advised? **3.** Why might it have been better for Absalom to have followed Ahithophel's advice (17:7–13)? **4.** What word does Hushai send to David (17:15–16,21)? Why (17:16)? **5.** Why does Ahithophel commit suicide: His pride was wounded? He had lost his place of power? He figured David would win and his "goose was cooked"? **6.** What kind of support does David seem to have among the populace (17:17,27–29)?

APPLY 1. When have you followed the wrong advice, to your own detriment or the detriment of others? **2.** When you have taken the wrong path, are you most likely to: Languish in despair? "Throw good money after bad" trying to make it right? Just figure it as one more course

---

16:21 Lie with your father's concubines whom he left. This act irrevocably finalized the division between Absalom and David. It signified that Absalom was claiming royal power and made it impossible for father and son to reconcile. This act also fulfilled Nathan's prophecy (12:11–12).

16:22 pitched a tent. This was probably a bridal tent. Its location on the roof ensured that word would be spread so that all of Israel would be aware of Absalom's claim to power.

17:1–3 set out tonight in pursuit of David. Ahithophel painted a picture of an easy victory. He underestimated the loyalty of David's soldiers, assuming that with David out of the picture, his armies would scatter. His advice sounded so good—get rid of David quickly without weakening the nation. And in fact, they probably would have been successful in killing David if they had caught him off guard, but his soldiers probably would not have given up as easily as Ahithophel made it sound.

17:7–13 The advice Ahithophel has given is not good this time. Hushai, who was secretly loyal to David, cleverly convinced Absalom to disregard Ahithophel's advice. He told Absalom to amass a huge army before attacking, hoping that buying David some time would give him a chance against Absalom.

father is an experienced fighter; he will not spend the night with the
troops. [9]Even now, he is hidden in a cave or some other place. If he
should attack your troops first,[a] whoever hears about it will say,
'There has been a slaughter among the troops who follow Absalom.'
[10]Then even the bravest soldier, whose heart is like the heart of a lion,
will melt with fear, for all Israel knows that your father is a fighter and
that those with him are brave.

[11]"So I advise you: Let all Israel, from Dan to Beersheba—as
numerous as the sand on the seashore—be gathered to you, with you
yourself leading them into battle. [12]Then we will attack him wherever
he may be found, and we will fall on him as dew settles on the
ground. Neither he nor any of his men will be left alive. [13]If he with-
draws into a city, then all Israel will bring ropes to that city, and we
will drag it down to the valley until not even a piece of it can be
found."

[14]Absalom and all the men of Israel said, "The advice of Hushai the
Arkite is better than that of Ahithophel." For the LORD had determined
to frustrate the good advice of Ahithophel in order to bring disaster
on Absalom.

[15]Hushai told Zadok and Abiathar, the priests, "Ahithophel has
advised Absalom and the elders of Israel to do such and such, but I
have advised them to do so and so. [16]Now send a message immediately and tell David, 'Do not spend the night at the fords in the desert;
cross over without fail, or the king and all the people with him will be
swallowed up.' "

[17]Jonathan and Ahimaaz were staying at En Rogel. A servant girl
was to go and inform them, and they were to go and tell King David,
for they could not risk being seen entering the city. [18]But a young
man saw them and told Absalom. So the two of them left quickly and
went to the house of a man in Bahurim. He had a well in his courtyard, and they climbed down into it. [19]His wife took a covering and
spread it out over the opening of the well and scattered grain over it.
No one knew anything about it.

[20]When Absalom's men came to the woman at the house, they
asked, "Where are Ahimaaz and Jonathan?"

The woman answered them, "They crossed over the brook."[b] The
men searched but found no one, so they returned to Jerusalem.

[21]After the men had gone, the two climbed out of the well and went
to inform King David. They said to him, "Set out and cross the river at
once; Ahithophel has advised such and such against you." [22]So David
and all the people with him set out and crossed the Jordan. By daybreak, no one was left who had not crossed the Jordan.

[23]When Ahithophel saw that his advice had not been followed, he
saddled his donkey and set out for his house in his hometown. He put

[a]9 Or *When some of the men fall at the first attack* [b]20 Or *"They passed by the sheep pen toward the water."*

in the "school of hard knocks"? Admit your mistake and make a U-turn? **3.** What does it mean to you to believe in a God who allows U-turns?

17:14 frustrate the good advice of Ahithophel. As always, the results were completely in God's hands.

17:16 cross over without fail. Hushai warned David to cross the Jordan in case Absalom changed his mind and followed Ahithophel's advice to set out after him immediately.

17:17 A servant girl. In order to avoid suspicion, a message was sent to Jonathan and Ahimaaz by means of a servant girl.

17:18 a young man saw them. Unfortunately, the two men were discovered and had to flee to the house of a man in Bahurim. There, a courageous woman saved their lives by hiding the two men in a well.

his house in order and then hanged himself. So he died and was buried in his father's tomb.

24David went to Mahanaim, and Absalom crossed the Jordan with all the men of Israel. 25Absalom had appointed Amasa over the army in place of Joab. Amasa was the son of a man named Jether,[a] an Israelite[b] who had married Abigail,[c] the daughter of Nahash and sister of Zeruiah the mother of Joab. 26The Israelites and Absalom camped in the land of Gilead.

27When David came to Mahanaim, Shobi son of Nahash from Rabbah of the Ammonites, and Makir son of Ammiel from Lo Debar, and Barzillai the Gileadite from Rogelim 28brought bedding and bowls and articles of pottery. They also brought wheat and barley, flour and roasted grain, beans and lentils,[d] 29honey and curds, sheep, and cheese from cows' milk for David and his people to eat. For they said, "The people have become hungry and tired and thirsty in the desert."

Absalom's Death

18 David mustered the men who were with him and appointed over them commanders of thousands and commanders of hundreds. 2David sent the troops out—a third under the command of Joab, a third under Joab's brother Abishai son of Zeruiah, and a third under Ittai the Gittite. The king told the troops, "I myself will surely march out with you."

3But the men said, "You must not go out; if we are forced to flee, they won't care about us. Even if half of us die, they won't care; but you are worth ten thousand of us.[e] It would be better now for you to give us support from the city."

4The king answered, "I will do whatever seems best to you."

So the king stood beside the gate while all the men marched out in units of hundreds and of thousands. 5The king commanded Joab, Abishai and Ittai, "Be gentle with the young man Absalom for my sake." And all the troops heard the king giving orders concerning Absalom to each of the commanders.

6The army marched into the field to fight Israel, and the battle took place in the forest of Ephraim. 7There the army of Israel was defeated by David's men, and the casualties that day were great—twenty thousand men. 8The battle spread out over the whole countryside, and the forest claimed more lives that day than the sword.

9Now Absalom happened to meet David's men. He was riding his mule, and as the mule went under the thick branches of a large oak,

[a]25 Hebrew *Ithra,* a variant of *Jether* [b]25 Hebrew and some Septuagint manuscripts; other Septuagint manuscripts (see also 1 Chron. 2:17) *Ishmaelite* or *Jezreelite* [c]25 Hebrew *Abigal,* a variant of *Abigail* [d]28 Most Septuagint manuscripts and Syriac; Hebrew *lentils, and roasted grain* [e]3 Two Hebrew manuscripts, some Septuagint manuscripts and Vulgate; most Hebrew manuscripts *care; for now there are ten thousand like us*

OPEN 1. What was your biggest confrontation you remember in high school? Was it in sports, music, debate, drama, school performance, vying for a person of the opposite sex or just in a power struggle? **2.** Who won this confrontation and how did you feel about it?

STUDY The hostility between David and his son Absalom has been brewing for some time and finally results in a showdown. David's forces win, but we will see that he feels like anything but a winner. **1.** What is the rationale for David staying behind and not being part of the battle? What might have been some other unspoken motivations for not having David go along with them? **2.** What command does David give to his generals concerning Absalom? Is David's command too realistic, given the nature of war and the hostility Absalom had shown to him? **3.** In what ways might a forest have claimed more lives than the swords of battle (v. 8)? Which would you credit Absalom's death to: Forest or sword? **4.** How does the man who spotted Absalom respond to Joab's rebuke (vv. 11–13)? Would you have reacted any differently? How so? **5.** Why does Joab disregard David's command concerning Absalom? **6.**

18:3 you are worth ten thousand of us. David was eager to accompany his men in battle, but they convinced him to stay behind. They wanted to ensure his safety, and they would be safer without him as well.

18:5 Be gentle with the young man Absalom. Before they left, David commanded his officers not to harm Absalom. He still loved his son, despite his evil deeds.

18:8 the forest claimed more lives that day than the sword. The rough terrain of the forest caused more deaths than the fighting. Some deaths may have been caused by men getting lost in the dense woods, or by wild animals.

18:9 Absalom's head. Ironically, Absalom's beautiful hair (14:25) became his undoing. It was caught in the branches of a tree as he rode underneath it, leaving him helpless and vulnerable.

Absalom's head got caught in the tree. He was left hanging in midair, while the mule he was riding kept on going.
[10]When one of the men saw this, he told Joab, "I just saw Absalom hanging in an oak tree."
[11]Joab said to the man who had told him this, "What! You saw him? Why didn't you strike him to the ground right there? Then I would have had to give you ten shekels[a] of silver and a warrior's belt."
[12]But the man replied, "Even if a thousand shekels[b] were weighed out into my hands, I would not lift my hand against the king's son. In our hearing the king commanded you and Abishai and Ittai, 'Protect the young man Absalom for my sake.[c]'
[13]And if I had put my life in jeopardy[d]—and nothing is hidden from the king—you would have kept your distance from me."
[14]Joab said, "I'm not going to wait like this for you." So he took three javelins in his hand and plunged them into Absalom's heart while Absalom was still alive in the oak tree.
[15]And ten of Joab's armor-bearers surrounded Absalom, struck him and killed him.
[16]Then Joab sounded the trumpet, and the troops stopped pursuing Israel, for Joab halted them.
[17]They took Absalom, threw him into a big pit in the forest and piled up a large heap of rocks over him. Meanwhile, all the Israelites fled to their homes.
[18]During his lifetime Absalom had taken a pillar and erected it in the King's Valley as a monument to himself, for he thought, "I have no son to carry on the memory of my name." He named the pillar after himself, and it is called Absalom's Monument to this day.

David Mourns

[19]Now Ahimaaz son of Zadok said, "Let me run and take the news to the king that the LORD has delivered him from the hand of his enemies."
[20]"You are not the one to take the news today," Joab told him. "You may take the news another time, but you must not do so today, because the king's son is dead."
[21]Then Joab said to a Cushite, "Go, tell the king what you have seen." The Cushite bowed down before Joab and ran off.
[22]Ahimaaz son of Zadok again said to Joab, "Come what may, please let me run behind the Cushite."
But Joab replied, "My son, why do you want to go? You don't have any news that will bring you a reward."
[23]He said, "Come what may, I want to run."
So Joab said, "Run!" Then Ahimaaz ran by way of the plain[e] and outran the Cushite.

[a]*11* That is, about 4 ounces (about 115 grams) [b]*12* That is, about 25 pounds (about 11 kilograms) [c]*12* A few Hebrew manuscripts, Septuagint, Vulgate and Syriac; most Hebrew manuscripts may be translated *Absalom, whoever you may be.* [d]*13* Or *Otherwise, if I had acted treacherously toward him* [e]*23* That is, the plain of the Jordan

What do you think might have happened had Absalom been taken captive instead of killed? Could there have been any hope at all for a happier ending? **7.** Were you given the task of saying something at Absalom's funeral that was both honest and compassionate, what might you have said?

APPLY 1. When have you been in a battle where it felt like everyone in it was a loser: In a divorce? In a family inheritance squabble? In a power struggle with a rebellious child? **2.** If you could go back and do things differently in that battle, what would you do? **3.** Are the wounds of that battle still sore? What hope do you hold for healing?

OPEN 1. In which of the following good news/bad news situations have you been torn between: Your child announced he or she was getting married? You found you were going to be a grandparent? You got a promotion that meant moving? Close relatives announced they were coming for an extended visit? **2.** When news is both good and bad, are you most likely to: Emphasize the positive? Dwell on the negative? Vacillate between positive and negative feelings?

STUDY Absalom, who led a rebellion against his father, David, has been killed in battle with David's forces. Now the task becomes telling David about this event. **1.** Why does Ahimaaz persist in his request (vv. 19–23)? **2.** Why does Joab at first choose a different messenger, the Cushite: Joab thought it best to send

18:11 Why didn't you strike him to the ground ... ? Joab wanted Absalom dead, despite David's strict instructions that no one harm him. To this end, Joab had even offered a reward (half an ounce of silver and a warrior's belt) for anyone who killed Absalom.

18:15 surrounded Absalom, struck him and killed him. The soldiers' brutality against Absalom was excessive. With Joab's three javelins in his heart, he was dead anyway. But anger propelled their violence.

18:17 threw him into a big pit in the forest. Joab refused Absalom the honor of a proper burial in Jerusalem. **large heap of rocks.** The pile of stones may have been a memorial ridiculing the memorial Absalom made for himself (v. 18). Or it may have been symbolic of a stoning, the legal punishment for rebellious sons.

someone less eager to tell the message? David had a habit of killing messengers and the foreigner was expendable? Ahimaaz was a good guy and Joab didn't want to send a good guy with bad news (v. 27)? **3.** Why does Ahimaaz hedge when it comes to telling David about Absalom's death (v. 29)? **4.** Why does David mourn so heavily for the son who sought to overthrow him? **5.** Do you think David would really have preferred to die instead of Absalom? **6.** Is Joab justified in his rebuke of David? Why or why not? **7.** What would you have done and said had you been in Joab's place when David was mourning?

APPLY 1. When have you mourned for someone or something with the intensity David shows in this story? **2.** Who or what helped you most in dealing with your grief and facing the world again?

24While David was sitting between the inner and outer gates, the watchman went up to the roof of the gateway by the wall. As he looked out, he saw a man running alone. 25The watchman called out to the king and reported it.

The king said, "If he is alone, he must have good news." And the man came closer and closer.

26Then the watchman saw another man running, and he called down to the gatekeeper, "Look, another man running alone!"

The king said, "He must be bringing good news, too."

27The watchman said, "It seems to me that the first one runs like Ahimaaz son of Zadok."

"He's a good man," the king said. "He comes with good news."

28Then Ahimaaz called out to the king, "All is well!" He bowed down before the king with his face to the ground and said, "Praise be to the LORD your God! He has delivered up the men who lifted their hands against my lord the king."

29The king asked, "Is the young man Absalom safe?"

Ahimaaz answered, "I saw great confusion just as Joab was about to send the king's servant and me, your servant, but I don't know what it was."

30The king said, "Stand aside and wait here." So he stepped aside and stood there.

31Then the Cushite arrived and said, "My lord the king, hear the good news! The LORD has delivered you today from all who rose up against you."

32The king asked the Cushite, "Is the young man Absalom safe?"

The Cushite replied, "May the enemies of my lord the king and all who rise up to harm you be like that young man."

33The king was shaken. He went up to the room over the gateway and wept. As he went, he said: "O my son Absalom! My son, my son Absalom! If only I had died instead of you—O Absalom, my son, my son!"

19 Joab was told, "The king is weeping and mourning for Absalom." 2And for the whole army the victory that day was turned into mourning, because on that day the troops heard it said, "The king is grieving for his son." 3The men stole into the city that day as men steal in who are ashamed when they flee from battle. 4The king covered his face and cried aloud, "O my son Absalom! O Absalom, my son, my son!"

5Then Joab went into the house to the king and said, "Today you have humiliated all your men, who have just saved your life and the lives of your sons and daughters and the lives of your wives and concubines. 6You love those who hate you and hate those who love you. You have made it clear today that the commanders and their men mean nothing to you. I see that you would be pleased if Absalom

18:27 a good man … with good news. Messengers were chosen based on what type of news was being delivered. *David didn't* think Joab would send Ahimaaz with bad news.

18:29 great confusion. Ahimaaz was aware that Absalom was dead, but he evaded David's question. Perhaps he feared David's response, or he just didn't want to be the bearer of bad news.

18:33 my son Absalom! At the news of his son's death, David was overcome with grief. He loved Absalom so deeply—despite all his son had done to hurt him—that he wished he had died in Absalom's place.

19:5 Joab went into the house to the king. Apparently David was unaware of Joab's role in Absalom's death at this time. Otherwise Joab would not have dared to enter David's presence in the middle of his grief.

were alive today and all of us were dead. 7Now go out and encourage
your men. I swear by the LORD that if you don't go out, not a man will
be left with you by nightfall. This will be worse for you than all the
calamities that have come upon you from your youth till now."
8So the king got up and took his seat in the gateway. When the
men were told, "The king is sitting in the gateway," they all came
before him.

David Returns to Jerusalem

Meanwhile, the Israelites had fled to their homes. 9Throughout the
tribes of Israel, the people were all arguing with each other, saying,
"The king delivered us from the hand of our enemies; he is the one
who rescued us from the hand of the Philistines. But now he has fled
the country because of Absalom; 10and Absalom, whom we anointed
to rule over us, has died in battle. So why do you say nothing about
bringing the king back?"
11King David sent this message to Zadok and Abiathar, the priests:
"Ask the elders of Judah, 'Why should you be the last to bring the king
back to his palace, since what is being said throughout Israel has
reached the king at his quarters? 12You are my brothers, my own flesh
and blood. So why should you be the last to bring back the king?'
13And say to Amasa, 'Are you not my own flesh and blood? May God
deal with me, be it ever so severely, if from now on you are not the
commander of my army in place of Joab.' "
14He won over the hearts of all the men of Judah as though they
were one man. They sent word to the king, "Return, you and all your
men." 15Then the king returned and went as far as the Jordan.
Now the men of Judah had come to Gilgal to go out and meet the
king and bring him across the Jordan. 16Shimei son of Gera, the Benjamite from Bahurim, hurried down with the men of Judah to meet
King David. 17With him were a thousand Benjamites, along with Ziba,
the steward of Saul's household, and his fifteen sons and twenty servants. They rushed to the Jordan, where the king was. 18They crossed
at the ford to take the king's household over and to do whatever he
wished.
When Shimei son of Gera crossed the Jordan, he fell prostrate
before the king 19and said to him, "May my lord not hold me guilty.
Do not remember how your servant did wrong on the day my lord the
king left Jerusalem. May the king put it out of his mind. 20For I your
servant know that I have sinned, but today I have come here as the
first of the whole house of Joseph to come down and meet my lord
the king."
21Then Abishai son of Zeruiah said, "Shouldn't Shimei be put to
death for this? He cursed the LORD's anointed."

OPEN 1. Of all the places you have been in your life, where would you most want to return? **2.** Who in this place would you most want to greet and what would you want to talk to him or her about?

STUDY David had been forced to flee Jerusalem because of the rebellion of his son, Absalom. But with Absalom dead, the country reunites under David's leadership, and David returns to Jerusalem. **1.** What would you say is the closest modern parallel to this story: When people line up for jobs after a presidential election? When the press that has been criticizing the coach all year finally becomes his biggest supporters after the big victory? When peers who have been critical of you suddenly "kiss up" to you after your promotion? Other? **2.** What overtures does David make to reunite the country? **3.** Why does David decide to forgive the insolent Shimei (16:5–14)? Is his willingness because of theological, personal or political reasons? **4.** What is David gaining by being so forgiving with those who had opposed him? What is he risking? **5.** Why does David decide to have Mephibosheth and Ziba divide the fields he had given originally to Mephibosheth (9:7) and later transferred to Ziba (16:4): He couldn't decide whom to trust? He wanted everyone to be happy? **6.** Why does David seek to reward Barzillai? Why is that offer refused? **7.** Why are the men of Israel so upset (v. 41)? What's at stake here besides hurt pride?

19:9 the people were all arguing with each other. The Israelites, many of whom had supported Absalom, now must decide who was king. On the one hand, David was an effective leader who accomplished great things for them in the past. On the other hand, he fled from the land—not a very kingly thing to do.

19:11 Why should you be the last to bring the king back to his palace ... ? In order to ensure public support for his return to the throne, David appealed to his faithful priests, Zadok and Abiathar, to take the initiative in inviting him back to the throne. His appeal was successful; he regained the throne with the support of the nation.

19:13 Amasa. As a further means of gaining support, particularly from Judah, David appointed Amasa commander of his army in place of Joab. Amasa had been commander of Absalom's army, so this appointment gained for David the allegiance of the rebel army. Apparently Joab's disagreements with David's policies and his killing of Absalom had made David distrust him.

19:17 Benjamites. This large contingent probably feared that they would be associated with Shimei's cursing. They were a sign to David that Saul's family had at last accepted him as king.

APPLY 1. What reward would you give the people who have stood by you in your hour of need? What would you want the reward to be? **2.** What "nay-sayer" from your past are you most challenged to forgive? What might you do to express that forgiveness?

22 David replied, "What do you and I have in common, you sons of
Zeruiah? This day you have become my adversaries! Should anyone
be put to death in Israel today? Do I not know that today I am king
over Israel?" 23 So the king said to Shimei, "You shall not die." And the
king promised him on oath.

24 Mephibosheth, Saul's grandson, also went down to meet the
king. He had not taken care of his feet or trimmed his mustache or
washed his clothes from the day the king left until the day he returned safely. 25 When he came from Jerusalem to meet the king, the
king asked him, "Why didn't you go with me, Mephibosheth?"

26 He said, "My lord the king, since I your servant am lame, I said, 'I
will have my donkey saddled and will ride on it, so I can go with the
king.' But Ziba my servant betrayed me. 27 And he has slandered your
servant to my lord the king. My lord the king is like an angel of God;
so do whatever pleases you. 28 All my grandfather's descendants
deserved nothing but death from my lord the king, but you gave your
servant a place among those who eat at your table. So what right do
I have to make any more appeals to the king?"

29 The king said to him, "Why say more? I order you and Ziba to
divide the fields."

30 Mephibosheth said to the king, "Let him take everything, now
that my lord the king has arrived home safely."

31 Barzillai the Gileadite also came down from Rogelim to cross the
Jordan with the king and to send him on his way from there. 32 Now
Barzillai was a very old man, eighty years of age. He had provided for
the king during his stay in Mahanaim, for he was a very wealthy man.
33 The king said to Barzillai, "Cross over with me and stay with me in
Jerusalem, and I will provide for you."

34 But Barzillai answered the king, "How many more years will I
live, that I should go up to Jerusalem with the king? 35 I am now eighty
years old. Can I tell the difference between what is good and what is
not? Can your servant taste what he eats and drinks? Can I still hear
the voices of men and women singers? Why should your servant be
an added burden to my lord the king? 36 Your servant will cross over
the Jordan with the king for a short distance, but why should the king
reward me in this way? 37 Let your servant return, that I may die in my
own town near the tomb of my father and mother. But here is your
servant Kimham. Let him cross over with my lord the king. Do for him
whatever pleases you."

38 The king said, "Kimham shall cross over with me, and I will do for
him whatever pleases you. And anything you desire from me I will do
for you."

39 So all the people crossed the Jordan, and then the king crossed

---

19:23 Shimei, you shall not die. David kept the pledge he made that day. However, Shimei eventually paid for his sin at the hand of Solomon, at David's request (1 Kin. 2:8,9,36–46).

19:25 Why didn't you go with me ... ? Remembering *Ziba's accusations* against Mephibosheth (16:3), David questioned Mephibosheth's allegiance. Mephibosheth's haggard appearance was intended to be a sign of mourning at David's absence.

19:27 do whatever pleases you. Mephibosheth proclaimed his innocence and politely asked David to reconsider giving all his property to Ziba.

19:29 Ziba to divide the fields. Unsure of who was telling the truth, David told them to divide the land. In this way, he did not have to determine whose story was true. Mephibosheth submitted to David's initial judgment in the matter.

19:35 I am now eighty years old. David urged Barzillai, who had given David supplies when he crossed into the Transjordan, to come live in Jerusalem. Barzillai refused, saying he was too old to enjoy all that palace life would offer.

19:37 your servant Kimham. Since Barzillai refused the king's offer, he chose to send Kimham, probably a son, in his place.

over. The king kissed Barzillai and gave him his blessing, and Barzillai returned to his home.
[40]When the king crossed over to Gilgal, Kimham crossed with him.
All the troops of Judah and half the troops of Israel had taken the king over.
[41]Soon all the men of Israel were coming to the king and saying to
him, "Why did our brothers, the men of Judah, steal the king away and bring him and his household across the Jordan, together with all his men?"
[42]All the men of Judah answered the men of Israel, "We did this
because the king is closely related to us. Why are you angry about it? Have we eaten any of the king's provisions? Have we taken anything for ourselves?"
[43]Then the men of Israel answered the men of Judah, "We have ten
shares in the king; and besides, we have a greater claim on David than you have. So why do you treat us with contempt? Were we not the first to speak of bringing back our king?"

But the men of Judah responded even more harshly than the men of Israel.

Sheba Rebels Against David

20 Now a troublemaker named Sheba son of Bicri, a Benjamite,
happened to be there. He sounded the trumpet and shouted,

"We have no share in David,
no part in Jesse's son!
Every man to his tent, O Israel!"

[2]So all the men of Israel deserted David to follow Sheba son of
Bicri. But the men of Judah stayed by their king all the way from the Jordan to Jerusalem.
[3]When David returned to his palace in Jerusalem, he took the ten
concubines he had left to take care of the palace and put them in a house under guard. He provided for them, but did not lie with them. They were kept in confinement till the day of their death, living as widows.
[4]Then the king said to Amasa, "Summon the men of Judah to come
to me within three days, and be here yourself." [5]But when Amasa
went to summon Judah, he took longer than the time the king had set for him.
[6]David said to Abishai, "Now Sheba son of Bicri will do us more
harm than Absalom did. Take your master's men and pursue him, or

OPEN 1. Who was the biggest troublemaker in your neighborhood when you were a child? What kind of things did he or she do to cause disruption? **2.** In your childhood home, what could someone have done to cause trouble: Mess up the TV reception? Monopolize the bathroom in the morning? Try to change the schedule of who did what chores? Question a decision of a parent? Play the stereo too loud? Other?

STUDY Absalom was not the last person to rebel against David's authority. In this story, Sheba led a rebellion that sought to divide the nation once again. **1.** In what ways do events of the previous chapter (19:41–43) fuel Sheba's revolt? **2.** Why does David treat his concubines as he does (16:21–22)? Was he being unfair in blaming them? **3.** Why does Joab kill Amasa (17:25; 19:13): Jealousy and ambition? Amasa's slowness of action when the kingdom

---

19:41 steal the king away. The Israelites were afraid when more Judahites accompanied David on his return to Jerusalem. They appeared less loyal, maybe even reluctant, to restore David to the throne.

19:43 a greater claim on David. Since it formed ten of the 12 tribes, Israel claimed a greater share in David's kingship. The argument showed how fickle these troops were. Only a short time before, they had supported Absalom, and now they were arguing over who played a more important role in David's kingdom.

20:1 Benjamite. Judah's claim of close relation to the king (19:42) stirred the Benjamites to jealousy. The royal house had once been theirs, under Saul, but was forfeited by his actions. The quarrels of 19:41–43 opened the door for a troublemaker like Sheba. **We have no share in David.** Sheba played on Israel's fear of being treated with contempt (19:43).

20:3 took the ten concubines. The concubines reminded everyone of the tragic consequences of Absalom's sin (15:16; 16:22). Afterwards, David took responsibility to protect and provide for them.

20:6 Abishai. David bypassed Joab again (v. 4) and gave Abishai charge over "Joab's men" (v. 7). David knew the merciless manner of Joab (3:26–30) and of his disobedience in the killing of Absalom (18:12–14).

was at stake? Suspicion of treason? Other? **4.** What impact do the blood and guts of Amasa have on Joab's men? What impact do such lurid details have on you? **5.** How does the woman in Abel Beth Maacah show her wisdom? **6.** What would you rate this story if it were a modern movie: PG? PG-13? R? **7.** How do you feel about the fact that the Bible has such graphic violence?

APPLY 1. What force is presently assaulting the walls of your home and keeping it from being peaceful (choose the one that is disturbing you the most): The crime around you? Societal pressures on your children's values? Financial pressure? Hate and bigotry? **2.** What strategy are you using to halt or ease this assault: Hiding behind walls, hoping it will go away? Making alliances with others under assault? Looking for a palatable "deal" with those assaulting you? Looking to God for protection? Other?

he will find fortified cities and escape from us." 7So Joab's men and
the Kerethites and Pelethites and all the mighty warriors went out
under the command of Abishai. They marched out from Jerusalem to
pursue Sheba son of Bicri.
8While they were at the great rock in Gibeon, Amasa came to meet
them. Joab was wearing his military tunic, and strapped over it at his
waist was a belt with a dagger in its sheath. As he stepped forward, it
dropped out of its sheath.
9Joab said to Amasa, "How are you, my brother?" Then Joab took
Amasa by the beard with his right hand to kiss him. 10Amasa was not
on his guard against the dagger in Joab's hand, and Joab plunged it
into his belly, and his intestines spilled out on the ground. Without
being stabbed again, Amasa died. Then Joab and his brother Abishai
pursued Sheba son of Bicri.
11One of Joab's men stood beside Amasa and said, "Whoever favors
Joab, and whoever is for David, let him follow Joab!" 12Amasa lay wallowing in his blood in the middle of the road, and the man saw that
all the troops came to a halt there. When he realized that everyone
who came up to Amasa stopped, he dragged him from the road into a
field and threw a garment over him. 13After Amasa had been removed
from the road, all the men went on with Joab to pursue Sheba son of
Bicri.
14Sheba passed through all the tribes of Israel to Abel Beth
Maacah[a] and through the entire region of the Berites, who gathered
together and followed him. 15All the troops with Joab came and besieged Sheba in Abel Beth Maacah. They built a siege ramp up to the
city, and it stood against the outer fortifications. While they were battering the wall to bring it down, 16a wise woman called from the city,
"Listen! Listen! Tell Joab to come here so I can speak to him." 17He
went toward her, and she asked, "Are you Joab?"
"I am," he answered.
She said, "Listen to what your servant has to say."
"I'm listening," he said.
18She continued, "Long ago they used to say, 'Get your answer at
Abel,' and that settled it. 19We are the peaceful and faithful in Israel.
You are trying to destroy a city that is a mother in Israel. Why do you
want to swallow up the LORD's inheritance?"
20"Far be it from me!" Joab replied, "Far be it from me to swallow up
or destroy! 21That is not the case. A man named Sheba son of Bicri,
from the hill country of Ephraim, has lifted up his hand against the
king, against David. Hand over this one man, and I'll withdraw from
the city."

[a]14 Or *Abel, even Beth Maacah*; also in verse 15

20:7 Joab's men and the Kerethites and Pelethites. Joab, though not in charge, went on the mission and had great influence over his men (vv. 11,15). **mighty warriors.** This select group of Special Forces was deployed for top priority missions (23:8–39).

20:10 Joab plunged it into his belly. Joab had done this before (3:27). David would not let Joab's actions be forgotten or go unpunished (1 Kin. 2:5–6). Even with enemies, there is a way to fight honorably. **Joab and his brother.** At this point in the action, Joab had already forced his way into equal status with David's appointed commander.

20:11 Whoever favors Joab ... David. Joab's men, though they had declared allegiance to David, seem to have ignored his chain of command. Certainly, they were for David, not Sheba. However, they were not for David's appointed leader, Abishai.

20:14 Israel to Abel Beth Maacah. Sheba recruited many from the tribes of Israel as he fled to this hideout in the northernmost part of Israel. He hoped to be far from the reach of David's army.

The woman said to Joab, "His head will be thrown to you from
the wall."
22Then the woman went to all the people with her wise advice, and
they cut off the head of Sheba son of Bicri and threw it to Joab. So he
sounded the trumpet, and his men dispersed from the city, each
returning to his home. And Joab went back to the king in Jerusalem.
23Joab was over Israel's entire army; Benaiah son of Jehoiada was
over the Kerethites and Pelethites; 24Adoniram[a] was in charge of
forced labor; Jehoshaphat son of Ahilud was recorder; 25Sheva was
secretary; Zadok and Abiathar were priests; 26and Ira the Jairite was
David's priest.

The Gibeonites Avenged

21 During the reign of David, there was a famine for three
successive years; so David sought the face of the LORD. The
LORD said, "It is on account of Saul and his blood-stained house; it is
because he put the Gibeonites to death."
2The king summoned the Gibeonites and spoke to them. (Now the
Gibeonites were not a part of Israel but were survivors of the
Amorites; the Israelites had sworn to ⌊spare⌋ them, but Saul in his
zeal for Israel and Judah had tried to annihilate them.) 3David asked
the Gibeonites, "What shall I do for you? How shall I make amends so
that you will bless the LORD's inheritance?"
4The Gibeonites answered him, "We have no right to demand silver
or gold from Saul or his family, nor do we have the right to put anyone in Israel to death."
"What do you want me to do for you?" David asked.
5They answered the king, "As for the man who destroyed us and
plotted against us so that we have been decimated and have no place
anywhere in Israel, 6let seven of his male descendants be given to us

[a]24 Some Septuagint manuscripts (see also 1 Kings 4:6 and 5:14); Hebrew *Adoram*

OPEN Which of the following "famines" would affect you the most: A "famine" of quality movies? A stockmarket "famine" (recession)? A "famine" of quality restaurants in your area? A famine of quality religious broadcasting? Your favorite singing artist going through a "creativity famine"?

STUDY A famine throughout the land causes David to inquire of God as to its cause. God says it is a punishment for acts of violence done when Saul was king, against a group called the Gibeonites, and so David gives them a chance for revenge against Saul's descendants. **1.** Why did Israel make a treaty with the Gibeonites ("Hivites") in the first place (Josh. 9)? **2.** How do you feel about the request of the Gibeonites (vv. 5–6) and how David granted it: Justice was done? Unduly vengeful? Superstition? It worked, so it must

---

20:23 Joab was over Israel's entire army. Joab did not like having his command and his men taken from him (vv. 6,7). By the end of the chapter, he had already pushed his way back to the top.

21:1–24:25 During the reign of David. The final chapters of 2 Samuel are not chronological, but summarize David's life. The bookends of this section paint David as a man who struggled with the sins of others (vv.1–14) as well as his own (24:1–25). Bordering these sections, David's mighty men appear to be the instruments God used to bring about great victories for the king (vv.15–22 and 23:8–39). At the center of this section (22:1–23:7), David's heart beats for the God who saves (v. 28; 23:5).

21:1–14 for three successive years. (16:7–8). Shimei mentioned the future consequences of Saul's bloodshed and spoke of Absalom as still being alive. Therefore, these years of famine must have occurred between Shimei's curse and Absalom's rebellion.

21:1 because he put the Gibeonites to death. In Saul's mind, his zeal for Israel justified ignoring the promises made by God (v. 2). Though Joshua had been tricked by the Gibeonites into this treaty (Josh. 9:14–15), to God a promise is a promise and must not be broken.

21:2 Amorites. A name used for the inhabitants of Canaan before Israel arrived in the land (Josh. 24:18). **tried to annihilate them.** God prevented Israel's attempt to exterminate the Amorite race.

21:3 bless the LORD's inheritance. David understood that the tables of blessing had been turned. Israel was told by God that through them all the peoples (nations) would be blessed (Gen. 12:3). Here David asked another nation to bless Israel. Clearly David is an example of one who proved his innocence by his "godly sorrow" (2 Cor. 7:11).

21:4 What do you want me to do for you? Though Saul had given the Gibeonites no rights, David was willing to do all that was necessary to make amends and prevent further consequences in Israel.

21:5 the man who destroyed us. That would be Saul. **we have been decimated.** Many Gibeonites had escaped with their lives, but their race had suffered irreparable damage.

21:6 seven. The number is symbolic of completeness. No further payment would be needed by the Israelites nor requested by the Gibeonites. The agreement showed a great commitment by Israel to make things right, and by Gibeon to forgive and forget.

to be killed and exposed before the LORD at Gibeah of Saul—the
LORD'S chosen one."
So the king said, "I will give them to you."
7The king spared Mephibosheth son of Jonathan, the son of Saul,
because of the oath before the LORD between David and Jonathan son
of Saul. 8But the king took Armoni and Mephibosheth, the two sons
of Aiah's daughter Rizpah, whom she had borne to Saul, together
with the five sons of Saul's daughter Merab,[a] whom she had borne to
Adriel son of Barzillai the Meholathite. 9He handed them over to the
Gibeonites, who killed and exposed them on a hill before the LORD.
All seven of them fell together; they were put to death during the first
days of the harvest, just as the barley harvest was beginning.
10Rizpah daughter of Aiah took sackcloth and spread it out for herself on a rock. From the beginning of the harvest till the rain poured
down from the heavens on the bodies, she did not let the birds of the
air touch them by day or the wild animals by night. 11When David was
told what Aiah's daughter Rizpah, Saul's concubine, had done, 12he
went and took the bones of Saul and his son Jonathan from the citizens of Jabesh Gilead. (They had taken them secretly from the public
square at Beth Shan, where the Philistines had hung them after they
struck Saul down on Gilboa.) 13David brought the bones of Saul and
his son Jonathan from there, and the bones of those who had been
killed and exposed were gathered up.
14They buried the bones of Saul and his son Jonathan in the tomb
of Saul's father Kish, at Zela in Benjamin, and did everything the king
commanded. After that, God answered prayer in behalf of the land.

Wars Against the Philistines

15Once again there was a battle between the Philistines and Israel.
David went down with his men to fight against the Philistines, and he
became exhausted. 16And Ishbi-Benob, one of the descendants of
Rapha, whose bronze spearhead weighed three hundred shekels[b]
and who was armed with a new ⌞sword⌟, said he would kill David.
17But Abishai son of Zeruiah came to David's rescue; he struck the
Philistine down and killed him. Then David's men swore to him, saying, "Never again will you go out with us to battle, so that the lamp of
Israel will not be extinguished."
18In the course of time, there was another battle with the Philistines, at Gob. At that time Sibbecai the Hushathite killed Saph, one of
the descendants of Rapha.
19In another battle with the Philistines at Gob, Elhanan son of

[a]8 Two Hebrew manuscripts, some Septuagint manuscripts and Syriac (see also 1 Samuel 18:19); most Hebrew and Septuagint manuscripts *Michal* [b]16 That is, about 7 1/2 pounds (about 3.5 kilograms)

have been what God wanted? **3.** What is the significance of the fact that these executions occurred during the first days of the harvest (remember v. 1)? **4.** How do you respond to Rizpah's action in verse 10? What feelings do you think she was experiencing? How do her actions seem to affect David? **5.** Why does David move the bones of Saul and Jonathan? How do you think he felt, moving the bones of his old friend Jonathan (1 Sam. 18:1–4)?

APPLY 1. When have you, like Rizpah, felt the need to stand by the side of a loved one who was suffering the judgment of the community you were in? What did you do to defend that person's dignity? **2.** How has your experience affected your views of judgment and mercy?

OPEN What did you do when you were younger that you no longer have the stamina to do now?

STUDY David continues to lead his people in a series of military victories, particularly against their arch-enemies, the Philistines. But on one occasion, David himself becomes exhausted and he has to be rescued. **1.** Who has to rescue David? **2.** Why do David's men now advise that he not go with them into their battles? **3.** How do you think David felt about the rescue and resultant advice from the men? **4.** How do you think David dealt with this advice?

APPLY When have you felt like you have had to confront

21:7 because of the oath. David would not break one oath of mercy to fix another (1 Sam. 18:3).

21:9 All seven. David himself made the difficult choice of these seven men. Israel would remember this tragic moment every year at the beginning of the barley harvest.

21:12 bones of Saul. The people of Jabesh Gilead had rescued the bodies of Saul and his sons from the Philistines and had buried the bones under a tamarisk tree (1 Sam. 31:11–13). From start to finish, David acted honorably toward the house of Saul.

21:15–22 The four divisions of this section (vv. 15–17; 18; 19; and 20–21) read like plaques in Israel's Hall of Fame. Each Hall of Famer earned his stripes by slaying a descendant of Rapha (v. 22).

21:16 Rapha. The Raphaites were strong, tall, numerous and also called Zamzummites (Deut. 2:20–21).

21:19 killed Goliath. This may have been the brother of Goliath that David killed at Socoh in Judah (1 Sam.17:1–3, 50–54; 1 Chr. 20:5).

Jaare-Oregim[a] the Bethlehemite killed Goliath[b] the Gittite, who had a
spear with a shaft like a weaver's rod.
20In still another battle, which took place at Gath, there was a huge
man with six fingers on each hand and six toes on each foot—twenty-
four in all. He also was descended from Rapha. 21When he taunted
Israel, Jonathan son of Shimeah, David's brother, killed him.
22These four were descendants of Rapha in Gath, and they fell at
the hands of David and his men.

David's Song of Praise

22 David sang to the LORD the words of this song when the LORD delivered him from the hand of all his enemies and from the hand of Saul. 2He said:

"The LORD is my rock, my fortress and my deliverer;
3 my God is my rock, in whom I take refuge,
my shield and the horn[c] of my salvation.
He is my stronghold, my refuge and my savior—
from violent men you save me.
4 I call to the LORD, who is worthy of praise,
and I am saved from my enemies.

5 "The waves of death swirled about me;
the torrents of destruction overwhelmed me.
6 The cords of the grave[d] coiled around me;
the snares of death confronted me.
7 In my distress I called to the LORD;
I called out to my God.
From his temple he heard my voice;
my cry came to his ears.

8 "The earth trembled and quaked,
the foundations of the heavens[e] shook;
they trembled because he was angry.
9 Smoke rose from his nostrils;
consuming fire came from his mouth,
burning coals blazed out of it.
10 He parted the heavens and came down;
dark clouds were under his feet.
11 He mounted the cherubim and flew;
he soared[f] on the wings of the wind.
12 He made darkness his canopy around him—
the dark[g] rain clouds of the sky.

[a]19 Or *son of Jair the weaver* [b]19 Hebrew and Septuagint; 1 Chron. 20:5 *son of Jair killed Lahmi the brother of Goliath* [c]3 *Horn* here symbolizes strength. [d]6 Hebrew *Sheol* [e]8 Hebrew; Vulgate and Syriac (see also Psalm 18:7) *mountains* [f]11 Many Hebrew manuscripts (see also Psalm 18:10); most Hebrew manuscripts *appeared* [g]12 Septuagint and Vulgate (see also Psalm 18:11); Hebrew *massed*

your own mortality? What has helped you to do so?

____

OPEN 1. Where do you go when you are feeling really low? **2.** How does going there help?

STUDY Tradition has attributed many of the psalms in the book of Psalms to David. But here we find one that for one reason or another it was not mentioned here. It thanks God for delivering him from such difficulties as he confronted in 21:15–22. **1.** If you had to express the emotions of David's song in music, what type of music would you pick and why? What refrains would you dramatize? Where would you signal the musical crescendo? **2.** Choose three of the following words to describe David, as you see him through this song: Egotistical? Grateful? Cold-hearted? Single-minded? Powerful? Self-righteous? Obedient? Power-hungry? Self-focused? **3.** What near encounters with death might he have been referring to in verses 5–7? **4.** What are the central qualities of God that David is extolling in verses 8–16? **5.** In verses 21–25, David speaks as though he were sinless, yet elsewhere he is very aware of his failures (Ps. 32; 51). How do you account for this difference? How could David make such claims about himself (22:21)? **6.** In verses 21–25, is David praising himself or praising God? Is he placing himself in danger of being judged by the principles of verse 28? Why or why not? **7.** In verses 31–37 and 47–51, what qualities of God do you see through the eyes of David? What effect does God have on him? **8.** In referring to his qualities as a warrior and king (vv. 38–46), what new insights do you gain into David?

22:1 the words of this song. Repeated in Psalm 18. David's words boasted of his confidence in victory by God's hand. He wrote this song soon after God delivered him from the hand of Saul (1 Sam. 31:8) but it was before his humiliating sin with Bathsheba (12:9–10).

22:2 my rock. David aligned himself with Moses in describing God as his rock (Deut. 32:4,15,18,30). Rocks had provided a fortress, a refuge, a shield and a stronghold for David against Saul.

22:9 Smoke rose from his nostrils. David compared God's power to that of a mighty beast. God needs no outside weapons, for his strength (fire) comes from within himself.

22:11 He mounted the cherubim. These heavenly creatures seem to be escorts and guards of the throne room of God (Gen. 3:24).

APPLY **1.** When has God reached down to draw you "out of deep waters" (v. 17)? In what ways have you shown your gratitude for this? **2.** As you look ahead to the path that is in front of you, how would you like God to "broaden that path ... so that your ankles do not turn" (v. 37)? **3.** In those times where the path cannot be made easier, in what ways would you like God to "arm you with strength for battle"?

13 Out of the brightness of his presence
bolts of lightning blazed forth.
14 The LORD thundered from heaven;
the voice of the Most High resounded.
15 He shot arrows and scattered ⌞the enemies⌟,
bolts of lightning and routed them.
16 The valleys of the sea were exposed
and the foundations of the earth laid bare
at the rebuke of the LORD,
at the blast of breath from his nostrils.

17 "He reached down from on high and took hold of me;
he drew me out of deep waters.
18 He rescued me from my powerful enemy,
from my foes, who were too strong for me.
19 They confronted me in the day of my disaster,
but the LORD was my support.
20 He brought me out into a spacious place;
he rescued me because he delighted in me.

21 "The LORD has dealt with me according to my righteousness;
according to the cleanness of my hands he has rewarded me.
22 For I have kept the ways of the LORD;
I have not done evil by turning from my God.
23 All his laws are before me;
I have not turned away from his decrees.
24 I have been blameless before him
and have kept myself from sin.
25 The LORD has rewarded me according to my righteousness,
according to my cleanness[a] in his sight.

26 "To the faithful you show yourself faithful,
to the blameless you show yourself blameless,
27 to the pure you show yourself pure,
but to the crooked you show yourself shrewd.
28 You save the humble,
but your eyes are on the haughty to bring them low.
29 You are my lamp, O LORD;
the LORD turns my darkness into light.
30 With your help I can advance against a troop[b];
with my God I can scale a wall.

[a]25 Hebrew; Septuagint and Vulgate (see also Psalm 18:24) *to the cleanness of my hands* [b]30 Or *can run through a barricade*

22:14 The LORD thundered from heaven. The voice of God, like thunder, strikes fear in people's hearts (Deut. 5:25–26). By his powerful voice, God created the world (Gen.1) and by it he can shake the world (Ps. 29).

22:17 He reached down. In verse 5, David said he was drowning. Now David is delivered much like the parting of the Red Sea when the people left Egypt (Ex. 14:21–22).

22:21 according to my righteousness ... to the cleanness. David's statement was not a claim of sinlessness, but an observation that up to that time—after Saul had been killed—he had been faithful to all his duties as a king (v. 51).

22:26–30 David spoke here about one's perspective of God. When a person is faithful to God, then God's faithfulness is more clearly seen. Morally corrupted people see God as nothing but shrewd. Indeed, the only way to know God is to follow him.

22:28 the haughty to bring them low. "Coming down" is not always punishment. God humbled Nebuchadnezzar and blessed him with new insight (Dan. 4:33–34).

22:29 You are my lamp O LORD. His men thought David to be the lamp of Israel (21:17). The Lord was the one who turned David's darkness into light.

[31]"As for God, his way is perfect;
the word of the LORD is flawless.
He is a shield
for all who take refuge in him.
[32]For who is God besides the LORD?
And who is the Rock except our God?
[33]It is God who arms me with strength[a]
and makes my way perfect.
[34]He makes my feet like the feet of a deer;
he enables me to stand on the heights.
[35]He trains my hands for battle;
my arms can bend a bow of bronze.
[36]You give me your shield of victory;
you stoop down to make me great.
[37]You broaden the path beneath me,
so that my ankles do not turn.

[38]"I pursued my enemies and crushed them;
I did not turn back till they were destroyed.
[39]I crushed them completely, and they could not rise;
they fell beneath my feet.
[40]You armed me with strength for battle;
you made my adversaries bow at my feet.
[41]You made my enemies turn their backs in flight,
and I destroyed my foes.
[42]They cried for help, but there was no one to save them—
to the LORD, but he did not answer.
[43]I beat them as fine as the dust of the earth;
I pounded and trampled them like mud in the streets.

[44]"You have delivered me from the attacks of my people;
you have preserved me as the head of nations.
People I did not know are subject to me,
[45] and foreigners come cringing to me;
as soon as they hear me, they obey me.
[46]They all lose heart;
they come trembling[b] from their strongholds.

[47]"The LORD lives! Praise be to my Rock!
Exalted be God, the Rock, my Savior!
[48]He is the God who avenges me,
who puts the nations under me,
[49] who sets me free from my enemies.
You exalted me above my foes;
from violent men you rescued me.
[50]Therefore I will praise you, O LORD, among the nations;
I will sing praises to your name.

[a]33 Dead Sea Scrolls, some Septuagint manuscripts, Vulgate and Syriac (see also Psalm 18:32); Masoretic Text *who is my strong refuge* [b]46 Some Septuagint manuscripts and Vulgate (see also Psalm 18:45); Masoretic Text *they arm themselves.*

22:31 his way is perfect. In the past, David had many doubts and fears amid his troubles. Looking back, David was able to observe that God's way of allowing him to experience those troubles was the right and perfect plan.

22:47 The LORD lives! Praise be. David, seeing the results of God's work, knew God was alive.

22:50 I will praise you, O LORD. David was a man overcome with the mercy of God. All nations were to hear the good news about God's salvation (Rom. 1:5; 16:26).

[51] He gives his king great victories;
he shows unfailing kindness to his anointed,
to David and his descendants forever."

OPEN Which of the following words or phrases would you most want said in your eulogy when you die: "__________ never met a stranger"? "__________ was a person of their word"? "__________ always gave their best"? "__________ never stopped learning? "__________ made the world a better place by being here"? "__________ helped people see the humor in life"?

STUDY David, now well-advanced in years, shares an oracle that speaks of how he sought to live his life. **1.** In these last words, how does David underscore the divine inspiration of *all* his recorded words (vv. 2–3)? **2.** What do the images of verse 4 say about life under a righteous ruler? **3.** How does David know all is right with his house (v. 5; 7:12–16)? **4.** How do evil men compare with him (vv. 6–7)?

APPLY 1. When have you felt like God has spoken through you, whether in one-on-one conversation or before a group? **2.** What were some of the feelings you had about God using you in this way?

____

The Last Words of David

23 These are the last words of David:

"The oracle of David son of Jesse,
the oracle of the man exalted by the Most High,
the man anointed by the God of Jacob,
Israel's singer of songs[a]:

[2] "The Spirit of the LORD spoke through me;
his word was on my tongue.
[3] The God of Israel spoke,
the Rock of Israel said to me:
'When one rules over men in righteousness,
when he rules in the fear of God,
[4] he is like the light of morning at sunrise
on a cloudless morning,
like the brightness after rain
that brings the grass from the earth.'

[5] "Is not my house right with God?
Has he not made with me an everlasting covenant,
arranged and secured in every part?
Will he not bring to fruition my salvation
and grant me my every desire?
[6] But evil men are all to be cast aside like thorns,
which are not gathered with the hand.
[7] Whoever touches thorns
uses a tool of iron or the shaft of a spear;
they are burned up where they lie."

[a] 1 Or *Israel's beloved singer*

22:51 to his anointed. David's third-person reference teaches two lessons: 1) He was saved and blessed because of his position as king, not because he was better than all others; 2) All great victories (salvation) are administered by God through David's descendants. Believers declare that all the blessings of salvation come through David's son, Jesus Christ (Rom. 1:3; 2 Tim. 2:8; Rev. 22:16).

23:2 The Spirit of the LORD spoke. David's claim means that God "breathed" his words into and through *David*, who is credited with 73 of the 150 psalms. Second Peter 1:21 confirms that God gave biblical writers the thoughts he wanted included in his Word.

23:3 Rock. David often refers to God as his rock, for example, "my rock and my redeemer" (Ps. 19:14). It is also a reference to his descendant Jesus Christ. **When one rules over men.** This is a key theme of this section. God both establishes and brings down rulers, his appointed leaders on earth. David reminds us that upright rulers benefit their people. **when he rules in the fear of God.** The fear of God is a healthy respect for who God is. We don't cringe before him in terror, but we bow in awe of his greatness.

23:4 like the light of morning. Continuing the theme of the righteous ruler, David likened him to light and favor, as contrasted with the darkness and harm of an evil ruler. The righteous leader also inspires goodness in his people.

23:5 Is not my house right?... everlasting covenant. While David wasn't perfect, he is described as a man after God's own heart. He confessed his sins and longed for closeness with God. God's covenants are ironclad. He doesn't break them.

23:6 evil men ... cast aside like thorns. David knew that God would ultimately deal justly with evil men. While they may seem to prosper for a time, they will eventually be destroyed (Ps. 37).

David's Mighty Men

8These are the names of David's mighty men:
Josheb-Basshebeth,[a] a Tahkemonite,[b] was chief of the Three; he
raised his spear against eight hundred men, whom he killed[c] in one
encounter.
9Next to him was Eleazar son of Dodai the Ahohite. As one of the
three mighty men, he was with David when they taunted the Philistines gathered ⌞at Pas Dammim⌟[d] for battle. Then the men of Israel
retreated, 10but he stood his ground and struck down the Philistines
till his hand grew tired and froze to the sword. The LORD brought
about a great victory that day. The troops returned to Eleazar, but
only to strip the dead.
11Next to him was Shammah son of Agee the Hararite. When the
Philistines banded together at a place where there was a field full of
lentils, Israel's troops fled from them. 12But Shammah took his stand
in the middle of the field. He defended it and struck the Philistines
down, and the LORD brought about a great victory.
13During harvest time, three of the thirty chief men came down to
David at the cave of Adullam, while a band of Philistines was encamped in the Valley of Rephaim. 14At that time David was in the
stronghold, and the Philistine garrison was at Bethlehem. 15David
longed for water and said, "Oh, that someone would get me a drink of
water from the well near the gate of Bethlehem!" 16So the three
mighty men broke through the Philistine lines, drew water from the
well near the gate of Bethlehem and carried it back to David. But he
refused to drink it; instead, he poured it out before the LORD. 17"Far
be it from me, O LORD, to do this!" he said. "Is it not the blood of men
who went at the risk of their lives?" And David would not drink it.
Such were the exploits of the three mighty men.
18Abishai the brother of Joab son of Zeruiah was chief of the Three.[e]
He raised his spear against three hundred men, whom he killed, and
so he became as famous as the Three. 19Was he not held in greater
honor than the Three? He became their commander, even though he
was not included among them.
20Benaiah son of Jehoiada was a valiant fighter from Kabzeel, who
performed great exploits. He struck down two of Moab's best men.
He also went down into a pit on a snowy day and killed a lion. 21And
he struck down a huge Egyptian. Although the Egyptian had a spear
in his hand, Benaiah went against him with a club. He snatched the

[a]8 Hebrew; some Septuagint manuscripts suggest *Ish-Bosheth,* that is, *Esh-Baal* (see also 1 Chron. 11:11 *Jashobeam*). [b]8 Probably a variant of *Hacmonite* (see 1 Chron. 11:11) [c]8 Some Septuagint manuscripts (see also 1 Chron. 11:11); Hebrew and other Septuagint manuscripts *Three; it was Adino the Eznite who killed eight hundred men* [d]9 See 1 Chron. 11:13; Hebrew *gathered there.* [e]18 Most Hebrew manuscripts (see also 1 Chron. 11:20); two Hebrew manuscripts and Syriac *Thirty*

OPEN 1. Which of the following was your favorite character when you were younger, and why: Superman? Batman? Spider Man? Indiana Jones? Princess Leah? James Bond? Zorro? **2.** If you could have a superpower of one of these heroes yourself, which one would you choose, and why: The ability to fly? Super coolness under stress? The ability to see through things? Invulnerability (except to maybe Kryptonite!)? The ability to always appear at the moment you're needed? Other?

STUDY Like a list of acknowledgements at the end of a book, here we learn of some mighty men of valor who helped many of David's great victories happen. **1.** What kind of person do you imagine the typical "mighty man of David" was? How do you think they would fare against the superheroes of your childhood? **2.** Which exploit by the men in this passage impresses you the most? Do you think any of these were "fish stories"? **3.** What do you think made David's mighty men so mighty: Steroids? A team spirit? Brutish strength? Will power and determination? The Spirit of God? A rigorous work-out schedule? "It's got to be the shoes!"? **4.** For what was Abishai famous (vv. 18–19)? Why do you think he was commander of "the Three," but *not* among them? **5.** What names do you recognize among "the Thirty" (vv. 24–39)? What biblical events do their names bring to mind for you?

APPLY 1. If you could choose three "mighty persons" who have fought by your side over the course of your life, who would they be? **2.** What victories have they helped you win? **3.** What can we learn from these "mighty persons" as we seek to be supportive of each other in this group?

23:8–39 *These 37 elite soldiers may have served as David's bodyguards.* They were brave, highly skilled and known for excellence above and beyond their duty.

23:8–11 Josheb-Basshebeth, a Tahkemonite. Chief of the captains, he outshone the rest. In battle, he killed 800 men at one time. **Eleazar.** He knew that persistence pays. Even after Israel retreated from the enemy, Eleazar attacked and defeated them. He persevered until his hand became frozen to his sword because he had clutched it so long. **Shammah.** He, too, fought the Philistines when the troops were retreating, and he won. These three men were examples for the rest.

23:13 Valley of Rephaim. The Philistines spread out in this valley on the route to Jerusalem to do battle with David's men. The Philistine garrison was at Bethlehem, David's hometown, six miles south of Jerusalem.

23:20 Benaiah … valiant fighter. An army commander with a division of 24,000 men, he was also in charge of David's personal bodyguards.

spear from the Egyptian's hand and killed him with his own spear.
[22]Such were the exploits of Benaiah son of Jehoiada; he too was as
famous as the three mighty men. [23]He was held in greater honor than
any of the Thirty, but he was not included among the Three. And
David put him in charge of his bodyguard.

[24]Among the Thirty were:
Asahel the brother of Joab,
Elhanan son of Dodo from Bethlehem,
[25]Shammah the Harodite,
Elika the Harodite,
[26]Helez the Paltite,
Ira son of Ikkesh from Tekoa,
[27]Abiezer from Anathoth,
Mebunnai[a] the Hushathite,
[28]Zalmon the Ahohite,
Maharai the Netophathite,
[29]Heled[b] son of Baanah the Netophathite,
Ithai son of Ribai from Gibeah in Benjamin,
[30]Benaiah the Pirathonite,
Hiddai[c] from the ravines of Gaash,
[31]Abi-Albon the Arbathite,
Azmaveth the Barhumite,
[32]Eliahba the Shaalbonite,
the sons of Jashen,
Jonathan [33]son of[d] Shammah the Hararite,
Ahiam son of Sharar[e] the Hararite,
[34]Eliphelet son of Ahasbai the Maacathite,
Eliam son of Ahithophel the Gilonite,
[35]Hezro the Carmelite,
Paarai the Arbite,
[36]Igal son of Nathan from Zobah,
the son of Hagri,[f]
[37]Zelek the Ammonite,
Naharai the Beerothite, the armor-bearer of Joab son of Zeruiah,
[38]Ira the Ithrite,
Gareb the Ithrite
[39]and Uriah the Hittite.
There were thirty-seven in all.

[a]27 Hebrew; some Septuagint manuscripts (see also 1 Chron. 11:29) *Sibbecai* [b]29 Some Hebrew manuscripts and Vulgate (see also 1 Chron. 11:30); most Hebrew manuscripts *Heleb* [c]30 Hebrew; some Septuagint manuscripts (see also 1 Chron. 11:32) *Hurai* [d]33 Some Septuagint manuscripts (see also 1 Chron. 11:34); Hebrew does not have *son of.* [e]33 Hebrew; some Septuagint manuscripts (see also 1 Chron. 11:35) *Sacar* [f]36 Some Septuagint manuscripts (see also 1 Chron. 11:38); Hebrew *Haggadi*

23:24 Among the Thirty. The number of active soldiers in this small military contingent called "The Thirty" was kept at around thirty men. The number varies in this and other passages, perhaps including members who had died in battle.

23:34 Eliam. Bathsheba's father and the son of Ahithophel, David's counselor, who joined Absalom's plot to unseat David and take the throne for himself.

23:39 Uriah. David went to great lengths to cover his sin against Uriah, Bathsheba's husband and a dedicated soldier whom David caused to be killed in battle. Not until Nathan confronted David did he admit his sin and repent (12:11–13). His sin would have great consequences.

David Counts the Fighting Men

24 Again the anger of the LORD burned against Israel, and he
incited David against them, saying, "Go and take a census of
Israel and Judah."
2So the king said to Joab and the army commanders[a] with him, "Go
throughout the tribes of Israel from Dan to Beersheba and enroll the
fighting men, so that I may know how many there are."
3But Joab replied to the king, "May the LORD your God multiply the
troops a hundred times over, and may the eyes of my lord the king see
it. But why does my lord the king want to do such a thing?"
4The king's word, however, overruled Joab and the army commanders; so they left the presence of the king to enroll the fighting
men of Israel.
5After crossing the Jordan, they camped near Aroer, south of the
town in the gorge, and then went through Gad and on to Jazer. 6They
went to Gilead and the region of Tahtim Hodshi, and on to Dan Jaan
and around toward Sidon. 7Then they went toward the fortress of
Tyre and all the towns of the Hivites and Canaanites. Finally, they
went on to Beersheba in the Negev of Judah.
8After they had gone through the entire land, they came back to Jerusalem at the end of nine months and twenty days.
9Joab reported the number of the fighting men to the king: In Israel
there were eight hundred thousand able-bodied men who could handle a sword, and in Judah five hundred thousand.
10David was conscience-stricken after he had counted the fighting
men, and he said to the LORD, "I have sinned greatly in what I have
done. Now, O LORD, I beg you, take away the guilt of your servant. I
have done a very foolish thing."
11Before David got up the next morning, the word of the LORD had
come to Gad the prophet, David's seer: 12"Go and tell David, 'This is
what the LORD says: I am giving you three options. Choose one of
them for me to carry out against you.' "
13So Gad went to David and said to him, "Shall there come upon
you three[b] years of famine in your land? Or three months of fleeing
from your enemies while they pursue you? Or three days of plague in
your land? Now then, think it over and decide how I should answer
the one who sent me."
14David said to Gad, "I am in deep distress. Let us fall into the

[a]2 Septuagint (see also verse 4 and 1 Chron. 21:2); Hebrew *Joab the army commander* [b]13 Septuagint (see also 1 Chron. 21:12); Hebrew *seven*

OPEN 1. Which of the following were you most likely to take a census of when you were in grade school: Your baseball trading cards? Your stuffed animals? Your marbles? Your friends? Your records or tapes? A collection like stamps or coins? **2.** What would you be most likely to need to inventory today: Items in your garage or attic? Files in your computer? Pairs of shoes in your closet? Tools you've borrowed from neighbors? Wasted opportunities in your life? The number of tasks you have to do this week?

STUDY David had been thriving because of his trust in the Lord. But in this story he acts in a way that shows distrust of the Lord's power—he counts the fighting men under his charge. **1.** Why does David decide to count the fighting men: Boredom? To feed his ego? To gauge his strength against his enemies? He was into statistics? He thought it was what God wanted? **2.** Why does Joab advise against this act? **3.** Who is put in charge of this task of counting the fighting men? **4.** How many fighting men did they find? Which part of the country had more fighting men—Israel or Judah? **5.** Why do you think God's anger "burned against Israel" (v. 1)? **6.** Why do you think David felt he had sinned (v. 10)? **7.** What punishment options does God give? Which does David choose? Which would you have chosen?

APPLY 1. Where are you tempted to lean upon the strength of your assets rather than upon the promises of God? **2.** If you truly trusted the promises of God for your future, what would you do differently?

24:1 Again the anger of the LORD burned. May refer to the Lord's anger at Saul's killing of the Gibeonites in 21:1. The reason for God's anger against Israel this time is not specified, but it may have resulted from the support many people gave Absalom against David. Just as God allowed Satan to afflict Job, he also allowed him to tempt David to take a census with sinful motives. **Go and take a census of Israel and Judah.** It was not the census that displeased God, but rather the condition of David's heart. He seemed to be relying on human strength and military muscle to defend Israel, rather than on God alone.

24:3 Joab. He challenged the wisdom of taking the census by asking David why he wanted to count his troops. Joab knew that God was able to provide the necessary manpower, and he believed David should trust in God rather than in military might.

24:9 men who could handle a sword. David counted only men of military age. The counters began east of the Jordan River, went counterclockwise until they reached Beersheba in the south, and reported to David in Jerusalem nearly ten months later.

24:12 giving you three options. Although God forgave David, there were still consequences resulting from his sin. Moses warned of these punishments for those who broke God's covenant.

24:14 Let us fall into the hands of the LORD. David's reliance on the goodness and mercy of God and his understanding of the human heart are

hands of the LORD, for his mercy is great; but do not let me fall into the hands of men."

15So the LORD sent a plague on Israel from that morning until the end of the time designated, and seventy thousand of the people from Dan to Beersheba died. 16When the angel stretched out his hand to destroy Jerusalem, the LORD was grieved because of the calamity and said to the angel who was afflicting the people, "Enough! Withdraw your hand." The angel of the LORD was then at the threshing floor of Araunah the Jebusite.

17When David saw the angel who was striking down the people, he said to the LORD, "I am the one who has sinned and done wrong. These are but sheep. What have they done? Let your hand fall upon me and my family."

David Builds an Altar

18On that day Gad went to David and said to him, "Go up and build an altar to the LORD on the threshing floor of Araunah the Jebusite." 19So David went up, as the LORD had commanded through Gad. 20When Araunah looked and saw the king and his men coming toward him, he went out and bowed down before the king with his face to the ground.

21Araunah said, "Why has my lord the king come to his servant?"

"To buy your threshing floor," David answered, "so I can build an altar to the LORD, that the plague on the people may be stopped."

22Araunah said to David, "Let my lord the king take whatever pleases him and offer it up. Here are oxen for the burnt offering, and here are threshing sledges and ox yokes for the wood. 23O king, Araunah gives all this to the king." Araunah also said to him, "May the LORD your God accept you."

24But the king replied to Araunah, "No, I insist on paying you for it. I will not sacrifice to the LORD my God burnt offerings that cost me nothing."

OPEN What could have been the biggest sacrifice you could have made when you were in high school?

STUDY Because of David's sin, there was a plague in the land. To end the plague, the prophet Gad calls David to build an altar and make a sacrifice. **1.** What do you think Araunah's feeling was when he saw the king coming to his threshing floor: Humility? Fear? Pride? Surprise? **2.** Why is it important to David that he pay a fair price for Araunah's property that would be used in sacrifice? **3.** What is most surprising to you about this story: That the plague didn't stop after three days (v. 13)? That Araunah was so generous with his property? That the king of the land could be ordered to do things by a prophet? That the sacrifice was effective in stopping the plague? **4.** How

---

evident in his choice among the three punishments. He chose God's mercy rather than the ill treatment of men.

24:16 angel stretched out. God stopped the angel carrying out the punishment from destroying the people of Jerusalem. Angels' duties range from delivering joyful messages ("He is not here; he has risen," Matt. 28:6), to guarding God's people ("to guard you in all your ways," Ps. 91:11), to caring for Jesus in the desert ("angels came and attended him," Matt. 4:11), to destroying people ("annihilated all the fighting men and the leaders and officers in the camp of the Assyrian king," 2 Chr. 32:21). **threshing floor.** A wide, smooth, hard surface where wheat is crushed to separate kernels from straw.

24:17 Let your hand fall upon me. David assumed responsibility for his sin, in keeping with the concept of the righteous leader bringing good and not evil to his people. David asked God not to punish the people for his sin.

24:19 David went up as the LORD had commanded. David obeyed the instructions received through Gad. He went to build an altar to atone for his sin, as God had specifically required.

24:21 To buy your threshing floor. A further example of David's acceptance of responsibility for his sin. The property owner offered to give David whatever he needed for the altar and the burnt offerings. But David insisted on paying, illustrating an important principle for all worship and service. Without cost, there is no real sacrifice.

24:24 sacrifice ... burnt offerings. The primary type of atoning sacrifice for unintentional sins. **David bought the threshing floor and the oxen.** He also bought the land surrounding the threshing floor for 600 shekels or 15 pounds of gold. This spot, Mount Moriah, was where Abraham had offered Isaac and where Solomon later built his splendid temple. Since he was far from his own herds, David needed the oxen to use as sacrifices, as well as the necessary tools. **fifty shekels.** The price David paid to Araunah for the threshing floor, the oxen and the tools. It is equal to about 1-1/4 pounds of silver.

So David bought the threshing floor and the oxen and paid fifty shekels[a] of silver for them. 25 David built an altar to the LORD there and sacrificed burnt offerings and fellowship offerings.[b] Then the LORD answered prayer in behalf of the land, and the plague on Israel was stopped.

[a]24 That is, about 1 1/4 pounds (about 0.6 kilogram) [b]25 Traditionally *peace offerings*

does this story about sin and offering relate to what Jesus said about sin, repentance and the cause of sickness (Luke 13:1–5; John 9:1–4)?

APPLY In light of what David says in verse 24, what can we learn about following God?

24:25 the plague on Israel was stopped. David's atonement, sacrifice and intercessory prayer for himself and on behalf of his people resulted in God answering his prayer, healing the land and stopping the plague.

1 Kings

Author. At one time, Jeremiah was considered the author, but some events listed in 2 Kings occurred after Jeremiah's death. Ezra is a likely candidate, but no one knows for certain who wrote 1 or 2 Kings. These books could have been compiled with records from several sources.

Personal Reading	Group Study Topic and Reading	
1:1–2:12	Solomon Made King	1:28–53
2:13–3:28	Solomon Gets Wisdom	3:1–28
4:1–6:38	Temple Built	6:1–38
7:1–8:66	Temple Dedicated	8:22–66
9:1–10:13	Queen of Sheba	10:1–13
10:14–11:13	Solomon's Wives	10:23–11:13
11:14–12:24	House Divided	12:1–24
12:25–14:31	Jeroboam Doomed	14:1–20
15:1–17:24	Widow at Zarephath	17:1–24
18:1–46	Elijah vs. Baal	18:16–40
19:1–20:43	God's Whisper	19:1–18
21:1–29	Ahab vs. Naboth	21:1–29
22:1–53	Micaiah vs. Ahab	22:1–28

Date. In their final form, 1 and 2 Kings were probably written between 560–540 B.C. The events of 1 Kings cover about 120 years, from David's reign to Jehoshaphat's death.

Purpose. The history of the Hebrew nation records cycles of obedience and disobedience. After they left Egypt, the people alternated between worshipping God faithfully and then rebelling against him. With the life of each king, the kingdom adopted a new spiritual outlook. First Kings traces the contours of the progression and stands as a warning to each reader that faith must be based on the God who never changes, rather than on circumstances that certainly do.

Historical Background. The book of 1 Kings recounts the history of Israel's monarchy from the last days of David's reign (in the united kingdom) to the reigns of Jehoshaphat in Judah and Ahaziah in Israel (in the divided kingdom). This time period began in hope, encompassed a time of splendor under Solomon and then deteriorated. Solomon continued his father's work in centralizing Israel's power in Jerusalem. He undertook many building projects, including a magnificent palace and the temple. Through alliances with foreign rulers and through tributes from other nations and merchants, Israel grew prosperous and powerful under Solomon's reign.

However, Solomon was not a vigilant king. The outside influence of foreign religions and customs eroded the national unity that David and Solomon had once fostered. Upon Solomon's death, the country split into two kingdoms, Israel to the north and Judah to the south, over the issue of the king's successor. The northern kingdom, near the trade routes, became increasingly influenced by outside forces. The gap between the two Hebrew nations grew wider and wider.

King Solomon's Reign. Solomon, David's son, reigned in opulence and grandeur. His riches, the temple, his palace, his wives and harem—none were half-hearted or unremarkable. In his day and time, Solomon was probably the most famous of all of Israel's kings. By the end of his reign, his faith was watered down to the point of confusion and disillusionment. His people were worn out from the work required of them to fund Solomon's luxury and Israel's reputation. His son lacked the wisdom to lead and kept only a small remnant of the kingdom when civil war broke out. Solomon succeeded in creating temporary political success but failed his people spiritually.

Adonijah Sets Himself Up as King

1 When King David was old and well advanced in years, he could
not keep warm even when they put covers over him. [2]So his
servants said to him, "Let us look for a young virgin to attend the
king and take care of him. She can lie beside him so that our lord the
king may keep warm."
[3]Then they searched throughout Israel for a beautiful girl and
found Abishag, a Shunammite, and brought her to the king. [4]The girl
was very beautiful; she took care of the king and waited on him, but
the king had no intimate relations with her.
[5]Now Adonijah, whose mother was Haggith, put himself forward
and said, "I will be king." So he got chariots and horses[a] ready, with
fifty men to run ahead of him. [6](His father had never interfered with
him by asking, "Why do you behave as you do?" He was also very
handsome and was born next after Absalom.)
[7]Adonijah conferred with Joab son of Zeruiah and with Abiathar
the priest, and they gave him their support. [8]But Zadok the priest,
Benaiah son of Jehoiada, Nathan the prophet, Shimei and Rei[b] and
David's special guard did not join Adonijah.
[9]Adonijah then sacrificed sheep, cattle and fattened calves at the
Stone of Zoheleth near En Rogel. He invited all his brothers, the
king's sons, and all the men of Judah who were royal officials, [10]but
he did not invite Nathan the prophet or Benaiah or the special guard
or his brother Solomon.
[11]Then Nathan asked Bathsheba, Solomon's mother, "Have you not
heard that Adonijah, the son of Haggith, has become king without
our lord David's knowing it? [12]Now then, let me advise you how you
can save your own life and the life of your son Solomon. [13]Go in to
King David and say to him, 'My lord the king, did you not swear to me
your servant: "Surely Solomon your son shall be king after me, and
he will sit on my throne"? Why then has Adonijah become king?'

[a]... charioteers [b]8 Or and his friends

OPEN **1.** *Which of the following is most likely to keep you from sleeping well:* Being too warm? Being too cold? Too much noise? Too quiet? Too much light? Too dark? Mattress too hard? Mattress too soft? **2.** When you have trouble sleeping, what is your most effective sleeping aid: Counting sheep? A good massage from your spouse? Soft music? Low background noise? Warm milk? A sleeping pill? A good book? A boring book?

STUDY David is now old, and he is having trouble staying warm as a result. A consequence of his old age is that his son Adonijah feels he can now challenge his aging father for the throne. **1.** Which of the following is closest to your reaction to the proposal to find a young virgin to keep the old king warm: Obviously a man's idea? What was wrong with all the wives he already had? It was just one of those privileges that went with being king? He was too old to care, anyway? **2.** Of the information given to us in verse 6, which is most relevant for Adonijah's political aspirations: That his father never challenged his behavior? He had the looks to get the people's attention? He was next in line after Absalom who had also rebelled? **3.** Joab had been with David through many conflicts. Why do you think he now joins Adonijah? **4.** Why do you think Nathan sides in with Bathsheba and Solomon: He knew Solomon was David's choice? He

1:1 David ... advanced in years. David was about seventy when he died ... many years of physical hardship in ... He had reigned over Israel for forty years, seven years in Hebron and ... years in Jerusalem.

1:3 Shunammite. Abishag came from Shunem, seven miles northwest of Nazareth, to nurse David. Adonijah, David's son, asked to marry her after his father's death.

1:5 Adonijah. David's fourth son, whose name means "the Lord is my Lord." **I will be king.** Despite David's choice of Solomon as his successor, Adonijah exalted himself and set out to become king. **fifty men to run ahead.** Adonijah prepared to fight against his father, if necessary, and also sought to impress the people with his entourage.

1:6 father had never interfered. Although David loved God and was a capable leader, he neglected to properly parent his children. Adonijah was spoiled and willful, and he didn't hesitate to disobey his father's wishes.

1:7 Joab. David's nephew who sided with Adonijah against the king. Joab had been a brave warrior and David had made him commander-in-chief. But Joab didn't always obey David's orders; for example, he executed David's son Absalom despite David's instructions to spare his life.

1:11 Nathan. This prophet had been David's spiritual advisor for years. Nathan had relayed to David God's promise to establish a kingdom through his descendants (2 Sam. 7:4–17). Nathan had also exposed David's sin of killing Uriah to cover the sin with Bathsheba (2 Sam. 12:1–14). **has become king.** Adonijah was David's oldest surviving son. He evidently believed that it was his right to become king. He had not been anointed or crowned king, but may have already proclaimed himself king.

1:12 save your own life. Perhaps God prompted Nathan to plan with Bathsheba to defeat Adonijah's rebellion. It is likely that both Bathsheba and her son Solomon, heir to the throne, would be killed if Adonijah became king. Nathan knew that they would have to act quickly because David was dying.

1:13 did you not swear to me? Nathan arranged for the two witnesses required under Mosaic Law when he sent Bathsheba to the king and followed himself. Both would witness David's pledge to make Solomon king.

thought Adonijah was too much flash and too little substance? He thought he would have more influence with Adonijah? Other? **5.** What does Nathan risk by taking the side he does? **6.** Why do you think David had not been more publicly forthright to this point about his desire for who would succeed him? **7.** How would you have felt in this situation had you been David: Angry? Pressured? Embarrassed? Confused? Other?

APPLY **1.** What bothers you most about facing your own aging: Declining health? Loss of sexual appeal? Loss of independence? So many of your friends dying? Facing the inevitability of death? **2.** What is most consoling to you as you face your own aging: My spiritual self is just getting better and better? God's promise of eternal life? The belief that God will send good, competent people to fill my shoes? The peace that comes from knowing God? Other?

OPEN **1.** What is the most important thing that your father or mother passed on to you: Their business or farm? Their values? A family heirloom? Personality traits, like a sense of humor? Certain physical traits? **2.** What would you like to pass on to your own children?

STUDY When David's son Adonijah seeks to grasp the throne, Nathan and Bathsheba come to remind David of his promise that Bathsheba's son, Solomon, would be the next king. David now decisively reaffirms that promise, and Solomon is given the throne. **1.** What is Bathsheba's mood as she comes before David (vv. 28–31)? On hearing David's

14While you are still there talking to the king, I will come in and
confirm what you have said."
15So Bathsheba went to see the aged king in his room, where
Abishag the Shunammite was attending him. 16Bathsheba bowed low
and knelt before the king.
"What is it you want?" the king asked.
17She said to him, "My lord, you yourself swore to me your servant
by the LORD your God: 'Solomon your son shall be king after me, and
he will sit on my throne.' 18But now Adon ah has become king, and
you, my lord the king, do not know about i 19He has sacrificed great
numbers of cattle, fattened calves, and shep, and has invited all the
king's sons, Abiatha the priest and Joab thcommander of the army,
but he has not invited olomon your serva 20My lord the king, the
eyes of all Israel are on u, to learn fron ou who will sit on the
throne of my lord the king a r him. 21Othe se, as soon as my lord
the king is laid to rest with his lathers, I and son Solomon will be
treated as criminals."
22While she was still speaking with the ki Na an the prophet
arrived. 23And they told the king, "Nathan the phe is here." So he
went before the king and bowed with his face he round.
24Nathan said, "Have you, my lord the king, d re that Adonijah
shall be king after you, and that he will sit on yo roe? 25Today he
has gone down and sacrificed great numbers c le, fattened
calves, and sheep. He has invited all the king's son he ommanders
of the army and Abiathar the priest. Right now th a eating and
drinking with him and saying, 'Long live King Ad a 26But me
your servant, and Zadok the priest, and Benaiah son Je ada, and
your servant Solomon he did not invite. 27Is this som my lord
the king has done without tting his servants know w uld sit
on the throne of my lord the k g after him?"

David Makes Solomon King

28Then King David said, Call in Bathsheba." So she ca
king's presence and stood fore him. he
29The king then took an oat "As surely as the LORD live
delivered me out of every troub 30I will surely cary out t
I swore to you by the LORD, the G of Israel: Solomon you
be king after me, and he will sit o y throne in my place."
31Then Bathsheba bowed low w h he e to the gro
kneeling before the king, said, "May y lord King David live
32King David said, "Call in Zadok the priest, Na
and Benaiah son of Jehoiada." When they came before the k
said to them: "Take your lord's servants with you and set Solom
son on my own mule and take him down to Gihon. 34There ha e Z
dok the priest and Nathan the prophet anoint him king over Israel.
Blow the trumpet and shout, 'Long live King Solomon!' 35Then

1:17 you yourself swore to me. After the king invited her to speak, Bathsheba stated the facts of Adonijah's rebellion and asked David to act to preserve his promise to her, reminding *him of his solemn oath.*

1:24 Have you … declared that Adonijah shall be king. By asking this question, Nathan graciously left the response up to David. He confirmed Bathsheba's statements and indicated the urgency of the situation to David.

1:34 anoint him king. Just as Samuel had anointed David by pouring oil on his head and dedicating him as king (1 Sam. 16:13), th prophet and the priest were to anoin Solomon at a spring near where Adonijah's rebels were gathered. Anoiting signified the coming of the Spirit of God on his chosen leader.

David. [11]He had reigned forty years over Israel—seven years in
Hebron and thirty-three in Jerusalem. [12]So Solomon sat on the
throne of his father David, and his rule was firmly established.

Solomon's Throne Established

[13]Now Adonijah, the son of Haggith, went to Bathsheba, Solomon's
mother. Bathsheba asked him, "Do you come peacefully?"
He answered, "Yes, peacefully." [14]Then he added, "I have something to say to you."
"You may say it," she replied.
[15]"As you know," he said, "the kingdom was mine. All Israel looked
to me as their king. But things changed, and the kingdom has gone to
my brother; for it has come to him from the LORD. [16]Now I have one
request to make of you. Do not refuse me."
"You may make it," she said.
[17]So he continued, "Please ask King Solomon—he will not refuse
you—to give me Abishag the Shunammite as my wife."
[18]"Very well," Bathsheba replied, "I will speak to the king for you."
[19]When Bathsheba went to King Solomon to speak to him for
Adonijah, the king stood up to meet her, bowed down to her and sat
down on his throne. He had a throne brought for the king's mother,
and she sat down at his right hand.
[20]"I have one small request to make of you," she said. "Do not
refuse me."
The king replied, "Make it, my mother; I will not refuse you."
[21]So she said, "Let Abishag the Shunammite be given in marriage
to your brother Adonijah."
[22]King Solomon answered his mother, "Why do you request
Abishag the Shunammite for Adonijah? You might as well request the
kingdom for him—after all, he is my older brother—yes, for him and
for Abiathar the priest and Joab son of Zeruiah!"
[23]Then King Solomon swore by the LORD: "May God deal with me,
be it ever so severely, if Adonijah does not pay with his life for this
request! [24]And now, as surely as the LORD lives—he who has established me securely on the throne of my father David and has founded
a dynasty for me as he promised—Adonijah shall be put to death
today!" [25]So King Solomon gave orders to Benaiah son of Jehoiada,
and he struck down Adonijah and he died.
[26]To Abiathar the priest the king said, "Go back to your fields in
Anathoth. You deserve to die, but I will not put you to death now,
because you carried the ark of the Sovereign LORD before my father

OPEN **1.** When you were in high school and were interested in a person of the opposite sex, who were you most likely to approach: The person themself? The person's best friend? A mutual friend? The person's parent or family member? Nobody (too shy!)? **2.** When you were in high school, what person of the opposite sex were you attracted to, but were never able to get together with? What thwarted you?

STUDY Adonijah, still plotting to have David's throne, seeks to gain a foothold by marrying David's former concubine, Abishag. Solomon refuses his request and has him killed. He also has Joab and Shimei killed. **1.** Why does Adonijah want Abishag killed? (v.17)? **2.** Why does Adonijah make his request through Bathsheba? What does Solomon see behind his brother's request? **3.** Why does Solomon punish Abiathar and Joab immediately after Adonijah's request? **4.** Where does Joab go for refuge and why? Why does Solomon have him killed anyway (v. 28)? **5.** Is Solomon acting righteously or is he simply eliminating the opposition to his government? Have you ever been in an organization while it has undergone leadership change? Does that help you understand the difficult relationships in this passage? **6.** Why doesn't Solomon just have Shimei put under house arrest instead of having him killed right way? **7.** Why do you think Shimei pursued the slaves when he had been told to stay in Jerusalem: He had forgotten the ban? He was being defiant? He didn't think Solomon would follow through with his threat? **8.** Compared to when this chapter

---

2:13 Adonijah. Here Adonijah again began to move against Solomon's kingship to take the throne himself.

2:15 kingdom was mine ... Israel looked to me as their king. Adonijah had deceived himself that his looks and popularity would make him king. This statement shows his mindset. He believed he should have been king, and he was now asking for compensation for not receiving the crown. **come to him from the LORD.** He pretended to acknowledge Solomon's rightful place on the throne as God's will (Dan. 2:21).

2:17 give me Abishag. Abishag had cared for David in his last illness. Although he had not had sexual relations with her, she had become a part of his harem, entitled to part of his inheritance. Adonijah's request to marry her was another attempt to make a claim to the throne.

2:22 request the kingdom for him. In his wisdom, Solomon realized that the people would interpret Adonijah's marriage to Abishag as a claim to the throne. Since Adonijah was older than Solomon, the people might view this as another reason Adonijah should be king. Solomon refused his mother's request because he saw it as a plot.

2:26 Abiathar ... you carried the ark. Abiathar, the high priest, had carried the Ark of the Covenant during David's reign. He had served David faithfully when Saul was pursuing David (1 Sam. 22:20–23).

began, is Solomon's kingdom now more secure or less so?

APPLY 1. When was the last time you felt you had to fight to defend your interests? **2.** When it comes to defending your interests, what influence does the fact that you are a follower of Christ have on how you fight for what you think is right?

David and shared all my father's hardships." 27So Solomon removed
Abiathar from the priesthood of the LORD, fulfilling the word the LORD
had spoken at Shiloh about the house of Eli.

28When the news reached Joab, who had conspired with Adonijah
though not with Absalom, he fled to the tent of the LORD and took
hold of the horns of the altar. 29King Solomon was told that Joab had
fled to the tent of the LORD and was beside the altar. Then Solomon
ordered Benaiah son of Jehoiada, "Go, strike him down!"

30So Benaiah entered the tent of the LORD and said to Joab, "The
king says, 'Come out!' "

But he answered, "No, I will die here."

Benaiah reported to the king, "This is how Joab answered me."

31Then the king commanded Benaiah, "Do as he says. Strike him
down and bury him, and so clear me and my father's house of the
guilt of the innocent blood that Joab shed. 32The LORD will repay him
for the blood he shed, because without the knowledge of my father
David he attacked two men and killed them with the sword. Both of
them—Abner son of Ner, commander of Israel's army, and Amasa son
of Jether, commander of Judah's army—were better men and more
upright than he. 33May the guilt of their blood rest on the head of
Joab and his descendants forever. But on David and his descendants,
his house and his throne, may there be the LORD's peace forever."

34So Benaiah son of Jehoiada went up and struck down Joab and
killed him, and he was buried on his own land[a] in the desert. 35The
king put Benaiah son of Jehoiada over the army in Joab's position
and replaced Abiathar with Zadok the priest.

36Then the king sent for Shimei and said to him, "Build yourself a
house in Jerusalem and live there, but do not go anywhere else. 37The
day you leave and cross the Kidron Valley, you can be sure you will
die; your blood will be on your own head."

38Shimei answered the king, "What you say is good. Your servant
will do as my lord the king has said." And Shimei stayed in Jerusalem
for a long time.

39But three years later, two of Shimei's slaves ran off to Achish son
of Maacah, king of Gath, and Shimei was told, "Your slaves are in
Gath." 40At this, he saddled his donkey and went to Achish at Gath in
search of his slaves. So Shimei went away and brought the slaves
back from Gath.

41When Solomon was told that Shimei had gone from Jerusalem to
Gath and had returned, 42the king summoned Shimei and said to
him, "Did I not make you swear by the LORD and warn you, 'On the
day you leave to go anywhere else, you can be sure you will die'? At

[a]34 *Or buried in his tomb*

2:27 fulfilling the word ... spoken at Shiloh. Solomon removed Abiathar from his office and sent him home, rather than having him killed for plotting with Adonijah. Abiathar was from Eli's line of priests, a line God had said would be cut off because of their wickedness (1 Sam. 2:30–35).

2:28 took hold of the horns. As Adonijah had done (1:50), Joab fled to the tent of the Lord to beg for mercy, but the refuge was only for those who had committed unintentional sins (Ex. 21:14).

2:32 he attacked two men. Solomon carried out David's instructions about Joab because he had killed Abner and Amasa (v. 5).

2:36 Build yourself a house ... do not go anywhere else. Shimei was from the same clan as Saul's family. In the midst of Absalom's rebellion, David did not execute Shimei for his traitorous behavior (v. 8), although his men asked permission to kill him. Solomon confined him to his home, again acknowledging David's final warning about Shimei.

that time you said to me, 'What you say is good. I will obey.' [43]Why then did you not keep your oath to the LORD and obey the command I gave you?"

[44]The king also said to Shimei, "You know in your heart all the wrong you did to my father David. Now the LORD will repay you for your wrongdoing. [45]But King Solomon will be blessed, and David's throne will remain secure before the LORD forever."

[46]Then the king gave the order to Benaiah son of Jehoiada, and he went out and struck Shimei down and killed him.

The kingdom was now firmly established in Solomon's hands.

Solomon Asks for Wisdom

3 Solomon made an alliance with Pharaoh king of Egypt and married his daughter. He brought her to the City of David until he finished building his palace and the temple of the LORD, and the wall around Jerusalem. [2]The people, however, were still sacrificing at the high places, because a temple had not yet been built for the Name of the LORD. [3]Solomon showed his love for the LORD by walking according to the statutes of his father David, except that he offered sacrifices and burned incense on the high places.

[4]The king went to Gibeon to offer sacrifices, for that was the most important high place, and Solomon offered a thousand burnt offerings on that altar. [5]At Gibeon the LORD appeared to Solomon during the night in a dream, and God said, "Ask for whatever you want me to give you."

[6]Solomon answered, "You have shown great kindness to your servant, my father David, because he was faithful to you and righteous and upright in heart. You have continued this great kindness to him and have given him a son to sit on his throne this very day.

[7]"Now, O LORD my God, you have made your servant king in place of my father David. But I am only a little child and do not know how to carry out my duties. [8]Your servant is here among the people you have chosen, a great people, too numerous to count or number. [9]So give your servant a discerning heart to govern your people and to distinguish between right and wrong. For who is able to govern this great people of yours?"

[10]The Lord was pleased that Solomon had asked for this. [11]So God said to him, "Since you have asked for this and not for long life or wealth for yourself, nor have asked for the death of your enemies but for discernment in administering justice, [12]I will do what you have asked. I will give you a wise and discerning heart, so that there will

OPEN 1. When you have dreams at night, what are you most likely to dream about: Weird, nonsensical things happening to you? Embarrassing things (like walking around in your underwear)? Frightening things (like being pursued)? Achieving great things or receiving great honors? Romantic encounters? **2.** When you have such a dream, when is it that you realize you are dreaming?

STUDY Solomon has a dream in which God says he will give him anything he wants, and Solomon asks for wisdom. God is pleased with this request and promises much more. **1.** How does Solomon show his love for the Lord? **2.** What is the problem with sacrificing in the "high places" (v. 2)? **3.** Why does Solomon ask for a discerning heart? Would you have asked for a discerning heart or for your personal desires? **4.** Why do you think Solomon desired wisdom above anything else? **5.** What else does God promise him besides a discerning heart? **6.** What are the preconditions that Solomon must fulfill in order to be granted a long life?

APPLY 1. When have you faced a decision or task so large that you felt like a child in the face of it? **2.** What do you see as the next step you need to make in order

---

2:46 struck Shimei. It sounds like Shimei left his home unintentionally, despite Solomon's orders. But in executing Shimei, Solomon judged his previous sins against David and also fulfilled David's final instructions.

3:1 Solomon made an alliance. The Pharaohs of Egypt usually did not observe the custom of ratifying an alliance by the marriage of the son of one king to the daughter of another. This ensured peace between Israel and Egypt and signified the growing importance of Solomon.

3:2 sacrificing at the high places. These hilltop areas were sites of Canaanite religious ceremonies. The higher up, the closer to their gods, they believed. The Law forbade sacrificing anywhere besides in the tabernacle, but Solomon and the Israelites sacrificed at the high places nevertheless.

3:3 showed his love for the LORD. Solomon generally followed in David's example in walking with God, except for sacrificing at the Canaanites' high places, opening the way for the Canaanites' religion to creep into Israel.

3:5 LORD appeared ... in a dream. In ancient Israel, God often revealed his will to individuals in a dream. In this way, he spoke to Solomon, Jacob (Gen. 28:10–15; 31:11), Joseph (Gen. 37:5–8) and Nebuchadnezzar (Dan. 2:28–30), among others.

3:7 a little child ... do not know. Solomon, about twenty years old when he became king, humbly admitted his inexperience and immaturity. He acknowledged his dependence on God.

to have the wisdom to face the challenges you face right now?

never have been anyone like you, nor will there ever be. 13Moreover, I
will give you what you have not asked for—both riches and honor—
so that in your lifetime you will have no equal among kings. 14And if
you walk in my ways and obey my statutes and commands as David
your father did, I will give you a long life." 15Then Solomon awoke—
and he realized it had been a dream.

He returned to Jerusalem, stood before the ark of the Lord's covenant and sacrificed burnt offerings and fellowship offerings.[a] Then
he gave a feast for all his court.

A Wise Ruling

16Now two prostitutes came to the king and stood before him.
17One of them said, "My lord, this woman and I live in the same
house. I had a baby while she was there with me. 18The third day after
my child was born, this woman also had a baby. We were alone; there
was no one in the house but the two of us.
19"During the night this woman's son died because she lay on him.
20So she got up in the middle of the night and took my son from my
side while I your servant was asleep. She put him by her breast and
put her dead son by my breast. 21The next morning, I got up to nurse
my son—and he was dead! But when I looked at him closely in the
morning light, I saw that it wasn't the son I had borne."

22The other woman said, "No! The living one is my son; the dead
one is yours."

But the first one insisted, "No! The dead one is yours; the living one
is mine." And so they argued before the king.

23The king said, "This one says, 'My son is alive and your son is
dead,' while that one says, 'No! Your son is dead and mine is alive.'"

24Then the king said, "Bring me a sword." So they brought a sword
for the king. 25He then gave an order: "Cut the living child in two and
give half to one and half to the other."

26The woman whose son was alive was filled with compassion for
her son and said to the king, "Please, my lord, give her the living
baby! Don't kill him!"

But the other said, "Neither I nor you shall have him. Cut him in
two!"

27Then the king gave his ruling: "Give the living baby to the first
woman. Do not kill him; she is his mother."

28When all Israel heard the verdict the king had given, they held the
king in awe, because they saw that he had wisdom from God to administer justice.

OPEN How did your parents settle disputes you had with your siblings?

STUDY The "discerning heart" that Solomon was granted in the first part of this chapter is illustrated here in the second half. He decides a tough case brought by two mothers over a dead child, and his decision inspires the people's confidence in him. **1.** What surprises you most about this case brought before Solomon: That a dispute between prostitutes would be brought before the king? That Solomon would even propose such a violent resolution? That the other mother didn't see through this ruse? That a prostitute would be such a devoted mother? **2.** For what quality was Solomon testing the women? **3.** Why was the second woman willing to have the child cut in two: She just didn't want to be the "loser"? She didn't want to mourn alone? She would do anything not to admit her lie? **4.** Would this decision have filled you with awe (v. 28)? Why do you think Israel was so impressed?

APPLY In what area of your life are you most likely to have to make a tough decision like Solomon had to make: With arguing children? With employees in a dispute? With a dispute in your family?

[a]15 Traditionally *peace offerings*

3:13 give you ... riches and honor. Solomon's request for wisdom pleased God. Instead of asking for riches or power, Solomon knew his greatest need was for discernment from God. In his generosity, God said he would give *Solomon riches and honor in addition to* the wisdom he requested.

3:15 stood before the ark of the LORD's covenant and sacrificed. Instead of making an offering to God at the high place, Solomon went to the tabernacle. Since only the high priest could enter there once a year, the king stood outside, facing the ark and made burnt offerings to show his dedication to God. He also made fellowship offerings to symbolize the relationship people can enjoy with God and others through God's grace.

3:17 this woman and I live in the same house. Two prostitutes who shared a house, perhaps a brothel, were able to approach the king asking that he judge a dispute between them.

3:28 saw that he had wisdom. The people knew from this incident that God had given Solomon great discernment so that he could administer justice wisely.

Solomon's Officials and Governors

4 So King Solomon ruled over all Israel. ²And these were his chief officials:

Azariah son of Zadok—the priest;
³Elihoreph and Ahijah, sons of Shisha—secretaries;
Jehoshaphat son of Ahilud—recorder;
⁴Benaiah son of Jehoiada—commander in chief;
Zadok and Abiathar—priests;
⁵Azariah son of Nathan—in charge of the district officers;
Zabud son of Nathan—a priest and personal adviser to the king;
⁶Ahishar—in charge of the palace;
Adoniram son of Abda—in charge of forced labor.

⁷Solomon also had twelve district governors over all Israel, who supplied provisions for the king and the royal household. Each one had to provide supplies for one month in the year. ⁸These are their names:

Ben-Hur—in the hill country of Ephraim;
⁹Ben-Deker—in Makaz, Shaalbim, Beth Shemesh and Elon Bethhanan;
¹⁰Ben-Hesed—in Arubboth (Socoh and all the land of Hepher were his);
¹¹Ben-Abinadab—in Naphoth Dor[a] (he was married to Taphath daughter of Solomon);
¹²Baana son of Ahilud—in Taanach and Megiddo, and in all of Beth Shan next to Zarethan below Jezreel, from Beth Shan to Abel Meholah across to Jokmeam;
¹³Ben-Geber—in Ramoth Gilead (the settlements of Jair son of Manasseh in Gilead were his, as well as the district of Argob in Bashan and its sixty large walled cities with bronze gate bars);
¹⁴Ahinadab son of Iddo—in Mahanaim;
¹⁵Ahimaaz—in Naphtali (he had married Basemath daughter of Solomon);
¹⁶Baana son of Hushai—in Asher and in Aloth;
¹⁷Jehoshaphat son of Paruah—in Issachar;
¹⁸Shimei son of Ela—in Benjamin;
¹⁹Geber son of Uri—in Gilead (the country of Sihon king of the Amorites and the country of Og king of Bashan). He was the only governor over the district.

[a]11 Or *in the heights of Dor*

OPEN If someone were in charge of providing you with supplies for a month, what would you want to most make sure that they provided: Plenty of chocolate? Enough beer to drink while watching football? Healthy, fat-free options? Tissues for when I watch heart-wrenching movies? Lots of red meat? Interesting desserts? Other?

STUDY No ruler rules alone, and here we have a list of those officials who helped Solomon rule. **1.** Which names do you recognize? Who seem to be carry-overs from David's administration (vv. 2–6; 1:32–33; 2 Sam. 8:16)? **2.** Which ones carry on the professions of their parents, and which ones seem determined to do otherwise (vv. 2,5)? **3.** What officials might have been accused of getting their jobs by "marrying the boss's daughter"? **4.** For what major projects will the king use "forced labor" (v. 6; 5:13–14)? **5.** How do you think the district governors will "supply provisions" for the royal court each month? How do you think the people felt about provisions from their region supplying the royal court? How does this compare with the taxes you pay? Do you agree with the way they are used?

APPLY Have you ever been accused of getting a position by some other means than by your ability? How did such an accusation make you feel?

4:1 Solomon ruled over all Israel. Israel's borders expanded under Solomon's leadership, another manifestation of his wisdom in ruling.

4:4 Benaiah. Commander in chief of the entire army. As one of David's mighty men, he did not participate in Adonijah's plots. He had participated in Solomon's anointment at Gihon. Benaiah is also the soldier who executed Adonijah upon Solomon's command.

4:5 Azariah. He was in charge of the 12 district officers in verses 8–19. This is not Azariah the priest in verse 2. **Zabud.** A priest of the priestly line and a personal advisor to Solomon.

4:6 Ahishar—in charge of the palace. Ahishar supervised the servants and other workers of the palace. Adoniram supervised non-Israelites living in Israel who were conscripted to work as forced labor for the king.

4:7 had twelve district governors. Solomon needed revenues to support his military forces. He divided Israel into 12 districts with a governor for each who collected taxes for the royal household. Two of the governors were Solomon's sons-in-law. Judah was not included in the districts.

4:13 sixty large walled cities. The Israelites had captured these from Og, king of Bashan (Deut. 3:3–5).

OPEN If you had to choose one period of your life as the happiest, what period would it be? What made it so happy?

STUDY After Solomon established his rule there came an idyllic time in Israel's history. Material goods were abundant because of the vastness of Solomon's kingdom, and Solomon's wisdom made justice equally abundant. **1.** What does verse 20 say about the national mood of Israel under Solomon? **2.** How does the size of Solomon's kingdom (v. 21) compare to Israel today? **3.** How would you describe Solomon's lifestyle: Indulgent? Luxurious? Wasteful? Garish and opulent? **4.** What *two* things does this section compare to "sand on the seashore" (vv. 20,29)? **5.** If you compared Solomon's wisdom to someone today, who might that person be? **6.** What were some areas where Solomon had particularly great expertise? **7.** What effect do you think Solomon's wisdom had on national identity and pride?

APPLY What is the source of your greatest pride right now: Possessions? Education? Family life? Appearance? Status? Accomplishments? The strides you have made spiritually? Other?

OPEN 1. What kinds of things did you trade as a child: Marbles? Dolls? Baseball cards? Books? Lunch? **2.** What trade or trades do you remember as a particularly good deal?

STUDY Solomon now turns his attention to building a temple, and he makes a deal for timber

Solomon's Daily Provisions

20The people of Judah and Israel were as numerous as the sand on
the seashore; they ate, they drank and they were happy. 21And Solomon ruled over all the kingdoms from the River[a] to the land of the
Philistines, as far as the border of Egypt. These countries brought
tribute and were Solomon's subjects all his life.
22Solomon's daily provisions were thirty cors[b] of fine flour and sixty cors[c] of meal, 23ten head of stall-fed cattle, twenty of pasture-fed
cattle and a hundred sheep and goats, as well as deer, gazelles, roe-
bucks and choice fowl. 24For he ruled over all the kingdoms west of
the River, from Tiphsah to Gaza, and had peace on all sides. 25During
Solomon's lifetime Judah and Israel, from Dan to Beersheba, lived in
safety, each man under his own vine and fig tree.
26Solomon had four[d] thousand stalls for chariot horses, and twelve
thousand horses.[e]
27The district officers, each in his month, supplied provisions for
King Solomon and all who came to the king's table. They saw to it
that nothing was lacking. 28They also brought to the proper place
their quotas of barley and straw for the chariot horses and the other
horses.

Solomon's Wisdom

29God gave Solomon wisdom and very great insight, and a breadth
of understanding as measureless as the sand on the seashore. 30Sol-
omon's wisdom was greater than the wisdom of all the men of the
East, and greater than all the wisdom of Egypt. 31He was wiser than
any other man, including Ethan the Ezrahite—wiser than Heman,
Calcol and Darda, the sons of Mahol. And his fame spread to all the
surrounding nations. 32He spoke three thousand proverbs and his
songs numbered a thousand and five. 33He described plant life, from
the cedar of Lebanon to the hyssop that grows out of walls. He also
taught about animals and birds, reptiles and fish. 34Men of all nations
came to listen to Solomon's wisdom, sent by all the kings of the
world, who had heard of his wisdom.

Preparations for Building the Temple

5 When Hiram king of Tyre heard that Solomon had been anointed
king to succeed his father David, he sent his envoys to Solomon,
because he had always been on friendly terms with David. 2Solomon
sent back this message to Hiram:

[a]*21* That is, the Euphrates; also in verse 24 [b]*22* That is, probably about 185 bushels (about 6.6 kiloliters) [c]*22* That is, probably about 375 bushels (about 13.2 kiloliters) [d]*26* Some Septuagint manuscripts (see also 2 Chron. 9:25); Hebrew *forty* [e]*26* Or *charioteers*

4:21 from the River to the land of the Philistines. Solomon's kingdom reached from the Euphrates River on the east and north to Egypt on the south and to the land of the Philistines on the west, although not all of these lands were incorporated into Israel's boundaries.

4:31 wiser ... man. Solomon's well-known wisdom surpassed that of the men of the East, probably from Mesopotamia, as well as the legendary wisdom of Egypt.

4:32 spoke three thousand proverbs. The book of Proverbs contains several hundred of Solomon's proverbs, and a few also appear in Ecclesiastes. One of his compositions is the Song of Songs.

4:34 all nations came to listen. Not every king sent a representative to visit Solomon, but many distinguished visitors from distant lands traveled to visit Solomon and his legendary wisdom. He received guests gladly. God's promise that he would be the wisest man was fulfilled (3:12).

5:1 Hiram. An ally of David, he had ruled Tyre for 34 years. From this important port city on the Mediterranean, he had provided workers and supplies, including cedars from the western slopes

3"You know that because of the wars waged against my father
David from all sides, he could not build a temple for the Name of
the LORD his God until the LORD put his enemies under his feet.
4But now the LORD my God has given me rest on every side, and
there is no adversary or disaster. 5I intend, therefore, to build a
temple for the Name of the LORD my God, as the LORD told my
father David, when he said, 'Your son whom I will put on the
throne in your place will build the temple for my Name.'
6"So give orders that cedars of Lebanon be cut for me. My men
will work with yours, and I will pay you for your men whatever
wages you set. You know that we have no one so skilled in felling
timber as the Sidonians."

7When Hiram heard Solomon's message, he was greatly pleased
and said, "Praise be to the LORD today, for he has given David a wise
son to rule over this great nation."
8So Hiram sent word to Solomon:

"I have received the message you sent me and will do all you
want in providing the cedar and pine logs. 9My men will haul
them down from Lebanon to the sea, and I will float them in rafts
by sea to the place you specify. There I will separate them and
you can take them away. And you are to grant my wish by providing food for my royal household."

10In this way Hiram kept Solomon supplied with all the cedar and
pine logs he wanted, 11and Solomon gave Hiram twenty thousand
cors[a] of wheat as food for his household, in addition to twenty thousand baths[b,c] of pressed olive oil. Solomon continued to do this for
Hiram year after year. 12The LORD gave Solomon wisdom, just as he
had promised him. There were peaceful relations between Hiram and
Solomon, and the two of them made a treaty.
13King Solomon conscripted laborers from all Israel—thirty thousand men. 14He sent them off to Lebanon in shifts of ten thousand a
month, so that they spent one month in Lebanon and two months at
home. Adoniram was in charge of the forced labor. 15Solomon had
seventy thousand carriers and eighty thousand stonecutters in the
hills, 16as well as thirty-three hundred[d] foremen who supervised the
project and directed the workmen. 17At the king's command they removed from the quarry large blocks of quality stone to provide a

[a]*11* That is, probably about 125,000 bushels (about 4,400 kiloliters) [b]*11* Septuagint (see also 2 Chron. 2:10); Hebrew *twenty cors* [c]*11* That is, about 115,000 gallons (about 440 kiloliters) [d]*16* Hebrew; some Septuagint manuscripts (see also 2 Chron. 2:2, 18) *thirty-six hundred*

with the king of Tyre. He then proceeds to conscript labor for the building process. **1.** Why does Hiram send a delegation to Solomon: To keep communication lines open? To honor him? To appease him? **2.** How much choice do you think Hiram had in going along with Solomon's proposal: Completely free? It was that or be invaded? Free choice—but it would have strained relations if he had done otherwise? **3.** Why did Hiram think Solomon's proposal was particularly wise: It was a win-win? He felt Israel needed a temple? Solomon affirmed and relied on the skills of Hiram's people (v. 6)? The proposal promoted peace? **4.** What work schedule does Solomon arrange for his conscripted labor? Is it fair? **5.** After Solomon's death, the people complained about how hard his work projects were on them (12:1–17), and these issues were influential in dividing the kingdom. Do you think this project fulfilled the hardships introduced?

APPLY 1. What are you seeking to "build" in your life right now: A safe and happy family? A portfolio of stocks and investments? A better world—at least in your corner? A business that truly serves people? A group where others can come? **2.** Who can you partner with in order to build more effectively? What do you need to do to make such a partnership win-win?

---

of the Lebanon Mountains east of Tyre, to build David's palace.

5:3 David ... could not build a temple. David made preparations for the temple even though God would not allow him to build it. David had spent most of his life at war. But God had promised David that his son would build God's temple (2 Sam. 7:1–17).

5:7 Praise be to the LORD. Here Hiram acknowledged Solomon's God to express his approval of Solomon's plans and his enthusiastic agreement with the treaty between the two kings.

5:9 grant my wish by providing food. Solomon agreed to provide food for Hiram's royal household in exchange for the materials supplied. Wheat and olive oil were not plentiful in or around Tyre.

5:13 laborers. Solomon drafted thousands of non-Israelite men into temporary service for him, which they performed along with their other responsibilities.

5:17 removed from the quarry large blocks of quality stone. Stonecutters cut massive limestone blocks out of the quarry in the hills north of Jerusalem. Carriers hauled them from place to place with great difficulty.

foundation of dressed stone for the temple. [18]The craftsmen of Solomon and Hiram and the men of Gebal[a] cut and prepared the timber and stone for the building of the temple.

Solomon Builds the Temple

6 In the four hundred and eightieth[b] year after the Israelites had come out of Egypt, in the fourth year of Solomon's reign over Israel, in the month of Ziv, the second month, he began to build the temple of the LORD.

[2]The temple that King Solomon built for the LORD was sixty cubits long, twenty wide and thirty high.[c] [3]The portico at the front of the main hall of the temple extended the width of the temple, that is twenty cubits,[d] and projected ten cubits[e] from the front of the temple. [4]He made narrow clerestory windows in the temple. [5]Against the walls of the main hall and inner sanctuary he built a structure around the building, in which there were side rooms. [6]The lowest floor was five cubits[f] wide, the middle floor six cubits[g] and the third floor seven.[h] He made offset ledges around the outside of the temple so that nothing would be inserted into the temple walls.

[7]In building the temple, only blocks dressed at the quarry were used, and no hammer, chisel or any other iron tool was heard at the temple site while it was being built.

[8]The entrance to the lowest[i] floor was on the south side of the temple; a stairway led up to the middle level and from there to the third. [9]So he built the temple and completed it, roofing it with beams and cedar planks. [10]And he built the side rooms all along the temple. The height of each was five cubits, and they were attached to the temple by beams of cedar.

[11]The word of the LORD came to Solomon: [12]"As for this temple you are building, if you follow my decrees, carry out my regulations and keep all my commands and obey them, I will fulfill through you the promise I gave to David your father. [13]And I will live among the Israelites and will not abandon my people Israel."

[14]So Solomon built the temple and completed it. [15]He lined its interior walls with cedar boards, paneling them from the floor of the temple to the ceiling, and covered the floor of the temple with planks of pine. [16]He partitioned off twenty cubits[d] at the rear of the temple with

[a]*18* That is, Byblos [b]*1* Hebrew; Septuagint *four hundred and fortieth* [c]*2* That is, about 90 feet (about 27 meters) long and 30 feet (about 9 meters) wide and 45 feet (about 13.5 meters) high [d]*3,16* That is, about 30 feet (about 9 meters) [e]*3* That is, about 15 feet (about 4.5 meters) [f]*6* That is, about 7 1/2 feet (about 2.3 meters); also in verses 10 and 24 [g]*6* That is, about 9 feet (about 2.7 meters) [h]*6* That is, about 10 1/2 feet (about 3.1 meters) [i]*8* Septuagint; Hebrew *middle*

OPEN 1. What do you remember of the building where you went to church (or which was in your neighborhood) as a child? What drew your eye: Stained glass windows? A steeple? Stone work or unusual architecture? How did going in that building make you feel? **2.** If someone were to ask, what special thing would you want in a new church building, what would you say?

STUDY Solomon builds the temple of the finest materials available at the time—the best cedars and the finest gold. It is an artistic accomplishment with many fine carvings. **1.** Why do you think they would have dated the building of the temple in relationship to the exodus? **2.** How does the size of the temple compare to the building where your church meets? **3.** Have you ever lived or worked in a building that was under construction? Why do you think it was important that no hammer, chisel or iron tool was heard at the building site? **4.** What agreement does God reaffirm in relationship to the building of this temple (vv. 11–13)? **5.** What art adorns the temple? What significance do you see, if any, in what is depicted? **6.** How long does it take to build the temple? **7.** What do you think Solomon was seeking to express about the character of God by the way he built this temple?

APPLY 1. In what environment do you feel you can best worship God: In an intimate little chapel? In a grand cathedral with high arching ceilings and visual art? Outdoors with no building of any kind around? **2.** What does your choice say about the aspects of God you most

---

5:18 The craftsmen of Solomon and Hiram and the men of Gebal. These men worked together to ready the timber and stone for various uses in the construction of the temple. Gebal was located 13 miles north of modern-day Beirut and sixty miles north of Tyre.

6:1 fourth year of Solomon's reign. This verse adds weight to the dates of Solomon's reign as being 971-931 B.C., as established in ancient writings. Solomon's death and the division of the kingdom occurred in 930 B.C. The years set out in this verse also help set the time of the exodus from Egypt at 1446 B.C.

6:2 temple. The temple was twice the size of the tabernacle and of similar design. It was about ninety feet long, thirty feet wide and 45 feet high, with 2,700 square feet of floor space, divided into the Most Holy Place, the Holy Place, and an outer courtyard.

6:12 if you follow my decrees. God reaffirms the promise he had already made to David to establish David's descendants on the throne forever (2 Sam. 7:13). God would fulfill the promise through Solomon and also protect the nation, if he would obey God. A righteous king would bring blessing on his nation.

6:13 live among the Israelites ... not abandon my people. God said that the nation would enjoy fellowship with him if Solomon were faithful to God. Israel lost out on some of this experience because of Solomon's later sin.

6:16 inner sanctuary, the Most Holy Place. The Most Holy Place was

cedar boards from floor to ceiling to form within the temple an inner
sanctuary, the Most Holy Place. 17The main hall in front of this room
was forty cubits[a] long. 18The inside of the temple was cedar, carved
with gourds and open flowers. Everything was cedar; no stone was to
be seen.
19He prepared the inner sanctuary within the temple to set the ark
of the covenant of the LORD there. 20The inner sanctuary was twenty
cubits long, twenty wide and twenty high.[b] He overlaid the inside
with pure gold, and he also overlaid the altar of cedar. 21Solomon
covered the inside of the temple with pure gold, and he extended gold
chains across the front of the inner sanctuary, which was overlaid
with gold. 22So he overlaid the whole interior with gold. He also overlaid with gold the altar that belonged to the inner sanctuary.
23In the inner sanctuary he made a pair of cherubim of olive wood,
each ten cubits[c] high. 24One wing of the first cherub was five cubits
long, and the other wing five cubits—ten cubits from wing tip to wing
tip. 25The second cherub also measured ten cubits, for the two cherubim were identical in size and shape. 26The height of each cherub was
ten cubits. 27He placed the cherubim inside the innermost room of
the temple, with their wings spread out. The wing of one cherub
touched one wall, while the wing of the other touched the other wall,
and their wings touched each other in the middle of the room. 28He
overlaid the cherubim with gold.
29On the walls all around the temple, in both the inner and outer
rooms, he carved cherubim, palm trees and open flowers. 30He also
covered the floors of both the inner and outer rooms of the temple
with gold.
31For the entrance of the inner sanctuary he made doors of olive
wood with five-sided jambs. 32And on the two olive wood doors he
carved cherubim, palm trees and open flowers, and overlaid the cherubim and palm trees with beaten gold. 33In the same way he made
four-sided jambs of olive wood for the entrance to the main hall. 34He
also made two pine doors, each having two leaves that turned in
sockets. 35He carved cherubim, palm trees and open flowers on them
and overlaid them with gold hammered evenly over the carvings.
36And he built the inner courtyard of three courses of dressed stone
and one course of trimmed cedar beams.
37The foundation of the temple of the LORD was laid in the fourth
year, in the month of Ziv. 38In the eleventh year in the month of Bul,

[a]17 That is, about 60 feet (about 18 meters) [b]20 That is, about 30 feet (about 9 meters) long, wide and high
[c]23 That is, about 15 feet (about 4.5 meters)

hunger for: A God who is close at all times? A God who is grand, powerful and glorious? A God who links you with all of creation? Why do you think you chose what you chose?

a thirty-foot cube covered with 21 tons of pure gold. It held the Ark of the Covenant and the mercy seat guarded by two cherubim. In front of the Most Holy Place, and separated from it by a veil, was the Holy Place (the main hall).

6:19 ark of the covenant. This symbolized God's presence among his people and contained the two stone tablets of the Ten Commandments (Deut. 10:1–5).

6:20 inner sanctuary ... pure gold. Gold symbolized wealth and, along with silver, was abundant during Solomon's reign. In the Old Testament, most references to gold refer to the tabernacle or to Solomon's temple.

6:23 pair of cherubim. The only likeness allowed in the worship of the Lord were these creatures with the body of a lion, a face like a human face and the wings of a huge bird (Ex. 25:18). Their wings spanned the width of the room.

6:31 doors. Olive wood doors leading from the Holy Place had five-sided jambs or doorframes. They may have been sliding doors. The cypress doors leading from the porch into the main hall (the Holy Place) had four-sided jambs and folded in half to open. The doors were decorated with carved cherubim, palm trees and flowers.

6:36 built the inner courtyard. Only the priests could use the upper inner courtyard. It was an open plaza surrounding the temple. A wall divided it from the lower and larger outer courtyard.

the eighth month, the temple was finished in all its details according to its specifications. He had spent seven years building it.

Solomon Builds His Palace

7 It took Solomon thirteen years, however, to complete the construction of his palace. 2He built the Palace of the Forest of Lebanon a hundred cubits long, fifty wide and thirty high,[a] with four rows of cedar columns supporting trimmed cedar beams. 3It was roofed with cedar above the beams that rested on the columns—forty-five beams, fifteen to a row. 4Its windows were placed high in sets of three, facing each other. 5All the doorways had rectangular frames; they were in the front part in sets of three, facing each other.[b]

6He made a colonnade fifty cubits long and thirty wide.[c] In front of it was a portico, and in front of that were pillars and an overhanging roof.

7He built the throne hall, the Hall of Justice, where he was to judge, and he covered it with cedar from floor to ceiling.[d] 8And the palace in which he was to live, set farther back, was similar in design. Solomon also made a palace like this hall for Pharaoh's daughter, whom he had married.

9All these structures, from the outside to the great courtyard and from foundation to eaves, were made of blocks of high-grade stone cut to size and trimmed with a saw on their inner and outer faces. 10The foundations were laid with large stones of good quality, some measuring ten cubits[e] and some eight.[f] 11Above were high-grade stones, cut to size, and cedar beams. 12The great courtyard was surrounded by a wall of three courses of dressed stone and one course of trimmed cedar beams, as was the inner courtyard of the temple of the LORD with its portico.

The Temple's Furnishings

13King Solomon sent to Tyre and brought Huram,[g] 14whose mother was a widow from the tribe of Naphtali and whose father was a man of Tyre and a craftsman in bronze. Huram was highly skilled and experienced in all kinds of bronze work. He came to King Solomon and did all the work assigned to him.

15He cast two bronze pillars, each eighteen cubits high and twelve

[a]2 That is, about 150 feet (about 46 meters) long, 75 feet (about 23 meters) wide and 45 feet (about 13.5 meters) high [b]5 The meaning of the Hebrew for this verse is uncertain. [c]6 That is, about 75 feet (about 23 meters) long and 45 feet (about 13.5 meters) wide [d]7 Vulgate and Syriac; Hebrew *floor* [e]10 That is, about 15 feet (about 4.5 meters) [f]10 That is, about 12 feet (about 3.6 meters) [g]13 Hebrew *Hiram,* a variant of *Huram;* also in verses 40 and 45

OPEN **1.** Where did you live when you were ten years old? What do you especially remember about that home? **2.** If you were to build your "dream home" today, where would it be?

STUDY After building the temple, Solomon proceeds to build his palace, which was both his home and place from which to govern. He also includes a special palace for his wife, the daughter of Pharaoh. **1.** Which took longer to build—the temple or Solomon's palace? Which was larger? **2.** Does the relative size of the palace over the temple say anything of Solomon's priorities? **3.** If you were Pharaoh's daughter, how would you feel about having your own palace: Honored? Alienated—from your husband? In Fantasy Land? **4.** How would you have felt in such a palace if you were bringing an issue before Solomon to judge?

APPLY How are you feeling right now about the blessings God has given you in your life?

OPEN **1.** What do you remember making that was displayed in your home when you were a child: A piece of art work? A bookshelf or pottery? A weaving or wall-hanging? How did you feel about making it and having it displayed? **2.** What have you made to furnish or spruce up your present home?

STUDY Solomon has Huram, a metal craftsman from Tyre come and make a variety of furnishings and finishing touches for the

---

7:2 built the Palace of the Forest of Lebanon. The palace was located in Jerusalem, and Lebanese cedar was used extensively throughout. It measured 150 feet by 75 feet and was 45 feet high with 11,250 square feet of floor space, four times the size of the temple. It probably consisted of several connected buildings.

7:8 the palace in which he was to live. Solomon's residence and a residence for Pharaoh's daughter, his wife. Both were of a design compatible with the palace. They were all attached.

7:9 blocks of high-grade stone. The best quality limestone was used, hand-cut with a saw. It had to be cut and trimmed right after it was quarried, because it hardens after exposure to the elements. All of the buildings were made of stone on stone foundations.

7:12 great courtyard was surrounded. A surrounding wall like the one around the inner courtyard of the temple protected the great courtyard. The courtyard enclosed all of the temple and palace buildings.

7:14 widow. Huram's mother was an Israelite widow. His father was a Phoenician from Tyre. He was a skilled craftsman who came to do bronze work for the palace.

7:15 He cast two bronze pillars. These beautiful pillars may have been freestanding, each 27 feet high and 18 feet in circumference, near the temple entrance on both sides of the portico

cubits around,[a] by line. 16He also made two capitals of cast bronze to
set on the tops of the pillars; each capital was five cubits[b] high. 17A
network of interwoven chains festooned the capitals on top of the
pillars, seven for each capital. 18He made pomegranates in two rows[c]
encircling each network to decorate the capitals on top of the pillars.[d]
He did the same for each capital. 19The capitals on top of the pillars in
the portico were in the shape of lilies, four cubits[e] high. 20On the
capitals of both pillars, above the bowl-shaped part next to the network, were the two hundred pomegranates in rows all around. 21He
erected the pillars at the portico of the temple. The pillar to the south
he named Jakin[f] and the one to the north Boaz.[g] 22The capitals on top
were in the shape of lilies. And so the work on the pillars was completed.

23He made the Sea of cast metal, circular in shape, measuring ten
cubits[h] from rim to rim and five cubits high. It took a line of thirty
cubits[i] to measure around it. 24Below the rim, gourds encircled it—ten
to a cubit. The gourds were cast in two rows in one piece with the Sea.

25The Sea stood on twelve bulls, three facing north, three facing
west, three facing south and three facing east. The Sea rested on top
of them, and their hindquarters were toward the center. 26It was a
handbreadth[j] in thickness, and its rim was like the rim of a cup, like a
lily blossom. It held two thousand baths.[k]

27He also made ten movable stands of bronze; each was four cubits
long, four wide and three high.[l] 28This is how the stands were made:
They had side panels attached to uprights. 29On the panels between
the uprights were lions, bulls and cherubim—and on the uprights as
well. Above and below the lions and bulls were wreaths of hammered
work. 30Each stand had four bronze wheels with bronze axles, and
each had a basin resting on four supports, cast with wreaths on each
side. 31On the inside of the stand there was an opening that had a circular frame one cubit[m] deep. This opening was round, and with its
basework it measured a cubit and a half.[n] Around its opening there
was engraving. The panels of the stands were square, not round.
32The four wheels were under the panels, and the axles of the wheels
were attached to the stand. The diameter of each wheel was a cubit
and a half. 33The wheels were made like chariot wheels; the axles,
rims, spokes and hubs were all of cast metal.

[a]*15* That is, about 27 feet (about 8.1 meters) high and 18 feet (about 5.4 meters) around [b]*16* That is, about 7 1/2 feet (about 2.3 meters); also in verse 23 [c]*18* Two Hebrew manuscripts and Septuagint; most Hebrew manuscripts *made the pillars, and there were two rows* [d]*18* Many Hebrew manuscripts and Syriac; most Hebrew manuscripts *pomegranates* [e]*19* That is, about 6 feet (about 1.8 meters); also in verse 38 [f]*21 Jakin* probably means *he establishes.* [g]*21 Boaz* probably means *in him is strength.* [h]*23* That is, about 15 feet (about 4.5 meters) [i]*23* That is, about 45 feet (about 13.5 meters) [j]*26* That is, about 3 inches (about 8 centimeters) [k]*26* That is, probably about 11,500 gallons (about 44 kiloliters); the Septuagint does not have this sentence. [l]*27* That is, about 6 feet (about 1.8 meters) long and wide and about 4 1/2 feet (about 1.3 meters) high [m]*31* That is, about 1 1/2 feet (about 0.5 meter) [n]*31* That is, about 2 1/4 feet (about 0.7 meter); also in verse 32

temple. He also brings to the temple some items dedicated by his father David. **1.** Why is Huram an ideal worker for this project? What would he bring from the Israelite side of his family (v. 14)? From the foreign side? **2.** Since they do not seem to hold anything up, what do you think is the purpose of the pillars? Why name them (vv. 15,21)? **3.** What is the function of the bronze "Sea"? What was the purpose of the ten movable stands (v. 26; 2 Chr. 4:6)? **4.** How was the golden altar used (Ex 30:6–10)? **5.** What silver and gold "things" had David dedicated (2 Sam. 8:9–12)? **6.** Why do you think the writer went to so much trouble describing so precisely what went into the temple: Because of what it symbolized? In case it later needed to be replaced? To feed trivia buffs?

APPLY 1. What item in your home has the most meaning to you right now? **2.** What item in your home would serve as the best symbol of who God is to you: Refrigerator—provider of good things? Fire place—provider of warmth and comfort? Fine antique furniture—spiritual roots and tradition? Window—a way of seeing the world? Washing machine—removes the soil of our sin and imperfection? Other? **3.** What do you need to do to bring God into your home in more than a symbolic way?

(front porch). They represented God's power and might.

7:21 Jakin and ... Boaz. Jakin, the name of the south pillar, means "he will establish," and Boaz means "in him is strength." The names symbolize God's security and strength available to the nation in obedience to him.

7:23 Sea of cast metal ... thirty cubits. This was a laver, or a large basin to wash in. This basin was 15 feet across and 7.5 feet high, holding 11,500 gallons of water. It also served as a reservoir for the temple. The circumference, or distance around the circular rim of the basin was 3 cubits. In 2 Chronicles 4:5 this basin holds 17,500 gallons.

7:27 made ten movable stands. The stands were used to kill the animal sacrifices. Each was six feet square and 5.5 feet high. A basin holding 230 gallons of water rested on the surface of each. Each stand was decorated with panels on each side and had four bronze wheels. These stands or charts appear only here (2 Chr. 4).

34 Each stand had four handles, one on each corner, projecting from
the stand. 35 At the top of the stand there was a circular band half a
cubit[a] deep. The supports and panels were attached to the top of the
stand. 36 He engraved cherubim, lions and palm trees on the surfaces
of the supports and on the panels, in every available space, with
wreaths all around. 37 This is the way he made the ten stands. They
were all cast in the same molds and were identical in size and shape.
38 He then made ten bronze basins, each holding forty baths[b] and
measuring four cubits across, one basin to go on each of the ten
stands. 39 He placed five of the stands on the south side of the temple
and five on the north. He placed the Sea on the south side, at the
southeast corner of the temple. 40 He also made the basins and shovels
and sprinkling bowls.

So Huram finished all the work he had undertaken for King Solomon in the temple of the LORD:

41 the two pillars;
the two bowl-shaped capitals on top of the pillars;
the two sets of network decorating the two bowl-shaped capitals
on top of the pillars;
42 the four hundred pomegranates for the two sets of network (two
rows of pomegranates for each network, decorating the bowl-
shaped capitals on top of the pillars);
43 the ten stands with their ten basins;
44 the Sea and the twelve bulls under it;
45 the pots, shovels and sprinkling bowls.

All these objects that Huram made for King Solomon for the temple
of the LORD were of burnished bronze. 46 The king had them cast in
clay molds in the plain of the Jordan between Succoth and Zarethan.
47 Solomon left all these things unweighed, because there were so
many; the weight of the bronze was not determined.
48 Solomon also made all the furnishings that were in the LORD's
temple:

the golden altar;
the golden table on which was the bread of the Presence;
49 the lampstands of pure gold (five on the right and five on the left,
in front of the inner sanctuary);
the gold floral work and lamps and tongs;
50 the pure gold basins, wick trimmers, sprinkling bowls, dishes
and censers;
and the gold sockets for the doors of the innermost room, the
Most Holy Place, and also for the doors of the main hall of the
temple.

[a] *35* That is, about 3/4 foot (about 0.2 meter) [b] *38* That is, about 230 gallons (about 880 liters)

7:40 basins ... shovels ... sprinkling bowls. A second basin on each stand drained into a tank below the surface through an opening. Burnt offerings could be rinsed and the water drained from the surface. The stands and basins were not only decorative but functional. Like today's fireplace shovels, these were used to remove ashes from the altar.

7:46 clay molds. The bronze items were made in clay molds in the Jordan Valley about 35 miles north of the Dead Sea, east of the Jordan River.

7:48 golden altar ... table. This corresponded to and replaced the altar of incense in the tabernacle (Ex. 30:2–4). The ten golden tables replaced the table of the presence in the tabernacle. It may have consisted of one larger table and nine smaller ones.

[51]When all the work King Solomon had done for the temple of
the LORD was finished, he brought in the things his father David had
dedicated—the silver and gold and the furnishings—and he placed
them in the treasuries of the LORD's temple.

The Ark Brought to the Temple

8 Then King Solomon summoned into his presence at Jerusalem
the elders of Israel, all the heads of the tribes and the chiefs of
the Israelite families, to bring up the ark of the LORD's covenant from
Zion, the City of David. [2]All the men of Israel came together to King
Solomon at the time of the festival in the month of Ethanim, the seventh month.
[3]When all the elders of Israel had arrived, the priests took up the
ark, [4]and they brought up the ark of the LORD and the Tent of Meeting
and all the sacred furnishings in it. The priests and Levites carried
them up, [5]and King Solomon and the entire assembly of Israel that
had gathered about him were before the ark, sacrificing so many
sheep and cattle that they could not be recorded or counted.
[6]The priests then brought the ark of the LORD's covenant to its
place in the inner sanctuary of the temple, the Most Holy Place, and
put it beneath the wings of the cherubim. [7]The cherubim spread their
wings over the place of the ark and overshadowed the ark and its
carrying poles. [8]These poles were so long that their ends could be
seen from the Holy Place in front of the inner sanctuary, but not from
outside the Holy Place; and they are still there today. [9]There was
nothing in the ark except the two stone tablets that Moses had placed
in it at Horeb, where the LORD made a covenant with the Israelites
after they came out of Egypt.
[10]When the priests withdrew from the Holy Place, the cloud filled
the temple of the LORD. [11]And the priests could not perform their service because of the cloud, for the glory of the LORD filled his temple.
[12]Then Solomon said, "The LORD has said that he would dwell in a
dark cloud; [13]I have indeed built a magnificent temple for you, a place
for you to dwell forever."

OPEN 1. What is the closest thing you have to a "holy place": Retreat you have in the mountains? Place in your home where you go for your quiet times? Place that has special memories for you and your family? **2.** If you could designate one thing (piece of furniture, memento, picture, etc.) to symbolize how God has been present with you in your life, what would it be?

STUDY With the temple complete, Solomon brings in the Ark of the Covenant. **1.** Where does Solomon move the ark (v. 1)? **2.** Look at 2 Samuel 6:1–7. What has Solomon learned from David's mistakes in moving the ark (vv. 3–5)? In that context, what might have been the purpose of sacrificing so many sheep and cattle? **3.** What was in the ark? **4.** What filled the temple of the Lord after the priests withdrew from the Holy Place? What was its significance? **5.** To whom does Solomon give credit for the successful building of the temple (vv. 14–21)? **6.** Why do you think it was so important to Solomon and the people to have a home for the ark? Do you think that they believed that God would literally live there?

APPLY 1. What have you been able to accomplish that your parents were not able to do?

7:51 David had dedicated. David had already prepared and dedicated furnishings for the temple he had wanted to build for God (2 Sam. 8:11). They had been stored until the temple was built.

8:1 Solomon summoned ... Israel ... bring up the ark. This moving day was cause for great rejoicing. From now on, the temple would be the permanent center of worship. After all the furnishings for the temple were in place, the ark was brought from its temporary shelter in Jerusalem.

8:2 time of the festival. The temple was dedicated at the Feast of Tabernacles in the period corresponding with September–October (Lev. 23:33–36). The feast commemorated God's granting rest to his people in the Promised Land and also renewal of the covenant. Solomon called all the people to come for the dedication, and the feast time was lengthened to two weeks.

8:4 priests and Levites carried them up. God had required that the ark be carried by the priests on long poles. The ark was the only piece of furniture that was not newly made for the temple. As the people worshiped at the temple dedication, the priests sacrificed many burnt offerings.

8:8 poles ... could be seen. The poles by which the priests carried the ark passed through golden rings on the sides of the ark. God had commanded the priests to leave the poles in the rings (Ex. 25:15). When the doors into the Most Holy Place were open, the poles could be seen from the Holy Place but not from outside.

8:9 two stone tablets. The tablets containing the Ten Commandments were kept in the ark to remind Israel of its blessings and responsibilities under Mosaic Law. The pot of manna (Ex. 16:33–34) and Aaron's rod that had budded (Num. 17:10), also kept in the ark, may have been lost by Solomon's time.

8:10 the cloud. Just as a cloud had covered the tabernacle, now a cloud, the symbol of God's glory, filled the temple. This is sometimes called "shekinah glory," a visible representation of God's presence with his people.

8:12 dwell in a dark cloud. This means that God was both near and far, both within and above (Ex. 20:21). He was hidden by a dark cloud, but he was also present in his temple.

14While the whole assembly of Israel was standing there, the king
turned around and blessed them. 15Then he said:

"Praise be to the LORD, the God of Israel, who with his own
hand has fulfilled what he promised with his own mouth to my
father David. For he said, 16'Since the day I brought my people
Israel out of Egypt, I have not chosen a city in any tribe of Israel
to have a temple built for my Name to be there, but I have chosen
David to rule my people Israel.'

17"My father David had it in his heart to build a temple for the
Name of the LORD, the God of Israel. 18But the LORD said to my
father David, 'Because it was in your heart to build a temple for
my Name, you did well to have this in your heart. 19Nevertheless,
you are not the one to build the temple, but your son, who is
your own flesh and blood—he is the one who will build the temple for my Name.'

20"The LORD has kept the promise he made: I have succeeded
David my father and now I sit on the throne of Israel, just as the
LORD promised, and I have built the temple for the Name of
the LORD, the God of Israel. 21I have provided a place there for
the ark, in which is the covenant of the LORD that he made with
our fathers when he brought them out of Egypt."

Solomon's Prayer of Dedication

22Then Solomon stood before the altar of the LORD in front of the
whole assembly of Israel, spread out his hands toward heaven 23and
said:

"O LORD, God of Israel, there is no God like you in heaven
above or on earth below—you who keep your covenant of love
with your servants who continue wholeheartedly in your way.
24You have kept your promise to your servant David my father;
with your mouth you have promised and with your hand you
have fulfilled it—as it is today.

25"Now LORD, God of Israel, keep for your servant David my father the promises you made to him when you said, 'You shall
never fail to have a man to sit before me on the throne of Israel,
if only your sons are careful in all they do to walk before me as
you have done.' 26And now, O God of Israel, let your word that
you promised your servant David my father come true.

27"But will God really dwell on earth? The heavens, even the
highest heaven, cannot contain you. How much less this temple
I have built! 28Yet give attention to your servant's prayer and his
plea for mercy, O LORD my God. Hear the cry and the prayer that
your servant is praying in your presence this day. 29May your
eyes be open toward this temple night and day, this place of

2. In what ways has God helped you with this accomplishment?

____

OPEN 1. How comfortable are you with saying a public prayer at this point in your spiritual journey: Not if your life depended on it? Only if Jesus himself appeared in a vision and demanded it? If people were desperate for someone to do it? Anytime, if there is time to prepare? Anytime, at the spur of the moment? **2.** If you were to say a prayer for our nation right now, what would be the number one concern you would want to pray about?

STUDY With the temple built and the ark brought into it, Solomon now feels led to say a public prayer of dedication. In this prayer he calls on God to bless the temple and fulfill his promises to his people. **1.** Which of God's promises has Solomon seen fulfilled already (vv. 23–24)? **2.** What promises does Solomon hope to see fulfilled in the future (vv. 25–26)? **3.** Given what Solomon says in verse 27, why has he built the temple anyway: For his own ego? As a worship aid for the people? As a

8:23 no God like you in heaven above or on earth below. Solomon acknowledged God's uniqueness and his faithfulness (Ex. 9:14). This was an especially good reminder in view of the pagan deities of the surrounding Canaanites.

8:25 sons ... walk before me. Solomon prayed for his people, that God would continue to fulfill his promises to David and hear their prayers. As he interceded for his people, he emphasized the need for them to be faithful to God.

8:27 this temple I have built! Since God is infinite, no building, even a magnificent one, can contain him. And yet God chooses to dwell among his people.

8:28 Hear. The word appears five times in verses 28–30. Solomon knew that God hears and answers the prayers of obedient people. Thus, Solomon's prayer was also an exhortation to obedience.

which you said, 'My Name shall be there,' so that you will hear
the prayer your servant prays toward this place. 30 Hear the supplication of your servant and of your people Israel when they
pray toward this place. Hear from heaven, your dwelling place,
and when you hear, forgive.
31 "When a man wrongs his neighbor and is required to take an
oath and he comes and swears the oath before your altar in this
temple, 32 then hear from heaven and act. Judge between your
servants, condemning the guilty and bringing down on his own
head what he has done. Declare the innocent not guilty, and so
establish his innocence.
33 "When your people Israel have been defeated by an enemy
because they have sinned against you, and when they turn back
to you and confess your name, praying and making supplication
to you in this temple, 34 then hear from heaven and forgive the sin
of your people Israel and bring them back to the land you gave to
their fathers.
35 "When the heavens are shut up and there is no rain because
your people have sinned against you, and when they pray toward
this place and confess your name and turn from their sin
because you have afflicted them, 36 then hear from heaven and
forgive the sin of your servants, your people Israel. Teach them
the right way to live, and send rain on the land you gave your
people for an inheritance.
37 "When famine or plague comes to the land, or blight or
mildew, locusts or grasshoppers, or when an enemy besieges
them in any of their cities, whatever disaster or disease may
come, 38 and when a prayer or plea is made by any of your people
Israel—each one aware of the afflictions of his own heart, and
spreading out his hands toward this temple— 39 then hear from
heaven, your dwelling place. Forgive and act; deal with each man
according to all he does, since you know his heart (for you alone
know the hearts of all men), 40 so that they will fear you all the
time they live in the land you gave our fathers.
41 "As for the foreigner who does not belong to your people Israel but has come from a distant land because of your name—
42 for men will hear of your great name and your mighty hand and

symbolic residence where God could be honored? Other? **4.** What possible disasters does Solomon foresee coming as a result of the people's sin? What does he ask God to do in relation to these moral failures? **5.** Why is Solomon concerned that God hear the prayers of foreigners (v. 43)? **6.** When Solomon is blessing the people, what does he say about God's promises (v. 56)? **7.** What does Solomon say is Israel's side of the bargain, in relation to the promises of God (v. 61)?

APPLY 1. Which of God's promises is most important to you right now: The promise of eternal life (John 3:16)? The promise that Jesus is with you always (Matt. 28:20)? The promise of a peace the world cannot give (John 14:27)? The promise that all things work together for good for those who love God (Rom. 8:28)? The promise that nothing will separate us from the love of Christ (Rom. 8:35–39)? Other? **2.** Which of the promises listed above is hardest for you to accept and claim?

8:30 Hear from heaven, your dwelling place. God is everywhere at once. He is in heaven, and yet he also dwelt in the temple. Prayer was to be directed toward the temple because God was present there.

8:33 defeated by an enemy. Sin *against God caused defeat in battle* (Lev. 26:36–39). Solomon asked God to forgive when his people repent and confess their sins.

8:34 Israel ... to the land. One of the consequences of sin against God was being scattered in foreign lands (Lev. 26:41–45).

8:35 heavens are shut up ... there is no rain. Solomon told God the people confessed his name and turned from the sins that caused drought (Deut. 11:16–17).

8:37 disaster or disease. God allows his people to suffer trouble in order to restore relationships and renew their commitment to him. Good things result from that. Not all disasters or diseases are the result of sin (John 9:3), but this verse lists some of the troubles brought on by sin.

8:39 deal with each man. Perhaps a reference to his father David who, although he sinned, had an overall life of devotion to God. Solomon also knew that God's dealings with people were designed to bring them to himself and to righteous living.

8:40 fear you all the time. Experiencing God and his forgiveness produces a sense of awe, or fear, in human beings (Ps. 128:1). This reverence helps us to obey God.

8:41 foreigner. Solomon prayed for non-Israelites who had come because they had heard about God. These people were distinguished from resident (nonbelieving) aliens within the country (Deut. 10:18–19).

8:42 your great name ... mighty hand. Solomon knew that those who heard of God's power would be

your outstretched arm—when he comes and prays toward this
temple, 43then hear from heaven, your dwelling place, and do
whatever the foreigner asks of you, so that all the peoples of the
earth may know your name and fear you, as do your own people
Israel, and may know that this house I have built bears your
Name.

44"When your people go to war against their enemies, wherever you send them, and when they pray to the LORD toward the
city you have chosen and the temple I have built for your Name,
45then hear from heaven their prayer and their plea, and uphold
their cause.

46"When they sin against you—for there is no one who does
not sin—and you become angry with them and give them over to
the enemy, who takes them captive to his own land, far away or
near; 47and if they have a change of heart in the land where they
are held captive, and repent and plead with you in the land of
their conquerors and say, 'We have sinned, we have done wrong,
we have acted wickedly'; 48and if they turn back to you with all
their heart and soul in the land of their enemies who took them
captive, and pray to you toward the land you gave their fathers,
toward the city you have chosen and the temple I have built for
your Name; 49then from heaven, your dwelling place, hear their
prayer and their plea, and uphold their cause. 50And forgive your
people, who have sinned against you; forgive all the offenses
they have committed against you, and cause their conquerors to
show them mercy; 51for they are your people and your inheritance, whom you brought out of Egypt, out of that iron-smelting
furnace.

52"May your eyes be open to your servant's plea and to the
plea of your people Israel, and may you listen to them whenever
they cry out to you. 53For you singled them out from all the nations of the world to be your own inheritance, just as you declared through your servant Moses when you, O Sovereign LORD,
brought our fathers out of Egypt."

54When Solomon had finished all these prayers and supplications
to the LORD, he rose from before the altar of the LORD, where he had
been kneeling with his hands spread out toward heaven. 55He stood
and blessed the whole assembly of Israel in a loud voice, saying:

56"Praise be to the LORD, who has given rest to his people Israel just as he promised. Not one word has failed of all the good
promises he gave through his servant Moses. 57May the LORD our
God be with us as he was with our fathers; may he never leave us
nor forsake us. 58May he turn our hearts to him, to walk in all his
ways and to keep the commands, decrees and regulations he

impressed and would believe (Deut. 3:24). In this way, Solomon hoped that news of God's greatness would spread all over the earth.

8:52 whenever they cry out to you. Solomon summarized his prayer by asking God to always listen to his people, despite their sin. When they cry out in calamities and pain, Solomon prayed, forgive them and restore them.

8:53 to be your own inheritance. Another reference to God's special love for Israel (Ex. 19:5–6, Ps. 135:4).

8:58 commands, decrees and regulations he gave our fathers. Solomon's desire is that God remain with him and his people as God had with their ancestors. He knew that the people's conduct would determine whether they received blessings or curses. Their hearts must be right with God.

gave our fathers. 59And may these words of mine, which I have
prayed before the LORD, be near to the LORD our God day and
night, that he may uphold the cause of his servant and the cause
of his people Israel according to each day's need, 60so that all
the peoples of the earth may know that the LORD is God and that
there is no other. 61But your hearts must be fully committed to
the LORD our God, to live by his decrees and obey his commands,
as at this time."

The Dedication of the Temple

62Then the king and all Israel with him offered sacrifices before the
LORD. 63Solomon offered a sacrifice of fellowship offerings[a] to the
LORD: twenty-two thousand cattle and a hundred and twenty thousand sheep and goats. So the king and all the Israelites dedicated the
temple of the LORD.
64On that same day the king consecrated the middle part of the
courtyard in front of the temple of the LORD, and there he offered
burnt offerings, grain offerings and the fat of the fellowship offerings,
because the bronze altar before the LORD was too small to hold the
burnt offerings, the grain offerings and the fat of the fellowship offerings.
65So Solomon observed the festival at that time, and all Israel with
him—a vast assembly, people from Lebo[b] Hamath to the Wadi of
Egypt. They celebrated it before the LORD our God for seven days and
seven days more, fourteen days in all. 66On the following day he sent
the people away. They blessed the king and then went home, joyful
and glad in heart for all the good things the LORD had done for his
servant David and his people Israel.

The LORD Appears to Solomon

9 When Solomon had finished building the temple of the LORD and
the royal palace, and had achieved all he had desired to do, 2the
LORD appeared to him a second time, as he had appeared to him at
Gibeon. 3The LORD said to him:

"I have heard the prayer and plea you have made before me; I
have consecrated this temple, which you have built, by putting
my Name there forever. My eyes and my heart will always be
there.
4"As for you, if you walk before me in integrity of heart and uprightness, as David your father did, and do all I command and
observe my decrees and laws, 5I will establish your royal throne

[a]63 Traditionally *peace offerings*; also in verse 64 [b]65 Or *from the entrance to*

OPEN What is your favorite holiday?

STUDY Solomon wastes little time in making large-scale sacrifices in the temple. **1.** How do you react to the sacrifice of so many animals? **2.** Why was the bronze altar, which they had just completed, too small for all their offerings? **3.** What festival were they celebrating (8:2; Lev. 23:34,41–43)?

APPLY What are you most thankful for at this point in your life?

OPEN When you were a teenager, what did your parents have to warn you against most frequently: Staying out past curfew? Smoking? Drugs and alcohol? Driving too fast? Talking back? Skipping school? Other?

STUDY God talks to Solomon to once more warn him against actions that could make him lose his dynasty and make Israel lose his favor—actions like idolatry. **1.** What happened when God appeared to Solomon at Gibeon (3:5–15)? **2.** What does God promise to Solomon concerning the temple Solomon built?

8:59 the cause of his servant. The righteous ruler exalts his people. Solomon knew that his position was established by God. When he finished speaking, fire from heaven burned up the sacrifice on the altar (2 Chr. 7:1–3).

8:62 offered sacrifices before the LORD. Large numbers of animals were sacrificed: 22,000 cattle and 120,000 sheep and goats. Thousands of priests sacrificed on many auxiliary altars, and the celebration lasted for two weeks.

9:2 appeared ... at Gibeon. As God had revealed himself to Solomon at Gibeon in a dream (3:4–5), he appeared to him again in Jerusalem.

9:3 there forever. God assured Solomon of continued presence in the temple. God said the people could count on his watching over them and loving them with compassion (Ps. 10:17).

9:4–5 walk before me in integrity of heart. This involved attitudes, actions and words that were submissive to God's instructions. God said he would provide rulers of Israel through Solomon if he would obey God.

3. What are the conditions for God establishing Solomon's royal throne forever? Are these reasonable conditions? **4.** What disasters will occur if Israel forsakes God?

APPLY 1. When have you ignored a warning to your own detriment: Parent's warning against dangerous behavior? Your body's warning about a disease you had? Highway warning sign before you crashed? Other? **2.** What do you think God might be seeking to warn you about right now?

OPEN 1. What was the most unusual wedding gift you received when you were married? **2.** If you could give your son or daughter anything you wanted to as a wedding gift, what would you give them?

STUDY In this section we read of various miscellaneous activities, including a gift of twenty towns Solomon gave to Hiram of Tyre, and a gift of a town Pharaoh gave his daughter, Solomon's wife, for a wedding present. We also read of Solomon's sacrifices and ship-building activity. **1.** How has Hiram helped Solomon with his building projects (5:8–9)? **2.** Why does Hiram name the areas Solomon gave him the Land of Cabul (vv. 12–13)? **3.** What were Solomon's building projects (v. 15)? **4.** What people did Solomon conscript as slave labor? **5.** How does what is said here about the Israelites not being conscripted laborers compare with what is said in 5:13–18 and 2 Chronicles 10:1–19? **6.** How many times a year did Solomon sacrifice burnt offerings?

over Israel forever, as I promised David your father when I said,
'You shall never fail to have a man on the throne of Israel.'
6"But if you[a] or your sons turn away from me and do not observe the commands and decrees I have given you[a] and go off to
serve other gods and worship them, 7then I will cut off Israel
from the land I have given them and will reject this temple I have
consecrated for my Name. Israel will then become a byword and
an object of ridicule among all peoples. 8And though this temple
is now imposing, all who pass by will be appalled and will scoff
and say, 'Why has the LORD done such a thing to this land and to
this temple?' 9People will answer, 'Because they have forsaken
the LORD their God, who brought their fathers out of Egypt, and
have embraced other gods, worshiping and serving them—that
is why the LORD brought all this disaster on them.' "

Solomon's Other Activities

10At the end of twenty years, during which Solomon built these two
buildings—the temple of the LORD and the royal palace— 11King Solomon gave twenty towns in Galilee to Hiram king of Tyre, because
Hiram had supplied him with all the cedar and pine and gold he
wanted. 12But when Hiram went from Tyre to see the towns that Solomon had given him, he was not pleased with them. 13"What kind of
towns are these you have given me, my brother?" he asked. And he
called them the Land of Cabul,[b] a name they have to this day. 14Now
Hiram had sent to the king 120 talents[c] of gold.
15Here is the account of the forced labor King Solomon conscripted
to build the LORD's temple, his own palace, the supporting terraces,[d]
the wall of Jerusalem, and Hazor, Megiddo and Gezer. 16(Pharaoh
king of Egypt had attacked and captured Gezer. He had set it on fire.
He killed its Canaanite inhabitants and then gave it as a wedding gift
to his daughter, Solomon's wife. 17And Solomon rebuilt Gezer.) He
built up Lower Beth Horon, 18Baalath, and Tadmor[e] in the desert,
within his land, 19as well as all his store cities and the towns for his
chariots and for his horses[f]—whatever he desired to build in Jerusalem, in Lebanon and throughout all the territory he ruled.
20All the people left from the Amorites, Hittites, Perizzites, Hivites
and Jebusites (these peoples were not Israelites), 21that is, their descendants remaining in the land, whom the Israelites could not

[a]6 The Hebrew is plural. [b]13 *Cabul* sounds like the Hebrew for *good-for-nothing.* [c]14 That is, about 4 1/2 tons (about 4 metric tons) [d]15 Or *the Millo*; also in verse 24 [e]18 The Hebrew may also be read *Tamar.* [f]19 Or *charioteers*

9:9 Because they have forsaken the LORD their God. People would know that Israel suffered because of its idolatry. God's warnings were clear. He knew how easy it would be for Solomon and his descendants, and the people of Israel, to be seduced by other gods.

9:11 Solomon gave ... king of Tyre. Hiram had provided cedar and pine and the equivalent of 9,000 pounds of gold for the temple. Twenty years after finishing the temple, Solomon gave Hiram twenty villages.

9:12 he was not pleased with them. The towns were near unproductive land and did not meet with Hiram's approval. The name he gave them sounds like the Hebrew phrase for "good-for-nothing."

9:15 supporting terraces. Probably large level areas between hills. He also built the wall of Jerusalem, which doubled the size of the city.

9:16 killed its Canaanite inhabitants. When Pharaoh captured Gezer, a key city west of Jerusalem, he killed its residents and burned the city. He gave it to Solomon as a wedding gift, and Solomon rebuilt and strengthened it.

9:20 Amorites ... Jebusites ... not Israelites. These were descendants of the conquered Canaanites. The Israelites acted as supervisors over thousands of slave laborers working on public projects.

exterminate[a]—these Solomon conscripted for his slave labor force,
as it is to this day. 22But Solomon did not make slaves of any of the
Israelites; they were his fighting men, his government officials, his
officers, his captains, and the commanders of his chariots and charioteers. 23They were also the chief officials in charge of Solomon's
projects—550 officials supervising the men who did the work.
24After Pharaoh's daughter had come up from the City of David to
the palace Solomon had built for her, he constructed the supporting
terraces.
25Three times a year Solomon sacrificed burnt offerings and
fellowship offerings[b] on the altar he had built for the LORD, burning
incense before the LORD along with them, and so fulfilled the temple
obligations.
26King Solomon also built ships at Ezion Geber, which is near Elath
in Edom, on the shore of the Red Sea.[c] 27And Hiram sent his men—
sailors who knew the sea—to serve in the fleet with Solomon's men.
28They sailed to Ophir and brought back 420 talents[d] of gold, which
they delivered to King Solomon.

The Queen of Sheba Visits Solomon

10 When the queen of Sheba heard about the fame of Solomon
and his relation to the name of the LORD, she came to test
him with hard questions. 2Arriving at Jerusalem with a very great
caravan—with camels carrying spices, large quantities of gold, and
precious stones—she came to Solomon and talked with him about all
that she had on her mind. 3Solomon answered all her questions;
nothing was too hard for the king to explain to her. 4When the queen
of Sheba saw all the wisdom of Solomon and the palace he had built,
5the food on his table, the seating of his officials, the attending servants in their robes, his cupbearers, and the burnt offerings he made
at[e] the temple of the LORD, she was overwhelmed.
6She said to the king, "The report I heard in my own country about
your achievements and your wisdom is true. 7But I did not believe
these things until I came and saw with my own eyes. Indeed, not even
half was told me; in wisdom and wealth you have far exceeded the
report I heard. 8How happy your men must be! How happy your officials, who continually stand before you and hear your wisdom!
9Praise be to the LORD your God, who has delighted in you and placed
you on the throne of Israel. Because of the LORD's eternal love for
Israel, he has made you king, to maintain justice and righteousness."
10And she gave the king 120 talents[f] of gold, large quantities of

[a] *21* The Hebrew term refers to the irrevocable giving over of things or persons to the LORD, often by totally destroying them. [b] *25* Traditionally *peace offerings* [c] *26* Hebrew *Yam Suph*; that is, Sea of Reeds [d] *28* That is, about 16 tons (about 14.5 metric tons) [e] *5* Or *the ascent by which he went up to* [f] *10* That is, about 4 1/2 tons (about 4 metric tons)

APPLY How are you likely to react when something you say or do for a friend disappoints them: Apologize profusely? Get defensive and call them "nit-picky"? Give them something better? Shrug it off?

OPEN **1.** Who can you depend on to ask you the "hard questions" when you are struggling with a decision: Your spouse? Your best friend? Your spiritual leaders? A therapist? **2.** How do you generally react when hard questions are asked of you: Defensive? Confident? Challenged or stimulated? Confused?

STUDY The reputation of Solomon, had become known far and wide. One of those who came to visit him from afar was the queen of Sheba. **1.** If you were the queen of Sheba what "hard questions" would you most want to ask Solomon? **2.** What impresses you the most about the queen of Sheba: She had the knowledge to test Solomon with hard questions? She saw the connection between Solomon's wisdom and his God? She was a woman of means and resources? **3.** Why does the queen say Solomon's wisdom compares to his reputation? **4.** Why does the queen of Sheba give gifts to Solomon: As a sign of respect? To gain his favor? So he would give even more to her? To keep him from attacking her country? **5.** Why does Solomon give so much back to her: He had money to burn?

9:25 Three times a year ... burnt offerings. The occasions were the Feast of Unleavened Bread, the Feast of Harvest, and the Feast of Tabernacles—the major feasts of Israel (Ex. 23:14–16). Solomon led his people in worship and saw to it that the temple was properly maintained.

10:1 queen of Sheba. This is modern Yemen in Arabia, about 1,200 miles from Jerusalem. It was a prosperous trading country that dealt in gold, gems, perfumes and rare spices. Solomon's traders were able to go east and south by water and probably brought him news of this country. **his relation to ... the LORD.** Solomon's legendary wisdom attracted many people. Sages from many countries visited him and learned that his wisdom came from God. The queen of Sheba came to see if his famed knowledge was genuine.

10:9 Praise be. The queen of Sheba acknowledged Solomon's God, as Hiram had done in 5:7. Whether she became a worshiper, or merely admired Solomon's giftedness, is unknown.

It's embarrassing to give less expensive gifts than you get? He also wanted peace and good will?

APPLY What hard questions can this group help you with right now? ____________

____

OPEN 1. What possessions bring you the greatest pleasure and pride? **2.** If you were to add one piece of fine furniture to what you already own, and money was no object, what would you want that piece of furniture to be made of: Mahogany? Ebony? Ivory? Walnut? Gold? Silver? Marble? A combination of these? Other?

STUDY Solomon's reign was a time of great affluence in the land. Much of this wealth came from gifts from those who visited, while seeking advice from the wise king. **1.** If Solomon were on "Lifestyles of the Rich and Famous" what aspect of his lifestyle do you think they would focus on the most? **2.** What impression does this passage make on you: A picture of materialistic excess? A tribute to the rewards of righteous living? An in-your-face flaunting of success? An exaggeration that has probably built up over time? **3.** How is God true to his promises to Solomon (3:12–13)? Is wisdom a money-maker (v. 25)? **4.** What exotic animals apparently had great value in Israel at this time? **5.** Where did Solomon get his horses?

APPLY 1. What are you most likely to turn to when you are trying to impress people: Your appearance? Your wealth? Your knowledge or expertise in a given area? Your charm? Your cooking? **2.** If Christ came to your home, how would your behavior differ from what you do when you want to impress people?

____

spices, and precious stones. Never again were so many spices brought in as those the queen of Sheba gave to King Solomon.

11(Hiram's ships brought gold from Ophir; and from there they brought great cargoes of almugwood[a] and precious stones. 12The king used the almugwood to make supports for the temple of the LORD and for the royal palace, and to make harps and lyres for the musicians. So much almugwood has never been imported or seen since that day.)

13King Solomon gave the queen of Sheba all she desired and asked for, besides what he had given her out of his royal bounty. Then she left and returned with her retinue to her own country.

Solomon's Splendor

14The weight of the gold that Solomon received yearly was 666 talents,[b] 15not including the revenues from merchants and traders and from all the Arabian kings and the governors of the land.

16King Solomon made two hundred large shields of hammered gold; six hundred bekas[c] of gold went into each shield. 17He also made three hundred small shields of hammered gold, with three minas[d] of gold in each shield. The king put them in the Palace of the Forest of Lebanon.

18Then the king made a great throne inlaid with ivory and overlaid with fine gold. 19The throne had six steps, and its back had a rounded top. On both sides of the seat were armrests, with a lion standing beside each of them. 20Twelve lions stood on the six steps, one at either end of each step. Nothing like it had ever been made for any other kingdom. 21All King Solomon's goblets were gold, and all the household articles in the Palace of the Forest of Lebanon were pure gold. Nothing was made of silver, because silver was considered of little value in Solomon's days. 22The king had a fleet of trading ships[e] at sea along with the ships of Hiram. Once every three years it returned, carrying gold, silver and ivory, and apes and baboons.

23King Solomon was greater in riches and wisdom than all the other kings of the earth. 24The whole world sought audience with Solomon to hear the wisdom God had put in his heart. 25Year after year, everyone who came brought a gift—articles of silver and gold, robes, weapons and spices, and horses and mules.

26Solomon accumulated chariots and horses; he had fourteen hundred chariots and twelve thousand horses,[f] which he kept in the chariot cities and also with him in Jerusalem. 27The king made silver as common in Jerusalem as stones, and cedar as plentiful as sycamore-fig trees in the foothills. 28Solomon's horses were imported from Egypt[g] and from Kue[h]—the royal merchants purchased them from Kue. 29They imported a chariot from Egypt for six hundred shekels[i] of silver, and a horse for a hundred and fifty.[j] They also exported them to all the kings of the Hittites and of the Arameans.

[a]*11* Probably a variant of *algumwood;* also in verse 12 [b]*14* That is, about 25 tons (about 23 metric tons) [c]*16* That is, about 7 1/2 pounds (about 3.5 kilograms) [d]*17* That is, about 3 3/4 pounds (about 1.7 kilograms) [e]*22* Hebrew *of ships of Tarshish* [f]*26* Or *charioteers* [g]*28* Or possibly *Muzur,* a region in Cilicia; also in verse 29 [h]*28* Probably *Cilicia* [i]*29* That is, about 15 pounds (about 7 kilograms) [j]*29* That is, about 3 3/4 pounds (about 1.7 kilograms)

10:13 King Solomon gave the queen ... all she desired and asked for. The queen was wealthy also. She gave Solomon the equivalent of 4.5 tons of gold as well as many spices and precious stones. He, too, gave her many gifts.

Solomon's Wives

11 King Solomon, however, loved many foreign women besides
Pharaoh's daughter—Moabites, Ammonites, Edomites, Sidonians and Hittites. 2They were from nations about which the LORD
had told the Israelites, "You must not intermarry with them, because
they will surely turn your hearts after their gods." Nevertheless, Solomon held fast to them in love. 3He had seven hundred wives of royal
birth and three hundred concubines, and his wives led him astray. 4As
Solomon grew old, his wives turned his heart after other gods, and
his heart was not fully devoted to the LORD his God, as the heart of
David his father had been. 5He followed Ashtoreth the goddess of the
Sidonians, and Molech[a] the detestable god of the Ammonites. 6So
Solomon did evil in the eyes of the LORD; he did not follow the LORD
completely, as David his father had done.

7On a hill east of Jerusalem, Solomon built a high place for Chemosh the detestable god of Moab, and for Molech the detestable god
of the Ammonites. 8He did the same for all his foreign wives, who
burned incense and offered sacrifices to their gods.

9The LORD became angry with Solomon because his heart had
turned away from the LORD, the God of Israel, who had appeared to
him twice. 10Although he had forbidden Solomon to follow other
gods, Solomon did not keep the LORD's command. 11So the LORD said
to Solomon, "Since this is your attitude and you have not kept my
covenant and my decrees, which I commanded you, I will most certainly tear the kingdom away from you and give it to one of your subordinates. 12Nevertheless, for the sake of David your father, I will not
do it during your lifetime. I will tear it out of the hand of your son.
13Yet I will not tear the whole kingdom from him, but will give him
one tribe for the sake of David my servant and for the sake of Jerusalem, which I have chosen."

Solomon's Adversaries

14Then the LORD raised up against Solomon an adversary, Hadad
the Edomite, from the royal line of Edom. 15Earlier when David was
fighting with Edom, Joab the commander of the army, who had gone
up to bury the dead, had struck down all the men in Edom. 16Joab and
all the Israelites stayed there for six months, until they had destroyed
all the men in Edom. 17But Hadad, still only a boy, fled to Egypt with
some Edomite officials who had served his father. 18They set out from

[a]5 Hebrew *Milcom;* also in verse 33

OPEN Which of the following have you felt compelled to neglect because of your relationship with your spouse: Your love of the opera? Your passion for the outdoors? Your ability to follow your favorite sports teams? Other?

STUDY While most of us have to make compromises to the tastes of our spouse, friends and family, for Solomon the compromise he chose to make was in his faith in the Lord. He allowed and even provided for sacrifices to foreign deities. **1.** What do you think drove Solomon to have so many wives? **2.** Why had God told the Israelites to not marry women from the countries listed (Deut. 7:1–4)? **3.** Would Israel have been better off had their men never married foreign women? How does it affect your answer when you remember that David himself was descended from the marriage of Boaz to Ruth, a Moabite woman (Ruth 1:4; 4:14–22)? **4.** Why was the worship of Molech so detestable (Lev. 20:1–5; 2 Kin. 23:10)? **5.** Why does God soften the judgment on Solomon (2 Sam. 7:11–16)?

APPLY 1. How have you compromised your beliefs in a way you now regret? **2.** How has God "softened the judgment" on you for that error?

OPEN Who was your adversary in each of the following areas: Your favorite areas of achievement in high school? Gaining the love of your spouse or significant other? Making a name for yourself in your profession?

STUDY Because Solomon had displeased the Lord by allowing his wives to sacrifice to foreign gods, God raised up adversar-

11:1 loved many foreign women. God established monogamy in Genesis 2:24 and forbade a king to marry many wives (Deut. 17:17). He also forbade marrying foreign women because they worshiped false gods. But Solomon had 700 wives and 300 concubines. His pagan wives led him into idolatry.

11:4 his wives turned his heart. Solomon still trusted God and loved him, but he was drawn into disobedience and even worshiped other gods. He built high places east of Jerusalem for these gods.

11:5 Ashtoreth. A Canaanite goddess of sex, fertility and war, whose worship involved sexual rites. **Molech.** Worship of this god included human sacrifices, especially children, strictly forbidden by God's Law (Lev. 18:21).

11:6 Solomon did evil ... he did not follow the LORD. David had remained true to God and had never worshiped false gods. David had always repented of his sin and returned to obedience.

11:11 my covenant. Even though God had warned Solomon again and again, and Solomon had instructed his people repeatedly, he was still lured away from God as he tried to please his wives by worshiping their deities. His attitude toward God had changed.

11:16 all the Israelites. Hadad, a prince of Edom, wanted revenge against David for killing Edomites in battle. Hadad had escaped and was living in Egypt.

ies to give him a hard time. **1.** What does it mean that God "raised up" adversaries against Solomon? **2.** Why does Hadad give up Egypt's comforts for a guerrilla fighter's life? **3.** Why does Pharaoh try to dissuade Hadad? **4.** Why did these rebels apparently wait until David was dead to start making trouble?

APPLY Who do you consider to be your adversaries? How might God be using the hard time these adversaries are giving you?

OPEN When you were a child, which of the following kingdoms would you have most wanted a part of: Never-never land (where you never grow up)? Disneyland? Wonderland (where Alice finds nothing is as it seems)? Camelot (where chivalry still reigns)?

STUDY While adversaries like Hadad and Rezon were irritants during Solomon's reign, a more serious threat was that of Jeroboam. Here we find that he is promised a kingdom that will include ten of the twelve tribes of Israel. **1.** What commends Jeroboam for the position he's given (vv. 26–28)? **2.** How do Ahijah's actions embody God's plans? Hasn't the "cloak" been divided for some time (2 Sam. 19:41–20:2)? **3.** What tribe will Solomon's heir keep? **4.** What causes Jeroboam to flee to Egypt? **5.** What written

Midian and went to Paran. Then taking men from Paran with them,
they went to Egypt, to Pharaoh king of Egypt, who gave Hadad a
house and land and provided him with food.
[19]Pharaoh was so pleased with Hadad that he gave him a sister of
his own wife, Queen Tahpenes, in marriage. [20]The sister of Tahpenes
bore him a son named Genubath, whom Tahpenes brought up in the
royal palace. There Genubath lived with Pharaoh's own children.
[21]While he was in Egypt, Hadad heard that David rested with his
fathers and that Joab the commander of the army was also dead.
Then Hadad said to Pharaoh, "Let me go, that I may return to my own
country."
[22]"What have you lacked here that you want to go back to your own
country?" Pharaoh asked.

"Nothing," Hadad replied, "but do let me go!"
[23]And God raised up against Solomon another adversary, Rezon
son of Eliada, who had fled from his master, Hadadezer king of
Zobah. [24]He gathered men around him and became the leader of a
band of rebels when David destroyed the forces[a] ⌞of Zobah⌟; the rebels
went to Damascus, where they settled and took control. [25]Rezon was
Israel's adversary as long as Solomon lived, adding to the trouble
caused by Hadad. So Rezon ruled in Aram and was hostile toward
Israel.

Jeroboam Rebels Against Solomon

[26]Also, Jeroboam son of Nebat rebelled against the king. He was
one of Solomon's officials, an Ephraimite from Zeredah, and his
mother was a widow named Zeruah.
[27]Here is the account of how he rebelled against the king: Solomon
had built the supporting terraces[b] and had filled in the gap in the wall
of the city of David his father. [28]Now Jeroboam was a man of standing,
and when Solomon saw how well the young man did his work,
he put him in charge of the whole labor force of the house of Joseph.
[29]About that time Jeroboam was going out of Jerusalem, and Ahijah
the prophet of Shiloh met him on the way, wearing a new cloak. The
two of them were alone out in the country, [30]and Ahijah took hold of
the new cloak he was wearing and tore it into twelve pieces. [31]Then
he said to Jeroboam, "Take ten pieces for yourself, for this is what the
LORD, the God of Israel, says: 'See, I am going to tear the kingdom out
of Solomon's hand and give you ten tribes. [32]But for the sake of my
servant David and the city of Jerusalem, which I have chosen out of
all the tribes of Israel, he will have one tribe. [33]I will do this because

[a]24 Hebrew *destroyed them* [b]27 Or *the Millo*

11:21 Let me go. Hadad knew that David and Joab, one of David's military leaders, were both dead. He asked Pharaoh for permission to return to Edom to fight the Israelites.

11:22 What have you lacked? Pharaoh considered *Hadad the Edomite* as a future ally strategically located on Israel's border. But with peace existing between Egypt and Israel, Pharaoh didn't want Hadad stirring up trouble.

11:24 band of rebels. Rezon was from Zobah, south of Damascus. He had led rebels against David and now opposed Solomon.

11:26 Jeroboam ... rebelled against the king. Solomon trusted *Jeroboam, an official* who supervised the labor force of the tribes of Ephraim and Manasseh. Jeroboam knew of discontent among the laborers, whom Solomon worked very hard.

11:31–32 ten tribes. The prediction by Ahijah the prophet must have made quite an impression on Jeroboam. Ahijah promised ten tribes to Jeroboam. The twelfth tribe may be Simeon, which became part of Judah. Benjamin may have served as a buffer area between Israel and Judah, linked occasionally with the northern kingdom. God had warned Solomon that his heir would lose all but one tribe (v. 13) because of his unfaithfulness. Once again, a sinful

they have[a] forsaken me and worshiped Ashtoreth the goddess of the Sidonians, Chemosh the god of the Moabites, and Molech the god of the Ammonites, and have not walked in my ways, nor done what is right in my eyes, nor kept my statutes and laws as David, Solomon's father, did.

34" 'But I will not take the whole kingdom out of Solomon's hand; I have made him ruler all the days of his life for the sake of David my servant, whom I chose and who observed my commands and statutes.
35I will take the kingdom from his son's hands and give you ten tribes.
36I will give one tribe to his son so that David my servant may always have a lamp before me in Jerusalem, the city where I chose to put my Name.
37However, as for you, I will take you, and you will rule over all that your heart desires; you will be king over Israel.
38If you do whatever I command you and walk in my ways and do what is right in my eyes by keeping my statutes and commands, as David my servant did, I will be with you. I will build you a dynasty as enduring as the one I built for David and will give Israel to you.
39I will humble David's descendants because of this, but not forever.' "

40Solomon tried to kill Jeroboam, but Jeroboam fled to Egypt, to Shishak the king, and stayed there until Solomon's death.

Solomon's Death

41As for the other events of Solomon's reign—all he did and the wisdom he displayed—are they not written in the book of the annals of Solomon?
42Solomon reigned in Jerusalem over all Israel forty years.
43Then he rested with his fathers and was buried in the city of David his father. And Rehoboam his son succeeded him as king.

Israel Rebels Against Rehoboam

12 Rehoboam went to Shechem, for all the Israelites had gone there to make him king.
2When Jeroboam son of Nebat heard this (he was still in Egypt, where he had fled from King Solomon), he returned from[b] Egypt.
3So they sent for Jeroboam, and he and the whole assembly of Israel went to Rehoboam and said to him:
4"Your

[a]33 Hebrew; Septuagint, Vulgate and Syriac *because he has* [b]2 Or *he remained in*

source concerning the acts of Solomon no longer exists (v. 41)? **6.** How long did Solomon reign?

APPLY 1. Which of the following have you lost because of your own negligence or foolishness: The love of a friend? An important position? Valued property? Prestige or respect? **2.** Did someone else profit because of your loss? **3.** What has God taught you through this experience?

OPEN 1. When you were an adolescent, whose advice did you value the most: Your father's? Your mother's? A grandparent's? That of a teacher? A best friend's? An advice columnist? **2.** When did you follow advice that you later regretted following?

---

leader (Solomon) brought harm to his nation.

11:36 David ... have a lamp before me in Jerusalem. As forerunners of Jesus, the Light of the World, the kings in ancient Israel were to act as light in a dark pagan world. God remembered his promise to David—that his descendants would continue to have a right to rule Israel—despite the chastening Solomon had brought on himself and the nation.

11:38 I will build you a dynasty. God gave the same instructions to Jeroboam as he had given to David and Solomon. But this time his promise was conditional: it would happen only if Jeroboam obeyed God and walked with him. But Jeroboam also gave up the promise through disobedience.

11:39 David's descendants. Solomon's sin brought judgment to the nation, as God had warned. **but not forever.** Always faithful to his promises, God would restore David's line to the throne in Jesus Christ (Jer. 30:8–10).

11:41 are they not written in the book of the annals of Solomon? This book is only mentioned here, unlike references to the books of the Chronicles of the Kings of Israel and the Chronicles of the Kings of Judah (2 Chr. 9:29; 12:15; 13:22).

12:1 Shechem. Rehoboam went to Shechem to be crowned even though Jerusalem was his capital and the temple of God was there. Why did he go to Shechem? **the Israelites had gone there.** Very likely, the ten northern tribes had informed Rehoboam that they would meet him there. Shechem was a northern city. It was also famous as a place where covenants were made (Josh. 24:1,25). The northern tribes let Rehoboam know they were willing to accept him as king, but he had to meet them halfway.

12:2 Jeroboam, hiding in Egypt, heard the news of Solomon's death and decided to return to Israel. He was in the delegation that met Rehoboam in Shechem (v. 3).

12:4 we will serve you. In later years, Solomon's reign had become oppressive. He had weighted the Israelites down with heavy taxes and pressed them into labor gangs (4:27–28; 5:13–16). Despite this, the northern

STUDY **1.** Where does Rehoboam go to gain the support of the northern tribes for his kingship? **2.** What complaint do the Israelites have against how Solomon treated them? **3.** What is the significance of the fact that the older people advised being easy on the people, while the younger advisors called for toughness? **4.** Why do you think Rehoboam chose the young men's counsel: He didn't trust anyone over 30? The younger men were his peers and he didn't want to lose their friendship? He didn't want to look like a wimp? **5.** What is meant by attributing this to the Lord (v. 15; 11:9–13)? **6.** Why does the word of Shemaiah so easily carry the day: The people of Judah really didn't want to fight their brothers anyway? They were afraid to go to war without God's blessing? The people thought Rehoboam deserved to lose the northern tribes? **7.** How do you think Rehoboam felt about his response to the Israelites request for work relief; after all was said and done: "It would have worked fine if God hadn't stepped in!"? "I still think I was right!"? "Hey, everyone has 20-20 hindsight!"? "I didn't want those guys in my kingdom anyway!"? "It's too late to turn back now"? "I wish Dad were still around!"?

APPLY **1.** In what area of your life do you feel oppressed to the point of rebellion: Time pressures put upon you? Unreasonable demands of the government? Expectations of your boss? Expectations of a demanding parent or spouse? Expectations of God? **2.** Where do you think "God's doing" is in the midst of these feelings of rebellion?

father put a heavy yoke on us, but now lighten the harsh labor and
the heavy yoke he put on us, and we will serve you."
[5]Rehoboam answered, "Go away for three days and then come
back to me." So the people went away.
[6]Then King Rehoboam consulted the elders who had served his
father Solomon during his lifetime. "How would you advise me to
answer these people?" he asked.
[7]They replied, "If today you will be a servant to these people and
serve them and give them a favorable answer, they will always be
your servants."
[8]But Rehoboam rejected the advice the elders gave him and consulted the young men who had grown up with him and were serving
him. [9]He asked them, "What is your advice? How should we answer
these people who say to me, 'Lighten the yoke your father put on us'?"
[10]The young men who had grown up with him replied, "Tell these
people who have said to you, 'Your father put a heavy yoke on us, but
make our yoke lighter'—tell them, 'My little finger is thicker than my
father's waist. [11]My father laid on you a heavy yoke; I will make it
even heavier. My father scourged you with whips; I will scourge you
with scorpions.'"
[12]Three days later Jeroboam and all the people returned to Rehoboam, as the king had said, "Come back to me in three days." [13]The
king answered the people harshly. Rejecting the advice given him by
the elders, [14]he followed the advice of the young men and said, "My
father made your yoke heavy; I will make it even heavier. My father
scourged you with whips; I will scourge you with scorpions." [15]So the
king did not listen to the people, for this turn of events was from the
LORD, to fulfill the word the LORD had spoken to Jeroboam son of
Nebat through Ahijah the Shilonite.
[16]When all Israel saw that the king refused to listen to them, they
answered the king:

"What share do we have in David,
 what part in Jesse's son?
To your tents, O Israel!
 Look after your own house, O David!"

So the Israelites went home. [17]But as for the Israelites who were living in the towns of Judah, Rehoboam still ruled over them.
[18]King Rehoboam sent out Adoniram,[a] who was in charge of forced
labor, but all Israel stoned him to death. King Rehoboam, however,

[a]18 Some Septuagint manuscripts and Syriac (see also 1 Kings 4:6 and 5:14); Hebrew *Adoram*

tribes were still willing to accept Solomon's son as their king—with this condition: Less work, more time off.

12:8 the young men. Rehoboam was 41 when he became king (14:21). He and his friends were young compared to *the elders*. ***were serving him.*** Rehoboam had not even been crowned, yet he had already removed older, wiser officials from their positions and installed inexperienced friends in their places.

12:11 I will make it even heavier. Rehoboam and his advisors were arrogant and out of touch with the people's suffering. Rehoboam was loathe to lighten the heavy taxes and see his revenues drop. If anything, he would increase taxes. He met the people's complaints by speaking to them harshly (v. 13).

12:15 turn of events. When Solomon turned from God to worship idols, God declared that Solomon's sins would cost him most of the kingdom (11:9–13). The prophet Ahijah then promised Jeroboam that God would make him king over the northern tribes (11:29–39). That day had come. God did not approve of Rehoboam's harshness and pride, nor of the northern tribes' rebellion, but he used these events to fulfill his word.

12:18 in charge of forced labor. Adoniram, the man in charge of Solomon's forced labor gangs, was a hated

managed to get into his chariot and escape to Jerusalem. [19]So Israel
has been in rebellion against the house of David to this day.
[20]When all the Israelites heard that Jeroboam had returned, they
sent and called him to the assembly and made him king over all
Israel. Only the tribe of Judah remained loyal to the house of David.
[21]When Rehoboam arrived in Jerusalem, he mustered the whole
house of Judah and the tribe of Benjamin—a hundred and eighty
thousand fighting men—to make war against the house of Israel and
to regain the kingdom for Rehoboam son of Solomon.
[22]But this word of God came to Shemaiah the man of God: [23]"Say to
Rehoboam son of Solomon king of Judah, to the whole house of
Judah and Benjamin, and to the rest of the people, [24]'This is what the
LORD says: Do not go up to fight against your brothers, the Israelites.
Go home, every one of you, for this is my doing.' " So they obeyed the
word of the LORD and went home again, as the LORD had ordered.

Golden Calves at Bethel and Dan

[25]Then Jeroboam fortified Shechem in the hill country of Ephraim
and lived there. From there he went out and built up Peniel.[a]
[26]Jeroboam thought to himself, "The kingdom will now likely revert
to the house of David. [27]If these people go up to offer sacrifices at the
temple of the LORD in Jerusalem, they will again give their allegiance
to their lord, Rehoboam king of Judah. They will kill me and return to
King Rehoboam."
[28]After seeking advice, the king made two golden calves. He said to
the people, "It is too much for you to go up to Jerusalem. Here are
your gods, O Israel, who brought you up out of Egypt." [29]One he set
up in Bethel, and the other in Dan. [30]And this thing became a sin; the
people went even as far as Dan to worship the one there.
[31]Jeroboam built shrines on high places and appointed priests from
all sorts of people, even though they were not Levites. [32]He instituted

[a]25 Hebrew *Penuel*, a variant of *Peniel*

OPEN When you have turned from God or have been less devoted, what has come closest to being your "house of worship"?

STUDY Jeroboam decides that if the Israelites go down to Jerusalem to worship, they might give their loyalty to Rehoboam, who is king there. So he builds some altars in Israel to false gods and encourages the people to worship there. **1.** At what other time did the people worship a golden calf (Ex. 32:1–6)? **2.** If Jeroboam was just trying to keep the people from going down to Jerusalem, why didn't he just build altars to the true God in his territory? **3.** What other changes did Jeroboam make to the accepted way of worshipping?

man of oppression. The crowd was in an ugly mood, so when he tried to enforce obedience, they killed him.

12:21 to make war. Rehoboam was still determined to show that he was in charge, still unconcerned for the people. First he threatened to oppress them. Then he prepared to wage war against them. **to regain the kingdom.** The northern tribes had rebelled in King David's day (2 Sam. 20) and he had fought to restore control. Rehoboam assumed that God would help him do the same.

12:24 they obeyed the word of the LORD. Rehoboam may have had a change of heart and decided to obey God. However, "they" most likely refers to the people, whom Shemaiah had also warned. After the people were told that God would not fight on their side, Rehoboam could not persuade them to go to battle.

12:26 Jeroboam thought. Jeroboam had been promised that if he served God, God would build him a lasting dynasty (11:37–38). But Jeroboam did not trust God to establish his kingdom. He thought that if his people continued making pilgrimages to the temple in Jerusalem, he would lose control over them. To prevent that from happening, he decided to lead his people into idolatry.

12:28 king made two golden calves. Aaron had built a golden calf in Moses' day, then declared a festival to the Lord (Ex. 32:4–5). Like Aaron, Jeroboam may not have intended to worship the calves as pagan gods, but as symbols of the power of God. **It is too much for you to go.** Even if this were true, the Israelites could have still worshiped God at his many altars throughout Israel (3:2–4). That would not have been ideal (Deut 12:13–14), but better than calf worship. Even Elijah would later pray at an altar in Israel (18:19,30–32).

12:30 became a sin. When Aaron built the golden calf, Moses destroyed it in anger (Ex. 32:19–20), and for good reason. Building any idol broke the second commandment (Ex. 20:4) and rapidly led to outright idol worship.

12:31 shrines on high places. The Israelites had built altars to God on the tops of hills, and it was also common for the pagans to build shrines to their gods on the highest peaks. **appointed priests ... not Levites.** Jeroboam rejected God's priesthood and appointed priests from his followers. He then drove out the Levites who abandoned their homes and lands and headed to Judah in a mass exodus (2 Chr. 11:13–17; 13:9).

12:32 He instituted a festival. The Israelites were required to worship God

APPLY How do you tell true religion from false religion? What should a person do to keep tuned to God's guidance rather than going off on their own?

OPEN **1.** In your past, which of your friends would basically tell you what you wanted to hear? Which of your friends would tell you the truth, no matter how hard? **2.** On a scale of "1" ("if it ain't good, I don't want it" to "10" ("hit me with your best shot—I can take it!"), how would you grade yourself right now in your receptivity to hard truths?

STUDY After Jeroboam starts sacrificing to false gods, a man of God comes down from Judah and makes an ominous pronouncement against him. Jeroboam tries to convince him to stay and talk about it all, but he is on orders from God to leave without eating or drinking. However, another prophet tricks the man of God into eating, and for this the man of God is himself punished with death. **1.** What happens when Jeroboam tries to have the man of God seized and punished? **2.** Why do you think the king then invites the man of God to his home? Would you have gone? **3.** Why do you think the man of God was ordered by God to return without eating or drinking: To test his spiritual discipline? It's like traveling to any foreign area—don't drink the water!? Eating or fellowshipping with sinners was a "no-no"? It was part of the symbolic condemnation—as if even their food were polluted by their evil? **4.** What motivates the old prophet to lie to the man of God? **5.** How is the old prophet affected by the death of the man of God: Worried he will be

a festival on the fifteenth day of the eighth month, like the festival
held in Judah, and offered sacrifices on the altar. This he did in
Bethel, sacrificing to the calves he had made. And at Bethel he also
installed priests at the high places he had made. 33On the fifteenth
day of the eighth month, a month of his own choosing, he offered
sacrifices on the altar he had built at Bethel. So he instituted the festival for the Israelites and went up to the altar to make offerings.

The Man of God From Judah

13 By the word of the LORD a man of God came from Judah to
Bethel, as Jeroboam was standing by the altar to make an
offering. 2He cried out against the altar by the word of the LORD:
"O altar, altar! This is what the LORD says: 'A son named Josiah will be
born to the house of David. On you he will sacrifice the priests of the
high places who now make offerings here, and human bones will be
burned on you.' " 3That same day the man of God gave a sign: "This is
the sign the LORD has declared: The altar will be split apart and the
ashes on it will be poured out."
4When King Jeroboam heard what the man of God cried out against
the altar at Bethel, he stretched out his hand from the altar and said,
"Seize him!" But the hand he stretched out toward the man shriveled
up, so that he could not pull it back. 5Also, the altar was split apart
and its ashes poured out according to the sign given by the man of
God by the word of the LORD.
6Then the king said to the man of God, "Intercede with the LORD
your God and pray for me that my hand may be restored." So the man
of God interceded with the LORD, and the king's hand was restored
and became as it was before.
7The king said to the man of God, "Come home with me and have
something to eat, and I will give you a gift."
8But the man of God answered the king, "Even if you were to give
me half your possessions, I would not go with you, nor would I eat
bread or drink water here. 9For I was commanded by the word of the
LORD: 'You must not eat bread or drink water or return by the way you
came.' " 10So he took another road and did not return by the way he
had come to Bethel.
11Now there was a certain old prophet living in Bethel, whose sons
came and told him all that the man of God had done there that day.
They also told their father what he had said to the king. 12Their father
asked them, "Which way did he go?" And his sons showed him which

at the temple in Jerusalem during three great feasts every year. Jeroboam's festival didn't coincide with any of these feasts. Since it took place in the fall, it was probably intended as a harvest feast.

13:1 man of God came from Judah. This prophet had a powerful message and performed mighty miracles, yet he was not even named.

13:3 a sign. When this prophecy was fulfilled before Jeroboam's eyes, he would know that the full prophecy of judgment would also happen.

13:5 ashes poured out. These were the ashes of animals that had been sacrificed to the golden calf. God dumped them onto the ground to show their worthlessness.

13:6 Intercede with the LORD. In one second, Jeroboam had gone from king and high priest to leper and social outcast. He instantly knew that God was all-powerful. In asking the man of God to pray for him, he acknowledged the prophet's authority and the truth of his message (Acts 8:24).

13:7 I will give you a gift. Jeroboam was shaken but not repentant (v. 33). His fear, however, made him eager to somehow placate God. Had the prophet accepted a gift, Jeroboam's guilty conscience would have been eased. That is why the prophet refused (2 Kin 5:13–16 tells of a similar refusal).

13:8 I would not. God did not want his prophet to eat or drink in the northern kingdom. Sharing a meal with someone was tantamount to declaring that God (whom the prophet represented) was at peace with that person. It was like saying, "Everything is fine between us." But everything was not fine.

road the man of God from Judah had taken. [13]So he said to his sons,
"Saddle the donkey for me." And when they had saddled the donkey
for him, he mounted it [14]and rode after the man of God. He found him
sitting under an oak tree and asked, "Are you the man of God who
came from Judah?"
"I am," he replied.
[15]So the prophet said to him, "Come home with me and eat."
[16]The man of God said, "I cannot turn back and go with you, nor
can I eat bread or drink water with you in this place. [17]I have been
told by the word of the LORD: 'You must not eat bread or drink water
there or return by the way you came.' "
[18]The old prophet answered, "I too am a prophet, as you are. And
an angel said to me by the word of the LORD: 'Bring him back with you
to your house so that he may eat bread and drink water.' " (But he
was lying to him.) [19]So the man of God returned with him and ate and
drank in his house.
[20]While they were sitting at the table, the word of the LORD came to
the old prophet who had brought him back. [21]He cried out to the man
of God who had come from Judah, "This is what the LORD says: 'You
have defied the word of the LORD and have not kept the command the
LORD your God gave you. [22]You came back and ate bread and drank
water in the place where he told you not to eat or drink. Therefore
your body will not be buried in the tomb of your fathers.' "
[23]When the man of God had finished eating and drinking, the
prophet who had brought him back saddled his donkey for him. [24]As
he went on his way, a lion met him on the road and killed him, and his
body was thrown down on the road, with both the donkey and the
lion standing beside it. [25]Some people who passed by saw the body
thrown down there, with the lion standing beside the body, and they
went and reported it in the city where the old prophet lived.
[26]When the prophet who had brought him back from his journey
heard of it, he said, "It is the man of God who defied the word of the
LORD. The LORD has given him over to the lion, which has mauled him
and killed him, as the word of the LORD had warned him."
[27]The prophet said to his sons, "Saddle the donkey for me," and
they did so. [28]Then he went out and found the body thrown down on
the road, with the donkey and the lion standing beside it. The lion
had neither eaten the body nor mauled the donkey. [29]So the prophet
picked up the body of the man of God, laid it on the donkey, and
brought it back to his own city to mourn for him and bury him. [30]Then
he laid the body in his own tomb, and they mourned over him and
said, "Oh, my brother!"
[31]After burying him, he said to his sons, "When I die, bury me in the
grave where the man of God is buried; lay my bones beside his bones.

next? Feeling guilty about his role in the death? Nostalgic for when God had spoken through him in such a way? **6.** Why does the prophet think of the man of God as his brother? **7.** Why is Jeroboam so stubborn after such a show of God's power: He figured it all to be coincidental? He didn't know how to admit he was wrong? He figured God would never take him back anyway? Other?

APPLY 1. What hard truth about yourself are you having trouble facing right now? **2.** What would most help you to face this truth: The reassurance from friends that they still love and accept me? The reassurance of God's forgiveness of me? Friends who don't let me run away or hide from the truth?

13:18 *I* too am a prophet. In his younger days, the old man had been a true prophet. He had apparently lost his former zeal and love for God (Rev. 2:4) but was still "religious" and eager to boast of former days.

13:19 returned with him. The man of God was tired (v. 14), hungry and thirsty. He probably wished God hadn't forbidden him to eat or drink. When the old prophet said he could now do both; it was what the man of God wanted to hear.

13:24 a lion ... killed him. God had swiftly judged Jeroboam and the altar (vv. 4–5). Now he swiftly judged the disobedient prophet. This may seem harsh, but the fate of an entire nation was at stake. The death of the prophet was an example to Israel. **standing beside it.** The donkey didn't flee and the lion didn't eat the man or attack the donkey. This sign proved that the young prophet's death was a divine judgment. This story was told in Bethel (v. 25), and served notice to Jeroboam that God would judge him as well.

[32]For the message he declared by the word of the LORD against the altar in Bethel and against all the shrines on the high places in the towns of Samaria will certainly come true."

[33]Even after this, Jeroboam did not change his evil ways, but once more appointed priests for the high places from all sorts of people. Anyone who wanted to become a priest he consecrated for the high places. [34]This was the sin of the house of Jeroboam that led to its downfall and to its destruction from the face of the earth.

Ahijah's Prophecy Against Jeroboam

14 At that time Abijah son of Jeroboam became ill, [2]and Jeroboam said to his wife, "Go, disguise yourself, so you won't be recognized as the wife of Jeroboam. Then go to Shiloh. Ahijah the prophet is there—the one who told me I would be king over this people. [3]Take ten loaves of bread with you, some cakes and a jar of honey, and go to him. He will tell you what will happen to the boy." [4]So Jeroboam's wife did what he said and went to Ahijah's house in Shiloh.

Now Ahijah could not see; his sight was gone because of his age. [5]But the LORD had told Ahijah, "Jeroboam's wife is coming to ask you about her son, for he is ill, and you are to give her such and such an answer. When she arrives, she will pretend to be someone else."

[6]So when Ahijah heard the sound of her footsteps at the door, he said, "Come in, wife of Jeroboam. Why this pretense? I have been sent to you with bad news. [7]Go, tell Jeroboam that this is what the LORD, the God of Israel, says: 'I raised you up from among the people and made you a leader over my people Israel. [8]I tore the kingdom away from the house of David and gave it to you, but you have not been like my servant David, who kept my commands and followed me with all his heart, doing only what was right in my eyes. [9]You have done more evil than all who lived before you. You have made for yourself other gods, idols made of metal; you have provoked me to anger and thrust me behind your back.

[10]" 'Because of this, I am going to bring disaster on the house of Jeroboam. I will cut off from Jeroboam every last male in Israel—slave or free. I will burn up the house of Jeroboam as one burns dung,

OPEN When younger, were you most likely to try to disguise who you were: When making prank calls? When trying to sneak into an "R" rated movie or drinking establishment? When trying to impress someone of the opposite sex?

STUDY When Jeroboam's son gets ill, he sends his wife to Ahijah, an old prophet, to see whether or not he will get better. Ahijah gives her the bad news that not only will the son die, but it will be the beginning of a harsh judgment on Jeroboam's family. **1.** Why does Jeroboam send his wife to Ahijah in disguise: So she wouldn't be harassed along the way? Because he knew Ahijah didn't like him because of his behavior? To see if Ahijah was in touch enough with God to see through the disguise? **2.** What irony is there in the fact that Jeroboam's wife has disguised herself to go see a man who cannot see? **3.** If you were Jeroboam's wife how would you have felt about Ahijah's greeting (v. 6)? **4.** Why are Jeroboam's sins particularly grievous to God (vv. 7–9)? **5.** Why is Abijah the only one of Jeroboam's family who will have the dignity of a burial? **6.** How would you feel if you were told that your family members would all be

---

13:32 message he declared ... will certainly come true. The old prophet was shaken out of his spiritual lethargy and declared his faith in the young prophet's message. By doing so, he took a clear stand against idolatry in Israel.

14:2 so you won't be recognized. The prophet Ahijah was now blind (v. 4), but his attendants would have recognized the queen.

14:3 He will tell you what will happen. Jeroboam recognized that *Ahijah*, a true prophet, would know whether his son would live or die. It is unlikely that Jeroboam thought he could trick the blind prophet into blessing his son, like Jacob had tricked Isaac (Gen. 27:1–33). Jeroboam simply wanted to know whether his son would survive.

14:5 But the LORD had told Ahijah. Contrary to Jeroboam's views, Ahijah did not have psychic ability to foretell events. Whatever Ahijah knew was a result of his relationship with the living God.

14:6 wife of Jeroboam. Jeroboam's wife was shocked when the blind prophet knew who she was *before* she even came in the door. This helped her believe the message that followed. **Why this pretense?** Ahijah knew the answer, of course: Jeroboam was hiding from God and had hoped to avoid another confrontation.

14:9 thrust me behind your back. Jeroboam had willfully turned his back on God. The word "thrust" implies a forceful, determined decision. Jeroboam had his mind made up. Even miraculous signs would not convince him to change his evil ways (13:33).

14:10 burn up the house of Jeroboam. God had once offered to make Jeroboam a dynasty. Because Jeroboam had chosen evil, God decided to utterly eradicate his family's claim to the throne. God allows people freedom of choice, but warns that he will respond to their choices (Ezek. 18:21–29).

until it is all gone. [11]Dogs will eat those belonging to Jeroboam who
die in the city, and the birds of the air will feed on those who die in
the country. The LORD has spoken!'

[12]"As for you, go back home. When you set foot in your city, the boy
will die. [13]All Israel will mourn for him and bury him. He is the only
one belonging to Jeroboam who will be buried, because he is the only
one in the house of Jeroboam in whom the LORD, the God of Israel,
has found anything good.

[14]"The LORD will raise up for himself a king over Israel who will cut
off the family of Jeroboam. This is the day! What? Yes, even now.[a]
[15]And the LORD will strike Israel, so that it will be like a reed swaying
in the water. He will uproot Israel from this good land that he gave to
their forefathers and scatter them beyond the River,[b] because they
provoked the LORD to anger by making Asherah poles.[c] [16]And he will
give Israel up because of the sins Jeroboam has committed and has
caused Israel to commit."

[17]Then Jeroboam's wife got up and left and went to Tirzah. As soon
as she stepped over the threshold of the house, the boy died. [18]They
buried him, and all Israel mourned for him, as the LORD had said
through his servant the prophet Ahijah.

[19]The other events of Jeroboam's reign, his wars and how he ruled,
are written in the book of the annals of the kings of Israel. [20]He
reigned for twenty-two years and then rested with his fathers. And
Nadab his son succeeded him as king.

Rehoboam King of Judah

[21]Rehoboam son of Solomon was king in Judah. He was forty-one
years old when he became king, and he reigned seventeen years in
Jerusalem, the city the LORD had chosen out of all the tribes of Israel
in which to put his Name. His mother's name was Naamah; she was
an Ammonite.

[22]Judah did evil in the eyes of the LORD. By the sins they committed
they stirred up his jealous anger more than their fathers had done.
[23]They also set up for themselves high places, sacred stones and
Asherah poles on every high hill and under every spreading tree.

[a]*14* The meaning of the Hebrew for this sentence is uncertain. [b]*15* That is, the Euphrates [c]*15* That is, symbols of the goddess Asherah; here and elsewhere in 1 Kings

devoured by animals upon their deaths? **7.** What does the future hold for Israel (vv. 15–16)? Why are the people so easily led astray by their rulers?

APPLY 1. What does it mean to you to "die with dignity"? **2.** As you think ahead to the time you will die, which of the following would add to your feeling that your death would have dignity, and which would detract: Knowing your organs would be donated to another? Knowing your body would be cremated? Having to go through a long period of suffering or mental incapacitation prior to your death? Knowing your friends and family would mark your death with a festive party? Knowing that something would be done to carry on your life's most important work? **3.** How does this whole discussion make you feel?

OPEN What are three "treasures" you have in your home that you would most want to protect from being carried off by thieves?

STUDY Solomon's son Rehoboam has let the country turn in an evil direction by allowing the people to worship foreign gods and goddesses. As a result they are invaded by the king of Egypt who carries off some of their most important treasures. **1.** Why does the text mention Rehoboam's ancestral lineage twice (vv. 21,31; 11:1–2)? **2.** In what

---

14:11 Dogs will eat ... and the birds. The Law of Moses warned that precisely this would happen if God's people did evil and ignored him (Deut. 28:26).

14:13 All Israel will mourn for him. Abijah was very likely the crown prince, well known and liked by the nation. God saw good in Abijah, as did the people.

14:14 a king over Israel who will cut off the family. This prophecy was fulfilled to the letter when Baasha became king and killed all the descendants of Jeroboam (15:27–30).

14:15 He will uproot Israel from this good land. God's plan had been for a godly dynasty to rule over the northern kingdom. Jeroboam was given a golden opportunity. When he chose evil, the seeds of the entire nation's destruction were sown. This was demonstrated in the great signs when the prophet warned Jeroboam (13:1–6) and in the severe judgment of the prophet when he disobeyed (13:24). A brief window of hope for the nation had now passed. Israel was doomed.

14:16 he will give Israel up. Jeroboam had created the golden calves. God, who sees human history from beginning to end, knew that once calf worship took root in Israel, it would not be swept away till the fall of the kingdom. Despite this, God preserved the godly people in Israel. Many who could not stand the idolatry moved south to Judah (2 Chr. 11:16–17; 15:8–9).

14:21 he reigned seventeen years. Rehoboam was, compared to the elders, a young man at 41 when he began to reign. **put his Name.** God had "put his name" in Jerusalem when the temple was built there. The temple was where his name was worshiped (8:20).

14:23 set up ... high places. Hilltop altars and shrines. **sacred stones.** Stone pillars intended to symbolize a god. **Asherah poles.** These carved wooden poles were probably intended to imitate trees, growing and full of life.

24 There were even male shrine prostitutes in the land; the people engaged in all the detestable practices of the nations the LORD had driven out before the Israelites.

25 In the fifth year of King Rehoboam, Shishak king of Egypt attacked Jerusalem. 26 He carried off the treasures of the temple of the LORD and the treasures of the royal palace. He took everything, including all the gold shields Solomon had made. 27 So King Rehoboam made bronze shields to replace them and assigned these to the commanders of the guard on duty at the entrance to the royal palace. 28 Whenever the king went to the LORD's temple, the guards bore the shields, and afterward they returned them to the guardroom.

29 As for the other events of Rehoboam's reign, and all he did, are they not written in the book of the annals of the kings of Judah? 30 There was continual warfare between Rehoboam and Jeroboam. 31 And Rehoboam rested with his fathers and was buried with them in the City of David. His mother's name was Naamah; she was an Ammonite. And Abijah[a] his son succeeded him as king.

Abijah King of Judah

15 In the eighteenth year of the reign of Jeroboam son of Nebat, Abijah[b] became king of Judah, 2 and he reigned in Jerusalem three years. His mother's name was Maacah daughter of Abishalom.[c]

3 He committed all the sins his father had done before him; his heart was not fully devoted to the LORD his God, as the heart of David his forefather had been. 4 Nevertheless, for David's sake the LORD his God gave him a lamp in Jerusalem by raising up a son to succeed him and by making Jerusalem strong. 5 For David had done what was right in the eyes of the LORD and had not failed to keep any of the LORD's commands all the days of his life—except in the case of Uriah the Hittite.

6 There was war between Rehoboam[d] and Jeroboam throughout ⌊Abijah's⌋ lifetime. 7 As for the other events of Abijah's reign, and all he did, are they not written in the book of the annals of the kings of Judah? There was war between Abijah and Jeroboam. 8 And Abijah rested with his fathers and was buried in the City of David. And Asa his son succeeded him as king.

[a] *31* Some Hebrew manuscripts and Septuagint (see also 2 Chron. 12:16); most Hebrew manuscripts *Abijam*
[b] *1* Some Hebrew manuscripts and Septuagint (see also 2 Chron. 12:16); most Hebrew manuscripts *Abijam*; also in verses 7 and 8 [c] *2* A variant of *Absalom*; also in verse 10 [d] *6* Most Hebrew manuscripts; some Hebrew manuscripts and Syriac *Abijam* (that is, Abijah)

ways has Solomon's sin born fruit in the life of his son and in Israel? **3.** What effect do you think the invasion and thefts had on the national pride of Israel? What effect did it have replacing gold shields with bronze? **4.** Who does the writer imply is to blame for the pillage: Shishak? Rehoboam? The people of Israel? God?

APPLY If someone were making a line graph of your own family history, what would your life look like: Big dip? Downward slope? Upward slope? Steep upward hill? Roller coaster?

OPEN 1. In what ways are you like your dad? In what ways are you unlike him? **2.** What chapter from your life would you rewrite if you could?

STUDY Rehoboam's son Abijah continues his story of rebelling against God. Still, God maintains the kingdom because of his promise to David. **1.** For what is Abijah's reign remembered? **2.** Why does God continue his line "for David's sake" (v. 4)? **3.** What struggle does Abijah inherit?

APPLY Which of your parents' beliefs did you hold on to? Which ones did you reject? Which ones are you still examining as we speak?

They were most often images of the goddess Asherah.

14:24 male shrine prostitutes in the land. Ritual prostitution was part of the fertility cults of Canaan. The Israelites learned these things from the Canaanites whom their forefathers had left in the land (Ps. 106:34–39). The *Israelites did these things even though* God had forbidden them (Deut. 18:9–13; 23:17).

14:26 He took everything. God had blessed Solomon with more riches than any man on earth. But Solomon turned from God, and his son, Rehoboam, followed his example. While obedience brings God's blessings, disobedience often causes blessings to be removed.

15:1 Abijah became king of Judah. After Rehoboam died, his son Abijah took the throne. Abijah was a common name. It had been the name of Jeroboam's son who died years earlier.

15:2 Maacah. Maacah was also the name of the mother of Absalom, David's son (2 Sam. 3:3), and Abishalom and Absalom were probably the same person. This would mean that Maacah was Absalom's daughter or, more likely, his granddaughter. She was a leading influence for evil.

15:3 not fully devoted to the LORD. Abijah was not a total idolater. Judah was plunging into idolatry, but worship of the true God was still an integral part of their culture. Although Abijah tolerated idols, he still publicly declared his devotion to God (2 Chr. 13:4,10–12).

Asa King of Judah

9In the twentieth year of Jeroboam king of Israel, Asa became king
of Judah, 10and he reigned in Jerusalem forty-one years. His
grandmother's name was Maacah daughter of Abishalom.
11Asa did what was right in the eyes of the LORD, as his father David
had done. 12He expelled the male shrine prostitutes from the land and
got rid of all the idols his fathers had made. 13He even deposed his
grandmother Maacah from her position as queen mother, because
she had made a repulsive Asherah pole. Asa cut the pole down and
burned it in the Kidron Valley. 14Although he did not remove the high
places, Asa's heart was fully committed to the LORD all his life. 15He
brought into the temple of the LORD the silver and gold and the articles that he and his father had dedicated.
16There was war between Asa and Baasha king of Israel throughout
their reigns. 17Baasha king of Israel went up against Judah and fortified Ramah to prevent anyone from leaving or entering the territory
of Asa king of Judah.
18Asa then took all the silver and gold that was left in the treasuries
of the LORD's temple and of his own palace. He entrusted it to his
officials and sent them to Ben-Hadad son of Tabrimmon, the son of
Hezion, the king of Aram, who was ruling in Damascus. 19"Let there
be a treaty between me and you," he said, "as there was between my
father and your father. See, I am sending you a gift of silver and gold.
Now break your treaty with Baasha king of Israel so he will withdraw
from me."
20Ben-Hadad agreed with King Asa and sent the commanders of his
forces against the towns of Israel. He conquered Ijon, Dan, Abel Beth
Maacah and all Kinnereth in addition to Naphtali. 21When Baasha
heard this, he stopped building Ramah and withdrew to Tirzah.
22Then King Asa issued an order to all Judah—no one was exempt—
and they carried away from Ramah the stones and timber Baasha had
been using there. With them King Asa built up Geba in Benjamin, and
also Mizpah.

OPEN 1. What is the biggest personal reform you have had to make in your life to this point: Stopping smoking? Eating more healthy food? "Settling down" when you got married? Learning to be "a responsible adult"? **2.** Who supported you in making this reform? Who gave you a hard time or tried to pull you backwards?

STUDY Asa becomes king in Judah and institutes religious reforms, influencing the nation away from foreign deities and back toward God. Hostility between Israel and Judah, however, continued under his reign. **1.** What do you think might have helped Asa break the chain of evil forged by his father and grandfather? **2.** What were some of the specific things Asa did to bring reform? **3.** Who stands in the way of Asa's reforms (v. 13)? **4.** What is Asa's strategy for national defense (vv. 16–20)? What short-term benefit might the alliance provide? What might be some long-term risks of such an alliance?

APPLY 1. When have you felt like your obedience to God has alienated a family member from you? **2.** Is there any way you might find reconciliation without selling out your principles?

15:13 grandmother Maacah. Maacah (vv. 2,9) was the queen mother. Her son, Abijah, had followed God only half-heartedly, likely due to her influence. Asa was free from her control. **repulsive Asherah pole.** Now King Asa had just initiated a national rededication to God (2 Chr. 15:10–15) and it appears that Maacah made her Asherah pole in a deliberate, brazen stand against God. Asa quickly cut down her idol, burned it and deposed her.

15:14 the high places. Asa cleaned house (2 Chr. 14:3). He completely destroyed the high places where idols were worshiped. The high places he did not destroy were the altars of the Lord. These had been legitimate places of worship during the days of the Patriarchs and were tolerated before the temple was built (3:2–4), but now that the temple existed they were obsolete (Deut. 12:13–14).

15:16 war between Asa and Baasha. These were not full-scale battles, but ongoing hostilities throughout their reigns.

15:17 to prevent anyone from leaving or entering. Asa took a wholehearted stand for God, destroyed the idols and made his kingdom great. Many godly people in Israel were so inspired about this that they moved south to Judah. Baasha was alarmed by the amount of people heading south and built the border town of Ramah into a huge guard post to stop the cross-border traffic.

15:19 a treaty. Asa's father had had a treaty with the former king of Aram, Tabrimmon. The new king of Aram, however, had made a treaty with Baasha of Israel. Now Asa was worried about Baasha building up Ramah, only six miles north of Jerusalem. It looked as if Baasha was preparing for war. Asa decided to stop Baasha by paying the Arameans to attack Israel's northern border.

15:21 Baasha ... stopped building Ramah. Asa's plan worked, but God was not pleased. Instead of trusting God to protect him, Asa had relied on the armies of a pagan nation. Up till now, Asa's godliness and popular appeal had transcended national politics and many Israelites had flocked to Judah (2 Chr. 15:9). Then they learned that Asa had paid foreigners to attack their nation.

15:22 an order to all Judah. Asa forced the nation of Judah into a giant labor gang to carry building materials away from Ramah. He became a tyrant, and began to brutally oppress some of his citizens (2 Chr. 16:10).

23As for all the other events of Asa's reign, all his achievements, all
he did and the cities he built, are they not written in the book of the
annals of the kings of Judah? In his old age, however, his feet became
diseased. 24Then Asa rested with his fathers and was buried with
them in the city of his father David. And Jehoshaphat his son succeeded him as king.

Nadab King of Israel

25Nadab son of Jeroboam became king of Israel in the second year
of Asa king of Judah, and he reigned over Israel two years. 26He did
evil in the eyes of the LORD, walking in the ways of his father and in
his sin, which he had caused Israel to commit.
27Baasha son of Ahijah of the house of Issachar plotted against
him, and he struck him down at Gibbethon, a Philistine town, while
Nadab and all Israel were besieging it. 28Baasha killed Nadab in the
third year of Asa king of Judah and succeeded him as king.
29As soon as he began to reign, he killed Jeroboam's whole family.
He did not leave Jeroboam anyone that breathed, but destroyed them
all, according to the word of the LORD given through his servant Ahijah the Shilonite— 30because of the sins Jeroboam had committed
and had caused Israel to commit, and because he provoked the LORD,
the God of Israel, to anger.
31As for the other events of Nadab's reign, and all he did, are they
not written in the book of the annals of the kings of Israel? 32There
was war between Asa and Baasha king of Israel throughout their
reigns.

Baasha King of Israel

33In the third year of Asa king of Judah, Baasha son of Ahijah became king of all Israel in Tirzah, and he reigned twenty-four years.
34He did evil in the eyes of the LORD, walking in the ways of Jeroboam
and in his sin, which he had caused Israel to commit.
16 Then the word of the LORD came to Jehu son of Hanani
against Baasha: 2"I lifted you up from the dust and made you
leader of my people Israel, but you walked in the ways of Jeroboam
and caused my people Israel to sin and to provoke me to anger by
their sins. 3So I am about to consume Baasha and his house, and I
will make your house like that of Jeroboam son of Nebat. 4Dogs will
eat those belonging to Baasha who die in the city, and the birds of the
air will feed on those who die in the country."
5As for the other events of Baasha's reign, what he did and his
achievements, are they not written in the book of the annals of the

OPEN Who was the biggest "backstabber" among your "friends" in high school?

STUDY Nadab became king of Israel after Jeroboam's death, but his reign only lasted two years. He was assassinated by Baasha, who then became king himself. **1.** What was the sin of Nadab's father, Jeroboam, (12:26–33)? **2.** Baasha was likely a military leader. How does his military coup fit in with God's plan (14:10–16)? **3.** Why would Baasha feel it necessary to kill everyone in Jeroboam's family?

APPLY In what ways is your family suffering because of things you have done wrong?

OPEN On a scale of 1–10, what kind of student of history are you, if "1" is "If they didn't make it into a movie, I don't know it" and "10" is "I ace the history categories on *Jeopardy*"?

STUDY Baasha shows he has not learned from history by following in the footsteps of Jeroboam and receiving his same fate. **1.** Are you surprised Baasha lasts 24 years in power? Why do you think God tolerates him that long? **2.** Was Baasha an improvement over the king he replaced? Why or why not? **3.** Is it fair to punish Baasha for destroying the house of Jeroboam when that apparently was God's plan (14:10–16)?

15:23 Asa's reign. Much more was written about this truly remarkable man, both about his achievements and his failures. Some of this information was preserved in 2 Chronicles 14–16.

15:25 Nadab son of Jeroboam. The author of the book of Kings now backtracks some years to describe the kings that had ruled in Israel during this same period. Nadab became king, but his days were numbered. He ruled only two years.

15:26 walking in the ways of his father. Jeroboam had angered God by instituting calf worship, and Nadab upheld this idolatry as the state religion.

15:29 according to the word of the LORD. Ahijah had prophesied that Jeroboam's sins would bring death to every male in his family. Baasha may or may not have known this prophecy. In his mind, these ruthless measures were simply a way to secure his throne.

16:1 Jehu son of Hanani. Jehu, like his father Hanani, was a prophet of Judah. His father had boldly rebuked a king and been imprisoned for it (2 Chr. 16:7–10). This didn't deter Jehu. When God told him to go to Israel to warn Baasha, he went. Jehu's ministry as a prophet would last some fifty years.

kings of Israel? [6]Baasha rested with his fathers and was buried in Tirzah. And Elah his son succeeded him as king.
[7]Moreover, the word of the LORD came through the prophet Jehu son of Hanani to Baasha and his house, because of all the evil he had done in the eyes of the LORD, provoking him to anger by the things he did, and becoming like the house of Jeroboam—and also because he destroyed it.

Elah King of Israel

[8]In the twenty-sixth year of Asa king of Judah, Elah son of Baasha became king of Israel, and he reigned in Tirzah two years.
[9]Zimri, one of his officials, who had command of half his chariots, plotted against him. Elah was in Tirzah at the time, getting drunk in the home of Arza, the man in charge of the palace at Tirzah. [10]Zimri came in, struck him down and killed him in the twenty-seventh year of Asa king of Judah. Then he succeeded him as king.
[11]As soon as he began to reign and was seated on the throne, he killed off Baasha's whole family. He did not spare a single male, whether relative or friend. [12]So Zimri destroyed the whole family of Baasha, in accordance with the word of the LORD spoken against Baasha through the prophet Jehu— [13]because of all the sins Baasha and his son Elah had committed and had caused Israel to commit, so that they provoked the LORD, the God of Israel, to anger by their worthless idols.
[14]As for the other events of Elah's reign, and all he did, are they not written in the book of the annals of the kings of Israel?

Zimri King of Israel

[15]In the twenty-seventh year of Asa king of Judah, Zimri reigned in Tirzah seven days. The army was encamped near Gibbethon, a Philistine town. [16]When the Israelites in the camp heard that Zimri had plotted against the king and murdered him, they proclaimed Omri, the commander of the army, king over Israel that very day there in the camp. [17]Then Omri and all the Israelites with him withdrew from Gibbethon and laid siege to Tirzah. [18]When Zimri saw that the city was taken, he went into the citadel of the royal palace and set the palace on fire around him. So he died, [19]because of the sins he had committed, doing evil in the eyes of the LORD and walking in the ways of Jeroboam and in the sin he had committed and had caused Israel to commit.
[20]As for the other events of Zimri's reign, and the rebellion he

APPLY In what ways has God "lifted you out of the dust" as he did with Baasha? What response from you does this call for?

OPEN What job, paid or volunteer, did you hold for the shortest period of time? What caused you to lose it or give it up?

STUDY Becoming king of Israel is like being head coach of a struggling football team which constantly changes coaching staff. One king, Zimri, reigns only seven days. Ahab becomes king of Israel and raises evil to a whole new level. **1.** What does this succession of short, virtually meaningless reigns say to you: There was a void of leadership? Evil and unbelief creates more evil and unbelief? Violent overthrow begets violent overthrow? **2.** How is Zimri's rise to power like Baasha's? **3.** How does Zimri help fulfill Jehu's prophecy (vv. 1–3)? **4.** Why does Zimri execute the friends, as well as the family, of Baasha? How is the contagion of violence spreading? **5.** What position does Omri have before being proclaimed king? **6.** What determines who becomes king between rivals Omri and Tibni? **7.** What does Ahab do that goes even further in showing evil than his predecessors? **8.** What was wrong with rebuilding Jericho (Josh. 6:17–19,26)? **9.** Who paid with their lives for Heil's decision to rebuild this city?

APPLY 1. Which of the following best indicates the level of violence used in settling disputes in your family: Fists swing, things are thrown? Sometimes there is pushing and shoving? Violent words are thrown around? We mostly solve

---

16:7 because he destroyed it. God did not condone Baasha's brutal murder of Jeroboam's family. God knew the future and saw exactly what was going to happen, but Baasha was responsible for his violent deeds (Matt. 26:24).

16:9 Elah ... getting drunk. While his army was laying seige to Gibbethon (v. 15), Elah was in the palace getting drunk. Zimri and the other officers likely had little respect for such a king.

16:11 Baasha's whole family. Zimri was an opportunist. When he saw the king vulnerable, he decided to kill him. Zimri had not given much thought to his coup d'etat. He was now king, but he had little popular support. Desperate to consolidate his power, he eliminated his competitors in a bloody purge.

16:12 the word of the LORD. Zimri had acted in his own selfish interests. Yet in doing so, he unwittingly fulfilled the prophecy of Jehu (vv. 1–4).

16:18 set the palace on fire. When Zimri realized he would not be king, he committed suicide. In his final act of selfishness, he burned down the palace to ensure that Omri would have neither palace nor throne.

16:19 walking in the ways of Jeroboam. Not a single king of Israel turned from calf worship.

things with non-violent words? 2. Do you need help to "disarm" violent tendencies in solving disputes?

carried out, are they not written in the book of the annals of the kings of Israel?

Omri King of Israel

[21]Then the people of Israel were split into two factions; half supported Tibni son of Ginath for king, and the other half supported Omri. [22]But Omri's followers proved stronger than those of Tibni son of Ginath. So Tibni died and Omri became king.

[23]In the thirty-first year of Asa king of Judah, Omri became king of Israel, and he reigned twelve years, six of them in Tirzah. [24]He bought the hill of Samaria from Shemer for two talents[a] of silver and built a city on the hill, calling it Samaria, after Shemer, the name of the former owner of the hill.

[25]But Omri did evil in the eyes of the LORD and sinned more than all those before him. [26]He walked in all the ways of Jeroboam son of Nebat and in his sin, which he had caused Israel to commit, so that they provoked the LORD, the God of Israel, to anger by their worthless idols.

[27]As for the other events of Omri's reign, what he did and the things he achieved, are they not written in the book of the annals of the kings of Israel? [28]Omri rested with his fathers and was buried in Samaria. And Ahab his son succeeded him as king.

Ahab Becomes King of Israel

[29]In the thirty-eighth year of Asa king of Judah, Ahab son of Omri became king of Israel, and he reigned in Samaria over Israel twenty-two years. [30]Ahab son of Omri did more evil in the eyes of the LORD than any of those before him. [31]He not only considered it trivial to commit the sins of Jeroboam son of Nebat, but he also married Jezebel daughter of Ethbaal king of the Sidonians, and began to serve Baal and worship him. [32]He set up an altar for Baal in the temple of Baal that he built in Samaria. [33]Ahab also made an Asherah pole and did more to provoke the LORD, the God of Israel, to anger than did all the kings of Israel before him.

[34]In Ahab's time, Hiel of Bethel rebuilt Jericho. He laid its founda-

[a]24 That is, about 150 pounds (about 70 kilograms)

16:22 Omri's followers proved stronger. Most of the army, it appears, supported Omri, but a man named Tibni was also proclaimed king. Tibni may have enjoyed popular support, but Omri's military advantage was decisive. The power struggle erupted into a four-year civil war (vv. 15,23). Tibni likely died in battle. **became king.** All Israel was now forced to accept Omri as king.

16:24 hill of Samaria. After four years of civil war, Israel was in ruins. Omri built a completely new capital to inspire the nation with a new beginning. He had another reason as well: to the north, Galilee was open to Aramean attacks; to the west Philistines held Israelite cities; to the south, Judah was strong. Omri needed an easily-defended capital. The hill of Samaria was in the middle of a broad valley, and a city there would be nearly impregnable. It also stood on the main north-south road. **calling it Samaria, after Shemer.** In Israel, land remained in a family and was rarely sold, even to a king (21:1–4). Omri facilitated the sale with a shrewd diplomatic move: he named the city after Shemer.

16:25 But Omri did evil. Omri was a decisive, able leader who built Israel back up into a strong nation. He desired to unite the nation, and since Israel's religion from its beginning had been calf worship, Omri placed great emphasis on it.

16:31 married Jezebel. The Assyrian empire, an ever-present threat of attack, was rumbling in the north. An alliance with the Phoenicians seemed like a good idea. A desire for better trade relations probably also influenced Ahab's decision to marry Jezebel, daughter of Ethbaal. **Baal.** Baal means "lord," and Ethbaal was not only the king of Sidon, but high priest of the local Baal, a god named Melquart. Ethbaal's daughter, Jezebel, was utterly devoted to Baal, and she brought Baal worship to Israel. As angered as God was by the golden calves, Baal worship was even worse.

16:34 rebuilt Jericho. After the walls of Jericho fell flat and the Israelites conquered the city, God wanted Jericho to remain without walls as an eternal memorial of his power. Joshua prophesied that if Jericho were rebuilt, the builder's

tions at the cost of his firstborn son Abiram, and he set up its gates at
the cost of his youngest son Segub, in accordance with the word of
the LORD spoken by Joshua son of Nun.

Elijah Fed by Ravens

17 Now Elijah the Tishbite, from Tishbe[a] in Gilead, said to Ahab,
"As the LORD, the God of Israel, lives, whom I serve, there will
be neither dew nor rain in the next few years except at my word."
2Then the word of the LORD came to Elijah: 3"Leave here, turn eastward and hide in the Kerith Ravine, east of the Jordan. 4You will drink
from the brook, and I have ordered the ravens to feed you there."
5So he did what the LORD had told him. He went to the Kerith
Ravine, east of the Jordan, and stayed there. 6The ravens brought him
bread and meat in the morning and bread and meat in the evening,
and he drank from the brook.

The Widow at Zarephath

7Some time later the brook dried up because there had been no
rain in the land. 8Then the word of the LORD came to him: 9"Go at
once to Zarephath of Sidon and stay there. I have commanded a
widow in that place to supply you with food." 10So he went to Zarephath. When he came to the town gate, a widow was there gathering
sticks. He called to her and asked, "Would you bring me a little water
in a jar so I may have a drink?" 11As she was going to get it, he called,
"And bring me, please, a piece of bread."
12"As surely as the LORD your God lives," she replied, "I don't have
any bread—only a handful of flour in a jar and a little oil in a jug. I am
gathering a few sticks to take home and make a meal for myself and
my son, that we may eat it—and die."
13Elijah said to her, "Don't be afraid. Go home and do as you have
said. But first make a small cake of bread for me from what you have
and bring it to me, and then make something for yourself and your
son. 14For this is what the LORD, the God of Israel, says: 'The jar of

[a]1 Or *Tishbite, of the settlers*

OPEN 1. If you knew that you would have just one last meal before you died, what would you want for that meal? **2.** Who would you want to share that meal with?

STUDY As Israel is led by Ahab, an evil king, the prophet Elijah appears on the scene. Elijah delivers God's word to Ahab that there will be a drought. God sends Elijah to the Kerith Ravine and then to Zarephath. **1.** Why does God send this drought (16:29–17:1)? **2.** Why do you think God sent Elijah out of Israel to stay with a Gentile: To keep him safe from Ahab? As a symbol of Israel's rejection of God? To be provided for by the widow? To provide for the widow? To make God known to the people of Zarephath? **3.** What does the provision by the ravens for Elijah demonstrate? **4.** What do you think was the greater miracle—the provision for Elijah by ravens or the provision for Elijah by a starving widow? **5.** If you were the widow, how would you have responded to Elijah's words in verses 13–14? **6.** What does the woman assume when her son dies? **7.** What impact does her son's recovery have on the widow? What effect do you think this event had on her future faith?

APPLY 1. When has God provided for you, when you saw no way that such provision could

---

oldest and youngest sons would die (Josh. 6:26). Jericho had been inhabited as an unwalled town since Joshua's day, and when Hiel rebuilt Jericho's walls and gates, his oldest and youngest sons died, fulfilling the curse.

17:1 Elijah. After Moses, Elijah was the greatest prophet in the Old Testament. When the northern kingdom was in its greatest spiritual darkness, Elijah appeared like a flash of lightning, suddenly and with great power. His power was not due to his own goodness or charisma. Elijah was very human (James 5:17). His power came from his relationship with God. Elijah's name ("Jehovah is my God") described his life and his message perfectly. He immediately obeyed every command that God gave him. He was utterly uncompromising in his message, totally resolved to turn Israel back to God. The fate of Israel as a nation was already sealed (14:15–16), but God wanted to spare as many of its people as he could.

17:3 Leave here ... and hide. Elijah became known for his sudden appearances and disappearances (18:12), and the effect was unnerving. Ahab would have killed Elijah, but Elijah had disappeared and Ahab was left with the prophet's words ringing in his ears.

17:4 ordered the ravens to feed you there. Ravens were considered an "unclean" bird (Deut. 14:14), but they were bold scavengers. Nevertheless, it took a miracle to direct them to bring their pickings to Elijah, and to do so faithfully (v. 6). This miracle was similar to God providing food for the children of Israel in the desert.

17:10 So he went to Zarephath. It took great faith for Elijah to go to Zarephath in Phoenecia. Ahab had searched all Israel for Elijah and even made other nations look for him (18:10). Sidon was Jezebel's hometown, and Zarephath was a mere eight miles away. It was probably the last place Ahab thought Elijah would go.

17:12 As surely as the LORD your God lives. The widow recognized Elijah as an Israelite, probably by his clothing or accent, and may simply have been honoring him with this statement. Likely, however, she already respected and had faith in Israel's God (v. 1).

17:14 For this is what the LORD ... says. Elijah then gave the Phoenecian widow a promise. The nation of Israel, with whom God had made a covenant,

come? **2.** What "jars and jugs" are running dry for you right now? What does God's past provision say to you in the midst of this situation?

flour will not be used up and the jug of oil will not run dry until the
day the LORD gives rain on the land.' "
15She went away and did as Elijah had told her. So there was food
every day for Elijah and for the woman and her family. 16For the jar of
flour was not used up and the jug of oil did not run dry, in keeping
with the word of the LORD spoken by Elijah.
17Some time later the son of the woman who owned the house became ill. He grew worse and worse, and finally stopped breathing.
18She said to Elijah, "What do you have against me, man of God? Did
you come to remind me of my sin and kill my son?"
19"Give me your son," Elijah replied. He took him from her arms,
carried him to the upper room where he was staying, and laid him on
his bed. 20Then he cried out to the LORD, "O LORD my God, have you
brought tragedy also upon this widow I am staying with, by causing
her son to die?" 21Then he stretched himself out on the boy three
times and cried to the LORD, "O LORD my God, let this boy's life return
to him!"
22The LORD heard Elijah's cry, and the boy's life returned to him,
and he lived. 23Elijah picked up the child and carried him down from
the room into the house. He gave him to his mother and said, "Look,
your son is alive!"
24Then the woman said to Elijah, "Now I know that you are a man
of God and that the word of the LORD from your mouth is the truth."

Elijah and Obadiah

OPEN 1. What person alive today do you admire more than anyone else? **2.** If you met that person face to face, what would you like to say to him or her?

STUDY The prophet Obadiah meets Elijah whom he respects highly. However, it turns into a somewhat frightening encounter for

18 After a long time, in the third year, the word of the LORD came
to Elijah: "Go and present yourself to Ahab, and I will send
rain on the land." 2So Elijah went to present himself to Ahab.
Now the famine was severe in Samaria, 3and Ahab had summoned
Obadiah, who was in charge of his palace. (Obadiah was a devout believer in the LORD. 4While Jezebel was killing off the LORD's prophets,
Obadiah had taken a hundred prophets and hidden them in two

---

had rejected God's word. Now a foreigner was given a chance to believe God's word and be blessed as a result (Ezek. 3:4–7).

17:15 She . . . did as Elijah had told her. In doing so, she was not only obeying Elijah, but the command of God (v. 9). In one of the most touching scenes in the Bible, a dying widow shared her family's last meal with a stranger, because she believed that the God of Israel cared for her. Jesus himself commended her in Luke 4:25–26.

17:16 For the jar of flour was not used up. For three years, day after day, God repeated the miracle, replenishing the widow's flour and oil. Despite the terrible famine, she always had enough.

17:18 remind me of my sin and kill my son? Like so many people when tragedy strikes, the widow assumed that God was judging her for sin in her life. Up till this point, she had rejoiced that God cared for her. Now she asked, "If God cares for me, why did he kill my son?" Elijah asked God this same question (v. 20).

17:21 cried to the LORD. Elijah stretched himself out on the boy three times, but that in itself is not what brought the boy back to life (2 Kin. 13:20–21). Nor was it simply Elijah's great faith crying out to God, though that was surely vital (James 5:14–17).

17:24 Now I know that you are a man of God. This miracle increased the widow's faith dramatically. This was God's purpose during the entire ordeal. Jesus raising Lazarus from the dead achieved similar results (John 11:1–4,40–45). **the word of the LORD from your mouth.** God's entire message to the widow was that he cared for her. Miraculously providing food proved that. During the years Elijah stayed with her, he would surely have told her that God was a caring, just and life-giving God. Now she knew that everything Elijah told her was true.

18:1 the third year. The drought had now lasted three and a half years (James 5:17). **Go and present yourself to Ahab.** Elijah needed not only faith but courage to obey this message. Ahab was out to kill him and Elijah had been in hiding all this time. Now he was to walk boldly up to his worst enemy. **I will send rain on the land.** As the drought stretched on year after year, the Israelites had prayed for Baal, the god of rain, to bring water from the heavens. Nothing. By now, love for Baal was at an all-time low. The drought had accomplished God's purpose. Now it was time for God to send rain.

18:4 killing off the LORD's prophets. Within days, Elijah would command the Israelites to slay the false prophets of Baal (v. 40). That may seem harsh, but it must be remembered that these same followers of Baal had consented

caves, fifty in each, and had supplied them with food and water.)
[5]Ahab had said to Obadiah, "Go through the land to all the springs and valleys. Maybe we can find some grass to keep the horses and mules alive so we will not have to kill any of our animals." [6]So they divided the land they were to cover, Ahab going in one direction and Obadiah in another.

[7]As Obadiah was walking along, Elijah met him. Obadiah recognized him, bowed down to the ground, and said, "Is it really you, my lord Elijah?"

[8]"Yes," he replied. "Go tell your master, 'Elijah is here.'"

[9]"What have I done wrong," asked Obadiah, "that you are handing your servant over to Ahab to be put to death? [10]As surely as the LORD your God lives, there is not a nation or kingdom where my master has not sent someone to look for you. And whenever a nation or kingdom claimed you were not there, he made them swear they could not find you. [11]But now you tell me to go to my master and say, 'Elijah is here.'
[12]I don't know where the Spirit of the LORD may carry you when I leave you. If I go and tell Ahab and he doesn't find you, he will kill me. Yet I your servant have worshiped the LORD since my youth. [13]Haven't you heard, my lord, what I did while Jezebel was killing the prophets of the LORD? I hid a hundred of the LORD's prophets in two caves, fifty in each, and supplied them with food and water. [14]And now you tell me to go to my master and say, 'Elijah is here.' He will kill me!"

[15]Elijah said, "As the LORD Almighty lives, whom I serve, I will surely present myself to Ahab today."

Elijah on Mount Carmel

[16]So Obadiah went to meet Ahab and told him, and Ahab went to meet Elijah. [17]When he saw Elijah, he said to him, "Is that you, you troubler of Israel?"

[18]"I have not made trouble for Israel," Elijah replied. "But you and your father's family have. You have abandoned the LORD's commands and have followed the Baals. [19]Now summon the people from all over Israel to meet me on Mount Carmel. And bring the four hundred and fifty prophets of Baal and the four hundred prophets of Asherah, who eat at Jezebel's table."

[20]So Ahab sent word throughout all Israel and assembled the prophets on Mount Carmel. [21]Elijah went before the people and said, "How long will you waver between two opinions? If the LORD is God, follow him; but if Baal is God, follow him."

But the people said nothing.

him, as Elijah wants him to convey to Ahab a message that Obadiah thinks might endanger his own life. **1.** What do you find most perplexing about this story: That the king and a high official are out scouting for good pasture instead of delegating someone else to do it? That Obadiah's act of hiding the prophets is well known, and yet Ahab hasn't killed him? That Obadiah was brave in hiding the prophets, but seems less brave about conveying Elijah's message? **2.** Why might Ahab kill Obadiah? **3.** What has Ahab tried in order to find and kill Elijah? **4.** Why might Obadiah tend to trust Elijah's reassurance in verse 15?

APPLY 1. When was the last time that trusting someone that was telling you the truth was a big risk for you? **2.** What helps you trust someone even when the stakes are high?

OPEN 1. When you were in high school, what kind of contest were you most likely to engage in with your rivals: Drag racing? Arm wrestling? A "gossip war"? A shouting contest? Challenging each other for an elected student office? A "war of wits"? **2.** What do you remember as your greatest triumph?

STUDY After announcing to wicked King Ahab the beginning of a severe drought, the prophet Elijah left Israel. Now, about three years later, Elijah returns to win a great victory over his rivals, the false prophets of Baal. **1.** Why does Ahab think Elijah is the "troubler of Israel"? Why does Elijah reverse the charges?

---

to the murder of God's prophets. Many probably had blood on their hands (Rev. 6:9–10). They also sacrificed young children in religious rituals.

18:5 keep the horses and mules alive. Ahab was unrepentant. He cared nothing that the prophets of God had been murdered. Yet now he was frantically searching for grass to spare his animals.

18:12 the Spirit of the LORD may carry you. Elijah's sudden appearances and disappearances had many people convinced that God was miraculously picking him up and carrying him away. Even other prophets were convinced of it (2 Kin. 2:15–17).

18:18 abandoned the LORD's commands. Ahab, not Elijah, had brought trouble to Israel. Elijah was referring to the evil of forsaking God and of worshiping Baal. The drought was not the main problem. The drought was God's punishment on Israel for abandoning his commands (Deut. 28:15–24).

18:19 summon the people from all over Israel. Elijah wanted a huge audience to see with their own eyes what would soon happen. Ahab, more than ready for a showdown, complied (v. 20). **bring the ... prophets of Baal.** The prophets of Baal sat around in Samaria, supported by the state, eating at Jezebel's table. Ahab was ordered to bring them to Mount Carmel.

Would you be considered to be a "troubler"? **2.** Which of the following modern phrases closest approximates what Elijah was telling the people in verse 21: "Stop straddling the fence"? "You can't have your cake and eat it too"? "It's time to make a commitment"? **3.** Why don't the people say anything in response to Elijah? **4.** What was Elijah pointing out through his not-so-subtle sarcasm in verse 27? **5.** How do you think the prophets of Baal were feeling: At the beginning of the day? At midday? By evening? When the fire of the Lord came down on Elijah's altar? **6.** How would you describe Elijah based on this story: Bold in his faith? Cocky? Decisive? Violent? Devoted? Larger than life? Other? **7.** After the signs of the sacrifice and the bringing of rain, how would you expect Ahab to react? Why do you think he remains stubborn and hostile (19:1–2)?

APPLY 1. In what ways, if any, do you find yourself "wavering between two opinions" instead of fully committing to God? **2.** What kind of "signs" would it take to bring you to a fuller commitment?

22 Then Elijah said to them, "I am the only one of the LORD's prophets left, but Baal has four hundred and fifty prophets. 23 Get two bulls
for us. Let them choose one for themselves, and let them cut it into
pieces and put it on the wood but not set fire to it. I will prepare the
other bull and put it on the wood but not set fire to it. 24 Then you call
on the name of your god, and I will call on the name of the LORD. The
god who answers by fire—he is God."
Then all the people said, "What you say is good."
25 Elijah said to the prophets of Baal, "Choose one of the bulls and
prepare it first, since there are so many of you. Call on the name of
your god, but do not light the fire." 26 So they took the bull given them
and prepared it.
Then they called on the name of Baal from morning till noon.
"O Baal, answer us!" they shouted. But there was no response; no
one answered. And they danced around the altar they had made.
27 At noon Elijah began to taunt them. "Shout louder!" he said.
"Surely he is a god! Perhaps he is deep in thought, or busy, or traveling. Maybe he is sleeping and must be awakened." 28 So they shouted
louder and slashed themselves with swords and spears, as was their
custom, until their blood flowed. 29 Midday passed, and they continued their frantic prophesying until the time for the evening sacrifice.
But there was no response, no one answered, no one paid attention.
30 Then Elijah said to all the people, "Come here to me." They came
to him, and he repaired the altar of the LORD, which was in ruins.
31 Elijah took twelve stones, one for each of the tribes descended from
Jacob, to whom the word of the LORD had come, saying, "Your name
shall be Israel." 32 With the stones he built an altar in the name of the
LORD, and he dug a trench around it large enough to hold two seahs[a]
of seed. 33 He arranged the wood, cut the bull into pieces and laid it on
the wood. Then he said to them, "Fill four large jars with water and
pour it on the offering and on the wood."
34 "Do it again," he said, and they did it again.
"Do it a third time," he ordered, and they did it the third time. 35 The
water ran down around the altar and even filled the trench.
36 At the time of sacrifice, the prophet Elijah stepped forward and
prayed: "O LORD, God of Abraham, Isaac and Israel, let it be known
today that you are God in Israel and that I am your servant and have
done all these things at your command. 37 Answer me, O LORD, answer

[a] *32* That is, probably about 13 quarts (about 15 liters)

18:22 the only one of the LORD's prophets left. Elijah knew of other prophets of God in Israel, but they were in hiding (v. 4). Elijah was the only prophet left with the courage to do what a prophet should do. No one stood with him that day on Mount Carmel.

18:24 answers by fire—he is God. The choice was clear: both God and Baal claimed the same divine power, but only one of them could be God.

18:26 there was no response. For years, Baal had failed to send rain. Now he failed to send fire. **they danced around the altar.** Such dances were a regular part of pagan worship to get a pagan god's attention and some answers to prayer. The dances put worshipers in a trance-like state.

18:30 he repaired the altar of the LORD. The altar was one of many ancient places of worship built before Solomon finished the temple (3:2). It had fallen down out of neglect or been destroyed by the followers of Baal (19:10).

18:33 Fill ... with water. By drenching the altar, the offering and the wood with buckets of water, Elijah deliberately made it difficult for his sacrifice to burn. He wanted to demonstrate to the crowd just how powerful the Lord was.

18:36 Elijah ... prayed. Elijah's brief, simple prayer was in direct contrast to the prophets of Baal, who had desperately prayed, chanted, danced and mutilated themselves for hours. **God of Abraham, Isaac and Israel**. Elijah reminded God of the covenant he had made with their forefathers, but he also reminded the people that Israel, after whom they were named, followed God.

me, so these people will know that you, O LORD, are God, and that
you are turning their hearts back again."
38Then the fire of the LORD fell and burned up the sacrifice, the
wood, the stones and the soil, and also licked up the water in
the trench.
39When all the people saw this, they fell prostrate and cried, "The
LORD—he is God! The LORD—he is God!"
40Then Elijah commanded them, "Seize the prophets of Baal. Don't
let anyone get away!" They seized them, and Elijah had them brought
down to the Kishon Valley and slaughtered there.
41And Elijah said to Ahab, "Go, eat and drink, for there is the sound
of a heavy rain." 42So Ahab went off to eat and drink, but Elijah
climbed to the top of Carmel, bent down to the ground and put his
face between his knees.
43"Go and look toward the sea," he told his servant. And he went up
and looked.
"There is nothing there," he said.
Seven times Elijah said, "Go back."
44The seventh time the servant reported, "A cloud as small as a
man's hand is rising from the sea."
So Elijah said, "Go and tell Ahab, 'Hitch up your chariot and go
down before the rain stops you.'"
45Meanwhile, the sky grew black with clouds, the wind rose, a
heavy rain came on and Ahab rode off to Jezreel. 46The power of the
LORD came upon Elijah and, tucking his cloak into his belt, he ran
ahead of Ahab all the way to Jezreel.

Elijah Flees to Horeb

19 Now Ahab told Jezebel everything Elijah had done and how
he had killed all the prophets with the sword. 2So Jezebel
sent a messenger to Elijah to say, "May the gods deal with me, be it
ever so severely, if by this time tomorrow I do not make your life like
that of one of them."
3Elijah was afraid[a] and ran for his life. When he came to Beersheba
in Judah, he left his servant there, 4while he himself went a day's

[a]3 Or *Elijah saw*

OPEN In each of the pairs of situations that follow, choose which one you are more likely to feel in touch with God: In the quietness of a moment alone or in the excitement of a big Christian rally? In a powerful thunderstorm or a gentle rain? In a group like this one or a worship service? In an eloquent sermon or in the loving presence of a friend?

18:39 The LORD—he is God! Utterly convinced, shaking with awe, the entire multitude fell to the ground to worship God.

18:40 They seized them. The crowd, which had earlier wavered, rushed to obey Elijah. **slaughtered.** According to the Law of God (Deut. 13:13–17), these idolatrous prophets were to be slain. Ahab made no move to stop the slaughter.

18:42 bent down to the ground. The altar of God was no longer there. It had been vaporized. So Elijah knelt on the ground and prayed. Now that God had turned the people's hearts back to him (v. 37), and they had confessed his name (v. 39), Elijah implored God to remove the curse (Deut. 28:20,24) and send rain (8:35–36).

18:46 power of the LORD. Elijah ran 14 miles through heavy rain, faster than a racing chariot. As Ahab drove to Jezreel, this final miracle was a reminder of how powerful God was. **ran ahead of Ahab.** When Ahab arrived in Jezreel, Elijah *was there.* When Ahab told the people that God had sent down fire, then had sent rain that was now falling around them, Elijah was there to reinforce the story.

19:2 Jezebel sent a messenger to Elijah. Elijah was no longer in hiding. The messenger found Elijah because he now walked boldly among the people.

19:3 Elijah was afraid. The news of God's victory swept through the land and Elijah now enjoyed great popular support. But when Jezebel's threat came, the people deserted Elijah. First the prophets had been afraid to stand with him. Now the people who had boldly slain the prophets of Baal fled in fear. Elijah was devastated. Elijah had been critical of other prophets who had not taken a stand (18:22). Now he ran in fear.

19:4 prayed that he might die. Elijah's entire life's work had culminated in a great victory that seemed poised to cause a national revival. When the victory vaporized, Elijah felt exhausted. He felt that everything he had accomplished amounted to nothing and that there was no point in living.

STUDY After "showing up" and killing the prophets of Baal, the favorites of Ahab and Jezebel, Elijah flees because of threats against his life by Jezebel. While on this flight, Elijah finds God in a quiet moment in a cave, and is spiritually nourished and revived. **1.** Why is Elijah afraid of Jezebel when he has just demonstrated the impotence of her gods? **2.** Why does Elijah want to die: Tired of running and feeling afraid? Tired of feeling alone against the crowd of Baal-worshipers? Disappointed he had not been able to turn the people away from the Baals and to God? **3.** What is significant about the 40 days and nights, at Mount Horeb? (Deut. 4:10–14)? **4.** How would you describe Elijah's mood in verse 10: Self-pity? Despair? Panicky? Angry? **5.** Why is it significant that God was not in the powerful wind, the earthquake or the fire, but rather came in a gentle whisper? In which of these had Moses found God (Ex. 3:1–2)? **6.** Why was it important for God to point out the number of knees that had not bowed to Baal? **7.** What's the point of Elijah throwing his cloak to the young Elisha? **8.** Why does Elisha slaughter his oxen and burn his plow, before joining Elijah?

APPLY 1. Where are you right now in terms of Elijah's journey: Feeling your moment of triumph turning to despair? Fleeing from your "enemies"? Searching for God, in whatever form God will appear? Learning how many people stand with you in your fight? Ready to pass your mantle on to someone else? **2.** Where is a place you could go to hear God's voice in the quiet? **3.** Were God to speak to you right now, what do you think he would say?

journey into the desert. He came to a broom tree, sat down under it
and prayed that he might die. "I have had enough, LORD," he said.
"Take my life; I am no better than my ancestors." 5Then he lay down
under the tree and fell asleep.
All at once an angel touched him and said, "Get up and eat." 6He
looked around, and there by his head was a cake of bread baked over
hot coals, and a jar of water. He ate and drank and then lay down
again.
7The angel of the LORD came back a second time and touched him
and said, "Get up and eat, for the journey is too much for you." 8So he
got up and ate and drank. Strengthened by that food, he traveled
forty days and forty nights until he reached Horeb, the mountain of
God. 9There he went into a cave and spent the night.

The Lord Appears to Elijah

And the word of the LORD came to him: "What are you doing here,
Elijah?"
10He replied, "I have been very zealous for the LORD God Almighty.
The Israelites have rejected your covenant, broken down your altars,
and put your prophets to death with the sword. I am the only one left,
and now they are trying to kill me too."
11The LORD said, "Go out and stand on the mountain in the presence of the LORD, for the LORD is about to pass by."
Then a great and powerful wind tore the mountains apart and
shattered the rocks before the LORD, but the LORD was not in the
wind. After the wind there was an earthquake, but the LORD was not
in the earthquake. 12After the earthquake came a fire, but the LORD
was not in the fire. And after the fire came a gentle whisper. 13When
Elijah heard it, he pulled his cloak over his face and went out and
stood at the mouth of the cave.
Then a voice said to him, "What are you doing here, Elijah?"
14He replied, "I have been very zealous for the LORD God Almighty.
The Israelites have rejected your covenant, broken down your altars,
and put your prophets to death with the sword. I am the only one left,
and now they are trying to kill me too."
15The LORD said to him, "Go back the way you came, and go to the
Desert of Damascus. When you get there, anoint Hazael king over
Aram. 16Also, anoint Jehu son of Nimshi king over Israel, and anoint
Elisha son of Shaphat from Abel Meholah to succeed you as prophet.

19:7 The angel of the LORD. God often sends his angels to strengthen and support those who are weak or discouraged (Matt. 4:11; Luke 22:43). **the journey.** Elijah had decided to go to Mount Horeb (another name for Mount Sinai) because there God had given his laws to Israel. Elijah was going through a deep personal crisis and had to talk to God. In his despair he refused to eat. Concerned for Elijah, God told him to eat.

19:10 I have been very zealous. Elijah had been driven by intense devotion for God. He had been zealous to the point of burnout, but in his uncompromising stand against idolatry, he had lost his patience and empathy. **rejected your covenant.** The people had sinned and Elijah wanted God to judge them—now. **I am the only one.** Elijah knew there were other prophets (18:13), but he had little respect for people who would not take a stand for God.

19:12 a gentle whisper. When God sent a destructive wind, an earthquake and fire, he was showing ability to speak in power and judge his people. But God wanted to touch people's hearts with the voice of his Spirit rather than drive them to obey out of fear. Gentleness was a trait that Elijah lacked.

19:15 anoint Hazael king over Aram. God would indeed judge Israel. Vengeance was his. But judgment was not for God's servants to pray for (Rom. 12:19–20). Hazael would be such a merciless enemy of Israel that Elisha, who fulfilled this command, literally wept for Israel as he anointed Hazael king (2 Kin. 8:7–15).

19:16 anoint Jehu ... king over Israel. Jehu would be a zealous sword

17Jehu will put to death any who escape the sword of Hazael, and
Elisha will put to death any who escape the sword of Jehu. 18Yet I
reserve seven thousand in Israel—all whose knees have not bowed
down to Baal and all whose mouths have not kissed him."

The Call of Elisha

19So Elijah went from there and found Elisha son of Shaphat. He
was plowing with twelve yoke of oxen, and he himself was driving the
twelfth pair. Elijah went up to him and threw his cloak around him.
20Elisha then left his oxen and ran after Elijah. "Let me kiss my father
and mother good-by," he said, "and then I will come with you."
"Go back," Elijah replied. "What have I done to you?"
21So Elisha left him and went back. He took his yoke of oxen and
slaughtered them. He burned the plowing equipment to cook the
meat and gave it to the people, and they ate. Then he set out to follow
Elijah and became his attendant.

Ben-Hadad Attacks Samaria

20 Now Ben-Hadad king of Aram mustered his entire army.
Accompanied by thirty-two kings with their horses and
chariots, he went up and besieged Samaria and attacked it. 2He sent
messengers into the city to Ahab king of Israel, saying, "This is what
Ben-Hadad says: 3'Your silver and gold are mine, and the best of your
wives and children are mine.' "
4The king of Israel answered, "Just as you say, my lord the king. I
and all I have are yours."
5The messengers came again and said, "This is what Ben-Hadad
says: 'I sent to demand your silver and gold, your wives and your children. 6But about this time tomorrow I am going to send my officials
to search your palace and the houses of your officials. They will seize
everything you value and carry it away.' "
7The king of Israel summoned all the elders of the land and said to
them, "See how this man is looking for trouble! When he sent for my
wives and my children, my silver and my gold, I did not refuse him."
8The elders and the people all answered, "Don't listen to him or
agree to his demands."
9So he replied to Ben-Hadad's messengers, "Tell my lord the king,
'Your servant will do all you demanded the first time, but this demand
I cannot meet.' " They left and took the answer back to Ben-Hadad.
10Then Ben-Hadad sent another message to Ahab: "May the gods

OPEN 1. Who were the biggest bullies when you were in school? What did they try to take from you? **2.** What did your parents counsel you about dealing with bullies: Tell the teacher? Stand and fight? Run? Form alliances with friends? Give in? Other?

STUDY Ben-Hadad, King of Aram, attacks King Ahab of Israel, and makes heavy demands for tribute. Ahab ultimately decides to resist. **1.** What are Ben-Hadad's initial demands? What does he add to these demands later? **2.** Why does Ben-Hadad increase the demands? **3.** Why does Ahab balk at the increased demands: His property was more important to him than his wives and children? He figured it wouldn't stop there? It was the straw that broke the camel's back? **4.** What point is Ahab making in verse 11? **5.** What were the kings doing when they heard Ahab's response? How might that have affected their behavior?

---

of vengeance in the Lord's hand. He would finish the job Elijah had started and completely destroy Baal worship from Israel (2 Kin. 10:18–28) Judgment was coming, but it was not to happen in Elijah's day. **anoint Elisha ... to succeed you as prophet.** Elijah had not finished God's work, but he now learned that it didn't depend just on him. God could, and now did, raise up someone to take Elijah's place.

19:17 Jehu will put to death any who escape ... Hazael. This is exactly what happened years later. King Joram was wounded in battle against Hazael, but escaped, only to be killed by Jehu (2 Kin. 9:14–24).

19:18 Yet I reserve seven thousand in Israel. God told Elijah that thousands of Israelites still loved him. Though Elijah did not esteem them highly, God did. Elijah was both humbled and encouraged, and left Sinai with renewed resolve.

19:19 found Elisha son of Shaphat. This was not difficult, since God had told Elijah where Elisha lived (v. 16). Elijah may even have known Elisha previously, but not given him much thought. **threw his cloak around him.** This immediately told Elisha that he had been chosen to succeed Elijah in ministry.

19:21 he set out to follow Elijah. Elijah accepted Elisha as a follower and eventually as a replacement. After this, many other prophets began to associate with Elijah and Elisha (20:13,35; 22:8; 2 Kin. 2:7,15).

APPLY What is so important to you that you would be willing to die to defend it?

---

deal with me, be it ever so severely, if enough dust remains in Samaria to give each of my men a handful."

[11]The king of Israel answered, "Tell him: 'One who puts on his armor should not boast like one who takes it off.' "

[12]Ben-Hadad heard this message while he and the kings were drinking in their tents,[a] and he ordered his men: "Prepare to attack." So they prepared to attack the city.

Ahab Defeats Ben-Hadad

OPEN 1. In sports, who are you most likely to root for: The favorite or the underdog? **2.** What wins by an underdog have excited you the most?

STUDY In the battle between Ben-Hadad and his allies and King Ahab's tiny little army, Israel is definitely the underdog. But an unnamed prophet comes and promises a victory from God. **1.** Why do you suppose the prophet here is never named? **2.** What result is the prophet expecting when the people recognized that God is helping Ahab (v. 13)? **3.** What makes Ahab nervous about the prophet's advice? Would you have been suspicious? **4.** Who takes the offensive in this battle? How might that have helped? **5.** What do Ben-Hadad's advisors tell him about why they think Israel defeated them in the first battle? **6.** What was the comparative size of the two armies in the second battle (v. 27)? **7.** What do you think happened for six days at the camp at Aphek? **8.** What message do the sackcloth and ropes convey? **9.** Why does Ahab let Ben-Hadad live: He's a merciful person? He liked the way Ben-Hadad groveled? He thought it was a good treaty? He didn't want to gamble on Ben-Hadad having a stronger successor? Other?

APPLY 1. When did you learn that God is not just a God who is with you on the hills (the high points of life), but when you are in the valleys (the low points of life) as well? **2.** What great victory has God brought to you when you were "down in the valley"?

[13]Meanwhile a prophet came to Ahab king of Israel and announced, "This is what the LORD says: 'Do you see this vast army? I will give it into your hand today, and then you will know that I am the LORD.' "

[14]"But who will do this?" asked Ahab.

The prophet replied, "This is what the LORD says: 'The young officers of the provincial commanders will do it.' "

"And who will start the battle?" he asked.

The prophet answered, "You will."

[15]So Ahab summoned the young officers of the provincial commanders, 232 men. Then he assembled the rest of the Israelites, 7,000 in all. [16]They set out at noon while Ben-Hadad and the 32 kings allied with him were in their tents getting drunk. [17]The young officers of the provincial commanders went out first.

Now Ben-Hadad had dispatched scouts, who reported, "Men are advancing from Samaria."

[18]He said, "If they have come out for peace, take them alive; if they have come out for war, take them alive."

[19]The young officers of the provincial commanders marched out of the city with the army behind them [20]and each one struck down his opponent. At that, the Arameans fled, with the Israelites in pursuit. But Ben-Hadad king of Aram escaped on horseback with some of his horsemen. [21]The king of Israel advanced and overpowered the horses and chariots and inflicted heavy losses on the Arameans.

[22]Afterward, the prophet came to the king of Israel and said, "Strengthen your position and see what must be done, because next spring the king of Aram will attack you again."

[23]Meanwhile, the officials of the king of Aram advised him, "Their gods are gods of the hills. That is why they were too strong for us. But if we fight them on the plains, surely we will be stronger than they. [24]Do this: Remove all the kings from their commands and replace them with other officers. [25]You must also raise an army like the one you lost—horse for horse and chariot for chariot—so we can fight Israel on the plains. Then surely we will be stronger than they." He agreed with them and acted accordingly.

[a]12 Or *in Succoth;* also in verse 16

20:11 This is a proverb or cliché of the day. It can be interpreted, "Save your bragging until after you win."

20:13 I will give it ... and then you will know that I am the LORD. God's purpose never changed. He wanted Ahab to know and recognize him (which Ahab did not do). God shows his presence in our lives for the same reasons.

20:15 7,000. This was not a large army for going after someone as powerful as Ben-Hadad, who had 32 city-states on his side. The smaller the Israelite army, though, the more obvious it was to all that victory belonged to the Lord.

20:20 horseback. This probably refers to chariots rather than actually riding on a horse's back.

20:22 next spring. This was the favorite time for kings to go to war (2 Sam. 11:1).

26 The next spring Ben-Hadad mustered the Arameans and went up
to Aphek to fight against Israel. 27 When the Israelites were also
mustered and given provisions, they marched out to meet them. The
Israelites camped opposite them like two small flocks of goats, while
the Arameans covered the countryside.
28 The man of God came up and told the king of Israel, "This is what
the LORD says: 'Because the Arameans think the LORD is a god of the
hills and not a god of the valleys, I will deliver this vast army into your
hands, and you will know that I am the LORD.' "
29 For seven days they camped opposite each other, and on the seventh day the battle was joined. The Israelites inflicted a hundred
thousand casualties on the Aramean foot soldiers in one day. 30 The
rest of them escaped to the city of Aphek, where the wall collapsed on
twenty-seven thousand of them. And Ben-Hadad fled to the city and
hid in an inner room.
31 His officials said to him, "Look, we have heard that the kings of
the house of Israel are merciful. Let us go to the king of Israel with
sackcloth around our waists and ropes around our heads. Perhaps he
will spare your life."
32 Wearing sackcloth around their waists and ropes around their
heads, they went to the king of Israel and said, "Your servant Ben-
Hadad says: 'Please let me live.' "
The king answered, "Is he still alive? He is my brother."
33 The men took this as a good sign and were quick to pick up his
word. "Yes, your brother Ben-Hadad!" they said.
"Go and get him," the king said. When Ben-Hadad came out, Ahab
had him come up into his chariot.
34 "I will return the cities my father took from your father," Ben-
Hadad offered. "You may set up your own market areas in Damascus,
as my father did in Samaria."
⌞Ahab said,⌟ "On the basis of a treaty I will set you free." So he made
a treaty with him, and let him go.

A Prophet Condemns Ahab

35 By the word of the LORD one of the sons of the prophets said to
his companion, "Strike me with your weapon," but the man refused.
36 So the prophet said, "Because you have not obeyed the LORD, as
soon as you leave me a lion will kill you." And after the man went
away, a lion found him and killed him.
37 The prophet found another man and said, "Strike me, please." So
the man struck him and wounded him. 38 Then the prophet went and
stood by the road waiting for the king. He disguised himself with
his headband down over his eyes. 39 As the king passed by, the prophet called out to him, "Your servant went into the thick of the battle,
and someone came to me with a captive and said, 'Guard this man.
If he is missing, it will be your life for his life, or you must pay a

OPEN When you were in grade school, which of the following disguises would you have most enjoyed putting on: Elvis? A famous political figure? A movie star? A famous singer?

STUDY Ahab has let Ben-Hadad live after defeating his forces in battle. A prophet now disguises himself in order to let Ahab know that God would judge him for that action. **1.** Why does this prophet want to be wounded? **2.** Why such a punishment for the well-meaning soul in verse 36? **3.** In what other famous

20:28 man of God came up. This same prophet talked with Ahab earlier (vv. 13, 22).

20:32 Your servant Ben-Hadad. The tables now were turned. In verse 4, Ahab had offered all he owned to Ben-Hadad. Now Ben-Hadad offered his own self (which meant all that he owned as well) to Ahab. **brother.** This does not mean a literal brother. It means "not an enemy."

20:34 your father. This phrase probably did not refer to Ahab's father, Omri, but to his predecessor, Baasha, who once had a treaty with Ben-Hadad.

20:35 one of the sons of the prophets. The prophets were organized into schools where they trained and studied the Law of Moses. Groups of prophets were often described as companies.

talent[a] of silver.' 40 While your servant was busy here and there, the man disappeared."

"That is your sentence," the king of Israel said. "You have pronounced it yourself."

41 Then the prophet quickly removed the headband from his eyes, and the king of Israel recognized him as one of the prophets. 42 He said to the king, "This is what the LORD says: 'You have set free a man I had determined should die.[b] Therefore it is your life for his life, your people for his people.' " 43 Sullen and angry, the king of Israel went to his palace in Samaria.

Naboth's Vineyard

21 Some time later there was an incident involving a vineyard belonging to Naboth the Jezreelite. The vineyard was in Jezreel, close to the palace of Ahab king of Samaria. 2 Ahab said to Naboth, "Let me have your vineyard to use for a vegetable garden, since it is close to my palace. In exchange I will give you a better vineyard or, if you prefer, I will pay you whatever it is worth."

3 But Naboth replied, "The LORD forbid that I should give you the inheritance of my fathers."

4 So Ahab went home, sullen and angry because Naboth the Jezreelite had said, "I will not give you the inheritance of my fathers." He lay on his bed sulking and refused to eat.

5 His wife Jezebel came in and asked him, "Why are you so sullen? Why won't you eat?"

6 He answered her, "Because I said to Naboth the Jezreelite, 'Sell me your vineyard; or if you prefer, I will give you another vineyard in its place.' But he said, 'I will not give you my vineyard.' "

7 Jezebel his wife said, "Is this how you act as king over Israel? Get up and eat! Cheer up. I'll get you the vineyard of Naboth the Jezreelite."

8 So she wrote letters in Ahab's name, placed his seal on them, and sent them to the elders and nobles who lived in Naboth's city with him. 9 In those letters she wrote:

> "Proclaim a day of fasting and seat Naboth in a prominent place among the people. 10 But seat two scoundrels opposite him and have them testify that he has cursed both God and the king. Then take him out and stone him to death."

11 So the elders and nobles who lived in Naboth's city did as Jezebel directed in the letters she had written to them. 12 They proclaimed a fast and seated Naboth in a prominent place among the people. 13 Then two scoundrels came and sat opposite him and brought

[a]*39* That is, about 75 pounds (about 34 kilograms) [b]*42* The Hebrew term refers to the irrevocable giving over of things or persons to the LORD, often by totally destroying them.

story does a prophet get a king to pronounce judgment on himself (2 Sam. 12:1–14)? **4.** Is it fair that Ahab should die for *not* killing someone?

APPLY When, if ever, have you gotten "angry and sullen" toward God? What happened that started you feeling that way?

OPEN 1. What do you treasure that was given to you by a parent, grandparent or other relative? **2.** What would be your reaction if someone tried to buy this "treasure" from you? Would you sell it at normal retail, at a premium or not at all?

STUDY Ahab tries to buy a vineyard from Naboth, who had received it as an inheritance. When Naboth refuses, he is killed in a plot by Jezebel; and so God announces judgment on both Ahab and Jezebel. **1.** Why does Ahab want this vineyard? As king, why doesn't he just confiscate it (Deut. 17:18–29)? **2.** Why does Naboth refuse his king this request (Num. 36:7)? Would you have refused the king? **3.** What impression do you get of Ahab from his reaction to Naboth's refusal: Whining wimp? Spoiled brat? A weak leader? **4.** What impression do you get of Jezebel from how she handles this situation: A strong woman? The power behind the throne? A conniving woman? A get-things-done type? A person without heart or principle? **5.** Was Naboth a brave man, or just a man naïve to the dangers of refusing an evil ruler? **6.** What helps a prophet like Elijah have the courage to confront violent, evil rulers like Ahab and Jezebel? **7.** Why might the sentence of being eaten by dogs, be a particularly repulsive way to die for royalty? **8.** Why does God decide to soften Ahab's punishment?

20:42 This confrontation between the prophet and Ahab is similar to a confrontation between the prophet Nathan and King David. Nathan allowed David to pass judgment on a fictitious man who stole a lamb, then Nathan applied the judgment to David who had stolen another man's wife (2 Sam. 12:1–7). **your life for his life.** Ahab had spared Ben-Hadad in order to form a treaty. This was a sign that Ahab still had not learned that God was his provider. Ahab was still wheeling and dealing, taking care of himself.

21:7 Jezebel. Jezebel has stood throughout history on the notoriety of her evil. Here, she treated Ahab much as the mother of a spoiled child, making evil plans to give him whatever he wanted.

21:9 fasting. This gave the impression of a sacred event. **seat Naboth.** Jezebel had the power to command anyone to help her frame Naboth.

21:10 two scoundrels. In order to frame Naboth, the law required two witnesses. **cursed both God and the king.** Mosaic Law did prescribe death as a punishment for cursing God, but not cursing the king.

charges against Naboth before the people, saying, "Naboth has
cursed both God and the king." So they took him outside the city and
stoned him to death. 14Then they sent word to Jezebel: "Naboth has
been stoned and is dead."
15As soon as Jezebel heard that Naboth had been stoned to death,
she said to Ahab, "Get up and take possession of the vineyard of Naboth the Jezreelite that he refused to sell you. He is no longer alive,
but dead." 16When Ahab heard that Naboth was dead, he got up and
went down to take possession of Naboth's vineyard.
17Then the word of the LORD came to Elijah the Tishbite: 18"Go
down to meet Ahab king of Israel, who rules in Samaria. He is now in
Naboth's vineyard, where he has gone to take possession of it. 19Say
to him, 'This is what the LORD says: Have you not murdered a man
and seized his property?' Then say to him, 'This is what the LORD
says: In the place where dogs licked up Naboth's blood, dogs will lick
up your blood—yes, yours!' "
20Ahab said to Elijah, "So you have found me, my enemy!"
"I have found you," he answered, "because you have sold yourself
to do evil in the eyes of the LORD. 21'I am going to bring disaster on
you. I will consume your descendants and cut off from Ahab every
last male in Israel—slave or free. 22I will make your house like that of
Jeroboam son of Nebat and that of Baasha son of Ahijah, because you
have provoked me to anger and have caused Israel to sin.'
23"And also concerning Jezebel the LORD says: 'Dogs will devour
Jezebel by the wall of[a] Jezreel.'
24"Dogs will eat those belonging to Ahab who die in the city, and
the birds of the air will feed on those who die in the country."
25(There was never a man like Ahab, who sold himself to do evil in
the eyes of the LORD, urged on by Jezebel his wife. 26He behaved in
the vilest manner by going after idols, like the Amorites the LORD
drove out before Israel.)
27When Ahab heard these words, he tore his clothes, put on sackcloth and fasted. He lay in sackcloth and went around meekly.
28Then the word of the LORD came to Elijah the Tishbite: 29"Have
you noticed how Ahab has humbled himself before me? Because he
has humbled himself, I will not bring this disaster in his day, but I will
bring it on his house in the days of his son."

Micaiah Prophesies Against Ahab

22 For three years there was no war between Aram and Israel.
2But in the third year Jehoshaphat king of Judah went down
to see the king of Israel. 3The king of Israel had said to his officials,
"Don't you know that Ramoth Gilead belongs to us and yet we are
doing nothing to retake it from the king of Aram?"
4So he asked Jehoshaphat, "Will you go with me to fight against
Ramoth Gilead?"

[a]23 Most Hebrew manuscripts; a few Hebrew manuscripts, Vulgate and Syriac (see also 2 Kings 9:26) *the plot of ground at*

APPLY 1. When, if ever, have you let someone else: "Do your dirty work for you"? Have someone else confront someone you were "too polite" to confront? Look the other way while a company did something unethical to save your job? Have your spouse discipline the kids so you could stay Mr./Mrs. Nice Guy? **2.** What is God calling you to do in this story: Stop sulking? Do your own "dirty work"? Humble yourself to receive God's direction and discipline? Other?

OPEN In which of the following situations are you most likely to be a lone voice against the crowd: In the team you root for? In the kind of music you want played at work? In the kind of restaurant you want to go to when you go out with your family or friends? In your political beliefs in your extended family? In what you want to watch on television?

STUDY Ahab wants to ally with Judah to make war

22:1 three years ... no war. During this three-year period, Ahab and Ben-Hadad together faced the Assyrian foe Shalmaneser in the Battle of Qarqar.

22:2 Jehoshaphat. Jehoshaphat was a godly king, while Ahab was not.

22:4 go with me. Ahab was quickly prepared to create an alliance with Judah against Aram. This switch of loyalties happened generation after generation. Jehoshaphat's father had made an alliance with the king of Aram against Israel. **Ramoth Gilead.** Ramoth in Gilead was directly east (across the Jordan River) of Jezreel, where Ahab's palace was located.

against Aram, but Jehosophat, King of Judah, wants to hear the guidance of one of God's legitimate prophets first. They find Micaiah, who, in contrast to the false prophets, predicts such a war would end in defeat. For giving such a negative prophecy, Micaiah is put in prison by Ahab, the king of Israel. **1.** Why does Ahab want to go to war? **2.** Who does Ahab bring at first to predict whether war will be successful? **3.** Why is Jehoshaphat not happy with just getting the view of the 400 prophets Ahab brings? **4.** Why does Ahab hate Micaiah? **5.** Why does Micaiah tell Ahab what he wants to hear at first? **6.** Why would God want to "entice" Ahab to going into a losing battle? **7.** Why does Zedekiah slap Micaiah and ask a sarcastic question? **8.** What is the test of the validity of Micaiah's message (vv. 25–28; Deut. 18:21–22)?

APPLY **1.** In which of the following situations do you find it most difficult to speak up for what you believe against the crowd: When people around you are telling racist jokes? When you are with people who are expressing anti-Christian sentiments? When people at work want to go to a strip joint or similar place where you would not feel comfortable? When other Christians are advocating political positions you believe are wrong? **2.** What helps you to take a stand in these difficult situations?

Jehoshaphat replied to the king of Israel, "I am as you are, my people as your people, my horses as your horses." 5But Jehoshaphat also
said to the king of Israel, "First seek the counsel of the LORD."
6So the king of Israel brought together the prophets—about four
hundred men—and asked them, "Shall I go to war against Ramoth
Gilead, or shall I refrain?"
"Go," they answered, "for the Lord will give it into the king's
hand."
7But Jehoshaphat asked, "Is there not a prophet of the LORD here
whom we can inquire of?"
8The king of Israel answered Jehoshaphat, "There is still one man
through whom we can inquire of the LORD, but I hate him because he
never prophesies anything good about me, but always bad. He is
Micaiah son of Imlah."
"The king should not say that," Jehoshaphat replied.
9So the king of Israel called one of his officials and said, "Bring
Micaiah son of Imlah at once."
10Dressed in their royal robes, the king of Israel and Jehoshaphat
king of Judah were sitting on their thrones at the threshing floor by
the entrance of the gate of Samaria, with all the prophets prophesying before them. 11Now Zedekiah son of Kenaanah had made iron
horns and he declared, "This is what the LORD says: 'With these you
will gore the Arameans until they are destroyed.' "
12All the other prophets were prophesying the same thing. "Attack
Ramoth Gilead and be victorious," they said, "for the LORD will give it
into the king's hand."
13The messenger who had gone to summon Micaiah said to him,
"Look, as one man the other prophets are predicting success for the
king. Let your word agree with theirs, and speak favorably."
14But Micaiah said, "As surely as the LORD lives, I can tell him only
what the LORD tells me."
15When he arrived, the king asked him, "Micaiah, shall we go to
war against Ramoth Gilead, or shall I refrain?"
"Attack and be victorious," he answered, "for the LORD will give it
into the king's hand."
16The king said to him, "How many times must I make you swear to
tell me nothing but the truth in the name of the LORD?"
17Then Micaiah answered, "I saw all Israel scattered on the hills
like sheep without a shepherd, and the LORD said, 'These people have
no master. Let each one go home in peace.' "
18The king of Israel said to Jehoshaphat, "Didn't I tell you that he
never prophesies anything good about me, but only bad?"
19Micaiah continued, "Therefore hear the word of the LORD: I saw
the LORD sitting on his throne with all the host of heaven standing
around him on his right and on his left. 20And the LORD said, 'Who will

---

22:5 the counsel of the LORD. Even though Jehoshaphat gave lip service to confirming his decisions with God, he made a poor choice in this case. Later, the prophet Jehu confronted Jehoshaphat about this choice (2 Chr. 19:2).

22:7 a prophet of the LORD. Jehoshaphat was right to ask. Ahab tended to dislike prophets who spoke the truth because they didn't tell him what he wanted to hear.

22:8 always bad. This was Ahab's rule of thumb for how favorably he assessed a prophet: Did the prophet tell him good things or bad things? It was not truth Ahab was interested in. Later he became enemies with the great prophet, Elijah, for this very reason.

22:16 How many times? According to Ahab's life thus far, this probably was not a true statement. He probably had not demanded truth of Micaiah previously, unless it was in response to sarcastic remarks on Micaiah's part.

entice Ahab into attacking Ramoth Gilead and going to his death there?'

"One suggested this, and another that. 21Finally, a spirit came
forward, stood before the LORD and said, 'I will entice him.'
22" 'By what means?' the LORD asked.

" 'I will go out and be a lying spirit in the mouths of all his prophets,' he said.

" 'You will succeed in enticing him,' said the LORD. 'Go and do it.'
23"So now the LORD has put a lying spirit in the mouths of all these prophets of yours. The LORD has decreed disaster for you."
24Then Zedekiah son of Kenaanah went up and slapped Micaiah in the face. "Which way did the spirit from[a] the LORD go when he went from me to speak to you?" he asked.
25Micaiah replied, "You will find out on the day you go to hide in an inner room."
26The king of Israel then ordered, "Take Micaiah and send him back
to Amon the ruler of the city and to Joash the king's son 27and say,
'This is what the king says: Put this fellow in prison and give him nothing but bread and water until I return safely.' "
28Micaiah declared, "If you ever return safely, the LORD has not spoken through me." Then he added, "Mark my words, all you people!"

Ahab Killed at Ramoth Gilead

29So the king of Israel and Jehoshaphat king of Judah went up to
Ramoth Gilead. 30The king of Israel said to Jehoshaphat, "I will enter the battle in disguise, but you wear your royal robes." So the king of Israel disguised himself and went into battle.
31Now the king of Aram had ordered his thirty-two chariot commanders, "Do not fight with anyone, small or great, except the king of
Israel." 32When the chariot commanders saw Jehoshaphat, they
thought, "Surely this is the king of Israel." So they turned to attack
him, but when Jehoshaphat cried out, 33the chariot commanders saw that he was not the king of Israel and stopped pursuing him.
34But someone drew his bow at random and hit the king of Israel between the sections of his armor. The king told his chariot driver, "Wheel around and get me out of the fighting. I've been wounded."
35All day long the battle raged, and the king was propped up in his chariot facing the Arameans. The blood from his wound ran onto the
floor of the chariot, and that evening he died. 36As the sun was setting, a cry spread through the army: "Every man to his town; everyone to his land!"
37So the king died and was brought to Samaria, and they buried

[a]24 Or *Spirit of*

OPEN When have you been mistaken for someone else or have mistaken someone else yourself? What embarrassing things happened as a result of this mistaken identity?

STUDY Ahab and Jehosophat go into battle against Aram, and Ahab disguises himself, so as not to be recognized by the opposing army. This backfires when he is mortally wounded anyway. **1.** Why does Ahab disguise himself (vv. 29–30)? Why would Jehoshaphat go along? **2.** Why does the King of Aram give the command of verse 31? **3.** What is the significance of a random arrow killing Ahab (v. 34)? **4.** How does the end of this story fulfill the prophecy of Micaiah (vv. 20,28)? Of Elijah (21:19–21,29)?

APPLY 1. What "wound" is currently draining the life from you: A bad experience from childhood? A rejection by someone important in your life? A failure you cannot seem

22:23 lying spirit. There are other times in the Old Testament when an evil or unrighteous spirit seems to be sent from God (for instance, when King Saul was tormented by an evil spirit, 1 Sam. 16:14). **decreed disaster.** Again, the prophet confirmed that the news from God about the battle was not hopeful.

22:31 the king of Israel. It was (and is) an excellent war strategy to attack the leadership so that the soldiers are disoriented and cannot finish the battle well.

22:34 at random. Ahab's disguise didn't protect him when it counted. The consequences of his actions found him no matter who he was trying to fool. **the king told his chariot driver.** During battle at this time, two and even three men rode in a chariot. One drove and the other fought; the third often commanded the other chariots.

to get over? **2.** What do you need to do right now to find God's healing from that wound?

____

him there. 38They washed the chariot at a pool in Samaria (where the prostitutes bathed),[a] and the dogs licked up his blood, as the word of the LORD had declared.

39As for the other events of Ahab's reign, including all he did, the palace he built and inlaid with ivory, and the cities he fortified, are they not written in the book of the annals of the kings of Israel? 40Ahab rested with his fathers. And Ahaziah his son succeeded him as king.

OPEN 1. In what two ways are you like, and unlike, your father? Your mother? **2.** If a biographer were writing the events of your life, what source documents and eyewitnesses would be invaluable?

STUDY Jehoshaphat continues the good of his father's reign in Judah, while Ahaziah continues the evil of his father's reign in Israel. **1.** What are Jehoshaphat's big accomplishments? What could he have done better? **2.** Why do you think it was important to record the wreck of Jehoshaphat's trading ships: To show he was a good man, but with less than competent "help"? To show that he was punished for not destroying all the altars? To show the evil of going after gold? **3.** What is Ahaziah's problem? Who is to blame for this repeated sin?

APPLY What has recently "wrecked" your life? What support do you need in recovering your losses?

____

Jehoshaphat King of Judah

41Jehoshaphat son of Asa became king of Judah in the fourth year of Ahab king of Israel. 42Jehoshaphat was thirty-five years old when he became king, and he reigned in Jerusalem twenty-five years. His mother's name was Azubah daughter of Shilhi. 43In everything he walked in the ways of his father Asa and did not stray from them; he did what was right in the eyes of the LORD. The high places, however, were not removed, and the people continued to offer sacrifices and burn incense there. 44Jehoshaphat was also at peace with the king of Israel.

45As for the other events of Jehoshaphat's reign, the things he achieved and his military exploits, are they not written in the book of the annals of the kings of Judah? 46He rid the land of the rest of the male shrine prostitutes who remained there even after the reign of his father Asa. 47There was then no king in Edom; a deputy ruled.

48Now Jehoshaphat built a fleet of trading ships[b] to go to Ophir for gold, but they never set sail—they were wrecked at Ezion Geber. 49At that time Ahaziah son of Ahab said to Jehoshaphat, "Let my men sail with your men," but Jehoshaphat refused.

50Then Jehoshaphat rested with his fathers and was buried with them in the city of David his father. And Jehoram his son succeeded him.

Ahaziah King of Israel

51Ahaziah son of Ahab became king of Israel in Samaria in the seventeenth year of Jehoshaphat king of Judah, and he reigned over Israel two years. 52He did evil in the eyes of the LORD, because he walked in the ways of his father and mother and in the ways of Jeroboam son of Nebat, who caused Israel to sin. 53He served and worshiped Baal and provoked the LORD, the God of Israel, to anger, just as his father had done.

[a]38 Or *Samaria and cleaned the weapons* [b]48 Hebrew *of ships of Tarshish*

22:38 dogs licked. Elijah had pronounced this prophecy (21:19) after Ahab and Jezebel had Naboth killed. Ahab would die a death of shame in that the dogs would lick his blood, rather than his body being carefully prepared for a ceremonial burial.

22:42 became king. Jehoshaphat actually became king while his father (King Asa) was still alive. Because of King Asa's failing health, he and his son shared rule for three years. King David and his son Solomon had shared leadership as well. It was called a "co-regency."

22:44 king of Israel. Three kings ruled Israel during Jehoshaphat's reign in Judah: Ahab, Ahaziah and Joram. This statement probably meant that Jehoshaphat's kingdom lived peaceably with Israel's kingdom, whoever was king at the time.

2 Kings

Author. Jeremiah has been considered the author, but some events listed in 2 Kings occurred after his death. Ezra is another likely candidate. No one knows for certain who wrote 1 or 2 Kings. These books could have been compiled from records from several sources.

Date. In their final form, 1 and 2 Kings were probably written between 560–540 B.C. The events of 2 Kings cover about 430 years, from the death of Ahab through the Babylonian captivity of Judah.

Personal Reading	Group Study Topic and Reading	
1:1–2:25	Elisha Succeeds Elijah	2:1–18
3:1–4:7	The Widow's Oil	4:1–7
4:8–4:44	Elisha Resurrects Boy	4:8–37
5:1–5:27	Naaman Healed	5:1–27
6:1–23	Elisha Traps Arameans	6:8–23
6:24–8:15	Aramean Siege Lifted	7:3–20
8:16–10:17	Ahab Curse Fulfilled	10:1–17
10:18–14:29	Jehoash With Elisha	13:10–25
15:1–16:20	Ahaz Does Evil	16:1–20
17:1–18:16	Israel Suffers Exile	17:7–23
18:17–20:21	Sennacherib Warns	18:17–37
21:1–23:35	Covenant Renewed	23:1–25
23:36–25:30	Jerusalem Falls	25:1–26

Purpose. The book of 2 Kings alternates between the divided kingdoms of Israel and Judah. It takes a brief, chronological look at the rule of each king, integrating the kingdoms together. In this way, it refuses to allow the kingdoms to dissolve into completely different entities. Second Kings reminds us that as a government leads, so will its people follow. It also reminds us that while a king of spiritual integrity may not always create the most prosperous kingdom, he will establish a kind of security for his people that only comes from God's protection.

Historical Background. The book of 2 Kings recounts the history of the kingship in the divided kingdoms, from the reigns of Ahaziah in Israel and Jehoshaphat in Judah to the fall of Jerusalem and the Babylonian exile. It tells a story of two capitals, Samaria in the north and Jerusalem in the south, and how the leaders in those cities failed to maintain the religious and cultural standards of their countries. The northern kingdom deteriorated more rapidly, and this time period was characterized by a succession of kings who were corrupt and ungodly, broken sporadically by a king who tried to "do what was right in the eyes of the LORD."

This era was also characterized by the influence of prophets, such as Elijah and Elisha, who called both nations to repent from their idol worship and turn back to God. The role of outside cultures reached a terrible peak in Israel when its people were exiled to Assyria; Judah's exile to Babylon came later.

The Divided Kingdom. When the kingdom divided, the northern ten tribes formed Israel, which later became known as Samaria. The remaining southern tribes formed Judah, which was the more geographically isolated of the two kingdoms. The Mediterranean Sea was Israel's western border, with ports of call along major trade routes. On the north, Israel bordered Assyria, a ruthless nation. This geographical difference undoubtedly contributed to the stronger cultural influence on Israel by other nations. Israel was thus the first of the two kingdoms to be occupied by foreign government and exiled from their homeland. In Jesus' day, the civil division between Israel and Judah was apparent, for no proper Jewish man would set foot in Samaria. The disciples were amazed when Jesus went through Samaria, even sitting by a well and having a conversation with a Samaritan woman.

OPEN **1.** If you had a chance to know how and when you would die, would you want to know? **2.** If you could choose *how* you were going to die, what would you choose: Quietly in bed, of old age? While doing something active, like sky-diving? While making love to your spouse? While doing something valiant, like defending someone from a criminal?

STUDY Ahab's son, Ahaziah, is injured in a fall, and sends for a foreign god to learn if he will recover. Because he has sent for a foreign god, God sends Elijah to let him know he will die in his bed. **1.** To what name used in the New Testament does the name for the god of Ekron bear resemblance (Luke 11:14–15)? **2.** Why does Ahaziah choose to consult the god of Ekron instead of the God of Israel: He figured this other god would tell him what he wanted to hear? Foreign gods were a family tradition? He didn't like Elijah, God's prophet? **3.** What New Testament figure does Elijah dress like (Matt. 3:4)? **4.** Why does Ahaziah want Elijah to come down off the hill: So he could kill him? To give his message in person? So he can talk Elijah out of his fate? **5.** Why does the third captain succeed? What attitude does this captain show toward Elijah? **6.** What would you say God is like if this chapter were your starting point?

APPLY **1.** When you are uncertain and grasping for answers, whom do you go to: God? An advice columnist? A professional counselor? A friend? **2.** If you could ask someone who talked directly to God like Elijah, what would you like to know about your future?

The Lord's Judgment on Ahaziah

1 After Ahab's death, Moab rebelled against Israel. [2]Now Ahaziah
had fallen through the lattice of his upper room in Samaria and
injured himself. So he sent messengers, saying to them, "Go and
consult Baal-Zebub, the god of Ekron, to see if I will recover from this
injury."
[3]But the angel of the LORD said to Elijah the Tishbite, "Go up and
meet the messengers of the king of Samaria and ask them, 'Is it
because there is no God in Israel that you are going off to consult
Baal-Zebub, the god of Ekron?' [4]Therefore this is what the LORD says:
'You will not leave the bed you are lying on. You will certainly die!' "
So Elijah went.
[5]When the messengers returned to the king, he asked them, "Why
have you come back?"
[6]"A man came to meet us," they replied. "And he said to us, 'Go back
to the king who sent you and tell him, "This is what the LORD says: Is
it because there is no God in Israel that you are sending men to consult
Baal-Zebub, the god of Ekron? Therefore you will not leave the
bed you are lying on. You will certainly die!" ' "
[7]The king asked them, "What kind of man was it who came to meet
you and told you this?"
[8]They replied, "He was a man with a garment of hair and with a
leather belt around his waist."
The king said, "That was Elijah the Tishbite."
[9]Then he sent to Elijah a captain with his company of fifty men. The
captain went up to Elijah, who was sitting on the top of a hill, and
said to him, "Man of God, the king says, 'Come down!' "
[10]Elijah answered the captain, "If I am a man of God, may fire come
down from heaven and consume you and your fifty men!" Then fire
fell from heaven and consumed the captain and his men.
[11]At this the king sent to Elijah another captain with his fifty men.
The captain said to him, "Man of God, this is what the king says,
'Come down at once!' "
[12]"If I am a man of God," Elijah replied, "may fire come down from
heaven and consume you and your fifty men!" Then the fire of God
fell from heaven and consumed him and his fifty men.
[13]So the king sent a third captain with his fifty men. This third
captain went up and fell on his knees before Elijah. "Man of God," he
begged, "please have respect for my life and the lives of these fifty
men, your servants! [14]See, fire has fallen from heaven and consumed
the first two captains and all their men. But now have respect for my
life!"

1:1 Moab rebelled against Israel. David had been able to conquer and control the Moabites. The rebellion of the northern tribes and the tribes east of the Jordan River caused such political instability that the time was right for a rebellion against Israel.

1:4 You will not leave. Though Ahaziah had not asked God about his future, God used Elijah to carry the message. Ironically, Ahaziah's inquiry of Baal-Zebub sealed his fate instead of revealing it.

1:5 the king ... asked. The king knew something was wrong. The trip to Ekron should have taken much longer. The messengers were back too soon.

1:10 fire fell from heaven. Elijah called upon God again to execute a trial by fire, as he had on Mount Carmel (1 Kin. 18:36–39).

1:11 another captain with his fifty men. Ahaziah was stubborn. He wanted to change his fate by forcing Elijah to change his prediction. Though he valued his own life as precious, the lives of his soldiers meant nothing.

1:13 lives of these fifty men, your servants. Fearing the worst, this third captain understood the covenant better than his commander. A soldier's duty is to carry out the wishes of the king, but these were "servants" of the prophet first, which meant they feared God more than Ahaziah, as they should.

15The angel of the LORD said to Elijah, "Go down with him; do not
be afraid of him." So Elijah got up and went down with him to the
king.
16He told the king, "This is what the LORD says: Is it because there
is no God in Israel for you to consult that you have sent messengers
to consult Baal-Zebub, the god of Ekron? Because you have done
this, you will never leave the bed you are lying on. You will certainly
die!" 17So he died, according to the word of the LORD that Elijah had
spoken.
Because Ahaziah had no son, Joram[a] succeeded him as king in the
second year of Jehoram son of Jehoshaphat king of Judah. 18As for all
the other events of Ahaziah's reign, and what he did, are they not
written in the book of the annals of the kings of Israel?

Elijah Taken Up to Heaven

2 When the LORD was about to take Elijah up to heaven in a whirlwind, Elijah and Elisha were on their way from Gilgal. 2Elijah
said to Elisha, "Stay here; the LORD has sent me to Bethel."
But Elisha said, "As surely as the LORD lives and as you live, I will
not leave you." So they went down to Bethel.
3The company of the prophets at Bethel came out to Elisha and
asked, "Do you know that the LORD is going to take your master from
you today?"
"Yes, I know," Elisha replied, "but do not speak of it."
4Then Elijah said to him, "Stay here, Elisha; the LORD has sent me
to Jericho."
And he replied, "As surely as the LORD lives and as you live, I will
not leave you." So they went to Jericho.
5The company of the prophets at Jericho went up to Elisha and
asked him, "Do you know that the LORD is going to take your master
from you today?"
"Yes, I know," he replied, "but do not speak of it."
6Then Elijah said to him, "Stay here; the LORD has sent me to the
Jordan."
And he replied, "As surely as the LORD lives and as you live, I will
not leave you." So the two of them walked on.
7Fifty men of the company of the prophets went and stood at a
distance, facing the place where Elijah and Elisha had stopped at the
Jordan. 8Elijah took his cloak, rolled it up and struck the water with
it. The water divided to the right and to the left, and the two of them
crossed over on dry ground.

[a]17 Hebrew *Jehoram*, a variant of *Joram*

OPEN **1.** When you were in high school, who did you look up to more than anyone else? What about them did you particularly admire? **2.** Who that you admired in the past has since died? How did you react to their death?

STUDY The prophet Elijah has had a long and illustrious career and now the rumor is that God is going to take him directly to heaven. His disciple Elisha follows him everywhere to make sure it doesn't happen when he isn't around. He also asks Elijah for "a double-share" of his spirit. **1.** Why does Elijah continue to ask Elisha to stay behind? Why does he keep refusing? What does it tell about each man and their relationship? **2.** Why does Elisha not want people to speak of God taking Elijah: It was a depressing thought? He thought if nobody spoke of it, it might not happen? He just wanted to think of the good times? **3.** What is the dividing of the waters reminiscent of (Ex. 14:21–22)? **4.** What does Elisha mean by "a double portion of your spirit" (v. 9)? Is this a presumptuous request? **5.** Which of the following words or phrases best expresses what you think Elisha was feeling when Elijah was taken to heaven: An intense mixture of joy and sorrow? Euphoria?

1:17 died. Ahaziah's death confirmed God's word as the true revelation. God's message had turned out to be true. Elijah was no mere fortune-teller. Pagan "fate" had no part in the king's death, it was the result of sin.

2:2 Elisha said ... I will not leave you. Elisha made a total commitment to Elijah. He knew that Elijah's work was nearly finished and that soon the great prophet would be gone. He wanted to be at Elijah's side until the end.

2:3 company of the prophets. Several different companies of prophets lived at Bethel (v. 3), Jericho (v. 5) and Gilgal (4:38). Before being taken up into heaven, Elijah visited his fellow prophets.

2:7 Fifty men of the company of the prophets. These groups of prophets must have been quite large since fifty members of the company at Jericho were gathered to witness the miraculous crossing of the Jordan River.

2:8 Elijah took his cloak, rolled it up and struck the water with it. The ministries of Moses and Elijah are remarkably similar. For example, the death of the king's soldiers by fire (1:10–12) parallels several incidents in Moses' life (Lev. 10:2; Num. 16:35). This miracle at the Jordan River reads like Moses' parting of the Red Sea (Ex. 14:15–25). Elijah rolled up his cloak and used it like Moses used his staff.

Abandonment? Fear? Anxiety? **6.** What is the closest you have come to experiencing what Elisha felt at this time? **7.** What is the significance of Elisha picking up Elijah's cloak and using it to divide the waters? **8.** Why does Elisha think it unwise to go looking for Elijah?

APPLY 1. If you could inherit "a double-portion" of the spirit of someone who is alive or who has recently died, what person's spirit would you choose? **2.** How do you think having that person's spirit would affect how you live and what you do? What would be the "sign" that you had that spirit? **3.** Do you believe that God could give you that spirit even now?

OPEN What aspect of your appearance are you most sensitive about?

STUDY Showing powers that are every bit as great as his mentor Elijah, Elisha makes bad water good, and calls down a curse on some youth who jeer at him. **1.** What does Elisha use to "heal" the water? **2.** What aspect of Elisha's appearance do the youth make fun of? **3.** How do you react to the severe punishment of these youth?

9When they had crossed, Elijah said to Elisha, "Tell me, what can I
do for you before I am taken from you?"
"Let me inherit a double portion of your spirit," Elisha replied.
10"You have asked a difficult thing," Elijah said, "yet if you see me
when I am taken from you, it will be yours—otherwise not."
11As they were walking along and talking together, suddenly a
chariot of fire and horses of fire appeared and separated the two of
them, and Elijah went up to heaven in a whirlwind. 12Elisha saw this
and cried out, "My father! My father! The chariots and horsemen of
Israel!" And Elisha saw him no more. Then he took hold of his own
clothes and tore them apart.
13He picked up the cloak that had fallen from Elijah and went back
and stood on the bank of the Jordan. 14Then he took the cloak that
had fallen from him and struck the water with it. "Where now is the
LORD, the God of Elijah?" he asked. When he struck the water, it
divided to the right and to the left, and he crossed over.
15The company of the prophets from Jericho, who were watching,
said, "The spirit of Elijah is resting on Elisha." And they went to meet
him and bowed to the ground before him. 16"Look," they said, "we
your servants have fifty able men. Let them go and look for your
master. Perhaps the Spirit of the LORD has picked him up and set him
down on some mountain or in some valley."
"No," Elisha replied, "do not send them."
17But they persisted until he was too ashamed to refuse. So he said,
"Send them." And they sent fifty men, who searched for three days
but did not find him. 18When they returned to Elisha, who was staying
in Jericho, he said to them, "Didn't I tell you not to go?"

Healing of the Water

19The men of the city said to Elisha, "Look, our lord, this town is
well situated, as you can see, but the water is bad and the land is
unproductive."
20"Bring me a new bowl," he said, "and put salt in it." So they
brought it to him.
21Then he went out to the spring and threw the salt into it, saying,
"This is what the LORD says: 'I have healed this water. Never again
will it cause death or make the land unproductive.' " 22And the water
has remained wholesome to this day, according to the word Elisha
had spoken.

2:9 Let me inherit a double portion of your spirit. A double portion was the rightful inheritance of a firstborn son.

2:10 asked a difficult thing. Appointing a successor was not Elijah's prerogative. God had told Elijah that Elisha would succeed him, but the appointment as such was up to God, not Elijah.

2:12 chariots and horsemen. Elisha recognized the chariot of fire as a manifestation of God. In the proper covenant relationship, Israel's power emanated from God, was articulated by the prophets and was carried out by the king.

2:14 When he struck the water. Elisha's inheritance and right of succession were confirmed when he replicated Elijah's miracle. Now he stood in the line of Moses and Elijah.

2:16 the Spirit of the LORD has picked him up. The prophets, showing both faith and doubt, knew that the Spirit of God had done something miraculous, but they could not fathom that Elijah would be spared the most universal of human experiences, death.

2:17 Send them. Elisha's first trial came quickly. The prophets acknowledged Elisha's right of succession (v. 15), but they still wanted to do things their own way.

2:20 Bring me a new bowl. A new bowl meant a new spiritual start. It was not contaminated by prior use and could be dedicated solely to service to God—new bowl, new heart.

Elisha Is Jeered

23 From there Elisha went up to Bethel. As he was walking along the
road, some youths came out of the town and jeered at him. "Go on
up, you baldhead!" they said. "Go on up, you baldhead!" 24 He turned
around, looked at them and called down a curse on them in the name
of the LORD. Then two bears came out of the woods and mauled forty-
two of the youths. 25 And he went on to Mount Carmel and from there
returned to Samaria.

Moab Revolts

3 Joram[a] son of Ahab became king of Israel in Samaria in the eighteenth year of Jehoshaphat king of Judah, and he reigned twelve
years. 2 He did evil in the eyes of the LORD, but not as his father and
mother had done. He got rid of the sacred stone of Baal that his
father had made. 3 Nevertheless he clung to the sins of Jeroboam son
of Nebat, which he had caused Israel to commit; he did not turn away
from them.

4 Now Mesha king of Moab raised sheep, and he had to supply the
king of Israel with a hundred thousand lambs and with the wool of a
hundred thousand rams. 5 But after Ahab died, the king of Moab
rebelled against the king of Israel. 6 So at that time King Joram set out
from Samaria and mobilized all Israel. 7 He also sent this message to
Jehoshaphat king of Judah: "The king of Moab has rebelled against
me. Will you go with me to fight against Moab?"

"I will go with you," he replied. "I am as you are, my people as your
people, my horses as your horses."

8 "By what route shall we attack?" he asked.

"Through the Desert of Edom," he answered.

9 So the king of Israel set out with the king of Judah and the king of
Edom. After a roundabout march of seven days, the army had no
more water for themselves or for the animals with them.

10 "What!" exclaimed the king of Israel. "Has the LORD called us
three kings together only to hand us over to Moab?"

11 But Jehoshaphat asked, "Is there no prophet of the LORD here,
that we may inquire of the LORD through him?"

An officer of the king of Israel answered, "Elisha son of Shaphat is
here. He used to pour water on the hands of Elijah.[b]"

12 Jehoshaphat said, "The word of the LORD is with him." So the

[a] 1 Hebrew *Jehoram*, a variant of *Joram*; also in verse 6 [b] 11 That is, he was Elijah's personal servant.

APPLY **1.** When it comes to disciplining youth, are you more likely to be too soft or too harsh? **2.** What most irritates you about the behavior of teens? What would help you have greater patience with them?

OPEN Which of the following would most likely cause you to revolt: Having to listen to rap music all day long? Having to eat nothing but healthy food for a month? A full year of political ads on TV? Having to spend your entire day off shopping with your spouse?

STUDY After Ahab dies, the king of Moab revolts against Israel. In response to the revolt, Israel and Judah form an alliance, but only after God, acting through Elisha, miraculously provides them water. **1.** What one reform does Joram make? **2.** What tribute does the king of Moab have to pay Israel at this time? **3.** Which of the three kings in the alliance does Elisha respect? **4.** How do you think Elisha's advice sets with the soldiers awaiting relief from thirst (vv. 16–18)? **5.** What would be the effect of throwing stones on the good fields of the Moabites? **6.** Why does the king of Moab sacrifice his son and heir (v. 27)? Why might this sacrifice have actually been effective?

APPLY **1.** When you are feeling "surrounded" by trouble, what desperate measures have you sometimes tried for relief? **2.** How could you use the strength of God and the support of Christian friends in lieu of these desperate measures?

2:23 Go on up, you baldhead! The youths had no respect whatsoever for the prophet. Baldness was seen as powerlessness. (Samson's story in Judges 13–16 is an extreme example.) Since Elisha was God's representative, an insult directed at Elisha was an insult thrown at God.

3:2 He did evil ... Joram's father and mother were Ahab and Jezebel, whose sins were judged worse than those of any before them (1 Kin. 16:30–33). Though it was little consolation, Joram broke a line of progressively evil kings that had begun with Omri (1 Kin. 16:25).

3:3 sins of Jeroboam. Frightened and insecure, Jeroboam turned the people of Israel away from God and toward idols, wrongly believing that allegiance to God would translate into greater power for his rival, Rehoboam.

3:7 message to Jehoshaphat ... Joram hoped that the bad blood between the northern and southern kingdoms would not prevent an alliance against a growing common threat, the Moabites. Jehoshaphat had already been condemned by the prophets for cooperating with the northern kings Ahab and Ahaziah (2 Chr. 18:1; 19:1–2; 20:35–37). Now Jehoshaphat believed an alliance with Joram was the right military move.

3:11 no prophet of the LORD ... The rulers had followed their own wisdom nearly to destruction. Now desperate, they wanted God's help. This was a recurring pattern, for rulers and almost everyone else.

king of Israel and Jehoshaphat and the king of Edom went down to him.

13Elisha said to the king of Israel, "What do we have to do with each other? Go to the prophets of your father and the prophets of your mother."

"No," the king of Israel answered, "because it was the LORD who called us three kings together to hand us over to Moab."

14Elisha said, "As surely as the LORD Almighty lives, whom I serve, if I did not have respect for the presence of Jehoshaphat king of Judah, I would not look at you or even notice you. 15But now bring me a harpist."

While the harpist was playing, the hand of the LORD came upon Elisha 16and he said, "This is what the LORD says: Make this valley full of ditches. 17For this is what the LORD says: You will see neither wind nor rain, yet this valley will be filled with water, and you, your cattle and your other animals will drink. 18This is an easy thing in the eyes of the LORD; he will also hand Moab over to you. 19You will overthrow every fortified city and every major town. You will cut down every good tree, stop up all the springs, and ruin every good field with stones."

20The next morning, about the time for offering the sacrifice, there it was—water flowing from the direction of Edom! And the land was filled with water.

21Now all the Moabites had heard that the kings had come to fight against them; so every man, young and old, who could bear arms was called up and stationed on the border. 22When they got up early in the morning, the sun was shining on the water. To the Moabites across the way, the water looked red—like blood. 23"That's blood!" they said. "Those kings must have fought and slaughtered each other. Now to the plunder, Moab!"

24But when the Moabites came to the camp of Israel, the Israelites rose up and fought them until they fled. And the Israelites invaded the land and slaughtered the Moabites. 25They destroyed the towns, and each man threw a stone on every good field until it was covered. They stopped up all the springs and cut down every good tree. Only Kir Hareseth was left with its stones in place, but men armed with slings surrounded it and attacked it as well.

26When the king of Moab saw that the battle had gone against him, he took with him seven hundred swordsmen to break through to the king of Edom, but they failed. 27Then he took his firstborn son, who

---

3:14 if I did not have respect for ... king of Judah. The kings of Israel had fallen into apostasy—blatant disregard for God's covenant and active pursuit of false gods. Joram was not as bad as his father and grandfather (v. 2), but neither was he a king after God's heart.

3:17 this valley will be filled with water. The word of God provided a simple solution: "obey my instructions with faith and you will receive my blessing." God was willing to provide for his people, but he expected them to respond thankfully and obediently.

3:19 cut down ... stop up ... and ruin. God demanded the devastation of rebellious Moab. He was willing to provide for his people, even "not-very-righteous" Joram, in order to protect his covenant nation from invasion or rebellion.

3:23 Those kings must have fought and slaughtered each other. The Moabites came to a logical, though inaccurate, conclusion. They saw water where there had been desert, and it looked like blood. Surely, they thought, the weak alliance opposing them had come to blows.

3:26 to break through to the king of Edom. In a last-ditch effort to break up the tenuous three-way alliance, the king of Moab tried to separate what he considered the weakest party. After all, the "king" of Edom was a puppet to the kings of Israel and Judah. The king of Moab assumed Edom would change sides if pressured enough.

3:27 offered him as a sacrifice. Desperate for a turn in the battle, the king of Moab sacrificed his own son as a burnt offering to the Moabite god Chemosh, and the scheme worked. Though Chemosh made no appearance

was to succeed him as king, and offered him as a sacrifice on the city wall. The fury against Israel was great; they withdrew and returned to their own land.

The Widow's Oil

4 The wife of a man from the company of the prophets cried out to Elisha, "Your servant my husband is dead, and you know that he revered the LORD. But now his creditor is coming to take my two boys as his slaves."
[2]Elisha replied to her, "How can I help you? Tell me, what do you have in your house?"
"Your servant has nothing there at all," she said, "except a little oil."
[3]Elisha said, "Go around and ask all your neighbors for empty jars.
Don't ask for just a few. [4]Then go inside and shut the door behind you and your sons. Pour oil into all the jars, and as each is filled, put it to one side."
[5]She left him and afterward shut the door behind her and her sons.
They brought the jars to her and she kept pouring. [6]When all the jars
were full, she said to her son, "Bring me another one."
But he replied, "There is not a jar left." Then the oil stopped flowing.
[7]She went and told the man of God, and he said, "Go, sell the oil and pay your debts. You and your sons can live on what is left."

The Shunammite's Son Restored to Life

[8]One day Elisha went to Shunem. And a well-to-do woman was there, who urged him to stay for a meal. So whenever he came by, he
stopped there to eat. [9]She said to her husband, "I know that this man
who often comes our way is a holy man of God. [10]Let's make a small room on the roof and put in it a bed and a table, a chair and a lamp for him. Then he can stay there whenever he comes to us."
[11]One day when Elisha came, he went up to his room and lay down
there. [12]He said to his servant Gehazi, "Call the Shunammite." So he
called her, and she stood before him. [13]Elisha said to him, "Tell her, 'You have gone to all this trouble for us. Now what can be done for you? Can we speak on your behalf to the king or the commander of the army?' "
She replied, "I have a home among my own people."
[14]"What can be done for her?" Elisha asked.
Gehazi said, "Well, she has no son and her husband is old."
[15]Then Elisha said, "Call her." So he called her, and she stood in the
doorway. [16]"About this time next year," Elisha said, "you will hold a son in your arms."

OPEN If your creditors suddenly called in all your loans, including what you owe on credit cards, what would you have to sell to pay them off?

STUDY A widow who is about to lose her sons as slaves appeals to Elisha for help, and he arranges for the little amount of oil she has to multiply. **1.** If a person could lose children to creditors today, how would it affect our economy and the way we live? **2.** Why does Elisha tell the widow not to ask for just a few jars, when seeking jars to fill with oil?

APPLY What resource would you most like to see God multiply in order to help you face the challenges you face today?

OPEN Which of the following statements best expresses the attitude toward hospitality that prevailed in the home in which you were raised: "There's always room for one more"? "Our home is your home"? "Visitors, like fish, stink after three days"? "Our home was our castle—and the drawbridge was always raised"?

STUDY The life of a woman in the town of Shunem changes dramatically when she befriends and cares for the prophet Elisha. She experiences great joy when she has a long-awaited son, and then she has bitter distress when her son dies. **1.** Why do you think the Shunammite woman showed such hospitality to Elisha: She figured it would earn her special favors later? She respected his work and wanted to support it? She liked the company?

(remember Baal's absence at Mount Carmel, 1 Kin. 18:26), the sight of the sacrifice may have enraged the Moabites sufficiently to drive Israel away.

4:1 two boys as his slaves. Mosaic law allowed servitude as a means to repay a debt. The intent was to allow a person in debt to "work off" that debt and therefore not endanger his family or possessions. The law was frequently abused and became a means of harming or enslaving the debtor, not helping him (Neh. 5:5).

4:12 servant Gehazi. Elisha's servant is mentioned here for the first time. He probably served Elisha as Elisha had served Elijah.

4:14 no son and her husband is old. The woman would soon be without means to survive. To take advantage of widows was a crime against God's Law (Ex. 22:22), but a widow without sons had no means of support. Moreover, her family's possessions would go to others, and the family would cease to exist.

4:16 Don't mislead your servant. Predictions of unlikely pregnancies caused strong reactions in the Old

2. When Elisha promised this woman that she will have a son, why does she object? 3. Why do you think the Shunammite woman told both her husband and Elisha's servant, Gehazi, that things were "all right": She was in denial? She didn't want to be emotionally vulnerable? She had faith that God would heal their son? 4. Why does Elisha first send his servant ahead with his staff to try to raise the boy (v. 29)? 5. What was most important in raising the boy to life: The woman's faith, shown by her coming to Elisha? The power of Elisha's prayers (v. 33)? A primitive form of CPR (v. 34)? 6. Why might God raise this boy and not the many others who died before and since?

APPLY 1. In what area of need like the Shunammite woman, have you been afraid to have your hopes raised? 2. What does this story say to you in the midst of this area of need: Don't be afraid to hope? God will provide? Nothing is impossible with God? Whatever dies in your life God can restore?

"No, my lord," she objected. "Don't mislead your servant, O man
of God!"
17 But the woman became pregnant, and the next year about that
same time she gave birth to a son, just as Elisha had told her.
18 The child grew, and one day he went out to his father, who was
with the reapers. 19 "My head! My head!" he said to his father.
His father told a servant, "Carry him to his mother." 20 After the
servant had lifted him up and carried him to his mother, the boy sat
on her lap until noon, and then he died. 21 She went up and laid him
on the bed of the man of God, then shut the door and went out.
22 She called her husband and said, "Please send me one of the servants and a donkey so I can go to the man of God quickly and return."
23 "Why go to him today?" he asked. "It's not the New Moon or the
Sabbath."
"It's all right," she said.
24 She saddled the donkey and said to her servant, "Lead on; don't
slow down for me unless I tell you." 25 So she set out and came to the
man of God at Mount Carmel.
When he saw her in the distance, the man of God said to his servant Gehazi, "Look! There's the Shunammite! 26 Run to meet her and
ask her, 'Are you all right? Is your husband all right? Is your child all
right?' "
"Everything is all right," she said.
27 When she reached the man of God at the mountain, she took
hold of his feet. Gehazi came over to push her away, but the man of
God said, "Leave her alone! She is in bitter distress, but the LORD has
hidden it from me and has not told me why."
28 "Did I ask you for a son, my lord?" she said. "Didn't I tell you,
'Don't raise my hopes'?"
29 Elisha said to Gehazi, "Tuck your cloak into your belt, take my
staff in your hand and run. If you meet anyone, do not greet him, and
if anyone greets you, do not answer. Lay my staff on the boy's face."
30 But the child's mother said, "As surely as the LORD lives and as
you live, I will not leave you." So he got up and followed her.
31 Gehazi went on ahead and laid the staff on the boy's face, but
there was no sound or response. So Gehazi went back to meet Elisha
and told him, "The boy has not awakened."
32 When Elisha reached the house, there was the boy lying dead on
his couch. 33 He went in, shut the door on the two of them and prayed

---

Testament. Sarah laughed at the news that she would bear Isaac (Gen. 18:12). The Shunammite woman reacted with incredulity. Her exclamation was due less to lack of faith than to fear of disappointment.

4:17 gave birth to a son, just as Elisha had told her. The woman not only delivered a child, but did so exactly as Elisha had predicted.

4:20 the boy ... *died*. *The child was* a gift from God in response to the woman's faith. The child's death tested that faith. Her actions validate Elisha's belief in her integrity.

4:21 laid him on the bed ... shut the door. Elisha's prophecy about this child was between the Shunammite woman and Elisha only. When the child died, she kept the death private as well by placing the boy's body in the prophet's room.

4:26 Everything is all right. Although Gehazi had been present when Elisha predicted the son's birth, the woman was determined, as an act of faith, to keep his death a private matter until she had spoken to Elisha. Perhaps she was also concerned that a public announcement might hinder Elisha's remedy.

4:28 Didn't I tell you. The woman's greatest fear had been realized (v. 16). She had acted in faith, and God had given her a miracle child. Now she was devastated.

4:29 take my staff ... Lay my staff. Elisha assumed that the special powers he had from God could be transferred through his staff. Not that the staff was magical—it was a symbol of Elisha's special relationship with God and could be used as an extension of God's power.

4:33 shut the door ... and prayed. Elisha may have remembered a similar

to the LORD. 34Then he got on the bed and lay upon the boy, mouth to
mouth, eyes to eyes, hands to hands. As he stretched himself out
upon him, the boy's body grew warm. 35Elisha turned away and
walked back and forth in the room and then got on the bed and
stretched out upon him once more. The boy sneezed seven times and
opened his eyes.

36Elisha summoned Gehazi and said, "Call the Shunammite." And
he did. When she came, he said, "Take your son." 37She came in, fell
at his feet and bowed to the ground. Then she took her son and went
out.

Death in the Pot

38Elisha returned to Gilgal and there was a famine in that region.
While the company of the prophets was meeting with him, he said to
his servant, "Put on the large pot and cook some stew for these men."
39One of them went out into the fields to gather herbs and found a
wild vine. He gathered some of its gourds and filled the fold of his
cloak. When he returned, he cut them up into the pot of stew, though
no one knew what they were. 40The stew was poured out for the men,
but as they began to eat it, they cried out, "O man of God, there is
death in the pot!" And they could not eat it.

41Elisha said, "Get some flour." He put it into the pot and said,
"Serve it to the people to eat." And there was nothing harmful in the
pot.

Feeding of a Hundred

42A man came from Baal Shalishah, bringing the man of God twenty loaves of barley bread baked from the first ripe grain, along with
some heads of new grain. "Give it to the people to eat," Elisha said.

43"How can I set this before a hundred men?" his servant asked.

But Elisha answered, "Give it to the people to eat. For this is what
the LORD says: 'They will eat and have some left over.' " 44Then he set
it before them, and they ate and had some left over, according to the
word of the LORD.

Naaman Healed of Leprosy

5 Now Naaman was commander of the army of the king of Aram.
He was a great man in the sight of his master and highly

OPEN What kind of food would you have said as a child would kill you: Broccoli? Brussel Sprouts? Liver? Okra? Vegetables in general? Other?

STUDY Elisha's powers extended to food preparation. In these stories he rescues a potentially poisonous stew and provides a miraculous supply of bread. **1.** What does it show about the famine that one of the company of prophets was willing to put the gourds into the stew even though nobody knew what they were? **2.** How did the others know there was "death in the pot"? **3.** How would the flour neutralize the poison in the stew?

APPLY 1. What is there a famine of in your life right now: Love? Faith? Hope? Self-worth? **2.** What would it mean for you to believe that God can supply all you need in this area?

OPEN 1. When you were a teenager, what was the most repulsive disease you felt you had: Zits? "Foot-in-mouth" disease when

---

incident involving Elijah (1 Kin. 17:19). Surely Elisha shared the woman's sense that the prediction of the boy's birth was private, and his healing should be private. Without permitting himself a moment of doubt, he sought God's will, *then acted on it.*

4:38 there was a famine in that region. Just as God provided for his people, he showed displeasure by sending famine and other trouble (Lev. 26:19–20; Deut. 28:18,23–24). In ancient times, famine meant hunger at best, but often widespread death.

4:39 found a wild vine. Desperate times force people to desperate acts. Not everything that might survive a drought is healthy to eat. God had provided his people with food, land and prosperity. Yet they had turned away from his gifts to worship Baal. Just like *Baal worship,* the wild vine was native to the land, but the food it provided was deadly.

4:41 there was nothing harmful in the pot. The flour was not magic dust, just as the salt earlier was not magic (2:19–22). The salt and the flour were common items that God used to represent goodness and grace. Those who violated the covenant were left to suffer the consequences of disobedience. The faithful, however, enjoyed the benefits of God's provision.

4:42 bread ... from the first ripe grain. The man brought the firstfruits of the harvest as commanded by covenant law (Lev. 2), but he gave the bread to the prophet, not the priests, which the law required. Faithful people in the northern kingdom had lost confidence in a corrupt priesthood, so their offerings went to prophets who still spoke God's truth.

5:1 the LORD had given victory to Aram. Although God's focus was on

talking to the opposite sex? Terminal shyness? Eating too much—being overweight? Eating too little—anorexia? **2.** How did your friends support you in the midst of this "disease"?

STUDY When this story takes place, the people of Aram and Israel were officially at peace, though border skirmishes were not uncommon. Here Naaman, a commander of Aram, is sent to be healed of leprosy by Elisha, a prophet of the God of Israel. Then one of the prophets drops a borrowed ax head in the water, but Elisha retrieves it when he makes it float. **1.** Why might the pagan king of Aram agree to have his top soldier travel to the heart of Israel for an unlikely cure? **2.** Who shows greater faith—the pagan king of Aram in sending Naaman, or the king of Israel in receiving him? **3.** Why does the king of Israel tear his robes? **4.** Why does Naaman get angry at Elisha's instructions: They were too easy? He didn't like that they were conveyed by a messenger instead of Elisha himself? He was prissy about bathing in a river? He was a superpatriot and didn't want to believe a foreign river could be better than one in his own country? **5.** How would you describe the relationship between Naaman and his servants? Did they care for him or serve him grudgingly (vv. 3,13)? **6.** What restores Naaman to health: The waters of the Jordan or his own obedience? **7.** Why does Naaman want earth from Israel to take home with him? **8.** How does the comparative behavior of Naaman and Gehazi show that faith (and God) was not the exclusive property of Israel and that foreigners could sometimes outshine the people of Israel (Luke 4:24–27)? **9.** Why all the worry over a lost ax head? What message does this story convey?

regarded, because through him the LORD had given victory to Aram.
He was a valiant soldier, but he had leprosy.[a]
2Now bands from Aram had gone out and had taken captive a
young girl from Israel, and she served Naaman's wife. 3She said to
her mistress, "If only my master would see the prophet who is in
Samaria! He would cure him of his leprosy."
4Naaman went to his master and told him what the girl from Israel
had said. 5"By all means, go," the king of Aram replied. "I will send a
letter to the king of Israel." So Naaman left, taking with him ten
talents[b] of silver, six thousand shekels[c] of gold and ten sets of clothing. 6The letter that he took to the king of Israel read: "With this letter
I am sending my servant Naaman to you so that you may cure him of
his leprosy."
7As soon as the king of Israel read the letter, he tore his robes and
said, "Am I God? Can I kill and bring back to life? Why does this fellow
send someone to me to be cured of his leprosy? See how he is trying
to pick a quarrel with me!"
8When Elisha the man of God heard that the king of Israel had torn
his robes, he sent him this message: "Why have you torn your robes?
Have the man come to me and he will know that there is a prophet in
Israel." 9So Naaman went with his horses and chariots and stopped
at the door of Elisha's house. 10Elisha sent a messenger to say to him,
"Go, wash yourself seven times in the Jordan, and your flesh will be
restored and you will be cleansed."
11But Naaman went away angry and said, "I thought that he would
surely come out to me and stand and call on the name of the LORD his
God, wave his hand over the spot and cure me of my leprosy. 12Are
not Abana and Pharpar, the rivers of Damascus, better than any of the
waters of Israel? Couldn't I wash in them and be cleansed?" So he
turned and went off in a rage.
13Naaman's servants went to him and said, "My father, if the
prophet had told you to do some great thing, would you not have
done it? How much more, then, when he tells you, 'Wash and be
cleansed'!" 14So he went down and dipped himself in the Jordan
seven times, as the man of God had told him, and his flesh was restored and became clean like that of a young boy.

[a]*1* The Hebrew word was used for various diseases affecting the skin—not necessarily leprosy; also in verses 3, 6, 7, 11 and 27. [b]*5* That is, about 750 pounds (about 340 kilograms) [c]*5* That is, about 150 pounds (about 70 kilograms)

---

the covenant people, God was at work among other nations too. All of creation was working out God's plans for humanity. The ebb and flow of power among pagan nations was in God's hands and under God's control.

5:2 young girl from Israel. Sometimes God's goodness spreads through the work and word of unlikely people. This passage contrasted the corrupt *ruler and priests of the northern king*dom with one young girl of faith, a slave with a heart and a voice.

5:8 Why have you torn your robes? Elisha scolded the king for fear and faithlessness. The king of Aram had given Joram a perfect opportunity to demonstrate God's greatness. But faithless Joram was stymied. Elisha was quick to recognize this situation not as a political crisis but as an opportunity to demonstrate God's power and grace to a pagan ruler. This opportunity was not to be missed.

5:10 wash ... in the Jordan. There was nothing magical about washing in the Jordan River. People did that all the time. What Elisha demanded was obedience. Naaman could be cured only by humbly obeying God's instructions.

5:11 wave his hand over the spot. Naaman expected a ceremony more inline with his position. In reality, he got just that. When he become a servant to God and acknowledged God's sovereignty, Naaman was healed.

5:14 his flesh was restored and became clean. When Naaman obeyed God's commands spoken by the prophet Elisha, this "pagan" commander was healed.

[15]Then Naaman and all his attendants went back to the man of God. He stood before him and said, "Now I know that there is no God in all the world except in Israel. Please accept now a gift from your servant."

[16]The prophet answered, "As surely as the LORD lives, whom I serve, I will not accept a thing." And even though Naaman urged him, he refused.

[17]"If you will not," said Naaman, "please let me, your servant, be given as much earth as a pair of mules can carry, for your servant will never again make burnt offerings and sacrifices to any other god but the LORD. [18]But may the LORD forgive your servant for this one thing: When my master enters the temple of Rimmon to bow down and he is leaning on my arm and I bow there also—when I bow down in the temple of Rimmon, may the LORD forgive your servant for this."

[19]"Go in peace," Elisha said.

After Naaman had traveled some distance, [20]Gehazi, the servant of Elisha the man of God, said to himself, "My master was too easy on Naaman, this Aramean, by not accepting from him what he brought. As surely as the LORD lives, I will run after him and get something from him."

[21]So Gehazi hurried after Naaman. When Naaman saw him running toward him, he got down from the chariot to meet him. "Is everything all right?" he asked.

[22]"Everything is all right," Gehazi answered. "My master sent me to say, 'Two young men from the company of the prophets have just come to me from the hill country of Ephraim. Please give them a talent[a] of silver and two sets of clothing.' "

[23]"By all means, take two talents," said Naaman. He urged Gehazi to accept them, and then tied up the two talents of silver in two bags, with two sets of clothing. He gave them to two of his servants, and they carried them ahead of Gehazi. [24]When Gehazi came to the hill, he took the things from the servants and put them away in the house. He sent the men away and they left. [25]Then he went in and stood before his master Elisha.

"Where have you been, Gehazi?" Elisha asked.

"Your servant didn't go anywhere," Gehazi answered.

[26]But Elisha said to him, "Was not my spirit with you when the man got down from his chariot to meet you? Is this the time to take money, or to accept clothes, olive groves, vineyards, flocks, herds, or menservants and maidservants? [27]Naaman's leprosy will cling to you and to your descendants forever." Then Gehazi went from Elisha's presence and he was leprous, as white as snow.

[a]*22* That is, about 75 pounds (about 34 kilograms)

APPLY 1. When have you, like Naaman, felt like the promises of God were too simple to be true? **2.** Who has acted like Naaman's servants to convince you to trust those promises?

5:15 *there is no God in all the world except in Israel.* God's gift of grace to Naaman evoked a powerful profession of faith from him. At a time when many of Israel's people were debating the existence and power of other gods, it was left to a pagan to declare the singular power and presence of the true and only God.

5:16 I will not accept a thing. Elisha recognized Naaman's healing as an act of God. He could not accept a reward for something God had done.

5:22 give them a talent ... clothing. Gehazi's flaw: he liked money. That led to other sins, coveting and lying. Gehazi was well aware that his actions were sinful, or he would not have misrepresented himself to Naaman and Elisha.

5:26 time to take money. Elisha's question went to the heart of Gehazi's offense. Naaman's healing was a wonderful opportunity to demonstrate God's goodness to a pagan people, and Gehazi had acted no better than the pagan soothsayers, the prophets for profit (Num. 22).

An Axhead Floats

6 The company of the prophets said to Elisha, "Look, the place where we meet with you is too small for us. [2]Let us go to the Jordan, where each of us can get a pole; and let us build a place there for us to live."

And he said, "Go."

[3]Then one of them said, "Won't you please come with your servants?"

"I will," Elisha replied. [4]And he went with them.

They went to the Jordan and began to cut down trees. [5]As one of them was cutting down a tree, the iron axhead fell into the water. "Oh, my lord," he cried out, "it was borrowed!"

[6]The man of God asked, "Where did it fall?" When he showed him the place, Elisha cut a stick and threw it there, and made the iron float. [7]"Lift it out," he said. Then the man reached out his hand and took it.

Elisha Traps Blinded Arameans

[8]Now the king of Aram was at war with Israel. After conferring with his officers, he said, "I will set up my camp in such and such a place."

[9]The man of God sent word to the king of Israel: "Beware of passing that place, because the Arameans are going down there." [10]So the king of Israel checked on the place indicated by the man of God. Time and again Elisha warned the king, so that he was on his guard in such places.

[11]This enraged the king of Aram. He summoned his officers and demanded of them, "Will you not tell me which of us is on the side of the king of Israel?"

[12]"None of us, my lord the king," said one of his officers, "but Elisha, the prophet who is in Israel, tells the king of Israel the very words you speak in your bedroom."

[13]"Go, find out where he is," the king ordered, "so I can send men and capture him." The report came back: "He is in Dothan." [14]Then he sent horses and chariots and a strong force there. They went by night and surrounded the city.

[15]When the servant of the man of God got up and went out early the next morning, an army with horses and chariots had surrounded the city. "Oh, my lord, what shall we do?" the servant asked.

[16]"Don't be afraid," the prophet answered. "Those who are with us are more than those who are with them."

OPEN If you were suddenly to become blind, what would you most miss seeing: Sunsets, rainbows and other natural beauty? The faces of your family and friends? The familiar sights in and around your home that give you comfort?

STUDY Repeated evidence that Israel knew in advance about Aramean military movements causes the king of Aram to suspect a traitor among his officers. When the king finds out about the prophet Elisha's powers, he sends a strong armed force to capture him. **1.** What about this story do you find the most amazing: Elisha's knowledge of the Arameans every move? The presence of the heavenly hosts around Elisha? That God blinds the Arameans at Elisha's request? That the Israelites have a feast for their enemies rather than killing them? **2.** What makes the king of Aram suspect a spy? **3.** What does Elisha want his servant to have his eyes opened to? **4.** In what other story involving Elisha do we hear of "chariots of fire" (2:11–12)? **5.** Why

---

6:1 The company of the prophets. Several groups of prophets clustered around the cities of Bethel, Jericho and Gilgal (2:1,3,5). They were not understudies to Elijah and Elisha, but they acknowledged the leadership of these two great prophets.

6:2 build a place there for us to live. Some evidence suggests that these prophets lived communally. However, the story *in 4:1–7 implies* that the prophets lived separately with their families. If so, then they were actually in need of a place to meet, not to live. For that purpose, the description in verse one, "the place where we meet with you," is the proper one.

6:5 borrowed. This company of prophets was not wealthy. An iron ax head was very expensive in those days, and the company had been forced to borrow one. Under the law, the man who lost the ax head was liable for it, and its loss could have meant a long term as a servant to repay the debt.

6:9 The man of God sent word to the king of Israel. Elisha took his role as a spiritual leader and advisor to the king seriously, despite Joram's faithlessness. Elisha's advice, normally spiritual, could raise any issue affecting the life of the country. In this instance, he advised the king on military intelligence.

6:13 send men and capture him. The king of Aram did not know how Elisha possessed special military knowledge. But Aram would capture him, interrogate him and keep him from offering any further assistance to Joram.

6:16 Don't be afraid. Elisha was not afraid. He had faith that the continuing, sustaining power of God surrounded him at all times. In fact, he had seen the

[17]And Elisha prayed, "O LORD, open his eyes so he may see." Then
the LORD opened the servant's eyes, and he looked and saw the hills
full of horses and chariots of fire all around Elisha.
[18]As the enemy came down toward him, Elisha prayed to the LORD,
"Strike these people with blindness." So he struck them with blindness, as Elisha had asked.
[19]Elisha told them, "This is not the road and this is not the city.
Follow me, and I will lead you to the man you are looking for." And he
led them to Samaria.
[20]After they entered the city, Elisha said, "LORD, open the eyes of
these men so they can see." Then the LORD opened their eyes and
they looked, and there they were, inside Samaria.
[21]When the king of Israel saw them, he asked Elisha, "Shall I kill
them, my father? Shall I kill them?"
[22]"Do not kill them," he answered. "Would you kill men you have
captured with your own sword or bow? Set food and water before
them so that they may eat and drink and then go back to their
master." [23]So he prepared a great feast for them, and after they had
finished eating and drinking, he sent them away, and they returned to
their master. So the bands from Aram stopped raiding Israel's territory.

Famine in Besieged Samaria

[24]Some time later, Ben-Hadad king of Aram mobilized his entire
army and marched up and laid siege to Samaria. [25]There was a great
famine in the city; the siege lasted so long that a donkey's head sold
for eighty shekels[a] of silver, and a quarter of a cab[b] of seed pods[c] for
five shekels.[d]
[26]As the king of Israel was passing by on the wall, a woman cried to
him, "Help me, my lord the king!"
[27]The king replied, "If the LORD does not help you, where can I get
help for you? From the threshing floor? From the winepress?" [28]Then
he asked her, "What's the matter?"
She answered, "This woman said to me, 'Give up your son so we
may eat him today, and tomorrow we'll eat my son.' [29]So we cooked
my son and ate him. The next day I said to her, 'Give up your son so
we may eat him,' but she had hidden him."

[a]25 That is, about 2 pounds (about 1 kilogram) [b]25 That is, probably about 1/2 pint (about 0.3 liter)
[c]25 Or *of dove's dung* [d]25 That is, about 2 ounces (about 55 grams)

does Elisha tell the king of Israel to hold a feast for the Arameans rather than kill them: It was a new military strategy? He wanted it to be a witness to God's mercy? He wanted Israel to "turn the other cheek"? **6.** What effect do you think these events had on the Aramean army?

APPLY 1. When have you felt like you were "cornered" but someone "let you off the hook"? How did it affect how you related to that person? **2.** Who do you feel God may be wanting you to "let off the hook" right now?

OPEN 1. If you knew that alL shipments into your hometown were to be stopped for a month, and you could stock up on just two items, what would you choose to stock up on? **2.** Who would you be willing to share your stockpile with?

STUDY The peace after Elisha's act of mercy did not prevail forever, and the king of Aram once again attacks Israel. This time the siege creates a terrible famine in Israel. **1.** What does the price of a donkey's head show about how terrible the famine was (v. 25)? **2.** What more gruesome indicator of the famine becomes evident later in the story (vv. 28–29)? **3.** Why does the king of Israel blame Elisha for the famine? **4.** With all of the power Elisha has shown, why hasn't he relieved the

heavenly host when Elijah was taken up in a whirlwind (2:11–12). He knew that no man could overcome the forces of God.

6:18 blindness. First Elisha prayed that his servant would be able to see the unseen. Second, he prayed that the *normally visible would become hidden* from the Aramean soldiers. The first prayer sought to reveal the truth, the second to conceal it temporarily.

6:19 Follow me, and I will lead you to the man you are looking for. Blindness made soldiers willing to follow anyone. They were seeking Elisha, who would be in Samaria when they arrived. The fact that the speaker was also the man they were seeking was a detail Elisha conveniently omitted.

6:22 Do not kill them. Elisha's advice held several advantages. Since God's power had blinded the soldiers, they were really God's captives. Joram had no right to harm them. Killing the prisoners would inflame already volatile relations between Israel and Aram. Finally, treating the captured soldiers well would show their king that Israel was not afraid and that further aggression against Israel was futile because the God of Israel would protect and preserve his people.

6:24 Ben-Hadad king of Aram. This same Aramean king had besieged Samaria in the past. After initial success, his army was defeated by Ahab, with help from God (1 Kin. 20:1–34). Afterward, he had agreed to the truce that was technically in effect until this attack.

6:25 donkey's head sold. Samaria was desperate. The law called donkeys unclean; they could not be eaten (Deut. 14:4–8). And the head was the least desirable part of a very undesirable animal. Yet this chunk of animal commanded a huge price.

people's suffering sooner? **5.** What would the prices in 7:1 indicate about the famine? **6.** Why would the officer not be allowed to eat any of the soon to be abundant food after the famine? For what act or attitude was he going to be punished?

APPLY **1.** What are you most starving for right now: Acceptance? Achievement? Forgiveness? Inner peace? Reconciliation with a loved one? Reconciliation with God? **2.** What would it mean for you to trust God's provision for this need?

OPEN **1.** When did you take what seemed like a big risk because in reality you had nothing to lose? How did it work out for you? **2.** Normally, how likely are you to take risks: Like a gambler? Like a stuntman? Nothing riskier than a CD in a federally insured bank?

STUDY Four lepers from Samaria decide they have nothing to lose by venturing to the camp of the Arameans to get something to eat. When they get there, they find the Arameans have fled, ending the siege and the famine. **1.** Would you have gone along with the logic of the lepers (vv. 3–4)? **2.** What does the hasty Aramean's retreat show about their army? **3.** Would you have been as suspicious about the good report as the king of Israel was (v. 12)? Why or why not? **4.** What does the king mean when he says of the men sent

30 When the king heard the woman's words, he tore his robes. As he
went along the wall, the people looked, and there, underneath, he
had sackcloth on his body. 31 He said, "May God deal with me, be it
ever so severely, if the head of Elisha son of Shaphat remains on his
shoulders today!"
32 Now Elisha was sitting in his house, and the elders were sitting
with him. The king sent a messenger ahead, but before he arrived,
Elisha said to the elders, "Don't you see how this murderer is sending
someone to cut off my head? Look, when the messenger comes, shut
the door and hold it shut against him. Is not the sound of his
master's footsteps behind him?"
33 While he was still talking to them, the messenger came down to
him. And ⌊the king⌋ said, "This disaster is from the LORD. Why should
I wait for the LORD any longer?"

7 Elisha said, "Hear the word of the LORD. This is what the LORD
says: About this time tomorrow, a seah[a] of flour will sell for a
shekel[b] and two seahs[c] of barley for a shekel at the gate of Samaria."
2 The officer on whose arm the king was leaning said to the man of
God, "Look, even if the LORD should open the floodgates of the heavens, could this happen?"
"You will see it with your own eyes," answered Elisha, "but you will
not eat any of it!"

The Siege Lifted

3 Now there were four men with leprosy[d] at the entrance of the city
gate. They said to each other, "Why stay here until we die? 4 If we say,
'We'll go into the city'—the famine is there, and we will die. And if we
stay here, we will die. So let's go over to the camp of the Arameans
and surrender. If they spare us, we live; if they kill us, then we die."
5 At dusk they got up and went to the camp of the Arameans. When
they reached the edge of the camp, not a man was there, 6 for the Lord
had caused the Arameans to hear the sound of chariots and horses
and a great army, so that they said to one another, "Look, the king of
Israel has hired the Hittite and Egyptian kings to attack us!" 7 So they
got up and fled in the dusk and abandoned their tents and their
horses and donkeys. They left the camp as it was and ran for their
lives.
8 The men who had leprosy reached the edge of the camp and entered one of the tents. They ate and drank, and carried away silver,

[a]1 That is, probably about 7 quarts (about 7.3 liters); also in verses 16 and 18 [b]1 That is, about 2/5 ounce (about 11 grams); also in verses 16 and 18 [c]1 That is, probably about 13 quarts (about 15 liters); also in verses 16 and 18 [d]3 The Hebrew word is used for various diseases affecting the skin—not necessarily leprosy; also in verse 8.

6:30 king ... tore his robes. Normally this act was associated with grief. However, in this case, Joram was expressing his anger toward God and Elisha, whom he held responsible for the famine.

***6:33 This disaster is from the* LORD.** Joram placed the blame for the terrible conditions in the city on God and Elisha. He felt that Elisha had somehow deceived him and that God was actually responsible for the famine. Despite his unwillingness to be a faithful, covenant king, he expected the prophet and God to act as if he were.

7:1 a seah of flour. This price was double the normal cost.

7:3 four men ... entrance of the city gate. These four men were not necessarily lepers. The Hebrew word used here was applied to a number of different skin diseases. The law prohibited these men from living in the city with these medical conditions, so they were forced to live on the outskirts.

7:6 the Hittite and Egyptian kings. God had confounded the Arameans with fear. The Hittite kings were rulers of small city-states in northern Aram. These states and their rulers were remnants of the Hittite empire that had ruled that region until its fall around 1200 B.C.

gold and clothes, and went off and hid them. They returned and
entered another tent and took some things from it and hid them also.
9Then they said to each other, "We're not doing right. This is a day
of good news and we are keeping it to ourselves. If we wait until daylight, punishment will overtake us. Let's go at once and report this to
the royal palace."
10So they went and called out to the city gatekeepers and told
them, "We went into the Aramean camp and not a man was there—
not a sound of anyone—only tethered horses and donkeys, and the
tents left just as they were." 11The gatekeepers shouted the news, and
it was reported within the palace.
12The king got up in the night and said to his officers, "I will tell you
what the Arameans have done to us. They know we are starving; so
they have left the camp to hide in the countryside, thinking, 'They will
surely come out, and then we will take them alive and get into the
city.' "
13One of his officers answered, "Have some men take five of the
horses that are left in the city. Their plight will be like that of all the
Israelites left here—yes, they will only be like all these Israelites who
are doomed. So let us send them to find out what happened."
14So they selected two chariots with their horses, and the king sent
them after the Aramean army. He commanded the drivers, "Go and
find out what has happened." 15They followed them as far as the
Jordan, and they found the whole road strewn with the clothing and
equipment the Arameans had thrown away in their headlong flight.
So the messengers returned and reported to the king. 16Then the
people went out and plundered the camp of the Arameans. So a seah
of flour sold for a shekel, and two seahs of barley sold for a shekel, as
the LORD had said.
17Now the king had put the officer on whose arm he leaned in
charge of the gate, and the people trampled him in the gateway, and
he died, just as the man of God had foretold when the king came
down to his house. 18It happened as the man of God had said to the
king: "About this time tomorrow, a seah of flour will sell for a shekel
and two seahs of barley for a shekel at the gate of Samaria."
19The officer had said to the man of God, "Look, even if the LORD
should open the floodgates of the heavens, could this happen?" The
man of God had replied, "You will see it with your own eyes, but you
will not eat any of it!" 20And that is exactly what happened to him, for
the people trampled him in the gateway, and he died.

The Shunammite's Land Restored

8 Now Elisha had said to the woman whose son he had restored to
life, "Go away with your family and stay for a while wherever you
can, because the LORD has decreed a famine in the land that will last
seven years." 2The woman proceeded to do as the man of God said.

to check the situation out, "Their plight will be like that of all the Israelites left here"? **5.** How did these events fulfill the prophecy of Elisha (vv. 1–2)?

APPLY 1. How willing are you to trust God's promises at this point in your life: Like the trampled officer—it's hard to believe what doesn't seem logical? Like the lepers—I can believe if I have nothing to lose? Like the king—I have to check things out first? Like Elisha—I believe God's promises completely? **2.** What step could you take to "stretch" your confidence in God's promises just a little?

OPEN Where was "home" for you when you were in grade school? Why did your family leave from there?

7:12 I will tell you what the Arameans have done to us. Joram's anger and faithlessness led him to see intrigue where there was none. Instead of recognizing God's provision and the fulfillment of Elisha's prophecy, Joram saw only deception. Without faith, he had lost the ability to recognize the truth.

8:2 She and her family went away and stayed in the land. The Shunammite woman was obedient to Elisha's warning. Obedience saved her from the privations of the famine. The lesson of her action was clear: Obedience was the way to enjoy God's protection and provision. Disobedience was the way to suffering.

STUDY The Shunammite woman had left Israel at Elisha's instruction in order to avoid the famine. When she returns, her land must be restored by the king. **1.** Why has God sent this famine to Israel (Lev. 26:18–20)? **2.** What was the king speaking about when the woman returned? Was that coincidence? **3.** Why does the king treat this woman well?

APPLY What have you lost that you would like to have someone help you recover?

OPEN When do you remember being so sick that you didn't know if you were going to recover? Who ministered to you during that time?

STUDY When Ben-Hadad becomes very ill, he sends Hazael to Elisha to ask if he will recover. Elisha says he will, but then predicts that Hazael will then murder him and become king. **1.** Why does a foreign king seek the counsel of a Hebrew prophet (1 Kin. 19:15)? **2.** Why does Hazael feel ashamed when Elisha stares at him? **3.** Does Elisha's prediction avert the disaster, bring it on, or rationalize it after the fact? **4.** Why doesn't Hazael warn Ben-Hadad?

APPLY **1.** When you are doing or planning to do wrong, how easy is it for other people to read it in your eyes or demeanor? **2.** If you could, would you choose to be better at hiding what is in your heart, or would you rather be one

She and her family went away and stayed in the land of the Philistines seven years.
3At the end of the seven years she came back from the land of the
Philistines and went to the king to beg for her house and land. 4The
king was talking to Gehazi, the servant of the man of God, and had
said, "Tell me about all the great things Elisha has done." 5Just as
Gehazi was telling the king how Elisha had restored the dead to life,
the woman whose son Elisha had brought back to life came to beg
the king for her house and land.
Gehazi said, "This is the woman, my lord the king, and this is her
son whom Elisha restored to life." 6The king asked the woman about
it, and she told him.
Then he assigned an official to her case and said to him, "Give back everything that belonged to her, including all the income from her land from the day she left the country until now."

Hazael Murders Ben-Hadad

7Elisha went to Damascus, and Ben-Hadad king of Aram was ill.
When the king was told, "The man of God has come all the way up
here," 8he said to Hazael, "Take a gift with you and go to meet the
man of God. Consult the LORD through him; ask him, 'Will I recover
from this illness?' "
9Hazael went to meet Elisha, taking with him as a gift forty camel-loads of all the finest wares of Damascus. He went in and stood before him, and said, "Your son Ben-Hadad king of Aram has sent me to ask, 'Will I recover from this illness?' "
10Elisha answered, "Go and say to him, 'You will certainly recover';
but[a] the LORD has revealed to me that he will in fact die." 11He stared
at him with a fixed gaze until Hazael felt ashamed. Then the man of God began to weep.
12"Why is my lord weeping?" asked Hazael.
"Because I know the harm you will do to the Israelites," he answered. "You will set fire to their fortified places, kill their young men with the sword, dash their little children to the ground, and rip open their pregnant women."
13Hazael said, "How could your servant, a mere dog, accomplish
such a feat?"

[a]10 The Hebrew may also be read *Go and say, 'You will certainly not recover,' for.*

8:3 went to the king to beg for her house and land. In her absence, someone had illegally taken the Shunammite woman's property.

8:4 Tell ... the great things Elisha has done. This phrase probably places this story at a later date. The king in this story was probably Jehu, who succeeded Joram as king of Israel. Joram would have had no need to ask Gehazi about Elisha, since the king and his *prophet had many conflicts with each other.*

8:6 Give back everything that belonged to her, including all the income. God's blessing was not limited to restoration of lost property but included all the income her property had generated.

8:7 Elisha went. On Mount Horeb, God had instructed Elijah to do three things, including anointing Elisha as his successor (1 Kin. 19:15–18). Elisha now journeyed to Damascus to complete one of his former master's tasks.

8:8 Consult the LORD. Ironically, as the pagan king faced death, he wanted to know his fate from Israel's God. This was a reversal of Ahaziah's actions in 1:1–3.

8:12 I know the harm you will do to the Israelites. God had given Elisha the terrible vision of Hazael's aggression against Israel. This vision did not imply that God would turn his back on Israel. Rather, Elisha saw that God would use Hazael as an instrument of judgment against Israel.

8:13 How could your servant ... accomplish such a feat? Hazael was not bothered by the scenes of violence Elisha described. While his question is an attempt at self-effacing incredulity, his later action revealed an aggressive thirst for power.

"The LORD has shown me that you will become king of Aram," answered Elisha.
[14]Then Hazael left Elisha and returned to his master. When Ben-Hadad asked, "What did Elisha say to you?" Hazael replied, "He told me that you would certainly recover." [15]But the next day he took a thick cloth, soaked it in water and spread it over the king's face, so that he died. Then Hazael succeeded him as king.

Jehoram King of Judah

[16]In the fifth year of Joram son of Ahab king of Israel, when Jehoshaphat was king of Judah, Jehoram son of Jehoshaphat began his reign as king of Judah. [17]He was thirty-two years old when he became king, and he reigned in Jerusalem eight years. [18]He walked in the ways of the kings of Israel, as the house of Ahab had done, for he married a daughter of Ahab. He did evil in the eyes of the LORD. [19]Nevertheless, for the sake of his servant David, the LORD was not willing to destroy Judah. He had promised to maintain a lamp for David and his descendants forever.
[20]In the time of Jehoram, Edom rebelled against Judah and set up its own king. [21]So Jehoram[a] went to Zair with all his chariots. The Edomites surrounded him and his chariot commanders, but he rose up and broke through by night; his army, however, fled back home. [22]To this day Edom has been in rebellion against Judah. Libnah revolted at the same time.
[23]As for the other events of Jehoram's reign, and all he did, are they not written in the book of the annals of the kings of Judah? [24]Jehoram rested with his fathers and was buried with them in the City of David. And Ahaziah his son succeeded him as king.

Ahaziah King of Judah

[25]In the twelfth year of Joram son of Ahab king of Israel, Ahaziah son of Jehoram king of Judah began to reign. [26]Ahaziah was twenty-two years old when he became king, and he reigned in Jerusalem one year. His mother's name was Athaliah, a granddaughter of Omri king of Israel. [27]He walked in the ways of the house of Ahab and did evil in the eyes of the LORD, as the house of Ahab had done, for he was related by marriage to Ahab's family.

[a]21 Hebrew *Joram,* a variant of *Jehoram;* also in verses 23 and 24

whom others can "see through"? Why?

____

OPEN In which of the following areas would you be a BAD example: Organizing your desk? Eating healthily? Having a regular exercise schedule? Managing finances? Talking positively to your kids? Singing the national anthem?

STUDY The two kings we meet in this section had someone well suited to be a bad example as king—Ahab. They followed in his ways, doing evil. **1.** What does Jehoram have going for, and against him (vv. 16–18; 1 Kin. 22:41–44)? **2.** Of what importance is it that Jehoram and Ahaziah both married into the family of Ahab? **3.** Why does God not destroy Judah, in spite of the evil of its kings? **4.** How are Jehoram and Ahaziah not like Jehoshaphat, their father and grandfather, respectively? What factors might have influenced them to be more like Ahab, than Jehoshaphat? **5.** What other factors sometimes lead to a good person having a not-so-good offspring? Do you know any people like this today? **6.** What other good persons from the Old Testament had not-so good offsprings (1 Sam. 2:27–36; 2 Sam. 15:1–12)?

APPLY 1. In what behaviors might you have done better to follow your parents? **2.** In what behaviors are you glad that you "charted

---

8:15 spread it over the king's face, so that he died. Elisha's prophecy must not be seen as moral justification for Ben-Hadad's murder. Rather, the prophecy notes God's role in Hazael's life. Hazael's assassination of Ben-Hadad, foretold by Elisha, was the action of a wicked man, not a man led by God. The story illustrates, however, that God is in control of the entire world, not just Israel. In this case, God chose a brutal pagan as the instrument of divine judgment (Isa. 10:5–19; Amos 1:4).

8:16 In the fifth year of Joram. The writer dated the succession of kingship in the southern kingdom in relation to that in the northern kingdom. The year described was 848 B.C.

8:19 for the sake of his servant David. The Lord spared Judah's royal house, despite its unfaithfulness, only because of the promise made to David that his house would endure forever (2 Sam. 7:16).

8:20 Edom rebelled ... and set up its own king. Judah had ruled over Edom for many years through a governor appointed by Judah's king. That governor had even been an ally to Judah on occasion (3:9; 1 Kin. 22:47).

8:21 he rose up and broke through by night. The rebel Edomites soundly defeated Jehoram's army, whose hasty retreat was in sharp contrast to Joram and Jehoshaphat's thrashing of the Moabites (3:24–26). In that instance, Jehoshaphat's presence caused the Lord to bless Israel and Judah (3:14). God allowed Jehoram's army to escape annihilation (to keep alive his promise to David in 2 Sam. 7:16), but the Edomite rebellion was a success.

8:25 In the twelfth year of Joram. Here, the year of Joram's accession was counted as his first year. In 9:29 that year was not counted, and his second year was counted as his first. Ahaziah ascended the throne of the southern kingdom in 841 B.C.

your own course" instead of being like your parents?

---

[28]Ahaziah went with Joram son of Ahab to war against Hazael king of Aram at Ramoth Gilead. The Arameans wounded Joram; [29]so King Joram returned to Jezreel to recover from the wounds the Arameans had inflicted on him at Ramoth[a] in his battle with Hazael king of Aram.

Then Ahaziah son of Jehoram king of Judah went down to Jezreel to see Joram son of Ahab, because he had been wounded.

OPEN Which of the following surprise announcements has most changed your life: The announcement that you and your spouse were pregnant? That you were being given a promotion you didn't know you were up for? That you had won a contest you had forgotten you entered?

STUDY Elisha sends a young prophet to anoint Jehu as king, a position to which he had apparently not given previous consideration. **1.** Why does Elisha send a younger prophet to do this task? Why must this prophet "anoint and run"? **2.** Who will Jehu avenge (1 Kin. 18:4,13; 19:10; 21:13)? **3.** How will the house of Ahab be like the houses of Jeroboam and Baasha (1 Kin. 15:29–30; 16:11–13)? **4.** What do verses 11–13 tell you about the mixed feelings people had toward prophets? **5.** How would you describe the reaction of the other officers to Jehu's report that the prophet had declared him king?

APPLY **1.** When have you received a challenge that you feared might be bigger than you could handle? **2.** In responding to this task, what help do you feel you received from God?

Jehu Anointed King of Israel

9 The prophet Elisha summoned a man from the company of the prophets and said to him, "Tuck your cloak into your belt, take this flask of oil with you and go to Ramoth Gilead. [2]When you get there, look for Jehu son of Jehoshaphat, the son of Nimshi. Go to him, get him away from his companions and take him into an inner room. [3]Then take the flask and pour the oil on his head and declare, 'This is what the LORD says: I anoint you king over Israel.' Then open the door and run; don't delay!"

[4]So the young man, the prophet, went to Ramoth Gilead. [5]When he arrived, he found the army officers sitting together. "I have a message for you, commander," he said.

"For which of us?" asked Jehu.

"For you, commander," he replied.

[6]Jehu got up and went into the house. Then the prophet poured the oil on Jehu's head and declared, "This is what the LORD, the God of Israel, says: 'I anoint you king over the LORD's people Israel. [7]You are to destroy the house of Ahab your master, and I will avenge the blood of my servants the prophets and the blood of all the LORD's servants shed by Jezebel. [8]The whole house of Ahab will perish. I will cut off from Ahab every last male in Israel—slave or free. [9]I will make the house of Ahab like the house of Jeroboam son of Nebat and like the house of Baasha son of Ahijah. [10]As for Jezebel, dogs will devour her on the plot of ground at Jezreel, and no one will bury her.' " Then he opened the door and ran.

[11]When Jehu went out to his fellow officers, one of them asked him, "Is everything all right? Why did this madman come to you?"

"You know the man and the sort of things he says," Jehu replied.

[12]"That's not true!" they said. "Tell us."

Jehu said, "Here is what he told me: 'This is what the LORD says: I anoint you king over Israel.' "

[13]They hurried and took their cloaks and spread them under him on the bare steps. Then they blew the trumpet and shouted, "Jehu is king!"

[a]29 Hebrew *Ramah,* a variant of *Ramoth*

8:28 Ahaziah went ... to war against Hazael. First Kings 22 told the story of Jehoshaphat uniting with Ahab to fight the Arameans at Ramoth Gilead. In a similar situation, the kings of Israel and Judah united again to fight the Arameans led by Hazael. In the first battle, Ahab *had been killed.* Though neither of the Israelite kings perished in the second battle, Joram was wounded.

9:7 destroy the house of Ahab your master. Jehu learned that he was appointed to be king and would be the instrument of God's judgment on Ahab's royal house. Elijah had warned Ahab of this judgment (1 Kin. 21:21–22), because Ahab had led Israel into the sins for which he himself was also guilty.

9:11 You know the man and the sort of things he says. Jehu tried to take advantage of the traditional contempt between the army and the prophets in order to deflect the question. His reticence seemed genuine. As a man of action and a military commander, he was reluctant to believe the prophecy. As an ambitious leader, however, he was intrigued by the prophecy.

Jehu Kills Joram and Ahaziah

14So Jehu son of Jehoshaphat, the son of Nimshi, conspired against
Joram. (Now Joram and all Israel had been defending Ramoth Gilead
against Hazael king of Aram, 15but King Joram[a] had returned to Jezreel to recover from the wounds the Arameans had inflicted on him in
the battle with Hazael king of Aram.) Jehu said, "If this is the way you
feel, don't let anyone slip out of the city to go and tell the news in
Jezreel." 16Then he got into his chariot and rode to Jezreel, because
Joram was resting there and Ahaziah king of Judah had gone down to
see him.

17When the lookout standing on the tower in Jezreel saw Jehu's
troops approaching, he called out, "I see some troops coming."

"Get a horseman," Joram ordered. "Send him to meet them and
ask, 'Do you come in peace?' "

18The horseman rode off to meet Jehu and said, "This is what the
king says: 'Do you come in peace?' "

"What do you have to do with peace?" Jehu replied. "Fall in
behind me."

The lookout reported, "The messenger has reached them, but he
isn't coming back."

19So the king sent out a second horseman. When he came to them
he said, "This is what the king says: 'Do you come in peace?' "

Jehu replied, "What do you have to do with peace? Fall in
behind me."

20The lookout reported, "He has reached them, but he isn't coming
back either. The driving is like that of Jehu son of Nimshi—he drives
like a madman."

21"Hitch up my chariot," Joram ordered. And when it was hitched
up, Joram king of Israel and Ahaziah king of Judah rode out, each in
his own chariot, to meet Jehu. They met him at the plot of ground that
had belonged to Naboth the Jezreelite. 22When Joram saw Jehu he
asked, "Have you come in peace, Jehu?"

"How can there be peace," Jehu replied, "as long as all the idolatry
and witchcraft of your mother Jezebel abound?"

23Joram turned about and fled, calling out to Ahaziah, "Treachery,
Ahaziah!"

24Then Jehu drew his bow and shot Joram between the shoulders.
The arrow pierced his heart and he slumped down in his chariot.
25Jehu said to Bidkar, his chariot officer, "Pick him up and throw him
on the field that belonged to Naboth the Jezreelite. Remember how
you and I were riding together in chariots behind Ahab his father
when the LORD made this prophecy about him: 26'Yesterday I saw the
blood of Naboth and the blood of his sons, declares the LORD, and I
will surely make you pay for it on this plot of ground, declares the

[a]15 Hebrew *Jehoram*, a variant of *Joram*; also in verses 17 and 21-24

OPEN 1. Has there ever been a rival group that you couldn't stand to be around? **2.** What is the biggest grudge you held against someone?

STUDY Jehu follows up on the prophecy given through a young prophet, by rising in rebellion against Joram. He kills Joram in a manner that fulfills Elijah's earlier prophecy. **1.** Why do the messengers sent by Joram fail to return and report to him: They are tired of Joram also? They see Jehu's strength and decide to go with a winner? They realize that God is with Jehu? **2.** Why do Joram and Ahaziah go out to check Jehu's motives in person: They were naïve? They were tired of messengers who didn't come back? They were blind to the risks? God was setting them up? **3.** What is it that Jehu cannot make peace with (v. 22)? **4.** How does Jehu's killing of Joram his king, contrast with David's unwillingness to kill Saul his king (1 Sam. 24:1–22; 26:1–25)? When God had prophesied their deaths and the loss of their kingdoms, was he being more godly to act to bring it about, as Jehu did, or to let things take their course, as David did? **5.** Why is Ahaziah also a target? Is Jehu truly a "madman" (v. 20) going too far? **6.** What prophecy does the manner of Joram's death fulfill (1 Kin. 21:1–29)?

APPLY 1. Which of the following is most likely to turn you into a "madman" or "mad woman": The pressures of a hectic schedule? People who don't listen to you? Insolent teenagers? Manipulative behavior? Sexist or racist behavior? **2.** How has God strengthened you to deal with these kind of people and situations?

9:15 don't let anyone slip out of the city ... tell the news. To succeed, Jehu's coup attempt had to be a total surprise. While the celebration of verse 13 seemed sincere, it was also a means to generate support for Jehu's rebellion.

9:22 idolatry and witchcraft of your mother. Jehu accused Joram of two sins, each punishable by death. Thus he was claiming the right of holy executioner as well as the right to the throne. In fact, God had appointed him to serve both roles (vv. 6–10).

9:25 throw him on the field. Jehu saw his actions as the fulfillment of God's prophecy against Ahab (1 Kin. 21:18–24). God had not carried out the prophecy directly against Ahab because the king had humbled himself before God. But the prophecy was never revoked, and now Ahab's descendants paid the price.

LORD.'[a] Now then, pick him up and throw him on that plot, in accordance with the word of the LORD."

27When Ahaziah king of Judah saw what had happened, he fled up the road to Beth Haggan.[b] Jehu chased him, shouting, "Kill him too!" They wounded him in his chariot on the way up to Gur near Ibleam, but he escaped to Megiddo and died there. 28His servants took him by chariot to Jerusalem and buried him with his fathers in his tomb in the City of David. 29(In the eleventh year of Joram son of Ahab, Ahaziah had become king of Judah.)

Jezebel Killed

30Then Jehu went to Jezreel. When Jezebel heard about it, she painted her eyes, arranged her hair and looked out of a window. 31As Jehu entered the gate, she asked, "Have you come in peace, Zimri, you murderer of your master?"[c]

32He looked up at the window and called out, "Who is on my side? Who?" Two or three eunuchs looked down at him. 33"Throw her down!" Jehu said. So they threw her down, and some of her blood spattered the wall and the horses as they trampled her underfoot.

34Jehu went in and ate and drank. "Take care of that cursed woman," he said, "and bury her, for she was a king's daughter." 35But when they went out to bury her, they found nothing except her skull, her feet and her hands. 36They went back and told Jehu, who said, "This is the word of the LORD that he spoke through his servant Elijah the Tishbite: On the plot of ground at Jezreel dogs will devour Jezebel's flesh.[d] 37Jezebel's body will be like refuse on the ground in the plot at Jezreel, so that no one will be able to say, 'This is Jezebel.' "

Ahab's Family Killed

10 Now there were in Samaria seventy sons of the house of Ahab. So Jehu wrote letters and sent them to Samaria: to the officials of Jezreel,[e] to the elders and to the guardians of Ahab's children. He said, 2"As soon as this letter reaches you, since your master's sons are with you and you have chariots and horses, a fortified city and weapons, 3choose the best and most worthy of your master's sons and set him on his father's throne. Then fight for your master's house."

4But they were terrified and said, "If two kings could not resist him, how can we?"

[a]26 See 1 Kings 21:19. [b]27 *Or fled by way of the garden house* [c]31 *Or "Did Zimri have peace, who murdered his master?"* [d]36 See 1 Kings 21:23. [e]1 Hebrew; some Septuagint manuscripts and Vulgate *of the city*

OPEN 1. When you were a child, what was your preferred way to choose up sides? **2.** Who did you always want to have on your side?

STUDY When Jehu is provoked by Jezebel, he looks to find who is on his side, and finds two eunuchs willing to throw her out her window. **1.** Why does Jezebel make herself up before yelling at Jehu: Vanity? A love-hate feeling for Jehu? **2.** How does her death confirm Elijah's prophecy (1 Kin. 21:23)?

APPLY How do you face confrontation: Guns blazing? Peace at any price? Change the subject?

OPEN When you are competing in a contest or election, are you more the type that wants to eliminate the competition so you have smooth sailing to victory, or the type who likes to have vigorous competition right up to the finish?

STUDY After having killed Joram and Jezebel, Jehu now proceeds to kill off all of their family members and friends so as to eliminate any competition for the throne. **1.** Why does Jehu at first encourage the elders of Samaria to put one of Ahab's sons on the throne: To test their loyalties? To provide himself a

9:27 Kill him too! Ahaziah's mother was Ahab's daughter. Thus Ahaziah may have been included in the curse against Ahab's descendants (1 Kin. 21:21). However, Ahaziah was also descended from David through his father, Jehoram. While Ahab's house had been cursed, David's had been blessed with the promise forever (2 Sam. 7:16). Jehu's right to kill Ahaziah was not clear.

9:31 Zimri. Jezebel compared Jehu to Zimri, who had similarly killed Elah to become king but whose reign lasted only seven days before he was overthrown by Ahab's father, Omri. Jezebel's challenge to Jehu's right of succession was also a threat.

9:36 This is the word of the LORD. Elijah had prophesied the terrible way that Jezebel would die (1 Kin. 21:23). God's word in that prophecy had been fulfilled. Jezebel had brought great hardship and death to people faithful to God, but her own miserable end came just as God had said. (1 Kin. 16:31–33; 18:13; 21:7–14.)

10:1 in Samaria seventy sons of the house of Ahab. Killing the king was just the first step in taking the throne of Israel. Jehu would have to consolidate power and capture Samaria. With Jezebel dead, he turned his effort toward Ahab's sons (probably grandsons as well) and deputies.

10:4 they were terrified. Jehu's strategy succeeded. The city leaders had depended on Ahab's strength. With Ahab gone, the leaders were more interested in surviving than succeeding.

5 So the palace administrator, the city governor, the elders and the
guardians sent this message to Jehu: "We are your servants and we
will do anything you say. We will not appoint anyone as king; you do
whatever you think best."
6 Then Jehu wrote them a second letter, saying, "If you are on my
side and will obey me, take the heads of your master's sons and come
to me in Jezreel by this time tomorrow."
Now the royal princes, seventy of them, were with the leading men
of the city, who were rearing them. 7 When the letter arrived, these
men took the princes and slaughtered all seventy of them. They put
their heads in baskets and sent them to Jehu in Jezreel. 8 When the
messenger arrived, he told Jehu, "They have brought the heads of the
princes."
Then Jehu ordered, "Put them in two piles at the entrance of the
city gate until morning."
9 The next morning Jehu went out. He stood before all the people
and said, "You are innocent. It was I who conspired against my master and killed him, but who killed all these? 10 Know then, that not a
word the LORD has spoken against the house of Ahab will fail. The
LORD has done what he promised through his servant Elijah." 11 So
Jehu killed everyone in Jezreel who remained of the house of Ahab, as
well as all his chief men, his close friends and his priests, leaving him
no survivor.
12 Jehu then set out and went toward Samaria. At Beth Eked of the
Shepherds, 13 he met some relatives of Ahaziah king of Judah and
asked, "Who are you?"
They said, "We are relatives of Ahaziah, and we have come down to
greet the families of the king and of the queen mother."
14 "Take them alive!" he ordered. So they took them alive and
slaughtered them by the well of Beth Eked—forty-two men. He left no
survivor.
15 After he left there, he came upon Jehonadab son of Recab, who
was on his way to meet him. Jehu greeted him and said, "Are you in
accord with me, as I am with you?"
"I am," Jehonadab answered.
"If so," said Jehu, "give me your hand." So he did, and Jehu helped
him up into the chariot. 16 Jehu said, "Come with me and see my zeal
for the LORD." Then he had him ride along in his chariot.
17 When Jehu came to Samaria, he killed all who were left there of

challenge? To tease them since he knew they would be too chicken? **2.** How do you think the leading men of the city who had reared these sons felt when they had to turn them over to be executed? **3.** Why does Jehu have the princes' heads put at the entrance of the city gate? **4.** Why does Jehu decide to slaughter the relatives of King Ahaziah of Judah: Just to show he could do it? Ahaziah had also worshiped false gods? He also wanted Ahaziah's throne? Ahaziah had been a friend of Ahab's? **5.** How does Jehu describe his purge (v. 16)? How do you think others might have described it?

APPLY 1. When have you felt like you had to be part of sacrificing human compassion for practical, political or business goals? **2.** In the end, did you feel that achieving the goals was worth it? Would you do anything differently if you had to do it over again?

10:6 If you ... will obey me, take the heads. Jehu made the executions a test of loyalty. He played on the worst traits of the city leaders: their fear and selfish desire to survive at all costs.

10:7 took the princes and slaughtered all seventy of them. The leaders were all too ready to commit this mass murder in order to save themselves. Ironically, they were willing to murder but not to travel to Jezreel with the severed heads.

10:9 who killed all these? Jehu's unabashed responsibility for the king's death made him a man to fear (v. 4). His letter to Samaria's leaders about the slaughter of Ahab's seventy offspring was ambiguous enough to relieve Jehu of direct responsibility. He put the blame on Samaria's leaders, established himself as the only person fit to rule and laid the groundwork for eliminating anyone close to Ahab.

10:10 The LORD has done what he promised through his servant Elijah. Jehu used Elijah's prophecy against Ahab (1 Kin. 21:20–24) as the justification for his actions against Joram as well as his continuing destruction of Ahab's family.

10:13 met some relatives of Ahaziah. These people, relatives of the assassinated king of Judah, were traveling to see Joram and Jezebel and had obviously not heard of their deaths.

10:15 Jehonadab. Jehonadab, a conservative reformer, opposed the worship of Baal and the settled, agricultural way of life that was emerging in the Middle East. He opposed planting crops, building permanent houses and the use of wine. The cultivation of grapes for wine was one of the first signs of stable rural life, and members of his movement were prohibited from drinking it. Two centuries later, adherents of the movement begun by Jehonadab were called Recabites (Jer. 35:6–10).

OPEN Which of the following signs might be a "shrine" that represents something you would benefit by eliminating from your life: McDonald's golden arches (junk food)? The big "Hollywood" sign (motives with negative values)? The dollar sign (materialism)? The internet explorer icon (addiction to the internet and high tech stuff)? The Nike checkmark logo (preoccupation with the physical to the detriment of the spiritual)? The Tommy Hilfiger logo (addiction to fashion)?

STUDY Jehu continues his "housecleaning" by slaughtering the prophets of Baal and tearing down the shrine to Baal. He falls short of complete religious reform, however. **1.** How would the followers of Yahweh have felt when Jehu declared his passion for Baal? **2.** What details help Jehu pull off this deception? **3.** Should the priests of Baal have been suspicious at Jehu's request that they make sure no servants of the Lord (Yahweh) were there? What might they have thought the motivation for this was? **4.** Elijah had killed the prophets of Baal earlier. What does this tell you about the attraction to false religion that Jehu again must eliminate the worship of Baal? **5.** Why might someone who was so zealous to destroy the worship of Baal not also end other worship of foreign gods (vv. 28–29)? **6.** What was the significance of the fact that God "began to reduce the size of Israel"?

APPLY **1.** What might it mean to bring reform to our nation today? What would Jehu do were he alive today? **2.** What role do you feel God is calling YOU to play? What strength and support would you need to fill that role?

Ahab's family; he destroyed them, according to the word of the LORD
spoken to Elijah.

Ministers of Baal Killed

18 Then Jehu brought all the people together and said to them,
"Ahab served Baal a little; Jehu will serve him much. 19 Now summon
all the prophets of Baal, all his ministers and all his priests. See that
no one is missing, because I am going to hold a great sacrifice for
Baal. Anyone who fails to come will no longer live." But Jehu was acting deceptively in order to destroy the ministers of Baal.
20 Jehu said, "Call an assembly in honor of Baal." So they proclaimed it. 21 Then he sent word throughout Israel, and all the ministers of Baal came; not one stayed away. They crowded into the temple
of Baal until it was full from one end to the other. 22 And Jehu said to
the keeper of the wardrobe, "Bring robes for all the ministers of
Baal." So he brought out robes for them.
23 Then Jehu and Jehonadab son of Recab went into the temple of
Baal. Jehu said to the ministers of Baal, "Look around and see that no
servants of the LORD are here with you—only ministers of Baal." 24 So
they went in to make sacrifices and burnt offerings. Now Jehu had
posted eighty men outside with this warning: "If one of you lets any
of the men I am placing in your hands escape, it will be your life for
his life."
25 As soon as Jehu had finished making the burnt offering, he ordered the guards and officers: "Go in and kill them; let no one escape." So they cut them down with the sword. The guards and
officers threw the bodies out and then entered the inner shrine of the
temple of Baal. 26 They brought the sacred stone out of the temple of
Baal and burned it. 27 They demolished the sacred stone of Baal and
tore down the temple of Baal, and people have used it for a latrine to
this day.
28 So Jehu destroyed Baal worship in Israel. 29 However, he did not
turn away from the sins of Jeroboam son of Nebat, which he had
caused Israel to commit—the worship of the golden calves at Bethel
and Dan.
30 The LORD said to Jehu, "Because you have done well in accomplishing what is right in my eyes and have done to the house of Ahab
all I had in mind to do, your descendants will sit on the throne of
Israel to the fourth generation." 31 Yet Jehu was not careful to keep the
law of the LORD, the God of Israel, with all his heart. He did not turn
away from the sins of Jeroboam, which he had caused Israel to
commit.
32 In those days the LORD began to reduce the size of Israel. Hazael
overpowered the Israelites throughout their territory 33 east of the

---

10:18 Ahab served Baal ... Jehu ... much. Jehu had great political skill. Among the rural, more conservative people he portrayed himself as one of them. After capturing Samaria, he portrayed himself to the people there as a zealot for Baal.

10:30 Because you have done well. God had chosen Jehu to carry out his holy vengeance on the house of Ahab. Despite Jehu's faults, he had accomplished what God "had in mind to do" concerning Ahab's descendants. The prophet Hosea condemned Jehu for the massacre at Jezreel (Hos. 1:4); however, God blessed Jehu with the longest dynasty (one hundred years) of any leader of the northern kingdom.

10:32 reduce the size of Israel. God continued to afflict the northern kingdom with the covenant curses during Jehu's rule (Lev. 26:14–35). Though Jehu curbed the worship of Baal, he continued to worship idols, and the people continued to disobey God's law.

10:33 east of the Jordan. Hazael, king of Aram, led his country to capture

Jordan in all the land of Gilead (the region of Gad, Reuben and Manasseh), from Aroer by the Arnon Gorge through Gilead to Bashan.
[34]As for the other events of Jehu's reign, all he did, and all his achievements, are they not written in the book of the annals of the kings of Israel?
[35]Jehu rested with his fathers and was buried in Samaria. And Jehoahaz his son succeeded him as king. [36]The time that Jehu reigned over Israel in Samaria was twenty-eight years.

Athaliah and Joash

11 When Athaliah the mother of Ahaziah saw that her son was dead, she proceeded to destroy the whole royal family. [2]But Jehosheba, the daughter of King Jehoram[a] and sister of Ahaziah, took Joash son of Ahaziah and stole him away from among the royal princes, who were about to be murdered. She put him and his nurse in a bedroom to hide him from Athaliah; so he was not killed. [3]He remained hidden with his nurse at the temple of the LORD for six years while Athaliah ruled the land.
[4]In the seventh year Jehoiada sent for the commanders of units of a hundred, the Carites and the guards and had them brought to him at the temple of the LORD. He made a covenant with them and put them under oath at the temple of the LORD. Then he showed them the king's son. [5]He commanded them, saying, "This is what you are to do: You who are in the three companies that are going on duty on the Sabbath—a third of you guarding the royal palace, [6]a third at the Sur Gate, and a third at the gate behind the guard, who take turns guarding the temple— [7]and you who are in the other two companies that normally go off Sabbath duty are all to guard the temple for the king. [8]Station yourselves around the king, each man with his weapon in his hand. Anyone who approaches your ranks[b] must be put to death. Stay close to the king wherever he goes."
[9]The commanders of units of a hundred did just as Jehoiada the priest ordered. Each one took his men—those who were going on duty on the Sabbath and those who were going off duty—and came to Jehoiada the priest. [10]Then he gave the commanders the spears and shields that had belonged to King David and that were in the temple of the LORD. [11]The guards, each with his weapon in his hand,

[a]2 Hebrew *Joram*, a variant of *Jehoram* [b]8 *Or approaches the precincts*

OPEN 1. What responsibilities were you given around the home when you were seven years old? **2.** What did you most enjoy doing at that age?

STUDY After Ahaziah, king of Judah, was killed by Jehu, a power struggle ensued, with Ahaziah's mother Athaliah trying to kill off candidates for the throne. Ahaziah's seven-year old son Joash was preserved, however, and he became king. **1.** What is Athaliah's motivation for killing off Ahaziah's heirs (v. 1)? Does it surprise you that she is killing off her own grandchildren? **2.** How long does Athaliah rule? **3.** What risks does Jehoiada take in this conspiracy (vv. 4–11)? What precautions? Why should the soldiers cooperate? **4.** What does Jehoiada give the king when he proclaims him king? What is the significance of that? **5.** Why did Jehoiada not want to put Ahaziah to death in the temple? **6.** What do the people do to show that they are returning to the worship of the Lord?

APPLY 1. Has there been a period of your life when you turned away from worshiping God? What did you "worship" during that period? **2.** Who or what turned you back to God? Did you do anything to symbolize your turning back to God?

---

all of the Transjordan from Israel. Elisha had prophesied that Hazael would become a terrible enemy of Israel, and the loss of the land east of the Jordan River fulfilled that prophecy. Like many others, Hazael was an instrument in God's hand to punish Israel (8:7–15).

10:34 the other events of Jehu's reign. Archeological sources indicate that Jehu paid tribute to the Assyrian king Shalmaneser III. This evidence is a reminder that the rulers in 1 and 2 Kings lived in turbulent times. As the power of Israel waned, other kingdoms and empires were gaining strength. Israel's decline affected not only its citizens but also the balance of power in the entire region.

11:1 Athaliah ... proceeded to destroy the whole royal family. The royal family of Judah had already been decimated. Jehoram had killed all his brothers when he succeeded Jehoshaphat (2 Chr. 21:4). Jehu had killed another forty-two men of Judah's royal house by the well at Beth Eked (10:14). Arabs had killed Ahaziah's brothers when they attacked Judah (2 Chr. 21:17; 22:1).

11:2 But Jehosheba ... took Joash. Athaliah was determined to kill all heirs to the throne of Judah. Joash, the son of the king, was hidden from his grandmother's scheme by his father's half-sister.

11:4 commanders of units. The conspiracy to install Joash as king was organized by a priest, Jehoiada. His conspiracy included all the people needed to make it successful. Five native Israelite commanders led the military guards; the Carites were mercenaries from Caria who had served as royal bodyguards. The Levites and heads of the Israelite families in all the towns gave the coup wide acceptance (2 Chr. 23:1–3).

stationed themselves around the king—near the altar and the temple,
from the south side to the north side of the temple.
[12]Jehoiada brought out the king's son and put the crown on him;
he presented him with a copy of the covenant and proclaimed him
king. They anointed him, and the people clapped their hands and
shouted, "Long live the king!"
[13]When Athaliah heard the noise made by the guards and the people, she went to the people at the temple of the LORD. [14]She looked
and there was the king, standing by the pillar, as the custom was. The
officers and the trumpeters were beside the king, and all the people
of the land were rejoicing and blowing trumpets. Then Athaliah tore
her robes and called out, "Treason! Treason!"
[15]Jehoiada the priest ordered the commanders of units of a hundred, who were in charge of the troops: "Bring her out between the
ranks[a] and put to the sword anyone who follows her." For the priest
had said, "She must not be put to death in the temple of the LORD."
[16]So they seized her as she reached the place where the horses enter
the palace grounds, and there she was put to death.
[17]Jehoiada then made a covenant between the LORD and the king
and people that they would be the LORD's people. He also made a
covenant between the king and the people. [18]All the people of the
land went to the temple of Baal and tore it down. They smashed the
altars and idols to pieces and killed Mattan the priest of Baal in front
of the altars.
Then Jehoiada the priest posted guards at the temple of the LORD.
[19]He took with him the commanders of hundreds, the Carites, the
guards and all the people of the land, and together they brought the
king down from the temple of the LORD and went into the palace, entering by way of the gate of the guards. The king then took his place
on the royal throne, [20]and all the people of the land rejoiced. And the
city was quiet, because Athaliah had been slain with the sword at the
palace.
[21]Joash[b] was seven years old when he began to reign.

Joash Repairs the Temple

12 In the seventh year of Jehu, Joash[c] became king, and he
reigned in Jerusalem forty years. His mother's name was
Zibiah; she was from Beersheba. [2]Joash did what was right in the
eyes of the LORD all the years Jehoiada the priest instructed him. [3]The

[a]*15 Or out from the precincts* [b]*21* Hebrew *Jehoash,* a variant of *Joash* [c]*1* Hebrew *Jehoash,* a variant of *Joash;* also in verses 2, 4, 6, 7 and 18

OPEN 1. On which of the following are you spending the most energy maintaining: Your home? Your yard? Your faith? Your car, boat or recreational vehicle? Your profession (continuing education)? **2.** Is this maintenance work progressing or standing still?

11:12 put the crown on him ... proclaimed him king. The coup was staged as an official coronation. Joash was given the symbol of earthly kingship, the crown. He was given the holy document that would govern his actions, the covenant. He was proclaimed king, and then he was anointed.

11:17 covenant between the LORD and the king and people. The old Mosaic covenant had to be renewed for Judah to move forward as a godly nation under Joash. This covenant defined the Israelites as God's people, his holy nation (Deut. 4:20). Also important was a renewal of covenant between king and people, to accompany a new accord between the people and God (1 Sam. 10:25).

11:21 seven years old. The new king, who would carry on the lineage of David in the royal house of Judah, was a mere child who had been hidden away for six of his seven years.

12:2 Joash did what was right ... all the years Jehoiada the priest instructed him. Under the priest's tutelage, Joash was a good ruler who adhered to his covenant responsibilities. After Jehoiada died, Joash listened to the leaders of Judah, and Baal worship began to flourish again.

high places, however, were not removed; the people continued to offer sacrifices and burn incense there.
4Joash said to the priests, "Collect all the money that is brought as
sacred offerings to the temple of the LORD—the money collected in
the census, the money received from personal vows and the money
brought voluntarily to the temple. 5Let every priest receive the money
from one of the treasurers, and let it be used to repair whatever damage is found in the temple."
6But by the twenty-third year of King Joash the priests still had not
repaired the temple. 7Therefore King Joash summoned Jehoiada the
priest and the other priests and asked them, "Why aren't you repairing the damage done to the temple? Take no more money from your
treasurers, but hand it over for repairing the temple." 8The priests
agreed that they would not collect any more money from the people
and that they would not repair the temple themselves.
9Jehoiada the priest took a chest and bored a hole in its lid. He
placed it beside the altar, on the right side as one enters the temple of
the LORD. The priests who guarded the entrance put into the chest all
the money that was brought to the temple of the LORD. 10Whenever
they saw that there was a large amount of money in the chest, the
royal secretary and the high priest came, counted the money that had
been brought into the temple of the LORD and put it into bags. 11When
the amount had been determined, they gave the money to the men
appointed to supervise the work on the temple. With it they paid
those who worked on the temple of the LORD—the carpenters and
builders, 12the masons and stonecutters. They purchased timber and
dressed stone for the repair of the temple of the LORD, and met all the
other expenses of restoring the temple.
13The money brought into the temple was not spent for making
silver basins, wick trimmers, sprinkling bowls, trumpets or any other
articles of gold or silver for the temple of the LORD; 14it was paid to
the workmen, who used it to repair the temple. 15They did not require
an accounting from those to whom they gave the money to pay the
workers, because they acted with complete honesty. 16The money
from the guilt offerings and sin offerings was not brought into the
temple of the LORD; it belonged to the priests.
17About this time Hazael king of Aram went up and attacked Gath

STUDY King Joash sets up a plan to fund the repair of the temple, but for some reason the maintenance project is placed on hold for a while. Finally, however, it goes forward and becomes the central event of Joash's reign. **1.** Why do you think it took the priests so long to get going on the repair project: They were looking for "a bigger piece of the action"? They were just being lazy? They were too busy with priest work? They were waiting for government permits? **2.** Why did it take Joash so long to notice the slow down? **3.** Was Joash naïve not to require an accounting of the money (v. 15)? Is such trust found anywhere today? Should it be? **4.** What are Joash's apparent weaknesses (vv. 17–18; 2 Chr. 24:17–25)? **5.** Why would a king so eager to rebuild the temple give so much away to a foreign tyrant?

APPLY What reform have you not followed through on in your life? What is holding you back?

12:4 money. Joash had a new financial plan for the temple. Money to support temple restoration would come from census taxes, personal vows and voluntary offerings.

12:5 Let every priest receive. Under Joash's plan, money for temple work was handled by treasurers who would allocate funds back to priests to keep the temple in good repair.

12:7 Take no more money. Basically, priests were removed from Joash's plan for restoring the temple.

12:8 priests agreed. The priests agreed that they would no longer be allocated money by the treasurers and would no longer be responsible for repairing the temple.

12:9 priests ... put into the chest all the money. Previous offerings appeared to have been squandered, since no repairs were evident. When the chest was put in the temple and people could see their money collected and guarded, public confidence in the process grew. So did the offerings.

12:10 royal secretary and the high priest. Originally, temple priests and officers handled the cash. Under the new plan, Joash placed the process under direct royal supervision, reducing the likelihood of theft or mismanagement.

12:13 money ... was not spent for. The money coming into the temple was designated strictly for repair and restoration. This specific prohibition implied that some of the money previously collected had been spent on ornamentation, not repair.

12:16 guilt offerings ... sin offerings. Income from these sources did not go into the temple fund but was instead controlled by priests.

12:17 Hazael ... turned to attack Jerusalem. With the virtual collapse of real power in the northern kingdom, the Arameans were free to ravage the area. They captured the important Philistine city of Gath, then turned toward

and captured it. Then he turned to attack Jerusalem. [18]But Joash king
of Judah took all the sacred objects dedicated by his fathers—
Jehoshaphat, Jehoram and Ahaziah, the kings of Judah—and the gifts
he himself had dedicated and all the gold found in the treasuries of
the temple of the LORD and of the royal palace, and he sent them to
Hazael king of Aram, who then withdrew from Jerusalem.
[19]As for the other events of the reign of Joash, and all he did, are
they not written in the book of the annals of the kings of Judah? [20]His
officials conspired against him and assassinated him at Beth Millo,
on the road down to Silla. [21]The officials who murdered him were
Jozabad son of Shimeath and Jehozabad son of Shomer. He died and
was buried with his fathers in the City of David. And Amaziah his son
succeeded him as king.

Jehoahaz King of Israel

13 In the twenty-third year of Joash son of Ahaziah king of
Judah, Jehoahaz son of Jehu became king of Israel in Samaria, and he reigned seventeen years. [2]He did evil in the eyes of the
LORD by following the sins of Jeroboam son of Nebat, which he had
caused Israel to commit, and he did not turn away from them. [3]So the
LORD's anger burned against Israel, and for a long time he kept them
under the power of Hazael king of Aram and Ben-Hadad his son.
[4]Then Jehoahaz sought the LORD's favor, and the LORD listened to
him, for he saw how severely the king of Aram was oppressing Israel.
[5]The LORD provided a deliverer for Israel, and they escaped from the
power of Aram. So the Israelites lived in their own homes as they had
before. [6]But they did not turn away from the sins of the house of
Jeroboam, which he had caused Israel to commit; they continued in
them. Also, the Asherah pole[a] remained standing in Samaria.
[7]Nothing had been left of the army of Jehoahaz except fifty horsemen, ten chariots and ten thousand foot soldiers, for the king of
Aram had destroyed the rest and made them like the dust at threshing
time.
[8]As for the other events of the reign of Jehoahaz, all he did and his
achievements, are they not written in the book of the annals of the

[a]6 That is, a symbol of the goddess Asherah; here and elsewhere in 2 Kings

OPEN Who would you have listed as your "oppressors" when you were in the eighth grade: Your teachers? Some peers who teased you? Your parents? Persons of another race or group?

STUDY Jehoahaz, king of Israel, is a wicked king and so God gives the nation over to be oppressed by Aram. He repents, however, and so God helps them escape from the oppression of Aram. **1.** How does Jehoahaz strike you: Resourceful? Compromiser? Sincere? Victim? Half-hearted? Under-achiever? Why? **2.** Is God soft on Israel, giving them too many chances to turn things around, or is he too harsh? **3.** With their depleted resources, how prepared for war is Israel (v. 7; 1 Kin. 20:29)?

APPLY In the midst of the "battles" you face, what resource is running low: Energy? Supportive friends? Courage? Hope? Direction?

Jerusalem. The writer of 2 Chronicles makes it clear that this attack on Jerusalem was the result of Joash turning away from the Lord (2 Chr. 24:17–25).

12:18 sacred objects ... gifts ... gold. Joash used the temple treasuries to ransom Jerusalem and forestall the attack. In ancient times, this practice was widespread. Wars were begun for the express purpose of extracting ransoms. Note that Joash, who controlled temple money (v. 10), chose to use the riches of the temple rather than the wealth his own royal treasury had accumulated.

12:20 His officials conspired against him and assassinated him. The writer of 2 Kings chose to delete several crucial pieces of the Joash story. After Jehoaida's death, Joash had turned away from the Lord and led Judah into apostasy. When Jehoaida's son, Zechariah, spoke out against this disobedience of God's commands, Joash ordered his death. This act enraged the king's officials, who conspired and killed Joash in his bed.

12:21 officials who murdered him. The men who killed Joash were not native Israelites but sons of Moabite and Ammonite women (2 Chr. 24:26). This suggests that the murderers were hired mercenaries.

13:2 following the sins of Jeroboam. Jeroboam had led Israel into apostasy by making two golden calves, by building shrines in high places and by instituting pagan religious festivals.

13:3 Ben-Hadad. He became king of Aram in either 806 or 796 B.C. Like his father, Ben-Hadad aggressively confronted Israel and was used as an instrument of God to punish rebellious Israel. (8:10–15.)

13:5 The LORD provided a deliverer for Israel. God answered Jehoahaz's prayers. The covenant people were oppressed by the Arameans, and God responded by empowering the Assyrians to become a much larger threat to the Arameans than was Israel. With the Arameans distracted, Israel was able to break their stranglehold during the reigns of Jehoash son of Jehoahaz and Jeroboam II.

kings of Israel? [9]Jehoahaz rested with his fathers and was buried in
Samaria. And Jehoash[a] his son succeeded him as king.

Jehoash King of Israel

[10]In the thirty-seventh year of Joash king of Judah, Jehoash son of
Jehoahaz became king of Israel in Samaria, and he reigned sixteen
years. [11]He did evil in the eyes of the LORD and did not turn away from
any of the sins of Jeroboam son of Nebat, which he had caused Israel
to commit; he continued in them.

[12]As for the other events of the reign of Jehoash, all he did and his
achievements, including his war against Amaziah king of Judah, are
they not written in the book of the annals of the kings of Israel? [13]Je-
hoash rested with his fathers, and Jeroboam succeeded him on the
throne. Jehoash was buried in Samaria with the kings of Israel.

[14]Now Elisha was suffering from the illness from which he died.
Jehoash king of Israel went down to see him and wept over him. "My
father! My father!" he cried. "The chariots and horsemen of Israel!"

[15]Elisha said, "Get a bow and some arrows," and he did so. [16]"Take
the bow in your hands," he said to the king of Israel. When he had
taken it, Elisha put his hands on the king's hands.

[17]"Open the east window," he said, and he opened it. "Shoot!"
Elisha said, and he shot. "The LORD's arrow of victory, the arrow of
victory over Aram!" Elisha declared. "You will completely destroy the
Arameans at Aphek."

[18]Then he said, "Take the arrows," and the king took them. Elisha
told him, "Strike the ground." He struck it three times and stopped.
[19]The man of God was angry with him and said, "You should have
struck the ground five or six times; then you would have defeated
Aram and completely destroyed it. But now you will defeat it only
three times."

[20]Elisha died and was buried.

Now Moabite raiders used to enter the country every spring.
[21]Once while some Israelites were burying a man, suddenly they saw
a band of raiders; so they threw the man's body into Elisha's tomb.
When the body touched Elisha's bones, the man came to life and
stood up on his feet.

[22]Hazael king of Aram oppressed Israel throughout the reign of
Jehoahaz. [23]But the LORD was gracious to them and had compassion

[a]9 Hebrew *Joash,* a variant of *Jehoash;* also in verses 12-14 and 25

OPEN 1. What person whose advice you valued has since died? How did that death affect you? **2.** What did this person teach you that you still try to hold on to?

STUDY When Elisha is near death he has Jehoash go through a ritual that will assure him of victory over Aram. However, Jehoash partially botches the ritual, which will make the victory less than complete. **1.** How do you think Jehoash is feeling as Elisha is facing death: Sad about how he has acted as king? Remorseful over the death of a man he respects? Hopeful that he would get some "favor" from the spiritually powerful man? **2.** Where else do we find the phrase Jehoash uses in verse 14 (2:12)? Of what significance is it? **3.** Why does Elisha have Jehoash go through this complex and specific ritual (vv. 15–19): To see how obedient he is willing to be? Because it's a magic formula? Because it was very symbolic? **4.** How do you view the story of Elisha's bones: Colorful myth? A testimony to the spiritual power of the man? A reminder of God's complete power over life and death? **5.** What would you say was Elisha's legacy?

APPLY If you could ensure a victory for your children and grandchildren as your last bequest, what victory would you most want to give them: A victory over financial stress? A victory over self-doubt and poor self-image? A victory over the fear of death? A victory over the oppression of prejudice, racism and sexism? Other?

13:14 My father! My father! ... The chariots and horsemen of Israel! Jehoash used the same words to honor Elisha that Elisha had used on the occasion of Elijah's ascent to heaven in a whirlwind (2:12). As in the earlier instance, the exclamation recognized that Israel's real military power rested in the hands of God and that the prophets were God's pipeline to the king.

13:16 Elisha put his hands on the king's hands. By holding the bow with Jehoash, Elisha symbolically demonstrated that God was going to be with him and bless his efforts against the Arameans. God had already blessed this effort when Jehoahaz sought the Lord's help for his people (v. 4).

13:18 He struck it three times and stopped. God was prepared to bless Jehoash in his war against the Arameans to the extent that the king had zeal for the task. Even in the presence of Elisha, the man of God, Jehoash showed little enthusiasm for driving the Arameans from his land.

13:19 you will defeat it only three times. Striking the ground with arrows was more than a symbolic act. It was a test of Jehoash's commitment to defeat the Arameans and indicated the success he would have driving the Arameans from Israel's territory.

13:21 the man came to life and stood up. Even in death, Elisha's bones were able to transmit God's power and grace (4:32–35).

13:23 gracious ... compassion ... concern. Despite Israel's deserving the full measure of punishment prescribed in the law for disobedience to the covenant, God was full of mercy and grace toward the people. To those who

and showed concern for them because of his covenant with Abraham, Isaac and Jacob. To this day he has been unwilling to destroy them or banish them from his presence.

[24]Hazael king of Aram died, and Ben-Hadad his son succeeded him as king. [25]Then Jehoash son of Jehoahaz recaptured from Ben-Hadad son of Hazael the towns he had taken in battle from his father Jehoahaz. Three times Jehoash defeated him, and so he recovered the Israelite towns.

Amaziah King of Judah

14 In the second year of Jehoash[a] son of Jehoahaz king of Israel, Amaziah son of Joash king of Judah began to reign. [2]He was twenty-five years old when he became king, and he reigned in Jerusalem twenty-nine years. His mother's name was Jehoaddin; she was from Jerusalem. [3]He did what was right in the eyes of the LORD, but not as his father David had done. In everything he followed the example of his father Joash. [4]The high places, however, were not removed; the people continued to offer sacrifices and burn incense there.

[5]After the kingdom was firmly in his grasp, he executed the officials who had murdered his father the king. [6]Yet he did not put the sons of the assassins to death, in accordance with what is written in the Book of the Law of Moses where the LORD commanded: "Fathers shall not be put to death for their children, nor children put to death for their fathers; each is to die for his own sins."[b]

[7]He was the one who defeated ten thousand Edomites in the Valley of Salt and captured Sela in battle, calling it Joktheel, the name it has to this day.

[8]Then Amaziah sent messengers to Jehoash son of Jehoahaz, the son of Jehu, king of Israel, with the challenge: "Come, meet me face to face."

[9]But Jehoash king of Israel replied to Amaziah king of Judah: "A thistle in Lebanon sent a message to a cedar in Lebanon, 'Give your daughter to my son in marriage.' Then a wild beast in Lebanon came along and trampled the thistle underfoot. [10]You have indeed defeated Edom and now you are arrogant. Glory in your victory, but stay at home! Why ask for trouble and cause your own downfall and that of Judah also?"

[11]Amaziah, however, would not listen, so Jehoash king of Israel attacked. He and Amaziah king of Judah faced each other at Beth Shemesh in Judah. [12]Judah was routed by Israel, and every man fled to his home. [13]Jehoash king of Israel captured Amaziah king of Judah, the son of Joash, the son of Ahaziah, at Beth Shemesh. Then Jehoash

[a] *1* Hebrew *Joash,* a variant of *Jehoash;* also in verses 13, 23 and 27 [b] *6* Deut. 24:16

OPEN 1. When as a teenager do you remember "biting more off than you could chew": Planning a school project that turned out to be too much? Fighting someone who was too tough? Taking on a job that left you with too little study time? **2.** How likely are you to "bite off more than you can chew" today: Happens all the time? Happens occasionally? Never happens—I take very conservative bites?

STUDY Amaziah is basically a good king, who also has an important military victory over the Edomites. However, when he challenges Israel, he finds he has extended himself too far. **1.** What tells you that Amaziah might bring a breath of fresh air to Judah (vv. 1–5)? **2.** Why should Amaziah respect the law against punishing sons for the sins of their fathers, when Amaziah's predecessors did not? **3.** What was the main point of Jehoash's riddle (vv. 9–10)? **4.** If Jehoash was an evil king (13:11), and Amaziah was a good king (v. 3), why would God not give victory to Amaziah over Jehoash? **5.** What does Amaziah not do that David would have done in this situation (2 Sam. 5:19)? **6.** What did Amaziah's military mistake cost him and his nation?

APPLY 1. When has pride or arrogance gotten the better of your judgment? What happened as a result? **2.** If you consulted God before taking on any major challenge, how do you think it might affect you and your success rate: It might slow you down? It would make you feel tenta-

---

had forgotten or neglected their obligations to God, the Lord showed mercy, remembering all his promises to them.

14:3 but not as his father David had done. Jeroboam served as a prototype king who allowed or promoted idol worship. In this passage, David was the prototype king who was faithful to God in all ways, especially in worship.

14:7 the one who defeated ten thousand Edomites. Edom had rebelled successfully against Judah under Jehoram. Amaziah was able to subdue the Edomites temporarily.

14:8 Come, meet me face to face. Feeling bold after his victory over the Edomites and provoked by the terrible acts of northern mercenaries, Amaziah challenged the northern kingdom to battle. These mercenaries, furious at being sent home at the Valley of Salt and thus kept from sharing in the spoils of victory, raided Judean towns, killing three thousand people and plundering property (2 Chr. 25:10–17).

went to Jerusalem and broke down the wall of Jerusalem from the
Ephraim Gate to the Corner Gate—a section about six hundred feet
long.[a] 14He took all the gold and silver and all the articles found in the
temple of the LORD and in the treasuries of the royal palace. He also
took hostages and returned to Samaria.
15As for the other events of the reign of Jehoash, what he did and
his achievements, including his war against Amaziah king of Judah,
are they not written in the book of the annals of the kings of Israel?
16Jehoash rested with his fathers and was buried in Samaria with the
kings of Israel. And Jeroboam his son succeeded him as king.
17Amaziah son of Joash king of Judah lived for fifteen years after
the death of Jehoash son of Jehoahaz king of Israel. 18As for the other
events of Amaziah's reign, are they not written in the book of the
annals of the kings of Judah?
19They conspired against him in Jerusalem, and he fled to Lachish,
but they sent men after him to Lachish and killed him there. 20He was
brought back by horse and was buried in Jerusalem with his fathers,
in the City of David.
21Then all the people of Judah took Azariah,[b] who was sixteen years
old, and made him king in place of his father Amaziah. 22He was the
one who rebuilt Elath and restored it to Judah after Amaziah rested
with his fathers.

Jeroboam II King of Israel

23In the fifteenth year of Amaziah son of Joash king of Judah, Jeroboam son of Jehoash king of Israel became king in Samaria, and he
reigned forty-one years. 24He did evil in the eyes of the LORD and did
not turn away from any of the sins of Jeroboam son of Nebat, which
he had caused Israel to commit. 25He was the one who restored the
boundaries of Israel from Lebo[c] Hamath to the Sea of the Arabah,[d] in
accordance with the word of the LORD, the God of Israel, spoken
through his servant Jonah son of Amittai, the prophet from Gath
Hepher.
26The LORD had seen how bitterly everyone in Israel, whether slave
or free, was suffering; there was no one to help them. 27And since the
LORD had not said he would blot out the name of Israel from under
heaven, he saved them by the hand of Jeroboam son of Jehoash.
28As for the other events of Jeroboam's reign, all he did, and his
military achievements, including how he recovered for Israel both
Damascus and Hamath, which had belonged to Yaudi,[e] are they not
written in the book of the annals of the kings of Israel? 29Jeroboam

[a]13 Hebrew *four hundred cubits* (about 180 meters) [b]21 Also called *Uzziah* [c]25 Or *from the entrance to* [d]25 That is, the Dead Sea [e]28 Or *Judah*

tive and unsure, making you less effective? It would help you to act with better judgment, ensuring greater success? It's what you do already?

OPEN 1. What kind of help were you most likely to need when you were in Jr. High: Help with bullies? Help with school work? Help with the opposite sex? Help with chores? **2.** Who was most likely to give you that help?

STUDY The people of Israel were needing help, and God supplies through the unlikely source of the evil king Jeroboam II. **1.** Why is Israel not punished because of the evil of Jeroboam? Why instead are they relieved of suffering and allowed to expand boundaries **2.** How would expansion of boundaries benefit Israel? **3.** What prophet promised these restored boundaries?

APPLY When has God used someone you would never have expected to help you?

14:14 all the articles. *During Solomon's reign the temple was filled with amazing wealth and treasures. The articles referred to here were minimal, though. Former King Joash had used the temple wealth to pay tribute to Hazael of Damascus (12:17–18).*

14:19 fled to Lachish. A border fortress in Judah, Lachish held a strategic position in a valley twenty-five *miles* southwest of Jerusalem. It had been a Canaanite royal city before Israel reinhabited the land.

14:21 Amaziah and his son, Azariah, probably served as co-regents for a substantial number of years before Amaziah's death in Lachish.

14:22 Elath. Elath functioned as a key seaport for each nation that controlled it. Restoring this port was one of Azariah's most significant accomplishments.

14:28 recovered for Israel both Damascus and Hamath. These cities had been under David's rule but were lost to Syria. Jeroboam's father had begun reclaiming the cities, but Jeroboam brought them finally back under Israel's rule.

OPEN What was your biggest concern at age 16?

STUDY Azariah becomes king of Judah at age 16. Although he basically does what is right, he is inflicted with leprosy his entire reign. **1.** By what other name is Azariah known (2 Chr. 26)? Why does he have leprosy (v. 5)? **2.** What happened the year Azariah died (Isa. 6:1)?

APPLY 1. What "leprosy" is eating away at you right now: Guilt? Jealousy? Bitterness? **2.** Where are you looking for a cure?

OPEN What were you most likely to have taken away from you by force when you were in the fourth grade: Lunch money? A cool toy? Stuff YOU had taken from someone else? Books? Love note?

STUDY Israel's turbulent political history continues as king after king is assassinated. **1.** What is the significance that Shallum attacked Zechariah "in front of the people"? Does this say anything about the political climate? **2.** If Shallum's act fulfilled prophecy, should he still be considered guilty of murder? **3.** What social conditions breed conspiracies? When is being in power dangerous? Is it ever safe? **4.** Does Shallum get his justice? **5.** What particularly gruesome act does Menahem commit (v. 16)? **6.** When violence starts to multiply in a culture, what can the people do to turn things around? What might Jesus have said about this?

APPLY 1. When have you felt like you had been "ripped open" by an act of violence (physical

rested with his fathers, the kings of Israel. And Zechariah his son
succeeded him as king.

Azariah King of Judah

15 In the twenty-seventh year of Jeroboam king of Israel,
Azariah son of Amaziah king of Judah began to reign. 2He
was sixteen years old when he became king, and he reigned in
Jerusalem fifty-two years. His mother's name was Jecoliah; she was
from Jerusalem. 3He did what was right in the eyes of the LORD, just
as his father Amaziah had done. 4The high places, however, were not
removed; the people continued to offer sacrifices and burn incense
there.
5The LORD afflicted the king with leprosy[a] until the day he died, and
he lived in a separate house.[b] Jotham the king's son had charge of the
palace and governed the people of the land.
6As for the other events of Azariah's reign, and all he did, are they
not written in the book of the annals of the kings of Judah? 7Azariah
rested with his fathers and was buried near them in the City of David.
And Jotham his son succeeded him as king.

Zechariah King of Israel

8In the thirty-eighth year of Azariah king of Judah, Zechariah son of
Jeroboam became king of Israel in Samaria, and he reigned six
months. 9He did evil in the eyes of the LORD, as his fathers had done.
He did not turn away from the sins of Jeroboam son of Nebat, which
he had caused Israel to commit.
10Shallum son of Jabesh conspired against Zechariah. He attacked
him in front of the people,[c] assassinated him and succeeded him as
king. 11The other events of Zechariah's reign are written in the book
of the annals of the kings of Israel. 12So the word of the LORD spoken
to Jehu was fulfilled: "Your descendants will sit on the throne of Israel
to the fourth generation."[d]

Shallum King of Israel

13Shallum son of Jabesh became king in the thirty-ninth year of
Uzziah king of Judah, and he reigned in Samaria one month. 14Then
Menahem son of Gadi went from Tirzah up to Samaria. He attacked
Shallum son of Jabesh in Samaria, assassinated him and succeeded
him as king.
15The other events of Shallum's reign, and the conspiracy he led,
are written in the book of the annals of the kings of Israel.

[a]5 The Hebrew word was used for various diseases affecting the skin—not necessarily leprosy. [b]5 Or *in a house where he was relieved of responsibility* [c]10 Hebrew; some Septuagint manuscripts *in Ibleam* [d]12 2 Kings 10:30

15:5 *afflicted.* *Leprosy was Azariah's* punishment for burning incense on the altar in the temple (2 Chr. 26:16–18). Burning incense was a task to be performed only by a priest.

15:6 Azariah's reign, and all he did. Azariah's reign was noted for his military victories. He also increased Judah's military strength and improved the organization of her government.

15:12 was fulfilled. Jehu had destroyed the worshipers of Baal in Ahab's wicked kingdom. Because of that, God promised Jehu that his dynasty would continue for four generations, and it did.

16 At that time Menahem, starting out from Tirzah, attacked Tiphsah
and everyone in the city and its vicinity, because they refused to open
their gates. He sacked Tiphsah and ripped open all the pregnant
women.

Menahem King of Israel

17 In the thirty-ninth year of Azariah king of Judah, Menahem son of
Gadi became king of Israel, and he reigned in Samaria ten years. 18 He
did evil in the eyes of the LORD. During his entire reign he did not turn
away from the sins of Jeroboam son of Nebat, which he had caused
Israel to commit.
19 Then Pul[a] king of Assyria invaded the land, and Menahem gave
him a thousand talents[b] of silver to gain his support and strengthen
his own hold on the kingdom. 20 Menahem exacted this money from
Israel. Every wealthy man had to contribute fifty shekels[c] of silver to
be given to the king of Assyria. So the king of Assyria withdrew and
stayed in the land no longer.
21 As for the other events of Menahem's reign, and all he did, are
they not written in the book of the annals of the kings of Israel?
22 Menahem rested with his fathers. And Pekahiah his son succeeded
him as king.

Pekahiah King of Israel

23 In the fiftieth year of Azariah king of Judah, Pekahiah son of Menahem became king of Israel in Samaria, and he reigned two years.
24 Pekahiah did evil in the eyes of the LORD. He did not turn away from
the sins of Jeroboam son of Nebat, which he had caused Israel to
commit. 25 One of his chief officers, Pekah son of Remaliah, conspired
against him. Taking fifty men of Gilead with him, he assassinated
Pekahiah, along with Argob and Arieh, in the citadel of the royal palace at Samaria. So Pekah killed Pekahiah and succeeded him as king.
26 The other events of Pekahiah's reign, and all he did, are written in
the book of the annals of the kings of Israel.

Pekah King of Israel

27 In the fifty-second year of Azariah king of Judah, Pekah son of
Remaliah became king of Israel in Samaria, and he reigned twenty
years. 28 He did evil in the eyes of the LORD. He did not turn away from
the sins of Jeroboam son of Nebat, which he had caused Israel to
commit.
29 In the time of Pekah king of Israel, Tiglath-Pileser king of Assyria
came and took Ijon, Abel Beth Maacah, Janoah, Kedesh and Hazor.
He took Gilead and Galilee, including all the land of Naphtali, and

[a]19 Also called *Tiglath-Pileser* [b]19 That is, about 37 tons (about 34 metric tons) [c]20 That is, about 1 1/4 pounds (about 0.6 kilogram)

or emotional)? **2.** What has helped you find healing?

OPEN Who was your favorite villain growing up: Bonnie and Clyde? Darth Vader? The Joker? Other?

STUDY Israel is going into a nose-dive in terms of the quality of their kings, as king after king is evil. One king, Menahem exacts money from the citizenry to keep King Pul (better known as Tiglath-Pileser) out of Israel; while he and others get their start by assassinating their predecessors. **1.** What do you think of Menahem's "fifty-shekel solution": Smart politics or a humiliating act of cowardice? What other choice might he have had? **2.** What hints do you see that despite Menahem, the country is enjoying prosperity? **3.** What does the quick turnaround in kings say about life in Israel?

APPLY What does it mean to you to be free? What have you had to pay to have that freedom? What kind of payment is acceptable when it comes to freedom, and what kind is unacceptable?

OPEN When as a child or teenager do you remember being "sent away" (out of the house or to live with someone else) in the midst of a crisis: When someone died? When your parents were having marriage trouble? When "adult things" needed to be discussed?

STUDY Israel's trouble intensifies as Assyria invades again, this time starting the process of deporting some of the people to Assyria. **1.** What happened the last

15:19 Pul king of Assyria. Otherwise known as Tiglath-Pileser III. **Menahem.** Menahem's kingdom was not a righteous one. He obtained the throne by assassinating his predecessor.

15:20 Every wealthy man had to contribute. Rather than fight Assyria, Menahem paid them off with a bribe. In this way he kept his throne, even if he didn't maintain his honor.

15:25–28 Pekah. Pekah's reign was characterized by the unrighteousness. The strength of his reign rested in two alliances. He aligned himself with Gilead against Assyria. He also aligned himself with Damascus against Judah.

time Assyria attacked (15:19)? **2.** With the national treasury empty, the army shoeless and the temple bare, what resource is left to extract? **3.** What does Tiglath-Pileser expect to gain by this victory? **4.** Which tribe gains the distinction of being the first deported to Assyria (v. 29; Isa. 9:1) **5.** Meanwhile in Judah, what does Jotham have going for him (vv. 32–34)? **6.** Who most likely destroyed the Upper Gate that Jotham here rebuilds (v. 35; 14:13)?

APPLY **1.** What struggles are you going through right now that seem like "deja vu"—struggles you have gone through before with little sense of progress? **2.** What hope do you have for this changing?

OPEN When you were a teenager, what did you want to be: Astronaut? Entertainer? Athlete? Actor/Actress? Other?

STUDY When Ahaz the king of Judah feels threatened by Israel and Aram, he appeals to the king of Assyria, Tiglath-Pileser. To win this king's favor he sends treasures from the temple. He also seeks to duplicate an altar he sees in Damascus when meeting the Assyrian king. **1.** What new standards for sinning does Ahaz set (vv. 3–4; Ex. 13:1–2,11–13; Lev. 18:21; Deut. 12:2)? **2.** Who else could Ahaz have appealed to for deliverance from Israel and Aram? **3.** Why do you think Ahaz meets with Tiglath-Pileser after he defeats Aram? **4.** Why does Ahaz want to copy the temple in Damascus (vv. 11–12)? **5.** What does Ahaz say he will now be using for

deported the people to Assyria. [30]Then Hoshea son of Elah conspired
against Pekah son of Remaliah. He attacked and assassinated him,
and then succeeded him as king in the twentieth year of Jotham son
of Uzziah.
[31]As for the other events of Pekah's reign, and all he did, are they
not written in the book of the annals of the kings of Israel?

Jotham King of Judah

[32]In the second year of Pekah son of Remaliah king of Israel,
Jotham son of Uzziah king of Judah began to reign. [33]He was twenty-
five years old when he became king, and he reigned in Jerusalem
sixteen years. His mother's name was Jerusha daughter of Zadok.
[34]He did what was right in the eyes of the LORD, just as his father
Uzziah had done. [35]The high places, however, were not removed; the
people continued to offer sacrifices and burn incense there. Jotham
rebuilt the Upper Gate of the temple of the LORD.
[36]As for the other events of Jotham's reign, and what he did, are
they not written in the book of the annals of the kings of Judah? [37](In
those days the LORD began to send Rezin king of Aram and Pekah son
of Remaliah against Judah.) [38]Jotham rested with his fathers and was
buried with them in the City of David, the city of his father. And Ahaz
his son succeeded him as king.

Ahaz King of Judah

16 In the seventeenth year of Pekah son of Remaliah, Ahaz son
of Jotham king of Judah began to reign. [2]Ahaz was twenty
years old when he became king, and he reigned in Jerusalem sixteen
years. Unlike David his father, he did not do what was right in the
eyes of the LORD his God. [3]He walked in the ways of the kings of Israel
and even sacrificed his son in[a] the fire, following the detestable ways
of the nations the LORD had driven out before the Israelites. [4]He offered sacrifices and burned incense at the high places, on the hilltops
and under every spreading tree.
[5]Then Rezin king of Aram and Pekah son of Remaliah king of Israel
marched up to fight against Jerusalem and besieged Ahaz, but they
could not overpower him. [6]At that time, Rezin king of Aram recovered
Elath for Aram by driving out the men of Judah. Edomites then moved
into Elath and have lived there to this day.
[7]Ahaz sent messengers to say to Tiglath-Pileser king of Assyria, "I
am your servant and vassal. Come up and save me out of the hand of

[a]3 *Or even made his son pass through*

15:30 Hoshea aligned himself with Assyria. In fact, the king of Assyria claimed to have established Hoshea's rule.

15:32–33 Jotham. Jotham's reign was characterized by righteousness. He reigned for 16 years during the ministry of Isaiah, the prophet.

15:35 Upper Gate. The restoration of the upper gate of the temple was one of Jotham's most famous accomplishments. He still failed to remove the high places—areas designated for the worship of false gods.

15:37 Rezin ... Pekah. Pekah's alliance with Rezin strengthened his position against Judah.

16:2 Unlike David. King David was the bar of excellence as far as kings in Judah went. Ahaz definitely did not measure up. In fact, he began a series of foreign alliances that eventually led to his people's exile.

16:3 sacrificed his son in the fire. God had directly forbidden his people to take part in the "detestable" practice of child sacrifice, yet the king of Judah succumbed. Ahaz did not offer all his sons, though, because his son Hezekiah succeeded him as king.

16:7 Ahaz sent messengers. Since Aram and Israel were uniting against Assyria, the nation was a likely candidate for an alignment with Judah.

the king of Aram and of the king of Israel, who are attacking me."
[8]And Ahaz took the silver and gold found in the temple of the LORD
and in the treasuries of the royal palace and sent it as a gift to the
king of Assyria. [9]The king of Assyria complied by attacking Damascus
and capturing it. He deported its inhabitants to Kir and put Rezin to
death.
[10]Then King Ahaz went to Damascus to meet Tiglath-Pileser king of
Assyria. He saw an altar in Damascus and sent to Uriah the priest a
sketch of the altar, with detailed plans for its construction. [11]So Uriah
the priest built an altar in accordance with all the plans that King
Ahaz had sent from Damascus and finished it before King Ahaz
returned. [12]When the king came back from Damascus and saw the
altar, he approached it and presented offerings[a] on it. [13]He offered up
his burnt offering and grain offering, poured out his drink offering,
and sprinkled the blood of his fellowship offerings[b] on the altar. [14]The
bronze altar that stood before the LORD he brought from the front of
the temple—from between the new altar and the temple of the
LORD—and put it on the north side of the new altar.
[15]King Ahaz then gave these orders to Uriah the priest: "On the
large new altar, offer the morning burnt offering and the evening
grain offering, the king's burnt offering and his grain offering, and
the burnt offering of all the people of the land, and their grain offering and their drink offering. Sprinkle on the altar all the blood of the
burnt offerings and sacrifices. But I will use the bronze altar for seeking guidance." [16]And Uriah the priest did just as King Ahaz had ordered.
[17]King Ahaz took away the side panels and removed the basins
from the movable stands. He removed the Sea from the bronze bulls
that supported it and set it on a stone base. [18]He took away the Sabbath canopy[c] that had been built at the temple and removed the royal
entryway outside the temple of the LORD, in deference to the king of
Assyria.
[19]As for the other events of the reign of Ahaz, and what he did, are
they not written in the book of the annals of the kings of Judah?
[20]Ahaz rested with his fathers and was buried with them in the City of
David. And Hezekiah his son succeeded him as king.

[a]12 Or *and went up* [b]13 Traditionally *peace offerings* [c]18 Or *the dais of his throne* (see Septuagint)

seeking guidance (v. 15)? **6.** Whose will has now become central over the Lord's (v. 18)?

APPLY 1. What "altar" are you now looking to most for guidance in your life: Science? Pop psychology? Supermarket tabloids? Astrological charts? Scripture? **2.** Is there a difference between where you feel you ought to be looking for guidance, and where you look in practice? What can you do to line your practice up with how you feel it ought to be?

16:8 found in the temple. Ahaz followed the example of former King Joash, who used the temple wealth to pay tribute to Hazael of Damascus *(12:17–18). The silver and gold Ahaz* used had probably been restored by King Jotham.

16:9 Kir. The location is unknown, but it is the origination point for the people of Aram.

16:10 Ahaz went. Ahaz's actions demonstrated his submission to the king of Assyria. Both his visit and the reproduction of the altar (probably an altar to the Assyrian king) showed his acquiescence.

16:13 He offered up. Ahaz offered the same offerings outlined in Leviticus. The offerings were made on an altar dedicated to a king, though, not to the Lord.

16:14 the new altar. Ahaz placed the new altar in the most prominent place in the temple. This reflected the priority he placed on his alliance with Assyria over his covenant with God.

16:15 Uriah the priest. Uriah seemed to cooperate readily in building the new altar and in offering sacrifices on it. This seemed to demonstrate the weakened state of the priesthood during Ahaz's reign.

16:17 took away ... removed. Ahaz's actions were more than rearranging furniture. He was taking liberty with holy places, and he wasn't doing this to honor God.

16:18 royal entryway. The king entered the temple through a special ramp or stairway. **in deference.** In removing the royal entry, Ahaz removed a symbol of his own leadership.

OPEN Choose two of the following events that ended an era and share how they affected you: (a) The fall of the Berlin Wall; (b) Johnny Carson's last night on *The Tonight Show*; (c) The last U.S. troops withdrawn from Vietnam; (d) The last M.A.S.H. show; (e) The end of the last millennium.

STUDY To this point Israel, the people God chose as his own, has consisted of twelve tribes divided into the two nations of Israel and Judah. That ends with the events of this chapter as the people of the northern kingdom of Israel are carried off into captivity in Assyria. It is truly the end of an era. **1.** How did Hoshea come to reign (15:29–30)? **2.** Why does Shalmaneser attack Hoshea? **3.** What were some of the sins the people of Israel did that resulted in their exile? Which ones seem particularly bad to you? **4.** What specific commands did Israel violate (vv. 12,15)? **5.** What is left now of the original twelve tribes of Israel? **6.** What king is blamed for sending Israel down the wrong path in the first place (vv. 21–23)?

APPLY 1. In what areas of your life has God particularly shown patience with you? What might it be like if that patience suddenly ended? **2.** How is God calling you to respond to his patience (Rom. 2:4)?

Hoshea Last King of Israel

17 In the twelfth year of Ahaz king of Judah, Hoshea son of Elah
became king of Israel in Samaria, and he reigned nine years.
2He did evil in the eyes of the LORD, but not like the kings of Israel
who preceded him.
3Shalmaneser king of Assyria came up to attack Hoshea, who had
been Shalmaneser's vassal and had paid him tribute. 4But the king of
Assyria discovered that Hoshea was a traitor, for he had sent envoys
to So[a] king of Egypt, and he no longer paid tribute to the king of Assyria, as he had done year by year. Therefore Shalmaneser seized him
and put him in prison. 5The king of Assyria invaded the entire land,
marched against Samaria and laid siege to it for three years. 6In the
ninth year of Hoshea, the king of Assyria captured Samaria and deported the Israelites to Assyria. He settled them in Halah, in Gozan on
the Habor River and in the towns of the Medes.

Israel Exiled Because of Sin

7All this took place because the Israelites had sinned against the
LORD their God, who had brought them up out of Egypt from under
the power of Pharaoh king of Egypt. They worshiped other gods 8and
followed the practices of the nations the LORD had driven out before
them, as well as the practices that the kings of Israel had introduced.
9The Israelites secretly did things against the LORD their God that
were not right. From watchtower to fortified city they built themselves high places in all their towns. 10They set up sacred stones and
Asherah poles on every high hill and under every spreading tree. 11At
every high place they burned incense, as the nations whom the LORD
had driven out before them had done. They did wicked things that
provoked the LORD to anger. 12They worshiped idols, though the LORD
had said, "You shall not do this."[b] 13The LORD warned Israel and Judah through all his prophets and seers: "Turn from your evil ways.
Observe my commands and decrees, in accordance with the entire
Law that I commanded your fathers to obey and that I delivered to
you through my servants the prophets."
14But they would not listen and were as stiff-necked as their fa-

[a]4 Or *to Sais, to the; So* is possibly an abbreviation for *Osorkon*. [b]12 Exodus 20:4, 5

17:1 the twelfth year of Ahaz king of Judah. Ahaz's reign developed in stages. He spent nine years as a vice-regent. Then he spent four years as a co-regent with his father, Jotham. After that, he ruled as principal king for sixteen years.

17:5 laid seige to it for three years. Samaria was not easy to conquer. When Omri built the city of Samaria, he fortified it with a wall on all sides.

17:6 deported. The deportation had been prophesied to Jeroboam, the first ruler of the northern kingdom. The prophet Ahijah told Jeroboam's wife that the kingdom would be taken away (1 Kin. 14:5–11).

17:7–23 The northern kingdom of Israel kept their covenant to no one. They betrayed Assyria by refusing to pay their tributes. They dishonored God by refusing to worship him as the one true God. While their exile could be explained by Assyria's betrayal, their downfall was actually a product of their spiritual unfaithfulness.

17:7 They worshiped other gods. Idolatry was Israel's chief betrayal in their covenant with God. He had faithfully delivered them to their homeland. Yet, they failed to faithfully honor the first of his commands: "Have no other gods before me" (Ex. 20:3).

17:10 high hill. Often referred to as the "high places," where idol worshipers were considered closest to their gods. **spreading tree.** Trees were seen as signs of fertility. Some gods were worshiped around them for that reason.

17:11 they did wicked things. The Old Testament records several wicked practices among the inhabitants of Canaan, including temple prostitution and child sacrifices.

17:13 the entire Law. God first outlined his commands through Moses. Then he sent the prophets to apply God's commands and call the people back to obedience.

17:14 stiff-necked as their fathers. To be stiff-necked is to be

thers, who did not trust in the LORD their God. 15 They rejected his
decrees and the covenant he had made with their fathers and the
warnings he had given them. They followed worthless idols and
themselves became worthless. They imitated the nations around
them although the LORD had ordered them, "Do not do as they do,"
and they did the things the LORD had forbidden them to do.
16 They forsook all the commands of the LORD their God and made
for themselves two idols cast in the shape of calves, and an Asherah
pole. They bowed down to all the starry hosts, and they worshiped
Baal. 17 They sacrificed their sons and daughters in[a] the fire. They
practiced divination and sorcery and sold themselves to do evil in the
eyes of the LORD, provoking him to anger.
18 So the LORD was very angry with Israel and removed them from
his presence. Only the tribe of Judah was left, 19 and even Judah did
not keep the commands of the LORD their God. They followed the
practices Israel had introduced. 20 Therefore the LORD rejected all the
people of Israel; he afflicted them and gave them into the hands of
plunderers, until he thrust them from his presence.
21 When he tore Israel away from the house of David, they made Jeroboam son of Nebat their king. Jeroboam enticed Israel away from
following the LORD and caused them to commit a great sin. 22 The Israelites persisted in all the sins of Jeroboam and did not turn away
from them 23 until the LORD removed them from his presence, as he
had warned through all his servants the prophets. So the people of
Israel were taken from their homeland into exile in Assyria, and they
are still there.

Samaria Resettled

24 The king of Assyria brought people from Babylon, Cuthah, Avva,
Hamath and Sepharvaim and settled them in the towns of Samaria to
replace the Israelites. They took over Samaria and lived in its towns.
25 When they first lived there, they did not worship the LORD; so he
sent lions among them and they killed some of the people. 26 It was
reported to the king of Assyria: "The people you deported and
resettled in the towns of Samaria do not know what the god of that
country requires. He has sent lions among them, which are killing
them off, because the people do not know what he requires."
27 Then the king of Assyria gave this order: "Have one of the priests
you took captive from Samaria go back to live there and teach the
people what the god of the land requires." 28 So one of the priests who

[a]17 Or *They made their sons and daughters pass through*

OPEN In which of the following areas do you like to "have it both ways": Worship style—drums, guitars! Home decor—mix those antiques in with the contemporary stuff? Cuisine—like Mexican pizza! Wardrobe—conservative suit with a wild tie, or jeans with faux fur! Politics—casting a split vote?

STUDY In some areas of life, we can have it both ways, but in others we have to choose. The people brought in from Assyria to populate Samaria wanted to have it both ways in their worship. **1.** How would a resettlement program build Assyria's empire? **2.** What problems

stubborn and uncooperative. God first described the Israelites this way when they worshiped a golden calf while God was giving the Ten Commandments to Moses (Ex. 32:9).

17:16–17 forsook all the commands. God consistently reminded the people not to take on the worship practices of the Canaanites. Yet, this description revealed what really happened: golden calves for idols, Asherah poles, worshiping the heavens and Baal.

17:18 removed them. God actually deported the people to Assyria. **Judah.** Remnants of the tribes of Benjamin and Simeon were included, but Judah was the only group that still maintained full identity as a tribe.

17:24 to replace the Israelites. Sargon, Assyria's king, resettled the land by following his government's policy—he did a people-swap. He deported the most influential Israelites and replaced them with citizens loyal to Assyria.

17:25 lions. To the new inhabitants of Samaria, the lions represented a plague from God as surely as the frogs had been in Egypt (Ex. 8) and the rats in Philistia (1 Sam. 5–6).

17:28 Bethel. Before the deportation, worship in Samaria was less than pure. Even with its shortcomings, Bethel was the center for the worship of God.

do the settlers face (vv. 25–28)? **3.** What did the Assyrian king believe about God's power (v. 27)? **4.** What were some of the gods the people in Samaria worshiped? **5.** What command was part of the covenant that God made with Israel (v. 35)? **6.** How persistent was the idolatry of the people in Samaria?

APPLY 1. In what ways have you tried to accommodate your faith to the culture around you? **2.** In what areas do you now think your accommodation was appropriate and in what areas do you now think your accommodation was wrong?

OPEN 1. Which leaving home experience was most traumatic for you: When you went away to college? When you got married? When you took a trip and were separated from your spouse for the first time? When you moved from a place you had lived a long time? **2.** What helped you make this transition?

had been exiled from Samaria came to live in Bethel and taught them
how to worship the LORD.
29Nevertheless, each national group made its own gods in the
several towns where they settled, and set them up in the shrines the
people of Samaria had made at the high places. 30The men from Babylon made Succoth Benoth, the men from Cuthah made Nergal, and
the men from Hamath made Ashima; 31the Avvites made Nibhaz and
Tartak, and the Sepharvites burned their children in the fire as sacrifices to Adrammelech and Anammelech, the gods of Sepharvaim.
32They worshiped the LORD, but they also appointed all sorts of their
own people to officiate for them as priests in the shrines at the high
places. 33They worshiped the LORD, but they also served their own
gods in accordance with the customs of the nations from which they
had been brought.
34To this day they persist in their former practices. They neither
worship the LORD nor adhere to the decrees and ordinances, the laws
and commands that the LORD gave the descendants of Jacob, whom
he named Israel. 35When the LORD made a covenant with the Israelites, he commanded them: "Do not worship any other gods or bow
down to them, serve them or sacrifice to them. 36But the LORD, who
brought you up out of Egypt with mighty power and outstretched
arm, is the one you must worship. To him you shall bow down and to
him offer sacrifices. 37You must always be careful to keep the decrees
and ordinances, the laws and commands he wrote for you. Do not
worship other gods. 38Do not forget the covenant I have made with
you, and do not worship other gods. 39Rather, worship the LORD your
God; it is he who will deliver you from the hand of all your enemies."
40They would not listen, however, but persisted in their former
practices. 41Even while these people were worshiping the LORD, they
were serving their idols. To this day their children and grandchildren
continue to do as their fathers did.

Hezekiah King of Judah

18 In the third year of Hoshea son of Elah king of Israel, Hezekiah son of Ahaz king of Judah began to reign. 2He was
twenty-five years old when he became king, and he reigned in Jerusalem twenty-nine years. His mother's name was Abijah[a] daughter of
Zechariah. 3He did what was right in the eyes of the LORD, just as his

[a]2 Hebrew *Abi,* a variant of *Abijah*

17:29 each national group. Samaria became a melting-pot culture. In Jesus' day, racial tension between Judah and Samaria was deeply rooted. The woman at the well revealed it in her surprise that a Jew would even ask a Samaritan for water (John 4:9).

17:33 but they *also served.* *Much* like we do today, Samaria combined the truth of God with popular religions of the day. This combination never works. Either God is sovereign, or he is not.

17:35 worship. God's requirement was purity of worship. The first commandment was to have no other gods before God. The people failed over and over again. Break the first, and all the others will fall.

17:41 children and grandchildren *continue.* God commanded his people to pass down their faith, to teach their children about his deliverance (Deut. 6:4–9).

18:1 Hezekiah. Hezekiah first ruled as a vice-regent under his father, Ahaz. He then ruled alone for 18 years before his own son Manasseh served as vice-regent under him.

18:2 twenty-five years old. At eleven years of age, Hezekiah began serving under his father.

18:3 as his father David had done. Few kings compare favorably with David. Of those (Asa, Jehoshaphat, Josiah), Hezekiah went a step further in purifying his nation in their worship.

father David had done. 4He removed the high places, smashed the
sacred stones and cut down the Asherah poles. He broke into pieces
the bronze snake Moses had made, for up to that time the Israelites
had been burning incense to it. (It was called[a] Nehushtan.[b])
5Hezekiah trusted in the LORD, the God of Israel. There was no one
like him among all the kings of Judah, either before him or after him.
6He held fast to the LORD and did not cease to follow him; he kept the
commands the LORD had given Moses. 7And the LORD was with him;
he was successful in whatever he undertook. He rebelled against the
king of Assyria and did not serve him. 8From watchtower to fortified
city, he defeated the Philistines, as far as Gaza and its territory.
9In King Hezekiah's fourth year, which was the seventh year of Hoshea son of Elah king of Israel, Shalmaneser king of Assyria marched
against Samaria and laid siege to it. 10At the end of three years the
Assyrians took it. So Samaria was captured in Hezekiah's sixth year,
which was the ninth year of Hoshea king of Israel. 11The king of Assyria deported Israel to Assyria and settled them in Halah, in Gozan
on the Habor River and in towns of the Medes. 12This happened because they had not obeyed the LORD their God, but had violated his
covenant—all that Moses the servant of the LORD commanded. They
neither listened to the commands nor carried them out.
13In the fourteenth year of King Hezekiah's reign, Sennacherib king
of Assyria attacked all the fortified cities of Judah and captured them.
14So Hezekiah king of Judah sent this message to the king of Assyria
at Lachish: "I have done wrong. Withdraw from me, and I will pay
whatever you demand of me." The king of Assyria exacted from
Hezekiah king of Judah three hundred talents[c] of silver and thirty
talents[d] of gold. 15So Hezekiah gave him all the silver that was found
in the temple of the LORD and in the treasuries of the royal palace.
16At this time Hezekiah king of Judah stripped off the gold with
which he had covered the doors and doorposts of the temple of the
LORD, and gave it to the king of Assyria.

Sennacherib Threatens Jerusalem

17The king of Assyria sent his supreme commander, his chief officer
and his field commander with a large army, from Lachish to King
Hezekiah at Jerusalem. They came up to Jerusalem and stopped at

[a]4 Or *He called it* [b]4 *Nehushtan* sounds like the Hebrew for *bronze* and *snake* and *unclean thing.*
[c]14 That is, about 11 tons (about 10 metric tons) [d]14 That is, about 1 ton (about 1 metric ton)

STUDY Hezekiah becomes king of Judah and is a good king. But there are some victories, the northern kingdom of Israel is carried from their homeland, and Hezekiah is forced into paying tribute. **1.** What victories did Hezekiah have? **2.** What is the significance of the bronze snake (v. 4; Num. 21:8–9; John 3:14–15)? Why might it become an object of worship? **3.** This author seems to rank Hezekiah as greater than David, Solomon and Josiah. Was he exaggerating or is Hezekiah simply underappreciated? **4.** The deportation referred to in verse 11 essentially ended the existence of the northern kingdom. How might this have been traumatic for both the people deported and those left behind? **5.** How could Hezekiah be "successful in whatever he understood" (v. 7), and still be forced to pay an expensive tribute to Assyria (vv. 13–16)?

APPLY 1. Do you presently feel "at home" where you live, or do you feel like you are living your life in "exile" from where your true home is—where you were raised or a place where you spent your happiest times? **2.** What would make the place where you now live feel more like "home" to you?

OPEN 1. Who taunted you the most when you were younger? **2.** What was this person most likely to tease you about: Your appearance? Your school performance? Your lack of social skills? Your faith? Your lack of athleticism? Other?

18:4 bronze snake. Other righteous kings of Judah had destroyed the idols used in false worship. Hezekiah destroyed even this artifact made by *Moses himself. It had become an idol* to the Israelites.

18:7 rebelled against ... Assyria. During former King Ahaz's reign, Judah became a vassal of Assyria. The alliance included annual tributes paid and a ceremonial recognition of Assyria's national gods. Hezekiah refused to do either.

18:8 From watchtower to fortified city. In other words, Hezekiah couldn't lose for winning. Gaza was the southernmost city in Philistia. When he defeated the Philistines there, there were no more Philistines left to defeat.

18:13 the fortified cities of Judah. According to Sennacherib's records he conquered 46 strong cities plus villages. He did not win a victory over Jerusalem, though.

18:14 I will pay. Hezekiah had previously refused to pay the annual tribute that his predecessor had sent to keep peace with Assyria. These tributes were the ancient equivalent of extortion.

18:15–16 Hezekiah raided his own house as well as the temple to pacify his Assyrian overseers. Several kings before him, including Hezekiah's father, Ahaz, had ransomed the riches of the temple (2 Chr. 28:21).

18:17 aqueduct. One of Hezekiah's most famous accomplishments was a tunnel that carried water from outside the wall of Jerusalem into the city. Because of this tunnel, the city under siege would not go thirsty.

STUDY In spite of the tribute paid by Hezekiah, the king of Assyria sends his supreme commander to assault Jerusalem. He begins by challenging Hezekiah and the people of Jerusalem and urging them to surrender, saying that no one can help them, even God. **1.** This passage is repeated verbatim in Isaiah 36. What advice had Isaiah given Hezekiah on the Assyrian invasion (Isa. 31:1–3)? **2.** Why isn't paying the tribute enough (vv. 14–16)? **3.** What does the field commander of the Assyrians say about where the people of Judah can put their confidence? **4.** Why do Hezekiah's men want the Assyrians to speak in Aramaic? What reason do the Assyrians give for continuing in Hebrew? What is he implying will happen? **5.** How do the Assyrians view: The God of Judah (vv. 22,32–35)? Assyrian power compared to deity-power? **6.** How do the people show their loyalty to Hezekiah (v. 36)? **7.** Why do the three palace messengers tear their clothes?

APPLY 1. What danger do you presently feel is "right outside your gate" threatening you: Financial ruin? The ruin of your reputation? Family disintegration? Emotional collapse? **2.** On what are you putting your confidence to avert that ruin? How firm is the ground do you feel you are standing on in that regard?

---

the aqueduct of the Upper Pool, on the road to the Washerman's
Field. 18They called for the king; and Eliakim son of Hilkiah the palace
administrator, Shebna the secretary, and Joah son of Asaph the
recorder went out to them.
19The field commander said to them, "Tell Hezekiah:

" 'This is what the great king, the king of Assyria, says: On
what are you basing this confidence of yours? 20You say you have
strategy and military strength—but you speak only empty words.
On whom are you depending, that you rebel against me? 21Look
now, you are depending on Egypt, that splintered reed of a staff,
which pierces a man's hand and wounds him if he leans on it!
Such is Pharaoh king of Egypt to all who depend on him. 22And if
you say to me, "We are depending on the LORD our God"—isn't
he the one whose high places and altars Hezekiah removed, saying to Judah and Jerusalem, "You must worship before this altar
in Jerusalem"?
23" 'Come now, make a bargain with my master, the king of
Assyria: I will give you two thousand horses—if you can put riders on them! 24How can you repulse one officer of the least of my
master's officials, even though you are depending on Egypt for
chariots and horsemen[a]? 25Furthermore, have I come to attack
and destroy this place without word from the LORD? The LORD
himself told me to march against this country and destroy it.' "

26Then Eliakim son of Hilkiah, and Shebna and Joah said to the
field commander, "Please speak to your servants in Aramaic, since we
understand it. Don't speak to us in Hebrew in the hearing of the people on the wall."
27But the commander replied, "Was it only to your master and you
that my master sent me to say these things, and not to the men sitting
on the wall—who, like you, will have to eat their own filth and drink
their own urine?"
28Then the commander stood and called out in Hebrew: "Hear the
word of the great king, the king of Assyria! 29This is what the king
says: Do not let Hezekiah deceive you. He cannot deliver you from my
hand. 30Do not let Hezekiah persuade you to trust in the LORD when
he says, 'The LORD will surely deliver us; this city will not be given
into the hand of the king of Assyria.'
31"Do not listen to Hezekiah. This is what the king of Assyria says:
Make peace with me and come out to me. Then every one of you will
eat from his own vine and fig tree and drink water from his own cistern, 32until I come and take you to a land like your own, a land of

[a]24 Or *charioteers*

18:19 confidence. Hezekiah's strength was his trust in God (v. 5).

18:23 will give you two thousand horses—if you can put riders on them. This statement implies that Judah's army was inferior in quality and quantity to the Assyrian army.

18:26 speak to your servants in Aramaic. Only the most educated people understood Aramaic. The leaders were hoping that if they switched to Aramaic, the townspeople listening from the wall wouldn't be able to understand the conversation. Their enemies wanted everyone to hear and be discouraged.

18:27–30 The commander's words were intended for the people listening. He wanted to break their confidence so that they would surrender in fear. But he had not studied his adversary, for he attacked Hezekiah at his strong point—his trust in God.

18:31 eat from his own vine. In this culture, an image of prosperity and wealth.

18:32 to a land like your own. A euphemistic description of deportation. **Choose life.** The Assyrian

grain and new wine, a land of bread and vineyards, a land of olive
trees and honey. Choose life and not death!
"Do not listen to Hezekiah, for he is misleading you when he says,
'The LORD will deliver us.' 33Has the god of any nation ever delivered
his land from the hand of the king of Assyria? 34Where are the gods of
Hamath and Arpad? Where are the gods of Sepharvaim, Hena and
Ivvah? Have they rescued Samaria from my hand? 35Who of all the
gods of these countries has been able to save his land from me? How
then can the LORD deliver Jerusalem from my hand?"
36But the people remained silent and said nothing in reply, because
the king had commanded, "Do not answer him."
37Then Eliakim son of Hilkiah the palace administrator, Shebna the
secretary and Joah son of Asaph the recorder went to Hezekiah, with
their clothes torn, and told him what the field commander had said.

Jerusalem's Deliverance Foretold

19 When King Hezekiah heard this, he tore his clothes and put
on sackcloth and went into the temple of the LORD. 2He sent
Eliakim the palace administrator, Shebna the secretary and the leading priests, all wearing sackcloth, to the prophet Isaiah son of Amoz.
3They told him, "This is what Hezekiah says: This day is a day of distress and rebuke and disgrace, as when children come to the point of
birth and there is no strength to deliver them. 4It may be that the
LORD your God will hear all the words of the field commander, whom
his master, the king of Assyria, has sent to ridicule the living God, and
that he will rebuke him for the words the LORD your God has heard.
Therefore pray for the remnant that still survives."
5When King Hezekiah's officials came to Isaiah, 6Isaiah said to
them, "Tell your master, 'This is what the LORD says: Do not be afraid
of what you have heard—those words with which the underlings of
the king of Assyria have blasphemed me. 7Listen! I am going to put
such a spirit in him that when he hears a certain report, he will return
to his own country, and there I will have him cut down with the
sword.' "
8When the field commander heard that the king of Assyria had left
Lachish, he withdrew and found the king fighting against Libnah.
9Now Sennacherib received a report that Tirhakah, the Cushite[a] king
⌊of Egypt⌋, was marching out to fight against him. So he again sent
messengers to Hezekiah with this word: 10"Say to Hezekiah king of
Judah: Do not let the god you depend on deceive you when he says,
'Jerusalem will not be handed over to the king of Assyria.' 11Surely you
have heard what the kings of Assyria have done to all the countries,

[a]9 That is, from the upper Nile region

OPEN When you were in high school, which of the following would you have regarded as a "scary report": That the principal wanted to see your parents? That the school was going to adopt a dress code? That they were going to close the local mall? That the linebackers of the team you would be playing on Friday had all just been granted parole?

STUDY King Hezekiah has just received the report that Sennacherib was just outside Jerusalem threatening him and his people. He goes to God for reassurance. **1.** What is Hezekiah worried about (vv. 1–4)? What does he do to win over worry? **2.** What good report does the prophet Isaiah give to Hezekiah (vv. 6–7)? **3.** What might Sennacherib suspect when he learned that the king of Egypt is marching against him just as he is preparing to assault Jerusalem: An alliance has been made? God is acting against him? Coincidence? **4.** What does Hezekiah do with the threatening letter from Sennacherib and why? **5.** What do Hezekiah and Sennacherib agree on (vv. 18–19)? **6.** To what motivation does Hezekiah appeal in asking God to intercede for them (v. 19)?

APPLY 1. What need or fear has inspired your most ear-

commander used Moses' words to compel the people to follow the Lord (Deut. 30:19).

18:33–35 The commander manipulated well by pointing out each national god and its lack of ability to deliver. He was particularly clever to mention Samaria. Historically Samaria and Judah were the same nation worshiping the same God. If God had not delivered Samaria, why would he deliver Judah?

19:2 Isaiah. The writer of the book of Isaiah. He was a prophet during the reigns of Uzziah, Jotham and Ahaz.

19:3 when children come to the point of birth. In other words, this was a "do or die" situation—a huge threat.

19:4 Hezekiah's hope seemed to be based more on God's protection of his own reputation than God's compassion for Judah.

19:7 The report Isaiah described may have been that Tirhakah, king of Egypt, was marching against Assyria (v. 9).

destroying them completely. And will you be delivered? [12]Did the gods
of the nations that were destroyed by my forefathers deliver them: the
gods of Gozan, Haran, Rezeph and the people of Eden who were in Tel
Assar? [13]Where is the king of Hamath, the king of Arpad, the king of the
city of Sepharvaim, or of Hena or Ivvah?"

Hezekiah's Prayer

[14]Hezekiah received the letter from the messengers and read it.
Then he went up to the temple of the LORD and spread it out before
the LORD. [15]And Hezekiah prayed to the LORD: "O LORD, God of Israel,
enthroned between the cherubim, you alone are God over all the
kingdoms of the earth. You have made heaven and earth. [16]Give ear,
O LORD, and hear; open your eyes, O LORD, and see; listen to the
words Sennacherib has sent to insult the living God.

[17]"It is true, O LORD, that the Assyrian kings have laid waste these
nations and their lands. [18]They have thrown their gods into the fire
and destroyed them, for they were not gods but only wood and stone,
fashioned by men's hands. [19]Now, O LORD our God, deliver us from
his hand, so that all kingdoms on earth may know that you alone,
O LORD, are God."

Isaiah Prophesies Sennacherib's Fall

[20]Then Isaiah son of Amoz sent a message to Hezekiah: "This is
what the LORD, the God of Israel, says: I have heard your prayer concerning Sennacherib king of Assyria. [21]This is the word that the LORD
has spoken against him:

" 'The Virgin Daughter of Zion
  despises you and mocks you.
The Daughter of Jerusalem
  tosses her head as you flee.
[22]Who is it you have insulted and blasphemed?
  Against whom have you raised your voice
and lifted your eyes in pride?
  Against the Holy One of Israel!
[23]By your messengers
  you have heaped insults on the Lord.
And you have said,
  "With my many chariots
I have ascended the heights of the mountains,
  the utmost heights of Lebanon.
I have cut down its tallest cedars,
  the choicest of its pines.
I have reached its remotest parts,
  the finest of its forests.
[24]I have dug wells in foreign lands
  and drunk the water there.

nest prayer in these past few weeks? **2.** How confident do you feel that God will bring an answer to this need? **3.** How can this group help support you in prayer in relation to this need?

OPEN Who would you most like to see "cut down to size": A politician who seems drunk with power? The IRS? A multi-million dollar athlete? An obnoxious talk show host? Whoever writes these obnoxious questions?

STUDY God answers Hezekiah's prayer through the prophet Isaiah. He both prophesies that Sennacherib will never enter Jerusalem and that even when Jerusalem does fall, a remnant of the people will return. God destroys a large number of the Assyrian army, causing Sennacherib to withdraw from Jerusalem, and later his sons assassinate him, fulfilling the first part of Isaiah's prophecy. **1.** Why is the mocking of young virgins a particularly appropriate way of cutting Sennacherib down to size (vv. 21–22)? **2.** Who does Sennacherib credit for Assyria's conquests? Who does God credit? **3.** What reassurances does God give Hezekiah concerning the prosperity of the land: The immediate threat of Sennacherib? The long-term future of Jerusalem? **4.** What meaning did early Christians attach to this remnant idea (v. 31; Rom. 11:5)? **5.** How do you

---

19:18 for they were not gods. *Hezekiah answers the accusations of* the Assyrian commander (18:33–35) and affirms that Jehovah is the only true God.

19:20 The record makes no indication that Hezekiah asked Isaiah for an *answer. Yet God* responded to Hezekiah's prayer through Isaiah.

19:22 Against the Holy One. Assyria's offense was not simply against the city of Jerusalem or the nation of Judah. It was against God himself. "Holy One" occurs 26 times in the book of Isaiah.

19:24 Egypt. Assyria had not conquered Egypt yet, so this report was an exaggeration.

With the soles of my feet
I have dried up all the streams of Egypt."

25" 'Have you not heard?
Long ago I ordained it.
In days of old I planned it;
now I have brought it to pass,
that you have turned fortified cities
into piles of stone.
26 Their people, drained of power,
are dismayed and put to shame.
They are like plants in the field,
like tender green shoots,
like grass sprouting on the roof,
scorched before it grows up.

27" 'But I know where you stay
and when you come and go
and how you rage against me.
28 Because you rage against me
and your insolence has reached my ears,
I will put my hook in your nose
and my bit in your mouth,
and I will make you return
by the way you came.'

29 "This will be the sign for you, O Hezekiah:

"This year you will eat what grows by itself,
and the second year what springs from that.
But in the third year sow and reap,
plant vineyards and eat their fruit.
30 Once more a remnant of the house of Judah
will take root below and bear fruit above.
31 For out of Jerusalem will come a remnant,
and out of Mount Zion a band of survivors.

The zeal of the LORD Almighty will accomplish this.

32 "Therefore this is what the LORD says concerning the king of Assyria:

"He will not enter this city
or shoot an arrow here.
He will not come before it with shield
or build a siege ramp against it.
33 By the way that he came he will return;
he will not enter this city,

declares the LORD.

think God killed those 185,000 men? What do you think the Assyrians thought had happened to them? **6.** What curse befalls Sennacherib, just as he hopes to secure the blessing of his own pagan idols (v. 37)? Why is this timing particularly appropriate?

APPLY 1. What could God do for you right now that would be most reassuring: Cut an enemy of yours down to size? Assure you of your financial future (vv. 30–31)? Assure you that he will protect you from danger (v. 34)? **2.** What would it take for you to truly accept the reassurance you seek: An audible voice from God? The words conveyed by a trusted person? Just a feeling inside of you? A miraculous sign, like when God destroyed the soldiers?

19:25 I ordained it. The Bible affirms over and over that God is in control of world events as well as individual destinies (Prov. 16:9; Rom. 13:1). Assyria won its victories in a God-controlled area.

19:28 will put my hook in your nose. Some ancient monuments picture Assyria's enemies being led around with hooks in their noses. Isaiah's prophecy sharply reversed the image.

19:30–31 remnant of the house of Judah. Attacks on Samaria and Judah had forced survivors to settle in this last piece of the original nation of Israel.

19:32 He will not enter. God sometimes delivered his people through mighty military victories. In this case, it was a simple administrative shift in Sennacherib's schedule that showed God's provision.

34I will defend this city and save it,
for my sake and for the sake of David my servant."

35That night the angel of the LORD went out and put to death a hundred and eighty-five thousand men in the Assyrian camp. When the
people got up the next morning—there were all the dead bodies! 36So
Sennacherib king of Assyria broke camp and withdrew. He returned
to Nineveh and stayed there.
37One day, while he was worshiping in the temple of his god Nisroch, his sons Adrammelech and Sharezer cut him down with the
sword, and they escaped to the land of Ararat. And Esarhaddon his
son succeeded him as king.

Hezekiah's Illness

20 In those days Hezekiah became ill and was at the point of
death. The prophet Isaiah son of Amoz went to him and said,
"This is what the LORD says: Put your house in order, because you are
going to die; you will not recover."
2Hezekiah turned his face to the wall and prayed to the LORD, 3"Remember, O LORD, how I have walked before you faithfully and with
wholehearted devotion and have done what is good in your eyes."
And Hezekiah wept bitterly.
4Before Isaiah had left the middle court, the word of the LORD came
to him: 5"Go back and tell Hezekiah, the leader of my people, 'This is
what the LORD, the God of your father David, says: I have heard your
prayer and seen your tears; I will heal you. On the third day from now
you will go up to the temple of the LORD. 6I will add fifteen years to
your life. And I will deliver you and this city from the hand of the king
of Assyria. I will defend this city for my sake and for the sake of my
servant David.' "
7Then Isaiah said, "Prepare a poultice of figs." They did so and
applied it to the boil, and he recovered.
8Hezekiah had asked Isaiah, "What will be the sign that the LORD
will heal me and that I will go up to the temple of the LORD on the
third day from now?"
9Isaiah answered, "This is the LORD's sign to you that the LORD will
do what he has promised: Shall the shadow go forward ten steps, or
shall it go back ten steps?"
10"It is a simple matter for the shadow to go forward ten steps,"
said Hezekiah. "Rather, have it go back ten steps."
11Then the prophet Isaiah called upon the LORD, and the LORD
made the shadow go back the ten steps it had gone down on the
stairway of Ahaz.

OPEN What are you most likely to cry over?

STUDY When Isaiah reports that Hezekiah is about to die, he begins to cry, and pray to God. God hears his prayer and gives him 15 more years of life and deliverance from Assyria. **1.** How do you react to how Hezekiah takes the news of his impending death: "What a cry-baby?" *or* "It sounds natural—what I might do"? **2.** Why does God decide to give Hezekiah 15 more years? **3.** Why does Isaiah have Hezekiah's servants prepare a poultice of figs? **4.** What is the significance of the sign of the shadow moving backwards (v. 9)?

APPLY Which of the following indicates your heart's reaction to this story: If God could do this for Hezekiah, why couldn't he do it for my loved one? I wish God would give ME clearer signs of his promises? God has done great things—and he will do great things in my life too!

19:37 One day. Years later, around 681 B.C. **Nisroch.** An idol, part eagle and part human. The temple was probably in Nineveh, the capital city of Assyria where Jonah once preached.

20:6 for the sake of my servant David. King David established Jerusalem as his capital, his residence and the site for Solomon's temple. God had made a similar promise to Solomon (1 Kin. 11:13).

20:7 poultice of figs. God healed in a variety of ways. Naaman had to wash seven times in the Jordan River to be healed of leprosy (5:9–10). Jesus put mud on a man's eyes to correct blindness (John 9:6).

20:9-11 the shadow. Isaiah and Hezekiah were talking about time. Should shadows recede down the stairway of Ahaz, time would be moving backward.

Envoys From Babylon

[12]At that time Merodach-Baladan son of Baladan king of Babylon sent Hezekiah letters and a gift, because he had heard of Hezekiah's illness. [13]Hezekiah received the messengers and showed them all that was in his storehouses—the silver, the gold, the spices and the fine oil—his armory and everything found among his treasures. There was nothing in his palace or in all his kingdom that Hezekiah did not show them.

[14]Then Isaiah the prophet went to King Hezekiah and asked, "What did those men say, and where did they come from?"

"From a distant land," Hezekiah replied. "They came from Babylon."

[15]The prophet asked, "What did they see in your palace?"

"They saw everything in my palace," Hezekiah said. "There is nothing among my treasures that I did not show them."

[16]Then Isaiah said to Hezekiah, "Hear the word of the LORD: [17]The time will surely come when everything in your palace, and all that your fathers have stored up until this day, will be carried off to Babylon. Nothing will be left, says the LORD. [18]And some of your descendants, your own flesh and blood, that will be born to you, will be taken away, and they will become eunuchs in the palace of the king of Babylon."

[19]"The word of the LORD you have spoken is good," Hezekiah replied. For he thought, "Will there not be peace and security in my lifetime?"

[20]As for the other events of Hezekiah's reign, all his achievements and how he made the pool and the tunnel by which he brought water into the city, are they not written in the book of the annals of the kings of Judah? [21]Hezekiah rested with his fathers. And Manasseh his son succeeded him as king.

Manasseh King of Judah

21 Manasseh was twelve years old when he became king, and he reigned in Jerusalem fifty-five years. His mother's name was Hephzibah. [2]He did evil in the eyes of the LORD, following the detestable practices of the nations the LORD had driven out before the Israelites. [3]He rebuilt the high places his father Hezekiah had destroyed; he also erected altars to Baal and made an Asherah pole, as Ahab king of Israel had done. He bowed down to all the starry hosts and worshiped them. [4]He built altars in the temple of the LORD, of which the LORD had said, "In Jerusalem I will put my Name." [5]In

OPEN When you were in grade school, what were you most likely to show off: Your home? Your parents' car or boat? Your athletic or musical skills? Your bicycle or toys?

STUDY Hezekiah shows off what is in his storehouses to messengers of the king of Babylon. Isaiah tells him that Babylon will end up claiming these items—and the freedom of his descendants as well. **1.** Why does Hezekiah show the envoys everything: Näive hospitality? Protocol? If you've got it, flaunt it? **2.** What is Isaiah's mood as he probes him: Nonchalant? Alarmed? Incredulous? Angry? **3.** Is Isaiah saying that the exile is a punishment for Hezekiah's foolhardy action, or is he just pointing out the irony of what would have happened anyway? **4.** Why is Hezekiah so accepting of this pronouncement by Isaiah?

APPLY What problem or need are you most worried about passing on to your children and grandchildren: Ecological disaster? A world with fewer principles and values? An economy that will collapse? A world where terrorism is on the rise?

OPEN 1. When you were 12 years old, what was the temptation that was hardest for you to face: Lying to your parents? Shoplifting? Looking at sexually-oriented magazines and books? Smoking? Gossiping about peers? Drug or alcohol use? Using violence to solve problems? **2.** Who helped you most in facing this temptation?

STUDY Manasseh becomes king of Judah at the age of 12.

20:12 Merodach-Baladan ... sent Hezekiah letters and a gift. This was more than a "get well" card. Merodach's gifts invited Hezekiah to join a political alliance.

20:13 showed them all. Hezekiah was trying to impress his guests. If he appeared wealthy and powerful he would stand a better chance of appearing useful as an ally against Assyria.

20:14–15 Hezekiah was transparent with Isaiah in reporting his actions but held back mention of an alliance.

20:17 The time will surely come. Hezekiah's plan eventually backfired. Judah was exiled to Babylon 115 years later.

20:18 will be taken away. The book of Daniel describes the era when Hezekiah's tribe was exiled to Babylon.

20:20 the tunnel. Hezekiah's tunnel, 1777 feet long through solid rock, connected Jerusalem to an outside water source so that during battle the people could drink without leaving the city.

21:1 fifty-five years. Includes his vice-regency with his father, Hezekiah. Manasseh's reign is the longest of any monarch in Israel or Judah.

21:2 evil. Manasseh took after his grandfather, the wicked King Ahaz. He rebuilt the pagan worship sites that his father had torn down. He reverted to the worship of Canaanite idols.

both courts of the temple of the LORD, he built altars to all the starry
hosts. [6]He sacrificed his own son in[a] the fire, practiced sorcery and
divination, and consulted mediums and spiritists. He did much evil in
the eyes of the LORD, provoking him to anger.

[7]He took the carved Asherah pole he had made and put it in the
temple, of which the LORD had said to David and to his son Solomon,
"In this temple and in Jerusalem, which I have chosen out of all the
tribes of Israel, I will put my Name forever. [8]I will not again make the
feet of the Israelites wander from the land I gave their forefathers, if
only they will be careful to do everything I commanded them and will
keep the whole Law that my servant Moses gave them." [9]But the people did not listen. Manasseh led them astray, so that they did more
evil than the nations the LORD had destroyed before the Israelites.

[10]The LORD said through his servants the prophets: [11]"Manasseh
king of Judah has committed these detestable sins. He has done more
evil than the Amorites who preceded him and has led Judah into sin
with his idols. [12]Therefore this is what the LORD, the God of Israel,
says: I am going to bring such disaster on Jerusalem and Judah that
the ears of everyone who hears of it will tingle. [13]I will stretch out
over Jerusalem the measuring line used against Samaria and the
plumb line used against the house of Ahab. I will wipe out Jerusalem
as one wipes a dish, wiping it and turning it upside down. [14]I will forsake the remnant of my inheritance and hand them over to their enemies. They will be looted and plundered by all their foes, [15]because
they have done evil in my eyes and have provoked me to anger from
the day their forefathers came out of Egypt until this day."

[16]Moreover, Manasseh also shed so much innocent blood that he
filled Jerusalem from end to end—besides the sin that he had caused
Judah to commit, so that they did evil in the eyes of the LORD.

[17]As for the other events of Manasseh's reign, and all he did, including the sin he committed, are they not written in the book of the
annals of the kings of Judah? [18]Manasseh rested with his fathers and
was buried in his palace garden, the garden of Uzza. And Amon his
son succeeded him as king.

Amon King of Judah

[19]Amon was twenty-two years old when he became king, and he
reigned in Jerusalem two years. His mother's name was Meshulle-
meth daughter of Haruz; she was from Jotbah. [20]He did evil in the
eyes of the LORD, as his father Manasseh had done. [21]He walked in all
the ways of his father; he worshiped the idols his father had wor-

[a]6 *Or He made his own son pass through*

Being human he struggled with temptations. But there is really nobody to help him with his temptations because his father has died and there is much evil in the land. Manasseh's evil exceeds even that of other kings, and God says that Judah will soon pay the penalty. **1.** After what experience did Hezekiah sire his son Manasseh (v. 1; 20:5–6)? **2.** Who would have been king had Hezekiah died from the boil? Viewing Manasseh's reign in retrospect, should God have let Hezekiah die? **3.** Which of the sins that Manasseh committed do you find most revolting (vv. 3–9,16)? **4.** What is a plumb line (v. 13)? What message does this warning convey? **5.** In a parallel account in 2 Chronicles 33:1–17, it says that Manasseh had a change of heart toward the end of his life and started worshipping the Lord again. Should that have changed the judgment God pronounces here? **6.** Why does God let some evil kings rule 55 years, like Manasseh, and some he only lets stay in power two years, like Amon?

APPLY 1. When have you had to "pay for" a sin that you had committed even after you repented of it: When you drove foolishly and caused an accident? When you were caught stealing or cheating? When you said something hateful that you couldn't take back? **2.** What has this incident taught you?

21:13 plumb line. An instrument used to measure vertical surfaces. The prophets Isaiah (Isa. 28:17), Amos (Amos 7:7) and Zechariah (Zech. 4:10) used the image of a plumb line to indicate a measure of judgment.

21:14 forsake. In this case, God let his people suffer the consequences of their own choices.

21:15 From the time of the exodus, the Hebrews lived in cycles of obedience and disobedience. Their exile would be the harshest judgment of their spotty history.

21:16 innocent blood. Manasseh engaged in child sacrifices, even that of his own son (v. 6). Tradition holds that during Manasseh's reign, Isaiah was killed by being sawed in two.

21:17 the other events. Manasseh was eventually taken captive to Babylon. He returned to Jerusalem and cleaned up some of the idolatry there. He was unable, though, to reverse the damage he had done.

21:19–20 Amon. Amon reestablished the idolatry that his father, Manasseh, had abolished at the end of his reign.

shiped, and bowed down to them. [22]He forsook the LORD, the God of his fathers, and did not walk in the way of the LORD.

[23]Amon's officials conspired against him and assassinated the king in his palace. [24]Then the people of the land killed all who had plotted against King Amon, and they made Josiah his son king in his place.

[25]As for the other events of Amon's reign, and what he did, are they not written in the book of the annals of the kings of Judah? [26]He was buried in his grave in the garden of Uzza. And Josiah his son succeeded him as king.

The Book of the Law Found

22 Josiah was eight years old when he became king, and he reigned in Jerusalem thirty-one years. His mother's name was Jedidah daughter of Adaiah; she was from Bozkath. [2]He did what was right in the eyes of the LORD and walked in all the ways of his father David, not turning aside to the right or to the left.

[3]In the eighteenth year of his reign, King Josiah sent the secretary, Shaphan son of Azaliah, the son of Meshullam, to the temple of the LORD. He said: [4]"Go up to Hilkiah the high priest and have him get ready the money that has been brought into the temple of the LORD, which the doorkeepers have collected from the people. [5]Have them entrust it to the men appointed to supervise the work on the temple. And have these men pay the workers who repair the temple of the LORD— [6]the carpenters, the builders and the masons. Also have them purchase timber and dressed stone to repair the temple. [7]But they need not account for the money entrusted to them, because they are acting faithfully."

[8]Hilkiah the high priest said to Shaphan the secretary, "I have found the Book of the Law in the temple of the LORD." He gave it to Shaphan, who read it. [9]Then Shaphan the secretary went to the king and reported to him: "Your officials have paid out the money that was in the temple of the LORD and have entrusted it to the workers and supervisors at the temple." [10]Then Shaphan the secretary informed the king, "Hilkiah the priest has given me a book." And Shaphan read from it in the presence of the king.

[11]When the king heard the words of the Book of the Law, he tore his robes. [12]He gave these orders to Hilkiah the priest, Ahikam son of Shaphan, Acbor son of Micaiah, Shaphan the secretary and Asaiah the king's attendant: [13]"Go and inquire of the LORD for me and for the people and for all Judah about what is written in this book that has been found. Great is the LORD's anger that burns against us because our fathers have not obeyed the words of this book; they have not acted in accordance with all that is written there concerning us."

[14]Hilkiah the priest, Ahikam, Acbor, Shaphan and Asaiah went to

OPEN 1. If you could find an old treasure from your past that you have lost, what would you most like to find: Your old class ring? A lock of your baby hair? A letter from an old boyfriend or girlfriend? A lost yearbook? A lost treasure given to you or your family from a relative now dead? Other? **2.** What treasure of yours would you most want to be passed on to your grandchildren?

STUDY When King Josiah decides to repair the temple, the Book of the Law is found. He mourns when he finds how much the people of Judah have violated the Law. **1.** What top priority does Josiah share with another boy king (vv. 4–7; 12:1–16; 2 Chr. 24:1)? **2.** How does the process of repairing the temple used under Josiah compare with the previous time it was repaired (12:1–16)? **3.** How do you suppose the Book of the Law got lost in the first place: People stopped reading it and so it got buried under other stuff? Someone hid it to protect it during the idolatry years? Someone hid it so people wouldn't pay attention to it? **4.** Why does Josiah tear his robes? **5.** Who does Josiah consult concerning the Book of the Law and what God now says about it? **6.** How will Judah be punished for turning from this Law? **7.** What concession will be made by God toward Josiah because of his righteousness? Would this console you if you were Josiah?

APPLY 1. When was there a time in your life when you "rediscovered" the Bible and its mes-

---

21:23 conspired. Amon's conspiracy involved both religion and politics, which were inseparable in the ancient world. Judah suffered both in spirit and in national administration. These were hard times.

22:1 Josiah. He was the last righteous king from the line of David, before Judah's exile. Jeremiah and Zephaniah prophesied during Josiah's reign.

22:3 eighteenth year. Josiah was eight when he became king and at 26 years of age was busily purging his kingdom of idolatry.

22:4 the money. This money had been collected specifically for the restoration of the temple.

22:8 Book of the Law in the temple. Either the complete writings of Moses (Genesis through Deuteronomy) or a portion of the book of Deuteronomy alone.

22:14 Huldah. Huldah enjoyed immense credibility and influence in Judah. The men took her word as a message from God and acted on it.

sage for you? **2.** When you "rediscovered" the Bible, was your reaction more one of mourning or of rejoicing? How did the rediscovery change your life?

speak to the prophetess Huldah, who was the wife of Shallum son of
Tikvah, the son of Harhas, keeper of the wardrobe. She lived in Jerusalem, in the Second District.
15 She said to them, "This is what the LORD, the God of Israel, says:
Tell the man who sent you to me, 16 'This is what the LORD says: I am
going to bring disaster on this place and its people, according to everything written in the book the king of Judah has read. 17 Because
they have forsaken me and burned incense to other gods and provoked me to anger by all the idols their hands have made,[a] my anger
will burn against this place and will not be quenched.' 18 Tell the king
of Judah, who sent you to inquire of the LORD, 'This is what the LORD,
the God of Israel, says concerning the words you heard: 19 Because
your heart was responsive and you humbled yourself before the LORD
when you heard what I have spoken against this place and its people,
that they would become accursed and laid waste, and because you
tore your robes and wept in my presence, I have heard you, declares
the LORD. 20 Therefore I will gather you to your fathers, and you will be
buried in peace. Your eyes will not see all the disaster I am going to
bring on this place.' "
So they took her answer back to the king.

Josiah Renews the Covenant

23 Then the king called together all the elders of Judah and
Jerusalem. 2 He went up to the temple of the LORD with the
men of Judah, the people of Jerusalem, the priests and the prophets—
all the people from the least to the greatest. He read in their hearing
all the words of the Book of the Covenant, which had been found in
the temple of the LORD. 3 The king stood by the pillar and renewed the
covenant in the presence of the LORD—to follow the LORD and keep
his commands, regulations and decrees with all his heart and all his
soul, thus confirming the words of the covenant written in this book.
Then all the people pledged themselves to the covenant.
4 The king ordered Hilkiah the high priest, the priests next in rank
and the doorkeepers to remove from the temple of the LORD all the
articles made for Baal and Asherah and all the starry hosts. He
burned them outside Jerusalem in the fields of the Kidron Valley and
took the ashes to Bethel. 5 He did away with the pagan priests appointed by the kings of Judah to burn incense on the high places of
the towns of Judah and on those around Jerusalem—those who
burned incense to Baal, to the sun and moon, to the constellations
and to all the starry hosts. 6 He took the Asherah pole from the temple
of the LORD to the Kidron Valley outside Jerusalem and burned it
there. He ground it to powder and scattered the dust over the graves
of the common people. 7 He also tore down the quarters of the male
shrine prostitutes, which were in the temple of the LORD and where
women did weaving for Asherah.

OPEN **1.** When it comes to cleaning house, are you more of a "keeper" or a "tosser"? What about your spouse or other person you live with? **2.** What have you kept that you wished you had tossed, or tossed that you wished you would have kept?

STUDY In response to finding the Book of the Law, Josiah now seeks to "clean house" by tossing all the paraphernalia, priests and other people associated with worship of other gods. Nevertheless, the judgment of God against Judah will still stand, and Josiah himself dies in battle with Pharaoh Neco. **1.** Why does Josiah read the entire Book of the Covenant to the people of Judah? **2.** What modern practice might be closest to the idea of "renewing the covenant" between God and Judah: Renewing wedding vows? Reenlisting in the army? Renegotiating a contract? **3.** Why was renewing the covenant so important at this time? **4.** Why were the people so willing to give up their idolatry: They feared the wrath of God? Josiah's convictions inspired and motivated them? They did whatever the king said? **5.** Who is the man of God who foretold these things and whose bones were left undis-

[a] 17 Or *by everything they have done*

22:20 Your eyes will not see. Josiah received the same comfort as Hezekiah. Judgment was coming, but he would not be around to watch the ax fall.

23:2 all the words of the Book of the Covenant. Most likely they read sections of Deuteronomy 27–28 where God set the terms of his covenant. There would be blessings for obedience and punishment for disobedience.

23:4 Bethel. The site where Jeroboam wrongly established an alternate festival and place of worship (10:29).

[8]Josiah brought all the priests from the towns of Judah and desecrated the high places, from Geba to Beersheba, where the priests had burned incense. He broke down the shrines[a] at the gates—at the entrance to the Gate of Joshua, the city governor, which is on the left of the city gate. [9]Although the priests of the high places did not serve at the altar of the LORD in Jerusalem, they ate unleavened bread with their fellow priests.

[10]He desecrated Topheth, which was in the Valley of Ben Hinnom, so no one could use it to sacrifice his son or daughter in[b] the fire to Molech. [11]He removed from the entrance to the temple of the LORD the horses that the kings of Judah had dedicated to the sun. They were in the court near the room of an official named Nathan-Melech. Josiah then burned the chariots dedicated to the sun.

[12]He pulled down the altars the kings of Judah had erected on the roof near the upper room of Ahaz, and the altars Manasseh had built in the two courts of the temple of the LORD. He removed them from there, smashed them to pieces and threw the rubble into the Kidron Valley. [13]The king also desecrated the high places that were east of Jerusalem on the south of the Hill of Corruption—the ones Solomon king of Israel had built for Ashtoreth the vile goddess of the Sidonians, for Chemosh the vile god of Moab, and for Molech[c] the detestable god of the people of Ammon. [14]Josiah smashed the sacred stones and cut down the Asherah poles and covered the sites with human bones.

[15]Even the altar at Bethel, the high place made by Jeroboam son of Nebat, who had caused Israel to sin—even that altar and high place he demolished. He burned the high place and ground it to powder, and burned the Asherah pole also. [16]Then Josiah looked around, and when he saw the tombs that were there on the hillside, he had the bones removed from them and burned on the altar to defile it, in accordance with the word of the LORD proclaimed by the man of God who foretold these things.

[17]The king asked, "What is that tombstone I see?"

The men of the city said, "It marks the tomb of the man of God who came from Judah and pronounced against the altar of Bethel the very things you have done to it."

[18]"Leave it alone," he said. "Don't let anyone disturb his bones." So they spared his bones and those of the prophet who had come from Samaria.

[19]Just as he had done at Bethel, Josiah removed and defiled all the shrines at the high places that the kings of Israel had built in the towns of Samaria that had provoked the LORD to anger. [20]Josiah slaughtered

[a]8 Or *high places* [b]10 Or *to make his son or daughter pass through* [c]13 Hebrew *Milcom*

turbed (1 Kin. 13:1–2,31–32)? **6.** How long does the author say it has been since the people celebrated Passover? **7.** Why did all of Josiah's effort and reform not result in God changing his judgment against Judah: He didn't think it was sincere? He didn't think it went much beyond Josiah? He was still too angry over what had been done before? He figured the nation needed a more long-term lesson?

APPLY 1. What would it mean for you to "renew your own covenant," your own commitment to God? What spiritual disciplines would need to be added to or strengthened in your life? What behaviors would you need to change? **2.** What help or support would you need from this group to truly follow through with such a personal "renewal"?

23:9 did not serve at the altar. Josiah honored the priests of the high places (those who led in pagan worship) by allowing them to fraternize with priests who led in the worship of God. Their only restrictions were similar to those placed on handicapped priests.

23:11 the horses. Horses that pulled idols in processionals. These horses were stabled in the temple courtyard.

23:14 human bones. The bones rendered the sites unclean and thus useless for any kind of worship.

23:15 high place made by Jeroboam. When Jeroboam built this altar, he received a prophecy about its destruction. The prophecy even mentioned Josiah's name (1 Kin. 13:2).

23:18 Samaria. The country of Samaria, not the city. The unknown prophet may have been from Bethel.

23:20 slaughtered all the priests. Pagan priests, not the levitical priests who were incorporated back into Jerusalem. **burned human bones.** To desecrate the altar.

all the priests of those high places on the altars and burned human
bones on them. Then he went back to Jerusalem.
21 The king gave this order to all the people: "Celebrate the Passover
to the LORD your God, as it is written in this Book of the Covenant."
22 Not since the days of the judges who led Israel, nor throughout the
days of the kings of Israel and the kings of Judah, had any such Passover been observed. 23 But in the eighteenth year of King Josiah, this
Passover was celebrated to the LORD in Jerusalem.
24 Furthermore, Josiah got rid of the mediums and spiritists, the
household gods, the idols and all the other detestable things seen in
Judah and Jerusalem. This he did to fulfill the requirements of the law
written in the book that Hilkiah the priest had discovered in the temple of the LORD. 25 Neither before nor after Josiah was there a king like
him who turned to the LORD as he did—with all his heart and with all
his soul and with all his strength, in accordance with all the Law of
Moses.
26 Nevertheless, the LORD did not turn away from the heat of his
fierce anger, which burned against Judah because of all that Manasseh had done to provoke him to anger. 27 So the LORD said, "I will
remove Judah also from my presence as I removed Israel, and I will
reject Jerusalem, the city I chose, and this temple, about which I said,
'There shall my Name be.'[a]"
28 As for the other events of Josiah's reign, and all he did, are they
not written in the book of the annals of the kings of Judah?
29 While Josiah was king, Pharaoh Neco king of Egypt went up to
the Euphrates River to help the king of Assyria. King Josiah marched
out to meet him in battle, but Neco faced him and killed him at Megiddo. 30 Josiah's servants brought his body in a chariot from Megiddo
to Jerusalem and buried him in his own tomb. And the people of the
land took Jehoahaz son of Josiah and anointed him and made him
king in place of his father.

OPEN Which are you: Make quick decisions? Mull over every decision I make? Can't decide if I'm indecisive?

STUDY Pharaoh makes Eliakim (whom he renamed Jehoiakim) king in Judah, and Jehoiakim does what he is told—collect taxes to send to Egypt. For a while he still does what he is told when Babylon takes over. But then he rebels and Babylon comes to make him pay the

Jehoahaz King of Judah

31 Jehoahaz was twenty-three years old when he became king, and
he reigned in Jerusalem three months. His mother's name was Hamutal daughter of Jeremiah; she was from Libnah. 32 He did evil in the
eyes of the LORD, just as his fathers had done. 33 Pharaoh Neco put
him in chains at Riblah in the land of Hamath[b] so that he might not
reign in Jerusalem, and he imposed on Judah a levy of a hundred
talents[c] of silver and a talent[d] of gold. 34 Pharaoh Neco made Eliakim

[a]27 1 Kings 8:29 [b]33 Hebrew; Septuagint (see also 2 Chron. 36:3) *Neco at Riblah in Hamath removed him*
[c]33 That is, about 3 3/4 tons (about 3.4 metric tons) [d]33 That is, about 75 pounds (about 34 kilograms)

23:21 as it is written. Deuteronomy 16:1–8 outlined the Passover as a community celebration at the sanctuary, rather than a family event in homes.

23:22 any such Passover. Josiah's *attention to detail made this Passover* quite special. Josiah made sure that only Levites slaughtered the sacrificial lambs, and he brought people from Israel and Judah together for the celebration.

23:29 Because Judah lay between Assyria and Egypt, Josiah opposed any alliance between those two nations.

23:30 Jehoahaz, the third son of Josiah, opposed any alliance with Egypt and won the people's support. After a short reign he was taken captive to Egypt, whose leaders placed an older brother on the throne.

23:33 he imposed on Judah. When Neco killed Josiah, he took control of Judah. That's why Jehoahaz, Egypt's vassal king, when summoned to Riblah, had no choice but to go, even though it meant captivity and death in Egypt.

23:34 Jehoiakim. Jehoahaz was formerly named Shallum. Jehoiakim was formerly named Eliakim. Jehoiakim no doubt complied with greater enthusiasm to Egyptian control.

son of Josiah king in place of his father Josiah and changed Eliakim's
name to Jehoiakim. But he took Jehoahaz and carried him off to
Egypt, and there he died. 35Jehoiakim paid Pharaoh Neco the silver
and gold he demanded. In order to do so, he taxed the land and
exacted the silver and gold from the people of the land according to
their assessments.

Jehoiakim King of Judah

36Jehoiakim was twenty-five years old when he became king, and
he reigned in Jerusalem eleven years. His mother's name was
Zebidah daughter of Pedaiah; she was from Rumah. 37And he did evil
in the eyes of the LORD, just as his fathers had done.

24 During Jehoiakim's reign, Nebuchadnezzar king of Babylon
invaded the land, and Jehoiakim became his vassal for three
years. But then he changed his mind and rebelled against Nebuchadnezzar. 2The LORD sent Babylonian,[a] Aramean, Moabite and
Ammonite raiders against him. He sent them to destroy Judah, in
accordance with the word of the LORD proclaimed by his servants the
prophets. 3Surely these things happened to Judah according to the
LORD's command, in order to remove them from his presence
because of the sins of Manasseh and all he had done, 4including the
shedding of innocent blood. For he had filled Jerusalem with innocent blood, and the LORD was not willing to forgive.
5As for the other events of Jehoiakim's reign, and all he did, are
they not written in the book of the annals of the kings of Judah?
6Jehoiakim rested with his fathers. And Jehoiachin his son succeeded
him as king.
7The king of Egypt did not march out from his own country again,
because the king of Babylon had taken all his territory, from the Wadi
of Egypt to the Euphrates River.

Jehoiachin King of Judah

8Jehoiachin was eighteen years old when he became king, and he
reigned in Jerusalem three months. His mother's name was Nehushta daughter of Elnathan; she was from Jerusalem. 9He did evil in the
eyes of the LORD, just as his father had done.
10At that time the officers of Nebuchadnezzar king of Babylon
advanced on Jerusalem and laid siege to it, 11and Nebuchadnezzar
himself came up to the city while his officers were besieging it.
12Jehoiachin king of Judah, his mother, his attendants, his nobles and
his officials all surrendered to him.
In the eighth year of the reign of the king of Babylon, he took
Jehoiachin prisoner. 13As the LORD had declared, Nebuchadnezzar

[a]2 Or *Chaldean*

price. **1.** Why do you think Pharaoh Neco replaces Jehoahaz with Eliakim? **2.** Why might Pharaoh change the name of Eliakim (which means "my God will raise up" and is related to a generic name for God) to Jehoiakim (which refers to the name "Yahweh" for God and means "the LORD will raise")? **3.** Why might Jehoiakim have rebelled, given the overwhelming odds against him? **4.** Nebuchadnezzar invades Judah. Who was warning Jehoiakim about this impending disaster all along, but to no avail (Jer. 36:1–3,22–25)?

APPLY 1. What oppressive circumstance have you been putting up with lately? **2.** How far are you from rebelling against this oppression? **3.** If rebelling is a battle you don't seem to have the resources to win, what can you do to get strength and support?

OPEN 1. What has been the closest you came to being "banished from the presence" of someone? **2.** What got you back in good stead?

STUDY Judah's long history of rebellion against God finally results in God allowing Babylon to come in and take over. When they are deported to Babylon, it is like they are being banished from the presence of God. **1.** How does Jehoiachin continue his father's policies toward God and Babylon (vv. 8–11)? **2.** What prophecy is fulfilled when the treasures are taken from the temple (20:16–18)?

24:1 Nebuchadnezzar king of Babylon. When Babylon conquered Egypt, Judah came under Nebuchadnezzar's rule. Eventually Nebuchadnezzar took captives from Judah to Babylon, including Daniel (Dan. 1).

24:2 Babylon commanded such power at the time that all these countries were at Nebuchadnezzar's disposal to attack Judah.

24:6 Jeremiah prophesied that Jehoiakim would not be given a royal burial (Jer. 22:19).

24:7 did not march out. Babylon had become so strong that even Egypt would not take a stand. Babylon controlled Egypt's resources.

24:11–15 Jehoiakim had fought against Babylon, but his son Jehoiachin quickly surrendered.

24:13–16 carried into exile. Nebuchadnezzar took the finest riches of

3. Why does Babylon not bother to deport the poorest people of the land? **4.** What was left for Zedekiah to be king of? **5.** What does it mean that God thrust the people of Judah from his presence: He was only present in Israel and Judah? He knew they would feel alienated from him in a foreign land? He was withdrawing his Spirit from them so that they would have the feeling of abandonment?

APPLY If you could rate your own sense of God's presence with you right now, on a scale of 1 to 10, how would you rate it, if "1" is "feeling totally abandoned, like the people being carried off to Babylon" and "10" were "on a spiritual high, like those with Jesus on the Mount of Transfiguration"?

OPEN **1.** When you were in high school, in what area of life did you suffer your biggest loss: On the athletic field? In competition for a person of the opposite sex? In academic competition? In competing with a sibling for your parents' attention? **2.** Who or what consoled you in your loss?

STUDY The final defeat of Judah is assured when Zedekiah rebels against Babylon. Jerusalem and the temple are destroyed, Zedekiah is blinded and more of the people are carried off to Babylon. The sole consolation is that King Jehoiachin is released from prison and given a place of honor. **1.** How long does the siege of Jerusalem last (vv. 1–2)? **2.** What does Jeremiah advise when the famine strikes (Jer. 38:17–23)? **3.** Why are Zedekiah's sons signaled out for execution? **4.** Who is appointed as governor of what is left of Judah? What will be his biggest challenge? **5.** What does Gedaliah advise the men left concerning how to behave? Was it good advice

removed all the treasures from the temple of the LORD and from the royal palace, and took away all the gold articles that Solomon king of Israel had made for the temple of the LORD. 14He carried into exile all Jerusalem: all the officers and fighting men, and all the craftsmen and artisans—a total of ten thousand. Only the poorest people of the land were left.

15Nebuchadnezzar took Jehoiachin captive to Babylon. He also took from Jerusalem to Babylon the king's mother, his wives, his officials and the leading men of the land. 16The king of Babylon also deported to Babylon the entire force of seven thousand fighting men, strong and fit for war, and a thousand craftsmen and artisans. 17He made Mattaniah, Jehoiachin's uncle, king in his place and changed his name to Zedekiah.

Zedekiah King of Judah

18Zedekiah was twenty-one years old when he became king, and he reigned in Jerusalem eleven years. His mother's name was Hamutal daughter of Jeremiah; she was from Libnah. 19He did evil in the eyes of the LORD, just as Jehoiakim had done. 20It was because of the LORD's anger that all this happened to Jerusalem and Judah, and in the end he thrust them from his presence.

The Fall of Jerusalem

Now Zedekiah rebelled against the king of Babylon.

25 So in the ninth year of Zedekiah's reign, on the tenth day of the tenth month, Nebuchadnezzar king of Babylon marched against Jerusalem with his whole army. He encamped outside the city and built siege works all around it. 2The city was kept under siege until the eleventh year of King Zedekiah. 3By the ninth day of the ⌞fourth⌟[a] month the famine in the city had become so severe that there was no food for the people to eat. 4Then the city wall was broken through, and the whole army fled at night through the gate between the two walls near the king's garden, though the Babylonians[b] were surrounding the city. They fled toward the Arabah,[c] 5but the Babylonian[d] army pursued the king and overtook him in the plains of Jericho. All his soldiers were separated from him and scattered, 6and he was captured. He was taken to the king of Babylon at Riblah, where sentence was pronounced on him. 7They killed the sons of Zedekiah before his eyes. Then they put out his eyes, bound him with bronze shackles and took him to Babylon.

8On the seventh day of the fifth month, in the nineteenth year of Nebuchadnezzar king of Babylon, Nebuzaradan commander of the imperial guard, an official of the king of Babylon, came to Jerusalem.

[a]3 See Jer. 52:6. [b]4 Or *Chaldeans*; also in verses 13, 25 and 26 [c]4 Or *the Jordan Valley* [d]5 Or *Chaldean*; also in verses 10 and 24

Judah and the most able people. The prophet Ezekiel continued to preach to his people while in exile.

24:15 Jehoiachin's captivity fulfilled a prophecy of Jeremiah (Jer. 22:24–25).

24:17 Mattaniah. Josiah's people named his third son king after Josiah's death. Then, another son was named king by Egypt. When Babylon came to power, Nebuchadnezzar named Josiah's youngest son as king and changed his name to Zedekiah.

24:18–19 Zedekiah. Zedekiah (formerly Mattaniah) was an evil and weak king who "ruled" over a remnant of the former nation.

25:7 Jeremiah had warned Zedekiah to surrender rather than rebel, but Zedekiah did not listen (Jer. 38:1–28). He suffered greatly for his rebellion.

[9]He set fire to the temple of the LORD, the royal palace and all the
houses of Jerusalem. Every important building he burned down.
[10]The whole Babylonian army, under the commander of the imperial
guard, broke down the walls around Jerusalem. [11]Nebuzaradan the
commander of the guard carried into exile the people who remained
in the city, along with the rest of the populace and those who
had gone over to the king of Babylon. [12]But the commander left
behind some of the poorest people of the land to work the vineyards
and fields.

[13]The Babylonians broke up the bronze pillars, the movable stands
and the bronze Sea that were at the temple of the LORD and they carried the bronze to Babylon. [14]They also took away the pots, shovels,
wick trimmers, dishes and all the bronze articles used in the temple
service. [15]The commander of the imperial guard took away the censers and sprinkling bowls—all that were made of pure gold or silver.
[16]The bronze from the two pillars, the Sea and the movable stands,
which Solomon had made for the temple of the LORD, was more than
could be weighed. [17]Each pillar was twenty-seven feet[a] high. The
bronze capital on top of one pillar was four and a half feet[b] high and
was decorated with a network and pomegranates of bronze all
around. The other pillar, with its network, was similar.

[18]The commander of the guard took as prisoners Seraiah the chief
priest, Zephaniah the priest next in rank and the three doorkeepers.
[19]Of those still in the city, he took the officer in charge of the fighting
men and five royal advisers. He also took the secretary who was chief
officer in charge of conscripting the people of the land and sixty of
his men who were found in the city. [20]Nebuzaradan the commander
took them all and brought them to the king of Babylon at Riblah.
[21]There at Riblah, in the land of Hamath, the king had them executed.

So Judah went into captivity, away from her land.

[22]Nebuchadnezzar king of Babylon appointed Gedaliah son of Ahikam, the son of Shaphan, to be over the people he had left behind in
Judah. [23]When all the army officers and their men heard that the king
of Babylon had appointed Gedaliah as governor, they came to Gedaliah at Mizpah—Ishmael son of Nethaniah, Johanan son of Kareah, Seraiah son of Tanhumeth the Netophathite, Jaazaniah the son of the
Maacathite, and their men. [24]Gedaliah took an oath to reassure them
and their men. "Do not be afraid of the Babylonian officials," he said.
"Settle down in the land and serve the king of Babylon, and it will go
well with you."

[25]In the seventh month, however, Ishmael son of Nethaniah, the
son of Elishama, who was of royal blood, came with ten men and assassinated Gedaliah and also the men of Judah and the Babylonians

[a]17 Hebrew *eighteen cubits* (about 8.1 meters) [b]17 Hebrew *three cubits* (about 1.3 meters)

for the situation? **6.** Why might Ishmael have assassinated Gedaliah? **7.** What do you suppose might have earned Jehoiachin his good treatment in Babylon?

APPLY 1. The popular "Serenity Prayer" asks God for the courage to change the things we can, the grace to accept the things we cannot change and the wisdom to know the difference. What difficult circumstance are you feeling the need to change? **2.** What difficult circumstance are you presently feeling you may have to accept? **3.** What would help you accept this difficult circumstance? How could this group help?

25:18 Seraiah. An ancestor of the exile leader, Ezra. Priests were taken so they would not lead another revolt.

25:21 Judah went into captivity. This judgment had been announced since Manasseh's kingdom. It was the worst possible fate for the Hebrews, since their whole covenant with God that was situated in the Land of Promise was now gone.

25:22–23 Gedaliah at Mizpah. A friend of Jeremiah, the prophet, and a descendant of Shaphan, Josiah's secretary of state. Shaphan had implemented Josiah's righteous reforms. Jerusalem was in ruins. Mizpah was located eight miles north of Jerusalem.

25:24 serve the king of Babylon. Gedaliah made use of Jeremiah's advice that his predecessor, Zedekiah, had ignored (v. 7).

who were with him at Mizpah. 26At this, all the people from the least
to the greatest, together with the army officers, fled to Egypt for fear
of the Babylonians.

Jehoiachin Released

27In the thirty-seventh year of the exile of Jehoiachin king of Judah,
in the year Evil-Merodach[a] became king of Babylon, he released
Jehoiachin from prison on the twenty-seventh day of the twelfth
month. 28He spoke kindly to him and gave him a seat of honor higher
than those of the other kings who were with him in Babylon. 29So
Jehoiachin put aside his prison clothes and for the rest of his life ate
regularly at the king's table. 30Day by day the king gave Jehoiachin a
regular allowance as long as he lived.

[a]27 Also called *Amel-Marduk*

1 Chronicles

Author. Because the style of writing is so consistent from one book to the next, 1 and 2 Chronicles were probably written by one author. No evidence suggests who that author might be. Some Jewish traditions consider Ezra a likely candidate.

Personal Reading	Group Study Topic and Reading	
1:1–5:26	God in History	5:11–26
6:1–9:1	God Inspires Worship	6:31–49
9:2–34	The Returned Exiles	9:2–34
9:35–10:14	The Death of Saul	10:1–14
11:1–12:40	David Crowned As King	11:1–9
13:1–14:17	The Ark Returns	13:1–14
15:1–16:43	David's Gratitude	16:7–43
17:1–18:17	God Promises David	17:1–15
19:1–22:1	The Fighting Men	21:1–22:1
22:2–24:31	Preparing for Worship	22:2–19
25:1–26:32	Temple Singers	25:1–31
27:1–34	The King's Officials	27:25–34
28:1–29:30	Solomon Enthroned	29:21–30

Date. First and 2 Chronicles were probably written around 400 B.C. No descendant of David is listed who lived after that date. Also, the words and customs mentioned in the Chronicles date to that time. First Chronicles covers the events of David's reign.

Purpose. The Chronicles were written for the Hebrews after they returned from their exile. The books review much of the historical data found in 2 Samuel and in 1 and 2 Kings, but from a different perspective. Rather than a historical account, Chronicles offers a religious or spiritual history of the same time period. Several omissions are glaring, such as David's sin with Bathsheba. The purpose of the Chronicles is not historical or biographical, but spiritual, to reveal the condition of the kingdom and to give hope to readers.

Historical Background. The book of 1 Chronicles focuses primarily on the reign of King David. Long genealogies, beginning with Adam, provide a panoramic view of history. For a nation that had just returned to their homeland from exile, it was important to position their present circumstances in the context of a long, established and illustrious past. As a nation in exile, the Hebrews had lost much of their national identity and pride. First Chronicles reflects on the Davidic kingship as a source of dignity. David, while certainly not perfect, was an admired, beloved and successful king.

Whereas 1 and 2 Kings portray the inevitable destruction that repeated sin brought on Israel and Judah, 1 and 2 Chronicles highlight a more heroic past. The central characters in that past are David and Solomon. For the small remnant that returned after the exile, God's promise that David's throne "will be established forever" (2 Sam. 7:16) became the cornerstone of their faith and government.

Exile. Both Judah and Israel were taken away. In this era, a conquering nation often scattered the subdued inhabitants so that they would have less opportunity for any kind of revolt. Israel was assimilated by Assyria. Some Hebrews settled around Samaria, which is why they were later referred to as Samaritans.

The people of Judah were exiled to Babylon to the south and Egypt to the west. This exile took the form of a series of deportations, while Judah still had kings and existed as a nation. When Nebuchadnezzar destroyed Jerusalem, though, the nation of Judah crumbled. The Hebrews that were resettled in Babylon maintained some semblance of their faith and history. Eventually, after more than 50 years, they were allowed to return to their homeland to reestablish residency. The time just before the exile forms the backdrop for the Chronicles. The period after the exile forms the backdrop for books such as Ezra, Nehemiah and some of the prophets.

OPEN 1. What kind of lists do you depend on (grocery, personal organizer, telephone, Christmas, "to do," etc.) to keep your life organized and efficient? **2.** What changes would be forced on you if one of your most used lists were lost forever?

STUDY 1. Genealogies often introduce stories, but in 1 Chronicles, genealogies seem to be the story. What do you think is the purpose behind these lists: To trace one's family tree and the property won? To value the struggles of bygone days? To see God guiding his chosen through thick and thin, heroism and villainy? To show children God's loving kindness to all generations? **2.** The chronicler (the person who wrote the Chronicles) highlights past events by arranging "linear genealogies" (a list devoted to a single line from ancestor to descendant) and "segmented genealogies" (a list tracing several lines of descent from a common ancestor). Where do you see the two kinds of lists here? **3.** Why so few names with any description? What major events are brought to mind by merely listing names associated with the events? **4.** Who is Nimrod (v. 10; Gen. 10:8–12)? Why might Nimrod be closely connected with a bunch of "ites" (tribal groups)? **5.** What strange events are linked with Peleg's era (vv. 19–20; Gen. 10:21–11:9)? **6.** What troubles and triumphs of history are embraced here? What kind of God (yet unnamed) is implicit in this narrative?

APPLY 1. Which of those listed were "household names" to you? **2.** Likely some important names listed here are virtual unknowns. For example, Seth: Like a substitute player, he takes the field in a world burned by murder and greed (Gen. 4:25). Yet through him, God establishes a chosen nation! For all who live fairly humble, non-descript lives, why should we think our life still counts for something?

Historical Records From Adam to Abraham

To Noah's Sons

1 Adam, Seth, Enosh, [2]Kenan, Mahalalel, Jared, [3]Enoch, Methuselah, Lamech, Noah.

[4]The sons of Noah:[a]
Shem, Ham and Japheth.

The Japhethites

[5]The sons[b] of Japheth:
Gomer, Magog, Madai, Javan, Tubal, Meshech and Tiras.
[6]The sons of Gomer:
Ashkenaz, Riphath[c] and Togarmah.
[7]The sons of Javan:
Elishah, Tarshish, the Kittim and the Rodanim.

The Hamites

[8]The sons of Ham:
Cush, Mizraim,[d] Put and Canaan.
[9]The sons of Cush:
Seba, Havilah, Sabta, Raamah and Sabteca.
The sons of Raamah:
Sheba and Dedan.
[10]Cush was the father[e] of
Nimrod, who grew to be a mighty warrior on earth.
[11]Mizraim was the father of
the Ludites, Anamites, Lehabites, Naphtuhites, [12]Pathrusites,
Casluhites (from whom the Philistines came) and Caphtorites.
[13]Canaan was the father of
Sidon his firstborn,[f] and of the Hittites, [14]Jebusites, Amorites,
Girgashites, [15]Hivites, Arkites, Sinites, [16]Arvadites, Zemarites
and Hamathites.

The Semites

[17]The sons of Shem:
Elam, Asshur, Arphaxad, Lud and Aram.
The sons of Aram[g]:
Uz, Hul, Gether and Meshech.
[18]Arphaxad was the father of Shelah,
and Shelah the father of Eber.

[a]4 Septuagint; Hebrew does not have *The sons of Noah:* [b]5 *Sons* may mean *descendants* or *successors* or *nations;* also in verses 6-10, 17 and 20. [c]6 Many Hebrew manuscripts and Vulgate (see also Septuagint and Gen. 10:3); most Hebrew manuscripts *Diphath* [d]8 That is, Egypt; also in verse 11 [e]10 *Father* may mean *ancestor* or *predecessor* or *founder;* also in verses 11, 13, 18 and 20. [f]13 Or *of the Sidonians, the foremost* [g]17 One Hebrew manuscript and some Septuagint manuscripts (see also Gen. 10:23); most Hebrew manuscripts do not have this line.

1:1–9:44 The chronicler uses genealogies as family photo albums—volumes of family history captured in names and faces. Israel's history is traced from Saul (9:35–44) back to Adam (vv. 1–4). The purpose of the genealogies is to show the continuum of God's faithfulness. The chronicler's contemporaries had returned from the Exile. A review of the past helped secure their faith in God's presence in the future. Therefore, emphasizing David and the Davidic line is a major theme of both Chronicles.

1:1–2:1 The lineage between Adam and Jacob is a brief stop on the roadmap to the chronicler's ultimate destination—David. The chronicler leaves out side street names that do not directly contribute to the royal route between Adam and David.

[19]Two sons were born to Eber:
One was named Peleg,[a] because in his time the earth was divided; his brother was named Joktan.
[20]Joktan was the father of
Almodad, Sheleph, Hazarmaveth, Jerah, [21]Hadoram, Uzal,
Diklah, [22]Obal,[b] Abimael, Sheba, [23]Ophir, Havilah and Jobab.
All these were sons of Joktan.

[24]Shem, Arphaxad,[c] Shelah,
[25]Eber, Peleg, Reu,
[26]Serug, Nahor, Terah
[27]and Abram (that is, Abraham).

The Family of Abraham

[28]The sons of Abraham:
Isaac and Ishmael.

Descendants of Hagar

[29]These were their descendants:
Nebaioth the firstborn of Ishmael, Kedar, Adbeel, Mibsam,
[30]Mishma, Dumah, Massa, Hadad, Tema, [31]Jetur, Naphish and
Kedemah. These were the sons of Ishmael.

Descendants of Keturah

[32]The sons born to Keturah, Abraham's concubine:
Zimran, Jokshan, Medan, Midian, Ishbak and Shuah.
The sons of Jokshan:
Sheba and Dedan.
[33]The sons of Midian:
Ephah, Epher, Hanoch, Abida and Eldaah.
All these were descendants of Keturah.

Descendants of Sarah

[34]Abraham was the father of Isaac.
The sons of Isaac:
Esau and Israel.

Esau's Sons

[35]The sons of Esau:
Eliphaz, Reuel, Jeush, Jalam and Korah.
[36]The sons of Eliphaz:
Teman, Omar, Zepho,[d] Gatam and Kenaz;
by Timna: Amalek.[e]
[37]The sons of Reuel:
Nahath, Zerah, Shammah and Mizzah.

[a]19 *Peleg* means *division.* [b]22 Some Hebrew manuscripts and Syriac (see also Gen. 10:28); most Hebrew manuscripts *Ebal* [c]24 Hebrew; some Septuagint manuscripts *Arphaxad, Cainan* (see also note at Gen. 11:10) [d]36 Many Hebrew manuscripts, some Septuagint manuscripts and Syriac (see also Gen. 36:11); most Hebrew manuscripts *Zephi* [e]36 Some Septuagint manuscripts (see also Gen. 36:12); Hebrew *Gatam, Kenaz, Timna and Amalek*

OPEN 1. If you were compiling a family tree, how would you decide who gets included and who doesn't? Would you include pirates and other "low-lifes"? Or would you skip them to highlight some high moral purpose? **2.** What family embarrassments would give you pause if you were to share that "tree" with your group?

STUDY 1. Why does the chronicler always call Jacob by his "other" name (v. 34)? **2.** This section includes some "firsts" for women in the book of Chronicles. Let's see if you genealogy sleuths can find: The first mention of a woman? Of a daughter? Of a grandmother? **3.** What political leader (town or movement) takes on the name of a woman? Why are their names omitted? **4.** What developments in the institution of marriage does chapter 1 recount? What happened to Hagar (v. 29; Gen. 21)? Likewise, Sarah (v. 34; Gen. 23)? And Keturah (vv. 32–33; Gen. 25:1–4)? **5.** Like a good baseball manager, the chronicler has a strategy in the way he makes out his line-up card of names. From his list of Abraham's sons (vv. 28–34), who seem to be regarded as the most important players? Why are they so vital? **6.** In verses 35–54 and Genesis 36:10–14,20–43, why is such unusual detail devoted to people and places having little role in Israel's development? **7.** Will the real "Timna" please stand up (vv. 36,39,51 and footnote to v. 36)? Is "she" a wife of Eliphaz? Or is "he" his son? And what kind of mom was she if her son's tribe, the Amalekites, became Israel's chief enemy (1 Sam. 15)? **8.** What's significant about the kings mentioned

1:29–36 Abraham's descendants are grouped according to their mothers: Hagar, Keturah and Sarah. **Timna.** Timna served Eliphaz as his concubine. Their son, Amalek, led the Amalekites (1 Sam. 15).

here (vv. 43–54)? **9.** What does Esau's lineage tell us about God's care for his people?

APPLY 1. Of all the groups (teams, associations, families) you belong to, which two most define who you are? Which will help you decide what neighborhood to live in? Or which group is an indicator of how much income you will declare on your income tax forms? Which groups influence your choice of clothes, hairstyle, leisure pursuits? **2.** How might the strange listing of the Edomites make you think twice about which people you view as offensive and unattractive outside your circles? **3.** Do you think marriage was taken more seriously in Abraham's day than today? Why or why not? Today we have ways of dissolving marriages which insure that the parties of a previous marriage are cared for. By today's standard of equal rights, would Abraham's effort to provide for Hagar have passed muster? If the exiled Hagar and her brood had moved next door to you, would you or your church be ready to assist her? Why or why not?

The People of Seir in Edom

38 The sons of Seir:
Lotan, Shobal, Zibeon, Anah, Dishon, Ezer and Dishan.
39 The sons of Lotan:
Hori and Homam. Timna was Lotan's sister.
40 The sons of Shobal:
Alvan,[a] Manahath, Ebal, Shepho and Onam.
The sons of Zibeon:
Aiah and Anah.
41 The son of Anah:
Dishon.
The sons of Dishon:
Hemdan,[b] Eshban, Ithran and Keran.
42 The sons of Ezer:
Bilhan, Zaavan and Akan.[c]
The sons of Dishan[d]:
Uz and Aran.

The Rulers of Edom

43 These were the kings who reigned in Edom before any Israelite
king reigned[e]:
Bela son of Beor, whose city was named Dinhabah.
44 When Bela died, Jobab son of Zerah from Bozrah succeeded him
as king.
45 When Jobab died, Husham from the land of the Temanites succeeded him as king.
46 When Husham died, Hadad son of Bedad, who defeated Midian
in the country of Moab, succeeded him as king. His city was
named Avith.
47 When Hadad died, Samlah from Masrekah succeeded him as
king.
48 When Samlah died, Shaul from Rehoboth on the river[f] succeeded him as king.
49 When Shaul died, Baal-Hanan son of Acbor succeeded him as
king.
50 When Baal-Hanan died, Hadad succeeded him as king. His city
was named Pau,[g] and his wife's name was Mehetabel daughter
of Matred, the daughter of Me-Zahab. 51 Hadad also died.

The chiefs of Edom were:
Timna, Alvah, Jetheth, 52 Oholibamah, Elah, Pinon, 53 Kenaz, Te-
man, Mibzar, 54 Magdiel and Iram. These were the chiefs of
Edom.

[a] *40* Many Hebrew manuscripts and some Septuagint manuscripts (see also Gen. 36:23); most Hebrew manuscripts *Alian* [b] *41* Many Hebrew manuscripts and some Septuagint manuscripts (see also Gen. 36:26); most Hebrew manuscripts *Hamran* [c] *42* Many Hebrew and Septuagint manuscripts (see also Gen. 36:27); most Hebrew manuscripts *Zaavan, Jaakan* [d] *42* Hebrew *Dishon,* a variant of *Dishan* [e] *43* Or *before an Israelite king reigned over them* [f] *48* Possibly the Euphrates [g] *50* Many Hebrew manuscripts, some Septuagint manuscripts, Vulgate and Syriac (see also Gen. 36:39); most Hebrew manuscripts *Pai*

1:43–51 Kings. The chronicler reveals the longstanding relationship between the Edomites and Israel with their appearance here (Gen. 36:31–43).

1:51–54 chiefs of Edom. These are the military leaders.

Israel's Sons

2 These were the sons of Israel:
Reuben, Simeon, Levi, Judah, Issachar, Zebulun, [2]Dan, Joseph,
Benjamin, Naphtali, Gad and Asher.

Judah

To Hezron's Sons

[3]The sons of Judah:
Er, Onan and Shelah. These three were born to him by a Canaanite woman, the daughter of Shua. Er, Judah's firstborn,
was wicked in the LORD's sight; so the LORD put him to death.
[4]Tamar, Judah's daughter-in-law, bore him Perez and Zerah.
Judah had five sons in all.

[5]The sons of Perez:
Hezron and Hamul.
[6]The sons of Zerah:
Zimri, Ethan, Heman, Calcol and Darda[a]—five in all.
[7]The son of Carmi:
Achar,[b] who brought trouble on Israel by violating the ban on
taking devoted things.[c]
[8]The son of Ethan:
Azariah.
[9]The sons born to Hezron were:
Jerahmeel, Ram and Caleb.[d]

From Ram Son of Hezron

[10]Ram was the father of
Amminadab, and Amminadab the father of Nahshon, the lead-
er of the people of Judah. [11]Nahshon was the father of
Salmon,[e] Salmon the father of Boaz, [12]Boaz the father of Obed
and Obed the father of Jesse.
[13]Jesse was the father of
Eliab his firstborn; the second son was Abinadab, the third
Shimea, [14]the fourth Nethanel, the fifth Raddai, [15]the sixth
Ozem and the seventh David. [16]Their sisters were Zeruiah and
Abigail. Zeruiah's three sons were Abishai, Joab and Asahel.
[17]Abigail was the mother of Amasa, whose father was Jether
the Ishmaelite.

[a]6 Many Hebrew manuscripts, some Septuagint manuscripts and Syriac (see also 1 Kings 4:31); most Hebrew manuscripts *Dara* [b]7 *Achar* means *trouble; Achar* is called *Achan* in Joshua. [c]7 The Hebrew term refers to the irrevocable giving over of things or persons to the LORD, often by totally destroying them. [d]9 Hebrew *Kelubai,* a variant of *Caleb* [e]11 Septuagint (see also Ruth 4:21); Hebrew *Salma*

OPEN 1. What politician's fall from public grace do you remember most clearly? **2.** What about a politician's or clan's "rise and fall" most intrigues you? What do you imagine it must be like to be famous and powerful one moment in history, only to be disgraced and banished the next?

STUDY 1. Much of the Old Testament "Hall of Fame" is contained here. In a quick, first read-through, which names are familiar to you? What stories of God's deliverance and human weakness do these footnotes to history bring to mind? **2.** Now take a closer look at verses 1–9: Of the 12 sons listed in verse 1, why is just one (Judah) explored further? **3.** What harm comes to the house of Judah with his first two sons, Er and Onan (v. 3; Gen. 38:7–10)? They are the first people since the Flood whose death is a direct result of their disobedience to God. What qualities of God would "Er and Onan" recall? **4.** Tamar prostitutes herself (Gen. 38), but is here the first woman in the royal line to be named by the chronicler. What do you recall about the convoluted moral drama she faced? What qualities of God would "Tamar" instantly recall for God's redeemed people? **5.** Achar (v. 7; alias "Achan," Josh. 7) also lives a troubled life; so much so, that his name change is recorded for all time by the chronicler: Why? What purpose was served by reminding people of their troubled past? **6.** In the midst of these examples of shame, "Azariah" reminds us "God has helped." What message is Ethan leaving his heirs with this name for his son (which name occurs 24 times in the Old Testament)? **7.** Where do you see the first direct mention of "the LORD" and any explicit qualities attributed to him? What does this tell you about the on-going relationship God has had with all the sons of Judah thus far? **8.** In verses 10–17, we see David's forefathers and family listed. At their family reunions, what

---

2:3–9 Perez emerges to carry on the royal line amid the sordid tales of Judah's other sons.

2:7 Achar. Achar (or Achan) bookmarks a lesson learned from the tragedy of disobedience (Josh. 7).

2:10–3:24 Like a pilot cleared for landing, the chronicler zeroes in on the genealogy related to David. The lineage begins with David's immediate family and half sisters (2:13–17). It concludes with a focus on the sons of David himself (3:1–9).

2:10–17 David's line of faith reaches through many family members. David was the eighth son of Jesse, but only seven are mentioned. However, betrayal lurked behind the bonds of family (see one example in 2 Sam. 17:25).

tales were likely told and retold about each? Take Eliab, for example (1 Sam. 16:6–7). What famous saying was first told to the expectant Eliab, and what might Eliab have learned about discipleship from his disappointment? Or Asahel (2 Sam. 2:18–32): What mix of qualities did he possess above his peers which, for lack of wisdom, led to his premature death? And which members of David's own family take up arms against him, teaching David (and us) valuable lessons in faith and trust (3:2; 2 Sam. 15:10–12; 17:25)? **9.** Of the names listed in verses 18–32, some are linked with stories of faith, such as Bezalel (v. 20; Ex. 31:1–11). He was a peer with Caleb (the one who spied out the land with Joshua and is the great-grandson of the Caleb listed here). Other names are linked with stories of sex (Hezron), money and power (Jair, Geshur, Aram). What does this tell you about how and why God gives good gifts to his people?

APPLY 1. It can be assumed that Ashhur was born into a single-parent family (v. 24). What would Ashhur's lot in life have been like? How many "Ashhur's" have you known—children of one parent? What resources today help such children grow to maturity? How can churches or Bible study groups help? **2.** Of what profit to the Ashhur's of this world would be a chronicle of their family history? **3.** How has your family overcome disadvantage or hardship in giving birth to their children? In giving birth to their dreams of making a "name" for themselves? **4.** Who in your family is like Bezalel—filled with the Spirit of God *and* with skill, ability and knowledge in all kinds of crafts? How do you respond to those who "have it all"? **5.** In the composite picture of your group, do you have more "Ashhur's" or "Bezalel's"? Any with the shenanigans of "Sheshan"?

Caleb Son of Hezron

18 Caleb son of Hezron had children by his wife Azubah (and by Jer-
ioth). These were her sons: Jesher, Shobab and Ardon. 19 When
Azubah died, Caleb married Ephrath, who bore him Hur. 20 Hur
was the father of Uri, and Uri the father of Bezalel.
21 Later, Hezron lay with the daughter of Makir the father of Gilead
(he had married her when he was sixty years old), and she
bore him Segub. 22 Segub was the father of Jair, who controlled
twenty-three towns in Gilead. 23 (But Geshur and Aram captured Havvoth Jair,[a] as well as Kenath with its surrounding
settlements—sixty towns.) All these were descendants of
Makir the father of Gilead.
24 After Hezron died in Caleb Ephrathah, Abijah the wife of Hezron
bore him Ashhur the father[b] of Tekoa.

Jerahmeel Son of Hezron

25 The sons of Jerahmeel the firstborn of Hezron:
Ram his firstborn, Bunah, Oren, Ozem and[c] Ahijah. 26 Jerah-
meel had another wife, whose name was Atarah; she was the
mother of Onam.
27 The sons of Ram the firstborn of Jerahmeel:
Maaz, Jamin and Eker.
28 The sons of Onam:
Shammai and Jada.
The sons of Shammai:
Nadab and Abishur.
29 Abishur's wife was named Abihail, who bore him Ahban and
Molid.
30 The sons of Nadab:
Seled and Appaim. Seled died without children.
31 The son of Appaim:
Ishi, who was the father of Sheshan.
Sheshan was the father of Ahlai.
32 The sons of Jada, Shammai's brother:
Jether and Jonathan. Jether died without children.
33 The sons of Jonathan:
Peleth and Zaza.
These were the descendants of Jerahmeel.
34 Sheshan had no sons—only daughters.
He had an Egyptian servant named Jarha. 35 Sheshan gave his
daughter in marriage to his servant Jarha, and she bore him
Attai.
36 Attai was the father of Nathan,
Nathan the father of Zabad,
37 Zabad the father of Ephlal,
Ephlal the father of Obed,
38 Obed the father of Jehu,

[a]23 Or *captured the settlements of Jair* [b]24 *Father* may mean *civic leader* or *military leader*; also in verses 42, 45, 49-52 and possibly elsewhere. [c]25 Or *Oren and Ozem, by*

2:34–41 Subtle reference to God's favor is implied in those names rendered childless (vv. 30, 32). In contrast, Sheshan's initially jeopardized status continues through his daughter's son, Attai (v. 34).

Jehu the father of Azariah,
39 Azariah the father of Helez,
Helez the father of Eleasah,
40 Eleasah the father of Sismai,
Sismai the father of Shallum,
41 Shallum the father of Jekamiah,
and Jekamiah the father of Elishama.

The Clans of Caleb

42 The sons of Caleb the brother of Jerahmeel:
Mesha his firstborn, who was the father of Ziph, and his son
Mareshah,[a] who was the father of Hebron.
43 The sons of Hebron:
Korah, Tappuah, Rekem and Shema. 44 Shema was the father of
Raham, and Raham the father of Jorkeam. Rekem was the
father of Shammai. 45 The son of Shammai was Maon, and
Maon was the father of Beth Zur.
46 Caleb's concubine Ephah was the mother of Haran, Moza and
Gazez. Haran was the father of Gazez.
47 The sons of Jahdai:
Regem, Jotham, Geshan, Pelet, Ephah and Shaaph.
48 Caleb's concubine Maacah was the mother of Sheber and Tirhanah.
49 She also gave birth to Shaaph the father of Madmannah
and to Sheva the father of Macbenah and Gibea. Caleb's
daughter was Acsah. 50 These were the descendants of Caleb.

The sons of Hur the firstborn of Ephrathah:
Shobal the father of Kiriath Jearim, 51 Salma the father of Bethlehem,
and Hareph the father of Beth Gader.
52 The descendants of Shobal the father of Kiriath Jearim were:
Haroeh, half the Manahathites, 53 and the clans of Kiriath
Jearim: the Ithrites, Puthites, Shumathites and Mishraites.
From these descended the Zorathites and Eshtaolites.
54 The descendants of Salma:
Bethlehem, the Netophathites, Atroth Beth Joab, half the Manahathites,
the Zorites, 55 and the clans of scribes[b] who lived at
Jabez: the Tirathites, Shimeathites and Sucathites. These are
the Kenites who came from Hammath, the father of the house
of Recab.[c]

The Sons of David

3 These were the sons of David born to him in Hebron:
The firstborn was Amnon the son of Ahinoam of Jezreel;
the second, Daniel the son of Abigail of Carmel;
2 the third, Absalom the son of Maacah daughter of Talmai king of Geshur;
the fourth, Adonijah the son of Haggith;
3 the fifth, Shephatiah the son of Abital;
and the sixth, Ithream, by his wife Eglah.

[a]42 The meaning of the Hebrew for this phrase is uncertain. [b]55 Or *of the Sopherites* [c]55 Or *father of Beth Recab*

OPEN 1. If tragedy is the bookmark of history, separating chapters into lessons learned and unlearned, then what tragic-type "bookmarks" have shaped your life? Any casualties of war? Any natural disaster striking close to home? **2.** What family tragedy has had the most impact on your life?

STUDY This chapter divides neatly into three parts, but those who lived in the divisions likely did not think life was too neat at all.

3:1–9 David's complex family unit is recorded (2 Sam. 3:2–5; 5:13–16; 13:1). Solomon, as the bearer of the royal lineage, stands out among David's other children. Obviously omitted is Bathsheba's son who died at birth (2 Sam. 12:18).

1. From verses 1–9 (2 Sam. 3:2–5; 5:13–16), what can you tell about David's family life? What must relations among the 19 named siblings and the 7+ sets of half-brothers have been like? **2.** Why do you think the lists vary in name and number between Samuel's account and the chronicler's? **3.** From the story of David's sin with Bathsheba, Solomon seems to be the first child of that union (2 Sam. 12:24–25). In 1 Chronicles, what is Solomon's apparent place? **4.** Why are children of concubines named in other royal family lines (1:32; 2:46), but not in David's (v. 9; 14:3–6)? And why list Tamar alone of all his daughters (14:3–6)? **5.** David was a "parent in pain," with open disdain, rebellion and sibling rivalry rampant among his sons. How is that evident in the stories of Amnon (2 Sam. 13), Absalom (2 Sam. 16:15–23; 18:31–33) and Adonijah (1 Kin. 1)? **6.** In verses 10–14, we are introduced to the kings of Judah, any of whom could provide interesting tangents to pursue in 1 and 2 Kings. From the heavy-handed reign of Rehoboam, "Israel has been in rebellion against the house of David to this day" (1 Kin. 12:19). Forced labor, foreign invaders, idol worship, assimilation of their neighbors' worldly values, foreign alliances—all such "evil in the sight of the LORD" spelled doom for Israel. What parallels in modern history seem to replay this reign of folly, tyranny and evil? **7.** Now we come back to Jehoiachin (v. 17): What has happened to him, to Jerusalem and to the royal line thereafter?

APPLY **1.** As did many of the Israelites after Solomon died, what legacy of family troubles did you inherit? What have you in turn passed along to others? **2.** When facing conflicts, what kind of bird are you: *Hawk*, flying above it all and ready to pounce? *Dove*, waging peace instead of war? *Ostrich*, your head in the sand? *Turkey*, easily ruffled, always squawking? **3.** What troubles have you tried tackling this year: Any of your own making? Any you've inherited? What help have you had? What disappointments? What will you do differently from here on?

4 These six were born to David in Hebron, where he reigned
seven years and six months.
David reigned in Jerusalem thirty-three years, 5 and these were the
children born to him there:
Shammua,[a] Shobab, Nathan and Solomon. These four were by
Bathsheba[b] daughter of Ammiel. 6 There were also Ibhar,
Elishua,[c] Eliphelet, 7 Nogah, Nepheg, Japhia, 8 Elishama, Eliada
and Eliphelet—nine in all. 9 All these were the sons of David,
besides his sons by his concubines. And Tamar was their
sister.

The Kings of Judah

10 Solomon's son was Rehoboam,
Abijah his son,
Asa his son,
Jehoshaphat his son,
11 Jehoram[d] his son,
Ahaziah his son,
Joash his son,
12 Amaziah his son,
Azariah his son,
Jotham his son,
13 Ahaz his son,
Hezekiah his son,
Manasseh his son,
14 Amon his son,
Josiah his son.
15 The sons of Josiah:
Johanan the firstborn,
Jehoiakim the second son,
Zedekiah the third,
Shallum the fourth.
16 The successors of Jehoiakim:
Jehoiachin[e] his son,
and Zedekiah.

The Royal Line After the Exile

17 The descendants of Jehoiachin the captive:
Shealtiel his son, 18 Malkiram, Pedaiah, Shenazzar, Jekamiah,
Hoshama and Nedabiah.
19 The sons of Pedaiah:
Zerubbabel and Shimei.
The sons of Zerubbabel:
Meshullam and Hananiah.
Shelomith was their sister.

[a]5 Hebrew *Shimea,* a variant of *Shammua* [b]5 One Hebrew manuscript and Vulgate (see also Septuagint and 2 Samuel 11:3); most Hebrew manuscripts *Bathshua* [c]6 Two Hebrew manuscripts (see also 2 Samuel 5:15 and 1 Chron. 14:5); most Hebrew manuscripts *Elishama* [d]11 Hebrew *Joram,* a variant of *Jehoram* [e]16 Hebrew *Jeconiah,* a variant of *Jehoiachin;* also in verse 17

3:9 Tamar. Only one of David's daughters is listed. She is here because of the injustice done to her by brother Amnon (2 Sam. 13:14–16). This sin brought shame on the family and resulted in a murder (2 Sam. 13:18–29).

3:17–20 None of Jehoiachin's sons succeeded him as king. Babylon took Judah captive at that time.

[20]There were also five others:
Hashubah, Ohel, Berekiah, Hasadiah and Jushab-Hesed.
[21]The descendants of Hananiah:
Pelatiah and Jeshaiah, and the sons of Rephaiah, of Arnan, of Obadiah and of Shecaniah.
[22]The descendants of Shecaniah:
Shemaiah and his sons:
Hattush, Igal, Bariah, Neariah and Shaphat—six in all.
[23]The sons of Neariah:
Elioenai, Hizkiah and Azrikam—three in all.
[24]The sons of Elioenai:
Hodaviah, Eliashib, Pelaiah, Akkub, Johanan, Delaiah and Anani—seven in all.

Other Clans of Judah

4 The descendants of Judah:
Perez, Hezron, Carmi, Hur and Shobal.
[2]Reaiah son of Shobal was the father of Jahath, and Jahath the father of Ahumai and Lahad. These were the clans of the Zorathites.
[3]These were the sons[a] of Etam:
Jezreel, Ishma and Idbash. Their sister was named Hazzelelponi. [4]Penuel was the father of Gedor, and Ezer the father of Hushah.
These were the descendants of Hur, the firstborn of Ephrathah and father[b] of Bethlehem.
[5]Ashhur the father of Tekoa had two wives, Helah and Naarah.
[6]Naarah bore him Ahuzzam, Hepher, Temeni and Haahashtari. These were the descendants of Naarah.
[7]The sons of Helah:
Zereth, Zohar, Ethnan, [8]and Koz, who was the father of Anub and Hazzobebah and of the clans of Aharhel son of Harum.

[9]Jabez was more honorable than his brothers. His mother had
named him Jabez,[c] saying, "I gave birth to him in pain." [10]Jabez cried
out to the God of Israel, "Oh, that you would bless me and enlarge my
territory! Let your hand be with me, and keep me from harm so that I
will be free from pain." And God granted his request.

[11]Kelub, Shuhah's brother, was the father of Mehir, who was the father of Eshton. [12]Eshton was the father of Beth Rapha, Paseah and Tehinnah the father of Ir Nahash.[d] These were the men of Recah.

[13]The sons of Kenaz:
Othniel and Seraiah.
The sons of Othniel:
Hathath and Meonothai.[e] [14]Meonothai was the father of Ophrah.

[a]3 Some Septuagint manuscripts (see also Vulgate); Hebrew *father* [b]4 *Father* may mean *civic leader* or *military leader*; also in verses 12, 14, 17, 18 and possibly elsewhere. [c]9 *Jabez* sounds like the Hebrew for *pain*. [d]12 Or *of the city of Nahash* [e]13 Some Septuagint manuscripts and Vulgate; Hebrew does not have *and Meonothai*.

OPEN **1.** What period or people of history do you enjoy reading about? Of those now in power, whose family history, royal lineage or cultural roots would you like to explore further? Why? **2.** Who in your group can trace their roots back the furthest?

STUDY **1.** Verses 1–8 are a curious replay of an earlier 1 Chronicles listing: Can you "geneatectives" find it? (Note: This coined term depicts astute Bible students who can find treasure in trivia and master God's purpose for these kingdom genealogies.) **2.** In verses 9–10, geneatectives will find the first direct quotation, the first prayer, and the first specific description of God's activity in this book. What do you learn about God's intentions for human life from the strange occurrence of these "firsts"? **3.** How is Jabez's life different due to his prayer? How might Jabez's prayer be related to his mother's pain? What lessons about prayer does Jabez's life exemplify? **4.** What most unusual marriage wins a mention here? What kinds of problems do you imagine Miriam, Shammai and Ishbah might have had with other kids at school? What special problems does Mered likely face by choosing to marry royalty? **5.** What professional groups are singled out for special mention here? What does their mention suggest about the way extended families learned and practiced certain crafts?

APPLY **1.** How have family relations and social institutions changed since grandparents, parents and children all lived and worked together? Did your mom or dad

4:1–23 The chronicler focuses in detail on Judah—David's royal tribe.

4:9–10 The chronicler reminds the reader of the God behind the genealogies. Jabez's short story is a lesson in God's goodness.

want you to follow in their footsteps family-wise, career-wise or otherwise? How so? **2.** Mixed marriages violated the law, yet evidence here suggests that all kinds of family units make up the chosen people. What "odd" families do you admit to your chosen circle of friends (group or church)? **3.** What expectations do you have of your children and their careers? If your extended family or your group joined together to maximize your resources, focus expenses, and train successive generations to do likewise, what might you specialize in? What might you achieve with time?

OPEN 1. How many hands contribute to a loaf of bread getting to the grocery store? **2.** How many workers were involved in making your last hotel stay so pleasant? **3.** Why doesn't the little guy ever hear, "What a great sandwich" or "What a good night's sleep"?

STUDY 1. The little clan of Simeon was absorbed by the bigger tribe of Judah some 400 years after the Exodus. Yet by this genealogy, the chronicler keeps their memory alive. What impresses you from this record of "lost Simeon"? **2.** From other lists of Simeon's sons (Gen. 46; Ex. 6; Num. 26), you geneatectives face these conundrums: Will the real third

Seraiah was the father of Joab,
the father of Ge Harashim.[a] It was called this because its people were craftsmen.
15 The sons of Caleb son of Jephunneh:
Iru, Elah and Naam.
The son of Elah:
Kenaz.
16 The sons of Jehallelel:
Ziph, Ziphah, Tiria and Asarel.
17 The sons of Ezrah:
Jether, Mered, Epher and Jalon. One of Mered's wives gave birth to Miriam, Shammai and Ishbah the father of Eshtemoa.
18 (His Judean wife gave birth to Jered the father of Gedor, Heber the father of Soco, and Jekuthiel the father of Zanoah.) These were the children of Pharaoh's daughter Bithiah, whom Mered had married.
19 The sons of Hodiah's wife, the sister of Naham:
the father of Keilah the Garmite, and Eshtemoa the Maacathite.
20 The sons of Shimon:
Amnon, Rinnah, Ben-Hanan and Tilon.
The descendants of Ishi:
Zoheth and Ben-Zoheth.
21 The sons of Shelah son of Judah:
Er the father of Lecah, Laadah the father of Mareshah and the clans of the linen workers at Beth Ashbea,
22 Jokim, the men of Cozeba, and Joash and Saraph, who ruled in Moab and Jashubi Lehem. (These records are from ancient times.)
23 They were the potters who lived at Netaim and Gederah; they stayed there and worked for the king.

Simeon

24 The descendants of Simeon:
Nemuel, Jamin, Jarib, Zerah and Shaul;
25 Shallum was Shaul's son, Mibsam his son and Mishma his son.
26 The descendants of Mishma:
Hammuel his son, Zaccur his son and Shimei his son.
27 Shimei had sixteen sons and six daughters, but his brothers did not have many children; so their entire clan did not become as numerous as the people of Judah.
28 They lived in Beersheba, Moladah, Hazar Shual,
29 Bilhah, Ezem, Tolad,
30 Bethuel, Hormah, Ziklag,
31 Beth Marcaboth, Hazar Susim, Beth Biri and Shaaraim. These were their towns until the reign of David.
32 Their surrounding villages were Etam, Ain, Rimmon, Token and Ashan—five towns—
33 and all the

[a] 14 *Ge Harashim* means *valley of craftsmen.*

4:17 Mered. *Unusual marriages* were a part of the family line in vv. 1–21. These unusual marriages were part of the culture. Mered chose to marry Bithiah, daughter of an Egyption Pharaoh.

4:21, 23 Families in Near Eastern society passed along generations of trade and craft secrets to their descendants.

4:24–43 The chronicler mentions Simeon as a part of the nation of Judah. With no land of their own (Josh .19:1–9), these people were taken in by the larger tribe of Judah. They lost their own identity by David's time.

villages around these towns as far as Baalath.[a] These were their
settlements. And they kept a genealogical record.

34 Meshobab, Jamlech, Joshah son of Amaziah, 35 Joel, Jehu son of
Joshibiah, the son of Seraiah, the son of Asiel, 36 also Elioenai,
Jaakobah, Jeshohaiah, Asaiah, Adiel, Jesimiel, Benaiah, 37 and
Ziza son of Shiphi, the son of Allon, the son of Jedaiah, the son of
Shimri, the son of Shemaiah.

38 The men listed above by name were leaders of their clans. Their
families increased greatly, 39 and they went to the outskirts of Gedor
to the east of the valley in search of pasture for their flocks. 40 They
found rich, good pasture, and the land was spacious, peaceful and
quiet. Some Hamites had lived there formerly.

41 The men whose names were listed came in the days of Hezekiah
king of Judah. They attacked the Hamites in their dwellings and also
the Meunites who were there and completely destroyed[b] them, as is
evident to this day. Then they settled in their place, because there was
pasture for their flocks. 42 And five hundred of these Simeonites, led
by Pelatiah, Neariah, Rephaiah and Uzziel, the sons of Ishi, invaded
the hill country of Seir. 43 They killed the remaining Amalekites who
had escaped, and they have lived there to this day.

Reuben

5 The sons of Reuben the firstborn of Israel (he was the firstborn,
but when he defiled his father's marriage bed, his rights as firstborn were given to the sons of Joseph son of Israel; so he could not
be listed in the genealogical record in accordance with his birthright,
2 and though Judah was the strongest of his brothers and a ruler came
from him, the rights of the firstborn belonged to Joseph)— 3 the sons
of Reuben the firstborn of Israel:

Hanoch, Pallu, Hezron and Carmi.

4 The descendants of Joel:
Shemaiah his son, Gog his son,
Shimei his son, 5 Micah his son,
Reaiah his son, Baal his son,
6 and Beerah his son, whom Tiglath-Pileser[c] king of Assyria
took into exile. Beerah was a leader of the Reubenites.

7 Their relatives by clans, listed according to their genealogical
records:
Jeiel the chief, Zechariah, 8 and Bela son of Azaz, the son of
Shema, the son of Joel. They settled in the area from Aroer to
Nebo and Baal Meon. 9 To the east they occupied the land up to
the edge of the desert that extends to the Euphrates River,
because their livestock had increased in Gilead.

10 During Saul's reign they waged war against the Hagrites,
who were defeated at their hands; they occupied the dwellings of
the Hagrites throughout the entire region east of Gilead.

Gad

11 The Gadites lived next to them in Bashan, as far as Salecah:
12 Joel was the chief, Shapham the second, then Janai and Shaphat, in Bashan.

[a]33 Some Septuagint manuscripts (see also Joshua 19:8); Hebrew *Baal* [b]41 The Hebrew term refers to the irrevocable giving over of things or persons to the LORD, often by totally destroying them. [c]6 Hebrew *Tilgath-Pilneser,* a variant of *Tiglath-Pileser*; also in verse 26

son of Simeon please stand up? How long before the Simeon clan intermarries with native women? Why do Shaul's sons seem so familiar (1:29–30)? **3.** What benefits came to the tribe of Judah by their taking in the loyal Simeonites?

APPLY 1. How would you feel if all your heritage was lost in a bigger crowd, as was Simeon's? **2.** What would you do to recover your lost identity?

OPEN 1. How important are your family photos? **2.** Do you keep photos of distant relatives you've never met? Why?

STUDY Chapter 5 records the tribes who settled east of the Jordan, while Joshua led the Hebrews west into Canaan. **1.** What privilege did big brother Reuben forfeit? What does this say about God's justice and mercy? **2.** Imagine Beerah, cut off from the bulk of Israel by a water barrier, defeated by a pagan king and taken captive: How does he explain his share in the covenant to his children? **3.** What do the Reubenites possess (vv. 9–10)?

APPLY 1. How has your spiritual inheritance been affected, for good and for bad, by your actions? By your parents' decisions? **2.** Your family may also have felt cut off by natural boundaries: How so?

OPEN 1. If you could choose your neighbor, would you prefer: Sheriff's deputy? Retirees? Car mechanic? Newlyweds? **2.** Describe your most friendly neighbor ever.

STUDY 1. What kind of neighbors were Gadites to Reubenites (vv. 18–19)? **2.** Given their

valiant bravery and accumulated wealth, how did their history as a tribe end (v. 22)? **3.** Even in defeat, how might the Gadites have found faith and hope during their exile? **4.** How is God portrayed here? **5.** Of the qualities which typify the half-tribe of Manasseh, which do you admire? Despise? Why? **6.** How is the Manasseh clan like, and unlike, the Gad clan?

APPLY 1. Are periods of prosperity or lack of it a part of your family's life cycle? How so? How would you feel about working hard only to have someone take (or tax) it all away? **2.** From what self-imposed or personal "exiles" have you had to recover? How did you recover?

OPEN 1. Which spiritual leader has meant the most to you personally? **2.** Have you ever aspired to be a pastor or priest? Why or why not?

STUDY 1. What two neat halves does this section divide into? Why does the chronicler seem to begin again in verse 16? **2.** What names in this list are familiar to you? Why? **3.** The Levites are given as much prominence as what other tribe? Why is that (Num. 3:5–10)?

13 Their relatives, by families, were:
Michael, Meshullam, Sheba, Jorai, Jacan, Zia and Eber—seven in all.
14 These were the sons of Abihail son of Huri, the son of Jaroah, the son of Gilead, the son of Michael, the son of Jeshishai, the son of Jahdo, the son of Buz.
15 Ahi son of Abdiel, the son of Guni, was head of their family.
16 The Gadites lived in Gilead, in Bashan and its outlying villages, and on all the pasturelands of Sharon as far as they extended.
17 All these were entered in the genealogical records during the reigns of Jotham king of Judah and Jeroboam king of Israel.

18 The Reubenites, the Gadites and the half-tribe of Manasseh had
44,760 men ready for military service—able-bodied men who could
handle shield and sword, who could use a bow, and who were trained
for battle. 19 They waged war against the Hagrites, Jetur, Naphish and
Nodab. 20 They were helped in fighting them, and God handed the
Hagrites and all their allies over to them, because they cried out to
him during the battle. He answered their prayers, because they
trusted in him. 21 They seized the livestock of the Hagrites—fifty thousand camels, two hundred fifty thousand sheep and two thousand
donkeys. They also took one hundred thousand people captive, 22 and
many others fell slain, because the battle was God's. And they occupied the land until the exile.

The Half-Tribe of Manasseh

23 The people of the half-tribe of Manasseh were numerous; they settled in the land from Bashan to Baal Hermon, that is, to Senir (Mount Hermon).

24 These were the heads of their families: Epher, Ishi, Eliel, Azriel,
Jeremiah, Hodaviah and Jahdiel. They were brave warriors, famous
men, and heads of their families. 25 But they were unfaithful to the
God of their fathers and prostituted themselves to the gods of the
peoples of the land, whom God had destroyed before them. 26 So
the God of Israel stirred up the spirit of Pul king of Assyria (that is,
Tiglath-Pileser king of Assyria), who took the Reubenites, the Gadites
and the half-tribe of Manasseh into exile. He took them to Halah,
Habor, Hara and the river of Gozan, where they are to this day.

Levi

6 The sons of Levi:
Gershon, Kohath and Merari.
2 The sons of Kohath:
Amram, Izhar, Hebron and Uzziel.
3 The children of Amram:
Aaron, Moses and Miriam.
The sons of Aaron:
Nadab, Abihu, Eleazar and Ithamar.
4 Eleazar was the father of Phinehas,
Phinehas the father of Abishua,

5:18–22 He answered their prayers. Again, the chronicler inserts a sound byte for God's faithfulness throughout the generations.

5:23–26 Manasseh was uniquely gifted. However, its irreverent idolatry gave the tribe an all-too-common fate: divine discipline.

6:1–3 The office of high priest was a family business. There was no job application or interview—a person could only be born into the role.

[5]Abishua the father of Bukki,
Bukki the father of Uzzi,
[6]Uzzi the father of Zerahiah,
Zerahiah the father of Meraioth,
[7]Meraioth the father of Amariah,
Amariah the father of Ahitub,
[8]Ahitub the father of Zadok,
Zadok the father of Ahimaaz,
[9]Ahimaaz the father of Azariah,
Azariah the father of Johanan,
[10]Johanan the father of Azariah (it was he who served as priest in the temple Solomon built in Jerusalem),
[11]Azariah the father of Amariah,
Amariah the father of Ahitub,
[12]Ahitub the father of Zadok,
Zadok the father of Shallum,
[13]Shallum the father of Hilkiah,
Hilkiah the father of Azariah,
[14]Azariah the father of Seraiah,
and Seraiah the father of Jehozadak.

[15]Jehozadak was deported when the LORD sent Judah and Jerusalem into exile by the hand of Nebuchadnezzar.

[16]The sons of Levi:
Gershon,[a] Kohath and Merari.
[17]These are the names of the sons of Gershon:
Libni and Shimei.
[18]The sons of Kohath:
Amram, Izhar, Hebron and Uzziel.
[19]The sons of Merari:
Mahli and Mushi.

These are the clans of the Levites listed according to their fathers:

[20]Of Gershon:
Libni his son, Jehath his son,
Zimmah his son, [21]Joah his son,
Iddo his son, Zerah his son
and Jeatherai his son.
[22]The descendants of Kohath:
Amminadab his son, Korah his son,
Assir his son, [23]Elkanah his son,
Ebiasaph his son, Assir his son,
[24]Tahath his son, Uriel his son,
Uzziah his son and Shaul his son.
[25]The descendants of Elkanah:
Amasai, Ahimoth,
[26]Elkanah his son,[b] Zophai his son,
Nahath his son, [27]Eliab his son,

[a]*16* Hebrew *Gershom,* a variant of *Gershon*; also in verses 17, 20, 43, 62 and 71 [b]*26* Some Hebrew manuscripts, Septuagint and Syriac; most Hebrew manuscripts *Ahimoth* [26]*and Elkanah. The sons of Elkanah:*

4. What trouble did the first chief priest, Aaron, have with his two oldest sons (Lev. 10:1–3)? What attitude does Aaron show after their demise? **5.** If Aaron is the first high priest, what is the chronicler's intention in this genealogy? **6.** Two of the priests listed here are briefly described (vv. 10,15): Which had the tougher job? **7.** Geneatectives may search the following texts (29:22; 2 Kin. 22; Ezra 3:2; Neh. 11:11;) for clues to these four riddles: Which high priest would be remembered as a martyr? Which high priest led a reformation in the worship of God by discovering a long-lost book? Which served Israel the longest following the greatest time-gap in their formal worship? Which served Israel's most famous king? **8.** While the terrible Nebuchadnezzar may have seemed invincible to Israel, he is a player in a larger drama according to the chronicler. Who writes the script for that drama? **9.** In verses 16 and following, what new information is provided? What info is given two or more versions within this section? **10.** For geneatectives only: What well-known person, listed here as a Levite, is linked to a different tribe in the introduction to the Bible book which bears his name?

APPLY 1. Can you think of a person in your genealogy that you would most want to be like? Who and why? **2.** What trait do you have that your children or grandchildren will most want? **3.** What in your personality would you most like to change?

6:4–15 Aaron was the patriarchal priest (Ex. 28:1). His lineage languished when Jehozadak was taken captive (v. 15).

6:27 Samuel. Samuel faithfully served in the tabernacle as an influential priest and leader. Samuel's family was described as Ephraimites (1 Sam. 1:1). He was clearly a Levite and was dedicated to service in the tabernacle (1 Sam. 2:11).

Jeroham his son, Elkanah his son
and Samuel his son.[a]
28 The sons of Samuel:
Joel[b] the firstborn
and Abijah the second son.
29 The descendants of Merari:
Mahli, Libni his son,
Shimei his son, Uzzah his son,
30 Shimea his son, Haggiah his son
and Asaiah his son.

The Temple Musicians

31 These are the men David put in charge of the music in the house
of the LORD after the ark came to rest there. 32 They ministered with
music before the tabernacle, the Tent of Meeting, until Solomon built
the temple of the LORD in Jerusalem. They performed their duties
according to the regulations laid down for them.
33 Here are the men who served, together with their sons:
From the Kohathites:
Heman, the musician,
the son of Joel, the son of Samuel,
34 the son of Elkanah, the son of Jeroham,
the son of Eliel, the son of Toah,
35 the son of Zuph, the son of Elkanah,
the son of Mahath, the son of Amasai,
36 the son of Elkanah, the son of Joel,
the son of Azariah, the son of Zephaniah,
37 the son of Tahath, the son of Assir,
the son of Ebiasaph, the son of Korah,
38 the son of Izhar, the son of Kohath,
the son of Levi, the son of Israel;
39 and Heman's associate Asaph, who served at his right hand:
Asaph son of Berekiah, the son of Shimea,
40 the son of Michael, the son of Baaseiah,[c]
the son of Malkijah, 41 the son of Ethni,
the son of Zerah, the son of Adaiah,
42 the son of Ethan, the son of Zimmah,
the son of Shimei, 43 the son of Jahath,
the son of Gershon, the son of Levi;
44 and from their associates, the Merarites, at his left hand:
Ethan son of Kishi, the son of Abdi,
the son of Malluch, 45 the son of Hashabiah,
the son of Amaziah, the son of Hilkiah,
46 the son of Amzi, the son of Bani,
the son of Shemer, 47 the son of Mahli,
the son of Mushi, the son of Merari,
the son of Levi.

48 Their fellow Levites were assigned to all the other duties of the
tabernacle, the house of God. 49 But Aaron and his descendants were
the ones who presented offerings on the altar of burnt offering and

[a]*27* Some Septuagint manuscripts (see also 1 Samuel 1:19,20 and 1 Chron. 6:33,34); Hebrew does not have *and Samuel his son.* [b]*28* Some Septuagint manuscripts and Syriac (see also 1 Samuel 8:2 and 1 Chron. 6:33); Hebrew does not have *Joel.* [c]*40* Most Hebrew manuscripts; some Hebrew manuscripts, one Septuagint manuscript and Syriac *Maaseiah*

OPEN **1.** What kind of music gets the most air-time in your home? What instruments make most of that music? **2.** What differences in musical taste are apparent in your family? What accounts for those differences: Generational gap? Influence of rock culture? God-given abilities and preferences? Church-dictated no-no's?

STUDY **1.** What does David do here (v. 31)? Up to now, what has he been chiefly concerned about (3:1–9)? **2.** Knowing their new king cared much about music and could make music himself (1 Sam. 16:14–23), how might that affect "Mr. and Mrs. Benjamite"? **3.** Compare this list of Kohathites (vv. 33–38) with the previous ones. What differences do you observe? Why trace Heman's contribution to the musicians' guild? **4.** Likewise, what is the meaning of Asaph's contribution among the Gershonites (vv. 38–43)? What do you know about the career of this leading vocalist/instrumentalist of Israel's golden age (16:4–7,37; 25:5–6; 2 Chr. 5:12; 29:30; 35:15; Neh. 12:45–47)? What works of this composer do you know (Ps(s). 50,73–83)? **5.** The third group is the Merarites, featuring Ethan. How many generations of training did Ethan have behind him (vv. 44–47)? **6.** What separates the priestly line of Aaron from the rest of the Levites (vv. 48–49)? To whom does the chronicler trace all "rules and regulations" of worship? **7.** Verses 54–81 list what resources? Why is the author so careful to list property outside the city limits? What kind of resources might be attached to such a list of "tax-exempt" real estate today? How might this list have been used to solve legal disputes? **8.** What cities are described? See Numbers 35:5–34 for details about the special status of those cities: Who needed them? What problems did they solve? Why would the Levites be ideal caretakers for such sanctuaries? **9.** The Levites received all their property from

on the altar of incense in connection with all that was done in the Most Holy Place, making atonement for Israel, in accordance with all that Moses the servant of God had commanded.

[50]These were the descendants of Aaron:
Eleazar his son, Phinehas his son,
Abishua his son, [51]Bukki his son,
Uzzi his son, Zerahiah his son,
[52]Meraioth his son, Amariah his son,
Ahitub his son, [53]Zadok his son
and Ahimaaz his son.

[54]These were the locations of their settlements allotted as their territory (they were assigned to the descendants of Aaron who were from the Kohathite clan, because the first lot was for them):
[55]They were given Hebron in Judah with its surrounding
pasturelands. [56]But the fields and villages around the city were
given to Caleb son of Jephunneh.
[57]So the descendants of Aaron were given Hebron (a city of
refuge), and Libnah,[a] Jattir, Eshtemoa, [58]Hilen, Debir, [59]Ashan,
Juttah[b] and Beth Shemesh, together with their pasturelands.
[60]And from the tribe of Benjamin they were given Gibeon,[c] Geba,
Alemeth and Anathoth, together with their pasturelands.
These towns, which were distributed among the Kohathite clans, were thirteen in all.
[61]The rest of Kohath's descendants were allotted ten towns from the clans of half the tribe of Manasseh.
[62]The descendants of Gershon, clan by clan, were allotted thirteen towns from the tribes of Issachar, Asher and Naphtali, and from the part of the tribe of Manasseh that is in Bashan.
[63]The descendants of Merari, clan by clan, were allotted twelve towns from the tribes of Reuben, Gad and Zebulun.
[64]So the Israelites gave the Levites these towns and their pasture-
lands. [65]From the tribes of Judah, Simeon and Benjamin they allotted
the previously named towns.
[66]Some of the Kohathite clans were given as their territory towns from the tribe of Ephraim.
[67]In the hill country of Ephraim they were given Shechem (a
city of refuge), and Gezer,[d] [68]Jokmeam, Beth Horon, [69]Aijalon and
Gath Rimmon, together with their pasturelands.
[70]And from half the tribe of Manasseh the Israelites gave Aner and Bileam, together with their pasturelands, to the rest of the Kohathite clans.

[71]The Gershonites received the following:
From the clan of the half-tribe of Manasseh
they received Golan in Bashan and also Ashtaroth, together with their pasturelands;
[72]from the tribe of Issachar
they received Kedesh, Daberath, [73]Ramoth and Anem, together with their pasturelands;
[74]from the tribe of Asher
they received Mashal, Abdon, [75]Hukok and Rehob, together

[a]57 See Joshua 21:13; Hebrew *given the cities of refuge: Hebron, Libnah.* [b]59 Syriac (see also Septuagint and Joshua 21:16); Hebrew does not have *Juttah.* [c]60 See Joshua 21:17; Hebrew does not have *Gibeon.* [d]67 See Joshua 21:21; Hebrew *given the cities of refuge: Shechem, Gezer.*

allotments given to (or won by) other tribes. In some cases, this meant armed tribes must conquer and bequeath that area for the Levites. What special bonds and resentments could this cause?

APPLY 1. Given the generations of training in music built into Heman, Asaph and Ethan, what kind of pressure from the laity are they laboring under? When have you faced similar pressure to perform and live up to your family name? **2.** The Levite's resources were widely known (once the chronicler published them). For what resources have you been given stewardship duties? Would you mind making them public to your church or even your group? Why? **3.** If the church is to continue the Levites' role in providing sanctuary, what role would your church be prepared to take regarding: Criminal refugees? Child abuse refugees? Political refugees? **4.** The armed tribes of Israel were to give a portion of their property to the Levites (and possibly also do battle for them), causing some indebtedness and resentment. We see this today in similar laity and clergy tensions. Which of today's abuses need attention where you live and worship? Why would you share your personal gains with your "Levite" minister?

with their pasturelands;
76 and from the tribe of Naphtali
they received Kedesh in Galilee, Hammon and Kiriathaim,
together with their pasturelands.

77 The Merarites (the rest of the Levites) received the following:
From the tribe of Zebulun
they received Jokneam, Kartah,[a] Rimmono and Tabor, together
with their pasturelands;
78 from the tribe of Reuben across the Jordan east of Jericho
they received Bezer in the desert, Jahzah, 79 Kedemoth and
Mephaath, together with their pasturelands;
80 and from the tribe of Gad
they received Ramoth in Gilead, Mahanaim, 81 Heshbon and
Jazer, together with their pasturelands.

Issachar

7 The sons of Issachar:
Tola, Puah, Jashub and Shimron—four in all.
2 The sons of Tola:
Uzzi, Rephaiah, Jeriel, Jahmai, Ibsam and Samuel—heads of
their families. During the reign of David, the descendants of
Tola listed as fighting men in their genealogy numbered
22,600.
3 The son of Uzzi:
Izrahiah.
The sons of Izrahiah:
Michael, Obadiah, Joel and Isshiah. All five of them were
chiefs. 4 According to their family genealogy, they had 36,000
men ready for battle, for they had many wives and children.
5 The relatives who were fighting men belonging to all the clans of
Issachar, as listed in their genealogy, were 87,000 in all.

Benjamin

6 Three sons of Benjamin:
Bela, Beker and Jediael.
7 The sons of Bela:
Ezbon, Uzzi, Uzziel, Jerimoth and Iri, heads of families—five in
all. Their genealogical record listed 22,034 fighting men.
8 The sons of Beker:
Zemirah, Joash, Eliezer, Elioenai, Omri, Jeremoth, Abijah, Anathoth and Alemeth. All these were the sons of Beker. 9 Their genealogical record listed the heads of families and 20,200
fighting men.
10 The son of Jediael:
Bilhan.
The sons of Bilhan:
Jeush, Benjamin, Ehud, Kenaanah, Zethan, Tarshish and

[a]77 See Septuagint and Joshua 21:34; Hebrew does not have *Jokneam, Kartah.*

OPEN **1.** In your family tree, are there any branches that had only daughters? Who in your group comes from a line that produces mostly females? **2.** What names (maiden name, spouse's pet name, childhood nicknames) do you go by in various circles? Would a later generation be able to recognize the one person behind all the names? Why or why not?

STUDY **1.** Comparing these numbers to earlier surveys (Gen. 46:13; Num. 26:25), is Issachar a "growth clan" or a "declining tribe"? **2.** Compare this list of Benjamin's three sons with other lists (8:1–2; Gen. 46:21; Num. 26:38–39). How do you account for the differences? What does Bela's repeated mention say about the significance of firstborn sons? **3.** Compare the same lists for the sons of that firstborn Bela. Why are no two names the same? What purpose is served by such variable lists? Or do verses 6–12 more suitably fit the clans of Zebulun and Dan (as vv. 6–12 does not match with what is known of Benjamin's lineage)? **4.** How might Manasseh qualify for "My Most Unforgettable Character" in *Readers' Digest* or at least in Joseph's clan (Gen. 41:51)? **5.** Manasseh's clan seems dominated by women: What does that suggest? A wife and sister with the same name (vv. 15–16) implies what? To dismiss one son who "had only daughters" not worth naming (Num. 26:33) implies what? **6.** Of what famous grandparents can Ephraim's clan brag (Gen. 41:51–52;

7:1–5 The chronicler details Issachar's strength in numbers during its most populated era.

7:6–12 Other lists give varying figures for the number of Benjamin's sons (8:1–2; Gen. 46:21). Genealogies provided various functions for the people, which is why the chronicler likely slanted his count to include only those in the military.

Ahishahar. [11]All these sons of Jediael were heads of families.
There were 17,200 fighting men ready to go out to war.
[12]The Shuppites and Huppites were the descendants of Ir, and the
Hushites the descendants of Aher.

Naphtali

[13]The sons of Naphtali:
Jahziel, Guni, Jezer and Shillem[a]—the descendants of Bilhah.

Manasseh

[14]The descendants of Manasseh:
Asriel was his descendant through his Aramean concubine.
She gave birth to Makir the father of Gilead. [15]Makir took a wife
from among the Huppites and Shuppites. His sister's name was
Maacah.
Another descendant was named Zelophehad, who had only
daughters.
[16]Makir's wife Maacah gave birth to a son and named him
Peresh. His brother was named Sheresh, and his sons were Ulam
and Rakem.
[17]The son of Ulam:
Bedan.
These were the sons of Gilead son of Makir, the son of Manasseh. [18]His sister Hammoleketh gave birth to Ishhod, Abiezer
and Mahlah.
[19]The sons of Shemida were:
Ahian, Shechem, Likhi and Aniam.

Ephraim

[20]The descendants of Ephraim:
Shuthelah, Bered his son,
Tahath his son, Eleadah his son,
Tahath his son, [21]Zabad his son
and Shuthelah his son.
Ezer and Elead were killed by the native-born men of Gath,
when they went down to seize their livestock. [22]Their father
Ephraim mourned for them many days, and his relatives came to
comfort him. [23]Then he lay with his wife again, and she became
pregnant and gave birth to a son. He named him Beriah,[b] because there had been misfortune in his family. [24]His daughter
was Sheerah, who built Lower and Upper Beth Horon as well as
Uzzen Sheerah.
[25]Rephah was his son, Resheph his son,[c]
Telah his son, Tahan his son,
[26]Ladan his son, Ammihud his son,
Elishama his son, [27]Nun his son
and Joshua his son.

[a]13 Some Hebrew and Septuagint manuscripts (see also Gen. 46:24 and Num. 26:49); most Hebrew manuscripts *Shallum* [b]23 *Beriah* sounds like the Hebrew for *misfortune.* [c]25 Some Septuagint manuscripts; Hebrew does not have *his son.*

46:20)? And of what favorite son, ten generations (400 years) removed from Joseph (vv. 25–27)? **7.** How has Ephraim's clan felt the misfortune of two "cattle thieves" and "frontier justice" (vv. 21–24)? **8.** If Ephraim's clan is noted for its grief and its favorite son Joshua, what are "Asher" (Gen. 30:9–13) and his clan noted for (v. 40)? **9.** Of all the genealogies in chapter 7, which ones are "linear" (tracing a single line of descent) and which are "segmented" (tracing several lines)? What does this say about the chronicler's purpose?

APPLY 1. With this chapter reading like a military roster or draft lottery, the protection function surely dominates the chronicler's concerns. How willing are you to be counted among the protectors of your people? Who in your town could use "fighting men" to escort them? How can you help others feel safe where you live? **2.** How have you learned, like Makir and other descendants of "unforgettable" Manasseh, to forget the troubles of the past (no sons, no eligible women) and make the best of the hand you are dealt? What griefs do you need to forget? What can this group specifically pray for? **3.** What grief-stricken families does Ephraim's clan bring to mind for you? How might their "Beriah" (child of misfortune) find a home in your group or church fellowship? What are you all doing to help families recover a sense of hope after suffering loss and grief?

7:12 It seems the Hushites are descendants of Dan (Gen. 46:23).

7:14–19 For a document of this period highlighting women was an unusual, though legitimate, function of a genealogy.

28 Their lands and settlements included Bethel and its surrounding
villages, Naaran to the east, Gezer and its villages to the west, and
Shechem and its villages all the way to Ayyah and its villages. 29 Along
the borders of Manasseh were Beth Shan, Taanach, Megiddo and Dor,
together with their villages. The descendants of Joseph son of Israel
lived in these towns.

Asher

30 The sons of Asher:
Imnah, Ishvah, Ishvi and Beriah. Their sister was Serah.
31 The sons of Beriah:
Heber and Malkiel, who was the father of Birzaith.
32 Heber was the father of Japhlet, Shomer and Hotham and of their sister Shua.
33 The sons of Japhlet:
Pasach, Bimhal and Ashvath.
These were Japhlet's sons.
34 The sons of Shomer:
Ahi, Rohgah,[a] Hubbah and Aram.
35 The sons of his brother Helem:
Zophah, Imna, Shelesh and Amal.
36 The sons of Zophah:
Suah, Harnepher, Shual, Beri, Imrah, 37 Bezer, Hod, Shamma,
Shilshah, Ithran[b] and Beera.
38 The sons of Jether:
Jephunneh, Pispah and Ara.
39 The sons of Ulla:
Arah, Hanniel and Rizia.

40 All these were descendants of Asher—heads of families, choice
men, brave warriors and outstanding leaders. The number of men
ready for battle, as listed in their genealogy, was 26,000.

The Genealogy of Saul the Benjamite

8 Benjamin was the father of Bela his firstborn,
Ashbel the second son, Aharah the third,
2 Nohah the fourth and Rapha the fifth.
3 The sons of Bela were:
Addar, Gera, Abihud,[c] 4 Abishua, Naaman, Ahoah, 5 Gera, She-
phuphan and Huram.
6 These were the descendants of Ehud, who were heads of families of those living in Geba and were deported to Manahath:
7 Naaman, Ahijah, and Gera, who deported them and who was the father of Uzza and Ahihud.
8 Sons were born to Shaharaim in Moab after he had divorced his
wives Hushim and Baara. 9 By his wife Hodesh he had Jobab,
Zibia, Mesha, Malcam, 10 Jeuz, Sakia and Mirmah. These were

[a]34 Or *of his brother Shomer: Rohgah* [b]37 Possibly a variant of *Jether* [c]3 Or *Gera the father of Ehud*

OPEN 1. When have you been jealous of a younger sibling who got more press than you did? **2.** What did your parents almost name you but didn't? **3.** What is the strangest name you have heard?

STUDY 1. Only Judah and Levi get more press coverage of their descendants by the chronicler. What does the inclusion of this extensive genealogy of Benjamin imply about the purpose of the chronicler? Who from this tribe is he interested in? Why extend his line from the Patriarchs all the way to the Exile? **2.** What likely embarrassing social arrangements and family blessings do you see in verses 8–11? From the

7:30–40 Asher. Asher stood out from the clan. It was a tribe of leaders and outstanding warriors (Gen. 30:9–13). Asher was the son of Jacob. His mother was Leah's servant Zilpah.

8:1–40 Benjamin's tribe, the tribe of Saul, earns a second helping of highlights (7:6–12). Understanding Saul's historical context early on allows the chronicler to pick up the story at Saul's death in chapter ten.

his sons, heads of families. [11]By Hushim he had Abitub and Elpaal.

[12]The sons of Elpaal:

Eber, Misham, Shemed (who built Ono and Lod with its surrounding villages), [13]and Beriah and Shema, who were heads of families of those living in Aijalon and who drove out the inhabitants of Gath.

[14]Ahio, Shashak, Jeremoth, [15]Zebadiah, Arad, Eder, [16]Michael, Ishpah and Joha were the sons of Beriah.

[17]Zebadiah, Meshullam, Hizki, Heber, [18]Ishmerai, Izliah and Jobab were the sons of Elpaal.

[19]Jakim, Zicri, Zabdi, [20]Elienai, Zillethai, Eliel, [21]Adaiah, Beraiah and Shimrath were the sons of Shimei.

[22]Ishpan, Eber, Eliel, [23]Abdon, Zicri, Hanan, [24]Hananiah, Elam, Anthothijah, [25]Iphdeiah and Penuel were the sons of Shashak.

[26]Shamsherai, Shehariah, Athaliah, [27]Jaareshiah, Elijah and Zicri were the sons of Jeroham.

[28]All these were heads of families, chiefs as listed in their genealogy, and they lived in Jerusalem.

[29]Jeiel[a] the father[b] of Gibeon lived in Gibeon.

His wife's name was Maacah, [30]and his firstborn son was Abdon, followed by Zur, Kish, Baal, Ner,[c] Nadab, [31]Gedor, Ahio, Zeker [32]and Mikloth, who was the father of Shimeah. They too lived near their relatives in Jerusalem.

[33]Ner was the father of Kish, Kish the father of Saul, and Saul the father of Jonathan, Malki-Shua, Abinadab and Esh-Baal.[d]

[34]The son of Jonathan:

Merib-Baal,[e] who was the father of Micah.

[35]The sons of Micah:

Pithon, Melech, Tarea and Ahaz.

[36]Ahaz was the father of Jehoaddah, Jehoaddah was the father of Alemeth, Azmaveth and Zimri, and Zimri was the father of Moza. [37]Moza was the father of Binea; Raphah was his son, Eleasah his son and Azel his son.

[38]Azel had six sons, and these were their names:

Azrikam, Bokeru, Ishmael, Sheariah, Obadiah and Hanan. All these were the sons of Azel.

[39]The sons of his brother Eshek:

Ulam his firstborn, Jeush the second son and Eliphelet the third. [40]The sons of Ulam were brave warriors who could handle the bow. They had many sons and grandsons—150 in all.

All these were the descendants of Benjamin.

[a]29 Some Septuagint manuscripts (see also 1 Chron. 9:35); Hebrew does not have *Jeiel.* [b]29 *Father* may mean *civic leader* or *military leader.* [c]30 Some Septuagint manuscripts (see also 1 Chron. 9:36); Hebrew does not have *Ner.* [d]33 Also known as *Ish-Bosheth* [e]34 Also known as *Mephibosheth*

hints offered here, why do you think Shaharaim divorced not one wife, but two? Could he have acted within his rights? How so? **3.** What relationship do Ner and Kish share here (vv. 31,33)? How does that compare with the record in 1 Samuel 9:1 and 1 Samuel 14:51? Why the variance? **4.** Loyal Israelites despised the pagan god Baal. How then do you account for Baal-names given to Saul's sons and grandsons (vv. 33–34), names which were later changed (2 Sam. 2:8; 4:4)? **5.** What is the "weakest link" in the chain of Saul's descendants? What does this say about God's enduring love for the Benjamite tribe?

APPLY 1. Who do you know who has changed his or her given name? Under what conditions would you change yours? **2.** The fortunes of families often change rapidly, being just one generation away from extinction. In the line of King Saul, this is true career-wise, biologically and spiritually. How is that true of your family? Who will inherit the family business? Any male heirs to pass along the family name? Any spiritual heirs to spread God's name? **3.** What's in a name, yours or your children's? How can one overdo the meaning of a name and saddle a kid for life?

8:28 they lived in Jerusalem. These are families of Benjamin that lived in Jerusalem. It is interesting to note that Jerusalem was not occupied until David's time. With this representation of Saul's tribe, Benjamin, in Jerusalem it is evident that David did not exclude Saul's relations from favorable positions in Israel.

8:33 Esh-Baal. Also known as Ish-Bosheth was Saul's youngest son and ruled over Israel (2 Sam. 2:8–10). Esh-Baal was a pagan name and illustrates the influence of paganism into the best families.

9

All Israel was listed in the genealogies recorded in the book of
the kings of Israel.

The People in Jerusalem

The people of Judah were taken captive to Babylon because of their
unfaithfulness. 2 Now the first to resettle on their own property in
their own towns were some Israelites, priests, Levites and temple
servants.
3 Those from Judah, from Benjamin, and from Ephraim and Manasseh who lived in Jerusalem were:
4 Uthai son of Ammihud, the son of Omri, the son of Imri, the son
of Bani, a descendant of Perez son of Judah.
5 Of the Shilonites:
Asaiah the firstborn and his sons.
6 Of the Zerahites:
Jeuel.
The people from Judah numbered 690.
7 Of the Benjamites:
Sallu son of Meshullam, the son of Hodaviah, the son of Hassenuah;
8 Ibneiah son of Jeroham; Elah son of Uzzi, the son of Micri; and
Meshullam son of Shephatiah, the son of Reuel, the son of
Ibnijah.
9 The people from Benjamin, as listed in their genealogy, numbered 956. All these men were heads of their families.
10 Of the priests:
Jedaiah; Jehoiarib; Jakin;
11 Azariah son of Hilkiah, the son of Meshullam, the son of
Zadok, the son of Meraioth, the son of Ahitub, the official in
charge of the house of God;
12 Adaiah son of Jeroham, the son of Pashhur, the son of Malkijah; and Maasai son of Adiel, the son of Jahzerah, the son of
Meshullam, the son of Meshillemith, the son of Immer.
13 The priests, who were heads of families, numbered 1,760.
They were able men, responsible for ministering in the house
of God.
14 Of the Levites:
Shemaiah son of Hasshub, the son of Azrikam, the son of
Hashabiah, a Merarite; 15 Bakbakkar, Heresh, Galal and Mattaniah son of Mica, the son of Zicri, the son of Asaph; 16 Obadiah
son of Shemaiah, the son of Galal, the son of Jeduthun; and
Berekiah son of Asa, the son of Elkanah, who lived in the villages of the Netophathites.
17 The gatekeepers:
Shallum, Akkub, Talmon, Ahiman and their brothers, Shallum
their chief 18 being stationed at the King's Gate on the east, up
to the present time. These were the gatekeepers belonging to

OPEN 1. How do you benefit from "many hands" or "shared work" to get tasks done: Carpooling kids? Difficult tasks at work? Co-parenting? Childcare? Church work? Other? **2.** When have you suffered because you didn't have the needed help?

STUDY 1. What is the time gap between verses 1 and 2? After years in captivity, and suffering great personal and material loss, what problems must the Israelites deal with in recovering their grand heritage? For example, how did they settle the issue of who owned what property? And what resources could they rely upon to begin again? **2.** Why do you think "some Israelites, priests, Levites and temple servants" (v. 2) were the first to resettle the land? What services would they add to nation-building that valiant warriors or clever architects could not? **3.** Where else do the returnees come from (v. 3)? How does this migration from north and south flesh out the meaning of "all Israel" (v. 1; 11:1–4)? **4.** Why mention here all the gatekeepers and their duties? Can you think of people in your church or group that might be overlooked in a listing of church workers? **5.** Which of the job assignments seem menial? Which require special skill, the right connections or the trust of VIPs? Which were performed "day and night"? Which required weekly shift rotations? Who had the graveyard shift? **6.** Carrying forward "something old and something new" helps many couples forge a new identity and begin again in married life. How was this true for the returning Israelites who had to forge a new identity out of resources from the past? Have you ever had a chance to start something over again? **7.** Where have you seen these names before? Why dredge up Saul's family line one more time? Why is it repeated in this context?

APPLY 1. Why did the Israelites take such precautions about guarding the "Tent of God"? Today, what sacred buildings are guarded heavily? **2.** In what sense have you inherited charge of the key

---

9:2–34 All who returned to their homeland after the Exile are *identified within their respective social* categories.

9:4–6 The chronicler's records served as an important "who's who" directory for the returnees. Genealogy played a *crucial role in restoring* individual identity, family role and social class to a lost people.

9:10–13 A match was made between historical record (6:12–13) and contemporary record and headcount here and in Nehemiah 11:10–14. The people's ties with the past gave them a perspective on the present and hope for the future.

the camp of the Levites. 19Shallum son of Kore, the son of Ebiasaph, the son of Korah, and his fellow gatekeepers from his
family (the Korahites) were responsible for guarding the
thresholds of the Tent[a] just as their fathers had been responsible for guarding the entrance to the dwelling of the LORD.
20In earlier times Phinehas son of Eleazar was in charge of the
gatekeepers, and the LORD was with him. 21Zechariah son of
Meshelemiah was the gatekeeper at the entrance to the Tent of
Meeting.
22Altogether, those chosen to be gatekeepers at the thresholds
numbered 212. They were registered by genealogy in their villages.
The gatekeepers had been assigned to their positions of trust by David and Samuel the seer. 23They and their descendants were in charge
of guarding the gates of the house of the LORD—the house called the
Tent. 24The gatekeepers were on the four sides: east, west, north and
south. 25Their brothers in their villages had to come from time to time
and share their duties for seven-day periods. 26But the four principal
gatekeepers, who were Levites, were entrusted with the responsibility for the rooms and treasuries in the house of God. 27They would
spend the night stationed around the house of God, because they had
to guard it; and they had charge of the key for opening it each
morning.
28Some of them were in charge of the articles used in the temple
service; they counted them when they were brought in and when they
were taken out. 29Others were assigned to take care of the furnishings and all the other articles of the sanctuary, as well as the flour
and wine, and the oil, incense and spices. 30But some of the priests
took care of mixing the spices. 31A Levite named Mattithiah, the firstborn son of Shallum the Korahite, was entrusted with the responsibility for baking the offering bread. 32Some of their Kohathite
brothers were in charge of preparing for every Sabbath the bread set
out on the table.
33Those who were musicians, heads of Levite families, stayed in
the rooms of the temple and were exempt from other duties because
they were responsible for the work day and night.
34All these were heads of Levite families, chiefs as listed in their genealogy, and they lived in Jerusalem.

The Genealogy of Saul

35Jeiel the father[b] of Gibeon lived in Gibeon.
His wife's name was Maacah, 36and his firstborn son was
Abdon, followed by Zur, Kish, Baal, Ner, Nadab, 37Gedor, Ahio,
Zechariah and Mikloth. 38Mikloth was the father of Shimeam.
They too lived near their relatives in Jerusalem.
39Ner was the father of Kish, Kish the father of Saul, and Saul the
father of Jonathan, Malki-Shua, Abinadab and Esh-Baal.[c]

[a]19 That is, the temple; also in verses 21 and 23 [b]35 *Father* may mean *civic leader* or *military leader.*
[c]39 Also known as *Ish-Bosheth*

to the house of God? Who are you letting in ... or keeping out? **3.** Who carries responsibilities for rules, rituals, receipts and recipes in your place of worship? **4.** How does your fellowship encourage delegation of its leadership roles and full participation by its members? What reentry points do you have for people disoriented by great personal and material loss?

9:19 Korah. These were descendants of Kohath who were close relations to the priests.

9:22–27 The gatekeepers served as the neighborhood block watch. Refugees rebuilt their lives amid ruin.

9:28–34 This division of the Levites consisted of civic duty specialists. They cared for the house of God.

40 The son of Jonathan:
Merib-Baal,[a] who was the father of Micah.
41 The sons of Micah:
Pithon, Melech, Tahrea and Ahaz.[b]
42 Ahaz was the father of Jadah, Jadah[c] was the father of Alemeth,
Azmaveth and Zimri, and Zimri was the father of Moza. 43 Moza
was the father of Binea; Rephaiah was his son, Eleasah his son
and Azel his son.
44 Azel had six sons, and these were their names:
Azrikam, Bokeru, Ishmael, Sheariah, Obadiah and Hanan.
These were the sons of Azel.

Saul Takes His Life

10 Now the Philistines fought against Israel; the Israelites fled
before them, and many fell slain on Mount Gilboa. 2 The
Philistines pressed hard after Saul and his sons, and they killed his
sons Jonathan, Abinadab and Malki-Shua. 3 The fighting grew fierce
around Saul, and when the archers overtook him, they wounded him.
4 Saul said to his armor-bearer, "Draw your sword and run me
through, or these uncircumcised fellows will come and abuse me."
But his armor-bearer was terrified and would not do it; so Saul
took his own sword and fell on it. 5 When the armor-bearer saw that
Saul was dead, he too fell on his sword and died. 6 So Saul and his
three sons died, and all his house died together.
7 When all the Israelites in the valley saw that the army had fled and
that Saul and his sons had died, they abandoned their towns and
fled. And the Philistines came and occupied them.
8 The next day, when the Philistines came to strip the dead, they
found Saul and his sons fallen on Mount Gilboa. 9 They stripped him
and took his head and his armor, and sent messengers throughout
the land of the Philistines to proclaim the news among their idols and
their people. 10 They put his armor in the temple of their gods and
hung up his head in the temple of Dagon.
11 When all the inhabitants of Jabesh Gilead heard of everything the
Philistines had done to Saul, 12 all their valiant men went and took the
bodies of Saul and his sons and brought them to Jabesh. Then they
buried their bones under the great tree in Jabesh, and they fasted
seven days.
13 Saul died because he was unfaithful to the LORD; he did not keep
the word of the LORD and even consulted a medium for guidance,
14 and did not inquire of the LORD. So the LORD put him to death and
turned the kingdom over to David son of Jesse.

David Becomes King Over Israel

11 All Israel came together to David at Hebron and said, "We are
your own flesh and blood. 2 In the past, even while Saul was
king, you were the one who led Israel on their military campaigns.

[a] *40* Also known as *Mephibosheth* [b] *41* Vulgate and Syriac (see also Septuagint and 1 Chron. 8:35); Hebrew does not have *and Ahaz.* [c] *42* Some Hebrew manuscripts and Septuagint (see also 1 Chron. 8:36); most Hebrew manuscripts *Jarah, Jarah*

OPEN 1. What death of a famous person has personally impacted you the most? **2.** Which way do you think you might die: "Rust out" (old age)? "Burn out" (in your prime)? Or "dropout" (in some accident)?

STUDY 1. Put yourself in this story, amid slain comrades, fiercely defending your king: How do you feel when the enemy catches up with Saul and his sons? How do you react to his death? Why do you abandon your homestead just because your king has died? Why do you risk taking Saul's head and armor to a place of honor? **2.** As Saul, why do you ask your armor-bearer to kill you? As Saul's armor-bearer, why do you refuse to take Saul's life (2 Sam. 1:14), but take your own? **3.** Why does the chronicler say "all his house died together," when one son survives to succeed Saul (v. 6; 2 Sam. 2:8–10)? **4.** What view of Saul's history and God's will does the chronicler offer?

APPLY 1. The Puritans stressed "dying well" as a Christian witness. How can you be prepared to die well? **2.** What is the relation between living well and dying well as typified by Saul? Why is Saul's story sad?

OPEN 1. How many times have you backed the eventual winning President? What big losers will you admit voting for? **2.** What up-hill battle have you won in recent years? How did that make you feel?

10:11 Saul. He had been chosen by God to lead Israel. His disobedience led to his downfall and ultimately his death.

11:1–3 David accepts Israel's landslide nomination for king.

And the LORD your God said to you, 'You will shepherd my people
Israel, and you will become their ruler.' "
3When all the elders of Israel had come to King David at Hebron, he
made a compact with them at Hebron before the LORD, and they
anointed David king over Israel, as the LORD had promised through
Samuel.

David Conquers Jerusalem

4David and all the Israelites marched to Jerusalem (that is, Jebus).
The Jebusites who lived there 5said to David, "You will not get in
here." Nevertheless, David captured the fortress of Zion, the City of
David.
6David had said, "Whoever leads the attack on the Jebusites will
become commander-in-chief." Joab son of Zeruiah went up first, and
so he received the command.
7David then took up residence in the fortress, and so it was called
the City of David. 8He built up the city around it, from the supporting
terraces[a] to the surrounding wall, while Joab restored the rest of the
city. 9And David became more and more powerful, because the LORD
Almighty was with him.

David's Mighty Men

10These were the chiefs of David's mighty men—they, together with
all Israel, gave his kingship strong support to extend it over the whole
land, as the LORD had promised— 11this is the list of David's mighty
men:
Jashobeam,[b] a Hacmonite, was chief of the officers[c]; he raised his
spear against three hundred men, whom he killed in one encounter.
12Next to him was Eleazar son of Dodai the Ahohite, one of the
three mighty men. 13He was with David at Pas Dammim when the
Philistines gathered there for battle. At a place where there was a
field full of barley, the troops fled from the Philistines. 14But they took
their stand in the middle of the field. They defended it and struck the
Philistines down, and the LORD brought about a great victory.
15Three of the thirty chiefs came down to David to the rock at the
cave of Adullam, while a band of Philistines was encamped in the Valley of Rephaim. 16At that time David was in the stronghold, and the
Philistine garrison was at Bethlehem. 17David longed for water and
said, "Oh, that someone would get me a drink of water from the well
near the gate of Bethlehem!" 18So the Three broke through the Philistine lines, drew water from the well near the gate of Bethlehem and
carried it back to David. But he refused to drink it; instead, he poured
it out before the LORD. 19"God forbid that I should do this!" he said.
"Should I drink the blood of these men who went at the risk of their
lives?" Because they risked their lives to bring it back, David would
not drink it.
Such were the exploits of the three mighty men.

[a]8 Or *the Millo* [b]11 Possibly a variant of *Jashob-Baal* [c]11 Or *Thirty*; some Septuagint manuscripts *Three* (see also 2 Samuel 23:8)

STUDY 1. What unanimous ballot does the chronicler cast for David where a split kingdom was indicated (2 Sam. 5:4–5)? **2.** What does David do that others said couldn't be done? What managerial and motivational techniques does David use to reach his impossible goal? **3.** Do you know of someone who has risen to a prominent position like David? Could that also be attributed to God?

APPLY Do you think God's will has anything to do with national elections or prosperity?

OPEN 1. What do you consider one of your greatest accomplishments? Why? What obstacles did you have to overcome to do it? **2.** Who was your favorite "superhero": Superman? Batman? Luke Skywalker? Indiana Jones? Other?

STUDY 1. What in this chapter suggests that David knew he could not fulfill *by himself* God's will for the nation? Do you know of any person who might be of the stature of David's "mighty men"? **2.** Which men do you think were "the Three" at the top of his list (vv. 12,15,18–19,21,24–25; 2 Sam. 23:9–11)? **3.** When in David's lifetime do you think the event of verses 15–19 occurred (1 Sam. 22:1 or 2 Sam. 5:17)? Why would a great military hero like David be hiding out in a cave? How do you think David felt when his three mighty men offered him the water? How would his men have felt when he then poured it on the ground? **4.** What do Abishai and Jashobeam have in common (vv. 11,20–21)? Why do you think Abishai was "doubly honored," commander of "the Three," but not among them (1 Sam. 26:6–11)? Who should get the greater honor for their victories? **5.** For what was Benaiah famous (vv. 22–25)? How are his exploits like David's? How was he honored? **6.** What names

---

11:10–41 Israel wholeheartedly accepts David as king. They demonstrate their support by a tremendous military showing (2 Sam. 23:8–39).

11:15–19 David's warriors demonstrate their unselfish devotion. Their efforts prompt David to demonstrate his ultimate devotion to God.

do you recognize among "the Thirty" (vv. 26–47)? What biblical events do their names bring to mind for you (e.g., Uriah the Hittite)? **7.** How many names are listed here (compare 2 Sam. 23:24–39)? What does the longer list here suggest about the fluidity of David's "thirty" best warriors? (Note, too, who else had "thirty with him.") Why would new officers be needed from time to time? **8.** What does such a loyal following of "chiefs" suggest about the common support David's kingship enjoyed from "all Israel" (v. 10)? What does all this tell you about God's support for David?

APPLY **1.** Who are the "three mighty men" in your life who have given of themselves to make you the person you are today? **2.** What was it about these people that so influenced your development? **3.** Whose life do you have great influence on? What can you do to be a more significant influence on their lives?

20 Abishai the brother of Joab was chief of the Three. He raised his
spear against three hundred men, whom he killed, and so he became
as famous as the Three. 21 He was doubly honored above the Three
and became their commander, even though he was not included
among them.

22 Benaiah son of Jehoiada was a valiant fighter from Kabzeel, who
performed great exploits. He struck down two of Moab's best men.
He also went down into a pit on a snowy day and killed a lion. 23 And
he struck down an Egyptian who was seven and a half feet[a] tall.
Although the Egyptian had a spear like a weaver's rod in his hand,
Benaiah went against him with a club. He snatched the spear from
the Egyptian's hand and killed him with his own spear. 24 Such were
the exploits of Benaiah son of Jehoiada; he too was as famous as the
three mighty men. 25 He was held in greater honor than any of the
Thirty, but he was not included among the Three. And David put him
in charge of his bodyguard.

26 The mighty men were:
Asahel the brother of Joab,
Elhanan son of Dodo from Bethlehem,
27 Shammoth the Harorite,
Helez the Pelonite,
28 Ira son of Ikkesh from Tekoa,
Abiezer from Anathoth,
29 Sibbecai the Hushathite,
Ilai the Ahohite,
30 Maharai the Netophathite,
Heled son of Baanah the Netophathite,
31 Ithai son of Ribai from Gibeah in Benjamin,
Benaiah the Pirathonite,
32 Hurai from the ravines of Gaash,
Abiel the Arbathite,
33 Azmaveth the Baharumite,
Eliahba the Shaalbonite,
34 the sons of Hashem the Gizonite,
Jonathan son of Shagee the Hararite,
35 Ahiam son of Sacar the Hararite,
Eliphal son of Ur,
36 Hepher the Mekerathite,
Ahijah the Pelonite,
37 Hezro the Carmelite,
Naarai son of Ezbai,
38 Joel the brother of Nathan,
Mibhar son of Hagri,
39 Zelek the Ammonite,
Naharai the Berothite, the armor-bearer of Joab son of Zeruiah,
40 Ira the Ithrite,
Gareb the Ithrite,
41 Uriah the Hittite,

[a]23 Hebrew *five cubits* (about 2.3 meters)

11:20 Abishai. He was listed as bravest of the brave.

11:41–12:40 The theme is not necessarily military might, but David's unanimous support throughout the entire nation.

Zabad son of Ahlai,
42 Adina son of Shiza the Reubenite, who was chief of the Reubenites, and the thirty with him,
43 Hanan son of Maacah,
Joshaphat the Mithnite,
44 Uzzia the Ashterathite,
Shama and Jeiel the sons of Hotham the Aroerite,
45 Jediael son of Shimri,
his brother Joha the Tizite,
46 Eliel the Mahavite,
Jeribai and Joshaviah the sons of Elnaam,
Ithmah the Moabite,
47 Eliel, Obed and Jaasiel the Mezobaite.

Warriors Join David

12 These were the men who came to David at Ziklag, while he
was banished from the presence of Saul son of Kish (they
were among the warriors who helped him in battle; 2 they were armed
with bows and were able to shoot arrows or to sling stones right-
handed or left-handed; they were kinsmen of Saul from the tribe of
Benjamin):

3 Ahiezer their chief and Joash the sons of Shemaah the Gibeath-
ite; Jeziel and Pelet the sons of Azmaveth; Beracah, Jehu the
Anathothite, 4 and Ishmaiah the Gibeonite, a mighty man among
the Thirty, who was a leader of the Thirty; Jeremiah, Jahaziel,
Johanan, Jozabad the Gederathite, 5 Eluzai, Jerimoth, Bealiah,
Shemariah and Shephatiah the Haruphite; 6 Elkanah, Isshiah,
Azarel, Joezer and Jashobeam the Korahites; 7 and Joelah and
Zebadiah the sons of Jeroham from Gedor.

8 Some Gadites defected to David at his stronghold in the desert.
They were brave warriors, ready for battle and able to handle the
shield and spear. Their faces were the faces of lions, and they were as
swift as gazelles in the mountains.

9 Ezer was the chief,
Obadiah the second in command, Eliab the third,
10 Mishmannah the fourth, Jeremiah the fifth,
11 Attai the sixth, Eliel the seventh,
12 Johanan the eighth, Elzabad the ninth,
13 Jeremiah the tenth and Macbannai the eleventh.

14 These Gadites were army commanders; the least was a match for
a hundred, and the greatest for a thousand. 15 It was they who crossed
the Jordan in the first month when it was overflowing all its banks,
and they put to flight everyone living in the valleys, to the east and to
the west.

16 *Other Benjamites and some* men from Judah also came to David
in his stronghold. 17 David went out to meet them and said to them,
"If you have come to me in peace, to help me, I am ready to have you
unite with me. But if you have come to betray me to my enemies
when my hands are free from violence, may the God of our fathers
see it and judge you."

18 Then the Spirit came upon Amasai, chief of the Thirty, and he said:
"We are yours, O David!

OPEN **1.** Who is your favorite villain: Joker? Bonnie and Clyde? Darth Vader? **2.** For you, what makes some renegades into villains and others into folk heroes: Folk heroes rob from the rich; villains from the poor? Folk heroes kill in self-defense; villains simply kill?

STUDY **1.** What tells you this is a "flashback," predating the events of chapter 11? **2.** What is notable about Saul's own kinsmen coming over to David's side before "all Israel" did so (v. 2)? **3.** Where else do the defectors come from? Are they "political dissidents," "proven winners" or "cast offs"? What is their claim to fame? What do you suppose made the Gadite commanders so effective for David? **4.** Why is David cautious about some renegades who join his side (vv. 16–17)? How are his suspicions laid to rest? Have you ever had someone you worked with that you felt cautious about trusting? **5.** Was invoking God's witness enough to cement ties between these two men (vv. 17–18)? Or were careful contractual negotiations between David and Amasai also necessary? Note that Amasai's (Amasa's) treason years later gives David "20/20 hindsight" to confirm his suspicions here (2 Sam. 17:25). **6.** What leads David to marvel at God's guidance during this time in exile (v. 22)? Can you see God's guidance in some events in your life?

APPLY **1.** For what reasons might someone be suspicious of you and withhold their trust? How do you win over those who are suspicious of you? **2.** Like these defectors from Saul pledging themselves to David, to whom have you felt inspired to pledge your service (with heart and will open to God)? What normally prevents such commitment? **3.** Adnah,

Jozabad and the others had to surrender loyalty to Saul in order to side with David. How do you decide which way to go when divided loyalties force a choice? **4.** Do you have a situation now in which you are torn between two sides?

OPEN 1. What event in your life has swelled in importance over the years? Does it now seem as if *everyone* was there? **2.** What events in your social calendar require special catering vs. paper plates for all the guests invited? **3.** Have you ever seen a ticker tape parade? What was it like?

STUDY 1. What do you think is the chronicler's point in recounting the numbers and nature of those joining David at Hebron, including the two priests named? **2.** What do you make of such *large* numbers (340,800 total men)? **3.** Do you think that having the fighting men support David influenced the "rest of Israel" to make David king? **4.** Do you know people like Naphtali that are known for always showing up with the stuff for a good party? Is that a spiritual gift?

APPLY 1. While huge numbers eating and drinking at David's three-day coronation may seem problematic, what does such imagery say about the *joy* that attended this banquet? **2.** When have you partied for three days? What was the occasion? Why is it we often feel guilty about such time-consuming pleasure? **3.** As a Christian anticipating the final banquet crowning your coming King (Luke 13:28–30; 14:16–24), what will you do with the limitless opportunity for enjoying your King?

We are with you, O son of Jesse!
Success, success to you,
and success to those who help you,
for your God will help you."

So David received them and made them leaders of his raiding
bands.
19Some of the men of Manasseh defected to David when he went
with the Philistines to fight against Saul. (He and his men did not
help the Philistines because, after consultation, their rulers sent him
away. They said, "It will cost us our heads if he deserts to his master
Saul.") 20When David went to Ziklag, these were the men of Manasseh who defected to him: Adnah, Jozabad, Jediael, Michael, Jozabad,
Elihu and Zillethai, leaders of units of a thousand in Manasseh.
21They helped David against raiding bands, for all of them were brave
warriors, and they were commanders in his army. 22Day after day
men came to help David, until he had a great army, like the army
of God.[a]

Others Join David at Hebron

23These are the numbers of the men armed for battle who came to
David at Hebron to turn Saul's kingdom over to him, as the LORD had
said:
24men of Judah, carrying shield and spear—6,800 armed for battle;
25men of Simeon, warriors ready for battle—7,100;
26men of Levi—4,600, 27including Jehoiada, leader of the family of
Aaron, with 3,700 men, 28and Zadok, a brave young warrior,
with 22 officers from his family;
29men of Benjamin, Saul's kinsmen—3,000, most of whom had
remained loyal to Saul's house until then;
30men of Ephraim, brave warriors, famous in their own clans—
20,800;
31men of half the tribe of Manasseh, designated by name to come
and make David king—18,000;
32men of Issachar, who understood the times and knew what
Israel should do—200 chiefs, with all their relatives under
their command;
33men of Zebulun, experienced soldiers prepared for battle with
every type of weapon, to help David with undivided loyalty—
50,000;
34men of Naphtali—1,000 officers, together with 37,000 men carrying shields and spears;
35men of Dan, ready for battle—28,600;
36men of Asher, experienced soldiers prepared for battle—40,000;
37and from east of the Jordan, men of Reuben, Gad and the half-
tribe of Manasseh, armed with every type of weapon—
120,000.

38All these were fighting men who volunteered to serve in the
ranks. They came to Hebron fully determined to make David king

[a]22 Or *a great and mighty army*

12:23–37 David warmly received the help of Saul's defectors. He made many of the volunteers leaders of his army (v. 18). His army continued to grow as word got out about his exploits.

over all Israel. All the rest of the Israelites were also of one mind to
make David king. 39The men spent three days there with David, eating
and drinking, for their families had supplied provisions for them.
40Also, their neighbors from as far away as Issachar, Zebulun and
Naphtali came bringing food on donkeys, camels, mules and oxen.
There were plentiful supplies of flour, fig cakes, raisin cakes, wine,
oil, cattle and sheep, for there was joy in Israel.

Bringing Back the Ark

13 David conferred with each of his officers, the commanders of
thousands and commanders of hundreds. 2He then said to
the whole assembly of Israel, "If it seems good to you and if it is the
will of the LORD our God, let us send word far and wide to the rest of
our brothers throughout the territories of Israel, and also to the
priests and Levites who are with them in their towns and pasturelands, to come and join us. 3Let us bring the ark of our God back to
us, for we did not inquire of[a] it[b] during the reign of Saul." 4The whole
assembly agreed to do this, because it seemed right to all the people.
5So David assembled all the Israelites, from the Shihor River in
Egypt to Lebo[c] Hamath, to bring the ark of God from Kiriath Jearim.
6David and all the Israelites with him went to Baalah of Judah (Kiriath
Jearim) to bring up from there the ark of God the LORD, who is
enthroned between the cherubim—the ark that is called by the Name.
7They moved the ark of God from Abinadab's house on a new cart,
with Uzzah and Ahio guiding it. 8David and all the Israelites were celebrating with all their might before God, with songs and with harps,
lyres, tambourines, cymbals and trumpets.
9When they came to the threshing floor of Kidon, Uzzah reached
out his hand to steady the ark, because the oxen stumbled. 10The
LORD's anger burned against Uzzah, and he struck him down because
he had put his hand on the ark. So he died there before God.
11Then David was angry because the LORD's wrath had broken out
against Uzzah, and to this day that place is called Perez Uzzah.[d]
12David was afraid of God that day and asked, "How can I ever
bring the ark of God to me?" 13He did not take the ark to be with
him in the City of David. Instead, he took it aside to the house of
Obed-Edom the Gittite. 14The ark of God remained with the family of
Obed-Edom in his house for three months, and the LORD blessed his
household and everything he had.

David's House and Family

14 Now Hiram king of Tyre sent messengers to David, along
with cedar logs, stonemasons and carpenters to build a palace for him. 2And David knew that the LORD had established him as
king over Israel and that his kingdom had been highly exalted for the
sake of his people Israel.

[a]3 Or *we neglected* [b]3 Or *him* [c]5 Or *to the entrance to* [d]11 *Perez Uzzah* means *outbreak against Uzzah.*

OPEN Recall when a party-pooper (parents, spouse, little brother) once killed the mood of your party; what did you do then?

STUDY 1. Who made the decision to bring back the ark? Where has it been (1 Sam. 7:1–2)? Why such high priority on bringing it back? **2.** How did they move it (v. 7)? Why a "new cart" (1 Sam. 6:7)? What's wrong with that? How's the ark supposed to be moved (Ex. 25:14)? And by whom (15:2,13–15; Num. 4:15)? **3.** How is Uzzah's act "the last straw"? Who then intervenes (vv. 10–12)? Do you think this punishment was fair? **4.** What does such anger show about God's holiness? About David's character and sense of responsibility? **5.** If you had been given this deadly ark, as was Obed-Edom (vv. 13–14), how would you feel?

APPLY 1. Do you treat God with more reverential awe or more familiarity? Why? **2.** Like Uzzah, when have you slipped and acted irreverently? When you fall, who intercedes? **3.** In what area of your life are you more likely to take God for granted?

OPEN 1. In what order have you established these priorities: Get married? Have kids? Build a new home? Establish God as the focal point? Prove yourself in your career? **2.** If you could do something to radically change your life, what would it be?

13:1–4 David issues his first spiritual directive: Bring back the ark. The Philistines had captured and then returned the ark years earlier. However, it remained in a warehouse and forgotten.

13:7 moved the ark. The ark was irreverently transported on a cart. The Levites alone were allowed to carry the ark—even then only on poles inserted in its corner rings (Ex. 25:13–15).

13:10 put his hand on the ark. Uzzah's death was the consequence of a series of careless errors. Divine discipline was in order.

14:1 palace. David's palace would establish his permanency as king both in Israel and abroad.

3In Jerusalem David took more wives and became the father of more sons and daughters. 4These are the names of the children born to him there: Shammua, Shobab, Nathan, Solomon, 5Ibhar, Elishua, Elpelet, 6Nogah, Nepheg, Japhia, 7Elishama, Beeliada[a] and Eliphelet.

David Defeats the Philistines

8When the Philistines heard that David had been anointed king over all Israel, they went up in full force to search for him, but David heard about it and went out to meet them. 9Now the Philistines had come and raided the Valley of Rephaim; 10so David inquired of God: "Shall I go and attack the Philistines? Will you hand them over to me?"

The LORD answered him, "Go, I will hand them over to you."

11So David and his men went up to Baal Perazim, and there he defeated them. He said, "As waters break out, God has broken out against my enemies by my hand." So that place was called Baal Perazim.[b] 12The Philistines had abandoned their gods there, and David gave orders to burn them in the fire.

13Once more the Philistines raided the valley; 14so David inquired of God again, and God answered him, "Do not go straight up, but circle around them and attack them in front of the balsam trees. 15As soon as you hear the sound of marching in the tops of the balsam trees, move out to battle, because that will mean God has gone out in front of you to strike the Philistine army." 16So David did as God commanded him, and they struck down the Philistine army, all the way from Gibeon to Gezer.

17So David's fame spread throughout every land, and the LORD made all the nations fear him.

The Ark Brought to Jerusalem

15 After David had constructed buildings for himself in the City of David, he prepared a place for the ark of God and pitched a tent for it. 2Then David said, "No one but the Levites may carry the ark of God, because the LORD chose them to carry the ark of the LORD and to minister before him forever."

3David assembled all Israel in Jerusalem to bring up the ark of the LORD to the place he had prepared for it. 4He called together the descendants of Aaron and the Levites:

5From the descendants of Kohath,
Uriel the leader and 120 relatives;
6from the descendants of Merari,
Asaiah the leader and 220 relatives;
7from the descendants of Gershon,[c]
Joel the leader and 130 relatives;
8from the descendants of Elizaphan,
Shemaiah the leader and 200 relatives;

[a]7 A variant of *Eliada* [b]11 *Baal Perazim* means *the lord who breaks out.* [c]7 Hebrew *Gershom,* a variant of *Gershon*

STUDY 1. What two events and two blessings recorded here are symbolic of David's truly becoming king of Israel? What political and redemptive purpose do they serve? **2.** How does this list of the king's kids compare with 3:5–8 and 2 Samuel 5:14–15? **3.** What priority does David take on next? What political platform do you notice in the king's First 100 Days in office? **4.** What strategic steps did David take to ensure success against the Philistines? What significance for a revived Israel do you see in his action, prayers, speech, removal of pagan idols, obedience to God and fame among the nations?

APPLY 1. When David was recognized by Hiram, this helped to secure David's sense that God had indeed called him. In this regard, whose recognition is important to you? **2.** David's first victory was insufficient. How do you react when your best shot requires a second effort? Try the same thing? Try something new? **3.** For what things do you "inquire of God"? How do you get your answer?

OPEN 1. What have you had to try more than once before you succeeded? **2.** What would it take to get you "dancing in the streets": Peace in the Middle East? A World Series or Super Bowl win for the home team? School let out early for the year? "It's a Boy!" The recipe actually worked!? She said, "I do"?

STUDY 1. What suggests that David has learned a valuable lesson about not playing loose with the rules for worship given by God through Moses? What blame-shifting by the chronicler do you also detect? **2.** What suggests that David is now the leader of all the people and no longer a mere challenger to the incumbent, Saul? **3.** What three clans of Levites are represented at this religious processional? What all is involved in David's ordering them to "consecrate yourselves" (vv. 12–15;

14:12 their gods. Destroying an enemy's idols symbolized dominance over their entire society.

14:17 spread throughout every land. David quickly rises to power throughout Israel. He gains a reputation as a devout warrior, a passionate leader of people and follower of God.

9from the descendants of Hebron,
Eliel the leader and 80 relatives;
10from the descendants of Uzziel,
Amminadab the leader and 112 relatives.
11Then David summoned Zadok and Abiathar the priests, and Uriel,
Asaiah, Joel, Shemaiah, Eliel and Amminadab the Levites. 12He said
to them, "You are the heads of the Levitical families; you and your
fellow Levites are to consecrate yourselves and bring up the ark of
the LORD, the God of Israel, to the place I have prepared for it. 13It was
because you, the Levites, did not bring it up the first time that the
LORD our God broke out in anger against us. We did not inquire of
him about how to do it in the prescribed way." 14So the priests and
Levites consecrated themselves in order to bring up the ark of the
LORD, the God of Israel. 15And the Levites carried the ark of God with
the poles on their shoulders, as Moses had commanded in accordance with the word of the LORD.
16David told the leaders of the Levites to appoint their brothers as
singers to sing joyful songs, accompanied by musical instruments:
lyres, harps and cymbals.
17So the Levites appointed Heman son of Joel; from his brothers,
Asaph son of Berekiah; and from their brothers the Merarites, Ethan
son of Kushaiah; 18and with them their brothers next in rank:
Zechariah,[a] Jaaziel, Shemiramoth, Jehiel, Unni, Eliab, Benaiah, Maaseiah, Mattithiah, Eliphelehu, Mikneiah, Obed-Edom and Jeiel,[b] the
gatekeepers.
19The musicians Heman, Asaph and Ethan were to sound the
bronze cymbals; 20Zechariah, Aziel, Shemiramoth, Jehiel, Unni, Eliab,
Maaseiah and Benaiah were to play the lyres according to *alamoth*,[c]
21and Mattithiah, Eliphelehu, Mikneiah, Obed-Edom, Jeiel and
Azaziah were to play the harps, directing according to *sheminith*.[c]
22Kenaniah the head Levite was in charge of the singing; that was his
responsibility because he was skillful at it.
23Berekiah and Elkanah were to be doorkeepers for the ark.
24Shebaniah, Joshaphat, Nethanel, Amasai, Zechariah, Benaiah and
Eliezer the priests were to blow trumpets before the ark of God.
Obed-Edom and Jehiah were also to be doorkeepers for the ark.
25So David and the elders of Israel and the commanders of units of
a thousand went to bring up the ark of the covenant of the LORD from
the house of Obed-Edom, with rejoicing. 26Because God had helped
the Levites who were carrying the ark of the covenant of the LORD,
seven bulls and seven rams were sacrificed. 27Now David was clothed
in a robe of fine linen, as were all the Levites who were carrying the
ark, and as were the singers, and Kenaniah, who was in charge of the
singing of the choirs. David also wore a linen ephod. 28So all Israel
brought up the ark of the covenant of the LORD with shouts, with the

[a]18 Three Hebrew manuscripts and most Septuagint manuscripts (see also verse 20 and 1 Chron. 16:5); most Hebrew manuscripts *Zechariah son and* or *Zechariah, Ben and* [b]18 Hebrew; Septuagint (see also verse 21) *Jeiel and Azaziah* [c]20,21 Probably a musical term

Ex. 29:1–37)? **4.** How does David organize them for worship (vv. 16–28)? **5.** How does Obed-Edom likely feel about getting the ark out of his house after three months? **6.** In what sense does God "help" the Levites carry the ark this time around, whereas before he had opposed them (v. 26)? **7.** As the ark is being moved to Jerusalem, what is the response of the people (vv. 25,28; 16:1)? Of David (vv. 25,27; 16:2–3)? Of the Levites (16:1,4–6) **8.** By contrast, how does Michal respond? Why is she so upset with David (v. 29; 2 Sam. 6:20)? **9.** If "clothes make the man," and if David "dresses for success," what do you make of his attire in verse 27 (1 Sam. 2:18; 22:18)? How is David by his costume thus redefining the role of the king?

APPLY 1. What would a worship service led by David be like in your church? What sights and sounds would surprise you? How would he be received? What would he have to wear? Why? **2.** When you think of coming to your group, do you prepare: What you will wear? What food you will bring? Your mind and heart for interaction and growth? **3.** Which of the following would characterize your group: Reverential awe? Childlike joy? Special clothing? Conversational prayer? David's serendipity-like dancing?

15:12 consecrate yourselves. David makes sure he does not repeat history. The Levites are to be spiritually prepared for their assignment to move the ark (Ex. 29:1–37).

15:13–15 The Levites' attention to detail revives their devotion to God. The move to Jerusalem is a success in more ways than one with all of life centered together.

15:27 linen ephod. The ephod was a chest covering reserved for the office of priest. As a sort of priest-king, David exercises a new form of spiritual leadership over Israel.

sounding of rams' horns and trumpets, and of cymbals, and the playing of lyres and harps.
29As the ark of the covenant of the LORD was entering the City of
David, Michal daughter of Saul watched from a window. And when
she saw King David dancing and celebrating, she despised him in her
heart.

16 They brought the ark of God and set it inside the tent that
David had pitched for it, and they presented burnt offerings
and fellowship offerings[a] before God. 2After David had finished sacrificing the burnt offerings and fellowship offerings, he blessed the
people in the name of the LORD. 3Then he gave a loaf of bread, a cake
of dates and a cake of raisins to each Israelite man and woman.
4He appointed some of the Levites to minister before the ark of the
LORD, to make petition, to give thanks, and to praise the LORD, the
God of Israel: 5Asaph was the chief, Zechariah second, then Jeiel,
Shemiramoth, Jehiel, Mattithiah, Eliab, Benaiah, Obed-Edom and
Jeiel. They were to play the lyres and harps, Asaph was to sound the
cymbals, 6and Benaiah and Jahaziel the priests were to blow the
trumpets regularly before the ark of the covenant of God.

David's Psalm of Thanks

7That day David first committed to Asaph and his associates this
psalm of thanks to the LORD:

8Give thanks to the LORD, call on his name;
make known among the nations what he has done.
9Sing to him, sing praise to him;
tell of all his wonderful acts.
10Glory in his holy name;
let the hearts of those who seek the LORD rejoice.
11Look to the LORD and his strength;
seek his face always.
12Remember the wonders he has done,
his miracles, and the judgments he pronounced,
13O descendants of Israel his servant,
O sons of Jacob, his chosen ones.

14He is the LORD our God;
his judgments are in all the earth.
15He remembers[b] his covenant forever,
the word he commanded, for a thousand generations,
16the covenant he made with Abraham,
the oath he swore to Isaac.
17He confirmed it to Jacob as a decree,
to Israel as an everlasting covenant:
18"To you I will give the land of Canaan
as the portion you will inherit."

[a]1 Traditionally *peace offerings;* also in verse 2 [b]15 Some Septuagint manuscripts (see also Psalm 105:8); Hebrew *Remember*

OPEN 1. What about your past, your dream life or your future vacation plans would you characterize as *awesome*? **2.** What era of your country's history or of world history would you like to visit in a time machine? Why? **3.** Are you the type to relive and reflect on the past? Or do you forget about the past, living only for now? Why?

STUDY 1. How is David's kingdom further strengthened by giving thanks to the Lord with this psalm? How would this psalm bring the 12 tribes closer together as one people? Have you ever been in a group that was brought closer together through a thanksgiving service? **2.** In the song's first stanza (vv. 8–13), What does the psalmist urge us to do and why? What memories for Israel are evoked by reference to God's "wonders," "miracles" or "judgments"? **3.** In the second stanza (vv. 14–18), who first understands God's mission in the world? What is the mission? The covenant? **4.** In the third stanza (vv. 19–22), who are the VIPs esteemed by God? How were they protected? **5.** In the majestic fourth stanza (vv. 23–33), what actions are we instructed to take (list the verbs)? Who or what is called upon to participate and why? Why "all the earth"? Why "day

15:29 Michal. *Human nature worms its way into the celebration. Michal, the daughter of Saul, could not accept her father's replacement.*

16:8–36 The chronicler embellishes the celebration in Jerusalem by the addition of a compilation of psalms not found in the book of Samuel (Ps. 96:1–13; 105:1–15; 106:1,47–48). David compiles events from the past into a merry celebration of the present.

[19]When they were but few in number,
few indeed, and strangers in it,
[20]they[a] wandered from nation to nation,
from one kingdom to another.
[21]He allowed no man to oppress them;
for their sake he rebuked kings:
[22]"Do not touch my anointed ones;
do my prophets no harm."

[23]Sing to the LORD, all the earth;
proclaim his salvation day after day.
[24]Declare his glory among the nations,
his marvelous deeds among all peoples.
[25]For great is the LORD and most worthy of praise;
he is to be feared above all gods.
[26]For all the gods of the nations are idols,
but the LORD made the heavens.
[27]Splendor and majesty are before him;
strength and joy in his dwelling place.
[28]Ascribe to the LORD, O families of nations,
ascribe to the LORD glory and strength,
[29] ascribe to the LORD the glory due his name.
Bring an offering and come before him;
worship the LORD in the splendor of his[b] holiness.
[30]Tremble before him, all the earth!
The world is firmly established; it cannot be moved.
[31]Let the heavens rejoice, let the earth be glad;
let them say among the nations, "The LORD reigns!"
[32]Let the sea resound, and all that is in it;
let the fields be jubilant, and everything in them!
[33]Then the trees of the forest will sing,
they will sing for joy before the LORD,
for he comes to judge the earth.

[34]Give thanks to the LORD, for he is good;
his love endures forever.
[35]Cry out, "Save us, O God our Savior;
gather us and deliver us from the nations,
that we may give thanks to your holy name,
that we may glory in your praise."
[36]Praise be to the LORD, the God of Israel,
from everlasting to everlasting.

Then all the people said "Amen" and "Praise the LORD."

[37]David left Asaph and his associates before the ark of the covenant
of the LORD to minister there regularly, according to each day's requirements. [38]He also left Obed-Edom and his sixty-eight associates
to minister with them. Obed-Edom son of Jeduthun, and also Hosah,
were gatekeepers.

[39]David left Zadok the priest and his fellow priests before the tabernacle of the LORD at the high place in Gibeon [40]to present burnt offerings to the LORD on the altar of burnt offering regularly, morning and

[a]*18-20* One Hebrew manuscript, Septuagint and Vulgate (see also Psalm 105:12); most Hebrew manuscripts *inherit, / [19]though you are but few in number, / few indeed, and strangers in it." / [20]They* [b]*29* Or LORD *with the splendor of*

after day"? Have you ever been in a service like this? How did it make you feel? **6.** If all these actions are to achieve their purpose, what will have to happen and when? **7.** In the fifth stanza (vv. 34–36), what common human needs are addressed? How will the Lord meet them, as no one else can? **8.** What familiar names appear after the benediction to this psalm? What roles are they given and why? Why does David wait until the end to resume his role as father and husband?

APPLY 1. The occasion for this psalm was the return of the ark and the establishment of David's reign. For what occasions might Israel and the church have used this psalm? How might you use it today? **2.** What qualities of Israel's God mentioned in this psalm of praise, are most comforting to you? What about this God do you find most disturbing? Which divine attribute applies to a current worry or problem of yours? **3.** If your church were to model its worship service after this multi-pattern, what skills would you have to import? What skills could you grow internally? What do you think would be the affect on your spiritual life if you were a part of a worship service like this? What can you do to contribute to group worship?

evening, in accordance with everything written in the Law of the LORD, which he had given Israel. 41With them were Heman and Jeduthun and the rest of those chosen and designated by name to give thanks to the LORD, "for his love endures forever." 42Heman and Jeduthun were responsible for the sounding of the trumpets and cymbals and for the playing of the other instruments for sacred song. The sons of Jeduthun were stationed at the gate.

43Then all the people left, each for his own home, and David returned home to bless his family.

God's Promise to David

17 After David was settled in his palace, he said to Nathan the prophet, "Here I am, living in a palace of cedar, while the ark of the covenant of the LORD is under a tent."

2Nathan replied to David, "Whatever you have in mind, do it, for God is with you."

3That night the word of God came to Nathan, saying:

4"Go and tell my servant David, 'This is what the LORD says: You are not the one to build me a house to dwell in. 5I have not dwelt in a house from the day I brought Israel up out of Egypt to this day. I have moved from one tent site to another, from one dwelling place to another. 6Wherever I have moved with all the Israelites, did I ever say to any of their leaders[a] whom I commanded to shepherd my people, "Why have you not built me a house of cedar?"'

7"Now then, tell my servant David, 'This is what the LORD Almighty says: I took you from the pasture and from following the flock, to be ruler over my people Israel. 8I have been with you wherever you have gone, and I have cut off all your enemies from before you. Now I will make your name like the names of the greatest men of the earth. 9And I will provide a place for my people Israel and will plant them so that they can have a home of their own and no longer be disturbed. Wicked people will not oppress them anymore, as they did at the beginning 10and have done ever since the time I appointed leaders over my people Israel. I will also subdue all your enemies.

" 'I declare to you that the LORD will build a house for you: 11When your days are over and you go to be with your fathers, I will raise up your offspring to succeed you, one of your own sons, and I will establish his kingdom. 12He is the one who will build a house for me, and I will establish his throne forever. 13I will be his father, and he will be my son. I will never take my love away from him, as I took it away from your predecessor. 14I will set him over my house and my kingdom forever; his throne will be established forever.' "

15Nathan reported to David all the words of this entire revelation.

[a]6 Traditionally *judges*; also in verse 10

OPEN Compare the house you grew up in with yours now. What do you like most about each house?

STUDY 1. What about David's house bothers him? How is Nathan's reply like a blank check? How does his open-ended counsel change (v. 2)? Have you ever been in a situation when the godly counsel has changed as dramatically as Nathan's? **2.** What is God's attitude toward his own house of cedar (v. 6)? Why is David reminded of his debt to God (vv. 7–8)? **3.** What kind of "house" does God promise David (v. 10)? What kind will God get (v. 12)? Should this news surprise or irk David? **4.** In what sense is God's kingdom "established forever" (v. 14; Isa. 9:6–7; Luke 1:32–33)?

APPLY 1. When have you felt like doing something for God? **2.** Which do you find motivates you more in your worship: God's promises, which are not dependent on your performance? God's conditional clauses, where obedience is expected to fully realize the terms of the covenant? Explain. **3.** What life dream or goal are you beginning to see that you will not accomplish yourself? Will a successor of yours be responsible for this? Are you trusting God to work his will in this matter?

17:1, 10 Enjoying a time of peace, David has more time to devote to his spiritual, non-military leadership. God assures David he will subdue his enemies in the meantime.

17:12–14 While David is blessed by God as a military leader and a king, God reveals that his son Solomon will now become the architect and contractor of God's house.

17:14 established forever. God implies a heavenly, eternal reign through his own son, Jesus (Isa. 9:6–7; Luke 1:32–33). This was a promise made to David (Ps. 89:35–37).

David's Prayer

16Then King David went in and sat before the LORD, and he said:
"Who am I, O LORD God, and what is my family, that you have
brought me this far? 17And as if this were not enough in your
sight, O God, you have spoken about the future of the house of
your servant. You have looked on me as though I were the most
exalted of men, O LORD God.
18"What more can David say to you for honoring your servant?
For you know your servant, 19O LORD. For the sake of your
servant and according to your will, you have done this great
thing and made known all these great promises.
20"There is no one like you, O LORD, and there is no God but
you, as we have heard with our own ears. 21And who is like your
people Israel—the one nation on earth whose God went out to
redeem a people for himself, and to make a name for yourself,
and to perform great and awesome wonders by driving out nations from before your people, whom you redeemed from Egypt?
22You made your people Israel your very own forever, and you,
O LORD, have become their God.
23"And now, LORD, let the promise you have made concerning
your servant and his house be established forever. Do as you
promised, 24so that it will be established and that your name will
be great forever. Then men will say, 'The LORD Almighty, the God
over Israel, is Israel's God!' And the house of your servant David
will be established before you.
25"You, my God, have revealed to your servant that you will
build a house for him. So your servant has found courage to pray
to you. 26O LORD, you are God! You have promised these good
things to your servant. 27Now you have been pleased to bless the
house of your servant, that it may continue forever in your sight;
for you, O LORD, have blessed it, and it will be blessed forever."

David's Victories

18 In the course of time, David defeated the Philistines and subdued them, and he took Gath and its surrounding villages from the control of the Philistines.
2David also defeated the Moabites, and they became subject to him
and brought tribute.
3Moreover, David fought Hadadezer king of Zobah, as far as Hamath, when he went to establish his control along the Euphrates
River. 4David captured a thousand of his chariots, seven thousand
charioteers and twenty thousand foot soldiers. He hamstrung all but
a hundred of the chariot horses.
5When the Arameans of Damascus came to help Hadadezer king of
Zobah, David struck down twenty-two thousand of them. 6He put
garrisons in the Aramean kingdom of Damascus, and the Arameans
became subject to him and brought tribute. The LORD gave David victory everywhere he went.
7David took the gold shields carried by the officers of Hadadezer

OPEN 1. When overwhelmed with generosity or a prestigious honor, what do you do? When have you been "twice blessed"? **2.** Is "reverence" necessary in work or worship? Do you like reverent folk?

STUDY 1. What motivates David to pray? To which of God's promises in this chapter is David answering in verse 16? In verse 17? **2.** How is God's sovereignty underscored in the way David addresses him in this prayer? **3.** Likewise, how is Israel's uniqueness underscored here? **4.** Why does David want so badly to see God's promise "kept forever" (vv. 23–24)? What gives him the courage to pray like this?

APPLY 1. How do you respond to the promises of our trustworthy God? How do you most often address God? Do you more often ask, or thank, God for things? What does that say about your rapport with him? **2.** Rank 1 to 5 these five activities in spiritual satisfaction: corporate worship; table grace; pre-game prayer; solitary prayer; group prayer. **3.** What does David's prayer inspire you and your group to pray for?

OPEN 1. What do you think of when you recall the good old days? What made them so good? **2.** What do you do for the sheer joy of it, regardless of its cost?

STUDY 1. How do you explain his winning streak? "The LORD gave David victory wherever he went." Does that say it all? Or does that only beg more questions for you? **2.** What does David do with captured soldiers, horses, equipment and articles? Why kill off good horses (Deut. 17:16), but dedicate the articles? What does this say about David? **3.** What gruesome story connected to these campaigns does Samuel tell, but is omitted here (2 Sam. 8:2)?

APPLY 1. How do you feel about armies praying for

18:1–20:8 David's foreign affairs comprise the chronicler's focus. His victories assure God's blessings on David's reign. He defeated Israel's archenemies: the Philistines and the Moabites.

God's blessing and for victory in battle? Is God to blame, win, lose or draw? **2.** Over what enemy has God given you victory? Where have you yet to experience his victory? **3.** What possessions, abilities or resources would you like to dedicate anew to God, as does David in this story?

OPEN 1. What's your favorite risk game? Can you put vast fortunes of play money on the line? Are you the "double or nothing" type? **2.** How do you feel about beards: They look attractive? Feel scratchy? Cover up acne? Save on razor blades? Proof of manliness? Offset baldness? The boss won't like it? Could catch a certain girl? Couldn't grow one if I tried?

STUDY 1. Who are the Ammonites (Gen. 19:38; Deut. 2:19)? Why are they a particular threat to Israel (Judg. 11:4–32)? Why does David send messengers to their new king (vv. 1–2)? What suspicions does that raise? **2.** What was Hanun trying to prove by stripping and shaving David's emissaries? What was the stench all about (vv. 5–6)? Have you ever had someone embarrass you in public? How did it make you feel? **3.** Who starts the war? Was it accidental? On purpose? Or "accidentally on purpose"? **4.** How does Joab manage the war on two fronts (vv. 10–13)? Who wins the war? **5.** How does Hadadezer think he can outmaneuver

and brought them to Jerusalem. 8From Tebah[a] and Cun, towns that belonged to Hadadezer, David took a great quantity of bronze, which Solomon used to make the bronze Sea, the pillars and various bronze articles.

9When Tou king of Hamath heard that David had defeated the entire army of Hadadezer king of Zobah, 10he sent his son Hadoram to King David to greet him and congratulate him on his victory in battle over Hadadezer, who had been at war with Tou. Hadoram brought all kinds of articles of gold and silver and bronze.

11King David dedicated these articles to the LORD, as he had done with the silver and gold he had taken from all these nations: Edom and Moab, the Ammonites and the Philistines, and Amalek.

12Abishai son of Zeruiah struck down eighteen thousand Edomites in the Valley of Salt. 13He put garrisons in Edom, and all the Edomites became subject to David. The LORD gave David victory everywhere he went.

David's Officials

14David reigned over all Israel, doing what was just and right for all his people. 15Joab son of Zeruiah was over the army; Jehoshaphat son of Ahilud was recorder; 16Zadok son of Ahitub and Ahimelech[b] son of Abiathar were priests; Shavsha was secretary; 17Benaiah son of Jehoiada was over the Kerethites and Pelethites; and David's sons were chief officials at the king's side.

The Battle Against the Ammonites

19 In the course of time, Nahash king of the Ammonites died, and his son succeeded him as king. 2David thought, "I will show kindness to Hanun son of Nahash, because his father showed kindness to me." So David sent a delegation to express his sympathy to Hanun concerning his father.

When David's men came to Hanun in the land of the Ammonites to express sympathy to him, 3the Ammonite nobles said to Hanun, "Do you think David is honoring your father by sending men to you to express sympathy? Haven't his men come to you to explore and spy out the country and overthrow it?" 4So Hanun seized David's men, shaved them, cut off their garments in the middle at the buttocks, and sent them away.

5When someone came and told David about the men, he sent messengers to meet them, for they were greatly humiliated. The king said, "Stay at Jericho till your beards have grown, and then come back."

6When the Ammonites realized that they had become a stench in David's nostrils, Hanun and the Ammonites sent a thousand talents[c] of silver to hire chariots and charioteers from Aram Naharaim,[d] Aram Maacah and Zobah. 7They hired thirty-two thousand chariots and charioteers, as well as the king of Maacah with his troops, who came

[a]8 Hebrew *Tibhath,* a variant of *Tebah* [b]16 Some Hebrew manuscripts, Vulgate and Syriac (see also 2 Samuel 8:17); most Hebrew manuscripts *Abimelech* [c]6 That is, about 37 tons (about 34 metric tons) [d]6 That is, Northwest Mesopotamia

19:1–20:3 David's risky battle against the Ammonites and their reinforcements pays off in a secured victory. David began by showing kindness at the death of Nahash, who ruled some 50 years.

and camped near Medeba, while the Ammonites were mustered
from their towns and moved out for battle.
8 On hearing this, David sent Joab out with the entire army of
fighting men. 9 The Ammonites came out and drew up in battle formation at the entrance to their city, while the kings who had come
were by themselves in the open country.
10 Joab saw that there were battle lines in front of him and behind
him; so he selected some of the best troops in Israel and deployed
them against the Arameans. 11 He put the rest of the men under the
command of Abishai his brother, and they were deployed against the
Ammonites. 12 Joab said, "If the Arameans are too strong for me,
then you are to rescue me; but if the Ammonites are too strong for
you, then I will rescue you. 13 Be strong and let us fight bravely for
our people and the cities of our God. The LORD will do what is
good in his sight."
14 Then Joab and the troops with him advanced to fight the Arameans, and they fled before him. 15 When the Ammonites saw that
the Arameans were fleeing, they too fled before his brother Abishai and went inside the city. So Joab went back to Jerusalem.
16 After the Arameans saw that they had been routed by Israel, they
sent messengers and had Arameans brought from beyond the River,[a]
with Shophach the commander of Hadadezer's army leading them.
17 When David was told of this, he gathered all Israel and crossed
the Jordan; he advanced against them and formed his battle lines
opposite them. David formed his lines to meet the Arameans in
battle, and they fought against him. 18 But they fled before Israel,
and David killed seven thousand of their charioteers and forty
thousand of their foot soldiers. He also killed Shophach the commander of their army.
19 When the vassals of Hadadezer saw that they had been defeated
by Israel, they made peace with David and became subject to him.
So the Arameans were not willing to help the Ammonites anymore.

The Capture of Rabbah

20 In the spring, at the time when kings go off to war, Joab led
out the armed forces. He laid waste the land of the Ammonites and went to Rabbah and besieged it, but David remained in
Jerusalem. Joab attacked Rabbah and left it in ruins. 2 David took the
crown from the head of their king[b]—its weight was found to be a
talent[c] of gold, and it was set with precious stones—and it was
placed on David's head. He took a great quantity of plunder from the
city 3 and brought out the people who were there, consigning them to
labor with saws and with iron picks and axes. David did this to all the
Ammonite towns. Then David and his entire army returned to Jerusalem.

War With the Philistines

4 In the course of time, war broke out with the Philistines, at Gezer.
At that time Sibbecai the Hushathite killed Sippai, one of the descendants of the Rephaites, and the Philistines were subjugated.
5 In another battle with the Philistines, Elhanan son of Jair killed

[a] *16* That is, the Euphrates [b] *2* Or *of Milcom,* that is, Molech [c] *2* That is, about 75 pounds (about 34 kilograms)

David (vv. 16–18)? When does he finally raise the white flag? **6.** What variations do you find between this account and the parallel one in 2 Samuel 10? What do you make of them? Which numbers make David look like he took the greater risk and won a greater victory?

APPLY 1. In what area of your life are you feeling the need for reinforcements? How might your group come to your rescue? **2.** How confident are you in taking risks? In escalating risky confrontations (as David did), even when you're in the right? What's the difference between "stepping out in faith" and risk-taking? **3.** How can children learn loyalty and trust, so that their parents' friends can become their genuine friends as well?

OPEN Apart from your parents, spouse or God, to whom do you owe the biggest debt of gratitude for your position in life?

STUDY 1. Who is the hero in the capture of Rabbah? Who actually gets the credit? **2.** What measure of mercy do you see here? **3.** What does the chronicler omit from his version of this battle (2 Sam. 11:1–12:31)? Why? **4.** What is the main point of these undated wars (vv. 4–8)? **5.** What trouble does David encounter here which the chronicler passes over (2 Sam. 21:15–17)? Why such embellishment?

APPLY 1. Do you feel you are getting proper credit for the jobs you do well? What reward are you working for? **2.** What giants have you fought for your King? What giants are

---

19:9 The battlefield consisted of a heavy Ammonite front at the entrance to the city. The Arameans' reinforcements lay waiting in the open fields.

20:2–3 placed on David's head. Crowning himself with an enemy's royalty was the ultimate sign of victory.

you preparing for? Training others for? How might the group help you?

OPEN 1. How well can you keep a secret: My smile gives it away? Sleepless until someone knows? Future career as a double agent? **2.** If you could travel back in history as the invisible person, what private conversations would you sit in on?

STUDY 1. What prompts David to take a census: God's anger (2 Sam. 24:1)? Satan's ruse? David's pride or insecurity? Some external threat? To keep his men busy between wars? To win power over Joab? Rationale for the temple property (vv. 28–30)? **2.** What does your answer say about who lies behind evil acts (v. 15; Job 1:12; James 1:13–15)? How could a "man after God's own heart" be duped by Satan? What should this tell us about the problem of pride? **3.** How does Joab remain true to his own conscience while taking David's census? Was his secret (v. 6) a lie? Was it justified by circumstances? Have you ever been in a situation where you were forced to do something that you felt was wrong? **4.** In the actual census-taking, what time, money and manpower are involved (vv. 4–6; 2 Sam. 24:8)? **5.** How does David discover his error (2 Sam. 24:10)? How do we know that David confessed his error to his advisors, that he was not trying for a cover-up? **6.** Is God working at cross-purposes when he grieves over what he inflicted on Israel? Why does he punish Israel for what David ordered? **7.** After the plague is over, David builds an altar (vv. 18–22:1). Where? Why there? What does David's prayer have to do with that? **8.** The plague reaches Araunah's threshing floor, and David wants to buy it to build an altar there. Why? For what price (1 Sam. 8:14)? What results?

Lahmi the brother of Goliath the Gittite, who had a spear with a shaft
like a weaver's rod.
6In still another battle, which took place at Gath, there was a huge
man with six fingers on each hand and six toes on each foot—twenty-
four in all. He also was descended from Rapha. 7When he taunted
Israel, Jonathan son of Shimea, David's brother, killed him.
8These were descendants of Rapha in Gath, and they fell at the
hands of David and his men.

David Numbers the Fighting Men

21 Satan rose up against Israel and incited David to take a
census of Israel. 2So David said to Joab and the commanders
of the troops, "Go and count the Israelites from Beersheba to Dan.
Then report back to me so that I may know how many there are."
3But Joab replied, "May the LORD multiply his troops a hundred
times over. My lord the king, are they not all my lord's subjects? Why
does my lord want to do this? Why should he bring guilt on Israel?"
4The king's word, however, overruled Joab; so Joab left and went
throughout Israel and then came back to Jerusalem. 5Joab reported
the number of the fighting men to David: In all Israel there were one
million one hundred thousand men who could handle a sword,
including four hundred and seventy thousand in Judah.
6But Joab did not include Levi and Benjamin in the numbering,
because the king's command was repulsive to him. 7This command
was also evil in the sight of God; so he punished Israel.
8Then David said to God, "I have sinned greatly by doing this. Now,
I beg you, take away the guilt of your servant. I have done a very foolish thing."
9The LORD said to Gad, David's seer, 10"Go and tell David, 'This is
what the LORD says: I am giving you three options. Choose one of
them for me to carry out against you.' "
11So Gad went to David and said to him, "This is what the LORD
says: 'Take your choice: 12three years of famine, three months of being swept away[a] before your enemies, with their swords overtaking
you, or three days of the sword of the LORD—days of plague in the
land, with the angel of the LORD ravaging every part of Israel.' Now
then, decide how I should answer the one who sent me."
13David said to Gad, "I am in deep distress. Let me fall into the
hands of the LORD, for his mercy is very great; but do not let me fall
into the hands of men."
14So the LORD sent a plague on Israel, and seventy thousand men of
Israel fell dead. 15And God sent an angel to destroy Jerusalem. But as
the angel was doing so, the LORD saw it and was grieved because of
the calamity and said to the angel who was destroying the people,
"Enough! Withdraw your hand." The angel of the LORD was then
standing at the threshing floor of Araunah[b] the Jebusite.
16David looked up and saw the angel of the LORD standing between

[a]12 Hebrew; Septuagint and Vulgate (see also 2 Samuel 24:13) *of fleeing* [b]15 Hebrew *Ornan,* a variant of *Araunah;* also in verses 18-28

21:1–22:1 In the midst of military momentum, David takes stock of his might through the use of a census. David's conceit and foolishness angers God (2 Sam. 24:1). He uses Satan's scheme to punish Israel.

21:5 Joab. Joab, ever loyal to David, has the complex job of tallying the totals for David's census.

heaven and earth, with a drawn sword in his hand extended over
Jerusalem. Then David and the elders, clothed in sackcloth, fell facedown.
17David said to God, "Was it not I who ordered the fighting men to
be counted? I am the one who has sinned and done wrong. These are
but sheep. What have they done? O LORD my God, let your hand fall
upon me and my family, but do not let this plague remain on your
people."
18Then the angel of the LORD ordered Gad to tell David to go up and
build an altar to the LORD on the threshing floor of Araunah the
Jebusite. 19So David went up in obedience to the word that Gad had
spoken in the name of the LORD.
20While Araunah was threshing wheat, he turned and saw the
angel; his four sons who were with him hid themselves. 21Then David
approached, and when Araunah looked and saw him, he left the
threshing floor and bowed down before David with his face to the
ground.
22David said to him, "Let me have the site of your threshing floor so
I can build an altar to the LORD, that the plague on the people may be
stopped. Sell it to me at the full price."
23Araunah said to David, "Take it! Let my lord the king do whatever
pleases him. Look, I will give the oxen for the burnt offerings, the
threshing sledges for the wood, and the wheat for the grain offering.
I will give all this."
24But King David replied to Araunah, "No, I insist on paying the full
price. I will not take for the LORD what is yours, or sacrifice a burnt
offering that costs me nothing."
25So David paid Araunah six hundred shekels[a] of gold for the site.
26David built an altar to the LORD there and sacrificed burnt offerings
and fellowship offerings.[b] He called on the LORD, and the LORD
answered him with fire from heaven on the altar of burnt offering.
27Then the LORD spoke to the angel, and he put his sword back into
its sheath. 28At that time, when David saw that the LORD had answered him on the threshing floor of Araunah the Jebusite, he offered
sacrifices there. 29The tabernacle of the LORD, which Moses had made
in the desert, and the altar of burnt offering were at that time on the
high place at Gibeon. 30But David could not go before it to inquire of
God, because he was afraid of the sword of the angel of the LORD.

22 Then David said, "The house of the LORD God is to be here,
and also the altar of burnt offering for Israel."

Preparations for the Temple

2So David gave orders to assemble the aliens living in Israel, and
from among them he appointed stonecutters to prepare dressed
stone for building the house of God. 3He provided a large amount of
iron to make nails for the doors of the gateways and for the fittings,
and more bronze than could be weighed. 4He also provided more

[a]25 That is, about 15 pounds (about 7 kilograms) [b]26 Traditionally *peace offerings*

APPLY 1. How are you like David—proud but insecure in "numbers"? When are you tempted to lean upon your superior assets, rather than in weakness depend on God? When have you, like David, pulled rank instead of listening to your "Joab"? **2.** Taking a cue from Israel's emphasis on body language (falling face down, etc.), how could you nonverbally express your fear, penitence or needs? **3.** What does this story say about the link between sin and suffering? Between sin and sacrifice? Between humility and service? Between wrath and mercy? What bearing does this have on your confidence that God brings good out of the trials we endure? How is that true for you? Is there a situation like this in your life right now?

OPEN 1. When have you ever been taken off a job that you very much wanted to complete yourself? How did you feel at the time? **2.** When have you had to replace someone at a task who, for one reason or another, was not the right person for the job? How did you feel, having to break the bad news? How

21:20–21 Although Araunah was willing to provide a ready-made sacrifice free of charge, David insists on purchasing it. David senses he must atone for his own error.

22:2–19 Resigned to the fact that he will not actually build the temple, David makes its spiritual and material preparations. His intimate connection with the temple is a major theme of both 1 and 2 Chronicles.

did you feel installing a person of your own choosing?

STUDY 1. What task has David yielded? Was he too defiled by war to build the temple himself (vv. 7–10; 17:10; 1 Kin. 5:3)? Why would God not allow David to build a temple when he had blessed him so in battle? **2.** What feelings can you read between the lines? Is David able to let go (of his dream and of his son)? Is he looking forward to retirement or an empty nest? **3.** What resources (material and spiritual) does David provide his son? Would that make it easier, or tougher, on Solomon? What burdens does Solomon inherit because of all David's preparations? **4.** How does David greet his son? How does he bid him farewell? What verbal assurances seem most significant in motivating a son to fulfill the assigned task? What virtues does he insist that Solomon cultivate? How will the Lord help in that? **5.** Are David and Solomon cast from the same mold?

APPLY 1. When have you "passed on the torch" to another person at work? To an heir in the family? **2.** What preparations have you made for passing on your life's work or family values? Would you "arrange" a child's life, as David did for Solomon? **3.** What kind of a head start in life did you get, materially, from your parents? Have you told them thank you?

cedar logs than could be counted, for the Sidonians and Tyrians had
brought large numbers of them to David.
5 David said, "My son Solomon is young and inexperienced, and the
house to be built for the LORD should be of great magnificence and
fame and splendor in the sight of all the nations. Therefore I will
make preparations for it." So David made extensive preparations
before his death.
6 Then he called for his son Solomon and charged him to build a
house for the LORD, the God of Israel. 7 David said to Solomon: "My
son, I had it in my heart to build a house for the Name of the LORD my
God. 8 But this word of the LORD came to me: 'You have shed much
blood and have fought many wars. You are not to build a house for
my Name, because you have shed much blood on the earth in my
sight. 9 But you will have a son who will be a man of peace and rest,
and I will give him rest from all his enemies on every side. His name
will be Solomon,[a] and I will grant Israel peace and quiet during his
reign. 10 He is the one who will build a house for my Name. He will be
my son, and I will be his father. And I will establish the throne of his
kingdom over Israel forever.'
11 "Now, my son, the LORD be with you, and may you have success
and build the house of the LORD your God, as he said you would.
12 May the LORD give you discretion and understanding when he puts
you in command over Israel, so that you may keep the law of the
LORD your God. 13 Then you will have success if you are careful to observe the decrees and laws that the LORD gave Moses for Israel. Be
strong and courageous. Do not be afraid or discouraged.
14 "I have taken great pains to provide for the temple of the LORD a
hundred thousand talents[b] of gold, a million talents[c] of silver, quantities of bronze and iron too great to be weighed, and wood and stone.
And you may add to them. 15 You have many workmen: stonecutters,
masons and carpenters, as well as men skilled in every kind of work
16 in gold and silver, bronze and iron—craftsmen beyond number.
Now begin the work, and the LORD be with you."
17 Then David ordered all the leaders of Israel to help his son Solomon. 18 He said to them, "Is not the LORD your God with you? And
has he not granted you rest on every side? For he has handed the
inhabitants of the land over to me, and the land is subject to the LORD
and to his people. 19 Now devote your heart and soul to seeking the
LORD your God. Begin to build the sanctuary of the LORD God, so that
you may bring the ark of the covenant of the LORD and the sacred
articles belonging to God into the temple that will be built for the
Name of the LORD."

The Levites

23 When David was old and full of years, he made his son
Solomon king over Israel.

OPEN Who in your group has the most siblings? The most kids? Most grandkids? Share photos, if you wish.

STUDY 1. How is David handling old age? What troubles

[a] *9 Solomon* sounds like and may be derived from the Hebrew for *peace.* [b] *14* That is, about 3,750 tons (about 3,450 metric tons) [c] *14* That is, about 37,500 tons (about 34,500 metric tons)

22:8–9 Where David was a man of war, Solomon's name described him as a man of peace. Therefore, Solomon (undefiled by bloodshed) would be the one to build the temple.

23:1 full of years, he made his son Solomon king. The chronicler smoothes the tough transition between David and Solomon's reign by leaving out the political implications (1 Kin. 1–2).

[2]He also gathered together all the leaders of Israel, as well as the
priests and Levites. [3]The Levites thirty years old or more were counted,
and the total number of men was thirty-eight thousand. [4]David said,
"Of these, twenty-four thousand are to supervise the work of the temple of the LORD and six thousand are to be officials and judges. [5]Four
thousand are to be gatekeepers and four thousand are to praise the
LORD with the musical instruments I have provided for that purpose."
[6]David divided the Levites into groups corresponding to the sons of
Levi: Gershon, Kohath and Merari.

Gershonites

[7]Belonging to the Gershonites:
Ladan and Shimei.
[8]The sons of Ladan:
Jehiel the first, Zetham and Joel—three in all.
[9]The sons of Shimei:
Shelomoth, Haziel and Haran—three in all.
These were the heads of the families of Ladan.
[10]And the sons of Shimei:
Jahath, Ziza,[a] Jeush and Beriah.
These were the sons of Shimei—four in all.
[11]Jahath was the first and Ziza the second, but Jeush and Beriah
did not have many sons; so they were counted as one family
with one assignment.

Kohathites

[12]The sons of Kohath:
Amram, Izhar, Hebron and Uzziel—four in all.
[13]The sons of Amram:
Aaron and Moses.
Aaron was set apart, he and his descendants forever, to consecrate the most holy things, to offer sacrifices before the LORD,
to minister before him and to pronounce blessings in his name
forever. [14]The sons of Moses the man of God were counted as
part of the tribe of Levi.
[15]The sons of Moses:
Gershom and Eliezer.
[16]The descendants of Gershom:
Shubael was the first.
[17]The descendants of Eliezer:
Rehabiah was the first.
Eliezer had no other sons, but the sons of Rehabiah were very
numerous.
[18]The sons of Izhar:
Shelomith was the first.
[19]The sons of Hebron:
Jeriah the first, Amariah the second, Jahaziel the third and Jekameam the fourth.

[a]10 One Hebrew manuscript, Septuagint and Vulgate (see also verse 11); most Hebrew manuscripts *Zina*

does David face among senior management (1 Kin. 1–2)? Why does the chronicler omit such bloody details? **2.** What other provisions for worship does David give? **3.** Study verses 7–11. How does this list compare with the one in chapter 6? Is Shimei the son of Libni and/or Gershon and/or Merari? And how many sons does Shimei seem to have (vv. 9–10)? Why reduce the assignment for two of his sons? As Beriah's heir, would you be pleased or resentful?

APPLY 1. How hard is it to turn over power? For David? For you? Do you remember giving up responsibility or a position? **2.** David delegated extensively at this stage in his career. Are you able to share responsibility or authority? How can this group help you?

OPEN Who is the most famous person you ever got to shake hands with, get an autograph from or actually visit with? What shirt-tail relative of some renown do you claim?

STUDY 1. Levi's tree has three branches. Which one is more famous and why? **2.** Is Aaron given busy work, or a creative outlet (v. 13)? What skills would he need to perform that role with excellence?

APPLY 1. What fights or political debates would you be spared today, if leaders were appointed "for life," as were the Hebrew priests? **2.** What lifelong duties or irrevocable callings have come your way? **3.** Who can you look to as your spiritual role model?

23:3 Levites. In further preparation for Solomon's reign, David assembles the Levites. David showed his concern for Israel's worship with his emphasis on his son's spiritual as well as royal readiness.

20The sons of Uzziel:
Micah the first and Isshiah the second.

Merarites

21The sons of Merari:
Mahli and Mushi.
The sons of Mahli:
Eleazar and Kish.
22Eleazar died without having sons: he had only daughters.
Their cousins, the sons of Kish, married them.
23The sons of Mushi:
Mahli, Eder and Jerimoth—three in all.

24These were the descendants of Levi by their families—the heads
of families as they were registered under their names and counted
individually, that is, the workers twenty years old or more who served
in the temple of the LORD. 25For David had said, "Since the LORD, the
God of Israel, has granted rest to his people and has come to dwell in
Jerusalem forever, 26the Levites no longer need to carry the tabernacle or any of the articles used in its service." 27According to the last
instructions of David, the Levites were counted from those twenty
years old or more.
28The duty of the Levites was to help Aaron's descendants in the
service of the temple of the LORD: to be in charge of the courtyards,
the side rooms, the purification of all sacred things and the performance of other duties at the house of God. 29They were in charge of
the bread set out on the table, the flour for the grain offerings, the
unleavened wafers, the baking and the mixing, and all measurements
of quantity and size. 30They were also to stand every morning to
thank and praise the LORD. They were to do the same in the evening
31and whenever burnt offerings were presented to the LORD on Sabbaths and at New Moon festivals and at appointed feasts. They were
to serve before the LORD regularly in the proper number and in the
way prescribed for them.
32And so the Levites carried out their responsibilities for the Tent of
Meeting, for the Holy Place and, under their brothers the descendants of Aaron, for the service of the temple of the LORD.

The Divisions of Priests

24 These were the divisions of the sons of Aaron:
The sons of Aaron were Nadab, Abihu, Eleazar and Ithamar.
2But Nadab and Abihu died before their father did, and they had no
sons; so Eleazar and Ithamar served as the priests. 3With the help of
Zadok a descendant of Eleazar and Ahimelech a descendant of Ithamar, David separated them into divisions for their appointed order of
ministering. 4A larger number of leaders were found among Eleazar's
descendants than among Ithamar's, and they were divided accordingly: sixteen heads of families from Eleazar's descendants and eight
heads of families from Ithamar's descendants. 5They divided them
impartially by drawing lots, for there were officials of the sanctuary

OPEN 1. "When I relax, I feel guilty"—does that describe you? How so? **2.** Who among your friends is an expert at having fun?

STUDY 1. Of the Merarites, David and the Levites, how did each succeed in their own way? Who seems most successful? **2.** What possible misunderstandings might the Hebrews have attached to the "rest" granted to them (vv. 25–26)? How would you rephrase David's intent here? **3.** Why the apparent changes in the age of eligibility for priests (vv. 24,27; 23:3; Num. 4:1–3; 8:23–24)? **4.** What here hints that the Hebrews enjoyed fun and fellowship in their work?

APPLY 1. For you, is your day of worship (Saturday, Sunday, Tuesday or whatever day that may be) restful, workful, or worshipful? **2.** The Levites had two teams, and membership was a matter of birth, not performance. If you were the chief Levite, what pep talk of yours would get the most out of your team? **3.** At age 20, where were you in relation to an organized church: Taking a four-year vacation? Attending when it was convenient? Getting actively involved?

OPEN 1. In your family, how do members decide what joint activity or common cause to engage in: By political or church ties? By geographic locale? By generations? By marriage? **2.** Who got you the job you are in now? Did you apply for it? Earn it? Or were you "volunteered"? How so?

STUDY 1. In the family line of Aaron, what divisions are evident? On the basis of what moral, inherited, and impartial grounds? **2.** What is the story behind the two

---

23:28–32 David encourages teamwork between the Levites and the priests. Lowering the minimum age ensures greater participation in worship service.

24:4 larger number. The division of labor was purely practical. Each division (consisting of 24) served about two weeks a year.

and officials of God among the descendants of both Eleazar and
Ithamar.
[6]The scribe Shemaiah son of Nethanel, a Levite, recorded their
names in the presence of the king and of the officials: Zadok the
priest, Ahimelech son of Abiathar and the heads of families of the
priests and of the Levites—one family being taken from Eleazar and
then one from Ithamar.

[7]The first lot fell to Jehoiarib,
the second to Jedaiah,
[8]the third to Harim,
the fourth to Seorim,
[9]the fifth to Malkijah,
the sixth to Mijamin,
[10]the seventh to Hakkoz,
the eighth to Abijah,
[11]the ninth to Jeshua,
the tenth to Shecaniah,
[12]the eleventh to Eliashib,
the twelfth to Jakim,
[13]the thirteenth to Huppah,
the fourteenth to Jeshebeab,
[14]the fifteenth to Bilgah,
the sixteenth to Immer,
[15]the seventeenth to Hezir,
the eighteenth to Happizzez,
[16]the nineteenth to Pethahiah,
the twentieth to Jehezkel,
[17]the twenty-first to Jakin,
the twenty-second to Gamul,
[18]the twenty-third to Delaiah
and the twenty-fourth to Maaziah.

[19]This was their appointed order of ministering when they entered
the temple of the LORD, according to the regulations prescribed for
them by their forefather Aaron, as the LORD, the God of Israel, had
commanded him.

The Rest of the Levites

[20]As for the rest of the descendants of Levi:
from the sons of Amram: Shubael;
from the sons of Shubael: Jehdeiah.
[21]As for Rehabiah, from his sons:
Isshiah was the first.
[22]From the Izharites: Shelomoth;
from the sons of Shelomoth: Jahath.
[23]The sons of Hebron: Jeriah the first,[a] Amariah the second, Jahaziel the third and Jekameam the fourth.
[24]The son of Uzziel: Micah;
from the sons of Micah: Shamir.
[25]The brother of Micah: Isshiah;
from the sons of Isshiah: Zechariah.

[a]23 Two Hebrew manuscripts and some Septuagint manuscripts (see also 1 Chron. 23:19); most Hebrew manuscripts *The sons of Jeriah:*

sons who are excluded on moral grounds (v. 2; Lev. 10:1–3)? **3.** Who is given the lion's share of the ministerial appointments (vv. 3–4)? On what grounds? **4.** By what means are the further divisions made, so as to balance out the natural advantage enjoyed by the more fruitful Eleazar? **5.** What might be the purpose of 24 evenly divided shifts? What rotation of duty would that allow them to do? **6.** What petty jealousies or party politics might this strategy avert? What might someone chosen first, second, last or second to last feel? **7.** What authorities (scribe, temporal and ultimate) stood behind this appointment process? How might that authority assure its rightness, control rumors and squelch any rebellion against these priestly divisions?

APPLY 1. Do you know someone who quietly serves the Lord for no apparent gain? Do you want to serve in this manner? **2.** Whether you were elected, appointed, or inherited your present job, what difference does that make in your job security? In your incentive to excel on the job? What difference does it make knowing God was in that selection process?

OPEN What venture or business partnership would you, a sibling or friend consider doing together? How would your sibling or friend complement you in this venture?

STUDY 1. Why do you suppose the chronicler was so concerned that no one should feel excluded (v. 20), and even repeated lists within the same book? Where have you seen these names before? **2.** For geneatectives only: How many generations separate Amram from Shubael? Who was Shubael's famous grandfather? How many generations separate Shelomoth from Levi? What change has happened to Shelomoth's name in only one chapter? Was Eleazar childless? Why is he listed next to Kish? **3.** What means is again used to

[26]The sons of Merari: Mahli and Mushi.
The son of Jaaziah: Beno.
[27]The sons of Merari:
from Jaaziah: Beno, Shoham, Zaccur and Ibri.
[28]From Mahli: Eleazar, who had no sons.
[29]From Kish: the son of Kish:
Jerahmeel.
[30]And the sons of Mushi: Mahli, Eder and Jerimoth.

These were the Levites, according to their families. [31]They also cast
lots, just as their brothers the descendants of Aaron did, in the
presence of King David and of Zadok, Ahimelech, and the heads of
families of the priests and of the Levites. The families of the oldest
brother were treated the same as those of the youngest.

The Singers

25 David, together with the commanders of the army, set apart some of the sons of Asaph, Heman and Jeduthun for the ministry of prophesying, accompanied by harps, lyres and cymbals. Here is the list of the men who performed this service:

[2]From the sons of Asaph:
Zaccur, Joseph, Nethaniah and Asarelah. The sons of Asaph were under the supervision of Asaph, who prophesied under the king's supervision.
[3]As for Jeduthun, from his sons:
Gedaliah, Zeri, Jeshaiah, Shimei,[a] Hashabiah and Mattithiah, six in all, under the supervision of their father Jeduthun, who prophesied, using the harp in thanking and praising the LORD.
[4]As for Heman, from his sons:
Bukkiah, Mattaniah, Uzziel, Shubael and Jerimoth; Hananiah, Hanani, Eliathah, Giddalti and Romamti-Ezer; Joshbekashah, Mallothi, Hothir and Mahazioth.
[5]All these were sons of Heman the king's seer. They were given him through the promises of God to exalt him.[b] God gave Heman fourteen sons and three daughters.

[6]All these men were under the supervision of their fathers for the music of the temple of the LORD, with cymbals, lyres and harps, for the ministry at the house of God. Asaph, Jeduthun and Heman were under the supervision of the king.
[7]Along with their relatives—all of them trained and skilled in music for the LORD—they numbered 288.
[8]Young and old alike, teacher as well as student, cast lots for their duties.

[9]The first lot, which was for Asaph, fell to Joseph,
his sons and relatives,[c] 12[d]
the second to Gedaliah,
he and his relatives and sons, 12

[a]3 One Hebrew manuscript and some Septuagint manuscripts (see also verse 17); most Hebrew manuscripts do not have *Shimei.* [b]5 Hebrew *exalt the horn* [c]9 See Septuagint; Hebrew does not have *his sons and relatives.* [d]9 See the total in verse 7; Hebrew does not have *twelve.*

ensure fairness and minimize power plays and party politics? Why all the witnesses?

APPLY By what means do you distribute privileges or chores evenly in the family? In church?

OPEN 1. What specific training or experience have you had in singing or playing a musical instrument in public? **2.** Would you ever consider using your talent in church? Why or why not?

STUDY 1. David is often portrayed as a hero without equal. Whom does David regularly depend on to get God's work accomplished? What three families are set apart by David and his Top Brass? Of these three families, who appears more equal than the rest? **2.** What instruments are designated here for special use? How might music serve as "prophesying"? **3.** Why would the music be of interest to "army commanders"? To David? To the people? Might this place the singers' songs on a par with Hebrew prophets and priests? Why or why not? **4.** The prophecy of musicians in ancient Israel was key to certain military decisions. How does that compare to the relative importance attached to the music program of your school or church? What role do your musicians play in discerning or conveying God's will for the church? **5.** What "skills in music for the Lord" were required in this temple service ensemble? What training was likely given young Hebrews in preparation for such temple music? Who likely did the teaching? **6.** What method of assigning roles and duties did David use? What problems did this avoid? What risks did this entail?

APPLY 1. In ancient Israel men of military *and* musical ability were needed to serve their

25:1 together with the commanders of the army. Far from an autocrat, David pulls together a cabinet of decision makers. **set apart ... ministry of prophesying.** During David's reign, musically gifted priests were encouraged to add their gifts to the people's worship experience. David also had a love for music.

[10] the third to Zaccur,
his sons and relatives, 12
[11] the fourth to Izri,[a]
his sons and relatives, 12
[12] the fifth to Nethaniah,
his sons and relatives, 12
[13] the sixth to Bukkiah,
his sons and relatives, 12
[14] the seventh to Jesarelah,[b]
his sons and relatives, 12
[15] the eighth to Jeshaiah,
his sons and relatives, 12
[16] the ninth to Mattaniah,
his sons and relatives, 12
[17] the tenth to Shimei,
his sons and relatives, 12
[18] the eleventh to Azarel,[c]
his sons and relatives, 12
[19] the twelfth to Hashabiah,
his sons and relatives, 12
[20] the thirteenth to Shubael,
his sons and relatives, 12
[21] the fourteenth to Mattithiah,
his sons and relatives, 12
[22] the fifteenth to Jerimoth,
his sons and relatives, 12
[23] the sixteenth to Hananiah,
his sons and relatives, 12
[24] the seventeenth to Joshbekashah,
his sons and relatives, 12
[25] the eighteenth to Hanani,
his sons and relatives, 12
[26] the nineteenth to Mallothi,
his sons and relatives, 12
[27] the twentieth to Eliathah,
his sons and relatives, 12
[28] the twenty-first to Hothir,
his sons and relatives, 12
[29] the twenty-second to Giddalti,
his sons and relatives, 12
[30] the twenty-third to Mahazioth,
his sons and relatives, 12
[31] the twenty-fourth to Romamti-Ezer,
his sons and relatives, 12

[a] *11* A variant of *Zeri* [b] *14* A variant of *Asarelah* [c] *18* A variant of *Uzziel*

nation. Today, what role does music play in military affairs: Encouraging the morale of the troops? Signaling troop movements? Recruiting volunteers? Encouraging loyalty back home? Prophesying and serving in places of worship? **2.** What advantages and disadvantages do you suppose a Minister of Music in David's era would have over today's music ministry? What would your church do with David's 288 trained singers? **3.** Are you able to let go with voice and heart in joyful singing? Or do you feel bashful, untrained, unmelodic? What would it take for you to move from the bashful stage to the kind of leadership shown by Gedaliah, Izri and Joshbekashah? Optional: Try a group sing-along to see what joyful noises and gifted resources you can share.

25:10–13 Throughout this chapter is name after name of the families who bore the responsibility for music in the house of the Lord. Filling the temple with music of praise was a very real priority for the nation. Like the tribal leaders, the great warriors and the priest, the musicians are recorded with a place of honor. For the nation to prosper, it needed to be obediently serving God. The future was determined by the devotion of the people to God. Worship was essential.

OPEN **1.** Where you live, do you lock up at night? During the day? Your car, too? Is your property fenced in? Is that locked, too? What does that say about your need for, or lack of, security? **2.** What experience have you had giving or receiving "guard duty": Pool lifeguard? Kid's babysitter? Night watchman? VIP's bodyguard? National Guard? Palace gatekeeper? Bailiff? Parole officer? Airport security?

STUDY **1.** What is this third most important function in Hebrew temple worship? (What were the other two?) What specifically did a gatekeeper do (v. 12; 9:22–29)? **2.** How many gatekeepers in all were there (vv. 6–11; compare 23:5)? Why the vast difference in numbers? **3.** Genealogies are loaded with name changes. What variation in Meshelemiah's name occurs in this very section? Likewise, in Ebiasaph's name (6:23, 9:19)? **4.** What do you remember about Obed-Edom (13:13–14)? Though not officially a Levite, how might his being "faithful in little" qualify him for adoption into this honored levitical duty of full-time temple service? Do you know anyone like this? **5.** How do you picture these guards: Lone Ranger types? All brawn, no brain? Ice in their veins? Stuffy country club types? Heartless tin woodsmen? Or what? **6.** How did they avoid petty jealousies, like who got duty at the south gate (the one most often used by the king)?

APPLY **1.** Are you responsible for safeguarding something? Who are you responsible to? **2.** What qualities are needed in someone who would be trusted to guard your most loved things or people? **3.** How can you be more trusted?

The Gatekeepers

26 The divisions of the gatekeepers:

From the Korahites: Meshelemiah son of Kore, one of the sons of Asaph.
2 Meshelemiah had sons:
Zechariah the firstborn,
Jediael the second,
Zebadiah the third,
Jathniel the fourth,
3 Elam the fifth,
Jehohanan the sixth
and Eliehoenai the seventh.
4 Obed-Edom also had sons:
Shemaiah the firstborn,
Jehozabad the second,
Joah the third,
Sacar the fourth,
Nethanel the fifth,
5 Ammiel the sixth,
Issachar the seventh
and Peullethai the eighth.
(For God had blessed Obed-Edom.)

6 His son Shemaiah also had sons, who were leaders in their
father's family because they were very capable men. 7 The sons
of Shemaiah: Othni, Rephael, Obed and Elzabad; his relatives
Elihu and Semakiah were also able men. 8 All these were
descendants of Obed-Edom; they and their sons and their
relatives were capable men with the strength to do the work—
descendants of Obed-Edom, 62 in all.
9 Meshelemiah had sons and relatives, who were able men—18 in
all.

10 Hosah the Merarite had sons: Shimri the first (although he was
not the firstborn, his father had appointed him the first), 11 Hilkiah the second, Tabaliah the third and Zechariah the fourth.
The sons and relatives of Hosah were 13 in all.
12 These divisions of the gatekeepers, through their chief men, had
duties for ministering in the temple of the LORD, just as their relatives
had. 13 Lots were cast for each gate, according to their families, young
and old alike.
14 The lot for the East Gate fell to Shelemiah.[a] Then lots were cast
for his son Zechariah, a wise counselor, and the lot for the North Gate
fell to him. 15 The lot for the South Gate fell to Obed-Edom, and the lot
for the storehouse fell to his sons. 16 The lots for the West Gate and
the Shalleketh Gate on the upper road fell to Shuppim and Hosah.
Guard was alongside of guard: 17 There were six Levites a day on
the east, four a day on the north, four a day on the south and two at

[a]14 A variant of *Meshelemiah*

26:1–19 The gatekeepers, formed from over 4,000 participants (23:5), served in a group of 22 at a time. The assignments are made through lots, similar to the way musicians were called to perform.

a time at the storehouse. 18 As for the court to the west, there were
four at the road and two at the court itself.

19 These were the divisions of the gatekeepers who were descendants of Korah and Merari.

The Treasurers and Other Officials

20 Their fellow Levites were[a] in charge of the treasuries of the house
of God and the treasuries for the dedicated things.

21 The descendants of Ladan, who were Gershonites through Ladan
and who were heads of families belonging to Ladan the Gershonite,
were Jehieli, 22 the sons of Jehieli, Zetham and his brother Joel. They
were in charge of the treasuries of the temple of the LORD.

23 From the Amramites, the Izharites, the Hebronites and the Uzzielites:

24 Shubael, a descendant of Gershom son of Moses, was the officer
in charge of the treasuries. 25 His relatives through Eliezer:
Rehabiah his son, Jeshaiah his son, Joram his son, Zicri his
son and Shelomith his son. 26 Shelomith and his relatives were
in charge of all the treasuries for the things dedicated by King
David, by the heads of families who were the commanders of
thousands and commanders of hundreds, and by the other
army commanders. 27 Some of the plunder taken in battle they
dedicated for the repair of the temple of the LORD. 28 And everything dedicated by Samuel the seer and by Saul son of Kish,
Abner son of Ner and Joab son of Zeruiah, and all the other
dedicated things were in the care of Shelomith and his relatives.

29 From the Izharites: Kenaniah and his sons were assigned duties
away from the temple, as officials and judges over Israel.

30 From the Hebronites: Hashabiah and his relatives—seventeen
hundred able men—were responsible in Israel west of the
Jordan for all the work of the LORD and for the king's service.
31 As for the Hebronites, Jeriah was their chief according to the
genealogical records of their families. In the fortieth year of
David's reign a search was made in the records, and capable
men among the Hebronites were found at Jazer in Gilead.
32 Jeriah had twenty-seven hundred relatives, who were able
men and heads of families, and King David put them in charge
of the Reubenites, the Gadites and the half-tribe of Manasseh
for every matter pertaining to God and for the affairs of the
king.

Army Divisions

27 This is the list of the Israelites—heads of families, commanders of thousands and commanders of hundreds, and their
officers, who served the king in all that concerned the army divisions

[a]20 Septuagint; Hebrew *As for the Levites, Ahijah was*

OPEN 1. Where do you hide extra cash: Shoe box? Refrigerator? **2.** Are you ever tempted to go on a shopping spree, using that college fund you've been saving? How do you protect long-range savings from short-term whims?

STUDY 1. What special service do the Levites offer here? What are these "treasuries" (vv. 20,26–28)? What do the other officials do (vv. 29–32)? **2.** How do these "last of the Levites" sustain their enthusiasm at a duller task? **3.** What job pressures do you think faced Shubael? What character qualities and job skills would be required for excellence in his field? **4.** How many officials and judges are required to administer justice outside Jerusalem (vv. 29–32; 23:4)? **5.** Is there any position in modern churches that parallels the work of these Levites? How essential is it to the work of the ministry?

APPLY 1. What view of the future *promotes* long-term financial planning in the church? What viewpoint *retards* such interest? **2.** Should ministries plan for the future? **3.** Should your group use its financial resources in ministry?

OPEN Of all you do each week, what would you gladly stop doing for a whole month? What would be impossible to stop for a month?

26:20 dedicated things. Temple officers served to receive and administrate the plunder from battles. The silver and gold from enemy cities would be dedicated to God's glory.

26:29–32 The remaining Levites operate in a more civic role as officials and judges.

26:30, 32 The complexity of the civic arrangements concludes with the role of those who work outside of Jerusalem. These traveling legal experts help keep the peace, and administer justice throughout the land

STUDY 1. What monthly duties are parceled out here? What advantage might this rotation of commanders have for David? For the privates and corporals? **2.** Review time for geneatectives (ch. 11): Who among the army commanders is already known for bravery? For foolhardy pursuit of personal enemies? For killing 300 enemy with a spear in one battle? Who appears by lineage to be a clergy-under-arms? Who also is listed among the roll call of David's "mighty men"? **3.** In delegating authority, is David trusting only hometown buddies and relatives? Or is he rewarding loyalty and experience? **4.** Just how large is this standing army? (Note: The Hebrew word for "1000" may mean "squad" or "squad leader." A squad was likely about 10 men.) **5.** The stress here seems to be on *symmetry* (to complement one another) rather than on *size*. How would this help ensure healthy Levitical divisions?

APPLY 1. In listing the physically powerful jobs last (ch. 27) and the artistic and liturgical jobs first (ch. 24–26), what does that suggest to young Hebrews who need heroes and role models? **2.** How satisfied are you with today's role models for children?

OPEN Who in your group can name your local, state and national representatives? What officials are hardest to remember?

STUDY 1. Which names in this list do you recognize from before? What "double duty" are some of them now doing? **2.** What two tribes, normally included in the roll call of "all Israel," are absent here? How many are present? **3.** What can you infer from verses 23–24 about the kind of work these officers tried to do? **4.** What new insight into David's

that were on duty month by month throughout the year. Each division consisted of 24,000 men.

2 In charge of the first division, for the first month, was Jashobeam son of Zabdiel. There were 24,000 men in his division. 3 He was a descendant of Perez and chief of all the army officers for the first month.
4 In charge of the division for the second month was Dodai the Ahohite; Mikloth was the leader of his division. There were 24,000 men in his division.
5 The third army commander, for the third month, was Benaiah son of Jehoiada the priest. He was chief and there were 24,000 men in his division. 6 This was the Benaiah who was a mighty man among the Thirty and was over the Thirty. His son Ammizabad was in charge of his division.
7 The fourth, for the fourth month, was Asahel the brother of Joab; his son Zebadiah was his successor. There were 24,000 men in his division.
8 The fifth, for the fifth month, was the commander Shamhuth the Izrahite. There were 24,000 men in his division.
9 The sixth, for the sixth month, was Ira the son of Ikkesh the Tekoite. There were 24,000 men in his division.
10 The seventh, for the seventh month, was Helez the Pelonite, an Ephraimite. There were 24,000 men in his division.
11 The eighth, for the eighth month, was Sibbecai the Hushathite, a Zerahite. There were 24,000 men in his division.
12 The ninth, for the ninth month, was Abiezer the Anathothite, a Benjamite. There were 24,000 men in his division.
13 The tenth, for the tenth month, was Maharai the Netophathite, a Zerahite. There were 24,000 men in his division.
14 The eleventh, for the eleventh month, was Benaiah the Pirathonite, an Ephraimite. There were 24,000 men in his division.
15 The twelfth, for the twelfth month, was Heldai the Netophathite, from the family of Othniel. There were 24,000 men in his division.

Officers of the Tribes

16 The officers over the tribes of Israel:

over the Reubenites: Eliezer son of Zicri;
over the Simeonites: Shephatiah son of Maacah;
17 over Levi: Hashabiah son of Kemuel;
over Aaron: Zadok;
18 over Judah: Elihu, a brother of David;
over Issachar: Omri son of Michael;
19 over Zebulun: Ishmaiah son of Obadiah;
over Naphtali: Jerimoth son of Azriel;
20 over the Ephraimites: Hoshea son of Azaziah;
over half the tribe of Manasseh: Joel son of Pedaiah;

27:2–20 David rotates his soldiers through the use of divisions. Each unit, consisting of 24,000 men, goes on active duty one month each year.

27:16–22 Each tribe of Israel symbolizes its loyalty to King David through the representation of its officer.

[21] over the half-tribe of Manasseh in Gilead: Iddo son of Zechariah;
over Benjamin: Jaasiel son of Abner;
[22] over Dan: Azarel son of Jeroham.
These were the officers over the tribes of Israel.

[23] David did not take the number of the men twenty years old or
less, because the LORD had promised to make Israel as numerous as
the stars in the sky. [24] Joab son of Zeruiah began to count the men but
did not finish. Wrath came on Israel on account of this numbering,
and the number was not entered in the book[a] of the annals of King
David.

The King's Overseers

[25] Azmaveth son of Adiel was in charge of the royal storehouses.
Jonathan son of Uzziah was in charge of the storehouses in the outlying districts, in the towns, the villages and the watchtowers.
[26] Ezri son of Kelub was in charge of the field workers who farmed
the land.
[27] Shimei the Ramathite was in charge of the vineyards.
Zabdi the Shiphmite was in charge of the produce of the vineyards for the wine vats.
[28] Baal-Hanan the Gederite was in charge of the olive and
sycamore-fig trees in the western foothills.
Joash was in charge of the supplies of olive oil.
[29] Shitrai the Sharonite was in charge of the herds grazing in Sharon.
Shaphat son of Adlai was in charge of the herds in the valleys.
[30] Obil the Ishmaelite was in charge of the camels.
Jehdeiah the Meronothite was in charge of the donkeys.
[31] Jaziz the Hagrite was in charge of the flocks.
All these were the officials in charge of King David's property.
[32] Jonathan, David's uncle, was a counselor, a man of insight and a
scribe. Jehiel son of Hacmoni took care of the king's sons.
[33] Ahithophel was the king's counselor.
Hushai the Arkite was the king's friend. [34] Ahithophel was succeeded by Jehoiada son of Benaiah and by Abiathar.
Joab was the commander of the royal army.

David's Plans for the Temple

28 David summoned all the officials of Israel to assemble at Jerusalem: the officers over the tribes, the commanders of the divisions in the service of the king, the commanders of thousands and commanders of hundreds, and the officials in charge of all the property and livestock belonging to the king and his sons, together with the palace officials, the mighty men and all the brave warriors.
[2] King David rose to his feet and said: "Listen to me, my brothers

[a]24 Septuagint; Hebrew *number*

wrong-headed census is provided here?

APPLY 1. Some jobs are better left undone, like David's ill-advised census. What projects have you unwisely started and wisely aborted? **2.** Do you keep a "book of annals"? Does your church?

OPEN 1. Fill in these blanks: "I am in charge of ______. I want to be in charge of ______, but only for one day." **2.** Are you a "take charge" person? Or more laid back? Would you ever take charge of your small group? Or family property?

STUDY 1. Write one job description for the property overseers (vv. 25–31); a second one for the royal cabinet (vv. 32–34). Include "key objectives" and "skills required." How do the two compare? **2.** Why would this "man after God's own heart" need a professional friend or spiritual leader (1 Kin. 2)?

APPLY 1. These good people began their careers entrusted with royal resources. Where did you begin your career? Where has it led you? **2.** What is your basic job description? Anything like these men? Who is your "friend," counselor or protector?

OPEN 1. Which PK's (President's Kids) are unforgettable for you? How many former First Family sons or daughters do you know anything about? **2.** In what ways are you known by reference to your dad: Same looks? Same career? Same Lord? Same virtues and vices?

STUDY 1. From clues in just this chapter, what kind of king was David? What kind of father was

27:23 numerous as the stars. The chronicler's phrase is reminiscent of God's promise to Abraham (Gen. 12:2). Inspired by God's assurance, David does not need to include the younger warriors in order to boost his confidence.

27:24 the number was not entered. David's military strength needs no fixed number. David counts on God's assurance.

27:25–31 The property overseers dealt with the complexities related to David's real estate and royal resources.

28:1 David finally proclaims the succession of his son Solomon. Every official is summoned to hear David's plans for the temple and the future of Israel.

he? How are the two roles related? **2.** How is this account of David and Solomon like and unlike the one in chapter 22? Which one is private? Public? **3.** How does this combined account compare to the transition between Moses and Joshua: Who failed to attain their goals? Why? Who succeeds in bringing the people to "rest"? Who has a direct pipeline to God for detailed plans (of tabernacle and temple)? What verbal assurances are given in parallel manner? **4.** Enlightening, as well, is the comparison between the version here and the one in 1 Kings 1–2. They present contrasting portraits of David's transition to retirement and Solomon's succession to power. Which one is peaceful and smooth? Uncertain and rocky? Where do you see cynical realism? Or cautious optimism? Bittersweet sorrow? Bloodless coup attempt and bloody rebel purge? **5.** What picture of God is drawn here? To whom does the temple belong? And the people? And the kingdom? What difference should that make to Solomon? To Mr. and Mrs. Fig-Farmer? To the remnant of Israel, who were the first readers of the chronicler's book? **6.** Are there any lasting truths that we can apply to leadership and to parenting?

APPLY 1. What can you do to become a "David" to some "Solomon" whom God has chosen to receive blessing through you? **2.** How might you apply God's powerful promise (v. 20) to your life's work? How about your group? **3.** List three things you should work on in your life? How can this group help you make these changes?

---

and my people. I had it in my heart to build a house as a place of rest for the ark of the covenant of the LORD, for the footstool of our God, and I made plans to build it. 3But God said to me, 'You are not to build a house for my Name, because you are a warrior and have shed blood.'

4"Yet the LORD, the God of Israel, chose me from my whole family to be king over Israel forever. He chose Judah as leader, and from the house of Judah he chose my family, and from my father's sons he was pleased to make me king over all Israel. 5Of all my sons—and the LORD has given me many—he has chosen my son Solomon to sit on the throne of the kingdom of the LORD over Israel. 6He said to me: 'Solomon your son is the one who will build my house and my courts, for I have chosen him to be my son, and I will be his father. 7I will establish his kingdom forever if he is unswerving in carrying out my commands and laws, as is being done at this time.'

8"So now I charge you in the sight of all Israel and of the assembly of the LORD, and in the hearing of our God: Be careful to follow all the commands of the LORD your God, that you may possess this good land and pass it on as an inheritance to your descendants forever.

9"And you, my son Solomon, acknowledge the God of your father, and serve him with wholehearted devotion and with a willing mind, for the LORD searches every heart and understands every motive behind the thoughts. If you seek him, he will be found by you; but if you forsake him, he will reject you forever. 10Consider now, for the LORD has chosen you to build a temple as a sanctuary. Be strong and do the work."

11Then David gave his son Solomon the plans for the portico of the temple, its buildings, its storerooms, its upper parts, its inner rooms and the place of atonement. 12He gave him the plans of all that the Spirit had put in his mind for the courts of the temple of the LORD and all the surrounding rooms, for the treasuries of the temple of God and for the treasuries for the dedicated things. 13He gave him instructions for the divisions of the priests and Levites, and for all the work of serving in the temple of the LORD, as well as for all the articles to be used in its service. 14He designated the weight of gold for all the gold articles to be used in various kinds of service, and the weight of silver for all the silver articles to be used in various kinds of service: 15the weight of gold for the gold lampstands and their lamps, with the weight for each lampstand and its lamps; and the weight of silver for each silver lampstand and its lamps, according to the use of each lampstand; 16the weight of gold for each table for consecrated bread; the weight of silver for the silver tables; 17the weight of pure gold for the forks, sprinkling bowls and pitchers; the weight of gold for each gold dish; the weight of silver for each silver dish; 18and the weight of the refined gold for the altar of incense. He also gave him the plan for the chariot, that is, the cherubim of gold that spread their wings and shelter the ark of the covenant of the LORD.

19"All this," David said, "I have in writing from the hand of the LORD upon me, and he gave me understanding in all the details of the plan."

28:5 he has chosen. David emphasizes God's selection of the next king. Like his father, Solomon enjoyed the assurance of being divinely appointed to his throne. The call of David was extended to his descendants.

20 David also said to Solomon his son, "Be strong and courageous,
and do the work. Do not be afraid or discouraged, for the LORD God,
my God, is with you. He will not fail you or forsake you until all the
work for the service of the temple of the LORD is finished. 21 The divisions of the priests and Levites are ready for all the work on the
temple of God, and every willing man skilled in any craft will help you
in all the work. The officials and all the people will obey your every
command."

Gifts for Building the Temple

29 Then King David said to the whole assembly: "My son
Solomon, the one whom God has chosen, is young and inexperienced. The task is great, because this palatial structure is not
for man but for the LORD God. 2 With all my resources I have provided
for the temple of my God—gold for the gold work, silver for the silver,
bronze for the bronze, iron for the iron and wood for the wood, as
well as onyx for the settings, turquoise,[a] stones of various colors, and
all kinds of fine stone and marble—all of these in large quantities.
3 Besides, in my devotion to the temple of my God I now give my personal treasures of gold and silver for the temple of my God, over and
above everything I have provided for this holy temple: 4 three thousand talents[b] of gold (gold of Ophir) and seven thousand talents[c] of
refined silver, for the overlaying of the walls of the buildings, 5 for the
gold work and the silver work, and for all the work to be done by
the craftsmen. Now, who is willing to consecrate himself today to the
LORD?"

6 Then the leaders of families, the officers of the tribes of Israel, the
commanders of thousands and commanders of hundreds, and the officials in charge of the king's work gave willingly. 7 They gave toward
the work on the temple of God five thousand talents[d] and ten thousand darics[e] of gold, ten thousand talents[f] of silver, eighteen thousand talents[g] of bronze and a hundred thousand talents[h] of iron. 8 Any
who had precious stones gave them to the treasury of the temple of
the LORD in the custody of Jehiel the Gershonite. 9 The people rejoiced
at the willing response of their leaders, for they had given freely and
wholeheartedly to the LORD. David the king also rejoiced greatly.

David's Prayer

10 David praised the LORD in the presence of the whole assembly,
saying,

"Praise be to you, O LORD,
God of our father Israel,
from everlasting to everlasting.
11 Yours, O LORD, is the greatness and the power
and the glory and the majesty and the splendor,

[a]2 The meaning of the Hebrew for this word is uncertain. [b]4 That is, about 110 tons (about 100 metric tons) [c]4 That is, about 260 tons (about 240 metric tons) [d]7 That is, about 190 tons (about 170 metric tons) [e]7 That is, about 185 pounds (about 84 kilograms) [f]7 That is, about 375 tons (about 345 metric tons) [g]7 That is, about 675 tons (about 610 metric tons) [h]7 That is, about 3,750 tons (about 3,450 metric tons)

OPEN How do you gauge *loyalty* to a grocery store? To a TV network? To a national football or soccer team? To your small group? Are you "loyal"?

STUDY 1. How does David's use of money become a model of loyalty? To what three things is David most loyal? **2.** To what top priorities are the people loyal (vv. 6–9)? Do their hearts follow their money? Or vice-versa? Why? **3.** As Solomon is still "young and inexperienced," where is David placing his faith (and gifts): In missions? Bricks and mortar? People? Worship? Education? Or what?

APPLY 1. How does David's fund-raising strategy rate against all the financial appeals you receive? **2.** If outside auditors were to look over your checkbook, what would they conclude about your top loyalties? How would you like to change that?

OPEN 1. Do you have a hard time taking a gift? Do you feel embarrassed when you sense that you have a need? **2.** Who gave to you last week? How did you express your gratitude: Returned the favor? Thank-you note? IOU? Took it for granted? Other?

STUDY This is the transition from David's rule to the reign of Solomon. With this change the book closes. David gives a farewell address and the people throw a party. **1.** As David nears retirement, what three things are uppermost on his mind? What fears may lurk behind those

29:2–9 The capstone of David's reign is the initiation of the building of the temple. David dedicates his personal wealth to its construction. The people gladly respond to his leadership, and voluntarily give their gifts.

priorities? **2.** What is David's view of how a nation prospers? Of who leads a nation? What seems to be his formula for "life, liberty and the pursuit of happiness"? **3.** How does David view God: Privately, as his own Savior? Corporately, as Israel's Deliverer and Provider? Cosmically, as Lord of the universe? Or what? **4.** By what gesture, rare today, do the people respond to David's prayer? **5.** What signs of party unity and total support does the chronicler portray here? Why has he neglected Adonijah's rebellion, which led aides and sons of the king to openly rebel (1 Kin. 1:9,19,25)? Is that why the chronicler refers to "a second time" (v. 22)? If so, when was the "first time"?

APPLY 1. What aspects of this prayer are useful to Christians today? What parts seem outdated? (What about bowing low? Falling prostrate? Praising God aloud?) Paraphrase this prayer in the language and concerns of your group. **2.** Like David, are you "without hope"? Where do you place your hope? What area of your life do you feel hopeless or needy in? **3.** Option: Throw a party yourself, to celebrate the unity your group has achieved in pursuit of truth, treasure and trivia in Chronicles! Dedicate one of each (truth, treasure and trivia) to the Lord.

for everything in heaven and earth is yours.
Yours, O LORD, is the kingdom;
you are exalted as head over all.
12 Wealth and honor come from you;
you are the ruler of all things.
In your hands are strength and power
to exalt and give strength to all.
13 Now, our God, we give you thanks,
and praise your glorious name.

14 "But who am I, and who are my people, that we should be able to
give as generously as this? Everything comes from you, and we have
given you only what comes from your hand. 15 We are aliens and
strangers in your sight, as were all our forefathers. Our days on earth
are like a shadow, without hope. 16 O LORD our God, as for all this
abundance that we have provided for building you a temple for your
Holy Name, it comes from your hand, and all of it belongs to you.
17 I know, my God, that you test the heart and are pleased with integrity. All these things have I given willingly and with honest intent. And
now I have seen with joy how willingly your people who are here
have given to you. 18 O LORD, God of our fathers Abraham, Isaac and
Israel, keep this desire in the hearts of your people forever, and keep
their hearts loyal to you. 19 And give my son Solomon the wholehearted devotion to keep your commands, requirements and decrees
and to do everything to build the palatial structure for which I have
provided."

20 Then David said to the whole assembly, "Praise the LORD your
God." So they all praised the LORD, the God of their fathers; they
bowed low and fell prostrate before the LORD and the king.

Solomon Acknowledged as King

21 The next day they made sacrifices to the LORD and presented
burnt offerings to him: a thousand bulls, a thousand rams and a
thousand male lambs, together with their drink offerings, and other
sacrifices in abundance for all Israel. 22 They ate and drank with great
joy in the presence of the LORD that day.

Then they acknowledged Solomon son of David as king a second
time, anointing him before the LORD to be ruler and Zadok to be
priest. 23 So Solomon sat on the throne of the LORD as king in place of
his father David. He prospered and all Israel obeyed him. 24 All the
officers and mighty men, as well as all of King David's sons, pledged
their submission to King Solomon.

25 The LORD highly exalted Solomon in the sight of all Israel and
bestowed on him royal splendor such as no king over Israel ever had
before.

The Death of David

26 David son of Jesse was king over all Israel. 27 He ruled over Israel
forty years—seven in Hebron and thirty-three in Jerusalem. 28 He died

---

29:22 a second time. Nearly two years prior, David had appointed Solomon to be king (23:1). However, the time had come for the official transition of power.

29:24 All the officers and mighty men. David's officers continue the chronicler's theme of unity among Israel in support for the king.

at a good old age, having enjoyed long life, wealth and honor. His son
Solomon succeeded him as king.
29 As for the events of King David's reign, from beginning to end,
they are written in the records of Samuel the seer, the records of
Nathan the prophet and the records of Gad the seer, 30 together with
the details of his reign and power, and the circumstances that surrounded him and Israel and the kingdoms of all the other lands.

2 Chronicles

Author. Both 1 Chronicles and 2 Chronicles were probably written by the same author, because of the similarity of style. Ezra is considered to be the author in Jewish tradition.

Date. First and 2 Chronicles were probably written around 400 B.C. Second Chronicles covers the events of Solomon's reign and the kings of Judah after him.

Purpose. The book reviews much of the historical data found in 1 and 2 Kings, but from a different perspective. As in 1 Chronicles, this book offers a spiritual history of the period. Rather than giving historical facts or even lessons from them, it describes the spiritual condition of the kingdom and gives hope to readers.

Personal Reading	Group Study Topic and Reading	
1–2	Solomon's Wisdom	1:1–17
3–7	Dedicating the Temple	7:1–10
8–9	Solomon's Splendor	9:13–28
10–12	The Great Divide	10:1–11:4
13–16	Asa's Reform	15:1–19
17:1–21:3	Jehoshaphat's Reform	20:1–30
21:4–22:9	Jehoram's Evil Ways	21:4–20
22:10–24:27	Fickle Joash	24:1–4,17–27
25–26	Uzziah's Reform	26:1–23
27–28	Ahaz's "Unjust War"	28:1–27
29–32	Hezekiah's Reform	30:1–31:1
33:1–36:1	Josiah's Reform	34:14–33
36:2–23	Jerusalem's Fall	36:15–23

Historical Background. The writer of 2 Chronicles reflects on the period of the kings, from Solomon to the exile, with a different set of priorities than the writer of 1 and 2 Kings. Historically, the period of the kings was characterized by repeated disobedience of the law, particularly in worshipping other gods and idols. The writer of 1 and 2 Kings focuses on these failures as the causes for Israel and Judah's fall and exile. The writer of 2 Chronicles describes the same years yet tends to brush over the failures and concentrate on the successes. Likewise, the author clearly focuses on the kings of Judah and not Israel. Israel was closer to the trade routes and was therefore susceptible to corrupting, outside influences. Judah, on the other hand, slid more slowly into disobedience. Second Chronicles focuses on the kings of Judah and their efforts to reform their wayward people.

Historically and spiritually, the kingship initiated by David and continued in Judah was the focal point of Israel's success and power. Second Chronicles offers hope from that period against the despair and insecurity that the post-exilic remnant felt when they returned home.

The Reforms. The highlights of 2 Chronicles are the reforms of the kings who tried to do right in the eyes of God. In Judah, the most famous of these kings were Asa, Jehoshaphat, Hezekiah and Josiah. Asa began his reign by deposing his wicked grandmother and her idolatrous priests. Jehoshaphat established formal religious education for his people in only the third year of his reign. Hezekiah reopened and cleansed the temple and celebrated the Passover feast. Josiah rediscovered the law of Moses and led sweeping reforms among the religious leadership. Other kings instituted periods of reform as well, but these four stand above the rest.

Solomon Asks for Wisdom

1 Solomon son of David established himself firmly over his
kingdom, for the LORD his God was with him and made him
exceedingly great.
[2]Then Solomon spoke to all Israel—to the commanders of thousands and commanders of hundreds, to the judges and to all the
leaders in Israel, the heads of families— [3]and Solomon and the
whole assembly went to the high place at Gibeon, for God's Tent of
Meeting was there, which Moses the LORD's servant had made in the
desert. [4]Now David had brought up the ark of God from Kiriath Jearim
to the place he had prepared for it, because he had pitched a tent for
it in Jerusalem. [5]But the bronze altar that Bezalel son of Uri, the son
of Hur, had made was in Gibeon in front of the tabernacle of the LORD;
so Solomon and the assembly inquired of him there. [6]Solomon went
up to the bronze altar before the LORD in the Tent of Meeting and
offered a thousand burnt offerings on it.
[7]That night God appeared to Solomon and said to him, "Ask for
whatever you want me to give you."
[8]Solomon answered God, "You have shown great kindness to
David my father and have made me king in his place. [9]Now, LORD
God, let your promise to my father David be confirmed, for you have
made me king over a people who are as numerous as the dust of the
earth. [10]Give me wisdom and knowledge, that I may lead this people,
for who is able to govern this great people of yours?"
[11]God said to Solomon, "Since this is your heart's desire and you
have not asked for wealth, riches or honor, nor for the death of your
enemies, and since you have not asked for a long life but for wisdom
and knowledge to govern my people over whom I have made you
king, [12]therefore wisdom and knowledge will be given you. And I will
also give you wealth, riches and honor, such as no king who was
before you ever had and none after you will have."
[13]Then Solomon went to Jerusalem from the high place at Gibeon,
from before the Tent of Meeting. And he reigned over Israel.
[14]Solomon accumulated chariots and horses; he had fourteen
hundred chariots and twelve thousand horses,[a] which he kept in the
chariot cities and also with him in Jerusalem. [15]The king made silver
and gold as common in Jerusalem as stones, and cedar as plentiful as
sycamore-fig trees in the foothills. [16]Solomon's horses were imported from Egypt[b] and from Kue[c]—the royal merchants purchased
them from Kue. [17]They imported a chariot from Egypt for six hundred
shekels[d] of silver, and a horse for a hundred and fifty.[e] They also
exported them to all the kings of the Hittites and of the Arameans.

[a]14 Or *charioteers* [b]16 Or possibly *Muzur,* a region in Cilicia; also in verse 17 [c]16 Probably Cilicia [d]17 That is, about 15 pounds (about 7 kilograms) [e]17 That is, about 3 3/4 pounds (about 1.7 kilograms)

OPEN 1. What moment over the past few months would you label as "exceedingly great" in your life? **2.** What outside of work, family and church is most important to you?

STUDY The book begins with Solomon, newly established in office, seeking after God. The chronicler (the person who wrote the book of Chronicles) makes it clear that Solomon began his reign on the right foot, eliminating some of the more sordid details of Solomon's life as related in 1 Kings 1–2. **1.** If you had to choose one word to describe your first impression of Solomon, what word would it be: Powerful? Spiritual? Wealthy? Wise? Humble? Blessed? Extravagant? Generous? **2.** Note Solomon's response to God's question in verse 7. How do you think God would have responded if Solomon had asked for wealth, riches and honor instead of wisdom and knowledge? **3.** Why do you think God goes beyond the original offer? **4.** Jesus said, "Seek first his kingdom and his righteousness, and all these things will be given to you as well" (Matt. 6:33). Do you think that is the principle at work here? **5.** What do you learn about Solomon in verses 14–17? **6.** Based solely on this chapter, how would you evaluate Solomon's character? How about his relationship with God? So far, do you think he deserves to be called "exceedingly great" (v. 1)?

APPLY 1. If you could ask God for anything right now, for what would you ask? **2.** Looking back over your life as a whole, do you feel that you have received more than you asked for from God or less than you asked for from God?

1:1 made him exceedingly great. Solomon became known as one of the greatest leaders in Israel's history. The nation enjoyed widespread stability and prosperity during his reign. Solomon's widsom enabled him to accomplish much.

1:7 whatever you want me to give you. As a sign of his blessing, God gives Solomon a blank check. Anything he requests would be granted.

1:9 dust of the earth. God promised Abraham a nation so large he would not be able to count the people (Gen. 13:16). Solomon now requests wisdom for the daunting task of leading the large population promised to Abraham.

OPEN **1.** Share a time in your life when you did not feel "qualified" or "up" for a task. **2.** For what would you come closest to receiving an "award for excellence": Singing? Making soup? Encouraging others? Sewing? Writing? Gardening? Woodworking? Staying positive?

STUDY Lacking the skilled craftsmen and cedar logs, Solomon enlists foreign help with the construction of the temple and his palace. The construction of the temple will be his greatest accomplishment, and a portion of it (The Wailing Wall) continues to stand today. **1.** How does Solomon describe the temple he wants to build to King Hiram of Tyre? Why do you think its construction was so important to Solomon? **2.** Hiram would have worshiped Phoenician deities. How do you suppose Solomon's saying, "Our God is greater than all other gods," set with him (v. 5)? **3.** How would you characterize Solomon's relationship with Hiram: Solomon was Hiram's vassal? Hiram was Solomon's vassal? They were friendly allies? They were equals in status and power? **4.** How did Solomon procure the necessary labor to build the temple? Compare verse 17 with 1 Kings 5:13–18. What do the words "forced labor" and "aliens" suggest to you about the work force? **5.** If you had been Huram-Abi, the master craftsman sent by Hiram to Solomon, how would you have felt about your new job assignment? **6.** Considering the entire chapter, what grade (A, B, C, D, F) would you give Solomon in the following areas: Administration? Foreign diplomacy? Civil Rights? Religion? **7.** Is there someone in your group or church that would be like Huram-Abi in building the temple?

APPLY **1.** Where could you use some help with a project: At home? At church? At the office? **2.** If you could do something significant for God, what would it be? **3.** Is there a major project that your church or your group should be a part of?

Preparations for Building the Temple

2 Solomon gave orders to build a temple for the Name of the LORD
and a royal palace for himself. 2 He conscripted seventy thousand
men as carriers and eighty thousand as stonecutters in the hills and
thirty-six hundred as foremen over them.
3 Solomon sent this message to Hiram[a] king of Tyre:

"Send me cedar logs as you did for my father David when you
sent him cedar to build a palace to live in. 4 Now I am about to
build a temple for the Name of the LORD my God and to dedicate
it to him for burning fragrant incense before him, for setting out
the consecrated bread regularly, and for making burnt offerings
every morning and evening and on Sabbaths and New Moons
and at the appointed feasts of the LORD our God. This is a lasting
ordinance for Israel.
5 "The temple I am going to build will be great, because our
God is greater than all other gods. 6 But who is able to build a
temple for him, since the heavens, even the highest heavens,
cannot contain him? Who then am I to build a temple for him,
except as a place to burn sacrifices before him?
7 "Send me, therefore, a man skilled to work in gold and silver,
bronze and iron, and in purple, crimson and blue yarn, and experienced
in the art of engraving, to work in Judah and Jerusalem
with my skilled craftsmen, whom my father David provided.
8 "Send me also cedar, pine and algum[b] logs from Lebanon, for
I know that your men are skilled in cutting timber there. My men
will work with yours 9 to provide me with plenty of lumber, because
the temple I build must be large and magnificent. 10 I will
give your servants, the woodsmen who cut the timber, twenty
thousand cors[c] of ground wheat, twenty thousand cors of barley,
twenty thousand baths[d] of wine and twenty thousand baths of
olive oil."

11 Hiram king of Tyre replied by letter to Solomon:

"Because the LORD loves his people, he has made you their
king."

12 And Hiram added:

"Praise be to the LORD, the God of Israel, who made heaven
and earth! He has given King David a wise son, endowed with intelligence
and discernment, who will build a temple for the LORD
and a palace for himself.
13 "I am sending you Huram-Abi, a man of great skill, 14 whose
mother was from Dan and whose father was from Tyre. He is
trained to work in gold and silver, bronze and iron, stone and
wood, and with purple and blue and crimson yarn and fine linen.

[a] 3 Hebrew *Huram,* a variant of *Hiram;* also in verses 11 and 12 [b] 8 Probably a variant of *almug;* possibly juniper [c] *10* That is, probably about 125,000 bushels (about 4,400 kiloliters) [d] *10* That is, probably about 115,000 gallons (about 440 kiloliters)

2:1 temple. Solomon begins the construction of the temple according to God's promise. It would be the greatest accomplishment of his reign.

2:3–10 Solomon sends the king of Tyre, Hiram, a specific order concerning Hiram's contribution to the construction of the temple. Hiram's participation would have spiritual and material significance. Solomon and Hiram had a close relationship, both were respected world leaders.

He is experienced in all kinds of engraving and can execute any design given to him. He will work with your craftsmen and with those of my lord, David your father.

15 "Now let my lord send his servants the wheat and barley and the olive oil and wine he promised, 16 and we will cut all the logs from Lebanon that you need and will float them in rafts by sea down to Joppa. You can then take them up to Jerusalem."

17 Solomon took a census of all the aliens who were in Israel, after the census his father David had taken; and they were found to be 153,600. 18 He assigned 70,000 of them to be carriers and 80,000 to be stonecutters in the hills, with 3,600 foremen over them to keep the people working.

Solomon Builds the Temple

3 Then Solomon began to build the temple of the LORD in Jerusalem on Mount Moriah, where the LORD had appeared to his father David. It was on the threshing floor of Araunah[a] the Jebusite, the place provided by David. 2 He began building on the second day of the second month in the fourth year of his reign.

3 The foundation Solomon laid for building the temple of God was sixty cubits long and twenty cubits wide[b] (using the cubit of the old standard). 4 The portico at the front of the temple was twenty cubits[c] long across the width of the building and twenty cubits[d] high.

He overlaid the inside with pure gold. 5 He paneled the main hall with pine and covered it with fine gold and decorated it with palm tree and chain designs. 6 He adorned the temple with precious stones. And the gold he used was gold of Parvaim. 7 He overlaid the ceiling beams, doorframes, walls and doors of the temple with gold, and he carved cherubim on the walls.

8 He built the Most Holy Place, its length corresponding to the width of the temple—twenty cubits long and twenty cubits wide. He overlaid the inside with six hundred talents[e] of fine gold. 9 The gold nails weighed fifty shekels.[f] He also overlaid the upper parts with gold.

10 In the Most Holy Place he made a pair of sculptured cherubim and overlaid them with gold. 11 The total wingspan of the cherubim was twenty cubits. One wing of the first cherub was five cubits[g] long and touched the temple wall, while its other wing, also five cubits long, touched the wing of the other cherub. 12 Similarly one wing of the second cherub was five cubits long and touched the other temple wall, and its other wing, also five cubits long, touched the wing of the first cherub. 13 The wings of these cherubim extended twenty cubits. They stood on their feet, facing the main hall.[h]

[a] *1* Hebrew *Ornan*, a variant of *Araunah* [b] *3* That is, about 90 feet (about 27 meters) long and 30 feet (about 9 meters) wide [c] *4* That is, about 30 feet (about 9 meters); also in verses 8, 11 and 13 [d] *4* Some Septuagint and Syriac manuscripts; Hebrew *and a hundred and twenty* [e] *8* That is, about 23 tons (about 21 metric tons) [f] *9* That is, about 1 1/4 pounds (about 0.6 kilogram) [g] *11* That is, about 7 1/2 feet (about 2.3 meters); also in verse 15 [h] *13* Or *facing inward*

OPEN 1. Describe the decor of your bedroom when you were 12. **2.** What is one of the most impressive buildings you have ever had the pleasure of entering?

STUDY After conscripting a workforce and obtaining the necessary building materials, Solomon begins constructing the temple. The construction commences in his fourth year as king of Israel. He will spare no expense on the project. **1.** What is your initial impression of the temple: Awesome? A waste of money? Different strokes for different folks? Classy? Over the top? **2.** What do you think Solomon had in mind by locating the temple on Mount Moriah (Gen. 22)? On the threshing floor of Araunah (1 Chr. 21:20–22:1)? **3.** One cubit equals approximately 1 1/2 feet. How does the foundation of the building (90 feet by 30 feet) correspond to the size you may have first had in mind? **4.** What were the three main parts of the temple? What special decorations would you have seen as you approached the temple? What message would they convey? **5.** Given the Hebrew insistence on bringing the best to God such as the firstfruits of crops, unblemished animals, and full tithes, do you think Solomon was right in spending so much on the temple? Do you think God would have been satisfied with less?

APPLY 1. Where is one of your favorite places to meet God? **2.** Where might God be calling you to be extravagant? **3.** What could your group do to make the place you

2:17–18 Solomon ensures that those who enjoy the bounty of his kingdom pay some of the freight. As a result, non-Israelites are enlisted to work at the temple site.

3:1 temple of the LORD. The temple would rise over the spot where Abraham and his son, Isaac, learned the importance of an obedient sacrifice (Gen. 22).

3:8 Picture a perfect cube when imagining the Most Holy Place. This proportionately square room would house the presence of God himself.

meet or the environment of your meeting more focused on the Lord?

OPEN 1. What piece of furniture do you particularly remember from your childhood home? **2.** How would you describe the furnishings in your home: A touch of class? Garage-sale steals? Eclectic ensemble? Child and pet tested? Well-worn? An interior decorator's delight? Early dorm life? Manly? A walk on the wild side? Vanilla? Knock your socks off? Frilly?

STUDY Now that the building is up, the task of furnishing the temple begins. A dazzling display of earthly treasures will be used for worship. Some of the items will be placed in the temple courtyard rather than within the temple itself. The 17,500 gallon basin for ceremonial washing is particularly impressive. **1.** In verses 1–11, what objects did Solomon have made to furnish the temple? How was each to be used? Which of them would you have wanted to examine closely? **2.** The Sea of cast metal is also described in 1 Kings 7:23–26. What are the differences between that description and the one in this chapter? How might you account for these differences? **3.** The master craftsman on loan from the king of Tyre, Huram-Abi, was first mentioned in 3:13–16. From the way his work is described here, how many stars (one star being the lowest and five stars being the highest) would you give him for his work? **4.** What temple-like furnishings do you notice still being used in churches today? What furnishings seem to have dropped by the wayside? **5.** Solomon brought the things his father dedicated into the temple. What do you think that says about Solomon's relationship with his father? **6.** How important are beautiful things for your own worship of

14 He made the curtain of blue, purple and crimson yarn and fine linen, with cherubim worked into it.

15 In the front of the temple he made two pillars, which ⌞together⌟ were thirty-five cubits[a] long, each with a capital on top measuring five cubits. 16 He made interwoven chains[b] and put them on top of the pillars. He also made a hundred pomegranates and attached them to the chains. 17 He erected the pillars in the front of the temple, one to the south and one to the north. The one to the south he named Jakin[c] and the one to the north Boaz.[d]

The Temple's Furnishings

4 He made a bronze altar twenty cubits long, twenty cubits wide and ten cubits high.[e] 2 He made the Sea of cast metal, circular in shape, measuring ten cubits from rim to rim and five cubits[f] high. It took a line of thirty cubits[g] to measure around it. 3 Below the rim, figures of bulls encircled it—ten to a cubit.[h] The bulls were cast in two rows in one piece with the Sea.

4 The Sea stood on twelve bulls, three facing north, three facing west, three facing south and three facing east. The Sea rested on top of them, and their hindquarters were toward the center. 5 It was a handbreadth[i] in thickness, and its rim was like the rim of a cup, like a lily blossom. It held three thousand baths.[j]

6 He then made ten basins for washing and placed five on the south side and five on the north. In them the things to be used for the burnt offerings were rinsed, but the Sea was to be used by the priests for washing.

7 He made ten gold lampstands according to the specifications for them and placed them in the temple, five on the south side and five on the north.

8 He made ten tables and placed them in the temple, five on the south side and five on the north. He also made a hundred gold sprinkling bowls.

9 He made the courtyard of the priests, and the large court and the doors for the court, and overlaid the doors with bronze. 10 He placed the Sea on the south side, at the southeast corner.

11 He also made the pots and shovels and sprinkling bowls.

So Huram finished the work he had undertaken for King Solomon in the temple of God:

12 the two pillars;
the two bowl-shaped capitals on top of the pillars;
the two sets of network decorating the two bowl-shaped capitals
on top of the pillars;

[a] *15* That is, about 52 feet (about 16 meters) [b] *16* Or possibly *made chains in the inner sanctuary*; the meaning of the Hebrew for this phrase is uncertain. [c] *17* *Jakin* probably means *he establishes.* [d] *17* *Boaz* probably means *in him is strength.* [e] *1* That is, about 30 feet (about 9 meters) long and wide, and about 15 feet (about 4.5 meters) high [f] *2* That is, about 7 1/2 feet (about 2.3 meters) [g] *2* That is, about 45 feet (about 13.5 meters) [h] *3* That is, about 1 1/2 feet (about 0.5 meter) [i] *5* That is, about 3 inches (about 8 centimeters) [j] *5* That is, about 17,500 gallons (about 66 kiloliters)

4:1 made a bronze altar. The bronze altar is located in the courtyard. Steps stretch across it in front of the temple.

4:2 Sea of cast metal, circular in shape. A huge round basin is erected for ceremonial washings. The "sea" contains about 17,500 gallons of water. A parallel reference says the basin contained about 11,000 gallons (1 Kin. 7:23–24).

4:4 Sea stood on twelve bulls. Twelve tribes are symbolized in the detailed statues, which face all four directions. In this way, Israel could see itself always in worship.

[13] the four hundred pomegranates for the two sets of network (two
rows of pomegranates for each network, decorating the bowl-
shaped capitals on top of the pillars);
[14] the stands with their basins;
[15] the Sea and the twelve bulls under it;
[16] the pots, shovels, meat forks and all related articles.

All the objects that Huram-Abi made for King Solomon for the temple of the LORD were of polished bronze. [17] The king had them cast in
clay molds in the plain of the Jordan between Succoth and Zarethan.[a]
[18] All these things that Solomon made amounted to so much that the
weight of the bronze was not determined.

[19] Solomon also made all the furnishings that were in God's temple:

the golden altar;
the tables on which was the bread of the Presence;
[20] the lampstands of pure gold with their lamps, to burn in front of
the inner sanctuary as prescribed;
[21] the gold floral work and lamps and tongs (they were solid gold);
[22] the pure gold wick trimmers, sprinkling bowls, dishes and
censers; and the gold doors of the temple: the inner doors to
the Most Holy Place and the doors of the main hall.

5 When all the work Solomon had done for the temple of the LORD
was finished, he brought in the things his father David had dedicated—the silver and gold and all the furnishings—and he placed
them in the treasuries of God's temple.

The Ark Brought to the Temple

[2] Then Solomon summoned to Jerusalem the elders of Israel, all the
heads of the tribes and the chiefs of the Israelite families, to bring up
the ark of the LORD's covenant from Zion, the City of David. [3] And all
the men of Israel came together to the king at the time of the festival
in the seventh month.

[4] When all the elders of Israel had arrived, the Levites took up the
ark, [5] and they brought up the ark and the Tent of Meeting and all the
sacred furnishings in it. The priests, who were Levites, carried them
up; [6] and King Solomon and the entire assembly of Israel that had
gathered about him were before the ark, sacrificing so many sheep
and cattle that they could not be recorded or counted.

[7] The priests then brought the ark of the LORD's covenant to its
place in the inner sanctuary of the temple, the Most Holy Place, and
put it beneath the wings of the cherubim. [8] The cherubim spread their
wings over the place of the ark and covered the ark and its carrying
poles. [9] These poles were so long that their ends, extending from the
ark, could be seen from in front of the inner sanctuary, but not from
outside the Holy Place; and they are still there today. [10] There was
nothing in the ark except the two tablets that Moses had placed in it

[a] 17 Hebrew *Zeredatha,* a variant of *Zarethan*

God? Does a beautifully decorated church or chapel tend to help or hinder your worship?

APPLY 1. Huram-Abi was remembered by later generations for his craftsmanship. How would you like to be remembered by later generations? **2.** Solomon brought his father's things to the temple. How do you remember your parents? **3.** What would you set aside of yours or make to be used in your church's worship?

OPEN 1. What musical instrument do you play or wish you could play? **2.** What was the best celebration you ever attended?

STUDY The temple is built. The furnishings have been strategically and artfully placed in and around the temple. Next comes the Ark of the Covenant, containing the stone tablets Moses had placed in it. For years the ark had symbolized God's presence with the people of Israel. **1.** Had you received an invitation from Solomon to attend the celebration described in this chapter, why would you have gone: To get a few days off from work? To be a part of an important event? To hear superb music? To hobnob with the rich and famous? To sneak a peak at what was inside the ark? **2.** Who did Solomon invite to this event? Of the different groups of invitees, who do you think had the best time? **3.** What do you make of the ark (Num. 10:33–36; 14:44–45; Josh. 3:3–4; 6:6–11; 1

5:2 Solomon summoned to … bring up the ark. For the first time, the ark is housed in a permanent, glorious dwelling. Its significance in the temple makes the seven years of labor worth every moment—God's presence is among them.

5:10 nothing in the ark except the two tablets. The Israelites recognize the significance of God's commands on the stone tablets inside the ark (Ex. 32:15–16). Though the ark had changed hands with Israel's enemies, God's commandments are miraculously undisturbed.

Sam. 4:1–11; 5:1–6:16)? What role did it play in the history of the people? Why do you suppose the people were so excited about having it placed in the inner sanctuary of the temple? **4.** What do you particularly like about the events described here? What, if anything, troubles you? **5.** Imagine Solomon's statement in 6:1 as a sound byte on the national news. What do you think the political pundits would say about his words? **6.** In Solomon's speech to the people (6:4–11), what do you learn about God? About Solomon's father, King David? About Solomon himself? What main point do you think Solomon tried to make in this speech?

APPLY 1. When, if ever, have you felt keenly aware of the Lord's presence? Were you with a group or alone? **2.** What kind of music helps you most consistently in your praise and worship of God: Hymns? Spirituals? Praise choruses? Camp songs? Chants? What song or songs were particularly important to you on your spiritual journey?

OPEN 1. When you were a child on what occasions did you or someone else in your family pray: Before meals? Before bed? In times of crisis? At church? Never? **2.** On a scale of one to ten, how would you assess your prayer life?

at Horeb, where the LORD made a covenant with the Israelites after
they came out of Egypt.
[11]The priests then withdrew from the Holy Place. All the priests
who were there had consecrated themselves, regardless of their divisions. [12]All the Levites who were musicians—Asaph, Heman, Jeduthun and their sons and relatives—stood on the east side of the altar,
dressed in fine linen and playing cymbals, harps and lyres. They were
accompanied by 120 priests sounding trumpets. [13]The trumpeters
and singers joined in unison, as with one voice, to give praise and
thanks to the LORD. Accompanied by trumpets, cymbals and other
instruments, they raised their voices in praise to the LORD and sang:

"He is good;
his love endures forever."

Then the temple of the LORD was filled with a cloud, [14]and the
priests could not perform their service because of the cloud, for the
glory of the LORD filled the temple of God.

6 Then Solomon said, "The LORD has said that he would dwell in a
dark cloud; [2]I have built a magnificent temple for you, a place for
you to dwell forever."
[3]While the whole assembly of Israel was standing there, the king
turned around and blessed them. [4]Then he said:

"Praise be to the LORD, the God of Israel, who with his hands
has fulfilled what he promised with his mouth to my father David. For he said, [5]'Since the day I brought my people out of Egypt,
I have not chosen a city in any tribe of Israel to have a temple
built for my Name to be there, nor have I chosen anyone to be
the leader over my people Israel. [6]But now I have chosen Jerusalem for my Name to be there, and I have chosen David to rule my
people Israel.'
[7]"My father David had it in his heart to build a temple for the
Name of the LORD, the God of Israel. [8]But the LORD said to my father David, 'Because it was in your heart to build a temple for my
Name, you did well to have this in your heart. [9]Nevertheless, you
are not the one to build the temple, but your son, who is your
own flesh and blood—he is the one who will build the temple for
my Name.'
[10]"The LORD has kept the promise he made. I have succeeded
David my father and now I sit on the throne of Israel, just as the
LORD promised, and I have built the temple for the Name of the
LORD, the God of Israel. [11]There I have placed the ark, in which is
the covenant of the LORD that he made with the people of Israel."

Solomon's Prayer of Dedication

[12]Then Solomon stood before the altar of the LORD in front of the
whole assembly of Israel and spread out his hands. [13]Now he had
made a bronze platform, five cubits[a] long, five cubits wide and three
cubits[b] high, and had placed it in the center of the outer court. He

[a] *13* That is, about 7 1/2 feet (about 2.3 meters) [b] *13* That is, about 4 1/2 feet (about 1.3 meters)

5:14 glory of the LORD. A supernatural cloud symbolizes the Lord's presence (Ex. 40:34–35) and God's pleasure with the new "home."

6:13 before the whole assembly. Solomon strategically places himself

stood on the platform and then knelt down before the whole assembly of Israel and spread out his hands toward heaven. [14]He said:

"O LORD, God of Israel, there is no God like you in heaven or on
earth—you who keep your covenant of love with your servants
who continue wholeheartedly in your way. [15]You have kept your
promise to your servant David my father; with your mouth you
have promised and with your hand you have fulfilled it—as it is
today.

[16]"Now LORD, God of Israel, keep for your servant David my
father the promises you made to him when you said, 'You shall
never fail to have a man to sit before me on the throne of Israel,
if only your sons are careful in all they do to walk before me
according to my law, as you have done.' [17]And now, O LORD, God
of Israel, let your word that you promised your servant David
come true.

[18]"But will God really dwell on earth with men? The heavens,
even the highest heavens, cannot contain you. How much less
this temple I have built! [19]Yet give attention to your servant's
prayer and his plea for mercy, O LORD my God. Hear the cry and
the prayer that your servant is praying in your presence. [20]May
your eyes be open toward this temple day and night, this place of
which you said you would put your Name there. May you hear
the prayer your servant prays toward this place. [21]Hear the supplications of your servant and of your people Israel when they
pray toward this place. Hear from heaven, your dwelling place;
and when you hear, forgive.

[22]"When a man wrongs his neighbor and is required to take an
oath and he comes and swears the oath before your altar in this
temple, [23]then hear from heaven and act. Judge between your
servants, repaying the guilty by bringing down on his own head
what he has done. Declare the innocent not guilty and so establish his innocence.

[24]"When your people Israel have been defeated by an enemy
because they have sinned against you and when they turn back
and confess your name, praying and making supplication before
you in this temple, [25]then hear from heaven and forgive the sin of
your people Israel and bring them back to the land you gave to
them and their fathers.

[26]"When the heavens are shut up and there is no rain because
your people have sinned against you, and when they pray toward
this place and confess your name and turn from their sin
because you have afflicted them, [27]then hear from heaven and
forgive the sin of your servants, your people Israel. Teach them
the right way to live, and send rain on the land you gave your
people for an inheritance.

[28]"When famine or plague comes to the land, or blight or mildew, locusts or grasshoppers, or when enemies besiege them in
any of their cities, whatever disaster or disease may come, [29]and

STUDY The temple is newly built and furnished. With the people of Israel gathered before him, Solomon offers a prayer of dedication. Some have called Solomon's prayer, one of the most moving supplications in the Old Testament. **1.** What do you think of Solomon's body position in prayer? If you had been in the crowd, would someone praying in that position make you comfortable or uncomfortable? **2.** After reading through the prayer, would you agree that this might be one of the most moving prayers found in the Bible? How does it stack up when you compare it to Jesus' prayer for his disciples in John 17? **3.** Let's examine the prayer. Solomon begins by praising God in verses 14–15. Why do you suppose Solomon begins here instead of getting right down to his list of requests? **4.** Solomon utters his first request in verses 16–17. What is the request? What do you think of Solomon's reminder? How do you think God felt about the reminder? **5.** In verses 18–21 Solomon utters request number two: Hear my prayer. Do you think God always hears our prayers? Does God always answer our prayers? **6.** In verses 32–39, Solomon envisions seven different occasions that call for prayer in or toward the temple (each is introduced by the word when). How would you summarize the seven occasions? **7.** What do you think of Solomon's hope in verses 32–33 about foreigners and the temple? Given that the Israelites often looked down on Gentiles, what do you think got into Solomon at this point? **8.** This prayer is also recorded in 1 Kings 8:22–50, but the end is different. Which ending do you prefer, 1 Kings 8:52–53 or what is in verses 40–42? **9.** When you pray do you feel like you are always saying the same words? Do you sense that you are communicating with God? Do you think God is paying as close attention to you as he did to Solomon?

APPLY **1.** Would you say that you have a high batting average or a low batting average when it comes to having your prayers answered? **2.** Which specific situation mentioned by Solomon do you feel the need to pray for as a group? **3.** Which of the following is the most important

---

front and center as Israel's leader. However, his position is that of humility, not showmanship. He kneels before God in worship.

6:26–31 As spiritually focused as his people are at present, a weaker moment is on the horizon. He requests God's mercy in advance of their inevitable mistakes. He reminds God that the land is a gift. He calls on God to show mercy so all will fear him.

characteristic about God when you pray: God's nearness? God's faithfulness? God's forgiveness? God's tenderness? ______

when a prayer or plea is made by any of your people Israel—each
one aware of his afflictions and pains, and spreading out his
hands toward this temple— 30then hear from heaven, your
dwelling place. Forgive, and deal with each man according to all
he does, since you know his heart (for you alone know the
hearts of men), 31so that they will fear you and walk in your ways
all the time they live in the land you gave our fathers.
32"As for the foreigner who does not belong to your people
Israel but has come from a distant land because of your great
name and your mighty hand and your outstretched arm—when
he comes and prays toward this temple, 33then hear from
heaven, your dwelling place, and do whatever the foreigner asks
of you, so that all the peoples of the earth may know your name
and fear you, as do your own people Israel, and may know that
this house I have built bears your Name.
34"When your people go to war against their enemies, wherever you send them, and when they pray to you toward this city
you have chosen and the temple I have built for your Name,
35then hear from heaven their prayer and their plea, and uphold
their cause.
36"When they sin against you—for there is no one who does
not sin—and you become angry with them and give them over to
the enemy, who takes them captive to a land far away or near;
37and if they have a change of heart in the land where they are
held captive, and repent and plead with you in the land of their
captivity and say, 'We have sinned, we have done wrong and
acted wickedly'; 38and if they turn back to you with all their heart
and soul in the land of their captivity where they were taken, and
pray toward the land you gave their fathers, toward the city you
have chosen and toward the temple I have built for your Name;
39then from heaven, your dwelling place, hear their prayer and
their pleas, and uphold their cause. And forgive your people,
who have sinned against you.
40"Now, my God, may your eyes be open and your ears attentive to the prayers offered in this place.

41"Now arise, O LORD God, and come to your resting place,
you and the ark of your might.
May your priests, O LORD God, be clothed with salvation,
may your saints rejoice in your goodness.
42O LORD God, do not reject your anointed one.
Remember the great love promised to David your servant."

OPEN 1. Which "big event" would you most want to attend and why: The Super Bowl? A presidential inauguration? The Cannes Film Festival? **2.** What have you done recently that surely put a smile on God's face?

The Dedication of the Temple

7 When Solomon finished praying, fire came down from heaven
and consumed the burnt offering and the sacrifices, and the
glory of the LORD filled the temple. 2The priests could not enter the
temple of the LORD because the glory of the LORD filled it. 3When all

6:34–35 Solomon describes another needy "what-if" scenario. He asks for God's protection in response to prayer.

6:40–42 These same verses are in Psalm 132:8–10. The Israelites would earnestly hope in Solomon's words. Solomon asks God to come among them, reminding him of his promise to David. Solomon had brought the ark to the temple (5:2–14).

7:1–3 God concludes the ceremonies in a firework display of heavenly power. God consumes the sacrifice on the altar, showing he accepts the praise and prayers from his people.

the Israelites saw the fire coming down and the glory of the LORD
above the temple, they knelt on the pavement with their faces to the
ground, and they worshiped and gave thanks to the LORD, saying,

"He is good;
his love endures forever."

4Then the king and all the people offered sacrifices before the LORD.
5And King Solomon offered a sacrifice of twenty-two thousand head
of cattle and a hundred and twenty thousand sheep and goats. So the
king and all the people dedicated the temple of God. 6The priests took
their positions, as did the Levites with the LORD's musical instruments, which King David had made for praising the LORD and which
were used when he gave thanks, saying, "His love endures forever."
Opposite the Levites, the priests blew their trumpets, and all the Israelites were standing.
7Solomon consecrated the middle part of the courtyard in front of
the temple of the LORD, and there he offered burnt offerings and the
fat of the fellowship offerings,[a] because the bronze altar he had made
could not hold the burnt offerings, the grain offerings and the fat
portions.
8So Solomon observed the festival at that time for seven days, and
all Israel with him—a vast assembly, people from Lebo[b] Hamath to
the Wadi of Egypt. 9On the eighth day they held an assembly, for they
had celebrated the dedication of the altar for seven days and the
festival for seven days more. 10On the twenty-third day of the seventh
month he sent the people to their homes, joyful and glad in heart for
the good things the LORD had done for David and Solomon and for
his people Israel.

The Lord Appears to Solomon

11When Solomon had finished the temple of the LORD and the royal
palace, and had succeeded in carrying out all he had in mind to do in
the temple of the LORD and in his own palace, 12the LORD appeared to
him at night and said:

"I have heard your prayer and have chosen this place for myself as a temple for sacrifices.
13"When I shut up the heavens so that there is no rain, or command locusts to devour the land or send a plague among my
people, 14if my people, who are called by my name, will humble
themselves and pray and seek my face and turn from their
wicked ways, then will I hear from heaven and will forgive their
sin and will heal their land. 15Now my eyes will be open and my
ears attentive to the prayers offered in this place. 16I have chosen
and consecrated this temple so that my Name may be there forever. My eyes and my heart will always be there.
17"As for you, if you walk before me as David your father did,

[a]7 Traditionally *peace offerings* [b]8 Or *from the entrance to*

STUDY Solomon receives a spectacular answer to his prayer of dedication when a divine fire consumes the burnt offering and God's glory fills the temple. **1.** What particularly impresses you about this story? **2.** What do you make of verse 2? In what way would the glory of the Lord prevent the priests from entering the temple? **3.** If you had been the timekeeper at the festival, and you had 14 days to sacrifice 14,200 animals, how many animals would need to be sacrificed an hour? How does this practice strike you? **4.** What thoughts and feelings do you think the people took home with them from this great festival? How high would Solomon's approval rating be at this point?

APPLY 1. What thoughts and feelings did you take home with you the last time you were at church? **2.** Share a time when you experienced God's "goodness."

OPEN 1. What were some "do's" and "don'ts" in your childhood home? **2.** What is one of your more memorable nighttime dreams? What meaning, if any, did it have for you?

STUDY Shortly after the dedication of the temple, God appears a second time to Solomon in a dream. God's words to Solomon are often quoted today on National Day of Prayer. **1.** Compare God's first dream appearance (vv. 1:7–12) with this second appearance. What similarities do you see? What differences? Do you think God still speaks to people in dreams? **2.** How many positive promises can you identify in God's nighttime visit to Solomon? How many dire warnings? **3.** How does God's "carrot" and "stick" message sit with you? How do you think it set with Solomon? How do you think it set with

---

7:6 musical instruments. Israel rises to its feet in celebration. The Levites render praise to God for his goodness.

7:14–18 After communal labor and celebration, God comes to Solomon alone at night. God recounts the reciprocal relationship he desires with his people. There would be blessings for obedience (vv. 17–18) and disaster for disobedience (vv. 19–20).

and do all I command, and observe my decrees and laws, [18]I will establish your royal throne, as I covenanted with David your father when I said, 'You shall never fail to have a man to rule over Israel.'

[19]"But if you[a] turn away and forsake the decrees and commands I have given you[a] and go off to serve other gods and worship them, [20]then I will uproot Israel from my land, which I have given them, and will reject this temple I have consecrated for my Name. I will make it a byword and an object of ridicule among all peoples. [21]And though this temple is now so imposing, all who pass by will be appalled and say, 'Why has the LORD done such a thing to this land and to this temple?' [22]People will answer, 'Because they have forsaken the LORD, the God of their fathers, who brought them out of Egypt, and have embraced other gods, worshiping and serving them—that is why he brought all this disaster on them.' "

Solomon's Other Activities

8 At the end of twenty years, during which Solomon built the temple of the LORD and his own palace, [2]Solomon rebuilt the villages that Hiram[b] had given him, and settled Israelites in them. [3]Solomon then went to Hamath Zobah and captured it. [4]He also built up Tadmor in the desert and all the store cities he had built in Hamath. [5]He rebuilt Upper Beth Horon and Lower Beth Horon as fortified cities, with walls and with gates and bars, [6]as well as Baalath and all his store cities, and all the cities for his chariots and for his horses[c]—whatever he desired to build in Jerusalem, in Lebanon and throughout all the territory he ruled.

[7]All the people left from the Hittites, Amorites, Perizzites, Hivites and Jebusites (these peoples were not Israelites), [8]that is, their descendants remaining in the land, whom the Israelites had not destroyed—these Solomon conscripted for his slave labor force, as it is to this day. [9]But Solomon did not make slaves of the Israelites for his work; they were his fighting men, commanders of his captains, and commanders of his chariots and charioteers. [10]They were also King Solomon's chief officials—two hundred and fifty officials supervising the men.

[11]Solomon brought Pharaoh's daughter up from the City of David to the palace he had built for her, for he said, "My wife must not live in the palace of David king of Israel, because the places the ark of the LORD has entered are holy."

[12]On the altar of the LORD that he had built in front of the portico, Solomon sacrificed burnt offerings to the LORD, [13]according to the daily requirement for offerings commanded by Moses for Sabbaths, New Moons and the three annual feasts—the Feast of Unleavened

[a]19 The Hebrew is plural. [b]2 Hebrew *Huram,* a variant of *Hiram;* also in verse 18 [c]6 Or *charioteers*

the people of Israel? **4.** What might God say if he appeared to your nation's leader tonight as he did to Solomon? **5.** Do any of your nation's problems happen because people "serve other gods and worship them" (v. 19)?

APPLY 1. If God came to you in a dream tonight, what would he likely talk to you about? **2.** If you could have a face-to-face talk with God, what would be the topic of discussion?

OPEN 1. What do you hope to be doing twenty years from now? **2.** If you won $1,000,000, how would you spend it?

STUDY Solomon not only used his considerable wealth to build the temple, but he also used it to rebuild the countryside. Unfortunately, he did so on the back of foreigners forced into slave labor. In addition, Solomon opens the door for the worship of foreign gods by marrying Pharaoh's daughter. **1.** After skimming through this chapter, how many major projects did Solomon accomplish in his career as king? What do you think Solomon did best? **2.** Why do you suppose Solomon used slaves instead of the Israelites for his work (v. 9)? How does the chronicler seem to feel about this arrangement? **3.** Does Solomon's treatment of his wife (v. 11) seem right to you? What dangers lurk behind his situation (1 Kin. 11:1–3)? **4.** How do you assess Solomon's concern for worship as demonstrated in verses 12–16? **5.** What do you find admirable in Solomon's accomplishments as king. What would you wish he hadn't done? Why?

APPLY 1. Looking back on your life, what is something you wish you had not done? **2.** Name three accomplishments of yours of

8:1–2 In contrast to his battle-weary father, Solomon enjoys a peaceful reign. Solomon originally gave Hiram 20 cities as partial payment for his help. Hiram wasn't pleased and eventually returned them (1 Kin. 9:10–14).

8:11 the places the ark ... has entered are holy. Solomon is all too aware of the spiritual conflict represented in his idol-worshiping Egyptian wife. His care to remove her from David's palace betrays his better sense (1 Kin. 11:1–4).

8:12–16 Solomon demonstrates the detail of his religious success in the form of numerous sacrifices. He keeps pace with his father's outward religious acts, though he ultimately fails to replicate David's devotion (1 Kin. 11:4).

Bread, the Feast of Weeks and the Feast of Tabernacles. 14In keeping
with the ordinance of his father David, he appointed the divisions of
the priests for their duties, and the Levites to lead the praise and to
assist the priests according to each day's requirement. He also
appointed the gatekeepers by divisions for the various gates, because
this was what David the man of God had ordered. 15They did not
deviate from the king's commands to the priests or to the Levites in
any matter, including that of the treasuries.
16All Solomon's work was carried out, from the day the foundation
of the temple of the LORD was laid until its completion. So the temple
of the LORD was finished.
17Then Solomon went to Ezion Geber and Elath on the coast of
Edom. 18And Hiram sent him ships commanded by his own officers,
men who knew the sea. These, with Solomon's men, sailed to Ophir
and brought back four hundred and fifty talents[a] of gold, which they
delivered to King Solomon.

The Queen of Sheba Visits Solomon

9 When the queen of Sheba heard of Solomon's fame, she came to
Jerusalem to test him with hard questions. Arriving with a very
great caravan—with camels carrying spices, large quantities of gold,
and precious stones—she came to Solomon and talked with him
about all she had on her mind. 2Solomon answered all her questions;
nothing was too hard for him to explain to her. 3When the queen of
Sheba saw the wisdom of Solomon, as well as the palace he had
built, 4the food on his table, the seating of his officials, the attending
servants in their robes, the cupbearers in their robes and the burnt
offerings he made at[b] the temple of the LORD, she was overwhelmed.
5She said to the king, "The report I heard in my own country about
your achievements and your wisdom is true. 6But I did not believe
what they said until I came and saw with my own eyes. Indeed, not
even half the greatness of your wisdom was told me; you have far
exceeded the report I heard. 7How happy your men must be! How
happy your officials, who continually stand before you and hear your
wisdom! 8Praise be to the LORD your God, who has delighted in you
and placed you on his throne as king to rule for the LORD your God.
Because of the love of your God for Israel and his desire to uphold
them forever, he has made you king over them, to maintain justice
and righteousness."
9Then she gave the king 120 talents[c] of gold, large quantities of
spices, and precious stones. There had never been such spices as
those the queen of Sheba gave to King Solomon.
10(The men of Hiram and the men of Solomon brought gold from
Ophir; they also brought algumwood[d] and precious stones. 11The
king used the algumwood to make steps for the temple of the LORD

[a]18 That is, about 17 tons (about 16 metric tons) [b]4 Or *the ascent by which he went up to* [c]9 That is, about 4 1/2 tons (about 4 metric tons) [d]10 Probably a variant of *almugwood*

which you are very proud. If you can't come up with three, name two. If you can't come up with two, name one! What can this group do to help one another accomplish great things?

OPEN 1. Who or what ever exceeded your expectations? **2.** If you could meet and get to know anyone in the world today, who would that person be?

STUDY When royalties visited each other's courts, it was the custom to take and receive gifts. The queen of Sheba's visit to Solomon was no exception. She brings gifts and she receives gifts. Her visit to Solomon's royal court is one of the best-known stories in the Old Testament. **1.** The queen of Sheba and her retinue probably traveled over 1,000 miles to Jerusalem. What reasons can you discover in verses 1–12 for such a spectacular visit? **2.** What kinds of things about Solomon and his capital impressed the queen? What about Solomon impresses you the most? **3.** How did the queen show her admiration for Solomon? Do you feel her words of praise in verses 5–8 had any political motivation? Personal attraction? **4.** What do you suppose would be a comparable visit between heads of state in today's world?

APPLY 1. Solomon answered all the queen's questions. What one question would you want Solomon to answer for you? **2.** Have you felt more like a giver or a receiver recently? Explain. What spiritual gift do you need right now?

8:17–18 The chronicler completes Solomon's success profile by including his economic achievements. King Hiram once again proves to be a royal relationship worth keeping. Tyre's navy became an important resource.

9:1–12 The queen of Sheba enters the economic success story and contributes much towards Solomon's portfolio (1 Kin. 10). This fulfills God's promise (1:12).

9:8 delighted ... placed you on his throne. The chronicler frames the queen's speech to affirm Solomon's divinely appointed rule. God enabled and enlightened this obscure but resplendent queen to speak courteously of the competition.

and for the royal palace, and to make harps and lyres for the musicians. Nothing like them had ever been seen in Judah.)
[12]King Solomon gave the queen of Sheba all she desired and asked
for; he gave her more than she had brought to him. Then she left and
returned with her retinue to her own country.

Solomon's Splendor

[13]The weight of the gold that Solomon received yearly was 666
talents,[a] [14]not including the revenues brought in by merchants and
traders. Also all the kings of Arabia and the governors of the land
brought gold and silver to Solomon.
[15]King Solomon made two hundred large shields of hammered
gold; six hundred bekas[b] of hammered gold went into each shield.
[16]He also made three hundred small shields of hammered gold, with
three hundred bekas[c] of gold in each shield. The king put them in the
Palace of the Forest of Lebanon.
[17]Then the king made a great throne inlaid with ivory and overlaid
with pure gold. [18]The throne had six steps, and a footstool of gold
was attached to it. On both sides of the seat were armrests, with a
lion standing beside each of them. [19]Twelve lions stood on the six
steps, one at either end of each step. Nothing like it had ever been
made for any other kingdom. [20]All King Solomon's goblets were gold,
and all the household articles in the Palace of the Forest of Lebanon
were pure gold. Nothing was made of silver, because silver was considered of little value in Solomon's day. [21]The king had a fleet of trading ships[d] manned by Hiram's[e] men. Once every three years it
returned, carrying gold, silver and ivory, and apes and baboons.
[22]King Solomon was greater in riches and wisdom than all the
other kings of the earth. [23]All the kings of the earth sought audience
with Solomon to hear the wisdom God had put in his heart. [24]Year
after year, everyone who came brought a gift—articles of silver and
gold, and robes, weapons and spices, and horses and mules.
[25]Solomon had four thousand stalls for horses and chariots, and
twelve thousand horses,[f] which he kept in the chariot cities and also
with him in Jerusalem. [26]He ruled over all the kings from the River[g] to
the land of the Philistines, as far as the border of Egypt. [27]The king
made silver as common in Jerusalem as stones, and cedar as plentiful
as sycamore-fig trees in the foothills. [28]Solomon's horses were imported from Egypt[h] and from all other countries.

Solomon's Death

[29]As for the other events of Solomon's reign, from beginning to
end, are they not written in the records of Nathan the prophet, in the
prophecy of Ahijah the Shilonite and in the visions of Iddo the seer
concerning Jeroboam son of Nebat? [30]Solomon reigned in Jerusalem
over all Israel forty years. [31]Then he rested with his fathers and was

[a]13 That is, about 25 tons (about 23 metric tons) [b]15 That is, about 7 1/2 pounds (about 3.5 kilograms) [c]16 That is, about 3 3/4 pounds (about 1.7 kilograms) [d]21 Hebrew *of ships that could go to Tarshish* [e]21 Hebrew *Huram,* a variant of *Hiram* [f]25 Or *charioteers* [g]26 That is, the Euphrates [h]28 Or possibly *Muzur,* a region in Cilicia

OPEN 1. What gold or silver item of yours do you especially treasure? **2.** If you could go out and buy anything today, what one thing would you buy?

STUDY Solomon's life comes to a close. He certainly ranks in the hall of fame of the rich and the famous. His treasure ships ventured as far as India and East Africa. **1.** Solomon's wealth is legendary. According to verses 13–28, what can you identify as sources of this wealth? **2.** How do you feel about Solomon's use of his wealth? In your opinion, what is the coolest thing he made out of gold? **3.** According to the chronicler, why was Solomon greater than all the other kings of the earth (v. 22)? How do you think this "world status" benefited Israel as a people? Hurt them? **4.** The chronicler sees Solomon's reign as an unqualified success. Do you? Why or why not?

APPLY 1. Solomon experienced a number of "high points" in his life. What would you consider to be a handful of high points in your life? **2.** When it comes to money, do you feel you have enough? At what point in your life were you the happiest? Compared to now, how wealthy were you?

9:28 Solomon's picture-perfect conclusion conveys the chronicler's biographical bias. The happy ending serves to contrast to the heritage of rebellion that came from his many foreign wives (1 Kin. 11:1–40).

buried in the city of David his father. And Rehoboam his son succeeded him as king.

Israel Rebels Against Rehoboam

10 Rehoboam went to Shechem, for all the Israelites had gone
there to make him king. 2When Jeroboam son of Nebat heard
this (he was in Egypt, where he had fled from King Solomon), he
returned from Egypt. 3So they sent for Jeroboam, and he and all Israel
went to Rehoboam and said to him: 4"Your father put a heavy yoke on
us, but now lighten the harsh labor and the heavy yoke he put on us,
and we will serve you."
5Rehoboam answered, "Come back to me in three days." So the
people went away.
6Then King Rehoboam consulted the elders who had served his
father Solomon during his lifetime. "How would you advise me to
answer these people?" he asked.
7They replied, "If you will be kind to these people and please them
and give them a favorable answer, they will always be your servants."
8But Rehoboam rejected the advice the elders gave him and consulted the young men who had grown up with him and were serving
him. 9He asked them, "What is your advice? How should we answer
these people who say to me, 'Lighten the yoke your father put
on us'?"
10The young men who had grown up with him replied, "Tell the
people who have said to you, 'Your father put a heavy yoke on us, but
make our yoke lighter'—tell them, 'My little finger is thicker than my
father's waist. 11My father laid on you a heavy yoke; I will make it
even heavier. My father scourged you with whips; I will scourge you
with scorpions.' "
12Three days later Jeroboam and all the people returned to Rehoboam, as the king had said, "Come back to me in three days." 13The
king answered them harshly. Rejecting the advice of the elders, 14he
followed the advice of the young men and said, "My father made your
yoke heavy; I will make it even heavier. My father scourged you with
whips; I will scourge you with scorpions." 15So the king did not listen
to the people, for this turn of events was from God, to fulfill the word
the LORD had spoken to Jeroboam son of Nebat through Ahijah the
Shilonite.
16When all Israel saw that the king refused to listen to them, they
answered the king:

"What share do we have in David,
what part in Jesse's son?
To your tents, O Israel!
Look after your own house, O David!"

So all the Israelites went home. 17But as for the Israelites who were
living in the towns of Judah, Rehoboam still ruled over them.

OPEN 1. To what person would you love to give advice if only he or she would listen? **2.** On a scale of 1 to 10 how would you rate yourself as a rebel?

STUDY In the following verses, we witness Solomon's kingdom split into north (Israel) and south (Judah). Heavily taxed and forced into labor for Solomon's lavish building program, the people of Israel rebel. Ten tribes align themselves with Jeroboam and two tribes with Solomon's son Rehoboam. Due to the chronicler's emphasis on the history of Judah, one needs to read 1 Kings 11:26–40 to hear "the rest of the story." **1.** What important details does the chronicler leave out? Do you think Jeroboam should be blamed for forcing a rebellion? If he is not to blame, where would you place it? **2.** When it comes to this battle of heavyweights, Jeroboam and Rehoboam, what would you say each has going for them? What clout does Jeroboam yield? Rehoboam? **3.** Why do you think Rehoboam rejected the counsel of elders and adopted the council of young men? **4.** Is it always true that "a gentle answer turns away wrath" (Prov. 15:1)? In a similar vein, is it always true that "if you give them an inch, they will take a mile"? What would you say are the risks inherent in a gentle answer? What are the risks in a tough answer? **5.** What reasons, in your opinion, would justify a nation to split? How about a church? How about a family? **6.** What point do you think the chronicler is attempting to hammer home here: The sins of the parents are passed to future generations? God is calling the shots? Listen to your elders? Take grievances seriously? Serve people and do not "lord it" over them?

APPLY 1. If you had it to do all over again, what would you like to do better the second time around? **2.** When it comes to conflict are you: A teddy bear? A grizzly bear? A polar bear? Explain. **3.** What do you

---

10:1–36:23 A tragic story of a divided kingdom follows this peaceful period in Israel's history. The chronicler shifts his focus to Judah and the southern kingdom's demise.

10:1–19 Rehoboam receives bad advice from younger, inexperienced cohorts. His cavalier attitude toward the northern kingdom's labor woes backfires. The kingdom officially splits north and south (1 Kin. 12:1–20).

18 King Rehoboam sent out Adoniram,[a] who was in charge of forced
labor, but the Israelites stoned him to death. King Rehoboam, however, managed to get into his chariot and escape to Jerusalem. 19 So
Israel has been in rebellion against the house of David to this day.

11 When Rehoboam arrived in Jerusalem, he mustered the
house of Judah and Benjamin—a hundred and eighty thousand fighting men—to make war against Israel and to regain the
kingdom for Rehoboam.
2 But this word of the LORD came to Shemaiah the man of God:
3 "Say to Rehoboam son of Solomon king of Judah and to all the Israelites in Judah and Benjamin, 4 'This is what the LORD says: Do not go
up to fight against your brothers. Go home, every one of you, for this
is my doing.' " So they obeyed the words of the LORD and turned back
from marching against Jeroboam.

Rehoboam Fortifies Judah

5 Rehoboam lived in Jerusalem and built up towns for defense in Judah: 6 Bethlehem, Etam, Tekoa, 7 Beth Zur, Soco, Adullam, 8 Gath, Mareshah, Ziph, 9 Adoraim, Lachish, Azekah, 10 Zorah, Aijalon and
Hebron. These were fortified cities in Judah and Benjamin. 11 He
strengthened their defenses and put commanders in them, with supplies of food, olive oil and wine. 12 He put shields and spears in all the
cities, and made them very strong. So Judah and Benjamin were his.
13 The priests and Levites from all their districts throughout Israel
sided with him. 14 The Levites even abandoned their pasturelands and
property, and came to Judah and Jerusalem because Jeroboam and
his sons had rejected them as priests of the LORD. 15 And he appointed
his own priests for the high places and for the goat and calf idols he
had made. 16 Those from every tribe of Israel who set their hearts on
seeking the LORD, the God of Israel, followed the Levites to Jerusalem
to offer sacrifices to the LORD, the God of their fathers. 17 They
strengthened the kingdom of Judah and supported Rehoboam son of
Solomon three years, walking in the ways of David and Solomon during this time.

Rehoboam's Family

18 Rehoboam married Mahalath, who was the daughter of David's
son Jerimoth and of Abihail, the daughter of Jesse's son Eliab. 19 She
bore him sons: Jeush, Shemariah and Zaham. 20 Then he married
Maacah daughter of Absalom, who bore him Abijah, Attai, Ziza and
Shelomith. 21 Rehoboam loved Maacah daughter of Absalom more
than any of his other wives and concubines. In all, he had eighteen
wives and sixty concubines, twenty-eight sons and sixty daughters.
22 Rehoboam appointed Abijah son of Maacah to be the chief prince
among his brothers, in order to make him king. 23 He acted wisely,
dispersing some of his sons throughout the districts of Judah and

[a] 18 Hebrew *Hadoram*, a variant of *Adoniram*

need to change about the way you handle conflict?

OPEN 1. If you had a backyard bomb shelter, what three things would you want to take in it (excluding family and pets)? **2.** Which brother or sister was most difficult for you to get along with?

STUDY One of the chronicler's themes centers on the existence of faithful Israelites in the north. The Levites were but one example of such faithful people. According to the chronicler, the Levites were so loyal to Solomon's son, Rehoboam, that they suffered persecution at the hands of his northern rival, Jeroboam. The Levites eventually sold their property and moved south. **1.** What do you think of Rehoboam's strategy to protect his kingdom from Jeroboam to the north and Egypt to the south (vv. 5–12,23)? **2.** How do you suppose the Levites moving to Judah affected Rehoboam? Jeroboam? The southern kingdom as a whole? **3.** What do you think might be the spiritual ramifications of replacing the Levites with Jeroboam's own priests?

APPLY 1. The Levites abandoned their pasturelands and property because of their faith in God. What people, attitudes, behaviors or possessions have you left behind as a result of your faith? **2.** How do you need to be fortified today? How can your group help?

11:5–10 Rehoboam faces great opposition but is armed with only two tribes: Benjamin and Judah. Despite great odds, Rehoboam prepares his forces for a fight. He fortified the cities and brought the priests into them. Many supported him and strengthened the kingdom (v. 17).

11:23 Rehoboam thinks ahead to the succession of his favored son, Abijah. As a consolation, his remaining sons are given political prestige.

Benjamin, and to all the fortified cities. He gave them abundant
provisions and took many wives for them.

Shishak Attacks Jerusalem

12 After Rehoboam's position as king was established and he
had become strong, he and all Israel[a] with him abandoned
the law of the LORD. [2]Because they had been unfaithful to the LORD,
Shishak king of Egypt attacked Jerusalem in the fifth year of King
Rehoboam. [3]With twelve hundred chariots and sixty thousand horsemen and the innumerable troops of Libyans, Sukkites and Cushites[b]
that came with him from Egypt, [4]he captured the fortified cities of
Judah and came as far as Jerusalem.
[5]Then the prophet Shemaiah came to Rehoboam and to the leaders
of Judah who had assembled in Jerusalem for fear of Shishak, and he
said to them, "This is what the LORD says, 'You have abandoned me;
therefore, I now abandon you to Shishak.' "
[6]The leaders of Israel and the king humbled themselves and said,
"The LORD is just."
[7]When the LORD saw that they humbled themselves, this word of
the LORD came to Shemaiah: "Since they have humbled themselves, I
will not destroy them but will soon give them deliverance. My wrath
will not be poured out on Jerusalem through Shishak. [8]They will,
however, become subject to him, so that they may learn the difference between serving me and serving the kings of other lands."
[9]When Shishak king of Egypt attacked Jerusalem, he carried off the
treasures of the temple of the LORD and the treasures of the royal
palace. He took everything, including the gold shields Solomon had
made. [10]So King Rehoboam made bronze shields to replace them and
assigned these to the commanders of the guard on duty at the entrance to the royal palace. [11]Whenever the king went to the LORD's
temple, the guards went with him, bearing the shields, and afterward
they returned them to the guardroom.
[12]Because Rehoboam humbled himself, the LORD's anger turned
from him, and he was not totally destroyed. Indeed, there was some
good in Judah.
[13]King Rehoboam established himself firmly in Jerusalem and
continued as king. He was forty-one years old when he became king,
and he reigned seventeen years in Jerusalem, the city the LORD had
chosen out of all the tribes of Israel in which to put his Name. His
mother's name was Naamah; she was an Ammonite. [14]He did evil
because he had not set his heart on seeking the LORD.
[15]As for the events of Rehoboam's reign, from beginning to end, are
they not written in the records of Shemaiah the prophet and of Iddo
the seer that deal with genealogies? There was continual warfare between Rehoboam and Jeroboam. [16]Rehoboam rested with his fathers
and was buried in the City of David. And Abijah his son succeeded
him as king.

[a] *1* That is, Judah, as frequently in 2 Chronicles [b] *3* That is, people from the upper Nile region

OPEN 1. What is the total number of times the members of your group have talked their way out of traffic tickets? **2.** What's some bad news you received in the past?

STUDY We come upon a story of punishment and deliverance and a story of human humbleness and God's mercy. God uses a foreign nation to discipline his people. The glory days of Solomon's kingdom are now a thing of the past. **1.** When times were good, Rehoboam and the Israelites (Judah) abandoned God. Why do you think that often happens with God's people? **2.** What prompted Rehoboam to wake-up and smell the coffee? What do you make of his response after he woke up (v. 6)? **3.** When bad things happen to you, is it a result of God disciplining you? Why or why not? **4.** What do you think of Rehoboam's punishment and deliverance: Too soft for a holy God? Too bitter a pill to swallow? A perfect mix of God's wrath and mercy? **5.** How does the story of the guardsman and their shields in verses 9–11 strike you: Heartwarming? Silly? Pathetic? **6.** What example does Rehoboam leave you to follow? To avoid? **7.** If this chapter was your point for discovering God, what would you learn about God's character and purpose?

APPLY 1. How many Shemaiahs (people who keep you in line by explaining the meaning of things that are happening to you) do you have in your life? Name them. **2.** In the spite of tough times there was some good in Judah (v. 12). Share some "good" that is happening in your life today.

12:1 all Israel ... abandoned the law. The divided kingdom is represented in terms of Judah (to the south) and Israel (to the north). The chronicler implies the reference is to Israelites living in Judah who abandon God's ways.

OPEN **1.** What was the last jam you found yourself in? **2.** Share a time when the odds were definitely against you.

STUDY In the following verses the chronicler makes it clear that the northern kingdom of Israel was wrong to have rebelled against Rehoboam. Rehoboam's successor, Abijah, will be God's instrument to chastise the rebels. **1.** How would you describe Abijah's leadership style: Cautious? Timid? Foolhardy? Righteous? Compare the picture of Abijah in 1 Kings 15:1–8 with this chapter. What differences do you see in the accounts? How do you account for these differences? **2.** What reason can you find for the armies of Abijah and Jeroboam facing off? **3.** Though Jeroboam has twice the fighting force, Abijah appears confident. Where do you believe his confidence comes? **4.** Do a little research on the term "covenant of salt" mentioned in verse 5 (Lev. 2:13; Num. 18:19). What did you discover about its meaning? What might it mean to Abijah? **5.** If you lived in Israel, would Abijah's speech convince you of the errors of Jeroboam? Explain. **6.** How does this passage leave you feeling about Jeroboam? About Abijah? **7.** Many Bible stories tell how God routed enemies when his people were outnumbered. What are God's people supposed to derive from such accounts: God helps underdogs? Put your trust in God and everything will turn out fine? It's not the size of the battle, it's the size of your God?

APPLY **1.** Where do you need to put your trust in God today? **2.** Name a time when you saw the error of your ways? How did it feel to come to such an awareness? What did you do in response to that new insight?

Abijah King of Judah

13 In the eighteenth year of the reign of Jeroboam, Abijah
became king of Judah, 2and he reigned in Jerusalem three
years. His mother's name was Maacah,[a] a daughter[b] of Uriel of Gibeah.
There was war between Abijah and Jeroboam. 3Abijah went into
battle with a force of four hundred thousand able fighting men, and
Jeroboam drew up a battle line against him with eight hundred thousand able troops.
4Abijah stood on Mount Zemaraim, in the hill country of Ephraim,
and said, "Jeroboam and all Israel, listen to me! 5Don't you know that
the LORD, the God of Israel, has given the kingship of Israel to David
and his descendants forever by a covenant of salt? 6Yet Jeroboam son
of Nebat, an official of Solomon son of David, rebelled against his
master. 7Some worthless scoundrels gathered around him and opposed Rehoboam son of Solomon when he was young and indecisive
and not strong enough to resist them.
8"And now you plan to resist the kingdom of the LORD, which is in
the hands of David's descendants. You are indeed a vast army and
have with you the golden calves that Jeroboam made to be your gods.
9But didn't you drive out the priests of the LORD, the sons of Aaron,
and the Levites, and make priests of your own as the peoples of other
lands do? Whoever comes to consecrate himself with a young bull
and seven rams may become a priest of what are not gods.
10"As for us, the LORD is our God, and we have not forsaken him.
The priests who serve the LORD are sons of Aaron, and the Levites
assist them. 11Every morning and evening they present burnt offerings and fragrant incense to the LORD. They set out the bread on the
ceremonially clean table and light the lamps on the gold lampstand
every evening. We are observing the requirements of the LORD our
God. But you have forsaken him. 12God is with us; he is our leader.
His priests with their trumpets will sound the battle cry against you.
Men of Israel, do not fight against the LORD, the God of your fathers,
for you will not succeed."
13Now Jeroboam had sent troops around to the rear, so that while
he was in front of Judah the ambush was behind them. 14Judah
turned and saw that they were being attacked at both front and rear.
Then they cried out to the LORD. The priests blew their trumpets 15and
the men of Judah raised the battle cry. At the sound of their battle cry,
God routed Jeroboam and all Israel before Abijah and Judah. 16The Israelites fled before Judah, and God delivered them into their hands.
17Abijah and his men inflicted heavy losses on them, so that there
were five hundred thousand casualties among Israel's able men.
18The men of Israel were subdued on that occasion, and the men of
Judah were victorious because they relied on the LORD, the God of
their fathers.
19Abijah pursued Jeroboam and took from him the towns of Bethel,
Jeshanah and Ephron, with their surrounding villages. 20Jeroboam

[a]2 Most Septuagint manuscripts and Syriac (see also 2 Chron. 11:20 and 1 Kings 15:2); Hebrew *Micaiah*
[b]2 Or *granddaughter*

13:1–14:1 The story in 1 Kings 15:1–8 parallels the details of Abijah's reign in 2 Chronicles, only with a different twist. First Kings' more negative portrayal is balanced by the chronicler's illustration of Abijah's battlefield plea.

did not regain power during the time of Abijah. And the LORD struck
him down and he died.
[21]But Abijah grew in strength. He married fourteen wives and had
twenty-two sons and sixteen daughters.
[22]The other events of Abijah's reign, what he did and what he said,
are written in the annotations of the prophet Iddo.

14 And Abijah rested with his fathers and was buried in the City
of David. Asa his son succeeded him as king, and in his days
the country was at peace for ten years.

Asa King of Judah

[2]Asa did what was good and right in the eyes of the LORD his God.
[3]He removed the foreign altars and the high places, smashed the
sacred stones and cut down the Asherah poles.[a] [4]He commanded Judah to seek the LORD, the God of their fathers, and to obey his laws
and commands. [5]He removed the high places and incense altars in
every town in Judah, and the kingdom was at peace under him. [6]He
built up the fortified cities of Judah, since the land was at peace. No
one was at war with him during those years, for the LORD gave him
rest.
[7]"Let us build up these towns," he said to Judah, "and put walls
around them, with towers, gates and bars. The land is still ours, because we have sought the LORD our God; we sought him and he has
given us rest on every side." So they built and prospered.
[8]Asa had an army of three hundred thousand men from Judah,
equipped with large shields and with spears, and two hundred and
eighty thousand from Benjamin, armed with small shields and with
bows. All these were brave fighting men.
[9]Zerah the Cushite marched out against them with a vast army[b]
and three hundred chariots, and came as far as Mareshah. [10]Asa went
out to meet him, and they took up battle positions in the Valley of
Zephathah near Mareshah.
[11]Then Asa called to the LORD his God and said, "LORD, there is no
one like you to help the powerless against the mighty. Help us,
O LORD our God, for we rely on you, and in your name we have come
against this vast army. O LORD, you are our God; do not let man prevail against you."
[12]The LORD struck down the Cushites before Asa and Judah. The
Cushites fled, [13]and Asa and his army pursued them as far as Gerar.
Such a great number of Cushites fell that they could not recover; they
were crushed before the LORD and his forces. The men of Judah
carried off a large amount of plunder. [14]They destroyed all the villages
around Gerar, for the terror of the LORD had fallen upon them. They
plundered all these villages, since there was much booty there.

[a]3 That is, symbols of the goddess Asherah; here and elsewhere in 2 Chronicles [b]9 Hebrew *with an army of a thousand thousands* or *with an army of thousands upon thousands*

OPEN 1. When recently have you felt peaceful? **2.** When it comes to your present energy level, is your tank: Full? Three-quarters full? Half full? Quarter full? Running on fumes?

STUDY Solomon, Rehoboam, Abijah and now Asa. With Asa the house of David continues the upward trend which Abijah began. Asa is one of the southern kingdom's good kings. **1.** Compare Asa's accomplishments in verses 2–6 with those outlined in 1 Kings 15:12–15. Which accomplishments do you think required the most moral fiber? **2.** How did God reward Asa's faithfulness? Which of these rewards would you most covet? **3.** How would you evaluate Asa's prayer in verse 11? How does one know if he or she is fighting on God's side? **4.** How do the actions in verses 12–15 affect you? How do you reconcile the actions here with a loving merciful God?

APPLY 1. If you were to go on a rampage against modern "Asherah poles," what are your top two or three targets? **2.** Asa relied on the Lord to help fight his battle. What battle are you currently fighting? How can you rely on the Lord to fight it with you?

14:1 the country was at peace for ten years. In contrast to his predecessor, Asa is fairly righteous. As a result, he enjoys peace as a sign of God's favor.

14:2–16:14 The chronicler uses the reign of Asa as a test case for the reciprocal relationship God promised Solomon (7:17–20). During most of his 41 years, Asa destroys heathen altars and leads people back to God. As a result, he prospers. However, at the moment his faith falters (16:2–10)—so does his kingdom.

14:5 removed the high places and incense altars. He attempts to reinstate worshiping in Judah. His mission is short-lived in the wake of overwhelming odds (15:17), and he isn't able to remove the high places (1 Kin. 15:14).

15They also attacked the camps of the herdsmen and carried off
droves of sheep and goats and camels. Then they returned to Jerusalem.

Asa's Reform

15 The Spirit of God came upon Azariah son of Oded. 2He went
out to meet Asa and said to him, "Listen to me, Asa and all
Judah and Benjamin. The LORD is with you when you are with him. If
you seek him, he will be found by you, but if you forsake him, he will
forsake you. 3For a long time Israel was without the true God, without a priest to teach and without the law. 4But in their distress they
turned to the LORD, the God of Israel, and sought him, and he was
found by them. 5In those days it was not safe to travel about, for all
the inhabitants of the lands were in great turmoil. 6One nation was
being crushed by another and one city by another, because God was
troubling them with every kind of distress. 7But as for you, be strong
and do not give up, for your work will be rewarded."

8When Asa heard these words and the prophecy of Azariah son of[a]
Oded the prophet, he took courage. He removed the detestable idols
from the whole land of Judah and Benjamin and from the towns he
had captured in the hills of Ephraim. He repaired the altar of the LORD
that was in front of the portico of the LORD's temple.

9Then he assembled all Judah and Benjamin and the people from
Ephraim, Manasseh and Simeon who had settled among them, for
large numbers had come over to him from Israel when they saw that
the LORD his God was with him.

10They assembled at Jerusalem in the third month of the fifteenth
year of Asa's reign. 11At that time they sacrificed to the LORD seven
hundred head of cattle and seven thousand sheep and goats from the
plunder they had brought back. 12They entered into a covenant to
seek the LORD, the God of their fathers, with all their heart and soul.
13All who would not seek the LORD, the God of Israel, were to be put
to death, whether small or great, man or woman. 14They took an oath
to the LORD with loud acclamation, with shouting and with trumpets
and horns. 15All Judah rejoiced about the oath because they had
sworn it wholeheartedly. They sought God eagerly, and he was found
by them. So the LORD gave them rest on every side.

16King Asa also deposed his grandmother Maacah from her position as queen mother, because she had made a repulsive Asherah
pole. Asa cut the pole down, broke it up and burned it in the Kidron
Valley. 17Although he did not remove the high places from Israel,
Asa's heart was fully committed ⌊to the LORD⌋ all his life. 18He brought
into the temple of God the silver and gold and the articles that he and
his father had dedicated.

19There was no more war until the thirty-fifth year of Asa's reign.

[a]8 Vulgate and Syriac (see also Septuagint and verse 1); Hebrew does not have *Azariah son of*.

OPEN 1. If money were no object, where would you like to go on your next vacation? **2.** What is a sermon or a message that stays with you to this day?

STUDY In response to a message from the prophet Azariah, Asa purges the land of polytheistic deities. This passage is another example of one of the chroniclers themes: People of Judah do not forget that there are a number of good Israelites. If former rebels from the north want to return to the fold, welcome them with open arms. **1.** Azariah delivers a dynamite message and gets results! What would you say is his main point? How does it affect Asa? The people? **2.** Do you think the command in verse 13 was fair? Why or why not (Deut. 7:1–4; 13:6–10)? **3.** In your opinion, what threat does belief in other gods pose to a Christian fellowship? What do you think our attitude should be to people of other faiths? **4.** In verse 15 we read, "they sought God eagerly." What do you think that means? How does one "seek" after God? What has worked for you? **5.** What would it mean for God to be "found" by your nation? By your church? By you?

APPLY 1. On a continuum with "lost" at one end and "found" at the other, where would you place your relationship with God at this moment? **2.** God called Asa to rid the nation of foreign idols. What do you sense God calling you to do?

15:1–19 A prophet's encouragement goes a long way with Asa. He resumes his search-and-destroy mission against idols with great zeal.

15:13 put to death. Religious expression has significant social and political implications. Rebellion against God is taken as a serious offense against the state. In keeping with the Law, "all who would not seek the LORD were to be put to death" (Deut. 13:6–9).

Asa's Last Years

16 In the thirty-sixth year of Asa's reign Baasha king of Israel
went up against Judah and fortified Ramah to prevent anyone from leaving or entering the territory of Asa king of Judah.
[2]Asa then took the silver and gold out of the treasuries of the
LORD's temple and of his own palace and sent it to Ben-Hadad king of
Aram, who was ruling in Damascus. [3]"Let there be a treaty between
me and you," he said, "as there was between my father and your
father. See, I am sending you silver and gold. Now break your treaty
with Baasha king of Israel so he will withdraw from me."
[4]Ben-Hadad agreed with King Asa and sent the commanders of his
forces against the towns of Israel. They conquered Ijon, Dan, Abel
Maim[a] and all the store cities of Naphtali. [5]When Baasha heard this,
he stopped building Ramah and abandoned his work. [6]Then King Asa
brought all the men of Judah, and they carried away from Ramah the
stones and timber Baasha had been using. With them he built up
Geba and Mizpah.
[7]At that time Hanani the seer came to Asa king of Judah and said to
him: "Because you relied on the king of Aram and not on the LORD
your God, the army of the king of Aram has escaped from your hand.
[8]Were not the Cushites[b] and Libyans a mighty army with great
numbers of chariots and horsemen[c]? Yet when you relied on the
LORD, he delivered them into your hand. [9]For the eyes of the LORD
range throughout the earth to strengthen those whose hearts are
fully committed to him. You have done a foolish thing, and from now
on you will be at war."
[10]Asa was angry with the seer because of this; he was so enraged
that he put him in prison. At the same time Asa brutally oppressed
some of the people.
[11]The events of Asa's reign, from beginning to end, are written in
the book of the kings of Judah and Israel. [12]In the thirty-ninth year of
his reign Asa was afflicted with a disease in his feet. Though his disease was severe, even in his illness he did not seek help from the
LORD, but only from the physicians. [13]Then in the forty-first year of
his reign Asa died and rested with his fathers. [14]They buried him in
the tomb that he had cut out for himself in the City of David. They laid
him on a bier covered with spices and various blended perfumes, and
they made a huge fire in his honor.

Jehoshaphat King of Judah

17 Jehoshaphat his son succeeded him as king and strengthened
himself against Israel. [2]He stationed troops in all the fortified
cities of Judah and put garrisons in Judah and in the towns of Ephraim that his father Asa had captured.
[3]The LORD was with Jehoshaphat because in his early years he

[a]4 Also known as *Abel Beth Maacah* [b]8 That is, people from the upper Nile region [c]8 Or *charioteers*

OPEN 1. Share one of your more foolish decisions or moments. **2.** When it comes to accepting help are you: Open to it? Closed to it? Depends on the help? Depends on the helper?

STUDY Good King Asa's life comes to an end. The chronicler criticizes Asa's decision to align himself with Ben-Hadad of Aram. He saw it as a lack of faith in God. In 1 Kings 15:16–24 we hear no such criticism. **1.** What is your impression of Baasha, king of Israel? **2.** What do you think of Asa's plan to protect his people? **3.** According to the chronicler, Asa made a handful of mistakes at the end of his life. What were they? Do you agree with the chronicler's assessment of Asa? Also, how do you explain that in 1 Kings 15 Asa dies with a good report, but here Asa dies after making foolish decisions? **4.** What were the consequences of Asa's foolish decision? Do you agree with the punishment? **5.** Where would you rank Asa as a person and as a leader in relation to those he followed (Solomon, Rehoboam and Abijah): First, second, third or fourth?

APPLY 1. When you are criticized how do you usually respond: Get defensive? Get angry at the criticizer? Beat yourself up? Welcome the input? Get depressed? Logically evaluate the criticism to see if it is warranted? **2.** Where in your life do you need to rely a little more on God and less on other people or yourself? How can this group hold you accountable?

OPEN 1. If you could go back to school to learn anything, what subject would you choose? Why? **2.** If "you are what you read" what would that make you?

STUDY Jehoshaphat, a man of outstanding virtue, follows his father Asa. He will experience tre-

16:1 Baasha. Baasha seeks to stop the Israelites from encroaching. He builds a border checkpoint at Ramah.

16:2–9 Asa wins the battle but loses the war. Dependence on foreign strength taints his faith in God.

17:1–21:3 Jehoshaphat receives high marks from the chronicler for his general devotion to God and his denouncement of idolatrous worship (vv. 3–4, 6). The king also institutes a noteworthy emphasis on religious education (vv. 7–9). This account is longer than the parallel in 1 Kings 22:1–46 to emphasize retribution during Jehoshaphat's reign.

mendous success. His story will also be filled with great drama and danger. **1.** From the first six verses, what would you say was the key to Jehoshaphat's success? **2.** What marks would you give Jehoshaphat for his spiritual enrichment program as described in verses 7–9? **3.** Do you think the spiritual enrichment program had any effect on how Judah's neighbors perceived them? Explain. **4.** Why do you suppose other neighboring nations would voluntarily bring gifts to Jehoshaphat? **5.** Do the math. How many fighting men did Jehoshaphat keep in Jerusalem? In relation to that, do you think that more often might makes right or right makes might? How so? **6.** What do you think of Jehoshaphat thus far? To what modern day leader might you link him?

APPLY 1. If an itinerant teaching team like Jehoshaphat's came to your church, what would you most like them to teach you: The Bible? Basic Theology? Church History? Relationships Jesus' Way? How to Share Christ with Others? Discovering Your Spiritual Gifts and Ministry? **2.** If someone brought you a gift, like they brought Jehoshaphat a gift, what would you really like to receive today? **3.** If you were to give a gift, what would it be?

OPEN 1. Did you ever tell a big lie as a child? Were you caught? What happened? **2.** Do you have any basement people in your life, who grab you by the ankles and consistently drag you down? Without naming names, describe the person and what he or she does to you.

STUDY The chronicler's attention turns briefly to the northern kingdom of Israel. He tells the story as a lead into what he will relate later—the dreadful corruption of

walked in the ways his father David had followed. He did not consult
the Baals 4but sought the God of his father and followed his commands rather than the practices of Israel. 5The LORD established the
kingdom under his control; and all Judah brought gifts to Jehoshaphat, so that he had great wealth and honor. 6His heart was devoted
to the ways of the LORD; furthermore, he removed the high places and
the Asherah poles from Judah.

7In the third year of his reign he sent his officials Ben-Hail, Obadiah,
Zechariah, Nethanel and Micaiah to teach in the towns of Judah. 8With
them were certain Levites—Shemaiah, Nethaniah, Zebadiah, Asahel,
Shemiramoth, Jehonathan, Adonijah, Tobijah and Tob-Adonijah—
and the priests Elishama and Jehoram. 9They taught throughout
Judah, taking with them the Book of the Law of the LORD; they went
around to all the towns of Judah and taught the people.

10The fear of the LORD fell on all the kingdoms of the lands surrounding Judah, so that they did not make war with Jehoshaphat.
11Some Philistines brought Jehoshaphat gifts and silver as tribute,
and the Arabs brought him flocks: seven thousand seven hundred
rams and seven thousand seven hundred goats.

12Jehoshaphat became more and more powerful; he built forts and
store cities in Judah 13and had large supplies in the towns of Judah.
He also kept experienced fighting men in Jerusalem. 14Their enroll-
ment by families was as follows:

From Judah, commanders of units of 1,000:
Adnah the commander, with 300,000 fighting men;
15next, Jehohanan the commander, with 280,000;
16next, Amasiah son of Zicri, who volunteered himself for the service of the LORD, with 200,000.
17From Benjamin:
Eliada, a valiant soldier, with 200,000 men armed with bows and shields;
18next, Jehozabad, with 180,000 men armed for battle.

19These were the men who served the king, besides those he stationed in the fortified cities throughout Judah.

Micaiah Prophesies Against Ahab

18 Now Jehoshaphat had great wealth and honor, and he allied
himself with Ahab by marriage. 2Some years later he went
down to visit Ahab in Samaria. Ahab slaughtered many sheep and
cattle for him and the people with him and urged him to attack Ramoth Gilead. 3Ahab king of Israel asked Jehoshaphat king of Judah,
"Will you go with me against Ramoth Gilead?"

Jehoshaphat replied, "I am as you are, and my people as your people; we will join you in the war." 4But Jehoshaphat also said to the
king of Israel, "First seek the counsel of the LORD."

5So the king of Israel brought together the prophets—four hundred

---

17:6 His heart was devoted. Jehoshaphat is lauded for his good intentions. However, like others before him, he falls short of even his own goals. He allows the idols to be restored during his reign (20:33).

18:1 allied himself. This subtle reference to a family alliance would prove near disastrous for Judah on more than one occasion. First, Jehoshaphat nearly loses his life, but he learns his lesson and recovers quickly (19:1–3). However, the Davidic line itself would be at stake (22:10–23:21).

men—and asked them, "Shall we go to war against Ramoth Gilead, or shall I refrain?"

"Go," they answered, "for God will give it into the king's hand."

6But Jehoshaphat asked, "Is there not a prophet of the LORD here whom we can inquire of?"

7The king of Israel answered Jehoshaphat, "There is still one man through whom we can inquire of the LORD, but I hate him because he never prophesies anything good about me, but always bad. He is Micaiah son of Imlah."

"The king should not say that," Jehoshaphat replied.

8So the king of Israel called one of his officials and said, "Bring Micaiah son of Imlah at once."

9Dressed in their royal robes, the king of Israel and Jehoshaphat king of Judah were sitting on their thrones at the threshing floor by the entrance to the gate of Samaria, with all the prophets prophesying before them.
10Now Zedekiah son of Kenaanah had made iron horns, and he declared, "This is what the LORD says: 'With these you will gore the Arameans until they are destroyed.' "

11All the other prophets were prophesying the same thing. "Attack Ramoth Gilead and be victorious," they said, "for the LORD will give it into the king's hand."

12The messenger who had gone to summon Micaiah said to him, "Look, as one man the other prophets are predicting success for the king. Let your word agree with theirs, and speak favorably."

13But Micaiah said, "As surely as the LORD lives, I can tell him only what my God says."

14When he arrived, the king asked him, "Micaiah, shall we go to war against Ramoth Gilead, or shall I refrain?"

"Attack and be victorious," he answered, "for they will be given into your hand."

15The king said to him, "How many times must I make you swear to tell me nothing but the truth in the name of the LORD?"

16Then Micaiah answered, "I saw all Israel scattered on the hills like sheep without a shepherd, and the LORD said, 'These people have no master. Let each one go home in peace.' "

17The king of Israel said to Jehoshaphat, "Didn't I tell you that he never prophesies anything good about me, but only bad?"

18Micaiah continued, "Therefore hear the word of the LORD: I saw the LORD sitting on his throne with all the host of heaven standing on his right and on his left.
19And the LORD said, 'Who will entice Ahab king of Israel into attacking Ramoth Gilead and going to his death there?'

"One suggested this, and another that.
20Finally, a spirit came forward, stood before the LORD and said, 'I will entice him.'

" 'By what means?' the LORD asked.

21" 'I will go and be a lying spirit in the mouths of all his prophets,' he said.

" 'You will succeed in enticing him,' said the LORD. 'Go and do it.'

22"So now the LORD has put a lying spirit in the mouths of these prophets of yours. The LORD has decreed disaster for you."

23Then Zedekiah son of Kenaanah went up and slapped Micaiah in the face. "Which way did the spirit from[a] the LORD go when he went from me to speak to you?" he asked.

[a]23 Or *Spirit of*

Judah's dynasty through the marriage of Jehoshaphat's son to the daughter of Ahab and Jezebel. **1.** Notice the change between Judah and Israel. Instead of enemies, they are now allies. From what you read here, what brought them together? How close do you sense the two kingdoms were at this point in history? **2.** What do you think of Ahab's request? Of Jehoshaphat's response? **3.** Note Jehoshaphat's response in verse 6 to the counsel of the 400 prophets. Why do you think he asked what he did? **4.** What is your impression of Micaiah? What does he tell Ahab? How does Ahab respond? **5.** What do you make of God's sending a lying spirit to the prophets? How does this square with the ninth commandment: You shall not bear false witness? If God is truth, how could God endorse the telling of a lie? Do you think if one lies for the greater good, that the ends justify the means? **6.** What best describes your thoughts on how Ahab treats Micaiah (v. 25) after hearing his report: Sad? Humorous? Ticks me off? Tragic? **7.** Rank the characters in the story from whom you like best to whom you like least: Ahab, Jehoshaphat, Micaiah, Zedekiah, the messenger.

APPLY 1. Has there ever been a time when you went along with the crowd, against your better judgment? When was it? What happened? Has there ever been a time when you were a lone voice of opposition? **2.** Who is a valued friend who consistently tells you "like it is" instead of how you would like it to be?

[24]Micaiah replied, "You will find out on the day you go to hide in an
inner room."
[25]The king of Israel then ordered, "Take Micaiah and send him back
to Amon the ruler of the city and to Joash the king's son, [26]and say,
'This is what the king says: Put this fellow in prison and give him
nothing but bread and water until I return safely.' "
[27]Micaiah declared, "If you ever return safely, the LORD has not spoken through me." Then he added, "Mark my words, all you people!"

Ahab Killed at Ramoth Gilead

[28]So the king of Israel and Jehoshaphat king of Judah went up to
Ramoth Gilead. [29]The king of Israel said to Jehoshaphat, "I will enter
the battle in disguise, but you wear your royal robes." So the king of
Israel disguised himself and went into battle.
[30]Now the king of Aram had ordered his chariot commanders, "Do
not fight with anyone, small or great, except the king of Israel."
[31]When the chariot commanders saw Jehoshaphat, they thought,
"This is the king of Israel." So they turned to attack him, but Jehoshaphat cried out, and the LORD helped him. God drew them away from
him, [32]for when the chariot commanders saw that he was not the
king of Israel, they stopped pursuing him.
[33]But someone drew his bow at random and hit the king of Israel
between the sections of his armor. The king told the chariot driver,
"Wheel around and get me out of the fighting. I've been wounded."
[34]All day long the battle raged, and the king of Israel propped himself
up in his chariot facing the Arameans until evening. Then at sunset he
died.

19 When Jehoshaphat king of Judah returned safely to his palace
in Jerusalem, [2]Jehu the seer, the son of Hanani, went out to
meet him and said to the king, "Should you help the wicked and love[a]
those who hate the LORD? Because of this, the wrath of the LORD is
upon you. [3]There is, however, some good in you, for you have rid the
land of the Asherah poles and have set your heart on seeking God."

Jehoshaphat Appoints Judges

[4]Jehoshaphat lived in Jerusalem, and he went out again among the
people from Beersheba to the hill country of Ephraim and turned
them back to the LORD, the God of their fathers. [5]He appointed judges
in the land, in each of the fortified cities of Judah. [6]He told them,
"Consider carefully what you do, because you are not judging for
man but for the LORD, who is with you whenever you give a verdict.
[7]Now let the fear of the LORD be upon you. Judge carefully, for with
the LORD our God there is no injustice or partiality or bribery."

[a]2 Or *and make alliances with*

OPEN What Halloween costume do you remember wearing when you were a child?

STUDY Jehoshaphat's relationship with King Ahab of Israel ends when Ahab is killed in battle. **1.** Do you think Ahab disguised himself to save his own neck or to better fight alongside his troops? Explain. **2.** What do you think of the king of Aram's military strategy? **3.** Why would Jehoshaphat not disguise himself as well? In your opinion was he: Naïve? Brave? Gullible? Foolish? Cowardly? **4.** Why did he chew out Jehoshaphat? In your opinion, was it warranted? What do you hope Jehoshaphat learned through his alliance with Ahab?

APPLY **1.** What was a good thing you did recently? What was a not-so-good thing? **2.** Share a mistake that ended up teaching you something.

OPEN Which would you prefer to judge and why: Figure skating? Beauty pageant? County fair pie contest? Texas chili contest? Kennel club competition?

STUDY The chronicler continues stressing the superiority of Judah and the importance of bringing the wayward Israelites back into the fold **1.** In Chapter 17 Jehoshaphat set up a teaching mission and here he begins judicial reform through-

18:29 disguised himself. Ahab arranges *for his rival to become an easy* target, and Jehoshaphat falls for it.

18:31 God drew them away. God intervenes despite human foolishness. Jehoshaphat narrowly escapes death.

19:2 Jehu the seer. Jehu carries a precautionary message to Jehoshaphat. The next time he might not be so lucky!

19:5 appointed judges ... in each city. The postexilic refugees reading the chronicler's message would refer to Jehoshaphat's system as a model to rebuild the civil and judicial systems necessary to function as a nation.

19:7 no injustice. God's perfect, personal example is the standard for justice.

8In Jerusalem also, Jehoshaphat appointed some of the Levites,
priests and heads of Israelite families to administer the law of the
LORD and to settle disputes. And they lived in Jerusalem. 9He gave
them these orders: "You must serve faithfully and wholeheartedly in
the fear of the LORD. 10In every case that comes before you from your
fellow countrymen who live in the cities—whether bloodshed or
other concerns of the law, commands, decrees or ordinances—you
are to warn them not to sin against the LORD; otherwise his wrath will
come on you and your brothers. Do this, and you will not sin.
11"Amariah the chief priest will be over you in any matter concerning the LORD, and Zebadiah son of Ishmael, the leader of the tribe of
Judah, will be over you in any matter concerning the king, and the
Levites will serve as officials before you. Act with courage, and may
the LORD be with those who do well."

Jehoshaphat Defeats Moab and Ammon

20 After this, the Moabites and Ammonites with some of the
Meunites[a] came to make war on Jehoshaphat.
2Some men came and told Jehoshaphat, "A vast army is coming
against you from Edom,[b] from the other side of the Sea.[c] It is already
in Hazazon Tamar" (that is, En Gedi). 3Alarmed, Jehoshaphat resolved to inquire of the LORD, and he proclaimed a fast for all Judah.
4The people of Judah came together to seek help from the LORD;
indeed, they came from every town in Judah to seek him.
5Then Jehoshaphat stood up in the assembly of Judah and Jerusalem at the temple of the LORD in the front of the new courtyard 6and
said:

"O LORD, God of our fathers, are you not the God who is in
heaven? You rule over all the kingdoms of the nations. Power
and might are in your hand, and no one can withstand you.
7O our God, did you not drive out the inhabitants of this land
before your people Israel and give it forever to the descendants
of Abraham your friend? 8They have lived in it and have built in it
a sanctuary for your Name, saying, 9'If calamity comes upon us,
whether the sword of judgment, or plague or famine, we will
stand in your presence before this temple that bears your Name
and will cry out to you in our distress, and you will hear us and
save us.'

10"But now here are men from Ammon, Moab and Mount Seir,
whose territory you would not allow Israel to invade when they
came from Egypt; so they turned away from them and did not destroy them. 11See how they are repaying us by coming to drive us
out of the possession you gave us as an inheritance. 12O our
God, will you not judge them? For we have no power to face this
vast army that is attacking us. We do not know what to do, but
our eyes are upon you."

[a]*1* Some Septuagint manuscripts; Hebrew *Ammonites* [b]*2* One Hebrew manuscript; most Hebrew manuscripts, Septuagint and Vulgate *Aram* [c]*2* That is, the Dead Sea

out Judah. What do you think of the guiding principle he offers to the judges? How do you think that would play in today's judicial system? **2.** What similarities are there between the judicial system in Jerusalem and in the rest of Judah? What differences? **3.** What are the qualifications of a judge? Would you add anything to that list? **4.** Do you believe God is with us in every decision we make?

APPLY What was a tough "judgment" call you had to make in the past? What tough call are you facing today?

OPEN 1. How long has it been since something "terrific" happened to you and what was it? **2.** When you are asked to give a public speech, what is your reaction: "Not on your life"? "Depends on the crowd"? "I hope they don't hear my knees knocking"? "Line up the loudspeakers"?

STUDY Jehoshaphat obviously learned a lesson after being chewed out by Jehu the seer, a prophet of God (19:2). The wrath of God comes upon Jehoshaphat's enemies and not Jehoshaphat. **1.** What would you say Jehoshaphat learned from his close calls in chapters 18 and 19? **2.** Have you ever fasted? Why did you do it? Why did Jehoshaphat proclaim one? **3.** Evaluate Jehoshaphat's prayer. Who does he blame for the invasion? What does he think about Judah's chances in battle? What do you think of his prayer? **4.** What picture do you get from the terse description of verse 13? **5.** How does God get his message to Jehoshaphat and Judah? How does the messenger's ancestry lend credibility to his words? How was the message received? If you had been in the crowd that day, what would have likely gone through your mind when you heard God's solution to the invasion? **6.** What do you make of Jehoshaphat's words prior to going into battle: "Have faith in the LORD your God and you will be upheld: Have faith in his prophets and you will be successful." Do you agree with that statement? Are those words just as true today as they were

---

19:8 appointed some of the Levites. The Levites would oversee the fairness of this supreme court. Thus, a balance between religion and state would be achieved.

20:1–30 The mere mention of Moab caused worry and fear. A record of Jehoshaphat's decisive victory over the Moabites and Ammonites would be cause for celebration.

20:5–12 Jehoshaphat wrestles in prayer before battling in the field. In answer to his prayer, God grants Judah victory.

back then? Why or why not? **7.** Picture the battle. What do you think really happened that day? **8.** What role did music play in the battle? In victory? What role does it play in your life? **9.** What are some good ways to fix your eyes on the Lord rather than on yourself or on the battle?

APPLY **1.** For what are you singing praises to God today? **2.** Compare the "serendipity" (happy discovery) in this chapter with experiences of your own. Can you identify a "serendipity" from your own life? **3.** What would you like to see happen in your life that only God can do?

[13]All the men of Judah, with their wives and children and little
ones, stood there before the LORD.
[14]Then the Spirit of the LORD came upon Jahaziel son of Zechariah,
the son of Benaiah, the son of Jeiel, the son of Mattaniah, a Levite
and descendant of Asaph, as he stood in the assembly.
[15]He said: "Listen, King Jehoshaphat and all who live in Judah and
Jerusalem! This is what the LORD says to you: 'Do not be afraid or discouraged because of this vast army. For the battle is not yours, but
God's. [16]Tomorrow march down against them. They will be climbing
up by the Pass of Ziz, and you will find them at the end of the gorge in
the Desert of Jeruel. [17]You will not have to fight this battle. Take up
your positions; stand firm and see the deliverance the LORD will give
you, O Judah and Jerusalem. Do not be afraid; do not be discouraged.
Go out to face them tomorrow, and the LORD will be with you.' "
[18]Jehoshaphat bowed with his face to the ground, and all the people of Judah and Jerusalem fell down in worship before the LORD.
[19]Then some Levites from the Kohathites and Korahites stood up and
praised the LORD, the God of Israel, with very loud voice.
[20]Early in the morning they left for the Desert of Tekoa. As they set
out, Jehoshaphat stood and said, "Listen to me, Judah and people of
Jerusalem! Have faith in the LORD your God and you will be upheld;
have faith in his prophets and you will be successful." [21]After consulting the people, Jehoshaphat appointed men to sing to the LORD and
to praise him for the splendor of his[a] holiness as they went out at the
head of the army, saying:

"Give thanks to the LORD,
for his love endures forever."

[22]As they began to sing and praise, the LORD set ambushes against
the men of Ammon and Moab and Mount Seir who were invading Judah, and they were defeated. [23]The men of Ammon and Moab rose up
against the men from Mount Seir to destroy and annihilate them. After they finished slaughtering the men from Seir, they helped to destroy one another.
[24]When the men of Judah came to the place that overlooks the
desert and looked toward the vast army, they saw only dead bodies
lying on the ground; no one had escaped. [25]So Jehoshaphat and his
men went to carry off their plunder, and they found among them a
great amount of equipment and clothing[b] and also articles of value—
more than they could take away. There was so much plunder that it
took three days to collect it. [26]On the fourth day they assembled in
the Valley of Beracah, where they praised the LORD. This is why it is
called the Valley of Beracah[c] to this day.
[27]Then, led by Jehoshaphat, all the men of Judah and Jerusalem returned joyfully to Jerusalem, for the LORD had given them cause to

[a]*21 Or him with the splendor of* [b]*25* Some Hebrew manuscripts and Vulgate; most Hebrew manuscripts *corpses* [c]*26 Beracah* means *praise.*

20:20 Have faith. As a military leader, Jehoshaphat might have instructed his warriors to hit first and hit hardest. However, his military strategy is spiritual—supporting all whom God has sent to guide them.

20:22 the LORD set ambushes. While Judah celebrates, the enemies grow more confused. They ambush each other, securing the victory for the Israelites who have yet to draw their weapons.

rejoice over their enemies. [28]They entered Jerusalem and went to the
temple of the LORD with harps and lutes and trumpets.
[29]The fear of God came upon all the kingdoms of the countries
when they heard how the LORD had fought against the enemies of
Israel. [30]And the kingdom of Jehoshaphat was at peace, for his God
had given him rest on every side.

The End of Jehoshaphat's Reign

[31]So Jehoshaphat reigned over Judah. He was thirty-five years old
when he became king of Judah, and he reigned in Jerusalem twenty-
five years. His mother's name was Azubah daughter of Shilhi. [32]He
walked in the ways of his father Asa and did not stray from them; he
did what was right in the eyes of the LORD. [33]The high places, however, were not removed, and the people still had not set their hearts
on the God of their fathers.
[34]The other events of Jehoshaphat's reign, from beginning to end,
are written in the annals of Jehu son of Hanani, which are recorded in
the book of the kings of Israel.
[35]Later, Jehoshaphat king of Judah made an alliance with Ahaziah
king of Israel, who was guilty of wickedness. [36]He agreed with him to
construct a fleet of trading ships.[a] After these were built at Ezion Geber, [37]Eliezer son of Dodavahu of Mareshah prophesied against Jehoshaphat, saying, "Because you have made an alliance with
Ahaziah, the LORD will destroy what you have made." The ships were
wrecked and were not able to set sail to trade.[b]

21 Then Jehoshaphat rested with his fathers and was buried with
them in the City of David. And Jehoram his son succeeded him
as king. [2]Jehoram's brothers, the sons of Jehoshaphat, were Azariah,
Jehiel, Zechariah, Azariahu, Michael and Shephatiah. All these were
sons of Jehoshaphat king of Israel.[c] [3]Their father had given them
many gifts of silver and gold and articles of value, as well as fortified
cities in Judah, but he had given the kingdom to Jehoram because he
was his firstborn son.

Jehoram King of Judah

[4]When Jehoram established himself firmly over his father's kingdom, he put all his brothers to the sword along with some of the
princes of Israel. [5]Jehoram was thirty-two years old when he became
king, and he reigned in Jerusalem eight years. [6]He walked in the ways
of the kings of Israel, as the house of Ahab had done, for he married

[a]36 Hebrew *of ships that could go to Tarshish* [b]37 Hebrew *sail for Tarshish* [c]2 That is, Judah, as frequently in 2 Chronicles

OPEN **1.** Share a memorable boating or cruising experience. **2.** When have you experienced taking three steps forward and two steps back?

STUDY Just when we think Jehoshaphat has learned his lesson about relying on God and not foreign alliances, he strikes up a questionable business deal with another wicked king from Israel. **1.** Following a story in which the whole nation is united in praise to God (vv. 13,27), does verse 33 seem unusual to you? Why or why not? **2.** Where does this dismal spirituality lead (vv. 35–37)? Would you agree that dismal spirituality leads to trouble? Can you be a good person without being spiritual? **3.** What evidence from this section would lead you to believe Jehoshaphat was blessed by God? **4.** What legacy does Jehoshaphat try to leave his nation? His family? What does he leave with you?

APPLY If you could leave "unwrapped" gifts for the next generation, what three gifts would you like to leave?

OPEN **1.** What famous "bad guy" is especially interesting to you and why: Jesse James? Dracula? Darth Vader? Hannibal Lector? Jack the Ripper? Al Capone? Judas? Benedict Arnold? **2.** What's the sickest you have ever felt?

STUDY In 2 Kings 8:16–24 the author briefly dismisses

20:30 at peace. After a weaponless victory, Judah's reputation for godly assistance keeps the enemy at bay. God's peace signifies his blessing upon Judah during the king's reign.

20:33 The king seems to have lost his momentum for destroying idols (17:6). Like a bad habit, the idols keep returning despite the king's initial efforts.

20:35–37 Despite Jehoshaphat's battlefield success, he proves to be an inept entrepreneur. He fails to carry the same godly trust into his business efforts, choosing instead to seek a failed alliance with a pagan partner.

21:2 sons. Jehoshaphat blessed one son with his throne and the other six with money and property.

21:4–20 Jehoram tests the limits of God's merciful protection of the line of David. Apart from God's commitment to David, the evil king's family would have been entirely obliterated (2 Kin. 8:16–24).

21:4 Jehoram was likely inspired by his wife's evil heritage. He brutally snuffs out all the competition in the false belief that this treachery would secure his empire.

21:6 walked in the ways. Jehoram is a political prodigy with an arranged marriage of convenience. Like his wife's side of the family, his whole life revolves around his personal kingdom.

Jehoram by saying, he "rested with his fathers and was buried with them." The chronicler does not let him off the hook so easily. The chronicler thought him so contemptible a ruler that he died in agony, and was dishonored in death by not being buried in the tombs of the kings. **1.** What do you think of Jehoram's method of establishing himself in power (v. 4)? **2.** Read 21:1–3. Based on these verses would you hold Jehoshaphat partly to blame for Jehoram's reign? How could such a bad apple fall from such a good tree? **3.** Judah had to endure eight years of Jehoram's reign. What would you say to someone who said, "Why did God take so long to wipe out the evil Jehoram?" **4.** After Elijah's letter arrived, do you think it was too late for Jehoram to change his ways? Was the handwriting already on the wall for him? In terms of forgiveness and getting right with God, how late is too late? **5.** What do you think of Jehoram's punishment: Too Severe? Too soft? Just right? **6.** "He passed away to no one's regret." How does that statement sit with you? Do you believe everyone eventually gets what he or she deserves? **7.** What does this passage teach you about God? **8.** What does the passage teach you about the nature of people? Why didn't they reject evil leadership?

APPLY **1.** Have you ever felt like you were in the presence of some form of evil? Explain. **2.** Where in your life does it seem that God is moving a little slower than you would like?

OPEN **1.** What three words would you use to describe your mother? **2.** What is a significant personality trait that your parents passed on to you?

STUDY Young, inexperienced and as bankrupt spiritually as

a daughter of Ahab. He did evil in the eyes of the LORD. [7]Nevertheless,
because of the covenant the LORD had made with David, the LORD was
not willing to destroy the house of David. He had promised to maintain a lamp for him and his descendants forever.

[8]In the time of Jehoram, Edom rebelled against Judah and set up its
own king. [9]So Jehoram went there with his officers and all his chariots. The Edomites surrounded him and his chariot commanders, but
he rose up and broke through by night. [10]To this day Edom has been
in rebellion against Judah.

Libnah revolted at the same time, because Jehoram had forsaken
the LORD, the God of his fathers. [11]He had also built high places on
the hills of Judah and had caused the people of Jerusalem to prostitute themselves and had led Judah astray.

[12]Jehoram received a letter from Elijah the prophet, which said:

"This is what the LORD, the God of your father David, says: 'You
have not walked in the ways of your father Jehoshaphat or of Asa
king of Judah. [13]But you have walked in the ways of the kings of
Israel, and you have led Judah and the people of Jerusalem to
prostitute themselves, just as the house of Ahab did. You have
also murdered your own brothers, members of your father's
house, men who were better than you. [14]So now the LORD is
about to strike your people, your sons, your wives and everything that is yours, with a heavy blow. [15]You yourself will be very
ill with a lingering disease of the bowels, until the disease causes
your bowels to come out.' "

[16]The LORD aroused against Jehoram the hostility of the Philistines
and of the Arabs who lived near the Cushites. [17]They attacked Judah,
invaded it and carried off all the goods found in the king's palace, together with his sons and wives. Not a son was left to him except
Ahaziah,[a] the youngest.

[18]After all this, the LORD afflicted Jehoram with an incurable disease of the bowels. [19]In the course of time, at the end of the second
year, his bowels came out because of the disease, and he died in great
pain. His people made no fire in his honor, as they had for his fathers.

[20]Jehoram was thirty-two years old when he became king, and he
reigned in Jerusalem eight years. He passed away, to no one's regret,
and was buried in the City of David, but not in the tombs of the kings.

Ahaziah King of Judah

22 The people of Jerusalem made Ahaziah, Jehoram's youngest
son, king in his place, since the raiders, who came with the
Arabs into the camp, had killed all the older sons. So Ahaziah son of
Jehoram king of Judah began to reign.

[a]17 Hebrew *Jehoahaz,* a variant of *Ahaziah*

21:10 God of his fathers. Jehoram's *lean toward* evil is not consistent with his family tree. He is from David's *line,* and his propensity toward evil is his own personal choice.

21:12–15 Elijah's wake-up call could not have come at a better time. Yet Jehoram ignores this word of warning and suffers the consequences.

21:20 passed away ... not in the tombs of the kings. Death has the final word on Jehoram's life. No funeral. No procession. Nothing is done to honor this relentlessly evil king.

22:1–9 Another deposed king. Ahaziah's brief rule repeats the lessons yet unlearned from Judah's history. Elijah had announced Ahaziah's death (2 Kin. 1:2–17).

2Ahaziah was twenty-two[a] years old when he became king, and he
reigned in Jerusalem one year. His mother's name was Athaliah, a
granddaughter of Omri.
3He too walked in the ways of the house of Ahab, for his mother
encouraged him in doing wrong. 4He did evil in the eyes of the LORD,
as the house of Ahab had done, for after his father's death they became his advisers, to his undoing. 5He also followed their counsel
when he went with Joram[b] son of Ahab king of Israel to war against
Hazael king of Aram at Ramoth Gilead. The Arameans wounded
Joram; 6so he returned to Jezreel to recover from the wounds they
had inflicted on him at Ramoth[c] in his battle with Hazael king of
Aram.
Then Ahaziah[d] son of Jehoram king of Judah went down to Jezreel
to see Joram son of Ahab because he had been wounded.
7Through Ahaziah's visit to Joram, God brought about Ahaziah's
downfall. When Ahaziah arrived, he went out with Joram to meet Jehu
son of Nimshi, whom the LORD had anointed to destroy the house of
Ahab. 8While Jehu was executing judgment on the house of Ahab, he
found the princes of Judah and the sons of Ahaziah's relatives, who
had been attending Ahaziah, and he killed them. 9He then went in
search of Ahaziah, and his men captured him while he was hiding in
Samaria. He was brought to Jehu and put to death. They buried him,
for they said, "He was a son of Jehoshaphat, who sought the LORD
with all his heart." So there was no one in the house of Ahaziah powerful enough to retain the kingdom.

Athaliah and Joash

10When Athaliah the mother of Ahaziah saw that her son was dead,
she proceeded to destroy the whole royal family of the house of Judah. 11But Jehosheba,[e] the daughter of King Jehoram, took Joash son
of Ahaziah and stole him away from among the royal princes who
were about to be murdered and put him and his nurse in a bedroom.
Because Jehosheba,[e] the daughter of King Jehoram and wife of the
priest Jehoiada, was Ahaziah's sister, she hid the child from Athaliah
so she could not kill him. 12He remained hidden with them at the
temple of God for six years while Athaliah ruled the land.

23 In the seventh year Jehoiada showed his strength. He made a
covenant with the commanders of units of a hundred:
Azariah son of Jeroham, Ishmael son of Jehohanan, Azariah son of

[a]2 Some Septuagint manuscripts and Syriac (see also 2 Kings 8:26); Hebrew *forty-two* [b]5 Hebrew *Jehoram*, a variant of *Joram*; also in verses 6 and 7 [c]6 Hebrew *Ramah*, a variant of *Ramoth* [d]6 Some Hebrew manuscripts, Septuagint, Vulgate and Syriac (see also 2 Kings 8:29); most Hebrew manuscripts *Azariah* [e]11 Hebrew *Jehoshabeath*, a variant of *Jehosheba*

his father, Ahaziah's reign is mercifully short. His death leaves the throne of Judah in shambles. **1.** What would you list as the positives when Ahaziah took the throne? What would you list as the negatives? **2.** Why do you think Ahaziah's mother was such a dominant force in his life? (Remember: Athaliah was the daughter of Ahab and Jezebel, 21:6) **3.** Once again, a Judean king enters into an "unholy alliance" with a king of Israel. Why do you suppose they keep making the same mistake? Do we ever learn from history? **4.** Name the individuals responsible for Ahaziah's downfall. **5.** What would you have put on Ahaziah's tombstone? In your opinion, why wasn't his grandfather's faith passed on?

APPLY 1. What spiritual impact did your parents have on your life? **2.** When were you ever in the wrong place at the wrong time?

OPEN 1. As a child, did you and your gang play hide and seek, sardines or both? What was a great place to hide in your neighborhood? **2.** Who was one of your childhood mentors?

STUDY In a story fit for a Hollywood script, the forces of good and evil collide. With the Davidic line of kings hanging by a thread, a courageous aunt and uncle help to restore the rightful king to the throne of Judah. The line of David endures. **1.** Given the fact that God had promised to keep the Davidic line in tact, do you think Athaliah's plan ever stood a chance? **2.** Who are the principal actors in this drama? Who do you like best? Why? **3.** What was

22:2 Ahaziah was twenty-two. Ahaziah's youth and inexperience play into his quick demise.

22:3–4 Ahaziah allows himself to be made a puppet of the northern kingdom. Unfortunately, his own mother is pulling the strings.

22:7 Ahaziah's downfall. Jehu, Israel's next king, assassinates Ahaziah, yet all is according to God's plan.

22:9 Ahaziah's end leaves the story in suspense. An occupied tomb leaves an empty throne. The only successor in Judah is a mere infant.

22:10–12 Like husband, like wife. Athaliah, like Jehoram, attempts to eradicate every inch of the Davidic line. However, her efforts are thwarted by the ingenuity of a quick-thinking girl.

23:1–24:27 Joash leans on Jehoiada for inspiration. Under his influence, the king restores the temple and combats idol worship. However, when Jehoiada dies, Joash's success soon sours.

23:1 Jehoiada showed his strength. Jehoiada goes from zero to hero as he shares the weight of a king's mantle with a seven-year-old. Jehoiada's decisions become royal rule.

Jehoiada's plan? Why do you think he relied so much on priests and Levites to make it work? **4.** How did Athaliah get wind of the coup against her? Does it sound to you that she was: Popular? Tolerated? Hated? **5.** With Athaliah dead and King Joash only a boy, who really made the decisions in Jerusalem? What kinds of things did he do to insure proper rule and worship? Which of his qualities do you admire? **6.** What do you see as the balance between "trusting the Lord" and "taking matters in your own hands?" Would you say Jehoiada trusted more or took matters into his own hands? **7.** As followers of Christ, and being aware of his statement, "blessed are the peacemakers," should we ever involve ourselves in a violent revolution? If yes, when? If no, why not?

APPLY 1. Whom might God be calling you to take under your wing? **2.** In addition to your parents, what relative has had a positive impact on you?

Obed, Maaseiah son of Adaiah, and Elishaphat son of Zicri. 2They
went throughout Judah and gathered the Levites and the heads of Israelite families from all the towns. When they came to Jerusalem, 3the
whole assembly made a covenant with the king at the temple of God.
Jehoiada said to them, "The king's son shall reign, as the LORD
promised concerning the descendants of David. 4Now this is what
you are to do: A third of you priests and Levites who are going on
duty on the Sabbath are to keep watch at the doors, 5a third of you at
the royal palace and a third at the Foundation Gate, and all the other
men are to be in the courtyards of the temple of the LORD. 6No one is
to enter the temple of the LORD except the priests and Levites on duty;
they may enter because they are consecrated, but all the other men
are to guard what the LORD has assigned to them.[a] 7The Levites are to
station themselves around the king, each man with his weapons in
his hand. Anyone who enters the temple must be put to death. Stay
close to the king wherever he goes."
8The Levites and all the men of Judah did just as Jehoiada the priest
ordered. Each one took his men—those who were going on duty on
the Sabbath and those who were going off duty—for Jehoiada the
priest had not released any of the divisions. 9Then he gave the commanders of units of a hundred the spears and the large and small
shields that had belonged to King David and that were in the temple
of God. 10He stationed all the men, each with his weapon in his hand,
around the king—near the altar and the temple, from the south side
to the north side of the temple.
11Jehoiada and his sons brought out the king's son and put the
crown on him; they presented him with a copy of the covenant and
proclaimed him king. They anointed him and shouted, "Long live the
king!"
12When Athaliah heard the noise of the people running and cheering the king, she went to them at the temple of the LORD. 13She
looked, and there was the king, standing by his pillar at the entrance.
The officers and the trumpeters were beside the king, and all the people of the land were rejoicing and blowing trumpets, and singers with
musical instruments were leading the praises. Then Athaliah tore her
robes and shouted, "Treason! Treason!"
14Jehoiada the priest sent out the commanders of units of a hundred, who were in charge of the troops, and said to them: "Bring her
out between the ranks[b] and put to the sword anyone who follows
her." For the priest had said, "Do not put her to death at the temple of
the LORD." 15So they seized her as she reached the entrance of the
Horse Gate on the palace grounds, and there they put her to death.
16Jehoiada then made a covenant that he and the people and the
king[c] would be the LORD's people. 17All the people went to the temple
of Baal and tore it down. They smashed the altars and idols and killed
Mattan the priest of Baal in front of the altars.
18Then Jehoiada placed the oversight of the temple of the LORD in
the hands of the priests, who were Levites, to whom David had made

[a]6 Or *to observe the LORD's command* ⌞*not to enter*⌟ [b]14 Or *out from the precincts* [c]16 Or *covenant between the LORD*⌞ *and the people and the king that they* (see 2 Kings 11:17)

23:13 Treason! Athaliah could not believe her ears. The sound of celebration suffocates her dream for royal power. Joash, the boy-king, would take her place. Her plan failed and God's plan came into play.

assignments in the temple, to present the burnt offerings of the LORD
as written in the Law of Moses, with rejoicing and singing, as David
had ordered. 19He also stationed doorkeepers at the gates of the
LORD's temple so that no one who was in any way unclean might
enter.
20He took with him the commanders of hundreds, the nobles, the
rulers of the people and all the people of the land and brought the
king down from the temple of the LORD. They went into the palace
through the Upper Gate and seated the king on the royal throne,
21and all the people of the land rejoiced. And the city was quiet,
because Athaliah had been slain with the sword.

Joash Repairs the Temple

24 Joash was seven years old when he became king, and he
reigned in Jerusalem forty years. His mother's name was
Zibiah; she was from Beersheba. 2Joash did what was right in the
eyes of the LORD all the years of Jehoiada the priest. 3Jehoiada chose
two wives for him, and he had sons and daughters.
4Some time later Joash decided to restore the temple of the LORD.
5He called together the priests and Levites and said to them, "Go to
the towns of Judah and collect the money due annually from all
Israel, to repair the temple of your God. Do it now." But the Levites
did not act at once.
6Therefore the king summoned Jehoiada the chief priest and said
to him, "Why haven't you required the Levites to bring in from Judah
and Jerusalem the tax imposed by Moses the servant of the LORD and
by the assembly of Israel for the Tent of the Testimony?"
7Now the sons of that wicked woman Athaliah had broken into the
temple of God and had used even its sacred objects for the Baals.
8At the king's command, a chest was made and placed outside, at
the gate of the temple of the LORD. 9A proclamation was then issued
in Judah and Jerusalem that they should bring to the LORD the tax that
Moses the servant of God had required of Israel in the desert. 10All
the officials and all the people brought their contributions gladly,
dropping them into the chest until it was full. 11Whenever the chest
was brought in by the Levites to the king's officials and they saw that
there was a large amount of money, the royal secretary and the officer of the chief priest would come and empty the chest and carry it
back to its place. They did this regularly and collected a great amount
of money. 12The king and Jehoiada gave it to the men who carried out
the work required for the temple of the LORD. They hired masons and
carpenters to restore the LORD's temple, and also workers in iron and
bronze to repair the temple.
13The men in charge of the work were diligent, and the repairs pro-
gressed under them. They rebuilt the temple of God according to its
original design and reinforced it. 14When they had finished, they
brought the rest of the money to the king and Jehoiada, and with it
were made articles for the LORD's temple: articles for the service and

OPEN 1. Which of these organizations do you give to regularly: Your church? Your alma mater? A world mission? The United Way? A conservation organization? A political party? A para-church group? **2.** Where did you live at the age of 7? Where did you go to school?

STUDY At the age of seven Joash begins his reign as king of Judah. He does well as long as he has the priest and his mentor Jehoiada at his side. **1.** Joash's reign as king is divided into two parts: The good part (vv. 1–16) and the bad part (vv. 17–32). What would you say was the difference between the two? **2.** According to the chronicler, what was Joash's greatest accomplishment? Why do you suppose he chose that as a project? **3.** Why do you think the Levites were hesitant to help him at first? **4.** Even though they were taxed, why do you think the people gave so joyfully? Do you feel joy when you give? Explain. **5.** How should a church motivate people to give joyfully? **6.** What would you put on Jehoiada's tombstone? In your opinion, did he deserve to be buried with the kings?

APPLY 1. Rank your top three spiritual mentors. How did they help you to remain faithful to God as Jehoiada helped Joash? **2.** Where do you finding yourself dragging your feet: At home? At work? At church? With diet? With exercise? With relationships?

24:2 all the years of Jehoiada. With Jehoiada in the picture, King Joash could not go wrong. However, he forfeits his borrowed enthusiasm for God at Jehoiada's death.

24:4 Joash ... restore the temple. Athaliah had left true worship in disarray. Restoring the temple was job number one.

24:5 Joash sends his Levitical priests in search of long overdue tax monies (Ex. 30:12–16).

for the burnt offerings, and also dishes and other objects of gold and
silver. As long as Jehoiada lived, burnt offerings were presented continually in the temple of the LORD.
15 Now Jehoiada was old and full of years, and he died at the age of
a hundred and thirty. 16 He was buried with the kings in the City of
David, because of the good he had done in Israel for God and his
temple.

The Wickedness of Joash

17 After the death of Jehoiada, the officials of Judah came and paid
homage to the king, and he listened to them. 18 They abandoned the
temple of the LORD, the God of their fathers, and worshiped Asherah
poles and idols. Because of their guilt, God's anger came upon Judah
and Jerusalem. 19 Although the LORD sent prophets to the people to
bring them back to him, and though they testified against them, they
would not listen.
20 Then the Spirit of God came upon Zechariah son of Jehoiada the
priest. He stood before the people and said, "This is what God says:
'Why do you disobey the LORD's commands? You will not prosper. Because you have forsaken the LORD, he has forsaken you.' "
21 But they plotted against him, and by order of the king they stoned
him to death in the courtyard of the LORD's temple. 22 King Joash did
not remember the kindness Zechariah's father Jehoiada had shown
him but killed his son, who said as he lay dying, "May the LORD see
this and call you to account."
23 At the turn of the year,[a] the army of Aram marched against Joash;
it invaded Judah and Jerusalem and killed all the leaders of the people. They sent all the plunder to their king in Damascus. 24 Although
the Aramean army had come with only a few men, the LORD delivered
into their hands a much larger army. Because Judah had forsaken the
LORD, the God of their fathers, judgment was executed on Joash.
25 When the Arameans withdrew, they left Joash severely wounded.
His officials conspired against him for murdering the son of Jehoiada
the priest, and they killed him in his bed. So he died and was buried
in the City of David, but not in the tombs of the kings.
26 Those who conspired against him were Zabad,[b] son of Shimeath
an Ammonite woman, and Jehozabad, son of Shimrith[c] a Moabite
woman. 27 The account of his sons, the many prophecies about him,
and the record of the restoration of the temple of God are written in
the annotations on the book of the kings. And Amaziah his son succeeded him as king.

Amaziah King of Judah

25 Amaziah was twenty-five years old when he became king,
and he reigned in Jerusalem twenty-nine years. His mother's

[a]23 Probably in the spring [b]26 A variant of *Jozabad* [c]26 A variant of *Shomer*

OPEN 1. When did you first feel you were on your own as an adult? What age were you: 16? 18? 21? Older? **2.** Whose death marked a turning point in your life?

STUDY How quickly the mighty fall. Joash's life is a tragic story of rags to riches to rags once again. **1.** How did Joash's reign as king differ from the first part of his life when Jehoiada the priest was alive? Did Joash lose his faith or never have much of it in the first place? **2.** Given his relationship with Jehoiada, how could Joash treat Zechariah so cruelly? Do you think Joash had inferiority problems or just wanted to step out of Jehoiada's shadow? **3.** If the repair of the temple were Joash's major accomplishment, what would you say was the major disaster of his reign? Why did it happen? How could it have been avoided? **4.** How does Joash's death summarize his reign? Why do you think he is left out of the list of Jesus' ancestors in Matthew 1:8?

APPLY 1. Joash was severely wounded in battle. Were you ever "severely wounded"? **2.** What are you doing to maintain deep, long lasting spiritual transformation in your faith?

OPEN 1. Where were your parents from? **2.** What was your heart not quite into recently?

STUDY Emboldened by his defeat of Edom, King Amazi-

24:15–22 Zechariah's dying words seem to roll off Joash. The king shrugs when reminded of Jehoiada's kindness to him.

24:18, 20, 24 The theme in Joash's second half of life is his complete renouncement of his former godliness. His destruction, therefore, is certain.

24:24 judgment was executed. The king pays for the sins of the people. Joash suffers an inexplicable defeat at the hands of a smaller army.

24:25 Joash ... killed ... buried ... not in the tombs of the kings. Like Jehoram before him, Joash's undignified burial marks the dishonor of his evil life.

25:1 Amaziah. His reign is basically good but not wholeheartedly godly.

name was Jehoaddin[a]; she was from Jerusalem. 2He did what was
right in the eyes of the LORD, but not wholeheartedly. 3After the
kingdom was firmly in his control, he executed the officials who had
murdered his father the king. 4Yet he did not put their sons to death,
but acted in accordance with what is written in the Law, in the Book
of Moses, where the LORD commanded: "Fathers shall not be put to
death for their children, nor children put to death for their fathers;
each is to die for his own sins."[b]

5Amaziah called the people of Judah together and assigned them
according to their families to commanders of thousands and commanders of hundreds for all Judah and Benjamin. He then mustered
those twenty years old or more and found that there were three hundred thousand men ready for military service, able to handle the
spear and shield. 6He also hired a hundred thousand fighting men
from Israel for a hundred talents[c] of silver.

7But a man of God came to him and said, "O king, these troops
from Israel must not march with you, for the LORD is not with Israel—
not with any of the people of Ephraim. 8Even if you go and fight courageously in battle, God will overthrow you before the enemy, for God
has the power to help or to overthrow."

9Amaziah asked the man of God, "But what about the hundred talents I paid for these Israelite troops?"

The man of God replied, "The LORD can give you much more than
that."

10So Amaziah dismissed the troops who had come to him from
Ephraim and sent them home. They were furious with Judah and left
for home in a great rage.

11Amaziah then marshaled his strength and led his army to the Valley of Salt, where he killed ten thousand men of Seir. 12The army of
Judah also captured ten thousand men alive, took them to the top of
a cliff and threw them down so that all were dashed to pieces.

13Meanwhile the troops that Amaziah had sent back and had not
allowed to take part in the war raided Judean towns from Samaria to
Beth Horon. They killed three thousand people and carried off great
quantities of plunder.

14When Amaziah returned from slaughtering the Edomites, he
brought back the gods of the people of Seir. He set them up as his
own gods, bowed down to them and burned sacrifices to them. 15The
anger of the LORD burned against Amaziah, and he sent a prophet to
him, who said, "Why do you consult this people's gods, which could
not save their own people from your hand?"

16While he was still speaking, the king said to him, "Have we appointed you an adviser to the king? Stop! Why be struck down?"

So the prophet stopped but said, "I know that God has determined
to destroy you, because you have done this and have not listened to
my counsel."

[a]*1* Hebrew *Jehoaddan,* a variant of *Jehoaddin* [b]*4* Deut. 24:16 [c]*6* That is, about 3 3/4 tons (about 3.4 metric tons); also in verse 9

ah unwisely challenges the king of Israel to battle, and is soundly defeated. After defeat, Amaziah flees to Lachish, but is extradited and brought back to be slain by his own people. **1.** After reading the entire chapter, do you agree with the chronicler's assessment of Amaziah in verse 2? Explain. **2.** What does a wholehearted follower of God look like? In your opinion what does such a person say or do? How about a half-hearted follower? **3.** Amaziah starts off by doing two good things: Obeying the law (v. 4) and listening to the man of God (vv. 7–10). What do you think got him off track? **4.** Why does God get so angry with Amaziah? Why is wholeheartedness so important to God. Wouldn't you say a little faith is better than no faith at all? How are you and those around you not wholehearted? **5.** In Amaziah's response to the prophet in verse 16, do you think that Amaziah's military success had gone to his head? Why or why not? **6.** How does Amaziah challenge Jehoash, king of Israel? Would you say Jehoash is trying to avoid bloodshed or coaxing Amaziah into a fury by his response? Could a proud king have just stayed at home after a reply like Jehoash sent? **7.** What did Jehoash do to Amaziah after he defeated him? Do you think Jehoash's treatment of Amaziah was merciful or cruel? **8.** Why do you suppose people in Jerusalem conspired against Amaziah? Why did they want him out of the way? **9.** What would you list as Amaziah's good points? His failures?

APPLY 1. Amaziah thought better of his decision to hire Israelite troops and was willing to lose his investment in order to follow God. What was something you thought better of and are now glad you changed your mind? What caused you to change your mind? **2.** How has your pride ever gotten you into trouble or caused you to act in a way you later regretted?

25:2 Amaziah avenges his father's death (vv. 3–4). However, he battles idolatry with lesser zeal. Even though he was doing "what was right in the eyes of the LORD, but not wholeheartedly."

25:7 the LORD is not with Israel. Hosting Israel's troops within his ranks would be inviting a curse. Amaziah wisely dismisses them.

25:14–25 Amaziah is so taken with the spoils of victory that he actually worships his plunder. In heavenly irony, God uses a taunting northern king to punish Amaziah's foolishness.

17After Amaziah king of Judah consulted his advisers, he sent this
challenge to Jehoash[a] son of Jehoahaz, the son of Jehu, king of Israel:
"Come, meet me face to face."
18But Jehoash king of Israel replied to Amaziah king of Judah: "A
thistle in Lebanon sent a message to a cedar in Lebanon, 'Give your
daughter to my son in marriage.' Then a wild beast in Lebanon came
along and trampled the thistle underfoot. 19You say to yourself that
you have defeated Edom, and now you are arrogant and proud. But
stay at home! Why ask for trouble and cause your own downfall and
that of Judah also?"
20Amaziah, however, would not listen, for God so worked that he
might hand them over to ⌞Jehoash⌟, because they sought the gods of
Edom. 21So Jehoash king of Israel attacked. He and Amaziah king of
Judah faced each other at Beth Shemesh in Judah. 22Judah was routed
by Israel, and every man fled to his home. 23Jehoash king of Israel
captured Amaziah king of Judah, the son of Joash, the son of
Ahaziah,[b] at Beth Shemesh. Then Jehoash brought him to Jerusalem
and broke down the wall of Jerusalem from the Ephraim Gate to the
Corner Gate—a section about six hundred feet[c] long. 24He took all the
gold and silver and all the articles found in the temple of God that
had been in the care of Obed-Edom, together with the palace treasures and the hostages, and returned to Samaria.
25Amaziah son of Joash king of Judah lived for fifteen years after
the death of Jehoash son of Jehoahaz king of Israel. 26As for the other
events of Amaziah's reign, from beginning to end, are they not written in the book of the kings of Judah and Israel? 27From the time that
Amaziah turned away from following the LORD, they conspired
against him in Jerusalem and he fled to Lachish, but they sent men
after him to Lachish and killed him there. 28He was brought back by
horse and was buried with his fathers in the City of Judah.

Uzziah King of Judah

26 Then all the people of Judah took Uzziah,[d] who was sixteen
years old, and made him king in place of his father Amaziah.
2He was the one who rebuilt Elath and restored it to Judah after Amaziah rested with his fathers.
3Uzziah was sixteen years old when he became king, and he
reigned in Jerusalem fifty-two years. His mother's name was Jecoliah; she was from Jerusalem. 4He did what was right in the eyes of the
LORD, just as his father Amaziah had done. 5He sought God during the
days of Zechariah, who instructed him in the fear[e] of God. As long as
he sought the LORD, God gave him success.
6He went to war against the Philistines and broke down the walls of

[a]17 Hebrew *Joash,* a variant of *Jehoash;* also in verses 18, 21, 23 and 25 [b]23 Hebrew *Jehoahaz,* a variant of *Ahaziah* [c]23 Hebrew *four hundred cubits* (about 180 meters) [d]1 Also called *Azariah* [e]5 Many Hebrew manuscripts, Septuagint and Syriac; other Hebrew manuscripts *vision*

OPEN 1. Recently, what ticked you off and got under your skin? **2.** Where would you place yourself on a "strong-weak" continuum today? Are you feeling strong? Weak? Somewhere in between?

STUDY With no great international political threat, both Uzziah in the south and Jeroboam II in the north experience 40 years of prosperity. From the prophets Amos, Hosea and Isaiah, however, we learn that the prosperity of the few led to great miseries for the majority. **1.** What strengths and weaknesses do you see in Uzziah, the teenage king? Why does the chronicler rate him so

26:1–23 The good. The bad. The ugly. Uzziah's reign proves that obedience brings prosperity (vv. 4–15), and disobedience results in destruction (vv. 16–21).

26:1 Uzziah ... sixteen years old. He starts his reign as an adolescent and ends as a convalescent, fifty-two years later.

26:5 As long as he sought the LORD. Uzziah's secret to success is no surprise. Obedience is the consistent key in the Davidic line.

26:6–8 Uzziah's military brilliance stretches his reputation to the borders of Egypt. He impresses his Ammonite enemies and threatens his northern neighbors.

Gath, Jabneh and Ashdod. He then rebuilt towns near Ashdod and elsewhere among the Philistines. 7God helped him against the Philistines and against the Arabs who lived in Gur Baal and against the Meunites. 8The Ammonites brought tribute to Uzziah, and his fame spread as far as the border of Egypt, because he had become very powerful.

9Uzziah built towers in Jerusalem at the Corner Gate, at the Valley Gate and at the angle of the wall, and he fortified them. 10He also built towers in the desert and dug many cisterns, because he had much livestock in the foothills and in the plain. He had people working his fields and vineyards in the hills and in the fertile lands, for he loved the soil.

11Uzziah had a well-trained army, ready to go out by divisions according to their numbers as mustered by Jeiel the secretary and Maaseiah the officer under the direction of Hananiah, one of the royal officials. 12The total number of family leaders over the fighting men was 2,600. 13Under their command was an army of 307,500 men trained for war, a powerful force to support the king against his enemies. 14Uzziah provided shields, spears, helmets, coats of armor, bows and slingstones for the entire army. 15In Jerusalem he made machines designed by skillful men for use on the towers and on the corner defenses to shoot arrows and hurl large stones. His fame spread far and wide, for he was greatly helped until he became powerful.

16But after Uzziah became powerful, his pride led to his downfall. He was unfaithful to the LORD his God, and entered the temple of the LORD to burn incense on the altar of incense. 17Azariah the priest with eighty other courageous priests of the LORD followed him in. 18They confronted him and said, "It is not right for you, Uzziah, to burn incense to the LORD. That is for the priests, the descendants of Aaron, who have been consecrated to burn incense. Leave the sanctuary, for you have been unfaithful; and you will not be honored by the LORD God."

19Uzziah, who had a censer in his hand ready to burn incense, became angry. While he was raging at the priests in their presence before the incense altar in the LORD's temple, leprosy[a] broke out on his forehead. 20When Azariah the chief priest and all the other priests looked at him, they saw that he had leprosy on his forehead, so they hurried him out. Indeed, he himself was eager to leave, because the LORD had afflicted him.

21King Uzziah had leprosy until the day he died. He lived in a separate house[b]—leprous, and excluded from the temple of the LORD. Jotham his son had charge of the palace and governed the people of the land.

22The other events of Uzziah's reign, from beginning to end, are recorded by the prophet Isaiah son of Amoz. 23Uzziah rested with his fathers and was buried near them in a field for burial that belonged to the kings, for people said, "He had leprosy." And Jotham his son succeeded him as king.

[a]*19* The Hebrew word was used for various diseases affecting the skin—not necessarily leprosy; also in verses 20, 21 and 23. [b]*21 Or in a house where he was relieved of responsibilities*

highly (v. 4), when he spends his latter years under divine punishment? **2.** Would you say Uzziah was a self-made man or did he get a little help? **3.** What are Uzziah's accomplishments (vv. 6–15)? Which one stands out to you as the headliner for this king's resumé? **4.** What happens to Uzziah midway through life? Why do you think Judean kings seem to falter at the halfway mark? **5.** Do you think Uzziah's mistake was an innocent blunder? Why or why not? **6.** What do you think of Uzziah's punishment? Does God allow too little time for punishment? Is it fair? **7.** Uzziah not only became leprous but also had to leave the palace and was excluded from the temple. Even in death he was not restored to his former place of honor (v. 23). What lessons were the people of Judah to learn from this tragedy? Where can you see God's mercy at work, as well? **8.** Is success oftentimes a danger to our relationship with God? What does Uzziah's story say to you about this?

APPLY 1. When it comes to your temper would others say you have: A long fuse? A short fuse? No fuse? How do you feel about the way you handle your anger? **2.** Where have you experienced God's mercy at work in your life? What is he leading you to change in your character?

26:23 in a field. In deference to leprosy—the physically and socially devastating disease that separated people from the rest of society—even in death. Uzziah is buried apart from the royal treatment.

Jotham King of Judah

27 Jotham was twenty-five years old when he became king, and he reigned in Jerusalem sixteen years. His mother's name was Jerusha daughter of Zadok. 2He did what was right in the eyes of the LORD, just as his father Uzziah had done, but unlike him he did not enter the temple of the LORD. The people, however, continued their corrupt practices. 3Jotham rebuilt the Upper Gate of the temple of the LORD and did extensive work on the wall at the hill of Ophel. 4He built towns in the Judean hills and forts and towers in the wooded areas.

5Jotham made war on the king of the Ammonites and conquered them. That year the Ammonites paid him a hundred talents[a] of silver, ten thousand cors[b] of wheat and ten thousand cors of barley. The Ammonites brought him the same amount also in the second and third years.

6Jotham grew powerful because he walked steadfastly before the LORD his God.

7The other events in Jotham's reign, including all his wars and the other things he did, are written in the book of the kings of Israel and Judah. 8He was twenty-five years old when he became king, and he reigned in Jerusalem sixteen years. 9Jotham rested with his fathers and was buried in the City of David. And Ahaz his son succeeded him as king.

Ahaz King of Judah

28 Ahaz was twenty years old when he became king, and he reigned in Jerusalem sixteen years. Unlike David his father, he did not do what was right in the eyes of the LORD. 2He walked in the ways of the kings of Israel and also made cast idols for worshiping the Baals. 3He burned sacrifices in the Valley of Ben Hinnom and sacrificed his sons in the fire, following the detestable ways of the nations the LORD had driven out before the Israelites. 4He offered sacrifices and burned incense at the high places, on the hilltops and under every spreading tree.

5Therefore the LORD his God handed him over to the king of Aram. The Arameans defeated him and took many of his people as prisoners and brought them to Damascus.

He was also given into the hands of the king of Israel, who inflicted heavy casualties on him. 6In one day Pekah son of Remaliah killed a hundred and twenty thousand soldiers in Judah—because Judah had forsaken the LORD, the God of their fathers. 7Zicri, an Ephraimite warrior, killed Maaseiah the king's son, Azrikam the officer in charge of the palace, and Elkanah, second to the king. 8The Israelites took captive from their kinsmen two hundred thousand wives, sons and

[a]5 That is, about 3 3/4 tons (about 3.4 metric tons) [b]5 That is, probably about 62,000 bushels (about 2,200 kiloliters)

OPEN If you could change where you live and what you are doing, what would you do?

STUDY The period of international peace continues. During Jotham's reign the great Isaiah was a prophet in Jerusalem. **1.** Finally, a king who stays true to the Lord. Why do you suppose so few verses are allotted to him? What strengths and weaknesses do you see in Jotham? **2.** The chronicler mentions the corruptness of the people. What do you think contributes the most to the greatness of a nation: Great people or great leaders? **3.** What would you say accounts for Jotham's success beyond his steadfastness and diligence? **4.** What does it mean, "He walked steadfastly before the LORD his God?" How does one do that today?

APPLY Where are you being steadfast? Where do you need to be a little more steadfast?

OPEN 1. What gifts do you like to receive anytime: Clothes? Jewelry? Electronic gadgets? Perfume? Music? Videos? Candy? **2.** What is about the angriest your parents ever were with you?

STUDY Things have changed internationally. Assyria now looms as a major threat, and will ultimately bring the northern kingdom of Israel to an end. **1.** Describe your opinion of Ahaz in one word. **2.** If you had been there, which of the punishments from God would have been the most severe (vv. 5–8). **3.** What do you think of Obed's message from God? What had the Israelites done wrong? What was the Israelites' response? **4.** Ahaz doesn't learn the lesson and God sends punishment number two. What nations does God use to deliver this punishment? Why don't you think God used Israel against Judah once again? **5.** Ahaz asks Tiglath-Pileser (a powerful adversary in the seventh century B.C.) to be his ally. How did Ahaz try to win Tiglath-Pileser's cooperation.

27:1 sixteen years. Jotham begins his rule alongside his incapacitated father during the *last years of his leprosy-ridden* reign.

27:2 people ... continued their corrupt practices. Jotham's middle-weight leadership is commendable. However, it cannot turn the tide of evil sweeping across his kingdom.

27:3–6 Jotham is one more example in the chronicler's record. Steadfast obedience is a sure thing.

28:1–27 Ahaz's life is riddled with reprehensible behavior (2 Kin. 16:1–20). Although evil kings preceded him, the chronicler points out that Ahaz is out of his own league. Ahaz is more akin to the wretchedness of the northern kingdom.

daughters. They also took a great deal of plunder, which they carried back to Samaria.

[9]But a prophet of the LORD named Oded was there, and he went out to meet the army when it returned to Samaria. He said to them, "Because the LORD, the God of your fathers, was angry with Judah, he gave them into your hand. But you have slaughtered them in a rage that reaches to heaven. [10]And now you intend to make the men and women of Judah and Jerusalem your slaves. But aren't you also guilty of sins against the LORD your God? [11]Now listen to me! Send back your fellow countrymen you have taken as prisoners, for the LORD's fierce anger rests on you."

[12]Then some of the leaders in Ephraim—Azariah son of Jehohanan, Berekiah son of Meshillemoth, Jehizkiah son of Shallum, and Amasa son of Hadlai—confronted those who were arriving from the war. [13]"You must not bring those prisoners here," they said, "or we will be guilty before the LORD. Do you intend to add to our sin and guilt? For our guilt is already great, and his fierce anger rests on Israel."

[14]So the soldiers gave up the prisoners and plunder in the presence of the officials and all the assembly. [15]The men designated by name took the prisoners, and from the plunder they clothed all who were naked. They provided them with clothes and sandals, food and drink, and healing balm. All those who were weak they put on donkeys. So they took them back to their fellow countrymen at Jericho, the City of Palms, and returned to Samaria.

[16]At that time King Ahaz sent to the king[a] of Assyria for help. [17]The Edomites had again come and attacked Judah and carried away prisoners, [18]while the Philistines had raided towns in the foothills and in the Negev of Judah. They captured and occupied Beth Shemesh, Aijalon and Gederoth, as well as Soco, Timnah and Gimzo, with their surrounding villages. [19]The LORD had humbled Judah because of Ahaz king of Israel,[b] for he had promoted wickedness in Judah and had been most unfaithful to the LORD. [20]Tiglath-Pileser[c] king of Assyria came to him, but he gave him trouble instead of help. [21]Ahaz took some of the things from the temple of the LORD and from the royal palace and from the princes and presented them to the king of Assyria, but that did not help him.

[22]In his time of trouble King Ahaz became even more unfaithful to the LORD. [23]He offered sacrifices to the gods of Damascus, who had defeated him; for he thought, "Since the gods of the kings of Aram have helped them, I will sacrifice to them so they will help me." But they were his downfall and the downfall of all Israel.

[24]Ahaz gathered together the furnishings from the temple of God and took them away.[d] He shut the doors of the LORD's temple and set up altars at every street corner in Jerusalem. [25]In every town in Judah he built high places to burn sacrifices to other gods and provoked the LORD, the God of his fathers, to anger.

[a]*16* One Hebrew manuscript, Septuagint and Vulgate (see also 2 Kings 16:7); most Hebrew manuscripts *kings* [b]*19* That is, Judah, as frequently in 2 Chronicles [c]*20* Hebrew *Tilgath-Pilneser,* a variant of *Tiglath-Pileser* [d]*24* Or *and cut them up*

What do you see as the differences and similarities between the chronicler's telling of this alliance and the telling of it in 2 Kings 16:7–18 and Isaiah 7:3–17? **6.** After verse 24 it looks like worship of the true God is outlawed in Judah. What do you suppose faithful Judeans did to continue their worship of God? If the doors of churches were barred today, what might faithful Christians do? **7.** Did times of trouble drive Ahaz toward the Lord or away from the Lord? How about most people? Do you think times of trouble generally drive people to God or away from God? **8.** Do you feel the people around you are being drawn toward God or away from him?

APPLY 1. In what area of your life do you feel like a prisoner? **2.** As the Israelites cared for those who had been taken captive, who has shown extra care to you recently?

28:17–18 Just when Ahaz thought things could not get worse, they do. His enemies declare open season on Judah.

28:20 Tiglath-Pileser king of Assyria. Assyria answers Ahaz's cry for help. Yet Assyria brings more harm than good.

28:24–25 Not only does Ahaz bar the temple shut, he goes one step further. He prohibits worshiping God—the faith of his fathers is now a crime.

OPEN 1. Which of the following most needs to be cleaned out right now: Your garage? Your purse or wallet? Your clothes closet? Your desk? Your refrigerator? Your car? **2.** Your first official act as president or prime minister of your country would be …?

STUDY Things could not have been much worse under Ahaz's reign. Child sacrifice and the closing of the temple mark all-time lows in the history of Judah. Now, however, we meet a king who is just the opposite. The author of 2 Kings said of Ahaz's successor, Hezekiah: "There was no king like him among all the kings of Judah, either before him or after him" (2 Kin. 18.5). **1.** Note Hezekiah's introduction in verses 1 and 2? Given his father's reign, does this surprise you or relieve you? Explain. **2.** What actions did Hezekiah take in the very first month of his reign? What does this say to you about Hezekiah's priorities as king? **3.** If you had been a priest or Levite in Hezekiah's time, how would you have responded to Hezekiah's orders? How did they respond? **4.** After its purification, note the different roles the city officials, the priests, the king, the whole assembly and the Levites played in the dedication of the temple. Given their different roles, what would you have rather been? **5.** How did the people respond to the opening of the temple? What problem did this cause? Who does the chronicler indirectly blame for the problem? What do you think it means that one group was more consecrated than the other? Were they: Better prepared? More holy? Did a better job with the task at hand? Other? **6.** In the final analysis, who was really respon-

26 The other events of his reign and all his ways, from beginning to
end, are written in the book of the kings of Judah and Israel. 27 Ahaz
rested with his fathers and was buried in the city of Jerusalem, but he
was not placed in the tombs of the kings of Israel. And Hezekiah his
son succeeded him as king.

Hezekiah Purifies the Temple

29 Hezekiah was twenty-five years old when he became king,
and he reigned in Jerusalem twenty-nine years. His mother's
name was Abijah daughter of Zechariah. 2 He did what was right in the
eyes of the LORD, just as his father David had done.
3 In the first month of the first year of his reign, he opened the
doors of the temple of the LORD and repaired them. 4 He brought in
the priests and the Levites, assembled them in the square on the east
side 5 and said: "Listen to me, Levites! Consecrate yourselves now and
consecrate the temple of the LORD, the God of your fathers. Remove
all defilement from the sanctuary. 6 Our fathers were unfaithful; they
did evil in the eyes of the LORD our God and forsook him. They turned
their faces away from the LORD's dwelling place and turned their
backs on him. 7 They also shut the doors of the portico and put out
the lamps. They did not burn incense or present any burnt offerings
at the sanctuary to the God of Israel. 8 Therefore, the anger of the
LORD has fallen on Judah and Jerusalem; he has made them an object
of dread and horror and scorn, as you can see with your own eyes.
9 This is why our fathers have fallen by the sword and why our sons
and daughters and our wives are in captivity. 10 Now I intend to make
a covenant with the LORD, the God of Israel, so that his fierce anger
will turn away from us. 11 My sons, do not be negligent now, for the
LORD has chosen you to stand before him and serve him, to minister
before him and to burn incense."
12 Then these Levites set to work:
from the Kohathites,
Mahath son of Amasai and Joel son of Azariah;
from the Merarites,
Kish son of Abdi and Azariah son of Jehallelel;
from the Gershonites,
Joah son of Zimmah and Eden son of Joah;
13 from the descendants of Elizaphan,
Shimri and Jeiel;
from the descendants of Asaph,
Zechariah and Mattaniah;
14 from the descendants of Heman,
Jehiel and Shimei;

28:27 Ahaz … buried … not placed in the tombs. He is ousted from the royal cemetery—a sign that he could not eradicate religion completely.

29:1–32:33 Hezekiah's rule is refreshing. Finally, a king with stamina to stand up against the rule of evil. He is noted for his religious reforms and restoration of the temple worship.

29:1 Hezekiah … reigned … twenty-nine years. Halfway into his reign Hezekiah became deathly ill (2 Kin. 20:1). The Lord was gracious and allowed him to rule another fifteen years (2 Kin. 20:6).

29:3 first month … first year. Hezekiah shuns procrastination. He restores the temple as top priority.

29:5–11 Hezekiah knows how to read the signs. He speaks the chronicler's language, explaining the simple history lesson in terms of cause and effect.

29:7 burn incense … burnt offerings. Solomon's solemn religious orders seem almost like ancient history (2:4; 4:7). However, they are just the remedy needed to rejuvenate Judah's languishing faith.

from the descendants of Jeduthun,
Shemaiah and Uzziel.

15When they had assembled their brothers and consecrated themselves, they went in to purify the temple of the LORD, as the king had
ordered, following the word of the LORD. 16The priests went into the
sanctuary of the LORD to purify it. They brought out to the courtyard
of the LORD's temple everything unclean that they found in the temple
of the LORD. The Levites took it and carried it out to the Kidron Valley.
17They began the consecration on the first day of the first month, and
by the eighth day of the month they reached the portico of the LORD.
For eight more days they consecrated the temple of the LORD itself,
finishing on the sixteenth day of the first month.

18Then they went in to King Hezekiah and reported: "We have purified the entire temple of the LORD, the altar of burnt offering with all
its utensils, and the table for setting out the consecrated bread, with
all its articles. 19We have prepared and consecrated all the articles
that King Ahaz removed in his unfaithfulness while he was king. They
are now in front of the LORD's altar."

20Early the next morning King Hezekiah gathered the city officials
together and went up to the temple of the LORD. 21They brought seven
bulls, seven rams, seven male lambs and seven male goats as a sin
offering for the kingdom, for the sanctuary and for Judah. The king
commanded the priests, the descendants of Aaron, to offer these on
the altar of the LORD. 22So they slaughtered the bulls, and the priests
took the blood and sprinkled it on the altar; next they slaughtered the
rams and sprinkled their blood on the altar; then they slaughtered
the lambs and sprinkled their blood on the altar. 23The goats for the
sin offering were brought before the king and the assembly, and they
laid their hands on them. 24The priests then slaughtered the goats
and presented their blood on the altar for a sin offering to atone for
all Israel, because the king had ordered the burnt offering and the sin
offering for all Israel.

25He stationed the Levites in the temple of the LORD with cymbals,
harps and lyres in the way prescribed by David and Gad the king's
seer and Nathan the prophet; this was commanded by the LORD
through his prophets. 26So the Levites stood ready with David's
instruments, and the priests with their trumpets.

27Hezekiah gave the order to sacrifice the burnt offering on the
altar. As the offering began, singing to the LORD began also, accompanied by trumpets and the instruments of David king of Israel. 28The
whole assembly bowed in worship, while the singers sang and the
trumpeters played. All this continued until the sacrifice of the burnt
offering was completed.

29When the offerings were finished, the king and everyone present
with him knelt down and worshiped. 30King Hezekiah and his officials ordered the Levites to praise the LORD with the words of David
and of Asaph the seer. So they sang praises with gladness and bowed
their heads and worshiped.

31Then Hezekiah said, "You have now dedicated yourselves to the
LORD. Come and bring sacrifices and thank offerings to the temple of
the LORD." So the assembly brought sacrifices and thank offerings,
and all whose hearts were willing brought burnt offerings.

32The number of burnt offerings the assembly brought was seventy
bulls, a hundred rams and two hundred male lambs—all of them for

sible for reopening the temple? Why is this important for us to remember? **7.** What do you learn from this chapter about Hezekiah's character? His leadership?

APPLY 1. If you could borrow something from Hezekiah's life and make it a part of yours, what would that be? **2.** What is God leading you to rededicate to him? Why is this difficult for you to do?

burnt offerings to the LORD. 33The animals consecrated as sacrifices amounted to six hundred bulls and three thousand sheep and goats. 34The priests, however, were too few to skin all the burnt offerings; so their kinsmen the Levites helped them until the task was finished and until other priests had been consecrated, for the Levites had been more conscientious in consecrating themselves than the priests had been. 35There were burnt offerings in abundance, together with the fat of the fellowship offerings[a] and the drink offerings that accompanied the burnt offerings.

So the service of the temple of the LORD was reestablished. 36Hezekiah and all the people rejoiced at what God had brought about for his people, because it was done so quickly.

OPEN 1. How would you rank each of these events as the days of the year you like to celebrate most: Birthday? Valentine's Day? Easter? Fourth of July? Halloween? Thanksgiving? Christmas? New Year's Day? **2.** What was an extremely important letter you received? What made this letter so important to you?

STUDY Hezekiah sends a letter to the fallen nation of Israel inviting subjugated Hebrews to come to Jerusalem to celebrate Passover. Chafing under the Assyrian's ban to worship Yahweh, many Israelites accept the invitation. **1.** Hezekiah's second major act is to reinstate the Passover (Ex. 12:1–28). Why do you suppose he reached out to people in the northern kingdom of Israel? Has anyone reached out to you or to the people you are close to? **2.** What do you think of Hezekiah's invitation to the Passover (vv. 6–9)? Do you think the tone is a little harsh? **3.** What were the various responses to Hezekiah's proclamation? How do you account for the differences? Pride? Politics? Or what? **4.** How did "the very large crowd of people assembled in Jerusalem" prepare for the feast? What effect did this have on the priests and Levites? What do you see as wrong with those religious leaders? **5.** Where were the rules "bent" in order for many to celebrate the Passover? Why do you think Hezekiah was confident that his deviation from the Law was okay

Hezekiah Celebrates the Passover

30 Hezekiah sent word to all Israel and Judah and also wrote letters to Ephraim and Manasseh, inviting them to come to the temple of the LORD in Jerusalem and celebrate the Passover to the LORD, the God of Israel. 2The king and his officials and the whole assembly in Jerusalem decided to celebrate the Passover in the second month. 3They had not been able to celebrate it at the regular time because not enough priests had consecrated themselves and the people had not assembled in Jerusalem. 4The plan seemed right both to the king and to the whole assembly. 5They decided to send a proclamation throughout Israel, from Beersheba to Dan, calling the people to come to Jerusalem and celebrate the Passover to the LORD, the God of Israel. It had not been celebrated in large numbers according to what was written.

6At the king's command, couriers went throughout Israel and Judah with letters from the king and from his officials, which read:

> "People of Israel, return to the LORD, the God of Abraham, Isaac and Israel, that he may return to you who are left, who have escaped from the hand of the kings of Assyria. 7Do not be like your fathers and brothers, who were unfaithful to the LORD, the God of their fathers, so that he made them an object of horror, as you see. 8Do not be stiff-necked, as your fathers were; submit to the LORD. Come to the sanctuary, which he has consecrated forever. Serve the LORD your God, so that his fierce anger will turn away from you. 9If you return to the LORD, then your brothers and your children will be shown compassion by their captors and will come back to this land, for the LORD your God is gracious and compassionate. He will not turn his face from you if you return to him."

[a]35 Traditionally *peace offerings*

29:35 offerings. These personal offerings express the repentance of the individual, not just the corporate response of the nation.

30:1–27 Now Hezekiah is getting somewhere. He celebrates his monumental progress with a Passover feast. The people of Judah and remnants of Israel witness an unprecedented spiritual renewal.

30:2 the Passover. The people plan a nationwide celebration, inviting refugees of the northern kingdom and Ephraim and Manasseh for this feast. They are celebrating unity.

30:9 captors. The Assyrians now dominate the northern kingdom, having captured most of its inhabitants. Those who remain are challenged to demonstrate their allegiance to God by attending the feast.

10 The couriers went from town to town in Ephraim and Manasseh, as far as Zebulun, but the people scorned and ridiculed them. 11 Nevertheless, some men of Asher, Manasseh and Zebulun humbled themselves and went to Jerusalem. 12 Also in Judah the hand of God was on the people to give them unity of mind to carry out what the king and his officials had ordered, following the word of the LORD.

13 A very large crowd of people assembled in Jerusalem to celebrate the Feast of Unleavened Bread in the second month. 14 They removed the altars in Jerusalem and cleared away the incense altars and threw them into the Kidron Valley.

15 They slaughtered the Passover lamb on the fourteenth day of the second month. The priests and the Levites were ashamed and consecrated themselves and brought burnt offerings to the temple of the LORD. 16 Then they took up their regular positions as prescribed in the Law of Moses the man of God. The priests sprinkled the blood handed to them by the Levites. 17 Since many in the crowd had not consecrated themselves, the Levites had to kill the Passover lambs for all those who were not ceremonially clean and could not consecrate their lambs to the LORD. 18 Although most of the many people who came from Ephraim, Manasseh, Issachar and Zebulun had not purified themselves, yet they ate the Passover, contrary to what was written. But Hezekiah prayed for them, saying, "May the LORD, who is good, pardon everyone 19 who sets his heart on seeking God—the LORD, the God of his fathers—even if he is not clean according to the rules of the sanctuary." 20 And the LORD heard Hezekiah and healed the people.

21 The Israelites who were present in Jerusalem celebrated the Feast of Unleavened Bread for seven days with great rejoicing, while the Levites and priests sang to the LORD every day, accompanied by the LORD's instruments of praise.[a]

22 Hezekiah spoke encouragingly to all the Levites, who showed good understanding of the service of the LORD. For the seven days they ate their assigned portion and offered fellowship offerings[b] and praised the LORD, the God of their fathers.

23 The whole assembly then agreed to celebrate the festival seven more days; so for another seven days they celebrated joyfully. 24 Hezekiah king of Judah provided a thousand bulls and seven thousand sheep and goats for the assembly, and the officials provided them with a thousand bulls and ten thousand sheep and goats. A great number of priests consecrated themselves. 25 The entire assembly of Judah rejoiced, along with the priests and Levites and all who had assembled from Israel, including the aliens who had come from Israel

[a] 21 Or *priests praised the LORD every day with resounding instruments belonging to the LORD*
[b] 22 Traditionally *peace offerings*

with God? Do you see a similar line of thought in Psalm 51:10–19? **6.** What would you say is the overall tone of this revived Passover celebration? How did Hezekiah keep it going for the first week? For the second week? Who does Hezekiah remind you of in the history of Israel (hint: 7:8–10)? **7.** What were some of the remarkable results of this Passover celebration in Jerusalem? In Judah? In Israel? In your opinion, were these responses just emotional froth, or were they motivated by a new desire to obey the Lord? Have you ever experienced renewed zeal for God after hearing a message or going to a meeting or retreat? **8.** If you had been an Israelite in Hezekiah's time, what would have moved you to travel to Jerusalem for the Passover? What would have impressed you the most about it? **9.** Is it okay to "bend" some of the rules to include people in your church? If so, which ones?

APPLY 1. What celebration or practice would you like to reinstate in your life? In your church? **2.** What prayer of yours would you like to reach heaven? What prayer seems to be falling short of heavenly realms? What are you going to do about it?

30:15 priests and Levites. In order to maintain the spiritual momentum, Hezekiah turns to those commissioned to be holy examples among the people.

30:17 Passover lambs. The Levites eagerly serve the people who come to the Passover unprepared. Just like in old times, the Levites slay the lambs for the people's sacrifice.

30:18–19 Hezekiah, ever the diplomat, smoothes the transition from heathen to holiness for those who attend the Passover.

and those who lived in Judah. 26There was great joy in Jerusalem, for
since the days of Solomon son of David king of Israel there had been
nothing like this in Jerusalem. 27The priests and the Levites stood to
bless the people, and God heard them, for their prayer reached
heaven, his holy dwelling place.

31 When all this had ended, the Israelites who were there went
out to the towns of Judah, smashed the sacred stones and cut
down the Asherah poles. They destroyed the high places and the altars throughout Judah and Benjamin and in Ephraim and Manasseh.
After they had destroyed all of them, the Israelites returned to their
own towns and to their own property.

Contributions for Worship

2Hezekiah assigned the priests and Levites to divisions—each of
them according to their duties as priests or Levites—to offer burnt
offerings and fellowship offerings,[a] to minister, to give thanks and to
sing praises at the gates of the LORD's dwelling. 3The king contributed from his own possessions for the morning and evening burnt offerings and for the burnt offerings on the Sabbaths, New Moons and
appointed feasts as written in the Law of the LORD. 4He ordered the
people living in Jerusalem to give the portion due the priests and
Levites so they could devote themselves to the Law of the LORD. 5As
soon as the order went out, the Israelites generously gave the firstfruits of their grain, new wine, oil and honey and all that the fields
produced. They brought a great amount, a tithe of everything. 6The
men of Israel and Judah who lived in the towns of Judah also brought
a tithe of their herds and flocks and a tithe of the holy things dedicated to the LORD their God, and they piled them in heaps. 7They began
doing this in the third month and finished in the seventh month.
8When Hezekiah and his officials came and saw the heaps, they
praised the LORD and blessed his people Israel.

9Hezekiah asked the priests and Levites about the heaps; 10and
Azariah the chief priest, from the family of Zadok, answered, "Since
the people began to bring their contributions to the temple of the
LORD, we have had enough to eat and plenty to spare, because the
LORD has blessed his people, and this great amount is left over."

11Hezekiah gave orders to prepare storerooms in the temple of the
LORD, and this was done. 12Then they faithfully brought in the contributions, tithes and dedicated gifts. Conaniah, a Levite, was in charge
of these things, and his brother Shimei was next in rank. 13Jehiel, Azaziah, Nahath, Asahel, Jerimoth, Jozabad, Eliel, Ismakiah, Mahath
and Benaiah were supervisors under Conaniah and Shimei his
brother, by appointment of King Hezekiah and Azariah the official in
charge of the temple of God.

14Kore son of Imnah the Levite, keeper of the East Gate, was in

[a]2 Traditionally *peace offerings*

OPEN 1. What person comes to mind when you hear the word "generous"? **2.** What food item do you like to consume in generous portions?

STUDY Now that the temple has been purified and the Passover reinstated, a problem arises as to how to support the clergy in their ministry. Hezekiah devises a plan and the people buy into it wholeheartedly. **1.** What specific things did King Hezekiah do in verses 2–4 to continue the revival of worship? Do you see these actions as important? Why or why not? **2.** How did people respond to Hezekiah's order in verse 5? Why do you think they responded in this way? What did Azariah the priest believe was the reason for the people's response? **3.** What does the term "first fruits" imply to you? For those not living in an agrarian society, how does one become a "firstfruits" giver? **4.** How did Hezekiah plan to handle the "heaps" of things given to the Lord? Who was provided for under the plan? What do you think of the plan? **5.** What most impresses you about Hezekiah from these verses? What was the secret of his success? **6.** Do you believe that obedience to the Lord insures prosperity for an individual? A church? A nation? Explain.

APPLY 1. What do you have "heaps" and "heaps" of? What would the Lord have you do with your "heaps"? **2.** Who has been a significant spiritual leader on your spiritual journey?

30:26 great joy ... since the days of Solomon. The chronicler cannot resist drawing the parallels between the overt religious emphasis of Hezekiah and that of Solomon.

31:2 *Hezekiah single-handedly motivates the people to an inspired movement. Then he directs the details of the operation among his staff.*

***31:3* king contributed from his own possessions.** David showed the power of example (1 Chr. 29:3–9). Hezekiah discovers its motivational strength by giving generously toward his own project.

31:5–6 Hezekiah closely follows God's commands to restore proper protocol for worship. The people respond with equal attentiveness.

charge of the freewill offerings given to God, distributing the contributions made to the LORD and also the consecrated gifts. 15Eden,
Miniamin, Jeshua, Shemaiah, Amariah and Shecaniah assisted him
faithfully in the towns of the priests, distributing to their fellow
priests according to their divisions, old and young alike.
16In addition, they distributed to the males three years old or more
whose names were in the genealogical records—all who would enter
the temple of the LORD to perform the daily duties of their various
tasks, according to their responsibilities and their divisions. 17And
they distributed to the priests enrolled by their families in the genealogical records and likewise to the Levites twenty years old or more,
according to their responsibilities and their divisions. 18They included all the little ones, the wives, and the sons and daughters of the
whole community listed in these genealogical records. For they were
faithful in consecrating themselves.
19As for the priests, the descendants of Aaron, who lived on the
farm lands around their towns or in any other towns, men were designated by name to distribute portions to every male among them
and to all who were recorded in the genealogies of the Levites.
20This is what Hezekiah did throughout Judah, doing what was
good and right and faithful before the LORD his God. 21In everything
that he undertook in the service of God's temple and in obedience to
the law and the commands, he sought his God and worked wholeheartedly. And so he prospered.

Sennacherib Threatens Jerusalem

32 After all that Hezekiah had so faithfully done, Sennacherib
king of Assyria came and invaded Judah. He laid siege to the
fortified cities, thinking to conquer them for himself. 2When Hezekiah saw that Sennacherib had come and that he intended to make
war on Jerusalem, 3he consulted with his officials and military staff
about blocking off the water from the springs outside the city, and
they helped him. 4A large force of men assembled, and they blocked
all the springs and the stream that flowed through the land. "Why
should the kings[a] of Assyria come and find plenty of water?" they
said. 5Then he worked hard repairing all the broken sections of the
wall and building towers on it. He built another wall outside that one
and reinforced the supporting terraces[b] of the City of David. He also
made large numbers of weapons and shields.
6He appointed military officers over the people and assembled
them before him in the square at the city gate and encouraged them
with these words: 7"Be strong and courageous. Do not be afraid or
discouraged because of the king of Assyria and the vast army with
him, for there is a greater power with us than with him. 8With him is
only the arm of flesh, but with us is the LORD our God to help us and
to fight our battles." And the people gained confidence from what
Hezekiah the king of Judah said.

[a]4 Hebrew; Septuagint and Syriac *king* [b]5 Or *the Millo*

OPEN 1. What is a favorite body of water for you: Your pool? Secret fishing hole? Stretch of white-water rapids? Secluded seashore or lake? **2.** Who picked on you when you were a child?

STUDY 2 Kings 18:13–16 relates a different story. In 2 Kings, the Assyrians capture Judean towns and King Hezekiah of Judah winds up paying tribute to appease King Sennacherib of Assyria. **1.** Did the chronicler alter the tale because he did not want such a great king as Hezekiah to suffer humiliation at the end of his reign or did the author of 2 Kings get it wrong? **2.** After all King Hezekiah's piety and obedience, here comes King Sennacherib of Assyrian with his powerful army. Does that seem fair to you? **3.** How did King Hezekiah prepare for this crisis? What strikes you about these preparations? **4.** What tactics did Sennacherib use to undermine the morale of Hezekiah and his people? What did Sennacherib say about Hezekiah? About himself? About the Lord? From what you read

31:20–21 Hezekiah's life marks another chapter in the chronicle of cause and effect. His reign is summarized with a sweeping statement about the power of diligence and obedience.

32:1–23 Hezekiah encounters an Assyrian king with an attitude. It is one thing to challenge a godly king. However, Sennacherib defies God himself (vv. 10–15). The result is humiliating disaster for Assyria (vv. 20–21).

here, how effective were these tactics? **5.** How was Sennacherib's invasion actually defeated? Who got credit for the defeat? For additional insight into the situation, see Isaiah 37. **6.** Is the resolution of this situation easy or difficult for you to believe? What do you believe about miracles? Do they actually occur? What does this say about your view of God? **7.** Does the fact that 2 Kings and 2 Chronicles tell the story differently concern you? Explain.

APPLY 1. Are you facing any Sennacheribs in your life right now? How is the situation affecting you? What are you doing to prepare yourself? **2.** Has God ever miraculously rescued you from a terrible situation or person? How did it happen?

OPEN 1. What were the most difficult tests for you in school: Math? History? English? Science? Foreign language? **2.** Where do you want to be buried when you die? Why?

9 Later, when Sennacherib king of Assyria and all his forces were laying siege to Lachish, he sent his officers to Jerusalem with this message for Hezekiah king of Judah and for all the people of Judah who were there:

10 "This is what Sennacherib king of Assyria says: On what are you basing your confidence, that you remain in Jerusalem under siege? 11 When Hezekiah says, 'The LORD our God will save us from the hand of the king of Assyria,' he is misleading you, to let you die of hunger and thirst. 12 Did not Hezekiah himself remove this god's high places and altars, saying to Judah and Jerusalem, 'You must worship before one altar and burn sacrifices on it'? 13 Do you not know what I and my fathers have done to all the peoples of the other lands? Were the gods of those nations ever able to deliver their land from my hand? 14 Who of all the gods of these nations that my fathers destroyed has been able to save his people from me? How then can your god deliver you from my hand? 15 Now do not let Hezekiah deceive you and mislead you like this. Do not believe him, for no god of any nation or kingdom has been able to deliver his people from my hand or the hand of my fathers. How much less will your god deliver you from my hand!"

16 Sennacherib's officers spoke further against the LORD God and against his servant Hezekiah. 17 The king also wrote letters insulting the LORD, the God of Israel, and saying this against him: "Just as the gods of the peoples of the other lands did not rescue their people from my hand, so the god of Hezekiah will not rescue his people from my hand." 18 Then they called out in Hebrew to the people of Jerusalem who were on the wall, to terrify them and make them afraid in order to capture the city. 19 They spoke about the God of Jerusalem as they did about the gods of the other peoples of the world—the work of men's hands.

20 King Hezekiah and the prophet Isaiah son of Amoz cried out in prayer to heaven about this. 21 And the LORD sent an angel, who annihilated all the fighting men and the leaders and officers in the camp of the Assyrian king. So he withdrew to his own land in disgrace. And when he went into the temple of his god, some of his sons cut him down with the sword.

22 So the LORD saved Hezekiah and the people of Jerusalem from the hand of Sennacherib king of Assyria and from the hand of all others. He took care of them[a] on every side. 23 Many brought offerings to Jerusalem for the LORD and valuable gifts for Hezekiah king of Judah. From then on he was highly regarded by all the nations.

Hezekiah's Pride, Success and Death

24 In those days Hezekiah became ill and was at the point of death. He prayed to the LORD, who answered him and gave him a miraculous

[a]22 Hebrew; Septuagint and Vulgate *He gave them rest*

32:9 Sennacherib begins his battle with a war of words. He insults Judah's king and Judah's God. His aim is to demoralize his enemy, to intimidate them into submission. The chronicler eliminates Hezekiah's response (2 Kin. 18:14–16).

32:21 Sennacherib blows on and off the scene in a ragged breath. The chronicler puts an end to his sarcastic taunts, rendering the rest of his rule and reign as insignificant.

sign. 25But Hezekiah's heart was proud and he did not respond to the
kindness shown him; therefore the LORD's wrath was on him and on
Judah and Jerusalem. 26Then Hezekiah repented of the pride of his
heart, as did the people of Jerusalem; therefore the LORD's wrath did
not come upon them during the days of Hezekiah.
27Hezekiah had very great riches and honor, and he made treasuries for his silver and gold and for his precious stones, spices, shields
and all kinds of valuables. 28He also made buildings to store the harvest of grain, new wine and oil; and he made stalls for various kinds
of cattle, and pens for the flocks. 29He built villages and acquired
great numbers of flocks and herds, for God had given him very great
riches.
30It was Hezekiah who blocked the upper outlet of the Gihon spring
and channeled the water down to the west side of the City of David.
He succeeded in everything he undertook. 31But when envoys were
sent by the rulers of Babylon to ask him about the miraculous sign
that had occurred in the land, God left him to test him and to know
everything that was in his heart.
32The other events of Hezekiah's reign and his acts of devotion are
written in the vision of the prophet Isaiah son of Amoz in the book of
the kings of Judah and Israel. 33Hezekiah rested with his fathers and
was buried on the hill where the tombs of David's descendants are.
All Judah and the people of Jerusalem honored him when he died.
And Manasseh his son succeeded him as king.

Manasseh King of Judah

33 Manasseh was twelve years old when he became king, and
he reigned in Jerusalem fifty-five years. 2He did evil in the
eyes of the LORD, following the detestable practices of the nations the
LORD had driven out before the Israelites. 3He rebuilt the high places
his father Hezekiah had demolished; he also erected altars to the
Baals and made Asherah poles. He bowed down to all the starry hosts
and worshiped them. 4He built altars in the temple of the LORD, of
which the LORD had said, "My Name will remain in Jerusalem forever." 5In both courts of the temple of the LORD, he built altars to all
the starry hosts. 6He sacrificed his sons in[a] the fire in the Valley of Ben
Hinnom, practiced sorcery, divination and witchcraft, and consulted
mediums and spiritists. He did much evil in the eyes of the LORD,
provoking him to anger.
7He took the carved image he had made and put it in God's temple,
of which God had said to David and to his son Solomon, "In this
temple and in Jerusalem, which I have chosen out of all the tribes of
Israel, I will put my Name forever. 8I will not again make the feet of
the Israelites leave the land I assigned to your forefathers, if only they
will be careful to do everything I commanded them concerning all the
laws, decrees and ordinances given through Moses." 9But Manasseh

[a]6 Or *He made his sons pass through*

STUDY In summarizing King Hezekiah's life, the chronicler says, "God left him to test him" (v. 31). **1.** What point do you think the chronicler is trying to make in verses 24–26? Do you agree with it? **2.** Of all the noteworthy accomplishments listed in verses 24–26, which is most impressive to you? **3.** Why do you think God tested Hezekiah after all these years? Do you think Hezekiah passed the test or failed the test? Why? **4.** Where does the chronicler rank Hezekiah among the kings of Judah? Where would you? Why? **5.** Hezekiah is criticized for his pride. Do you think pride is always bad?

APPLY **1.** Has God ever "left" you for a time? What were the circumstances? **2.** Where are you feeling tested today?

OPEN **1.** If you had a monument dedicated to your memory, what kind of monument would you prefer: Highway? Building? Park? Stadium? Street? Library? Airport? **2.** What do you think of body piercing? Do you like it or hate it?

STUDY The evil King Manasseh follows the great King Hezekiah. Manasseh's 55-year reign marks the longest evil reign in Judah. He was the most evil king in the history of Judah. **1.** List Manasseh's offenses. Which do you find most despicable? **2.** What finally turned Manasseh around? How does Manasseh show that he really was changed? Do you think God should have let him off the hook? Is there anything God won't forgive if you are truly repentant? **3.** How does this story of Manasseh compare to the story in 2 Kings 21:1–18? How do you account for the difference in the moral verdict on Manasseh? **4.** What, if any, similarities do you see between Manasseh and Hezekiah? **5.** Amon learned some

32:25–26 Hezekiah experiences corporate success yet personal failure. He loses sight of his faith when he loses his health. His disobedience brings God's wrath.

32:27–29 The chronicler concludes Hezekiah's life with a summary of his economic success and material wealth.

33:1–20 According to the chronicler, Manasseh was no less evil for having repented. However, 2 Kings 21:1–18 leaves out his repentance altogether. Regardless, the outcome is the longest evil reign in Judah's history.

lessons and rejected others from the life of his father. Which ones? What would you say was the big difference between father and son? **6.** Who assassinated Amon? What happened to his assassins? Do you think God approved or disapproved of the assassination? **7.** What would you say is the lesson of this chapter?

APPLY 1. When did God first become real in your life? What concrete ways did your life begin to change? **2.** Who might God be calling you to give another chance?

led Judah and the people of Jerusalem astray, so that they did more
evil than the nations the LORD had destroyed before the Israelites.
10The LORD spoke to Manasseh and his people, but they paid no attention. 11So the LORD brought against them the army commanders
of the king of Assyria, who took Manasseh prisoner, put a hook in his
nose, bound him with bronze shackles and took him to Babylon. 12In
his distress he sought the favor of the LORD his God and humbled
himself greatly before the God of his fathers. 13And when he prayed to
him, the LORD was moved by his entreaty and listened to his plea; so
he brought him back to Jerusalem and to his kingdom. Then Manasseh knew that the LORD is God.

14Afterward he rebuilt the outer wall of the City of David, west of
the Gihon spring in the valley, as far as the entrance of the Fish Gate
and encircling the hill of Ophel; he also made it much higher. He stationed military commanders in all the fortified cities in Judah.

15He got rid of the foreign gods and removed the image from the
temple of the LORD, as well as all the altars he had built on the temple
hill and in Jerusalem; and he threw them out of the city. 16Then he restored the altar of the LORD and sacrificed fellowship offerings[a] and
thank offerings on it, and told Judah to serve the LORD, the God of
Israel. 17The people, however, continued to sacrifice at the high
places, but only to the LORD their God.

18The other events of Manasseh's reign, including his prayer to his
God and the words the seers spoke to him in the name of the LORD,
the God of Israel, are written in the annals of the kings of Israel.[b]
19His prayer and how God was moved by his entreaty, as well as all
his sins and unfaithfulness, and the sites where he built high places
and set up Asherah poles and idols before he humbled himself—all
are written in the records of the seers.[c] 20Manasseh rested with his
fathers and was buried in his palace. And Amon his son succeeded
him as king.

Amon King of Judah

21Amon was twenty-two years old when he became king, and he
reigned in Jerusalem two years. 22He did evil in the eyes of the LORD,
as his father Manasseh had done. Amon worshiped and offered sacrifices to all the idols Manasseh had made. 23But unlike his father Manasseh, he did not humble himself before the LORD; Amon increased
his guilt.

24Amon's officials conspired against him and assassinated him in
his palace. 25Then the people of the land killed all who had plotted
against King Amon, and they made Josiah his son king in his place.

[a]16 Traditionally *peace offerings* [b]18 That is, Judah, as frequently in 2 Chronicles [c]19 One Hebrew manuscript and Septuagint; most Hebrew manuscripts *of Hozai*

33:10 paid no attention. God gives Manasseh the dignity of a warning. However, Manasseh's evil behavior deafens his ear to divine precaution.

33:11–17 It takes a ring in his nose and bars in front of his face for Manasseh to call upon God, who always responds to sincere repentance.

33:11 took Manasseh prisoner ... took him to Babylon. Babylon was the preferred province of Assyria—a fine exile for an evil king.

33:20 Manasseh ... buried in his palace. Manasseh's burial plot is not among the kings. He remains outside of God's favor even in death. Five kings (Ahaz, Jehoram, Joash, Uzziah and Manasseh) had this kind of burial.

Josiah's Reforms

34 Josiah was eight years old when he became king, and he
reigned in Jerusalem thirty-one years. 2He did what was
right in the eyes of the LORD and walked in the ways of his father
David, not turning aside to the right or to the left.
3In the eighth year of his reign, while he was still young, he began
to seek the God of his father David. In his twelfth year he began to
purge Judah and Jerusalem of high places, Asherah poles, carved
idols and cast images. 4Under his direction the altars of the Baals
were torn down; he cut to pieces the incense altars that were above
them, and smashed the Asherah poles, the idols and the images.
These he broke to pieces and scattered over the graves of those who
had sacrificed to them. 5He burned the bones of the priests on their
altars, and so he purged Judah and Jerusalem. 6In the towns of
Manasseh, Ephraim and Simeon, as far as Naphtali, and in the ruins
around them, 7he tore down the altars and the Asherah poles and
crushed the idols to powder and cut to pieces all the incense altars
throughout Israel. Then he went back to Jerusalem.
8In the eighteenth year of Josiah's reign, to purify the land and the
temple, he sent Shaphan son of Azaliah and Maaseiah the ruler of the
city, with Joah son of Joahaz, the recorder, to repair the temple of
the LORD his God.
9They went to Hilkiah the high priest and gave him the money that
had been brought into the temple of God, which the Levites who were
the doorkeepers had collected from the people of Manasseh, Ephraim and the entire remnant of Israel and from all the people of Judah
and Benjamin and the inhabitants of Jerusalem. 10Then they entrusted it to the men appointed to supervise the work on the LORD's
temple. These men paid the workers who repaired and restored the
temple. 11They also gave money to the carpenters and builders to
purchase dressed stone, and timber for joists and beams for the
buildings that the kings of Judah had allowed to fall into ruin.
12The men did the work faithfully. Over them to direct them were
Jahath and Obadiah, Levites descended from Merari, and Zechariah
and Meshullam, descended from Kohath. The Levites—all who were
skilled in playing musical instruments— 13had charge of the laborers
and supervised all the workers from job to job. Some of the Levites
were secretaries, scribes and doorkeepers.

The Book of the Law Found

14While they were bringing out the money that had been taken into
the temple of the LORD, Hilkiah the priest found the Book of the Law
of the LORD that had been given through Moses. 15Hilkiah said to
Shaphan the secretary, "I have found the Book of the Law in the
temple of the LORD." He gave it to Shaphan.

OPEN 1. What song was popular when you were 16? **2.** What do you remember doing as a child that got you a lot of praise?

STUDY King Josiah follows in the footsteps of his great grandfather Hezekiah. Like Hezekiah, Josiah initiated sweeping reforms that got the nation focused on God once again. **1.** How old was Josiah when he began to seek the Lord? How old were you? How old was he when he began his reforms? How old when he turned his attention to the temple? **2.** What reforms did Josiah institute? Do you sense that these reforms were accomplished with ease or with some difficulty? Explain. **3.** Why do you think the repair of the temple was not attended to first? What point might Josiah be trying to press? **4.** How did Josiah fund the repair of the temple? Who administered the funds and supervised the work? If you had been one of the workers, what job would you have liked to do? **5.** How would you assess the spirit of the work crew: Excellent? Good? Fair? Poor? Atrocious? Why do you think that? **6.** How do you account for Josiah being so different from his father (Amon) and grandfather (Manasseh)?

APPLY 1. What clean-up program do you need to give top priority: Spiritual? Emotional? Physical? Mental? How can the group be of help? **2.** What are some good qualities you got from your father? How about bad qualities?

OPEN 1. Rummaging through an attic you happen upon a big chest covered with dust. What would you prefer to find inside: Old letters? Old baseball cards? Old newspaper clippings? Old scrapbooks? A treasure map? Old books? Old clothes?

34:1–36:1 Josiah initiates religious reform that sweeps across the nation of Judah and into Israel (vv. 3–7). When he discovers the book of Moses and its long forgotten Laws, his reform becomes revival (vv. 14,29–32).

34:3–7 Josiah follows in great grandfather Hezekiah's steps. All his national reforms flow from his intimate relationship with God.

34:6 as far as Naphtali. Josiah's zeal knows no bounds. His reforms sweep to the northern borders by sheer spiritual momentum.

34:9 money. The people give toward repairing and refurbishing the temple.

Family Bible with family tree? What makes your choice so interesting to you? **2.** What was the place of the Bible in your childhood home?

STUDY The nation has fallen so far that they have misplaced the Book of the Law. The rediscovery of God's Word will bring a spiritual revival into the land. **1.** Who finds the Book of the Law? In your opinion, when do they get excited about the find? Right away or down the road a bit? **2.** How do you account for Josiah's strange and intense reaction to the Book? **3.** Who is Huldah? What role does she play? What is her message? Do you think they understood the entire message or just part of it? **4.** How does Josiah respond to her message? What does he have the people do? **5.** Do you think it would be difficult to celebrate the recovery of the Law, given the fact that God said through Huldah that the end is near? **6.** What do you make of the people's commitment to the Lord? Do you think Josiah forced them into it or do you believe they are on the same page as Josiah?

APPLY **1.** What role does the Bible play in your life today: Prominent? Sporadic? Casual? Nearly non-existent? **2.** Complete the sentence: "I would make the Bible a bigger part of my life if ... "

16 Then Shaphan took the book to the king and reported to him: "Your officials are doing everything that has been committed to them. 17 They have paid out the money that was in the temple of the LORD and have entrusted it to the supervisors and workers." 18 Then Shaphan the secretary informed the king, "Hilkiah the priest has given me a book." And Shaphan read from it in the presence of the king.

19 When the king heard the words of the Law, he tore his robes. 20 He gave these orders to Hilkiah, Ahikam son of Shaphan, Abdon son of Micah,[a] Shaphan the secretary and Asaiah the king's attendant: 21 "Go and inquire of the LORD for me and for the remnant in Israel and Judah about what is written in this book that has been found. Great is the LORD's anger that is poured out on us because our fathers have not kept the word of the LORD; they have not acted in accordance with all that is written in this book."

22 Hilkiah and those the king had sent with him[b] went to speak to the prophetess Huldah, who was the wife of Shallum son of Tokhath,[c] the son of Hasrah,[d] keeper of the wardrobe. She lived in Jerusalem, in the Second District.

23 She said to them, "This is what the LORD, the God of Israel, says: Tell the man who sent you to me, 24 'This is what the LORD says: I am going to bring disaster on this place and its people—all the curses written in the book that has been read in the presence of the king of Judah. 25 Because they have forsaken me and burned incense to other gods and provoked me to anger by all that their hands have made,[e] my anger will be poured out on this place and will not be quenched.' 26 Tell the king of Judah, who sent you to inquire of the LORD, 'This is what the LORD, the God of Israel, says concerning the words you heard: 27 Because your heart was responsive and you humbled yourself before God when you heard what he spoke against this place and its people, and because you humbled yourself before me and tore your robes and wept in my presence, I have heard you, declares the LORD. 28 Now I will gather you to your fathers, and you will be buried in peace. Your eyes will not see all the disaster I am going to bring on this place and on those who live here.' "

So they took her answer back to the king.

29 Then the king called together all the elders of Judah and Jerusalem. 30 He went up to the temple of the LORD with the men of Judah, the people of Jerusalem, the priests and the Levites—all the people from the least to the greatest. He read in their hearing all the words of the Book of the Covenant, which had been found in the temple of the LORD. 31 The king stood by his pillar and renewed the covenant in the presence of the LORD—to follow the LORD and keep his commands, regulations and decrees with all his heart and all his soul, and to obey the words of the covenant written in this book.

32 Then he had everyone in Jerusalem and Benjamin pledge themselves to it; the people of Jerusalem did this in accordance with the covenant of God, the God of their fathers.

33 Josiah removed all the detestable idols from all the territory belonging to the Israelites, and he had all who were present in Israel serve the LORD their God. As long as he lived, they did not fail to follow the LORD, the God of their fathers.

[a]20 Also called *Acbor son of Micaiah* [b]22 One Hebrew manuscript, Vulgate and Syriac; most Hebrew manuscripts do not have *had sent with him.* [c]22 Also called *Tikvah* [d]22 Also called *Harhas* [e]25 Or *by everything they have done*

Josiah Celebrates the Passover

35 Josiah celebrated the Passover to the LORD in Jerusalem, and
the Passover lamb was slaughtered on the fourteenth day of
the first month. [2]He appointed the priests to their duties and encouraged them in the service of the LORD's temple. [3]He said to the Levites,
who instructed all Israel and who had been consecrated to the LORD:
"Put the sacred ark in the temple that Solomon son of David king of
Israel built. It is not to be carried about on your shoulders. Now serve
the LORD your God and his people Israel. [4]Prepare yourselves by families in your divisions, according to the directions written by David
king of Israel and by his son Solomon.
[5]"Stand in the holy place with a group of Levites for each sub-
division of the families of your fellow countrymen, the lay people.
[6]Slaughter the Passover lambs, consecrate yourselves and prepare
⌞the lambs⌟ for your fellow countrymen, doing what the LORD commanded through Moses."
[7]Josiah provided for all the lay people who were there a total of
thirty thousand sheep and goats for the Passover offerings, and also
three thousand cattle—all from the king's own possessions.
[8]His officials also contributed voluntarily to the people and the
priests and Levites. Hilkiah, Zechariah and Jehiel, the administrators
of God's temple, gave the priests twenty-six hundred Passover offerings and three hundred cattle. [9]Also Conaniah along with Shemaiah
and Nethanel, his brothers, and Hashabiah, Jeiel and Jozabad, the
leaders of the Levites, provided five thousand Passover offerings and
five hundred head of cattle for the Levites.
[10]The service was arranged and the priests stood in their places
with the Levites in their divisions as the king had ordered. [11]The
Passover lambs were slaughtered, and the priests sprinkled the blood
handed to them, while the Levites skinned the animals. [12]They set
aside the burnt offerings to give them to the subdivisions of the families of the people to offer to the LORD, as is written in the Book of
Moses. They did the same with the cattle. [13]They roasted the Passover
animals over the fire as prescribed, and boiled the holy offerings in
pots, caldrons and pans and served them quickly to all the people.
[14]After this, they made preparations for themselves and for the
priests, because the priests, the descendants of Aaron, were sacrificing the burnt offerings and the fat portions until nightfall. So the
Levites made preparations for themselves and for the Aaronic priests.
[15]The musicians, the descendants of Asaph, were in the places
prescribed by David, Asaph, Heman and Jeduthun the king's seer. The
gatekeepers at each gate did not need to leave their posts, because
their fellow Levites made the preparations for them.
[16]So at that time the entire service of the LORD was carried out for
the celebration of the Passover and the offering of burnt offerings on
the altar of the LORD, as King Josiah had ordered. [17]The Israelites who
were present celebrated the Passover at that time and observed the
Feast of Unleavened Bread for seven days. [18]The Passover had not

OPEN 1. Friends want to give a large banquet in your honor. You decide the menu. What will you have? **2.** On the celebrating-boohooing continuum, where would you place yourself today?

STUDY King Josiah was quite a leader. He threw the best Passover celebration in years, and when he died the great prophet Jeremiah greatly laments his death. **1.** One gets the impression after reading this section that tons of preparation went into the Passover celebration. Why do you think Josiah went to so much trouble? **2.** What were Josiah's specific instructions? Who provided the main dish? What does this tell you about the provider? **3.** Such a Passover! How good was it (v. 18)? **4.** The last event to be recorded in Josiah's life was his death. How did Josiah meet his end? What did King Neco of Egypt urge Josiah to do? What do you think of Josiah's decision to engage in the battle? **5.** If pious kings succeed in battle, and evil kings do not, why do you think Josiah gets shot? **6.** For what previous leaders have the Israelites mourned so greatly? How high would you rank Josiah in terms of the great kings of Judah? Who would you rank ahead of him?

APPLY 1. If you could take one thing from Josiah's character and make it a part of your character, what would it be: His piety? His generosity? His courage? His leadership skills? His attention to details? His love of the Word of God? **2.** If you knew your death was imminent, what, if anything, would you do differently?

35:1–19 Josiah culminates his reform with a Passover feast fit for royalty and shared by all the people.

35:3 Put the sacred ark in the temple that Solomon ... built. The ark symbolizes God's presence among his people. Placing it back in the temple communicates security and stability.

35:4 according to the directions. Josiah is a traditionalist. He takes his orders for religious reform from David and Solomon. Two other passages support this thought (7:10; 11:17).

been observed like this in Israel since the days of the prophet Samuel;
and none of the kings of Israel had ever celebrated such a Passover as
did Josiah, with the priests, the Levites and all Judah and Israel who
were there with the people of Jerusalem. 19This Passover was celebrated in the eighteenth year of Josiah's reign.

The Death of Josiah

20After all this, when Josiah had set the temple in order, Neco king
of Egypt went up to fight at Carchemish on the Euphrates, and Josiah
marched out to meet him in battle. 21But Neco sent messengers to
him, saying, "What quarrel is there between you and me, O king of
Judah? It is not you I am attacking at this time, but the house with
which I am at war. God has told me to hurry; so stop opposing God,
who is with me, or he will destroy you."

22Josiah, however, would not turn away from him, but disguised
himself to engage him in battle. He would not listen to what Neco
had said at God's command but went to fight him on the plain of
Megiddo.

23Archers shot King Josiah, and he told his officers, "Take me away;
I am badly wounded." 24So they took him out of his chariot, put him
in the other chariot he had and brought him to Jerusalem, where he
died. He was buried in the tombs of his fathers, and all Judah and
Jerusalem mourned for him.

25Jeremiah composed laments for Josiah, and to this day all the
men and women singers commemorate Josiah in the laments. These
became a tradition in Israel and are written in the Laments.

26The other events of Josiah's reign and his acts of devotion,
according to what is written in the Law of the LORD— 27all the events,
from beginning to end, are written in the book of the kings of Israel
and Judah. 1And the people of the land took Jehoahaz son of
36 Josiah and made him king in Jerusalem in place of his father.

Jehoahaz King of Judah

2Jehoahaz[a] was twenty-three years old when he became king, and
he reigned in Jerusalem three months. 3The king of Egypt dethroned
him in Jerusalem and imposed on Judah a levy of a hundred talents[b]
of silver and a talent[c] of gold. 4The king of Egypt made Eliakim, a
brother of Jehoahaz, king over Judah and Jerusalem and changed
Eliakim's name to Jehoiakim. But Neco took Eliakim's brother Jehoahaz and carried him off to Egypt.

Jehoiakim King of Judah

5Jehoiakim was twenty-five years old when he became king, and he
reigned in Jerusalem eleven years. He did evil in the eyes of the LORD

[a]2 Hebrew *Joahaz,* a variant of *Jehoahaz;* also in verse 4 [b]3 That is, about 3 3/4 tons (about 3.4 metric tons)
[c]3 That is, about 75 pounds (about 34 kilograms)

OPEN 1. If someone were to carry you off to a foreign land, what would be a great place to be carried? A terrible place? **2.** Given the unenviable choice between being taken off into captivity or dying by the sword, which would you choose?

STUDY In rapid succession, the chronicler mentions the kings of Judah during its final 22 years of independence. None of them put a smile on God's face. **1.** Name each of the four remaining kings and in one sentence tell something about them. **2.** What prophets were around at this time? Why didn't the people listen to them? **3.** What kings carried out God's

35:21–22 Even Josiah could not dare thwart God's mysterious providence. Josiah insists on challenging a pagan ruler in battle, despite God's warnings—warnings that came from Neco himself.

35:25 The shocking news of Josiah's death causes the prophet Jeremiah to express his emotions in written laments. These laments remained popular even in the chronicler's day.

36:2–14 Josiah's offspring are neither as righteous nor influential as their ancestor. Evil snowballs among the succeeding kings.

36:5–8 Jehoiakim watches the nation change hands from Egypt to Babylon. His weak leadership cannot influence these changes.

his God. 6 Nebuchadnezzar king of Babylon attacked him and bound
him with bronze shackles to take him to Babylon. 7 Nebuchadnezzar
also took to Babylon articles from the temple of the LORD and put
them in his temple[a] there.
8 The other events of Jehoiakim's reign, the detestable things he did
and all that was found against him, are written in the book of the
kings of Israel and Judah. And Jehoiachin his son succeeded him as
king.

Jehoiachin King of Judah

9 Jehoiachin was eighteen[b] years old when he became king, and he
reigned in Jerusalem three months and ten days. He did evil in the
eyes of the LORD. 10 In the spring, King Nebuchadnezzar sent for him
and brought him to Babylon, together with articles of value from the
temple of the LORD, and he made Jehoiachin's uncle,[c] Zedekiah, king
over Judah and Jerusalem.

Zedekiah King of Judah

11 Zedekiah was twenty-one years old when he became king, and
he reigned in Jerusalem eleven years. 12 He did evil in the eyes of the
LORD his God and did not humble himself before Jeremiah the
prophet, who spoke the word of the LORD. 13 He also rebelled against
King Nebuchadnezzar, who had made him take an oath in God's
name. He became stiff-necked and hardened his heart and would not
turn to the LORD, the God of Israel. 14 Furthermore, all the leaders of
the priests and the people became more and more unfaithful, following all the detestable practices of the nations and defiling the temple
of the LORD, which he had consecrated in Jerusalem.

The Fall of Jerusalem

15 The LORD, the God of their fathers, sent word to them through his
messengers again and again, because he had pity on his people and
on his dwelling place. 16 But they mocked God's messengers, despised
his words and scoffed at his prophets until the wrath of the LORD was
aroused against his people and there was no remedy. 17 He brought up
against them the king of the Babylonians,[d] who killed their young
men with the sword in the sanctuary, and spared neither young man
nor young woman, old man or aged. God handed all of them over to
Nebuchadnezzar. 18 He carried to Babylon all the articles from the
temple of God, both large and small, and the treasures of the LORD's
temple and the treasures of the king and his officials. 19 They set fire
to God's temple and broke down the wall of Jerusalem; they burned
all the palaces and destroyed everything of value there.
20 He carried into exile to Babylon the remnant, who escaped from
the sword, and they became servants to him and his sons until the

[a] *7* Or *palace* [b] *9* One Hebrew manuscript, some Septuagint manuscripts and Syriac (see also 2 Kings 24:8); most Hebrew manuscripts *eight* [c] *10* Hebrew *brother,* that is, relative (see 2 Kings 24:17) [d] *17* Or *Chaldeans*

punishment for Judah? Do you agree with the punishment? Is it a logical consequence or too severe? **4.** Who were the remnants? What happened to them? What would you say was the quality of their lives? **5.** How do the people get back to Jerusalem? Why do you think God let them return? **6.** Do you see an irony in Cyrus' appointment to build a temple for God? If so, what? **7.** Does this chapter depress you or give you hope for the future of Israel? For your own life? How so?

APPLY 1. Where are you feeling somewhat like an exile: At work? At church? At home? With family? What is causing this feeling? **2.** Has God remained present with you through tough times? What does this tell you about God and yourself? How can you apply these observations to your present situation?

36:20–21 The chronicler concludes with Nebuchadnezzar. This foreigner terminates the royal kingdom, taking Judah's people captive. The authors of 1 and 2 Samuel and 1 and 2 Kings shared these reasons for why Israel was taken into exile, while the chronicler looks at the exile as a new beginning.

kingdom of Persia came to power. 21The land enjoyed its sabbath
rests; all the time of its desolation it rested, until the seventy years
were completed in fulfillment of the word of the LORD spoken by
Jeremiah.

22In the first year of Cyrus king of Persia, in order to fulfill the word
of the LORD spoken by Jeremiah, the LORD moved the heart of Cyrus
king of Persia to make a proclamation throughout his realm and to
put it in writing:

> 23"This is what Cyrus king of Persia says:
>
> " 'The LORD, the God of heaven, has given me all the kingdoms of the earth and he has appointed me to build a temple for him at Jerusalem in Judah. Anyone of his people among you—may the LORD his God be with him, and let him go up.' "

36:22–23 The Davidic dynasty does not die. A broken and contrite people arise from the rubble of ruined dreams. The coming King of Israel would be their newfound hope. God would never forget his covenant.

Ezra

Author. Ezra has traditionally been cited as the author of this book. While his authorship is not stated explicitly, he obviously writes in the first person.

Personal Reading	Group Study Topic and Reading	
1:1–2:70	Returning Exiles	1:1–11
3:1–13	Rebuilding the Altar	3:1–6
4:1–24	Rebuilding Delayed	4:6–24
5:1–6:22	Darius' Decree	6:1–12
7:1–8:36	Artaxerxes' Letter	7:11–28
9:1–15	Ezra's Prayer	9:1–15
10:1–44	Confession of Sin	10:1–17

Date. The book of Ezra could not have been written any earlier than 450 B.C. The book covers events from 538–458 B.C.

Purpose. Ezra's story reveals an amazing act of God. God had made a covenant with Abraham that the Hebrews would inhabit the land of Canaan, later called Israel and then Palestine. When the people were exiled, that covenant seemed broken forever. Yet the book of Ezra chronicles the return of a remnant of Hebrews to their land. This return began after more than 50 years of exile and continued for the next 90 years. Generations had passed. Many Hebrews had never even lived in their homeland. There was no human reason for King Cyrus to grant the decree that enabled the return. Ezra's story testifies that God will keep his promises, regardless of time.

Historical Background. Cyrus, king of Persia, captured Babylon while the Jews were exiled there. In 538 B.C., he began letting the Jews return to their homeland and rebuild the temple in Jerusalem. The temple was completed and dedicated around 516 B.C. Some 58 years later, in 458 B.C., King Artaxerxes allowed another remnant of Jews, led by Ezra, to return to Palestine, and another 14 years later Nehemiah returned.

These events comprise the centerpiece of the book of Ezra. The book is not a description of the exile but an account of the return to the homeland God had promised. The pieces of history fit together perfectly for this return. The capture of Babylon by the Persians under Cyrus was crucial. Cyrus' foreign policy vastly differed from that of the Babylonians and Assyrians. He believed that it was wiser to placate the gods of the people he conquered than to destroy their temples and idols. Thus, he allowed the Jews to rebuild the temple in Jerusalem. Almost 60 years later, Ezra led the spiritual rebirth of the nation.

Rebuilding the Temple. Since the days of the Exodus, when God gave Moses the first plans for the tabernacle (a mobile temple), the place of worship had been the focus of Hebrew culture. At the temple, sacrifices were made, the Law was expounded on and God's presence was seen most fully in the Holy Place, the central room that housed the Ark, a chest of sacred artifacts. Throughout the history of the Hebrews, the temple was central to major events. When the Hebrews returned to their homeland, then, they believed that rebuilding the temple was imperative.

OPEN **1.** What big event has most shaped your family history? How did it change your family? **2.** How old were you when it happened? What difference did it make for you?

STUDY After living in captivity for more than a generation the Jews are allowed to return to their homeland by Cyrus, the ruling king. Some chose to leave, some chose to stay in their adopted homeland. **1.** If you were a Jew in Babylon, how would you have felt hearing Cyrus' decree (vv. 2–4): Astonished? Bewildered? Sorry to leave? Excited beyond words? Would you have volunteered to leave the place you now knew as "home"? **2.** What do you think was causing Cyrus to return the Jews to Jerusalem and restore their temple? **3.** Why do you think the neighbors gave gifts to the Jews who were leaving? Was this garage-sale season or something deeper? **4.** How do you think God was setting the stage for the return to Jerusalem? What step by Cyrus was the most important for getting God's plan done? Why?

APPLY Looking back is often the best view to realize that God has acted in our lives. How would you compare God working through the Cyrus story with God working in your life.

Cyrus Helps the Exiles to Return

1 In the first year of Cyrus king of Persia, in order to fulfill the word
of the LORD spoken by Jeremiah, the LORD moved the heart of
Cyrus king of Persia to make a proclamation throughout his realm
and to put it in writing:

2"This is what Cyrus king of Persia says:
" 'The LORD, the God of heaven, has given me all the kingdoms
of the earth and he has appointed me to build a temple for him at
Jerusalem in Judah. 3Anyone of his people among you—may his
God be with him, and let him go up to Jerusalem in Judah and
build the temple of the LORD, the God of Israel, the God who is in
Jerusalem. 4And the people of any place where survivors may
now be living are to provide him with silver and gold, with goods
and livestock, and with freewill offerings for the temple of God in
Jerusalem.' "

5Then the family heads of Judah and Benjamin, and the priests and
Levites—everyone whose heart God had moved—prepared to go up
and build the house of the LORD in Jerusalem. 6All their neighbors
assisted them with articles of silver and gold, with goods and
livestock, and with valuable gifts, in addition to all the freewill offerings. 7Moreover, King Cyrus brought out the articles belonging to the
temple of the LORD, which Nebuchadnezzar had carried away from
Jerusalem and had placed in the temple of his god.[a] 8Cyrus king of
Persia had them brought by Mithredath the treasurer, who counted
them out to Sheshbazzar the prince of Judah.

9This was the inventory:

gold dishes	30
silver dishes	1,000
silver pans[b]	29
10gold bowls	30
matching silver bowls	410
other articles	1,000

11In all, there were 5,400 articles of gold and of silver. Sheshbazzar
brought all these along when the exiles came up from Babylon to
Jerusalem.

[a]7 Or *gods* [b]9 The meaning of the Hebrew for this word is uncertain.

1:1 first year of Cyrus king of Persia. Cyrus the Great, founder of the greater Persian Empire, conquered Babylon without a struggle in 539 B.C. **to fulfill the word ... spoken by Jeremiah.** Cyrus brought the Jews back to Jerusalem to establish strong, loyal buffer states around his empire. God used Cyrus to fulfill Jeremiah's prophecy that *the Jewish captivity in Babylon would* last seventy years (Jer. 25:11–12). By the time the people returned and built the altar in 536 B.C., seventy years were nearly fulfilled (2 Chr. 36:22–23; Isa. 44:28).

1:2 the LORD, the God of heaven. Cyrus, a worshiper of Bel and Nebo, was not a true believer in the God of the Jews. He showed fidelity to pagan deities and hoped that the gods of the people he had resettled in their sacred cities would pray to Bel and Nebo for him.

1:3 build the temple of the LORD, the God of Israel. God is also referred to as "the God of heaven" nine times in the book of Ezra. Isaiah had referred to Cyrus by name 150 years earlier as the one who would rebuild the temple in Jerusalem (Isa. 44:28).

1:7 articles belonging to the temple of the LORD. Since the Israelites had no image of their God, Nebuchadnezzar, in the custom of conquering kings, carried away the temple articles. Cyrus ordered these articles returned.

1:11 5,400 articles. The list in verses 9 and 10 totals 2,499 and probably refers to only the larger and more important items returned to Jerusalem.

The List of the Exiles Who Returned

2 Now these are the people of the province who came up from the
captivity of the exiles, whom Nebuchadnezzar king of Babylon
had taken captive to Babylon (they returned to Jerusalem and Judah,
each to his own town, [2]in company with Zerubbabel, Jeshua, Nehemiah, Seraiah, Reelaiah, Mordecai, Bilshan, Mispar, Bigvai, Rehum
and Baanah):

The list of the men of the people of Israel:

[3]the descendants of Parosh	2,172
[4]of Shephatiah	372
[5]of Arah	775
[6]of Pahath-Moab (through the line of Jeshua and Joab)	2,812
[7]of Elam	1,254
[8]of Zattu	945
[9]of Zaccai	760
[10]of Bani	642
[11]of Bebai	623
[12]of Azgad	1,222
[13]of Adonikam	666
[14]of Bigvai	2,056
[15]of Adin	454
[16]of Ater (through Hezekiah)	98
[17]of Bezai	323
[18]of Jorah	112
[19]of Hashum	223
[20]of Gibbar	95
[21]the men of Bethlehem	123
[22]of Netophah	56
[23]of Anathoth	128
[24]of Azmaveth	42
[25]of Kiriath Jearim,[a] Kephirah and Beeroth	743
[26]of Ramah and Geba	621
[27]of Micmash	122
[28]of Bethel and Ai	223
[29]of Nebo	52
[30]of Magbish	156
[31]of the other Elam	1,254
[32]of Harim	320
[33]of Lod, Hadid and Ono	725
[34]of Jericho	345
[35]of Senaah	3,630

[36]The priests:

the descendants of Jedaiah (through the family of Jeshua)	973

[a]25 See Septuagint (see also Neh. 7:29); Hebrew *Kiriath Arim.*

OPEN **1.** When it comes to organization, are you a "list-maker" or a "free-wheeler"? **2.** In your group, who is the most committed to keeping records? Who can name the birthdays of your neighbor's kids?

STUDY This chapter gives us a census by group type of the people who traveled back to Jerusalem. **1.** When was the last time you participated in a census or roll call? What was the most difficult question to answer? **2.** What is the first thought that comes to your mind when you scan through these verses of chapter 2? Who do you think the leaders were? What group is the most surprising to you? **3.** Imagine that your family decided to join this group for the four-month trip. Which group would you have wanted to travel with? Why? **4.** Chapter 2 and Nehemiah 7 agree on the priestly and Levite family names, their order and the numbers assigned to each (vv. 36–40). What might that say about their importance? **5.** What is the ratio of priests and Levites to the total number of people (v. 64). How might the priests' and Levites' significance in the restored Jerusalem community compare to that of other professional groups, listed with smaller numbers? **6.** How do you think the people felt who could not find their family records? **7.** After 70 years of exile, what towns did the people settle in (v. 70)? How did they know where to go: Homing instincts? Good family trees? God's guidance? Good maps?

APPLY **1.** Do you keep a family tree or other form of record such as a diary, photo album or memorabilia? Why are they important to you? If a stranger looked through them, what would they find out about the kind of person you are? **2.** This chapter emphasizes the importance of spiritual ancestors. Who is a spiritual ancestor to you? What quality have they passed on to you? What one spiritual quality do you hope to pass on to those who follow you? How are you developing it as one of God's people?

2:2 Zerubbabel. He was listed in the genealogy of David in 1 Chronicles 3:19. **Jeshua.** This was Joshua, the high priest (Hag. 1:1). The men listed in this verse were leaders of the expedition to Jerusalem.

2:2–20 The list of the. Ezra listed people by their families and clans, totaling 15,604. Next came a list of inhabitants from nearby towns totaling 8,540, followed by 4,289 priests and 341 Levites.

37 of Immer 1,052
38 of Pashhur 1,247
39 of Harim 1,017

40 The Levites:
the descendants of Jeshua and Kadmiel
(through the line of Hodaviah) 74

41 The singers:
the descendants of Asaph 128

42 The gatekeepers of the temple:
the descendants of
Shallum, Ater, Talmon,
Akkub, Hatita and Shobai 139

43 The temple servants:
the descendants of
Ziha, Hasupha, Tabbaoth,
44 Keros, Siaha, Padon,
45 Lebanah, Hagabah, Akkub,
46 Hagab, Shalmai, Hanan,
47 Giddel, Gahar, Reaiah,
48 Rezin, Nekoda, Gazzam,
49 Uzza, Paseah, Besai,
50 Asnah, Meunim, Nephussim,
51 Bakbuk, Hakupha, Harhur,
52 Bazluth, Mehida, Harsha,
53 Barkos, Sisera, Temah,
54 Neziah and Hatipha

55 The descendants of the servants of Solomon:
the descendants of
Sotai, Hassophereth, Peruda,
56 Jaala, Darkon, Giddel,
57 Shephatiah, Hattil,
Pokereth-Hazzebaim and Ami

58 The temple servants and the descendants
of the servants of Solomon 392

59 The following came up from the towns of Tel Melah, Tel
Harsha, Kerub, Addon and Immer, but they could not show that
their families were descended from Israel:

60 The descendants of
Delaiah, Tobiah and Nekoda 652

2:40 Levites. During the time of David, 24,000 Levites were involved in the worship of God by assisting the temple priests and teaching the Law. At the time of the return to Jerusalem, the number of Levites was small compared to priests.

2:42 gatekeepers of the temple. The returning group included 139 gatekeepers, who were Levites charged with preventing unauthorized people from entering the restricted area of the temple. During Solomon's reign, 4,000 gatekeepers did this work (1 Chr. 23:5; 2 Chr. 8:14).

2:59 they could not show that their families were descended from Israel. According to the Law of Moses, people who could not prove their Jewish origin by genealogy were excluded from the priesthood. They were, however, allowed to return to Jerusalem.

61And from among the priests:

The descendants of
Hobaiah, Hakkoz and Barzillai (a man who had married a
daughter of Barzillai the Gileadite and was called by that
name).
62These searched for their family records, but they could not
find them and so were excluded from the priesthood as unclean.
63The governor ordered them not to eat any of the most sacred
food until there was a priest ministering with the Urim and
Thummim.

64The whole company numbered 42,360, 65besides their 7,337
menservants and maidservants; and they also had 200 men and
women singers. 66They had 736 horses, 245 mules, 67435 camels
and 6,720 donkeys.

68When they arrived at the house of the LORD in Jerusalem, some of
the heads of the families gave freewill offerings toward the rebuilding
of the house of God on its site. 69According to their ability they gave
to the treasury for this work 61,000 drachmas[a] of gold, 5,000 minas[b]
of silver and 100 priestly garments.
70The priests, the Levites, the singers, the gatekeepers and the temple servants settled in their own towns, along with some of the other
people, and the rest of the Israelites settled in their towns.

Rebuilding the Altar

3 When the seventh month came and the Israelites had settled in
their towns, the people assembled as one man in Jerusalem.
2Then Jeshua son of Jozadak and his fellow priests and Zerubbabel
son of Shealtiel and his associates began to build the altar of the God
of Israel to sacrifice burnt offerings on it, in accordance with what is
written in the Law of Moses the man of God. 3Despite their fear of the
peoples around them, they built the altar on its foundation and sacrificed burnt offerings on it to the LORD, both the morning and evening
sacrifices. 4Then in accordance with what is written, they celebrated
the Feast of Tabernacles with the required number of burnt offerings
prescribed for each day. 5After that, they presented the regular burnt
offerings, the New Moon sacrifices and the sacrifices for all the appointed sacred feasts of the LORD, as well as those brought as freewill
offerings to the LORD. 6On the first day of the seventh month they

[a]69 That is, about 1,100 pounds (about 500 kilograms) [b]69 That is, about 3 tons (about 2.9 metric tons)

OPEN What's number one on your project to-do list?

STUDY 1. If you were a nationally syndicated columnist hiding behind a pillar in Jerusalem, what headline would you give to this scene of rebuilding the altar? **2.** Why do you think Jeshua wanted to get the altar built so quickly? Does it seem strange that they started offering sacrifices before laying the temple foundation? **3.** What is the significance of building the altar according to the Law and on its original foundation (vv. 2–4)?

APPLY On what "foundation" are you building your altar to God? What do you sacrifice?

2:64 whole company numbered 42,360. This figure may include women, who were not named in the lists in verses 3–60, which totaled 29,818.

2:65 singers. Many Jews achieved prosperity in Babylon and could afford to hire professional singers for banquets, feasts and funerals (2 Chr. 35:25).

2:66 736 horses. The large number of horses indicates affluence among those returning to Jerusalem. Before this time, horses had been used only for war and ceremonies. **6,720 donkeys.** Even the donkeys, commonly used for riding, were counted. The 900-mile trip from Babylon to Israel took about four months.

2:69 they gave to the treasury. When the Jews returned to Jerusalem, they gave of their possessions to help rebuild the temple. This list of precious metals and materials differs from the account in Nehemiah 7:70–72, perhaps because of scribal error or because Nehemiah's list gives more precise detail. Another possibility is that the two lists may give totals from different times of collection.

3:2 altar. The first job was to rebuild the altar of burnt offerings essential for reestablishing the sacrificial system that set the Jews apart as a people. The altar was located east of where the temple building would be.

OPEN Who in your group looks most like a general contractor—someone who gets the job done?

STUDY The altar is in place and it's time to build the temple. The Levite brothers order the materials, organize the workers and lay the foundation. **1.** Read 1 Kings 5:1–6:1. How did the preparation for this temple compare to the preparation that Solomon did in the first temple? Why do you think Ezra points out the altar was built "in accordance with the Law of Moses" (v. 2)? **2.** As the new temple foundation was laid, a great celebration began (vv. 11–13). How would you have felt as a young person watching all this happen? What must it have been like to be an old person remembering the "glory days"? **3.** What does this passage teach us about second chances?

APPLY Can you think back to a "cornerstone experience"—one that signaled a new beginning in some part of your life? Where was it: In your marriage? In your work? Your retirement? Your life with God?

OPEN Can you remember a time in your childhood when the playground bully "drove you crazy" with teasing or threats?

STUDY **1.** If you had been Zerubbabel or Jeshua, what would you have done to counteract this long-term opposition? **2.** What subtle tools did the enemies of Judah

began to offer burnt offerings to the LORD, though the foundation of the LORD's temple had not yet been laid.

Rebuilding the Temple

7 Then they gave money to the masons and carpenters, and gave food and drink and oil to the people of Sidon and Tyre, so that they would bring cedar logs by sea from Lebanon to Joppa, as authorized by Cyrus king of Persia.

8 In the second month of the second year after their arrival at the house of God in Jerusalem, Zerubbabel son of Shealtiel, Jeshua son of Jozadak and the rest of their brothers (the priests and the Levites and all who had returned from the captivity to Jerusalem) began the work, appointing Levites twenty years of age and older to supervise the building of the house of the LORD. 9 Jeshua and his sons and brothers and Kadmiel and his sons (descendants of Hodaviah[a]) and the sons of Henadad and their sons and brothers—all Levites—joined together in supervising those working on the house of God.

10 When the builders laid the foundation of the temple of the LORD, the priests in their vestments and with trumpets, and the Levites (the sons of Asaph) with cymbals, took their places to praise the LORD, as prescribed by David king of Israel. 11 With praise and thanksgiving they sang to the LORD:

"He is good;
  his love to Israel endures forever."

And all the people gave a great shout of praise to the LORD, because the foundation of the house of the LORD was laid. 12 But many of the older priests and Levites and family heads, who had seen the former temple, wept aloud when they saw the foundation of this temple being laid, while many others shouted for joy. 13 No one could distinguish the sound of the shouts of joy from the sound of weeping, because the people made so much noise. And the sound was heard far away.

Opposition to the Rebuilding

4 When the enemies of Judah and Benjamin heard that the exiles were building a temple for the LORD, the God of Israel, 2 they came to Zerubbabel and to the heads of the families and said, "Let us help you build because, like you, we seek your God and have been sacrificing to him since the time of Esarhaddon king of Assyria, who brought us here."

[a]9 Hebrew *Yehudah,* probably a variant of *Hodaviah*

3:7 Sidon and Tyre. When Solomon built the first temple, he purchased materials from Sidon and Tyre in Lebanon, well known for cedar forests and expert woodworkers (2 Chr. 2:10–16). For the rebuilt temple, Cyrus authorized the sale of cedar logs to the Jews, paid for with food, drink and oil.

3:10 trumpets. The people followed their forefathers' traditions when dedicating the temple as its foundations were laid. When David had brought the ark to Jerusalem, priests blew trumpets and Asaph had sounded cymbals (1 Chr. 16:5–6). This order was later followed when the ark was brought to the temple Solomon built. Here the same ceremonial order was followed, with descendants of Asaph playing the cymbals.

3:11 With praise and thanksgiving they sang. The priests and Levites sang words nearly identical to those used in the temple dedication in Solomon's reign. **He is good; his love to Israel endures forever.** This song of praise acknowledged that God had again established his loving protection over Israel. The two parts of the song were probably sung responsively.

3:13 No one could distinguish ... shouts of joy ... sound of weeping. The old men could remember the splendor of Solomon's temple, destroyed fifty years earlier in 586 B.C., and they wept. Younger travelers felt joy in other

[3]But Zerubbabel, Jeshua and the rest of the heads of the families of Israel answered, "You have no part with us in building a temple to our God. We alone will build it for the LORD, the God of Israel, as King Cyrus, the king of Persia, commanded us."

[4]Then the peoples around them set out to discourage the people of Judah and make them afraid to go on building.[a] [5]They hired counselors to work against them and frustrate their plans during the entire reign of Cyrus king of Persia and down to the reign of Darius king of Persia.

Later Opposition Under Xerxes and Artaxerxes

[6]At the beginning of the reign of Xerxes,[b] they lodged an accusation against the people of Judah and Jerusalem.

[7]And in the days of Artaxerxes king of Persia, Bishlam, Mithredath, Tabeel and the rest of his associates wrote a letter to Artaxerxes. The letter was written in Aramaic script and in the Aramaic language.[c,d]

[8]Rehum the commanding officer and Shimshai the secretary wrote a letter against Jerusalem to Artaxerxes the king as follows:

[9]Rehum the commanding officer and Shimshai the secretary, together with the rest of their associates—the judges and officials over the men from Tripolis, Persia,[e] Erech and Babylon, the Elamites of Susa, [10]and the other people whom the great and honorable Ashurbanipal[f] deported and settled in the city of Samaria and elsewhere in Trans-Euphrates.

[11](This is a copy of the letter they sent him.)

To King Artaxerxes,

From your servants, the men of Trans-Euphrates:

[12]The king should know that the Jews who came up to us from you have gone to Jerusalem and are rebuilding that rebellious and wicked city. They are restoring the walls and repairing the foundations.

[13]Furthermore, the king should know that if this city is built and its walls are restored, no more taxes, tribute or duty will be paid, and the royal revenues will suffer. [14]Now since we are under obligation to the palace and it is not proper for us to see the king dishonored, we are sending this message to inform the

[a]4 *Or and troubled them as they built* [b]6 *Hebrew Ahasuerus, a variant of Xerxes' Persian name*
[c]7 *Or written in Aramaic and translated* [d]7 *The text of Ezra 4:8—6:18 is in Aramaic.* [e]9 *Or officials, magistrates and governors over the men from* [f]10 *Aramaic Osnappar, a variant of Ashurbanipal*

and Benjamin use to undermine the rebuilding? **3.** How and why do you think the families of Israel could remain so persistent?

APPLY Do you see a principle for overcoming/resisting opposition?

OPEN 1. When was the last time you lodged a complaint? Who were you complaining about: A passing driver? A parent? A company? A friend? A child? **2.** Do you express concerns or complaints better verbally or in writing?

STUDY The opposition didn't end with the reign of Cyrus. It continued on through the reigns of Darius, Xerxes and Artaxerxes. **1.** Why do you think the letter writers were so intent on "dropping names" (vv. 9–10) in the greeting to their letter? **2.** When was the last time you caught yourself dropping names? Why do you think you did it? **3.** Ashurbanipal squelched a major revolt in Babylonia (652–648 B.C.), destroyed the town of Susa (v. 9) and deported the rebels (v. 10). What irony do you see in what Rehum and the other descendants of those rebels are now doing two centuries later? How do you think the treatment of Rehum's ancestors affects his opposition to the Israelites? What kind of feelings might be buried deep in their tribal history? **4.** What was their letter designed to do? If you were teaching a communication class on letter writing, what various appeals to the king would you want your students to notice? What emotions are the writers of the letter trying to raise in Artaxerxes? What inflammatory words do they use? **5.** Check out Nehemiah 1:3. Some scholars believe that this episode is what Nehemiah is

---

ways because the temple and their covenantal relationship with God were being reestablished.

4:3 You have no part with us. The Samaritans, who opposed rebuilding the temple and city walls, offered their help in order to subvert the effort. Their religious practices blended worship of God with worship of false idols. The Jewish leaders rejected their help.

4:9 associates—the judges and officials. The letter represented the views of people in various parts of the Persian Empire, as well as the judges and officials. This letter and the response from the king are out of place chronologically, but they show continued opposition to the rebuilding project.

4:10 honorable Ashurbanipal. This Assyrian king had deported people to Samaria (in Israel) during 669–626 B.C. (2 Kin. 17:24). Descendants of the deported Babylonians living in Israel opposed the Jews' return.

4:13 taxes. The city walls were far from complete. The writers of the letter tried to persuade the king that if Jerusalem's walls were rebuilt, the city would no longer pay taxes and Jews would capture part of his territory.

4:14 under obligation to the palace. Appealing to a king's worst fears, the writers told him that their own loyalty motivated their sending this warning.

hearing about. What unintended effect do you think this letter had on the long-term rebuilding of Jerusalem? **6.** Can you find a life-principle in this passage? How would you summarize it in ten words or less?

APPLY 1. Rehum's complaints against Israel remind us that our past sometimes comes back to haunt us. Can you think of traits in your family that you would like to stop with you, so others don't have to deal with them? **2.** The Jews proclaimed themselves as the only true worshippers of God to people who were a mixed race. What opposition might we expect when we express our faith as the only way? Who might we expect opposition from?

OPEN 1. Are you a "pack-rat," selective saver or toss-it-all person? **2.** Who in your group has the oldest item in their purse or billfold? Why do they still have it? Why is it important?

STUDY The opening verses of this passage seem to represent a new start for the Jews as they get back to work on the temple construction. **1.** Look at this passage through the eyes of a detective. What key pieces of information do you see right away? **2.** Why might it be important that the "prophets of God were with them" (v. 2)? How does that com-

king, [15]so that a search may be made in the archives of your
predecessors. In these records you will find that this city is a
rebellious city, troublesome to kings and provinces, a place of
rebellion from ancient times. That is why this city was destroyed.
[16]We inform the king that if this city is built and its walls are restored, you will be left with nothing in Trans-Euphrates.

[17]The king sent this reply:

To Rehum the commanding officer, Shimshai the secretary and the rest of their associates living in Samaria and elsewhere in Trans-Euphrates:

Greetings.

[18]The letter you sent us has been read and translated in my
presence. [19]I issued an order and a search was made, and it was
found that this city has a long history of revolt against kings and
has been a place of rebellion and sedition. [20]Jerusalem has had
powerful kings ruling over the whole of Trans-Euphrates, and
taxes, tribute and duty were paid to them. [21]Now issue an order
to these men to stop work, so that this city will not be rebuilt
until I so order. [22]Be careful not to neglect this matter. Why let
this threat grow, to the detriment of the royal interests?

[23]As soon as the copy of the letter of King Artaxerxes was read to
Rehum and Shimshai the secretary and their associates, they went
immediately to the Jews in Jerusalem and compelled them by force to
stop.

[24]Thus the work on the house of God in Jerusalem came to a stand-
still until the second year of the reign of Darius king of Persia.

Tattenai's Letter to Darius

5 Now Haggai the prophet and Zechariah the prophet, a descendant
of Iddo, prophesied to the Jews in Judah and Jerusalem in the
name of the God of Israel, who was over them. [2]Then Zerubbabel son
of Shealtiel and Jeshua son of Jozadak set to work to rebuild the
house of God in Jerusalem. And the prophets of God were with them,
helping them.
[3]At that time Tattenai, governor of Trans-Euphrates, and Shethar-
Bozenai and their associates went to them and asked, "Who
authorized you to rebuild this temple and restore this structure?"
[4]They also asked, "What are the names of the men constructing this
building?"[a] [5]But the eye of their God was watching over the elders of

[a]4 See Septuagint; Aramaic [4]*We told them the names of the men constructing this building.*

4:15 search ... archives. The official historical records of the empire (Est. 2:23).

4:21 Now issue an order. The archival search revealed that the people of Jerusalem had revolted against the Babylonians. Although the king ordered the rebuilding to stop, he left the way open for future completion. The project was resumed in the second year of Darius's reign in 520 B.C.

4:23 by force. Upon receiving the king's order, the officials stopped the work, probably destroying sections of the wall already repaired (Neh. 2:12–16).

5:1 Haggai the prophet and Zechariah the prophet. Two important prophets who preached in favor of resuming work on the temple (Hag. 1:1–3, Zech. 1:1,16).

5:5 the eye of their God. God protected the workers, allowing the project to continue despite opposition. An-

the Jews, and they were not stopped until a report could go to Darius and his written reply be received.

6This is a copy of the letter that Tattenai, governor of Trans-Euphrates, and Shethar-Bozenai and their associates, the officials of Trans-Euphrates, sent to King Darius. 7The report they sent him read as follows:

To King Darius:
Cordial greetings.

8The king should know that we went to the district of Judah, to the temple of the great God. The people are building it with large stones and placing the timbers in the walls. The work is being carried on with diligence and is making rapid progress under their direction.

9We questioned the elders and asked them, "Who authorized you to rebuild this temple and restore this structure?" 10We also asked them their names, so that we could write down the names of their leaders for your information.

11This is the answer they gave us:

"We are the servants of the God of heaven and earth, and we are rebuilding the temple that was built many years ago, one that a great king of Israel built and finished. 12But because our fathers angered the God of heaven, he handed them over to Nebuchadnezzar the Chaldean, king of Babylon, who destroyed this temple and deported the people to Babylon.

13"However, in the first year of Cyrus king of Babylon, King Cyrus issued a decree to rebuild this house of God. 14He even removed from the temple[a] of Babylon the gold and silver articles of the house of God, which Nebuchadnezzar had taken from the temple in Jerusalem and brought to the temple[a] in Babylon.

"Then King Cyrus gave them to a man named Sheshbazzar, whom he had appointed governor, 15and he told him, 'Take these articles and go and deposit them in the temple in Jerusalem. And rebuild the house of God on its site.' 16So this Sheshbazzar came and laid the foundations of the house of God in Jerusalem. From that day to the present it has been under construction but is not yet finished."

17Now if it pleases the king, let a search be made in the royal archives of Babylon to see if King Cyrus did in fact issue a decree to rebuild this house of God in Jerusalem. Then let the king send us his decision in this matter.

The Decree of Darius

6 King Darius then issued an order, and they searched in the archives stored in the treasury at Babylon. 2A scroll was found in

[a]14 Or *palace*

pare to "the eye of their God was watching" them (v. 5)? Do you get the feeling that there is a bigger plan at work here? What evidence of God's timing do you see? **3.** If you had been one of the workers would you have given your name to Tattenai (vv. 3–5)? Why or why not? How did the Jews respond? **4.** Why do you think the Jews told such a complete history of the building process (vv. 11–16)? Are you surprised that Tattenai and Shethar-Bozenai included it in the letter to Darius? Would you have? **5.** Do you think Tattenai really wanted the true story from "the royal archives" (v. 17) or was he hoping to get evidence against the Jews? **6.** How might this entire event be a blessing from God? How might the letter be God's blessing? What are the negative possibilities? **7.** Look back over the chapter. What key verse or phrase captures you?

APPLY 1. What is the most recent delay in your life? How did you handle it? **2.** As you look back now, would you consider that delay a blessing from God or not? Why or why not? **3.** How might you experience delays differently in the future?

OPEN 1. When have you been expecting bad news and the report came back great? What was your response? Was it better than if you had known good news was com-

other, common expression of God's care appearing in Ezra and Nehemiah is "the hand of the LORD."

5:6 King Darius. The governor inquired whether Darius had authorized the work in order to verify what the Jewish leaders had told him.

5:11 rebuilding the temple. The Jews told Tattenai about Solomon and the temple he had built. They said it had been destroyed and they had been deported because of their sin. They wanted the decree issued by King Darius to be found so that the temple could be completed. They were allowed to continue working while waiting.

ing? **2.** Would you rather have the joy of telling someone good news or the joy of receiving the good news yourself? Why?

STUDY King Darius did his research and found that King Cyrus had ordered the rebuilding of the Jewish temple, as the Jews had reported in the letter from Tattenai. So King Darius actually added to the order of King Cyrus, turning the tables on those attempting to delay the temple construction. **1.** Put yourself in the shoes of the Jewish builders when they heard Darius' decree. What would you have done: Started a celebration party? Tried to get even with Tattenai? Speeded up the work plan? Other? **2.** Compare Cyrus's original decree (1:2–4) with this one (vv. 3–5). What is the difference in the details reported? Why do you think the difference is important in each situation? **3.** In Darius' additional comments (vv. 11–12) one might get the idea that Darius is a worshiper of the Jewish God. Try to read between the lines in the decree. What do you think is going on here? Was this just his way of making a point to the opposition parties or was he seeking favor from the Jews? Why? **4.** Do you think God was just using this pagan king to get God's will done or was this king moving closer to becoming a "God-follower" as demonstrated by his actions?

APPLY **1.** How are you praying for those in authority over you? Are you seeking God's will to be done through them, even if you don't agree with them? **2.** Are you supporting a project that brings restoration to others?

OPEN Are you more a project starter or a project completer? How do you handle delays in a project?

STUDY The temple was finally finished after 29 years of building—70 years after its destruction. **1.** Since many of those who lived through the temple's destruction were

the citadel of Ecbatana in the province of Media, and this was written on it:

Memorandum:

[3]In the first year of King Cyrus, the king issued a decree concerning the temple of God in Jerusalem:

Let the temple be rebuilt as a place to present sacrifices, and let its foundations be laid. It is to be ninety feet[a] high and ninety feet wide, [4]with three courses of large stones and one of timbers. The costs are to be paid by the royal treasury. [5]Also, the gold and silver articles of the house of God, which Nebuchadnezzar took from the temple in Jerusalem and brought to Babylon, are to be returned to their places in the temple in Jerusalem; they are to be deposited in the house of God.

[6]Now then, Tattenai, governor of Trans-Euphrates, and Shethar-Bozenai and you, their fellow officials of that province, stay away from there. [7]Do not interfere with the work on this temple of God. Let the governor of the Jews and the Jewish elders rebuild this house of God on its site.

[8]Moreover, I hereby decree what you are to do for these elders of the Jews in the construction of this house of God:

The expenses of these men are to be fully paid out of the royal treasury, from the revenues of Trans-Euphrates, so that the work will not stop. [9]Whatever is needed—young bulls, rams, male lambs for burnt offerings to the God of heaven, and wheat, salt, wine and oil, as requested by the priests in Jerusalem—must be given them daily without fail, [10]so that they may offer sacrifices pleasing to the God of heaven and pray for the well-being of the king and his sons.

[11]Furthermore, I decree that if anyone changes this edict, a beam is to be pulled from his house and he is to be lifted up and impaled on it. And for this crime his house is to be made a pile of rubble. [12]May God, who has caused his Name to dwell there, overthrow any king or people who lifts a hand to change this decree or to destroy this temple in Jerusalem.

I Darius have decreed it. Let it be carried out with diligence.

Completion and Dedication of the Temple

[13]Then, because of the decree King Darius had sent, Tattenai, governor of Trans-Euphrates, and Shethar-Bozenai and their associates carried it out with diligence. [14]So the elders of the Jews continued to build and prosper under the preaching of Haggai the prophet and Zechariah, a descendant of Iddo. They finished building the temple

[a]3 Aramaic *sixty cubits* (about 27 meters)

6:7 Do not interfere. After reading *the official record of Cyrus's decree,* Darius instructed the government to stop opposing the work. He said work on the temple was to be funded by taxes and that animals, wheat, salt and oil were to be supplied for sacrifices.

6:10 pray for ... the king and his sons. When Darius requested prayer, he probably thought of Yahweh as a local deity.

6:12 May God ... overthrow any king. Darius's curse was fulfilled. Antiochus Epiphanes desecrated the temple in 167 B.C. and died insane three years later. Herod the Great, who had added to the temple to glorify himself, died of disease. The Romans destroyed the temple in 70 A.D., and their empire was later destroyed.

according to the command of the God of Israel and the decrees of
Cyrus, Darius and Artaxerxes, kings of Persia. [15]The temple was completed on the third day of the month Adar, in the sixth year of the
reign of King Darius.
[16]Then the people of Israel—the priests, the Levites and the rest of
the exiles—celebrated the dedication of the house of God with joy.
[17]For the dedication of this house of God they offered a hundred
bulls, two hundred rams, four hundred male lambs and, as a sin
offering for all Israel, twelve male goats, one for each of the tribes of
Israel. [18]And they installed the priests in their divisions and the
Levites in their groups for the service of God at Jerusalem, according
to what is written in the Book of Moses.

The Passover

[19]On the fourteenth day of the first month, the exiles celebrated the
Passover. [20]The priests and Levites had purified themselves and were
all ceremonially clean. The Levites slaughtered the Passover lamb for
all the exiles, for their brothers the priests and for themselves. [21]So
the Israelites who had returned from the exile ate it, together with all
who had separated themselves from the unclean practices of their
Gentile neighbors in order to seek the LORD, the God of Israel. [22]For
seven days they celebrated with joy the Feast of Unleavened Bread,
because the LORD had filled them with joy by changing the attitude of
the king of Assyria, so that he assisted them in the work on the house
of God, the God of Israel.

Ezra Comes to Jerusalem

7 After these things, during the reign of Artaxerxes king of Persia,
Ezra son of Seraiah, the son of Azariah, the son of Hilkiah, [2]the
son of Shallum, the son of Zadok, the son of Ahitub, [3]the son of Amariah, the son of Azariah, the son of Meraioth, [4]the son of Zerahiah,
the son of Uzzi, the son of Bukki, [5]the son of Abishua, the son of
Phinehas, the son of Eleazar, the son of Aaron the chief priest— [6]this
Ezra came up from Babylon. He was a teacher well versed in the Law
of Moses, which the LORD, the God of Israel, had given. The king had
granted him everything he asked, for the hand of the LORD his God
was on him. [7]Some of the Israelites, including priests, Levites, singers, gatekeepers and temple servants, also came up to Jerusalem in
the seventh year of King Artaxerxes.
[8]Ezra arrived in Jerusalem in the fifth month of the seventh year of

probably now dead or too old to return to Jerusalem from Babylon, what do you think kept the enthusiasm alive for the rebuilding? **2.** How do you think Tattenai and Shethar-Bozenai could carry out the king's decree (to support the rebuilding) "with diligence" (v. 13) after opposing it in the first place? **3.** How would you have written the headline to cover the day's events in the *Jerusalem Times*? **4.** With the temple's completion came the Jews' opportunity to finally celebrate the Passover together. What pattern do you see that led to their separating themselves from the "unclean practices of their Gentile neighbors" and caused them to confess their sins to God?

APPLY What principles do you find in this passage that might lead you to move closer to God?

OPEN Who in your group is carrying on a family business?

STUDY "After these things," (v. 1) means about 60 years later. We have a new king—Artaxerxes—on the scene and he's sending another group of Israelites back to Jerusalem. **1.** Note that Ezra just completed the four-month journey from Babylon. As you think about what his role might be in Jerusalem, why do you think it's important for him to be "a teacher well versed in the Law of Moses"? **2.** How do you think his heritage qualified him for the ministry God sent him to do?

6:15 The temple was completed. God worked through the orders of the Persian kings to accomplish his purposes. The temple was completed in 515 B.C., seventy years and six months after it had been destroyed and 21 years after reconstruction had begun.

6:16 celebrated ... with joy. Psalms 145–148 may have been used in celebrating the completed temple (Neh. 12:27). For the first time since captivity, the people could celebrate Passover according to the Law, with sacrifices offered in the temple.

6:17 bulls ... rams ... lambs ... goats. The numbers of sheep and oxen sacrificed were much smaller than the number of sacrifices in Solomon's temple dedication (1 Kin. 8:63) due to the relative poverty of the community.

6:20 The priests and Levites had purified themselves. Before priests and Levites could perform temple duties, they were required to offer sacrifices for forgiveness of sin.

6:21 together with all who had separated themselves. This probably refers to Jews who had remained in the land during the captivity and practiced idolatry and intermarriage with foreigners. They now repented of their sinful activities.

7:1 during the reign of Artaxerxes. A gap of 57 years separates the end of chapter six from the start of chapter seven. The events of the book of Esther occurred during this gap. **Ezra.** He was the leader of the second return to Jerusalem. His lineage goes back to Aaron, the first priest.

APPLY When is your family history/heritage most helpful and when is it most hurtful?

OPEN 1. When have you received a recommendation, commendation or your picture in the news? What was it for? How did you feel to have someone say good things about you publicly? **2.** How did others respond to your notoriety?

STUDY King Artaxerxes' letter opened the doors for Ezra to return with the people, supplies and authority he needed to do his ministry. **1.** If you had been Ezra, what would you have done with the king's letter **2.** Does it appear that Ezra will over use his authority? Why or why not? **3.** How is each part of the letter important as it describes: The people who could go? The supplies, animals, etc.? Ezra's authority to appoint leaders? **4.** What is the king up to when he refers to "your God," "the God of Jerusalem," "the God of heaven" as if he doesn't believe in the God of Israel himself? Note the clues in verses 24 and 27. Is this whole letter a way for the king to appease a God he fears might hurt him? **5.** What does Ezra's response (vv. 27–28) show you about his character and his understanding of who's really in charge? **6.** How does knowing "the hand of the Lord my God was on me" (v. 28) make a difference for Ezra and for you?

APPLY 1. How have the members of your group seen the hand of God in their lives? **2.** Where in your life do you need to know that "the hand of the Lord" is upon you? How will that area be changed? What risky thing might you be willing to try?

the king. [9]He had begun his journey from Babylon on the first day of
the first month, and he arrived in Jerusalem on the first day of the
fifth month, for the gracious hand of his God was on him. [10]For Ezra
had devoted himself to the study and observance of the Law of the
LORD, and to teaching its decrees and laws in Israel.

King Artaxerxes' Letter to Ezra

[11]This is a copy of the letter King Artaxerxes had given to Ezra the
priest and teacher, a man learned in matters concerning the commands and decrees of the LORD for Israel:

[12][a]Artaxerxes, king of kings,

To Ezra the priest, a teacher of the Law of the God of heaven:

Greetings.

[13]Now I decree that any of the Israelites in my kingdom,
including priests and Levites, who wish to go to Jerusalem with
you, may go. [14]You are sent by the king and his seven advisers to
inquire about Judah and Jerusalem with regard to the Law of
your God, which is in your hand. [15]Moreover, you are to take
with you the silver and gold that the king and his advisers have
freely given to the God of Israel, whose dwelling is in Jerusalem,
[16]together with all the silver and gold you may obtain from the
province of Babylon, as well as the freewill offerings of the
people and priests for the temple of their God in Jerusalem.
[17]With this money be sure to buy bulls, rams and male lambs,
together with their grain offerings and drink offerings, and sacrifice them on the altar of the temple of your God in Jerusalem.
[18]You and your brother Jews may then do whatever seems best
with the rest of the silver and gold, in accordance with the will of
your God. [19]Deliver to the God of Jerusalem all the articles
entrusted to you for worship in the temple of your God. [20]And
anything else needed for the temple of your God that you may
have occasion to supply, you may provide from the royal treasury.
[21]Now I, King Artaxerxes, order all the treasurers of Trans-Euphrates to provide with diligence whatever Ezra the priest, a
teacher of the Law of the God of heaven, may ask of you—[22]up
to a hundred talents[b] of silver, a hundred cors[c] of wheat, a hundred baths[d] of wine, a hundred baths[d] of olive oil, and salt without limit. [23]Whatever the God of heaven has prescribed, let it be

[a] *12* The text of Ezra 7:12-26 is in Aramaic. [b] *22* That is, about 3 3/4 tons (about 3.4 metric tons) [c] *22* That is, probably about 600 bushels (about 22 kiloliters) [d] *22* That is, probably about 600 gallons (about 2.2 kiloliters)

7:10 teaching its decrees and laws in Israel. "Teacher" also meant recorder, scribe, writer or learned man able to teach God's Law. Ezra enjoyed the *king's favor as well as the blessing of* God. He used the king's favor to advance the cause of God among the people.

7:11 letter. King Artaxerxes's letter to Ezra permitted him to take a group back to Israel, specifying freedoms and privileges they would enjoy.

7:16 freewill offerings of the people. Voluntary gifts from the Jewish people who remained in Babylon. God accepts gifts from those who do not know him (the king and his counselors in verse 15 and the people of Babylon in verse 16) and from his followers. But he rejects gifts from people who appear to know him but whose hearts are far from him (Isa. 1:10–15).

7:22 hundred talents of silver. The king ordered generous supplies of gold, silver, wine and olive oil from provincial treasuries for Ezra's group.

done with diligence for the temple of the God of heaven. Why
should there be wrath against the realm of the king and of his
sons? [24]You are also to know that you have no authority to impose taxes, tribute or duty on any of the priests, Levites, singers,
gatekeepers, temple servants or other workers at this house of
God.

[25]And you, Ezra, in accordance with the wisdom of your God,
which you possess, appoint magistrates and judges to administer justice to all the people of Trans-Euphrates—all who know
the laws of your God. And you are to teach any who do not know
them. [26]Whoever does not obey the law of your God and the law
of the king must surely be punished by death, banishment, confiscation of property, or imprisonment.

[27]Praise be to the LORD, the God of our fathers, who has put it into
the king's heart to bring honor to the house of the LORD in Jerusalem
in this way [28]and who has extended his good favor to me before the
king and his advisers and all the king's powerful officials. Because
the hand of the LORD my God was on me, I took courage and gathered
leading men from Israel to go up with me.

List of the Family Heads Returning With Ezra

8 These are the family heads and those registered with them who came up with me from Babylon during the reign of King Artaxerxes:

[2]of the descendants of Phinehas, Gershom;
of the descendants of Ithamar, Daniel;
of the descendants of David, Hattush [3]of the descendants of Shecaniah;

of the descendants of Parosh, Zechariah, and with him were registered 150 men;
[4]of the descendants of Pahath-Moab, Eliehoenai son of Zerahiah, and with him 200 men;
[5]of the descendants of Zattu,[a] Shecaniah son of Jahaziel, and with him 300 men;
[6]of the descendants of Adin, Ebed son of Jonathan, and with him 50 men;
[7]of the descendants of Elam, Jeshaiah son of Athaliah, and with him 70 men;
[8]of the descendants of Shephatiah, Zebadiah son of Michael, and with him 80 men;
[9]of the descendants of Joab, Obadiah son of Jehiel, and with him 218 men;
[10]of the descendants of Bani,[b] Shelomith son of Josiphiah, and with him 160 men;

[a]5 Some Septuagint manuscripts (also 1 Esdras 8:32); Hebrew does not have *Zattu*. [b]10 Some Septuagint manuscripts (also 1 Esdras 8:36); Hebrew does not have *Bani*.

OPEN 1. How far back can you trace your family tree before you come to a person born in another country? **2.** What is the longest time you have been away from home and/or family? When did you get homesick?

STUDY 1. If you had been one of the travelers starting out with Ezra how would you have felt about his leadership? On a scale of 1 to 5 (1 being "can't stand to follow him," 5 being "this guy can lead me anywhere") how would you rate his leadership/management skills? **2.** Would you have reconsidered the trip when he turned down protective troops? What do you think about his replacing the soldiers with prayer and fasting? **3.** What do you note about Ezra's financial wisdom (and his understanding of financial principles) in the way he divided up the large amounts of money for travel? **4.** Why do you think the genealogical record in verses 2–14 is important to Ezra? What did he discover about the positions he needed to fill? What is most interesting about his job recruiting? **5.** Why do you think the story-teller's viewpoint changes to the first person (me) from 7:27 through chapter 9. Paraphrase this passage in a four-line

7:26 Whoever does not obey ... punished by death ... imprisonment. The king gave Ezra authority to administer justice to the Jews in Jerusalem, Syria, Phoenicia and Palestine. Ezra later used this authority to punish sin.

8:1 These are the family heads. There were 1,496 heads of families who returned to Jerusalem with Ezra. Including women and children, the group probably numbered 5,000 people, far fewer than the 50,000 on the first return.

poem that summarizes your understanding and Ezra's understanding of dependence on God. **6.** What is the most important life-principle you got from Ezra in this passage? Do you think God's hand is more directly involved in the lives of people when they go out on a limb or is it just more obvious that God is at work then?

APPLY 1. Trying to get 5,000 people to walk the 900 mile road must have seemed to take an eternity for most of the travelers. How many times do you think Ezra heard, "Are we there yet?" When have you felt that the spiritual progress you are making is "taking forever"? How might this affect your patience in bringing others along with you in your vision? **2.** Ezra trusted 24 men with millions of dollars, holding them accountable for safe-guarding it. Over what parts of your world has God made you accountable? How are you caring for it? **3.** How is your group helping one another remain accountable in their spiritual journeys? Where does the group need to be more intentional?

11 of the descendants of Bebai, Zechariah son of Bebai, and with him 28 men;
12 of the descendants of Azgad, Johanan son of Hakkatan, and with him 110 men;
13 of the descendants of Adonikam, the last ones, whose names were Eliphelet, Jeuel and Shemaiah, and with them 60 men;
14 of the descendants of Bigvai, Uthai and Zaccur, and with them 70 men.

The Return to Jerusalem

15 I assembled them at the canal that flows toward Ahava, and we
camped there three days. When I checked among the people and the
priests, I found no Levites there. 16 So I summoned Eliezer, Ariel, Shemaiah, Elnathan, Jarib, Elnathan, Nathan, Zechariah and Meshullam,
who were leaders, and Joiarib and Elnathan, who were men of
learning, 17 and I sent them to Iddo, the leader in Casiphia. I told them
what to say to Iddo and his kinsmen, the temple servants in Casiphia,
so that they might bring attendants to us for the house of our God.
18 Because the gracious hand of our God was on us, they brought us
Sherebiah, a capable man, from the descendants of Mahli son of Levi,
the son of Israel, and Sherebiah's sons and brothers, 18 men; 19 and
Hashabiah, together with Jeshaiah from the descendants of Merari,
and his brothers and nephews, 20 men. 20 They also brought 220 of
the temple servants—a body that David and the officials had established to assist the Levites. All were registered by name.

21 There, by the Ahava Canal, I proclaimed a fast, so that we might
humble ourselves before our God and ask him for a safe journey for
us and our children, with all our possessions. 22 I was ashamed to ask
the king for soldiers and horsemen to protect us from enemies on the
road, because we had told the king, "The gracious hand of our God is
on everyone who looks to him, but his great anger is against all who
forsake him." 23 So we fasted and petitioned our God about this, and
he answered our prayer.

24 Then I set apart twelve of the leading priests, together with Sherebiah, Hashabiah and ten of their brothers, 25 and I weighed out to
them the offering of silver and gold and the articles that the king, his
advisers, his officials and all Israel present there had donated for the
house of our God. 26 I weighed out to them 650 talents[a] of silver, silver
articles weighing 100 talents,[b] 100 talents[b] of gold, 27 20 bowls of gold
valued at 1,000 darics,[c] and two fine articles of polished bronze, as
precious as gold.

28 I said to them, "You as well as these articles are consecrated to

[a]26 That is, about 25 tons (about 22 metric tons) [b]26 That is, about 3 3/4 tons (about 3.4 metric tons)
[c]27 That is, about 19 pounds (about 8.5 kilograms)

8:15 I found no Levites. Ezra discovered the group included no Levites, who could conduct temple ministry and teach the Law. Levites were also responsible for taking the precious metals and utensils back to Jerusalem.

8:17 bring attendants to us for the house of our God. Ezra sent a group of leaders to Casiphia, probably on the Tigris River near modern Baghdad, to recruit Levites and temple servants. There may have been a Jewish temple in Casiphia.

8:18 Sherebiah. They found 38 Levites from the families of Sherebiah and Jeshaiah, as well as 220 temple servants, willing to go to Jerusalem.

8:22 I was ashamed to ask the king. Ezra did not want to ask for soldiers and horsemen to protect the group on the journey because he had publicly said that God would take care of his people. Later Nehemiah accepted a military escort for his return to Jerusalem.

the LORD. The silver and gold are a freewill offering to the LORD, the
God of your fathers. 29Guard them carefully until you weigh them out
in the chambers of the house of the LORD in Jerusalem before the
leading priests and the Levites and the family heads of Israel." 30Then
the priests and Levites received the silver and gold and sacred articles that had been weighed out to be taken to the house of our God
in Jerusalem.
31On the twelfth day of the first month we set out from the Ahava
Canal to go to Jerusalem. The hand of our God was on us, and he protected us from enemies and bandits along the way. 32So we arrived in
Jerusalem, where we rested three days.
33On the fourth day, in the house of our God, we weighed out the
silver and gold and the sacred articles into the hands of Meremoth
son of Uriah, the priest. Eleazar son of Phinehas was with him, and
so were the Levites Jozabad son of Jeshua and Noadiah son of Binnui. 34Everything was accounted for by number and weight, and the
entire weight was recorded at that time.
35Then the exiles who had returned from captivity sacrificed burnt
offerings to the God of Israel: twelve bulls for all Israel, ninety-six
rams, seventy-seven male lambs and, as a sin offering, twelve male
goats. All this was a burnt offering to the LORD. 36They also delivered
the king's orders to the royal satraps and to the governors of Trans-
Euphrates, who then gave assistance to the people and to the house
of God.

Ezra's Prayer About Intermarriage

9 After these things had been done, the leaders came to me and
said, "The people of Israel, including the priests and the Levites,
have not kept themselves separate from the neighboring peoples
with their detestable practices, like those of the Canaanites, Hittites,
Perizzites, Jebusites, Ammonites, Moabites, Egyptians and Amorites.
2They have taken some of their daughters as wives for themselves
and their sons, and have mingled the holy race with the peoples
around them. And the leaders and officials have led the way in this
unfaithfulness."
3When I heard this, I tore my tunic and cloak, pulled hair from my
head and beard and sat down appalled. 4Then everyone who trembled at the words of the God of Israel gathered around me because of
this unfaithfulness of the exiles. And I sat there appalled until the
evening sacrifice.
5Then, at the evening sacrifice, I rose from my self-abasement, with
my tunic and cloak torn, and fell on my knees with my hands spread
out to the LORD my God 6and prayed:

"O my God, I am too ashamed and disgraced to lift up my face
to you, my God, because our sins are higher than our heads and

OPEN **1.** What picture comes to your mind when you hear the word "confession": A confessional box? A letter to a "Dear Jane" column? A trusted friend? Bad public relations? Losing your job? **2.** If you thought no one would find out about a wrong you've done, would you confess it anyway (to clear your conscience) or bury it deep (and take a chance on getting away with it)? Why?

STUDY Ezra has just arrived on the scene in Jerusalem and finds that the people are sinning just as they had before the exile. In fact, the leaders put in place by God are leading the people into disobedience. **1.** What is your first impression of the passage? Does this remind you of any experience that you have come through? **2.** If you had been God what would you have done? Is God too easy on the Israelites or have they suffered enough? **3.** How widespread does this

9:1 After these things had been done. Jewish leaders told Ezra that some Israelites had participated in their pagan neighbors' idol worship and intermarriage. Ezra was devoted to careful teaching of the Law. He knew that disobedience to God would only bring trouble.

9:2 leaders ... led the way in this unfaithfulness. The Law of Moses expressly forbade marrying Israel's pagan neighbors (Ex. 34:16). This practice often led Jews to worship the pagan gods of their spouses.

9:6 ashamed and disgraced to lift up my face. Ezra confessed sin among the people. He knew that the sin of intermarriage and idol worship had caused the captivity as a form of discipline. **our sins.** Although Ezra had not participated in this sin himself, he was appalled by it, perhaps fearing God would send the people into captivity again.

problem of intermarriage seem to be? What's the big deal here, anyway? Is Ezra just a bigot against people who are not Jews? **4.** Ezra was hoping to establish a holy nation with pure marriages. What seemed to happen most of the time, in the mixed marriages, to the Jew's faith? **5.** Can you find five themes in Ezra's prayer (vv. 6,8,10,13,15)? What does this prayer teach us about the nature of God? What hope do you find here? **6.** Why do you think he confessed for the people, even before they had come together to confess for themselves? **7.** From this passage do you think God is more: Angry or merciful? Seeking justice or giving grace? Vengeful or loving? Why?

APPLY 1. How did Ezra's public prayer affect the Jews? How does it affect you? Do you pray more "I-prayers" or more "we-prayers"? Why? **2.** About 25 years later when Nehemiah came to Jerusalem he found the same problem of marriage outside the faith. Why do the Israelites seem not to learn their lesson? Are there areas in your life that you vow to change and then find yourself back in the same pattern again and again? Why?

OPEN What was the last New Year's resolution that you made and actually kept for six months or more? When was it?

STUDY While Ezra lies on the ground, praying and grieving for his people, a crowd gathers. They join in the weeping for their sin, taking responsibility for what they've done. In fact they ask Ezra to get up

our guilt has reached to the heavens. 7From the days of our forefathers until now, our guilt has been great. Because of our sins,
we and our kings and our priests have been subjected to the
sword and captivity, to pillage and humiliation at the hand of
foreign kings, as it is today.
8"But now, for a brief moment, the LORD our God has been
gracious in leaving us a remnant and giving us a firm place in his
sanctuary, and so our God gives light to our eyes and a little
relief in our bondage. 9Though we are slaves, our God has not
deserted us in our bondage. He has shown us kindness in the
sight of the kings of Persia: He has granted us new life to rebuild
the house of our God and repair its ruins, and he has given us a
wall of protection in Judah and Jerusalem.
10"But now, O our God, what can we say after this? For we
have disregarded the commands 11you gave through your servants the prophets when you said: 'The land you are entering to
possess is a land polluted by the corruption of its peoples. By
their detestable practices they have filled it with their impurity
from one end to the other. 12Therefore, do not give your daughters in marriage to their sons or take their daughters for your
sons. Do not seek a treaty of friendship with them at any time,
that you may be strong and eat the good things of the land and
leave it to your children as an everlasting inheritance.'
13"What has happened to us is a result of our evil deeds and
our great guilt, and yet, our God, you have punished us less than
our sins have deserved and have given us a remnant like this.
14Shall we again break your commands and intermarry with the
peoples who commit such detestable practices? Would you not
be angry enough with us to destroy us, leaving us no remnant or
survivor? 15O LORD, God of Israel, you are righteous! We are left
this day as a remnant. Here we are before you in our guilt,
though because of it not one of us can stand in your presence."

The People's Confession of Sin

10 While Ezra was praying and confessing, weeping and throwing himself down before the house of God, a large crowd of
Israelites—men, women and children—gathered around him. They
too wept bitterly. 2Then Shecaniah son of Jehiel, one of the descendants of Elam, said to Ezra, "We have been unfaithful to our God by
marrying foreign women from the peoples around us. But in spite of
this, there is still hope for Israel. 3Now let us make a covenant before
our God to send away all these women and their children, in accor-

---

9:8 giving us a firm place. God had allowed the remnant to be established in his chosen place. **God gives light to our eyes.** God gave the light of his will to those in the darkness of sin. Not only were they free from the Babylonian captivity, but also from the bondage of sin. Ezra warned against choosing to go back into bondage.

9:10 what can we say after this? Ezra acknowledged that the Jews had no excuse for disobeying God's commands to remain pure from the idolatrous practices of their neighbors.

9:15 before you in our guilt. When people disobey God, they deserve his wrath (Dan. 9:14). **not one of us can stand.** Ezra threw himself and his people on God's mercy.

10:1 a large crowd of Israelites. Many were grieved over sin in the community. Previously they had been afraid to speak out, but they now joined in Ezra's grief.

10:2 Shecaniah. He spoke on behalf of the weeping people and acknowledged their sin. He clung to hope for Israel, suggesting divorce from foreign wives, sending them away with their children (Neh. 13:23–27).

dance with the counsel of my lord and of those who fear the
commands of our God. Let it be done according to the Law. [4]Rise up;
this matter is in your hands. We will support you, so take courage and
do it."

[5]So Ezra rose up and put the leading priests and Levites and all
Israel under oath to do what had been suggested. And they took the
oath. [6]Then Ezra withdrew from before the house of God and went to
the room of Jehohanan son of Eliashib. While he was there, he ate no
food and drank no water, because he continued to mourn over the
unfaithfulness of the exiles.

[7]A proclamation was then issued throughout Judah and Jerusalem
for all the exiles to assemble in Jerusalem. [8]Anyone who failed to appear within three days would forfeit all his property, in accordance
with the decision of the officials and elders, and would himself be
expelled from the assembly of the exiles.

[9]Within the three days, all the men of Judah and Benjamin had
gathered in Jerusalem. And on the twentieth day of the ninth month,
all the people were sitting in the square before the house of God,
greatly distressed by the occasion and because of the rain. [10]Then
Ezra the priest stood up and said to them, "You have been unfaithful;
you have married foreign women, adding to Israel's guilt. [11]Now
make confession to the LORD, the God of your fathers, and do his will.
Separate yourselves from the peoples around you and from your
foreign wives."

[12]The whole assembly responded with a loud voice: "You are right!
We must do as you say. [13]But there are many people here and it is the
rainy season; so we cannot stand outside. Besides, this matter
cannot be taken care of in a day or two, because we have sinned
greatly in this thing. [14]Let our officials act for the whole assembly.
Then let everyone in our towns who has married a foreign woman
come at a set time, along with the elders and judges of each town,
until the fierce anger of our God in this matter is turned away from
us." [15]Only Jonathan son of Asahel and Jahzeiah son of Tikvah, supported by Meshullam and Shabbethai the Levite, opposed this.

[16]So the exiles did as was proposed. Ezra the priest selected men
who were family heads, one from each family division, and all of
them designated by name. On the first day of the tenth month they
sat down to investigate the cases, [17]and by the first day of the first
month they finished dealing with all the men who had married foreign women.

and help them get their relationship right with God. **1.** Why do you think the people so willingly followed Ezra's example in grieving for their sin: They saw his seriousness? They were afraid God would get them again? They were reminded of their sin and truly grieved? Other? **2.** What do you think about sending all these women and children away? Why such drastic measures when the men seemed to have led in the sinning? **3.** Does Ezra seem to be pulling rank on the people or taking his rightful role as spiritual leader? What are the pros and cons of his leadership here? Who is your spiritual leader? How does he or she demonstrate their deep commitment to follow God, and help you follow God, too? **4.** What do you think about Ezra's willingness to compromise with the people when they said that they were "greatly distressed by the occasion and because of the rain?" Do you think God grinned because they wanted to get out of the rain? Why do you think this statement is included in the Bible? **5.** Do you think the plan to investigate the problem was fair to the couples and children? Why or why not?

APPLY **1.** Do you find it easier to make a decision and act immediately or do you need processing time before acting? Can you give an example? **2.** From this passage, what connection do you see between: Repentance and hope? Prayer and action?

10:5 Ezra ... the leading priests ... under oath. A covenant was the most binding form of agreement. While divorce was not preferable, intermarriage led the Israelites into worship of false deities and seduced them away from God. The Law permitted marriage with outside women only if they became worshipers of the true God.

10:7 proclamation. Under the king's authority, Ezra called all the exiles to Jerusalem. Whoever ignored the proclamation would be stripped of legal rights.

10:8 within three days. Even though it was the rainy season, the people gathered in the square east of the temple. They feared both God's wrath and family breakups. **forfeit.** Confiscated property was sold; proceeds went into the temple treasury.

10:15 opposed. Two men, supported by two Levites, opposed Ezra's plan. The rest of the people agreed to deport foreign wives who had not become true believers in God.

10:16 investigate the cases. The elders and judges of each town knew whether the women worshiped the Lord or idols. All the marriages were examined within three months.

Those Guilty of Intermarriage

18 Among the descendants of the priests, the following had married
foreign women:

From the descendants of Jeshua son of Jozadak, and his brothers: Maaseiah, Eliezer, Jarib and Gedaliah. 19 (They all gave
their hands in pledge to put away their wives, and for their
guilt they each presented a ram from the flock as a guilt offering.)

20 From the descendants of Immer:
Hanani and Zebadiah.
21 From the descendants of Harim:
Maaseiah, Elijah, Shemaiah, Jehiel and Uzziah.
22 From the descendants of Pashhur:
Elioenai, Maaseiah, Ishmael, Nethanel, Jozabad and Elasah.

23 Among the Levites:

Jozabad, Shimei, Kelaiah (that is, Kelita), Pethahiah, Judah and Eliezer.
24 From the singers:
Eliashib.
From the gatekeepers:
Shallum, Telem and Uri.

25 And among the other Israelites:

From the descendants of Parosh:
Ramiah, Izziah, Malkijah, Mijamin, Eleazar, Malkijah and Benaiah.
26 From the descendants of Elam:
Mattaniah, Zechariah, Jehiel, Abdi, Jeremoth and Elijah.
27 From the descendants of Zattu:
Elioenai, Eliashib, Mattaniah, Jeremoth, Zabad and Aziza.
28 From the descendants of Bebai:
Jehohanan, Hananiah, Zabbai and Athlai.
29 From the descendants of Bani:
Meshullam, Malluch, Adaiah, Jashub, Sheal and Jeremoth.
30 From the descendants of Pahath-Moab:
Adna, Kelal, Benaiah, Maaseiah, Mattaniah, Bezalel, Binnui and Manasseh.
31 From the descendants of Harim:
Eliezer, Ishijah, Malkijah, Shemaiah, Shimeon, 32 Benjamin,
Malluch and Shemariah.
33 From the descendants of Hashum:
Mattenai, Mattattah, Zabad, Eliphelet, Jeremai, Manasseh and Shimei.
34 From the descendants of Bani:
Maadai, Amram, Uel, 35 Benaiah, Bedeiah, Keluhi, 36 Vaniah,
Meremoth, Eliashib, 37 Mattaniah, Mattenai and Jaasu.

OPEN 1. What is an embarrassing thing you got caught doing as a child? **2.** Who has a "file" on you that you would like to keep sealed forever: Your elementary teacher? Your high school? A friend? The IRS? A doctor? A former sweetheart? Other? **3.** How would it feel to have your private information made public?

STUDY The Jews completed the investigation of all the couples who were intermarried then posted the names of those who were guilty. **1.** Try to put yourself in the place of one of the men listed. What would have been hardest to do: Face your extended family members again or say goodbye to your wife and children? How do you think knowing that you were forgiven by God helped to ease the pain? **2.** How do you feel when you see a list of 111 guilty men knowing they represent ex-wives, children and broken homes? How would your sentiment overshadow the principles involved? Why do you think children were an insufficient reason for stopping the divorces? **3.** Why do you think there was such furor over few transgressors (27 clergy and 84 laity)? What might have been the reason for only one singer and three gatekeepers to be named among the 111? **4.** As you look back over this chapter, how do you see God's love and forgiveness being shown, even through the difficult consequences for sin?

APPLY 1. What lesson can you get from this passage that connects to your world? How do you think God wants purity lived out today? **2.** What have you learned about God in the book of Ezra that makes you want to look further for answers? What encourages you in your walk of faith?

10:19 gave their hands in pledge. Many Israelites, including priests, Levites and gatekeepers, had married foreign women. Some had children by these women. While the separation of families was painful, the serious sin of intermarriage often turned people's hearts away from God as they worshiped their spouses' idols. Spiritual priorities prevailed here in a rigorous demonstration of obedience and emotional upheaval.

38 From the descendants of Binnui:[a]
Shimei, 39 Shelemiah, Nathan, Adaiah, 40 Macnadebai, Shashai,
Sharai, 41 Azarel, Shelemiah, Shemariah, 42 Shallum, Amariah
and Joseph.
43 From the descendants of Nebo:
Jeiel, Mattithiah, Zabad, Zebina, Jaddai, Joel and Benaiah.

44 All these had married foreign women, and some of them had children by these wives.[b]

[a] *37,38* See Septuagint (also 1 Esdras 9:34); Hebrew *Jaasu* [38] *and Bani and Binnui,* [b] *44* Or *and they sent them away with their children*

Nehemiah

Personal Reading	Group Study Topic and Reading	
1:1–1:11	Nehemiah's Passion	1:1–1:11
2:1–20	Artaxerxes's Permission	2:1–20
3:1–32	Builders of the Wall	3:1–32
4:1–23	Opposition to the Rebuilding	4:1–23
5:1–19	Nehemiah Helps the Poor	5:1–19
6:1–7:3	Rebuilding Opposed, Completed	6:1–7:3
7:4–73a	List of Exiles Who Returned	7:4–73a
7:73b–8:18	Ezra Reads the Law	7:73b–8:18
9:1–37	Israelites Confess Their Sins	9:1–37
9:38–10:39	Agreement of the People	9:38–10:39
11:1–36	Residents of Jerusalem	11:1–36
12:1–47	Leaders and Wall Dedicated	12:1–47
13:1–31	Nehemiah's Final Reform	13:1–31

Author. Some of the book of Nehemiah is written in the first person, while other parts are written in the third person. Nevertheless, Nehemiah is credited with writing the complete manuscript. Ezra has been considered a possible contributor.

Date. The book of Nehemiah was probably written very soon after the events that it describes, possibly around 430 B.C. The events of this book span 12 to 15 years.

Purpose. The book of Nehemiah offers a rich message for both the readers of that day and for contemporary culture. It is an organizational treatise, a call to spiritual purity and a blow-by-blow description of God at work in the everyday events of life. Nehemiah's determination to repair the wall that protected the city stands as a testimony of a man who discerned God's call in his life and trusted God for the strength to follow through without distraction.

Historical Background. In 538 B.C., Cyrus, king of Persia, began letting the Jews return to their homeland and rebuild the temple in Jerusalem. The temple was completed and dedicated around 516 B.C. Some 58 years later, in 458 B.C., King Artaxerxes allowed another remnant of Jews, led by Ezra, to return to Palestine. When Ezra arrived, he found the Jews in Israel living ungodly lives, intermarrying with other peoples and practicing pagan rituals. His passion was to reform the lives of the Jews in Israel.

In 444 B.C., about 14 years after Ezra arrived, Nehemiah returned to Jerusalem to rebuild the city's wall. His rebuilding plans had a broader scope, however. Whereas Ezra had focused on the renewal of the religious spirit of the Jews, Nehemiah focused on rebuilding the country's social and economic life. Both Ezra and Nehemiah played significant roles in the rebirth of the nation of Judah. The exile had stripped the people of their identity, their pride and their commitment to their faith. Both Ezra and Nehemiah helped reestablish the faith and the nation.

Intermarrying. When Ezra read the Law to the people (8:1–18), they became aware of a problem in their culture: intermarriage. From the time of the exodus, God had warned them against marrying into another culture. It is important to understand why. In that day, the Hebrews were the one nation dedicated to the worship of only Jehovah. The first of the Ten Commandments confirmed it: Have no other gods before me. When a Hebrew married a person of another culture, the marriage diluted his or her faith.

Throughout the rest of Old Testament Hebrew history, the trend became more certain. Even a man as influential as Solomon was seduced from his faith by the idolatry of his wives. Many more kings made the same mistake. At that time, intermarrying involved much more than the choice of a spouse. It dramatically affected purity of worship.

Nehemiah's Prayer

1 The words of Nehemiah son of Hacaliah:
In the month of Kislev in the twentieth year, while I was in the citadel of Susa, [2]Hanani, one of my brothers, came from Judah with
some other men, and I questioned them about the Jewish remnant
that survived the exile, and also about Jerusalem.
[3]They said to me, "Those who survived the exile and are back in the
province are in great trouble and disgrace. The wall of Jerusalem is
broken down, and its gates have been burned with fire."
[4]When I heard these things, I sat down and wept. For some days I
mourned and fasted and prayed before the God of heaven. [5]Then I
said:

"O LORD, God of heaven, the great and awesome God, who
keeps his covenant of love with those who love him and obey his
commands, [6]let your ear be attentive and your eyes open to hear
the prayer your servant is praying before you day and night for
your servants, the people of Israel. I confess the sins we Israelites, including myself and my father's house, have committed
against you. [7]We have acted very wickedly toward you. We have
not obeyed the commands, decrees and laws you gave your servant Moses.
[8]"Remember the instruction you gave your servant Moses,
saying, 'If you are unfaithful, I will scatter you among the nations, [9]but if you return to me and obey my commands, then
even if your exiled people are at the farthest horizon, I will
gather them from there and bring them to the place I have chosen as a dwelling for my Name.'
[10]"They are your servants and your people, whom you redeemed by your great strength and your mighty hand. [11]O Lord,
let your ear be attentive to the prayer of this your servant and to
the prayer of your servants who delight in revering your name.
Give your servant success today by granting him favor in the
presence of this man."

I was cupbearer to the king.

OPEN 1. What do you think of when you hear the word "home"? **2.** If you could build/create the world's greatest "spiritual care-center," with no financial limits, what would you create?

STUDY Nehemiah got the bad news about the broken condition of Jerusalem from his brother. The news crushed him but not to the point of giving up. He immediately started an action plan to bring a solution to the problem. **1.** If you had been Nehemiah and received this news about Jerusalem what would you have done first? Why do you think Nehemiah didn't go directly to the king for help? **2.** On a scale of 1–10 (1 = lowest; 10 = highest), how important do you think prayer was to Nehemiah? How often do you think he prayed? If you can imagine yourself in his shoes, why do you think prayer was so important? **3.** As you read through the prayer (vv. 5–11) what do you see about Nehemiah's understanding of God? What do you see about Nehemiah's understanding of himself? **4.** Why do you think Nehemiah needed to go through the "mourning, fasting and praying" (v. 4) before he went to the king?

APPLY When was the last time you saw a deep need that caused you to grieve? What was the situation?

1:1 Nehemiah. Probably born in Persia, he served as King Artaxerxes's personal cupbearer. He was also an important statesman who helped Ezra reestablish the Jews in Jerusalem. His name means "the Lord comforts." His great-grandparents may have been taken into captivity when the Babylonians captured Jerusalem.

1:2 Hanani, one of my brothers. Nehemiah's brother who brought him a message at the Persian palace. The troubling report said Jerusalem's wall was broken down and its gates were burned, making it vulnerable to attack. Nehemiah later appointed Hanani to an important position in Jerusalem (7:2).

1:4 fasted and prayed. Going without food often indicated grief or an especially fervent prayer request (Ps. 35:13; 109:24).

1:6 servant is praying before you day and night. Nehemiah wept, fasted and prayed continuously for several days over the condition of Jerusalem. He knew he could not solve the problem without God's help. **sins ... myself and my father's house, have committed.** He included himself and his family when he confessed the sins of the Israelites. He shared the responsibility for Israel's disobedience.

1:8 If you are unfaithful, I will scatter you. He reminded God of his covenant in Leviticus 26:27–45: If Israel were unfaithful, God would send them from their homeland to various places; but if they obeyed, he would regather them to Jerusalem (Deut. 30:1–5). Nehemiah recalled God's own words in his plea for help.

1:10 by your great strength and your mighty hand. Recalling God's work in the past (Ex. 32:11), Nehemiah asked him to help the people again. They belonged to God, and God would hear their prayer and help them. They needed God's power in their lives (Deut. 9:29).

OPEN 1. What risky thing have you done, that you can share with the group, that scared you spitless? 2. Who first broke your heart?

STUDY Three months after hearing the news of Jerusalem's plight, Nehemiah appeared again before the king. This is his request for help. 1. What do you think Nehemiah had been doing for the intervening three months, between the end of chapter one and the beginning of chapter two? Note his request to the king. 2. How do you think the king could tell that Nehemiah's sadness was "sadness of the heart" (v. 2)? How would you define sadness of the heart?

APPLY 1. Have you ever experienced "heart sadness"? What caused it? Why? 2. Can you tell when people close to you are sad inside? What clues do you look for? How do you respond to them?

OPEN 1. Have you ever witnessed a hurricane, earthquake or tornado? How did you feel seeing the destruction? 2. If you were able to walk through the wreckage, did it feel different than viewing it at a distance or on TV?

STUDY Nehemiah finally arrived in Jerusalem and secretly surveyed the damage firsthand. Gradually and strategically he then unveiled his vision to the resident Jews. 1. If you had been Nehemiah,

Artaxerxes Sends Nehemiah to Jerusalem

2 In the month of Nisan in the twentieth year of King Artaxerxes,
when wine was brought for him, I took the wine and gave it to
the king. I had not been sad in his presence before; [2]so the king asked
me, "Why does your face look so sad when you are not ill? This can
be nothing but sadness of heart."
I was very much afraid, [3]but I said to the king, "May the king live
forever! Why should my face not look sad when the city where my
fathers are buried lies in ruins, and its gates have been destroyed by
fire?"
[4]The king said to me, "What is it you want?"
Then I prayed to the God of heaven, [5]and I answered the king, "If it
pleases the king and if your servant has found favor in his sight, let
him send me to the city in Judah where my fathers are buried so that
I can rebuild it."
[6]Then the king, with the queen sitting beside him, asked me, "How
long will your journey take, and when will you get back?" It pleased
the king to send me; so I set a time.
[7]I also said to him, "If it pleases the king, may I have letters to the
governors of Trans-Euphrates, so that they will provide me safe-
conduct until I arrive in Judah? [8]And may I have a letter to Asaph,
keeper of the king's forest, so he will give me timber to make beams
for the gates of the citadel by the temple and for the city wall and for
the residence I will occupy?" And because the gracious hand of my
God was upon me, the king granted my requests. [9]So I went to the
governors of Trans-Euphrates and gave them the king's letters. The
king had also sent army officers and cavalry with me.
[10]When Sanballat the Horonite and Tobiah the Ammonite official
heard about this, they were very much disturbed that someone had
come to promote the welfare of the Israelites.

Nehemiah Inspects Jerusalem's Walls

[11]I went to Jerusalem, and after staying there three days [12]I set out
during the night with a few men. I had not told anyone what my God
had put in my heart to do for Jerusalem. There were no mounts with
me except the one I was riding on.
[13]By night I went out through the Valley Gate toward the Jackal[a]
Well and the Dung Gate, examining the walls of Jerusalem, which had
been broken down, and its gates, which had been destroyed by fire.
[14]Then I moved on toward the Fountain Gate and the King's Pool, but
there was not enough room for my mount to get through; [15]so I went

[a]13 Or *Serpent* or *Fig*

2:3 May the king live forever! A servant was never to display negative emotions in front of the king lest they be interpreted as dissatisfaction or criticism of the king. A servant's job and life could be jeopardized as a result. Yet Artaxerxes noticed Nehemiah's expression and inquired. Although afraid, Nehemiah boldly answered the king.

2:4 I prayed to the God of heaven. Nehemiah had prepared himself for this opportunity by prayer and fasting. He courteously revealed the desire of his heart to the king.

2:11 after staying there three days. He prepared himself with prayer, thought and research before trusting a few men with his plans.

2:13 examining the walls of Jerusalem. He surveyed the walls at night, perhaps to make plans before he let others know his intentions. Either he inspected the entire wall or turned back when piles of rubble made the route impassable.

2:15 reentered through the Valley Gate. This was Nehemiah's starting point in the southwest wall, traveling through the gate into the Hinnon Valley.

up the valley by night, examining the wall. Finally, I turned back and reentered through the Valley Gate. [16]The officials did not know where I had gone or what I was doing, because as yet I had said nothing to the Jews or the priests or nobles or officials or any others who would be doing the work.

[17]Then I said to them, "You see the trouble we are in: Jerusalem lies in ruins, and its gates have been burned with fire. Come, let us rebuild the wall of Jerusalem, and we will no longer be in disgrace." [18]I also told them about the gracious hand of my God upon me and what the king had said to me.

They replied, "Let us start rebuilding." So they began this good work.

[19]But when Sanballat the Horonite, Tobiah the Ammonite official and Geshem the Arab heard about it, they mocked and ridiculed us. "What is this you are doing?" they asked. "Are you rebelling against the king?"

[20]I answered them by saying, "The God of heaven will give us success. We his servants will start rebuilding, but as for you, you have no share in Jerusalem or any claim or historic right to it."

Builders of the Wall

3 Eliashib the high priest and his fellow priests went to work and rebuilt the Sheep Gate. They dedicated it and set its doors in place, building as far as the Tower of the Hundred, which they dedicated, and as far as the Tower of Hananel. [2]The men of Jericho built the adjoining section, and Zaccur son of Imri built next to them.

[3]The Fish Gate was rebuilt by the sons of Hassenaah. They laid its beams and put its doors and bolts and bars in place. [4]Meremoth son of Uriah, the son of Hakkoz, repaired the next section. Next to him Meshullam son of Berekiah, the son of Meshezabel, made repairs, and next to him Zadok son of Baana also made repairs. [5]The next section was repaired by the men of Tekoa, but their nobles would not put their shoulders to the work under their supervisors.[a]

[6]The Jeshanah[b] Gate was repaired by Joiada son of Paseah and Meshullam son of Besodeiah. They laid its beams and put its doors and bolts and bars in place. [7]Next to them, repairs were made by men from Gibeon and Mizpah—Melatiah of Gibeon and Jadon of Meronoth—places under the authority of the governor of Trans-Euphrates.

[a]5 *Or their Lord or the governor* [b]6 *Or Old*

what would you have done first when arriving at Jerusalem? Why all the secrecy? **2.** At this point in the story, what is Nehemiah's greatest asset? His greatest weakness? **3.** Evaluate Nehemiah's speech in verses 17–18. What three key points does he make?

APPLY When is it hardest for you to act: When your project is in ruins? When your helpers are few? When others mock or ridicule your idea? When you have to buck "city hall"?

OPEN 1. Do you like to watch individual or team sports the most? Which do you like to play most? Why? **2.** What are five advantages of creating a project as a group? What are two or three potential difficulties?

STUDY The Jewish people were assigned areas of the Jerusalem wall to rebuild, mostly close to their personal dwellings. So, the families jumped into the work with diligence. **1.** Note the group of people who did the building. How many were professional builders? How many were working outside their "comfort zones"? What part of the wall would you have wanted to help repair? Why? **2.** Why do you think the people were assigned repair areas close to home: To cut down on travel expenses? To save time on lunch breaks? To make the work personal (they were helping to protect their own homes)? To keep mutiny at a minimum? **3.** The nobles of Tekoa (v. 5) refused to work. Why?

2:17 Jerusalem lies in ruins. The walls and gates had been destroyed by Nebuchadnezzar in 586 B.C. Although attempts had been made to repair them, the work had not been completed.

2:18 gracious hand of my God. Nehemiah combined challenge with encouragement. He urged the people to rebuild the wall, noting the disgrace and trouble resulting from its ruin. He reminded them that God would enable the work in the same way he had given Nehemiah favor with King Artaxerxes.

3:1 Eliashib the high priest and his fellow priests. A grandson of Jeshua, the high priest in Zerubbabel's day (Ezra 3:2). He and the other priests, as leaders of the people, started rebuilding the city walls. **rebuilt the Sheep Gate.** Used to bring sheep to the temple for sacrifice. The gate was on the city's northeast side, just north of the temple. **Tower of the Hundred ... Tower of Hananel.** Located between the Sheep Gate and the Fish Gate, the towers protected the city's northern approaches.

3:3 Fish Gate was rebuilt. Perhaps the gate through which people of Tyre brought fish to market. It may have been located near the site of the modern Damascus Gate.

3:5 men of Tekoa. Amos's hometown, about 12 miles south of Jerusalem. **but their nobles.** These men disdained manual labor and did not help with the work.

Why do you think Nehemiah published their names? How did their refusal affect the remaining Tekoa workers (vv. 5,27)? **4.** As you read this chapter, do you think Nehemiah would be a successful CEO at Microsoft or another Fortune 500 company? Why or why not? **5.** Nehemiah's name is left off the worker list. What was he probably doing while the people worked on the wall? **6.** Review this chapter as a group. Can you find three principles of working together that your group might adapt in reaching out to those who should be attending your group?

APPLY 1. When were you last asked to serve in a way that you didn't feel prepared for? What did you do? If you served, how were you trained? **2.** What attitudes or actions of Nehemiah's wall-builders fit followers of Christ who want to build his church? Which attitudes and actions should followers of Christ avoid? Which of those actions or attitudes should you demonstrate: At home? At work/school? At church? **3.** Is God calling you as a group to minister together? What might that ministry look like? How can each group member find a place on the team?

[8]Uzziel son of Harhaiah, one of the goldsmiths, repaired the next
section; and Hananiah, one of the perfume-makers, made repairs
next to that. They restored[a] Jerusalem as far as the Broad Wall.
[9]Rephaiah son of Hur, ruler of a half-district of Jerusalem, repaired
the next section. [10]Adjoining this, Jedaiah son of Harumaph made
repairs opposite his house, and Hattush son of Hashabneiah made
repairs next to him. [11]Malkijah son of Harim and Hasshub son of
Pahath-Moab repaired another section and the Tower of the Ovens.
[12]Shallum son of Hallohesh, ruler of a half-district of Jerusalem,
repaired the next section with the help of his daughters.

[13]The Valley Gate was repaired by Hanun and the residents of
Zanoah. They rebuilt it and put its doors and bolts and bars in place.
They also repaired five hundred yards[b] of the wall as far as the Dung
Gate.

[14]The Dung Gate was repaired by Malkijah son of Recab, ruler of
the district of Beth Hakkerem. He rebuilt it and put its doors and bolts
and bars in place.

[15]The Fountain Gate was repaired by Shallun son of Col-Hozeh, ruler of the district of Mizpah. He rebuilt it, roofing it over and putting its
doors and bolts and bars in place. He also repaired the wall of the Pool
of Siloam,[c] by the King's Garden, as far as the steps going down from
the City of David. [16]Beyond him, Nehemiah son of Azbuk, ruler of a
half-district of Beth Zur, made repairs up to a point opposite the
tombs[d] of David, as far as the artificial pool and the House of the
Heroes.
[17]Next to him, the repairs were made by the Levites under Rehum
son of Bani. Beside him, Hashabiah, ruler of half the district of Keilah, carried out repairs for his district. [18]Next to him, the repairs were
made by their countrymen under Binnui[e] son of Henadad, ruler of the
other half-district of Keilah. [19]Next to him, Ezer son of Jeshua, ruler
of Mizpah, repaired another section, from a point facing the ascent to
the armory as far as the angle. [20]Next to him, Baruch son of Zabbai
zealously repaired another section, from the angle to the entrance of
the house of Eliashib the high priest. [21]Next to him, Meremoth son of
Uriah, the son of Hakkoz, repaired another section, from the entrance of Eliashib's house to the end of it.
[22]The repairs next to him were made by the priests from the
surrounding region. [23]Beyond them, Benjamin and Hasshub made
repairs in front of their house; and next to them, Azariah son of Maaseiah, the son of Ananiah, made repairs beside his house. [24]Next to
him, Binnui son of Henadad repaired another section, from Azariah's
house to the angle and the corner, [25]and Palal son of Uzai worked
opposite the angle and the tower projecting from the upper palace

[a]8 Or *They left out part of* [b]13 Hebrew *a thousand cubits* (about 450 meters) [c]15 Hebrew *Shelah,* a variant of *Shiloah,* that is, Siloam [d]16 Hebrew; Septuagint, some Vulgate manuscripts and Syriac *tomb* [e]18 Two Hebrew manuscripts and Syriac (see also Septuagint and verse 24); most Hebrew manuscripts *Bavvai*

3:8 Broad Wall. Probably built by Hezekiah in the seventh century B.C. to accommodate the refugees arriving after the fall of Samaria in 722 B.C. (2 Chr. 32:5).

3:10 made repairs opposite his house. It would seem sensible to have the workers make the repairs closest to their homes. Even the priests were involved in the repairs (vv. 20,21).

3:28 Horse Gate. Located in the easternmost part of the city, this gate led to the Kidron Valley. It may have been an entrance for horses coming to the palace area.

near the court of the guard. Next to him, Pedaiah son of Parosh [26]and
the temple servants living on the hill of Ophel made repairs up to a
point opposite the Water Gate toward the east and the projecting
tower. [27]Next to them, the men of Tekoa repaired another section,
from the great projecting tower to the wall of Ophel.

[28]Above the Horse Gate, the priests made repairs, each in front of
his own house. [29]Next to them, Zadok son of Immer made repairs
opposite his house. Next to him, Shemaiah son of Shecaniah, the
guard at the East Gate, made repairs. [30]Next to him, Hananiah son of
Shelemiah, and Hanun, the sixth son of Zalaph, repaired another section. Next to them, Meshullam son of Berekiah made repairs opposite
his living quarters. [31]Next to him, Malkijah, one of the goldsmiths,
made repairs as far as the house of the temple servants and the merchants, opposite the Inspection Gate, and as far as the room above
the corner; [32]and between the room above the corner and the Sheep
Gate the goldsmiths and merchants made repairs.

Opposition to the Rebuilding

4 When Sanballat heard that we were rebuilding the wall, he became angry and was greatly incensed. He ridiculed the Jews,
[2]and in the presence of his associates and the army of Samaria, he
said, "What are those feeble Jews doing? Will they restore their wall?
Will they offer sacrifices? Will they finish in a day? Can they bring the
stones back to life from those heaps of rubble—burned as they are?"
[3]Tobiah the Ammonite, who was at his side, said, "What they are
building—if even a fox climbed up on it, he would break down their
wall of stones!"

[4]Hear us, O our God, for we are despised. Turn their insults back on
their own heads. Give them over as plunder in a land of captivity. [5]Do
not cover up their guilt or blot out their sins from your sight, for they
have thrown insults in the face of[a] the builders.

[6]So we rebuilt the wall till all of it reached half its height, for the
people worked with all their heart.
[7]But when Sanballat, Tobiah, the Arabs, the Ammonites and the
men of Ashdod heard that the repairs to Jerusalem's walls had gone
ahead and that the gaps were being closed, they were very angry.
[8]They all plotted together to come and fight against Jerusalem and
stir up trouble against it. [9]But we prayed to our God and posted a
guard day and night to meet this threat.
[10]Meanwhile, the people in Judah said, "The strength of the laborers

[a]5 *Or have provoked you to anger before*

OPEN What nickname did your childhood "friends" give you that was embarrassing? Was it something you did or the way you looked (such as "four-eyes" because you wore glasses) that caused the name-calling to start? How did the taunting affect you? What happened to stop the name-calling?

STUDY Each time the Jews started rebuilding, opposition came upon them. Sometimes the opposition was verbal, other times, such as in this chapter, the opposition included physical threats. **1.** Why do you think Sanballat was so opposed to the rebuilding of Jerusalem? How many different weapons did Sanballat's people use against the Jews? Which were probably most effective? **2.** Are you surprised at the tone of Nehemiah's prayer (vv. 4–5)? Why or why not? What do you think its impact was on the workers? **3.** Not only are there outside threats against the work, there are internal threats. What are they? Which type of threat is hardest to overcome? How does Nehemiah respond? How is he able to encourage the people? **4.** How does Nehemiah's strategy (vv. 13–23) foil

4:1 Sanballat. Probably from Beth-Horon, 15 miles northeast of Jerusalem, he was later called "governor of Samaria." He may have objected to Nehemiah's return and the reconstruction project because he wanted to gain control of Judah.

4:2 presence of his associates ... he said. Sanballat was upset when Nehemiah arrived in Jerusalem (2:10). He angrily ridiculed the Jews and accused them of rebelling against the king. **burned.** In his derisive tirade, Sanballat referred to burned, weakened bricks from the old, demolished wall.

4:4 Hear us, O our God. Nehemiah's consistent pattern was prayer before action. He immediately turned to God in the face of opposition.

4:9 prayed to our God and posted a guard. All those working on the wall joined in Nehemiah's prayer and then prepared to resist the attack.

4:10 strength ... is giving out. Posting a guard did not end the problem. The workers were exhausted, and the job was only half done. Discouragement set in.

both the internal and the external threats? How is defense of their own homes an important part of the strategy? Do you think Nehemiah was more a good manipulator or a good human resource person? **5.** When you read verse 23 what first thoughts come to your mind: The sweat smell—the need for a laundry? Nehemiah's commitment to "get down and dirty" with the people? A diligent leader in action? Why?

APPLY 1. When have you had a dream so big that it could only be accomplished if God performed a miracle? What was it? What happened to it? **2.** Are you more a "juggler" (trying to multi-task your life) or a "one-at-a-timer" (doing one thing at a time, in an orderly way)? Which juggling acts in verses 17 and 23 would have been the hardest for you to do? Why? **3.** What area of your life has so much "rubble" that you wonder if it can ever be repaired? How are you trying to cooperate with God and others to help build something beautiful out of your "rubble"?

is giving out, and there is so much rubble that we cannot rebuild the wall."

11 Also our enemies said, "Before they know it or see us, we will be right there among them and will kill them and put an end to the work."

12 Then the Jews who lived near them came and told us ten times over, "Wherever you turn, they will attack us."

13 Therefore I stationed some of the people behind the lowest points of the wall at the exposed places, posting them by families, with their swords, spears and bows.
14 After I looked things over, I stood up and said to the nobles, the officials and the rest of the people, "Don't be afraid of them. Remember the Lord, who is great and awesome, and fight for your brothers, your sons and your daughters, your wives and your homes."

15 When our enemies heard that we were aware of their plot and that God had frustrated it, we all returned to the wall, each to his own work.

16 From that day on, half of my men did the work, while the other half were equipped with spears, shields, bows and armor. The officers posted themselves behind all the people of Judah
17 who were building the wall. Those who carried materials did their work with one hand and held a weapon in the other,
18 and each of the builders wore his sword at his side as he worked. But the man who sounded the trumpet stayed with me.

19 Then I said to the nobles, the officials and the rest of the people, "The work is extensive and spread out, and we are widely separated from each other along the wall.
20 Wherever you hear the sound of the trumpet, join us there. Our God will fight for us!"

21 So we continued the work with half the men holding spears, from the first light of dawn till the stars came out.
22 At that time I also said to the people, "Have every man and his helper stay inside Jerusalem at night, so they can serve us as guards by night and workmen by day."
23 Neither I nor my brothers nor my men nor the guards with me took off our clothes; each had his weapon, even when he went for water.[a]

[a] 23 The meaning of the Hebrew for this clause is uncertain.

4:11 our enemies said. The opposition started rumors among the Jews to produce fear and weaken their resolve to complete the task. The rumors contained threats of a secret attack.

4:13 posting them by families. Placing whole families together, including women and children, was dangerous, but Nehemiah knew fathers would fight to protect their families. The Jews had no formal army to defend themselves.

4:14 Don't be afraid of them. Remember the LORD. Nehemiah encouraged the frightened people to remember God's strength and power. The enemies did not attack, and the work on the wall resumed.

4:17 work with one hand. Nehemiah armed the workers. Those who carried baskets of rubble on their heads held their weapons in one hand and balanced the baskets with the other. Half the men worked on the wall while the other half stood guard.

4:20 Our God will fight for us! Nehemiah combined faith and effort, trusting God to protect the workers. The trumpeter accompanied Nehemiah as he supervised the work. The trumpet blast served as a battle cry, summoning the people to the place of attack.

4:21 first light of dawn. The workers living outside the city did not return to their homes to sleep. They worked until well after sunset, and traveling at night was too dangerous.

4:23 even when he went for water. The urgency of the project required constant diligence and long, hard hours. The workers toiled night and day and remained armed at all times.

Nehemiah Helps the Poor

5 Now the men and their wives raised a great outcry against their
Jewish brothers. [2]Some were saying, "We and our sons and
daughters are numerous; in order for us to eat and stay alive, we
must get grain."
[3]Others were saying, "We are mortgaging our fields, our vineyards
and our homes to get grain during the famine."
[4]Still others were saying, "We have had to borrow money to pay the
king's tax on our fields and vineyards. [5]Although we are of the same
flesh and blood as our countrymen and though our sons are as good
as theirs, yet we have to subject our sons and daughters to slavery.
Some of our daughters have already been enslaved, but we are
powerless, because our fields and our vineyards belong to others."
[6]When I heard their outcry and these charges, I was very angry. [7]I
pondered them in my mind and then accused the nobles and officials.
I told them, "You are exacting usury from your own countrymen!" So
I called together a large meeting to deal with them [8]and said: "As far
as possible, we have bought back our Jewish brothers who were sold
to the Gentiles. Now you are selling your brothers, only for them to
be sold back to us!" They kept quiet, because they could find nothing
to say.
[9]So I continued, "What you are doing is not right. Shouldn't you
walk in the fear of our God to avoid the reproach of our Gentile enemies? [10]I and my brothers and my men are also lending the people
money and grain. But let the exacting of usury stop! [11]Give back to
them immediately their fields, vineyards, olive groves and houses,
and also the usury you are charging them—the hundredth part of the
money, grain, new wine and oil."
[12]"We will give it back," they said. "And we will not demand anything more from them. We will do as you say."
Then I summoned the priests and made the nobles and officials
take an oath to do what they had promised. [13]I also shook out the
folds of my robe and said, "In this way may God shake out of his
house and possessions every man who does not keep this promise.
So may such a man be shaken out and emptied!"
At this the whole assembly said, "Amen," and praised the LORD. And
the people did as they had promised.
[14]Moreover, from the twentieth year of King Artaxerxes, when I was
appointed to be their governor in the land of Judah, until his thirty-
second year—twelve years—neither I nor my brothers ate the food
allotted to the governor. [15]But the earlier governors—those preceding me—placed a heavy burden on the people and took forty shekels[a]

[a]15 That is, about 1 pound (about 0.5 kilogram)

OPEN In your growing up years, what kind of fighter were you (with siblings and others): Scrapper? Underdog? Topdog? Pit bull terrier?

STUDY Nehemiah discovered that the poorer Jews are being misused by their Jewish kin. Some were deep in debt, others in slavery. He challenged their system of usury and called for immediate restoration. **1.** What may have brought on the economic crisis facing the people in Jerusalem? Who was most affected by the crisis? How and when do you think this economic crisis became a "people crisis"? **2.** What would it feel like to be in debt to your sister or brother? What would it feel like to be a wealthy brother, holding the loan on your sister or brother? How would the debt affect your relationship? **3.** Try to put yourself in the place of those who were slaves. Even if your brother or sister treated you well, what might it feel like to know you were a slave to them? **4.** Why do you think Nehemiah was so adamant about resolving the problem? What impact would this problem have on finishing the wall? On building community? **5.** Are you surprised at the quick willingness of the rulers to follow Nehemiah's direction? Were they cowards? Were they afraid of Nehemiah's soldiers? Did they feel guilty? **6.** Nehemiah made major changes in the governor's office. What examples do you see of his wisdom? Would you have been more suspicious (wondering what he was trying to prove) or impressed (believing that he was setting a genuine example) by Nehemiah's actions? **7.** What "take away" principle or idea do you get from watching Nehemiah work through this difficult situation with his people?

APPLY **1.** In your life this past year, what crisis or problem (personal, financial, politics) has hindered your service to God and others? **2.** Nehemiah shows us an

5:1 men and their wives. Stress produced complaints. While working on the wall, families were unable to tend their crops. Complaints from within a group were as hard for leaders to deal with as outside opposition.

5:3 mortgaging our fields. Some workers had mortgaged their fields and vineyards to buy grain. The Jews charged each other exorbitant interest rates.

5:9 walk in the fear of our God to avoid the reproach. Nehemiah became angry, but instead of taking immediate action, he reflected on the problem and cooled down. He was then able to decide on a course of action. He exhorted the people to honor God during the difficult work.

5:10 But let the exacting of usury stop! As governor, Nehemiah could have acquired real estate and sold it at a profit. Instead, he lent money and grain to the people out of his personal resources. He did not ask the people to sacrifice for the work without setting an example of sacrifice.

5:14 twelve years. During his 12 years as governor, Nehemiah collected no taxes from the people, as he could have done.

example of serving God and others through personal sacrifice. When was the last time your beliefs really cost you something?

OPEN 1. When were you first able to tell the difference between the truth and a lie? **2.** Have you ever had someone start an untrue rumor about you? How did you stop it, or could you?

STUDY The wall was nearly completed so the enemies of the Jews made one last attempt to sabotage the project. Since they couldn't stop the building they seemed bent on killing Nehemiah the leader. **1.** If you had been Sanballat and his friends, why would you have been so desperate to "get" Nehemiah? What plan would you have put together? How would Nehemiah's death impact the people? **2.** How do you think Nehemiah knew that Sanballat was not really wanting to hold a peace conference? **3.** Note that Nehemiah kept focused on what was most important, refusing to be distracted by the opposition. What do you think helped him from getting sidetracked? Do you think his ability to stay focused was a personality strength or something else? How would you compare your ability to stay focused amid distractions? **4.**

of silver from them in addition to food and wine. Their assistants also lorded it over the people. But out of reverence for God I did not act like that. [16]Instead, I devoted myself to the work on this wall. All my men were assembled there for the work; we[a] did not acquire any land.

[17]Furthermore, a hundred and fifty Jews and officials ate at my table, as well as those who came to us from the surrounding nations. [18]Each day one ox, six choice sheep and some poultry were prepared for me, and every ten days an abundant supply of wine of all kinds. In spite of all this, I never demanded the food allotted to the governor, because the demands were heavy on these people.

[19]Remember me with favor, O my God, for all I have done for these people.

Further Opposition to the Rebuilding

6 When word came to Sanballat, Tobiah, Geshem the Arab and the rest of our enemies that I had rebuilt the wall and not a gap was left in it—though up to that time I had not set the doors in the gates—[2]Sanballat and Geshem sent me this message: "Come, let us meet together in one of the villages[b] on the plain of Ono."

But they were scheming to harm me; [3]so I sent messengers to them with this reply: "I am carrying on a great project and cannot go down. Why should the work stop while I leave it and go down to you?" [4]Four times they sent me the same message, and each time I gave them the same answer.

[5]Then, the fifth time, Sanballat sent his aide to me with the same message, and in his hand was an unsealed letter [6]in which was written:

> "It is reported among the nations—and Geshem[c] says it is true—that you and the Jews are plotting to revolt, and therefore you are building the wall. Moreover, according to these reports you are about to become their king [7]and have even appointed prophets to make this proclamation about you in Jerusalem: 'There is a king in Judah!' Now this report will get back to the king; so come, let us confer together."

[a]*16* Most Hebrew manuscripts; some Hebrew manuscripts, Septuagint, Vulgate and Syriac *I* [b]*2* Or *in Kephirim* [c]*6* Hebrew *Gashmu,* a variant of *Geshem*

5:16 devoted myself. He could have lent money with real estate as security, and then foreclosed when the people could not repay their debts. But Nehemiah remembered that his purpose was to help the people, not to exploit them. He was careful not to abuse his position as governor.

5:17 officials ate at my table. A ruler was expected to entertain lavishly. Nehemiah *served visiting officials from* his own food and wine.

5:18 the food allotted to the governor. Aware of the deprivations of his people, Nehemiah did not use the provisions to which he, as governor, would have been entitled.

6:2 let us meet together. When Nehemiah's enemies heard that the wall was nearly completed, they set a trap for him as another attempt to stop the work (Prov. 26:24–25). They invited him to meet them 25 miles northwest of Jerusalem, a day's *journey.*

6:3 Why should the work stop? Nehemiah wisely refused to leave the work unsupervised for he didn't want to be distracted, but he did not accuse his enemies outright of planning harm.

6:4 Four times they sent me. The adversaries were persistent and unyielding, and they revealed their true motives. If they sincerely wanted peace, they could have come to Jerusalem to meet him.

6:5 his hand was an unsealed letter. Failing to entice Nehemiah into their trap, the enemies resorted to accusations that Nehemiah planned to overthrow King Artaxerxes. Since the letter was unsealed, it was obviously meant to be read, and the rumor spread.

[8]I sent him this reply: "Nothing like what you are saying is happening; you are just making it up out of your head."

[9]They were all trying to frighten us, thinking, "Their hands will get too weak for the work, and it will not be completed."

⌊But I prayed,⌋ "Now strengthen my hands."

[10]One day I went to the house of Shemaiah son of Delaiah, the son of Mehetabel, who was shut in at his home. He said, "Let us meet in the house of God, inside the temple, and let us close the temple doors, because men are coming to kill you—by night they are coming to kill you."

[11]But I said, "Should a man like me run away? Or should one like me go into the temple to save his life? I will not go!" [12]I realized that God had not sent him, but that he had prophesied against me because Tobiah and Sanballat had hired him. [13]He had been hired to intimidate me so that I would commit a sin by doing this, and then they would give me a bad name to discredit me.

[14]Remember Tobiah and Sanballat, O my God, because of what they have done; remember also the prophetess Noadiah and the rest of the prophets who have been trying to intimidate me.

The Completion of the Wall

[15]So the wall was completed on the twenty-fifth of Elul, in fifty-two days. [16]When all our enemies heard about this, all the surrounding nations were afraid and lost their self-confidence, because they realized that this work had been done with the help of our God.

[17]Also, in those days the nobles of Judah were sending many letters to Tobiah, and replies from Tobiah kept coming to them. [18]For many in Judah were under oath to him, since he was son-in-law to Shecaniah son of Arah, and his son Jehohanan had married the daughter of Meshullam son of Berekiah. [19]Moreover, they kept reporting to me his good deeds and then telling him what I said. And Tobiah sent letters to intimidate me.

7 After the wall had been rebuilt and I had set the doors in place, the gatekeepers and the singers and the Levites were appointed. [2]I put in charge of Jerusalem my brother Hanani, along with[a] Hananiah the commander of the citadel, because he was a man of integrity and feared God more than most men do. [3]I said to them, "The gates of Jerusalem are not to be opened until the sun is hot. While the gatekeepers are still on duty, have them shut the doors and bar them. Also

[a]2 Or *Hanani, that is,*

What do you think was the point of the unsealed letter (vv. 5–7)? Do you think Nehemiah was intimidated by it? Why or why not? How did he respond to the threats and rumors?

APPLY Reviewing Nehemiah's response to rumors and slander, what principles do you discover for handling the situation when it comes to you next time?

OPEN What was the last project you completed that you thought would never get done?

STUDY It's done! And in record time. The wall was completed and gates installed in only 52 days. **1.** Reading between the lines, what do you think accounts for the amazing speed with which the wall was completed? **2.** Note the plan and the people that Nehemiah put into place to provide Jerusalem's security. What about his plan is well thought out and timely for the situation? What wisdom do you see in Nehemiah's choices?

APPLY How do you set your daily priorities for God, family, work, school? Where do you need God's and the group's help to be more accountable?

6:8 you are just making it up. Nehemiah's response is bold and direct. He explained the lie to the Jewish workers. He also prayed for strength.

6:10 Shemaiah ... was shut in. To lure Nehemiah into the temple, his enemies hired this priest who claimed to be a prophet. He tried to frighten Nehemiah into hiding from assassins in the holy place, which was forbidden by the Law (Num. 3:10; 18:7).

6:11 I will not go! He realized that God would not tell him to flee when the wall was nearly completed.

6:12 God had not sent him. Nehemiah knew that a true prophet would not advise someone to desecrate the sanctuary by disobeying the Law.

6:13 discredit me. Nehemiah recognized the danger to the project if he were to run and hide out of fear. Morale among the people would have plummeted.

6:15 wall was completed. After lying in ruins for almost 150 years, the walls were rebuilt in less than two months. Nehemiah's trip to Jerusalem probably took longer than the building project itself.

6:17 Tobiah. Many Jews traded with Tobiah and tried to convince Nehemiah of his loyalty to the project. Both his father-in-law, Shecaniah son of Arah, and his daughter-in-law, daughter of Meshullam son of Berekiah (3:4,30), worked on two sections of the wall. But Tobiah opposed the work.

appoint residents of Jerusalem as guards, some at their posts and
some near their own houses."

The List of the Exiles Who Returned

[4]Now the city was large and spacious, but there were few people in
it, and the houses had not yet been rebuilt. [5]So my God put it into my
heart to assemble the nobles, the officials and the common people
for registration by families. I found the genealogical record of those
who had been the first to return. This is what I found written there:

[6]These are the people of the province who came up from the
captivity of the exiles whom Nebuchadnezzar king of Babylon
had taken captive (they returned to Jerusalem and Judah, each to
his own town, [7]in company with Zerubbabel, Jeshua, Nehemiah,
Azariah, Raamiah, Nahamani, Mordecai, Bilshan, Mispereth,
Bigvai, Nehum and Baanah):

The list of the men of Israel:

[8]the descendants of Parosh	2,172
[9]of Shephatiah	372
[10]of Arah	652
[11]of Pahath-Moab (through the line of Jeshua and Joab)	2,818
[12]of Elam	1,254
[13]of Zattu	845
[14]of Zaccai	760
[15]of Binnui	648
[16]of Bebai	628
[17]of Azgad	2,322
[18]of Adonikam	667
[19]of Bigvai	2,067
[20]of Adin	655
[21]of Ater (through Hezekiah)	98
[22]of Hashum	328
[23]of Bezai	324
[24]of Hariph	112
[25]of Gibeon	95
[26]the men of Bethlehem and Netophah	188
[27]of Anathoth	128
[28]of Beth Azmaveth	42
[29]of Kiriath Jearim, Kephirah and Beeroth	743
[30]of Ramah and Geba	621
[31]of Micmash	122
[32]of Bethel and Ai	123
[33]of the other Nebo	52
[34]of the other Elam	1,254
[35]of Harim	320
[36]of Jericho	345
[37]of Lod, Hadid and Ono	721
[38]of Senaah	3,930

[39]The priests:

the descendants of Jedaiah (through the family of Jeshua)	973

OPEN 1. Who were you named after? When you gave your name to the teacher on the first day of seventh grade were you embarrassed or proud? Why? **2.** Have you explored your family tree? What is the best part? To what part do you wish you were not related?

STUDY Now that the city walls were completed, there were not many people to live in the city. So, Nehemiah developed a repopulation plan. He started by digging out the old genealogical records to find out where past generations had lived. **1.** If you were a Jew in the time of Nehemiah, why do you think a family record would be important? **2.** The record reported here is almost the same as that in Ezra 2. (Note: Some variance in the names and numbers between the two lists may be due to the different functions of the genealogies.) As you compare the two lists, what difference in the function of the genealogies do you notice? What does this tell you about the importance of Jerusalem to God and his people? **3.** As you read through the list of names do you feel more like you're walking through a cemetery or you're connecting to people who will make a difference in history? **4.** If you were trying to repopulate a city what kinds of people would you want and what skills would you want them to have? How does this list compare to yours? **5.** Why do you think it was important to count the livestock, precious metals and utensils: To impress the investors supporting this project? To check the tax potential of each person's "financial holdings"? To get enough barns built? To evaluate God's blessing? **6.** What would you have done if you couldn't find your family record like the families in verse 64? How would you have felt? Would you have stayed in Jerusalem or gone back to your village?

APPLY 1. Do you keep a record of your family, memorabilia or pictures? Why are they important to you? What do they tell you about your heritage? **2.** Who has been a mentor in your spiritual journey? What has been their influence on you? *Who are you influencing spiritually?* What is the one most important thing to pass on to them? How are you being intentional in passing it on?

[40]of Immer 1,052
[41]of Pashhur 1,247
[42]of Harim 1,017

[43]The Levites:

the descendants of Jeshua (through Kadmiel through the line of Hodaviah) 74

[44]The singers:

the descendants of Asaph 148

[45]The gatekeepers:

the descendants of
Shallum, Ater, Talmon, Akkub, Hatita and Shobai 138

[46]The temple servants:

the descendants of
Ziha, Hasupha, Tabbaoth,
[47]Keros, Sia, Padon,
[48]Lebana, Hagaba, Shalmai,
[49]Hanan, Giddel, Gahar,
[50]Reaiah, Rezin, Nekoda,
[51]Gazzam, Uzza, Paseah,
[52]Besai, Meunim, Nephussim,
[53]Bakbuk, Hakupha, Harhur,
[54]Bazluth, Mehida, Harsha,
[55]Barkos, Sisera, Temah,
[56]Neziah and Hatipha

[57]The descendants of the servants of Solomon:

the descendants of
Sotai, Sophereth, Perida,
[58]Jaala, Darkon, Giddel,
[59]Shephatiah, Hattil,
Pokereth-Hazzebaim and Amon

[60]The temple servants and the descendants of the servants of Solomon 392

[61]The following came up from the towns of Tel Melah, Tel Harsha, Kerub, Addon and Immer, but they could not show that their families were descended from Israel:

[62]the descendants of
Delaiah, Tobiah and Nekoda 642

[63]And from among the priests:

the descendants of
Hobaiah, Hakkoz and Barzillai (a man who had married a daughter of Barzillai the Gileadite and was called by that name).

[64]These searched for their family records, but they could not find them and so were excluded from the priesthood as unclean.
[65]The governor, therefore, ordered them not to eat any of the most sacred food until there should be a priest ministering with the Urim and Thummim.

66 The whole company numbered 42,360, 67 besides their 7,337 menservants and maidservants; and they also had 245 men and women singers. 68 There were 736 horses, 245 mules,[a] 69 435 camels and 6,720 donkeys.

70 Some of the heads of the families contributed to the work. The governor gave to the treasury 1,000 drachmas[b] of gold, 50 bowls and 530 garments for priests. 71 Some of the heads of the families gave to the treasury for the work 20,000 drachmas[c] of gold and 2,200 minas[d] of silver. 72 The total given by the rest of the people was 20,000 drachmas of gold, 2,000 minas[e] of silver and 67 garments for priests.

73 The priests, the Levites, the gatekeepers, the singers and the temple servants, along with certain of the people and the rest of the Israelites, settled in their own towns.

Ezra Reads the Law

When the seventh month came and the Israelites had settled in their towns,

8 1 all the people assembled as one man in the square before the Water Gate. They told Ezra the scribe to bring out the Book of the Law of Moses, which the LORD had commanded for Israel.

2 So on the first day of the seventh month Ezra the priest brought the Law before the assembly, which was made up of men and women and all who were able to understand. 3 He read it aloud from daybreak till noon as he faced the square before the Water Gate in the presence of the men, women and others who could understand. And all the people listened attentively to the Book of the Law.

4 Ezra the scribe stood on a high wooden platform built for the occasion. Beside him on his right stood Mattithiah, Shema, Anaiah, Uriah, Hilkiah and Maaseiah; and on his left were Pedaiah, Mishael, Malkijah, Hashum, Hashbaddanah, Zechariah and Meshullam.

5 Ezra opened the book. All the people could see him because he was standing above them; and as he opened it, the people all stood up. 6 Ezra praised the LORD, the great God; and all the people lifted their hands and responded, "Amen! Amen!" Then they bowed down and worshiped the LORD with their faces to the ground.

7 The Levites—Jeshua, Bani, Sherebiah, Jamin, Akkub, Shabbethai, Hodiah, Maaseiah, Kelita, Azariah, Jozabad, Hanan and Pelaiah—instructed the people in the Law while the people were standing there. 8 They read from the Book of the Law of God, making it clear[f] and giving the meaning so that the people could understand what was being read.

[a] *68* Some Hebrew manuscripts (see also Ezra 2:66); most Hebrew manuscripts do not have this verse. [b] *70* That is, about 19 pounds (about 8.5 kilograms) [c] *71* That is, about 375 pounds (about 170 kilograms); also in verse 72 [d] *71* That is, about 1 1/3 tons (about 1.2 metric tons) [e] *72* That is, about 1 1/4 tons (about 1.1 metric tons) [f] *8* Or *God, translating it*

OPEN **1.** Have you attended a high school or college reunion? What do you notice most about your former classmates? Who has changed the most from the yearbook picture, you or them? Why do you think so? **2.** When you meet old friends after a long time apart, what do you talk about: Family? Job? Politics? Spiritual faith?

STUDY Life was back to normal in the old homeland so the Israelites came together for a great feast. But before the party could get started the people called for Ezra, the prophet, to read God's Law to them. **1.** Why do you think the people were intent on hearing God's Law read? Why didn't they read it for themselves? How could Ezra be heard with no microphone? What kept his voice from tiring out? **2.** As you read verses 4–9, what things do the people do that are like a worship service at your church? How are they different? How do you think the years of building the temple and the wall, together, affected the Jews deep emotions in response to hearing God's Law? **3.** Part of this account (vv. 8–9) sounds like a great Bible study? Why do you think the people had to be instructed? Could they not have learned on their own? How does this remind you of your group time, except on a large-scale? **4.** When the second gathering happened (vv. 13–15), who came to

---

8:1 all the people assembled as one man. The people from the cities *and countryside of Judah* gathered together to hear Ezra read and teach the Law in the five books of Moses (Deut. 31:11-12). **Water Gate.** They met in an open square between the southeast part of the temple and the eastern wall.

8:2 first day of the seventh month Ezra the priest. Taking place in the September-October period, this was the Feast of Trumpets, where work stopped and a sacred assembly took place.

8:3 read it aloud from daybreak till noon. Adults and children who were old enough to understand (vv. 2-3) stood and listened attentively all morning.

9 Then Nehemiah the governor, Ezra the priest and scribe, and the
Levites who were instructing the people said to them all, "This day is
sacred to the LORD your God. Do not mourn or weep." For all the
people had been weeping as they listened to the words of the Law.
10 Nehemiah said, "Go and enjoy choice food and sweet drinks, and
send some to those who have nothing prepared. This day is sacred to
our Lord. Do not grieve, for the joy of the LORD is your strength."
11 The Levites calmed all the people, saying, "Be still, for this is a
sacred day. Do not grieve."
12 Then all the people went away to eat and drink, to send portions
of food and to celebrate with great joy, because they now understood
the words that had been made known to them.
13 On the second day of the month, the heads of all the families,
along with the priests and the Levites, gathered around Ezra the
scribe to give attention to the words of the Law. 14 They found written
in the Law, which the LORD had commanded through Moses, that the
Israelites were to live in booths during the feast of the seventh month
15 and that they should proclaim this word and spread it throughout
their towns and in Jerusalem: "Go out into the hill country and bring
back branches from olive and wild olive trees, and from myrtles,
palms and shade trees, to make booths"—as it is written.[a]
16 So the people went out and brought back branches and built
themselves booths on their own roofs, in their courtyards, in the
courts of the house of God and in the square by the Water Gate and
the one by the Gate of Ephraim. 17 The whole company that had returned from exile built booths and lived in them. From the days of
Joshua son of Nun until that day, the Israelites had not celebrated it
like this. And their joy was very great.
18 Day after day, from the first day to the last, Ezra read from the
Book of the Law of God. They celebrated the feast for seven days, and
on the eighth day, in accordance with the regulation, there was an
assembly.

The Israelites Confess Their Sins

9 On the twenty-fourth day of the same month, the Israelites
gathered together, fasting and wearing sackcloth and having
dust on their heads. 2 Those of Israelite descent had separated themselves from all foreigners. They stood in their places and confessed
their sins and the wickedness of their fathers. 3 They stood where they
were and read from the Book of the Law of the LORD their God for a
quarter of the day, and spent another quarter in confession and in
worshiping the LORD their God. 4 Standing on the stairs were the

[a] *15* See Lev. 23:37-40.

it? Why do you think the crowd was different? What do you think about the plan to "distribute the information"? Was it more effective than the first gathering or not? Why? **5.** If you and your family had come home from a distant prison camp, how would your attitudes and actions have been compared with that of the Jews? Can you identify with their deep joy? What "life-application" idea do you find in this chapter?

APPLY 1. How important is study and reading of the Bible in your spiritual journey? Which is most helpful: Personal or group study? Why? **2.** Can you think of a time when you were studying the Bible alone or with a group and you experienced great grief or great joy? What happened? What difference did those moments make in your long-term spiritual life? **3.** What three activities described in this chapter could be foundational in the renewal of your own life? Your church? How might your group help make it happen?

OPEN 1. What comes to your mind when you think of confession: A chance to start over? Spine-tingling dread? A special room? An important person? A fear of God? **2.** Have you ever written down a prayer? Why? If so, what made the moment important enough to preserve it in writing?

STUDY After separating themselves from the non-Jews, the Israelites gathered, wearing

8:10 Go and enjoy choice food. When they heard the Law read and explained, the people wept and repented of their sins. While Nehemiah was undoubtedly pleased by their response, he reminded them that it was a time to celebrate with feasting.

8:16 courts ... square. The priests and Levites built their booths in the courts of the temple. Residents of the cities built booths (temporary shelters for the feast) on the flat roofs of their houses or in the courtyards. People from the countryside set up huts in the streets. Booths commemorated the time of wandering in the wilderness when the people had no permanent homes (Lev. 23:43).

8:17 the days of Joshua ... until that day. The joy and involvement of this celebration was unmatched since Joshua's day, since the people themselves had helped reconstruct the walls.

9:1 fasting ... sackcloth ... dust. These actions symbolized remorse and grief over sin. Sackcloth was a dark, coarse cloth made from goat's hair (Ps. 30:11; 35:13). Dust referred to ashes (1 Sam. 4:12).

sackcloth and ashes as a symbol of sorrow for their sins. The leaders then guided them through a day of reading the Law, praying and worship. **1.** As you read through the prayer, what emotions do you feel? If you were to write a song describing this day, what would you title it? Would it contain a celebration of God's goodness or grief for the people's sin? **2.** The prayer recounts God's hand at work throughout history. Why do you think they retold the story as part of this prayer: God needed reminding? The people needed reminding? Both? Note the contrast between God's goodness and the people's rebellion. Why do you think the people kept turning against God when God continued to care for them? **3.** How do you think God should respond to the plight of the Jews? Should he say, "I've had enough" or should he forgive and forget, again? What restrictions should he put on the people this time if he removes the kings who rule their land? **4.** Do you think the Jews are truly repentant this time? Why or why not? **5.** What new thoughts about God's care have you learned by reading this passage? What old ideas, that you once knew, have been brought back to memory?

APPLY 1. Can you tell the group about the last time you needed to ask forgiveness but didn't want to: Were you afraid to do it because you didn't want to get caught or were you too embarrassed for doing something "stupid"? Neither? What happened to bring resolution? **2.** As a group, write a prayer that includes ways that you have seen God work, from creation until today. Then include those things that you as group members have done wrong or against God. Close with a celebration in God's love and forgiveness.

Levites—Jeshua, Bani, Kadmiel, Shebaniah, Bunni, Sherebiah, Bani
and Kenani—who called with loud voices to the LORD their God.
5And the Levites—Jeshua, Kadmiel, Bani, Hashabneiah, Sherebiah,
Hodiah, Shebaniah and Pethahiah—said: "Stand up and praise the
LORD your God, who is from everlasting to everlasting.[a]"

"Blessed be your glorious name, and may it be exalted above
all blessing and praise. 6You alone are the LORD. You made the
heavens, even the highest heavens, and all their starry host, the
earth and all that is on it, the seas and all that is in them. You
give life to everything, and the multitudes of heaven worship
you.

7"You are the LORD God, who chose Abram and brought him
out of Ur of the Chaldeans and named him Abraham. 8You found
his heart faithful to you, and you made a covenant with him to
give to his descendants the land of the Canaanites, Hittites, Amorites, Perizzites, Jebusites and Girgashites. You have kept your
promise because you are righteous.

9"You saw the suffering of our forefathers in Egypt; you heard
their cry at the Red Sea.[b] 10You sent miraculous signs and wonders against Pharaoh, against all his officials and all the people
of his land, for you knew how arrogantly the Egyptians treated
them. You made a name for yourself, which remains to this day.
11You divided the sea before them, so that they passed through it
on dry ground, but you hurled their pursuers into the depths, like
a stone into mighty waters. 12By day you led them with a pillar of
cloud, and by night with a pillar of fire to give them light on the
way they were to take.

13"You came down on Mount Sinai; you spoke to them from
heaven. You gave them regulations and laws that are just and
right, and decrees and commands that are good. 14You made
known to them your holy Sabbath and gave them commands,
decrees and laws through your servant Moses. 15In their hunger
you gave them bread from heaven and in their thirst you brought
them water from the rock; you told them to go in and take possession of the land you had sworn with uplifted hand to give
them.

16"But they, our forefathers, became arrogant and stiff-necked,
and did not obey your commands. 17They refused to listen and
failed to remember the miracles you performed among them.
They became stiff-necked and in their rebellion appointed a
leader in order to return to their slavery. But you are a forgiving
God, gracious and compassionate, slow to anger and abounding
in love. Therefore you did not desert them, 18even when they cast
for themselves an image of a calf and said, 'This is your god, who
brought you up out of Egypt,' or when they committed awful
blasphemies.

[a]5 Or *God for ever and ever* [b]9 Hebrew *Yam Suph*; that is, Sea of Reeds

9:5 your glorious name. The importance of God's name is based in the Law. The Levites recited historical instances of God's goodness to the Jews. They recalled the covenant and its stipulation of obedience.

9:16 our forefathers became arrogant and stiff-necked. The Levites' prayer extolled God's graciousness and compassion, even in the face of disobedience and idol worship (Ex. 32). The priests emphasized that although God's people had rebelled, God mercifully forgave them and restored them to the land.

19"Because of your great compassion you did not abandon them in the desert. By day the pillar of cloud did not cease to guide them on their path, nor the pillar of fire by night to shine on the way they were to take. 20You gave your good Spirit to instruct them. You did not withhold your manna from their mouths, and you gave them water for their thirst. 21For forty years you sustained them in the desert; they lacked nothing, their clothes did not wear out nor did their feet become swollen.

22"You gave them kingdoms and nations, allotting to them even the remotest frontiers. They took over the country of Sihon[a] king of Heshbon and the country of Og king of Bashan. 23You made their sons as numerous as the stars in the sky, and you brought them into the land that you told their fathers to enter and possess. 24Their sons went in and took possession of the land. You subdued before them the Canaanites, who lived in the land; you handed the Canaanites over to them, along with their kings and the peoples of the land, to deal with them as they pleased. 25They captured fortified cities and fertile land; they took possession of houses filled with all kinds of good things, wells already dug, vineyards, olive groves and fruit trees in abundance. They ate to the full and were well-nourished; they reveled in your great goodness.

26"But they were disobedient and rebelled against you; they put your law behind their backs. They killed your prophets, who had admonished them in order to turn them back to you; they committed awful blasphemies. 27So you handed them over to their enemies, who oppressed them. But when they were oppressed they cried out to you. From heaven you heard them, and in your great compassion you gave them deliverers, who rescued them from the hand of their enemies.

28"But as soon as they were at rest, they again did what was evil in your sight. Then you abandoned them to the hand of their enemies so that they ruled over them. And when they cried out to you again, you heard from heaven, and in your compassion you delivered them time after time.

29"You warned them to return to your law, but they became arrogant and disobeyed your commands. They sinned against your ordinances, by which a man will live if he obeys them. Stubbornly they turned their backs on you, became stiff-necked and refused to listen. 30For many years you were patient with them. By your Spirit you admonished them through your prophets. Yet they paid no attention, so you handed them over to the neighboring peoples. 31But in your great mercy you did not put an end to them or abandon them, for you are a gracious and merciful God.

32"Now therefore, O our God, the great, mighty and awesome God, who keeps his covenant of love, do not let all this hardship seem trifling in your eyes—the hardship that has come upon us, upon our kings and leaders, upon our priests and prophets, upon our fathers and all your people, from the days of the kings of Assyria until today. 33In all that has happened to us, you have been just; you have acted faithfully, while we did wrong. 34Our

[a]22 One Hebrew manuscript and Septuagint; most Hebrew manuscripts *Sihon, that is, the country of the*

kings, our leaders, our priests and our fathers did not follow
your law; they did not pay attention to your commands or the
warnings you gave them. 35Even while they were in their kingdom, enjoying your great goodness to them in the spacious and
fertile land you gave them, they did not serve you or turn from
their evil ways.

36"But see, we are slaves today, slaves in the land you gave our
forefathers so they could eat its fruit and the other good things it
produces. 37Because of our sins, its abundant harvest goes to the
kings you have placed over us. They rule over our bodies and our
cattle as they please. We are in great distress.

The Agreement of the People

38"In view of all this, we are making a binding agreement, putting it
in writing, and our leaders, our Levites and our priests are affixing
their seals to it."

10 Those who sealed it were:

Nehemiah the governor, the son of Hacaliah.

Zedekiah, 2Seraiah, Azariah, Jeremiah,
3Pashhur, Amariah, Malkijah,
4Hattush, Shebaniah, Malluch,
5Harim, Meremoth, Obadiah,
6Daniel, Ginnethon, Baruch,
7Meshullam, Abijah, Mijamin,
8Maaziah, Bilgai and Shemaiah.
These were the priests.

9The Levites:

Jeshua son of Azaniah, Binnui of the sons of Henadad, Kadmiel,
10and their associates: Shebaniah,
Hodiah, Kelita, Pelaiah, Hanan,
11Mica, Rehob, Hashabiah,
12Zaccur, Sherebiah, Shebaniah,
13Hodiah, Bani and Beninu.

14The leaders of the people:

Parosh, Pahath-Moab, Elam, Zattu, Bani,
15Bunni, Azgad, Bebai,
16Adonijah, Bigvai, Adin,
17Ater, Hezekiah, Azzur,
18Hodiah, Hashum, Bezai,
19Hariph, Anathoth, Nebai,
20Magpiash, Meshullam, Hezir,
21Meshezabel, Zadok, Jaddua,
22Pelatiah, Hanan, Anaiah,
23Hoshea, Hananiah, Hasshub,
24Hallohesh, Pilha, Shobek,
25Rehum, Hashabnah, Maaseiah,

OPEN **1.** What is the most important contract you've ever signed? How did you feel after the reality of signing settled in? Were you more delighted (because the deal was closed) or sick (because you'd spent all that money)? **2.** Was it important to you that the contract was written and signed rather than a verbal agreement? Why?

STUDY At the conclusion of worship and confession the people put down in writing their commitment to follow the Law given by God. They "bind themselves" (v. 29) together with a contract to not only follow God's ways in life and family but to care for the temple. **1.** Compare the list of names here with the list in chapter seven. What do you think these lists tell us about the commitment of all the people to follow God? Why is it important for the whole community to join in this contract? **2.** When you read the specific details in verses 30–39, what first comes to mind? Why do you think it was important to put so much into writing? Didn't the people already have the Law which Ezra had read to them? **3.** What do you think the people were learning about stewardship of life by promising to take turns in caring for the temple (vv. 32–39)? How might this plan affect their children's view of God, particularly the boys (v. 36)? **4.** Do you think the people complained about this tax of their money and crops? Why or why not? How does participation by the whole group make it easier to join in? **5.** Can you find three principles in this covenant that you think could work in today's world, to make it better?

APPLY **1.** Are there any agreements like the *one in*

10:1-8 Those who sealed it were. Twenty-four heads of families signed the agreement to obey the Law. A distinctive seal authenticating the document was pressed into soft clay, similar to the later use of sealing wax.

[26]Ahiah, Hanan, Anan,
[27]Malluch, Harim and Baanah.

[28]"The rest of the people—priests, Levites, gatekeepers, singers, temple servants and all who separated themselves from the
neighboring peoples for the sake of the Law of God, together
with their wives and all their sons and daughters who are able to
understand— [29]all these now join their brothers the nobles, and
bind themselves with a curse and an oath to follow the Law of
God given through Moses the servant of God and to obey carefully all the commands, regulations and decrees of the LORD our
Lord.
[30]"We promise not to give our daughters in marriage to the
peoples around us or take their daughters for our sons.
[31]"When the neighboring peoples bring merchandise or grain
to sell on the Sabbath, we will not buy from them on the Sabbath
or on any holy day. Every seventh year we will forgo working the
land and will cancel all debts.
[32]"We assume the responsibility for carrying out the commands to give a third of a shekel[a] each year for the service of the
house of our God: [33]for the bread set out on the table; for the
regular grain offerings and burnt offerings; for the offerings on
the Sabbaths, New Moon festivals and appointed feasts; for the
holy offerings; for sin offerings to make atonement for Israel;
and for all the duties of the house of our God.
[34]"We—the priests, the Levites and the people—have cast lots
to determine when each of our families is to bring to the house
of our God at set times each year a contribution of wood to burn
on the altar of the LORD our God, as it is written in the Law.
[35]"We also assume responsibility for bringing to the house of
the LORD each year the firstfruits of our crops and of every fruit
tree.
[36]"As it is also written in the Law, we will bring the firstborn of
our sons and of our cattle, of our herds and of our flocks to the
house of our God, to the priests ministering there.
[37]"Moreover, we will bring to the storerooms of the house of
our God, to the priests, the first of our ground meal, of our ⌞grain⌟
offerings, of the fruit of all our trees and of our new wine and oil.
And we will bring a tithe of our crops to the Levites, for it is the
Levites who collect the tithes in all the towns where we work. [38]A
priest descended from Aaron is to accompany the Levites when
they receive the tithes, and the Levites are to bring a tenth of the
tithes up to the house of our God, to the storerooms of the treasury. [39]The people of Israel, including the Levites, are to bring

[a]32 That is, about 1/8 ounce (about 4 grams)

this chapter that we as followers of Christ enter into (such as pledges, doctrinal statements, marriage vows, etc.)? Are any of these agreements done in writing? Would it make a difference in how seriously they are followed? **2.** As you look back over the verses on giving (vv. 32–39) how do you think the ideas described there could be lived out in the church today? How might it affect your personal life? Do you think stewardship of your possessions is an accurate barometer of your commitment to God? **3.** Where does your church need your help? The help of your group?

10:31–33 Sabbath. The agreement spelled out the leaders' commitment to avoid intermarriage, keep the Sabbath by refraining from work (Ex. 20:10) and provide for the needs of the temple. **seventh year ... forgo working the land ... cancel all debts.** Fields were to be left uncultivated and debts forgiven every seventh year (Lev. 25:1–7).

10:35 firstfruits of our crops. This means giving to the Lord from the first and best crops to acknowledge that God owns the land. Firstfruits of the trees meant giving over and above what the Law required to provide wood to keep the altar fire burning constantly (Lev. 6:12-13).

10:37 bring to the storerooms. The precious metals and temple articles were stored in rooms in the temple courts.

OPEN 1. When did you last volunteer for community service? What was it for? When you think of volunteering again: Are you more like a cheetah ("not again, let me out of here")? Pet dog ("sure, I'll be here no matter what")? Someplace in between? **2.** Have you ever lived in a setting (college dorm, rough neighborhood, etc.) where you thought you deserved "hazardous duty" pay?

STUDY The people were reluctant to leave their villages and towns to repopulate the newly rebuilt Jerusalem so Nehemiah instituted a form of "draft." **1.** Why do you think Nehemiah wanted the newly walled city filled with people? Do you think his plan is fair to the people, even though they got great recognition by having their names listed in the Bible? Who do you feel sorry for the most: Those who had to move or the families left behind? Why? **2.** What types of people seemed to "volunteer" to move back to the city: Mostly men? Temple workers? Mostly women? Young urban professionals? Stockbrokers? Why was it important for the various groups to be there? **3.** Many more priests, the leaders of worship, moved back into the city than Levites, (the temple custodians). Why do you think that happened? Did the Levites prefer the "good life" out in the villages or was it something else? **4.** Most of the people stayed in the villages and rural settings. When you compare their setting to the rural people of your country, why do you think it was important for most people to stay outside of Jerusalem? **5.** Do you think the people who moved back to Jerusalem were more committed to God than those who stayed in the villages? Why or why not?

APPLY 1. If God asked you to relocate so you could be more effective in your ministry, where would be the hardest place to go? Why? How do you think you would respond? **2.** What is the "city" in your area that

their contributions of grain, new wine and oil to the storerooms where the articles for the sanctuary are kept and where the ministering priests, the gatekeepers and the singers stay.

"We will not neglect the house of our God."

The New Residents of Jerusalem

11 Now the leaders of the people settled in Jerusalem, and the rest of the people cast lots to bring one out of every ten to live in Jerusalem, the holy city, while the remaining nine were to stay in their own towns. 2 The people commended all the men who volunteered to live in Jerusalem.

3 These are the provincial leaders who settled in Jerusalem (now some Israelites, priests, Levites, temple servants and descendants of Solomon's servants lived in the towns of Judah, each on his own property in the various towns, 4 while other people from both Judah and Benjamin lived in Jerusalem):

From the descendants of Judah:

Athaiah son of Uzziah, the son of Zechariah, the son of Amariah, the son of Shephatiah, the son of Mahalalel, a descendant of Perez; 5 and Maaseiah son of Baruch, the son of Col-Hozeh, the son of Hazaiah, the son of Adaiah, the son of Joiarib, the son of Zechariah, a descendant of Shelah. 6 The descendants of Perez who lived in Jerusalem totaled 468 able men.

7 From the descendants of Benjamin:

Sallu son of Meshullam, the son of Joed, the son of Pedaiah, the son of Kolaiah, the son of Maaseiah, the son of Ithiel, the son of Jeshaiah, 8 and his followers, Gabbai and Sallai—928 men. 9 Joel son of Zicri was their chief officer, and Judah son of Hassenuah was over the Second District of the city.

10 From the priests:

Jedaiah; the son of Joiarib; Jakin; 11 Seraiah son of Hilkiah, the son of Meshullam, the son of Zadok, the son of Meraioth, the son of Ahitub, supervisor in the house of God, 12 and their associates, who carried on work for the temple—822 men; Adaiah son of Jeroham, the son of Pelaliah, the son of Amzi, the son of Zechariah, the son of Pashhur, the son of Malkijah, 13 and his associates, who were heads of families—242 men; Amashsai son of Azarel, the son of Ahzai, the son of Meshillemoth, the son of Immer, 14 and his[a] associates, who were able men—128. Their chief officer was Zabdiel son of Haggedolim.

15 From the Levites:

Shemaiah son of Hasshub, the son of Azrikam, the son of Hashabiah, the son of Bunni; 16 Shabbethai and Jozabad, two of the

[a] 14 Most Septuagint manuscripts; Hebrew *their*

11:1 one out of every ten. Along with the leaders, one-tenth of the people were to populate Jerusalem to make it a strong and vital city.

11:10–18 priests ... Levites. The priests, from six family heads, totaled 1,192 (vv. 10–14). The number given in 1 Chronicles 9:13 is 1,760. There were many fewer Levites, only 284 (vv. 15–18). Many fewer Levites returned. Maybe they didn't want the hard work of rebuilding.

heads of the Levites, who had charge of the outside work of the house of God; [17]Mattaniah son of Mica, the son of Zabdi, the son of Asaph, the director who led in thanksgiving and prayer; Bakbukiah, second among his associates; and Abda son of Shammua, the son of Galal, the son of Jeduthun. [18]The Levites in the holy city totaled 284.

[19]The gatekeepers:

Akkub, Talmon and their associates, who kept watch at the gates—172 men.

[20]The rest of the Israelites, with the priests and Levites, were in all
the towns of Judah, each on his ancestral property.
[21]The temple servants lived on the hill of Ophel, and Ziha and Gishpa were in charge of them.
[22]The chief officer of the Levites in Jerusalem was Uzzi son of Bani,
the son of Hashabiah, the son of Mattaniah, the son of Mica. Uzzi was one of Asaph's descendants, who were the singers responsible for
the service of the house of God. [23]The singers were under the king's
orders, which regulated their daily activity.
[24]Pethahiah son of Meshezabel, one of the descendants of Zerah
son of Judah, was the king's agent in all affairs relating to the people.
[25]As for the villages with their fields, some of the people of Judah
lived in Kiriath Arba and its surrounding settlements, in Dibon and its
settlements, in Jekabzeel and its villages, [26]in Jeshua, in Moladah, in
Beth Pelet, [27]in Hazar Shual, in Beersheba and its settlements, [28]in
Ziklag, in Meconah and its settlements, [29]in En Rimmon, in Zorah, in
Jarmuth, [30]Zanoah, Adullam and their villages, in Lachish and its
fields, and in Azekah and its settlements. So they were living all the
way from Beersheba to the Valley of Hinnom.
[31]The descendants of the Benjamites from Geba lived in Micmash,
Aija, Bethel and its settlements, [32]in Anathoth, Nob and Ananiah, [33]in
Hazor, Ramah and Gittaim, [34]in Hadid, Zeboim and Neballat, [35]in Lod
and Ono, and in the Valley of the Craftsmen.
[36]Some of the divisions of the Levites of Judah settled in Benjamin.

Priests and Levites

12 These were the priests and Levites who returned with Zerubbabel son of Shealtiel and with Jeshua:

Seraiah, Jeremiah, Ezra,
[2]Amariah, Malluch, Hattush,
[3]Shecaniah, Rehum, Meremoth,
[4]Iddo, Ginnethon,[a] Abijah,
[5]Mijamin,[b] Moadiah, Bilgah,
[6]Shemaiah, Joiarib, Jedaiah,
[7]Sallu, Amok, Hilkiah and Jedaiah.

These were the leaders of the priests and their associates in the days of Jeshua.

[8]The Levites were Jeshua, Binnui, Kadmiel, Sherebiah, Judah, and
also Mattaniah, who, together with his associates, was in charge of
the songs of thanksgiving. [9]Bakbukiah and Unni, their associates,
stood opposite them in the services.

[a]4 Many Hebrew manuscripts and Vulgate (see also Neh. 12:16); most Hebrew manuscripts *Ginnethoi*
[b]5 A variant of *Miniamin*

you and your church need to be ministering in? How might you help the ministry get started? How might your group get involved?

OPEN 1. Do you consider yourself young, middle-aged or older? Are you more a contemporary or a traditionalist? Do you want change or to keep things the same? **2.** What season of the year most makes you want to have older family members around? What event reminds you most of family members who are no longer alive?

STUDY Nehemiah listed the priests and Levites from the past generation (vv. 1–7) who had returned from Babylon. Then he followed with a listing of his contemporaries. **1.** Why do you think it was important for Nehemiah to remember the past generation of priests and Levites? How must he have felt to complete the rebuilding job they had started? What do you notice that is similar and different in the two lists? **2.** How do you

see God's faithfulness expressed as you look through the two lists? How do you see human loyalty expressed? **3.** If you had been a Jew listening to the reading of these names, what difference would it have made to you? How do you think remembering all these people affected the upcoming dedication ceremony for the wall?

APPLY 1. How do you want your children to remember you? What should they write for your epitaph? **2.** As you think back over the generations connected to you (either biologically or spiritually) what important life principle has been carried through? How will you make sure that it carries on to the next generations?

OPEN 1. What is your favorite "musical extravaganza": A symphony orchestra? A boom-box concert? A Super Bowl half-time show? A concert by your favorite singer/band? **2.** How do you express gratitude to God most effectively? To family? To other people?

STUDY The wall is completed and it's time to celebrate with a great festival of thanksgiving. So the whole nation gathered and "cut loose." *1. As the governor, Nehemiah* manages the city and all its events. Does he appear to be more of a "manager of the details" or a "guide to fulfill the

[10]Jeshua was the father of Joiakim, Joiakim the father of Eliashib,
Eliashib the father of Joiada, [11]Joiada the father of Jonathan, and
Jonathan the father of Jaddua.

[12]In the days of Joiakim, these were the heads of the priestly
families:

of Seraiah's family, Meraiah;
of Jeremiah's, Hananiah;
[13]of Ezra's, Meshullam;
of Amariah's, Jehohanan;
[14]of Malluch's, Jonathan;
of Shecaniah's,[a] Joseph;
[15]of Harim's, Adna;
of Meremoth's,[b] Helkai;
[16]of Iddo's, Zechariah;
of Ginnethon's, Meshullam;
[17]of Abijah's, Zicri;
of Miniamin's and of Moadiah's, Piltai;
[18]of Bilgah's, Shammua;
of Shemaiah's, Jehonathan;
[19]of Joiarib's, Mattenai;
of Jedaiah's, Uzzi;
[20]of Sallu's, Kallai;
of Amok's, Eber;
[21]of Hilkiah's, Hashabiah;
of Jedaiah's, Nethanel.

[22]The family heads of the Levites in the days of Eliashib, Joiada,
Johanan and Jaddua, as well as those of the priests, were recorded in
the reign of Darius the Persian. [23]The family heads among the
descendants of Levi up to the time of Johanan son of Eliashib were
recorded in the book of the annals. [24]And the leaders of the Levites
were Hashabiah, Sherebiah, Jeshua son of Kadmiel, and their associates, who stood opposite them to give praise and thanksgiving,
one section responding to the other, as prescribed by David the man
of God.

[25]Mattaniah, Bakbukiah, Obadiah, Meshullam, Talmon and Akkub
were gatekeepers who guarded the storerooms at the gates. [26]They
served in the days of Joiakim son of Jeshua, the son of Jozadak, and
in the days of Nehemiah the governor and of Ezra the priest and
scribe.

Dedication of the Wall of Jerusalem

[27]At the dedication of the wall of Jerusalem, the Levites were
sought out from where they lived and were brought to Jerusalem to
celebrate joyfully the dedication with songs of thanksgiving and with
the music of cymbals, harps and lyres. [28]The singers also were
brought together from the region around Jerusalem—from the villages of the Netophathites, [29]from Beth Gilgal, and from the area of
Geba and Azmaveth, for the singers had built villages for themselves
around Jerusalem. [30]When the priests and Levites had purified themselves ceremonially, they purified the people, the gates and the wall.
[31]I had the leaders of Judah go up on top[c] of the wall. I also

[a] *14* Very many Hebrew manuscripts, some Septuagint manuscripts and Syriac (see also Neh. 12:3); most Hebrew manuscripts *Shebaniah's* [b] *15* Some Septuagint manuscripts (see also Neh. 12:3); Hebrew *Meraioth's* [c] *31* *Or go alongside*

assigned two large choirs to give thanks. One was to proceed on top[a]
of the wall to the right, toward the Dung Gate. 32Hoshaiah and half
the leaders of Judah followed them, 33along with Azariah, Ezra,
Meshullam, 34Judah, Benjamin, Shemaiah, Jeremiah, 35as well as
some priests with trumpets, and also Zechariah son of Jonathan, the
son of Shemaiah, the son of Mattaniah, the son of Micaiah, the son of
Zaccur, the son of Asaph, 36and his associates—Shemaiah, Azarel,
Milalai, Gilalai, Maai, Nethanel, Judah and Hanani—with musical
instruments ⌞prescribed by⌟ David the man of God. Ezra the scribe led
the procession. 37At the Fountain Gate they continued directly up the
steps of the City of David on the ascent to the wall and passed above
the house of David to the Water Gate on the east.

38The second choir proceeded in the opposite direction. I followed
them on top[b] of the wall, together with half the people—past the
Tower of the Ovens to the Broad Wall, 39over the Gate of Ephraim, the
Jeshanah[c] Gate, the Fish Gate, the Tower of Hananel and the Tower of
the Hundred, as far as the Sheep Gate. At the Gate of the Guard they
stopped.

40The two choirs that gave thanks then took their places in the
house of God; so did I, together with half the officials, 41as well as the
priests—Eliakim, Maaseiah, Miniamin, Micaiah, Elioenai, Zechariah
and Hananiah with their trumpets— 42and also Maaseiah, Shemaiah,
Eleazar, Uzzi, Jehohanan, Malkijah, Elam and Ezer. The choirs sang
under the direction of Jezrahiah. 43And on that day they offered great
sacrifices, rejoicing because God had given them great joy. The wom-
en and children also rejoiced. The sound of rejoicing in Jerusalem
could be heard far away.

44At that time men were appointed to be in charge of the storerooms for the contributions, firstfruits and tithes. From the fields
around the towns they were to bring into the storerooms the portions
required by the Law for the priests and the Levites, for Judah was
pleased with the ministering priests and Levites. 45They performed
the service of their God and the service of purification, as did also the
singers and gatekeepers, according to the commands of David and
his son Solomon. 46For long ago, in the days of David and Asaph,
there had been directors for the singers and for the songs of praise
and thanksgiving to God. 47So in the days of Zerubbabel and of Nehemiah, all Israel contributed the daily portions for the singers and
gatekeepers. They also set aside the portion for the other Levites, and
the Levites set aside the portion for the descendants of Aaron.

Nehemiah's Final Reforms

13 On that day the Book of Moses was read aloud in the hearing
of the people and there it was found written that no Ammonite or Moabite should ever be admitted into the assembly of God,
2because they had not met the Israelites with food and water but had

[a]31 Or *proceed alongside* [b]38 Or *them alongside* [c]39 Or *Old*

vision"? How would you evaluate his managing of this giant celebration? Should the Olympic Committee hire him for the next opening ceremonies? Why or why not? **2.** What music group would you have wanted to join? How might you have felt if your choir was sent to sing at the Dung Gate? How does this dedication compare to any big event you've participated in? How is it different? **3.** Look through the passage and note how many things were happening "off camera" during the public celebration. Which was most important, the public or the private events? Why? **4.** Compare Nehemiah's lonely tour of the city in chapter 2 with this grand procession. What do you think he wrote on this day's entry in his diary?

APPLY **1.** Do you have a "before" and "after" story in your life? Can you share it with the group? Who has been instrumental in your getting from the "before" to the "after"? **2.** How are you, like Ezra and Nehemiah, discovering, developing and using your gifts/abilities to build God's kingdom?

OPEN **1.** When was the last time you were caught with your "hand in the cookie jar" either literally or figuratively? What was your first thought when you knew you were caught? What excuses did you make? What action did you take? **2.** What day do you observe as

12:44 Judah was pleased with the ministering priests. The joy of the celebration overflowed into generous provision for the temple. The priests and Levites followed David's pattern of worship from 500 years earlier (1 Chr. 22–26), including the prominent role of music.

12:47 all Israel contributed. According to the agreement, giving firstfruits and tithes was to be a continual practice rather than a one-time event. Every person participated in this contribution.

hired Balaam to call a curse down on them. (Our God, however,
turned the curse into a blessing.) 3When the people heard this law,
they excluded from Israel all who were of foreign descent.
4Before this, Eliashib the priest had been put in charge of the storerooms of the house of our God. He was closely associated with
Tobiah, 5and he had provided him with a large room formerly used to
store the grain offerings and incense and temple articles, and also
the tithes of grain, new wine and oil prescribed for the Levites, singers and gatekeepers, as well as the contributions for the priests.
6But while all this was going on, I was not in Jerusalem, for in the
thirty-second year of Artaxerxes king of Babylon I had returned to the
king. Some time later I asked his permission 7and came back to
Jerusalem. Here I learned about the evil thing Eliashib had done in
providing Tobiah a room in the courts of the house of God. 8I was
greatly displeased and threw all Tobiah's household goods out of the
room. 9I gave orders to purify the rooms, and then I put back into
them the equipment of the house of God, with the grain offerings and
the incense.
10I also learned that the portions assigned to the Levites had not
been given to them, and that all the Levites and singers responsible
for the service had gone back to their own fields. 11So I rebuked the
officials and asked them, "Why is the house of God neglected?" Then
I called them together and stationed them at their posts.
12All Judah brought the tithes of grain, new wine and oil into the
storerooms. 13I put Shelemiah the priest, Zadok the scribe, and a
Levite named Pedaiah in charge of the storerooms and made Hanan
son of Zaccur, the son of Mattaniah, their assistant, because these
men were considered trustworthy. They were made responsible for
distributing the supplies to their brothers.

14Remember me for this, O my God, and do not blot out what I have
so faithfully done for the house of my God and its services.

15In those days I saw men in Judah treading winepresses on the
Sabbath and bringing in grain and loading it on donkeys, together
with wine, grapes, figs and all other kinds of loads. And they were
bringing all this into Jerusalem on the Sabbath. Therefore I warned
them against selling food on that day. 16Men from Tyre who lived in
Jerusalem were bringing in fish and all kinds of merchandise and
selling them in Jerusalem on the Sabbath to the people of Judah. 17I
rebuked the nobles of Judah and said to them, "What is this wicked

the Sabbath or Lord's Day? What do you do to make it a worshipful, different, restful, restorative day?

STUDY Nehemiah returned to Babylon, leaving others in charge. When he returned "some time later" (v. 6) he found that the people were no longer tithing nor caring for the temple. **1.** Nehemiah ran directly into the same issues and sins of the people that Ezra had confronted some 25 years earlier (Ezra 9). If you had ridden back into town and found the people returning to their old sins, what would you have done? How would your response compare with Nehemiah's? **2.** Why do you think it was so hard for the people to continue proper care of the temple and to keep bringing their tithes? What does it take to keep a good habit going when no one is looking over your shoulder? **3.** What made the marriages with foreign women so wicked? If you were a marriage counselor, how would you have guided Nehemiah in his response to the intermarriage? Would his response in verse 29 have been part of your plan? Why do you think the men kept marrying outside the Jewish culture: There were no female Jews? The foreign women were better looking? The grass is always greener on the other side of the fence? The men didn't want to follow God? Other? **4.** Amid Nehemiah's harsh responses to the sins of the people, where do you see God's hand of care and love? How do you think the Jews knew that God loved them?

APPLY **1.** Which of the sins that Nehemiah confronts is most prominent in our culture? Why do you think so? **2.** If you were going to "clean house," bringing followers of Christ back into right relationship with God and one another, where would you start? Whose hair would you pull

---

13:5 provided him with a large room … to store … offerings. When Nehemiah returned to Jerusalem after an absence of several months, he discovered that the high priest Eliashib had allowed one of Nehemiah's enemies and his family to occupy one of the large temple storerooms used normally for storing grain offerings.

13:8 greatly displeased. Since Tobiah had opposed the restoration of the city walls, Nehemiah was angry that he had moved into the temple. He threw Tobiah's belongings out of the rooms, ordered that the rooms be cleaned, and refilled them with grain.

13:10 portions assigned to the Levites had not been given to them. Nehemiah found that the people had not brought their tithes and offerings to support the temple as promised, forcing the Levites to work in the fields. He reprimanded the leaders for not enforcing the tithes and offerings.

13:13 these men were considered trustworthy. Nehemiah appointed a priest, a scribe, a Levite and an assistant to oversee the tithes of grain, new wine and oil. He stationed the Levites at their proper posts. He knew that neglect could undo the reforms already accomplished.

13:17 rebuked the nobles of Judah. Another part of the written commitment was to honor the Sabbath (10:31). But in Jerusalem Nehemiah found the people carrying on trade on the Sabbath. He confronted the leaders who were responsible for enforcing the agreement.

thing you are doing—desecrating the Sabbath day? 18Didn't your
forefathers do the same things, so that our God brought all this
calamity upon us and upon this city? Now you are stirring up more
wrath against Israel by desecrating the Sabbath."
19When evening shadows fell on the gates of Jerusalem before the
Sabbath, I ordered the doors to be shut and not opened until the
Sabbath was over. I stationed some of my own men at the gates so
that no load could be brought in on the Sabbath day. 20Once or twice
the merchants and sellers of all kinds of goods spent the night outside Jerusalem. 21But I warned them and said, "Why do you spend the
night by the wall? If you do this again, I will lay hands on you." From
that time on they no longer came on the Sabbath. 22Then I commanded the Levites to purify themselves and go and guard the gates
in order to keep the Sabbath day holy.

Remember me for this also, O my God, and show mercy to me according to your great love.

23Moreover, in those days I saw men of Judah who had married
women from Ashdod, Ammon and Moab. 24Half of their children
spoke the language of Ashdod or the language of one of the other
peoples, and did not know how to speak the language of Judah. 25I
rebuked them and called curses down on them. I beat some of the
men and pulled out their hair. I made them take an oath in God's
name and said: "You are not to give your daughters in marriage to
their sons, nor are you to take their daughters in marriage for your
sons or for yourselves. 26Was it not because of marriages like these
that Solomon king of Israel sinned? Among the many nations there
was no king like him. He was loved by his God, and God made him
king over all Israel, but even he was led into sin by foreign women.
27Must we hear now that you too are doing all this terrible wickedness and are being unfaithful to our God by marrying foreign
women?"

28One of the sons of Joiada son of Eliashib the high priest was son-
in-law to Sanballat the Horonite. And I drove him away from me.

29Remember them, O my God, because they defiled the priestly
office and the covenant of the priesthood and of the Levites.
30So I purified the priests and the Levites of everything foreign, and
assigned them duties, each to his own task. 31I also made provision
for contributions of wood at designated times, and for the firstfruits.

Remember me with favor, O my God.

out: Your own (like Ezra) or other's (like Nehemiah)? What would you want God to remember you for? **3.** What principle from Nehemiah's life do you most need to apply to your life? How can your group help you be faithful to follow-through?

13:19 When evening shadows. Nehemiah took action to stop trading on the Sabbath by shutting the city doors on Friday evening and posting guards. Days were counted from sunset to sunset. He coupled his action with prayer.

13:23 men of Judah who had married women from Ashdod, Ammon and Moab. Ezra had dealt with the problem of intermarriage thirty years earlier (Ezra 9:1–4), and the people had made a covenant vow not to marry foreign wives again.

13:24 children spoke the language of Ashdod. Nehemiah knew that if the people did not speak and understand Hebrew, they could not learn the Law or worship in the temple. The Jews were raising children who did not know God.

13:25 You are not to give your daughters in marriage. Nehemiah did not dissolve the foreign marriages like Ezra had done, but he reacted passionately, realizing that intermarriage was the sin that had led to Israel's captivity by Babylon.

13:26 Solomon king of Israel. Nehemiah reminded the people of Solomon, whose stellar beginning was ruined when he married foreign women (1 Kin. 11:1–8). **he was led into sin.** Solomon worshiped his foreign wives' idols, which drew his heart away from God. He even built high places to the false gods (1 Kin. 11:7).

Esther

Author. While some have hypothesized that Ezra or Nehemiah wrote the book of Esther, the author has never been revealed or confirmed.

Date. The events described in this book fit the culture in Persia around 470 B.C. The book was probably written around then.

Personal Reading	Group Study Topic and Reading	
1:1–22	Queen Vashti Deposed	1:1–22
2:1–23	Esther Made Queen	2:1–18
3:1–15	Haman's Evil Plot	3:1–15
4:1–17	Mordecai's Appeal	4:1–17
5:1–14	Esther's Request	5:1–8
6:1–14	Mordecai Honored	6:1–14
7:1–10	Haman Hanged	7:1–10
8:1–17	The King's Edict	8:1–17
9:1–17	The Jews Triumph	9:1–17
9:18–10:3	Purim Celebrated	9:18–32

Purpose. The book of Esther is a puzzling book. God is not explicitly mentioned in the book, nor is prayer. The characters in the book are not great spiritual leaders, nor are they profound thinkers or speakers of God's Word. Quite the contrary is true. Despite those basic contradictions, the book teaches a lesson of grace. It teaches that God is faithful, even when people are not. It teaches that God has a commitment to save and preserve his people, though they may not even know it. It teaches that God has a plan for his people that he carries out even when they are disobedient or lax in their holiness. It shows us clearly that while we may forget God, he never forgets us.

Historical Background. The book of Esther provides a unique, close-up look at the Persian court during the exile of the Jews in Babylon. As such, the book of Esther may be more useful as a picture of history than an account of it. Xerxes was a tremendously powerful ruler. His domain stretched over 127 ancient provinces. He had a palace at Susa and a large harem there. The book of Esther gives a portrait of his life and household consistent with the collateral historical evidence.

Esther also gives readers a glimpse into a non-spiritual Jewish family during the exile. However, the book of Esther does provide the reason behind the Feast of Purim, which appears to have been very important in post-exilic Jewish life.

Feasts. One of the unique features of the book of Esther is the inauguration of a new feast. Feasts played an important role in Hebrew history. They did not function merely as holidays, such as Christmas and New Years do today. The Jewish feasts were religious festivals, object lessons of God's provision and guidance. The feast of the Sabbath was a weekly feast, but the Jews also celebrated several yearly feasts. These included the Feast of the Passover (commemorating the last plague before the exodus from Egypt), the Feast of Pentecost (coinciding with the end of the wheat harvest), the Feast of Trumpets (a kind of spiritual New Year), the Day of Atonement (confession of national sin) and the Feast of Tabernacles (remembering the time in the wilderness). The feast instituted by Esther and Mordecai was a yearly feast commemorating the failure of Haman's plot to destroy the Jews.

Queen Vashti Deposed

1 This is what happened during the time of Xerxes,[a] the Xerxes
who ruled over 127 provinces stretching from India to Cush[b]: 2At
that time King Xerxes reigned from his royal throne in the citadel of
Susa, 3and in the third year of his reign he gave a banquet for all his
nobles and officials. The military leaders of Persia and Media, the
princes, and the nobles of the provinces were present.
4For a full 180 days he displayed the vast wealth of his kingdom
and the splendor and glory of his majesty. 5When these days were
over, the king gave a banquet, lasting seven days, in the enclosed garden of the king's palace, for all the people from the least to the greatest, who were in the citadel of Susa. 6The garden had hangings of
white and blue linen, fastened with cords of white linen and purple
material to silver rings on marble pillars. There were couches of gold
and silver on a mosaic pavement of porphyry, marble, mother-of-
pearl and other costly stones. 7Wine was served in goblets of gold,
each one different from the other, and the royal wine was abundant,
in keeping with the king's liberality. 8By the king's command each
guest was allowed to drink in his own way, for the king instructed all
the wine stewards to serve each man what he wished.
9Queen Vashti also gave a banquet for the women in the royal palace of King Xerxes.
10On the seventh day, when King Xerxes was in high spirits from
wine, he commanded the seven eunuchs who served him—Mehu-
man, Biztha, Harbona, Bigtha, Abagtha, Zethar and Carcas— 11to
bring before him Queen Vashti, wearing her royal crown, in order
to display her beauty to the people and nobles, for she was lovely to
look at. 12But when the attendants delivered the king's command,
Queen Vashti refused to come. Then the king became furious and
burned with anger.
13Since it was customary for the king to consult experts in matters
of law and justice, he spoke with the wise men who understood the
times 14and were closest to the king—Carshena, Shethar, Admatha,
Tarshish, Meres, Marsena and Memucan, the seven nobles of Persia
and Media who had special access to the king and were highest in the
kingdom.
15"According to law, what must be done to Queen Vashti?" he
asked. "She has not obeyed the command of King Xerxes that the
eunuchs have taken to her."
16Then Memucan replied in the presence of the king and the
nobles, "Queen Vashti has done wrong, not only against the king but
also against all the nobles and the peoples of all the provinces of King
Xerxes. 17For the queen's conduct will become known to all the
women, and so they will despise their husbands and say, 'King Xerxes

[a]*1* Hebrew *Ahasuerus,* a variant of Xerxes' Persian name; here and throughout Esther [b]*1* That is, the upper Nile region

OPEN 1. Have you thrown a big banquet or an open house party? What were you celebrating? **2.** What is the biggest bash you have attended in the last few years, and who was invited? **3.** Whose pictures do you keep in your wallet? Share a few.

STUDY Over 100 years after Daniel and Ezekiel have been taken captive to Babylon and Jeremiah to Egypt; and, 30 years after the temple has been rebuilt in Jerusalem, Esther comes to center stage. This is still 25 years before Ezra and 40 years before Nehemiah led their groups back to Jerusalem. The king of Persia (King Xerxes) throws a party that will last 180 days. **1.** What might be the occasion for this opulent banquet thrown by King Xerxes (vv. 3–8)? Who is invited? **2.** What do you make of all the architectural, fashion and wine detail given here? **3.** Why do you think his wife, Queen Vashti, throws a separate party (v. 9)? Why does he send for her (v. 11)? When she refuses, how does the king react? **4.** Who advises the king what to do and why? What is their advice? **5.** What is at stake here: The king's honor? Male supremacy? Potential anarchy? Obeying authority? **6.** What would cause a government to establish a law that could not be repealed (v. 19; 8:8): Trapping a king in a moment of weakness (v. 10; 2:1)? Keeping women in their place? Trying to preserve "family values"? Explain. **7.** With which of the characters do you most identify? Why? Where in your life are you: Obeying authority? Mutual respect? Sharing (not showing) your wealth? Being the host with the most?

APPLY 1. What important decision is pending for you? What input from the group would you like for this? **2.** In decisions affecting other people, who is your "Memucan" (someone who likes to give advice)? Who would you feel free to call in the middle of the night? **3.** The nobles feared anarchy would result if women were as "independent" as Vashti. At home, how do you work out disagreements?

1:1 Xerxes who ruled. His name is also written as Ahasuerus. Xerxes succeeded his father, Darius, as king. Xerxes ruled the Persian Empire for 21 years from 486 to 465 B.C.

1:9 Queen Vashti. Xerxes gave one banquet for his nobles, officials and military leaders, and a second for all the people in Susa. Queen Vashti simultaneously gave a banquet for the women in the royal palace.

1:13 he spoke with the wise men who understood the times. Astrologers and magicians who served in the court by giving advice and attempting to predict the future. God's prophets viewed them with scorn (Isa. 44:24-25).

commanded Queen Vashti to be brought before him, but she would not come.' [18]This very day the Persian and Median women of the nobility who have heard about the queen's conduct will respond to all the king's nobles in the same way. There will be no end of disrespect and discord.

[19]"Therefore, if it pleases the king, let him issue a royal decree and let it be written in the laws of Persia and Media, which cannot be repealed, that Vashti is never again to enter the presence of King Xerxes. Also let the king give her royal position to someone else who is better than she. [20]Then when the king's edict is proclaimed throughout all his vast realm, all the women will respect their husbands, from the least to the greatest."

[21]The king and his nobles were pleased with this advice, so the king did as Memucan proposed. [22]He sent dispatches to all parts of the kingdom, to each province in its own script and to each people in its own language, proclaiming in each people's tongue that every man should be ruler over his own household.

Esther Made Queen

2 Later when the anger of King Xerxes had subsided, he remembered Vashti and what she had done and what he had decreed about her. [2]Then the king's personal attendants proposed, "Let a search be made for beautiful young virgins for the king. [3]Let the king appoint commissioners in every province of his realm to bring all these beautiful girls into the harem at the citadel of Susa. Let them be placed under the care of Hegai, the king's eunuch, who is in charge of the women; and let beauty treatments be given to them. [4]Then let the girl who pleases the king be queen instead of Vashti." This advice appealed to the king, and he followed it.

[5]Now there was in the citadel of Susa a Jew of the tribe of Benjamin, named Mordecai son of Jair, the son of Shimei, the son of Kish, [6]who had been carried into exile from Jerusalem by Nebuchadnezzar king of Babylon, among those taken captive with Jehoiachin[a] king of Judah. [7]Mordecai had a cousin named Hadassah, whom he had brought up because she had neither father nor mother. This girl, who was also known as Esther, was lovely in form and features, and Mordecai had taken her as his own daughter when her father and mother died.

[8]When the king's order and edict had been proclaimed, many girls were brought to the citadel of Susa and put under the care of Hegai.

[a]6 Hebrew *Jeconiah,* a variant of *Jehoiachin*

OPEN 1. If invited for a private audience with the prime minister or president, would you go? What might she or he want to talk to you about? What questions would you pose? How would you dress and prepare yourself? **2.** What contest have you ever won? Who was your competition?

STUDY 1. Verse 1 is a hinge verse, spanning four years (v. 16; 1:3). What has happened to the king's anger? His memory? His decree? To Vashti? **2.** As this king's search unfolds, how does it compare to the Joseph story (Gen. 37–41)? **3.** How do Mordecai and Esther fit in to that model? Who are Mordecai's ancestors (1 Sam. 9:1)? How are Mordecai and Esther related to each other? How do they fit the man-woman household rule in 1:22? **4.** What might have happened if Esther had not obeyed Mordecai? How did she manage to keep her ethnic background secret from the king? **5.** Of what significance is the year-long preparation period? What in your culture roughly corre-

1:19 never again to enter the presence of King Xerxes. One of Xerxes's wise men suggested deposing the queen so that the women of the kingdom would not follow Vashti's example and disobey their husbands. He issued a royal decree demoting Vashti from her position of queen and banishing her *from his sight.*

2:1 Later when the anger. Apparently, after his anger cooled, the king regretted his actions toward Vashti. The wise men did not want Vashti brought back because she would retaliate against them.

2:4 the girl who pleases the king. Xerxes's advisors suggested the king find a new queen from among the beautiful young girls of the kingdom. He already had a harem in Susa.

2:7 cousin named Hadassah. Esther's Hebrew name means "myrtle." Esther is a Persian name, meaning "star." Her parents died when she was young, and her cousin Mordecai raised her.

2:8 Esther also was taken to the King's palace. Selected women had no choice but to enter the harem. She received special treatment, including seven maids, special food and beauty treatments. She waited in the harem 12 months before seeing the king.

Esther also was taken to the king's palace and entrusted to Hegai, who had charge of the harem.
9The girl pleased him and won his favor. Immediately he provided her with her beauty treatments and special food. He assigned to her seven maids selected from the king's palace and moved her and her maids into the best place in the harem.
10Esther had not revealed her nationality and family background, because Mordecai had forbidden her to do so.
11Every day he walked back and forth near the courtyard of the harem to find out how Esther was and what was happening to her.
12Before a girl's turn came to go in to King Xerxes, she had to complete twelve months of beauty treatments prescribed for the women, six months with oil of myrrh and six with perfumes and cosmetics.
13And this is how she would go to the king: Anything she wanted was given her to take with her from the harem to the king's palace.
14In the evening she would go there and in the morning return to another part of the harem to the care of Shaashgaz, the king's eunuch who was in charge of the concubines. She would not return to the king unless he was pleased with her and summoned her by name.
15When the turn came for Esther (the girl Mordecai had adopted, the daughter of his uncle Abihail) to go to the king, she asked for nothing other than what Hegai, the king's eunuch who was in charge of the harem, suggested. And Esther won the favor of everyone who saw her.
16She was taken to King Xerxes in the royal residence in the tenth month, the month of Tebeth, in the seventh year of his reign.
17Now the king was attracted to Esther more than to any of the other women, and she won his favor and approval more than any of the other virgins. So he set a royal crown on her head and made her queen instead of Vashti.
18And the king gave a great banquet, Esther's banquet, for all his nobles and officials. He proclaimed a holiday throughout the provinces and distributed gifts with royal liberality.

Mordecai Uncovers a Conspiracy

19When the virgins were assembled a second time, Mordecai was sitting at the king's gate.
20But Esther had kept secret her family background and nationality just as Mordecai had told her to do, for she continued to follow Mordecai's instructions as she had done when he was bringing her up.
21During the time Mordecai was sitting at the king's gate, Bigthana[a] and Teresh, two of the king's officers who guarded the doorway, became angry and conspired to assassinate King Xerxes.
22But Mordecai found out about the plot and told Queen Esther, who in turn reported it to the king, giving credit to Mordecai.
23And when the report was investigated and found to be true, the two officials were hanged on a gallows.[b] All this was recorded in the book of the annals in the presence of the king.

[a]21 Hebrew *Bigthan, a variant of Bigthana* [b]23 Or *were hung* (or *impaled*) *on poles*; similarly elsewhere in Esther

sponds to it? **6.** Nothing is said here about the morality of King Xerxes seizing or sampling the women as he does. Why is that? **7.** Who do you identify with in this story: A queen fit for a king? A runner-up? A personal attendant? A fretful, fatherly Mordecai?

APPLY 1. How would you feel if God, as King, took four years to fill a "vacancy" or solve some other problem in your life? How important (to you and God) is time and timing? **2.** How do you feel God is using you? What unique gift do you have or unique place in someone else's life do you hold? What is your responsibility?

OPEN 1. In your zealous years, did you march, rally, picket, obstruct, or otherwise "protest"? For what cause? Break any laws? Get in trouble? **2.** In what ways have your views changed?

STUDY 1. The plot twists! Four more years elapse between chapters (v. 7; 2:16) in this TV-like "mini-series." Who now comes on the scene as a star? Why not Mordecai? **2.** The three characters: Esther, Mordecai and Haman all have secrets. What are each keeping quiet about? **3.** Why won't Mordecai kneel? And why is Haman intent on killing all of Mordecai's race? Is this a clash of: Priorities? People? Personalities? Perception? **4.** What is a "pur" (v. 7)?

2:10 nationality and family background. Mordecai had warned her not to reveal her nationality. Jews were forbidden to marry pagans (Deut. 7:1–4) or have sexual relations outside of marriage (Ex. 20:14). Joining the king's harem violated these rules, but God protected and used Esther and Mordecai to save their people.

2:19 sitting at the king's gate. The gate was where commercial and legal transactions were made. Mordecai probably held an official position in the judicial system, which helped him uncover the assassination plot against the king. He stayed at the gate to find out how Esther was doing in the palace.

What is the significance of the 11-month delay secured "by lot" (vv. 7,12)? Was providence overruling coincidence? **5.** If Haman the Agagite is a descendant of King Agag (1 Sam. 15) and the hated Amalekites, what does that mean for the Israelites? How is King Saul's failure to extinguish all the Amalekites coming back, 500 years later, to haunt Israel? **6.** What does this chapter add to your picture of King Xerxes? What half-truths does he agree with (vv. 8–9)? What does he disavow (v. 11; 4:7; 7:4)? What do his own people think (v. 15)?

APPLY 1. Think of someone whose customs are different from yours. How does that affect your fellowship? Do you build on the similarities, or bridge the differences? Why? **2.** In conflicts of conscience, are you more like: Mordecai, a pacifist protester? Haman, an enraged politician? King Xerxes, easily swayed or pacified? The couriers, dutifully bearing whatever news they are given? The people, bewildered by it all? **3.** Where do you need to show more courage in your life?

Haman's Plot to Destroy the Jews

3 After these events, King Xerxes honored Haman son of Hammedatha, the Agagite, elevating him and giving him a seat of
honor higher than that of all the other nobles. 2 All the royal officials
at the king's gate knelt down and paid honor to Haman, for the king
had commanded this concerning him. But Mordecai would not kneel
down or pay him honor.
3 Then the royal officials at the king's gate asked Mordecai, "Why do
you disobey the king's command?" 4 Day after day they spoke to him
but he refused to comply. Therefore they told Haman about it to see
whether Mordecai's behavior would be tolerated, for he had told
them he was a Jew.
5 When Haman saw that Mordecai would not kneel down or pay
him honor, he was enraged. 6 Yet having learned who Mordecai's people were, he scorned the idea of killing only Mordecai. Instead Haman looked for a way to destroy all Mordecai's people, the Jews,
throughout the whole kingdom of Xerxes.
7 In the twelfth year of King Xerxes, in the first month, the month of
Nisan, they cast the *pur* (that is, the lot) in the presence of Haman to
select a day and month. And the lot fell on[a] the twelfth month, the
month of Adar.
8 Then Haman said to King Xerxes, "There is a certain people dispersed and scattered among the peoples in all the provinces of your
kingdom whose customs are different from those of all other people
and who do not obey the king's laws; it is not in the king's best interest to tolerate them. 9 If it pleases the king, let a decree be issued to
destroy them, and I will put ten thousand talents[b] of silver into the
royal treasury for the men who carry out this business."
10 So the king took his signet ring from his finger and gave it to
Haman son of Hammedatha, the Agagite, the enemy of the Jews.
11 "Keep the money," the king said to Haman, "and do with the people
as you please."
12 Then on the thirteenth day of the first month the royal secretaries
were summoned. They wrote out in the script of each province and in
the language of each people all Haman's orders to the king's satraps,
the governors of the various provinces and the nobles of the various
peoples. These were written in the name of King Xerxes himself and
sealed with his own ring. 13 Dispatches were sent by couriers to all the

[a] 7 Septuagint; Hebrew does not have *And the lot fell on.* [b] 9 That is, about 375 tons (about 345 metric tons)

3:1 After these events. Four years after Mordecai saved the king from assassination, Haman was promoted to the highest position in the land. **Haman ... the Agagite.** Haman was an Amalekite, among the descendants of Esau. Ever since Saul had captured an Amalekite king, hostility between Jews and Amalekites was business as usual.

3:2 knelt down and paid honor to Haman. This was an act of respect, not worship (unlike the requirement to worship the image of Nebuchadnezzar in Dan. 3:8-15). Mordecai's refusal was more from pride than religious beliefs, because Jews were permitted to bow in respect to kings or other high officials.

3:7 In the twelfth year ... first month. Corresponds to April or May, 474 B.C., the fifth year after Esther became queen. **cast the pur.** A Babylonian word for "the lot," the system used by Haman to decide when the Jews should be killed. Lots were often cast at the beginning of the year because Babylonians believed the gods gathered at the beginning of each year to establish human destiny. The Feast of Purim (9:24–26) was later established to celebrate God's deliverance from this threat of destruction and ruin.

3:8 who do not obey the king's laws. Haman slyly omitted the name of the people he wished to destroy when he falsely accused them of rebellion against the king.

3:9 for the men who carry out this business. Haman's offer to pay the equivalent of millions of dollars to crush the supposed rebellion was meant to show his devotion to the king.

3:13 destroy, kill and annihilate all the Jews. The proclamation was sent

king's provinces with the order to destroy, kill and annihilate all the
Jews—young and old, women and little children—on a single day, the
thirteenth day of the twelfth month, the month of Adar, and to plunder their goods. [14]A copy of the text of the edict was to be issued as
law in every province and made known to the people of every nationality so they would be ready for that day.
[15]Spurred on by the king's command, the couriers went out, and
the edict was issued in the citadel of Susa. The king and Haman sat
down to drink, but the city of Susa was bewildered.

Mordecai Persuades Esther to Help

4 When Mordecai learned of all that had been done, he tore his
clothes, put on sackcloth and ashes, and went out into the city,
wailing loudly and bitterly. [2]But he went only as far as the king's gate,
because no one clothed in sackcloth was allowed to enter it. [3]In every
province to which the edict and order of the king came, there was
great mourning among the Jews, with fasting, weeping and wailing.
Many lay in sackcloth and ashes.
[4]When Esther's maids and eunuchs came and told her about
Mordecai, she was in great distress. She sent clothes for him to put
on instead of his sackcloth, but he would not accept them. [5]Then
Esther summoned Hathach, one of the king's eunuchs assigned to
attend her, and ordered him to find out what was troubling Mordecai
and why.
[6]So Hathach went out to Mordecai in the open square of the city in
front of the king's gate. [7]Mordecai told him everything that had happened to him, including the exact amount of money Haman had
promised to pay into the royal treasury for the destruction of the
Jews. [8]He also gave him a copy of the text of the edict for their annihilation, which had been published in Susa, to show to Esther and
explain it to her, and he told him to urge her to go into the king's
presence to beg for mercy and plead with him for her people.
[9]Hathach went back and reported to Esther what Mordecai had
said. [10]Then she instructed him to say to Mordecai, [11]"All the king's
officials and the people of the royal provinces know that for any man
or woman who approaches the king in the inner court without being
summoned the king has but one law: that he be put to death. The
only exception to this is for the king to extend the gold scepter to him
and spare his life. But thirty days have passed since I was called to go
to the king."
[12]When Esther's words were reported to Mordecai, [13]he sent back
this answer: "Do not think that because you are in the king's house
you alone of all the Jews will escape. [14]For if you remain silent at this
time, relief and deliverance for the Jews will arise from another place,

OPEN 1. When have you "cried your eyes out"? Over what issue, hurt or loss? **2.** In your family, who cries like an open spigot? Like a drippy faucet? Who pouts? Fasts?

STUDY 1. By now this story is front page news in the *Persia Herald*. As a reporter, to whom in Susa would you go for an "inside scoop"? For your "gossip column"? Would you name your sources? Why or why not? **2.** Mordecai's crying and penitence were culturally accepted (vv. 1,3). What was Esther's motivation for sending letters to Mordecai? **3.** As for Esther, what options are open to her as: Queen? Jew? At what cost? **4.** Which option does Esther finally settle on (vv. 15–16)? What hope does she have for success? What else is she feeling? **5.** What does fasting involve? Where is God in this? **6.** Why do you think Mordecai would break his silence about who Esther is? If she remains silent, what hope is there? **7.** Do you think Esther was either innocent or helpless? What did Mordecai think?

APPLY 1. Can you imagine a crisis in which you would go "against the law," as Esther does, to find a solution? **2.** Have you ever fasted? How long? What for? What was the result? How do you show your readiness to do God's will? **3.** Is there something in your life where fasting and prayer might be in order?

---

to all the provinces in various languages. The order included all Jewish women and children. The Jews' property was also to be confiscated.

3:15 the city of Susa was bewildered. Such a decree had never before come from the royal court. As the king and Haman drank to celebrate the issuance of the decree, Jews mourned and fasted (4:1–3, 15-16).

4:1 wailing loudly and bitterly. Mordecai's feud with Haman had brought the threat of annihilation to his people. His public grief signified his mourning. He may have regretted revealing his nationality and placing his people in this type of jeopardy.

4:4 instead of his sackcloth. Esther heard of Mordecai's wailing and sent him clothes so he could enter the palace gate. She wanted to know why he was grieving. He refused the clothes, even though no one could enter the gate dressed in mourning.

but you and your father's family will perish. And who knows but that
you have come to royal position for such a time as this?"
15Then Esther sent this reply to Mordecai: 16"Go, gather together all
the Jews who are in Susa, and fast for me. Do not eat or drink for
three days, night or day. I and my maids will fast as you do. When this
is done, I will go to the king, even though it is against the law. And if
I perish, I perish."
17So Mordecai went away and carried out all of Esther's instructions.

OPEN 1. Did it help to "dress for success" in your last job interview? How so? 2. When you want someone to do a special favor for you, how do you convince them?

STUDY 1. "On the third day"—of what? Why is that detail relevant to the plot? 2. What might be the purpose of Esther's delaying tactics: Fear? Intriguing the king? Buying time? Waiting for him to up his offer? Building suspense for the reader? Or what? 3. What is the king's response so far to her requests? What does this imply? 4. As the tension mounts, so do tempers. Why is Haman in "high spirits"? What is the toasting all about? 5. What infuriates Haman most about Mordecai? What irony do you see here (3:2–6)? What does this say about Haman? About human nature?

APPLY 1. If any request could be granted, as was done for Esther, for what would you ask? Why that? 2. What assurances do you have that when you ask God for something, it will be granted? 3. What issue do you have in your life that you need to trust God to answer your prayers?

Esther's Request to the King

5 On the third day Esther put on her royal robes and stood in the
inner court of the palace, in front of the king's hall. The king was
sitting on his royal throne in the hall, facing the entrance. 2When he
saw Queen Esther standing in the court, he was pleased with her and
held out to her the gold scepter that was in his hand. So Esther
approached and touched the tip of the scepter.
3Then the king asked, "What is it, Queen Esther? What is your
request? Even up to half the kingdom, it will be given you."
4"If it pleases the king," replied Esther, "let the king, together with
Haman, come today to a banquet I have prepared for him."
5"Bring Haman at once," the king said, "so that we may do what
Esther asks."
So the king and Haman went to the banquet Esther had prepared.
6As they were drinking wine, the king again asked Esther, "Now what
is your petition? It will be given you. And what is your request? Even
up to half the kingdom, it will be granted."
7Esther replied, "My petition and my request is this: 8If the king regards me with favor and if it pleases the king to grant my petition and
fulfill my request, let the king and Haman come tomorrow to the banquet I will prepare for them. Then I will answer the king's question."

Haman's Rage Against Mordecai

9Haman went out that day happy and in high spirits. But when he
saw Mordecai at the king's gate and observed that he neither rose
nor showed fear in his presence, he was filled with rage against Mordecai. 10Nevertheless, Haman restrained himself and went home.
Calling together his friends and Zeresh, his wife, 11Haman boasted
to them about his vast wealth, his many sons, and all the ways the

4:15 fast. She asked for the support of her people in fasting for three days before she approached the king. She didn't mention praying, but fasting normally included earnestly seeking God in prayer.

4:16 if I perish, I perish. Esther was well aware that the king could execute anyone, including the queen, who approached him without an appointment. She resolved to approach the king on behalf of her people, even if it meant her death.

5:2 he was pleased with her. Although Esther had not seen the king in a month, he held out the gold scepter toward her, granting permission to approach him. He offered to grant her request even up to half the kingdom (Herod made this offer to Herodias's daughter in Mark 6:23).

5:4 If it pleases the king. This polite expression appears throughout the book. Her request was an invitation to a banquet for the king and Haman.

5:6 what is your petition? Esther's reason for not revealing Haman's plot at the first banquet is not given. She may have been afraid, or she may have felt that the king was not in the mood for such news. God used the delay to remind the king that Mordecai had never been thanked for saving the king's life.

5:9 rage against Mordecai. Haman's good fortune in banqueting with the king and queen was spoiled for him by Mordecai's refusal to bow down to him.

5:10 Zeresh. Haman and his wife were well suited to each other. After his whining about Mordecai and his boasting about his favor with the king, she encouraged her husband to murder Mordecai as an example to everyone that Haman was in control.

king had honored him and how he had elevated him above the other
nobles and officials. 12"And that's not all," Haman added. "I'm the
only person Queen Esther invited to accompany the king to the
banquet she gave. And she has invited me along with the king tomorrow. 13But all this gives me no satisfaction as long as I see that Jew
Mordecai sitting at the king's gate."
14His wife Zeresh and all his friends said to him, "Have a gallows
built, seventy-five feet[a] high, and ask the king in the morning to have
Mordecai hanged on it. Then go with the king to the dinner and be
happy." This suggestion delighted Haman, and he had the gallows
built.

Mordecai Honored

6 That night the king could not sleep; so he ordered the book of
the chronicles, the record of his reign, to be brought in and read
to him. 2It was found recorded there that Mordecai had exposed
Bigthana and Teresh, two of the king's officers who guarded the
doorway, who had conspired to assassinate King Xerxes.
3"What honor and recognition has Mordecai received for this?" the
king asked.
"Nothing has been done for him," his attendants answered.
4The king said, "Who is in the court?" Now Haman had just entered
the outer court of the palace to speak to the king about hanging
Mordecai on the gallows he had erected for him.
5His attendants answered, "Haman is standing in the court."
"Bring him in," the king ordered.
6When Haman entered, the king asked him, "What should be done
for the man the king delights to honor?"
Now Haman thought to himself, "Who is there that the king would
rather honor than me?" 7So he answered the king, "For the man the
king delights to honor, 8have them bring a royal robe the king has
worn and a horse the king has ridden, one with a royal crest placed
on its head. 9Then let the robe and horse be entrusted to one of the
king's most noble princes. Let them robe the man the king delights to
honor, and lead him on the horse through the city streets, proclaiming before him, 'This is what is done for the man the king delights to
honor!' "
10"Go at once," the king commanded Haman. "Get the robe and the
horse and do just as you have suggested for Mordecai the Jew, who
sits at the king's gate. Do not neglect anything you have recommended."
11So Haman got the robe and the horse. He robed Mordecai, and
led him on horseback through the city streets, proclaiming before
him, "This is what is done for the man the king delights to honor!"

[a]14 Hebrew *fifty cubits* (about 23 meters)

OPEN What brings on sleep the quickest for you: Hard day's work? Hard day's fun? Big meal? Bible reading? Soft music? Watching TV? What delays sleep for you?

STUDY 1. Ironies abound! What was keeping the king awake (5:14)? What does he do when he can't sleep? **2.** Whose hand print is on these events: The king's insomnia? The appearance of Mordecai's heroism in the reading? Haman's entrance into the court? Why can't King Xerxes and Haman see this? **3.** What other ironies or coincidences do you see in the hidden identity? In the robe? In the friends' counsel? **4.** What do you make of Haman's wife changing her advice (v. 13; 5:14)? **5.** What do the actions and resulting rewards for Haman and Mordecai teach us?

APPLY 1. Is there an area of your life where you have a blind spot like Haman: Prejudice? Unfairness towards an individual? An area you haven't turned over to God? **2.** Who can you show honor to who has been overlooked?

6:3 honor and recognition. God used a sleepless night to accomplish his purpose. The king read the official records and discovered that Mordecai had never been honored for saving his life five years before.

6:6 the man the king delights to honor. As Haman had hidden the Jews' name from the king, Xerxes did not reveal to Haman who it was he wished to honor. Arrogant Haman naturally assumed it must be himself. Haman had just finished having the gallows for Mordecai erected.

6:8 bring a royal robe the king has worn. Haman recited his wish list, designed to gain more respect for himself. The king granted his wish, but with Mordecai as the honoree. Haman's fury at leading Mordecai through the streets must have been obvious to everyone.

12Afterward Mordecai returned to the king's gate. But Haman rushed home, with his head covered in grief, 13and told Zeresh his wife and all his friends everything that had happened to him.

His advisers and his wife Zeresh said to him, "Since Mordecai, before whom your downfall has started, is of Jewish origin, you cannot stand against him—you will surely come to ruin!" 14While they were still talking with him, the king's eunuchs arrived and hurried Haman away to the banquet Esther had prepared.

Haman Hanged

7 So the king and Haman went to dine with Queen Esther, 2and as they were drinking wine on that second day, the king again asked, "Queen Esther, what is your petition? It will be given you. What is your request? Even up to half the kingdom, it will be granted."

3Then Queen Esther answered, "If I have found favor with you, O king, and if it pleases your majesty, grant me my life—this is my petition. And spare my people—this is my request. 4For I and my people have been sold for destruction and slaughter and annihilation. If we had merely been sold as male and female slaves, I would have kept quiet, because no such distress would justify disturbing the king.[a]"

5King Xerxes asked Queen Esther, "Who is he? Where is the man who has dared to do such a thing?"

6Esther said, "The adversary and enemy is this vile Haman."

Then Haman was terrified before the king and queen. 7The king got up in a rage, left his wine and went out into the palace garden. But Haman, realizing that the king had already decided his fate, stayed behind to beg Queen Esther for his life.

8Just as the king returned from the palace garden to the banquet hall, Haman was falling on the couch where Esther was reclining.

The king exclaimed, "Will he even molest the queen while she is with me in the house?"

As soon as the word left the king's mouth, they covered Haman's face. 9Then Harbona, one of the eunuchs attending the king, said, "A gallows seventy-five feet[b] high stands by Haman's house. He had it made for Mordecai, who spoke up to help the king."

The king said, "Hang him on it!" 10So they hanged Haman on the gallows he had prepared for Mordecai. Then the king's fury subsided.

The King's Edict in Behalf of the Jews

8 That same day King Xerxes gave Queen Esther the estate of Haman, the enemy of the Jews. And Mordecai came into the presence of the king, for Esther had told how he was related to her.

[a]4 *Or quiet, but the compensation our adversary offers cannot be compared with the loss the king would suffer* [b]9 Hebrew *fifty cubits* (about 23 meters)

OPEN "Make your words sweet, you may have to eat them some day"—When have you seen the truth of that proverb in your life?

STUDY 1. "The king again asked" implies a previous inquiry (v. 2). When? Why? What has led up to this dramatic banquet? **2.** What does it reveal about Esther's character: Self-preservation? Selfless loyalty? Royal respect? Sweet revenge? **3.** What about Haman is: Vile? Foolish? Pitiful? Pitiless? **4.** What lessons are there in this story about appearance of evil, respect for others, honesty, etc.? **5.** What role does Harbona play (v. 9; 1:10)? **6.** While this chapter ends with Haman's death, what issues remain unresolved?

APPLY 1. If you were Esther, would you have handled the situation any differently? How so? **2.** What enemy threatens you and your goals or your church and its goals: Prejudice? Apathy? Politics? **3.** What application can you take from this story and put into practice?

OPEN What is the toughest part of seeking a raise: The asking? The amount? Waiting for an answer? When have you had to do that? What answer did you get? How will you approach the boss next time?

7:3 spare my people. In Esther's impassioned plea she disclosed her true identity to the king for the first time. She had no idea how the king would respond.

7:5 Who is he? Imagine Haman's terror as he realized he was about to be exposed and executed.

7:8 Haman was ... where Esther was reclining. The reason the king went out into the palace garden is not known. But Haman begged her for his life after the king left. He was not assaulting her, but he may have been grasping at her in desperation.

7:9 gallows. The eunuch informed the king of Haman's plot and reminded the king of Mordecai's bravery. The tables were turned as Haman was executed on the gallows he had prepared for Mordecai.

8:1 gave Queen Esther the estate. Ironically, all of Haman's property was given to the Jews, whom Haman had planned to strip of their property.

2The king took off his signet ring, which he had reclaimed from Haman, and presented it to Mordecai. And Esther appointed him over
Haman's estate.
3Esther again pleaded with the king, falling at his feet and weeping.
She begged him to put an end to the evil plan of Haman the Agagite,
which he had devised against the Jews. 4Then the king extended the
gold scepter to Esther and she arose and stood before him.
5"If it pleases the king," she said, "and if he regards me with favor
and thinks it the right thing to do, and if he is pleased with me, let an
order be written overruling the dispatches that Haman son of Hammedatha, the Agagite, devised and wrote to destroy the Jews in all the
king's provinces. 6For how can I bear to see disaster fall on my
people? How can I bear to see the destruction of my family?"
7King Xerxes replied to Queen Esther and to Mordecai the Jew,
"Because Haman attacked the Jews, I have given his estate to Esther,
and they have hanged him on the gallows. 8Now write another decree
in the king's name in behalf of the Jews as seems best to you, and
seal it with the king's signet ring—for no document written in the
king's name and sealed with his ring can be revoked."
9At once the royal secretaries were summoned—on the twenty-
third day of the third month, the month of Sivan. They wrote out all
Mordecai's orders to the Jews, and to the satraps, governors and
nobles of the 127 provinces stretching from India to Cush.[a] These
orders were written in the script of each province and the language of
each people and also to the Jews in their own script and language.
10Mordecai wrote in the name of King Xerxes, sealed the dispatches
with the king's signet ring, and sent them by mounted couriers, who
rode fast horses especially bred for the king.
11The king's edict granted the Jews in every city the right to assemble and protect themselves; to destroy, kill and annihilate any armed
force of any nationality or province that might attack them and their
women and children; and to plunder the property of their enemies.
12The day appointed for the Jews to do this in all the provinces of King
Xerxes was the thirteenth day of the twelfth month, the month of
Adar. 13A copy of the text of the edict was to be issued as law in every
province and made known to the people of every nationality so that
the Jews would be ready on that day to avenge themselves on their
enemies.
14The couriers, riding the royal horses, raced out, spurred on by the
king's command. And the edict was also issued in the citadel of Susa.
15Mordecai left the king's presence wearing royal garments of blue
and white, a large crown of gold and a purple robe of fine linen. And
the city of Susa held a joyous celebration. 16For the Jews it was a time
of happiness and joy, gladness and honor. 17In every province and in
every city, wherever the edict of the king went, there was joy and
gladness among the Jews, with feasting and celebrating. And many

[a]9 That is, the upper Nile region

STUDY **1.** "It's all over but the shouting"—How might that gleeful commentary from the sports world fit this chapter? What is almost over? What's the shouting all about? **2.** Before the victors dispatch Haman's estate (vv. 1–2; 5:11), what must be dispatched first? Why the anguish for Esther, who is now quite secure in the king's favor (vv. 1–6)? What is the problem with getting the king to reverse the death sentence on the Jews (v. 8)? **3.** What does the new decree do for the Jews? For others? What seems like "deja vu" or "same song, second verse" about this edict (1:19; 3:1–4:3; 6:10)? What is particularly symmetrical about its timing (v. 12; 3:7,13)? **4.** Verse 17 starts a new theme song. What is it? What is the principle for evangelism here?

APPLY **1.** The Jews had nine months to prepare their defense (vv. 9–12). What could you accomplish in the next nine months that would put your life in better order? What part of that reordering will you do this month? **2.** If you were in a position to destroy your enemy without fear of the consequences to you, would you take advantage of the situation? Why or why not? **3.** If the rules of the game are switched on you at halftime, how do you react: Cry foul? Suit up for battle anyway? If you can't fight 'em, join 'em? Would your response give honor to God?

8:3 the evil plan of Haman. Although Haman was dead, his decree was still in effect. When Esther again approached the king without permission, he held out his gold scepter to her.

8:8 write another decree. While Haman's decree could not be revoked, a second one could override it. Xerxes authorized Mordecai to write another decree and authenticate it with the king's signet ring. The new decree gave the Jews the right to protect themselves against anyone who sought to attack them. God had used Esther to help her people.

people of other nationalities became Jews because fear of the Jews
had seized them.

Triumph of the Jews

9 On the thirteenth day of the twelfth month, the month of Adar,
the edict commanded by the king was to be carried out. On this
day the enemies of the Jews had hoped to overpower them, but now
the tables were turned and the Jews got the upper hand over those
who hated them. 2The Jews assembled in their cities in all the provinces of King Xerxes to attack those seeking their destruction. No one
could stand against them, because the people of all the other nationalities were afraid of them. 3And all the nobles of the provinces, the
satraps, the governors and the king's administrators helped the Jews,
because fear of Mordecai had seized them. 4Mordecai was prominent
in the palace; his reputation spread throughout the provinces, and he
became more and more powerful.
5The Jews struck down all their enemies with the sword, killing and
destroying them, and they did what they pleased to those who hated
them. 6In the citadel of Susa, the Jews killed and destroyed five
hundred men. 7They also killed Parshandatha, Dalphon, Aspatha,
8Poratha, Adalia, Aridatha, 9Parmashta, Arisai, Aridai and Vaizatha,
10the ten sons of Haman son of Hammedatha, the enemy of the Jews.
But they did not lay their hands on the plunder.
11The number of those slain in the citadel of Susa was reported to
the king that same day. 12The king said to Queen Esther, "The Jews
have killed and destroyed five hundred men and the ten sons of
Haman in the citadel of Susa. What have they done in the rest of the
king's provinces? Now what is your petition? It will be given you.
What is your request? It will also be granted."
13"If it pleases the king," Esther answered, "give the Jews in Susa
permission to carry out this day's edict tomorrow also, and let
Haman's ten sons be hanged on gallows."
14So the king commanded that this be done. An edict was issued in
Susa, and they hanged the ten sons of Haman. 15The Jews in Susa
came together on the fourteenth day of the month of Adar, and they
put to death in Susa three hundred men, but they did not lay their
hands on the plunder.
16Meanwhile, the remainder of the Jews who were in the king's
provinces also assembled to protect themselves and get relief from
their enemies. They killed seventy-five thousand of them but did not
lay their hands on the plunder. 17This happened on the thirteenth day
of the month of Adar, and on the fourteenth they rested and made it a
day of feasting and joy.

OPEN **1.** What have you won (a job, a game, a mate, an appeal) that you were not expecting to win? Did you crow about it? Make others eat humble pie? Or what? **2.** How often do you cheer for the "underdog"? The "topdog"? When on top, do you ever "pour it on"? Why or why not?

STUDY **1.** To what do you compare the distinct *tone* of this chapter: Nostalgic newsreel of WW II? Teaser for an upcoming horror show? Notes on the jacket of a war novel? Other? **2.** How and why were the Jews able to triumph? Who "turned the tables"? When the Jews got the upper hand, how did they handle it: Cruelly? Mercifully? As expected in war? **3.** In what sense is this defeat of the Amalekites the very opposite of what happened in 1 Samuel 15? Why do the Jews seem intent this time to "take no prisoners" and "take no plunder" (vv. 10,15–16)? **4.** What does this chapter reveal about the character of Esther? Of God? **5.** What do you think about King Xerxes' complete change of heart: He didn't know what was happening? He wanted to right a wrong? He was captivated by Esther?

APPLY **1.** How do you square this story of annihilating and humiliating one's enemy with what Jesus stood for: namely, to "love your enemy"? Would it make a difference to you if it were "kill or be killed"? When, if ever, have you faced such a dilemma? **2.** Do you know of an injustice that needs to be corrected? What can you do about it?

9:5 struck down all their enemies. The Jews gathered in various cities to face their attackers, and government authorities helped them as well. On the day of battle they killed 500 men plus Haman's ten sons. The Jews took no plunder, although the king had given them permission to do so.

9:16 assembled to protect ... relief from their enemies. After defeating their enemies, the Jews experienced peace, and Mordecai became a powerful leader. In Deuteronomy 25:17–19, Moses linked rest from their enemies with the command to blot out the Amalekites, Haman's people.

Purim Celebrated

[18]The Jews in Susa, however, had assembled on the thirteenth and fourteenth, and then on the fifteenth they rested and made it a day of feasting and joy.

[19]That is why rural Jews—those living in villages—observe the fourteenth of the month of Adar as a day of joy and feasting, a day for giving presents to each other.

[20]Mordecai recorded these events, and he sent letters to all the
Jews throughout the provinces of King Xerxes, near and far, [21]to have
them celebrate annually the fourteenth and fifteenth days of the
month of Adar [22]as the time when the Jews got relief from their enemies, and as the month when their sorrow was turned into joy and their mourning into a day of celebration. He wrote them to observe the days as days of feasting and joy and giving presents of food to one another and gifts to the poor.

[23]So the Jews agreed to continue the celebration they had begun,
doing what Mordecai had written to them. [24]For Haman son of Hammedatha, the Agagite, the enemy of all the Jews, had plotted against the Jews to destroy them and had cast the *pur* (that is, the lot) for
their ruin and destruction. [25]But when the plot came to the king's
attention,[a] he issued written orders that the evil scheme Haman had devised against the Jews should come back onto his own head, and
that he and his sons should be hanged on the gallows. [26](Therefore
these days were called Purim, from the word *pur*.) Because of everything written in this letter and because of what they had seen and
what had happened to them, [27]the Jews took it upon themselves to
establish the custom that they and their descendants and all who join them should without fail observe these two days every year, in the
way prescribed and at the time appointed. [28]These days should be
remembered and observed in every generation by every family, and in every province and in every city. And these days of Purim should never cease to be celebrated by the Jews, nor should the memory of them die out among their descendants.

[29]So Queen Esther, daughter of Abihail, along with Mordecai the Jew, wrote with full authority to confirm this second letter concerning Purim. [30]And Mordecai sent letters to all the Jews in the 127 prov-
inces of the kingdom of Xerxes—words of goodwill and assurance—
[31]to establish these days of Purim at their designated times, as Mordecai the Jew and Queen Esther had decreed for them, and as they had established for themselves and their descendants in regard
to their times of fasting and lamentation. [32]Esther's decree con-
firmed these regulations about Purim, and it was written down in the records.

The Greatness of Mordecai

10 King Xerxes imposed tribute throughout the empire, to its
distant shores. [2]And all his acts of power and might, together

[a]25 Or *when Esther came before the king*

OPEN **1.** What national day of celebration do you enjoy the most? What makes it so special? **2.** Birthdays aside, which event in your life is an annual personal day of celebration? Why?

STUDY **1.** *Purim* is a most revered Jewish festival, celebrated to this day. (*Purim* is "a day for giving ... to one another and ... the poor.") Why is that? How was it first established? Where did it get its name? **2.** Why is *Purim* celebrated for two days (v. 27)? What customs make *Purim* different from the other feast days of the Jews? **3.** In recounting the story (vv. 23–28), why do you suppose the narrator chose to start with Haman's plot, instead of "at the beginning," with Esther's rise to prominence in a foreign monarchy (reminiscent of Joseph)? **4.** What was the great turning point of the story? **5.** Is there such a moment in your life?

APPLY **1.** What event in your life has turned sorrow into joy? How have you commemorated that event? How have you shared it with others so that they could join you? **2.** What prompts you to give to others, especially the poor: Times of tragedy? Only at Christmas? More often than that? How regularly? **3.** What "relief from your enemies" have you received lately? What relief are you still seeking? How can your group be a "relief agency" for you and others?

OPEN **1.** Who are your top three heroes (past or present)? **2.** What do your three heroes have in common?

9:19 a day of joy and feasting. The Feast of Purim was commanded by Mordecai and Esther to remember God's goodness in protecting his people from destruction. It was to be an annual event celebrated with eating, rejoicing and sharing with the poor. It was called Purim because of Haman's use of the *pur* (the lot) to determine the time for the Jews' execution (3:7). The *pur* became a symbol of God's rescue from desperate and dangerous events.

STUDY **1.** For what was Mordecai honored: Character? Behavior? Results? How are those three related? **2.** Using anecdotes from Mordecai's life, illustrate the point that he "worked for the good of his people" and "spoke up for the welfare of all the Jews." **3.** What is the central theological point of this book? How is that point accented by the narrator's use of duplication and symmetry? **4.** Why would a book, so obviously Jewish, be devoid of any reference to the Lord? Does the total lack of any reference to God (prayer or any specific religious activity) make the main point more obvious? Why do you think such a "secular" book is in the Bible?

APPLY **1.** How would your personal history sound if it was told without any proper references to God? Try it. What audience reaction do you get? **2.** How do you see yourself: As consciously guided and used of God? As an unwitting pawn? Illustrate. **3.** What do you need to do to be like Esther and Mordecai and follow God?

with a full account of the greatness of Mordecai to which the king
had raised him, are they not written in the book of the annals of the
kings of Media and Persia? 3Mordecai the Jew was second in rank to
King Xerxes, preeminent among the Jews, and held in high esteem by
his many fellow Jews, because he worked for the good of his people
and spoke up for the welfare of all the Jews.

Author. Everyone from Job to Moses to Elihu (Job's fourth friend) has been suggested as possible authors for this book, but no one knows the real identity of the author.

Date. The date of the writing is uncertain, as well. The events it describes are most easily placed within the Patriarchal Period.

Purpose. Job is typically considered a book about suffering. It disconnects the notion that human suffering is tied to God's displeasure. Job is also a book about God. It reveals God's presence, his watchful eye and his organization of both life here on earth and in heaven. It reveals his sovereignty above any evil forces or earthly circumstances.

Personal Reading	Group Study Topic and Reading	
1	Job's First Test	1:1–22
2	Job's Second Test	2:1–10
3–5	Job's Misery	3:1–26
6–8	Job Must Have Sinned	8:1–22
9–11	Job Is Self-Deceived	11:1–20
12–15	Job Is Misunderstood	13:1–28
16–18	Job Finds No Relief	16:1–22
19–22	Job Ponders the Wicked	21:1–34
23–25	Job: A Mere Worm?	25:1–6
26–31	"I Am Innocent!"	31:1–40
32–37	Job Must Be Guilty	32:1–22
38–41	God Reveals His Glory	40:1–24
42	Job Is Restored	42:7–17

Historical Background. The book of Job is set in an ancient world. Though the book of Job is placed after the books of the post-exile period (Ezra and Nehemiah), the story of the man Job does not belong to that era. The setting has much in common with the Patriarchal Period in the Near East. Job has the long lifespan of the patriarchs (over one hundred years); his wealth is measured as much as Issac's or Jacob's would have been in relation to his livestock; there is no designated priesthood and Job serves as the priest for his household. Part of that dating is due to internal evidence. Iron is mentioned in 19:24, and iron was not common in the Near East until the twelfth century B.C.

A Mystery. Job is a very difficult book to summarize because it offers no simple answers. It speaks volumes about faith, about the nature of evil in the world, about suffering, about friendship and about the true nature of human existence. Job is a good man who still sins. He suffers, but his suffering is caused not by sin but by other things. Job responds to suffering in the right way.

All of these contradictions make up the complex portrait of Job, and by extension, of all humans. None of us suffer quite like Job did, but we all suffer in our own ways. The book of Job offers us little consolation or encouragement, but it does offer empathy. We are not alone. Others are suffering with us, and God is always there. Job offers readers those gems of hope. As we struggle through feelings of pain and isolation, we can be confident that Job would understand.

OPEN 1. When do you remember getting some really bad news as a kid? 2. What tragedy has happened recently in your community that has caused people to ask the question "why"?

STUDY 1. What made Job "the greatest man among all the people of the East" (v. 3)? 2. How does God describe Job to Satan? How would you paraphrase this in modern-day terms? 3. What is the assumption behind the challenge that Satan puts to God (vv. 9–11)? 4. How do you feel about the Lord allowing Satan to put Job through a test? 5. What would be a comparable series of disasters today to what Job experienced in this story? 6. What does Satan want to prove? How would you describe Job's response to the news of the events (vv. 20–21)? 7. What are three or four questions that immediately come to mind as you read this story? How would you answer your own questions?

APPLY 1. What is the closest you have come to experiencing the kind of personal losses that Job experienced? What was your immediate response? 2. As you look back upon the traumatic and painful events in your life, how do you look upon these events now? 3. How has your faith in God affected the way you look at the day-to-day events in your life?

Prologue

1 In the land of Uz there lived a man whose name was Job. This
man was blameless and upright; he feared God and shunned
evil. 2He had seven sons and three daughters, 3and he owned seven
thousand sheep, three thousand camels, five hundred yoke of oxen
and five hundred donkeys, and had a large number of servants. He
was the greatest man among all the people of the East.
4His sons used to take turns holding feasts in their homes, and
they would invite their three sisters to eat and drink with them.
5When a period of feasting had run its course, Job would send and
have them purified. Early in the morning he would sacrifice a burnt
offering for each of them, thinking, "Perhaps my children have sinned
and cursed God in their hearts." This was Job's regular custom.

Job's First Test

6One day the angels[a] came to present themselves before the LORD,
and Satan[b] also came with them. 7The LORD said to Satan, "Where
have you come from?"
Satan answered the LORD, "From roaming through the earth and
going back and forth in it."
8Then the LORD said to Satan, "Have you considered my servant
Job? There is no one on earth like him; he is blameless and upright, a
man who fears God and shuns evil."
9"Does Job fear God for nothing?" Satan replied. 10"Have you not
put a hedge around him and his household and everything he has?
You have blessed the work of his hands, so that his flocks and herds
are spread throughout the land. 11But stretch out your hand and
strike everything he has, and he will surely curse you to your face."
12The LORD said to Satan, "Very well, then, everything he has is in
your hands, but on the man himself do not lay a finger."
Then Satan went out from the presence of the LORD.

[a]6 Hebrew *the sons of God* [b]6 *Satan means accuser.*

1:1 land of Uz there lived a man. Some scholars believe that Uz was in Bashan, south of Damascus; others say Uz was east of Edom in northern Arabia. Although near a desert, the land was fertile for agriculture and raising livestock. **blameless and upright.** Job was morally mature and did not readily deviate from God's standards. He was not sinless, but strong in his faith. His relationship with God motivated him to turn away from evil.

1:5 feasting. Feasts were held to celebrate various occasions, including birthdays. **have them purified.** Job sought to make his ten children ceremonially clean from known or unknown *sins.* ***he would sacrifice a burnt*** **offering.** He interceded on behalf of his children, presenting a burnt offering for each of them and asking for God's forgiveness of their sins.

1:7 Where have you come from? God did not ask from a need to find out, but as part of a conversation, similar to his asking Adam in the garden, "Where are you?" Satan had been roaming the earth, evidently looking for people to dominate. As the god of this age (2 Cor. 4:4), the world is Satan's domain for evil (1 John 5:19).

1:8 Have you considered my servant Job? God pointed to Job as an example of character and loyalty. **my servant.** This is the proper relationship between a joyful, trusting, obedient believer and God. **shuns evil.** As stated in verse one, Job deliberately avoided evil.

1:9 Satan. Satan questioned the motives of an upright man, saying Job only loved and obeyed God because of the benefits he received from God. Satan challenged God by asking if anyone would obey God without getting good things in return.

1:10 put a hedge. No harm could come to Job or his family unless God permitted it, because God had placed a shield of protection around them. God has always protected his people, sometimes by a cloud, a wall of fire or guardian angels, and he continues to do so today.

1:11 he will surely curse you to your face. Satan addressed God with bold disrespect, trying to demean him by saying man's only motive in loving God is selfish and by implying that God must buy human love with good gifts.

1:12 everything he has ... but on the man himself do not lay a finger. God limited Satan's power so that the devil could not act without God's permission. God is sovereign over the world and its inhabitants (Isa. 45:5–7).

[13]One day when Job's sons and daughters were feasting and
drinking wine at the oldest brother's house, [14]a messenger came to
Job and said, "The oxen were plowing and the donkeys were grazing
nearby, [15]and the Sabeans attacked and carried them off. They put
the servants to the sword, and I am the only one who has escaped to
tell you!"

[16]While he was still speaking, another messenger came and said,
"The fire of God fell from the sky and burned up the sheep and the
servants, and I am the only one who has escaped to tell you!"

[17]While he was still speaking, another messenger came and said,
"The Chaldeans formed three raiding parties and swept down on
your camels and carried them off. They put the servants to the sword,
and I am the only one who has escaped to tell you!"

[18]While he was still speaking, yet another messenger came and
said, "Your sons and daughters were feasting and drinking wine at
the oldest brother's house, [19]when suddenly a mighty wind swept in
from the desert and struck the four corners of the house. It collapsed
on them and they are dead, and I am the only one who has escaped to
tell you!"

[20]At this, Job got up and tore his robe and shaved his head. Then he
fell to the ground in worship [21]and said:

"Naked I came from my mother's womb,
  and naked I will depart.[a]
The LORD gave and the LORD has taken away;
  may the name of the LORD be praised."

[22]In all this, Job did not sin by charging God with wrongdoing.

Job's Second Test

2 On another day the angels[b] came to present themselves before
the LORD, and Satan also came with them to present himself before him. [2]And the LORD said to Satan, "Where have you come from?"

Satan answered the LORD, "From roaming through the earth and
going back and forth in it."

[3]Then the LORD said to Satan, "Have you considered my servant
Job? There is no one on earth like him; he is blameless and upright, a
man who fears God and shuns evil. And he still maintains his
integrity, though you incited me against him to ruin him without any
reason."

[4]"Skin for skin!" Satan replied. "A man will give all he has for his

[a]21 Or *will return there* [b]1 Hebrew *the sons of God*

OPEN 1. Who is your favorite: TV courtroom attorney? Your favorite TV judge? What do you like about them? **2.** What experience have you had in court as a witness, defendant or plaintiff?

STUDY 1. In this heavenly courtroom scene, how would you characterize the defendant? His wife? The prosecuting attorney? The judge? The three witnesses? **2.** How does this judge respond to the tactics of the accuser and the rights of the defendant the first time around (v. 3)? And the second time (vv. 4–6)? Is Satan still on a leash, or given more free

---

1:20 At this, Job got up and tore his robe and shaved his head. Job grieved over his stunning and swift losses (Jer. 48:37). But rather than shaking his fist angrily at God or questioning him, he fell to the ground in worship.

1:21 depart. Job acknowledged that he was born with nothing and would die with nothing. Everything he had was from God. **The LORD gave and the LORD has taken away.** He again recognized God's sovereignty, and he submitted to it rather than blaming God or becoming bitter. **may the name of the LORD be praised.** Job proved that his love for God was not based on material prosperity. His response demonstrated genuine faith.

2:2 Where have you come from? This passage is nearly identical to 1:6–7, where Satan came before God to stir up trouble. God knew exactly where Satan had been when he asked the question that began their conversation.

2:3 though you incited me. God again pointed to Job's integrity even in the face of Satan's attack, reminding Satan that Job had done nothing to deserve the calamities that had befallen him. God knew that Job could endure the test.

2:4 Skin for skin! Satan points to Job's breaking point: not the retirement fund or bank account or even his children, but deep personal pain and suffering. The proverbial phrase referred

reign? **3.** What part does Job's wife play in this courtroom scene? If Job did curse God, what would that prove about Job? About God? About Satan? **4.** Instead, how does Job respond? How do his three friends respond? What do you find commendable in their responses?

APPLY 1. Recall the last time you "sat among the ashes." What questions were you asking God then? Who else listened to you? What answers did you get? **2.** When bad things happen to good people, whom do you blame? **3.** When are you most comfortable with silence? Why? When is silence more preferable, even more powerful, than words?

own life. [5]But stretch out your hand and strike his flesh and bones,
and he will surely curse you to your face."
[6]The LORD said to Satan, "Very well, then, he is in your hands; but
you must spare his life."
[7]So Satan went out from the presence of the LORD and afflicted
Job with painful sores from the soles of his feet to the top of his head.
[8]Then Job took a piece of broken pottery and scraped himself with it
as he sat among the ashes.
[9]His wife said to him, "Are you still holding on to your integrity?
Curse God and die!"
[10]He replied, "You are talking like a foolish[a] woman. Shall we
accept good from God, and not trouble?"
In all this, Job did not sin in what he said.

Job's Three Friends

[11]When Job's three friends, Eliphaz the Temanite, Bildad the
Shuhite and Zophar the Naamathite, heard about all the troubles that
had come upon him, they set out from their homes and met together
by agreement to go and sympathize with him and comfort him.
[12]When they saw him from a distance, they could hardly recognize
him; they began to weep aloud, and they tore their robes and
sprinkled dust on their heads. [13]Then they sat on the ground with him
for seven days and seven nights. No one said a word to him, because
they saw how great his suffering was.

Job Speaks

3 After this, Job opened his mouth and cursed the day of his birth.
[2]He said:

[3]"May the day of my birth perish,
  and the night it was said, 'A boy is born!'
[4]That day—may it turn to darkness;
  may God above not care about it;

OPEN 1. Imagine if your closest family member or friend had never been born—how would your life be different? **2.** What day qualifies as the worst day of your life? Explain briefly.

STUDY 1. Note the change in the text from prose to poetry. What does this change mean? Should poetry be interpreted just like prose,

[a]10 The Hebrew word rendered *foolish* denotes moral deficiency.

---

to either bartering animal skins or to the "eye for an eye" concept of Exodus 21:23–25.

2:6 but you must spare his life. Only one restriction kept Satan from going all the way. God is sovereign, even on Job's worst day. The relationship between God and Job could stand the hard test of prolonged agony.

2:7 painful sores from the soles of his feet to the top of his head. The two Hebrew words used for "painful sores" were also used to describe the plague of festering boils in Egypt (Ex. 9:8–11). In Deuteronomy 28:35, "painful boils" is one of the curses for disobedience and refers to an incurable disease.

2:9 Curse God and die! When Job needed comfort from his wife, he received instead a mocking suggestion, parallel to what Satan had predicted Job himself would do. Her bitterness toward God was evident; her advice was cynical and crushing.

2:10 Shall we accept good ... not trouble? Job again modeled a faithful response to adversity. Without any answers to his "whys," he trusted God, proving Satan wrong.

2:12 could hardly recognize him. Job was so disfigured that his friends had trouble recognizing him. His maladies included ulcerous sores, itching, degenerative changes in facial skin, blackened skin, loss of appetite, depression, worms in the boils, weight loss, running sores and difficulty breathing. **weep aloud, and they tore their robes and sprinkled dust on their heads.** These responses indicate the depth of grief, emotional shock and sorrow (1:20; 1 Sam. 4:12).

2:13 sat on the ground with him for seven days. Job's friends grieved with him silently for seven days and seven nights. Then Job spoke first.

3:1 cursed the day of his birth. After a week of silent contemplation, Job despaired of life itself (Jer. 15:10). Yet he did not curse God, nor threaten suicide.

3:3 May ... my birth perish. Although Job did not blaspheme, he regretted his birth and longed to die. He felt miserable. Pain and loss had driven him to a very low point, yet he obeyed God.

3:4 day—may it turn to darkness. Job wished that his birth date had been eclipsed—never happened—so that he would never have existed. No Job, no suffering.

may no light shine upon it.
[5] May darkness and deep shadow[a] claim it once more;
may a cloud settle over it;
may blackness overwhelm its light.
[6] That night—may thick darkness seize it;
may it not be included among the days of the year
nor be entered in any of the months.
[7] May that night be barren;
may no shout of joy be heard in it.
[8] May those who curse days[b] curse that day,
those who are ready to rouse Leviathan.
[9] May its morning stars become dark;
may it wait for daylight in vain
and not see the first rays of dawn,
[10] for it did not shut the doors of the womb on me
to hide trouble from my eyes.

[11] "Why did I not perish at birth,
and die as I came from the womb?
[12] Why were there knees to receive me
and breasts that I might be nursed?
[13] For now I would be lying down in peace;
I would be asleep and at rest
[14] with kings and counselors of the earth,
who built for themselves places now lying in ruins,
[15] with rulers who had gold,
who filled their houses with silver.
[16] Or why was I not hidden in the ground like a stillborn child,
like an infant who never saw the light of day?
[17] There the wicked cease from turmoil,
and there the weary are at rest.
[18] Captives also enjoy their ease;
they no longer hear the slave driver's shout.
[19] The small and the great are there,
and the slave is freed from his master.

[20] "Why is light given to those in misery,
and life to the bitter of soul,
[21] to those who long for death that does not come,
who search for it more than for hidden treasure,
[22] who are filled with gladness
and rejoice when they reach the grave?
[23] Why is life given to a man
whose way is hidden,
whom God has hedged in?

[a]5 Or *and the shadow of death* [b]8 Or *the sea*

or are the rules different? **2.** After *what* (v. 1) does Job speak? What is the relation between their prolonged silence and his eventual speech? **3.** Is Job speaking logically? Theologically? Emotionally? How can you tell? **4.** Why does Job curse the day of his birth, rather than God? Is cursing God's creation equivalent to cursing God? **5.** In verses 11–26, instead of cursing, what is Job doing? Who is he questioning? What does he prefer to the status quo? **6.** By cursing and questioning his own existence, how does this implicate God? What statement of Job's comes closest to challenging God's power, wisdom and goodness? **7.** In light of chapter 1, what irony do you see in verse 23? Who was "hedging" before? Who is hedging now? **8.** What does this chapter tell you about Job's health—emotionally, physically and spiritually? What does it tell you, if anything, about his sense of loss? Does that surprise you? How so?

APPLY 1. When, if ever, have you felt like life was not worth living? What were you feeling? What were the circumstances? What did you end up doing about that? Where was God for you when it hurt the most? **2.** How do *you* respond to rhetorical questions, such as Job asks (vv. 11–12,16,20–23)? **3.** What three friends of yours are better listeners than most? What might you want to share with them now?

3:10 to hide trouble from my eyes. Job did not blame God, curse God or contemplate taking his own life. But emotional and physical agony caused him to wish he had never been born.

3:16 like a stillborn child. Job again expressed his desire to have never been born. He imagined the peace he would experience in death, as contrasted with the restlessness and pain of the moment. Nonexistence was Job's only wish for escape. His lament has poetic elements, as he portrayed his misery by using several similes and metaphors.

3:23 whom God has hedged in. Job understood God's protective hedge around his life, but wondered if that hedge could be trimmed enough to allow a merciful death. Earlier, God's hedge produced bounty and all good things; now it kept Job in pain.

²⁴For sighing comes to me instead of food;
my groans pour out like water.
²⁵What I feared has come upon me;
what I dreaded has happened to me.
²⁶I have no peace, no quietness;
I have no rest, but only turmoil."

Eliphaz

4 Then Eliphaz the Temanite replied:

²"If someone ventures a word with you, will you be impatient?
But who can keep from speaking?
³Think how you have instructed many,
how you have strengthened feeble hands.
⁴Your words have supported those who stumbled;
you have strengthened faltering knees.
⁵But now trouble comes to you, and you are discouraged;
it strikes you, and you are dismayed.
⁶Should not your piety be your confidence
and your blameless ways your hope?

⁷"Consider now: Who, being innocent, has ever perished?
Where were the upright ever destroyed?
⁸As I have observed, those who plow evil
and those who sow trouble reap it.
⁹At the breath of God they are destroyed;
at the blast of his anger they perish.
¹⁰The lions may roar and growl,
yet the teeth of the great lions are broken.
¹¹The lion perishes for lack of prey,
and the cubs of the lioness are scattered.

¹²"A word was secretly brought to me,
my ears caught a whisper of it.
¹³Amid disquieting dreams in the night,
when deep sleep falls on men,
¹⁴fear and trembling seized me
and made all my bones shake.
¹⁵A spirit glided past my face,
and the hair on my body stood on end.
¹⁶It stopped,

OPEN 1. When you were an adolescent, whose criticism did you have the hardest time with: Your dad's? Your mom's? Your friend's? **2.** What unjustified criticism have you received lately? What justified criticism? How do you tell the difference?

STUDY 1. After seven days of mourning, Eliphaz speaks up. How do his first words strike you: Sympathetic? Instructive? Well-meaning? Dogmatic? Or what? **2.** What neat theological formula does Eliphaz urge upon Job as the proper basis for his hope (vv. 6–11)? How does that view of the "blameless" and the "evildoers" compare with the prevailing theology of that day (Ps. 1)? Is Eliphaz's theology correct? How so? **3.** What is Eliphaz's source for his authoritative viewpoint (vv. 12–16)? How does he describe his spiritual experience? Does that hair-raising, mystical experience sound reliable to you? **4.** What does Eliphaz say God told him (vv. 17–21)? **5.** Who would serve as a mediator to help plead Job's case (5:1; 9:33; 16:19–20)? Who are these "holy ones" (1:6; 2:1)? Why does Job need a mediator (5:2–7)? **6.** What is the gist of Eliphaz's advice (5:8-16)? What is his concept of God? His view of God working in history? What, if anything, is wrong with Eliphaz's views? **7.** What does Eliphaz imply is the reason for suffering (5:17–26)? How would these words likely be received by Job, a "blameless and upright man," a man who has lost his security and children? **8.** What is Job

---

4:1 Eliphaz. Probably the oldest of the three friends, he spoke first, in response to what he viewed as Job's tirade against his troubles. Eliphaz firmly but wrongly believed that God was punishing Job for sin.

4:2 ventures a word with you. Eliphaz was afraid that his words would provoke another outburst from Job, but *he felt he must confront him.*

4:3 Think how you have instructed many. Eliphaz affirmed Job's support and help toward others in their times of need (Isa. 35:3), but he reminded Job how he had advised others who were suffering to be patient under trial. The implication was that he should follow his own advice.

4:7 Who, being innocent, has ever perished? Eliphaz believed that suffering was the result of sin and that righteousness yielded protection from disaster. He did not understand that many times the innocent person also suffers (John 9:1–3; 1 Peter 2:19–20).

4:8 those who sow trouble reap it. "You reap what you sow" appears throughout the Bible (Ps. 7:14–16; Prov. 11:18). Eliphaz had certainly seen that principle at work in his own life. But Scripture is also clear that not all suffering is the result of personal sin.

4:10 the teeth of the great lions are broken. Implied here is that Job, once strong, had sinned and brought his calamities upon himself. Just as the mighty lion can be brought low by God's anger, so Job suffered because God was punishing his sin.

but I could not tell what it was.
A form stood before my eyes,
and I heard a hushed voice:
[17]'Can a mortal be more righteous than God?
Can a man be more pure than his Maker?
[18]If God places no trust in his servants,
if he charges his angels with error,
[19]how much more those who live in houses of clay,
whose foundations are in the dust,
who are crushed more readily than a moth!
[20]Between dawn and dusk they are broken to pieces;
unnoticed, they perish forever.
[21]Are not the cords of their tent pulled up,
so that they die without wisdom?'[a]

5 "Call if you will, but who will answer you?
To which of the holy ones will you turn?
[2]Resentment kills a fool,
and envy slays the simple.
[3]I myself have seen a fool taking root,
but suddenly his house was cursed.
[4]His children are far from safety,
crushed in court without a defender.
[5]The hungry consume his harvest,
taking it even from among thorns,
and the thirsty pant after his wealth.
[6]For hardship does not spring from the soil,
nor does trouble sprout from the ground.
[7]Yet man is born to trouble
as surely as sparks fly upward.

[8]"But if it were I, I would appeal to God;
I would lay my cause before him.
[9]He performs wonders that cannot be fathomed,
miracles that cannot be counted.
[10]He bestows rain on the earth;
he sends water upon the countryside.
[11]The lowly he sets on high,
and those who mourn are lifted to safety.
[12]He thwarts the plans of the crafty,
so that their hands achieve no success.

[a]21 Some interpreters end the quotation after verse 17.

supposed to do with Eliphaz's advice (5:27)? What part of Eliphaz's advice is field-tested as true and applicable to Job?

APPLY 1. How did your closest friend react the last time you faced personal difficulty? How was he or she most helpful? Unhelpful? **2.** What about when the tables were turned and your friend was facing difficulty? What kind of friend did you prove to be? **3.** What are you more comfortable doing—giving comfort and support to others or receiving it when you are in need (vv. 4–5)?

4:19 in houses of clay. This refers to human mortality, the human body made from delicate substances (Rom. 9:21). **whose foundations are in the dust.** God the Potter who fashioned the humans from clay (Gen. 2:7), can reduce people to dust when he chooses. Eliphaz again implied that Job's pain was caused by sin.

4:21 so that they die without wisdom. At the time, to die without finding wisdom was a terrible disaster. According to Eliphaz, Job was obviously not wise or he would not be undergoing such calamities.

5:1 To which of the holy ones will you turn? Eliphaz warned Job that angels would not be able to intervene on his behalf. Job later desired a mediator to go between himself and God (9:33; 16:19–21).

5:2 fool. A fool is one who ignores God (Ps. 14:1). Eliphaz mercilessly portrayed Job as someone who had prospered through right living and then suddenly fell under God's curse because of his sin, losing wealth and children.

5:11 The lowly he sets on high. God sometimes disciplines people for their sin through pain and suffering (Heb. 12:7). Eliphaz incorrectly concluded that Job's misfortunes were God's discipline. He encouraged Job to submit to this adversity and reminded him that God shows mercy to the humble (1 Sam. 2:7–8).

[13]He catches the wise in their craftiness,
and the schemes of the wily are swept away.
[14]Darkness comes upon them in the daytime;
at noon they grope as in the night.
[15]He saves the needy from the sword in their mouth;
he saves them from the clutches of the powerful.
[16]So the poor have hope,
and injustice shuts its mouth.

[17]"Blessed is the man whom God corrects;
so do not despise the discipline of the Almighty.[a]
[18]For he wounds, but he also binds up;
he injures, but his hands also heal.
[19]From six calamities he will rescue you;
in seven no harm will befall you.
[20]In famine he will ransom you from death,
and in battle from the stroke of the sword.
[21]You will be protected from the lash of the tongue,
and need not fear when destruction comes.
[22]You will laugh at destruction and famine,
and need not fear the beasts of the earth.
[23]For you will have a covenant with the stones of the field,
and the wild animals will be at peace with you.
[24]You will know that your tent is secure;
you will take stock of your property and find nothing missing.
[25]You will know that your children will be many,
and your descendants like the grass of the earth.
[26]You will come to the grave in full vigor,
like sheaves gathered in season.

[27]"We have examined this, and it is true.
So hear it and apply it to yourself."

Job

6 Then Job replied:

[2]"If only my anguish could be weighed
and all my misery be placed on the scales!
[3]It would surely outweigh the sand of the seas—
no wonder my words have been impetuous.
[4]The arrows of the Almighty are in me,
my spirit drinks in their poison;

[a]17 Hebrew *Shaddai*; here and throughout Job

OPEN 1. In what areas of life are you a noted "heavyweight": Heavy thinker? Heavy player? Heavy worker? Heavy sleeper? Heavy talker? Other? **2.** In what areas of life are you considered a "lightweight"?

STUDY 1. In 6:2–6 and 7:1–6, does Job describe his anguish more in physical terms? Emotional tones? Spiritual ideas? Or what? **2.** What images or word pictures carry more of the weight of Job's anguish

---

5:17 Blessed is the man whom God corrects. As a father disciplines a beloved child, so God disciplines his beloved children (Heb. 12:6). Eliphaz told Job that if he had the right attitude and welcomed God's discipline, God would bless him. **Almighty.** This *translation of the divine title Shaddai* is found 31 times in the book of Job and only 17 times in the rest of the Old Testament.

5:24–25 your tent is secure ... your children will be many. In view of Job's recent losses, Eliphaz's assurance must have only heightened Job's pain. His misguided theological inferences and advice sounded more like condemnation than comfort.

5:27 hear it and apply it to yourself. Eliphaz concluded his speech by reiterating his belief that Job was being disciplined and must repent.

6:1 If only my anguish could be weighed. Job replied to Eliphaz's lofty advice in lamentation and anguish, rather than direct response to Eliphaz. The dialogue reads like a speech contest rather than a conversation.

6:2–3 A little sympathy went a long way with Job. He defended his rash words (ch. 3) by emphasizing his pain.

God's terrors are marshaled against me.
5 Does a wild donkey bray when it has grass,
or an ox bellow when it has fodder?
6 Is tasteless food eaten without salt,
or is there flavor in the white of an egg[a]?
7 I refuse to touch it;
such food makes me ill.

8 "Oh, that I might have my request,
that God would grant what I hope for,
9 that God would be willing to crush me,
to let loose his hand and cut me off!
10 Then I would still have this consolation—
my joy in unrelenting pain—
that I had not denied the words of the Holy One.

11 "What strength do I have, that I should still hope?
What prospects, that I should be patient?
12 Do I have the strength of stone?
Is my flesh bronze?
13 Do I have any power to help myself,
now that success has been driven from me?

14 "A despairing man should have the devotion of his friends,
even though he forsakes the fear of the Almighty.
15 But my brothers are as undependable as intermittent streams,
as the streams that overflow
16 when darkened by thawing ice
and swollen with melting snow,
17 but that cease to flow in the dry season,
and in the heat vanish from their channels.
18 Caravans turn aside from their routes;
they go up into the wasteland and perish.
19 The caravans of Tema look for water,
the traveling merchants of Sheba look in hope.
20 They are distressed, because they had been confident;
they arrive there, only to be disappointed.
21 Now you too have proved to be of no help;
you see something dreadful and are afraid.
22 Have I ever said, 'Give something on my behalf,
pay a ransom for me from your wealth,
23 deliver me from the hand of the enemy,
ransom me from the clutches of the ruthless'?

24 "Teach me, and I will be quiet;
show me where I have been wrong.
25 How painful are honest words!

[a]6 The meaning of the Hebrew for this phrase is uncertain.

than any of the others? **3.** Who does Job view as the source of his suffering? According to chapters 1–2, is he right? **4.** How does Job regard the food for thought offered by Eliphaz (vv. 5–6)? **5.** What is Job's request in verses 8–10? Is he thinking of suicide? **6.** What does his "consolation" prize (v. 10) say about his priorities? **7.** Is Job being too hard on his friends (vv. 14–30)? What does he expect of his "brothers" (compare Gal. 6:1–2)? How have they proven to be of no help? What false accusations does he want them to take back? **8.** What does Job's "integrity" consist of (v. 29; 2:9–10)? Why does he think his integrity is at stake here?

APPLY 1. Have you ever experienced anything like Job's misery, as described in 7:3–4: Months? Several nights? Even one night? What were the circumstances and your response to them? **2.** When have you felt like your personal integrity was at stake? What did you do to defend yourself from false accusations? **3.** What consolation have you experienced from the hand of God?

6:5–6 Job was hurting, and the words of his friends were as comforting as tasteless food. Comparing himself to animals that cry in need, Job justified his outrage.

6:14–15 Ideally, close friends would comfort Job in his misfortune. However, their behavior was disappointing at best.

6:15 my brothers. Instead of helping and trusting him, as true brothers would, Job's friends disappointed him (Gal. 6:1). They were not dependable.

6:22–23 Job could not expect friends to remove his pain, but to "be there" in his suffering. These friends were only a disappointment to Job (12:1–3; 21:1–6; 26:1–4).

But what do your arguments prove?
26 Do you mean to correct what I say,
and treat the words of a despairing man as wind?
27 You would even cast lots for the fatherless
and barter away your friend.

28 "But now be so kind as to look at me.
Would I lie to your face?
29 Relent, do not be unjust;
reconsider, for my integrity is at stake.[a]
30 Is there any wickedness on my lips?
Can my mouth not discern malice?

7 "Does not man have hard service on earth?
Are not his days like those of a hired man?
2 Like a slave longing for the evening shadows,
or a hired man waiting eagerly for his wages,
3 so I have been allotted months of futility,
and nights of misery have been assigned to me.
4 When I lie down I think, 'How long before I get up?'
The night drags on, and I toss till dawn.
5 My body is clothed with worms and scabs,
my skin is broken and festering.

6 "My days are swifter than a weaver's shuttle,
and they come to an end without hope.
7 Remember, O God, that my life is but a breath;
my eyes will never see happiness again.
8 The eye that now sees me will see me no longer;
you will look for me, but I will be no more.
9 As a cloud vanishes and is gone,
so he who goes down to the grave[b] does not return.
10 He will never come to his house again;
his place will know him no more.

11 "Therefore I will not keep silent;
I will speak out in the anguish of my spirit,
I will complain in the bitterness of my soul.
12 Am I the sea, or the monster of the deep,
that you put me under guard?
13 When I think my bed will comfort me
and my couch will ease my complaint,
14 even then you frighten me with dreams
and terrify me with visions,
15 so that I prefer strangling and death,
rather than this body of mine.
16 I despise my life; I would not live forever.
Let me alone; my days have no meaning.

[a]29 *Or my righteousness still stands* [b]9 Hebrew *Sheol*

OPEN If your under-your-breath conversations were monitored for a day, what would that likely reveal about you: Lots of self-talk, berating myself? Many pep-talks, encouraging myself? Unmentionable cursing? Talk-back sessions? Prayers too deep for words? Last laughs? Imaginary friends?

STUDY **1.** To whom is Job speaking now? Why pray now? **2.** In praying, is Job trying to get God to pay more attention to him? Or is Job trying to get rid of God, who now terrifies him? **3.** Is Job's complaint frivolous, or well founded (vv. 11–16)? **4.** Why does Job doubt his self-worth (vv. 15–17)? Why does he think God created him (vv. 18–21)? **5.** What does it mean to be examined by God, according to Job? According to the psalmist (Ps. 8:4–8; 139)? How are their situations different?

APPLY **1.** What do you struggle with the most in regard to your own self-image: How you view

6:27 Job exaggerated their cruelty to make his point.

6:29 Falsely accused, Job urged his friends to take back their words.

7:1–21 Job was disillusioned. How could God treat him this way?

7:7 never see happiness again. Going. Going. Gone. Job was losing sight of hope for a better tomorrow.

7:13–14 Job's dreaming turned to nightmares—terror without escape.

[17]"What is man that you make so much of him,
that you give him so much attention,
[18]that you examine him every morning
and test him every moment?
[19]Will you never look away from me,
or let me alone even for an instant?
[20]If I have sinned, what have I done to you,
O watcher of men?
Why have you made me your target?
Have I become a burden to you?[a]
[21]Why do you not pardon my offenses
and forgive my sins?
For I will soon lie down in the dust;
you will search for me, but I will be no more."

Bildad

8 Then Bildad the Shuhite replied:

[2]"How long will you say such things?
Your words are a blustering wind.
[3]Does God pervert justice?
Does the Almighty pervert what is right?
[4]When your children sinned against him,
he gave them over to the penalty of their sin.
[5]But if you will look to God
and plead with the Almighty,
[6]if you are pure and upright,
even now he will rouse himself on your behalf
and restore you to your rightful place.
[7]Your beginnings will seem humble,
so prosperous will your future be.

[8]"Ask the former generations
and find out what their fathers learned,
[9]for we were born only yesterday and know nothing,
and our days on earth are but a shadow.
[10]Will they not instruct you and tell you?
Will they not bring forth words from their understanding?
[11]Can papyrus grow tall where there is no marsh?
Can reeds thrive without water?

[a]20 A few manuscripts of the Masoretic Text, an ancient Hebrew scribal tradition and Septuagint; most manuscripts of the Masoretic Text *I have become a burden to myself.*

your body (v. 15)? Your sense of purpose (v. 16)? Your moral life (vv. 17–21)? **2.** What do you most need to feel better about yourself: God's forgiveness? Affirming friends? A new vocation?

OPEN 1. Who among your family knows the most: The one who has lived the longest? The one with the most formal education? The one who graduated from the "school of hard knocks"? **2.** What invaluable lesson have you learned from your grandparents?

STUDY 1. How does the tone of Bildad's argument compare to Eliphaz's argument (ch. 4)? What kind of friend does he appear to be? **2.** What is Bildad's view of justice? What "If ..., then ..." formula does he use on Job? **3.** In the eyes of Bildad, what is Job: An evil hypocrite (pretending to be something he is not)? Self-deceived? All talk, no show? "Pure, upright, blameless"? How can you tell (vv. 2,6,13,20)? **4.** At what point is Bildad's prophecy more accurate than he thinks (vv. 6,20; 42:10–17)? **5.** What source does Bildad draw upon for his authoritative view (vv. 8–10)? Does this seem any more reliable to you than Eliphaz's source (4:12–16)? How so? **6.** What age-old wisdom of former generations does Bildad offer (vv. 11–19)? How does that extended proverb apply to Job's situation (vv. 20–22)?

7:17 attention. Convinced his life was pointless, Job had lost interest in himself. He wondered why God had not done the same.

7:20 If I have sinned. Job was not blameless, but did he deserve this kind of treatment? He hinted that God should forgive his imperfections.

7:21 pardon ... forgive. Pardon would bring peace. Job urged God to get on with it and forgive him.

8:2 such things. Bildad spewed out impatience with Job. Irritated, he attempted to dispel what seemed like nonsense to him.

8:3 Bildad's rhetorical questions set the stage for his explanation. According to Bildad, Job was only getting his due.

8:5–6 Bildad betrayed his bad listening skills. Job had already pleaded with God on his own behalf (7:20–21), yet God had not given any relief.

8:6 if you are pure and upright. A sliver of sarcasm accompanied Bildad's reasoning. If Job were really innocent, his healing would not be delayed.

8:8 former generations. Where Eliphaz turned to mysticism for insight (4:12–21), Bildad found straightforward wisdom in the pages of history.

APPLY **1.** What proverbial wisdom has been effectively passed down in your family by those who have graduated from life's "school of hard knocks"? How would that wisdom apply to Job's situation? To your current situation? **2.** What view would Bildad likely have of you and your situation, as compared to Job's? How would you respond to a friend like Bildad?

---

[12]While still growing and uncut,
they wither more quickly than grass.
[13]Such is the destiny of all who forget God;
so perishes the hope of the godless.
[14]What he trusts in is fragile[a];
what he relies on is a spider's web.
[15]He leans on his web, but it gives way;
he clings to it, but it does not hold.
[16]He is like a well-watered plant in the sunshine,
spreading its shoots over the garden;
[17]it entwines its roots around a pile of rocks
and looks for a place among the stones.
[18]But when it is torn from its spot,
that place disowns it and says, 'I never saw you.'
[19]Surely its life withers away,
and[b] from the soil other plants grow.

[20]"Surely God does not reject a blameless man
or strengthen the hands of evildoers.
[21]He will yet fill your mouth with laughter
and your lips with shouts of joy.
[22]Your enemies will be clothed in shame,
and the tents of the wicked will be no more."

Job

9

Then Job replied:

[2]"Indeed, I know that this is true.
But how can a mortal be righteous before God?
[3]Though one wished to dispute with him,
he could not answer him one time out of a thousand.
[4]His wisdom is profound, his power is vast.
Who has resisted him and come out unscathed?
[5]He moves mountains without their knowing it
and overturns them in his anger.
[6]He shakes the earth from its place
and makes its pillars tremble.
[7]He speaks to the sun and it does not shine;
he seals off the light of the stars.
[8]He alone stretches out the heavens
and treads on the waves of the sea.
[9]He is the Maker of the Bear and Orion,
the Pleiades and the constellations of the south.
[10]He performs wonders that cannot be fathomed,
miracles that cannot be counted.

[a]14 The meaning of the Hebrew for this word is uncertain. [b]19 Or *Surely all the joy it has / is that*

OPEN **1.** When have you felt small and most overwhelmed by an awesome natural wonder: On top of a mountain or canyon? Flying? Inside a mammoth cave? Sailing the ocean? Gazing at stars? **2.** By contrast, when do you feel big? **3.** Which did you feel last week—small or big? How come?

STUDY **1.** Why does Job ask the same question as Eliphaz (v. 2; 4:17): Mockery? Flattery? Pursuit of truth? Self-defense? **2.** In what respects does Job agree with his friends on the character of God? On his own character? Where does he go beyond what the others believe? Where is he more modest (vv. 10–11; 4:15–16)? **3.** If God is undeniably, infinitely *great* (vv. 5–10), does Job believe God's greatness is controlled at all by *goodness* or *justice*? Why or why not? **4.** What would Job like to say to God if granted a day in court with him (vv. 3,14–24)? Who would be on trial? In the witness stand? Who would be the blind-folded judge? The

---

8:20 Bildad invited Job to read between the lines and recognize himself as a hypocrite. Why else would God reject Job?

9:2–3 Job recognized that Bildad was right: the wicked deserve punishment. However, Job was hardly wicked. Therefore, Job disputed the fairness of his situation.

9:3 dispute with him. Job described his plight in legal terms (vv. 3,15–16,20,24,32). He took his case to an imaginary courtroom in search of justice.

9:5–10 Sitting across the courtroom from Job was God himself: majestic, awesome and powerful. No wonder Job felt inadequate to bring a case against him.

11 When he passes me, I cannot see him;
when he goes by, I cannot perceive him.
12 If he snatches away, who can stop him?
Who can say to him, 'What are you doing?'
13 God does not restrain his anger;
even the cohorts of Rahab cowered at his feet.

14 "How then can I dispute with him?
How can I find words to argue with him?
15 Though I were innocent, I could not answer him;
I could only plead with my Judge for mercy.
16 Even if I summoned him and he responded,
I do not believe he would give me a hearing.
17 He would crush me with a storm
and multiply my wounds for no reason.
18 He would not let me regain my breath
but would overwhelm me with misery.
19 If it is a matter of strength, he is mighty!
And if it is a matter of justice, who will summon him[a]?
20 Even if I were innocent, my mouth would condemn me;
if I were blameless, it would pronounce me guilty.

21 "Although I am blameless,
I have no concern for myself;
I despise my own life.
22 It is all the same; that is why I say,
'He destroys both the blameless and the wicked.'
23 When a scourge brings sudden death,
he mocks the despair of the innocent.
24 When a land falls into the hands of the wicked,
he blindfolds its judges.
If it is not he, then who is it?

25 "My days are swifter than a runner;
they fly away without a glimpse of joy.
26 They skim past like boats of papyrus,
like eagles swooping down on their prey.
27 If I say, 'I will forget my complaint,
I will change my expression, and smile,'
28 I still dread all my sufferings,
for I know you will not hold me innocent.
29 Since I am already found guilty,
why should I struggle in vain?
30 Even if I washed myself with soap[b]
and my hands with washing soda,

[a] 19 See Septuagint; Hebrew *me.* [b] 30 Or *snow*

prosecuting attorney? **5.** In Job's case, what would be the reasonable verdict? The morally indifferent verdict? **6.** In what tone of voice can you hear Job setting forth his case: Angry? Bitter? Sarcastic? Humble? Begging? **7.** How does Job think sin and suffering are related? How is that different from his friends? **8.** According to Jesus, who gets the greater share of justice or mercy (Matt. 5:45)?

APPLY 1. In verses 4–10 Job speaks of how God shows his power. What manifestation of God's power in nature has most impressed you?. **2.** How does God's power in nature make you feel: Insignificant? Afraid? Reassured? Awed? **3.** Does knowing this power make you more or less prone to go to him with a need or complaint?

OPEN 1. In your no-holds-barred family arguments, who tends to be the position-taker? The conflict-avoider? The negotiator? The scapegoat? Who generally wins and why? **2.** What "moment's joy" were you given last week?

STUDY 1. In verses 25–31, Job shifts focus—to what? What feelings can you discern? What flights of fancy? What unsound reasoning? **2.** What puzzling problem comes into sharp focus in verses 32–33? **3.** Is Job eager to make intellectual sense of the problem of suffering? Or is he more eager to

9:17 for no reason. Job concluded that his suffering was nonsensical, though he was unaware of the heavenly drama that preceded all his troubles (1:6–12).

9:21 Although I am blameless. Although innocence ought to bring relief, Job was convinced otherwise. To be blameless had no payoff, he believed.

9:22–24 God does not rule a fair universe, Job surmised. Wicked people rightly mock the idea that righteous people can expect justice. Moral innocence is no guarantee against calamity.

9:28 you will not hold me innocent. No matter how Job reacted, God's guilty verdict remained steadfast.

9:29 struggle in vain. In fatalistic fashion, Job presumed he was guilty. So, why try?

attain or preserve a right relationship with God, which makes suffering acceptable, if not intelligible? Is he looking for forgiveness from some divine mediator (Heb. 9:15), or is he desiring someone to attest his innocence? **4.** In the "complaint" of 10:1–7, what is Job appealing to God for? **5.** If God's intentions in creating life were good, why would Job go on to conclude that very same life is not worth living (10:18–22)? Why would God create at all if he was only going to destroy later? **6.** From his description of it, is Job eagerly awaiting the joy of life after death, as his one hope of escaping the pain of this life? Or does his "moment's joy" lie somewhere, sometime only on this side of the grave?

APPLY 1. Job saw himself, as we might say, "caught between a rock and a hard place" (10:14–17). When have you felt likewise? How did you solve the riddle of your dilemma? **2.** In the future, how is Christ to be the answer to the questions raised by Job (10:1–7)? How has Christ the Mediator solved the unsolvable dilemmas of your life? **3.** When have you simply laid out your miserable options before God in a "complaint"? What happened as a result?

31 you would plunge me into a slime pit
so that even my clothes would detest me.

32 "He is not a man like me that I might answer him,
that we might confront each other in court.
33 If only there were someone to arbitrate between us,
to lay his hand upon us both,
34 someone to remove God's rod from me,
so that his terror would frighten me no more.
35 Then I would speak up without fear of him,
but as it now stands with me, I cannot.

10 "I loathe my very life;
therefore I will give free rein to my complaint
and speak out in the bitterness of my soul.
2 I will say to God: Do not condemn me,
but tell me what charges you have against me.
3 Does it please you to oppress me,
to spurn the work of your hands,
while you smile on the schemes of the wicked?
4 Do you have eyes of flesh?
Do you see as a mortal sees?
5 Are your days like those of a mortal
or your years like those of a man,
6 that you must search out my faults
and probe after my sin—
7 though you know that I am not guilty
and that no one can rescue me from your hand?

8 "Your hands shaped me and made me.
Will you now turn and destroy me?
9 Remember that you molded me like clay.
Will you now turn me to dust again?
10 Did you not pour me out like milk
and curdle me like cheese,
11 clothe me with skin and flesh
and knit me together with bones and sinews?
12 You gave me life and showed me kindness,
and in your providence watched over my spirit.

13 "But this is what you concealed in your heart,
and I know that this was in your mind:
14 If I sinned, you would be watching me
and would not let my offense go unpunished.
15 If I am guilty—woe to me!
Even if I am innocent, I cannot lift my head,

9:33 lay his hand upon us both. Job sought in vain for an impartial arbiter. Who better for this job than God *himself? But trust in God had not spared* Job the loss of everything.

10:1 give free rein to my complaint. Job unabashedly spoke his mind about the condition of his soul.

10:3 spurn the work of your hands. Job assigned cruel intentions to God. Depressed and utterly discouraged, Job began to believe his ranting, though his ideas denied everything that Job had always believed about God.

10:8–17 As if addressing the witness stand, Job questioned God's motives.

10:8–11 Job accused God of being doubleminded: lovingly creating him only to cruelly crush him.

10:15–16 Job believed he could not win, despite all efforts. Innocence and wickedness share the same fate.

for I am full of shame
and drowned in[a] my affliction.
16 If I hold my head high, you stalk me like a lion
and again display your awesome power against me.
17 You bring new witnesses against me
and increase your anger toward me;
your forces come against me wave upon wave.

18 "Why then did you bring me out of the womb?
I wish I had died before any eye saw me.
19 If only I had never come into being,
or had been carried straight from the womb to the grave!
20 Are not my few days almost over?
Turn away from me so I can have a moment's joy
21 before I go to the place of no return,
to the land of gloom and deep shadow,[b]
22 to the land of deepest night,
of deep shadow and disorder,
where even the light is like darkness."

Zophar

11 Then Zophar the Naamathite replied:

2 "Are all these words to go unanswered?
Is this talker to be vindicated?
3 Will your idle talk reduce men to silence?
Will no one rebuke you when you mock?
4 You say to God, 'My beliefs are flawless
and I am pure in your sight.'
5 Oh, how I wish that God would speak,
that he would open his lips against you
6 and disclose to you the secrets of wisdom,
for true wisdom has two sides.
Know this: God has even forgotten some of your sin.

7 "Can you fathom the mysteries of God?
Can you probe the limits of the Almighty?
8 They are higher than the heavens—what can you do?
They are deeper than the depths of the grave[c]—what can you know?
9 Their measure is longer than the earth
and wider than the sea.

[a]15 Or *and aware of* [b]21 Or *and the shadow of death*; also in verse 22 [c]8 Hebrew *than Sheol*

OPEN 1. What favorite saying in your family like ("Time heals all wounds") is quoted to those who hit bottom and need a pick-me-up? **2.** What do you do when you want to wipe out the memory of a bad day: Sleep? Play music? Eat? Talk to God? Read a book? Write a book? Workout? Call a friend? Other?

STUDY 1. Which theological formula of Eliphaz and Bildad does Zophar now carry forward, even more forcefully? **2.** Is Zophar "all wet" in this thinking, or is he right in some respects? At what points do you think he is right? And wrong? **3.** Compared to the other two, what tone of voice do you hear in Zophar's speech? Why does Zophar seem more eager to rebuke Job? **4.** What presumptions does he make about Job (vv. 3–4,13–20)? When has Job ever mocked God? Or claimed "flawless" beliefs and "pure" behavior? **5.** In what ways does Zophar misrepresent God (vv. 6,17,19; compare Ps. 73, where the psalmist disagrees with Zophar's "bed of roses" theology)?

11:1–20 Eliphaz started it. Bildad elaborated on it. Now, Zophar reiterated their finger-pointing theme: Poor Job was being punished for his own sin.

11:2–3 Zophar accused Job of mocking God. However, he mistook Job's questioning for belligerence.

11:4 I am pure in your sight. Job never claimed to be perfect (9:21). Nonetheless, Zophar used Job's words against him.

11:5 open his lips against you. Zophar wanted to put words in God's mouth, presuming God's words would put Job in his place. Instead, God eventually spoke against Zophar himself (42:7).

11:6 secrets of wisdom. Zophar assumed that Job had it all wrong. He wished God would set him straight.

11:7 Zophar prompted Job to give up this courtroom procedure (10:2). Against such a formidable opponent—God—who could win?

11:8–9 Zophar's portrait of God resembles God's self-description (38:1–42:6).

APPLY **1.** What "prison" do you feel confined in right now (v. 10)? **2.** Do you see God as the one who has imprisoned you, or the one with the key?

---

[10]"If he comes along and confines you in prison
and convenes a court, who can oppose him?
[11]Surely he recognizes deceitful men;
and when he sees evil, does he not take note?
[12]But a witless man can no more become wise
than a wild donkey's colt can be born a man.[a]

[13]"Yet if you devote your heart to him
and stretch out your hands to him,
[14]if you put away the sin that is in your hand
and allow no evil to dwell in your tent,
[15]then you will lift up your face without shame;
you will stand firm and without fear.
[16]You will surely forget your trouble,
recalling it only as waters gone by.
[17]Life will be brighter than noonday,
and darkness will become like morning.
[18]You will be secure, because there is hope;
you will look about you and take your rest in safety.
[19]You will lie down, with no one to make you afraid,
and many will court your favor.
[20]But the eyes of the wicked will fail,
and escape will elude them;
their hope will become a dying gasp."

Job

12 Then Job replied:

[2]"Doubtless you are the people,
and wisdom will die with you!
[3]But I have a mind as well as you;
I am not inferior to you.
Who does not know all these things?

[4]"I have become a laughingstock to my friends,
though I called upon God and he answered—
a mere laughingstock, though righteous and blameless!
[5]Men at ease have contempt for misfortune
as the fate of those whose feet are slipping.
[6]The tents of marauders are undisturbed,
and those who provoke God are secure—
those who carry their god in their hands.[b]

[a]12 *Or wild donkey can be born tame* [b]6 *Or secure / in what God's hand brings them*

OPEN **1.** Describe the counselor or spiritual leader who has been the most help to you over the years. What about that person was most helpful? **2.** When have you been more helped by the counsel of friends, not professionals? What about their friendship meant the most?

STUDY **1.** What tone of voice do you hear in Job's reply here? Where is sarcasm most evident? **2.** What superior knowledge do the three friends claim to have, that Job and all of creation know as well (vv. 2–3,7–12; 13:1–2)? **3.** On what basis does Job make this claim to know as much as they (vv. 3,22; 13:1)? **4.** What distinguishes Job from criminals and idolaters (vv. 4–6)? **5.** What does Job hope his three friends will learn from God's random activity in creation (vv. 7–10,14–25)? **6.** In creation and his-

---

11:11–12 Zophar resorted to insult. He mocked Job's feeble understanding.

11:13–20 Despite his good intentions, Zophar offered unrealistic assurances *related to godly living. Although many* would like to follow his formula for happiness (vv. 16–17), it does not match up to reality (Ps. 73).

12:1–14:22 The bulk of the book of Job is dialogue among Job and his three friends. He responds to them in his longest speech thus far (12:1–13:19). Finally, his attention turns again to God (13:20–14:22).

12:2 wisdom will die with you. Job sneered at his friends' supposed monopoly on wisdom.

12:3 I have a mind as well as you. His friends' lengthy epiphanies were not news to Job. Job did not cease to think when he began to hurt.

12:6 undisturbed. Crime may not pay, but in Job's mind, it did not seem to hurt either. Why should he suffer while criminals had it easy?

[7] "But ask the animals, and they will teach you,
or the birds of the air, and they will tell you;
[8] or speak to the earth, and it will teach you,
or let the fish of the sea inform you.
[9] Which of all these does not know
that the hand of the LORD has done this?
[10] In his hand is the life of every creature
and the breath of all mankind.
[11] Does not the ear test words
as the tongue tastes food?
[12] Is not wisdom found among the aged?
Does not long life bring understanding?

[13] "To God belong wisdom and power;
counsel and understanding are his.
[14] What he tears down cannot be rebuilt;
the man he imprisons cannot be released.
[15] If he holds back the waters, there is drought;
if he lets them loose, they devastate the land.
[16] To him belong strength and victory;
both deceived and deceiver are his.
[17] He leads counselors away stripped
and makes fools of judges.
[18] He takes off the shackles put on by kings
and ties a loincloth[a] around their waist.
[19] He leads priests away stripped
and overthrows men long established.
[20] He silences the lips of trusted advisers
and takes away the discernment of elders.
[21] He pours contempt on nobles
and disarms the mighty.
[22] He reveals the deep things of darkness
and brings deep shadows into the light.
[23] He makes nations great, and destroys them;
he enlarges nations, and disperses them.
[24] He deprives the leaders of the earth of their reason;
he sends them wandering through a trackless waste.
[25] They grope in darkness with no light;
he makes them stagger like drunkards.

13 "My eyes have seen all this,
my ears have heard and understood it.
[2] What you know, I also know;
I am not inferior to you.

[a]18 Or *shackles of kings / and ties a belt*

tory, is there a *moral* pattern: Do the righteous suffer, regardless of God's presence? Does the punishment always fit the crime? **7.** In verses 17–25, who parades forth in Job's view of human history? **8.** Is God whimsical or arbitrary? Is God seen as detached from it all, or responsible for it all? What does Job say to either defend, or indict, God's nature? **9.** How does this contrast with Eliphaz's "simple" understanding of the way God works in nature and history (5:10–16)? **10.** Is merely "knowing" the ways of God enough to satisfy Job (13:1–5)? Why or why not? What more does he want from God? From his "wise" friends (Prov. 17:28)?

APPLY 1. When have you felt you were a "laughing-stock" to your friends or to other people around you? **2.** When you feel "alone against the crowd" do you view God as a comforter on your side, or as one of those laughing at you? How so?

12:7–12 Even the animals know the gist of all that his friends had told him. Job insinuated that wisdom had not accompanied age in their case (8:8–10).

12:7 ask the animals, and they will teach you. The most primitive creatures understood the most basic principles of life.

12:9 hand of the LORD. Life's trials ultimately come under God's authority.

12:13–25 If only life were as simple as Eliphaz suggested (5:10–16). In contrast, Job neither oversimplified nor understated life's complexities. He cited examples of the powerful turned powerless (v. 21) and the wise turned simple (v. 24). However, God is the one constant among many variables.

13:1–12 Job asserted that his friends had done more damage than good (v. 4). They had misconstrued Job's case and misrepresented God. As self-appointed spokespersons for God, they had failed (vv. 7–8).

OPEN **1.** When you were a child, what was on the very top of your wish list? **2.** When you became an adult, how did that wish list change?

STUDY **1.** In verses 6–12, how does Job, the defendant, turn the tables on the three friends? **2.** What is so wrong with the way they have been arguing their case (vv. 7–8)? By what standards will they in turn be judged (vv. 9–12)? **3.** What risks is Job taking in bypassing his friends and appealing his case directly to God (vv. 13–19)? Of what is he most certain? Why? **4.** What do you see here in Job's character: Spunk? Spite? Courage? Arrogance? Hope? Foolishness? **5.** Of the many issues he takes up with God (vv. 20–27), what are the "two things" Job desires most from him? **6.** In what ways does Job lay himself wide open for yet more "bitter things" from God? With what mistaken notion about sins and suffering is Job still burdened?

APPLY **1.** If you could make two requests of God, with the prospect of them both coming true, what would they be? How might they change if you were facing extreme hardship? **2.** Compared to Job, with what attitudes do you approach God? When does seeking after God become "risky" for you? Are you willing to take that risk, now? Why or why not?

---

[3] But I desire to speak to the Almighty
and to argue my case with God.
[4] You, however, smear me with lies;
you are worthless physicians, all of you!
[5] If only you would be altogether silent!
For you, that would be wisdom.
[6] Hear now my argument;
listen to the plea of my lips.
[7] Will you speak wickedly on God's behalf?
Will you speak deceitfully for him?
[8] Will you show him partiality?
Will you argue the case for God?
[9] Would it turn out well if he examined you?
Could you deceive him as you might deceive men?
[10] He would surely rebuke you
if you secretly showed partiality.
[11] Would not his splendor terrify you?
Would not the dread of him fall on you?
[12] Your maxims are proverbs of ashes;
your defenses are defenses of clay.

[13] "Keep silent and let me speak;
then let come to me what may.
[14] Why do I put myself in jeopardy
and take my life in my hands?
[15] Though he slay me, yet will I hope in him;
I will surely[a] defend my ways to his face.
[16] Indeed, this will turn out for my deliverance,
for no godless man would dare come before him!
[17] Listen carefully to my words;
let your ears take in what I say.
[18] Now that I have prepared my case,
I know I will be vindicated.
[19] Can anyone bring charges against me?
If so, I will be silent and die.

[20] "Only grant me these two things, O God,
and then I will not hide from you:
[21] Withdraw your hand far from me,
and stop frightening me with your terrors.
[22] Then summon me and I will answer,
or let me speak, and you reply.
[23] How many wrongs and sins have I committed?
Show me my offense and my sin.

[a]15 Or *He will surely slay me; I have no hope — / yet I will*

13:5 Friends who wish to help people in need should listen first and speak later (vv. 6,13,17,19). The wisest thing his well-intentioned friends could say now was nothing at all.

13:15 Confident of his innocence, Job would present his case before God if it were his last living act. Come what may, Job would put his hope in God.

13:17 Listen carefully. Like an attorney presenting opening remarks, Job began his self-defense.

13:20 grant me these two things. Job asked for a stay to his torment (v. 21), and then, a fair trial where God would hear his case and respond (v. 22).

13:23 Job led with his strongest argument: What had he done wrong to deserve such punishment?

24 Why do you hide your face
and consider me your enemy?
25 Will you torment a windblown leaf?
Will you chase after dry chaff?
26 For you write down bitter things against me
and make me inherit the sins of my youth.
27 You fasten my feet in shackles;
you keep close watch on all my paths
by putting marks on the soles of my feet.

28 "So man wastes away like something rotten,
like a garment eaten by moths.

14 "Man born of woman
is of few days and full of trouble.
2 He springs up like a flower and withers away;
like a fleeting shadow, he does not endure.
3 Do you fix your eye on such a one?
Will you bring him[a] before you for judgment?
4 Who can bring what is pure from the impure?
No one!
5 Man's days are determined;
you have decreed the number of his months
and have set limits he cannot exceed.
6 So look away from him and let him alone,
till he has put in his time like a hired man.

7 "At least there is hope for a tree:
If it is cut down, it will sprout again,
and its new shoots will not fail.
8 Its roots may grow old in the ground
and its stump die in the soil,
9 yet at the scent of water it will bud
and put forth shoots like a plant.
10 But man dies and is laid low;
he breathes his last and is no more.
11 As water disappears from the sea
or a riverbed becomes parched and dry,
12 so man lies down and does not rise;
till the heavens are no more, men will not awake
or be roused from their sleep.

13 "If only you would hide me in the grave[b]
and conceal me till your anger has passed!

[a]3 Septuagint, Vulgate and Syriac; Hebrew *me* [b]13 Hebrew *Sheol*

OPEN In tending your garden (if you have one), do you prefer annuals (which bloom all summer long, but then die forever) or perennials (which bloom only briefly, but spring to life again the next year)? Which flowers in the annuals/perennials categories are your favorites?

STUDY 1. What are the four major poetic images in this chapter (vv. 1–6,7–13,14–17,18–22)? What mixed metaphors do you see here? **2.** What do these poems say about the human condition? About God's link to humankind? **3.** What mood swings in Job do you detect as he moves through the various stanzas? Where do you see waves of despair? Renewal of hope? Certainty of faith? **4.** What is the movement here: Is Job regressing? Or progressing? What is the "bottom line" for him? (Note: Job is speaking *poetically*, often circling around the main point, *not logically*, in step-wise sequence, as if each new line of thought built upon or superseded the previous one.) **5.** What will God do with Job's sin (vv. 13–17)? When? To what does Job owe his continued existence, now and hereafter: To some immortal element relating to his soul? Or some act and gift of God? **6.** What impression has Job made on you so far? Would you want him for a dinner guest? A missionary project? A best friend in time of need? **7.** Has Job cursed God yet, as Satan says he surely will? If so where? If not, how close does he come?

13:24 enemy. Job believed his change in circumstances was due to a change in his relationship with God. Instead of a child of God, he was now considered an enemy!

13:26 write down bitter things. Job supposed that God had meticulously recorded his vendetta against him (7:19–20; 10:14; 31:4).

14:2–6 Job tried a bit of poetic psychology. He suggested that a mere mortal is not worth the time or effort of a magnificent God. So why doesn't God just leave him alone (v. 6)?

14:2 fleeting shadow. Job's current state of suffering seemed an eternity. However, life itself is short.

14:7–12 Job longed to escape his suffering. He was as certain to die as a cut flower.

14:13–17 Job looked toward death as a hiding place from God's wrath. There he would be safe until God chose to revive him.

APPLY 1. Which of the poems best captures your present mood? **2.** Where on the continuum between suicidal despair and resurrection hope are you? Where are most of your friends? How might Job speak to their condition?

If only you would set me a time
and then remember me!
14 If a man dies, will he live again?
All the days of my hard service
I will wait for my renewal[a] to come.
15 You will call and I will answer you;
you will long for the creature your hands have made.
16 Surely then you will count my steps
but not keep track of my sin.
17 My offenses will be sealed up in a bag;
you will cover over my sin.

18 "But as a mountain erodes and crumbles
and as a rock is moved from its place,
19 as water wears away stones
and torrents wash away the soil,
so you destroy man's hope.
20 You overpower him once for all, and he is gone;
you change his countenance and send him away.
21 If his sons are honored, he does not know it;
if they are brought low, he does not see it.
22 He feels but the pain of his own body
and mourns only for himself."

OPEN 1. Who was voted "Most Likely to Succeed" in your graduating class? Who is the most successful person you have ever met since that time? How would you account for their success: Born great? Achieved greatness? Greatness was thrust upon them? **2.** At what age did you first say, "I know more than my teachers (or parents)"? In what areas do you now think of yourself as knowledgeable? As ignorant?

STUDY 1. How does this scene compare with the scene where the four men sat together in silence (2:11–13). What is happening to the sympathy which Eliphaz used to express to Job (4:3–4; 5:17–19)? **2.** Why is he so offended with Job? Of what is he accusing Job (vv. 7–9)? **3.** What does Job "know" that his friends don't know? What type of knowledge do they possess (v. 10)? Whose words do they claim to be speaking? **4.** What is Eliphaz's view of humanity (vv. 14–16)? How does that compare with Job's view (10:12–13)? **5.** How does Eliphaz describe the

Eliphaz

15 Then Eliphaz the Temanite replied:

2 "Would a wise man answer with empty notions
or fill his belly with the hot east wind?
3 Would he argue with useless words,
with speeches that have no value?
4 But you even undermine piety
and hinder devotion to God.
5 Your sin prompts your mouth;
you adopt the tongue of the crafty.
6 Your own mouth condemns you, not mine;
your own lips testify against you.

7 "Are you the first man ever born?
Were you brought forth before the hills?
8 Do you listen in on God's council?
Do you limit wisdom to yourself?
9 What do you know that we do not know?
What insights do you have that we do not have?
10 The gray-haired and the aged are on our side,
men even older than your father.

[a]14 Or *release*

14:18–22 Hope may await Job at death, but what about the here and now? *The chore of daily living had worn* him out. Job had no hope in life.

15:1–6 Eliphaz served a second helping of advice. He was less compassionate and more impatient this time around.

15:7–10 When it came to wisdom, Job claimed equality with his elders, not superiority (12:3; 13:2). However, Eliphaz was indignant. Who did Job think he was, anyway? Did he know more than they did?

15:10 Eliphaz counted on the calendar for his right to speak. Likely the eldest of the four men, Eliphaz exercised his seniority.

11 Are God's consolations not enough for you,
words spoken gently to you?
12 Why has your heart carried you away,
and why do your eyes flash,
13 so that you vent your rage against God
and pour out such words from your mouth?

14 "What is man, that he could be pure,
or one born of woman, that he could be righteous?
15 If God places no trust in his holy ones,
if even the heavens are not pure in his eyes,
16 how much less man, who is vile and corrupt,
who drinks up evil like water!

17 "Listen to me and I will explain to you;
let me tell you what I have seen,
18 what wise men have declared,
hiding nothing received from their fathers
19 (to whom alone the land was given
when no alien passed among them):
20 All his days the wicked man suffers torment,
the ruthless through all the years stored up for him.
21 Terrifying sounds fill his ears;
when all seems well, marauders attack him.
22 He despairs of escaping the darkness;
he is marked for the sword.
23 He wanders about—food for vultures[a];
he knows the day of darkness is at hand.
24 Distress and anguish fill him with terror;
they overwhelm him, like a king poised to attack,
25 because he shakes his fist at God
and vaunts himself against the Almighty,
26 defiantly charging against him
with a thick, strong shield.

27 "Though his face is covered with fat
and his waist bulges with flesh,
28 he will inhabit ruined towns
and houses where no one lives,
houses crumbling to rubble.
29 He will no longer be rich and his wealth will not endure,
nor will his possessions spread over the land.
30 He will not escape the darkness;
a flame will wither his shoots,
and the breath of God's mouth will carry him away.
31 Let him not deceive himself by trusting what is worthless,
for he will get nothing in return.

[a]23 Or *about, looking for food*

plight of the evil man in verses 20–35? In what ways do evil people suffer? (And are they aware of it?) In what ways do they prosper? **6.** In denying that the evil always prosper, is Eliphaz answering Job's real question, or avoiding it? How so? **7.** Is Eliphaz accurate in his view of the human plight? How does Eliphaz compare to the psalmist in his views on the prosperity of the wicked (Ps. 73)? How do you reconcile the two descriptions of the plight of the evil person? **8.** Why do *you* think the wicked prosper? Why aren't good people honored and evil persons shown for who they really are?

APPLY 1. When have you found yourself "trusting what is worthless" (v. 31)? **2.** How did you suffer because of this misplaced trust? **3.** What helped you to reorient your priorities?

15:11–13 A self-righteous Eliphaz criticized Job's response to his friends and to God. At the same time, he subtly defended their failed attempts at consoling Job.

15:14–16 Once more, Eliphaz attempted to force Job to a confession (4:17). How can a man be pure compared to God, if even angels are not pure? How much more sinful Job must be than the angels!

15:20–35 Eliphaz described a clear-cut moral world of cause and effect. Calamity befalls only the wicked (vv. 20–24); Job was foolish not to see that (9:22). Job must be evil, since he was suffering so severely.

32 Before his time he will be paid in full,
and his branches will not flourish.
33 He will be like a vine stripped of its unripe grapes,
like an olive tree shedding its blossoms.
34 For the company of the godless will be barren,
and fire will consume the tents of those who love bribes.
35 They conceive trouble and give birth to evil;
their womb fashions deceit."

Job

16

Then Job replied:

2 "I have heard many things like these;
miserable comforters are you all!
3 Will your long-winded speeches never end?
What ails you that you keep on arguing?
4 I also could speak like you,
if you were in my place;
I could make fine speeches against you
and shake my head at you.
5 But my mouth would encourage you;
comfort from my lips would bring you relief.

6 "Yet if I speak, my pain is not relieved;
and if I refrain, it does not go away.
7 Surely, O God, you have worn me out;
you have devastated my entire household.
8 You have bound me—and it has become a witness;
my gauntness rises up and testifies against me.
9 God assails me and tears me in his anger
and gnashes his teeth at me;
my opponent fastens on me his piercing eyes.
10 Men open their mouths to jeer at me;
they strike my cheek in scorn
and unite together against me.
11 God has turned me over to evil men
and thrown me into the clutches of the wicked.
12 All was well with me, but he shattered me;
he seized me by the neck and crushed me.
He has made me his target;
13 his archers surround me.
Without pity, he pierces my kidneys
and spills my gall on the ground.
14 Again and again he bursts upon me;
he rushes at me like a warrior.

15 "I have sewed sackcloth over my skin
and buried my brow in the dust.

OPEN 1. Which role best describes the image of God you had as you were growing up: Grandfather? Executioner? Benefactor? Politician? Coach? Lifeguard? Spy? Scrooge? Other? **2.** Today, what roles would you use to describe God to an unchurched friend? **3.** How would your unchurched friend depict God?

STUDY 1. How does Job feel about his friends now (vv. 1–5). What kind of comforters have they proven to be? Could he do any better? **2.** Who does Job see as his real enemy and why (vv. 7–8)? What four pictures of God does he paint in verses 8–14? What is his attitude toward God: Irreverent? Hateful? Bitter? **3.** Is there any question in Job's mind who is the source of his suffering? Is Job cursing God here? Why or why not? **4.** What picture does Job paint of himself in verses 15–17? Does he admit guilt? Does he feel the need to perform sacrifices to God as he does in 1:5? Why or why not? **5.** What does he want in (16:18–17:1): Death? Heavenly intercession? Human comfort? Vindication before his peers while there's still time?

APPLY 1. When have you blamed God for something in your life? What were the circumstances? Were you justified in your accusations, or was your case "thrown out of court"? On what grounds? **2.** When have you felt accused by God? Were you feeling real, objective guilt, or was it self-inflicted, psychological guilt? How so?

16:2–5 *Job's frustration was growing.* If roles were reversed, Job would comfort instead of condemn.

16:2 miserable comforters are you all! To Job, these friends had become a nuisance. They had brought him misery instead of comfort.

16:10–14 Despite Eliphaz's accusation, Job did not see himself on the offensive with God (15:25). Instead, just the opposite: God was on the offensive against *him*.

16:15–17 Job was physically and emotionally defeated. Nevertheless, his claim to moral innocence was undimmed.

[16]My face is red with weeping,
deep shadows ring my eyes;
[17]yet my hands have been free of violence
and my prayer is pure.

[18]"O earth, do not cover my blood;
may my cry never be laid to rest!
[19]Even now my witness is in heaven;
my advocate is on high.
[20]My intercessor is my friend[a]
as my eyes pour out tears to God;
[21]on behalf of a man he pleads with God
as a man pleads for his friend.

[22]"Only a few years will pass
before I go on the journey of no return.

17 My spirit is broken,
my days are cut short,
the grave awaits me.
[2]Surely mockers surround me;
my eyes must dwell on their hostility.

[3]"Give me, O God, the pledge you demand.
Who else will put up security for me?
[4]You have closed their minds to understanding;
therefore you will not let them triumph.
[5]If a man denounces his friends for reward,
the eyes of his children will fail.

[6]"God has made me a byword to everyone,
a man in whose face people spit.
[7]My eyes have grown dim with grief;
my whole frame is but a shadow.
[8]Upright men are appalled at this;
the innocent are aroused against the ungodly.
[9]Nevertheless, the righteous will hold to their ways,
and those with clean hands will grow stronger.

[10]"But come on, all of you, try again!
I will not find a wise man among you.
[11]My days have passed, my plans are shattered,
and so are the desires of my heart.
[12]These men turn night into day;
in the face of darkness they say, 'Light is near.'
[13]If the only home I hope for is the grave,[b]

[a]20 Or *My friends treat me with scorn* [b]13 Hebrew *Sheol*

OPEN We all have our moments when we fly so high with hope "we scrape the ceiling" or feel so sad someone has to "scrape us off the floor." What scraping experiences have you had most recently?

STUDY **1.** What tone of voice do you hear in verses: 3? 6? 8–10? 12–16? **2.** Who are the mockers (v. 2), the denouncing man (v. 5), the upright and innocent (v. 8), the righteous (v. 9), and the worm (v. 14)? **3.** Does Job's claim to righteousness provide genuine hope or wishful thinking during his suffering? How can he be so sure he's right? **4.** How low is Job here? Can he get any lower? Is this a case of it always being "darkest before the dawn"? Or is darkness alone the end in view? Explain.

APPLY **1.** Have you (or anyone you know) ever felt that suicide was an option? What kept you going? **2.** How would you intercede for a person this close to hitting rock bottom? Where would you turn for help?

16:18–21 Job sought heavenly assistance in his pursuit of a just verdict (v. 20). Was there anyone who would be a true friend and testify to his innocence (9:33)?

17:3 pledge. Job asked God to post bail for him as a sign of Job's innocence (Ps. 119:121–122). He certainly could not ask his friends for that kind of help.

17:5 denounces his friends for reward. Job was confident his friends' judgmental behavior would be punished. He quoted an ancient proverb in predicting that his friends' children would become blind on account of their parents' sin.

17:6–9 An exasperated Job sarcastically called his counselors innocent, if only to emphasize their heartless and self-righteous behavior. He would persevere despite their taunts and accusations (v. 9).

17:10–16 So much for the promised dawn of deliverance (11:17). Job saw only the certain darkness of death (v. 13).

if I spread out my bed in darkness,
[14]if I say to corruption, 'You are my father,'
and to the worm, 'My mother' or 'My sister,'
[15]where then is my hope?
Who can see any hope for me?
[16]Will it go down to the gates of death[a]?
Will we descend together into the dust?"

OPEN Think of a time in your childhood when you did wrong and got away with it. How did you feel about it then? How do you feel about it now?

STUDY **1.** In what ways has Bildad's mood changed from his first speech (ch. 8)? Who does he now view as wicked? Why? **2.** How does Bildad respond to Job's words in 12:7–10? What is he suggesting that Job is trying to do (vv. 3–4)? **3.** What is so wrong with Bildad's theology in verses 5–21? Which of his assertions is tainted: Evil persons have to live with the consequences of their sin? Evil is a trap? Evil brings calamity? The wages of sin is death (Rom. 6:23)? **4.** But to whom is Bildad applying this theology? In what circumstances? What is of primary concern to Bildad, the traditionalist? **5.** Can one be right in theory and wrong in practice? How so? **6.** When someone is living with the consequences of their sin, how should we treat them?

APPLY **1.** When have you felt like you had suffered because of your sin? **2.** If you later experienced forgiveness, who conveyed it to you? Was it complete or did you feel continuing guilt?

Bildad

18 Then Bildad the Shuhite replied:

[2]"When will you end these speeches?
Be sensible, and then we can talk.
[3]Why are we regarded as cattle
and considered stupid in your sight?
[4]You who tear yourself to pieces in your anger,
is the earth to be abandoned for your sake?
Or must the rocks be moved from their place?

[5]"The lamp of the wicked is snuffed out;
the flame of his fire stops burning.
[6]The light in his tent becomes dark;
the lamp beside him goes out.
[7]The vigor of his step is weakened;
his own schemes throw him down.
[8]His feet thrust him into a net
and he wanders into its mesh.
[9]A trap seizes him by the heel;
a snare holds him fast.
[10]A noose is hidden for him on the ground;
a trap lies in his path.
[11]Terrors startle him on every side
and dog his every step.
[12]Calamity is hungry for him;
disaster is ready for him when he falls.
[13]It eats away parts of his skin;
death's firstborn devours his limbs.
[14]He is torn from the security of his tent
and marched off to the king of terrors.
[15]Fire resides[b] in his tent;
burning sulfur is scattered over his dwelling.
[16]His roots dry up below
and his branches wither above.
[17]The memory of him perishes from the earth;
he has no name in the land.
[18]He is driven from light into darkness
and is banished from the world.

[a]16 Hebrew *Sheol* [b]15 Or *Nothing he had remains*

18:1–4 *Bildad, once remotely comforting,* changed his tactics. Although he was incensed at Job's four-footed insults (12:7–9), he adopted Job's manner, sarcastically implying that the earth did not revolve around Job (v. 4).

18:5–21 Bildad could not tolerate Job's insistence that innocent people suffer for inexplicable reasons. In his universe all people receive their due: the wicked suffer, the righteous prosper. With poetic flourish, Bildad believed that Job's sins would return to him one way or another.

[19]He has no offspring or descendants among his people,
no survivor where once he lived.
[20]Men of the west are appalled at his fate;
men of the east are seized with horror.
[21]Surely such is the dwelling of an evil man;
such is the place of one who knows not God."

Job

19

Then Job replied:

[2]"How long will you torment me
and crush me with words?
[3]Ten times now you have reproached me;
shamelessly you attack me.
[4]If it is true that I have gone astray,
my error remains my concern alone.
[5]If indeed you would exalt yourselves above me
and use my humiliation against me,
[6]then know that God has wronged me
and drawn his net around me.

[7]"Though I cry, 'I've been wronged!' I get no response;
though I call for help, there is no justice.
[8]He has blocked my way so I cannot pass;
he has shrouded my paths in darkness.
[9]He has stripped me of my honor
and removed the crown from my head.
[10]He tears me down on every side till I am gone;
he uproots my hope like a tree.
[11]His anger burns against me;
he counts me among his enemies.
[12]His troops advance in force;
they build a siege ramp against me
and encamp around my tent.

[13]"He has alienated my brothers from me;
my acquaintances are completely estranged from me.
[14]My kinsmen have gone away;
my friends have forgotten me.
[15]My guests and my maidservants count me a stranger;
they look upon me as an alien.
[16]I summon my servant, but he does not answer,
though I beg him with my own mouth.
[17]My breath is offensive to my wife;
I am loathsome to my own brothers.
[18]Even the little boys scorn me;
when I appear, they ridicule me.

OPEN 1. If you were poised over your own tombstone with chisel in hand, what words would you inscribe to summarize your life? How would you want people to remember you? **2.** What are your favorite lines from Handel's *Messiah*?

STUDY 1. Surely now (vv. 6–20) Job has cursed God, or has he? What does cursing God mean for Job: To claim righteousness for himself (vv. 4–9)? To blame God as his enemy (v. 6)? To be lonely, rejected by loved ones and in despair rather than to "trust" God (vv. 13–20)? Other? **2.** Could it be that God has cursed or "wronged" Job? How so? **3.** Is Job here refuting Bildad's notion that man brings evil on himself (18:8–10)? Or is he only denying that in his case, suffering is not the consequence of evil? And if not Job, then who else but God can he blame? **4.** In contrast to friends and family who are all alienated from him, to whom does Job turn in verses 23–27? What is it that Job wants inscribed and for what reason? For what does he yearn? **5.** God has wronged, struck and alienated Job (vv. 6–22). How can he also be Job's "Redeemer" (v. 25): Job is speaking of Christ who redeems from guilt and sin? Job wants someone to plead his case before God. Job thinks of God alone as his Kinsman-Redeemer (akin to Boaz in the story of Ruth). What else could Job have in mind here?

APPLY 1. Is there a sharper pain than rejection by your loved ones? When have you been a parent in pain? A person in pain? A spouse in pain? A child in pain? **2.** When have you found it easier to depend upon your good works rather than to hope in a Kinsman-Redeemer who lives and cares for his own? How

---

19:4 my error remains my concern alone. Job politely told his friends not to get involved.

19:6 God has wronged me. Job answered Bildad's question (8:3) by drawing on his own experience as an example where God had skewed justice and punished the innocent. **drawn his net around me.** Like a wild animal caught in a trap, Job felt cornered.

19:8–12 Job was like an enemy forfeiting the spoils of war. His wealth, possessions, family and health—all were gone (1:16–19; 2:7).

19:13–19 Job looked terrible and had lost everything. Even Job's remaining loved ones and companions had left him lonely.

could you use a living Kinsman-Redeemer right now?

OPEN What is the "sure-fire" way of starting an argument: In your home? On the job? With your in-laws? Your best friend? What is your "sure-fire" way of ending one?

STUDY 1. What seems to bother Zophar the most about Job's earlier remarks (19:28–29), as reflected here (vv. 1–3)? Are Zophar's arguments (vv. 4–11) now just theoretical? What else is at stake for him and his source of authority? **2.** According to Zophar, what immediate consequences befall the wicked (vv. 4–11)? What images help to make his point? **3.** What disasters are prepared for the wicked (vv. 23–29)? **4.** In your own experience, is Zophar right here? Do you see the wicked getting "what they deserve"? Or do you see them prospering in spite of (or because of) their wickedness? **5.** How might the

19 All my intimate friends detest me;
those I love have turned against me.
20 I am nothing but skin and bones;
I have escaped with only the skin of my teeth.[a]

21 "Have pity on me, my friends, have pity,
for the hand of God has struck me.
22 Why do you pursue me as God does?
Will you never get enough of my flesh?

23 "Oh, that my words were recorded,
that they were written on a scroll,
24 that they were inscribed with an iron tool on[b] lead,
or engraved in rock forever!
25 I know that my Redeemer[c] lives,
and that in the end he will stand upon the earth.[d]
26 And after my skin has been destroyed,
yet[e] in[f] my flesh I will see God;
27 I myself will see him
with my own eyes—I, and not another.
How my heart yearns within me!

28 "If you say, 'How we will hound him,
since the root of the trouble lies in him,[g]'
29 you should fear the sword yourselves;
for wrath will bring punishment by the sword,
and then you will know that there is judgment.[h]"

Zophar

20 Then Zophar the Naamathite replied:

2 "My troubled thoughts prompt me to answer
because I am greatly disturbed.
3 I hear a rebuke that dishonors me,
and my understanding inspires me to reply.

4 "Surely you know how it has been from of old,
ever since man[i] was placed on the earth,
5 that the mirth of the wicked is brief,
the joy of the godless lasts but a moment.
6 Though his pride reaches to the heavens
and his head touches the clouds,
7 he will perish forever, like his own dung;
those who have seen him will say, 'Where is he?'

[a]20 Or *only my gums* [b]24 Or *and* [c]25 Or *defender* [d]25 Or *upon my grave* [e]26 Or *And after I awake, / though this ⌊body⌋ has been destroyed, / then* [f]26 Or */ apart from* [g]28 Many Hebrew manuscripts, Septuagint and Vulgate; most Hebrew manuscripts *me* [h]29 Or */ that you may come to know the Almighty* [i]4 Or *Adam*

19:23–27 From the bottom, Job suddenly catapulted to great confidence. His sorry situation had caused him to rely on God *alone* for deliverance (v. 26).

19:23 recorded. Job wanted future generations to know his hopeful revelation (vv. 23–24).

19:25 my Redeemer lives. Though Job was ready to die, he confidently believed that God himself would tell of Job's innocence. **in the end he will stand.** Job was referring to the end of his physical life.

20:4–11 According to Zophar, wickedness always gets punished immediately (v. 5). Job would soon perish if he did not repent (v. 8). Somewhere along the way, Job had sinned, and God had revoked Job's wealth, just like the wealth of all who set themselves against God.

8 Like a dream he flies away, no more to be found,
banished like a vision of the night.
9 The eye that saw him will not see him again;
his place will look on him no more.
10 His children must make amends to the poor;
his own hands must give back his wealth.
11 The youthful vigor that fills his bones
will lie with him in the dust.

12 "Though evil is sweet in his mouth
and he hides it under his tongue,
13 though he cannot bear to let it go
and keeps it in his mouth,
14 yet his food will turn sour in his stomach;
it will become the venom of serpents within him.
15 He will spit out the riches he swallowed;
God will make his stomach vomit them up.
16 He will suck the poison of serpents;
the fangs of an adder will kill him.
17 He will not enjoy the streams,
the rivers flowing with honey and cream.
18 What he toiled for he must give back uneaten;
he will not enjoy the profit from his trading.
19 For he has oppressed the poor and left them destitute;
he has seized houses he did not build.

20 "Surely he will have no respite from his craving;
he cannot save himself by his treasure.
21 Nothing is left for him to devour;
his prosperity will not endure.
22 In the midst of his plenty, distress will overtake him;
the full force of misery will come upon him.
23 When he has filled his belly,
God will vent his burning anger against him
and rain down his blows upon him.
24 Though he flees from an iron weapon,
a bronze-tipped arrow pierces him.
25 He pulls it out of his back,
the gleaming point out of his liver.
Terrors will come over him;
26 total darkness lies in wait for his treasures.
A fire unfanned will consume him
and devour what is left in his tent.
27 The heavens will expose his guilt;
the earth will rise up against him.
28 A flood will carry off his house,
rushing waters[a] on the day of God's wrath.

[a]28 Or *The possessions in his house will be carried off, / washed away*

author of Ecclesiastes respond to Zophar (Eccl. 7:15)?

APPLY 1. When was the last time a sweet, healthy family discussion turned into a sour, vicious argument? Did it start with good intentions? What went wrong? Why did it turn personal? What drama was going on beneath the spoken words? How did the discussion end? **2.** What was going on in your own mouth and stomach as you chewed on what Zophar had to say in verses 12–23?

20:10,19 At least on this they agreed: Oppressing the poor is wicked (31:16–23).

20:20–25 The wicked are greedy for more wealth. But God will punish them for their full stomachs.

20:28 flood. God would cause the rivers and streams to overflow, causing destruction of houses.

29 Such is the fate God allots the wicked,
the heritage appointed for them by God."

Job

21

Then Job replied:

2 "Listen carefully to my words;
let this be the consolation you give me.
3 Bear with me while I speak,
and after I have spoken, mock on.

4 "Is my complaint directed to man?
Why should I not be impatient?
5 Look at me and be astonished;
clap your hand over your mouth.
6 When I think about this, I am terrified;
trembling seizes my body.
7 Why do the wicked live on,
growing old and increasing in power?
8 They see their children established around them,
their offspring before their eyes.
9 Their homes are safe and free from fear;
the rod of God is not upon them.
10 Their bulls never fail to breed;
their cows calve and do not miscarry.
11 They send forth their children as a flock;
their little ones dance about.
12 They sing to the music of tambourine and harp;
they make merry to the sound of the flute.
13 They spend their years in prosperity
and go down to the grave[a] in peace.[b]
14 Yet they say to God, 'Leave us alone!
We have no desire to know your ways.
15 Who is the Almighty, that we should serve him?
What would we gain by praying to him?'
16 But their prosperity is not in their own hands,
so I stand aloof from the counsel of the wicked.

17 "Yet how often is the lamp of the wicked snuffed out?
How often does calamity come upon them,
the fate God allots in his anger?
18 How often are they like straw before the wind,
like chaff swept away by a gale?
19 ⌊It is said,⌋ 'God stores up a man's punishment for his sons.'
Let him repay the man himself, so that he will know it!

[a]13 Hebrew *Sheol* [b]13 Or *in an instant*

OPEN What best describes your ideas on prosperity: "The one with the most toys in the end wins"? "You can't take it with you"? "Eat, drink and be merry, for tomorrow we die(t)"? "Everything that goes around, comes around," so no one gets away with anything? "God sends rain on the just and the unjust," so both their parades get wet? "The righteous shall prosper"? "Everyone gets what they deserve, nothing more, nothing less"? "What the mind can conceive and the will believe, you can and will achieve, so think and grow rich"?

STUDY 1. To whom is Job directing his complaint in verse 4 and why? **2.** How does Job view the happiness of the wicked (vv. 7–16)? How does it compare to Eliphaz's account of the happiness of the righteous in 5:17–27? **3.** How does Job perceive the fate of the wicked (vv. 17–21)? How does Job's view compare to his friend's (8:11–19; 15:20–35; 18:5–21; 20)? In what ways is Job right? In what ways are his three friends right? **4.** In contrast to his friends, what is Job saying in verses 22–26? In what ways is God bigger than the teaching of his three friends (Isa. 40:14; Matt. 5:45)? Is Job focusing here on a principle of equality, fickleness, absurdity, mystery or what? Explain. **5.** What nonsense and falsehood is Job speaking of in verse 34? How does that relate to his opening remarks in verses 2–3? **6.** If no one can instruct God (v. 22), then why does the church try to neatly define its dogma? Why do we say God adheres to certain inviolable spiritual laws of the universe?

APPLY 1. How do you respond to someone who has an answer for everything? Do they really? **2.** Relative to your parents, are you more, or less, prosperous than they? Are you paying your dues and getting "just deserts," or being "short-

---

20:29 Such is the fate. With this self-assured summary of the fate of the wicked, Zophar brought his second speech to a close.

21:4 impatient. Job had good reason to be impatient. He rebuffed his counselors, preferring to address God himself, knowing God was responsible.

21:7–15 Contrary to the theology of his companions, Job's mind was not threatened by reality. The wicked may grow powerful (v. 7), not powerless (20:11). They may be blessed with offspring (v. 8, 11), not barren (18:19). Outwardly, the righteous and wicked may share a common happiness (5:17–27).

21:16 In pointing out the similarities between the righteous and the wicked, Job noted one difference. He did not buy into the wicked lifestyle.

20 Let his own eyes see his destruction;
let him drink of the wrath of the Almighty.[a]
21 For what does he care about the family he leaves behind
when his allotted months come to an end?

22 "Can anyone teach knowledge to God,
since he judges even the highest?
23 One man dies in full vigor,
completely secure and at ease,
24 his body[b] well nourished,
his bones rich with marrow.
25 Another man dies in bitterness of soul,
never having enjoyed anything good.
26 Side by side they lie in the dust,
and worms cover them both.

27 "I know full well what you are thinking,
the schemes by which you would wrong me.
28 You say, 'Where now is the great man's house,
the tents where wicked men lived?'
29 Have you never questioned those who travel?
Have you paid no regard to their accounts—
30 that the evil man is spared from the day of calamity,
that he is delivered from[c] the day of wrath?
31 Who denounces his conduct to his face?
Who repays him for what he has done?
32 He is carried to the grave,
and watch is kept over his tomb.
33 The soil in the valley is sweet to him;
all men follow after him,
and a countless throng goes[d] before him.

34 "So how can you console me with your nonsense?
Nothing is left of your answers but falsehood!"

Eliphaz

22

Then Eliphaz the Temanite replied:

2 "Can a man be of benefit to God?
Can even a wise man benefit him?
3 What pleasure would it give the Almighty if you were righteous?
What would he gain if your ways were blameless?

4 "Is it for your piety that he rebukes you
and brings charges against you?

[a]*17-20* Verses 17 and 18 may be taken as exclamations and 19 and 20 as declarations. [b]*24* The meaning of the Hebrew for this word is uncertain. [c]*30* Or *man is reserved for the day of calamity, / that he is brought forth to* [d]*33* Or */ as a countless throng went*

changed"? **3.** To what extent do you allow God to make sense out of your life? Does he explain every detail? What do you do with all the "loose ends"?

OPEN 1. Who is your favorite advice columnist? **2.** What is the best advice you have ever read in their column? When did you feel the columnist really missed the mark?

STUDY 1. Chapters 22–26 constitute the third cycle of dialogue. Compared with Eliphaz's first speech (4:3-6; 5:17–19, for example), what kind of friend has he become? Why the change? **2.** What is Eliphaz saying about the character of God and humanity in verses 2–4? What irony is Eliphaz unwittingly contributing to

22:1–26:14 For the third and final round of speeches, Eliphaz gave it his best shot, Bildad came up short and Zophar gave up entirely. Neither Job nor his friends were willing to concede on the issues. The friends resorted to specific accusations, which Job resolutely refuted.

22:2–4 Eliphaz erroneously concluded that God is indifferent to personal purity. In fact, the purity of the worshiper was at the heart of the heavenly question behind Job's suffering (1:8–12; 2:3–6).

the story of Job (1:8–12; 2:3–6)? **3.** In verses 5–11, why is he claiming Job is evil? Is he being fair, or libelous? **4.** In verses 12–20, in what ways has Eliphaz overstated his case? **5.** In verses 21–30, in what ways is he theologically "correct" in his last attempt to reach Job? How does this speech of Eliphaz compare with the song of David in 2 Samuel 22:20–28? **6.** Good theology can be harmful if applied to the wrong situation. How are the situations different for David and Job?

APPLY 1. When have you misapplied truth in counseling another? **2.** What does it mean to "walk a mile in the moccasins of another"? Have you? When and with whom? How did it change you or your attitude toward the other person? How did it affect the other person? **3.** Eliphaz and Job agree on at least this much—the appalling treatment received by the fatherless, the widowed, the hungry. How can you help the single-parent household in your neighborhood?

5 Is not your wickedness great?
Are not your sins endless?
6 You demanded security from your brothers for no reason;
you stripped men of their clothing, leaving them naked.
7 You gave no water to the weary
and you withheld food from the hungry,
8 though you were a powerful man, owning land—
an honored man, living on it.
9 And you sent widows away empty-handed
and broke the strength of the fatherless.
10 That is why snares are all around you,
why sudden peril terrifies you,
11 why it is so dark you cannot see,
and why a flood of water covers you.

12 "Is not God in the heights of heaven?
And see how lofty are the highest stars!
13 Yet you say, 'What does God know?
Does he judge through such darkness?
14 Thick clouds veil him, so he does not see us
as he goes about in the vaulted heavens.'
15 Will you keep to the old path
that evil men have trod?
16 They were carried off before their time,
their foundations washed away by a flood.
17 They said to God, 'Leave us alone!
What can the Almighty do to us?'
18 Yet it was he who filled their houses with good things,
so I stand aloof from the counsel of the wicked.

19 "The righteous see their ruin and rejoice;
the innocent mock them, saying,
20 'Surely our foes are destroyed,
and fire devours their wealth.'

21 "Submit to God and be at peace with him;
in this way prosperity will come to you.
22 Accept instruction from his mouth
and lay up his words in your heart.
23 If you return to the Almighty, you will be restored:
If you remove wickedness far from your tent
24 and assign your nuggets to the dust,
your gold of Ophir to the rocks in the ravines,
25 then the Almighty will be your gold,
the choicest silver for you.
26 Surely then you will find delight in the Almighty
and will lift up your face to God.
27 You will pray to him, and he will hear you,
and you will fulfill your vows.

22:5–11 Oppressing the poor is the worst crime Eliphaz could conceive (20:10). With flawless logic, he assigned that crime to Job to account for his punitive suffering. But Job's reputation refuted the accusation (1:1–5).

22:12–20 Concern turned to callousness. Eliphaz assigned Job a dishonorable place in the evil hall of fame (v. 15).

22:21–30 If Job needed to repent of a specific sin, Eliphaz provided a formula to follow.

[28]What you decide on will be done,
and light will shine on your ways.
[29]When men are brought low and you say, 'Lift them up!'
then he will save the downcast.
[30]He will deliver even one who is not innocent,
who will be delivered through the cleanness of your hands."

Job

23 Then Job replied:

[2]"Even today my complaint is bitter;
his hand[a] is heavy in spite of[b] my groaning.
[3]If only I knew where to find him;
if only I could go to his dwelling!
[4]I would state my case before him
and fill my mouth with arguments.
[5]I would find out what he would answer me,
and consider what he would say.
[6]Would he oppose me with great power?
No, he would not press charges against me.
[7]There an upright man could present his case before him,
and I would be delivered forever from my judge.

[8]"But if I go to the east, he is not there;
if I go to the west, I do not find him.
[9]When he is at work in the north, I do not see him;
when he turns to the south, I catch no glimpse of him.
[10]But he knows the way that I take;
when he has tested me, I will come forth as gold.
[11]My feet have closely followed his steps;
I have kept to his way without turning aside.
[12]I have not departed from the commands of his lips;
I have treasured the words of his mouth more than my daily bread.

[13]"But he stands alone, and who can oppose him?
He does whatever he pleases.
[14]He carries out his decree against me,
and many such plans he still has in store.
[15]That is why I am terrified before him;
when I think of all this, I fear him.
[16]God has made my heart faint;
the Almighty has terrified me.
[17]Yet I am not silenced by the darkness,
by the thick darkness that covers my face.

[a]2 Septuagint and Syriac; Hebrew / *the hand on me* [b]2 Or *heavy on me in*

OPEN 1. Did you enjoy playing "hide-and-seek" as a child (or as a parent with a child)? Which did you like more—hiding or seeking? If you were "it," what motivated you to keep seeking? **2.** If you were to bring a malpractice suit against God for the bad way things turned out one particular day, what would be the charges? What compensation would you want?

STUDY 1. Job dares seek a day in court with God. What would he do in God's presence (vv. 3–7)? What does he wish from God in return? **2.** Why can't Job find God (vv. 8–9; compare Ps. 139:7–10): Looking in the wrong places? Not looking with faith or humility? Veiled from seeing what we can see? God can stay in hiding as long as he pleases? **3.** How do verses 10–12 resolve this paradox of God's silence? **4.** What does Job mean when he says, "when he has tested me, I will come forth as gold" (v. 10; compare also 1 Peter 1:7)? **5.** In verses 13–17, what does Job fear? What does he hope?

APPLY 1. When you, like Job, can't sense God in your life, what do you feel most: Disorientation? Guilt? Loneliness? Alienation? Explain. **2.** Why does God sometimes choose to "hide"? At such times, is he hiding from you, or are you hiding from him? **3.** How does God take the initiative in finding *you*?

23:6 oppose me. Despite fluctuating emotions, Job's convictions remained secure. God would not and could not find him guilty.

23:8,10 But he knows the way that I take. Job's friends were wordy, verbose and rhetorically eloquent, but God had yet to speak. However, Job knew that if he could not find God, God would find him (Ps. 139:7–10).

23:13 whatever he pleases. Although his friends portrayed him otherwise, Job was respectfully resigned to God's sovereignty.

23:15 I am terrified. Job revered God and was humbled by God's authority.

23:17 darkness. Hope beamed through the darkness of misery around him. He remained hopeful throughout his troubles.

OPEN 1. Desk tops can be quite revealing ("Clean desks are the province of a sick mind"). What does yours say about you: "Creative clutter" or "Well-ordered paranoia"? What would your closest family member say and why? **2.** Would you want Judgment Day to come *sooner* (while everything is still in order) or *later* (to give you time to clean house)?

STUDY 1. Job still wants to know where in the world God is when it hurts. What is the implication behind his questions in verse 1? **2.** What does the prosperity of the wicked say about God's system of justice (vv. 1–12)? What does Job think God is doing about crimes committed against the poor (vv. 2–4)? The unfulfilled needs of the poor and oppressed (vv. 5–12)? The crimes of the wicked (vv. 13–17)? **3.** Does Job seem more concerned about the victims of crime, the perpetrators of crime, or the God who seemingly does nothing about either? In questioning him in this manner, is Job cursing God now? **4.** Does it please Job (and his friends) that the wicked do get their dues (vv. 18–25), or does that only increase the severity of Job's dilemma? How so? **5.** How is Job limited by *time* (vv. 1,21–24)? How is God unlimited by this constraint?

APPLY 1. Where has the injustice of the world touched you most personally? **2.** When you experience injustice, are you more likely to fantasize about revenge or to seek a forgiving heart? **3.** What do you need to do to make your attitude more like Christ in this area?

24 "Why does the Almighty not set times for judgment?
Why must those who know him look in vain for such days?
2 Men move boundary stones;
they pasture flocks they have stolen.
3 They drive away the orphan's donkey
and take the widow's ox in pledge.
4 They thrust the needy from the path
and force all the poor of the land into hiding.
5 Like wild donkeys in the desert,
the poor go about their labor of foraging food;
the wasteland provides food for their children.
6 They gather fodder in the fields
and glean in the vineyards of the wicked.
7 Lacking clothes, they spend the night naked;
they have nothing to cover themselves in the cold.
8 They are drenched by mountain rains
and hug the rocks for lack of shelter.
9 The fatherless child is snatched from the breast;
the infant of the poor is seized for a debt.
10 Lacking clothes, they go about naked;
they carry the sheaves, but still go hungry.
11 They crush olives among the terraces[a];
they tread the winepresses, yet suffer thirst.
12 The groans of the dying rise from the city,
and the souls of the wounded cry out for help.
But God charges no one with wrongdoing.

13 "There are those who rebel against the light,
who do not know its ways
or stay in its paths.
14 When daylight is gone, the murderer rises up
and kills the poor and needy;
in the night he steals forth like a thief.
15 The eye of the adulterer watches for dusk;
he thinks, 'No eye will see me,'
and he keeps his face concealed.
16 In the dark, men break into houses,
but by day they shut themselves in;
they want nothing to do with the light.
17 For all of them, deep darkness is their morning[b];
they make friends with the terrors of darkness.[c]

18 "Yet they are foam on the surface of the water;
their portion of the land is cursed,
so that no one goes to the vineyards.
19 As heat and drought snatch away the melted snow,

[a] 11 Or *olives between the millstones;* the meaning of the Hebrew for this word is uncertain.
[b] 17 Or *them, their morning is like the shadow of death* [c] 17 Or *of the shadow of death*

24:1–12 Job outlined several outlandish injustices. Orphans and widows were robbed of their minimal possessions (v.3,9), leaving them hungry and homeless (vv. 4–8; 10–11). However, the gap between the actual crime and the ensuing retribution makes a mockery of justice.

24:13–17 Job identified the criminals and their love for evil activity.

24:18–20 Those who disobey God and disregard his commands will be ultimately undone.

so the grave[a] snatches away those who have sinned.
20The womb forgets them,
the worm feasts on them;
evil men are no longer remembered
but are broken like a tree.
21They prey on the barren and childless woman,
and to the widow show no kindness.
22But God drags away the mighty by his power;
though they become established, they have no assurance of life.
23He may let them rest in a feeling of security,
but his eyes are on their ways.
24For a little while they are exalted, and then they are gone;
they are brought low and gathered up like all others;
they are cut off like heads of grain.

25"If this is not so, who can prove me false
and reduce my words to nothing?"

Bildad

25

Then Bildad the Shuhite replied:

2"Dominion and awe belong to God;
he establishes order in the heights of heaven.
3Can his forces be numbered?
Upon whom does his light not rise?
4How then can a man be righteous before God?
How can one born of woman be pure?
5If even the moon is not bright
and the stars are not pure in his eyes,
6how much less man, who is but a maggot—
a son of man, who is only a worm!"

Job

26

Then Job replied:

2"How you have helped the powerless!
How you have saved the arm that is feeble!
3What advice you have offered to one without wisdom!
And what great insight you have displayed!
4Who has helped you utter these words?
And whose spirit spoke from your mouth?

5"The dead are in deep anguish,
those beneath the waters and all that live in them.
6Death[a] is naked before God;
Destruction[b] lies uncovered.

[a]19,6 Hebrew *Sheol* [b]6 Hebrew *Abaddon*

OPEN 1. Which of the following are you most repulsed by: Worms? Spiders? Cockroaches? Mice? Maggots? **2.** What about people repulses you?

STUDY 1. Compare Bildad's words in 25:2–3 to Job's words in 26:7–14. If they agree about so much, what are they arguing about? **2.** What is Bildad saying about human nature in verses 4–6? Do you agree with this view? **3.** If all people are unrighteous, what happens to the argument that Job is suffering because he has sinned? Is it supported or undercut? **4.** Review the figures of speech in 26:6–14. What pictures do they paint for you of God in relation to his creation? **5.** What attributes of God are plainly evident in creation? Which can only be faintly discerned (26:14)?

APPLY 1. If you were to choose just one thing in creation that impresses you the most, what would it be? **2.** Apart from what you have been taught, what do you *feel* your own place is in creation right now: An insignificant little dot in a backwater of the universe? A central part of a magnificent work of art? Something in between?

24:21–24 For a little while. In contrast to his companions, Job affirmed the eventual, not necessarily immediate, punishment of the wicked.

25:1–6 Bildad made one last attempt to convince Job of his folly.

25:2 heights of heaven. Bildad was wrongly stating that God is too righteously removed to endure the pip-squeak personal arguments of the likes of Job.

26:2–4 Job launched into his longest speech yet. He tersely responded to Bildad and then moved on to engage God.

26:5–14 Job described God in all his magnificence. Job's powerful prose depicted his God-centered confidence, despite his condition.

7 He spreads out the northern ⌊skies⌋ over empty space;
he suspends the earth over nothing.
8 He wraps up the waters in his clouds,
yet the clouds do not burst under their weight.
9 He covers the face of the full moon,
spreading his clouds over it.
10 He marks out the horizon on the face of the waters
for a boundary between light and darkness.
11 The pillars of the heavens quake,
aghast at his rebuke.
12 By his power he churned up the sea;
by his wisdom he cut Rahab to pieces.
13 By his breath the skies became fair;
his hand pierced the gliding serpent.
14 And these are but the outer fringe of his works;
how faint the whisper we hear of him!
Who then can understand the thunder of his power?"

27 And Job continued his discourse:

2 "As surely as God lives, who has denied me justice,
the Almighty, who has made me taste bitterness of soul,
3 as long as I have life within me,
the breath of God in my nostrils,
4 my lips will not speak wickedness,
and my tongue will utter no deceit.
5 I will never admit you are in the right;
till I die, I will not deny my integrity.
6 I will maintain my righteousness and never let go of it;
my conscience will not reproach me as long as I live.

7 "May my enemies be like the wicked,
my adversaries like the unjust!
8 For what hope has the godless when he is cut off,
when God takes away his life?
9 Does God listen to his cry
when distress comes upon him?
10 Will he find delight in the Almighty?
Will he call upon God at all times?

11 "I will teach you about the power of God;
the ways of the Almighty I will not conceal.
12 You have all seen this yourselves.
Why then this meaningless talk?

13 "Here is the fate God allots to the wicked,
the heritage a ruthless man receives from the Almighty:
14 However many his children, their fate is the sword;
his offspring will never have enough to eat.

OPEN **1.** In disputed matters, how easy is it for you to admit someone else is in the right: During the first round of the conflict? Second? Fifteenth? **2.** Ever lock horns in a never-ending dispute? What was it like?

STUDY **1.** Is Job appealing to his own rights or to God's justice (vv. 2–6)? If he were appealing to his rights what would be his case? **2.** How far has Job come here from his response to his wife in 2:9–10? Has he compromised an inch? A foot? A mile? What is still most important to him? What does hanging onto his integrity have to do with cursing or not cursing God? **3.** Who are Job's enemies? What does he wish for them? What are the implications? **4.** What is the fate of the wicked (vv. 13–23)? How does this description compare with Zophar's description in chapter 20? **5.** To what extent does Job fit this description?

APPLY **1.** When have you wanted something so much that you were willing to do anything in order to get it? How might the saying, "No pain, no gain," fit Job? How might that describe your last year? **2.** Have you ever complained about God or to God? How did you feel about doing so? **3.** Did struggling with

---

26:14 whisper ... thunder. Job knew only what God had revealed to *him.* If God revealed all his glory, the experience would be thunderous and overwhelming.

27:1–23 His companions may question *his innocence*, but they could not doubt Job's convictions about his innocence (vv. 2–6). As if to frame his argument one more time, Job summarized his theology about the way of the wicked (vv. 13–23).

27:11 I will not conceal. Job had nothing to hide. He protected his righteous reputation without denigrating God's decrees.

15The plague will bury those who survive him,
and their widows will not weep for them.
16Though he heaps up silver like dust
and clothes like piles of clay,
17what he lays up the righteous will wear,
and the innocent will divide his silver.
18The house he builds is like a moth's cocoon,
like a hut made by a watchman.
19He lies down wealthy, but will do so no more;
when he opens his eyes, all is gone.
20Terrors overtake him like a flood;
a tempest snatches him away in the night.
21The east wind carries him off, and he is gone;
it sweeps him out of his place.
22It hurls itself against him without mercy
as he flees headlong from its power.
23It claps its hands in derision
and hisses him out of his place.

28 "There is a mine for silver
and a place where gold is refined.
2Iron is taken from the earth,
and copper is smelted from ore.
3Man puts an end to the darkness;
he searches the farthest recesses
for ore in the blackest darkness.
4Far from where people dwell he cuts a shaft,
in places forgotten by the foot of man;
far from men he dangles and sways.
5The earth, from which food comes,
is transformed below as by fire;
6sapphires[a] come from its rocks,
and its dust contains nuggets of gold.
7No bird of prey knows that hidden path,
no falcon's eye has seen it.
8Proud beasts do not set foot on it,
and no lion prowls there.
9Man's hand assaults the flinty rock
and lays bare the roots of the mountains.
10He tunnels through the rock;
his eyes see all its treasures.
11He searches[b] the sources of the rivers
and brings hidden things to light.

12"But where can wisdom be found?
Where does understanding dwell?
13Man does not comprehend its worth;
it cannot be found in the land of the living.
14The deep says, 'It is not in me';
the sea says, 'It is not with me.'

[a]6 Or *lapis lazuli*; also in verse 16 [b]11 Septuagint, Aquila and Vulgate; Hebrew *He dams up*

God make you closer to him in the end?

OPEN 1. If you were looking for "wisdom" in your hometown, where would you look first: The community college? The den of your house? The bar scene? Your relatives? Your group? How would you know when you found it? **2.** Recall a time when you were looking to master a certain subject matter in school. Where did you go to find what you were looking for?

STUDY 1. Where, if anywhere, has Job found wisdom in the words of his friends: Through mystical experience? Theology and historical precedent? Common sense? Why not just call God's actions a mystery and leave it at that? **2.** If a monetary figure could assess how precious wisdom and understanding are to Job (vv. 13–19), what figure would you pick? **3.** How does one answer Job's question, "Where then does wisdom come from?" (vv. 12,20)? Does it appear to be easily available? Plainly seen? Mysteriously hidden? Divinely revealed? Spiritually discerned? Commonly overlooked? **4.** With what price tag does wisdom come (vv. 15–19)? **5.** What does it mean that God *looked, appraised, confirmed* and *tested* wisdom (v. 27)? How is wisdom apparent in one's life (v. 28)?

APPLY 1. How understanding are you of the way God is working in your life? If you could see

28:1–28 The self-assured trio seemed to enjoy a monopoly on wisdom. However, Job showed that wisdom is a mystery at best. His elusive description of wisdom foreshadows God's own response (38:1–41:34).

behind heaven's curtain to behold the purpose and rationale behind all the things happening to you, would you keep your eyes open, or would you turn away? **2.** All modesty aside, are you considered a wise person? In what ways? How will you strive to be a wiser and more understanding person this month?

OPEN "Oh, for the good ol' days!" What slice of life in your past are you yearning to taste once again? What made it so good? Was it really all that good?

STUDY 1. How does Job characterize his past relationship with God (vv. 1–6)? How does his memory of the "good ol' days" compare with what was said of him back then (1:1–5)? Has God's relationship with Job changed? How so? **2.** How would you portray Job's role in the community: Wealthy banker? Civic-minded mayor? Benevolent physician? Community activist? Pious leader? In a word, characterize his reputation. Is Job being boastful here, or just realistic? **3.** What were Job's expectations

15 It cannot be bought with the finest gold,
nor can its price be weighed in silver.
16 It cannot be bought with the gold of Ophir,
with precious onyx or sapphires.
17 Neither gold nor crystal can compare with it,
nor can it be had for jewels of gold.
18 Coral and jasper are not worthy of mention;
the price of wisdom is beyond rubies.
19 The topaz of Cush cannot compare with it;
it cannot be bought with pure gold.

20 "Where then does wisdom come from?
Where does understanding dwell?
21 It is hidden from the eyes of every living thing,
concealed even from the birds of the air.
22 Destruction[a] and Death say,
'Only a rumor of it has reached our ears.'
23 God understands the way to it
and he alone knows where it dwells,
24 for he views the ends of the earth
and sees everything under the heavens.
25 When he established the force of the wind
and measured out the waters,
26 when he made a decree for the rain
and a path for the thunderstorm,
27 then he looked at wisdom and appraised it;
he confirmed it and tested it.
28 And he said to man,
'The fear of the Lord—that is wisdom,
and to shun evil is understanding.' "

29

Job continued his discourse:

2 "How I long for the months gone by,
for the days when God watched over me,
3 when his lamp shone upon my head
and by his light I walked through darkness!
4 Oh, for the days when I was in my prime,
when God's intimate friendship blessed my house,
5 when the Almighty was still with me
and my children were around me,
6 when my path was drenched with cream
and the rock poured out for me streams of olive oil.

7 "When I went to the gate of the city
and took my seat in the public square,

[a]22 Hebrew *Abaddon*

28:18 price of wisdom. Job was uniquely qualified to attest to wisdom's value. *Why calamity comes to a righteous person such as Job is one of life's great mysteries.*

28:25–27 Answers to life can be traced to God himself. The only one who intimately knows life is God.

28:28 that is wisdom. Although his accusers had depicted Job as rebellious and wicked, Job provided evidence that proved just the opposite. He both feared the Lord and shunned evil (1:1,8; 2:3).

29:4 intimate friendship. Job's relationship with God was still intact. However, his circumstances had prevented his feeling God's presence as he had felt it during better times.

8 the young men saw me and stepped aside
and the old men rose to their feet;
9 the chief men refrained from speaking
and covered their mouths with their hands;
10 the voices of the nobles were hushed,
and their tongues stuck to the roof of their mouths.
11 Whoever heard me spoke well of me,
and those who saw me commended me,
12 because I rescued the poor who cried for help,
and the fatherless who had none to assist him.
13 The man who was dying blessed me;
I made the widow's heart sing.
14 I put on righteousness as my clothing;
justice was my robe and my turban.
15 I was eyes to the blind
and feet to the lame.
16 I was a father to the needy;
I took up the case of the stranger.
17 I broke the fangs of the wicked
and snatched the victims from their teeth.

18 "I thought, 'I will die in my own house,
my days as numerous as the grains of sand.
19 My roots will reach to the water,
and the dew will lie all night on my branches.
20 My glory will remain fresh in me,
the bow ever new in my hand.'

21 "Men listened to me expectantly,
waiting in silence for my counsel.
22 After I had spoken, they spoke no more;
my words fell gently on their ears.
23 They waited for me as for showers
and drank in my words as the spring rain.
24 When I smiled at them, they scarcely believed it;
the light of my face was precious to them.[a]
25 I chose the way for them and sat as their chief;
I dwelt as a king among his troops;
I was like one who comforts mourners.

30 "But now they mock me,
men younger than I,
whose fathers I would have disdained
to put with my sheep dogs.
2 Of what use was the strength of their hands to me,
since their vigor had gone from them?
3 Haggard from want and hunger,

[a] 24 The meaning of the Hebrew for this clause is uncertain.

and goals in life (vv. 18–20)? Did he have every right to hold these expectations? What right did Job have to expect anything good from God?

APPLY 1. What memories of your past are especially meaningful to you? Why? How have these memories sustained you in difficult times? In what ways can memories be viewed as gifts from God? **2.** Looking to the future, what right do we have to expect only good things from God? Doesn't God always give us "the desires of our heart" (Ps. 20:4)? What does God promise that we can expect? What doesn't he promise?

OPEN 1. When you were in grade school, what about you did other kids sometimes make fun of? **2.** How did you react to being made fun of: Laughed along with them? Made fun of them? Vowed to never let it happen again?

STUDY 1. Demonstrating the truth of 1:21, "the LORD gave" (ch. 29) and "the LORD has taken

29:12–13 Once again, Eliphaz's accusatory arrows missed the mark. Job did not oppress the poor (22:6–7); he blessed them.

29:21–25 Job appeared to be the perfect foil to this disastrous trio of counselors. When he spoke, people listened and were blessed (vv. 21–23).

30:1–31 Job followed a description of the best of times with that of the unparalleled worst (vv. 1–19). The haunting contrast of past and present made reliving the agony all the more painful for Job (vv. 20–31).

away" (ch. 30). In chapter 30, what has been taken away? What was Job most concerned about losing? What about his children, his possessions, his health? **2.** Why is his reputation so important (vv. 9–15) to him? **3.** As those who understand the events of chapters 1–2, how do you respond to Job's comments in verses 16–23? What is Job claiming God has done with his divine power? Is he right? **4.** Why doesn't God answer Job when he calls (v. 20)? Is Job being ignored by God? Why aren't Job's sincerity and righteousness enough (vv. 24–25)? Is it a matter of praying harder? **5.** What larger "celestial" issues are at stake here of which Job is not aware? How would the cause-and-effects of Job's life make more sense if he, too, had the bigger picture? **6.** Didn't Job show a great lack of faith by not simply trusting that God had a bigger plan and that he needn't worry? Explain.

APPLY 1. If you had access to the "larger picture" in your life how would it affect your attitude heading into next week? How would it affect your relationship with God? What one corner of the larger picture would you like to know? **2.** What would you guess are the larger issues going on between God and Satan that are presently shaping the cause-and-effects of your life and your world right now? **3.** Does questioning God mean you are lacking in faith, or exercising faith? Do problems in your life result from lack of faith on your part, or because your faith is deemed worthy? In light of Job, what else could be the cause of problems in your life?

they roamed[a] the parched land
in desolate wastelands at night.
4 In the brush they gathered salt herbs,
and their food[b] was the root of the broom tree.
5 They were banished from their fellow men,
shouted at as if they were thieves.
6 They were forced to live in the dry stream beds,
among the rocks and in holes in the ground.
7 They brayed among the bushes
and huddled in the undergrowth.
8 A base and nameless brood,
they were driven out of the land.

9 "And now their sons mock me in song;
I have become a byword among them.
10 They detest me and keep their distance;
they do not hesitate to spit in my face.
11 Now that God has unstrung my bow and afflicted me,
they throw off restraint in my presence.
12 On my right the tribe[c] attacks;
they lay snares for my feet,
they build their siege ramps against me.
13 They break up my road;
they succeed in destroying me—
without anyone's helping them.[d]
14 They advance as through a gaping breach;
amid the ruins they come rolling in.
15 Terrors overwhelm me;
my dignity is driven away as by the wind,
my safety vanishes like a cloud.

16 "And now my life ebbs away;
days of suffering grip me.
17 Night pierces my bones;
my gnawing pains never rest.
18 In his great power ⌞God⌟ becomes like clothing to me[e];
he binds me like the neck of my garment.
19 He throws me into the mud,
and I am reduced to dust and ashes.

20 "I cry out to you, O God, but you do not answer;
I stand up, but you merely look at me.
21 You turn on me ruthlessly;
with the might of your hand you attack me.
22 You snatch me up and drive me before the wind;
you toss me about in the storm.
23 I know you will bring me down to death,
to the place appointed for all the living.

[a]3 Or *gnawed* [b]4 Or *fuel* [c]12 The meaning of the Hebrew for this word is uncertain. [d]13 Or *me. / 'No one can help him,' ⌞they say⌟.* [e]18 Hebrew; Septuagint *⌞God⌟ grasps my clothing*

30:19 throws me into the mud. Perhaps God had been silent because he was ashamed of Job. Dust, ashes and mud were symbols of shame.

30:20–23 If only Job could have known the prologue of his own story (1:6–12). God's power was responsible for restraining further suffering, not causing it (1:12; 2:6). He felt his pleas to God had been unheard. God allowed Satan to inflict suffering on Job; only to a certain point.

24 "Surely no one lays a hand on a broken man
when he cries for help in his distress.
25 Have I not wept for those in trouble?
Has not my soul grieved for the poor?
26 Yet when I hoped for good, evil came;
when I looked for light, then came darkness.
27 The churning inside me never stops;
days of suffering confront me.
28 I go about blackened, but not by the sun;
I stand up in the assembly and cry for help.
29 I have become a brother of jackals,
a companion of owls.
30 My skin grows black and peels;
my body burns with fever.
31 My harp is tuned to mourning,
and my flute to the sound of wailing.

31 "I made a covenant with my eyes
not to look lustfully at a girl.
2 For what is man's lot from God above,
his heritage from the Almighty on high?
3 Is it not ruin for the wicked,
disaster for those who do wrong?
4 Does he not see my ways
and count my every step?

5 "If I have walked in falsehood
or my foot has hurried after deceit—
6 let God weigh me in honest scales
and he will know that I am blameless—
7 if my steps have turned from the path,
if my heart has been led by my eyes,
or if my hands have been defiled,
8 then may others eat what I have sown,
and may my crops be uprooted.

9 "If my heart has been enticed by a woman,
or if I have lurked at my neighbor's door,
10 then may my wife grind another man's grain,
and may other men sleep with her.
11 For that would have been shameful,
a sin to be judged.
12 It is a fire that burns to Destruction[a];
it would have uprooted my harvest.

13 "If I have denied justice to my menservants and maidservants

[a]12 Hebrew *Abaddon*

OPEN 1. When you were in high school, what things that the other kids were doing did you take pride in NOT doing: Smoking? Drinking? Cheating? Drugs? Sex? Cutting class? Kissing up to the teachers? **2.** Looking back at those times, would you do things any differently?

STUDY 1. In Job's final claim to uphold his integrity, before whom is he making his defense? Who is his adversary at law (v. 35)? What kind of courtroom is this, in Job's mind, where the judge and the prosecutor are the same person (v. 35)? Is this true justice or blind perception? Explain. **2.** Who would you guess is standing silently on one side of the courtroom and why? **3.** Upon what basis does Job claim his innocence in verses 5–7? In verses 1,9? In verses 13–21? In verses 24–27? In verses 29–33? In verses 38–39? **4.** What is the implicit answer to each of these "if-clauses"? How can Job be so confident before God? What can you assume from this about Job's understanding of God's character? **5.** What strategy does Job use for his defense? Is he claiming sinless perfection? If not, what? **6.** How does Job wish to confirm his oath-taking. How is this oath related to his wish of 19:23? **7.** In the end, what has Job claimed in this chapter that has already been

30:24 in his distress. Job strains for an inkling of insight. Why does God kick him when he is down?

30:29 companion of owls. With no friends or family, Job found solace among the creatures of darkness.

31:1–40 Job issued his strongest denial yet. If he were guilty of any listed sin, then he would gladly accept the consequence. Job was not trying to demonstrate perfection.

31:1–12 Job denied sexual longing (vv. 1–4) as well as sexual immorality (vv. 9–12). He professed upright business practices as well (vv. 5–8).

31:13–23 Job moved from matters of the heart to social issues. Justice guided him, and mercy motivated him.

claimed for him by God in 1:3? From the perspective of chapters 1–2, is Job right in his defense of himself? If so, upon what grounds?

APPLY 1. How will you claim your innocence before God when your "day in court" comes? Of what sins will you quickly claim yourself innocent? What sins (of omission or commission) will you, more than likely, not want to bring up? **2.** How confident will you be before the divine Judge? Who will be your accuser? Upon what ground can anyone come confidently before the throne of Judgment? Who will be at your side? In this matter, how is our situation different from Job's?

when they had a grievance against me,
14 what will I do when God confronts me?
What will I answer when called to account?
15 Did not he who made me in the womb make them?
Did not the same one form us both within our mothers?

16 "If I have denied the desires of the poor
or let the eyes of the widow grow weary,
17 if I have kept my bread to myself,
not sharing it with the fatherless—
18 but from my youth I reared him as would a father,
and from my birth I guided the widow—
19 if I have seen anyone perishing for lack of clothing,
or a needy man without a garment,
20 and his heart did not bless me
for warming him with the fleece from my sheep,
21 if I have raised my hand against the fatherless,
knowing that I had influence in court,
22 then let my arm fall from the shoulder,
let it be broken off at the joint.
23 For I dreaded destruction from God,
and for fear of his splendor I could not do such things.

24 "If I have put my trust in gold
or said to pure gold, 'You are my security,'
25 if I have rejoiced over my great wealth,
the fortune my hands had gained,
26 if I have regarded the sun in its radiance
or the moon moving in splendor,
27 so that my heart was secretly enticed
and my hand offered them a kiss of homage,
28 then these also would be sins to be judged,
for I would have been unfaithful to God on high.

29 "If I have rejoiced at my enemy's misfortune
or gloated over the trouble that came to him—
30 I have not allowed my mouth to sin
by invoking a curse against his life—
31 if the men of my household have never said,
'Who has not had his fill of Job's meat?'—
32 but no stranger had to spend the night in the street,
for my door was always open to the traveler—
33 if I have concealed my sin as men do,[a]
by hiding my guilt in my heart
34 because I so feared the crowd
and so dreaded the contempt of the clans
that I kept silent and would not go outside

35 ("Oh, that I had someone to hear me!

[a]33 Or *as Adam did*

31:24–28 Job's friends had accused him of secret covetousness (22:24). In fact, Job had forthrightly denounced greed.

31:35–37 Job's life was an open book.

31:35 accuser. Job assumed that his counselors, or even God himself, had filed a complaint against him. He wanted to know the wording of that complaint.

I sign now my defense—let the Almighty answer me;
let my accuser put his indictment in writing.
36 Surely I would wear it on my shoulder,
I would put it on like a crown.
37 I would give him an account of my every step;
like a prince I would approach him.)—

38 "if my land cries out against me
and all its furrows are wet with tears,
39 if I have devoured its yield without payment
or broken the spirit of its tenants,
40 then let briers come up instead of wheat
and weeds instead of barley."

The words of Job are ended.

Elihu

32 So these three men stopped answering Job, because he was
righteous in his own eyes. 2 But Elihu son of Barakel the
Buzite, of the family of Ram, became very angry with Job for justifying himself rather than God. 3 He was also angry with the three
friends, because they had found no way to refute Job, and yet had
condemned him.[a] 4 Now Elihu had waited before speaking to Job because they were older than he. 5 But when he saw that the three men
had nothing more to say, his anger was aroused.
6 So Elihu son of Barakel the Buzite said:

"I am young in years,
and you are old;
that is why I was fearful,
not daring to tell you what I know.
7 I thought, 'Age should speak;
advanced years should teach wisdom.'
8 But it is the spirit[b] in a man,
the breath of the Almighty, that gives him understanding.
9 It is not only the old[c] who are wise,
not only the aged who understand what is right.

10 "Therefore I say: Listen to me;
I too will tell you what I know.
11 I waited while you spoke,
I listened to your reasoning;
while you were searching for words,

[a]3 Masoretic Text; an ancient Hebrew scribal tradition *Job, and so had condemned God* [b]8 Or *Spirit*; also in verse 18 [c]9 Or *many*; or *great*

OPEN 1. At what times have you found yourself speechless? Why? (Were you awed, outwitted, fumbling for words, suffering from a sore throat, or what?) **2.** If "age before beauty" were the ground rule, who would go first in your group? Who would go last?

STUDY 1. From his actions and words in chapter 32, how would you describe Elihu as a person? Would you want him for a good friend? Why or why not? **2.** Why has he not spoken up until now? What might have happened if he had to listen any longer in silence? What finally motivates him to speak? Does what he has to say come from his head, his heart or both? **3.** Why should Job listen to Elihu rather than his three friends? **4.** At what points does Elihu restate Job's position most accurately (33:9–11,13)? At what points does he slant Job's position? Has Job ever claimed to be "pure and without sin" (7:21; 13:26)? Does he think God never speaks to man? Or that God is his enemy? What has Job claimed? **5.** In what ways does Elihu show that God speaks (33:14–22)? Which of these ways seems most intelligible and credible to you? **6.** What does Elihu view as the benefits of suffering (33:23–28)? How can something good

31:40 The words of Job. *His speech* ended with a barely audible sigh. He had presented his case well. The defense rested.

32:1–37:24 Elihu, to this point silent before his elders, now spoke. His tone was tactful, compared to the exasperated trio. In his view, all four men were off base. The trio had rushed to judgment without fully considering the facts of Job's case (32:12). Job, for his part, seemed prideful in his pronouncements against God (40:2). Elihu addressed the different sides through four levels of speeches (32:5–33:33; chs.34–35; chs.36–37).

32:1 stopped answering. The trio surrendered their arguments. They could not change Job's mind.

32:2–3 justifying himself. Elihu thought Job discredited God with his self-focused overtures. Elihu brought balance to his friends' condemnations and to Job's pleas of innocence.

32:6,10,17 what I know. He had waited. He had listened. And now Elihu confidently added his points and perspective.

come from something evil? **7.** How can sinful humanity be spared from going to the pit or grave (33:18, 24,30)? What does he claim God promises, even in the midst of sin? **8.** Why should Job listen to Elihu (33:31,33)? According to Elihu, what will it take for Job to be cleared (33:32)?

APPLY 1. In your group life together, how have you heard God speak—"now one way, now another" (33:14)? How do you account for the variety of ways each of you hears God? **2.** What has God used to catch your attention: A 2x4 between the eyes? Bouts with suffering? Prophetic rebukes? Group Bible study? Other? **3.** Think of a time in your life when you have suffered. In what ways did it change you? How did it affect your relationship with God? Were you ultimately "a better person for it" or were you devastated by it?

12 I gave you my full attention.
But not one of you has proved Job wrong;
none of you has answered his arguments.
13 Do not say, 'We have found wisdom;
let God refute him, not man.'
14 But Job has not marshaled his words against me,
and I will not answer him with your arguments.

15 "They are dismayed and have no more to say;
words have failed them.
16 Must I wait, now that they are silent,
now that they stand there with no reply?
17 I too will have my say;
I too will tell what I know.
18 For I am full of words,
and the spirit within me compels me;
19 inside I am like bottled-up wine,
like new wineskins ready to burst.
20 I must speak and find relief;
I must open my lips and reply.
21 I will show partiality to no one,
nor will I flatter any man;
22 for if I were skilled in flattery,
my Maker would soon take me away.

33 "But now, Job, listen to my words;
pay attention to everything I say.
2 I am about to open my mouth;
my words are on the tip of my tongue.
3 My words come from an upright heart;
my lips sincerely speak what I know.
4 The Spirit of God has made me;
the breath of the Almighty gives me life.
5 Answer me then, if you can;
prepare yourself and confront me.
6 I am just like you before God;
I too have been taken from clay.
7 No fear of me should alarm you,
nor should my hand be heavy upon you.

8 "But you have said in my hearing—
I heard the very words—
9 'I am pure and without sin;
I am clean and free from guilt.
10 Yet God has found fault with me;
he considers me his enemy.
11 He fastens my feet in shackles;
he keeps close watch on all my paths.'

32:14 marshaled his words. Patience pays. Unlike those who spoke before him, *Elihu could speak to the* issues without rebutting Job's reply.

32:18 full of words. Elihu hardly knew where to begin. He was passionate about his perspective and eager to share.

33:1–33 In his speeches, Elihu addressed all of Job's major points. He began by refuting Job's charge concerning God's apparent silence. In fact, God sometimes speaks through dreams (v. 15) and personal pain (v. 19).

33:8 heard the very words. Elihu proved that he was a good listener. He used Job's own words to express Job's concern about God's silence (vv. 8–11).

12"But I tell you, in this you are not right,
for God is greater than man.
13Why do you complain to him
that he answers none of man's words[a]?
14For God does speak—now one way, now another—
though man may not perceive it.
15In a dream, in a vision of the night,
when deep sleep falls on men
as they slumber in their beds,
16he may speak in their ears
and terrify them with warnings,
17to turn man from wrongdoing
and keep him from pride,
18to preserve his soul from the pit,[b]
his life from perishing by the sword.[c]
19Or a man may be chastened on a bed of pain
with constant distress in his bones,
20so that his very being finds food repulsive
and his soul loathes the choicest meal.
21His flesh wastes away to nothing,
and his bones, once hidden, now stick out.
22His soul draws near to the pit,[d]
and his life to the messengers of death.[e]

23"Yet if there is an angel on his side
as a mediator, one out of a thousand,
to tell a man what is right for him,
24to be gracious to him and say,
'Spare him from going down to the pit[f];
I have found a ransom for him'—
25then his flesh is renewed like a child's;
it is restored as in the days of his youth.
26He prays to God and finds favor with him,
he sees God's face and shouts for joy;
he is restored by God to his righteous state.
27Then he comes to men and says,
'I sinned, and perverted what was right,
but I did not get what I deserved.
28He redeemed my soul from going down to the pit,[g]
and I will live to enjoy the light.'

29"God does all these things to a man—
twice, even three times—
30to turn back his soul from the pit,[h]
that the light of life may shine on him.

[a]13 Or that he does not answer for any of his actions [b]18 Or preserve him from the grave [c]18 Or from crossing the River [d]22 Or He draws near to the grave [e]22 Or to the dead [f]24 Or grave [g]28 Or redeemed me from going down to the grave [h]30 Or turn him back from the grave

33:12 in this you are not right. Though Job had never claimed to be sinless (7:21; 13:26), Elihu misinterpreted Job's profession of purity as a claim to perfection (v. 9). If Job's own self-concept were wrong, who was he to question God's character (vv. 10–11)?

33:19 chastened. For the first time, pain is cast in a positive light. Elihu believed that pain could be a means of personal growth, not necessarily punishment.

33:23–28 Eliphaz thought Job was a lost cause (5:1). Elihu, however, envisioned an angel mediating on Job's behalf.

33:30 turn back his soul. Elihu emphasized repentance as a way to escape God's wrath and experience mercy instead.

[31]"Pay attention, Job, and listen to me;
be silent, and I will speak.
[32]If you have anything to say, answer me;
speak up, for I want you to be cleared.
[33]But if not, then listen to me;
be silent, and I will teach you wisdom."

34

Then Elihu said:

[2]"Hear my words, you wise men;
listen to me, you men of learning.
[3]For the ear tests words
as the tongue tastes food.
[4]Let us discern for ourselves what is right;
let us learn together what is good.

[5]"Job says, 'I am innocent,
but God denies me justice.
[6]Although I am right,
I am considered a liar;
although I am guiltless,
his arrow inflicts an incurable wound.'
[7]What man is like Job,
who drinks scorn like water?
[8]He keeps company with evildoers;
he associates with wicked men.
[9]For he says, 'It profits a man nothing
when he tries to please God.'

[10]"So listen to me, you men of understanding.
Far be it from God to do evil,
from the Almighty to do wrong.
[11]He repays a man for what he has done;
he brings upon him what his conduct deserves.
[12]It is unthinkable that God would do wrong,
that the Almighty would pervert justice.
[13]Who appointed him over the earth?
Who put him in charge of the whole world?
[14]If it were his intention
and he withdrew his spirit[a] and breath,
[15]all mankind would perish together
and man would return to the dust.

[16]"If you have understanding, hear this;
listen to what I say.

[a]14 Or *Spirit*

OPEN 1. Which of the following fictional characters best embodies your idea of innocence: Gomer Pyle? Charlie Brown? Woody (on "Cheers")? Radar O'Reily (M.A.S.H.)? **2.** How long would a truly innocent person last in your neighborhood? Where you work?

STUDY 1. The self-appointed arbitrator, Elihu, summons Job to an earthly court to judge what is justice (v. 4). Since it is not appropriate for God to appear in a human court (v. 23), who does he use as judges? What are the charges brought against Job (vv. 5–9)? And the verdict (vv. 34–37)? **2.** Why does Elihu rush to God's defense (vv. 10–15)? From Elihu's perspective, who sets the ground rules for justice? Upon what basis does God determine what is just? According to Elihu, does man have an "inalienable right" to God's justice, or is it a divine gift? **3.** How does Elihu characterize the way that God administers justice in this world (vv. 16–30): As democratic leader? Totalitarian tyrant? Enlightened ruler with power? Human rights activist? To what extent does man have an active part in administering God's justice? **4.** What "right" does man have to experience the presence of God? From Elihu's perspective, if God so chooses to hide himself, what does this silence say about God? About man? Does God's silence mean judgment? What else could it mean?

APPLY 1. What period of your life do you look upon as a time of relative innocence? **2.** If you could point to one event in your life that truly stripped you of your sense of innocence, what would it be? **3.** What guilt would you especially

33:32 speak up, for I want you to be cleared. Elihu's motive was refreshingly compassionate. He urged Job to *repent.*

34:1–37 Satisfied that he had defended God's silence, Elihu next took on the issue of God's fairness, or lack thereof. He systematically addressed the so-called wise companions (vv. 2–15), then Job (vv. 16–33) and then himself (vv. 34–37).

34:5,9 In Elihu's imaginary courtroom, Job was tried for blasphemy against God's nature. Job had charged God with injustice and indifference.

34:10 Far be it from God. How dare Job insinuate God's wrongdoing (27:2)! Who was Job to argue against the Almighty?

34:16 If you have understanding. Elihu's carefully crafted arguments made sense. God's purpose is justice (v. 17); why question him?

17 Can he who hates justice govern?
Will you condemn the just and mighty One?
18 Is he not the One who says to kings, 'You are worthless,'
and to nobles, 'You are wicked,'
19 who shows no partiality to princes
and does not favor the rich over the poor,
for they are all the work of his hands?
20 They die in an instant, in the middle of the night;
the people are shaken and they pass away;
the mighty are removed without human hand.

21 "His eyes are on the ways of men;
he sees their every step.
22 There is no dark place, no deep shadow,
where evildoers can hide.
23 God has no need to examine men further,
that they should come before him for judgment.
24 Without inquiry he shatters the mighty
and sets up others in their place.
25 Because he takes note of their deeds,
he overthrows them in the night and they are crushed.
26 He punishes them for their wickedness
where everyone can see them,
27 because they turned from following him
and had no regard for any of his ways.
28 They caused the cry of the poor to come before him,
so that he heard the cry of the needy.
29 But if he remains silent, who can condemn him?
If he hides his face, who can see him?
Yet he is over man and nation alike,
30 to keep a godless man from ruling,
from laying snares for the people.

31 "Suppose a man says to God,
'I am guilty but will offend no more.
32 Teach me what I cannot see;
if I have done wrong, I will not do so again.'
33 Should God then reward you on your terms,
when you refuse to repent?
You must decide, not I;
so tell me what you know.

34 "Men of understanding declare,
wise men who hear me say to me,
35 'Job speaks without knowledge;
his words lack insight.'
36 Oh, that Job might be tested to the utmost
for answering like a wicked man!
37 To his sin he adds rebellion;
scornfully he claps his hands among us
and multiplies his words against God."

want God to take away from you right now? ______

34:35 words lack insight. Insufficient insight is a common theme running throughout the book of Job. Each person has part of the puzzle, but God alone fits the pieces together (38:2; 42:3).

OPEN 1. When you were a child, who did you have the hardest time getting to listen to you: Your dad? Your mom? A sibling? Your teachers? **2.** If someone did not listen to you at this age, what did you do: Stop talking? Talk louder? Act up?

STUDY 1. God is seen by some as familiar and personal and by others as transcendent and detached. According to Elihu, why is that? **2.** How does sin affect our relationship and righteousness with God (vv. 5–7)? What difference does it make whether we sin or not (v. 3)? **3.** Why does Elihu say that God hasn't answered some prayers (vv. 12–15)? **4.** Does his description of God strike you as quite intimately involved, or does Elihu's god detach himself from Job? Why no answers to prayer?

APPLY 1. Have you ever thought that God didn't care, or that he was judging you for some sin or lack of faith in your life? What was that period of silence like? **2.** When in your life has it seemed that God was just not answering a prayer of yours? What did you do then? What reasons were you given? **3.** What tells you that you've "made contact" with God?

35

Then Elihu said:

2 "Do you think this is just?
You say, 'I will be cleared by God.[a]'
3 Yet you ask him, 'What profit is it to me,[b]
and what do I gain by not sinning?'

4 "I would like to reply to you
and to your friends with you.
5 Look up at the heavens and see;
gaze at the clouds so high above you.
6 If you sin, how does that affect him?
If your sins are many, what does that do to him?
7 If you are righteous, what do you give to him,
or what does he receive from your hand?
8 Your wickedness affects only a man like yourself,
and your righteousness only the sons of men.

9 "Men cry out under a load of oppression;
they plead for relief from the arm of the powerful.
10 But no one says, 'Where is God my Maker,
who gives songs in the night,
11 who teaches more to us than to[c] the beasts of the earth
and makes us wiser than[d] the birds of the air?'
12 He does not answer when men cry out
because of the arrogance of the wicked.
13 Indeed, God does not listen to their empty plea;
the Almighty pays no attention to it.
14 How much less, then, will he listen
when you say that you do not see him,
that your case is before him
and you must wait for him,
15 and further, that his anger never punishes
and he does not take the least notice of wickedness.[e]
16 So Job opens his mouth with empty talk;
without knowledge he multiplies words."

OPEN 1. If it is true that "to spare the rod is to spoil the child," how did you make it through your childhood: By the skin of your teeth? With flying colors and a sore bottom? Counting your blessings? Spoiled and thankful? **2.** Would you discipline or reward your children differently than you were disciplined and rewarded? How so?

STUDY 1. Is Elihu being virtuous or presumptuous in claiming to speak for God, and to

36

Elihu continued:

2 "Bear with me a little longer and I will show you
that there is more to be said in God's behalf.
3 I get my knowledge from afar;
I will ascribe justice to my Maker.
4 Be assured that my words are not false;
one perfect in knowledge is with you.

5 "God is mighty, but does not despise men;

[a]2 Or *My righteousness is more than God's* [b]3 Or *you* [c]11 Or *teaches us by* [d]11 Or *us wise by*
[e]15 Symmachus, Theodotion and Vulgate; the meaning of the Hebrew for this word is uncertain.

35:5 *Look up at the heavens.* *Like* Bildad (18:4), Elihu encouraged Job to see the big picture. God is concerned about creation, but, according to Elihu, God's heavenly position insulates him from earthly affairs.

35:9 plead for relief. Elihu criticized Job's foxhole prayer. No wonder God was silent when people prayed so inconsistently.

36:5 God's great capacity for justice is balanced by his infinite supply of mercy.

he is mighty, and firm in his purpose.
6 He does not keep the wicked alive
but gives the afflicted their rights.
7 He does not take his eyes off the righteous;
he enthrones them with kings
and exalts them forever.
8 But if men are bound in chains,
held fast by cords of affliction,
9 he tells them what they have done—
that they have sinned arrogantly.
10 He makes them listen to correction
and commands them to repent of their evil.
11 If they obey and serve him,
they will spend the rest of their days in prosperity
and their years in contentment.
12 But if they do not listen,
they will perish by the sword[a]
and die without knowledge.

13 "The godless in heart harbor resentment;
even when he fetters them, they do not cry for help.
14 They die in their youth,
among male prostitutes of the shrines.
15 But those who suffer he delivers in their suffering;
he speaks to them in their affliction.

16 "He is wooing you from the jaws of distress
to a spacious place free from restriction,
to the comfort of your table laden with choice food.
17 But now you are laden with the judgment due the wicked;
judgment and justice have taken hold of you.
18 Be careful that no one entices you by riches;
do not let a large bribe turn you aside.
19 Would your wealth
or even all your mighty efforts
sustain you so you would not be in distress?
20 Do not long for the night,
to drag people away from their homes.[b]
21 Beware of turning to evil,
which you seem to prefer to affliction.

22 "God is exalted in his power.
Who is a teacher like him?
23 Who has prescribed his ways for him,
or said to him, 'You have done wrong'?
24 Remember to extol his work,

[a] *12 Or will cross the River* [b] *20* The meaning of the Hebrew for verses 18-20 is uncertain.

speak for him so perfectly (vv. 2–4)? Upon what grounds does he defend God? Why is he striving to prove God innocent? **2.** From Elihu's perspective (vv. 5–21), why is humanity endowed with the divine rights of kings? Why are we treated as captains of our own fate, getting exactly what we deserve, even what we choose? **3.** Elihu says that the righteous are rewarded and sinners are punished (vv. 11–12). How does that contrast with what Job has been claiming? **4.** What are the benefits of God's discipline? What is the fate of those who respond positively to God's correction? Likewise, to those who ignore God's correction? **5.** What new reason, hope and warning with regard to suffering does Elihu introduce in this section (vv. 16–21)? What does Elihu say here that distinguishes him from the other three friends who have given up on Job? What does he say here that contradicts God's view of Job (1:8; 2:3)? **6.** In verses 22–33, what does Elihu say about God that is true and worthy of full acceptance?

APPLY 1. When have you been in a situation where you have felt stretched by God in order to learn something from him? What were the circumstances and what did you learn? **2.** Was the pain worth the gain? Why didn't God just "tell" you what he wanted you to know and leave the agony to those who aren't listening anyway?

36:10 listen to correction. God uses trouble like a father disciplining a wayward child. His motive is correction, not punishment.

36:13–15 speaks to them in their affliction. Many are unwilling to use pain to their advantage. However, God often achieves his purposes in people's lives through a painful process.

36:16–21 Elihu encouraged Job not to miss God's purpose in his pain. Too much concern about how his life would turn out might cause Job to miss opportunities for growth along the way.

36:21 turning to evil. Elihu wrongly emphasized Job's propensity toward evil. However, God knew Job's true character (1:8; 2:3).

which men have praised in song.
25 All mankind has seen it;
men gaze on it from afar.
26 How great is God—beyond our understanding!
The number of his years is past finding out.

27 "He draws up the drops of water,
which distill as rain to the streams[a];
28 the clouds pour down their moisture
and abundant showers fall on mankind.
29 Who can understand how he spreads out the clouds,
how he thunders from his pavilion?
30 See how he scatters his lightning about him,
bathing the depths of the sea.
31 This is the way he governs[b] the nations
and provides food in abundance.
32 He fills his hands with lightning
and commands it to strike its mark.
33 His thunder announces the coming storm;
even the cattle make known its approach.[c]

37 "At this my heart pounds
and leaps from its place.
2 Listen! Listen to the roar of his voice,
to the rumbling that comes from his mouth.
3 He unleashes his lightning beneath the whole heaven
and sends it to the ends of the earth.
4 After that comes the sound of his roar;
he thunders with his majestic voice.
When his voice resounds,
he holds nothing back.
5 God's voice thunders in marvelous ways;
he does great things beyond our understanding.
6 He says to the snow, 'Fall on the earth,'
and to the rain shower, 'Be a mighty downpour.'
7 So that all men he has made may know his work,
he stops every man from his labor.[d]
8 The animals take cover;
they remain in their dens.
9 The tempest comes out from its chamber,
the cold from the driving winds.
10 The breath of God produces ice,
and the broad waters become frozen.
11 He loads the clouds with moisture;
he scatters his lightning through them.
12 At his direction they swirl around
over the face of the whole earth

[a]27 Or *distill from the mist as rain* [b]31 Or *nourishes* [c]33 Or *announces his coming— / the One zealous against evil* [d]7 Or / *he fills all men with fear by his power*

OPEN 1. What motivates you more: A well-timed whisper full of wisdom? A mighty shout that knocks you off your feet? A radical change in circumstances? **2.** Are you more of a fall, winter, spring or summer person? Why?

STUDY 1. Why does Elihu's heart "leap"? How does he describe God's voice? **2.** How does God grab our attention (vv. 6–13)? How does God "show his love" (v. 13)? **3.** In what condition is Job now as Elihu addresses him (vv. 14–18)? Could Job use a chilling north wind (v. 10) or a warm southerly wind (v. 17) right about now? **4.** According to Elihu, is God oppressing Job (v. 23)? Why or why not? **5.** Why do people worship God (v. 24)? How does that fit Job's situation?

APPLY 1. On a scale of one to 10, how would you describe your "LQ" (listening quotient) in your relationship with God? What needs to happen for you to become a better listener to God? **2.** How have you experienced the "awesome majesty" of God recently (v. 22)? What did God say to you through that experience?

36:26 beyond our understanding. Faith accepts some things without the benefit of understanding (Phil. 4:7). Elihu was comfortable not knowing all the answers. Our plans are not the same as God's plans.

37:1–13 Elihu established the function of God's sovereignty. God uses power to get people's attention (v. 7). God's awesome works are those of love (v. 13).

to do whatever he commands them.
[13]He brings the clouds to punish men,
or to water his earth[a] and show his love.

[14]"Listen to this, Job;
stop and consider God's wonders.
[15]Do you know how God controls the clouds
and makes his lightning flash?
[16]Do you know how the clouds hang poised,
those wonders of him who is perfect in knowledge?
[17]You who swelter in your clothes
when the land lies hushed under the south wind,
[18]can you join him in spreading out the skies,
hard as a mirror of cast bronze?

[19]"Tell us what we should say to him;
we cannot draw up our case because of our darkness.
[20]Should he be told that I want to speak?
Would any man ask to be swallowed up?
[21]Now no one can look at the sun,
bright as it is in the skies
after the wind has swept them clean.
[22]Out of the north he comes in golden splendor;
God comes in awesome majesty.
[23]The Almighty is beyond our reach and exalted in power;
in his justice and great righteousness, he does not oppress.
[24]Therefore, men revere him,
for does he not have regard for all the wise in heart?[b]"

The LORD Speaks

38 Then the LORD answered Job out of the storm. He said:

[2]"Who is this that darkens my counsel
with words without knowledge?
[3]Brace yourself like a man;
I will question you,
and you shall answer me.

[4]"Where were you when I laid the earth's foundation?
Tell me, if you understand.
[5]Who marked off its dimensions? Surely you know!
Who stretched a measuring line across it?
[6]On what were its footings set,
or who laid its cornerstone—
[7]while the morning stars sang together
and all the angels[c] shouted for joy?

[8]"Who shut up the sea behind doors
when it burst forth from the womb,

[a]13 Or *to favor them* [b]24 Or *for he does not have regard for any who think they are wise.* [c]7 Hebrew *the sons of God*

OPEN 1. Think of a time in your life when you have received the wrong answer because you asked the wrong question. Silly you, what happened? When did you finally wake up? **2.** What about the natural world is for you a most awesome experience: Scary things, like snowstorms? Tall things, like mountain peaks? Powerful things, like waterfalls? Little things, like sprouting grass? Vast things, like the starry constellations? Give one example of being overwhelmed by God's creation.

STUDY 1. Does God reveal himself here as a distant, transcendent entity under whom Job should cower, or as a personal God who is willing to reveal himself? **2.** What does it mean for Job to meet God in the storm? Is this what either Job (31:35) or Elihu expected (37:22)? How is Job proven wrong about what would happen if he were to meet God face-to-face (9:14–20)? **3.** From the

37:14–18 Elihu used rhetorical questions to further demonstrate how little Job (or anyone for that matter) knew about God, or his magnificent power.

37:19 Job's case was signed, sealed and ready for delivery (31:35). Yet, in light of Elihu's evidence, caution had replaced haste.

peculiar way that God chooses to answer Job, who really is on trial? Which, if any, of Job's charges against God does God choose to answer? **4.** Is God skirting the issues, or getting to the main point? Is God trying to humiliate Job with a list of his grave sins or of God's great accomplishments? Explain. **5.** What do you think is the net effect on Job of God's dumfounding questions? Pick a few of these ponderous questions and consider how Job would have answered them. **6.** What is God trying to teach Job about his divine nature? What does it say about human nature in general, and the nature of Job in particular, that God is communicating with him in this manner? **7.** Does God reveal the specific answers for why Job suffered? What does he reveal? **8.** How does God's response to Job reflect Job's concerns throughout? Has Job ever asked for specific answers to the "whys" behind the loss of children, possessions, health? What has always been his concern instead? **9.** To what extent are God's concerns here the same concerns Job has had all along?

APPLY 1. What kind of questions do you ask God when you don't understand circumstances in your life? What do you pray for? Does God always give you solutions to your problems or answers to your questions? **2.** What else might God want to be revealing to you? Any "reasons why" certain things happen to you? Or is it enough to know God is good and God is great?

9 when I made the clouds its garment
and wrapped it in thick darkness,
10 when I fixed limits for it
and set its doors and bars in place,
11 when I said, 'This far you may come and no farther;
here is where your proud waves halt'?

12 "Have you ever given orders to the morning,
or shown the dawn its place,
13 that it might take the earth by the edges
and shake the wicked out of it?
14 The earth takes shape like clay under a seal;
its features stand out like those of a garment.
15 The wicked are denied their light,
and their upraised arm is broken.

16 "Have you journeyed to the springs of the sea
or walked in the recesses of the deep?
17 Have the gates of death been shown to you?
Have you seen the gates of the shadow of death[a]?
18 Have you comprehended the vast expanses of the earth?
Tell me, if you know all this.

19 "What is the way to the abode of light?
And where does darkness reside?
20 Can you take them to their places?
Do you know the paths to their dwellings?
21 Surely you know, for you were already born!
You have lived so many years!

22 "Have you entered the storehouses of the snow
or seen the storehouses of the hail,
23 which I reserve for times of trouble,
for days of war and battle?
24 What is the way to the place where the lightning is dispersed,
or the place where the east winds are scattered over the earth?
25 Who cuts a channel for the torrents of rain,
and a path for the thunderstorm,
26 to water a land where no man lives,
a desert with no one in it,
27 to satisfy a desolate wasteland
and make it sprout with grass?
28 Does the rain have a father?
Who fathers the drops of dew?
29 From whose womb comes the ice?
Who gives birth to the frost from the heavens
30 when the waters become hard as stone,
when the surface of the deep is frozen?

31 "Can you bind the beautiful[b] Pleiades?
Can you loose the cords of Orion?
32 Can you bring forth the constellations in their seasons[c]
or lead out the Bear[d] with its cubs?

[a] *17 Or gates of deep shadows* [b] *31 Or the twinkling; or the chains of the* [c] *32 Or the morning star in its season* [d] *32 Or out Leo*

work harder? **2.** If you had full confidence in God's sovereignty, how would it change the way you behave in the coming week??

OPEN What animal do you think God had the most fun designing? What features about this animal strike you as funny?

STUDY 1. In God's second speech, *who is on trial* (40:8–41:34)? What common refrains link this speech to the first one (38:1–40:2)? Once again, how does God

13"The wings of the ostrich flap joyfully,
but they cannot compare with the pinions and feathers of the stork.
14She lays her eggs on the ground
and lets them warm in the sand,
15unmindful that a foot may crush them,
that some wild animal may trample them.
16She treats her young harshly, as if they were not hers;
she cares not that her labor was in vain,
17for God did not endow her with wisdom
or give her a share of good sense.
18Yet when she spreads her feathers to run,
she laughs at horse and rider.

19"Do you give the horse his strength
or clothe his neck with a flowing mane?
20Do you make him leap like a locust,
striking terror with his proud snorting?
21He paws fiercely, rejoicing in his strength,
and charges into the fray.
22He laughs at fear, afraid of nothing;
he does not shy away from the sword.
23The quiver rattles against his side,
along with the flashing spear and lance.
24In frenzied excitement he eats up the ground;
he cannot stand still when the trumpet sounds.
25At the blast of the trumpet he snorts, 'Aha!'
He catches the scent of battle from afar,
the shout of commanders and the battle cry.

26"Does the hawk take flight by your wisdom
and spread his wings toward the south?
27Does the eagle soar at your command
and build his nest on high?
28He dwells on a cliff and stays there at night;
a rocky crag is his stronghold.
29From there he seeks out his food;
his eyes detect it from afar.
30His young ones feast on blood,
and where the slain are, there is he."

40 The LORD said to Job:

2"Will the one who contends with the Almighty correct him?
Let him who accuses God answer him!"

3Then Job answered the LORD:

4"I am unworthy—how can I reply to you?
I put my hand over my mouth.

40:1–2 answer him. This is the end of the first speech by God. Job's request returned to haunt him. He now received the terrifying opportunity to dialogue with God.

40:3–5 put my hand over my mouth. Now roles are reversed. God spoke and Job was silent.

[33]Do you know the laws of the heavens?
Can you set up ⌊God's[a]⌋ dominion over the earth?

[34]"Can you raise your voice to the clouds
and cover yourself with a flood of water?
[35]Do you send the lightning bolts on their way?
Do they report to you, 'Here we are'?
[36]Who endowed the heart[b] with wisdom
or gave understanding to the mind[c]?
[37]Who has the wisdom to count the clouds?
Who can tip over the water jars of the heavens
[38]when the dust becomes hard
and the clods of earth stick together?

[39]"Do you hunt the prey for the lioness
and satisfy the hunger of the lions
[40]when they crouch in their dens
or lie in wait in a thicket?
[41]Who provides food for the raven
when its young cry out to God
and wander about for lack of food?

39 "Do you know when the mountain goats give birth?
Do you watch when the doe bears her fawn?
[2]Do you count the months till they bear?
Do you know the time they give birth?
[3]They crouch down and bring forth their young;
their labor pains are ended.
[4]Their young thrive and grow strong in the wilds;
they leave and do not return.

[5]"Who let the wild donkey go free?
Who untied his ropes?
[6]I gave him the wasteland as his home,
the salt flats as his habitat.
[7]He laughs at the commotion in the town;
he does not hear a driver's shout.
[8]He ranges the hills for his pasture
and searches for any green thing.

[9]"Will the wild ox consent to serve you?
Will he stay by your manger at night?
[10]Can you hold him to the furrow with a harness?
Will he till the valleys behind you?
[11]Will you rely on him for his great strength?
Will you leave your heavy work to him?
[12]Can you trust him to bring in your grain
and gather it to your threshing floor?

[a]33 Or *his*; or *their* [b]36 The meaning of the Hebrew for this word is uncertain.

OPEN 1. Which animals are you more fascinated with—those on a farm, in a zoo or in the wilderness? Of those animals, which is your favorite? What details of that animal's behavior have you most enjoyed observing? **2.** Would you make a better zookeeper, veterinarian or forest ranger? Why?

STUDY 1. How does the animal imagery in this chapter affect you? **2.** Which of these miracles of nature have you personally witnessed? What effect did that have on you at the time? **3.** In looking at both the intricate order and balance of creation, as well as its mystery and paradox, what can be said about the Creator? About the similar ways God may govern both the animal kingdom and humanity? **4.** What, if anything, does God say here about Job's suffering? About divine justice? About Job's innocence or guilt? Why is that? **5.** How does God's active involvement with creation redefine our Job-like questions?

APPLY 1. Does knowing God is sovereign comfort you or scare you? Why? Knowing God is always at work, do you relax more or

38:39–39:30 God deals with the intricacy of the animal kingdom in the same manner he dealt with Job: in his way and in his time. Just as God's authority is unchallenged in nature, along with inanimate creation, so must it be with Job.

39:9–12 If taming a wild ox would be a challenge for Job, how did he expect to fare against God himself?

39:11 rely on him for his great strength. A wild ox would prove too much for Job. His confident attempts to tackle God in court now seemed silly.

[5]I spoke once, but I have no answer—
twice, but I will say no more."

[6]Then the LORD spoke to Job out of the storm:

[7]"Brace yourself like a man;
I will question you,
and you shall answer me.

[8]"Would you discredit my justice?
Would you condemn me to justify yourself?
[9]Do you have an arm like God's,
and can your voice thunder like his?
[10]Then adorn yourself with glory and splendor,
and clothe yourself in honor and majesty.
[11]Unleash the fury of your wrath,
look at every proud man and bring him low,
[12]look at every proud man and humble him,
crush the wicked where they stand.
[13]Bury them all in the dust together;
shroud their faces in the grave.
[14]Then I myself will admit to you
that your own right hand can save you.

[15]"Look at the behemoth,[a]
which I made along with you
and which feeds on grass like an ox.
[16]What strength he has in his loins,
what power in the muscles of his belly!
[17]His tail[b] sways like a cedar;
the sinews of his thighs are close-knit.
[18]His bones are tubes of bronze,
his limbs like rods of iron.
[19]He ranks first among the works of God,
yet his Maker can approach him with his sword.
[20]The hills bring him their produce,
and all the wild animals play nearby.
[21]Under the lotus plants he lies,
hidden among the reeds in the marsh.
[22]The lotuses conceal him in their shadow;
the poplars by the stream surround him.
[23]When the river rages, he is not alarmed;
he is secure, though the Jordan should surge against his mouth.
[24]Can anyone capture him by the eyes,[c]
or trap him and pierce his nose?

[a]15 Possibly the hippopotamus or the elephant [b]17 Possibly trunk [c]24 Or *by a water hole*

reverse the roles of prosecutor and defendant in this trial? **2.** What else do you learn about God's character from the manner in which he answers Job? Is God being coy? Caring? Abrasive? Just? **3.** In the prologue to this speech (vv. 8–14), what does God say about Job's suffering or God's justice? **4.** *Justice* can mean both "claim or right" on man's part and "sovereign rule" on God's part. Depending on which way one uses the term *justice*, the problem of Job's suffering looks very different. Which way do you see the problem? As the term is used in verse 8, is God's justice an inalienable right for Job, or a sovereign act for God? In either event, who needs justification—God or Job? Why? **5.** In the follow-up question (v. 9), what is God saying to Job about Job's ability to comprehend the suffering and evil that is around him? **6.** In verses 15–24, what is the point about the behemoth (a large animal—a beast)? **7.** We live life on the back side of a woven tapestry, from which we can see only knots, loose ends and a faint, obscured outline of the picture on the front side. What picture is God weaving for Job in these last three chapters?

APPLY **1.** What new insights does this chapter give you into the place of suffering in your own life? **2.** How can the events of your life be used by God for reasons you might not be aware of? From what perspective can you say, "the pain is worth the gain"?

40:8–14 God had become tired of Job's backseat driving. If Job were prepared to take God's place, he could. However, God demonstrated that Job wasn't up to the job.

40:15–24 Job was unequipped to take on earth's most massive creature. How then could he challenge a heavenly force, far greater than anything on earth?

40:15 behemoth, which I made. What was the behemoth? Suggestions include hippopotamus, elephant or dinosaur. The identity is unclear, but the word means "great beast."

OPEN **1.** As a child, or as a parent-reading-to-children, what is your favorite monster story? Were you raised to believe in any particular monsters of mythical proportions—hiding under your bed or in your closet? **2.** Did (or do) you have much interest in dinosaurs? Reptiles? Snakes?

STUDY **1.** Look closely at the behemoth (a large animal—a beast) (40:15–24) and especially the leviathan here (vv. 1–34). What mental images of each come to mind? What points of similarity do you see? **2.** What sections of the leviathan's portrait seem literal enough to refer to a large marine animal (as in Ps. 104:26)? Which references here are obviously figurative (as in 3:8 and Isa. 27:1)? How did you make that distinction between literal and figurative language? **3.** Nowhere after chapter 2 is Satan mentioned. Does this seem strange to you? In what ways can you see Satan symbolized in the figurative language describing the leviathan? What characteristics do Satan and this leviathan possess in common? How do they rate in power? To what extent can humanity control them? **4.** What is God saying here about Job's ability to control the accuser (Satan) and to comprehend evil, as typified by this leviathan? **5.** Job is allowed the privilege of participating in the heavenly battle between good and evil. What does that say about God's view of Job?

APPLY **1.** What "monsters" in your life seem uncontrollable? **2.** What spiritual weapons have the greatest potential to help you battle these "monsters": Prayer? Bible study? Devotional reading? Music? Being part of a group in your church?

41 "Can you pull in the leviathan[a] with a fishhook
or tie down his tongue with a rope?
2 Can you put a cord through his nose
or pierce his jaw with a hook?
3 Will he keep begging you for mercy?
Will he speak to you with gentle words?
4 Will he make an agreement with you
for you to take him as your slave for life?
5 Can you make a pet of him like a bird
or put him on a leash for your girls?
6 Will traders barter for him?
Will they divide him up among the merchants?
7 Can you fill his hide with harpoons
or his head with fishing spears?
8 If you lay a hand on him,
you will remember the struggle and never do it again!
9 Any hope of subduing him is false;
the mere sight of him is overpowering.
10 No one is fierce enough to rouse him.
Who then is able to stand against me?
11 Who has a claim against me that I must pay?
Everything under heaven belongs to me.

12 "I will not fail to speak of his limbs,
his strength and his graceful form.
13 Who can strip off his outer coat?
Who would approach him with a bridle?
14 Who dares open the doors of his mouth,
ringed about with his fearsome teeth?
15 His back has[b] rows of shields
tightly sealed together;
16 each is so close to the next
that no air can pass between.
17 They are joined fast to one another;
they cling together and cannot be parted.
18 His snorting throws out flashes of light;
his eyes are like the rays of dawn.
19 Firebrands stream from his mouth;
sparks of fire shoot out.
20 Smoke pours from his nostrils
as from a boiling pot over a fire of reeds.
21 His breath sets coals ablaze,
and flames dart from his mouth.
22 Strength resides in his neck;
dismay goes before him.
23 The folds of his flesh are tightly joined;
they are firm and immovable.
24 His chest is hard as rock,

[a]1 Possibly the crocodile [b]15 Or *His pride is his*

41:1 leviathan. The word means "sea serpent." Some have suggested this could be a crocodile. In Job's time, this vicious marine animal commonly symbolized chaotic evil and was more ferocious than the behemoth. God focused on the human inability control evil in this world. Only God can subdue it.

hard as a lower millstone.
25When he rises up, the mighty are terrified;
they retreat before his thrashing.
26The sword that reaches him has no effect,
nor does the spear or the dart or the javelin.
27Iron he treats like straw
and bronze like rotten wood.
28Arrows do not make him flee;
slingstones are like chaff to him.
29A club seems to him but a piece of straw;
he laughs at the rattling of the lance.
30His undersides are jagged potsherds,
leaving a trail in the mud like a threshing sledge.
31He makes the depths churn like a boiling caldron
and stirs up the sea like a pot of ointment.
32Behind him he leaves a glistening wake;
one would think the deep had white hair.
33Nothing on earth is his equal—
a creature without fear.
34He looks down on all that are haughty;
he is king over all that are proud."

Job

42 Then Job replied to the LORD:

2"I know that you can do all things;
no plan of yours can be thwarted.
3⌊You asked,⌋ 'Who is this that obscures my counsel without knowledge?'
Surely I spoke of things I did not understand,
things too wonderful for me to know.
4⌊"You said,⌋ 'Listen now, and I will speak;
I will question you,
and you shall answer me.'
5My ears had heard of you
but now my eyes have seen you.
6Therefore I despise myself
and repent in dust and ashes."

Epilogue

7After the LORD had said these things to Job, he said to Eliphaz the Temanite, "I am angry with you and your two friends, because you

OPEN 1. When you got hurt as a kid, what did your parents do to make it better? **2.** When reading a book, do you sometimes read the last chapter first?

STUDY 1. What caused Job to "repent in dust and ashes"(v. 6)? What exactly did he repent of? **2.** Why do you think Job's three friends were told to sacrifice "seven bulls and seven rams" and ask Job to intercede for them? **3.** What is the lesson in verse 10, "after Job prayed for his friends, the LORD made him prosperous again"? **4.** How would you describe the "brothers and sisters and everyone who had known him" who came to comfort Job (v. 11)? What motivated them to show up now? **5.** What do you think is the primary theme in the story of Job: Suffering? Justice? Patience? Sovereignty? Faith? Other? How does your choice of theme best summarize this book? **6.** What have you learned from

---

41:34 king over all. God put an end to the rumor of his incompetence. As the Creator, God subdues all of his prideful creation.

42:1–6 Job had changed from contentious to contrite. His renewed understanding enabled him to repent.

42:2 you can do all things. At first, Job had merely recognized God's authority (40:3–5). Finally, Job rested in God's sovereignty and majesty.

42:3 Who is this. After a litany of more than seventy rhetorical questions, Job's ears still burned with God's initial inquiry (38:2).

42:4 Listen now. Job affirmed God's initial advice to him (38:3).

42:5 ears had heard of you. Job expressed the difference between knowing God and merely knowing about him. **my eyes have seen you.** A dream had come true (19:26).

42:6 I despise myself. New understanding washed over Job, resulting in humility.

42:7–9 Job profited from his persistence—he never cursed God and never succumbed to evil. Meanwhile, his friends were held accountable for their

your study of Job: About God? About suffering and pain?

APPLY 1. How would you compare the suffering in your life to the sufferings of Job? **2.** How would you compare your faith in God in the midst of pain and suffering to the faith of Job?

have not spoken of me what is right, as my servant Job has. 8So now
take seven bulls and seven rams and go to my servant Job and
sacrifice a burnt offering for yourselves. My servant Job will pray for
you, and I will accept his prayer and not deal with you according to
your folly. You have not spoken of me what is right, as my servant
Job has." 9So Eliphaz the Temanite, Bildad the Shuhite and Zophar
the Naamathite did what the LORD told them; and the LORD accepted
Job's prayer.

10After Job had prayed for his friends, the LORD made him prosperous again and gave him twice as much as he had before. 11All his
brothers and sisters and everyone who had known him before came
and ate with him in his house. They comforted and consoled him
over all the trouble the LORD had brought upon him, and each one
gave him a piece of silver[a] and a gold ring.

12The LORD blessed the latter part of Job's life more than the first.
He had fourteen thousand sheep, six thousand camels, a thousand
yoke of oxen and a thousand donkeys. 13And he also had seven sons
and three daughters. 14The first daughter he named Jemimah, the
second Keziah and the third Keren-Happuch. 15Nowhere in all the
land were there found women as beautiful as Job's daughters, and
their father granted them an inheritance along with their brothers.

16After this, Job lived a hundred and forty years; he saw his children
and their children to the fourth generation. 17And so he died, old and
full of years.

[a]*11* Hebrew *him a kesitah;* a kesitah was a unit of money of unknown weight and value.

accusations. Now the one they had belittled blessed and restored them (v. 9).

42:7–8 my servant Job. God lavished the well-deserved title on Job (1:8; 2:3).

42:10 After Job had prayed. His repentant attitude had initiated his restoration, but his willingness to forgive his companions completed it. **made him prosperous again.** He enjoyed double his previous prosperity.

42:12–16 Job's prosperity was a gift from God. He had not earned God's favor; he had received God's grace.

42:12 Satan's scheme had failed (ch. 1). God multiplied Job's blessings beyond what he had lost.

42:13 seven sons and three daughters. Job went through his suffering virtually alone (30:29). He would enjoy companionship the rest of his life.

42:16 After this. Job once thought his life had come to an end (10:18–22). But in God's grace, Job prospered again.

Psalms

Author. David wrote the majority of the psalms. Seventy-three are clearly attributed to him. Others were written by Moses, Asaph, Solomon, Ethan and the sons of Korah. Fifty have no author assigned.

Personal Reading	Group Study Topic and Reading	
1,32,34,65,84	True Happiness	1
4-5,7,13–14,17,22,53,64,69,88,143	Suffering	22
3,31,36,39,42–44,49,54,57,79,142	Discouragement	42–43
11,15,23,27,40,41,46,52,56,62-63,107,131	Trust	63
25–26,51,90,102,106	Confession	51
35,58–59,129,137	Anger	58
2,21,24,29–30,45,47–48,70–72,75–76,78,110	The King's Glory	72
10,12,20,28,55,73–74,77,132,140–143	Despair and Hope	73
16,18,31,61,86,91,112,121–122,124–125,127,133	Security	91
50,60,80,82–83,87,93–99	God's Universal Reign	99
6,38,85,103,123,130	Forgiveness	130
8,19,37,89,139	God's Sovereignty	139
9,33,66–68,81,92,100–101,104–105,108–109,111, 113–120,126,128,134–136,138,144–150	Praise the Lord!	145

Date. The psalms were written over a long span of time, probably from around 1400 B.C. to 400 B.C. The compilation was probably finalized around 400 B.C.

Purpose. Worshiping God in every part of life is the theme of the book of Psalms. Psalms functioned as a hymnal for ancient Israel. Today, it reveals that our relationship with God relates to every dimension of life, not just the religious parts. The individual writers of the psalms wrote for personal reasons. They wrote from their hearts. Together, as a collection, the psalms connect readers to God, in times of joy, sorrow, thanksgiving, suffering and celebration.

Historical Background. The book of Psalms are living history. Some of them can easily be identified with known historical events. Many cannot be placed in any time frame. Psalms are part of the worship liturgy, and so their development probably parallels the development of the tabernacle and temple worship. Each individual psalm provides a picture of the time when it was written. Some reflect the deeply personal tone of one author and time, while others are stylized and ritualistic. The psalms were not meant as historical records; rather, they illuminate the concerns and feelings of their writers. In this way, they provide first-hand history lessons on what people thought was important, whether it was political conflict, war, personal crises or troubles among the faithful. From the personal tears and joys of David, to the public cries of an exiled nation, the psalms make personal history openly public.

Psalms and Old Testament Law. For the modern Bible reader, the book of Psalms provide a sharp contrast to books about ritual, such as Exodus, Leviticus, Numbers and Deuteronomy. The poems in Psalms are filled with imagery and emotion. Whether the reader is in hiding with David or by the rivers of Babylon with the exiles, the book of Psalms often seem closer and more relevant than the books of the law. These poems and songs reflect the hearts of the Jewish people and their relationships with God. The acts of offering, sacrifice, feasting and fasting may seem foreign to readers, but the emotions of the Psalms do not seem foreign at all. The book of Psalms offer a personal, artistic and human perspective of the law and the history of the time.

OPEN 1. What is the most impressive tree you have seen in your life? What made it grand? 2. When you were a child, who in your family represented stability to you?

STUDY 1. When you read about the "blessed man," how does this person come across to you? 2. What practical problems result from habitually "walking," "standing," and "sitting" with bad people? 3. How can a person keep up with 21st century life and still "delight in the law of the LORD"? 4. Do you think "the wicked" are unstable because God opposes them or because their lives can't hold together? 5. Do you think the righteous are stable because God looks out for them or because their lives have substance?

APPLY 1. Did your day today feel more like a rooted tree or wind-blown chaff? 2. If you could ask God for one thing to make your life more fruitful, what would it be?

OPEN 1. What is the worst trouble you ever got into when you were in school? 2. What is your boss like: A tyrant? A friend? A limp stalk of celery?

STUDY 1. What is there about power that seems to cause people who have it to be at odds with God? 2. This psalm is about David as God's anointed representative to rule Israel. What was the big deal about opposing him (vv. 2,3,6,12)? 3. David, "the anointed one," pictures Christ, "the Anointed One." What promises did God make David and Christ (vv. 7–9)? What qualities do you think these two need to keep them from being tyrants? 4. Why is it natural to feel like rebelling against an absolute ruler? Why is it right to ac-

BOOK I

Psalms 1–41

Psalm 1

1 Blessed is the man
who does not walk in the counsel of the wicked
or stand in the way of sinners
or sit in the seat of mockers.
2 But his delight is in the law of the LORD,
and on his law he meditates day and night.
3 He is like a tree planted by streams of water,
which yields its fruit in season
and whose leaf does not wither.
Whatever he does prospers.

4 Not so the wicked!
They are like chaff
that the wind blows away.
5 Therefore the wicked will not stand in the judgment,
nor sinners in the assembly of the righteous.

6 For the LORD watches over the way of the righteous,
but the way of the wicked will perish.

Psalm 2

1 Why do the nations conspire[a]
and the peoples plot in vain?
2 The kings of the earth take their stand
and the rulers gather together
against the LORD
and against his Anointed One.[b]
3 "Let us break their chains," they say,
"and throw off their fetters."

4 The One enthroned in heaven laughs;
the Lord scoffs at them.
5 Then he rebukes them in his anger
and terrifies them in his wrath, saying,
6 "I have installed my King[c]
on Zion, my holy hill."

[a]1 Hebrew; Septuagint *rage* [b]2 Or *anointed one* [c]6 Or *king*

1:1 Blessed is the man. Blessed people enjoy a happy state of mind because they are obedient. **way of sinners.** In contrast, sinful people have no use for God's ways. **seat of mockers.** Some people go one step further. They actually make light of godly living.

1:2 meditates day and night. The blessed person relishes God's Law—the first five books of the Bible. More than mere study material or a "good read," God's ways are a necessary part of daily living.

1:3 Whatever he does prospers. The psalmist describes the rewards of godly living: strength, security and prosperity. The picture of a godly person's life is like a tree blessing others with fruit and shade.

1:6 the LORD watches over. A clear distinction determines the destiny of the wicked and the righteous. God protects the path of the righteous. But the unguarded way of the wicked ends abruptly.

2:2 take their stand. One side is the Lord (God) and his Anointed One (Israel's king and more specifically the Messiah, Jesus). On the other side, the nations gather against the king of the universe, against God's Anointed, Jesus.

2:4–6 the LORD scoffs at them. God reigns over all earthly institutions.

[7]I will proclaim the decree of the LORD:
He said to me, "You are my Son[a];
today I have become your Father.[b]
[8]Ask of me,
and I will make the nations your inheritance,
the ends of the earth your possession.
[9]You will rule them with an iron scepter[c];
you will dash them to pieces like pottery."
[10]Therefore, you kings, be wise;
be warned, you rulers of the earth.
[11]Serve the LORD with fear
and rejoice with trembling.
[12]Kiss the Son, lest he be angry
and you be destroyed in your way,
for his wrath can flare up in a moment.
Blessed are all who take refuge in him.

Psalm 3

A psalm of David. When he fled from his son Absalom.

[1]O LORD, how many are my foes!
How many rise up against me!
[2]Many are saying of me,
"God will not deliver him." *Selah*[d]
[3]But you are a shield around me, O LORD;
you bestow glory on me and lift[e] up my head.
[4]To the LORD I cry aloud,
and he answers me from his holy hill. *Selah*
[5]I lie down and sleep;
I wake again, because the LORD sustains me.
[6]I will not fear the tens of thousands
drawn up against me on every side.
[7]Arise, O LORD!
Deliver me, O my God!
Strike all my enemies on the jaw;
break the teeth of the wicked.

[a]7 Or *son*; also in verse 12 [b]7 Or *have begotten you* [c]9 Or *will break them with a rod of iron*
[d]2 A word of uncertain meaning, occurring frequently in the Psalms; possibly a musical term [e]3 Or *LORD, / my Glorious One, who lifts*

cept the absolute rule of God through his king? **5.** How do you react to the idea of fearing the Lord (v. 11)? **6.** What is there about God that fills you with awe? **7.** What kinds of things do you think would make God angry "in a moment"?

APPLY **1.** How are you relating to the "King": Like a rebel? Like a loyal subject? **2.** What are some ways an individual can "kiss the Son"? How can a group express love and devotion to him?

OPEN **1.** How much sleep have you "lost" this week? Why? **2.** Which of your parents could you more easily cry with? Why?

STUDY **1.** Who are David's "foes" (2 Sam. 15:13–30)? Why does he flee the city rather than fight? **2.** Why does David praise God so much for his protectors: To make sure they keep coming or because God is worthy of such praise? Why do you think so? **3.** What does it mean that God "lifted up David's head"? **4.** From where does his peace, victory and blessing come (vv. 6–8)? Likewise, his anger and anxiety?

APPLY **1.** When did you last feel abandoned by friends? By God? What happened? **2.** What "foes" are you facing? From what are you praying for deliverance? How will you know when that prayer is answered?

He muses at the nations' futile battle plans.

2:7 my Son ... become your Father. The psalmist implies the succession of rule from father to son. The king recognized God as his higher authority, like a father to a son (2 Sam. 7:12–16).

Ps. 3 David penned this psalm while running from his son Absalom (2 Sam. 15:13–30). First he focuses on the urgency of his problem (vv. 1–2). Then he asserts his unfailing trust (vv. 3–6), all the while soliciting God's help (vv. 7–8).

3:3 shield around me. Nothing impresses a warrior more than comparing God to a shield (84:11; 91:4). David gains confidence knowing he is completely protected.

3:7 Deliver me. David does not fight battles depending on his own might. He depends on God to fight for him.

[8] From the LORD comes deliverance.
May your blessing be on your people. *Selah*

Psalm 4

For the director of music. With stringed instruments.
A psalm of David.

[1] Answer me when I call to you,
O my righteous God.
Give me relief from my distress;
be merciful to me and hear my prayer.

[2] How long, O men, will you turn my glory into shame[a]?
How long will you love delusions and seek false gods[b]? *Selah*

[3] Know that the LORD has set apart the godly for himself;
the LORD will hear when I call to him.

[4] In your anger do not sin;
when you are on your beds,
search your hearts and be silent. *Selah*
[5] Offer right sacrifices
and trust in the LORD.

[6] Many are asking, "Who can show us any good?"
Let the light of your face shine upon us, O LORD.
[7] You have filled my heart with greater joy
than when their grain and new wine abound.
[8] I will lie down and sleep in peace,
for you alone, O LORD,
make me dwell in safety.

Psalm 5

For the director of music. For flutes. A psalm of David.

[1] Give ear to my words, O LORD,
consider my sighing.
[2] Listen to my cry for help,
my King and my God,
for to you I pray.
[3] In the morning, O LORD, you hear my voice;
in the morning I lay my requests before you
and wait in expectation.

[a]2 Or *you dishonor my Glorious One* [b]2 Or *seek lies*

OPEN 1. Which are you: Defeatist? Optimist? Realist? 2. How does faith in God influence that perspective?

STUDY 1. What four things does David ask of God (v. 1)? What might be causing him this distress and shame (v. 2)? 2. What outcome does David expect? Why is he so confident? Why is he "set apart"? 3. While wavering loyalty grieves David (v. 2), what counsel does he give those whose loyalty burns too fierce (vv. 4–5)? 4. What's his answer to the defeatist (vv. 6–8)? 5. Given his prior mood (vv. 1–2), why is David now joyful, peaceful and secure?

APPLY 1. When you are angry, how are you tempted to show it in a sinful way (v. 4)? 2. What is your biggest source of stress? Where lies your confidence? 3. Do disloyal people get you down? What does it mean to yield your rights, needs and feelings to God?

OPEN 1. Who gave you the most comfort growing up: Mom? Dad? Grandparent? Siblings? Your pets or stuffed toys? Your spiritual leader? The telephone? Why? 2. What schoolyard bully did you just hate?

STUDY 1. What do verses 1–3 sound like? Look like? Feel like? What is David losing sleep over? 2. What is the focus of verses 4–6? Where does the focus shift in the next stanza (vv. 7–8)? Verses 9–10? 3. Why does David plea for justice one minute and mercy the next? What does it say about his guilt? 4. How

---

3:8 From the LORD. David's confidence is in the Lord, and prayer makes him sure of victory (6:8–10).

4:1 Answer me. Like someone calling for help in an emergency, David is desperate for God's aid. He likely penned this psalm to follow the previous psalm.

4:2–3 David criticizes his enemies who are intent on ruining his reputation. He reminds them the Lord will respond to his cries for help.

4:4–5 We tend to look at problems with anger or worry. David encourages trust as the antidote to stress.

4:4 anger do not sin ... search your hearts. David describes a fine balance concerning anger's proper place (Eph. 4:26). Anger is inappropriate when it substitutes for trust in God.

4:6 Many are asking. As a leader on the run, David admits his people are uncertain and afraid. He prays God will bless them with the security of his presence.

Ps. 5 When his enemies verbally assault him, David turns to prayer. David

[4]You are not a God who takes pleasure in evil;
with you the wicked cannot dwell.
[5]The arrogant cannot stand in your presence;
you hate all who do wrong.
[6]You destroy those who tell lies;
bloodthirsty and deceitful men
the LORD abhors.

[7]But I, by your great mercy,
will come into your house;
in reverence will I bow down
toward your holy temple.
[8]Lead me, O LORD, in your righteousness
because of my enemies—
make straight your way before me.

[9]Not a word from their mouth can be trusted;
their heart is filled with destruction.
Their throat is an open grave;
with their tongue they speak deceit.
[10]Declare them guilty, O God!
Let their intrigues be their downfall.
Banish them for their many sins,
for they have rebelled against you.

[11]But let all who take refuge in you be glad;
let them ever sing for joy.
Spread your protection over them,
that those who love your name may rejoice in you.
[12]For surely, O LORD, you bless the righteous;
you surround them with your favor as with a shield.

Psalm 6

For the director of music. With stringed instruments.
According to *sheminith.*[a] A psalm of David.

[1]O LORD, do not rebuke me in your anger
or discipline me in your wrath.
[2]Be merciful to me, LORD, for I am faint;
O LORD, heal me, for my bones are in agony.
[3]My soul is in anguish.
How long, O LORD, how long?

[4]Turn, O LORD, and deliver me;
save me because of your unfailing love.

[a]Title: Probably a musical term

dare David come before God knowing that he is a man with sin like any other man? He is known for the great sin with Bathsheba (2 Sam. 11–12). Given that, how can he consider himself "the righteous" (v. 12)? **5.** What contrasts are drawn between "rebels" against God (v. 10) and "refugees" who come to God (v. 11)?

APPLY 1. In terms of this psalm, how are you feeling about your status before God: Relying on his mercy to come into his house (v. 7)? Or feeling you "cannot stand in his presence" (v. 5)? **2.** How (when? where?) could you build this "morning watch" (v. 3) into your daily routine? Is it a routine for everyone? **3.** What situation are you now facing, where you could use help from God and your group?

OPEN Did (or does) your family express negative emotions very well? How so?

STUDY 1. Why is David so sick with grief? Is God punishing him for sin, or is David just afraid that God is against him (vv. 1–2)? Why has God not answered him? **2.** What does David believe about death (v. 5)? **3.** Why do David's eyes fail (v. 7): He's in the dark? Justice is blind? No end in sight? Seeing is believing? **4.** Why the different tone in verses 8–10? How does he know God has answered him?

---

begins his day with a petition for the Lord to act on his behalf.

5:4–6 David describes the faults of his enemies. They are ruthless rebels whose hearts are intent on disobedience.

5:7–8 In contrast, David appears humble and respectful toward God. He hopes God will gladly guide him as a result of his reverence.

5:8 Lead me ... in righteousness. David submits to God and depends on his direction.

5:9 filled with destruction. Again, David alternates the contrast between the wicked and the righteous. God's favor makes David righteous (v. 7). In comparison, the wicked are filled with evil.

6:1–3 David fears his failing health is a sign of God's wrath (v. 1). He asks for mercy; he cannot hold out much longer (vv. 2–3).

APPLY **1.** Have you ever worried about your health, prayed for healing and not received it, or been sick with grief? How so? **2.** What in your life makes you cry out "How long, O LORD"? Why is God waiting? **3.** Do you ever see God as an "angry judge"? Does this psalm add to your despair or your hope? How can you turn your pain over to God?

OPEN **1.** In school, were you more likely the one picking on others or the one getting picked on? How did that feel? **2.** It's 3:00 a.m. You are being pursued or caught in a jam. Who do you call first? Second?

STUDY **1.** Why was the tribe of Benjamin hostile to David (2 Sam. 16:5–8; 20:1–2)? What is David accused of in verses 3–4? Why? **2.** In verses 6–11, how does David broaden his appeal for personal vindication? With what images of God? **3.** What is meant by "my righteousness" (v. 8): David is sinless? Right? Sincere? **4.** Does David's appeal stand (or fall) on his righteousness, or on God's? Why is that? **5.** From verses 11–12, how is evil done in: By a personal judge? By self-destruction? In a purely anonymous way? Compare this with verses 14–16. Why the difference, if any? **6.** What is David's attitude toward the way God expresses his wrath? Is he frightened or reassured by it? How does this compare to your own attitude about God's wrath?

APPLY **1.** When have you felt falsely accused? How did you appeal your case? Like David? **2.** Would you want God to judge you according to your righteousness or the integrity of your heart? Why? **3.** What "pit" of your own making have you fallen into lately? Are you digging out? Or piling it down on your head?

5 No one remembers you when he is dead.
Who praises you from the grave[a]?

6 I am worn out from groaning;
all night long I flood my bed with weeping
and drench my couch with tears.
7 My eyes grow weak with sorrow;
they fail because of all my foes.

8 Away from me, all you who do evil,
for the LORD has heard my weeping.
9 The LORD has heard my cry for mercy;
the LORD accepts my prayer.
10 All my enemies will be ashamed and dismayed;
they will turn back in sudden disgrace.

Psalm 7

A *shiggaion*[b] of David, which he sang to the LORD concerning Cush, a Benjamite.

1 O LORD my God, I take refuge in you;
save and deliver me from all who pursue me,
2 or they will tear me like a lion
and rip me to pieces with no one to rescue me.

3 O LORD my God, if I have done this
and there is guilt on my hands—
4 if I have done evil to him who is at peace with me
or without cause have robbed my foe—
5 then let my enemy pursue and overtake me;
let him trample my life to the ground
and make me sleep in the dust. *Selah*

6 Arise, O LORD, in your anger;
rise up against the rage of my enemies.
Awake, my God; decree justice.
7 Let the assembled peoples gather around you.
Rule over them from on high;
8 let the LORD judge the peoples.
Judge me, O LORD, according to my righteousness,
according to my integrity, O Most High.
9 O righteous God,
who searches minds and hearts,
bring to an end the violence of the wicked
and make the righteous secure.

10 My shield[c] is God Most High,
who saves the upright in heart.

[a]5 Hebrew *Sheol* [b]Title: Probably a literary or musical term [c]10 Or *sovereign*

6:5 *The* psalmist rationalizes he cannot praise *God when he is dead.* Therefore, God must save him.

6:7 eyes grow weak. David has made himself even more ill because of his grieving. He strains to see God's deliverance, but foes fill his vision.

6:8–10 Regaining his second *wind,* David defiantly addresses his enemies. His concluding confidence in God is a common theme in many psalms (7:10–17; 10:16–18; 12:7).

7:6 Arise. David encourages God's quick and *decisive* action.

11 God is a righteous judge,
a God who expresses his wrath every day.
12 If he does not relent,
he[a] will sharpen his sword;
he will bend and string his bow.
13 He has prepared his deadly weapons;
he makes ready his flaming arrows.

14 He who is pregnant with evil
and conceives trouble gives birth to disillusionment.
15 He who digs a hole and scoops it out
falls into the pit he has made.
16 The trouble he causes recoils on himself;
his violence comes down on his own head.

17 I will give thanks to the LORD because of his righteousness
and will sing praise to the name of the LORD Most High.

Psalm 8

For the director of music. According to *gittith*.[b]
A psalm of David.

1 O LORD, our Lord,
how majestic is your name in all the earth!

You have set your glory
above the heavens.
2 From the lips of children and infants
you have ordained praise[c]
because of your enemies,
to silence the foe and the avenger.

3 When I consider your heavens,
the work of your fingers,
the moon and the stars,
which you have set in place,
4 what is man that you are mindful of him,
the son of man that you care for him?
5 You made him a little lower than the heavenly beings[d]
and crowned him with glory and honor.

6 You made him ruler over the works of your hands;
you put everything under his feet:
7 all flocks and herds,
and the beasts of the field,
8 the birds of the air,

[a]12 Or *If a man does not repent, / God* [b]Title: Probably a musical term [c]2 Or *strength* [d]5 Or *than God*

OPEN Rank the following as to which you'd most and least prefer to be: Starry-eyed lover? Entertainer? Professional athlete? Environmentalist? King of ___? Astronaut? Other?

STUDY 1. Where is "above the heavens" (Gen. 1:6–8)? What is David saying about God? **2.** How might "majestic name" be linked to "infant praise" (v. 2)? How does "baby talk" silence God's foes? **3.** How are humans a "little lower" than heavenly beings (v. 5)? **4.** How does "star-gazing" make David feel about himself? **5.** What is the job of the "ruler" (v. 6; Gen. 1:28; 2:15)? Does this mean we can do anything we want with God's creation? What responsibilities go with this position?

APPLY 1. What experience has made you question your own importance to God: Star-gazing? Experiencing suffering? Being depressed about a failure? **2.** What has reassured you in the midst of this questioning: Scripture? Contemplating Christ's sacrifice for you? The love of a friend? **3.** Have you ever wondered, gazing at a starry sky, how God could be "mindful" of your little life? Do you feel important to God?

7:11 judge. His image is of a judge bringing a swift sentence (vv. 8,11).

7:14–16 Crime carries a consequence. God, the righteous judge, ordains each consequence.

8:1–5 God's majesty is so secure even the praiseworthy babble of babes is powerful. Praise is not powerful in itself. God alone holds power. While the psalmist can understand God's care for the celestial creations, he cannot understand God's concern with human frailty (144:3). Why would God care for the likes of him?

8:5 little lower than the heavenly beings. David marvels at his privileged position.

8:6–8 ruler. With privilege comes responsibility. The psalmist applies the job description given in the Garden of Eden (Gen. 1:28; 2:15).

and the fish of the sea,
all that swim the paths of the seas.

9 O LORD, our Lord,
how majestic is your name in all the earth!

OPEN 1. If you were a judge, which crime would you punish more severely than is usual? Which crime would you go easier on than usual? **2.** Digging a pit for someone else and then falling in it yourself can be embarrassing. When has that happened to you?

STUDY 1. What might be some of the "wonders" David refers to in verse 1 (v. 3; 2 Sam. 8:1–14)? **2.** David sings of God dispensing justice for "the world" and for "ever and ever." Has God already brought justice or is David just confident his prayer will be answered (v. 7)? In what sense does God reign? **3.** How are worship and witness related for David (v. 11)? For you? **4.** Who are the "wicked" (vv. 5,16–17)? What three names are given in contrast (vv. 9,12,18)? **5.** In what way is the Lord "known by his justice" (v. 16)? Does God bring justice by divine intervention or by "the work of our hands"? **6.** Skim the next psalm to see how Psalm 10 once may have been an extension of Psalm 9. Why might it have been later separated into the two psalms we now have? **7.** Does God carry out judgments in this life or does he wait for a future "Judgment Day"? Why has God waited so long? **8.** What hope does this psalm give people suffering injustice? What is your advice to them?

APPLY 1. Which of God's wonders have you felt like singing about this week? **2.** What word best describes you: Oppressed? Afflicted? Needy? Wicked? Wonderful? Why? **3.** Does your private worship affect your public witness? How has your public witness affected your desire to pray, plead and sing?

Psalm 9[a]

For the director of music. To the tune of,
"The Death of the Son." A psalm of David.

1 I will praise you, O LORD, with all my heart;
I will tell of all your wonders.
2 I will be glad and rejoice in you;
I will sing praise to your name, O Most High.

3 My enemies turn back;
they stumble and perish before you.
4 For you have upheld my right and my cause;
you have sat on your throne, judging righteously.
5 You have rebuked the nations and destroyed the wicked;
you have blotted out their name for ever and ever.
6 Endless ruin has overtaken the enemy,
you have uprooted their cities;
even the memory of them has perished.

7 The LORD reigns forever;
he has established his throne for judgment.
8 He will judge the world in righteousness;
he will govern the peoples with justice.
9 The LORD is a refuge for the oppressed,
a stronghold in times of trouble.
10 Those who know your name will trust in you,
for you, LORD, have never forsaken those who seek you.

11 Sing praises to the LORD, enthroned in Zion;
proclaim among the nations what he has done.
12 For he who avenges blood remembers;
he does not ignore the cry of the afflicted.

13 O LORD, see how my enemies persecute me!
Have mercy and lift me up from the gates of death,
14 that I may declare your praises
in the gates of the Daughter of Zion
and there rejoice in your salvation.
15 The nations have fallen into the pit they have dug;

[a]Psalms 9 and 10 may have been originally a single acrostic poem, the stanzas of which begin with the successive letters of the Hebrew alphabet. In the Septuagint they constitute one psalm.

Ps. 9 David records his thanks for God's righteous rule among evil nations. His lyrical words are filled with gratitude for God's greatness.

9:1–2 David fine-tunes an attitude of praise.

9:1 tell of all your wonders. Whenever David's enemies retreated, it was cause to celebrate (v. 3; 2 Sam. 8:1–14). David believes his victories are miraculous and worthy of praise.

9:3–6 Each victory carried national as well as personal meaning. David considers his victory personal vindication among his enemies.

9:7–10 Before the psalm concludes, David extols God's righteous judgment. In David's faithful eyes, God's justice has already overcome his enemies.

9:11 proclaim among the nations. The news is too good to keep inside. Others will testify far and wide of God's greatness.

their feet are caught in the net they have hidden.
16The LORD is known by his justice;
the wicked are ensnared by the work of their hands.
Higgaion.[a] *Selah*
17The wicked return to the grave,[b]
all the nations that forget God.
18But the needy will not always be forgotten,
nor the hope of the afflicted ever perish.

19Arise, O LORD, let not man triumph;
let the nations be judged in your presence.
20Strike them with terror, O LORD;
let the nations know they are but men. *Selah*

Psalm 10[c]

1Why, O LORD, do you stand far off?
Why do you hide yourself in times of trouble?

2In his arrogance the wicked man hunts down the weak,
who are caught in the schemes he devises.
3He boasts of the cravings of his heart;
he blesses the greedy and reviles the LORD.
4In his pride the wicked does not seek him;
in all his thoughts there is no room for God.
5His ways are always prosperous;
he is haughty and your laws are far from him;
he sneers at all his enemies.
6He says to himself, "Nothing will shake me;
I'll always be happy and never have trouble."
7His mouth is full of curses and lies and threats;
trouble and evil are under his tongue.
8He lies in wait near the villages;
from ambush he murders the innocent,
watching in secret for his victims.
9He lies in wait like a lion in cover;
he lies in wait to catch the helpless;
he catches the helpless and drags them off in his net.
10His victims are crushed, they collapse;
they fall under his strength.
11He says to himself, "God has forgotten;
he covers his face and never sees."

12Arise, LORD! Lift up your hand, O God.
Do not forget the helpless.
13Why does the wicked man revile God?
Why does he say to himself,

[a]*16* Or *Meditation*; possibly a musical notation [b]*17* Hebrew *Sheol* [c]Psalms 9 and 10 may have been originally a single acrostic poem, the stanzas of which begin with the successive letters of the Hebrew alphabet. In the Septuagint they constitute one psalm.

OPEN 1. Where do you hide in times of trouble: Under the bed covers? Behind a smoke screen? Behind a veil of humor? With face covered ("hear no evil, see no evil")? Explain. **2.** When you were in high school, who was the biggest boaster you knew? How did that make you feel?

STUDY 1. This continuation of Psalm 9 seems to make contradictory statements within itself: How can both verses 1 and 14 be true? Or verses 11 and 17? **2.** What is the basis for this wicked man's practical atheism? Does he sound "far away" from God, or is God far removed from him? Or is God actually "too close for comfort" (vv. 6,11,13)? Why do you think so? **3.** How does this man victimize his prey? Who does he remind you of? Does he arouse your compassion or revulsion? **4.** When, if ever, does justice catch up with him? **5.** What does the helpless victim want God to do (vv. 12,15)? What does God do instead? Why? **6.** Who in the world today seems similar to the wicked man in this psalm? What would you like to say to him or her? What do you think God wants to say? **7.** Paul applies verse 7 to all of us (Rom. 3:14). What's his point?

APPLY 1. Have you ever felt like the king does here? What happened? Why is God sometimes so silent in the face of great needs? **2.** When God does not appear to answer your prayers, as in this psalmist's plight, do you persevere in faith anyway? If so, how? If not, why not?

9:18 needy will not always be forgotten. In contrast to the wicked, the godly who are afflicted will eventually find help. God's timing is always right, though help may seem an eternity in coming.

9:19–20 David prompts God to awaken his enemies to a harsh reality. Mere mortals cannot oppose a great God.

10:11 God has forgotten. Wicked people conveniently wink at evil and erroneously believe God does the same. Just because God may not act immediately does not mean he is indifferent to injustice (v. 14).

"He won't call me to account"?
14 But you, O God, do see trouble and grief;
you consider it to take it in hand.
The victim commits himself to you;
you are the helper of the fatherless.
15 Break the arm of the wicked and evil man;
call him to account for his wickedness
that would not be found out.

16 The LORD is King for ever and ever;
the nations will perish from his land.
17 You hear, O LORD, the desire of the afflicted;
you encourage them, and you listen to their cry,
18 defending the fatherless and the oppressed,
in order that man, who is of the earth, may terrify no more.

Psalm 11

For the director of music. Of David.

1 In the LORD I take refuge.
How then can you say to me:
"Flee like a bird to your mountain.
2 For look, the wicked bend their bows;
they set their arrows against the strings
to shoot from the shadows
at the upright in heart.
3 When the foundations are being destroyed,
what can the righteous do[a]?"

4 The LORD is in his holy temple;
the LORD is on his heavenly throne.
He observes the sons of men;
his eyes examine them.
5 The LORD examines the righteous,
but the wicked[b] and those who love violence
his soul hates.
6 On the wicked he will rain
fiery coals and burning sulfur;
a scorching wind will be their lot.

7 For the LORD is righteous,
he loves justice;
upright men will see his face.

[a]3 Or *what is the Righteous One doing* [b]5 Or *The LORD, the Righteous One, examines the wicked, /*

OPEN 1. What made you feel secure as a child? **2.** As an adult, do you have a "getaway" place? When do you go there?

STUDY 1. What advice is David receiving here (vv. 1–3)? What attitudes does such advice reflect? **2.** What is David's response (vv. 4–6)? Was he wrong to "head for the hills" at other times (1 Sam. 23:14)? **3.** "Fire and brimstone" is an enduring image. What do you see as the lot of the wicked (v. 6)?

APPLY 1. What hiding places or "getaways" does the world urge upon you? How do you seek refuge in the Lord instead? **2.** What can your group do to help each other, when the "foundations around us are being destroyed"?

10:14 you are the helper of the fatherless. Those with no other source of assistance find their help in God (27:10).

10:15 *evil man ... for his wickedness.* The psalmist demands justice. Offenders must pay for their wickedness.

10:16–18 Nations are destroyed and prideful people are humbled—as in the previous psalm (9:19–20). The two psalms link together, portraying the whole of God's awesome power.

11:1–3 David's enemies are armed and dangerous. Yet, when others run for cover, David's faith remains firm.

11:2 bend their bows. Even the threat of attack is frightening. As enemy archers prepare for the onslaught, those around David succumb to worry.

11:4–7 In response, David does not bend a bow. He does not sharpen a sword. He reminds the people not to worry. God himself will destroy their enemies (v. 6).

Psalm 12

For the director of music. According to *sheminith*.[a]
A psalm of David.

[1] Help, LORD, for the godly are no more;
the faithful have vanished from among men.
[2] Everyone lies to his neighbor;
their flattering lips speak with deception.

[3] May the LORD cut off all flattering lips
and every boastful tongue
[4] that says, "We will triumph with our tongues;
we own our lips[b]—who is our master?"

[5] "Because of the oppression of the weak
and the groaning of the needy,
I will now arise," says the LORD.
"I will protect them from those who malign them."
[6] And the words of the LORD are flawless,
like silver refined in a furnace of clay,
purified seven times.

[7] O LORD, you will keep us safe
and protect us from such people forever.
[8] The wicked freely strut about
when what is vile is honored among men.

OPEN When something important must be said, do you write, call or visit in person? Why?

STUDY 1. What three types of "lip service" does David lament in verses 2–4? **2.** How do these hurt the weak (v. 5)? **3.** What is meant by "the words of the LORD" (v. 6)? Who wins this battle of words? Why? How? **4.** In what way is it true today that "what is vile is honored among men" (v. 8)?

APPLY 1. What is your biggest "speech impediment": Withholding the truth? Flattery? Boasting? Not listening? **2.** Do you consider yourself a good communicator? What do your friends think? **3.** When did a small word hurt a lot? Encourage a lot?

Psalm 13

For the director of music. A psalm of David.

[1] How long, O LORD? Will you forget me forever?
How long will you hide your face from me?
[2] How long must I wrestle with my thoughts
and every day have sorrow in my heart?
How long will my enemy triumph over me?

[3] Look on me and answer, O LORD my God.
Give light to my eyes, or I will sleep in death;
[4] my enemy will say, "I have overcome him,"
and my foes will rejoice when I fall.

[5] But I trust in your unfailing love;
my heart rejoices in your salvation.
[6] I will sing to the LORD,
for he has been good to me.

OPEN Have you ever been forgotten by someone who was supposed to pick you up? How did you feel? What were you thinking?

STUDY 1. What are the three stages in this uphill prayer? What makes David so low? So high? **2.** Who is responsible for the fact that David "must wrestle with his thoughts"? Who does David see as responsible? **3.** What is David's tension? Why does he become hopeful at the end of his prayer?

APPLY 1. Have you felt anger or despair like David does here? For how long? What helped? **2.** When do you feel like singing? When is God's goodness most real?

[a]Title: Probably a musical term [b]4 Or / *our lips are our plowshares*

12:3 cut off all flattering lips. David intends for God to interrupt and silence everyone who speaks nonsense against him.

12:6 words of the LORD are flawless. To trust God's word is to put one's life in his hands. Those in battle know the value of reliability. God is dependable; he will do what he says.

12:8 freely strut about. The wicked boast of victory at half time—before the game is over and the Lord proves them wrong.

Ps. 13 Similar to other psalms of lament, David details his distress. He feels forsaken (vv.1–2), yet he unashamedly asks for deliverance (vv. 3–4). He musters his strength to end on a confident note (vv. 5–6).

13:1 Will you forget me. David senses his prayers are merely bouncing off the ceiling, going nowhere. Just when he needs him most, God seems to ignore him.

13:5 trust in your unfailing love. His feelings tell him he is unloved. But his faith reminds him God's love is unfailing. His face may be temporarily saddened, but his heart rejoices.

OPEN Who played the "fool" in your senior class? What antics of your class clown were outrageous?

STUDY **1.** Why is it "foolish" to say "there is no God"? In what way is this fool an atheist (vv. 1–3)? **2.** Is David's sweeping indictment a bit exaggerated? Or exceptionally accurate? Explain. **3.** What are the implications of the view that "there is no one who does good"? **4.** What does this psalm say about God's view of evil? What does God plan to do about it?

APPLY **1.** When have you been so devastated by a tragedy or unjustice that you concluded that there is no God? **2.** What if anything, happened to help you see your original conclusion as foolish?

Psalm 14

For the director of music. Of David.

1 The fool[a] says in his heart,
"There is no God."
They are corrupt, their deeds are vile;
there is no one who does good.

2 The LORD looks down from heaven
on the sons of men
to see if there are any who understand,
any who seek God.
3 All have turned aside,
they have together become corrupt;
there is no one who does good,
not even one.

4 Will evildoers never learn—
those who devour my people as men eat bread
and who do not call on the LORD?
5 There they are, overwhelmed with dread,
for God is present in the company of the righteous.
6 You evildoers frustrate the plans of the poor,
but the LORD is their refuge.

7 Oh, that salvation for Israel would come out of Zion!
When the LORD restores the fortunes of his people,
let Jacob rejoice and Israel be glad!

OPEN **1.** Where would your dream house be? **2.** What special features would you want to have?

STUDY **1.** Who gets to live on God's "holy hill"? Why isn't God's dwelling available on an "equal housing opportunity" basis? **2.** Why "despise" the vile (v. 4)? **3.** What is "usury" (v. 5; Ex. 22:25)? Why was it considered to be wrong? **4.** How would it affect our society to outlaw usury?

APPLY **1.** In applying for God's dwelling, would your references say you have the required good character? Words? Works? Dealings? Why or why not? **2.** Does Paul have a different landlord than David (Eph. 2:8–10)? Explain.

Psalm 15

A psalm of David.

1 LORD, who may dwell in your sanctuary?
Who may live on your holy hill?

2 He whose walk is blameless
and who does what is righteous,
who speaks the truth from his heart
3 and has no slander on his tongue,
who does his neighbor no wrong
and casts no slur on his fellowman,
4 who despises a vile man
but honors those who fear the LORD,
who keeps his oath
even when it hurts,

[a] 1 The Hebrew words rendered *fool* in Psalms denote one who is morally deficient.

14:1 the fool. The fool may be intelligent but morally bankrupt. This kind of *fool believes* God is irrelevant to the practicality of life (10:4).

14:4 devour. David is amazed at the audacity of evil. Wicked people attack God's people, not realizing they bring God's wrath upon themselves.

15:1 dwell in your sanctuary. The psalmist wonders who is qualified to be on God's guest list for worshiping at the temple.

15:4 who fear the LORD. Those who are faithful and obedient are eligible to enter God's presence. The first to enter is God's Son—whose gift of righteousness saves a spot for the forgiven (Eph. 2:8–10).

5 who lends his money without usury
and does not accept a bribe against the innocent.

He who does these things
will never be shaken.

Psalm 16

A *miktam*[a] of David.

1 Keep me safe, O God,
for in you I take refuge.

2 I said to the LORD, "You are my Lord;
apart from you I have no good thing."
3 As for the saints who are in the land,
they are the glorious ones in whom is all my delight.[b]
4 The sorrows of those will increase
who run after other gods.
I will not pour out their libations of blood
or take up their names on my lips.

5 LORD, you have assigned me my portion and my cup;
you have made my lot secure.
6 The boundary lines have fallen for me in pleasant places;
surely I have a delightful inheritance.

7 I will praise the LORD, who counsels me;
even at night my heart instructs me.
8 I have set the LORD always before me.
Because he is at my right hand,
I will not be shaken.

9 Therefore my heart is glad and my tongue rejoices;
my body also will rest secure,
10 because you will not abandon me to the grave,[c]
nor will you let your Holy One[d] see decay.
11 You have made[e] known to me the path of life;
you will fill me with joy in your presence,
with eternal pleasures at your right hand.

OPEN 1. Have you inherited anything from a relative? What do you wish would be left to you? **2.** Are you a night person? If so, what do you do late at night?

STUDY 1. What two types of Israelites did David see (vv. 3–4)? **2.** For what blessings does he praise God (vv. 5–8)? What exactly do you think he means by each? **3.** What helps David to feel secure (v. 5)? **4.** Did David's hope come true (v. 10)? In what way?

APPLY 1. Judging from your appointment calendar or your daydreams this past week, what do you "delight" in? **2.** What "gods" are you tempted to pursue? What sorrows do they bring? **3.** In this psalm, David moves from being a refugee to an heir of God's kingdom: Which do you feel more like now? Why?

Psalm 17

A prayer of David.

1 Hear, O LORD, my righteous plea;
listen to my cry.

OPEN 1. When have you felt singled out for punishment by your parents, teacher or boss? Was it for something you didn't do? How did you feel then? **2.** When did you feel really terrified? Did your worst fears come true?

[a]Title: Probably a literary or musical term [b]3 Or *As for the pagan priests who are in the land / and the nobles in whom all delight, I said:* [c]10 Hebrew *Sheol* [d]10 Or *your faithful one* [e]11 Or *You will make*

15:5 lends his money without usury. Lending money was a helpful gesture. Using excessive interest as a means to get ahead was condemned (Ex. 22:25).

16:4 I will not ... take up. No matter how many are tempted to worship other gods (v. 4), David will not go along. Count him with the saints instead (v. 3). The Lord is his God.

16:5–6 delightful inheritance. David found pleasure in the land of promise where his people lived (vv. 5–6). But greater still was his relationship with the landowner, God himself (vv. 7–8).

16:8 he is at my right hand, I will not be shaken. God is the secret to David's success—the source of every victory.

16:9–11 Any way David looks at life, he knows he cannot lose. God guides his life now (v. 11). Even death cannot rob his joyful confidence in God's presence (v. 10).

STUDY 1. Does David think he is without sin (vv. 3–5)? Or is he merely contrasting himself with his enemies (vv. 9–12)? What else might he be saying? **2.** Although he calls on God as a judge (vv. 1–5), how does David relate to him (vv. 6–9)? **3.** Of the three things that he prays for—justice (vv. 1–5), protection (vv. 6–9) and God's fellowship (v. 15)—what does David desire most? Why do you think so? **4.** "When I awake" (v. 15) may be a metaphor for resurrection (Isa. 26:19; Dan. 12:2). What reward does David wish for his enemies (v. 14)?

APPLY 1. On what basis do you make your plea before God: Your integrity? The heartlessness of your enemies? God's love? Some combination? Or do you rarely see God as judge? **2.** What makes the biggest difference in how and why you live compared with people who do not know God: God's love? God's righteousness? God's reward? **3.** In what situation do you need deliverance from people or forces that seem out to get you?

Give ear to my prayer—
it does not rise from deceitful lips.
2 May my vindication come from you;
may your eyes see what is right.

3 Though you probe my heart and examine me at night,
though you test me, you will find nothing;
I have resolved that my mouth will not sin.
4 As for the deeds of men—
by the word of your lips
I have kept myself
from the ways of the violent.
5 My steps have held to your paths;
my feet have not slipped.

6 I call on you, O God, for you will answer me;
give ear to me and hear my prayer.
7 Show the wonder of your great love,
you who save by your right hand
those who take refuge in you from their foes.
8 Keep me as the apple of your eye;
hide me in the shadow of your wings
9 from the wicked who assail me,
from my mortal enemies who surround me.

10 They close up their callous hearts,
and their mouths speak with arrogance.
11 They have tracked me down, they now surround me,
with eyes alert, to throw me to the ground.
12 They are like a lion hungry for prey,
like a great lion crouching in cover.

13 Rise up, O LORD, confront them, bring them down;
rescue me from the wicked by your sword.
14 O LORD, by your hand save me from such men,
from men of this world whose reward is in this life.

You still the hunger of those you cherish;
their sons have plenty,
and they store up wealth for their children.
15 And I—in righteousness I will see your face;
when I awake, I will be satisfied with seeing your likeness.

OPEN 1. Picture God as you did when you were a child. What did the face look like? The body? Did God hold anything? What color was God? What words did God say? **2.** What images do you have of God today? What color? Emotions? Sounds?

Psalm 18

For the director of music. Of David the servant of the LORD. He sang to the LORD the words of this song when the LORD delivered him from the hand of all his enemies and from the hand of Saul. He said:

1 I love you, O LORD, my strength.

2 The LORD is my rock, my fortress and my deliverer;
my God is my rock, in whom I take refuge.

17:3–5 you will find nothing. David contrasts the purity (not perfection) of his life with the evil people around him (vv. 9–12). He asks God to vindicate his innocence, to "search his heart" (v. 2; 139:23).

17:10–12 David implies God cannot allow such vile people to overtake him.

17:15 I will see your face when I awake. In David's time, sleep was a euphemism for death. He awakes to the glorious presence of God (Dan. 12:2).

He is my shield and the horn[a] of my salvation, my stronghold.
[3] I call to the LORD, who is worthy of praise,
and I am saved from my enemies.

[4] The cords of death entangled me;
the torrents of destruction overwhelmed me.
[5] The cords of the grave[b] coiled around me;
the snares of death confronted me.
[6] In my distress I called to the LORD;
I cried to my God for help.
From his temple he heard my voice;
my cry came before him, into his ears.

[7] The earth trembled and quaked,
and the foundations of the mountains shook;
they trembled because he was angry.
[8] Smoke rose from his nostrils;
consuming fire came from his mouth,
burning coals blazed out of it.
[9] He parted the heavens and came down;
dark clouds were under his feet.
[10] He mounted the cherubim and flew;
he soared on the wings of the wind.
[11] He made darkness his covering, his canopy around him—
the dark rain clouds of the sky.
[12] Out of the brightness of his presence clouds advanced,
with hailstones and bolts of lightning.
[13] The LORD thundered from heaven;
the voice of the Most High resounded.[c]
[14] He shot his arrows and scattered ⌞the enemies⌟,
great bolts of lightning and routed them.
[15] The valleys of the sea were exposed
and the foundations of the earth laid bare
at your rebuke, O LORD,
at the blast of breath from your nostrils.

[16] He reached down from on high and took hold of me;
he drew me out of deep waters.
[17] He rescued me from my powerful enemy,
from my foes, who were too strong for me.
[18] They confronted me in the day of my disaster,
but the LORD was my support.

[a]2 *Horn* here symbolizes strength. [b]5 Hebrew *Sheol* [c]13 Some Hebrew manuscripts and Septuagint (see also 2 Samuel 22:14); most Hebrew manuscripts *resounded, / amid hailstones and bolts of lightning*

STUDY 1. If you had to express the emotions of this psalm in music, what types of music would you choose? What refrains would you dramatize? What solo parts stand out? Where would you signal the musical crescendo? **2.** This psalm appears in 2 Samuel 22, as a summary of David's life. How accurate a summary is it? Does it gloss over some of David's less noble deeds? **3.** David spent much time hiding from Saul in rocks and caves. What insight does this give you into the meaning of God as "fortress" or "stronghold" or "rock"? What names could you give God based on your experiences? **4.** Nowhere in 1 or 2 Samuel are the cosmic events of verses 4–19 recorded. Why does David use such dramatic language to describe God saving him? To what other redemptive experiences in Israel's history is he alluding (vv. 16–17)? **5.** What does the linking of God's rescue of David to God's actions for Israel at the Red Sea or Mount Sinai say about God's love for the individual? What else does this dramatic picture say about God's justice? **6.** In several psalms David speaks as though he were sinless (vv. 20–24). In others he is very aware of his failure (32:5). How do you account for this? **7.** Is David boasting or praising God in verses 20–29? What "decrees" had God given him? How did David perform? How much of his appeal is based on God's promises and peculiar delight in him? Why do you think so? **8.** What image of God is most prominent in the eyes of David, according to verses 30–36 and 46–50? Do we tend to "make God" in our own image?

APPLY 1. Is it easy or hard for you to say "I love you, Lord"? When are you most aware of God's love for you? **2.** Habakkuk 3:19 quotes verse 33 to build up hope in the face of a national crisis. What verse would you choose to describe how you want to see God work in your own crisis? In your nation's crisis?

18:4–6 David penned this psalm when King Saul's army was closing in. Just in time, God hears David's cry for help (v. 6).

18:4–5 David gets his point across in dramatic fashion. His enemies are too close for comfort (vv. 4–5).

18:5 cords of the grave. Powerful enemies cause David to fear for his life.

18:8 consuming fire. Like an inferno, God rises up as the formidable opponent of David's enemies. His strength is unmatched.

18:10 mounted the cherubim and flew. The angel is poised to deliver God to the battle scene (80:1; 99:1).

18:16–19 David fantasizes the ultimate destruction of his foes. He borrows elements from his people's past for dramatic effect (Ex. 14).

Why that verse? **3.** Members may hold a short time of praise, offering short prayers beginning like this psalm: "I love you, O LORD, because ..."

[19]He brought me out into a spacious place;
he rescued me because he delighted in me.

[20]The LORD has dealt with me according to my righteousness;
according to the cleanness of my hands he has rewarded me.
[21]For I have kept the ways of the LORD;
I have not done evil by turning from my God.
[22]All his laws are before me;
I have not turned away from his decrees.
[23]I have been blameless before him
and have kept myself from sin.
[24]The LORD has rewarded me according to my righteousness,
according to the cleanness of my hands in his sight.

[25]To the faithful you show yourself faithful,
to the blameless you show yourself blameless,
[26]to the pure you show yourself pure,
but to the crooked you show yourself shrewd.
[27]You save the humble
but bring low those whose eyes are haughty.
[28]You, O LORD, keep my lamp burning;
my God turns my darkness into light.
[29]With your help I can advance against a troop[a];
with my God I can scale a wall.

[30]As for God, his way is perfect;
the word of the LORD is flawless.
He is a shield
for all who take refuge in him.
[31]For who is God besides the LORD?
And who is the Rock except our God?
[32]It is God who arms me with strength
and makes my way perfect.
[33]He makes my feet like the feet of a deer;
he enables me to stand on the heights.
[34]He trains my hands for battle;
my arms can bend a bow of bronze.
[35]You give me your shield of victory,
and your right hand sustains me;
you stoop down to make me great.
[36]You broaden the path beneath me,
so that my ankles do not turn.

[37]I pursued my enemies and overtook them;
I did not turn back till they were destroyed.
[38]I crushed them so that they could not rise;
they fell beneath my feet.

[a]29 Or *can run through a barricade*

18:19 brought me out into a *spacious place ... delighted in me.* David compares the confines of his previous dilemma (vv. 4–6) to the deep breath he takes in the wide-open spaces of God's deliverance. God's motive to rescue David is pure pleasure. David was a man "after his own heart" (1 Sam. 13:14).

18:30–36 David rolls the credits at the conclusion of his dramatic display. To God be the glory!

18:30 shield ... to take refuge. God's battle plan focuses on a defensive strategy. He will be the protector for his people while he battles in their place.

39 You armed me with strength for battle;
you made my adversaries bow at my feet.
40 You made my enemies turn their backs in flight,
and I destroyed my foes.
41 They cried for help, but there was no one to save them—
to the LORD, but he did not answer.
42 I beat them as fine as dust borne on the wind;
I poured them out like mud in the streets.

43 You have delivered me from the attacks of the people;
you have made me the head of nations;
people I did not know are subject to me.
44 As soon as they hear me, they obey me;
foreigners cringe before me.
45 They all lose heart;
they come trembling from their strongholds.

46 The LORD lives! Praise be to my Rock!
Exalted be God my Savior!
47 He is the God who avenges me,
who subdues nations under me,
48 who saves me from my enemies.
You exalted me above my foes;
from violent men you rescued me.
49 Therefore I will praise you among the nations, O LORD;
I will sing praises to your name.
50 He gives his king great victories;
he shows unfailing kindness to his anointed,
to David and his descendants forever.

Psalm 19

For the director of music. A psalm of David.

1 The heavens declare the glory of God;
the skies proclaim the work of his hands.
2 Day after day they pour forth speech;
night after night they display knowledge.
3 There is no speech or language
where their voice is not heard.[a]
4 Their voice[b] goes out into all the earth,
their words to the ends of the world.

[a]3 Or *They have no speech, there are no words; / no sound is heard from them* [b]4 Septuagint, Jerome and Syriac; Hebrew *line*

OPEN 1. What's your favorite dessert? When's the last time you had it? **2.** Do you like to read? What would you rather do?

STUDY 1. Who speaks in verses 1–4? What do "they" say? Is the truth about God in nature obvious to everyone? Why don't some people "hear" it? **2.** What five names does David give the Jewish Law (vv. 7–10)? What eight words describe this Law? What phrases describe its effect on our lives? **3.** What does the revelation through Scripture do for us that the revelation in creation does not

18:43–45 The spoils of victory belong to David. He is victorious beyond measure.

18:43 head of nations. David rises from certain death (vv. 4–6) to command conquered nations.

18:46 my Rock! God is a solid place, high above all trouble. The image is safety and unthreatened security.

18:50 his king. David's victories signal future spiritual victories under Christ the King (2:2,6). **unfailing kindness.** David concludes with an image of God's benevolent nature.

Ps. 19 Psalm 19 is a hymn of praise celebrating the glory of God. God's glory is not only evident in the beauty of the starry heavens, it is also revealed by his law. In combination with Psalm 18, God's glory is revealed through three aspects of his character. Psalm 18 highlights glory revealed by God's mercy for his people. Psalm 19 presents God's glory in creation and the justice which makes creation secure.

19:1–4 declare ... their voice goes out. The lights of the heavens proclaim God's glory. Though the heavens seem to be silent, they speak through sheer beauty.

19:4–6 a tent for the sun. For many ancient people, the sky was a canopy over the earth spreading from horizon to horizon. The psalmist takes that

(v. 11)? **4.** David uses the name "God" ("El") in verse 1, then switches to "the LORD" ("Yahweh") in verses 7–9. Why the change? Note: "El" is the least specific Hebrew word for God, whereas "Yahweh" is God's personal name (Ex. 3:14–15). **5.** How does David's confession and prayer (vv. 12–14) square with his claims to blamelessness in the previous psalm (18:20–24)?

APPLY **1.** What in creation fills you most with a sense of God's glory? **2.** Which of David's "one-liners" about God's Law best matches your experience with Scripture? Or should you write your own? How does your sense of its value translate into the time you spend reading it? **3.** Which would nurture your faith most: Meditation on creation? Meditation on the Word? A combination? Other? Why?

OPEN **1.** What are you least looking forward to in the upcoming week? Why? **2.** How do you psych yourself for a challenge? A conflict?

STUDY **1.** This psalm is a prayer before war (1 Kin. 8:44–45). Picture the scene in verses 1–5, people gathered around their

In the heavens he has pitched a tent for the sun,
5 which is like a bridegroom coming forth from his pavilion,
like a champion rejoicing to run his course.
6 It rises at one end of the heavens
and makes its circuit to the other;
nothing is hidden from its heat.

7 The law of the LORD is perfect,
reviving the soul.
The statutes of the LORD are trustworthy,
making wise the simple.
8 The precepts of the LORD are right,
giving joy to the heart.
The commands of the LORD are radiant,
giving light to the eyes.
9 The fear of the LORD is pure,
enduring forever.
The ordinances of the LORD are sure
and altogether righteous.
10 They are more precious than gold,
than much pure gold;
they are sweeter than honey,
than honey from the comb.
11 By them is your servant warned;
in keeping them there is great reward.

12 Who can discern his errors?
Forgive my hidden faults.
13 Keep your servant also from willful sins;
may they not rule over me.
Then will I be blameless,
innocent of great transgression.

14 May the words of my mouth and the meditation of my heart
be pleasing in your sight,
O LORD, my Rock and my Redeemer.

Psalm 20

For the director of music. A psalm of David.

1 May the LORD answer you when you are in distress;
may the name of the God of Jacob protect you.
2 May he send you help from the sanctuary
and grant you support from Zion.
3 May he remember all your sacrifices

---

image one step further and portrays the sky as a royal tent for the sun. The sun itself was not divine, although it was widely worshiped in pagan societies. It was merely one of God's creations. The magnificence of the sun was pale in relation to its creator.

19:11–13 The Law provides guideposts for living in God's will. Human conscience alone cannot guide people to a life pleasing to God. Thus God gave us divine law as both warning and promise. It warns that certain actions are errors that require forgiveness. It promises that faithfulness to the Law would bring great reward. Willful disregard for the Law meant deliberately ignoring its warnings. The result of such disregard is separation from God's people (Num. 15:30).

Ps. 20 The liturgy of this psalm is meant to prepare a king for battle. The people sing the psalm to encourage their king to face the enemy. Verses 1–5 ask God to bless the king by hearing his prayers, helping him and giving the king the success he desires. The second part, verses 6–9, is a confession of faith in God's willingness and power to help the king and army in battle.

and accept your burnt offerings. *Selah*
4 May he give you the desire of your heart
and make all your plans succeed.
5 We will shout for joy when you are victorious
and will lift up our banners in the name of our God.
May the LORD grant all your requests.

6 Now I know that the LORD saves his anointed;
he answers him from his holy heaven
with the saving power of his right hand.
7 Some trust in chariots and some in horses,
but we trust in the name of the LORD our God.
8 They are brought to their knees and fall,
but we rise up and stand firm.

9 O LORD, save the king!
Answer[a] us when we call!

Psalm 21

For the director of music. A psalm of David.

1 O LORD, the king rejoices in your strength.
How great is his joy in the victories you give!
2 You have granted him the desire of his heart
and have not withheld the request of his lips. *Selah*
3 You welcomed him with rich blessings
and placed a crown of pure gold on his head.
4 He asked you for life, and you gave it to him—
length of days, for ever and ever.
5 Through the victories you gave, his glory is great;
you have bestowed on him splendor and majesty.
6 Surely you have granted him eternal blessings
and made him glad with the joy of your presence.
7 For the king trusts in the LORD;
through the unfailing love of the Most High
he will not be shaken.

8 Your hand will lay hold on all your enemies;
your right hand will seize your foes.
9 At the time of your appearing
you will make them like a fiery furnace.
In his wrath the LORD will swallow them up,
and his fire will consume them.
10 You will destroy their descendants from the earth,
their posterity from mankind.

[a]9 Or *save! / O King, answer*

army. How can they be so confident? **2.** "Chariots and horses" were the potent technology at the time: what is the equivalent today? **3.** Is it practical to trust in God if the other side has the firepower and technology? Why or why not?

APPLY 1. What "war" are you preparing for in your life, for which you need this kind of "pep talk"? **2.** What would it mean for you to trust God for the victory?

OPEN 1. What is the biggest victory you've ever won? The most recent? Do you feel exhilarated, exhausted or what? **2.** How do you celebrate your victories?

STUDY 1. This psalm is the "morning after" complement to chapter 20. What must have happened between the two chapters? Does God take sides in war (vv. 1,5)? **2.** What has God done for the king (vv. 3–6)? What does this tell you about what God will do for those who trust in him? **3.** Do verses 8–12 strike you as a realistic picture of the battle past? Is the psalmist referring to more than just David (v. 10)?

APPLY 1. The last time you overcame a major obstacle, what were you inclined to do: Give yourself a pat on the back? Give thanks to God? Rally the troops who prayed for you? Why? **2.** When have you prayed and not received the victory? How did it affect the way you prayed and faced your big test the next time? **3.** What difference does it make, knowing ultimate victory belongs to God?

20:7–8 Some trust in chariots. A good army does not guarantee success. God's help is the only assurance of victory.

Ps. 21 Psalm 20 prays for victory in battle, and Psalm 21 celebrates victory. The victorious king receives great honor, but the greater glory belongs to God. Indeed, more victories are in sight here. The king who trusts God will be given even greater success in battle.

21:6 eternal blessings. God is the source of all blessings. The greatest blessing is God's continuing presence in the king's life, through which the king receives an unending bounty of enduring blessings.

21:8–12 With God's aid, the king's enemies will be defeated and destroyed. The enemies will become cowards when they are confronted by the power of God.

[11] Though they plot evil against you
and devise wicked schemes, they cannot succeed;
[12] for you will make them turn their backs
when you aim at them with drawn bow.

[13] Be exalted, O LORD, in your strength;
we will sing and praise your might.

Psalm 22

For the director of music. To the tune of, "The Doe of the Morning." A psalm of David.

[1] My God, my God, why have you forsaken me?
Why are you so far from saving me,
so far from the words of my groaning?
[2] O my God, I cry out by day, but you do not answer,
by night, and am not silent.

[3] Yet you are enthroned as the Holy One;
you are the praise of Israel.[a]
[4] In you our fathers put their trust;
they trusted and you delivered them.
[5] They cried to you and were saved;
in you they trusted and were not disappointed.

[6] But I am a worm and not a man,
scorned by men and despised by the people.
[7] All who see me mock me;
they hurl insults, shaking their heads:
[8] "He trusts in the LORD;
let the LORD rescue him.
Let him deliver him,
since he delights in him."

[9] Yet you brought me out of the womb;
you made me trust in you
even at my mother's breast.
[10] From birth I was cast upon you;
from my mother's womb you have been my God.
[11] Do not be far from me,
for trouble is near
and there is no one to help.

[12] Many bulls surround me;
strong bulls of Bashan encircle me.

[a]3 Or *Yet you are holy, / enthroned on the praises of Israel*

OPEN 1. When you were a child, what "enemy" did you feel you were surrounded by: Angry adults? Giddy girls? Bratty boys? **2.** Who did you look to for rescue?

STUDY 1. What is David's basic struggle (vv. 1–2,6–8)? What seems worse: God's distance or people's mocking? **2.** Where is David's faith in the midst of these struggles (vv. 3–5)? What does he recall about God's past action that leads to the words of verses 1 and 11? **3.** What is David's claim in verse 10? How is this true? **4.** How would you describe the mood shift between verses 1–21 and verses 22–31? What may have happened between verses 21 and 22? **5.** Who is invited to David's assembly (vv. 26–29)? Why does he want to host this world-wide feast? **6.** Jesus quoted the first line of this psalm on the cross (Matt. 27:46). What does the fact that he did say about his experience on the cross? **7.** What other details of this psalm turn up in the crucifixion narratives (Mark 15, Luke 23 and John 19)? How do these help you to understand this psalm?

APPLY 1. When you are stricken with grief, feeling abandoned even by God, how do you express yourself: Disbelief? Tears? Anger? Woe is me? Wanting to crawl back into the womb? Thinking about your death? Bargaining with God? Faith in spite of a bleak outlook? **2.** At such times, does it help to know that Jesus experienced human emotions and troubles while on this earth? **3.** Verses 1–21 shift between faith and despair. If "faith" was on the wall to your right, "despair" on the wall to

---

Ps. 22 David is under siege by enemies. He feels hopeless and alone, even deserted by God who had helped him in the past. Psalm 22 reflects the despair he is feeling at that time. *While he recognizes that God has rescued him in the past,* that is little consolation now. David is under siege through no fault of his own. This psalm is the cry of a righteous sufferer. Gospel writers find striking parallels between David in this psalm and Christ at his crucifixion (Matt. 27:35,39,43; John 19:23–24).

22:1 Jesus quotes this verse during his crucifixion (Matt. 27:46; Mark 15:34).

22:3–5 they trusted and you delivered them. The psalmist recalls that God is faithful. The Israelites cried out and God saved them.

22:9–10 you brought me out of the womb. David recalls what God has done for him. God had chosen David in the same manner as God's choice of Israel.

22:12–18 bulls ... evil men. The psalmist uses a series of powerful

[13]Roaring lions tearing their prey
open their mouths wide against me.
[14]I am poured out like water,
and all my bones are out of joint.
My heart has turned to wax;
it has melted away within me.
[15]My strength is dried up like a potsherd,
and my tongue sticks to the roof of my mouth;
you lay me[a] in the dust of death.
[16]Dogs have surrounded me;
a band of evil men has encircled me,
they have pierced[b] my hands and my feet.
[17]I can count all my bones;
people stare and gloat over me.
[18]They divide my garments among them
and cast lots for my clothing.

[19]But you, O LORD, be not far off;
O my Strength, come quickly to help me.
[20]Deliver my life from the sword,
my precious life from the power of the dogs.
[21]Rescue me from the mouth of the lions;
save[c] me from the horns of the wild oxen.

[22]I will declare your name to my brothers;
in the congregation I will praise you.
[23]You who fear the LORD, praise him!
All you descendants of Jacob, honor him!
Revere him, all you descendants of Israel!
[24]For he has not despised or disdained
the suffering of the afflicted one;
he has not hidden his face from him
but has listened to his cry for help.

[25]From you comes the theme of my praise in the great assembly;
before those who fear you[d] will I fulfill my vows.
[26]The poor will eat and be satisfied;
they who seek the LORD will praise him—
may your hearts live forever!

[a]15 Or / *I am laid* [b]16 Some Hebrew manuscripts, Septuagint and Syriac; most Hebrew manuscripts / *like the lion,* [c]21 Or / *you have heard* [d]25 Hebrew *him*

your left, where would you position yourself in the room to show where you are spiritually? Why?

images to portray both his enemies (bulls, lions, dogs and evil men) and his own weakness to deal with them (water, wax, potsherd and dust).

22:20–21 The four images of the psalmist's attackers are portrayed in reverse order from verses 12–18. The "sword" probably relates back to the image of verse 16. The evil men who wield the sword could have been robbers or enemy soldiers. Regardless, they are the personification of violent death.

22:21 save me. Alternatively, this phrase could be translated, "you have heard me." The meaning of the verse shifts dramatically if that translation is adopted. The translation, "save me," provides a parallel to "rescue me" and the verse becomes a plea for help. If "you have heard me" is meant, then the tone of the psalm turns from despair to hope. Since verse 22 introduces the theme of praising and thanking God for deliverance, the alternate translation must be considered.

22:22–31 I will praise you. Regardless of the translation of verse 21, these verses present vows to praise and glorify God in response to the psalmist's deliverance. This praise would spread from the psalmist himself (v. 22) to Israel (vv. 23–25), and from Israel to the entire world (vv. 26–31). The psalmist's vision anticipates the outpouring of God's saving grace through Christ as it spread from person to person, community to community and nation to nation.

[27]All the ends of the earth
will remember and turn to the LORD,
and all the families of the nations
will bow down before him,
[28]for dominion belongs to the LORD
and he rules over the nations.

[29]All the rich of the earth will feast and worship;
all who go down to the dust will kneel before him—
those who cannot keep themselves alive.
[30]Posterity will serve him;
future generations will be told about the Lord.
[31]They will proclaim his righteousness
to a people yet unborn—
for he has done it.

Psalm 23

A psalm of David.

[1]The LORD is my shepherd, I shall not be in want.
[2] He makes me lie down in green pastures,
he leads me beside quiet waters,
[3] he restores my soul.
He guides me in paths of righteousness
for his name's sake.
[4]Even though I walk
through the valley of the shadow of death,[a]
I will fear no evil,
for you are with me;
your rod and your staff,
they comfort me.

[5]You prepare a table before me
in the presence of my enemies.
You anoint my head with oil;
my cup overflows.
[6]Surely goodness and love will follow me
all the days of my life,
and I will dwell in the house of the LORD
forever.

[a]4 Or *through the darkest valley*

OPEN With what formulas for dealing with stress were you raised? "Forget it"? "Pray about it"? "Sleep on it"?

STUDY 1. David now departs from the "rock" and "stronghold" images of God. From what part of his life does this psalm come (1 Sam. 16:10–12)? **2.** Why might a "rod" and "staff" (tools to keep sheep "in line") be comforting? **3.** What second image is used (vv. 5–6)? What are the possible meanings of "anointment" (1 Sam. 16:13; Luke 7:46)?

APPLY 1. Read this psalm again in the negative ("The LORD is not my shepherd ..."). What verse is most disturbing? **2.** What dark valley do you walk now? Has God rescued or protected you with his "rod and staff"? What "green pastures and still waters" has he brought your way? **3.** Who are your "enemies" today? What would you like your cup to overflow with?

22:27 All the ends of the earth. All the earth would be told of God's saving acts. As a result, the God of Israel would become the God of salvation for all people who would turn to him.

23:1 shepherd. Although Israel became an increasingly urban nation after it settled Canaan, rural people still practiced the lifestyle of their ancestors. This was true in David's time, in Christ's time and is even true in modern times. In the Psalms, the shepherd was a widely used metaphor for the king (78:71–72; 2 Sam. 5:2). In this psalm, King David acknowledges that God is his shepherd-king. Jesus is the shepherd of his people, and by implication, their shepherd-king (John 10:14).

23:3 He guides me. The shepherd must determine the wise path for his flock and seek to keep it within the path's boundaries. That good path would lead to food and water where the flock could be refreshed and restored.

23:4 for you are with me ... comfort me. God is present with his people. His presence guides their survival in a dangerous, fallen world. God's staff is a support that his people can lean upon when their walk is difficult. God's people should be comforted by the knowledge that God's rod is there to protect and to save them and his staff to support them. Rod and staff are, of course, metaphors for God's presence and power in our lives. God's Word gives us promises we can lean on, and commandments we must follow.

23:5 You prepare a table before me. God, the shepherd-king, receives David at his table and gives him protection. Their relationship is based on a covenant. In the ancient Near East, covenants were often concluded with a meal (Gen. 31:54).

23:6 goodness and love. Goodness and love are two outcomes of a proper covenant relationship with God.

Psalm 24

Of David. A psalm.

[1]The earth is the LORD's, and everything in it,
the world, and all who live in it;
[2]for he founded it upon the seas
and established it upon the waters.

[3]Who may ascend the hill of the LORD?
Who may stand in his holy place?
[4]He who has clean hands and a pure heart,
who does not lift up his soul to an idol
or swear by what is false.[a]
[5]He will receive blessing from the LORD
and vindication from God his Savior.
[6]Such is the generation of those who seek him,
who seek your face, O God of Jacob.[b] *Selah*

[7]Lift up your heads, O you gates;
be lifted up, you ancient doors,
that the King of glory may come in.
[8]Who is this King of glory?
The LORD strong and mighty,
the LORD mighty in battle.
[9]Lift up your heads, O you gates;
lift them up, you ancient doors,
that the King of glory may come in.
[10]Who is he, this King of glory?
The LORD Almighty—
he is the King of glory. *Selah*

Psalm 25[c]

Of David.

[1]To you, O LORD, I lift up my soul;
[2] in you I trust, O my God.
Do not let me be put to shame,

[a]4 Or *swear falsely* [b]6 Two Hebrew manuscripts and Syriac (see also Septuagint); most Hebrew manuscripts *face, Jacob* [c]This psalm is an acrostic poem, the verses of which begin with the successive letters of the Hebrew alphabet.

OPEN 1. What was the toughest hike or climb you ever made? How did you prepare for it? **2.** Do you like answering machines? What message do you like best?

STUDY 1. What lines of this psalm indicate a procession into the city (1 Chr. 15:25–29)? **2.** What does David stress about God in verses 1–2? How does that relate to his question and answer (vv. 3–4)? **3.** What is meant by "clean hands and a pure heart"? **4.** What is stressed about God in verses 7–10? What three names would you give God from this psalm? **5.** How does Paul apply this psalm to freedom in Christ (v. 1; 1 Cor. 10:25–26)?

APPLY 1. How do you prepare for worship? What might help you prepare this week? **2.** What modern "idols" tempt you to live for them instead of the true God? What does God's reign call you to be and do?

OPEN 1. When lost in a strange city or new store, do you: Ask for help? Consult the map? Find your own way? **2.** Were you a rebel as a child? Teenager? Adult? Senior? What did you do? **3.** What "sins of your youth" do you especially hope God forgets?

STUDY 1. In which verses does David ask God for

Ps. 24 This psalm celebrates the Lord's entrance into Zion. It was probably composed to celebrate the arrival of the Ark of the Covenant in Jerusalem or to commemorate that event. God is portrayed entering the temple, the holy place of his people. By extension, the Christian church has adopted this psalm as a representation of Jesus' ascension into the holy city of New Jerusalem.

24:2 founded ... established. The psalmist uses the language usually applied to the founding of a city or a temple. Both cities and temples were described as having foundations (Josh. 6:26; 1 Kin. 5:17). Like cities and temples, the earth itself has foundations (1 Sam. 2:8). With the foundation image, the psalmist creates parallels between the temple and Jerusalem which we extend today to foreshadow the heavenly kingdom of God.

24:4 pure heart. Having a pure heart does not imply moral perfection. Instead, it points to freedom from sinful motives and intentionally sinful attitudes. In the Sermon on the Mount Jesus said, "Blessed are the pure in heart, for they will see God" (Matt. 5:8).

24:5 blessing from the LORD. The products of righteousness ("clean hands and a pure heart") are blessings from God. All the struggles of the righteous person, and all the effort to keep life pure, are finally vindicated when God smiles with approval on that life. No one earns God's forgiveness through moral perfection, but in Christ, here anticipated, all people's sins are covered and the righteous life is given divine help.

24:7–10 Lift up your heads ... gates ... doors. All of creation sings and shouts as God enters the temple of Jerusalem. If gates and doors rejoice, how much more so the people who know God as deliverer and helper against all foes.

protection from his enemies? What sort of enemies did he face? **2.** In which verses does David ask for guidance? What characterizes God's "path" (v. 4)? Who will God guide? **3.** In which verses does David ask for forgiveness? Does God have a bad memory (v. 7)? To what aspect of God does David make his appeal? **4.** For whose sake does David ask God to forgiven his iniquity (v. 11)? Why would forgiving David elevate or honor God's name? **5.** How is David's personal plea also a congregational prayer (v. 22)?

APPLY **1.** What are you most in need of today: protection, guidance or forgiveness? Do you feel you will receive it? Why or why not? **2.** What quality needed for finding God's guidance will you work to develop this week? How could this psalm answer the question, "How can I know God's will"? **3.** What about God's character gives you the most hope as you face tough times ahead?

nor let my enemies triumph over me.
3 No one whose hope is in you
will ever be put to shame,
but they will be put to shame
who are treacherous without excuse.

4 Show me your ways, O LORD,
teach me your paths;
5 guide me in your truth and teach me,
for you are God my Savior,
and my hope is in you all day long.
6 Remember, O LORD, your great mercy and love,
for they are from of old.
7 Remember not the sins of my youth
and my rebellious ways;
according to your love remember me,
for you are good, O LORD.

8 Good and upright is the LORD;
therefore he instructs sinners in his ways.
9 He guides the humble in what is right
and teaches them his way.
10 All the ways of the LORD are loving and faithful
for those who keep the demands of his covenant.
11 For the sake of your name, O LORD,
forgive my iniquity, though it is great.
12 Who, then, is the man that fears the LORD?
He will instruct him in the way chosen for him.
13 He will spend his days in prosperity,
and his descendants will inherit the land.
14 The LORD confides in those who fear him;
he makes his covenant known to them.
15 My eyes are ever on the LORD,
for only he will release my feet from the snare.

16 Turn to me and be gracious to me,
for I am lonely and afflicted.
17 The troubles of my heart have multiplied;
free me from my anguish.
18 Look upon my affliction and my distress
and take away all my sins.
19 See how my enemies have increased
and how fiercely they hate me!
20 Guard my life and rescue me;
let me not be put to shame,
for I take refuge in you.
21 May integrity and uprightness protect me,
because my hope is in you.

22 Redeem Israel, O God,
from all their troubles!

25:6–7 according to your love remember me. A scrapbook contains many images and memories, but most scrapbooks help to recall positive, happy times. The writer asks God to be merciful in remembering his promises, and forget (put away, do not hold against the writer) sins committed long ago.

Psalm 26

Of David.

[1]Vindicate me, O LORD,
for I have led a blameless life;
I have trusted in the LORD
without wavering.
[2]Test me, O LORD, and try me,
examine my heart and my mind;
[3]for your love is ever before me,
and I walk continually in your truth.
[4]I do not sit with deceitful men,
nor do I consort with hypocrites;
[5]I abhor the assembly of evildoers
and refuse to sit with the wicked.
[6]I wash my hands in innocence,
and go about your altar, O LORD,
[7]proclaiming aloud your praise
and telling of all your wonderful deeds.
[8]I love the house where you live, O LORD,
the place where your glory dwells.

[9]Do not take away my soul along with sinners,
my life with bloodthirsty men,
[10]in whose hands are wicked schemes,
whose right hands are full of bribes.
[11]But I lead a blameless life;
redeem me and be merciful to me.

[12]My feet stand on level ground;
in the great assembly I will praise the LORD.

Psalm 27

Of David.

[1]The LORD is my light and my salvation—
whom shall I fear?
The LORD is the stronghold of my life—
of whom shall I be afraid?
[2]When evil men advance against me
to devour my flesh,[a]
when my enemies and my foes attack me,

[a]2 Or *to slander me*

OPEN Do you tend to sit in the same place at the dinner table? In church? In this group? Next to whom? Why?

STUDY 1. What does "blameless" mean (vv. 1,11)? Faultless? Sincere? How does David's life contrast with those pictured here (vv. 4–5,9–10)? **2.** How does "love" motivate David (vv. 3,8)? How is that love expressed? **3.** From what you know of David, what "grade" would you give him on the Lord's "test" (v. 2)? Why would you grant his request (vv. 1,9,11)?

APPLY 1. Given a "sincerity scale" of 1 to 10, how would you score on the Lord's test? Why? **2.** David's "crib sheet" (it helped him pass the test) was God's love and truth: What "crib sheet" do you rely on? How can you follow David's example to improve your "grade"? **3.** What changes in your "seating preferences" would help you conform with verses 4–5, without becoming proud or pompous?

OPEN 1. If you could ask "one thing" of the Lord, and have it granted, what would it be? Why don't you ask? **2.** How good are you at remembering faces? Why?

STUDY 1. What three qualities of God does David recall in verse 1? What do you think he means by each? How does each relate to David's confidence (vv. 2–3)? **2.** In what ways might these verses reflect David's life experiences? **3.** What clue does the oft-repeated

26:1 blameless life. The blameless part of this life is not moral perfection. The writer, probably David, is all too aware of past sins. Here "blameless" refers to David's passionate and lifelong devotion to God. He has not worshiped false gods. He trusts God alone.

26:4–5 sit with. David knows that evil companions can lead a person into sin. He also knows that one's environment can be morally rotten, depending on one's choice of company. But David has surrounded himself with honorable men, and with them, he seeks the company of God. David could not hope that God would be his friend if other companions were rotten and corrupt.

26:8 where your glory dwells. The tabernacle was originally built as a tangible sign of the presence of the Lord among the Israelites. God's glory dwelt in the tent (Ex. 40:35) and later in the temple (1 Kin. 8:11). The glory of God dwelling in the tabernacle assures Israel that God's covenant with them is still in place.

26:12 level ground. David is confident that with God's continuing presence he will not stumble on the rocky, pitted paths of life.

"seek" (vv. 4,8) give you into David's deepest desire: Does he desire to be a priest? Receive sanctuary? Do God's will? What does it mean to you to seek God's face? **4.** What "one thing" does David seek above all else? **5.** What is the relationship between "seeking" and "waiting" for God (v. 14)? What does this tell you about the believer's life? **6.** Given David's experience with rejection, what seems to be most comforting about God's presence?

APPLY 1. How has the Lord been like a "light" or a "stronghold" in your life this past month? What situation has driven you to him to find shelter? What words describe your sense of his presence at the point of need? **2.** "Seek his face" is echoed by Jesus: "Seek first his kingdom and his righteousness and all these other things will be given to you as well" (Matt. 6:33). Is seeking God's face (or kingdom) first for you? Second or third? What distracts you from "putting first things first"? **3.** In your love life with God, where does he stand: Closer to you than your own parents? More like a distant relative you've only heard about? Somewhere in between? Why?

they will stumble and fall.
3 Though an army besiege me,
my heart will not fear;
though war break out against me,
even then will I be confident.

4 One thing I ask of the LORD,
this is what I seek:
that I may dwell in the house of the LORD
all the days of my life,
to gaze upon the beauty of the LORD
and to seek him in his temple.
5 For in the day of trouble
he will keep me safe in his dwelling;
he will hide me in the shelter of his tabernacle
and set me high upon a rock.
6 Then my head will be exalted
above the enemies who surround me;
at his tabernacle will I sacrifice with shouts of joy;
I will sing and make music to the LORD.

7 Hear my voice when I call, O LORD;
be merciful to me and answer me.
8 My heart says of you, "Seek his[a] face!"
Your face, LORD, I will seek.
9 Do not hide your face from me,
do not turn your servant away in anger;
you have been my helper.
Do not reject me or forsake me,
O God my Savior.
10 Though my father and mother forsake me,
the LORD will receive me.
11 Teach me your way, O LORD;
lead me in a straight path
because of my oppressors.
12 Do not turn me over to the desire of my foes,
for false witnesses rise up against me,
breathing out violence.

13 I am still confident of this:
I will see the goodness of the LORD
in the land of the living.
14 Wait for the LORD;

[a]8 Or *To you, O my heart, he has said, "Seek my*

27:4–6 dwell in the house of the LORD. David recognizes that his source of power is God. He draws his strength from a higher king; as a steward-king under God, he can look to the Lord's "palace" as a place of refuge and wise counsel. David's only security is the Lord, and his only real place of safety is in the Lord's house.

27:7–12 Hear my voice. David prays for deliverance from his enemies. First, however, he asks that the Lord hear him. He asks God to show him the right way to handle his problem after he has put forward his request to be heard.

27:11 Teach me your way. Real deliverance comes from learning God's will and doing it. The process of learning God's will is often difficult, even for David (2 Sam. 7:14,15).

27:14 Wait for the LORD. David recognizes that a person must often wait for answers to prayers. God reveals his will in his own time; part of the process of obedience is to have faith ("take heart") and wait.

be strong and take heart
and wait for the LORD.

Psalm 28

Of David.

[1] To you I call, O LORD my Rock;
do not turn a deaf ear to me.
For if you remain silent,
I will be like those who have gone down to the pit.
[2] Hear my cry for mercy
as I call to you for help,
as I lift up my hands
toward your Most Holy Place.

[3] Do not drag me away with the wicked,
with those who do evil,
who speak cordially with their neighbors
but harbor malice in their hearts.
[4] Repay them for their deeds
and for their evil work;
repay them for what their hands have done
and bring back upon them what they deserve.
[5] Since they show no regard for the works of the LORD
and what his hands have done,
he will tear them down
and never build them up again.

[6] Praise be to the LORD,
for he has heard my cry for mercy.
[7] The LORD is my strength and my shield;
my heart trusts in him, and I am helped.
My heart leaps for joy
and I will give thanks to him in song.

[8] The LORD is the strength of his people,
a fortress of salvation for his anointed one.
[9] Save your people and bless your inheritance;
be their shepherd and carry them forever.

Psalm 29

A psalm of David.

[1] Ascribe to the LORD, O mighty ones,
ascribe to the LORD glory and strength.

OPEN When you call on your best friend for help, what do you need most: A listening ear? A certain voice? A handout? A detailed game plan? Companionship?

STUDY **1.** What is David's main concern (vv. 1–5): A premature death? A miscarriage of justice? A plea for mercy? Why do you think so? **2.** What images does he associate with God? Why? What experiences do they reflect upon? What meaning do they convey for you? **3.** What must have happened for David to turn his personal plea (vv. 1–7) into a prayer for the people as a whole (vv. 8–9)?

APPLY **1.** When have you been as desperate as David (vv. 1–5)? As confident as David (vv. 6–7)? **2.** Music helps David better express his feelings to God (v. 7; 26:7). How about for you? What words or song best sums up how you are feeling about God now? **3.** Which image means more to you now: God as your fortress? Or God as your shepherd? Why?

OPEN How does a thunderstorm make you feel? Does it make you think of God?

STUDY **1.** What is the impact of this thunderous Lord on

Ps. 28 This psalm is a prayer for deliverance from malicious enemies that surround Israel. David puts the focus not on enemies' malice but on God's ability to deliver his people and confidence in prayer.

28:5 the works of the LORD. David's enemies are God's enemies too. Their "evil work" (v. 4) is a failure to recognize God's covenant with Israel (Ex. 19–24) and God' selection of David to rule over Israel (2 Sam. 7).

28:9 Save ... bless ... be their shepherd. The psalmist summarizes God's shepherdlike care for his people: God rescues from danger and destruction; blesses to make lives more fruitful; protects and guides the people.

nature? On the people? On you? **2.** What path does the storm take (vv. 5–8)? Trace it on a map. **3.** Why is the name Yahweh ("the LORD") repeated 18 times? **4.** When the storm passes (v. 10), what then?

APPLY 1. What storm is blowing through your life now? Are you responding like the people—giving glory to God for ruling over the storm? Or are you like nature—in uproar? Why? **2.** Would you find peace by recognizing the Lord of the storm? Why or why not?

OPEN Do you like roller-coasters? Is your life like a roller-coaster? A ferris wheel? The merry-go-round?

STUDY 1. For what reasons does David praise God (vv. 1–3)? How does he account for why the Lord allowed these hard times to come upon him? **2.** What do you learn about the Lord's anger (v. 5)? About his favor? **3.** What error did David make (vv. 6–7)? Is it wrong to feel secure? **4.** How does David argue that God should spare him (v. 9)? What does this indicate about his view of the afterlife? **5.** Why would this psalm be written for the dedication of the temple (1 Kin. 8:2–66)?

2 Ascribe to the LORD the glory due his name;
worship the LORD in the splendor of his[a] holiness.

3 The voice of the LORD is over the waters;
the God of glory thunders,
the LORD thunders over the mighty waters.
4 The voice of the LORD is powerful;
the voice of the LORD is majestic.
5 The voice of the LORD breaks the cedars;
the LORD breaks in pieces the cedars of Lebanon.
6 He makes Lebanon skip like a calf,
Sirion[b] like a young wild ox.
7 The voice of the LORD strikes
with flashes of lightning.
8 The voice of the LORD shakes the desert;
the LORD shakes the Desert of Kadesh.
9 The voice of the LORD twists the oaks[c]
and strips the forests bare.
And in his temple all cry, "Glory!"

10 The LORD sits[d] enthroned over the flood;
the LORD is enthroned as King forever.
11 The LORD gives strength to his people;
the LORD blesses his people with peace.

Psalm 30

A psalm. A song. For the dedication
of the temple.[e] Of David.

1 I will exalt you, O LORD,
for you lifted me out of the depths
and did not let my enemies gloat over me.
2 O LORD my God, I called to you for help
and you healed me.
3 O LORD, you brought me up from the grave[f];
you spared me from going down into the pit.

4 Sing to the LORD, you saints of his;
praise his holy name.

[a]2 Or *LORD with the splendor of* [b]6 That is, Mount Hermon [c]9 Or *LORD makes the deer give birth* [d]10 Or *sat* [e]Title: Or *palace* [f]3 Hebrew *Sheol*

29:3–9 David describes the voice of God using images of nature's power: God's voice thunders, strikes like lightning; is the wind that breaks cedars and strips forests; is in the earthquakes that shake the desert. God's voice creates and controls everything.

29:9 temple. The temple can be understood on three levels here. The faithful who worship at the temple (tabernacle) in Jerusalem praise God. But verses 3–9 also point to the heavenly temple of God (Isa. 6:1). In addition, all of creation is God's temple, and nature itself proclaims God's glory.

29:10–11 The Lord is the king of all creation. God strengthens his people so they might endure and blesses them so they might prosper.

Ps. 30 This psalm praises God for delivering the king from death. It begins and ends with personal vows to praise God. Verses 4 and 5 expand on the king's praise of God and call the worshippers to join him.

30:1 out of the depths. God's saving power reaches down from heaven into the misery of human existence. The "depths" are the human condition at its worst. Here the depths are related to death and the place of eternal torment, Sheol. God's great love rescues people not at their zenith but at their lowest point.

30:4–5 Sing to the LORD. David testifies to the gathered worshipers that God has saved him (vv. 1–3). Now he calls them to join him in praising God.

5 For his anger lasts only a moment,
but his favor lasts a lifetime;
weeping may remain for a night,
but rejoicing comes in the morning.

6 When I felt secure, I said,
"I will never be shaken."
7 O LORD, when you favored me,
you made my mountain[a] stand firm;
but when you hid your face,
I was dismayed.

8 To you, O LORD, I called;
to the Lord I cried for mercy:
9 "What gain is there in my destruction,[b]
in my going down into the pit?
Will the dust praise you?
Will it proclaim your faithfulness?
10 Hear, O LORD, and be merciful to me;
O LORD, be my help."

11 You turned my wailing into dancing;
you removed my sackcloth and clothed me with joy,
12 that my heart may sing to you and not be silent.
O LORD my God, I will give you thanks forever.

Psalm 31

For the director of music. A psalm of David.

1 In you, O LORD, I have taken refuge;
let me never be put to shame;
deliver me in your righteousness.
2 Turn your ear to me,
come quickly to my rescue;
be my rock of refuge,
a strong fortress to save me.
3 Since you are my rock and my fortress,
for the sake of your name lead and guide me.

[a]7 Or *hill country* [b]9 Or *there if I am silenced*

APPLY 1. Is security important to you? How much of your money goes toward buying a house? Medical and life insurance? Savings? Where does security lie? **2.** Has God turned a time of wailing into a time of dancing for you? Was it "overnight," surprising you with joy? Or did your mood swings level out more gradually? **3.** How is the theme of "sorrow producing joy" developed in the New Testament (John 16:19–22; 2 Cor. 4:16–18)? For what are you "mourning"? How long has your "night" been? How long until "morning" comes?

OPEN 1. When do you feel most "trapped" or stuck at home: Sick in bed? No one called for a Saturday night date? Somebody called, but you had no baby-sitter? **2.** Is there someone you would hide from if you saw him or her on the street today? Why?

STUDY 1. How do you picture David's "trap" (vv. 1–5)? **2.** What turn do verses 6–8 take? How is David's trust rewarded? **3.** What causes David's sorrow in verses 9–18? Hasn't God rescued him (v. 8)? What might have happened to cause such fluctuations in his feelings?

David's survival symbolizes the nation's survival; David's success is an event for everyone to celebrate.

30:5 anger ... favor. God spends more "time" loving and blessing than punishing his people. God's anger flashes quickly, but God's favor is long lasting. When God becomes angry with his people, he is anxious to forgive and resume pouring out the blessings of spiritual prosperity.

30:6–7 when you favored ... when you hid. The psalmist's well-being is not affected by his own strength but by God's favor. Like most people, the psalmist would like to control his own happiness, but God has taught him otherwise.

30:6 never be shaken. At times, people can believe that they have all the answers. Their arrogance obscures the real source of strength and breaks their prayer connection to God. Strength bottoms out. They burn out.

30:8–10 O LORD, be my help. With self-assurance shattered, the psalmist faces death (the pit) powerless to help himself. Desperately he cries to God for mercy.

30:11–12 God answers David's cries. The Lord turns wailing into singing. Despair ("sackcloth") becomes joy. David, reminded that God is the source of all blessings, vows to praise God forever.

31:1–5 rock of refuge. Psalm 30 describes God as "the deliverer." Psalm 31 portrays God as the psalmist's refuge—a place of safety, a fortress.

31:3 for the sake of your name. Enemies who attack David are attacking God's servant. God's honor is being assaulted, but David's rescue preserves God's glory.

4. What feelings are expressed in verses 9–18 which are not present in verses 1–5? What new situation is David likely facing? **5.** This time, how does David break through in faith (vv. 14–18) and praise (vv. 19–24)? What words and acts prove this faith? How is God's goodness evident? To whom? **6.** Both Jesus and Stephen quoted verse 5 as they were about to die (Luke 23:46; Acts 7:59). Were their situations similar to David's? **7.** What action from verses 19–24 do you most need to take: Fear God? Take refuge in God? Call out to God? Be faithful? Place hope in God?

APPLY 1. Where are you feeling "trapped": By your enemies? By your desires? By loneliness? How will you "escape"? **2.** Can you express feelings of abandonment or rejection by God? Does it show a lack of faith? Why or why not? **3.** Like David, have you ever felt joy in God, then felt the joy slip away unpredictably? **4.** In what situation do you need to "be strong and take heart"? What from this psalm can help you do just that?

4 Free me from the trap that is set for me,
for you are my refuge.
5 Into your hands I commit my spirit;
redeem me, O LORD, the God of truth.

6 I hate those who cling to worthless idols;
I trust in the LORD.
7 I will be glad and rejoice in your love,
for you saw my affliction
and knew the anguish of my soul.
8 You have not handed me over to the enemy
but have set my feet in a spacious place.

9 Be merciful to me, O LORD, for I am in distress;
my eyes grow weak with sorrow,
my soul and my body with grief.
10 My life is consumed by anguish
and my years by groaning;
my strength fails because of my affliction,[a]
and my bones grow weak.
11 Because of all my enemies,
I am the utter contempt of my neighbors;
I am a dread to my friends—
those who see me on the street flee from me.
12 I am forgotten by them as though I were dead;
I have become like broken pottery.
13 For I hear the slander of many;
there is terror on every side;
they conspire against me
and plot to take my life.

14 But I trust in you, O LORD;
I say, "You are my God."
15 My times are in your hands;
deliver me from my enemies
and from those who pursue me.
16 Let your face shine on your servant;

[a]10 Or *guilt*

31:4 trap that is set for me. David's enemies have set a trap for him. His only escape is through God's intervention.

31:5 Into your hands I commit my spirit. This phrase, quoted by Jesus in Luke 23:46, expresses total commitment to the Lord. That commitment is based on a powerful trust that God can and will protect and deliver regardless of their situation. In Hebrew the word translated "commit" literally means "to deposit." David gives up control of his life and places it in God's hands for safekeeping.

31:6–8 David really trusts God. His faith is based on experience. He has trusted God in the past and has confidence now in God's care for the present.

31:8 spacious place. Being rescued is like being freed from captivity. God's refuge is safe like a fortress but not confining like a prison (18:19; Job 36:16).

31:9–13 David explains his distress. He is the object of slander and the target of assassination. Because his enemies are so strong, all his friends have forsaken him. If the enemy's scheming does not kill him, anguish over his situation will.

31:11–12 those who see me ... flee from me. Befriending David is not good for your health. At the least you will be slandered, but you may also find yourself in the midst of an assassination attempt. Others have abandoned David, hurting him politically. He complains he is too dangerous for friendship (38:11; 41:9; 88:8).

31:14–18 But I trust in you, O LORD. David's rescue can only come from God. David has cried to the Lord for help and trusted God to answer his cries. God's help will surely come soon.

31:15 My times are in your hands. David commits his spirit to God—soul, mind, goals, passions (v. 5)—but all his daily needs too. Spirit and life—all are God's.

save me in your unfailing love.
17 Let me not be put to shame, O LORD,
for I have cried out to you;
but let the wicked be put to shame
and lie silent in the grave.[a]
18 Let their lying lips be silenced,
for with pride and contempt
they speak arrogantly against the righteous.

19 How great is your goodness,
which you have stored up for those who fear you,
which you bestow in the sight of men
on those who take refuge in you.
20 In the shelter of your presence you hide them
from the intrigues of men;
in your dwelling you keep them safe
from accusing tongues.

21 Praise be to the LORD,
for he showed his wonderful love to me
when I was in a besieged city.
22 In my alarm I said,
"I am cut off from your sight!"
Yet you heard my cry for mercy
when I called to you for help.

23 Love the LORD, all his saints!
The LORD preserves the faithful,
but the proud he pays back in full.
24 Be strong and take heart,
all you who hope in the LORD.

Psalm 32

Of David. A *maskil*.[b]

1 Blessed is he
whose transgressions are forgiven,
whose sins are covered.
2 Blessed is the man
whose sin the LORD does not count against him
and in whose spirit is no deceit.

[a]17 Hebrew *Sheol* [b]Title: Probably a literary or musical term

OPEN How do you compare to a horse: Not much understanding, but lots of horse sense? Hot-tempered, must be broken in? Lazy and stubborn, must be led by bit and bridle? Love to take people for a ride? Why are you that way?

STUDY **1.** What is the source of blessedness or happiness in this psalm? How does this compare with Psalm 1:1? **2.** What does "in whose spirit is no deceit" mean? How

31:19 stored up. Because David has deposited his life with God, he can share in the goodness that God has stored up for the faithful.

31:21–22 David may be praising God for something in the past or anticipating rescue from his present predicament.

31:23–24 Love the LORD, all his saints. David's despair in verses 9–13 has turned to hope, and hope to praise. As the psalm ends, his praise expands from his own experience to blessings given to all faithful. He encourages the faithful to love God, to be strong and to hope.

32:1–2 Blessed is he. Happiness is being forgiven. The psalmist uses repetition as a poetic technique to express the depth of his happiness. Jesus used the same technique in the Beatitudes to underscore traits found among people who are forgiven and who share in the kingdom of God (Matt. 5:3–10).

32:2 in whose spirit is no deceit. Forgiveness is the product of an honest relationship with God. An honest spirit acknowledges sins and accepts forgiveness.

does it relate to the struggle expressed in verses 3–5? Why do you think he would refuse to confess his sin for so long? What happened when he did? **3.** What has David realized about God (vv. 6–7)? **4.** How does the Lord's counsel (vv. 8–9) relate to David's struggle (vv. 3–4)? How is he like a mule? **5.** What's the punch line of this psalm for you? **6.** What does Paul try to prove with this psalm (Rom. 4:7–8)?

APPLY 1. God freely forgives those who trust him: How has that message been driven home to you recently? How has that forgiveness spilled over into your other relationships? How do you see yourself differently? **2.** Have you felt like God is not to be found? What "waters" rise and obscure God?

---

[3] When I kept silent,
my bones wasted away
through my groaning all day long.
[4] For day and night
your hand was heavy upon me;
my strength was sapped
as in the heat of summer. *Selah*
[5] Then I acknowledged my sin to you
and did not cover up my iniquity.
I said, "I will confess
my transgressions to the LORD"—
and you forgave
the guilt of my sin. *Selah*

[6] Therefore let everyone who is godly pray to you
while you may be found;
surely when the mighty waters rise,
they will not reach him.
[7] You are my hiding place;
you will protect me from trouble
and surround me with songs of deliverance. *Selah*

[8] I will instruct you and teach you in the way you should go;
I will counsel you and watch over you.
[9] Do not be like the horse or the mule,
which have no understanding
but must be controlled by bit and bridle
or they will not come to you.
[10] Many are the woes of the wicked,
but the LORD's unfailing love
surrounds the man who trusts in him.

[11] Rejoice in the LORD and be glad, you righteous;
sing, all you who are upright in heart!

Psalm 33

OPEN 1. What helps you worship best: Music? Loud shouts? Nature? Silence? Ritual? Why? **2.** What distracts you from worship: Silence? A baby's cry? Talking? Loud noises? **3.** As we are all different in how we like to worship,

[1] Sing joyfully to the LORD, you righteous;
it is fitting for the upright to praise him.
[2] Praise the LORD with the harp;
make music to him on the ten-stringed lyre.

32:3–5 The psalmist shares his personal experience with hidden sin. The kind of sin is not specified, but the effects of sin are devastating. Sin brings misery like a festering sore. Sin drains life away, but confession brings relief—good riddance to guilt.

32:4 strength was sapped. God's disapproval of the psalmist's sin is like a heavy hand that holds him down. Though he might fight against it, that *heavy hand is a burden he must carry.* Under that burden he wilts like a plant in the hot summer sun.

32:6 The psalmist changes focus from his own sin to the sin of his fellow worshipers. The psalmist was wrong not to confess earlier. Indeed, his fellow worshipers should confess sin now, while God is near. Failure to confess will bring misery and the debilitating effects of God's "heavy hand."

32:7 surround me with songs of deliverance. God has delivered David, and David has shared the news of that deliverance with other worshipers. As a result, many will join David in praising the Lord.

32:8–10 The psalm moves from confession to priestly instruction. Whether David is the speaker or the recipient of this instruction is not clear. Regardless, these verses teach that all people must trust God and obey God's instructions. If not, then the miseries that hurt David will befall them.

32:9 horse or the mule. Farm animals obey because they have learned to respond unquestioningly to the superior power of the master, having felt his whip many times. God can control people in the same way, but God prefers the more intimate and personal control that follows from trust and covenant love.

[3] Sing to him a new song;
play skillfully, and shout for joy.

[4] For the word of the LORD is right and true;
he is faithful in all he does.
[5] The LORD loves righteousness and justice;
the earth is full of his unfailing love.

[6] By the word of the LORD were the heavens made,
their starry host by the breath of his mouth.
[7] He gathers the waters of the sea into jars[a];
he puts the deep into storehouses.
[8] Let all the earth fear the LORD;
let all the people of the world revere him.
[9] For he spoke, and it came to be;
he commanded, and it stood firm.
[10] The LORD foils the plans of the nations;
he thwarts the purposes of the peoples.
[11] But the plans of the LORD stand firm forever,
the purposes of his heart through all generations.

[12] Blessed is the nation whose God is the LORD,
the people he chose for his inheritance.
[13] From heaven the LORD looks down
and sees all mankind;
[14] from his dwelling place he watches
all who live on earth—
[15] he who forms the hearts of all,
who considers everything they do.
[16] No king is saved by the size of his army;
no warrior escapes by his great strength.
[17] A horse is a vain hope for deliverance;
despite all its great strength it cannot save.
[18] But the eyes of the LORD are on those who fear him,
on those whose hope is in his unfailing love,
[19] to deliver them from death
and keep them alive in famine.

[20] We wait in hope for the LORD;
he is our help and our shield.
[21] In him our hearts rejoice,
for we trust in his holy name.
[22] May your unfailing love rest upon us, O LORD,
even as we put our hope in you.

[a]7 Or *sea as into a heap*

how do we let others around us worship as they like and still not become distracted ourselves?

STUDY 1. What aids to worship do you see employed in this psalm? **2.** How are both the love and the power of God evident in creation? If verses 4–9 focus on God's creative power, what is the focus of verses 10–19? **3.** How might verses 16–19 bring hope to people in hard times? **4.** What response does the Lord expect from all the earth (v. 8)? From all nations, especially his own people (v. 12)? What is incompatible about trust in "horses" and trust in God (vv. 16–18)? **5.** How does God's "unfailing love" apply to justice (v. 5)? Worship (v. 18)? Hope (v. 22)?

APPLY 1. What are two things about creation that have impressed you about God's power? About his love? Do these things help you to worship God? **2.** Do you believe that God controls even "the plans of the nations"? In what sense? Does that comfort you? **3.** In what would an outside observer conclude that you place your hope: "horses" or the Lord?

33:4–11 The Lord spoke and all of creation appeared—God's plan was wonderful and perfect. Faced with a God who speaks such a powerful word, what can people do to thwart or subvert God's stated intention to save his people? Absolutely nothing.

33:12–19 Israel is the blessed beneficiary of God's plan, chosen as a witness of God's saving power. God's protection of Israel is assured, for he is the Lord of creation and he will not be frustrated (vv. 6–11). God's plan for their care is carefully orchestrated.

33:18,22 unfailing love. The love described here is God's passion for his covenant people.

33:20–22 The people respond to God's unfailing love. They wait upon the Lord in trust. They hope in God.

OPEN **1.** What commercial could you rewrite to recommend God? **2.** Do your grudges last long? How do you get rid of them?

STUDY **1.** Read 1 Samuel 21:10–15 to see what prompted this psalm ("Abimelech", not to be confused with Ahimelech of 1 Sam. 21, may be a title used by King Achish). If you were David, would you write a psalm praising God for deliverance, or one congratulating yourself for a clever ploy? **2.** This psalm has two parts. Where do you think the dividing line is? What subtitle would you give the first half? The rest? **3.** How could David "taste and see" that the Lord is good? Is he saying the righteous will never die of hunger (v. 10)? **4.** What promises do you see in this psalm? Which one has your name on it? **5.** What destroys the wicked (v. 21)? Why doesn't God intervene? **6.** Peter uses verses 8 and 12–16 to comfort those who suffer for doing good (1 Peter 2:3; 3:10–12). How do you reconcile the "good things" the Lord promises with the acute suffering experienced by some followers of Christ? **7.** What does it mean to "seek peace and pursue it" (v. 14)? How does it apply to God? Others? Society? Would "casual" or "relentless" better describe your pursuit of peace this week? Why?

APPLY **1.** How does your journey as a believer "taste" to you: Sweet? Sour? Spicy? Salty? Bitter? Bland? Why is that? **2.** In what way is this psalm also your testimony (v. 22, Rom. 8:1)?

Psalm 34[a]

Of David. When he pretended to be insane before
Abimelech, who drove him away, and he left.

1 I will extol the LORD at all times;
his praise will always be on my lips.
2 My soul will boast in the LORD;
let the afflicted hear and rejoice.
3 Glorify the LORD with me;
let us exalt his name together.

4 I sought the LORD, and he answered me;
he delivered me from all my fears.
5 Those who look to him are radiant;
their faces are never covered with shame.
6 This poor man called, and the LORD heard him;
he saved him out of all his troubles.
7 The angel of the LORD encamps around those who fear him,
and he delivers them.

8 Taste and see that the LORD is good;
blessed is the man who takes refuge in him.
9 Fear the LORD, you his saints,
for those who fear him lack nothing.
10 The lions may grow weak and hungry,
but those who seek the LORD lack no good thing.

11 Come, my children, listen to me;
I will teach you the fear of the LORD.
12 Whoever of you loves life
and desires to see many good days,
13 keep your tongue from evil
and your lips from speaking lies.
14 Turn from evil and do good;
seek peace and pursue it.

15 The eyes of the LORD are on the righteous
and his ears are attentive to their cry;
16 the face of the LORD is against those who do evil,
to cut off the memory of them from the earth.

17 The righteous cry out, and the LORD hears them;
he delivers them from all their troubles.

[a]This psalm is an acrostic poem, the verses of which begin with the successive letters of the Hebrew alphabet.

34:1–7 The psalmist praises God for answering prayer and delivering him. He calls others to join in his praise (v. 3), then describes the story of his deliverance (vv. 4–7).

34:1–3 I will extol. The psalmist promises to praise God *continually,* and then instructs his fellow worshipers to join in his praising.

34:4–7 he delivered me. The psalmist faced real trouble, prayed for deliverance and God answered. Such deliverance is available to "those who fear" God, if they will ask.

34:8–14 The psalmist moves from praise to instruction, concentrating on human senses and emotions. Often, the senses are considered to be breeding grounds for sin. In this case, however, they are the means to obey God. By tasting (v. 8), fearing (v. 9), listening (v. 11), loving and desiring (v. 12) and speaking (v. 13), a person learns to fear God and do his will.

34:15–18 eyes of the LORD are on the righteous. Senses and emotions are also part of God's help to the righteous and condemnation of the wicked. The Lord sees the righteous (v. 15) and hears their cry (vv. 15,17). The wicked are defeated so thoroughly that not even a memory of them remains.

18 The LORD is close to the brokenhearted
and saves those who are crushed in spirit.
19 A righteous man may have many troubles,
but the LORD delivers him from them all;
20 he protects all his bones,
not one of them will be broken.

21 Evil will slay the wicked;
the foes of the righteous will be condemned.
22 The LORD redeems his servants;
no one will be condemned who takes refuge in him.

Psalm 35

Of David.

1 Contend, O LORD, with those who contend with me;
fight against those who fight against me.
2 Take up shield and buckler;
arise and come to my aid.
3 Brandish spear and javelin[a]
against those who pursue me.
Say to my soul,
"I am your salvation."

4 May those who seek my life
be disgraced and put to shame;
may those who plot my ruin
be turned back in dismay.
5 May they be like chaff before the wind,
with the angel of the LORD driving them away;
6 may their path be dark and slippery,
with the angel of the LORD pursuing them.
7 Since they hid their net for me without cause
and without cause dug a pit for me,
8 may ruin overtake them by surprise—
may the net they hid entangle them,
may they fall into the pit, to their ruin.
9 Then my soul will rejoice in the LORD
and delight in his salvation.
10 My whole being will exclaim,
"Who is like you, O LORD?
You rescue the poor from those too strong for them,
the poor and needy from those who rob them."

11 Ruthless witnesses come forward;
they question me on things I know nothing about.

[a]3 Or *and block the way*

OPEN 1. Salt on the tail catches the bird, but what catches a person? If you wanted to "trap" somebody who has tried to do you in, how would you do it? **2.** If "spear throwing" were your sport, which enemy of yours would you want to be your "spear catcher"?

STUDY 1. What seems to be the occasion for this psalm? How might his plea be related to the events of David's life? **2.** What hurts David the most: The pain of injustice? The one-sidedness of it all? The Lord's delay in judgment? **3.** What does he want the Lord to do to these people? What do you think of the "poetic justice" in David's plea (v. 8)? **4.** How will David respond when God acts (vv. 9–10)? How do you account for his rejoicing at another's downfall? **5.** Is David recalling accurately his record of behavior (vv. 13–14)? Is he justified in praying "against" his enemies? **6.** What is the significance of a "wink" (v. 19; Prov. 6:13)?

APPLY 1. How do you respond when people treat you unfairly? In what situation do you wish the Lord would fight for you? **2.** Are you comfortable with David's many cries for vengeance? How can we pray "against" our enemies? **3.** What injustice around you hurts enough to move you to pray against it? If nothing does, what does that say about your compassion and concern for justice for other people?

34:19–22 Evil will slay the wicked. A righteous person can be delivered from troubles and saved from sin. The wicked must suffer the consequence of sin: death (Rom. 6:23).

35:4–10 David asks God to match and surpass his enemies' might. As enemies seek to ensnare David, God should ensnare them. As they dig a pit for David, God should make them fall into it. David wants God to be an ally.

35:11–18 David explains the troubles he has suffered. His enemies were once his friends. In the past David had suffered with them and even prayed for them (v. 13). Yet, when David's fortunes were low, these people had seized the opportunity to slander him. With these facts laid out before God, David appeals

12 They repay me evil for good
and leave my soul forlorn.
13 Yet when they were ill, I put on sackcloth
and humbled myself with fasting.
When my prayers returned to me unanswered,
14 I went about mourning
as though for my friend or brother.
I bowed my head in grief
as though weeping for my mother.
15 But when I stumbled, they gathered in glee;
attackers gathered against me when I was unaware.
They slandered me without ceasing.
16 Like the ungodly they maliciously mocked[a];
they gnashed their teeth at me.
17 O Lord, how long will you look on?
Rescue my life from their ravages,
my precious life from these lions.
18 I will give you thanks in the great assembly;
among throngs of people I will praise you.

19 Let not those gloat over me
who are my enemies without cause;
let not those who hate me without reason
maliciously wink the eye.
20 They do not speak peaceably,
but devise false accusations
against those who live quietly in the land.
21 They gape at me and say, "Aha! Aha!
With our own eyes we have seen it."

22 O LORD, you have seen this; be not silent.
Do not be far from me, O Lord.
23 Awake, and rise to my defense!
Contend for me, my God and Lord.
24 Vindicate me in your righteousness, O LORD my God;
do not let them gloat over me.
25 Do not let them think, "Aha, just what we wanted!"
or say, "We have swallowed him up."

26 May all who gloat over my distress
be put to shame and confusion;
may all who exalt themselves over me
be clothed with shame and disgrace.
27 May those who delight in my vindication
shout for joy and gladness;
may they always say, "The LORD be exalted,
who delights in the well-being of his servant."
28 My tongue will speak of your righteousness
and of your praises all day long.

[a] 16 Septuagint; Hebrew may mean *ungodly circle of mockers.*

for God's help (v. 17) and promises to praise God publicly for deliverance (v. 18).

35:15 stumbled. David stumbled morally at times, causing him grief and suffering. The tumble here was the kind of decline anyone, even the righteous, might suffer.

Psalm 36

For the director of music.
Of David the servant of the LORD.

1 An oracle is within my heart
concerning the sinfulness of the wicked:[a]
There is no fear of God
before his eyes.
2 For in his own eyes he flatters himself
too much to detect or hate his sin.
3 The words of his mouth are wicked and deceitful;
he has ceased to be wise and to do good.
4 Even on his bed he plots evil;
he commits himself to a sinful course
and does not reject what is wrong.

5 Your love, O LORD, reaches to the heavens,
your faithfulness to the skies.
6 Your righteousness is like the mighty mountains,
your justice like the great deep.
O LORD, you preserve both man and beast.
7 How priceless is your unfailing love!
Both high and low among men
find[b] refuge in the shadow of your wings.
8 They feast on the abundance of your house;
you give them drink from your river of delights.
9 For with you is the fountain of life;
in your light we see light.

10 Continue your love to those who know you,
your righteousness to the upright in heart.
11 May the foot of the proud not come against me,
nor the hand of the wicked drive me away.
12 See how the evildoers lie fallen—
thrown down, not able to rise!

Psalm 37[c]

Of David.

1 Do not fret because of evil men
or be envious of those who do wrong;

[a]1 Or *heart: / Sin proceeds from the wicked.* [b]7 Or *love, O God! / Men find*; or *love! / Both heavenly beings and men / find* [c]This psalm is an acrostic poem, the stanzas of which begin with the successive letters of the Hebrew alphabet.

OPEN Where do you go to get refreshed or live it up?

STUDY 1. From verses 1–4, what qualities characterize the wicked? What is meant by verse 2? **2.** What difference do you see in the thoughts of the "wicked" and the "righteous"? How do thoughts give birth to actions? **3.** David's thoughts about the wicked (vv. 1–4) suddenly move him to reflect upon God's character: Why is that? What is the point of each word picture in verses 5–9? **4.** Using your own literary license, rewrite verses 5–6 in terms of your own experience of God. To what can you compare God's love? His faithfulness? His justice? **5.** How does verse 12 flow out of verses 10–11? Is this a fitting end to the psalm? Why or why not?

APPLY 1. In the book of Psalms the "righteous" seem to be those who may do evil but are generally seeking to please God. The "wicked" are those who, despite good they may do, are generally rejecting God's ways. What aspects of each do you see in your own life? **2.** Have you tasted of God's "feast" recently? How has he refreshed or enlivened you?

OPEN 1. What do you consider your "home turf"? Why? **2.** What do you worry about the most?

STUDY 1. Is the psalmist addressing himself, God or man? What problem is David addressing (v. 7)? **2.** What different answers does David give to the fact that the wicked often go unpunished (vv.

36:1–4 The wicked do not fear the Lord. They judge their own behavior and so act as their own god. They live under the false assumption of moral perfection. Nothing good can come from them, and they have no fear of choosing wrong over right.

36:4 on his bed. A wicked person even uses leisure time to plot wickedness. Why waste time meditating on God's Law (1:2) or praying (42:8) when evil is your goal?

36:5–6 love ... faithfulness ... righteousness ... justice. The psalmist sees these four virtues, which are central to God's character, evident in all of nature, top to bottom. All of creation reflects the creator God.

36:10–11 This psalm of pain and discouragement from David's enemies concludes with a prayer and a request. David has praised God's love and righteousness. Now he asks that this love be given to those who know God, and that righteousness be given to those with pure hearts. Then David asks for protection from the proud and the wicked.

2,9,13,15,17)? **3.** Instead of worrying about the short-lived success of evil, what qualities should shape their lives (vv. 3–8)? What is meant by "be still ... and wait patiently for the LORD" (v. 7)? **4.** What does David mean by "the meek" (v. 11)? Why do you think "inheriting" or "dwelling in" the land is mentioned eight times in this psalm? How would that comfort disenfranchised or dispossessed people? **5.** How does Jesus use the idea that the meek will inherit the land (Matt. 5:5)? **6.** The wicked being "cut off" is mentioned five times. What other images portray how they will be frustrated eventually in their plans (vv. 2,9–10,12–17,20,35–36)? **7.** What proverbial wisdom do you see here with regard to money matters (vv. 16–21,25–26)? How is generosity with money an indicator of trust and waiting on the Lord to uphold? **8.** Is verse 25 always true? Or was this just David's experience, for which there are many exceptions? Why do you think so?

APPLY 1. What do you secretly want to see happen to those who do evil and enjoy momentary success? How does their success and your reaction to it make you feel about God? **2.** Give an example of how you are postponing an immediate good for a future, greater gain? Does society encourage "delayed gratification"? **3.** Are you currently frustrated because "evil" people are getting their way? How can you apply verses 3–8 this week? Which of those biblical qualities would a best friend tell you to work on? **4.** Since Job, good people have been asking why bad things happen to them. How would you sensitively encourage others who suffer oppression? How does the suffering of Jesus relate to these times?

2 for like the grass they will soon wither,
like green plants they will soon die away.

3 Trust in the LORD and do good;
dwell in the land and enjoy safe pasture.
4 Delight yourself in the LORD
and he will give you the desires of your heart.

5 Commit your way to the LORD;
trust in him and he will do this:
6 He will make your righteousness shine like the dawn,
the justice of your cause like the noonday sun.

7 Be still before the LORD and wait patiently for him;
do not fret when men succeed in their ways,
when they carry out their wicked schemes.

8 Refrain from anger and turn from wrath;
do not fret—it leads only to evil.
9 For evil men will be cut off,
but those who hope in the LORD will inherit the land.

10 A little while, and the wicked will be no more;
though you look for them, they will not be found.
11 But the meek will inherit the land
and enjoy great peace.

12 The wicked plot against the righteous
and gnash their teeth at them;
13 but the Lord laughs at the wicked,
for he knows their day is coming.

14 The wicked draw the sword
and bend the bow
to bring down the poor and needy,
to slay those whose ways are upright.
15 But their swords will pierce their own hearts,
and their bows will be broken.

16 Better the little that the righteous have
than the wealth of many wicked;
17 for the power of the wicked will be broken,
but the LORD upholds the righteous.

18 The days of the blameless are known to the LORD,
and their inheritance will endure forever.
19 In times of disaster they will not wither;
in days of famine they will enjoy plenty.

37:8 anger ... wrath. Getting tied in knots over the success of the wicked can be dangerous. If righteous people allow themselves to get angry at the prosperity of evil people, they sink to the same level as the wicked and will share their destruction.

37:10 a little while. This phrase points with certainty to something that will happen soon (58:9; Job 20:5–11).

37:11 meek will inherit the land. This phrase is quoted by Jesus in the Beatitudes (Matt. 5:5). The meek are those who are humble before the Lord, and who, without bloated ego, acknowledge their dependence on God. All who faithfully depend on God—his children by faith—will receive a full inheritance.

20But the wicked will perish:
The LORD's enemies will be like the beauty of the fields,
they will vanish—vanish like smoke.

21The wicked borrow and do not repay,
but the righteous give generously;
22those the LORD blesses will inherit the land,
but those he curses will be cut off.

23If the LORD delights in a man's way,
he makes his steps firm;
24though he stumble, he will not fall,
for the LORD upholds him with his hand.

25I was young and now I am old,
yet I have never seen the righteous forsaken
or their children begging bread.
26They are always generous and lend freely;
their children will be blessed.

27Turn from evil and do good;
then you will dwell in the land forever.
28For the LORD loves the just
and will not forsake his faithful ones.

They will be protected forever,
but the offspring of the wicked will be cut off;
29the righteous will inherit the land
and dwell in it forever.

30The mouth of the righteous man utters wisdom,
and his tongue speaks what is just.
31The law of his God is in his heart;
his feet do not slip.

32The wicked lie in wait for the righteous,
seeking their very lives;
33but the LORD will not leave them in their power
or let them be condemned when brought to trial.

34Wait for the LORD
and keep his way.
He will exalt you to inherit the land;
when the wicked are cut off, you will see it.

35I have seen a wicked and ruthless man
flourishing like a green tree in its native soil,
36but he soon passed away and was no more;
though I looked for him, he could not be found.

37:21 borrow ... give. The wicked borrow in order to advance their goals. Borrowing makes them subservient to the lenders. The righteous are given blessings by God and are free to share because they have confidence the Lord will continue to supply their needs (Deut. 15:6).

37:29 forever. God's blessings to his people are eternal. In contrast, the prosperity of the wicked is temporary (vv. 10,28).

37:32 lie in wait ... seeking their very lives. The wicked are predatory but cowardly. They prefer ambush but will use whatever means necessary to steal the blessings of the righteous (10:8–9). They will even bring false charges in court against the righteous in an attempt to seize their livelihood (v. 33).

37 Consider the blameless, observe the upright;
there is a future[a] for the man of peace.
38 But all sinners will be destroyed;
the future[b] of the wicked will be cut off.

39 The salvation of the righteous comes from the LORD;
he is their stronghold in time of trouble.
40 The LORD helps them and delivers them;
he delivers them from the wicked and saves them,
because they take refuge in him.

Psalm 38

A psalm of David. A petition.

1 O LORD, do not rebuke me in your anger
or discipline me in your wrath.
2 For your arrows have pierced me,
and your hand has come down upon me.
3 Because of your wrath there is no health in my body;
my bones have no soundness because of my sin.
4 My guilt has overwhelmed me
like a burden too heavy to bear.

5 My wounds fester and are loathsome
because of my sinful folly.
6 I am bowed down and brought very low;
all day long I go about mourning.
7 My back is filled with searing pain;
there is no health in my body.
8 I am feeble and utterly crushed;
I groan in anguish of heart.

9 All my longings lie open before you, O Lord;
my sighing is not hidden from you.
10 My heart pounds, my strength fails me;
even the light has gone from my eyes.
11 My friends and companions avoid me because of my wounds;
my neighbors stay far away.
12 Those who seek my life set their traps,
those who would harm me talk of my ruin;
all day long they plot deception.

13 I am like a deaf man, who cannot hear,
like a mute, who cannot open his mouth;

[a]37 *Or there will be posterity* [b]38 *Or posterity*

OPEN 1. What is the first part of your body to serve as an alarm clock that "something's wrong"? **2.** How do you get rid of hiccups?

STUDY 1. How has God's hand come down on David (vv. 1–8)? What did people believe caused illness in David's day (v. 3)? Why does it follow that friends avoid him (v. 11)? **2.** What adds insult to injury for David (vv. 9–12)? In light of his compounded suffering, how do you account for David's continued trust in God: A placid or stoic disposition? A pleasant turn of events? He trusts in God for the bigger picture? **3.** Who does David feel is responsible for his suffering? If this same God is seen as the one who punishes sin, why trust him for future deliverance? **4.** Think of this psalm as written at a time of great illness. What illnesses are caused by ignoring God's Laws? What did Jesus say to the notion of illness as punishment (John 9:1–3)? **5.** Think of this psalm as written at a time of great awareness of sin. Is David's guilt healthy? Why or why not?

APPLY 1. When have you felt punished by God? What happened at that time of crisis? How did you relate to God then? **2.** What part of David's faith can you relate to from your own experience? How so? Where do you need to exert such faith now?

37:39–40 Despite all the efforts of the wicked, the righteous will prevail. The Lord provides for them, saves them and protects them. Their inheritance is sure, guaranteed by the eternal love of God.

Ps. 38 David begs the Lord to heal him of an illness that is having terrible effects on him physically, socially and politically. The illness is a rebuke from God, a form of discipline for a sin that is not specified in the psalm. David suffers pain and misery (vv. 3–8), social alienation (v. 11) and political turmoil (v. 12).

38:9–12 David explains the devastating effects of his illness. God's discipline has made him a physical weakling, a social outcast and an easy political target.

38:11 David often finds himself abandoned by friends and under attack by enemies (31:11–12).

38:13–16 David has no retorts for his enemies. Like a deaf-mute, he will not make any response to them. God alone will be David's advocate.

14 I have become like a man who does not hear,
whose mouth can offer no reply.
15 I wait for you, O LORD;
you will answer, O Lord my God.
16 For I said, "Do not let them gloat
or exalt themselves over me when my foot slips."

17 For I am about to fall,
and my pain is ever with me.
18 I confess my iniquity;
I am troubled by my sin.
19 Many are those who are my vigorous enemies;
those who hate me without reason are numerous.
20 Those who repay my good with evil
slander me when I pursue what is good.

21 O LORD, do not forsake me;
be not far from me, O my God.
22 Come quickly to help me,
O Lord my Savior.

Psalm 39

For the director of music. For Jeduthun.
A psalm of David.

1 I said, "I will watch my ways
and keep my tongue from sin;
I will put a muzzle on my mouth
as long as the wicked are in my presence."
2 But when I was silent and still,
not even saying anything good,
my anguish increased.
3 My heart grew hot within me,
and as I meditated, the fire burned;
then I spoke with my tongue:

4 "Show me, O LORD, my life's end
and the number of my days;
let me know how fleeting is my life.
5 You have made my days a mere handbreadth;
the span of my years is as nothing before you.
Each man's life is but a breath. *Selah*
6 Man is a mere phantom as he goes to and fro:
He bustles about, but only in vain;
he heaps up wealth, not knowing who will get it.

7 "But now, Lord, what do I look for?
My hope is in you.
8 Save me from all my transgressions;
do not make me the scorn of fools.

OPEN 1. Would you want to know the exact date you'll die? Why or why not? **2.** If you had only two weeks to live, what is one thing you must do? Why that one?

STUDY 1. Why does David ask to know the "number of my days" (v. 4)? What does this say about his mood? **2.** Who imposes the silence: David (vv. 1–3) or God (vv. 9–11)? Both? Why? **3.** What are David's burdens (vv. 6,8)? What would he prefer from God, silence or severity? **4.** Why does David ask God to "look away from me" (v. 13)? What does he think the Lord's "departure" will do for him?

APPLY 1. How is David's shame like Peter's (Luke 5:8)? Have you ever felt ashamed before God? **2.** Perhaps David is angry when God seems unfair. Do you ever feel like God "gangs up" on you? Can you express hard questions or doubts about what God is doing? **3.** Does life sometimes seem short and empty? How does that awareness affect your priorities? **4.** Compare verse 13 with Job 7:16–20: When have you felt God was demanding "too much" from you? What happened to push you to the brink? Will this psalm give you hope in God when hard times next occur?

38:17–20 David grows weaker because of his illness and guilt. His enemies grow stronger.

39:1 keep my tongue from sin. As spiritual leader and king, David must control his anger and not speak evil words, which would give the wicked even more ammunition against him and would betray the righteous (73:15).

39:4–6 let me know. David prays for understanding. He recognizes the brevity of human life and wants to understand and accept it.

9 I was silent; I would not open my mouth,
for you are the one who has done this.
10 Remove your scourge from me;
I am overcome by the blow of your hand.
11 You rebuke and discipline men for their sin;
you consume their wealth like a moth—
each man is but a breath. *Selah*

12 "Hear my prayer, O LORD,
listen to my cry for help;
be not deaf to my weeping.
For I dwell with you as an alien,
a stranger, as all my fathers were.
13 Look away from me, that I may rejoice again
before I depart and am no more."

Psalm 40

For the director of music. Of David. A psalm.

1 I waited patiently for the LORD;
he turned to me and heard my cry.
2 He lifted me out of the slimy pit,
out of the mud and mire;
he set my feet on a rock
and gave me a firm place to stand.
3 He put a new song in my mouth,
a hymn of praise to our God.
Many will see and fear
and put their trust in the LORD.

4 Blessed is the man
who makes the LORD his trust,
who does not look to the proud,
to those who turn aside to false gods.[a]
5 Many, O LORD my God,
are the wonders you have done.
The things you planned for us
no one can recount to you;
were I to speak and tell of them,
they would be too many to declare.

6 Sacrifice and offering you did not desire,
but my ears you have pierced[b,c];
burnt offerings and sin offerings
you did not require.

[a]4 Or *to falsehood* [b]6 Hebrew; Septuagint *but a body you have prepared for me* (see also Symmachus and Theodotion) [c]6 Or *opened*

OPEN 1. As a child, what "big deal" do you remember waiting for Dad to do with you or for you? How did you feel when the planned event actually happened? **2.** Are you good at waiting? How long do you wait before giving up?

STUDY 1. Compare the first and last verses. What subtitle would you give the first half of the psalm (vv. 1–10)? The last half? Why the two moods? Do you suppose these were written at the same time or at different times? **2.** From what "slimy pit" has the psalmist been rescued: Sickness? Sin? Peril? Or does it matter? **3.** What sacrifice does God desire (vv. 6–8)? Then why did God command burnt offerings? What is David referring to as "your Law"? **4.** How do you account for David's recurring problems? For David's renewed waiting? Wherein lies his hope? **5.** The New Testament puts verses 6–8 into the mouth of Jesus (Heb. 10:5–9). Do you see any other foretastes of Jesus in the psalm?

APPLY 1. When God seems to take too long to help you, what "false gods" offer tempting alternative solutions? What happened the last time you relied on one of those gods? **2.** What in your life feels like a "slimy pit"? Where are you: Knee-deep? Waist-deep? One foot out?

Ps. 40 David faces troubles and prays for help. His prayer begins with a review of God's help in the past (vv. 1–5). *David then praises the faithfulness to* God, in a sense, making a case for the help just requested. Verses 1–10 are a preface to his actual appeal for help in verses 11–17.

40:1–3 David describes an incident in the past when God had helped him. At that time, David had responded to God's *mercy* with praise. That praise had spread to others and brought honor to God.

40:6 did not desire ... did not require. Though the Law demands sacrifice and offerings, God really desires obedience (1 Sam. 15:22). God demands obedience from his servants. If David (or any other person) were perfectly obedient, then sacrifice and offerings would not be necessary. David devoted his life to serving the Lord.

[7]Then I said, "Here I am, I have come—
it is written about me in the scroll.[a]
[8]I desire to do your will, O my God;
your law is within my heart."

[9]I proclaim righteousness in the great assembly;
I do not seal my lips,
as you know, O LORD.
[10]I do not hide your righteousness in my heart;
I speak of your faithfulness and salvation.
I do not conceal your love and your truth
from the great assembly.

[11]Do not withhold your mercy from me, O LORD;
may your love and your truth always protect me.
[12]For troubles without number surround me;
my sins have overtaken me, and I cannot see.
They are more than the hairs of my head,
and my heart fails within me.

[13]Be pleased, O LORD, to save me;
O LORD, come quickly to help me.
[14]May all who seek to take my life
be put to shame and confusion;
may all who desire my ruin
be turned back in disgrace.
[15]May those who say to me, "Aha! Aha!"
be appalled at their own shame.
[16]But may all who seek you
rejoice and be glad in you;
may those who love your salvation always say,
"The LORD be exalted!"

[17]Yet I am poor and needy;
may the Lord think of me.
You are my help and my deliverer;
O my God, do not delay.

Psalm 41

For the director of music. A psalm of David.

[1]Blessed is he who has regard for the weak;
the LORD delivers him in times of trouble.
[2]The LORD will protect him and preserve his life;

[a]7 Or *come / with the scroll written for me*

Standing up to it? **3.** Which helps you most with present troubles: Remembering God's actions in the past? Or claiming God's promises for the future? Why? **4.** Which is the greater pressure on you right now: The external opposition of others? Or the internal weight of your sin? What from this psalm most helps you in dealing with this pressure?

OPEN 1. Are you sick and tired of being sick and tired? Do you tend to be sick or tired? **2.** What is your most recurrent illness? The most effective cure?

STUDY 1. What's promised in verses 1–3? Why is David's experience so different (vv. 4–9)?

40:8 I desire. Desire frames this stanza. Some things God does not desire (v. 6); some things David does desire (v. 8). The point is clear: God desires obedience from David, and David wants to be obedient.

40:9–10 proclaim righteousness. Though he sins, David's life is characterized by his frequent praise of God. God desires praise more than sacrifices and offerings.

40:12 troubles ... sins. David's troubles are products of sin. David compares his sins and troubles to the hair on his head. David was apparently not a bald-headed man.

40:14–15 Using David's many troubles, his enemies want to seize the advantage of his weakness. This theme occurs often in Psalms (38:12; 39:8).

41:1–3 Blessed is he. Persons who have regard for the weak can be assured of similar treatment from God when they are weak. The Lord will restore those who try to do the same for others in need.

2. The "close friend" of verse 9 may be David's counselor, Ahithophel (2 Sam. 16:23–17:4). What light does this throw on the psalm? 3. What hope sustains David through his trials? 4. Given his confession of sin (v. 4), what does he mean by invoking his "integrity" (v. 12)? How does he know he is "right"?

APPLY 1. Do you consider yourself strong or weak? What does it mean to you to show regard for the weak? 2. Have you secretly rejoiced at another's trouble? What does that say about you? 3. What one word describes your life in relation to God's promises: Incongruity? Integrity? Blessed? Never-say-die? Illustrate with an experience.

---

he will bless him in the land
and not surrender him to the desire of his foes.
3 The LORD will sustain him on his sickbed
and restore him from his bed of illness.

4 I said, "O LORD, have mercy on me;
heal me, for I have sinned against you."
5 My enemies say of me in malice,
"When will he die and his name perish?"
6 Whenever one comes to see me,
he speaks falsely, while his heart gathers slander;
then he goes out and spreads it abroad.

7 All my enemies whisper together against me;
they imagine the worst for me, saying,
8 "A vile disease has beset him;
he will never get up from the place where he lies."
9 Even my close friend, whom I trusted,
he who shared my bread,
has lifted up his heel against me.

10 But you, O LORD, have mercy on me;
raise me up, that I may repay them.
11 I know that you are pleased with me,
for my enemy does not triumph over me.
12 In my integrity you uphold me
and set me in your presence forever.

13 Praise be to the LORD, the God of Israel,
from everlasting to everlasting.
Amen and Amen.

BOOK II

Psalms 42–72

Psalm 42[a]

For the director of music.
A *maskil*[b] of the Sons of Korah.

OPEN 1. What do you find best quenches your thirst? 2. When were you homesick? What would your correspondence from that time reveal about your innermost yearnings and fears?

STUDY 1. These two psalms form one unified whole: What refrains and themes are common to each? 2. From 2 Kings 14:11–14, we see hostages being taken captive from

1 As the deer pants for streams of water,
so my soul pants for you, O God.
2 My soul thirsts for God, for the living God.
When can I go and meet with God?

[a]In many Hebrew manuscripts Psalms 42 and 43 constitute one psalm. [b]Title: Probably a literary or musical term

---

41:9 close friend ... shared my bread. A king's intimate friends share his table. Here one of David's inner circle has betrayed him. In John 13:18, Jesus quotes this passage to predict his own betrayal by Judas. As heir of David's royal house, Jesus suffered the same treatment as his forefather.

41:10 that I may repay them. David the king wants to call his enemies to account and "balance the books" with them, not for revenge but justice.

42:1 deer pants for water. The psalmist is "on the run" from enemies like a deer fleeing hunters. As the deer needs water, the psalmist must have God's restoring power to stand against oppressors.

42:2 When can I go and meet with God? Because of his troubles, the psalmist is unable to go to the temple to worship and commune with God.

[3] My tears have been my food
day and night,
while men say to me all day long,
"Where is your God?"
[4] These things I remember
as I pour out my soul:
how I used to go with the multitude,
leading the procession to the house of God,
with shouts of joy and thanksgiving
among the festive throng.

[5] Why are you downcast, O my soul?
Why so disturbed within me?
Put your hope in God,
for I will yet praise him,
my Savior and [6] my God.

My[a] soul is downcast within me;
therefore I will remember you
from the land of the Jordan,
the heights of Hermon—from Mount Mizar.
[7] Deep calls to deep
in the roar of your waterfalls;
all your waves and breakers
have swept over me.

[8] By day the LORD directs his love,
at night his song is with me—
a prayer to the God of my life.

[9] I say to God my Rock,
"Why have you forgotten me?
Why must I go about mourning,
oppressed by the enemy?"
[10] My bones suffer mortal agony
as my foes taunt me,
saying to me all day long,
"Where is your God?"

[11] Why are you downcast, O my soul?
Why so disturbed within me?
Put your hope in God,
for I will yet praise him,
my Savior and my God.

Psalm 43[b]

[1] Vindicate me, O God,
and plead my cause against an ungodly nation;

[a]5,6 A few Hebrew manuscripts, Septuagint and Syriac; most Hebrew manuscripts *praise him for his saving help. /* [6]O my God, my [b]In many Hebrew manuscripts Psalms 42 and 43 constitute one psalm.

Judah: How might such a situation give birth to these psalms (vv. 1–3)? **3.** From the descriptive words and phrases, what diagnosis best fits this psalmist's condition: Thirsty? Depressed? Exiled? Homesick? Hopeful? Plagued by spiritual doubts? **4.** What prescription does the psalmist recommend (vv. 5,11)? Is this a realistic way to handle grief? Why or why not? **5.** In dealing with his depression, this man freely cried (v. 3), talked to himself (vv. 5,11; 43:5), reminded himself of God's nature (vv. 6,8) and prayed honestly (v. 9; 43:2). By comparison, how do you deal with depression? **6.** Although the psalmist asks the same question in verse 9 that his foes ask in verses 3 and 10, what is the difference in how these questions are put? What does this say about the dark side of faith and the sunny side of doubt? **7.** He wants to be back in God's house in Jerusalem, but what is he learning about God from where he is right now? (What does the difference between what's happening "day and night" in verses 3 and 8 tell you)? **8.** What progression of faith or mood swing do you see in Psalm 43? Does his prayer in 43:3–4 express a conviction that he will soon be released by his enemies? Or is this a spiritual homecoming?

APPLY 1. What causes God to seem far away at times? Who moved, God or you? How might these two psalms help you in times when you wonder where God is? **2.** Of the adjectives and titles which this man ascribed to God, which ones best describe your relationship with God? Is the possessive pronoun "my" one that you readily use in relation to God? Why or why not? How has God been "yours" in recent weeks?

42:5 This stanza, repeated in verse 11, serves as the refrain of the psalm. Its theme: To overcome difficulty, praise God. Great encouragement follows acts of praise, and the hope thus generated leads to more praise. Discouragement and doubt drag us down during trouble. Praising God will lift our spirits and prepare us for God's deliverance.

43:1–4 The psalmist prays for deliverance from enemies who are "deceitful

rescue me from deceitful and wicked men.
[2] You are God my stronghold.
Why have you rejected me?
Why must I go about mourning,
oppressed by the enemy?
[3] Send forth your light and your truth,
let them guide me;
let them bring me to your holy mountain,
to the place where you dwell.
[4] Then will I go to the altar of God,
to God, my joy and my delight.
I will praise you with the harp,
O God, my God.

[5] Why are you downcast, O my soul?
Why so disturbed within me?
Put your hope in God,
for I will yet praise him,
my Savior and my God.

Psalm 44

For the director of music.
Of the Sons of Korah. A *maskil.*[a]

[1] We have heard with our ears, O God;
our fathers have told us
what you did in their days,
in days long ago.
[2] With your hand you drove out the nations
and planted our fathers;
you crushed the peoples
and made our fathers flourish.
[3] It was not by their sword that they won the land,
nor did their arm bring them victory;
it was your right hand, your arm,
and the light of your face, for you loved them.

[4] You are my King and my God,
who decrees[b] victories for Jacob.
[5] Through you we push back our enemies;
through your name we trample our foes.
[6] I do not trust in my bow,
my sword does not bring me victory;
[7] but you give us victory over our enemies,

[a]Title: Probably a literary or musical term [b]4 Septuagint, Aquila and Syriac; Hebrew *King, O God; / command*

OPEN 1. What is the most amazing story your parents or grandparents told you about in regards to the era in which they lived? **2.** What amazing story about your life or era do you most want to tell your children or grandchildren?

STUDY 1. This might be the prayer of a Judean king. What about God does he recall in verses 1–8? What does this king realize about his own limitations? **2.** What problem is the king facing (vv. 9–16)? How does he see God related to this problem? **3.** Beyond the physical pain, the social stigma and the emotional turmoil lies the real problem bothering the psalmist (vv. 17–22): What is it? **4.** Compare verse 22 with Romans 8:31–39. Might Paul see the sufferings of the king as a battle scar resulting from loyalty? A punishment for sin? Why? **5.** This king felt like God was sleeping on the job, as did Jesus' disciples (Mark 4:35–38). Have you felt like this? What did you do to rouse God?

APPLY 1. What is one "bad thing" that has happened to you recently that you didn't deserve?

and wicked." He longs to return safely to the temple where God dwells so he can properly commune with God and praise him.

43:3 light ... truth. God's light and truth are personified as God's messengers who will guide the psalmist back to the temple where restoration will take place. Jesus used light and truth in much the same way in John 8:12 and John 14:6. Light and truth actively lead people toward a vital relationship with God.

44:1–8 Israel has suffered a terrible defeat. Before crying out for help, the psalmist reviews how God has helped the Israelites in the past. Verses 1–3 recall how God aided the Israelites in capturing the Promised Land. Verses 4–8 review how God has helped them keep the land given them. Having stated his case, the psalmist can appeal to God to resume his help.

you put our adversaries to shame.
8In God we make our boast all day long,
and we will praise your name forever. *Selah*

9But now you have rejected and humbled us;
you no longer go out with our armies.
10You made us retreat before the enemy,
and our adversaries have plundered us.
11You gave us up to be devoured like sheep
and have scattered us among the nations.
12You sold your people for a pittance,
gaining nothing from their sale.

13You have made us a reproach to our neighbors,
the scorn and derision of those around us.
14You have made us a byword among the nations;
the peoples shake their heads at us.
15My disgrace is before me all day long,
and my face is covered with shame
16at the taunts of those who reproach and revile me,
because of the enemy, who is bent on revenge.

17All this happened to us,
though we had not forgotten you
or been false to your covenant.
18Our hearts had not turned back;
our feet had not strayed from your path.
19But you crushed us and made us a haunt for jackals
and covered us over with deep darkness.

20If we had forgotten the name of our God
or spread out our hands to a foreign god,
21would not God have discovered it,
since he knows the secrets of the heart?
22Yet for your sake we face death all day long;
we are considered as sheep to be slaughtered.

23Awake, O Lord! Why do you sleep?
Rouse yourself! Do not reject us forever.
24Why do you hide your face
and forget our misery and oppression?

25We are brought down to the dust;
our bodies cling to the ground.
26Rise up and help us;
redeem us because of your unfailing love.

2. How is your faith in God's justice and love affected when it appears that God is neglecting you in your situation? **3.** Write a group "psalm of distress" about unanswered questions facing you. Follow the shape of this psalm: You have helped us in the past, but you seem to be asleep now. We're not aware we have sinned, so please help us again now!

44:9–16 Israel knew victory in the past, but Israel lies defeated here. God has forsaken his people, the psalmist says, causing them to suffer defeat (vv. 9–12) and shaming them among other nations (vv. 13–16).

44:17–22 The psalmist struggles with the question, "Why do the righteous suffer?". He says Israel has not deserved this, to be forsaken and left ripe for destruction. Israel has been true to the covenant (vv. 17–19). Why hasn't God acted? The people have not worshiped foreign gods.

44:19 deep darkness. God has forsaken them and taken his light away. The people feel desolation and despair. Whereas light draws people to God, darkness represents separation from God.

44:22 for your sake we face death. Being a chosen people of God has made Israel nearly everyone's enemy. Paul applies this verse to Christians in Romans 8:36.

44:24 hide your face. Psalmists often use God's face as the metaphor for his presence or absence. When God is present, the light of his face brings joy and deliverance (4:6; 31:16). When God's face is not present, there is darkness and despair (30:7; 44:24).

OPEN 1. Who was one of your favorite comic book or TV heroes? Why? **2.** What was the most extravagant wedding you ever attended or witnessed?

STUDY 1. This is a royal wedding song which celebrates the groom (vv. 1–9), the bride (vv. 10–15) and their future (vv. 16–17). For what is the groom praised? **2.** What are the most appealing qualities of the bride? Do these two sound like a good match? **3.** The king is called "God" in verses 6–7. Who else is likened to God (Ex. 7:1; Isa. 9:6; Zech. 12:8)? What is being said? **4.** How does the New Testament make sense out of verses 6–7 (Heb. 1:8–9)? What is being said about Jesus and the church (Eph. 5:25–27)? **5.** What does the "Daughter of Tyre" represent (v. 12)? What future did the Jews hope for the Gentiles (Isa. 60:3)?

APPLY 1. Taking verses 2–7 as applying to Jesus, which royal qualities about him mean the most to you now? Why? **2.** What place does "truth, humility and righteousness" have in your life? Where do white lies, false humility and self-justification still hold sway? **3.** How does someone truly loving you help you "forget" all other relationships? What are some of the things in your past that you must "forget" in order to truly honor Jesus as Lord?

Psalm 45

For the director of music. To ⌊the tune of⌋ "Lilies." Of the Sons of Korah. A *maskil.*[a] A wedding song.

1 My heart is stirred by a noble theme
as I recite my verses for the king;
my tongue is the pen of a skillful writer.

2 You are the most excellent of men
and your lips have been anointed with grace,
since God has blessed you forever.
3 Gird your sword upon your side, O mighty one;
clothe yourself with splendor and majesty.
4 In your majesty ride forth victoriously
in behalf of truth, humility and righteousness;
let your right hand display awesome deeds.
5 Let your sharp arrows pierce the hearts of the king's enemies;
let the nations fall beneath your feet.
6 Your throne, O God, will last for ever and ever;
a scepter of justice will be the scepter of your kingdom.
7 You love righteousness and hate wickedness;
therefore God, your God, has set you above your companions
by anointing you with the oil of joy.
8 All your robes are fragrant with myrrh and aloes and cassia;
from palaces adorned with ivory
the music of the strings makes you glad.
9 Daughters of kings are among your honored women;
at your right hand is the royal bride in gold of Ophir.

10 Listen, O daughter, consider and give ear:
Forget your people and your father's house.
11 The king is enthralled by your beauty;
honor him, for he is your lord.
12 The Daughter of Tyre will come with a gift,[b]
men of wealth will seek your favor.

13 All glorious is the princess within ⌊her chamber⌋;
her gown is interwoven with gold.
14 In embroidered garments she is led to the king;
her virgin companions follow her

[a]Title: Probably a literary or musical term [b]12 Or *A Tyrian robe is among the gifts*

45:1 noble theme. At the king's wedding the psalmist praises the king and reminds him of his place before God.

45:2 most excellent of men. The king displays all the positive traits of manhood, as well he should, for the king embodies the best in his people (1 Sam. 9:2).

45:3–5 Gird your sword. The psalmist encourages the king to be a warrior for good, to go out and fight on behalf of "truth, humility and righteousness." The glory the king gains by these acts will have a splendor that surpasses even these wedding day celebrations.

45:8–9 The psalmist gives a "gossip-column" description of the wedding. He tells who is there and what the king is wearing. The psalmist seeks to bring honor and prestige to the event and thus to the king.

45:10–15 After advising the king (vv. 3–9), the psalmist turns his attention to the royal bride and offers advice to her.

45:10–11 The royal bride is a foreigner. She must forget her people and be loyal to the king. Though the details of this marriage are not revealed, royal marriages were often political alliances. Whether that is true here, the psalmist advises the bride (with a hint of warning) that her loyalty is now to Israel and its king.

45:12–15 In another "gossip column" passage, the psalmist describes the bride. She is beautiful; she will bring esteem and honor to her husband, the king.

and are brought to you.
[15]They are led in with joy and gladness;
they enter the palace of the king.

[16]Your sons will take the place of your fathers;
you will make them princes throughout the land.
[17]I will perpetuate your memory through all generations;
therefore the nations will praise you for ever and ever.

Psalm 46

For the director of music. Of the Sons of Korah.
According to *alamoth.*[a] A song.

[1]God is our refuge and strength,
an ever-present help in trouble.
[2]Therefore we will not fear, though the earth give way
and the mountains fall into the heart of the sea,
[3]though its waters roar and foam
and the mountains quake with their surging. *Selah*

[4]There is a river whose streams make glad the city of God,
the holy place where the Most High dwells.
[5]God is within her, she will not fall;
God will help her at break of day.
[6]Nations are in uproar, kingdoms fall;
he lifts his voice, the earth melts.

[7]The LORD Almighty is with us;
the God of Jacob is our fortress. *Selah*

[8]Come and see the works of the LORD,
the desolations he has brought on the earth.
[9]He makes wars cease to the ends of the earth;
he breaks the bow and shatters the spear,
he burns the shields[b] with fire.
[10]"Be still, and know that I am God;
I will be exalted among the nations,
I will be exalted in the earth."

[11]The LORD Almighty is with us;
the God of Jacob is our fortress. *Selah*

[a]Title: Probably a musical term [b]9 Or *chariots*

OPEN What is the most frightening natural disaster you have ever witnessed?

STUDY 1. Biblical writers often used apocalyptic pictures to describe a national crisis. What might be happening to Israel here (vv. 2,3,6)? **2.** Why does the writer feel immune to disaster (vv. 4–5)? Did Israel prove to be immune? **3.** What seven phrases describe God? Which of these have proven true? **4.** How does being still help a person know that God is indeed God (v. 10)? The church today faces problems with the benefit of the Holy Spirit and the truth of the New Testament. What forces threaten the church today?

APPLY 1. Could verses 2–3 and 5–6 portray any crisis in your life? How did you respond to that crisis? **2.** What difference does it make to you to know Jesus is Lord over all those chaotic events? How is he a fortress to you? Where do you feel a need for his special protection right now? **3.** Spend some time in prayer. As each group member shares a trouble, one member can read verse 10 in response.

45:16 take the place of your fathers. The psalmist pronounces a subtle blessing on the king by assuming his new bride will bear him sons. The king will pass on his dynasty through these sons.

46:1–3 The psalmist confesses his complete trust in God. That trust is so great that even the destruction of creation itself will not cause him to fear. The powerful imagery is reminiscent of the creation process itself. He says that even if creation were to fall apart God would still stand.

46:4–6 The psalmist continues the water images of verses 1–3. Jerusalem has no actual river. The "river" in these verses is the current of blessings that emanate from God and flow to Israel. These blessings sustain God's people through the chaos around them.

46:10 "Be still, and know that I am God." God interrupts the psalmist and "lifts his voice" to the nations. God will be exalted by all nations because God saves his people. This is a frequent theme in Psalms (47:9; 65:8; 66:1–7).

OPEN **1.** Have you ever seen a famous person in the flesh? Did he or she seem different than you imagined? **2.** How often do you clap your hands or shout for joy in church: Always? Sometimes? Never?

STUDY **1.** "Nations" and "all the earth" are repeated 7 times here. Who are the "nations"? What's the psalmist saying about them? **2.** What might verse 5 refer to (2 Sam. 6:12–15)? **3.** What Jewish hope is expressed in verse 9 (Gen. 12:3)? **4.** In what way is God king of all the earth when so many people ignore and disobey him? **5.** Judaism does not teach that all should become Jews. Do you think God wants everyone to become a believer? Even Jews? What is your vision of the messianic assembly (v. 9)?

APPLY What has God done in our life recently that makes you want to stand and clap your hands?

Psalm 47

For the director of music.
Of the Sons of Korah. A psalm.

[1] Clap your hands, all you nations;
shout to God with cries of joy.
[2] How awesome is the LORD Most High,
the great King over all the earth!
[3] He subdued nations under us,
peoples under our feet.
[4] He chose our inheritance for us,
the pride of Jacob, whom he loved. *Selah*

[5] God has ascended amid shouts of joy,
the LORD amid the sounding of trumpets.
[6] Sing praises to God, sing praises;
sing praises to our King, sing praises.

[7] For God is the King of all the earth;
sing to him a psalm[a] of praise.
[8] God reigns over the nations;
God is seated on his holy throne.
[9] The nobles of the nations assemble
as the people of the God of Abraham,
for the kings[b] of the earth belong to God;
he is greatly exalted.

OPEN **1.** Where is "God's country" for you? **2.** What town or city do you see as the most beautiful or attractive place to be?

STUDY **1.** Mount Zion (Jerusalem) is idealized in verse 2. What verses are down to earth? How must the people be feeling? **2.** How was the city delivered (2 Kin. 18:17–36; 19:35–37)? Was it "secure forever" (v. 8)? **3.** How did the Jews recall God's deeds to the "next generation"? **4.** What wider conflict or war when the kings joined forces (v. 4) does the sweeping language of this psalm anticipate? **5.** Why was it encouraging to the people to be able to count the towers and ramparts of the city?

Psalm 48

A song. A psalm of the Sons of Korah.

[1] Great is the LORD, and most worthy of praise,
in the city of our God, his holy mountain.
[2] It is beautiful in its loftiness,
the joy of the whole earth.
Like the utmost heights of Zaphon[c] is Mount Zion,
the[d] city of the Great King.
[3] God is in her citadels;
he has shown himself to be her fortress.

[4] When the kings joined forces,
when they advanced together,
[5] they saw ⌞her⌟ and were astounded;
they fled in terror.

[a]7 Or *a maskil* (probably a literary or musical term) [b]9 Or *shields* [c]2 *Zaphon* can refer to a sacred mountain or the direction north. [d]2 Or *earth, / Mount Zion, on the northern side / of the*

47:1–4 These verses expand on the idea in 46:10 that God will be exalted among all nations. Verses 1–4 call to those other nations and invite them to participate in praising God. The psalmist does a little "chest thumping" here by reminding other nations that God had been Israel's ally in conquering and subduing their enemies.

47:9 the kings of the earth belong to God. In fulfillment of the promise to Abraham (Gen. 12:2–3), all nations will be blessed through Israel. The psalmist describes a new kingdom of many nations that are ruled by God (46:10).

48:2 beautiful in its loftiness. Jerusalem (often referred to as Mount Zion) is God's "holy hill" (2:6). It had neither the highest elevation in the area nor the most beautiful location, but the temple was the center of Israel's religious and political life. The city commands a wide view, which made it difficult to attack. More importantly, however, the city was lofty in a spiritual sense. God was worshiped there; festivals and sacrifices were offered there.

6 Trembling seized them there,
pain like that of a woman in labor.
7 You destroyed them like ships of Tarshish
shattered by an east wind.

8 As we have heard,
so have we seen
in the city of the LORD Almighty,
in the city of our God:
God makes her secure forever.
Selah

9 Within your temple, O God,
we meditate on your unfailing love.
10 Like your name, O God,
your praise reaches to the ends of the earth;
your right hand is filled with righteousness.
11 Mount Zion rejoices,
the villages of Judah are glad
because of your judgments.

12 Walk about Zion, go around her,
count her towers,
13 consider well her ramparts,
view her citadels,
that you may tell of them to the next generation.
14 For this God is our God for ever and ever;
he will be our guide even to the end.

Psalm 49

For the director of music.
Of the Sons of Korah. A psalm.

1 Hear this, all you peoples;
listen, all who live in this world,
2 both low and high,
rich and poor alike:
3 My mouth will speak words of wisdom;
the utterance from my heart will give understanding.
4 I will turn my ear to a proverb;
with the harp I will expound my riddle:
5 Why should I fear when evil days come,
when wicked deceivers surround me—

APPLY 1. How have you seen God guide you through a crisis which threatened your city? **2.** Who was significant in passing God's love on to you? How can you pass God's love on?

OPEN 1. How would you complete the phrase: "Man is the only animal that ..."? **2.** What would you want named after you: Children or grandchildren? Town? Park or building? Scholarship fund? Scientific discovery? What would others associate with your name?

STUDY 1. How does the psalmist get your attention in verses 1–4? What is his "riddle"? **2.** Is the message for the rich alone? In what things do these people trust (vv. 6,11)? What reality do they refuse to see? How is that world view expressed today? **3.** How does the psalmist account for the unfairness in

---

48:8 God makes her secure forever. This verse states the principal theme of the psalm. God makes the city secure, protecting it against all threats. The psalmist is convinced of this security by worshiping at the temple.Though he had heard how God protected his own, only through worshiping at the temple does he see how God is the true source of security.

48:9–11 we meditate. The psalmist leads fellow worshipers in joyful meditation, celebrating how God's love has brought about mighty acts on their behalf.

49:1–2 The psalmist calls the world's people to hear his words. His tone anticipates the prophets: "I have something to say that you must hear." These verses also introduce the conflict between high and low, rich and poor—the subject of the psalm.

49:4 turn my ear. A figure of speech for listening. Just as he asks the people to listen to him, the psalmist says he did the same when God revealed the truth to him. He claims to speak with wisdom, so he must acknowledge that his enlightenment came from God, the only source of knowledge.

49:5–11 Why should I fear? Death is the great leveler. The rich and powerful may enjoy a lavish earthly life, but they too will suffer the ignominy of death. The poor and the weak may be

life (v. 15)? What is the basis for his viewing reality that way? How can God solve the problem stated in verses 7–9? **4.** What picture does the psalmist paint of the hereafter (vv. 16–19)? What verses indicate a heaven and hell? What verses indicate no afterlife at all? **5.** If money cannot buy eternity, what can? Why is money ultimately over-rated? **6.** If all perish like the beasts (v. 12), what is the benefit of doing right? If there were no heaven or hell, would you agree with modern sentiments like "just do it," or "he who dies with the most toys, wins"?

APPLY 1. Has the death of a loved one caused a "big chill" on your or your friends' world views? **2.** This psalm is echoed in Jesus' teaching (Matt. 6:25–34). How do both teachings challenge your current lifestyle and priorities? How can you avoid being "like the beasts"?

6 those who trust in their wealth
and boast of their great riches?
7 No man can redeem the life of another
or give to God a ransom for him—
8 the ransom for a life is costly,
no payment is ever enough—
9 that he should live on forever
and not see decay.

10 For all can see that wise men die;
the foolish and the senseless alike perish
and leave their wealth to others.
11 Their tombs will remain their houses[a] forever,
their dwellings for endless generations,
though they had[b] named lands after themselves.

12 But man, despite his riches, does not endure;
he is[c] like the beasts that perish.

13 This is the fate of those who trust in themselves,
and of their followers, who approve their sayings. *Selah*
14 Like sheep they are destined for the grave,[d]
and death will feed on them.
The upright will rule over them in the morning;
their forms will decay in the grave,[d]
far from their princely mansions.
15 But God will redeem my life[e] from the grave;
he will surely take me to himself. *Selah*

16 Do not be overawed when a man grows rich,
when the splendor of his house increases;
17 for he will take nothing with him when he dies,
his splendor will not descend with him.
18 Though while he lived he counted himself blessed—
and men praise you when you prosper—
19 he will join the generation of his fathers,
who will never see the light of life.

20 A man who has riches without understanding
is like the beasts that perish.

[a]*11* Septuagint and Syriac; Hebrew *In their thoughts their houses will remain* [b]*11* Or / *for they have* [c]*12* Hebrew; Septuagint and Syriac read verse 12 the same as verse 20. [d]*14* Hebrew *Sheol*; also in verse 15 [e]*15* Or *soul*

oppressed for a time, but eventually all share the grave.

49:7–9 No man can redeem the life. Life cannot be purchased. Even if someone is redeemed or ransomed (Ex. 21:30), the respite is temporary. God is the only hope of redemption from the grave (v. 15).

49:11 tombs will remain their houses. The wealthy spend lots of money on their tombs trying to attain immortality and fame. But expensive graves do not comfort the dead.

49:15 God will redeem my life. Is there hope anywhere? Can the cycle of life and death be broken and meaning to life restored? God is the answer.

49:16–19 his splendor will not descend with him. All earthly success and prosperity is temporal. It does not go with the dead into another life. Far better to be poor and redeemed than rich, wicked and condemned.

Psalm 50

A psalm of Asaph.

1 The Mighty One, God, the LORD,
speaks and summons the earth
from the rising of the sun to the place where it sets.
2 From Zion, perfect in beauty,
God shines forth.
3 Our God comes and will not be silent;
a fire devours before him,
and around him a tempest rages.
4 He summons the heavens above,
and the earth, that he may judge his people:
5 "Gather to me my consecrated ones,
who made a covenant with me by sacrifice."
6 And the heavens proclaim his righteousness,
for God himself is judge. *Selah*

7 "Hear, O my people, and I will speak,
O Israel, and I will testify against you:
I am God, your God.
8 I do not rebuke you for your sacrifices
or your burnt offerings, which are ever before me.
9 I have no need of a bull from your stall
or of goats from your pens,
10 for every animal of the forest is mine,
and the cattle on a thousand hills.
11 I know every bird in the mountains,
and the creatures of the field are mine.
12 If I were hungry I would not tell you,
for the world is mine, and all that is in it.
13 Do I eat the flesh of bulls
or drink the blood of goats?
14 Sacrifice thank offerings to God,
fulfill your vows to the Most High,
15 and call upon me in the day of trouble;
I will deliver you, and you will honor me."

16 But to the wicked, God says:

"What right have you to recite my laws

OPEN 1. Does your mind wander during church? At what part of the service do you daydream the most? **2.** Have you ever heard God speak like a voice in your head? An audible voice outside your head? What did God say?

STUDY 1. What picture of God is drawn in verses 1–6? Whom is he addressing and judging here? Why summon the heavens and the earth to witness this trial? **2.** What is God's message to the religious in verses 7–15? Is it wrong to offer sacrifices as decreed in the Law? For whose benefit were they decreed? God's? **3.** Why is God so harsh with his own people (Amos 3:2)? What does God want (vv. 14–15)? **4.** What is God's message to the "wicked" (vv. 16–21)? How do they differ from the first group? Who has the right words? The right actions? What does each group lack? **5.** What is the threat and promise in verses 22–23? Why is God so fierce? **6.** If God were to address your church today through this psalm, what would he more likely attack: mindless ritualism or lip service? Why? What forms of empty religion would he rail against? What forms of hypocrisy?

APPLY 1. Do you ever picture God as an angry judge? How does it make you feel? Did your parents give you this image? **2.** What comes first in your spirituality: Action? Sacrifice? Prayer? Talk? Why? What comes second? **3.** In this psalm, God first warned the people, then reissued his call to follow him: How has he done that for you? **4.** What "thank offerings" do you give to God? How can this group give a "thank offering"?

50:1–6 The Lord converts the temple into a courtroom where he will judge. The issue is Israel's behavior in relation to the covenant established at Sinai (Ex. 19:4–8). God has come to praise those who are righteous and live in accord with the covenant.

50:1 The Mighty One, God, the LORD. This sequence of names occurs only two places in the Bible, here and in Joshua 22:22. The many titles for God in this psalm serve to accent his ability and right to judge Israel. In a sense, this verse introduces God as Israel's judge in the same way that any judge is introduced entering a courtroom. Whereas a judge presides in a courtroom, God presides in the temple.

50:4 the heavens above and the earth. In Deuteronomy 30:19 and 31:28, Moses calls on the heavens and earth to witness a renewal of the covenant between God and Israel. In this verse God calls down these witnesses to testify that the covenant stands and justice prevails.

50:7–15 God clarifies the role of offerings and sacrifices in worship. While offerings and sacrifices please God, they are not required. God's requirements are simple: give thanks that demonstrate a sincere gratitude for God's blessings and call on God for help in times of trouble.

50:14–15 thank offerings. God is the source of all blessings, and he wants those blessings to be acknowledged. Just as important, the thank offering allows Israel to acknowledge its total dependence on God—an acknowledgment God desires. God also wants us to pray in times of need. He promises to answer those prayers.

50:16–23 The Lord reproves the

OPEN Do you recall getting caught with your "hand in the cookie jar" as a child? As an adult? What happened each time?

STUDY **1.** In how many ways did David sin in the Bathsheba affair (2 Sam. 11:1–27)? **2.** In light of his arrogance, adultery, deception and murder, how does he dare approach God? What does he feel? **3.** Murder is a capital crime under Jewish law. Why also adultery (Deut. 22:22)? **4.** Since such sins involve others, what is the meaning of verse 4? What does this show about the nature of sin? **5.** Are there really any victimless crimes? How do personal failings affect God? Others? Self? Society? **6.** How can an unborn child be considered "sinful" (v. 5)? If God created all things "good," why does mankind tend to sin (Rom. 5:12–14)? **7.** In light of all this, what does David ask God to do (vv. 7–12)? What is "cleansing with hyssop" (Lev. 14:4–

or take my covenant on your lips?
17 You hate my instruction
and cast my words behind you.
18 When you see a thief, you join with him;
you throw in your lot with adulterers.
19 You use your mouth for evil
and harness your tongue to deceit.
20 You speak continually against your brother
and slander your own mother's son.
21 These things you have done and I kept silent;
you thought I was altogether[a] like you.
But I will rebuke you
and accuse you to your face.

22 "Consider this, you who forget God,
or I will tear you to pieces, with none to rescue:
23 He who sacrifices thank offerings honors me,
and he prepares the way
so that I may show him[b] the salvation of God."

Psalm 51

For the director of music. A psalm of David.
When the prophet Nathan came to him after David
had committed adultery with Bathsheba.

1 Have mercy on me, O God,
according to your unfailing love;
according to your great compassion
blot out my transgressions.
2 Wash away all my iniquity
and cleanse me from my sin.

3 For I know my transgressions,
and my sin is always before me.
4 Against you, you only, have I sinned
and done what is evil in your sight,
so that you are proved right when you speak
and justified when you judge.
5 Surely I was sinful at birth,
sinful from the time my mother conceived me.

[a]21 *Or thought the 'I AM' was* [b]23 *Or and to him who considers his way / I will show*

wicked for sinful behavior, especially their hypocrisy (vv. 16–17), thievery (v. 18), adultery (v. 18) and lying (vv. 19–20).

50:21 I kept silent. The wicked mistakenly interpret God's silence about their evil as approval.

Ps. 51 *This psalm is a humble prayer* for forgiveness—the proper response of a sinner to Psalm 50. The psalmist recognizes that the way back into a proper relationship with God lies through a contrite heart and utter dependence on him. Only after God has fixed the broken places in people's lives can the redeemed make thank offerings which truly please God.

51:1–2 Have mercy. Only God's mercy can restore David, who can do nothing to erase his sins. Jesus confirmed this lesson in Luke 18:13–14.

51:4 Against you, you only, have I sinned. David wrote this psalm in response to Nathan's rebuke for his adultery with Bathsheba. That sin would seem to be against another person, Bathsheba's husband at least. David recognizes, however, that his sin is a violation first against God and then against Uriah.

51:5 sinful at birth. David cannot claim that his sin is a onetime blip in an otherwise holy life. His nature is to be sinful. No one is born pure and lives blamelessly except Christ (Rom. 3:23).

[6]Surely you desire truth in the inner parts[a];
you teach[b] me wisdom in the inmost place.
[7]Cleanse me with hyssop, and I will be clean;
wash me, and I will be whiter than snow.
[8]Let me hear joy and gladness;
let the bones you have crushed rejoice.
[9]Hide your face from my sins
and blot out all my iniquity.

[10]Create in me a pure heart, O God,
and renew a steadfast spirit within me.
[11]Do not cast me from your presence
or take your Holy Spirit from me.
[12]Restore to me the joy of your salvation
and grant me a willing spirit, to sustain me.

[13]Then I will teach transgressors your ways,
and sinners will turn back to you.
[14]Save me from bloodguilt, O God,
the God who saves me,
and my tongue will sing of your righteousness.
[15]O Lord, open my lips,
and my mouth will declare your praise.
[16]You do not delight in sacrifice, or I would bring it;
you do not take pleasure in burnt offerings.
[17]The sacrifices of God are[c] a broken spirit;
a broken and contrite heart,
O God, you will not despise.

[18]In your good pleasure make Zion prosper;
build up the walls of Jerusalem.
[19]Then there will be righteous sacrifices,
whole burnt offerings to delight you;
then bulls will be offered on your altar.

[a]6 The meaning of the Hebrew for this phrase is uncertain. [b]6 Or *you desired . . . ; / you taught*
[c]17 Or *My sacrifice, O God, is*

7)? Why does David request this? **8.** How does David hope to escape God's wrath (vv. 13–17)? On what basis does he hope for a restored relationship? **9.** Why does David generalize his prayer to include the whole nation (vv. 18–19)? What does this say about the nature of sin? **10.** What kinds of sacrifices does the Lord desire in verses 16–17? In verse 19? When is a broken spirit or contrite heart enough? When are acts of sacrifice due?

APPLY 1. Has covering up sin backfired in your life? How have you seen God's mercy when you owned up to your sin? **2.** Are you more sensitive to sin and brokenness in yourself as a follower of Christ than beforehand? Why?

51:6 truth in the inner parts. David speaks as though the self were an onion. As far back as he peels, there is still rottenness and filth. Nowhere can David find goodness. Yet even to the deepest layer, God standards apply. Who can do this, apart from God's own strength and power.

51:7 cleanse ... clean ... wash. Sin has left him dirty. In order to attain goodness in his inner parts (v. 6), he must first be cleaned from the spiritual filth of sin. He must be ritually cleansed with hyssop, which was used to ceremonially clean the doorways at the first Passover (Ex. 12:22). He must also be washed by God.

51:8 hear joy and gladness. When clean, he will again be able to participate with other righteous people as they rejoice and praise God. Rejoicing and praising God will help him be restored to spiritual health.

51:10 Create in me. Only God is described in the Old Testament as creating. The psalmist prays for a new, pure heart to be a new man, free of the burden and stain of sin. In the same way, forgiveness requires a new heart that can live passionately for God. Paul tells us that God makes us a new creation in Christ (2 Cor. 5:17).

51:17 broken spirit ... a broken and contrite heart. God fixes broken hearts. Jesus said that the "poor in spirit" will receive God's greatest gifts (Matt. 5:3).

OPEN When you were a child, did any three words strike more terror than "I'm gonna tell"? Did you tend to get told on or were you the tattler?

STUDY 1. What type of man was Doeg the Edomite (1 Sam. 22:6–23)? What was he willing to do that Jewish soldiers were not? **2.** What was Doeg's boast (v. 1)? How does David account for Doeg's success (v. 7)? **3.** Why are the righteous often compared to trees (v. 8; 1:3)? What did olive trees provide in David's time? **4.** What does David trust (vv. 8–9)? How is that trust in God evident in what David does? **5.** Doeg was someone who used people and loved things. Where do you see that attitude in others or in yourself today?

APPLY 1. Has anyone ever suffered for helping or taking a risk for you? What happened? What did you feel: Guilt? Regret? Shame? Nonchalance? **2.** Are you "flourishing in the house of God"? What is lacking in your spiritual commitment? What helps you flourish?

Psalm 52

For the director of music. A *maskil*[a] of David.
When Doeg the Edomite had gone to Saul and told him:
"David has gone to the house of Ahimelech."

1 Why do you boast of evil, you mighty man?
Why do you boast all day long,
you who are a disgrace in the eyes of God?
2 Your tongue plots destruction;
it is like a sharpened razor,
you who practice deceit.
3 You love evil rather than good,
falsehood rather than speaking the truth. *Selah*
4 You love every harmful word,
O you deceitful tongue!

5 Surely God will bring you down to everlasting ruin:
He will snatch you up and tear you from your tent;
he will uproot you from the land of the living. *Selah*
6 The righteous will see and fear;
they will laugh at him, saying,
7 "Here now is the man
who did not make God his stronghold
but trusted in his great wealth
and grew strong by destroying others!"

8 But I am like an olive tree
flourishing in the house of God;
I trust in God's unfailing love
for ever and ever.
9 I will praise you forever for what you have done;
in your name I will hope, for your name is good.
I will praise you in the presence of your saints.

OPEN Who is your favorite TV, movie or fictional "fool"? What makes him or her foolish?

STUDY 1. Does this psalm seem familiar (ch. 14)? What accounts for this? **2.** Why is it foolish to say "there is no God"? In what way is this fool an atheist (vv. 1–3)? **3.** Is David's sweeping indictment a bit exaggerated? Or exceptionally accurate? Explain. **4.** What does this psalm say about God's view of evil? What does God plan to do about it?

APPLY 1. Have you ever been one of these fools: The

Psalm 53

For the director of music. According
to *mahalath*.[b] A *maskil*[a] of David.

1 The fool says in his heart,
"There is no God."
They are corrupt, and their ways are vile;
there is no one who does good.

2 God looks down from heaven
on the sons of men
to see if there are any who understand,
any who seek God.

[a]Title: Probably a literary or musical term [b]Title: Probably a musical term

52:8 like an olive tree. Olive trees live for hundreds of years and can withstand harsh conditions (v. 5). As an olive tree produces good fruit, the righteous person produces praise for God.

[3] Everyone has turned away,
they have together become corrupt;
there is no one who does good,
not even one.

[4] Will the evildoers never learn—
those who devour my people as men eat bread
and who do not call on God?
[5] There they were, overwhelmed with dread,
where there was nothing to dread.
God scattered the bones of those who attacked you;
you put them to shame, for God despised them.

[6] Oh, that salvation for Israel would come out of Zion!
When God restores the fortunes of his people,
let Jacob rejoice and Israel be glad!

Psalm 54

For the director of music. With stringed instruments.
A *maskil*[a] of David. When the Ziphites had gone to
Saul and said, "Is not David hiding among us?"

[1] Save me, O God, by your name;
vindicate me by your might.
[2] Hear my prayer, O God;
listen to the words of my mouth.

[3] Strangers are attacking me;
ruthless men seek my life—
men without regard for God. *Selah*

[4] Surely God is my help;
the Lord is the one who sustains me.

[5] Let evil recoil on those who slander me;
in your faithfulness destroy them.

[6] I will sacrifice a freewill offering to you;
I will praise your name, O LORD,
for it is good.
[7] For he has delivered me from all my troubles,
and my eyes have looked in triumph on my foes.

[a]Title: Probably a literary or musical term

intellectual seeker? The practical atheist? Self-destructive? Unhealthy in relationships? **2.** What tempts you to think "there is no God"? Does distance from God affect your behavior? **3.** What part of your life runs without regard to God? How will you put your faith to work today?

OPEN How do you feel when members of a religious sect come to your door? Do you talk with them or hide?

STUDY 1. What strangers are seeking to attack David (v. 3; 1 Sam. 23:1–20)? Why do they betray the man who saved them from the Philistines? **2.** How does David feel? How do you account for the switch in tone in verses 6–7 (1 Sam. 23:26–29)? **3.** What is the purpose of the offering mentioned in verse 6: To thank God ahead of time or get God on his side?

APPLY 1. Has your faith ever been attacked? Was the attack: Intellectual? Theological? Emotional? Social? How do you respond? **2.** Have you seen evil recoil back on those who promote it? When has this happened to you?

53:4–6 Verses 4 and 6 are identical to 14:4,7. Verse 5 is quite different however. In 14:5 the psalmist portrays evildoers as afraid because of the presence of God. In verse 5 here, evildoers are afraid without reason. They lack security because they lack faith.

54:3 ruthless men. David's enemies, whether political rivals or foreign invaders, are men who have become enemies of God and seek to destroy the righteous.

54:4 David is confident that the Lord will rescue, protect and sustain him. In this particular instance it is clear that God would side with David. David expects God to share his desire to destroy a wicked enemy. David could expect that defeating the wicked would fit into God's will.

54:7 he has delivered me. In verse 4, David is confident that God will help him now and sustain him in the future. Verse 7 shows that David's confidence is based on how God has delivered him in the past.

OPEN 1. Where would you fly if you had the "wings of a dove"? How far south? With what other love bird? Where would you nest? **2.** What age do you figure will be your halfway point in life: 17? 27? 37? 47?

STUDY 1. Is David troubled by internal or external strife (vv. 1–3)? What is he afraid of (vv. 4–5)? **2.** Does David feel like facing his problems head on (vv. 6–8)? He has had "escapist" feelings before (11:1). Why not fight his enemies (vv. 9–11)? What does he want God to do? **3.** What makes David's present trouble terrifying (vv. 12–14)? Do you think this psalm fits Ahithophel's defection to Saul (2 Sam. 15:12–31)? **4.** What fate does David wish on his enemies beyond mere "confusion" (v. 15)? What do you think of his other curses (vv. 19,23)? **5.** David's betrayer is a good speaker (vv. 20–21). What do his words hide? What else do words often hide? **6.** Faced with open rebellion, what does it mean for David to be "sustained" by God?

APPLY 1. How do you tend to respond to troubles: Deny they exist? Blame someone else? Avoid the problem or person? Escape? Tackle them head on? Pray? How are you handling your biggest problem today? **2.** To whom would you like to pass the message of verse 22 (1 Peter 5:7)? **3.** Do the streets of your city resemble verses 10–11? How do you handle the increasing deterioration of urban life? Where lies hope? **4.** When do you use speech as described in verse 21? What feelings do you cover up with deceitful words: Anger? Hatred? Jealousy? Envy? Love? Praise? Sexual interest? What does that do to your sense of who you are?

Psalm 55

For the director of music. With stringed instruments.
A *maskil*[a] of David.

1 Listen to my prayer, O God,
do not ignore my plea;
2 hear me and answer me.
My thoughts trouble me and I am distraught
3 at the voice of the enemy,
at the stares of the wicked;
for they bring down suffering upon me
and revile me in their anger.

4 My heart is in anguish within me;
the terrors of death assail me.
5 Fear and trembling have beset me;
horror has overwhelmed me.
6 I said, "Oh, that I had the wings of a dove!
I would fly away and be at rest—
7 I would flee far away
and stay in the desert; *Selah*
8 I would hurry to my place of shelter,
far from the tempest and storm."

9 Confuse the wicked, O Lord, confound their speech,
for I see violence and strife in the city.
10 Day and night they prowl about on its walls;
malice and abuse are within it.
11 Destructive forces are at work in the city;
threats and lies never leave its streets.

12 If an enemy were insulting me,
I could endure it;
if a foe were raising himself against me,
I could hide from him.
13 But it is you, a man like myself,
my companion, my close friend,
14 with whom I once enjoyed sweet fellowship
as we walked with the throng at the house of God.

[a]Title: Probably a literary or musical term

55:1–3 Psalm 55 shows David very close to the breaking point. Both his life and his political title are under serious assault. In fear and anguish he cries out to God. He has fallen so low. Will God please answer the call?

55:4–8 My heart is in anguish. David is in terrible emotional pain. His present enemy is a former friend. David feels betrayed and fears for his life (v. 4). And he fears that the present conflict will destroy all the work he has done as king (vv. 9–11). His first thought is just to escape and have some peace.

55:6–8 flee far away. For David, the most appealing solution is just to run away from his problems. Though he cannot leave problems behind, he can run to the Lord for refuge and deliverance.

55:9–11 violence and strife in the city. The conspiracy against the king has affected the lives of Jerusalem's people. In response to this spreading violence, David prays for God to take action against those who oppose him. As a good king, he is responsible for his people's welfare.

55:9 Confuse ... confound their speech. At the center of any conspiracy plans are being discussed, plots are being hatched. David prays that God will disrupt enemy communication and render the conspiracy harmless, as happened at the Tower of Babel (Gen. 11:5–9). Without a common language, the efforts of the Babel builders came to a halt. David hopes the same will be true for him.

15 Let death take my enemies by surprise;
let them go down alive to the grave,[a]
for evil finds lodging among them.

16 But I call to God,
and the LORD saves me.
17 Evening, morning and noon
I cry out in distress,
and he hears my voice.
18 He ransoms me unharmed
from the battle waged against me,
even though many oppose me.
19 God, who is enthroned forever,
will hear them and afflict them— *Selah*
men who never change their ways
and have no fear of God.

20 My companion attacks his friends;
he violates his covenant.
21 His speech is smooth as butter,
yet war is in his heart;
his words are more soothing than oil,
yet they are drawn swords.

22 Cast your cares on the LORD
and he will sustain you;
he will never let the righteous fall.
23 But you, O God, will bring down the wicked
into the pit of corruption;
bloodthirsty and deceitful men
will not live out half their days.

But as for me, I trust in you.

Psalm 56

For the director of music. To ⌞the tune of⌟ "A Dove on Distant Oaks." Of David. A *miktam.*[b] When the Philistines had seized him in Gath.

1 Be merciful to me, O God, for men hotly pursue me;
all day long they press their attack.
2 My slanderers pursue me all day long;
many are attacking me in their pride.

[a]15 Hebrew *Sheol* [b]Title: Probably a literary or musical term

OPEN 1. If you collected all the tears you shed in recent years, how much water would you have: A glass? Bucket? Swimming pool? Niagara Falls? **2.** What is the silliest thing you are afraid of?

STUDY 1. This psalm reflects 1 Samuel 21:10–15, where David flees Saul by escaping to Gath, Goliath's hometown. How desperate must David be to jump out of the frying pan into the fire? Where do you

55:15 This time it is not enough for David to just be delivered from enemies. The betrayal he has suffered causes him to want revenge.

Ps. 56 David is in deep trouble. His very life is in danger. His enemies pursue him, slander him and erode his reputation. The psalmist begins with an appeal for help (v. 1) and concludes with a statement of assurance that help is coming (v. 13). In the middle section, David describes the nature of the problem and proposes a solution.

56:2 My slanderers. Slander is the primary weapon of David's enemies. They seek to ruin his reputation and diminish his position. They are confident in their strength and even plot to kill him (vv. 5–6). Their whole campaign against David is based on cunning and cleverness.

see that despair reflected in this psalm? **2.** What's happening to David (vv. 5–6)? How would you feel in his place, hunted by your former friends? **3.** What does it mean that God "records your tears" (v. 8)? **4.** Is David invincible (vv. 4,11)? What does it mean to trust God in fearful circumstances? How is such trust demonstrated? How is it rewarded?

APPLY 1. Does being afraid lead you to trust God more, or less? Conversely, does not trusting God lead you to be more afraid? Less? Why? How can you choose faith when you are afraid? **2.** Which gets more notice from God: Your tears? Sins? Praises? Petitions? Why? If not God, in front of whom can you cry openly? **3.** If God is with you, why do you fear human threats so much? Can head knowledge of God alleviate fears, which are emotional? How do you overcome fear?

OPEN When you were a child, what did you want to be when you grew up? Now that you are grown what do you want to be?

STUDY 1. To which cave hideout does this psalm heading refer? Form two groups: one read 1 Samuel 21:10–22:2, the other 1 Samuel 24. Present a case for your cave. **2.** David cries to God to fulfill "his purpose for me" (v. 2). What is God's purpose (1 Sam. 16:1–13)? **3.** As one hated and hunted by Saul, the Lord's current "anointed one," how might David come to view that job? Is

3 When I am afraid,
 I will trust in you.
4 In God, whose word I praise,
 in God I trust; I will not be afraid.
 What can mortal man do to me?

5 All day long they twist my words;
 they are always plotting to harm me.
6 They conspire, they lurk,
 they watch my steps,
 eager to take my life.

7 On no account let them escape;
 in your anger, O God, bring down the nations.
8 Record my lament;
 list my tears on your scroll[a]—
 are they not in your record?

9 Then my enemies will turn back
 when I call for help.
 By this I will know that God is for me.
10 In God, whose word I praise,
 in the LORD, whose word I praise—
11 in God I trust; I will not be afraid.
 What can man do to me?

12 I am under vows to you, O God;
 I will present my thank offerings to you.
13 For you have delivered me[b] from death
 and my feet from stumbling,
that I may walk before God
 in the light of life.[c]

Psalm 57

For the director of music. ⌞To the tune of⌟ "Do Not Destroy."
Of David. A *miktam*.[d] When he had fled from Saul into the cave.

1 Have mercy on me, O God, have mercy on me,
 for in you my soul takes refuge.
I will take refuge in the shadow of your wings
 until the disaster has passed.

2 I cry out to God Most High,
 to God, who fulfills ⌞his purpose⌟ for me.

[a]8 Or / *put my tears in your wineskin* [b]13 Or *my soul* [c]13 Or *the land of the living* [d]Title: Probably a literary or musical term

---

56:3–4 David confesses his trust in God and poses the ironic question, "If God is for me, what do I have to fear from anyone?"

56:4 word. In this context, God's word is the covenant promise to be the God of his people and help them when they ask.

56:5–7 bring down the nations. David asks God to act against his enemies out of righteous anger. It is not enough to teach them a lesson; God must destroy them.

56:8 Record ... list ... on your scroll. David wants God to document his troubles so there can be no doubt that redress against David's enemies is the right thing to do.

56:9 If David's tears were documented, there could be no doubt that God would see the terrible way he is being treated. Since David is blessed by God, that documentation would certainly mean that God would rescue him.

57:2 God Most High ... who fulfills his purpose for me. God appointed David as king with a divine purpose. He

3 He sends from heaven and saves me,
rebuking those who hotly pursue me; *Selah*
God sends his love and his faithfulness.

4 I am in the midst of lions;
I lie among ravenous beasts—
men whose teeth are spears and arrows,
whose tongues are sharp swords.

5 Be exalted, O God, above the heavens;
let your glory be over all the earth.

6 They spread a net for my feet—
I was bowed down in distress.
They dug a pit in my path—
but they have fallen into it themselves. *Selah*

7 My heart is steadfast, O God,
my heart is steadfast;
I will sing and make music.
8 Awake, my soul!
Awake, harp and lyre!
I will awaken the dawn.

9 I will praise you, O Lord, among the nations;
I will sing of you among the peoples.
10 For great is your love, reaching to the heavens;
your faithfulness reaches to the skies.

11 Be exalted, O God, above the heavens;
let your glory be over all the earth.

Psalm 58

For the director of music. ⌞To the tune of⌟ "Do Not Destroy." Of David. A *miktam*.[a]

1 Do you rulers indeed speak justly?
Do you judge uprightly among men?
2 No, in your heart you devise injustice,
and your hands mete out violence on the earth.
3 Even from birth the wicked go astray;
from the womb they are wayward and speak lies.
4 Their venom is like the venom of a snake,
like that of a cobra that has stopped its ears,

[a]Title: Probably a literary or musical term

David deterred from, or spurred on, to see that purpose fulfilled? Why do you think so? **4.** Where do you see an abrupt change in mood in this psalm? What must have occurred? **5.** Verses 5 and 11 are the same except for their context: verse 5 expresses faith in hard times, verse 11 expresses joy after deliverance. Which context is yours right now?

APPLY 1. What promises of God do you lean on in hard time? Can you expect God's protection from every disaster? Why or why not? **2.** What do you feel is God's purpose for you? How far along are you in seeing God's purpose fulfilled: In the research stage? Stalled in a production snag? Back to the drawing boards? Already useful in the marketplace?

OPEN 1. How do you react to violent, bloody movies: Ho-hum? More! More!? Get me out of here? **2.** What is most likely to make you "out for blood": An act of treachery? Being lied about? An attack on your family? Other?

STUDY 1. With whom is David angry (vv. 1–2)? What is their problem? **2.** Are the wicked predestined to evil (vv. 3–5)? Who are the "charmers and enchanters" of life? **3.** What does David wish for unjust rulers (vv. 6–8)? What does this say about God's abhorrence of injustice? **4.** What do people say about God

---

will not allow David's enemies to thwart that purpose or disrupt the plans he has for David and his lineage.

57:6–11 David is confident God will help him, so he pledges to remain steadfast to the Lord and to praise him for deliverance.

57:6 They dug a pit ... but. The psalmist described his enemies as lions (v. 4). Here those enemies had set a net and dug a pit as if they were hunters and David a lion. But God changes the roles, and the enemies fall into the trap. The lions fall prey to David and God.

58:1–5 As king, David may be powerful, but responsibility for justice is still in the hands of judges. Many are wicked and dispense injustice.

58:3 from birth. The judges' corruption is so ingrained and so natural that it seems they have been corrupt since birth. Their deeds are that consistent and pervasive.

58:4 venom. Snakes have been suspicious creatures since the Garden of Eden (Gen. 3). There the snake turned goodness into disobedience. Likewise the words of these wicked judges bring misery to their subjects. Their words are like poison.

when injustice and cruelty continually occur? What would David like us to believe (v. 11)? **5.** Is David being "bloodthirsty" in verse 10? **6.** Compare this psalm with Jesus' words in Matthew 23:33–36. When are such words appropriate today?

APPLY 1. What social injustice or tyranny gets you stirred up? Why? How is that reflected in your prayers? **2.** Could you use the cries for vengeance in verses 6–9 as your own? Why or why not? **3.** What can this group do to help bring justice in the community?

OPEN 1. Did you ever write a letter in the heat of the moment and then choose not to mail it? Why? Did you send a revised version instead? **2.** Have people thrown a surprise party for you? Did you suspect? Did you play along with it?

STUDY 1. Who does David credit for his escape (vv. 1–2; 1 Sam. 19:11–18)? Is he out of danger yet? **2.** Why does David include all Gentiles in his plea (vv. 5,8)? Is he getting paranoid? **3.** What are his enemies like (vv. 6–7)? What is their attitude towards God? **4.** In verses 11–13, what does David pray for "my people"? For the "ends of the earth"? What does "consume them" mean? Is this David the fugitive praying, or David the king? Why do you think so? **5.** What comfort and hope does David draw from the promise of God's personal and worldwide judgment? What does judgment show about God's view of injustice in the world? What would it mean if God did not judge evil? **6.** What words change in verses 9 and

5 that will not heed the tune of the charmer,
however skillful the enchanter may be.

6 Break the teeth in their mouths, O God;
tear out, O LORD, the fangs of the lions!
7 Let them vanish like water that flows away;
when they draw the bow, let their arrows be blunted.
8 Like a slug melting away as it moves along,
like a stillborn child, may they not see the sun.

9 Before your pots can feel ⌞the heat of⌟ the thorns—
whether they be green or dry—the wicked will be swept away.[a]
10 The righteous will be glad when they are avenged,
when they bathe their feet in the blood of the wicked.
11 Then men will say,
"Surely the righteous still are rewarded;
surely there is a God who judges the earth."

Psalm 59

For the director of music. ⌞To the tune of⌟ "Do Not Destroy."
Of David. A *miktam*.[b] When Saul had sent men
to watch David's house in order to kill him.

1 Deliver me from my enemies, O God;
protect me from those who rise up against me.
2 Deliver me from evildoers
and save me from bloodthirsty men.

3 See how they lie in wait for me!
Fierce men conspire against me
for no offense or sin of mine, O LORD.
4 I have done no wrong, yet they are ready to attack me.
Arise to help me; look on my plight!
5 O LORD God Almighty, the God of Israel,
rouse yourself to punish all the nations;
show no mercy to wicked traitors. *Selah*

6 They return at evening,
snarling like dogs,
and prowl about the city.

[a]9 The meaning of the Hebrew for this verse is uncertain. [b]Title: Probably a literary or musical term

58:6–8 David prays that Israel will be purged of such evil judges. The tone of the verses is much more like a curse than a prayer.

58:8 slug. The slug is usually viewed with disdain and distaste. Here, the psalmist refers to the way it will dry up to nothing in the hot sun.

58:9–11 The judges will themselves be judged, found guilty and punished. The righteous will rejoice that evil in their midst has been destroyed, and that their God controls the earth.

58:11 there is a God who judges the earth. Usually, judgment is frightening. For the righteous however, it is the opposite. The punishment of the wicked is evidence that a just God controls this fallen world.

59:1 protect me. The Hebrew for this phrase literally means "raise me to a high, secure place." The psalmist is asking to be raised higher than his enemies can reach. That place is with God, who can protect from any harm that might befall.

59:3–5 I have done no wrong. Though others lie (v. 12) and slander (v. 10), the psalmist proclaims innocence. He asks God to judge these enemies and to punish them for wickedness.

59:5 show no mercy. The psalmist makes an ironic request of God. Without God's mercy no one could pass God's judgment, neither the enemy nor the psalmist.

[7]See what they spew from their mouths—
they spew out swords from their lips,
and they say, "Who can hear us?"
[8]But you, O LORD, laugh at them;
you scoff at all those nations.

[9]O my Strength, I watch for you;
you, O God, are my fortress, [10]my loving God.

God will go before me
and will let me gloat over those who slander me.
[11]But do not kill them, O Lord our shield,[a]
or my people will forget.
In your might make them wander about,
and bring them down.
[12]For the sins of their mouths,
for the words of their lips,
let them be caught in their pride.
For the curses and lies they utter,
[13] consume them in wrath,
consume them till they are no more.
Then it will be known to the ends of the earth
that God rules over Jacob. *Selah*

[14]They return at evening,
snarling like dogs,
and prowl about the city.
[15]They wander about for food
and howl if not satisfied.
[16]But I will sing of your strength,
in the morning I will sing of your love;
for you are my fortress,
my refuge in times of trouble.

[17]O my Strength, I sing praise to you;
you, O God, are my fortress, my loving God.

[a]11 Or *sovereign*

17? What does this show about David's progression in faith between then and now? **7.** How did God answer David's prayer (1 Sam. 19:19–24)? Is this what David had in mind? **8.** How would you relate this psalm to the New Testament teaching that suffering is redemptive (Col. 1:24; 1 Peter 4:12–13)?

APPLY 1. How do you balance hatred of evil with love for enemies? **2.** Where in your life right now do you most feel surrounded by "snarling dogs": At work? Among extended family? While involved in political activity? **3.** In what way can God be your refuge amid these "snarling dogs"?

59:10–13 The psalmist harbors no doubt that God will do as requested in verse 5 and punish Israel's enemies. Confidently he asks God to prolong the destruction of the enemy to make sure that Israel learns the lesson of God's deliverance once and for all.

59:12 sins of their mouths. Sometimes the sharpest weapons are lies and slanders (31:13; 35:15; 56:2).

59:13 known to the ends of the earth. Psalm 22:22–31 proclaims that God will be known throughout the world for the way he delivers his people from trouble. Psalm 46:8,9 says essentially the same thing except the focus is on the warlike destruction of Israel's enemies. In these verses, the psalmist claims that God will be known throughout the earth for his destruction of the wicked.

59:14–16 snarling like dogs. Enemies who snarl like dogs are not to be feared. God laughs at them (v. 8); the psalmist will sing of God's strength and love at their destruction (vv. 14–16).

OPEN **1.** Were you ever in a fist fight at school? What happened? Who won? **2.** Can you recall a pep talk from a teacher, parent or coach that deeply affected you?

STUDY **1.** While David was securing his borders on the far northeast corner of his kingdom, Edom attacked on the far south (2 Sam. 8:2–3,13). How did David respond to this behind-the-back blow? Does this psalm paint as glorious a picture as the Samuel account (vv. 1–3)? Why does he blame God? **2.** Armies "raised a banner" to regroup fleeing, disorganized soldiers. For whom does God raise a banner (v. 4)? Why? **3.** How do you account for the confident tone of verse 5? What did God promise (vv. 6–8)? **4.** Why David's growing sense of hope (vv. 9–12)? What is David's part and God's part in this upcoming battle?

APPLY **1.** Have you ever felt scattered or unorganized? What serves as God's rallying banner for you? **2.** What "Edom" is attacking you now from your blind side? What lesson in this psalm can help you face problems head on? **3.** How are the battles that you have to face different from the wars of God's Old Testament people? How are they similar?

Psalm 60

For the director of music. To ⌊the tune of⌋ "The Lily of the Covenant." A *miktam*[a] of David. For teaching. When he fought Aram Naharaim[b] and Aram Zobah,[c] and when Joab returned and struck down twelve thousand Edomites in the Valley of Salt.

1 You have rejected us, O God, and burst forth upon us;
you have been angry—now restore us!
2 You have shaken the land and torn it open;
mend its fractures, for it is quaking.
3 You have shown your people desperate times;
you have given us wine that makes us stagger.

4 But for those who fear you, you have raised a banner
to be unfurled against the bow. *Selah*

5 Save us and help us with your right hand,
that those you love may be delivered.
6 God has spoken from his sanctuary:
"In triumph I will parcel out Shechem
and measure off the Valley of Succoth.
7 Gilead is mine, and Manasseh is mine;
Ephraim is my helmet,
Judah my scepter.
8 Moab is my washbasin,
upon Edom I toss my sandal;
over Philistia I shout in triumph."

9 Who will bring me to the fortified city?
Who will lead me to Edom?
10 Is it not you, O God, you who have rejected us
and no longer go out with our armies?
11 Give us aid against the enemy,
for the help of man is worthless.
12 With God we will gain the victory,
and he will trample down our enemies.

[a]Title: Probably a literary or musical term [b]Title: That is, Arameans of Northwest Mesopotamia
[c]Title: That is, Arameans of central Syria

60:1 rejected us. Israel has been defeated. That could only happen if God were absent. Therefore, the psalmist assumes that God has temporarily cast Israel aside. The covenant bond is not broken, however, so the psalmist can still call upon the Lord to ask for help.

60:4 banner. In the middle of battle, banners were used to establish a rallying point, a place where an army could regroup and counterattack. The psalmist calls upon God to raise that banner so Israel can gather together and counter its defeat with victory.

60:5 those you love. Though God may have temporarily rejected Israel, he truly loves his holy nation and will help them.

60:6–8 In triumph. The psalmist recalls an oracle, probably already old at this time, that portrays God as the warrior-king who leads his people to victory.

60:10–12 The psalmist is confident that the Lord's rejection of Israel is temporary. God is faithful to his people and will lead them again into battle.

60:12 gain the victory. With God's help, the people of Israel can do mighty things, and will defeat the enemy.

Psalm 61

For the director of music.
With stringed instruments. Of David.

[1]Hear my cry, O God;
listen to my prayer.

[2]From the ends of the earth I call to you,
I call as my heart grows faint;
lead me to the rock that is higher than I.
[3]For you have been my refuge,
a strong tower against the foe.

[4]I long to dwell in your tent forever
and take refuge in the shelter of your wings. *Selah*

[5]For you have heard my vows, O God;
you have given me the heritage of those who fear your name.

[6]Increase the days of the king's life,
his years for many generations.
[7]May he be enthroned in God's presence forever;
appoint your love and faithfulness to protect him.

[8]Then will I ever sing praise to your name
and fulfill my vows day after day.

OPEN 1. Which parent gave you rock-like security? How so? **2.** What is the longest long-distance phone call you've ever made?

STUDY 1. How far away from home is David (v. 2)? In what state of health? **2.** What kind of fellowship with God does David want (vv. 3–5)? What vows has he taken? What does he inherit? **3.** Is David praying for himself (vv. 6–7)? What else is he thinking about (2 Sam. 7:8–16)?

APPLY 1. When have you felt exiled? How do you pray when faint from exhaustion? **2.** Do believers inherit anything like David (Eph. 1:3–6)? What vow could you make this coming week to help you grow stronger in faith?

Psalm 62

For the director of music. For Jeduthun. A psalm of David.

[1]My soul finds rest in God alone;
my salvation comes from him.
[2]He alone is my rock and my salvation;
he is my fortress, I will never be shaken.

OPEN 1. What is the most restful vacation you have taken in the last 10 years? What made it so? **2.** What is the best reward someone could give you for a job well done?

STUDY 1. What two evils prompt David to write this psalm (vv. 3–4)? **2.** What is the refrain

---

Ps. 61 This psalm and the three that follow (Ps. 61–64) are united by a common theme of trusting God in threatening times. Psalm 61 begins with a plea to God to hear (v. 1) and ends with a vow to praise God (v. 8). The psalmist, perhaps David, prays that he might experience God's presence because of his vows of faith. David may have had in mind the events of 2 Samuel 17:21–29 when he escaped after Absalom's uprising. The king also looks ahead to the King to come.

61:2 ends of the earth. The language is hyperbolic, but David nevertheless feels he is a great distance from God—either physically (having fled from a threat; 42:6) or spiritually (facing death and sensing God's absence; 63:9). **rock that is higher.** God is pictured as solid rock—an image first used by Moses (Deut.32:4) and echoed elsewhere in the Psalms (62:2; 71:3; 91:1,2; 144:1).

61:4 I long to dwell in your tent forever. The psalmist expresses his commitment and determination to worship God and live acceptably to him.

61:5 you have heard. David is confident that God will hear his prayer. His confidence is based either on his past experiences with God, or on his faith that God will satisfy his longing this time. **my vows.** The psalmist makes his requests to God on the basis of his vows to God (50:14; 66:14). **heritage.** The psalmist knows he is part of God's people, living in the land God promised, where God dwells with his people. He also realizes God has given him a great responsibility to rule over it (16:6; 135:12; 136:21,22).

61:6–7 The psalmist prays that the king would live long. Of course, the king himself, David, is noted as the writer of the psalm. Speaking about oneself in the third person was common in ancient Near Eastern literature. On the other hand, he could be quoting a prayer of the people led by a priest. The prayer itself—which was applied to the Messiah by later Jewish scholars—is fulfilled in Christ, David's ultimate heir and king of all.

Ps. 62 As in Psalm 61, the psalmist (who is clearly a king) faces opposition and treachery from traitors who seek to overthrow him, and he turns to God for protection. If the writer was David, the events prompting this wisdom psalm could be the attempt of Saul's family to remove David from the throne. The writer feels weak (v. 3), perhaps due to his age, and seeks God's strength. David offers a supreme description of pure trust in God (Ps. 31). Structurally the psalm has three parts. The first part confesses reliance on God, the second part speaks of trust and hope, and the last part explains why that is possible.

62:1–2 A beautiful declaration of David's total dependence upon God.

of the song? What is the difference between "salvation" and "honor" (v. 7)? **3.** In what does David urge us to "trust" and "not trust" (vv. 8–10)? **4.** How can people know if they are trusting in God, people or money? **5.** What two things has David heard about God? (vv. 11–12)? How will God judge?

APPLY 1. What circumstances, people or forces are pressuring you now? What are you learning from their pressure? **2.** Who do you bless with your lips but curse in your heart? Is this hypocrisy? What can you most readily change, lips or heart? **3.** In what do you trust first: God, yourself, people or money? What do you trust second? Third? **4.** How does it feel to know you will be rewarded according to what you have done (Matt. 16:27; Rom. 2:6–8; 2 Cor. 5:10)? To what hope do you hold?

---

3 How long will you assault a man?
Would all of you throw him down—
this leaning wall, this tottering fence?
4 They fully intend to topple him
from his lofty place;
they take delight in lies.
With their mouths they bless,
but in their hearts they curse. *Selah*

5 Find rest, O my soul, in God alone;
my hope comes from him.
6 He alone is my rock and my salvation;
he is my fortress, I will not be shaken.
7 My salvation and my honor depend on God[a];
he is my mighty rock, my refuge.
8 Trust in him at all times, O people;
pour out your hearts to him,
for God is our refuge. *Selah*

9 Lowborn men are but a breath,
the highborn are but a lie;
if weighed on a balance, they are nothing;
together they are only a breath.
10 Do not trust in extortion
or take pride in stolen goods;
though your riches increase,
do not set your heart on them.

11 One thing God has spoken,
two things have I heard:
that you, O God, are strong,
12 and that you, O Lord, are loving.
Surely you will reward each person
according to what he has done.

OPEN 1. Describe the object, person or activity you were most devoted to as a teenager. How has your obsession or first love changed since then? **2.** When your mind starts to wander from what you're doing, where does it go? What do your daydreams zero in on?

STUDY 1. Why is David in the desert (2 Sam. 15:13–14, 23–25)? What dangers wait there

Psalm 63

A psalm of David.
When he was in the Desert of Judah.

1 O God, you are my God,
earnestly I seek you;
my soul thirsts for you,
my body longs for you,

[a]7 Or / *God Most High is my salvation and my honor*

62:3 leaning wall ... tottering fence. The psalmist wonders if his tormentors will ever stop. He describes himself with metaphors of fragility, noting that he has no strength to carry on by himself and realizing his opponents see *him as unable to put* up a fight.

62:8 Trust. David speaks to the righteous, encouraging them to rely on God. What is true of the king (in v. 7) is expanded to include the whole family of God.

62:10 Do not trust. In an echo of Psalm 49, the psalmist warns those *who trust in* themselves rather than God to achieve their goals.

62:12 you will reward each person. Ultimately God will judge each person according to his or her actions (Eccl. 12:13,14).

Ps. 63 This royal psalm follows the same theme as the previous two. The psalmist, David, according to the ascription, longs for God's presence and protection—a longing likened to hunger (v. 5) and thirst (v. 1). David probably refers to the time when Saul chased him in the wilderness (1 Sam. 22–24).

in a dry and weary land
where there is no water.

2 I have seen you in the sanctuary
and beheld your power and your glory.
3 Because your love is better than life,
my lips will glorify you.
4 I will praise you as long as I live,
and in your name I will lift up my hands.
5 My soul will be satisfied as with the richest of foods;
with singing lips my mouth will praise you.

6 On my bed I remember you;
I think of you through the watches of the night.
7 Because you are my help,
I sing in the shadow of your wings.
8 My soul clings to you;
your right hand upholds me.

9 They who seek my life will be destroyed;
they will go down to the depths of the earth.
10 They will be given over to the sword
and become food for jackals.

11 But the king will rejoice in God;
all who swear by God's name will praise him,
while the mouths of liars will be silenced.

Psalm 64

For the director of music.
A psalm of David.

1 Hear me, O God, as I voice my complaint;
protect my life from the threat of the enemy.
2 Hide me from the conspiracy of the wicked,
from that noisy crowd of evildoers.

3 They sharpen their tongues like swords
and aim their words like deadly arrows.
4 They shoot from ambush at the innocent man;
they shoot at him suddenly, without fear.

(vv. 1,6–7,10)? **2.** What memories keep David going (vv. 2–5)? What is better than life? How can David devote himself to the love of God at a time and place like this? **3.** Can you think of anything in your life that would make you think, like David, that the love of God is better than life? **4.** What does it mean to "swear by God's name" (v. 11)? **5.** Is it ever appropriate to swear by God's name? When (compare to Matt. 5:33–37)?

APPLY 1. What "desert" have you been through recently? What did you long for the most? Did you find it? **2.** Which verse of this psalm best fits your relationship with God? How might you deepen your first love with God? **3.** St. John Chrysostom advised reading this psalm daily. Try it for the next week and share any impact.

OPEN What is your biggest complaint about work or school? With whom are you most free to share?

STUDY 1. While chapter 63 focused almost exclusively on God, what does this one focus on? **2.** What are the weapons and tactics of David's opponents (vv. 2–6)? Are people really as bad as he makes them out here? Do you know anyone this wicked? **3.** What does it mean "shoot from ambush"? Do you know anyone who does this? **4.** How will God judge

---

63:2–5 The writer remembers the comfort of God's presence in the sanctuary and refreshes his trust in God's faithful love.

63:2 The sanctuary. David had sought God's presence at Nob (1 Sam. 21:1). Later the sanctuary was moved to Jerusalem.

63:6 On my bed. The psalmist is experiencing sleeplessness because of threats against him. In the darkness he turns to God and anticipates the morning when God will rescue him. **watches of the night.** The Jews divided the night into three watches, so the psalmist is up all night (119:148; Lam. 2:19).

63:8 your right hand. The right hand of God refers to his power and authority—the same power that delivered Israel from Egypt (Ex. 15:6). God's power is available to David and to all believers every day.

63:9–10 will be destroyed. The psalmist's adversaries will get their just desserts. Because they have attempted to destroy David's life, they will lose their own (Gen. 9:5; Deut. 19:21).

Ps. 64 The psalmist, David, faces a conspiracy, and again he puts his trust in God. Here the attacks are more verbal than physical, but no less painful (vv. 3,4). God will "turn their own tongues against them" (vv. 7,8). Unlike Psalm 62, the king here is not described as weak. David prays for God's protection from his conspirators. This is a wisdom psalm with lament and warning.

64:3 tongues. Psalmists often complain about one weapon used against them: the tongue, which is more painful than the sword (5:9). **swords ... deadly arrows.** The enemies' curses and lies (59:7,12).

64:4 without fear. Those who

evil (vv. 7–8)? What will others think (vv. 8–9)? Does this happen, then or now?

APPLY 1. Do you feel ambushed? Threatened? How so? Does anyone think of you as "the enemy"? **2.** What is most important to you about God's judgment: Its certainty? Swiftness? "Tit-for-tat" fairness? It foils the cleverest of plans?

OPEN 1. Which season brings out the best in you? Why? **2.** What would you want on the menu of your last meal?

STUDY 1. List the verbs associated with God in this psalm. Which describe God as Creator? As Redeemer? As Provider? **2.** Which verses support the possible origins of the psalm: Harvest festival? Spring celebration of first fruits? National deliverance from drought or famine? God's forgiveness? **3.** How did the Israelites see their God, Yahweh, as different than other tribal or national gods (vv. 5–8)? In what sense is God the "hope of all the ends of the earth"? **4.** If this psalm was first written after an abundant harvest, what did such plenty signify to David (v. 3)?

APPLY 1. What aspect of God is most exciting to you today: Creator? Provider? Redeemer?

5 They encourage each other in evil plans,
they talk about hiding their snares;
they say, "Who will see them[a]?"
6 They plot injustice and say,
"We have devised a perfect plan!"
Surely the mind and heart of man are cunning.

7 But God will shoot them with arrows;
suddenly they will be struck down.
8 He will turn their own tongues against them
and bring them to ruin;
all who see them will shake their heads in scorn.

9 All mankind will fear;
they will proclaim the works of God
and ponder what he has done.
10 Let the righteous rejoice in the LORD
and take refuge in him;
let all the upright in heart praise him!

Psalm 65

For the director of music. A psalm of David. A song.

1 Praise awaits[b] you, O God, in Zion;
to you our vows will be fulfilled.
2 O you who hear prayer,
to you all men will come.
3 When we were overwhelmed by sins,
you forgave[c] our transgressions.
4 Blessed are those you choose
and bring near to live in your courts!
We are filled with the good things of your house,
of your holy temple.

5 You answer us with awesome deeds of righteousness,
O God our Savior,
the hope of all the ends of the earth
and of the farthest seas,

[a]5 Or *us* [b]1 Or *befits;* the meaning of the Hebrew for this word is uncertain. [c]3 Or *made atonement for*

threaten David do not consider what might happen to them as a result—unfortunately for them (vv. 7,8).

64:7–8 The psalmist expresses his certain trust in God's justice. God will surely act with righteousness, doing to them what they planned to do to him (63:9,10).

64:9–10 David looks joyfully to the outcome of God's justice. Outsiders will "fear ... proclaim ... and ponder" the works of the Lord, but God's people will "rejoice ... take refuge ... praise."

Ps. 65 The psalmist, apparently David, praises God for his amazing acts on behalf of his people. When the people faithfully pray, God is quick to forgive their sin so they can worship him in the temple (vv. 3,4). God will also control the world to bring about peace and security for the nation (vv. 5–8) and to bless the Promised Land with bounty and beauty. This wisdom psalm (with prophetic elements) is the first of several with similar themes.

65:1 awaits. The Hebrew word here could mean "befits" or "is silent before." The psalmist seems to personify praise as one who dwells in the temple, resting and waiting for the people to come, worship and fulfill their vows to God (57:8).

65:3 forgave our transgressions. The people offered God the prescribed sacrifices for atonement. As a result God forgave them (32:1,2; 78:38; 79:9).

65:5–8 Israel has prayed for security and peace; God answers. He quiets the noisy nations around Israel and protects her.

65:5 awesome deeds. A reference to the many works of God on the nation's behalf—including Israel's exodus from Egypt and conquest of the Promised

2 that your ways may be known on earth,
your salvation among all nations.

3 May the peoples praise you, O God;
may all the peoples praise you.
4 May the nations be glad and sing for joy,
for you rule the peoples justly
and guide the nations of the earth. *Selah*
5 May the peoples praise you, O God;
may all the peoples praise you.

6 Then the land will yield its harvest,
and God, our God, will bless us.
7 God will bless us,
and all the ends of the earth will fear him.

Psalm 68

For the director of music. Of David.
A psalm. A song.

1 May God arise, may his enemies be scattered;
may his foes flee before him.
2 As smoke is blown away by the wind,
may you blow them away;
as wax melts before the fire,
may the wicked perish before God.
3 But may the righteous be glad
and rejoice before God;
may they be happy and joyful.

4 Sing to God, sing praise to his name,
extol him who rides on the clouds[a]—
his name is the LORD—
and rejoice before him.
5 A father to the fatherless, a defender of widows,
is God in his holy dwelling.
6 God sets the lonely in families,[b]
he leads forth the prisoners with singing;
but the rebellious live in a sun-scorched land.

[a]4 Or *I prepare the way for him who rides through the deserts* [b]6 Or *the desolate in a homeland*

STUDY 1. What famous blessing has shaped this psalm (Num. 6:24–26)? **2.** Israel seeks God's blessing (vv. 1–2) for what reasons (vv. 6–7)? **3.** What vision of a Messiah is echoed in this psalm (Isa. 66:18–23)? **4.** Do verses 2–7 indicate a belief that all nations will worship the Lord one day? Or simply that all nations will realize Israel has a powerful God?

APPLY What blessings has God brought into your life? For whose benefit? For what wider purpose?

OPEN 1. Do you prefer a church with a large congregation for its resources, or a small one for its intimacy? What do you like most about your church? **2.** On a scale of 1–10, how much do you like parades? Do you watch them at street level, or from your living room? Why?

STUDY 1. This psalm may be based on the return of the ark to Jerusalem (1 Chr. 15). Why did poets and preachers recount Israel's history at such events? **2.** Which phrases in the prelude (vv. 1–6) sing of God as Judge? Creator? Redeemer? Parent? **3.** What event is referred to in verse 7? When did the "earth shake" (Ex. 19:16–19)? What miracles occurred in the wilderness (vv. 9–10)? **4.** The periods of Joshua and the Judges are covered in verses 11–14. What kings fled (Judg. 5:19)? What plunder did the Israelites divide besides silver and gold (Judg. 5:30)? What happened at Mount Zalmon (Judg. 9:48–49)? **5.** Israel eventually wanted a king instead of judges. What mountain did David acquire for God's dwelling (vv. 15–16)? Is it high or rug-

psalmist uses Aaron's benediction (Num. 6:24–26), calling on God to bless his people.

67:2 that your ways may be known. The congregation desires God's blessing in order to show the world his wonderful ways (46:10).

67:3–5 These verses expand on verse 2. They pray that God's acts on their behalf would be so amazing that not only his own people, but other nations too, would praise God.

67:6 land will yield its harvest. The nation would experience all the bounty God had promised them through the land he gave them (65:9–13).

Ps. 68 This psalm, based partly on Deborah's song in Judges 5, was likely used as a processional in worship. It offers praise to God for his wonderful reign over Israel. Nine stanzas are included, with the first introducing the procession and the last picturing God enthroned in the temple.

68:3 righteous. Here the Israelites are seen as God's committed, obedient people—unlike the enemies of God (the "wicked," v. 2).

68:4 who rides on the clouds. This description, used often of the Canaanite god Baal, is applied to the true God who rules over all (v. 33; 104:3; Matt. 26:64).

68:5–6 father ... defender. God protects and cares for those who cannot do so for themselves (10:14; 146:7–9; 147:6).

ged? Can you think of other times when God chose the unimpressive to show his glory? **6.** What were the "chariots of God" (2 Kin. 6:15–17; 7:5–6)? **7.** What would this rapid review of their redemption by God do for the worshippers as they draw near to Jerusalem with the ark of God? From your reviewing stand (vv. 24–27), what in this parade do you see? Hear? Feel? **8.** What is significant about Zebulun and Naphtali joining the ceremonies (Isa. 9:1; Matt. 4:13–16)? **9.** The psalmist expands his vision from the renegade Galileans to the neighboring pagans (vv. 28–31). What does he want God to do? How big is his vision (vv. 32–34)?

APPLY 1. Give a brief review of your personal salvation history. What was your Egypt? Exodus? Desert? Promised land? Kingdom expansion? What evil had to be rooted out of your life? **2.** Who or what are some mighty "mountains of Bashan" that threaten or intimidate you? What does it mean to you that God chooses the "weak and the small" (such as Zion) to confound the strong and accomplish his purpose? **3.** Do you experience an awesome God in your place of worship? How does worship affect your mission in life?

7 When you went out before your people, O God,
when you marched through the wasteland, *Selah*

8 the earth shook,
the heavens poured down rain,
before God, the One of Sinai,
before God, the God of Israel.
9 You gave abundant showers, O God;
you refreshed your weary inheritance.
10 Your people settled in it,
and from your bounty, O God, you provided for the poor.

11 The Lord announced the word,
and great was the company of those who proclaimed it:
12 "Kings and armies flee in haste;
in the camps men divide the plunder.
13 Even while you sleep among the campfires,[a]
the wings of ⌊my⌋ dove are sheathed with silver,
its feathers with shining gold."
14 When the Almighty[b] scattered the kings in the land,
it was like snow fallen on Zalmon.

15 The mountains of Bashan are majestic mountains;
rugged are the mountains of Bashan.
16 Why gaze in envy, O rugged mountains,
at the mountain where God chooses to reign,
where the LORD himself will dwell forever?
17 The chariots of God are tens of thousands
and thousands of thousands;
the Lord ⌊has come⌋ from Sinai into his sanctuary.
18 When you ascended on high,
you led captives in your train;
you received gifts from men,
even from[c] the rebellious—
that you,[d] O LORD God, might dwell there.

[a] 13 Or *saddlebags* [b] 14 Hebrew *Shaddai* [c] 18 Or *gifts for men, / even* [d] 18 Or *they*

68:7–10 When you went out before your people. The psalmist remembers God leading the nation through the desert to the Promised Land (Judg. 5:4,5).

68:8 earth shook. God's presence caused Mount Sinai to quake (Ex. 19:18). **heavens poured down rain.** The books of Moses make no reference to heavy rain during the desert sojourn. Here rain is a part of the earthquake signifying the majesty of God poured out (Judg. 5:4). Exodus 19:16 refers to "thunder and lightning, with a thick cloud" upon the mountain, and perhaps rain is part of that display of power. But verse 9 indicates occasional rain showers along the way which refreshed God's weary people on their journey.

68:9 your ... inheritance. This is a reference to the nation, God's people whom he possessed (Deut. 9:29).

68:10 bounty. The word literally means "goodness" (65:11). **provided.** God met the people's needs with the produce of the land (Josh. 5:11,12).

68:11 announced the word. God clearly revealed beforehand that he would defeat the Canaanites in order to give his people the land (Ex. 23:22–31; Deut. 7:10–24). **proclaimed it.** The people praised God and spread word of his victories (2 Chr. 20:26–28).

68:14 the Almighty. The Hebrew name is "Shaddai," referring to God's strength and majesty (91:1).

68:15–16 mountains of Bashan. These mountains, which included Hermon, surrounded Bashan, a fertile area to the northeast of the Sea of Galilee. They are pictured here as envious over God's choice of Mount Zion as his throne—thus making it the "highest" of all mountains (48:2).

68:17 chariots of God. A reference to the vast host of God's angelic beings, likened to a powerful force of charioteers (2 Kin. 6:17; Hab. 3:8).

68:18 ascended on high. God went up to his throne on Mount Zion (7:7). **that you ... might dwell there.** The purpose of God's ascension on high. This verse was used of the risen Christ (Eph. 4:8–10), revealing that Jesus fulfilled God's kingship in Jerusalem.

6 who formed the mountains by your power,
having armed yourself with strength,
7 who stilled the roaring of the seas,
the roaring of their waves,
and the turmoil of the nations.
8 Those living far away fear your wonders;
where morning dawns and evening fades
you call forth songs of joy.

9 You care for the land and water it;
you enrich it abundantly.
The streams of God are filled with water
to provide the people with grain,
for so you have ordained it.[a]
10 You drench its furrows
and level its ridges;
you soften it with showers
and bless its crops.
11 You crown the year with your bounty,
and your carts overflow with abundance.
12 The grasslands of the desert overflow;
the hills are clothed with gladness.
13 The meadows are covered with flocks
and the valleys are mantled with grain;
they shout for joy and sing.

Psalm 66

For the director of music. A song. A psalm.

1 Shout with joy to God, all the earth!
2 Sing the glory of his name;
make his praise glorious!
3 Say to God, "How awesome are your deeds!
So great is your power
that your enemies cringe before you.
4 All the earth bows down to you;
they sing praise to you,
they sing praise to your name." *Selah*

5 Come and see what God has done,
how awesome his works in man's behalf!
6 He turned the sea into dry land,

[a]9 Or *for that is how you prepare the land*

What does it mean to you that God not only forgives your sin but brings you near to "live in his courts" (vv. 3–4)? **2.** David expressed God's provision in terms of a harvest: How would you rewrite verses 9–13 to praise God's provision for you? **3.** How would you explain these verses to a people living in drought or famine? Why doesn't God provide for them? What can the group do to help them?

OPEN 1. What feelings does a noisy child stir up within you: Irritation? Attention? Affection? **2.** Have you ever been in prison, either as a resident or visitor? What was it like?

STUDY 1. Who does the psalmist call to worship (vv. 1,4)? What types of things can mankind "come and see" (v. 5)? **2.** On what event does he reflect (vv. 6–7)? What does it reveal about God? In what ways have Jews and Christians memorialized it? **3.** What tests did the people go through (vv. 10–12)? What is the purpose of "refining"? **4.** What kind of vows did the psalmist make (vv. 13–14)? **5.** Why does the psalmist think God answered his prayers (vv. 18–19)? **6.** All the earth does not

Land (106:22; 145:6; 2 Sam. 7:23). **hope of all.** This is true despite most of the nations not knowing God.

65:8 Those living far away. Eventually God's merciful acts will be recognized by all the world—prompting a response of awe and fear.

65:9–10 You care for the land and water it. Rain is God's blessing upon the land, in keeping with his covenant to provide all of Israel's needs (Deut. 28:12).

Ps. 66 The psalmist—perhaps a king—praises God for answering his prayer, probably for protection from an enemy. The writer has apparently made a vow which he fulfills now in the temple (vv. 13,14), calling on the whole nation to join him.

66:1 all the earth. Not only Israel but all nations are invited to join in the praise of almighty God (100:1).

66:5 Come and see. The results of God's merciful acts of salvation can be witnessed in the lives of those who have experienced them, who retell them and celebrate them continually (48:8,9).

66:6 waters. A reference to the Jordan, though crossing of the Red Sea by Israel is also possible.

bow to God. What is the point of saying so (v. 4)? What is your vision of a world at peace with God?

APPLY 1. What could you say God has done for you lately? What about God and his ways of dealing with all people would we learn from your testimony? **2.** Do you feel God is testing you? How? Why? What "abundant place" do you hope for? **3.** What sacrifices should you make this week for the Lord? What would be your equivalent to "bulls and goats"?

OPEN What is most likely to make your face "shine": A romantic evening? Seeing grandchildren? Going shopping? Your team winning? Promotion?

they passed through the waters on foot—
come, let us rejoice in him.
7 He rules forever by his power,
his eyes watch the nations—
let not the rebellious rise up against him. *Selah*

8 Praise our God, O peoples,
let the sound of his praise be heard;
9 he has preserved our lives
and kept our feet from slipping.
10 For you, O God, tested us;
you refined us like silver.
11 You brought us into prison
and laid burdens on our backs.
12 You let men ride over our heads;
we went through fire and water,
but you brought us to a place of abundance.

13 I will come to your temple with burnt offerings
and fulfill my vows to you—
14 vows my lips promised and my mouth spoke
when I was in trouble.
15 I will sacrifice fat animals to you
and an offering of rams;
I will offer bulls and goats. *Selah*

16 Come and listen, all you who fear God;
let me tell you what he has done for me.
17 I cried out to him with my mouth;
his praise was on my tongue.
18 If I had cherished sin in my heart,
the Lord would not have listened;
19 but God has surely listened
and heard my voice in prayer.
20 Praise be to God,
who has not rejected my prayer
or withheld his love from me!

Psalm 67

For the director of music. With stringed instruments.
A psalm. A song.

1 May God be gracious to us and bless us
and make his face shine upon us, *Selah*

66:10 tested ... refined. Difficult trials in life test a believer's faith in God. Precious metals were refined by fire to remove any impurities and increase their value. The psalmist uses the metaphor for the process all believers go through as they approach maturity (12:6; 17:3).

66:16–20 all you who fear God. To those worshiping with him, the psalmist recounts God's acts and praises God for them.

66:17 his praise. Old Testament believers considered prayer and praise to be two kinds of communication with God. They would praise God even in the face of the difficulties from which they were seeking his deliverance (Phil. 4:6; 1 Tim. 2:1).

Ps. 67 The psalmist prays for God's blessing on behalf of the nation in this praise psalm. This was likely a congregational prayer used in liturgical worship, perhaps just before the priest's closing prayer. The prayer notes that all nations will witness God's works on behalf of Israel and turn to him as a result (65:2). Its structure is symmetrical—with an introductory prayer (vv. 1,2) and a concluding recognition of God's answer to the prayer (vv. 6,7). The heart of the psalm reflects the people's desire to experience God's answer to their prayer so the nations will turn to him.

67:1 make his face shine. The

[19]Praise be to the Lord, to God our Savior,
who daily bears our burdens. *Selah*
[20]Our God is a God who saves;
from the Sovereign LORD comes escape from death.

[21]Surely God will crush the heads of his enemies,
the hairy crowns of those who go on in their sins.
[22]The Lord says, "I will bring them from Bashan;
I will bring them from the depths of the sea,
[23]that you may plunge your feet in the blood of your foes,
while the tongues of your dogs have their share."

[24]Your procession has come into view, O God,
the procession of my God and King into the sanctuary.
[25]In front are the singers, after them the musicians;
with them are the maidens playing tambourines.
[26]Praise God in the great congregation;
praise the LORD in the assembly of Israel.
[27]There is the little tribe of Benjamin, leading them,
there the great throng of Judah's princes,
and there the princes of Zebulun and of Naphtali.

[28]Summon your power, O God[a];
show us your strength, O God, as you have done before.
[29]Because of your temple at Jerusalem
kings will bring you gifts.
[30]Rebuke the beast among the reeds,
the herd of bulls among the calves of the nations.
Humbled, may it bring bars of silver.
Scatter the nations who delight in war.
[31]Envoys will come from Egypt;
Cush[b] will submit herself to God.

[32]Sing to God, O kingdoms of the earth,
sing praise to the Lord, *Selah*
[33]to him who rides the ancient skies above,
who thunders with mighty voice.
[34]Proclaim the power of God,
whose majesty is over Israel,
whose power is in the skies.
[35]You are awesome, O God, in your sanctuary;
the God of Israel gives power and strength to his people.

Praise be to God!

[a]28 Many Hebrew manuscripts, Septuagint and Syriac; most Hebrew manuscripts *Your God has summoned power for you* [b]31 That is, the upper Nile region

68:24–27 Your procession. This may refer to carrying the Ark of the Covenant in the wilderness, to God's leadership of Israel's army or to the procession of the Savior King when he comes to earth to establish his rule (Rev. 19:4–21).

68:27 All the tribes of Israel join together, from the little tribe of Benjamin to the large and powerful tribe of Judah, and from the north and the south. **Benjamin, leading them.** The small tribe has a prominent role perhaps because the first king of Israel, Saul, came from it. Saul began the conquest of Israel's foes (1 Sam. 11:11; 14:20–23).

68:29 bring you gifts. Gifts of homage were made to Solomon (1 Kin. 10:1–10), but this also may look forward to the time kings would bring gifts to the baby Jesus (Matt. 2:1–12). Ultimately, the kings of the world will show their submission to Christ in this way (2:10–12).

68:33–35 The psalm ends with a crescendo of praise for God who dwells in power among his people, the God above all.

OPEN **1.** If your life were the subject of a political cartoon, what traits (physical, clothing, mannerisms) would be exaggerated to make sport of you or to make a humorous point? **2.** What's your favorite thirst-quencher? Are you thirsty now? Are there any of your favorite thirst-quenchers on hand?

STUDY **1.** David has become the butt of jokes in Israel. Why do people hate him (v. 4)? Is David over-stating his innocence or is all the trouble really unjustified (v. 5)? What groups of people opposing David can you identify in verses 4–12? **2.** What does David fear might happen to those who look up to him (v. 6)? **3.** Why does David think he is being subjected to such abuse in the media (vv. 7–11)? Who has written a song about him (v. 12)? **4.** "Help!" seems to sum up David's prayer in verses 13–18. Where do flashfloods occur? What must be David's spiritual condition? On what basis does he appeal to God for help? **5.** What does David wish for his enemies (vv. 22–28)? Do such prayers shock you? Why does he feel this way (vv. 19–21)? **6.** Verse 29 serves as a hinge to this psalm: How so? From the context, what must have happened to turn David's curse of men into praise of God? **7.** What does the phrase "captive people" tell us about when this psalm was composed (v. 33)? What does the psalmist hope for the exiles (v. 35)? Without a temple, what sacrifices can the people make (vv. 30–31)? **8.** How might recalling the experiences of David help the people at such a time of exile? **9.** The New Testament applies three verses in this psalm to Jesus (vv. 4,9,21). In what ways might Jesus have felt like David? Why wouldn't Jesus drink the wine he was offered, knowing it would ease his pain (v. 21; Matt. 27:34,48)?

Psalm 69

For the director of music.
To the tune of "Lilies." Of David.

1 Save me, O God,
for the waters have come up to my neck.
2 I sink in the miry depths,
where there is no foothold.
I have come into the deep waters;
the floods engulf me.
3 I am worn out calling for help;
my throat is parched.
My eyes fail,
looking for my God.
4 Those who hate me without reason
outnumber the hairs of my head;
many are my enemies without cause,
those who seek to destroy me.
I am forced to restore
what I did not steal.

5 You know my folly, O God;
my guilt is not hidden from you.

6 May those who hope in you
not be disgraced because of me,
O Lord, the LORD Almighty;
may those who seek you
not be put to shame because of me,
O God of Israel.
7 For I endure scorn for your sake,
and shame covers my face.
8 I am a stranger to my brothers,
an alien to my own mother's sons;
9 for zeal for your house consumes me,
and the insults of those who insult you fall on me.
10 When I weep and fast,
I must endure scorn;
11 when I put on sackcloth,
people make sport of me.
12 Those who sit at the gate mock me,
and I am the song of the drunkards.

Ps. 69 The psalmist, a king (perhaps David or his descendant), asks God for mercy and protection from his enemies in this lament psalm with messianic references. Similar to Psalm 22, which anticipates Christ's physical distress, this psalm focuses on his deep emotional and spiritual pain.

69:1–2 waters ... miry depths ... deep waters ... floods. This figurative language is used to describe deep pain and distress. The cause of the pain is enemy attacks (vv. 14,15,29), but also God's own "wounding" of the psalmist (v. 26).

69:4 without reason ... without cause. The psalmist has done nothing to deserve the treatment he is receiving, but enemies have conspired against him (35:19).

69:5–12 The psalmist's prayer acknowledges that his sin is worthy of God's discipline (his "wounding" in v. 26), but asks that other believers not be disgraced because of his failures. His sin was not against his enemies, so their attacks on him are unwarranted, though they mock him because of his distress (22:6–8). His prayer seeks God's restoration and vindication because of his faith and trust.

69:12 Those who sit at the gate ... drunkards. Everyone, from elders at the city gates to drunkards, mock him.

13 But I pray to you, O LORD,
in the time of your favor;
in your great love, O God,
answer me with your sure salvation.
14 Rescue me from the mire,
do not let me sink;
deliver me from those who hate me,
from the deep waters.
15 Do not let the floodwaters engulf me
or the depths swallow me up
or the pit close its mouth over me.
16 Answer me, O LORD, out of the goodness of your love;
in your great mercy turn to me.
17 Do not hide your face from your servant;
answer me quickly, for I am in trouble.
18 Come near and rescue me;
redeem me because of my foes.

19 You know how I am scorned, disgraced and shamed;
all my enemies are before you.
20 Scorn has broken my heart
and has left me helpless;
I looked for sympathy, but there was none,
for comforters, but I found none.
21 They put gall in my food
and gave me vinegar for my thirst.

22 May the table set before them become a snare;
may it become retribution and[a] a trap.
23 May their eyes be darkened so they cannot see,
and their backs be bent forever.
24 Pour out your wrath on them;
let your fierce anger overtake them.
25 May their place be deserted;
let there be no one to dwell in their tents.
26 For they persecute those you wound
and talk about the pain of those you hurt.
27 Charge them with crime upon crime;
do not let them share in your salvation.
28 May they be blotted out of the book of life
and not be listed with the righteous.

[a]22 Or *snare / and their fellowship become*

APPLY 1. When you feel up to your neck in hot water: Do you keep it to yourself? Do you cry on someone's shoulder? Do you tell everybody in sight? What response do you want from others: Good biblical answers? Advice? "I know how you feel"? No response, just a listening ear? **2.** Jesus never cursed his accusers as David did; instead, Jesus forgave his persecutors from the cross (Luke 23:34) and urged us to do the same (Matt. 5:10–12). How are you like David? Like Jesus? **3.** How do people today substitute formal religion ("an ox and bull") for heartfelt gratitude? What tips you off when this is happening to you? What can you do to keep the heart in your worship?

69:13–18 The psalmist continues to pray in spite of the mockery of him and his faith.

69:22–28 The psalmist asks God, in light of the wrongs done against him, to respond and vindicate him.

69:22–23 Paul applied these verses to Jews who turned away from Christ (Rom. 11:9,10).

69:23 The psalmist's enemies made fun of him because of his pain. Now he asks God to give them the same painful blind eyes (v. 3) and bent backs (38:5–8). **May ... their backs be bent.** Literally this is "May ... their loins give way," referring to the midsection which was considered the back's source of strength.

69:24–28 Pour out your wrath. The writer asks God to judge his enemies in a display of anger. Verse 25 was fulfilled by Judas Iscariot (Acts 1:20 combines these words with those of 109:8).

69:27 crime upon crime. The psalmist has been falsely charged with crimes (v. 4) and asks God to charge his enemies with the true crimes they have committed against him.

69:28 The psalmist seeks what he considers a fair solution: Since his enemies sought his death, they should experience death themselves. **book of life.** The Old Testament refers to this

29 I am in pain and distress;
may your salvation, O God, protect me.

30 I will praise God's name in song
and glorify him with thanksgiving.
31 This will please the LORD more than an ox,
more than a bull with its horns and hoofs.
32 The poor will see and be glad—
you who seek God, may your hearts live!
33 The LORD hears the needy
and does not despise his captive people.

34 Let heaven and earth praise him,
the seas and all that move in them,
35 for God will save Zion
and rebuild the cities of Judah.
Then people will settle there and possess it;
36 the children of his servants will inherit it,
and those who love his name will dwell there.

Psalm 70

For the director of music. Of David. A petition.

1 Hasten, O God, to save me;
O LORD, come quickly to help me.
2 May those who seek my life
be put to shame and confusion;
may all who desire my ruin
be turned back in disgrace.
3 May those who say to me, "Aha! Aha!"
turn back because of their shame.
4 But may all who seek you
rejoice and be glad in you;
may those who love your salvation always say,
"Let God be exalted!"

5 Yet I am poor and needy;
come quickly to me, O God.
You are my help and my deliverer;
O LORD, do not delay.

Psalm 71

1 In you, O LORD, I have taken refuge;
let me never be put to shame.

OPEN Are you a poor loser or good one? Under what situations have you recently found out?

STUDY 1. This psalm also appears at the end of Psalm 40. Why make it a separate song? **2.** David's enemies are poor losers, seeking his ruin and belittling God: How does David counteract them? **3.** How can King David see himself as "poor and needy" (v. 5)? Is he a bit of a whiner, or what?

APPLY What prayers of yours are marked "rush order"? Why? Is God obliging you? If not, do you exalt him, or do you grow impatient, even spiteful?

OPEN 1. Which would you rather keep and why: The mind of a 20-year-old, while your body ages? The body of a 20-year-old, while

frequently as God's divine list of all the righteous who enjoy his blessing of life (37:17,29; 55:22; 75:10). The New Testament use of the term includes those who have received God's gift of eternal life (Phil. 4:3; Rev. 3:5).

69:29 *The psalmist reprises his prayer* before he vows to praise God for deliverance (vv. 30–33). **protect me.** Literally this means "raise me to a high, safe place."

69:34–36 The psalmist calls on all to praise God, knowing that he will restore Judah's fortunes in the Promised Land.

Ps. 70 This brief "emergency" prayer for God's rescue in the face of enemy threat is similar to 40:13–17 and is related to Psalm 71. Requests for God to "come quickly" frame the lament (vv. 1,5).

70:2 be put to shame and confusion. David asks God to prove wrong those who take pleasure in his misery and assume God is unable to rescue his people.

70:4 God's rescue of the psalmist will not only restore him but will make all God's children glad with a reminder of their own sure salvation. **Let God be exalted!** This contrasts with the enemy's "Aha! Aha!" in verse 3 and proposes that God's salvation is certain.

[2] Rescue me and deliver me in your righteousness;
turn your ear to me and save me.
[3] Be my rock of refuge,
to which I can always go;
give the command to save me,
for you are my rock and my fortress.
[4] Deliver me, O my God, from the hand of the wicked,
from the grasp of evil and cruel men.

[5] For you have been my hope, O Sovereign LORD,
my confidence since my youth.
[6] From birth I have relied on you;
you brought me forth from my mother's womb.
I will ever praise you.
[7] I have become like a portent to many,
but you are my strong refuge.
[8] My mouth is filled with your praise,
declaring your splendor all day long.

[9] Do not cast me away when I am old;
do not forsake me when my strength is gone.
[10] For my enemies speak against me;
those who wait to kill me conspire together.
[11] They say, "God has forsaken him;
pursue him and seize him,
for no one will rescue him."
[12] Be not far from me, O God;
come quickly, O my God, to help me.
[13] May my accusers perish in shame;
may those who want to harm me
be covered with scorn and disgrace.

[14] But as for me, I will always have hope;
I will praise you more and more.
[15] My mouth will tell of your righteousness,
of your salvation all day long,
though I know not its measure.
[16] I will come and proclaim your mighty acts, O Sovereign LORD;
I will proclaim your righteousness, yours alone.
[17] Since my youth, O God, you have taught me,
and to this day I declare your marvelous deeds.
[18] Even when I am old and gray,
do not forsake me, O God,

your mind ages? **2.** What gets better with age? What gets worse?

STUDY 1. An elder statesman, perhaps David, wrote this psalm. What was his upbringing like (vv. 5–6,17)? What other circumstances sound similar to David's life? **2.** What does he now fear (vv. 9,18)? Why? How might he be a "portent" (someone who foreshadows; v. 7)? **3.** What would "righteousness" of God be (v. 19)? Why would the psalmist see it reaching up to the sky, when most people are unaware of it? **4.** What is the center of the psalmist's life (vv. 8,14–16, 22–24)? How does he hope God will reward him for this (vv. 13,21)? **5.** How can God "restore" the life of the old man? **6.** Can people see that you are redeemed, and would that put them to shame (v. 24)? **7.** Why would the psalmist be afraid of being rejected by God, when he knew he was redeemed?

APPLY 1. What do you fear most about growing older: Failing health? Failing mind? Becoming dependent? Death of family members? Your own death? **2.** Were you raised a Christian, or did you come to faith later in life? What are the advantages and disadvantages of either experience? **3.** What experience with God in the past gives you confidence now that he will be with you in the future? **4.** What would you like to declare to "the next generation"? Why not start this week?

71:5–8 Following an appeal to God for deliverance in verses 1–4, these verses *are a statement of confidence that the* Lord has always been the psalmist's hope.

71:5 since my youth. Even in his youth the writer put his hope and confidence in the Lord (22:9–10).

71:7 like a portent. Many wondered at him, thinking that God's help was a special sign of power similar to those God gave Moses. **strong refuge.** God gave shelter from danger throughout all the struggles of his life.

71:9–13 The psalmist's enemies assume that God has forsaken him. Now they will harm him. The psalmist asks God to continue to protect him in his later years as in the past. God's reputation was on the line, not just the psalmist's comfort. If God did not save him, the enemies' mockery of God's power would be vindicated.

71:13 He prays for justice—the demise of his enemies. After all, his enemies are also God's enemies.

71:14 This verse marks the turning point of the psalm. After his plea for help in verses 1–13, the psalmist here determines to hope in God as he has since his youth. He confidently expects God will deliver him.

71:15–18 This section of the psalm expresses the poet's determination to

your mind ages? 2. What gets better with age? What gets worse?

OPEN 1. To get your vote, what one characteristic must a candidate for the highest office in the land exhibit? What second trait? Third? **2.** Do you like your national anthem? With what lines do you agree or disagree most strongly?

STUDY 1. This psalm is dedicated to Solomon. To what other king does it allude (Isa. 9:6–7; Zech. 9:9–10)? **2.** What three qualities will the king bring his people (vv. 1–4)? What should he do about oppression? Why aren't middle or upper classes mentioned? **3.** How long

till I declare your power to the next generation,
your might to all who are to come.

19 Your righteousness reaches to the skies, O God,
you who have done great things.
Who, O God, is like you?
20 Though you have made me see troubles, many and bitter,
you will restore my life again;
from the depths of the earth
you will again bring me up.
21 You will increase my honor
and comfort me once again.

22 I will praise you with the harp
for your faithfulness, O my God;
I will sing praise to you with the lyre,
O Holy One of Israel.
23 My lips will shout for joy
when I sing praise to you—
I, whom you have redeemed.
24 My tongue will tell of your righteous acts
all day long,
for those who wanted to harm me
have been put to shame and confusion.

Psalm 72

Of Solomon.

1 Endow the king with your justice, O God,
the royal son with your righteousness.
2 He will[a] judge your people in righteousness,
your afflicted ones with justice.
3 The mountains will bring prosperity to the people,
the hills the fruit of righteousness.
4 He will defend the afflicted among the people
and save the children of the needy;
he will crush the oppressor.

[a]2 Or *May he;* similarly in verses 3-11 and 17

proclaim the Lord's righteousness and power. He has praised God since his youth. Now in old age, he pleads with God not to forsake him.

71:20 restore my life. The one who created him will renew his life, replacing bitter troubles with joy. **depths of the earth.** This metaphor expresses the psalmist's desperation. He feels as *though he were in the realm of the* dead, cast down beyond the grave.

71:22–24 The psalmist sums up with a vow to praise God as he anticipates God's answer to his prayer for deliverance. He is so confident of God's help that he even speaks in the past tense—as if God has already put his enemies to shame.

Ps. 72 This psalm is a prayer for the king. The nation wants God to appoint a king who is just and righteous, obedient to God in all he does. This is an *idealized* king who rules during a time of peace and glory for the nation. It could describe Solomon's kingdom, but it also prophesies the Messiah's coming kingdom, when Christ will return to rule the new heavens and new earth in perfect righteousness.

72:1 The entire prayer may be summed up in this verse. May the king be endowed with the ability to rule justly, making righteous decisions in accordance with God's will. Indeed, if Solomon is so blessed, his reign will reflect the rule of God himself. Solomon did, in fact, ask God to give him wisdom (1 Kin. 3:9–12).

72:3 A king ruling in righteousness would bring God's blessing of prosperity.

[5] He will endure[a] as long as the sun,
as long as the moon, through all generations.
[6] He will be like rain falling on a mown field,
like showers watering the earth.
[7] In his days the righteous will flourish;
prosperity will abound till the moon is no more.

[8] He will rule from sea to sea
and from the River[b] to the ends of the earth.[c]
[9] The desert tribes will bow before him
and his enemies will lick the dust.
[10] The kings of Tarshish and of distant shores
will bring tribute to him;
the kings of Sheba and Seba
will present him gifts.
[11] All kings will bow down to him
and all nations will serve him.

[12] For he will deliver the needy who cry out,
the afflicted who have no one to help.
[13] He will take pity on the weak and the needy
and save the needy from death.
[14] He will rescue them from oppression and violence,
for precious is their blood in his sight.

[15] Long may he live!
May gold from Sheba be given him.
May people ever pray for him
and bless him all day long.
[16] Let grain abound throughout the land;
on the tops of the hills may it sway.
Let its fruit flourish like Lebanon;
let it thrive like the grass of the field.
[17] May his name endure forever;
may it continue as long as the sun.

All nations will be blessed through him,
and they will call him blessed.

[18] Praise be to the LORD God, the God of Israel,
who alone does marvelous deeds.
[19] Praise be to his glorious name forever;
may the whole earth be filled with his glory.
Amen and Amen.

[20] This concludes the prayers of David son of Jesse.

[a]5 Septuagint; Hebrew *You will be feared* [b]8 That is, the Euphrates [c]8 Or *the end of the land*

will he rule (vv. 5–7)? Over what boundaries (v. 8)? How will the nations respond (vv. 9–11)? **4.** Since no Israelite king ever ruled such vast territory, what is the author saying in this royal extravagance? **5.** How does verse 17 relate to Abraham (Gen. 12:3)? To Christ? **6.** This psalm is regarded in Jewish and Christian tradition as "messianic." Given only this psalm to work with, how would you explain the Messiah to someone else?

APPLY 1. How do you feel about nationalism? Who rules you? Why have human government? Does God approve of all world leaders and their actions? **2.** Could you honestly say that God is your ruler? If not, who is? If so, what about your life reveals God's rule?

72:6 A righteous king is refreshing to the people, just like rain that causes plants to flourish.

72:8–11 lick the dust. His authority will extend all around the world. Even his enemies will submit to him.

72:17 name endure forever. This verse either refers to God, whose rule is eternal, or to a human king, whose reputation endures for generations. **All nations will be blessed.** The wording of this verse reminds of God's promise to Abraham in Genesis 12:3 and 22:18. Here the promise will be fulfilled through the Son of David—the Messiah.

OPEN If you had to choose between being (a) prosperous and wicked, or (b) poverty-stricken and pure in heart, what would you be? Why?

STUDY 1. Asaph is credited with chapters 50 and 73–83. He was most likely a poet associated with the temple. What is his nagging doubt in this psalm (vv. 2–3)? **2.** What has he seen (vv. 4–12)? What attitudes may be undermining his faith? **3.** Do you think Asaph is objective in what he sees? Why or why not? What does he find both attractive and negative in the lifestyle, world-view and agnosticism of the rich? **4.** What was he hoping his "pure heart" would get him (vv. 13–14)? What causes him to change his mind (vv. 15–17)? To what might the "sanctuary of God" refer? What new insight does he gain? Why does Asaph feel like God sleeps (v. 20; 35:23; 44:23)? **5.** What "glory" does Asaph have in mind (vv. 24–25; 16:9–11)? What path will he take toward it (vv. 23–28)? **6.** What constant hope literally surrounds Asaph's envy and despair (vv. 1,28)?

APPLY 1. Imagine your life now is just a dream (or a nightmare), and when you awake, all will return to normal. What heavy burden, human ill or gross injustice would you like to wish away, as if it were but a dream? Do you ever share Asaph's envy? Does his insight satisfy you? Why or why not? **2.** When your feet have stumbled, how have you recovered your balance? What could you do to let others know in your group that you are ready to help them when they stumble? **3.** Have you had a "sanctuary" experience? When?

BOOK III

Psalms 73–89

Psalm 73

A psalm of Asaph.

1 Surely God is good to Israel,
to those who are pure in heart.

2 But as for me, my feet had almost slipped;
I had nearly lost my foothold.
3 For I envied the arrogant
when I saw the prosperity of the wicked.

4 They have no struggles;
their bodies are healthy and strong.[a]
5 They are free from the burdens common to man;
they are not plagued by human ills.
6 Therefore pride is their necklace;
they clothe themselves with violence.
7 From their callous hearts comes iniquity[b];
the evil conceits of their minds know no limits.
8 They scoff, and speak with malice;
in their arrogance they threaten oppression.
9 Their mouths lay claim to heaven,
and their tongues take possession of the earth.
10 Therefore their people turn to them
and drink up waters in abundance.[c]
11 They say, "How can God know?
Does the Most High have knowledge?"

12 This is what the wicked are like—
always carefree, they increase in wealth.

13 Surely in vain have I kept my heart pure;
in vain have I washed my hands in innocence.
14 All day long I have been plagued;
I have been punished every morning.

15 If I had said, "I will speak thus,"
I would have betrayed your children.

[a]4 With a different word division of the Hebrew; Masoretic Text *struggles at their death; / their bodies are healthy* [b]7 Syriac (see also Septuagint); Hebrew *Their eyes bulge with fat* [c]10 The meaning of the Hebrew for this verse is uncertain.

Ps. 73 This is the first of eleven psalms (73–83) attributed to Asaph. He and his descendants were the leaders of one of David's Levitical choirs. The theme of most of these psalms is God's rule over the world. This psalm is a word of instruction contrasting the destinies of the righteous and the wicked. It answers the question, "Why do evil people prosper while many good *people suffer?" This psalm has many* similarities with Psalm 49.

73:1–14 Asaph is almost overwhelmed by doubts as he compares his own life to that of worldly people. His crisis of faith is triggered by the prosperity of the wicked.

73:4–12 A graphic picture of prosperous evildoers, these verses are clearly exaggerations for poetic effect. We see the prosperity of these success-oriented people in verses 4–5, and then the behavior that results from their prosperity in verses 6–9. Verses 10–12 show how the world views them.

73:6 pride is their necklace; clothe ... violence. These powerful images suggest that these people cover themselves with pride and violence. Rather than hiding these sins as most people would, they actually display them.

73:13–14 Asaph is plagued with doubts about the value of his salvation. He wonders if he has lived a pure life in vain, since the wicked seem to be better off than he is.

73:15–28 The turning point in Asaph's struggle comes when he goes to the temple to worship God (v. 17). His faith is renewed as he sees that the wicked

16 When I tried to understand all this,
it was oppressive to me
17 till I entered the sanctuary of God;
then I understood their final destiny.

18 Surely you place them on slippery ground;
you cast them down to ruin.
19 How suddenly are they destroyed,
completely swept away by terrors!
20 As a dream when one awakes,
so when you arise, O Lord,
you will despise them as fantasies.

21 When my heart was grieved
and my spirit embittered,
22 I was senseless and ignorant;
I was a brute beast before you.

23 Yet I am always with you;
you hold me by my right hand.
24 You guide me with your counsel,
and afterward you will take me into glory.
25 Whom have I in heaven but you?
And earth has nothing I desire besides you.
26 My flesh and my heart may fail,
but God is the strength of my heart
and my portion forever.

27 Those who are far from you will perish;
you destroy all who are unfaithful to you.
28 But as for me, it is good to be near God.
I have made the Sovereign LORD my refuge;
I will tell of all your deeds.

Psalm 74

A *maskil*[a] of Asaph.

1 Why have you rejected us forever, O God?
Why does your anger smolder against the sheep of your pasture?
2 Remember the people you purchased of old,

[a]Title: Probably a literary or musical term

Where? What happened? What are you doing to keep that faith perspective alive?

OPEN 1. How is it appropriate to use your hands at your church: Praying? Greeting? Raised in worship? Asking "why" with raised hands? **2.** Would you say you are a "summer" or "winter" person? In what way? What does the group think?

STUDY 1. Where in history must we place this psalm (vv.

will get their just desserts at the judgment.

73:18–20 This is the first solution to Asaph's doubts: *the wicked are in a* precarious position. Without warning they will come to ruin.

73:20 fantasies. When God rises up to punish the wicked, they will vanish like a dream and will turn out to be nothing but counterfeits of reality.

73:21–26 Here is the second solution to Asaph's dilemma: in contrast to the destruction facing evil people: his destiny will be glorious. For this reason, none of the evildoers' earthly prosperity looks attractive—nothing is more desirable than God.

Ps. 74 This psalm is a prayer for God to come to the aid of his people in the face of persecution from enemies. It was written during the time of the exile, when Israel was destroyed, the Promised Land devastated, and the temple in ruins. Verses 1–11 tell why the people needed help, and verses 13–23 are a statement of confidence in God's power and a call for God to rise up against the enemy.

74:1 Why. The first word of the psalm introduces a lament—a cry to God, and then a definition of the problem. The invasion of Israel was thought to be a sign of God's anger. It looked as though God had deserted the people.

74:2 Remember. The psalm is framed with pleas for God to "remember" (vv. 2,22). Here Asaph focuses on God's past faithfulness. **Mount Zion.** The wording of this verse and verses 12–17

3,7)? What crisis of faith does Jerusalem's destruction bring (vv. 1–2)? **2.** Why is this so perplexing to the "sheep of God's pasture"? What had the prophets said (v. 9; Jer. 6:6–8)? What "sign" proved them right (2 Kin. 25:1–21)? **3.** Why does the destruction of Jerusalem bring mockery to God (v. 10)? What do the people want God to do? **4.** Which verse serves as the "watershed" verse, on either side of which flow the two major streams of thought in this psalm? **5.** What event in Israel's history does the psalmist cite as evidence for his case (vv. 13–15)? What event in world history (vv. 16–17)? If God is so powerful, why doesn't he save the people from their enemies? **6.** What does the psalmist appeal to in the end? What does he think God cares about (vv. 19–21)? What "clamor" does he think God will want to silence (vv. 18,22–23)?

APPLY 1. On which side of the "watershed" are you: Focused on the "they" who ruined life for you? Or the "you" who can do something about it? **2.** Have you ever felt like God had forgotten you or your cause forever? What triggered your tears? Your anger? Or do you keep all such emotion inside? **3.** Can you be yourself with the group? With God? What would God do in your situation now if you freely expressed your feelings? What is God likely to do if you're not honest?

the tribe of your inheritance, whom you redeemed—
Mount Zion, where you dwelt.
3 Turn your steps toward these everlasting ruins,
all this destruction the enemy has brought on the sanctuary.

4 Your foes roared in the place where you met with us;
they set up their standards as signs.
5 They behaved like men wielding axes
to cut through a thicket of trees.
6 They smashed all the carved paneling
with their axes and hatchets.
7 They burned your sanctuary to the ground;
they defiled the dwelling place of your Name.
8 They said in their hearts, "We will crush them completely!"
They burned every place where God was worshiped in the land.
9 We are given no miraculous signs;
no prophets are left,
and none of us knows how long this will be.

10 How long will the enemy mock you, O God?
Will the foe revile your name forever?
11 Why do you hold back your hand, your right hand?
Take it from the folds of your garment and destroy them!

12 But you, O God, are my king from of old;
you bring salvation upon the earth.
13 It was you who split open the sea by your power;
you broke the heads of the monster in the waters.
14 It was you who crushed the heads of Leviathan
and gave him as food to the creatures of the desert.
15 It was you who opened up springs and streams;
you dried up the ever flowing rivers.
16 The day is yours, and yours also the night;
you established the sun and moon.
17 It was you who set all the boundaries of the earth;
you made both summer and winter.

18 Remember how the enemy has mocked you, O LORD,
how foolish people have reviled your name.

---

recalls the victory song of Exodus 15. The Israelites saw the destruction of Zion as a reversal of God's victory over Egypt.

74:3–8 These verses detail the Babylonians' methods for destroying the temple. The demolition was complete—every place of worship was destroyed.

74:9 no prophets are left. Most troubling to Asaph was the absence of prophets to give the people hope and tell them when these troubles would end. At this time *Jeremiah had been taken to* Egypt (Jer. 43:6–7), and Ezekiel had been deported to Babylon (Ezek. 1:1).

74:12 This is the center verse, the statement of confidence in God that conveys a truth presupposed by the rest of the psalm: God is Israel's king and he will bring salvation.

74:13–17 These verses form a section that outlines God's mighty acts of the past. The emphatic "you" of these verses contrasts with the "they" of verses 4–8.

74:13–14 Asaph recalls God the creator's deliverance of his people from Egypt. The image of a great sea monster comes from Near Eastern creation myths, in which the creator battled a many-headed sea monster before establishing order in creation. Leviathan is a symbol for Satan. Thus we see the interweaving of God's creative power with the salvation of the Israelites from the Egyptians and God's eventual rescue of believers from Satan. God opened the Red Sea for the Hebrews but destroyed the Egyptians when they tried to follow. God overcomes hostile powers, both spiritual and human, to establish order in the world.

74:15 God performed many water miracles. He gave the Israelites water in the wilderness (Ex. 17:5,6; Num. 20:8–13), enabled them to cross the Red Sea (Ex. 14) and the Jordan River (Josh. 3).

74:16–17 God established order in creation and is therefore ruler over all things. So if God is in control, why are bad things happening to Israel?

19 Do not hand over the life of your dove to wild beasts;
do not forget the lives of your afflicted people forever.
20 Have regard for your covenant,
because haunts of violence fill the dark places of the land.
21 Do not let the oppressed retreat in disgrace;
may the poor and needy praise your name.

22 Rise up, O God, and defend your cause;
remember how fools mock you all day long.
23 Do not ignore the clamor of your adversaries,
the uproar of your enemies, which rises continually.

Psalm 75

For the director of music. To the tune of "Do Not Destroy." A psalm of Asaph. A song.

1 We give thanks to you, O God,
we give thanks, for your Name is near;
men tell of your wonderful deeds.

2 You say, "I choose the appointed time;
it is I who judge uprightly.
3 When the earth and all its people quake,
it is I who hold its pillars firm. *Selah*
4 To the arrogant I say, 'Boast no more,'
and to the wicked, 'Do not lift up your horns.
5 Do not lift your horns against heaven;
do not speak with outstretched neck.' "

6 No one from the east or the west
or from the desert can exalt a man.
7 But it is God who judges:
He brings one down, he exalts another.
8 In the hand of the LORD is a cup
full of foaming wine mixed with spices;
he pours it out, and all the wicked of the earth
drink it down to its very dregs.

9 As for me, I will declare this forever;
I will sing praise to the God of Jacob.
10 I will cut off the horns of all the wicked,
but the horns of the righteous will be lifted up.

OPEN Which best describes you: Stiff neck? Rubber neck? Long neck? Stick your neck out? No neck?

STUDY **1.** What is the mood of this psalm: Triumphant? Desperate? Impatient? Other? **2.** When will the proud and defiant get their due (vv. 2–5)? Why not now? How bad does it have to get before God acts? What purpose of God could possibly be served by waiting any longer? **3.** What does the LORD's cup represent (v. 8)? **4.** For what does the psalmist praise God (v. 9)?

APPLY **1.** What has held the world together for you in hard times? Give an example. **2.** Does "because I said so" satisfy you? How do you deal with the mysteries of God's relationship to life's events? **3.** For what do you praise God today? Wondrous deeds? Upright judgment? Firm hold on the world? Uplifting righteousness? Other?

74:20 have regard for your covenant. Asaph pleads with God to remember his covenant with Israel. God had promised to be their God and to establish them securely in the Promised Land (Ex. 19:5–6; Lev. 26:11–12; Deut. 28:1–14).

74:22–23 defend your cause. In the end, the reason God should save his people is for his own glory. Israel is his nation, so its suffering causes God's name to be mocked—as if he isn't powerful enough to save them. Israel's enemies are God's enemies.

75:1 This psalm begins with the congregation praising God for his wonderful deeds and his presence with them. Note the contrast with 74:1 in which the people wondered why God had rejected and deserted them. Some scholars believe this psalm answers the questions in Psalm 74.

75:2–5 God is determined to judge the arrogant.

75:2 God will judge all people, but his judgment comes in his time, not ours. When he judges, no one on earth can help those under his wrath (v. 6).

75:4 arrogant ... wicked. God warns those who misinterpret his delay. Make no mistake—judgment will come. These arrogant people are described in Psalm 73:4–12.

75:6–9 The people affirm that God is judge and vow to praise him forever. God as judge controls the destinies of people. To some he gives authority, while others are brought low.

OPEN How did your parents show anger: A protruding vein? Invoking your full name? Invoking God's name? Giving a talking to? A spanking?

STUDY **1.** What local judgment has God just performed (vv. 3–6)? Does verse 5 fit Assyria's retreat (2 Kin. 19:35–36)? **2.** What does this show Israel about God (vv. 7–9)? Who does God judge? For what purpose? **3.** How does "wrath against men" bring God praise? Who are the "survivors"? **4.** What do particular judgments imply of God's wrath to come? **5.** Does God prevent wars today (vv. 3,6)? Why or why not? Does God care about those who suffer from invading armies?

APPLY **1.** How well do you know God as an angry judge: All too well? Casually? Never met on that basis? What does it mean to "fear God"? **2.** What vows have you taken? What vow do you want to make to the Lord today? Should it be private or should this group know and hold you to it?

OPEN **1.** What song always seems to bring back memories? Are they pleasant memories of fulfilled promise? Or painful memories of a failed one? **2.** If someone were to put your life story to song, would it most likely be: Jazz? Hard rock? Pop? Country-western? Gospel?

Psalm 76

For the director of music. With stringed instruments.
A psalm of Asaph. A song.

1 In Judah God is known;
his name is great in Israel.
2 His tent is in Salem,
his dwelling place in Zion.
3 There he broke the flashing arrows,
the shields and the swords, the weapons of war. *Selah*

4 You are resplendent with light,
more majestic than mountains rich with game.
5 Valiant men lie plundered,
they sleep their last sleep;
not one of the warriors
can lift his hands.
6 At your rebuke, O God of Jacob,
both horse and chariot lie still.
7 You alone are to be feared.
Who can stand before you when you are angry?
8 From heaven you pronounced judgment,
and the land feared and was quiet—
9 when you, O God, rose up to judge,
to save all the afflicted of the land. *Selah*
10 Surely your wrath against men brings you praise,
and the survivors of your wrath are restrained.[a]

11 Make vows to the LORD your God and fulfill them;
let all the neighboring lands
bring gifts to the One to be feared.
12 He breaks the spirit of rulers;
he is feared by the kings of the earth.

Psalm 77

For the director of music. For Jeduthun.
Of Asaph. A psalm.

1 I cried out to God for help;
I cried out to God to hear me.

[a] 10 Or *Surely the wrath of men brings you praise, / and with the remainder of wrath you arm yourself*

76:1–3 God has defeated enemies in Jerusalem and Zion, his dwelling places. Celebrate!

76:1 God is known. The good news of God's truth and power will be known particularly after the defeat of the enemies of Judah and Israel, his covenant people.

76:2 tent. Refers to the temple. The poet may be using an image of the temple as a campaign tent, such as would be used during battle.

76:4–6 These verses declare God's majesty. His power is greater than that of the enemy.

76:6 rebuke. Refers to either the power of God's sovereign majesty wielded over his enemies (9:5; Job 26:11) or the sheer force of his wrath (Isa. 66:15).

76:7–10 God's wrath accomplishes his sovereign purposes. The whole earth fears him.

76:10 brings you praise. God's wrath causes those he rescues to praise him. In the end, God is glorified when his righteous judgments are carried out.

77:1–9 Asaph is perplexed over God's lack of response to his prayers. He remembers days when he could sing in the night about God's deliverance. Now he has no reason to praise God.

2 When I was in distress, I sought the Lord;
at night I stretched out untiring hands
and my soul refused to be comforted.

3 I remembered you, O God, and I groaned;
I mused, and my spirit grew faint. *Selah*
4 You kept my eyes from closing;
I was too troubled to speak.
5 I thought about the former days,
the years of long ago;
6 I remembered my songs in the night.
My heart mused and my spirit inquired:

7 "Will the Lord reject forever?
Will he never show his favor again?
8 Has his unfailing love vanished forever?
Has his promise failed for all time?
9 Has God forgotten to be merciful?
Has he in anger withheld his compassion?" *Selah*

10 Then I thought, "To this I will appeal:
the years of the right hand of the Most High."
11 I will remember the deeds of the LORD;
yes, I will remember your miracles of long ago.
12 I will meditate on all your works
and consider all your mighty deeds.

13 Your ways, O God, are holy.
What god is so great as our God?
14 You are the God who performs miracles;
you display your power among the peoples.
15 With your mighty arm you redeemed your people,
the descendants of Jacob and Joseph. *Selah*

16 The waters saw you, O God,
the waters saw you and writhed;
the very depths were convulsed.
17 The clouds poured down water,
the skies resounded with thunder;
your arrows flashed back and forth.
18 Your thunder was heard in the whirlwind,
your lightning lit up the world;
the earth trembled and quaked.
19 Your path led through the sea,
your way through the mighty waters,
though your footprints were not seen.

20 You led your people like a flock
by the hand of Moses and Aaron.

STUDY 1. What modern titles could describe the psalmist's condition (vv. 1–4)? **2.** What question is at the bottom of his despair (vv. 7–9)? What do you think he remembers about God (vv. 3,6)? What "promise" seems to have failed? **3.** Where do his thoughts wander (vv. 10–12)? What are the "years of the right hand" (18:35; 139:10)? How can a meditation on the past help him? How does it answer his questions (vv. 7–9)? **4.** What specific acts of God does the poet recall (vv. 13–20)? What hints can you find of: The exodus? Moses at Sinai? Seven years of famine? The Flood? Creation? **5.** What is the difference between the remembering in verses 3–6 and verses 11–15? In this renewal of his faith, what new affirmations about God does he make? **6.** How would you try to comfort someone feeling like Asaph does? Would you point to the past, present or future? **7.** What does this poet's experience suggest is the interplay between physical, emotional and spiritual forces in managing stress?

APPLY 1. Are you feeling close to God, or do you long for "the good old days"? Could these days someday seem like the "good old days"? How do you keep your relationship with God fresh? **2.** What event in your past do you call to mind in times of trouble? How often do you think of past things? Do you tend to live in the past?

77:7–9 Asaph believes God has deserted him. He wonders: Is God angry? Has anger extinguished God's favor, love, mercy and compassion?

77:10–15 Asaph appeals to God's character and past faithfulness. He makes a conscious decision, in faith, to focus on God rather than on his troubles.

77:16–19 In vivid language, the poet describes God's display of power in delivering the Israelites from the Egyptians at the Red Sea (Ex. 14). The thunderstorm and earthquake, not mentioned in Exodus, were signs of God's power often associated by the Hebrew poets with the Lord's coming. God who displays his power through thunderstorm and earthquake made a way through the water to deliver his people from bondage.

OPEN 1. What were your favorite stories when you were young: Mother Goose? Aesop's Fables? Grimm's Fairy Tales? Homespun stories? Bible stories? Others? What are the favorite stories for any children you may have (at home, in school, in church)? **2.** Who is the keeper of your family stories and traditions? Do you ever hear of times when your folks or grandparents were young? What warning to future generations is implicit in their oft-repeated stories?

STUDY 1. People in biblical times did not have universal access to Scripture. What took the place of history books, schools and seminaries (vv. 1–8)? **2.** What does this believer want future believers to know and not forget about God? What would happen if the next generation forgets? Whose responsibility is it to see that they remember (Deut. 6:6–9)? **3.** Who are the men of Ephraim (vv. 9–11; Jer. 31:5–6)? Who does Ephraim come to symbolize as the list of sins grows (vv. 8–11)? **4.** How could anyone forget such acts of God? What difference should these miracles of the past make in their present lives? **5.** What test do they put to God (vv. 18–20)? What test does God put to them (Ex. 16:16–20)? Why do they demand further proofs of God's covenant love? **6.** What moods does God alternate between (vv. 21–24,30–31)? Why does God save them only to kill them (Num. 11:33–34)? What limits to divine patience do you see here? **7.** How would you characterize the role Israel relegated to God (vv. 32–39)? What name would you give to the "game" Israel plays with God: The spirit is willing, the flesh is weak? Flattery will get you anywhere? Lip service only? Insincerity? Let's buy some time? Good start, but no follow through? All head, no heart? **8.** Why does God have mercy on humans (vv. 38–39)? Is it fair for God to expect more from "a passing breeze"? **9.** What is Israel urged

Psalm 78

A *maskil*[a] of Asaph.

1 O my people, hear my teaching;
listen to the words of my mouth.
2 I will open my mouth in parables,
I will utter hidden things, things from of old—
3 what we have heard and known,
what our fathers have told us.
4 We will not hide them from their children;
we will tell the next generation
the praiseworthy deeds of the LORD,
his power, and the wonders he has done.
5 He decreed statutes for Jacob
and established the law in Israel,
which he commanded our forefathers
to teach their children,
6 so the next generation would know them,
even the children yet to be born,
and they in turn would tell their children.
7 Then they would put their trust in God
and would not forget his deeds
but would keep his commands.
8 They would not be like their forefathers—
a stubborn and rebellious generation,
whose hearts were not loyal to God,
whose spirits were not faithful to him.

9 The men of Ephraim, though armed with bows,
turned back on the day of battle;
10 they did not keep God's covenant
and refused to live by his law.
11 They forgot what he had done,
the wonders he had shown them.
12 He did miracles in the sight of their fathers
in the land of Egypt, in the region of Zoan.
13 He divided the sea and led them through;
he made the water stand firm like a wall.
14 He guided them with the cloud by day
and with light from the fire all night.
15 He split the rocks in the desert

[a]Title: Probably a literary or musical term

Ps. 78 This psalm, like Psalm 77, focuses on God saving his people. Stories of God's faithfulness and of the people's stubborn rebellion instruct and warn the people not to repeat Israel's past sins. Trusting and obeying God are covenant matters, a result of remembering God's saving acts. While Psalm 77 *focuses on God's faithfulness* to Israel under Moses' leadership, Psalm 78 speaks of both Moses's and David's leadership. This combination is appropriate. David was Israel's shepherd when the nation was clearly established under the leadership of a strong king. This completed the goals of the Exodus, begun under Moses, when the people moved out of bondage toward the Promised Land.

78:1–8 News of God's praiseworthy deeds and covenantal commands must be passed from generation to generation so that children will be faithful to him.

78:2 parables ... hidden things. Many biblical teachings have deeper meanings under the surface. Matthew 13:35 uses this verse as a prophecy of Jesus' teaching.

78:8 rebellious generation. The people of Israel are depicted as prodigal children of God (Deut. 9:6–7).

78:9–16 Ephraim, the northern kingdom, had forgotten God's miraculous acts and had broken God's covenantal Law.

and gave them water as abundant as the seas;
16 he brought streams out of a rocky crag
and made water flow down like rivers.

17 But they continued to sin against him,
rebelling in the desert against the Most High.
18 They willfully put God to the test
by demanding the food they craved.
19 They spoke against God, saying,
"Can God spread a table in the desert?
20 When he struck the rock, water gushed out,
and streams flowed abundantly.
But can he also give us food?
Can he supply meat for his people?"
21 When the LORD heard them, he was very angry;
his fire broke out against Jacob,
and his wrath rose against Israel,
22 for they did not believe in God
or trust in his deliverance.
23 Yet he gave a command to the skies above
and opened the doors of the heavens;
24 he rained down manna for the people to eat,
he gave them the grain of heaven.
25 Men ate the bread of angels;
he sent them all the food they could eat.
26 He let loose the east wind from the heavens
and led forth the south wind by his power.
27 He rained meat down on them like dust,
flying birds like sand on the seashore.
28 He made them come down inside their camp,
all around their tents.
29 They ate till they had more than enough,
for he had given them what they craved.
30 But before they turned from the food they craved,
even while it was still in their mouths,
31 God's anger rose against them;
he put to death the sturdiest among them,
cutting down the young men of Israel.

32 In spite of all this, they kept on sinning;
in spite of his wonders, they did not believe.
33 So he ended their days in futility
and their years in terror.
34 Whenever God slew them, they would seek him;
they eagerly turned to him again.
35 They remembered that God was their Rock,
that God Most High was their Redeemer.
36 But then they would flatter him with their mouths,
lying to him with their tongues;

to remember (vv. 40–55)? What plagues of Egypt underscore the psalmist's point? **10.** What events from the times of Joshua and Samuel are recalled (vv. 54–66)? Why does the psalmist say the Lord "abandoned the tabernacle of Shiloh" (v. 60; 1 Sam. 4:1–11)? How did God put the Philistines "to everlasting shame" (v. 66; 1 Sam. 5:6–10)? **11.** In the psalmist's mind, why did God have the temple built in Judah (vv. 67–69)? Since the temple was built by Solomon, why does the psalmist sing the praises of David? **12.** What is Asaph's message to Ephraim? To Judah? Will his generation avoid the mistakes of the past?

APPLY 1. How do you feel about God's involvement in the staging of your own continuing story: God has written every chapter? God is seen between the lines only? God is the audience? God is the director? God is hogging center stage? **2.** Would you like your part or God's part in that script to be rewritten? What ending would you prefer? Does the group play a part in it? **3.** What lesson would you like to pass along to the next generation? What historical example would you use to make your point? **4.** When does your patience run out? When do you feel like "abandoning your people"? How do you resolve the problem of your people going "the wrong way": Let the people go? Increase the consequences? Withdraw your blessing? Keep forgiving? Begin again? No good resolution yet?

78:32–39 Israel followed a pattern of rebelling against God, suffering his wrath, obeying for a time, then forgetting God's powerful punishment and rebelling again. From their earliest days in the desert, they continually broke their covenant with God. Yet God forgave them time after time.

78:32 did not believe. God's miracles did not convince the Israelites that he would help them conquer the Canaanites (Num. 14:11).

37 their hearts were not loyal to him,
they were not faithful to his covenant.
38 Yet he was merciful;
he forgave their iniquities
and did not destroy them.
Time after time he restrained his anger
and did not stir up his full wrath.
39 He remembered that they were but flesh,
a passing breeze that does not return.

40 How often they rebelled against him in the desert
and grieved him in the wasteland!
41 Again and again they put God to the test;
they vexed the Holy One of Israel.
42 They did not remember his power—
the day he redeemed them from the oppressor,
43 the day he displayed his miraculous signs in Egypt,
his wonders in the region of Zoan.
44 He turned their rivers to blood;
they could not drink from their streams.
45 He sent swarms of flies that devoured them,
and frogs that devastated them.
46 He gave their crops to the grasshopper,
their produce to the locust.
47 He destroyed their vines with hail
and their sycamore-figs with sleet.
48 He gave over their cattle to the hail,
their livestock to bolts of lightning.
49 He unleashed against them his hot anger,
his wrath, indignation and hostility—
a band of destroying angels.
50 He prepared a path for his anger;
he did not spare them from death
but gave them over to the plague.
51 He struck down all the firstborn of Egypt,
the firstfruits of manhood in the tents of Ham.
52 But he brought his people out like a flock;
he led them like sheep through the desert.
53 He guided them safely, so they were unafraid;
but the sea engulfed their enemies.
54 Thus he brought them to the border of his holy land,
to the hill country his right hand had taken.
55 He drove out nations before them
and allotted their lands to them as an inheritance;
he settled the tribes of Israel in their homes.

56 But they put God to the test
and rebelled against the Most High;

78:40–55 Israel quickly forgot God's powerful acts that saved them from Egyptian oppression. Yet God brought them through the sea and the desert, eventually establishing them in the Promised Land.

78:44–51 These verses recount the plagues God brought on Egypt (Ex. 7-12). Only the first and last are mentioned in order. Four of the plagues are omitted from this list.

78:56–64 Israel's next generation continued the rebellious disconnect from God, so God finally rejected them.

they did not keep his statutes.
57 Like their fathers they were disloyal and faithless,
as unreliable as a faulty bow.
58 They angered him with their high places;
they aroused his jealousy with their idols.
59 When God heard them, he was very angry;
he rejected Israel completely.
60 He abandoned the tabernacle of Shiloh,
the tent he had set up among men.
61 He sent ⌊the ark of⌋ his might into captivity,
his splendor into the hands of the enemy.
62 He gave his people over to the sword;
he was very angry with his inheritance.
63 Fire consumed their young men,
and their maidens had no wedding songs;
64 their priests were put to the sword,
and their widows could not weep.

65 Then the Lord awoke as from sleep,
as a man wakes from the stupor of wine.
66 He beat back his enemies;
he put them to everlasting shame.
67 Then he rejected the tents of Joseph,
he did not choose the tribe of Ephraim;
68 but he chose the tribe of Judah,
Mount Zion, which he loved.
69 He built his sanctuary like the heights,
like the earth that he established forever.
70 He chose David his servant
and took him from the sheep pens;
71 from tending the sheep he brought him
to be the shepherd of his people Jacob,
of Israel his inheritance.
72 And David shepherded them with integrity of heart;
with skillful hands he led them.

Psalm 79

A psalm of Asaph.

1 O God, the nations have invaded your inheritance;
they have defiled your holy temple,
they have reduced Jerusalem to rubble.
2 They have given the dead bodies of your servants
as food to the birds of the air,
the flesh of your saints to the beasts of the earth.

OPEN 1. If your house were on fire, what one possession would you save? What would you make sure got left behind? **2.** Before facing a firing squad, what would be your last request?

STUDY 1. What does this psalm lament (vv. 1–4; 2 Kin. 25:8–12)? **2.** Did God feel like the people of Jerusalem had been "servants"

78:60 Shiloh. Located in Ephraim, Shiloh was the center of worship during the latter period of the judges.

78:61 his might ... his splendor. These words refer to the Ark of the Covenant and emphasize its role as the sign of God's dominion over Israel. The ark was lost when the Philistines won the battle of Aphek (1 Sam. 4:1–11,21–22).

79:1–4 The psalm opens with a review of the nations' sin. Asaph laments the devastation of Jerusalem by foreign nations. God's temple had been defiled and reduced to rubble. God's people lay slaughtered, their bodies eaten by animals because no one was alive to bury the dead. God's chosen people were being mocked by the world.

79:2 your servants. Although the Israelites were rejected by God and banished from the Promised Land, they still claim a covenantal relationship with God (v. 13).

(v. 10; Jer. 5:1–2)? How did the exile make the God of the Jews look (v. 4)? **3.** Is the people's plea, "How long, O LORD" an expression of trust or self-pity (v. 5)? **4.** What two things do they ask God to do (vv. 6–8)? Are they responsible for what has happened (vv. 8–9)? Who is? **5.** What is an "avenger of blood" (v. 10; Num. 35:19–21)? In Israel's view, how would avenging their blood be in God's best interest (v. 12)? **6.** How much space is given to repentance? Praising God? Seeking vengeance? How would you react to such prayers if you were God?

APPLY 1. How would you react if the events recorded in verses 1–4 were happening in your church or community? Has distress ever given your church, family or friends the opportunity to pull together? **2.** In what ways does the world ask "Where is your God?" What answer can you give? Where can you point to the power of God? **3.** Are you asking: How long? Right now? What makes you impatient? Can the group step in for you?

OPEN 1. What would you say you have "planted" in your life to this point: Nothing but weeds? A little sapling? A fruit tree? A giant Sequoia? **2.** How is that planting doing right now: Suffering from drought? Bug-infested? Thriving? Being cut down by others?

STUDY 1. Why is Joseph mentioned (vv. 1–2; Gen. 46:19–21)? Who do these names rep-

3 They have poured out blood like water
all around Jerusalem,
and there is no one to bury the dead.
4 We are objects of reproach to our neighbors,
of scorn and derision to those around us.

5 How long, O LORD? Will you be angry forever?
How long will your jealousy burn like fire?
6 Pour out your wrath on the nations
that do not acknowledge you,
on the kingdoms
that do not call on your name;
7 for they have devoured Jacob
and destroyed his homeland.
8 Do not hold against us the sins of the fathers;
may your mercy come quickly to meet us,
for we are in desperate need.

9 Help us, O God our Savior,
for the glory of your name;
deliver us and forgive our sins
for your name's sake.
10 Why should the nations say,
"Where is their God?"
Before our eyes, make known among the nations
that you avenge the outpoured blood of your servants.
11 May the groans of the prisoners come before you;
by the strength of your arm
preserve those condemned to die.

12 Pay back into the laps of our neighbors seven times
the reproach they have hurled at you, O Lord.
13 Then we your people, the sheep of your pasture,
will praise you forever;
from generation to generation
we will recount your praise.

Psalm 80

For the director of music. To ⌊the tune of⌋ "The Lilies of the Covenant." Of Asaph. A psalm.

1 Hear us, O Shepherd of Israel,
you who lead Joseph like a flock;
you who sit enthroned between the cherubim, shine forth
2 before Ephraim, Benjamin and Manasseh.
Awaken your might;
come and save us.

79:5–8 With the familiar lament "How long?" Israel begs God to forgive them and judge the nations who do not acknowledge him.

79:6 Pour out your wrath. A prayer for curses on one's enemies is often part of psalms of lament. These prayers are based on God's covenant promise to Abraham to curse those who curse him (Gen. 12:2,3).

79:9–11 A prayer for God to help, forgive his people and punish their enemies. The appeal is based on God's character and reputation among the nations. A plea for God's power.

80:1 God is portrayed as a shepherd of Israel. The same image is used by Christ to describe his relationship with Christians in John 10. God leads Israel like a shepherd leads a flock. **Joseph.** Here refers to the northern kingdom.

3 Restore us, O God;
make your face shine upon us,
that we may be saved.

4 O LORD God Almighty,
how long will your anger smolder
against the prayers of your people?
5 You have fed them with the bread of tears;
you have made them drink tears by the bowlful.
6 You have made us a source of contention to our neighbors,
and our enemies mock us.

7 Restore us, O God Almighty;
make your face shine upon us,
that we may be saved.

8 You brought a vine out of Egypt;
you drove out the nations and planted it.
9 You cleared the ground for it,
and it took root and filled the land.
10 The mountains were covered with its shade,
the mighty cedars with its branches.
11 It sent out its boughs to the Sea,[a]
its shoots as far as the River.[b]

12 Why have you broken down its walls
so that all who pass by pick its grapes?
13 Boars from the forest ravage it
and the creatures of the field feed on it.
14 Return to us, O God Almighty!
Look down from heaven and see!
Watch over this vine,
15 the root your right hand has planted,
the son[c] you have raised up for yourself.

16 Your vine is cut down, it is burned with fire;
at your rebuke your people perish.
17 Let your hand rest on the man at your right hand,
the son of man you have raised up for yourself.
18 Then we will not turn away from you;
revive us, and we will call on your name.

[a] 11 Probably the Mediterranean [b] 11 That is, the Euphrates [c] 15 Or *branch*

resent? From what do they need to be saved (2 Kin. 17:7–8)? **2.** What does "make your face shine upon us" mean (v. 3; Num. 6:24–26)? **3.** What is their affliction? What do you think is most painful about their trial of faith (vv. 4–6)? **4.** How do you read the symbols in the allegory of the vine (vv. 8–16)? Is the "vine" the northern kingdom? What does its great size mean? What is the removal of the walls (Isa. 5:5–6)? The boar (v. 13)? The son (v. 15)? **5.** How is the change in the refrain significant (v. 14)? Is this psalm saying that only God can close the distance the people feel? **6.** Who is the "son of man" mentioned in verse 17: The nation of Israel (Ex. 4:22)? The king of the returning exiles? A future Davidic king? What three images in this psalm did Jesus apply to himself (John 10:11; 15:1; 17:1)?

APPLY 1. What do you do in times of trouble and need: Pray for God's restoration? Turn to other people? Go it on your own? Retreat in frustration? Does God want you to respond differently? **2.** What is your "bowl of tears"? Is there any relief in sight? How can you keep from being overwhelmed? Can the group help? **3.** How do you work through conflicts when you are angry at someone? Do you let anger out or hide it inside?

80:3 make your face shine upon us. The phrasing of this verse echoes the priestly benediction "The LORD make his face shine upon you" (Num. 6:25).

80:4–7 Asaph laments God's severe punishment of his people. He feels that their prayers for deliverance have gone unanswered.

80:5 bread of tears. A reference to the manna and water that God provided for Israel in the wilderness (Ex. 16:4; Num. 20:1–13). Asaph's point is that God provided nourishment for past generations, but to the people of this generation he has only given tears.

80:8–16 The metaphor of God as a gardener caring for Israel, the vine, graphically contrasts Israel's former condition with the present. The psalmist reminds God of his tender care for Israel in the past and how pitiful Israel's present condition is (Isa. 5:1–7; Hos. 10:1; John 15).

80:12 broken down its walls. The Lord removed his hand of protection from Israel, making it vulnerable to attacks from enemies.

80:14 Look down from heaven. Asaph begs God to observe the sorry state of Israel and have compassion on his people.

80:17 man at your right hand. This phrase may refer to Israel's king honored in God's presence, or to Israel itself being God's right hand because it has been planted and raised up by God.

80:18 In response to God's revival, the poet vows to trust and worship God alone.

19 Restore us, O LORD God Almighty;
make your face shine upon us,
that we may be saved.

Psalm 81

For the director of music.
According to *gittith.*[a] Of Asaph.

1 Sing for joy to God our strength;
shout aloud to the God of Jacob!
2 Begin the music, strike the tambourine,
play the melodious harp and lyre.

3 Sound the ram's horn at the New Moon,
and when the moon is full, on the day of our Feast;
4 this is a decree for Israel,
an ordinance of the God of Jacob.
5 He established it as a statute for Joseph
when he went out against Egypt,
where we heard a language we did not understand.[b]

6 He says, "I removed the burden from their shoulders;
their hands were set free from the basket.
7 In your distress you called and I rescued you,
I answered you out of a thundercloud;
I tested you at the waters of Meribah. *Selah*

8 "Hear, O my people, and I will warn you—
if you would but listen to me, O Israel!
9 You shall have no foreign god among you;
you shall not bow down to an alien god.
10 I am the LORD your God,
who brought you up out of Egypt.
Open wide your mouth and I will fill it.

11 "But my people would not listen to me;
Israel would not submit to me.
12 So I gave them over to their stubborn hearts
to follow their own devices.

13 "If my people would but listen to me,
if Israel would follow my ways,
14 how quickly would I subdue their enemies
and turn my hand against their foes!
15 Those who hate the LORD would cringe before him,

[a]Title: Probably a musical term [b]5 Or / *and we heard a voice we had not known*

OPEN 1. What food or drink would really "hit the spot"? **2.** How do you feel about going to the dentist: Fear? Jaw clenches? Mouth quivers? You're glad someone is taking care of you?

STUDY 1. What festival begins after the first full moon of the Jewish New Year (vv. 1–3; Lev. 23:34–36)? What is the purpose of the celebration (Lev. 23:42–43)? **2.** From what "basket" are the people free (v. 6)? What test did God give them at Meribah (v. 7; Num. 20:1–13)? **3.** Does God's mood fit the party spirit (vv. 8–12)? What does God want the people to do? How should reliving the past for seven days help get the message through? **4.** How else would Israel benefit by listening to the Lord (vv. 13–16)? What is "honey from the rock" (v. 16; Deut. 32:13–14)?

APPLY 1. What excites you about your relationship with God? Have you experienced the freedom and spontaneity expressed in this psalm? If so, how? If not, why not? **2.** Has God ever lifted a burden from your shoulders? What was it? What happened? Are you carrying a burden now? **3.** How can stubborness be a good quality and also be a trap? How do stubbornness and persistence differ?

Ps. 81 This festival psalm begins as a psalm of praise and becomes a psalm of admonition. It was probably used at the festival of tabernacles (v. 3) that commemorated God's care of his *people during the desert journey.* This festival was also a feast of thanksgiving for the harvest.

81:4 The psalmist calls the congregation to come to the festival. God's Law and their national law require their attendance.

81:6 I removed the burden. God delivered his people from forced labor in Egypt (Ex. 1).

81:7 I answered. God revealed himself to Moses on Mount Sinai.

I tested you. A reference to Israel's wandering in the desert, which was commemorated in the Feast of Tabernacles.

81:10 Open wide your mouth. The people are admonished to trust God alone for their needs. God will respond by taking care of them, as he did in the desert.

and their punishm ould last forever.
16 But you would be the finest of wheat;
with honey fro ck I would satisfy you."

Psalm 82

A psalm of Asaph.

1 God p eat assembly;
h among the "gods":

2 defend the unjust
ty to the wicked? *Selah*
f the weak and fatherless;
nts of the poor and oppressed.
and needy;
om the hand of the wicked.

ning, they understand nothing.
out in darkness;
ations of the earth are shaken.

ou are "gods";
are all sons of the Most High.'
ut you will die like mere men;
you will fall like every other ruler."

8 Rise up, O God, judge the earth,
for all the nations are your inheritance.

Psalm 83

A song. A psalm of Asaph.

1 O God, do not keep silent;
be not quiet, O God, be not still.
2 See how your enemies are astir,
how your foes rear their heads.
3 With cunning they conspire against your people;
they plot against those you cherish.
4 "Come," they say, "let us destroy them as a nation,
that the name of Israel be remembered no more."

[a]2 The Hebrew is plural.

OPEN What trial is making the news right now? Is the accused guilty as far as you can tell?

STUDY 1. Who are the "gods" (v. 1)? Angels and devils (1 Kin. 22:19; Job 1:6)? Rulers and judges in Israel (Ex. 21:6, 22:8–9,28)? **2.** Of what does God accuse them (vv. 2–4)? Why is God so concerned about those with the least power? **3.** Why does God call them "gods" when he thinks so little of them (v. 5)? **4.** Why do the "gods" misuse power (vv. 6–7)? What incorrect assumption have they made? **5.** How did Jesus use this psalm when he was "on trial" (John 10:30–39)?

APPLY 1. What responsibility do you have to the weak and needy? Can the group help? **2.** In what ways do you feel you "walk about in darkness"?

OPEN What war, past or present, do you follow? Why does it interest you? Why are wars intriguing?

STUDY 1. What is Asaph's problem (vv. 2–4)? How does he try to interest God in his cause (vv. 2,5)? **2.** Why are these enemies so ruthless? What could Israel have done to make them want to wipe out their memory? **3.** What happened to the Hagrites (v. 6; 1 Chr. 5:10)? To Gebal, Philistia and Tyre (v. 7; Josh. 13:1–7)? Who now fuels the wave of

---

81:16 finest of wheat ... honey from the rock. God promised that if *the people* obey him, he would subdue their enemies *and give them prosperity*. Wheat and honey (which often came from hives built among rocks) were symbols of prosperity.

82:1 great assembly. God presides over the court of the great assembly in heaven. The rulers and judges of the earth are called before him to give account of their judgments. **gods.** A sarcastic reference to the judges of the earth.

82:3–4 God reviews his commands to the judges of the earth: to administer true justice and provide the defenseless with a place of protection against their oppressors.

82:5 They know nothing. The indictment against these judges is that they live in moral darkness. They do not take their responsibility seriously, so God's Law is undermined.

82:7 die like mere men. No matter how exalted their position on earth, corrupt judges will suffer the same fate as other men.

Ps. 83 In a prayer intended to vindicate the glory of God, Asaph uses strong words against the wicked.

83:1–4 Asaph calls on God to judge the wicked and to protect Israel in the face of grave danger.

83:4 let us destroy them. Israel's enemies want to wipe them out.

revenge (v. 8)? **4.** From what did the judges protect the people of Israel (vv. 9–12; Judg. 4:1-7; 7:19–8:21)? Who are these people and why were they punished? **5.** What does the psalmist want God to do to enemies present (vv. 9–18)? How does this cry for vengeance sit with Jesus' belief about loving enemies?

APPLY 1. Are you generally quiet or talkative? When do you go against your norm: speaking out for once or finally shutting up? How do you feel about periods of silence in conversations? **2.** When have you wanted God to be more "talkative" in your life? How do you communicate your desire to God to "break the silence"? **3.** Who are your opponents in the "game of life" right now? Are your enemies also God's? Do you pray for vengeance or the grace to love your enemy?

OPEN 1. Do you like "roughing it"? Backpacks and tents? Or do you prefer hotels and bathrooms? **2.** With whom do you feel "at home"? Why? What do you like to do to make someone feel "at home" with you?

STUDY 1. Who were the sons of Korah, to whom this

5 With one mind they plot together;
they form an alliance against you—
6 the tents of Edom and the Ishmaelites,
of Moab and the Hagrites,
7 Gebal,[a] Ammon and Amalek,
Philistia, with the people of Tyre.
8 Even Assyria has joined them
to lend strength to the descendants of Lot.

9 Do to them as you did to Midian,
as you did to Sisera and Jabin at the river Kishon,
10 who perished at Endor
and became like refuse on the ground.
11 Make their nobles like Oreb and Zeeb,
all their princes like Zebah and Zalmunna,
12 who said, "Let us take possession
of the pasturelands of God."

13 Make them like tumbleweed, O my God,
like chaff before the wind.
14 As fire consumes the forest
or a flame sets the mountains ablaze,
15 so pursue them with your tempest
and terrify them with your storm.
16 Cover their faces with shame
so that men will seek your name, O LORD.

17 May they ever be ashamed and dismayed;
may they perish in disgrace.
18 Let them know that you, whose name is the LORD—
that you alone are the Most High over all the earth.

Psalm 84

For the director of music. According to *gittith*.[b]
Of the Sons of Korah. A psalm.

1 How lovely is your dwelling place,
O LORD Almighty!
2 My soul yearns, even faints,

[a]7 That is, Byblos [b]Title: Probably a musical term

83:5–8 These verses rehearse the acts of these evil enemies. The threat is from a huge alliance of nations, all set against Israel.

83:6 Hagrites. This refers either to Ishmaelites (descendants of Hagar) or a confederacy of Arabians.

83:8 Assyria. At this time, Assyria was a declining power.

83:9–12 *Recalling God's acts of judgment, this section refers to the time of* the judges. Threats to God's kingdom on earth must be crushed so that his kingdom may shape the destiny of the world (Judg. 4,7).

83:13–18 Asaph calls on God to judge the wicked, wiping them out just as they have plotted to do to Israel.

83:15 God, pictured here as a heavenly warrior, uses natural disasters as a weapon against enemies.

83:18 Asaph's motive in asking God to wipe out Israel's enemies *is that God's name will be glorified.* He longs for the entire earth to acknowledge the one true God and submit to his rule.

Ps. 84 This psalm uses the occasion of a pilgrimage to the temple to expound on the delight of worshiping God. It covers the psalmist's responses to the temple as he arrives there (vv. 2–4), the joy of journeying there (vv. 5–7), a prayer uttered at the temple (vv. 8–9) and the concluding feelings of the worshiper (vv. 10–12). Throughout the poem, home is used as a metaphor for the temple.

84:1 The psalmist speaks of the temple, God's dwelling, as a beloved place. At that time God's people had to go to Jerusalem to draw near to God. Today we draw near to God in prayer, from anywhere at all.

for the courts of the LORD;
my heart and my flesh cry out
for the living God.

[3]Even the sparrow has found a home,
and the swallow a nest for herself,
where she may have her young—
a place near your altar,
O LORD Almighty, my King and my God.
[4]Blessed are those who dwell in your house;
they are ever praising you. *Selah*

[5]Blessed are those whose strength is in you,
who have set their hearts on pilgrimage.
[6]As they pass through the Valley of Baca,
they make it a place of springs;
the autumn rains also cover it with pools.[a]
[7]They go from strength to strength,
till each appears before God in Zion.

[8]Hear my prayer, O LORD God Almighty;
listen to me, O God of Jacob. *Selah*
[9]Look upon our shield,[b] O God;
look with favor on your anointed one.

[10]Better is one day in your courts
than a thousand elsewhere;
I would rather be a doorkeeper in the house of my God
than dwell in the tents of the wicked.
[11]For the LORD God is a sun and shield;
the LORD bestows favor and honor;
no good thing does he withhold
from those whose walk is blameless.

[12]O LORD Almighty,
blessed is the man who trusts in you.

[a]6 Or *blessings* [b]9 Or *sovereign*

psalm is attributed (1 Chr. 26:1–19)? With what are they enamored (vv. 1–2)? **2.** Why does the psalmist mention birds in verse 3? Why do the Korahites love their job (v. 4)? **3.** Verses 5–7 describe one of the three annual pilgrimages to the Jerusalem Temple. Which one might meet with "autumn rains" (Lev. 23:39–43)? **4.** "Baca" is Hebrew for "balsam tree" and also comes from the root "to weep." What happened to David in this valley (2 Sam. 5:22–25)? What image does the poet give you of the pilgrims (vv. 6–7)? **5.** What do they pray in the temple (vv. 8–9)? Who is the "shield" or "anointed one"? **6.** What could be so good about being in the temple courts (vv. 10–12)? What keeps it from getting repetitious? **7.** Whose walk is "blameless" (v. 11)?

APPLY 1. What makes worship either dull or exciting for you? **2.** Are you more of a "settler" or a "pilgrim"? Why? What does insecurity do to you? How does this psalm make you feel about God's role in your life choices?

84:3 The psalmist longs to have the same unhindered access to God's temple that birds have as they nest in the temple. The image shows that God cares for even the lowliest parts of his creation. Nesting birds highlight the temple as home for *all* who worship God.

84:5–7 The psalmist recalls the joyful journey of those who make a pilgrimage to Zion. No matter how difficult the journey, the joy of coming to God's presence strengthens the weary.

84:5 those whose strength is in you. These are the people who trust in God for deliverance and sustenance. **who have set their hearts on pilgrimage.** These travelers come to Zion not so much from obligation as joy at drawing near to God.

84:6 Valley of Baca. Also translated Valley of Weeping, this phrase refers to the difficulties pilgrims face on their journey. Even the desert areas become as springs to them because their joyful anticipation of the temple refreshes them.

84:8–9 As part of his worship in the temple, the psalmist prays for God to bless the king in Jerusalem.

84:9 our shield. Refers to the king in Jerusalem, the one God anointed to rule over his people.

84:10–12 The worshiper expresses his feelings at the conclusion of his worship experience. With eloquent words of antithesis (one day versus a thousand days, God's courts versus other places, doorkeeper versus an owner of tents, God's house versus human tents), the poet subverts conventional standards of value and shows us what is truly worthwhile.

84:10 doorkeeper. A humble servant in the temple.

OPEN Relatives excluded, who gave you your first kiss? Was it what you expected? Did you try again?

STUDY **1.** Which verses are about the past? The present? The future? What are the restored fortunes of Jacob (v. 1)? **2.** How is the present going? What tension do verses 1–3 and 4–7 create? How would you explain the word "revive" in verse 6? **3.** What do verses 4–7 give as the cause of God's anger? What is a sign of revival, both personal and corporate (v. 6)? **4.** What is dangerous about a crisis of faith (v. 8)? What does it mean for God's glory to dwell in the land (v. 9; Ezek. 11:22–24)? **5.** What truth is expressed in verses 10–12? What is God's part of the deal? What is the people's? **6.** What's the meaning of verse 13? How might this be a messianic promise?

APPLY **1.** Are you disappointed that something didn't turn out the way you hoped it would? How might this psalm help you? **2.** What pattern of faith unfolds in this psalm? In your life? **3.** What does it mean to let God's glory dwell in your life?

Psalm 85

For the director of music.
Of the Sons of Korah. A psalm.

1 You showed favor to your land, O LORD;
you restored the fortunes of Jacob.
2 You forgave the iniquity of your people
and covered all their sins. *Selah*
3 You set aside all your wrath
and turned from your fierce anger.

4 Restore us again, O God our Savior,
and put away your displeasure toward us.
5 Will you be angry with us forever?
Will you prolong your anger through all generations?
6 Will you not revive us again,
that your people may rejoice in you?
7 Show us your unfailing love, O LORD,
and grant us your salvation.

8 I will listen to what God the LORD will say;
he promises peace to his people, his saints—
but let them not return to folly.
9 Surely his salvation is near those who fear him,
that his glory may dwell in our land.

10 Love and faithfulness meet together;
righteousness and peace kiss each other.
11 Faithfulness springs forth from the earth,
and righteousness looks down from heaven.
12 The LORD will indeed give what is good,
and our land will yield its harvest.
13 Righteousness goes before him
and prepares the way for his steps.

OPEN **1.** What "sign of goodness" do you look forward to receiving from your parents that lets you know you are special? **2.** Did you ever need a lifeguard? Ever wish you could be one?

Psalm 86

A prayer of David.

1 Hear, O LORD, and answer me,
for I am poor and needy.

85:1 restored the fortunes of Jacob. This psalm is a prayer for renewal written when God restored the people following a catastrophe—perhaps the Babylonian captivity.

85:3 set aside all your wrath. God forgave the people's sins and turned his wrath aside. Surely God loves them.

85:4–7 These verses are a petition for revival. The poet knows that Israel's troubles are a sign of God's displeasure.

85:8–9 The psalmist expects that God will act soon to restore his people.

85:8 I will listen. The psalmist will wait for a word from the Lord. He expects God to send the promised peace.

85:9 glory. The manifestation of God's presence is called his glory. Wherever God's mercy is displayed, his glory is revealed.

85:10–13 God will restore his people.

85:10 Love and faithfulness ... righteousness and peace. God's attributes will be perfectly unified when he restores his people. These words express God's favor toward his people and are perhaps a vision of the coming kingdom of God.

85:11 Faithfulness springs forth. This image connotes prosperity for God's people. **righteousness looks down.** In other words, God's covenant blessing of righteousness rests on Israel.

Ps. 86 Enemy attacks on the psalmist prompt this lament and prayer for God's rescue. The psalmist, who identifies himself as God's "servant" (v. 2), may have been David. If not David, then a king who had a close relationship with God. His enemies may have been other nations seeking to overthrow Israel or traitors within his own kingdom

86:1 poor and needy. Often in the psalms the "poor" are those not neces-

[2] Guard my life, for I am devoted to you.
You are my God; save your servant
who trusts in you.
[3] Have mercy on me, O Lord,
for I call to you all day long.
[4] Bring joy to your servant,
for to you, O Lord,
I lift up my soul.

[5] You are forgiving and good, O Lord,
abounding in love to all who call to you.
[6] Hear my prayer, O LORD;
listen to my cry for mercy.
[7] In the day of my trouble I will call to you,
for you will answer me.

[8] Among the gods there is none like you, O Lord;
no deeds can compare with yours.
[9] All the nations you have made
will come and worship before you, O Lord;
they will bring glory to your name.
[10] For you are great and do marvelous deeds;
you alone are God.

[11] Teach me your way, O LORD,
and I will walk in your truth;
give me an undivided heart,
that I may fear your name.
[12] I will praise you, O Lord my God, with all my heart;
I will glorify your name forever.
[13] For great is your love toward me;
you have delivered me from the depths of the grave.[a]

[14] The arrogant are attacking me, O God;
a band of ruthless men seeks my life—

[a]13 Hebrew *Sheol*

STUDY **1.** What four reasons does David give for God to answer him (vv. 1–4)? Is he boasting in his own piety? Why or why not? Which reason do you think would be most convincing to God? **2.** What fifth reason does he give (v. 7)? Does he sound confident or wishful? **3.** What do verses 8–10 affirm about God? On what basis does David say all nations will worship Yahweh? Has this ever been the case? **4.** Why is David now moved to make promises to God (vv. 11–13)? What does he pledge? What is an undivided heart? What feeling underlies his praise (v. 13)? **5.** Why is he still bothered (v. 14)? What kind of "sign" is he asking for (v. 17)?

APPLY **1.** Does God answer all of your prayers? What would you say is the biggest reason God should answer them? **2.** On a scale of 1 to 10, how do you rate on self-esteem: "I am a worm" (1) to "I am God's gift to the world" (10)? How would you complete the phrase, "I am ..."? How would you rate the attitude in this psalm? **3.** Do you have an undivided heart? What divides it? How many "pieces" of heart do you carry inside? What can restore your internal unity?

---

sarily destitute, but people who realize they cannot deliver themselves in their own power and resources. They are totally dependent on God (see 34:6; 35:10)..

86:2 You are my God. The psalmist (David) acknowledges that God has chosen him as his servant, not that he has chosen God (1 Sam. 13:14; 2 Sam. 7:8). So here we have both sides of commitment: David's commitment to God and God's commitment to him.

86:3 The psalmist prays for mercy and protection. He acknowledges God's supremacy and his own humility and need.

86:5–7 In the middle of trouble David trusts God. He knows that God in his loving mercy answers prayer.

86:8–10 David prays to the one true God, who alone can act with sovereign authority (115:3–7; 135:13–17). Ultimately all nations will worship God.

86:9 All the nations. God's work on behalf of Israel will cause the whole world to acknowledge him—a prominent theme throughout Psalms (22:27; 47:9; 66:1–7; 86:9) and the Old Testament itself (Ex. 7:5; Lev. 26:45; 1 Sam. 17:46; 1 Kin. 8:41–43; Ezek. 20:41). This middle verse of the psalm offers a heartfelt expression of faith in God's sovereign rule over all creation.

86:11 Teach me ... give me. David looks beyond rescue from his enemies to ask for rescue from himself—his own sin and doubt. Alert to his own weakness, David depends totally on God (25:5; 51:7,10). God will shower his love, power and aid on those who are truly devoted to him (v. 12).

86:13 you have delivered me. David looks forward to the time when his prayer will be answered. The psalms frequently end on a note of confidence that God will hear and answer prayer (3:8; 6:8–10; 7:10–17; 10:16–18; 12:7; 13:5,6).

86:14 ruthless. The Hebrew word includes the concept of ferocious violence. **men without regard for you.** The enemies arrogantly ignore David's God, who will defend David and punish them (Jer. 20:11). Throughout the Psalms, God is described as the enemy of the proud and the helper of the humble (138:6; 147:6).

men without regard for you.
15 But you, O Lord, are a compassionate and gracious God,
slow to anger, abounding in love and faithfulness.
16 Turn to me and have mercy on me;
grant your strength to your servant
and save the son of your maidservant.[a]
17 Give me a sign of your goodness,
that my enemies may see it and be put to shame,
for you, O LORD, have helped me and comforted me.

Psalm 87

Of the Sons of Korah. A psalm. A song.

1 He has set his foundation on the holy mountain;
2 the LORD loves the gates of Zion
more than all the dwellings of Jacob.
3 Glorious things are said of you,
O city of God: *Selah*
4 "I will record Rahab[b] and Babylon
among those who acknowledge me—
Philistia too, and Tyre, along with Cush[c]—
and will say, 'This[d] one was born in Zion.' "

5 Indeed, of Zion it will be said,
"This one and that one were born in her,
and the Most High himself will establish her."
6 The LORD will write in the register of the peoples:
"This one was born in Zion." *Selah*
7 As they make music they will sing,
"All my fountains are in you."

[a]16 Or *save your faithful son* [b]4 A poetic name for Egypt [c]4 That is, the upper Nile region
[d]4 Or *"O Rahab and Babylon, / Philistia, Tyre and Cush, / I will record concerning those who acknowledge me: / 'This*

OPEN How do you feel about that part of the country or world where you were born?

STUDY **1.** Why is Jerusalem the center of the world for the psalmist (vv. 1–2)? **2.** What future does he see for Israel's former enemies (vv. 3–4)? Will Jews and Gentiles be treated differently (vv. 5–6)? **3.** How would this idea strike nationalists?

APPLY In what ways do you find yourself being tempted toward ethnocentrism? What can you do to open yourself to other cultures?

86:16 grant your strength. David asks for divine power to be exercised on his behalf. **son of your maidservant.** David may be saying that since his mother was so godly, God should therefore care for David (116:16).

86:17 goodness. God's blessings as promised in the covenant (27:13). **may see it.** David asks that God show his enemies the full force of divine power (31:19).

87:1 his foundation. God himself established the foundations of the city (48:2; 68:15–16; Isa. 14:32), including the temple Solomon built.

87:2 the LORD loves. The verb includes the idea of choice as well as the emotion of affection (Deut. 6:5).

87:4 I will record ... This one was born in Zion. This verse looks ahead to a future time when all nations gather in Zion to worship God and calls upon those nations to turn to God now. All who *worship God will* be recorded in God's royal register, whether native or foreign-born, and all will enjoy the full blessings of the kingdom of God. The listing in God's register, however, could also serve as a warning to enemy nations that each person listed is under God's protection, so that if any harm comes to them the perpetrators will be punished (105:15; Isa. 14:28–32). **Rahab.** A reference to Egypt (Isa. 30:7) rather than to the legendary sea monster.

87:5 This one and that one. While God's people will be found here and there in the world, their "hometown" is Zion no matter where they were born.

87:7 fountains. This refers to God as a refreshing spring, the only source of salvation.

Psalm 88

A song. A psalm of the Sons of Korah. For the director of music. According to *mahalath leannoth*.[a] A *maskil*[b] of Heman the Ezrahite.

1 O LORD, the God who saves me,
day and night I cry out before you.
2 May my prayer come before you;
turn your ear to my cry.

3 For my soul is full of trouble
and my life draws near the grave.[c]
4 I am counted among those who go down to the pit;
I am like a man without strength.
5 I am set apart with the dead,
like the slain who lie in the grave,
whom you remember no more,
who are cut off from your care.

6 You have put me in the lowest pit,
in the darkest depths.
7 Your wrath lies heavily upon me;
you have overwhelmed me with all your waves. *Selah*
8 You have taken from me my closest friends
and have made me repulsive to them.
I am confined and cannot escape;
9 my eyes are dim with grief.

I call to you, O LORD, every day;
I spread out my hands to you.
10 Do you show your wonders to the dead?
Do those who are dead rise up and praise you? *Selah*
11 Is your love declared in the grave,
your faithfulness in Destruction[d]?
12 Are your wonders known in the place of darkness,
or your righteous deeds in the land of oblivion?

[a]Title: Possibly a tune, "The Suffering of Affliction" [b]Title: Probably a literary or musical term [c]3 Hebrew *Sheol* [d]11 Hebrew *Abaddon*

OPEN 1. Can you think of a movie that made you cry? Was it sad or happy? Were you glad to be in a dark theater? **2.** Did you ever "ditch" a friend? How did you feel about playing the game? How does it feel to be the "ditchee"?

STUDY 1. With what glimmer of hope does the sick and discouraged psalmist begin (vv. 1–2)? **2.** What hints do we have that the psalmist, Heman, has leprosy (vv. 5–9,15)? How has illness affected his spirits? Has God been very comforting? How might his experiences in prayer be the source of his deepest frustration? Why? **3.** What kind of place is Sheol? What is Heman's argument in verses 10–12? What does he want God to do? **4.** Who does he blame for his afflictions (vv. 6–9)? Why does he think God is angry with him? **5.** How does the psalmist experience God (vv. 13–14)? **6.** On what note does the psalm end? Has there been any development or growth? Why or why not?

APPLY 1. Do you fear or suffer from illness? Do you see God as a healer? Of what would you like to be healed? **2.** Have you ever been treated like a "leper"? Have you treated someone like that? Who are the "lepers" in your life? What can you do to help them? **3.** Can you be both a committed realist and optimist? Which do you tend to be? Do you feel the need to grow in one area? What steps can you take?

Ps. 88 An honest lament written by one experiencing the depths of pain, near death—one whose life has been marked by trouble and difficulty. He seems familiar only with God's wrath (v. 7); even those closest to him have forsaken him (v. 8). Unlike most psalms, this one offers little hope—other than the opening line: "O LORD, the God who saves me." Even though lives of godly people can be filled with pain (73:14), still God is their Savior.

88:1–2 The psalmist appeals to God as the One "who saves me." This is the lone note of hope in the psalm. **I cry out.** The verb indicates a loud scream or desperate weeping.

88:3–5 The psalmist seems to face either literal physical death or (if a figure of speech is the point here) deep emotional distress.

88:5 remember no more. From the vantage point of human life, God's care appears to end at death, after which God no longer needs to rescue the suffering one (25:7; 106:4). The psalmist's mood is totally bleak.

88:6–9 The psalmist blames God for his predicament. He knows of no fault which could have caused his troubles (v. 14)—this is all God's doing (Amos 3:6). Already hopeless, his focus on God's wrath only makes his pain and hopelessness worse.

88:9–12 The psalmist cries to his Savior God for help before it is too late, and he falls away "in the land of oblivion" (v. 12).

88:10,12 wonders. God's miraculous acts of salvation (9:1). The writer assumes that the answer to his questions is "no"; he pleads for God's wonders before it is too late.

OPEN 1. Have you ever been forced to break an important promise? How was it taken by the "promisee"? 2. What part of yourself was most mature in your early teenage years: body, soul or spirit?

STUDY 1. How does Ethan define love in this psalm (vv. 1–2)? To what covenant is he referring (vv. 3–4; 2 Sam. 7:8–17)? 2. Why do you think Ethan launches into a lengthy hymn to the Creator at this point (vv. 5–18)? Who are "the holy ones" (Dan. 4:13; Job 15:15–16)? 3. What is the connection between God's faithfulness and might? 4. Are verses 9–13 about creation? What battle is hinted at (v. 10)? Do you think "Rahab" refers to the mythical sea monster or Egypt (87:4; Job 7:12)? 5. The psalmist's God has power to create and defend. What other power does Yahweh wield (vv. 14–16)? How is the Jewish God different from the pagan gods (Ex. 34:6–7)? 6. To what theme does the psalmist finally return (vv. 19–29)? To whom did God speak in a vision (v. 19; 2 Sam. 7:16–17)? 7. What promises were made to David? How did he respond (v. 26)? What

[13]But I cry to you for help, O LORD;
in the morning my prayer comes before you.
[14]Why, O LORD, do you reject me
and hide your face from me?

[15]From my youth I have been afflicted and close to death;
I have suffered your terrors and am in despair.
[16]Your wrath has swept over me;
your terrors have destroyed me.
[17]All day long they surround me like a flood;
they have completely engulfed me.
[18]You have taken my companions and loved ones from me;
the darkness is my closest friend.

Psalm 89

A *maskil*[a] of Ethan the Ezrahite.

[1]I will sing of the LORD's great love forever;
with my mouth I will make your faithfulness known through all generations.
[2]I will declare that your love stands firm forever,
that you established your faithfulness in heaven itself.

[3]You said, "I have made a covenant with my chosen one,
I have sworn to David my servant,
[4]'I will establish your line forever
and make your throne firm through all generations.' " *Selah*

[5]The heavens praise your wonders, O LORD,
your faithfulness too, in the assembly of the holy ones.
[6]For who in the skies above can compare with the LORD?
Who is like the LORD among the heavenly beings?
[7]In the council of the holy ones God is greatly feared;
he is more awesome than all who surround him.
[8]O LORD God Almighty, who is like you?
You are mighty, O LORD, and your faithfulness surrounds you.

[9]You rule over the surging sea;
when its waves mount up, you still them.

[a]Title: Probably a literary or musical term

88:14 hide your face. A common complaint of the psalmist when God's absence is sensed (13:1).

88:15–18 The psalmist notes that his God-ordained troubles have persisted since his youth.

88:18 companions and loved ones. In verse 8 the psalmist says his friends have been taken from him and repeats the charge here. He feels alone *and abandoned, despite the consistent* message of Psalms that God answers those who call upon him (28:6).

Ps. 89 The psalmist begs God to restore the Davidic kingdom, which has fallen because of unfaithfulness. This fall is so shocking to the writer that he wrestles with the idea of God's abandoning his nation and king to the point that they become a mockery to the world. This psalm starts as a praise psalm but ends as a lament.

89:1 love ... faithfulness. These two charactersitics of God are paralleled here and combined in verse 14 (vv. 2,33,49). **love.** The psalmist uses both words, love and faithfulness, seven times (in v. 14 the Hebrew for "faithfulness" is a different word) and then asks "What happened?" These traits of God seem to have been absent when God rejected the Davidic ruler (vv. 38–45).

89:5–8 The Lord God is incomparable in might and faithfulness. God is over and above all powers of the heavenly realm, who fear and reverence him.

89:9–13 The psalmist describes God's creative power displayed in heavens and on earth.

89:9–10 This passage shares language and poetic imagery with ancient Near East creation hymns. The psalmist praises God for his power in

[10]You crushed Rahab like one of the slain;
with your strong arm you scattered your enemies.
[11]The heavens are yours, and yours also the earth;
you founded the world and all that is in it.
[12]You created the north and the south;
Tabor and Hermon sing for joy at your name.
[13]Your arm is endued with power;
your hand is strong, your right hand exalted.

[14]Righteousness and justice are the foundation of your throne;
love and faithfulness go before you.
[15]Blessed are those who have learned to acclaim you,
who walk in the light of your presence, O LORD.
[16]They rejoice in your name all day long;
they exult in your righteousness.
[17]For you are their glory and strength,
and by your favor you exalt our horn.[a]
[18]Indeed, our shield[b] belongs to the LORD,
our king to the Holy One of Israel.

[19]Once you spoke in a vision,
to your faithful people you said:
"I have bestowed strength on a warrior;
I have exalted a young man from among the people.
[20]I have found David my servant;
with my sacred oil I have anointed him.
[21]My hand will sustain him;
surely my arm will strengthen him.
[22]No enemy will subject him to tribute;
no wicked man will oppress him.
[23]I will crush his foes before him
and strike down his adversaries.
[24]My faithful love will be with him,
and through my name his horn[c] will be exalted.
[25]I will set his hand over the sea,
his right hand over the rivers.
[26]He will call out to me, 'You are my Father,
my God, the Rock my Savior.'
[27]I will also appoint him my firstborn,
the most exalted of the kings of the earth.

[a]*17 Horn* here symbolizes strong one. [b]*18* Or *sovereign* [c]*24 Horn* here symbolizes strength.

position would Israel hold among the peoples of the world (v. 27)? **8.** What conditions were on the agreement (vv. 30–31)? How could God be "faithful" and still reserve the right to correct the erring king? What is the psalmist thinking has happened (v. 38)? **9.** What event has shattered the psalmist's faith (vv. 40–45)? What are the neighboring people saying (v. 50)? Has the covenant really been broken?

APPLY **1.** Does God seem to keep promises with you or have you felt misled or confused? What situation of life has called God's promises into question? **2.** When you experience setbacks what is your first reaction: Emotional? Focus on the problem? Affirm God's control? What is the psalmist's approach? **3.** Do you see God at work in the adversities you face now? Do you feel free to go to God in the "hard times" or do you think you have to "be at your best"? How do you keep yourself hidden from God? **4.** What has God created in your life? What battles has God won for you? Your church? Your group? **5.** Does God's faithfulness excite you? Why or why not? Do you make the Lord's faithfulness known "through all generations"? What do you want others to know? How can you become a more effective witness?

---

establishing the primordial waters which led to the whole creation (74:13,14; Gen. 1:6–10).

89:14 Righteousness and justice. The foundation stones on which God's throne sits. **love and faithfulness.** The psalmist pictures these traits as attending messengers proclaiming God's arrival and forward movement (23:6).

89:15 Blessed. This word, also used in verse 1, means "manifest happiness."

89:19–29 The psalmist recounts God's eternal covenant with David as king and steward of God's people. In this section God notes his anointing of his servant (vv. 20,21) and his promise to destroy all foes (vv. 22,23), expand his borders (vv. 24,25), place him above all other kings (vv. 26,27) and extend his dynasty forever (vv. 28,29). All these promises were fulfilled in Christ's everlasting reign (John 12:34).

89:19 A reminder that God intervened miraculously in David's life because of his covenant. **vision.** This probably refers to God's revelation to Samuel (1 Sam. 16:1–12) or Nathan (2 Sam. 7:4–17). **from among the people.** David, an ordinary shepherd, had humble beginnings (2 Sam. 7:18) much like Jesus.

89:27 firstborn. Firstborn sons enjoyed the highest position in God's royal kingdom, so he was the "most exalted of the kings of the earth" (Rev. 1:5). The concept of universal rule is in view—which Christ would eventually fulfill.

28 I will maintain my love to him forever,
and my covenant with him will never fail.
29 I will establish his line forever,
his throne as long as the heavens endure.

30 "If his sons forsake my law
and do not follow my statutes,
31 if they violate my decrees
and fail to keep my commands,
32 I will punish their sin with the rod,
their iniquity with flogging;
33 but I will not take my love from him,
nor will I ever betray my faithfulness.
34 I will not violate my covenant
or alter what my lips have uttered.
35 Once for all, I have sworn by my holiness—
and I will not lie to David—
36 that his line will continue forever
and his throne endure before me like the sun;
37 it will be established forever like the moon,
the faithful witness in the sky." *Selah*

38 But you have rejected, you have spurned,
you have been very angry with your anointed one.
39 You have renounced the covenant with your servant
and have defiled his crown in the dust.
40 You have broken through all his walls
and reduced his strongholds to ruins.
41 All who pass by have plundered him;
he has become the scorn of his neighbors.
42 You have exalted the right hand of his foes;
you have made all his enemies rejoice.
43 You have turned back the edge of his sword
and have not supported him in battle.
44 You have put an end to his splendor
and cast his throne to the ground.
45 You have cut short the days of his youth;
you have covered him with a mantle of shame. *Selah*

46 How long, O LORD? Will you hide yourself forever?
How long will your wrath burn like fire?
47 Remember how fleeting is my life.
For what futility you have created all men!
48 What man can live and not see death,
or save himself from the power of the grave[a]? *Selah*

[a]48 Hebrew *Sheol*

89:30–37 God's unconditional covenant with David *was eternal* (v. 28). However, God makes it clear that any unfaithful descendant would be disciplined—and the whole nation would suffer as a result.

89:38–45 The psalmist relates God's rejection of David's son because of unfaithfulness and recounts terrible consequences. All God promised was unraveling. Military defeat left the people in despair and disillusionment.

89:46–51 The psalm ends without a resolution; the king and people remain distressed. Despite all that has happened, however, the psalmist clings to hope, begging God to remain faithful to the Davidic covenant.

[49]O Lord, where is your former great love,
which in your faithfulness you swore to David?
[50]Remember, Lord, how your servant has[a] been mocked,
how I bear in my heart the taunts of all the nations,
[51]the taunts with which your enemies have mocked, O LORD,
with which they have mocked every step of your anointed one.

[52]Praise be to the LORD forever!
Amen and Amen.

BOOK IV

Psalms 90–106

Psalm 90

A prayer of Moses the man of God.

[1]Lord, you have been our dwelling place
throughout all generations.
[2]Before the mountains were born
or you brought forth the earth and the world,
from everlasting to everlasting you are God.

[3]You turn men back to dust,
saying, "Return to dust, O sons of men."
[4]For a thousand years in your sight
are like a day that has just gone by,
or like a watch in the night.
[5]You sweep men away in the sleep of death;
they are like the new grass of the morning—
[6]though in the morning it springs up new,
by evening it is dry and withered.

[7]We are consumed by your anger
and terrified by your indignation.
[8]You have set our iniquities before you,
our secret sins in the light of your presence.
[9]All our days pass away under your wrath;
we finish our years with a moan.

[a]50 Or *your servants have*

OPEN 1. What is your earliest memory? Why do you think this incident has stuck in your mind? **2.** Who do you consider a wise person? Who do you think is just a "wise guy"? What's the difference?

STUDY 1. At what point in his life do you think Moses wrote this psalm? What country did he consider home (v. 1)? **2.** How do God and humans differ (vv. 3–6)? **3.** Life is short. What else is wrong with it (vv. 7–9)? What picture of God comes in verse 7? Why is humanity full of "trouble and sorrow"? **4.** Why is God so angry (v. 11)? How should Moses feel, being barred from the Promised Land (Num. 20:6–13; Deut. 32:50–52)? Do you think his mood would be different if he knew of the resurrection and afterlife? **5.** What does it mean to "number our days aright"? **6.** What different requests are made of God (vv. 13–17)? Does the final request remove the futility? What gives ultimate purpose to our endeavors?

APPLY 1. Would you call this psalm: Pessimistic? Realistic? Encouraging? Why? Do you consider

89:52 This verse was added later to conclude Book III of the Psalms on a note of praise.

Ps. 90 In this lament the psalmist prays on behalf of the nation that God, the eternal Creator, would bestow love, joy and compassion on his servants, who live in the shadow of his wrath until they die. The writer presents God as sovereign, above time, angry at sin, while his servants toil in fear and count their days yearning for significance. Yet there is hope and not frustration, faith and not fear in the psalmist's heart. He knows he is guilty, but he also knows God feels "unfailing love" for him (v. 14). Only this psalm is attributed to Moses, who wrote two other poems in the Pentateuch (Ex. 15; Deut. 32).

90:1 dwelling place. The same Hebrew word is translated "refuge" in 71:3.

90:3–6 From the dust of creation to the dust of the grave, humanity exists under a divine death sentence (v. 3; Gen. 3:19).

90:7–10 Not only must we face death, but during our brief lives we must deal with trials and tribulations, the result of God's righteous wrath toward sin.

90:8 light of your presence. God's holiness shines into the dark corners of the human heart, exposing its wickedness.

life something God has "afflicted" you with? **2.** Are you "teachable"? When are you most able to receive instruction? When are you most resistant? **3.** How do you "number your days": One day at a time? Make each one count? With a clock and calendar? Lost count?

OPEN 1. How do you feel when someone gives you a hug? What kind of "hugger" are you: Bear hugger? Three-light-pats-on-the-back hugger? Non-hugger? **2.** What does the word shelter bring to mind? What person, place, thing or institution is shelter for you?

STUDY 1. What four names of God does the psalmist use (vv. 1–2)? What other names can you think of? **2.** What types of disasters are discussed (vv. 3–8)? What image of God do you prefer: Mother hen? Shield? Fortress? Immune system? Force field? **3.** What is the "terror of the night" (v. 5)? **4.** Is God's protection available to everyone (vv. 9–10)? Who does all the work (v. 11)? How

10 The length of our days is seventy years—
or eighty, if we have the strength;
yet their span[a] is but trouble and sorrow,
for they quickly pass, and we fly away.

11 Who knows the power of your anger?
For your wrath is as great as the fear that is due you.
12 Teach us to number our days aright,
that we may gain a heart of wisdom.

13 Relent, O LORD! How long will it be?
Have compassion on your servants.
14 Satisfy us in the morning with your unfailing love,
that we may sing for joy and be glad all our days.
15 Make us glad for as many days as you have afflicted us,
for as many years as we have seen trouble.
16 May your deeds be shown to your servants,
your splendor to their children.

17 May the favor[b] of the Lord our God rest upon us;
establish the work of our hands for us—
yes, establish the work of our hands.

Psalm 91

1 He who dwells in the shelter of the Most High
will rest in the shadow of the Almighty.[c]
2 I will say[d] of the LORD, "He is my refuge and my fortress,
my God, in whom I trust."

3 Surely he will save you from the fowler's snare
and from the deadly pestilence.
4 He will cover you with his feathers,
and under his wings you will find refuge;
his faithfulness will be your shield and rampart.
5 You will not fear the terror of night,
nor the arrow that flies by day,
6 nor the pestilence that stalks in the darkness,
nor the plague that destroys at midday.

[a]10 *Or yet the best of them* [b]17 *Or beauty* [c]1 Hebrew *Shaddai* [d]2 *Or He says*

90:10 seventy ... eighty. Rather than setting a standard length for life here, the writer is demonstrating that, in context, human life is brief and death is inevitable.

90:11–12 Who knows ... Teach us. God's anger cannot be measured, but human life can be. Knowing the limits of life is wise, and living within them, understanding one's mortality and accountability to God, is wiser still (Ps. 49; 73:4–12). ***number our days.*** The psalmist urges more than just a recognition of mortality; he encourages God's children to value time and use it for God's eternal glory.

90:13–17 The psalmist asks God for compassion, joy and gladness in life.

90:14 in the morning. After a dark night of fear of God's anger, the psalmist yearns for a bright morning of love and joy. If Moses indeed wrote this psalm, he may be yearning for the Promised Land after forty hard years of wandering (Ex. 33:14; Deut. 12:9). Finally, the prayer is answered in the Resurrection (Rom. 5:2–5; 8:18; 2 Cor. 4:16–18).

90:16–17 your deeds ... your splendor. Moses desires a sense of significance that will continue to the generations that follow.

91:3 fowler's snare. This "snare" pictured danger from an enemy. Because God is a "refuge" and a "fortress" (v. 2), he can be trusted to protect his people from those who seek to harm them.

91:5 terror. As God will protect from the "snares" of the enemies (v. 3), so he will protect his people from outright attacks (such as through warfare, hence the reference to *the arrow*). Whether the attack comes at *night* or *by day*, God promises to protect his people from harm (v. 10).

7 A thousand may fall at your side,
ten thousand at your right hand,
but it will not come near you.
8 You will only observe with your eyes
and see the punishment of the wicked.

9 If you make the Most High your dwelling—
even the LORD, who is my refuge—
10 then no harm will befall you,
no disaster will come near your tent.
11 For he will command his angels concerning you
to guard you in all your ways;
12 they will lift you up in their hands,
so that you will not strike your foot against a stone.
13 You will tread upon the lion and the cobra;
you will trample the great lion and the serpent.

14 "Because he loves me," says the LORD, "I will rescue him;
I will protect him, for he acknowledges my name.
15 He will call upon me, and I will answer him;
I will be with him in trouble,
I will deliver him and honor him.
16 With long life will I satisfy him
and show him my salvation."

Psalm 92

A psalm. A song. For the Sabbath day.

1 It is good to praise the LORD
and make music to your name, O Most High,
2 to proclaim your love in the morning
and your faithfulness at night,
3 to the music of the ten-stringed lyre
and the melody of the harp.

4 For you make me glad by your deeds, O LORD;
I sing for joy at the works of your hands.
5 How great are your works, O LORD,
how profound your thoughts!
6 The senseless man does not know,
fools do not understand,

do they show motherly care (v. 12)? **5.** Is God's favor shown by spiritual blessing or material (vv. 14–16)?

APPLY 1. If God promises such perfect protection, why does evil befall believers? Didn't it befall Jesus? The Apostles? The early church? **2.** What does it mean to make God your refuge? **3.** Is God calling you to take some risks? How can you avail yourself of God's protection?

OPEN 1. What's your idea of an ideal day? When's the last time it happened? **2.** What is your favorite movie "good guy"? Your favorite "bad guy"? Who do you like to see triumph? Why?

STUDY 1. What kind of day does the psalmist have on the Sabbath (vv. 1–3)? Since he cannot work, what "work" becomes the focus (vv. 4–5)? **2.** Although he praises God's deeds, what does he find most profound? What thought do fools fail to grasp (vv. 6–7)? Are they victims of low I.Q., or are they responsible for their ignorance (Prov. 1:7)? Why could we say God's greatest deed is justice? **3.** How does the psalmist express faith

---

91:12 against a stone. God constantly watches over his people, sending angels to guard and protect them even from common mishaps. This does not mean believers won't ever have difficulties; instead, this pictures God's constant concern and care for his people. Satan quoted this verse to Jesus when he tried to tempt Jesus to jump off the temple so that the angels could catch him (Matt. 4:5–6).

91:13 lion ... cobra ... great lion ... serpent. These deadly beasts round out the list of situations in which God's people can expect his protection (including war, pestilence, terror and mishaps). Lions, cobras and snakes are common in the Middle East and posed a deadly threat to people. Yet even these cannot harm God's people when he intervenes to protect them.

91:14–16 This encouraging psalm about God's great love and care for his people closes with a prophecy. Believers can claim this promise of God's rescue, protection, presence in trouble, deliverance, honor and salvation. God cares about each person individually; he promises to be with his people in their times of greatest need. Those who trust in God are secure in him, forever.

92:4–5 God's works on behalf of his people have been, and should continue to be, a source of great joy. **how profound your thoughts.** God's great deeds reveal the depth of his thoughts toward his people.

92:6 senseless ... fools. Referring to the "wicked," "evildoers" (v. 7) and God's "enemies" (v. 9), these senseless, foolish people do not understand that the Lord is "exalted forever" (v. 8) and they themselves will "perish" (v. 9). The

in the future (vv. 8–9)? How has the Lord blessed him (v. 10)? **4.** What promises are made to the "righteous" (vv. 12–14)? What does it mean to be "planted in the house of the LORD"?

APPLY 1. Which of God's deeds brings you joy? How do you express spiritual joy? **2.** How can you stay "fresh and green" as the years go by? What "fruit" can you bear?

[7] that though the wicked spring up like grass
and all evildoers flourish,
they will be forever destroyed.

[8] But you, O LORD, are exalted forever.

[9] For surely your enemies, O LORD,
surely your enemies will perish;
all evildoers will be scattered.
[10] You have exalted my horn[a] like that of a wild ox;
fine oils have been poured upon me.
[11] My eyes have seen the defeat of my adversaries;
my ears have heard the rout of my wicked foes.

[12] The righteous will flourish like a palm tree,
they will grow like a cedar of Lebanon;
[13] planted in the house of the LORD,
they will flourish in the courts of our God.
[14] They will still bear fruit in old age,
they will stay fresh and green,
[15] proclaiming, "The LORD is upright;
he is my Rock, and there is no wickedness in him."

Psalm 93

OPEN Do you admire people who have: Physical strength? Physical beauty? Physical mind? Which of these are you working on now for yourself?

STUDY 1. For what, other than creation, does the psalmist praise God (v. 5)? How did the Jewish concept of God differ from neighboring countries? **2.** Is God "mightier than the breakers" through creative or moral power? Why does the psalm end with praise for God's statutes?

APPLY 1. What is most important to you: might or right? Is it because you gain power or because you seek truth? Both? Neither? **2.** Is it sometimes hard to believe that God controls nature and history? What does this belief imply? What might obscure it?

[1] The LORD reigns, he is robed in majesty;
the LORD is robed in majesty
and is armed with strength.
The world is firmly established;
it cannot be moved.
[2] Your throne was established long ago;
you are from all eternity.

[3] The seas have lifted up, O LORD,
the seas have lifted up their voice;
the seas have lifted up their pounding waves.
[4] Mightier than the thunder of the great waters,
mightier than the breakers of the sea—
the LORD on high is mighty.

[5] Your statutes stand firm;
holiness adorns your house
for endless days, O LORD.

[a] *10 Horn* here symbolizes strength.

wicked may flourish for a time, but their ultimate punishment is certain.

92:8 exalted forever. God is eternal. He will be exalted (honored, praised, glorified) forever and ever. This offers assurance to his people that he will have the final victory over his enemies. As he will be "exalted forever," so his enemies *"will be forever destroyed"* (v. 7).

92:9 enemies. The "senseless man," the "fools," the "wicked," and the "evildoers" mentioned in verses 6–7.

92:10–11 exalted my horn. The psalm writer has praised God for his great deeds (vv. 4–5), and here thanks God for helping him in victory. The "horn" symbolized strength, and so the writer is grateful to God for exalting him with strength like that of an ox. The **fine oils** poured on his head picture prosperity, peace and joy because of God's defeat of his enemies.

92:12–15 In contrast to the wicked who will be "forever destroyed" (v. 7), the righteous have a secure and glorious future "in the house of the LORD" (v. 13).

93:1–2 Not only is God exalted forever into the future (92:8), but his "throne was established long ago." God has existed "from all eternity." The world God created in Genesis one is "firmly established." God controls all of time and all of creation.

93:5 statutes. The God of creation, the God who established the earth, the God

Psalm 94

1 O LORD, the God who avenges,
O God who avenges, shine forth.
2 Rise up, O Judge of the earth;
pay back to the proud what they deserve.
3 How long will the wicked, O LORD,
how long will the wicked be jubilant?

4 They pour out arrogant words;
all the evildoers are full of boasting.
5 They crush your people, O LORD;
they oppress your inheritance.
6 They slay the widow and the alien;
they murder the fatherless.
7 They say, "The LORD does not see;
the God of Jacob pays no heed."

8 Take heed, you senseless ones among the people;
you fools, when will you become wise?
9 Does he who implanted the ear not hear?
Does he who formed the eye not see?
10 Does he who disciplines nations not punish?
Does he who teaches man lack knowledge?
11 The LORD knows the thoughts of man;
he knows that they are futile.

12 Blessed is the man you discipline, O LORD,
the man you teach from your law;
13 you grant him relief from days of trouble,
till a pit is dug for the wicked.
14 For the LORD will not reject his people;
he will never forsake his inheritance.
15 Judgment will again be founded on righteousness,
and all the upright in heart will follow it.

16 Who will rise up for me against the wicked?
Who will take a stand for me against evildoers?
17 Unless the LORD had given me help,
I would soon have dwelt in the silence of death.
18 When I said, "My foot is slipping,"
your love, O LORD, supported me.
19 When anxiety was great within me,
your consolation brought joy to my soul.

OPEN 1. Were your parents strict or easy-going? How do you feel about the kind and amount of discipline you received as a child? **2.** Are you sure-footed or a bit of a "klutz"? What is the most clumsy thing you've ever done?

STUDY 1. How would you describe the tone of verses 1–3: Vengeful and bitter? Self-righteous? Pleading? Confident and direct? Why? **2.** What is the psalmist's complaint (v. 3)? What is the sin of the wicked (vv. 4–7)? How do they misuse power? Why do they oppress the powerless (v. 7)? **3.** What is the psalmist's warning (vv. 8–11)? What is his argument? If God created man, what can we deduce about God? About man? Has the psalmist found an answer for verse 3? **4.** How does the focus change in verse 12? How is God addressed differently? Why? If wickedness goes unpunished, what can the psalmist hope for the righteous (vv. 12–13)? **5.** What kind of "run in" has this writer had with the wicked (vv. 16–21)? Is he poor? Siding with the poor? A victim of politics? What keeps him going? Has he found peace of mind yet?

APPLY 1. Have you ever continued doing wrong because no punishment or ill consequences seemed to come? How did you become aware of your misdeeds? Should the group help keep you accountable? **2.** What is your feeling about injustice? Why doesn't God just end it? Is it our job or do we wait for God to intervene and "set the record straight"? **3.** When does God seem to come to your rescue: When the wave of trouble is approaching? When your feet get wet? When you're shivering and worn out? When you're just about to drown? How has God rescued you?

---

who reigns from eternity past to eternity future has given his people life directives to guide them as *they live for him on this* earth. Who would dare to ignore the statutes of the eternal God who loves his people enough to give them rules for living well? See Psalm 119 for more about the value of God's laws.

94:1 avenges. God will punish those who have opposed him and his people. Vengeance is God's job, not ours (Deut. 32:35,41; Rom. 12:19; Heb. 10:30).

94:4–7 These verses indict evildoers. Such people may think they can get away with evil acts against God's people. One day, however, God "will repay them for their sins" (v. 23).

94:12–15 In contrast to the coming punishment of the wicked, God's people are blessed. Why? Because God loves them enough to discipline them. The words *discipline* and *teach* point to God's patient love for his people as he instructs and corrects them according to his laws. God's love is further manifested as he gives his people "relief from days of trouble," and promises never to reject or forsake them.

94:14 his people ... his inheritance. These words are synonymous, describing God's people, Israel. In response to verse 5, God promises that he will not abandon his people to their evil oppressors, nor would injustice prevail against them.

OPEN **1.** Complete this sentence: "I belong to the ______ generation." Why give your generation that title? **2.** What could your generation give to the next generation?

STUDY **1.** Why use music to rejoice (vv. 1–2)? What dimension does music add to words? **2.** What does bowing or kneeling represent (v. 6)? **3.** What happened at Meribah and Massah (v. 8; Ex. 17:1–7)? How was God on trial? **4.** What is God's response (vv. 10–11)? What is the meaning of "rest"? **5.** What is the New Testament notion of "entering God's rest" (Heb. 4:1–3)?

APPLY **1.** Does your relationship with God feel like rest or is there more work to be done? **2.** Is your heart "hard" today? How can it be softened? **3.** How do you live like "your fathers"? Or have you left the beliefs of your parents?

20 Can a corrupt throne be allied with you—
one that brings on misery by its decrees?
21 They band together against the righteous
and condemn the innocent to death.
22 But the LORD has become my fortress,
and my God the rock in whom I take refuge.
23 He will repay them for their sins
and destroy them for their wickedness;
the LORD our God will destroy them.

Psalm 95

1 Come, let us sing for joy to the LORD;
let us shout aloud to the Rock of our salvation.
2 Let us come before him with thanksgiving
and extol him with music and song.

3 For the LORD is the great God,
the great King above all gods.
4 In his hand are the depths of the earth,
and the mountain peaks belong to him.
5 The sea is his, for he made it,
and his hands formed the dry land.

6 Come, let us bow down in worship,
let us kneel before the LORD our Maker;
7 for he is our God
and we are the people of his pasture,
the flock under his care.

Today, if you hear his voice,
8 do not harden your hearts as you did at Meribah,[a]
as you did that day at Massah[b] in the desert,
9 where your fathers tested and tried me,
though they had seen what I did.
10 For forty years I was angry with that generation;
I said, "They are a people whose hearts go astray,
and they have not known my ways."

[a]8 *Meribah* means *quarreling.* [b]8 *Massah* means *testing.*

94:20–23 corrupt throne. This pictures injustice at the very highest levels. The world may be filled with evil and injustice but, in the end, God's justice will prevail. The Lord will protect his people and repay evildoers for their wickedness.

95:3–5 This psalm is a call to worship the Lord. God's people are to praise him because he is "above all gods" and Creator of land and sea. All of creation is "in his hand." While many ancient religions had gods that ruled over various aspects of creation (the sea, fire, the skies), Israel's God alone rules all of creation.

95:6–11 True worship of God involves both submission and obedience. The psalmist first calls for the people to "bow down in worship" and then pleads with them to not "harden" their hearts in disobedience against the Lord. The writer of Hebrews reflects on these verses in Hebrews 3:7–4:13.

95:8 Meribah ... Massah. The psalmist reminds the readers of their ancestors' disobedience against God. After all the wonderful miracles the nation had experienced in being freed from Egypt, here the people complained and longed to return to Egypt because they were thirsty. At Meribah and Massah, God told Moses to strike a rock with his staff and give water to the people (Ex. 17:1–7).

95:10 forty years. Israel's complaint about water (v. 8) was only one of many complaints against Moses and against God. The people's lack of faith in God was seen again as the people were on the very brink of the Promised Land. They were afraid of the inhabitants of the land and did not have faith that God would give them the land as he had promised (Num. 14:1–38). So God "was angry with that generation" and sent them to wander forty years in the desert until almost an entire generation died.

11 So I declared on oath in my anger,
"They shall never enter my rest."

Psalm 96

1 Sing to the LORD a new song;
sing to the LORD, all the earth.
2 Sing to the LORD, praise his name;
proclaim his salvation day after day.
3 Declare his glory among the nations,
his marvelous deeds among all peoples.

4 For great is the LORD and most worthy of praise;
he is to be feared above all gods.
5 For all the gods of the nations are idols,
but the LORD made the heavens.
6 Splendor and majesty are before him;
strength and glory are in his sanctuary.

7 Ascribe to the LORD, O families of nations,
ascribe to the LORD glory and strength.
8 Ascribe to the LORD the glory due his name;
bring an offering and come into his courts.
9 Worship the LORD in the splendor of his[a] holiness;
tremble before him, all the earth.

10 Say among the nations, "The LORD reigns."
The world is firmly established, it cannot be moved;
he will judge the peoples with equity.
11 Let the heavens rejoice, let the earth be glad;
let the sea resound, and all that is in it;
12 let the fields be jubilant, and everything in them.
Then all the trees of the forest will sing for joy;
13 they will sing before the LORD, for he comes,
he comes to judge the earth.

[a]9 Or *LORD with the splendor of*

OPEN 1. What's your favorite new song? **2.** When is the last time you changed a long-held opinion of yours? What do you now believe?

STUDY 1. Why does this psalm appear in 1 Chronicles 16:8–33? Why do you think one version is longer? **2.** To whom are verses 1–6 directed? Verses 7–10? Verses 11–13? **3.** Why is "new" important (v. 1; Isa. 43:18–19)? What "new thing" is God doing? **4.** What 10 things does the psalmist want the Israelites to include in their worship of God (vv. 1–10)? What does "ascribe" mean (vv. 7–8)? **5.** What's the importance of the international appeal? What is the psalmist's vision of the one to come? Why is that? Why is "for he comes" a cause of joy (v. 13)?

APPLY 1. What new thing would you like God to do in your life? How do old habits, limitations or people interfere with your singing a new song? How could it start today? **2.** Does it seem to you that God reigns?

95:11 on oath. In Numbers 14:28 God had vowed that, because of the people's lack of faith, he would do to the nation everything they feared. **They shall never enter my rest.** The Promised Land had been called a place where God would give his people rest (Ex. 33:14). Because of their disobedience, however, that generation would never enter the land.

96:1–3 The psalmist calls *all* people to give the Lord the glory due him (v. 8). The triple repetition of the word "sing," like other triple repetitions, gives the utmost emphasis to the word or phrase being repeated (vv. 7–9; 103:20–22; 118:2–4). **all the earth,** quoted again in verse 9, pictures the psalmist's vision that not just Israel, but all people everywhere, would one day worship the Lord.

96:4–6 Why is the Lord alone "most worthy of praise"? He is greater than the idols of all the nations for he alone **made the heavens;** he alone is the Creator. While many gods of the nations were said to live in the heavens, the Lord alone *made* the heavens. Thus he is above all gods.

96:6 Splendor and majesty ... strength and glory. These two pairs of adjectives are personified as beings in God's sanctuary, always waiting before him. Similar personification of adjectives is found in 23:6.

96:7–9 The threefold use of the word *ascribe* matches the threefold use of the word "sing" in verses 1–2. The psalmist calls to the nations to attribute to the Lord the glory, strength and holiness that are truly his. The appropriate response is for all the earth to worship and tremble before him.

96:11–12 As a result of the fall, all of nature, including mankind, was made subject to evil. Creation was "subjected to frustration" and waits to one day "be liberated from its bondage to decay" (Rom. 8:20–21). The writer pictures the heavens, the earth, the sea, the fields and the trees of the forest singing for joy when God sets up his righteous kingdom.

96:13 The hope of God's people is expressed in the word *comes*. The promise of God's return to reign over all things and to bring judgment on sin and wickedness gave the people hope in times of trial and difficulty. One day God will *judge the world in righteousness* and all will be made right.

He will judge the world in righteousness
and the peoples in his truth.

OPEN 1. If you were king or queen for a day, how would you speed up justice? 2. What was the last party you really liked? Who, besides yourself, was the life of the party?

STUDY 1. In the psalmist's opinion, how far-reaching is the power of the Lord (v. 1)? Why does he think the God of the Jews is so powerful (vv. 3–6)? When did God make such fantastic appearances (Judg. 5:5; 1 Kin. 8:10–12)? 2. Why are the Gentiles ashamed at God's appearance (v. 7)? Why does Judah rejoice (vv. 8–9)? 3. How does one keep on receiving God's blessings (vv. 10–12)? What blessings are promised? 4. Can rejoicing be commanded? Why or why not?

APPLY 1. What word pictures describe God's presence in your life? 2. Which describes you the closest: Hater of evil? Faithful? Righteous? Upright in heart? Which would you like to be?

Psalm 97

1 The LORD reigns, let the earth be glad;
let the distant shores rejoice.

2 Clouds and thick darkness surround him;
righteousness and justice are the foundation of his throne.
3 Fire goes before him
and consumes his foes on every side.
4 His lightning lights up the world;
the earth sees and trembles.
5 The mountains melt like wax before the LORD,
before the Lord of all the earth.
6 The heavens proclaim his righteousness,
and all the peoples see his glory.

7 All who worship images are put to shame,
those who boast in idols—
worship him, all you gods!

8 Zion hears and rejoices
and the villages of Judah are glad
because of your judgments, O LORD.
9 For you, O LORD, are the Most High over all the earth;
you are exalted far above all gods.

10 Let those who love the LORD hate evil,
for he guards the lives of his faithful ones
and delivers them from the hand of the wicked.
11 Light is shed upon the righteous
and joy on the upright in heart.
12 Rejoice in the LORD, you who are righteous,
and praise his holy name.

OPEN Who is your favorite singer, musician or group? Why?

STUDY 1. Why should we sing a new song: don't the old ones apply (v. 1)? 2. What three titles for God could you derive from this psalm (vv. 3,6,9)? 3. What do "his right hand and his holy arm" say about

Psalm 98

A psalm.

1 Sing to the LORD a new song,
for he has done marvelous things;
his right hand and his holy arm
have worked salvation for him.
2 The LORD has made his salvation known

97:1 distant shores. The Lord reigns not just in the land of Israel. The psalmist calls those distant lands to join in and *rejoice* as well.

97:2–6 The Lord's great might and power are displayed in many ways in creation. *Here the psalmist* uses the awesome power of a thunderstorm to describe God's majesty.

97:4 In another example of personification, the psalmist pictures the physical earth trembling before the power of God.

97:7 The contrast is unmistakable: Those who trust in the Lord will find joy; those who worship idols will be put to shame. With a touch of irony, the writer calls upon all those supposed "gods" to bow down and worship the one true God.

97:8–12 The only ones who will truly rejoice over the Lord's righteous rule are those who love righteousness and hate evil. **Zion.** This is another name for Jerusalem, the holy city and they will rejoice, along with all the villages of Judah, when God is exalted.

98:2 God does not try to hide his salvation from anyone; on the contrary, he is "not wanting anyone to perish, but everyone to come to repentance" (2 Peter 3:9). **revealed.** His saving acts

and revealed his righteousness to the nations.
[3]He has remembered his love
and his faithfulness to the house of Israel;
all the ends of the earth have seen
the salvation of our God.

[4]Shout for joy to the LORD, all the earth,
burst into jubilant song with music;
[5]make music to the LORD with the harp,
with the harp and the sound of singing,
[6]with trumpets and the blast of the ram's horn—
shout for joy before the LORD, the King.

[7]Let the sea resound, and everything in it,
the world, and all who live in it.
[8]Let the rivers clap their hands,
let the mountains sing together for joy;
[9]let them sing before the LORD,
for he comes to judge the earth.
He will judge the world in righteousness
and the peoples with equity.

Psalm 99

[1]The LORD reigns,
let the nations tremble;
he sits enthroned between the cherubim,
let the earth shake.
[2]Great is the LORD in Zion;
he is exalted over all the nations.
[3]Let them praise your great and awesome name—
he is holy.

[4]The King is mighty, he loves justice—
you have established equity;
in Jacob you have done
what is just and right.
[5]Exalt the LORD our God
and worship at his footstool;
he is holy.

[6]Moses and Aaron were among his priests,
Samuel was among those who called on his name;

God's need for assistance (44:3)? **4.** How is Israel's salvation an opportunity for the nations (vv. 3,9)? **5.** Can creation praise God, or is this just a poetic metaphor (vv. 7–9; Luke 19:39–40)?

APPLY 1. Do you expect God to do new things in your life? Or do you think a lot about how God should change the next person? **2.** Do you ever "cut loose" in joyful expression? Or do you sing your songs to God like a quiet ballad?

OPEN Where do you feel most in touch with the holiness of God: On a mountaintop? In a beautiful sanctuary? In a small chapel? In the countryside at night, while looking at the stars?

STUDY 1. What does it mean to call God "holy" (v. 3)? Why would this lead someone to worship God? **2.** How is God's holiness expressed in verses 1–3? In verses 4–5? How has God's righteousness been worked out "in Jacob" (v. 4)? **3.** How can a holy God get his "hands dirty" dealing with humans (vv. 6–7)? How did God respond to intercessors (v. 8)? In what way is God more than just a mighty being?

APPLY 1. How can God forgive and still punish us for our misdeeds? What actions and attitudes deserve punishment? What would it

have been *made known* to the nations (Isa. 52:10).

98:9 comes to judge. For God's people, the day when he judges will not be a day of sorrow, but a day of rejoicing because he will judge in righteousness and fairness.

99:1–2 The Lord reigns over all the nations and over all of creation. The nations, in turn, should acknowledge his great power.

99:3 Let them praise. The great name and holiness of the Lord should result in praise from all the nations.

99:4 just and right. The nation of Israel (here called *Jacob*) had experienced God's righteousness through his saving acts on their behalf. Everything God does is just and right.

99:6–7 God gave priests to the nation of Israel to serve as intermediaries between him and the people. The priests performed the sacrifices, interceded for the people with God, and in turn, brought God's instructions to them.

99:6 Moses ... Aaron ... Samuel. These three men had served as priests to the nation of Israel. Moses served as the first priest, anointing Aaron to serve as Israel's high priest (Ex. 24:1–7; 28:1). Samuel was both a priest and a prophet who also served Israel during a time when they had no strong leaders (1 Sam. 7:2–17). These men are listed as representatives of all those who served Israel as priests throughout the nation's history. **called on his name.** God answered them. Now, however, all believers can call upon God and he will answer (1 Peter 2:9).

mean to you to love justice more? **2.** "God knows, we're only human." True enough, but does that really excuse us (Lev. 19:2; Matt. 5:48)? How can love for holiness be seen in your life?

OPEN 1. What is the most joyful song you know? **2.** When do you most feel like singing a joyful song: When heading home from work or school? When going to worship? When your team wins? When you find a bargain when shopping?

STUDY 1. What six reasons does the psalmist give to praise God? Do these apply to "all the earth" or just to "his people"? **2.** What responsibilities are involved in knowing that the Lord is God (100:3)? **3.** What attitude characterizes God's people (100:4–5)? Why is thanksgiving a public, communal event? **4.** What is David's resolution (101:2)? Why must he be careful? Are rulers known for their blameless lives? **5.** Where does purity of heart begin (101:3)? Is conscious effort involved? **6.** What public standards grow from a blameless heart (101:5–7)? What kind of advisors will lose their jobs?

APPLY 1. Which reason most motivates you to praise God? **2.** Is your expression of joy too limited? Too private? Do you need the freedom to have a more joyful life? **3.** How can surrendering to "vile things" (101:3) take away your joy?

---

they called on the LORD
and he answered them.
7 He spoke to them from the pillar of cloud;
they kept his statutes and the decrees he gave them.

8 O LORD our God,
you answered them;
you were to Israel[a] a forgiving God,
though you punished their misdeeds.[b]
9 Exalt the LORD our God
and worship at his holy mountain,
for the LORD our God is holy.

Psalm 100

A psalm. For giving thanks.

1 Shout for joy to the LORD, all the earth.
2 Worship the LORD with gladness;
come before him with joyful songs.
3 Know that the LORD is God.
It is he who made us, and we are his[c];
we are his people, the sheep of his pasture.

4 Enter his gates with thanksgiving
and his courts with praise;
give thanks to him and praise his name.
5 For the LORD is good and his love endures forever;
his faithfulness continues through all generations.

Psalm 101

Of David. A psalm.

1 I will sing of your love and justice;
to you, O LORD, I will sing praise.
2 I will be careful to lead a blameless life—
when will you come to me?

I will walk in my house
with blameless heart.

[a] *8 Hebrew* them [b] *8 Or / an avenger of the wrongs done to them* [c] *3 Or* and not we ourselves

---

99:7 When these priests called to him, God answered and spoke to them. The reference to the pillar of cloud recalls the days in the desert when God led his people with a pillar of cloud by day and a pillar of fire by night. God's presence was in the cloud, and spoke to Moses (Ex. 33:9) and Aaron (Num. 12:5–6). While Samuel was not alive at that time, Samuel was spoken to directly by God from his presence in the Ark of the Covenant in the tabernacle (1 Sam. 3:1–21).

99:8–9 Israel had sinned many times and, although God had punished them for their sins, he had also forgiven them. Therefore, God deserves to be worshiped and exalted.

100 This short psalm calls "all the earth" to worship the Lord. This psalm closes a series of psalms that began with Psalm 93.

100:1 all the earth. Although God has a special relationship with Israel, the psalmist sends out a call to all nations to joyfully acknowledge God for what he has done on behalf of his people.

100:3 Know. This means to acknowledge that the Lord alone is God.

100:5 the LORD is good. A basic attribute of God—goodness (Luke 18:19).

101:1 love and justice. These are two key qualities of God's rule (6:4; 99:4). God is always loving and always just. God will never act contrary to these attributes.

101:2–5 David, writer of this psalm, calls upon God to come to him for he is trying to lead a blameless life. David understood that obedience is a matter of the heart, so he needed to carefully guard both his heart and eyes. Old Testament writers understood people's

3 I will set before my eyes
no vile thing.

The deeds of faithless men I hate;
they will not cling to me.
4 Men of perverse heart shall be far from me;
I will have nothing to do with evil.

5 Whoever slanders his neighbor in secret,
him will I put to silence;
whoever has haughty eyes and a proud heart,
him will I not endure.

6 My eyes will be on the faithful in the land,
that they may dwell with me;
he whose walk is blameless
will minister to me.

7 No one who practices deceit
will dwell in my house;
no one who speaks falsely
will stand in my presence.

8 Every morning I will put to silence
all the wicked in the land;
I will cut off every evildoer
from the city of the LORD.

Psalm 102

A prayer of an afflicted man. When he is faint
and pours out his lament before the LORD.

1 Hear my prayer, O LORD;
let my cry for help come to you.
2 Do not hide your face from me
when I am in distress.
Turn your ear to me;
when I call, answer me quickly.

3 For my days vanish like smoke;
my bones burn like glowing embers.

OPEN 1. What is your favorite cure for the blues: TV? Sleep? Food? Exercise? Talk? How does it help? **2.** What two books (besides the Bible) would you want to pass on to the next generation?

STUDY 1. What hint can you find that this psalm was written during the Exile in Babylon (v. 16)? **2.** List the psalmist's afflictions (vv. 3–11). What modern diagnoses would you give? What ailments are physical and psychological? **3.** Why does he liken himself to a desert owl (v. 6; Lev.

actions to result from following their hearts (inward compulsion) or eyes (external influences). (Num. 15:39; Job 31:7; Prov. 21:4.) In addition, he needed to be careful about who would be in his circle of friends, avoiding those who would be a bad influence.

101:4 perverse. Wicked, corrupt. Because David sought to live a blameless life, he would not keep company with such people.

101:5 David pledged that he would remove from his presence not only perverse people (v. 4), but also slanderous and arrogant people. To slander means to defame others through malicious or false reports. Arrogant people have a law unto themselves and may be ruthless.

Ps. 102 This psalm is unique because no author is named and there are no liturgical or historical notes. Instead, the title identifies the author's life circumstance and the kind of life situation in which this psalm would be most helpful. The writer is indeed afflicted personally, but verses 12–22 indicate the affliction of his entire nation. The physical affliction of the writer may be the result of national affliction. This may have been written during the nation's exile, evidenced by the writer's desire that the Lord would rebuild Zion (v. 16).

102:3–11 The distress is so deep that it wearies both body and spirit. This has occurred because of God's anger against his people (v. 10); as a result, the people's enemies seem to be getting away with their pokes and jabs (v. 8). Because of God's wrath against them, the people feel hopeless. Yet the writer is not completely without hope, for he knows of God's great compassion, and will call upon that compassion at the end of the psalm (v. 13).

102:3 The writer describes his days vanishing like smoke and his bones burning like glowing embers. His life is wasting away and the pain is so intense that he feels as if his bones are on fire.

11:13 –18)? What feeling does this and verse 7 underscore? What ails him socially (v. 8)? **4.** Who does he think is responsible for the trouble (v. 10)? What is the tone of this section? **5.** How does the tone and content change in verses 12 –17? Why does he bring up God's immortality? What is his argument? **6.** What is his vision for Jerusalem (v. 15)? **7.** If this poet has had it so bad, why does he recommend telling future generations about God (v. 18)? Why does he continue his lament in verses 23 and 24? What role has God played in his affliction? **8.** How is God different from creation? What promise is reiterated in the closing verse?

APPLY 1. Would the story of your spiritual life be beneficial to future generations? Or should you be forgotten? Why? **2.** Are you afflicted, depressed, alone or distressed in any way? Do you feel free to express it to God? A special friend? The group? Or do you bear it all alone? How can this group help you keep your faith alive? What is your prayer request?

---

4 My heart is blighted and withered like grass;
I forget to eat my food.
5 Because of my loud groaning
I am reduced to skin and bones.
6 I am like a desert owl,
like an owl among the ruins.
7 I lie awake; I have become
like a bird alone on a roof.
8 All day long my enemies taunt me;
those who rail against me use my name as a curse.
9 For I eat ashes as my food
and mingle my drink with tears
10 because of your great wrath,
for you have taken me up and thrown me aside.
11 My days are like the evening shadow;
I wither away like grass.

12 But you, O LORD, sit enthroned forever;
your renown endures through all generations.
13 You will arise and have compassion on Zion,
for it is time to show favor to her;
the appointed time has come.
14 For her stones are dear to your servants;
her very dust moves them to pity.
15 The nations will fear the name of the LORD,
all the kings of the earth will revere your glory.
16 For the LORD will rebuild Zion
and appear in his glory.
17 He will respond to the prayer of the destitute;
he will not despise their plea.

18 Let this be written for a future generation,
that a people not yet created may praise the LORD:
19 "The LORD looked down from his sanctuary on high,
from heaven he viewed the earth,

102:6 owl. The repetition of the word *owl* actually translates two different words in Hebrew, for there are several different types of owls (Lev. 11:16–18). For the writer to compare himself to an owl pictures his desolation, for the owls were associated with desert areas and ruins (Isa. 34:8–15; Jer. 50:39).

102:12–17 The psalm writers often move from lament to trust, and that is the case here. The writer understands that his suffering, and that of his nation, is the result of God's anger against sin. He also knows, however, that God is compassionate and will keep his promises. He will restore the nation (v. 16) and hear the prayers of the destitute (v. 17).

102:12 sit enthroned forever. The theme of God's eternal reign runs throughout the psalms, especially in Psalms 92–100. Because God is enthroned forever and remains the same forever (v. 27), his people can count on his compassion, his mercy and his unfailing promises.

102:13 Verses 13 and 16 form a frame around verses 14–15. Verses 13 and 16 speak of the writer's trust in God to have compassion on his people and to rebuild their city, Zion. The intervening verses picture the distress of the people that the city lies in dust and their hope that one day all nations will fear God when they see what he has done for his people. Perhaps the writer has heard about this promise through a prophet of the Lord. The *dust* of the city gives a clue that this may have been written during the Babylonian Exile after Jerusalem had been destroyed.

102:14 dear to your servants. God's people dearly loved Zion (Jerusalem), the city of God. It was their capital city, the home of their temple, the center of their worship. The city symbolized the nation's prosperity and relationship with God (2 Sam. 5:6–12; Ps. 48). Jesus expressed love for the city and its people (Matt. 23:37). The city was dear to the people, and it was dear to God as well.

102:18–22 a future generation. So certain is the writer of God's deliverance of his people and restoration of Jerusalem and the temple that he records the fact so that they might praise God when they worship there.

102:18 written. History was often handed down orally through songs and poems (22:30; 44:1; 78:1–4). Here, however, the writer calls for these words to be *written* so that they can be remembered.

20 to hear the groans of the prisoners
and release those condemned to death."
21 So the name of the LORD will be declared in Zion
and his praise in Jerusalem
22 when the peoples and the kingdoms
assemble to worship the LORD.

23 In the course of my life[a] he broke my strength;
he cut short my days.
24 So I said:
"Do not take me away, O my God, in the midst of my days;
your years go on through all generations.
25 In the beginning you laid the foundations of the earth,
and the heavens are the work of your hands.
26 They will perish, but you remain;
they will all wear out like a garment.
Like clothing you will change them
and they will be discarded.
27 But you remain the same,
and your years will never end.
28 The children of your servants will live in your presence;
their descendants will be established before you."

Psalm 103

Of David.

1 Praise the LORD, O my soul;
all my inmost being, praise his holy name.
2 Praise the LORD, O my soul,
and forget not all his benefits—
3 who forgives all your sins
and heals all your diseases,
4 who redeems your life from the pit
and crowns you with love and compassion,
5 who satisfies your desires with good things
so that your youth is renewed like the eagle's.

6 The LORD works righteousness
and justice for all the oppressed.

7 He made known his ways to Moses,
his deeds to the people of Israel:
8 The LORD is compassionate and gracious,
slow to anger, abounding in love.
9 He will not always accuse,

[a]23 Or *By his power*

OPEN 1. What is most likely to make you feel young again: Going to a dance? Taking a walk on a nice day? Getting a compliment from the opposite sex? **2.** If you could revisit your youth what would you most look forward to? What would you least look forward to?

STUDY 1. Who does David address in verses 1–5? How has he benefited from God's favor? **2.** Why does he say the eagle's youth is renewed (v. 5)? How does God renew our youth? **3.** To where does the focus shift in verses 6–14? What "ways" were made known to Moses and Israel? Is a loving and forgiving God known only from the New Testament (v. 8; Ex. 34:6–7)? **4.** Which word picture of forgiveness do you like best (vv. 11–13)? **5.** Why does God bother with such temporary beings as humans? What seems to be most important: personal souls or impersonal principles (vv. 17–18)? Is God "talking to himself" somehow? **6.** What is the focus of verses 19–22? What

102:26–27 wear out like a garment. God is more enduring than all of his creation. He created the heavens and the earth (v. 25), but they will one day be discarded. The first creation will be replaced with a new creation (Matt. 24:35; 2 Peter 3:7,10–13; Rev. 21:1). But God will *remain the same;* his *years will never end.*

103:1–2 O my soul. This is a common phrase in Hebrew, used as a way of addressing oneself (42:5; 43:5; 62:5; 116:7).

103:5 like the eagle's. God's benefits (v. 2), forgiveness, healing (v. 3), redemption, love, compassion (v. 4) and satisfying of all desires with good things will bring renewal to every person. That renewal will be like the proverbial strength of an eagle (Isa. 40:31).

103:6 Along with verse 19, this pictures God's righteous and just reign under which Israel has been blessed.

nor will he harbor his anger forever;
10 he does not treat us as our sins deserve
or repay us according to our iniquities.
11 For as high as the heavens are above the earth,
so great is his love for those who fear him;
12 as far as the east is from the west,
so far has he removed our transgressions from us.
13 As a father has compassion on his children,
so the LORD has compassion on those who fear him;
14 for he knows how we are formed,
he remembers that we are dust.
15 As for man, his days are like grass,
he flourishes like a flower of the field;
16 the wind blows over it and it is gone,
and its place remembers it no more.
17 But from everlasting to everlasting
the LORD's love is with those who fear him,
and his righteousness with their children's children—
18 with those who keep his covenant
and remember to obey his precepts.

19 The LORD has established his throne in heaven,
and his kingdom rules over all.

20 Praise the LORD, you his angels,
you mighty ones who do his bidding,
who obey his word.
21 Praise the LORD, all his heavenly hosts,
you his servants who do his will.
22 Praise the LORD, all his works
everywhere in his dominion.

Praise the LORD, O my soul.

Psalm 104

1 Praise the LORD, O my soul.

O LORD my God, you are very great;
you are clothed with splendor and majesty.
2 He wraps himself in light as with a garment;
he stretches out the heavens like a tent
3 and lays the beams of his upper chambers on their waters.
He makes the clouds his chariot
and rides on the wings of the wind.

takes "center stage": God's will or God's creation? What do you think of the last line? **7.** Like other ancient Jews, David believed prosperity to be a sign of God's favor and illness a sign of personal sin. Do you think healing is a sign of forgiveness? Is disease a result of unconfessed sin? Why or why not?

APPLY 1. Which do you tend to be: Complainer or a praiser? Satisfied or dissatisfied? Why? Has affliction made you positive or negative? Why? **2.** Does your experience with your father or mother resemble the picture of God in verse 13? Does this image help you? Can God's knowing how you are formed comfort you (v. 14)? **3.** When have you experienced God's grace firsthand? How have you benefited from it?

OPEN 1. Are you a "detail person" or a "big picture thinker"? What evidence do you have to support this claim? **2.** Do you like books or documentaries on nature? What part of nature interests you the most?

STUDY 1. How closely does this psalm follow the creation sequence in Genesis 1? What segments correspond to which "days" of

---

103:10–12 as far as the east is from the west. God justly punishes people's sins; as the psalmist noted, however, he does not punish as people's sins deserve. Instead, so great is his love that he forgives; so great is his forgiveness that he removes our sins. Our sins are not just forgiven—they are forgotten.

103:17 God's love is infinite; man's time on earth is finite. God's love overarches our time frame and extends across all generations past and future and on into eternity.

103:20–22 This concluding call to praise encompasses all the hosts of heaven and all of humanity.

Ps. 104 This psalm glorifies God as Creator. The psalmist may have been inspired by the account of creation recorded in Genesis 1 but was not concerned for following the order set down in Genesis. Instead, the writer looked at the beauty of creation around him and glorified its Creator and Sustainer.

104:2 light. The reference to light pictures that first day of creation when God said, "Let there be light" (Gen. 1:3). The stretching out of the heavens pictures that second day of creation when God separated the sky from the water (Gen. 1:6–8).

[4] He makes winds his messengers,[a]
flames of fire his servants.

[5] He set the earth on its foundations;
it can never be moved.
[6] You covered it with the deep as with a garment;
the waters stood above the mountains.
[7] But at your rebuke the waters fled,
at the sound of your thunder they took to flight;
[8] they flowed over the mountains,
they went down into the valleys,
to the place you assigned for them.
[9] You set a boundary they cannot cross;
never again will they cover the earth.

[10] He makes springs pour water into the ravines;
it flows between the mountains.
[11] They give water to all the beasts of the field;
the wild donkeys quench their thirst.
[12] The birds of the air nest by the waters;
they sing among the branches.
[13] He waters the mountains from his upper chambers;
the earth is satisfied by the fruit of his work.
[14] He makes grass grow for the cattle,
and plants for man to cultivate—
bringing forth food from the earth:
[15] wine that gladdens the heart of man,
oil to make his face shine,
and bread that sustains his heart.
[16] The trees of the LORD are well watered,
the cedars of Lebanon that he planted.
[17] There the birds make their nests;
the stork has its home in the pine trees.
[18] The high mountains belong to the wild goats;
the crags are a refuge for the coneys.[b]

[19] The moon marks off the seasons,
and the sun knows when to go down.

[a] 4 Or *angels* [b] 18 That is, the hyrax or rock badger

creation? **2.** What's the psalmist's picture of the heavens (Isa. 40:22)? What are the "upper chambers" (Amos 9:6)? How are they held up? What's the purpose of the clouds, wind, and fire (vv. 3–4)? **3.** What holds up the flat, table-like earth (v. 5; 75:3)? What waters "stood above the mountains" (v. 6; Gen. 1:6–9)? How did God harness the waters (vv. 7–9; Job 38:8–11)? **4.** For what four things does water set the stage (vv. 10–14)? What are three fruits of the earth (v. 15)? How have these become enduring religious symbols? **5.** Does God seem concerned about the small things? How does this give confidence in God's ability to sustain creation? **6.** Why do you think the sun and moon were created on the "fourth day" (vv. 19–23; Gen. 1:16–19)? **7.** How does God's wise control of space and time affect the world? How are man and beast able to coexist? **8.** Why is "in wisdom you made them all" a pivotal phrase (v. 24; Prov. 3:19)? What other part of nature displays God's handiwork (vv. 25–26)? **9.** What do all creatures have in common (vv. 27–30)? How does God provide? How total is God's care (vv. 29–30)? What's the creature's greatest fear? **10.** What is the ultimate purpose of creation and the writing of this psalm (v. 31)? **11.** What does God's creation inspire the psalmist to do (vv. 33–34)? What commitment does it arouse? What motivates the strong statement in verse 35?

APPLY **1.** How does God provide for you physically, spiritually and emotionally? Is it enough or are you left wanting more? Is it good or mixed with bad? Why? **2.** When has God's provision come at just the right time? Have you ever thought God was tardy?

104:3 upper chambers. Pictures God's heavenly abode, his home. The reference to the *waters* above God's home is from Genesis 1:7, which says that God "separated the water under the expanse from the water above it." From the "waters above" God sends rain to water the earth (v. 13).

104:4 These picturesque words refer to God's heavenly host.

104:5 foundations. In ancient times, learned people wondered what held the earth in place. Often they viewed the earth as a giant building which needed foundations just like any other building. Here the earth is made firm by God, created with solid foundations that no one can move, except God himself, when he so chooses (93:1; 96:10; 1 Chr. 16:30).

104:9 set a boundary. God set in place boundaries for the waters so that they would never again cover the earth. This promise is recorded in Genesis 9:15.

104:10–18 These verses picture the creatures God created to live in the sky and on the land. This compares with the fifth and sixth days of creation (Gen. 1:20–31).

104:10–16 God had divided the water into two great expanses above and below (Gen. 1:7). The water below, on the earth, fills lakes and ravines, providing water for the creatures of the earth. The water above, from the heavens, brings rain to the earth and waters the mountains, the cultivated fields and the trees.

104:15 As the rains bring lushness to the fields, people can cultivate grapes to make wine, olives to make the oil and grain to make bread. The oil that makes a person's face shine could refer either to putting the oil on the face or to health that comes from eating good food.

104:19–23 The continuation of day and night and the certainty of the seasons reveal a world created by a loving Creator and Sustainer. The reference to the moon and the sun is a reminder of the fourth day of creation (Gen. 1:14–19).

20 You bring darkness, it becomes night,
and all the beasts of the forest prowl.
21 The lions roar for their prey
and seek their food from God.
22 The sun rises, and they steal away;
they return and lie down in their dens.
23 Then man goes out to his work,
to his labor until evening.

24 How many are your works, O LORD!
In wisdom you made them all;
the earth is full of your creatures.
25 There is the sea, vast and spacious,
teeming with creatures beyond number—
living things both large and small.
26 There the ships go to and fro,
and the leviathan, which you formed to frolic there.

27 These all look to you
to give them their food at the proper time.
28 When you give it to them,
they gather it up;
when you open your hand,
they are satisfied with good things.
29 When you hide your face,
they are terrified;
when you take away their breath,
they die and return to the dust.
30 When you send your Spirit,
they are created,
and you renew the face of the earth.

31 May the glory of the LORD endure forever;
may the LORD rejoice in his works—
32 he who looks at the earth, and it trembles,
who touches the mountains, and they smoke.

33 I will sing to the LORD all my life;
I will sing praise to my God as long as I live.
34 May my meditation be pleasing to him,
as I rejoice in the LORD.
35 But may sinners vanish from the earth
and the wicked be no more.

104:24–26 As if finishing the thought from verses 10–16, the writer completes the story of creation by noting the vast variety of creatures that live in the sea. This is recorded in the fifth day of creation (Gen. 1:20–23).

104:27–30 God's care over creation causes it to be sustained and to flourish. Creation continues in its cycles of days and nights, seasons and years, because of God's presence and loving care for it.

104:31 glory of the LORD. Referring to all of creation.

104:32 God created all things and lovingly sustains them. But he is always greater than that which he creates; so much so that God's glance or touch could destroy it if God so chose.

104:33 The writer has marveled at the beauty of creation and vowed to praise God as long as he has breath.

104:35 Creation, for all its beauty, has been marred by sin. The writer looks forward to the day when all sin and all sinners *vanish from the earth.* God promises that this will one day happen (Rev. 21:1,4,27).

Praise the LORD, O my soul.

Praise the LORD.[a]

Psalm 105

[1]Give thanks to the LORD, call on his name;
make known among the nations what he has done.
[2]Sing to him, sing praise to him;
tell of all his wonderful acts.
[3]Glory in his holy name;
let the hearts of those who seek the LORD rejoice.
[4]Look to the LORD and his strength;
seek his face always.

[5]Remember the wonders he has done,
his miracles, and the judgments he pronounced,
[6]O descendants of Abraham his servant,
O sons of Jacob, his chosen ones.
[7]He is the LORD our God;
his judgments are in all the earth.

[8]He remembers his covenant forever,
the word he commanded, for a thousand generations,
[9]the covenant he made with Abraham,
the oath he swore to Isaac.
[10]He confirmed it to Jacob as a decree,
to Israel as an everlasting covenant:
[11]"To you I will give the land of Canaan
as the portion you will inherit."

[12]When they were but few in number,
few indeed, and strangers in it,
[13]they wandered from nation to nation,
from one kingdom to another.
[14]He allowed no one to oppress them;
for their sake he rebuked kings:
[15]"Do not touch my anointed ones;
do my prophets no harm."

[a]35 Hebrew *Hallelu Yah;* in the Septuagint this line stands at the beginning of Psalm 105.

OPEN **1.** What period of history interests you most? What about it attracts you? **2.** Test yourself: What did you do two days ago? Five years ago this month? Which was easier to recall?

STUDY **1.** Like Psalm 78, this psalm is a lengthy run-down of Israel's ancient history. Why are the Jewish people frequently called to "remember" (vv. 1–7)? **2.** What is the gist of God's covenant with Abraham (vv. 5–7; Gen. 15:18–21)? Why would the promise of land be so important? Why didn't God promise spiritual blessings such as great enlightenment or grace? **3.** When they were a small and insignificant group of nomads, how did God esteem them (vv. 12–15)? In what nations did they wander (Gen. 12:1,10; 13:1,18; 20:1; 21:34; 28:10; 33:18–19; 35:1)? Why does God call them "prophets" (v. 15)? **4.** Who does the psalmist think is responsible for the famine (v. 16)? Who planned Joseph's slavery? Who made the Egyptians "hate" the Israelites (vv. 23–25)? Do you think God really controls all this? Do humans have no choices? **5.** What plagues of Egypt are not mentioned in this psalm (Ex. 7–11)? What ultimate purpose did the plagues serve? What was Egypt's response to the exodus (v. 38)? **6.** Why did God make a covenant with Abraham about some land (vv. 42–45)? What is God's higher purpose? What did God want to do for all people through Israel?

APPLY **1.** How can focusing your thoughts on God positively affect your attitude? Your

---

Ps. 105 This psalm was composed by David and "committed to Asaph and his associates" (1 Chr. 16:7) to sing to the nation on one of the annual religious festivals. The first 15 verses of the psalm are the same as the song recorded in 1 Chronicles 16:8–22. The entire psalm rehearses Israel's history, giving thanks to the Lord for all he has done on the nation's behalf. Similar reminders of God's work in Israel's history are recorded (78; 106; Josh. 24:2–13; Neh. 9:7–25).

105:1 Give thanks. The writer gives thanks through praising God for all that he has done for Israel. **call on his name.** People call on God through prayer. The twin imperatives of praise and prayer show the people how to rightly demonstrate their devotion to God for his saving acts in the past and for promises yet to happen.

105:5 Remember. This is important for all believers, just as it was important for Israel. Whenever we face difficult times, whenever we praise God, whenever we seek God's face in prayer—we should remember what he has done for us in the past. When people remember the past, they can more easily trust him for the future.

105:8–11 covenant. God's covenant with Abraham is recorded in Genesis 15:9–21. This covenant promised that Abraham would receive *the land of Canaan*, which Israel possessed at the time of the writing of this psalm. God's covenants are forever. As his promises of the past have always come true, so will his promises for events yet to occur.

105:12–41 This section of the psalm describes God's fulfillment of his covenant to Abraham—from the days of the patriarchs who were nomads in the land, to the days of God's protection of the people through the leadership of Moses.

emotions? How can it give you a sense of control over your life? Do you find comfort in remembering God's wonders? What are one or two recent wonders in your life? **2.** What does God think about those to whom he extends the covenant promise? Is anyone insignificant to God? What causes you to feel unimportant at times? Can this psalm help? **3.** How has God come through for you when you saw no way out? What has turned out for good? What did you learn?

16 He called down famine on the land
and destroyed all their supplies of food;
17 and he sent a man before them—
Joseph, sold as a slave.
18 They bruised his feet with shackles,
his neck was put in irons,
19 till what he foretold came to pass,
till the word of the LORD proved him true.
20 The king sent and released him,
the ruler of peoples set him free.
21 He made him master of his household,
ruler over all he possessed,
22 to instruct his princes as he pleased
and teach his elders wisdom.

23 Then Israel entered Egypt;
Jacob lived as an alien in the land of Ham.
24 The LORD made his people very fruitful;
he made them too numerous for their foes,
25 whose hearts he turned to hate his people,
to conspire against his servants.
26 He sent Moses his servant,
and Aaron, whom he had chosen.
27 They performed his miraculous signs among them,
his wonders in the land of Ham.
28 He sent darkness and made the land dark—
for had they not rebelled against his words?
29 He turned their waters into blood,
causing their fish to die.
30 Their land teemed with frogs,
which went up into the bedrooms of their rulers.
31 He spoke, and there came swarms of flies,
and gnats throughout their country.
32 He turned their rain into hail,
with lightning throughout their land;
33 he struck down their vines and fig trees
and shattered the trees of their country.
34 He spoke, and the locusts came,
grasshoppers without number;
35 they ate up every green thing in their land,
ate up the produce of their soil.
36 Then he struck down all the firstborn in their land,
the firstfruits of all their manhood.

37 He brought out Israel, laden with silver and gold,
and from among their tribes no one faltered.

105:25 whose hearts he turned to hate. God is sovereign. Even when evil people turn their dark purposes against God's people, God is in control of that evil and will ultimately work it for good. This refers to Pharaoh, whose heart God hardened "so that he will not let the people go" (Ex. 4:21). This allowed God to show the Egyptians his powerful signs and wonders on behalf of his enslaved people.

105:26–36 God sent Moses and Aaron to do great wonders in Egypt. The ten plagues visited upon Egypt (Ex. 7:14–12:30) are symbolically described here as only seven (the number symbolizing completeness). The Egyptians were devastated by these plagues both physically and spiritually. Each plague was directed at one of the Egyptians' gods, showing those gods to be powerless before the God of Israel. For example, the chief Egyptian god, Ra, god of the sun, was powerless to stop darkness from settling over the entire land (except over where the Hebrews lived) for three days.

38 Egypt was glad when they left,
because dread of Israel had fallen on them.
39 He spread out a cloud as a covering,
and a fire to give light at night.
40 They asked, and he brought them quail
and satisfied them with the bread of heaven.
41 He opened the rock, and water gushed out;
like a river it flowed in the desert.

42 For he remembered his holy promise
given to his servant Abraham.
43 He brought out his people with rejoicing,
his chosen ones with shouts of joy;
44 he gave them the lands of the nations,
and they fell heir to what others had toiled for—
45 that they might keep his precepts
and observe his laws.

Praise the LORD.[a]

Psalm 106

1 Praise the LORD.[b]

Give thanks to the LORD, for he is good;
his love endures forever.
2 Who can proclaim the mighty acts of the LORD
or fully declare his praise?
3 Blessed are they who maintain justice,
who constantly do what is right.
4 Remember me, O LORD, when you show favor to your people,
come to my aid when you save them,
5 that I may enjoy the prosperity of your chosen ones,
that I may share in the joy of your nation
and join your inheritance in giving praise.

6 We have sinned, even as our fathers did;
we have done wrong and acted wickedly.
7 When our fathers were in Egypt,
they gave no thought to your miracles;
they did not remember your many kindnesses,
and they rebelled by the sea, the Red Sea.[c]
8 Yet he saved them for his name's sake,
to make his mighty power known.
9 He rebuked the Red Sea, and it dried up;
he led them through the depths as through a desert.
10 He saved them from the hand of the foe;

[a]45 Hebrew *Hallelu Yah* [b]1 Hebrew *Hallelu Yah*; also in verse 48 [c]7 Hebrew *Yam Suph*; that is, Sea of Reeds; also in verses 9 and 22

OPEN 1. What period of history are you glad you weren't around for? Why was it so bad? **2.** Did you ever rebel as a teenager? As a preteen? Young adult? Older adult? What was or is the issue that most concerns you with regard to this?

STUDY 1. Chapter 105 focused on God's covenant. What does this one bring to light (v. 6)? For what "salvation" is the psalmist waiting (vv. 4–5)? At what point in time was this written (v. 41)? **2.** Eight examples of rebellion are given. Is the psalmist taking responsibility for his sins (v. 6)? Why does he link himself up with the sins of his ancestors? What sin comes first (v. 7; Ex. 14:10–12)? Why did God save them (v. 8)? Does their opposition hinder God's power in any way? **3.** Why is Israel so forgetful (v. 13)? How could anyone doubt God after having passed through the Red Sea? **4.** What did the people crave (vv. 14–15; Num. 11:4–5, 32–34)? Why do people get cravings? Are they wrong? Why did God punish them for this one? **5.** Who were Dathan and Abiram (vv. 16–18; Num. 16:12–14,26–33)? What sin deserved so severe a punishment? **6.** What rebellion led God to say he would destroy the people (vv. 19–23)?

105:45 precepts. God keeps his promises and expects his people to keep theirs. The word *"precepts"* here is the same Hebrew word as "decree" in verse 10. God's work of redeeming a people for himself through fulfilling his covenant promises has as its goal to guide those people to love him and conform their lives to his will. The people should praise God, but they should do more—they should obey him (1 Sam. 15:22).

106:6–43 The previous psalm focused on God's great works on behalf of Israel; this psalm chronicles Israel's history of rebellion that occurred despite God's care for the nation.

106:10 redeemed. This word is often used as a synonym for "delivered."

Why does the psalmist locate this at Horeb? What is at the heart of Moses' intercession (Ex. 32:11–13)? What difference does it make? **7.** What report did 10 of the 12 spies give on the land of Canaan (Num. 13:25–29)? In what sense was the land filled with "giants" or was this a metaphor? What is so wrong about believing the majority report (vv. 25–27)? **8.** What "trouble" came to Moses because of the rebellion at Meribah (vv. 32–33; Deut. 32:48–52)? What happened (Num. 20:2–13)? **9.** Over the course of 600 years in Canaan, what did the Israelites fail to do (vv. 34–39)? How did they "sacrifice" their children (Jer. 7:30–31)? **10.** What punishment befits their disobedience (vv. 40–43)? Where was God during the sentence of judgment? How is Yahweh's loyalty and love contrasted with Israel's? How does God's love prevail? **11.** How does this full confession of sin give the psalmist confidence in God's power to save (vv. 47–48)? What attitude comes after confession?

APPLY 1. Are you experiencing God's favor now? Is unconfessed sin standing in the way? Why is it important to confess sins to other believers (James 5:16)? Why do we not confess our sins to others when God instructs us? **2.** Is it hard for you to take full responsibility for your mistakes and failures? Are other people, things or circumstances usually to blame? **3.** Does forgiveness ever remove the consequences of sin? Why or why not? When have you suffered serious consequences even after being forgiven? **4.** How do you feel about making mistakes? Do you "rake yourself over the coals," or do you see them as opportunities to grow? What's good about taking your share of the blame?

from the hand of the enemy he redeemed them.
11 The waters covered their adversaries;
not one of them survived.
12 Then they believed his promises
and sang his praise.

13 But they soon forgot what he had done
and did not wait for his counsel.
14 In the desert they gave in to their craving;
in the wasteland they put God to the test.
15 So he gave them what they asked for,
but sent a wasting disease upon them.

16 In the camp they grew envious of Moses
and of Aaron, who was consecrated to the LORD.
17 The earth opened up and swallowed Dathan;
it buried the company of Abiram.
18 Fire blazed among their followers;
a flame consumed the wicked.

19 At Horeb they made a calf
and worshiped an idol cast from metal.
20 They exchanged their Glory
for an image of a bull, which eats grass.
21 They forgot the God who saved them,
who had done great things in Egypt,
22 miracles in the land of Ham
and awesome deeds by the Red Sea.
23 So he said he would destroy them—
had not Moses, his chosen one,
stood in the breach before him
to keep his wrath from destroying them.

24 Then they despised the pleasant land;
they did not believe his promise.
25 They grumbled in their tents
and did not obey the LORD.
26 So he swore to them with uplifted hand
that he would make them fall in the desert,
27 make their descendants fall among the nations
and scatter them throughout the lands.

28 They yoked themselves to the Baal of Peor
and ate sacrifices offered to lifeless gods;
29 they provoked the LORD to anger by their wicked deeds,
and a plague broke out among them.
30 But Phinehas stood up and intervened,
and the plague was checked.
31 This was credited to him as righteousness
for endless generations to come.

106:13 did not wait for his counsel. Not long after Israel had experienced God's awesome power in delivering them through the Red Sea, the people began to complain against God. Hungry and thirsty, they complained against Moses, demanding to return to Egypt where at least they had received food and water. They did not wait for God's "counsel" (his divine plan and power), but instead they gave in to fear and rebelled.

[32]By the waters of Meribah they angered the LORD,
and trouble came to Moses because of them;
[33]for they rebelled against the Spirit of God,
and rash words came from Moses' lips.[a]

[34]They did not destroy the peoples
as the LORD had commanded them,
[35]but they mingled with the nations
and adopted their customs.
[36]They worshiped their idols,
which became a snare to them.
[37]They sacrificed their sons
and their daughters to demons.
[38]They shed innocent blood,
the blood of their sons and daughters,
whom they sacrificed to the idols of Canaan,
and the land was desecrated by their blood.
[39]They defiled themselves by what they did;
by their deeds they prostituted themselves.

[40]Therefore the LORD was angry with his people
and abhorred his inheritance.
[41]He handed them over to the nations,
and their foes ruled over them.
[42]Their enemies oppressed them
and subjected them to their power.
[43]Many times he delivered them,
but they were bent on rebellion
and they wasted away in their sin.

[44]But he took note of their distress
when he heard their cry;
[45]for their sake he remembered his covenant
and out of his great love he relented.
[46]He caused them to be pitied
by all who held them captive.

[47]Save us, O LORD our God,
and gather us from the nations,
that we may give thanks to your holy name
and glory in your praise.

[a]33 Or *against his spirit, / and rash words came from his lips*

106:34–39 These words are a general description of the most heinous of Israel's sins. At their worst, the people worshiped idols and even sacrificed their children to false gods. This occurred because they intermingled with the Canaanites against God's command. Ultimately, these sins would lead them into exile.

106:40–43 The people's sins always had devastating consequences. From the time of the judges, their constant turning to idols caused them to be ruled by their enemies. The most severe case was the exile to Babylon. At that time their enemies not only ruled over them—they destroyed their nation, their temple, their cities and took the people away from the land and into captivity. God had promised to punish them if they turned away from him (Lev. 26:1–13—blessings; 14–13—curses; Deut. 28:15–68).

106:44–46 Even though God punished their sin, he never forgot his covenant with his people. When they cried out to him, God heard and answered them.

106:46 pitied by all who held them captive. This refers especially to the captivity in Babylon (2 Chr. 30:9; 36:22–23; Ezra 1:1–8; 9:6–9).

48Praise be to the LORD, the God of Israel,
from everlasting to everlasting.
Let all the people say, "Amen!"

Praise the LORD.

BOOK V

Psalms 107–150

Psalm 107

1Give thanks to the LORD, for he is good;
his love endures forever.
2Let the redeemed of the LORD say this—
those he redeemed from the hand of the foe,
3those he gathered from the lands,
from east and west, from north and south.[a]

4Some wandered in desert wastelands,
finding no way to a city where they could settle.
5They were hungry and thirsty,
and their lives ebbed away.
6Then they cried out to the LORD in their trouble,
and he delivered them from their distress.
7He led them by a straight way
to a city where they could settle.
8Let them give thanks to the LORD for his unfailing love
and his wonderful deeds for men,
9for he satisfies the thirsty
and fills the hungry with good things.

10Some sat in darkness and the deepest gloom,
prisoners suffering in iron chains,
11for they had rebelled against the words of God
and despised the counsel of the Most High.
12So he subjected them to bitter labor;
they stumbled, and there was no one to help.
13Then they cried to the LORD in their trouble,
and he saved them from their distress.
14He brought them out of darkness and the deepest gloom
and broke away their chains.

[a]3 Hebrew *north and the sea*

OPEN 1. What do you do when you get lost while driving: Stop at a gas station? Ask people on the street for directions? Drive around in hope of finding your destination? Panic? Make a phone call? **2.** Have you attended some kind of reunion? What was it like seeing old friends? Do you avoid reunions? Why?

STUDY 1. Who is invited to thank God (vv. 1–3)? What four groups of "redeemed" people are mentioned? How should each group respond to God's unfailing love (vv. 8,15,21,31)? **2.** Of what time in Israel's history do the lost travelers remind you (vv. 4–9)? What do they symbolize? What is their basic problem (v. 5)? **3.** What is the plight of the prisoners (vv. 10–16)? Of what time in Judah's history do they remind you (Isa. 45:2)? Why are they subjected to this plight? What belief of the times undergirds the reason given (Job 36:8–9)? **4.** In the same way, how are the physically ill viewed (v. 17)? What are their symptoms? How does the Lord answer their cry (vv. 19–20)? **5.** What is the sailor's greatest need (vv. 23–30)? What kind of seas are described (v. 26)? Who seems to be in charge of calm seas?

APPLY 1. With which of these four groups of people do you most identify? From what condition or state of trouble has God redeemed you: Aimlessness? Bondage? Illness? Danger? **2.** Who are the needy in your neighborhood? Your

---

107:1 Give thanks to the LORD, for he is good. These words form a traditional call to praise (106:1; 118:1,29; 136:1; 1 Chr. 16:34; Jer. 33:11). Praise to God often begins with giving thanks to God, for he is indeed good to his people.

107:3 from the lands. The writer rejoices in Israel's return from the Babylonian Exile. The people who had been dispersed had been gathered and returned to rebuild the land, the city of Jerusalem and the temple (Ezra 2; Neh. 1:8–9; Isa. 11:12; 43:5–6).

107:4–9 This psalm celebrates how the Lord had heard the prayers of his people in various times of need. These verses picture those rescued from wandering in the desert. Although God was punishing them for sin, he also protected them during that time (Deut. 29:2–5).

107:10–16 These verses picture God hearing the prayers of those enslaved in foreign countries. As noted in verses 4–9, although their time in captivity was punishment for sin, God still cared for his people and delivered them.

107:10 prisoners. This reference to prisoners refers to foreign bondage, but may also refer to other forms of distress in which people feel like suffering prisoners (Job 36:8).

10 Who will bring me to the fortified city?
Who will lead me to Edom?
11 Is it not you, O God, you who have rejected us
and no longer go out with our armies?
12 Give us aid against the enemy,
for the help of man is worthless.
13 With God we will gain the victory,
and he will trample down our enemies.

Psalm 109

For the director of music.
Of David. A psalm.

1 O God, whom I praise,
do not remain silent,
2 for wicked and deceitful men
have opened their mouths against me;
they have spoken against me with lying tongues.
3 With words of hatred they surround me;
they attack me without cause.
4 In return for my friendship they accuse me,
but I am a man of prayer.
5 They repay me evil for good,
and hatred for my friendship.

6 Appoint[a] an evil man[b] to oppose him;
let an accuser[c] stand at his right hand.
7 When he is tried, let him be found guilty,
and may his prayers condemn him.
8 May his days be few;
may another take his place of leadership.
9 May his children be fatherless
and his wife a widow.
10 May his children be wandering beggars;
may they be driven[d] from their ruined homes.
11 May a creditor seize all he has;
may strangers plunder the fruits of his labor.
12 May no one extend kindness to him
or take pity on his fatherless children.
13 May his descendants be cut off,
their names blotted out from the next generation.
14 May the iniquity of his fathers be remembered before the LORD;

[a]6 Or *They say:* "*Appoint* (with quotation marks at the end of verse 19) [b]6 Or *the Evil One* [c]6 Or *let Satan* [d]10 Septuagint; Hebrew *sought*

OPEN 1. On a scale of 1("Hey, go for it") to 10 ("Let's set up a committee"), rate your impulsiveness/caution. What would your rule of thumb be? **2.** If someone gave you $1,000 to satisfy an urgent personal need, how would you spend it?

STUDY 1. What motivates these attacks on David as far as he's concerned (v. 3)? Do you think he's completely innocent? How well do they know him (v. 5)? How is David different from them (v. 4)? **2.** What is the tone of verses 6–19? Is David: Cursing his enemies? Quoting their accusations against him (v. 6; Deut. 19:16–21)? **3.** What do you think was the water that brings a curse (v. 18; Num. 5:23–31)? **4.** How could David, the king, claim to be "poor and needy" (vv. 22–25)? Why would people "shake their heads" when they saw him? **5.** Does David lighten up at the end (vv. 28–29)? How will God "bless" these accusers? Why does he conclude with a vow (vv. 30–31)? **6.** How does this psalm agree with Jesus' attitude toward false persecution (Matt. 5:11–12)? Which verse of the psalm seems closest to his teaching? **7.** Peter saw verse 8 of this psalm fulfilled in Judas (Acts 1:20). What does this psalm have to do with choosing an apostolic replacement for Judas? What irony do you see in Judas receiving this curse he intended for Jesus?

APPLY 1. Have you ever been a victim in an intense conflict? What hurt did you sustain? What did you do with your feelings?

109:1–5 wicked and deceitful men. This psalm is an appeal to God to deliver the writer from false accusers, who are telling lies about him and attacking him without cause.

109:4 I am a man of prayer. David contrasts himself with his enemies. Either he has prayed and acted as he thought he should, or he is saying that he has prayed for these enemies. In any case, the writer has tried to be a friend and to do good, but these men are returning only evil and hatred.

109:6–15 Appealing for justice in the courts, David prays that God would deal with his malicious enemy and halt the unjust oppression.

109:7 prayers. Referring to petitions the enemy offers on his own behalf, David asks that the enemy's own self-defense would condemn him.

109:14–15 iniquity of his fathers. The Old Testament placed the guilt for sin not only on the sinner but also on all his or her family and possessions (Josh. 7:24). Punishment was often extended to the family (Ex. 20:5). David asks that his enemy's sins be punished, as well as the sins of his enemy's parents.

2. Do you tend to feel guilty: Too much? Only when you're wrong? Not enough? Even when it's mostly someone else's responsibility? 3. Are you responsible for your parents' mistakes? Has God "visited" the sins of the past generation on you and your family? What role does confession and self-awareness play? 4. How do you wrongly accuse yourself? How does the "accuser" take over God's place at your right hand? How can you let God have his rightful place there? Can the group help?

may the sin of his mother never be blotted out.
15 May their sins always remain before the LORD,
that he may cut off the memory of them from the earth.

16 For he never thought of doing a kindness,
but hounded to death the poor
and the needy and the brokenhearted.
17 He loved to pronounce a curse—
may it[a] come on him;
he found no pleasure in blessing—
may it be[b] far from him.
18 He wore cursing as his garment;
it entered into his body like water,
into his bones like oil.
19 May it be like a cloak wrapped about him,
like a belt tied forever around him.
20 May this be the LORD's payment to my accusers,
to those who speak evil of me.

21 But you, O Sovereign LORD,
deal well with me for your name's sake;
out of the goodness of your love, deliver me.
22 For I am poor and needy,
and my heart is wounded within me.
23 I fade away like an evening shadow;
I am shaken off like a locust.
24 My knees give way from fasting;
my body is thin and gaunt.
25 I am an object of scorn to my accusers;
when they see me, they shake their heads.

26 Help me, O LORD my God;
save me in accordance with your love.
27 Let them know that it is your hand,
that you, O LORD, have done it.
28 They may curse, but you will bless;
when they attack they will be put to shame,
but your servant will rejoice.
29 My accusers will be clothed with disgrace
and wrapped in shame as in a cloak.

30 With my mouth I will greatly extol the LORD;
in the great throng I will praise him.
31 For he stands at the right hand of the needy one,
to save his life from those who condemn him.

[a] 17 Or *curse, / and it has* [b] 17 Or *blessing, / and it is*

109:17–18 curse ... cursing. This *referred not to* "bad words" but to pronouncements of evil upon someone. David asks that his enemy's curses would return on his enemy's own head. This enemy's curses were so prevalent that they were like clothing and food to him; the enemy thoroughly enjoyed cursing others.

109:23 These words may describe a debilitating sickness that David was experiencing, or this poetically describes David's feelings of desolation in the face of his enemy's taunts.

109:30–31 from those who condemn him. David knows that he is upright and that God will come to his aid. So at the end of the psalm, he promises to praise the Lord.

Psalm 110

Of David. A psalm.

[1]The LORD says to my Lord:
"Sit at my right hand
until I make your enemies
a footstool for your feet."

[2]The LORD will extend your mighty scepter from Zion;
you will rule in the midst of your enemies.
[3]Your troops will be willing
on your day of battle.
Arrayed in holy majesty,
from the womb of the dawn
you will receive the dew of your youth.[a]

[4]The LORD has sworn
and will not change his mind:
"You are a priest forever,
in the order of Melchizedek."

[5]The Lord is at your right hand;
he will crush kings on the day of his wrath.
[6]He will judge the nations, heaping up the dead
and crushing the rulers of the whole earth.
[7]He will drink from a brook beside the way[b];
therefore he will lift up his head.

Psalm 111[c]

[1]Praise the LORD.[d]

I will extol the LORD with all my heart
in the council of the upright and in the assembly.

[a]3 Or / *your young men will come to you like the dew* [b]7 Or / *The One who grants succession will set him in authority* [c]This psalm is an acrostic poem, the lines of which begin with the successive letters of the Hebrew alphabet. [d]1 Hebrew *Hallelu Yah*

OPEN What is the most unusual first name you've ever heard?

STUDY 1. The New Testament applies this psalm to Jesus. If you lived in David's day, what sense would it make? Who is the first "LORD" in verse 1? The second? What will the first Lord do while the second Lord waits? **2.** Who is Melchizedek (v. 4; Gen. 14:17–20)? Was he a Hebrew? What two offices did he combine? Why are these roles conferred on the Davidic line (Heb. 7:1–19)? **3.** Would you apply verses 5–7 to David? What do you make of verse 7? **4.** What point did Jesus make with this psalm (Luke 20:41–44)?

APPLY What would you most like God to do to help you deal with your "enemies": Crush them? Change them? Help you understand them? Help you love them?

OPEN What job or career looks pretty good compared to your present one? Why is it attractive? What's wrong with the one you've got?

STUDY 1. Why is the author praising the Lord (v. 2)? How did God cause his works to be

---

Ps. 110 This psalm, written by David, is a prophetic picture of the coming Messiah-King who would rule over the nations. Verses 1 and 4 are quoted in the New Testament as referring to Jesus Christ (Matt. 22:41–46; Mark 12:35–37; Luke 20:41–44; Heb. 1:13; 5:6; 7:11–28). Like Psalm 2, this appears to have been a coronation psalm, written to be used at the crowning of a new king. David, writing as a prophet, not only composed a coronation song for a human descendant but was actually composing a song for his greatest descendant of all—Jesus Christ—who will one day rule as King of kings.

110:1 my Lord. King David wrote these words, indicating that he was addressing a sovereign, someone superior to himself. His descendant would be greater—so great, in fact, that David addressed him as "Lord." Jesus made a point of this statement to the religious leaders when he asked them whose son the Messiah would be. They answered that the Messiah would be the son of David. So Jesus, quoting from this psalm, asked why David, speaking of his son, would call him "Lord" (Matt. 22:41–46; Mark 12:35–37; Luke 20:41–44). Jesus' point was that David's descendant would be more than a human king, he would be God himself. This descendant will *sit* enthroned at God's *right hand,* referring to the place of highest honor (Matt. 26:64).

110:4 a priest forever, in the order of Melchizedek. The kings of Judah functioned in many worship-related activities. David had planned the construction of the temple and the worship service by the priests and Levites (1 Chr. 22–29). However, the king could not serve as the priest; in fact, King Uzziah was afflicted with leprosy for performing a function reserved for the priest (2 Chr. 26:16–21). This coming king, however, will also be a priest, in the order of Melchizedek, the king-priest of God Most High whom Abraham had met (Gen. 14:17–20). This is explained in Hebrews 7 and this verse is quoted in Hebrews 7:17.

110:5–6 The Lord is at your right hand. A picture of David's descendant who will have a place at the right hand of God (Matt. 26:64) and will one day be victorious (Rev. 19:11–21).

110:7 drink from a brook. Nothing will stop this king from completing the task of crushing the rulers of the whole earth (v. 6). He will find refreshment even in the heat of battle and will be reinvigorated to continue the battle until victory is sure.

"remembered" (v. 4; Ex. 23:14–17)? **2.** When did God provide food (v. 5)? How did God show power (v. 6)? What "works" of God show faithfulness and justice (v. 7)? **3.** What does the psalmist mean by the term "redemption" (v. 9)?

APPLY 1. How has God worked in your recent personal history? Can you think of any "works" you could ponder? **2.** The Hebrew acrostic starts each line with the next letter in the alphabet. Try writing your own acrostic psalm, using the letters of the words WORKS, FEAR or WISDOM to start the lines.

OPEN 1. What were you afraid of when you were a child? Dogs? Big trucks? The doctor? Did you outgrow it? **2.** What are you afraid of now?

STUDY 1. Using the same acrostic device as the previous one, how does this psalm flow out of the last one? To what "commands" does the psalmist refer (v. 1)? What does fearing God mean? **2.** What external signs point to the righteous man being blessed (vv. 2–3)? What kind of blessing is implied in verse 4? **3.** What two traits characterize his dealings with people (vv. 4–5)? **4.** What internal blessings are available (vv. 7–8)? Why does disastrous news fail to shake him?

2 Great are the works of the LORD;
they are pondered by all who delight in them.
3 Glorious and majestic are his deeds,
and his righteousness endures forever.
4 He has caused his wonders to be remembered;
the LORD is gracious and compassionate.
5 He provides food for those who fear him;
he remembers his covenant forever.
6 He has shown his people the power of his works,
giving them the lands of other nations.
7 The works of his hands are faithful and just;
all his precepts are trustworthy.
8 They are steadfast for ever and ever,
done in faithfulness and uprightness.
9 He provided redemption for his people;
he ordained his covenant forever—
holy and awesome is his name.

10 The fear of the LORD is the beginning of wisdom;
all who follow his precepts have good understanding.
To him belongs eternal praise.

Psalm 112[a]

1 Praise the LORD.[b]

Blessed is the man who fears the LORD,
who finds great delight in his commands.

2 His children will be mighty in the land;
the generation of the upright will be blessed.
3 Wealth and riches are in his house,
and his righteousness endures forever.
4 Even in darkness light dawns for the upright,
for the gracious and compassionate and righteous man.[c]
5 Good will come to him who is generous and lends freely,
who conducts his affairs with justice.

[a] This psalm is an acrostic poem, the lines of which begin with the successive letters of the Hebrew alphabet. [b] 1 Hebrew *Hallelu Yah* [c] 4 Or / *for* ⌞*the* LORD⌟ *is gracious and compassionate and righteous*

111:2 Psalms 111–118 are a collection of "hallelujah" psalms expressing praise to the Lord. Psalm 111 focuses on what God has done for his people. **works of the LORD.** These include his grace and compassion (v. 4), his covenant (v. 5), the Promised Land (v. 6) and, above all, redemption (v. 9).

111:5 provides food. God cares for the basic needs of his people. Jesus taught his disciples to pray for God to provide for their daily needs (Matt. 6:11) and said that God cares for people's most basic needs (Matt. 6:31–32).

111:7 faithful ... just ... trustworthy. These attributes of God are to be praised by his people.

111:9 provided redemption. God's greatest gift to his people is redemption—buying them back to be his own. He did this through the sacrifice of his Son, Jesus Christ, on the cross (Rom. 3:22–24; Eph. 1:7; Col. 1:14; Heb. 9:12).

112:1 This psalm focuses on the blessings given to those who fear the Lord. Verse 10 describes the punishment awaiting the wicked. This psalm is much like Psalm 1, which describes the ways of the godly and the wicked.

112:2 children. Godly parents who seek to raise their children in the fear of the Lord can trust that their children will be blessings to them and to others (127:3–5). God will honor the faithfulness of those who lead a godly life.

112:4 darkness. Refers to times of difficulty and calamity. For God's people, even times of darkness will eventually give way to the light of dawn because God is gracious and compassionate.

112:5 Good. Refers to well-being and prosperity. Such statements in the Bible are to be seen as general truths. This does not mean that God's people will not, at times, face difficulty. As a general principle, however, God's people can trust that he cares about their needs (111:5) and will always work for their ultimate good.

[6]Surely he will never be shaken;
a righteous man will be remembered forever.
[7]He will have no fear of bad news;
his heart is steadfast, trusting in the LORD.
[8]His heart is secure, he will have no fear;
in the end he will look in triumph on his foes.
[9]He has scattered abroad his gifts to the poor,
his righteousness endures forever;
his horn[a] will be lifted high in honor.

[10]The wicked man will see and be vexed,
he will gnash his teeth and waste away;
the longings of the wicked will come to nothing.

Psalm 113

[1]Praise the LORD.[b]

Praise, O servants of the LORD,
praise the name of the LORD.
[2]Let the name of the LORD be praised,
both now and forevermore.
[3]From the rising of the sun to the place where it sets,
the name of the LORD is to be praised.

[4]The LORD is exalted over all the nations,
his glory above the heavens.
[5]Who is like the LORD our God,
the One who sits enthroned on high,
[6]who stoops down to look
on the heavens and the earth?

[7]He raises the poor from the dust
and lifts the needy from the ash heap;
[8]he seats them with princes,
with the princes of their people.
[9]He settles the barren woman in her home
as a happy mother of children.

Praise the LORD.

[a]9 *Horn* here symbolizes dignity. [b]1 Hebrew *Hallelu Yah*; also in verse 9

APPLY 1. Do any of the lines in this psalm fit someone you admire? Do any fit yourself? Which one do you wish fit you? **2.** Is life really this smooth for the "nice guy"? Do you know any good people who aren't rich and carefree? Do you know any bad people who are? Why bother with this simplistic poem? **3.** Would you say you are generous? Give a recent example.

OPEN Do you ever give money to strangers on the street? Who would most likely get your money?

STUDY 1. Why praise the Lord's name (vv. 1–3)? **2.** What two extremes does God bridge? Where is God in relation to the heavens and the earth? **3.** Why does Hannah quote verses 7–8 in her prayer (1 Sam. 2:8)? Or Mary's (Luke 1:52)? Were they like the woman of verse 9?

APPLY 1. What name of God means the most to you? Why? Based on your life, what name could be added to the biblical ones? **2.** In what respect are you poor? In what respect are you barren? How might God lift you up?

112:7–8 heart is steadfast ... secure. The "heart" means one's emotions. No matter how people feel or how outward circumstances are affecting them, *they can remain steadfast in faith and secure in God's promises.*

113:2 now and forevermore. Those who love God and sing his praises will not rest until all the world is singing praises into eternity.

113:4 exalted. God is greater than all the nations of the earth; in fact, he controls them (Ps. 2). By extension, he is also greater than the gods of all those nations. God is greater than even the greatest parts of creation—he is above even the heavens.

113:7–9 In many religions, the lowly and poor were considered to have been abandoned by the gods while the rich were considered blessed by the gods. However, God cares about the lowly and needy and meets their deepest needs. Hannah (1 Sam. 2:3–10), Naomi (Ruth 1:11–13), and Mary (Luke 1:46–55) understood this.

113:9 barren woman. In ancient cultures, childlessness was the greatest of tragedies (Gen. 30:1; 1 Sam. 1:2–8). Some even thought barrenness indicated God's displeasure with the woman or her family. God, who controls all of creation, can provide a barren woman with children, as with Sarah (Gen. 21:2), Rebekah (Gen. 25:21), Rachel (Gen. 30:23), Hannah (1 Sam. 1:19–20) and Elizabeth (Luke 1:7,13).

OPEN Ever forded or waded across a river? What happened?

STUDY **1.** What ripple effect do you notice in the structure of the psalm? **2.** Why are the events at the Red Sea and the Jordan associated (v. 3; Josh. 4:23–24)? **3.** How is Sinai depicted? How does the psalmist's approach to events differ from the approach in Moses' song (Ex. 15)?

APPLY **1.** When did God first begin to speak to you? How did he draw you to himself? What main events would you retell in a personal psalm? **2.** What in your life was: Egypt? The Red Sea? The Jordan? Sinai? Water from the rock?

OPEN **1.** What brings out the artist in you? What kind of art do you appreciate? **2.** What modern gadget is conspicuously missing from your house? Why? Or do you have everything you need?

STUDY **1.** What trouble is written between the lines (vv. 1–2)? Why do the pagans ask where Yahweh is? **2.** What kind of gods are the pagans used to (vv. 4–7)? Why do they worship idols if they have no power? Why do the Jews refuse to represent God in sculpture or painting (Ex. 20:4–5)? What would be wrong with making an image of Yahweh? **3.** What do you think of religious statues and paintings? Is it wrong to depict Jesus in art? Why do you think the early church departed from the Jewish interpretation of the Second Commandment? **4.** Why do idolaters receive the fate in verse 8? **5.** Who are the three groups ad-

Psalm 114

1 When Israel came out of Egypt,
the house of Jacob from a people of foreign tongue,
2 Judah became God's sanctuary,
Israel his dominion.

3 The sea looked and fled,
the Jordan turned back;
4 the mountains skipped like rams,
the hills like lambs.

5 Why was it, O sea, that you fled,
O Jordan, that you turned back,
6 you mountains, that you skipped like rams,
you hills, like lambs?

7 Tremble, O earth, at the presence of the Lord,
at the presence of the God of Jacob,
8 who turned the rock into a pool,
the hard rock into springs of water.

Psalm 115

1 Not to us, O LORD, not to us
but to your name be the glory,
because of your love and faithfulness.

2 Why do the nations say,
"Where is their God?"
3 Our God is in heaven;
he does whatever pleases him.
4 But their idols are silver and gold,
made by the hands of men.
5 They have mouths, but cannot speak,
eyes, but they cannot see;
6 they have ears, but cannot hear,
noses, but they cannot smell;
7 they have hands, but cannot feel,
feet, but they cannot walk;
nor can they utter a sound with their throats.
8 Those who make them will be like them,
and so will all who trust in them.

Ps. 114 This psalm celebrates God's deliverance of his people from Egypt. This was a milestone in the nation's history. After delivering the Israelites from slavery, God gave them Laws and made a covenant with them as his own people (Ex. 19:4–6).

114:3 sea ... Jordan. These words refer to the parting of the Red Sea, which allowed the Israelites to escape from Egypt (Ex. 14:21–22) and the parting of the Jordan River to allow entrance to the Promised Land (Josh. 3:14–17).

114:7–8 presence of the Lord. As the Lord was with his people, guiding and protecting them, so he is present with his people today through the Holy Spirit. **God of Jacob.** It is a synonym for Israel. Jacob was the grandson of Abraham and son of Isaac. God changed his name to Israel (Gen. 32:28).

115:2 "Where is their God?" The psalmist quoted taunts made by evil nations that had fought and enslaved Israel. When Israel and its temple were destroyed, their enemies mocked them (79:10; Joel 2:17; Mic. 7:10).

115:3–7 Israel's God is in heaven and controls all things. The gods of the nations are merely *silver and gold.* Although these idols are fashioned with mouths, eyes, ears, noses, hands and feet, they cannot speak, see, hear, smell, touch or walk. Because they are fashioned by people, they are no more powerful than the inanimate silver and gold from which they are made (1 Sam. 12:21; Isa. 57:13; Jer. 14:22). They are worthless.

[9]O house of Israel, trust in the LORD—
he is their help and shield.
[10]O house of Aaron, trust in the LORD—
he is their help and shield.
[11]You who fear him, trust in the LORD—
he is their help and shield.

[12]The LORD remembers us and will bless us:
He will bless the house of Israel,
he will bless the house of Aaron,
[13]he will bless those who fear the LORD—
small and great alike.

[14]May the LORD make you increase,
both you and your children.
[15]May you be blessed by the LORD,
the Maker of heaven and earth.

[16]The highest heavens belong to the LORD,
but the earth he has given to man.
[17]It is not the dead who praise the LORD,
those who go down to silence;
[18]it is we who extol the LORD,
both now and forevermore.

Praise the LORD.[a]

Psalm 116

[1]I love the LORD, for he heard my voice;
he heard my cry for mercy.
[2]Because he turned his ear to me,
I will call on him as long as I live.

[3]The cords of death entangled me,
the anguish of the grave[b] came upon me;
I was overcome by trouble and sorrow.
[4]Then I called on the name of the LORD:
"O LORD, save me!"

[5]The LORD is gracious and righteous;
our God is full of compassion.
[6]The LORD protects the simplehearted;
when I was in great need, he saved me.

[a]18 Hebrew *Hallelu Yah* [b]3 Hebrew *Sheol*

dressed in verses 9–11? Who are "those who fear the LORD" (v. 13)? **6.** What kinds of blessings are promised (vv. 14–15)? **7.** What view of the afterlife does the psalmist hold (vv. 16–18)?

APPLY 1. Have you ever been asked "where is your God?" Has your faith been ridiculed? Not taken seriously? How did you respond? **2.** What are some idols? In what sense do you become what you worship? Are there any ideas, things, people that you trust more readily than God?

OPEN 1. Has your experience in dating or business made you feel people cannot be trusted? If not, what percentage would you say are honest? **2.** Do you owe anyone a lot of money? How do you plan to pay it off?

STUDY 1. Why is the psalmist so devoted to God (vv. 1–2)? Is this a good reason? What trouble had apparently befallen him (vv. 3–4)? **2.** What does the psalmist mean by "simplehearted" (v. 6; 19:7; Prov. 1:4)? Who was perhaps responsible for his "great need"? **3.** What clues do you find in verses 8–11 about the psalmist's problems? What did he "believe" (v. 10)? **4.** How will the psalmist try to repay the Lord (vv. 12–14,17–19)? What is the "cup of

115:9–11 house of Israel ... Aaron ... who fear him. In this triple repetition, the focus has been on the Israelite nation, the special group of priests and Levites, and another group, perhaps proselytes who were not born Jews but converted to Judaism. The three groups are addressed in verses 12–13.

115:14 make you increase. Referring to wealth, numbers and strength.

116:1–6 This psalm praises God for deliverance from death (vv. 3,8). This could refer to times of oppression and slavery. The writer praises God for hearing his fearful cries and saving him.

116:2 I will call on him. God holds power over life and death. The author experienced God's care for him in a time of great fear and certain death, so he declared his trust in God forever.

116:3 cords of death. This could refer to a severe sickness or to the fear of death experienced in times of war or bondage.

116:6 simplehearted. Those who are simple hearted are childlike in their complete trust in God. Jesus said that the kingdom of heaven would be made up of those with childlike faith (Matt. 19:13–15).

[7]Be at rest once more, O my soul,
for the LORD has been good to you.

[8]For you, O LORD, have delivered my soul from death,
my eyes from tears,
my feet from stumbling,
[9]that I may walk before the LORD
in the land of the living.
[10]I believed; therefore[a] I said,
"I am greatly afflicted."
[11]And in my dismay I said,
"All men are liars."

[12]How can I repay the LORD
for all his goodness to me?
[13]I will lift up the cup of salvation
and call on the name of the LORD.
[14]I will fulfill my vows to the LORD
in the presence of all his people.

[15]Precious in the sight of the LORD
is the death of his saints.
[16]O LORD, truly I am your servant;
I am your servant, the son of your maidservant[b];
you have freed me from my chains.

[17]I will sacrifice a thank offering to you
and call on the name of the LORD.
[18]I will fulfill my vows to the LORD
in the presence of all his people,
[19]in the courts of the house of the LORD—
in your midst, O Jerusalem.

Praise the LORD.[c]

Psalm 117

[1]Praise the LORD, all you nations;
extol him, all you peoples.

[a]*10 Or believed even when* [b]*16 Or servant, your faithful son* [c]*19 Hebrew Hallelu Yah*

salvation" (v. 13; Gen. 14:18; 1 Cor. 10:16)? What vows are fulfilled in public (vv. 14,18; Lev. 7:12–15)? **5.** What do you make of verse 15 (72:14)? Why do you think the psalmist put it here? **6.** What choices were given to slaves upon release (v. 16; Deut. 15:12–17)? What choice does the psalmist make? **7.** Who are the "nations" in chapter 117? Does the fact that they are being called on to praise the Lord indicate a more universal view of God than we find in the book of Psalms?

APPLY 1. What does God's "turned ear" (v. 2) say about how he feels about you? How can you strive to imitate God's readiness to listen? **2.** What thank offerings could you give to God?

116:7–14 The author thanks God for his personal care and love. He then considers in what ways he can repay God. Of course, nothing can be done to repay God, but the writer knows that the best way to show appreciation is to speak of God's salvation, call on God continually and fulfill his vow to obey God.

116:7 be at rest. This "rest" refers not to inactivity, but to a state of trust and contentment as a result of one's relationship with God. When one has peace with God, the soul is not restless but instead knows the peace of God and "rests" in God's truth and love.

116:10 I believed. Because the author had faith—he believed in God—he knew that he could call upon the Lord when facing difficulty. When in trouble or simply discouraged, he called upon God, trusting that God would answer his needs.

116:12–14 repay. Nothing a person does can repay God for all God has done. However, the author knows what expressions of devotions would please God. So he speaks of salvation, calls on the Lord and fulfills his promise of obedience.

116:13 lift up the cup of salvation. This may refer to a special part of a ceremonial meal, perhaps the thank offering celebrating God's deliverance.

116:14 vows. The author promises to honor his word as a way of showing his love for God.

116:15 Precious ... is the death of his saints. The word "precious" means that God carefully watches over his people, caring for them as precious ones at the time of their death (72:14).

116:16 The psalmist identifies himself only as a *servant* of the Lord and a son of a mother who was also a servant of the Lord.

117:1–2 With only two verses, this is the shortest psalm in the entire book and the shortest chapter in the Bible. All nations and peoples are called upon to

2 For great is his love toward us,
and the faithfulness of the LORD endures forever.

Praise the LORD.[a]

Psalm 118

1 Give thanks to the LORD, for he is good;
his love endures forever.

2 Let Israel say:
"His love endures forever."
3 Let the house of Aaron say:
"His love endures forever."
4 Let those who fear the LORD say:
"His love endures forever."

5 In my anguish I cried to the LORD,
and he answered by setting me free.
6 The LORD is with me; I will not be afraid.
What can man do to me?
7 The LORD is with me; he is my helper.
I will look in triumph on my enemies.

8 It is better to take refuge in the LORD
than to trust in man.
9 It is better to take refuge in the LORD
than to trust in princes.

10 All the nations surrounded me,
but in the name of the LORD I cut them off.
11 They surrounded me on every side,
but in the name of the LORD I cut them off.
12 They swarmed around me like bees,
but they died out as quickly as burning thorns;
in the name of the LORD I cut them off.

13 I was pushed back and about to fall,
but the LORD helped me.

[a]2 Hebrew *Hallelu Yah*

OPEN 1. Who was your favorite childhood hero? What did you admire about him or her? **2.** What is your favorite holiday? What makes it special? Which holiday would you rather drop?

STUDY 1. What clues can you find that this psalm describes the Feast of Tabernacles (vv. 19–20,27; Lev. 23:33–36,39–44)? What do these three groups represent (vv. 1–4)? What do they mean by "love"? **2.** What has the Lord done for the psalmist (v. 5)? Based on the attitude in verses 6–7, from what do you think he is free? **3.** In verses 10–12, what does it mean to cut off the nations? Is this the psalmist's personal story, or the story of the whole people? **4.** What do you make of verse 14? Is there a process being described, or simply two ways of saying the same thing? **5.** What is the psalmist's mood about being chastened (vv. 17–18)? **6.** Why does the psalmist call himself "righteous" (vv. 19–20)? Why does he feel worthy to enter the "gates of righteousness"? **7.** Who are the "builders" (v. 22)? What "stone" do they reject? Who did the New Testament writers see in this allegory (Acts 4:8–11)? **8.** "Hosanna" is Hebrew for "O grant salvation." Who do you think is "he who comes in the name of the LORD" (vv. 25–26)? How does this thanksgiving procession end (v. 27; Neh. 8:15–18)?

APPLY 1. Have you ever felt like a "stone the builders

praise the Lord for his love and faithfulness toward Israel. The destiny of all peoples is inextricably bound up in what God is doing for Israel (Gen. 12:3; Isa. 2:2–4; 14:1–2; 25:6–7; 56:1–8; Jer. 16:19–21; 33:9; Hag. 2:6–9; Zech. 2:10–11; 8:20–23; 9:9–10; Mal 3:12). **all you nations ... all you peoples.** Paul had this verse in mind when he wrote his letter to the church in Rome (Rom. 15:11) to show that salvation was offered not just to Jews, but also to Gentiles (all nations).

Ps. 118 This is the last of the hallelujah psalms (Ps. 111–118). It is a song of thanksgiving for God's help in delivering his people from enemies. As the last song of that liturgy, this may have been the hymn sung by Jesus and the disciples at the conclusion of the Last Supper (Matt. 26:30). Some interpretors think that a king of Judah wrote this psalm as thanksgiving for deliverance in battle. Verses 10–13 picture a battle in which Israel's army was vastly outnumbered, but God gave them victory. A second interpretation is that this is a song of thanksgiving for Israel's deliverance from Egypt and victories in the Promised Land. A third view interprets this as a song sung by the Jews after the Exile, perhaps when they rebuilt the temple or Jerusalem's walls. In all three of these situations, God graciously protected his people, and they had reason to offer thanks for abundant provision.

118:1 These are common words calling people to praise God (106:1; 107:1; 136:1; 1 Chr. 16:34; Jer. 33:11). God's people ought to continually *give thanks,* for their God is good and loves them forever.

118:2–4 Israel ... house of Aaron ... who fear the LORD. As in 115:9–13, the author uses triple repetition yet focuses on three different groups: the nation, the special group of priests and Levites and others, perhaps proselytes who had converted to Judaism.

118:5 setting me free. The word "free" literally means "in a broad place" or a "spacious place," as opposed to being in bondage.

rejected"? How did you handle it? Why do you suppose Martin Luther called this his favorite psalm? **2.** Do you feel part of a spiritual community that has gone through "chastening"? Or must you "go it alone" spiritually? Who is the "us" in "LORD, save us"? **3.** Where do you need: Help right now? Joy? Victory? Success? What promise do you hold on to?

14 The LORD is my strength and my song;
he has become my salvation.

15 Shouts of joy and victory
resound in the tents of the righteous:
"The LORD's right hand has done mighty things!
16 The LORD's right hand is lifted high;
the LORD's right hand has done mighty things!"

17 I will not die but live,
and will proclaim what the LORD has done.
18 The LORD has chastened me severely,
but he has not given me over to death.

19 Open for me the gates of righteousness;
I will enter and give thanks to the LORD.
20 This is the gate of the LORD
through which the righteous may enter.
21 I will give you thanks, for you answered me;
you have become my salvation.

22 The stone the builders rejected
has become the capstone;
23 the LORD has done this,
and it is marvelous in our eyes.
24 This is the day the LORD has made;
let us rejoice and be glad in it.

25 O LORD, save us;
O LORD, grant us success.
26 Blessed is he who comes in the name of the LORD.
From the house of the LORD we bless you.[a]
27 The LORD is God,
and he has made his light shine upon us.
With boughs in hand, join in the festal procession
up[b] to the horns of the altar.

[a]26 The Hebrew is plural. [b]27 Or *Bind the festal sacrifice with ropes / and take it*

118:14 This verse has become a song of praise for many who have discovered faith in God and the salvation he offers. This truly brings strength and joy to all who love God. (Isa. 12:2.)

118:18 chastened me severely. The writer realizes that the difficulty he has experienced was God's chastening work in his life, teaching him faith, humility and godliness.

118:19–20 gates of righteousness. This song, situated at the end of the hallelujah psalms, may have been the final song sung as pilgrims approached *the city of Jerusalem on* festival days (v. 27). The call to "open for me the gates of righteousness" could be a call to open the gates of the city and of the temple.

118:22–27 The people praise God for his care for them.

118:22 The stone the builders rejected. People of that day may have interpreted the "stone" as their king who was scorned by other nations but emerged victorious. It may also have been seen as the nation of Israel itself, also scorned by many powerful nations, but cared for by God as his own special people. **Capstone.** This was the stone at the top of an arch or at the corner of a building's foundation. In both cases, the stone was vital to the building's strength. The capstone is the keystone in an arch holding both sides in place; the cornerstone anchors and aligns the walls of a building. The nation of Israel and its kings had been despised and "tossed aside" by many in the world, but ultimately, God's plan for the entire world is brought about through Israel. Jesus applied this verse to himself as the one rejected by many but the most important of all (Matt. 21:42–44; Acts 4:8–12; 1 Peter 2:7).

118:24 The people were rejoicing because of God's deliverance. They have seen God's love for them in marvelous deeds of rescue and care (v. 23). For God's people, every day is a day that the Lord has made; every day is a day of rejoicing and being glad.

118:26 he who comes in the name of the LORD. The writer had defeated his enemies "in the name of the LORD" (vv. 10–12) and so came to praise God along with the others.

[28]You are my God, and I will give you thanks;
you are my God, and I will exalt you.

[29]Give thanks to the LORD, for he is good;
his love endures forever.

Psalm 119[a]

א Aleph

[1]Blessed are they whose ways are blameless,
who walk according to the law of the LORD.
[2]Blessed are they who keep his statutes
and seek him with all their heart.
[3]They do nothing wrong;
they walk in his ways.
[4]You have laid down precepts
that are to be fully obeyed.
[5]Oh, that my ways were steadfast
in obeying your decrees!
[6]Then I would not be put to shame
when I consider all your commands.
[7]I will praise you with an upright heart
as I learn your righteous laws.
[8]I will obey your decrees;
do not utterly forsake me.

ב Beth

[9]How can a young man keep his way pure?
By living according to your word.
[10]I seek you with all my heart;
do not let me stray from your commands.

[a]This psalm is an acrostic poem; the verses of each stanza begin with the same letter of the Hebrew alphabet.

OPEN 1. What do teenage boys you know do for fun? **2.** What teacher or friend helped you enjoy a subject of study you once disliked? How did this person encourage you?

STUDY 1. What is the positive intention of God's Law? What promise is implied in seeking the Lord wholeheartedly? Can only "perfect" people be blessed? Why or why not? **2.** Does the psalmist truly believe it is possible to "do nothing wrong"? Or is he speaking relatively? **3.** What deeper devotion underlies devotion to the Law? How is such commitment shown? What is the Law's final purpose? **4.** Can youthful indiscretion be avoided? Must one "sow their wild oats" in order to learn, or is there a better way? **5.** What practical steps can you take to pattern your life after God's Word? **6.** What attitude is a hallmark of following the Law? What does this say about the psalmist's perception of the Law?

APPLY 1. What or whom do you love so much that no language adequately expresses your devotion? **2.** What eight words that begin with "A" or "B" describe your group?

Ps. 119 This is the longest psalm—indeed, the longest chapter in the Bible—and an outstanding example of an acrostic (alphabetical) poem. This carefully constructed psalm has 22 stanzas, each one headed by a letter of the Hebrew alphabet. Each stanza contains eight verses, and the first word of each verse begins with the Hebrew letter for that section. This poetic form was not someone's attempt to be clever. People then did not have personal copies of the Scriptures, so they memorized God's Word and shared it with others orally. The repetitive structure of this psalm, with built-in memory aids, allowed them to do that easily. Psalm 119 expresses a passionate love for God's Word and a desire to live its truth. The author lived in poverty and was torn between his temptation to compromise for material gain and his desire to remain true to God. In the day it was written, this psalm was a rallying cry: "I will be faithful to God's Word!" It remains exactly that today. Who wrote this stirring eulogy to the Word of God? The author was most likely a priest or Levite who had returned from the Exile in Babylon and was suffering "trouble and disgrace" in Judea (Ezra 9:7; Neh. 1:3). Possibly it was written by Ezra, who devoted his life to teaching the Law (Ezra 7:10). The author personally experienced the poverty, hostility and ridicule he describes but may also have been describing the sufferings of others he knew.

119:2 statutes. The Hebrew word for "statutes" is a specifically covenant term. From the beginning, the author reminded his readers that obeying the Law was what made them God's special, blessed covenant people. **and seek him.** Meticulous obedience is not enough. People must have a personal relationship with the living God himself.

119:3 ways. The Hebrew for "ways" is common in the Mosaic Law as a reference to God's covenant requirements.

119:9 young man. In Jewish society, scribes only taught boys to read and write. The main reason for the Jewish educational system was to learn God's Word. **pure.** Hillel, one of the greatest Jewish teachers, declared, "An ignorant man cannot be pious."

119:10 I seek you. When God's people love him and spend time in prayer, they get to know God personally and are motivated to obey his Word. **do not let me stray.** The psalmist asked God to keep him on the straight and narrow. When people try to obey the Bible in their own strength, they eventually become either weak or legalistic.

OPEN **1.** When were you last feeling down in the dumps? **2.** What is your idea of something good?

STUDY **1.** Why does the psalmist's life depend on God's word? What does it mean to be a "stranger on earth"? **2.** When have you longed to know God's will? Are you longing for it now? **3.** How can you be in a position to have your eyes opened by God? Are good people immune from slander? **4.** Are those who follow God's Word exempt from stress? Depression? What does suffering motivate the psalmist to do? **5.** What is your attitude toward those around you who suffer? **6.** What three things does he ask God to supply (vv. 27–29)? How has he prepared himself to receive God's help?

APPLY What eight words that begin with "D" or "G" describe your group?

11 I have hidden your word in my heart
that I might not sin against you.
12 Praise be to you, O LORD;
teach me your decrees.
13 With my lips I recount
all the laws that come from your mouth.
14 I rejoice in following your statutes
as one rejoices in great riches.
15 I meditate on your precepts
and consider your ways.
16 I delight in your decrees;
I will not neglect your word.

ג Gimel

17 Do good to your servant, and I will live;
I will obey your word.
18 Open my eyes that I may see
wonderful things in your law.
19 I am a stranger on earth;
do not hide your commands from me.
20 My soul is consumed with longing
for your laws at all times.
21 You rebuke the arrogant, who are cursed
and who stray from your commands.
22 Remove from me scorn and contempt,
for I keep your statutes.
23 Though rulers sit together and slander me,
your servant will meditate on your decrees.
24 Your statutes are my delight;
they are my counselors.

ד Daleth

25 I am laid low in the dust;
preserve my life according to your word.
26 I recounted my ways and you answered me;
teach me your decrees.
27 Let me understand the teaching of your precepts;
then I will meditate on your wonders.
28 My soul is weary with sorrow;
strengthen me according to your word.
29 Keep me from deceitful ways;

119:13 recount. The Jews committed great portions of Scripture to memory—wrote them on their hearts (Prov. 7:3)—and could quote them at length to teach and encourage others.

119:17–24 God's servants are dedicated to obeying his Word. God blesses them for this but the ungodly and arrogant look on them with scorn.

119:17 I will obey. The psalmist knew that God provided and cared for him. He was grateful for this and wanted to obey God out of love.

119:18 wonderful things. There are wonderful treasures of truth hidden in God's Word. Believers need to pray for the Holy Spirit to open their eyes so they can see them and be inspired.

119:21 You rebuke the arrogant. Powerful, ruling Jews who had abandoned the Law lorded it over the poor believers. The poor could not rebuke them but took comfort in God's rebuke of these rulers.

119:23 slander me. Believers should continue to be devoted to God's Word despite scorn and contempt, despite being slandered by the "in" crowd.

119:25 laid low in the dust. The faithful but impoverished Jews were trodden underfoot by the arrogant rich. They were "weary with sorrow" (v. 28) because of oppression and slander. Powerless to resist, they could only cry out to God to rescue them.

119:29 deceitful ways. In Hebrew,

be gracious to me through your law.
30 I have chosen the way of truth;
I have set my heart on your laws.
31 I hold fast to your statutes, O LORD;
do not let me be put to shame.
32 I run in the path of your commands,
for you have set my heart free.

ה He

33 Teach me, O LORD, to follow your decrees;
then I will keep them to the end.
34 Give me understanding, and I will keep your law
and obey it with all my heart.
35 Direct me in the path of your commands,
for there I find delight.
36 Turn my heart toward your statutes
and not toward selfish gain.
37 Turn my eyes away from worthless things;
preserve my life according to your word.[a]
38 Fulfill your promise to your servant,
so that you may be feared.
39 Take away the disgrace I dread,
for your laws are good.
40 How I long for your precepts!
Preserve my life in your righteousness.

ו Waw

41 May your unfailing love come to me, O LORD,
your salvation according to your promise;
42 then I will answer the one who taunts me,
for I trust in your word.
43 Do not snatch the word of truth from my mouth,
for I have put my hope in your laws.

[a]37 Two manuscripts of the Masoretic Text and Dead Sea Scrolls; most manuscripts of the Masoretic Text *life in your way*

OPEN 1. What do you desire with all your heart? **2.** How would you describe your attempts at witnessing?

STUDY 1. What teaching does the psalmist want from God: Theory or practice? To what might "selfish gain" refer? **2.** What "worthless things" distract you from following God? **3.** Although he longs for God's Law, what "disgrace" threatens him? How does his poverty or disease make God look? Can he expect longevity and wealth from obeying God? **4.** To what "promise" does the psalmist refer? What commitment is necessary to effectively speak God's truth? **5.** Does the Jewish Law seem like a burden to him (v. 45)? Can anyone dispute the justice of God's Law? **6.** How can seeking God's precepts bring freedom (v. 45)?

APPLY What eight words that begin with "H" or "W" describe your group?

"the way of lying." The writer prays to not be like those who deceive themselves and depart from God's Law. **through your law.** God is gracious to his people, but not always by removing hardships. He often helps them by giving hope and strength with his Word.

119:32 set my heart free. Literally "enlarged my heart," caused my heart to swell with joy. The writer had gone from "weary with sorrow" (v. 28) to bursting with joy. How? By believing God's promises and finding strength in them.

119:33–40 The writer didn't merely pray to understand the Law, but for God to give him the desire to follow and obey it. He wanted to truly follow God.

119:37 worthless things. Surrounded by those seeking "selfish gain" (v. 36), the writer was also tempted by materialism and worthless luxuries. He prayed for God to keep his heart faithful to his word.

119:38 Fulfill your promise. The psalmist turned his back on the pursuit of riches and determined to obey God's Word. In the Law, God repeatedly promised to bless those who obeyed him. The writer now asked God to fulfill those promises (Matt. 6:33).

119:39 disgrace I dread. God's people were often poor, sick or forced into debt. Their healthy, wealthy oppressors would then boast that God was blessing them and cursing those who tried to serve God. David and Job struggled with this same issue (73:28; Job 21:7–16) and concluded that it was still better to serve God.

119:41–48 Taunted, called on the rug before kings, the psalmist had one prayer: to not be deprived of the Word of God. Why? Because with God's Word, he would be able to answer his oppressors.

119:41 unfailing love. The Law repeatedly stated God's unfailing love for his covenant people. It promised that God would deliver them. The writer now reminds God of those promises.

119:42 then I will answer. The writer did not seek prosperity and security. He merely wanted to be able to stand and say, "God has provided for me and protected me just as he promised he would if I trusted him."

OPEN 1. What do you find most comforting: A bowl of ice cream? Cookies and milk? A soothing song? A warm, cozy bed? Being with "warm and fuzzy" critters? **2.** What was most likely to get you "tied up in knots" when you were in high school: The opposite sex? Tests? Dealing with parents?

STUDY 1. What "promise" keeps the psalmist going in crisis? **2.** What two irritants threaten his hope (vv. 51,53)? **3.** What's the theme of his song? What's your song? How do you practice it? **4.** To what did "portion" refer to for the Israelite (16:5–6)? What does it mean to have the Lord as your portion? How might introspection help? **5.** Is the psalmist bound with physical "ropes"? What in society "ties you up"? **6.** How involved is the commitment to remember God's Law? How involved are you?

APPLY What eight words that begin with "Z" or "Ch" describe your group?

44 I will always obey your law,
for ever and ever.
45 I will walk about in freedom,
for I have sought out your precepts.
46 I will speak of your statutes before kings
and will not be put to shame,
47 for I delight in your commands
because I love them.
48 I lift up my hands to[a] your commands, which I love,
and I meditate on your decrees.

ז Zayin

49 Remember your word to your servant,
for you have given me hope.
50 My comfort in my suffering is this:
Your promise preserves my life.
51 The arrogant mock me without restraint,
but I do not turn from your law.
52 I remember your ancient laws, O LORD,
and I find comfort in them.
53 Indignation grips me because of the wicked,
who have forsaken your law.
54 Your decrees are the theme of my song
wherever I lodge.
55 In the night I remember your name, O LORD,
and I will keep your law.
56 This has been my practice:
I obey your precepts.

ח Heth

57 You are my portion, O LORD;
I have promised to obey your words.
58 I have sought your face with all my heart;
be gracious to me according to your promise.
59 I have considered my ways
and have turned my steps to your statutes.
60 I will hasten and not delay
to obey your commands.
61 Though the wicked bind me with ropes,

[a]48 Or *for*

119:45 walk about in freedom. Literally, "a wide space." The writer knew that if he put God first, God would give him space to breathe and would not allow him to be trampled under by sickness, debt or oppression.

119:48 I lift up my hands. Despite his poverty, the writer rejoiced in God's Word. He loved it so much that he raised his hands to praise it. What gratitude!

119:45–56 Whatever I suffer, whoever mocks me, I will be faithful to your Law, O God.

119:53 Indignation grips me. The psalmist was fervently dedicated to God's Word. He did not burn with anger at the wicked for oppressing him, nor for their proud boasts; he was indignant because by mocking everything he stood for, they were mocking the Word of God.

119:54 wherever I lodge. Literally, "in my temporary house." Due to poverty, he may have not owned his dwelling place or land. Another explanation is that he may have been referring to his brief stay on this earth (v. 19).

119:57 You are my portion. This verse is believed to identify the writer as a Levite who "had no inheritance among the Israelites" (Num. 18:23–24). It also shows his utter dedication to God.

119:61 bind me with ropes. Rich oppressors were in power. Justice

I will not forget your law.
62 At midnight I rise to give you thanks
for your righteous laws.
63 I am a friend to all who fear you,
to all who follow your precepts.
64 The earth is filled with your love, O LORD;
teach me your decrees.

ט Teth

65 Do good to your servant
according to your word, O LORD.
66 Teach me knowledge and good judgment,
for I believe in your commands.
67 Before I was afflicted I went astray,
but now I obey your word.
68 You are good, and what you do is good;
teach me your decrees.
69 Though the arrogant have smeared me with lies,
I keep your precepts with all my heart.
70 Their hearts are callous and unfeeling,
but I delight in your law.
71 It was good for me to be afflicted
so that I might learn your decrees.
72 The law from your mouth is more precious to me
than thousands of pieces of silver and gold.

י Yodh

73 Your hands made me and formed me;
give me understanding to learn your commands.
74 May those who fear you rejoice when they see me,
for I have put my hope in your word.
75 I know, O LORD, that your laws are righteous,
and in faithfulness you have afflicted me.
76 May your unfailing love be my comfort,
according to your promise to your servant.
77 Let your compassion come to me that I may live,
for your law is my delight.
78 May the arrogant be put to shame for wronging me without cause;
but I will meditate on your precepts.
79 May those who fear you turn to me,
those who understand your statutes.
80 May my heart be blameless toward your decrees,
that I may not be put to shame.

OPEN 1. Describe a time when you were glad that you were caught doing something wrong? **2.** Describe a time when you were wrongly judged.

STUDY 1. How many times does the psalmist use the word "good"? **2.** What does he assume about God's discipline? What character changes are evident? How does he assess the Law's value? **3.** Do you welcome God's discipline? How about "constructive criticism" from others? **4.** What is the purpose of the intellect? With whom does the psalmist hope to be popular? Why? **5.** Against whom will they be his allies (vv. 78–79)? **6.** Is it realistic to try to be "blameless"? What happens if you set a lower goal?

APPLY What eight words that begin with "Th" or "J" describe your group?

seemed to be on their side. They ruled the courts and imprisoned the "guilty." The poor, driven into debt, were also forced into servitude (Neh. 5:1–7).

119:65–72 The arrogant have lied about me and trampled me into the dust, but this has been good for me. Weak mortal that I am, I was going astray. God, you allowed me to suffer affliction so I would learn to obey your Law. I now realize that your Word is more precious than riches or any other thing I possess.

119:67 I was afflicted. Literally, "lowered, humbled." God's servant had been trodden underfoot, "laid low in the dust" (v. 25). He had endured suffering and pain.

119:73 give me understanding. The author recognized that the God who had the wisdom and power to create him could surely give insight into his Word.

119:74 those who fear you. The community of faithful Jews rejoiced whenever someone declared their determination to live God's Word.

OPEN Were your eyes to fail, what would you most miss seeing?

STUDY **1.** What mood is the psalmist in? Why does he feel blind? Have you ever felt this way? **2.** What is a "wineskin in the smoke" (v. 83)? Is his resolve fading? **3.** What does he still hope obedience will bring him? **4.** What bargain does he offer God (v. 88)? Have you ever made a deal with God? Did God come through? Did you keep your part? **5.** Is the "eternal Word" referring to the Law (Prov. 8:22–23)? From what do the commandments flow? **6.** Is it important to see a limit to "all perfection"? How does it affect your search for excellence?

APPLY What eight words that begin with "K" or "L" describe your group?

OPEN With nothing to do, what do you tend to meditate on or mull over in your mind?

כ Kaph

81 My soul faints with longing for your salvation,
 but I have put my hope in your word.
82 My eyes fail, looking for your promise;
 I say, "When will you comfort me?"
83 Though I am like a wineskin in the smoke,
 I do not forget your decrees.
84 How long must your servant wait?
 When will you punish my persecutors?
85 The arrogant dig pitfalls for me,
 contrary to your law.
86 All your commands are trustworthy;
 help me, for men persecute me without cause.
87 They almost wiped me from the earth,
 but I have not forsaken your precepts.
88 Preserve my life according to your love,
 and I will obey the statutes of your mouth.

ל Lamedh

89 Your word, O LORD, is eternal;
 it stands firm in the heavens.
90 Your faithfulness continues through all generations;
 you established the earth, and it endures.
91 Your laws endure to this day,
 for all things serve you.
92 If your law had not been my delight,
 I would have perished in my affliction.
93 I will never forget your precepts,
 for by them you have preserved my life.
94 Save me, for I am yours;
 I have sought out your precepts.
95 The wicked are waiting to destroy me,
 but I will ponder your statutes.
96 To all perfection I see a limit;
 but your commands are boundless.

מ Mem

97 Oh, how I love your law!
 I meditate on it all day long.

119:81–82 My soul faints. The author had remained faithful to the Law. He had endured oppression, poverty and persecution. But now he was exhausted (Heb. 12:3), literally, "fatigued."

119:83 wineskin in the smoke. The psalmist felt as if he had been blackened and shriveled through affliction (Lam. 3:1–4; 4:7–8). Still, he refused to take his eyes off God's decrees.

119:84 When will you punish my persecutors? The tone of Psalm 119 is one of humility, patience and trust. Though the writer had been persecuted "without cause" (v. 86), he chose to continue to obey the Lord. Instead, he left judgment in God's hands. He just wanted to know how soon it would happen (Rev. 6:9–10).

119:89 Your word. "By the word of the LORD were the heavens made" (33:6). John 1:1–3,14 clarifies this, saying that Jesus is God, he is the Word and he created all things. **is eternal.** The "eternal word" is not the Jewish law. Jesus said the Law would last "until *everything is accomplished*" (Matt. 5:18). Hebrews 8:13 says that the Law is now obsolete and "will soon disappear." The eternal Word is Jesus Christ. **firm in the heavens.** Jesus' power created all things and still holds everything together (Col.1:16–17).

119:92 would have perished in my affliction. If he had not been encouraged by God's Word, the psalmist would have lost hope and gone under.

119:96 perfection. All created things are "perfect" in that they are complete and finished. **your commands are boundless.** Literally, "very broad." God's Word is an inexhaustible source of wisdom.

119:97–104 Dear Lord, meditating on your Law gives me more wisdom than

98 Your commands make me wiser than my enemies,
for they are ever with me.
99 I have more insight than all my teachers,
for I meditate on your statutes.
100 I have more understanding than the elders,
for I obey your precepts.
101 I have kept my feet from every evil path
so that I might obey your word.
102 I have not departed from your laws,
for you yourself have taught me.
103 How sweet are your words to my taste,
sweeter than honey to my mouth!
104 I gain understanding from your precepts;
therefore I hate every wrong path.

נ Nun

105 Your word is a lamp to my feet
and a light for my path.
106 I have taken an oath and confirmed it,
that I will follow your righteous laws.
107 I have suffered much;
preserve my life, O LORD, according to your word.
108 Accept, O LORD, the willing praise of my mouth,
and teach me your laws.
109 Though I constantly take my life in my hands,
I will not forget your law.
110 The wicked have set a snare for me,
but I have not strayed from your precepts.
111 Your statutes are my heritage forever;
they are the joy of my heart.
112 My heart is set on keeping your decrees
to the very end.

ס Samekh

113 I hate double-minded men,
but I love your law.
114 You are my refuge and my shield;
I have put my hope in your word.
115 Away from me, you evildoers,

STUDY **1.** What do his enemies, teachers and elders have in common? What is the heart of his boast? **2.** How do you tell the difference between "right" and "wrong" paths? What role does the Law play? **3.** Has acting in a just but unpopular way ever left a sweet taste in your mouth? A bitter one? **4.** What are the functions and images in the word "lamp"? What does it illuminate? How does it direct us? **5.** With what oil does the psalmist keep it burning? What threatens to extinguish it? **6.** For what would he risk his life (v. 109)? How do you keep your lamp on? Have you gotten "burned out"?

APPLY What eight words that begin with "M" or "W" describe your group?

OPEN **1.** Apart from God's Word, what most sustains you? **2.** When do you feel most oppressed or overwhelmed?

STUDY **1.** Who are "double-minded" men (1 Kin. 18:21)? Have you ever wanted "the best of

my enemies, more than my teachers, more than the elders. This is because when I meditate deeply on your Word, you yourself teach me.

119:98 wiser than my enemies. His *enemies were worldly wise* and arrogant. They knew what to do to stay on top. However, the humble man of God with an intimate knowledge of God's Word had true wisdom. **they.** God's commands.

119:99 teachers. His teachers had been able scholars, but the writer had given himself *completely* to the Word "all day long" (v. 97). He truly tried to live these promises on a daily basis.

119:100 elders. Old men with many years of experience and practical wisdom.

119:105 light for my path. This verse echos Proverbs 6:23, which says that God's commands show clearly which moral choices lead to life and which do not.

119:109 take my life in my hands. He had already suffered much and his life was in constant danger (v. 107). This was more than poverty or hardships. He was in danger of being killed.

119:111 heritage. Literally, "inheritance." Again, likely identifying the author as a Levite. The Israelites were to support the Levites but had failed to do so, and the Levites were desperately poor (Neh. 13:13).

119:113 double-minded men. Such people were compromising, trying to "serve both God and money" (Matt. 6:24). They had strayed from the truth and God would discard them (vv. 118–119). A double-minded person is "unstable in all he does" (James 1:8).

both worlds"? **2.** What gives the psalmist peace of mind in his struggles with evildoers? What "hope" is he afraid might be dashed (v. 116)? **3.** How does the tension between belief and uncertainty leave him feeling? How well do you handle uncertainty? **4.** What situation has thrown the psalmist into confusion? What does he seek to understand or discern (v. 126)? Does his plea sound confident? **5.** On what does he rest his case: in his own merit or something else? **6.** What do you seek when the wicked around you prosper: more money or better insight?

APPLY What eight words that begin with "S" or "O" describe your group?

that I may keep the commands of my God!
116 Sustain me according to your promise, and I will live;
do not let my hopes be dashed.
117 Uphold me, and I will be delivered;
I will always have regard for your decrees.
118 You reject all who stray from your decrees,
for their deceitfulness is in vain.
119 All the wicked of the earth you discard like dross;
therefore I love your statutes.
120 My flesh trembles in fear of you;
I stand in awe of your laws.

ע Ayin

121 I have done what is righteous and just;
do not leave me to my oppressors.
122 Ensure your servant's well-being;
let not the arrogant oppress me.
123 My eyes fail, looking for your salvation,
looking for your righteous promise.
124 Deal with your servant according to your love
and teach me your decrees.
125 I am your servant; give me discernment
that I may understand your statutes.
126 It is time for you to act, O LORD;
your law is being broken.
127 Because I love your commands
more than gold, more than pure gold,
128 and because I consider all your precepts right,
I hate every wrong path.

פ Pe

129 Your statutes are wonderful;
therefore I obey them.
130 The unfolding of your words gives light;
it gives understanding to the simple.
131 I open my mouth and pant,
longing for your commands.
132 Turn to me and have mercy on me,
as you always do to those who love your name.
133 Direct my footsteps according to your word;
let no sin rule over me.
134 Redeem me from the oppression of men,
that I may obey your precepts.

OPEN 1. What is most likely to bring tears to your eyes? **2.** What have you been most zealous about over the past year: Politics? Building relationships with your unchurched friends? Sports?

STUDY 1. Why does the psalmist obey God's Law? What kind of world would we have if everyone acted in love and mercy? **2.** What name does he give those who ignore God's Law (vv. 118–119)? Why are their deeds especially painful for the psalmist? **3.** Does injustice and inhumanity ever bring you to tears? Give an example. **4.** Why does the psalm-

119:116 hopes be dashed. The psalmist trusted that God would keep his promise to bless the faithful and judge the oppressors. Until now, however, nothing had changed and his hope was nearly gone.

119:121–128 Lord, my oppressors have broken your law. They crush the righteous. It looks like they are winning! Don't leave me in their hands. I *know* you love me, so please do something. Rescue me!

119:126 time for you to act. God had warned that he would judge those who broke the Law. It had now been broken. The psalmist reminded God: "It's time to rise up and take action."

119:130 unfolding of your words. Think of a bud slowly and majestically opening up and unfolding into a beautiful bloom. When God reveals the mysteries of his Word to his people, they gaze into its beautiful depths.

119:133 let no sin rule over me. The psalmist was painfully aware of his own sins and shortcomings. He knew that only living the Word could keep him from falling into sin (v. 9).

[135]Make your face shine upon your servant
and teach me your decrees.
[136]Streams of tears flow from my eyes,
for your law is not obeyed.

צ Tsadhe

[137]Righteous are you, O LORD,
and your laws are right.
[138]The statutes you have laid down are righteous;
they are fully trustworthy.
[139]My zeal wears me out,
for my enemies ignore your words.
[140]Your promises have been thoroughly tested,
and your servant loves them.
[141]Though I am lowly and despised,
I do not forget your precepts.
[142]Your righteousness is everlasting
and your law is true.
[143]Trouble and distress have come upon me,
but your commands are my delight.
[144]Your statutes are forever right;
give me understanding that I may live.

ק Qoph

[145]I call with all my heart; answer me, O LORD,
and I will obey your decrees.
[146]I call out to you; save me
and I will keep your statutes.
[147]I rise before dawn and cry for help;
I have put my hope in your word.
[148]My eyes stay open through the watches of the night,
that I may meditate on your promises.
[149]Hear my voice in accordance with your love;
preserve my life, O LORD, according to your laws.
[150]Those who devise wicked schemes are near,
but they are far from your law.
[151]Yet you are near, O LORD,
and all your commands are true.
[152]Long ago I learned from your statutes
that you established them to last forever.

ר Resh

[153]Look upon my suffering and deliver me,
for I have not forgotten your law.
[154]Defend my cause and redeem me;
preserve my life according to your promise.
[155]Salvation is far from the wicked,
for they do not seek out your decrees.

ist grow weary (v. 139)? Is he trying too hard to change other people? Is he sensitive to people being treated unjustly? Is he too interested in being proven right? Has his zeal for the Law faded? Is he stubborn? Trusting? **5.** Have you persevered in an unpopular cause because you felt it was right?

APPLY What eight words that begin with "P" or "T" describe your group?

OPEN 1. What quest or questions would keep you up at night? **2.** When have you experienced rejection for something other than the cause of Christ? Likewise, when have you experienced redemption?

STUDY 1. What deal does the psalmist make with God? Does it seem like a fair bargain? Why is he having a hard time sleeping? What does he do with the insomnia? **2.** What do you do with time spent waiting in lines and traffic? **3.** The writer says both the wicked and God are near. In your experience who is closer: the wicked or God (vv. 150–151)? Why will God prevail? **4.** What does the psalmist hope obeying God's Law will bring him? **5.** Why does the poet "loathe" the faithless? Is it right to hate anyone? Is the lack of visible rewards getting to him?

APPLY What eight words that begin with "Q" and "R" describe your group?

119:145–152 I'm crying to you with my whole heart, Lord! I'm up before sunrise, begging you to help. The wicked are plotting to kill me. If you love me, please protect me.

119:150–151 wicked ... are near. The wicked were nearby. They were close to God's servant and ready to kill him. He was in real danger. **Yet you are near.** The one thought that comforted him was that God was also near and could protect him.

119:152 last forever. His word will endure forever.

OPEN 1. At whose word might you shake? Why? **2.** When was the last time your tongue got you in trouble?

STUDY 1. How much stake in earthly society does the psalmist have? **2.** Is it important to remember the Lord "seven times a day"? What benefit does the psalmist find in it (vv. 164–165)? Where do you need God's peace now? Are you waiting for the Lord's salvation? **3.** How honest are you with God about "all your ways"? With yourself? Others? **4.** God gave a specific code of Law to the Jews. How can God's "Laws" actively guide your day? What does it mean to delight in God's Laws? What doesn't it mean? **5.** How can you follow God's Word without "living by the book"? **6.** Do you find the end of this psalm a surprise (v. 176)? Is the psalmist satisfied yet? Do you think he ever will be?

APPLY What eight words that begin with "Sh" or "T" describe your group?

156 Your compassion is great, O LORD;
preserve my life according to your laws.
157 Many are the foes who persecute me,
but I have not turned from your statutes.
158 I look on the faithless with loathing,
for they do not obey your word.
159 See how I love your precepts;
preserve my life, O LORD, according to your love.
160 All your words are true;
all your righteous laws are eternal.

ש Sin and Shin

161 Rulers persecute me without cause,
but my heart trembles at your word.
162 I rejoice in your promise
like one who finds great spoil.
163 I hate and abhor falsehood
but I love your law.
164 Seven times a day I praise you
for your righteous laws.
165 Great peace have they who love your law,
and nothing can make them stumble.
166 I wait for your salvation, O LORD,
and I follow your commands.
167 I obey your statutes,
for I love them greatly.
168 I obey your precepts and your statutes,
for all my ways are known to you.

ת Taw

169 May my cry come before you, O LORD;
give me understanding according to your word.
170 May my supplication come before you;
deliver me according to your promise.
171 May my lips overflow with praise,
for you teach me your decrees.
172 May my tongue sing of your word,
for all your commands are righteous.
173 May your hand be ready to help me,
for I have chosen your precepts.
174 I long for your salvation, O LORD,
and your law is my delight.
175 Let me live that I may praise you,
and may your laws sustain me.
176 I have strayed like a lost sheep.

119:164 Seven times a day. Seven is a number signifying completeness. The psalmist was in constant communion with God, praising him throughout the day.

119:165 Great peace. Even when the world is in chaos around them, God's people trust that he is in control. This gives them peace. **stumble.** "Though he stumble, he will not fall" (37:24; 1 John 2:10).

119:171 overflow with praise. In the midst of crying out to God for protection, the psalmist repeated his intense love for God's Word, independent of whether God delivered him or not.

119:176 I have strayed. Despite his deep devotion to God's Law, the author humbly confessed his own shortcomings. He prayed, "Do not let me stray" (v. 10) but he *had* longed for the wealth that others enjoyed. The proud had strayed from God's Law in their scramble for things (v. 113), but the psalmist was not sinless either. In his last

Seek your servant,
for I have not forgotten your commands.

Psalm 120

A song of ascents.

[1] I call on the LORD in my distress,
and he answers me.
[2] Save me, O LORD, from lying lips
and from deceitful tongues.

[3] What will he do to you,
and what more besides, O deceitful tongue?
[4] He will punish you with a warrior's sharp arrows,
with burning coals of the broom tree.

[5] Woe to me that I dwell in Meshech,
that I live among the tents of Kedar!
[6] Too long have I lived
among those who hate peace.
[7] I am a man of peace;
but when I speak, they are for war.

Psalm 121

A song of ascents.

[1] I lift up my eyes to the hills—
where does my help come from?
[2] My help comes from the LORD,
the Maker of heaven and earth.

[3] He will not let your foot slip—
he who watches over you will not slumber;
[4] indeed, he who watches over Israel
will neither slumber nor sleep.

[5] The LORD watches over you—
the LORD is your shade at your right hand;
[6] the sun will not harm you by day,
nor the moon by night.

OPEN What "peace pipe" has helped you get back in the graces of an offended one?

STUDY 1. Called "ascents," chapters 120–134 were sung as pilgrims climbed to Jerusalem. Of what is the psalmist a victim (vv. 1–2)? **2.** How powerful is the tongue (vv. 3–4; James 3:6)? **3.** Among what kind of people have the pilgrims lived (vv. 5–6; Isa. 21:16–17)?

APPLY Do you "wear your heart on your sleeve"? Or do you keep your emotional guard up? Why?

OPEN Are you more of a "night owl" or a "morning lark"? What are your most creative hours?

STUDY 1. What is the mood of pilgrims on a winding road through hills? To what are they vulnerable (vv. 1–3)? How much more after nightfall? **2.** What comfort does the traveler receive for the journey (vv. 3,5–8)?

APPLY 1. Do you like to travel or dread it? What dangers lie on the road on inward journeys? **2.** Does God protect you? Do you feel invincible? What form has God's protection taken for you?

---

breath, he declared that his own efforts had not kept him faithful, but God is merciful.

Ps. 120 This psalm is the first of a group of psalms (120 through 134) which have the heading "A song of ascents." Some take "ascents" to mean the stairs leading up to the temple. The generally accepted view, however, is that these psalms were sung by pilgrims as they "ascended up" to the temple in Jerusalem for the annual Jewish festivals (Ex. 23:14–17; Mic. 4:2). Crowds of pilgrims traveling to Jerusalem often rejoiced, sang and played musical instruments as they went (Isa. 30:29). This group of psalms is known in Jewish liturgy as the Great Hallel (from *halal*, "to praise").

120:2 Save me, O LORD. The Jewish people who lived far from God's temple in Judah were often surrounded by foes. They needed God's protection.

120:5 I dwell in Meshech ... Kedar. After the Exile, Jews lived throughout the Persian Empire (Est. 3:8). They lived from Meshech (central Asia Minor) in the north to Kedar in Arabia to the south.

121:1 the hills. Refers to the group of hills on which Jerusalem is situated. Because the temple was there, help was to come from the temple, from God.

121:3 not let your foot slip. This can refer to physical protection (91:9–12) as well as spiritual protection. God will help believers keep walking in the way of truth.

121:4 he who watches over Israel. God loves his people and protects them.

3. When do you feel most vulnerable? How do you protect yourself?

OPEN In what way, small or large, did you "make peace" with someone this past week?

STUDY **1.** Why does David rejoice (v. 1)? What is the mood of the pilgrim crowd (vv. 3–5)? **2.** What does it mean that Jerusalem is "compacted" (v. 3; Neh. 7:4)? **3.** For what two reasons do the tribes come here (vv. 4–5; Deut. 16:16–17, 17:8)? **4.** How are the pilgrims asked to show concern for Jerusalem (vv. 6–9)?

APPLY **1.** On a scale of 1–10, rate your own eagerness for worship when that time comes around, if "1" is "Oh no, again!" and "10" is "I can't wait!" **2.** What helps you look forward to worship? What makes you desire other activity?

OPEN Toward what do your eyes turn most readily: The opposite sex? Beautiful art? A fancy car? Any sign that says "SALE!"?

STUDY **1.** What "contempt" have the pilgrims faced (123:3; Neh. 4:1–3)? **2.** For what do

7 The LORD will keep you from all harm—
he will watch over your life;
8 the LORD will watch over your coming and going
both now and forevermore.

Psalm 122

A song of ascents. Of David.

1 I rejoiced with those who said to me,
"Let us go to the house of the LORD."
2 Our feet are standing
in your gates, O Jerusalem.

3 Jerusalem is built like a city
that is closely compacted together.
4 That is where the tribes go up,
the tribes of the LORD,
to praise the name of the LORD
according to the statute given to Israel.
5 There the thrones for judgment stand,
the thrones of the house of David.

6 Pray for the peace of Jerusalem:
"May those who love you be secure.
7 May there be peace within your walls
and security within your citadels."
8 For the sake of my brothers and friends,
I will say, "Peace be within you."
9 For the sake of the house of the LORD our God,
I will seek your prosperity.

Psalm 123

A song of ascents.

1 I lift up my eyes to you,
to you whose throne is in heaven.
2 As the eyes of slaves look to the hand of their master,
as the eyes of a maid look to the hand of her mistress,

121:8 your coming and going. Originally this referred to the Jews coming up to the feasts, then going back home. God still protects believers today in all their comings and goings.

122:1 I rejoiced. Great rejoicing greeted pilgrims arriving safely in Jerusalem at the temple of God.

122:3–5 To the scattered Jews, Jerusalem was a holy city, the center of their faith.

122:3 closely compacted together. Jerusalem was a small, tight, well-fortified city. Jesus compared Christians to "a city on a hill" (Matt. 5:14). The church is also compared to a temple in which believers, like stones, are "built together" (Eph. 2:20–22).

122:4 to praise. The Jews praised God wherever they lived, but "according to the statute given to Israel," three times a year they were to go to Jerusalem to worship God.

122:6 In Hebrew a beautiful wordplay unites the words "pray," "peace," "Jerusalem" and "be secure." **those who *love you.*** Most Jews lived in distant lands and could not stay in Jerusalem. The question was, did they *love* Jerusalem? If so, God would be with them and bless them wherever they lived.

Ps.123 As God's people worship in his presence, they acknowledge their dependence upon him. They also ask him to have mercy upon them and protect them from their enemies.

123:1 throne is in heaven. Now that they stood in the very temple of God, believers still had to look up, for God's throne is in heaven, not on earth. God's name was in his temple, but his throne was not (2 Chr. 6:18; Acts 7:48).

123:2 slaves ... maid. Humble, faithful men and women of God are utterly dependent upon God. Just as slaves and maids look to their masters, God's people look to him for mercy.

so our eyes look to the LORD our God,
till he shows us his mercy.

3 Have mercy on us, O LORD, have mercy on us,
for we have endured much contempt.
4 We have endured much ridicule from the proud,
much contempt from the arrogant.

Psalm 124

A song of ascents. Of David.

1 If the LORD had not been on our side—
let Israel say—
2 if the LORD had not been on our side
when men attacked us,
3 when their anger flared against us,
they would have swallowed us alive;
4 the flood would have engulfed us,
the torrent would have swept over us,
5 the raging waters
would have swept us away.

6 Praise be to the LORD,
who has not let us be torn by their teeth.
7 We have escaped like a bird
out of the fowler's snare;
the snare has been broken,
and we have escaped.
8 Our help is in the name of the LORD,
the Maker of heaven and earth.

Psalm 125

A song of ascents.

1 Those who trust in the LORD are like Mount Zion,
which cannot be shaken but endures forever.
2 As the mountains surround Jerusalem,
so the LORD surrounds his people
both now and forevermore.

3 The scepter of the wicked will not remain
over the land allotted to the righteous,
for then the righteous might use
their hands to do evil.

slaves look to their masters? The psalmist to God? **3.** Why do the proud ridicule? Is it due to: Superiority or hidden inferiority? **4.** Jerusalem has never been threatened by flood. What foes might David be describing (124:1)? **5.** What realization leads to praise (124:6)? **6.** How do verses 7 and 8 of chapter 124 further underscore Israel's helplessness and God's helpfulness?

APPLY 1. What "flood" threatens to engulf you right now? **2.** In the midst of what threatens you now, do you feel more like a soaring bird or a dead duck?

OPEN What has been one of your wisest purchases in terms of durability and quality?

STUDY 1. How do these pilgrims feel going up the mountain pass (vv. 1–2)? Are the trusting immune from shaking? **2.** What does the poet fear might happen if foreign domination isn't removed (v. 3)?

APPLY 1. What tempts you at home, work, school or in society? How do you stay "true"? **2.** When is it hardest for you to trust the Lord? Why is that?

124:2–5 when men attacked. Enemies had tried to annihilate Israel many times during her history. God had saved Israel each time. Haman's recent genocidal attack had also failed (Est. 3:12–13; 8:10–11).

124:6 torn by their teeth. The enemies of God's people were seen as vicious beasts.

124:7 snare has been broken. Haman had set a snare to catch the Jews, but the snare had been broken and the Jews had "escaped like a bird."

125:1,2 Those who trust in the LORD. Foreign oppressors tried to push the Jews around, but trusting in God made Israel as unmovable as a mountain. **The LORD surrounds.** God is able to put a ring of protection and blessing around his people that the enemy cannot penetrate (Job 1:10).

125:3 scepter of the wicked. This probably refers to Persian rulers (Neh. 9:36–37). **land allotted to the righteous.** God had given the land to his people. Foreign control of it was only temporary. **the righteous might.** Some Jews had learned how to "use the system" and prosper through unjust and fraudulent practices. Faithful Jews were tempted to do the same.

OPEN What period could you describe as your "golden years"? Why?

STUDY **1.** What mood does "we were like men who dreamed" capture? What verses show the exiles have mixed feelings? **2.** On what do they agree (vv. 2–3)? **3.** What problems do they still face (vv. 4–6; Neh. 5:1–5)? How do the two parables of God answering prayer differ?

APPLY **1.** Has God ever done something so great you had to pinch yourself to see if you were dreaming? **2.** How does God tend to answer your prayers: A flash flood or a long growing season?

OPEN Were you to build a new house today, what would you want to make sure you include?

STUDY **1.** What work does Solomon renounce (v. 1)? **2.** How do those who rely on their own efforts see their work (v. 2)? **3.** Is the beginning tied to the end? What is said about large families? Do you agree? What happens "in the gate" (v. 5)?

APPLY **1.** How often do you rise early or stay up late to get work done? How is this affecting you? **2.** What stresses most frequently rob you of sleep? **3.** How can God help us with this?

---

4 Do good, O LORD, to those who are good,
to those who are upright in heart.
5 But those who turn to crooked ways
the LORD will banish with the evildoers.

Peace be upon Israel.

Psalm 126

A song of ascents.

1 When the LORD brought back the captives to[a] Zion,
we were like men who dreamed.[b]
2 Our mouths were filled with laughter,
our tongues with songs of joy.
Then it was said among the nations,
"The LORD has done great things for them."
3 The LORD has done great things for us,
and we are filled with joy.

4 Restore our fortunes,[c] O LORD,
like streams in the Negev.
5 Those who sow in tears
will reap with songs of joy.
6 He who goes out weeping,
carrying seed to sow,
will return with songs of joy,
carrying sheaves with him.

Psalm 127

A song of ascents. Of Solomon.

1 Unless the LORD builds the house,
its builders labor in vain.
Unless the LORD watches over the city,
the watchmen stand guard in vain.
2 In vain you rise early
and stay up late,
toiling for food to eat—
for he grants sleep to[d] those he loves.

3 Sons are a heritage from the LORD,

[a]1 Or *LORD restored the fortunes of* [b]1 Or *men restored to health* [c]4 Or *Bring back our captives*
[d]2 Or *eat— / for while they sleep he provides for*

126:1 like men who dreamed. For years the Jews had dreamed of returning to Israel. When they finally returned, they were so overcome with joy they could scarcely believe it was happening.

126:2 filled with laughter. As the returning exiles caught sight of Mount Zion, they laughed and whooped with joy. ***among the nations.*** The surrounding nations knew what had happened to the Jews. Now they looked on in awe as God fulfilled his word and brought his people back.

126:4 Restore our fortunes. They returned to their land to find it neglected and overgrown and strangers occupying the best fields. They prayed for God to restore their lands and livelihoods. **like streams in the Negev.** These desert wadis were dry and empty in the summer but filled with water when the winter rains came.

127:1–2 Unless the LORD builds. God blesses hard work but warns that anxious, frantic labor is futile. If his people fail to trust him as their ultimate source of shelter, security and food, they become workaholics and burn out.

127:3 Sons. Children are not just by-products of sexual relations. Like all else, they too are gifts given by God. **heritage.** In Israelite society, a man's chief inheritance was the land his father passed down to him. Children were a part of the heritage because without sons to inherit the land, it would pass out of a family's possession.

children a reward from him.
4 Like arrows in the hands of a warrior
are sons born in one's youth.
5 Blessed is the man
whose quiver is full of them.
They will not be put to shame
when they contend with their enemies in the gate.

Psalm 128

A song of ascents.

1 Blessed are all who fear the LORD,
who walk in his ways.
2 You will eat the fruit of your labor;
blessings and prosperity will be yours.
3 Your wife will be like a fruitful vine
within your house;
your sons will be like olive shoots
around your table.
4 Thus is the man blessed
who fears the LORD.

5 May the LORD bless you from Zion
all the days of your life;
may you see the prosperity of Jerusalem,
6 and may you live to see your children's children.

Peace be upon Israel.

Psalm 129

A song of ascents.

1 They have greatly oppressed me from my youth—
let Israel say—
2 they have greatly oppressed me from my youth,
but they have not gained the victory over me.
3 Plowmen have plowed my back
and made their furrows long.
4 But the LORD is righteous;
he has cut me free from the cords of the wicked.

5 May all who hate Zion
be turned back in shame.

OPEN Describe your domestic happiness from a fruit picker's perspective: Out of season? Ripening? Ripe and juicy? Rotting?

STUDY **1.** What type of blessings are promised the "man who fears the LORD"? Why not blessings of a more spiritual nature? **2.** How are the individual blessings bound up with national prosperity (vv. 5–6)? **3.** What family-related blessing was especially valued at this time (v. 6)?

APPLY **1.** What blessed event do you most want to live to see? **2.** If you were to liken your own family relationships to a plant, would it be more like a fruitful vine (v. 3) or a thornbush? **3.** What needs to happen to nurture your family into a healthier plant?

OPEN What chore would you prefer: mowing the lawn, putting on a new roof or cleaning house? Other?

STUDY **1.** Why has Israel been oppressed and hated throughout history (vv. 1–3)? How have the Jews managed to outlive every oppressor (v. 4)? **2.** What does the psalmist wish for the "haters of Zion" (vv. 5–8)? Do you like this attitude? **3.** What is freedom? Does it lie in political sovereignty? What internal menace always plagued Israel?

127:5 contend with their enemies. When falsely accused in court, a man with many children would have lots of zealous character witnesses to testify on his behalf. **in the gate.** In the Old Testament, courts were held in public just inside the city gates (Ruth 4:1–2).

128:2 the fruit of your labor. God's people of all ages have longed to receive a full reward for their hard work, unhindered by oppression, fraud or theft.

128:3 Your wife. Psalm 128 is called the marriage prayer as it was often sung at Jewish weddings. Marital bliss has always been one of the greatest blessings.

128:5–6 bless you. All the preceding blessings, including long life to enjoy them, are now wished upon the faithful. **prosperity of Jerusalem.** A prosperous capital meant a prosperous people. Jerusalem was also the heart of the Jews' faith and national identity. When that prospered, the nation was spiritually healthy.

129:2 have not gained the victory. God guards his people. He allows them to go through hard times to test their faith, but usually does not allow their enemies to destroy or overcome them or to be held in captivity more than God would allow (2 Cor. 4:8–9).

APPLY 1. Have you ever suffered harsh treatment? Are you emotionally tied up? How? Has God cut the cords for you before? 2. Can this group become "freedom fighters" for you?

OPEN 1. Have you ever lost sleep anticipating the next day's events? Did it turn out like you hoped or like you had feared? 2. What kind of child were you: Quiet and well-behaved or active and mischievous?

STUDY 1. Where are "the depths" (v. 1)? 2. What disrupted his relationship with God (v. 3)? How does forgiveness lead to revering God (v. 4)? 3. With what attitude does he await forgiveness (vv. 5–6)? What is God's attitude? 4. Why do you think chapter 131 is a standard for funerals of believers? 5. What does David avoid (v. 1)? Why? 6. What does the "weaned child" image suggest? 7. What's important to David?

APPLY 1. To what kind of infant would you compare your soul right now: One peacefully sleeping? One smiling and making cute noises? One with colic? 2. How do you "still your soul"? 3. To what "weaning" has spiritual growth called you?

6 May they be like grass on the roof,
which withers before it can grow;
7 with it the reaper cannot fill his hands,
nor the one who gathers fill his arms.
8 May those who pass by not say,
"The blessing of the LORD be upon you;
we bless you in the name of the LORD."

Psalm 130

A song of ascents.

1 Out of the depths I cry to you, O LORD;
2 O Lord, hear my voice.
Let your ears be attentive
to my cry for mercy.

3 If you, O LORD, kept a record of sins,
O Lord, who could stand?
4 But with you there is forgiveness;
therefore you are feared.

5 I wait for the LORD, my soul waits,
and in his word I put my hope.
6 My soul waits for the Lord
more than watchmen wait for the morning,
more than watchmen wait for the morning.

7 O Israel, put your hope in the LORD,
for with the LORD is unfailing love
and with him is full redemption.
8 He himself will redeem Israel
from all their sins.

Psalm 131

A song of ascents. Of David.

1 My heart is not proud, O LORD,
my eyes are not haughty;
I do not concern myself with great matters
or things too wonderful for me.
2 But I have stilled and quieted my soul;

129:6 withers before it can grow. Grass cannot take deep root on a hard, sunbaked roof. It is scorched before it bears fruit. The psalmist prays that God will stop those who hate Zion before they can carry out their plans.

130:1 I cry to you. This psalm of repentance may have been quoted during the day of atonement, the feast at which the Israelites confessed their sins (Lev. 16:29–30).

130:4 there is forgiveness. If God resolutely punished every sin and infraction of the Law, no one would be left standing. The good news is that God forgives his people and blots out their sins. **feared.** Honored, reverenced and worshiped as the one true God.

130:5–8 I wait. The Bible promises that God will help his people. When times are tough or situations intolerable, that hope gives believers faith to wait for God to act. **unfailing love.** God doesn't give up on his people. He is always there for them.

131:1 proud ... haughty. People become proud when they focus on their own virtues and strengths, and forget how much they need God. Humility comes from a recognition of inadequacy (Prov. 3:34).

131:2 quieted my soul. It takes a conscious effort for people to "still" their souls and allow God to calm them. Mature believers are no longer fussy nursing infants. Like a weaned child content to simply be with its mother, close to her, so they are content to simply be in God's presence and close to him.

like a weaned
like a wea with its mother,
is my soul within me.

[3] O Israel, ope in the LORD
both orevermore.

Psalm 132

A song of ascents.

...ember David
...e hardships he endured.

... an oath to the LORD
...ade a vow to the Mighty One of Jacob:
...ot enter my house
or go to my bed—
[4] I will allow no sleep to my eyes,
no slumber to my eyelids,
[5] till I find a place for the LORD,
a dwelling for the Mighty One of Jacob."

[6] We heard it in Ephrathah,
we came upon it in the fields of Jaar[a]:[b]
[7] "Let us go to his dwelling place;
let us worship at his footstool—
[8] arise, O LORD, and come to your resting place,
you and the ark of your might.
[9] May your priests be clothed with righteousness;
may your saints sing for joy."

[10] For the sake of David your servant,
do not reject your anointed one.

[11] The LORD swore an oath to David,
a sure oath that he will not revoke:
"One of your own descendants
I will place on your throne—
[12] if your sons keep my covenant
and the statutes I teach them,
then their sons will sit
on your throne for ever and ever."

[a]6 That is, Kiriath Jearim [b]6 Or *heard of it in Ephrathah, / we found it in the fields of Jaar.* (And no quotes around verses 7-9)

OPEN 1. Who are your two closest friends? Why are you close? Is your time together prearranged or does it "just happen"? **2.** Have you ever had to spend the night in a car? Airport or train station? Out in the brush or on a hillside? Why?

STUDY 1. What "hardships" has David endured (v. 1)? What does he promise Yahweh? Does God need an earthly "dwelling"? **2.** Where was the Ark of the Covenant prior to David's conquest of Jerusalem (v. 6; 1 Sam. 6:21–7:2)? Why does he want it in his city? **3.** What does the Lord swear to David (v. 11; 2 Sam. 7:16)? What condition is placed on the promise (v. 12)? Based on what happened to Israel, how would you say his sons did? **4.** On what is the permanence of David's dynasty based (v. 13)? How will Israel be blessed (vv. 14–18)? **5.** What do you make of the fact that there is no longer a king in Israel and that Jerusalem was conquered? Is God unable to keep his promises? Or did the people bring it on themselves?

APPLY 1. Do you give yourself deadlines? Is it good to put time limits on goals? **2.** What need does God want you to fill in your church? At home? At work? In the neighborhood? How committed are you to the project(s)? Have you made so many promises, you can't fulfill them all?

132:1 hardships. *David wrote this psalm near the end of his life, and reminded God that he had remained faithful despite every hardship.*

132:2 He swore an oath. David passionately loved God. He had a special relationship with him. When God committed himself to David and his descendants (v. 11), David responded by committing himself to the work of God (v. 8). The events are found in (2 Sam. 6–7).

132:6 We heard it. David was a youth in Ephrathah (Bethlehem) when he heard of the ark not having a "house." **we came upon it.** The ark spent twenty years in "the fields of Jaar" (Kiriath Jearim). David moved it from there to Jerusalem (1 Sam. 7:1–2; 2 Sam. 6:1–3).

132:11 swore an oath. Many of David's descendants were unworthy rulers or even idolaters. This sure, unbreakable oath (2 Sam. 7:11–16) was the reason that they nevertheless reigned in a continuous dynasty.

132:12 keep my covenant. This covenant was the Law of Moses, given at Mount Sinai. When Israelites agreed to obey it, the terms of this "contract" were made binding upon them.

[13]For the LORD has chosen Zion,
he has desired it for his dwelling:
[14]"This is my resting place for ever and ever;
here I will sit enthroned, for I have desired it—
[15]I will bless her with abundant provisions;
her poor will I satisfy with food.
[16]I will clothe her priests with salvation,
and her saints will ever sing for joy.

[17]"Here I will make a horn[a] grow for David
and set up a lamp for my anointed one.
[18]I will clothe his enemies with shame,
but the crown on his head will be resplendent."

OPEN How did you get along with your siblings (or cousins) when you were a child?

STUDY 1. How is unity like the oil used to anoint priests (Ex. 30:22–30)? Like a morning dew? **2.** What does "life forevermore" mean here? **3.** What night workers does the poet have in mind (Isa. 30:29)? Why minister at night?

APPLY 1. What is the last thing you do before going to sleep? **2.** How can you "bless" others in your group? Take group time to do this.

Psalm 133

A song of ascents. Of David.

[1]How good and pleasant it is
when brothers live together in unity!
[2]It is like precious oil poured on the head,
running down on the beard,
running down on Aaron's beard,
down upon the collar of his robes.
[3]It is as if the dew of Hermon
were falling on Mount Zion.
For there the LORD bestows his blessing,
even life forevermore.

Psalm 134

A song of ascents.

[1]Praise the LORD, all you servants of the LORD
who minister by night in the house of the LORD.
[2]Lift up your hands in the sanctuary
and praise the LORD.

[3]May the LORD, the Maker of heaven and earth,
bless you from Zion.

OPEN 1. Have you ever inherited anything? What would you like to inherit some day? **2.** What great person, alive or dead, do you admire? Why?

Psalm 135

[1]Praise the LORD.[b]

Praise the name of the LORD;

[a]17 *Horn* here symbolizes strong one, that is, king. [b]1 Hebrew *Hallelu Yah*; also in verses 3 and 21

132:13 desired it for his dwelling. When David built an altar on Mount Moriah, he declared, "The house of the LORD God is to be here" (1 Chr. 22:1). He was speaking prophetically because that was indeed God's will (Deut. 12:4–5).

133:1 good and pleasant. God desires that his people love one another and live in peace with one another (1 Cor. 1:10). In Israel, this unity was most evident when the entire nation came together to celebrate the feasts.

133:3 dew of Hermon ... on Mount Zion. Israel was a dry land and the Jews depended on dew to water the ground and sustain life. Dew was therefore a symbol of the blessing of God on Israel (Gen. 27:28; Hos. 14:5). Mount Hermon was a tall, cold mountain, so heavy dew fell upon it. God compared that to the blessings which drenched Mount Zion.

134:1–2 who minister by night. This is the final Psalm of Ascent. As night falls the departing pilgrims call upon the Levites to continue worshiping God (1 Chr. 9:33). The Levites then respond with a blessing (v. 3).

135:1–2 praise him. The first call to praise God was addressed to the priests

praise him, you servants of the LORD,
[2]you who minister in the house of the LORD,
in the courts of the house of our God.

[3]Praise the LORD, for the LORD is good;
sing praise to his name, for that is pleasant.
[4]For the LORD has chosen Jacob to be his own,
Israel to be his treasured possession.

[5]I know that the LORD is great,
that our Lord is greater than all gods.
[6]The LORD does whatever pleases him,
in the heavens and on the earth,
in the seas and all their depths.
[7]He makes clouds rise from the ends of the earth;
he sends lightning with the rain
and brings out the wind from his storehouses.

[8]He struck down the firstborn of Egypt,
the firstborn of men and animals.
[9]He sent his signs and wonders into your midst, O Egypt,
against Pharaoh and all his servants.
[10]He struck down many nations
and killed mighty kings—
[11]Sihon king of the Amorites,
Og king of Bashan
and all the kings of Canaan—
[12]and he gave their land as an inheritance,
an inheritance to his people Israel.

[13]Your name, O LORD, endures forever,
your renown, O LORD, through all generations.
[14]For the LORD will vindicate his people
and have compassion on his servants.

[15]The idols of the nations are silver and gold,
made by the hands of men.
[16]They have mouths, but cannot speak,
eyes, but they cannot see;
[17]they have ears, but cannot hear,
nor is there breath in their mouths.
[18]Those who make them will be like them,
and so will all who trust in them.

STUDY 1. This psalm borrows verses from several other psalms. To whom is the call of worship addressed (vv. 1–2)? What three reasons are given for praising the Lord (vv. 3–4)? **2.** What title for God would you draw from verses 5–7? From verses 8–12? Why does the psalmist praise God for the slaughter of Egyptians and Canaanites? How do you feel praising God for such events? **3.** What does it mean to "vindicate his people" (v. 14; Deut. 32:36)? **4.** What is the difference between the Lord and idols (vv. 15–17)? If idols are so impotent, why would anyone worship them? How does the worshipper—of God or idol—become like the object of worship? **5.** What is the significance of the four groups called to praise God (vv. 19–20)?

APPLY 1. What's pleasant about praising God? Does this mean you always have to feel like doing it? Can worship be pleasant when you're not in the mood for it? Why or why not? **2.** Are you one of God's people? Do you always feel like you are? Why or why not? **3.** How could you come to view yourself as a treasure in God's eyes? Would a stronger assurance of God's high esteem of you give you new attitudes and behaviors?

---

and Levites who served God full-time. Today's spiritual leaders are likewise called to lead in praising God.

135:3–4 the LORD is good. God has been good to his people. This is the first and greatest reason for them to praise him. **treasured possession.** Believers praise God because of the special relationship they have with him: He loves them and treasures them above all other things (1 Peter 2:9).

135:5–7 LORD does whatever pleases him. God is not only good but all-powerful. God's power knows no limits; God's plans cannot be frustrated. Whatever God *wants* to happen *will* happen.

135:8–12 He struck down. The psalmist doesn't boast of Israel's great accomplishments. He recognizes clearly that it was God who loved them and who defended them. Therefore, God is to be praised.

135:14 vindicate his people. God will do justice on behalf of his people. He will protect them, validating their claim that he is the one true God and they are his chosen people.

135:15–18 idols of the nations. Hostile nations cannot prevail against God's people. Pagan gods are lifeless and powerless. They are worthless. God's people worship the true, all-powerful God. **like them.** People who depend on a powerless image become powerless themselves.

19 O house of Israel, praise the LORD;
O house of Aaron, praise the LORD;
20 O house of Levi, praise the LORD;
you who fear him, praise the LORD.
21 Praise be to the LORD from Zion,
to him who dwells in Jerusalem.

Praise the LORD.

Psalm 136

1 Give thanks to the LORD, for he is good.
His love endures forever.
2 Give thanks to the God of gods.
His love endures forever.
3 Give thanks to the Lord of lords:
His love endures forever.

4 to him who alone does great wonders,
His love endures forever.
5 who by his understanding made the heavens,
His love endures forever.
6 who spread out the earth upon the waters,
His love endures forever.
7 who made the great lights—
His love endures forever.
8 the sun to govern the day,
His love endures forever.
9 the moon and stars to govern the night;
His love endures forever.

10 to him who struck down the firstborn of Egypt
His love endures forever.
11 and brought Israel out from among them
His love endures forever.
12 with a mighty hand and outstretched arm;
His love endures forever.

13 to him who divided the Red Sea[a] asunder
His love endures forever.
14 and brought Israel through the midst of it,
His love endures forever.
15 but swept Pharaoh and his army into the Red Sea;
His love endures forever.

16 to him who led his people through the desert,
His love endures forever.
17 who struck down great kings,
His love endures forever.
18 and killed mighty kings—
His love endures forever.

[a]13 Hebrew *Yam Suph*; that is, Sea of Reeds; also in verse 15

OPEN 1. As you think back over your life, what are you most thankful for? **2.** How do you know the Lord is good?

STUDY 1. This psalm is called "the Great Hallel" and is recited at Jewish Passover meals. What is the purpose of a "call and response" prayer? **2.** What types of "wonders" are listed? In what different spheres of life has the Lord been actively involved? **3.** How are the acts of verses 10 and 17–20 signs of God's enduring love? **4.** Is the refrain monotonous or does it center your thoughts?

APPLY 1. What are some modern day "gods" and "lords"? Which most vies for your attention? **2.** Which of the wonders listed especially moves you to thanksgiving? What wonder from your own life would you add to the prayer? **3.** How do you feel when those who are evil suffer? Do you rejoice that justice is done? Are you sad when anyone suffers? Do you have mixed feelings?

Ps. 136 This psalm, repeating many of the themes of Psalm 135, was intended for public worship. A Levite or song leader would sing one verse after another, and the choir or worshipers would respond with, "His love endures forever" (2 Chr. 5:12–14). God's love for his people is the reason he blesses and protects them.

[19]Sihon king of the Amorites
His love endures forever.
[20]and Og king of Bashan—
His love endures forever.
[21]and gave their land as an inheritance,
His love endures forever.
[22]an inheritance to his servant Israel;
His love endures forever.
[23]to the One who remembered us in our low estate
His love endures forever.
[24]and freed us from our enemies,
His love endures forever.
[25]and who gives food to every creature.
His love endures forever.
[26]Give thanks to the God of heaven.
His love endures forever.

Psalm 137

[1]By the rivers of Babylon we sat and wept
when we remembered Zion.
[2]There on the poplars
we hung our harps,
[3]for there our captors asked us for songs,
our tormentors demanded songs of joy;
they said, "Sing us one of the songs of Zion!"
[4]How can we sing the songs of the LORD
while in a foreign land?
[5]If I forget you, O Jerusalem,
may my right hand forget its skill.
[6]May my tongue cling to the roof of my mouth
if I do not remember you,
if I do not consider Jerusalem
my highest joy.
[7]Remember, O LORD, what the Edomites did
on the day Jerusalem fell.
"Tear it down," they cried,
"tear it down to its foundations!"
[8]O Daughter of Babylon, doomed to destruction,
happy is he who repays you
for what you have done to us—

OPEN Have you ever sung a solo? Is it harder to sing in front of a group of people or speak to them? Why?

STUDY 1. When does this psalm take place? What is the mood of the exiled musicians (vv. 1–3)? **2.** Why do their captors demand songs (v. 3)? Why is this an offensive request? Why is remembering Jerusalem so important to the psalmist? **3.** What had Edom done (v. 7; Obad. 8–14)? What does he wish for them in return? What does he wish for Babylon? **4.** What must the Babylonians have done to the Jews?

APPLY 1. Have you or a loved one experienced deep grief? Did you "hang your harps"? Or were you pressured to keep playing and singing as before? When is it okay to "hang our harps"? **2.** Do you feel a sense of belonging in this group, or are you in a "foreign land"? What would help you feel more at home?

137:1 rivers of Babylon. The Tigris and Euphrates Rivers and the great network of canals between them. **sat and wept.** God had banished the Jews from their homeland because they had turned from him to worship idols. Now they not only wept in grief over all they had lost, but they wept tears of repentance.

137:2,3 we hung our harps. Overcome with grief, the exiled Jews had no heart for music (Lam. 5:14–18). **songs of Zion.** These were worship songs sung in the temple on Mount Zion. The Israelites could not bring themselves to sing happy songs of victory and praise.

137:7 Edomites Like the Israelites, the Edomites descended from Abraham and Isaac. God had told the Israelites to respect the Edomites as brothers (Deut. 23:7), so it was especially painful to know that the Edomites had urged the Babylonians to mercilessly attack the Israelites (Obad. 8–15).

OPEN Who was the best friend you ever had? What was special about him or her?

STUDY 1. In the context of the psalm, before what "gods" does David sing (v. 1): Angels? Idols? Earthly rulers? What "word" has God exalted (v. 2)? **2.** How does David tie his own life into something greater (vv. 4–5)? What possible picture captures his attention (Isa. 40:5)? **3.** What mood underlies the thanksgiving (vv. 6–8)? How does God help the "lowly"? **4.** How does God's cause become the psalmist's own (v. 8)? **5.** Why is humility a prerequisite for asking God to grant a request (v. 6)? How do humility and weakness differ?

APPLY 1. What exterior factors encourage you to praise God? What interior ones? **2.** Do you feel that God is fulfilling a purpose in you? What purpose? How do you find it? Can the group help?

OPEN 1. If you found out the government was bugging your home, what would you immediately stop saying or doing? **2.** Break into pairs and jot down as many positive facts about your partner as you can in three minutes. Then tell your partner something he or she doesn't already know.

9 he who seizes your infants
and dashes them against the rocks.

Psalm 138

Of David.

1 I will praise you, O LORD, with all my heart;
before the "gods" I will sing your praise.
2 I will bow down toward your holy temple
and will praise your name
for your love and your faithfulness,
for you have exalted above all things
your name and your word.
3 When I called, you answered me;
you made me bold and stouthearted.

4 May all the kings of the earth praise you, O LORD,
when they hear the words of your mouth.
5 May they sing of the ways of the LORD,
for the glory of the LORD is great.

6 Though the LORD is on high, he looks upon the lowly,
but the proud he knows from afar.
7 Though I walk in the midst of trouble,
you preserve my life;
you stretch out your hand against the anger of my foes,
with your right hand you save me.
8 The LORD will fulfill ⌞his purpose⌟ for me;
your love, O LORD, endures forever—
do not abandon the works of your hands.

Psalm 139

For the director of music. Of David. A psalm.

1 O LORD, you have searched me
and you know me.
2 You know when I sit and when I rise;
you perceive my thoughts from afar.
3 You discern my going out and my lying down;
you are familiar with all my ways.

137:9 your infants. This verse, with its vivid image of cruelty, has often troubled believers. However, it must be remembered that the Israelites did not take such vengeance into their own hands. The psalmist was not even crying out to God to execute vengeance. He was warning Babylon what *their* enemies would do. Hundreds of years before, Isaiah had given a prophecy to Babylon, and the psalmist was now *repeating Isaiah's prophecy* (Isa. 13:1,16–18). Ancient warfare was brutal (2 Kin. 8:11–12; Hos. 13:16), and the Israelites had suffered horrors at the hands of the Babylonians. Their children had died or become slaves (Deut. 28:32–34; Lam. 2:11–12). The Babylonians mocked these grieving survivors, demanding they sing happy songs. The psalmist warned that Babylon's enemies would be the "happy" ones—as they judged Babylon.

138:1 gods. Possibly "gods" referred to angels or pagan kings who represented their gods. More likely, however, David was praising the true God in the midst of a world full of worthless idols.

138:2 your name. Out of the endless list of so-called gods, one name rises above all others—Yahweh, the God of Israel. **your word.** The Law was God's Word, his covenant with Israel. Within the Law are many promises of blessing. These two things, God's word and his name, are worth more than anything else.

139:1–6 God, you know everything about me. You know my habits, my special personal ways. You know everything I do and every word I speak. You know every thought I think. I can't even begin to understand how this is possible. Truly, you are God.

4 Before a word is on my tongue
you know it completely, O LORD.

5 You hem me in—behind and before;
you have laid your hand upon me.
6 Such knowledge is too wonderful for me,
too lofty for me to attain.

7 Where can I go from your Spirit?
Where can I flee from your presence?
8 If I go up to the heavens, you are there;
if I make my bed in the depths,[a] you are there.
9 If I rise on the wings of the dawn,
if I settle on the far side of the sea,
10 even there your hand will guide me,
your right hand will hold me fast.

11 If I say, "Surely the darkness will hide me
and the light become night around me,"
12 even the darkness will not be dark to you;
the night will shine like the day,
for darkness is as light to you.

13 For you created my inmost being;
you knit me together in my mother's womb.
14 I praise you because I am fearfully and wonderfully made;
your works are wonderful,
I know that full well.
15 My frame was not hidden from you
when I was made in the secret place.
When I was woven together in the depths of the earth,
16 your eyes saw my unformed body.
All the days ordained for me
were written in your book
before one of them came to be.

17 How precious to[b] me are your thoughts, O God!
How vast is the sum of them!
18 Were I to count them,
they would outnumber the grains of sand.
When I awake,
I am still with you.

[a]8 Hebrew *Sheol* [b]17 Or *concerning*

STUDY 1. How does David feel about God's total knowledge of him (vv. 1–6)? Is he restricted or protected? Free or oppressed? **2.** Why does he bother to pray (v. 4)? Is he free to choose his own actions (v. 6)? **3.** Why does David think about escaping God (vv. 7–12)? What directions are mentioned (vv. 8–9)? What do verses 11 and 12 say about God's ability to transform the most hopeless situations? **4.** The ancients spoke of child-bearing in mysterious terms (vv. 13–16). Has science added or subtracted from the mystery of life? What do you think of David's conclusion (v. 16)? **5.** To what "thoughts" do you think David refers (vv. 17–18)? What thought plagues him in particular (v. 19)? **6.** What do you think of David's "hatred" (vv. 21–22)? Is the mood of personal animosity or concern for God's honor? **7.** Why does he ask God to search his thoughts? How does he show an awareness of his own limitations (vv. 23–24)? **8.** If God is so omnipresent, why do so many people not believe in God? Can nonbelievers escape God more easily than believers?

APPLY 1. How does this psalm make you feel about yourself and your value to God? **2.** Is there a "dark" situation in your life? How can it be brought into God's light? **3.** Do you ask God to check your motives? Does God correct you with an internal voice or do you need the feedback of others?

139:6 too wonderful for me. Human beings with finite minds cannot begin to understand how God can know everything. But that's what makes God awesome and worthy of worship.

139:7–12 Can I go anywhere on earth where you are not present? Is there any distant land where you won't be right beside me, showing me the way? Is there any galaxy in the distant reaches of heaven where you have never been? No. You are everywhere. You "fill the whole universe" (Eph. 4:10).

139:11–12 No place in all creation is a hiding place from God. Even complete darkness hides nothing from him.

139:13 you created. God is the one who creates the unique mental and physical attributes of each individual. **inmost being.** Mental attributes, emotions**. knit me together.** Physical makeup: skeletal and muscular systems, etc.

139:16 your eyes saw. God sees absolutely everything. He even sees every human being as he or she is being formed in the womb. **days ordained.** God has determined the length of each person's life. **your book.** The blueprint for everything is in the mind of God.

139:17 How precious. God is all-knowing, but not impersonal and distant. His thoughts are loving. **How vast.** If God knows every detail about everything, his thoughts are immense beyond imagining. Man cannot measure his thoughts.

OPEN 1. Do you like action movies with lots of fighting and gore? Why or why not? What is attractive about violence? **2.** If you were elected king or queen of the world for a day, what one thing would you do to promote peace? Why?

STUDY 1. What characterizes "evil men" (vv. 1–3)? Is David opposed to violence in general or just when it's aimed at him (vv. 4–5)? **2.** How does David contrast his character with his enemies' (vv. 6–7)? What argument does he make (v. 8)? Why would the wicked become proud? **3.** What does David want God to do (vv. 9–11)? Should God answer such a prayer? **4.** Why the change in mood between verses 11 and 12? What might God have said to David to change his tone? **5.** In what circumstances is violence appropriate?

APPLY 1. Who or what is your greatest enemy? **2.** What ensnares you, keeps you from following the path God has set out for you? From reaching your own goals and dreams? What would you like God to do?

19 If only you would slay the wicked, O God!
Away from me, you bloodthirsty men!
20 They speak of you with evil intent;
your adversaries misuse your name.
21 Do I not hate those who hate you, O LORD,
and abhor those who rise up against you?
22 I have nothing but hatred for them;
I count them my enemies.

23 Search me, O God, and know my heart;
test me and know my anxious thoughts.
24 See if there is any offensive way in me,
and lead me in the way everlasting.

Psalm 140

For the director of music. A psalm of David.

1 Rescue me, O LORD, from evil men;
protect me from men of violence,
2 who devise evil plans in their hearts
and stir up war every day.
3 They make their tongues as sharp as a serpent's;
the poison of vipers is on their lips. *Selah*
4 Keep me, O LORD, from the hands of the wicked;
protect me from men of violence
who plan to trip my feet.
5 Proud men have hidden a snare for me;
they have spread out the cords of their net
and have set traps for me along my path. *Selah*
6 O LORD, I say to you, "You are my God."
Hear, O LORD, my cry for mercy.
7 O Sovereign LORD, my strong deliverer,
who shields my head in the day of battle—
8 do not grant the wicked their desires, O LORD;
do not let their plans succeed,
or they will become proud. *Selah*
9 Let the heads of those who surround me
be covered with the trouble their lips have caused.
10 Let burning coals fall upon them;
may they be thrown into the fire,
into miry pits, never to rise.

139:19 If only. David was besieged with wicked enemies and was impatient for God to judge them. Nevertheless, he left their fate in God's hands.

139:23–24 God, you're the one who created my inmost being. I couldn't hold a secret back from you even if I tried. But I won't try. Instead, I invite you to search me. Tell me what you see in my life. If there's anything that offends you, I want to know about it. Then show me how to overcome it.

140:1–3 Lord, my enemies are violent and cruel. Every day they plot my death. Protect me from their evil machinations.

140:45 Lord, the wicked have set traps for me that I can't see. But you see them. Point them out to me. Protect me from lurking danger.

140:10 fire ... miry pits. This is similar to the "fiery coals and burning sulfur" (11:6) which God rains on the wicked. It foreshadows the "fiery lake of burning sulfur" (Rev. 19:20), the final place of punishment for the wicked.

[11]Let slanderers not be established in the land;
may disaster hunt down men of violence.

[12]I know that the LORD secures justice for the poor
and upholds the cause of the needy.
[13]Surely the righteous will praise your name
and the upright will live before you.

Psalm 141

A psalm of David.

[1]O LORD, I call to you; come quickly to me.
Hear my voice when I call to you.
[2]May my prayer be set before you like incense;
may the lifting up of my hands be like the evening sacrifice.

[3]Set a guard over my mouth, O LORD;
keep watch over the door of my lips.
[4]Let not my heart be drawn to what is evil,
to take part in wicked deeds
with men who are evildoers;
let me not eat of their delicacies.

[5]Let a righteous man[a] strike me—it is a kindness;
let him rebuke me—it is oil on my head.
My head will not refuse it.

Yet my prayer is ever against the deeds of evildoers;
[6] their rulers will be thrown down from the cliffs,
and the wicked will learn that my words were well spoken.
[7]⌊They will say,⌋ "As one plows and breaks up the earth,
so our bones have been scattered at the mouth of the grave.[b]"

[8]But my eyes are fixed on you, O Sovereign LORD;
in you I take refuge—do not give me over to death.
[9]Keep me from the snares they have laid for me,
from the traps set by evildoers.
[10]Let the wicked fall into their own nets,
while I pass by in safety.

[a]5 Or *Let the Righteous One* [b]7 Hebrew *Sheol*

OPEN From whom can you accept constructive criticism gracefully? Why that person? Why not others?

STUDY 1. What clues do we have that David wrote this "on the run" (vv. 1–2)? What does he need (vv. 3–4)? Why? What awareness undergirds the request (Prov. 13:3)? **2.** Why would a righteous man "strike" David (v. 5)? What would be kind about it (Prov. 9:8)? **3.** What do you think verse 6 means? **4.** Of what is David most afraid (v. 8)? Where does he focus his attention to overcome temptation?

APPLY 1. What temptations are hard for you to overcome? Can God actually "guard" you and "keep watch" over you? Or do you tend to go it alone? Who else can help you keep your heart from being drawn to evil? **2.** Do you get defensive easily? How can you receive good feedback on your spiritual growth?

140:11 disaster hunt down. It is a Law of God that "misfortune pursues the sinner" (Prov. 13:21). It happens eventually. David asked God to stop his enemies before they could do any more violence.

140:12–13 God will bring about justice for the needy, but often justice only triumphs when powerful oppressors are judged.

141:1–2 David was beset by the wicked and turned to God in desperate prayer.

141:4 Let not my heart. With cruel men all around him, David was tempted to resort to cruel tactics himself. He knew this was wrong and asked God to curb his angry impulses.

141:5 Let a righteous man strike me. An authentic friend is kind when he or she gives an honest, stern rebuke, even if it hurts (Prov. 27:6). **will not refuse it.** The wise person accepts honest advice.

141:6–7 the wicked will learn. Sometimes it is so clear that *God* protected the innocent and judged the guilty that even the wicked get the point. **breaks up ... scattered.** Their strength is broken apart like hard earth under a plow. Like dry bones they are broken, scattered and brought to nothing.

141:8 do not give me over. David asked God to judge the wicked, but knew that he was not altogether innocent himself (v. 4). He asked God to spare him, not because of his righteousness, but because of his steady trust in God.

OPEN If God kept a complaint box, what grievance would you put in it?

STUDY 1. In which cave do you think this psalm was written (1 Sam. 22:1–2; 24:1–7)? What is the tone of this lament (vv. 1–3)? How free is David to express his true feelings? **2.** What's painful about the immediate circumstances (v. 4)? Is this an exaggeration? **3.** What does David mean by "portion" (v. 5; Num. 18:20)? **4.** Why will the righteous "gather about" (v. 7)? What do the righteous tend to do and say when the chips are down (Job 36: 8–9)?

APPLY 1. Are there complaints you keep from God? Feelings you consider inappropriate to bring up? Do you feel this group is a safe place to speak your true feelings? Or only the positive ones? **2.** Is the Lord your "portion"? Or are you seeking an earthly inheritance? Both? Where do you want to be?

OPEN 1. How old were you when you got your first job? What was it? **2.** Have you ever fainted? What happened? How did you feel when you came to again?

STUDY 1. What kind of calamity do you think David faces (vv. 1–4)? Is he making excuses by saying "I'm only human" in verse 2? **2.** What brings a glimmer of hope into his dark days (vv. 5–6)? What attitude motivates him? **3.** Who are "those who go down to the pit" (v. 7)? Is David afraid of dying? **4.** What "deal" does he strike with God (vv. 8–10)? What's his concluding argument to

Psalm 142

A *maskil*[a] of David.
When he was in the cave. A prayer.

[1] I cry aloud to the LORD;
I lift up my voice to the LORD for mercy.
[2] I pour out my complaint before him;
before him I tell my trouble.

[3] When my spirit grows faint within me,
it is you who know my way.
In the path where I walk
men have hidden a snare for me.
[4] Look to my right and see;
no one is concerned for me.
I have no refuge;
no one cares for my life.

[5] I cry to you, O LORD;
I say, "You are my refuge,
my portion in the land of the living."
[6] Listen to my cry,
for I am in desperate need;
rescue me from those who pursue me,
for they are too strong for me.
[7] Set me free from my prison,
that I may praise your name.

Then the righteous will gather about me
because of your goodness to me.

Psalm 143

A psalm of David.

[1] O LORD, hear my prayer,
listen to my cry for mercy;
in your faithfulness and righteousness
come to my relief.
[2] Do not bring your servant into judgment,
for no one living is righteous before you.

[3] The enemy pursues me,
he crushes me to the ground;
he makes me dwell in darkness

[a] Title: Probably a literary or musical term

142:3–4 David declares his weakness (v. 6) and his utter dependence on God.

142:3 spirit grows faint. David was overwhelmed from being daily beset with "trouble" (v. 2), plots and danger. **know my way.** David knew that enemies were all around and didn't know which way to turn. He needed God's wisdom to proceed.

142:5 portion. A person's share of the things of this life. David had power, fame and wealth but he viewed them as inconsequential. God alone was important.

142:7 gather about me. David had said, "No one is concerned for me" (v. 4). He asked God to show concern for him. When God vindicated him, others would rally around him.

143:2 no one living is righteous. This is one of David's most beautiful prayers and begins with an honest admission of his own sinfulness. David asks God to answer him, not because David is righteous or for the fact that David deserves God's righteousness, but because God is righteous.

like those long dead.
4 So my spirit grows faint within me;
my heart within me is dismayed.
5 I remember the days of long ago;
I meditate on all your works
and consider what your hands have done.
6 I spread out my hands to you;
my soul thirsts for you like a parched land. *Selah*

7 Answer me quickly, O LORD;
my spirit fails.
Do not hide your face from me
or I will be like those who go down to the pit.
8 Let the morning bring me word of your unfailing love,
for I have put my trust in you.
Show me the way I should go,
for to you I lift up my soul.
9 Rescue me from my enemies, O LORD,
for I hide myself in you.
10 Teach me to do your will,
for you are my God;
may your good Spirit
lead me on level ground.

11 For your name's sake, O LORD, preserve my life;
in your righteousness, bring me out of trouble.
12 In your unfailing love, silence my enemies;
destroy all my foes,
for I am your servant.

Psalm 144

Of David.

1 Praise be to the LORD my Rock,
who trains my hands for war,
my fingers for battle.
2 He is my loving God and my fortress,
my stronghold and my deliverer,
my shield, in whom I take refuge,
who subdues peoples[a] under me.

3 O LORD, what is man that you care for him,
the son of man that you think of him?

[a]2 Many manuscripts of the Masoretic Text, Dead Sea Scrolls, Aquila, Jerome and Syriac; most manuscripts of the Masoretic Text *subdues my people*

"persuade" God to hear his plea? **5.** Is mankind all that bad? Are people really "sinful" or just ignorant? Irrational? Who made us this way, anyway?

APPLY 1. When you experience calamity, can you direct your thoughts to God and keep from becoming despondent? What do you focus on? **2.** Do you consider yourself teachable? When did you last change your mind on an important matter? **3.** When's the last time you felt you were walking on "level ground"? Are you usually climbing upwards or going "downhill"?

OPEN 1. Did you ever protect a childhood friend? How? Did you need defending as a child? **2.** Do you like war films? Which war? Why do you find it intriguing?

STUDY 1. For what does David give thanks (vv. 1–2)? Why does he rejoice in war-making abilities? **2.** Do you think a country has to be strongly defended in order to enjoy safety and peace? Do you train your hands for war or endorse others to do so? Under what conditions would you go to battle? **3.** Why do David's thoughts turn to his insignificance (vv. 3–4)? If he is feeling so puny, why does he launch into a string of

143:5–6 I remember. God had helped and protected David repeatedly through the years. David reminded himself of all that God had done. Surely God would be with him now.

143:7 my spirit fails. David said, "My spirit grows faint" (v. 4); now his spiritual reserves were nearly dry. He was like "parched land" (v. 6), desperate for God to answer his prayer.

143:12 for I am your servant. David could ask God to destroy his foes because he stood for the principles of God. Those who fought him made themselves enemies of the God he served.

144:2 He is my loving God. Literally, "my unfailing love." God's love never ends, never fails. In the midst of battle, David declared that the source of his strength was God's unfailing love.

144:3–4 what is man. David marveled that a God so powerful cared for insignificant humans. Why take the time

requests (vv. 5–8)? Is his humility genuine? Or is he "buttering God up"? What promise does he make (vv. 9–10)? **4.** What hints can you find that this psalm was written after the Exile in Babylon (vv. 11,14)? Did David live before or after the Exile? **5.** What kind of prosperity does David desire for the people (vv. 12–14)? Why not ask for great wisdom and spiritual strength? What view of the afterlife is implied here?

APPLY 1. Why do you think God cares about fleeting "shadows"? Do you ever feel so small as to be insignificant to God? **2.** Does humility lead you to greater confidence before God? When do you feel most confident? Least? Can this group help? **3.** Do you see yourself as a fighter, well-nurtured plant or carved pillar? What one blessing would you seek for yourself? **4.** Are followers of Christ the only "people whose God is the Lord"? Who can expect God's favor today?

OPEN Have you ever seen a modern day monarch? What is the purpose of royalty? How do they differ from presidents or prime ministers?

STUDY 1. Why does God deserve praise (vv. 1–3)? What method will be used to spread the divine King's fame (vv. 4–7)? Won't it be obvious to everyone? **2.** Is the

4 Man is like a breath;
his days are like a fleeting shadow.

5 Part your heavens, O LORD, and come down;
touch the mountains, so that they smoke.
6 Send forth lightning and scatter ⌊the enemies⌋;
shoot your arrows and rout them.
7 Reach down your hand from on high;
deliver me and rescue me
from the mighty waters,
from the hands of foreigners
8 whose mouths are full of lies,
whose right hands are deceitful.

9 I will sing a new song to you, O God;
on the ten-stringed lyre I will make music to you,
10 to the One who gives victory to kings,
who delivers his servant David from the deadly sword.

11 Deliver me and rescue me
from the hands of foreigners
whose mouths are full of lies,
whose right hands are deceitful.

12 Then our sons in their youth
will be like well-nurtured plants,
and our daughters will be like pillars
carved to adorn a palace.
13 Our barns will be filled
with every kind of provision.
Our sheep will increase by thousands,
by tens of thousands in our fields;
14 our oxen will draw heavy loads.[a]
There will be no breaching of walls,
no going into captivity,
no cry of distress in our streets.

15 Blessed are the people of whom this is true;
blessed are the people whose God is the LORD.

Psalm 145[b]

A psalm of praise. Of David.

1 I will exalt you, my God the King;
I will praise your name for ever and ever.
2 Every day I will praise you
and extol your name for ever and ever.

[a] 14 Or *our chieftains will be firmly established* [b] This psalm is an acrostic poem, the verses of which (including verse 13b) begin with the successive letters of the Hebrew alphabet.

---

to be concerned for someone whose entire life is like a single breath or a fleeting shadow? Yet God *does* care.

144:11 foreigners. David repeats his prayer of verses 7–8. Clearly, this pressing issue was the reason for his psalm. David most likely composed this as a foreign power prepared to battle him (v. 1).

[3]Great is the LORD and most worthy of praise;
his greatness no one can fathom.
[4]One generation will commend your works to another;
they will tell of your mighty acts.
[5]They will speak of the glorious splendor of your majesty,
and I will meditate on your wonderful works.[a]
[6]They will tell of the power of your awesome works,
and I will proclaim your great deeds.
[7]They will celebrate your abundant goodness
and joyfully sing of your righteousness.

[8]The LORD is gracious and compassionate,
slow to anger and rich in love.
[9]The LORD is good to all;
he has compassion on all he has made.
[10]All you have made will praise you, O LORD;
your saints will extol you.
[11]They will tell of the glory of your kingdom
and speak of your might,
[12]so that all men may know of your mighty acts
and the glorious splendor of your kingdom.
[13]Your kingdom is an everlasting kingdom,
and your dominion endures through all generations.

The LORD is faithful to all his promises
and loving toward all he has made.[b]
[14]The LORD upholds all those who fall
and lifts up all who are bowed down.
[15]The eyes of all look to you,
and you give them their food at the proper time.
[16]You open your hand
and satisfy the desires of every living thing.

[17]The LORD is righteous in all his ways
and loving toward all he has made.
[18]The LORD is near to all who call on him,
to all who call on him in truth.
[19]He fulfills the desires of those who fear him;
he hears their cry and saves them.
[20]The LORD watches over all who love him,
but all the wicked he will destroy.

[21]My mouth will speak in praise of the LORD.
Let every creature praise his holy name
for ever and ever.

[a]5 Dead Sea Scrolls and Syriac (see also Septuagint); Masoretic Text *On the glorious splendor of your majesty / and on your wonderful works I will meditate* [b]13 One manuscript of the Masoretic Text, Dead Sea Scrolls and Syriac (see also Septuagint); most manuscripts of the Masoretic Text do not have the last two lines of verse 13.

King's good repute merely the result of effective propaganda or is there more substance to it? List all the reasons given for praising God. Which is most exciting to you? What is the divine King's true greatness (v. 8)? **3.** How does God treat subjects (v. 9)? And the subjects treat God (v. 10)? Do all subjects respond equally (vv. 10–13)? **4.** How does the Lord return the loyalty given (vv. 13–16)? What kind of king is this? What two characteristics does the Lord hold in balance (v. 17)? **5.** What does the divine king promise to give those who call on him earnestly (vv. 18–20)? What can one's only response to these gifts be (v. 21)?

APPLY 1. What kind of ruler is God to you: Benevolent king? Harsh dictator? Ceremonial monarch? Democratic leader? Prime minister? What has influenced your picture of God? Does it need adjusting? **2.** Picture yourself as one of the divine King's subjects. What's good about living in this kingdom? Why would spending time with the King one-on-one within the palace walls be the greatest reward for a citizen? **3.** What does God want to give you? How do your eyes look to God the King? What promise is contained in the phrase "at the proper time"? **4.** Has God fulfilled your desires? Which ones? If you are unfulfilled in some way, does this indicate you are not right with God? What does it mean to call on God "in truth"?

145:3–7 They will tell. Israel's history was a long list of miracles that God had done to protect them. Jewish parents were instructed to tell God's mighty acts to their children, so they too would be in awe of God (Ex. 13:14–15).

145:8–13 God's compassion, goodness and love cause his people to praise him and to tell others about him.

145:21 speak in praise. After declaring God's virtues, David realized how worthy God was to be praised.

OPEN Apart from eating, drinking and sleeping, what can you look back and say you've done "all your life"?

STUDY 1. Is the psalmist being pious or is this really his daily experience (vv. 1–2)? **2.** What is "trust in princes" (vv. 3–4)? Is it wrong to seek human help? **3.** Is the psalmist plagued by a low view of himself or is he blessed with realism and courage? How so? **4.** At what two types of power does the psalmist marvel (vv. 5–9)? Who does God seem to be most concerned about?

APPLY 1. Ask the members of your group to comment on what they think makes you tick. What two or three goals are evident from how you spend your time and talents? What do they see in your life that glorifies God? **2.** How does this psalm speak to you when you're feeling betrayed or on your own?

OPEN 1. Do you prefer thinking, talking or doing? Demonstrate from your activities today. **2.** How do you express creativity? What squelches it? What inspires it?

STUDY 1. List the verbs describing God's activity. Which are: Thinking? Speaking? Doing? **2.** When was this psalm probably written (vv. 2–3)? How has God chosen to respond to the needs at hand? On what two qualities is our attention focused (vv. 5–6)? **3.** What's the cause of thanksgiving in verses 7 through 9? Why do we need to be reminded to give thanks? What does God see as strength (vv. 10–11)? **4.** What two blessings are in store for

Psalm 146

1 Praise the LORD.[a]

Praise the LORD, O my soul.
2 I will praise the LORD all my life;
I will sing praise to my God as long as I live.

3 Do not put your trust in princes,
in mortal men, who cannot save.
4 When their spirit departs, they return to the ground;
on that very day their plans come to nothing.

5 Blessed is he whose help is the God of Jacob,
whose hope is in the LORD his God,
6 the Maker of heaven and earth,
the sea, and everything in them—
the LORD, who remains faithful forever.
7 He upholds the cause of the oppressed
and gives food to the hungry.
The LORD sets prisoners free,
8 the LORD gives sight to the blind,
the LORD lifts up those who are bowed down,
the LORD loves the righteous.
9 The LORD watches over the alien
and sustains the fatherless and the widow,
but he frustrates the ways of the wicked.

10 The LORD reigns forever,
your God, O Zion, for all generations.

Praise the LORD.

Psalm 147

1 Praise the LORD.[b]

How good it is to sing praises to our God,
how pleasant and fitting to praise him!

2 The LORD builds up Jerusalem;
he gathers the exiles of Israel.
3 He heals the brokenhearted
and binds up their wounds.

4 He determines the number of the stars
and calls them each by name.
5 Great is our Lord and mighty in power;
his understanding has no limit.

[a] 1 Hebrew *Hallelu Yah*; also in verse 10 [b] 1 Hebrew *Hallelu Yah*; also in verse 20

146:3–4 Believers are not to trust mortals, for even powerful princes die and can help no more.

146:5–9 God, who created heaven and earth, alone has power to truly help. God's infinite compassion motivates his use of power to stop oppressors and help those oppressed, discouraged, hungry, orphans and widows.

Ps. 147 This joyful psalm was likely composed and sung when Nehemiah and the Jews finished rebuilding the walls of Jerusalem (vv. 2,13; Neh. 12:27–43).

147:4–6 stars ... by name. Untold numbers of galaxies comprise the universe, each one containing billions of stars. God, who created all these stars,

[6]The LORD sustains the humble
but casts the wicked to the ground.

[7]Sing to the LORD with thanksgiving;
make music to our God on the harp.
[8]He covers the sky with clouds;
he supplies the earth with rain
and makes grass grow on the hills.
[9]He provides food for the cattle
and for the young ravens when they call.

[10]His pleasure is not in the strength of the horse,
nor his delight in the legs of a man;
[11]the LORD delights in those who fear him,
who put their hope in his unfailing love.

[12]Extol the LORD, O Jerusalem;
praise your God, O Zion,
[13]for he strengthens the bars of your gates
and blesses your people within you.
[14]He grants peace to your borders
and satisfies you with the finest of wheat.

[15]He sends his command to the earth;
his word runs swiftly.
[16]He spreads the snow like wool
and scatters the frost like ashes.
[17]He hurls down his hail like pebbles.
Who can withstand his icy blast?
[18]He sends his word and melts them;
he stirs up his breezes, and the waters flow.

[19]He has revealed his word to Jacob,
his laws and decrees to Israel.
[20]He has done this for no other nation;
they do not know his laws.

Praise the LORD.

Psalm 148

[1]Praise the LORD.[a]

Praise the LORD from the heavens,
praise him in the heights above.
[2]Praise him, all his angels,
praise him, all his heavenly hosts.

[a]1 Hebrew *Hallelu Yah*; also in verse 14

Jerusalem (vv. 12–14)? What is this "word" that "runs swiftly" (v. 15)? **5.** Does the psalmist sound burdened by the Jewish law here (vv. 19–20)? Why is the Law so important to Jews?

APPLY 1. What comes to mind when you think power: Physical strength? Beauty? Ability to influence events? Moral truth? Compassion? Other? Do you feel powerful in any way? **2.** Has God ever surprised you with a creative alternative to an "impossible" situation? Is a new creation waiting to be born in your life now?

OPEN 1. Who is your favorite composer, song writer, conductor or group? **2.** What color seems to go best with praising God? What taste? Kind of weather?

STUDY 1. Can you trace the psalmist's call to worship from the "top down"? Where are the "highest heavens" (1 Kin. 8:27; 2 Cor.

knows each one by name. He also knows each downtrodden believer by name and has the power to help him or her.

147:7–11 God blesses hard work but is not pleased when people take pride in self-sufficiency and exclude God from their lives. God is the source of all supply and wants believers to realize that they are dependent on him.

147:15 sends his command. This does not refer only to the Law which God had already given to Israel, but to his ongoing care and concern for his people. Whatever God wants done, he has but to speak the word and it is done "swiftly"—divine order.

147:19–20 no other nation. God chose Israel, gave them his Law and made a covenant with them. God did not create this relationship with any other nation (Ezra 4:1–4). Through Israel, salvation would come to all (John 4:22).

12:2)? What different parts of creation join in this symphony of praise? **2.** Are any instructions given on how to play your instrument? Who gets the attention and applause? Why (vv. 5–6,13)? **3.** What do all creatures have in common? **4.** What is the "horn" raised up (v. 14)? **5.** It is taken for granted in the psalm that creation knows "how to" praise God. How do inanimate objects praise God? Animals and plants?

APPLY 1. What helped you praise God in the past? How could your church or group explore new and different avenues of worship? **2.** Do you enjoy nature? What is your response to man's slow destruction of it? Do you feel this is a problem for God to solve? What role do you see yourself taking?

3 Praise him, sun and moon,
praise him, all you shining stars.
4 Praise him, you highest heavens
and you waters above the skies.
5 Let them praise the name of the LORD,
for he commanded and they were created.
6 He set them in place for ever and ever;
he gave a decree that will never pass away.

7 Praise the LORD from the earth,
you great sea creatures and all ocean depths,
8 lightning and hail, snow and clouds,
stormy winds that do his bidding,
9 you mountains and all hills,
fruit trees and all cedars,
10 wild animals and all cattle,
small creatures and flying birds,
11 kings of the earth and all nations,
you princes and all rulers on earth,
12 young men and maidens,
old men and children.

13 Let them praise the name of the LORD,
for his name alone is exalted;
his splendor is above the earth and the heavens.
14 He has raised up for his people a horn,[a]
the praise of all his saints,
of Israel, the people close to his heart.

Praise the LORD.

OPEN Do you like to dance? What kind of dance? Or do you prefer to watch others do it?

STUDY 1. What four activities are done to praise God (vv. 1–3)? What is God doing to praise the people (v. 4)? **2.** What is meant by singing for joy "on their beds" (v. 5; 63:6)? In a land with few private bedrooms, wouldn't this be a nuisance? **3.** What's the flipside of this kingdom of joy (vv. 6–9)? Why vengeance? How is this type of activity "the glory" of all saints?

APPLY 1. In your church's worship, can you see God joining in with delight and spontaneity or nodding off in boredom? How about you? What kind of celebration

Psalm 149

1 Praise the LORD.[b]

Sing to the LORD a new song,
his praise in the assembly of the saints.

2 Let Israel rejoice in their Maker;
let the people of Zion be glad in their King.
3 Let them praise his name with dancing
and make music to him with tambourine and harp.
4 For the LORD takes delight in his people;
he crowns the humble with salvation.
5 Let the saints rejoice in this honor
and sing for joy on their beds.

6 May the praise of God be in their mouths
and a double-edged sword in their hands,

[a]14 *Horn* here symbolizes strong one, that is, king. [b]1 Hebrew *Hallelu Yah*; also in verse 9

148:8–10 clouds. All of nature praises God by declaring his glory (19:1–4). **cedars, wild animals.** All living things, by their very existence, praise God. Their complex design declares the existence of an intelligent Creator.

149:4 crowns ... salvation. Here these words mean deliverance or victory, both physically and spiritually. They also have the deeper spiritual meaning of eternal life (Matt. 5:3; James 1:12).

149:5 on their beds. Night is an excellent time to pray (42:8).

149:6–9 When battling enemies, the Israelites knew that strength was not primarily in the swords they held but in

[7]to inflict vengeance on the nations
and punishment on the peoples,
[8]to bind their kings with fetters,
their nobles with shackles of iron,
[9]to carry out the sentence written against them.
This is the glory of all his saints.

Praise the LORD.

Psalm 150

[1]Praise the LORD.[a]

Praise God in his sanctuary;
praise him in his mighty heavens.
[2]Praise him for his acts of power;
praise him for his surpassing greatness.
[3]Praise him with the sounding of the trumpet,
praise him with the harp and lyre,
[4]praise him with tambourine and dancing,
praise him with the strings and flute,
[5]praise him with the clash of cymbals,
praise him with resounding cymbals.

[6]Let everything that has breath praise the LORD.

Praise the LORD.

[a]1 Hebrew *Hallelu Yah*; also in verse 6

does God delight in? **2.** What "double-edged sword" do you wield against the "kings" of this world? Are you binding the evil in the world or are you bound yourself?

OPEN Do you play a musical instrument?

STUDY 1. Of what is the temple an earthly symbol (v. 1)? **2.** What instruments provide the rhythm? Melody? Chords? Do people sit politely? **3.** What is significant about "breath" (v. 6; Gen. 2:7)?

APPLY 1. Is your worship mostly mental or emotional? **2.** How could you worship God more?

the God they trusted and praised (Rev. 19:14–15).

150:1,2 Praise the LORD. This triumphant, joyous psalm gives a rousing call to believers to praise God. It is a fitting finale to the book of Psalms. **for his acts of power.** Because of the miracles God has done for his people. **for his surpassing greatness.** Because of who God is—the powerful, great and glorious God.

150:3 Praise him with. Worship is often quiet, even silent. But sometimes worship should be a rousing, loud celebration accompanied by a full array of musical instruments—worthy of what God has done for us.

Proverbs

Author. Writers include Solomon, Agur and Lemuel.

Personal Reading	Group Study Topic and Reading	
1:1–2:22	Purpose and Theme	1:1–7
3:1–4:27	Wisdom Is Supreme	4:1–27
5:1–7:27	Warnings Against Folly	6:1–19
8:1–9:18	Wisdom Personified	8:1–36
10:1–11:31	Consequences of Life	11:1–31
12:1–14:35	Power of Words	14:1–35
15:1–16:33	Sovereignty of God	16:1–33
17:1–19:29	Relationships	17:1–28
20:1–22:16	Worthy Advice	22:1–16
22:17–24:34	Social Climbing	23:1–35
25:1–26:28	Power of Words	25:1–28
27:1–29:27	Relationships	27:1–27
30:1–31:31	Virtuous Woman	31:10–31

Date. The sections by Solomon were written during his reign in the tenth century B.C. Other sections were probably compiled later.

Purpose. According to the first chapter, Proverbs is intended to offer practical wisdom (based on obedience to God's commands) that will help in everyday living.

Historical Background. Most cultures of Solomon's day had their own libraries of wisdom literature and common sense expressions, similar to those found in Proverbs. The important distinction that sets apart the Hebrews' wisdom literature was the belief that true wisdom is rooted in God. In fact, Proverbs opens with the truth that fearing God is the very beginning of wisdom.

The original word for *wisdom* used most often in Proverbs is a word that connotes a skill developed through experience, as a craftsman masters his craft over years of practice. In that same way, Proverbs reminds us that the wisdom that makes a person morally upright is the practice of making good choices repeatedly throughout life.

Hebrew Poetry. Hebrew poetry was not typically written with lines ending in rhyming words. Their poetry was more a product of the symmetry of profound thoughts. It was called poetry because of its structure and style of language. Psalms, Proverbs, Ecclesiastes and Song of Songs are considered poetry. This type of literature is also called wisdom writing. Although wisdom literature is true, its purpose is not purely informational. Rather, it should be pondered and applied in many ways.

The Proverbs contain many good examples of Hebrew poetry in the form of couplets (two-line pairs) that express the same concept but from two different perspectives. Sometimes the second line restates the first but with a twist. In other instances, the second line reinforces the first using an opposite point of view; for example, "The fear of the LORD *is* the beginning of knowledge: *but* fools despise wisdom and discipline" (1:7).

Prologue: Purpose and Theme

1 The proverbs of Solomon son of David, king of Israel:

[2]for attaining wisdom and discipline;
for understanding words of insight;
[3]for acquiring a disciplined and prudent life,
doing what is right and just and fair;
[4]for giving prudence to the simple,
knowledge and discretion to the young—
[5]let the wise listen and add to their learning,
and let the discerning get guidance—
[6]for understanding proverbs and parables,
the sayings and riddles of the wise.

[7]The fear of the LORD is the beginning of knowledge,
but fools[a] despise wisdom and discipline.

Exhortations to Embrace Wisdom

Warning Against Enticement

[8]Listen, my son, to your father's instruction
and do not forsake your mother's teaching.
[9]They will be a garland to grace your head
and a chain to adorn your neck.

[10]My son, if sinners entice you,
do not give in to them.
[11]If they say, "Come along with us;
let's lie in wait for someone's blood,
let's waylay some harmless soul;
[12]let's swallow them alive, like the grave,[b]
and whole, like those who go down to the pit;
[13]we will get all sorts of valuable things
and fill our houses with plunder;
[14]throw in your lot with us,
and we will share a common purse"—
[15]my son, do not go along with them,
do not set foot on their paths;
[16]for their feet rush into sin,
they are swift to shed blood.

[a]7 The Hebrew words rendered *fool* in Proverbs, and often elsewhere in the Old Testament, denote one who is morally deficient. [b]12 Hebrew *Sheol*

OPEN One of the wisest things I have ever done was ...?

STUDY 1. What greets you in this prologue? What grips you? Why? **2.** What do you think "fear of the LORD" means? Do you agree that it is the beginning of knowledge? Explain. **3.** What does Solomon say are the marks of a fool? Do you agree with his assessment? Would you add anything?

APPLY 1. Where are you on the road to wisdom: Stuck in traffic? Backtracking? Fast lane? Fool's Alley? Wrong way on a one way street? Why? **2.** Where do you need an extra dose of wisdom?

OPEN 1. What two things did your father teach you? What two things did your mother teach you? **2.** How would your friends rank you as a listener: Great? Good? Average? Fair? Poor? What would you say?

STUDY 1. In light of verses 8 and 9, if someone were to ask you, "Why is it good to heed one's parents?" How would you answer? Do you agree with Solomon about parental instruction? **2.** How would you define the term "sinner"? What are the "sinners" asking the son to do here? **3.** In your opinion, what is appealing about get-rich-quick schemes? What is wrong with them? **4.** Would this advice keep a son from getting into trouble, or get him out of trouble? Why? **5.** What is the end of all wrongdoing? What does Jesus say about gaining the world but losing one's soul (Mark 8:36)?

APPLY 1. When did you go along with the crowd and later regret it? **2.** What did you find particularly enticing as a child? In your youth? As an adult?

1:2 attaining wisdom. Proverbs' theme is wisdom, the nature of it and how to get it. The proverbs are common-sense guidelines for living the good life well, which begins with fearing the Lord (v. 7).

1:7 fear of the LORD. The fear of the Lord involves acknowledging God's power and sovereignty, then offering our obedience in light of it. The fool disregards God's presence and power, acting as if nothing mattered but the satisfaction of appetites.

1:8 listen. The writer often introduces a new section with "Listen" (8:6,32). **son.** Probably Solomon's actual son.

1:11 lie in wait for someone's blood. Murder. The "sinners" described here have complete disregard for human life. They use others for what they can receive from them.

1:13 all sorts of valuable things. This is almost an oxymoron since Proverbs is really a book about what "things" in life are really valuable. These thieves disregard what matters (life lived in the fear of the Lord) for stolen trinkets produced by wasted lives.

[17]How useless to spread a net
in full view of all the birds!
[18]These men lie in wait for their own blood;
they waylay only themselves!
[19]Such is the end of all who go after ill-gotten gain;
it takes away the lives of those who get it.

Warning Against Rejecting Wisdom

[20]Wisdom calls aloud in the street,
she raises her voice in the public squares;
[21]at the head of the noisy streets[a] she cries out,
in the gateways of the city she makes her speech:

[22]"How long will you simple ones[b] love your simple ways?
How long will mockers delight in mockery
and fools hate knowledge?
[23]If you had responded to my rebuke,
I would have poured out my heart to you
and made my thoughts known to you.
[24]But since you rejected me when I called
and no one gave heed when I stretched out my hand,
[25]since you ignored all my advice
and would not accept my rebuke,
[26]I in turn will laugh at your disaster;
I will mock when calamity overtakes you—
[27]when calamity overtakes you like a storm,
when disaster sweeps over you like a whirlwind,
when distress and trouble overwhelm you.

[28]"Then they will call to me but I will not answer;
they will look for me but will not find me.
[29]Since they hated knowledge
and did not choose to fear the LORD,
[30]since they would not accept my advice
and spurned my rebuke,
[31]they will eat the fruit of their ways
and be filled with the fruit of their schemes.
[32]For the waywardness of the simple will kill them,
and the complacency of fools will destroy them;
[33]but whoever listens to me will live in safety
and be at ease, without fear of harm."

[a]*21* Hebrew; Septuagint / *on the tops of the walls* [b]*22* The Hebrew word rendered *simple* in Proverbs generally denotes one without moral direction and inclined to evil.

OPEN 1. The nosiest place in my world is ... **2.** Name something you hate.

STUDY 1. If you were a reporter covering "Wisdom's" speech in the town square, what would you say about: The content? The tone? The impact? Would your report be approving or disapproving? **2.** How would this speech play in your town? Would people stand and cheer or tune out? **3.** How will God laugh (vv. 26–27): With tears? Smiles? Derision? Vindication? Does this laughter strike you positively or negatively? Explain. **4.** What is the result of rejecting wisdom (v. 32)? Of receiving wisdom (v. 33)? Does that seem fair to you? Why or why not? **5.** In your opinion, if wisdom is so publicly available, why are so many so foolish?

APPLY 1. When have you heard "wisdom crying" to you recently? How did you discern what you heard was truly wisdom? **2.** Where is your good advice falling on deaf ears?

1:17–18 spread a net. A typical trap for a bird, effective only if the bird doesn't see the net being laid out.

1:18 waylay only themselves. The writer humorously compares those who live their lives apart from God with buffoons who spread a trap only to catch themselves in it. That is the height of folly—living without wisdom.

1:26 laugh ... mock. If people reject wisdom, they face consequences that have no regard for their intentions. But widsom takes joy in the works of God and ridicules those that reject wisdom.

1:32 kill ... destroy. Living outside of God's wisdom eventually brings death and destruction. This message in Proverbs is repeated often in the New Testament (Rom. 6:23).

1:33 be at ease. While obedience may seem like a burden, it is really the most comfortable way to live. Consider the difference between honesty and deception—living transparently before others as opposed to keeping track of lies and half-truths.

Moral Benefits of Wisdom

2 My son, if you accept my words
and store up my commands within you,
[2] turning your ear to wisdom
and applying your heart to understanding,
[3] and if you call out for insight
and cry aloud for understanding,
[4] and if you look for it as for silver
and search for it as for hidden treasure,
[5] then you will understand the fear of the LORD
and find the knowledge of God.
[6] For the LORD gives wisdom,
and from his mouth come knowledge and understanding.
[7] He holds victory in store for the upright,
he is a shield to those whose walk is blameless,
[8] for he guards the course of the just
and protects the way of his faithful ones.

[9] Then you will understand what is right and just
and fair—every good path.
[10] For wisdom will enter your heart,
and knowledge will be pleasant to your soul.
[11] Discretion will protect you,
and understanding will guard you.

[12] Wisdom will save you from the ways of wicked men,
from men whose words are perverse,
[13] who leave the straight paths
to walk in dark ways,
[14] who delight in doing wrong
and rejoice in the perverseness of evil,
[15] whose paths are crooked
and who are devious in their ways.

[16] It will save you also from the adulteress,
from the wayward wife with her seductive words,
[17] who has left the partner of her youth
and ignored the covenant she made before God.[a]
[18] For her house leads down to death
and her paths to the spirits of the dead.
[19] None who go to her return
or attain the paths of life.

[20] Thus you will walk in the ways of good men
and keep to the paths of the righteous.

[a]17 Or *covenant of her God*

OPEN 1. What collectible item do you especially treasure? Why that one? **2.** What career path did you want to take as a child? At age 21?

STUDY 1. In chapter 1:20–33, wisdom clamors to be heard. Who is clamoring now? What would you say is the person's tone of voice? **2.** Note the verbs in verses 1–4. According to these verbs, what do you need to do to attain wisdom? How doable would you say this is? **3.** What would you say is the goal of this treasure hunt (vv. 5–6): Head knowledge? Moral knowledge? Change in behavior? Conversion? Why do you think so? **4.** Is such a relationship with God discovered or given? If a little of both, what percentage would you assign to each? Is it more God or more us? **5.** How does God help you in this (vv. 7–8)? What further benefits attend the awe and intimacy of knowing God (vv. 9–11)? **6.** From what will wisdom save us (vv. 12–19)? What protection (vv. 12–19) and provision (vv. 20–22) can you expect from wisdom? **7.** What attracts you about the "ways of good men" (v. 20): Looks? Means? Results (vv. 21–22)? **8.** Since pleasures of sin are compelling, what must righteousness and wisdom counter-offer for you to follow them instead?

APPLY 1. How's your search for wisdom coming along: "I found it"? "I lost it"? Or, "I give up, where is it?" What two clues from this passage can help you find the source and benefits of wisdom? **2.** Is the path of your life taking you where you've always dreamed of going? Or are you off-course somewhere? How can knowing God better help you get back on track? Likewise, how can your group help?

2:1–3 Over and over the writer appeals to his son to live a life of wisdom: accept, store up, turn, apply, call out, cry aloud.

2:4 search for ... treasure. An apt comparison. To find a treasure we have to hunt, search, dig, excavate. To find wisdom requires the same kind of activity. The effort required of the journey will be worth great rewards.

2:5 then you will ... find. Here is the treasure mentioned in verse 4. When we search for wisdom, we find God himself and our relationship with him.

2:12–19 Wisdom is protection. We are protected from both evil men and women who would lure us into self-destruction.

2:12 perverse. The original word translated as "perverse" simply means "to turn away from the upright." Throughout Proverbs this word describes someone who chooses wickedness over wisdom (8:13; 10:31).

[21]For the upright will live in the land,
and the blameless will remain in it;
[22]but the wicked will be cut off from the land,
and the unfaithful will be torn from it.

Further Benefits of Wisdom

3 My son, do not forget my teaching,
but keep my commands in your heart,
[2]for they will prolong your life many years
and bring you prosperity.

[3]Let love and faithfulness never leave you;
bind them around your neck,
write them on the tablet of your heart.
[4]Then you will win favor and a good name
in the sight of God and man.

[5]Trust in the LORD with all your heart
and lean not on your own understanding;
[6]in all your ways acknowledge him,
and he will make your paths straight.[a]

[7]Do not be wise in your own eyes;
fear the LORD and shun evil.
[8]This will bring health to your body
and nourishment to your bones.

[9]Honor the LORD with your wealth,
with the firstfruits of all your crops;
[10]then your barns will be filled to overflowing,
and your vats will brim over with new wine.

[11]My son, do not despise the LORD's discipline
and do not resent his rebuke,
[12]because the LORD disciplines those he loves,
as a father[b] the son he delights in.

[13]Blessed is the man who finds wisdom,
the man who gains understanding,
[14]for she is more profitable than silver
and yields better returns than gold.

[a]6 Or *will direct your paths* [b]12 Hebrew; Septuagint / *and he punishes*

OPEN 1. What is something or someone you recently forgot? **2.** What nicknames were you given as a child? How did you get them?

STUDY 1. How does this chapter strike you: The ramblings of an old man? The insight of a philosopher? The logic of a scholar? The warm counsel of concerned father? Why? **2.** What three sections do you observe (introduced my "My Son")? What instructions, benefits and exhortation accompany that lead-in address? Within each section, what verses best sum up what the teaching is all about? **3.** How does one know if God is trustworthy (vv. 5–6)? Does such faith involve a "blind leap"? Or is faith predicted on understanding based on sound teaching (vv. 1–4)? Why do you think that? **4.** "Poetic parallelism" is a literary devise wherein the second line or verse repeats, extends or contrasts with the first. What examples of each kind of parallelism can you find here? **5.** A good name (honor and reputation) is highly prized in most cultures. How does this chapter suggest you gain it (vv. 4,32–33)? How might you lose it? **6.** This chapter introduces us to the first use of short, isolated, seemingly unrelated bits of wisdom called "proverbs." Verse 10 is a case in point. What is the promise based on? What does it mean to honor the Lord with your finances: Gratitude? Trust? Tithing from the cream of the crop? Investing in the Lord's work? **7.** How does the Lord's discipline (vv. 11–12) relate to his blessing? Do you agree with this state-

2:21 upright will live in the land. A powerful image for this Jewish audience. Their whole history involved a journey back to the land God had promised their ancestor Abraham. The land was their reward for following God obediently.

3:2 prosperity. *This word is often* translated "peace." It suggests wholeness, health and harmony.

3:5 with all your heart. The Bible uses this phrase to express total commitment. One of the earliest calls to love God was the great "Shema" in Deuteronomy. There the people are encouraged to love God with all their heart, mind and soul. Jesus described this as the first and greatest commandment.

3:6 will make your paths straight. This implies more than guidance. It means God intentionally removing obstacles from our path.

3:10 vats will brim over. Plenty of wine meant prosperity to Old Testament worshipers. Often the wealth of a land was described in terms of its vineyards, grapes or wine. **new wine.** In this case, "freshly squeezed grape juice."

3:11–12 discipline. Discipline has a role to play in the prosperity God promises. God disciplines his children. God disciplined the Hebrew nation with forty years of wandering through the desert. Discipline leads to prosperity.

15 She is more precious than rubies;
nothing you desire can compare with her.
16 Long life is in her right hand;
in her left hand are riches and honor.
17 Her ways are pleasant ways,
and all her paths are peace.
18 She is a tree of life to those who embrace her;
those who lay hold of her will be blessed.

19 By wisdom the LORD laid the earth's foundations,
by understanding he set the heavens in place;
20 by his knowledge the deeps were divided,
and the clouds let drop the dew.

21 My son, preserve sound judgment and discernment,
do not let them out of your sight;
22 they will be life for you,
an ornament to grace your neck.
23 Then you will go on your way in safety,
and your foot will not stumble;
24 when you lie down, you will not be afraid;
when you lie down, your sleep will be sweet.
25 Have no fear of sudden disaster
or of the ruin that overtakes the wicked,
26 for the LORD will be your confidence
and will keep your foot from being snared.

27 Do not withhold good from those who deserve it,
when it is in your power to act.
28 Do not say to your neighbor,
"Come back later; I'll give it tomorrow"—
when you now have it with you.

29 Do not plot harm against your neighbor,
who lives trustfully near you.
30 Do not accuse a man for no reason—
when he has done you no harm.

31 Do not envy a violent man
or choose any of his ways,
32 for the LORD detests a perverse man
but takes the upright into his confidence.

33 The LORD's curse is on the house of the wicked,
but he blesses the home of the righteous.
34 He mocks proud mockers
but gives grace to the humble.
35 The wise inherit honor,
but fools he holds up to shame.

Wisdom Is Supreme

4 Listen, my sons, to a father's instruction;
pay attention and gain understanding.
2 I give you sound learning,
so do not forsake my teaching.

ment? Explain. **8.** What kind of person does the Lord take into "his confidence"? At what price? For whose benefit? In your opinion is the price impossible to pay? **9.** With verses 1–2 in mind, what would you say to the saddened parents of an 8-year old who was killed by a drunk driver?

APPLY 1. Which one of the promises, proverbs or warnings seem to have "your name" on it? Why that one? **2.** Whose name comes to mind as you read verses 27–28: A charitable organization? A government program? A friend? A neighbor? Your church? Yourself? **3.** Have you ever felt that God was indicating to you or guiding you to do something specific as in verses 5 and 6? Let someone in the group share his or her story. How does the story make you feel? At what points can you relate to it?

OPEN 1. What was it like growing up in your parent's house: A laugh a minute? Warm and tender? Tense? Cold as ice? A roller coaster ride? Strict? **2.** Are you a morning person or a night person? Explain.

STUDY **1.** This particular passage draws from the author's (traditionally Solomon is considered to be the author) family background (1 Kin. 1:28–30; 2:1–4). Who was his dad? His mom? What do you suppose their father-son talks were like: Monologue? Dialogue? Q & A? What was David's charge to Solomon? How is it reflected here (vv. 4–9)? **2.** In passing along wisdom from one generation to another (vv. 1,3–4), what would you say is most important: Setting a good example? Being good with words? Minding your P's and Q's? Long lists of "Do's and Don'ts"? **3.** In this proverb would you say there are more "Do's" or "Don'ts"? Why might that be? How well is Solomon doing on selling his "sons" on the value of wisdom? **4.** What does the travel motif imply about the nature of biblical wisdom? Is the way to wisdom well-traveled, or is it less-traveled? Can you stay at home in an ivory tower and still learn it? Do you dare leave home without it? Why or why not? **5.** After reading this chapter (and possibly the previous chapters) how would you define "wisdom"? Has this chapter, or the previous chapters, changed how you look at wisdom? If so, how?

APPLY **1.** Using the travel motif as it applies to your pursuit of biblical wisdom these days, what would you say you are: Lonely trailblazer? Crazy "off-road" driver? Sleepless over-the-road 18-wheeler? Teenage hot rodder? Demolition derby buff? Chugging along in your compact car? Touring the USA in your convertible? Strictly thumbing and bumming? Explain. **2.** In what area of your life do you need the counsel of verses 25–27? How can your group help you to do this? **3.** Of all the father-son or mother-daughter talks you've had, which one stands out as particularly helpful in the long run? Why so?

---

3 When I was a boy in my father's house,
still tender, and an only child of my mother,
4 he taught me and said,
"Lay hold of my words with all your heart;
keep my commands and you will live.
5 Get wisdom, get understanding;
do not forget my words or swerve from them.
6 Do not forsake wisdom, and she will protect you;
love her, and she will watch over you.
7 Wisdom is supreme; therefore get wisdom.
Though it cost all you have,[a] get understanding.
8 Esteem her, and she will exalt you;
embrace her, and she will honor you.
9 She will set a garland of grace on your head
and present you with a crown of splendor."

10 Listen, my son, accept what I say,
and the years of your life will be many.
11 I guide you in the way of wisdom
and lead you along straight paths.
12 When you walk, your steps will not be hampered;
when you run, you will not stumble.
13 Hold on to instruction, do not let it go;
guard it well, for it is your life.
14 Do not set foot on the path of the wicked
or walk in the way of evil men.
15 Avoid it, do not travel on it;
turn from it and go on your way.
16 For they cannot sleep till they do evil;
they are robbed of slumber till they make someone fall.
17 They eat the bread of wickedness
and drink the wine of violence.

18 The path of the righteous is like the first gleam of dawn,
shining ever brighter till the full light of day.
19 But the way of the wicked is like deep darkness;
they do not know what makes them stumble.

20 My son, pay attention to what I say;
listen closely to my words.
21 Do not let them out of your sight,
keep them within your heart;
22 for they are life to those who find them
and health to a man's whole body.
23 Above all else, guard your heart,

[a]7 Or *Whatever else you get*

4:3 in my father's house. Solomon's father was King David. Because Solomon was "young and inexperienced" (*1 Chr. 22:5*), David handled the preparations for the grand temple whose construction became Solomon's great achievement.

4:4 he taught me. Solomon is passing down the wisdom of his father to his sons, from generation to generation.

4:10 years of your life. The Bible often equates obedience with long life, yet we only have to look around to see that the best people are not always those who live longest. A long life is measured by quality as well as quantity. Certainly, in those terms, obedience makes our lives better.

4:18–19 Throughout the Bible, righteousness and wickedness are compared to light and darkness. God's presence and guidance are described in terms of light. Jesus was called the Light of the World (John 8:12).

for it is the wellspring of life.
[24]Put away perversity from your mouth;
keep corrupt talk far from your lips.
[25]Let your eyes look straight ahead,
fix your gaze directly before you.
[26]Make level[a] paths for your feet
and take only ways that are firm.
[27]Do not swerve to the right or the left;
keep your foot from evil.

Warning Against Adultery

5 My son, pay attention to my wisdom,
listen well to my words of insight,
[2]that you may maintain discretion
and your lips may preserve knowledge.
[3]For the lips of an adulteress drip honey,
and her speech is smoother than oil;
[4]but in the end she is bitter as gall,
sharp as a double-edged sword.
[5]Her feet go down to death;
her steps lead straight to the grave.[b]
[6]She gives no thought to the way of life;
her paths are crooked, but she knows it not.

[7]Now then, my sons, listen to me;
do not turn aside from what I say.
[8]Keep to a path far from her,
do not go near the door of her house,
[9]lest you give your best strength to others
and your years to one who is cruel,
[10]lest strangers feast on your wealth
and your toil enrich another man's house.
[11]At the end of your life you will groan,
when your flesh and body are spent.
[12]You will say, "How I hated discipline!
How my heart spurned correction!
[13]I would not obey my teachers
or listen to my instructors.
[14]I have come to the brink of utter ruin
in the midst of the whole assembly."

[15]Drink water from your own cistern,
running water from your own well.
[16]Should your springs overflow in the streets,
your streams of water in the public squares?
[17]Let them be yours alone,
never to be shared with strangers.

[a]26 Or *Consider the* [b]5 Hebrew *Sheol*

OPEN 1. Who was one of your favorite elementary school teachers? **2.** How did you learn about the "birds and the bees"?

STUDY 1. This chapter is filled with word pictures. Do they enhance the point of the passage for you or detract from it? **2.** Why does adultery appeal (vv. 3–4,7–8,12–13,20–22)? What helps us to resist? **3.** What consequences does this permissive lifestyle reap (vv. 9–11,14)? What benefits accrue to those who "drink from their own cistern" (vv. 15–19)? **4.** The adulteress does not even realize that "her paths are crooked" (v. 6). Why do you suppose that is: Denial? Rebellion? Moral depravity? Foolishness? **5.** What do you think causes a person to think, "The grass is always greener on the other side of the fence"? Are wives tempted by the same things as men? Why? **6.** Martin Luther said of sexual temptation: "We can't do anything about the birds flying over our head, but we can prevent them building a nest in our hair." How does that metaphor fit your experience and chapter 5? **7.** Does verse 21 cause you comfort or pain? Explain. **8.** In your opinion, what has been most influential in our culture's understanding of sexual behavior: TV? Sitcoms? Movies? The availability of pornographic material?

APPLY 1. If you were going down the wrong path would you want someone to correct you? Who? How? **2.** Taking the wrong path (vv. 8–11) leads to disaster. What do you hope to be doing and where do you hope to be living at the end of your life?

5:3 honey. When Proverbs was written, honey was the sweetest substance in Israel. Some think this refers to kisses as well as speech. **Oil.** Olive oil was the smoothest substance in that culture.

5:7–14 Sexual infidelity carries a price. In the end, Solomon says, you will lose everything, including self-respect.

5:11 you will groan. This may be simply a reference to old age, but more likely to the cumulative, debilitating effects of living immorally.

5:13 my teachers. Could possibly be "parents."

[18]May your fountain be blessed,
and may you rejoice in the wife of your youth.
[19]A loving doe, a graceful deer—
may her breasts satisfy you always,
may you ever be captivated by her love.
[20]Why be captivated, my son, by an adulteress?
Why embrace the bosom of another man's wife?

[21]For a man's ways are in full view of the LORD,
and he examines all his paths.
[22]The evil deeds of a wicked man ensnare him;
the cords of his sin hold him fast.
[23]He will die for lack of discipline,
led astray by his own great folly.

Warnings Against Folly

6 My son, if you have put up security for your neighbor,
if you have struck hands in pledge for another,
[2]if you have been trapped by what you said,
ensnared by the words of your mouth,
[3]then do this, my son, to free yourself,
since you have fallen into your neighbor's hands:
Go and humble yourself;
press your plea with your neighbor!
[4]Allow no sleep to your eyes,
no slumber to your eyelids.
[5]Free yourself, like a gazelle from the hand of the hunter,
like a bird from the snare of the fowler.

[6]Go to the ant, you sluggard;
consider its ways and be wise!
[7]It has no commander,
no overseer or ruler,
[8]yet it stores its provisions in summer
and gathers its food at harvest.

[9]How long will you lie there, you sluggard?
When will you get up from your sleep?
[10]A little sleep, a little slumber,
a little folding of the hands to rest—
[11]and poverty will come on you like a bandit
and scarcity like an armed man.[a]

[12]A scoundrel and villain,
who goes about with a corrupt mouth,
[13] who winks with his eye,
signals with his feet

[a]11 *Or like a vagrant / and scarcity like a beggar*

OPEN 1. On a scale of 1 (I'll get to it tomorrow) to 10 (I did it yesterday), where would you place yourself on "The Procrastination Scale"? **2.** What would be on your "top seven" list of things you hate?

STUDY 1. How would you describe the "intensity" of this passage: Fireside chat? Fiery sermon? Political filibuster? Ad for a TV mini-series? Or what? **2.** How would you summarize Solomon's point? In your opinion, how well does he present it? How effective are his figures of speech? **3.** If he were writing for a modern audience, would he have to change anything? If so, what? Why? **4.** From verses 1–5, what are the dangers of co-signing for a loan? Do you agree with these dangers? **5.** Does "humility" (v. 3) work in getting out of a tough situation? Why or why not? Has it ever worked for you? **6.** According to verses 6–11, why work? Why do you think he chose an ant to make his point? **7.** What's the difference between a "scoundrel" and a "villain"? What is the final end for such a person? Is this a natural consequence or the judgment of God? Why do you think so? **8.** Solomon gives a list (vv. 16–19) of what the Lord hates and detests. Do you think the list is exhaustive? Explain.

APPLY 1. In what way can you be more "ant-like" this week? **2.** When have you pledged yourself to something you later regret-

6:1 security ... pledge. The equivalent of co-signing a loan and being responsible for someone else's debt. Among the Hebrews charging interest on loans to fellow countrymen was not considered an honorable way to make money.

6:6 you sluggard. Probably a rhetorical question rather than a direct address to Solomon's son. A "sluggard" was lazy and shiftless, someone who chose a lifestyle of irresponsibility over doing the right thing energetically.

6:12 scoundrel ... villain. A worthless and wicked person (Judg. 19:22; 1 Sam. 25:25). One who would also be a troublemaker. Eventually this term became associated with Satan himself (2 Cor. 6:14–15).

and motions with his fingers,
14 who plots evil with deceit in his heart—
he always stirs up dissension.
15 Therefore disaster will overtake him in an instant;
he will suddenly be destroyed—without remedy.

16 There are six things the LORD hates,
seven that are detestable to him:
17 haughty eyes,
a lying tongue,
hands that shed innocent blood,
18 a heart that devises wicked schemes,
feet that are quick to rush into evil,
19 a false witness who pours out lies
and a man who stirs up dissension among brothers.

Warning Against Adultery

20 My son, keep your father's commands
and do not forsake your mother's teaching.
21 Bind them upon your heart forever;
fasten them around your neck.
22 When you walk, they will guide you;
when you sleep, they will watch over you;
when you awake, they will speak to you.
23 For these commands are a lamp,
this teaching is a light,
and the corrections of discipline
are the way to life,
24 keeping you from the immoral woman,
from the smooth tongue of the wayward wife.
25 Do not lust in your heart after her beauty
or let her captivate you with her eyes,
26 for the prostitute reduces you to a loaf of bread,
and the adulteress preys upon your very life.
27 Can a man scoop fire into his lap
without his clothes being burned?
28 Can a man walk on hot coals
without his feet being scorched?
29 So is he who sleeps with another man's wife;
no one who touches her will go unpunished.

30 Men do not despise a thief if he steals
to satisfy his hunger when he is starving.
31 Yet if he is caught, he must pay sevenfold,
though it costs him all the wealth of his house.
32 But a man who commits adultery lacks judgment;
whoever does so destroys himself.
33 Blows and disgrace are his lot,

ted? What would you like to get out of right now?

____

OPEN 1. What were you disciplined for most often? How were you disciplined? **2.** What's your favorite kind of bread: Sourdough? Wheat? Rye? White? French? Marble? Other?

STUDY 1. What images help picture what the "commands" and "teaching" are like? Have you found this to be true in your life? How? **2.** What is sexual sin like? What do you think it means that a "prostitute reduces you to a loaf of bread"? **3.** How dumb does Solomon think it is to commit adultery or frequent a prostitute (vv. 27–29)? What's the consequence of doing so (vv. 29,32–35)? **4.** What do you see in verses 30–31: Situational ethics? Moral relativity? Justice? Something else? **5.** Do you think God's judgment (vv. 32–35) is brought on by ourselves, or exacted by others? Why? **6.** If parental instruction (vv. 20–22) is wrong, or not of God, must you still obey? Why?

APPLY 1. A time in my life I should have listened to my parents was ... **2.** Where do you especially need God's light to shine in your life?

____

6:17 haughty eyes. A proud look. God does not reward pride. Later Proverbs teaches that pride leads only to destruction (16:18; 18:12).

6:23 lamp ... light. This writer describes parents teaching truth to their children in the same way the psalmist describes the Word of God: "A lamp to my feet and a light to my path" (Ps. 119:105).

6:31 sevenfold. Seven is a number of completion. Hebrew law doesn't require more than a fivefold return for theft. "Sevenfold" implies "until it is done" or "whatever it takes." The price he would pay would be paid in full. As harsh as this penalty was for theft, no penalty could pardon adultery.

and his shame will never be wiped away;
[34]for jealousy arouses a husband's fury,
and he will show no mercy when he takes revenge.
[35]He will not accept any compensation;
he will refuse the bribe, however great it is.

OPEN 1. Who considered you the "apple of their eye"? **2.** For a fun night out on the town, what would you do? Where would you go? With whom?

STUDY 1. If you were to set this chapter to music, what would you underscore? Where would you introduce dissonance? Cymbals? Drum roll? Violins? Resolution? **2.** What is meant by the "apple of your eye"? Why is it used here (v. 2)? **3.** What is meant by "write them on the tablet of your heart" (v. 3; Jer. 31:33)? How do you write on it? What do you write? Why (Ps. 119:9,11)? **4.** How does the prostitute show "crafty intent" (v. 10)? On a scale of 1 to 10, how high would you rank her skills as a temptress (vv. 14–21)? **5.** Solomon seems to be quite concerned about adultery and prostitution (chs. 2; 5; 6; 7). Why do you suppose that is? How did sexual sin affect Solomon's own life, heritage, integrity and parenting (1 Kin. 11:1–6)? **6.** Can adultery and prostitution also be symbolic of all wrongdoing, which leads one astray from God? Why do you think so?

APPLY 1. When was the last time some smooth talker convinced you to do or buy something that was against your better judgment? What did you learn from the experience? What did the lesson learned really cost you? **2.** What is the lesson to be learned from this passage?

Warning Against the Adulteress

7 My son, keep my words
and store up my commands within you.
[2]Keep my commands and you will live;
guard my teachings as the apple of your eye.
[3]Bind them on your fingers;
write them on the tablet of your heart.
[4]Say to wisdom, "You are my sister,"
and call understanding your kinsman;
[5]they will keep you from the adulteress,
from the wayward wife with her seductive words.

[6]At the window of my house
I looked out through the lattice.
[7]I saw among the simple,
I noticed among the young men,
a youth who lacked judgment.
[8]He was going down the street near her corner,
walking along in the direction of her house
[9]at twilight, as the day was fading,
as the dark of night set in.

[10]Then out came a woman to meet him,
dressed like a prostitute and with crafty intent.
[11](She is loud and defiant,
her feet never stay at home;
[12]now in the street, now in the squares,
at every corner she lurks.)
[13]She took hold of him and kissed him
and with a brazen face she said:

[14]"I have fellowship offerings[a] at home;
today I fulfilled my vows.
[15]So I came out to meet you;
I looked for you and have found you!
[16]I have covered my bed
with colored linens from Egypt.
[17]I have perfumed my bed
with myrrh, aloes and cinnamon.
[18]Come, let's drink deep of love till morning;
let's enjoy ourselves with love!
[19]My husband is not at home;

[a]14 Traditionally *peace offerings*

7:2 apple. This word means "center." It is used sometimes to refer to the middle of the night (v. 9). Here it refers to the pupil of the eye.

7:3 bind them. Moses' last charge to the Hebrews was to bind God's Law to their foreheads and hands (Deut. 6:8). Solomon echoes that here.

7:19 The woman's logic shows premeditation, an effort at deception that goes beyond an impulsive mistake and speaks more of a lifestyle.

he has gone on a long journey.
[20]He took his purse filled with money
and will not be home till full moon."

[21]With persuasive words she led him astray;
she seduced him with her smooth talk.
[22]All at once he followed her
like an ox going to the slaughter,
like a deer[a] stepping into a noose[b]
[23] till an arrow pierces his liver,
like a bird darting into a snare,
little knowing it will cost him his life.

[24]Now then, my sons, listen to me;
pay attention to what I say.
[25]Do not let your heart turn to her ways
or stray into her paths.
[26]Many are the victims she has brought down;
her slain are a mighty throng.
[27]Her house is a highway to the grave,[c]
leading down to the chambers of death.

Wisdom's Call

8 Does not wisdom call out?
Does not understanding raise her voice?
[2]On the heights along the way,
where the paths meet, she takes her stand;
[3]beside the gates leading into the city,
at the entrances, she cries aloud:
[4]"To you, O men, I call out;
I raise my voice to all mankind.
[5]You who are simple, gain prudence;
you who are foolish, gain understanding.
[6]Listen, for I have worthy things to say;
I open my lips to speak what is right.
[7]My mouth speaks what is true,
for my lips detest wickedness.
[8]All the words of my mouth are just;
none of them is crooked or perverse.
[9]To the discerning all of them are right;
they are faultless to those who have knowledge.
[10]Choose my instruction instead of silver,
knowledge rather than choice gold,
[11]for wisdom is more precious than rubies,
and nothing you desire can compare with her.

[12]"I, wisdom, dwell together with prudence;
I possess knowledge and discretion.
[13]To fear the LORD is to hate evil;
I hate pride and arrogance,

[a]22 Syriac (see also Septuagint); Hebrew *fool* [b]22 The meaning of the Hebrew for this line is uncertain.
[c]27 Hebrew *Sheol*

OPEN 1. What's your favorite piece of jewelry? **2.** Where are you in the birth order of your family? How has that affected you?

STUDY 1. As you listen to "wisdom" call out, what does she sound like: Talk show host? Football coach? TV evangelist? Kindly grandma? Other? **2.** "Listen, for I have worthy things to say" (v. 6)—how many times have you heard that line before? From whom? Was it worthy? How did you discern that it was true? **3.** With what is wisdom equated or likened? How many different comparisons can you find here? **4.** From verses 12–21, what results from finding wisdom? Which fruit of wisdom do you most want? **5.** Verses 22–31 are a hymn personifying wisdom as an attribute of God, active in creation (1:20–33; 3:15–18; 9:1–12). If "Christ" could be substituted for "wisdom" in this chapter, how would that affect your view or application of its main points? **6.** Verses 32–36 drive home the appeal of wisdom with the ultimate sanctions of life and death. It's as if the Lord Jesus himself were talking. How might these be considered a promise of the Savior? Can one find "wisdom" or "life" apart from Christ?

APPLY 1. When in your life have you harmed yourself by

7:21 persuasive ... seduced. An accurate picture of sin and temptation. The motive is clear. This woman sets out to cause a man to fall, to draw him into sin. It is deliberate and premeditated.

failing to find the wisdom you needed? What wisdom has come to you since? 2. Where are you feeling "fully" alive? Where are you feeling less than alive?

evil behavior and perverse speech.
14 Counsel and sound judgment are mine;
I have understanding and power.
15 By me kings reign
and rulers make laws that are just;
16 by me princes govern,
and all nobles who rule on earth.[a]
17 I love those who love me,
and those who seek me find me.
18 With me are riches and honor,
enduring wealth and prosperity.
19 My fruit is better than fine gold;
what I yield surpasses choice silver.
20 I walk in the way of righteousness,
along the paths of justice,
21 bestowing wealth on those who love me
and making their treasuries full.

22 "The LORD brought me forth as the first of his works,[b,c]
before his deeds of old;
23 I was appointed[d] from eternity,
from the beginning, before the world began.
24 When there were no oceans, I was given birth,
when there were no springs abounding with water;
25 before the mountains were settled in place,
before the hills, I was given birth,
26 before he made the earth or its fields
or any of the dust of the world.
27 I was there when he set the heavens in place,
when he marked out the horizon on the face of the deep,
28 when he established the clouds above
and fixed securely the fountains of the deep,
29 when he gave the sea its boundary
so the waters would not overstep his command,
and when he marked out the foundations of the earth.
30 Then I was the craftsman at his side.
I was filled with delight day after day,
rejoicing always in his presence,
31 rejoicing in his whole world
and delighting in mankind.

32 "Now then, my sons, listen to me;
blessed are those who keep my ways.
33 Listen to my instruction and be wise;
do not ignore it.

[a]16 Many Hebrew manuscripts and Septuagint; most Hebrew manuscripts *and nobles—all righteous rulers*
[b]22 Or *way*; or *dominion* [c]22 Or *The LORD possessed me at the beginning of his work*; or *The LORD brought me forth at the beginning of his work* [d]23 Or *fashioned*

8:14 Following the description of sin's debilitating effects, wisdom is highlighted here as a source of strength. This chapter draws a stark contrast between the wise person and the helpless victim caught in sin's web.

8:22–31 Wisdom is personified in this hymn-like passage. New Testament writers describe Jesus in similar terms: the Word that was with God during creation (John 1:1–3) and the "wisdom of God" (1 Cor. 1:24,30).

8:32 blessed ... who keep my ways. Blessings that follow wisdom are not so much mystical rewards as the natural consequences of good choices and a well-lived life.

34 Blessed is the man who listens to me,
watching daily at my doors,
waiting at my doorway.
35 For whoever finds me finds life
and receives favor from the LORD.
36 But whoever fails to find me harms himself;
all who hate me love death."

Invitations of Wisdom and of Folly

9 Wisdom has built her house;
she has hewn out its seven pillars.
2 She has prepared her meat and mixed her wine;
she has also set her table.
3 She has sent out her maids, and she calls
from the highest point of the city.
4 "Let all who are simple come in here!"
she says to those who lack judgment.
5 "Come, eat my food
and drink the wine I have mixed.
6 Leave your simple ways and you will live;
walk in the way of understanding.

7 "Whoever corrects a mocker invites insult;
whoever rebukes a wicked man incurs abuse.
8 Do not rebuke a mocker or he will hate you;
rebuke a wise man and he will love you.
9 Instruct a wise man and he will be wiser still;
teach a righteous man and he will add to his learning.

10 "The fear of the LORD is the beginning of wisdom,
and knowledge of the Holy One is understanding.
11 For through me your days will be many,
and years will be added to your life.
12 If you are wise, your wisdom will reward you;
if you are a mocker, you alone will suffer."

13 The woman Folly is loud;
she is undisciplined and without knowledge.
14 She sits at the door of her house,
on a seat at the highest point of the city,

OPEN 1. Describe a memorable dinner party. What made it so memorable: The food? The people? The occasion? **2.** Which of life's simple pleasures do you especially enjoy: A good night's sleep? A conversation with a friend? A good meal? A great laugh? A walk in the park? A quiet evening? Other?

STUDY 1. Compare and contrast "Wisdom and Folly": What are their personalities? Lifestyles? Residences? Messages? Results? **2.** In practical terms, what is the difference between a "mocker" and a "wise man" (vv. 7–9)? When have you tried to correct one or the other? What happened? **3.** The first nine chapters serve as an introduction to this whole book (10:1). Why do you think Solomon closes his introduction as he does? Why is choice so important in a person's life? **4.** If you made this chapter into a movie who would you cast as "Wisdom"? Who would you cast as "Folly"?

APPLY 1. How do you usually respond to criticism? How easy is it to correct? What would make it easier for you to hear the input your critics have to offer? **2.** Where are you feeling prepared? Where are you feeling undisciplined?

8:36 harms himself. Sin, choosing our own way over God's, is characterized in the Bible as self-destruction.

9:1 house ... seven pillars. Many theories have surfaced regarding the meaning of "seven" pillars. They could be the seven days of creation or perhaps the seven constellations known at that time. Every interpreter agrees that with seven pillars, wisdom's house is fine and spacious, revealing the kind of life wisdom brings.

9:5 eat ... drink. Spiritual blessings are often described in terms of edibles (Isa. 55:1–2; John 6:27,35). Here wisdom is like homemade wine and food.

9:7 mocker. A wicked person cannot be taught. He will lash out at correction. **abuse.** A blotch or defect. A wicked person throws back a rebuke in retaliation.

9:8 he will love you. A wise person is teachable. Even a rebuke is a pleasant thing in the end because the wise person can learn from it.

9:9 wiser still. Wisdom leads to wisdom. Because a person wisely maintains a teachable attitude, he learns from everything that happens. No matter the immediate outcome, he only grows wiser.

9:10 beginning. Prerequisite. This is the theme of Proverbs, to have wisdom you must fear and obey God.

9:11 years will be added. Everyone can see exceptions to this rule. Nevertheless, wisdom adds to the quality and often the quantity of life.

9:12 The rewards of wisdom and folly work on the same principle that Paul described in Galatians 6:7. What a person sows, he or she will reap.

[15]calling out to those who pass by,
who go straight on their way.
[16]"Let all who are simple come in here!"
she says to those who lack judgment.
[17]"Stolen water is sweet;
food eaten in secret is delicious!"
[18]But little do they know that the dead are there,
that her guests are in the depths of the grave.[a]

Proverbs of Solomon

10 The proverbs of Solomon:

A wise son brings joy to his father,
but a foolish son grief to his mother.

[2]Ill-gotten treasures are of no value,
but righteousness delivers from death.

[3]The LORD does not let the righteous go hungry
but he thwarts the craving of the wicked.

[4]Lazy hands make a man poor,
but diligent hands bring wealth.

[5]He who gathers crops in summer is a wise son,
but he who sleeps during harvest is a disgraceful son.

[6]Blessings crown the head of the righteous,
but violence overwhelms the mouth of the wicked.[b]

[7]The memory of the righteous will be a blessing,
but the name of the wicked will rot.

[8]The wise in heart accept commands,
but a chattering fool comes to ruin.

[9]The man of integrity walks securely,
but he who takes crooked paths will be found out.

[10]He who winks maliciously causes grief,
and a chattering fool comes to ruin.

[11]The mouth of the righteous is a fountain of life,
but violence overwhelms the mouth of the wicked.

[12]Hatred stirs up dissension,
but love covers over all wrongs.

[13]Wisdom is found on the lips of the discerning,
but a rod is for the back of him who lacks judgment.

[a]18 Hebrew *Sheol* [b]6 *Or but the mouth of the wicked conceals violence;* also in verse 11

OPEN 1. What did you do as a child that put a smile on your parent's face? **2.** If your tongue were entered in a prize fight in what class would it fight: Heavyweight? Light heavyweight? Middleweight? Lightweight? Flyweight? Explain.

STUDY 1. According to Webster a proverb is a "short, pithy, popular wise saying or precept, often in picturesque language." How do these proverbs of Solomon fit that definition? How else would you define what you see here? **2.** What do you see here that relates to hard work? Do you agree with the proverbs on this subject? Why? **3.** What aspects of the "righteous" and the "wicked" are conveyed here by the images of head? Of memory? Mouth or lips? Wages? Desires? Destinies? **4.** We usually reserve discipline for children or people who do bad things. What here suggests otherwise (vv. 8,13,17,25; Heb. 12:4–13)? **5.** How do you understand verses 6 and 11: The tongue conceals violence? The tongue gets us in trouble? The tongue only reflects what enters through the eyes and the ears, as in "garbage in" "garbage out"? **6.** How can love "cover up all wrongs"? Is love blind, innocent, forgiving or what? Has this been your experience? **7.** What is Solomon affirming here? What does the alternative imply? How does this relate to the "chattering fool" (vv. 8,10,14, 18)? **8.** What do you learn here about the material and spiritual results of righteousness? What is long-term? Immediate? Temporary? How can you "nourish many" (v. 21) with your righteousness? **9.** Which proverbs here have a New Testament

10:1 The proverbs of Solomon. Chapters 10–22 are included under this title. While the previous chapters were written in sections of verses, the upcoming chapters are collections of individual proverbs without a centering theme. Yet chapters 10–15 continue to contrast wisdom with folly, doing right with doing evil.

10:4 poor. Poverty in Proverbs is usually associated with laziness or a lack of discipline.

10:5 harvest. Solomon's culture was agricultural. He often uses the image of harvest to picture a person who understands the discipline of taking care of himself. In chapter 6 he used the image of the ant to make the same comparison (6:6–8).

10:13 rod. Beatings were a form of punishment in this era. Even in Jesus' day, beatings accompanied capital punishment (Matt. 27:26).

14 Wise men store up knowledge,
but the mouth of a fool invites ruin.

15 The wealth of the rich is their fortified city,
but poverty is the ruin of the poor.

16 The wages of the righteous bring them life,
but the income of the wicked brings them punishment.

17 He who heeds discipline shows the way to life,
but whoever ignores correction leads others astray.

18 He who conceals his hatred has lying lips,
and whoever spreads slander is a fool.

19 When words are many, sin is not absent,
but he who holds his tongue is wise.

20 The tongue of the righteous is choice silver,
but the heart of the wicked is of little value.

21 The lips of the righteous nourish many,
but fools die for lack of judgment.

22 The blessing of the LORD brings wealth,
and he adds no trouble to it.

23 A fool finds pleasure in evil conduct,
but a man of understanding delights in wisdom.

24 What the wicked dreads will overtake him;
what the righteous desire will be granted.

25 When the storm has swept by, the wicked are gone,
but the righteous stand firm forever.

26 As vinegar to the teeth and smoke to the eyes,
so is a sluggard to those who send him.

27 The fear of the LORD adds length to life,
but the years of the wicked are cut short.

28 The prospect of the righteous is joy,
but the hopes of the wicked come to nothing.

29 The way of the LORD is a refuge for the righteous,
but it is the ruin of those who do evil.

30 The righteous will never be uprooted,
but the wicked will not remain in the land.

31 The mouth of the righteous brings forth wisdom,
but a perverse tongue will be cut out.

32 The lips of the righteous know what is fitting,
but the mouth of the wicked only what is perverse.

11 The LORD abhors dishonest scales,
but accurate weights are his delight.

ring to them? For example, what proverb is the equivalent of Matthew 7:24-27? Romans 6:23? James 5:20?

APPLY 1. Which of these proverbs would your parents want you to read? Which one of these has your name on it? **2.** When has God's rod disciplined you? What were the results? Does it still hurt? **3.** What storms are passing through your life right now? How are you holding up? Where are you seeking refuge? How can your group help?

OPEN 1. Which modern proverb would your family

10:25 Jesus may have had this proverb in mind when he told the parable of the wise man who built his house on rock and thus withstood a fierce storm, while the foolish man built on the sand (Matt. 7:24–29).

members or friends use to describe your philosophy of money management: "A penny saved is a penny earned? "Don't be penny wise and pound foolish? "You can't take it with you"? "Eat, drink, and be merry for tomorrow we die"? "The one who dies with the most toys wins"? Other? **2.** What is one of the smarter things you've done with your money? What is one of the more foolish things?

STUDY 1. What proverbs do you see here that develop the theme of generosity? Taken together, how do they shape Solomon's view of giving: Generosity pays? Money misers are miserable? Neither a borrower, nor a lender be? I got mine the old fashioned way—I earned it? God helps those who help themselves? **2.** What is the end result of those who trust in their wealth (vv. 4,7,28)? Who benefits from the prosperity of the righteous (vv. 10–11,17,24–25)? **3.** How does Solomon's view of riches and stewardship compare with Jesus' view (what we are unwilling to part with will keep us from the kingdom of God)? And with Paul's view (a generous sower will reap generously)? Do you agree with these views on money and possessions? Why or why not? **4.** What proverbs do you see here that develop the theme of honesty? Taken together, how do they shape Solomon's view of honesty: Scales never lie, even if people do? Honesty hurts, but it's the best policy? Honesty does not always pay, but it's still worth it? It doesn't matter what you believe as long as you have integrity? The heart is exceedingly corrupt? **5.** What is the end of those who betray truth (vv. 3,6,11,19,21,31)? Do you believe the wicked will get their due? Explain. **6.** What do you learn here about admitting your mistakes (v. 2)? About keeping secrets (v. 13)? About seeking guidance (v. 14)? About seeking good (vv. 23,27)? About pig-like behavior (v. 22)? **7.** What do you think it means here to "win souls" (v. 30)? How does a person do this? How well do you do this?

APPLY 1. When it comes to talking about money do you: Love it? Despise it? Wish they would

2 When pride comes, then comes disgrace,
but with humility comes wisdom.

3 The integrity of the upright guides them,
but the unfaithful are destroyed by their duplicity.

4 Wealth is worthless in the day of wrath,
but righteousness delivers from death.

5 The righteousness of the blameless makes a straight way for
them,
but the wicked are brought down by their own wickedness.

6 The righteousness of the upright delivers them,
but the unfaithful are trapped by evil desires.

7 When a wicked man dies, his hope perishes;
all he expected from his power comes to nothing.

8 The righteous man is rescued from trouble,
and it comes on the wicked instead.

9 With his mouth the godless destroys his neighbor,
but through knowledge the righteous escape.

10 When the righteous prosper, the city rejoices;
when the wicked perish, there are shouts of joy.

11 Through the blessing of the upright a city is exalted,
but by the mouth of the wicked it is destroyed.

12 A man who lacks judgment derides his neighbor,
but a man of understanding holds his tongue.

13 A gossip betrays a confidence,
but a trustworthy man keeps a secret.

14 For lack of guidance a nation falls,
but many advisers make victory sure.

15 He who puts up security for another will surely suffer,
but whoever refuses to strike hands in pledge is safe.

16 A kindhearted woman gains respect,
but ruthless men gain only wealth.

17 A kind man benefits himself,
but a cruel man brings trouble on himself.

18 The wicked man earns deceptive wages,
but he who sows righteousness reaps a sure reward.

19 The truly righteous man attains life,
but he who pursues evil goes to his death.

20 The LORD detests men of perverse heart
but he delights in those whose ways are blameless.

11:4 in the day of wrath. Probably a reference to death.

11:7 hope perishes. Beyond this life, wealth and power mean nothing. To trade righteousness or wisdom for either is a futile attempt at happiness.

11:16 This proverb cleverly makes its point by comparing "respect" to "only wealth." The reader is left with no doubt which is the prize.

[21]Be sure of this: The wicked will not go unpunished,
but those who are righteous will go free.

[22]Like a gold ring in a pig's snout
is a beautiful woman who shows no discretion.

[23]The desire of the righteous ends only in good,
but the hope of the wicked only in wrath.

[24]One man gives freely, yet gains even more;
another withholds unduly, but comes to poverty.

[25]A generous man will prosper;
he who refreshes others will himself be refreshed.

[26]People curse the man who hoards grain,
but blessing crowns him who is willing to sell.

[27]He who seeks good finds goodwill,
but evil comes to him who searches for it.

[28]Whoever trusts in his riches will fall,
but the righteous will thrive like a green leaf.

[29]He who brings trouble on his family will inherit only wind,
and the fool will be servant to the wise.

[30]The fruit of the righteous is a tree of life,
and he who wins souls is wise.

[31]If the righteous receive their due on earth,
how much more the ungodly and the sinner!

12 Whoever loves discipline loves knowledge,
but he who hates correction is stupid.

[2]A good man obtains favor from the LORD,
but the LORD condemns a crafty man.

[3]A man cannot be established through wickedness,
but the righteous cannot be uprooted.

[4]A wife of noble character is her husband's crown,
but a disgraceful wife is like decay in his bones.

[5]The plans of the righteous are just,
but the advice of the wicked is deceitful.

[6]The words of the wicked lie in wait for blood,
but the speech of the upright rescues them.

[7]Wicked men are overthrown and are no more,
but the house of the righteous stands firm.

change the subject? Tolerate it? Welcome it? Benefit from it? Why do you suppose you respond to this subject as you do? **2.** Of all the proverbs mentioned in this chapter, which one do you want to tape to the door of your refrigerator? Why is that one so special to you?

OPEN 1. If God would grant you one of your fantasies or dreams, what would you like to come true? **2.** If your use of words were compared to the way you drive a car, what sort of driver were you over the past 24 hours: Cautious, looking both ways? Speeding, driving a little too fast? Egocentric, tooting your own horn? Distracted, watching the gals or guys go by? Reckless, with a few fender-benders? Faultless, never in danger of getting a ticket.

STUDY 1. Which proverbs in this passage would you label "absolutely true"? Which ones "absolutely false"? Why? **2.** How many proverbs can you find here which refer to speech? Why do you think Solomon spends so much time on this

---

11:24 gives freely, yet gains. A paradox. Generosity, not hoarding, is the path to prosperity.

11:28 trusts. The problem is not having the riches, but *trusting* in them. Jesus touched on the same topic (Matt. 19:23–24). The second line doesn't mean that right living leads to wealth. It is all about attitude.

11:31 their due. This phrase can be interpreted both in terms of blessings and consequences. Many scenarios in Scripture show the righteous receiving their penalty for sin. David suffered because of his sin with Bathsheba (2 Sam. 12:7–10). Moses suffered because of his lack of trust in the Lord (Num. 20:9–12). This verse functions as a summary for verses 29–30.

subject? **3.** All together, what do these proverbs say positively or negatively about the power of words? About the value of true talk? The venom of sinful talk? **4.** Verse 14 links words to the theme of work (14:23). What do you see as the connection? How might a career built on lies and a career built on honesty illustrate this point? **5.** Regarding this theme of work, what does Solomon say to your culture about: Dreamers who chase "fantastic" ideas? Get-rich-quick-schemes? Sound financial planners? Welfare recipients? Workaholics? **6.** How are we to handle advice (v. 15), insults (v. 16) and anxiety (v. 25)? How would that help you on the job? At home? **7.** "Working hard" and "diligence" contrast with "chasing fantasies" and "laziness" (vv. 11,24,27; 10:4; 19:24; 28:19). What's the point of each contrast? When is it okay to rest from our labors? When is it okay to let our money or our employees work in our stead? When is it okay to enjoy our possessions?

APPLY **1.** What do you love about your "work"? What is one thing you would like to change if you could? **2.** What "favor from the Lord" (v. 2) are you thankful for? What other favor do you seek? Why?

8 A man is praised according to his wisdom,
but men with warped minds are despised.

9 Better to be a nobody and yet have a servant
than pretend to be somebody and have no food.

10 A righteous man cares for the needs of his animal,
but the kindest acts of the wicked are cruel.

11 He who works his land will have abundant food,
but he who chases fantasies lacks judgment.

12 The wicked desire the plunder of evil men,
but the root of the righteous flourishes.

13 An evil man is trapped by his sinful talk,
but a righteous man escapes trouble.

14 From the fruit of his lips a man is filled with good things
as surely as the work of his hands rewards him.

15 The way of a fool seems right to him,
but a wise man listens to advice.

16 A fool shows his annoyance at once,
but a prudent man overlooks an insult.

17 A truthful witness gives honest testimony,
but a false witness tells lies.

18 Reckless words pierce like a sword,
but the tongue of the wise brings healing.

19 Truthful lips endure forever,
but a lying tongue lasts only a moment.

20 There is deceit in the hearts of those who plot evil,
but joy for those who promote peace.

21 No harm befalls the righteous,
but the wicked have their fill of trouble.

22 The LORD detests lying lips,
but he delights in men who are truthful.

23 A prudent man keeps his knowledge to himself,
but the heart of fools blurts out folly.

24 Diligent hands will rule,
but laziness ends in slave labor.

25 An anxious heart weighs a man down,
but a kind word cheers him up.

26 A righteous man is cautious in friendship,[a]
but the way of the wicked leads them astray.

[a]26 Or *man is a guide to his neighbor*

12:14 fruit of his lips. The words he speaks (25:11). **filled with good things.** Benefits. The good things we do and say bring benefits to us.

12:16 overlooks. Sometimes this word is translated "covers." The concept is diplomacy and tact, rather than avoidance.

[27]The lazy man does not roast[a] his game,
but the diligent man prizes his possessions.

[28]In the way of righteousness there is life;
along that path is immortality.

13 A wise son heeds his father's instruction,
but a mocker does not listen to rebuke.

[2]From the fruit of his lips a man enjoys good things,
but the unfaithful have a craving for violence.

[3]He who guards his lips guards his life,
but he who speaks rashly will come to ruin.

[4]The sluggard craves and gets nothing,
but the desires of the diligent are fully satisfied.

[5]The righteous hate what is false,
but the wicked bring shame and disgrace.

[6]Righteousness guards the man of integrity,
but wickedness overthrows the sinner.

[7]One man pretends to be rich, yet has nothing;
another pretends to be poor, yet has great wealth.

[8]A man's riches may ransom his life,
but a poor man hears no threat.

[9]The light of the righteous shines brightly,
but the lamp of the wicked is snuffed out.

[10]Pride only breeds quarrels,
but wisdom is found in those who take advice.

[11]Dishonest money dwindles away,
but he who gathers money little by little makes it grow.

[12]Hope deferred makes the heart sick,
but a longing fulfilled is a tree of life.

[13]He who scorns instruction will pay for it,
but he who respects a command is rewarded.

[14]The teaching of the wise is a fountain of life,
turning a man from the snares of death.

[15]Good understanding wins favor,
but the way of the unfaithful is hard.[b]

[16]Every prudent man acts out of knowledge,
but a fool exposes his folly.

[a]27 The meaning of the Hebrew for this word is uncertain. [b]15 Or *unfaithful does not endure*

OPEN 1. Who was your best childhood friend? What did you enjoy doing together? **2.** For what have you been hoping for a long, long, long time?

STUDY 1. What recurring themes do you see here? Which proverbs pick up themes from previous chapters? **2.** What does this chapter sound like to you: Sweet pillow talk? Tough parent-child talk? Parent-teacher conference talk? Grandparent-grandchild talk? Smooth life insurance talk? Do you see examples of each in this chapter? Where? **3.** On the riches/poverty theme (vv. 7,8,11,18,21–23), what point of contrast does each verse make? Why do you suppose rich and poor alike pretend to be what they are not (v. 7)? **4.** In the face of robbers, blackmailers or big fiscal commitments, what edge do the poor have over the rich (v. 8)? In terms of the best justice money can buy, how is that advantage reversed (v. 23)? **5.** What happens to the "get-rich-quick" scheme or the shady business person (v. 11)? What profit do diligence and discipline bring (vv. 4,11,18)? Do you think what Solomon says here is "take-it-to-the-bank true," "generally true," "moderately true," or "I wish it were true"? **6.** Proverbs stresses the general rule that righteous living leads to prosperity. What percentage of the time do you think that is true: 100%? 75%? 50%? 25% 10%? **7.** Discipline links the material and spiritual aspects of prosperity and poverty. How is that evident in verses 4,13,18,25? How many "sluggards" (v. 4.) or "wicked stomachs" (v. 25) do you see go hungry? To what kind of "hunger" do you think Solomon is referring? What does "prospering" mean here? **8.** How does the company you keep (v. 20) affect you? Why? **9.** You are a talk-show host discussing the spanking of children. How does

12:27 roast. May refer to the preparation of food or preparation for the hunt. Whichever, the lazy person won't even put effort into providing for himself and his family.

13:3 guards his lips. Words we speak matter. James reinforced the wisdom in taming the tongue (James 3:5–9).

13:7 Both of the scenarios are folly and subterfuge. Any attempt to project a false impression is silly and wasted.

13:8 A humorous proverb. Which is the greater protection, to have the money to ransom yourself or to have so little no thief would try to bilk you?

13:11 Dishonest money. Money gained illegitimately (10:2, Jer. 17:11), for instance, by extortion (Ps. 62:10) or deceit (Prov. 21:6). **little by little.** Through savings and safe investments.

your three-generation panel each react to verse 24?

APPLY 1. Where in life are you feeling satisfied and full? Where are you feeling "hungry": At home? At work? At church? At school? With friends? **2.** What do you believe about leaving large inheritances to your children or grandchildren: Let them earn it the hard way? Spend it all on your retirement? Leave as much as possible for others? Giving money creates more problems than it solves?

OPEN 1. Of all the houses in which you have lived, what is one of your favorites? Why that particular house? **2.** If you would allow yourself to do so, what might you become bitter about?

STUDY 1. How might verse 1 serve as a good "subtitle" for this chapter? Explain. **2.** Some proverbs arrest our attention due to a figure of speech that is ambiguous. Such is the case with verse 4. What do you think it means: Growth is never neat, but often messy —like an ox? Take care of your means of production if you want a rich harvest? Be kind to animals and they will be kind to you? **3.** Do you agree with verses 2, 26–27? How would you define the term "fear of the LORD"? In your opinion, how prevalent is a "fear of the LORD" mindset in your church and community? **4.** What does it mean to "stay away" from a fool (v. 7)? How does one avoid worshipping, working, or socializing with a "fool"? **5.** Does verse

17 A wicked messenger falls into trouble,
but a trustworthy envoy brings healing.

18 He who ignores discipline comes to poverty and shame,
but whoever heeds correction is honored.

19 A longing fulfilled is sweet to the soul,
but fools detest turning from evil.

20 He who walks with the wise grows wise,
but a companion of fools suffers harm.

21 Misfortune pursues the sinner,
but prosperity is the reward of the righteous.

22 A good man leaves an inheritance for his children's children,
but a sinner's wealth is stored up for the righteous.

23 A poor man's field may produce abundant food,
but injustice sweeps it away.

24 He who spares the rod hates his son,
but he who loves him is careful to discipline him.

25 The righteous eat to their hearts' content,
but the stomach of the wicked goes hungry.

14

The wise woman builds her house,
but with her own hands the foolish one tears hers down.

2 He whose walk is upright fears the LORD,
but he whose ways are devious despises him.

3 A fool's talk brings a rod to his back,
but the lips of the wise protect them.

4 Where there are no oxen, the manger is empty,
but from the strength of an ox comes an abundant harvest.

5 A truthful witness does not deceive,
but a false witness pours out lies.

6 The mocker seeks wisdom and finds none,
but knowledge comes easily to the discerning.

7 Stay away from a foolish man,
for you will not find knowledge on his lips.

8 The wisdom of the prudent is to give thought to their ways,
but the folly of fools is deception.

9 Fools mock at making amends for sin,
but goodwill is found among the upright.

13:22 inheritance. Throughout Proverbs the long-term legacy of the righteous is compared to the short life of the unrighteous (10:27).

13:24 the rod. In this culture the rod was used for spanking. The truth underlying the verse applies to all forms of discipline. Proverbs consistently reinforces the importance of discipline (10:13; 22:15; 29:15).

14:1 builds her house. Providing a solid foundation for her family is one of the great achievements of a wise woman.

14:4 manger. Food trough. **abundant harvest.** In order to see a harvest, the farmer must invest time, money, effort and put up with a lot of inconvenience. An empty manger doesn't require much effort, nor does it bring much benefit.

14:8 folly. The belief that nothing matters, that no thought is required, is child's play. Only a fool believes it.

[10]Each heart knows its own bitterness,
and no one else can share its joy.

[11]The house of the wicked will be destroyed,
but the tent of the upright will flourish.

[12]There is a way that seems right to a man,
but in the end it leads to death.

[13]Even in laughter the heart may ache,
and joy may end in grief.

[14]The faithless will be fully repaid for their ways,
and the good man rewarded for his.

[15]A simple man believes anything,
but a prudent man gives thought to his steps.

[16]A wise man fears the LORD and shuns evil,
but a fool is hotheaded and reckless.

[17]A quick-tempered man does foolish things,
and a crafty man is hated.

[18]The simple inherit folly,
but the prudent are crowned with knowledge.

[19]Evil men will bow down in the presence of the good,
and the wicked at the gates of the righteous.

[20]The poor are shunned even by their neighbors,
but the rich have many friends.

[21]He who despises his neighbor sins,
but blessed is he who is kind to the needy.

[22]Do not those who plot evil go astray?
But those who plan what is good find[a] love and faithfulness.

[23]All hard work brings a profit,
but mere talk leads only to poverty.

[24]The wealth of the wise is their crown,
but the folly of fools yields folly.

[25]A truthful witness saves lives,
but a false witness is deceitful.

[26]He who fears the LORD has a secure fortress,
and for his children it will be a refuge.

[27]The fear of the LORD is a fountain of life,
turning a man from the snares of death.

[28]A large population is a king's glory,
but without subjects a prince is ruined.

[a]22 *Or show*

13 make sense to you? Have you ever experienced this yourself? **6.** How should we relate to our neighbors in need (vv. 21,31)? What happens if we follow this advice? How does shabby treatment of the unfortunate reflect on one's relationship with God? How does the good we do for the poor honor God and exalt one's nation as morally righteous? Why do you think that is so? Is yours an exalted nation, or a disgraced one (v. 34)? Explain. **7.** What alone provides true security (v. 26)? Have you found security there? Why or why not? **8.** Look at verse 30. Does envy get a bad rap? Why? In what way does envy "rot the bones"?

APPLY 1. Comparing your life to a "house," what condition is it in: Good foundation, but tacky additions? Fancy exterior, but shabby interior? Under priced fixer-upper? Well lived in? Ready for resale? A bargain at any price? **2.** If you had a choice of the following, which would you like to work on and why: Strong back? Wise lips? Rich friends? Caring heart? Discerning heart? Quick temper? King's delight? Nation's righteousness? **3.** On a scale of one to ten, how are you doing with envy?

14:19 Evil men will bow down. Sometimes evil triumphs, but the hope is that good will triumph.

14:21 despises. Holds in contempt, belittles, ridicules. God held the whole nation responsible for their poor.

14:22 love and faithfulness. The New Testament equivalent would be "grace and truth." It could be called "true love".

29 A patient man has great understanding,
but a quick-tempered man displays folly.

30 A heart at peace gives life to the body,
but envy rots the bones.

31 He who oppresses the poor shows contempt for their Maker,
but whoever is kind to the needy honors God.

32 When calamity comes, the wicked are brought down,
but even in death the righteous have a refuge.

33 Wisdom reposes in the heart of the discerning
and even among fools she lets herself be known.[a]

34 Righteousness exalts a nation,
but sin is a disgrace to any people.

35 A king delights in a wise servant,
but a shameful servant incurs his wrath.

15 A gentle answer turns away wrath,
but a harsh word stirs up anger.

2 The tongue of the wise commends knowledge,
but the mouth of the fool gushes folly.

3 The eyes of the LORD are everywhere,
keeping watch on the wicked and the good.

4 The tongue that brings healing is a tree of life,
but a deceitful tongue crushes the spirit.

5 A fool spurns his father's discipline,
but whoever heeds correction shows prudence.

6 The house of the righteous contains great treasure,
but the income of the wicked brings them trouble.

7 The lips of the wise spread knowledge;
not so the hearts of fools.

8 The LORD detests the sacrifice of the wicked,
but the prayer of the upright pleases him.

9 The LORD detests the way of the wicked
but he loves those who pursue righteousness.

[a] 33 Hebrew; Septuagint and Syriac / *but in the heart of fools she is not known*

OPEN 1. Who would get the reward for best peacemaking efforts in your family? Why did you select that person? **2.** What's your favorite vegetable? Your least favorite?

STUDY 1. As a key is used to unlock the door to a house, what key words do you find here that unlock the meaning of the chapter? What is the key to "joy"? To "success"? To "keeping peace"? To "healing hurts"? If you had to pick a "master key" from this chapter, what would it be? **2.** How does it strike you that God is always, everywhere "keeping watch" (v. 3)? Would this make the average person: Uneasy? Scared? Relieved? Secure? How about you? **3.** You have heard the phrase, "Talk is cheap." Would Solomon agree or disagree with that? Why do you think so? What value does he place on the tongue, lips, mouth, words? **4.** What does the Lord detest here? In what sense can "sacrifice" be detestable? Could something as good as going to church and saying your prayers actually offend God? How so? What does

14:29 quick-tempered. James wrote about this problem when he encouraged his readers to be slow to speak and slow to anger (James 1:19).

14:31 God is a protector of the poor (22:22–23). Our actions toward the poor reflect our attitude toward God.

14:32 a refuge. When tragedy strikes, where do you look for hope? God is in control, even in death. People who worship God truly can find their hope in him.

14:34 Righteousness and sinfulness affect a nation in much the same way they do an individual.

15:1 Proverbs makes the point, much like James, that the way we use speech tells a lot about what kind of people we are (James 3:5–8). Whether we use gentle or harsh words has everything to do with character.

15:3 keeping watch. That God sees everyone at all times evokes different responses in people: to the righteous it is comfort; to the wicked, a threat.

15:4 deceitful. Subversive or duplicitous. We have the power through our words to influence those around us, to be an agent of change.

15:8 sacrifice. Even in the Old Testament, God made it clear that he wanted devoted hearts more than cold obedience. Samuel, a priest to Solomon's father David, taught this same concept (1 Sam. 15:22).

[10]Stern discipline awaits him who leaves the path;
he who hates correction will die.

[11]Death and Destruction[a] lie open before the LORD—
how much more the hearts of men!

[12]A mocker resents correction;
he will not consult the wise.

[13]A happy heart makes the face cheerful,
but heartache crushes the spirit.

[14]The discerning heart seeks knowledge,
but the mouth of a fool feeds on folly.

[15]All the days of the oppressed are wretched,
but the cheerful heart has a continual feast.

[16]Better a little with the fear of the LORD
than great wealth with turmoil.

[17]Better a meal of vegetables where there is love
than a fattened calf with hatred.

[18]A hot-tempered man stirs up dissension,
but a patient man calms a quarrel.

[19]The way of the sluggard is blocked with thorns,
but the path of the upright is a highway.

[20]A wise son brings joy to his father,
but a foolish man despises his mother.

[21]Folly delights a man who lacks judgment,
but a man of understanding keeps a straight course.

[22]Plans fail for lack of counsel,
but with many advisers they succeed.

[23]A man finds joy in giving an apt reply—
and how good is a timely word!

[24]The path of life leads upward for the wise
to keep him from going down to the grave.[b]

[25]The LORD tears down the proud man's house
but he keeps the widow's boundaries intact.

[26]The LORD detests the thoughts of the wicked,
but those of the pure are pleasing to him.

[27]A greedy man brings trouble to his family,
but he who hates bribes will live.

[a]*11 Hebrew Sheol and Abaddon* [b]*24 Hebrew Sheol*

please the Lord? **5.** What is the interplay between the "heart" and other aspects of the personality mentioned here (vv. 7,11,13–15,28, 30)? Does what's on the inside come through to the outside (v. 13)? Or does seeing and putting on a cheerful face determine how the heart feels (v. 30)? Which would you say contributes the most: inside to outside or outside to inside? Why? **6.** What is to be our response to correction or rebuke (vv. 5,10,12,31–32)? If we listen to it, what happens? If we ignore it, what happens? Do you believe it's that simple? Why or why not? **7.** If this chapter were a book for sale, which verse would be on the cover as a "come on" to persuade you to buy it?

APPLY 1. How would you assess the condition of your "heart" right now: Light hearted? Heavy hearted? Heart broken? Heart throbbing? Heart aching? Heart burning? Other? Explain. **2.** Do you think anyone else has your same "heart" condition? Why not share your condition with someone to see if they can offer some wisdom.

15:11 Death and Destruction. Probably an allusion to seeing the dead in their graves or in their eternal homes. How much more should God be able to see the hearts of living people?

15:13 happy heart. Inner joy and contentment. **heartache.** Depression.

15:15 the oppressed. Those who are bowed down under their affliction; the needy. Those who cannot overcome their circumstances.

28 The heart of the righteous weighs its answers,
but the mouth of the wicked gushes evil.

29 The LORD is far from the wicked
but he hears the prayer of the righteous.

30 A cheerful look brings joy to the heart,
and good news gives health to the bones.

31 He who listens to a life-giving rebuke
will be at home among the wise.

32 He who ignores discipline despises himself,
but whoever heeds correction gains understanding.

33 The fear of the LORD teaches a man wisdom,[a]
and humility comes before honor.

16 To man belong the plans of the heart,
but from the LORD comes the reply of the tongue.

2 All a man's ways seem innocent to him,
but motives are weighed by the LORD.

3 Commit to the LORD whatever you do,
and your plans will succeed.

4 The LORD works out everything for his own ends—
even the wicked for a day of disaster.

5 The LORD detests all the proud of heart.
Be sure of this: They will not go unpunished.

6 Through love and faithfulness sin is atoned for;
through the fear of the LORD a man avoids evil.

7 When a man's ways are pleasing to the LORD,
he makes even his enemies live at peace with him.

8 Better a little with righteousness
than much gain with injustice.

9 In his heart a man plans his course,
but the LORD determines his steps.

[a]33 Or *Wisdom teaches the fear of the LORD*

OPEN 1. What do you plan to do this week? This month? This year? **2.** Where have your experienced an extra dose of pleasure recently? **3.** Are you a person who would rather "go with the flow" or "chart the flow"? Explain.

STUDY 1. What does this chapter sound like to you: Personal testimony? History lesson? Philosophy class? Parental lecture? Career counseling? What elements of each do you see here? **2.** Compare verses 1–9 with 10–15. What do you observe as the roles and character of the Lord? Of the king? How do they compare? **3.** What principles for decision-making, goal-setting, and knowing God's will do you see here (vv. 1-4,9-10,17,20,25,33)? What role should feelings, circumstances, counsel, conscience, casting lots (v. 33), and oracles (v. 10) each play in knowing and doing God's will? Which should be determinative? Confirming? Suspect? **4.** It has been said, "Man proposes, God disposes." How is that viewpoint illustrated here? Likewise,

15:30 cheerful look. Literally, "bright eyes." **health to the bones.** Several times Proverbs associates emotional health with physical well-being (v. 13).

15:32 discipline. Throughout the Bible, God's discipline or moral correction is included as part of his love. Moses reminded the people in Deuteronomy *that God disciplines them as children.* Hebrews, as well as other New Testament books, repeats that truth (Heb. 12:7–11). We are to heed discipline or regret foolishness (5:11–12).

16:1 plans. Several proverbs juxtapose human plans with God's sovereignty. Even with our best efforts, God's plans take priority. That can be a comfort when we are unsure of which way to go with a decision.

16:4 disaster. God's justice is punishment for wickedness as well as rewards for righteousness.

16:6 love and faithfulness. This is *God's* love and *God's* faithfulness. It is through God's saving grace and then our ongoing relationship with God that we avoid evil.

16:7 pleasing to the LORD. Habits that please God include pure thoughts (15:26) and honesty (20:23).

16:9 a man plans his course. God's sovereignty over our lives should not discourage us from planning and setting goals. Rather, it gives us reassurance that the outcome is not ours alone. Someone much bigger is watching out for us.

[10]The lips of a king speak as an oracle,
and his mouth should not betray justice.

[11]Honest scales and balances are from the LORD;
all the weights in the bag are of his making.

[12]Kings detest wrongdoing,
for a throne is established through righteousness.

[13]Kings take pleasure in honest lips;
they value a man who speaks the truth.

[14]A king's wrath is a messenger of death,
but a wise man will appease it.

[15]When a king's face brightens, it means life;
his favor is like a rain cloud in spring.

[16]How much better to get wisdom than gold,
to choose understanding rather than silver!

[17]The highway of the upright avoids evil;
he who guards his way guards his life.

[18]Pride goes before destruction,
a haughty spirit before a fall.

[19]Better to be lowly in spirit and among the oppressed
than to share plunder with the proud.

[20]Whoever gives heed to instruction prospers,
and blessed is he who trusts in the LORD.

[21]The wise in heart are called discerning,
and pleasant words promote instruction.[a]

[22]Understanding is a fountain of life to those who have it,
but folly brings punishment to fools.

[23]A wise man's heart guides his mouth,
and his lips promote instruction.[b]

[24]Pleasant words are a honeycomb,
sweet to the soul and healing to the bones.

[25]There is a way that seems right to a man,
but in the end it leads to death.

[26]The laborer's appetite works for him;
his hunger drives him on.

[27]A scoundrel plots evil,
and his speech is like a scorching fire.

[a]21 Or words make a man persuasive *[b]23 Or mouth / and makes his lips persuasive*

to what extent does Solomon say we are "free" to set goals and reach for them? Do you agree with his counsel? Explain. **5.** If "God works out everything for his own ends" (v. 4), does that make God responsible for evil? If not, then does evil always serve God's purposes? How so? **6.** Which aspect of God seems to be uppermost in these proverbs: Just? Sovereign? Caring? Judging? Guiding? Blessing? Which have you observed most strongly in your life this past year? **7.** What new themes have been introduced in this chapter? Which proverbs in the chapter raise a question or two in your mind? Which do you find particularly comforting?

APPLY 1. Where are you struggling to discern God's will? How can the group be of help to you in this matter? **2.** What have you done in your life that you are certain put a smile on God's face?

16:10 king. Originally the nation of Israel was a theocracy, governed by God. Then Israel was ruled by judges, and finally by kings. The first two kings were chosen by God: Saul and David (Solomon's father). Even though these early kings were political rulers, they were also seen as God's representatives.

16:12 righteousness. The history of Israel was an on-again, off-again struggle between righteous kings and evil kings. The nation eventually fell to exile because of loss of worship and disobedience.

[28]A perverse man stirs up dissension,
and a gossip separates close friends.

[29]A violent man entices his neighbor
and leads him down a path that is not good.

[30]He who winks with his eye is plotting perversity;
he who purses his lips is bent on evil.

[31]Gray hair is a crown of splendor;
it is attained by a righteous life.

[32]Better a patient man than a warrior,
a man who controls his temper than one who takes a city.

[33]The lot is cast into the lap,
but its every decision is from the LORD.

17 Better a dry crust with peace and quiet
than a house full of feasting,[a] with strife.

[2]A wise servant will rule over a disgraceful son,
and will share the inheritance as one of the brothers.

[3]The crucible for silver and the furnace for gold,
but the LORD tests the heart.

[4]A wicked man listens to evil lips;
a liar pays attention to a malicious tongue.

[5]He who mocks the poor shows contempt for their Maker;
whoever gloats over disaster will not go unpunished.

[6]Children's children are a crown to the aged,
and parents are the pride of their children.

[7]Arrogant[b] lips are unsuited to a fool—
how much worse lying lips to a ruler!

[8]A bribe is a charm to the one who gives it;
wherever he turns, he succeeds.

[9]He who covers over an offense promotes love,
but whoever repeats the matter separates close friends.

[10]A rebuke impresses a man of discernment
more than a hundred lashes a fool.

[11]An evil man is bent only on rebellion;
a merciless official will be sent against him.

[12]Better to meet a bear robbed of her cubs
than a fool in his folly.

[13]If a man pays back evil for good,
evil will never leave his house.

[a]1 Hebrew *sacrifices* [b]7 Or *Eloquent*

OPEN **1.** If money and time where no object, what would you do for a little "peace and quiet"? **2.** One of the most peaceful moments of my life was …

STUDY **1.** From this chapter, do you get the idea the author was: Poor but respectful? Rich and resentful? Young and restless? A grief-stricken parent? A proud grandparent? Why do you think so? Where in these proverbs do you see elements of each? **2.** What conflict management ideas do you see in verses 1,4,9,11,14,17,19? How practical or useful do you think they are? **3.** In what sense is verse 2 true? How did this come true for Solomon's servant and son (1 Kin. 11:28–40)? **4.** If the Lord detests the injustice of acquitting the guilty (v. 15), why does God acquit us of our sin (Rom. 3:26; 4:5)? How does God remain just in doing that? **5.** In what sense is verse 22 true (15:13,30)? What about the grief-stricken "father of a fool" (vv. 21,25)? How does he get a cheerful heart (James 1:2–12)? **6.** What principles for justice and justification do you see here (vv. 8,13,15,23,26)? How does God deal with the perpetrators and victims of injustice? How should we? **7.** When corrected by the Lord, how does it feel? Are you ever in the doghouse very long? What does it take to get out?

APPLY **1.** In what ways can you identify with the author's experience of family strife (v. 1), grief

17:2 wise servant. The truth of this proverb is revealed in Solomon's own life. His disgraceful son Rehoboam was rejected by the northern tribe which became Israel and he was left only with Judah.

17:9 covers. To cover a sin is to literally overwhelm it with forgiveness and love.

[14]Starting a quarrel is like breaching a dam;
so drop the matter before a dispute breaks out.

[15]Acquitting the guilty and condemning the innocent—
the LORD detests them both.

[16]Of what use is money in the hand of a fool,
since he has no desire to get wisdom?

[17]A friend loves at all times,
and a brother is born for adversity.

[18]A man lacking in judgment strikes hands in pledge
and puts up security for his neighbor.

[19]He who loves a quarrel loves sin;
he who builds a high gate invites destruction.

[20]A man of perverse heart does not prosper;
he whose tongue is deceitful falls into trouble.

[21]To have a fool for a son brings grief;
there is no joy for the father of a fool.

[22]A cheerful heart is good medicine,
but a crushed spirit dries up the bones.

[23]A wicked man accepts a bribe in secret
to pervert the course of justice.

[24]A discerning man keeps wisdom in view,
but a fool's eyes wander to the ends of the earth.

[25]A foolish son brings grief to his father
and bitterness to the one who bore him.

[26]It is not good to punish an innocent man,
or to flog officials for their integrity.

[27]A man of knowledge uses words with restraint,
and a man of understanding is even-tempered.

[28]Even a fool is thought wise if he keeps silent,
and discerning if he holds his tongue.

18 An unfriendly man pursues selfish ends;
he defies all sound judgment.

[2]A fool finds no pleasure in understanding
but delights in airing his own opinions.

[3]When wickedness comes, so does contempt,
and with shame comes disgrace.

(vv. 21,25), disgrace (v. 2), and pride (v. 6)? What would you like your group to pray concerning your family ties? **2.** Who do you know that deserves the "appearance of wisdom" award (vv. 27–28)?

OPEN 1. In terms of longevity, who has been one of your closest friends? When did you meet? How have you kept the relationship alive for so long? **2.** What's a memorable gift you remember giving or receiving?

17:17 friend ... brother. This verse does not focus on the difference between a friend and a brother, but rather on the commitment that either shows. Solomon may have heard stories about his father David's friendship with Jonathan, a friendship that illustrated this verse (1 Sam. 18:1). Paul calls for this love in the church (1 Cor. 13).

17:19 high gate. Either a door that is physically tall to show off wealth or a symbol for boasting.

17:22 good medicine. Proverbs is a practical book that connects our inner and outer worlds. Verses like this make the connection between emotional and physical health long before modern medicine did the same thing.

17:26 flog officials. Only kings or judges could make this happen. The perversion to the justice system described here happened to Daniel when officials of the Persian government set out to catch him in a legal loophole that would result in his execution (Dan. 6:4–5).

STUDY **1.** Following chapter 17:27–28, what does chapter 18 say about a fool's tongue, lips, mouth? How do these proverbs relate to the forming and articulating of opinions? In your opinion, which one best sums up the others? **2.** What is the meaning of "deep waters" (v. 4; 20:5)? How does the "bubbling brook" differ from the obscurity or secrecy of "deep waters"? **3.** Which proverbs convey principles for rich and poor alike (vv. 5,16–17,19,23)? Why do you think favoritism of any kind is uniformly condemned in the Scriptures? How might the Lord deal justly with the "fortified cities" of verses 11 and 19? **4.** What does this chapter say about finding and keeping your brothers, sisters, friends, even your life mate? **5.** Verse 10 has been set to music. Why do you think it has become a popular song of praise? **6.** The tongue (speech) has the "power of life and death" (v. 21). What examples have you seen of speech bringing "life"? Bringing "death"? **7.** What is the main point of verses 13 and 17? As a guiding principle, how would you apply this to raising children? To formulating doctrine? Deliberating legal cases? Conducting scientific experiments? Making public policy? What difference would it make in your group study? In personal relationships?

APPLY **1.** When in your life did you come close to or actually have a "crushed spirit" (v. 14)? How did it affect you? What helped you recover? **2.** What words from your past have "stung" you? What words have "empowered" you?

4The words of a man's mouth are deep waters,
but the fountain of wisdom is a bubbling brook.

5It is not good to be partial to the wicked
or to deprive the innocent of justice.

6A fool's lips bring him strife,
and his mouth invites a beating.

7A fool's mouth is his undoing,
and his lips are a snare to his soul.

8The words of a gossip are like choice morsels;
they go down to a man's inmost parts.

9One who is slack in his work
is brother to one who destroys.

10The name of the LORD is a strong tower;
the righteous run to it and are safe.

11The wealth of the rich is their fortified city;
they imagine it an unscalable wall.

12Before his downfall a man's heart is proud,
but humility comes before honor.

13He who answers before listening—
that is his folly and his shame.

14A man's spirit sustains him in sickness,
but a crushed spirit who can bear?

15The heart of the discerning acquires knowledge;
the ears of the wise seek it out.

16A gift opens the way for the giver
and ushers him into the presence of the great.

17The first to present his case seems right,
till another comes forward and questions him.

18Casting the lot settles disputes
and keeps strong opponents apart.

19An offended brother is more unyielding than a fortified city,
and disputes are like the barred gates of a citadel.

20From the fruit of his mouth a man's stomach is filled;
with the harvest from his lips he is satisfied.

18:4 bubbling brook. Implies fresh, moving water. Wise words refresh and illuminate our lives.

18:5 partial. Favoritism, particularly toward the wicked, was condemned throughout the Old and New Testaments. God is just and fair (Rom. 2:11), and God expects us to be.

18:8 choice morsels. Like eating a delicacy. An apt description of a "juicy" piece of gossip. Just as a delicacy is digested, then, gossip becomes a part of who we are and how we see people. It affects our frame of reference.

18:11 they imagine it an unscalable wall. The deceit of trusting money is the myth that it can really take care of us. Jesus addressed this same issue with the rich young ruler who would not give up his wealth even for the kingdom of God (Matt. 19:21–24).

18:17 "Hearing both sides of the story before making a decision" is wisdom that extends beyond the courtroom walls. Here it is a warning to a judge, but the same is true of parents, friends, organizational leaders and community members.

[21]The tongue has the power of life and death,
and those who love it will eat its fruit.

[22]He who finds a wife finds what is good
and receives favor from the LORD.

[23]A poor man pleads for mercy,
but a rich man answers harshly.

[24]A man of many companions may come to ruin,
but there is a friend who sticks closer than a brother.

19 Better a poor man whose walk is blameless
than a fool whose lips are perverse.

[2]It is not good to have zeal without knowledge,
nor to be hasty and miss the way.

[3]A man's own folly ruins his life,
yet his heart rages against the LORD.

[4]Wealth brings many friends,
but a poor man's friend deserts him.

[5]A false witness will not go unpunished,
and he who pours out lies will not go free.

[6]Many curry favor with a ruler,
and everyone is the friend of a man who gives gifts.

[7]A poor man is shunned by all his relatives—
how much more do his friends avoid him!

Though he pursues them with pleading,
they are nowhere to be found.[a]

[8]He who gets wisdom loves his own soul;
he who cherishes understanding prospers.

[9]A false witness will not go unpunished,
and he who pours out lies will perish.

[10]It is not fitting for a fool to live in luxury—
how much worse for a slave to rule over princes!

[11]A man's wisdom gives him patience;
it is to his glory to overlook an offense.

[12]A king's rage is like the roar of a lion,
but his favor is like dew on the grass.

[13]A foolish son is his father's ruin,
and a quarrelsome wife is like a constant dripping.

[a]7 The meaning of the Hebrew for this sentence is uncertain.

OPEN 1. Are you more likely to read the instructions before putting something together, or refer to them only when you run into trouble? **2.** What are you zealous about these days? Where are you lacking in zeal?

STUDY 1. What recurring themes and key words do you see highlighted here? **2.** Solomon often uses two contrasting statements to emphasize a point. In which proverb do you feel the contrast is most pronounced? How does this help you to understand the main point? **3.** Some couplets use comparison more than contrast to make a point. What examples do you see of this? What point is made by these comparisons using "better than," "worse than" and "like"? **4.** Which proverbs in this chapter put a smile on your face? Which caused you to furrow your brow? **5.** Women, what do you think of verse 13? Men, what do you think of it? If a quarrelsome wife is like "a constant dripping," what would a quarrelsome husband be like? **6.** Have you ever seen an example of the person described in verse 3? Why do you suppose some people blame God rather than themselves for the way their lives turn out? **7.** What do you make of verse 21? Does it mean: God always has the last word? What God wants done, God gets done? God will always show you the right way? Other? Explain.

APPLY 1. Share a time when your hastiness outdistanced your good sense. In what area of your life today do you want to make sure you think things through before you act? **2.** How have you experienced the

19:2 zeal. Ambitious drive. Many modern proverbs parallel this one, including "Haste makes waste" and "Getting nowhere in record time."

19:3 his heart rages. Cain, son of Adam and Eve, was an example of this. His sacrifice was not accepted by God. Rather than adjusting his sacrifice, he became angry with God and killed his brother (Heb. 11:4; 1 John 3:12).

19:13 ruin. The ruin that a foolish son brings is like a "chasm" in the life of his father. It is a deep pit of despair. **quarrelsome**. Though translated different ways, this word is used more in Proverbs than in any other Old Testament book. Sometimes it appears as "dissension" (10:12) or "strife" (23:29).

truth in verses 5 and 9? Have you ever been hurt by a false witness? Was it intentional or unintentional? Share your story.

---

[14]Houses and wealth are inherited from parents,
but a prudent wife is from the LORD.

[15]Laziness brings on deep sleep,
and the shiftless man goes hungry.

[16]He who obeys instructions guards his life,
but he who is contemptuous of his ways will die.

[17]He who is kind to the poor lends to the LORD,
and he will reward him for what he has done.

[18]Discipline your son, for in that there is hope;
do not be a willing party to his death.

[19]A hot-tempered man must pay the penalty;
if you rescue him, you will have to do it again.

[20]Listen to advice and accept instruction,
and in the end you will be wise.

[21]Many are the plans in a man's heart,
but it is the LORD's purpose that prevails.

[22]What a man desires is unfailing love[a];
better to be poor than a liar.

[23]The fear of the LORD leads to life:
Then one rests content, untouched by trouble.

[24]The sluggard buries his hand in the dish;
he will not even bring it back to his mouth!

[25]Flog a mocker, and the simple will learn prudence;
rebuke a discerning man, and he will gain knowledge.

[26]He who robs his father and drives out his mother
is a son who brings shame and disgrace.

[27]Stop listening to instruction, my son,
and you will stray from the words of knowledge.

[28]A corrupt witness mocks at justice,
and the mouth of the wicked gulps down evil.

[29]Penalties are prepared for mockers,
and beatings for the backs of fools.

OPEN 1. What was the place of alcohol in your childhood home? What is the place of alcohol now? **2.** When you were a child, what was one forbidden activity? Did you ever do it? Did your parents ever find out? What did they do?

20

Wine is a mocker and beer a brawler;
whoever is led astray by them is not wise.

[2]A king's wrath is like the roar of a lion;
he who angers him forfeits his life.

[a]22 Or *A man's greed is his shame*

19:26 robs. Assaults or mistreatments. In this culture the care of elderly parents fell squarely on sons and daughters.

20:1 Wine ... beer. Wine refers to fermented grape juice here, but at times in the Bible, the same term refers to unfermented juice. **beer.** Strong drinks made from barley, dates or pomegranates. Priests were forbidden to drink this because it was so intoxicating.

[3]It is to a man's honor to avoid strife,
but every fool is quick to quarrel.

[4]A sluggard does not plow in season;
so at harvest time he looks but finds nothing.

[5]The purposes of a man's heart are deep waters,
but a man of understanding draws them out.

[6]Many a man claims to have unfailing love,
but a faithful man who can find?

[7]The righteous man leads a blameless life;
blessed are his children after him.

[8]When a king sits on his throne to judge,
he winnows out all evil with his eyes.

[9]Who can say, "I have kept my heart pure;
I am clean and without sin"?

[10]Differing weights and differing measures—
the LORD detests them both.

[11]Even a child is known by his actions,
by whether his conduct is pure and right.

[12]Ears that hear and eyes that see—
the LORD has made them both.

[13]Do not love sleep or you will grow poor;
stay awake and you will have food to spare.

[14]"It's no good, it's no good!" says the buyer;
then off he goes and boasts about his purchase.

[15]Gold there is, and rubies in abundance,
but lips that speak knowledge are a rare jewel.

[16]Take the garment of one who puts up security for a stranger;
hold it in pledge if he does it for a wayward woman.

[17]Food gained by fraud tastes sweet to a man,
but he ends up with a mouth full of gravel.

[18]Make plans by seeking advice;
if you wage war, obtain guidance.

[19]A gossip betrays a confidence;
so avoid a man who talks too much.

[20]If a man curses his father or mother,
his lamp will be snuffed out in pitch darkness.

STUDY 1. If you were promoting this chapter during a 10-second sneak preview TV commercial, which verse(s) would you use as a tease to attract an audience? Why? **2.** Do you think verse 1 is a little over the top or right on the money? Explain. **3.** What do you think Solomon is saying in verse 6: Faithful people are rare? No one is faithful? Actions speak louder than words? Do not trust anyone? **4.** How would you answer the rhetorical question posed in verse 9? How does Job (Job 14:4)? The psalmist (Ps. 24:4; 119:9,11)? The Apostle Paul (Rom. 3:23)? **5.** What does this chapter say about the Lord (vv. 10,12, 22,24,27)? Do these statements coincide with your picture of God? Explain. **6.** What do you make out of verse 30? Is this an endorsement for corporal punishment or is Solomon saying something else? If so, what?

APPLY 1. In what do you "glory" (v. 29): Grandchildren? Job? House? Intelligence? Strength? Physical attractiveness? Church? Other? **2.** Of the qualities of God mentioned in this chapter, which brings you special comfort today? Why?

20:3 avoid strife. It is easy to get pulled into quarrels, to prove you're right. But the wise person stays out of that competition.

20:9 without sin. Paul, in the book of Romans, corroborates that no one is without sin (Rom. 3:12).

20:17 gravel. An apt picture of the long-term consequences of sin. At first, getting away with something is sweet, but in the end we are left with the remains of our broken character.

20:20 snuffed out. Death. **pitch darkness.** The darkest part of the night when you cannot see your hand in front of your face. Cursing your father and mother was punishable by death (Lev. 20:9).

[21]An inheritance quickly gained at the beginning
will not be blessed at the end.

[22]Do not say, "I'll pay you back for this wrong!"
Wait for the LORD, and he will deliver you.

[23]The LORD detests differing weights,
and dishonest scales do not please him.

[24]A man's steps are directed by the LORD.
How then can anyone understand his own way?

[25]It is a trap for a man to dedicate something rashly
and only later to consider his vows.

[26]A wise king winnows out the wicked;
he drives the threshing wheel over them.

[27]The lamp of the LORD searches the spirit of a man[a];
it searches out his inmost being.

[28]Love and faithfulness keep a king safe;
through love his throne is made secure.

[29]The glory of young men is their strength,
gray hair the splendor of the old.

[30]Blows and wounds cleanse away evil,
and beatings purge the inmost being.

21 The king's heart is in the hand of the LORD;
he directs it like a watercourse wherever he pleases.

[2]All a man's ways seem right to him,
but the LORD weighs the heart.

[3]To do what is right and just
is more acceptable to the LORD than sacrifice.

[4]Haughty eyes and a proud heart,
the lamp of the wicked, are sin!

[5]The plans of the diligent lead to profit
as surely as haste leads to poverty.

[a]27 Or *The spirit of man is the LORD's lamp*

OPEN 1. If you could play any character in a movie, what character would you like to play: Hero or heroine? Villain? Trusty sidekick? Comic sidekick? Stunt person? Narrator? Tragic victim? Love interest? Other? **2.** If you could live anywhere in the world, where would you live?

STUDY 1. If this chapter were a play, who would be the cast of characters? Who would have the lead? Which would receive standing ovations? Why? **2.** Verse 1 tells us that God uses the hand or actions of a national leader, even an

20:21 quickly gained. The inheritance described here could be gained by deceit, or by request, like the prodigal son (Luke 15:12–13). That parable reflects the truth of this verse.

20:22 Wait for the LORD. Knowing *what belongs to God and what* belongs to a person is a wisdom repeated in Proverbs. In this case, vengeance belongs to God. For a person to take revenge is sin.

20:25 dedicate something rashly. Jephthah is a prime example of a rash vow. For a military victory he promised God to sacrifice the first thing he saw at home. Unfortunately that was his daughter (Judg. 11:34–35).

20:27 searches out. King David prayed for this very thing. He asked God to search him out (Ps. 139:23). See Hebrews 4:12 for another way of being "found" by God.

21:1 watercourse. A farmer digs canals and controls the direction and amount of water that runs into canals. Likewise, God controls government.

21:3 sacrifice. While the sacrificial system was an important part of Hebrew life, God's greatest desire was for his people to honor him by doing justly and showing mercy. The prophets Hosea (Hos. 6:6) and Micah (Mic. 6:7–8) emphasized this point.

[6]A fortune made by a lying tongue
is a fleeting vapor and a deadly snare.[a]

[7]The violence of the wicked will drag them away,
for they refuse to do what is right.

[8]The way of the guilty is devious,
but the conduct of the innocent is upright.

[9]Better to live on a corner of the roof
than share a house with a quarrelsome wife.

[10]The wicked man craves evil;
his neighbor gets no mercy from him.

[11]When a mocker is punished, the simple gain wisdom;
when a wise man is instructed, he gets knowledge.

[12]The Righteous One[b] takes note of the house of the wicked
and brings the wicked to ruin.

[13]If a man shuts his ears to the cry of the poor,
he too will cry out and not be answered.

[14]A gift given in secret soothes anger,
and a bribe concealed in the cloak pacifies great wrath.

[15]When justice is done, it brings joy to the righteous
but terror to evildoers.

[16]A man who strays from the path of understanding
comes to rest in the company of the dead.

[17]He who loves pleasure will become poor;
whoever loves wine and oil will never be rich.

[18]The wicked become a ransom for the righteous,
and the unfaithful for the upright.

[19]Better to live in a desert
than with a quarrelsome and ill-tempered wife.

[20]In the house of the wise are stores of choice food and oil,
but a foolish man devours all he has.

[21]He who pursues righteousness and love
finds life, prosperity[c] and honor.

[22]A wise man attacks the city of the mighty
and pulls down the stronghold in which they trust.

[a]6 Some Hebrew manuscripts, Septuagint and Vulgate; most Hebrew manuscripts *vapor for those who seek death* [b]12 Or *The righteous man* [c]21 Or *righteousness*

unrighteous one, to correct the people (Isa. 10:6–7). Do you agree with this truth? If so, where do you see this principle in force today? How does that affect your view of those in authority, even those outside our faith? **3.** Why do you think the Lord regards "sacrifice" (vv. 3,27) as unacceptable, even detestable? What does God want instead (15:8; Mic. 6:7-8)? What, if anything, does this say about mere ritual or orthodox belief? Why are spiritual reality and practical justice more acceptable? **4.** The pursuit of justice brings "joy" (v. 15) among other blessings (v. 21), but the direct pursuit of "pleasure" leads to poverty (v. 17). How do you explain that paradox? **5.** As for the poor, what happens when we ignore and when we heed their cry for justice and mercy (vv. 13;14, 21,31)? Positively restated, what does this proverb and related ones suggest we do for the poor? **6.** What thoughts and feelings do verses 9 and 19 arouse in your group? Why?

APPLY 1. What "cry" of the poor particularly tugs at your heart strings? What have you done or what would you like to do about it? **2.** We tend to exert authority as kings and queens in our own right, but in reality we are subject to God's heart-searching authority (vv. 2,30–31). How have you attempted to prevail against the Lord? What was the result?

21:13 he too. In several places Scripture reveals a "reap what you sow" mentality. In this case a person will receive the same treatment that they give to the poor. Jesus taught that a person will be forgiven by God according to how he or she forgives.

21:14 bribe. The purpose of this verse is not to condone bribery. Instead, it is to admit the power of a gift, in whatever form it comes (18:16; 19:6).

21:17 loves wine and oil. Both were associated with luxury and expense. Wine and oil easily eat up any pennies saved.

[23]He who guards his mouth and his tongue
keeps himself from calamity.

[24]The proud and arrogant man—"Mocker" is his name;
he behaves with overweening pride.

[25]The sluggard's craving will be the death of him,
because his hands refuse to work.
[26]All day long he craves for more,
but the righteous give without sparing.

[27]The sacrifice of the wicked is detestable—
how much more so when brought with evil intent!

[28]A false witness will perish,
and whoever listens to him will be destroyed forever.[a]

[29]A wicked man puts up a bold front,
but an upright man gives thought to his ways.

[30]There is no wisdom, no insight, no plan
that can succeed against the LORD.

[31]The horse is made ready for the day of battle,
but victory rests with the LORD.

22

A good name is more desirable than great riches;
to be esteemed is better than silver or gold.

[2]Rich and poor have this in common:
The LORD is the Maker of them all.

[3]A prudent man sees danger and takes refuge,
but the simple keep going and suffer for it.

[4]Humility and the fear of the LORD
bring wealth and honor and life.

[5]In the paths of the wicked lie thorns and snares,
but he who guards his soul stays far from them.

[6]Train[b] a child in the way he should go,
and when he is old he will not turn from it.

[7]The rich rule over the poor,
and the borrower is servant to the lender.

[8]He who sows wickedness reaps trouble,
and the rod of his fury will be destroyed.

[9]A generous man will himself be blessed,
for he shares his food with the poor.

[a]28 Or / *but the words of an obedient man will live on* [b]6 Or *Start*

OPEN 1. If you were ever to choose an "alias," what name would you choose for yourself? **2.** What "dangerous" or "adventurous" things have you attempted?

STUDY 1. How can a good name be more valuable than riches? **2.** How should we view the rich and the poor (vv. 2,7,9,16)? What do they have in common? How do they differ? How might they depend on one another? Who does God bless and why? **3.** What distinguishes the "wicked," the "simple," the "mocker," the "sluggard," and the "adulteress" from the "prudent" and the "pure in heart"? **4.** What child-rearing principles and promises do you see in verses 6 and 15? Does this general rule offer an absolute guarantee? Why? **5.** Someone has said of verse 6 and related texts: "You can't raise a Christian, only sinners exposed to the Gospel." And ... "Before, I had three sure-fire child-rearing principles, but no kids; now I have three kids but no sure-fire principles." What do such statements assume about human na-

---

22:1 good name ... desirable. A reputation for having honorable character is to be sought after. The way to have a "good name" is through love and faithfulness (3:3–4). God's riches are better than the world's riches (3:14; Ps. 19:9–10).

22:7 servant. Often in ancient culture people had to enslave themselves to pay off debts. The servant referred to in this verse is not literal, though. Rather, anyone in debt puts himself in a difficult and inferior position.

22:9 himself be blessed. This theme recurs through Scripture: we are to give because we have received, and we can only expect to receive by giving. Giving and receiving are repeatedly linked.

[10]Drive out the mocker, and out goes strife;
quarrels and insults are ended.

[11]He who loves a pure heart and whose speech is gracious
will have the king for his friend.

[12]The eyes of the LORD keep watch over knowledge,
but he frustrates the words of the unfaithful.

[13]The sluggard says, "There is a lion outside!"
or, "I will be murdered in the streets!"

[14]The mouth of an adulteress is a deep pit;
he who is under the LORD's wrath will fall into it.

[15]Folly is bound up in the heart of a child,
but the rod of discipline will drive it far from him.

[16]He who oppresses the poor to increase his wealth
and he who gives gifts to the rich—both come to poverty.

Sayings of the Wise

[17]Pay attention and listen to the sayings of the wise;
apply your heart to what I teach,
[18]for it is pleasing when you keep them in your heart
and have all of them ready on your lips.
[19]So that your trust may be in the LORD,
I teach you today, even you.
[20]Have I not written thirty[a] sayings for you,
sayings of counsel and knowledge,
[21]teaching you true and reliable words,
so that you can give sound answers
to him who sent you?

[22]Do not exploit the poor because they are poor
and do not crush the needy in court,
[23]for the LORD will take up their case
and will plunder those who plunder them.

[24]Do not make friends with a hot-tempered man,
do not associate with one easily angered,
[25]or you may learn his ways
and get yourself ensnared.

[26]Do not be a man who strikes hands in pledge
or puts up security for debts;
[27]if you lack the means to pay,
your very bed will be snatched from under you.

[28]Do not move an ancient boundary stone
set up by your forefathers.

[a]20 Or *not formerly written;* or *not written excellent*

ture? Parenting? God's grace? Do you agree or disagree? Why? **6.** Verse 13 smacks of "excuses, excuses." Why do you think some people procrastinate? How is it cured?

APPLY 1. Looking back on your life, what have you done to make a "good name" for yourself? **2.** Was there a time when you turned from the things your parents taught you? Was it for the good or bad? Have you come back to reclaim any of their teachings?

OPEN 1. Name three people who have been mentors/teachers in your life. In what way did each impact you? **2.** What particularly pleasing event did you experience in the past few days?

STUDY 1. What do these "sayings of the wise" sound like: Empathy? Game rules? Parent talk? Candid confessions? **2.** Why do they strike you that way: Tone? Context? Or what? **3.** Toward what end is this instruction in wisdom given (vv. 17–21)? What three-step process gets you there? By whom is one held accountable for this? **4.** What is the wise course of action with regard to the poor and needy? Your friends and associates? Your vows and debts? **5.** With which of these proverbs do you most agree? Are there any you would like to question? **6.** What do verses 28–29 say about getting ahead honestly?

APPLY 1. Where would you put yourself in the three-step process of verses 17–21: First stepper? Second stepper? Third stepper? How prepared do you feel when it comes to giving "sound answers"? **2.** Where do you feel particularly "skilled" (v. 29)? Where do you feel unprepared?

22:13 sluggard. A lazy, irresponsible person. The excuses listed here are ridiculous. The irony is: a sluggard will go to great lengths to get out of work.

22:14 mouth. Not just her kisses, but also her empty promises, a deep pit. All of that belies the consequence of God's wrath.

22:15 rod. The importance of this phrase is the organized discipline of the parent, whether it includes spankings, verbal correction, or instruction.

[29]Do you see a man skilled in his work?
He will serve before kings;
he will not serve before obscure men.

23

When you sit to dine with a ruler,
note well what[a] is before you,
[2]and put a knife to your throat
if you are given to gluttony.
[3]Do not crave his delicacies,
for that food is deceptive.

[4]Do not wear yourself out to get rich;
have the wisdom to show restraint.
[5]Cast but a glance at riches, and they are gone,
for they will surely sprout wings
and fly off to the sky like an eagle.

[6]Do not eat the food of a stingy man,
do not crave his delicacies;
[7]for he is the kind of man
who is always thinking about the cost.[b]
"Eat and drink," he says to you,
but his heart is not with you.
[8]You will vomit up the little you have eaten
and will have wasted your compliments.

[9]Do not speak to a fool,
for he will scorn the wisdom of your words.

[10]Do not move an ancient boundary stone
or encroach on the fields of the fatherless,
[11]for their Defender is strong;
he will take up their case against you.

[12]Apply your heart to instruction
and your ears to words of knowledge.

[13]Do not withhold discipline from a child;
if you punish him with the rod, he will not die.
[14]Punish him with the rod
and save his soul from death.[c]

[15]My son, if your heart is wise,
then my heart will be glad;

[a]1 Or *who* [b]7 Or *for as he thinks within himself, / so he is*; or *for as he puts on a feast, / so he is*
[c]14 Hebrew *Sheol*

OPEN 1. If you could choose the perfect meal, what would be on the menu? **2.** On the generous-stingy continuum, where would you fall?

STUDY 1. Where do you think the conversation of this chapter would best take place: Family dinner table? 21st birthday? Woodshed? Walk in the park? Other? Why? **2.** How many don'ts can you count in this chapter? How many do's? What positive alternatives are given for someone who chooses "not to"? **3.** What is it about the king's fare, a stingy man's offering or strong drink that we are to avoid (vv. 1–8; 30–34)? What is the point of such abstinence? If we are not to "linger over wine" why did Jesus turn water into wine (John 2:1-11)? **4.** How are we to regard the fool? The poor and fatherless? Drunkards? **5.** Who is the "defender" of those who lose property and lose their fathers (vv. 10–11); see Kinsman-Redeemer in Lev. 25:25; Ruth 3:12–13; 4:1–6 and the "deliverer" in Gen. 48:16; Ex. 6.6)? **6.** What is the rod of discipline (vv. 13–14)? What is the result of using it? Of not doing it? **7.** On a scale of 1–10, how much do you agree with verses 13 and 14? Are such teachings realistic in light of the problem of child abuse? **8.** What makes a parent happy (vv. 15–16,24–25)? Which of these would especially put a smile on your face? **9.** What do you think the "future hope" is (v. 18)? How confident do you think people generally are about this hope?

APPLY 1. If getting "wisdom, discipline and understanding" were compared to a football game, where are you: Still in the locker room, getting suited up? On the bench, resting from your turn on defense?

22:29 Everyday life testifies to the truth of this practical principle. A skilled craftsman rises in the ranks based on his craft.

23:1–3 A guest should show restraint in order to honor the host but also to protect himself until he is *sure of the* intent of the host.

23:4 wear yourself out. The modern term is workaholism. It is often honored in Western culture.

23:6 stingy. While a stingy host will offer food to appear generous, he is counting the cost. The rules of the game are changed. Rather than being complimented by his guests enjoying *the meal, he* may resent it.

23:10 move ... boundary stone. This is the equivalent of stealing land. It means moving boundary markers. **fatherless.** Throughout the Old Testament Law, God made provisions for the fatherless. These included grain left in the fields after harvest and portions of sacrifices held aside.

23:11 Defender is strong. God is a defender of the fatherless, and a defender of widows. "Defender" also alludes to a "Kinsman-Redeemer," someone who steps in to care for the family of a dead relative.

[16]my inmost being will rejoice
when your lips speak what is right.

[17]Do not let your heart envy sinners,
but always be zealous for the fear of the LORD.
[18]There is surely a future hope for you,
and your hope will not be cut off.

[19]Listen, my son, and be wise,
and keep your heart on the right path.
[20]Do not join those who drink too much wine
or gorge themselves on meat,
[21]for drunkards and gluttons become poor,
and drowsiness clothes them in rags.

[22]Listen to your father, who gave you life,
and do not despise your mother when she is old.
[23]Buy the truth and do not sell it;
get wisdom, discipline and understanding.
[24]The father of a righteous man has great joy;
he who has a wise son delights in him.
[25]May your father and mother be glad;
may she who gave you birth rejoice!

[26]My son, give me your heart
and let your eyes keep to my ways,
[27]for a prostitute is a deep pit
and a wayward wife is a narrow well.
[28]Like a bandit she lies in wait,
and multiplies the unfaithful among men.

[29]Who has woe? Who has sorrow?
Who has strife? Who has complaints?
Who has needless bruises? Who has bloodshot eyes?
[30]Those who linger over wine,
who go to sample bowls of mixed wine.
[31]Do not gaze at wine when it is red,
when it sparkles in the cup,
when it goes down smoothly!
[32]In the end it bites like a snake
and poisons like a viper.
[33]Your eyes will see strange sights
and your mind imagine confusing things.
[34]You will be like one sleeping on the high seas,
lying on top of the rigging.
[35]"They hit me," you will say, "but I'm not hurt!
They beat me, but I don't feel it!
When will I wake up
so I can find another drink?"

24 Do not envy wicked men,
do not desire their company;

Stopping for a break? Running with the ball on offense? Sacked behind the line of scrimmage? **2.** Look at verse 29. Where would you place yourself right now: In woe? In sorrow? In strife? With complaints? Needlessly bruised? With bloodshot eyes? What brought on this condition? How might wisdom lead you away from it?

OPEN 1. What do you remember about your first

24:1 envy wicked men. Too often righteous people envy an evil person's freedom from restraint and the seeming lack of penalty for sin. God warns us not to follow that deceptive path (1:15; 12:26).

²for their hearts plot violence,
and their lips talk about making trouble.

³By wisdom a house is built,
and through understanding it is established;
⁴through knowledge its rooms are filled
with rare and beautiful treasures.

⁵A wise man has great power,
and a man of knowledge increases strength;
⁶for waging war you need guidance,
and for victory many advisers.

⁷Wisdom is too high for a fool;
in the assembly at the gate he has nothing to say.

⁸He who plots evil
will be known as a schemer.
⁹The schemes of folly are sin,
and men detest a mocker.

¹⁰If you falter in times of trouble,
how small is your strength!

¹¹Rescue those being led away to death;
hold back those staggering toward slaughter.
¹²If you say, "But we knew nothing about this,"
does not he who weighs the heart perceive it?
Does not he who guards your life know it?
Will he not repay each person according to what he has done?

¹³Eat honey, my son, for it is good;
honey from the comb is sweet to your taste.
¹⁴Know also that wisdom is sweet to your soul;
if you find it, there is a future hope for you,
and your hope will not be cut off.

¹⁵Do not lie in wait like an outlaw against a righteous man's house,
do not raid his dwelling place;
¹⁶for though a righteous man falls seven times, he rises again,
but the wicked are brought down by calamity.

¹⁷Do not gloat when your enemy falls;
when he stumbles, do not let your heart rejoice,
¹⁸or the LORD will see and disapprove
and turn his wrath away from him.

¹⁹Do not fret because of evil men
or be envious of the wicked,

house/apartment? What color was it? How many rooms? **2.** If you gave into it, where might envy creep into your life?

STUDY 1. Advertising encourages us to envy. What does this chapter imply about envy (vv. 1,19–20)? What or who should we follow instead? **2.** How are we to wield power wisely (vv. 5–7)? Compassionately (vv. 11–12)? How are the two related? **3.** The person compares honey and wisdom (vv. 13–14). How are they alike? What differences do you see? **4.** Do God's people "fall"? What difference is there then between God's people "falling" and the ungodly "falling"? **5.** What happens when God's people seem to be defeated (vv. 10,16)? What is supposed to be our hope? **6.** What do you think is meant by defeating evil powers and deferring to the Lord's justice (vv. 17–22)? How can we not gloat (vv. 17–18) when drug dealers, rapists, terrorists and the like get their due?

APPLY 1. Reread verse 10, and think of a trouble you are currently facing. With what would you compare your strength in relation to this difficulty: A grain of sand? A pebble? A rock? A boulder? A mountain? **2.** Look at verses 11 and 12. Who rescued you from spiritual death? Who would you like to rescue?

24:11 those being led away. Probably refers to people who have been unjustly accused.

24:12 we knew nothing. God judges those who are aware of injustice but do nothing about it. They may believe they can feign innocence and ignorance. They are as deceived as Adam and Eve who believed they could hide from God in the garden.

24:13–14 honey ... wisdom. Honey was the sweetest substance known in this ancient culture. Likewise, wisdom is the most valuable trait.

24:17–18 gloat. An attitude of superiority. God detests this attitude even when we gloat over adversaries.

20for the evil man h… future hope,
and the lamp… wicked will be snuffed out.
21Fear the Lo… e king, my son,
and do… ith the rebellious,
22for thos… end sudden destruction upon them,
an… what calamities they can bring?

Further Sayings of the Wise

…re sayings of the wise:

…iality in judging is not good:
…ys to the guilty, "You are innocent"—
… will curse him and nations denounce him.
… go well with those who convict the guilty,
…ch blessing will come upon them.

… honest answer
is like a kiss on the lips.

27Finish your outdoor work
and get your fields ready;
after that, build your house.

28Do not testify against your neighbor without cause,
or use your lips to deceive.
29Do not say, "I'll do to him as he has done to me;
I'll pay that man back for what he did."

30I went past the field of the sluggard,
past the vineyard of the man who lacks judgment;
31thorns had come up everywhere,
the ground was covered with weeds,
and the stone wall was in ruins.
32I applied my heart to what I observed
and learned a lesson from what I saw:
33A little sleep, a little slumber,
a little folding of the hands to rest—
34and poverty will come on you like a bandit
and scarcity like an armed man.[a]

More Proverbs of Solomon

25 These are more proverbs of Solomon, copied by the men of Hezekiah king of Judah:

2It is the glory of God to conceal a matter;
to search out a matter is the glory of kings.

[a]34 *Or like a vagrant / and scarcity like a beggar*

OPEN 1. What do you remember about your first kiss? Who was it? When did it happen? **2.** Share a time when you were accused of something you did not do.

STUDY 1. How do these "sayings of the wise" extend the themes set forth in the first part of the chapter? How do the wise approach their life and learning (v. 32)? **2.** What is the difference between judging rightly and wrongly? When have you witnessed examples of this? **3.** Expand on verse 26. In what way would you say that an honest answer is like "a kiss on the lips"? **4.** What does verse 27 imply about priorities? Do you agree with the principle here? Explain. **5.** Consider verse 33. Do you agree with this philosophy? If taken too far, what might be the danger?

APPLY 1. Where have you become a little lazy in life: At home? At work? In your marriage? With your children? With your parents? At church? **2.** Share a time when you were less than honest with someone. Why did you withhold the truth? Would you do it differently today? Why?

OPEN 1. Share a refreshing moment from the past week. **2.** If you could visit anyone in the world, to whose house would you go?

STUDY 1. Many of Solomon's proverbs are but "variations on a theme." What major themes do you see? What variations

---

24:20 evil man has no future hope. No matter how prosperous the wicked may seem for the short-term, their future is without God and therefore dismal and hopeless.

24:21 the LORD and the king. Both civil and religious obedience was expected. Solomon, who wrote many of the proverbs, was only the third king of Israel, so the kingship was still closely associated with God's leadership.

24:27 after that. Since the culture was agrarian, the first priority was establishing the land and planting the seed. **build your house.** May mean a literal house, or establishing your family.

25:2 search out a matter. Only a king has the power to investigate a situation. God can hide matters from kings, however, and so retains ultimate control.

are significant to you? **2.** What do the repeated themes in the book of Proverbs do for you: Drive home a point I may have missed? Suggest new areas for application? Bore me to tears? Develop a habit from reinforced ideas? **3.** What sorts of things does God conceal from us? Do you think this is a good thing or a bad thing? Explain. **4.** How do leaders "remove wickedness from their presence" (vv. 4–5,26)? What does this achieve? In your opinion, why does that seem so hard to do? **5.** Why is it so crucial to settle out of court (v. 8)? To keep a confidence (vv. 9-10)? Do you agree with Solomon's counsel on these matters? Why? **6.** What variations do you see here on the power of the spoken word, for good and evil (vv. 9-15,20,23,25)? **7.** When does quiet persistence win out? What other actions speak louder than words? **8.** What does it mean (v. 22) to "heap coals on his head"? Would you say that Jesus (Luke 6:27–36) expands this counsel or merely says the same thing but in different words? Why? **9.** What variation on the "honey" theme, do you see here (vv. 16,27; 24:13)? What rules of thumb does this suggest for any who wishes not to overstay their welcome, or not indulge in too much of a good thing?

APPLY **1.** What area of your life would you compare to a "broken down wall" (v. 28)? What do you need to do to fix it? How might others in your group help you shore up structure? **2.** What "good news from a distant land" (v. 25) would be refreshing to your soul right now?

---

3 As the heavens are high and the earth is dee
so the hearts of kings are unsearchable.

4 Remove the dross from the silver,
and out comes material for[a] the silversmith;
5 remove the wicked from the king's presence,
and his throne will be established through righteo

6 Do not exalt yourself in the king's presence,
and do not claim a place among great men;
7 it is better for him to say to you, "Come up here,"
than for him to humiliate you before a nobleman.

What you have seen with your eyes
8 do not bring[b] hastily to court,
for what will you do in the end
if your neighbor puts you to shame?

9 If you argue your case with a neighbor,
do not betray another man's confidence,
10 or he who hears it may shame you
and you will never lose your bad reputation.

11 A word aptly spoken
is like apples of gold in settings of silver.

12 Like an earring of gold or an ornament of fine gold
is a wise man's rebuke to a listening ear.

13 Like the coolness of snow at harvest time
is a trustworthy messenger to those who send him;
he refreshes the spirit of his masters.

14 Like clouds and wind without rain
is a man who boasts of gifts he does not give.

15 Through patience a ruler can be persuaded,
and a gentle tongue can break a bone.

16 If you find honey, eat just enough—
too much of it, and you will vomit.
17 Seldom set foot in your neighbor's house—
too much of you, and he will hate you.

18 Like a club or a sword or a sharp arrow
is the man who gives false testimony against his neighbor.

19 Like a bad tooth or a lame foot
is reliance on the unfaithful in times of trouble.

[a]4 Or *comes a vessel from* [b]7,8 Or *nobleman / on whom you had set your eyes. /* [8]*Do not go*

25:4 dross. The impurities that must be removed from silver before beautiful and useful things are made. A kingdom must also be purified.

25:8 hastily. Before going to court, ask yourself, "Do you *really* know what you are doing?" Before you file, count the cost of losing.

25:9–10 argue your case. When you make your accusation public, the court of public opinion will make its judgment and you will be held accountable.

25:11 word aptly spoken. This "word" can be an encouragement or a rebuke. Either way, when spoken in good timing and the right spirit, it's a beautiful thing. Words from our lips have power. Used correctly, we are wise—used incorrectly, we are fools.

[20] Like one who takes away a garment on a cold day,
or like vinegar poured on soda,
is one who sings songs to a heavy heart.

[21] If your enemy is hungry, give him food to eat;
if he is thirsty, give him water to drink.
[22] In doing this, you will heap burning coals on his head,
and the LORD will reward you.

[23] As a north wind brings rain,
so a sly tongue brings angry looks.

[24] Better to live on a corner of the roof
than share a house with a quarrelsome wife.

[25] Like cold water to a weary soul
is good news from a distant land.

[26] Like a muddied spring or a polluted well
is a righteous man who gives way to the wicked.

[27] It is not good to eat too much honey,
nor is it honorable to seek one's own honor.

[28] Like a city whose walls are broken down
is a man who lacks self-control.

26 Like snow in summer or rain in harvest,
honor is not fitting for a fool.

[2] Like a fluttering sparrow or a darting swallow,
an undeserved curse does not come to rest.

[3] A whip for the horse, a halter for the donkey,
and a rod for the backs of fools!

[4] Do not answer a fool according to his folly,
or you will be like him yourself.

[5] Answer a fool according to his folly,
or he will be wise in his own eyes.

[6] Like cutting off one's feet or drinking violence
is the sending of a message by the hand of a fool.

[7] Like a lame man's legs that hang limp
is a proverb in the mouth of a fool.

OPEN **1.** Are you a "cat" person or a "dog" person or neither? Why do you prefer one to the other? **2.** Share a time in your life when you were surprised by the weather.

STUDY **1.** What three one-word titles can your group come up with to fit the three main divisions of this chapter? **2.** Verses 4–5 seem self-contradictory. What is Solomon's point? What good might result from not arguing with a fool? What bad might come from not arguing? **3.** To what is a "proverb in the mouth of a fool" compared (v. 9)? Why this analogy? What would you say would be a modern equivalent? **4.** What does verse 10 tell employers about their next hire? What general principle is at work here? **5.** In what ways can words

---

25:21 if your enemy. Jesus taught this same "give even when you don't have to" mentality. He said to love your enemy, to give when you won't receive, to offer more than a person asks for (Luke 6:27–31).

25:22 heap burning coals. When a fire went out, the homeowner would often borrow burning coals from a neighbor to start the fire again. In Egyptian culture carrying burning coals on one's head was a ritual of repentance. Paul quoted this proverb in Romans 12:20.

25:22 the LORD will reward you. Jesus confirmed this truth in his Sermon on the Mount. Our true reward comes from God, not others. That is why we should give to the needy without expectation of repayment (Matt. 6:1–6).

25:23 sly. A person of secrecy or slanderous words.

26:2 fluttering sparrow. An apt picture for an undeserved lie that will not stick. This proverb was lived out in the life of Balaam, a prophet who was asked by a foreign king to curse Israel but warned by God to bless rather than curse (Num. 22:12).

26:4 you will be like him. A modern proverb would say, "Don't stoop to his level."

26:5 answer a fool. Verses 4 and 5 go together as two tactics for facing foolishness. Sometimes a person must refuse to stoop to a foolish level. Other times a confrontation is the only way to deal with foolishness.

"stoke the fire" of conflict (vv. 20–21)? How do the words of these proverbs compare to James 3:5–12? **6.** If a malicious person can disguise himself (vv. 24–26), how can he or she be "exposed"? **7.** What "life principle" is implied in verse 27? Do you agree with it? Why or why not? **8.** How does this chapter leave you: Uplifted? Slapped down? Laughing at yourself in a mirror? What lies behind this feeling?

APPLY **1.** Which proverb in this chapter hits closest to home? How so? **2.** Who is causing the most trouble in your life today: A fool? A sluggard? A person of malice? A liar?

8 Like tying a stone in a sling
is the giving of honor to a fool.

9 Like a thornbush in a drunkard's hand
is a proverb in the mouth of a fool.

10 Like an archer who wounds at random
is he who hires a fool or any passer-by.

11 As a dog returns to its vomit,
so a fool repeats his folly.

12 Do you see a man wise in his own eyes?
There is more hope for a fool than for him.

13 The sluggard says, "There is a lion in the road,
a fierce lion roaming the streets!"

14 As a door turns on its hinges,
so a sluggard turns on his bed.

15 The sluggard buries his hand in the dish;
he is too lazy to bring it back to his mouth.

16 The sluggard is wiser in his own eyes
than seven men who answer discreetly.

17 Like one who seizes a dog by the ears
is a passer-by who meddles in a quarrel not his own.

18 Like a madman shooting
firebrands or deadly arrows
19 is a man who deceives his neighbor
and says, "I was only joking!"

20 Without wood a fire goes out;
without gossip a quarrel dies down.

21 As charcoal to embers and as wood to fire,
so is a quarrelsome man for kindling strife.

22 The words of a gossip are like choice morsels;
they go down to a man's inmost parts.

23 Like a coating of glaze[a] over earthenware
are fervent lips with an evil heart.

24 A malicious man disguises himself with his lips,
but in his heart he harbors deceit.

25 Though his speech is charming, do not believe him,
for seven abominations fill his heart.

[a]23 With a different word division of the Hebrew; Masoretic Text *of silver dross*

26:9 Today we might say: A little knowledge in the wrong hands is a dangerous thing. The point of Proverbs is how to get and handle wisdom. A fool is someone who knows neither.

26:10 he who hires. Sound business advice. Today we talk about this principle in terms of "warm bodies," just having the people but not concerning ourselves with their aptitude for the job.

26:14 door turns on its hinges. The point is not the way a sluggard twists and turns, but the fact that a door never separates itself from its hinges. A sluggard never gets up.

26:17 meddles in. Gets excited about.

26:18–19 only joking. This describes damage being done, but then declaring it a prank. The damage is still done.

[26]His malice may be concealed by deception,
but his wickedness will be exposed in the assembly.

[27]If a man digs a pit, he will fall into it;
if a man rolls a stone, it will roll back on him.

[28]A lying tongue hates those it hurts,
and a flattering mouth works ruin.

27 Do not boast about tomorrow,
for you do not know what a day may bring forth.

[2]Let another praise you, and not your own mouth;
someone else, and not your own lips.

[3]Stone is heavy and sand a burden,
but provocation by a fool is heavier than both.

[4]Anger is cruel and fury overwhelming,
but who can stand before jealousy?

[5]Better is open rebuke
than hidden love.

[6]Wounds from a friend can be trusted,
but an enemy multiplies kisses.

[7]He who is full loathes honey,
but to the hungry even what is bitter tastes sweet.

[8]Like a bird that strays from its nest
is a man who strays from his home.

[9]Perfume and incense bring joy to the heart,
and the pleasantness of one's friend springs from his earnest counsel.

[10]Do not forsake your friend and the friend of your father,
and do not go to your brother's house when disaster strikes you—
better a neighbor nearby than a brother far away.

[11]Be wise, my son, and bring joy to my heart;
then I can answer anyone who treats me with contempt.

[12]The prudent see danger and take refuge,
but the simple keep going and suffer for it.

[13]Take the garment of one who puts up security for a stranger;
hold it in pledge if he does it for a wayward woman.

[14]If a man loudly blesses his neighbor early in the morning,
it will be taken as a curse.

OPEN 1. What do you hope to accomplish tomorrow? **2.** When were you recently affirmed? What was the affirmation? Who gave it?

STUDY 1. Some proverbs are simple observations of life; some are advice on living. How can you tell the difference? From this chapter, what key concepts distinguish them both? **2.** What's the point of boasting or praising (vv. 1–2,21)? How does the New Testament expand that (Matt. 6:34; Luke 12:19–20; John 12:43; 2 Cor. 10:12–18)? **3.** What choices are implicit in each of the comparisons in verses 3–6? Which of these do you need further clarified? With which do you most heartedly agree? **4.** What distinguishes true friends (vv. 5–6,9–10,14,17)? Would you add anything to this list? What? **5.** What reveals true character (vv. 19–22)? What can be done to satisfy a person's restlessness or change a fool's character? If verse 22 is true, what hope is there for a fool? **6.** What is the proper balance between hard work and God's provision (vv. 23–27)? **7.** Your local high school has invited you to be a guest lecturer on "friendship," and you have chosen this chapter as your text. How would you start? What illustrations would you use? What stories from personal experience come to mind of someone who has rebuked you, sharpened you, earnestly counseled you, or been a good neighbor?

APPLY 1. What personal or national "danger" lurks on the horizon (v. 12)? What is the "prudent" thing for you to do in relation to the

---

26:27 Haman from the book of Esther is an excellent example of this verse. He prepared gallows to execute Esther's cousin Mordecai. He spent much energy manipulating the situation. But in the end, Haman died on his own gallows (Est. 9:24–25).

26:28 a lying tongue hates. Lying and hating are connected. When we lie we disregard the person we are lying to.

27:6 friend. One who loves. **enemy.** One who hates.

27:7 What we have determines what we want.

27:8 man who strays. Whether this man is a husband or a son, when he leaves home he leaves not only responsibility but protection behind.

27:10 This proverb is more about friends than family. Family ties are important, but often friends become our family of choice.

27:14 Bad timing makes all the difference between a blessing and a curse.

danger? How can your group help? **2.** Who in your life "sharpens" you like iron? Do you think you may be that to someone else? Does the idea of being such a person make you feel good, or cause a little fear? Why?

---

[15]A quarrelsome wife is like
a constant dripping on a rainy day;
[16]restraining her is like restraining the wind
or grasping oil with the hand.

[17]As iron sharpens iron,
so one man sharpens another.

[18]He who tends a fig tree will eat its fruit,
and he who looks after his master will be honored.

[19]As water reflects a face,
so a man's heart reflects the man.

[20]Death and Destruction[a] are never satisfied,
and neither are the eyes of man.

[21]The crucible for silver and the furnace for gold,
but man is tested by the praise he receives.

[22]Though you grind a fool in a mortar,
grinding him like grain with a pestle,
you will not remove his folly from him.

[23]Be sure you know the condition of your flocks,
give careful attention to your herds;
[24]for riches do not endure forever,
and a crown is not secure for all generations.
[25]When the hay is removed and new growth appears
and the grass from the hills is gathered in,
[26]the lambs will provide you with clothing,
and the goats with the price of a field.
[27]You will have plenty of goats' milk
to feed you and your family
and to nourish your servant girls.

28

The wicked man flees though no one pursues,
but the righteous are as bold as a lion.

[2]When a country is rebellious, it has many rulers,
but a man of understanding and knowledge maintains order.

[3]A ruler[b] who oppresses the poor
is like a driving rain that leaves no crops.

[4]Those who forsake the law praise the wicked,
but those who keep the law resist them.

[a]20 Hebrew *Sheol and Abaddon* [b]3 Or *A poor man*

OPEN 1. Generally speaking, what is more appealing to you: trying something new or sticking to what you already know? Explain. **2.** Of all the "bosses" you have had, which one warmed your heart? Which one drove you nuts?

STUDY 1. What does the rambling of this chapter sound like: Learned political science professor? Wise grandparent? Police captain? Drill sergeant? Other? **2.**

27:17 iron sharpens iron. A modern image would be a knife sharpener, metal against metal.

27:19 reflects. Jesus said something similar to this proverb when he talked about a person's character being revealed by what is inside rather than outside (Luke 11:39–41).

27:23–27 This passage celebrates the security and the cycle of an agricultural society. In the mind of this writer being fed and clothed by the land is much more secure than making a living through politics.

27:23 flocks. Sheep. **herds.** Cattle or goats. Ancient ranchers raised these livestock.

28:3 ruler who oppresses. In this case the ruler is a strong and desperate man. In oppressing the poor, he hurts people who are actually like him.

[5]Evil men do not understand justice,
but those who seek the LORD understand it fully.

[6]Better a poor man whose walk is blameless
than a rich man whose ways are perverse.

[7]He who keeps the law is a discerning son,
but a companion of gluttons disgraces his father.

[8]He who increases his wealth by exorbitant interest
amasses it for another, who will be kind to the poor.

[9]If anyone turns a deaf ear to the law,
even his prayers are detestable.

[10]He who leads the upright along an evil path
will fall into his own trap,
but the blameless will receive a good inheritance.

[11]A rich man may be wise in his own eyes,
but a poor man who has discernment sees through him.

[12]When the righteous triumph, there is great elation;
but when the wicked rise to power, men go into hiding.

[13]He who conceals his sins does not prosper,
but whoever confesses and renounces them finds mercy.

[14]Blessed is the man who always fears the LORD,
but he who hardens his heart falls into trouble.

[15]Like a roaring lion or a charging bear
is a wicked man ruling over a helpless people.

[16]A tyrannical ruler lacks judgment,
but he who hates ill-gotten gain will enjoy a long life.

[17]A man tormented by the guilt of murder
will be a fugitive till death;
let no one support him.

[18]He whose walk is blameless is kept safe,
but he whose ways are perverse will suddenly fall.

[19]He who works his land will have abundant food,
but the one who chases fantasies will have his fill of poverty.

[20]A faithful man will be richly blessed,
but one eager to get rich will not go unpunished.

[21]To show partiality is not good—
yet a man will do wrong for a piece of bread.

What is the point of all this "law and order" talk? Who do you think is the intended audience: Top brass? The ruling class? The under class? Victims of injustice? Teachers? Parents? Why do you think so? **3.** What law is to be upheld? What abuses of that law and their victims are singled out here? **4.** Who are the wicked? What is their behavior like? What impact do they have on others (vv. 1,4–5,12,15,28)? What will be their retribution (vv. 8–11,13–15, 17–18,22,27)? **5.** Which parts of verses 6, 19 and 20 ring true with you? In what way is it better to be poor? In what way can one be rich and blameless, or rich and unpunished? **6.** What is the message in all this for those in authority and the people they lead (vv. 2,7,10,13,16,18, 20,24)? **7.** If someone came up to you and asked, "Why confess and renounce sins?" How would you answer? What help do you receive from verses 13, 14, and 17? **8.** How would you explain the difference between: Trusting in self (v. 26)? Self-confidence? Trusting in the Lord (v. 25)?

APPLY 1. Where would you place yourself today on the "trusting self/trusting God" continuum? Explain. **2.** What behavior of yours would you like to renounce today? How can the group keep you accountable in this regard?

28:5 Wickedness perverts a sense of right and wrong. When Solomon became king he prayed to understand right from wrong (1 Kin. 3:9).

28:11 wise in his own eyes. To be unteachable or proud. Proverbs describes the fool (26:5) and the sluggard (26:16) this way.

28:13 conceals his sins. Solomon's father, David, had learned this lesson firsthand. After committing adultery with Solomon's mother, Bathsheba, David tried to hide his mistake by murdering a man (2 Sam. 12:7–9).

28:17 tormented by the guilt of murder. Judas Iscariot lived out this proverb. After turning Jesus over to authorities, he returned the money and then took his own life.

28:20 eager to get rich. Get-rich-quick schemes are definitely not the way to God's blessing. Proverbs listed others who will not go unpunished including the adulterer (6:29), the wicked (11:21), the proud (16:5), the one who mocks the poor (17:5) and the false witness (19:9).

[22]A stingy man is eager to get rich
and is unaware that poverty awaits him.

[23]He who rebukes a man will in the end gain more favor
than he who has a flattering tongue.

[24]He who robs his father or mother
and says, "It's not wrong"—
he is partner to him who destroys.

[25]A greedy man stirs up dissension,
but he who trusts in the LORD will prosper.

[26]He who trusts in himself is a fool,
but he who walks in wisdom is kept safe.

[27]He who gives to the poor will lack nothing,
but he who closes his eyes to them receives many curses.

[28]When the wicked rise to power, people go into hiding;
but when the wicked perish, the righteous thrive.

29 A man who remains stiff-necked after many rebukes
will suddenly be destroyed—without remedy.

[2]When the righteous thrive, the people rejoice;
when the wicked rule, the people groan.

[3]A man who loves wisdom brings joy to his father,
but a companion of prostitutes squanders his wealth.

[4]By justice a king gives a country stability,
but one who is greedy for bribes tears it down.

[5]Whoever flatters his neighbor
is spreading a net for his feet.

[6]An evil man is snared by his own sin,
but a righteous one can sing and be glad.

[7]The righteous care about justice for the poor,
but the wicked have no such concern.

[8]Mockers stir up a city,
but wise men turn away anger.

[9]If a wise man goes to court with a fool,
the fool rages and scoffs, and there is no peace.

[10]Bloodthirsty men hate a man of integrity
and seek to kill the upright.

[11]A fool gives full vent to his anger,
but a wise man keeps himself under control.

OPEN **1.** On a scale of 1 to 10, what number would you give to your "stubbornness" factor? **2.** What's a song you often hum to yourself?

STUDY **1.** If you were to put mood music to the reading of this chapter what would it be: Rolling Stones? Beethoven? Celine Dion? Alanis Morissette? Carlos Santana? Creed? Other? **2.** If "mere words" (v. 19) or "rebukes" are not enough to correct someone, what else would you suggest? **3.** What marks the righteous (vv. 2,6–7,16,27)? Which mark especially resonates with you? **4.** Verses 8-9,11,20 and 22 again raise the twin issues of anger and fools. How do you deal with the temperament of a fool? What hope does Solomon offer here? **5.** What is the result of dishonesty in leadership (v. 12)? Are "lies" (v. 12) more powerful than "rebukes" (v. 1) or "mere words" (v. 19)? Why might that be? **6.** How might "discipline" (v. 17) give meaning to "words" (v. 19)? When do you think "leaving a child to himself" (v. 15) is a healthy corrective? When is it too permissive? **7.** If "from the LORD we get justice" (v. 26), what does this say to you about civil and church courts? Does God work through a judicial system? How so?

28:23 According to many proverbs, rebukes are welcomed when they fall on the ear of the wise. But flattery is never effective with the wise and discerning. So in the end, truth, even the form of a rebuke, is a more effective way to achieve favor.

29:7 poor. Feeble, weak or helpless. A sign of righteousness is a concern for others. A sign of wickedness is a lack of that concern. A person reveals his level of concern when the poor are involved.

29:9 rages and scoffs. Rants. To go to court with a fool is to try to fight fair with someone who will not follow any rules. He will feed the turmoil of the situation rather than settling the dispute.

[12]If a ruler listens to lies,
all his officials become wicked.

[13]The poor man and the oppressor have this in common:
The LORD gives sight to the eyes of both.

[14]If a king judges the poor with fairness,
his throne will always be secure.

[15]The rod of correction imparts wisdom,
but a child left to himself disgraces his mother.

[16]When the wicked thrive, so does sin,
but the righteous will see their downfall.

[17]Discipline your son, and he will give you peace;
he will bring delight to your soul.

[18]Where there is no revelation, the people cast off restraint;
but blessed is he who keeps the law.

[19]A servant cannot be corrected by mere words;
though he understands, he will not respond.

[20]Do you see a man who speaks in haste?
There is more hope for a fool than for him.

[21]If a man pampers his servant from youth,
he will bring grief[a] in the end.

[22]An angry man stirs up dissension,
and a hot-tempered one commits many sins.

[23]A man's pride brings him low,
but a man of lowly spirit gains honor.

[24]The accomplice of a thief is his own enemy;
he is put under oath and dare not testify.

[25]Fear of man will prove to be a snare,
but whoever trusts in the LORD is kept safe.

[26]Many seek an audience with a ruler,
but it is from the LORD that man gets justice.

[27]The righteous detest the dishonest;
the wicked detest the upright.

Sayings of Agur

30 The sayings of Agur son of Jakeh—an oracle[b]:

This man declared to Ithiel,
to Ithiel and to Ucal:[c]

[a]21 The meaning of the Hebrew for this word is uncertain. [b]1 Or *Jakeh of Massa* [c]1 Masoretic Text; with a different word division of the Hebrew *declared, "I am weary, O God; / I am weary, O God, and faint.*

APPLY 1. Which proverb here penetrates an area of your life? Why that proverb? **2.** What's causing you to "sing" today? What's bringing you "low"?

OPEN 1. Complete the sentence: Three things that I find utterly amazing are ... **2.** Complete the sentence: One thing about which I am totally ignorant is ... **3.** To what vehicle would you compare yourself or your lifestyle: Four-wheel drive truck? Nine-passenger van? Speedy sports car? Classic roadster? Sports

29:18 no revelation. Prophecy from God. Where people are not hearing God's truth, they live lawless lives.

29:19 servant. Training a servant is different than training a child. One must use different training techniques.

30:1 oracle. A weighty message. The identities of the three men in this verse are unknown.

utility vehicle? Chauffeur-driven limo? Ambulance? Fire truck? Basic sedan?

STUDY Chapter 30 is attributed to Agur, a non-Hebrew teacher. **1.** In what ways are the "Sayings of Agur" like Solomon's proverbs? What do you see as differences? **2.** After viewing Agur's humble, artistic impressions, how do you feel: "I know where this guy's coming from"? "I'm totally confused"? "There ... but for the grace of God go I"? "I wish the guy wasn't so poetic"? "Why doesn't he just say what he means"? **3.** What do you learn about Agur from verses 2–4? From verses 7–9? What assumptions about human nature and money underlie his two-fold request? Why doesn't he pray to use poverty and riches rightly? **4.** What do you learn of God from the agnostic's questions in verse 4? From the answer in verses 5–6? From Agur's prayer in verses 7–9? From the arrogant "eyes" of verses 11–14? **5.** How does the character of "those" pictured in verses 11–14 contrast with Agur at prayer? What will happen to the "eyes" of those who arrogantly leech off others (vv. 15–17)? **6.** What do you think of Agur's amazing list (vv. 18–20)? Are there any you would eliminate from this list? Which one and why? **7.** What do you make of Agur's "unbearable" list (vv. 21–23)? Once again, are there any you would remove? Which one? **8.** What is so "wise" about the four "small" creatures (vv. 21–23)? **9.** What is "stately" about the next four things (vv. 29–31)? Any of these not make your list?

APPLY 1. Which of the following words from this chapter comes closest to capturing you today: Unsatisfied (v. 15)? Feeling amazing (v. 18)? Feeling ignorant (v. 18)? Trembling (v. 21)? Extremely wise (v. 24)? Little strength (v. 25)? Stately

2 "I am the most ignorant of men;
I do not have a man's understanding.
3 I have not learned wisdom,
nor have I knowledge of the Holy One.
4 Who has gone up to heaven and come down?
Who has gathered up the wind in the hollow of his hands?
Who has wrapped up the waters in his cloak?
Who has established all the ends of the earth?
What is his name, and the name of his son?
Tell me if you know!

5 "Every word of God is flawless;
he is a shield to those who take refuge in him.
6 Do not add to his words,
or he will rebuke you and prove you a liar.

7 "Two things I ask of you, O LORD;
do not refuse me before I die:
8 Keep falsehood and lies far from me;
give me neither poverty nor riches,
but give me only my daily bread.
9 Otherwise, I may have too much and disown you
and say, 'Who is the LORD?'
Or I may become poor and steal,
and so dishonor the name of my God.

10 "Do not slander a servant to his master,
or he will curse you, and you will pay for it.

11 "There are those who curse their fathers
and do not bless their mothers;
12 those who are pure in their own eyes
and yet are not cleansed of their filth;
13 those whose eyes are ever so haughty,
whose glances are so disdainful;
14 those whose teeth are swords
and whose jaws are set with knives
to devour the poor from the earth,
the needy from among mankind.

15 "The leech has two daughters.
'Give! Give!' they cry.

30:2–3 ignorant. Stupid or dull-minded. Agur comes up lacking when he compares his knowledge with the knowledge of God (9:10).

30:5–6 Do not add. Do not add human speculation or imagination. Let God's Word stand on its own authority and be its own interpreter.

30:7–8 neither poverty nor riches. In other words, Agur prayed for "just enough." His words were similar to Christ's model prayer, "Give us each day our daily bread" (Luke 11:3).

30:9 Who is the LORD? When Israel prospered, the people strayed from God.

30:12 pure in their own eyes. People who believe themselves to be morally pure are blind to the danger they face. The young man who asked Jesus how to get eternal life faced this challenge (Matt. 19:17–22).

30:14 An apt description of those who prey on the misfortune of others.

30:15–29 Agur favors lists, as seen in this passage. Note how God's inspiration of Scripture works through the natural style of the Bible writers.

"There are three things that are never satisfied,
four that never say, 'Enough!':
16 the grave,[a] the barren womb,
land, which is never satisfied with water,
and fire, which never says, 'Enough!'

17 "The eye that mocks a father,
that scorns obedience to a mother,
will be pecked out by the ravens of the valley,
will be eaten by the vultures.

18 "There are three things that are too amazing for me,
four that I do not understand:
19 the way of an eagle in the sky,
the way of a snake on a rock,
the way of a ship on the high seas,
and the way of a man with a maiden.

20 "This is the way of an adulteress:
She eats and wipes her mouth
and says, 'I've done nothing wrong.'

21 "Under three things the earth trembles,
under four it cannot bear up:
22 a servant who becomes king,
a fool who is full of food,
23 an unloved woman who is married,
and a maidservant who displaces her mistress.

24 "Four things on earth are small,
yet they are extremely wise:
25 Ants are creatures of little strength,
yet they store up their food in the summer;
26 coneys[b] are creatures of little power,
yet they make their home in the crags;
27 locusts have no king,
yet they advance together in ranks;
28 a lizard can be caught with the hand,
yet it is found in kings' palaces.

29 "There are three things that are stately in their stride,
four that move with stately bearing:

[a]16 Hebrew *Sheol* [b]26 That is, the hyrax or rock badger

(v. 29)? **2.** What two things (v. 7) would you like to ask of God today?

30:16 barren womb. Women without children in Solomon's day were desperate to prove their worth. Bearing children was the key to self-value.

30:17 pecked out. This probably means that the child will be left unburied (a great shame) and so become food for the scavengers.

30:18–19 All four things are following their own path. Each includes some form of a mystery.

30:19 a man with a maiden. Probably, the mystery of a courtship.

30:20 I've done nothing wrong. The adulteress takes her conquests casually. Her sexual appetite is no more complicated than eating a meal.

30:23 an unloved woman. Leah, Jacob's wife, was a good example. Jacob was tricked into marrying her in order to have the wife he really loved, Rachel (Gen. 29:23–31). **maidservant who displaces.** Sarah's maid, Hagar, was a prime example of this kind of relationship (Gen. 16:1–2).

30:27 locusts. Locusts were known to destroy whole crops in their path. Joel 2:3–9 portrays them as an army.

30:28 lizards. On one hand they are weak and controllable. On the other, they have the run of the palace. Strength takes many forms.

[30]a lion, mighty among beasts,
who retreats before nothing;
[31]a strutting rooster, a he-goat,
and a king with his army around him.[a]

[32]"If you have played the fool and exalted yourself,
or if you have planned evil,
clap your hand over your mouth!
[33]For as churning the milk produces butter,
and as twisting the nose produces blood,
so stirring up anger produces strife."

OPEN What favorite saying of your mother's can you recite?

STUDY Chapter 31 is attributed to Lemuel, probably a non-Hebrew author of whom we know nothing other than his name. **1.** How would you characterize the king's relationship with his mother: Great? Good? Fair? Poor? Why? **2.** If the *Jerusalem Times* decided to print each of these paragraphs (vv. 2–3,4-7,8–9) as separate articles, with you as its editor, what headline would you give each one? What accompanying pictures do they bring to mind? What section of the paper do they fit in best? **3.** Other than women (v. 3), who are "those who ruin kings"? Would you agree they ruin more than kings?

APPLY To whom do you want to give a bit of advice or counsel? What would you say to him or her? How do you think it would be received?

OPEN 1. Who was your favorite TV or movie wife? Did you secretly want her to be your mother? What did you like most about her? **2.** If you have been married, where and when did you get married? If you have yet to be married, where

Sayings of King Lemuel

31 The sayings of King Lemuel—an oracle[b] his mother taught him:

[2]"O my son, O son of my womb,
O son of my vows,[c]
[3]do not spend your strength on women,
your vigor on those who ruin kings.

[4]"It is not for kings, O Lemuel—
not for kings to drink wine,
not for rulers to crave beer,
[5]lest they drink and forget what the law decrees,
and deprive all the oppressed of their rights.
[6]Give beer to those who are perishing,
wine to those who are in anguish;
[7]let them drink and forget their poverty
and remember their misery no more.

[8]"Speak up for those who cannot speak for themselves,
for the rights of all who are destitute.
[9]Speak up and judge fairly;
defend the rights of the poor and needy."

Epilogue: The Wife of Noble Character

[10][d]A wife of noble character who can find?
She is worth far more than rubies.

[a]31 Or *king secure against revolt* [b]1 Or *of Lemuel king of Massa, which* [c]2 Or *I the answer to my prayers*
[d]10 Verses 10-31 are an acrostic, each verse beginning with a successive letter of the Hebrew alphabet.

30:30 lion. Here the lion is described as stately and powerful. Jesus is sometimes called the Lion of Judah (Rev. 5:5).

30:31 rooster ... king. All appear confident and even invincible.

31:1–9 A section on wise women taught by a queen mother.

31:1 Lemuel. Lemuel was a non-Israelite king. The teachings here came from his mother.

31:2 vows. Perhaps this mother had committed Lemuel to God much as Hannah did Samuel before she was even pregnant with him (1 Sam. 1:11).

31:3 do not spend your strength. A king's strength would have been badly spent if all he did was chase women.

31:4–5 wine ... beer. An alcoholic king posed a double danger. His people and his politics depended on judgment and memory. Alcohol could debilitate both.

31:6–7 Some people use alcohol to escape decision making or difficulties. For a king, that kind of escape was not an option.

31:8–9 defend the rights. While politics might require a king to cater to the powerful, here the king is encouraged to spend his energies representing the weak and disenfranchised, those who probably will have nothing to give back to him. It's character over politics.

31:10 noble character. This phrase was used to describe Ruth (Ruth 3:11). It means capable or skilled.

[11]Her husband has full confidence in her
and lacks nothing of value.
[12]She brings him good, not harm,
all the days of her life.
[13]She selects wool and flax
and works with eager hands.
[14]She is like the merchant ships,
bringing her food from afar.
[15]She gets up while it is still dark;
she provides food for her family
and portions for her servant girls.
[16]She considers a field and buys it;
out of her earnings she plants a vineyard.
[17]She sets about her work vigorously;
her arms are strong for her tasks.
[18]She sees that her trading is profitable,
and her lamp does not go out at night.
[19]In her hand she holds the distaff
and grasps the spindle with her fingers.
[20]She opens her arms to the poor
and extends her hands to the needy.
[21]When it snows, she has no fear for her household;
for all of them are clothed in scarlet.
[22]She makes coverings for her bed;
she is clothed in fine linen and purple.
[23]Her husband is respected at the city gate,
where he takes his seat among the elders of the land.
[24]She makes linen garments and sells them,
and supplies the merchants with sashes.
[25]She is clothed with strength and dignity;
she can laugh at the days to come.
[26]She speaks with wisdom,
and faithful instruction is on her tongue.
[27]She watches over the affairs of her household

and how would you like to get married?

STUDY 1. Verses 10–31 form an "acrostic"; that is, each verse in succession begins with the next letter of the 22-character Hebrew alphabet. How might this carefully crafted epilogue relate to the prologue (1:1–7)? **2.** How could anyone become like this woman? What does verse 10 imply? Do you think she is just a symbol for the perfect wife or an actual flesh and blood person? Or both? **3.** Would the author of this epilogue be applauded by feminists and traditionalists? Would the woman described here support equal rights for women or sex defined roles? What makes you think so? Which verses support your view? **4.** In addition to being a person of "noble character" (v. 10), how many more of her "qualities" can you identify? **5.** What abilities make her praiseworthy in the eyes of her husband? Her children? The city fathers and mothers? The poor and the needy? **6.** If she represents "God's ideal woman," should the "average" woman (single or married) aspire to her qualities? **7.** How does this woman who "does it all" compare with your image of the woman today who "does it all"? What are the differences? The similarities? **8.** What would you think of a person who aspired to these qualities, but came up "a buck short"? What if she came up "woefully short"?

31:10–31 In its original language this passage was an acrostic poem. Each line began with the next letter of the Hebrew alphabet.

31:12 brings him good. A wife can make life miserable. Proverbs has described wives who are liabilities, as irritating as dripping faucets. This passage describes a woman who is an asset, not a liability.

31:13 flax. Plant used to make linen. **eager hands.** A good wife delights to work with her hands.

31:14 merchant ships. She is a wise and creative consumer, an expert in home management.

31:15 gets up while it is still dark. This woman is the opposite of the sluggard who loves to sleep (6:9; 20:13).

31:16 buys it. Where women were not allowed to own property, this was a feat. This woman evidently had resources that the average woman of her day did not.

31:18 her lamp does not go out. This image indicated that the woman planned well, managed her resources well, that she would prosper. An extinguished lamp was a sign of calamity and misfortune.

31:19 spindle. She worked with cloth and probably some form of weaving and sewing.

31:20 opens her arms. She is generous. She looks beyond her own survival to the survival of others.

31:21 scarlet. Scarlet connotes expensive garments. This woman has cared for her family lavishly.

31:22 fine linen and purple. Her own clothes reflect her family's strong position. Purple was a color for royalty made from a dye from shellfish.

31:23 respected at the city gate. Where the wise men of the town gathered to share wisdom, settle disputes and transact business.

31:24 makes ... and sells. She not only supplies her home, she is productive enough to supply merchants with her wares. She is ahead of the game rather than running to catch up.

31:25 laugh. She has hope and confidence to face whatever circumstances come her way.

31:26 wisdom, and faithful instruction. Certainly her wisdom is shared with her children and servants. Paul wrote to Titus about women of the church sharing wisdom as this woman does (Titus 2:3–4).

APPLY **1.** In verses 10–31, what would be the modern application of all that a woman does? **2.** What one character trait of this woman do you need more of in your life right now? **3.** Why does a woman feel, she needs to "do it all" in order to be "God's ideal woman"? **4.** How can you as a group help each other this week with not trying to "do it all"?

and does not eat the bread of idleness.
[28]Her children arise and call her blessed;
her husband also, and he praises her:
[29]"Many women do noble things,
but you surpass them all."
[30]Charm is deceptive, and beauty is fleeting;
but a woman who fears the LORD is to be praised.
[31]Give her the reward she has earned,
and let her works bring her praise at the city gate.

31:28–29 noble. This woman enjoys a good reputation not only in the community but also in her own household where everyone's weaknesses are evident.

31:30 to be praised. This woman is lauded for her character and her life of wisdom. She has lived the book of Proverbs.

31:31 city gate. A place where only men received recognition. This woman proves that good character and wisdom surpass gender and cultural bias.

Ecclesiates

Author. Solomon is traditionally considered the author of Ecclesiastes. Solomon was the wealthiest king of Israel. He was also the last king of unified Israel before the political split between Israel (in the north) and Judah (in the south).

Personal Reading	Group Study Topic and Reading	
1:1–18	Life's Meaninglessness	1:1–11
2:1–26	Wealth's Passing Value	2:1–16
3:1–22	God's Sovereignty	3:1–15
4:1–5:7	Change and Honesty	4:13–5:7
5:8–6:9	Riches	5:8–6:9
6:10–7:14	The Truly Good	6:10–7:14
7:15–8:1	Extremism and Sin	7:15–8:1
8:2–17	Response to Injustice	8:2–17
9:1–12	Chance and Destiny	9:1–12
9:13–10:15	Wisdom and Folly	9:13–10:15
10:16–11:6	Investing Wisely	11:1–6
11:7–12:8	Life's Backside	11:7–12:8
12:9–14	Conclusion	12:9–14

Date. Solomon probably wrote Ecclesiastes toward the end of his life. If so, the date would be just before 930 B.C.

Purpose. Many people spend their lives thinking that they would be happy if they just had something else. Ecclesiastes is Solomon's response to that idea. He was the man who had everything. In his final years, he wrote about the meaning and futility of life. Solomon had everything, yet at some point, he wandered from his faith. Solomon shares that without God, all else loses meaning.

Historical Background. Life in the tenth century B.C. was fragile. Though the rich lived lavishly, their life expectancy was short. In addition, their world was often dominated by famine, disease, war and pestilence. The great political powers of the world were ruled by men who did not value the lives of their subjects. The consequences of losing a war were national slavery and bondage worse than death. History had already taught that even powerful kingdoms such as Egypt and Babylon were just a few military defeats (or famines or plagues) from decline. Small kingdoms such as Israel rose to power and then fell again, swept along in the historical current created by the great empires of the region.

Though Solomon's kingdom was prosperous, the world outside his borders was turbulent politically and socially. Assyria, a ruthless nation, was rising to regional dominance. Egypt was under the rule of a Libyan commander who would later raid Israel in 926 B.C.

Theme. Solomon had power and wealth as the king of Israel. While he hoped and planned for continued prosperity in Israel after his death, he knew that earthly peace and success are never guaranteed. Ecclesiastes is brutally frank in its assessment of life and life's potential. It concludes that all of life is meaningless without God. All the things for which people may strive—wisdom, pleasure, advancement and riches—are meaningless. Even those things that are regarded as virtuous, such as work, are meaningless, too. The meaning that life holds for humanity is simply the gift of God, the opportunity to "eat and drink, and find satisfaction in all his toil" (3:13).

The word "meaningless" appears in Ecclesiastes over and over again. Solomon's one conclusion was that all the things that the contemporary culture assumes will bring meaning to life simply do not fulfill the longings of the human spirit.

OPEN 1. What is your favorite style of clothing? What type of clothing would you not be caught dead in? **2.** What was the first large thing you saved your pennies for?

STUDY 1. The word for "meaningless" (v. 2) can also mean "breath" or "vapor." What, then, is meant by the motto, "everything is meaningless"? **2.** What does the phrase "under the sun" (vv. 3,9) tell you about the perspective of this thesis? **3.** How does mankind's labor compare with the earth's cycle (vv. 3–7)? **4.** What problem does verse 8 point out? **5.** What's the theme of verses 9–10? What qualifies as "something new" by this Teacher's definition? **6.** In verse 11, what tone of voice do you hear? What logic do you see? Is verse 11 the logical extension or inevitable conclusion of careful reasoning? Or is this an emotional lament of an embittered old man?

APPLY 1. On a scale of 1–10, how would you rate the satisfaction you get from your present job, if "1" is "It's just a paycheck" and "10" is "It's what I live for"? **2.** What, if anything, are you doing in your life that truly "makes a difference"? **3.** For what would you like to be remembered after you are gone?

OPEN 1. In which subject did (or do) you get the best grades? **2.** At what age did you first say, "I know more than my teachers (or parents)"?

Everything Is Meaningless

1 The words of the Teacher,[a] son of David, king in Jerusalem:

2 "Meaningless! Meaningless!"
says the Teacher.
"Utterly meaningless!
Everything is meaningless."
3 What does man gain from all his labor
at which he toils under the sun?
4 Generations come and generations go,
but the earth remains forever.
5 The sun rises and the sun sets,
and hurries back to where it rises.
6 The wind blows to the south
and turns to the north;
round and round it goes,
ever returning on its course.
7 All streams flow into the sea,
yet the sea is never full.
To the place the streams come from,
there they return again.
8 All things are wearisome,
more than one can say.
The eye never has enough of seeing,
nor the ear its fill of hearing.
9 What has been will be again,
what has been done will be done again;
there is nothing new under the sun.
10 Is there anything of which one can say,
"Look! This is something new"?
It was here already, long ago;
it was here before our time.
11 There is no remembrance of men of old,
and even those who are yet to come
will not be remembered
by those who follow.

Wisdom Is Meaningless

12 I, the Teacher, was king over Israel in Jerusalem. 13 I devoted myself to study and to explore by wisdom all that is done under heaven.

[a]1 Or *leader of the assembly*; also in verses 2 and 12

1:2 This verse sums up the message of the whole book. **Meaningless.** This word occurs 35 times in the book. The thrust of the word is "breath" or "vapor," a concrete image for the brevity, emptiness and futility of life. **Everything.** Anything humans undertake apart from God.

1:3 The rhetorical question in this verse demands the answer "nothing." All the work people do on earth amounts to nothing. Jesus expands on this concept in Mark 8:36–38. **under the sun.** This key phrase is used 29 times in this book to refer to the limitations of this present world.

1:4 As proof that labors of men and women on earth are unprofitable, the author points to the never ending cycles of life and of nature. The earth may remain forever, but human life (one generation after another), like the cycles of the sun, wind and water, produces nothing permanent.

1:10–11 This is something new. What may appear new to us is really just an old idea in a new guise. Things only appear new because we have forgotten the ages past. Humankind is subject to the futility of relearning the same lessons generation after generation because we are so forgetful.

1:12–18 Relentlessly unhappy, the writer goes on a quest for satisfaction. Here he demonstrates the futility of human wisdom.

What a heavy burden God has laid on men! [14]I have seen all the things
that are done under the sun; all of them are meaningless, a chasing
after the wind.

[15]What is twisted cannot be straightened;
what is lacking cannot be counted.

[16]I thought to myself, "Look, I have grown and increased in wisdom more than anyone who has ruled over Jerusalem before me; I
have experienced much of wisdom and knowledge." [17]Then I applied
myself to the understanding of wisdom, and also of madness and
folly, but I learned that this, too, is a chasing after the wind.

[18]For with much wisdom comes much sorrow;
the more knowledge, the more grief.

Pleasures Are Meaningless

2 I thought in my heart, "Come now, I will test you with pleasure to
find out what is good." But that also proved to be meaningless.
[2]"Laughter," I said, "is foolish. And what does pleasure accomplish?"
[3]I tried cheering myself with wine, and embracing folly—my mind
still guiding me with wisdom. I wanted to see what was worthwhile
for men to do under heaven during the few days of their lives.

[4]I undertook great projects: I built houses for myself and planted
vineyards. [5]I made gardens and parks and planted all kinds of fruit
trees in them. [6]I made reservoirs to water groves of flourishing trees.
[7]I bought male and female slaves and had other slaves who were
born in my house. I also owned more herds and flocks than anyone
in Jerusalem before me. [8]I amassed silver and gold for myself, and the
treasure of kings and provinces. I acquired men and women singers,
and a harem[a] as well—the delights of the heart of man. [9]I became
greater by far than anyone in Jerusalem before me. In all this my wisdom stayed with me.

[10]I denied myself nothing my eyes desired;
I refused my heart no pleasure.
My heart took delight in all my work,
and this was the reward for all my labor.
[11]Yet when I surveyed all that my hands had done
and what I had toiled to achieve,
everything was meaningless, a chasing after the wind;
nothing was gained under the sun.

[a]8 The meaning of the Hebrew for this phrase is uncertain.

STUDY 1. Where has the Teacher searched for wisdom? **2.** What is the "burden" in verse 13? Why is God blamed for it? **3.** Why does wisdom bring sorrow and knowledge bring grief?

APPLY 1. Where "under heaven" have you searched for meaning? Where have you found it? **2.** In what instances has knowledge caused you sorrow?

OPEN 1. What crazy stunt in high school are you remembered for? **2.** What creative science project do you remember from those days? **3.** What material goods are on your all-time wish list?

STUDY 1. What paradox does the Teacher find in hedonism (vv. 1–3)? **2.** What do these key phrases tell you about the perspective of this passage: "During the few days of their lives" (v. 3)? "Under the sun" (v. 11)? "In days to come" (v. 16)? **3.** What "great projects" does he undertake (vv. 4–8)? What desires were such projects meant to satisfy? **4.** During these projects, what is the Teacher's relation to wisdom (vv. 3,9,12–13)? **5.** In verses 12–16, to what does "wisdom" refer: Spiritual insight? Street smarts? Survival skills? Upright behavior? **6.** Does "folly" here mean something similar to wisdom, or something opposite? **7.** How is light better than darkness? What does this say about the difference between wisdom and folly? **8.** Why is this Teacher so unhappy with what so many would call success?

APPLY 1. What is the most important project you have undertaken in the last year? How do

1:13 God. The name used for God throughout Ecclesiastes emphasizes divine sovereignty over all things.

1:15 Humans are incapable of controlling their destiny, so human effort is meaningless. We should instead learn to accept the situation God has put us in.

1:18 Knowledge leads to sorrow and grief on several levels. The more we learn, the more we realize how much we don't know, a painful discovery. In addition, knowledge of the world allows us to see how hopeless we are. Without the hope God offers, the troubles of the world truly are overwhelming and impossible to solve.

2:1–11 Since wisdom leads to a dead end, the teacher next looks to pleasure. He drinks wine, then acquires real estate, gardens, slaves and herds of animals. He enjoys entertainment. But this, too, is meaningless (v. 11).

2:3 still guiding me with wisdom. The teacher did not surrender to his appetites, but instead exercised temperance in his test of pleasure.

you measure your success in that? **2.** Do you regard death as the final tragedy or the final triumph? Is the death of the fool different from that of the wise? How can you prepare yourself for death? **3.** How does a passage like this help you focus on the truly important things in life? What are they?

OPEN What is your most valued possession? Who would you like to leave it to when you die?

STUDY 1. Why did the Teacher hate life? **2.** Who is said to be the real beneficiary of someone's work (vv. 18–21)? Why is that? **3.** How do verses 24–26 contrast with the preceding? **4.** What does it mean to "please God" in this context? **5.** What does God have to do with satisfaction in work? **6.** Who is the "sinner"? Why does God favor the one over the other?

APPLY 1. Why do you work? When do you most feel like not working? **2.** Do you see your work as a gift from God, as drudgery, or both? Does that make you grateful, even for the drudgery, or hateful? Why?

Wisdom and Folly Are Meaningless

12 Then I turned my thoughts to consider wisdom,
 and also madness and folly.
What more can the king's successor do
 than what has already been done?
13 I saw that wisdom is better than folly,
 just as light is better than darkness.
14 The wise man has eyes in his head,
 while the fool walks in the darkness;
but I came to realize
 that the same fate overtakes them both.

15 Then I thought in my heart,

"The fate of the fool will overtake me also.
 What then do I gain by being wise?"
I said in my heart,
 "This too is meaningless."
16 For the wise man, like the fool, will not be long remembered;
 in days to come both will be forgotten.
Like the fool, the wise man too must die!

Toil Is Meaningless

17 So I hated life, because the work that is done under the sun was
grievous to me. All of it is meaningless, a chasing after the wind. 18 I
hated all the things I had toiled for under the sun, because I must
leave them to the one who comes after me. 19 And who knows
whether he will be a wise man or a fool? Yet he will have control over
all the work into which I have poured my effort and skill under the
sun. This too is meaningless. 20 So my heart began to despair over all
my toilsome labor under the sun. 21 For a man may do his work with
wisdom, knowledge and skill, and then he must leave all he owns to
someone who has not worked for it. This too is meaningless and a
great misfortune. 22 What does a man get for all the toil and anxious
striving with which he labors under the sun? 23 All his days his work is
pain and grief; even at night his mind does not rest. This too is meaningless.

24 A man can do nothing better than to eat and drink and find satisfaction in his work. This too, I see, is from the hand of God, 25 for
without him, who can eat or find enjoyment? 26 To the man who
pleases him, God gives wisdom, knowledge and happiness, but to the
sinner he gives the task of gathering and storing up wealth to hand it
over to the one who pleases God. This too is meaningless, a chasing
after the wind.

2:13–14 is better than folly. Wisdom is better than foolishness, but both the wise person and the foolish person *eventually die.* The superiority of wisdom is canceled by the common fate of all people, whether wise or not.

2:24–25 Suddenly the teacher changes tone and asserts that life is meaningful, even in areas he previously found unfulfilling. The difference is that he is now describing life above the sun—life lived in relationship with God. We will never find joy in eating, drinking and working if we seek these things as an end in themselves. Life under the sun is meaningful only if God's plan lies behind all of its many joys and sorrows.

2:26 the task of gathering and storing up wealth to hand it over. The teacher notes that often unbelievers store up earthly wealth only to find it turned over to people who follow God. This makes labor for labor's sake meaninglessness.

A Time for Everything

3 There is a time for everything,
and a season for every activity under heaven:
2 a time to be born and a time to die,
a time to plant and a time to uproot,
3 a time to kill and a time to heal,
a time to tear down and a time to build,
4 a time to weep and a time to laugh,
a time to mourn and a time to dance,
5 a time to scatter stones and a time to gather them,
a time to embrace and a time to refrain,
6 a time to search and a time to give up,
a time to keep and a time to throw away,
7 a time to tear and a time to mend,
a time to be silent and a time to speak,
8 a time to love and a time to hate,
a time for war and a time for peace.

9 What does the worker gain from his toil? 10 I have seen the burden
God has laid on men. 11 He has made everything beautiful in its time.
He has also set eternity in the hearts of men; yet they cannot fathom
what God has done from beginning to end. 12 I know that there is
nothing better for men than to be happy and do good while they live.
13 That everyone may eat and drink, and find satisfaction in all his
toil—this is the gift of God. 14 I know that everything God does will
endure forever; nothing can be added to it and nothing taken from it.
God does it so that men will revere him.

15 Whatever is has already been,
and what will be has been before;
and God will call the past to account.[a]

16 And I saw something else under the sun:

In the place of judgment—wickedness was there,
in the place of justice—wickedness was there.

17 I thought in my heart,

"God will bring to judgment
both the righteous and the wicked,
for there will be a time for every activity,
a time for every deed."

[a]15 Or *God calls back the past*

OPEN 1. Of the following activities mentioned here, which do you most enjoy taking time for: Planting? Building? Dancing? Embracing? Keeping (collecting things)? Cleaning? **2.** Which are you like at a party: Party animal? Party pooper? Hostess helper? Wall flower? **3.** What was your favorite season as a child? Why? Which is your favorite now?

STUDY 1. In the list of opposites (vv. 1–8), is the Teacher describing what is, or prescribing what one should do? Why do you think so? **2.** What is "the burden God has laid on man" (v. 10)? **3.** What does it mean to "set eternity in the hearts of men" (v. 11)? **4.** What is the Teacher encouraging in verses 12–13: Hedonism? Gratitude? Or what? **5.** Toward what end does all of this point (vv. 14–15)? **6.** What is meant by "God will call the past to account" (v. 15)?

APPLY 1. Would you rather spend your time: Fathoming God's work (v. 11)? Doing good (v. 12)? Eating and drinking (v. 13)? Why? **2.** Can you just "eat, drink and be merry" without feeling guilt? When is such carefree living good, and when is it inappropriate? **3.** Does belief in God's sovereignty free you to enjoy life? How so?

OPEN Which childhood pet do you miss most? Is your dead pet in the ground or in "animal heaven"? Why do you think so?

STUDY 1. How does the theme of this passage (vv. 16–17) relate to the previous one? **2.** How are humans like, and unlike, animals? **3.** How does the "wickedness" in verse 16 relate to this comparison with animals? **4.** What does this passage teach concerning the destiny of humans? Or animals?

3:1–22 The teacher proves that humans are unable to alter God's sovereign plan. He first gives the human view of time (vv. 1–8), then God's view of time (vv. 9–22).

3:1–8 This famous poem deals with the problem of time viewed from a human perspective. Does life roll out like a premade carpet? Are we just actors on a stage reciting a script? Can anything original happen?

3:11 He has also set eternity in the hearts of men. Humans are made for eternity. Our capacity to comprehend immortality leads us to want it, and therefore to seek God. In the words of Augustine, "Our souls are restless till they rest in thee."

3:14 In contrast to fleeting human efforts, God's works are eternal.

3:16–18 Injustice penetrates all parts of the world. But God has a plan for achieving justice and a purpose for all the current injustice. God will judge in his time. What appears to escape God's judgment here on earth will face it on a final judgment day. In the meantime, injustice demonstrates that we, like the animals, are mortal.

APPLY **1.** When do you find yourself most acting "like an animal": When challenged by a hostile person? When you see someone attractive? When in a competitive situation? **2.** How do you feel about acting in such a way? **3.** How does the promise of eternal life (John 5:24) help you deal with injustice?

[18]I also thought, "As for men, God tests them so that they may see
that they are like the animals. [19]Man's fate is like that of the animals;
the same fate awaits them both: As one dies, so dies the other. All
have the same breath[a]; man has no advantage over the animal. Everything is meaningless. [20]All go to the same place; all come from dust,
and to dust all return. [21]Who knows if the spirit of man rises upward
and if the spirit of the animal[b] goes down into the earth?"

[22]So I saw that there is nothing better for a man than to enjoy his
work, because that is his lot. For who can bring him to see what will
happen after him?

Oppression, Toil, Friendlessness

OPEN **1.** When in life were you most in need of a friend? Did one come? **2.** Which of your neighbor's possessions do you most covet?

STUDY **1.** Who are the "oppressed" in verse 1? The "oppressors"? **2.** Why does the Teacher say that the dead are happier than the living? **3.** What does he say is the primary motivation for mankind (v. 4)? **4.** What is the meaning of each of the proverbs in verses 5–6? What do they imply is the Teacher's view of labor and competition?

APPLY **1.** Do you see yourself more often in the role of the "oppressed" or the "oppressor"? How so? **2.** How much does someone's wealth or status affect the way you treat him? **3.** Do you presently have "one handful" or "two" (v. 6)?

4 Again I looked and saw all the oppression that was taking place
under the sun:

I saw the tears of the oppressed—
and they have no comforter;
power was on the side of their oppressors—
and they have no comforter.
[2]And I declared that the dead,
who had already died,
are happier than the living,
who are still alive.
[3]But better than both
is he who has not yet been,
who has not seen the evil
that is done under the sun.

[4]And I saw that all labor and all achievement spring from man's envy
of his neighbor. This too is meaningless, a chasing after the wind.

[5]The fool folds his hands
and ruins himself.
[6]Better one handful with tranquillity
than two handfuls with toil
and chasing after the wind.

[7]Again I saw something meaningless under the sun:

OPEN What job have you tackled by yourself that you should have asked someone to help you do?

STUDY **1.** What is the status of the man in verse 8? How materially successful is he? At what cost? What is he questioning? **2.** Why does the Teacher see the "business" in verse 8 as "meaningless"? **3.** What are the benefits of "two" in verses 9–12? **4.** How is the proverb in verse 12 a fitting conclusion?

[8]There was a man all alone;
he had neither son nor brother.
There was no end to his toil,
yet his eyes were not content with his wealth.
"For whom am I toiling," he asked,
"and why am I depriving myself of enjoyment?"
This too is meaningless—
a miserable business!

[a]19 Or *spirit* [b]21 Or *Who knows the spirit of man, which rises upward, or the spirit of the animal, which*

3:18–19 same fate. Both humans and animals will die. The difference is that humans are responsible for making moral choices.

4:1–8 The teacher meditates on various social groups: the poor and oppressed (v. 1), the powerful oppressor (v. 1), the successful competitor (v. 4), the lazy worker (v. 5) and the lonely miser (vv. 7–8).

4:4 Labor is certainly meaningless if it is done simply to compete for prestige.

4:5 The idle person is consistently portrayed in Scripture as coming to ruin (10:18; Prov. 6:6–11; 24:30–34).

4:6 The alternative to the empty hands of the lazy person (v. 5) and the two handfuls of the competitor (v. 4) is one handful of peacefulness. Paul elaborates on this in Philippians 4:11–13.

[9] Two are better than one,
because they have a good return for their work:
[10] If one falls down,
his friend can help him up.
But pity the man who falls
and has no one to help him up!
[11] Also, if two lie down together, they will keep warm.
But how can one keep warm alone?
[12] Though one may be overpowered,
two can defend themselves.
A cord of three strands is not quickly broken.

Advancement Is Meaningless

[13] Better a poor but wise youth than an old but foolish king who no
longer knows how to take warning. [14] The youth may have come from
prison to the kingship, or he may have been born in poverty within
his kingdom. [15] I saw that all who lived and walked under the sun
followed the youth, the king's successor. [16] There was no end to all
the people who were before them. But those who came later were not
pleased with the successor. This too is meaningless, a chasing after
the wind.

Stand in Awe of God

5 Guard your steps when you go to the house of God. Go near to
listen rather than to offer the sacrifice of fools, who do not know
that they do wrong.

[2] Do not be quick with your mouth,
do not be hasty in your heart
to utter anything before God.
God is in heaven
and you are on earth,
so let your words be few.
[3] As a dream comes when there are many cares,
so the speech of a fool when there are many words.

[4] When you make a vow to God, do not delay in fulfilling it. He has
no pleasure in fools; fulfill your vow. [5] It is better not to vow than to
make a vow and not fulfill it. [6] Do not let your mouth lead you into sin.
And do not protest to the ⌞temple⌟ messenger, "My vow was a mistake." Why should God be angry at what you say and destroy the
work of your hands? [7] Much dreaming and many words are meaningless. Therefore stand in awe of God.

APPLY **1.** For whom (yourself, God, others) do you toil in the different areas of life (work, home, school, church)? How much satisfaction do you derive from your toil and your companions? **2.** How easy is it for you to allow someone to help you? Or, to let someone know that you need help? **3.** Where would you be spiritually were it not for the help of others?

OPEN **1.** How do you react to a new spiritual leader? **2.** What "hasty promise" have you later regretted making?

STUDY **1.** These two passages (4:13–16; 5:1–7) focus on our relationship to lordship. What type of lordship is the focus in the first passage? In the second? **2.** In 4:13–16, why is the old king so unpopular? The successor so popular? Why are those who come "later" displeased with the successor (4:16)? **3.** In 5:1–7, what is the fool's error? What is meant by the exhortations to "listen," "keep silent," and "not delay"? What are the potential results of "quick" mouths? **4.** How does 5:7 summarize the message of 4:13–16; 5:1–7?

APPLY **1.** When facing poor or evil leadership in a particular group, are you: Most patient? Most prayerful? Most pushy for change? Most "quick with your mouth"? **2.** How do you become part of the solution instead of the problem? **3.** What do you do when you make a hasty promise you cannot keep?

4:9–12 The human solution to life's misery is companionship. This oft-quoted passage is not entirely positive. Life is better with a companion, but one still experiences work, falls, cold and attacks from outsiders. Even with intimate friendship, we still live under the sun, subject to all the troubles life brings.

4:13–16 Fame is transitory. The king may become foolish and lose his power. Likewise, the young upstart with throngs of admirers will one day be forgotten.

5:1–7 This more up-beat section of the book gives commands about how to worship God properly. The writer encourages readers to worship God sincerely, to not merely talk of faith, but to humbly obey the Lord. He also warns that making vows to the Lord can be dangerous—if we vow to give God money, we must give it.

5:2 Do not be quick with your mouth. We should not be hasty to make vows before the Lord. Jesus gave this same advice in Matthew 5:33–37.

5:3 This verse, like verse 7, condemns thoughtless worship that contains many words but no sincerity or obedience. Words that may be spoken carelessly.

OPEN **1.** What was the most physically exhausting job you ever did? **2.** What effect does your work have on you: Invigoration? Frustration? Exhaustion? Boredom? **3.** What pleasure in life do you not get enough time for?

STUDY **1.** What is the reason for the oppression in verses 8–9? Why should we not be surprised by this? **2.** In what way do the three proverbs (5:10,11,12) describe situations that are meaningless? **3.** What about money is he bemoaning here: The addiction to money? Its emptiness? The indulgence of money? **4.** What is the "grievous evil" of 5:13–17? How do "wealth hoarded" and "wealth lost" fit into this observation? **5.** What isn't "right" about going out as naked as we arrive? Is the Teacher asking of life more than it can ever give? **6.** What does the Teacher conclude is "good and proper"? Why (2:24–26)? **7.** Why is it a blessing not to "reflect" with the mind but to "enjoy" with the heart? What might the Teacher be saying about himself here? **8.** What is the other evil in 6:1–2 and verses 3–6? What belief influences the Teacher's conclusions (6:6)?

APPLY **1.** What priority does the pursuit of wealth and work have in your life? Is this necessary? What are you expecting your life's work will give you in the end? **2.** How much "gladness of heart" do you presently experience in your "labor under the sun" (6:18)? What would help you enjoy your work more? **3.** In the Old Testament, the "dream of a lifetime" was hundreds of children and thousands of years on earth (6:3,6). What is your life's dream? When might you most enjoy your life's attainments?

Riches Are Meaningless

8If you see the poor oppressed in a district, and justice and rights
denied, do not be surprised at such things; for one official is eyed by
a higher one, and over them both are others higher still. 9The increase from the land is taken by all; the king himself profits from the
fields.

10Whoever loves money never has money enough;
whoever loves wealth is never satisfied with his income.
This too is meaningless.

11As goods increase,
so do those who consume them.
And what benefit are they to the owner
except to feast his eyes on them?
12The sleep of a laborer is sweet,
whether he eats little or much,
but the abundance of a rich man
permits him no sleep.

13I have seen a grievous evil under the sun:

wealth hoarded to the harm of its owner,
14 or wealth lost through some misfortune,
so that when he has a son
there is nothing left for him.
15Naked a man comes from his mother's womb,
and as he comes, so he departs.
He takes nothing from his labor
that he can carry in his hand.

16This too is a grievous evil:

As a man comes, so he departs,
and what does he gain,
since he toils for the wind?
17All his days he eats in darkness,
with great frustration, affliction and anger.

18Then I realized that it is good and proper for a man to eat and
drink, and to find satisfaction in his toilsome labor under the sun
during the few days of life God has given him—for this is his lot.
19Moreover, when God gives any man wealth and possessions, and
enables him to enjoy them, to accept his lot and be happy in his
work—this is a gift of God. 20He seldom reflects on the days of his
life, because God keeps him occupied with gladness of heart.

6 I have seen another evil under the sun, and it weighs heavily on
men: 2God gives a man wealth, possessions and honor, so that

5:8–9 These verses begin a section (vv. 8–17) that attacks wealth. Here the teacher points to a hierarchy of corruption. The fruits of our labor may be lost through a rash vow (vv. 1–7) or to corrupt authorities.

5:10 People greedy for wealth will never be satisfied with the money they have. Money is never able to satisfy human longings anyway.

5:13–14 In the end, money destroys the owner, partly because the owner must worry about protecting all those possessions.

5:20 A truly successful person will feel that life goes by quickly. This is the person who can truly enjoy wealth, unlike those in verses 8–17 who were so absorbed in gathering and keeping wealth that they were unable to enjoy it.

6:2–3 Here we see the opposite of the person described at the end of chapter 5. This person has not been given the

he lacks nothing his heart desires, but God does not enable him to enjoy them, and a stranger enjoys them instead. This is meaningless, a grievous evil.

[3]A man may have a hundred children and live many years; yet no
matter how long he lives, if he cannot enjoy his prosperity and does
not receive proper burial, I say that a stillborn child is better off than
he. [4]It comes without meaning, it departs in darkness, and in darkness its name is shrouded. [5]Though it never saw the sun or knew
anything, it has more rest than does that man— [6]even if he lives a
thousand years twice over but fails to enjoy his prosperity. Do not all
go to the same place?

[7]All man's efforts are for his mouth,
yet his appetite is never satisfied.
[8]What advantage has a wise man
over a fool?
What does a poor man gain
by knowing how to conduct himself before others?
[9]Better what the eye sees
than the roving of the appetite.
This too is meaningless,
a chasing after the wind.

[10]Whatever exists has already been named,
and what man is has been known;
no man can contend
with one who is stronger than he.
[11]The more the words,
the less the meaning,
and how does that profit anyone?

[12]For who knows what is good for a man in life, during the few and
meaningless days he passes through like a shadow? Who can tell him
what will happen under the sun after he is gone?

Wisdom

7 A good name is better than fine perfume,
and the day of death better than the day of birth.
[2]It is better to go to a house of mourning
than to go to a house of feasting,
for death is the destiny of every man;
the living should take this to heart.
[3]Sorrow is better than laughter,
because a sad face is good for the heart.
[4]The heart of the wise is in the house of mourning,
but the heart of fools is in the house of pleasure.
[5]It is better to heed a wise man's rebuke
than to listen to the song of fools.
[6]Like the crackling of thorns under the pot,

OPEN 1. If you compared your life to a product in a catalog, which item is it most like: Power tool? Sofa? Lawn ornament? Grey flannel pajamas? Other? Would you be the good, better or best model? **2.** Who was the last person to "tell you off"? Why? How did you react? **3.** Dream a bit: If all goes well, what do you predict for yourself next year?

STUDY 1. In 6:10–12, the Teacher gives some observations and questions that introduce the next section. What are the observations? The questions? **2.** In 7:1–12, how does the Teacher go about searching for answers to his question, "What is good"? Is anything absolutely good, or are some things only relatively better? **3.** In each of the couplets or comparisons in 7:1–4, which is the better thing and why? **4.** What is the reason behind the advice given in 7:5–7? **5.** Why is the question in 7:10 so unwise (7:8–10; 1:9)? **6.** In 7:11–12, what is meant by comparing wisdom to "an inheritance"? To a "shelter"? How does wisdom preserve life?

gift of God that enables enjoyment of wealth. In some cases, other people enjoy the wealth. In other cases, the person has simply not been empowered by God to enjoy wealth. The writer sees the inability to enjoy wealth as a great tragedy.

7:1–8 Here a series of proverbs encourages a realistic outlook on life. It is wiser to see life as mainly negative than to have a foolish optimism that denies life's difficulties. Difficult times teach us more than good times do. Life's meaning can be found in Christ (Phil. 1:21).

APPLY **1.** When you are confused, how do you decide who to listen to? How do you know when to give advice? Rebuke? Praise? **2.** As compared to dwelling on the past or longing for the future, how much do you live in the present? How much do you enjoy it? What can you do to enjoy the "here and now" more? **3.** Would you say these days are good times or bad times for you? Is your answer based on nostalgia (for the past) or hope (for the future)?

so is the laughter of fools.
This too is meaningless.

7 Extortion turns a wise man into a fool,
and a bribe corrupts the heart.
8 The end of a matter is better than its beginning,
and patience is better than pride.
9 Do not be quickly provoked in your spirit,
for anger resides in the lap of fools.

10 Do not say, "Why were the old days better than these?"
For it is not wise to ask such questions.

11 Wisdom, like an inheritance, is a good thing
and benefits those who see the sun.
12 Wisdom is a shelter
as money is a shelter,
but the advantage of knowledge is this:
that wisdom preserves the life of its possessor.

13 Consider what God has done:

Who can straighten
what he has made crooked?
14 When times are good, be happy;
but when times are bad, consider:
God has made the one
as well as the other.
Therefore, a man cannot discover
anything about his future.

15 In this meaningless life of mine I have seen both of these:

a righteous man perishing in his righteousness,
and a wicked man living long in his wickedness.
16 Do not be overrighteous,
neither be overwise—
why destroy yourself?
17 Do not be overwicked,
and do not be a fool—
why die before your time?
18 It is good to grasp the one
and not let go of the other.
The man who fears God will avoid all extremes.[a]

[a] 18 *Or will follow them both*

OPEN **1.** What gossip about yourself got back to you and made your blood boil? How did you react? **2.** In trying new things, which are you: Cautious? Venturesome? Uninterested? In what areas are you most likely to experiment?

STUDY **1.** What observations inspire these warnings (vv. 15–18)? What is meant by "overrighteous" (v. 16)? By "overwicked" (v. 17)? **2.** Would the Teacher ever say, "Nothing to excess, everything in moderation"? How does such a view square with genuine fear of God (v. 18)? **3.** Is verse 20 a confession,

7:9–10 Neither bitterness nor nostalgia are proper response to life's sorrows.

7:13–14 True wisdom is the ability to *place earthly sorrows in the context of* God's sovereignty. We cannot control our circumstances to avoid difficult times, so we might as well submit to God's control and trust him to orchestrate the circumstances of our lives.

7:15–16 The writer tells us not to rely on our own righteousness or wisdom to guarantee God's blessing. Righteous people do not always live long, and some wicked people do. Yet the writer is not implying that we should be half-hearted in our obedience to God.

7:17 That God does not always punish sin on earth is not a license to sin. We should live in the light of God's judgment and keep in mind that God sometimes judges people by causing them to die before their time. To the writer, God's judgment comes on earth, not so much in an afterlife.

7:18 We should avoid the extremes of depending on our own righteousness (legalism) or abandoning all standards (hedonism). It is best to lead a balanced life.

19Wisdom makes one wise man more powerful
than ten rulers in a city.

20There is not a righteous man on earth
who does what is right and never sins.

21Do not pay attention to every word people say,
or you may hear your servant cursing you—
22for you know in your heart
that many times you yourself have cursed others.

23All this I tested by wisdom and I said,

"I am determined to be wise"—
but this was beyond me.
24Whatever wisdom may be,
it is far off and most profound—
who can discover it?
25So I turned my mind to understand,
to investigate and to search out wisdom and the scheme of things
and to understand the stupidity of wickedness
and the madness of folly.

26I find more bitter than death
the woman who is a snare,
whose heart is a trap
and whose hands are chains.
The man who pleases God will escape her,
but the sinner she will ensnare.

27"Look," says the Teacher,[a] "this is what I have discovered:

"Adding one thing to another to discover the scheme of things—
28 while I was still searching
but not finding—
I found one ⌞upright⌟ man among a thousand,
but not one ⌞upright⌟ woman among them all.
29This only have I found:
God made mankind upright,
but men have gone in search of many schemes."

8 Who is like the wise man?
Who knows the explanation of things?
Wisdom brightens a man's face
and changes its hard appearance.

Obey the King

2Obey the king's command, I say, because you took an oath before
God. 3Do not be in a hurry to leave the king's presence. Do not stand

[a]27 Or *leader of the assembly*

an excuse or an accusation? What light does verse 20 shed on verse 19? **4.** What is the danger in paying attention to gossip or hearsay (v. 21)? What theme unites verses 19–22? **5.** In verses 23 and 25, what are the Teacher's goals? How do they differ? What does he conclude about these goals? What is meant by "the scheme of things" (vv. 25,27)? **6.** How do the two stories about "a woman" (vv. 26,28–29) differ? What is the basis for his pessimism: Sampling of "a thousand" wives (v. 28; 1 Kin. 11:3)? Experience with human nature (v. 20)? Revealed truth of creation and the fall (v. 29)? **7.** Is the "search of many schemes" (v. 29) our fault or our fate? Why? **8.** In light of verse 24, how is 8:1 best understood? What is the advantage of wisdom in this verse?

APPLY 1. When do you wish you hadn't "paid attention to every word people say" (v. 21)? How can paying attention to God's Word help you put the words of people in proper perspective? **2.** Do you have a harder time trusting men or women (v. 28)? How can God's Word help you get past gender-based conflict (Gal. 3:28)?

OPEN 1. Who was the first "bully" you stood up against? With what results? **2.** When you hear the phrase "the good die young," whom do you think of? At such times, are you: Sorrowful? Angry? Disgusted? Disillusioned?

STUDY 1. What reasons are given for obedience in verses 2–5? How will the "wise heart" know "the proper time and procedure" (vv.

7:23–24 Wisdom is also limited: It is unattainable and incapable of rightly interpreting the past. Verse 24 reminds us that whatever happens lies beyond what people can fathom.

7:26 Wickedness is personified here as a woman. Falling into folly is a fate worse than death. Only those who please God are able to escape her clutches.

7:29 God is not to blame for troubles on earth. God created humans perfectly, but we chose to disobey. Adam was the first to disobey God (Rom. 3:23; 5:12).

5–6; 3:1–15)? **2.** Who would you substitute for "no man" in verses 7–8? In every sentence? **3.** Who seems to be the subject in verses 9–10? How does the "lording it over" in verse 9 contrast to having "power over" in verse 8? **4.** What is the problem in verse 11, and who is to blame for it? In verses 12–13, what injustice does the Teacher see? In what ways will it "go better" for the God-fearer (vv. 12–13)? Why? **5.** How is the injustice depicted in verse 14 meaningless? How does verse 15 strike you: Realistic? Sarcastic? Cop-out? Joyful? What is the link between verses 14 and 15? **6.** What is the difference between seeing "all that God has done" and grasping "what goes on" (v. 17)? What advice is implied in the Teacher's realization (vv. 16–17)?

APPLY 1. What sort of injustices (personal, family, global) are most likely to arouse you to act? Where do you draw the line? **2.** How does your search for answers to life's problems affect your relationship with God? How easy is it for you to trust him when the answers are unattainable? What can be done to develop such trust?

OPEN 1. Everyone knows the phrase, "You can't take it with you." If you could, what one exception to this rule would you like, when your time comes? **2.** What oaths or vows have you ever taken (scouts, marriage, secrecy, etc.)? How easy is it for you to keep them?

up for a bad cause, for he will do whatever he pleases. 4Since a king's
word is supreme, who can say to him, "What are you doing?"

5Whoever obeys his command will come to no harm,
and the wise heart will know the proper time and procedure.
6For there is a proper time and procedure for every matter,
though a man's misery weighs heavily upon him.

7Since no man knows the future,
who can tell him what is to come?
8No man has power over the wind to contain it[a];
so no one has power over the day of his death.
As no one is discharged in time of war,
so wickedness will not release those who practice it.

9All this I saw, as I applied my mind to everything done under the
sun. There is a time when a man lords it over others to his own[b] hurt.
10Then too, I saw the wicked buried—those who used to come and go
from the holy place and receive praise[c] in the city where they did this.
This too is meaningless.

11When the sentence for a crime is not quickly carried out, the
hearts of the people are filled with schemes to do wrong. 12Although
a wicked man commits a hundred crimes and still lives a long time, I
know that it will go better with God-fearing men, who are reverent
before God. 13Yet because the wicked do not fear God, it will not go
well with them, and their days will not lengthen like a shadow.

14There is something else meaningless that occurs on earth: righteous men who get what the wicked deserve, and wicked men who
get what the righteous deserve. This too, I say, is meaningless. 15So I
commend the enjoyment of life, because nothing is better for a man
under the sun than to eat and drink and be glad. Then joy will accompany him in his work all the days of the life God has given him
under the sun.

16When I applied my mind to know wisdom and to observe man's
labor on earth—his eyes not seeing sleep day or night— 17then I saw
all that God has done. No one can comprehend what goes on under
the sun. Despite all his efforts to search it out, man cannot discover
its meaning. Even if a wise man claims he knows, he cannot really
comprehend it.

A Common Destiny for All

9 So I reflected on all this and concluded that the righteous and
the wise and what they do are in God's hands, but no man
knows whether love or hate awaits him. 2All share a common desti-

[a]8 *Or over his spirit to retain it* [b]9 Or *to their* [c]10 Some Hebrew manuscripts and Septuagint (Aquila); most Hebrew manuscripts *and are forgotten*

8:10–14 The writer poses a problem and then offers a solution. The problem (vv. 10–11) is that wicked people are *often praised* and punishment is often delayed. The solution (vv. 12–13) is that in the end wickedness will be punished and those who fear God will be saved.

8:15 Here we are encouraged to "eat, drink and be glad." This is not a license for thoughtless hedonism but encouragement for humbly enjoying the life God has given us, whatever it holds.

8:17 No one can comprehend what goes on under the sun. God allows us to know a little about his will but keeps other things from us (Deut. 29:29).

9:2 All share a common destiny. Through a series of opposites, we see that all people share the common destiny of death. The playing field is level—all die no matter how privileged or oppressed they are on earth.

ny—the righteous and the wicked, the good and the bad,[a] the clean
and the unclean, those who offer sacrifices and those who do not.

As it is with the good man,
so with the sinner;
as it is with those who take oaths,
so with those who are afraid to take them.

3This is the evil in everything that happens under the sun: The
same destiny overtakes all. The hearts of men, moreover, are full of
evil and there is madness in their hearts while they live, and afterward they join the dead. 4Anyone who is among the living has
hope[b]—even a live dog is better off than a dead lion!

5For the living know that they will die,
but the dead know nothing;
they have no further reward,
and even the memory of them is forgotten.
6Their love, their hate
and their jealousy have long since vanished;
never again will they have a part
in anything that happens under the sun.

7Go, eat your food with gladness, and drink your wine with a joyful
heart, for it is now that God favors what you do. 8Always be clothed in
white, and always anoint your head with oil. 9Enjoy life with your
wife, whom you love, all the days of this meaningless life that God
has given you under the sun— all your meaningless days. For this is
your lot in life and in your toilsome labor under the sun. 10Whatever
your hand finds to do, do it with all your might, for in the grave,[c]
where you are going, there is neither working nor planning nor
knowledge nor wisdom.

11I have seen something else under the sun:

The race is not to the swift
or the battle to the strong,
nor does food come to the wise
or wealth to the brilliant
or favor to the learned;
but time and chance happen to them all.

12Moreover, no man knows when his hour will come:

As fish are caught in a cruel net,
or birds are taken in a snare,
so men are trapped by evil times
that fall unexpectedly upon them.

Wisdom Better Than Folly

13I also saw under the sun this example of wisdom that greatly impressed me: 14There was once a small city with only a few people in it.

[a]2 Septuagint (Aquila), Vulgate and Syriac; Hebrew does not have *and the bad.* [b]4 Or *What then is to be chosen? With all who live, there is hope* [c]10 Hebrew *Sheol*

STUDY 1. What does the Teacher conclude about human destiny (vv. 1–2)? What people "take oaths" and who are "afraid to" (v. 2)? **2.** What theme unifies verses 3–6? How is death described here? In this context, what is the "madness in their hearts" (v. 3): Evil? Craziness? Aliveness? Hope? Love? Hate? Jealousy? **3.** To whom is this madness ascribed? In this context, are you "mad"? **4.** To what actions does the Teacher exhort us in verses 7–10? To what attitude? What motivation does he suggest for such a lifestyle? What does it mean to be "clothed in white" (v. 8)? **5.** What explanation is offered for the apparent contradictions in verse 11? How does this relate to the "evil times" in verse 12?

APPLY 1. Do you feel you deserve a reward in life for your righteousness? Or would a kick-in-the-pants be more appropriate? What trophy, prize or punishment do you feel you deserve? **2.** In what ways do you feel you receive the benefits of faith in this life? Are there benefits that you have ignored or rejected? Why? What are they? **3.** Given the unexpected nature of life (vv. 11–12), how do you prepare yourself for such disruptions? How can you best help others through them?

OPEN 1. In games of strategy, how would you rate yourself: Ruthless? Reluctant? First one out? **2.** If you could learn any instrument, what would it be? What song would you like to play on it?

9:11 Two other things all people have in common are the limitations of time and chance. Because we have no ultimate control over the events of our lives, good things do not always happen to those we think deserve it.

3. What was the last time you got lost? Where were you going? Did you ever get there?

STUDY 1. The Teacher derives two morals from the example story in 9:13–16. What are they? **2.** How does the first pair of proverbs (9:17–18) correspond to the preceding example story? What themes are similar? Do they agree with, or take issue with, the story? Why doesn't wisdom win out? **3.** What two things are contrasted in 10:1–3? What is the main point here? **4.** In this context, what's wrong with leaving your post (10:3–5)? **5.** What is the "evil" in 10:5–7? Where is it found? **6.** In 10:6–11, where do you see poetic justice? Random events? Cause and effect? Dry humor? How does the "skill" in 10:10 relate to wisdom? **7.** What topic is addressed in 10:12–15? What progression is evident in 10:12–14? How does the contention in 10:14 add to the problem of the fool? What hope, if any, is there for the lost fool?

APPLY 1. How does someone's social position affect your respect for his opinions? In what ways could that person's "wisdom" help you? **2.** How "skilled" are you in the various areas of life (family, friendships, work, ministry)? In which areas do you need to develop greater skills? How can this best be done? How can your group help in this? **3.** How has something foolish you said affected others and yourself? To whom do you need to apologize because of it (no names)? What practical steps can you take to avoid such "foolish" conversation?

And a powerful king came against it, surrounded it and built huge
siegeworks against it. 15 Now there lived in that city a man poor but
wise, and he saved the city by his wisdom. But nobody remembered
that poor man. 16 So I said, "Wisdom is better than strength." But the
poor man's wisdom is despised, and his words are no longer heeded.

17 The quiet words of the wise are more to be heeded
than the shouts of a ruler of fools.
18 Wisdom is better than weapons of war,
but one sinner destroys much good.

10 As dead flies give perfume a bad smell,
so a little folly outweighs wisdom and honor.
2 The heart of the wise inclines to the right,
but the heart of the fool to the left.
3 Even as he walks along the road,
the fool lacks sense
and shows everyone how stupid he is.
4 If a ruler's anger rises against you,
do not leave your post;
calmness can lay great errors to rest.

5 There is an evil I have seen under the sun,
the sort of error that arises from a ruler:
6 Fools are put in many high positions,
while the rich occupy the low ones.
7 I have seen slaves on horseback,
while princes go on foot like slaves.
8 Whoever digs a pit may fall into it;
whoever breaks through a wall may be bitten by a snake.
9 Whoever quarries stones may be injured by them;
whoever splits logs may be endangered by them.

10 If the ax is dull
and its edge unsharpened,
more strength is needed
but skill will bring success.

11 If a snake bites before it is charmed,
there is no profit for the charmer.

12 Words from a wise man's mouth are gracious,
but a fool is consumed by his own lips.
13 At the beginning his words are folly;
at the end they are wicked madness—
14 and the fool multiplies words.

No one knows what is coming—
who can tell him what will happen after him?

15 A fool's work wearies him;
he does not know the way to town.

10:1 This catalog of proverbs serves two functions: praise of wisdom through practical examples, and glimpses of the folly of life under the sun.

10:2 inclines to the right. The right may refer to the right hand, the place of protection, or maybe simply a simple contrast between the way of good and the way of evil.

10:12–14 Here the writer reminds us of the importance of being wise in our choice of words. The book of James gives us instructions in taming our tongues.

[16]Woe to you, O land whose king was a servant[a]
and whose princes feast in the morning.
[17]Blessed are you, O land whose king is of noble birth
and whose princes eat at a proper time—
for strength and not for drunkenness.

[18]If a man is lazy, the rafters sag;
if his hands are idle, the house leaks.

[19]A feast is made for laughter,
and wine makes life merry,
but money is the answer for everything.

[20]Do not revile the king even in your thoughts,
or curse the rich in your bedroom,
because a bird of the air may carry your words,
and a bird on the wing may report what you say.

Bread Upon the Waters

11 Cast your bread upon the waters,
for after many days you will find it again.
[2]Give portions to seven, yes to eight,
for you do not know what disaster may come upon the land.

[3]If clouds are full of water,
they pour rain upon the earth.
Whether a tree falls to the south or to the north,
in the place where it falls, there will it lie.
[4]Whoever watches the wind will not plant;
whoever looks at the clouds will not reap.

[5]As you do not know the path of the wind,
or how the body is formed[b] in a mother's womb,
so you cannot understand the work of God,
the Maker of all things.

[6]Sow your seed in the morning,
and at evening let not your hands be idle,
for you do not know which will succeed,
whether this or that,
or whether both will do equally well.

Remember Your Creator While Young

[7]Light is sweet,
and it pleases the eyes to see the sun.

[a]16 Or *king is a child* [b]5 Or *know how life* (or *the spirit*) */ enters the body being formed*

OPEN Ever quit a job due to the boss? What made the boss hard to work for?

STUDY 1. What makes a leader good or bad (vv. 16–17)? **2.** What do verses 18–19 say about government? How is money the "answer" (v. 19)? **3.** Why should we not revile those in power?

APPLY 1. As a leader, how conscientious are you? How generous? **2.** What is your duty to those over you? Under you?

OPEN What is the worst investment (time, money, etc.) you ever made? Why?

STUDY 1. What does "bread" symbolize? What happens when you "cast your bread" (v. 1)? How will the giving of "portions" help in a time of disaster (v. 2)? **2.** What do the matter-of-fact observations in verse 3 imply? **3.** Why are those who just "watch" so unproductive and ignorant (vv. 4–5)? **4.** How do the observations in verses 3–5 lead to the concluding advice (v. 6)? How does this relate to the advice in verse 1?

APPLY 1. When have you spent too much time "watching the winds" and "looking at clouds" (analyzing), when you should have been "planting" (acting)? **2.** What "seed" is God calling you to sow right now?

OPEN 1. Who was the wildest classmate when you were growing up? What has happened to that person? **2.** As you grow older, which do you want to hold on to most: Youthful body? Youthful mind?

10:19 money ... everything. This statement is part of a portrait (vv. 18–20) of undisciplined, incompetent and lazy leaders who think money can satisfy by providing the means to feast and drink. We are warned not to curse these misguided leaders, even in our thoughts.

11:1–6 Since many circumstances are beyond our control, we need practical advice about ordering our daily lives. This section is set up in pairs of verses: 1–2 deal with how to handle wealth; 3–4 urge us to work diligently and not be paralyzed by fate; and 5–6 remind that God's ways transcend human comprehension. We should work decisively and diligently in the face of our questions and dilemmas.

11:1 bread upon the waters. Be generous because in giving away we receive much more than we give.

11:2 portions to seven. Since wealth is meaningless and uncertain, be generous with money. Since disaster is always possible, make investments in several different areas. Don't put all your eggs in one basket.

Youthful heart? **3.** What do you imagine you'll be like at age 100?

STUDY 1. What are "the days of darkness" (11:8) and why does the Teacher want us to "remember" them? What light do the other exhortations to "remember" (12:1,6) shed on this? **2.** What does the Teacher encourage in 11:9–10? What qualifies the joy we experience? How are youth and vigor "meaningless"? **3.** What does the long sentence in 12:1–5 describe? What sort of description is this: Positive, negative or neutral? Realistic or imaginary? Vain regrets or pipe dreams? **4.** What event is described in 12:5–7? Is this akin to a believer's hope of eternal life? Or is he speaking merely of finality? Which fits the book as a whole? **5.** In 12:8 the motto is repeated (1:2). What does this signal? What does it reveal about any change of perspective by the Teacher?

APPLY 1. How much do "eternal concerns" affect your daily decisions? Which areas of your life are least influenced by your faith in God? Which are most? **2.** How free do you feel to "be happy" and enjoy life? **3.** How can you "remember your Creator in the days of your youth"? How can you help children to do so?

8 However many years a man may live,
let him enjoy them all.
But let him remember the days of darkness,
for they will be many.
Everything to come is meaningless.

9 Be happy, young man, while you are young,
and let your heart give you joy in the days of your youth.
Follow the ways of your heart
and whatever your eyes see,
but know that for all these things
God will bring you to judgment.
10 So then, banish anxiety from your heart
and cast off the troubles of your body,
for youth and vigor are meaningless.

12 Remember your Creator
in the days of your youth,
before the days of trouble come
and the years approach when you will say,
"I find no pleasure in them"—
2 before the sun and the light
and the moon and the stars grow dark,
and the clouds return after the rain;
3 when the keepers of the house tremble,
and the strong men stoop,
when the grinders cease because they are few,
and those looking through the windows grow dim;
4 when the doors to the street are closed
and the sound of grinding fades;
when men rise up at the sound of birds,
but all their songs grow faint;
5 when men are afraid of heights
and of dangers in the streets;
when the almond tree blossoms
and the grasshopper drags himself along
and desire no longer is stirred.
Then man goes to his eternal home
and mourners go about the streets.

6 Remember him—before the silver cord is severed,
or the golden bowl is broken;
before the pitcher is shattered at the spring,

11:8 days of darkness. Darkness is a metaphor for death. The days of darkness will be eternal.

11:9 Young people are urged to do and enjoy whatever their hearts desire, but to temper their desires with an awareness of God's judgment.

12:1–8 The writer uses a variety of images to describe old age.

12:2 Darkness and clouds are metaphors for weakening eyesight.

12:3–4 Age is compared to a disintegrating house. The writer describes the trembling hands, stooping shoulders, lost teeth, poor eyesight, loss of hearing, sleeplessness and confused speech of the elderly.

12:5 Old people increasingly fear going out, partly because their waning vigor and feebleness make movement dangerous. **almond tree blossoms.** Refers to gray hair. **grasshopper drags himself along.** People previously as agile as grasshoppers become stiff and frail in old age. **desire no longer is stirred.** Sex eventually carries no more appeal. **eternal home.** This refers to the grave, not to the afterlife.

12:6 Remember God before your life is broken and it comes to an end, like the household objects described in this verse.

or the wheel broken at the well,
[7]and the dust returns to the ground it came from,
and the spirit returns to God who gave it.

[8]"Meaningless! Meaningless!" says the Teacher.[a]
"Everything is meaningless!"

The Conclusion of the Matter

[9]Not only was the Teacher wise, but also he imparted knowledge to
the people. He pondered and searched out and set in order many
proverbs. [10]The Teacher searched to find just the right words, and
what he wrote was upright and true.

[11]The words of the wise are like goads, their collected sayings like
firmly embedded nails—given by one Shepherd. [12]Be warned, my
son, of anything in addition to them.

Of making many books there is no end, and much study wearies the body.

[13]Now all has been heard;
here is the conclusion of the matter:
Fear God and keep his commandments,
for this is the whole ⌊duty⌋ of man.
[14]For God will bring every deed into judgment,
including every hidden thing,
whether it is good or evil.

[a]8 *Or the leader of the assembly;* also in verses 9 and 10

OPEN Name one of the best books you ever read. Why did you enjoy it? What is one of the worst?

STUDY **1.** Who is speaking in verses 9–14? **2.** How is the Teacher described (vv. 9–10)? What work has he done? **3.** Goads and nails create pain. How were the sayings of Ecclesiastes like that? **4.** What do verses 11–12 warn against? Who is the "Shepherd" in verse 11? **5.** How does the speaker summarize his interpretation of the book (vv. 13–14)? How does this compare to the teachings in the rest of the book?

APPLY **1.** When has wisdom come to you like a "goad," bringing pain? **2.** How does it affect your perspective to know that the source of the "goad" is a loving Shepherd?

12:8 The writer repeats the opening theme of the book. Life apart from God lacks meaning.

12:9–10 The writer has sought true wisdom and written it down in delightful words.

12:11–12 given by one Shepherd. The writer affirms that Scripture, unlike any other book, is full of wisdom. Earthly wisdom, through the study of many books, is tiring. But the Bible is full of spiritual wisdom and is not lacking anything necessary for gaining wisdom.

12:13–14 The writer summarizes what he has found to be the secret of fulfillment and true wisdom: reverence and obedience to God. Proverbs tells us this is our responsibility in light of our accountability to God for everything we do (3:17; 8:12–13; 11:9).

Song of Songs

Personal Reading	Group Study Topic and Reading	
1:1–2:7	"The Bud of Romance"	1:1–2:7
2:8–3:5	"The Blossom of Courtship"	2:8–3:5
3:6–11	"The Wedding Song"	3:6–11
4:1–5:1	"Some Enchanted Evening"	4:1–5:1
5:2–6:3	"The Absence"	5:2–6:3
6:4–7:9a	"The Return of Love"	6:4–7:9a
7:9b–8:14	"A Romp in the Woods"	7:9b–8:14

Author. The Song of Songs itself acknowledges Solomon as the author.

Date. Solomon probably wrote this book during his reign. If so, it was written between 971–931 B.C. He probably wrote this poem as a young man.

Purpose. On the surface, it appears that Solomon was prompted to write this poem purely for the glory of love. It beautifully celebrates the love between a man and a woman. Throughout the ages, though, scholars and interpreters have disagreed on the actual purpose of the poem. Some have defined the love described in Song of Songs as purely spiritual, allegorical for God's love for humanity, or allegorical for love between Christ and the church. Others have argued that the love in Song of Songs is simply carnal and that the book does not belong in the Bible. The book itself gives no basis to believe that Solomon's purpose in writing was any other than to express and expound on his current experience.

Historical Background. While King David established a royal court at Jerusalem, it was King Solomon who expanded it. The court was much like that of other rulers of the tenth century B.C. Luxury abounded, even in the size of the palace and its furnishings. The court itself was a busy place, filled with scurrying courtiers, retainers and members of the royal household, including concubines. Literature appears to have flourished in that court. The books of Proverbs and Ecclesiastes would have been written in that setting, and the opulence surrounding Solomon had a profound influence on each book. It had an impact on the Song of Songs as well.

Poetry and songs held places of importance in royal courts throughout history. Poets and songwriters were often the entertainers of the day. Love poetry has always been a favorite, and for the most part, the Song of Songs falls into that historical, literary category. The imagery and themes of the book are consistent with the other wisdom literature of the age, including Solomon's other writings, especially Proverbs. Likewise, the book has similarities to other love songs from ancient Babylon and Egypt.

Form. The Song of Songs is a poem, but it is a form of poetry unfamiliar to us today. The essence of this poetry is found not in its rhyme scheme but in its imagery. The text jumps from character to character. The voices are those of the king, his beloved, and a chorus that functions as response to the couple in love. At times, it can get a little confusing who is talking to whom. (Some who have studied this poem even wonder if there is actually a fourth speaker—a shepherd to whom the woman was betrothed when Solomon met her.) Like other poems of its day, the Song of Songs uses images from everyday life to describe the affection the writer feels toward the one he loves.

1 Solomon's Song of Songs.

Beloved[a]

²Let him kiss me with the kisses of his mouth—
for your love is more delightful than wine.
³Pleasing is the fragrance of your perfumes;
your name is like perfume poured out.
No wonder the maidens love you!
⁴Take me away with you—let us hurry!
Let the king bring me into his chambers.

Friends

We rejoice and delight in you[b];
we will praise your love more than wine.

Beloved

How right they are to adore you!

⁵Dark am I, yet lovely,
O daughters of Jerusalem,
dark like the tents of Kedar,
like the tent curtains of Solomon.[c]
⁶Do not stare at me because I am dark,
because I am darkened by the sun.
My mother's sons were angry with me
and made me take care of the vineyards;
my own vineyard I have neglected.
⁷Tell me, you whom I love, where you graze your flock
and where you rest your sheep at midday.
Why should I be like a veiled woman
beside the flocks of your friends?

[a]Primarily on the basis of the gender of the Hebrew pronouns used, male and female speakers are indicated in the margins by the captions *Lover* and *Beloved* respectively. The words of others are marked *Friends*. In some instances the divisions and their captions are debatable. [b]4 The Hebrew is masculine singular. [c]5 Or *Salma*

OPEN 1. When did you get interested in the opposite sex? **2.** How did you meet your spouse?

STUDY Here are three considerations for leaders of groups studying Song of Songs for a course on sexual intimacy in marriage: (1) Ask each couple to bring to the next session a few snapshots—of their dating days, wedding, honeymoon, etc.; (2) Ask for volunteers to read the different parts. Be aware of embarrassing words; (3) Be sensitive to the group's preference to discuss some questions only with their spouses. **1.** Why do you think God included a book about sex in the Bible: It's illustrative of God's love? God wanted to affirm the beauty of human sexual love? The Bible speaks to all areas of life? Other? **2.** What portrayal of the Lover most impresses you: He's a good lover? He smells good? He's popular with women? He's loved by the Beloved? Other? **3.** What impression do you get of the Beloved: She's swept off her feet? She's self-conscious? She's tanned? She's beautiful? **4.** How did your parents handle the subject of sex: They avoided the subject? They stumbled their way through the subject with me? They were open and helpful? They left it to the school? Other?

APPLY 1. What first struck you about your future mate: Striking good looks? Dashing wit? Brilliant mind? Shared values? Similar interests? Great personality? Other?

1:1 Solomon's Song of Songs. The title of this book, attributed to Solomon the king, means the "greatest song," in the same vein as "King of kings" or "Holy of Holies." Solomon wrote more than 1,000 songs (1 Kin. 4:32).

1:2 him ... his. Solomon, the lover, is the reference here. **love.** In Hebrew the noun (in the plural denoting intensity) refers to divinely blessed sexual love. Delight is experienced in various physical expressions of the love (v. 4; 4:10; 7:12; Prov. 7:18; Ezek. 16:8). **your love is more delightful than wine.** This is echoed by the chorus in verse 4. The lover returns the compliment in 4:10.

1:3 your name is like perfume. Even the mention of the lover's name brings a pleasing fragrance to the air. The aroma of his personality and reputation attracts numerous women. In Hebrew, "name" and "perfume" sound similar. **love.** Unlike the word used in verse 2, this Hebrew word refers to romantic feelings.

1:5 Dark am I. Because of her work outside in the vineyard, the beloved's skin has been deeply tanned by the sun (v. 6), a condition which was not considered attractive because it revealed her common background, unlike the maidens of the court, who were pampered and pale. **tent curtains.** These were usually woven with the dark hair of goats.

1:6 my own vineyard. She admits neglecting her own body because of the work she had done (2:15; 8:12). Even so, her beauty had captivated Solomon. A vineyard is the source of wine, to which love's delights are compared (v. 2). She provides her lover with precious fruits (4:12–16).

1:7 Tell me . . . where you graze your flock. Her lover, the king, is likened to a shepherd, and she herself is described as a shepherdess in verse 8. **like a veiled woman.** Prostitutes of the time wore veils (Gen. 38:14,15). The beloved fears other shepherds would mistake her for a prostitute if she were to pursue her lover among his flocks. This poetic language may refer to her frustration regarding Solomon's time-consuming responsibilities as a head of state and his dealings with other officials.

2. What would you call sex: A gift from God? A gift I give my spouse? A celebration of love? Overemphasized? The glue of a marriage? None of your business? **3.** What brought you to this group: My spouse brought me? This is my favorite subject? I want to know more of what the Bible says about sex? Other? **4.** How do you feel about discussing sexual intimacy in this group?

OPEN **1.** What is something you appreciate about your spouse? **2.** What would you say is your spouse's best feature?

STUDY Leaders should be sensitive to the group's preference to discuss some questions only with their spouses. **1.** In the next series of snapshots (1:15–2:3), the scene shifts from the palace to a quiet walk and talk in the woods. What do you make of their exchange of compliments? What makes such dialogue possible? How has her self-image changed from 1:6? Is their love blinding or enabling them to see truly? Why? **2.** Back at the palace (2:4–7), what tells you the beloved woman is feeling more and more secure in her man's love? What does the banner (used to signal large troop movements in battle) signify here? What does she

Friends

8 If you do not know, most beautiful of women,
follow the tracks of the sheep
and graze your young goats
by the tents of the shepherds.

Lover

9 I liken you, my darling, to a mare
harnessed to one of the chariots of Pharaoh.
10 Your cheeks are beautiful with earrings,
your neck with strings of jewels.
11 We will make you earrings of gold,
studded with silver.

Beloved

12 While the king was at his table,
my perfume spread its fragrance.
13 My lover is to me a sachet of myrrh
resting between my breasts.
14 My lover is to me a cluster of henna blossoms
from the vineyards of En Gedi.

Lover

15 How beautiful you are, my darling!
Oh, how beautiful!
Your eyes are doves.

Beloved

16 How handsome you are, my lover!
Oh, how charming!
And our bed is verdant.

Lover

17 The beams of our house are cedars;
our rafters are firs.

Beloved[a]

2 I am a rose[b] of Sharon,
a lily of the valleys.

[a]1 Or *Lover* [b]1 Possibly a member of the crocus family

1:8 follow ... graze ... by the tents of the shepherds. Her friends encourage the beloved to seek her lover among the shepherds in the fields, rather than pine away in the palace.

1:9 my darling, to a mare. A term of endearment used only of the beloved. This was a compliment, referring to her grace and strength of beauty. **harnessed to one of the chariots of Pharaoh.** Among the many stallions of the Egyptian charioteers, a mare would certainly stand out—in the same way as the beloved's beauty attracts attention. Solomon apparently purchased horses from Egypt (1 Kin. 10:28).

1:13 sachet of myrrh. Balsam trees that grew in Arabia, Ethiopia and India exuded from their bark an aromatic sap kept in a small pouch around a woman's neck for use as a perfume (Est. 2:12; Prov. 7:17). Royal wedding clothes were also perfumed with myrrh (Ps. 45:8). Of course, myrrh was one of the gifts the magi brought to Jesus—one fit for a king (Matt. 2:2,11). And it was one of the aromatic ingredients in anointing oil (Ex. 30:23).

1:15 Your eyes are doves. A reference to her beauty and innocence (4:1; 5:12).

2:1–2 a lily ... among thorns. Referring to the beloved's self-description in verse 1, the lover compares her favorably to the court maidens.

Lover

[2] Like a lily among thorns
is my darling among the maidens.

Beloved

[3] Like an apple tree among the trees of the forest
is my lover among the young men.
I delight to sit in his shade,
and his fruit is sweet to my taste.
[4] He has taken me to the banquet hall,
and his banner over me is love.
[5] Strengthen me with raisins,
refresh me with apples,
for I am faint with love.
[6] His left arm is under my head,
and his right arm embraces me.
[7] Daughters of Jerusalem, I charge you
by the gazelles and by the does of the field:
Do not arouse or awaken love
until it so desires.

[8] Listen! My lover!
Look! Here he comes,
leaping across the mountains,
bounding over the hills.
[9] My lover is like a gazelle or a young stag.
Look! There he stands behind our wall,
gazing through the windows,
peering through the lattice.
[10] My lover spoke and said to me,
"Arise, my darling,
my beautiful one, and come with me.
[11] See! The winter is past;
the rains are over and gone.
[12] Flowers appear on the earth;
the season of singing has come,
the cooing of doves
is heard in our land.
[13] The fig tree forms its early fruit;
the blossoming vines spread their fragrance.
Arise, come, my darling;
my beautiful one, come with me."

do with her aroused feelings? **3.** Which compliment do you like best in this passage: "How beautiful you are, my darling!" (1:15)? "Your eyes are doves" (1:15)? "How handsome you are, my lover!" (1:16)? "My lover is like a gazelle" (2:9)? Other? **4.** The Lover and Beloved obviously felt attracted to each other. Which of the following does your spouse most often do? Which would you like him to do more often: Tells me how nice I look? Brings me romantic gifts? Brags about me to others? Displays affection for me? Writes me love notes or cards? Other?

APPLY 1. What compliments do you most like to receive from your spouse? **2.** How would you characterize you and your spouse's communication about sex: What communication? We talk when there's a problem? Communicating about sex is an important part of our love life? Other? **3.** This couple was aware of the "little foxes" (2:15) that can ruin love. What do you think are the most common problems that couples face today in the area of sexual intimacy: Bad experiences in the past? False expectations? Physical problems? Difficulty talking about sex? Other? **4.** How can this group support you in prayer now and in the coming week?

2:4 banner. The king boldly displays his love for all to see, like the large flag identifying military forces. Even today Jewish weddings are held under a banner or covering. The banner imagery is repeated in 6:4 as a battle flag (Num. 2:2; Ps. 20:5).

2:5–6 A poetic description of joyful, marital sexual love. **raisins ... apples.** Symbols of sexual passion in the ancient Near East.

2:7 This refrain is repeated (3:5; 5:8; 8:4) by the beloved while describing her physical pleasure with the king. **gazelles ... does.** These beautiful and graceful animals serve as witnesses to the beloved's charge—a picture that fits well with the writer's many imaginative references to nature in the Song. **until it so desires.** The beloved has learned a lesson from her love life: Don't force love or manipulate it. Instead, avoid premarital physical relations and let love be open and spontaneous at its own pace.

2:11–13 Spring is when a young person's thoughts turn to love, and here the first signs of spring are evident (6:11; 7:12).

Lover

14 My dove in the clefts of the rock,
in the hiding places on the mountainside,
show me your face,
let me hear your voice;
for your voice is sweet,
and your face is lovely.
15 Catch for us the foxes,
the little foxes
that ruin the vineyards,
our vineyards that are in bloom.

Beloved

16 My lover is mine and I am his;
he browses among the lilies.
17 Until the day breaks
and the shadows flee,
turn, my lover,
and be like a gazelle
or like a young stag
on the rugged hills.[a]

3 All night long on my bed
I looked for the one my heart loves;
I looked for him but did not find him.
2 I will get up now and go about the city,
through its streets and squares;
I will search for the one my heart loves.
So I looked for him but did not find him.
3 The watchmen found me
as they made their rounds in the city.
"Have you seen the one my heart loves?"
4 Scarcely had I passed them
when I found the one my heart loves.
I held him and would not let him go
till I had brought him to my mother's house,
to the room of the one who conceived me.
5 Daughters of Jerusalem, I charge you
by the gazelles and by the does of the field:
Do not arouse or awaken love
until it so desires.

6 Who is this coming up from the desert

[a]17 Or *the hills of Bether*

OPEN 1. How often are you and your spouse apart? **2.** What's the longest you've ever been apart from your spouse?

STUDY Leaders should be sensitive to the group's preference to discuss some questions only with their spouses. **1.** How does the bride react when she and her lover are apart: Afraid? Unable to sleep? Insecure? Other? **2.** What did the woman mean in 3:5 when she said, "Do not arouse or awaken love until it so desires": Don't try to make love happen—be patient until you know it's right? Don't put yourself in a compromising position? Love and desire go together? Keep yourself sexually pure until married? Other? **3.** How are sexual desire and self-restraint healthy and beneficial to a married couple growing in love: Lack of desire kills romance? Abstinence makes the heart grow fonder? Self-control for the sake of your spouse is an important part of sexuality? I don't see that self-restraint is particularly beneficial? Other?

APPLY 1. In terms of romance, what do you value most: Flowers (or other gifts)? Special dates? Verbal affection? Physical affection? Quality time together? Thoughtful acts of service? Open communication? Other? **2.** When you were first married, how would you compare your relationship to the couple's in Song of Songs: Ours was every bit as

2:15 This verse may more likely have been spoken by the beloved. **vineyards.** This picture language (1:6) may refer to the couple's physical beauty, which must be protected from anything that might ruin it.

2:16 My lover is mine. This sentiment is repeated in 6:3 and 7:10, indicating a close, strong relationship.

3:1 All night long on my bed. This section recounts a dream that occurred before the marriage. A night without her lover leaves the beloved lonely, her heart preoccupied with finding him—perhaps fearful about the realities of marriage to a king.

3:5 Do not arouse or awaken love. Before the marriage, the beloved warns against premarital relations (2:7).

3:6–11 This chorus may have been spoken by the friends (8:5). In this case, they could be describing the wedding procession of the king and his bride as they neared the city.

like a column of smoke,
perfumed with myrrh and incense
made from all the spices of the merchant?
7 Look! It is Solomon's carriage,
escorted by sixty warriors,
the noblest of Israel,
8 all of them wearing the sword,
all experienced in battle,
each with his sword at his side,
prepared for the terrors of the night.
9 King Solomon made for himself the carriage;
he made it of wood from Lebanon.
10 Its posts he made of silver,
its base of gold.
Its seat was upholstered with purple,
its interior lovingly inlaid
by[a] the daughters of Jerusalem.
11 Come out, you daughters of Zion,
and look at King Solomon wearing the crown,
the crown with which his mother crowned him
on the day of his wedding,
the day his heart rejoiced.

Lover

4 How beautiful you are, my darling!
Oh, how beautiful!
Your eyes behind your veil are doves.
Your hair is like a flock of goats
descending from Mount Gilead.
2 Your teeth are like a flock of sheep just shorn,
coming up from the washing.
Each has its twin;
not one of them is alone.
3 Your lips are like a scarlet ribbon;
your mouth is lovely.
Your temples behind your veil
are like the halves of a pomegranate.
4 Your neck is like the tower of David,
built with elegance[b];
on it hang a thousand shields,
all of them shields of warriors.
5 Your two breasts are like two fawns,
like twin fawns of a gazelle

[a]10 *Or its inlaid interior a gift of love / from* [b]4 The meaning of the Hebrew for this word is uncertain.

romantic? Our relationship was much more subdued? Our relationship is still this way? Other? **3.** What helps keep your love alive: Dreaming together? Times apart? Having supportive friends? Private time together? Other? **4.** What positive steps can you take to continue to nurture your love life: Have a date night? Schedule time to be alone together? Get away for a romantic weekend every so often? Other?

OPEN Where did you go on your honeymoon? (Or, where would you like to go?) Why there?

STUDY 1. Assuming this section refers to the couple's wedding night, what is memorable about it (4:1–5:1)? What do you make of these compliments? Do you ever compliment someone you adore? How does your "beloved" react? **2.** The husband praises seven different aspects of his wife's beauty. What makes her beauty and personality flawless to him? In the long run, what will bring out all the wife's beauty: Praise or Criticism? Why? **3.** What effect does his intimate foreplay have on his wife? How does she reciprocate (vv. 10–11,16)? **4.** How does the king deal with her fears about marriage and thoughts of home (v. 8)? What role does such reassurance and foreplay serve in the love-making which follows? **5.** How is the extended metaphor of the garden used here? Where do you see restraint and freedom expressed? **6.** What is

3:7–10 Solomon's carriage. This may have been a beautiful, specially built sedan chair on which the beloved was carried by bearers to the wedding.

4:1 eyes behind your veil. The beloved's face may be covered by a veil, but the lover still sees the beauty underneath, as well as in her eyes. **a flock of goats descending.** Goats common in Canaan were generally black; the lover sees his beloved's dark hair cascading down.

4:2 sheep just shorn. The sheep would thus have been clean and white.

4:3 Your lips ... scarlet. Egyptian women often painted their lips, so perhaps the beloved followed their example.

4:4 Your neck is like the tower. Her neck, adorned with beautiful necklaces, was long, strong and straight.

4:5 two fawns. Fawns are young, sweet, delicate and not fully grown (8:8).

the meaning here for those who question the beauty, playfulness and joy of sex?

APPLY 1. If God's view of sex in marriage is conveyed here, then why do so many couples experience nothing like it? What does this Song have to say to a divorced person? To macho men? To prudish women? **2.** If single: How might a beautiful courtship, like the one here, better equip you for marriage? What do you learn from this passage that you might ask from God so you will have a good courtship? **3.** If married: Using the garden metaphor as it applies to love, what are you now growing: Nothing? Weeds? Desert? Annuals? Perennials? A new garden? **4.** Reflecting on the winds of change since your wedding day, what is now blowing your way: A cold northerly or warm southerly wind? Breezy or gusty? Clearing up or clouding over? Does this happen to all couples? Why do we not share it with each other? **5.** Applying this lovers' poem allegorically to Christ and the church, how does Christ's royal love for the church inspire your devotion and self-surrender? If your "garden" is barren, how can the chief Gardener restore it?

that browse among the lilies.
6 Until the day breaks
and the shadows flee,
I will go to the mountain of myrrh
and to the hill of incense.
7 All beautiful you are, my darling;
there is no flaw in you.

8 Come with me from Lebanon, my bride,
come with me from Lebanon.
Descend from the crest of Amana,
from the top of Senir, the summit of Hermon,
from the lions' dens
and the mountain haunts of the leopards.
9 You have stolen my heart, my sister, my bride;
you have stolen my heart
with one glance of your eyes,
with one jewel of your necklace.
10 How delightful is your love, my sister, my bride!
How much more pleasing is your love than wine,
and the fragrance of your perfume than any spice!
11 Your lips drop sweetness as the honeycomb, my bride;
milk and honey are under your tongue.
The fragrance of your garments is like that of Lebanon.
12 You are a garden locked up, my sister, my bride;
you are a spring enclosed, a sealed fountain.
13 Your plants are an orchard of pomegranates
with choice fruits,
with henna and nard,
14 nard and saffron,
calamus and cinnamon,
with every kind of incense tree,
with myrrh and aloes
and all the finest spices.
15 You are[a] a garden fountain,
a well of flowing water
streaming down from Lebanon.

Beloved

16 Awake, north wind,
and come, south wind!

[a]15 Or *I am* (spoken by the *Beloved*)

4:6 Until the day breaks. Their wedding night was long and passionate.

4:9 stolen my heart, my sister. As Solomon's wife she was now part of his royal family. Love poetry of the ancient Near East often had lovers call each other "brother" and "sister" (vv. 10,12; 5:1).

4:11 Your lips drop sweetness as the honeycomb. Her words of love are rich and sweet to him (Prov. 5:3; 16:24). Love's delights are often described with images of sweetness in the ancient Near East.

4:12 garden. A garden is full of beauty, refreshment and sensual delight—a beautiful description of love (v. 16; 5:1; 6:2). **locked up ... enclosed ... sealed.** References to the beloved's virginity before the wedding night, or perhaps her exclusive relationship with her lover, the king.

4:14–15 The perfumed aromas are sensual and rich, and many of them are used in anointing oil. The beloved desires the winds to blow her charming fragrances to her lover, drawing him to her.

4:16 Let my lover come into his garden. The beloved bride invites her lover to enjoy her sexual pleasures for the first time. He expresses his complete satisfaction as a result in 5:1.

Blow on my garden,
 that its fragrance may spread abroad.
Let my lover come into his garden
 and taste its choice fruits.

Lover

5 I have come into my garden, my sister, my bride;
 I have gathered my myrrh with my spice.
I have eaten my honeycomb and my honey;
 I have drunk my wine and my milk.

Friends

Eat, O friends, and drink;
 drink your fill, O lovers.

Beloved

²I slept but my heart was awake.
 Listen! My lover is knocking:
"Open to me, my sister, my darling,
 my dove, my flawless one.
My head is drenched with dew,
 my hair with the dampness of the night."
³I have taken off my robe—
 must I put it on again?
I have washed my feet—
 must I soil them again?
⁴My lover thrust his hand through the latch-opening;
 my heart began to pound for him.
⁵I arose to open for my lover,
 and my hands dripped with myrrh,
my fingers with flowing myrrh,
 on the handles of the lock.
⁶I opened for my lover,
 but my lover had left; he was gone.
 My heart sank at his departure.[a]
I looked for him but did not find him.
 I called him but he did not answer.
⁷The watchmen found me
 as they made their rounds in the city.
They beat me, they bruised me;
 they took away my cloak,
 those watchmen of the walls!
⁸O daughters of Jerusalem, I charge you—
 if you find my lover,
what will you tell him?
 Tell him I am faint with love.

[a]6 Or *heart had gone out to him when he spoke*

OPEN If married: How long did your honeymoon last: 7 days? 7 weeks? 7 years? How did you know that your honeymoon had ended and new realities had set in? Who do you know who seems to have enjoyed a perpetual honeymoon?

STUDY 1. The next significant event is either a dream or reality. What support can you find for each view (vv. 2–8)? **2.** How do you account for the wife not rushing to the door at her lover's knock (vv. 2–3): Playful? Sleepy? Lethargic? **3.** In either event, how does her lover respond (v. 6): Hurt by the rebuff? Playing hide and seek? Believes that she is asleep? Is being respectful of her desires? **4.** What impact do you suppose her run-away lover and run-in with "police" had on her (vv. 6–8): Roused her from a nightmare? Brought her back to her senses? Made her heart grow fonder? **5.** What is the spirit behind the friends' first question (v. 9): To replace her apathy with gratitude? To challenge her love? To calm their fear of love and the agony of parting? **6.** How much does he evidently mean to her, after all (vv. 10–16)? What strikes you about her sensuous desire for her "lover and friend"? **7.** If the friends' first question prepares her attitude, to what does the second question lead (6:1–3)? What paves the way for reunion with her beloved: A place to talk privately? A sense of mutual belonging? A time to make up?

5:2 I slept. This section may recount another dream. Love is always awake, aware and alive even when asleep—in much the same way as a parent sleeps with an ear on alert for a child's cry.

5:5 my hands dripped with myrrh. The beloved's hands are oiled with perfume for her lover's arrival.

APPLY 1. How would you describe the level of friendship with you and your lover? Are you your mate's *best* friend? Was your love first based in friendship, or did friendship really develop only after the fires of passion settled down? **2.** How are you ensuring that neither friendship nor love will be neglected in the future? What is the next date on the calendar for just the two of you? **3.** With your beloved, as with the two in this story, what keeps your love alive: Playful teasing? Dreaming together? Times apart? Caring friends? Private reunion times? **4.** What would a reminder list of his or her attributes do for your relationship? What three things about your mate do you most appreciate? Write them down and exchange lists. **5.** Rank in order the following needs for yourself and your mate: Admiration, affection, attractive spouse, honesty and trust, family commitment, open conversation, domestic support, financial security, recreational companionship, sexual fulfillment. Which needs are the top five on both lists? **6.** Knowing this, how can you better meet each other's needs to celebrate what God has given you and to strengthen your marriage?

Friends

9 How is your beloved better than others,
most beautiful of women?
How is your beloved better than others,
that you charge us so?

Beloved

10 My lover is radiant and ruddy,
outstanding among ten thousand.
11 His head is purest gold;
his hair is wavy
and black as a raven.
12 His eyes are like doves
by the water streams,
washed in milk,
mounted like jewels.
13 His cheeks are like beds of spice
yielding perfume.
His lips are like lilies
dripping with myrrh.
14 His arms are rods of gold
set with chrysolite.
His body is like polished ivory
decorated with sapphires.[a]
15 His legs are pillars of marble
set on bases of pure gold.
His appearance is like Lebanon,
choice as its cedars.
16 His mouth is sweetness itself;
he is altogether lovely.
This is my lover, this my friend,
O daughters of Jerusalem.

Friends

6 Where has your lover gone,
most beautiful of women?
Which way did your lover turn,
that we may look for him with you?

Beloved

2 My lover has gone down to his garden,
to the beds of spices,
to browse in the gardens
and to gather lilies.
3 I am my lover's and my lover is mine;
he browses among the lilies.

[b]14 Or *lapis lazuli*

5:9 The friends give the beloved her only opportunity to describe her lover's beauty (vv. 10–16), in the Song.

6:2–3 gather lilies. Imaginative language that portrays the lover as a gazelle (2:7) nibbling on the alluring lilies in the exotic garden, thus enjoying intimate moments with his beloved.

Lover

[4]You are beautiful, my darling, as Tirzah,
lovely as Jerusalem,
majestic as troops with banners.
[5]Turn your eyes from me;
they overwhelm me.
Your hair is like a flock of goats
descending from Gilead.
[6]Your teeth are like a flock of sheep
coming up from the washing.
Each has its twin,
not one of them is alone.
[7]Your temples behind your veil
are like the halves of a pomegranate.
[8]Sixty queens there may be,
and eighty concubines,
and virgins beyond number;
[9]but my dove, my perfect one, is unique,
the only daughter of her mother,
the favorite of the one who bore her.
The maidens saw her and called her blessed;
the queens and concubines praised her.

Friends

[10]Who is this that appears like the dawn,
fair as the moon, bright as the sun,
majestic as the stars in procession?

Lover

[11]I went down to the grove of nut trees
to look at the new growth in the valley,
to see if the vines had budded
or the pomegranates were in bloom.
[12]Before I realized it,
my desire set me among the royal chariots of my people.[a]

Friends

[13]Come back, come back, O Shulammite;
come back, come back, that we may gaze on you!

Lover

Why would you gaze on the Shulammite
as on the dance of Mahanaim?

[a]12 Or *among the chariots of Amminadab*; or *among the chariots of the people of the prince*

OPEN 1. Was *sex* a wholesome word, or a dirty word, for you growing up? Who embarrasses more easily about questions of sex: You, your parents or your kids? Why is that? **2.** How did your parents resolve conflicts: An eye for an eye? Repetitive round robins? Mount Vesuvius temper tantrums? Hit-and-run attacks? Peace at any price? No fights allowed? Fighting fair? How did you feel when they fought?

STUDY 1. When might the woman have heard something akin to this adoration (compare 6:4–9 with 4:1–7)? What does he omit this time? Why the aversion to being aroused by her eyes? What do you suspect that he wants? **2.** Lovers always prefer each other above all others (vv. 8–9). So what do you make of the "sixty queens, ... eighty concubines and countless virgins" (v. 8; 1 Kin. 11:3, where 1000 women are listed in his harem)? Has Solomon lost *count?* Has he lost his *integrity* as a one-woman man? Or has he lost *interest in all others* for her sake? (Note: The 60 "queens" may be nobles' wives or maids of honor escorted by the 60 warriors in 3:7, and thus *not* a sign of any current promiscuity by Solomon.) **3.** What is implied by her passing by in one of his famous chariots (vv. 10–12)? How does she use this chariot to seek a "new growth" in their budding romance? **4.** Since "Shulammite" (v. 13) was once the feminine form of "Solomon" (as in Don and Donna), what does this say about her fitness as his mate? **5.** After expressing how in love they truly are, what follows next (7:1–9)? What new detail do you see in his description of her beauty this time around? Why would that be?

APPLY 1. God is a jealous lover. So were these two. Do *you* ever get jealous or arouse your mate's jealousy? How so? **2.** When celebrating "after hours" the body that God has given you and its capacity to bring pleasure to another, what thoughts and prayers come to mind?

6:5 Turn your eyes. The lover is captivated by the deep love he sees through his beloved's eyes—and it is almost too wonderful to bear (4:9).

6:8 queens ... concubines, and virgins. The lover, Solomon, may be referring to his own royal harem or to all the women in the kingdom.

6:12 chariots. Solomon had a reputation widely held among the nations for maintaining a substantial force of horses and chariots.

6:13 O Shulammite. The friends refer to the beloved with a name that either refers to her origin as a girl from Shunem ("Shunammite," Josh. 19:18, 1 Kin. 1:3) or uses a feminine version of Solomon's name to mean "Solomon's girl."

3. Does your hope for true married love spring eternal? Or has it wilted? Where does it need the nourishment and security of God's true love, renewed every morning? 4. What serendipitous event has kept alive the love between you and yours? 5. Do you and your lover still see each other as you were when you first declared your love? Is that unconditional acceptance: Romantic? Paternal? Fraternal? Divine? Or what?

OPEN 1. Where did you first meet your "one and only"? 2. Complete this sentence: "Love is ...." Compare your definitions for what they have in common.

STUDY 1. What "love potion" seems to be a favorite of this couple? Is their marriage any less sacred for their playfulness? Why do you think so? 2. What does it tell you about the equal role a woman has in the dance of love and sex (7:11–13)? 3. Why the repeated charge to the daughters of Jerusalem (8:4; 2:7; 3:5)? Is this meant to warn any who may have lustful interests aroused by this candid love story? 4. Many of the lovers' metaphors deserve a second look (8:6–7). How is married love like an owner's *seal*? Like *death*? Or like *fire*? (For example, would a death-like

7 How beautiful your sandaled feet,
O prince's daughter!
Your graceful legs are like jewels,
the work of a craftsman's hands.
2 Your navel is a rounded goblet
that never lacks blended wine.
Your waist is a mound of wheat
encircled by lilies.
3 Your breasts are like two fawns,
twins of a gazelle.
4 Your neck is like an ivory tower.
Your eyes are the pools of Heshbon
by the gate of Bath Rabbim.
Your nose is like the tower of Lebanon
looking toward Damascus.
5 Your head crowns you like Mount Carmel.
Your hair is like royal tapestry;
the king is held captive by its tresses.
6 How beautiful you are and how pleasing,
O love, with your delights!
7 Your stature is like that of the palm,
and your breasts like clusters of fruit.
8 I said, "I will climb the palm tree;
I will take hold of its fruit."
May your breasts be like the clusters of the vine,
the fragrance of your breath like apples,
9 and your mouth like the best wine.

Beloved

May the wine go straight to my lover,
flowing gently over lips and teeth.[a]
10 I belong to my lover,
and his desire is for me.
11 Come, my lover, let us go to the countryside,
let us spend the night in the villages.[b]
12 Let us go early to the vineyards
to see if the vines have budded,
if their blossoms have opened,
and if the pomegranates are in bloom—
there I will give you my love.
13 The mandrakes send out their fragrance,
and at our door is every delicacy,
both new and old,
that I have stored up for you, my lover.

[a]9 Septuagint, Aquila, Vulgate and Syriac; Hebrew *lips of sleepers* [b]11 Or *henna bushes*

7:4 neck ... an ivory tower. This description mixes the two images to describe the shape, color and smoothness of the beloved's neck.

7:7–8 palm tree. The imagery is sexual. Palm trees were often pollinated by taking some of its flowers and tying them to the female tree.

7:9 May the wine go ... to my lover. The wine is a word picture describing the beloved's love, which she gladly offers the king (5:1).

7:12 there I will give you my love. The beloved commits herself fully, offering herself to her lover.

7:13 mandrakes. These flowering herbs with a pungent fragrance were used for fertility.

8 If only you were to me like a brother,
who was nursed at my mother's breasts!
Then, if I found you outside,
I would kiss you,
and no one would despise me.
2 I would lead you
and bring you to my mother's house—
she who has taught me.
I would give you spiced wine to drink,
the nectar of my pomegranates.
3 His left arm is under my head
and his right arm embraces me.
4 Daughters of Jerusalem, I charge you:
Do not arouse or awaken love
until it so desires.

Friends

5 Who is this coming up from the desert
leaning on her lover?

Beloved

Under the apple tree I roused you;
there your mother conceived you,
there she who was in labor gave you birth.
6 Place me like a seal over your heart,
like a seal on your arm;
for love is as strong as death,
its jealousy[a] unyielding as the grave.[b]
It burns like blazing fire,
like a mighty flame.[c]
7 Many waters cannot quench love;
rivers cannot wash it away.
If one were to give
all the wealth of his house for love,
it[d] would be utterly scorned.

Friends

8 We have a young sister,
and her breasts are not yet grown.
What shall we do for our sister
for the day she is spoken for?

[a]6 Or *ardor* [b]6 Hebrew *Sheol* [c]6 Or / *like the very flame of the* LORD [d]7 Or *he*

love be a fatal attraction, or unbearable, or irreversible? Likewise, would a fire-like love be dangerous, or unquenchable, or capable of burning hot and then dying out?) **5.** What is the point about the price of love (8:7): The one with the most toys wins the girl? Sex can be cheaply bought? Love must be freely given? Other? **6.** In 8:8–14, we have a series of flashbacks to bring closure to this story. How does her family both encourage and discipline her to save herself for marriage? **7.** What lover's freedom does she assert in the end? What is memorable about their last words to each other?

APPLY 1. Take time to think about the degree of exclusiveness in your relationship with the one you love. Do you actively and openly prefer your beloved to all others? Do you work to make yourself preferable? How so? When were you last jealous for the good of your beloved? Ask the "Author" of love for the gift of single-minded love today. **2.** What makes sexual freedom within marriage possible: Time spent together? Reassurances from each other? Environmental factors? Internal factors? Explain. **3.** How important is the *sizzle factor* in friendship that leads to marriage? Even if *all* other systems indicate "Go for it," should two friends marry who do *not* have irresistible physical chemistry? What's wrong with experimenting beforehand to see if the sexual compatibility is there? Would such an experiment even be valid without a *commitment factor* secured only in marriage blessed by God? **4.** This story only speaks of the woman saving herself for marriage (8:8–9). Isn't sexual purity equally incumbent upon men? Why or why not? **5.** How would you compare the Song of Songs in its approach to love, sex and marriage with today's culture? What healthy antidotes to casual sex, emotional insecurity and self-destructive thinking does this Song offer? **6.** Using the allegorical approach,

8:1 like a brother. Her love for Solomon is so intense that the beloved wishes she had known him since his birth.

8:6–7 love is ... grave. Three proverbs or wisdom statements describe the love of husband and wife as strong, unyielding and mighty—more so than anything else in human experience. These statements, the book's climax, reveal the Song's purpose and underlying message.

8:6 seal over your heart. An official seal symbolized ownership. The beloved wants her husband, who is completely committed to her as she is to him, to possess her. **jealousy unyielding as the grave.** Once buried, a person must remain in the grave; he or she cannot escape. In the same way, the beloved will never give up her relationship with her lover. **burns like ... mighty flame.** In Hebrew the text indicates a raging blaze, with a suggestion that God himself kindled it.

8:8–14 The final verses of the Song seem to echo the initial lines (1:2–7), perhaps recalling the beloved's coming of age and the kindling of her love for Solomon leading to their marriage. Note particularly her brothers' comments (vv. 8–9), her closing description of the king (vv. 11–12) and her reference to her own "vineyard" (v. 12).

how is Christ's love for you like the king's love for his bride? Where have you experienced his painful, possessive, persevering and priceless love?

---

[9] If she is a wall,
we will build towers of silver on her.
If she is a door,
we will enclose her with panels of cedar.

Beloved

[10] I am a wall,
and my breasts are like towers.
Thus I have become in his eyes
like one bringing contentment.
[11] Solomon had a vineyard in Baal Hamon;
he let out his vineyard to tenants.
Each was to bring for its fruit
a thousand shekels[a] of silver.
[12] But my own vineyard is mine to give;
the thousand shekels are for you, O Solomon,
and two hundred[b] are for those who tend its fruit.

Lover

[13] You who dwell in the gardens
with friends in attendance,
let me hear your voice!

Beloved

[14] Come away, my lover,
and be like a gazelle
or like a young stag
on the spice-laden mountains.

[a] *11* That is, about 25 pounds (about 11.5 kilograms); also in verse 12 [b] *12* That is, about 5 pounds (about 2.3 kilograms)

8:9 The beloved's brothers picturesquely express their desire to protect their younger sister until the time is right for a love relationship. This verse could also describe their desire that she is properly prepared and adorned for her wedding.

8:12 my own vineyard is mine to give. A poetic reference to her own body (1:6). The lover is master of his own vineyard, and the beloved also is responsible for hers, with the responsibility to offer it as she chooses. Here she makes the owner's portion of her vineyard available to Solomon.

8:13 dwell in the gardens. The beloved had earlier invited Solomon to her vineyards in the country (7:11–12). Now they are together in the garden.

8:14 like a gazelle or ... young stag. The beloved desires her lover to be graceful, virile, strong and agile with her as he quickly returns to her loving embrace (1:13; 4:6).

Isaiah

Author. The book of Isaiah is named for its author, the prophet Isaiah.

Date. Isaiah's prophecy was probably recorded during his ministry, between 739–681 B.C.

Purpose. Isaiah seemed to have several reasons for addressing his nation. First, he encouraged them toward holy living. Then he presented God's plan for redemption by foretelling the coming Messiah. Isaiah also prepared his people for the inevitable Babylonian captivity. Isaiah's mission was much like the mission of the other prophets. He tried to call his people back to God before they suffered the inevitable consequences for their lack of faith and obedience.

Personal Reading	Group Study Topic and Reading	
1:1–5:30	True and False Faith	1:1–31
6:1–10:34	Call of Isaiah	6:1–13
11:1–12:6	Kingdom of Peace	11:1–16
13:1–21:17	People in Pain	15:1–16:13
22:1–26:21	Song of Praise	26:1–21
27:1–33:24	Woes on Jerusalem	29:1–24
34:1–39:8	Salvation From God	37:1–38
40:1–44:5	The Comfort of God	40:1–31
44:6–48:22	God and Idols	44:6–23
49:1–55:13	God's Invitation	55:1–13
56:1–59:21	True and False Fasting	58:1–14
60:1–66:24	The Coming Glory	60:1–22
42,49,50,53	Review the Four "Servant Songs"	42,49,50,53

Historical Background. Isaiah wrote during a terrible time in Israel's history. The Assyrians, Israel's cruel neighbor to the east, were growing into an empire and expanding westward. This expansion under King Tiglath-Pileser III (745–727 B.C.) stretched across Aram and reached to Canaan. Around 733 B.C., the king of Israel asked Ahaz, king of Judah, to form an alliance in order to defeat the Assyrians. Ahaz refused to join with Israel. Instead, he formed an alliance with Tiglath-Pileser himself, leading to Israel's defeat. This alliance saved Judah temporarily, until Assyria threatened Judah under the reign of Assyrian King Sennacherib.

The entire backdrop of the book of Isaiah is the collapse of the kingdoms of Israel and Judah and the ascendancy of foreign powers over them. The volatility of national power is an underlying theme of Isaiah's prophecy. Israel and Judah struggled to survive, and both fell. The Assyrians wielded great political power, but only briefly. The Babylonians had a period of weakness, but they rose and conquered Judah. The Babylonians eventually fell to the Persians. Such was the life and death of nations in Isaiah's day in the millennium before Christ.

The Writing. Isaiah's writing is some of the best in the Old Testament. He used both poetry and prose, and both come alive with unforgettable imagery. His Song of the Vineyard (5:1–7) combines elements of a love poem and an allegory to describe the destruction of Judah. Chapter 14 contains a taunting song against the king of Babylon. Chapter 24 is an apocalyptic portrait of the Lord's destruction of the earth that seems very modern in its imagery of people who are partying as the world unravels toward destruction.

Isaiah's prophecy is vibrant and visual. Even nature assumes human traits. The desert and parched land rejoice (35:1), and the trees "clap their hands" (55:12). Isaiah's writing ranges from despair to elation, from the desolation of the earth to astounding victory. His ability to use poetry and prose with great skill brings his writing to life.

OPEN **1.** Who was the leader of your country when you were born? What were your mom and dad doing for a living then? **2.** As a teenager, over what issues would you rebel against your parents: Curfew? Car? Phone? Dates? Church? Money? How long did your rebellion last? When did you grow out of it? (Or did you ever?)

STUDY Chapters 1–5 contain sermons that at some time Isaiah preached to the people. Though not arranged chronologically, they introduce major themes to be developed throughout the book, as when Isaiah begins (v. 2) and ends (66:24) by condemning rebels against God. **1.** Isaiah's ministry spanned the reigns of four kings of Judah, almost 50 years. What do you know about the reign of Uzziah (2 Chr. 26:3–5,16–20)? Of Jotham (2 Chr. 27:1–9)? Of Ahaz (2 Chr. 28:1–8,22–25)? Of Hezekiah (2 Chr. 29:1–11; 31:20–21; 32:24–26)? How would you sum up what was going on in Judah during their reigns? **2.** What is the purpose of God calling heaven and earth to witness his complaint against his covenant people? What is his case against them (vv. 2–4)? **3.** What is their pitiable condition like? What sympathy do they get (vv. 5–6)? What is going on in their country (vv. 7–9; 2 Kin. 16:5–6; 18:9–16)? **4.** God compares the people of Judah with Sodom and Gomorrah (vv. 9–20). What is the point of the comparison? **5.** The Jews loved the feasts, ceremonies and sacrifices (such as Passover). Why did God take no pleasure in their sacrifices? Why are they "meaningless" and "evil"? **6.** What does God call the people to do (vv. 16–17)? What does God promise in accordance with their repentance? What's happening in

1 The vision concerning Judah and Jerusalem that Isaiah son of Amoz saw during the reigns of Uzziah, Jotham, Ahaz and Hezekiah, kings of Judah.

A Rebellious Nation

2 Hear, O heavens! Listen, O earth!
For the LORD has spoken:
"I reared children and brought them up,
but they have rebelled against me.
3 The ox knows his master,
the donkey his owner's manger,
but Israel does not know,
my people do not understand."

4 Ah, sinful nation,
a people loaded with guilt,
a brood of evildoers,
children given to corruption!
They have forsaken the LORD;
they have spurned the Holy One of Israel
and turned their backs on him.

5 Why should you be beaten anymore?
Why do you persist in rebellion?
Your whole head is injured,
your whole heart afflicted.
6 From the sole of your foot to the top of your head
there is no soundness—
only wounds and welts
and open sores,
not cleansed or bandaged
or soothed with oil.

7 Your country is desolate,
your cities burned with fire;
your fields are being stripped by foreigners
right before you,
laid waste as when overthrown by strangers.
8 The Daughter of Zion is left
like a shelter in a vineyard,

1:1 kings of Judah. The nation of Israel has been divided into Judah in the south and Israel in the north. Isaiah focuses his message on Judah, listing the four kings who ruled from 792 to 686 B.C., when he received God's prophetic visions and words.

1:2 they have rebelled. Isaiah summarizes the core message God wants his people to hear (echoed at the end of the book, 66:24). Despite his loving care for them, God's people have rebelled against him, refusing to submit to his authority and rule. Isaiah calls the heavens and the earth as witnesses to this situation because they also witnessed the forging of God's covenant with his people (Deut. 30:19; 31:28; 32:1).

1:3 my people do not understand. Even the ox and the donkey know their master and their place, but not God's stubborn people. As a result, Judah will be forced to leave her land in exile (5:13).

1:5–6 injured ... afflicted. Israel's rebellion has resulted in deep spiritual and emotional wounds—later the suffering servant is described as voluntarily receiving rather similar treatment (53:4–5).

1:6 Just as Job (2:7) suffered from head to toe, so the nation is thoroughly diseased morally and spiritually.

1:7–9 The land of Judah has suffered intensely as a result of invasions by foreign powers including Aram, Edom and Philistia (2 Chr. 28:5–18), as well as later by Assyria under Sennacherib (701 B.C.; see 36:1,2) and Babylonia under Nebuchadnezzar (605–586 B.C.).

1:8 Daughter of Zion is left. The city of Jerusalem is personified in this lovely but slightly confusing phrase: The daughter *is* Zion (37:22; 60:14).

like a hut in a field of melons,
like a city under siege.
9 Unless the LORD Almighty
had left us some survivors,
we would have become like Sodom,
we would have been like Gomorrah.

10 Hear the word of the LORD,
you rulers of Sodom;
listen to the law of our God,
you people of Gomorrah!
11 "The multitude of your sacrifices—
what are they to me?" says the LORD.
"I have more than enough of burnt offerings,
of rams and the fat of fattened animals;
I have no pleasure
in the blood of bulls and lambs and goats.
12 When you come to appear before me,
who has asked this of you,
this trampling of my courts?
13 Stop bringing meaningless offerings!
Your incense is detestable to me.
New Moons, Sabbaths and convocations—
I cannot bear your evil assemblies.
14 Your New Moon festivals and your appointed feasts
my soul hates.
They have become a burden to me;
I am weary of bearing them.
15 When you spread out your hands in prayer,
I will hide my eyes from you;
even if you offer many prayers,
I will not listen.
Your hands are full of blood;
16 wash and make yourselves clean.
Take your evil deeds
out of my sight!
Stop doing wrong,
17 learn to do right!
Seek justice,
encourage the oppressed.[a]
Defend the cause of the fatherless,
plead the case of the widow.

[a]17 Or / *rebuke the oppressor*

Judah that accounts for this call and promise (vv. 15,21–23)? **7.** Given their religious rituals (vv. 11–15), how does the secular image of adultery (v. 21) fit their spiritual state? Likewise, how do "scarlet" and "red" fit? What is the condition upon which the forgiveness of their sins rests? **8.** What is the purpose of the judgment awaiting those who forsake the Lord (vv. 24–31)? What is the future for those who are penitent? How will it be different from their present situation?

APPLY 1. Was there a time in your life when religion was meaningless? What changed your mind, or does it tend to be that way now? Why? **2.** Who do you identify with most in this passage: God—because you too know what it's like to have rebellious children (v. 2)? The people of Israel—because you feel you've been beaten down by life (vv. 5–6)? God—because you are outraged by the injustices you see (vv. 15–17)? **3.** Who is God calling you to encourage, plead for or defend (v. 17)?

1:9–10 Sodom ... Gomorrah. So far Judah has escaped total destruction, but the precedent has already been set by these sinful cities God utterly destroyed (3:9; Gen. 13:13; 18:20,21; 19:5,24,25). Isaiah likens the Judeans to the sin-stenched rulers of Sodom and Gomorrah.

1:11–15 Motive is vital when worshiping God. Ritual is meaningless—in fact, detestable—to God unless the heart honestly seeks God and his will (66:3; 1 Sam. 15:22,23; Jer. 7:21–26; Hos. 6:6; Amos 5:21–24; Mic. 6:6–8).

1:17 Defend ... fatherless, plead ... widow. This guidance is echoed in Jeremiah 22:16 and James 1:27. These types of people are symbolic of all oppressed people in society. Their treatment by the nation as a whole was a barometer for the nation's spiritual and moral health, and rulers were not to take advantage of them (v. 23; 10:2; Jer. 22:3).

18 "Come now, let us reason together,"
says the LORD.
"Though your sins are like scarlet,
they shall be as white as snow;
though they are red as crimson,
they shall be like wool.
19 If you are willing and obedient,
you will eat the best from the land;
20 but if you resist and rebel,
you will be devoured by the sword."
For the mouth of the LORD has spoken.

21 See how the faithful city
has become a harlot!
She once was full of justice;
righteousness used to dwell in her—
but now murderers!
22 Your silver has become dross,
your choice wine is diluted with water.
23 Your rulers are rebels,
companions of thieves;
they all love bribes
and chase after gifts.
They do not defend the cause of the fatherless;
the widow's case does not come before them.
24 Therefore the Lord, the LORD Almighty,
the Mighty One of Israel, declares:
"Ah, I will get relief from my foes
and avenge myself on my enemies.
25 I will turn my hand against you;
I will thoroughly purge away your dross
and remove all your impurities.
26 I will restore your judges as in days of old,
your counselors as at the beginning.
Afterward you will be called
the City of Righteousness,
the Faithful City."

27 Zion will be redeemed with justice,
her penitent ones with righteousness.
28 But rebels and sinners will both be broken,
and those who forsake the LORD will perish.

29 "You will be ashamed because of the sacred oaks
in which you have delighted;

1:18 let us reason together. Not an invitation to compromise, but to come to a legal decision in alignment with God's perfect will regarding their sin. **scarlet.** God has caught his people *"red handed." Blood covers their hands* as it would a murderer's (vv. 15,21). **as snow.** God's forgiveness provides complete cleansing (Ps. 51:7)—but the offer depends on the people's receptiveness and their true repentance (v. 19).

1:21 faithful city ... harlot. Jerusalem is pictured as a cheating wife, spiritually speaking, because she has pursued false idols rather than God (v. 4; Jer. 3:6–14; Ezek. 16:25,26).

1:25 my hand. The hand of God had protectively guided Israel from bondage in Egypt; now it was raised against the people in judgment.

1:27–28 The nation as a whole (represented by Zion or Jerusalem) will be redeemed, meaning "ransomed" or "freed from slavery through payment of a price," but the same may not be true of stubborn, sinful individuals. This argument is examined further in 65:8–16.

you will be disgraced because of the gardens
that you have chosen.
30 You will be like an oak with fading leaves,
like a garden without water.
31 The mighty man will become tinder
and his work a spark;
both will burn together,
with no one to quench the fire."

The Mountain of the Lord

2 This is what Isaiah son of Amoz saw concerning Judah and Jerusalem:

2 In the last days

the mountain of the LORD's temple will be established
as chief among the mountains;
it will be raised above the hills,
and all nations will stream to it.

3 Many peoples will come and say,

"Come, let us go up to the mountain of the LORD,
to the house of the God of Jacob.
He will teach us his ways,
so that we may walk in his paths."
The law will go out from Zion,
the word of the LORD from Jerusalem.
4 He will judge between the nations
and will settle disputes for many peoples.
They will beat their swords into plowshares
and their spears into pruning hooks.
Nation will not take up sword against nation,
nor will they train for war anymore.

5 Come, O house of Jacob,
let us walk in the light of the LORD.

The Day of the Lord

6 You have abandoned your people,
the house of Jacob.
They are full of superstitions from the East;
they practice divination like the Philistines
and clasp hands with pagans.
7 Their land is full of silver and gold;
there is no end to their treasures.

OPEN In your family, who is the explorer? The warrior? Peacemaker? Idealist? Realist?

STUDY 1. "The mountain of the LORD" refers to the site upon which the temple in Jerusalem was built (11:9; 24:23; 27:13; 56:6–7). What picture does Isaiah envision? **2.** Why are so many coming to the temple? What will God do for them? **3.** What is meant by "the last days" (v. 2; Acts 2:17; Heb. 1:2)? **4.** Why does Isaiah call Judah to come to the temple at this time? **5.** What does the New Testament make of Isaiah's vision? Did, or will, Jesus inaugurate this era of peace? If so, when will it be fulfilled? Why do you think so?

APPLY 1. Which of your swords and spears (i.e., mean streak, angry outbursts, cutting tongue) has God transformed into tools for peace? **2.** How might this vision of God's kingdom shape your hope? Prayers? Values?

OPEN 1. Of what "all by myself" project were you most proud as a child? Of what trophies are you most proud? Which ones are still on display? **2.** Did you have a favorite hiding place in the house you grew up in? Or a getaway place now? Under what circumstances would you go there?

2:2–4 Isaiah often refers to the "mountain of the LORD," which is quite similar to Micah 4:1–3. This theme often refers to the last days when both Jews and Gentiles come to Jerusalem (11:9; 27:13; 56:7; 57:13; 65:25; 66:20; Zech. 14:16). This looks ahead to every era in which the rule of Christ spreads over the earth, especially to the end of time when all of God's kingdom is complete.

2:2 last days. This phrase can refer to the future in general (Gen. 49:1), but its primary use involves the final events of human history. In many ways the "last days" were inaugurated by Christ when he first came to earth (Acts 2:17; Heb. 1:2) and will culminate with his second coming.

2:7 land is full of silver and gold. While a healthy surplus sounds reasonable for a king to have, God specifically forbade the accumulation of vast hordes of such riches (Deut. 17:16–17) because it tended to cause the king, and the nation, to put their trust in money rather than in God (31:1).

STUDY 1. Isaiah returns from the vision of the future (vv. 1–5), to the reality of the present. What do verses 6–8 add to Isaiah's catalogue of sins in 1:21–23? **2.** What makes the pagan practices (v. 6) so awful to God (Deut. 7:1–6; 18:9–13 and 2 Kin. 16:7–18, where King Ahaz is guilty of clasping hands with pagans)?What's wrong with kings accumulating horses, silver or gold (v. 7; Deut. 17:16–20)? **3.** What is significant about Judah prostrating itself before idols (vv. 8–9; Deut. 31:16–18)? **4.** Verses 10–21 are a song of judgment against the people described in verses 6–8. What is the root cause of their sin? **5.** What will the "Day of the LORD" be like for the proud (vv. 10,19,21)? What is their essential problem (v. 22)?

APPLY 1. Which of the following American idols disturbs you the most: Commercialism and greed? Sex? Power? Fame? Which one lures you the most? **2.** When has pride come between you and your relationship to others? When has it come between you and God?

Their land is full of horses;
there is no end to their chariots.
8 Their land is full of idols;
they bow down to the work of their hands,
to what their fingers have made.
9 So man will be brought low
and mankind humbled—
do not forgive them.[a]

10 Go into the rocks,
hide in the ground
from dread of the LORD
and the splendor of his majesty!
11 The eyes of the arrogant man will be humbled
and the pride of men brought low;
the LORD alone will be exalted in that day.

12 The LORD Almighty has a day in store
for all the proud and lofty,
for all that is exalted
(and they will be humbled),
13 for all the cedars of Lebanon, tall and lofty,
and all the oaks of Bashan,
14 for all the towering mountains
and all the high hills,
15 for every lofty tower
and every fortified wall,
16 for every trading ship[b]
and every stately vessel.
17 The arrogance of man will be brought low
and the pride of men humbled;
the LORD alone will be exalted in that day,
18 and the idols will totally disappear.

19 Men will flee to caves in the rocks
and to holes in the ground
from dread of the LORD
and the splendor of his majesty,
when he rises to shake the earth.
20 In that day men will throw away
to the rodents and bats
their idols of silver and idols of gold,
which they made to worship.
21 They will flee to caverns in the rocks
and to the overhanging crags

[a] 9 Or *not raise them up* [b] 16 Hebrew *every ship of Tarshish*

2:10 rocks. Israelites would hide themselves in caves and crevices in times of attack or oppression (Judg. 6:1,2; 1 Sam. 13:6). **splendor of his majesty!** The same Hebrew word is translated "pride" when applied to humans, who become full of pride when they try to be their own god (14:13–14).

2:11,17,20 exalted in that day. This phrase pointing to the day of judgment is used seven times in chapters 2–4 (3:7,18; 4:1,2). On the day of the Lord, God will judge or bless depending on the nations' situation (Zeph. 1:14–2:3). God would use Assyria and Babylon to bring his judgment on Judah (5:26–30).

2:13–16 Isaiah lists examples of proud, lofty and exalted things (v. 12) humans would look to. Compared to God himself they will all be brought low, so that arrogant humanity will acknowledge God's greatness.

from dread of the LORD
and the splendor of his majesty,
when he rises to shake the earth.

22 Stop trusting in man,
who has but a breath in his nostrils.
Of what account is he?

Judgment on Jerusalem and Judah

3 See now, the Lord,
the LORD Almighty,
is about to take from Jerusalem and Judah
both supply and support:
all supplies of food and all supplies of water,
2 the hero and warrior,
the judge and prophet,
the soothsayer and elder,
3 the captain of fifty and man of rank,
the counselor, skilled craftsman and clever enchanter.

4 I will make boys their officials;
mere children will govern them.
5 People will oppress each other—
man against man, neighbor against neighbor.
The young will rise up against the old,
the base against the honorable.

6 A man will seize one of his brothers
at his father's home, and say,
"You have a cloak, you be our leader;
take charge of this heap of ruins!"
7 But in that day he will cry out,
"I have no remedy.
I have no food or clothing in my house;
do not make me the leader of the people."

8 Jerusalem staggers,
Judah is falling;
their words and deeds are against the LORD,
defying his glorious presence.
9 The look on their faces testifies against them;
they parade their sin like Sodom;
they do not hide it.
Woe to them!
They have brought disaster upon themselves.

10 Tell the righteous it will be well with them,
for they will enjoy the fruit of their deeds.

OPEN 1. Which of the following best describes how you dress: A fashion trend-setter? A rebel who dresses to make a "statement"? A throw-back to a previous fashion era? A slob and proud of it? **2.** What piece of clothing or fashion accessory would you do without?

STUDY 1. The first part of this sermon is a more specific prophecy of the judgment that is coming upon Judah. What things make up their "supply and support" that the Lord is going to take away? **2.** The soothsayer and clever enchanter should never have existed in a faithful Judah. What would happen to a society where all their partners in crime were removed as well (3:1–3)? **3.** What types of social chaos would come about as a result of God's judgment (3:4–7)? **4.** If you lived during a time like this, what would you expect to see around you? How would you feel about your future? Your family? Your money? **5.** What attitudes and actions precipitate God's judgment (3:8–15)? By what "legal" means might the leaders "plunder the poor"? **6.** How are the women pictured in 3:16–24? What reference to their captivity do you see here? **7.** What contrasts do you see between 3:16–24 and 4:1? **8.** Is the "Branch of the LORD" the remnant of people who survive God's judgment (4:2–6)? How does the remnant contrast with the leaders and women described in chapter 3? What will the Lord do for them? What does this show about God's purpose in judgment? **9.** What is meant by "cloud ... fire ... shelter" (4:5–6; Ex. 13:21–22; 40:34–38)? What is the purpose of the canopy God will spread over those who come to him? What does Isaiah mean by being safe from

2:22 Stop trusting. In Hebrew this literally means "Give up on man" or "Cease from man." Ironically, the Messiah, the one man God's people should have trusted, was later rejected or "given up on." He alone is worthy of the trust and esteem the Israelites squandered on their weak leaders.

3:1–3 God would remove the nation's leaders, either through death or exile (2 Kin. 24:14; 25:18–21).

3:2–3 Leaders of Judah filled four roles: warriors, counselors, religious mediums and craftsmen. **soothsayer ... enchanter.** God condemned those who drew power and influence from the occult (Deut. 18:10; Jer. 8:17). Punishment for this type of folly would cleanse the people of paganism, but also of God's help and assistance. The results would be all loss of "supply and support."

"the heat of the day" and the "storm and rain"? **10.** What does that say about who the true Branch of the Lord is? How do we become part of this Branch?

APPLY 1. What national or world injustice most causes you to cry out in frustration, "I have no remedy" (3:7)? **2.** In what ways are you seeking to beautify your inner self? How do your efforts in this area compare to the time and effort you spend on keeping your outer self looking nice? **3.** What "filth" in your life would you like to see the Lord wash away (4:4)?

11 Woe to the wicked! Disaster is upon them!
They will be paid back for what their hands have done.

12 Youths oppress my people,
women rule over them.
O my people, your guides lead you astray;
they turn you from the path.

13 The LORD takes his place in court;
he rises to judge the people.
14 The LORD enters into judgment
against the elders and leaders of his people:
"It is you who have ruined my vineyard;
the plunder from the poor is in your houses.
15 What do you mean by crushing my people
and grinding the faces of the poor?"
declares the Lord, the LORD Almighty.

16 The LORD says,
"The women of Zion are haughty,
walking along with outstretched necks,
flirting with their eyes,
tripping along with mincing steps,
with ornaments jingling on their ankles.
17 Therefore the Lord will bring sores on the heads of the women of Zion;
the LORD will make their scalps bald."

18 In that day the Lord will snatch away their finery: the bangles and
headbands and crescent necklaces, 19 the earrings and bracelets and
veils, 20 the headdresses and ankle chains and sashes, the perfume
bottles and charms, 21 the signet rings and nose rings, 22 the fine robes
and the capes and cloaks, the purses 23 and mirrors, and the linen
garments and tiaras and shawls.

24 Instead of fragrance there will be a stench;
instead of a sash, a rope;
instead of well-dressed hair, baldness;
instead of fine clothing, sackcloth;
instead of beauty, branding.
25 Your men will fall by the sword,
your warriors in battle.
26 The gates of Zion will lament and mourn;
destitute, she will sit on the ground.

4 In that day seven women
will take hold of one man

3:12 Ancient Near Eastern culture looked down on the exercise of leadership by women or youth.

3:14 ruined my vineyard. The nation Israel (5:1–7) is described as "poor" here because the nation's leaders had plundered fields and populace.

3:15 crushing ... grinding. Just as grain was crushed by millstones, the nation's poor have been ground down by their leaders.

3:16 walking ... flirting ... tripping along. Filled with pretension, women often wore ornaments and accessories on their ankles and feet, affecting the way they walked. In the ancient Near East, one's gait expressed an attitude.

3:21 signet rings and nose rings. Signet rings, worn by those in authority, featured an official seal (Gen. 41:42). Nose rings made of gold or other precious metals were worn by brides.

3:24 rope ... branding. Those taken captive would be herded and roughly treated like cattle—a far cry from the opulent ease they were accustomed to.

and say, "We will eat our own food
 and provide our own clothes;
only let us be called by your name.
 Take away our disgrace!"

The Branch of the Lord

2In that day the Branch of the LORD will be beautiful and glorious,
and the fruit of the land will be the pride and glory of the survivors in
Israel. 3Those who are left in Zion, who remain in Jerusalem, will be
called holy, all who are recorded among the living in Jerusalem. 4The
Lord will wash away the filth of the women of Zion; he will cleanse
the bloodstains from Jerusalem by a spirit[a] of judgment and a spirit[a]
of fire. 5Then the LORD will create over all of Mount Zion and over
those who assemble there a cloud of smoke by day and a glow of
flaming fire by night; over all the glory will be a canopy. 6It will be a
shelter and shade from the heat of the day, and a refuge and hiding
place from the storm and rain.

The Song of the Vineyard

5 I will sing for the one I love
 a song about his vineyard:
My loved one had a vineyard
 on a fertile hillside.
2He dug it up and cleared it of stones
 and planted it with the choicest vines.
He built a watchtower in it
 and cut out a winepress as well.
Then he looked for a crop of good grapes,
 but it yielded only bad fruit.

3"Now you dwellers in Jerusalem and men of Judah,
 judge between me and my vineyard.
4What more could have been done for my vineyard
 than I have done for it?
When I looked for good grapes,
 why did it yield only bad?
5Now I will tell you
 what I am going to do to my vineyard:
I will take away its hedge,
 and it will be destroyed;
I will break down its wall,
 and it will be trampled.
6I will make it a wasteland,
 neither pruned nor cultivated,
 and briers and thorns will grow there.

[a]4 Or *the Spirit*

OPEN 1. When you start a project (term paper, remodeling a house), with high hopes but it fails repeatedly, what do you do: Give up? Try again? Wait 'til next year? Why? **2.** What does your garden grow?

STUDY 1. Put yourself in the place of the gardener in this song: What do you expect from your labors (v. 2)? How do you feel about the results? What would you do next year? **2.** If you were a gardener with an annual crop, how long would it take you to give up on that plot of land? What is God's purpose in asking the people to judge for themselves what he should do to the vineyard (vv. 3–4)? **3.** Verse 7 explains the song. What are some of the ways God cultivated and cared for Judah, the garden of his delight? **4.** What is one chief quality God expects to see in his people (1:17)? How is the "fruit" that has grown different from what he expected? **5.** What are some of the "fruits" people use today to evaluate how spiritual a person is? How do these compare with what God looks for (Matt. 21:33–44; John 15:1–3; Gal. 5:22–23)?

APPLY How would you assess the "fruit" in your life:

4:2 Branch of the LORD. This title is used of the Messiah because he will be the "shoot" or "Branch" and often referred to as "the stump" (11:1; 53:2), a descendant of David. However, some scholars take this reference to be Judah rather than the Messiah.

4:5–6 cloud of smoke ... shelter. When Israel wandered in the desert following their escape from Egypt, God led them with a pillar of cloud by day and of fire by night, protecting and guiding them (Ex. 13:21–22; 14:21–22). The exodus theme is found throughout Isaiah (11:15–16; 31:5; 51:10).

4:6 In the same way God led and protected the wandering Israelites, he will watch over Mount Zion which he will redeem (Ps. 121:5–6).

Just budding? Still premature? Developing on schedule? Ripe for enjoyment? Diseased?

OPEN 1. When someone "let you have it" for all the things they held against you, how did you feel? What did you do? **2.** Where you live and work, are you among the "nobles" or the "masses"? Why?

STUDY 1. This sermon elaborates what God said about the condition of the people in verse 7. What have the people in the first woe (v. 8) done that is so offensive to the Lord (3:14–15)? **2.** How would you react if you reaped only a tenth of what you had sown (v. 10)? How does this curse contrast with the promise of blessing in Amos 9:13–15? Why will judgment come upon these people? **3.** Who gets hit with the second woe and why (vv. 11–17)? How contemporary does their lifestyle sound to you? Does their judgment seem appropriate? **4.** What role reversal do you see in the fate of the "arrogant" (v. 15) and that of the "lambs" and "sheep" (v. 17)? Who's who in this portrait of justice? **5.** Who gets hit with the third woe and why (vv. 18–19)? **6.** How would you describe the sin of those deserving the fourth woe (v. 20)? The fifth woe (v. 21)? How do they relate? What effect would these woeful people have on others who tried to follow after God's ways? **7.** Although the sixth woe (vv. 22–24) starts off in a similar way to that in verses 11–17, what is the focus of God's judgment here? How does Isaiah emphasize the completeness of the judgment they will face? **8.** Verse 25 sums up God's anger against all the "bad fruit" described so far. If judgment has already come

I will command the clouds
  not to rain on it."

7 The vineyard of the LORD Almighty
  is the house of Israel,
and the men of Judah
  are the garden of his delight.
And he looked for justice, but saw bloodshed;
  for righteousness, but heard cries of distress.

Woes and Judgments

8 Woe to you who add house to house
  and join field to field
till no space is left
  and you live alone in the land.

9 The LORD Almighty has declared in my hearing:

"Surely the great houses will become desolate,
  the fine mansions left without occupants.
10 A ten-acre[a] vineyard will produce only a bath[b] of wine,
  a homer[c] of seed only an ephah[d] of grain."

11 Woe to those who rise early in the morning
  to run after their drinks,
who stay up late at night
  till they are inflamed with wine.
12 They have harps and lyres at their banquets,
  tambourines and flutes and wine,
but they have no regard for the deeds of the LORD,
  no respect for the work of his hands.
13 Therefore my people will go into exile
  for lack of understanding;
their men of rank will die of hunger
  and their masses will be parched with thirst.
14 Therefore the grave[e] enlarges its appetite
  and opens its mouth without limit;
into it will descend their nobles and masses
  with all their brawlers and revelers.
15 So man will be brought low
  and mankind humbled,
  the eyes of the arrogant humbled.
16 But the LORD Almighty will be exalted by his justice,

[a] *10* Hebrew *ten-yoke,* that is, the land plowed by 10 yoke of oxen in one day [b] *10* That is, probably about 6 gallons (about 22 liters) [c] *10* That is, probably about 6 bushels (about 220 liters) [d] *10* That is, probably about 3/5 bushel (about 22 liters) [e] *14* Hebrew *Sheol*

5:7 This verse provides the interpretation of verses 1–6, the "song of the vineyard." The vineyard belongs to God ("my," v. 4). In Hebrew the words for "justice" and "bloodshed" are similar, as are the words for "righteousness" and "distress."

5:8 house to house ... field to field till no space is left. The land of Israel had been given permanently to specific families, so it could only be rented to others, not sold (Num. 27:7–11; 1 Kin. 21:1–3). God declared the land "mine" (Lev. 25:23) but greedy *landowners* sought to control the best plots of land in Israel for themselves.

5:10 homer ... ephah. Poor results, as an ephah (the amount of harvested grain) is only one-tenth of a homer (the original amount of seed). One of the results of a nation's sin is poor farming (Deut. 28:38–39; Hag. 2:16–17).

5:11–13 Drunkenness and decadence are also decried by the prophet Amos (Amos 4:1–3; 6:6–7).

and the holy God will show himself holy by his righteousness.
[17]Then sheep will graze as in their own pasture;
lambs will feed[a] among the ruins of the rich.

[18]Woe to those who draw sin along with cords of deceit,
and wickedness as with cart ropes,
[19]to those who say, "Let God hurry,
let him hasten his work
so we may see it.
Let it approach,
let the plan of the Holy One of Israel come,
so we may know it."

[20]Woe to those who call evil good
and good evil,
who put darkness for light
and light for darkness,
who put bitter for sweet
and sweet for bitter.
[21]Woe to those who are wise in their own eyes
and clever in their own sight.

[22]Woe to those who are heroes at drinking wine
and champions at mixing drinks,
[23]who acquit the guilty for a bribe,
but deny justice to the innocent.
[24]Therefore, as tongues of fire lick up straw
and as dry grass sinks down in the flames,
so their roots will decay
and their flowers blow away like dust;
for they have rejected the law of the LORD Almighty
and spurned the word of the Holy One of Israel.
[25]Therefore the LORD's anger burns against his people;
his hand is raised and he strikes them down.
The mountains shake,
and the dead bodies are like refuse in the streets.

Yet for all this, his anger is not turned away,
his hand is still upraised.
[26]He lifts up a banner for the distant nations,
he whistles for those at the ends of the earth.
Here they come,
swiftly and speedily!
[27]Not one of them grows tired or stumbles,
not one slumbers or sleeps;
not a belt is loosened at the waist,

[a]17 Septuagint; Hebrew / *strangers will eat*

to Judah, why is more punishment necessary (1:5–7)? What will be the climactic judgment they have to face (vv. 26–30)?

APPLY 1. Which of these woes make you most uneasy: The woe against land-grabbing (v. 8)? The woe against being deceitful (v. 18)? The woe against conceit (v. 21)? The woe against being a champion partier/drinker (v. 22) The woe against acts of injustice (v. 23)? **2.** In what areas of life are you most tempted to call "evil good and good evil"?

5:18 cords of deceit. The people are bound to their sin, drawing it along with them. By contrast, God leads his people with "cords of human kindness" (Hos. 11:4).

5:20 call evil good. The life of the wicked is upside down, inside out—exactly opposite of what it should be.

5:25 The mountains shake. All of God's creation trembles before his wrath (64:3; Jer. 4:24–26). This is an example of a theophany, an appearance of God in human appearance.

5:26 he whistles. The Lord, in control of the armies of judgment, will whistle for them as a master calls his dog, as a signal to invade.

not a sandal thong is broken.
28Their arrows are sharp,
all their bows are strung;
their horses' hoofs seem like flint,
their chariot wheels like a whirlwind.
29Their roar is like that of the lion,
they roar like young lions;
they growl as they seize their prey
and carry it off with no one to rescue.
30In that day they will roar over it
like the roaring of the sea.
And if one looks at the land,
he will see darkness and distress;
even the light will be darkened by the clouds.

OPEN 1. When were you last called into the office of your chief principal or boss's boss? What for? How did that affect you? **2.** What volunteer ministries have you been involved with? How were you recruited?

STUDY 1. If King Uzziah represents stability to Judah, what does his death mean? Why does God choose this time to reveal himself to Isaiah? **2.** Imagine you are Isaiah. What do you tell a friend about what you saw, heard, felt and smelled in verses 1–4? **3.** What questions about God's nature and purpose does this encounter raise for you? **4.** What makes Isaiah despair for his life and confess his sin (v. 5; Ex. 20:19)? **5.** Animals were burned on the altar as a substitute for the death of the sinner. What is the significance of Isaiah's lips being touched with a coal from this altar? **6.** Compare Isaiah's re-

Isaiah's Commission

6 In the year that King Uzziah died, I saw the Lord seated on a throne,
high and exalted, and the train of his robe filled the temple.
2Above him were seraphs, each with six wings: With two wings they
covered their faces, with two they covered their feet, and with two
they were flying. 3And they were calling to one another:

"Holy, holy, holy is the LORD Almighty;
the whole earth is full of his glory."

4At the sound of their voices the doorposts and thresholds shook and
the temple was filled with smoke.
5"Woe to me!" I cried. "I am ruined! For I am a man of unclean lips,
and I live among a people of unclean lips, and my eyes have seen the
King, the LORD Almighty."
6Then one of the seraphs flew to me with a live coal in his hand,
which he had taken with tongs from the altar. 7With it he touched my
mouth and said, "See, this has touched your lips; your guilt is taken
away and your sin atoned for."
8Then I heard the voice of the Lord saying, "Whom shall I send?
And who will go for us?"

6:1 King Uzziah died. Uzziah, a good king who ruled well, reigned from 792 until he died in 740 B.C. He contracted leprosy as a judgment upon his insistence on burning incense in God's temple and died with that condition (2 Chr. 26:16–21). He was also known as Azariah (2 Kin. 14:21; 2 Chr. 26:1). This section describing Isaiah's commission likely occurred before his prophetic work began. The author probably placed it here after the initial prophecies to provide proof that he was a trustworthy spokesman for God.

6:2 seraphs. These angels are mentioned only here in the Bible. Their name comes from a Hebrew word meaning "burn," possibly speaking of God's purity (v. 6; Rev. 4:6–9). Note the contrast between their worship of God and the rebellious pride of humanity.

6:3 holy, holy, holy. Repeating a word three times in Hebrew means it is supremely important. God's holiness is indescribably perfect and transcendent. God is completely above us and different from us, and yet in his mercy he reaches us and cares for us.

6:5 my eyes have seen the King, the LORD. Isaiah expresses concern because whoever sees God is expected to die, since humans are incapable of surviving the sight of God's majesty and glory (Gen. 16:13; 32:30; Ex. 33:20). In the light of God's perfect holiness, Isaiah's sinful humanness stands in stark contrast.

6:6 live coal. These were found in the temple on the Day of Atonement when they were taken by the high priest into the Most Holy Place (Lev. 16:12).

6:7 he touched my mouth. God touches Isaiah's mouth to purify it in order to communicate his word (Jer. 1:9).

6:8 who will go for us. The plural could refer to God speaking on behalf of himself and his angelic host (Gen. 1:26; 3:22; 11:7) or referring to himself in the plural of majesty alluding to the Trinity: Father, Son and Holy Spirit. In this case, Isaiah the prophet is made part of the divine decision. This prophetic honor was also given to Micaiah (1 Kin. 22:19–20) and Jeremiah (23:18,22; Amos 3:7). **Here am I.** Like Abraham, Moses and Samuel, Isaiah answers as a servant when God called him by name (Gen. 22:1; Ex. 3:4; 1 Sam. 3:4,6,8). They all were willing to be available to whatever God wanted them to be.

And I said, "Here am I. Send me!"
[9]He said, "Go and tell this people:

" 'Be ever hearing, but never understanding;
be ever seeing, but never perceiving.'
[10]Make the heart of this people calloused;
make their ears dull
and close their eyes.[a]
Otherwise they might see with their eyes,
hear with their ears,
understand with their hearts,
and turn and be healed."

[11]Then I said, "For how long, O Lord?"
And he answered:

"Until the cities lie ruined
and without inhabitant,
until the houses are left deserted
and the fields ruined and ravaged,
[12]until the LORD has sent everyone far away
and the land is utterly forsaken.
[13]And though a tenth remains in the land,
it will again be laid waste.
But as the terebinth and oak
leave stumps when they are cut down,
so the holy seed will be the stump in the land."

The Sign of Immanuel

7 When Ahaz son of Jotham, the son of Uzziah, was king of Judah,
King Rezin of Aram and Pekah son of Remaliah king of Israel
marched up to fight against Jerusalem, but they could not
overpower it.
[2]Now the house of David was told, "Aram has allied itself with[b]
Ephraim"; so the hearts of Ahaz and his people were shaken, as the
trees of the forest are shaken by the wind.
[3]Then the LORD said to Isaiah, "Go out, you and your son Shear-
Jashub,[c] to meet Ahaz at the end of the aqueduct of the Upper Pool,
on the road to the Washerman's Field. [4]Say to him, 'Be careful, keep
calm and don't be afraid. Do not lose heart because of these
two smoldering stubs of firewood—because of the fierce anger of
Rezin and Aram and of the son of Remaliah. [5]Aram, Ephraim and

[a]9,10 Hebrew; Septuagint *'You will be ever hearing, but never understanding; / you will be ever seeing, but never perceiving.' / [10]This people's heart has become calloused; / they hardly hear with their ears, / and they have closed their eyes* [b]2 Or *has set up camp in* [c]3 *Shear-Jashub* means *a remnant will return.*

sponse in verse 8 with verse 5. What is significant about that? **7.** What is Isaiah's new mission (vv. 9–10). What effect will it have on Judah? **8.** What does "but" signify (v. 13)? How does the stump in verse 13 relate to the Branch (4:2–6)? **9.** John 12:40–41 relates this vision to Jesus. How is Jesus' glory like the suffering and healing Isaiah saw?

APPLY 1. How is your experience with God like Isaiah's: Awestruck? Guilt-ridden? Cleansed? Are you willing to serve anywhere, anytime? **2.** God's holiness and universal reign awed Isaiah. Which of God's attributes most impresses you? Why? **3.** What is the closest you have come to experiencing a sense of calling like Isaiah felt?

OPEN 1. Picture yourself at age 12–13: Where were you living? Who were your heroes? **2.** What experience, if any, have you had with special diets? K-rations? Dorm food? Foraging for food? Surviving without much food?

STUDY The events here occur in Ahaz' reign, some 10–16 years after those of chapter 6 (2 Kin. 16:5–18)? (Note: this is known in history books as the Syro-Ephraimite War of 735/734 B.C.) **1.** What danger was threatening him now (vv. 1–6)? **2.** Ahaz was known as an evil king, so what do you make of his response here (v. 12)? Was this unbelief or humility? What was his alternative plan (2 Kin. 16:7–9)? **3.** What is the sign that the Lord will

6:9–10 Jesus made use of this passage in the parable of the sower (Matt. 13:14–15; Mark 4:12; Luke 8:10; Rom. 11:7–10,25).

6:10 Make the heart ... ears ... eyes. Common in the Old Testament, this inverted construction (abc/cba) is called a "chiasm," a poetic form that emphasizes a point. **ears dull ... close their eyes.** Israel refuses to see or hear God, a condition also noted in 29:9; 42:18; 43:8. The time will come, however, when their ears and eyes will be opened again (29:18; 35:5).

7:1 This attack on Jerusalem by the kings of Aram (Syria) and Israel (Ephraim), known as the Syro-Ephraimite War, occurred probably in 735-34 B.C. The two kings tried without success to encourage Ahaz to join them in a coalition against Assyria, which was seeking to expand its borders to the west. Isaiah attempted to prevent Ahaz from allying instead with Assyria (2 Kin. 16:5–18; 2 Chr. 28:16–21).

7:3 your son Shear-Jashub. Isaiah's son's name alludes to the coming exile and subsequent return of the remnant, which will occur long after Isaiah's death.

give to Ahaz anyway? How does this sign fit the crisis? Can a comforting sign also warn? Instead of peace, what will happen once Israel and Aram are out of the picture? **4.** What images does Isaiah use in verses 18–25 to show what Assyria will do to Judah? Which one is the most graphic to you? What do you make of the "curds and honey" imagery?

APPLY 1. What situation are you facing that frightens you now? What forces are involved? How trusting of God are you in that situation? What makes it difficult for you to trust God in such fearful times? **2.** When have you found that your solution to a problem, rather than God's, only made the problem worse? **3.** Matthew 1:23 shows that Jesus fulfilled the prophecy in verse 14 far more than any child in Ahaz' day could have. When facing a challenging crisis, how have you seen Jesus as "Immanuel" ("God with us")?

Remaliah's son have plotted your ruin, saying, 6"Let us invade Judah;
let us tear it apart and divide it among ourselves, and make the son of
Tabeel king over it." 7Yet this is what the Sovereign LORD says:

" 'It will not take place,
it will not happen,
8for the head of Aram is Damascus,
and the head of Damascus is only Rezin.
Within sixty-five years
Ephraim will be too shattered to be a people.
9The head of Ephraim is Samaria,
and the head of Samaria is only Remaliah's son.
If you do not stand firm in your faith,
you will not stand at all.' "

10Again the LORD spoke to Ahaz, 11"Ask the LORD your God for a
sign, whether in the deepest depths or in the highest heights."
12But Ahaz said, "I will not ask; I will not put the LORD to the test."
13Then Isaiah said, "Hear now, you house of David! Is it not enough
to try the patience of men? Will you try the patience of my God also?
14Therefore the Lord himself will give you[a] a sign: The virgin will be
with child and will give birth to a son, and[b] will call him Immanuel.[c]
15He will eat curds and honey when he knows enough to reject the
wrong and choose the right. 16But before the boy knows enough to
reject the wrong and choose the right, the land of the two kings
you dread will be laid waste. 17The LORD will bring on you and on
your people and on the house of your father a time unlike any since
Ephraim broke away from Judah—he will bring the king of Assyria."
18In that day the LORD will whistle for flies from the distant streams
of Egypt and for bees from the land of Assyria. 19They will all come
and settle in the steep ravines and in the crevices in the rocks, on all
the thornbushes and at all the water holes. 20In that day the Lord will
use a razor hired from beyond the River[d]—the king of Assyria—to
shave your head and the hair of your legs, and to take off your beards
also. 21In that day, a man will keep alive a young cow and two goats.
22And because of the abundance of the milk they give, he will have
curds to eat. All who remain in the land will eat curds and honey. 23In
that day, in every place where there were a thousand vines worth a
thousand silver shekels,[e] there will be only briers and thorns. 24Men

[a]14 The Hebrew is plural. [b]14 Masoretic Text; Dead Sea Scrolls *and he* or *and they* [c]14 *Immanuel* means *God with us.* [d]20 That is, the Euphrates [e]23 That is, about 25 pounds (about 11.5 kilograms)

7:9 Remaliah's son. This king, named Pekah, was a weak threat to king Ahaz (in the line of David) because he had usurped his throne. Whereas Aram and Israel had human kings, Judah's king was God (vv. 8–9,14; 8:8,10).

7:14 will give you a sign. Usually signs were realized within only a few years, so those who received the sign also witnessed its fulfillment (8:18; 20:3–4; 37:30). **virgin.** The word means "a young woman of marriageable age," with the *assumption that the woman is* a virgin. In the Septuagint it is translated with a Greek word that specifically means "virgin." In Matthew 1:23 this verse is taken as a foreshadowing of the Virgin Mary. Here Isaiah may be referring to a young woman to whom he was betrothed (his first wife probably died after the birth of Shear-Jashub). The same word (*'almah*) is used of a betrothed woman in Genesis 24:43 (Prov. 30:19). **Immanuel.** The name means "God with us," thus assuring king Ahaz that God would protect him from enemy nations (Num. 14:9; 2 Chr. 13:12; Ps. 46:7). The same name appears in 8:8,10, perhaps in reference to Maher-Shalal-Hash-Baz, whose name means "quick to the plunder, swift to the spoil" (8:3); the combined names speak of the nation's divinely empowered victory over enemies. Of course, the final application of the name is to Jesus Christ who truly became "God with us" (9:6–7; Matt. 1:23).

7:19 settle ... in the crevices in the rocks. Under attack, Israelites would often flee to caves or crevices (2:10); but here such escape will not be possible.

7:20 shave. Conquerors would often shave the head and beards of the defeated in order to further humiliate them (2 Sam. 10:4–5).

7:23–25 will be only briers and thorns. The repetition of this

will go there with bow and arrow, for the land will be covered with
briers and thorns. [25]As for all the hills once cultivated by the hoe, you
will no longer go there for fear of the briers and thorns; they will become places where cattle are turned loose and where sheep run.

Assyria, the Lord's Instrument

8 The LORD said to me, "Take a large scroll and write on it with an
ordinary pen: Maher-Shalal-Hash-Baz.[a] [2]And I will call in Uriah
the priest and Zechariah son of Jeberekiah as reliable witnesses
for me."

[3]Then I went to the prophetess, and she conceived and gave birth
to a son. And the LORD said to me, "Name him Maher-Shalal-Hash-
Baz. [4]Before the boy knows how to say 'My father' or 'My mother,'
the wealth of Damascus and the plunder of Samaria will be carried
off by the king of Assyria."

[5]The LORD spoke to me again:

[6]"Because this people has rejected
the gently flowing waters of Shiloah
and rejoices over Rezin
and the son of Remaliah,
[7]therefore the Lord is about to bring against them
the mighty floodwaters of the River[b]—
the king of Assyria with all his pomp.
It will overflow all its channels,
run over all its banks
[8]and sweep on into Judah, swirling over it,
passing through it and reaching up to the neck.
Its outspread wings will cover the breadth of your land,
O Immanuel[c]!"

[9]Raise the war cry,[d] you nations, and be shattered!
Listen, all you distant lands.
Prepare for battle, and be shattered!
Prepare for battle, and be shattered!
[10]Devise your strategy, but it will be thwarted;
propose your plan, but it will not stand,
for God is with us.[e]

Fear God

[11]The LORD spoke to me with his strong hand upon me, warning me
not to follow the way of this people. He said:

[12]"Do not call conspiracy
everything that these people call conspiracy[f];
do not fear what they fear,

[a]1 *Maher-Shalal-Hash-Baz* means *quick to the plunder, swift to the spoil*; also in verse 3. [b]7 That is, the Euphrates [c]8 *Immanuel* means *God with us.* [d]9 Or *Do your worst* [e]10 Hebrew *Immanuel* [f]12 Or *Do not call for a treaty / every time these people call for a treaty*

OPEN 1. Whom were you named after? What does your full name mean? **2.** When have you been afraid of water and why?

STUDY 1. What is the meaning of Judah "rejecting" Shiloah and "rejoicing" over Rezin (vv. 6–7; 7:1)? **2.** Why does Judah prefer Assyrian help over God's as they face this crisis (2 Kin. 16:7–9)? Why would idolatry lead to destructive political alliances? **3.** Is "O Immanuel!" (v. 8) a cry of despair or of hope? Why? What is the prophet's hope for Judah, even as he considers the coming siege from Assyria (chs. 36–37)?

APPLY 1. How has the Lord been like a gently flowing stream to you? **2.** When has your choice of allies resulted in a flood of overwhelming trouble? When has God stopped the flood of wrong choices from overwhelming you?

OPEN 1. When have you been afraid of the dark and why? How did you get over that fear? **2.** What funny or fearful experience have you had with blackouts?

STUDY 1. What is the "way of this people" God told Isaiah not to follow (v. 11)? What do they fear contrasted with what Isaiah fears? **2.** What effects do these fears have on the way each acts? On God's

phrase is emphatic: As part of God's judgment the land can no longer be cultivated.

8:3 prophetess ... son. This may initially fulfill the prophecy of 7:14. Note that Isaiah's wife was a prophetess in her own right.

8:10 propose your plan, but it will not stand. Human strategies cannot succeed if they oppose God's purposes.

8:11 The LORD spoke ... his strong hand upon me. The prophets were clearly aware that their word was inspired and that God was using them for divine purposes (Ezek. 1:3; 37:1; 40:1).

response? **3.** How does Isaiah respond to Judah's rejection of his message? How is his family a sign and symbol from the Lord (v. 18; 7:3,14)? **4.** How does Isaiah bring out the contrast between mediums, spiritists and God? **5.** What should the people be seeking? What "blackout" will result from their refusal to do so?

APPLY 1. From watching your life this week, what would someone say it means for you to fear God? What does it really mean to fear God? **2.** How is Jesus both a "sanctuary" and a "stumbling block" (v. 14; Rom. 9:33; 1 Peter 2:6–8)? Which is he to you right now?

OPEN 1. When were you most in need of, or grateful for, a flashlight? **2.** When have you gotten up early to greet the sunrise? What "dawn of a new day" are you anticipating on this year's calendar?

STUDY 1. What do you think Isaiah meant by the "darkness" in which the people walk (v. 2)? What suffering had Zebulun and Naphtali (in Israel) experienced (2 Kin. 15:29)? **2.** How does Isaiah describe the effects of the dawning light (vv. 3–5; for Midian's defeat)? The

and do not dread it.
13 The LORD Almighty is the one you are to regard as holy,
he is the one you are to fear,
he is the one you are to dread,
14 and he will be a sanctuary;
but for both houses of Israel he will be
a stone that causes men to stumble
and a rock that makes them fall.
And for the people of Jerusalem he will be
a trap and a snare.
15 Many of them will stumble;
they will fall and be broken,
they will be snared and captured."

16 Bind up the testimony
and seal up the law among my disciples.
17 I will wait for the LORD,
who is hiding his face from the house of Jacob.
I will put my trust in him.

18 Here am I, and the children the LORD has given me. We are signs
and symbols in Israel from the LORD Almighty, who dwells on Mount
Zion.
19 When men tell you to consult mediums and spiritists, who whisper and mutter, should not a people inquire of their God? Why
consult the dead on behalf of the living? 20 To the law and to the testimony! If they do not speak according to this word, they have no light
of dawn. 21 Distressed and hungry, they will roam through the land;
when they are famished, they will become enraged and, looking
upward, will curse their king and their God. 22 Then they will look
toward the earth and see only distress and darkness and fearful
gloom, and they will be thrust into utter darkness.

To Us a Child Is Born

9 Nevertheless, there will be no more gloom for those who were in distress. In the past he humbled the land of Zebulun and the land of Naphtali, but in the future he will honor Galilee of the Gentiles, by the way of the sea, along the Jordan—

2 The people walking in darkness
have seen a great light;
on those living in the land of the shadow of death[a]
a light has dawned.
3 You have enlarged the nation

[a]2 Or *land of darkness*

8:17 wait ... trust. Isaiah still hopes in God, confidently expecting that the people will ultimately be delivered. Of course, ultimate hope is found in Jesus Christ.

8:19 consult mediums and spiritists. In threatening, fearful conditions the people sought help through the practice of necromancy (contact with the spirits of dead people in an effort to influence present reality). King Saul consulted the deceased Samuel to ascertain what would happen to him (1 Sam. 28:8–11). God abhorred this practice because it demonstrated a lack of trust *in him.*

8:21 curse their king and their God. Frustrated with their present suffering, the people will lash out against those they consider responsible, despite warnings of terrible punishment for anyone who does this (Ex. 22:28; Lev. 24:15–16).

9:2 have seen a great light. A reference to God's truth, blessing and presence. Later Isaiah would refer to the Messiah as a "light for the Gentiles" (42:6; 49:6).

and increased their joy;
they rejoice before you
as people rejoice at the harvest,
as men rejoice
when dividing the plunder.
4 For as in the day of Midian's defeat,
you have shattered
the yoke that burdens them,
the bar across their shoulders,
the rod of their oppressor.
5 Every warrior's boot used in battle
and every garment rolled in blood
will be destined for burning,
will be fuel for the fire.
6 For to us a child is born,
to us a son is given,
and the government will be on his shoulders.
And he will be called
Wonderful Counselor,[a] Mighty God,
Everlasting Father, Prince of Peace.
7 Of the increase of his government and peace
there will be no end.
He will reign on David's throne
and over his kingdom,
establishing and upholding it
with justice and righteousness
from that time on and forever.
The zeal of the LORD Almighty
will accomplish this.

The Lord's Anger Against Israel

8 The Lord has sent a message against Jacob;
it will fall on Israel.
9 All the people will know it—
Ephraim and the inhabitants of Samaria—
who say with pride
and arrogance of heart,
10 "The bricks have fallen down,
but we will rebuild with dressed stone;
the fig trees have been felled,
but we will replace them with cedars."
11 But the LORD has strengthened Rezin's foes against them
and has spurred their enemies on.

[a]6 Or *Wonderful, Counselor*

gloom is the threat of Assyria. What relation does the light (v. 2) have to the child (7:13–17)? What will be the light? How is he defined in verses 6–7? **3.** What expectations would this arouse in you if you had first heard Isaiah pronounce it? What type of son or ruler would you expect to arise? How would his future rule and counsel compare with past alliances and plans (8:7–10)? How would this make you feel? **4.** How does the New Testament interpret what this prophecy means (Matt. 4:12–17; Luke 1:32; John 8:12)? Of the titles given in verse 6, which fits Jesus as you know him?

APPLY 1. Where has gloom come into your life in recent months? **2.** How can the light of Jesus Christ help dispel that gloom?

OPEN 1. When have you boastfully thought something would turn out fine, but it didn't? **2.** Have you ever felt a decision was rigged against you: "Heads I win, tails you lose"?

STUDY 1. The repetition in verses 12,17,21 and 10:4 shows that this is a poem or song. What do you think the song is about? **2.** What must have happened in Israel? (Note: The opposition of King Rezin of Aram in vv. 11–12 indicates this prophecy was given prior to the alliance described in 7:1.) How did the people of Israel (Ephraim and Samaria) respond to these attacks

9:6 he will be called Wonderful Counselor. The first of four "throne names" each of which combine two key aspects of the Messiah and his rule and speak of his combined humanity and divinity. This phrase describes him as a king (Mic. 4:8) who prudently plans and performs his responsibilities (14:27). As a result of his reign (described in chapters 11, 24–27; "marvelous things, things planned long ago," 25:1), the whole world will stand in awe of his wisdom and power. **Mighty God.** As a warrior he will be supreme (10:21). **Everlasting Father.** God will lovingly provide and protect forever (40:9–11). **Prince of Peace.** Under his reign the people will experience "shalom," peace, well-being and wholeness.

9:7 David's throne ... forever. Unlike the human kings of Israel, even the good ones like Ahaz, the Messiah will rule with perfect wisdom, justice and righteousness eternally (11:3–5; 2 Sam. 7:12,13,16; Jer. 33:15,20–22).

(vv. 9,10,13)? How should they have responded? **3.** Hence, what will God do to their leaders (vv. 14–17)? With what result? **4.** What pictures come to mind as Isaiah describes the wickedness of the people (vv. 18–20)? What is the point of comparing their wickedness to a raging forest fire or people eating up their own family? **5.** What are the specific charges God lays against the leaders of Israel (10:1–2)? What will be the result of refusing to provide justice and peace for the people?

APPLY 1. From this song, what attitudes and actions do you see that are particularly offensive to God? Which ones do you feel are evident in your life? In the life of your nation? **2.** God's final judgment came only after many attempts to warn the people about the consequences of their deeds. How has God tried to warn you in the past of the consequences of where you were heading? How did you respond to those warnings? **3.** What is one area of injustice or neglect of the poor in your community or nation that you could work on correcting: Tax reform? Housing? Health care? Race relations? Abuse victims? Or what? What keeps you from doing so?

---

12 Arameans from the east and Philistines from the west
have devoured Israel with open mouth.

Yet for all this, his anger is not turned away,
his hand is still upraised.

13 But the people have not returned to him who struck them,
nor have they sought the LORD Almighty.
14 So the LORD will cut off from Israel both head and tail,
both palm branch and reed in a single day;
15 the elders and prominent men are the head,
the prophets who teach lies are the tail.
16 Those who guide this people mislead them,
and those who are guided are led astray.
17 Therefore the Lord will take no pleasure in the young men,
nor will he pity the fatherless and widows,
for everyone is ungodly and wicked,
every mouth speaks vileness.

Yet for all this, his anger is not turned away,
his hand is still upraised.

18 Surely wickedness burns like a fire;
it consumes briers and thorns,
it sets the forest thickets ablaze,
so that it rolls upward in a column of smoke.
19 By the wrath of the LORD Almighty
the land will be scorched
and the people will be fuel for the fire;
no one will spare his brother.
20 On the right they will devour,
but still be hungry;
on the left they will eat,
but not be satisfied.
Each will feed on the flesh of his own offspring[a]:
21 Manasseh will feed on Ephraim, and Ephraim on Manasseh;
together they will turn against Judah.

Yet for all this, his anger is not turned away,
his hand is still upraised.

10 Woe to those who make unjust laws,
to those who issue oppressive decrees,
2 to deprive the poor of their rights
and withhold justice from the oppressed of my people,
making widows their prey
and robbing the fatherless.

[a]20 *Or arm*

9:12 hand is still upraised. The *picture of God with his hand raised in* wrath is first used in 5:25, and recurs in verses 17, 21, and also in 10:4 as a climax of the passage.

9:14 cut off ... head and tail ... palm branch and reed. A reference to Israel's corrupt leaders (3:1–3). The same two descriptions are applied to Egypt's leaders in 19:15.

9:17 nor will he pity the fatherless and widows. Leaders (1:17) often took advantage of these victims. But now even the disadvantaged are being judged because they are depraved.

[3]What will you do on the day of reckoning,
when disaster comes from afar?
To whom will you run for help?
Where will you leave your riches?
[4]Nothing will remain but to cringe among the captives
or fall among the slain.

Yet for all this, his anger is not turned away,
his hand is still upraised.

God's Judgment on Assyria

[5]"Woe to the Assyrian, the rod of my anger,
in whose hand is the club of my wrath!
[6]I send him against a godless nation,
I dispatch him against a people who anger me,
to seize loot and snatch plunder,
and to trample them down like mud in the streets.
[7]But this is not what he intends,
this is not what he has in mind;
his purpose is to destroy,
to put an end to many nations.
[8]'Are not my commanders all kings?' he says.
[9] 'Has not Calno fared like Carchemish?
Is not Hamath like Arpad,
and Samaria like Damascus?
[10]As my hand seized the kingdoms of the idols,
kingdoms whose images excelled those of Jerusalem and
Samaria—
[11]shall I not deal with Jerusalem and her images
as I dealt with Samaria and her idols?' "

[12]When the Lord has finished all his work against Mount Zion and
Jerusalem, he will say, "I will punish the king of Assyria for the willful
pride of his heart and the haughty look in his eyes. [13]For he says:

" 'By the strength of my hand I have done this,
and by my wisdom, because I have understanding.
I removed the boundaries of nations,
I plundered their treasures;
like a mighty one I subdued[a] their kings.
[14]As one reaches into a nest,
so my hand reached for the wealth of the nations;
as men gather abandoned eggs,
so I gathered all the countries;

[a]13 Or / *I subdued the mighty,*

OPEN Who was the bully in your grade school, neighborhood or family who pushed you around with apparent impunity? How did you feel about that? Whatever became of that person?

STUDY 1. While 9:8–10:4 conveys God's judgment against Israel, what is the focus of his judgment here? What was God's purpose in allowing Assyria to overrun Israel and Judah (vv. 5–6; 7:17)? **2.** The cities listed in verse 9 are all conquered by the Assyrian army en route to Jerusalem. What attitudes have these victories produced in the Assyrian leaders (vv. 10–11)? Why do they think Jerusalem ought to be an easy victory? What does this show about their deep misunderstanding of the Lord? **3.** Read aloud verses 13–14, accenting the tone of voice and attitude expressed in the many times "I" and "my" are used. What root problem does this reveal? According to the absurd picture in verse 15, what have they got backwards? **4.** What is the Lord's response to their pride? Compare verse 16 with 37:36. What do you think happened here? **5.** How is God both like a light and a fire (vv. 16–19)? What truth about God is expressed in each idea?

APPLY 1. When have you taken the credit for what was really God's work and you were merely his instrument? How do you practice giving credit where credit is due? **2.** Does God seem more like a guiding light, or a consuming fire to you right now? How so? When have you

10:5 rod of my anger. God will ultimately destroy the weapons of the oppressor, Assyria (9:4). Babylon also was used by God as a club of punishment against rebellious nations (Jer. 50:23; 51:20; Hab. 1:6). Although God uses these godless nations, eventually they will be judged.

10:10 images. Despite God's clear word concerning idols, Israelites routinely worshiped them (2:8). Just as God had chastened Samaria because of idolatry (through defeat by Shalmaneser V and Sargon II in 722–21 B.C.), God would be forced to do the same to Israel.

10:12 willful pride. God announced his judgment on pride through the prophet in 2:11,17.

10:13–14 I have done this. Marked by hubris, Assyria's king refers to himself arrogantly nine times in these two verses (14:13,14; Ezek. 28:2–5).

experienced him in the other way? What have you learned about God from these experiences?

---

not one flapped a wing,
 or opened its mouth to chirp.' "

15 Does the ax raise itself above him who swings it,
 or the saw boast against him who uses it?
As if a rod were to wield him who lifts it up,
 or a club brandish him who is not wood!
16 Therefore, the Lord, the LORD Almighty,
 will send a wasting disease upon his sturdy warriors;
under his pomp a fire will be kindled
 like a blazing flame.
17 The Light of Israel will become a fire,
 their Holy One a flame;
in a single day it will burn and consume
 his thorns and his briers.
18 The splendor of his forests and fertile fields
 it will completely destroy,
 as when a sick man wastes away.
19 And the remaining trees of his forests will be so few
 that a child could write them down.

The Remnant of Israel

20 In that day the remnant of Israel,
 the survivors of the house of Jacob,
will no longer rely on him
 who struck them down
but will truly rely on the LORD,
 the Holy One of Israel.
21 A remnant will return,[a] a remnant of Jacob
 will return to the Mighty God.
22 Though your people, O Israel, be like the sand by the sea,
 only a remnant will return.
Destruction has been decreed,
 overwhelming and righteous.
23 The Lord, the LORD Almighty, will carry out
 the destruction decreed upon the whole land.

24 Therefore, this is what the Lord, the LORD Almighty, says:

"O my people who live in Zion,
 do not be afraid of the Assyrians,
who beat you with a rod
 and lift up a club against you, as Egypt did.
25 Very soon my anger against you will end
 and my wrath will be directed to their destruction."

[a] 21 Hebrew *shear-jashub*; also in verse 22

OPEN 1. What remnants do you have more of in your house: Food? Carpets? Clothing? Other? What do you plan on doing with them? **2.** If you could save only a remnant of your possessions in a disaster, what would you most want to save?

STUDY 1. Judah originally looked to Assyria to help them (2 Kin. 16:7). What will result from this experience? What price is paid for this object lesson? **2.** The "remnant" theme has appeared before (1:9; 4:3; 6:13). How does this theme show both God's judgment and his mercy? What attitudes characterize the "remnant of Israel"? **3.** In verses 24–27, what hope does Isaiah provide for the people even before these events occur? How do the stories of Gideon (Judg. 7) and Moses (Ex. 14:21) boost their hope? **4.** Verses 28–32 recount an army's hypothetical approach from a point about 10 miles north of Jerusalem. Substitute names of cities and towns near you. How does this help you to understand what the author wants the people of Jerusalem to feel? To do? **5.** What will God do to this army (vv. 33–34)? How do you feel after God's intervention?

10:16 will send a wasting disease. This probably refers to a plague, as happened to Sennacherib when 185,000 Assyrian soldiers were put to death by an angel of God in 701 B.C. (37:36; 2 Sam. 24:15,16; 1 Chr. 21:22,27).

10:20–22 remnant of Israel. Isaiah frequently refers to the righteous remnant who will survive God's judgment on Israel (1:9; 4:3; 11:11; 46:3). In fact, Isaiah's firstborn son was named "a remnant will return" (7:3). Indeed, Hezekiah would lead a remnant who survived Assyria's invasion of 701 B.C. (37:4). Later a remnant would return to the land from exile in Babylon.

10:25 Very soon. From a human point of view the present difficulty would be long and hard, but in the

will lash them with a whip,
ck down Midian at the rock of Oreb;
his staff over the waters,
gypt.
ir burden will be lifted from your shoulders,
from your neck;
l be broken
you have grown so fat.[a]

r Aiath;
ass through Migron;
store supplies at Micmash.
go over the pass, and say,
We will camp overnight at Geba."
amah trembles;
Gibeah of Saul flees.
30 Cry out, O Daughter of Gallim!
Listen, O Laishah!
Poor Anathoth!
31 Madmenah is in flight;
the people of Gebim take cover.
32 This day they will halt at Nob;
they will shake their fist
at the mount of the Daughter of Zion,
at the hill of Jerusalem.

33 See, the Lord, the LORD Almighty,
will lop off the boughs with great power.
The lofty trees will be felled,
the tall ones will be brought low.
34 He will cut down the forest thickets with an ax;
Lebanon will fall before the Mighty One.

The Branch From Jesse

11 A shoot will come up from the stump of Jesse;
from his roots a Branch will bear fruit.
2 The Spirit of the LORD will rest on him—
the Spirit of wisdom and of understanding,
the Spirit of counsel and of power,
the Spirit of knowledge and of the fear of the LORD—
3 and he will delight in the fear of the LORD.

[a]27 Hebrew; Septuagint *broken / from your shoulders*

APPLY 1. Isaiah looked back to the stories of Moses and Gideon to provide hope for the people. What stories of God's grace and deliverance—both Biblical and contemporary—can you look back upon to find hope in times when it is hard to trust God? **2.** How have you seen God cut down an army that has threatened to overwhelm you? What army seems to be breathing down your neck now?

OPEN 1. Who was your hero when you were 10 years old? Was he or she fictional or real? What was your hero able to do that you couldn't? **2.** What do you like most about coming home after being away a long time?

STUDY 1. Whereas the mighty tree of Assyria was destroyed (10:33–34), what will happen to the Root of Jesse (Israel)? How

context of eternity the time would be very brief.

10:28–32 Isaiah describes the Assyrian army's movements toward Jerusalem from north of the city as though he were literally witnessing it.

11:1 stump of Jesse. The figurative stump of David's father Jesse is all that remained of David's dynasty after Judah was exiled to Babylon in 586 B.C. The shoot or branch represents Jesus Christ, David's descendant who will fulfill God's covenant with David and rule over a greater kingdom forever (Zech. 6:12; Acts 13:23).

11:2 The Spirit of the LORD will rest on him. Like David, the Messiah would be empowered by the Holy Spirit (Luke 3:22; John 1:32–34) and characterized by wisdom, understanding, counsel, power, knowledge and fear of the Lord, making him the Wonderful Counselor of 9:6. Isaiah refers to the Holy Spirit more than any other Old Testament prophet (16 times). The Holy Spirit would enable the Messiah to complete his mission.

is this "Branch" different from that mentioned in 4:2? **2.** What does it mean that "the Spirit of the LORD will rest on him" (vv. 2–3; 2 Kin. 2:15)? What supernatural knowledge, ability or motivation do you see here? **3.** What will his reign be like (vv. 3–5; compare 9:6–7; contrast 1:17–23 and 5:12–23)? **4.** Verses 6–9 figuratively portray the peaceable kingdom. What types of people or situations may Isaiah have in mind here (19:23–25)? What does this scene tell you about human relationships under the rule of this King? About the cause and extent of his reign? **5.** Armies rally round a raised banner. Who will rally here? What will be the result (v. 12; 32:16–18)? Once before, God saved his people by the exodus. How will this happen a second time? **6.** Comparing verse 12 with John 12:32, could it be that the "banner" raised by the promised Messiah is ultimately the cross of Christ? Why do you think so? **7.** How might verses 11–12 relate to the imagery of verses 6–9? To the promise of 19:24–25? How certain will all this be (9:7)? Why? **8.** This picture of the Messiah's reign is both deeply personal and social. What would a new society look like under the Messiah's reign (be specific)?

APPLY 1. The New Testament interprets the "Branch" as the Messiah, Jesus (Rom. 15:12; Rev. 5:5). What stories, teachings or sayings about Jesus come to mind as you consider the qualities described in verses 2–5? Which of these qualities of Jesus has particularly made a difference in your life? **2.** Do you see yourself at this time more like a wolf or a lamb? Who do you see as your opposite in this regard? Why? What does it mean for the two of you that God does not change wolves into sheep, or vice versa, but transforms them so they can live in peace with one another? **3.** How would you like to grow under the Lordship of Christ?

He will not judge by what he sees with his eye
 or decide by what he hears with his ears;
4 but with righteousness he will judge the needy,
 with justice he will give decisions for the poor
He will strike the earth with the rod of his mouth;
 with the breath of his lips he will slay the wicked.
5 Righteousness will be his belt
 and faithfulness the sash around his waist.

6 The wolf will live with the lamb,
 the leopard will lie down with the goat,
the calf and the lion and the yearling[a] together;
 and a little child will lead them.
7 The cow will feed with the bear,
 their young will lie down together,
 and the lion will eat straw like the ox.
8 The infant will play near the hole of the cobra,
 and the young child put his hand into the viper's nest.
9 They will neither harm nor destroy
 on all my holy mountain,
for the earth will be full of the knowledge of the LORD
 as the waters cover the sea.

10 In that day the Root of Jesse will stand as a banner for the peoples; the nations will rally to him, and his place of rest will be glorious. 11 In that day the Lord will reach out his hand a second time to
reclaim the remnant that is left of his people from Assyria, from Lower Egypt, from Upper Egypt,[b] from Cush,[c] from Elam, from Babylonia,[d]
from Hamath and from the islands of the sea.

12 He will raise a banner for the nations
 and gather the exiles of Israel;
he will assemble the scattered people of Judah
 from the four quarters of the earth.
13 Ephraim's jealousy will vanish,
 and Judah's enemies[e] will be cut off;
Ephraim will not be jealous of Judah,
 nor Judah hostile toward Ephraim.
14 They will swoop down on the slopes of Philistia to the west;
 together they will plunder the people to the east.
They will lay hands on Edom and Moab,
 and the Ammonites will be subject to them.
15 The LORD will dry up
 the gulf of the Egyptian sea;
with a scorching wind he will sweep his hand
 over the Euphrates River.[f]

[a] 6 Hebrew; Septuagint *lion will feed* [b] 11 Hebrew *from Pathros* [c] 11 That is, the upper Nile region [d] 11 Hebrew *Shinar* [e] 13 Or *hostility* [f] 15 Hebrew *the River*

11:4 righteousness he will judge. Jesus Christ will not be *an ordinary human judge with limited abilities. Since he sees straight into the heart, he will be able to judge* impartiality and to end injustice. **rod of his mouth.** By his speech, the Messiah will sentence the wicked and protect the innocent and oppressed (Heb. 4:12–13).

11:6 a little child. In the Messianic kingdom children will not be harmed (Hos. 2:18).

He will break it up into seven streams
so that men can cross over in sandals.
16 There will be a highway for the remnant of his people
that is left from Assyria,
as there was for Israel
when they came up from Egypt.

Songs of Praise

12 In that day you will say:

"I will praise you, O LORD.
Although you were angry with me,
your anger has turned away
and you have comforted me.
2 Surely God is my salvation;
I will trust and not be afraid.
The LORD, the LORD, is my strength and my song;
he has become my salvation."
3 With joy you will draw water
from the wells of salvation.

4 In that day you will say:

"Give thanks to the LORD, call on his name;
make known among the nations what he has done,
and proclaim that his name is exalted.
5 Sing to the LORD, for he has done glorious things;
let this be known to all the world.
6 Shout aloud and sing for joy, people of Zion,
for great is the Holy One of Israel among you."

A Prophecy Against Babylon

13 An oracle concerning Babylon that Isaiah son of Amoz saw:

2 Raise a banner on a bare hilltop,
shout to them;
beckon to them
to enter the gates of the nobles.
3 I have commanded my holy ones;

OPEN 1. How would you share good news with a loved one: Phone? Write a letter? Sing a song? **2.** What is the best thing that happened to you last week?

STUDY 1. How does this song of God's deliverance from Assyria compare with the way Israel celebrated God's deliverance from Egypt (Ex. 15)? **2.** How deeply does Israel respond to the Lord's salvation in verses 1–3? In verses 4–6? **3.** What is the real deliverance—of which Assyria is only an example—that God has in view here? What is the ultimate reason for Israel's joy?

APPLY 1. How well does your joy match your walk and your talk for God? **2.** When have you most keenly felt God's anger? God's goodness?

OPEN 1. What was the most dramatic or true-to-life war movie you ever saw? How did it affect you as you watched it? **2.** What warring nation in real life gets your "Evil Empire" award and why?

STUDY Chapters 13–23 bring together several prophetic judgments against the nations

12:1 I will praise you. The people who have returned from Babylon praise God because his anger has turned to comfort. This hymn is similar to Moses and Miriam's hymn of praise after the Exodus from Egypt (Ex. 15).

12:2 The LORD ... has become my salvation. From the Lord comes strength, salvation and song. Israel's salvation will include spiritual peace of mind, deliverance from bondage and prosperity.

12:3 wells of salvation. Hebrew poets often associate water with salvation, a divine provision in the desert. This metaphor depicts living according to God's instructions and enjoying the blessings God provides.

12:4 make known ... proclaim. Praise means "give public acknowledgment." Several imperatives in verses 4–6 (sing, let this be known to all the world, shout aloud, sing for joy) designate public, vocal acknowledgment of God's work among the people. Eventually, the whole world will know of God's glory.

12:6 people of Zion. Refers to the people who returned from captivity in Babylon (Zeph. 3:14–15).

13:1 oracle concerning Babylon. Sometimes translated "burden," as in a weighty message to deliver. Isaiah's oracle concerned Babylon, which had been a pagan city ever since Genesis 11:1–9. This is significant because Isaiah made this prophecy before the fall of Babylon occurred. The book of Isaiah takes a major turn at 13:1 and focuses on God's judgments against the nations.

13:3 I have commanded my holy ones. God calls this army from many places. The army's purpose is to serve as an instrument of God's judgment upon sinful nations (Joel 3:11).

surrounding Judah. This new section, together with the world-visions in chapters 24–27, serves as an interlude between the promised Assyrian crisis (chs. 1–12) and its onset (chs. 28–39). **1.** What is the intended audience of these prophecies? **2.** Why might God lead Isaiah to pronounce judgment upon all these nations if only Judah, and not the nations themselves, would have heard them? What does this say about Judah's tendency to trust in alliances with lesser nations for protection against greater enemies? **3.** Since Babylon was not the dominant world power until a century after this prophecy in chapters 13–14, what does this city symbolize that is timeless and bigger than itself (vv. 5,9,11)? What characterizes this Babylon (vv. 11,19; 14:13–14)? **4.** What is the "day of the LORD" like for Babylon (vv. 6,9; 2:11,17,20)? What poetic and cosmic images in verses 4–16 graphically communicate its power to you? **5.** What should the Judeans have learned about God from this prophecy against such a powerful nation? **6.** The Medes, from what is today part of Iran, had a reputation as fighters even in the days of the Assyrian dominance. How will they be used as God's agents against Babylon (as they eventually were)? **7.** What is the ultimate destiny of any endeavor built upon human pride (vv. 19–22)? **8.** What is the positive side and real purpose of this judgment (14:1–2)? **9.** What is the basis for God acting on Israel's behalf (12:1; 40:1–2)? On the Gentiles' behalf? What do you think this imagery of tables turned actually means (2:3–4; 11:11; 19:24–25)?

APPLY **1.** What is most likely to cause "your hands to go limp" and "your heart to melt" (v. 7): A stock market dive? A military confrontation between the U.S. and a hostile country? A violent storm? The anger of your spouse when you've let him/her down? **2.** If God were to judge you today by taking away what you treasure the most, what would it be? **3.** What helps you keep God's values primary? In what area is that especially hard for you right now? How can your group help in this regard?

I have summoned my warriors to carry out my wrath—
those who rejoice in my triumph.

4 Listen, a noise on the mountains,
like that of a great multitude!
Listen, an uproar among the kingdoms,
like nations massing together!
The LORD Almighty is mustering
an army for war.
5 They come from faraway lands,
from the ends of the heavens—
the LORD and the weapons of his wrath—
to destroy the whole country.

6 Wail, for the day of the LORD is near;
it will come like destruction from the Almighty.[a]
7 Because of this, all hands will go limp,
every man's heart will melt.
8 Terror will seize them,
pain and anguish will grip them;
they will writhe like a woman in labor.
They will look aghast at each other,
their faces aflame.

9 See, the day of the LORD is coming
—a cruel day, with wrath and fierce anger—
to make the land desolate
and destroy the sinners within it.
10 The stars of heaven and their constellations
will not show their light.
The rising sun will be darkened
and the moon will not give its light.
11 I will punish the world for its evil,
the wicked for their sins.
I will put an end to the arrogance of the haughty
and will humble the pride of the ruthless.
12 I will make man scarcer than pure gold,
more rare than the gold of Ophir.
13 Therefore I will make the heavens tremble;
and the earth will shake from its place
at the wrath of the LORD Almighty,
in the day of his burning anger.

14 Like a hunted gazelle,
like sheep without a shepherd,
each will return to his own people,
each will flee to his native land.
15 Whoever is captured will be thrust through;

[a]6 Hebrew *Shaddai*

13:6 the day of the LORD is near. The time of God's judgment on the wicked and deliverance of his people. The political upheaval resulting in the fall of Babylon to the Assyrians in 689 B.C. parallels the turmoil coming upon the world just before God establishes a kingdom of peace.

13:13 heavens tremble ... earth ... shake. Figures of speech suggesting total destruction, similar to the final judgment of the world (Hag. 2:6–7).

all who are caught will fall by the sword.
[16]Their infants will be dashed to pieces before their eyes;
their houses will be looted and their wives ravished.

[17]See, I will stir up against them the Medes,
who do not care for silver
and have no delight in gold.
[18]Their bows will strike down the young men;
they will have no mercy on infants
nor will they look with compassion on children.
[19]Babylon, the jewel of kingdoms,
the glory of the Babylonians'[a] pride,
will be overthrown by God
like Sodom and Gomorrah.
[20]She will never be inhabited
or lived in through all generations;
no Arab will pitch his tent there,
no shepherd will rest his flocks there.
[21]But desert creatures will lie there,
jackals will fill her houses;
there the owls will dwell,
and there the wild goats will leap about.
[22]Hyenas will howl in her strongholds,
jackals in her luxurious palaces.
Her time is at hand,
and her days will not be prolonged.

14 The LORD will have compassion on Jacob;
once again he will choose Israel
and will settle them in their own land.
Aliens will join them
and unite with the house of Jacob.
[2]Nations will take them
and bring them to their own place.
And the house of Israel will possess the nations
as menservants and maidservants in the LORD's land.
They will make captives of their captors
and rule over their oppressors.

[3]On the day the LORD gives you relief from suffering and turmoil
and cruel bondage, [4]you will take up this taunt against the king of
Babylon:

How the oppressor has come to an end!
How his fury[b] has ended!
[5]The LORD has broken the rod of the wicked,

[a]19 Or *Chaldeans'* [b]4 Dead Sea Scrolls, Septuagint and Syriac; the meaning of the word in the Masoretic Text is uncertain.

OPEN In your childhood relationships, what taunts were used to anger you? Which of your taunts were used to get the best of others? Which taunts among your children (if any) are most mischievous or upsetting?

STUDY The taunt song here (vv. 4–21) is comprised of four stanzas which celebrate the overthrow

13:19 glory ... pride. The city of Babylon would be overthrown in 689 B.C. by the Assyrians, God's instrument of wrath. Just as Sodom and Gomorrah had been destroyed for their wickedness, beautiful, wealthy Babylon would lie desolate and uninhabited.

14:1 will have compassion ... will settle them. When God destroys Babylon, he will restore Israel (Ps. 102:13). His choosing of Israel is a major Old Testament theme, particularly in 1 and 2 Chronicles and the Psalms.

of the ruler of Babylon, who personifies the pride that marked the nation as a whole. **1.** In the first stanza (vv. 4–8), how is this king described? What was his rule like? What happens now that his rule is ended? **2.** In the second stanza (vv. 9–11), what grave matter should concern this king but doesn't? How does this stanza demonstrate the folly of laying up treasure on earth? **3.** In the third stanza (vv. 12–15), Isaiah makes use of pagan mythology to ridicule the king. What primarily motivates this king? How does his destiny compare with his ambition? **4.** The "morning star" is probably Venus, which appears bright on the horizon until the sun rises and it disappears from view. What does this tell you about human pride that asserts itself against God? **5.** In the final stanza (vv. 16–21), what is the contrast between the king's early power and final condition? Unable to have his power endure, what is the final judgment upon this king? **6.** There is no known Babylonian or Assyrian king who suffered this type of disgrace. What then is the idea which verses 22–23 reinforce? Is all that is said about this king really a symbol for God's judgment upon the people of Babylon as a whole? Upon human pride as a whole? Or what?

APPLY **1.** What personal "fall from heaven" have you experienced that has caused you to lose face in the eyes of others and re-evaluate your life: Divorce? Bankruptcy? Being fired or laid off? Being publically censored or criticized? Other? **2.** With whom do you identify more in this taunt: The defeated people who were glad to see the tables turned on Babylon? Or Babylon, the one who saw her victories turn to defeat? **3.** When you suffer a humiliating setback, how does it change the way you look at the role of God in your life?

the scepter of the rulers,
6 which in anger struck down peoples
with unceasing blows,
and in fury subdued nations
with relentless aggression.
7 All the lands are at rest and at peace;
they break into singing.
8 Even the pine trees and the cedars of Lebanon
exult over you and say,
"Now that you have been laid low,
no woodsman comes to cut us down."

9 The grave[a] below is all astir
to meet you at your coming;
it rouses the spirits of the departed to greet you—
all those who were leaders in the world;
it makes them rise from their thrones—
all those who were kings over the nations.
10 They will all respond,
they will say to you,
"You also have become weak, as we are;
you have become like us."
11 All your pomp has been brought down to the grave,
along with the noise of your harps;
maggots are spread out beneath you
and worms cover you.

12 How you have fallen from heaven,
O morning star, son of the dawn!
You have been cast down to the earth,
you who once laid low the nations!
13 You said in your heart,
"I will ascend to heaven;
I will raise my throne
above the stars of God;
I will sit enthroned on the mount of assembly,
on the utmost heights of the sacred mountain.[b]
14 I will ascend above the tops of the clouds;
I will make myself like the Most High."
15 But you are brought down to the grave,
to the depths of the pit.

16 Those who see you stare at you,
they ponder your fate:
"Is this the man who shook the earth
and made kingdoms tremble,

[a]9 Hebrew *Sheol*; also in verses 11 and 15 [b]13 Or *the north*; Hebrew *Zaphon*

14:9 it makes them rise from their thrones. *The grave is pictured as a* throne room in hell where kings of the earth go upon death (Ezek. 32:21). Other kings, seeing the tyrant Sennacherib *among them,* were amazed that he had been defeated.

14:12 laid low the nations. Mighty Sennacherib had defeated Phoenicia, Philistia, Egypt, Moab, Edom, Cilicia, part of Judah and northern Arabia. He desired eternal world domination, believing himself to be a god. Sennacherib believed he was undestructable.

17 the man who made the world a desert,
  who overthrew its cities
  and would not let his captives go home?"

18 All the kings of the nations lie in state,
  each in his own tomb.
19 But you are cast out of your tomb
  like a rejected branch;
 you are covered with the slain,
  with those pierced by the sword,
  those who descend to the stones of the pit.
 Like a corpse trampled underfoot,
20 you will not join them in burial,
 for you have destroyed your land
  and killed your people.

 The offspring of the wicked
  will never be mentioned again.
21 Prepare a place to slaughter his sons
  for the sins of their forefathers;
 they are not to rise to inherit the land
  and cover the earth with their cities.

22 "I will rise up against them,"
  declares the LORD Almighty.
 "I will cut off from Babylon her name and survivors,
  her offspring and descendants,"
   declares the LORD.
23 "I will turn her into a place for owls
  and into swampland;
 I will sweep her with the broom of destruction,"
  declares the LORD Almighty.

A Prophecy Against Assyria

24 The LORD Almighty has sworn,

 "Surely, as I have planned, so it will be,
  and as I have purposed, so it will stand.
25 I will crush the Assyrian in my land;
  on my mountains I will trample him down.
 His yoke will be taken from my people,
  and his burden removed from their shoulders."

26 This is the plan determined for the whole world;
  this is the hand stretched out over all nations.
27 For the LORD Almighty has purposed, and who can thwart him?
  His hand is stretched out, and who can turn it back?

OPEN What experience have you had with snakes?

STUDY 1. Here the previous taunt song is applied to Judah's immediate enemy, Assyria. What aspects of Babylon's judgment will be validated by Assyria's overthrow (10:5–34)? **2.** What qualities of God are stressed here? How does God's planning and counsel stand over "the whole world"? **3.** One tradition says Ahaz died in 715 B.C., when Assyria's control was weak and Philistia rebelled. What will result from this revolt (vv. 29–31)? **4.** Philistia

14:17 would not let his captives go home. King Cyrus had sent the exiles home to keep them from rebelling, but the king of Babylon kept them in captivity.

14:18 kings of the nations lie in state. The tyrant was not given an honorable burial, as due a king, but was assassinated by his sons Adrammelech and Sharezer.

14:21 a place to slaughter his sons. His sons had to run for their lives and could not succeed to the throne (2 Kin. 19:37). The verse is a reminder that all earthly kings, even powerful rulers, die.

wanted Judah as an ally against Assyria. Why would this message against Philistia be given to Judah? Where should Judah look for safety (vv. 30,32)?

APPLY What alliances (getting in with the "right" people, hoarding wealth, etc.) might keep you from fully trusting God? What does this prophecy tell you about those alliances?

OPEN 1. If you had to flee on foot from your home tonight because of the sudden invasion of an alien force, what three things would you grab to take with you? Why those three? **2.** From what you have seen of modern refugees, what strikes you most about their lot?

STUDY 1. Kir Hareseth, Dibon, Nebo, Medeba and Heshbon are all cities or mountains in Moab, a country to the immediate east of Judah. What do you imagine Isaiah foresees happening to these places that accounts for such wailing and mourning (15:1–4)? **2.** What do you imagine the scene was like for these refugees fleeing the warfare in Moab (15:5–8)? What do they look like? What are they carrying? What are they feeling? What future prospects do they have (15:9)? **3.** Sending lambs to a ruler was a common sign of submission to his authority. To whom are the Moabites to send these lambs (16:1–4)? What need prompts them to do so? What is their request of Judah? **4.** What hope is held out to them (16:4–5)? **5.** From God's perspective, what is the reason for Moab's destruction? What does it tell you about God that he, through Isaiah, weeps for their destruction even as he ordains it to occur (16:9–11)? **6.** Why is it futile for the Moabites to go to their "high *place*" or "*shrine*" (16:12) in Dibon,

A Prophecy Against the Philistines

28 This oracle came in the year King Ahaz died:

29 Do not rejoice, all you Philistines,
that the rod that struck you is broken;
from the root of that snake will spring up a viper,
its fruit will be a darting, venomous serpent.
30 The poorest of the poor will find pasture,
and the needy will lie down in safety.
But your root I will destroy by famine;
it will slay your survivors.

31 Wail, O gate! Howl, O city!
Melt away, all you Philistines!
A cloud of smoke comes from the north,
and there is not a straggler in its ranks.
32 What answer shall be given
to the envoys of that nation?
"The LORD has established Zion,
and in her his afflicted people will find refuge."

A Prophecy Against Moab

15 An oracle concerning Moab:

Ar in Moab is ruined,
destroyed in a night!
Kir in Moab is ruined,
destroyed in a night!
2 Dibon goes up to its temple,
to its high places to weep;
Moab wails over Nebo and Medeba.
Every head is shaved
and every beard cut off.
3 In the streets they wear sackcloth;
on the roofs and in the public squares
they all wail,
prostrate with weeping.
4 Heshbon and Elealeh cry out,
their voices are heard all the way to Jahaz.
Therefore the armed men of Moab cry out,
and their hearts are faint.

5 My heart cries out over Moab;
her fugitives flee as far as Zoar,
as far as Eglath Shelishiyah.
They go up the way to Luhith,
weeping as they go;
on the road to Horonaim
they lament their destruction.
6 The waters of Nimrim are dried up
and the grass is withered;

15:2 Every head is shaved. Shaving one's head and cutting off one's beard were signs of humiliation. Wearing sackcloth (coarse, dark cloth) symbolized mourning. The Moabities were lamenting the destruction of their cities.

the vegetation is gone
and nothing green is left.
7 So the wealth they have acquired and stored up
they carry away over the Ravine of the Poplars.
8 Their outcry echoes along the border of Moab;
their wailing reaches as far as Eglaim,
their lamentation as far as Beer Elim.
9 Dimon's[a] waters are full of blood,
but I will bring still more upon Dimon[a]—
a lion upon the fugitives of Moab
and upon those who remain in the land.

16 Send lambs as tribute
to the ruler of the land,
from Sela, across the desert,
to the mount of the Daughter of Zion.
2 Like fluttering birds
pushed from the nest,
so are the women of Moab
at the fords of the Arnon.

3 "Give us counsel,
render a decision.
Make your shadow like night—
at high noon.
Hide the fugitives,
do not betray the refugees.
4 Let the Moabite fugitives stay with you;
be their shelter from the destroyer."

The oppressor will come to an end,
and destruction will cease;
the aggressor will vanish from the land.
5 In love a throne will be established;
in faithfulness a man will sit on it—
one from the house[b] of David—
one who in judging seeks justice
and speeds the cause of righteousness.

6 We have heard of Moab's pride—
her overweening pride and conceit,
her pride and her insolence—
but her boasts are empty.
7 Therefore the Moabites wail,
they wail together for Moab.

[a]9 Masoretic Text; Dead Sea Scrolls, some Septuagint manuscripts and Vulgate *Dibon* [b]5 Hebrew *tent*

where they worshiped the god Chemosh (44:17–20)? **7.** From 16:13–14, this prophecy may be dated three years before Moab was destroyed. Since Judah would be tempted to look to Moab as an ally against Assyria, what would God desire them to learn from this prophecy? **8.** Isaiah held out the Messiah as the only real hope for his hearers and readers. In what way is the reign of Jesus Christ the only real hope for people suffering in the world? How does his rule serve as a model for how believers ought to respond now toward the poor, the homeless and the hungry?

APPLY 1. What part of your world suffers most because of political chaos and war? When you hear of the oppression and suffering people experience due to these situations, what do you feel? Say? Do? How do you think God responds to such misery? **2.** What is a false god you once trusted in? How did that god serve only to wear you out? How does that god look to you now, compared to the King described in 16:5?

15:9 Dimon's waters ... blood. Dimon may be Dibon (v. 2). So much death and destruction had occurred there that the water supply ran with blood.

16:1 send lambs as tribute. The Moabites fled to strongholds fifty miles away, but they should have fled to Jerusalem, sending lambs on ahead as gifts. Isaiah had already prophesied that Jerusalem would be saved from attacks by Assyria.

16:3 Give us counsel. Counsel can also be translated as making plans. The Moabites begged for help from Jerusalem.

16:6 heard of Moa was a small, boas thought they could d without God's help

Lament and grieve
for the men[a] of Kir Hareseth.
8 The fields of Heshbon wither,
the vines of Sibmah also.
The rulers of the nations
have trampled down the choicest vines,
which once reached Jazer
and spread toward the desert.
Their shoots spread out
and went as far as the sea.
9 So I weep, as Jazer weeps,
for the vines of Sibmah.
O Heshbon, O Elealeh,
I drench you with tears!
The shouts of joy over your ripened fruit
and over your harvests have been stilled.
10 Joy and gladness are taken away from the orchards;
no one sings or shouts in the vineyards;
no one treads out wine at the presses,
for I have put an end to the shouting.
11 My heart laments for Moab like a harp,
my inmost being for Kir Hareseth.
12 When Moab appears at her high place,
she only wears herself out;
when she goes to her shrine to pray,
it is to no avail.

13 This is the word the LORD has already spoken concerning Moab.
14 But now the LORD says: "Within three years, as a servant bound by
contract would count them, Moab's splendor and all her many people will be despised, and her survivors will be very few and feeble."

An Oracle Against Damascus

17 An oracle concerning Damascus:

"See, Damascus will no longer be a city
but will become a heap of ruins.
2 The cities of Aroer will be deserted
and left to flocks, which will lie down,
with no one to make them afraid.
3 The fortified city will disappear from Ephraim,
and royal power from Damascus;
the remnant of Aram will be
like the glory of the Israelites,"
declares the LORD Almighty.

[a]7 Or *"raisin cakes,"* a wordplay

OPEN What experience, if any, have you had with harvesting? What fascinates you about what grows in your garden and in the fields, and what retards or kills that growth?

STUDY 1. The previous two prophecies refer to events when the northern kingdom of Israel was allied with Aram (or Syria, of which Damascus was the leading city) against Assyria (ch. 7). Compare verses 1–3 with 7:4–9, what will be the future of Damascus and Israel (Ephraim)? **2.** What do verses 7–8 and 10 imply about Israel's spiritual condition during this time (2 Kin. 17:7–

16:9 weep ... for the vines. Due to *pride, Moab's harvests would be lost.* The combination of the invading army ~nd drought would wipe out its crops orchards. Isaiah had compassion ~n as they experienced judgment.

16:14 Within three years. Although Moab had already suffered extensively, Isaiah predicted more destruction in three years, or by 715 B.C. Unlike Babylon or Philistia, Moab would have a few survivors as a remnant.

17:3 Ephraim. This refers to northern Israel, which was allied with Damascus, Syria's capital. Isaiah predicted judgment against both nations. Assyria defeated Damascus in 732 B.C. and Israel in 722.

4 "In that day the glory of Jacob will fade;
the fat of his body will waste away.
5 It will be as when a reaper gathers the standing grain
and harvests the grain with his arm—
as when a man gleans heads of grain
in the Valley of Rephaim.
6 Yet some gleanings will remain,
as when an olive tree is beaten,
leaving two or three olives on the topmost branches,
four or five on the fruitful boughs,"
declares the LORD, the God of Israel.

7 In that day men will look to their Maker
and turn their eyes to the Holy One of Israel.
8 They will not look to the altars,
the work of their hands,
and they will have no regard for the Asherah poles[a]
and the incense altars their fingers have made.

9 In that day their strong cities, which they left because of the Israelites, will be like places abandoned to thickets and undergrowth.
And all will be desolation.

10 You have forgotten God your Savior;
you have not remembered the Rock, your fortress.
Therefore, though you set out the finest plants
and plant imported vines,
11 though on the day you set them out, you make them grow,
and on the morning when you plant them, you bring them to
bud,
yet the harvest will be as nothing
in the day of disease and incurable pain.

12 Oh, the raging of many nations—
they rage like the raging sea!
Oh, the uproar of the peoples—
they roar like the roaring of great waters!
13 Although the peoples roar like the roar of surging waters,
when he rebukes them they flee far away,
driven before the wind like chaff on the hills,
like tumbleweed before a gale.
14 In the evening, sudden terror!
Before the morning, they are gone!
This is the portion of those who loot us,
the lot of those who plunder us.

[a] 8 That is, symbols of the goddess Asherah

18)? Since Israel still worshiped the Lord (as well as other gods), what does it mean to "have forgotten God" (v. 10)? **3.** Verses 10–11 refer to a pagan fertility rite whereby plants were force-bloomed in hopes of persuading the gods to bless the harvest. How will this practice backfire on Israel? **4.** What does the farmer's image of harvesting and gleaning (vv. 4–6,9–11) mean for the cities of Israel? What will be the result of this destruction? **5.** What does the sailor's image ("raging sea") and the desert image ("chaff" and "tumbleweed") mean for the future of "many nations" (vv. 12–14)? What does such imagery mean for the future of Israel? **6.** Compare verses 12–13 with Psalm 2:1–6. What truth about God emerges from these descriptions? **7.** Where else have you seen Israel's powerful enemies so quickly cut down, as in verse 14? How is this depicted in 10:28–34 and 37:36–37?

APPLY **1.** In this section, God is described as the Maker, the Holy One, the Savior and the Rock. Which of these aspects do you tend to forget? What leads you to do so? Instead, what do you find yourself trusting in? What practices can help you remember God and live out your life accordingly? **2.** How might the story of Jesus calming the sea (Mark 4:35–41), together with the image of verse 13, affect you as you face a world full of confusion and tumult?

17:5 in the Valley of Rephaim. A fertile area west of Jerusalem where David had defeated the Philistines twice (2 Sam. 5:18–20,22–25). Rephaim is the Hebrew word for ghosts, so this is the Valley of Death.

17:8 Asherah poles. Wooden symbols of the Canaanite fertility goddess in the Baal worship system. Many Asherah-worshipers lived in the northern kingdom of Israel. But under Assyrian attack, Israel would realize that wooden idols could not help them.

17:13 chaff on the hills. Chaff is the lightweight and useless part of grain, which blows away during threshing, leaving the valuable wheat behind. The enemies of Israel would become like tumbleweed, and 185,000 Assyrian soldiers would be killed overnight.

OPEN 1. What would your life be like if you were a head taller? A head shorter? **2.** On hot summer days, how do you beat the heat?

STUDY 1. During 715 B.C., envoys of Cush (Ethiopia) tried to persuade Jerusalem to align with them against Assyria. How would you sum up God's answer (vv. 3–6), which they are to bring to the "aggressive nation" (likely Assyria)? **2.** What do the images of the summer heat, morning dew and the farmer pruning his garden show about the way God will work with Assyria? How do the events of 37:36–38 illustrate the lesson of verses 5–6? **3.** How does this message broadly apply to all the world (v. 3)? What banner will God raise (5:26; 11:10,12)? **4.** Beyond the Assyrian crisis, what ultimately will result from God's work among the nations (v. 7; 2:2–4; 9:6–7; 11:10–12; 14:1–2; 16:4–5; Ps. 68:31)?

APPLY 1. Which of the following forces "feared far and wide" intimidate you the most: Financial disaster? Violent crime? Drug abuse? Teenage rebellion? Racism? **2.** How do you see God taking the punch out of this intimidating force in your life? **3.** In your life, who has been God's "heat" and "dew"? How might you be like that to someone you know who is feared far and wide? What would it take for you to do so?

A Prophecy Against Cush

18 Woe to the land of whirring wings[a]
along the rivers of Cush,[b]
2 which sends envoys by sea
in papyrus boats over the water.

Go, swift messengers,
to a people tall and smooth-skinned,
to a people feared far and wide,
an aggressive nation of strange speech,
whose land is divided by rivers.

3 All you people of the world,
you who live on the earth,
when a banner is raised on the mountains,
you will see it,
and when a trumpet sounds,
you will hear it.
4 This is what the LORD says to me:
"I will remain quiet and will look on from my dwelling place,
like shimmering heat in the sunshine,
like a cloud of dew in the heat of harvest."
5 For, before the harvest, when the blossom is gone
and the flower becomes a ripening grape,
he will cut off the shoots with pruning knives,
and cut down and take away the spreading branches.
6 They will all be left to the mountain birds of prey
and to the wild animals;
the birds will feed on them all summer,
the wild animals all winter.

7 At that time gifts will be brought to the LORD Almighty

from a people tall and smooth-skinned,
from a people feared far and wide,
an aggressive nation of strange speech,
whose land is divided by rivers—

the gifts will be brought to Mount Zion, the place of the Name of the LORD Almighty.

OPEN 1. Who is the most unlikely convert you know? **2.** What would you miss most if there were no interstate highway system or paved roads? **3.** How has sibling rivalry affected you?

STUDY 1. Egypt was the most likely ally for Judah against Assyria (chs. 30–31). Why is

A Prophecy About Egypt

19 An oracle concerning Egypt:

See, the LORD rides on a swift cloud
and is coming to Egypt.
The idols of Egypt tremble before him,
and the hearts of the Egyptians melt within them.

[a] 1 Or *of locusts* [b] 1 That is, the upper Nile region

18:5 before the harvest. God would wait until the right time, after Assyria had taken Israel captive as punishment for its sins. They would expect a good harvest, which would expand their empire. God would then swiftly defeat them when they least expected it, showing who was in control.

[2] "I will stir up Egyptian against Egyptian—
brother will fight against brother,
neighbor against neighbor,
city against city,
kingdom against kingdom.
[3] The Egyptians will lose heart,
and I will bring their plans to nothing;
they will consult the idols and the spirits of the dead,
the mediums and the spiritists.
[4] I will hand the Egyptians over
to the power of a cruel master,
and a fierce king will rule over them,"
declares the Lord, the LORD Almighty.

[5] The waters of the river will dry up,
and the riverbed will be parched and dry.
[6] The canals will stink;
the streams of Egypt will dwindle and dry up.
The reeds and rushes will wither,
[7] also the plants along the Nile,
at the mouth of the river.
Every sown field along the Nile
will become parched, will blow away and be no more.
[8] The fishermen will groan and lament,
all who cast hooks into the Nile;
those who throw nets on the water
will pine away.
[9] Those who work with combed flax will despair,
the weavers of fine linen will lose hope.
[10] The workers in cloth will be dejected,
and all the wage earners will be sick at heart.

[11] The officials of Zoan are nothing but fools;
the wise counselors of Pharaoh give senseless advice.
How can you say to Pharaoh,
"I am one of the wise men,
a disciple of the ancient kings"?

[12] Where are your wise men now?
Let them show you and make known
what the LORD Almighty
has planned against Egypt.
[13] The officials of Zoan have become fools,
the leaders of Memphis[a] are deceived;
the cornerstones of her peoples
have led Egypt astray.

[a] 13 Hebrew *Noph*

that so foolish (vv. 1–4)? Given what happened during the exodus, why might Egyptian idols tremble? **2.** Zoan and Memphis were major cities in Upper and Lower Egypt. Compared to the Lord's power and wisdom, what are their famed wise men like? What effect has their leadership had upon the country? How is this related to their wayward spiritual ties (v. 3)? **3.** Since Egypt's plans (v. 3), natural resources (vv. 5–7) and leadership (vv. 11–12) are all dependent upon God, what should that have said to the Judeans who were looking to Egypt instead of God for help? **4.** Isaiah anticipates a tremendous change in Egypt (vv. 16–25). How and why will Egypt's sense of superiority over Judah change? **5.** What do you think is meant by the image of the five Egyptian cities? What could Isaiah have meant by that one city, the center for the worship of the chief Egyptian god, adopting the very language of the Jews (v. 18)? **6.** Compare verses 19–20 with Exodus 3:7–10. What does that tell you about God's judgments? **7.** What does the "highway" motif indicate about restored fellowship between Egypt, Assyria and Israel (v. 23; 11:16; 40:3–4)? **8.** How would Isaiah's fellow Jews feel about Assyrians? What effect would hearing verse 25 have on them? What does that show about God's attitude toward other nations?

APPLY 1. Someone has said, "Whatever we trust in place of God will eventually turn on us and destroy us." How have you seen that to be true so far in Isaiah? How about in your own experience? Where are you struggling with that now? **2.** In verses 16–22, Egypt moves from (a) fearing God, to (b) calling upon him for help, to (c) joyfully worshiping him. How far along are you on that a-b-c highway? **3.** What "pagan Assyrian" in your life do you presently disdain, as much as a Jew in Isaiah's day would? What will you do about changing your heart in this area? Can this group help?

19:3 consult the idols. Some Israelites hoped that Egypt would help, but Isaiah predicted God's judgment on Egypt. Its idols and mediums would be unable to help this once cruel master of the Israelites. Now Egypt would have its own cruel master in the Assyrians.

19:12 Where are your wise men now? Egypt was famous for its wisdom writings and its wise men. But their wisdom was foolishness compared to God, who would destroy Egypt (1 Cor. 1:20).

[14]The LORD has poured into them
a spirit of dizziness;
they make Egypt stagger in all that she does,
as a drunkard staggers around in his vomit.
[15]There is nothing Egypt can do—
head or tail, palm branch or reed.

[16]In that day the Egyptians will be like women. They will shudder
with fear at the uplifted hand that the LORD Almighty raises against
them. [17]And the land of Judah will bring terror to the Egyptians;
everyone to whom Judah is mentioned will be terrified, because of
what the LORD Almighty is planning against them.
[18]In that day five cities in Egypt will speak the language of Canaan
and swear allegiance to the LORD Almighty. One of them will be called
the City of Destruction.[a]
[19]In that day there will be an altar to the LORD in the heart of Egypt,
and a monument to the LORD at its border. [20]It will be a sign and witness to the LORD Almighty in the land of Egypt. When they cry out to
the LORD because of their oppressors, he will send them a savior and
defender, and he will rescue them. [21]So the LORD will make himself
known to the Egyptians, and in that day they will acknowledge the
LORD. They will worship with sacrifices and grain offerings; they will
make vows to the LORD and keep them. [22]The LORD will strike Egypt
with a plague; he will strike them and heal them. They will turn to the
LORD, and he will respond to their pleas and heal them.
[23]In that day there will be a highway from Egypt to Assyria. The Assyrians will go to Egypt and the Egyptians to Assyria. The Egyptians
and Assyrians will worship together. [24]In that day Israel will be the
third, along with Egypt and Assyria, a blessing on the earth. [25]The
LORD Almighty will bless them, saying, "Blessed be Egypt my people,
Assyria my handiwork, and Israel my inheritance."

A Prophecy Against Egypt and Cush

20 In the year that the supreme commander, sent by Sargon
king of Assyria, came to Ashdod and attacked and captured
it— [2]at that time the LORD spoke through Isaiah son of Amoz. He said
to him, "Take off the sackcloth from your body and the sandals from
your feet." And he did so, going around stripped and barefoot.

[a]18 Most manuscripts of the Masoretic Text; some manuscripts of the Masoretic Text, Dead Sea Scrolls and Vulgate *City of the Sun* (that is, Heliopolis)

OPEN Have you ever been in a situation where someone was wearing so little clothing that you were embarassed?

STUDY 1. Ashdod, a city in revolt against Assyria, was destroyed by Sargon in 711 B.C. What lesson was that meant to teach Judah? **2.** Why does God have Isaiah

19:18 five cities in Egypt. Probably meant the rest of the nation, which would recognize and worship the true God. The Egyptians would become fluent enough in Hebrew to worship God.

19:19 altar to the LORD. This monument will symbolize Egypt's national policy of worshiping God with the sacrificial worship system (Zech. 14:16–19).

19:20 oppressors ... savior. When the Egyptians turn to God and ask for help, God will give it. This will take place after the Messiah has returned and established his millennial kingdom (43:11).

19:23 highway from Egypt to Assyria. Egypt and Assyria had been enemies for centuries. People from both nations and from Israel will worship together peacefully in the millennial kingdom. This will fulfill part of God's promise to Abraham that all peoples would be blessed through him (Gen. 12:3).

19:25 my people ... my handiwork ... my inheritance. Here these titles for Israel are applied to believing Gentiles from all nations, symbolized by Egypt and Assyria.

20:1 Ashdod. The capture of this Philistine city by Assyrian king Sargon II demonstrated to Israel that foreign alliances could not protect them.

20:2 stripped and barefoot. To represent exile and captivity, Isaiah probably did not wear his outer garment (or maybe worse). This showed how Egypt and Cush would be treated by a victorious Assyria, a warning that Israel should not look to foreign allies for protection.

³Then the LORD said, "Just as my servant Isaiah has gone stripped
and barefoot for three years, as a sign and portent against Egypt and
Cush,[a] ⁴so the king of Assyria will lead away stripped and barefoot
the Egyptian captives and Cushite exiles, young and old, with buttocks bared—to Egypt's shame. ⁵Those who trusted in Cush and
boasted in Egypt will be afraid and put to shame. ⁶In that day the
people who live on this coast will say, 'See what has happened to
those we relied on, those we fled to for help and deliverance from the
king of Assyria! How then can we escape?' "

A Prophecy Against Babylon

21 An oracle concerning the Desert by the Sea:

Like whirlwinds sweeping through the southland,
  an invader comes from the desert,
  from a land of terror.

²A dire vision has been shown to me:
  The traitor betrays, the looter takes loot.
Elam, attack! Media, lay siege!
  I will bring to an end all the groaning she caused.

³At this my body is racked with pain,
  pangs seize me, like those of a woman in labor;
I am staggered by what I hear,
  I am bewildered by what I see.
⁴My heart falters,
  fear makes me tremble;
the twilight I longed for
  has become a horror to me.

⁵They set the tables,
  they spread the rugs,
  they eat, they drink!
Get up, you officers,
  oil the shields!

⁶This is what the Lord says to me:

"Go, post a lookout
  and have him report what he sees.
⁷When he sees chariots
  with teams of horses,
riders on donkeys
  or riders on camels,
let him be alert,
  fully alert."

⁸And the lookout[b] shouted,

"Day after day, my lord, I stand on the watchtower;
  every night I stay at my post.

[a]3 That is, the upper Nile region; also in verse 5 [b]8 Dead Sea Scrolls and Syriac; Masoretic Text *A lion*

strip down to give this message? **3.** Who will be put to shame as a result of God's action (vv. 4,5)?

APPLY When have you been so ashamed by a mistake you made that it was like walking around with "bare buttocks"?

OPEN 1. What scary theme recurs in your dreams: Bad school experience? Car accident? War casualties? End times? Other? How do you feel when you wake-up from a bad dream? **2.** When have you been a lookout?

STUDY 1. In Isaiah's day, Babylon sought allies among the other nations, including Judah (ch. 39), to help her resist Assyria. Why is that a faulty, even fatal hope? **2.** How does this "dire vision" affect Isaiah? Why is he so upset? What does that show you about him? **3.** What were the leaders of Babylon doing the very night of their final overthrow? **4.** Why post a watchman (vv. 6–10)? If Judah in Isaiah's day hoped that Babylon might protect them from Assyria, how would they react to the news "Babylon has fallen!" (v. 9)? **5.** Dumah, invaded by the Assyrians when they came against Babylon, was an oasis on a major trade route to Seir (Edom) and an ally of Babylon. In calling to the watchman (Isaiah) regarding these events (vv. 11–12), what are the Edomites really asking? **6.** What are the Arabian cities of Dedan and Tema told to do (vv. 13–14)? Which fugitives (or refugees) are they to care for? From verses 16–17 (Jer. 49:28–33), what does the future hold for Arabia (Kedar)? **7.** How might these three prophecies affect Judah's sense of hope as they consider the Assyrian threat? Why do you think God revealed these things to Judah?

APPLY 1. What "Babylon" are you betting on to shelter you from the uncertainties of life? Knowing that such temporal security will be swept away, like Babylon, how do you feel? What can you do to fill that God-shaped void of insecurity? **2.** When Isaiah envisions a suffering Babylon, even though it was a direct

21:5 eat ... drink. The Babylonians were living in confident self-assurance, but Isaiah warned them of coming battle (Dan. 5:4–5). **Get up.** He urged them to stop feasting and prepare for war.

judgment by God, he is moved with God's compassion. What model does that give you for how to respond to the sufferings of others? Does your television help you identify with the suffering of others, or does it harden you against it? Why?

9 Look, here comes a man in a chariot
with a team of horses.
And he gives back the answer:
'Babylon has fallen, has fallen!
All the images of its gods
lie shattered on the ground!' "

10 O my people, crushed on the threshing floor,
I tell you what I have heard
from the LORD Almighty,
from the God of Israel.

A Prophecy Against Edom

11 An oracle concerning Dumah[a]:

Someone calls to me from Seir,
"Watchman, what is left of the night?
Watchman, what is left of the night?"
12 The watchman replies,
"Morning is coming, but also the night.
If you would ask, then ask;
and come back yet again."

A Prophecy Against Arabia

13 An oracle concerning Arabia:

You caravans of Dedanites,
who camp in the thickets of Arabia,
14 bring water for the thirsty;
you who live in Tema,
bring food for the fugitives.
15 They flee from the sword,
from the drawn sword,
from the bent bow
and from the heat of battle.

16 This is what the Lord says to me: "Within one year, as a servant
bound by contract would count it, all the pomp of Kedar will come to
an end. 17 The survivors of the bowmen, the warriors of Kedar, will be
few." The LORD, the God of Israel, has spoken.

A Prophecy About Jerusalem

22 An oracle concerning the Valley of Vision:

What troubles you now,
that you have all gone up on the roofs,
2 O town full of commotion,
O city of tumult and revelry?

[a] *11 Dumah* means *silence* or *stillness,* a wordplay on *Edom.*

OPEN 1. When have you felt like crying even though everyone around you was partying? **2.** What might prompt you to tear your hair out? **3.** In your planning, are you nearsighted or far-sighted? Telescopic or microscopic? When have you failed to see what lays ahead because you kept looking down?

21:9 Babylon ... fallen. Israel hoped that Babylon would defeat the Assyrians, so this news was devastating (Jer. 51:8).

22:1 Valley of Vision. The Kidron Valley ran between two hills just east of Jerusalem. Here God revealed himself to Isaiah.

22:2 Your slain were not killed by the sword. Isaiah describes the rulers being captured while fleeing to save their lives (2 Kin. 25:4–6).

Your slain were not killed by the sword,
nor did they die in battle.
[3]All your leaders have fled together;
they have been captured without using the bow.
All you who were caught were taken prisoner together,
having fled while the enemy was still far away.
[4]Therefore I said, "Turn away from me;
let me weep bitterly.
Do not try to console me
over the destruction of my people."

[5]The Lord, the LORD Almighty, has a day
of tumult and trampling and terror
in the Valley of Vision,
a day of battering down walls
and of crying out to the mountains.
[6]Elam takes up the quiver,
with her charioteers and horses;
Kir uncovers the shield.
[7]Your choicest valleys are full of chariots,
and horsemen are posted at the city gates;
[8] the defenses of Judah are stripped away.

And you looked in that day
to the weapons in the Palace of the Forest;
[9]you saw that the City of David
had many breaches in its defenses;
you stored up water
in the Lower Pool.
[10]You counted the buildings in Jerusalem
and tore down houses to strengthen the wall.
[11]You built a reservoir between the two walls
for the water of the Old Pool,
but you did not look to the One who made it,
or have regard for the One who planned it long ago.

[12]The Lord, the LORD Almighty,
called you on that day
to weep and to wail,
to tear out your hair and put on sackcloth.
[13]But see, there is joy and revelry,
slaughtering of cattle and killing of sheep,
eating of meat and drinking of wine!

STUDY 1. In light of Judah's searching for worldly allies while rejecting God, what is the irony in how Isaiah addresses Jerusalem (vv. 1,8–11)? **2.** Judging from verses 2–3 and 6–8, what do you think had happened or would soon happen to Jerusalem? How would you describe the quality of leadership Jerusalem had? **3.** How would the people respond to the threat of enemy attack (vv. 8–11)? (Note: The Palace of the Forest was an armory in Jerusalem constructed of fine woods.) What is wrong with such stock-piling for war? **4.** With danger around them, why their "eat drink and be merry" attitude (v. 13)? What does such revelry show about their trust in God? Their hope for the future? Their inner character? Why are they no different than the people of Babylon (21:5)? **5.** How would their attitudes and actions be different if they had responded as God desired (v. 12)? What does God's final word on the matter indicate about the depth of their hard-heartedness? **6.** What is the shameful example of what Isaiah has been denouncing in verses 1–14 (vv. 15–25)? In view of impending national disaster, what is Shebna, the steward (a high administrative position in government), preoccupied with? How will God deal with such egocentric leadership? **7.** Eliakim had replaced Shebna as steward at least by the time of the Assyrian invasion (36:3). How do his qualities contrast with those of Shebna? In spite of his good leadership, what will ultimately happen?

APPLY 1. When have you experienced such stress that your response was like that of the people in verses 8–11? What would it mean for you to look to God instead? What could help you develop that trust? **2.** What leadership positions (in the home, work, church, community) do you have? When, if ever, have you

22:6 Elam ... Kir. Soldiers from Elam, east of Assyria, and the Assyrian province of Kir joined the Assyrian warriors, indicating that troops from all over Assyria were joining to attack Jerusalem.

22:9 City of David ... its defenses. The defense of the city depended upon available water. Hezekiah had repaired broken sections of the wall and also preserved the water supply (2 Chr. 32:1–5). **Lower Pool.** A reservoir in Jerusalem's southwestern valley. Hezekiah connected it, by a 1,777-foot tunnel carved out of rock under the city, to the Old Pool, the water source in the eastern valley.

22:11 the One who made it. Hezekiah's efforts were insufficient to protect the people. They refused to turn to God, who alone could save them.

22:13 Let us eat and drink ... for tomorrow we die! This has become a motto of pleasure-seeking hedonism. The statement signifies, both then and now, a refusal to believe that God can save people. Instead of revelry, the appropriate response would be repentance.

acted like a Shebna in that position? If Isaiah spoke to you, as you were busy glorifying your name, how would you react? How can you be more like an Eliakim?

"Let us eat and drink," you say,
"for tomorrow we die!"

[14]The LORD Almighty has revealed this in my hearing: "Till your
dying day this sin will not be atoned for," says the Lord, the LORD
Almighty.

[15]This is what the Lord, the LORD Almighty, says:

"Go, say to this steward,
to Shebna, who is in charge of the palace:
[16]What are you doing here and who gave you permission
to cut out a grave for yourself here,
hewing your grave on the height
and chiseling your resting place in the rock?

[17]"Beware, the LORD is about to take firm hold of you
and hurl you away, O you mighty man.
[18]He will roll you up tightly like a ball
and throw you into a large country.
There you will die
and there your splendid chariots will remain—
you disgrace to your master's house!
[19]I will depose you from your office,
and you will be ousted from your position.

[20]"In that day I will summon my servant, Eliakim son of Hilkiah. [21]I
will clothe him with your robe and fasten your sash around him and
hand your authority over to him. He will be a father to those who live
in Jerusalem and to the house of Judah. [22]I will place on his shoulder
the key to the house of David; what he opens no one can shut, and
what he shuts no one can open. [23]I will drive him like a peg into a firm
place; he will be a seat[a] of honor for the house of his father. [24]All the
glory of his family will hang on him: its offspring and offshoots—all
its lesser vessels, from the bowls to all the jars.

[25]"In that day," declares the LORD Almighty, "the peg driven into the
firm place will give way; it will be sheared off and will fall, and the
load hanging on it will be cut down." The LORD has spoken.

A Prophecy About Tyre

23

An oracle concerning Tyre:

Wail, O ships of Tarshish!
For Tyre is destroyed
and left without house or harbor.
From the land of Cyprus[b]
word has come to them.

OPEN 1. What loss would be most devastating to you and why: Your home? Your business? Your job? Your ability to communicate? Your car? **2.** How do you feel when introduced to one far more powerful and wealthy than you? Why do you react that way?

STUDY 1. Tyre was the main city of Phoenicia, a prosperous trading country on the Mediterranean

[a]23 Or *throne* [b]1 Hebrew *Kittim*

22:25 peg ... will give way. Eliakim was the palace administrator and a godly man. He would be a respected leader and a firm and stable foundation for the nation. But even he would come to an end, and the kingdom of Judah would be taken into captivity.

23:1 Tyre. This seaport city was captured several times over a period of four hundred years before being destroyed by Alexander the Great in 332 B.C. King Hiram of Tyre supplied the cedars and craftsmen for Solomon's temple.

2 Be silent, you people of the island
and you merchants of Sidon,
whom the seafarers have enriched.
3 On the great waters
came the grain of the Shihor;
the harvest of the Nile[a] was the revenue of Tyre,
and she became the marketplace of the nations.

4 Be ashamed, O Sidon, and you, O fortress of the sea,
for the sea has spoken:
"I have neither been in labor nor given birth;
I have neither reared sons nor brought up daughters."
5 When word comes to Egypt,
they will be in anguish at the report from Tyre.

6 Cross over to Tarshish;
wail, you people of the island.
7 Is this your city of revelry,
the old, old city,
whose feet have taken her
to settle in far-off lands?
8 Who planned this against Tyre,
the bestower of crowns,
whose merchants are princes,
whose traders are renowned in the earth?
9 The LORD Almighty planned it,
to bring low the pride of all glory
and to humble all who are renowned on the earth.

10 Till[b] your land as along the Nile,
O Daughter of Tarshish,
for you no longer have a harbor.
11 The LORD has stretched out his hand over the sea
and made its kingdoms tremble.
He has given an order concerning Phoenicia[c]
that her fortresses be destroyed.
12 He said, "No more of your reveling,
O Virgin Daughter of Sidon, now crushed!

"Up, cross over to Cyprus[d];
even there you will find no rest."
13 Look at the land of the Babylonians,[e]
this people that is now of no account!
The Assyrians have made it
a place for desert creatures;
they raised up their siege towers,
they stripped its fortresses bare
and turned it into a ruin.

14 Wail, you ships of Tarshish;
your fortress is destroyed!

[a]2,3 Masoretic Text; one Dead Sea Scroll *Sidon, / who cross over the sea; / your envoys [3]are on the great waters. / The grain of the Shihor, / the harvest of the Nile,* [b]10 Dead Sea Scrolls and some Septuagint manuscripts; Masoretic Text *Go through* [c]11 Hebrew *Canaan* [d]12 Hebrew *Kittim* [e]13 Or *Chaldeans*

Sea. What role did Tyre play in the economy of the surrounding nations (vv. 1–3)? What was the city like before the events of this prophecy (vv. 7–8)? **2.** Ships of Tarshish were capable of sailing to the ends of the known world. What message was given to their sailors as they were returning home? How did this message affect Tyre's trading partners? **3.** Isaiah may be anticipating here one of the Assyrian attacks upon Tyre or its final destruction by the Greeks. In either event, whom does he credit with planning the downfall of Tyre, the king-maker? How is God's control over the kings and nations evident (vv. 9–12)? **4.** Babylon, the symbol of strength and prestige in the East, was beaten by Assyria. What effect would recalling the destruction of both Babylon in the East and Tyre on the West have on Judah as they faced the Assyrians? What would they associate with the "70 years" (v. 15)? **5.** In what sense will the Lord "deal with" Tyre (vv. 17–18)? What will happen as a result of Tyre's restoration? How does this compare with what Isaiah said of Egypt and Assyria (19:23–25)? **6.** Since verse 18 has never happened literally, what is the figurative meaning behind this passage? What does it imply about God's plan for the world (Rev. 18:3)? **7.** If Babylon represented the height of the world's culture, and Tyre the apex of its wealth, how would you use Isaiah's message to challenge people dedicated to power and money? Does this mean power and wealth in themselves are wrong? Why or why not? How does this message serve as an on-going warning to the church in every age? To your church in particular?

APPLY 1. Chapters 13–23 reflect upon the foolishness of Judah depending upon alliances with the other nations rather than upon God to protect her from Assyria. What do you see as one implication of that loyalty principle for your life today? To what or to whom have you looked to fill that God-shaped void of insecurity in your life? **2.** How does the promise in verse 18 relate to Jesus' promise in Matthew 5:5? How would you picture the hope stirred up by these pictures and promises? What specific action will you take to embody that hope for a reconciled world loyal to God?

15 At that time Tyre will be forgotten for seventy years, the span of a
king's life. But at the end of these seventy years, it will happen to Tyre
as in the song of the prostitute:

16 "Take up a harp, walk through the city,
 O prostitute forgotten;
play the harp well, sing many a song,
 so that you will be remembered."

17 At the end of seventy years, the LORD will deal with Tyre. She will
return to her hire as a prostitute and will ply her trade with all the
kingdoms on the face of the earth. 18 Yet her profit and her earnings
will be set apart for the LORD; they will not be stored up or hoarded.
Her profits will go to those who live before the LORD, for abundant
food and fine clothes.

The Lord's Devastation of the Earth

24 See, the LORD is going to lay waste the earth
 and devastate it;
he will ruin its face
 and scatter its inhabitants—
2 it will be the same
 for priest as for people,
 for master as for servant,
 for mistress as for maid,
 for seller as for buyer,
 for borrower as for lender,
 for debtor as for creditor.
3 The earth will be completely laid waste
 and totally plundered.
 The LORD has spoken this word.

4 The earth dries up and withers,
 the world languishes and withers,
 the exalted of the earth languish.
5 The earth is defiled by its people;
 they have disobeyed the laws,
violated the statutes
 and broken the everlasting covenant.
6 Therefore a curse consumes the earth;
 its people must bear their guilt.
Therefore earth's inhabitants are burned up,
 and very few are left.

OPEN 1. Have you ever visited a ghost town? Where? What was it like? **2.** Have you ever been to a party that came to a crashing halt? (Was that when your parents came home?) What happened?

STUDY Chapters 24–27 present in universal terms the blessings and judgments prophesied for specific nations in chapters 13–23. **1.** What is the scope of the judgments in verses 1–6? Who gets hit? Who is left? **2.** What is the reason for this total devastation that is to come (vv. 5–6)? What "everlasting covenant" (from God's viewpoint) might the people have broken (Gen. 9:8–17)? What subsequent "curse" have the people brought on themselves? How has this been illustrated by some of the specific judgments (14:12–14; 16:6; 17:10; 22:11)? **3.** What will be the impact of this future judgment on the rural and urban sectors (vv. 7–13)? **4.** Who are "they" who rejoice in verses 14–16? How does their "song of glory" (v. 16) differ from the "sounds of silence" (v. 8)? How do you account for this flip-side of judgment in verses 14–16 (14:7; 16:5; 17:7–8; 18:7; 19:23–25; 23:18)? **5.** Verses 16–20 return to the theme of judgment. What

23:15 forgotten for seventy years. This represented a king's lifetime. The period referred to was probably from about 700 to 630 B.C. when Phoenicia's trade was reduced by the Assyrians. After 630 B.C. Assyria declined, and Tyre rebuilt its successful trading operations.

23:17 prostitute. Tyre's reestablished (and profitable) trade activities, often with unethical partners, is compared to a prostitute who stops her trade in illicit sex but returns to it more successful than ever.

23:18 earnings ... set apart for the LORD. Although Deuteronomy 23:18 forbade contributing a harlot's pay to the temple, Tyre's spoils would belong to God after this war against the unrighteous.

24:2 debtor. God's judgment of the wicked will level the world's playing field, ending special treatment for those with wealth, power or position (Hos. 4:9).

24:5 disobeyed ... broken the everlasting covenant. Probably referred to the implied covenant with God that people should obey him. God gave each person an innate sense of right or wrong—a conscience. Since the beginning people have rebelled against God's Word.(Gen. 2:16–17).

24:6 curse consumes the earth. God's judgment in consequence of sin. **few are left.** A remnant will be preserved (10:20).

[7]The new wine dries up and the vine withers;
all the merrymakers groan.
[8]The gaiety of the tambourines is stilled,
the noise of the revelers has stopped,
the joyful harp is silent.
[9]No longer do they drink wine with a song;
the beer is bitter to its drinkers.
[10]The ruined city lies desolate;
the entrance to every house is barred.
[11]In the streets they cry out for wine;
all joy turns to gloom,
all gaiety is banished from the earth.
[12]The city is left in ruins,
its gate is battered to pieces.
[13]So will it be on the earth
and among the nations,
as when an olive tree is beaten,
or as when gleanings are left after the grape harvest.

[14]They raise their voices, they shout for joy;
from the west they acclaim the LORD's majesty.
[15]Therefore in the east give glory to the LORD;
exalt the name of the LORD, the God of Israel,
in the islands of the sea.
[16]From the ends of the earth we hear singing:
"Glory to the Righteous One."

But I said, "I waste away, I waste away!
Woe to me!
The treacherous betray!
With treachery the treacherous betray!"
[17]Terror and pit and snare await you,
O people of the earth.
[18]Whoever flees at the sound of terror
will fall into a pit;
whoever climbs out of the pit
will be caught in a snare.

The floodgates of the heavens are opened,
the foundations of the earth shake.
[19]The earth is broken up,
the earth is split asunder,
the earth is thoroughly shaken.
[20]The earth reels like a drunkard,
it sways like a hut in the wind;
so heavy upon it is the guilt of its rebellion
that it falls—never to rise again.

[21]In that day the LORD will punish
the powers in the heavens above
and the kings on the earth below.
[22]They will be herded together

is the point of the dilemma that Isaiah presents here? Who is wasting away? Under whose treachery? How would you feel under such persecution? **6.** Pretend these pictures of the earth (vv. 18–20) are literal descriptions. What do you see happening? When has something like this happened before? What is the reality these pictures are meant to convey? What effect does that have upon you? **7.** What cosmic realities does God battle and bind "in that day" (v. 21)? What is the ultimate purpose of this judgment? Why, in spite of all the destruction foreseen here, is this really good news? **8.** What do you learn about God from considering his past judgments (such as Noah's flood, or the fall of specific nations)? In comparison, what do you learn when you consider God's future glory, which will eclipse even the sun and stars above?

APPLY 1. Both joy (v. 14) and sorrow (v. 16) will be the experience of the godly remnant who survive this judgment. When you see or hear about current disaster striking those who don't deserve it, what do you feel? **2.** When have you tried getting "out of the frying pan" only to find yourself "in the fire"? What did you learn about yourself in that situation? Did that experience drive you toward God, or away from God? Why?

24:14 They. Those who love God's Law and have suffered for righteousness will remain after the judgment. There will be shouting and praising that the earth will be finally cleansed from sin.

like prisoners bound in a dungeon;
they will be shut up in prison
and be punished[a] after many days.
23 The moon will be abashed, the sun ashamed;
for the LORD Almighty will reign
on Mount Zion and in Jerusalem,
and before its elders, gloriously.

Praise to the Lord

25 O LORD, you are my God;
I will exalt you and praise your name,
for in perfect faithfulness
you have done marvelous things,
things planned long ago.
2 You have made the city a heap of rubble,
the fortified town a ruin,
the foreigners' stronghold a city no more;
it will never be rebuilt.
3 Therefore strong peoples will honor you;
cities of ruthless nations will revere you.
4 You have been a refuge for the poor,
a refuge for the needy in his distress,
a shelter from the storm
and a shade from the heat.
For the breath of the ruthless
is like a storm driving against a wall
5 and like the heat of the desert.
You silence the uproar of foreigners;
as heat is reduced by the shadow of a cloud,
so the song of the ruthless is stilled.

6 On this mountain the LORD Almighty will prepare
a feast of rich food for all peoples,
a banquet of aged wine—
the best of meats and the finest of wines.
7 On this mountain he will destroy
the shroud that enfolds all peoples,
the sheet that covers all nations;
8 he will swallow up death forever.
The Sovereign LORD will wipe away the tears
from all faces;
he will remove the disgrace of his people
from all the earth.
The LORD has spoken.

9 In that day they will say,

[a]22 Or *released*

OPEN 1. As a child, where was the "heap of rubble" that you used to play on? What was one of the more useful pieces of junk you brought home? **2.** What was your safe place when a severe storm was brewing? Where was your emotional shelter when things were stormy? **3.** At what feast do you always overeat?

STUDY 1. What mood shift do you sense in this new chapter? What leads Isaiah (and his people) to exclaim, "O LORD, you are my God!"? **2.** The "city" and "fortified town" in verse 2 symbolize all the things in which people have placed their pride and confidence. What will be the result of God's judgment upon these things? How does this relate to 19:23–25? **3.** How is God's relationship to the poor and the needy pictured here? **4.** Kings would often hold inaugural and wedding feasts for their subjects. For whom is this feast on Mount Zion given? Who will be excluded from this feast? Why? **5.** What will be the effects of the Lord's reign on those who submit and those who don't? **6.** What applications does the New Testament make of this great feast (v. 6; Rev. 19:9; 21:4)? What will be the effect of Christ's coming in that day?

APPLY 1. What is the "storm" or "heat of the desert" that is affecting you right now? How has God sheltered you from that? Where do you need a shelter or cloud cover now? **2.** In coping with death, disappointment or disgrace, what does the promise of verses 7–8 mean to you? When has that promise been made real to you? Or does it seem so distant in its fulfillment that it is not much help to you, here and now?

25:4 refuge for the poor ... needy. God's protection was described as a shelter and a shade (Ps. 91:1–3). He will protect the needy from the storm and still the storms created by the ruthless.

25:6 a feast ... a banquet. God's deliverance of his people is pictured as a banquet on Mount Zion for people from all over the earth who will be saved (Dan. 7:14).

25:8 swallow up death ... wipe away the tears. This will take place at the end of the 1,000-year reign of Christ described in Revelation 21:4.

"Surely this is our God;
we trusted in him, and he saved us.
This is the LORD, we trusted in him;
let us rejoice and be glad in his salvation."

10 The hand of the LORD will rest on this mountain;
but Moab will be trampled under him
as straw is trampled down in the manure.
11 They will spread out their hands in it,
as a swimmer spreads out his hands to swim.
God will bring down their pride
despite the cleverness[a] of their hands.
12 He will bring down your high fortified walls
and lay them low;
he will bring them down to the ground,
to the very dust.

A Song of Praise

26 In that day this song will be sung in the land of Judah:

We have a strong city;
God makes salvation
its walls and ramparts.
2 Open the gates
that the righteous nation may enter,
the nation that keeps faith.
3 You will keep in perfect peace
him whose mind is steadfast,
because he trusts in you.
4 Trust in the LORD forever,
for the LORD, the LORD, is the Rock eternal.
5 He humbles those who dwell on high,
he lays the lofty city low;
he levels it to the ground
and casts it down to the dust.
6 Feet trample it down—
the feet of the oppressed,
the footsteps of the poor.

7 The path of the righteous is level;
O upright One, you make the way of the righteous smooth.
8 Yes, LORD, walking in the way of your laws,[b]
we wait for you;
your name and renown
are the desire of our hearts.
9 My soul yearns for you in the night;
in the morning my spirit longs for you.

[a] *11* The meaning of the Hebrew for this word is uncertain. [b] *8* Or *judgments*

OPEN 1. Are you more of a "daydreamer," "worry wart" or "bookworm"? Last week, did you daydream more, worry more, or read more? **2.** What do you do that keeps your mind sharp and glowing? Rested and peaceful?

STUDY 1. How does this "city of God" contrast with the "cities of the world" mentioned in 24:10–12 and 25:2–3? What characterizes the inhabitants of God's city (vv. 3–4,7–9)? What qualities mark those upon whom judgment comes (vv. 5,10–11)? **2.** What makes the Lord worthy of trust (vv. 4–6)? Does this reversal of human fortune underscore, or undermine, either God's justice or his love? How so? **3.** What do you learn about faith from the images of the ramparts (v. 1), the gates (v. 2), the steadfast mind (v. 3), the Rock (v. 4), level paths (v. 7), walking, waiting and yearning (vv. 8–9)? **4.** With these images in mind, is faith active, passive or both? How so? **5.** How is God contrasted to the "other lords" (Assyria and Egypt; vv. 12–15)? What image of faith is projected over against these foreign powers? **6.** What does the pain of childbirth imagery add to your understanding of faith—its pain and purpose (vv. 16–18)? **7.** In her failure to give birth and bring salvation to others, Israel has failed in her divine calling. Still, what hope is she given here (vv. 4–6,19; 25:7–8; Ezek. 37:11–12; contrast v. 14 with Dan. 12:2)?

26:1 a strong city. Refers to Jerusalem where the Messiah will reign. The humble will be exalted and oppressors vanquished, a reversal of the world's wicked system.

26:8 we wait for you ... your name and renown. The righteous trust in God's care (Ps. 40:1). Problems will certainly come, but God will lead the faithful through all of life's trials and reward them with goodness and joy at the end.

26:9 night ... morning. The prophet continually seeks God.

8. What does Isaiah mean by his advice in verse 20? What are they to hide from (24:21–22)? How long will the oppressor's tyranny and Judah's exile last? How is that related to waiting on the LORD (v. 8)?

APPLY 1. Of the qualities of God's people (vv. 3–4,7–9), what one or two do you yearn for now? **2.** What hope is held out to you in verse 19 as you consider your failures in life? How might this hope affect your view of yourself? Your willingness to take risks? Your sense of God's call and courage?

When your judgments come upon the earth,
 the people of the world learn righteousness.
10 Though grace is shown to the wicked,
 they do not learn righteousness;
even in a land of uprightness they go on doing evil
 and regard not the majesty of the LORD.
11 O LORD, your hand is lifted high,
 but they do not see it.
Let them see your zeal for your people and be put to shame;
 let the fire reserved for your enemies consume them.

12 LORD, you establish peace for us;
 all that we have accomplished you have done for us.
13 O LORD, our God, other lords besides you have ruled over us,
 but your name alone do we honor.
14 They are now dead, they live no more;
 those departed spirits do not rise.
You punished them and brought them to ruin;
 you wiped out all memory of them.
15 You have enlarged the nation, O LORD;
 you have enlarged the nation.
You have gained glory for yourself;
 you have extended all the borders of the land.

16 LORD, they came to you in their distress;
 when you disciplined them,
 they could barely whisper a prayer.[a]
17 As a woman with child and about to give birth
 writhes and cries out in her pain,
 so were we in your presence, O LORD.
18 We were with child, we writhed in pain,
 but we gave birth to wind.
We have not brought salvation to the earth;
 we have not given birth to people of the world.

19 But your dead will live;
 their bodies will rise.
You who dwell in the dust,
 wake up and shout for joy.
Your dew is like the dew of the morning;
 the earth will give birth to her dead.

20 Go, my people, enter your rooms
 and shut the doors behind you;
hide yourselves for a little while
 until his wrath has passed by.

[a] 16 The meaning of the Hebrew for this clause is uncertain.

26:10 grace. Unmerited favor shown by God to all people. The wicked show contempt for God's grace (Rom. 2:4) and only learn through God's judgment.

26:13 other lords besides you. Included rulers of Egypt in the past, Assyria in the present and Babylon in the future (2 Chr. 12:8).

26:19 dead will live ... bodies will rise. Isaiah assured the people that their believing dead will rise to life at Christ's second coming (Job 19:26; Dan. 12:2). **dew of the morning.** As dew refreshes grass, believers will experience new life and God's blessing (Ps. 133:3).

26:20 hide ... a little while ... wrath. Isaiah urged the future believing remnant to hide during the Tribulation when God pours out his anger and to wait for God to deliver them.

[21]See, the LORD is coming out of his dwelling
to punish the people of the earth for their sins.
The earth will disclose the blood shed upon her;
she will conceal her slain no longer.

Deliverance of Israel

27 In that day,

the LORD will punish with his sword,
his fierce, great and powerful sword,
Leviathan the gliding serpent,
Leviathan the coiling serpent;
he will slay the monster of the sea.

[2]In that day—

"Sing about a fruitful vineyard:
[3] I, the LORD, watch over it;
I water it continually.
I guard it day and night
so that no one may harm it.
[4] I am not angry.
If only there were briers and thorns confronting me!
I would march against them in battle;
I would set them all on fire.
[5]Or else let them come to me for refuge;
let them make peace with me,
yes, let them make peace with me."

[6]In days to come Jacob will take root,
Israel will bud and blossom
and fill all the world with fruit.

[7]Has ⌞the LORD⌟ struck her
as he struck down those who struck her?
Has she been killed
as those were killed who killed her?
[8]By warfare[a] and exile you contend with her—
with his fierce blast he drives her out,
as on a day the east wind blows.
[9]By this, then, will Jacob's guilt be atoned for,
and this will be the full fruitage of the removal of his sin:
When he makes all the altar stones
to be like chalk stones crushed to pieces,
no Asherah poles[b] or incense altars
will be left standing.

[a]8 See Septuagint; the meaning of the Hebrew for this word is uncertain. [b]9 That is, symbols of the goddess Asherah

OPEN 1. As a child, did you love or fear monsters? Were any "hidden" in your room? Where? **2.** Tell about your garden. Do you grow food or flowers? How much time do you lavish on it?

STUDY 1. The Leviathan was an evil monster in ancient Eastern mythology. What would God's slaying this familiar symbol accomplish (24:1–3,21–23; 26:20–21)? **2.** As God sings about his garden (vv. 2–6), what chords does he strike: Major or minor? Harmony or discord? High notes or low notes? **3.** How does this song of God's vineyard harmonize with that in 5:1–7? What accounts for the change in tune? **4.** How fruitful has Israel been? What is the "fruit" that will eventually "fill all the world" (2:1–5; 19:23–25; 26:18)? **5.** What has been the cause and purpose of God's judgments against Judah (vv. 7–11; compare 11:11)? **6.** Whether "the city" (v. 10) is Jerusalem, or is symbolic of any human endeavor pursued without regard for God (as in 24:10–12; 25:2–3), what is the future of all such plans?

APPLY 1. What "sea monsters" (pressures, temptations, opposing forces) seem to be chasing after you these days? How do you cope with them? Which one do you want God to slay first? **2.** Is the fruit of your life mostly taking root (present, but unseen)? Or is your fruit budding and blossoming (it's beginning to show its God-given potential)? **3.** This past year, have you sensed God singing about your garden (as in vv. 2–6)? Or have you felt God was disciplining you in some way (as in vv. 7–9)? Why? In retrospect (and in view of John 15), what do you see as the purpose of such discipline? What is your part, and God's part, in being fruitful and multiplying for God?

26:21 to punish. God will judge people for both open and secret sins. **conceal her slain no longer.** Since God knows all the bloodshed and evil on earth and will judge its perpetrators, this statement encourages believers to completely obey God.

27:1 sword ... Leviathan. God will triumph over all who oppose him, including this large sea creature (Ps. 74:13–14).

27:5 refuge ... peace. While God must judge sin, he prefers that believers repent and obey him, living in the proper covenant relationship and receiving his blessings (Job 22:21).

[10]The fortified city stands desolate,
an abandoned settlement, forsaken like the desert;
there the calves graze,
there they lie down;
they strip its branches bare.
[11]When its twigs are dry, they are broken off
and women come and make fires with them.
For this is a people without understanding;
so their Maker has no compassion on them,
and their Creator shows them no favor.

[12]In that day the LORD will thresh from the flowing Euphrates[a] to
the Wadi of Egypt, and you, O Israelites, will be gathered up one by
one. [13]And in that day a great trumpet will sound. Those who were
perishing in Assyria and those who were exiled in Egypt will come
and worship the LORD on the holy mountain in Jerusalem.

Woe to Ephraim

28 Woe to that wreath, the pride of Ephraim's drunkards,
to the fading flower, his glorious beauty,
set on the head of a fertile valley—
to that city, the pride of those laid low by wine!
[2]See, the Lord has one who is powerful and strong.
Like a hailstorm and a destructive wind,
like a driving rain and a flooding downpour,
he will throw it forcefully to the ground.
[3]That wreath, the pride of Ephraim's drunkards,
will be trampled underfoot.
[4]That fading flower, his glorious beauty,
set on the head of a fertile valley,
will be like a fig ripe before harvest—
as soon as someone sees it and takes it in his hand,
he swallows it.

[5]In that day the LORD Almighty
will be a glorious crown,
a beautiful wreath
for the remnant of his people.
[6]He will be a spirit of justice
to him who sits in judgment,
a source of strength
to those who turn back the battle at the gate.

[7]And these also stagger from wine
and reel from beer:
Priests and prophets stagger from beer
and are befuddled with wine;
they reel from beer,
they stagger when seeing visions,

[a]12 Hebrew *River*

OPEN 1. What household chore stands out as one that your parent or spouse has nagged you about? Why did you have to be nagged or coerced into doing that chore? Did you ever get away with waiting until someone else did it? In either event, how did that affect your relationship with your parent or spouse? **2.** Do you feel your parents set down "rules upon rules"? Or were they lax when it came to rules? Which would you have preferred?

STUDY While chapters 13–27 deal with God's authority over the nations in general, chapters 28–33 consist of six "woes" detailing God's judgment (chs. 28–31) and restoration (chs. 32–33) of Judah in particular. **1.** In verses 1–4, Isaiah singles out Samaria (a luxurious and decadent city in Israel at this time) as an example of God's judgment, comparing her to a head-wreath of flowers that party goers would wear. What will happen to this "wreath" in which the Israelites have taken such pride? What are the reasons for God's judgment upon Israel (1:12–17; 10:1–4)? **2.** What light does 2 Kings 17:1–6 shed on the fulfillment of this prophecy against Samaria? **3.** What will be different when God is truly the "crown" of his people (vv. 5–6)? **4.** What is Isaiah saying about the "visions" and "decisions" of the religious leadership of Israel by the severe way he describes them (vv. 7–8)? What is the effect on Israel of their drunken excesses? To what spiritual reality

27:10 desolate ... abandoned ... forsaken. Because of Israel's sin, Jerusalem was destroyed in 586 B.C.

27:12 the LORD will thresh. Refers to God's judgment of Israel's oppressors. He will bring the Israelites from Assyria and Egypt to Jerusalem where the Messiah will reign.

they stumble when rendering decisions.
[8]All the tables are covered with vomit
and there is not a spot without filth.

[9]"Who is it he is trying to teach?
To whom is he explaining his message?
To children weaned from their milk,
to those just taken from the breast?
[10]For it is:
Do and do, do and do,
rule on rule, rule on rule[a];
a little here, a little there."

[11]Very well then, with foreign lips and strange tongues
God will speak to this people,
[12]to whom he said,
"This is the resting place, let the weary rest";
and, "This is the place of repose"—
but they would not listen.
[13]So then, the word of the LORD to them will become:
Do and do, do and do,
rule on rule, rule on rule;
a little here, a little there—
so that they will go and fall backward,
be injured and snared and captured.

[14]Therefore hear the word of the LORD, you scoffers
who rule this people in Jerusalem.
[15]You boast, "We have entered into a covenant with death,
with the grave[b] we have made an agreement.
When an overwhelming scourge sweeps by,
it cannot touch us,
for we have made a lie our refuge
and falsehood[c] our hiding place."

[16]So this is what the Sovereign LORD says:

"See, I lay a stone in Zion,
a tested stone,
a precious cornerstone for a sure foundation;
the one who trusts will never be dismayed.
[17]I will make justice the measuring line
and righteousness the plumb line;
hail will sweep away your refuge, the lie,
and water will overflow your hiding place.
[18]Your covenant with death will be annulled;
your agreement with the grave will not stand.
When the overwhelming scourge sweeps by,

[a]10 Hebrew / *sav lasav sav lasav / kav lakav kav lakav* (possibly meaningless sounds; perhaps a mimicking of the prophet's words); also in verse 13 [b]15 Hebrew *Sheol*; also in verse 18 [c]15 Or *false gods*

does this vivid imagery point? **5.** How do these leaders receive Isaiah's message (vv. 9–10)? Why would they mock him and his warnings, much like a rebel teenager does his parents? **6.** How will they be forced to eat their mocking words (v. 13; 6:9–13)? **7.** What is God's basic message to Israel which they are ignoring to their detriment (v. 12)? What is meant by this "resting place" (30:15; 40:31; Josh. 1:13)? **8.** Isaiah now applies the lesson of Israel to Judah. What is their "covenant with death" (v. 15)? **9.** In contrast to lies and falsehood (v. 15), what is the "sure foundation" of God's kingdom (vv. 16–19)? What promise is given to those who will trust in that cornerstone? What is the warning given to those who do not? **10.** How will their covenant prove "too short" (vv. 20–22)? What was God's work at Mount Perazim and at Gibeon (1 Chr. 14:8–11; Josh. 10:10)? **11.** What is the point of the farmer parable (vv. 23–29)? What picture of God's ways do we get by appreciating the seemingly strange ways of this farmer? If Judah's leaders do not stop their mocking, what "strange" and yet "wonderful" work will God do (vv. 21–)?

APPLY 1. Judah's kings often lacked strength to oppose evil. Where do you need the Spirit of the Lord to strengthen you to "turn back the battle at the gate" of your life (vv. 5–6)? **2.** Have you ever responded to the Lord's message as the leaders did in verses 9–10? How long did that rebellious phase last? With what result? How did God break through your cynicism? **3.** What use has the New Testament made of verse 16 (1 Cor. 3:11; 1 Peter 2:4–8)? What are some of the implications of saying that Jesus is the foundation stone for your life? How will you demonstrate that in a practical way this week?

28:12 let the weary rest. Although God had offered Israel peace and rest, they refused to listen. If the people would not learn from God and obey him, they would be judged and oppressed by their enemies.

28:15,18 covenant with death. Isaiah's way of describing Israel's covenant with Egypt. Jerusalem's leaders trusted in other gods, such as the god of the underworld, to save them.

you will be beaten down by it.
19 As often as it comes it will carry you away;
morning after morning, by day and by night,
it will sweep through."

The understanding of this message
will bring sheer terror.
20 The bed is too short to stretch out on,
the blanket too narrow to wrap around you.
21 The LORD will rise up as he did at Mount Perazim,
he will rouse himself as in the Valley of Gibeon—
to do his work, his strange work,
and perform his task, his alien task.
22 Now stop your mocking,
or your chains will become heavier;
the Lord, the LORD Almighty, has told me
of the destruction decreed against the whole land.

23 Listen and hear my voice;
pay attention and hear what I say.
24 When a farmer plows for planting, does he plow continually?
Does he keep on breaking up and harrowing the soil?
25 When he has leveled the surface,
does he not sow caraway and scatter cummin?
Does he not plant wheat in its place,[a]
barley in its plot,[a]
and spelt in its field?
26 His God instructs him
and teaches him the right way.

27 Caraway is not threshed with a sledge,
nor is a cartwheel rolled over cummin;
caraway is beaten out with a rod,
and cummin with a stick.
28 Grain must be ground to make bread;
so one does not go on threshing it forever.
Though he drives the wheels of his threshing cart over it,
his horses do not grind it.
29 All this also comes from the LORD Almighty,
wonderful in counsel and magnificent in wisdom.

Woe to David's City

29 Woe to you, Ariel, Ariel,
the city where David settled!
Add year to year
and let your cycle of festivals go on.

[a]25 The meaning of the Hebrew for this word is uncertain.

OPEN 1. In what part of your family heritage do you take special pride? What part is less flattering, even embarrassing, to talk about? **2.** What things do you display around the house (or on the refrigerator) that you have made with your hands or that someone else has made

28:20 bed ... blanket. Looking for protection from false gods was as futile as trying to sleep in a small, uncomfortable bed with a thin blanket unable to keep out the cold.

28:24 a farmer. Isaiah compared God's judgment to the work of a farmer who must grind certain of his crops to get out the small seeds. Though God will judge sin, he will also save and restore.

28:29 wonderful in counsel ... wisdom. God gives the farmer wisdom in handling his crops. Isaiah urged Israel to submit to God, who knows how to handle his people (9:6).

29:1–2,7 Ariel, the city. Probably means "altar hearth" (Ezek. 43:15) and refers to Jerusalem, where so much

[2]Yet I will besiege Ariel;
she will mourn and lament,
she will be to me like an altar hearth.[a]
[3]I will encamp against you all around;
I will encircle you with towers
and set up my siege works against you.
[4]Brought low, you will speak from the ground;
your speech will mumble out of the dust.
Your voice will come ghostlike from the earth;
out of the dust your speech will whisper.

[5]But your many enemies will become like fine dust,
the ruthless hordes like blown chaff.
Suddenly, in an instant,
[6] the LORD Almighty will come
with thunder and earthquake and great noise,
with windstorm and tempest and flames of a devouring fire.
[7]Then the hordes of all the nations that fight against Ariel,
that attack her and her fortress and besiege her,
will be as it is with a dream,
with a vision in the night—
[8]as when a hungry man dreams that he is eating,
but he awakens, and his hunger remains;
as when a thirsty man dreams that he is drinking,
but he awakens faint, with his thirst unquenched.
So will it be with the hordes of all the nations
that fight against Mount Zion.

[9]Be stunned and amazed,
blind yourselves and be sightless;
be drunk, but not from wine,
stagger, but not from beer.
[10]The LORD has brought over you a deep sleep:
He has sealed your eyes (the prophets);
he has covered your heads (the seers).

[11]For you this whole vision is nothing but words sealed in a scroll.
And if you give the scroll to someone who can read, and say to him,
"Read this, please," he will answer, "I can't; it is sealed." [12]Or if you
give the scroll to someone who cannot read, and say, "Read this,
please," he will answer, "I don't know how to read."

[13]The Lord says:

"These people come near to me with their mouth
and honor me with their lips,

[a]2 The Hebrew for *altar hearth* sounds like the Hebrew for *Ariel*.

for you? Which creation do you treasure most?

STUDY 1. What happened regularly on the temple's altar that Isaiah is warning is merely lip service and unintelligible at that (vv. 4,13)? Who is being criticized in this mockery of the city's unwarranted hope in their immunity from God's judgment? **2.** Although it will be the Assyrian army outside their gates, who is really encamped against Jerusalem (v. 3; 28:21)? How would this realization affect the city's proud leaders (v. 4; compare 28:14–15)? What might they expect to happen next? **3.** Instead, what "serendipity" will God bring about, "in an instant" (vv. 5–8)? What will happen, like a dream in the night, to those who have been devastating Jerusalem (10:5–19 and 27:1, which refer to the destruction of Assyria's army)? **4.** Even though the 11th hour defeat of Judah's enemies has been foretold, what effect will these events have on the people (vv. 9–14)? What will the impact be, specifically, on the prophets and seers? On the uneducated? On the literate? On the wise and intelligent? **5.** How do you account for why they are so unable to grasp what Isaiah is saying to them (vv. 10–13; compare 26:8)? **6.** Verses 15–24 comprise another "woe" to the leaders of Jerusalem. What hidden agenda do you think was going on in their hearts or behind closed doors to bring on this woe (vv. 15–16)? What does such secrecy show about their view of God? **7.** What will be the future of these unjust leaders (vv. 20–21)? By contrast, what will become of their victims (vv. 17–19)? What irony do you see here (compare vv. 10–12)? **8.** What will be the net result of all that the Lord promises to do (vv. 22–24)?

APPLY 1. When was the last time you tried to sneak something past God so he wouldn't notice? What did the "potter" then say to the "clay"? What else would it take to break you out of such presumptuous thinking (that the potter is just like the

bloodshed would make the city appear like an altar where sacrifices had been slain (Ezek. 24:6,9).

29:4 voice will come ghostlike. Refers to the deceptive "voices" of the dead who supposedly spoke through mediums. A humbled Jerusalem will only be able to speak in a whisper.

29:6 the LORD Almighty will come. As God intervened and spared Jerusalem from destruction by Assyrian soldiers, God will come and destroy the nations attacking his people (Zech. 14:1–3).

29:13 their hearts are far from me. Professing to know God or engaging in acts of worship do not necessarily mean that a person's heart is turned toward God. The people of Jerusalem were legalistic. They followed rules well but ignored God's intention to remake their hearts (Col. 2:22).

clay)? **2.** Tell the group about a time when God turned things around for you "in an instant" (v. 5). What were you doing at the time you were "surprised by joy"? How did God show his love to you in a special, personal way? What does such a "serendipity" show you about God's grace? **3.** The apostle Paul echoes Isaiah in saying that the "wisdom of the wise," which advocates that people find spiritual reality in some other way than Christ, will perish (1 Cor. 1:19). Have you found Christ to be a more reliable ally in your spiritual life than the other alternatives people turn to? How so? What other ally still seems to appeal to you? Why? What does this ally do to your faith in God?

OPEN 1. When you are in need of a good rest, what do you like to do? **2.** Would your parents have ever called you obstinate or a "do-nothing"? For what reason? **3.** What was an embarrassing nickname for you? How did you get it?

but their hearts are far from me.
Their worship of me
is made up only of rules taught by men.[a]
14 Therefore once more I will astound these people
with wonder upon wonder;
the wisdom of the wise will perish,
the intelligence of the intelligent will vanish."
15 Woe to those who go to great depths
to hide their plans from the LORD,
who do their work in darkness and think,
"Who sees us? Who will know?"
16 You turn things upside down,
as if the potter were thought to be like the clay!
Shall what is formed say to him who formed it,
"He did not make me"?
Can the pot say of the potter,
"He knows nothing"?
17 In a very short time, will not Lebanon be turned into a fertile field
and the fertile field seem like a forest?
18 In that day the deaf will hear the words of the scroll,
and out of gloom and darkness
the eyes of the blind will see.
19 Once more the humble will rejoice in the LORD;
the needy will rejoice in the Holy One of Israel.
20 The ruthless will vanish,
the mockers will disappear,
and all who have an eye for evil will be cut down—
21 those who with a word make a man out to be guilty,
who ensnare the defender in court
and with false testimony deprive the innocent of justice.

22 Therefore this is what the LORD, who redeemed Abraham, says to
the house of Jacob:

"No longer will Jacob be ashamed;
no longer will their faces grow pale.
23 When they see among them their children,
the work of my hands,
they will keep my name holy;
they will acknowledge the holiness of the Holy One of Jacob,
and will stand in awe of the God of Israel.
24 Those who are wayward in spirit will gain understanding;
those who complain will accept instruction."

Woe to the Obstinate Nation

30 "Woe to the obstinate children,"
declares the LORD,
"to those who carry out plans that are not mine,

[a] 13 Hebrew; Septuagint *They worship me in vain; / their teachings are but rules taught by men*

29:22 the LORD, who redeemed. God renewed his covenant with Abraham, promising to deliver and bless Israel (Josh. 24:3; Acts 7:2–4). **No longer ... be ashamed.** God's deliverance from the Assyrian army was a preview of a future day when God's people will no longer be dominated by either foreign oppression or their own sin.

30:1 forming an alliance. King Hezekiah's advisors wanted to join

forming an alliance, but not by my Spirit,
heaping sin upon sin;
[2]who go down to Egypt
without consulting me;
who look for help to Pharaoh's protection,
to Egypt's shade for refuge.
[3]But Pharaoh's protection will be to your shame,
Egypt's shade will bring you disgrace.
[4]Though they have officials in Zoan
and their envoys have arrived in Hanes,
[5]everyone will be put to shame
because of a people useless to them,
who bring neither help nor advantage,
but only shame and disgrace."

[6]An oracle concerning the animals of the Negev:

Through a land of hardship and distress,
of lions and lionesses,
of adders and darting snakes,
the envoys carry their riches on donkeys' backs,
their treasures on the humps of camels,
to that unprofitable nation,
[7] to Egypt, whose help is utterly useless.
Therefore I call her
Rahab the Do-Nothing.

[8]Go now, write it on a tablet for them,
inscribe it on a scroll,
that for the days to come
it may be an everlasting witness.
[9]These are rebellious people, deceitful children,
children unwilling to listen to the LORD's instruction.
[10]They say to the seers,
"See no more visions!"
and to the prophets,
"Give us no more visions of what is right!
Tell us pleasant things,
prophesy illusions.
[11]Leave this way,
get off this path,
and stop confronting us
with the Holy One of Israel!"

[12]Therefore, this is what the Holy One of Israel says:

"Because you have rejected this message,
relied on oppression
and depended on deceit,
[13]this sin will become for you

STUDY 1. This is Isaiah's fourth "woe" message since 28:1. For what is he pronouncing God's judgment here? What is the basic problem with Israel's desire to form an alliance with Egypt against Assyria (vv. 1–7)? **2.** How would you feel as one of the envoys to Egypt when Isaiah approaches your caravan and gives this oracle? How does the nickname for Egypt ("Rahab the Do-Nothing") contrast with the description of God throughout these chapters? (Note: Rahab is a mythical sea dragon; its name means storm or arrogance.) **3.** What was the official response to Isaiah (vv. 8–11)? What inescapable logic do you see in God's judgment here? What does Isaiah mean by the image of the wall (vv. 13–14)? **4.** In contrast to their alliance with Egypt, what is Isaiah's plan for their deliverance (v. 15)? What will happen as a result of Israel rejecting this plan? **5.** In light of all the warnings throughout chapters 28–30, how do you account for the promises of God's grace here (vv. 18–26)? **6.** What do the agricultural images convey about God's grace? What would be equivalent industrial or technological images to convey the same idea today? **7.** Are salvation (vv. 18–26) and judgment (vv. 27–33) flip sides of the same action on God's part? How do they work together to achieve the same divine purpose? **8.** Some songs teach theology. This song of God's imminent judgment over Assyria is a case in point. What images, names and verbs are associated with God? What do these teach you about who God is, what he does and why? **9.** What will happen to Assyria at Topheth? **10.** What does this passage say to severely oppressed people (Jewish prisoners in a Nazi concentration camp, American Blacks, the Arab Palestinian, victims of ethnic cleansing in Bosnia or Rwanda, dissenters in Communist China)? Knowing God's judgment is certain, how does that strengthen you to keep following him?

APPLY 1. Judah's shame is repeated three times in verses 3–5. Judah looked for the right thing (security) but in the wrong place (Egypt instead of God). What are some

---

Egypt to fight against the Assyrians, although Egypt was then a weak player on the Near East scene.

30:8 write it ... inscribe it. Even though the people would not obey God's instructions, Isaiah was to write them down so the people could not say they had never known or heard. The written message would testify against their flimsy excuses.

30:13 sin ... like a high wall. The simile meant that judgment would come suddenly and completely (Jer. 19:11).

of the wrong places you have hoped to find the right things (security, love, acceptance)? As a result of your search, did you find what you were looking for? **2.** Israel was tired of hearing the Word of God, and wished to be left alone or listen to others as well. What in your life are the "pleasant things" or "illusions" (v. 10) you would rather listen to at times? How have they resulted in "high walls" (v. 13), fencing out God? **3.** When has God called you to repentance, rest and quietness, and you just kept running (v. 15) What role can rest and quietness play in bringing a busy person closer to God?

like a high wall, cracked and bulging,
that collapses suddenly, in an instant.
14It will break in pieces like pottery,
shattered so mercilessly
that among its pieces not a fragment will be found
for taking coals from a hearth
or scooping water out of a cistern."

15This is what the Sovereign LORD, the Holy One of Israel, says:

"In repentance and rest is your salvation,
in quietness and trust is your strength,
but you would have none of it.
16You said, 'No, we will flee on horses.'
Therefore you will flee!
You said, 'We will ride off on swift horses.'
Therefore your pursuers will be swift!
17A thousand will flee
at the threat of one;
at the threat of five
you will all flee away,
till you are left
like a flagstaff on a mountaintop,
like a banner on a hill."

18Yet the LORD longs to be gracious to you;
he rises to show you compassion.
For the LORD is a God of justice.
Blessed are all who wait for him!

19O people of Zion, who live in Jerusalem, you will weep no more.
How gracious he will be when you cry for help! As soon as he hears,
he will answer you. 20Although the Lord gives you the bread of adversity and the water of affliction, your teachers will be hidden no more;
with your own eyes you will see them. 21Whether you turn to the right
or to the left, your ears will hear a voice behind you, saying, "This is
the way; walk in it." 22Then you will defile your idols overlaid with
silver and your images covered with gold; you will throw them away
like a menstrual cloth and say to them, "Away with you!"

23He will also send you rain for the seed you sow in the ground,
and the food that comes from the land will be rich and plentiful. In
that day your cattle will graze in broad meadows. 24The oxen and
donkeys that work the soil will eat fodder and mash, spread out with
fork and shovel. 25In the day of great slaughter, when the towers fall,
streams of water will flow on every high mountain and every lofty
hill. 26The moon will shine like the sun, and the sunlight will be seven

---

30:15 quietness and trust. The peace and confidence available to people who trust totally in God's strength are part of the promise of the new life of faith.

30:18 longs to be gracious to you. God's mercy is part of, not the flip side of, God's judgment (Jer. 17:7). When God judges, it is an expression of mercy, though often harsh mercy.

30:26 binds up the bruises ... heals the wounds. God will restore and bless his people after purging and judging their sin. God will heal the people from their wickedness.

times brighter, like the light of seven full days, when the LORD binds up the bruises of his people and heals the wounds he inflicted.

27 See, the Name of the LORD comes from afar,
with burning anger and dense clouds of smoke;
his lips are full of wrath,
and his tongue is a consuming fire.
28 His breath is like a rushing torrent,
rising up to the neck.
He shakes the nations in the sieve of destruction;
he places in the jaws of the peoples
a bit that leads them astray.
29 And you will sing
as on the night you celebrate a holy festival;
your hearts will rejoice
as when people go up with flutes
to the mountain of the LORD,
to the Rock of Israel.
30 The LORD will cause men to hear his majestic voice
and will make them see his arm coming down
with raging anger and consuming fire,
with cloudburst, thunderstorm and hail.
31 The voice of the LORD will shatter Assyria;
with his scepter he will strike them down.
32 Every stroke the LORD lays on them
with his punishing rod
will be to the music of tambourines and harps,
as he fights them in battle with the blows of his arm.
33 Topheth has long been prepared;
it has been made ready for the king.
Its fire pit has been made deep and wide,
with an abundance of fire and wood;
the breath of the LORD,
like a stream of burning sulfur,
sets it ablaze.

Woe to Those Who Rely on Egypt

31 Woe to those who go down to Egypt for help,
who rely on horses,
who trust in the multitude of their chariots
and in the great strength of their horsemen,
but do not look to the Holy One of Israel,
or seek help from the LORD.
2 Yet he too is wise and can bring disaster;
he does not take back his words.
He will rise up against the house of the wicked,
against those who help evildoers.
3 But the Egyptians are men and not God;
their horses are flesh and not spirit.
When the LORD stretches out his hand,
he who helps will stumble,
he who is helped will fall;
both will perish together.

OPEN If you had to be a horse, lion or bird, which one would you choose and why? Which of their assets (speed, strength, appetite, quickness) would you like to have?

STUDY 1. How is this "woe" related to the one in chapter 30? What similarities do you see? What differences? What reasoning is given here for the warning in the previous "woe"? **2.** If you were a leader in Judah, why would you be seeking this alliance? What have these leaders overlooked as they have formed this alliance? **3.** In contrast to the stumbling of the Egyptians, how will God help Judah during the Assyrian attack (vv. 4–9)? How will God be like a lion? Like a mother bird? Like a fire?

4. How will this event be like another Passover for Judah (v. 5; Ex. 12:12–13)? What will be the result for the Assyrians? For the Jews? **5.** What does it mean that this deliverance doesn't depend upon whether they "return to him" first (v. 6)? What will happen as a result of this deliverance?

APPLY 1. What pressures have you felt lately? In practical terms, does relying on God in such times mean not involving the help of anyone else? **2.** God intended to deliver Judah even while she persisted in rebellion. What hope does that offer you (Rom. 5:8)? **3.** When have you actually lived as though God didn't matter? What did matter at that time? What difference does it make to you to realize that even in those times God is protecting you as a lion or a mother bird? What other images of God help you to embrace him?

OPEN What are you thirsty or hungry for, right now?

STUDY 1. What conditions marked the reign of the leaders who did not trust God (28:7–10, 14–15; 29:13,20–21)? **2.** By contrast, what will this kingdom of righteousness look like (vv. 2–4)? **3.** What will happen to the ways of the fool and the unjust? Why does foolishness flourish when there's no justice?

APPLY 1. When you need someone to be a shelter for you, to whom do you turn? Why? **2.** For whom could you be like a shelter or a stream of water today? How? What example can you think of where a person's power has been mistaken for true greatness? **3.** What marks of true greatness (v. 8) do you want to

4 This is what the LORD says to me:

"As a lion growls,
a great lion over his prey—
and though a whole band of shepherds
is called together against him,
he is not frightened by their shouts
or disturbed by their clamor—
so the LORD Almighty will come down
to do battle on Mount Zion and on its heights.
5 Like birds hovering overhead,
the LORD Almighty will shield Jerusalem;
he will shield it and deliver it,
he will 'pass over' it and will rescue it."

6 Return to him you have so greatly revolted against, O Israelites.
7 For in that day every one of you will reject the idols of silver and gold
your sinful hands have made.

8 "Assyria will fall by a sword that is not of man;
a sword, not of mortals, will devour them.
They will flee before the sword
and their young men will be put to forced labor.
9 Their stronghold will fall because of terror;
at sight of the battle standard their commanders will panic,"
declares the LORD,
whose fire is in Zion,
whose furnace is in Jerusalem.

The Kingdom of Righteousness

32 See, a king will reign in righteousness
and rulers will rule with justice.
2 Each man will be like a shelter from the wind
and a refuge from the storm,
like streams of water in the desert
and the shadow of a great rock in a thirsty land.

3 Then the eyes of those who see will no longer be closed,
and the ears of those who hear will listen.
4 The mind of the rash will know and understand,
and the stammering tongue will be fluent and clear.
5 No longer will the fool be called noble
nor the scoundrel be highly respected.
6 For the fool speaks folly,
his mind is busy with evil:
He practices ungodliness
and spreads error concerning the LORD;

31:4 lion. God was not intimidated by the Assyrians, just as a lion is not afraid of shepherds (Hos. 11:10).

31:5 birds ... will shield Jerusalem. A picture of God's protection of Jerusalem against the enemy. **pass over.** A reference to the destroying angel who passed over Israel when the firstborn of Egypt were killed (Ex. 12:13).

31:9 battle standard. A banner serving as the rallying point for battle. The Assyrian commanders would be terrified when they saw Judah's banner and the slaughter of their soldiers by God's angel.

32:1 king will reign in righteousness. The Messiah will reign in righteousness when God's justice is finally won over all the earth (Jer. 23:5).

32:5 fool. A senseless person who teaches falsehood and gives no thought to the needs of others.

the hungry he leaves empty
and from the thirsty he withholds water.
7 The scoundrel's methods are wicked,
he makes up evil schemes
to destroy the poor with lies,
even when the plea of the needy is just.
8 But the noble man makes noble plans,
and by noble deeds he stands.

The Women of Jerusalem

9 You women who are so complacent,
rise up and listen to me;
you daughters who feel secure,
hear what I have to say!
10 In little more than a year
you who feel secure will tremble;
the grape harvest will fail,
and the harvest of fruit will not come.
11 Tremble, you complacent women;
shudder, you daughters who feel secure!
Strip off your clothes,
put sackcloth around your waists.
12 Beat your breasts for the pleasant fields,
for the fruitful vines
13 and for the land of my people,
a land overgrown with thorns and briers—
yes, mourn for all houses of merriment
and for this city of revelry.
14 The fortress will be abandoned,
the noisy city deserted;
citadel and watchtower will become a wasteland forever,
the delight of donkeys, a pasture for flocks,
15 till the Spirit is poured upon us from on high,
and the desert becomes a fertile field,
and the fertile field seems like a forest.
16 Justice will dwell in the desert
and righteousness live in the fertile field.
17 The fruit of righteousness will be peace;
the effect of righteousness will be quietness and confidence
forever.
18 My people will live in peaceful dwelling places,
in secure homes,
in undisturbed places of rest.
19 Though hail flattens the forest
and the city is leveled completely,
20 how blessed you will be,

see growing in you? How can you cultivate that fruit (Matt. 6:33)?

OPEN In the morning, are you easy to wake up? Or do you need two alarms, a dog with a cold nose and someone to pull the covers off of you?

STUDY 1. Up to this point, how have the men responded to Isaiah's message (28:7–10)? Why might he be turning to the women at this juncture? What does he anticipate for them? **2.** What does he mean by the "thorns and briers" (v. 13; 5:6; 7:23; 27:4)? What is wrong with the revelry and merriment over which he calls the women to mourn (22:12–13)? **3.** What will restore Judah (vv. 15–20)? What will the restored kingdom look like? **4.** What does Isaiah feel the outpouring of the Spirit will be like on God's people (v. 15)? How does that compare to the disciples' question in Acts 1:5–6? **5.** How do these promises of God compare with those given earlier (vv. 1–8; 28:16; 29:17–24; 30:19–26)? What is distinctive about the imagery Isaiah uses to convey his message?

APPLY 1. What is the difference between the complacency of verse 9 and the quietness and confidence of verse 17? Which are you closest to in your own life? **2.** What "desert" in your life would you like to see God make into a "fertile field" (v. 15)? What change of attitude would this require in you?

---

scoundrel. A person who plots to take advantage of the poor and needy (Prov. 24:7–9).

32:9 women. A warning to the women of Judah who thought that judgment would not come (3:16–23).

complacent ... feel secure. Can mean "trusting" or "assured." The wicked relied on Egypt for security, while the righteous trusted in the Lord.

32:15 till the Spirit. The outpouring of God's Spirit will bring fertility, justice, productivity and security, as promised in the Deuteronomic covenant—if the people obeyed God (Deut. 5:2–3; 29:9; Joel 2:28).

sowing your seed by every stream,
and letting your cattle and donkeys range free.

Distress and Help

33 Woe to you, O destroyer,
you who have not been destroyed!
Woe to you, O traitor,
you who have not been betrayed!
When you stop destroying,
you will be destroyed;
when you stop betraying,
you will be betrayed.

2 O LORD, be gracious to us;
we long for you.
Be our strength every morning,
our salvation in time of distress.
3 At the thunder of your voice, the peoples flee;
when you rise up, the nations scatter.
4 Your plunder, O nations, is harvested as by young locusts;
like a swarm of locusts men pounce on it.

5 The LORD is exalted, for he dwells on high;
he will fill Zion with justice and righteousness.
6 He will be the sure foundation for your times,
a rich store of salvation and wisdom and knowledge;
the fear of the LORD is the key to this treasure.[a]

7 Look, their brave men cry aloud in the streets;
the envoys of peace weep bitterly.
8 The highways are deserted,
no travelers are on the roads.
The treaty is broken,
its witnesses[b] are despised,
no one is respected.
9 The land mourns[c] and wastes away,
Lebanon is ashamed and withers;
Sharon is like the Arabah,
and Bashan and Carmel drop their leaves.

10 "Now will I arise," says the LORD.
"Now will I be exalted;
now will I be lifted up.
11 You conceive chaff,
you give birth to straw;
your breath is a fire that consumes you.
12 The peoples will be burned as if to lime;
like cut thornbushes they will be set ablaze."

13 You who are far away, hear what I have done;
you who are near, acknowledge my power!

[a] 6 Or *is a treasure from him* [b] 8 Dead Sea Scrolls; Masoretic Text / *the cities* [c] 9 Or *dries up*

OPEN 1. "When the cat is away the mice will play." What playful thing do you try to get away with when the (boss, parent, teacher) is gone? **2.** Recall the three monkeys who "hear no evil, see no evil, and speak no evil." What current issues do you wish someone in office would notice and speak against?

STUDY 1. Although the earlier "woes" in chapters 28–32 were directed toward Judah in light of the Assyrian invasion, to whom is this one addressed? In verses 1–9, what four shifts in mood and speaker do you sense? **2.** How are the Jerusalem leaders reacting to the news that Egypt will not help in the fight against Assyria? What does it matter that Assyria rebuffs the envoys of peace with their payments of tribute (v. 7; 2 Kin. 18:14– 16)? **3.** As their city is besieged, how does Israel respond (vv. 2–3)? How does that compare with earlier responses in a national emergency (28:14–15; 31:1)? Are they any closer to demonstrating what God desired for them all along (30:15; 31:6)? How will they find in God what they have been mistakenly looking for in their alliance with Egypt? **4.** What will occur "now" that it is God's time to act (vv. 10–12)? How will the people of Jerusalem react to this outpouring of God's power in the defeat of her enemy? How does their reaction to God's holiness and power (v. 14) compare to Isaiah's reaction (6:5)? **5.** What is it that is heard, seen and spoken in God's answer (vv. 15–16; Ps. 15), in contrast to the proverbial deaf, blind and dumb monkeys? How does God's answer reflect both personal and social righteousness? **6.** Verses 17–24 conclude the series of prophecies begun in 28:1. What does this final picture of God's grace to Judah emphasize about God's plan for his people? Who do you think "the king in his beauty" (v. 17) refers to: Hezekiah (who was the king of Judah at this time)? Some Davidic king still to come? God as King? Why do you think so? Might this also be a picture of what the Gospel of Christ is all about? How so? **7.** What does it mean to you that the Lord Jesus is the fulfillment of verse 22? What aspects of his

33:2 our strength ... our salvation. Isaiah and the believing remnant longed for God's deliverance and defeat of their opponents. God has shown his power by defeating their opponents many times before (12.2; Ex. 15:2; Ps. 118:14).

[14]The sinners in Zion are terrified;
trembling grips the godless:
"Who of us can dwell with the consuming fire?
Who of us can dwell with everlasting burning?"
[15]He who walks righteously
and speaks what is right,
who rejects gain from extortion
and keeps his hand from accepting bribes,
who stops his ears against plots of murder
and shuts his eyes against contemplating evil—
[16]this is the man who will dwell on the heights,
whose refuge will be the mountain fortress.
His bread will be supplied,
and water will not fail him.

[17]Your eyes will see the king in his beauty
and view a land that stretches afar.
[18]In your thoughts you will ponder the former terror:
"Where is that chief officer?
Where is the one who took the revenue?
Where is the officer in charge of the towers?"
[19]You will see those arrogant people no more,
those people of an obscure speech,
with their strange, incomprehensible tongue.

[20]Look upon Zion, the city of our festivals;
your eyes will see Jerusalem,
a peaceful abode, a tent that will not be moved;
its stakes will never be pulled up,
nor any of its ropes broken.
[21]There the LORD will be our Mighty One.
It will be like a place of broad rivers and streams.
No galley with oars will ride them,
no mighty ship will sail them.
[22]For the LORD is our judge,
the LORD is our lawgiver,
the LORD is our king;
it is he who will save us.

[23]Your rigging hangs loose:
The mast is not held secure,
the sail is not spread.
Then an abundance of spoils will be divided
and even the lame will carry off plunder.
[24]No one living in Zion will say, "I am ill";
and the sins of those who dwell there will be forgiven.

earthly and future ministry come to mind when you picture Jesus as Judge? Lawgiver? King? Savior?

APPLY 1. When was one time God's power was so evident to you that by contrast your weakness was highlighted? In your experience of God now, does he seem more like a consuming fire or a fading candle? How can you keep on experiencing the fire? **2.** From what former "terror" has God delivered you? How? What effect has that had upon your view of God? On the way you worship or live?

33:16 heights ... mountain fortress. God's dwelling place, where the righteous will go to live with God forever in peace and safety high above their enemies.

33:17 in his beauty. Believers will see the Messiah face-to-face. In Christ's kingdom, "Jerusalem"—the center of God's covenant—will be peaceful and secure.

33:24 sins ... will be forgiven. Both sickness and sin will be removed in the coming kingdom (Jer. 31:34). The Messiah will be judge, lawgiver and king.

OPEN 1. What do you associate with the following words: War? Massacre? Meat slaughter house? Red Cross blood drive? Hospital surgery? Other? **2.** What's the bloodiest thing that's ever happened to you? What does the sight of lots of blood do to you? Have you ever fainted?

STUDY Chapters 34 and 35 conclude the series of prophecies about God's rule over the nations. **1.** If special effects recreated the cosmic and gory scenes depicted here for a movie, what would God's anger look like? Feel like? What would the movie be rated? **2.** Where would you place the drum roll? The crescendo? The discordant notes? The resolution? **3.** Why is the Lord this angry with "all nations" (v. 2; 10:5–19)? What modern political and military leaders does that example bring to mind? What is Isaiah's purpose in doing so in such graphic detail? **4.** How is God's vengeance related to his saving purpose (v. 8; 35:4)? **5.** Edom, a traditional enemy of Judah, represents all the nations as an object lesson here. What is the object lesson meted out to Edom for having refused to willingly offer sacrifice to the Lord (vv. 4–7)? **6.** After making them give their own blood in sacrifice to him, what will the resulting population and landscape be like for Edom (and all nations under judgment)? Are these images meant to be understood literally, figuratively or both? Explain.

APPLY 1. How do you feel about God after reading this passage? How might you feel if you read it from the viewpoint of an oppressed person reflecting on the fact that justice would one day overtake your oppressor? **2.** The "measuring line" and "plumb line" of verse 11 are images drawn from building construction, meant to symbolize judgment (Amos 7:7–9). If God measured what you have built in your life with such a line, do you feel like he would say: "Tear this building down!"? "Maybe some remodeling would suffice"? "Good enough for government work"?

Judgment Against the Nations

34 Come near, you nations, and listen;
pay attention, you peoples!
Let the earth hear, and all that is in it,
the world, and all that comes out of it!
2 The LORD is angry with all nations;
his wrath is upon all their armies.
He will totally destroy[a] them,
he will give them over to slaughter.
3 Their slain will be thrown out,
their dead bodies will send up a stench;
the mountains will be soaked with their blood.
4 All the stars of the heavens will be dissolved
and the sky rolled up like a scroll;
all the starry host will fall
like withered leaves from the vine,
like shriveled figs from the fig tree.

5 My sword has drunk its fill in the heavens;
see, it descends in judgment on Edom,
the people I have totally destroyed.
6 The sword of the LORD is bathed in blood,
it is covered with fat—
the blood of lambs and goats,
fat from the kidneys of rams.
For the LORD has a sacrifice in Bozrah
and a great slaughter in Edom.
7 And the wild oxen will fall with them,
the bull calves and the great bulls.
Their land will be drenched with blood,
and the dust will be soaked with fat.

8 For the LORD has a day of vengeance,
a year of retribution, to uphold Zion's cause.
9 Edom's streams will be turned into pitch,
her dust into burning sulfur;
her land will become blazing pitch!
10 It will not be quenched night and day;
its smoke will rise forever.
From generation to generation it will lie desolate;
no one will ever pass through it again.
11 The desert owl[b] and screech owl[b] will possess it;
the great owl[b] and the raven will nest there.
God will stretch out over Edom
the measuring line of chaos

[a] *2* The Hebrew term refers to the irrevocable giving over of things or persons to the LORD, often by totally destroying them; also in verse 5. [b] *11* The precise identification of these birds is uncertain.

34:2 angry ... wrath. God responds to sin by destroying it (13:5). Even the stars will be dissolved in his final judgment.

34:7 wild oxen ... great bulls. May symbolize Edom's soldiers or leaders who will attack Israel. God will destroy them at Bozrah, about 25 miles southeast of the Dead Sea.

34:8 day of vengeance ... retribution. God will punish the oppressors of his people (63:4).

34:9 pitch ... burning sulfur. Pitch is a tarlike substance that seems to burn forever. Sulfur burns with great heat and intensity. This may refer to the destruction of Sodom and Gomorrah.

and the plumb line of desolation.
12 Her nobles will have nothing there to be called a kingdom,
all her princes will vanish away.
13 Thorns will overrun her citadels,
nettles and brambles her strongholds.
She will become a haunt for jackals,
a home for owls.
14 Desert creatures will meet with hyenas,
and wild goats will bleat to each other;
there the night creatures will also repose
and find for themselves places of rest.
15 The owl will nest there and lay eggs,
she will hatch them, and care for her young under the shadow
of her wings;
there also the falcons will gather,
each with its mate.

16 Look in the scroll of the LORD and read:

None of these will be missing,
not one will lack her mate.
For it is his mouth that has given the order,
and his Spirit will gather them together.
17 He allots their portions;
his hand distributes them by measure.
They will possess it forever
and dwell there from generation to generation.

Joy of the Redeemed

35 The desert and the parched land will be glad;
the wilderness will rejoice and blossom.
Like the crocus, 2 it will burst into bloom;
it will rejoice greatly and shout for joy.
The glory of Lebanon will be given to it,
the splendor of Carmel and Sharon;
they will see the glory of the LORD,
the splendor of our God.

3 Strengthen the feeble hands,
steady the knees that give way;
4 say to those with fearful hearts,
"Be strong, do not fear;
your God will come,
he will come with vengeance;
with divine retribution
he will come to save you."

"More building should be done like this"? ____________

OPEN 1. After a long, cold winter, what is the first spring flower that you watch for? How do you feel when you see it? **2.** What was the last time you or your city "danced in the streets for joy"?

STUDY 1. In contrast to those God destroys (ch. 34), what will happen to the land and people he saves? What does the image of the crocus bursting into bloom convey to you? What does this show you about the ultimate purpose of God's judgment? **2.** What effect will this spring-like salvation have on the people (vv. 5–10)? When do you think such everlasting joy will come? **3.** Are such physical transformations meant to be taken literally, or figuratively (6:9; 32:3–4)? Would Isaiah have in view the work of the Messiah (Luke 7:22)?

34:16 Look in the scroll. This book of the Lord may refer to the prophecy in verses 1–15 where God will judge all nations hostile to Israel (Mal. 3:16).

34:17 from generation to generation. For a long and unspecified length of time, God will give Edom over to wild creatures. No humans will live in Edom's ruined condition.

35:3 Strengthen the feeble hands. Isaiah encouraged the believing remnant to live by God's instructions and to encourage the fainthearted and weak (Josh. 1:6; Heb. 12:12).

35:4 Be strong, do not fear. The Israelites' courage was not based on their own abilities, but on God's promise to protect and deliver them (Josh. 1:9).

APPLY **1.** What pressures are "causing your hands and knees to tremble" now? How might the message of verse 4 bring strength to you? When you have given up trying to reach God? How has he come to you? **2.** Is the water of God's Spirit more like a flooded spring or a plugged faucet in your life now? Why? What will it take to release all the joy of the redeemed in your life? **3.** Jesus claims to be "the Way" (John 14:6). What insight does that give you into the meaning of verse 8? How are you doing on this "Highway to Holiness": Cruising on auto-pilot? Running out of gas? Stuck in the breakdown lane? Still trying to find the entrance ramp? How can others in the group help you get on and stay on that "Way"?

OPEN **1.** When approached by solicitors with "an offer too good to refuse" are you an easy sell or a hard sell? **2.** When have you bought something "hook, line and sinker," only to regret it?

STUDY Chapters 36–37 climax all that has been foretold up to this point. The Assyrian army had already routed Egyptian forces 20 miles west of Jerusalem, and were fighting at Lachish, some 20 miles southwest. **1.** What would the people in Jerusalem feel as they saw this Assyrian army pincer movement? **2.** How does this event fulfill what Isaiah warned in 7:3,18–25 and 8:6–8? **3.** What arguments does the field commander offer for why Jerusalem should surrender (vv. 4–10)? Do you find them persuasive? **4.** How do Assyria and Isaiah compare in their view of Judah's alliance with Egypt

5 Then will the eyes of the blind be opened
and the ears of the deaf unstopped.
6 Then will the lame leap like a deer,
and the mute tongue shout for joy.
Water will gush forth in the wilderness
and streams in the desert.
7 The burning sand will become a pool,
the thirsty ground bubbling springs.
In the haunts where jackals once lay,
grass and reeds and papyrus will grow.

8 And a highway will be there;
it will be called the Way of Holiness.
The unclean will not journey on it;
it will be for those who walk in that Way;
wicked fools will not go about on it.[a]
9 No lion will be there,
nor will any ferocious beast get up on it;
they will not be found there.
But only the redeemed will walk there,
10 and the ransomed of the LORD will return.
They will enter Zion with singing;
everlasting joy will crown their heads.
Gladness and joy will overtake them,
and sorrow and sighing will flee away.

Sennacherib Threatens Jerusalem

36 In the fourteenth year of King Hezekiah's reign, Sennacherib
king of Assyria attacked all the fortified cities of Judah and
captured them. 2 Then the king of Assyria sent his field commander
with a large army from Lachish to King Hezekiah at Jerusalem. When
the commander stopped at the aqueduct of the Upper Pool, on the
road to the Washerman's Field, 3 Eliakim son of Hilkiah the palace administrator, Shebna the secretary, and Joah son of Asaph the recorder
went out to him.
4 The field commander said to them, "Tell Hezekiah,

" 'This is what the great king, the king of Assyria, says: On
what are you basing this confidence of yours? 5 You say you have
strategy and military strength—but you speak only empty words.
On whom are you depending, that you rebel against me? 6 Look
now, you are depending on Egypt, that splintered reed of a staff,
which pierces a man's hand and wounds him if he leans on it!
Such is Pharaoh king of Egypt to all who depend on him. 7 And if

[a] 8 Or / *the simple will not stray from it*

35:5 eyes ... opened ... ears ... unstopped. The Messiah will heal the people and the land. Jesus accomplished both spiritual and physical healing during his life on earth.

35:8 highway ... called the Way of Holiness. This highway will lead to God's city, Jerusalem, where his ways will be followed (Joel 3:17). Only the righteous will travel on this road.

36:4 king of Assyria. Sennacherib and his proud army believed themselves invincible. They believed they were gods. The field commander did not even acknowledge Hezekiah as king in this message.

36:7 high places and altars. High places were the locations of pagan worship. The Assyrian commander knew that Hezekiah had removed many pagan sites that his father Ahaz had built in Judah (2 Chr. 31:1–3). The commander may have thought Hezekiah had stopped trusting in any god altogether.

you say to me, "We are depending on the LORD our God"—isn't
he the one whose high places and altars Hezekiah removed,
saying to Judah and Jerusalem, "You must worship before this
altar"?
[8]" 'Come now, make a bargain with my master, the king of
Assyria: I will give you two thousand horses—if you can put
riders on them! [9]How then can you repulse one officer of the
least of my master's officials, even though you are depending on
Egypt for chariots and horsemen? [10]Furthermore, have I come to
attack and destroy this land without the LORD? The LORD himself
told me to march against this country and destroy it.' "

[11]Then Eliakim, Shebna and Joah said to the field commander,
"Please speak to your servants in Aramaic, since we understand it.
Don't speak to us in Hebrew in the hearing of the people on the wall."
[12]But the commander replied, "Was it only to your master and you
that my master sent me to say these things, and not to the men sitting
on the wall—who, like you, will have to eat their own filth and drink
their own urine?"
[13]Then the commander stood and called out in Hebrew, "Hear the
words of the great king, the king of Assyria! [14]This is what the king
says: Do not let Hezekiah deceive you. He cannot deliver you! [15]Do
not let Hezekiah persuade you to trust in the LORD when he says, 'The
LORD will surely deliver us; this city will not be given into the hand of
the king of Assyria.'
[16]"Do not listen to Hezekiah. This is what the king of Assyria says:
Make peace with me and come out to me. Then every one of you will
eat from his own vine and fig tree and drink water from his own
cistern, [17]until I come and take you to a land like your own—a land of
grain and new wine, a land of bread and vineyards.
[18]"Do not let Hezekiah mislead you when he says, 'The LORD will
deliver us.' Has the god of any nation ever delivered his land from the
hand of the king of Assyria? [19]Where are the gods of Hamath and
Arpad? Where are the gods of Sepharvaim? Have they rescued Samaria from my hand? [20]Who of all the gods of these countries has been
able to save his land from me? How then can the LORD deliver Jerusalem from my hand?"
[21]But the people remained silent and said nothing in reply, because
the king had commanded, "Do not answer him."
[22]Then Eliakim son of Hilkiah the palace administrator, Shebna the
secretary, and Joah son of Asaph the recorder went to Hezekiah, with
their clothes torn, and told him what the field commander had said.

(19:14–15; 30:3–5)? As a Judean leader, how would you feel, hearing this Assyrian commander repeat the same things Isaiah has been saying for years? **5.** How does the Assyrian king's account of Hezekiah's reforms (v. 7) differ from the account in 2 Kings 18:3–4? **6.** What is the meaning of his offer in verse 8? What is he implying by his final statement in verse 10 (10:6–7,12)? **7.** Why does the king speak in Hebrew to people on the city wall (vv. 13–20)? What alternatives does he offer them? Compared to the "gods," where is the Lord in all this? **8.** Do the people respond as expected? Why not panic in the face of such a clear threat from Assyria?

APPLY 1. How must the faith of Hezekiah have appeared to the Assyrians? In what situation has your faith in God's promises appeared equally foolish? **2.** Given your level of faith now, would you have clung to Isaiah's prophecies at this point, or would you have caved in to "reality"? Why? **3.** What "Assyrian threat" faces you now? To what promises of God are you clinging?

36:10 The LORD ... told me to march. Ancient conquerors often claimed that the gods of their defeated enemies had joined their side (2 Chr. 35:21). The commander used this tactic to intimidate the Israelites.

36:11 Don't speak ... in Hebrew. The negotiators thought panic might spread if the people heard the Assyrian demands in Hebrew. The confident commander went ahead and spoke in Hebrew anyway.

36:12 eat ... filth. The commander predicted that the Assyrian siege would cause famine in Judah. Famine would cause people to do horrific things.

36:18 Hezekiah mislead you. The commander tried to undermine the king of Judah by tempting the people with prosperity if they surrendered to Assyria. He reasoned that since the gods of other nations had not been able to protect them from Assyria, God could not protect his people either. The Assyrian King blamed Judah's losses on God (2 Kin. 18:33–35).

OPEN **1.** What is one of the most memorable reports you have ever received? **2.** What report, yet to come, would "make your day"?

STUDY **1.** What is the significance of Hezekiah tearing his clothes and wearing burlap? How would you react if a leader you revered did anything like that? **2.** How does his response to this threat differ from that of his father Ahaz (7:2–13)? On what basis does Hezekiah believe God will help him (2 Chr. 32:6–8)? **3.** What work is God doing to control events and undermine the smug king of Assyria (36:16–20)? **4.** What changes Sennacherib's plans: Spirit of compulsion from the Lord? News from abroad? Out-flanked army? How might his withdrawal affect those in Jerusalem? **5.** In terms of mocking God, how does Sennacherib outdo his field commander (vv. 10–13)? What's the point of reminding Hezekiah of the other kings' fates? **6.** How does Hezekiah's prayer compare to what God has been calling Judean leaders to do all along (1:15)? **7.** What truths about God does Hezekiah grasp? Why does he dwell on these? **8.** How is the point of his prayer like that of the exodus (Ex. 15:14–16)? **9.** What does Hezekiah's prayer have in common with that of the disciples in Acts 4:23–31? What do these prayers show about God's and Hezekiah's character? What do you see here as the proper focus of prayer?

APPLY Hezekiah models how to respond to intimidation. What big threat to you or your faith do you worry about? Is the threat real or imagined? How does Hezekiah's example help you deal with that threat?

OPEN **1.** How did you feel as a child when you played "king of the hill" and got to the top? What did you do to stay there? How did you feel when you were knocked off? **2.** What version of this same game do

Jerusalem's Deliverance Foretold

37 When King Hezekiah heard this, he tore his clothes and put on
sackcloth and went into the temple of the LORD. [2]He sent Eliakim the palace administrator, Shebna the secretary, and the leading
priests, all wearing sackcloth, to the prophet Isaiah son of Amoz.
[3]They told him, "This is what Hezekiah says: This day is a day of distress and rebuke and disgrace, as when children come to the point of
birth and there is no strength to deliver them. [4]It may be that the
LORD your God will hear the words of the field commander, whom his
master, the king of Assyria, has sent to ridicule the living God, and
that he will rebuke him for the words the LORD your God has heard.
Therefore pray for the remnant that still survives."
[5]When King Hezekiah's officials came to Isaiah, [6]Isaiah said to
them, "Tell your master, 'This is what the LORD says: Do not be afraid
of what you have heard—those words with which the underlings of
the king of Assyria have blasphemed me. [7]Listen! I am going to put a
spirit in him so that when he hears a certain report, he will return to
his own country, and there I will have him cut down with the
sword.' "
[8]When the field commander heard that the king of Assyria had left
Lachish, he withdrew and found the king fighting against Libnah.
[9]Now Sennacherib received a report that Tirhakah, the Cushite[a]
king of Egypt,, was marching out to fight against him. When he heard
it, he sent messengers to Hezekiah with this word: [10]"Say to Hezekiah
king of Judah: Do not let the god you depend on deceive you when he
says, 'Jerusalem will not be handed over to the king of Assyria.'
[11]Surely you have heard what the kings of Assyria have done to all the
countries, destroying them completely. And will you be delivered?
[12]Did the gods of the nations that were destroyed by my forefathers
deliver them—the gods of Gozan, Haran, Rezeph and the people of
Eden who were in Tel Assar? [13]Where is the king of Hamath, the king
of Arpad, the king of the city of Sepharvaim, or of Hena or Ivvah?"

Hezekiah's Prayer

[14]Hezekiah received the letter from the messengers and read it.
Then he went up to the temple of the LORD and spread it out before
the LORD. [15]And Hezekiah prayed to the LORD: [16]"O LORD Almighty,
God of Israel, enthroned between the cherubim, you alone are God
over all the kingdoms of the earth. You have made heaven and earth.
[17]Give ear, O LORD, and hear; open your eyes, O LORD, and see; listen
to all the words Sennacherib has sent to insult the living God.
[18]"It is true, O LORD, that the Assyrian kings have laid waste all
these peoples and their lands. [19]They have thrown their gods into the
fire and destroyed them, for they were not gods but only wood and
stone, fashioned by human hands. [20]Now, O LORD our God, deliver us
from his hand, so that all kingdoms on earth may know that you
alone, O LORD, are God.[b]"

Sennacherib's Fall

[21]Then Isaiah son of Amoz sent a message to Hezekiah: "This is
what the LORD, the God of Israel, says: Because you have prayed to

[a]9 That is, from the upper Nile region [b]20 Dead Sea Scrolls (see also 2 Kings 19:19); Masoretic Text *alone are the LORD*

me concerning Sennacherib king of Assyria, 22this is the word the
LORD has spoken against him:

"The Virgin Daughter of Zion
despises and mocks you.
The Daughter of Jerusalem
tosses her head as you flee.
23Who is it you have insulted and blasphemed?
Against whom have you raised your voice
and lifted your eyes in pride?
Against the Holy One of Israel!
24By your messengers
you have heaped insults on the Lord.
And you have said,
'With my many chariots
I have ascended the heights of the mountains,
the utmost heights of Lebanon.
I have cut down its tallest cedars,
the choicest of its pines.
I have reached its remotest heights,
the finest of its forests.
25I have dug wells in foreign lands[a]
and drunk the water there.
With the soles of my feet
I have dried up all the streams of Egypt.'

26"Have you not heard?
Long ago I ordained it.
In days of old I planned it;
now I have brought it to pass,
that you have turned fortified cities
into piles of stone.
27Their people, drained of power,
are dismayed and put to shame.
They are like plants in the field,
like tender green shoots,
like grass sprouting on the roof,
scorched[b] before it grows up.

28"But I know where you stay
and when you come and go
and how you rage against me.
29Because you rage against me
and because your insolence has reached my ears,
I will put my hook in your nose
and my bit in your mouth,

[a]25 Dead Sea Scrolls (see also 2 Kings 19:24); Masoretic Text does not have *in foreign lands.* [b]27 Some manuscripts of the Masoretic Text, Dead Sea Scrolls and some Septuagint manuscripts (see also 2 Kings 19:26); most manuscripts of the Masoretic Text *roof / and terraced fields*

you play at work or in society? Have you reached the top yet? Have you fallen yet?

STUDY 1. What is the intended impact of this woman taunting her attacker (v. 22)? How does this song suit the occasion? What is Isaiah asserting about God's relationship to Jerusalem by portraying him as the woman's defender? **2.** What insults have the Assyrians made against God (vv. 24–25; 36:18–20)? How will they end up eating their own words? In what way has Sennacherib misunderstood the reason for his past success (10:12–19)? **3.** In response to Hezekiah's prayer, by what images does God convey his authority over all nations (vv. 26–29)? What lesson is in this event for Assyria? For Judah? How might it pave the way for 19:23–25 to be fulfilled? **4.** What sign does God give Hezekiah (vv. 30–32)? Why give a sign that will be fulfilled only after the event it is meant to show? How does this sign relate to the promises of restoration (as in 10:20–23)? **5.** In what sense is God saving Jerusalem for his sake? For David's sake? **6.** Other ancient writings speak of Sennacherib's army being decimated by fear and panic perhaps because of a plague. How does this fulfill the earlier prophecies (10:33–34; 29:5–8; 30:31)? If you were living in Jerusalem, how would you react when you heard that 185,000 Assyrian soldiers had died? Would you be more likely to respond like those described in 33:14–15, or in 35:10? Why? **7.** Verse 38 records an event that occurred 20 years after the events of verses 36–37. As you compare the worship of Sennacherib in verse 38 and Hezekiah in 37:1–20, what lessons can be be drawn? **8.** Considering that every city in Judah, except Jerusalem, was destroyed, thousands of innocent people were killed and Judah was plunged into poverty for decades following this attack, do you think this is really a victory for Judah and a defeat for Assyria? Why or why not?

APPLY 1. When have you felt like Hezekiah—backed up against a wall with no recourse but to

37:23 lifted your eyes. In response to Hezekiah's prayer, God said that the Assyrians would be defeated because of their blasphemy and pride.

37:25 dug wells in foreign lands. The Assyrian king boasted that nothing could stand in his way. He claimed to have dug wells in the desert, dried up Egyptian streams and cut down the cedars of Lebanon. All to proclaim before the people his so-called power and domain.

pray? How have you seen God's affirmation of his love for you? **2.** Lachish wanted "last minute salvation" from God, but it didn't happen that way. When "11th hour" appeals to God seem to fall on deaf ears, how do you cope? What could be God's purpose in delaying or saying "No"?

OPEN 1. Would you like to know the exact date when you will die? What difference would it make in how you lived now: Buy more life insurance? Give more of your time and money? Spend more time with the children or grandchildren? Go after your dreams? **2.** What premonition do you have about when or how you will die?

and I will make you return
  by the way you came.

30"This will be the sign for you, O Hezekiah:

"This year you will eat what grows by itself,
  and the second year what springs from that.
But in the third year sow and reap,
  plant vineyards and eat their fruit.
31Once more a remnant of the house of Judah
  will take root below and bear fruit above.
32For out of Jerusalem will come a remnant,
  and out of Mount Zion a band of survivors.
The zeal of the LORD Almighty
  will accomplish this.

33"Therefore this is what the LORD says concerning the king of Assyria:

"He will not enter this city
  or shoot an arrow here.
He will not come before it with shield
  or build a siege ramp against it.
34By the way that he came he will return;
  he will not enter this city,"
    declares the LORD.
35"I will defend this city and save it,
  for my sake and for the sake of David my servant!"

36Then the angel of the LORD went out and put to death a hundred
and eighty-five thousand men in the Assyrian camp. When the people
got up the next morning—there were all the dead bodies! 37So Sennacherib king of Assyria broke camp and withdrew. He returned to
Nineveh and stayed there.
38One day, while he was worshiping in the temple of his god Nisroch, his sons Adrammelech and Sharezer cut him down with the
sword, and they escaped to the land of Ararat. And Esarhaddon his
son succeeded him as king.

Hezekiah's Illness

38 In those days Hezekiah became ill and was at the point of death.
The prophet Isaiah son of Amoz went to him and said, "This
is what the LORD says: Put your house in order, because you are going
to die; you will not recover."
2Hezekiah turned his face to the wall and prayed to the LORD, 3"Remember, O LORD, how I have walked before you faithfully and with
wholehearted devotion and have done what is good in your eyes."
And Hezekiah wept bitterly.

37:30 second ... third year. Any part of a year was counted as a year, so the third year could have been thirteen to fifteen months from that time. The third year is the normal time it takes for a vineyard to begin producing grapes.

37:38 worshiping in the temple. God slaughtered the Assyrians overnight, as Isaiah had predicted. Sennacherib was assassinated twenty years later in 681 B.C. by two of his sons.

38:1 you are going to die. Hezekiah's fatal illness included a boil (2 Chr. 32:24).

38:2 Hezekiah ... prayed. Self-preservation is a powerful motivator. Hezekiah did not explicitly ask God for longer life, but that was clearly his desire.

38:3 with wholehearted devotion. He asked God to remember the good

ORD came to Isaiah: 5"Go and tell Hezekiah,
he God of your father David, says: I have
n your tears; I will add fifteen years to your
u and this city from the hand of the king of
city.
gn to you that the LORD will do what he has
e shadow cast by the sun go back the ten
on the stairway of Ahaz.' " So the sunlight
t had gone down.

king of Judah after his illness and recovery:

my life
e gates of death[a]
he rest of my years?"
again see the LORD,
n the land of the living;
r will I look on mankind,
be with those who now dwell in this world.[b]
Like a shepherd's tent my house
has been pulled down and taken from me.
Like a weaver I have rolled up my life,
and he has cut me off from the loom;
day and night you made an end of me.
13I waited patiently till dawn,
but like a lion he broke all my bones;
day and night you made an end of me.
14I cried like a swift or thrush,
I moaned like a mourning dove.
My eyes grew weak as I looked to the heavens.
I am troubled; O Lord, come to my aid!"

15But what can I say?
He has spoken to me, and he himself has done this.
I will walk humbly all my years
because of this anguish of my soul.
16Lord, by such things men live;
and my spirit finds life in them too.
You restored me to health
and let me live.
17Surely it was for my benefit
that I suffered such anguish.

[a]*10* Hebrew *Sheol* [b]*11* A few Hebrew manuscripts; most Hebrew manuscripts *in the place of cessation*

STUDY Chapters 38–39 serve as a transition to chapters 40–66, which deal with the period, about 150 years later, when Jerusalem is destroyed and its people are captives in Babylon. **1.** Why is Hezekiah so distressed by the message from Isaiah: His house is a mess? He hadn't made out his will yet? He objects to bad things happening to good people? He objects to his father Ahaz, who had been a terrible king, getting to reign longer than him? His whole relationship with God is thrown into question by such a premature death? **2.** What is the track record of "wholehearted devotion" (v. 3) on which he appeals to the Lord to spare his life (2 Kin. 18:1–8)? **3.** Hezekiah asked Isaiah for a sign that his healing would occur (vv. 7–8; 2 Kin. 20:8–11). How does this contrast with Ahaz' response to Isaiah in 7:11–14, when Ahaz was told to ask for a sign but refused to do so? Which man—Ahaz or Hezekiah—demonstrates more faith? How so? What does God's response tell you about God and his mysterious ways? **4.** In the song (vv. 10–20), what images does Hezekiah use to talk about death (vv. 10–20)? What aspect of death and dying do they each convey? To what does he credit his temporary deliverance from death? What part does divine forgiveness play in his healing? What resolve does he make in light of that deliverance?

APPLY 1. Wicked people often live easy lives, or long lives, whereas those serving God often experience great hardships. How do you deal with the seeming unfairness? **2.** Have you known someone who serves God with much joy and yet deals with great hardships? What can you learn from them and how can you apply those lessons to your own life? **3.** What do you fear about death? What hope does the gospel give you that was unknown to Hezekiah?

---

things he had done as he grieved over his impending death (2 Kin. 18:5–8).

38:9 writing of Hezekiah. God granted Hezekiah an additional fifteen years of life and promised to prevent Assyria from capturing Jerusalem during that time. In response, Hezekiah wrote a thanksgiving song similar to the psalms of David and Asaph.

38:10 In the prime of my life. As Hezekiah recounted the misery of his illness, he expressed deep inner anguish. He had no male heir when he learned he was going to die.

38:12 rolled up my life. Hezekiah used similes to describe the impermanence of life (Job 7:6).

38:13 broke all my bones. Hezekiah was humbled as he realized that God had brought the illness upon him.

38:16 restored me to health. He was grateful for God's healing, and he realized that the illness had been used for good. God had not punished him as his sins deserved, and Hezekiah promised to use his new life to praise God.

38:17 you have put all my sins. Apparently Hezekiah's illness was connected to his sin, although not all sickness is the result of a personal sin (John 9:2–3). **behind your back.** When God forgives, he puts our sins far away forever (Ps. 103:12; Jer. 31:34).

4. How do you respond to the fact that suffering is part of God's plan for you? What role does suffering serve in your life?

In your love you kept me
  from the pit of destruction;
you have put all my sins
  behind your back.
18 For the grave[a] cannot praise you,
  death cannot sing your praise;
those who go down to the pit
  cannot hope for your faithfulness.
19 The living, the living—they praise you,
  as I am doing today;
fathers tell their children
  about your faithfulness.

20 The LORD will save me,
  and we will sing with stringed instruments
all the days of our lives
  in the temple of the LORD.

21 Isaiah had said, "Prepare a poultice of figs and apply it to the boil,
and he will recover."
22 Hezekiah had asked, "What will be the sign that I will go up to the
temple of the LORD?"

Envoys From Babylon

39 At that time Merodach-Baladan son of Baladan king of Babylon
sent Hezekiah letters and a gift, because he had heard of his
illness and recovery. 2 Hezekiah received the envoys gladly and
showed them what was in his storehouses—the silver, the gold, the
spices, the fine oil, his entire armory and everything found among his
treasures. There was nothing in his palace or in all his kingdom that
Hezekiah did not show them.
3 Then Isaiah the prophet went to King Hezekiah and asked, "What
did those men say, and where did they come from?"
"From a distant land," Hezekiah replied. "They came to me from
Babylon."
4 The prophet asked, "What did they see in your palace?"
"They saw everything in my palace," Hezekiah said. "There is nothing among my treasures that I did not show them."
5 Then Isaiah said to Hezekiah, "Hear the word of the LORD
Almighty: 6 The time will surely come when everything in your palace,
and all that your fathers have stored up until this day, will be carried
off to Babylon. Nothing will be left, says the LORD. 7 And some of your
descendants, your own flesh and blood who will be born to you, will

[a]18 Hebrew *Sheol*

OPEN 1. What treasure do you show off when you can: Trophy? Car? House? Kids? **2.** How do you feel towards someone whose treasures outshine yours?

STUDY 1. What treasure is Hezekiah showing off? Why is he strutting his stuff (2 Chr. 32:22–25)? **2.** How does this puffed-up Hezekiah compare with the Hezekiah in 38:15–19? What happened in the meantime? **3.** What hopes might such wealth stir up among patronizing people of Judah and Babylon? **4.** Isaiah was speaking of the removal of the best of the young men (vv. 5–7; Dan. 1:3–4). How did this turn out for the good of God's people?

APPLY 1. What hero (religious or political) have you idolized? How has seeing his or her faults forced you to look again to Jesus as the model for your life? **2.** Is it harder for you to be faithful to God during times of hardship or times of success? Why?

38:18 hope. While earthly life ends at death, eternal life continues forever (2 Tim. 1:10; 1 John 5:11–12).

38:21 Prepare a poultice ... and apply. This procedure was a common treatment for boils at that time. **he will recover.** In response to Hezekiah's prayer, God used medicinal procedures to heal Hezekiah.

39:2 storehouses ... treasures. Hezekiah proudly showed his riches, perhaps because he was trusting in his wealth and the armies of nations like Babylon, and not in God. The Babylonians saw that he could provide money to fight Assyria.

39:6 everything ... carried off to Babylon. Since the enemy at the time was Assyria, this prediction was surprising (Jer. 20:4). The rebel army of these envoys had been defeated repeatedly and hardly seemed like a threat. Second Kings 21:11–15, tells the story of the wicked King Manasseh (Hezekiah's son).

be taken away, and they will become eunuchs in the palace of the king of Babylon."

[8]"The word of the LORD you have spoken is good," Hezekiah replied. For he thought, "There will be peace and security in my lifetime."

Comfort for God's People

40 Comfort, comfort my people,
says your God.
[2]Speak tenderly to Jerusalem,
and proclaim to her
that her hard service has been completed,
that her sin has been paid for,
that she has received from the LORD's hand
double for all her sins.

[3]A voice of one calling:
"In the desert prepare
the way for the LORD[a];
make straight in the wilderness
a highway for our God.[b]
[4]Every valley shall be raised up,
every mountain and hill made low;
the rough ground shall become level,
the rugged places a plain.
[5]And the glory of the LORD will be revealed,
and all mankind together will see it.
For the mouth of the LORD has spoken."

[6]A voice says, "Cry out."
And I said, "What shall I cry?"

"All men are like grass,
and all their glory is like the flowers of the field.
[7]The grass withers and the flowers fall,
because the breath of the LORD blows on them.
Surely the people are grass.
[8]The grass withers and the flowers fall,
but the word of our God stands forever."

[9]You who bring good tidings to Zion,
go up on a high mountain.

[a]3 Or *A voice of one calling in the desert: / "Prepare the way for the LORD* [b]3 Hebrew; Septuagint *make straight the paths of our God*

OPEN **1.** What was the most exciting news you ever received? Why was it so welcome? **2.** What is the farthest distance you have ever run or walked? How did you feel at the end?

STUDY Jerusalem's deliverance in 701 B.C. from King Sennacherib (Isa. 37) climaxes the prophecies of chapters 1–39. Chapters 40–48 deal with events that occur some 150 years later. **1.** Jerusalem is sacked and its people deported by Babylon, the new world power (2 Kin. 25). Given this situation, what does Isaiah's emphatic comfort mean to Israel? What word of comfort do the three "voices" bring (vv. 3,6,9)? What images does the Lord use to assure his people of their forgiveness? **2.** In Isaiah's time the coming of a king was announced by a herald. People literally leveled the roads the king would travel. What "King" is in view in verses 3–5? What does it mean to prepare the way for him? **3.** How would this message affect you if you were one of these defeated people torn away from your home, your faith and your way of life? After all you'd been through at the hands of foreign kings, how would you feel toward the coming King? **4.** What then would the eternal Word of God mean to you (vv. 6–8)? What promises from Israel's history might be in view here (Gen. 12:1–3; 2 Sam. 7:8–16)? **5.** The Gospels quote verse 3 in reference to John the Baptist preparing the way for Jesus. What does that imply about the identity of Jesus?

APPLY **1.** How can you "prepare the way" in your life for

40:1 Comfort, comfort my people. Repetition of the word emphasizes its meaning. This prophecy was written 100 years before the Jews were taken to Babylon. It offered comfort and encouragement to the exiles from Judah by reminding them they would return to Jerusalem. It also referred to the salvation to be brought by Jesus Christ.

40:2 Jerusalem. Represented the exiles who would return to Jerusalem. **double for all her sins.** May mean the equivalent or the right amount of punishment for Israel's sins but not more punishment than was deserved.

40:3 voice of one calling. Prophets were voices delivering God's messages. They called the nation back into a proper relationship with God. Each gospel writer applied this verse to John the Baptist who prepared the way for Jesus Christ (Matt. 3:1–4; Mark 1:1–4; Luke 1:76–78; John 1:23).

40:5 the glory of the LORD. God's glory began to be revealed in the restoration of the Israelites from the Exile, but ultimately the glory of the Lord would be seen in Jesus Christ (Luke 2:29–32; John 1:14).

40:9 good tidings to Zion. Refers to God coming to rescue his enslaved

Jesus? What needs leveling or shoring up? **2.** Jesus comes as Shepherd as well as King. What sort of sheep do you feel like: Cradled? Content? Wandering? Caught? Lost? Why?

OPEN 1. During the past week what "speed" have you been on most of the time: Walking, running or soaring? **2.** What has been most important in renewing your strength this past week: Plenty of rest? Your devotional time? Time with supportive friends? Time with family?

STUDY 1. What is the intended effect of all these rhetorical questions? In each comparison (creation, knowledge, the nations), how does God fare? **2.** How do the works of our hands compare with those of God (vv. 12,19–20)? When do our own works become idols? **3.** How does God regard the power of nations, even today's superpowers (vv. 15–17,23–24)? **4.** Is any image or standard of comparison adequate to measure God's worth (vv. 18–25)? Why or why not? **5.** What is the complaint of the exiles (v. 27)? What must they still learn about God before they can be restored to their homeland (vv. 21, 28)? **6.** As a weary exile, which of these promises would you find most uplifting (vv. 28–31)?

APPLY 1. When have you most recently felt like God must have lost your address or phone number? What fears and thoughts arose in your mind? How might the truths of this chapter help restore

You who bring good tidings to Jerusalem,[a]
lift up your voice with a shout,
lift it up, do not be afraid;
say to the towns of Judah,
"Here is your God!"
10 See, the Sovereign LORD comes with power,
and his arm rules for him.
See, his reward is with him,
and his recompense accompanies him.
11 He tends his flock like a shepherd:
He gathers the lambs in his arms
and carries them close to his heart;
he gently leads those that have young.

12 Who has measured the waters in the hollow of his hand,
or with the breadth of his hand marked off the heavens?
Who has held the dust of the earth in a basket,
or weighed the mountains on the scales
and the hills in a balance?
13 Who has understood the mind[b] of the LORD,
or instructed him as his counselor?
14 Whom did the LORD consult to enlighten him,
and who taught him the right way?
Who was it that taught him knowledge
or showed him the path of understanding?

15 Surely the nations are like a drop in a bucket;
they are regarded as dust on the scales;
he weighs the islands as though they were fine dust.
16 Lebanon is not sufficient for altar fires,
nor its animals enough for burnt offerings.
17 Before him all the nations are as nothing;
they are regarded by him as worthless
and less than nothing.

18 To whom, then, will you compare God?
What image will you compare him to?
19 As for an idol, a craftsman casts it,
and a goldsmith overlays it with gold
and fashions silver chains for it.
20 A man too poor to present such an offering
selects wood that will not rot.

[a]9 *Or O Zion, bringer of good tidings, / go up on a high mountain. / O Jerusalem, bringer of good tidings*
[b]13 *Or Spirit*; or *spirit*

people. Isaiah believed that the return from the Exile would lead right into a renewal of God's kingdom, but in fact the final kingdom of God, where peace and justice will finally come, is still ahead. Isaiah and other prophets were looking ahead in terms of their history, but today we also apply these promises to the coming kingdom of God, when all God's work will be finished.

40:11 He gathers the lambs in his arms. A description of God's love for his people (Mic. 5:4; John 10:11,14–16). God carefully carries and leads the weak of his flock.

40:12 measured the waters. God, Creator of the universe and Israel's Lord, needed no help to save his people (Job 28:25).

40:17 nations are as nothing ... worthless. The same word used to describe the primeval chaos of Genesis 1:2.

40:19 idol. Many idols were made of wood overlaid with gold and held in place by silver chains. These gods were made by men from materials that the true God created.

He looks for a skilled craftsman
to set up an idol that will not topple.

21 Do you not know?
Have you not heard?
Has it not been told you from the beginning?
Have you not understood since the earth was founded?
22 He sits enthroned above the circle of the earth,
and its people are like grasshoppers.
He stretches out the heavens like a canopy,
and spreads them out like a tent to live in.
23 He brings princes to naught
and reduces the rulers of this world to nothing.
24 No sooner are they planted,
no sooner are they sown,
no sooner do they take root in the ground,
than he blows on them and they wither,
and a whirlwind sweeps them away like chaff.

25 "To whom will you compare me?
Or who is my equal?" says the Holy One.
26 Lift your eyes and look to the heavens:
Who created all these?
He who brings out the starry host one by one,
and calls them each by name.
Because of his great power and mighty strength,
not one of them is missing.

27 Why do you say, O Jacob,
and complain, O Israel,
"My way is hidden from the LORD;
my cause is disregarded by my God"?
28 Do you not know?
Have you not heard?
The LORD is the everlasting God,
the Creator of the ends of the earth.
He will not grow tired or weary,
and his understanding no one can fathom.
29 He gives strength to the weary
and increases the power of the weak.
30 Even youths grow tired and weary,
and young men stumble and fall;
31 but those who hope in the LORD
will renew their strength.
They will soar on wings like eagles;
they will run and not grow weary,
they will walk and not be faint.

strength to you? **2.** When has there been a time when all you could do was put one foot in front of the other, and God has helped you to "walk and not be faint"? **3.** When have you recently been so busy that the strength you needed was to "run and not grow weary"? **4.** When in your life has God brought you to such a spiritual high that it felt like your spirit could "soar like an eagle"?

40:21 from the beginning. Worship of God went back to Genesis, but many people chose to worship man-made idols over the living God.

40:25 the Holy One. God cannot be compared with other gods. Unlike lifeless statues of Babylon, God created the heavens, the earth and people and God will create the new heavens and new earth as well.

40:27 Jacob ... Israel. Represented all 12 tribes. Isaiah used the two words together 16 times. God's people should never think he does not see or remember them or fail to keep his promises.

40:31 hope in the LORD. Implies confident expectation rather than passive resignation (Ps. 40:1). Faith brings spiritual transformation. Weary captives returning from the Exile would be emotionally uplifted.

OPEN **1.** When you were afraid as a child, who would hold your hand? **2.** Have you ever won a game when the odds looked like it was impossible for you to do so? How did your opponent react?

STUDY The "one from the east" (v. 2) was Cyrus, the Persian king who overthrew Babylon in 538 B.C. (45:1). **1.** What is God asserting about himself by claiming that he is the one behind Cyrus' success? **2.** Why was the victory of Cyrus good news for the Jewish exiles in Babylon (2 Chr. 36:22–23)? How are the other nations reacting to this onward march of Cyrus' army (vv. 5–7)? **3.** What terms does he use to address the exiles in verses 8–10? How would these terms calm their fears? **4.** Why does God address the exiles as "worm Jacob" and "little Israel" (v. 14)? **5.** What is to be the fate of Babylon (vv. 11–16)? How would you react to these statements as you considered all the power and might of Babylon which was all around you? What would it mean to these humiliated exiles to consider that God was influencing all of world history in order to bring about their deliverance? **6.** What type of thirst is Isaiah referring to in verse 17 (Ps. 42:1–2)? How will their situation soon change? Why will the Lord restore his people (v. 20)? **7.** Of all the peoples conquered by Babylon, only the Jews retained their religious, ethnic and political identity. How might this be a witness to the other nations (v. 20)? How does this relate to Israel's call to be his servant?

APPLY **1.** If God moves heaven and earth in order to protect and save his people, how should that knowledge affect your prayers? Your worship? Your attitude in hard times? Your priorities and purpose in life? How might meditating upon the picture of God in chapters 40–41 help you grasp this truth? **2.** What "mountains" and "hills" are there in your life today? If you compare your faith to Israel's threshing sledge, how "new," "sharp" and "many" are your "teeth"?

The Helper of Israel

41 "Be silent before me, you islands!
Let the nations renew their strength!
Let them come forward and speak;
let us meet together at the place of judgment.

2 "Who has stirred up one from the east,
calling him in righteousness to his service[a]?
He hands nations over to him
and subdues kings before him.
He turns them to dust with his sword,
to windblown chaff with his bow.
3 He pursues them and moves on unscathed,
by a path his feet have not traveled before.
4 Who has done this and carried it through,
calling forth the generations from the beginning?
I, the LORD—with the first of them
and with the last—I am he."

5 The islands have seen it and fear;
the ends of the earth tremble.
They approach and come forward;
6 each helps the other
and says to his brother, "Be strong!"
7 The craftsman encourages the goldsmith,
and he who smooths with the hammer
spurs on him who strikes the anvil.
He says of the welding, "It is good."
He nails down the idol so it will not topple.

8 "But you, O Israel, my servant,
Jacob, whom I have chosen,
you descendants of Abraham my friend,
9 I took you from the ends of the earth,
from its farthest corners I called you.
I said, 'You are my servant';
I have chosen you and have not rejected you.
10 So do not fear, for I am with you;
do not be dismayed, for I am your God.
I will strengthen you and help you;
I will uphold you with my righteous right hand.

11 "All who rage against you
will surely be ashamed and disgraced;
those who oppose you
will be as nothing and perish.

[a]2 Or / *whom victory meets at every step*

41:1 nations renew their strength. This phrase contrasts the strength resulting from faith in God with mere *human strength.* The islands and nations refer to all the world's people whom God invites to come.

41:2 one from the east. Cyrus, king of Persia from 559–530 B.C. **calling him in righteousness.** Because of God's promise to Abraham, he brought the exiles back. Cyrus was to carry out God's righteous plan, fulfilling God's will, even if he was unaware of it.

41:8 whom I have chosen. God appointed Israel as his honored servant to administer and advance his kingdom.

41:10 do not fear ... do not be dismayed. God will be with Abraham's descendants (Deut. 31:6), bringing them back from the Exile. He punished Israel, but he did not cast her away.

[12]Though you search for your enemies,
you will not find them.
Those who wage war against you
will be as nothing at all.
[13]For I am the LORD, your God,
who takes hold of your right hand
and says to you, Do not fear;
I will help you.
[14]Do not be afraid, O worm Jacob,
O little Israel,
for I myself will help you," declares the LORD,
your Redeemer, the Holy One of Israel.
[15]"See, I will make you into a threshing sledge,
new and sharp, with many teeth.
You will thresh the mountains and crush them,
and reduce the hills to chaff.
[16]You will winnow them, the wind will pick them up,
and a gale will blow them away.
But you will rejoice in the LORD
and glory in the Holy One of Israel.

[17]"The poor and needy search for water,
but there is none;
their tongues are parched with thirst.
But I the LORD will answer them;
I, the God of Israel, will not forsake them.
[18]I will make rivers flow on barren heights,
and springs within the valleys.
I will turn the desert into pools of water,
and the parched ground into springs.
[19]I will put in the desert
the cedar and the acacia, the myrtle and the olive.
I will set pines in the wasteland,
the fir and the cypress together,
[20]so that people may see and know,
may consider and understand,
that the hand of the LORD has done this,
that the Holy One of Israel has created it.

[21]"Present your case," says the LORD.
"Set forth your arguments," says Jacob's King.
[22]"Bring in ⌊your idols⌋ to tell us
what is going to happen.
Tell us what the former things were,
so that we may consider them
and know their final outcome.
Or declare to us the things to come,

OPEN Have you ever predicted something would happen and nobody listened? Were you correct? How did you feel?

STUDY 1. Verses 21–29 resume God's address to the nations. To what competition does the Lord challenge the idols? Why do the idols fail when the Lord succeeds?

41:13 takes hold of your right hand. God showed his sovereignty and power when he brought the Hebrews out of Egypt (Ex. 15:6).

41:14 your Redeemer. Isaiah used this title for God 13 times. The redeemer was the family protector who helped distressed relatives, avenged murders and reclaimed indentured slaves.

41:20 Israel has created it. In the millennial kingdom, the climate will be changed so that even the desert is fertile. Only God can truly create.

41:22 Bring in your idols. God challenged the nations to determine whether their false gods could recall the events of history or predict the future.

What will be the outcome for those who had placed their trust in the idols? In the Lord? **2.** Cyrus is also called the "one from the north" (v. 25). Persia was to the east of Babylon, yet Cyrus marched against her from the north. Although Cyrus credited his victories to many "gods," what was the real truth about this period of history? **3.** How do the military conquests of Cyrus stand in contrast to those of Assyria (10:12–13)?

APPLY 1. In whose predictions of the future do you place your faith? Are there any "idols" in your life whose wisdom or advice you credit above God's? What will you do to change that attitude? **2.** Where do you see God at work in: Your own life? What new perspective have you gained from this chapter on God's wisdom? On his dependability?

OPEN As a kid, were you ever disciplined by having to remain in the house or in your bedroom for a period of time? How did you feel when you got out again?

STUDY This is the first of four "Servant Songs" (49:1–13; 50:4–9; 52:13–53:12). In Isaiah's time, a king's servant stood in a position of great importance. **1.** What terms express this servant's relationship to God (vv. 1–7)? His mission? His character? **2.** Who is the servant referred to here (41:9)? What kind of servant has he been? Why is the Lord singing to honor the servant? **3.** Why will God's servant "not shout or cry out" (v. 2; Prov. 8:1-4)? What is meant by a bruised reed and smoldering wick (v. 3; 36:6)? **4.** In what ways does Jesus fulfill this picture of God's servant?

APPLY 1. Acts 13:47 and 2 Timothy 2:24–26 extend

23 tell us what the future holds,
so we may know that you are gods.
Do something, whether good or bad,
so that we will be dismayed and filled with fear.
24 But you are less than nothing
and your works are utterly worthless;
he who chooses you is detestable.

25 "I have stirred up one from the north, and he comes—
one from the rising sun who calls on my name.
He treads on rulers as if they were mortar,
as if he were a potter treading the clay.
26 Who told of this from the beginning, so we could know,
or beforehand, so we could say, 'He was right'?
No one told of this,
no one foretold it,
no one heard any words from you.
27 I was the first to tell Zion, 'Look, here they are!'
I gave to Jerusalem a messenger of good tidings.
28 I look but there is no one—
no one among them to give counsel,
no one to give answer when I ask them.
29 See, they are all false!
Their deeds amount to nothing;
their images are but wind and confusion.

The Servant of the Lord

42 "Here is my servant, whom I uphold,
my chosen one in whom I delight;
I will put my Spirit on him
and he will bring justice to the nations.
2 He will not shout or cry out,
or raise his voice in the streets.
3 A bruised reed he will not break,
and a smoldering wick he will not snuff out.
In faithfulness he will bring forth justice;
4 he will not falter or be discouraged
till he establishes justice on earth.
In his law the islands will put their hope."

5 This is what God the LORD says—
he who created the heavens and stretched them out,
who spread out the earth and all that comes out of it,
who gives breath to its people,
and life to those who walk on it:
6 "I, the LORD, have called you in righteousness;
I will take hold of your hand.

41:25 one from the north. King Cyrus of Persia whose territories were both to the north and east of Israel. **calls on my name.** Although Cyrus did not know God, he called on God's name (2 Chr. 36:23).

42:1 my servant ... uphold. Refers to Jesus Christ who will bring universal justice and peace (Matt. 12:15–21), fulfilling God's will. When God upholds a person, nothing can bring him or her down.

42:3 bruised reed. The promise points to Christ when he will be gentle to those who are hurting, poor and needy. **smoldering wick.** People who have nearly lost their faith in God. Jesus will restore their hope.

I will keep you and will make you
to be a covenant for the people
and a light for the Gentiles,
7 to open eyes that are blind,
to free captives from prison
and to release from the dungeon those who sit in darkness.

8 "I am the LORD; that is my name!
I will not give my glory to another
or my praise to idols.
9 See, the former things have taken place,
and new things I declare;
before they spring into being
I announce them to you."

Song of Praise to the Lord

10 Sing to the LORD a new song,
his praise from the ends of the earth,
you who go down to the sea, and all that is in it,
you islands, and all who live in them.
11 Let the desert and its towns raise their voices;
let the settlements where Kedar lives rejoice.
Let the people of Sela sing for joy;
let them shout from the mountaintops.
12 Let them give glory to the LORD
and proclaim his praise in the islands.
13 The LORD will march out like a mighty man,
like a warrior he will stir up his zeal;
with a shout he will raise the battle cry
and will triumph over his enemies.

14 "For a long time I have kept silent,
I have been quiet and held myself back.
But now, like a woman in childbirth,
I cry out, I gasp and pant.
15 I will lay waste the mountains and hills
and dry up all their vegetation;
I will turn rivers into islands
and dry up the pools.
16 I will lead the blind by ways they have not known,
along unfamiliar paths I will guide them;
I will turn the darkness into light before them
and make the rough places smooth.
These are the things I will do;
I will not forsake them.
17 But those who trust in idols,
who say to images, 'You are our gods,'
will be turned back in utter shame.

this image of "the servant" to apply to all believers. In light of that, what does this passage say about your mission? Your family? Your work? Your priorities? Your character? **2.** How does this encourage and challenge you?

OPEN What new song has been running through your head lately?

STUDY 1. What places does the prophet call upon here? How does this widespread call relate to the mission of the servant in verses 6–7? **2.** How is God "like a mighty man" (v. 13)? How is he "like a woman in childbirth" (v. 14)? Why does he first "shout" the battle cry, then "gasp and pant"? **3.** Why does Isaiah finish the good promises of verses 14–16 with the warning of verse 17? **4.** How are we called to imitate God's actions in this song (Acts 26:18 and 1 Peter 2:9)?

APPLY 1. Who has helped you to see the light in the darkness? How can you help others turn from darkness to light? **2.** What "idols" are you tempted to look to in your life? How might this passage help you? **3.** Create a "new song" (v. 10) of praise to God, each person adding a verse or stanza based upon this section.

42:13 mighty man. God will be a conquering warrior on behalf of his people, just as God fought for them at the Red Sea (Ex. 15:3).

42:15 mountains and hills. Refers to all obstacles which could prevent Israel's return from the Exile to Jerusalem. **dry up.** Recalled the passage through the Red Sea on dry land (Ex. 14:16–29). God at any time can cause the land to become barren.

OPEN Have you ever misplaced something, only to discover it "right under your nose"? What and where was it? Why did you fail to see it right away?

STUDY 1. What things have the exiles seen and heard but failed to notice? What was the result? **2.** What did God originally plan that Israel should be? How have they failed to live up to this? What have they become instead? **3.** If you were an exile, what comfort would you find in this passage? What lesson for the future would you learn?

APPLY 1. Are there times in your past when you were deaf or blind to the obvious will of God? How was it obvious, now that you look back? Did God give up on you? **2.** If God needed to gain your attention today, where would you place yourself on the scale of 1 (deaf) to 5 (all ears)? Are there any areas of your life where you might still be turning a deaf ear or an intentional blind eye?

OPEN If your house were on fire, what three things would you save and why?

STUDY 1. If you were an exile, how would you feel if the prophet stopped with chapter 42? What would be your reaction to verses 1–7? **2.** On what occasions in Israel's history did they in fact "pass through" waters and rivers that did not sweep over them (v. 2; Ex. 14:5–31; Josh. 3:14–17)? **3.** Persia, under Cyrus, conquered Egypt, Cush and Seba. Based on Cyrus' treatment of the exiles, what might the Lord mean in verses 3 and 4? Why will he give "men in exchange" for Israel (v. 4)? **4.** Why are the exiles told not to fear (vv. 1,5)?

Israel Blind and Deaf

18 "Hear, you deaf;
look, you blind, and see!
19 Who is blind but my servant,
and deaf like the messenger I send?
Who is blind like the one committed to me,
blind like the servant of the LORD?
20 You have seen many things, but have paid no attention;
your ears are open, but you hear nothing."
21 It pleased the LORD
for the sake of his righteousness
to make his law great and glorious.
22 But this is a people plundered and looted,
all of them trapped in pits
or hidden away in prisons.
They have become plunder,
with no one to rescue them;
they have been made loot,
with no one to say, "Send them back."

23 Which of you will listen to this
or pay close attention in time to come?
24 Who handed Jacob over to become loot,
and Israel to the plunderers?
Was it not the LORD,
against whom we have sinned?
For they would not follow his ways;
they did not obey his law.
25 So he poured out on them his burning anger,
the violence of war.
It enveloped them in flames, yet they did not understand;
it consumed them, but they did not take it to heart.

Israel's Only Savior

43 But now, this is what the LORD says—
he who created you, O Jacob,
he who formed you, O Israel:
"Fear not, for I have redeemed you;
I have summoned you by name; you are mine.
2 When you pass through the waters,
I will be with you;
and when you pass through the rivers,
they will not sweep over you.
When you walk through the fire,
you will not be burned;
the flames will not set you ablaze.
3 For I am the LORD, your God,
the Holy One of Israel, your Savior;

42:24 Who handed Jacob over ... ? Since Israel was blind to her sin, God allowed her to be plundered and taken into captivity. The Messiah will open their eyes to their sin and to God's salvation.

42:25 poured out ... burning anger. God's anger against sin would destroy Jerusalem with flames; God's people already had a taste of his wrath (2 Kin. 25:9; Jer. 10:25).

43:3 your Savior. The name Jesus is derived from the Hebrew word for Savior (Matt. 1:21). Israel is precious because of God's love and protection, because God chose to favor this people.

I give Egypt for your ransom,
  Cush[a] and Seba in your stead.
4 Since you are precious and honored in my sight,
  and because I love you,
I will give men in exchange for you,
  and people in exchange for your life.
5 Do not be afraid, for I am with you;
  I will bring your children from the east
  and gather you from the west.
6 I will say to the north, 'Give them up!'
  and to the south, 'Do not hold them back.'
Bring my sons from afar
  and my daughters from the ends of the earth—
7 everyone who is called by my name,
  whom I created for my glory,
  whom I formed and made."

8 Lead out those who have eyes but are blind,
  who have ears but are deaf.
9 All the nations gather together
  and the peoples assemble.
Which of them foretold this
  and proclaimed to us the former things?
Let them bring in their witnesses to prove they were right,
  so that others may hear and say, "It is true."
10 "You are my witnesses," declares the LORD,
  "and my servant whom I have chosen,
so that you may know and believe me
  and understand that I am he.
Before me no god was formed,
  nor will there be one after me.
11 I, even I, am the LORD,
  and apart from me there is no savior.
12 I have revealed and saved and proclaimed—
  I, and not some foreign god among you.
You are my witnesses," declares the LORD, "that I am God.
13 Yes, and from ancient days I am he.
No one can deliver out of my hand.
  When I act, who can reverse it?"

God's Mercy and Israel's Unfaithfulness

14 This is what the LORD says—
  your Redeemer, the Holy One of Israel:
"For your sake I will send to Babylon
  and bring down as fugitives all the Babylonians,[b]
  in the ships in which they took pride.

[a]3 That is, the upper Nile region [b]14 Or *Chaldeans*

How will they know that God is with them? **5.** Although Israel has been blind and deaf to God in the past (42:18–20), what is the purpose for which he will lead them out of Babylon (41:20)? What will that act of deliverance communicate to the nations? With what attitude do you imagine this witness will be carried out?

APPLY 1. What "waters" or "fire" (v. 2) seem to be fearfully close to you at the moment? What does it mean to you that God says he will be with his people through these things? How have you experienced that in the past? **2.** During the "unromantic" times in your life, when life and relationships have lost their sparkle, how does this passage help you to put things in perspective? **3.** When has God worked good in your life despite your "blindness and deafness"? How would you explain to an unchurched friend what God has done for you?

OPEN Have you ever fallen asleep in church? Was it out of tiredness or boredom? What woke you up?

STUDY 1. What contrasting attitudes has God found in the Babylonians, in the wild animals, and in Israel (vv. 14,20,22)? **2.** What event in Israel's history do verses 16 and 17

43:3 Egypt ... Cush ... Seba. To reward Cyrus for releasing the Jewish captives, God allowed Persia to conquer these lands. Cush consisted of modern-day Sudan, southern Egypt and northern Ethiopia. Seba may be Sheba in southern Arabia.

43:14 bring down as fugitives ... in the ships. God would turn the Babylonians into conquered people, rather than conquerors (Jer. 51:1–44). The ships may have been trading vessels. This is a description of Babylonia's destruction.

refer to (Ex. 14:5–31)? Why would this event be important to God's people in exile in Babylon? **3.** With what attitude do you imagine the exiles carried out their religious practices (vv. 22–28)? What does that show about their view of God? Although God has not wearied them with his demands, how have they wearied him? **4.** In spite of their attitudes, what has God done for them? What does God say about himself in these verses? **5.** What does God mean by blotting out sins "for my own sake" (v. 25)?

APPLY 1. When has God seemed like a dusty memory to you? At those times, what helps you get in touch with him? How might recalling the acts of God in your past give you courage to face the present and future? **2.** What has God done in your past that you especially can look to as evidence of his presence with you? What "stream in the desert" is bubbling up for you now? **3.** In your worship life, are you lavishly giving yourself to God or callously wearying him with meaningless rituals? When has it been different? What accounts for the change?

---

15 I am the LORD, your Holy One,
Israel's Creator, your King."

16 This is what the LORD says—
he who made a way through the sea,
a path through the mighty waters,
17 who drew out the chariots and horses,
the army and reinforcements together,
and they lay there, never to rise again,
extinguished, snuffed out like a wick:
18 "Forget the former things;
do not dwell on the past.
19 See, I am doing a new thing!
Now it springs up; do you not perceive it?
I am making a way in the desert
and streams in the wasteland.
20 The wild animals honor me,
the jackals and the owls,
because I provide water in the desert
and streams in the wasteland,
to give drink to my people, my chosen,
21 the people I formed for myself
that they may proclaim my praise.

22 "Yet you have not called upon me, O Jacob,
you have not wearied yourselves for me, O Israel.
23 You have not brought me sheep for burnt offerings,
nor honored me with your sacrifices.
I have not burdened you with grain offerings
nor wearied you with demands for incense.
24 You have not bought any fragrant calamus for me,
or lavished on me the fat of your sacrifices.
But you have burdened me with your sins
and wearied me with your offenses.

25 "I, even I, am he who blots out
your transgressions, for my own sake,
and remembers your sins no more.
26 Review the past for me,
let us argue the matter together;
state the case for your innocence.
27 Your first father sinned;
your spokesmen rebelled against me.
28 So I will disgrace the dignitaries of your temple,
and I will consign Jacob to destruction[a]
and Israel to scorn.

[a] 28 The Hebrew term refers to the irrevocable giving over of things or persons to the LORD, often by totally destroying them.

43:20 jackals ... owls. *Although Israel would travel through desolate areas on the way back to Jerusalem, God would provide refreshment even in the desert.*

43:22 not called ... not wearied. The people had worshiped God only halfheartedly without troubling themselves with the sacrificial system God required.

43:25 for my own sake. God saves and forgives. God loves when people do not deserve it, a relationship we call "grace."

Israel the Chosen

44 "But now listen, O Jacob, my servant,
Israel, whom I have chosen.
²This is what the LORD says—
he who made you, who formed you in the womb,
and who will help you:
Do not be afraid, O Jacob, my servant,
Jeshurun, whom I have chosen.
³For I will pour water on the thirsty land,
and streams on the dry ground;
I will pour out my Spirit on your offspring,
and my blessing on your descendants.
⁴They will spring up like grass in a meadow,
like poplar trees by flowing streams.
⁵One will say, 'I belong to the LORD';
another will call himself by the name of Jacob;
still another will write on his hand, 'The LORD's,'
and will take the name Israel.

The LORD, Not Idols

⁶"This is what the LORD says—
Israel's King and Redeemer, the LORD Almighty:
I am the first and I am the last;
apart from me there is no God.
⁷Who then is like me? Let him proclaim it.
Let him declare and lay out before me
what has happened since I established my ancient people,
and what is yet to come—
yes, let him foretell what will come.
⁸Do not tremble, do not be afraid.
Did I not proclaim this and foretell it long ago?
You are my witnesses. Is there any God besides me?
No, there is no other Rock; I know not one."
⁹All who make idols are nothing,
and the things they treasure are worthless.
Those who would speak up for them are blind;
they are ignorant, to their own shame.
¹⁰Who shapes a god and casts an idol,
which can profit him nothing?
¹¹He and his kind will be put to shame;
craftsmen are nothing but men.
Let them all come together and take their stand;
they will be brought down to terror and infamy.

OPEN What affectionate nicknames do you have for people you care about?

STUDY 1. What is the prophet emphasizing by saying "but now" (v. 1)? **2.** How does God describe himself in verse 2? In what ways would this description reassure the people? **3.** Since the Spirit seems to have been given only to Israel's leaders in the past, what is the significance and hope of the promise in verse 3?

APPLY 1. Is the "flower" of your spiritual life still a seed? Breaking ground? In full bloom? How so? **2.** How do you typically let others know that you are a follower of Christ? What new idea does verse 5 suggest?

OPEN 1. What is one thing that you made as a child that you were really proud of? **2.** Have you ever worked hard toward a goal, only to discover that it wasn't worth the work? How did you feel?

STUDY 1. In verses 6–8, what are the ways that God claims to be unique? What titles and descriptions does God use of himself? What does each mean? In what ways is he different from the idols in verses 12–20? **2.** For what reasons is idolatry mocked in verses 9–20? In what ways do those who worship idols end up like the idols (vv. 18–20)? **3.** In contrast to the idols that can do nothing, what things has God done for Israel (vv. 21–23)? In turn, what does he call upon the people to do? What does he mean by it? **4.** God redeemed Israel before they returned to him. What does this show of God's nature?

APPLY 1. On what foundations have you sought to build your life other than the "Rock" who is the true God (v. 8)? When did these false foundations become shaky for

---

44:4 spring up like grass. A symbol of prosperity. When the Messiah comes, God will pour water on the land and pour his Holy Spirit on the people.

44:5 call himself by the name. Israel will grow in numbers and will want to be known as the Lord's obedient people. **write on his hand.** Signified ownership.

44:6 This is what the LORD says. These words emphasize the truthfulness of the statement to follow. **first ... last.** God is sovereign over time, and he is eternal.

44:9 nothing ... worthless. This warning to future generations condemned idolatry and noted the foolishness of worshiping a stone or metal image. **ignorant, to their own shame.** Idol worship will ultimately prove the worshipers to be blind and ignorant.

you? **2.** When have you looked at what you had built with your life and determined it was all a lie (v. 20)? **3.** What has God done for you that might call you to "burst into song" (v. 23)?

[12]The blacksmith takes a tool
and works with it in the coals;
he shapes an idol with hammers,
he forges it with the might of his arm.
He gets hungry and loses his strength;
he drinks no water and grows faint.
[13]The carpenter measures with a line
and makes an outline with a marker;
he roughs it out with chisels
and marks it with compasses.
He shapes it in the form of man,
of man in all his glory,
that it may dwell in a shrine.
[14]He cut down cedars,
or perhaps took a cypress or oak.
He let it grow among the trees of the forest,
or planted a pine, and the rain made it grow.
[15]It is man's fuel for burning;
some of it he takes and warms himself,
he kindles a fire and bakes bread.
But he also fashions a god and worships it;
he makes an idol and bows down to it.
[16]Half of the wood he burns in the fire;
over it he prepares his meal,
he roasts his meat and eats his fill.
He also warms himself and says,
"Ah! I am warm; I see the fire."
[17]From the rest he makes a god, his idol;
he bows down to it and worships.
He prays to it and says,
"Save me; you are my god."
[18]They know nothing, they understand nothing;
their eyes are plastered over so they cannot see,
and their minds closed so they cannot understand.
[19]No one stops to think,
no one has the knowledge or understanding to say,
"Half of it I used for fuel;
I even baked bread over its coals,
I roasted meat and I ate.
Shall I make a detestable thing from what is left?
Shall I bow down to a block of wood?"
[20]He feeds on ashes, a deluded heart misleads him;
he cannot save himself, or say,
"Is not this thing in my right hand a lie?"

[21]"Remember these things, O Jacob,
for you are my servant, O Israel.

44:13 shapes it in the form of man. Craftsmen made images of metal or wood, while God made the craftsmen, ores for metal and trees for wood (Rom. 1:23).

44:17 you are my god. The idolater prayed to an inanimate object incapable of helping him. Anything that comes before God in a person's life is his or her idol.

44:18 eyes are plastered ... minds closed. Possibly refers to a practice where mud was applied to a worshiper's eyes. False practices blinded people from knowing the true God.

I have made you, you are my servant;
O Israel, I will not forget you.
22 I have swept away your offenses like a cloud,
your sins like the morning mist.
Return to me,
for I have redeemed you."

23 Sing for joy, O heavens, for the LORD has done this;
shout aloud, O earth beneath.
Burst into song, you mountains,
you forests and all your trees,
for the LORD has redeemed Jacob,
he displays his glory in Israel.

Jerusalem to Be Inhabited

24 "This is what the LORD says—
your Redeemer, who formed you in the womb:

I am the LORD,
who has made all things,
who alone stretched out the heavens,
who spread out the earth by myself,

25 who foils the signs of false prophets
and makes fools of diviners,
who overthrows the learning of the wise
and turns it into nonsense,
26 who carries out the words of his servants
and fulfills the predictions of his messengers,

who says of Jerusalem, 'It shall be inhabited,'
of the towns of Judah, 'They shall be built,'
and of their ruins, 'I will restore them,'
27 who says to the watery deep, 'Be dry,
and I will dry up your streams,'
28 who says of Cyrus, 'He is my shepherd
and will accomplish all that I please;
he will say of Jerusalem, "Let it be rebuilt,"
and of the temple, "Let its foundations be laid."'

45

"This is what the LORD says to his anointed,
to Cyrus, whose right hand I take hold of
to subdue nations before him
and to strip kings of their armor,
to open doors before him
so that gates will not be shut:
2 I will go before you

OPEN 1. How would you have liked God to have made you differently: Better looking? Smarter? Less temperamental? More like one of your siblings? **2.** What needs to happen to make you more at peace with how God made you?

STUDY 1. What truth about God is stressed in verse 24? **2.** As an exile who had no freedom to leave Babylon, much less consider rebuilding Jerusalem would you have responded to these promises with hope or with cynicism? Why? **3.** In light of this prophecy, how might the exiles feel as they heard rumors of Cyrus' conquests and approach to Babylon? **4.** Cyrus entered Babylon by diverting the flow of the Euphrates River, which flowed through the city, so that his army could enter via the river bed. What does that imply about the relationship between God's actions and Cyrus' plans? **5.** In the past, only Israelite kings were called God's anointed. What is the significance of God using this title for a pagan king? **6.** Why does God give victory after victory to Cyrus (45:3–6)? Since no other deported people ever maintained their ethnic and religious heritage, how will the reestablishment of the Jews fulfill these purposes? **7.** Several times in this section God repeats that there is no god but him. Why is this being stressed? Does God's deliverance of the Jews from Babylon by the hand of a Persian prove this claim? **8.** Per-

---

44:22 swept away your offenses like a cloud. God offers total forgiveness (40:2; 43:25). Israel's punishment made forgiveness and restoration possible. **redeemed.** God will buy back his people.

44:27 watery deep. Refers either to the moat around Babylon or obstacles to the exiles' return to Jerusalem (Jer. 51:36).

45:1 his anointed. Means "appointed to an office," usually king. The word referred to the relationship of Kings Saul and David with God. The title Messiah comes from the Hebrew word for anointed. Cyrus' job would be to free the people and bring judgment on unbelievers.

sian religion taught that a god of light and a god of darkness were in perpetual warfare with each other. What light does this shed on (45:7)? Why does God bring about these judgments and blessings (45:6)? **9.** Evidently, some people objected to the prophet's declaration that God would use a pagan as the means of deliverance. How does God refute that objection (45:11–13)?

APPLY 1. What has God done in your life that has convinced you that he is Lord (v. 3)? **2.** If you could question God about how he works in this world, what one question would you want to ask (v. 11)? **3.** What would help you to be more trusting of how God works? **4.** Do you have any outstanding quarrels with your "Maker"? What are they? What should you do to resolve them?

and will level the mountains[a];
I will break down gates of bronze
and cut through bars of iron.
3 I will give you the treasures of darkness,
riches stored in secret places,
so that you may know that I am the LORD,
the God of Israel, who summons you by name.
4 For the sake of Jacob my servant,
of Israel my chosen,
I summon you by name
and bestow on you a title of honor,
though you do not acknowledge me.
5 I am the LORD, and there is no other;
apart from me there is no God.
I will strengthen you,
though you have not acknowledged me,
6 so that from the rising of the sun
to the place of its setting
men may know there is none besides me.
I am the LORD, and there is no other.
7 I form the light and create darkness,
I bring prosperity and create disaster;
I, the LORD, do all these things.

8 "You heavens above, rain down righteousness;
let the clouds shower it down.
Let the earth open wide,
let salvation spring up,
let righteousness grow with it;
I, the LORD, have created it.

9 "Woe to him who quarrels with his Maker,
to him who is but a potsherd among the potsherds on the ground.
Does the clay say to the potter,
'What are you making?'
Does your work say,
'He has no hands'?
10 Woe to him who says to his father,
'What have you begotten?'
or to his mother,
'What have you brought to birth?'

11 "This is what the LORD says—
the Holy One of Israel, and its Maker:
Concerning things to come,
do you question me about my children,
or give me orders about the work of my hands?
12 It is I who made the earth
and created mankind upon it.

[a]2 Dead Sea Scrolls and Septuagint; the meaning of the word in the Masoretic Text is uncertain.

45:9 potsherd. A broken, discarded piece of pottery. Without the work of the creator, the potsherd is only pottery. The thing created by another has no right to question its creator (Jer. 18:6).

My own hands stretched out the heavens;
  I marshaled their starry hosts.
13 I will raise up Cyrus[a] in my righteousness:
  I will make all his ways straight.
He will rebuild my city
  and set my exiles free,
but not for a price or reward,
  says the LORD Almighty."

14 This is what the LORD says:

"The products of Egypt and the merchandise of Cush,[b]
  and those tall Sabeans—
they will come over to you
  and will be yours;
they will trudge behind you,
  coming over to you in chains.
They will bow down before you
  and plead with you, saying,
'Surely God is with you, and there is no other;
  there is no other god.'"

15 Truly you are a God who hides himself,
  O God and Savior of Israel.
16 All the makers of idols will be put to shame and disgraced;
  they will go off into disgrace together.
17 But Israel will be saved by the LORD
  with an everlasting salvation;
you will never be put to shame or disgraced,
  to ages everlasting.

18 For this is what the LORD says—
he who created the heavens,
  he is God;
he who fashioned and made the earth,
  he founded it;
he did not create it to be empty,
  but formed it to be inhabited—
he says:
"I am the LORD,
  and there is no other.
19 I have not spoken in secret,
  from somewhere in a land of darkness;
I have not said to Jacob's descendants,
  'Seek me in vain.'
I, the LORD, speak the truth;
  I declare what is right.

20 "Gather together and come;
  assemble, you fugitives from the nations.

[a]13 Hebrew *him* [b]14 That is, the upper Nile region

OPEN Can you remember a political speech that impressed you? Why? Did any of the hopes and promises expressed come true?

STUDY **1.** Verse 14 describes a defeated people being led in chains to the land of their conquerors. Since Israel never even tried to conquer these people, what type of conquest is in view here? What "forces" are involved in the battle (vv. 15–17)? What effect will this deliverance have even upon nations that are far away? (Note: Egypt, Cush and Seba—all in Africa—were considered the farthest nations.) **2.** What lessons from 44:24–26 are repeated here? What is the purpose of this continual contrast between God and idols (vv. 16–18)? **3.** From this passage alone, what does God say about his character? His purposes? His desires? **4.** How do verses 22–25 form the backdrop for Philippians 2:10–11? Accordingly, who are the "descendants of Israel" (Gal. 3:29)? What do these verses indicate about the ultimate purpose of God's judgments and acts in history?

APPLY **1.** What is the closest you have come to "raging against" God (v. 24)? **2.** What happened that caused you to put that rage behind you and bow your knees to him in submission (v. 23)? Or if that has yet to happen, what would need to occur for you to make that change?

45:14 coming over to you ... bow down. People from Egypt and Cush would acknowledge the God of Israel as Lord. They would submit to God's truth and worship him (1 Cor. 14:25).

45:15 a God who hides himself. Although it seems as if God is hiding and unavailable as a result of human sin, God is in fact present as the Scriptures tell (Ps. 44:24). The hand of God is not always apparent.

Ignorant are those who carry about idols of wood,
who pray to gods that cannot save.
21 Declare what is to be, present it—
let them take counsel together.
Who foretold this long ago,
who declared it from the distant past?
Was it not I, the LORD?
And there is no God apart from me,
a righteous God and a Savior;
there is none but me.

22 "Turn to me and be saved,
all you ends of the earth;
for I am God, and there is no other.
23 By myself I have sworn,
my mouth has uttered in all integrity
a word that will not be revoked:
Before me every knee will bow;
by me every tongue will swear.
24 They will say of me, 'In the LORD alone
are righteousness and strength.' "
All who have raged against him
will come to him and be put to shame.
25 But in the LORD all the descendants of Israel
will be found righteous and will exult.

Gods of Babylon

46 Bel bows down, Nebo stoops low;
their idols are borne by beasts of burden.[a]
The images that are carried about are burdensome,
a burden for the weary.
2 They stoop and bow down together;
unable to rescue the burden,
they themselves go off into captivity.

3 "Listen to me, O house of Jacob,
all you who remain of the house of Israel,
you whom I have upheld since you were conceived,
and have carried since your birth.
4 Even to your old age and gray hairs
I am he, I am he who will sustain you.
I have made you and I will carry you;
I will sustain you and I will rescue you.

5 "To whom will you compare me or count me equal?
To whom will you liken me that we may be compared?
6 Some pour out gold from their bags
and weigh out silver on the scales;

[a] 1 *Or are but beasts and cattle*

OPEN Have you ever walked a long distance carrying a heavy load: In a backpack? Wheelbarrow? Appliance dolly? Describe the scene.

STUDY 1. Bel and Nebo were the names of the two principal gods in Babylon (v. 1). What burden are they carrying? What happens to them? How does this compare with the Lord (vv. 3–4)? What do they do for the people that worship and carry them? What things does God say here that "I" have done and will do for Israel? **2.** Who are the "rebels" and the "stubborn-hearted" (vv. 8,12; 42:18–25)? How does this relate to the promises in verses 3 and 4? What will the people learn once more through the events that are soon to occur? **3.** The man in verse 11 is Cyrus. Although Israel is currently "far from righteousness" how will God use Cyrus (whose standard was an eagle) to bring "righteousness near" to them? Why is God doing this?

45:24 All who have raged against him. Everyone is invited by God to repent of sin, yet many will continue to angrily oppose God. These people will have no part in his eternal kingdom.

46:2 they themselves go off into captivity. The idols were heavy burdens to carry around, and they could not help the Babylonians escape defeat. Instead, they were carried off into captivity along with the people.

they hire a goldsmith to make it into a god,
and they bow down and worship it.
7 They lift it to their shoulders and carry it;
they set it up in its place, and there it stands.
From that spot it cannot move.
Though one cries out to it, it does not answer;
it cannot save him from his troubles.

8 "Remember this, fix it in mind,
take it to heart, you rebels.
9 Remember the former things, those of long ago;
I am God, and there is no other;
I am God, and there is none like me.
10 I make known the end from the beginning,
from ancient times, what is still to come.
I say: My purpose will stand,
and I will do all that I please.
11 From the east I summon a bird of prey;
from a far-off land, a man to fulfill my purpose.
What I have said, that will I bring about;
what I have planned, that will I do.
12 Listen to me, you stubborn-hearted,
you who are far from righteousness.
13 I am bringing my righteousness near,
it is not far away;
and my salvation will not be delayed.
I will grant salvation to Zion,
my splendor to Israel.

The Fall of Babylon

47 "Go down, sit in the dust,
Virgin Daughter of Babylon;
sit on the ground without a throne,
Daughter of the Babylonians.[a]
No more will you be called
tender or delicate.
2 Take millstones and grind flour;
take off your veil.
Lift up your skirts, bare your legs,
and wade through the streams.
3 Your nakedness will be exposed
and your shame uncovered.
I will take vengeance;
I will spare no one."

4 Our Redeemer—the LORD Almighty is his name—
is the Holy One of Israel.

[a]1 Or *Chaldeans*; also in verse 5

APPLY 1. How have you experienced God as a father carrying you when you were weak? Or as a strong man sustaining you when you were tired? Or as a warrior rescuing you when you were trapped? **2.** How are you dealing with the signs of aging in your body? How does God help you deal with aging (v. 4)?

OPEN In your lifetime what famous person, who seemed to have it all, ended up in sorrow and tragedy? What did you learn from that situation?

STUDY 1. What does the picture of a queen reduced to slavery tell you about Babylon's past and future? Since Babylon was not destroyed, though literally conquered by Cyrus in a single day, what is the meaning of this image? What is the reason for this judgment (10:12)? What does this say about God? **2.** What do you learn about the spiritual beliefs and practices of Babylon (vv. 9–15)? What do you imagine they were doing as Cyrus came closer and closer? **3.** What will they inherit for all their activity? How does this highlight the truth proclaimed in chapter 40, that there is no other god but the Lord? Of what value would this truth be for the exiles?

46:12 Listen ... stubborn-hearted. Just as some Israelites wanted to stay in Egypt during the first Exodus (Num. 14:3), in the second exodus some would want to stay in the comfort and security of Babylon and Persia.

47:3 nakedness. Indicated disgrace, vulnerability and impropriety (Gen. 9:22–23). Babylon will be humbled and shamed. She will be like a prostitute who has been caught.

APPLY 1. In our sophisticated and cynical age, why do you think most major newspapers faithfully print astrological information day after day? Have you ever made a decision based on an astrological sign or chart? Do you think it is appropriate for followers of Christ to be involved in these things? Why or why not? **2.** In regard to what dilemma you have faced, could you have said, "All the counsel you have received has only worn you out" (v. 13)? Could direction from God have helped?

5 "Sit in silence, go into darkness,
Daughter of the Babylonians;
no more will you be called
queen of kingdoms.
6 I was angry with my people
and desecrated my inheritance;
I gave them into your hand,
and you showed them no mercy.
Even on the aged
you laid a very heavy yoke.
7 You said, 'I will continue forever—
the eternal queen!'
But you did not consider these things
or reflect on what might happen.

8 "Now then, listen, you wanton creature,
lounging in your security
and saying to yourself,
'I am, and there is none besides me.
I will never be a widow
or suffer the loss of children.'
9 Both of these will overtake you
in a moment, on a single day:
loss of children and widowhood.
They will come upon you in full measure,
in spite of your many sorceries
and all your potent spells.
10 You have trusted in your wickedness
and have said, 'No one sees me.'
Your wisdom and knowledge mislead you
when you say to yourself,
'I am, and there is none besides me.'
11 Disaster will come upon you,
and you will not know how to conjure it away.
A calamity will fall upon you
that you cannot ward off with a ransom;
a catastrophe you cannot foresee
will suddenly come upon you.

12 "Keep on, then, with your magic spells
and with your many sorceries,
which you have labored at since childhood.
Perhaps you will succeed,
perhaps you will cause terror.
13 All the counsel you have received has only worn you out!
Let your astrologers come forward,
those stargazers who make predictions month by month,
let them save you from what is coming upon you.
14 Surely they are like stubble;

47:9 loss of children and widowhood. Boastful Babylon believed she would never be defeated. But God would judge her, causing desolation in a single day.

47:10 wickedness ... wisdom ... knowledge. The leaders of Babylon believed they would rule forever, even called the empire "I am," a name appropriate only for the eternal God. Babylon's religions included sorcery and magic, practices forbidden by God (8:19; 44:24–25).

47:14 cannot ... save themselves.

the fire will burn them up.
They cannot even save themselves
from the power of the flame.
Here are no coals to warm anyone;
here is no fire to sit by.
15 That is all they can do for you—
these you have labored with
and trafficked with since childhood.
Each of them goes on in his error;
there is not one that can save you.

Stubborn Israel

48 "Listen to this, O house of Jacob,
you who are called by the name of Israel
and come from the line of Judah,
you who take oaths in the name of the LORD
and invoke the God of Israel—
but not in truth or righteousness—
2 you who call yourselves citizens of the holy city
and rely on the God of Israel—
the LORD Almighty is his name:
3 I foretold the former things long ago,
my mouth announced them and I made them known;
then suddenly I acted, and they came to pass.
4 For I knew how stubborn you were;
the sinews of your neck were iron,
your forehead was bronze.
5 Therefore I told you these things long ago;
before they happened I announced them to you
so that you could not say,
'My idols did them;
my wooden image and metal god ordained them.'
6 You have heard these things; look at them all.
Will you not admit them?

"From now on I will tell you of new things,
of hidden things unknown to you.
7 They are created now, and not long ago;
you have not heard of them before today.
So you cannot say,
'Yes, I knew of them.'
8 You have neither heard nor understood;
from of old your ear has not been open.
Well do I know how treacherous you are;
you were called a rebel from birth.
9 For my own name's sake I delay my wrath;
for the sake of my praise I hold it back from you,

OPEN When it comes to rebelliousness, which were you most like as a child: Always trying to do the right thing? Full of sass and backtalk? Always inventing mischief? Obedient, prim and proper?

STUDY 1. For what does the prophet rebuke the nation here? How might this attitude account for the Lord's ridicule of idolatry in chapters 40–48? **2.** Why has God gone to such lengths to announce this deliverance ahead of time (vv. 5–6)? **3.** Why does he bother to save them, anyway (44:8; 45:14)? If he had cut them off, what would the nations assume about God compared to the gods of Babylon?

APPLY 1. How have you been influenced by the rebellious attitude of other people? How has your rebellion at times affected others? What has it cost you in terms of God's peace and blessing in your life? **2.** When has God refined you "in the furnace of affliction"? In what way has that experience strengthened you?

Astrologers could not save Babylon any more than idols could. Some idols were carved out of firewood.

47:15 labored with and trafficked with since childhood. Referred to the merchants whose trade made Babylon wealthy.

48:6 tell you of new things. Israel had ignored previous prophecies, but now God said he would delay his wrath and free Israel from captivity. The new things included Cyrus' activities, the fall of Babylon and Israel's restoration. The new era of God's kingdom to be ushered in by the Messiah is also in view here.

so as not to cut you off.
[10]See, I have refined you, though not as silver;
I have tested you in the furnace of affliction.
[11]For my own sake, for my own sake, I do this.
How can I let myself be defamed?
I will not yield my glory to another.

Israel Freed

[12]"Listen to me, O Jacob,
Israel, whom I have called:
I am he;
I am the first and I am the last.
[13]My own hand laid the foundations of the earth,
and my right hand spread out the heavens;
when I summon them,
they all stand up together.

[14]"Come together, all of you, and listen:
Which of the idols has foretold these things?
The LORD's chosen ally
will carry out his purpose against Babylon;
his arm will be against the Babylonians.[a]
[15]I, even I, have spoken;
yes, I have called him.
I will bring him,
and he will succeed in his mission.

[16]"Come near me and listen to this:

"From the first announcement I have not spoken in secret;
at the time it happens, I am there."

And now the Sovereign LORD has sent me,
with his Spirit.

[17]This is what the LORD says—
your Redeemer, the Holy One of Israel:
"I am the LORD your God,
who teaches you what is best for you,
who directs you in the way you should go.
[18]If only you had paid attention to my commands,
your peace would have been like a river,
your righteousness like the waves of the sea.
[19]Your descendants would have been like the sand,
your children like its numberless grains;
their name would never be cut off
nor destroyed from before me."

[a]14 Or *Chaldeans*; also in verse 20

OPEN As a teen, did you pay more attention to your driving teacher or to your English teacher? Why?

STUDY 1. Who are the two people God has specifically "called" (vv. 12,15)? What has each been given to do? **2.** What message has God been communicating to the exiles (vv. 14–16)? In what way is Cyrus the Lord's chosen ally? **3.** What has Israel's history of rebellion and ignoring God cost the people (vv. 18–19)? How might history have been different if Israel had followed God's original plan? **4.** What have God's people lost through their exile in Babylon (vv. 18–22)? **5.** What about God will this deliverance communicate to all the nations? **6.** How does this show that God's concern for his people has not changed since the exodus?

APPLY 1. In what ways is Cyrus' deliverance of the Jews from Babylon like the deliverance from sin that Jesus has won for his people? How did you first respond to the news that, because of what Jesus has done, you are free from enslavement to sin (Rom. 8:1–3)? How do you respond now? Why? **2.** What are some bad reasons people witness to others about Christ? How might grasping the goodness of the Gospel encourage others to listen? **3.** Paul compares the water from the rock (v. 21; Ex. 17:6) to the life of the Spirit that flows from Christ (1 Cor. 10:3). In your life, is the water of the Spirit gushing, trickling, dripping or turned off? Why? What would help increase the flow?

48:10 furnace of affliction. The captivity in Babylon purified the people *like gold and silver are refined in high* heat. Slavery in Egypt also refined Israel.

48:14 The LORD's chosen ally. God called Cyrus to free Israel and defeat Babylon, and God helped him succeed.

48:16 LORD has sent me, with his Spirit. Just as God helped Cyrus accomplish his task, the Messiah, with the Holy Spirit on him, will accomplish his mission.

48:18 peace ... like a river ... the waves. The Israelites could have avoided captivity by obeying God's Law (Ps. 81:11–16). God had warned them of judgment for sin and had continually taught them the Law through prophets and priests.

[20]Leave Babylon,
flee from the Babylonians!
Announce this with shouts of joy
and proclaim it.
Send it out to the ends of the earth;
say, "The LORD has redeemed his servant Jacob."
[21]They did not thirst when he led them through the deserts;
he made water flow for them from the rock;
he split the rock
and water gushed out.

[22]"There is no peace," says the LORD, "for the wicked."

The Servant of the Lord

49 Listen to me, you islands;
hear this, you distant nations:
Before I was born the LORD called me;
from my birth he has made mention of my name.
[2]He made my mouth like a sharpened sword,
in the shadow of his hand he hid me;
he made me into a polished arrow
and concealed me in his quiver.
[3]He said to me, "You are my servant,
Israel, in whom I will display my splendor."
[4]But I said, "I have labored to no purpose;
I have spent my strength in vain and for nothing.
Yet what is due me is in the LORD's hand,
and my reward is with my God."

[5]And now the LORD says—
he who formed me in the womb to be his servant
to bring Jacob back to him
and gather Israel to himself,
for I am honored in the eyes of the LORD
and my God has been my strength—
[6]he says:
"It is too small a thing for you to be my servant
to restore the tribes of Jacob
and bring back those of Israel I have kept.
I will also make you a light for the Gentiles,
that you may bring my salvation to the ends of the earth."

[7]This is what the LORD says—
the Redeemer and Holy One of Israel—

OPEN During your childhood, who was your favorite hero? How did you show it?

STUDY 1. How might this servant speak to the people (v. 2)? How does that contrast with the servant's type of speech (42:2)? **2.** Why does the Lord call his servant by the name Israel (v. 3), if he is speaking to an individual with a mission to Israel (v. 5; 26:18)? **3.** How do you think the servant was received by Israel, the nation (vv. 4, 7)? How does this reflect the experience of Isaiah (30:9–11)? Of Jeremiah (Jer. 26:7–8)? Of Jesus (Luke 22:54–23:47)? **4.** What task that Israel had been struggling with does God tell them is "too small a thing" (v. 6)? **5.** How would you have felt if God said something you had struggled with was not too large a task, but too small of one? **6.** In his discouragement, what promises does the servant receive from God? How is this related to the prophecy of 11:10? What does this imply about the identity of the servant?

APPLY 1. When have you spent a lot of time and energy on something that turned out to be trivial? **2.** What "larger task" is God challenging you with right now?

48:20 redeemed. God brought his people out of slavery in Babylon, as he had out of Egypt. They were encouraged to leave quickly. Judgment was coming on Babylon.

48:21 did not thirst ... made water flow for them from the rock. After the Hebrews left Egypt, God provided water in the desert out of a rock (Ex. 17:1–7). God would provide for them as they left Babylon as well.

49:2 my mouth like a sharpened sword. Jesus Christ will conquer the earth through the gospel (Rev. 1:16; 2:12). God's Word is also depicted as a sword (Eph. 6:17; Heb. 4:12).

49:3 in whom I will display my splendor. The Messiah is called Israel because he epitomizes the nation, fulfilling what it failed to do (Zech. 3:8).

49:4 labored to no purpose ... strength in vain. This pointed to Christ's rejection by the nation of Israel and his suffering. But Jesus trusted God to ultimately accomplish divine will.

49:7 despised and abhorred. Although rejected by Israel (John 1:10–11), the servant would succeed in his ministry to the Gentiles. **chosen you.** At Christ's second coming, everyone on earth, even kings, will bow and acknowledge him as Messiah (Phil. 2:10–11).

to him who was despised and abhorred by the nation,
to the servant of rulers:
"Kings will see you and rise up,
princes will see and bow down,
because of the LORD, who is faithful,
the Holy One of Israel, who has chosen you."

Restoration of Israel

8 This is what the LORD says:

"In the time of my favor I will answer you,
and in the day of salvation I will help you;
I will keep you and will make you
to be a covenant for the people,
to restore the land
and to reassign its desolate inheritances,
9 to say to the captives, 'Come out,'
and to those in darkness, 'Be free!'

"They will feed beside the roads
and find pasture on every barren hill.
10 They will neither hunger nor thirst,
nor will the desert heat or the sun beat upon them.
He who has compassion on them will guide them
and lead them beside springs of water.
11 I will turn all my mountains into roads,
and my highways will be raised up.
12 See, they will come from afar—
some from the north, some from the west,
some from the region of Aswan.[a]"

13 Shout for joy, O heavens;
rejoice, O earth;
burst into song, O mountains!
For the LORD comforts his people
and will have compassion on his afflicted ones.

14 But Zion said, "The LORD has forsaken me,
the Lord has forgotten me."

15 "Can a mother forget the baby at her breast
and have no compassion on the child she has borne?
Though she may forget,
I will not forget you!
16 See, I have engraved you on the palms of my hands;
your walls are ever before me.
17 Your sons hasten back,
and those who laid you waste depart from you.
18 Lift up your eyes and look around;
all your sons gather and come to you.
As surely as I live," declares the LORD,

[a] 12 Dead Sea Scrolls; Masoretic Text *Sinim*

OPEN When hurt as a child, did you normally run to mom, to dad or to whom? Why? What was the best way they could help you feel better?

STUDY 1. What will happen for the exiles "in the day of salvation"? How will the nations learn of God's covenant promises (45:14, 22–24)? How does Israel reflect the mission of "the Servant" (42:6)? **2.** If the exiles are to return on a "highway" to Jerusalem (35:5–10; 43:19–20), what will the trip be like (vv. 9–12)? **3.** What are Israel's doubts (vv. 14,24)? How does this passage answer them? **4.** Having children was important, both as a sign of God's blessing and for provision for the future. What then does it mean that the people feel like a barren and widowed woman? What images does God use to respond to that feeling? **5.** Although we normally think of God as "our Father," what insight do you gain about God from considering the image of God as a mother (v. 15)? **6.** Verses 22 and 23 present a military image where the conquered bring their spoil and bow down before the victor. How does that fit in with God's work in the world (45:22–23)? **7.** The grotesque description in verse 26 describes civil strife within a nation (as in 9:20–21). How does this apply to the coming conquest of Babylon by Cyrus (45:1–7)? What is the ultimate purpose of it all (vv. 23,26)? **8.** What response is God looking for in Israel (v. 23)? What exactly do you think it means? **9.** How does verse 25 illuminate Jesus' comment about "binding the strong man" (Matt. 12:29)?

APPLY 1. Right now, do you feel more like a forsaken captive or like a person coming home to a long-awaited reunion? Why? **2.** Is the freeing of the exiles from Babylon by Cyrus at all like what Jesus has done for you? How so? **3.** What is one thing that convinces you that the Lord, and

49:8 time of my favor ... day of salvation. God's offer of salvation is always current. Then and now, God calls people to surrender their lives to his leadership, to repent of sin and to live in God's service.

"you will wear them all as ornaments;
you will put them on, like a bride.

19 "Though you were ruined and made desolate
and your land laid waste,
now you will be too small for your people,
and those who devoured you will be far away.
20 The children born during your bereavement
will yet say in your hearing,
'This place is too small for us;
give us more space to live in.'
21 Then you will say in your heart,
'Who bore me these?
I was bereaved and barren;
I was exiled and rejected.
Who brought these up?
I was left all alone,
but these—where have they come from?' "

22 This is what the Sovereign LORD says:

"See, I will beckon to the Gentiles,
I will lift up my banner to the peoples;
they will bring your sons in their arms
and carry your daughters on their shoulders.
23 Kings will be your foster fathers,
and their queens your nursing mothers.
They will bow down before you with their faces to the ground;
they will lick the dust at your feet.
Then you will know that I am the LORD;
those who hope in me will not be disappointed."

24 Can plunder be taken from warriors,
or captives rescued from the fierce[a]?

25 But this is what the LORD says:

"Yes, captives will be taken from warriors,
and plunder retrieved from the fierce;
I will contend with those who contend with you,
and your children I will save.
26 I will make your oppressors eat their own flesh;
they will be drunk on their own blood, as with wine.
Then all mankind will know
that I, the LORD, am your Savior,
your Redeemer, the Mighty One of Jacob."

Israel's Sin and the Servant's Obedience

50 This is what the LORD says:

"Where is your mother's certificate of divorce
with which I sent her away?
Or to which of my creditors
did I sell you?
Because of your sins you were sold;

[a]24 Dead Sea Scrolls, Vulgate and Syriac (see also Septuagint and verse 25); Masoretic Text *righteous*

not some other god or force, is indeed the one you can trust?

OPEN What is the first thing you hear in the morning: Alarm? Radio? Kids? Dog? How do you respond?

STUDY 1. What is the Lord emphasizing with the rhetorical questions in verses 1–2? Has he in fact divorced Israel (49:14)? **2.** Verses 4–9 present the third of four "Servant songs" (42:1-7; 49:1-13; 52:13–53:12). How would you

describe the servant's mission? His relationship to God? How does he differ from the nation of Israel (48:8)? **3.** What new element about the servant, not found in the previous two songs, is added in verses 6–9? What might cause the servant to be mistreated like this? What gives the servant confidence and hope in spite of such ill-treatment? **4.** Compare verse 6 to what Jesus says in Matthew 5:39. What significance do you find in this? **5.** Compare verses 8–9 with Romans 8:31–34. How would you summarize the message of these passages? **6.** What might the prophet mean by those "in the dark" (v. 10; 49:14)? What are they to do? How might the example of the servant encourage them? **7.** In view of the many rebukes against idolatry in chapters 40–48, what does he mean by those who "provide themselves with flaming torches"? What will happen to those who try to find solutions apart from God?

APPLY 1. How would you describe your current relationship with God: Casual date? Going steady? Engaged? Married? Divorced? Why? **2.** What would it mean for you to start your day by listening to God? How might you do so? **3.** Recently, has the voice of Jesus to you been one that sustains you when weary (v. 4), or one that cuts like a sharp sword (49:2)? Why? How is that related to your attitude of love and obedience to him?

OPEN Who is your favorite Bible character? Why? When do you find the most encouragement from that person's biography?

because of your transgressions your mother was sent away.
2 When I came, why was there no one?
When I called, why was there no one to answer?
Was my arm too short to ransom you?
Do I lack the strength to rescue you?
By a mere rebuke I dry up the sea,
I turn rivers into a desert;
their fish rot for lack of water
and die of thirst.
3 I clothe the sky with darkness
and make sackcloth its covering."

4 The Sovereign LORD has given me an instructed tongue,
to know the word that sustains the weary.
He wakens me morning by morning,
wakens my ear to listen like one being taught.
5 The Sovereign LORD has opened my ears,
and I have not been rebellious;
I have not drawn back.
6 I offered my back to those who beat me,
my cheeks to those who pulled out my beard;
I did not hide my face
from mocking and spitting.
7 Because the Sovereign LORD helps me,
I will not be disgraced.
Therefore have I set my face like flint,
and I know I will not be put to shame.
8 He who vindicates me is near.
Who then will bring charges against me?
Let us face each other!
Who is my accuser?
Let him confront me!
9 It is the Sovereign LORD who helps me.
Who is he that will condemn me?
They will all wear out like a garment;
the moths will eat them up.

10 Who among you fears the LORD
and obeys the word of his servant?
Let him who walks in the dark,
who has no light,
trust in the name of the LORD
and rely on his God.
11 But now, all you who light fires
and provide yourselves with flaming torches,
go, walk in the light of your fires
and of the torches you have set ablaze.
This is what you shall receive from my hand:
You will lie down in torment.

Everlasting Salvation for Zion

51 "Listen to me, you who pursue righteousness
and who seek the LORD:
Look to the rock from which you were cut
and to the quarry from which you were hewn;

2 look to Abraham, your father,
and to Sarah, who gave you birth.
When I called him he was but one,
and I blessed him and made him many.
3 The LORD will surely comfort Zion
and will look with compassion on all her ruins;
he will make her deserts like Eden,
her wastelands like the garden of the LORD.
Joy and gladness will be found in her,
thanksgiving and the sound of singing.

4 "Listen to me, my people;
hear me, my nation:
The law will go out from me;
my justice will become a light to the nations.
5 My righteousness draws near speedily,
my salvation is on the way,
and my arm will bring justice to the nations.
The islands will look to me
and wait in hope for my arm.
6 Lift up your eyes to the heavens,
look at the earth beneath;
the heavens will vanish like smoke,
the earth will wear out like a garment
and its inhabitants die like flies.
But my salvation will last forever,
my righteousness will never fail.

7 "Hear me, you who know what is right,
you people who have my law in your hearts:
Do not fear the reproach of men
or be terrified by their insults.
8 For the moth will eat them up like a garment;
the worm will devour them like wool.
But my righteousness will last forever,
my salvation through all generations."

9 Awake, awake! Clothe yourself with strength,
O arm of the LORD;
awake, as in days gone by,
as in generations of old.
Was it not you who cut Rahab to pieces,
who pierced that monster through?
10 Was it not you who dried up the sea,
the waters of the great deep,
who made a road in the depths of the sea
so that the redeemed might cross over?

STUDY Chapters 51:1–52:12 are an extended poem, summing up God's intent for the exiles. **1.** How is their current situation like that of Abraham and Sarah (vv. 1–3)? Since Abraham was old and his wife, Sarah, was barren, why would God use this example for the exiles? **2.** If verses 1–3 were meant to give hope to the exiles, what would verses 4–6 do for them? What effect will their deliverance have upon the other nations? What does this indicate about God's purpose in restoring Jerusalem? **3.** Compare verse 6 with Genesis 15:5. How does the "starry" lesson of the exiles compare with that of Abraham? What does this stress about God? **4.** How are the people here (vv. 1,7) different from those addressed in 48:1–4? What effect should the heavenly vision (v. 6) have upon these exiles as they face their oppressors (vv. 7–8)? **5.** Who is speaking in verses 9–11? For what nation was Rahab the nickname (30:7)? To what event is the speaker referring? What does the speaker mean by calling upon God to "do it again"? What effect would recalling this event have upon the exiles? **6.** What words or pictures are used to describe what the exile felt like to those people who loved God (vv. 12–16)? How would you sum up God's message to these people? What would that word do for you if you were a discouraged exile?

APPLY **1.** When have God's promises seemed to you like mere words? When you feel like that, how might the faith of Abraham, who waited 25 years to see one child born, encourage you? **2.** If you were in exile, what would it mean to you that God's promises are more enduring than the stars or the earth around you? How might meditating upon the lesson of the stars give you a new perspective on the problems that you face today? **3.** When feeling discouraged, what event in your personal history can you look back upon and call on God to do again? **4.** What promises of God especially encourage you to keep on following him even when things get hard?

51:3 Zion ... Eden. Both referred to places of fellowship with God that were free from sin and guarded by angels (Gen. 3:24). Zion will be fruitful and lush like the Garden of Eden.

51:4 law ... my justice will become a light. God's Law will be known and justice will prevail all over the world. **light to the nations.** Jesus Christ.

51:5 righteousness. God would bring Israel back to Jerusalem from the Exile. After the restoration of Israel, God's work would continue, offering all nations salvation through Christ.

51:9 Awake. While it appeared to the Israelites that God was asleep, God is ever vigilant on behalf of his people (Ps. 121:3–4).

[11]The ransomed of the LORD will return.
They will enter Zion with singing;
everlasting joy will crown their heads.
Gladness and joy will overtake them,
and sorrow and sighing will flee away.

[12]"I, even I, am he who comforts you.
Who are you that you fear mortal men,
the sons of men, who are but grass,
[13]that you forget the LORD your Maker,
who stretched out the heavens
and laid the foundations of the earth,
that you live in constant terror every day
because of the wrath of the oppressor,
who is bent on destruction?
For where is the wrath of the oppressor?
[14] The cowering prisoners will soon be set free;
they will not die in their dungeon,
nor will they lack bread.
[15]For I am the LORD your God,
who churns up the sea so that its waves roar—
the LORD Almighty is his name.
[16]I have put my words in your mouth
and covered you with the shadow of my hand—
I who set the heavens in place,
who laid the foundations of the earth,
and who say to Zion, 'You are my people.' "

The Cup of the Lord's Wrath

[17]Awake, awake!
Rise up, O Jerusalem,
you who have drunk from the hand of the LORD
the cup of his wrath,
you who have drained to its dregs
the goblet that makes men stagger.
[18]Of all the sons she bore
there was none to guide her;
of all the sons she reared
there was none to take her by the hand.
[19]These double calamities have come upon you—
who can comfort you?—
ruin and destruction, famine and sword—
who can[a] console you?
[20]Your sons have fainted;
they lie at the head of every street,
like antelope caught in a net.

[a]19 Dead Sea Scrolls, Septuagint, Vulgate and Syriac; Masoretic Text / *how can I*

OPEN What is the attraction to being drunk?

STUDY 1. Who is responsible for making Jerusalem drunk (51:17–23)? What would such a portrait of herself teach Israel? **2.** What six things does Zion (Jerusalem) need to do to change this picture (52:1–2)? What does each mean? What is God going to do to change it? **3.** This section continues the long poem begun in 51:1. Whereas in 51:9, God was called upon to awake, who is called upon in 51:17–23? What has been the effect of God's punishment upon the people? **4.** Why is God's anger turning upon the Babylonians (45:5–7)? What does this judgment show about God? **5.** In the third "awake" section (52:1–10), what promises are given to the exiles? **6.** What have the watchmen been faithfully saying? What will be their

51:14 prisoners will soon be set free. These were captives in exile in Babylon, yet meaning extends to everyone living in the darkness of sin, alienated from God.

51:17 cup ... drained. The empty cup referred to suffering God's judgment. In exile the Israelites truly felt God's punishment (Jer. 25:15–29; Lam. 4:21).

51:18 none to take her by the hand. Many young men of Jerusalem were killed during the destruction of the city. This phrase depicted Jerusalem as a sick woman with no sons to care for her.

They are filled with the wrath of the LORD
and the rebuke of your God.

[21]Therefore hear this, you afflicted one,
made drunk, but not with wine.
[22]This is what your Sovereign LORD says,
your God, who defends his people:
"See, I have taken out of your hand
the cup that made you stagger;
from that cup, the goblet of my wrath,
you will never drink again.
[23]I will put it into the hands of your tormentors,
who said to you,
'Fall prostrate that we may walk over you.'
And you made your back like the ground,
like a street to be walked over."

52 Awake, awake, O Zion,
clothe yourself with strength.
Put on your garments of splendor,
O Jerusalem, the holy city.
The uncircumcised and defiled
will not enter you again.
[2]Shake off your dust;
rise up, sit enthroned, O Jerusalem.
Free yourself from the chains on your neck,
O captive Daughter of Zion.

[3]For this is what the LORD says:

"You were sold for nothing,
and without money you will be redeemed."

[4]For this is what the Sovereign LORD says:

"At first my people went down to Egypt to live;
lately, Assyria has oppressed them.

[5]"And now what do I have here?" declares the LORD.

"For my people have been taken away for nothing,
and those who rule them mock,[a]"
declares the LORD.
"And all day long
my name is constantly blasphemed.
[6]Therefore my people will know my name;
therefore in that day they will know
that it is I who foretold it.
Yes, it is I."

[7]How beautiful on the mountains
are the feet of those who bring good news,

[a]5 Dead Sea Scrolls and Vulgate; Masoretic Text *wail*

reward for this? Who are the watchmen?

APPLY 1. What does Paul say about the "beautiful feet" (52:7; Rom. 10:14–15)? When you share your faith with others what image fits best: Messenger clicking your heels with joy? Messenger dragging your feet? Operator of travel booth just passing out information? Doomsday prophet? **2.** When have you sensed and conveyed real joy and peace in sharing your faith with others? How could you share more of the "good tidings" of the Gospel next week?

52:1 uncircumcised and defiled will not enter. Referred to Israel's pagan conquerors who, in the Millennium, would never again conquer her and pollute Jerusalem with their false religious practices.

52:7 feet ... bring good news. Messengers ran with news of battles to the king and people (2 Sam. 18:26).

who proclaim peace,
 who bring good tidings,
 who proclaim salvation,
who say to Zion,
 "Your God reigns!"
8 Listen! Your watchmen lift up their voices;
 together they shout for joy.
When the LORD returns to Zion,
 they will see it with their own eyes.
9 Burst into songs of joy together,
 you ruins of Jerusalem,
for the LORD has comforted his people,
 he has redeemed Jerusalem.
10 The LORD will lay bare his holy arm
 in the sight of all the nations,
and all the ends of the earth will see
 the salvation of our God.

11 Depart, depart, go out from there!
 Touch no unclean thing!
Come out from it and be pure,
 you who carry the vessels of the LORD.
12 But you will not leave in haste
 or go in flight;
for the LORD will go before you,
 the God of Israel will be your rear guard.

The Suffering and Glory of the Servant

13 See, my servant will act wisely[a];
 he will be raised and lifted up and highly exalted.
14 Just as there were many who were appalled at him[b]—
 his appearance was so disfigured beyond that of any man
 and his form marred beyond human likeness—
15 so will he sprinkle many nations,[c]
 and kings will shut their mouths because of him.
For what they were not told, they will see,
 and what they have not heard, they will understand.

53 Who has believed our message
 and to whom has the arm of the LORD been revealed?
2 He grew up before him like a tender shoot,

[a]13 Or *will prosper* [b]14 Hebrew *you* [c]15 Hebrew; Septuagint *so will many nations marvel at him*

OPEN 1. When you were growing up, who was the kid in school who everyone picked on? Why? Did you join in? How do you feel about that now? **2.** When you were in high school, what was most likely to attract others to you: Your physical appearance? Your sense of humor? Your athletic or musical talent? Your crazy behavior? Your ability to listen? **3.** On a scale of 1–10, how attractive did you feel at that time, if "1" is "like one from whom people hide their face" and "10" is on the list "of most beautiful people"? How did you handle this emotionally?

STUDY 1. This is the last of the four "Servant songs"

Your God reigns! The good news in this verse will be the joyful announcement that the Messiah is returning to Zion to reign in peace.

52:8 Listen ... watchmen. Those who long for salvation (62:6).

52:10 lay bare his holy arm. A phrase meaning "a show of God's power and strength "(40:10; 51:9).

52:13 lifted up and highly exalted. From this verse to 53:12, the servant's death for the sins of his people is predicted. This phrase referred to his resurrection, ascension into heaven and glorification (Rom. 4:24–25).

52:14 appalled at him. Possibly referred to Christ's appearance on the cross. Could also be translated "awestruck" or "astonished." Everyone who sees him at his second coming will be astounded.

52:15 sprinkle many nations and kings. Associated with cleansing from sin by the priest under Mosaic Law (Lev. 4:6). **shut their mouths.** Meant the stunned respect by the kings of the earth who had not considered Christ important. **For what ... understand.** The nations will finally understand that the Messiah is Lord. Romans 15:21 refers to this passage.

53:2 tender shoot ... a root out of dry ground. From a spiritually arid area

and like a root out of dry ground.
He had no beauty or majesty to attract us to him,
nothing in his appearance that we should desire him.
[3]He was despised and rejected by men,
a man of sorrows, and familiar with suffering.
Like one from whom men hide their faces
he was despised, and we esteemed him not.

[4]Surely he took up our infirmities
and carried our sorrows,
yet we considered him stricken by God,
smitten by him, and afflicted.
[5]But he was pierced for our transgressions,
he was crushed for our iniquities;
the punishment that brought us peace was upon him,
and by his wounds we are healed.
[6]We all, like sheep, have gone astray,
each of us has turned to his own way;
and the LORD has laid on him
the iniquity of us all.

[7]He was oppressed and afflicted,
yet he did not open his mouth;
he was led like a lamb to the slaughter,
and as a sheep before her shearers is silent,
so he did not open his mouth.
[8]By oppression[a] and judgment he was taken away.
And who can speak of his descendants?
For he was cut off from the land of the living;
for the transgression of my people he was stricken.[b]
[9]He was assigned a grave with the wicked,
and with the rich in his death,
though he had done no violence,
nor was any deceit in his mouth.

[10]Yet it was the LORD's will to crush him and cause him to suffer,
and though the LORD makes[c] his life a guilt offering,
he will see his offspring and prolong his days,
and the will of the LORD will prosper in his hand.
[11]After the suffering of his soul,
he will see the light ⌊of life⌋[d] and be satisfied[e];

[a]8 Or *From arrest* [b]8 Or *away. / Yet who of his generation considered / that he was cut off from the land of the living / for the transgression of my people, / to whom the blow was due?* [c]10 Hebrew *though you make* [d]11 Dead Sea Scrolls (see also Septuagint); Masoretic Text does not have *the light ⌊of life⌋*. [e]11 Or (with Masoretic Text) [11]*He will see the result of the suffering of his soul / and be satisfied*

(42:1–13; 49:1–13; 50:4–9). If all we had were 52:13–15, what would you imagine happened to this song that so many were appalled by? **2.** The songs in chapters 42 and 49 indicated that the servant would "be a light to the Gentiles." How is that idea communicated in these opening lines? **3.** If you had grown up next door to "the servant," how would you describe his childhood to a newspaper reporter who interviewed you about him (53:2–3)? How does that contrast with God's perspective of him (53:2)? **4.** If all you knew about the servant's adult life was summed up in 53:7–9, what would you assume must have happened to him? How does this relate to the picture of the servant in 50:6? **5.** What was the purpose of the servant's suffering (53:4–6)? What was the nature of his suffering? What benefits come to others because of his suffering and death? **6.** How do you account for the paradox between his death (53:9) and his seeing the "light of life" (53:11)? **7.** Chapter 53:7,10,12 use sacrificial imagery to speak of the servant. How does that make his death more than a mere martyr's death? **8.** The New Testament freely applies this song to Jesus (Matt. 27:38, 57–60; John 1:29; Acts 8:32–34; 1 Peter 2:22–23). From this song, how would you explain to someone else the meaning of Jesus' death and resurrection?

APPLY 1. Paul applies 53:1 to the ministry of a follower of Christ (Rom. 10:16). How have you experienced rejection from others because of your faith? Has obedience to God ever left you feeling "cut off from the land of the living" (53:8)? **2.** What spiritual wounds has Christ healed in you (53:5)?

where no fruit is expected to grow (his rejection by Israel), the Messiah comes from David's line.

53:4 he took up our infirmities. The nation of Israel will realize that the servant took upon himself the consequences of their sin, an illness of the soul.

53:5 crushed for our iniquities. The servant suffered in our place in order to reconcile us with God. He healed physical illnesses during his earthly ministry, and he heals spiritual sickness as well.

53:6 laid on him the iniquity of us all. The restored remnant, and all other believers, will admit their guilt and acknowledge that the Lord suffered punishment and death in their place.

53:9 the rich. The wealthy Joseph of Arimathea provided the tomb for Jesus' burial (Matt. 27:57–60).

53:10 it was the LORD's will. Referred to the doctrine of the atonement, or substitute sacrifice as payment for sin. Jesus' death satisfied the penalty for sin and allowed all who accept his sacrifice in faith to be reconciled to God (2 Cor. 5:21).

OPEN 1. If you discovered you were going to be the proud parent of quintuplets, what changes would that force on your budget? Your housing situation? Your emotions? **2.** Have you or a family member ever witnessed an earthquake? What was it like?

STUDY 1. In 51:2 Sarah was used as an example of faith for the exiles. How is her experience reflected in verses 1–3 as well (Gen. 18:9–14; 21:6–7)? What does the prophet mean by using this image? **2.** Since singleness and barrenness were causes of shame for a woman, how would that exemplify the experience of the exiles? How does this picture differ from that seen in Jeremiah 3:6–10? What is the point of each analogy? **3.** How was the captivity in Babylon like "the days of Noah" for the exiles? For God? **4.** Although Jerusalem was rebuilt, it had not regained the influence and status pictured in verses 11–15. In light of that, what does the prophet really mean? How does this relate to John's description of "the new Jerusalem" seen in Revelation 21:11–21? What promises are associated with it?

APPLY 1. What point is Isaiah making in verses 10,16 and 17? Have you felt the "ground" under your spiritual life quake? Can you trace God's control of events in your own life which seemed out of control? **2.** What circumstances have caused you to feel abandoned by God? At those times, how might you be helped by the picture of God as a husband renewing his vows? **3.** Of the promises in verses 11–17, which one means the most to you now? Why?

by his knowledge[a] my righteous servant will justify many,
and he will bear their iniquities.
12 Therefore I will give him a portion among the great,[b]
and he will divide the spoils with the strong[c]
because he poured out his life unto death,
and was numbered with the transgressors.
For he bore the sin of many,
and made intercession for the transgressors.

The Future Glory of Zion

54 "Sing, O barren woman,
you who never bore a child;
burst into song, shout for joy,
you who were never in labor;
because more are the children of the desolate woman
than of her who has a husband,"
says the LORD.

2 "Enlarge the place of your tent,
stretch your tent curtains wide,
do not hold back;
lengthen your cords,
strengthen your stakes.
3 For you will spread out to the right and to the left;
your descendants will dispossess nations
and settle in their desolate cities.

4 "Do not be afraid; you will not suffer shame.
Do not fear disgrace; you will not be humiliated.
You will forget the shame of your youth
and remember no more the reproach of your widowhood.
5 For your Maker is your husband—
the LORD Almighty is his name—
the Holy One of Israel is your Redeemer;
he is called the God of all the earth.
6 The LORD will call you back
as if you were a wife deserted and distressed in spirit—
a wife who married young,
only to be rejected," says your God.
7 "For a brief moment I abandoned you,
but with deep compassion I will bring you back.
8 In a surge of anger
I hid my face from you for a moment,
but with everlasting kindness
I will have compassion on you,"
says the LORD your Redeemer.

[a]11 *Or by knowledge of him* [b]12 *Or many* [c]12 *Or numerous*

53:12 divide the spoils with the strong. Depicted a victorious army general sharing the enemy's goods with his soldiers. Believers will share in the benefits of Christ's rewards.

54:1 who never bore a child. Children performed valuable services like helping with family chores and caring for aged parents. Bearing many children was considered a sign of God's blessing. Although the Israelites were reduced in number during the Exile, God would give the nation many children to repopulate the land. His covenant with Abraham would continue.

9 "To me this is like the days of Noah,
when I swore that the waters of Noah would never again cover
the earth.
So now I have sworn not to be angry with you,
never to rebuke you again.
10 Though the mountains be shaken
and the hills be removed,
yet my unfailing love for you will not be shaken
nor my covenant of peace be removed,"
says the LORD, who has compassion on you.

11 "O afflicted city, lashed by storms and not comforted,
I will build you with stones of turquoise,[a]
your foundations with sapphires.[b]
12 I will make your battlements of rubies,
your gates of sparkling jewels,
and all your walls of precious stones.
13 All your sons will be taught by the LORD,
and great will be your children's peace.
14 In righteousness you will be established:
Tyranny will be far from you;
you will have nothing to fear.
Terror will be far removed;
it will not come near you.
15 If anyone does attack you, it will not be my doing;
whoever attacks you will surrender to you.

16 "See, it is I who created the blacksmith
who fans the coals into flame
and forges a weapon fit for its work.
And it is I who have created the destroyer to work havoc;
17 no weapon forged against you will prevail,
and you will refute every tongue that accuses you.
This is the heritage of the servants of the LORD,
and this is their vindication from me,"
declares the LORD.

Invitation to the Thirsty

55 "Come, all you who are thirsty,
come to the waters;
and you who have no money,
come, buy and eat!
Come, buy wine and milk
without money and without cost.
2 Why spend money on what is not bread,

[a] *11* The meaning of the Hebrew for this word is uncertain. [b] *11* Or *lapis lazuli*

How will that hope make a difference in the way you live today? ________

OPEN What is your favorite junk food? How would you feel if that were all you had available to eat?

STUDY 1. What is God's message to poor exiles (v. 1) and rich exiles (v. 2)? How will this "class" distinction be removed? What is required of the exiles to receive this blessing from God? **2.** How does Isaiah's invitation relate to Jesus'

54:9 like the days of Noah. God promised Noah that he would never again destroy the earth by water (Gen. 9:11). The day is coming when he will never rebuke Israel again and the peace he promised will be permanent and strong.

54:17 servants of the LORD. Referred to all saints or believers, both Jews and Gentiles.

55:1 thirsty, come to the waters. Thirst speaks of the desire for spiritual answers to life's mysteries. Waters represent the satisfaction of knowing God as Savior and Provider (John 4:10–14).

55:2 spend money ... labor on what does not satisfy? Throughout history, people have tried to find satisfaction through many things other than

words in John 6:35? What does it mean to "feed" upon Jesus? **3.** How would the exiles respond to the disparity in verses 8 and 9? How might they have felt if the Lord had not reminded them of this? **4.** What is the expiration date of the covenant God is making with the exiles (v. 3)? What is its purpose (vv. 4–5)? What other sections from Isaiah 40–55 have stressed this same theme? What does that tell you about God's purpose for the world? **5.** What does it mean to "seek the LORD" (vv. 6–7)? What hopeful promise is associated with doing so? **6.** Why is God trying to impress the people with how much higher his ways are than theirs (vv. 8–9): To humiliate them? To reassure them of his wisdom and control? To "keep them in their place"? To let them know there will always be things they don't understand?

APPLY 1. How does the question in verse 2 strike you? What things have you spent your money or labor on that have ultimately proven to be unfulfilling? **2.** In light of verses 6–7, would you say you have been seeking the Lord or hiding from him this week? Why? **3.** Joy and peace are the fruit God's Word produces (vv. 11–12). At what stage of development is this fruit in your life: Buried seed? Just starting to sprout? Ripening fruit? In need of weeding? How might you be "fertilized" by the commands in verses 1–3 and 6–7?

and your labor on what does not satisfy?
Listen, listen to me, and eat what is good,
and your soul will delight in the richest of fare.
3 Give ear and come to me;
hear me, that your soul may live.
I will make an everlasting covenant with you,
my faithful love promised to David.
4 See, I have made him a witness to the peoples,
a leader and commander of the peoples.
5 Surely you will summon nations you know not,
and nations that do not know you will hasten to you,
because of the LORD your God,
the Holy One of Israel,
for he has endowed you with splendor."

6 Seek the LORD while he may be found;
call on him while he is near.
7 Let the wicked forsake his way
and the evil man his thoughts.
Let him turn to the LORD, and he will have mercy on him,
and to our God, for he will freely pardon.

8 "For my thoughts are not your thoughts,
neither are your ways my ways,"
declares the LORD.
9 "As the heavens are higher than the earth,
so are my ways higher than your ways
and my thoughts than your thoughts.
10 As the rain and the snow
come down from heaven,
and do not return to it
without watering the earth
and making it bud and flourish,
so that it yields seed for the sower and bread for the eater,
11 so is my word that goes out from my mouth:
It will not return to me empty,
but will accomplish what I desire
and achieve the purpose for which I sent it.
12 You will go out in joy
and be led forth in peace;
the mountains and hills
will burst into song before you,
and all the trees of the field
will clap their hands.
13 Instead of the thornbush will grow the pine tree,
and instead of briers the myrtle will grow.
This will be for the LORD's renown,
for an everlasting sign,
which will not be destroyed."

God. But the joy of salvation cannot be obtained except through God's free gift.

55:5 nations that do not know you. Many nations will recognize the splendor of the Lord and go to Israel to worship God. This is a reversal of the Exile when Israel was taken to a foreign nation.

Salvation for Others

56 This is what the LORD says:

"Maintain justice
and do what is right,
for my salvation is close at hand
and my righteousness will soon be revealed.
2 Blessed is the man who does this,
the man who holds it fast,
who keeps the Sabbath without desecrating it,
and keeps his hand from doing any evil."

3 Let no foreigner who has bound himself to the LORD say,
"The LORD will surely exclude me from his people."
And let not any eunuch complain,
"I am only a dry tree."

4 For this is what the LORD says:

"To the eunuchs who keep my Sabbaths,
who choose what pleases me
and hold fast to my covenant—
5 to them I will give within my temple and its walls
a memorial and a name
better than sons and daughters;
I will give them an everlasting name
that will not be cut off.
6 And foreigners who bind themselves to the LORD
to serve him,
to love the name of the LORD,
and to worship him,
all who keep the Sabbath without desecrating it
and who hold fast to my covenant—
7 these I will bring to my holy mountain
and give them joy in my house of prayer.
Their burnt offerings and sacrifices
will be accepted on my altar;
for my house will be called
a house of prayer for all nations."
8 The Sovereign LORD declares—
he who gathers the exiles of Israel:
"I will gather still others to them
besides those already gathered."

OPEN Have you ever moved into a new neighborhood? How long did it take to settle down and become a full member of the community?

STUDY 1. In light of the impending deliverance (55:12), what type of lifestyle ought to characterize the exiles? **2.** Given the fact that family life was central to Jewish identity, what types of losses would those Jewish men suffer who were castrated by the Babylonians (vv. 3–5; Deut. 23:1–3)? What hope is God extending to them? What must they do to receive it? **3.** How does the attitude toward foreigners that is expressed here (vv. 3,6–7), compare to that of Jesus? To the religious leaders of Jesus' day (Luke 4:24–30)? **4.** What is God's purpose in restoring Jerusalem (vv. 7–8)?

APPLY 1. Where do you sometimes feel like a "foreigner" or outsider: At work? In church? At social functions? In groups of a different ethnic culture? In groups where people are all older or younger than you? **2.** What can you do to help others who are different feel included in God's people (v. 3)?

56:2 the man ... who keeps the Sabbath. Keeping the Sabbath was an important part of the Law because it signified God's covenant with Israel. Refraining from work on that day showed trust in God to provide.

56:3 no foreigner. Gentiles, who were not part of the covenant, would also find God's peace if they turned to God in faith. **eunuch.** Eunuchs were excluded under the Mosaic Law (Deut. 23:1), but they would be part of Christ's kingdom.

56:7 house of prayer. Being included in the covenantal family of Israel meant intimate communication with and worship of God (Mark 11:17).

56:8 gather still others. God promised Abraham that through him all peoples of the world would be blessed (Gen. 12:3). People everywhere who repent and come to God are welcomed into his kingdom with joy.

OPEN Who is your favorite dog hero: Lassie? Benji? Snoopy? Eddie ("Frasier")? Beethoven? What in yourself do you see in your hero?

STUDY It is uncertain whether this section is addressed to the Jews before or during the exile. **1.** In what ways are the leaders as useless as gluttonous, sleeping watchdogs that can't even bark? What are their primary concerns (56:11–12)? In a situation like this, why is the death of a good person an act of mercy? **2.** How is the people's idolatry like adultery (57:3–10)? What is his point in using that image? Why has this happened? **3.** How are people today still "burning with lust" and "sacrificing their children" (57:5)? How are they "sending ambassadors far away" (57:9)? **4.** What is meant by the prophet's harsh words in 57:9? **5.** How will their fate contrast with the future of those who have taken refuge in God (57:11–13)?

APPLY **1.** In the positions of leadership you have held (at home, work, school, in the community or church), how have you felt the temptation to pursue your own goals regardless of the effects it could have on others (56:10–12)? **2.** If God asked you, "Whom have you so dreaded and feared that you have been false to me ...?" (57:11), how would you answer: Your boss—because he or she pressures you to be unethical? Your non-believing friends—because they might make fun of you? Bigots—because they pressure you to reject brothers and sisters of another race or culture? Other? **3.** How would you explain to someone what it means to take refuge in God (57:13)? What pressures are directing you to God's protection today?

God's Accusation Against the Wicked

9 Come, all you beasts of the field,
come and devour, all you beasts of the forest!
10 Israel's watchmen are blind,
they all lack knowledge;
they are all mute dogs,
they cannot bark;
they lie around and dream,
they love to sleep.
11 They are dogs with mighty appetites;
they never have enough.
They are shepherds who lack understanding;
they all turn to their own way,
each seeks his own gain.
12 "Come," each one cries, "let me get wine!
Let us drink our fill of beer!
And tomorrow will be like today,
or even far better."

57 The righteous perish,
and no one ponders it in his heart;
devout men are taken away,
and no one understands
that the righteous are taken away
to be spared from evil.
2 Those who walk uprightly
enter into peace;
they find rest as they lie in death.

3 "But you—come here, you sons of a sorceress,
you offspring of adulterers and prostitutes!
4 Whom are you mocking?
At whom do you sneer
and stick out your tongue?
Are you not a brood of rebels,
the offspring of liars?
5 You burn with lust among the oaks
and under every spreading tree;
you sacrifice your children in the ravines
and under the overhanging crags.
6 ⌊The idols⌋ among the smooth stones of the ravines are your portion;
they, they are your lot.
Yes, to them you have poured out drink offerings
and offered grain offerings.
In the light of these things, should I relent?
7 You have made your bed on a high and lofty hill;
there you went up to offer your sacrifices.

57:3 adulterers and prostitutes. Referred to the Canaanite fertility rites in which some Israelites participated. Supposedly, engaging in sexual relations with prostitutes in the temple helped guarantee fertility in crops, animals and families. The people had a history with this sin.

57:4 mocking ... sneer. Israelites who participated in the idolatrous religious rites mocked those who obeyed God, further demonstrating their rebellion.

[8]Behind your doors and your doorposts
you have put your pagan symbols.
Forsaking me, you uncovered your bed,
you climbed into it and opened it wide;
you made a pact with those whose beds you love,
and you looked on their nakedness.
[9]You went to Molech[a] with olive oil
and increased your perfumes.
You sent your ambassadors[b] far away;
you descended to the grave[c] itself!
[10]You were wearied by all your ways,
but you would not say, 'It is hopeless.'
You found renewal of your strength,
and so you did not faint.

[11]"Whom have you so dreaded and feared
that you have been false to me,
and have neither remembered me
nor pondered this in your hearts?
Is it not because I have long been silent
that you do not fear me?
[12]I will expose your righteousness and your works,
and they will not benefit you.
[13]When you cry out for help,
let your collection ⌞of idols⌟ save you!
The wind will carry all of them off,
a mere breath will blow them away.
But the man who makes me his refuge
will inherit the land
and possess my holy mountain."

Comfort for the Contrite

[14]And it will be said:

"Build up, build up, prepare the road!
Remove the obstacles out of the way of my people."
[15]For this is what the high and lofty One says—
he who lives forever, whose name is holy:
"I live in a high and holy place,
but also with him who is contrite and lowly in spirit,
to revive the spirit of the lowly
and to revive the heart of the contrite.
[16]I will not accuse forever,
nor will I always be angry,
for then the spirit of man would grow faint before me—
the breath of man that I have created.
[17]I was enraged by his sinful greed;

[a]9 Or *to the king* [b]9 Or *idols* [c]9 Hebrew *Sheol*

OPEN If the President or the Queen were coming to visit you, what repair jobs would you suddenly find time to do?

STUDY 1. What does God promise in verses 15, 18 and 19? What must the people do first? **2.** What does it mean to be lowly and contrite (v. 15)? **3.** What "obstacles" did the people need to clear out of God's way? What "road" needed building up (v. 14)?

APPLY 1. If the wicked are like the tossing sea, how would you picture those at peace with God? Which do you feel like? Why? What might you need to do to quiet things down? What word of peace might Jesus speak to calm you? **2.** In

57:9 you descended to the grave itself! Worship of the Ammonite gods sometimes involved child sacrifice. By engaging in false religion, rebellious participants chose the path that would lead to their distruction (Rom. 1:18–32).

57:10 It is hopeless. The people continued in sin, refusing to give up their false religious practices (Jer. 2:25).

57:11 long been silent. Israel appeared to forget God because he seemed silent to them (Ps. 50:21). He would be silent until it was time for his judgment (42:14).

what ways are you lowly and contrite (v. 15)? In what ways might you sometimes be "high and lofty"? **3.** What "obstacles" (v. 14) are hindering God's work in your life? What areas of your spiritual walk are in need of repair?

OPEN 1. Have you ever fasted? Why or why not? What benefits did you experience? **2.** What is your first reaction to TV or newspaper reports of homeless people: "They probably are just too lazy to work"? or "We ought to do something to help"? Why?

STUDY 1. In what ways did God's people seem to do the right thing (vv. 1–3)? How did they spoil it (vv. 3–5)? **2.** How did their view of fasting differ from God's? If their fasting were sincere, what would be different about their relationships with others? Their concern for the poor? **3.** What is the connection between religious exercises like this and a concern for justice (v. 13; 56:1–2)? How is personal spiritual renewal related to seeking justice for the poor (vv. 8–14)? Which do you think comes first? **4.** Although expressed in physical terms, what do these promises mean spiritually? **5.** Note the relationship between the "yoke of oppression" and the "pointing finger" (v. 9). Where should God's people be looking to discover and remove oppression?

APPLY 1. In which religious activities do you find yourself just going through the motions: Attending church? Reading the Bible? Prayer? Communion services? Fasting? **2.** How should these activities impact us individually and as a community? How are they affecting you now? What attitudes are needed for these activities to be acceptable to the

I punished him, and hid my face in anger,
yet he kept on in his willful ways.
18 I have seen his ways, but I will heal him;
I will guide him and restore comfort to him,
19 creating praise on the lips of the mourners in Israel.
Peace, peace, to those far and near,"
says the LORD. "And I will heal them."
20 But the wicked are like the tossing sea,
which cannot rest,
whose waves cast up mire and mud.
21 "There is no peace," says my God, "for the wicked."

True Fasting

58 "Shout it aloud, do not hold back.
Raise your voice like a trumpet.
Declare to my people their rebellion
and to the house of Jacob their sins.
2 For day after day they seek me out;
they seem eager to know my ways,
as if they were a nation that does what is right
and has not forsaken the commands of its God.
They ask me for just decisions
and seem eager for God to come near them.
3 'Why have we fasted,' they say,
'and you have not seen it?
Why have we humbled ourselves,
and you have not noticed?'

"Yet on the day of your fasting, you do as you please
and exploit all your workers.
4 Your fasting ends in quarreling and strife,
and in striking each other with wicked fists.
You cannot fast as you do today
and expect your voice to be heard on high.
5 Is this the kind of fast I have chosen,
only a day for a man to humble himself?
Is it only for bowing one's head like a reed
and for lying on sackcloth and ashes?
Is that what you call a fast,
a day acceptable to the LORD?

6 "Is not this the kind of fasting I have chosen:
to loose the chains of injustice
and untie the cords of the yoke,
to set the oppressed free
and break every yoke?

57:19 those far and near. God will give comfort to people from all nations, whether Gentiles or Jews (Eph. 2:13).

58:2 day after day they seek me out. Outwardly the people seemed to long for a deeper relationship with God by engaging in ritual worship.

58:3 fasted ... fasting. Refraining from food, repenting of sin and praying signified a humble people before God in times of national calamity. Here they continued in sin, going through the motions, without truly turning their hearts and minds toward God.

58:5 a day acceptable to the LORD? God exposed their hypocrisy. Their self-righteous behavior did not hide their exploitation of employees. Religious activity without obedience is never acceptable to God.

7 Is it not to share your food with the hungry
and to provide the poor wanderer with shelter—
when you see the naked, to clothe him,
and not to turn away from your own flesh and blood?
8 Then your light will break forth like the dawn,
and your healing will quickly appear;
then your righteousness[a] will go before you,
and the glory of the LORD will be your rear guard.
9 Then you will call, and the LORD will answer;
you will cry for help, and he will say: Here am I.

"If you do away with the yoke of oppression,
with the pointing finger and malicious talk,
10 and if you spend yourselves in behalf of the hungry
and satisfy the needs of the oppressed,
then your light will rise in the darkness,
and your night will become like the noonday.
11 The LORD will guide you always;
he will satisfy your needs in a sun-scorched land
and will strengthen your frame.
You will be like a well-watered garden,
like a spring whose waters never fail.
12 Your people will rebuild the ancient ruins
and will raise up the age-old foundations;
you will be called Repairer of Broken Walls,
Restorer of Streets with Dwellings.

13 "If you keep your feet from breaking the Sabbath
and from doing as you please on my holy day,
if you call the Sabbath a delight
and the LORD's holy day honorable,
and if you honor it by not going your own way
and not doing as you please or speaking idle words,
14 then you will find your joy in the LORD,
and I will cause you to ride on the heights of the land
and to feast on the inheritance of your father Jacob."
The mouth of the LORD has spoken.

Sin, Confession and Redemption

59 Surely the arm of the LORD is not too short to save,
nor his ear too dull to hear.
2 But your iniquities have separated
you from your God;
your sins have hidden his face from you,
so that he will not hear.
3 For your hands are stained with blood,
your fingers with guilt.
Your lips have spoken lies,
and your tongue mutters wicked things.

[a]8 Or *your righteous One*

Lord? **3.** Would you be willing to fast from food and other forms of self-fulfillment for one day this week? How can you use that spiritual activity to help satisfy the needs of the oppressed and hungry?

OPEN 1. What kind of stains was your mother most likely to find on your clothes when you were as child: Grass stains on your knees? Chocolate? Paint? Dirt? **2.** When your mother found these stains, how did you "plead your case": Blamed someone else? Pleaded ignorance? Said it would never happen again? Said, "Hey, it's what kids do!"?

STUDY 1. From 58:1–3, what question is on the minds of the people? How does their perception of the problem compare with God's? **2.** Of what sins does God

58:8 light will break. Inner righteousness manifests itself in a concern for others and in acts of justice and mercy. God would bless them with joy and prosperity when they were obedient to him.

accuse them (vv. 3–8)? What would life in this community be like? What does the image of the adder's eggs and spider's web say about the effect of all their sin? **3.** What does each image in verses 9–11 add to your understanding of what has happened as a result of the people's sins? **4.** What will God do about this situation? How does that relate to their confession in verses 12–15? How do you reconcile the picture of God as a warrior (vv. 15–19) with that of the redeemer (v. 20)? **5.** What will be the results of God's action on those who have opposed him? On those who repent? On the nations? **6.** What is the covenant Isaiah speaks of in verse 21? What is required of the people?

APPLY 1. When have you experienced blindness like that described in verse 10? What effective aids or artificial props did you use to grope through life's darkness? Did God break through to you in that dark time? How? **2.** Paul exhorts followers of Christ to wear the armor that God wears (v. 17; Eph. 6:13–17). How might this help you face evil and injustice? What is one way you can suit up and be God's instrument in bringing salvation to others this week?

---

4 No one calls for justice;
  no one pleads his case with integrity.
They rely on empty arguments and speak lies;
  they conceive trouble and give birth to evil.
5 They hatch the eggs of vipers
  and spin a spider's web.
Whoever eats their eggs will die,
  and when one is broken, an adder is hatched.
6 Their cobwebs are useless for clothing;
  they cannot cover themselves with what they make.
Their deeds are evil deeds,
  and acts of violence are in their hands.
7 Their feet rush into sin;
  they are swift to shed innocent blood.
Their thoughts are evil thoughts;
  ruin and destruction mark their ways.
8 The way of peace they do not know;
  there is no justice in their paths.
They have turned them into crooked roads;
  no one who walks in them will know peace.

9 So justice is far from us,
  and righteousness does not reach us.
We look for light, but all is darkness;
  for brightness, but we walk in deep shadows.
10 Like the blind we grope along the wall,
  feeling our way like men without eyes.
At midday we stumble as if it were twilight;
  among the strong, we are like the dead.
11 We all growl like bears;
  we moan mournfully like doves.
We look for justice, but find none;
  for deliverance, but it is far away.

12 For our offenses are many in your sight,
  and our sins testify against us.
Our offenses are ever with us,
  and we acknowledge our iniquities:
13 rebellion and treachery against the LORD,
  turning our backs on our God,
fomenting oppression and revolt,
  uttering lies our hearts have conceived.
14 So justice is driven back,
  and righteousness stands at a distance;
truth has stumbled in the streets,
  honesty cannot enter.

59:4 no one pleads his case with integrity. The poor received no fairness in the law courts, evidence of the nation's spiritual depravity.

59:7 Their feet rush ... to shed innocent blood. Used in Romans 3:15–17 to demonstrate the universality of sin.

evil thoughts. Sin begins in the mind (James 1:14–15).

59:9 all is darkness ... walk in deep shadows. Spiritual corruption leads to blindness to one's sin and to eventual death. Light and darkness contrast eternal life with death and truth with lies.

59:10 like men without eyes. This was part of the covenant curse on the disobedient (Deut. 28:29). Without God's light in our lives, we live in darkness, unable to see.

59:11 growl like bears. Expressed frustration and despair.

[15]Truth is nowhere to be found,
and whoever shuns evil becomes a prey.

The LORD looked and was displeased
that there was no justice.
[16]He saw that there was no one,
he was appalled that there was no one to intervene;
so his own arm worked salvation for him,
and his own righteousness sustained him.
[17]He put on righteousness as his breastplate,
and the helmet of salvation on his head;
he put on the garments of vengeance
and wrapped himself in zeal as in a cloak.
[18]According to what they have done,
so will he repay
wrath to his enemies
and retribution to his foes;
he will repay the islands their due.
[19]From the west, men will fear the name of the LORD,
and from the rising of the sun, they will revere his glory.
For he will come like a pent-up flood
that the breath of the LORD drives along.[a]
[20]"The Redeemer will come to Zion,
to those in Jacob who repent of their sins,"
declares the LORD.

[21]"As for me, this is my covenant with them," says the LORD. "My Spirit, who is on you, and my words that I have put in your mouth will not depart from your mouth, or from the mouths of your children, or from the mouths of their descendants from this time on and forever," says the LORD.

The Glory of Zion

60 "Arise, shine, for your light has come,
and the glory of the LORD rises upon you.
[2]See, darkness covers the earth
and thick darkness is over the peoples,
but the LORD rises upon you
and his glory appears over you.
[3]Nations will come to your light,
and kings to the brightness of your dawn.

[4]"Lift up your eyes and look about you:
All assemble and come to you;
your sons come from afar,
and your daughters are carried on the arm.

[a]19 *Or When the enemy comes in like a flood, / the Spirit of the LORD will put him to flight*

OPEN 1. What do you like best about a parade: Bands? Floats? Military displays? Have you ever felt tingles down your spine of pride or joy during such an event? Describe it. **2.** Have you ever witnessed a total eclipse of the sun or moon? How did you feel?

STUDY 1. How do you understand verses 1–3 in light of 59:10? In light of 9:1–2? How intense will that coming light be (vv. 19–20)? What does the prophet mean by this? **2.** Is the light prophesied by Isaiah a future hope, a present reality or both? Why do you think so (John 4:23; Rev. 21:23–25)? **3.** What are some of the major themes seen throughout Isaiah

59:17 put on righteousness as his breastplate. God fights for his people like a warrior. Believers need to put on Christ's armor in the fight against Satan (Eph. 6:14–17).

59:20 who repent of their sins. Jesus Christ will save all who turn from sin and put their faith in him (Rom. 11:26).

59:21 my covenant. The Messiah will return in judgment and enter into a new covenant with believing Israel (Jer. 31:31), pouring his spirit on them.

60:1 Arise, shine. Zion will both receive and reflect God's light and blessing. God is the light—his light will endure forever.

which this song ties together (2:2–3; 9:1; 14:1–2; 27:12; 30:26; 49:22–23)? **4.** From what directions will people come to Jerusalem? How will they do so? Why will they do so? What will change as a result for Jerusalem? For the nations? **5.** Since a city's gates were normally closed at night as a defense against enemies, what does verse 11 say about the new situation God will bring about? **6.** What does the Lord mean by "in its time I will do this swiftly" (v. 22)? When and how will this come to pass?

APPLY 1. Where in the range of "darkness" (v. 2) to "radiance" (v. 5) are you this week? What aspects of the Christian life have lost their shine since your salvation? Which have gained new sparkle? What can help you shine more brightly? **2.** How can this song encourage you at a time when peace and righteousness are missing from community life? What can you do to help nurture peace and righteousness within yourself and those around you? **3.** Daydream, as a group, about what it would be like if Jesus returned tomorrow and set up his throne in Jerusalem. What would it be like to see Jesus in person? How would you feel then about the important and urgent matters of your daily life? Spend some time together in praise and worship.

5 Then you will look and be radiant,
your heart will throb and swell with joy;
the wealth on the seas will be brought to you,
to you the riches of the nations will come.
6 Herds of camels will cover your land,
young camels of Midian and Ephah.
And all from Sheba will come,
bearing gold and incense
and proclaiming the praise of the LORD.
7 All Kedar's flocks will be gathered to you,
the rams of Nebaioth will serve you;
they will be accepted as offerings on my altar,
and I will adorn my glorious temple.

8 "Who are these that fly along like clouds,
like doves to their nests?
9 Surely the islands look to me;
in the lead are the ships of Tarshish,[a]
bringing your sons from afar,
with their silver and gold,
to the honor of the LORD your God,
the Holy One of Israel,
for he has endowed you with splendor.

10 "Foreigners will rebuild your walls,
and their kings will serve you.
Though in anger I struck you,
in favor I will show you compassion.
11 Your gates will always stand open,
they will never be shut, day or night,
so that men may bring you the wealth of the nations—
their kings led in triumphal procession.
12 For the nation or kingdom that will not serve you will perish;
it will be utterly ruined.

13 "The glory of Lebanon will come to you,
the pine, the fir and the cypress together,
to adorn the place of my sanctuary;
and I will glorify the place of my feet.
14 The sons of your oppressors will come bowing before you;
all who despise you will bow down at your feet
and will call you the City of the LORD,
Zion of the Holy One of Israel.

15 "Although you have been forsaken and hated,
with no one traveling through,
I will make you the everlasting pride
and the joy of all generations.

[a]9 Or *the trading ships*

60:5 wealth on the seas will be brought. At the beginning of the Millennium when Israel is restored to her land, redeemed people from other nations will bring great wealth to Israel.

60:11 gates will always stand open. Zion will be secure and won't need locked gates for protection. **wealth.** The gates will also be open to allow believers and their wealth into the city.

[16]You will drink the milk of nations
and be nursed at royal breasts.
Then you will know that I, the LORD, am your Savior,
your Redeemer, the Mighty One of Jacob.
[17]Instead of bronze I will bring you gold,
and silver in place of iron.
Instead of wood I will bring you bronze,
and iron in place of stones.
I will make peace your governor
and righteousness your ruler.
[18]No longer will violence be heard in your land,
nor ruin or destruction within your borders,
but you will call your walls Salvation
and your gates Praise.
[19]The sun will no more be your light by day,
nor will the brightness of the moon shine on you,
for the LORD will be your everlasting light,
and your God will be your glory.
[20]Your sun will never set again,
and your moon will wane no more;
the LORD will be your everlasting light,
and your days of sorrow will end.
[21]Then will all your people be righteous
and they will possess the land forever.
They are the shoot I have planted,
the work of my hands,
for the display of my splendor.
[22]The least of you will become a thousand,
the smallest a mighty nation.
I am the LORD;
in its time I will do this swiftly."

The Year of the Lord's Favor

61 The Spirit of the Sovereign LORD is on me,
because the LORD has anointed me
to preach good news to the poor.
He has sent me to bind up the brokenhearted,
to proclaim freedom for the captives
and release from darkness for the prisoners,[a]
[2]to proclaim the year of the LORD's favor
and the day of vengeance of our God,
to comfort all who mourn,
[3] and provide for those who grieve in Zion—
to bestow on them a crown of beauty
instead of ashes,
the oil of gladness
instead of mourning,
and a garment of praise

[a]1 Hebrew; Septuagint *the blind*

OPEN 1. In your family chores or in your work situation, what is the dirtiest job you have to do? What clothes do you wear to do it? **2.** When you celebrate special occasions, what clothes do you wear? How do these clothes affect your mood?

STUDY 1. What good news is the prophet bringing to the poor, broken-hearted and grief-stricken? **2.** What stories from the Gospels portray Jesus' ministry in terms of verses 1–3 (Luke 4:18–19)? **3.** During times of grief, people would put on sackcloth and cover themselves with ashes as a sign of their mourning. With what will God replace these garments? **4.** Are the promises in verses 4–7 primarily material or spiritual in nature? Why? Priests were supported by the

61:3 bestow on them a crown of beauty. In place of the ashes that signify mourning, the Israelites will wear a crown symbolizing joy (Ps. 30:11). This is to be a time of celebration—mourning period is over.

gifts of the worshippers, so what is the implication in verse 6? **5.** How extensive is this priesthood? Who are the worshippers? Why is God going to do this for the people (vv. 8–9)? **6.** Verses 10–11 present the people's response to the Lord's promises. In what way are they like a bride? A garden? What emotions are these images meant to convey?

APPLY 1. Do you feel as though you are "wearing ashes" or are you "trying on new clothes"? Why? In what way do you especially want to see God bring this freedom to you? **2.** How do each of the following key words in this passage apply to you spiritually: Poor? Brokenhearted? Captive? **3.** In your response to God's promises, are you like a person preparing for marriage, or one wondering whether to go out on a second date? Why?

OPEN 1. Do you know the meanings of your names? For what reason were you given your first and middle names? What did they mean to your parents? What do they mean to you? **2.** What was one of the more exuberant weddings you have attended? What made it so much fun?

instead of a spirit of despair.
They will be called oaks of righteousness,
a planting of the LORD
for the display of his splendor.

4 They will rebuild the ancient ruins
and restore the places long devastated;
they will renew the ruined cities
that have been devastated for generations.
5 Aliens will shepherd your flocks;
foreigners will work your fields and vineyards.
6 And you will be called priests of the LORD,
you will be named ministers of our God.
You will feed on the wealth of nations,
and in their riches you will boast.

7 Instead of their shame
my people will receive a double portion,
and instead of disgrace
they will rejoice in their inheritance;
and so they will inherit a double portion in their land,
and everlasting joy will be theirs.

8 "For I, the LORD, love justice;
I hate robbery and iniquity.
In my faithfulness I will reward them
and make an everlasting covenant with them.
9 Their descendants will be known among the nations
and their offspring among the peoples.
All who see them will acknowledge
that they are a people the LORD has blessed."

10 I delight greatly in the LORD;
my soul rejoices in my God.
For he has clothed me with garments of salvation
and arrayed me in a robe of righteousness,
as a bridegroom adorns his head like a priest,
and as a bride adorns herself with her jewels.
11 For as the soil makes the sprout come up
and a garden causes seeds to grow,
so the Sovereign LORD will make righteousness and praise
spring up before all nations.

Zion's New Name

62 For Zion's sake I will not keep silent,
for Jerusalem's sake I will not remain quiet,
till her righteousness shines out like the dawn,
her salvation like a blazing torch.
2 The nations will see your righteousness,
and all kings your glory;

61:4 restore the places long devastated. The cities of Israel, destroyed many years ago, will be rebuilt after the exile.

61:6 priests of the LORD. Along with Christ, the priests will intercede for the people, asking for forgiveness of their sins (1 Peter 2:9–10).

62:2 new name. Signified a new status and a new righteous character. Names often represented one's anticipated or present character.

you will be called by a new name
that the mouth of the LORD will bestow.
[3]You will be a crown of splendor in the LORD's hand,
a royal diadem in the hand of your God.
[4]No longer will they call you Deserted,
or name your land Desolate.
But you will be called Hephzibah,[a]
and your land Beulah[b];
for the LORD will take delight in you,
and your land will be married.
[5]As a young man marries a maiden,
so will your sons[c] marry you;
as a bridegroom rejoices over his bride,
so will your God rejoice over you.

[6]I have posted watchmen on your walls, O Jerusalem;
they will never be silent day or night.
You who call on the LORD,
give yourselves no rest,
[7]and give him no rest till he establishes Jerusalem
and makes her the praise of the earth.

[8]The LORD has sworn by his right hand
and by his mighty arm:
"Never again will I give your grain
as food for your enemies,
and never again will foreigners drink the new wine
for which you have toiled;
[9]but those who harvest it will eat it
and praise the LORD,
and those who gather the grapes will drink it
in the courts of my sanctuary."

[10]Pass through, pass through the gates!
Prepare the way for the people.
Build up, build up the highway!
Remove the stones.
Raise a banner for the nations.

[11]The LORD has made proclamation
to the ends of the earth:
"Say to the Daughter of Zion,
'See, your Savior comes!
See, his reward is with him,
and his recompense accompanies him.'"
[12]They will be called the Holy People,
the Redeemed of the LORD;
and you will be called Sought After,
the City No Longer Deserted.

[a]4 *Hephzibah* means *my delight is in her.* [b]4 *Beulah* means *married.* [c]5 Or *Builder*

STUDY 1. What is God's intent for his people (62:1–2)? What is the relationship between God's plan for the nations and the restoration of his people (62:2)? **2.** What does each new name indicate about God's new relationship with his people (62:4,12; 60:14,18)? Why is a new name so important for Zion? What names and words have been associated with her in the past? Why? Why will they no longer be appropriate? **3.** What things does the picture of marriage communicate about God's relationship to his people (62:5; compare 61:10)? **4.** Normally, watchmen were guards who kept a lookout for enemies approaching the city, but what is the purpose of the watchmen in this new Jerusalem? **5.** What are these watchmen like (62:6–7; compare 56:10)? What are they calling to God for? Why give him "no rest"? **6.** "Edom" (symbol for God's enemies) means red. What might the symbols used in 63:1–6 mean? How is this the flip side of the salvation coming to Jerusalem? **7.** What does this picture of God as a warrior add to the other images of God in (62:1–12)?

APPLY 1. Of the new names God gives to the people he saves, which one means the most to you right now? Why? **2.** Do you normally tend to think of God's relationship with you as that of a bride to her waiting bridegroom? Or a judge to a criminal? Why? How does each picture affect your view of God? Of yourself? What does it mean to you that the bride and bridegroom image is the one he invites us to consider in his relationship with us? **3.** Is there anything you want so much that you will neither rest, nor give God rest, until you see it come to pass? What does this mean for your prayer life?

62:6 watchmen on your walls. Guards stationed on city walls looked for any approaching enemy. Here it refers to prophets "who call on the Lord." **no rest.** The prophets who interceded for the people were to be vigilant on Jerusalem's behalf, continually praying for God's promised reestablishment of the city. Believers are to pray for things God has already promised, as Jesus taught his disciples in Matthew 6:10.

God's Day of Vengeance and Redemption

63 Who is this coming from Edom,
from Bozrah, with his garments stained crimson?
Who is this, robed in splendor,
striding forward in the greatness of his strength?

"It is I, speaking in righteousness,
mighty to save."

2 Why are your garments red,
like those of one treading the winepress?

3 "I have trodden the winepress alone;
from the nations no one was with me.
I trampled them in my anger
and trod them down in my wrath;
their blood spattered my garments,
and I stained all my clothing.
4 For the day of vengeance was in my heart,
and the year of my redemption has come.
5 I looked, but there was no one to help,
I was appalled that no one gave support;
so my own arm worked salvation for me,
and my own wrath sustained me.
6 I trampled the nations in my anger;
in my wrath I made them drunk
and poured their blood on the ground."

Praise and Prayer

7 I will tell of the kindnesses of the LORD,
the deeds for which he is to be praised,
according to all the LORD has done for us—
yes, the many good things he has done
for the house of Israel,
according to his compassion and many kindnesses.
8 He said, "Surely they are my people,
sons who will not be false to me";
and so he became their Savior.
9 In all their distress he too was distressed,
and the angel of his presence saved them.
In his love and mercy he redeemed them;
he lifted them up and carried them
all the days of old.
10 Yet they rebelled
and grieved his Holy Spirit.
So he turned and became their enemy
and he himself fought against them.

OPEN 1. What are the three most common emotions you feel when you come to God in prayer? **2.** When you were a teenager, did you ever get in trouble trying to rebel against your parents' authority? How did they respond? **3.** If you could have switched roles and been the parent, how would you have responded to this teenage rebellion?

STUDY This long prayer sums up the desires of the prophet as he anticipates the salvation God has promised. **1.** What things might the prophet be recalling as he considers "the many good things God has done for the house of Israel" (63:7–9)? What do these verses express about God's relationship to Israel? **2.** What might the prophet mean in 63:10 (Ps. 78:17–22)? **3.** In 63:11–19, the prophet moves from recalling the past to considering the

---

63:1 Bozrah. *The main town of Edom, an enemy of Israel that God would judge.*

63:5 wrath sustained me. In the final battle of Armageddon, God will defeat his enemies. Sin produces anger in God because it offends his holiness.

63:7 I will tell. As a representative of the people, Isaiah publicly proclaimed God's mercy, love and goodness. Recalling God's loving actions in the past helps believers to trust in his provision for the present and future.

[11]Then his people recalled[a] the days of old,
the days of Moses and his people—
where is he who brought them through the sea,
with the shepherd of his flock?
Where is he who set
his Holy Spirit among them,
[12]who sent his glorious arm of power
to be at Moses' right hand,
who divided the waters before them,
to gain for himself everlasting renown,
[13]who led them through the depths?
Like a horse in open country,
they did not stumble;
[14]like cattle that go down to the plain,
they were given rest by the Spirit of the LORD.
This is how you guided your people
to make for yourself a glorious name.

[15]Look down from heaven and see
from your lofty throne, holy and glorious.
Where are your zeal and your might?
Your tenderness and compassion are withheld from us.
[16]But you are our Father,
though Abraham does not know us
or Israel acknowledge us;
you, O LORD, are our Father,
our Redeemer from of old is your name.
[17]Why, O LORD, do you make us wander from your ways
and harden our hearts so we do not revere you?
Return for the sake of your servants,
the tribes that are your inheritance.
[18]For a little while your people possessed your holy place,
but now our enemies have trampled down your sanctuary.
[19]We are yours from of old;
but you have not ruled over them,
they have not been called by your name.[b]

64 Oh, that you would rend the heavens and come down,
that the mountains would tremble before you!
[2]As when fire sets twigs ablaze
and causes water to boil,
come down to make your name known to your enemies
and cause the nations to quake before you!
[3]For when you did awesome things that we did not expect,
you came down, and the mountains trembled before you.
[4]Since ancient times no one has heard,
no ear has perceived,

[a]11 Or *But may he recall* [b]19 Or *We are like those you have never ruled, / like those never called by your name*

present. What questions must be on the minds of the exiles as they face their present suffering? What does this prayer tell you about their emotional state? What things upset them? Do you see this as more a prayer of confession, or of complaint? Why? **4.** How would you compare the tone of the prayer in 64:1–4 to that in 63:15–19? What does that tell you about the emotional state of the prophet? About his real desire? **5.** In those days, women used strips of old cloth to catch their menstrual flow. What does that image (64:6) illustrate about the spiritual state of the exiles? What does the shriveled leaf illustrate? **6.** In view of their spiritual bankruptcy, to what truths does the prophet appeal as he asks for God's help (64:8–12)? Why does he think that now is the time for God to act?

APPLY **1.** What is the "exodus event" that you fondly recall in your life when it was clear that God was working in you? **2.** When have you felt that God is not involved in what you are going through? How do you account for his silence in those times? How do you pray then? **3.** Learning from the prophet, choose one area of your own prayer life which might benefit from attention: Repentance, faith, zeal, relationship, boldness, humility, contentedness, concern for God's honor. How will you strengthen this area?

63:17 make us wander from your ways. This phrase recalled wandering in the desert after the Hebrews left Egypt. **harden our hearts.** The Lord confirmed the people in their choice to sin.

64:1 rend the heavens and come down. The sky was depicted as a piece of cloth God would tear as he came to destroy Israel's enemies (Mic. 1:3–4).

no eye has seen any God besides you,
who acts on behalf of those who wait for him.
5 You come to the help of those who gladly do right,
who remember your ways.
But when we continued to sin against them,
you were angry.
How then can we be saved?
6 All of us have become like one who is unclean,
and all our righteous acts are like filthy rags;
we all shrivel up like a leaf,
and like the wind our sins sweep us away.
7 No one calls on your name
or strives to lay hold of you;
for you have hidden your face from us
and made us waste away because of our sins.

8 Yet, O LORD, you are our Father.
We are the clay, you are the potter;
we are all the work of your hand.
9 Do not be angry beyond measure, O LORD;
do not remember our sins forever.
Oh, look upon us, we pray,
for we are all your people.
10 Your sacred cities have become a desert;
even Zion is a desert, Jerusalem a desolation.
11 Our holy and glorious temple, where our fathers praised you,
has been burned with fire,
and all that we treasured lies in ruins.
12 After all this, O LORD, will you hold yourself back?
Will you keep silent and punish us beyond measure?

Judgment and Salvation

65 "I revealed myself to those who did not ask for me;
I was found by those who did not seek me.
To a nation that did not call on my name,
I said, 'Here am I, here am I.'
2 All day long I have held out my hands
to an obstinate people,
who walk in ways not good,
pursuing their own imaginations—
3 a people who continually provoke me
to my very face,
offering sacrifices in gardens
and burning incense on altars of brick;
4 who sit among the graves
and spend their nights keeping secret vigil;
who eat the flesh of pigs,

OPEN 1. Have you had a cherished possession that was broken, lost or stolen? How did you feel? How would you have felt if you had given it away? **2.** When you were a kid playing hide-and-seek, did you prefer being the hider or the seeker? Where was a favorite hiding place?

STUDY This section is God's reply to the prayer of chapter 64. **1.** What has been God's frustration in his relationship with Israel? How would he answer the questions of the people in 64:11–12? **2.** Verses 3–5 and 11 depict practices associated with idolatry. How does God react to these practices? Why did judgment have to come upon Israel (vv. 1–5)?

64:6 righteous acts are like filthy rags. *Sins were described as the color red—a warning of loss, of hurt, of defeat—in 1:18. Compared to God's righteousness, even our good behavior is nothing.*

65:1 did not ask ... did not seek. God allowed himself to be found as he continually reached out in love to Israel. He was ready to help them, but even though he was speaking they did not respond.

65:3 continually provoke me. The people disobeyed God by worshiping idols and consulting mediums and spiritists. **to my very face.** They did not hide their shameful activities, but they defiantly and boldly sacrificed to idols.

and whose pots hold broth of unclean meat;
5 who say, 'Keep away; don't come near me,
for I am too sacred for you!'
Such people are smoke in my nostrils,
a fire that keeps burning all day.

6 "See, it stands written before me:
I will not keep silent but will pay back in full;
I will pay it back into their laps—
7 both your sins and the sins of your fathers,"
says the LORD.
"Because they burned sacrifices on the mountains
and defied me on the hills,
I will measure into their laps
the full payment for their former deeds."

8 This is what the LORD says:

"As when juice is still found in a cluster of grapes
and men say, 'Don't destroy it,
there is yet some good in it,'
so will I do in behalf of my servants;
I will not destroy them all.
9 I will bring forth descendants from Jacob,
and from Judah those who will possess my mountains;
my chosen people will inherit them,
and there will my servants live.
10 Sharon will become a pasture for flocks,
and the Valley of Achor a resting place for herds,
for my people who seek me.

11 "But as for you who forsake the LORD
and forget my holy mountain,
who spread a table for Fortune
and fill bowls of mixed wine for Destiny,
12 I will destine you for the sword,
and you will all bend down for the slaughter;
for I called but you did not answer,
I spoke but you did not listen.
You did evil in my sight
and chose what displeases me."

13 Therefore this is what the Sovereign LORD says:

"My servants will eat,
but you will go hungry;
my servants will drink,
but you will go thirsty;
my servants will rejoice,
but you will be put to shame.
14 My servants will sing
out of the joy of their hearts,
but you will cry out

3. Although their sin of idolatry is the focus here, what other sins have led up to judgment (56:9–12; 58:3–4; 59:3–4)? How might these sins all stem from the practice of idolatry? **4.** Compare verses 8–12 with 10:20–23. What do they have in common? How is the emphasis of each different? What promises are here for those who have not followed the way of idolatry? **5.** What do the contrasts in verses 13–16 show about the quality of life God intends for his people (compare Luke 6:20–26)? What will happen to those who have placed their hope in other gods?

APPLY 1. When have you been so caught up with chasing after modern "idols" that you have been unable to hear God calling you? What did it take for him to finally break through? **2.** How can the promises of verses 13–16 be of help when you feel spiritually hungry, thirsty and ashamed? **3.** In terms of "hide and seek," do you see God in your own life as more the hider or the seeker? Is there any area in your life today where God is holding out his hands (v. 2) or calling, "Here am I" (v. 1)? How will you respond?

65:5 I am too sacred for you! Idolaters are like the Pharisees in the New Testament whom Jesus called children of the devil (John 8:44). They thought of themselves as better than others.

from anguish of heart
and wail in brokenness of spirit.
15 You will leave your name
to my chosen ones as a curse;
the Sovereign LORD will put you to death,
but to his servants he will give another name.
16 Whoever invokes a blessing in the land
will do so by the God of truth;
he who takes an oath in the land
will swear by the God of truth.
For the past troubles will be forgotten
and hidden from my eyes.

New Heavens and a New Earth

17 "Behold, I will create
new heavens and a new earth.
The former things will not be remembered,
nor will they come to mind.
18 But be glad and rejoice forever
in what I will create,
for I will create Jerusalem to be a delight
and its people a joy.
19 I will rejoice over Jerusalem
and take delight in my people;
the sound of weeping and of crying
will be heard in it no more.

20 "Never again will there be in it
an infant who lives but a few days,
or an old man who does not live out his years;
he who dies at a hundred
will be thought a mere youth;
he who fails to reach[a] a hundred
will be considered accursed.
21 They will build houses and dwell in them;
they will plant vineyards and eat their fruit.
22 No longer will they build houses and others live in them,
or plant and others eat.
For as the days of a tree,
so will be the days of my people;
my chosen ones will long enjoy
the works of their hands.
23 They will not toil in vain
or bear children doomed to misfortune;
for they will be a people blessed by the LORD,
they and their descendants with them.
24 Before they call I will answer;

[a]20 Or / *the sinner who reaches*

OPEN 1. Who is the oldest person you have ever known? What insight into life did you pick up from him or her? **2.** As a child, how did you picture what heaven must be like?

STUDY 1. What emotion will typify the relationship of the restored people to God? Of God to them? What accounts for this new state of affairs? **2.** What will life be like when the exiles are freed? What is the reality that lies behind each figure of speech? **3.** What promises, echoed elsewhere in Isaiah, are summed up in this section (2:4; 11:6–9; 14:1; 30:19; 32:18)? **4.** How does the account of the creation and fall figure as background to this passage? What do we learn here about God's purposes and plans? **5.** How does this new creation come into being for us (2 Cor. 5:17)? What will be the impact of this truth on our lifestyle (2 Peter 3:11–13)? What does this vision ultimately mean to us (Rev. 21:1–5)?

APPLY 1. Try to picture your life without any of the causes or results of grief, sin and pain. What would that free you to do? **2.** How might this vision of what God will bring about affect the way you deal with the struggles you face now?

65:15 my chosen ones as a curse. Believers will refer to rebellious Israelites as an example of those receiving judgment. The name of evil King Ahab was used as a curse. The restored remnant would receive both a new name and a new character as a blessing.

65:18 create Jerusalem to be a delight. God created the earth and heavens, and God will create a new world for the enjoyment of his people when Christ returns (Rev. 21:1).

while they are still speaking I will hear.
25 The wolf and the lamb will feed together,
and the lion will eat straw like the ox,
but dust will be the serpent's food.
They will neither harm nor destroy
on all my holy mountain,"
says the LORD.

Judgment and Hope

66 This is what the LORD says:

"Heaven is my throne,
and the earth is my footstool.
Where is the house you will build for me?
Where will my resting place be?
2 Has not my hand made all these things,
and so they came into being?"
declares the LORD.

"This is the one I esteem:
he who is humble and contrite in spirit,
and trembles at my word.
3 But whoever sacrifices a bull
is like one who kills a man,
and whoever offers a lamb,
like one who breaks a dog's neck;
whoever makes a grain offering
is like one who presents pig's blood,
and whoever burns memorial incense,
like one who worships an idol.
They have chosen their own ways,
and their souls delight in their abominations;
4 so I also will choose harsh treatment for them
and will bring upon them what they dread.
For when I called, no one answered,
when I spoke, no one listened.
They did evil in my sight
and chose what displeases me."

5 Hear the word of the LORD,
you who tremble at his word:
"Your brothers who hate you,
and exclude you because of my name, have said,
'Let the LORD be glorified,
that we may see your joy!'
Yet they will be put to shame.
6 Hear that uproar from the city,
hear that noise from the temple!
It is the sound of the LORD
repaying his enemies all they deserve.

OPEN 1. What is one of the most beautiful churches or cathedrals you have seen? What emotions did it evoke as you walked in? As you joined in the worship service? **2.** Did you ever do something to please your parents or teachers which invoked their displeasure instead? Tell about it. How did you feel?

STUDY Before the exile, the temple of Jerusalem was viewed as the proof of God's dwelling in the midst of Israel. The returning exiles were anxious to rebuild the temple that had been destroyed by the Babylonians. **1.** What is the significance of verses 1–2 as God's final word to the people? What would they mean to you as you signed on to work in the temple reconstruction program? **2.** Verses 3–6 indicate that the exiles looked forward to being able to resume offering the sacrifices commanded under the Mosaic Law. Why would God choose to disavow their cherished temple practices at this time? How does this relate to the warnings given much earlier (1:10–17)? Why does Isaiah warn them again at this point? **3.** The image of a mother is used here (vv. 7–13) to describe the new Jerusalem and the Lord giving birth and nursing their respective children. This contrasts with an earlier picture of Zion as barren (54:1) and with our usual view of God as Father. Who are these sons and daughters? Are they the same ones as in 49:18–22? Or as in 60:4–5? Why do you think so? **4.** What does the image of God as a mother convey about the renewed relationship God will establish with these people? **5.** Verses 14–18 and 24 focus on God's judgment. To whom is this directed (vv. 14–18,24)? What is God's purpose in ending this book with this final warning? **6.** Throughout Isaiah, God's ultimate concern has been for all nations. How does that come to its final expression in verses 19–

66:1 Where is the house? God cannot be contained in any building (1 Kin. 8:27). He is everywhere.

22? **7.** Looking at a map, in what directions will God's representatives be sent? (Note: Tubal was an area near the Black Sea.) Why? How is this prophecy to be fulfilled (Ezek. 6:8–9; Matt. 24:30; 28:18–20; Acts 1:8; Rev. 21)?

APPLY 1. In your background, what religious traditions do you especially value: Communion? Certain holidays? Certain mode of baptism? Saying the creeds? Special type of building? The Scriptures? Other? How important are these things to you now? **2.** How would you feel if you were suddenly forced (or asked by God) to stop practicing these traditions? How would you feel if, like the sons and daughters in this chapter, you were once again free to do so? **3.** When have you found yourself focusing on the forms of worship and missing the reality of what it's all about? What is worship all about (vv. 2–5)?

7 "Before she goes into labor,
she gives birth;
before the pains come upon her,
she delivers a son.
8 Who has ever heard of such a thing?
Who has ever seen such things?
Can a country be born in a day
or a nation be brought forth in a moment?
Yet no sooner is Zion in labor
than she gives birth to her children.
9 Do I bring to the moment of birth
and not give delivery?" says the LORD.
"Do I close up the womb
when I bring to delivery?" says your God.
10 "Rejoice with Jerusalem and be glad for her,
all you who love her;
rejoice greatly with her,
all you who mourn over her.
11 For you will nurse and be satisfied
at her comforting breasts;
you will drink deeply
and delight in her overflowing abundance."

12 For this is what the LORD says:

"I will extend peace to her like a river,
and the wealth of nations like a flooding stream;
you will nurse and be carried on her arm
and dandled on her knees.
13 As a mother comforts her child,
so will I comfort you;
and you will be comforted over Jerusalem."

14 When you see this, your heart will rejoice
and you will flourish like grass;
the hand of the LORD will be made known to his servants,
but his fury will be shown to his foes.
15 See, the LORD is coming with fire,
and his chariots are like a whirlwind;
he will bring down his anger with fury,
and his rebuke with flames of fire.
16 For with fire and with his sword
the LORD will execute judgment upon all men,
and many will be those slain by the LORD.

17 "Those who consecrate and purify themselves to go into the gardens, following the one in the midst of[a] those who eat the flesh of pigs and rats and other abominable things—they will meet their end together," declares the LORD.

[a] 17 *Or gardens behind one of your temples, and*

66:7 Before ... labor ... before the pains. Israel's return to the land will happen so quickly that it will occur without pain. Zion here is pictured as the mother of Israel, which is also the Messiah.

66:11 delight in her overflowing abundance. The people in Jerusalem will enjoy the city as an infant enjoys food provided by its mother. Everyone will rejoice.

[18]"And I, because of their actions and their imaginations, am about
to come[a] and gather all nations and tongues, and they will come and
see my glory.
[19]"I will set a sign among them, and I will send some of those who
survive to the nations—to Tarshish, to the Libyans[b] and Lydians (famous as archers), to Tubal and Greece, and to the distant islands that have not heard of my fame or seen my glory. They will proclaim my
glory among the nations. [20]And they will bring all your brothers, from
all the nations, to my holy mountain in Jerusalem as an offering to the LORD—on horses, in chariots and wagons, and on mules and camels," says the LORD. "They will bring them, as the Israelites bring their grain offerings, to the temple of the LORD in ceremonially clean
vessels. [21]And I will select some of them also to be priests and Levites," says the LORD.

[22]"As the new heavens and the new earth that I make will endure before me," declares the LORD, "so will your name and descendants
endure. [23]From one New Moon to another and from one Sabbath to another, all mankind will come and bow down before me," says the
LORD. [24]"And they will go out and look upon the dead bodies of those who rebelled against me; their worm will not die, nor will their fire be quenched, and they will be loathsome to all mankind."

[a] *18* The meaning of the Hebrew for this clause is uncertain. [b] *19* Some Septuagint manuscripts *Put* (Libyans); Hebrew *Pul*

66:20 clean vessels. This phrase referred to the Gentiles who, in the Old Testament, were considered pagan and outside the covenant (56:6–7).

66:23 all mankind. Referred to believing Jews and Gentiles from all nations, in contrast to those who reject God (Zech. 14:16).

Jeremiah

Author. Jeremiah is recognized as the author of this prophecy, as identified by his name in the very first verse.

Date. Jeremiah stated his prophecies throughout his ministry, from 626 B.C., during the reign of Josiah, until 560 B.C. Jeremiah wrote and compiled these prophecies with the help of Baruch, his secretary, probably during his exile in Egypt, but he did not compile them in chronological order.

Personal Reading	Group Study Topic and Reading	
1–2	Call of Jeremiah	1:1–19
3–4	Unfaithful Israel	3:6–4:4
5–7	Worthless Religion	7:1–29
8–11	Fountain of Tears	8:4–9:1
12–17	Jeremiah's Complaint	12:1–17
18–19	Potter and Clay	18:1–19:15
20–25	Pashur and Jeremiah	20:1–18
26–29	Jeremiah Threatened	26:1–24
30–32	Restoration of Israel	30:1–24
33–35	Promise of Renewal	33:1–26
36–38	Jeremiah in Prison	37:1–21
39–45	Jeremiah's Last Word	44:1–30
46–52	Fall of Jerusalem	52:1–30

Purpose. Jeremiah prophesied to his people in order to turn them from their sin. He prophesied to the leadership in Judah to influence the nation through them. Jeremiah hoped to see his people repent, turn back to God and escape some of the consequences of their sin. After years of disobedience, punishment was inevitable, and Jeremiah's message changed from warning to preparation. He was aware of the impending hardships and worked to prepare his people for that. Finally, he spoke about the eventual restoration through the Messiah, hoping to set their focus back on God's provision for them.

Historical Background. Jeremiah prophesied just before the collapse of Judah, its military occupation and its subsequent exile into Babylon. For hundreds of years, power in the Near East had been held by Babylon, Assyria and Egypt. These three empires grew and declined, fighting each other and the minor kingdoms in the region for territory and spoils. Israel fell to the Assyrians in 722 B.C. Except for an alliance between King Ahaz and the Assyrian king, Judah might have fallen as well.

By 626 B.C., when Jeremiah began his ministry, Assyria was declining rapidly. In 612 B.C., Assyria's capital city fell to the Babylonians and Medes. In 605 B.C., the Babylonians, led by Nebuchadnezzar, defeated the Egyptians and became the only remaining power in the Near East. They besieged Jerusalem in 605 B.C. and installed a puppet king. In 586 B.C., they took much of the Jerusalem population into captivity in Mesopotamia. Jeremiah was taken against his will to Egypt with a group fleeing the Babylonians. Jeremiah lived through much of this history. He saw the punishment of God at work through Judah's terrors and defeats.

Impending Punishment. Jeremiah called the people of Judah to repent and reject their idol worship. Religious disobedience was the cause of Judah's impending punishment. That punishment would take on the forms described in the covenant Judah made with God: famine, plague, pestilence and war. God had equipped the Assyrians and prepared them without their knowledge or permission to act as his tool of punishment. Assyria, the "destroyer of nations" (4:7), would bring "terrible destruction" (4:6) against Judah. As Jeremiah explained to his fellow Judeans, "Your own conduct and actions have brought this upon you. This is your punishment."

God had the right to punish disobedience. The punishment, like the crime, was not just individual but happened at a national level.

1 The words of Jeremiah son of Hilkiah, one of the priests at Anathoth in the territory of Benjamin. [2]The word of the LORD came to
him in the thirteenth year of the reign of Josiah son of Amon king of
Judah, [3]and through the reign of Jehoiakim son of Josiah king of Judah, down to the fifth month of the eleventh year of Zedekiah son of
Josiah king of Judah, when the people of Jerusalem went into exile.

The Call of Jeremiah

[4]The word of the LORD came to me, saying,

[5]"Before I formed you in the womb I knew[a] you,
before you were born I set you apart;
I appointed you as a prophet to the nations."

[6]"Ah, Sovereign LORD," I said, "I do not know how to speak; I am
only a child."
[7]But the LORD said to me, "Do not say, 'I am only a child.' You must
go to everyone I send you to and say whatever I command you. [8]Do
not be afraid of them, for I am with you and will rescue you," declares
the LORD.
[9]Then the LORD reached out his hand and touched my mouth and
said to me, "Now, I have put my words in your mouth. [10]See, today I
appoint you over nations and kingdoms to uproot and tear down, to
destroy and overthrow, to build and to plant."
[11]The word of the LORD came to me: "What do you see, Jeremiah?"
"I see the branch of an almond tree," I replied.
[12]The LORD said to me, "You have seen correctly, for I am watching[b]
to see that my word is fulfilled."
[13]The word of the LORD came to me again: "What do you see?"
"I see a boiling pot, tilting away from the north," I answered.

[a]5 Or *chose* [b]12 The Hebrew for *watching* sounds like the Hebrew for *almond tree.*

OPEN 1. Where were you born: At home? Hospital? Taxi? What stories about the event have you been told? **2.** Which relative made you feel wanted and safe as a child?

STUDY 1. What was Jeremiah's occupation (v. 1)? What can you deduce about his family and heritage? **2.** When did Josiah rule? When did Zedekiah? How long did Jeremiah prophesy? Through the reigns of which five kings? **3.** What kind of king was Josiah (2 Kin. 22:1–2)? What did he do to renew the worship of the Lord (2 Kin. 23)? **4.** How do you think the "word of the LORD" came to Jeremiah: Voice from the clouds? Human-sounding voice? Inner voice? **5.** How far back does God's relationship with Jeremiah go (v. 5)? How involved was God in preparing Jeremiah? **6.** How does God's call make Jeremiah feel (v. 6)? How old is Jeremiah? What does God say to Jeremiah to confirm his call (vv. 7–8)? **7.** What two object lessons does God give him (vv. 11–15)? Upon what pun does the first depend (see text footnote)? What does the second mean? Why is God going to punish his people (v. 16)? **8.** What opposition will Jeremiah face in his ministry (vv. 17–19)? What does he need to do to overcome it? What things does God promise to do for him?

1:2 Josiah. Josiah became king of Judah at eight years of age. When he matured, he became unhappy at how far his country had drifted from obedience to the Law (2 Kin. 22:11), so he started reforms to renew the nation's spiritual life. Josiah was the last godly king of Judah. After his rule, Judah fell into the terrible spiritual state that Jeremiah cried out against.

1:3 Jehoiakim son of Josiah. After Josiah was killed by Pharaoh Neco (2 Kin. 23:29), his successor lasted only three months, then Jehoiakim was named king by the pharaoh. Jehoiakim was evil, unlike his father Josiah.

1:5 I formed ... knew ... appointed you. God asserted his right to call Jeremiah into service as his prophet. God had made Jeremiah, chosen him and "set him apart" for that task. Jeremiah's calling was the culmination of God's plan for him that began even before his was conceived.

1:6 do not know how to speak. Jeremiah tried the same excuse as Moses had when God called him to service (Ex. 4:10). It did not work for Moses, and it did not work for Jeremiah either. In both cases, God had prepared the men for the roles they were to play (v. 5), and God would provide remedies for any shortcomings the men possessed.

1:7 I am only a child. Youthfulness was no excuse. God knew Jeremiah's shortcomings and called him anyway. Jeremiah is only responsible to go where God sends him and say what God tells him. The prophet need not be old, powerful and wise. He is called to do God's bidding, not his own teaching.

1:8 Do not be afraid. God understood that Jeremiah's objections had their roots in fear. The antidote to fear is the promise of God's presence and deliverance. No matter what their profession or talent, these promises are made to all believers, who are called to serve God.

1:9 touched my mouth. When Moses bemoaned his lack of speaking skill, God appointed Aaron his spokesman (Ex. 4:10–16). For Jeremiah, God simply reached down and placed his words in the prophet's mouth. Jeremiah is a conduit between God and the covenant people.

1:12 I am watching. God tested the verbal cleverness of his prophet with a "sounds like" question. The Hebrew word for "watching" sounds like the word for "almond tree." Prophets had to be able to interpret God's words no matter how subtle. To accentuate this point, God reminded Jeremiah that he would be watching to make sure his word was fulfilled.

1:13 boiling pot. Israel was heading toward difficult days. The "boiling pot" was a domestic image of terrible portent.

APPLY **1.** Do you trust that God has a wonderful plan for your life? Or do you feel somewhat like Jeremiah—dubious and fearful? **2.** When you were little, what did you want to be when you grew up? Which future plans did your parents encourage? Discourage? **3.** How does the Lord communicate with you: Are his plan's for you always clear, sometimes clear or never clear? What role does Scripture play? What about advice, hunches, prayer, circumstances? ______

OPEN **1.** For the never-married: Describe the perfect honeymoon. When, where and with whom? If you have married: Where did you go on your honeymoon? How was the: Travel? Lodging? Weather? What snapshot helps you best remember this time? **2.** Is it hard to maintain "friendship" with past loves? Why or why not?

STUDY Chapters 2–6 of Jeremiah's prophecy are considered to be among his earliest and were delivered midway during the reign of Josiah (3:6), who was the most favorable of all kings to Jeremiah's radical message. These chapters deal with the near total apostasy of Judah and the inevitable foreign invasion which serves as God's retribution. **1.** God pictures Israel as a bride. How did the marriage start out (vv. 2–3)? To what "desert" does he refer (vv. 6–7)? **2.** What went wrong (v. 5)? What did the powerful do that

14The LORD said to me, "From the north disaster will be poured out
on all who live in the land. 15I am about to summon all the peoples of
the northern kingdoms," declares the LORD.

"Their kings will come and set up their thrones
in the entrance of the gates of Jerusalem;
they will come against all her surrounding walls
and against all the towns of Judah.
16I will pronounce my judgments on my people
because of their wickedness in forsaking me,
in burning incense to other gods
and in worshiping what their hands have made.

17"Get yourself ready! Stand up and say to them whatever I command you. Do not be terrified by them, or I will terrify you before
them. 18Today I have made you a fortified city, an iron pillar and a
bronze wall to stand against the whole land—against the kings of
Judah, its officials, its priests and the people of the land. 19They will
fight against you but will not overcome you, for I am with you and
will rescue you," declares the LORD.

Israel Forsakes God

2 The word of the LORD came to me: 2"Go and proclaim in the hearing of Jerusalem:

" 'I remember the devotion of your youth,
how as a bride you loved me
and followed me through the desert,
through a land not sown.
3Israel was holy to the LORD,
the firstfruits of his harvest;
all who devoured her were held guilty,
and disaster overtook them,' "
declares the LORD.

4Hear the word of the LORD, O house of Jacob,
all you clans of the house of Israel.

5This is what the LORD says:

"What fault did your fathers find in me,
that they strayed so far from me?
They followed worthless idols
and became worthless themselves.

The Hebrew word translated "pot" is translated "cauldron" in Job 41:31. The troubles to come were huge.

1:16 pronounce my judgments on my people. God is sovereign over his covenant people. Though they have turned their back on him, God is still their ruler and will assert his power over them. God also has power over the rest of the world. He will use the Babylonians, mortal enemies of his people, to fulfill his divine plan of judgment and punishment.

1:17 terrified by them ... terrify you before them. God's calling had serious consequences for the prophet. He must give the people terrible news without fear. If he failed, God would hold him accountable. In essence, God told Jeremiah, "If you think the people can get angry, you ought to see me!"

2:2 as a bride you loved me. Marriage often illustrated the relationship between God and his people (Isa. 54:5; Hos. 2:16). During the Exodus, Israel had followed God like a young bride who is still enamored with her husband. In Jeremiah's time, that intimacy was just a memory. In the New Testament, Paul compared the husband/wife relationship to that of Jesus and his church (Eph. 5:23).

2:3 firstfruits of his harvest. The Law commanded that Israel sacrifice the first and the best of the harvest to God (Ex. 23:19). In the same way, Israel constituted God's firstfruits; they were his chosen and treasured people.

6 They did not ask, 'Where is the LORD,
who brought us up out of Egypt
and led us through the barren wilderness,
through a land of deserts and rifts,
a land of drought and darkness,[a]
a land where no one travels and no one lives?'
7 I brought you into a fertile land
to eat its fruit and rich produce.
But you came and defiled my land
and made my inheritance detestable.
8 The priests did not ask,
'Where is the LORD?'
Those who deal with the law did not know me;
the leaders rebelled against me.
The prophets prophesied by Baal,
following worthless idols.

9 "Therefore I bring charges against you again,"
declares the LORD.
"And I will bring charges against your children's children.
10 Cross over to the coasts of Kittim[b] and look,
send to Kedar[c] and observe closely;
see if there has ever been anything like this:
11 Has a nation ever changed its gods?
(Yet they are not gods at all.)
But my people have exchanged their[d] Glory
for worthless idols.
12 Be appalled at this, O heavens,
and shudder with great horror,"
declares the LORD.
13 "My people have committed two sins:
They have forsaken me,
the spring of living water,
and have dug their own cisterns,
broken cisterns that cannot hold water.
14 Is Israel a servant, a slave by birth?
Why then has he become plunder?
15 Lions have roared;
they have growled at him.
They have laid waste his land;
his towns are burned and deserted.
16 Also, the men of Memphis[e] and Tahpanhes
have shaved the crown of your head.[f]

[a]6 Or *and the shadow of death* [b]10 That is, Cyprus and western coastlands [c]10 The home of Bedouin tribes in the Syro-Arabian desert [d]11 Masoretic Text; an ancient Hebrew scribal tradition *my* [e]16 Hebrew *Noph* [f]16 Or *have cracked your skull*

was so contrary to God's intent (vv. 6–8)? Where was the Lord all this time? **3.** What charges does God bring? What is so impossible about changing gods (v. 11)? **4.** "Baal" is Hebrew for "master" or "lord." In what way is Baal-worship or idolatry really two sins in one (v. 13)? **5.** What role do "lions" (symbolic of Assyria) and the Egyptians (vv. 15–16; 44:1) play in humiliating and destroying Israel? What role does Israel play in this (vv. 17–19)? What role does God play in sealing Israel's fate (2:36–37)?

APPLY 1. When have you forsaken what you believed in and ended up feeling worthless (v. 5)? **2.** What "barren wilderness" (v. 6) has God led you through to get you where you are today? **3.** How have you acknowledged what God has done for you through how you've served him?

2:6 through the barren wilderness. God had led and nurtured his people through these ordeals during the forty-year journey from Egypt to the Promised Land. All the images of this verse are related to death in some way. Note how the exodus mirrors life: God's will is to deliver us from the bondage of sin, out of the desert of certain death, into the promised glory—the inheritance of God's children.

2:11 exchanged their Glory for worthless idols. It makes sense for a people who worship powerless gods to have idols as they search for some power greater than their own. Yet, how ironic that a people led by the true and powerful God should resort to the worship of idols.

2:13 broken cisterns. Note the contrast between God and the pagan deities represented by idols. God was the source of life-sustaining water while the cisterns could not hold even a drop for the people to drink.

17 Have you not brought this on yourselves
by forsaking the LORD your God
when he led you in the way?
18 Now why go to Egypt
to drink water from the Shihor[a]?
And why go to Assyria
to drink water from the River[b]?
19 Your wickedness will punish you;
your backsliding will rebuke you.
Consider then and realize
how evil and bitter it is for you
when you forsake the LORD your God
and have no awe of me,"
declares the Lord, the LORD Almighty.

20 "Long ago you broke off your yoke
and tore off your bonds;
you said, 'I will not serve you!'
Indeed, on every high hill
and under every spreading tree
you lay down as a prostitute.
21 I had planted you like a choice vine
of sound and reliable stock.
How then did you turn against me
into a corrupt, wild vine?
22 Although you wash yourself with soda
and use an abundance of soap,
the stain of your guilt is still before me,"
declares the Sovereign LORD.
23 "How can you say, 'I am not defiled;
I have not run after the Baals'?
See how you behaved in the valley;
consider what you have done.
You are a swift she-camel
running here and there,
24 a wild donkey accustomed to the desert,
sniffing the wind in her craving—
in her heat who can restrain her?
Any males that pursue her need not tire themselves;
at mating time they will find her.
25 Do not run until your feet are bare
and your throat is dry.
But you said, 'It's no use!

[a]18 That is, a branch of the Nile [b]18 That is, the Euphrates

OPEN **1.** Who is considered the "black sheep" or "wild vine" of your family? How and why did he or she become that way? **2.** Have you ever been accused of something and thought you were innocent? What happened? Did you later discover you were wrong?

STUDY **1.** What word-pictures does Jeremiah paint to describe Israel? How is Israel like a stubborn mule? Like a prostitute? A wild vine? A she-camel? A disgraced thief? A ravenous lion? **2.** How does this picture of prostitutes and animals in heat differ from the earlier one of Israel as the bride (2:2–3)? **3.** How has Israel treated the poor (v. 34)? Did Jewish law permit killing burglars in defense of property (Ex. 22:2–3)? **4.** What punishment of Israel is indicated in 2:35–37? For what reasons? By what means? **5.** What does the analogy of divorce mean in this context (3:1–5)? Who is the one properly entitled to seek divorce: God or Israel? **6.** Who is the one seeking reconciliation? Who is the one likely to reject that effort? Why is that?

APPLY **1.** How do you show your loyalty to God as your first love? How do you handle conflicts of loyalty between God and other loves (such as Israel found herself in)? **2.** How important is loyalty to you in your

2:18 to drink water. Jeremiah returned to the illustration in verse 13. God had provided spiritual and physical food in the desert (v. 6), yet the people *turned away and looked to enemies for* political and spiritual guidance.

2:19 wickedness ... backsliding. The Hebrew word translated "backsliding" implied repeated descents into apostasy. Passages such as 3:22, 5:6 and 14:7 further demonstrate Jeremiah's understanding of backsliding.

2:20 broke off your yoke. Jeremiah compared Judah to a stubborn draft animal that rebelled against its master. Judah would not submit to the yoke of service to God but was more than willing to degrade itself like a prostitute who served the one that paid her.

2:22 wash ... stain. The stain of sin cannot be removed by washing, either literally or figuratively, but only by the grace and forgiveness of God.

I love foreign gods,
and I must go after them.'

26"As a thief is disgraced when he is caught,
so the house of Israel is disgraced—
they, their kings and their officials,
their priests and their prophets.
27They say to wood, 'You are my father,'
and to stone, 'You gave me birth.'
They have turned their backs to me
and not their faces;
yet when they are in trouble, they say,
'Come and save us!'
28Where then are the gods you made for yourselves?
Let them come if they can save you
when you are in trouble!
For you have as many gods
as you have towns, O Judah.

29"Why do you bring charges against me?
You have all rebelled against me,"
declares the LORD.
30"In vain I punished your people;
they did not respond to correction.
Your sword has devoured your prophets
like a ravening lion.

31"You of this generation, consider the word of the LORD:

"Have I been a desert to Israel
or a land of great darkness?
Why do my people say, 'We are free to roam;
we will come to you no more'?
32Does a maiden forget her jewelry,
a bride her wedding ornaments?
Yet my people have forgotten me,
days without number.
33How skilled you are at pursuing love!
Even the worst of women can learn from your ways.
34On your clothes men find
the lifeblood of the innocent poor,
though you did not catch them breaking in.
Yet in spite of all this
35 you say, 'I am innocent;
he is not angry with me.'
But I will pass judgment on you
because you say, 'I have not sinned.'
36Why do you go about so much,

relationships apart from God? To what or whom do you feel most loyal? Why? How loyal do you feel toward your group? In what ways can you show your loyalty to them?

2:31 desert ... land of great darkness ... roam. God rescued the Israelites from bondage and brought them safely through the desert to Canaan. When they would not enter the Promised Land, they were forced to roam for forty years. The great irony of this verse was that the one who delivered Israel through the desert, and through their wandering, was now shunned because the people wanted to roam on their own.

2:35–36 God's constancy is the cornerstone of a godly life. In the midst of uncertainty, we know that God is always there. As Jeremiah warned, becoming attached to earthly powers always leads to disappointment. Others fail us many times. God is the only certainty. Even though Assyria and Egypt were mighty, their power was limited. God's power is limitless and will he not disappoint us.

changing your ways?
You will be disappointed by Egypt
as you were by Assyria.
37 You will also leave that place
with your hands on your head,
for the LORD has rejected those you trust;
you will not be helped by them.

3 "If a man divorces his wife
and she leaves him and marries another man,
should he return to her again?
Would not the land be completely defiled?
But you have lived as a prostitute with many lovers—
would you now return to me?"
declares the LORD.

2 "Look up to the barren heights and see.
Is there any place where you have not been ravished?
By the roadside you sat waiting for lovers,
sat like a nomad[a] in the desert.
You have defiled the land
with your prostitution and wickedness.
3 Therefore the showers have been withheld,
and no spring rains have fallen.
Yet you have the brazen look of a prostitute;
you refuse to blush with shame.
4 Have you not just called to me:
'My Father, my friend from my youth,
5 will you always be angry?
Will your wrath continue forever?'
This is how you talk,
but you do all the evil you can."

Unfaithful Israel

6 During the reign of King Josiah, the LORD said to me, "Have you
seen what faithless Israel has done? She has gone up on every high
hill and under every spreading tree and has committed adultery
there. 7 I thought that after she had done all this she would return to

[a]2 Or *an Arab*

OPEN Sometimes we must learn the hard way, by ourselves. Sometimes we learn from an elder sibling. What lesson do you remember learning "the hard way" for which you wish you had had an older brother or sister to learn from? What lesson did you spare a younger sibling from having to learn the hard way?

3:1 now return to me. Returning to the marriage analogy introduced in 2:2, Jeremiah put Judah's unfaithfulness to God on a very personal level. The people may have seen their relationship with God as contractual. As such, unfaithfulness was merely a violation of the Law. Jeremiah reminded the people, however, that the covenant relationship was a legal institution certainly, but one with emotion at its core. The faithlessness of Israel was bad enough (vv. 8ff), but Judah's sin was worse than that. She had prostituted herself with other gods. Would the men of Judah forgive and take back a wife that was unfaithful? The question rose above the Law and challenged the hearts of the people.

3:4 My Father, my friend. God is rarely called "Father" in the Old Testament. As this verse implied, Judah was trying to flatter God into forgiving the nation. They were calling on the father/child relationship that God had initiated at creation and confirmed with the covenant. Just as Judah had failed as the bride of God (v. 1), so had it failed as God's child.

3:5 Will your wrath continue forever? God's grace and forgiveness are greater than sin. God will forgive if his people repent.

3:6–6:30 What would be the consequences of Judah's unfaithfulness? God would use the Babylonians to judge his rebellious people.

3:7 unfaithful sister Judah. Jeremiah expanded on the theme of family to elaborate on the relationship between God and his people. Verses 2:2 and 3:1 used the husband/wife relationship, and verse 4 introduced the father/child relationship. Here Judah and Israel are presented as unfaithful sisters. Ezekiel expanded on this metaphor in Ezekiel 23.

me but she did not, and her unfaithful sister Judah saw it. [8]I gave
faithless Israel her certificate of divorce and sent her away because of
all her adulteries. Yet I saw that her unfaithful sister Judah had no
fear; she also went out and committed adultery. [9]Because Israel's
immorality mattered so little to her, she defiled the land and committed adultery with stone and wood. [10]In spite of all this, her unfaithful
sister Judah did not return to me with all her heart, but only in pretense," declares the LORD.

[11]The LORD said to me, "Faithless Israel is more righteous than unfaithful Judah. [12]Go, proclaim this message toward the north:

" 'Return, faithless Israel,' declares the LORD,
'I will frown on you no longer,
for I am merciful,' declares the LORD,
'I will not be angry forever.
[13]Only acknowledge your guilt—
you have rebelled against the LORD your God,
you have scattered your favors to foreign gods
under every spreading tree,
and have not obeyed me,' "
declares the LORD.

[14]"Return, faithless people," declares the LORD, "for I am your husband. I will choose you—one from a town and two from a clan—and
bring you to Zion. [15]Then I will give you shepherds after my own
heart, who will lead you with knowledge and understanding. [16]In
those days, when your numbers have increased greatly in the land,"
declares the LORD, "men will no longer say, 'The ark of the covenant
of the LORD.' It will never enter their minds or be remembered; it will
not be missed, nor will another one be made. [17]At that time they will
call Jerusalem The Throne of the LORD, and all nations will gather in
Jerusalem to honor the name of the LORD. No longer will they follow
the stubbornness of their evil hearts. [18]In those days the house of
Judah will join the house of Israel, and together they will come from
a northern land to the land I gave your forefathers as an inheritance.

[19]"I myself said,

" 'How gladly would I treat you like sons
and give you a desirable land,
the most beautiful inheritance of any nation.'
I thought you would call me 'Father'

STUDY 1. To what does God compare the northern kingdom of Israel and the southern kingdom of Judah (vv. 6–7)? The people of the north were attacked and deported by the Assyrians, a century before Jeremiah. Why did God allow that to happen (vv. 8–10)? **2.** What did God hope the people of Judah would do when they saw what happened to Israel? What did Judah do? **3.** Why was Israel "more righteous" (v. 11)? What is Jeremiah's message to the north (Northern Kingdom—Israel; vv. 12–14)? What do the "one ... two" represent? **4.** How does Jeremiah envision the future for all Israel (vv. 16–18)? Why will the Ark of the Covenant be irrelevant "in those days"? **5.** In what sense has Israel become like a disenfranchised firstborn son (v. 19)? Like an unfaithful woman (v. 20)? **6.** Under what conditions would God find Israel acceptable again (vv. 22–25)? **7.** If the northern tribes of Israel never regathered, what could we assume about Israel's answer to God's call (4:1–2)? **8.** What should Judah do now (4:3–4; Hosea 10:12)? What is a "circumcised heart" (Deut. 30:6)?

APPLY 1. Consider silently how you would feel and react if someone were unfaithful to you. What does it tell you about God's love that he wants to take Israel back? What does God want from us when someone has been unfaithful to us? **2.** Do you have trouble forgiving yourself for something you've done? Does it help knowing that God forgives you? What else is needed when you can't forgive yourself? How can this group help? **3.** Is it easy for you to feel responsible when things go wrong? Or do you feel most problems in your life are caused by other people? When is the last time you admitted you were wrong?

3:8 had no fear. Judah had watched the decline and fall of Israel (2 Kin. 15:17–17:41). Yet the southern kingdom never seemed to worry that the same fate might happen to them. Judah's sin and alienation, the nation apparently thought, would not reach a similar judgment.

3:9 committed adultery. As God's unfaithful wife, Israel had committed adultery by worshipping other gods.

3:10 did not return ... only in pretense. Judah had only pretended to embrace Josiah's reforms (2 Kin. 23:1–25).

3:12 toward the north. Many of Israel's citizens had been taken into exile by Assyria and removed to that empire's northern provinces. Those who remained in Israel lived north of Judah.

3:16 In those days ... it will not be missed. Jeremiah envisions a Messianic age in Israel when even the Ark of the Covenant will be irrelevant and forgotten. He did not imply that this coming age would be godless, but rather that the old covenant would be superseded for something better.

3:17 call Jerusalem The Throne. The Ark of the Covenant had contained the atonement cover. Golden cherubim sat on each end of this cover, and God was "enthroned between the cherubim" (2 Chr. 5:8). In the Messianic age, however, all of Jerusalem would be God's throne. By implication, Jerusalem would become the "holy of holies" which all people could enter to "honor the name of the LORD."

3:18 house of Judah will join ... Israel. God's people had become a divided nation (1 Kin. 11–12). Both Judah and Israel had turned away from their covenant relationship with God. In the Messianic age, God's people would be united again.

and not turn away from following me.
20 But like a woman unfaithful to her husband,
so you have been unfaithful to me, O house of Israel,"
declares the LORD.

21 A cry is heard on the barren heights,
the weeping and pleading of the people of Israel,
because they have perverted their ways
and have forgotten the LORD their God.

22 "Return, faithless people;
I will cure you of backsliding."

"Yes, we will come to you,
for you are the LORD our God.
23 Surely the ⌊idolatrous⌋ commotion on the hills
and mountains is a deception;
surely in the LORD our God
is the salvation of Israel.
24 From our youth shameful gods have consumed
the fruits of our fathers' labor—
their flocks and herds,
their sons and daughters.
25 Let us lie down in our shame,
and let our disgrace cover us.
We have sinned against the LORD our God,
both we and our fathers;
from our youth till this day
we have not obeyed the LORD our God."

4 "If you will return, O Israel,
return to me,"
declares the LORD.
"If you put your detestable idols out of my sight
and no longer go astray,
2 and if in a truthful, just and righteous way
you swear, 'As surely as the LORD lives,'
then the nations will be blessed by him
and in him they will glory."

3 This is what the LORD says to the men of Judah and to Jerusalem:

"Break up your unplowed ground
and do not sow among thorns.
4 Circumcise yourselves to the LORD,
circumcise your hearts,
you men of Judah and people of Jerusalem,
or my wrath will break out and burn like fire
because of the evil you have done—
burn with no one to quench it.

4:2 nations will be blessed by him. God promised Abram more than to make his descendants into a great nation (Gen. 12:2–3). He also promised that other nations would be blessed by Abram's descendants. For that promise to be fulfilled, however, Israel must repent and return to friendship with God.

Disaster From the North

[5] "Announce in Judah and proclaim in Jerusalem and say:
'Sound the trumpet throughout the land!'
Cry aloud and say:
'Gather together!
Let us flee to the fortified cities!'
[6] Raise the signal to go to Zion!
Flee for safety without delay!
For I am bringing disaster from the north,
even terrible destruction."

[7] A lion has come out of his lair;
a destroyer of nations has set out.
He has left his place
to lay waste your land.
Your towns will lie in ruins
without inhabitant.
[8] So put on sackcloth,
lament and wail,
for the fierce anger of the LORD
has not turned away from us.

[9] "In that day," declares the LORD,
"the king and the officials will lose heart,
the priests will be horrified,
and the prophets will be appalled."

[10] Then I said, "Ah, Sovereign LORD, how completely you have deceived this people and Jerusalem by saying, 'You will have peace,'
when the sword is at our throats."
[11] At that time this people and Jerusalem will be told, "A scorching
wind from the barren heights in the desert blows toward my people,
but not to winnow or cleanse; [12] a wind too strong for that comes
from me.[a] Now I pronounce my judgments against them."

[13] Look! He advances like the clouds,
his chariots come like a whirlwind,
his horses are swifter than eagles.
Woe to us! We are ruined!
[14] O Jerusalem, wash the evil from your heart and be saved.
How long will you harbor wicked thoughts?
[15] A voice is announcing from Dan,
proclaiming disaster from the hills of Ephraim.
[16] "Tell this to the nations,
proclaim it to Jerusalem:
'A besieging army is coming from a distant land,
raising a war cry against the cities of Judah.

[a] 12 Or *comes at my command*

OPEN 1. If you were warned that a nuclear strike would hit your area in 25 minutes, where would you go for safety? What would you take with you? What would you spend the time doing? **2.** What skill do you keep telling yourself you'll learn when you get a little extra time? Do you think you will ever acquire it?

STUDY 1. A terrible disaster is coming. Where will it come from (vv. 5–6; 6:1)? **2.** When did God "deceive" the people (v. 10; 14:13–14)? What do the people think will happen to them? **3.** What five word-pictures does Jeremiah use to describe the Babylonians (vv. 11–17)? Why has God brought them to attack his people (v. 18)? Can Jerusalem be saved (v. 14)? How so (3:23; 4:1–2)? **4.** How does Jeremiah feel when he learns his nation will be destroyed (vv. 18–21)? What does his pain reveal about him? **5.** What excuse, if any do the people have (v. 22)? Did they not know any better, or did they know only too well what they were doing? **6.** What vision does Jeremiah now have of life after the Babylonian invasion (vv. 23–26)? To what does Jeremiah compare the aftermath? **7.** Verses 29–31 depict three different responses to the invasion. What are they? What do the images represent?

APPLY 1. Have you experienced God as judge or avenger? How did the experience affect you? How do you square the pictures of God the loving parent with God the avenging judge? **2.** Think of a place that has been devastated recently by war or disaster. Do you ever experience something like Jeremiah's concern and agony when you learn of people's suffering? Why or why not?

4:10 completely you have deceived. God had not directly deceived his people. He had, however, allowed false prophets to promulgate untruths for various reasons. (1 Kin. 22:20–23.)

4:11 scorching wind ... blows. The Babylonians were speedily approaching with the goal of destroying Israel and Judah. The image of the desert sirocco captured the speed and inevitability of the coming onslaught.

4:12 a wind too strong for that. A light breeze was ideal for separating wheat from chaff. Winnowing is a metaphor for judgment. The good falls and the bad (chaff) is blown away. (Ps. 35:5.) The sirocco that Jeremiah predicted would not separate good from evil, but destroy them both.

17They surround her like men guarding a field,
because she has rebelled against me,' "
declares the LORD.

18"Your own conduct and actions
have brought this upon you.
This is your punishment.
How bitter it is!
How it pierces to the heart!"

19Oh, my anguish, my anguish!
I writhe in pain.
Oh, the agony of my heart!
My heart pounds within me,
I cannot keep silent.
For I have heard the sound of the trumpet;
I have heard the battle cry.
20Disaster follows disaster;
the whole land lies in ruins.
In an instant my tents are destroyed,
my shelter in a moment.
21How long must I see the battle standard
and hear the sound of the trumpet?

22"My people are fools;
they do not know me.
They are senseless children;
they have no understanding.
They are skilled in doing evil;
they know not how to do good."

23I looked at the earth,
and it was formless and empty;
and at the heavens,
and their light was gone.
24I looked at the mountains,
and they were quaking;
all the hills were swaying.
25I looked, and there were no people;
every bird in the sky had flown away.
26I looked, and the fruitful land was a desert;
all its towns lay in ruins
before the LORD, before his fierce anger.

27This is what the LORD says:

"The whole land will be ruined,
though I will not destroy it completely.

4:19–26 Jeremiah expressed his anguish at the vision of destruction God had given him. The images of this destruction (lion, sirocco, clouds, whirlwind, eagles) have been replaced by *real images of battle (vv. 19–21) and* apocalyptic images of the aftermath (vv. 23–26). In verse 22 God explained how Judah and Israel deserved the destruction that was coming.

4:23 earth ... was formless and empty. For Jeremiah, the destruction of Israel and Judah would return the world to the state of chaos that preceded creation. The description of that condition in Genesis 1:2 is the only other use of this phrase in the Bible.

4:25–26 I looked, and there were no people. The destruction that Jeremiah envisioned would reduce the world to the state which existed before God had created life (Gen. 1:1–10). The devastation of God's people would reverse the creation process (v. 23).

4:27 I will not destroy it completely. God corrected Jeremiah's apocalyptic vision. The coming devasta-

28 Therefore the earth will mourn
and the heavens above grow dark,
because I have spoken and will not relent,
I have decided and will not turn back."

29 At the sound of horsemen and archers
every town takes to flight.
Some go into the thickets;
some climb up among the rocks.
All the towns are deserted;
no one lives in them.

30 What are you doing, O devastated one?
Why dress yourself in scarlet
and put on jewels of gold?
Why shade your eyes with paint?
You adorn yourself in vain.
Your lovers despise you;
they seek your life.

31 I hear a cry as of a woman in labor,
a groan as of one bearing her first child—
the cry of the Daughter of Zion gasping for breath,
stretching out her hands and saying,
"Alas! I am fainting;
my life is given over to murderers."

Not One Is Upright

5 "Go up and down the streets of Jerusalem,
look around and consider,
search through her squares.
If you can find but one person
who deals honestly and seeks the truth,
I will forgive this city.
2 Although they say, 'As surely as the LORD lives,'
still they are swearing falsely."

3 O LORD, do not your eyes look for truth?
You struck them, but they felt no pain;
you crushed them, but they refused correction.
They made their faces harder than stone
and refused to repent.
4 I thought, "These are only the poor;
they are foolish,
for they do not know the way of the LORD,
the requirements of their God.
5 So I will go to the leaders

OPEN 1. What section of the newspaper do you read first or most attentively? What part of the TV news grips you? Where in your reading or viewing priorities is the report on violent crimes? **2.** Who are your favorite fictional villains? Why do you like them? Do you ever find yourself rooting for the bad guy?

STUDY 1. What is Jeremiah's quest (v. 1)? What will God do if Jeremiah succeeds? How does that compare to God's response to Abraham's plea for Sodom (Gen. 18:16–32)? **2.** Jeremiah finds a city full of evil. What evil actions does he find (vv. 2–31)? **3.** Is Jeremiah inclined to excuse the poor and blame the upper class (vv. 4–6)? Or are they equally at fault? **4.** How would you answer Jeremiah's rhetorical questions in verses 7 and 9? What answer is provided in verse 10? **5.** How is God going

---

tion would be terrible, but judgment would be tempered with mercy.

4:29 into the thickets ... up among the rocks. Though the ruin brought by the Babylonians would be terrible, it would not reverse creation, as Jeremiah feared (vv. 23–26). It would, however, reduce the social structure and architecture of Israel and Judah to rubble. The people would hide in thickets and rocks like small animals hiding from predators. They would be transformed from a proud, foolish nation (v. 22) to a fearful people with no land at all.

5:1 find but one person. In an echo of God's challenge to Abraham at the city of Sodom (Gen. 18:26–33), God made a similar challenge about Jerusalem. For the sake of ten righteous people God would spare Sodom. In Jerusalem God would spare the city for only one honest person. God is challenging the people to search their hearts and see their corruption.

to punish Judah (vv. 10,13–18)? How will the words of God differ from the words of the false prophets? Why won't the destruction be final? **6.** What has become the prevailing attitude about God (vv. 12,22–24)? Why should people fear God when the wicked grow rich? **7.** Which of Judah's failings do you think angers God the most? Do you think God gets as angry as Jeremiah tells it?

APPLY 1. Jeremiah lamented that not one person could be found who dealt honestly and sought the truth. How has it been in your life? What person has served as a model in your life for how to live with honesty and integrity? **2.** When is it easy for you to be truthful and when is it hard? In what area of life do you need to raise the level of honesty? **3.** People in Jeremiah's day were blind to their faults and easily led to presume their innocence. What accountability mechanisms do you have in place to help detect spiritual blindspots in your life? How can your group or family help in this?

and speak to them;
surely they know the way of the LORD,
the requirements of their God."
But with one accord they too had broken off the yoke
and torn off the bonds.
6 Therefore a lion from the forest will attack them,
a wolf from the desert will ravage them,
a leopard will lie in wait near their towns
to tear to pieces any who venture out,
for their rebellion is great
and their backslidings many.

7 "Why should I forgive you?
Your children have forsaken me
and sworn by gods that are not gods.
I supplied all their needs,
yet they committed adultery
and thronged to the houses of prostitutes.
8 They are well-fed, lusty stallions,
each neighing for another man's wife.
9 Should I not punish them for this?"
declares the LORD.
"Should I not avenge myself
on such a nation as this?

10 "Go through her vineyards and ravage them,
but do not destroy them completely.
Strip off her branches,
for these people do not belong to the LORD.
11 The house of Israel and the house of Judah
have been utterly unfaithful to me,"
declares the LORD.

12 They have lied about the LORD;
they said, "He will do nothing!
No harm will come to us;
we will never see sword or famine.
13 The prophets are but wind
and the word is not in them;
so let what they say be done to them."

14 Therefore this is what the LORD God Almighty says:

"Because the people have spoken these words,
I will make my words in your mouth a fire
and these people the wood it consumes.
15 O house of Israel," declares the LORD,
"I am bringing a distant nation against you—
an ancient and enduring nation,
a people whose language you do not know,
whose speech you do not understand.
16 Their quivers are like an open grave;

5:12 never see sword or famine. God's weapons are powerful. Jeremiah mentions two of them. The third was plague. (14:12). God wielded his power through control of nations, nature and disease. God would use these three instruments of judgment even against his own people if they refused to repent and turn away.

all of them are mighty warriors.
17 They will devour your harvests and food,
devour your sons and daughters;
they will devour your flocks and herds,
devour your vines and fig trees.
With the sword they will destroy
the fortified cities in which you trust.

18 "Yet even in those days," declares the LORD, "I will not destroy
you completely. 19 And when the people ask, 'Why has the LORD our
God done all this to us?' you will tell them, 'As you have forsaken me
and served foreign gods in your own land, so now you will serve foreigners in a land not your own.'

20 "Announce this to the house of Jacob
and proclaim it in Judah:
21 Hear this, you foolish and senseless people,
who have eyes but do not see,
who have ears but do not hear:
22 Should you not fear me?" declares the LORD.
"Should you not tremble in my presence?
I made the sand a boundary for the sea,
an everlasting barrier it cannot cross.
The waves may roll, but they cannot prevail;
they may roar, but they cannot cross it.
23 But these people have stubborn and rebellious hearts;
they have turned aside and gone away.
24 They do not say to themselves,
'Let us fear the LORD our God,
who gives autumn and spring rains in season,
who assures us of the regular weeks of harvest.'
25 Your wrongdoings have kept these away;
your sins have deprived you of good.

26 "Among my people are wicked men
who lie in wait like men who snare birds
and like those who set traps to catch men.
27 Like cages full of birds,
their houses are full of deceit;
they have become rich and powerful
28 and have grown fat and sleek.
Their evil deeds have no limit;
they do not plead the case of the fatherless to win it,
they do not defend the rights of the poor.
29 Should I not punish them for this?"
declares the LORD.
"Should I not avenge myself
on such a nation as this?

5:23 stubborn and rebellious hearts. The people of Israel and Judah had several obstacles between themselves and God. First, they had sin (adultery and idolatry, v. 7). Second, stubborn hearts that "refused correction" (v. 3). Third, rebellious hearts that would not stay within the moral and spiritual boundaries God had set (vv. 22–23).

5:28 evil deeds have no limit. People had become rich and powerful through wickedness (vv. 26–27), doubly terrible because they not only committed sins but also neglected to do right for the poor and unfortunate who needed it.

30 "A horrible and shocking thing
has happened in the land:
31 The prophets prophesy lies,
the priests rule by their own authority,
and my people love it this way.
But what will you do in the end?

Jerusalem Under Siege

6 "Flee for safety, people of Benjamin!
Flee from Jerusalem!
Sound the trumpet in Tekoa!
Raise the signal over Beth Hakkerem!
For disaster looms out of the north,
even terrible destruction.
2 I will destroy the Daughter of Zion,
so beautiful and delicate.
3 Shepherds with their flocks will come against her;
they will pitch their tents around her,
each tending his own portion."

4 "Prepare for battle against her!
Arise, let us attack at noon!
But, alas, the daylight is fading,
and the shadows of evening grow long.
5 So arise, let us attack at night
and destroy her fortresses!"

6 This is what the LORD Almighty says:

"Cut down the trees
and build siege ramps against Jerusalem.
This city must be punished;
it is filled with oppression.
7 As a well pours out its water,
so she pours out her wickedness.
Violence and destruction resound in her;
her sickness and wounds are ever before me.
8 Take warning, O Jerusalem,
or I will turn away from you
and make your land desolate
so no one can live in it."

9 This is what the LORD Almighty says:

"Let them glean the remnant of Israel
as thoroughly as a vine;
pass your hand over the branches again,
like one gathering grapes."

OPEN 1. How would you rate yourself as an optimist on a scale of 1 ("Everything that can go wrong will go wrong") to 10 ("Every cloud has a silver lining")? **2.** When you go on trips, are you a plan-it-for-months type, or a pick-up-and-go type? Is the rest of your family like you? Does this make travel easy or hard?

STUDY 1. Who is speaking to whom in verses 1–3? In verses 4–5? 6? 10–11? 11–23? 24–26? 27–30? Look for this change of speaker and audience throughout Jeremiah's prophecy. **2.** Why should people flee the walled city of Jerusalem (vv. 1–5; compare 4:6, where they are told to go to Zion/Jerusalem)? Why is it safer outside? What happens in a siege (v. 6)? **3.** Why does God want Jeremiah to warn Jerusalem (v. 8)? How eager is the city to hear God's word (v. 10)? What role have the religious leaders played in delivering the warning (vv. 13–15)? **4.** What are the "ancient paths" to Jeremiah's audience (v. 16)? Who are the "watchmen" (v. 17)? Why does God call the earth and the nations to witness the disaster (vv. 18–20)? **5.** What has Judah offered God instead of obedience (v. 20)? How do they respond to God's warning (vv. 24–25)? What response would God prefer? **6.** What is Jeremiah's role now (v. 27; Mal. 3:2–3)? Smelters purify silver ore by throwing it into molten lead: The pure silver floats, the dross sinks. What does Jeremiah observe as Jerusalem goes into the fire? **7.** What do you think was God's purpose in this warning? What does this tell you about God's character?

APPLY 1. When you look back at how you behaved in

6:1 Flee from Jerusalem. There would be no safe haven from the onslaught of Babylonians. There was a certain safety implied in the "fortified cities" (4:5), but even that refuge will be swept away by the invaders. God's people had refused to repent, and the Babylonians were instruments of the Lord's judgment.

6:4 Prepare for battle. The Babylonians speak in verses 4 and 5. In contrast to the panic felt by the people of Judah (v. 1), the invaders were calm and calculating about the upcoming battle. The Babylonians prepared themselves for war, but the people of Judah looked only to escape.

[10]To whom can I speak and give warning?
Who will listen to me?
Their ears are closed[a]
so they cannot hear.
The word of the LORD is offensive to them;
they find no pleasure in it.
[11]But I am full of the wrath of the LORD,
and I cannot hold it in.

"Pour it out on the children in the street
and on the young men gathered together;
both husband and wife will be caught in it,
and the old, those weighed down with years.
[12]Their houses will be turned over to others,
together with their fields and their wives,
when I stretch out my hand
against those who live in the land,"
declares the LORD.
[13]"From the least to the greatest,
all are greedy for gain;
prophets and priests alike,
all practice deceit.
[14]They dress the wound of my people
as though it were not serious.
'Peace, peace,' they say,
when there is no peace.
[15]Are they ashamed of their loathsome conduct?
No, they have no shame at all;
they do not even know how to blush.
So they will fall among the fallen;
they will be brought down when I punish them,"
says the LORD.

[16]This is what the LORD says:

"Stand at the crossroads and look;
ask for the ancient paths,
ask where the good way is, and walk in it,
and you will find rest for your souls.
But you said, 'We will not walk in it.'
[17]I appointed watchmen over you and said,
'Listen to the sound of the trumpet!'
But you said, 'We will not listen.'

[a]10 Hebrew *uncircumcised*

your youth, what especially makes you blush (v. 15)? **2.** What obstacles are you finding in your path these days (v. 2)? Do you believe those obstacles are: There to test your resolve? There to turn you in a different direction? There as a punishment from God? Just coincidental? **3.** Have you experienced God's refining fire? What "silver" came to the surface? What dross remains to be burnt away?

6:10 Their ears are closed. Jeremiah wanted to warn the people, but they were so caught up in their sin, they would not listen. In Hebrew, the word translated "closed" meant "uncircumcised." Though the people were physically circumcised, they acted like pagans.

6:11 full of the wrath of the LORD. Jeremiah had "ingested" the Word of God and seen God's visions. He had been filled like a bucket with the Lord's righteous anger. Now God called for wrath to be poured upon everyone—children, young men, husbands, wives and the elderly.

6:14 Peace, peace, ... when there is no peace. Corrupt priests and prophets taught a "feel-good" message that aimed to treat the symptoms of the people's spiritual disease instead of treating the disease itself. Instead of calling for repentance, they tried to console the people with lies. They wanted to make them feel better.

6:17 appointed watchmen. God appointed true prophets to serve his people so that his Word could be heard and his warnings understood. (Ezek. 3:17.)

18 Therefore hear, O nations;
observe, O witnesses,
what will happen to them.
19 Hear, O earth:
I am bringing disaster on this people,
the fruit of their schemes,
because they have not listened to my words
and have rejected my law.
20 What do I care about incense from Sheba
or sweet calamus from a distant land?
Your burnt offerings are not acceptable;
your sacrifices do not please me."

21 Therefore this is what the LORD says:

"I will put obstacles before this people.
Fathers and sons alike will stumble over them;
neighbors and friends will perish."

22 This is what the LORD says:

"Look, an army is coming
from the land of the north;
a great nation is being stirred up
from the ends of the earth.
23 They are armed with bow and spear;
they are cruel and show no mercy.
They sound like the roaring sea
as they ride on their horses;
they come like men in battle formation
to attack you, O Daughter of Zion."

24 We have heard reports about them,
and our hands hang limp.
Anguish has gripped us,
pain like that of a woman in labor.
25 Do not go out to the fields
or walk on the roads,
for the enemy has a sword,
and there is terror on every side.
26 O my people, put on sackcloth
and roll in ashes;
mourn with bitter wailing
as for an only son,
for suddenly the destroyer
will come upon us.

27 "I have made you a tester of metals
and my people the ore,
that you may observe
and test their ways.
28 They are all hardened rebels,

6:20 Your burnt offerings are not acceptable. Ritual sacrifices and offerings without devotion were unacceptable to God. God would rather see a spirit of repentance than hardened people doing rituals.

6:27–30 God appointed Jeremiah to test his people as a refiner tested metals, to determine the people's true composition and worth; if they could be pure like gold (Job 23:10).

going about to slander.
They are bronze and iron;
they all act corruptly.
29The bellows blow fiercely
to burn away the lead with fire,
but the refining goes on in vain;
the wicked are not purged out.
30They are called rejected silver,
because the LORD has rejected them."

False Religion Worthless

7 This is the word that came to Jeremiah from the LORD: 2"Stand at
the gate of the LORD's house and there proclaim this message:
" 'Hear the word of the LORD, all you people of Judah who come
through these gates to worship the LORD. 3This is what the LORD
Almighty, the God of Israel, says: Reform your ways and your actions,
and I will let you live in this place. 4Do not trust in deceptive words and
say, "This is the temple of the LORD, the temple of the LORD, the temple
of the LORD!" 5If you really change your ways and your actions and
deal with each other justly, 6if you do not oppress the alien, the fatherless or the widow and do not shed innocent blood in this place, and if
you do not follow other gods to your own harm, 7then I will let you
live in this place, in the land I gave your forefathers for ever and ever.
8But look, you are trusting in deceptive words that are worthless.
9" 'Will you steal and murder, commit adultery and perjury,[a] burn
incense to Baal and follow other gods you have not known, 10and
then come and stand before me in this house, which bears my Name,
and say, "We are safe"—safe to do all these detestable things? 11Has
this house, which bears my Name, become a den of robbers to you?
But I have been watching! declares the LORD.
12" 'Go now to the place in Shiloh where I first made a dwelling for
my Name, and see what I did to it because of the wickedness of my
people Israel. 13While you were doing all these things, declares the

[a]9 *Or and swear by false gods*

OPEN 1. Have you ever seen abandoned farms, a ghost town or ancient ruins? Where? How did it make you feel? **2.** Have you ever seen a protest or a labor strike? What was the issue? How did it make you feel?

STUDY This series of temple prophecies (chs. 7–10) may be dated to Jehoiakim's reign, due to similarities between chapters 7 and 26. **1.** How did Jehoiakim come to be king (2 Kin. 23:29–37)? What kind of king was he? **2.** Where does the prophet go to proclaim this message (v. 2)? Who would hear it there? **3.** How can Judah remain in the land (vv. 5–7)? What kind of crimes have the people committed? **4.** What have they done to the temple (vv. 8–11)? What happened a century earlier that makes them feel safe (2 Kin. 19:32–36)? But are they safe, despite what the other prophets say in verse 4? **5.** Israel had a tabernacle at Shiloh long before David conquered Jerusalem and Solomon built the temple. What happened to it (1 Sam. 4:3–11; Ps. 78:60–64)? What lesson does God

---

6:29 refining goes on in vain. To refine silver, the refiner would add lead to the silver, then melt the metals in a crucible. The lead would oxidize and take other impurities with it. The result was pure silver. In this refining however, the ore was so corrupt that its impurities cannot be purged.

6:30 rejected silver. The people failed the test. Their wickedness was so great that refining cannot make them useful to the Lord.

7:1–10:25 This section of Jeremiah contains a series of messages delivered by the prophet at the temple. In contrast with the fearful imagery and rhetoric of chapters 1–6, these messages are less emotional. The theme of "repent or perish" is still prevalent; however, the messages focus on specific concerns such as false religion, idolatry, sin and its punishment and obedience.

7:2 come through these gates. Jeremiah was told to stand in the gate between the inner and outer courts of the temple and proclaim the message God gave him. The business of the gate area commanded attention.

7:4 deceptive words ... the temple of the LORD. The corrupt priests and prophets, in accordance with their message that "everything will be all right," had proclaimed that God would not destroy Jerusalem because his temple was there. Judah had fallen so far away from the Lord that this idea was "worthless" (v. 8).

7:5–7 God laid out clearly how Judah could avoid disaster. Repentance was a first step, including a change in behavior. To abandon false worship was crucial, but the focus now was on dealing "with others justly." God demanded repentance and obedience to the social code that the covenant required.

7:12 place in Shiloh. After the conquest of Canaan, the tabernacle was set up at Shiloh (Josh. 18:1) and remained there through the period of the judges (1 Sam. 1:9). The tabernacle itself was moved at some later time (It's at Gibeon in David's reign, 1 Chr. 21:29.). Some auxiliary buildings had been erected at Shiloh and later destroyed. (It was probably these "doors of the house of the LORD" that Samuel opened in 1 Sam. 3:15.) Thus, God's warning about the destruction of the temple had a historical precedent.

want Judah to learn from that (vv. 12–15)? **6.** Why do you think God forbids Jeremiah to pray for Judah (v. 16)? What is the point of mentioning men, women and children involved in this idolatrous worship (vv. 18–19)? Who is really being hurt by this practice? **7.** How are they trying to appease God now (v. 21)? What's being neglected (vv. 22–24)? **8.** Will Jeremiah fare any better than the other prophets (vv. 25–27)? What will happen then (vv. 28–29)? **9.** How did Jesus see Jeremiah's words fulfilled in his day (Matt. 21:12–13)? What would Jeremiah and Jesus say about what goes on in churches today?

APPLY 1. Where are you in your spiritual journey? In "Egypt" feeling captive (v. 25)? Just released from "Egypt" (v. 25)? Thrust from God's presence (v. 15)? At the gate of the Lord's house, calling to others (v. 1)? **2.** In your relationship with God right now, who do you feel is doing the least listening, you (v. 13) or God (v. 16)? What can you do to change that?

LORD, I spoke to you again and again, but you did not listen; I called
you, but you did not answer. [14]Therefore, what I did to Shiloh I will
now do to the house that bears my Name, the temple you trust in, the
place I gave to you and your fathers. [15]I will thrust you from my presence, just as I did all your brothers, the people of Ephraim.'
[16]"So do not pray for this people nor offer any plea or petition for
them; do not plead with me, for I will not listen to you. [17]Do you not
see what they are doing in the towns of Judah and in the streets of
Jerusalem? [18]The children gather wood, the fathers light the fire, and
the women knead the dough and make cakes of bread for the Queen
of Heaven. They pour out drink offerings to other gods to provoke me
to anger. [19]But am I the one they are provoking? declares the LORD.
Are they not rather harming themselves, to their own shame?
[20]" 'Therefore this is what the Sovereign LORD says: My anger and
my wrath will be poured out on this place, on man and beast, on the
trees of the field and on the fruit of the ground, and it will burn and
not be quenched.
[21]" 'This is what the LORD Almighty, the God of Israel, says: Go
ahead, add your burnt offerings to your other sacrifices and eat the
meat yourselves! [22]For when I brought your forefathers out of Egypt
and spoke to them, I did not just give them commands about burnt
offerings and sacrifices, [23]but I gave them this command: Obey me,
and I will be your God and you will be my people. Walk in all the ways
I command you, that it may go well with you. [24]But they did not listen
or pay attention; instead, they followed the stubborn inclinations of
their evil hearts. They went backward and not forward. [25]From the
time your forefathers left Egypt until now, day after day, again and
again I sent you my servants the prophets. [26]But they did not listen to
me or pay attention. They were stiff-necked and did more evil than
their forefathers.'
[27]"When you tell them all this, they will not listen to you; when you
call to them, they will not answer. [28]Therefore say to them, 'This is the
nation that has not obeyed the LORD its God or responded to correction. Truth has perished; it has vanished from their lips. [29]Cut off your
hair and throw it away; take up a lament on the barren heights, for
the LORD has rejected and abandoned this generation that is under
his wrath.

The Valley of Slaughter

OPEN 1. What song would you like sung at your funeral? **2.** What is the most exciting thing you have seen in the heavens: UFO? Eclipse? Northern lights? Meteors?

[30]" 'The people of Judah have done evil in my eyes, declares the
LORD. They have set up their detestable idols in the house that bears
my Name and have defiled it. [31]They have built the high places of To-

7:16 do not pray for this people. Prophets always prayed for the people. God did not want these prayers, however. Jeremiah's prayers, without the repentance of the people, would not be enough to forestall their destruction.

7:22–23 God did not desire sacrifices *and offerings by themselves.* These rituals were meant to be part of a life of obedience and repentance (6:20).

7:25 my servants the prophets. The prophets held a unique place in the life of Israel. Like Moses, they were appointed to do God's work among the people. Though prophets would intercede with God on the people's behalf, their true role was to preach the Word of God and serve God faithfully. Jeremiah was part of a long roster of servants specially chosen for this role. (Deut. 18:15–22.)

7:30 set up their ... idols in the house that bears my Name. King Hezekiah tried to end paganism among the people (2 Kin. 18:3–4). His son Manasseh, however, built altars in the temple to pagan gods (2 Kin. 21:4). During Jeremiah's time, Josiah renewed the covenant (2 Kin. 23) and tried to stop idolatry (2 Kin. 23:24). These reforms failed as well. Less than twenty years after Jeremiah's death, Ezekiel reported that idols occupied the temple courts again (Ezek. 8:3,5–6).

7:31 to burn their sons and daugh-

pheth in the Valley of Ben Hinnom to burn their sons and daughters
in the fire—something I did not command, nor did it enter my mind.
32So beware, the days are coming, declares the LORD, when people
will no longer call it Topheth or the Valley of Ben Hinnom, but the
Valley of Slaughter, for they will bury the dead in Topheth until there
is no more room. 33Then the carcasses of this people will become
food for the birds of the air and the beasts of the earth, and there will
be no one to frighten them away. 34I will bring an end to the sounds of
joy and gladness and to the voices of bride and bridegroom in the
towns of Judah and the streets of Jerusalem, for the land will become
desolate.

8 " 'At that time, declares the LORD, the bones of the kings and officials of Judah, the bones of the priests and prophets, and the
bones of the people of Jerusalem will be removed from their graves.
2They will be exposed to the sun and the moon and all the stars of the
heavens, which they have loved and served and which they have
followed and consulted and worshiped. They will not be gathered up
or buried, but will be like refuse lying on the ground. 3Wherever I
banish them, all the survivors of this evil nation will prefer death to
life, declares the LORD Almighty.'

Sin and Punishment

4"Say to them, 'This is what the LORD says:

" 'When men fall down, do they not get up?
 When a man turns away, does he not return?
5Why then have these people turned away?
 Why does Jerusalem always turn away?
They cling to deceit;
 they refuse to return.
6I have listened attentively,
 but they do not say what is right.
No one repents of his wickedness,
 saying, "What have I done?"
Each pursues his own course
 like a horse charging into battle.
7Even the stork in the sky
 knows her appointed seasons,
and the dove, the swift and the thrush
 observe the time of their migration.

STUDY 1. What two crimes have the people committed (vv. 30–31)? Is child sacrifice new to Palestine (2 Kin. 16:3)? Why did God forbid it (Lev. 18:21; Deut. 12:31)? **2.** Why will God rename the Hinnom Valley (v. 32)? How is this ironic? **3.** What disgrace will the powerful face (8:1–2)? What punishment will the living suffer?

APPLY 1. What "stars" have you been most prone to follow and worship in your life: Hollywood stars? Actual stars (astrology)? Stars of the business world? Religious stars (televangelists, etc.)? **2.** What would it take for God to turn you away from this practice?

OPEN 1. What is your greatest accomplishment so far? How long did it take you to do it? What was so hard about it? **2.** If you were a migratory bird, where would you like to spend your winters? **3.** Are your trips to the doctor frequent or rare? Does the doctor usually know what's wrong, or could you have taken care of it yourself? What advice do you find easiest, and hardest, to obey?

STUDY 1. What about the people of Jerusalem amazes God (vv. 4–7)? How are even the birds smarter than they? **2.** Who preserved the written law of the Lord (vv. 8–12)? What have they done to deceive the people? What were their motives? How will God punish them? **3.** Is verse 13 a threat of physical destruction, or is the figless tree the spiritual condition God finds in Judah? **4.** How would

---

ters. Here trash was dumped and children were sacrificed to pagan gods. Though prohibited by the Law (Lev. 18:21), *child sacrifice was practiced by* Ahaz (2 Kin. 16:2–3) and Manasseh (2 Kin. 21:1,6). The Hebrew name for the Valley of Ben Hinnom ("ge' hinnom") became "Gehenna," which was translated in the New Testament as "hell." The fiery, terrible trash dump represented the place of eternal punishment for those who die unforgiven (Matt. 18:9).

7:32 Valley of Slaughter. God warned Judah that the Valley of Ben Hinnom would become a mass grave for people killed by the Babylonians.

8:1 bones ... removed from their graves. Even the dead would not be safe when the invaders arrived. The bones of the dead would be treated with scorn and their proper burial undone. Graveyard desecration was a gross violation of social and religious tradition.

8:2 exposed to the sun and the moon. The bones would disintegrate rapidly when exposed to the elements, leaving no evidence that the people ever lived. Many people worshiped the heavenly bodies (2 Kin. 21:3). The disintegration of the bones in the presence of the sun, moon and stars would demonstrate the powerlessness of those gods.

8:7 stork ... dove ... swift ... thrush. Birds follow instinct to fulfill their God-given natures. People, whom God has told the right things to do, rebel and refuse God's instruction.

you describe the people's feeling about the coming invasion (vv. 14–16): Frightened? Resolved? Nonchalant? Resigned? Mad at God? **5.** How does Jeremiah feel (vv. 8–9:1)? What seems to bother him the most? Where does he hope to find healing (46:11; 51:8)? Does his fountain of tears seem genuine to you, or is this for show?

APPLY 1. In what ways do you feel spiritually wounded right now? In what ways do you sometimes behave as though this wound is not as serious as it is (v. 11)? **2.** Who do you know who really seems to feel the pain of your wound (v. 21)? **3.** Where are you looking for healing for this wound (v. 22)? On a scale of 1–10, how frustrated are you in your search, if "1," is "totally frustrated" and "10" is "totally hopeful"?

But my people do not know
the requirements of the LORD.

8 " 'How can you say, "We are wise,
for we have the law of the LORD,"
when actually the lying pen of the scribes
has handled it falsely?
9 The wise will be put to shame;
they will be dismayed and trapped.
Since they have rejected the word of the LORD,
what kind of wisdom do they have?
10 Therefore I will give their wives to other men
and their fields to new owners.
From the least to the greatest,
all are greedy for gain;
prophets and priests alike,
all practice deceit.
11 They dress the wound of my people
as though it were not serious.
"Peace, peace," they say,
when there is no peace.
12 Are they ashamed of their loathsome conduct?
No, they have no shame at all;
they do not even know how to blush.
So they will fall among the fallen;
they will be brought down when they are punished,
says the LORD.

13 " 'I will take away their harvest,
declares the LORD.
There will be no grapes on the vine.
There will be no figs on the tree,
and their leaves will wither.
What I have given them
will be taken from them.[a] ' "

14 "Why are we sitting here?
Gather together!
Let us flee to the fortified cities
and perish there!
For the LORD our God has doomed us to perish
and given us poisoned water to drink,
because we have sinned against him.
15 We hoped for peace
but no good has come,
for a time of healing
but there was only terror.
16 The snorting of the enemy's horses

[a] 13 The meaning of the Hebrew for this sentence is uncertain.

8:8–9 we have the law of the LORD ... word of the LORD. The Law of God had been wrongly interpreted. Thus the true Law and teachings of the prophets were rejected.

8:13 Common agricultural images show that the upcoming invasion would destroy the fruit (the people) of the vine (the nation). (For an introduction to this image see 2:21.) Even the leaves would wither without nourishment.

ons
is heard from Dan
at the neighing of
the whole lan in it,
They have co there."
the land as snakes among you,
the city harmed,

declares the LORD.

17 "See,
rrow,
in me.
people
y:
on?
ger there?"
voked me to anger with their images,
thless foreign idols?"

st is past,
ummer has ended,
nd we are not saved."

Since my people are crushed, I am crushed;
I mourn, and horror grips me.
22 Is there no balm in Gilead?
Is there no physician there?
Why then is there no healing
for the wound of my people?

9 1 Oh, that my head were a spring of water
and my eyes a fountain of tears!
I would weep day and night
for the slain of my people.
2 Oh, that I had in the desert
a lodging place for travelers,
so that I might leave my people
and go away from them;
for they are all adulterers,
a crowd of unfaithful people.

[a]18 The meaning of the Hebrew for this word is uncertain.

OPEN 1. What is your favorite place to get away from it all? How often do you go there? **2.** Who in your group can twist their tongue or touch their nose with it? Try it and see.

STUDY 1. Having wept continuously, what does Jere-

8:18 my heart is faint within me. Jeremiah was overcome with grief and worry. Though his spirit was weak, he still called on God to save the people.

8:19 Is the LORD not in Zion ... no longer there? Jeremiah imagined the devastation of his people suffering in exile. In their turmoil the people could not identify the reasons for their tragedy. They wondered how their sovereign God-King could allow such a terrible fate to befall. The answer that eluded them was that God had always been with them, but they had not been "with" God. He had been their king, but they had been disloyal.

9:1–2 Jeremiah, the servant prophet of God, was caught squarely in the middle between God and his people. Verse 1 shows his deep love for the people, and verse 2 his vehement disgust at their actions. He loved his people, but he loved goodness because God had shown him the consequences of disobedience.

9:1 my eyes a fountain of tears. Jeremiah, the "weeping prophet," was a tenderhearted man. See also verse 10; 13:17 and the book of Lamentations.

9:2 leave my people and go away from them. The prophet wanted to get away from his wicked countrymen. He despised their unfaithfulness, and even used the term "adulterers" to describe their sin. In his eyes, they were committing adultery against God by desiring other gods.

miah now want to do? Why? **2.** What are their tongues capable of doing (vv. 3,8)? In what situations does deception prove effective? **3.** What does the prophet weep over in verse 10? What seems to bother Jeremiah the most about God bringing Jerusalem to ruins (vv. 11–12)? **4.** How does the Lord answer him (vv. 13–19)? **5.** In what sense is death the "grim reaper" (v. 22)? **6.** What do the wise, the strong and the rich stand to lose from the invasion? What does it mean to "boast" in wisdom, strength or riches? In what should one boast instead (v. 24; compare 1 Cor. 1:31)? **7.** Was circumcision the sole property of the Israelites (vv. 25–26)? What kind of circumcision matters to God and why (4:4; Gen. 17:10; Deut. 10:16)?

APPLY 1. What kinds of things do people today "boast" or take pride in? What do you tend to boast about? **2.** What has been a great sadness in your life? Would it feel good to have someone "wail" with you about it? How do people respond to your feelings of loss or sorrow? How has God treated you? **3.** Do you make friends easily, or are you a loner? Did betrayal by a friend or sibling make it hard for you to trust? How do you protect yourself from being hurt by people important to you?

---

3 "They make ready their tongue
like a bow, to shoot lies;
it is not by truth
that they triumph[a] in the land.
They go from one sin to another;
they do not acknowledge me,"
declares t
4 "Beware of your friends;
do not trust your brothers.
For every brother is a deceiver,[b]
and every friend a slanderer.
5 Friend deceives friend,
and no one speaks the truth.
They have taught their tongues to lie;
they weary themselves with sinning.
6 You[c] live in the midst of deception;
in their deceit they refuse to acknowledge me,"
declares the LORD.

7 Therefore this is what the LORD Almighty says:

"See, I will refine and test them,
for what else can I do
because of the sin of my people?
8 Their tongue is a deadly arrow;
it speaks with deceit.
With his mouth each speaks cordially to his neighbor,
but in his heart he sets a trap for him.
9 Should I not punish them for this?"
declares the LORD.
"Should I not avenge myself
on such a nation as this?"

10 I will weep and wail for the mountains
and take up a lament concerning the desert pastures.
They are desolate and untraveled,
and the lowing of cattle is not heard.
The birds of the air have fled
and the animals are gone.

11 "I will make Jerusalem a heap of ruins,
a haunt of jackals;
and I will lay waste the towns of Judah
so no one can live there."

12 What man is wise enough to understand this? Who has been
instructed by the LORD and can explain it? Why has the land been
ruined and laid waste like a desert that no one can cross?
13 The LORD said, "It is because they have forsaken my law, which I

[a]3 Or *lies; / they are not valiant for truth* [b]4 Or *a deceiving Jacob* [c]6 That is, Jeremiah (the Hebrew is singular)

9:12 What ... Who ... Why. The first two questions are rhetorical. God's answer could only be "You, Jeremiah." Jeremiah's task was to be wise about the ways of God, to be instructed by him, and to explain his Word to the people. But God did not answer these two questions. Verses 12–16 are God's answer to the third question.

9:13 forsaken my law. God is patient but still demands obedience. Ongoing

set before them; they have not obeyed me or followed my law. [14]In-
stead, they have followed the stubbornness of their hearts; they have
followed the Baals, as their fathers taught them." [15]Therefore, this is
what the LORD Almighty, the God of Israel, says: "See, I will make this
people eat bitter food and drink poisoned water. [16]I will scatter them
among nations that neither they nor their fathers have known, and I
will pursue them with the sword until I have destroyed them."

[17]This is what the LORD Almighty says:

"Consider now! Call for the wailing women to come;
  send for the most skillful of them.
[18]Let them come quickly
  and wail over us
till our eyes overflow with tears
  and water streams from our eyelids.
[19]The sound of wailing is heard from Zion:
  'How ruined we are!
  How great is our shame!
We must leave our land
  because our houses are in ruins.' "

[20]Now, O women, hear the word of the LORD;
  open your ears to the words of his mouth.
Teach your daughters how to wail;
  teach one another a lament.
[21]Death has climbed in through our windows
  and has entered our fortresses;
it has cut off the children from the streets
  and the young men from the public squares.

[22]Say, "This is what the LORD declares:

" 'The dead bodies of men will lie
  like refuse on the open field,
like cut grain behind the reaper,
  with no one to gather them.' "

[23]This is what the LORD says:

"Let not the wise man boast of his wisdom
  or the strong man boast of his strength
  or the rich man boast of his riches,
[24]but let him who boasts boast about this:
  that he understands and knows me,
that I am the LORD, who exercises kindness,
  justice and righteousness on earth,
  for in these I delight,"

declares the LORD.

---

disobedience without repentance was a breach in the covenant between God and Israel—with terrible consequences for the nation (11:9–13).

9:17 Call for the wailing women. The time for mourning had arrived. "Wailing women" were professionals who led mourners in expressing grief. (Amos 5:16.)

9:24 boast ... that he understands and knows me. Everything of this world is temporary and not worth adoring. Boasting is risky, but if one is going to boast, let it be in knowing and understanding the eternal God. Only heavenly things will endure time

[25]"The days are coming," declares the LORD, "when I will punish all
who are circumcised only in the flesh— [26]Egypt, Judah, Edom, Ammon, Moab and all who live in the desert in distant places.[a] For all
these nations are really uncircumcised, and even the whole house of
Israel is uncircumcised in heart."

God and Idols

10 Hear what the LORD says to you, O house of Israel. [2]This is
what the LORD says:

"Do not learn the ways of the nations
or be terrified by signs in the sky,
though the nations are terrified by them.
[3]For the customs of the peoples are worthless;
they cut a tree out of the forest,
and a craftsman shapes it with his chisel.
[4]They adorn it with silver and gold;
they fasten it with hammer and nails
so it will not totter.
[5]Like a scarecrow in a melon patch,
their idols cannot speak;
they must be carried
because they cannot walk.
Do not fear them;
they can do no harm
nor can they do any good."

[6]No one is like you, O LORD;
you are great,
and your name is mighty in power.
[7]Who should not revere you,
O King of the nations?
This is your due.
Among all the wise men of the nations
and in all their kingdoms,
there is no one like you.
[8]They are all senseless and foolish;
they are taught by worthless wooden idols.
[9]Hammered silver is brought from Tarshish
and gold from Uphaz.
What the craftsman and goldsmith have made
is then dressed in blue and purple—
all made by skilled workers.
[10]But the LORD is the true God;
he is the living God, the eternal King.

[a]26 Or *desert and who clip the hair by their foreheads*

OPEN 1. In choosing your Christmas tree, do you prefer it natural or artificial? Large or small? Big needle or small needle? **2.** In adorning your tree, do you prefer lots of bulbs and glitter? Only natural, handmade items? Only lights? **3.** Describe one of your favorite ornaments that gets hung on your Christmas tree every year, or the special one you made or received last year.

STUDY The word "nations" is from the Hebrew "Goyim," meaning "Gentiles" or non-Jews. **1.** From what two Gentile customs does God discourage Israel (vv. 2–3)? What feeling lies beneath these words about idols (vv. 4–5)? **2.** If idols are so impotent and worthless (Ps. 115:4–7), why do you think God's people constantly turn to them? Did idol worship play a part in the social and economic fabric of Palestine (v. 9; Acts 19:23–27)? **3.** How was the Jewish concept of God different from that of the pagans (vv. 10–13)? How easy would it be to combine the monotheism of Israel with worship of local cultic deities? Who ultimately is mocked by this attempt? **4.** The words "portion" and "inheritance" are similar in verse 16. What does it mean that Israel's portion or inheritance is God? That Israel is the "tribe of his inheritance"?

APPLY 1. What kinds of things do you idolize today—things that you are counting on to speak to you, carry you or do good for you, as only God can? **2.** How much time do you take to meditate on God's creation and power? What aspect of nature speaks most clearly to you of God's power? **3.** In what sense might verse 5 apply to you: Is there anything you fear that you need not? Is there a better way you could spend your prime waking hours and disposable income?

10:1–25 In the last of these temple messages, Jeremiah contrasts the powerlessness of idols with the mighty God. Idolatry creates a breach in the covenant (9:13) by forsaking trust in God alone (2:11). This is a terrible offense to God—a violation of the divine law and a personal betrayal (3:9).

10:4 adorn it with silver and gold. Wooden idols were often plated with silver or gold to make them more beautiful and to preserve them. At their core however, they would still all rot away—pretty packages with no permanence.

10:5 An idol was simply an empty image which could neither move nor act, an object neither to be feared nor revered, worthy only of disregard.

When he is angry, the earth trembles;
the nations cannot endure his wrath.

[11]"Tell them this: 'These gods, who did not make the heavens and the earth, will perish from the earth and from under the heavens.' "[a]

[12]But God made the earth by his power;
he founded the world by his wisdom
and stretched out the heavens by his understanding.
[13]When he thunders, the waters in the heavens roar;
he makes clouds rise from the ends of the earth.
He sends lightning with the rain
and brings out the wind from his storehouses.

[14]Everyone is senseless and without knowledge;
every goldsmith is shamed by his idols.
His images are a fraud;
they have no breath in them.
[15]They are worthless, the objects of mockery;
when their judgment comes, they will perish.
[16]He who is the Portion of Jacob is not like these,
for he is the Maker of all things,
including Israel, the tribe of his inheritance—
the LORD Almighty is his name.

Coming Destruction

[17]Gather up your belongings to leave the land,
you who live under siege.
[18]For this is what the LORD says:
"At this time I will hurl out
those who live in this land;
I will bring distress on them
so that they may be captured."

[19]Woe to me because of my injury!
My wound is incurable!
Yet I said to myself,
"This is my sickness, and I must endure it."
[20]My tent is destroyed;
all its ropes are snapped.
My sons are gone from me and are no more;
no one is left now to pitch my tent
or to set up my shelter.

[a]*11* The text of this verse is in Aramaic.

OPEN 1. What is the most time away from school or work which you have missed because of an illness or injury? How did you make up for the lost time? **2.** If you had to vacate your house before dawn, how many carloads would it take to move your belongings? Truckloads? What would you take if you could keep only what you could carry?

STUDY 1. What will happen to those who stay under siege? To those who flee the city? If Jeremiah's name means "the LORD throws," what possible pun do you see here? **2.** Who speaks in verses 19–22? What is the "incurable wound"? What happened to the leaders? **3.** How does Jeremiah feel about himself in this time of crisis (vv. 23–24)? For what two reasons is he angry with Judah's enemies (v. 25)? **4.** Is this prayer vengeful, or is it an appeal for God's

10:11 them. This verse was addressed to followers of pagan idols. It was written in Aramaic, the language of diplomacy during that period, and would have been used when addressing a non-Hebrew. The message was clear: idols were worthless in God's eyes, less than rubble (v. 5). Here Jeremiah calls the makers of idols worthless. Idols were valueless not only for God's people but also for the pagans who built and worshipped them.

10:13 God rules over all nature. He is the God of Israel and the master of the universe. Idols are powerless.

10:19–20 Jeremiah cries in pain because of the fate he and his countrymen suffer. To add to their misery, these people have no choice but to reconcile themselves to the coming destruction and exile. Jeremiah evoked the image of the old, pastoral-nomadic lifestyle to illustrate the disappearance of the culture the Israelites had planted in the Promised Land. Towns would become empty with no one left to even pitch a tent (v. 25).

justice? Why do you think so? **5.** Do you believe the fate of your country depends on whether the political leaders look to God for guidance? Why?

APPLY 1. Have you ever met a refugee? How would you feel if your home was destroyed and your country at war? **2.** Which would you rather receive: God's justice or anger? What determines who gets what?

OPEN 1. Think of one promise you have kept for a long time and one promise that was broken. How did (or do) you feel about a broken promise? **2.** Where would you live if you could choose anywhere in the world? What would you want there that would be the modern equivalent of the "milk and honey" promised to the ancient Israelites?

STUDY 1. When did God and Israel make "the terms of this covenant," especially those dealing with "cursed is the man" (vv. 1–5; Deut. 27:15–26)? What happened in the reign of Josiah to renew such interest in the covenant (2 Kin. 22:8–13; 23:1–3)? **2.** What did God promise to do for Israel (vv. 4–8)? What was their land of "milk and honey" (Ex 3:8)? **3.** What was their part of the bargain? How are the people of Judah responding to Josiah's and Jeremiah's call (vv. 9–13)? **4.** Again, Jeremiah is forbidden to pray for Israel (v. 14; 7:16)? Why (1 John 5:16–17)? **5.** What is the point of the covenant when Israel never keeps it? What curses are coming if they don't (Deut. 28:15–68)? **6.** What is Judah doing to win God's favor (v. 15; 7:10–11,21–24)? Can

21 The shepherds are senseless
and do not inquire of the LORD;
so they do not prosper
and all their flock is scattered.
22 Listen! The report is coming—
a great commotion from the land of the north!
It will make the towns of Judah desolate,
a haunt of jackals.

Jeremiah's Prayer

23 I know, O LORD, that a man's life is not his own;
it is not for man to direct his steps.
24 Correct me, LORD, but only with justice—
not in your anger,
lest you reduce me to nothing.
25 Pour out your wrath on the nations
that do not acknowledge you,
on the peoples who do not call on your name.
For they have devoured Jacob;
they have devoured him completely
and destroyed his homeland.

The Covenant Is Broken

11 This is the word that came to Jeremiah from the LORD: 2 "Listen
to the terms of this covenant and tell them to the people of
Judah and to those who live in Jerusalem. 3 Tell them that this is what
the LORD, the God of Israel, says: 'Cursed is the man who does not
obey the terms of this covenant— 4 the terms I commanded your forefathers when I brought them out of Egypt, out of the iron-smelting
furnace.' I said, 'Obey me and do everything I command you, and you
will be my people, and I will be your God. 5 Then I will fulfill the oath
I swore to your forefathers, to give them a land flowing with milk and
honey'—the land you possess today."

I answered, "Amen, LORD."

6 The LORD said to me, "Proclaim all these words in the towns of
Judah and in the streets of Jerusalem: 'Listen to the terms of this covenant and follow them. 7 From the time I brought your forefathers up
from Egypt until today, I warned them again and again, saying, "Obey
me." 8 But they did not listen or pay attention; instead, they followed
the stubbornness of their evil hearts. So I brought on them all the
curses of the covenant I had commanded them to follow but that they
did not keep.' "

9 Then the LORD said to me, "There is a conspiracy among the people of Judah and those who live in Jerusalem. 10 They have returned to
the sins of their forefathers, who refused to listen to my words. They
have followed other gods to serve them. Both the house of Israel and
the house of Judah have broken the covenant I made with their forefathers. 11 Therefore this is what the LORD says: 'I will bring on them a

---

11:3 Cursed is the man who does not obey. Jeremiah used the phrase repeated 12 times in Deuteronomy 27:15–26. There, Moses instructed the people that obedience resulted in blessings (Deut. 28:1–14), and disobedience, in curses (Deut. 28:15–68).

11:9 conspiracy among the people. King Josiah tried to reform the social and spiritual conditions of Judah. He was the last king who tried to do good. Many opposed him. Upon his death, his reforms were reversed and they returned to their wickedness.

disaster they cannot escape. Although they cry out to me, I will not
listen to them. 12The towns of Judah and the people of Jerusalem will
go and cry out to the gods to whom they burn incense, but they will
not help them at all when disaster strikes. 13You have as many gods
as you have towns, O Judah; and the altars you have set up to burn
incense to that shameful god Baal are as many as the streets of Jerusalem.'

14"Do not pray for this people nor offer any plea or petition for
them, because I will not listen when they call to me in the time of
their distress.

15"What is my beloved doing in my temple
as she works out her evil schemes with many?
Can consecrated meat avert ⌊your punishment⌋?
When you engage in your wickedness,
then you rejoice.[a]"

16The LORD called you a thriving olive tree
with fruit beautiful in form.
But with the roar of a mighty storm
he will set it on fire,
and its branches will be broken.

17The LORD Almighty, who planted you, has decreed disaster for you,
because the house of Israel and the house of Judah have done evil
and provoked me to anger by burning incense to Baal.

Plot Against Jeremiah

18Because the LORD revealed their plot to me, I knew it, for at that
time he showed me what they were doing. 19I had been like a gentle
lamb led to the slaughter; I did not realize that they had plotted
against me, saying,

"Let us destroy the tree and its fruit;
let us cut him off from the land of the living,
that his name be remembered no more."
20But, O LORD Almighty, you who judge righteously
and test the heart and mind,
let me see your vengeance upon them,
for to you I have committed my cause.

21"Therefore this is what the LORD says about the men of Anathoth
who are seeking your life and saying, 'Do not prophesy in the name of
the LORD or you will die by our hands'— 22therefore this is what the
LORD Almighty says: 'I will punish them. Their young men will die by
the sword, their sons and daughters by famine. 23Not even a remnant
will be left to them, because I will bring disaster on the men of Anathoth in the year of their punishment.' "

[a]15 *Or Could consecrated meat avert your punishment? / Then you would rejoice*

anything change God's mind at this point (vv. 11,14–15)? Is this fair?

APPLY 1. If your spiritual life were a tree, how would the tree be doing (vv. 16–17): Thriving and laddened with fruit? Bearing fruit, but underproducing? Surviving but blighted by insects and disease? Ready to be cut down and replaced? **2.** Does your group have a covenant with God? With each other? What promises need to be restated in the group?

OPEN 1. What were you noted for in your hometown? **2.** Tom Wolfe wrote, "You can't go home again." Has this been true for you?

STUDY 1. Jeremiah helps Josiah close local shrines. Does this play well in his hometown of Anathoth? Why does this distress him (12:2)? **2.** How does he discover the plot? Why did it take him so long to realize his peril? **3.** Why was the plot revealed?

APPLY 1. Jesus also had a "bad homecoming" (Matt. 13:53–58). Has obeying God ever alienated those closest to you? What happened? **2.** Are you comfortable in seeking God's vengeance? What would you request if you were Jeremiah?

11:15 my beloved doing in my temple. In Deuteronomy 33:12 Benjamin was called "beloved of the LORD." By extension, Judah (with its capital, Jerusalem, in Benjamite territory) is addressed by the same term. But note the irony: Judah had become so evil that God, who still loved his people, was bringing disaster on both the southern kingdom and Israel.

11:23 Not even a remnant. These men were from Jeremiah's own town. Only the conspirators of Anathoth were annihilated. After the Exile, 128 other men returned to the village (Ezra 2:23).

OPEN 1. If you were a lawyer, would you prefer to prosecute or defend? Would you prosecute someone you felt was innocent? Defend someone you thought was guilty? **2.** In your experience, do nice guys always finish last? Do bad guys always finish first? **3.** What member of your family or group would you nominate as "King of the World" for a day? What do you think he or she could do that other world leaders can't or won't?

STUDY 1. What is Jeremiah's bone of contention (v. 2)? Has this thought ever crossed your mind? **2.** What does Jeremiah want God to do (v. 3)? Why is Jeremiah so brutal? Why are the faithless so carefree (v. 4)? **3.** In Jeremiah's complaint, on what is he basing his appeal: Good guys always win in the end? Divine justice? Prophetic license? **4.** What is the point of the comparison in verses 5–6? What comfort can Jeremiah take in that? **5.** What is God's warning to Judah (vv. 7–13)? How does he seem to feel? How is this an answer for Jeremiah? **6.** What is God's warning to Judah's marauding neighbors (vv. 14–17; 2 Kin. 24:1–2)? **7.** What good news do you see here for the exiles, both Jewish and Gentile? What will determine how God treats them (vv. 16–17)? **8.** How would you describe God's response to Jeremiah's honesty: Angry? Glad? Disturbed? Sympathetic? Puzzled? Matter-of-fact? Other?

APPLY 1. Have you ever complained to God as honestly as Jeremiah did? What was God's response? **2.** What would our world be like if God instantly punished every sin? What would your life be like? **3.** Are you "on foot ... competing with horses" (v. 5)? Or are you "stumbling in safe country"? How do you prepare for tougher times? How can your group assist?

Jeremiah's Complaint

12 You are always righteous, O LORD,
when I bring a case before you.
Yet I would speak with you about your justice:
Why does the way of the wicked prosper?
Why do all the faithless live at ease?
2 You have planted them, and they have taken root;
they grow and bear fruit.
You are always on their lips
but far from their hearts.
3 Yet you know me, O LORD;
you see me and test my thoughts about you.
Drag them off like sheep to be butchered!
Set them apart for the day of slaughter!
4 How long will the land lie parched[a]
and the grass in every field be withered?
Because those who live in it are wicked,
the animals and birds have perished.
Moreover, the people are saying,
"He will not see what happens to us."

God's Answer

5 "If you have raced with men on foot
and they have worn you out,
how can you compete with horses?
If you stumble in safe country,[b]
how will you manage in the thickets by[c] the Jordan?
6 Your brothers, your own family—
even they have betrayed you;
they have raised a loud cry against you.
Do not trust them,
though they speak well of you.

7 "I will forsake my house,
abandon my inheritance;
I will give the one I love
into the hands of her enemies.
8 My inheritance has become to me
like a lion in the forest.
She roars at me;

[a]4 Or *land mourn* [b]5 Or *If you put your trust in a land of safety* [c]5 Or *the flooding of*

12:1 Why does the way of the wicked prosper? Jeremiah was not alone in asking this question. (Job 21:7–15, Mal. 3:15.) God answered that the wicked seem to prosper but will perish (vv. 7–13), and the invaders who seem to benefit from his people's misery will surely be destroyed in turn.

12:3 sheep to be butchered. Jeremiah requested that the same fate be given the wicked in Judah as was planned for him by his enemies (11:19). He was confident that his motives in this request were right and acknowledged that the Lord knew his thoughts.

12:5 how will you manage? God told Jeremiah that things would get worse for him, not better. The prophet was caught in the upheaval of invasion and exile, the descent of his people into apostasy and even a conspiracy to kill him. Here God makes the prophet look in a mirror. How would he manage these terrible events? In verse 3 Jeremiah acknowledges that God could test him.

12:6 your own family. Members of Jeremiah's own family were conspiring to kill him. (God said in v. 5 that things would get worse—they just did.) The Hebrew word translated as "family" means "house." Thus there is a direct connection to verse 7 in which Jeremiah disavows his family.

12:8 She roars ... I hate her. Jeremiah must give up his love for Judah

therefore I hate her.
[9]Has not my inheritance become to me
like a speckled bird of prey
that other birds of prey surround and attack?
Go and gather all the wild beasts;
bring them to devour.
[10]Many shepherds will ruin my vineyard
and trample down my field;
they will turn my pleasant field
into a desolate wasteland.
[11]It will be made a wasteland,
parched and desolate before me;
the whole land will be laid waste
because there is no one who cares.
[12]Over all the barren heights in the desert
destroyers will swarm,
for the sword of the LORD will devour
from one end of the land to the other;
no one will be safe.
[13]They will sow wheat but reap thorns;
they will wear themselves out but gain nothing.
So bear the shame of your harvest
because of the LORD's fierce anger."

[14]This is what the LORD says: "As for all my wicked neighbors who
seize the inheritance I gave my people Israel, I will uproot them from
their lands and I will uproot the house of Judah from among them.
[15]But after I uproot them, I will again have compassion and will bring
each of them back to his own inheritance and his own country. [16]And
if they learn well the ways of my people and swear by my name,
saying, 'As surely as the LORD lives'—even as they once taught my
people to swear by Baal—then they will be established among my
people. [17]But if any nation does not listen, I will completely uproot
and destroy it," declares the LORD.

A Linen Belt

13 This is what the LORD said to me: "Go and buy a linen belt and
put it around your waist, but do not let it touch water." [2]So I
bought a belt, as the LORD directed, and put it around my waist.
[3]Then the word of the LORD came to me a second time: [4]"Take the
belt you bought and are wearing around your waist, and go now to
Perath[a] and hide it there in a crevice in the rocks." [5]So I went and hid
it at Perath, as the LORD told me.
[6]Many days later the LORD said to me, "Go now to Perath and get
the belt I told you to hide there." [7]So I went to Perath and dug up the

[a]4 Or possibly *the Euphrates;* also in verses 5-7

OPEN When you were a child, where did you hide special things to keep them from parents or siblings?

STUDY 1. What metaphors do you see in this allegory (vv. 1–6)? Why a linen belt? The hiding? The spoiling? **2.** What does the allegory mean (vv. 6–11)? Why does God use an object lesson? **3.** What is the meaning of the wineskin metaphor (v. 12)? Why belabor the obvious? What should be obvious to Judah?

and give her up "into the hands of her enemies" (v. 7). Here, hate is more the absence of love than the presence of antipathy.

13:1–11 God instructs Jeremiah to perform certain acts and then interprets them. All the symbols God uses are familiar to Jeremiah. New Testament parables use symbols in the same way, to bring a lesson home to the listener.

13:1 linen belt. The priests' garments, made of linen, symbolized the nation as a "kingdom of priests" (Ex. 19:6). The new belt represented the former intimate relationship between God and this "kingdom."

13:7 it was ruined and completely useless. The linen belt was meant to be worn, symbolizing the close connection between God and his people. When taken off and hidden (exiled), it

belt and took it from the place where I had hidden it, but now it was
ruined and completely useless.

8Then the word of the LORD came to me: 9"This is what the LORD
says: 'In the same way I will ruin the pride of Judah and the great
pride of Jerusalem. 10These wicked people, who refuse to listen to my
words, who follow the stubbornness of their hearts and go after
other gods to serve and worship them, will be like this belt—completely useless! 11For as a belt is bound around a man's waist, so I
bound the whole house of Israel and the whole house of Judah to
me,' declares the LORD, 'to be my people for my renown and praise
and honor. But they have not listened.'

Wineskins

12"Say to them: 'This is what the LORD, the God of Israel, says:
Every wineskin should be filled with wine.' And if they say to you,
'Don't we know that every wineskin should be filled with wine?'
13then tell them, 'This is what the LORD says: I am going to fill with
drunkenness all who live in this land, including the kings who sit on
David's throne, the priests, the prophets and all those living in Jerusalem. 14I will smash them one against the other, fathers and sons
alike, declares the LORD. I will allow no pity or mercy or compassion
to keep me from destroying them.' "

Threat of Captivity

15Hear and pay attention,
do not be arrogant,
for the LORD has spoken.
16Give glory to the LORD your God
before he brings the darkness,
before your feet stumble
on the darkening hills.
You hope for light,
but he will turn it to thick darkness
and change it to deep gloom.
17But if you do not listen,
I will weep in secret
because of your pride;
my eyes will weep bitterly,
overflowing with tears,
because the LORD's flock will be taken captive.
18Say to the king and to the queen mother,
"Come down from your thrones,
for your glorious crowns
will fall from your heads."
19The cities in the Negev will be shut up,

4. Is Judah's drunkenness literal or spiritual (v. 13; 25:15–29)? What's the message in this for Judah to hear? For you?

APPLY 1. Have there been times in your life when God used actions, even a "belting," to speak louder than words? What happened? How did the message get through? **2.** Jeremiah obeyed God instantly, without questioning. How willing are you to go along with things that you don't understand? **3.** We try to convey God's message through words and deeds. Which is easier for you? In what ways might one without the other confuse people? How can you share God's message more clearly and openly?

OPEN 1. What precautions do you take when traveling at night, alone? When darkness falls, what do you fear might happen to you? **2.** When was the last time you were lost? What happened?

STUDY 1. Is there any hope for Judah, or is captivity inevitable (vv. 15–17)? Why would Jeremiah weep secretly (9:1)? **2.** Who are the "king and ... queen mother" (v. 18; 2 Kin. 24:8–12, which dates this prophecy c. 597 B.C.)? **3.** The defeated were often led naked into captivity. What sense of shame does this fate convey (vv. 22,26; Ezek. 16:36–38)? **4.** Is Judah unable to stop sinning (v. 23)? Is it fair to punish people for acts that Jeremiah seems to consider beyond their control? **5.** What had Judah done to deserve this fate (vv. 24–25)? **6.** How do you think Jeremiah felt delivering this kind of message again and again? Why didn't God just warn Judah once and then lower the boom? What do these repeated warnings tell you about God? **7.** Why did

---

became ruined and useless by the foreign elements it contacted.

13:12–14 These verses use the common wineskin to describe the destruction of Judah's leaders and people, who were no longer filled with God's Spirit. Empty wineskins are not the way things should be.

13:13 fill with drunkenness. God's people are like wineskins that should be filled with God's Spirit. But the people of Judah were empty. Instead of being filled with God's love through his Spirit, they will be filled with God's wrath, which will destroy them.

13:18 king and ... queen mother. If the king and queen mother are Jehoiachin and Nehushta (2 Kin. 24:8), then the year was 597 B.C., just before Nebuchadnezzar laid siege to Jerusalem.

and there will be no one to open them.
All Judah will be carried into exile,
carried completely away.

20 Lift up your eyes and see
those who are coming from the north.
Where is the flock that was entrusted to you,
the sheep of which you boasted?
21 What will you say when ⌊the LORD⌋ sets over you
those you cultivated as your special allies?
Will not pain grip you
like that of a woman in labor?
22 And if you ask yourself,
"Why has this happened to me?"—
it is because of your many sins
that your skirts have been torn off
and your body mistreated.
23 Can the Ethiopian[a] change his skin
or the leopard its spots?
Neither can you do good
who are accustomed to doing evil.

24 "I will scatter you like chaff
driven by the desert wind.
25 This is your lot,
the portion I have decreed for you,"
declares the LORD,
"because you have forgotten me
and trusted in false gods.
26 I will pull up your skirts over your face
that your shame may be seen—
27 your adulteries and lustful neighings,
your shameless prostitution!
I have seen your detestable acts
on the hills and in the fields.
Woe to you, O Jerusalem!
How long will you be unclean?"

Drought, Famine, Sword

14 This is the word of the LORD to Jeremiah concerning the drought:

2 "Judah mourns,
her cities languish;
they wail for the land,
and a cry goes up from Jerusalem.
3 The nobles send their servants for water;
they go to the cisterns

[a]23 Hebrew *Cushite* (probably a person from the upper Nile region)

God liken the worship of other gods to adultery? What does that tell you about the way he thinks of his relationship with us?

APPLY 1. How easily do you cry? What was the cause of your last tears? Has the state of your church or humanity ever upset you enough to weep? **2.** Imagining God as your spouse, do you feel: Head over heels? The honeymoon's over? All work, no play? Separation? Still going strong? Divorced? **3.** When have you felt especially frustrated in your efforts to change? How do you react emotionally to verse 23? Does Christ affect our ability to change (Rom. 7:21–25)?

OPEN 1. Are you usually early, on-time or late for appointments or meetings? Why? Would you consider breaking the mold by being the opposite (early for once, or late)? **2.** When was the last time you were too late for something? What happened? How did you feel? **3.** If you had to pick a torturous "fate worse than death," what would it be?

STUDY 1. What "triple whammy" from God finally gets Judah's attention (14:1–6)? How

13:22 skirts have been torn off. Defeat by the Babylonians would mean total humiliation. Judah and Babylon had been allies in the past (v. 21), but now defeat would reduce Judah to the status of a prostitute, a proper fate because Judah had acted like a prostitute in adultery with other gods.

14:1 drought. Drought was one of the curses of disobedience (Lev. 26:19–20). This drought was especially terrible because it came during the Babylonian invasion. No food, no water, no safety (v. 18).

do you imagine this "drought, famine and sword" would come about: All at once? In shifts of successive years? Or what? **2.** On what basis do the people hope God will rescue them (14:7–9)? What do you think was the most effective part of their appeal? **3.** Why is God fed up with them and their cries (14:10–13)? Why should Jeremiah pray for them, as a true prophet would (1 Sam. 7:8; 12:23)? **4.** What will happen to the false prophets (14:14–18)? What irony do you see here? **5.** Though told not to pray for the people, what is Jeremiah doing in 14:19–22? What is the basis of Jeremiah's appeal on behalf of the rejected people (Lev. 26:44–45)? **6.** Does God soften up (15:1–4)? What sins did King Manasseh commit (2 Kin. 21:1–18)? **7.** What is the focus of the poem in 15:5–9? What irony and tragedy do you see here?

APPLY **1.** The false prophets told the kings what they wanted to hear. Do you know someone who says "yes" to avoid rocking the boat? Are you ever a "yes-sayer"? Has it ever gotten you in trouble? What troubles do you see stemming from people who only tell others what they want to hear? **2.** On the other hand, some people like to make waves. Do you? What is one thing you have said that greatly upset some people's presumptuous thinking? What happened as a result? **3.** When have you reacted with scorn or persecution against someone who rocked your boat?

---

but find no water.
They return with their jars unfilled;
dismayed and despairing,
they cover their heads.
4 The ground is cracked
because there is no rain in the land;
the farmers are dismayed
and cover their heads.
5 Even the doe in the field
deserts her newborn fawn
because there is no grass.
6 Wild donkeys stand on the barren heights
and pant like jackals;
their eyesight fails
for lack of pasture."

7 Although our sins testify against us,
O LORD, do something for the sake of your name.
For our backsliding is great;
we have sinned against you.
8 O Hope of Israel,
its Savior in times of distress,
why are you like a stranger in the land,
like a traveler who stays only a night?
9 Why are you like a man taken by surprise,
like a warrior powerless to save?
You are among us, O LORD,
and we bear your name;
do not forsake us!

10 This is what the LORD says about this people:

"They greatly love to wander;
they do not restrain their feet.
So the LORD does not accept them;
he will now remember their wickedness
and punish them for their sins."

11 Then the LORD said to me, "Do not pray for the well-being of this
people. 12 Although they fast, I will not listen to their cry; though they
offer burnt offerings and grain offerings, I will not accept them.
Instead, I will destroy them with the sword, famine and plague."
13 But I said, "Ah, Sovereign LORD, the prophets keep telling them,
'You will not see the sword or suffer famine. Indeed, I will give you
lasting peace in this place.' "
14 Then the LORD said to me, "The prophets are prophesying lies in
my name. I have not sent them or appointed them or spoken to them.
They are prophesying to you false visions, divinations, idolatries[a] and
the delusions of their own minds. 15 Therefore, this is what the LORD

[a]14 Or *visions, worthless divinations*

14:4 there is no rain in the land. Judah and Israel occupy arid land. Normally enough rain falls to sustain life. Egypt could depend on the Nile as a water source, but Israel and Judah were dependent on rainfall to fill wells and cisterns to keep their water supply adequate.

14:10–11 this people ... wander. God had rejected "his people." They might offer offerings and sacrifices, but God would not accept them.

[14]I will enslave you to your enemies
in[a] a land you do not know,
for my anger will kindle a fire
that will burn against you."

[15]You understand, O LORD;
remember me and care for me.
Avenge me on my persecutors.
You are long-suffering—do not take me away;
think of how I suffer reproach for your sake.
[16]When your words came, I ate them;
they were my joy and my heart's delight,
for I bear your name,
O LORD God Almighty.
[17]I never sat in the company of revelers,
never made merry with them;
I sat alone because your hand was on me
and you had filled me with indignation.
[18]Why is my pain unending
and my wound grievous and incurable?
Will you be to me like a deceptive brook,
like a spring that fails?

[19]Therefore this is what the LORD says:

"If you repent, I will restore you
that you may serve me;
if you utter worthy, not worthless, words,
you will be my spokesman.
Let this people turn to you,
but you must not turn to them.
[20]I will make you a wall to this people,
a fortified wall of bronze;
they will fight against you
but will not overcome you,
for I am with you
to rescue and save you,"
declares the LORD.
[21]"I will save you from the hands of the wicked
and redeem you from the grasp of the cruel."

Day of Disaster

16 Then the word of the LORD came to me: [2]"You must not marry
and have sons or daughters in this place." [3]For this is what

[a]14 Some Hebrew manuscripts, Septuagint and Syriac (see also Jer. 17:4); most Hebrew manuscripts *I will cause your enemies to bring you / into*

APPLY 1. If you could go back and change anything in your life, what would you change? What do you wish could have happened instead? **2.** Do you think serving the Lord was a pleasant task for Jeremiah? Would you have liked his job? Do you ever feel unrewarded for your dedication? Unappreciated by God? By others? **3.** Do you receive enough encouragement and support from this group? How could the group provide more of what you need?

OPEN 1. Recall a really good wedding you have attended. What made it great? **2.** What was (or what do you imagine might be) the best part of your wedding? **3.** When was the last time you were invited to

15:15 You understand ... remember me. Judah had lost its connection with God, but Jeremiah called on his own relationship with the Lord to support his request for vengeance upon his persecutors.

15:18 Jeremiah asked two rhetorical questions concerning his emotional pain, the mission God had given him and God's faithfulness in light of Israel's doom. Was God the "spring of living water" (2:13) or a "spring that fails"?

15:19–21 If you repent, I will restore you. Jeremiah was not exempt from the temptation to sin or immune to its consequences. It was wrong for Jeremiah to doubt God, and God called him to repent. God understood him (v. 15) and encouraged him by promising protection from enemies and salvation from the wicked.

16:2 You must not marry. God prohibited Jeremiah from marrying and having children. The language here is

a celebration but could not go? Did the others miss you? How did you feel?

STUDY **1.** What three activities of normal human life does God forbid to Jeremiah (vv. 1–9)? Why? What is his abstinence from these things supposed to convey to the people? **2.** How do you suppose Jeremiah coped with the loneliness that came with his particular calling? **3.** How do verses 6 and 7 make you feel about the desolation in store for Judah? In what way will the people "serve other gods" (v. 13)? **4.** What rays of hope do you see in this otherwise dismal picture? What event will outshine the Exodus? **5.** What is so doubly detestable to God about idol worship, that "fisherman" and "hunters" were sent in after them (vv. 16–18)?

APPLY **1.** Have you ever decided not to go to someone's wedding or party in order to make a statement—perhaps to show disapproval of their behavior (vv. 1–9)? Do you think the statement was heard? How did you feel about it in the end? **2.** When has something happened to you that you wondered if God was trying to make a statement to *you* (v. 10)? Did you hear the message? How did you feel about it in the end?

OPEN To what tree or plant would you compare your life: Evergreen—tall and majestic? Weep-

the LORD says about the sons and daughters born in this land and
about the women who are their mothers and the men who are their
fathers: 4"They will die of deadly diseases. They will not be mourned
or buried but will be like refuse lying on the ground. They will perish
by sword and famine, and their dead bodies will become food for the
birds of the air and the beasts of the earth."

5For this is what the LORD says: "Do not enter a house where there
is a funeral meal; do not go to mourn or show sympathy, because I
have withdrawn my blessing, my love and my pity from this people,"
declares the LORD. 6"Both high and low will die in this land. They will
not be buried or mourned, and no one will cut himself or shave his
head for them. 7No one will offer food to comfort those who mourn
for the dead—not even for a father or a mother—nor will anyone give
them a drink to console them.

8"And do not enter a house where there is feasting and sit down to
eat and drink. 9For this is what the LORD Almighty, the God of Israel,
says: Before your eyes and in your days I will bring an end to the
sounds of joy and gladness and to the voices of bride and bridegroom
in this place.

10"When you tell these people all this and they ask you, 'Why has
the LORD decreed such a great disaster against us? What wrong have
we done? What sin have we committed against the LORD our God?'
11then say to them, 'It is because your fathers forsook me,' declares
the LORD, 'and followed other gods and served and worshiped them.
They forsook me and did not keep my law. 12But you have behaved
more wickedly than your fathers. See how each of you is following
the stubbornness of his evil heart instead of obeying me. 13So I will
throw you out of this land into a land neither you nor your fathers
have known, and there you will serve other gods day and night, for I
will show you no favor.'

14"However, the days are coming," declares the LORD, "when men
will no longer say, 'As surely as the LORD lives, who brought the Israelites up out of Egypt,' 15but they will say, 'As surely as the LORD lives,
who brought the Israelites up out of the land of the north and out of
all the countries where he had banished them.' For I will restore them
to the land I gave their forefathers.

16"But now I will send for many fishermen," declares the LORD,
"and they will catch them. After that I will send for many hunters, and
they will hunt them down on every mountain and hill and from the
crevices of the rocks. 17My eyes are on all their ways; they are not hidden from me, nor is their sin concealed from my eyes. 18I will repay
them double for their wickedness and their sin, because they have
defiled my land with the lifeless forms of their vile images and have
filled my inheritance with their detestable idols."

19O LORD, my strength and my fortress,
my refuge in time of distress,
to you the nations will come

---

the same as the absolute commands of the Ten Commandments (Ex. 20:3–4,7,13–17).

16:5 Do not enter a house where there is. The times would become so bad that Jeremiah was not to participate *in either* mourning or feasting. The present mourning was only a shadow of what was to come, and nothing warranted celebrating here. Destruction would soon come.

16:16 many fishermen ... many hunters. Fishermen and hunters were symbols of conquerors who snare their victims in a net (Ezek. 12:13) or hook the jaws of enemies (Ezek. 29:4).

from the ends of the earth and say,
"Our fathers possessed nothing but false gods,
worthless idols that did them no good.
20 Do men make their own gods?
Yes, but they are not gods!"

21 "Therefore I will teach them—
this time I will teach them
my power and might.
Then they will know
that my name is the LORD.

17 "Judah's sin is engraved with an iron tool,
inscribed with a flint point,
on the tablets of their hearts
and on the horns of their altars.
2 Even their children remember
their altars and Asherah poles[a]
beside the spreading trees
and on the high hills.
3 My mountain in the land
and your[b] wealth and all your treasures
I will give away as plunder,
together with your high places,
because of sin throughout your country.
4 Through your own fault you will lose
the inheritance I gave you.
I will enslave you to your enemies
in a land you do not know,
for you have kindled my anger,
and it will burn forever."

5 This is what the LORD says:

"Cursed is the one who trusts in man,
who depends on flesh for his strength
and whose heart turns away from the LORD.
6 He will be like a bush in the wastelands;
he will not see prosperity when it comes.
He will dwell in the parched places of the desert,
in a salt land where no one lives.

7 "But blessed is the man who trusts in the LORD,
whose confidence is in him.
8 He will be like a tree planted by the water
that sends out its roots by the stream.
It does not fear when heat comes;
its leaves are always green.
It has no worries in a year of drought
and never fails to bear fruit."

9 The heart is deceitful above all things

[a]2 That is, symbols of the goddess Asherah [b]2,3 Or *hills* / [3]*and the mountains of the land. / Your*

ing willow—bending with the wind? Desert cactus—a sole survivor? Oak—a bit nutty? Other?

STUDY 1. Upon what is Jeremiah relying? How does this contrast with the gods of other nations, "their altars and Asherah poles" (v. 2; Ex. 34:12–14)? **2.** In contrast to the cursed drought conditions that prevail, what blessed hope does Jeremiah cling to and hold forth for others (vv. 5–8)? **3.** Why does Jeremiah call the human heart "deceitful above all things" (v. 9)? What is the relationship between mind and action (v. 10)? What is the point of the related parable (v. 11)? **4.** What are Jeremiah's countrymen saying about his ability to prophesy (vv. 14–15)? How will the coming disaster bring both hope and terror to the prophet? **5.** Of what does Jeremiah need healing? How might he be confused with a false prophet? (Hint: What has not yet happened that he is predicting will?)

APPLY 1. What times of spiritual "drought" have you experienced? What keeps you going during those dry times? **2.** At present, are you feeling more like a "bush in the wastelands" (v. 6) or a "tree planted by the water" (v. 8)? Why? **3.** How honest are you with yourself? Could your heart be deceiving you about the motives of some of your actions at work? At home? In relationships?

17:9–10 heart is deceitful. Jeremiah referred to the heart as the seat of passion and will. The heart is the root where wickedness begins. God alone understands the heart. God alone can judge a person's motives.

and beyond cure.
Who can understand it?

10 "I the LORD search the heart
and examine the mind,
to reward a man according to his conduct,
according to what his deeds deserve."

11 Like a partridge that hatches eggs it did not lay
is the man who gains riches by unjust means.
When his life is half gone, they will desert him,
and in the end he will prove to be a fool.

12 A glorious throne, exalted from the beginning,
is the place of our sanctuary.
13 O LORD, the hope of Israel,
all who forsake you will be put to shame.
Those who turn away from you will be written in the dust
because they have forsaken the LORD,
the spring of living water.

14 Heal me, O LORD, and I will be healed;
save me and I will be saved,
for you are the one I praise.
15 They keep saying to me,
"Where is the word of the LORD?
Let it now be fulfilled!"
16 I have not run away from being your shepherd;
you know I have not desired the day of despair.
What passes my lips is open before you.
17 Do not be a terror to me;
you are my refuge in the day of disaster.
18 Let my persecutors be put to shame,
but keep me from shame;
let them be terrified,
but keep me from terror.
Bring on them the day of disaster;
destroy them with double destruction.

Keeping the Sabbath Holy

19 This is what the LORD said to me: "Go and stand at the gate of the
people, through which the kings of Judah go in and out; stand also at
all the other gates of Jerusalem. 20 Say to them, 'Hear the word of the
LORD, O kings of Judah and all people of Judah and everyone living in
Jerusalem who come through these gates. 21 This is what the LORD
says: Be careful not to carry a load on the Sabbath day or bring it
through the gates of Jerusalem. 22 Do not bring a load out of your

OPEN 1. What was your favorite activity as a kid? What sounds like an ideal day to you now? **2.** Would you keep your job if you inherited a fortune?

STUDY 1. Why doesn't Jeremiah make this announcement at the gates of the temple (vv. 20–22)? **2.** Where does the Sabbath

---

17:15 Where is the word of the LORD? *The proper test for a false prophet is that his prophecies do not come true* (Deut. 18:22). Jeremiah's enemies were applying that test but going too far. Their test was about God's power, not Jeremiah's status as a prophet.

17:16 your shepherd. "Shepherd" points to leadership and care for the master's flocks.

17:19 gate of the people. Probably the east gate of the temple. Many people gathered there, and kings often used that entrance. The prophet would have a large audience at that spot. Jeremiah was not to stay there, however. He must go to all the gates of the city. Everyone must hear his message. No one was to be excluded from the message.

houses or do any work on the Sabbath, but keep the Sabbath day
holy, as I commanded your forefathers. 23Yet they did not listen or pay
attention; they were stiff-necked and would not listen or respond to
discipline. 24But if you are careful to obey me, declares the LORD, and
bring no load through the gates of this city on the Sabbath, but keep
the Sabbath day holy by not doing any work on it, 25then kings who
sit on David's throne will come through the gates of this city with
their officials. They and their officials will come riding in chariots and
on horses, accompanied by the men of Judah and those living in Jerusalem, and this city will be inhabited forever. 26People will come from
the towns of Judah and the villages around Jerusalem, from the territory of Benjamin and the western foothills, from the hill country and
the Negev, bringing burnt offerings and sacrifices, grain offerings, incense and thank offerings to the house of the LORD. 27But if you do
not obey me to keep the Sabbath day holy by not carrying any load as
you come through the gates of Jerusalem on the Sabbath day, then I
will kindle an unquenchable fire in the gates of Jerusalem that will
consume her fortresses.' "

At the Potter's House

18 This is the word that came to Jeremiah from the LORD: 2"Go
down to the potter's house, and there I will give you my message." 3So I went down to the potter's house, and I saw him working
at the wheel. 4But the pot he was shaping from the clay was marred in
his hands; so the potter formed it into another pot, shaping it as
seemed best to him.
5Then the word of the LORD came to me: 6"O house of Israel, can I
not do with you as this potter does?" declares the LORD. "Like clay in
the hand of the potter, so are you in my hand, O house of Israel. 7If at
any time I announce that a nation or kingdom is to be uprooted, torn
down and destroyed, 8and if that nation I warned repents of its evil,
then I will relent and not inflict on it the disaster I had planned. 9And
if at another time I announce that a nation or kingdom is to be built
up and planted, 10and if it does evil in my sight and does not obey me,
then I will reconsider the good I had intended to do for it.
11"Now therefore say to the people of Judah and those living in Jerusalem, 'This is what the LORD says: Look! I am preparing a disaster
for you and devising a plan against you. So turn from your evil ways,
each one of you, and reform your ways and your actions.' 12But they
will reply, 'It's no use. We will continue with our own plans; each of
us will follow the stubbornness of his evil heart.' "

rank in Jewish law (Ex. 20:3–8; 31:12–17)? Why is "work" forbidden (v. 24; Num. 15:32–36; Neh. 13:15)? **3.** Why is God now demanding a formal religious practice (vv. 24–27)?

APPLY Do you need to put more worship, more leisure, or more spiritual growth into your day of worship? How can you begin doing that next week?

OPEN 1. Are you any good at making things or doing crafts? What have you made? What would you like to make? **2.** What "pot" best describes you: Kettle? Crackpot? Frying pan? Cast-iron? Flower pot? Fine china? Other?

STUDY 1. What does Jeremiah see at the potter's house (18:2–4)? **2.** How does the nature of the clay determine the quality of the pot and what it is used for? What point is God trying to make about the conditional nature of his promises and threats? (18:5–10) **3.** What is Judah's decision regarding God's warning (18:11–12)? Why do the people continually ignore God? What sense does Jeremiah try to make of their stubbornness (18:13–17)? **4.** What do the people want to do with Jeremiah and why (18:18)? In Jeremiah's confession, how does he come to terms with what is happening to him (18:19–23)? Can you fault Jeremiah for wanting to dish out punishment equal to what he

---

17:26 bringing burnt offerings and sacrifices, grain offerings, incense and thank offerings. Here faithfully observing the Sabbath was a sign of obedience. If the commandment were kept, peace and prosperity would come to the people.

18:2 Go down to the potter's house. The potter's workshop was probably located near the Potsherd Gate, so named because it stood near the main garbage dump (Valley of Ben Hinnom) where broken pottery would be thrown away—probably a dirty, smelly part of town.

18:3 at the wheel. The potters' wheel was an axle stuck in the ground with a large round stone attached near either end. The top stone provided a platform for the clay, and the bottom was turned by foot.

18:4 clay was marred. The potter's raw material was flawed. Bad clay could not produce excellent work.

18:6 Like clay ... so are you in my hand. God, like the potter, was working with flawed material. People, unlike clay, have a moral sense and conscience. As the potter made and remade the pot, so would God forgive and "remake" his people. But the people must cooperate with love and obedience or be rejected and discarded into the garbage dump like the broken pots and other unneeded items.

has had to take from his accusers? **5.** Who is supposed to see the lesson of the jar first (19:1–3)? Why do you suppose he goes to the Hinnom Valley near the Potsherd Gate? What would be happening there (19:4–9)? **6.** What does Jeremiah's action symbolize (19:10–13)? Do you think such cannibalism was merely symbolic, or could it actually have happened that way? (For some historical precedents, 2 Kin. 6:28–29; Lam. 2:20; 4:10; Ezek. 5:10.) **7.** What does Jerusalem have in common with Topheth (19:12–13), that her fate will be similar (19:5–6; 2 Kin. 23:10)? **8.** Why does Jeremiah repeat the warning in the temple court (19:14–15)? Do you think Judah deserves another spin on God's "potter's wheel," or does Judah deserve the scrap heap or total destruction?

APPLY 1. The prophets often dramatized their messages. What message do you want the world to hear today? How could you make the point through a symbolic action or dramatized parable? Could you see it being covered on national TV news? **2.** If God were to re-create you, what chip, crack or bulge in your life's jar would you like God to fix the second time around?

13 Therefore this is what the LORD says:

"Inquire among the nations:
Who has ever heard anything like this?
A most horrible thing has been done
by Virgin Israel.
14 Does the snow of Lebanon
ever vanish from its rocky slopes?
Do its cool waters from distant sources
ever cease to flow?[a]
15 Yet my people have forgotten me;
they burn incense to worthless idols,
which made them stumble in their ways
and in the ancient paths.
They made them walk in bypaths
and on roads not built up.
16 Their land will be laid waste,
an object of lasting scorn;
all who pass by will be appalled
and will shake their heads.
17 Like a wind from the east,
I will scatter them before their enemies;
I will show them my back and not my face
in the day of their disaster."

18 They said, "Come, let's make plans against Jeremiah; for the
teaching of the law by the priest will not be lost, nor will counsel from
the wise, nor the word from the prophets. So come, let's attack him
with our tongues and pay no attention to anything he says."

19 Listen to me, O LORD;
hear what my accusers are saying!
20 Should good be repaid with evil?
Yet they have dug a pit for me.
Remember that I stood before you
and spoke in their behalf
to turn your wrath away from them.
21 So give their children over to famine;
hand them over to the power of the sword.
Let their wives be made childless and widows;
let their men be put to death,
their young men slain by the sword in battle.
22 Let a cry be heard from their houses
when you suddenly bring invaders against them,
for they have dug a pit to capture me
and have hidden snares for my feet.
23 But you know, O LORD,
all their plots to kill me.

[a]14 The meaning of the Hebrew for this sentence is uncertain.

18:14–15 Nature conformed to the laws of God. Judah, however, had no regard for God's Law. While nature behaved as prescribed, Judah wandered from the path God set for the people.

18:23 Do not forgive ... Let them be overthrown. Jeremiah prayed that his enemies would suffer the punishment they deserved. One day they would face God's judgment without mercy.

word of the LORD, O king of Judah, you who sit on David's throne—
you, your officials and your people who come through these gates.
[3]This is what the LORD says: Do what is just and right. Rescue from
the hand of his oppressor the one who has been robbed. Do no
wrong or violence to the alien, the fatherless or the widow, and do
not shed innocent blood in this place. [4]For if you are careful to carry
out these commands, then kings who sit on David's throne will come
through the gates of this palace, riding in chariots and on horses,
accompanied by their officials and their people. [5]But if you do not
obey these commands, declares the LORD, I swear by myself that this
palace will become a ruin.' "

[6]For this is what the LORD says about the palace of the king of Judah:

"Though you are like Gilead to me,
like the summit of Lebanon,
I will surely make you like a desert,
like towns not inhabited.
[7]I will send destroyers against you,
each man with his weapons,
and they will cut up your fine cedar beams
and throw them into the fire.

[8]"People from many nations will pass by this city and will ask one
another, 'Why has the LORD done such a thing to this great city?' [9]And
the answer will be: 'Because they have forsaken the covenant of the
LORD their God and have worshiped and served other gods.' "

[10]Do not weep for the dead ⌞king⌟ or mourn his loss;
rather, weep bitterly for him who is exiled,
because he will never return
nor see his native land again.

[11]For this is what the LORD says about Shallum[a] son of Josiah, who
succeeded his father as king of Judah but has gone from this place:
"He will never return. [12]He will die in the place where they have led
him captive; he will not see this land again."

[13]"Woe to him who builds his palace by unrighteousness,
his upper rooms by injustice,
making his countrymen work for nothing,
not paying them for their labor.
[14]He says, 'I will build myself a great palace
with spacious upper rooms.'
So he makes large windows in it,
panels it with cedar
and decorates it in red.

[a]11 Also called *Jehoahaz*

STUDY 1. What message does Jeremiah repeat to the rulers (vv. 1–3)? Does this message seem like one addressed to a particular king, or a timeless message, applicable to all those in David's royal line? Why? **2.** What three oppressed groups of people are mentioned? What do they have in common (Ex. 22:21–24)? Why does the king's security depend upon how he treats them? **3.** Why is King Shallum, also called Jehoahaz, to be pitied more than his father, Josiah (vv. 10–12)? What happened to Jehoahaz (2 Kin. 23:34)? **4.** After his brother was deposed, Jehoiakim became king. For what did he use slave labor (vv. 13–14)? What was his father, Josiah, like (vv. 15–17)? How could such a good king have such nasty sons? **5.** How does God define what it means to know him (v. 16)? **6.** Jehoiachin next ruled as king. What will happen to him (vv. 24–27)? Did any of his descendants sit on the throne (vv. 28–30; 2 Kin. 24:15–17)? **7.** If you were Zedekiah, what would you conclude from this sad replay of your family history? Through how many reigns has God been patient? Why does God wait so long to end the line?

APPLY 1. Which leader (church, civic or world) has made a great impact on you by their life? By their death? **2.** How did you feel when a public champion of peace and justice (Gandhi, JFK, Martin Luther King, Mother Teresa) died? Do you hold any real hope that love is stronger than bullets? **3.** When do you respond to God more faithfully, when you are comfortable and secure (v. 21) or when you are under stress? How can you listen and respond more faithfully?

---

throne. The king was likely Zedekiah. (21:3.) The dynasty founded by David had endured, though the path was strewn with failures.

22:10 Do not weep for the dead king. Though his reforms were quickly reversed, the beloved King Josiah was mourned after his death (2 Chr. 35:25).

22:13 builds ... palace by unrighteousness. The king of Judah was authorized to build and rule as he pleased, but he was expected to administer justice and live righteously according to the Law. His profiting from unrighteousness violated the Law and undercut his legitimacy as king.

15"Does it make you a king
  to have more and more cedar?
Did not your father have food and drink?
  He did what was right and just,
  so all went well with him.
16He defended the cause of the poor and needy,
  and so all went well.
Is that not what it means to know me?"
  declares the LORD.
17"But your eyes and your heart
  are set only on dishonest gain,
on shedding innocent blood
  and on oppression and extortion."

18Therefore this is what the LORD says about Jehoiakim son of Josiah
king of Judah:

"They will not mourn for him:
  'Alas, my brother! Alas, my sister!'
They will not mourn for him:
  'Alas, my master! Alas, his splendor!'
19He will have the burial of a donkey—
  dragged away and thrown
  outside the gates of Jerusalem."

20"Go up to Lebanon and cry out,
  let your voice be heard in Bashan,
cry out from Abarim,
  for all your allies are crushed.
21I warned you when you felt secure,
  but you said, 'I will not listen!'
This has been your way from your youth;
  you have not obeyed me.
22The wind will drive all your shepherds away,
  and your allies will go into exile.
Then you will be ashamed and disgraced
  because of all your wickedness.
23You who live in 'Lebanon,[a]'
  who are nestled in cedar buildings,
how you will groan when pangs come upon you,
  pain like that of a woman in labor!

24"As surely as I live," declares the LORD, "even if you, Jehoiachin[b]
son of Jehoiakim king of Judah, were a signet ring on my right hand,
I would still pull you off. 25I will hand you over to those who seek
your life, those you fear—to Nebuchadnezzar king of Babylon and to
the Babylonians.[c] 26I will hurl you and the mother who gave you birth
into another country, where neither of you was born, and there you
both will die. 27You will never come back to the land you long to
return to."

[a]23 That is, the palace in Jerusalem (see 1 Kings 7:2) [b]24 Hebrew *Coniah,* a variant of *Jehoiachin;* also in verse 28 [c]25 Or *Chaldeans*

28Is this man Jehoiachin a despised, broken pot,
an object no one wants?
Why will he and his children be hurled out,
cast into a land they do not know?
29O land, land, land,
hear the word of the LORD!
30This is what the LORD says:
"Record this man as if childless,
a man who will not prosper in his lifetime,
for none of his offspring will prosper,
none will sit on the throne of David
or rule anymore in Judah."

The Righteous Branch

23 "Woe to the shepherds who are destroying and scattering the
sheep of my pasture!" declares the LORD. 2Therefore this is
what the LORD, the God of Israel, says to the shepherds who tend my
people: "Because you have scattered my flock and driven them away
and have not bestowed care on them, I will bestow punishment on
you for the evil you have done," declares the LORD. 3"I myself will
gather the remnant of my flock out of all the countries where I have
driven them and will bring them back to their pasture, where they will
be fruitful and increase in number. 4I will place shepherds over them
who will tend them, and they will no longer be afraid or terrified, nor
will any be missing," declares the LORD.

5"The days are coming," declares the LORD,
"when I will raise up to David[d] a righteous Branch,
a King who will reign wisely
and do what is just and right in the land.
6In his days Judah will be saved
and Israel will live in safety.
This is the name by which he will be called:
The LORD Our Righteousness.

7"So then, the days are coming," declares the LORD, "when people
will no longer say, 'As surely as the LORD lives, who brought the Israelites up out of Egypt,' 8but they will say, 'As surely as the LORD lives,
who brought the descendants of Israel up out of the land of the north
and out of all the countries where he had banished them.' Then they
will live in their own land."

Lying Prophets

9Concerning the prophets:

My heart is broken within me;
all my bones tremble.

[d]5 Or *up from David's line*

OPEN Which would you rather be and why: Politician or spiritual leader? Who is more likely to get their flock to follow their lead?

STUDY 1. Who are the "shepherds" (v. 1)? How are they scattering the "flock"? What will God do to them? **2.** What new shepherds and "righteous Branch" will God appoint (vv. 4–5; Isa. 11:1–2)? **3.** "Zedekiah" is Hebrew for "The LORD my righteousness." What is the significance of the future king's title in verse 6? **4.** What historical bench marks define Israel as a nation (vv. 7–8)? Why is one more significant?

APPLY 1. Jesus applied this shepherd imagery to himself (John 10:7–16). How does he fulfill this promise for you? Which title, name or role of Jesus is most special to you? **2.** Hope shines in even the most difficult chapters of Israel's history. How does hope shine for you?

OPEN 1. Do you remember your dreams? Describe a dream you had recently. Why does it stick in your memory? **2.** Do you ever read the horoscope section of the newspaper? Why or why not?

22:28 a despised, broken pot. Jeremiah returned to an image used in 18:1–10 and 19:1–15. A broken pot was worthless and should be thrown away. Jehoiachin was "cast away" and taken into exile where he became utterly irrelevant.

22:30 as if childless ... none of his offspring. Although Jehoiachin had at least seven children, none of them sat on the throne of Judah. Thus, Jehoiachin was the last king of the Davidic line to rule Judah. David's line continued, however, and was the family of the King of Kings—Jesus the Christ.

23:6 will be called: The LORD Our Righteousness. Jeremiah portrayed the flawless future King, Jesus Christ. Compared to sinful human kings, this King would rule in righteousness.

STUDY **1.** Why would Jeremiah feel "like a drunken man" upon finding out that the court prophets are false (v. 9)? What does God mean by calling the prophets "adulterers" (vv. 10,14)? **2.** What distinguishes the false prophet (vv. 13–17,21,27,32; Deut. 13:1–5)? How are Judah's prophets measuring up to these criteria? What false image of God do they project (vv. 23–24)? **3.** Compared to the source of the false prophet's word, where does a true prophet get God's word (vv. 18,22)? **4.** How will both the false and true prophets be exposed for what they are (vv. 25–32)? **5.** What is meant by "every man's own word becomes his oracle" (v. 36)? In what way do you see this attitude today? **6.** Who has become a "burden" to God? Why is he weary of all this? What will God do to unburden his people (vv. 39–40; 20:11)?

APPLY **1.** Who in our society has sold you "false hopes" (v. 16) Politicians? Advertisers? Popular self-help authors? What opened your eyes to the falseness of these hopes? **2.** In what ways have you sought to hide from the Lord? In the midst of such efforts, what do verses 23–24 say to you? **3.** For what do you have a burden today? Do you have a message to give? An action to take? A situation to remedy? In what way is that burdensome? Can the group help?

I am like a drunken man,
like a man overcome by wine,
because of the LORD
and his holy words.
10 The land is full of adulterers;
because of the curse[a] the land lies parched[b]
and the pastures in the desert are withered.
The ⌊prophets⌋ follow an evil course
and use their power unjustly.

11 "Both prophet and priest are godless;
even in my temple I find their wickedness,"
declares the LORD.

12 "Therefore their path will become slippery;
they will be banished to darkness
and there they will fall.
I will bring disaster on them
in the year they are punished,"
declares the LORD.

13 "Among the prophets of Samaria
I saw this repulsive thing:
They prophesied by Baal
and led my people Israel astray.
14 And among the prophets of Jerusalem
I have seen something horrible:
They commit adultery and live a lie.
They strengthen the hands of evildoers,
so that no one turns from his wickedness.
They are all like Sodom to me;
the people of Jerusalem are like Gomorrah."

15 Therefore, this is what the LORD Almighty says concerning the
prophets:

"I will make them eat bitter food
and drink poisoned water,
because from the prophets of Jerusalem
ungodliness has spread throughout the land."

16 This is what the LORD Almighty says:

"Do not listen to what the prophets are prophesying to you;
they fill you with false hopes.
They speak visions from their own minds,
not from the mouth of the LORD.
17 They keep saying to those who despise me,
'The LORD says: You will have peace.'
And to all who follow the stubbornness of their hearts
they say, 'No harm will come to you.'

[a]10 Or *because of these things* [b]10 Or *land mourns*

23:10 parched. A barren field symbolized God's judgment. In contrast, bounty was a sign of God's continued blessing.

23:16 speak visions from their own minds. True prophets were God's messengers. False prophets spoke their own mind, not the mind of God.

23:17 You will have peace ... No harm. False prophets lulled their listeners into a false assurance. God would punish them for their foolishness.

[18]But which of them has stood in the council of the LORD
to see or to hear his word?
Who has listened and heard his word?
[19]See, the storm of the LORD
will burst out in wrath,
a whirlwind swirling down
on the heads of the wicked.
[20]The anger of the LORD will not turn back
until he fully accomplishes
the purposes of his heart.
In days to come
you will understand it clearly.
[21]I did not send these prophets,
yet they have run with their message;
I did not speak to them,
yet they have prophesied.
[22]But if they had stood in my council,
they would have proclaimed my words to my people
and would have turned them from their evil ways
and from their evil deeds.

[23]"Am I only a God nearby,"
declares the LORD,
"and not a God far away?
[24]Can anyone hide in secret places
so that I cannot see him?"
declares the LORD.
"Do not I fill heaven and earth?"
declares the LORD.

[25]"I have heard what the prophets say who prophesy lies in my
name. They say, 'I had a dream! I had a dream!' [26]How long will this
continue in the hearts of these lying prophets, who prophesy the delusions of their own minds? [27]They think the dreams they tell one
another will make my people forget my name, just as their fathers
forgot my name through Baal worship. [28]Let the prophet who has a
dream tell his dream, but let the one who has my word speak it faithfully. For what has straw to do with grain?" declares the LORD. [29]"Is
not my word like fire," declares the LORD, "and like a hammer that
breaks a rock in pieces?

[30]"Therefore," declares the LORD, "I am against the prophets who
steal from one another words supposedly from me. [31]Yes," declares
the LORD, "I am against the prophets who wag their own tongues and
yet declare, 'The LORD declares.' [32]Indeed, I am against those who
prophesy false dreams," declares the LORD. "They tell them and lead
my people astray with their reckless lies, yet I did not send or appoint
them. They do not *benefit these people in the least,"* declares the
LORD.

23:23 nearby ... far away. There was nowhere to hide. God heard every word of their deceit.

23:31 prophets who wag ... declare. The false prophets enjoyed a prophetic position without heeding principles. They declared lies as truths. They gave "feel good" messages instead of truth.

False Oracles and False Prophets

33“When these people, or a prophet or a priest, ask you, ‘What is the oracle[a] of the LORD?’ say to them, ‘What oracle?[b] I will forsake you, declares the LORD.’ 34If a prophet or a priest or anyone else claims, ‘This is the oracle of the LORD,’ I will punish that man and his household. 35This is what each of you keeps on saying to his friend or relative: ‘What is the LORD’s answer?’ or ‘What has the LORD spoken?’ 36But you must not mention ‘the oracle of the LORD’ again, because every man’s own word becomes his oracle and so you distort the words of the living God, the LORD Almighty, our God. 37This is what you keep saying to a prophet: ‘What is the LORD’s answer to you?’ or ‘What has the LORD spoken?’ 38Although you claim, ‘This is the oracle of the LORD,’ this is what the LORD says: You used the words, ‘This is the oracle of the LORD,’ even though I told you that you must not claim, ‘This is the oracle of the LORD.’ 39Therefore, I will surely forget you and cast you out of my presence along with the city I gave to you and your fathers. 40I will bring upon you everlasting disgrace—everlasting shame that will not be forgotten.”

Two Baskets of Figs

24 After Jehoiachin[c] son of Jehoiakim king of Judah and the officials, the craftsmen and the artisans of Judah were carried into exile from Jerusalem to Babylon by Nebuchadnezzar king of Babylon, the LORD showed me two baskets of figs placed in front of the temple of the LORD. 2One basket had very good figs, like those that ripen early; the other basket had very poor figs, so bad they could not be eaten.

3Then the LORD asked me, “What do you see, Jeremiah?”

“Figs,” I answered. “The good ones are very good, but the poor ones are so bad they cannot be eaten.”

4Then the word of the LORD came to me: 5“This is what the LORD, the God of Israel, says: ‘Like these good figs, I regard as good the exiles from Judah, whom I sent away from this place to the land of the Babylonians.[d] 6My eyes will watch over them for their good, and I will bring them back to this land. I will build them up and not tear them down; I will plant them and not uproot them. 7I will give them a heart to know me, that I am the LORD. They will be my people, and I will be their God, for they will return to me with all their heart.

8“ ‘But like the poor figs, which are so bad they cannot be eaten,’ says the LORD, ‘so will I deal with Zedekiah king of Judah, his officials and the survivors from Jerusalem, whether they remain in this land or live in Egypt. 9I will make them abhorrent and an offense to all the kingdoms of the earth, a reproach and a byword, an object of ridicule and cursing, wherever I banish them. 10I will send the sword, famine and plague against them until they are destroyed from the land I gave to them and their fathers.’ ”

[a]33 Or *burden* (see Septuagint and Vulgate) [b]33 Hebrew; Septuagint and Vulgate *'You are the burden.* (The Hebrew for *oracle* and *burden* is the same.) [c]1 Hebrew *Jeconiah,* a variant of *Jehoiachin* [d]5 Or *Chaldeans*

OPEN 1. What is the grossest thing you have ever found in your refrigerator? **2.** How good are you at throwing out things that need to be thrown out?

STUDY The Babylonians under Nebuchadnezzar threatened Judah and deported many in the reign of Jehoiachin. **1.** Who was left in Judah for Zedekiah to rule (vv. 1–3,8; 2 Kin. 24:14–20)? What would their world look like? **2.** What does each basket of figs symbolize (vv. 5–8)? What is God going to do with the exiles? Why and when? What is he going to do with those left behind (vv. 9–10)? **3.** Why would God favor one group over another (2 Chr. 36:11–16)?

APPLY 1. Do you feel “at home” in your church? Or more like an out-of-place exile? Why? **2.** During what period of your life were you an “exile” from God? What did it take to bring you “home”?

23:33 oracle. The deceitfulness of the spiritual leaders weighed heavily in Jeremiah’s mind. Those who meant to be helpful created more harm.

24:1 carried into exile. Babylon selectively captured the influential leaders of Judah. **showed me.** Jeremiah had a meaningful vision from God.

24:5–6 Figs were a favored delicacy of this culture that they preserved. God’s people were a similar delight—well worth saving.

Seventy Years of Captivity

25 The word came to Jeremiah concerning all the people of
Judah in the fourth year of Jehoiakim son of Josiah king of
Judah, which was the first year of Nebuchadnezzar king of Babylon.
2So Jeremiah the prophet said to all the people of Judah and to all
those living in Jerusalem: 3For twenty-three years—from the thirteenth year of Josiah son of Amon king of Judah until this very day—
the word of the LORD has come to me and I have spoken to you again
and again, but you have not listened.
4And though the LORD has sent all his servants the prophets to you
again and again, you have not listened or paid any attention. 5They
said, "Turn now, each of you, from your evil ways and your evil practices, and you can stay in the land the LORD gave to you and your
fathers for ever and ever. 6Do not follow other gods to serve and
worship them; do not provoke me to anger with what your hands
have made. Then I will not harm you."
7"But you did not listen to me," declares the LORD, "and you have
provoked me with what your hands have made, and you have brought
harm to yourselves."
8Therefore the LORD Almighty says this: "Because you have not
listened to my words, 9I will summon all the peoples of the north and
my servant Nebuchadnezzar king of Babylon," declares the LORD,
"and I will bring them against this land and its inhabitants and
against all the surrounding nations. I will completely destroy[a] them
and make them an object of horror and scorn, and an everlasting
ruin. 10I will banish from them the sounds of joy and gladness, the
voices of bride and bridegroom, the sound of millstones and the light
of the lamp. 11This whole country will become a desolate wasteland,
and these nations will serve the king of Babylon seventy years.
12"But when the seventy years are fulfilled, I will punish the king of
Babylon and his nation, the land of the Babylonians,[b] for their guilt,"
declares the LORD, "and will make it desolate forever. 13I will bring
upon that land all the things I have spoken against it, all that are written in this book and prophesied by Jeremiah against all the nations.
14They themselves will be enslaved by many nations and great kings;
I will repay them according to their deeds and the work of their
hands."

The Cup of God's Wrath

15This is what the LORD, the God of Israel, said to me: "Take from
my hand this cup filled with the wine of my wrath and make all the
nations to whom I send you drink it. 16When they drink it, they will
stagger and go mad because of the sword I will send among them."

[a]9 The Hebrew term refers to the irrevocable giving over of things or persons to the LORD, often by totally destroying them. [b]12 Or *Chaldeans*

OPEN 1. When was the last time someone said to you: "I told you so"? Did you appreciate it? **2.** What title would you give your autobiography? What kind of movie would your life story make?

STUDY 1. The dovetailing of the two events in verse 1 dates this prophesy c. 605 B.C. How long has God been speaking through Jeremiah? Through other prophets (v. 4; 7:25)? How must Jeremiah and God be feeling at this point? **2.** Why does God call a pagan king his "servant" (v. 9)? What purpose will he serve? **3.** Is it fair to punish Babylon for performing God's will (v. 12)? What principle is at work here? What do you suppose was their crime (vv. 13–14)? **4.** In retrospect, which of Jeremiah's predictions have come true? Why does God reveal the length of the coming exile? **5.** Why did God warn the people for so long before taking action? Why did God's patience finally run out?

APPLY 1. How long would you persist in a task without seeing any success? Do you ever wonder about a direction you once took but abandoned? **2.** Is God warning you about anything? Are you paying more attention than Judah did? How so?

OPEN 1. Have you ever been caught doing something that others got away with? What happened? How did it make you feel? **2.** When have you been drunk or been around someone who was drunk? What was the worst part about it?

25:3 I have spoken ... you have not listened. Jeremiah's message had not changed for over two decades. Yet his warnings were not heeded.

25:9 Nebuchadnezzar. The king of Babylon was decidedly pagan. However, in God's grand scheme, even a pagan could be used as a tool to accomplish God's will.

25:11–12 nations will serve ... seventy years. Jeremiah's warnings concerned an extensive exile. The Babylonians punished the exiled people for over half a century.

25:12 punish. God used the Babylonians; he did not favor them. He would eventually punish them for brutalizing his people.

25:15 drink it. God's wrath is unavoidable. His enemies would be forced to undergo it.

STUDY 1. Why is God's wrath likened to a cup of wine (vv. 15–16; Isa. 51:17–23; Rev. 14:8; 18:6)? What effect will it have on those who drink it? Is this what they would suspect? **2.** Who drinks from the cup first and why (vv. 17–18)? Who next (v. 19)? Who last (v. 26; see text footnote)? **3.** Why will God punish the nations (vv. 27–33) with the "sword" and "mighty storm" of the Babylonian invasion? What "charges" will God bring (2:5–9,35)? **4.** What will happen to the world leaders (vv. 34–38)? How is their fate like that of Judah's leaders (21:1–23:7)?

APPLY 1. When in your life did you feel like you were "drinking from the cup of God's wrath"? Who "drank" with you? **2.** When you feel God is angry with you, how hard is it for you to repent?

17 So I took the cup from the LORD's hand and made all the nations to whom he sent me drink it: 18 Jerusalem and the towns of Judah, its kings and officials, to make them a ruin and an object of horror and scorn and cursing, as they are today; 19 Pharaoh king of Egypt, his attendants, his officials and all his people, 20 and all the foreign people there; all the kings of Uz; all the kings of the Philistines (those of Ashkelon, Gaza, Ekron, and the people left at Ashdod); 21 Edom, Moab and Ammon; 22 all the kings of Tyre and Sidon; the kings of the coastlands across the sea; 23 Dedan, Tema, Buz and all who are in distant places[a]; 24 all the kings of Arabia and all the kings of the foreign people who live in the desert; 25 all the kings of Zimri, Elam and Media; 26 and all the kings of the north, near and far, one after the other—all the kingdoms on the face of the earth. And after all of them, the king of Sheshach[b] will drink it too.

27 "Then tell them, 'This is what the LORD Almighty, the God of Israel, says: Drink, get drunk and vomit, and fall to rise no more because of the sword I will send among you.' 28 But if they refuse to take the cup from your hand and drink, tell them, 'This is what the LORD Almighty says: You must drink it! 29 See, I am beginning to bring disaster on the city that bears my Name, and will you indeed go unpunished? You will not go unpunished, for I am calling down a sword upon all who live on the earth, declares the LORD Almighty.'

30 "Now prophesy all these words against them and say to them:

" 'The LORD will roar from on high;
he will thunder from his holy dwelling
and roar mightily against his land.
He will shout like those who tread the grapes,
shout against all who live on the earth.
31 The tumult will resound to the ends of the earth,
for the LORD will bring charges against the nations;
he will bring judgment on all mankind
and put the wicked to the sword,' "
declares the LORD.

32 This is what the LORD Almighty says:

"Look! Disaster is spreading
from nation to nation;
a mighty storm is rising
from the ends of the earth."

33 At that time those slain by the LORD will be everywhere—from one end of the earth to the other. They will not be mourned or gathered up or buried, but will be like refuse lying on the ground.

34 Weep and wail, you shepherds;
roll in the dust, you leaders of the flock.
For your time to be slaughtered has come;
you will fall and be shattered like fine pottery.

[a] *23 Or who clip the hair by their foreheads* [b] *26 Sheshach* is a cryptogram for Babylon.

25:18 God's own people are the first to endure God's wrath (Ezek. 9:6; 1 Peter 4:17).

25:19–26 Babylon would punish all of the enemy nations. However, even Babylon could not escape God's wrath.

25:32 mighty storm. Like the wrath of God, Babylon is the destructive weapon of choice.

his grandson until the time for his land comes; then many nations
and great kings will subjugate him.
8" 'If, however, any nation or kingdom will not serve Nebuchadnezzar king of Babylon or bow its neck under his yoke, I will punish
that nation with the sword, famine and plague, declares the LORD,
until I destroy it by his hand. 9So do not listen to your prophets, your
diviners, your interpreters of dreams, your mediums or your sorcerers who tell you, 'You will not serve the king of Babylon.' 10They
prophesy lies to you that will only serve to remove you far from your
lands; I will banish you and you will perish. 11But if any nation will
bow its neck under the yoke of the king of Babylon and serve him, I
will let that nation remain in its own land to till it and to live there,
declares the LORD." ' "
12I gave the same message to Zedekiah king of Judah. I said, "Bow
your neck under the yoke of the king of Babylon; serve him and his
people, and you will live. 13Why will you and your people die by the
sword, famine and plague with which the LORD has threatened any
nation that will not serve the king of Babylon? 14Do not listen to the
words of the prophets who say to you, 'You will not serve the king of
Babylon,' for they are prophesying lies to you. 15'I have not sent
them,' declares the LORD. 'They are prophesying lies in my name.
Therefore, I will banish you and you will perish, both you and the
prophets who prophesy to you.' "
16Then I said to the priests and all these people, "This is what the
LORD says: Do not listen to the prophets who say, 'Very soon now the
articles from the LORD's house will be brought back from Babylon.'
They are prophesying lies to you. 17Do not listen to them. Serve the
king of Babylon, and you will live. Why should this city become a
ruin? 18If they are prophets and have the word of the LORD, let them
plead with the LORD Almighty that the furnishings remaining in the
house of the LORD and in the palace of the king of Judah and in Jerusalem not be taken to Babylon. 19For this is what the LORD Almighty
says about the pillars, the Sea, the movable stands and the other furnishings that are left in this city, 20which Nebuchadnezzar king of
Babylon did not take away when he carried Jehoiachin[a] son of Jehoiakim king of Judah into exile from Jerusalem to Babylon, along with
all the nobles of Judah and Jerusalem— 21yes, this is what the LORD
Almighty, the God of Israel, says about the things that are left in the
house of the LORD and in the palace of the king of Judah and in Jerusalem: 22'They will be taken to Babylon and there they will remain
until the day I come for them,' declares the LORD. 'Then I will bring
them back and restore them to this place.' "

The False Prophet Hananiah

28 In the fifth month of that same year, the fourth year, early in
the reign of Zedekiah king of Judah, the prophet Hananiah

[a]20 Hebrew *Jeconiah,* a variant of *Jehoiachin*

vise? **3.** Why does he give the same message to Zedekiah (vv. 12–15)? How are court prophets different than pagan mediums, if at all? **4.** What hope does Jeremiah hold out for them instead (vv. 7,16–22)? **5.** What sacrilegious use would Nebuchadnezzar and his heirs have for the temple gold (2 Kin. 24:12–13; Dan. 5:1–4)? **6.** Why does Jeremiah recommend surrender to a pagan, sacrilegious king? Why shouldn't Zedekiah and the other rulers band together against him?

APPLY 1. Ancient cultures saw the world run by many gods, each exercising power over a certain territory. In your world, how is God's sphere of influence limited? Do you look to God to reign over certain areas but not others? Explain. **2.** When have you experienced the fight-or-flight dilemma faced by Judah in this chapter? When do you know when to fight and when to surrender?

OPEN 1. Do you like to argue, or do you avoid conflict? When was the last time you went against your natural tendency? **2.** On a scale of 1 ("It'll never work.") to 10 ("Go for it!"), how do you rate on optimism?

27:12 Bow your neck. Jeremiah referred to his yoke to encourage Judah not to resist God's intentions.

27:18 plead. True prophets were instructed to pray about Judah's impending doom.

28:1 prophet Hananiah. This prophet's name means, "The LORD is gracious." However, Hananiah used his name as wishful thinking rather than a true revelation of God's plans. It would actually get worse before it got better.

STUDY 1. When does Hananiah predict that Babylon will fall (vv. 1–4)? Do you hear sincerity or sarcasm? Optimism or opportunism? **2.** Likewise, what tone in Jeremiah's voice do you hear in verse 6? Why is it easier to be a prophet of doom than a prophet of peace (vv. 7–9)? **3.** What does Hananiah do to illustrate his prophecy (vv. 10–11)? How long has Jeremiah been wearing it (v. 1; 27:1)? Why do you think he leaves rather than argues his case? **4.** What does the new message to Hananiah mean (vv. 12–14)? How does Jeremiah show he is a true prophet (vv. 15–17)?

APPLY 1. As with alleged prophets for ancient Israel, today's political advisors also give opposing advice, often to protect their vested interest. How do you know who to believe? What political opinion have you recently changed? **2.** Do you agree with the saying, "If you can't say something nice, don't say anything at all"? Why is it often easier to say something good (as did Hananiah) rather than the truth (as did Jeremiah)? **3.** Are you having trouble deciding something important right now? How can the group help out?

---

son of Azzur, who was from Gibeon, said to me in the house of the
LORD in the presence of the priests and all the people: [2]"This is what
the LORD Almighty, the God of Israel, says: 'I will break the yoke of the
king of Babylon. [3]Within two years I will bring back to this place all
the articles of the LORD's house that Nebuchadnezzar king of Babylon
removed from here and took to Babylon. [4]I will also bring back to this
place Jehoiachin[a] son of Jehoiakim king of Judah and all the other
exiles from Judah who went to Babylon,' declares the LORD, 'for I will
break the yoke of the king of Babylon.' "

[5]Then the prophet Jeremiah replied to the prophet Hananiah before
the priests and all the people who were standing in the house of the
LORD. [6]He said, "Amen! May the LORD do so! May the LORD fulfill the
words you have prophesied by bringing the articles of the LORD's
house and all the exiles back to this place from Babylon. [7]Neverthe-
less, listen to what I have to say in your hearing and in the hearing of
all the people: [8]From early times the prophets who preceded you and
me have prophesied war, disaster and plague against many countries
and great kingdoms. [9]But the prophet who prophesies peace will be
recognized as one truly sent by the LORD only if his prediction comes
true."

[10]Then the prophet Hananiah took the yoke off the neck of the
prophet Jeremiah and broke it, [11]and he said before all the people,
"This is what the LORD says: 'In the same way will I break the yoke of
Nebuchadnezzar king of Babylon off the neck of all the nations within two years.' " At this, the prophet Jeremiah went on his way.

[12]Shortly after the prophet Hananiah had broken the yoke off the
neck of the prophet Jeremiah, the word of the LORD came to Jeremiah:
[13]"Go and tell Hananiah, 'This is what the LORD says: You have broken
a wooden yoke, but in its place you will get a yoke of iron. [14]This is
what the LORD Almighty, the God of Israel, says: I will put an iron yoke
on the necks of all these nations to make them serve Nebuchadnezzar king of Babylon, and they will serve him. I will even give him control over the wild animals.' "

[15]Then the prophet Jeremiah said to Hananiah the prophet, "Listen,
Hananiah! The LORD has not sent you, yet you have persuaded this
nation to trust in lies. [16]Therefore, this is what the LORD says: 'I am
about to remove you from the face of the earth. This very year you are
going to die, because you have preached rebellion against the
LORD.' "

[17]In the seventh month of that same year, Hananiah the prophet
died.

a4 Hebrew *Jeconiah,* a variant of *Jehoiachin*

28:7 Nevertheless, listen. History hinted that Hananiah's predictions were false. Time would also tell who was right regarding Judah's future release from Babylon.

28:8 prophets who preceded you. Hananiah's predictions went against the tide of history. How could all the prior prophets of doom and destruction be wrong?

28:10 broke it. Hananiah came up with his own word-picture. He broke the yoke around Jeremiah's neck—a vivid symbol of Babylon's dominance.

28:16 you have preached rebellion. Hananiah preached what the people wanted to hear: good news. However, his message symbolized rebellion against God. Death was the punishment for such teaching.

28:17 same year. Jeremiah proved trustworthy once again. His prediction came true within the allotted time.

A Letter to the Exiles

29 This is the text of the letter that the prophet Jeremiah sent from Jerusalem to the surviving elders among the exiles and to the priests, the prophets and all the other people Nebuchadnezzar had carried into exile from Jerusalem to Babylon. [2](This was after King Jehoiachin[a] and the queen mother, the court officials and the leaders of Judah and Jerusalem, the craftsmen and the artisans had gone into exile from Jerusalem.) [3]He entrusted the letter to Elasah son of Shaphan and to Gemariah son of Hilkiah, whom Zedekiah king of Judah sent to King Nebuchadnezzar in Babylon. It said:

[4]This is what the LORD Almighty, the God of Israel, says to all those I carried into exile from Jerusalem to Babylon: [5]"Build houses and settle down; plant gardens and eat what they produce. [6]Marry and have sons and daughters; find wives for your sons and give your daughters in marriage, so that they too may have sons and daughters. Increase in number there; do not decrease. [7]Also, seek the peace and prosperity of the city to which I have carried you into exile. Pray to the LORD for it, because if it prospers, you too will prosper." [8]Yes, this is what the LORD Almighty, the God of Israel, says: "Do not let the prophets and diviners among you deceive you. Do not listen to the dreams you encourage them to have. [9]They are prophesying lies to you in my name. I have not sent them," declares the LORD.

[10]This is what the LORD says: "When seventy years are completed for Babylon, I will come to you and fulfill my gracious promise to bring you back to this place. [11]For I know the plans I have for you," declares the LORD, "plans to prosper you and not to harm you, plans to give you hope and a future. [12]Then you will call upon me and come and pray to me, and I will listen to you. [13]You will seek me and find me when you seek me with all your heart. [14]I will be found by you," declares the LORD, "and will bring you back from captivity.[b] I will gather you from all the nations and places where I have banished you," declares the LORD, "and will bring you back to the place from which I carried you into exile."

[15]You may say, "The LORD has raised up prophets for us in Babylon," [16]but this is what the LORD says about the king who sits on David's throne and all the people who remain in this city, your countrymen who did not go with you into exile— [17]yes, this is what the LORD Almighty says: "I will send the sword, famine and plague against them and I will make them like poor figs that are so bad they cannot be eaten. [18]I will pursue them with the sword, famine and plague and will make them abhorrent to all the kingdoms of the earth and an object of cursing and horror, of scorn and reproach, among all the nations where I drive them. [19]For they have not listened to my words," declares the LORD, "words

[a]2 Hebrew *Jeconiah,* a variant of *Jehoiachin* [b]14 Or *will restore your fortunes*

OPEN Are you a good letter writer? To how many people do you owe letters right now? Which correspondent of yours lives the farthest away?

STUDY 1. What do you think of the postal system in Jeremiah's day (vv. 1–3,25)? What effect do you think this written Word of God will have on the exiles, as compared with Jeremiah's other words from God, which were usually spoken, sometimes acted out? Why should they pay heed to it (vv. 4,19)? **2.** Why is it important for the people to pray for and support the city in which they will live as exiles (v. 7)? **3.** Why does Jeremiah debunk those prophesying an early return (vv. 8–9)? Why did God keep the nation in exile 70 years (vv. 10–14)? Is there a catch to this wonderful promise? If so, what? **4.** What must the exiles be feeling about those living in Jerusalem (vv. 15–19), as well as the false prophets Ahab and Zedekiah (vv. 20–23): "I told you so"? "Serves 'em right"? "But for the grace of God, there go I"? "What—me too!"? **5.** How do Jeremiah's superiors learn of his letter to the exiles (vv. 25–28)? Why is Jeremiah regarded a madman if his prophecies has finally come true? Should Shemaiah's letter come as any surprise to Zephaniah the priest? **6.** What do the two prophets, Hananiah and Shemaiah, have in common (vv. 31–32; 28:15–16)? What clues do you see as to how to spot false prophets?

APPLY 1. Have you ever seen God bring good out of bad situations in your life, as in verses 11–14? What happened? Could there have been an easier way to learn that lesson? **2.** Who might think of you in any sense as a "madman"? Or do you blend in pretty good? **3.** Is criticism hard to take? What makes it easier? When's the last time you gave criticism successfully?

29:4 The exiles received a message from God himself. He delivered encouragement to their Babylonian doorstep.

29:8 deceive you. False prophets were eager to draw an audience with their message of hope.

29:12–13 A restored relationship with God awaited the exiles at the end of the road. He alone was their hope.

that I sent to them again and again by my servants the prophets.
And you exiles have not listened either," declares the LORD.
[20]Therefore, hear the word of the LORD, all you exiles whom I
have sent away from Jerusalem to Babylon. [21]This is what the
LORD Almighty, the God of Israel, says about Ahab son of Kolaiah
and Zedekiah son of Maaseiah, who are prophesying lies to you
in my name: "I will hand them over to Nebuchadnezzar king of
Babylon, and he will put them to death before your very eyes.
[22]Because of them, all the exiles from Judah who are in Babylon
will use this curse: 'The LORD treat you like Zedekiah and Ahab,
whom the king of Babylon burned in the fire.' [23]For they have
done outrageous things in Israel; they have committed adultery
with their neighbors' wives and in my name have spoken lies,
which I did not tell them to do. I know it and am a witness to it,"
declares the LORD.

Message to Shemaiah

[24]Tell Shemaiah the Nehelamite, [25]"This is what the LORD Almighty,
the God of Israel, says: You sent letters in your own name to all the
people in Jerusalem, to Zephaniah son of Maaseiah the priest, and to
all the other priests. You said to Zephaniah, [26]'The LORD has appointed you priest in place of Jehoiada to be in charge of the house of the
LORD; you should put any madman who acts like a prophet into the
stocks and neck-irons. [27]So why have you not reprimanded Jeremiah
from Anathoth, who poses as a prophet among you? [28]He has sent
this message to us in Babylon: It will be a long time. Therefore build
houses and settle down; plant gardens and eat what they produce.' "
[29]Zephaniah the priest, however, read the letter to Jeremiah the
prophet. [30]Then the word of the LORD came to Jeremiah: [31]"Send this
message to all the exiles: 'This is what the LORD says about Shemaiah
the Nehelamite: Because Shemaiah has prophesied to you, even
though I did not send him, and has led you to believe a lie, [32]this is
what the LORD says: I will surely punish Shemaiah the Nehelamite
and his descendants. He will have no one left among this people, nor
will he see the good things I will do for my people, declares the LORD,
because he has preached rebellion against me.' "

Restoration of Israel

30 This is the word that came to Jeremiah from the LORD: [2]"This
is what the LORD, the God of Israel, says: 'Write in a book all
the words I have spoken to you. [3]The days are coming,' declares the
LORD, 'when I will bring my people Israel and Judah back from
captivity[a] and restore them to the land I gave their forefathers to possess,' says the LORD."

[a]3 Or *will restore the fortunes of my people Israel and Judah*

OPEN 1. What is your favorite book of the Bible? What is your favorite book apart from the Bible? How do each of your favorite books turn out in the end? **2.** How far back do you date your "days of old"? Is that a past you would sooner forget, or are they the "good ol' days"?

29:21 hand them over to Nebuchadnezzar. Once again, a pagan king was God's tool for assigning punishment. The false prophets were finally silenced.

29:31–32 God made it easier for his people to understand his true intentions. He identified and silenced the false prophets like Shemaiah.

30:1–33:26 Jeremiah balanced his message of doom with that of hope. He described a postexilic day of restoration that would serve as an encouraging reminder to the returning exiles.

30:1–31:40 Jeremiah used poetic language to describe the people's physical deliverance (30:1–11). Additionally, he described the ensuing spiritual healing (30:12–17) and joyful results (31:2–40).

30:3 days are coming. The first exiles would not return to their homeland until many years later (537 B.C.).

4These are the words the LORD spoke concerning Israel and Judah:
5"This is what the LORD says:

" 'Cries of fear are heard—
terror, not peace.
6Ask and see:
Can a man bear children?
Then why do I see every strong man
with his hands on his stomach like a woman in labor,
every face turned deathly pale?
7How awful that day will be!
None will be like it.
It will be a time of trouble for Jacob,
but he will be saved out of it.

8" 'In that day,' declares the LORD Almighty,
'I will break the yoke off their necks
and will tear off their bonds;
no longer will foreigners enslave them.
9Instead, they will serve the LORD their God
and David their king,
whom I will raise up for them.

10" 'So do not fear, O Jacob my servant;
do not be dismayed, O Israel,'
declares the LORD.
'I will surely save you out of a distant place,
your descendants from the land of their exile.
Jacob will again have peace and security,
and no one will make him afraid.
11I am with you and will save you,'
declares the LORD.
'Though I completely destroy all the nations
among which I scatter you,
I will not completely destroy you.
I will discipline you but only with justice;
I will not let you go entirely unpunished.'

12"This is what the LORD says:

" 'Your wound is incurable,
your injury beyond healing.
13There is no one to plead your cause,
no remedy for your sore,
no healing for you.
14All your allies have forgotten you;
they care nothing for you.
I have struck you as an enemy would
and punished you as would the cruel,
because your guilt is so great
and your sins so many.
15Why do you cry out over your wound,
your pain that has no cure?

STUDY 1. How do you suppose God conveyed this message to Jeremiah: By messenger? Audibly, giving dictation? In a dream (31:26)? **2.** What clues tell you this "book of consolation" is largely directed to all the tribes of Israel (vv. 2, 7,10,18; 31:1–22)? **3.** What had happened to Israel a century before Jeremiah (v. 8; 2 Kin. 17:5–6, 24–33), a situation which would be rectified (vv. 16–18)? **4.** Who is "David their king" (vv. 8–9)? What will he be like (v. 21; 23:5)? What had King Josiah of Judah done for the northerners early in Jeremiah's career (2 Kin. 23:15–20) to serve as a prototype for this righteous King to come? **5.** What were the "days of old" (v. 20) like for Israel, under the reign of David? What fortunes, songs of praise and covenant promises would be restored (vv. 18–22)? What will accomplish this turnabout?

APPLY 1. Is it easy for you to detach yourself emotionally from people who were once important to you? After a falling out, does "out of sight, out of mind" come naturally? Would you like a "restoration" with someone from your past? How could it happen? **2.** What and how could your fortunes be restored: More money, for less work? More friends, for less energy? More knowledge, for less time? Other? Explain how you are truly fortunate.

30:9 their king. The mere mention of David brought back memories of a golden era. However, the righteousness of their future king (Jesus Christ) would surpass David's reign and those that would rule after him.

Because of your great guilt and many sins
I have done these things to you.

16 " 'But all who devour you will be devoured;
all your enemies will go into exile.
Those who plunder you will be plundered;
all who make spoil of you I will despoil.
17 But I will restore you to health
and heal your wounds,'
declares the LORD,

'because you are called an outcast,
Zion for whom no one cares.'

18 "This is what the LORD says:

" 'I will restore the fortunes of Jacob's tents
and have compassion on his dwellings;
the city will be rebuilt on her ruins,
and the palace will stand in its proper place.
19 From them will come songs of thanksgiving
and the sound of rejoicing.
I will add to their numbers,
and they will not be decreased;
I will bring them honor,
and they will not be disdained.
20 Their children will be as in days of old,
and their community will be established before me;
I will punish all who oppress them.
21 Their leader will be one of their own;
their ruler will arise from among them.
I will bring him near and he will come close to me,
for who is he who will devote himself
to be close to me?'
declares the LORD.

22 " 'So you will be my people,
and I will be your God.' "

23 See, the storm of the LORD
will burst out in wrath,
a driving wind swirling down
on the heads of the wicked.
24 The fierce anger of the LORD will not turn back
until he fully accomplishes
the purposes of his heart.
In days to come
you will understand this.

OPEN 1. Right now, would you say your spiritual life is closer to a sunrise or a sunset? Is a new day dawning in your life? How so? **2.** "It's always darkest before the

31

"At that time," declares the LORD, "I will be the God of all the clans of Israel, and they will be my people."
2 This is what the LORD says:

"The people who survive the sword

30:20 as in days of old. In the midst of such a chaotic state, thoughts of David's peaceful past inspired a desire for a restored future. They longed for the peace and stability that David's rule brought to their nation.

will find favor in the desert;
I will come to give rest to Israel."

[3]The LORD appeared to us in the past,[a] saying:

"I have loved you with an everlasting love;
I have drawn you with loving-kindness.
[4]I will build you up again
and you will be rebuilt, O Virgin Israel.
Again you will take up your tambourines
and go out to dance with the joyful.
[5]Again you will plant vineyards
on the hills of Samaria;
the farmers will plant them
and enjoy their fruit.
[6]There will be a day when watchmen cry out
on the hills of Ephraim,
'Come, let us go up to Zion,
to the LORD our God.' "

[7]This is what the LORD says:

"Sing with joy for Jacob;
shout for the foremost of the nations.
Make your praises heard, and say,
'O LORD, save your people,
the remnant of Israel.'
[8]See, I will bring them from the land of the north
and gather them from the ends of the earth.
Among them will be the blind and the lame,
expectant mothers and women in labor;
a great throng will return.
[9]They will come with weeping;
they will pray as I bring them back.
I will lead them beside streams of water
on a level path where they will not stumble,
because I am Israel's father,
and Ephraim is my firstborn son.

[10]"Hear the word of the LORD, O nations;
proclaim it in distant coastlands:
'He who scattered Israel will gather them
and will watch over his flock like a shepherd.'
[11]For the LORD will ransom Jacob
and redeem them from the hand of those stronger than they.
[12]They will come and shout for joy on the heights of Zion;
they will rejoice in the bounty of the LORD—
the grain, the new wine and the oi,
the young of the flocks and herd.

[a]3 Or *LORD has appeared to us from afar*

dawn," the saying goes. How has this been true for you? **3.** What is the best news you heard last week? What made it so special?

STUDY 1. Verses 1–22 continue the consolation for Israel. By what other names is Israel called in this section (vv. 7,10,18)? **2.** What evidence do you see here that the promise of restoration is extended to the southern kingdom of Judah, as well (vv. 1,23–40)? **3.** What political vision does Jeremiah have of the restored nation (vv. 5–8)? Why would Israel be considered the "foremost of nations" (Deut. 7:6–8)? Why will they come "with weeping" (v. 9)? **4.** Who else is included in this vision and why (vv. 10–14)? **5.** Who are Rachel and her children (v. 15; Gen. 29:18,30; 46:19–20)? How and why does Jeremiah use the image of "Rachel weeping"? **6.** What other images of grieving and consolation give hope to the readers (vv. 16–20,23–25,27–28)? **7.** What relationship does God want to restore between himself and Israel (vv. 21–22; Hosea 2:18–20)? How can adulterous Israel become a "virgin" again? **8.** What is the meaning of the proverb quoted in verse 29 (Ezek. 18:2–4)? Is God changing the rules (Ex. 20:5; Num. 14:18) by which many thought of themselves as guilty (v. 30; Deut. 24:16)? **9.** What was the covenant God made with Israel's forefathers (vv. 31–32; Gen. 17:1–14; Ex. 19:1–6)? What was "wrong" or obsolete about this old or first covenant (Heb. 8:6–13; 9:13–15; 10:11–18, where Jeremiah is quoted)? **10.** How will the new covenant supersede or fulfill the old one (vv. 33–34)? In what way will it be a covenant? What seals or secures the covenant from God's side (vv. 35–37)? **11.** The exiles returned after 70 years to rebuild Jerusalem. The city did not prove invincible, but was sacked again, most notably by the Romans in A.D. 70 (Luke 21:6). What then does God's promise to Jerusalem of never being destroyed again really mean (vv. 38–40)?

APPLY 1. What have you been mourning the most over the past year? In what way might God be turning that mourning into gladness

---

31:7 The only way a rebellious nation could graduate to "foremost of the nations" was by God's favor (Deut. 7:6–8). Favored status was God's grace on a nati's notoriety not merit.

31:1 stronger than they. Judah was easy victory for Babylon, the ruling power of the day. God's people proved helpless against it. They would need God's power to help them overcome Babylon.

from the least of them to the greatest,"
declares the LORD.

"For I will forgive their wickedness
and will remember their sins no more."

35This is what the LORD says,

he who appoints the sun
to shine by day,
who decrees the moon and stars
to shine by night,
who stirs up the sea
so that its waves roar—
the LORD Almighty is his name:
36"Only if these decrees vanish from my sight,"
declares the LORD,
"will the descendants of Israel ever cease
to be a nation before me."

37This is what the LORD says:

"Only if the heavens above can be measured
and the foundations of the earth below be searched out
will I reject all the descendants of Israel
because of all they have done,"
declares the LORD.

38"The days are coming," declares the LORD, "when this city will be
rebuilt for me from the Tower of Hananel to the Corner Gate. 39The
measuring line will stretch from there straight to the hill of Gareb and
then turn to Goah. 40The whole valley where dead bodies and ashes
are thrown, and all the terraces out to the Kidron Valley on the east as
far as the corner of the Horse Gate, will be holy to the LORD. The city
will never again be uprooted or demolished."

Jeremiah Buys a Field

32 This is the word that came to Jeremiah from the LORD in the
tenth year of Zedekiah king of Judah, which was the eighteenth year of Nebuchadnezzar. 2The army of the king of Babylon was
then besieging Jerusalem, and Jeremiah the prophet was confined in
the courtyard of the guard in the royal palace of Judah.
3Now Zedekiah king of Judah had imprisoned him there, saying,
"Why do you prophesy as you do? You say, 'This is what the LORD
says: I am about to hand this city over to the king of Babylon, and
he will capture it. 4Zedekiah king of Judah will not escape out of the
hands of the Babylonians[a] but will certainly be handed over to the
king of Babylon, and will speak with him face to face and see him
with his own eyes. 5He will take Zedekiah to Babylon, where he will
remain until I deal with him, declares the LORD. If you fight against
the Babylonians, you will not succeed.' "
6Jeremiah said, "The word of the LORD came to me: 7Hanamel son

[a]4 Or *Chaldeans*; also in verses 5, 24, 25, 28, 29 and 43

OPEN 1. Are you better at spending money or making money? **2.** Have you ever bought any real estate? Was it easier or harder than you thought it would be? Would you do it again? **3.** What is the dumbest purchase you've made?

STUDY This chapter resumes stories from Jeremiah's history. **1.** How might it also be an extension of his Book of Consolation (chs. 31–32)? **2.** At the end of chapter 26, Jeremiah was last seen under arrest for preaching in the temple. As this chapter opens, what is happening to the city and to Jeremiah (vv. 1–5)? **3.** How then do you account for the intrusion and seeming irrelevance of Jeremiah's cousin and God's confirming word (vv. 6–8)? At this time is the real estate market

32:1 Jeremiah carefully noted the dates of his messages. The destruction of Judah was quickly approaching within a year.

32:7 right and duty. Jeremiah had to follow an ancient law (Lev. 25:23–25). It

of Shallum your uncle is going to come to you and say, 'Buy my field at Anathoth, because as nearest relative it is your right and duty to buy it.'

8"Then, just as the LORD had said, my cousin Hanamel came to me in the courtyard of the guard and said, 'Buy my field at Anathoth in the territory of Benjamin. Since it is your right to redeem it and possess it, buy it for yourself.'

"I knew that this was the word of the LORD; 9so I bought the field at Anathoth from my cousin Hanamel and weighed out for him seventeen shekels[a] of silver. 10I signed and sealed the deed, had it witnessed, and weighed out the silver on the scales. 11I took the deed of purchase—the sealed copy containing the terms and conditions, as well as the unsealed copy— 12and I gave this deed to Baruch son of Neriah, the son of Mahseiah, in the presence of my cousin Hanamel and of the witnesses who had signed the deed and of all the Jews sitting in the courtyard of the guard.

13"In their presence I gave Baruch these instructions: 14'This is what the LORD Almighty, the God of Israel, says: Take these documents, both the sealed and unsealed copies of the deed of purchase, and put them in a clay jar so they will last a long time. 15For this is what the LORD Almighty, the God of Israel, says: Houses, fields and vineyards will again be bought in this land.'

16"After I had given the deed of purchase to Baruch son of Neriah, I prayed to the LORD:

17"Ah, Sovereign LORD, you have made the heavens and the earth by your great power and outstretched arm. Nothing is too hard for you. 18You show love to thousands but bring the punishment for the fathers' sins into the laps of their children after them. O great and powerful God, whose name is the LORD Almighty, 19great are your purposes and mighty are your deeds. Your eyes are open to all the ways of men; you reward everyone according to his conduct and as his deeds deserve. 20You performed miraculous signs and wonders in Egypt and have continued them to this day, both in Israel and among all mankind, and have gained the renown that is still yours. 21You brought your people Israel out of Egypt with signs and wonders, by a mighty hand and an outstretched arm and with great terror. 22You gave them this land you had sworn to give their forefathers, a land flowing with milk and honey. 23They came in and took possession of it, but they did not obey you or follow your law; they did not do what you commanded them to do. So you brought all this disaster upon them.

24"See how the siege ramps are built up to take the city. Because of the sword, famine and plague, the city will be handed over to the Babylonians who are attacking it. What you said has happened, as you now see. 25And though the city will be handed over to the Babylonians, you, O Sovereign LORD, say to me, 'Buy the field with silver and have the transaction witnessed.' "

[a]9 That is, about 7 ounces (about 200 grams)

a buyer's market, or a seller's market? **4.** Why does Jeremiah have the "right and duty" to buy it (Lev. 25:23–25; Ruth 4:1–4)? Does he think it's a good deal, or does he feel stuck (vv. 24–25)? **5.** Why then does he purchase the field (vv. 8–12)? What proof did he have that it was the right thing to do? **6.** How do the parts played by Hanamel, the witnesses and Baruch serve the overall point of this passage? **7.** How does Jeremiah's prayer (vv. 17–25) serve that overall purpose? What themes from chapters 30–31 does he bring before God? Is this a prayer of affirmation or resignation? Why do you think so? **8.** What comfort does God offer in verses 26–29? In verses 36–41? In verses 42–44? **9.** If the spiritual health of Anathoth is at all like the other Israelite towns (vv. 30–35), what will probably be the fate of Jeremiah's newly-acquired property (11:21–23)? Why then does God ask Jeremiah to buy the field (vv. 42–44)? What do you think the rest of the city would have thought about this crazy real estate transaction?

APPLY 1. Of what comfort to you are long-range assurances of prosperity, when your present financial outlook is precarious (at best) or bankrupt (at worst)? **2.** What lessons of hope have you learned that could only have been taught you through adversity, doom and gloom? **3.** How "bullish" would you be if God were to call you to invest in the future of your country right now: No thanks—I don't do "junk bonds"? Only if I could diversify with some foreign investment? Well, if God says so, I'm gung ho!?

required Jeremiah to buy land from a financially struggling relative to keep it within the family.

32:25 Despite the city's inevitable fate, Jeremiah purchased the land as another word-picture. He put a down payment on Judah's eventual return to their homeland. While he was hesitant, he did obey God.

26Then the word of the LORD came to Jeremiah: 27"I am the LORD,
the God of all mankind. Is anything too hard for me? 28Therefore, this
is what the LORD says: I am about to hand this city over to the Babylonians and to Nebuchadnezzar king of Babylon, who will capture it.
29The Babylonians who are attacking this city will come in and set it
on fire; they will burn it down, along with the houses where the people provoked me to anger by burning incense on the roofs to Baal and
by pouring out drink offerings to other gods.
30"The people of Israel and Judah have done nothing but evil in my
sight from their youth; indeed, the people of Israel have done nothing
but provoke me with what their hands have made, declares the LORD.
31From the day it was built until now, this city has so aroused my
anger and wrath that I must remove it from my sight. 32The people of
Israel and Judah have provoked me by all the evil they have done—
they, their kings and officials, their priests and prophets, the men of
Judah and the people of Jerusalem. 33They turned their backs to me
and not their faces; though I taught them again and again, they
would not listen or respond to discipline. 34They set up their abominable idols in the house that bears my Name and defiled it. 35They
built high places for Baal in the Valley of Ben Hinnom to sacrifice
their sons and daughters[a] to Molech, though I never commanded,
nor did it enter my mind, that they should do such a detestable thing
and so make Judah sin.
36"You are saying about this city, 'By the sword, famine and plague
it will be handed over to the king of Babylon'; but this is what the
LORD, the God of Israel, says: 37I will surely gather them from all the
lands where I banish them in my furious anger and great wrath; I will
bring them back to this place and let them live in safety. 38They will be
my people, and I will be their God. 39I will give them singleness of
heart and action, so that they will always fear me for their own good
and the good of their children after them. 40I will make an everlasting
covenant with them: I will never stop doing good to them, and I will
inspire them to fear me, so that they will never turn away from me. 41I
will rejoice in doing them good and will assuredly plant them in this
land with all my heart and soul.
42"This is what the LORD says: As I have brought all this great calamity on this people, so I will give them all the prosperity I have
promised them. 43Once more fields will be bought in this land of
which you say, 'It is a desolate waste, without men or animals, for it
has been handed over to the Babylonians.' 44Fields will be bought for
silver, and deeds will be signed, sealed and witnessed in the territory
of Benjamin, in the villages around Jerusalem, in the towns of Judah
and in the towns of the hill country, of the western foothills and of
the Negev, because I will restore their fortunes,[b] declares the LORD."

Promise of Restoration

33 While Jeremiah was still confined in the courtyard of the
guard, the word of the LORD came to him a second time:
2"This is what the LORD says, he who made the earth, the LORD who

[a]35 *Or to make their sons and daughters pass through ⌞the fire⌟* [b]44 *Or will bring them back from captivity*

OPEN 1. When were you most homesick? When were you most sick of home? What happened? **2.** What current situations come to mind for you as you picture these fragments of dialogue express-

32:40 make an everlasting covenant. The former covenant was rendered useless because of the people's disobedience (Isa. 24:5). However, the new covenant would be eternal.

out—Lachish and Azekah. These were the only fortified cities left in Judah.

Freedom for Slaves

[8]The word came to Jeremiah from the LORD after King Zedekiah had
made a covenant with all the people in Jerusalem to proclaim freedom for the slaves. [9]Everyone was to free his Hebrew slaves, both
male and female; no one was to hold a fellow Jew in bondage. [10]So all
the officials and people who entered into this covenant agreed that
they would free their male and female slaves and no longer hold
them in bondage. They agreed, and set them free. [11]But afterward
they changed their minds and took back the slaves they had freed
and enslaved them again.

[12]Then the word of the LORD came to Jeremiah: [13]"This is what the
LORD, the God of Israel, says: I made a covenant with your forefathers
when I brought them out of Egypt, out of the land of slavery. I said,
[14]'Every seventh year each of you must free any fellow Hebrew who
has sold himself to you. After he has served you six years, you must
let him go free.'[a] Your fathers, however, did not listen to me or pay attention to me. [15]Recently you repented and did what is right in my
sight: Each of you proclaimed freedom to his countrymen. You even
made a covenant before me in the house that bears my Name. [16]But
now you have turned around and profaned my name; each of you has
taken back the male and female slaves you had set free to go where
they wished. You have forced them to become your slaves again.

[17]"Therefore, this is what the LORD says: You have not obeyed me;
you have not proclaimed freedom for your fellow countrymen. So I
now proclaim 'freedom' for you, declares the LORD—'freedom' to fall
by the sword, plague and famine. I will make you abhorrent to all the
kingdoms of the earth. [18]The men who have violated my covenant
and have not fulfilled the terms of the covenant they made before me,
I will treat like the calf they cut in two and then walked between its
pieces. [19]The leaders of Judah and Jerusalem, the court officials, the
priests and all the people of the land who walked between the pieces
of the calf, [20]I will hand over to their enemies who seek their lives.
Their dead bodies will become food for the birds of the air and the
beasts of the earth.

[21]"I will hand Zedekiah king of Judah and his officials over to their
enemies who seek their lives, to the army of the king of Babylon,
which has withdrawn from you. [22]I am going to give the order, declares the LORD, and I will bring them back to this city. They will fight
against it, take it and burn it down. And I will lay waste the towns of
Judah so no one can live there."

[a]*14* Deut. 15:12

OPEN 1. Has anyone gone back on a promise to you? When? How did it make you feel? **2.** What freedoms were you granted upon reaching the age of: 11? 13? 16? 18??

STUDY 1. Who became slaves in ancient Israel and why (vv. 8–9; Lev. 25:39–46)? Why was a limit set for the servitude of a fellow Jew (vv. 13–14)? **2.** Why do you think Zedekiah declares freedom for the slaves (vv. 8–10)? Why do the slave-holders renege on this (vv. 11,16,21–22; 37:5)? **3.** One ancient rite to "cut" a covenant had partners cut a calf in two and walk between the pieces. What might have been the significance of this (vv. 18–20; Gen. 15:8–11, 17)? **4.** Why fuss over the slaves? How would it feel to be freed, then enslaved again? How will God "free" those who break their vow (vv. 17–22)? **5.** If this were your only biblical basis for learning how God cares for the poor, what would you conclude about God? About the poor? About rich land-owners and office-holders?

APPLY 1. When have you made a promise, and then gone back on what you promised? Who was the main one victimized by this promise: Your spouse? Your kids? Your boss? God? Yourself? **2.** Is there a way you could make good on that promise even now? **3.** Do you feel "enslaved" in any way? What would freedom mean to you? What can you do for those enslaved as you once were (or still are)?

34:8 freedom. Zedekiah proclaimed freedom for the Hebrews who were slaves of their own people.

34:10 The people of Judah attempted to right as many wrongs as possible in light of their impending doom.

34:14 Unfortunately, Judah's attempts to reinstate the Law were halfhearted at best (Deut. 15:12). They eventually recaptured their slaves (v. 16).

34:18 Jeremiah used the graphic image of how a covenant was executed between two parties. God had passed through the sacrifice in making the covenant (Gen. 15:8–11,17). Their punishment was to be treated like the original sacrifice.

OPEN **1.** When it comes to parties, are you: A party animal? A party pooper? A wall flower? Prudish with food and drink? Enough food and drink to satisfy an army? **2.** What famous people would you invite to an "ideal" dinner party? What does your guest list (or last year's social calendar) say about you?

STUDY Chapters 35–36 flash back to the reign of Jehoiakim (v. 1), nearly 25 years earlier. **1.** What is the relationship between Judah and Babylon at this time (2 Kin. 24:1–2)? **2.** Why did God tell Jeremiah to offer the Recabites wine (vv. 2–5)? What two things made them different from other Israelites (vv. 6–10)? Why do you think they had been told to live so radically different (2 Kin. 10:15–23; compare the Nazirite's vow, Num. 6:2–4,20)? **3.** Why had they moved into Jerusalem (v. 11)? Why might they feel uneasy about the situation? **4.** What about the Recabites pleases God (vv. 13–16)? How will they be rewarded (vv. 18–19)? What is the object lesson in this for Judah (33:18)? For you?

APPLY **1.** Is yours an alternative lifestyle—distinct from that of your peers at work, school or neighborhood? What one thing distinguishes you? **2.** How should followers of Christ be separate from the rest of society, yet live so that others can tell what motivates us? In what respect is your group a pace-setter for those around you?

The Recabites

35 This is the word that came to Jeremiah from the LORD during
the reign of Jehoiakim son of Josiah king of Judah: 2"Go to
the Recabite family and invite them to come to one of the side rooms
of the house of the LORD and give them wine to drink."
3So I went to get Jaazaniah son of Jeremiah, the son of Habaz-
ziniah, and his brothers and all his sons—the whole family of the
Recabites. 4I brought them into the house of the LORD, into the room
of the sons of Hanan son of Igdaliah the man of God. It was next to
the room of the officials, which was over that of Maaseiah son of
Shallum the doorkeeper. 5Then I set bowls full of wine and some cups
before the men of the Recabite family and said to them, "Drink some
wine."
6But they replied, "We do not drink wine, because our forefather
Jonadab son of Recab gave us this command: 'Neither you nor your
descendants must ever drink wine. 7Also you must never build
houses, sow seed or plant vineyards; you must never have any of
these things, but must always live in tents. Then you will live a long
time in the land where you are nomads.' 8We have obeyed everything
our forefather Jonadab son of Recab commanded us. Neither we nor
our wives nor our sons and daughters have ever drunk wine 9or built
houses to live in or had vineyards, fields or crops. 10We have lived in
tents and have fully obeyed everything our forefather Jonadab commanded us. 11But when Nebuchadnezzar king of Babylon invaded
this land, we said, 'Come, we must go to Jerusalem to escape the
Babylonian[a] and Aramean armies.' So we have remained in Jerusalem."
12Then the word of the LORD came to Jeremiah, saying: 13"This is
what the LORD Almighty, the God of Israel, says: Go and tell the men
of Judah and the people of Jerusalem, 'Will you not learn a lesson and
obey my words?' declares the LORD. 14'Jonadab son of Recab ordered
his sons not to drink wine and this command has been kept. To this
day they do not drink wine, because they obey their forefather's command. But I have spoken to you again and again, yet you have not
obeyed me. 15Again and again I sent all my servants the prophets to
you. They said, "Each of you must turn from your wicked ways and
reform your actions; do not follow other gods to serve them. Then
you will live in the land I have given to you and your fathers." But you
have not paid attention or listened to me. 16The descendants of Jonadab son of Recab have carried out the command their forefather gave
them, but these people have not obeyed me.'
17"Therefore, this is what the LORD God Almighty, the God of Israel,
says: 'Listen! I am going to bring on Judah and on everyone living in
Jerusalem every disaster I pronounced against them. I spoke to them,
but they did not listen; I called to them, but they did not answer.' "
18Then Jeremiah said to the family of the Recabites, "This is what
the LORD Almighty, the God of Israel, says: 'You have obeyed the com-

[a]11 Or *Chaldean*

35:2 Recabite family. The Recabites were nomads with quirky traditions based on the instructions of their nomadic forefather, Jonadab.

35:6 We do not drink wine. The Recabites steadfastly refused the wine prohibited by their forefather. In so doing, they became an object lesson to Judah.

35:13 Will you not learn a lesson. If this nomadic tribe could be obedient to family tradition, why did Judah resist God's Laws?

mand of your forefather Jonadab and have followed all his instructions and have done everything he ordered.' 19Therefore, this is what the LORD Almighty, the God of Israel, says: 'Jonadab son of Recab will never fail to have a man to serve me.' "

Jehoiakim Burns Jeremiah's Scroll

36 In the fourth year of Jehoiakim son of Josiah king of Judah, this word came to Jeremiah from the LORD: 2"Take a scroll and write on it all the words I have spoken to you concerning Israel, Judah and all the other nations from the time I began speaking to you in the reign of Josiah till now. 3Perhaps when the people of Judah hear about every disaster I plan to inflict on them, each of them will turn from his wicked way; then I will forgive their wickedness and their sin."

4So Jeremiah called Baruch son of Neriah, and while Jeremiah dictated all the words the LORD had spoken to him, Baruch wrote them on the scroll. 5Then Jeremiah told Baruch, "I am restricted; I cannot go to the LORD's temple. 6So you go to the house of the LORD on a day of fasting and read to the people from the scroll the words of the LORD that you wrote as I dictated. Read them to all the people of Judah who come in from their towns. 7Perhaps they will bring their petition before the LORD, and each will turn from his wicked ways, for the anger and wrath pronounced against this people by the LORD are great."

8Baruch son of Neriah did everything Jeremiah the prophet told him to do; at the LORD's temple he read the words of the LORD from the scroll. 9In the ninth month of the fifth year of Jehoiakim son of Josiah king of Judah, a time of fasting before the LORD was proclaimed for all the people in Jerusalem and those who had come from the towns of Judah. 10From the room of Gemariah son of Shaphan the secretary, which was in the upper courtyard at the entrance of the New Gate of the temple, Baruch read to all the people at the LORD's temple the words of Jeremiah from the scroll.

11When Micaiah son of Gemariah, the son of Shaphan, heard all the words of the LORD from the scroll, 12he went down to the secretary's room in the royal palace, where all the officials were sitting: Elishama the secretary, Delaiah son of Shemaiah, Elnathan son of Acbor, Gemariah son of Shaphan, Zedekiah son of Hananiah, and all the other officials. 13After Micaiah told them everything he had heard Baruch read to the people from the scroll, 14all the officials sent Jehudi son of Nethaniah, the son of Shelemiah, the son of Cushi, to say to Baruch, "Bring the scroll from which you have read to the people and come." So Baruch son of Neriah went to them with the scroll in his hand. 15They said to him, "Sit down, please, and read it to us."

So Baruch read *it* to them. 16When they heard all these words, they looked at each other in fear and said to Baruch, "We must report all

OPEN 1. Have you ever been vandalized? What happened? How did it make you feel? **2.** If you wrote a book, who would be the last person you'd want to read it? Who is your harshest critic? Your easiest? **3.** How often have you tried excusing yourself for not turning in a paper by saying something like, "My dog ate it!"? Did that ever really happen?

STUDY 1. What roles did Jeremiah, Baruch and the Lord each play in producing the first version of the book of Jeremiah (vv. 1–4,17–18)? Why might a written account fare better than nearly 20 years of preaching? **2.** Why do you think Jeremiah is banned from the temple area (vv. 5–7; 26:7–11)? Who might have called the time of fasting (v. 9): The king? The priests? The Lord? **3.** Why do the officials tell Baruch and Jeremiah to hide (vv. 16–19)? How has the family of Shaphan treated Jeremiah in the past (26:24)? Why must they tell the king? **4.** What review does the king give Jeremiah's book (vv. 22–24)? How would you compare Jehoiakim's "critique" with what King Josiah did upon rediscovering God's Word (2 Kin. 22:11–23:3)? **5.** How must Jeremiah have felt when he heard the fate of the scroll? How did the Lord address that felt need and the cockiness of Jehoaikim (vv. 27–31; 2 Kin. 24:1)? **6.** What is the point of writing it all down again (vv. 28,32; compare Ex. 34:1)? What extra words might have appeared in the second version of the book of Jeremiah? **7.** Why do you think officials sympathetic to Jeremiah did not stand up to the king? What would decisive action have cost them?

APPLY 1. Have you ever persisted in a task for years despite legal opposition and a total lack of visible success? What motivated you to persist? **2.** When has someone brought you news that was so bad that

---

35:19 A simple man proved a simple truth. Obedience is rewarded.

36:1 The narrative now goes back to the fourth year of Jehoiakim's reign, which marks the beginning of the Babylonian siege.

36:2 scroll. This was Jeremiah's first attempt to pen his prophecies. A written record could be read aloud and hopefully warn more people.

36:5 I am restricted. Jeremiah found a way to propagate his message despite his own unpopularity (26:7–11); and for the fact that he had been threatened (20:2). His assistant, Baruch, took the message to the temple.

you were tempted to "kill the messenger"? What did you end up doing? **3.** How do people today show disdain for God's Word? Do you honor it? How so?

these words to the king." [17]Then they asked Baruch, "Tell us, how did
you come to write all this? Did Jeremiah dictate it?"
[18]"Yes," Baruch replied, "he dictated all these words to me, and I
wrote them in ink on the scroll."
[19]Then the officials said to Baruch, "You and Jeremiah, go and hide.
Don't let anyone know where you are."
[20]After they put the scroll in the room of Elishama the secretary,
they went to the king in the courtyard and reported everything to
him. [21]The king sent Jehudi to get the scroll, and Jehudi brought it
from the room of Elishama the secretary and read it to the king and
all the officials standing beside him. [22]It was the ninth month and the
king was sitting in the winter apartment, with a fire burning in the
firepot in front of him. [23]Whenever Jehudi had read three or four
columns of the scroll, the king cut them off with a scribe's knife and
threw them into the firepot, until the entire scroll was burned in the
fire. [24]The king and all his attendants who heard all these words
showed no fear, nor did they tear their clothes. [25]Even though Elnathan, Delaiah and Gemariah urged the king not to burn the scroll, he
would not listen to them. [26]Instead, the king commanded Jerahmeel,
a son of the king, Seraiah son of Azriel and Shelemiah son of Abdeel
to arrest Baruch the scribe and Jeremiah the prophet. But the LORD
had hidden them.
[27]After the king burned the scroll containing the words that Baruch
had written at Jeremiah's dictation, the word of the LORD came to Jeremiah: [28]"Take another scroll and write on it all the words that were
on the first scroll, which Jehoiakim king of Judah burned up. [29]Also
tell Jehoiakim king of Judah, 'This is what the LORD says: You burned
that scroll and said, "Why did you write on it that the king of Babylon
would certainly come and destroy this land and cut off both men and
animals from it?" [30]Therefore, this is what the LORD says about Jehoiakim king of Judah: He will have no one to sit on the throne of David;
his body will be thrown out and exposed to the heat by day and the
frost by night. [31]I will punish him and his children and his attendants
for their wickedness; I will bring on them and those living in Jerusalem and the people of Judah every disaster I pronounced against
them, because they have not listened.'"
[32]So Jeremiah took another scroll and gave it to the scribe Baruch
son of Neriah, and as Jeremiah dictated, Baruch wrote on it all the
words of the scroll that Jehoiakim king of Judah had burned in the
fire. And many similar words were added to them.

Jeremiah in Prison

37 Zedekiah son of Josiah was made king of Judah by Nebuchadnezzar king of Babylon; he reigned in place of Jehoiachin[a]
son of Jehoiakim. [2]Neither he nor his attendants nor the people of the

[a]1 Hebrew *Coniah*, a variant of *Jehoiachin*

OPEN 1. Have you ever been to jail or a prison? As a tourist, visitor or resident? How long were you "in for"? How did the place make you feel? **2.** What makes someone your best friend? How many best friends have you had?

36:19 go and hide. The news was so disturbing, the officials instructed Baruch to run for safety! They feared the king would react to the messenger as well as the message.

36:23 threw them into the firepot. Jeremiah's message was all but wasted on Judah's present king. Jehoiakim demonstrated his disdain by burning the message instead of heeding it.

36:30 Ultimately, Jehoiakim's indifference contributed to his son's insignificance. His son would succeed him for three months before being humiliated by the Babylonians.

land paid any attention to the words the LORD had spoken through Jeremiah the prophet.

3King Zedekiah, however, sent Jehucal son of Shelemiah with the priest Zephaniah son of Maaseiah to Jeremiah the prophet with this message: "Please pray to the LORD our God for us."

4Now Jeremiah was free to come and go among the people, for he had not yet been put in prison. 5Pharaoh's army had marched out of Egypt, and when the Babylonians[a] who were besieging Jerusalem heard the report about them, they withdrew from Jerusalem.

6Then the word of the LORD came to Jeremiah the prophet: 7"This is what the LORD, the God of Israel, says: Tell the king of Judah, who sent you to inquire of me, 'Pharaoh's army, which has marched out to support you, will go back to its own land, to Egypt. 8Then the Babylonians will return and attack this city; they will capture it and burn it down.'

9"This is what the LORD says: Do not deceive yourselves, thinking, 'The Babylonians will surely leave us.' They will not! 10Even if you were to defeat the entire Babylonian[b] army that is attacking you and only wounded men were left in their tents, they would come out and burn this city down."

11After the Babylonian army had withdrawn from Jerusalem because of Pharaoh's army, 12Jeremiah started to leave the city to go to the territory of Benjamin to get his share of the property among the people there. 13But when he reached the Benjamin Gate, the captain of the guard, whose name was Irijah son of Shelemiah, the son of Hananiah, arrested him and said, "You are deserting to the Babylonians!"

14"That's not true!" Jeremiah said. "I am not deserting to the Babylonians." But Irijah would not listen to him; instead, he arrested Jeremiah and brought him to the officials. 15They were angry with Jeremiah and had him beaten and imprisoned in the house of Jonathan the secretary, which they had made into a prison.

16Jeremiah was put into a vaulted cell in a dungeon, where he remained a long time. 17Then King Zedekiah sent for him and had him brought to the palace, where he asked him privately, "Is there any word from the LORD?"

"Yes," Jeremiah replied, "you will be handed over to the king of Babylon."

18Then Jeremiah said to King Zedekiah, "What crime have I committed against you or your officials or this people, that you have put me in prison? 19Where are your prophets who prophesied to you, 'The king of Babylon will not attack you or this land'? 20But now, my lord

[a]5 Or *Chaldeans*; also in verses 8, 9, 13 and 14 [b]10 Or *Chaldean*; also in verse 11

STUDY **1.** Chapter 37 moves forward 20 years, once again, to Jeremiah's sufferings under Zedekiah. What fulfilled prophecy links this chapter with the previous one (v. 1; 36:30; 2 Kin. 24:17–20)? **2.** What events led to the siege and later withdrawal by Babylon (vv. 5,7,11; 2 Kin. 25:1–2)? Where do you think Jeremiah stands in the public opinion polls of that day? **3.** How would you make sense of Zedekiah's feelings about the prophet (vv. 2–3,16–17)? Why does he respect him at times and ignore him at others? **4.** Why does Jeremiah try leaving the city (vv. 11–13; 32:8)? Why doesn't Irijah believe him (vv. 13–17; 21:8–10)? Would you have been suspicious, or trusting, of Jeremiah? **5.** How does God use evil events for Jeremiah's welfare and Zedekiah's downfall (vv. 14–21)? How does Jeremiah show his ability to think on his feet? Why is he persuasive?

APPLY **1.** At what points can you empathize with the main characters in this story: I predicted doom that did not come to pass? I warned people against a course of action, only to find them ignoring me and prospering as well? I once hoped someone would suffer so that I could be proved right? I feel my motives are often mistrusted? Choose one to explain further. **2.** How do you determine whether a message is truly God's will, or just what you want to hear?

37:1–38:28 With the threat of Babylon closing in on the inhabitants of Jerusalem, the unpopular prophet was falsely imprisoned for treason (37:11–16). King Zedekiah tried protecting the prisoner (37:17–21); however, Jeremiah ended up in a dark cistern (38:1–6). Jeremiah's rescue proved to be a timely turn of events (38:7–13).

37:3 Please pray. Zedekiah enjoyed a cafeteria-style relationship with Jeremiah—picking and choosing what he wanted to hear. With Babylon closing in on the city, Zedekiah turned to Jeremiah for prayer.

37:5 they withdrew from Jerusalem. The Babylonians were drawn away from attacking smaller prey to pursue the powerful pharaoh. The Egyptians proved an insufficient ally against the Babylonians.

37:17 asked him privately. Although Zedekiah held the most powerful position in the land, he was afraid. He made his inquiry in secret.

the king, please listen. Let me bring my petition before you: Do not send me back to the house of Jonathan the secretary, or I will die there."

21 King Zedekiah then gave orders for Jeremiah to be placed in the courtyard of the guard and given bread from the street of the bakers each day until all the bread in the city was gone. So Jeremiah remained in the courtyard of the guard.

Jeremiah Thrown Into a Cistern

38 Shephatiah son of Mattan, Gedaliah son of Pashhur, Jehucal[a] son of Shelemiah, and Pashhur son of Malkijah heard what Jeremiah was telling all the people when he said, 2 "This is what the LORD says: 'Whoever stays in this city will die by the sword, famine or plague, but whoever goes over to the Babylonians[b] will live. He will escape with his life; he will live.' 3 And this is what the LORD says: 'This city will certainly be handed over to the army of the king of Babylon, who will capture it.' "

4 Then the officials said to the king, "This man should be put to death. He is discouraging the soldiers who are left in this city, as well as all the people, by the things he is saying to them. This man is not seeking the good of these people but their ruin."

5 "He is in your hands," King Zedekiah answered. "The king can do nothing to oppose you."

6 So they took Jeremiah and put him into the cistern of Malkijah, the king's son, which was in the courtyard of the guard. They lowered Jeremiah by ropes into the cistern; it had no water in it, only mud, and Jeremiah sank down into the mud.

7 But Ebed-Melech, a Cushite,[c] an official[d] in the royal palace, heard that they had put Jeremiah into the cistern. While the king was sitting in the Benjamin Gate, 8 Ebed-Melech went out of the palace and said to him, 9 "My lord the king, these men have acted wickedly in all they have done to Jeremiah the prophet. They have thrown him into a cistern, where he will starve to death when there is no longer any bread in the city."

10 Then the king commanded Ebed-Melech the Cushite, "Take thirty men from here with you and lift Jeremiah the prophet out of the cistern before he dies."

11 So Ebed-Melech took the men with him and went to a room under the treasury in the palace. He took some old rags and worn-out clothes from there and let them down with ropes to Jeremiah in the cistern. 12 Ebed-Melech the Cushite said to Jeremiah, "Put these old rags and worn-out clothes under your arms to pad the ropes." Jeremiah did so, 13 and they pulled him up with the ropes and lifted him out of the cistern. And Jeremiah remained in the courtyard of the guard.

[a]1 Hebrew *Jucal,* a variant of *Jehucal* [b]2 Or *Chaldeans;* also in verses 18, 19 and 23 [c]7 Probably from the upper Nile region [d]7 Or *a eunuch*

OPEN 1. Has your car ever gotten stuck in the mud or snow? How did you get out? **2.** What is your favorite old item of clothing? Why are you attached to it?

STUDY 1. Why does this "gang of four" have it in for Jeremiah (vv. 1–4; 21:1; 37:3)? **2.** How and why does Zedekiah appear "wimpish" (vv. 5–6,10)? Why not just kill Jeremiah outright? In using a cistern so publicly accessible (v. 6), what might the king be secretly hoping? **3.** Who stands up for Jeremiah and why (vv. 7–9; 39:18)? Why the details about the 30 men and the old rags? **4.** Is this a retelling of the same story recorded in 37:16–21? Has Jeremiah been thrown in different cisterns, or the same one twice? Why do you think so?

APPLY 1. Are you "stuck in the mud" or "climbing the walls" right now? Is it from: An accident? All work, no play? Enemy? No friends? What would be solid ground to you? **2.** What has been your spiritual low point? Where did you receive help? Were any "old rags" or trusted friends used in your rescue?

38:5 He is in your hands. Zedekiah *eagerly released himself* from responsibility in a potentially volatile situation.

38:7 Ebed-Melech, a Cushite. His name means "king's servant." He actually became a servant by helping Jeremiah, who was about sixty years old at the time. Jeremiah would have died at the hands of unjust men apart from the protests of this appalled official. Ebed-Melech was rewarded for acting justly and rescuing Jeremiah (39:15–18).

38:12 Ebed-Melech exercised extra-mile effort. He managed the process with concern for Jeremiah's safety and comfort.

Zedekiah Questions Jeremiah Again

[14]Then King Zedekiah sent for Jeremiah the prophet and had him brought to the third entrance to the temple of the LORD. "I am going to ask you something," the king said to Jeremiah. "Do not hide anything from me."

[15]Jeremiah said to Zedekiah, "If I give you an answer, will you not kill me? Even if I did give you counsel, you would not listen to me."

[16]But King Zedekiah swore this oath secretly to Jeremiah: "As surely as the LORD lives, who has given us breath, I will neither kill you nor hand you over to those who are seeking your life."

[17]Then Jeremiah said to Zedekiah, "This is what the LORD God Almighty, the God of Israel, says: 'If you surrender to the officers of the king of Babylon, your life will be spared and this city will not be burned down; you and your family will live. [18]But if you will not surrender to the officers of the king of Babylon, this city will be handed over to the Babylonians and they will burn it down; you yourself will not escape from their hands.' "

[19]King Zedekiah said to Jeremiah, "I am afraid of the Jews who have gone over to the Babylonians, for the Babylonians may hand me over to them and they will mistreat me."

[20]"They will not hand you over," Jeremiah replied. "Obey the LORD by doing what I tell you. Then it will go well with you, and your life will be spared. [21]But if you refuse to surrender, this is what the LORD has revealed to me: [22]All the women left in the palace of the king of Judah will be brought out to the officials of the king of Babylon. Those women will say to you:

" 'They misled you and overcame you—
those trusted friends of yours.
Your feet are sunk in the mud;
your friends have deserted you.'

[23]"All your wives and children will be brought out to the Babylonians. You yourself will not escape from their hands but will be captured by the king of Babylon; and this city will[a] be burned down."

[24]Then Zedekiah said to Jeremiah, "Do not let anyone know about this conversation, or you may die. [25]If the officials hear that I talked with you, and they come to you and say, 'Tell us what you said to the king and what the king said to you; do not hide it from us or we will kill you,' [26]then tell them, 'I was pleading with the king not to send me back to Jonathan's house to die there.' "

[27]All the officials did come to Jeremiah and question him, and he told them everything the king had ordered him to say. So they said no more to him, for no one had heard his conversation with the king.

[28]And Jeremiah remained in the courtyard of the guard until the day Jerusalem was captured.

[a]23 Or *and you will cause this city to*

OPEN **1.** Do you find it easier to give or to receive advice? Why? What advice do you have on giving or asking for advice? **2.** Have you ever been entrusted with a secret which you (accidentally) passed on to others? Are there secrets you've never told? (Don't start now.) Any secrets of yours you hope someone else is keeping?

STUDY **1.** Is Jeremiah reluctant to answer Zedekiah, or is he simply negotiating (vv. 14–15; compare Jesus' encounter, Luke 22:66–67)? Why has Zedekiah neither killed him nor heeded his advice? What does he stand to lose either way? **2.** What question does the king actually ask (vv. 16–19)? What question do you deduce from Jeremiah's answer? Is this message different from others in the past (vv. 2–3; 21:9–10; 32:3–5)? **3.** Why is the king afraid to surrender (v. 19)? Who else is he afraid of (vv. 16,24–26)? What word fits Zedekiah's situation? **4.** Jeremiah says there is only one path to save the city (vv. 17–18,20–23). Which path do you think he'll take? **5.** Was it right for Jeremiah to tell the officials a half-truth (vv. 26–27)? What would you have done here?

APPLY **1.** Have you ever been in a no-win situation? If it looked like you'd be "damned if you did and damned if you didn't," how did you decide the best way to lose? **2.** When have you felt deserted by trusted friends (v. 22)? **3.** How has God's Word proven to be trustworthy to you at times when others weren't?

38:19 I am afraid. The king's powerful position was hindered by paranoia. He feared retribution from his own people.

38:27 no one had heard his conversation. Zedekiah instructed Jeremiah to not talk about their private conversation. In fact, when asked, Jeremiah merely repeated his earlier pleas to Zedekiah regarding his safekeeping (37:20). He was not obligated to share with them anything else.

The Fall of Jerusalem

39 This is how Jerusalem was taken: 1In the ninth year of Zedekiah king of Judah, in the tenth month, Nebuchadnezzar king of Babylon marched against Jerusalem with his whole army and laid siege to it. 2And on the ninth day of the fourth month of Zedekiah's eleventh year, the city wall was broken through. 3Then all the officials of the king of Babylon came and took seats in the Middle Gate: Nergal-Sharezer of Samgar, Nebo-Sarsekim[a] a chief officer, Nergal-Sharezer a high official and all the other officials of the king of Babylon. 4When Zedekiah king of Judah and all the soldiers saw them, they fled; they left the city at night by way of the king's garden, through the gate between the two walls, and headed toward the Arabah.[b]

5But the Babylonian[c] army pursued them and overtook Zedekiah in the plains of Jericho. They captured him and took him to Nebuchadnezzar king of Babylon at Riblah in the land of Hamath, where he pronounced sentence on him. 6There at Riblah the king of Babylon slaughtered the sons of Zedekiah before his eyes and also killed all the nobles of Judah. 7Then he put out Zedekiah's eyes and bound him with bronze shackles to take him to Babylon.

8The Babylonians[d] set fire to the royal palace and the houses of the people and broke down the walls of Jerusalem. 9Nebuzaradan commander of the imperial guard carried into exile to Babylon the people who remained in the city, along with those who had gone over to him, and the rest of the people. 10But Nebuzaradan the commander of the guard left behind in the land of Judah some of the poor people, who owned nothing; and at that time he gave them vineyards and fields.

11Now Nebuchadnezzar king of Babylon had given these orders about Jeremiah through Nebuzaradan commander of the imperial guard: 12"Take him and look after him; don't harm him but do for him whatever he asks." 13So Nebuzaradan the commander of the guard, Nebushazban a chief officer, Nergal-Sharezer a high official and all the other officers of the king of Babylon 14sent and had Jeremiah taken out of the courtyard of the guard. They turned him over to Gedaliah son of Ahikam, the son of Shaphan, to take him back to his home. So he remained among his own people.

15While Jeremiah had been confined in the courtyard of the guard, the word of the LORD came to him: 16"Go and tell Ebed-Melech the Cushite, 'This is what the LORD Almighty, the God of Israel, says: I am about to fulfill my words against this city through disaster, not prosperity. At that time they will be fulfilled before your eyes. 17But I will rescue you on that day, declares the LORD; you will not be handed over to those you fear. 18I will save you; you will not fall by the sword but will escape with your life, because you trust in me, declares the LORD.' "

[a]3 Or *Nergal-Sharezer, Samgar-Nebo, Sarsekim* [b]4 Or *the Jordan Valley* [c]5 Or *Chaldean*
[d]8 Or *Chaldeans*

OPEN 1. What movie have you seen recently that had far too much violence in your opinion? What about violence attracts (and repels) you? **2.** What is the longest you have gone without eating? Was it planned or forced on you? How did you "break fast"?

STUDY 1. Imagine living in Jerusalem during the two-year Babylonian siege (vv. 1–2; 2 Kin. 25:1–3). What would you fear the most: Giving up the stones in my house to buttress the walls? Not knowing when the end would come? Sure death by sword? Slow death by famine? **2.** Jeremiah has been predicting the fall of Jerusalem ever since he was first called by the Lord some 40 years earlier (vv. 1–3; compare 1:14–16). How many kings have heard his message since then (1:2–3; 2 Kin. 22:1; 23:31,36; 24:8,18)? **3.** What violence is Zedekiah forced to endure, which he would sooner have not seen (vv. 5–9)? Do you feel sympathy for him? Why or why not? **4.** Who does Nebuchadnezzar (and the Lord) spare and why (vv. 9–10,12–14,16–18)? Why does Babylon deport the ruling class and leave the poor people to tend the land (2 Kin. 24:12–14)? **5.** Why does Nebuchadnezzar treat Jeremiah so well? Has Jeremiah sold out (27:12; 37:13)? Or is he in debt only to the Shaphan family (v. 14)? **6.** Why is God sparing Ebed-Melech (vv. 15–18; 38:10)?

APPLY 1. From what has God rescued you? Do you feel it was because you deserved it or because of God's mercy? **2.** As you look to what is fearful in your future, how easy or hard is it to trust God to rescue you again?

39:2 A pile of rubble marked the beginning of the end for Jerusalem. After a two-month siege, the Babylonians captured the stalwart city.

39:14 among his own people. In the midst of preparing for deportation, Jeremiah was identified and released from his political imprisonment.

39:18 trust in me. Ebed-Melech's past heroism proved to be invaluable to his future (38:7–13). He escaped certain death.

Jeremiah Freed

40 The word came to Jeremiah from the LORD after Nebuzaradan commander of the imperial guard had released him at Ramah. He had found Jeremiah bound in chains among all the captives from Jerusalem and Judah who were being carried into exile to Babylon. 2When the commander of the guard found Jeremiah, he said to him, "The LORD your God decreed this disaster for this place. 3And now the LORD has brought it about; he has done just as he said he would. All this happened because you people sinned against the LORD and did not obey him. 4But today I am freeing you from the chains on your wrists. Come with me to Babylon, if you like, and I will look after you; but if you do not want to, then don't come. Look, the whole country lies before you; go wherever you please." 5However, before Jeremiah turned to go,[a] Nebuzaradan added, "Go back to Gedaliah son of Ahikam, the son of Shaphan, whom the king of Babylon has appointed over the towns of Judah, and live with him among the people, or go anywhere else you please."

Then the commander gave him provisions and a present and let him go. 6So Jeremiah went to Gedaliah son of Ahikam at Mizpah and stayed with him among the people who were left behind in the land.

Gedaliah Assassinated

7When all the army officers and their men who were still in the open country heard that the king of Babylon had appointed Gedaliah son of Ahikam as governor over the land and had put him in charge of the men, women and children who were the poorest in the land and who had not been carried into exile to Babylon, 8they came to Gedaliah at Mizpah—Ishmael son of Nethaniah, Johanan and Jonathan the sons of Kareah, Seraiah son of Tanhumeth, the sons of Ephai the Netophathite, and Jaazaniah[b] the son of the Maacathite, and their men. 9Gedaliah son of Ahikam, the son of Shaphan, took an oath to reassure them and their men. "Do not be afraid to serve the Babylonians,[c]" he said. "Settle down in the land and serve the king of Babylon, and it will go well with you. 10I myself will stay at Mizpah to represent you before the Babylonians who come to us, but you are to harvest the wine, summer fruit and oil, and put them in your storage jars, and live in the towns you have taken over."

11When all the Jews in Moab, Ammon, Edom and all the other countries heard that the king of Babylon had left a remnant in Judah and had appointed Gedaliah son of Ahikam, the son of Shaphan, as governor over them, 12they all came back to the land of Judah, to Gedaliah at Mizpah, from all the countries where they had been scattered. And they harvested an abundance of wine and summer fruit.

13Johanan son of Kareah and all the army officers still in the open country came to Gedaliah at Mizpah 14and said to him, "Don't you know that Baalis king of the Ammonites has sent Ishmael son of

[a]5 Or *Jeremiah answered* [b]8 Hebrew *Jezaniah,* a variant of *Jaazaniah* [c]9 Or *Chaldeans*; also in verse 10

OPEN Ever wish you could start over with a clean slate? Did you ever try it? What happened?

STUDY 1. What "word" comes to Jeremiah (v. 1; 39:11–14)? **2.** How has Jeremiah's prediction about Ramah (31:15) come true in his day? In Jesus' day (Matt. 2:18)? **3.** Why does Nebuzaradan grasp what no Judean king ever did (vv. 2–3)? Why would he host Jeremiah in Babylon (v. 4)? **4.** Why does Jeremiah say "no" (vv. 5–6)?

APPLY 1. How do you respond to unexpected setbacks: Complain? Fight? Rebound? Give up? Give a recent example. **2.** Ever been freed by a non-believer to pursue God's will? How did that feel?

OPEN 1. Of the assassinations that have occurred in your lifetime, which affected you the most? Why? **2.** Do you have any hobby collections? What lengths do you go to get these? **3.** Are you a "pack-rat," collecting everything? If you had to suddenly clear out all your stuff, what would be the last to go?

STUDY 1. What sort of governor was Gedaliah (40:7)? What were the Jewish guerrilla commanders concerned about (40:8–10)? **2.** Why do the Jewish refugees from the war return to Judah (40:11–12)? What are their alternatives? What alternative is Ishmael pursuing and why (40:14–41:1)? **3.** Why would Baalis support this assassination plot? Why does Gedaliah find such a plot incredible? What is Gedaliah's "fatal flaw"? **4.** Why do the 80 Samaritans come to Judah (41:5; 16:6–7)? Why does Ishmael ambush them (41:7–8)? What political statement is made in filling King Asa's cistern with the dead (41:9; 1 Kin. 15:16–22)? **5.** Ishmael could set up rule at Mizpah and declare war on Babylon. Why doesn't he (41:10–12)? Why is his leadership divided? **6.** Do you think Gedaliah was right not to make a preemptive strike at Ishmael?

40:1 The word came to Jeremiah. Jeremiah began another chapter of postprison prophecies. His job was not over yet. He continued the task at hand, even though he had just been given freedom.

40:2–3 Jeremiah's insightful prophecies against Judah were not lost on the pagan officials of Babylon. The first exiles likely spread the word as his predictions came true one by one.

40:10 represent you before the Babylonians. As governor, Gedaliah served as a national link between the remnants of Jews in Judah and the powerful Babylon.

Why or why not? What else could he have done to protect himself? **7.** To this day, Jews commemorate the assassination of Gedaliah with a day of fasting. Why do you think this event was so significant?

APPLY 1. Are you a good judge of character? What sorts of things influence your impressions? Have you ever seriously misjudged someone's intentions towards you? **2.** Is there any situation in which you are tempted to take matters into your own hands and rid yourself of the person you can't get along with? If violence only begets more violence, why do you do it? If running away from your problems or striking first doesn't solve your problems, what does?

Nethaniah to take your life?" But Gedaliah son of Ahikam did not believe them.
15Then Johanan son of Kareah said privately to Gedaliah in Mizpah,
"Let me go and kill Ishmael son of Nethaniah, and no one will know
it. Why should he take your life and cause all the Jews who are gathered around you to be scattered and the remnant of Judah to perish?"
16But Gedaliah son of Ahikam said to Johanan son of Kareah,
"Don't do such a thing! What you are saying about Ishmael is not
true."

41 In the seventh month Ishmael son of Nethaniah, the son of
Elishama, who was of royal blood and had been one of the
king's officers, came with ten men to Gedaliah son of Ahikam at
Mizpah. While they were eating together there, 2Ishmael son of Nethaniah and the ten men who were with him got up and struck down
Gedaliah son of Ahikam, the son of Shaphan, with the sword, killing
the one whom the king of Babylon had appointed as governor over
the land. 3Ishmael also killed all the Jews who were with Gedaliah at
Mizpah, as well as the Babylonian[a] soldiers who were there.
4The day after Gedaliah's assassination, before anyone knew about
it, 5eighty men who had shaved off their beards, torn their clothes
and cut themselves came from Shechem, Shiloh and Samaria, bringing grain offerings and incense with them to the house of the LORD.
6Ishmael son of Nethaniah went out from Mizpah to meet them,
weeping as he went. When he met them, he said, "Come to Gedaliah
son of Ahikam." 7When they went into the city, Ishmael son of Nethaniah and the men who were with him slaughtered them and threw
them into a cistern. 8But ten of them said to Ishmael, "Don't kill us!
We have wheat and barley, oil and honey, hidden in a field." So he let
them alone and did not kill them with the others. 9Now the cistern
where he threw all the bodies of the men he had killed along with
Gedaliah was the one King Asa had made as part of his defense
against Baasha king of Israel. Ishmael son of Nethaniah filled it with
the dead.
10Ishmael made captives of all the rest of the people who were in
Mizpah—the king's daughters along with all the others who were left
there, over whom Nebuzaradan commander of the imperial guard
had appointed Gedaliah son of Ahikam. Ishmael son of Nethaniah
took them captive and set out to cross over to the Ammonites.
11When Johanan son of Kareah and all the army officers who were
with him heard about all the crimes Ishmael son of Nethaniah had
committed, 12they took all their men and went to fight Ishmael son of
Nethaniah. They caught up with him near the great pool in Gibeon.
13When all the people Ishmael had with him saw Johanan son of Kareah and the army officers who were with him, they were glad. 14All
the people Ishmael had taken captive at Mizpah turned and went over
to Johanan son of Kareah. 15But Ishmael son of Nethaniah and eight
of his men escaped from Johanan and fled to the Ammonites.

[a]3 Or *Chaldean*

40:16 Don't do such a thing! The last thing Gedaliah wanted was to upset his peacekeeping position. Little did he know he would soon be a victim of violence himself (41:1–3). His life would soon be taken.

41:1 Gedaliah's first feast would be his last official event. Ishmael's mealtime murder caught Gedaliah off guard.

Flight to Egypt

16 Then Johanan son of Kareah and all the army officers who were
with him led away all the survivors from Mizpah whom he had recovered from Ishmael son of Nethaniah after he had assassinated Gedaliah son of Ahikam: the soldiers, women, children and court officials
he had brought from Gibeon. 17 And they went on, stopping at Geruth
Kimham near Bethlehem on their way to Egypt 18 to escape the
Babylonians.[a] They were afraid of them because Ishmael son of Nethaniah had killed Gedaliah son of Ahikam, whom the king of Babylon
had appointed as governor over the land.

42 Then all the army officers, including Johanan son of Kareah
and Jezaniah[b] son of Hoshaiah, and all the people from the
least to the greatest approached 2 Jeremiah the prophet and said to
him, "Please hear our petition and pray to the LORD your God for this
entire remnant. For as you now see, though we were once many, now
only a few are left. 3 Pray that the LORD your God will tell us where we
should go and what we should do."

4 "I have heard you," replied Jeremiah the prophet. "I will certainly
pray to the LORD your God as you have requested; I will tell you everything the LORD says and will keep nothing back from you."

5 Then they said to Jeremiah, "May the LORD be a true and faithful
witness against us if we do not act in accordance with everything the
LORD your God sends you to tell us. 6 Whether it is favorable or unfa-
vorable, we will obey the LORD our God, to whom we are sending you,
so that it will go well with us, for we will obey the LORD our God."

7 Ten days later the word of the LORD came to Jeremiah. 8 So he
called together Johanan son of Kareah and all the army officers who
were with him and all the people from the least to the greatest. 9 He
said to them, "This is what the LORD, the God of Israel, to whom you
sent me to present your petition, says: 10 'If you stay in this land, I will
build you up and not tear you down; I will plant you and not uproot
you, for I am grieved over the disaster I have inflicted on you. 11 Do
not be afraid of the king of Babylon, whom you now fear. Do not be
afraid of him, declares the LORD, for I am with you and will save you
and deliver you from his hands. 12 I will show you compassion so that
he will have compassion on you and restore you to your land.'

13 "However, if you say, 'We will not stay in this land,' and so disobey the LORD your God, 14 and if you say, 'No, we will go and live in
Egypt, where we will not see war or hear the trumpet or be hungry for
bread,' 15 then hear the word of the LORD, O remnant of Judah. This is
what the LORD Almighty, the God of Israel, says: 'If you are determined to go to Egypt and you do go to settle there, 16 then the sword
you fear will overtake you there, and the famine you dread will follow
you into Egypt, and there you will die. 17 Indeed, all who are determined to go to Egypt to settle there will die by the sword, famine and
plague; not one of them will survive or escape the disaster I will bring
on them.' 18 This is what the LORD Almighty, the God of Israel, says: 'As

[a] 18 Or *Chaldeans* [b] 1 Hebrew; Septuagint (see also 43:2) *Azariah*

OPEN 1. When lost, do you just keep driving, or do you stop to ask for directions? How long have you been lost before you finally decided to consult a map? **2.** What type of stone best describes you: Hefty boulder to block the way? Diamond in the rough? Bedrock that can't be penetrated? Brick for building? Pebble for a sling shot? Other? Explain.

STUDY 1. Why are the army officers afraid, even though they had nothing to do with Gedaliah's murder (41:16–18; 2 Kin. 25:25–26)? How might Nebuchadnezzar interpret the act? What are their options? What is "Plan A"? **2.** Are the people sincere in seeking guidance (42:2–6)? Why ask Jeremiah, if their minds are already made up? **3.** What do you suppose they were thinking about during the 10 day delay, waiting to hear from God (42:7)? What do you think Jeremiah did during those 10 days? **4.** What does God tell them and why (42:8–18)? What is wrong with the Jews following their natural instincts and "getting out of the kitchen if you can't stand the heat (the Babylonians)"? Why would they want to live in Egypt anyway? **5.** How does Jeremiah's counsel go over (43:2–3)? Does this surprise you after hearing all their promises? **6.** Why would they accuse Baruch of manipulating him? What do they think the Babylonians will do to them (43:3)? Why might they suspect Jeremiah and Baruch are not afraid? **7.** Do you suppose Jeremiah and Baruch go along to Egypt willingly or unwillingly (43:4–6)? What was Egypt's relationship with Babylon (37:5; 2 Kin. 24:7)? How would Nebuchadnezzar interpret a flight to Egypt? **8.** What message does God give Jeremiah at the Egyptian border and why (43:8–13)?

APPLY 1. In your decision-making process this past week, at what point did you seek God's counsel? The input of others? Did you truly want advice, or simply a blessing on your plans? **2.** When in doubt about someone's intentions, do you assume the best or the worst? Are you naturally trusting or skeptical? Has anyone ever doubted your integrity, as they did Jeremiah's? Why? **3.** Do you

---

42:6 The army officers' good intentions prove to be short-lived. Like many in the presence of a prophet, they heard only what they wanted (43:2).

42:7 Ten days later ... Jeremiah. Jeremiah had to spend ten days in prayer for the people. His message came as a result of his persistence.

prefer to call the shots in work situations? In relationships? What do you find objectionable about submitting to someone? When was the last time you deliberately surrendered control? What happened? **4.** Have you ever felt beyond God's reach? Did God reach you, after all? How so? Do you know anyone who feels "out of touch" with God? How can you help?

OPEN 1. What "famous last words" have you had to eat recently? How did you feel when the other person got the last laugh? **2.** When have you crowed, "I told you

my anger and wrath have been poured out on those who lived in
Jerusalem, so will my wrath be poured out on you when you go to
Egypt. You will be an object of cursing and horror, of condemnation
and reproach; you will never see this place again.'
19"O remnant of Judah, the LORD has told you, 'Do not go to Egypt.'
Be sure of this: I warn you today 20that you made a fatal mistake[a]
when you sent me to the LORD your God and said, 'Pray to the LORD
our God for us; tell us everything he says and we will do it.' 21I have
told you today, but you still have not obeyed the LORD your God in all
he sent me to tell you. 22So now, be sure of this: You will die by the
sword, famine and plague in the place where you want to go to
settle."

43 When Jeremiah finished telling the people all the words of the
LORD their God—everything the LORD had sent him to tell
them— 2Azariah son of Hoshaiah and Johanan son of Kareah and all
the arrogant men said to Jeremiah, "You are lying! The LORD our God
has not sent you to say, 'You must not go to Egypt to settle there.'
3But Baruch son of Neriah is inciting you against us to hand us over
to the Babylonians,[b] so they may kill us or carry us into exile to Babylon."
4So Johanan son of Kareah and all the army officers and all the
people disobeyed the LORD's command to stay in the land of Judah.
5Instead, Johanan son of Kareah and all the army officers led away all
the remnant of Judah who had come back to live in the land of Judah
from all the nations where they had been scattered. 6They also led
away all the men, women and children and the king's daughters
whom Nebuzaradan commander of the imperial guard had left with
Gedaliah son of Ahikam, the son of Shaphan, and Jeremiah the
prophet and Baruch son of Neriah. 7So they entered Egypt in disobedience to the LORD and went as far as Tahpanhes.
8In Tahpanhes the word of the LORD came to Jeremiah: 9"While the
Jews are watching, take some large stones with you and bury them in
clay in the brick pavement at the entrance to Pharaoh's palace in Tahpanhes.
10Then say to them, 'This is what the LORD Almighty, the God
of Israel, says: I will send for my servant Nebuchadnezzar king of
Babylon, and I will set his throne over these stones I have buried
here; he will spread his royal canopy above them. 11He will come and
attack Egypt, bringing death to those destined for death, captivity to
those destined for captivity, and the sword to those destined for the
sword. 12He[c] will set fire to the temples of the gods of Egypt; he will
burn their temples and take their gods captive. As a shepherd wraps
his garment around him, so will he wrap Egypt around himself and
depart from there unscathed. 13There in the temple of the sun[d] in
Egypt he will demolish the sacred pillars and will burn down the temples of the gods of Egypt.' "

Disaster Because of Idolatry

44 This word came to Jeremiah concerning all the Jews living in
Lower Egypt—in Migdol, Tahpanhes and Memphis[e]—and in

[a]20 Or *you erred in your hearts* [b]3 Or *Chaldeans* [c]12 Or *I* [d]13 Or *in Heliopolis* [e]1 Hebrew *Noph*

43:3 Despite their pleas and promises, the people could not accept Jeremiah's word. It was exactly opposite of what they had planned. They wanted to shift the blame to someone else, and not deal with the issue.

Upper Egypt[a]: 2"This is what the LORD Almighty, the God of Israel,
says: You saw the great disaster I brought on Jerusalem and on all the
towns of Judah. Today they lie deserted and in ruins 3because of the
evil they have done. They provoked me to anger by burning incense
and by worshiping other gods that neither they nor you nor your
fathers ever knew. 4Again and again I sent my servants the prophets,
who said, 'Do not do this detestable thing that I hate!' 5But they did
not listen or pay attention; they did not turn from their wickedness or
stop burning incense to other gods. 6Therefore, my fierce anger was
poured out; it raged against the towns of Judah and the streets of
Jerusalem and made them the desolate ruins they are today.
7"Now this is what the LORD God Almighty, the God of Israel, says:
Why bring such great disaster on yourselves by cutting off from Judah
the men and women, the children and infants, and so leave yourselves without a remnant? 8Why provoke me to anger with what your
hands have made, burning incense to other gods in Egypt, where you
have come to live? You will destroy yourselves and make yourselves
an object of cursing and reproach among all the nations on earth.
9Have you forgotten the wickedness committed by your fathers and
by the kings and queens of Judah and the wickedness committed by
you and your wives in the land of Judah and the streets of Jerusalem?
10To this day they have not humbled themselves or shown reverence,
nor have they followed my law and the decrees I set before you and
your fathers.
11"Therefore, this is what the LORD Almighty, the God of Israel,
says: I am determined to bring disaster on you and to destroy all
Judah. 12I will take away the remnant of Judah who were determined
to go to Egypt to settle there. They will all perish in Egypt; they will
fall by the sword or die from famine. From the least to the greatest,
they will die by sword or famine. They will become an object of cursing and horror, of condemnation and reproach. 13I will punish those
who live in Egypt with the sword, famine and plague, as I punished
Jerusalem. 14None of the remnant of Judah who have gone to live in
Egypt will escape or survive to return to the land of Judah, to which
they long to return and live; none will return except a few fugitives."
15Then all the men who knew that their wives were burning incense to other gods, along with all the women who were present—a
large assembly—and all the people living in Lower and Upper Egypt,[b]
said to Jeremiah, 16"We will not listen to the message you have
spoken to us in the name of the LORD! 17We will certainly do everything we said we would: We will burn incense to the Queen of Heaven
and will pour out drink offerings to her just as we and our fathers,
our kings and our officials did in the towns of Judah and in the streets
of Jerusalem. At that time we had plenty of food and were well off and
suffered no harm. 18But ever since we stopped burning incense to the
Queen of Heaven and pouring out drink offerings to her, we have had
nothing and have been perishing by sword and famine."
19The women added, "When we burned incense to the Queen of
Heaven and poured out drink offerings to her, did not our husbands

[a]1 Hebrew *in Pathros* [b]15 Hebrew *in Egypt and Pathros*

so," over a similar fate happening to someone else?

STUDY The Jews fleeing the scene of the crime (Gedaliah's murder) plus any who had been deported earlier (2 Kin. 23:34) make up the "large assembly" (vv. 1,15) to hear what would be Jeremiah's last recorded prophecy. **1.** In this word of the Lord, what does Jeremiah try to explain (vv. 2–6)? **2.** What have the Jews in Egypt done (vv. 7–10)? Does this surprise you, in light of all Judah has suffered? Why are they honoring the "Queen of Heaven" or the pagan goddess of war, Ishtar (vv. 17–18)? What must their opinion of Yahweh be? **3.** What does God promise in return (vv. 11–14)? Who will the "few fugitives" be? Does Jeremiah's prophecy surprise you? **4.** Why do you think this story of apostasy keeps playing over and over, with only the names or places changing? **5.** What prophecy does Jeremiah make as a sign (vv. 29–30)? Hophra was deposed and executed a few years later. What impact do you think Jeremiah's accurate prediction would have on the Jews? **6.** This chapter gives the end of Jeremiah's story as we know it. Was his 40-odd years of prophecy a failure? How would you gauge success as a prophet?

APPLY **1.** How can people hear God's Word, see God's power and yet still misunderstand the message? In what sense were you like that with your parents? In what sense are you like that with your Parent in Heaven? **2.** Would you say your life has been a success so far? On what basis? What constitutes a failure: Falling short of a goal? Not seeing any results for all your effort? Not trying hard enough? Making mistakes? Not making any mistakes? **3.** Martin Luther examined his conscience by contemplating the "regrets" in his life. What do you "regret"? What do you do with "regrets"?

44:18 we have had nothing ... perishing. The people were like defiant children as they voiced their rebellious intentions. Now they saw idolatry as their only hope for restoring prosperity.

know that we were making cakes like her image and pouring out
drink offerings to her?"
[20]Then Jeremiah said to all the people, both men and women, who
were answering him, [21]"Did not the LORD remember and think about
the incense burned in the towns of Judah and the streets of Jerusalem
by you and your fathers, your kings and your officials and the people
of the land? [22]When the LORD could no longer endure your wicked actions and the detestable things you did, your land became an object
of cursing and a desolate waste without inhabitants, as it is today.
[23]Because you have burned incense and have sinned against the LORD
and have not obeyed him or followed his law or his decrees or his
stipulations, this disaster has come upon you, as you now see."
[24]Then Jeremiah said to all the people, including the women, "Hear
the word of the LORD, all you people of Judah in Egypt. [25]This is what
the LORD Almighty, the God of Israel, says: You and your wives have
shown by your actions what you promised when you said, 'We will
certainly carry out the vows we made to burn incense and pour out
drink offerings to the Queen of Heaven.'
"Go ahead then, do what you promised! Keep your vows! [26]But hear
the word of the LORD, all Jews living in Egypt: 'I swear by my great
name,' says the LORD, 'that no one from Judah living anywhere in
Egypt will ever again invoke my name or swear, "As surely as the Sovereign LORD lives." [27]For I am watching over them for harm, not for
good; the Jews in Egypt will perish by sword and famine until they are
all destroyed. [28]Those who escape the sword and return to the land of
Judah from Egypt will be very few. Then the whole remnant of Judah
who came to live in Egypt will know whose word will stand—mine or
theirs.
[29]" 'This will be the sign to you that I will punish you in this place,'
declares the LORD, 'so that you will know that my threats of harm
against you will surely stand.' [30]This is what the LORD says: 'I am going to hand Pharaoh Hophra king of Egypt over to his enemies who
seek his life, just as I handed Zedekiah king of Judah over to Nebuchadnezzar king of Babylon, the enemy who was seeking his life.' "

A Message to Baruch

45 This is what Jeremiah the prophet told Baruch son of Neriah
in the fourth year of Jehoiakim son of Josiah king of Judah,
after Baruch had written on a scroll the words Jeremiah was then dic-
tating: [2]"This is what the LORD, the God of Israel, says to you, Baruch:
[3]You said, 'Woe to me! The LORD has added sorrow to my pain; I am
worn out with groaning and find no rest.'
[4]⌊The LORD said,⌋ "Say this to him: 'This is what the LORD says: I will
overthrow what I have built and uproot what I have planted, throughout the land. [5]Should you then seek great things for yourself? Seek
them not. For I will bring disaster on all people, declares the LORD,
but wherever you go I will let you escape with your life.' "

OPEN What do you find most helpful when you can't sleep: Counting sheep? Turning on the TV? A sleeping pill? Warm milk?

STUDY **1.** Why is Baruch so tired (36:4,27–28)? **2.** Is God very consoling to him? What "great things" might Baruch want? What "great thing" does God promise? **3.** Why this postscript here?

APPLY Are you ambitious for great things, or satisfied with very little? Illustrate.

45:5 Seek them not. God instructed Jeremiah to remind Baruch of the importance of priorities over personal self-seeking agendas. Baruch's true greatness would come from honoring God over himself.

A Message About Egypt

46 This is the word of the LORD that came to Jeremiah the prophet concerning the nations:

2 Concerning Egypt:

This is the message against the army of Pharaoh Neco king of Egypt, which was defeated at Carchemish on the Euphrates River by Nebuchadnezzar king of Babylon in the fourth year of Jehoiakim son of Josiah king of Judah:

3 "Prepare your shields, both large and small,
and march out for battle!
4 Harness the horses,
mount the steeds!
Take your positions
with helmets on!
Polish your spears,
put on your armor!
5 What do I see?
They are terrified,
they are retreating,
their warriors are defeated.
They flee in haste
without looking back,
and there is terror on every side,"
declares the LORD.
6 "The swift cannot flee
nor the strong escape.
In the north by the River Euphrates
they stumble and fall.

7 "Who is this that rises like the Nile,
like rivers of surging waters?
8 Egypt rises like the Nile,
like rivers of surging waters.
She says, 'I will rise and cover the earth;
I will destroy cities and their people.'
9 Charge, O horses!
Drive furiously, O charioteers!
March on, O warriors—
men of Cush[a] and Put who carry shields,
men of Lydia who draw the bow.
10 But that day belongs to the Lord, the LORD Almighty—
a day of vengeance, for vengeance on his foes.
The sword will devour till it is satisfied,
till it has quenched its thirst with blood.
For the Lord, the LORD Almighty, will offer sacrifice
in the land of the north by the River Euphrates.

[a] 9 That is, the upper Nile region

OPEN **1.** What image comes to mind at the word "Egypt"? Do you have any desire to visit there? **2.** How do you relate to a horse: Like horsing around? Could eat a horse? Workhorse? Other? **3.** How long does it take you to get ready for a night out? What takes the most time? What does this say about you?

STUDY This chapter resumes the oracles against the nations first introduced in chapter 25. **1.** Why does Neco march against Nebuchadnezzar (v. 8; 37:5–7)? Who would the people of Judah want to win and why? **2.** Why does Jeremiah prophesy defeat for Egypt? What is Egypt's problem (vv. 15,25)? Why does God favor the pagan Babylonians (Ezek. 29:19–20)? **3.** Apart from the immediate participants, who comes out the winner in this prophecy (Isa. 19:23–25)? Who stands to lose the most? **4.** Thirty years later Nebuchadnezzar carries the war back into Egypt (vv. 13–17, 19–21)? Why do many soldiers desert? **5.** Will Egypt be different after the dust settles (v. 26)? **6.** What does disciplined "only with justice" mean (v. 28)? What other types of discipline are there?

APPLY **1.** When have you lived through a trying time, learned lots of lessons and then gone to ways "as in times past" when the dust settled? How can you make a lesson once learned stick for all time? Can the group help? **2.** Do you "stumble repeatedly" over the same problem (v. 16)? Why is it hard to get up and walk straight? Is God the one "pushing you down" (v. 15; James 1:12–15, for the difference between a trial and a temptation)? **3.** Have you ever missed your opportunity when its time finally came (v. 17)? Why did you hesitate to follow through? Was it something you really didn't want, or something you thought you might not deserve?

46:10 belongs to the LORD ... day of vengeance. God earmarked a time to reverse Egypt's arrogance and superiority (v. 25). He would establish his sovereignty over the Egyptian pharaoh.

11 "Go up to Gilead and get balm,
O Virgin Daughter of Egypt.
But you multiply remedies in vain;
there is no healing for you.
12 The nations will hear of your shame;
your cries will fill the earth.
One warrior will stumble over another;
both will fall down together."

13 This is the message the LORD spoke to Jeremiah the prophet
about the coming of Nebuchadnezzar king of Babylon to attack
Egypt:

14 "Announce this in Egypt, and proclaim it in Migdol;
proclaim it also in Memphis[a] and Tahpanhes:
'Take your positions and get ready,
for the sword devours those around you.'
15 Why will your warriors be laid low?
They cannot stand, for the LORD will push them down.
16 They will stumble repeatedly;
they will fall over each other.
They will say, 'Get up, let us go back
to our own people and our native lands,
away from the sword of the oppressor.'
17 There they will exclaim,
'Pharaoh king of Egypt is only a loud noise;
he has missed his opportunity.'

18 "As surely as I live," declares the King,
whose name is the LORD Almighty,
"one will come who is like Tabor among the mountains,
like Carmel by the sea.
19 Pack your belongings for exile,
you who live in Egypt,
for Memphis will be laid waste
and lie in ruins without inhabitant.

20 "Egypt is a beautiful heifer,
but a gadfly is coming
against her from the north.
21 The mercenaries in her ranks
are like fattened calves.
They too will turn and flee together,
they will not stand their ground,
for the day of disaster is coming upon them,
the time for them to be punished.
22 Egypt will hiss like a fleeing serpent
as the enemy advances in force;
they will come against her with axes,
like men who cut down trees.

[a]14 Hebrew *Noph*; also in verse 19

46:16 to our own people. Warriors from smaller, nearby nations would turn their backs on the losing Egyptian army. They would rather return home alive with what they had, than continue losing and end up with nothing.

23 They will chop down her forest,"
declares the LORD,
"dense though it be.
They are more numerous than locusts,
they cannot be counted.
24 The Daughter of Egypt will be put to shame,
handed over to the people of the north."

25 The LORD Almighty, the God of Israel, says: "I am about to bring
punishment on Amon god of Thebes,[a] on Pharaoh, on Egypt and her
gods and her kings, and on those who rely on Pharaoh. 26 I will hand
them over to those who seek their lives, to Nebuchadnezzar king of
Babylon and his officers. Later, however, Egypt will be inhabited as in
times past," declares the LORD.

27 "Do not fear, O Jacob my servant;
do not be dismayed, O Israel.
I will surely save you out of a distant place,
your descendants from the land of their exile.
Jacob will again have peace and security,
and no one will make him afraid.
28 Do not fear, O Jacob my servant,
for I am with you," declares the LORD.
"Though I completely destroy all the nations
among which I scatter you,
I will not completely destroy you.
I will discipline you but only with justice;
I will not let you go entirely unpunished."

A Message About the Philistines

47 This is the word of the LORD that came to Jeremiah the prophet concerning the Philistines before Pharaoh attacked Gaza:

2 This is what the LORD says:

"See how the waters are rising in the north;
they will become an overflowing torrent.
They will overflow the land and everything in it,
the towns and those who live in them.
The people will cry out;
all who dwell in the land will wail
3 at the sound of the hoofs of galloping steeds,
at the noise of enemy chariots
and the rumble of their wheels.
Fathers will not turn to help their children;
their hands will hang limp.
4 For the day has come
to destroy all the Philistines
and to cut off all survivors
who could help Tyre and Sidon.
The LORD is about to destroy the Philistines,
the remnant from the coasts of Caphtor.[b]
5 Gaza will shave her head in mourning;
Ashkelon will be silenced.

OPEN 1. If you could have traded fathers when you were a kid, whose dad would you have taken? Why? **2.** What war interests you the most? Is war intriguing to you? In what way?

STUDY 1. What do your five senses tell you is happening in this prophecy? **2.** How were relations between Judah and Philistia in the past (Judg. 13:1; 1 Sam. 18:25–27)? **3.** Why has God ordered the sword against the Philistines (vv. 6–7; Ezek. 25:15–17)? (Note: Ashkelon was attacked by Nebuchadnezzar in partial fulfillment of this prophecy.)

APPLY 1. When have you felt helpless in the face of a tragedy you saw coming, as the Philistine fathers did (v. 3)? **2.** When you feel helpless, is prayer a consolation? In what way?

[a]25 Hebrew *No* [b]4 That is, Crete

O remnant on the plain,
how long will you cut yourselves?

6 " 'Ah, sword of the LORD,' ⌞you cry,⌟
'how long till you rest?
Return to your scabbard;
cease and be still.'
7 But how can it rest
when the LORD has commanded it,
when he has ordered it
to attack Ashkelon and the coast?"

A Message About Moab

48 Concerning Moab:

This is what the LORD Almighty, the God of Israel, says:

"Woe to Nebo, for it will be ruined.
Kiriathaim will be disgraced and captured;
the stronghold[a] will be disgraced and shattered.
2 Moab will be praised no more;
in Heshbon[b] men will plot her downfall:
'Come, let us put an end to that nation.'
You too, O Madmen,[c] will be silenced;
the sword will pursue you.
3 Listen to the cries from Horonaim,
cries of great havoc and destruction.
4 Moab will be broken;
her little ones will cry out.[d]
5 They go up the way to Luhith,
weeping bitterly as they go;
on the road down to Horonaim
anguished cries over the destruction are heard.
6 Flee! Run for your lives;
become like a bush[e] in the desert.
7 Since you trust in your deeds and riches,
you too will be taken captive,
and Chemosh will go into exile,
together with his priests and officials.
8 The destroyer will come against every town,
and not a town will escape.
The valley will be ruined
and the plateau destroyed,
because the LORD has spoken.
9 Put salt on Moab,
for she will be laid waste[f];
her towns will become desolate,
with no one to live in them.

[a] 1 Or / *Misgab* [b] 2 The Hebrew for *Heshbon* sounds like the Hebrew for *plot.* [c] 2 The name of the Moabite town Madmen sounds like the Hebrew for *be silenced.* [d] 4 Hebrew; Septuagint / *proclaim it to Zoar* [e] 6 Or *like Aroer* [f] 9 Or *Give wings to Moab, / for she will fly away*

OPEN 1. Where do you keep your family records: With a relative? In a family Bible? Safe deposit box? Museum of Natural History? **2.** What one fact or story do you think would distinguish your family tree from the others in your group? **3.** If you were a news reporter, which "beat" would you like to be assigned: Foreign War? Government intrigue? Movies & TV? Business? Sports? Love life? Other? Explain.

STUDY 1. How are Judah and Moab related (Gen. 19:36–38)? Where is Moab located? How many towns does Jeremiah mention (vv. 1–5, 21–24)? Why do you think he knows so much? **2.** Who is the "local god" of the Moabites (v. 7; 1 Kin. 11:7,33)? Although Yahweh has not given them the Jewish law, what does he expect from Moab (v. 13; 1 Kin. 12:26–30)? **3.** Besides worshiping Chemosh, what has Moab done to Judah (vv. 26–27; 2 Kin. 24:1–2)? What was the prevailing attitude about Judah's plight (v. 29)? **4.** What product was Moab particularly famous for (vv. 11–12,32–33)? What form of political domination is Moab going to suffer for the first time? When Moab was invaded by the Babylonians soon after the fall of Judah, who occupied their land (Ezek. 25:10)? **5.** Verses 36–38 describe an ancient Middle Eastern funeral. Why do you think these things were done? **6.** Around 150 years earlier, Isaiah prophesied against Moab (Isa. 15). Why do you think Jeremiah's language is so similar? **7.** How final does Moab's defeat sound to you? **8.** The Moabites no longer exist as a national group. What do you make of God's promise to "restore their fortunes"?

47:7 he has ordered it. Although Babylonian officers would give the army orders, God was the ultimate commander-in-chief. He used Babylon to fulfill his prophecies. Babylon was merely the weapon he used.

10 "A curse on him who is lax in doing the LORD's work!
A curse on him who keeps his sword from bloodshed!

11 "Moab has been at rest from youth,
like wine left on its dregs,
not poured from one jar to another—
she has not gone into exile.
So she tastes as she did,
and her aroma is unchanged.
12 But days are coming,"
declares the LORD,
"when I will send men who pour from jars,
and they will pour her out;
they will empty her jars
and smash her jugs.
13 Then Moab will be ashamed of Chemosh,
as the house of Israel was ashamed
when they trusted in Bethel.

14 "How can you say, 'We are warriors,
men valiant in battle'?
15 Moab will be destroyed and her towns invaded;
her finest young men will go down in the slaughter,"
declares the King, whose name is the LORD Almighty.
16 "The fall of Moab is at hand;
her calamity will come quickly.
17 Mourn for her, all who live around her,
all who know her fame;
say, 'How broken is the mighty scepter,
how broken the glorious staff!'

18 "Come down from your glory
and sit on the parched ground,
O inhabitants of the Daughter of Dibon,
for he who destroys Moab
will come up against you
and ruin your fortified cities.
19 Stand by the road and watch,
you who live in Aroer.
Ask the man fleeing and the woman escaping,
ask them, 'What has happened?'
20 Moab is disgraced, for she is shattered.
Wail and cry out!
Announce by the Arnon
that Moab is destroyed.
21 Judgment has come to the plateau—
to Holon, Jahzah and Mephaath,
22 to Dibon, Nebo and Beth Diblathaim,
23 to Kiriathaim, Beth Gamul and Beth Meon,
24 to Kerioth and Bozrah—
to all the towns of Moab, far and near.
25 Moab's horn[a] is cut off;
her arm is broken,"
declares the LORD.

[a] 25 *Horn* here symbolizes strength.

APPLY **1.** Are there any long-standing feuds in your family? What issues do relatives fight over? What punishments do they exact? Why is it so easy for family members to be so hard on each other? **2.** Does seeing and hearing about disasters from the media affect you anymore? What is the effect of broadcasting disaster after disaster every day? How can you keep from being hardened to the suffering of others in the world? **3.** Have you ever had the last laugh on a boss? Parent? Schoolyard bully? How did it feel? Has anyone had the last laugh on you? Is there ever a last laugh?

26 "Make her drunk,
for she has defied the LORD.
Let Moab wallow in her vomit;
let her be an object of ridicule.
27 Was not Israel the object of your ridicule?
Was she caught among thieves,
that you shake your head in scorn
whenever you speak of her?
28 Abandon your towns and dwell among the rocks,
you who live in Moab.
Be like a dove that makes its nest
at the mouth of a cave.

29 "We have heard of Moab's pride—
her overweening pride and conceit,
her pride and arrogance
and the haughtiness of her heart.
30 I know her insolence but it is futile,"
declares the LORD,
"and her boasts accomplish nothing.
31 Therefore I wail over Moab,
for all Moab I cry out,
I moan for the men of Kir Hareseth.
32 I weep for you, as Jazer weeps,
O vines of Sibmah.
Your branches spread as far as the sea;
they reached as far as the sea of Jazer.
The destroyer has fallen
on your ripened fruit and grapes.
33 Joy and gladness are gone
from the orchards and fields of Moab.
I have stopped the flow of wine from the presses;
no one treads them with shouts of joy.
Although there are shouts,
they are not shouts of joy.

34 "The sound of their cry rises
from Heshbon to Elealeh and Jahaz,
from Zoar as far as Horonaim and Eglath Shelishiyah,
for even the waters of Nimrim are dried up.
35 In Moab I will put an end
to those who make offerings on the high places
and burn incense to their gods,"
declares the LORD.

36 "So my heart laments for Moab like a flute;
it laments like a flute for the men of Kir Hareseth.
The wealth they acquired is gone.
37 Every head is shaved
and every beard cut off;
every hand is slashed

48:26 Make her drunk. The mighty Moab once brought fear to the inhabitants of Judah. Now, God would numb the nation with his wrath.

48:29 We have heard. Moab's prideful propensity brought God to tears (Isa. 16:7,11). Ultimately, the nation's arrogance incurred God's wrath as well.

and every waist is covered with sackcloth.
38On all the roofs in Moab
and in the public squares
there is nothing but mourning,
for I have broken Moab
like a jar that no one wants,"
declares the LORD.
39"How shattered she is! How they wail!
How Moab turns her back in shame!
Moab has become an object of ridicule,
an object of horror to all those around her."

40This is what the LORD says:

"Look! An eagle is swooping down,
spreading its wings over Moab.
41Kerioth[a] will be captured
and the strongholds taken.
In that day the hearts of Moab's warriors
will be like the heart of a woman in labor.
42Moab will be destroyed as a nation
because she defied the LORD.
43Terror and pit and snare await you,
O people of Moab,"
declares the LORD.
44"Whoever flees from the terror
will fall into a pit,
whoever climbs out of the pit
will be caught in a snare;
for I will bring upon Moab
the year of her punishment,"
declares the LORD.

45"In the shadow of Heshbon
the fugitives stand helpless,
for a fire has gone out from Heshbon,
a blaze from the midst of Sihon;
it burns the foreheads of Moab,
the skulls of the noisy boasters.
46Woe to you, O Moab!
The people of Chemosh are destroyed;
your sons are taken into exile
and your daughters into captivity.

47"Yet I will restore the fortunes of Moab
in days to come,"
declares the LORD.

Here ends the judgment on Moab.

[a]41 Or *The cities*

48:43 Terror and pit and snare await you. God's wrath would make a clean sweep throughout Moab. He would trap his enemy like a hunter.

48:44 There was no place to hide from God's wrath—all attempts to escape would be thwarted (Amos 5:18–20). There would be no turning back.

OPEN 1. Are you a world traveler or a homebody? Why? 2. If you could learn instantly, what new language would you learn? Why?

STUDY 1. How are Judah and Ammon related (Gen. 19:36–38)? What do you make of verse 1? Who is Molech (vv. 1,3; 2 Kin. 23:13–14)? Why do the Ammonites trust him (v. 4)? 2. How much are riches and prosperity the basis of military strength today? 3. Is the promised restoration an afterthought (v. 6; Ezek. 25:7) or the highlight? 4. Ammon enjoyed the "fruits" of land that belonged to someone else. Of which countries is that true today? Is it true of this country?

APPLY 1. If you could put a percentage on it, to what degree are you trusting in material possessions (v. 4) and to what degree are you trusting in God: 90%–10%? 75%–25%? 50%–50%? 25%–75%? 10%–90%? 2. What should you be doing to change this?

OPEN 1. If you could painlessly learn a foreign language and cheaply travel in a foreign country, where would you go? Which countries might you consider living in as a foreign ambassador? Which ones, due to their naked violence, would you be sure to avoid? 2. What is your favorite way of acquainting yourself with a foreign culture: Movies? Gourmet clubs? Host International students? Travel abroad? National Geographic specials? In this way which countries do you know best?

A Message About Ammon

49 Concerning the Ammonites:

This is what the LORD says:

"Has Israel no sons?
Has she no heirs?
Why then has Molech[a] taken possession of Gad?
Why do his people live in its towns?
2 But the days are coming,"
declares the LORD,
"when I will sound the battle cry
against Rabbah of the Ammonites;
it will become a mound of ruins,
and its surrounding villages will be set on fire.
Then Israel will drive out
those who drove her out,"
says the LORD.

3 "Wail, O Heshbon, for Ai is destroyed!
Cry out, O inhabitants of Rabbah!
Put on sackcloth and mourn;
rush here and there inside the walls,
for Molech will go into exile,
together with his priests and officials.
4 Why do you boast of your valleys,
boast of your valleys so fruitful?
O unfaithful daughter,
you trust in your riches and say,
'Who will attack me?'
5 I will bring terror on you
from all those around you,"
declares the Lord, the LORD Almighty.

"Every one of you will be driven away,
and no one will gather the fugitives.

6 "Yet afterward, I will restore the fortunes of the Ammonites,"
declares the LORD.

A Message About Edom

7 Concerning Edom:

This is what the LORD Almighty says:

"Is there no longer wisdom in Teman?
Has counsel perished from the prudent?
Has their wisdom decayed?
8 Turn and flee, hide in deep caves,
you who live in Dedan,
for I will bring disaster on Esau
at the time I punish him.

[a]1 Or *their king*; Hebrew *malcam*; also in verse 3

49:7 The people from Edom were known for their wisdom (Job 2:11). Ironically, it was their ignorance of the things of God (lack of wisdom) that brought God's wrath down on them.

9 If grape pickers came to you,
would they not leave a few grapes?
If thieves came during the night,
would they not steal only as much as they wanted?
10 But I will strip Esau bare;
I will uncover his hiding places,
so that he cannot conceal himself.
His children, relatives and neighbors will perish,
and he will be no more.
11 Leave your orphans; I will protect their lives.
Your widows too can trust in me."

12 This is what the LORD says: "If those who do not deserve to drink
the cup must drink it, why should you go unpunished? You will not go
unpunished, but must drink it. 13 I swear by myself," declares the
LORD, "that Bozrah will become a ruin and an object of horror, of reproach and of cursing; and all its towns will be in ruins forever."

14 I have heard a message from the LORD:
An envoy was sent to the nations to say,
"Assemble yourselves to attack it!
Rise up for battle!"

15 "Now I will make you small among the nations,
despised among men.
16 The terror you inspire
and the pride of your heart have deceived you,
you who live in the clefts of the rocks,
who occupy the heights of the hill.
Though you build your nest as high as the eagle's,
from there I will bring you down,"
declares the LORD.
17 "Edom will become an object of horror;
all who pass by will be appalled and will scoff
because of all its wounds.
18 As Sodom and Gomorrah were overthrown,
along with their neighboring towns,"
says the LORD,
"so no one will live there;
no man will dwell in it.

19 "Like a lion coming up from Jordan's thickets
to a rich pastureland,
I will chase Edom from its land in an instant.
Who is the chosen one I will appoint for this?
Who is like me and who can challenge me?
And what shepherd can stand against me?"
20 Therefore, hear what the LORD has planned against Edom,
what he has purposed against those who live in Teman:
The young of the flock will be dragged away;
he will completely destroy their pasture because of them.
21 At the sound of their fall the earth will tremble;

STUDY 1. From whom do the Edomites descend (Gen. 25:29–30; 36:6–8)? Where is their country? What kind of land is it? For what quality are they known (v. 7; Obad. 8, where this quality is typified in Job's friends)? **2.** The crimes of Edom are well known to Jeremiah's hearers, but they are only hinted at here. What have they done (vv. 12,16; Ezek. 25:12; Amos 1:11; Obad. 10–14)? **3.** How extensive would God's wrath be (Ezek. 25:13–14)? Why are orphans and widows exempt from this wrath (v. 11)? **4.** God is compared to a lion and an eagle (vv. 19,22). Which image do you think fits God best? **5.** Why do you think God makes the people no promise of restoration, as he does for the Egyptians, Moabites and Ammonites (v. 6; 46:26; 48:47)?

APPLY 1. Have you ever been afraid of God? When and why? What does it mean to "fear God" in the way Jeremiah advises? **2.** The flip side of every virtue is a vice, and so it was with Edom's wisdom. How can intellect hinder spiritual growth? How can it help? What is the role of intelligence in your spiritual life? **3.** Of the "orphans and widows" in your world, for whom can you be an instrument of God's mercy? **4.** What "eagle's nest" (fortress mentality) have you built to feel secure in your private world? How secure are you, really? How has God broken through that to bring you to himself?

49:16 deceived you. Edom was a powerful and respected nation. However, these well-intentioned accolades proved to be a disastrous disservice. Her pride was one of her downfalls that lead to defeat.

their cry will resound to the Red Sea.[a]
[22]Look! An eagle will soar and swoop down,
spreading its wings over Bozrah.
In that day the hearts of Edom's warriors
will be like the heart of a woman in labor.

A Message About Damascus

[23]Concerning Damascus:

"Hamath and Arpad are dismayed,
for they have heard bad news.
They are disheartened,
troubled like[b] the restless sea.
[24]Damascus has become feeble,
she has turned to flee
and panic has gripped her;
anguish and pain have seized her,
pain like that of a woman in labor.
[25]Why has the city of renown not been abandoned,
the town in which I delight?
[26]Surely, her young men will fall in the streets;
all her soldiers will be silenced in that day,"
declares the LORD Almighty.
[27]"I will set fire to the walls of Damascus;
it will consume the fortresses of Ben-Hadad."

A Message About Kedar and Hazor

[28]Concerning Kedar and the kingdoms of Hazor, which Nebuchadnezzar king of Babylon attacked:

This is what the LORD says:

"Arise, and attack Kedar
and destroy the people of the East.
[29]Their tents and their flocks will be taken;
their shelters will be carried off
with all their goods and camels.
Men will shout to them,
'Terror on every side!'

[30]"Flee quickly away!
Stay in deep caves, you who live in Hazor,"
declares the LORD.

"Nebuchadnezzar king of Babylon has plotted against you;
he has devised a plan against you.

[31]"Arise and attack a nation at ease,
which lives in confidence,"
declares the LORD,
"a nation that has neither gates nor bars;
its people live alone.

[a]21 Hebrew *Yam Suph*; that is, Sea of Reeds [b]23 Hebrew *on* or *by*

OPEN Ever sail the open seas? Ever get seasick? Are you pretty much a "landlubber"?

STUDY 1. Where is Damascus? In what state does Jeremiah see the cities of Syria? **2.** Who is behind the disaster? What have the Syrians done (2 Kin. 8:7–12; Amos 1:3)? **3.** Is there any sign of mercy here?

APPLY 1. What is the source of trouble in your life: God punishing you for sin? You reap what you sow? Rain falls on the just and the unjust? The devil made you do it? **2.** Has the group helped you in time of crisis? How so?

OPEN 1. What is the most desolate place you have ever visited? Would you ever want to go back there? **2.** What is the most awful overnight accommodation you have experienced?

STUDY 1. How would you characterize the lifestyle of these "people of the East" living at Kedar and Hazor? **2.** Who attacks them and why? (Hint: What had their ancestors done to the Israelites in Judg. 6:1–6)? **3.** Were they ready for it or taken off guard? Why are they so vulnerable? Who is behind the disaster?

APPLY 1. Are roots important to you? Do you consider yourself settled down, or do you tend to move around? Why? **2.** Do you feel you are at ease spiritually? Where are you now compared to where you used to be? Is there the need to move on to new places, spiritually? Where to?

49:22 eagle. God used a bird of prey to illustrate his watchful gaze over his enemy. High above, God seemed remote and removed; yet God would soon swoop down upon the prey as does the eagle.

32Their camels will become plunder,
and their large herds will be booty.
I will scatter to the winds those who are in distant places[a]
and will bring disaster on them from every side,"
declares the LORD.
33"Hazor will become a haunt of jackals,
a desolate place forever.
No one will live there;
no man will dwell in it."

A Message About Elam

34This is the word of the LORD that came to Jeremiah the prophet
concerning Elam, early in the reign of Zedekiah king of Judah:

35This is what the LORD Almighty says:

"See, I will break the bow of Elam,
the mainstay of their might.
36I will bring against Elam the four winds
from the four quarters of the heavens;
I will scatter them to the four winds,
and there will not be a nation
where Elam's exiles do not go.
37I will shatter Elam before their foes,
before those who seek their lives;
I will bring disaster upon them,
even my fierce anger,"
declares the LORD.
"I will pursue them with the sword
until I have made an end of them.
38I will set my throne in Elam
and destroy her king and officials,"
declares the LORD.

39"Yet I will restore the fortunes of Elam
in days to come,"
declares the LORD.

A Message About Babylon

50 This is the word the LORD spoke through Jeremiah the prophet
concerning Babylon and the land of the Babylonians[b]:

2"Announce and proclaim among the nations,
lift up a banner and proclaim it;
keep nothing back, but say,
'Babylon will be captured;
Bel will be put to shame,
Marduk filled with terror.
Her images will be put to shame
and her idols filled with terror.'

[a]32 Or *who clip the hair by their foreheads* [b]1 Or *Chaldeans*; also in verses 8, 25, 35 and 45

OPEN What weather forecast fits your disposition: Morning fog? Sunny day? Overcast? Scattered showers? Hot and humid?

STUDY 1. Where would you find Elam today? Who was their biblical patriarch (Gen. 10:22)? **2.** What was Elam's claim to fame? Their fate (9:16)? Who is to blame (Ezek. 32:24–25)? **3.** Why do you think God promises to restore them, but not the people of Edom, Damascus, Kedar and Hazor? Is restoration only for those nations specified (46:26; 48:47; 49:6), or is it implied for the others as well (Isa. 11:11–12)? **4.** Did these nations ever hear Jeremiah's prophecies? For whose benefit were they intended?

APPLY 1. What is your "claim to fame"? How would life look if God took that away from you? **2.** Do you learn from the hardships of others? What lesson did you pick up recently?

OPEN 1. Who is the meanest looking person you have seen? **2.** Is your person more like a velvet-covered brick (soft on the outside, tough on the inside), or like a pretty tough cookie (with a soft, creamy inside)? **3.** Did you see any of the "Star Wars" movies? What impression do you have of Darth Vader and the empire? Does that evil empire remind you of any contemporary nations?

STUDY This is by far the longest of Jeremiah's oracles of judgment against foreign nations.

49:35 Modern day Iran rests on the tragic site of Elam—a nation of notable archers.

50:2 Babylon. Finally, the conqueror gets conquered. The nation that enjoyed seemingly endless conquests was temporarily halted by many northern nations. All of Babylon was doomed to eventual defeat.

To make it possible to complete this study in your usual allotted time, assign different readers to each major grouping of verses: 50:1–20; 50:21–46, then answer the following questions from your respective sections. **1.** Just as he said in chapter 25, Jeremiah holds out the "cup of wrath" to Babylon. For what sins will they "drink the cup" (50:2,11,15,24,29, 32,36; Hab. 1:6–11)? Which sins seem most foul-tasting to you? **2.** Who will God use to punish Babylon (50:3, 9,41)? What does that tell you about what it will take to knock out this evil empire for good? **3.** How can God punish Babylon for invading Judah when he approved the invasion for his own purposes? What principle of retribution should any person or nation keep in mind when they go to war? **4.** What will be the effect on the nations of the world (50:2)? How do you account for the different responses? **5.** What will be the effect on the Jews (50:4–8,17–20, 28,33–34)? Why is it crucial that Israel and Judah take the initiative in seeking God?

APPLY What feelings and actions do you think God wanted to inspire here in the Jews in exile? What feelings and actions does he want them to inspire in you?

3 A nation from the north will attack her
and lay waste her land.
No one will live in it;
both men and animals will flee away.

4 "In those days, at that time,"
declares the LORD,
"the people of Israel and the people of Judah together
will go in tears to seek the LORD their God.
5 They will ask the way to Zion
and turn their faces toward it.
They will come and bind themselves to the LORD
in an everlasting covenant
that will not be forgotten.

6 "My people have been lost sheep;
their shepherds have led them astray
and caused them to roam on the mountains.
They wandered over mountain and hill
and forgot their own resting place.
7 Whoever found them devoured them;
their enemies said, 'We are not guilty,
for they sinned against the LORD, their true pasture,
the LORD, the hope of their fathers.'

8 "Flee out of Babylon;
leave the land of the Babylonians,
and be like the goats that lead the flock.
9 For I will stir up and bring against Babylon
an alliance of great nations from the land of the north.
They will take up their positions against her,
and from the north she will be captured.
Their arrows will be like skilled warriors
who do not return empty-handed.
10 So Babylonia[a] will be plundered;
all who plunder her will have their fill,"
declares the LORD.

11 "Because you rejoice and are glad,
you who pillage my inheritance,
because you frolic like a heifer threshing grain
and neigh like stallions,
12 your mother will be greatly ashamed;
she who gave you birth will be disgraced.
She will be the least of the nations—
a wilderness, a dry land, a desert.
13 Because of the LORD's anger she will not be inhabited
but will be completely desolate.
All who pass Babylon will be horrified and scoff
because of all her wounds.

[a]10 Or *Chaldea*

50:11 pillage my inheritance. God resented Babylon's indifference to the plight of Judah—his chosen people. The inheritance of God's people was promised by God himself. Babylon would suffer for her harshness.

14 "Take up your positions around Babylon,
all you who draw the bow.
Shoot at her! Spare no arrows,
for she has sinned against the LORD.
15 Shout against her on every side!
She surrenders, her towers fall,
her walls are torn down.
Since this is the vengeance of the LORD,
take vengeance on her;
do to her as she has done to others.
16 Cut off from Babylon the sower,
and the reaper with his sickle at harvest.
Because of the sword of the oppressor
let everyone return to his own people,
let everyone flee to his own land.

17 "Israel is a scattered flock
that lions have chased away.
The first to devour him
was the king of Assyria;
the last to crush his bones
was Nebuchadnezzar king of Babylon."

18 Therefore this is what the LORD Almighty, the God of Israel, says:

"I will punish the king of Babylon and his land
as I punished the king of Assyria.
19 But I will bring Israel back to his own pasture
and he will graze on Carmel and Bashan;
his appetite will be satisfied
on the hills of Ephraim and Gilead.
20 In those days, at that time,"
declares the LORD,
"search will be made for Israel's guilt,
but there will be none,
and for the sins of Judah,
but none will be found,
for I will forgive the remnant I spare.

21 "Attack the land of Merathaim
and those who live in Pekod.
Pursue, kill and completely destroy[a] them,"
declares the LORD.
"Do everything I have commanded you.
22 The noise of battle is in the land,
the noise of great destruction!
23 How broken and shattered
is the hammer of the whole earth!
How desolate is Babylon
among the nations!

[a] *21* The Hebrew term refers to the irrevocable giving over of things or persons to the LORD, often by totally destroying them; also in verse 26.

50:16 Because of the sword of the oppressor. Babylon no longer represented safety to foreigners. However, the entire fulfillment of this prophecy is in the future—many never returned to their homeland.

24I set a trap for you, O Babylon,
and you were caught before you knew it;
you were found and captured
because you opposed the LORD.
25The LORD has opened his arsenal
and brought out the weapons of his wrath,
for the Sovereign LORD Almighty has work to do
in the land of the Babylonians.
26Come against her from afar.
Break open her granaries;
pile her up like heaps of grain.
Completely destroy her
and leave her no remnant.
27Kill all her young bulls;
let them go down to the slaughter!
Woe to them! For their day has come,
the time for them to be punished.
28Listen to the fugitives and refugees from Babylon
declaring in Zion
how the LORD our God has taken vengeance,
vengeance for his temple.

29"Summon archers against Babylon,
all those who draw the bow.
Encamp all around her;
let no one escape.
Repay her for her deeds;
do to her as she has done.
For she has defied the LORD,
the Holy One of Israel.
30Therefore, her young men will fall in the streets;
all her soldiers will be silenced in that day,"
declares the LORD.

31"See, I am against you, O arrogant one,"
declares the Lord, the LORD Almighty,
"for your day has come,
the time for you to be punished.
32The arrogant one will stumble and fall
and no one will help her up;
I will kindle a fire in her towns
that will consume all who are around her."

33This is what the LORD Almighty says:

"The people of Israel are oppressed,
and the people of Judah as well.
All their captors hold them fast,
refusing to let them go.
34Yet their Redeemer is strong;
the LORD Almighty is his name.
He will vigorously defend their cause

50:25 weapons of his wrath. A great coalition of neighboring northern nations would bring God's punishment on Babylon. Those who Babylon had once fought would now be turning to conquer Babylon.

so that he may bring rest to their land,
but unrest to those who live in Babylon.

35 "A sword against the Babylonians!"
declares the LORD—
"against those who live in Babylon
and against her officials and wise men!
36 A sword against her false prophets!
They will become fools.
A sword against her warriors!
They will be filled with terror.
37 A sword against her horses and chariots
and all the foreigners in her ranks!
They will become women.
A sword against her treasures!
They will be plundered.
38 A drought on[a] her waters!
They will dry up.
For it is a land of idols,
idols that will go mad with terror.

39 "So desert creatures and hyenas will live there,
and there the owl will dwell.
It will never again be inhabited
or lived in from generation to generation.
40 As God overthrew Sodom and Gomorrah
along with their neighboring towns,"
declares the LORD,
"so no one will live there;
no man will dwell in it.

41 "Look! An army is coming from the north;
a great nation and many kings
are being stirred up from the ends of the earth.
42 They are armed with bows and spears;
they are cruel and without mercy.
They sound like the roaring sea
as they ride on their horses;
they come like men in battle formation
to attack you, O Daughter of Babylon.
43 The king of Babylon has heard reports about them,
and his hands hang limp.
Anguish has gripped him,
pain like that of a woman in labor.
44 Like a lion coming up from Jordan's thickets
to a rich pastureland,
I will chase Babylon from its land in an instant.
Who is the chosen one I will appoint for this?
Who is like me and who can challenge me?
And what shepherd can stand against me?"
45 Therefore, hear what the LORD has planned against Babylon,
what he has purposed against the land of the Babylonians:
The young of the flock will be dragged away;
he will completely destroy their pasture because of them.

[a]38 Or *A sword against*

OPEN What is the longest speech you have ever had to sit through? What is the most memorable speech you have ever heard?

STUDY We will now come to the study of this long oracle of Jeremiah. Have different people read the following sections of verses: 51:1–26; 51:27–39; 51:40–64. **1.** What sins are listed here (vv. 9,24,44,47,49,52)? Rank them from bad to worst. **2.** What does God say he will do to Babylon (vv. 11,14,27–28,53)? Should they be afraid? **3.** How will this affect other nations (vv. 9,27,44,48)? **4.** What is to be done with this message (51:59–64)? How would it comfort the exiles in Babylon? How is the fate of this scroll like the fate of Babylon (51:64)? **5.** If a fall is imminent, why did Jeremiah tell the exiles earlier to settle into society? Why no mention of the 70 years (25:12)? How and why were they supposed to pray about the Babylonians (29:7)? **6.** What overall picture of God do you get from this prophecy and the preceding ones? **7.** Why do you think Jeremiah's prophecy ends with God's judgment on Babylon? How is this a fitting conclusion to the book?

APPLY **1.** What do you need most in your life: Destruction of enemies? Restoration of fortunes? Raised banner in the field? What would you like to see happen in one of these areas? **2.** If God did to you as you have done to others, what would be your fate?

---

46 At the sound of Babylon's capture the earth will tremble;
its cry will resound among the nations.

51

This is what the LORD says:

"See, I will stir up the spirit of a destroyer
against Babylon and the people of Leb Kamai.[a]
2 I will send foreigners to Babylon
to winnow her and to devastate her land;
they will oppose her on every side
in the day of her disaster.
3 Let not the archer string his bow,
nor let him put on his armor.
Do not spare her young men;
completely destroy[b] her army.
4 They will fall down slain in Babylon,[c]
fatally wounded in her streets.
5 For Israel and Judah have not been forsaken
by their God, the LORD Almighty,
though their land[d] is full of guilt
before the Holy One of Israel.

6 "Flee from Babylon!
Run for your lives!
Do not be destroyed because of her sins.
It is time for the LORD's vengeance;
he will pay her what she deserves.
7 Babylon was a gold cup in the LORD's hand;
she made the whole earth drunk.
The nations drank her wine;
therefore they have now gone mad.
8 Babylon will suddenly fall and be broken.
Wail over her!
Get balm for her pain;
perhaps she can be healed.

9 " 'We would have healed Babylon,
but she cannot be healed;
let us leave her and each go to his own land,
for her judgment reaches to the skies,
it rises as high as the clouds.'

10 " 'The LORD has vindicated us;
come, let us tell in Zion
what the LORD our God has done.'

11 "Sharpen the arrows,
take up the shields!
The LORD has stirred up the kings of the Medes,

[a] *1 Leb Kamai* is a cryptogram for Chaldea, that is, Babylonia. [b] 3 The Hebrew term refers to the irrevocable giving over of things or persons to the LORD, often by totally destroying them. [c] 4 Or *Chaldea* [d] 5 Or */ and the land of the Babylonians*

51:6 Flee from Babylon! Earlier, Jeremiah instructed the people of Judah to surrender to Babylon. Even though God was going to discipline his people, he had a plan for restoration after the Exile.

because his purpose is to destroy Babylon.
The LORD will take vengeance,
vengeance for his temple.
12 Lift up a banner against the walls of Babylon!
Reinforce the guard,
station the watchmen,
prepare an ambush!
The LORD will carry out his purpose,
his decree against the people of Babylon.
13 You who live by many waters
and are rich in treasures,
your end has come,
the time for you to be cut off.
14 The LORD Almighty has sworn by himself:
I will surely fill you with men, as with a swarm of locusts,
and they will shout in triumph over you.

15 "He made the earth by his power;
he founded the world by his wisdom
and stretched out the heavens by his understanding.
16 When he thunders, the waters in the heavens roar;
he makes clouds rise from the ends of the earth.
He sends lightning with the rain
and brings out the wind from his storehouses.

17 "Every man is senseless and without knowledge;
every goldsmith is shamed by his idols.
His images are a fraud;
they have no breath in them.
18 They are worthless, the objects of mockery;
when their judgment comes, they will perish.
19 He who is the Portion of Jacob is not like these,
for he is the Maker of all things,
including the tribe of his inheritance—
the LORD Almighty is his name.

20 "You are my war club,
my weapon for battle—
with you I shatter nations,
with you I destroy kingdoms,
21 with you I shatter horse and rider,
with you I shatter chariot and driver,
22 with you I shatter man and woman,
with you I shatter old man and youth,
with you I shatter young man and maiden,
23 with you I shatter shepherd and flock,
with you I shatter farmer and oxen,
with you I shatter governors and officials.

24 "Before your eyes I will repay Babylon and all who live in Babylonia[a] for all the wrong they have done in Zion," declares the LORD.

25 "I am against you, O destroying mountain,
you who destroy the whole earth,"
declares the LORD.

[a] 24 Or *Chaldea*; also in verse 35

"I will stretch out my hand against you,
roll you off the cliffs,
and make you a burned-out mountain.
26 No rock will be taken from you for a cornerstone,
nor any stone for a foundation,
for you will be desolate forever,"
declares the LORD.

27 "Lift up a banner in the land!
Blow the trumpet among the nations!
Prepare the nations for battle against her;
summon against her these kingdoms:
Ararat, Minni and Ashkenaz.
Appoint a commander against her;
send up horses like a swarm of locusts.
28 Prepare the nations for battle against her—
the kings of the Medes,
their governors and all their officials,
and all the countries they rule.
29 The land trembles and writhes,
for the LORD's purposes against Babylon stand—
to lay waste the land of Babylon
so that no one will live there.
30 Babylon's warriors have stopped fighting;
they remain in their strongholds.
Their strength is exhausted;
they have become like women.
Her dwellings are set on fire;
the bars of her gates are broken.
31 One courier follows another
and messenger follows messenger
to announce to the king of Babylon
that his entire city is captured,
32 the river crossings seized,
the marshes set on fire,
and the soldiers terrified."

33 This is what the LORD Almighty, the God of Israel, says:

"The Daughter of Babylon is like a threshing floor
at the time it is trampled;
the time to harvest her will soon come."

34 "Nebuchadnezzar king of Babylon has devoured us,
he has thrown us into confusion,
he has made us an empty jar.
Like a serpent he has swallowed us
and filled his stomach with our delicacies,
and then has spewed us out.
35 May the violence done to our flesh[a] be upon Babylon,"
say the inhabitants of Zion.
"May our blood be on those who live in Babylonia,"
says Jerusalem.

36 Therefore, this is what the LORD says:

[a]35 Or *done to us and to our children*

59This is the message Jeremiah gave to the staff officer Seraiah
son of Neriah, the son of Mahseiah, when he went to Babylon with
Zedekiah king of Judah in the fourth year of his reign. 60Jeremiah had
written on a scroll about all the disasters that would come upon Babylon—all that had been recorded concerning Babylon. 61He said to
Seraiah, "When you get to Babylon, see that you read all these words
aloud. 62Then say, 'O LORD, you have said you will destroy this place,
so that neither man nor animal will live in it; it will be desolate forever.' 63When you finish reading this scroll, tie a stone to it and throw
it into the Euphrates. 64Then say, 'So will Babylon sink to rise no
more because of the disaster I will bring upon her. And her people
will fall.' "

The words of Jeremiah end here.

The Fall of Jerusalem

52 Zedekiah was twenty-one years old when he became king,
and he reigned in Jerusalem eleven years. His mother's name
was Hamutal daughter of Jeremiah; she was from Libnah. 2He did evil
in the eyes of the LORD, just as Jehoiakim had done. 3It was because
of the LORD's anger that all this happened to Jerusalem and Judah,
and in the end he thrust them from his presence.

Now Zedekiah rebelled against the king of Babylon.

4So in the ninth year of Zedekiah's reign, on the tenth day of the
tenth month, Nebuchadnezzar king of Babylon marched against
Jerusalem with his whole army. They camped outside the city and
built siege works all around it. 5The city was kept under siege until
the eleventh year of King Zedekiah.

6By the ninth day of the fourth month the famine in the city had
become so severe that there was no food for the people to eat. 7Then
the city wall was broken through, and the whole army fled. They left
the city at night through the gate between the two walls near the
king's garden, though the Babylonians[a] were surrounding the city.
They fled toward the Arabah,[b] 8but the Babylonian[c] army pursued
King Zedekiah and overtook him in the plains of Jericho. All his soldiers were separated from him and scattered, 9and he was captured.

He was taken to the king of Babylon at Riblah in the land of Hamath, where he pronounced sentence on him. 10There at Riblah the
king of Babylon slaughtered the sons of Zedekiah before his eyes; he
also killed all the officials of Judah. 11Then he put out Zedekiah's
eyes, bound him with bronze shackles and took him to Babylon,
where he put him in prison till the day of his death.

12On the tenth day of the fifth month, in the nineteenth year of
Nebuchadnezzar king of Babylon, Nebuzaradan commander of the
imperial guard, who served the king of Babylon, came to Jerusalem.
13He set fire to the temple of the LORD, the royal palace and all the

[a]7 Or *Chaldeans*; also in verse 17 [b]7 Or *the Jordan Valley* [c]8 Or *Chaldean*; also in verse 14

OPEN 1. Have you been particularly affected by any books or movies regarding war? Read or seen any more than once? Why? **2.** Have you personally witnessed the horrors of war or assassinations? Have family or friends? How did you react at the time? **3.** Have you ever picked a fight with someone, only to find out too late that you had bitten off more than you could chew? What happened?

STUDY 1. What family ties, political forces and spiritual influences seem to have motivated Zedekiah to rebel against the king of Babylon (vv. 1–4; 27:1–7; 37:5; Ezek. 17:15–16)? **2.** What had Jeremiah (and God) advised Zedekiah when he first thought of rebellion (27:12–14; 29:4–9)? How about during the siege of Jerusalem (38:14–23)? **3.** When does it dawn on Zedekiah that he was biting off more than he could chew in the final showdown with Babylon (vv. 4–7; 2 Chr. 36:12–13)? With tail between his legs, where does he go? **4.** What is the net effect of Zedekiah's revolt on him and his family? On the city itself? On the officials and the poor? On their beloved temple? What prophecy about the temple did this fulfill (26:1–6)? **5.** Why were some people singled out for execution (vv. 24–27), while others were spared? **6.** What was the reason for this disaster which fell upon Jerusalem (v. 3)? **7.** What lessons from the book of Jeremiah are brought to mind by this postscript or second reading

---

52:1–27,31–34 Baruch probably penned the addendum to Jeremiah's prophecies (see the parallel in 2 Kin. 24:18–25:21,27–30). Hindsight validated Jeremiah's prophecies against Jerusalem. The eventual fulfillment of his prophecies regarding the exiles' return was an encouragement to them. The plan of God was a help to the people as they endured in a foreign land.

52:1 Zedekiah. Baruch framed Zedekiah's ambition in the bigger picture of God's plan. Zedekiah's attempted heroism resulted in rebellion against God's design for his people.

about the fall of Jerusalem? What else in Jeremiah do you need to reread to make sure you get the point God wants you to get?

APPLY 1. Who is the "Jeremiah" (or "Ezekiel") in your life who warns you when you've made a wrong turn or bad decision? Are you trying to tune that person out (and God) in any way right now? **2.** What is your gut reaction to the wrath of God revealed in this passage? Does it make you yearn for a happier ending? Or do you feel satisfied that the punishment fit the crime?

---

houses of Jerusalem. Every important building he burned down. [14]The whole Babylonian army under the commander of the imperial guard broke down all the walls around Jerusalem. [15]Nebuzaradan the commander of the guard carried into exile some of the poorest people and those who remained in the city, along with the rest of the craftsmen[a] and those who had gone over to the king of Babylon. [16]But Nebuzaradan left behind the rest of the poorest people of the land to work the vineyards and fields.

[17]The Babylonians broke up the bronze pillars, the movable stands and the bronze Sea that were at the temple of the LORD and they carried all the bronze to Babylon. [18]They also took away the pots, shovels, wick trimmers, sprinkling bowls, dishes and all the bronze articles used in the temple service. [19]The commander of the imperial guard took away the basins, censers, sprinkling bowls, pots, lampstands, dishes and bowls used for drink offerings—all that were made of pure gold or silver.

[20]The bronze from the two pillars, the Sea and the twelve bronze bulls under it, and the movable stands, which King Solomon had made for the temple of the LORD, was more than could be weighed. [21]Each of the pillars was eighteen cubits high and twelve cubits in circumference[b]; each was four fingers thick, and hollow. [22]The bronze capital on top of the one pillar was five cubits[c] high and was decorated with a network and pomegranates of bronze all around. The other pillar, with its pomegranates, was similar. [23]There were ninety-six pomegranates on the sides; the total number of pomegranates above the surrounding network was a hundred.

[24]The commander of the guard took as prisoners Seraiah the chief priest, Zephaniah the priest next in rank and the three doorkeepers. [25]Of those still in the city, he took the officer in charge of the fighting men, and seven royal advisers. He also took the secretary who was chief officer in charge of conscripting the people of the land and sixty of his men who were found in the city. [26]Nebuzaradan the commander took them all and brought them to the king of Babylon at Riblah. [27]There at Riblah, in the land of Hamath, the king had them executed.

So Judah went into captivity, away from her land. [28]This is the number of the people Nebuchadnezzar carried into exile:

in the seventh year, 3,023 Jews;
[29]in Nebuchadnezzar's eighteenth year,
  832 people from Jerusalem;
[30]in his twenty-third year,
  745 Jews taken into exile by Nebuzaradan the commander of the imperial guard.
  There were 4,600 people in all.

[a]*15* Or *populace* [b]*21* That is, about 27 feet (about 8.1 meters) high and 18 feet (about 5.4 meters) in circumference [c]*22* That is, about 7 1/2 feet (about 2.3 meters)

52:28 number of people. The staged deportation represented the Babylonian's systematic conquest. Piece by piece, the nation of Judah was disassembled and taken away.

52:30 twenty-third year. This second deportation was probably a result of the assassination of the governor, Gedaliah (41:1–3). The numbers likely represent only the males. These, of course, were the best of the people.

Jehoiachin Released

[31]In the thirty-seventh year of the exile of Jehoiachin king of Judah, in the year Evil-Merodach[a] became king of Babylon, he released Jehoiachin king of Judah and freed him from prison on the twenty-fifth day of the twelfth month. [32]He spoke kindly to him and gave him a seat of honor higher than those of the other kings who were with him in Babylon. [33]So Jehoiachin put aside his prison clothes and for the rest of his life ate regularly at the king's table. [34]Day by day the king of Babylon gave Jehoiachin a regular allowance as long as he lived, till the day of his death.

[a]31 Also called *Amel-Marduk*

OPEN If you could award honors or medals to other members of your group, what would you give them and why?

STUDY 1. After building throughout the book to God's judgment upon Israel and Judah, are you surprised by the way in which the book ends? Why or why not? **2.** Why do you think this happier note of Jehoiachin's elevation follows the previous passage about Zedekiah's rebellion and imprisonment? **3.** What is the significance of eating at the king's table? What does this say about how God rewards faithful people, even those who wait 37 years for answered prayer? **4.** As you review the book, which promises of God did Jeremiah live to see fulfilled? Which were still to come?

APPLY 1. When have you had to wait a long time for an answer to prayer? What did you feel about God while you waited? How did you recognize the answer when it finally came? **2.** The King of Kings has asked you to put off your old clothes and come to eat with him at his table (Col. 3:5–12; Rev. 3:20). What is your response?

52:34 Jehoiachin. Jehoiachin represented the hope of the people. His release and restoration kindled the exiles' belief in Jeremiah's prophecies of future prosperity. Jehoiachin was treated well until his death.

Lamentations

Personal Reading	Group Study Topic and Reading	
1:1–22	Jerusalem: Unconsolable	1:1–22
2:1–22	The Desolate Daughter of Zion	2:1–22
3:1–66	Crushed, but Not Consumed	3:1–66
4:1–22	The Precious Has Become Profane	4:1–22
5:1–22	Lord, Remember and Restore	5:1–22

Author. The book of Lamentations does not name its author, but from the earliest traditions, Jeremiah has been considered the author.

Date. Jeremiah probably wrote Lamentations after Jerusalem fell to Babylon but before he was taken to Egypt as an exile himself. If so, he wrote Lamentations between 586 and 585 B.C.

Purpose. Jeremiah spoke to his people from a broken heart. His Lamentations expressed his own sorrow over his people's sin and gave a final attempt to call them to repentance. Whereas most of the prophets wrote to warn their people about the consequences of their sin, Jeremiah wrote after the consequences had already begun. Yet, the message still offers hope—the hope that God eventually brings salvation, no matter how unfaithful his children have been.

Historical Background. Lamentations records a historical event. Zedekiah was appointed king of Judah by Nebuchadnezzar in 597 B.C. When Zedekiah rebelled against the Babylonian king, Nebuchadnezzar besieged Jerusalem. The siege began in 588 B.C., and by 586 B.C., the city was facing starvation. Zedekiah and his army fled the city but were overtaken by the Babylonians on the plains of Jericho. One month later, Jerusalem itself fell and was ransacked and burned. Jerusalem's final fall prompted the five laments or dirges that make up Lamentations.

Since the days of Moses, the Hebrews had found their identity in their covenant with God. Part of that covenant involved an agreement between Abraham and God, in which God promised the land of Canaan to Abraham and his descendants. Centuries later, Jerusalem was the focal point of this agreement. The fall of Jerusalem dealt a severe blow to the life the Hebrews would have had if they had upheld their part of the covenant.

Lament Poetry. The lament poem is not unique to the book of Lamentations. The book of Psalms contains many poems of this kind, as do many of the prophetic books of the Old Testament. Lamentations is the only book, however, that consists solely of laments.

1[a] How deserted lies the city,
once so full of people!
How like a widow is she,
who once was great among the nations!
She who was queen among the provinces
has now become a slave.

2 Bitterly she weeps at night,
tears are upon her cheeks.
Among all her lovers
there is none to comfort her.
All her friends have betrayed her;
they have become her enemies.

3 After affliction and harsh labor,
Judah has gone into exile.
She dwells among the nations;
she finds no resting place.
All who pursue her have overtaken her
in the midst of her distress.

4 The roads to Zion mourn,
for no one comes to her appointed feasts.
All her gateways are desolate,
her priests groan,
her maidens grieve,
and she is in bitter anguish.

5 Her foes have become her masters;
her enemies are at ease.
The LORD has brought her grief
because of her many sins.
Her children have gone into exile,
captive before the foe.

6 All the splendor has departed
from the Daughter of Zion.
Her princes are like deer
that find no pasture;
in weakness they have fled
before the pursuer.

7 In the days of her affliction and wandering
Jerusalem remembers all the treasures
that were hers in days of old.
When her people fell into enemy hands,
there was no one to help her.
Her enemies looked at her
and laughed at her destruction.

[a]This chapter is an acrostic poem, the verses of which begin with the successive letters of the Hebrew alphabet.

OPEN 1. When you were a teenager, what was most likely to bring you to tears: Boy-girl conflicts? School frustration? Athletic failures? Conflict with parents? **2.** Who was most likely to comfort you?

STUDY 1. What does the title Lamentations suggest to you? Is this the grief of an individual or of a nation? Can you think of similar outpourings of grief in Scripture? **2.** From this, what overall picture of Judah comes to mind? What one word would you use to describe her situation? **3.** What has happened to Judah and her "lovers" (v. 2; Jer. 52:4–30 for background details of Jerusalem's fall)? What irony do you see here? What do you imagine Jerusalem looked like after these events? Compare this to her "glory days" (1 Chr. 14:17; 1 Kin. 10:1–9,23–25). **4.** What "reversals" of her fortunes has she suffered (vv. 1–7)? Why? What were some of her sins (2 Kin. 21:1–9,16)? **5.** How had Judah failed to "consider her future" (v. 9)? What warnings had she received as part of the covenant (Deut. 28:58–68)? How did she respond to the warnings of the prophets? What is especially tragic about this failure? **6.** What has happened to the sanctuary (v. 10)? What does it suggest about God's attitude toward Judah? **7.** Does the poet consider the Lord's treatment unjust (v. 18)? What resources or securities have proven futile against the Lord's anger? **8.** Jerusalem was under siege for about a year and a half (Jer. 52:4–6). What do you think life was like during the siege (vv. 20–21)? **9.** In his distress, to whom does the poet appeal? For what does he pray (vv. 21–22)? On what basis does he make this request?

APPLY 1. Think of your darkest hour. What kinds of emotions toward God did you feel? How did you deal with those feelings? How did you try to make sense out of what had happened? **2.** What warnings has God given you that you've failed to heed? With what result? Could you be living now on "borrowed time"? **3.** Could there be a "sin of presumption" in your life that threatens your

1:1 How deserted lies the city. Although anonymous, the author was likely an eyewitness to Babylon's devastating destruction and deportation of Jerusalem. The once bustling, thriving city was now empty.

1:2 Among all her lovers. Such destruction befell Judah as a consequence to the nation's passionate idolatry. Now, in Judah's time of need, their gods proved useless.

prosperity? How is the psalmist's attitude in Psalm 139:23–24 a necessary safeguard?

[8] Jerusalem has sinned greatly
and so has become unclean.
All who honored her despise her,
for they have seen her nakedness;
she herself groans
and turns away.

[9] Her filthiness clung to her skirts;
she did not consider her future.
Her fall was astounding;
there was none to comfort her.
"Look, O LORD, on my affliction,
for the enemy has triumphed."

[10] The enemy laid hands
on all her treasures;
she saw pagan nations
enter her sanctuary—
those you had forbidden
to enter your assembly.

[11] All her people groan
as they search for bread;
they barter their treasures for food
to keep themselves alive.
"Look, O LORD, and consider,
for I am despised."

[12] "Is it nothing to you, all you who pass by?
Look around and see.
Is any suffering like my suffering
that was inflicted on me,
that the LORD brought on me
in the day of his fierce anger?

[13] "From on high he sent fire,
sent it down into my bones.
He spread a net for my feet
and turned me back.
He made me desolate,
faint all the day long.

[14] "My sins have been bound into a yoke[a];
by his hands they were woven together.
They have come upon my neck
and the Lord has sapped my strength.
He has handed me over
to those I cannot withstand.

[15] "The Lord has rejected
all the warriors in my midst;
he has summoned an army against me
to[b] crush my young men.

[a] *14* Most Hebrew manuscripts; Septuagint *He kept watch over my sins* [b] *15* Or *has set a time for me / when he will*

1:9 filthiness. Like a homeless harlot, Judah paraded her uncleanness without any regard to her appearance.

In his winepress the Lord has trampled
the Virgin Daughter of Judah.

16 "This is why I weep
and my eyes overflow with tears.
No one is near to comfort me,
no one to restore my spirit.
My children are destitute
because the enemy has prevailed."

17 Zion stretches out her hands,
but there is no one to comfort her.
The LORD has decreed for Jacob
that his neighbors become his foes;
Jerusalem has become
an unclean thing among them.

18 "The LORD is righteous,
yet I rebelled against his command.
Listen, all you peoples;
look upon my suffering.
My young men and maidens
have gone into exile.

19 "I called to my allies
but they betrayed me.
My priests and my elders
perished in the city
while they searched for food
to keep themselves alive.

20 "See, O LORD, how distressed I am!
I am in torment within,
and in my heart I am disturbed,
for I have been most rebellious.
Outside, the sword bereaves;
inside, there is only death.

21 "People have heard my groaning,
but there is no one to comfort me.
All my enemies have heard of my distress;
they rejoice at what you have done.
May you bring the day you have announced
so they may become like me.

22 "Let all their wickedness come before you;
deal with them
as you have dealt with me
because of all my sins.
My groans are many
and my heart is faint."

1:20 Outside ... inside there is only death. Judah was in a no-win situation. For 18 months, the city was under Nebuchadnezzar's attack. Certain death awaited any escapees, while starvation stifled those within the city walls.

1:21 day you have announced. The author selfishly wished their Babylonian captor would share Judah's same fate—God's judgment would be severe (Jer. 25:15–38). He understood the impartiality of divine retribution for disobedience.

OPEN **1.** How would you feel if you organized a party or group activity, only to have nobody come? Has that ever happened to you or your friends? How did you feel? **2.** Have you ever seen a person or group get "what was coming to them"? What happened?

STUDY **1.** Compare 1:1 with 2:1. What is similar? What is different? **2.** What emotions does the poet attribute to God? What images does he use to describe God's treatment of the "Daughter of Zion" (vv. 4–5,8)? **3.** How extensive has the calamity been? List the things "torn down," "swallowed up" or "destroyed." **4.** In verses 6–7, what has the Lord done to "his dwelling"? Why would he treat his own things this way? **5.** What images of helplessness and hopelessness does the poet paint in verses 9–12? What do the gates and bars represent: The kings and princes? The law? The prophets? Or what? What is significant of the posture of the elders and young women (v. 10)? **6.** What emotions does the poet express when he sees the suffering of the children? Who has escaped the judgment of the Lord? Why? **7.** Why is the poet without words of comfort for Judah (v. 13)? Had anything like this happened in her history before? **8.** Where does the poet lay much of the blame for Judah's destruction (v. 14)? What "false and misleading" oracles have the prophets spoken (Jer. 14:13–16)? Why? **9.** What does Judah's downfall bring about in onlookers? In her enemies? What do both groups seem to forget about her punishment (v. 17)? **10.** Judah's punishment had been decreed by God much earlier, as recorded in Leviticus 26:27–46. How is God just in sending this calamity? How is he merciful? **11.** Why is Judah encouraged to "pour out" her heart to the Lord (vv. 18–19)? As she pleads her case, is she asking for justice or mercy (vv. 20–21)? **12.** What questions are especially troubling for Judah (v. 20)? What is she ultimately looking for (v. 22)?

APPLY **1.** In what ways have you become casual about sin? **2.** Does God seem like an "enemy" to

2

[a] How the Lord has covered the Daughter of Zion
with the cloud of his anger[b]!
He has hurled down the splendor of Israel
from heaven to earth;
he has not remembered his footstool
in the day of his anger.

2 Without pity the Lord has swallowed up
all the dwellings of Jacob;
in his wrath he has torn down
the strongholds of the Daughter of Judah.
He has brought her kingdom and its princes
down to the ground in dishonor.

3 In fierce anger he has cut off
every horn[c] of Israel.
He has withdrawn his right hand
at the approach of the enemy.
He has burned in Jacob like a flaming fire
that consumes everything around it.

4 Like an enemy he has strung his bow;
his right hand is ready.
Like a foe he has slain
all who were pleasing to the eye;
he has poured out his wrath like fire
on the tent of the Daughter of Zion.

5 The Lord is like an enemy;
he has swallowed up Israel.
He has swallowed up all her palaces
and destroyed her strongholds.
He has multiplied mourning and lamentation
for the Daughter of Judah.

6 He has laid waste his dwelling like a garden;
he has destroyed his place of meeting.
The LORD has made Zion forget
her appointed feasts and her Sabbaths;
in his fierce anger he has spurned
both king and priest.

7 The Lord has rejected his altar
and abandoned his sanctuary.
He has handed over to the enemy
the walls of her palaces;
they have raised a shout in the house of the LORD
as on the day of an appointed feast.

[a] This chapter is an acrostic poem, the verses of which begin with the successive letters of the Hebrew alphabet. [b] 1 Or *How the Lord in his anger / has treated the Daughter of Zion with contempt* [c] 3 Or / *all the strength*; or *every king*; *horn* here symbolizes strength.

2:1 How the LORD has covered. The divine director behind this tragic state of affairs was not the enemy army in charge. Babylon was God's discipline on Judah.

2:6 his dwelling ... his place of meeting. Judah recognized the temple as a sign of God's presence among them. Their spiritual indifference resulted in its destruction.

2:7 raised a shout. The pilfering pagans struck the author with sadness. Their irreverent and mocking shouts of victory in the temple added insult to injury.

8 The LORD determined to tear down
the wall around the Daughter of Zion.
He stretched out a measuring line
and did not withhold his hand from destroying.
He made ramparts and walls lament;
together they wasted away.

9 Her gates have sunk into the ground;
their bars he has broken and destroyed.
Her king and her princes are exiled among the nations,
the law is no more,
and her prophets no longer find
visions from the LORD.

10 The elders of the Daughter of Zion
sit on the ground in silence;
they have sprinkled dust on their heads
and put on sackcloth.
The young women of Jerusalem
have bowed their heads to the ground.

11 My eyes fail from weeping,
I am in torment within,
my heart is poured out on the ground
because my people are destroyed,
because children and infants faint
in the streets of the city.

12 They say to their mothers,
"Where is bread and wine?"
as they faint like wounded men
in the streets of the city,
as their lives ebb away
in their mothers' arms.

13 What can I say for you?
With what can I compare you,
O Daughter of Jerusalem?
To what can I liken you,
that I may comfort you,
O Virgin Daughter of Zion?
Your wound is as deep as the sea.
Who can heal you?

14 The visions of your prophets
were false and worthless;
they did not expose your sin
to ward off your captivity.
The oracles they gave you
were false and misleading.

15 All who pass your way
clap their hands at you;

you right now? Are there any sins with which you have "made friends"? **3.** In this chapter, the poet indicts the false prophets who did not expose the sins of Judah. When have you given ear to someone who turned out to be a "false prophet"? **4.** When spiritual leaders mess up, how should we react?

2:9 prophets no longer find visions from the LORD. God stopped wasting his breath on messages through the prophets. The only message left for Judah was mass destruction.

2:14 false and misleading. A true prophet, like Jeremiah, spoke only God's message. However, false prophets spread lies like weeds to choke out God's truth.

they scoff and shake their heads
at the Daughter of Jerusalem:
"Is this the city that was called
the perfection of beauty,
the joy of the whole earth?"

16 All your enemies open their mouths
wide against you;
they scoff and gnash their teeth
and say, "We have swallowed her up.
This is the day we have waited for;
we have lived to see it."

17 The LORD has done what he planned;
he has fulfilled his word,
which he decreed long ago.
He has overthrown you without pity,
he has let the enemy gloat over you,
he has exalted the horn[a] of your foes.

18 The hearts of the people
cry out to the Lord.
O wall of the Daughter of Zion,
let your tears flow like a river
day and night;
give yourself no relief,
your eyes no rest.

19 Arise, cry out in the night,
as the watches of the night begin;
pour out your heart like water
in the presence of the Lord.
Lift up your hands to him
for the lives of your children,
who faint from hunger
at the head of every street.

20 "Look, O LORD, and consider:
Whom have you ever treated like this?
Should women eat their offspring,
the children they have cared for?
Should priest and prophet be killed
in the sanctuary of the Lord?

21 "Young and old lie together
in the dust of the streets;
my young men and maidens
have fallen by the sword.
You have slain them in the day of your anger;
you have slaughtered them without pity.

22 "As you summon to a feast day,
so you summoned against me terrors on every side.

[a] *17 Horn* here symbolizes strength.

2:19 pour out your heart like water. The image pictures a full confession (Ps. 62:8). In the face of utter tragedy, Judah needed to be broken before God (v. 11). She needed to be truly repentant of her disobedience.

In the day of the LORD's anger
no one escaped or survived;
those I cared for and reared,
my enemy has destroyed."

3 [a]I am the man who has seen affliction
by the rod of his wrath.
2 He has driven me away and made me walk
in darkness rather than light;
3 indeed, he has turned his hand against me
again and again, all day long.

4 He has made my skin and my flesh grow old
and has broken my bones.
5 He has besieged me and surrounded me
with bitterness and hardship.
6 He has made me dwell in darkness
like those long dead.

7 He has walled me in so I cannot escape;
he has weighed me down with chains.
8 Even when I call out or cry for help,
he shuts out my prayer.
9 He has barred my way with blocks of stone;
he has made my paths crooked.

10 Like a bear lying in wait,
like a lion in hiding,
11 he dragged me from the path and mangled me
and left me without help.
12 He drew his bow
and made me the target for his arrows.

13 He pierced my heart
with arrows from his quiver.
14 I became the laughingstock of all my people;
they mock me in song all day long.
15 He has filled me with bitter herbs
and sated me with gall.

16 He has broken my teeth with gravel;
he has trampled me in the dust.
17 I have been deprived of peace;
I have forgotten what prosperity is.
18 So I say, "My splendor is gone
and all that I had hoped from the LORD."

19 I remember my affliction and my wandering,
the bitterness and the gall.
20 I well remember them,
and my soul is downcast within me.

[a]This chapter is an acrostic poem; the verses of each stanza begin with the successive letters of the Hebrew alphabet, and the verses within each stanza begin with the same letter.

OPEN 1. What sayings or homespun wisdom can you still hear your mom or dad reciting? How do these still affect you? **2.** How do you pass the time in a dentist's waiting room? What feelings do you experience there? **3.** What do you do to get an hour's reprieve from the hectic pace of your day? Where do you go to get away for a weekend?

STUDY 1. For whom is the poet speaking in the opening verses? How has God treated him (vv. 1–18)? How is he feeling? **2.** What has Judah focused her attention on (vv. 17,19)? What are the consequences of forgetting her past prosperity? **3.** How does the poet stem the tide of grief and despair (v. 21)? Is this an easy or natural thing to do in the midst of sorrow? What is the secret of redirecting one's focus this way? **4.** Where does the poet look to find hope (vv. 22–27)? Given the situation, do these words seem hollow? Insane? Unreal? Courageous? Noble? Explain. **5.** The phrases in verses 22–27 come from Psalms and Isaiah. Why were they familiar to the poet? How must he have prepared himself in the past to deal with his current depression? **6.** What attributes of the Lord are recalled in verses 22–33? How does this picture contrast with that in verses 1–18? Why is it necessary to balance both feelings (vv. 1–18) and faith (vv. 22–33)? **7.** To whom does the poet address his rhetorical questions in verses 34–39? What attributes of God do they establish? **8.** To what logical conclusion is the poet brought (vv. 40–42)? How was this conclusion arrived at? How does this begin to make sense out of Judah's suffering? **9.** Why does the poet list the sufferings of the people (vv. 43–54)? **10.** For what does the poet pray (vv. 55–66)? What hope of an answer does his own punishment give him? When and how had God heard and answered their plea in the past? What did the covenant and the prophets say about God's hearing (Jer. 30:10–11)? **11.** Briefly review the chapter. What kind of psychological and emotional progress has the poet

3:1–2 The author painfully describes for the entire community one sorry, sad, abandoned individual.

3:15 bitter herbs. The pungent taste of punishment plagued the nation of Judah (Jer. 9:15). Even food, their source for life, was bitterly unsatisfying. At Passover the herbs reminded them of hardship.

made from the beginning to the end? What have been the steps in that process? What spiritual "weapons" has the poet used to fight his way back to God?

APPLY 1. Have you ever felt like the poet in the opening section of this chapter (vv. 1–18)? Were you able to express those feelings to God? What kept you from giving up completely at that time? **2.** What portions of Scripture are especially helpful to you in difficult times? What songs are especially meaningful to you? **3.** When you're feeling forsaken and chastened how do you express your feelings? What is the danger of being too stoic or unemotional? What can you do to balance these two extremes? **4.** Do you grow more during easy times or during tough times? What help does verse 33 (Rom 5:3–5; James 1:2–4) teach you about affliction? **5.** What "compassions" or "faithfulness" (vv. 22–23) has the Lord shown you this week? How have you shown your love and gratitude to God?

21 Yet this I call to mind
and therefore I have hope:

22 Because of the LORD's great love we are not consumed,
for his compassions never fail.
23 They are new every morning;
great is your faithfulness.
24 I say to myself, "The LORD is my portion;
therefore I will wait for him."

25 The LORD is good to those whose hope is in him,
to the one who seeks him;
26 it is good to wait quietly
for the salvation of the LORD.
27 It is good for a man to bear the yoke
while he is young.

28 Let him sit alone in silence,
for the LORD has laid it on him.
29 Let him bury his face in the dust—
there may yet be hope.
30 Let him offer his cheek to one who would strike him,
and let him be filled with disgrace.

31 For men are not cast off
by the Lord forever.
32 Though he brings grief, he will show compassion,
so great is his unfailing love.
33 For he does not willingly bring affliction
or grief to the children of men.

34 To crush underfoot
all prisoners in the land,
35 to deny a man his rights
before the Most High,
36 to deprive a man of justice—
would not the Lord see such things?

37 Who can speak and have it happen
if the Lord has not decreed it?
38 Is it not from the mouth of the Most High
that both calamities and good things come?
39 Why should any living man complain
when punished for his sins?

3:22 we are not consumed. With a sudden glance toward the bright side, the author credited God for not eradicating them entirely. As bad as it was, things could be worse.

3:23 new every morning; great is your faithfulness. Although the destruction surrounding them was great, Judah knew that God was faithful. God's mercy is present along with his judgment.

3:24 portion. With nothing but rubble to call their own, Judah's only valuable belonging was God (Num. 18:20). **I will wait for him.** No hope for a second wind. No will for fighting back. There was nothing else Judah could do but wait on God.

3:27 bear the yoke. Like an ox bearing a yoke to accomplish a task, the author realized this overbearing trial (v. 1) might turn out for their good. He encouraged his people to endure the current hardship on to completion.

3:32 compassion, so great is his unfailing love. The same God whose wrath seemed unending (vv. 1–18) now demonstrated unfailing love. The author balanced a complete portrait of Judah's God.

3:36 deprive a man of justice. The author built a case for God's compassion through rhetorical questions. Judah could hardly call her situation unjust.

[40]Let us examine our ways and test them,
and let us return to the LORD.
[41]Let us lift up our hearts and our hands
to God in heaven, and say:
[42]"We have sinned and rebelled
and you have not forgiven.

[43]"You have covered yourself with anger and pursued us;
you have slain without pity.
[44]You have covered yourself with a cloud
so that no prayer can get through.
[45]You have made us scum and refuse
among the nations.

[46]"All our enemies have opened their mouths
wide against us.
[47]We have suffered terror and pitfalls,
ruin and destruction."
[48]Streams of tears flow from my eyes
because my people are destroyed.

[49]My eyes will flow unceasingly,
without relief,
[50]until the LORD looks down
from heaven and sees.
[51]What I see brings grief to my soul
because of all the women of my city.

[52]Those who were my enemies without cause
hunted me like a bird.
[53]They tried to end my life in a pit
and threw stones at me;
[54]the waters closed over my head,
and I thought I was about to be cut off.

[55]I called on your name, O LORD,
from the depths of the pit.
[56]You heard my plea: "Do not close your ears
to my cry for relief."
[57]You came near when I called you,
and you said, "Do not fear."

[58]O Lord, you took up my case;
you redeemed my life.
[59]You have seen, O LORD, the wrong done to me.
Uphold my cause!
[60]You have seen the depth of their vengeance,
all their plots against me.

[61]O LORD, you have heard their insults,
all their plots against me—
[62]what my enemies whisper and mutter
against me all day long.

3:57 when I called you. Jeremiah looks back to his personal experience and gives testimony to God's faithfulness. Crisis was met with compassion. God is real to those he loves (Ps. 145:18).

63 Look at them! Sitting or standing,
they mock me in their songs.

64 Pay them back what they deserve, O LORD,
for what their hands have done.
65 Put a veil over their hearts,
and may your curse be on them!
66 Pursue them in anger and destroy them
from under the heavens of the LORD.

4

[a] How the gold has lost its luster,
the fine gold become dull!
The sacred gems are scattered
at the head of every street.

2 How the precious sons of Zion,
once worth their weight in gold,
are now considered as pots of clay,
the work of a potter's hands!

3 Even jackals offer their breasts
to nurse their young,
but my people have become heartless
like ostriches in the desert.

4 Because of thirst the infant's tongue
sticks to the roof of its mouth;
the children beg for bread,
but no one gives it to them.

5 Those who once ate delicacies
are destitute in the streets.
Those nurtured in purple
now lie on ash heaps.

6 The punishment of my people
is greater than that of Sodom,
which was overthrown in a moment
without a hand turned to help her.

7 Their princes were brighter than snow
and whiter than milk,
their bodies more ruddy than rubies,
their appearance like sapphires.[b]

8 But now they are blacker than soot;
they are not recognized in the streets.
Their skin has shriveled on their bones;
it has become as dry as a stick.

[a]This chapter is an acrostic poem, the verses of which begin with the successive letters of the Hebrew alphabet. [b]7 Or *lapis lazuli*

OPEN 1. Are the stories from your parents' past "the good old days," or are they "those hard times"? What experiences of satisfaction and suffering do you recall from those stories? **2.** Have you ever dressed up only to find yourself doing some dirty job? What was the job? Did you keep your clothes clean? **3.** What is the hungriest or thirstiest you have ever been?

STUDY 1. What are the "gold" and "sacred gems" of verses 1–2? What is the difference between these items and the clay pots? What modern image is the equivalent of this comparison? **2.** What is the difference in child-rearing responsibility between the jackal and the ostrich? (Ostriches will abandon their eggs when confronted with danger.) What have the people of Judah done to deserve this comparison? **3.** How is Judah's punishment worse than that of Sodom (vv. 6–10)? **4.** Why did everyone assume that Jerusalem's gates were impregnable (Jer. 7:1–8)? What made the gates vulnerable (vv. 12–13)? **5.** Even as destruction approached, where did Judah look for help (v. 17)? Who is probably responsible for this "looking in vain"? **6.** Have the people lost confidence in their king (v. 20)? Why or why not (2 Kin. 25:1–7)? **7.** Why does the poet's attention shift to "the Daughter of Edom" in verses 21–22? Why is she rejoicing? What will be her end (Jer. 49:17–22)? **8.** What hope is given to the "Daughter of Zion" in verse 22? If you were one of the people of Judah, how would you feel at the end of this dirge?

APPLY 1. What are the "gold and sacred gems" in your life?

3:63 they mock me. In dire straits, Judah was the joke of many nations (vv. 46–47). Where was Judah's God now?

4:1 fine gold become dull. Jerusalem was a tragic before-and-after comparison. Before their calamity, the people were priceless. Now, sin had devalued them (v. 2). The great valuables from the Temple are gone and even the people, the greater treasure, are now almost worthless (v. 2).

4:6 Sodom ... overthrown in a moment. God's punishment on Sodom, although equally thorough, was mercifully quick (Gen. 19:24–29). By contrast, Jerusalem's painful siege went on month after month.

[9]Those killed by the sword are better off
than those who die of famine;
racked with hunger, they waste away
for lack of food from the field.

[10]With their own hands compassionate women
have cooked their own children,
who became their food
when my people were destroyed.

[11]The LORD has given full vent to his wrath;
he has poured out his fierce anger.
He kindled a fire in Zion
that consumed her foundations.

[12]The kings of the earth did not believe,
nor did any of the world's people,
that enemies and foes could enter
the gates of Jerusalem.

[13]But it happened because of the sins of her prophets
and the iniquities of her priests,
who shed within her
the blood of the righteous.

[14]Now they grope through the streets
like men who are blind.
They are so defiled with blood
that no one dares to touch their garments.

[15]"Go away! You are unclean!" men cry to them.
"Away! Away! Don't touch us!"
When they flee and wander about,
people among the nations say,
"They can stay here no longer."

[16]The LORD himself has scattered them;
he no longer watches over them.
The priests are shown no honor,
the elders no favor.

[17]Moreover, our eyes failed,
looking in vain for help;
from our towers we watched
for a nation that could not save us.

[18]Men stalked us at every step,
so we could not walk in our streets.
Our end was near, our days were numbered,
for our end had come.

[19]Our pursuers were swifter
than eagles in the sky;
they chased us over the mountains
and lay in wait for us in the desert.

If these were suddenly taken away, how would you feel? Where would you look for a sense of self-worth? **2.** Jerusalem's gates were, for Judah, a symbol of security. What are your symbols of security? **3.** If you do not resist the Lord's discipline, but submit to it, what can you hope for?

4:17 a nation that could not save us. Egypt proved to be an impotent ally against God's plan to use Babylon against Jerusalem. The author betrays his fatalistic disappointment with Egypt's attempt.

20 The LORD's anointed, our very life breath,
was caught in their traps.
We thought that under his shadow
we would live among the nations.

21 Rejoice and be glad, O Daughter of Edom,
you who live in the land of Uz.
But to you also the cup will be passed;
you will be drunk and stripped naked.

22 O Daughter of Zion, your punishment will end;
he will not prolong your exile.
But, O Daughter of Edom, he will punish your sin
and expose your wickedness.

5 Remember, O LORD, what has happened to us;
look, and see our disgrace.
2 Our inheritance has been turned over to aliens,
our homes to foreigners.
3 We have become orphans and fatherless,
our mothers like widows.
4 We must buy the water we drink;
our wood can be had only at a price.
5 Those who pursue us are at our heels;
we are weary and find no rest.
6 We submitted to Egypt and Assyria
to get enough bread.
7 Our fathers sinned and are no more,
and we bear their punishment.
8 Slaves rule over us,
and there is none to free us from their hands.
9 We get our bread at the risk of our lives
because of the sword in the desert.
10 Our skin is hot as an oven,
feverish from hunger.
11 Women have been ravished in Zion,
and virgins in the towns of Judah.
12 Princes have been hung up by their hands;
elders are shown no respect.
13 Young men toil at the millstones;
boys stagger under loads of wood.
14 The elders are gone from the city gate;
the young men have stopped their music.
15 Joy is gone from our hearts;
our dancing has turned to mourning.
16 The crown has fallen from our head.
Woe to us, for we have sinned!
17 Because of this our hearts are faint,

OPEN 1. Were you ever lured into wrongdoing, caught and punished while the ones who led you astray got away clean? What were the circumstances? How did you feel? **2.** Have you ever found yourself under the authority of someone who wasn't entitled to that authority? Summarize the situation and your reactions.

STUDY 1. Who is responsible for the punishment Judah is suffering (v. 7)? Is this a realistic view or blame-shifting (v. 16)? **2.** Who are the different groups mentioned in verses 11–14? What is said of each? What is the total impact of these verses? **3.** Describe the emotion you hear in verses 15–18. What is the climactic line of verses 1–18? How is this the beginning of Judah's return? **4.** What attribute of God does the poet mention (v. 19)? Why is that significant? **5.** For what does the poet pray throughout this chapter? Has God abandoned Judah or has Judah abandoned God? Both? Neither? Does the book end on a hopeful note or a despairing one? Why do you think so?

APPLY 1. When are you most apt to "consider your ways": During smooth sailing? In the midst of the storm? When you're going nowhere? **2.** In what sense are you bearing the punishment for the sins of your fathers? In what ways are you laying up punishment for your children? How can the cycle be broken? **3.** If repentance is the first step in re-

4:22 punishment will end. In the end, Judah's sole hope was in God's covenant with his people (Deut. 28–30) and his assurance of a new covenant (Jer. 31:31). Because of God's promises, the nation would be restored.

5:7 The people of Judah realized their present condition was the result of generations of sin. Their heritage was pain and disobedience.

5:16 crown has fallen. Jerusalem's royal destiny was displaced by rebellion. As a result, the golden city was ruined.

because of these things our eyes grow dim
[18]for Mount Zion, which lies desolate,
with jackals prowling over it.

[19]You, O LORD, reign forever;
your throne endures from generation to generation.
[20]Why do you always forget us?
Why do you forsake us so long?
[21]Restore us to yourself, O LORD, that we may return;
renew our days as of old
[22]unless you have utterly rejected us
and are angry with us beyond measure.

turning to God's favor, is that step easy or difficult for you? Where in your life is it most difficult to admit your failure and ask for God's help? What incentive does this book give you to do that?

5:22 utterly rejected. The author feared the one thing God would never do (Jer. 31:37). Despite Judah's rebellious streak, God would never abandon them completely. He was always near (Ps. 145:18).

Ezekiel

Author. The prophet and priest Ezekiel is considered the author of this prophecy, both by Jewish and Christian traditions and as stated in the text.

Personal Reading	Group Study Topic and Reading	
1	Glory of the Lord	1:1–28
2–3	Ezekiel's Call	2:1–3:15
4–5	Siege of Jerusalem	4:1–5:17
6–8	Idolatry in the Temple	8:1–18
9–16	Unfaithful Jerusalem	16:1–63
17–18	Sin and Death	18:1–32
19–22	Jerusalem's Sins	22:1–31
23–28	Nations in Prophecy	25:1–17
29–34	Shepherds and Sheep	34:1–31
35–36	Mountains of Israel	36:1–38
37–39	The Dry Bones	37:1–14
40–43	The New Temple	40:1–43:27
44–48	River From the Temple	47:1–12

Date. Ezekiel's ministry began during the reign of Jehoiachin in 593 B.C. His last dated prophecy was in 571 B.C. Sometime after that, Ezekiel compiled his prophecies in chronological order as he had given them.

Purpose. Ezekiel prophesied to his people to encourage them that God could still restore Israel. His message, though, was not one of mere inspiration. He confronted his people, calling them to repentance. His prophecies were not always verbal. Sometimes they came in the form of object lessons. Each one was meant to help the people see their mistakes and turn back to God.

Historical Background. In 612 B.C., an alliance of Babylonians and Medes captured the Assyrian capital of Nineveh. Three years later, Pharaoh Neco II of Egypt was en route to assist Assyria when he fought against Judah, led by King Josiah at Megiddo. Judah was defeated, and not long afterward, Neco II placed Jehoiakim as his royal vassal on the throne of Judah. In 605 B.C., Jehoiakim shifted his allegiance to Nebuchadnezzar of Babylon, then later back to Egypt. In 597 B.C., Nebuchadnezzar reacted to this switch and attacked Jerusalem, taking several thousand Jews captive. He was a prophet during the Babylonian exile. In 586 B.C., Jerusalem fell to another Babylonian siege and was destroyed.

Exile. The Babylonian exile was not just a single historical event but a chain of several events. The first exile occurred in 605 B.C., when Nebuchadnezzar besieged Jerusalem. The prophet Daniel was among these first exiles. Then in 597 B.C., Nebuchadnezzar took ten thousand captives back to his homeland. Finally, in 586 B.C., the Babylonians captured Jerusalem, destroyed the temple, and took many more captives. It is uncertain exactly where all these captives lived in Babylon. Ezekiel lived in a village on the Kebar River (1:1), but the location of that village is still a mystery. Hundreds of the captives taken after the fall of Jerusalem were taken to the city of Riblah "in the land of Hamath," to the north of Damascus.

The Prophet. Exiles themselves expressed that the exile was painful. The early exiles, such as Daniel and Ezekiel, could only watch from a distance as their nation was destroyed, their families murdered and their temple razed. As a nation whose identity had been established around their God-given homeland, the exile seemed the end of their story, even though the prophets claimed otherwise. For the individuals taken captive, it was a tragedy of the most personal kind because it involved not just nationalism but also faith.

The Living Creatures and the Glory of the Lord

1 In the[a] thirtieth year, in the fourth month on the fifth day, while I
was among the exiles by the Kebar River, the heavens were
opened and I saw visions of God.
2On the fifth of the month—it was the fifth year of the exile of King
Jehoiachin— 3the word of the LORD came to Ezekiel the priest, the
son of Buzi,[b] by the Kebar River in the land of the Babylonians.[c] There
the hand of the LORD was upon him.
4I looked, and I saw a windstorm coming out of the north—an immense cloud with flashing lightning and surrounded by brilliant light.
The center of the fire looked like glowing metal, 5and in the fire was
what looked like four living creatures. In appearance their form was
that of a man, 6but each of them had four faces and four wings. 7Their
legs were straight; their feet were like those of a calf and gleamed like
burnished bronze. 8Under their wings on their four sides they had the
hands of a man. All four of them had faces and wings, 9and their
wings touched one another. Each one went straight ahead; they did
not turn as they moved.
10Their faces looked like this: Each of the four had the face of a
man, and on the right side each had the face of a lion, and on the left
the face of an ox; each also had the face of an eagle. 11Such were their
faces. Their wings were spread out upward; each had two wings, one
touching the wing of another creature on either side, and two wings
covering its body. 12Each one went straight ahead. Wherever the spirit
would go, they would go, without turning as they went. 13The appearance of the living creatures was like burning coals of fire or like
torches. Fire moved back and forth among the creatures; it was
bright, and lightning flashed out of it. 14The creatures sped back and
forth like flashes of lightning.
15As I looked at the living creatures, I saw a wheel on the ground
beside each creature with its four faces. 16This was the appearance
and structure of the wheels: They sparkled like chrysolite, and all
four looked alike. Each appeared to be made like a wheel intersecting
a wheel. 17As they moved, they would go in any one of the four directions the creatures faced; the wheels did not turn about[d] as the creatures went. 18Their rims were high and awesome, and all four rims
were full of eyes all around.
19When the living creatures moved, the wheels beside them moved;
and when the living creatures rose from the ground, the wheels also
rose. 20Wherever the spirit would go, they would go, and the wheels

[a]1 Or *my* [b]3 Or *Ezekiel son of Buzi the priest* [c]3 Or *Chaldeans* [d]17 Or *aside*

OPEN 1. Think back to the time when you were age 30 (or project yourself into that time frame): Where are you living? Who with? What are you doing for a living? What lies ahead for you, five years down the road? **2.** When and where have you felt the closest to God? **3.** If you were the special effects director for a movie and had to portray God, how would you do it?

STUDY 1. When Ezekiel sees this vision, where is he (v. 1)? Why is he there? How old is he now? How long has he been there (v. 2)? **2.** What career might Ezekiel have entered at age 30 (v. 3; Num. 4:3), had it not been for exile? What new career has opened up to him instead (2:5)? **3.** How do you think the last five years in exile have prepared Ezekiel, emotionally and spiritually, for his new role? **4.** List the different elements which comprise Ezekiel's two-part vision. What does he see? Hear? **5.** To what does he liken the four attendants to the throne? What aspects of God's nature are revealed in other-worldly images? **6.** How does Ezekiel react to this multi-sensory experience (v. 28)? What must he be feeling on the inside?

APPLY 1. God obviously has Ezekiel's attention: What does God have to do to get yours? **2.** How does Ezekiel's description of God affect you emotionally: It scares me—this is a God you don't want to cross? It reassures me—what a mighty God we serve? It mesmerizes me—like a powerful thunderstorm? It inspires me—a bigger-than-life character in a divine drama? **3.** Had you been Ezekiel, what would you have done when you realized who this was: Run!? Shivered in my shoes? Praised God!? Just like Ezekiel—hit the deck, face down!

1:1 thirtieth year ... I saw visions of God. Ezekiel celebrated his thirtieth birthday in Babylonian exile. Under ordinary circumstances, this occasion would have marked the beginning of his priesthood (Num. 4:3). Ezekiel's privileged encounter with God's glory marked the beginning of his role as a prophet.

1:2 fifth year of the exile of King Jehoiachin. In 597 B.C., the Babylonians captured King Jehoiachin, Ezekiel, and many other Jews. Ezekiel's prophetic role began a few years later.

1:3 word of the LORD. Ezekiel did not preach his own passions. He relayed only God's message. **hand of the LORD.** Ezekiel prophesied under direct order from God himself.

1:4 I looked, and I saw. Ezekiel's bizarre experience began with the display of God's power in a rumbling storm.

1:5–6 four living creatures ... four faces and four wings. Although the creatures looked like humans, they were hardly earthly. They are later identified as cherubim—special angelic beings (ch.10).

1:7 gleamed like burnished bronze. The creatures were accentuated by an angelic glow.

1:12 The creatures effortlessly maneuvered in a number of directions, without having to turn their heads.

would rise along with them, because the spirit of the living creatures
was in the wheels. [21]When the creatures moved, they also moved;
when the creatures stood still, they also stood still; and when the
creatures rose from the ground, the wheels rose along with them,
because the spirit of the living creatures was in the wheels.
[22]Spread out above the heads of the living creatures was what
looked like an expanse, sparkling like ice, and awesome. [23]Under the
expanse their wings were stretched out one toward the other, and
each had two wings covering its body. [24]When the creatures moved, I
heard the sound of their wings, like the roar of rushing waters, like
the voice of the Almighty,[a] like the tumult of an army. When they
stood still, they lowered their wings.
[25]Then there came a voice from above the expanse over their heads
as they stood with lowered wings. [26]Above the expanse over their
heads was what looked like a throne of sapphire,[b] and high above on
the throne was a figure like that of a man. [27]I saw that from what appeared to be his waist up he looked like glowing metal, as if full of
fire, and that from there down he looked like fire; and brilliant light
surrounded him. [28]Like the appearance of a rainbow in the clouds on
a rainy day, so was the radiance around him.
This was the appearance of the likeness of the glory of the LORD.
When I saw it, I fell facedown, and I heard the voice of one speaking.

Ezekiel's Call

2 He said to me, "Son of man, stand up on your feet and I will speak
to you." [2]As he spoke, the Spirit came into me and raised me to
my feet, and I heard him speaking to me.
[3]He said: "Son of man, I am sending you to the Israelites, to a rebellious nation that has rebelled against me; they and their fathers
have been in revolt against me to this very day. [4]The people to whom
I am sending you are obstinate and stubborn. Say to them, 'This is
what the Sovereign LORD says.' [5]And whether they listen or fail to listen—for they are a rebellious house—they will know that a prophet
has been among them. [6]And you, son of man, do not be afraid of
them or their words. Do not be afraid, though briers and thorns are
all around you and you live among scorpions. Do not be afraid of
what they say or terrified by them, though they are a rebellious
house. [7]You must speak my words to them, whether they listen or fail
to listen, for they are rebellious. [8]But you, son of man, listen to what
I say to you. Do not rebel like that rebellious house; open your mouth
and eat what I give you."
[9]Then I looked, and I saw a hand stretched out to me. In it was a
scroll, [10]which he unrolled before me. On both sides of it were written
words of lament and mourning and woe.

3 And he said to me, "Son of man, eat what is before you, eat this
scroll; then go and speak to the house of Israel." [2]So I opened
my mouth, and he gave me the scroll to eat.

[a]24 Hebrew *Shaddai* [b]26 Or *lapis lazuli*

OPEN 1. What is the strangest thing you have been asked to eat? Did you do so willingly? Did you choke it down? **2.** When you were a child, how stubborn were you—like an immovable rock, or more like a marshmallow?

STUDY 1. What is significant about Ezekiel's current posture (1:28) and the position God wants him to assume (2:1–2)? **2.** What do you think God intends by repeatedly (93 times) calling him "son of man"? Addressed in his human weakness, where does Ezekiel get the strength to comply with God's request (2:2; 3:8,12, 14)? **3.** To whom does God send Ezekiel to speak (2:3–8; 3:5–9)? What are they like? Why might Ezekiel be afraid to take on this "mission impossible" (3:6–7)? **4.** How does God console him (2:6–7; 3:1–3,8 –12)? What seems to be required to get this job done: Thick skin? Strong stomach? Hard hat? Big ears? Soft heart? Foreign language? Flying machine? **5.** What is on the scroll that Ezekiel has to eat (2:10)? How does it taste to him (3:3)? What he thought would be sour or "bitter" (3:14) actually wasn't. What lesson do you think God is try-

1:26 on the throne. *Ezekiel* saw a picture of God's heavenly glory and authority.

1:28 I fell facedown. Ezekiel was understandably overwhelmed by the weighty vision. However, God called him to his feet (2:1–2).

2:1 Son of man. Ezekiel received a divine commission to address earthly prospects as equals. Perhaps God emphasized Ezekiel's humanness in order to stress humility. This phrase is used many times throughout Ezekiel.

[3]Then he said to me, "Son of man, eat this scroll I am giving you
and fill your stomach with it." So I ate it, and it tasted as sweet as
honey in my mouth.
[4]He then said to me: "Son of man, go now to the house of Israel
and speak my words to them. [5]You are not being sent to a people of
obscure speech and difficult language, but to the house of Israel—
[6]not to many peoples of obscure speech and difficult language,
whose words you cannot understand. Surely if I had sent you to
them, they would have listened to you. [7]But the house of Israel is not
willing to listen to you because they are not willing to listen to me, for
the whole house of Israel is hardened and obstinate. [8]But I will make
you as unyielding and hardened as they are. [9]I will make your forehead like the hardest stone, harder than flint. Do not be afraid of
them or terrified by them, though they are a rebellious house."
[10]And he said to me, "Son of man, listen carefully and take to heart
all the words I speak to you. [11]Go now to your countrymen in exile
and speak to them. Say to them, 'This is what the Sovereign LORD
says,' whether they listen or fail to listen."
[12]Then the Spirit lifted me up, and I heard behind me a loud rumbling sound—May the glory of the LORD be praised in his dwelling
place!— [13]the sound of the wings of the living creatures brushing
against each other and the sound of the wheels beside them, a loud
rumbling sound. [14]The Spirit then lifted me up and took me away, and
I went in bitterness and in the anger of my spirit, with the strong
hand of the LORD upon me. [15]I came to the exiles who lived at Tel Abib
near the Kebar River. And there, where they were living, I sat among
them for seven days—overwhelmed.

Warning to Israel

[16]At the end of seven days the word of the LORD came to me: [17]"Son
of man, I have made you a watchman for the house of Israel; so hear
the word I speak and give them warning from me. [18]When I say to a
wicked man, 'You will surely die,' and you do not warn him or speak
out to dissuade him from his evil ways in order to save his life, that
wicked man will die for[a] his sin, and I will hold you accountable for
his blood. [19]But if you do warn the wicked man and he does not turn
from his wickedness or from his evil ways, he will die for his sin; but
you will have saved yourself.
[20]"Again, when a righteous man turns from his righteousness and
does evil, and I put a stumbling block before him, he will die. Since
you did not warn him, he will die for his sin. The righteous things he
did will not be remembered, and I will hold you accountable for his
blood. [21]But if you do warn the righteous man not to sin and he does

[a]18 Or *in*; also in verses 19 and 20

ing to teach him in shaking up his taste buds (a lesson also taught to John—Rev. 10:9–10)? **6.** Ezekiel returns to his home in Tel Abib (3:14–15): How does he get there? How does he feel at first? How might his sitting among his fellow exiles compare with his having stood before the Lord?

APPLY 1. As you review your life's work, have you ever been aware of any special calling or "overwhelming" task from the Lord? **2.** What would be scarier for you—going as a missionary to a foreign country or being sent by God to boldly share your faith where you work? Why? **3.** What would God have to strengthen in order for you to successfully share your faith to those God is calling you: Like Ezekiel, my forehead—I'd have to be more "hardened" to deal with stubbornness (3:8–9)? My mouth—I can never find the words? My nerves—sharing faith is scary for me! My heart—it would take a lot of love for me to do that!

OPEN 1. Do you read the warning labels on the products you buy? What warning labels do you read, but choose to ignore as "that couldn't happen to me"? **2.** Recall a time when you were quite "tongue-tied" or speechless. What happened? How did you recover?

STUDY 1. What is the main point of God's warning to Ezekiel (vv. 18–21,24–26)? Of Ezekiel's warning to Israel (vv. 17,27)? Why is Ezekiel held accountable for their response? **2.** "Watchmen" were posted on farm and town walls to warn of thieves or attackers. What then does it mean for Ezekiel to be made a "spiritual watchman"? **3.** How does the hand of the Lord feel to Ezekiel (vv. 22–27)? What restraints does God

3:9 forehead ... stone. The forehead represented a person's determination or stubbornness (Isa. 48:4). Ezekiel would need to toughen up in order to deliver the bad news to an unreceptive people.

3:11 whether they listen or fail to listen. A prophet's success was not in a receptive hearing, but in the successful delivery of God's message.

3:15 Tel Abib. Ezekiel returned to his home in exile to consider his experience. **seven days.** Ezekiel spent the week in silence—still in shock over his encounter.

3:17 a watchman for the house of Israel. Ezekiel modeled his role after the watchmen of ancient times who were positioned on the city walls to warn of impending physical danger. Ezekiel, like other prophets, warned the people of spiritual danger and the consequences of one's behavior.

impose on him? How does this show God is serious?

APPLY 1. What message do you think God has for the people where you live? What is your role: To tell everyone, or only those who come to you? **2.** What would help them take you more seriously?

OPEN 1. As a child, did you ever set up true-to-life scenarios with dolls or little green army guys? What did you enjoy about such imaginative activity? **2.** Again, as a child, what food would you refuse to eat on principle: Anything with foreign-sounding names? Anything with onions and green peppers? Anything slimy?

STUDY 1. For each object lesson Ezekiel was to act out, answer the following: What equipment or props did he need for it? What were the lines scripted for him to speak? How long would it take? What did each prop, action or time span symbolize? **2.** What do you think Ezekiel would have done with a modern computer? **3.** What was the object lesson the audience was intended to learn? Do you think Israel got the point and repented? Or did they likely get angry and take out revenge on Ezekiel for "offending community standards of decency" by his outrageous street theatre? **4.** Given his priestly training, what object lesson was too offensive even for brazen Ezekiel to do (4:12–15)? Which would you, as an Israelite, find too much to stomach? **5.** In one column list all the things God says he will do in his wrath; in the other column list all of Israel's sins. How are they related? **6.** The particular judgments listed here represent God's anger "fully spent" (5:13; 6:12; 7:8;

not sin, he will surely live because he took warning, and you will have
saved yourself."
22The hand of the LORD was upon me there, and he said to me, "Get
up and go out to the plain, and there I will speak to you." 23So I got up
and went out to the plain. And the glory of the LORD was standing
there, like the glory I had seen by the Kebar River, and I fell facedown.
24Then the Spirit came into me and raised me to my feet. He spoke
to me and said: "Go, shut yourself inside your house. 25And you, son
of man, they will tie with ropes; you will be bound so that you cannot
go out among the people. 26I will make your tongue stick to the roof
of your mouth so that you will be silent and unable to rebuke them,
though they are a rebellious house. 27But when I speak to you, I will
open your mouth and you shall say to them, 'This is what the Sovereign LORD says.' Whoever will listen let him listen, and whoever will
refuse let him refuse; for they are a rebellious house.

Siege of Jerusalem Symbolized

4 "Now, son of man, take a clay tablet, put it in front of you and
draw the city of Jerusalem on it. 2Then lay siege to it: Erect siege
works against it, build a ramp up to it, set up camps against it and put
battering rams around it. 3Then take an iron pan, place it as an iron
wall between you and the city and turn your face toward it. It will be
under siege, and you shall besiege it. This will be a sign to the house
of Israel.
4"Then lie on your left side and put the sin of the house of Israel
upon yourself.[a] You are to bear their sin for the number of days you lie
on your side. 5I have assigned you the same number of days as the
years of their sin. So for 390 days you will bear the sin of the house of
Israel.
6"After you have finished this, lie down again, this time on your
right side, and bear the sin of the house of Judah. I have assigned you
40 days, a day for each year. 7Turn your face toward the siege of Jerusalem and with bared arm prophesy against her. 8I will tie you up with
ropes so that you cannot turn from one side to the other until you
have finished the days of your siege.
9"Take wheat and barley, beans and lentils, millet and spelt; put
them in a storage jar and use them to make bread for yourself. You
are to eat it during the 390 days you lie on your side. 10Weigh out
twenty shekels[b] of food to eat each day and eat it at set times. 11Also
measure out a sixth of a hin[c] of water and drink it at set times. 12Eat
the food as you would a barley cake; bake it in the sight of the people,
using human excrement for fuel." 13The LORD said, "In this way the
people of Israel will eat defiled food among the nations where I will
drive them."

[a]4 Or *your side* [b]10 That is, about 8 ounces (about 0.2 kilogram) [c]11 That is, about 2/3 quart (about 0.6 liter)

3:26 you will be silent and unable to rebuke them. Ezekiel was prohibited to speak *except during his specific* prophecies.

4:1 Ezekiel's visual aid modeled the inarguable demise of the city of Jerusalem.

4:5 you will bear the sin. Ezekiel drew attention as a living picture of pending punishment against God's people.

4:6 lie down ... on your right side. Like a compass, Ezekiel's prostrate positions symbolized God's concerns for both the northern and southern kingdoms of Israel.

4:9 Those within Jerusalem's besieged walls would have to scrape together a hodge-podge meal in order to survive.

14Then I said, "Not so, Sovereign LORD! I have never defiled myself. From my youth until now I have never eaten anything found dead or torn by wild animals. No unclean meat has ever entered my mouth."

15"Very well," he said, "I will let you bake your bread over cow manure instead of human excrement."

16He then said to me: "Son of man, I will cut off the supply of food in Jerusalem. The people will eat rationed food in anxiety and drink rationed water in despair, 17for food and water will be scarce. They will be appalled at the sight of each other and will waste away because of[a] their sin.

5 "Now, son of man, take a sharp sword and use it as a barber's razor to shave your head and your beard. Then take a set of scales and divide up the hair. 2When the days of your siege come to an end, burn a third of the hair with fire inside the city. Take a third and strike it with the sword all around the city. And scatter a third to the wind. For I will pursue them with drawn sword. 3But take a few strands of hair and tuck them away in the folds of your garment. 4Again, take a few of these and throw them into the fire and burn them up. A fire will spread from there to the whole house of Israel.

5"This is what the Sovereign LORD says: This is Jerusalem, which I have set in the center of the nations, with countries all around her. 6Yet in her wickedness she has rebelled against my laws and decrees more than the nations and countries around her. She has rejected my laws and has not followed my decrees.

7"Therefore this is what the Sovereign LORD says: You have been more unruly than the nations around you and have not followed my decrees or kept my laws. You have not even[b] conformed to the standards of the nations around you.

8"Therefore this is what the Sovereign LORD says: I myself am against you, Jerusalem, and I will inflict punishment on you in the sight of the nations. 9Because of all your detestable idols, I will do to you what I have never done before and will never do again. 10Therefore in your midst fathers will eat their children, and children will eat their fathers. I will inflict punishment on you and will scatter all your survivors to the winds. 11Therefore as surely as I live, declares the Sovereign LORD, because you have defiled my sanctuary with all your vile images and detestable practices, I myself will withdraw my favor; I will not look on you with pity or spare you. 12A third of your people will die of the plague or perish by famine inside you; a third will fall by the sword outside your walls; and a third I will scatter to the winds and pursue with drawn sword.

13"Then my anger will cease and my wrath against them will subside, and I will be avenged. And when I have spent my wrath upon them, they will know that I the LORD have spoken in my zeal.

14"I will make you a ruin and a reproach among the nations around you, in the sight of all who pass by. 15You will be a reproach and a taunt, a warning and an object of horror to the nations around you

[a]17 Or *away in* [b]7 Most Hebrew manuscripts; some Hebrew manuscripts and Syriac *You have*

13:15; 20:8,21). Why would God want to spend all of his anger on his chosen people?

APPLY 1. What things that are happening in this country do you feel so strongly about that you would "lay your body down" in protest about it? **2.** In what way have you "conformed to the nations around you" instead of doing what God has called you to do?

4:15 bake your bread over cow manure. Manure was used as a fuel for cooking. Ezekiel requested use of this instead of a morally compromising one.

5:1 sharp sword. Ezekiel symbolized Jerusalem's coming close encounter with the enemy's sword. His bald head symbolized the humiliation that would result.

5:10 I will inflict punishment on you. God reminded his people of their covenant relationship. Because of the people's sin, divine discipline was inevitable.

when I inflict punishment on you in anger and in wrath and with
stinging rebuke. I the LORD have spoken. 16When I shoot at you with
my deadly and destructive arrows of famine, I will shoot to destroy
you. I will bring more and more famine upon you and cut off your
supply of food. 17I will send famine and wild beasts against you, and
they will leave you childless. Plague and bloodshed will sweep
through you, and I will bring the sword against you. I the LORD have
spoken."

A Prophecy Against the Mountains of Israel

6 The word of the LORD came to me: 2"Son of man, set your face
against the mountains of Israel; prophesy against them 3and say:
'O mountains of Israel, hear the word of the Sovereign LORD. This is
what the Sovereign LORD says to the mountains and hills, to the ravines and valleys: I am about to bring a sword against you, and I will
destroy your high places. 4Your altars will be demolished and your
incense altars will be smashed; and I will slay your people in front of
your idols. 5I will lay the dead bodies of the Israelites in front of their
idols, and I will scatter your bones around your altars. 6Wherever you
live, the towns will be laid waste and the high places demolished, so
that your altars will be laid waste and devastated, your idols smashed
and ruined, your incense altars broken down, and what you have
made wiped out. 7Your people will fall slain among you, and you will
know that I am the LORD.

8" 'But I will spare some, for some of you will escape the sword
when you are scattered among the lands and nations. 9Then in the
nations where they have been carried captive, those who escape will
remember me—how I have been grieved by their adulterous hearts,
which have turned away from me, and by their eyes, which have
lusted after their idols. They will loathe themselves for the evil they
have done and for all their detestable practices. 10And they will know
that I am the LORD; I did not threaten in vain to bring this calamity on
them.

11" 'This is what the Sovereign LORD says: Strike your hands together and stamp your feet and cry out "Alas!" because of all the
wicked and detestable practices of the house of Israel, for they will
fall by the sword, famine and plague. 12He that is far away will die of
the plague, and he that is near will fall by the sword, and he that survives and is spared will die of famine. So will I spend my wrath upon
them. 13And they will know that I am the LORD, when their people lie
slain among their idols around their altars, on every high hill and on
all the mountaintops, under every spreading tree and every leafy
oak—places where they offered fragrant incense to all their idols.
14And I will stretch out my hand against them and make the land a
desolate waste from the desert to Diblah[a]—wherever they live. Then
they will know that I am the LORD.' "

[a]14 Most Hebrew manuscripts; a few Hebrew manuscripts *Riblah*

OPEN 1. For a vacation, would you rather go to the mountains or the seashore? Why? **2.** When you get really angry, does it show in your face, arms, legs or body? Demonstrate.

STUDY 1. Why does God want Ezekiel to prophesy against the mountains (Deut. 12:2–7)? What had happened on those "high places" that so displeased the Lord? What was so evil about burning incense to "idols" (a derisive term, meaning literally "dung pellets")? **2.** What are the different punishments God says he will bring against Israel? What effect will these punishments have on those who survive them? **3.** What do you think is implied by: "You will know that I am the LORD"? God is unique? Universal? Jealous? Sovereign? **4.** Why do you think Ezekiel talks so much about God's judgment? **5.** What is the ultimate purpose of God's judgment? Why is it sometimes selective? Why are people hit differently?

APPLY 1. Have you ever seen the effects of "sword, famine and plague," or other forms of God's judgment? How did it affect you? **2.** Have you ever "loathed" yourself (v. 9) because you had fallen short morally? Is loathing yourself appropriate in such a situation?

6:3 destroy your high places. God promised to destroy the pagan altars erected throughout the land.

6:11–14 Strike your hands together ... I will spend my wrath ... stretch out my hand. Ezekiel would be involved in personally proclaiming God's message, but at the same time God would personally bring destruction.

The End Has Come

7 The word of the LORD came to me: 2"Son of man, this is what the Sovereign LORD says to the land of Israel: The end! The end has come upon the four corners of the land. 3The end is now upon you and I will unleash my anger against you. I will judge you according to your conduct and repay you for all your detestable practices. 4I will not look on you with pity or spare you; I will surely repay you for your conduct and the detestable practices among you. Then you will know that I am the LORD.

5"This is what the Sovereign LORD says: Disaster! An unheard-of[a] disaster is coming. 6The end has come! The end has come! It has roused itself against you. It has come! 7Doom has come upon you—you who dwell in the land. The time has come, the day is near; there is panic, not joy, upon the mountains. 8I am about to pour out my wrath on you and spend my anger against you; I will judge you according to your conduct and repay you for all your detestable practices. 9I will not look on you with pity or spare you; I will repay you in accordance with your conduct and the detestable practices among you. Then you will know that it is I the LORD who strikes the blow.

10"The day is here! It has come! Doom has burst forth, the rod has budded, arrogance has blossomed! 11Violence has grown into[b] a rod to punish wickedness; none of the people will be left, none of that crowd—no wealth, nothing of value. 12The time has come, the day has arrived. Let not the buyer rejoice nor the seller grieve, for wrath is upon the whole crowd. 13The seller will not recover the land he has sold as long as both of them live, for the vision concerning the whole crowd will not be reversed. Because of their sins, not one of them will preserve his life. 14Though they blow the trumpet and get everything ready, no one will go into battle, for my wrath is upon the whole crowd.

15"Outside is the sword, inside are plague and famine; those in the country will die by the sword, and those in the city will be devoured by famine and plague. 16All who survive and escape will be in the mountains, moaning like doves of the valleys, each because of his sins. 17Every hand will go limp, and every knee will become as weak as water. 18They will put on sackcloth and be clothed with terror. Their faces will be covered with shame and their heads will be shaved. 19They will throw their silver into the streets, and their gold will be an unclean thing. Their silver and gold will not be able to save them in the day of the LORD's wrath. They will not satisfy their hunger or fill their stomachs with it, for it has made them stumble into sin. 20They were proud of their beautiful jewelry and used it to make their detestable idols and vile images. Therefore I will turn these into an unclean thing for them. 21I will hand it all over as plunder to foreigners and as loot to the wicked of the earth, and they will defile it. 22I will turn my face away from them, and they will desecrate my treasured place; robbers will enter it and desecrate it.

[a]5 Most Hebrew manuscripts; some Hebrew manuscripts and Syriac *Disaster after* [b]11 Or *The violent one has become*

OPEN 1. What things from last week did you put off until another day: Homework? Office work? Chores? Errands? Promised time with spouse or kids? **2.** What does such procrastination tell you about yourself? **3.** What would you do with the rest of today if you knew the world would end at midnight?

STUDY 1. What specifically has come to an end for Israel? What is "The end!" all about? **2.** What effect will God's punishment have on Israel militarily, financially, emotionally and spiritually? How will the world be affected (vv. 2,21,24)? **3.** What actions and attitudes of Israel have brought God's wrath upon them? What loop-hole or escape clause is provided? **4.** What end-time advice will the people be looking for? Where will they turn (vv. 25–26)? **5.** What does God say about the fairness of his actions against Israel? **6.** Does it surprise you that God's patience has an end? Why or why not? If God's patience were limitless, what would his justice look like?

APPLY 1. Would you like to be judged by the standards you use to evaluate others? Why or why not? **2.** In the context of relating to people you love, where is your patience being stretched the thinnest? How much more patience do you have left? What will happen when you run out? How might limiting your patience be the more loving thing to do?

7:2 end ... four corners of the land. Enough was enough! No one would escape God's punishment. The phrase four is used throughout Ezekiel. It refers to "four directions" (Gen. 13:14); "four quarters" (Isa. 11:12) and "four creatures" (Rev. 4:7).

7:14 they blow the trumpet. Devastation will be so complete they will not be able to defend themselves.

23"Prepare chains, because the land is full of bloodshed and the
city is full of violence. 24I will bring the most wicked of the nations to
take possession of their houses; I will put an end to the pride of the
mighty, and their sanctuaries will be desecrated. 25When terror
comes, they will seek peace, but there will be none. 26Calamity upon
calamity will come, and rumor upon rumor. They will try to get a
vision from the prophet; the teaching of the law by the priest will be
lost, as will the counsel of the elders. 27The king will mourn, the
prince will be clothed with despair, and the hands of the people of the
land will tremble. I will deal with them according to their conduct,
and by their own standards I will judge them. Then they will know
that I am the LORD."

Idolatry in the Temple

8 In the sixth year, in the sixth month on the fifth day, while I was
sitting in my house and the elders of Judah were sitting before
me, the hand of the Sovereign LORD came upon me there. 2I looked,
and I saw a figure like that of a man.[a] From what appeared to be his
waist down he was like fire, and from there up his appearance was as
bright as glowing metal. 3He stretched out what looked like a hand
and took me by the hair of my head. The Spirit lifted me up between
earth and heaven and in visions of God he took me to Jerusalem, to
the entrance to the north gate of the inner court, where the idol that
provokes to jealousy stood. 4And there before me was the glory of the
God of Israel, as in the vision I had seen in the plain.

5Then he said to me, "Son of man, look toward the north." So I
looked, and in the entrance north of the gate of the altar I saw this
idol of jealousy.

6And he said to me, "Son of man, do you see what they are doing—
the utterly detestable things the house of Israel is doing here, things
that will drive me far from my sanctuary? But you will see things that
are even more detestable."

7Then he brought me to the entrance to the court. I looked, and I
saw a hole in the wall. 8He said to me, "Son of man, now dig into the
wall." So I dug into the wall and saw a doorway there.

9And he said to me, "Go in and see the wicked and detestable
things they are doing here." 10So I went in and looked, and I saw portrayed all over the walls all kinds of crawling things and detestable
animals and all the idols of the house of Israel. 11In front of them
stood seventy elders of the house of Israel, and Jaazaniah son of Shaphan was standing among them. Each had a censer in his hand, and
a fragrant cloud of incense was rising.

12He said to me, "Son of man, have you seen what the elders of the
house of Israel are doing in the darkness, each at the shrine of his
own idol? They say, 'The LORD does not see us; the LORD has forsaken

[a]2 Or *saw a fiery figure*

OPEN 1. Recall the parody of three monkeys whose hands cover their eyes, ears and mouth so that they "see no evil, hear no evil, speak no evil." What neglected issues concern you, that you wish more people would see, hear or speak up about? **2.** Which are you?

STUDY 1. Where is Ezekiel when the vision begins? To what city is he taken? By whom? **2.** In each of Ezekiel's four visions he is shown a part of the temple. What about each vision is "more detestable" than the one before? Like the blind, deaf-mute monkey with its eyes opened and ears unplugged, what evil does he sense, as if for the first time? **3.** When else has Ezekiel seen a fiery "figure like that of a man" (v. 2; 1:26–27)? What is the prior history of the "idol of jealousy" (vv. 3,5; 2 Kin. 21:7; 2 Chr. 33:15). **4.** Tammuz (v. 14) is a Babylonian fertility god, and smelling branches (v. 17) was a form of nature worship. What do the peoples' actions reveal about what some Israelites really believed?

APPLY 1. The idol that made God jealous kept reappearing in the temple. What idol has the tendency to reappear in your heart? What can you do to keep it out? **2.** If Ezekiel were allowed to peep through "a hole in the wall" of your heart and mind, what would he see there? **3.** What can you do about anything there that displeases God?

8:1 elders of Judah. *Although they were in captivity, the elders enjoyed some religious assembly rights.*

8:2 figure like that of a man. An angelic representation of God summoned Ezekiel to a dreamlike day trip to the city of Jerusalem.

8:3 took me to Jerusalem, to the entrance. For Ezekiel, seeing was believing. He received a birds-eye view of the sin in Jerusalem. **jealousy.** God resented the idols that stole the affection of his own people.

the land.' " 13Again, he said, "You will see them doing things that are
even more detestable."
14Then he brought me to the entrance to the north gate of the
house of the LORD, and I saw women sitting there, mourning for Tammuz.
15He said to me, "Do you see this, son of man? You will see
things that are even more detestable than this."
16He then brought me into the inner court of the house of the LORD,
and there at the entrance to the temple, between the portico and the
altar, were about twenty-five men. With their backs toward the temple
of the LORD and their faces toward the east, they were bowing
down to the sun in the east.
17He said to me, "Have you seen this, son of man? Is it a trivial
matter for the house of Judah to do the detestable things they are
doing here? Must they also fill the land with violence and continually
provoke me to anger? Look at them putting the branch to their nose!
18Therefore I will deal with them in anger; I will not look on them
with pity or spare them. Although they shout in my ears, I will not listen to them."

Idolaters Killed

9 Then I heard him call out in a loud voice, "Bring the guards of
the city here, each with a weapon in his hand." 2And I saw six
men coming from the direction of the upper gate, which faces north,
each with a deadly weapon in his hand. With them was a man clothed
in linen who had a writing kit at his side. They came in and stood
beside the bronze altar.
3Now the glory of the God of Israel went up from above the cherubim,
where it had been, and moved to the threshold of the temple.
Then the LORD called to the man clothed in linen who had the writing
kit at his side 4and said to him, "Go throughout the city of Jerusalem
and put a mark on the foreheads of those who grieve and lament over
all the detestable things that are done in it."
5As I listened, he said to the others, "Follow him through the city
and kill, without showing pity or compassion. 6Slaughter old men,
young men and maidens, women and children, but do not touch anyone
who has the mark. Begin at my sanctuary." So they began with
the elders who were in front of the temple.
7Then he said to them, "Defile the temple and fill the courts with
the slain. Go!" So they went out and began killing throughout the city.
8While they were killing and I was left alone, I fell facedown, crying
out, "Ah, Sovereign LORD! Are you going to destroy the entire remnant
of Israel in this outpouring of your wrath on Jerusalem?"
9He answered me, "The sin of the house of Israel and Judah is
exceedingly great; the land is full of bloodshed and the city is full of
injustice. They say, 'The LORD has forsaken the land; the LORD does

OPEN 1. When have you been singled out from a group for distinguished service? **2.** Have you ever joined a group or team with a special mark, badge or uniform signifying membership?

STUDY 1. Where is Ezekiel in this vision and who is his guide (ch. 8)? **2.** Ezekiel sees seven men. What are they given to do and with what tools? **3.** Who gets the special "mark" and why? What do you think the people are like who do not get marks? **4.** When the men begin killing unmarked people (vv. 5–8), what does Ezekiel do? What is God's answer? Do you think that satisfies Ezekiel? Why?

APPLY 1. If you had lived in Jerusalem, would you have been marked? Why or why not? **2.** How do you think you are different from the people around you? If seven of your neighbors and coworkers were interviewed, what would they say is different about you? **3.** From John 13:35, 1 Corinthians 13 and Galatians 5:22–23, what is supposed to "mark" a believer? What can you do to make your "mark" more visible?

8:14 mourning for Tammuz. According to pagan culture, the death of a certain god would incur the devastation of their crops.

9:2 writing kit. The seventh man was dressed with dignity. He carried a case for reed pens and supplies.

9:4 mark on the foreheads. An "x," the last letter of the Hebrew alphabet, would mark those with a repentant, sorrowful attitude.

9:6 Begin. God would distinguish the repentant from the rebels, beginning at the most logical location—his own people with his temple.

9:8 outpouring of your wrath. The brutality overwhelmed Ezekiel. He reasoned with God about the severe nature of the punishment. Ezekiel wanted God to reconsider his punishment. He did this on several occasions (4:14; 11:13).

not see.' 10So I will not look on them with pity or spare them, but I
will bring down on their own heads what they have done."
11Then the man in linen with the writing kit at his side brought
back word, saying, "I have done as you commanded."

The Glory Departs From the Temple

10 I looked, and I saw the likeness of a throne of sapphire[a]
above the expanse that was over the heads of the cherubim.
2The LORD said to the man clothed in linen, "Go in among the wheels
beneath the cherubim. Fill your hands with burning coals from
among the cherubim and scatter them over the city." And as I
watched, he went in.
3Now the cherubim were standing on the south side of the temple
when the man went in, and a cloud filled the inner court. 4Then the
glory of the LORD rose from above the cherubim and moved to the
threshold of the temple. The cloud filled the temple, and the court
was full of the radiance of the glory of the LORD. 5The sound of the
wings of the cherubim could be heard as far away as the outer court,
like the voice of God Almighty[b] when he speaks.
6When the LORD commanded the man in linen, "Take fire from
among the wheels, from among the cherubim," the man went in and
stood beside a wheel. 7Then one of the cherubim reached out his
hand to the fire that was among them. He took up some of it and put
it into the hands of the man in linen, who took it and went out. 8(Under the wings of the cherubim could be seen what looked like the
hands of a man.)
9I looked, and I saw beside the cherubim four wheels, one beside
each of the cherubim; the wheels sparkled like chrysolite. 10As for
their appearance, the four of them looked alike; each was like a wheel
intersecting a wheel. 11As they moved, they would go in any one of
the four directions the cherubim faced; the wheels did not turn
about[c] as the cherubim went. The cherubim went in whatever direction the head faced, without turning as they went. 12Their entire bodies, including their backs, their hands and their wings, were
completely full of eyes, as were their four wheels. 13I heard the
wheels being called "the whirling wheels." 14Each of the cherubim
had four faces: One face was that of a cherub, the second the face of
a man, the third the face of a lion, and the fourth the face of an eagle.
15Then the cherubim rose upward. These were the living creatures I
had seen by the Kebar River. 16When the cherubim moved, the wheels
beside them moved; and when the cherubim spread their wings to
rise from the ground, the wheels did not leave their side. 17When the
cherubim stood still, they also stood still; and when the cherubim
rose, they rose with them, because the spirit of the living creatures
was in them.
18Then the glory of the LORD departed from over the threshold of
the temple and stopped above the cherubim. 19While I watched, the
cherubim spread their wings and rose from the ground, and as they

[a]1 Or *lapis lazuli* [b]5 Hebrew *El-Shaddai* [c]11 Or *aside*

OPEN **1.** What is the strangest dream you have ever had? Did you attach any meaning to what happened in the dream? **2.** Have you ever felt like God has spoken to you through a dream?

STUDY **1.** As in chapter 1, Ezekiel sees a vision of God's glory. From where has the glory of the Lord come (1 Kin. 8:10–11)? To where has Ezekiel seen the glory move (8:4; 9:3; 10:18–19; 11:23)? What do you think was symbolized by this departing, hovering glory? **2.** What order does the Lord give to "the man clothed in linen"? What do you think the coals represent (Gen. 19:24; Amos 7:4)? What do you think his action accomplishes? **3.** How does Ezekiel react this time around to this deja vu experience (compare 1:28)? How do you account for his relatively tranquil, matter-of-fact response? **4.** How do you reconcile the teaching of this chapter, that God is *not* always present with his people, with the promise of Jesus that he *is* always with us (Matt. 28:20)? What is *conditional*, and what is *unconditional*, about God's presence?

APPLY **1.** When have you felt like the presence of God has left your life? What do you feel caused that to happen? **3.** Do you sense the presence of God in your life now? How might your life be more welcoming of him? How would you react if told, "God has left your church"?

10:7 fire. God's fiery judgment was represented in the angel's cupped hand.

10:14 cherubim. There were ancient statues that were called "cherubs." This cherubim face is different than the face on the wheel in 1:10. In 1:10 the face resembled that of an ox.

went, the wheels went with them. They stopped at the entrance to the east gate of the LORD's house, and the glory of the God of Israel was above them.

[20]These were the living creatures I had seen beneath the God of Israel by the Kebar River, and I realized that they were cherubim.
[21]Each had four faces and four wings, and under their wings was what looked like the hands of a man. [22]Their faces had the same appearance as those I had seen by the Kebar River. Each one went straight ahead.

Judgment on Israel's Leaders

11 Then the Spirit lifted me up and brought me to the gate of the house of the LORD that faces east. There at the entrance to the gate were twenty-five men, and I saw among them Jaazaniah son of Azzur and Pelatiah son of Benaiah, leaders of the people. [2]The LORD
said to me, "Son of man, these are the men who are plotting evil and giving wicked advice in this city. [3]They say, 'Will it not soon be time to build houses?[a] This city is a cooking pot, and we are the meat.'
[4]Therefore prophesy against them; prophesy, son of man."
[5]Then the Spirit of the LORD came upon me, and he told me to say: "This is what the LORD says: That is what you are saying, O house of Israel, but I know what is going through your mind. [6]You have killed
many people in this city and filled its streets with the dead.
[7]"Therefore this is what the Sovereign LORD says: The bodies you have thrown there are the meat and this city is the pot, but I will drive you out of it. [8]You fear the sword, and the sword is what I will bring against you, declares the Sovereign LORD. [9]I will drive you out of the city and hand you over to foreigners and inflict punishment on you.
[10]You will fall by the sword, and I will execute judgment on you at the borders of Israel. Then you will know that I am the LORD. [11]This city
will not be a pot for you, nor will you be the meat in it; I will execute judgment on you at the borders of Israel. [12]And you will know that I
am the LORD, for you have not followed my decrees or kept my laws but have conformed to the standards of the nations around you."
[13]Now as I was prophesying, Pelatiah son of Benaiah died. Then I fell facedown and cried out in a loud voice, "Ah, Sovereign LORD! Will you completely destroy the remnant of Israel?"
[14]The word of the LORD came to me: [15]"Son of man, your brothers—your brothers who are your blood relatives[b] and the whole house of Israel—are those of whom the people of Jerusalem have said, 'They are[c] far away from the LORD; this land was given to us as our possession.'

Promised Return of Israel

[16]"Therefore say: 'This is what the Sovereign LORD says: Although I sent them far away among the nations and scattered them among the

[a]3 Or *This is not the time to build houses.* [b]15 Or *are in exile with you* (see Septuagint and Syriac)
[c]15 Or *those to whom the people of Jerusalem have said, 'Stay*

OPEN 1. How do you like your meat done? If not cooked that way, do you send it back? **2.** In renting, buying or building your own place, what's the best advice you've heard? What's the worst advice—information which proved bad or unreliable?

STUDY 1. Where is Ezekiel and who does he see? What role do these 25 men play in Jerusalem? **2.** What kind of leadership have they been offering? What effect has their leadership had (v. 6)? **3.** If the "cooking pot" implies security for Israel's top leaders, what does that say about how well the Lord's message has gotten through to them? **4.** If they view themselves as choice meat (v. 3), who do they think are the discarded bones (v. 15)? How does Ezekiel (and God) turn the tables on them to help them eat their own words (vv. 7–13; ch. 24)? **5.** How will they then *know* God is sovereign?

APPLY 1. When have you felt like "your goose was cooked"? **2.** What happened to deliver you?

OPEN Where do you consider "home"? What's the longest you've been away? What did it feel like to return?

11:3 build houses? Certain leaders were wishful thinkers concerning Jerusalem's future. **cooking pot.** Caught up in their own fantasy, these leaders regarded themselves as the lucky ones.

11:7 meat. God's select portions were, in contrast, the righteous people these rebellious leaders had killed. Ezekiel reversed their imagery and used it against them.

11:16 sanctuary. The people's prior conception of God's presence was tied to a place—the temple. Now, God's presence went outside the temple's physical limitations.

countries, yet for a little while I have been a sanctuary for them in the countries where they have gone.'

17"Therefore say: 'This is what the Sovereign LORD says: I will gather you from the nations and bring you back from the countries where you have been scattered, and I will give you back the land of Israel again.'

18"They will return to it and remove all its vile images and detestable idols. 19I will give them an undivided heart and put a new spirit in them; I will remove from them their heart of stone and give them a heart of flesh. 20Then they will follow my decrees and be careful to keep my laws. They will be my people, and I will be their God. 21But as for those whose hearts are devoted to their vile images and detestable idols, I will bring down on their own heads what they have done, declares the Sovereign LORD."

22Then the cherubim, with the wheels beside them, spread their wings, and the glory of the God of Israel was above them. 23The glory of the LORD went up from within the city and stopped above the mountain east of it. 24The Spirit lifted me up and brought me to the exiles in Babylonia[a] in the vision given by the Spirit of God.

Then the vision I had seen went up from me, 25and I told the exiles everything the LORD had shown me.

The Exile Symbolized

12 The word of the LORD came to me: 2"Son of man, you are living among a rebellious people. They have eyes to see but do not see and ears to hear but do not hear, for they are a rebellious people.

3"Therefore, son of man, pack your belongings for exile and in the daytime, as they watch, set out and go from where you are to another place. Perhaps they will understand, though they are a rebellious house. 4During the daytime, while they watch, bring out your belongings packed for exile. Then in the evening, while they are watching, go out like those who go into exile. 5While they watch, dig through the wall and take your belongings out through it. 6Put them on your shoulder as they are watching and carry them out at dusk. Cover your face so that you cannot see the land, for I have made you a sign to the house of Israel."

7So I did as I was commanded. During the day I brought out my things packed for exile. Then in the evening I dug through the wall with my hands. I took my belongings out at dusk, carrying them on my shoulders while they watched.

8In the morning the word of the LORD came to me: 9"Son of man, did not that rebellious house of Israel ask you, 'What are you doing?'

10"Say to them, 'This is what the Sovereign LORD says: This oracle concerns the prince in Jerusalem and the whole house of Israel who are there.' 11Say to them, 'I am a sign to you.'

"As I have done, so it will be done to them. They will go into exile as captives.

12"The prince among them will put his things on his shoulder at

STUDY **1.** In chapter 11, how does the fate of those who stayed in Jerusalem compare with those who were taken into exile? How is God himself a "sanctuary" (v. 16) for people who have always believed God's presence is linked to the temple? **2.** What changes does God promise to make in the hearts of his people (vv. 18–21)? **3.** How will their behavior change as a result?

APPLY **1.** Have you had this "sanctuary" experience? Where? When? Are you different? **2.** What was Christ's role in providing "a substitute temple" while you were in "exile"?

OPEN **1.** Where do you go when you just want to get away from it all for a day? What or who do you take with you? **2.** Who in your family packs for a week, even though it's just an overnite trip? **3.** What big trips have you taken recently?

STUDY **1.** What are the people like to whom Ezekiel prophesies (vv. 1–2; Isa. 6:9–10)? **2.** Because they don't listen or see, what way does God use to communicate his message? Do you think such *sign* language will work? Why or why not? **3.** In the timing and sequence of this unfolding revelation, what is significant about: "The word of the LORD" coming to Ezekiel? Ezekiel's unquestioning obedience? Israel's questioning response (v. 9)? How are these related? **4.** Of all the things God tells Ezekiel to do in verses 3–16, what part seems most eye-catching or poignant? What is its symbolic meaning? Read Jeremiah 39:1–10 to see to what extent Ezekiel's words came true. **5.** What revelation unfolds next in verses 17–20? What do Ezekiel's symbolic acts mean this time? **6.** What proverbs does God say are popular in Israel (vv. 22,27)? What do they mean? How will God put an end to such false visions

[a]24 Or *Chaldea*

11:19 undivided heart. The opportunity for loyalty loomed ahead—but only as a result of repentance (Ps. 86:11).

12:8 In the morning the word ... came. The very next day God promptly evaluated the success of Ezekiel's unusual demonstration of obedience. Ezekiel had followed through with God's instruction (v. 7).

dusk and leave, and a hole will be dug in the wall for him to go
through. He will cover his face so that he cannot see the land. [13]I will
spread my net for him, and he will be caught in my snare; I will bring
him to Babylonia, the land of the Chaldeans, but he will not see it,
and there he will die. [14]I will scatter to the winds all those around
him—his staff and all his troops—and I will pursue them with drawn
sword.

[15]"They will know that I am the LORD, when I disperse them among
the nations and scatter them through the countries. [16]But I will spare
a few of them from the sword, famine and plague, so that in the nations where they go they may acknowledge all their detestable practices. Then they will know that I am the LORD."

[17]The word of the LORD came to me: [18]"Son of man, tremble as you
eat your food, and shudder in fear as you drink your water. [19]Say to
the people of the land: 'This is what the Sovereign LORD says about
those living in Jerusalem and in the land of Israel: They will eat their
food in anxiety and drink their water in despair, for their land will be
stripped of everything in it because of the violence of all who live
there. [20]The inhabited towns will be laid waste and the land will be
desolate. Then you will know that I am the LORD.' "

[21]The word of the LORD came to me: [22]"Son of man, what is this
proverb you have in the land of Israel: 'The days go by and every vision comes to nothing'? [23]Say to them, 'This is what the Sovereign
LORD says: I am going to put an end to this proverb, and they will no
longer quote it in Israel.' Say to them, 'The days are near when every
vision will be fulfilled. [24]For there will be no more false visions or flattering divinations among the people of Israel. [25]But I the LORD will
speak what I will, and it shall be fulfilled without delay. For in your
days, you rebellious house, I will fulfill whatever I say, declares the
Sovereign LORD.' "

[26]The word of the LORD came to me: [27]"Son of man, the house of
Israel is saying, 'The vision he sees is for many years from now, and
he prophesies about the distant future.'

[28]"Therefore say to them, 'This is what the Sovereign LORD says:
None of my words will be delayed any longer; whatever I say will be
fulfilled, declares the Sovereign LORD.' "

False Prophets Condemned

13 The word of the LORD came to me: [2]"Son of man, prophesy
against the prophets of Israel who are now prophesying. Say
to those who prophesy out of their own imagination: 'Hear the word
of the LORD! [3]This is what the Sovereign LORD says: Woe to the
foolish[a] prophets who follow their own spirit and have seen nothing!
[4]Your prophets, O Israel, are like jackals among ruins. [5]You have not
gone up to the breaks in the wall to repair it for the house of Israel so
that it will stand firm in the battle on the day of the LORD. [6]Their
visions are false and their divinations a lie. They say, "The LORD

[a]3 Or *wicked*

and human procrastination? How does this prove God is the Sovereign Lord?

APPLY 1. Read 2 Peter 3:3–13 for another answer to the problem mentioned in verses 22 and 27. Do you find it hard to wait for God to fulfill his promises? Why do you think he delays? **2.** What about the future causes you to tremble and shudder (vv. 17–20)? What promises of God reassure you?

OPEN 1. List all the professions that your group can think of—from palm readers to economic forecasters to weathermen—whose job it is to predict the future. **2.** Whose advice or warnings do you pay most attention to? Why? **3.** Have you ever had someone's prediction for you come true? On what was that prediction based?

STUDY 1. What is the basic message of the false prophets? How does it differ from Ezekiel's

12:18 tremble. Anxiety would soon characterize even the most menial tasks of everyday living (4:16).

12:27 years from now. The people thought the fulfillment was far off; it wasn't.

13:6 their words to be fulfilled. Accuracy was the mark of true prophets. False prophets weren't as good.

message? **2.** God uses a number of powerful images or metaphors to condemn the false prophets. What is meant here by "whitewashed walls" and "torrential rains" (vv. 10–16)? **3.** What props do the female false prophets use in their occult practices? What is the random effect of their evil actions (vv. 19,22)? **4.** Why would anyone listen to "lies" of false prophets? In Deuteronomy 18:14–22, what criteria does God give for distinguishing true prophets from false? **5.** What will God do to intervene and put a stop to this (vv. 20–23)? How will this prove that God is the sovereign Lord? **6.** How did Jesus distinguish between true and false prophets (Matt. 7:15–23; 23:13–32; 24:23–27)? How do his warnings compare with Ezekiel's? **7.** Can you think of any false prophets who are operating today? What is their message? How do you know they are false?

APPLY 1. God objected to false prophets who were hiding falseness like someone covering a shoddy wall with whitewash. What areas of your life are you most likely to "cover with whitewash": Your emotions—washing over your "negative" emotions like your anger and your pain? Your moral life—trying to look purer than you really are? Your failures—trying to pretend perfection? Your social relationships—trying to make like you care for people you actually detest? **2.** Judging by your reading habits and whom you consult with, are you more concerned with "what the future holds" or "who holds the future"? What are you doing to reduce your anxiety level?

declares," when the LORD has not sent them; yet they expect their words to be fulfilled. [7]Have you not seen false visions and uttered lying divinations when you say, "The LORD declares," though I have not spoken?

[8]" 'Therefore this is what the Sovereign LORD says: Because of your false words and lying visions, I am against you, declares the Sovereign LORD. [9]My hand will be against the prophets who see false visions and utter lying divinations. They will not belong to the council of my people or be listed in the records of the house of Israel, nor will they enter the land of Israel. Then you will know that I am the Sovereign LORD.

[10]" 'Because they lead my people astray, saying, "Peace," when there is no peace, and because, when a flimsy wall is built, they cover it with whitewash, [11]therefore tell those who cover it with whitewash that it is going to fall. Rain will come in torrents, and I will send hailstones hurtling down, and violent winds will burst forth. [12]When the wall collapses, will people not ask you, "Where is the whitewash you covered it with?"

[13]" 'Therefore this is what the Sovereign LORD says: In my wrath I will unleash a violent wind, and in my anger hailstones and torrents of rain will fall with destructive fury. [14]I will tear down the wall you have covered with whitewash and will level it to the ground so that its foundation will be laid bare. When it[a] falls, you will be destroyed in it; and you will know that I am the LORD. [15]So I will spend my wrath against the wall and against those who covered it with whitewash. I will say to you, "The wall is gone and so are those who whitewashed it, [16]those prophets of Israel who prophesied to Jerusalem and saw visions of peace for her when there was no peace, declares the Sovereign LORD." '

[17]"Now, son of man, set your face against the daughters of your people who prophesy out of their own imagination. Prophesy against them [18]and say, 'This is what the Sovereign LORD says: Woe to the women who sew magic charms on all their wrists and make veils of various lengths for their heads in order to ensnare people. Will you ensnare the lives of my people but preserve your own? [19]You have profaned me among my people for a few handfuls of barley and scraps of bread. By lying to my people, who listen to lies, you have killed those who should not have died and have spared those who should not live.

[20]" 'Therefore this is what the Sovereign LORD says: I am against your magic charms with which you ensnare people like birds and I will tear them from your arms; I will set free the people that you ensnare like birds. [21]I will tear off your veils and save my people from your hands, and they will no longer fall prey to your power. Then you will know that I am the LORD. [22]Because you disheartened the righteous with your lies, when I had brought them no grief, and because you encouraged the wicked not to turn from their evil ways and so

[a]14 Or *the city*

13:10 cover it with whitewash. A laborer used white paste to cover inconsistencies in a rock-hewn wall. Likewise, God's people covered over their problems. They focused on the appearances on the outside rather than the inside. God is concerned about the heart (1 Sam. 16:7).

13:11 Rain will come in torrents ... hailstones. Reverting back to the storm imagery, Ezekiel described how their sin would be exposed (1:4).

save their lives, [23]therefore you will no longer see false visions or practice divination. I will save my people from your hands. And then you will know that I am the LORD.' "

Idolaters Condemned

14 Some of the elders of Israel came to me and sat down in front of me. [2]Then the word of the LORD came to me: [3]"Son of man, these men have set up idols in their hearts and put wicked stumbling blocks before their faces. Should I let them inquire of me at all? [4]Therefore speak to them and tell them, 'This is what the Sovereign LORD says: When any Israelite sets up idols in his heart and puts a wicked stumbling block before his face and then goes to a prophet, I the LORD will answer him myself in keeping with his great idolatry. [5]I will do this to recapture the hearts of the people of Israel, who have all deserted me for their idols.'

[6]"Therefore say to the house of Israel, 'This is what the Sovereign LORD says: Repent! Turn from your idols and renounce all your detestable practices!

[7]" 'When any Israelite or any alien living in Israel separates himself from me and sets up idols in his heart and puts a wicked stumbling block before his face and then goes to a prophet to inquire of me, I the LORD will answer him myself. [8]I will set my face against that man and make him an example and a byword. I will cut him off from my people. Then you will know that I am the LORD.

[9]" 'And if the prophet is enticed to utter a prophecy, I the LORD have enticed that prophet, and I will stretch out my hand against him and destroy him from among my people Israel. [10]They will bear their guilt—the prophet will be as guilty as the one who consults him. [11]Then the people of Israel will no longer stray from me, nor will they defile themselves anymore with all their sins. They will be my people, and I will be their God, declares the Sovereign LORD.' "

Judgment Inescapable

[12]The word of the LORD came to me: [13]"Son of man, if a country sins against me by being unfaithful and I stretch out my hand against it to cut off its food supply and send famine upon it and kill its men and their animals, [14]even if these three men—Noah, Daniel[a] and Job—were in it, they could save only themselves by their righteousness, declares the Sovereign LORD.

[15]"Or if I send wild beasts through that country and they leave it childless and it becomes desolate so that no one can pass through it because of the beasts, [16]as surely as I live, declares the Sovereign LORD, even if these three men were in it, they could not save their

[a]14 Or *Danel*; the Hebrew spelling may suggest a person other than the prophet Daniel; also in verse 20.

OPEN Ever had a speaking part in a play? What did you like best about it? And least? Ever stumble over your lines? What happened?

STUDY 1. Who comes to see Ezekiel? What do you think they want? Why is God angry with them? **2.** What do you think is meant by the "idols in their hearts"? By "wicked stumbling blocks before their faces" (vv. 3,4,7; 3:20; 7:19)? **3.** What's so wrong with consulting the Lord's prophet when you also worship idols (vv. 4–5,7–8)? **4.** Why is the prophet who is consulted also liable? If God would never speak to an idolater, who then is the prophecy for? **5.** What then is significant about this first warning to "Repent!"?

APPLY 1. What kind of idols do you have in your heart today? **2.** What effect is mixed loyalties having on your relationship with God? What action does God want you to take in this regard?

OPEN Who is your favorite hero from modern history? Why? How are you like that person?

STUDY 1. Why do you suppose God picks these three heroes from Israel's history? What did each one do to become famous? **2.** What point does God make by mentioning Noah, Daniel and Job in this context? What had the people in Jerusalem evidently thought would spare them from God's judgment? On what similar hope did Abraham base his plea for Sodom (Gen. 18:16–33)? **3.** Will everyone in Jerusalem be

---

14:3 inquire. Pagans seeking advice from Ezekiel seemed hypocritical. Why consult two opposing forces?

14:4 stumbling block. The idolatrous people seemed bent on self-sabotage. They tripped on their own sin which resulted in death.

14:6 Repent! Turn. Ezekiel urged repentance while there was still time.

14:9 destroy him. The fewer distractions, the better off God's people would be. The sudden death of a false prophet distinguished the righteous from the rebellious.

14:14,20 Noah, Daniel and Job. Ezekiel imagined a scenario where even favored biblical characters would have no saving influence over such a wicked society. They could only save themselves. These great men of faith were probably used as examples because they sought after God's heart.

killed? If not, where will the survivors go? **4.** What will those who see them say about the mercy and justice of God's punishment? Why? How will this object lesson prove God is the Sovereign Lord?

APPLY 1. Of these three—Noah, Daniel and Job—who seems more heroic to you? Why? **2.** On what hero in the political or religious arena are you pinning your hopes? Or, are you captain of your own ship? **3.** In this chapter, what hope does God give you for surviving his future judgment?

own sons or daughters. They alone would be saved, but the land
would be desolate.

17"Or if I bring a sword against that country and say, 'Let the sword
pass throughout the land,' and I kill its men and their animals, 18as
surely as I live, declares the Sovereign LORD, even if these three men
were in it, they could not save their own sons or daughters. They
alone would be saved.

19"Or if I send a plague into that land and pour out my wrath upon
it through bloodshed, killing its men and their animals, 20as surely as
I live, declares the Sovereign LORD, even if Noah, Daniel and Job were
in it, they could save neither son nor daughter. They would save only
themselves by their righteousness.

21"For this is what the Sovereign LORD says: How much worse will
it be when I send against Jerusalem my four dreadful judgments—
sword and famine and wild beasts and plague—to kill its men and
their animals! 22Yet there will be some survivors—sons and daughters who will be brought out of it. They will come to you, and when
you see their conduct and their actions, you will be consoled regarding the disaster I have brought upon Jerusalem—every disaster I have
brought upon it. 23You will be consoled when you see their conduct
and their actions, for you will know that I have done nothing in it
without cause, declares the Sovereign LORD."

OPEN If you were to be made of wood, what kind of wood would you want to be: Balsam? Cedar? Ebony? Mahogany? Oak?

STUDY 1. What is vine wood good for? Why is that so shocking? How else are God's people like a "vine" (Ps. 80:8–11; Hosea 14:5–8) or a "peg" (Isa. 22:23–25)? **2.** Though they survived the fire of 597 B.C., what "fire will yet consume them"? How will this prove God is sovereign?

APPLY 1. When do you feel most useful? **2.** How can commitment to God help you feel even more useful?

Jerusalem, A Useless Vine

15 The word of the LORD came to me: 2"Son of man, how is the
wood of a vine better than that of a branch on any of the
trees in the forest? 3Is wood ever taken from it to make anything useful? Do they make pegs from it to hang things on? 4And after it is
thrown on the fire as fuel and the fire burns both ends and chars the
middle, is it then useful for anything? 5If it was not useful for anything when it was whole, how much less can it be made into something useful when the fire has burned it and it is charred?

6"Therefore this is what the Sovereign LORD says: As I have given
the wood of the vine among the trees of the forest as fuel for the fire,
so will I treat the people living in Jerusalem. 7I will set my face against
them. Although they have come out of the fire, the fire will yet consume them. And when I set my face against them, you will know that
I am the LORD. 8I will make the land desolate because they have been
unfaithful, declares the Sovereign LORD."

OPEN 1. What recent book or magazine have you bought, mostly because of its cover appeal? Any romance novels or tabloids? **2.** Of the TV personalities you know, which ones would you like to meet in person to see what beauty lies beneath the surface? **3.** If married: How did you and your mate get engaged? If single:

An Allegory of Unfaithful Jerusalem

16 The word of the LORD came to me: 2"Son of man, confront
Jerusalem with her detestable practices 3and say, 'This is
what the Sovereign LORD says to Jerusalem: Your ancestry and birth
were in the land of the Canaanites; your father was an Amorite and
your mother a Hittite. 4On the day you were born your cord was not
cut, nor were you washed with water to make you clean, nor were

15:2 wood of a vine. Ezekiel used sarcasm to make a point.

15:4 useful. Cut off from their divine source, Israel was ineffective (Ps. 80:8–13).

15:7 fire will yet consume them. The remaining inhabitants of Jerusalem considered escaping the initial wave of capture in 597 B.C. a close call. Yet, Jerusalem's total destruction was only a few years away.

16:3 Jerusalem. This city was also called the fortress of Zion. In some ways, rebellion was in the city's blood. Jerusalem remained a Canaanite hotspot until David completely conquered it (1 Chr. 11:4-9).

you rubbed with salt or wrapped in cloths. 5No one looked on you
with pity or had compassion enough to do any of these things for
you. Rather, you were thrown out into the open field, for on the day
you were born you were despised.
6" 'Then I passed by and saw you kicking about in your blood, and
as you lay there in your blood I said to you, "Live!"[a] 7I made you grow
like a plant of the field. You grew up and developed and became the
most beautiful of jewels.[b] Your breasts were formed and your hair
grew, you who were naked and bare.
8" 'Later I passed by, and when I looked at you and saw that you
were old enough for love, I spread the corner of my garment over you
and covered your nakedness. I gave you my solemn oath and entered
into a covenant with you, declares the Sovereign LORD, and you became mine.
9" 'I bathed[c] you with water and washed the blood from you and
put ointments on you. 10I clothed you with an embroidered dress and
put leather sandals on you. I dressed you in fine linen and covered
you with costly garments. 11I adorned you with jewelry: I put bracelets on your arms and a necklace around your neck, 12and I put a ring
on your nose, earrings on your ears and a beautiful crown on your
head. 13So you were adorned with gold and silver; your clothes were
of fine linen and costly fabric and embroidered cloth. Your food was
fine flour, honey and olive oil. You became very beautiful and rose to
be a queen. 14And your fame spread among the nations on account of
your beauty, because the splendor I had given you made your beauty
perfect, declares the Sovereign LORD.
15" 'But you trusted in your beauty and used your fame to become a
prostitute. You lavished your favors on anyone who passed by and
your beauty became his.[d] 16You took some of your garments to make
gaudy high places, where you carried on your prostitution. Such
things should not happen, nor should they ever occur. 17You also took
the fine jewelry I gave you, the jewelry made of my gold and silver,
and you made for yourself male idols and engaged in prostitution
with them. 18And you took your embroidered clothes to put on them,
and you offered my oil and incense before them. 19Also the food I
provided for you—the fine flour, olive oil and honey I gave you to
eat—you offered as fragrant incense before them. That is what happened, declares the Sovereign LORD.
20" 'And you took your sons and daughters whom you bore to me
and sacrificed them as food to the idols. Was your prostitution not
enough? 21You slaughtered my children and sacrificed them[e] to the
idols. 22In all your detestable practices and your prostitution you did
not remember the days of your youth, when you were naked and
bare, kicking about in your blood.
23" 'Woe! Woe to you, declares the Sovereign LORD. In addition to
all your other wickedness, 24you built a mound for yourself and made

[a]6 A few Hebrew manuscripts, Septuagint and Syriac; most Hebrew manuscripts *"Live!" And as you lay there in your blood I said to you, "Live!"* [b]7 Or *became mature* [c]9 Or *I had bathed* [d]15 Most Hebrew manuscripts; one Hebrew manuscript (see some Septuagint manuscripts) *by. Such a thing should not happen* [e]21 Or *and made them pass through ⌊the fire⌋*

How do you imagine making or receiving the marriage proposal?

STUDY 1. Who are the characters in this allegorical love story? Who do they represent? **2.** What about this woman's "ancestry and birth" is significant (v. 3)? **3.** What does the man do for the woman in the beginning of this story? What reference do you see here to childbirth? Puberty? Marriage? What one word sums up his desire for her (and God's desire for all people)? **4.** How does the woman respond to the man? What does she do now (vv. 15–19) with all the gifts he once gave her (vv. 10–14)? **5.** To what physical involvement (with fertility gods) and spiritual attitude does the man's accusation refer? **6.** How does she treat his children (vv. 20–21)? Is this act literal or figurative? Why do you think so (2 Kin. 17:17)? **7.** What does she do (physically and spiritually) with her neighbors and strangers (vv. 25–34)? What does she do this for? **8.** How will the husband punish his wife for her deeds (vv. 35–42; Deut. 22:20–24)? How will these actions make him feel? **9.** What kind of a relationship will they have in the future? Why do you think the "like mother, like daughter" illustration is an apt one (vv. 3,44–48)? What does she have in common with her "sisters"? How is she worse off? **10.** Does all this mean the woman (Jerusalem) will never again remember, much less recover, the "days of her youth"? Who has the last laugh and why? **11.** Does this story have a happy ending or a sad one? How so? What hope is there that the love of her youth, if not her innocence, will be restored to this woman (vv. 53–58)? **12.** How does this extended parable show God is the Sovereign Lord?

APPLY 1. How would you treat a wife who behaved like the woman in this story? Does God's response surprise you? Why or why not? **2.** In what way has God rescued you from a time when, like this woman, you felt abandoned and despised? **3.** What does this story say about God's father-like relationship to you?

16:6 Live! Jerusalem's existence was not due to luck or tenacity. God himself commanded the city's survival.

16:7 Your breasts were formed. Jerusalem came into her own and was quite desireable.

16:15 trusted in your beauty. God's gift to Jerusalem became a pitfall as Jerusalem asserted independence.

a lofty shrine in every public square. 25At the head of every street you
built your lofty shrines and degraded your beauty, offering your body
with increasing promiscuity to anyone who passed by. 26You engaged
in prostitution with the Egyptians, your lustful neighbors, and provoked me to anger with your increasing promiscuity. 27So I stretched
out my hand against you and reduced your territory; I gave you over
to the greed of your enemies, the daughters of the Philistines, who
were shocked by your lewd conduct. 28You engaged in prostitution
with the Assyrians too, because you were insatiable; and even after
that, you still were not satisfied. 29Then you increased your promiscuity to include Babylonia,[a] a land of merchants, but even with this
you were not satisfied.

30" 'How weak-willed you are, declares the Sovereign LORD, when
you do all these things, acting like a brazen prostitute! 31When you
built your mounds at the head of every street and made your lofty
shrines in every public square, you were unlike a prostitute, because
you scorned payment.

32" 'You adulterous wife! You prefer strangers to your own husband! 33Every prostitute receives a fee, but you give gifts to all your
lovers, bribing them to come to you from everywhere for your illicit
favors. 34So in your prostitution you are the opposite of others; no
one runs after you for your favors. You are the very opposite, for you
give payment and none is given to you.

35" 'Therefore, you prostitute, hear the word of the LORD! 36This is
what the Sovereign LORD says: Because you poured out your wealth[b]
and exposed your nakedness in your promiscuity with your lovers,
and because of all your detestable idols, and because you gave them
your children's blood, 37therefore I am going to gather all your lovers, with whom you found pleasure, those you loved as well as those
you hated. I will gather them against you from all around and will
strip you in front of them, and they will see all your nakedness. 38I
will sentence you to the punishment of women who commit adultery
and who shed blood; I will bring upon you the blood vengeance of my
wrath and jealous anger. 39Then I will hand you over to your lovers,
and they will tear down your mounds and destroy your lofty shrines.
They will strip you of your clothes and take your fine jewelry and
leave you naked and bare. 40They will bring a mob against you, who
will stone you and hack you to pieces with their swords. 41They will
burn down your houses and inflict punishment on you in the sight of
many women. I will put a stop to your prostitution, and you will no
longer pay your lovers. 42Then my wrath against you will subside and
my jealous anger will turn away from you; I will be calm and no longer angry.

43" 'Because you did not remember the days of your youth but enraged me with all these things, I will surely bring down on your head
what you have done, declares the Sovereign LORD. Did you not add
lewdness to all your other detestable practices?

44" 'Everyone who quotes proverbs will quote this proverb about

[a] 29 Or *Chaldea* [b] 36 Or *lust*

16:37 gather them against you. God's sovereignty over the scenario allowed him to turn Jerusalem's so-called lovers into enemies.

16:44 Jerusalem was unable to shake its pagan past. Jerusalem shared a common bond with the rebellious people who first inhabited the land.

you: "Like mother, like daughter." 45 You are a true daughter of your
mother, who despised her husband and her children; and you are a
true sister of your sisters, who despised their husbands and their
children. Your mother was a Hittite and your father an Amorite. 46 Your
older sister was Samaria, who lived to the north of you with her
daughters; and your younger sister, who lived to the south of you
with her daughters, was Sodom. 47 You not only walked in their ways
and copied their detestable practices, but in all your ways you soon
became more depraved than they. 48 As surely as I live, declares the
Sovereign LORD, your sister Sodom and her daughters never did what
you and your daughters have done.

49 " 'Now this was the sin of your sister Sodom: She and her daughters were arrogant, overfed and unconcerned; they did not help the
poor and needy. 50 They were haughty and did detestable things before me. Therefore I did away with them as you have seen. 51 Samaria
did not commit half the sins you did. You have done more detestable
things than they, and have made your sisters seem righteous by all
these things you have done. 52 Bear your disgrace, for you have furnished some justification for your sisters. Because your sins were
more vile than theirs, they appear more righteous than you. So then,
be ashamed and bear your disgrace, for you have made your sisters
appear righteous.

53 " 'However, I will restore the fortunes of Sodom and her daughters and of Samaria and her daughters, and your fortunes along with
them, 54 so that you may bear your disgrace and be ashamed of all you
have done in giving them comfort. 55 And your sisters, Sodom with her
daughters and Samaria with her daughters, will return to what they
were before; and you and your daughters will return to what you
were before. 56 You would not even mention your sister Sodom in the
day of your pride, 57 before your wickedness was uncovered. Even so,
you are now scorned by the daughters of Edom[a] and all her neighbors and the daughters of the Philistines—all those around you who
despise you. 58 You will bear the consequences of your lewdness and
your detestable practices, declares the LORD.

59 " 'This is what the Sovereign LORD says: I will deal with you as
you deserve, because you have despised my oath by breaking the
covenant. 60 Yet I will remember the covenant I made with you in the
days of your youth, and I will establish an everlasting covenant with
you. 61 Then you will remember your ways and be ashamed when you
receive your sisters, both those who are older than you and those
who are younger. I will give them to you as daughters, but not on the
basis of my covenant with you. 62 So I will establish my covenant with
you, and you will know that I am the LORD. 63 Then, when I make
atonement for you for all you have done, you will remember and be
ashamed and never again open your mouth because of your humiliation, declares the Sovereign LORD.' "

[a]57 Many Hebrew manuscripts and Syriac; most Hebrew manuscripts, Septuagint and Vulgate *Aram*

16:47 more depraved than they. Comparing a city to the destruction in Sodom was the ultimate insult (Jer. 23:14). Ezekiel's graphic contrast put Jerusalem's sin in perspective.

16:49 they did not help the poor and needy. Social injustice was at the top of the list. Sodom focused completely on her own needs and didn't care for those who needed help.

16:56 your pride. Ezekiel reminisced about Jerusalem's sense of superiority over Sodom. The name Sodom was never even mentioned for fear of lowering itself to Sodom's standards.

OPEN **1.** What's your favorite fable of Aesop? Why do you like it? **2.** If you had to liken yourself to an animal to tell a fable about yourself, what animal would you pick and why?

STUDY **1.** Retell the fable of the two eagles and the vine in your own words. What does each element represent: Great eagle (vv. 3,12)? Lebanon (vv. 3,12)? Cedar (v. 3)? Topmost shoot (vv. 4,12)? Land of merchants (vv. 4,12; 16:29)? Seed planted (vv. 5,13)? Low, spreading vine (vv. 6,14; 15:2)? Another great eagle (vv. 7,17)? Sent out its roots toward him (vv. 7, 15)? East wind (vv. 10,21)? **2.** What is the punch line of this fable? Read 2 Chronicles 36 for another account of what happened. What was wrong with Zedekiah's actions? **3.** What new allegory does God develop from the elements of the previous story (vv. 22–24)? What does he promise to do with the very top of the cedar tree? What does this mean for Israel? **4.** What do you think Jesus meant by similar imagery in his kingdom parables (Matt. 13:31–32)?

APPLY **1.** As you consider the forces at work in the world today, what hope do you find in this parable? How might this help you deal with fear, cynicism and discouragement? **2.** What agreements are you party to that God might care about? Are you fulfilling them or forgetting them? How so? **3.** When has God helped you to flourish when you felt like "a dry tree" (v. 24)?

Two Eagles and a Vine

17 The word of the LORD came to me: 2"Son of man, set forth an
allegory and tell the house of Israel a parable. 3Say to them,
'This is what the Sovereign LORD says: A great eagle with powerful
wings, long feathers and full plumage of varied colors came to Lebanon. Taking hold of the top of a cedar, 4he broke off its topmost shoot
and carried it away to a land of merchants, where he planted it in a
city of traders.
5" 'He took some of the seed of your land and put it in fertile soil.
He planted it like a willow by abundant water, 6and it sprouted and
became a low, spreading vine. Its branches turned toward him, but its
roots remained under it. So it became a vine and produced branches
and put out leafy boughs.
7" 'But there was another great eagle with powerful wings and full
plumage. The vine now sent out its roots toward him from the plot
where it was planted and stretched out its branches to him for water.
8It had been planted in good soil by abundant water so that it would
produce branches, bear fruit and become a splendid vine.'
9"Say to them, 'This is what the Sovereign LORD says: Will it thrive?
Will it not be uprooted and stripped of its fruit so that it withers? All
its new growth will wither. It will not take a strong arm or many people to pull it up by the roots. 10Even if it is transplanted, will it thrive?
Will it not wither completely when the east wind strikes it—wither
away in the plot where it grew?' "
11Then the word of the LORD came to me: 12"Say to this rebellious
house, 'Do you not know what these things mean?' Say to them: 'The
king of Babylon went to Jerusalem and carried off her king and her
nobles, bringing them back with him to Babylon. 13Then he took a
member of the royal family and made a treaty with him, putting him
under oath. He also carried away the leading men of the land, 14so
that the kingdom would be brought low, unable to rise again, surviving only by keeping his treaty. 15But the king rebelled against him by
sending his envoys to Egypt to get horses and a large army. Will he
succeed? Will he who does such things escape? Will he break the
treaty and yet escape?
16" 'As surely as I live, declares the Sovereign LORD, he shall die in
Babylon, in the land of the king who put him on the throne, whose
oath he despised and whose treaty he broke. 17Pharaoh with his
mighty army and great horde will be of no help to him in war, when
ramps are built and siege works erected to destroy many lives. 18He
despised the oath by breaking the covenant. Because he had given
his hand in pledge and yet did all these things, he shall not escape.
19" 'Therefore this is what the Sovereign LORD says: As surely as I
live, I will bring down on his head my oath that he despised and my
covenant that he broke. 20I will spread my net for him, and he will be
caught in my snare. I will bring him to Babylon and execute judgment
upon him there because he was unfaithful to me. 21All his fleeing
troops will fall by the sword, and the survivors will be scattered to the
winds. Then you will know that I the LORD have spoken.

17:2–10 The prophet contrasted the imagery of a vine (Judah), two powerful eagles (Babylon (v. 3), and Egypt (v. 7)). He demonstrated how Judah's varying allegiances played a role in Judah's downfall. King Zedekiah (v. 15) recruited Egypt to help rebel against Babylon (2 Kin. 24:20) which proved a failure. Ezekiel predicted the king's revolt and the resulting Babylonian retribution nearly three years in advance (vv. 19–21).

22" 'This is what the Sovereign LORD says: I myself will take a shoot
from the very top of a cedar and plant it; I will break off a tender sprig
from its topmost shoots and plant it on a high and lofty mountain.
23On the mountain heights of Israel I will plant it; it will produce
branches and bear fruit and become a splendid cedar. Birds of every
kind will nest in it; they will find shelter in the shade of its branches.
24All the trees of the field will know that I the LORD bring down the tall
tree and make the low tree grow tall. I dry up the green tree and make
the dry tree flourish.

" 'I the LORD have spoken, and I will do it.' "

The Soul Who Sins Will Die

18 The word of the LORD came to me: 2"What do you people mean
by quoting this proverb about the land of Israel:

" 'The fathers eat sour grapes,
and the children's teeth are set on edge'?

3"As surely as I live, declares the Sovereign LORD, you will no longer
quote this proverb in Israel. 4For every living soul belongs to me, the
father as well as the son—both alike belong to me. The soul who sins
is the one who will die.

5"Suppose there is a righteous man
who does what is just and right.
6He does not eat at the mountain shrines
or look to the idols of the house of Israel.
He does not defile his neighbor's wife
or lie with a woman during her period.
7He does not oppress anyone,
but returns what he took in pledge for a loan.
He does not commit robbery
but gives his food to the hungry
and provides clothing for the naked.
8He does not lend at usury
or take excessive interest.[a]
He withholds his hand from doing wrong
and judges fairly between man and man.
9He follows my decrees
and faithfully keeps my laws.
That man is righteous;
he will surely live,
declares the Sovereign LORD.

10"Suppose he has a violent son, who sheds blood or does any of
these other things[b] 11(though the father has done none of them):

[a]8 Or *take interest*; similarly in verses 13 and 17 [b]10 Or *things to a brother*

OPEN 1. What quotable quote or favorite saying do (or did) your parents live by? What did it mean? **2.** If your philosophy of life were likewise summed up in a favorite slogan or saying of yours, what would that be? What do you like about it? **3.** In what two ways (proverbial or otherwise) are you like, and unlike, your dad or mom?

STUDY 1. What was the original meaning of this (still popular) saying about "eating sour grapes" and "setting your teeth on edge"? Why do you suppose that saying was so popular in Israel (Jer. 31:29)? **2.** How does this saying compare or contrast to an earlier one, "Like mother, like daughter" (16:44)? **3.** How might it relate to the people whose way of thinking is expressed in chapter 14? **4.** What false ideas put forth in this three-generation pattern does the Lord oppose with a divine oath (vv. 3–4)? **5.** What alternative standard for judgment does the Sovereign Lord swear by? (Note: "Soul," as used here, connotes "life" or "person," not something distinct from the body.) **6.** What point does listing both the deeds of the righteous and the wicked *affirm*? What point does it *refute*? Would a different listing of actions God rewards and punishes accomplish the same purpose? Why do you think so? **7.** In the lists given here, what is particularly germane to the thrust of Ezekiel's prophecy so far? **8.** What *guilt* does God want each party to assume? Why? What *action* does God want each party to take? Why? **9.** How does God remain just in forgiving sinners

17:22 I myself ... will break. God would prove to be the security Judah so desperately sought. **shoot.** Jesus Christ, from the Davidic line, would serve over this restored kingdom.

18:2 A popular saying that a child could suffer blame for a parent's sins.

18:4 every living soul belongs to me. God contrasted a common saying with his sovereign command. Individuals would be accountable to God for their own sin.

18:9 he will surely live. Ezekiel gives the decree of God about the physical, not eternal, context of life and death (Deut. 30:15–20). He goes on to further illustrate how righteousness is rewarded on its own merit, despite family history.

who repent? Instead, who is truly "unjust"? **10.** How do you think God feels when someone dies in his or her sins?

APPLY 1. When have you blamed your parent(s) for your own bad behavior? What different attitude does this chapter call you to have? **2.** In what ways have you blamed yourself for the behaviors of an adult child? What insight does this chapter have for you about that practice? **3.** Can a person acknowledge that faulty parenting influence misbehavior, and yet encourage people to take responsibility for their own actions? How easy or hard is it for you to take responsibility for your own actions and repent?

"He eats at the mountain shrines.
He defiles his neighbor's wife.
12 He oppresses the poor and needy.
He commits robbery.
He does not return what he took in pledge.
He looks to the idols.
He does detestable things.
13 He lends at usury and takes excessive interest.

Will such a man live? He will not! Because he has done all these
detestable things, he will surely be put to death and his blood will be
on his own head.

14 "But suppose this son has a son who sees all the sins his father
commits, and though he sees them, he does not do such things:

15 "He does not eat at the mountain shrines
  or look to the idols of the house of Israel.
He does not defile his neighbor's wife.
16 He does not oppress anyone
  or require a pledge for a loan.
He does not commit robbery
  but gives his food to the hungry
  and provides clothing for the naked.
17 He withholds his hand from sin[a]
  and takes no usury or excessive interest.
He keeps my laws and follows my decrees.

He will not die for his father's sin; he will surely live. 18 But his father
will die for his own sin, because he practiced extortion, robbed his
brother and did what was wrong among his people.

19 "Yet you ask, 'Why does the son not share the guilt of his father?'
Since the son has done what is just and right and has been careful to
keep all my decrees, he will surely live. 20 The soul who sins is the one
who will die. The son will not share the guilt of the father, nor will the
father share the guilt of the son. The righteousness of the righteous
man will be credited to him, and the wickedness of the wicked will be
charged against him.

21 "But if a wicked man turns away from all the sins he has committed and keeps all my decrees and does what is just and right, he will
surely live; he will not die. 22 None of the offenses he has committed
will be remembered against him. Because of the righteous things he
has done, he will live. 23 Do I take any pleasure in the death of the
wicked? declares the Sovereign LORD. Rather, am I not pleased when
they turn from their ways and live?

24 "But if a righteous man turns from his righteousness and commits sin and does the same detestable things the wicked man does,
will he live? None of the righteous things he has done will be remembered. Because of the unfaithfulness he is guilty of and because of
the sins he has committed, he will die.

[a]17 Septuagint (see also verse 8); Hebrew *from the poor*

18:21 he will not die. Through repentance, a wicked person changed course.

25 "Yet you say, 'The way of the Lord is not just.' Hear, O house of
Israel: Is my way unjust? Is it not your ways that are unjust? 26 If a
righteous man turns from his righteousness and commits sin, he will
die for it; because of the sin he has committed he will die. 27 But if a
wicked man turns away from the wickedness he has committed and
does what is just and right, he will save his life. 28 Because he considers all the offenses he has committed and turns away from them, he
will surely live; he will not die. 29 Yet the house of Israel says, 'The way
of the Lord is not just.' Are my ways unjust, O house of Israel? Is it
not your ways that are unjust?

30 "Therefore, O house of Israel, I will judge you, each one according to his ways, declares the Sovereign LORD. Repent! Turn away from
all your offenses; then sin will not be your downfall. 31 Rid yourselves
of all the offenses you have committed, and get a new heart and a
new spirit. Why will you die, O house of Israel? 32 For I take no pleasure in the death of anyone, declares the Sovereign LORD. Repent and
live!

A Lament for Israel's Princes

19 "Take up a lament concerning the princes of Israel 2 and say:

" 'What a lioness was your mother
among the lions!
She lay down among the young lions
and reared her cubs.
3 She brought up one of her cubs,
and he became a strong lion.
He learned to tear the prey
and he devoured men.
4 The nations heard about him,
and he was trapped in their pit.
They led him with hooks
to the land of Egypt.

5 " 'When she saw her hope unfulfilled,
her expectation gone,
she took another of her cubs
and made him a strong lion.
6 He prowled among the lions,
for he was now a strong lion.
He learned to tear the prey
and he devoured men.
7 He broke down[a] their strongholds
and devastated their towns.
The land and all who were in it
were terrified by his roaring.

[a]7 Targum (see Septuagint); Hebrew *He knew*

OPEN 1. Of all the stories you've heard your parents or grandparents tell about "the good ol' days," which one sticks in your mind? **2.** Who is your favorite political cartoonist? What satirical cartoon lamenting the signs of the times still sticks in your mind? Why?

STUDY 1. What is a "lament"? How might its use in funerals apply here? **2.** This chapter is also an allegory, similar in content to chapter 17, with an application in the events found in 2 Kings 23:31–24:20. What then is your best guess at the meaning of these symbolic elements: Lioness ... your mother ... a vine (vv. 2,10; 15:2; 17:7)? One of her cubs ... devoured men ... brought to Egypt (vv. 3–4; 2 Kin. 23:31–34)? Another of her cubs ... brought to Babylon (vv. 5–9; 2 Kin. 24:8,15)? East wind (v. 12; 17:10)? Desert (v. 13)? Fire ... one of its main branches (v. 14; 2 Kin. 24:20)? **3.** Put these puzzle pieces all together—is the picture you get just a sad funeral song about the destruction of Jerusalem and its last kings, or does this puzzling lament contain any hints that the tragedy was their fault and came as God's judgment on them? **4.** Why do you think God inspires a lament for a few evil kings? How might this lament be a particular illustration of the general teaching in chapter 18?

18:32 I take no pleasure in the death. In this summary statement, Ezekiel revealed the center of God's character. God is consistent, not capricious, in his judgment. God is not willing for any to perish (2 Peter 3:9).

19:1 princes of Israel. Ezekiel rehearsed a mournful poem lamenting the fate of all the wicked people in Jerusalem.

19:3–14 Ezekiel used a pair of allegories to illustrate Jerusalem's demise. The cubs symbolized kings Jehoahaz (v. 3) and Zedekiah (v. 5) who were taken into exile in Babylon. The story of the vine (vv. 10–14) parallels Judah's fiery rebellion that led to its uprooting.

5. How would you update the political cartoon or allegorical lament of chapter 19, so that it fits your current situation?

APPLY 1. What do *you* lament? What does God lament? What difference do you see between what breaks your heart and what breaks his? **2.** What can you do to be more a person "after God's own heart," even in your laments?

OPEN 1. How far back do you know your family tree? Who is your favorite ancestor? Why? **2.** What incident from your family history tells us what you'd like your family name to be noted for?

STUDY 1. What sets this chapter up as distinct from the five previous ones? As similar to chapters 1 and 8? **2.** Imagine this unfolding revelation as a four-act play: "Curtain rise" (vv. 1–4); "Act I" (vv. 5–9); "Act II" (vv. 10–17); "Act III" (vv. 18–26); "Act IV" (vv. 27–29). What titles would you give to each act? **3.** A full cycle of four "scenes" or seasons may be seen in all but the fourth act. What repeated pattern do you see in the first three acts? **4.** *When they were in Egypt* (vv. 5–9), how did God reveal himself to Israel? How did they rebel? What display of wrath resulted? Why didn't God de-

8 Then the nations came against him,
those from regions round about.
They spread their net for him,
and he was trapped in their pit.
9 With hooks they pulled him into a cage
and brought him to the king of Babylon.
They put him in prison,
so his roar was heard no longer
on the mountains of Israel.

10 " 'Your mother was like a vine in your vineyard[a]
planted by the water;
it was fruitful and full of branches
because of abundant water.
11 Its branches were strong,
fit for a ruler's scepter.
It towered high
above the thick foliage,
conspicuous for its height
and for its many branches.
12 But it was uprooted in fury
and thrown to the ground.
The east wind made it shrivel,
it was stripped of its fruit;
its strong branches withered
and fire consumed them.
13 Now it is planted in the desert,
in a dry and thirsty land.
14 Fire spread from one of its main[b] branches
and consumed its fruit.
No strong branch is left on it
fit for a ruler's scepter.'

This is a lament and is to be used as a lament."

Rebellious Israel

20 In the seventh year, in the fifth month on the tenth day, some
of the elders of Israel came to inquire of the LORD, and they
sat down in front of me.
2 Then the word of the LORD came to me: 3 "Son of man, speak to the
elders of Israel and say to them, 'This is what the Sovereign LORD
says: Have you come to inquire of me? As surely as I live, I will not let
you inquire of me, declares the Sovereign LORD.'
4 "Will you judge them? Will you judge them, son of man? Then confront them with the detestable practices of their fathers 5 and say to
them: 'This is what the Sovereign LORD says: On the day I chose
Israel, I swore with uplifted hand to the descendants of the house of
Jacob and revealed myself to them in Egypt. With uplifted hand I said
to them, "I am the LORD your God." 6 On that day I swore to them that
I would bring them out of Egypt into a land I had searched out for
them, a land flowing with milk and honey, the most beautiful of all
lands. 7 And I said to them, "Each of you, get rid of the vile images you

[a] *10* Two Hebrew manuscripts; most Hebrew manuscripts *your blood* [b] *14* Or *from under its*

have set your eyes on, and do not defile yourselves with the idols of Egypt. I am the LORD your God."

[8]" 'But they rebelled against me and would not listen to me; they did not get rid of the vile images they had set their eyes on, nor did they forsake the idols of Egypt. So I said I would pour out my wrath on them and spend my anger against them in Egypt. [9]But for the sake of my name I did what would keep it from being profaned in the eyes of the nations they lived among and in whose sight I had revealed myself to the Israelites by bringing them out of Egypt. [10]Therefore I led them out of Egypt and brought them into the desert. [11]I gave them my decrees and made known to them my laws, for the man who obeys them will live by them. [12]Also I gave them my Sabbaths as a sign between us, so they would know that I the LORD made them holy.

[13]" 'Yet the people of Israel rebelled against me in the desert. They did not follow my decrees but rejected my laws—although the man who obeys them will live by them—and they utterly desecrated my Sabbaths. So I said I would pour out my wrath on them and destroy them in the desert. [14]But for the sake of my name I did what would keep it from being profaned in the eyes of the nations in whose sight I had brought them out. [15]Also with uplifted hand I swore to them in the desert that I would not bring them into the land I had given them—a land flowing with milk and honey, most beautiful of all lands— [16]because they rejected my laws and did not follow my decrees and desecrated my Sabbaths. For their hearts were devoted to their idols. [17]Yet I looked on them with pity and did not destroy them or put an end to them in the desert. [18]I said to their children in the desert, "Do not follow the statutes of your fathers or keep their laws or defile yourselves with their idols. [19]I am the LORD your God; follow my decrees and be careful to keep my laws. [20]Keep my Sabbaths holy, that they may be a sign between us. Then you will know that I am the LORD your God."

[21]" 'But the children rebelled against me: They did not follow my decrees, they were not careful to keep my laws—although the man who obeys them will live by them—and they desecrated my Sabbaths. So I said I would pour out my wrath on them and spend my anger against them in the desert. [22]But I withheld my hand, and for the sake of my name I did what would keep it from being profaned in the eyes of the nations in whose sight I had brought them out. [23]Also with uplifted hand I swore to them in the desert that I would disperse them among the nations and scatter them through the countries, [24]because they had not obeyed my laws but had rejected my decrees and desecrated my Sabbaths, and their eyes ⌞lusted⌟ after their fathers' idols. [25]I also gave them over to statutes that were not good and laws they could not live by; [26]I let them become defiled through their gifts—the sacrifice of every firstborn[a]—that I might fill them with horror so they would know that I am the LORD.'

[a]26 Or *—making every firstborn pass through ⌞the fire⌟*

stroy them there? **5.** Likewise in the desert (vv. 10–26), what did God do for Israel? How did they treat him? What was God's response? Why did he reconsider pouring out his wrath? **6.** Were the children of that desert generation any different from their parents? How did God treat them? Why? **7.** What does it mean that those who keep or obey God's laws "will live by them" (vv. 11,13,21)? Is law-keeping a *way of salvation* for the *lost* (Rom. 10:5; Gal. 3:12)? Or is law-keeping *a way of life* for the *redeemed* (Ex. 19:6; Lev, 18:2–5)? **8.** In practical terms, what does it mean to "desecrate my Sabbath" (vv. 13,16,21,24)? What is the point of keeping the Sabbath? **9.** How does this timeless revelation prove God is sovereign?

APPLY 1. Why do you think God is so concerned for his name or reputation? How is God's name dragged through the mud every time his people rebel? **2.** What "practices of your parents" are you seeking to follow in your life? What "practices of your parents" are you seeking to avoid duplicating?

20:9 Other nations watched in curious fascination at the turn of events in Israel.

20:13 desecrated my Sabbaths. God established the Sabbath as a weekly gift of rest to his people (Ex. 20:8–11). However, the people proved ungrateful and unconcerned to use it the way God had intended.

20:26 fill them with horror. Child sacrifice represented the height of Judah's adherence to pagan religions. God's intent was for his people to become sickened by their own sin.

27"Therefore, son of man, speak to the people of Israel and say to them, 'This is what the Sovereign LORD says: In this also your fathers blasphemed me by forsaking me: 28When I brought them into the land I had sworn to give them and they saw any high hill or any leafy tree, there they offered their sacrifices, made offerings that provoked me to anger, presented their fragrant incense and poured out their drink offerings. 29Then I said to them: What is this high place you go to?' " (It is called Bamah[a] to this day.)

Judgment and Restoration

30"Therefore say to the house of Israel: 'This is what the Sovereign LORD says: Will you defile yourselves the way your fathers did and lust after their vile images? 31When you offer your gifts—the sacrifice of your sons in[b] the fire—you continue to defile yourselves with all your idols to this day. Am I to let you inquire of me, O house of Israel? As surely as I live, declares the Sovereign LORD, I will not let you inquire of me.

32" 'You say, "We want to be like the nations, like the peoples of the world, who serve wood and stone." But what you have in mind will never happen. 33As surely as I live, declares the Sovereign LORD, I will rule over you with a mighty hand and an outstretched arm and with outpoured wrath. 34I will bring you from the nations and gather you from the countries where you have been scattered—with a mighty hand and an outstretched arm and with outpoured wrath. 35I will bring you into the desert of the nations and there, face to face, I will execute judgment upon you. 36As I judged your fathers in the desert of the land of Egypt, so I will judge you, declares the Sovereign LORD. 37I will take note of you as you pass under my rod, and I will bring you into the bond of the covenant. 38I will purge you of those who revolt and rebel against me. Although I will bring them out of the land where they are living, yet they will not enter the land of Israel. Then you will know that I am the LORD.

39" 'As for you, O house of Israel, this is what the Sovereign LORD says: Go and serve your idols, every one of you! But afterward you will surely listen to me and no longer profane my holy name with your gifts and idols. 40For on my holy mountain, the high mountain of Israel, declares the Sovereign LORD, there in the land the entire house of Israel will serve me, and there I will accept them. There I will require your offerings and your choice gifts,[c] along with all your holy sacrifices. 41I will accept you as fragrant incense when I bring you out from the nations and gather you from the countries where you have been scattered, and I will show myself holy among you in the sight of the nations. 42Then you will know that I am the LORD, when I bring you into the land of Israel, the land I had sworn with uplifted hand to give to your fathers. 43There you will remember your conduct and all the actions by which you have defiled yourselves, and you will loathe

[a]29 *Bamah* means *high place.* [b]31 Or *—making your sons pass through* [c]40 Or *and the gifts of your firstfruits*

OPEN 1. What wears out your patience more: Training a dog to obey? Training your child to obey? Learning to obey yourself? **2.** After you've been impatient, how do you calm down?

STUDY 1. What is the point of the comparisons in verses 30–32 and the irony in verse 39: How is Israel like (or unlike) her "fathers"? And "the nations"? What sins of this generation truly provoke the Lord? **2.** In what ways will the future judgment of God be reminiscent of the Exodus (vv. 33–38)? **3.** Who is God telling, "Go and serve your idols" (v. 39): The rebels of verse 38? The purified Israel of verse 40? **4.** What will be different about the way God treats this generation from the ones that have gone before (vv. 40–44)? **5.** What, ultimately, will result from God's punishment? **6.** How will God's particular way of restoring Israel show him to be the Sovereign Lord? **7.** What do you learn from this passage (vv. 30–44) about God's character and plan of salvation? About God's *permissive* will and his *perfect* will? **8.** As "fire" commonly refers to an invading enemy, and "forest" refers to Judah in the south, what is God saying here (vv. 45–49)? How do "green" and "dry" trees fare (17:24)? **9.** Do the hearers heed this warning? Why not?

APPLY 1. Who are you trying to be like right now in your life (v. 32): Like your father or mother? Like a mentor? Like a famous personality? Is being like that person consistent with being like Christ? **2.** What have you seen in your life or in your country that calls you to take God's wrath seriously (v. 49)?

20:30 Judah's shaky family tree continued to produce bad fruit. Like generations before, rebellion was rampant.

20:32 will never happen. Forget it! God would not release his people from his loving grip.

20:39 But afterward. At the end of a rebellious streak, God expected the house of Israel to return to him.

yourselves for all the evil you have done. 44You will know that I am
the LORD, when I deal with you for my name's sake and not according
to your evil ways and your corrupt practices, O house of Israel, declares the Sovereign LORD.' "

Prophecy Against the South

45The word of the LORD came to me: 46"Son of man, set your face
toward the south; preach against the south and prophesy against the
forest of the southland. 47Say to the southern forest: 'Hear the word
of the LORD. This is what the Sovereign LORD says: I am about to set
fire to you, and it will consume all your trees, both green and dry. The
blazing flame will not be quenched, and every face from south to
north will be scorched by it. 48Everyone will see that I the LORD have
kindled it; it will not be quenched.' "

49Then I said, "Ah, Sovereign LORD! They are saying of me, 'Isn't he
just telling parables?' "

Babylon, God's Sword of Judgment

21 The word of the LORD came to me: 2"Son of man, set your face
against Jerusalem and preach against the sanctuary. Prophesy against the land of Israel 3and say to her: 'This is what the LORD
says: I am against you. I will draw my sword from its scabbard and
cut off from you both the righteous and the wicked. 4Because I am
going to cut off the righteous and the wicked, my sword will be
unsheathed against everyone from south to north. 5Then all people
will know that I the LORD have drawn my sword from its scabbard; it
will not return again.'

6"Therefore groan, son of man! Groan before them with broken
heart and bitter grief. 7And when they ask you, 'Why are you groaning?' you shall say, 'Because of the news that is coming. Every heart
will melt and every hand go limp; every spirit will become faint and
every knee become as weak as water.' It is coming! It will surely take
place, declares the Sovereign LORD."

8The word of the LORD came to me: 9"Son of man, prophesy and
say, 'This is what the Lord says:

" 'A sword, a sword,
sharpened and polished—
10sharpened for the slaughter,
polished to flash like lightning!

" 'Shall we rejoice in the scepter of my son ⌞Judah⌟? The sword despises every such stick.

11" 'The sword is appointed to be polished,
to be grasped with the hand;
it is sharpened and polished,
made ready for the hand of the slayer.
12Cry out and wail, son of man,
for it is against my people;
it is against all the princes of Israel.

OPEN 1. As a child, did you have "gun fights" and "sword fights"? **2.** What kind of things make you cry more: Birthdays, weddings or funerals? Saying good-bye or saying hello? Seeing bad news on TV or hearing good news? **3.** What accidents have you had with a sharp cutting instrument? What scars do you have to show for it?

STUDY 1. In these five "sword oracles," what is the overall intent and impact of this sharp metaphor on Ezekiel? On his audience? On God himself? **2.** To what or whom does the sword refer (vv. 3,19)? What does this tell you about God's use of human instruments to execute his divine purpose? **3.** Why will both the righteous and the wicked die in this invasion (v. 4)? How does this square with the teaching of chapter 18? How does John 11:25–26 help believers resolve this apparent contradiction? **4.** How will people respond to news of this invasion (vv. 6–7,12,15)? Compare their response to God's (18:23)? **5.** What symbols of royalty do you see (vv. 10,13)? What will the sword do to them? What do these actions represent? **6.** In verses 18–32, Ezekiel is supposed to make a model of a road with a fork in it. What lies at the end of each road? How will the king of Babylon decide which fork to take? What false hope do those in Judah loyal to Nebuchadnezzar cling to (vv. 10,23; 17:14–15)? Why are they guilty (v. 24)? **7.** What ruinous reversal will

---

21:3 my sword ... cut off ... the wicked. God would soon use Babylon to carry out his wrath. Jerusalem's destruction would be an impartial fate.

21:9 sword. Ezekiel referenced battle imagery to indicate Jerusalem's pending siege and destruction. This was actually written as a song.

happen later (586 B.C.) to the "prince" (vv. 25–27)? When will this Davidic kingship be restored? **8.** What will happen later to those Ammonites on the other fork (vv. 28–32)? By whom? Why at this time (25:1–7)?

APPLY 1. What do you see around you that causes you to have a "broken heart and bitter grief"? **2.** In what ways are you at a "fork in the road" right now wondering which way God will lead you? **3.** Have you ever experienced a punishment from God? Or are you hoping God's sword took the other turn at the fork in the road, never to return your way again? What is your basis for hoping that?

They are thrown to the sword
along with my people.
Therefore beat your breast.

13" 'Testing will surely come. And what if the scepter ⌊of Judah⌋, which the sword despises, does not continue? declares the Sovereign LORD.'

14"So then, son of man, prophesy
and strike your hands together.
Let the sword strike twice,
even three times.
It is a sword for slaughter—
a sword for great slaughter,
closing in on them from every side.
15So that hearts may melt
and the fallen be many,
I have stationed the sword for slaughter[a]
at all their gates.
Oh! It is made to flash like lightning,
it is grasped for slaughter.
16O sword, slash to the right,
then to the left,
wherever your blade is turned.
17I too will strike my hands together,
and my wrath will subside.
I the LORD have spoken."

18The word of the LORD came to me: 19"Son of man, mark out two
roads for the sword of the king of Babylon to take, both starting from
the same country. Make a signpost where the road branches off to the
city. 20Mark out one road for the sword to come against Rabbah of the
Ammonites and another against Judah and fortified Jerusalem. 21For
the king of Babylon will stop at the fork in the road, at the junction of
the two roads, to seek an omen: He will cast lots with arrows, he will
consult his idols, he will examine the liver. 22Into his right hand will
come the lot for Jerusalem, where he is to set up battering rams, to
give the command to slaughter, to sound the battle cry, to set battering rams against the gates, to build a ramp and to erect siege works.
23It will seem like a false omen to those who have sworn allegiance to
him, but he will remind them of their guilt and take them captive.
24"Therefore this is what the Sovereign LORD says: 'Because you
people have brought to mind your guilt by your open rebellion, revealing your sins in all that you do—because you have done this, you
will be taken captive.
25" 'O profane and wicked prince of Israel, whose day has come,
whose time of punishment has reached its climax, 26this is what the
Sovereign LORD says: Take off the turban, remove the crown. It will
not be as it was: The lowly will be exalted and the exalted will be

[a]15 Septuagint; the meaning of the Hebrew for this word is uncertain.

21:21 he will examine the liver. Sheep livers were studied to make predictions of future events.

21:25 prince of Israel. *The prince* here is Zedekiah. *His punishment* would soon *come for his* wickedness. **whose day has come.** Zedekiah (prince) would be king at the time of Jerusalem's fall.

"mob" or "terrorist" groups under the direction of Ezekiel? Could you go through with your violent assignment? Why or why not? ________

rank, all mounted on horses. 24 They will come against you with
weapons,[a] chariots and wagons and with a throng of people; they will
take up positions against you on every side with large and small
shields and with helmets. I will turn you over to them for punishment, and they will punish you according to their standards. 25 I will
direct my jealous anger against you, and they will deal with you in
fury. They will cut off your noses and your ears, and those of you who
are left will fall by the sword. They will take away your sons and
daughters, and those of you who are left will be consumed by fire.
26 They will also strip you of your clothes and take your fine jewelry.
27 So I will put a stop to the lewdness and prostitution you began in
Egypt. You will not look on these things with longing or remember
Egypt anymore.

28 "For this is what the Sovereign LORD says: I am about to hand you
over to those you hate, to those you turned away from in disgust.
29 They will deal with you in hatred and take away everything you have
worked for. They will leave you naked and bare, and the shame of
your prostitution will be exposed. Your lewdness and promiscuity
30 have brought this upon you, because you lusted after the nations
and defiled yourself with their idols. 31 You have gone the way of your
sister; so I will put her cup into your hand.

32 "This is what the Sovereign LORD says:

"You will drink your sister's cup,
a cup large and deep;
it will bring scorn and derision,
for it holds so much.
33 You will be filled with drunkenness and sorrow,
the cup of ruin and desolation,
the cup of your sister Samaria.
34 You will drink it and drain it dry;
you will dash it to pieces
and tear your breasts.

I have spoken, declares the Sovereign LORD.

35 "Therefore this is what the Sovereign LORD says: Since you have
forgotten me and thrust me behind your back, you must bear the
consequences of your lewdness and prostitution."

36 The LORD said to me: "Son of man, will you judge Oholah and
Oholibah? Then confront them with their detestable practices, 37 for
they have committed adultery and blood is on their hands. They committed adultery with their idols; they even sacrificed their children,
whom they bore to me,[b] as food for them. 38 They have also done this
to me: At that same time they defiled my sanctuary and desecrated my
Sabbaths. 39 On the very day they sacrificed their children to their
idols, they entered my sanctuary and desecrated it. That is what they
did in my house.

[a]24 The meaning of the Hebrew for this word is uncertain. [b]37 *Or even made the children they bore to me pass through* ⌞*the fire*⌟

23:31 cup. God' s judgment was contained in the cup. The guilty party drank in his wrath (Jer. 25:15–29).

23:37–38 sacrificed their children ... defiled my sanctuary. The people would not give up their pagan practices of idolatry and child sacrifice. They would compound the sin by doing it in God's temple.

Two Adulterous Sisters

23 The word of the LORD came to me: 2"Son of man, there were
two women, daughters of the same mother. 3They became
prostitutes in Egypt, engaging in prostitution from their youth. *In that*
land their breasts were fondled and their virgin bosoms caressed.
4The older was named Oholah, and her sister was Oholibah. They
were mine and gave birth to sons and daughters. Oholah is Samaria,
and Oholibah is Jerusalem.

5"Oholah engaged in prostitution while she was still mine; and she
lusted after her lovers, the Assyrians—warriors 6clothed in blue, governors and commanders, all of them handsome young men, and
mounted horsemen. 7She gave herself as a prostitute to all the elite of
the Assyrians and defiled herself with all the idols of everyone she
lusted after. 8She did not give up the prostitution she began in Egypt,
when during her youth men slept with her, caressed her virgin bosom
and poured out their lust upon her.

9"Therefore I handed her over to her lovers, the Assyrians, for
whom she lusted. 10They stripped her naked, took away her sons and
daughters and killed her with the sword. She became a byword
among women, and punishment was inflicted on her.

11"Her sister Oholibah saw this, yet in her lust and prostitution she
was more depraved than her sister. 12She too lusted after the Assyrians—governors and commanders, warriors in full dress, mounted
horsemen, all handsome young men. 13I saw that she too defiled herself; both of them went the same way.

14"But she carried her prostitution still further. She saw men portrayed on a wall, figures of Chaldeans[a] portrayed in red, 15with belts
around their waists and flowing turbans on their heads; all of them
looked like Babylonian chariot officers, natives of Chaldea.[b] 16As
soon as she saw them, she lusted after them and sent messengers to
them in Chaldea. 17Then the Babylonians came to her, to the bed of
love, and in their lust they defiled her. After she had been defiled by
them, she turned away from them in disgust. 18When she carried on
her prostitution openly and exposed her nakedness, I turned away
from her in disgust, just as I had turned away from her sister. 19Yet
she became more and more promiscuous as she recalled the days of
her youth, when she was a prostitute in Egypt. 20There she lusted after her lovers, whose genitals were like those of donkeys and whose
emission was like that of horses. 21So you longed for the lewdness of
your youth, when in Egypt your bosom was caressed and your young
breasts fondled.[c]

22"Therefore, Oholibah, this is what the Sovereign LORD says: I will
stir up your lovers against you, those you turned away from in
disgust, and I will bring them against you from every side— 23the
Babylonians and all the Chaldeans, the men of Pekod and Shoa and
Koa, and all the Assyrians with them, handsome young men, all of
them governors and commanders, chariot officers and men of high

[a]14 Or *Babylonians* [b]15 Or *Babylonia;* also in verse 16 [c]21 Syriac (see also verse 3); Hebrew *caressed because of your young breasts*

OPEN 1. What about your "younger days" would you like to relive? **2.** What about your "younger days" do you find disgusting (so much so, you can't imagine why you did any of those crazy things)? Why then did you? How do you account for your change of heart? **3.** How freely did your parents talk about sex when you were a child? Were there any aspects of sex that you were not to discuss?

STUDY 1. In this frank story about Israel and Judah, the sexual language is vivid, but figurative, implying political alliances not idolatrous worship (as in ch. 16). How is each people represented? Who is the true husband? **2.** Where do the adulterous sins begin for each sister (vv. 5–13)? What other partners are involved? **3.** What happens to each woman, figuratively and historically? What do their sins represent? Why is Oholibah's sin worse than that of Oholah? **4.** How does Oholibah "carry her prostitution still further" (vv. 14–21)? With what cruel and unusual punishment (vv. 22–28)? **5.** What is the "cup" that the two sisters share (vv. 31–34)? What will happen if and when they drink it? **6.** What word of instruction and explanation does God give Ezekiel privately (vv. 36–45)? **7.** What "mob-related" and "terrorist" activities is Ezekiel associated with? What will be the ultimate result of God's punishment (v. 49)? How will this prove God is the Sovereign Lord?

APPLY 1. Have you ever heard a sermon on this passage? Why do you think God uses such a graphic story with such explicit language? How would reading this story have gone over if read in the family in which you were brought up? How would you make the language of chapter 23 more palatable to your group? **2.** Do you ever get disgusted by sin? Yours or someone else's? Why is that? What makes you both calloused toward sin and sensitive to sin? **3.** Is there anything about your personal life or your nation's life which would come under the scrutiny of Ezekiel's indiscreet prophecy? What is it about the game of international politics that God is so dead set against it? **4.** What would you do if you were one of the

---

23:5 lusted after her lovers. Judah relied on foreign alliances for help instead of God, the nation's true love.

23:8 give up the prostitution ... in Egypt. Egypt, despite its efforts, proved to be an ineffective ally. Even so, God's people pursued a political relationship with it until the end (Ex. 17:3; Num. 11:5,18,20).

40"They even sent messengers for men who came from far away,
and when they arrived you bathed yourself for them, painted your
eyes and put on your jewelry. 41You sat on an elegant couch, with a
table spread before it on which you had placed the incense and oil
that belonged to me.

42"The noise of a carefree crowd was around her; Sabeans[a] were
brought from the desert along with men from the rabble, and they put
bracelets on the arms of the woman and her sister and beautiful
crowns on their heads. 43Then I said about the one worn out by adultery, 'Now let them use her as a prostitute, for that is all she is.' 44And
they slept with her. As men sleep with a prostitute, so they slept with
those lewd women, Oholah and Oholibah. 45But righteous men will
sentence them to the punishment of women who commit adultery
and shed blood, because they are adulterous and blood is on their
hands.

46"This is what the Sovereign LORD says: Bring a mob against them
and give them over to terror and plunder. 47The mob will stone them
and cut them down with their swords; they will kill their sons and
daughters and burn down their houses.

48"So I will put an end to lewdness in the land, that all women may
take warning and not imitate you. 49You will suffer the penalty for
your lewdness and bear the consequences of your sins of idolatry.
Then you will know that I am the Sovereign LORD."

The Cooking Pot

24 In the ninth year, in the tenth month on the tenth day, the
word of the LORD came to me: 2"Son of man, record this date,
this very date, because the king of Babylon has laid siege to Jerusalem this very day. 3Tell this rebellious house a parable and say to
them: 'This is what the Sovereign LORD says:

" 'Put on the cooking pot; put it on
and pour water into it.
4 Put into it the pieces of meat,
all the choice pieces—the leg and the shoulder.
Fill it with the best of these bones;
5 take the pick of the flock.
Pile wood beneath it for the bones;
bring it to a boil
and cook the bones in it.

6" 'For this is what the Sovereign LORD says:

" 'Woe to the city of bloodshed,
to the pot now encrusted,
whose deposit will not go away!

[a]42 Or *drunkards*

OPEN 1. Who's the best cook in your family? What's your favorite dish? (Be descriptive!) **2.** When was the last time someone burned something in your kitchen? What happened? **3.** Suppose you get an over-cooked fortune cookie that says, "You are about to jump from the frying pan into the fire." To what in your life situation might that saying refer?

STUDY 1. What sets this chapter up as conveying a revelation worth noting? What happens in Jerusalem on the same day this word comes to Ezekiel? **2.** What figures of speech does Ezekiel use to describe the city and its leadership? What does each part represent: The cooking pot (vv. 3,6; 11:3)? The choice pieces of meat (v. 4; 11:3)? The dirty deposit that has encrusted the pot (vv. 6,11–13)? **3.** What will happen to the city (vv. 9–13)? Why did the "choice pieces" mistakenly think their names would be omitted from this

24:2 laid siege. While hundreds of miles away in Babylon, Ezekiel received the news of Jerusalem's siege by way of a vision from God.

24:3 rebellious house. The house would soon receive its dues.

24:4 Put into it ... choice pieces. Those arrogant leaders who remained from the first exile thought they had opted out of the judgment. However, God revealed they were indeed special—special enough to be included on the menu (11:3).

24:6 Empty ... without casting lots for them. It seems that in the previous deportation the Babylonians had cast lots to determine who would go. No one would wait for the unlucky names to be called. This time, everyone would be deported to Babylon.

"pot-boiler" (11:1–8)? **4.** What does their uncovered blood represent (vv. 7–8; Gen. 4:10; Isa. 3:9; 26:21)? **5.** Here, as in the story of Jonah, God sometimes does not carry out his threats. What is God's reason for threatening Jerusalem (v. 13)? How do they respond? Can they hope for a similar change of heart on God's part this time (v. 14)?

APPLY 1. Are you feeling the heat anywhere? Is God warning you about anything? If you are on God's hot seat or in his cooking pot, what does he want you to do about that? **2.** As for the corruption of city government officials in your area, what are some "back-burner issues" which Ezekiel might be prompting you to bring to the front burner and "pile on the wood"?

OPEN 1. What is the saddest day of your life you can still recall with feeling? **2.** Who is your "heart's desire"? What would life be like without him or her?

STUDY 1. How does Ezekiel seem to react to his wife's death? **2.** What was Ezekiel's "grief" meant to signal by analogy? How does this analogy extend to God losing his "eye's delight" and "heart's desire"? **3.** By contrast, how would the Jews in Babylon react to their Temple's destruction and their children's captivity? Why does God not want them to grieve? **4.** What happens to Ezekiel here (v. 27; 33:21–22; compare in 3:26 when God silenced Ezekiel)?

Empty it piece by piece
without casting lots for them.

7 " 'For the blood she shed is in her midst:
She poured it on the bare rock;
she did not pour it on the ground,
where the dust would cover it.
8 To stir up wrath and take revenge
I put her blood on the bare rock,
so that it would not be covered.

9 " 'Therefore this is what the Sovereign LORD says:

" 'Woe to the city of bloodshed!
I, too, will pile the wood high.
10 So heap on the wood
and kindle the fire.
Cook the meat well,
mixing in the spices;
and let the bones be charred.
11 Then set the empty pot on the coals
till it becomes hot and its copper glows
so its impurities may be melted
and its deposit burned away.
12 It has frustrated all efforts;
its heavy deposit has not been removed,
not even by fire.

13 " 'Now your impurity is lewdness. Because I tried to cleanse you
but you would not be cleansed from your impurity, you will not be
clean again until my wrath against you has subsided.

14 " 'I the LORD have spoken. The time has come for me to act. I will
not hold back; I will not have pity, nor will I relent. You will be judged
according to your conduct and your actions, declares the Sovereign
LORD.' "

Ezekiel's Wife Dies

15 The word of the LORD came to me: 16 "Son of man, with one blow
I am about to take away from you the delight of your eyes. Yet do not
lament or weep or shed any tears. 17 Groan quietly; do not mourn for
the dead. Keep your turban fastened and your sandals on your feet;
do not cover the lower part of your face or eat the customary food ⌞of
mourners⌟."

18 So I spoke to the people in the morning, and in the evening my
wife died. The next morning I did as I had been commanded.

19 Then the people asked me, "Won't you tell us what these things
have to do with us?"

20 So I said to them, "The word of the LORD came to me: 21 Say to the
house of Israel, 'This is what the Sovereign LORD says: I am about to
desecrate my sanctuary—the stronghold in which you take pride, the
delight of your eyes, the object of your affection. The sons and

24:11 empty pot on the coals. The deserted city was burned and decimated. The fire would hopefully burn off the impurities and out of the impurities would come a more purified substance.

daughters you left behind will fall by the sword. 22And you will do as
I have done. You will not cover the lower part of your face or eat the
customary food ⌊of mourners⌋. 23You will keep your turbans on your
heads and your sandals on your feet. You will not mourn or weep but
will waste away because of[a] your sins and groan among yourselves.
24Ezekiel will be a sign to you; you will do just as he has done. When
this happens, you will know that I am the Sovereign LORD.'
25"And you, son of man, on the day I take away their stronghold,
their joy and glory, the delight of their eyes, their heart's desire, and
their sons and daughters as well— 26on that day a fugitive will come
to tell you the news. 27At that time your mouth will be opened; you
will speak with him and will no longer be silent. So you will be a sign
to them, and they will know that I am the LORD."

A Prophecy Against Ammon

25 The word of the LORD came to me: 2"Son of man, set your
face against the Ammonites and prophesy against them.
3Say to them, 'Hear the word of the Sovereign LORD. This is what the
Sovereign LORD says: Because you said "Aha!" over my sanctuary
when it was desecrated and over the land of Israel when it was laid
waste and over the people of Judah when they went into exile, 4there-
fore I am going to give you to the people of the East as a possession.
They will set up their camps and pitch their tents among you; they
will eat your fruit and drink your milk. 5I will turn Rabbah into a pasture for camels and Ammon into a resting place for sheep. Then you
will know that I am the LORD. 6For this is what the Sovereign LORD
says: Because you have clapped your hands and stamped your feet,
rejoicing with all the malice of your heart against the land of Israel,
7therefore I will stretch out my hand against you and give you as
plunder to the nations. I will cut you off from the nations and exterminate you from the countries. I will destroy you, and you will know
that I am the LORD.' "

A Prophecy Against Moab

8"This is what the Sovereign LORD says: 'Because Moab and Seir
said, "Look, the house of Judah has become like all the other nations," 9therefore I will expose the flank of Moab, beginning at its
frontier towns—Beth Jeshimoth, Baal Meon and Kiriathaim—the
glory of that land. 10I will give Moab along with the Ammonites to the
people of the East as a possession, so that the Ammonites will not be
remembered among the nations; 11and I will inflict punishment on
Moab. Then they will know that I am the LORD.' "

A Prophecy Against Edom

12"This is what the Sovereign LORD says: 'Because Edom took revenge on the house of Judah and became very guilty by doing so,
13therefore this is what the Sovereign LORD says: I will stretch out my
hand against Edom and kill its men and their animals. I will lay it

[a]23 Or *away in*

APPLY 1. Of all that God calls Ezekiel to do, what do you think is the hardest? Why? **2.** If obeying God sometimes made Ezekiel suffer, what about us? By obeying God, can you hope to escape Ezekiel's loss? **3.** How can you cultivate "his heart's desire"?

OPEN 1. Do you like "put down" jokes? Do you find them rude? (Is that your nose or are you eating a banana?) **2.** Is your family tightly knit or spread out all over all around the world? Socially? Religiously?

STUDY 1. Where were Ammon, Moab, Edom and Philistia? What was the origin of these nations (Gen. 19:36–38; 36:6–9)? Were the Philistines related to Israel? (Gen. 10:13) **2.** For what crime is each nation being punished? Had any of them been given the Ten Commandments or any part of God's Law? **3.** How will God punish each nation? **4.** What will be the effect of the punishments (vv. 7,11,14,17)?

APPLY 1. Do you recall a time when you learned "the Lord is God" through hard knocks? Does your faith grow best in good times or adversity? **2.** What is your attitude when you hear bad things are happening to bad people? What should it be? **3.** When have you rejoiced when someone you didn't like "got what was coming to them?" Does God judge such behavior when we do it, or only when enemies like the Ammonites do it?

24:27 you will be a sign to them. Ezekiel, the widower (his wife was taken in an instant by God—24:15–19), offered a living picture of the agony and grief that awaited all of Judah.

25:8 like all the other nations. The reckless insults of pagan nations would signal their own divine judgment.

waste, and from Teman to Dedan they will fall by the sword. 14I will
take vengeance on Edom by the hand of my people Israel, and they
will deal with Edom in accordance with my anger and my wrath; they
will know my vengeance, declares the Sovereign LORD.' "

A Prophecy Against Philistia

15"This is what the Sovereign LORD says: 'Because the Philistines
acted in vengeance and took revenge with malice in their hearts, and
with ancient hostility sought to destroy Judah, 16therefore this is
what the Sovereign LORD says: I am about to stretch out my hand
against the Philistines, and I will cut off the Kerethites and destroy
those remaining along the coast. 17I will carry out great vengeance on
them and punish them in my wrath. Then they will know that I am the
LORD, when I take vengeance on them.' "

A Prophecy Against Tyre

26 In the eleventh year, on the first day of the month, the word of
the LORD came to me: 2"Son of man, because Tyre has said of
Jerusalem, 'Aha! The gate to the nations is broken, and its doors have
swung open to me; now that she lies in ruins I will prosper,' 3there-
fore this is what the Sovereign LORD says: I am against you, O Tyre,
and I will bring many nations against you, like the sea casting up its
waves. 4They will destroy the walls of Tyre and pull down her towers;
I will scrape away her rubble and make her a bare rock. 5Out in the
sea she will become a place to spread fishnets, for I have spoken,
declares the Sovereign LORD. She will become plunder for the nations, 6and her settlements on the mainland will be ravaged by the
sword. Then they will know that I am the LORD.

7"For this is what the Sovereign LORD says: From the north I am
going to bring against Tyre Nebuchadnezzar[a] king of Babylon, king of
kings, with horses and chariots, with horsemen and a great army. 8He
will ravage your settlements on the mainland with the sword; he will
set up siege works against you, build a ramp up to your walls and
raise his shields against you. 9He will direct the blows of his battering
rams against your walls and demolish your towers with his weapons.
10His horses will be so many that they will cover you with dust. Your
walls will tremble at the noise of the war horses, wagons and chariots when he enters your gates as men enter a city whose walls have
been broken through. 11The hoofs of his horses will trample all your
streets; he will kill your people with the sword, and your strong pillars will fall to the ground. 12They will plunder your wealth and loot
your merchandise; they will break down your walls and demolish
your fine houses and throw your stones, timber and rubble into the
sea. 13I will put an end to your noisy songs, and the music of your
harps will be heard no more. 14I will make you a bare rock, and you
will become a place to spread fishnets. You will never be rebuilt, for I
the LORD have spoken, declares the Sovereign LORD.

[a]7 Hebrew *Nebuchadrezzar,* of which *Nebuchadnezzar* is a variant; here and often in Ezekiel and Jeremiah

OPEN 1. Have you ever come close to drowning? Have you ever saved somebody from drowning? What was it like? **2.** Have you ever been in an earthquake? Did it move buildings or furniture? Did it move you?

STUDY 1. Tyre was about 100 miles north of Jerusalem. How would Tyre prosper from Israel's destruction (v. 2)? How was Tyre's response like those of the nations back in chapter 25? **2.** What will Tyre's punishment be? Who will inflict it (v. 7)? Will it be thorough (vv. 9–14)? **3.** If God knows disaster is coming, what is the point of warning Tyre? Why not just let it happen? **4.** The "coastlands" are the countries and islands of the Mediterranean that Tyre engaged in trade. Why will they be so "shaken up" (vv. 15–18)? **5.** Is God going overboard in punishing those who rejoice in Israel's misfortune so harshly? What does this say about God's commitment to Israel?

APPLY 1. Whose fall made you stop and think: A famous rock star who overdosed? A preacher who was caught in shady activity? A politician caught in a scandal? **2.** What message did you get from this fall?

26:2 Aha! Tyre wasted no time laying claim to the monopoly of trade opportunities that became available after Jerusalem's demise. However, Tyre's greed would also bring grief.

26:7 Babylon. Babylon set its sights on Tyre to carry out divine retribution.

26:8 set up siege works. Babylon besieged the nation of Tyre for fifteen years. Tyre held out due to its navy—a constant supply source.

[15]"This is what the Sovereign LORD says to Tyre: Will not the coastlands tremble at the sound of your fall, when the wounded groan and
the slaughter takes place in you? [16]Then all the princes of the coast
will step down from their thrones and lay aside their robes and take
off their embroidered garments. Clothed with terror, they will sit on
the ground, trembling every moment, appalled at you. [17]Then they
will take up a lament concerning you and say to you:

" 'How you are destroyed, O city of renown,
 peopled by men of the sea!
You were a power on the seas,
 you and your citizens;
you put your terror
 on all who lived there.
[18]Now the coastlands tremble
 on the day of your fall;
the islands in the sea
 are terrified at your collapse.'

[19]"This is what the Sovereign LORD says: When I make you a desolate city, like cities no longer inhabited, and when I bring the ocean
depths over you and its vast waters cover you, [20]then I will bring you
down with those who go down to the pit, to the people of long ago. I
will make you dwell in the earth below, as in ancient ruins, with those
who go down to the pit, and you will not return or take your place[a] in
the land of the living. [21]I will bring you to a horrible end and you will
be no more. You will be sought, but you will never again be found,
declares the Sovereign LORD."

A Lament for Tyre

27 The word of the LORD came to me: [2]"Son of man, take up a lament concerning Tyre. [3]Say to Tyre, situated at the gateway to
the sea, merchant of peoples on many coasts, 'This is what the Sovereign LORD says:

" 'You say, O Tyre,
 "I am perfect in beauty."
[4]Your domain was on the high seas;
 your builders brought your beauty to perfection.
[5]They made all your timbers
 of pine trees from Senir[b];
they took a cedar from Lebanon
 to make a mast for you.
[6]Of oaks from Bashan
 they made your oars;
of cypress wood[c] from the coasts of Cyprus[d]
 they made your deck, inlaid with ivory.
[7]Fine embroidered linen from Egypt was your sail

[a]20 Septuagint; Hebrew *return, and I will give glory* [b]5 That is, Hermon [c]6 Targum; the Masoretic Text has a different division of the consonants. [d]6 Hebrew *Kittim*

OPEN 1. What is the most beautiful city you've ever visited? What impressed you the most? Have you been in a city you could describe as "clean"? **2.** Have you ever had anything beautiful which was ruined? How did it happen? How did you feel?

STUDY 1. To what is Tyre likened in this poem (vv. 4–9)? Do you find the image fitting? What parts of it are mentioned? From where did the supplies come? What words reveal the elegance of its construction? **2.** Where did this ship travel? Can you find the limits of its trade in each direction on a map? What were some of the goods it exchanged? Do you think Tyre had good reasons to be proud? **3.** What will happen to this great luxury ship (vv. 25–36)? What will cause the accident? **4.** What different groups will hear of the mishap (vv. 30–36)? Who is most upset? Why? **5.** What is the mood of this

27:3 O Tyre, I am perfect in beauty. Tyre was a city located on the coast and was known for its great navy, variety of goods and trading port. The city of Tyre believed it was invincible—even against a formidable foe such as Babylon. Chapter 28 refers to Tyre as a city of beauty and pride.

lament: Joy over a fallen foe? Regret over something lovely destroyed? Sorrow over a people crushed? What does this lament tell you about God's feelings? About God's regard for beauty?

APPLY 1. Is it wrong to feel pride in your achievements or attributes? Do you find a lot of false "humilities"? **2.** Who would be upset if you were broke? Friends? Family? Church members? Creditors? Would anyone even know? **3.** If you were writing a lament for your city, what items might appear in the verses?

and served as your banner;
your awnings were of blue and purple
from the coasts of Elishah.
8 Men of Sidon and Arvad were your oarsmen;
your skilled men, O Tyre, were aboard as your seamen.
9 Veteran craftsmen of Gebal[a] were on board
as shipwrights to caulk your seams.
All the ships of the sea and their sailors
came alongside to trade for your wares.

10 " 'Men of Persia, Lydia and Put
served as soldiers in your army.
They hung their shields and helmets on your walls,
bringing you splendor.
11 Men of Arvad and Helech
manned your walls on every side;
men of Gammad
were in your towers.
They hung their shields around your walls;
they brought your beauty to perfection.

12 " 'Tarshish did business with you because of your great wealth of
goods; they exchanged silver, iron, tin and lead for your merchandise.
13 " 'Greece, Tubal and Meshech traded with you; they exchanged
slaves and articles of bronze for your wares.
14 " 'Men of Beth Togarmah exchanged work horses, war horses
and mules for your merchandise.
15 " 'The men of Rhodes[b] traded with you, and many coastlands
were your customers; they paid you with ivory tusks and ebony.
16 " 'Aram[c] did business with you because of your many products;
they exchanged turquoise, purple fabric, embroidered work, fine lin-
en, coral and rubies for your merchandise.
17 " 'Judah and Israel traded with you; they exchanged wheat from
Minnith and confections,[d] honey, oil and balm for your wares.
18 " 'Damascus, because of your many products and great wealth of
goods, did business with you in wine from Helbon and wool from
Zahar.
19 " 'Danites and Greeks from Uzal bought your merchandise; they
exchanged wrought iron, cassia and calamus for your wares.
20 " 'Dedan traded in saddle blankets with you.
21 " 'Arabia and all the princes of Kedar were your customers; they
did business with you in lambs, rams and goats.
22 " 'The merchants of Sheba and Raamah traded with you; for your
merchandise they exchanged the finest of all kinds of spices and precious stones, and gold.
23 " 'Haran, Canneh and Eden and merchants of Sheba, Asshur and
Kilmad traded with you. 24 In your marketplace they traded with you

[a]9 That is, Byblos [b]15 Septuagint; Hebrew *Dedan* [c]16 Most Hebrew manuscripts; some Hebrew manuscripts and Syriac *Edom* [d]17 The meaning of the Hebrew for this word is uncertain.

27:12 wealth of goods. Tyre maintained excellent trade relations with a number of nations. Their range of goods made them the talk of the trade route.

27:17 Judah and Israel also traded with the pagan nation of Tyre.

beautiful garments, blue fabric, embroidered work and multicolored
rugs with cords twisted and tightly knotted.

25" 'The ships of Tarshish serve
as carriers for your wares.
You are filled with heavy cargo
in the heart of the sea.
26Your oarsmen take you
out to the high seas.
But the east wind will break you to pieces
in the heart of the sea.
27Your wealth, merchandise and wares,
your mariners, seamen and shipwrights,
your merchants and all your soldiers,
and everyone else on board
will sink into the heart of the sea
on the day of your shipwreck.
28The shorelands will quake
when your seamen cry out.
29All who handle the oars
will abandon their ships;
the mariners and all the seamen
will stand on the shore.
30They will raise their voice
and cry bitterly over you;
they will sprinkle dust on their heads
and roll in ashes.
31They will shave their heads because of you
and will put on sackcloth.
They will weep over you with anguish of soul
and with bitter mourning.
32As they wail and mourn over you,
they will take up a lament concerning you:
"Who was ever silenced like Tyre,
surrounded by the sea?"
33When your merchandise went out on the seas,
you satisfied many nations;
with your great wealth and your wares
you enriched the kings of the earth.
34Now you are shattered by the sea
in the depths of the waters;
your wares and all your company
have gone down with you.
35All who live in the coastlands
are appalled at you;
their kings shudder with horror
and their faces are distorted with fear.
36The merchants among the nations hiss at you;
you have come to a horrible end
and will be no more.' "

27:26 break you to pieces. Tyre's economic security sank suddenly and swiftly.

OPEN 1. What's your favorite status symbol? How do you let people know you are successful? Do you prefer to appear unsuccessful? **2.** To which celebrity would you give the "Most Conceited Person in the World Award"? What did he or she do to earn it?

STUDY 1. Why did the king consider himself wise (vv. 2–5)? How did he show it? **2.** Do you think other countries admired the king's "great skill in trading" (v. 5)? Did such skill help or hurt them? **3.** Who will God use to punish him (v. 7)? What will they do to him? **4.** In what exaggerated terms does Ezekiel describe the king's character, adornment, location and role (vv. 13–15)? Of which biblical character does this remind you? **5.** How does the lament describe his sin (vv. 15–18)? Do you think the king mattered to God? **6.** Why do you think God hates pride so much? Why is he so jealous of his role as the only God in the universe?

APPLY 1. Do you ever "play god" in your words, actions or attitudes? Who in your life would know? Have you asked them about your "pride status"? **2.** Who sits on the throne in your heart? Has the issue been decided or is there sometimes a struggle for power? Are there some areas in which your surrender is less than complete? How can your group help you change attitudes or actions?

A Prophecy Against the King of Tyre

28 The word of the LORD came to me: [2]"Son of man, say to the ruler of Tyre, 'This is what the Sovereign LORD says:

" 'In the pride of your heart
you say, "I am a god;
I sit on the throne of a god
in the heart of the seas."
But you are a man and not a god,
though you think you are as wise as a god.
[3]Are you wiser than Daniel[a]?
Is no secret hidden from you?
[4]By your wisdom and understanding
you have gained wealth for yourself
and amassed gold and silver
in your treasuries.
[5]By your great skill in trading
you have increased your wealth,
and because of your wealth
your heart has grown proud.

[6]" 'Therefore this is what the Sovereign LORD says:

" 'Because you think you are wise,
as wise as a god,
[7]I am going to bring foreigners against you,
the most ruthless of nations;
they will draw their swords against your beauty and wisdom
and pierce your shining splendor.
[8]They will bring you down to the pit,
and you will die a violent death
in the heart of the seas.
[9]Will you then say, "I am a god,"
in the presence of those who kill you?
You will be but a man, not a god,
in the hands of those who slay you.
[10]You will die the death of the uncircumcised
at the hands of foreigners.

I have spoken, declares the Sovereign LORD.' "

[11]The word of the LORD came to me: [12]"Son of man, take up a lament concerning the king of Tyre and say to him: 'This is what the Sovereign LORD says:

" 'You were the model of perfection,
full of wisdom and perfect in beauty.
[13]You were in Eden,
the garden of God;
every precious stone adorned you:

[a]3 Or *Danel;* the Hebrew spelling may suggest a person other than the prophet Daniel.

28:7 most ruthless of nations. Babylon was the unchallenged superpower among all nations.

28:13 Eden, the garden of God. The king's demise was contrasted against his original destiny (Gen. 2:15), when man first enjoyed fellowship with God, but because of sin life became a severe hardship.

ruby, topaz and emerald,
chrysolite, onyx and jasper,
sapphire,[a] turquoise and beryl.[b]
Your settings and mountings[c] were made of gold;
on the day you were created they were prepared.
14You were anointed as a guardian cherub,
for so I ordained you.
You were on the holy mount of God;
you walked among the fiery stones.
15You were blameless in your ways
from the day you were created
till wickedness was found in you.
16Through your widespread trade
you were filled with violence,
and you sinned.
So I drove you in disgrace from the mount of God,
and I expelled you, O guardian cherub,
from among the fiery stones.
17Your heart became proud
on account of your beauty,
and you corrupted your wisdom
because of your splendor.
So I threw you to the earth;
I made a spectacle of you before kings.
18By your many sins and dishonest trade
you have desecrated your sanctuaries.
So I made a fire come out from you,
and it consumed you,
and I reduced you to ashes on the ground
in the sight of all who were watching.
19All the nations who knew you
are appalled at you;
you have come to a horrible end
and will be no more.' "

A Prophecy Against Sidon

20The word of the LORD came to me: 21"Son of man, set your face
against Sidon; prophesy against her 22and say: 'This is what the Sovereign LORD says:

" 'I am against you, O Sidon,
and I will gain glory within you.
They will know that I am the LORD,
when I inflict punishment on her
and show myself holy within her.
23I will send a plague upon her
and make blood flow in her streets.
The slain will fall within her,

[a]13 Or *lapis lazuli* [b]13 The precise identification of some of these precious stones is uncertain. [c]13 The meaning of the Hebrew for this phrase is uncertain.

OPEN 1. Who is the best next- door neighbor you've ever had? The worst? **2.** Was there ever a time when you got some really good news after a long period of bad news? What happened?

STUDY 1. What is God going to do to Sidon (v. 23)? Why are neighbors often "briers and sharp thorns"? **2.** What is God going to do for Israel (vv. 24–26)? Why? **3.** What does God mean when he says both Sidon and Israel will know that he is the Lord? Will they both know him in the same way?

28:14 guardian cherub. Cherubim also guarded the entrance to the Garden of Eden (Gen. 3:24).

28:17 threw you to the earth. God cannot tolerate pride in his presence and drove him out.

28:20 Sidon. This was a sister city to Tyre. Sidon has similar commercial vitality and similar sins.

APPLY 1. When have you had difficulty loving a neighbor because they were like "a painful brier" or "sharp thorn" (v. 24)? **2.** Here God judges bad neighbors where Jesus calls us to love them (Matt. 5:43–47). How do you reconcile the two concepts?

---

with the sword against her on every side.
Then they will know that I am the LORD.

24 " 'No longer will the people of Israel have malicious neighbors
who are painful briers and sharp thorns. Then they will know that I
am the Sovereign LORD.
25 " 'This is what the Sovereign LORD says: When I gather the people
of Israel from the nations where they have been scattered, I will show
myself holy among them in the sight of the nations. Then they will
live in their own land, which I gave to my servant Jacob. 26 They will
live there in safety and will build houses and plant vineyards; they
will live in safety when I inflict punishment on all their neighbors
who maligned them. Then they will know that I am the LORD their
God.' "

OPEN 1. Which barnyard animal best describes this country? Which jungle animal? Is the world more like a barnyard or jungle? **2.** Has a good friend ever let you down? What happened? How did it feel?

STUDY 1. God depicted Tyre as a ship. How does he depict Egypt? Why is it appropriate? **2.** For what two things does God punish Pharaoh (vv. 3,6–7)? How reliable was Egypt as a military ally (2 Kin. 18:19–21)? **3.** How will God punish Egypt? When will God regather her? How does this compare with the fate of Ammon (25:7)? Tyre (26:14)? Israel (20:36–38)? **4.** Why might the "horn" in verse 21 symbolize strength (1 Sam. 2:1; Ps. 92:10)? **5.** Do you think Nebuchadnezzar attacked Tyre and Egypt out of conscious obedience to the Lord? What is the significance of your answer as you consider international conflicts today?

APPLY 1. Does God work in your life without your knowing it? On hindsight, when do you recall this happening? **2.** How does God reveal his actions and plans? How can you better understand and fit in with his purposes? **3.** What do you see happening in the world that convinces you that God is in control?

A Prophecy Against Egypt

29 In the tenth year, in the tenth month on the twelfth day, the
word of the LORD came to me: 2 "Son of man, set your face
against Pharaoh king of Egypt and prophesy against him and against
all Egypt. 3 Speak to him and say: 'This is what the Sovereign LORD
says:

" 'I am against you, Pharaoh king of Egypt,
you great monster lying among your streams.
You say, "The Nile is mine;
I made it for myself."
4 But I will put hooks in your jaws
and make the fish of your streams stick to your scales.
I will pull you out from among your streams,
with all the fish sticking to your scales.
5 I will leave you in the desert,
you and all the fish of your streams.
You will fall on the open field
and not be gathered or picked up.
I will give you as food
to the beasts of the earth and the birds of the air.

6 Then all who live in Egypt will know that I am the LORD.

" 'You have been a staff of reed for the house of Israel. 7 When they
grasped you with their hands, you splintered and you tore open their
shoulders; when they leaned on you, you broke and their backs were
wrenched.[a]
8 " 'Therefore this is what the Sovereign LORD says: I will bring a
sword against you and kill your men and their animals. 9 Egypt will
become a desolate wasteland. Then they will know that I am the
LORD.
" 'Because you said, "The Nile is mine; I made it," 10 therefore I am
against you and against your streams, and I will make the land of
Egypt a ruin and a desolate waste from Migdol to Aswan, as far as the

[a] 7 Syriac (see also Septuagint and Vulgate); Hebrew *and you caused their backs to stand*

28:24 painful briers and sharp thorns. Pagan nations would not be allowed to torment Israel anymore.

28:25 show myself holy. God would redeem his reputation before the nations by redeeming his people.

29:3 Pharaoh ... great monster. Ezekiel portrayed Egypt as a menacing force lying wait in the peaceful Nile.

border of Cush.[a] 11 No foot of man or animal will pass through it; no
one will live there for forty years. 12 I will make the land of Egypt desolate among devastated lands, and her cities will lie desolate forty
years among ruined cities. And I will disperse the Egyptians among
the nations and scatter them through the countries.

13 " 'Yet this is what the Sovereign LORD says: At the end of forty
years I will gather the Egyptians from the nations where they were
scattered. 14 I will bring them back from captivity and return them to
Upper Egypt,[b] the land of their ancestry. There they will be a lowly
kingdom. 15 It will be the lowliest of kingdoms and will never again
exalt itself above the other nations. I will make it so weak that it will
never again rule over the nations. 16 Egypt will no longer be a source
of confidence for the people of Israel but will be a reminder of their
sin in turning to her for help. Then they will know that I am the Sovereign LORD.' "

17 In the twenty-seventh year, in the first month on the first day, the
word of the LORD came to me: 18 "Son of man, Nebuchadnezzar king
of Babylon drove his army in a hard campaign against Tyre; every
head was rubbed bare and every shoulder made raw. Yet he and his
army got no reward from the campaign he led against Tyre. 19 Therefore this is what the Sovereign LORD says: I am going to give Egypt to
Nebuchadnezzar king of Babylon, and he will carry off its wealth. He
will loot and plunder the land as pay for his army. 20 I have given him
Egypt as a reward for his efforts because he and his army did it for
me, declares the Sovereign LORD.

21 "On that day I will make a horn[c] grow for the house of Israel, and
I will open your mouth among them. Then they will know that I am
the LORD."

A Lament for Egypt

30 The word of the LORD came to me: 2 "Son of man, prophesy
and say: 'This is what the Sovereign LORD says:

" 'Wail and say,
"Alas for that day!"
3 For the day is near,
the day of the LORD is near—
a day of clouds,
a time of doom for the nations.
4 A sword will come against Egypt,
and anguish will come upon Cush.[d]
When the slain fall in Egypt,
her wealth will be carried away
and her foundations torn down.

5 Cush and Put, Lydia and all Arabia, Libya[e] and the people of the covenant land will fall by the sword along with Egypt.

[a] 10 That is, the upper Nile region [b] 14 Hebrew *to Pathros* [c] 21 *Horn* here symbolizes strength. [d] 4 That is, the upper Nile region; also in verses 5 and 9 [e] 5 Hebrew *Cub*

OPEN 1. Have you ever broken a bone? Did it heal, good as new? **2.** Have you ever had to "break the news" to a friend? How do you approach a friend with criticism or bad news? **3.** What is your favorite form of escapism? How many times a week do you have to escape reality?

STUDY 1. What does the Lord say he is going to do to Egypt (v. 4)? What will be the effect on all its military allies (vv. 5–6)? **2.** Who will God use to punish Egypt (v. 10)? What kind of nation are they (v. 11)? **3.** What are some of the specific things God promises to do to Egypt (vv. 13–19)? **4.** While Ezekiel chanted this lament, the Babylonians laid siege to Jerusalem. Did Egypt save the day (Jer. 37:6–8)? Does God have a "bone to pick" with Pharaoh (vv. 21–22)? Why do you think the Lord did not want the people to de-

29:21 horn. When Egypt finally endured judgment, Israel would vicariously receive a "horn" of renewed strength.

30:4 A sword ... against Egypt. The sword is referring to Nebuchadnezzar.

pend on Egypt for deliverance? Could the city be saved from God's judgment anyway?

APPLY 1. The people in Jerusalem hoped that Ezekiel was wrong about the Babylonians and that Egypt would come to their rescue. Do you find yourself waiting for someone to rescue you? How do you feel broken and helpless? **2.** God had to take away Israel's false hope before he could help them. Is God doing this in any area to you? How are you responding? Are you listening or gripping your hopes more tightly?

6" 'This is what the LORD says:

" 'The allies of Egypt will fall
and her proud strength will fail.
From Migdol to Aswan
they will fall by the sword within her,
declares the Sovereign LORD.
7" 'They will be desolate
among desolate lands,
and their cities will lie
among ruined cities.
8 Then they will know that I am the LORD,
when I set fire to Egypt
and all her helpers are crushed.

9" 'On that day messengers will go out from me in ships to frighten
Cush out of her complacency. Anguish will take hold of them on the
day of Egypt's doom, for it is sure to come.

10" 'This is what the Sovereign LORD says:

" 'I will put an end to the hordes of Egypt
by the hand of Nebuchadnezzar king of Babylon.
11 He and his army—the most ruthless of nations—
will be brought in to destroy the land.
They will draw their swords against Egypt
and fill the land with the slain.
12 I will dry up the streams of the Nile
and sell the land to evil men;
by the hand of foreigners
I will lay waste the land and everything in it.

I the LORD have spoken.

13" 'This is what the Sovereign LORD says:

" 'I will destroy the idols
and put an end to the images in Memphis.[a]
No longer will there be a prince in Egypt,
and I will spread fear throughout the land.
14 I will lay waste Upper Egypt,[b]
set fire to Zoan
and inflict punishment on Thebes.[c]
15 I will pour out my wrath on Pelusium,[d]
the stronghold of Egypt,
and cut off the hordes of Thebes.
16 I will set fire to Egypt;
Pelusium will writhe in agony.
Thebes will be taken by storm;
Memphis will be in constant distress.
17 The young men of Heliopolis[e] and Bubastis[f]

[a] 13 Hebrew *Noph*; also in verse 16 [b] 14 Hebrew *waste Pathros* [c] 14 Hebrew *No*; also in verses 15 and 16 [d] 15 Hebrew *Sin*; also in verse 16 [e] 17 Hebrew *Awen* (or *On*) [f] 17 Hebrew *Pi Beseth*

30:11 Other previously conquered nations were the building blocks of Babylon's terrifying reputation. Babylon had a reputation of wickedness. Their methods were cruel and inhumane (2 Kin. 25:1–26).

will fall by the sword,
and the cities themselves will go into captivity.
18 Dark will be the day at Tahpanhes
when I break the yoke of Egypt;
there her proud strength will come to an end.
She will be covered with clouds,
and her villages will go into captivity.
19 So I will inflict punishment on Egypt,
and they will know that I am the LORD.' "

20 In the eleventh year, in the first month on the seventh day, the
word of the LORD came to me: 21 "Son of man, I have broken the arm
of Pharaoh king of Egypt. It has not been bound up for healing or put
in a splint so as to become strong enough to hold a sword. 22 Therefore this is what the Sovereign LORD says: I am against Pharaoh king
of Egypt. I will break both his arms, the good arm as well as the
broken one, and make the sword fall from his hand. 23 I will disperse
the Egyptians among the nations and scatter them through the countries. 24 I will strengthen the arms of the king of Babylon and put my
sword in his hand, but I will break the arms of Pharaoh, and he will
groan before him like a mortally wounded man. 25 I will strengthen
the arms of the king of Babylon, but the arms of Pharaoh will fall
limp. Then they will know that I am the LORD, when I put my sword
into the hand of the king of Babylon and he brandishes it against
Egypt. 26 I will disperse the Egyptians among the nations and scatter
them through the countries. Then they will know that I am the LORD."

A Cedar in Lebanon

31 In the eleventh year, in the third month on the first day, the
word of the LORD came to me: 2 "Son of man, say to Pharaoh
king of Egypt and to his hordes:

" 'Who can be compared with you in majesty?
3 Consider Assyria, once a cedar in Lebanon,
with beautiful branches overshadowing the forest;
it towered on high,
its top above the thick foliage.
4 The waters nourished it,
deep springs made it grow tall;
their streams flowed
all around its base
and sent their channels
to all the trees of the field.
5 So it towered higher
than all the trees of the field;
its boughs increased
and its branches grew long,
spreading because of abundant waters.
6 All the birds of the air
nested in its boughs,

OPEN 1. When was the last time you were in a forest? Why were you there? How did you feel? **2.** Who is the most successful person you know? What impresses you most about him or her?

STUDY 1. Who does God tell Pharaoh to consider (v. 3)? To what does God compare this country? How does God describe it? **2.** What was the sin of the cedar? How was it punished? By whom (vv. 10–12; 30:10–11)? What will be the impact on other trees (vv. 14,16–17)? **3.** Is pride always a sin? When should we be proud? When do we risk being "cut down" because of pride (vv. 10–12)? **4.** What lesson does God want Pharaoh to learn from this allegory of the cedar tree?

APPLY 1. What are you proud of in your life right now? What should you do to acknowledge God as the true source of your abilities and blessings? **2.** Has God ever acted in blessing or judgment in the

---

30:21 not been bound up for healing. A prior defeat by Nebuchadnezzar was only the beginning of Egypt's pain and suffering. Soon, Babylon would crush every bone.

31:3 Assyria. In case Egypt needed more proof of its pending punishment, God encouraged them to consider the defeat of Assyria. Like Egypt, it was once a powerful nation. Yet, it came to ruin under Babylon.

life of someone you know? What did you learn from that experience? Can you really learn from other peoples' mistakes, or must you make your own?

all the beasts of the field
gave birth under its branches;
all the great nations
lived in its shade.
7 It was majestic in beauty,
with its spreading boughs,
for its roots went down
to abundant waters.
8 The cedars in the garden of God
could not rival it,
nor could the pine trees
equal its boughs,
nor could the plane trees
compare with its branches—
no tree in the garden of God
could match its beauty.
9 I made it beautiful
with abundant branches,
the envy of all the trees of Eden
in the garden of God.

10 " 'Therefore this is what the Sovereign LORD says: Because it towered on high, lifting its top above the thick foliage, and because it
was proud of its height, 11 I handed it over to the ruler of the nations,
for him to deal with according to its wickedness. I cast it aside, 12 and
the most ruthless of foreign nations cut it down and left it. Its boughs
fell on the mountains and in all the valleys; its branches lay broken in
all the ravines of the land. All the nations of the earth came out from
under its shade and left it. 13 All the birds of the air settled on the fall-
en tree, and all the beasts of the field were among its branches.
14 Therefore no other trees by the waters are ever to tower proudly on
high, lifting their tops above the thick foliage. No other trees so well-
watered are ever to reach such a height; they are all destined for
death, for the earth below, among mortal men, with those who go
down to the pit.

15 " 'This is what the Sovereign LORD says: On the day it was
brought down to the grave[a] I covered the deep springs with mourning
for it; I held back its streams, and its abundant waters were restrained. Because of it I clothed Lebanon with gloom, and all the
trees of the field withered away. 16 I made the nations tremble at the
sound of its fall when I brought it down to the grave with those who
go down to the pit. Then all the trees of Eden, the choicest and best of
Lebanon, all the trees that were well-watered, were consoled in the
earth below. 17 Those who lived in its shade, its allies among the nations, had also gone down to the grave with it, joining those killed by
the sword.

18 " 'Which of the trees of Eden can be compared with you in splen-

[a]15 Hebrew *Sheol*; also in verses 16 and 17

31:12 Babylon felled the mighty cedar of Assyria.

31:16 nations ... were consoled. Lesser nations were consoled by the fact that even the mightiest nation could not withstand Babylon.

31:17 killed by the sword. Smaller nations preceded Assyria in defeat. They shared the same murderous fate.

31:18 God made sure the pharaoh got the message. His end was near.

dor and majesty? Yet you, too, will be brought down with the trees of Eden to the earth below; you will lie among the uncircumcised, with those killed by the sword.

" 'This is Pharaoh and all his hordes, declares the Sovereign LORD.' "

A Lament for Pharaoh

32 In the twelfth year, in the twelfth month on the first day, the
word of the LORD came to me: **2**"Son of man, take up a lament concerning Pharaoh king of Egypt and say to him:

" 'You are like a lion among the nations;
you are like a monster in the seas
thrashing about in your streams,
churning the water with your feet
and muddying the streams.

3" 'This is what the Sovereign LORD says:

" 'With a great throng of people
I will cast my net over you,
and they will haul you up in my net.
4I will throw you on the land
and hurl you on the open field.
I will let all the birds of the air settle on you
and all the beasts of the earth gorge themselves on you.
5I will spread your flesh on the mountains
and fill the valleys with your remains.
6I will drench the land with your flowing blood
all the way to the mountains,
and the ravines will be filled with your flesh.
7When I snuff you out, I will cover the heavens
and darken their stars;
I will cover the sun with a cloud,
and the moon will not give its light.
8All the shining lights in the heavens
I will darken over you;
I will bring darkness over your land,
declares the Sovereign LORD.
9I will trouble the hearts of many peoples
when I bring about your destruction among the nations,
among[a] lands you have not known.
10I will cause many peoples to be appalled at you,
and their kings will shudder with horror because of you
when I brandish my sword before them.
On the day of your downfall
each of them will tremble
every moment for his life.

[a]9 Hebrew; Septuagint *bring you into captivity among the nations, / to*

OPEN 1. What countries do you think will be world superpowers 50 years from now? Is your answer a hunch or do you have reasons? **2.** If you could live some time in the past, when and where would you choose? Why?

STUDY 1. What animals join the list of metaphors for Egypt and Pharaoh? What will God do to Pharaoh (vv. 3–8)? How will the "birds and beasts" react? The "moon and stars"? **2.** What is the ultimate destination of Pharaoh and his mighty army (v. 18)? Who will share this fate? What had these other nations been like in their prime? **3.** How would you define "terrorists"? How are they different than "freedom fighters"? **4.** Circumcision was thought to be a rite of purification. Why would it be particularly shameful to be buried with the uncircumcised? With those who had been killed by the sword? **5.** Why would Pharaoh "console" himself when he saw that his fate was the same as the great nations of the past (v. 31)?

APPLY 1. Would you bother being a follower of Christ if there was no afterlife? Why or why not? **2.** What do you fear most about dying? Why? What hope do you have about facing death? What hope does God want you to have?

32:2 lion. Lions were symbols of strength and dominance. Such was the apparent power of the pharaoh.

32:7 cover the heavens. Ezekiel described the magnitude of grief and sorrow that would darken the heavens on the Day of Judgment.

32:9 among lands you have not known. Even anonymous rulers of other nations would be alarmed by Egypt's fallen state. The widespread knowledge of Egypt's fall would humiliate the pharaoh.

OPEN 1. What countries do you think will be world superpowers 50 years from now? Is your answer a hunch or do you have reasons? 2. If you could live some time in the past, when and where would you choose? Why?

STUDY 1. What animals join the list of metaphors for Egypt and Pharaoh? What will God do to Pharaoh (vv. 3–8)? How will the "birds and beasts" react? The "moon and stars"? 2. What is the ultimate destination of Pharaoh and his mighty army (v. 18)? Who will share this fate? What had these other nations been like in their prime? 3. How would you define "terrorists"? How are they different from "freedom fighters"? 4. Circumcision was thought to be a rite of purification. Why would it be particularly shameful to be buried with the uncircumcised? With those who had been killed by the sword? 5. Why would Pharaoh "console" himself when he saw that his fate was the same as that great nations of the past (v. 31)?

APPLY 1. Would you bother being a follower of Christ if there was no afterlife? Why or why not? 2. What do you fear most about dying? Why? What hope do you have about facing death? What hope does God want you to have?

[11]" 'For this is what the Sovereign LORD says:

" 'The sword of the king of Babylon
will come against you.
[12]I will cause your hordes to fall
by the swords of mighty men—
the most ruthless of all nations.
They will shatter the pride of Egypt,
and all her hordes will be overthrown.
[13]I will destroy all her cattle
from beside abundant waters
no longer to be stirred by the foot of man
or muddied by the hoofs of cattle.
[14]Then I will let her waters settle
and make her streams flow like oil,
declares the Sovereign LORD.

[15]When I make Egypt desolate
and strip the land of everything in it,
when I strike down all who live there,
then they will know that I am the LORD.'

[16]"This is the lament they will chant for her. The daughters of the
nations will chant it; for Egypt and all her hordes they will chant it,
declares the Sovereign LORD."

[17]In the twelfth year, on the fifteenth day of the month, the word of
the LORD came to me: [18]"Son of man, wail for the hordes of Egypt and
consign to the earth below both her and the daughters of mighty
nations, with those who go down to the pit. [19]Say to them, 'Are you
more favored than others? Go down and be laid among the uncircumcised.' [20]They will fall among those killed by the sword. The
sword is drawn; let her be dragged off with all her hordes. [21]From
within the grave[a] the mighty leaders will say of Egypt and her allies,
'They have come down and they lie with the uncircumcised, with
those killed by the sword.'

[22]"Assyria is there with her whole army; she is surrounded by the
graves of all her slain, all who have fallen by the sword. [23]Their graves
are in the depths of the pit and her army lies around her grave. All
who had spread terror in the land of the living are slain, fallen by the
sword.

[24]"Elam is there, with all her hordes around her grave. All of them
are slain, fallen by the sword. All who had spread terror in the land of
the living went down uncircumcised to the earth below. They bear
their shame with those who go down to the pit. [25]A bed is made for
her among the slain, with all her hordes around her grave. All of them
are uncircumcised, killed by the sword. Because their terror had
spread in the land of the living, they bear their shame with those who
go down to the pit; they are laid among the slain.

[26]"Meshech and Tubal are there, with all their hordes around their
graves. All of them are uncircumcised, killed by the sword because
they spread their terror in the land of the living. [27]Do they not lie with
the other uncircumcised warriors who have fallen, who went down to
the grave with their weapons of war, whose swords were placed
under their heads? The punishment for their sins rested on their

[a]21 Hebrew *Sheol;* also in verse 27

bones, though the terror of these warriors had stalked through the
land of the living.
28"You too, O Pharaoh, will be broken and will lie among the uncircumcised, with those killed by the sword.
29"Edom is there, her kings and all her princes; despite their power,
they are laid with those killed by the sword. They lie with the uncircumcised, with those who go down to the pit.
30"All the princes of the north and all the Sidonians are there; they
went down with the slain in disgrace despite the terror caused by
their power. They lie uncircumcised with those killed by the sword
and bear their shame with those who go down to the pit.
31"Pharaoh—he and all his army—will see them and he will be
consoled for all his hordes that were killed by the sword, declares the
Sovereign LORD. 32Although I had him spread terror in the land of the
living, Pharaoh and all his hordes will be laid among the uncircumcised, with those killed by the sword, declares the Sovereign LORD."

Ezekiel a Watchman

33 The word of the LORD came to me: 2"Son of man, speak to
your countrymen and say to them: 'When I bring the sword
against a land, and the people of the land choose one of their men
and make him their watchman, 3and he sees the sword coming
against the land and blows the trumpet to warn the people, 4then if
anyone hears the trumpet but does not take warning and the sword
comes and takes his life, his blood will be on his own head. 5Since he
heard the sound of the trumpet but did not take warning, his blood
will be on his own head. If he had taken warning, he would have
saved himself. 6But if the watchman sees the sword coming and does
not blow the trumpet to warn the people and the sword comes and
takes the life of one of them, that man will be taken away because of
his sin, but I will hold the watchman accountable for his blood.'
7"Son of man, I have made you a watchman for the house of Israel;
so hear the word I speak and give them warning from me. 8When I say
to the wicked, 'O wicked man, you will surely die,' and you do not
speak out to dissuade him from his ways, that wicked man will die
for[a] his sin, and I will hold you accountable for his blood. 9But if you
do warn the wicked man to turn from his ways and he does not do so,
he will die for his sin, but you will have saved yourself.
10"Son of man, say to the house of Israel, 'This is what you are saying: "Our offenses and sins weigh us down, and we are wasting away
because of[b] them. How then can we live?"' 11Say to them, 'As surely
as I live, declares the Sovereign LORD, I take no pleasure in the death
of the wicked, but rather that they turn from their ways and live. Turn!
Turn from your evil ways! Why will you die, O house of Israel?'
12"Therefore, son of man, say to your countrymen, 'The righteousness of the righteous man will not save him when he disobeys, and

[a]8 Or *in*; also in verse 9 [b]10 Or *away in*

OPEN 1. Who is your favorite newscaster? What channel is he or she on? Why do you like him or her? **2.** Do you have an alarm system on your house or car? Has it ever scared away a crook? Does it ever give false alarms?

STUDY 1. What is the one way the watchman can fail in his job (v. 6)? What are those who hear the warning supposed to do? What will happen if people ignore the warning? **2.** What problem do the people of Israel have besides their sins (v. 10)? What does God say to encourage them (v. 11)? **3.** Verses 12–20 echo chapter 18's declaration of individual responsibility. Which actions will cause the righteous to die? Which will cause the wicked to live? By what standards will God judge each person's life (v. 20)?

APPLY 1. When have you been reluctant to bring bad news to persons you loved? What did you finally do and what was the result? **2.** People often get discouraged when they hear the bad news. Do you get discouraged when you fail the Lord? Does God want you to punish yourself or do something else? What does 2 Corinthians 7:10 say about your attitudes and actions in response to sin? **3.** If you could warn people about one danger today, what would it be? What prevents you from "sounding the trumpet"?

33:6 accountable for his blood. The watchman was held responsible for the safety of all the inhabitants inside the city walls. Likewise, the spiritual condition of Jerusalem was of vital importance.

33:10 offenses and sins weigh us down. The exiles finally made a significant spiritual breakthrough. They recognized their weighty sinfulness.

33:11 Turn from your evil ways! God's remedy is repentance.

33:12–20 In God's justice system, every person is held accountable for

the wickedness of the wicked man will not cause him to fall when he
turns from it. The righteous man, if he sins, will not be allowed to live
because of his former righteousness.' [13]If I tell the righteous man
that he will surely live, but then he trusts in his righteousness and
does evil, none of the righteous things he has done will be remembered; he will die for the evil he has done. [14]And if I say to the wicked
man, 'You will surely die,' but he then turns away from his sin and
does what is just and right— [15]if he gives back what he took in pledge
for a loan, returns what he has stolen, follows the decrees that give
life, and does no evil, he will surely live; he will not die. [16]None of the
sins he has committed will be remembered against him. He has done
what is just and right; he will surely live.

[17]"Yet your countrymen say, 'The way of the Lord is not just.' But it
is their way that is not just. [18]If a righteous man turns from his righteousness and does evil, he will die for it. [19]And if a wicked man turns
away from his wickedness and does what is just and right, he will live
by doing so. [20]Yet, O house of Israel, you say, 'The way of the Lord is
not just.' But I will judge each of you according to his own ways."

Jerusalem's Fall Explained

[21]In the twelfth year of our exile, in the tenth month on the fifth
day, a man who had escaped from Jerusalem came to me and said,
"The city has fallen!" [22]Now the evening before the man arrived, the
hand of the LORD was upon me, and he opened my mouth before the
man came to me in the morning. So my mouth was opened and I was
no longer silent.

[23]Then the word of the LORD came to me: [24]"Son of man, the people
living in those ruins in the land of Israel are saying, 'Abraham was
only one man, yet he possessed the land. But we are many; surely the
land has been given to us as our possession.' [25]Therefore say to
them, 'This is what the Sovereign LORD says: Since you eat meat with
the blood still in it and look to your idols and shed blood, should you
then possess the land? [26]You rely on your sword, you do detestable
things, and each of you defiles his neighbor's wife. Should you then
possess the land?'

[27]"Say this to them: 'This is what the Sovereign LORD says: As surely as I live, those who are left in the ruins will fall by the sword, those
out in the country I will give to the wild animals to be devoured, and
those in strongholds and caves will die of a plague. [28]I will make the
land a desolate waste, and her proud strength will come to an end,
and the mountains of Israel will become desolate so that no one will
cross them. [29]Then they will know that I am the LORD, when I have
made the land a desolate waste because of all the detestable things
they have done.'

[30]"As for you, son of man, your countrymen are talking together
about you by the walls and at the doors of the houses, saying to each
other, 'Come and hear the message that has come from the LORD.'
[31]My people come to you, as they usually do, and sit before you to lis-

OPEN What part of the body best describes you? Why?

STUDY **1.** What news comes from Jerusalem? How many years had Ezekiel waited for this (Compare 1:2 with v. 21)? **2.** Why was Ezekiel dumb (3:26–27; 24:27)? **3.** What false hope did the Jerusalemites entertain in comparing themselves to Abraham (v. 24)? Why wouldn't they possess the land (vv. 25–26)? **4.** What three groups remained in the Jerusalem area (v. 27)? What will happen to each? What will the effect be on those who witness the desolation (v. 29)? **5.** Did the exiles take Ezekiel seriously (vv. 30–32)? If they were no more serious than those in Jerusalem, why was their fate so different?

APPLY **1.** Are you, like the Israelites, ever tempted to think you can get God's blessing without obeying his commands? **2.** The exiles liked to listen to Ezekiel but didn't do what he said. What does Jesus say about such people (Matt. 7:24–27)? How would you describe yourself: A listener but no action? Easier said than done? A procrastinating doer? Not even a listener?

---

personal choices (18:21–29). Judgment is metered on a fair and equitable scale (vv. 17–20).

33:22 I was no longer silent. When Babylon finally took over Jerusalem, Ezekiel's restrictions were lifted (3:26).

33:24 only one man ... But we are many. The remaining Jews appealed to strength in numbers, hoping to change God's plans. Like homesick children, they wanted to stay in their homeland.

33:31 hearts are greedy. God

ten to your words, but they do not put them into practice. With their
mouths they express devotion, but their hearts are greedy for unjust
gain. 32Indeed, to them you are nothing more than one who sings
love songs with a beautiful voice and plays an instrument well, for
they hear your words but do not put them into practice.
33"When all this comes true—and it surely will—then they will
know that a prophet has been among them."

Shepherds and Sheep

34 The word of the LORD came to me: 2"Son of man, prophesy
against the shepherds of Israel; prophesy and say to them:
'This is what the Sovereign LORD says: Woe to the shepherds of Israel
who only take care of themselves! Should not shepherds take care of
the flock? 3You eat the curds, clothe yourselves with the wool and
slaughter the choice animals, but you do not take care of the flock.
4You have not strengthened the weak or healed the sick or bound up
the injured. You have not brought back the strays or searched for the
lost. You have ruled them harshly and brutally. 5So they were scattered because there was no shepherd, and when they were scattered
they became food for all the wild animals. 6My sheep wandered over
all the mountains and on every high hill. They were scattered over the
whole earth, and no one searched or looked for them.
7" 'Therefore, you shepherds, hear the word of the LORD: 8As surely
as I live, declares the Sovereign LORD, because my flock lacks a shepherd and so has been plundered and has become food for all the wild
animals, and because my shepherds did not search for my flock but
cared for themselves rather than for my flock, 9therefore,
O shepherds, hear the word of the LORD: 10This is what the Sovereign
LORD says: I am against the shepherds and will hold them accountable for my flock. I will remove them from tending the flock so that
the shepherds can no longer feed themselves. I will rescue my flock
from their mouths, and it will no longer be food for them.
11" 'For this is what the Sovereign LORD says: I myself will search
for my sheep and look after them. 12As a shepherd looks after his
scattered flock when he is with them, so will I look after my sheep. I
will rescue them from all the places where they were scattered on a
day of clouds and darkness. 13I will bring them out from the nations
and gather them from the countries, and I will bring them into their
own land. I will pasture them on the mountains of Israel, in the ravines and in all the settlements in the land. 14I will tend them in a
good pasture, and the mountain heights of Israel will be their grazing
land. There they will lie down in good grazing land, and there they
will feed in a rich pasture on the mountains of Israel. 15I myself will
tend my sheep and have them lie down, declares the Sovereign LORD.
16I will search for the lost and bring back the strays. I will bind up the

OPEN 1. Have you ever taken a field trip or gone on an outing with a large group? What happened? Did anyone get lost? Was it a restful experience? **2.** When was the last time you saw a sheep? Was it cute and cuddly or dirty and stupid? Was it by itself or in a flock?

STUDY 1. What were the shepherds doing (vv. 2–3)? Five different groups of sheep are mentioned. What care was needed by each? **2.** What has happened to the sheep because of the bad shepherds (vv. 5–8)? What will God do to the shepherds for this malpractice (v. 10)? **3.** What will God himself do for the sheep (vv. 11–16)? What will God do for those who have been scattered? How will God provide food and safety for them? **4.** After God rounds up the flock, what groups will be found among them (vv. 16–22)? How do the sheep treat one another? How will God treat each group? Who will be as a shepherd over them (vv. 23–24)? **5.** What will God do to the land on which he pastures his flock? How will this affect the sheep (vv. 25–31)? **6.** In the allegory of the sheep: Who are the sheep? The shepherds? What is God promising to do? Who is the coming Shepherd? **7.** In this parable, what do you learn about the mission of Jesus?

APPLY 1. What kind of sheep are you: Weak? Sick? Injured? Lost? Does it feel like God is taking care of you? **2.** The word "pastor" literally means "a shepherd." Are you getting good shepherding? Do you follow where your shepherd leads you or are you always running away? Are you growing in your ability to shep-

---

peered into the hearts of the elders and leaders who gathered at Ezekiel's feet. He alone realized each individual's true motivation.

34:2 shepherds of Israel. Leaders were often regarded as shepherds (Isa. 44:28). These misfit shepherds disregarded the physical well-being and spiritual condition of the people under their care.

34:5 scattered ... no shepherd. As a result of their leaders' selfishness, the entire flock would suffer. Ezekiel referred to the divide-and-conquer strategy of the Exile as a flock without a shepherd (Mark 6:34).

34:11 I myself will search. God intervened. He assumed the caring role that the leaders failed to execute.

34:16 the sleek and the strong. The tables were turned. The selfish leaders would now be destroyed. Then God would respond and tend to the discarded sheep himself.

herd others? **3.** What sorts of sheep come to your group: Tramplers? Drinkers? Muddy? Fat? Lean? How can you treat each other better?

---

injured and strengthen the weak, but the sleek and the strong I will
destroy. I will shepherd the flock with justice.
17 "'As for you, my flock, this is what the Sovereign LORD says: I will
judge between one sheep and another, and between rams and goats.
18 Is it not enough for you to feed on the good pasture? Must you also
trample the rest of your pasture with your feet? Is it not enough for
you to drink clear water? Must you also muddy the rest with your
feet? 19 Must my flock feed on what you have trampled and drink what
you have muddied with your feet?
20 "'Therefore this is what the Sovereign LORD says to them: See, I
myself will judge between the fat sheep and the lean sheep. 21 Because you shove with flank and shoulder, butting all the weak sheep
with your horns until you have driven them away, 22 I will save my
flock, and they will no longer be plundered. I will judge between one
sheep and another. 23 I will place over them one shepherd, my servant
David, and he will tend them; he will tend them and be their shepherd. 24 I the LORD will be their God, and my servant David will be
prince among them. I the LORD have spoken.
25 "'I will make a covenant of peace with them and rid the land of
wild beasts so that they may live in the desert and sleep in the forests
in safety. 26 I will bless them and the places surrounding my hill.[a] I will
send down showers in season; there will be showers of blessing.
27 The trees of the field will yield their fruit and the ground will yield
its crops; the people will be secure in their land. They will know that
I am the LORD, when I break the bars of their yoke and rescue them
from the hands of those who enslaved them. 28 They will no longer be
plundered by the nations, nor will wild animals devour them. They
will live in safety, and no one will make them afraid. 29 I will provide
for them a land renowned for its crops, and they will no longer be victims of famine in the land or bear the scorn of the nations. 30 Then
they will know that I, the LORD their God, am with them and that they,
the house of Israel, are my people, declares the Sovereign LORD.
31 You my sheep, the sheep of my pasture, are people, and I am your
God, declares the Sovereign LORD.'"

A Prophecy Against Edom

35 The word of the LORD came to me: 2 "Son of man, set your
face against Mount Seir; prophesy against it 3 and say: 'This
is what the Sovereign LORD says: I am against you, Mount Seir, and I
will stretch out my hand against you and make you a desolate waste.
4 I will turn your towns into ruins and you will be desolate. Then you
will know that I am the LORD.
5 "'Because you harbored an ancient hostility and delivered the Israelites over to the sword at the time of their calamity, the time their

[a]26 Or *I will make them and the places surrounding my hill a blessing*

OPEN 1. Is there a certain sports team or politician you really dislike? How do you feel when they lose? **2.** Were you ever envious of anyone when you were young? Who? Why?

STUDY 1. What does the capital Mount Seir represent? (vv. 2–3,7–8,15)? **2.** Who were the Edomites (Gen. 36:6–9)? How far back does their "ancient hostility" go (Gen. 25:19–34, Esau is also called Edom;

34:17 I will judge. God turned his attention to the individuals represented in the flock. Judgment would be metered out one by one.

34:23–24 Ezekiel described a future united kingdom with a divine king who would truly care for the sheep.

34:25 make a covenant of peace. The hallmark of this future kingdom is peace, in contrast to the present terror that surrounded Jerusalem.

35:2 Mount Seir. While on the subject of peace, God encouraged his people by judging one of their worst enemies, Edom (Gen. 32–33).

35:5 time of their calamity. Edom was a hostile nation and capitalized on Jerusalem's calamity. They showed their true colors and rushed in to raid the weakened city (Obad. 12–14).

punishment reached its climax, 6therefore as surely as I live, declares
the Sovereign LORD, I will give you over to bloodshed and it will pursue you. Since you did not hate bloodshed, bloodshed will pursue
you. 7I will make Mount Seir a desolate waste and cut off from it all
who come and go. 8I will fill your mountains with the slain; those
killed by the sword will fall on your hills and in your valleys and in all
your ravines. 9I will make you desolate forever; your towns will not be
inhabited. Then you will know that I am the LORD.

10" 'Because you have said, "These two nations and countries will
be ours and we will take possession of them," even though I the LORD
was there, 11therefore as surely as I live, declares the Sovereign LORD,
I will treat you in accordance with the anger and jealousy you
showed in your hatred of them and I will make myself known among
them when I judge you. 12Then you will know that I the LORD have
heard all the contemptible things you have said against the mountains of Israel. You said, "They have been laid waste and have been
given over to us to devour." 13You boasted against me and spoke
against me without restraint, and I heard it. 14This is what the Sovereign LORD says: While the whole earth rejoices, I will make you desolate. 15Because you rejoiced when the inheritance of the house of
Israel became desolate, that is how I will treat you. You will be desolate, O Mount Seir, you and all of Edom. Then they will know that I
am the LORD.' "

A Prophecy to the Mountains of Israel

36 "Son of man, prophesy to the mountains of Israel and say,
'O mountains of Israel, hear the word of the LORD. 2This is
what the Sovereign LORD says: The enemy said of you, "Aha! The ancient heights have become our possession." ' 3Therefore prophesy
and say, 'This is what the Sovereign LORD says: Because they ravaged
and hounded you from every side so that you became the possession
of the rest of the nations and the object of people's malicious talk
and slander, 4therefore, O mountains of Israel, hear the word of the
Sovereign LORD: This is what the Sovereign LORD says to the mountains and hills, to the ravines and valleys, to the desolate ruins and
the deserted towns that have been plundered and ridiculed by the
rest of the nations around you— 5this is what the Sovereign LORD
says: In my burning zeal I have spoken against the rest of the nations,
and against all Edom, for with glee and with malice in their hearts
they made my land their own possession so that they might plunder
its pastureland.' 6Therefore prophesy concerning the land of Israel
and say to the mountains and hills, to the ravines and valleys: 'This is
what the Sovereign LORD says: I speak in my jealous wrath because
you have suffered the scorn of the nations. 7Therefore this is what the
Sovereign LORD says: I swear with uplifted hand that the nations
around you will also suffer scorn.

8" 'But you, O mountains of Israel, will produce branches and fruit
for my people Israel, for they will soon come home. 9I am concerned

Obad. 11–14)? **3.** Why is God angry with the way Edom responded to Israel's calamity (vv. 5–6,10–13,15)? What will the Lord do to them? **4.** What will be the effect on the people of Edom and of Israel when they see the Lord's punishment (vv. 4,15)? **5.** Why do you think it was wrong for Edom to rejoice when God punished Israel?

APPLY 1. When has someone laughed when you were crying? **2.** What is your attitude when you see nasty people get what they deserve? What should it be? **3.** If you truly believed that God hears all you say, how would it affect how you talk about people this week (v. 12)?

OPEN 1. Are you afraid of heights? What is the highest spot you've visited? Was it man-made or natural? **2.** Have you or anyone you know had heart surgery? Was it a long ordeal or a quick operation? **3.** Which institution do you hate to deal with the most: Bank? Post office? Motor vehicles? IRS? Supermarket? Social security? Which bureaucrat gets the "Heart of Stone Award"?

STUDY 1. Ezekiel 6 was also directed to the mountains of Israel. What was the earlier message? What had happened in the mountains of Israel (6:13)? **2.** In light of the history of God's actions, why would the Israelites bother with idols in the "high places"? Why was idolatry a constant temptation? **3.** How would you summarize Ezekiel's new message to the mountains? Why did he use the same metaphor for both the good and bad news? **4.** What had Israel's enemies done (vv. 2–3)? What will God do to the nations which plundered Israel (vv. 6–7)? Wasn't this God's will (vv. 17–19)? Is God being fair to Israel's enemies? **5.** What did the nations say

35:6 hate bloodshed ... will pursue you. Edom would soon suffer the same fate it had once inflicted upon Jerusalem.

36:3 object of people's malicious talk. International humiliation had resulted in Jerusalem's humiliation. Now, those nations that scorned Jerusalem's weaknesses would be accountable to God.

36:5 made my land their own possession. Edom saw an opportunity to plunder a weakened city. However, God took the crime personally. They were actually plundering his land.

about God (vv. 20–21)? What motivated God to restore Israel (vv. 21–22)? **6.** Where will God perform "surgery" on the people of Israel (vv. 24–26)? What changes are "on the table"? What will happen to their land (vv. 29–30)? What will they remember (v. 31)? What did the people do to deserve God's actions (v. 32)? **7.** Would Israel become the kind of place you'd want to visit (vv. 35–38)? **8.** How do verses 24–27 shed light on the mission of Jesus (Jer. 31:33; Heb. 10:11–16)?

APPLY 1. Have you experienced any of God's promises to Israel: Cleansing? Stony heart transplant? Power to obey? Plentiful harvest? How did it happen? Which would you like to see happen? **2.** What shape is your heart in right now: Like a piece of granite? Being broken up by some hard blows? Being softened by the steady "rain" of the Spirit? Other? Why do you describe yourself like this? **3.** What fear keeps you from "climbing mountains"? Do you find your group a safe place to express your fears? Do the members: Listen and accept? Try to fix it? Analyze you? Approve or disapprove? What do you need when you're being vulnerable?

for you and will look on you with favor; you will be plowed and sown,
10and I will multiply the number of people upon you, even the whole
house of Israel. The towns will be inhabited and the ruins rebuilt. 11I
will increase the number of men and animals upon you, and they will
be fruitful and become numerous. I will settle people on you as in the
past and will make you prosper more than before. Then you will
know that I am the LORD. 12I will cause people, my people Israel, to
walk upon you. They will possess you, and you will be their inheritance; you will never again deprive them of their children.

13" 'This is what the Sovereign LORD says: Because people say to
you, "You devour men and deprive your nation of its children,"
14therefore you will no longer devour men or make your nation childless, declares the Sovereign LORD. 15No longer will I make you hear
the taunts of the nations, and no longer will you suffer the scorn of
the peoples or cause your nation to fall, declares the Sovereign
LORD.' "

16Again the word of the LORD came to me: 17"Son of man, when the
people of Israel were living in their own land, they defiled it by their
conduct and their actions. Their conduct was like a woman's monthly
uncleanness in my sight. 18So I poured out my wrath on them because they had shed blood in the land and because they had defiled it
with their idols. 19I dispersed them among the nations, and they were
scattered through the countries; I judged them according to their
conduct and their actions. 20And wherever they went among the nations they profaned my holy name, for it was said of them, 'These are
the LORD's people, and yet they had to leave his land.' 21I had concern
for my holy name, which the house of Israel profaned among the nations where they had gone.

22"Therefore say to the house of Israel, 'This is what the Sovereign
LORD says: It is not for your sake, O house of Israel, that I am going to
do these things, but for the sake of my holy name, which you have
profaned among the nations where you have gone. 23I will show the
holiness of my great name, which has been profaned among the nations, the name you have profaned among them. Then the nations
will know that I am the LORD, declares the Sovereign LORD, when I
show myself holy through you before their eyes.

24" 'For I will take you out of the nations; I will gather you from all
the countries and bring you back into your own land. 25I will sprinkle
clean water on you, and you will be clean; I will cleanse you from all
your impurities and from all your idols. 26I will give you a new heart
and put a new spirit in you; I will remove from you your heart of stone
and give you a heart of flesh. 27And I will put my Spirit in you and
move you to follow my decrees and be careful to keep my laws. 28You
will live in the land I gave your forefathers; you will be my people, and
I will be your God. 29I will save you from all your uncleanness. I will
call for the grain and make it plentiful and will not bring famine upon
you. 30I will increase the fruit of the trees and the crops of the field, so
that you will no longer suffer disgrace among the nations because of
famine. 31Then you will remember your evil ways and wicked deeds,
and you will loathe yourselves for your sins and detestable practices.

36:22 It is not for your sake ... Israel. God's restoration of his people was not a personal favor to the people. He recovered his nation for his own sake. This is the reason he gave for withholding wrath (20:9).

32 I want you to know that I am not doing this for your sake, declares the Sovereign LORD. Be ashamed and disgraced for your conduct, O house of Israel!

33 " 'This is what the Sovereign LORD says: On the day I cleanse you from all your sins, I will resettle your towns, and the ruins will be rebuilt. 34 The desolate land will be cultivated instead of lying desolate in the sight of all who pass through it. 35 They will say, "This land that was laid waste has become like the garden of Eden; the cities that were lying in ruins, desolate and destroyed, are now fortified and inhabited." 36 Then the nations around you that remain will know that I the LORD have rebuilt what was destroyed and have replanted what was desolate. I the LORD have spoken, and I will do it.'

37 "This is what the Sovereign LORD says: Once again I will yield to the plea of the house of Israel and do this for them: I will make their people as numerous as sheep, 38 as numerous as the flocks for offerings at Jerusalem during her appointed feasts. So will the ruined cities be filled with flocks of people. Then they will know that I am the LORD."

The Valley of Dry Bones

37 The hand of the LORD was upon me, and he brought me out by the Spirit of the LORD and set me in the middle of a valley; it was full of bones. 2 He led me back and forth among them, and I saw a great many bones on the floor of the valley, bones that were very dry. 3 He asked me, "Son of man, can these bones live?"

I said, "O Sovereign LORD, you alone know."

4 Then he said to me, "Prophesy to these bones and say to them, 'Dry bones, hear the word of the LORD! 5 This is what the Sovereign LORD says to these bones: I will make breath[a] enter you, and you will come to life. 6 I will attach tendons to you and make flesh come upon you and cover you with skin; I will put breath in you, and you will come to life. Then you will know that I am the LORD.' "

7 So I prophesied as I was commanded. And as I was prophesying, there was a noise, a rattling sound, and the bones came together, bone to bone. 8 I looked, and tendons and flesh appeared on them and skin covered them, but there was no breath in them.

9 Then he said to me, "Prophesy to the breath; prophesy, son of man, and say to it, 'This is what the Sovereign LORD says: Come from the four winds, O breath, and breathe into these slain, that they may live.' " 10 So I prophesied as he commanded me, and breath entered them; they came to life and stood up on their feet—a vast army.

11 Then he said to me: "Son of man, these bones are the whole house of Israel. They say, 'Our bones are dried up and our hope is gone; we are cut off.' 12 Therefore prophesy and say to them: 'This is

[a]5 The Hebrew for this word can also mean *wind* or *spirit* (see verses 6-14).

OPEN 1. Where have you gone where you've meditated on those who have gone before you: A cemetery? A national memorial? An ancient city like Athens or Rome? **2.** Where have you gone where you've contemplated your own past: A childhood home? Your alma mater? The site of a big decision you once made?

STUDY 1. Imagine a valley full of bones. Why might their dryness be significant (vv. 2, 4)? **2.** Hebrews uses the word "ruach" for "wind," "breath" and "spirit." How are these three related (vv. 5, 9, 14)? **3.** What are the two steps in raising these dead bones (vv. 7–10)? Why not do it all at once? **4.** How are the exiles feeling (v. 11)? What is God telling them about the future of: Israel? The individual? Humanity?

APPLY 1. If you could describe your own spiritual life in terms of this story, where would you be right now: In the "valley," wondering if the "old bones" of your life can ever live again? There's some rattling and things are starting to come together, but no real life yet? Alive and strong, standing with your "buds" in a

36:33 rebuilt. God promised to accomplish an otherwise impossible task (v. 36).

37:2 bones on the floor of the valley. The exposed bones were denied the dignity of a customary burial. In addition, the bones symbolized an extended time of neglect.

37:7 the bones came together. The bones were connected together to create form and shape.

37:8 but there was no breath. Similar to a balloon with no air, the lifeless shape lacked the mysterious and divine quality needed to bring it to life (Gen. 2:7).

37:11 our hope is gone. God wanted Israel to envision the possibilities. Yes, they could indeed be restored despite the desparity around them.

mighty army? **2.** What has God done recently to truly bring life to your spirit? **3.** How can group members help to raise each others' spirits?

OPEN 1. Do you learn best by hearing, seeing or doing? Give an example. **2.** Did you ever break something as a child and try to fix it without your parents finding out? Did it work?

STUDY The people of Israel split into northern and southern kingdoms after the death of Solomon. **1.** Which kingdom is the "stick of Judah" (1 Kin. 12:21–24)? Where was "Ephraim"? **2.** What is the "point" of Ezekiel's stick lesson to Israel? (vv. 22–23)? **3.** Who will be king of the united land (v. 24)? How long will his reign last? Who might this "David" represent? **4.** Do you think this prophecy has ever been fulfilled?

APPLY 1. What object lesson has illustrated God's truth to you recently? Have you been paying attention? **2.** Has your family been divided by: Sibling rivalry? Divorce? Long-standing feuds? Death? Can this brokenness be healed? How? **3.** Christendom is currently divided into hundreds of rival groups. Do you think God approves? What would it take to restore the unity of all believers as God intended (John 17:20–26)? Is your group open to other believers of different perspectives?

OPEN 1. Have you ever been given a nickname you couldn't stand? Would it embarrass you to tell the group? How does the name make you feel? **2.** Are your hunches about the future very reliable? Give an ex-

what the Sovereign LORD says: O my people, I am going to open your graves and bring you up from them; I will bring you back to the land of Israel. 13 Then you, my people, will know that I am the LORD, when I open your graves and bring you up from them. 14 I will put my Spirit in you and you will live, and I will settle you in your own land. Then you will know that I the LORD have spoken, and I have done it, declares the LORD.' "

One Nation Under One King

15 The word of the LORD came to me: 16 "Son of man, take a stick of wood and write on it, 'Belonging to Judah and the Israelites associated with him.' Then take another stick of wood, and write on it, 'Ephraim's stick, belonging to Joseph and all the house of Israel associated with him.' 17 Join them together into one stick so that they will become one in your hand.

18 "When your countrymen ask you, 'Won't you tell us what you mean by this?' 19 say to them, 'This is what the Sovereign LORD says: I am going to take the stick of Joseph—which is in Ephraim's hand—and of the Israelite tribes associated with him, and join it to Judah's stick, making them a single stick of wood, and they will become one in my hand.' 20 Hold before their eyes the sticks you have written on 21 and say to them, 'This is what the Sovereign LORD says: I will take the Israelites out of the nations where they have gone. I will gather them from all around and bring them back into their own land. 22 I will make them one nation in the land, on the mountains of Israel. There will be one king over all of them and they will never again be two nations or be divided into two kingdoms. 23 They will no longer defile themselves with their idols and vile images or with any of their offenses, for I will save them from all their sinful backsliding,[a] and I will cleanse them. They will be my people, and I will be their God.

24 " 'My servant David will be king over them, and they will all have one shepherd. They will follow my laws and be careful to keep my decrees. 25 They will live in the land I gave to my servant Jacob, the land where your fathers lived. They and their children and their children's children will live there forever, and David my servant will be their prince forever. 26 I will make a covenant of peace with them; it will be an everlasting covenant. I will establish them and increase their numbers, and I will put my sanctuary among them forever. 27 My dwelling place will be with them; I will be their God, and they will be my people. 28 Then the nations will know that I the LORD make Israel holy, when my sanctuary is among them forever.' "

A Prophecy Against Gog

38 The word of the LORD came to me: 2 "Son of man, set your face against Gog, of the land of Magog, the chief prince of[b]

[a] 23 Many Hebrew manuscripts (see also Septuagint); most Hebrew manuscripts *all their dwelling places where they sinned* [b] 2 Or *the prince of Rosh,*

37:14 I will settle you in your own land. God's promise was what his displaced people longed to hear. It gave them tremendous hope to return home.

37:17 together. Although Israel's past had been divided into two kingdoms for centuries, Ezekiel illustrated a united future.

37:19 become one in my hand. In the same way, God would just as easily join together his people under his rule.

37:24 David. When Israel imagined better times, David and his expansive rule came to mind. God used his example to stir their hopes for the future.

Meshech and Tubal; prophesy against him 3and say: 'This is what the
Sovereign LORD says: I am against you, O Gog, chief prince of[a]
Meshech and Tubal. 4I will turn you around, put hooks in your jaws
and bring you out with your whole army—your horses, your horsemen fully armed, and a great horde with large and small shields, all of
them brandishing their swords. 5Persia, Cush[b] and Put will be with
them, all with shields and helmets, 6also Gomer with all its troops,
and Beth Togarmah from the far north with all its troops—the many
nations with you.

7" 'Get ready; be prepared, you and all the hordes gathered about
you, and take command of them. 8After many days you will be called
to arms. In future years you will invade a land that has recovered
from war, whose people were gathered from many nations to the
mountains of Israel, which had long been desolate. They had been
brought out from the nations, and now all of them live in safety. 9You
and all your troops and the many nations with you will go up, advancing like a storm; you will be like a cloud covering the land.

10" 'This is what the Sovereign LORD says: On that day thoughts will
come into your mind and you will devise an evil scheme. 11You will
say, "I will invade a land of unwalled villages; I will attack a peaceful
and unsuspecting people—all of them living without walls and without gates and bars. 12I will plunder and loot and turn my hand against
the resettled ruins and the people gathered from the nations, rich in
livestock and goods, living at the center of the land." 13Sheba and
Dedan and the merchants of Tarshish and all her villages[c] will say to
you, "Have you come to plunder? Have you gathered your hordes to
loot, to carry off silver and gold, to take away livestock and goods
and to seize much plunder?" '

14"Therefore, son of man, prophesy and say to Gog: 'This is what
the Sovereign LORD says: In that day, when my people Israel are living
in safety, will you not take notice of it? 15You will come from your
place in the far north, you and many nations with you, all of them riding on horses, a great horde, a mighty army. 16You will advance
against my people Israel like a cloud that covers the land. In days to
come, O Gog, I will bring you against my land, so that the nations
may know me when I show myself holy through you before their
eyes.

17" 'This is what the Sovereign LORD says: Are you not the one I
spoke of in former days by my servants the prophets of Israel? At that
time they prophesied for years that I would bring you against them.
18This is what will happen in that day: When Gog attacks the land of
Israel, my hot anger will be aroused, declares the Sovereign LORD.
19In my zeal and fiery wrath I declare that at that time there shall be a

[a]3 Or *Gog, prince of Rosh,* [b]5 That is, the upper Nile region [c]13 Or *her strong lions*

ample of one that was either exactly right or laughably wrong. **3.** If you knew you were going to win, would that make playing a game more or less fun for you? Why?

STUDY 1. Gog is unknown to us outside this reference. Magog is Hebrew for "the place where Gog lives." What was the fate of Meshech and Tubal in 32:26? **2.** When will the invasion by Gog occur (vv. 8,14)? Is this an upcoming event or the distant future? **3.** What does Gog stand to gain from the attack (38:11–13)? Why is Israel "unwalled"? Who is really behind the attack (38:16–17)? Is God always behind wars? **4.** Will Gog win this war (38:18–22)? What will Israel do with Gog's weapons (39:9–10)? Wouldn't you keep a few for yourself? How long will it take to bury the dead (39:12)? Who do you think should spring for all the cemetery plots? **5.** What will God accomplish through this war? What will the whole world learn from it (39:21)? What will Israel learn (39:22)? **6.** What does Revelation 20:8–9 say about Gog? Do you think the books of Ezekiel and Revelation are describing the same event? Two events with similar characters? Is it all symbolic? Of what? **7.** Do you think prophecies concerning Israel in the "last days" refer to the Jewish people or the Christian church? How do you take them: Literally, complete with horses, shields and swords? Allegorically, with Gog and Magog representing actual countries? Symbolically, reflecting spiritual realities in believers' lives?

APPLY 1. How does the idea that God will ultimately destroy all evil make you feel? Sorry for those who are punished? Relieved? Vindicated? Scared? Expectant? Confident? Something else? All of the above? **2.** Do you feel that God is in control of your life? Your country? World destiny? How much depends on our human choices?

38:8 called to arms. Gog would be summoned to battle against Israel once God's people were finally resettled.

38:10 God would puppeteer Gog into play at a future time. Evil would once again be controlled by divine command.

38:11 unwalled villages. A peaceful and restored Israel would have no use for protective barriers. In this surreal future battle, Gog would take advantage of its vulnerability.

38:17 Are you not the one? Gog is identified as the subject of similar prophecies of days gone by (Joel 3:9–14).

38:19 great earthquake. God would intervene, announcing his presence in the form of a thunderous earthquake. He would shatter Gog's plans for victory. God would make his presence known.

great earthquake in the land of Israel. 20The fish of the sea, the birds
of the air, the beasts of the field, every creature that moves along the
ground, and all the people on the face of the earth will tremble at my
presence. The mountains will be overturned, the cliffs will crumble
and every wall will fall to the ground. 21I will summon a sword
against Gog on all my mountains, declares the Sovereign LORD. Every
man's sword will be against his brother. 22I will execute judgment
upon him with plague and bloodshed; I will pour down torrents of
rain, hailstones and burning sulfur on him and on his troops and on
the many nations with him. 23And so I will show my greatness and my
holiness, and I will make myself known in the sight of many nations.
Then they will know that I am the LORD.'

39 "Son of man, prophesy against Gog and say: 'This is what the
Sovereign LORD says: I am against you, O Gog, chief prince
of[a] Meshech and Tubal. 2I will turn you around and drag you along. I
will bring you from the far north and send you against the mountains
of Israel. 3Then I will strike your bow from your left hand and make
your arrows drop from your right hand. 4On the mountains of Israel
you will fall, you and all your troops and the nations with you. I will
give you as food to all kinds of carrion birds and to the wild animals.
5You will fall in the open field, for I have spoken, declares the Sovereign LORD. 6I will send fire on Magog and on those who live in safety
in the coastlands, and they will know that I am the LORD.

7" 'I will make known my holy name among my people Israel. I will
no longer let my holy name be profaned, and the nations will know
that I the LORD am the Holy One in Israel. 8It is coming! It will surely
take place, declares the Sovereign LORD. This is the day I have
spoken of.

9" 'Then those who live in the towns of Israel will go out and use
the weapons for fuel and burn them up—the small and large shields,
the bows and arrows, the war clubs and spears. For seven years they
will use them for fuel. 10They will not need to gather wood from the
fields or cut it from the forests, because they will use the weapons for
fuel. And they will plunder those who plundered them and loot those
who looted them, declares the Sovereign LORD.

11" 'On that day I will give Gog a burial place in Israel, in the valley
of those who travel east toward[b] the Sea.[c] It will block the way of
travelers, because Gog and all his hordes will be buried there. So it
will be called the Valley of Hamon Gog.[d]

12" 'For seven months the house of Israel will be burying them in
order to cleanse the land. 13All the people of the land will bury them,
and the day I am glorified will be a memorable day for them, declares
the Sovereign LORD.

14" 'Men will be regularly employed to cleanse the land. Some will
go throughout the land and, in addition to them, others will bury
those that remain on the ground. At the end of the seven months they
will begin their search. 15As they go through the land and one of them
sees a human bone, he will set up a marker beside it until the grave-

[a] 1 Or *Gog, prince of Rosh,* [b] 11 Or *of* [c] 11 That is, the Dead Sea [d] 11 *Hamon Gog* means *hordes of Gog.*

38:22 The enemy's internal confusion (v. 21) would be compounded by God's use of supernatural plagues and storms. Israel did not even need an army to assist him in accomplishing victory.

diggers have buried it in the Valley of Hamon Gog. 16(Also a town
called Hamonah[a] will be there.) And so they will cleanse the land.'
17"Son of man, this is what the Sovereign LORD says: Call out to
every kind of bird and all the wild animals: 'Assemble and come together from all around to the sacrifice I am preparing for you, the
great sacrifice on the mountains of Israel. There you will eat flesh
and drink blood. 18You will eat the flesh of mighty men and drink the
blood of the princes of the earth as if they were rams and lambs,
goats and bulls—all of them fattened animals from Bashan. 19At the
sacrifice I am preparing for you, you will eat fat till you are glutted
and drink blood till you are drunk. 20At my table you will eat your fill
of horses and riders, mighty men and soldiers of every kind,' declares
the Sovereign LORD.
21"I will display my glory among the nations, and all the nations
will see the punishment I inflict and the hand I lay upon them. 22From
that day forward the house of Israel will know that I am the LORD
their God. 23And the nations will know that the people of Israel went
into exile for their sin, because they were unfaithful to me. So I hid
my face from them and handed them over to their enemies, and they
all fell by the sword. 24I dealt with them according to their uncleanness and their offenses, and I hid my face from them.
25"Therefore this is what the Sovereign LORD says: I will now bring
Jacob back from captivity[b] and will have compassion on all the people of Israel, and I will be zealous for my holy name. 26They will forget
their shame and all the unfaithfulness they showed toward me when
they lived in safety in their land with no one to make them afraid.
27When I have brought them back from the nations and have gathered them from the countries of their enemies, I will show myself
holy through them in the sight of many nations. 28Then they will
know that I am the LORD their God, for though I sent them into exile
among the nations, I will gather them to their own land, not leaving
any behind. 29I will no longer hide my face from them, for I will pour
out my Spirit on the house of Israel, declares the Sovereign LORD."

The New Temple Area

40 In the twenty-fifth year of our exile, at the beginning of the
year, on the tenth of the month, in the fourteenth year after
the fall of the city—on that very day the hand of the LORD was upon
me and he took me there. 2In visions of God he took me to the land of
Israel and set me on a very high mountain, on whose south side were
some buildings that looked like a city. 3He took me there, and I saw a
man whose appearance was like bronze; he was standing in the gateway with a linen cord and a measuring rod in his hand. 4The man said
to me, "Son of man, look with your eyes and hear with your ears and
pay attention to everything I am going to show you, for that is why
you have been brought here. Tell the house of Israel everything you
see."

[a]*16 Hamonah* means *horde.* [b]*25* Or *now restore the fortunes of Jacob*

OPEN 1. Have you been in on the planning for any construction? Did you have your house built or were you part of a group that built or remodeled a church? What was the part you liked best? Least? **2.** When somebody "gives you the grand tour" through his or her new house, what do you notice? Are you usually envious of what they have? Smug that yours is better? Simply glad that they're happy?

STUDY 1. How many years passed between the fall of Jerusalem (33:21) and Ezekiel's vision of the temple (v. 1)? **2.** Solomon built the original temple around 950 B.C.

39:22–23 God's reputation is one of justice and mercy (v. 25) when it comes to his own people. He showed compassion and safeguarded his name.

40:2 set me on a very high mountain. Ezekiel was taken to a future restored Jerusalem and seated upon Mount Zion.

40:4 pay attention to everything I ... show you. A sketch of the new temple's dimensions was easily made from his descriptions.

The Babylonians destroyed it in 586 B.C. The exiles finished rebuilding it in 515 B.C. Why do you think the temple was so important to the Jewish people? **3.** Where will the new temple be located? In relation to the city (v. 2)? **4.** The long cubit was about 21 inches, making the man's measuring rod about 10 feet long. How high and thick is the outer wall (v. 5)? Why do you think Ezekiel records every "nook and cranny"? Is God this concerned about modern buildings of worship? **5.** Ezekiel can enter the outer court from three sides. How are these outer gates decorated (vv. 8–16)? What does this suggest about Hebrew religious art? **6.** There are three entrances to the inner court. What is the purpose of the rooms at the north and south inner gates? How are they furnished (for more detail on the description of the gates, see vv. 20–49)? What profession could the priests fall back on during an exile? **7.** What two groups of priests get the rooms inside the inner gates (vv. 45–46)? Who was Zadok (2 Sam. 8:17–18; 1 Kin. 1:38–39)?

APPLY 1. What physical place best draws you into worship? Do you prefer a large ornate sanctuary or a simple chapel? How much are the senses of sight and hearing involved? Smell? Taste? Touch? **2.** Imagine you are a temple. The outer court is your public life with casual friends, the inner court your private heart. Who are the "faithful few" who see that inner court? What "sacrifice" did they make to gain entrance? When do you feel you can "open the gates" in safety?

The East Gate to the Outer Court

5 I saw a wall completely surrounding the temple area. The length of the measuring rod in the man's hand was six long cubits, each of which was a cubit[a] and a handbreadth.[b] He measured the wall; it was one measuring rod thick and one rod high.

6 Then he went to the gate facing east. He climbed its steps and measured the threshold of the gate; it was one rod deep.[c] 7 The alcoves for the guards were one rod long and one rod wide, and the projecting walls between the alcoves were five cubits thick. And the threshold of the gate next to the portico facing the temple was one rod deep.

8 Then he measured the portico of the gateway; 9 it[d] was eight cubits deep and its jambs were two cubits thick. The portico of the gateway faced the temple.

10 Inside the east gate were three alcoves on each side; the three had the same measurements, and the faces of the projecting walls on each side had the same measurements. 11 Then he measured the width of the entrance to the gateway; it was ten cubits and its length was thirteen cubits. 12 In front of each alcove was a wall one cubit high, and the alcoves were six cubits square. 13 Then he measured the gateway from the top of the rear wall of one alcove to the top of the opposite one; the distance was twenty-five cubits from one parapet opening to the opposite one. 14 He measured along the faces of the projecting walls all around the inside of the gateway—sixty cubits. The measurement was up to the portico[e] facing the courtyard.[f] 15 The distance from the entrance of the gateway to the far end of its portico was fifty cubits. 16 The alcoves and the projecting walls inside the gateway were surmounted by narrow parapet openings all around, as was the portico; the openings all around faced inward. The faces of the projecting walls were decorated with palm trees.

The Outer Court

17 Then he brought me into the outer court. There I saw some rooms and a pavement that had been constructed all around the court; there were thirty rooms along the pavement. 18 It abutted the sides of the gateways and was as wide as they were long; this was the lower pavement. 19 Then he measured the distance from the inside of the lower gateway to the outside of the inner court; it was a hundred cubits on the east side as well as on the north.

The North Gate

20 Then he measured the length and width of the gate facing north, leading into the outer court. 21 Its alcoves—three on each side—its projecting walls and its portico had the same measurements as those of the first gateway. It was fifty cubits long and twenty-five cubits wide. 22 Its openings, its portico and its palm tree decorations had the same measurements as those of the gate facing east. Seven steps led up to it, with its portico opposite them. 23 There was a gate to the inner court facing the north gate, just as there was on the east. He measured from one gate to the opposite one; it was a hundred cubits.

[a]5 The common cubit was about 1 1/2 feet (about 0.5 meter). [b]5 That is, about 3 inches (about 8 centimeters) [c]6 Septuagint; Hebrew *deep, the first threshold, one rod deep* [d]8,9 Many Hebrew manuscripts, Septuagint, Vulgate and Syriac; most Hebrew manuscripts *gateway facing the temple; it was one rod deep. 9Then he measured the portico of the gateway; it* [e]14 Septuagint; Hebrew *projecting wall* [f]14 The meaning of the Hebrew for this verse is uncertain.

The South Gate

[24]Then he led me to the south side and I saw a gate facing south. He measured its jambs and its portico, and they had the same measurements as the others. [25]The gateway and its portico had narrow openings all around, like the openings of the others. It was fifty cubits long and twenty-five cubits wide. [26]Seven steps led up to it, with its portico opposite them; it had palm tree decorations on the faces of the projecting walls on each side. [27]The inner court also had a gate facing south, and he measured from this gate to the outer gate on the south side; it was a hundred cubits.

Gates to the Inner Court

[28]Then he brought me into the inner court through the south gate, and he measured the south gate; it had the same measurements as the others. [29]Its alcoves, its projecting walls and its portico had the same measurements as the others. The gateway and its portico had openings all around. It was fifty cubits long and twenty-five cubits wide. [30](The porticoes of the gateways around the inner court were twenty-five cubits wide and five cubits deep.) [31]Its portico faced the outer court; palm trees decorated its jambs, and eight steps led up to it.

[32]Then he brought me to the inner court on the east side, and he measured the gateway; it had the same measurements as the others. [33]Its alcoves, its projecting walls and its portico had the same measurements as the others. The gateway and its portico had openings all around. It was fifty cubits long and twenty-five cubits wide. [34]Its portico faced the outer court; palm trees decorated the jambs on either side, and eight steps led up to it.

[35]Then he brought me to the north gate and measured it. It had the same measurements as the others, [36]as did its alcoves, its projecting walls and its portico, and it had openings all around. It was fifty cubits long and twenty-five cubits wide. [37]Its portico[a] faced the outer court; palm trees decorated the jambs on either side, and eight steps led up to it.

The Rooms for Preparing Sacrifices

[38]A room with a doorway was by the portico in each of the inner gateways, where the burnt offerings were washed. [39]In the portico of the gateway were two tables on each side, on which the burnt offerings, sin offerings and guilt offerings were slaughtered. [40]By the outside wall of the portico of the gateway, near the steps at the entrance to the north gateway were two tables, and on the other side of the steps were two tables. [41]So there were four tables on one side of the gateway and four on the other—eight tables in all—on which the sacrifices were slaughtered. [42]There were also four tables of dressed stone for the burnt offerings, each a cubit and a half long, a cubit and a half wide and a cubit high. On them were placed the utensils for

[a]37 Septuagint (see also verses 31 and 34); Hebrew *jambs*

40:38 burnt offerings. Even in the new temple, burnt sacrifices were reinstated as a meaningful tradition.

slaughtering the burnt offerings and the other sacrifices. 43 And double-pronged hooks, each a handbreadth long, were attached to the wall all around. The tables were for the flesh of the offerings.

Rooms for the Priests

44 Outside the inner gate, within the inner court, were two rooms, one[a] at the side of the north gate and facing south, and another at the side of the south[b] gate and facing north. 45 He said to me, "The room facing south is for the priests who have charge of the temple, 46 and the room facing north is for the priests who have charge of the altar. These are the sons of Zadok, who are the only Levites who may draw near to the LORD to minister before him."

47 Then he measured the court: It was square—a hundred cubits long and a hundred cubits wide. And the altar was in front of the temple.

The Temple

48 He brought me to the portico of the temple and measured the jambs of the portico; they were five cubits wide on either side. The width of the entrance was fourteen cubits and its projecting walls were[c] three cubits wide on either side. 49 The portico was twenty cubits wide, and twelve[d] cubits from front to back. It was reached by a flight of stairs,[e] and there were pillars on each side of the jambs.

41 Then the man brought me to the outer sanctuary and measured the jambs; the width of the jambs was six cubits[f] on each side.[g] 2 The entrance was ten cubits wide, and the projecting walls on each side of it were five cubits wide. He also measured the outer sanctuary; it was forty cubits long and twenty cubits wide.

3 Then he went into the inner sanctuary and measured the jambs of the entrance; each was two cubits wide. The entrance was six cubits wide, and the projecting walls on each side of it were seven cubits wide. 4 And he measured the length of the inner sanctuary; it was twenty cubits, and its width was twenty cubits across the end of the outer sanctuary. He said to me, "This is the Most Holy Place."

5 Then he measured the wall of the temple; it was six cubits thick, and each side room around the temple was four cubits wide. 6 The side rooms were on three levels, one above another, thirty on each level. There were ledges all around the wall of the temple to serve as supports for the side rooms, so that the supports were not inserted into the wall of the temple. 7 The side rooms all around the temple were wider at each successive level. The structure surrounding the temple was built in ascending stages, so that the rooms widened as one went upward. A stairway went up from the lowest floor to the top floor through the middle floor.

8 I saw that the temple had a raised base all around it, forming the foundation of the side rooms. It was the length of the rod, six long cubits. 9 The outer wall of the side rooms was five cubits thick. The open area between the side rooms of the temple 10 and the ⌊priests'⌋ rooms was twenty cubits wide all around the temple. 11 There were entrances to the side rooms from the open area, one on the north and

[a]44 Septuagint; Hebrew *were rooms for singers, which were* [b]44 Septuagint; Hebrew *east* [c]48 Septuagint; Hebrew *entrance was* [d]49 Septuagint; Hebrew *eleven* [e]49 Hebrew; Septuagint *Ten steps led up to it*
[f]1 The common cubit was about 1 1/2 feet (about 0.5 meter). [g]1 One Hebrew manuscript and Septuagint; most Hebrew manuscripts *side, the width of the tent*

OPEN 1. Have you ever visited a cathedral? What impressed you the most? What didn't impress you? **2.** Do you know anyone who is two-faced? How did he or she earn such a description?

STUDY 1. Inside the inner court is the temple proper, consisting of an entrance portico, an outer sanctuary and an inner sanctuary. What is the inner sanctuary called (41: 4)? How big is it? **2.** What are dimensions of the entire temple (41:13–14)? Did you expect it to be this size? **3.** What kind of wall covering was inside the temple (41:15–16)? What figures adorn the wood (41:18–19)? How does this differ from Solomon's original decor (1 Kin. 6:29–30)? What might be the significance of these "two-faced" creatures? **4.** What are the dimensions of the wooden altar (41:22)? Do you find this impressive? **5.** Why do you think it was so important for Israel to know the temple would be rebuilt? What did it symbolize to them?

APPLY 1. What symbolizes the presence of God to you? How can you be more aware of his presence in your life? **2.** How would you design the ideal place for you to worship? Where would it be? What would have to be present?

another on the south; and the base adjoining the open area was five
cubits wide all around.
12The building facing the temple courtyard on the west side was
seventy cubits wide. The wall of the building was five cubits thick all
around, and its length was ninety cubits.
13Then he measured the temple; it was a hundred cubits long, and
the temple courtyard and the building with its walls were also a
hundred cubits long. 14The width of the temple courtyard on the east,
including the front of the temple, was a hundred cubits.
15Then he measured the length of the building facing the courtyard
at the rear of the temple, including its galleries on each side; it was a
hundred cubits.

The outer sanctuary, the inner sanctuary and the portico facing the
court, 16as well as the thresholds and the narrow windows and galleries around the three of them—everything beyond and including
the threshold was covered with wood. The floor, the wall up to the
windows, and the windows were covered. 17In the space above the
outside of the entrance to the inner sanctuary and on the walls at
regular intervals all around the inner and outer sanctuary 18were
carved cherubim and palm trees. Palm trees alternated with cherubim. Each cherub had two faces: 19the face of a man toward the palm
tree on one side and the face of a lion toward the palm tree on the
other. They were carved all around the whole temple. 20From the floor
to the area above the entrance, cherubim and palm trees were carved
on the wall of the outer sanctuary.
21The outer sanctuary had a rectangular doorframe, and the one at
the front of the Most Holy Place was similar. 22There was a wooden
altar three cubits high and two cubits square[a]; its corners, its base[b]
and its sides were of wood. The man said to me, "This is the table that
is before the LORD." 23Both the outer sanctuary and the Most Holy
Place had double doors. 24Each door had two leaves—two hinged
leaves for each door. 25And on the doors of the outer sanctuary were
carved cherubim and palm trees like those carved on the walls, and
there was a wooden overhang on the front of the portico. 26On the
sidewalls of the portico were narrow windows with palm trees carved
on each side. The side rooms of the temple also had overhangs.

Rooms for the Priests

42 Then the man led me northward into the outer court and
brought me to the rooms opposite the temple courtyard and
opposite the outer wall on the north side. 2The building whose door
faced north was a hundred cubits[c] long and fifty cubits wide. 3Both in
the section twenty cubits from the inner court and in the section
opposite the pavement of the outer court, gallery faced gallery at the
three levels. 4In front of the rooms was an inner passageway ten
cubits wide and a hundred cubits[d] long. Their doors were on the

[a]22 Septuagint; Hebrew *long* [b]22 Septuagint; Hebrew *length* [c]2 The common cubit was about 1 1/2 feet (about 0.5 meter). [d]4 Septuagint and Syriac; Hebrew *and one cubit*

OPEN 1. Have you ever visited a monastery? Met a monk? What are the common stereotypes of monks? **2.** Do you dress up for church? Why or why not?

STUDY 1. What did the priests do with the sacrifices of the people (v. 13)? What was the function of the three offerings: Grain (Num. 6:14–23; 15:2–4)? Sin (Lev. 4:27–31; 6:24–30)? Guilt (Lev. 5:14–16)? **2.** What garments did the priests have to wear in the sanctuary (Ex.

41:13 The temple was just over 87 feet wide and 175 feet long.

41:18 Two-faced angelic creatures provided a thorough guarding of the temple (11:22).

41:22 wooden altar. A large wooden altar served as the only furniture accessory listed. This altar may be where the Bread of Presence was placed (Ex. 25:30; 1 Kin. 6:20).

28:4)? Why couldn't they wear them home (v. 14)? How can clothes be holy? **3.** What is the purpose of the outside temple wall (v. 20)? What makes a place holy? Common? Why separate them? **4.** During the exile, Judaism was forced to develop new institutions, such as rabbis, synagogues, formal prayers, etc., as temporary substitutes for the temple, sacrifices, priests, etc. Many of the new institutions survive today within Judaism. In what ways have these institutions influenced Christianity (remember that Jesus and many of the early believers were rabbis)? Why bother reading about Jewish temple regulations?

APPLY 1. Priests acted as bridges between God and Israel. Do any of the following act as a bridge for God's love to you: The Bible? Other believers? A spiritual leader? The Lord's Supper? Nature? What else has been your "priest"? **2.** When were you a priest for someone else? What happened? **3.** In your life, do you have holy places? Times? People? Objects? What makes something holy?

OPEN What favorite entertainer of yours has made a big comeback? Who should make a "go-away"?

STUDY 1. Why did the glory of the Lord depart from the temple? Where did the Lord go (10:18–19; 11:22–23)? **2.** Where does Ezekiel encounter God (v. 5)? Can he see God? **3.** Why does God need to "a resting place" (Isa. 66:1)? Why is the

north. 5Now the upper rooms were narrower, for the galleries took
more space from them than from the rooms on the lower and middle
floors of the building. 6The rooms on the third floor had no pillars, as
the courts had; so they were smaller in floor space than those on the
lower and middle floors. 7There was an outer wall parallel to the
rooms and the outer court; it extended in front of the rooms for fifty
cubits. 8While the row of rooms on the side next to the outer court
was fifty cubits long, the row on the side nearest the sanctuary was a
hundred cubits long. 9The lower rooms had an entrance on the east
side as one enters them from the outer court.

10On the south side[a] along the length of the wall of the outer court,
adjoining the temple courtyard and opposite the outer wall, were
rooms 11with a passageway in front of them. These were like the
rooms on the north; they had the same length and width, with similar
exits and dimensions. Similar to the doorways on the north 12were
the doorways of the rooms on the south. There was a doorway at the
beginning of the passageway that was parallel to the corresponding
wall extending eastward, by which one enters the rooms.

13Then he said to me, "The north and south rooms facing the temple courtyard are the priests' rooms, where the priests who approach
the LORD will eat the most holy offerings. There they will put the most
holy offerings—the grain offerings, the sin offerings and the guilt
offerings—for the place is holy. 14Once the priests enter the holy precincts, they are not to go into the outer court until they leave behind
the garments in which they minister, for these are holy. They are to
put on other clothes before they go near the places that are for the
people."

15When he had finished measuring what was inside the temple
area, he led me out by the east gate and measured the area all
around: 16He measured the east side with the measuring rod; it was
five hundred cubits.[b] 17He measured the north side; it was five hundred cubits[c] by the measuring rod. 18He measured the south side; it
was five hundred cubits by the measuring rod. 19Then he turned to
the west side and measured; it was five hundred cubits by the measuring rod. 20So he measured the area on all four sides. It had a wall
around it, five hundred cubits long and five hundred cubits wide, to
separate the holy from the common.

The Glory Returns to the Temple

43 Then the man brought me to the gate facing east, 2and I saw
the glory of the God of Israel coming from the east. His voice
was like the roar of rushing waters, and the land was radiant with
his glory. 3The vision I saw was like the vision I had seen when he[d]
came to destroy the city and like the visions I had seen by the Kebar
River, and I fell facedown. 4The glory of the LORD entered the temple

[a]*10* Septuagint; Hebrew *Eastward* [b]*16* See Septuagint of verse 17; Hebrew *rods*; also in verses 18 and 19. [c]*17* Septuagint; Hebrew *rods* [d]*3* Some Hebrew manuscripts and Vulgate; most Hebrew manuscripts *I*

42:13 eat the most holy offerings. Ezekiel described images that were very close to home. The Jews recognized the priests' traditional sampling of the offerings as a familiar command (Lev. 6:16,26,29).

43:2 God, who previously abandoned the defiled temple in Jerusalem (11:22–23), now returned in triumphant procession to reclaim his place among his people.

through the gate facing east. 5 Then the Spirit lifted me up and
brought me into the inner court, and the glory of the LORD filled the
temple.
6 While the man was standing beside me, I heard someone speaking
to me from inside the temple. 7 He said: "Son of man, this is the place
of my throne and the place for the soles of my feet. This is where I will
live among the Israelites forever. The house of Israel will never again
defile my holy name—neither they nor their kings—by their
prostitution[a] and the lifeless idols[b] of their kings at their high places.
8 When they placed their threshold next to my threshold and their
doorposts beside my doorposts, with only a wall between me and
them, they defiled my holy name by their detestable practices. So I
destroyed them in my anger. 9 Now let them put away from me their
prostitution and the lifeless idols of their kings, and I will live among
them forever.
10 "Son of man, describe the temple to the people of Israel, that they
may be ashamed of their sins. Let them consider the plan, 11 and if
they are ashamed of all they have done, make known to them the
design of the temple—its arrangement, its exits and entrances—its
whole design and all its regulations[c] and laws. Write these down before them so that they may be faithful to its design and follow all its
regulations.
12 "This is the law of the temple: All the surrounding area on top of
the mountain will be most holy. Such is the law of the temple.

The Altar

13 "These are the measurements of the altar in long cubits, that cubit being a cubit[d] and a handbreadth[e]: Its gutter is a cubit deep and a
cubit wide, with a rim of one span[f] around the edge. And this is the
height of the altar: 14 From the gutter on the ground up to the lower
ledge it is two cubits high and a cubit wide, and from the smaller
ledge up to the larger ledge it is four cubits high and a cubit wide.
15 The altar hearth is four cubits high, and four horns project upward
from the hearth. 16 The altar hearth is square, twelve cubits long and
twelve cubits wide. 17 The upper ledge also is square, fourteen cubits
long and fourteen cubits wide, with a rim of half a cubit and a gutter
of a cubit all around. The steps of the altar face east."
18 Then he said to me, "Son of man, this is what the Sovereign LORD
says: These will be the regulations for sacrificing burnt offerings and
sprinkling blood upon the altar when it is built: 19 You are to give a
young bull as a sin offering to the priests, who are Levites, of the
family of Zadok, who come near to minister before me, declares the

[a]7 Or *their spiritual adultery*; also in verse 9 [b]7 Or *the corpses*; also in verse 9 [c]11 Some Hebrew manuscripts and Septuagint; most Hebrew manuscripts *regulations and its whole design* [d]13 The common cubit was about 1 1/2 feet (about 0.5 meter). [e]13 That is, about 3 inches (about 8 centimeters) [f]13 That is, about 9 inches (about 22 centimeters)

image of God at rest important? **4.** Solomon built his palace adjacent to the temple. What kind of neighbors were the Judean kings (v. 8)? **5.** Why would the exiles feel ashamed upon hearing of the new temple plan (vv. 10–11)? **6.** What is the law of the temple?

APPLY 1. How do you experience the "glory of the LORD?" **2.** When did God seem far away? Has God made a comeback or are you still feeling distant? **3.** Think of someone you were once close to but no longer have a relationship with. How would you renew it if you could?

OPEN 1. Have you served on a jury? What verdict did you give? Or did you arrange to be relieved from jury duty? **2.** What bad habit could you quit anytime? What habit would be harder to quit?

STUDY 1. Compare the altar dimensions in verses 13–17 with the description of 41:22. Why the difference? How was the small altar in the Most Holy Place used (Ex. 30:1–10)? How was the large altar used (1 Kin. 8:64)? **2.** What sacrifices were required the first week (vv. 18–26)? Why do you think this was necessary? **3.** What sacrifices were offered after the eighth day (v. 27)? What did these ceremonies mean to the people? **4.** List the three types of "fellowship offerings" (Lev. 7:11–20). Why couldn't some parts be eaten (Lev. 3:14–17)? **5.** Ezekiel says that animal sacrifices will make Israel acceptable. Does sacrifice play a role in Christian faith (Heb.

43:5 glory. The long-awaited day finally came. God's presence, symbolized in splendor and glory, filled the temple (v. 4).

43:8 Solomon built his palace close to the temple, blurring the distinction between what was holy and what was his (1 Kin. 7:1–12). God resented the confusion.

43:13–15 Ezekiel described the features involved in the religious services that will highlight the future temple. The altar of the new temple was considerably larger than that of Solomon's. The priests would arrive at the altar (the actual site of sacrifice) by a flight of steps.

43:19 sin offering to the priests. Similar to a christening, the first act of sacrifice at the new temple was sanctification—setting it apart as a holy place.

Sovereign LORD. [20]You are to take some of its blood and put it on the four horns of the altar and on the four corners of the upper ledge and all around the rim, and so purify the altar and make atonement for it. [21]You are to take the bull for the sin offering and burn it in the designated part of the temple area outside the sanctuary.

[22]"On the second day you are to offer a male goat without defect for a sin offering, and the altar is to be purified as it was purified with the bull. [23]When you have finished purifying it, you are to offer a young bull and a ram from the flock, both without defect. [24]You are to offer them before the LORD, and the priests are to sprinkle salt on them and sacrifice them as a burnt offering to the LORD.

[25]"For seven days you are to provide a male goat daily for a sin offering; you are also to provide a young bull and a ram from the flock, both without defect. [26]For seven days they are to make atonement for the altar and cleanse it; thus they will dedicate it. [27]At the end of these days, from the eighth day on, the priests are to present your burnt offerings and fellowship offerings[a] on the altar. Then I will accept you, declares the Sovereign LORD."

The Prince, the Levites, the Priests

44 Then the man brought me back to the outer gate of the sanctuary, the one facing east, and it was shut. [2]The LORD said to me, "This gate is to remain shut. It must not be opened; no one may enter through it. It is to remain shut because the LORD, the God of Israel, has entered through it. [3]The prince himself is the only one who may sit inside the gateway to eat in the presence of the LORD. He is to enter by way of the portico of the gateway and go out the same way."

[4]Then the man brought me by way of the north gate to the front of the temple. I looked and saw the glory of the LORD filling the temple of the LORD, and I fell facedown.

[5]The LORD said to me, "Son of man, look carefully, listen closely and give attention to everything I tell you concerning all the regulations regarding the temple of the LORD. Give attention to the entrance of the temple and all the exits of the sanctuary. [6]Say to the rebellious house of Israel, 'This is what the Sovereign LORD says: Enough of your detestable practices, O house of Israel! [7]In addition to all your other detestable practices, you brought foreigners uncircumcised in heart and flesh into my sanctuary, desecrating my temple while you offered me food, fat and blood, and you broke my covenant. [8]Instead of carrying out your duty in regard to my holy things, you put others in charge of my sanctuary. [9]This is what the Sovereign LORD says: No

[a]27 Traditionally *peace offerings*

10:12)? What is Paul's concept of a "living sacrifice" (Rom. 12:1)?

APPLY 1. What do you need to give up to be closer to God? Has it been hard to make the sacrifice? Why or why not? Can the group help? **2.** Is there anything you own that you would not "lay on the altar" if God demanded it?

OPEN 1. Have you ever known a leader or teacher who didn't "practice what he preached"? What effect did it have on you? **2.** Would you bother to pick up a penny from the gutter? Three pennies? A nickel? Dollar bill? What amount is worth the effort?

STUDY 1. Why is the eastern gateway sealed (vv. 1–3)? Why do you think the prince is the only person allowed to eat sacrifices in this area? **2.** Besides all the other sins mentioned in previous chapters, what had Israel done to dishonor the Lord (vv. 5–9)? What do you think it means to be uncircumcised in heart? **3.** Who were some famous members of the tribe of Levi (Ex. 2:1–10; 4:14)? What "put food on the table" in a Levite home (Deut. 18:1–5)? How had some of the Levites strayed from the Lord (v. 12)? How does their job description read (vv. 11,13–14)? How will the faithful Levites serve (vv. 15–16)? **4.** What might be wrong with wearing wool (vv. 17–18)? In what ways were the priests in the new temple to

43:21 The blood of the sacrifice was necessary to accomplish the offering. Then the animal carcasses were burned outside of the temple (Lev. 4:12,21).

43:27 *fellowship offerings.* A solemn week of sanctification passed before the jubilation could begin. Fellowship offerings allowed the people to share the bounty of meat.

44:2 gate. The sealed gate remained a symbol of God's holiness. No one else could enter through it, as God had when he first entered the temple (43:4).

44:3 eat. This prince is allowed to partake in the fellowship offerings of the people (Lev. 7:15–21). He eats in a separate area away from the people.

44:7 desecrating my temple. Ezekiel's careful review of the religious observances and traditions associated with the new temple served as a warning. God would forbid history to repeat itself. Israel could not disregard these new observances as they had before. They had ignored God and had allowed unbelieving foreigners to serve in the sanctuary.

foreigner uncircumcised in heart and flesh is to enter my sanctuary, not even the foreigners who live among the Israelites.

10 " 'The Levites who went far from me when Israel went astray and who wandered from me after their idols must bear the consequences of their sin. 11 They may serve in my sanctuary, having charge of the gates of the temple and serving in it; they may slaughter the burnt offerings and sacrifices for the people and stand before the people and serve them. 12 But because they served them in the presence of their idols and made the house of Israel fall into sin, therefore I have sworn with uplifted hand that they must bear the consequences of their sin, declares the Sovereign LORD. 13 They are not to come near to serve me as priests or come near any of my holy things or my most holy offerings; they must bear the shame of their detestable practices. 14 Yet I will put them in charge of the duties of the temple and all the work that is to be done in it.

15 " 'But the priests, who are Levites and descendants of Zadok and who faithfully carried out the duties of my sanctuary when the Israelites went astray from me, are to come near to minister before me; they are to stand before me to offer sacrifices of fat and blood, declares the Sovereign LORD. 16 They alone are to enter my sanctuary; they alone are to come near my table to minister before me and perform my service.

17 " 'When they enter the gates of the inner court, they are to wear linen clothes; they must not wear any woolen garment while ministering at the gates of the inner court or inside the temple. 18 They are to wear linen turbans on their heads and linen undergarments around their waists. They must not wear anything that makes them perspire. 19 When they go out into the outer court where the people are, they are to take off the clothes they have been ministering in and are to leave them in the sacred rooms, and put on other clothes, so that they do not consecrate the people by means of their garments.

20 " 'They must not shave their heads or let their hair grow long, but they are to keep the hair of their heads trimmed. 21 No priest is to drink wine when he enters the inner court. 22 They must not marry widows or divorced women; they may marry only virgins of Israelite descent or widows of priests. 23 They are to teach my people the difference between the holy and the common and show them how to distinguish between the unclean and the clean.

24 " 'In any dispute, the priests are to serve as judges and decide it according to my ordinances. They are to keep my laws and my decrees for all my appointed feasts, and they are to keep my Sabbaths holy.

25 " 'A priest must not defile himself by going near a dead person;

sanctify themselves (vv. 20–31)? What was the point of these regulations? **5.** Do you think any dispute in Israel could be considered a secular issue? **6.** Circumcision made a male a Jew. Why did God exclude non-Jews from his temple?

APPLY 1. What helps you discern the "holy" in the midst of the common (v. 23)? When have you recently experienced the "holy"? **2.** Does your life show the cleanness or holiness of God? **3.** What characterizes your tithes and offerings: Prime rib? Rump roast? Leftovers? How can you give God your first fruits? Is money the only acceptable sacrifice?

44:10 bear the consequences. The weight of the sins of the Levites was heavy indeed, for they were supposed to be the spiritual leader-priests (Deut. 33:8–11). As a result, all Levites (except those related to Zadok the priest (v. 15)) would be limited in their future role (vv. 13–14).

44:15 But the priests. The faithful priests descended from Zadok were allowed full access in the temple sacrifices as a reward for their devotion and purity (1 Sam. 2:27–36).

44:16 perform my service. Ezekiel's vision centered on a renewed sense of worship and commitment to the task. As a sign of renewal, priests would reintroduce their religious ordinances.

44:17 linen clothes. Linen often represented holiness and distinction (9:2).

44:20 hair. The priests would be separate from all other people. Therefore, they shared a common code of conduct and appearance (Lev. 21:1–5; Num. 6:5).

44:23 difference between the holy and the common. The restored Israelites would need remedial learning. Like children learning basic life-skills, they needed to learn the elemental aspects of holiness.

44:24 priests ... as judges. The priests' legal role was nothing new. Early on, they were commanded to settle disputes between the people (2 Chr. 19:8–11). These responsibilities were brought back again with Ezekiel's guidance.

however, if the dead person was his father or mother, son or daughter, brother or unmarried sister, then he may defile himself. 26After he
is cleansed, he must wait seven days. 27On the day he goes into the
inner court of the sanctuary to minister in the sanctuary, he is to offer
a sin offering for himself, declares the Sovereign LORD.
28" 'I am to be the only inheritance the priests have. You are to give
them no possession in Israel; I will be their possession. 29They will
eat the grain offerings, the sin offerings and the guilt offerings; and
everything in Israel devoted[a] to the LORD will belong to them. 30The
best of all the firstfruits and of all your special gifts will belong to the
priests. You are to give them the first portion of your ground meal so
that a blessing may rest on your household. 31The priests must not
eat anything, bird or animal, found dead or torn by wild animals.

Division of the Land

45 " 'When you allot the land as an inheritance, you are to present to the LORD a portion of the land as a sacred district,
25,000 cubits long and 20,000[b] cubits wide; the entire area will be
holy. 2Of this, a section 500 cubits square is to be for the sanctuary,
with 50 cubits around it for open land. 3In the sacred district, measure off a section 25,000 cubits[c] long and 10,000 cubits[d] wide. In it
will be the sanctuary, the Most Holy Place. 4It will be the sacred portion of the land for the priests, who minister in the sanctuary and
who draw near to minister before the LORD. It will be a place for their
houses as well as a holy place for the sanctuary. 5An area 25,000 cubits long and 10,000 cubits wide will belong to the Levites, who serve
in the temple, as their possession for towns to live in.[e]
6" 'You are to give the city as its property an area 5,000 cubits wide
and 25,000 cubits long, adjoining the sacred portion; it will belong to
the whole house of Israel.
7" 'The prince will have the land bordering each side of the area
formed by the sacred district and the property of the city. It will extend westward from the west side and eastward from the east side,
running lengthwise from the western to the eastern border parallel to
one of the tribal portions. 8This land will be his possession in Israel.
And my princes will no longer oppress my people but will allow the
house of Israel to possess the land according to their tribes.
9" 'This is what the Sovereign LORD says: You have gone far
enough, O princes of Israel! Give up your violence and oppression
and do what is just and right. Stop dispossessing my people, declares
the Sovereign LORD. 10You are to use accurate scales, an accurate

[a]29 The Hebrew term refers to the irrevocable giving over of things or persons to the LORD. [b]1 Septuagint (see also verses 3 and 5 and 48:9); Hebrew *10,000* [c]3 That is, about 7 miles (about 12 kilometers) [d]3 That is, about 3 miles (about 5 kilometers) [e]5 Septuagint; Hebrew *temple; they will have as their possession 20 rooms*

OPEN 1. Would you invest in real estate if you had the money? Why or why not? **2.** Have you ever been cheated by a service or sales person? What did you do?

STUDY 1. Palestine is to be redivided when the tribes return. How many square miles belong to the Lord (v. 1)? **2.** Why the "open land" surrounding the temple square (v. 2; 42:20)? Had the Levites ever owned land before (vv. 4–5; Josh. 13:33)? **3.** How does Ezekiel's plan keep the palace away from the temple (v. 7)? Why the separation of church and state (vv. 8–9; 43:8)? **4.** What other injustice does God prevent by assigning official values to weights and measures (vv. 10–12)? What was the state of money changing at the time of Jesus?

APPLY 1. Why does God care about land distribution, weights and measures? Should Christians be more concerned about people's "spiritual" needs? **2.** How do people in your line of work commonly "bend the rules"? Have you ever done this? **3.** Do people in power face more temptation than others, or does power simply attract corruptible people? How does power affect *you*?

45:1 The restored nation would need somewhere to live. The Lord divided the land among them, setting aside a holy lot for himself. It would serve as the building site for his temple and house the temple ministers.

45:2 open land. No building permits would be given out for the area around the sanctuary this time! God's holiness would be set apart.

45:4 sacred portion of the land for the priests. In Israel's history, the priests were peppered throughout the land as references of religious service and justice (Josh. 21:1–42). In the new temple era, they would be centralized around the sanctuary.

45:5 The priests lived off the holy section of land, but they did not own it. However, the Levites were allowed to own their own property in the new temple era.

45:7 prince will have the land. Unlike Solomon's time, the new palace would be separate from the new temple.

45:10 use accurate scales. God established common ground rules to guard against extortion. Following these

ephah[a] and an accurate bath.[b] 11The ephah and the bath are to be the
same size, the bath containing a tenth of a homer[c] and the ephah a
tenth of a homer; the homer is to be the standard measure for both.
12The shekel[d] is to consist of twenty gerahs. Twenty shekels plus
twenty-five shekels plus fifteen shekels equal one mina.[e]

Offerings and Holy Days

13" 'This is the special gift you are to offer: a sixth of an ephah from
each homer of wheat and a sixth of an ephah from each homer of
barley. 14The prescribed portion of oil, measured by the bath, is a
tenth of a bath from each cor (which consists of ten baths or one
homer, for ten baths are equivalent to a homer). 15Also one sheep is
to be taken from every flock of two hundred from the well-watered
pastures of Israel. These will be used for the grain offerings, burnt
offerings and fellowship offerings[f] to make atonement for the people,
declares the Sovereign LORD. 16All the people of the land will participate in this special gift for the use of the prince in Israel. 17It will be
the duty of the prince to provide the burnt offerings, grain offerings
and drink offerings at the festivals, the New Moons and the
Sabbaths—at all the appointed feasts of the house of Israel. He will
provide the sin offerings, grain offerings, burnt offerings and fellowship offerings to make atonement for the house of Israel.

18" 'This is what the Sovereign LORD says: In the first month on the
first day you are to take a young bull without defect and purify the
sanctuary. 19The priest is to take some of the blood of the sin offering
and put it on the doorposts of the temple, on the four corners of the
upper ledge of the altar and on the gateposts of the inner court. 20You
are to do the same on the seventh day of the month for anyone who
sins unintentionally or through ignorance; so you are to make atonement for the temple.

21" 'In the first month on the fourteenth day you are to observe the
Passover, a feast lasting seven days, during which you shall eat bread
made without yeast. 22On that day the prince is to provide a bull as a
sin offering for himself and for all the people of the land. 23Every day
during the seven days of the Feast he is to provide seven bulls and
seven rams without defect as a burnt offering to the LORD, and a male
goat for a sin offering. 24He is to provide as a grain offering an ephah
for each bull and an ephah for each ram, along with a hin[g] of oil for
each ephah.

25" 'During the seven days of the Feast, which begins in the seventh
month on the fifteenth day, he is to make the same provision for sin
offerings, burnt offerings, grain offerings and oil.

46 " 'This is what the Sovereign LORD says: The gate of the inner
court facing east is to be shut on the six working days, but on

[a]*10* An ephah was a dry measure. [b]*10* A bath was a liquid measure. [c]*11* A homer was a dry measure. [d]*12* A shekel weighed about 2/5 ounce (about 11.5 grams). [e]*12* That is, 60 shekels; the common mina was 50 shekels. [f]*15* Traditionally *peace offerings*; also in verse 17 [g]*24* That is, probably about 4 quarts (about 4 liters)

OPEN 1. What was your favorite holiday as a child? Now that you're older, has it changed? Why? **2.** If you had to lose one of your physical senses, which would be the hardest one to give up? Which would be the easiest?

STUDY 1. What kinds of things are offered to the Lord (45:13–15)? On what occasions does the prince pay for the sacrifices (45:17)? What were the three public "festivals" in Israel (Ex. 23:14–16)? **2.** What had to be done every New Moon, the first day of Israel's lunar month (45:18)? How often are Sabbaths celebrated? How do they celebrate Passover (45:21–24)? What Feast falls in the seventh month (45:25; Num. 29:12)? **3.** Why do you think the east gate is open only on Sabbaths and New Moons (46:1)? Why is the prince given special treatment (46:2–3)? Is it fair for him to "foot the bill" for so many animals (46:4–7)? In what way is he humbled (46:10)? **4.** Why do you think the animals had to be without defect (46:13)? What was the lesson to Israel? **5.** What rules does God give the prince about giving away land (46:16–17)? What is the "year of freedom" (Lev. 25:10)? Is it fair to force a poor servant to give land back to the children of kings? What had the kings intended to do (46:18)? **6.** Why did the priests cook the offerings (46:23–24)?

APPLY 1. Imagine you are an Israelite worshipping in the temple. What do you see, hear, smell and taste? What effect does such a service have on you? What effect do you think the Lord wants to produce? How does this effect compare to the one at your church? **2.** Israel worshiped the Lord by offering him *things*. What can you offer him? Could you afford one-tenth of your time every day (2.4 hours)? **3.** Does your relationship

guidelines, the people would not find themselves relearning old lessons against greed.

45:13 special gift you are to offer. The cycle of gifts went from the people to the prince and back to God.

45:17 appointed feasts. The ruler in this new age would graciously provide the offerings necessary for the traditional feasts of the Israelites.

45:25 Feast. The Feast of Tabernacles represented a crucial gathering of God's people (Num. 29:12; Deut. 16:16). It was a seven-day blowout celebration at the end of the year. These sacrifices were made on each of these seven days.

with God contain as much celebration as Israel's did? Should it? Do you have an idea for a special "group festival" you can celebrate together?

---

the Sabbath day and on the day of the New Moon it is to be opened.
2 The prince is to enter from the outside through the portico of the
gateway and stand by the gatepost. The priests are to sacrifice his
burnt offering and his fellowship offerings.[a] He is to worship at the
threshold of the gateway and then go out, but the gate will not be
shut until evening. 3 On the Sabbaths and New Moons the people of
the land are to worship in the presence of the LORD at the entrance to
that gateway. 4 The burnt offering the prince brings to the LORD on the
Sabbath day is to be six male lambs and a ram, all without defect.
5 The grain offering given with the ram is to be an ephah,[b] and the
grain offering with the lambs is to be as much as he pleases, along
with a hin[c] of oil for each ephah. 6 On the day of the New Moon he is
to offer a young bull, six lambs and a ram, all without defect. 7 He is to
provide as a grain offering one ephah with the bull, one ephah with
the ram, and with the lambs as much as he wants to give, along with
a hin of oil with each ephah. 8 When the prince enters, he is to go in
through the portico of the gateway, and he is to come out the same
way.

9 "'When the people of the land come before the LORD at the
appointed feasts, whoever enters by the north gate to worship is to
go out the south gate; and whoever enters by the south gate is to go
out the north gate. No one is to return through the gate by which
he entered, but each is to go out the opposite gate. 10 The prince is to
be among them, going in when they go in and going out when they
go out.

11 "'At the festivals and the appointed feasts, the grain offering is to
be an ephah with a bull, an ephah with a ram, and with the lambs as
much as one pleases, along with a hin of oil for each ephah. 12 When
the prince provides a freewill offering to the LORD—whether a burnt
offering or fellowship offerings—the gate facing east is to be opened
for him. He shall offer his burnt offering or his fellowship offerings as
he does on the Sabbath day. Then he shall go out, and after he has
gone out, the gate will be shut.

13 "'Every day you are to provide a year-old lamb without defect for
a burnt offering to the LORD; morning by morning you shall provide
it. 14 You are also to provide with it morning by morning a grain offering, consisting of a sixth of an ephah with a third of a hin of oil to
moisten the flour. The presenting of this grain offering to the LORD is
a lasting ordinance. 15 So the lamb and the grain offering and the oil
shall be provided morning by morning for a regular burnt offering.

16 "'This is what the Sovereign LORD says: If the prince makes a gift
from his inheritance to one of his sons, it will also belong to his descendants; it is to be their property by inheritance. 17 If, however, he
makes a gift from his inheritance to one of his servants, the servant
may keep it until the year of freedom; then it will revert to the prince.

[a] 2 Traditionally *peace offerings*; also in verse 12 [b] 5 That is, probably about 3/5 bushel (about 22 liters)
[c] 5 That is, probably about 4 quarts (about 4 liters)

46:2 prince ... stand by the gatepost. Although the prince was royalty, he was no priest. Therefore, he could not legally enter the inner court.

46:12 freewill offering. God was pleased with this offering of generosity. He marked the occasion by allowing the eastern gate to be opened.

46:16 property by inheritance. The royal line was not bound by God's command for land rights to be surrendered every fifty years (Lev. 25:10–13).

His inheritance belongs to his sons only; it is theirs. [18]The prince must not take any of the inheritance of the people, driving them off their property. He is to give his sons their inheritance out of his own property, so that none of my people will be separated from his property.' "

[19]Then the man brought me through the entrance at the side of the gate to the sacred rooms facing north, which belonged to the priests, and showed me a place at the western end. [20]He said to me, "This is the place where the priests will cook the guilt offering and the sin offering and bake the grain offering, to avoid bringing them into the outer court and consecrating the people."

[21]He then brought me to the outer court and led me around to its four corners, and I saw in each corner another court. [22]In the four corners of the outer court were enclosed[a] courts, forty cubits long and thirty cubits wide; each of the courts in the four corners was the same size. [23]Around the inside of each of the four courts was a ledge of stone, with places for fire built all around under the ledge. [24]He said to me, "These are the kitchens where those who minister at the temple will cook the sacrifices of the people."

The River From the Temple

47 The man brought me back to the entrance of the temple, and I saw water coming out from under the threshold of the temple toward the east (for the temple faced east). The water was coming down from under the south side of the temple, south of the altar. [2]He then brought me out through the north gate and led me around the outside to the outer gate facing east, and the water was flowing from the south side.

[3]As the man went eastward with a measuring line in his hand, he measured off a thousand cubits[b] and then led me through water that was ankle-deep. [4]He measured off another thousand cubits and led me through water that was knee-deep. He measured off another thousand and led me through water that was up to the waist. [5]He measured off another thousand, but now it was a river that I could not cross, because the water had risen and was deep enough to swim in—a river that no one could cross. [6]He asked me, "Son of man, do you see this?"

Then he led me back to the bank of the river. [7]When I arrived there, I saw a great number of trees on each side of the river. [8]He said to me, "This water flows toward the eastern region and goes down into the Arabah,[c] where it enters the Sea.[d] When it empties into the Sea,[d] the water there becomes fresh. [9]Swarms of living creatures will live wherever the river flows. There will be large numbers of fish, because this water flows there and makes the salt water fresh; so where the

[a]22 The meaning of the Hebrew for this word is uncertain. [b]3 That is, about 1,500 feet (about 450 meters) [c]8 Or *the Jordan Valley* [d]8 That is, the Dead Sea

OPEN 1. Do you like swimming? Do you prefer an ocean, lake or swimming pool? **2.** What's your favorite drink on a hot day?

STUDY 1. Where does the river start? Which direction does it flow (vv. 1–2)? **2.** What happens to the river as it gets farther from the temple (vv. 3–6)? **3.** As it flows into the Dead Sea, what happens to the animals, fish, trees and people of the region (vv. 7–12)? What would the river mean to a people dependent on wells and cisterns for water? **4.** What might Ezekiel's river represent? How do Jesus and the New Testament writers use the image of the river (John 4:14, Rev. 22:1–3)?

APPLY 1. What best describes your relationship with God: Dying of thirst? Man overboard? Treading water? Overflowing? Waterlogged? Smooth sailing? **2.** Does some part of your life feel like a parched desert? What could happen that would be like living water in the desert? **3.** Picture the spiritual life as a river that keeps getting deeper and deeper. Are you testing the waters? Ankle deep? Up to your waist? What is the

47:1 water. Ezekiel enticed his fellow exiled Jews with his vision of a free-flowing stream. Its waters were life-giving, as it originated from the temple.

47:5 a river that no one could cross. Ezekiel painted a portrait of abundance. The river is full; no one could cross its width or fathom its depth.

47:7–9 Not only is the river wide, it is full of life (Rev. 22:1). Freshwater sea life thrives inside it, and vegetation and trees grow beside it on the banks.

next step? Can the group help you take it?

OPEN 1. Would you ever live in a foreign country? Why or why not? Which one, if any, might attract you? **2.** Do you get along with your next-door neighbors? Why did Robert Frost say "good fences make good neighbors"?

STUDY 1. These boundaries resemble the boundaries of Solomon's golden age. Why is God so concerned to return the land to Israel (v. 14)? **2.** Why is God concerned about the non-Jewish inhabitants (vv. 22–23; Ex. 22:21)? What is the meaning of "inheritance" if aliens are entitled?

APPLY 1. How important is "settling down" to you? Do you need land? A house? An army to protect you? **2.** What people in your area are regarded as "aliens"? How open are you to these "aliens"? Does your church have the racial and social mix of the surrounding population? Does the group? **3.** Has God given you an inheritance or were you "left out of the will"? What is your inheritance?

---

river flows everything will live. [10]Fishermen will stand along the
shore; from En Gedi to En Eglaim there will be places for spreading
nets. The fish will be of many kinds—like the fish of the Great Sea.[a]
[11]But the swamps and marshes will not become fresh; they will be left
for salt. [12]Fruit trees of all kinds will grow on both banks of the river.
Their leaves will not wither, nor will their fruit fail. Every month they
will bear, because the water from the sanctuary flows to them. Their
fruit will serve for food and their leaves for healing."

The Boundaries of the Land

[13]This is what the Sovereign LORD says: "These are the boundaries
by which you are to divide the land for an inheritance among the
twelve tribes of Israel, with two portions for Joseph. [14]You are to
divide it equally among them. Because I swore with uplifted hand to
give it to your forefathers, this land will become your inheritance.

[15]"This is to be the boundary of the land:

"On the north side it will run from the Great Sea by the Hethlon
road past Lebo[b] Hamath to Zedad, [16]Berothah[c] and Sibraim
(which lies on the border between Damascus and Hamath), as far as Hazer Hatticon, which is on the border of
Hauran. [17]The boundary will extend from the sea to Hazar
Enan,[d] along the northern border of Damascus, with the
border of Hamath to the north. This will be the north
boundary.

18 "On the east side the boundary will run between Hauran
and Damascus, along the Jordan between Gilead and the
land of Israel, to the eastern sea and as far as Tamar.[e] This
will be the east boundary.

19 "On the south side it will run from Tamar as far as the
waters of Meribah Kadesh, then along the Wadi ⌞of Egypt⌟
to the Great Sea. This will be the south boundary.

20 "On the west side, the Great Sea will be the boundary to a
point opposite Lebo[f] Hamath. This will be the west boundary.

[21]"You are to distribute this land among yourselves according to
the tribes of Israel. [22]You are to allot it as an inheritance for yourselves and for the aliens who have settled among you and who have
children. You are to consider them as native-born Israelites; along
with you they are to be allotted an inheritance among the tribes of
Israel. [23]In whatever tribe the alien settles, there you are to give him
his inheritance," declares the Sovereign LORD.

[a]*10* That is, the Mediterranean; also in verses 15, 19 and 20 [b]*15* Or *past the entrance to* [c]*15,16* See Septuagint and Ezekiel 48:1; Hebrew *road to go into Zedad,* [16]*Hamath, Berothah* [d]*17* Hebrew *Enon,* a variant of *Enan* [e]*18* Septuagint and Syriac; Hebrew *Israel. You will measure to the eastern sea* [f]*20* Or *opposite the entrance to*

47:10 spreading nets. For the first time, fishermen would find their livelihood on the banks of the former Dead Sea.

47:14 divide it equally. Land distribution played an important cultural role in Ezekiel's time. God's careful instructions laid the groundwork for fulfilling the needs of a future society.

47:15 This is to be the boundary of the land. The boundaries of the future allotment would come close to the expanse of the glory days of David and Solomon. However, many Israelites would enjoy different territory than their ancestors did under Joshua's original allotment (Josh. 13–19).

47:22 aliens. All non-Jewish people were to be included in the distribution of land. In fact, they were considered part of the family.

The Division of the Land

48 "These are the tribes, listed by name: At the northern frontier,
Dan will have one portion; it will follow the Hethlon road to
Lebo[a] Hamath; Hazar Enan and the northern border of Damascus
next to Hamath will be part of its border from the east side to the west
side.
2 "Asher will have one portion; it will border the territory of Dan
from east to west.
3 "Naphtali will have one portion; it will border the territory of Asher from east to west.
4 "Manasseh will have one portion; it will border the territory of
Naphtali from east to west.
5 "Ephraim will have one portion; it will border the territory of Manasseh from east to west.
6 "Reuben will have one portion; it will border the territory of
Ephraim from east to west.
7 "Judah will have one portion; it will border the territory of Reuben
from east to west.
8 "Bordering the territory of Judah from east to west will be the portion you are to present as a special gift. It will be 25,000 cubits[b] wide,
and its length from east to west will equal one of the tribal portions;
the sanctuary will be in the center of it.
9 "The special portion you are to offer to the LORD will be 25,000
cubits long and 10,000 cubits[c] wide. 10 This will be the sacred portion
for the priests. It will be 25,000 cubits long on the north side, 10,000
cubits wide on the west side, 10,000 cubits wide on the east side and
25,000 cubits long on the south side. In the center of it will be the
sanctuary of the LORD. 11 This will be for the consecrated priests, the
Zadokites, who were faithful in serving me and did not go astray as
the Levites did when the Israelites went astray. 12 It will be a special
gift to them from the sacred portion of the land, a most holy portion,
bordering the territory of the Levites.
13 "Alongside the territory of the priests, the Levites will have an
allotment 25,000 cubits long and 10,000 cubits wide. Its total length
will be 25,000 cubits and its width 10,000 cubits. 14 They must not sell
or exchange any of it. This is the best of the land and must not pass
into other hands, because it is holy to the LORD.
15 "The remaining area, 5,000 cubits wide and 25,000 cubits long,
will be for the common use of the city, for houses and for pastureland. The city will be in the center of it 16 and will have these measurements: the north side 4,500 cubits, the south side 4,500 cubits, the
east side 4,500 cubits, and the west side 4,500 cubits. 17 The pastureland for the city will be 250 cubits on the north, 250 cubits on the
south, 250 cubits on the east, and 250 cubits on the west. 18 What

[a] *1 Or to the entrance to* [b] *8 That is, about 7 miles* (about 12 kilometers) [c] *9 That is, about 3 miles* (about 5 kilometers)

OPEN 1. How many children did your parents have? Did any of your relatives have 10–12 children? How did they manage? **2.** What are your most prized earthly assets? If you died tonight, who would you want to get them?

STUDY 1. Does God redistribute the land evenly (vv. 1–7,23–29)? Will some of the land be more fertile? More mountainous? Is this fair? **2.** There are 13 tribes listed here. Which son of Jacob sired two tribes (Gen. 48:5–6)? Which tribe gets land for the first time (vv. 13–14)? How does this land rank? Why can't they sell it? **3.** How does God treat the Zadokites differently from the rest of the Levites (vv. 10–13)? Why? **4.** Who will share the arable pastureland near the city (vv. 15–20)? In Ezekiel's vision, is land owned by private individuals or by the community?

APPLY 1. When you picture God's kingdom coming to this world, do you see economic justice as a central feature? Why or why not? Should it be? What do you imagine it will look like? **2.** When you consider what you have been allotted in life, what you have been given to work with, do you feel God has been fair with you: Less than fair? More than fair? How do you feel about this? **3.** How can you promote community in your group? What are the biggest barriers to community in your neighborhood? How can you promote community in the world?

48:1 The land was divided according to the names of the tribes of Israel—the descendants of the patriarch Jacob. Families were grouped according to tribal ancestry and received their land accordingly.

48:2 Asher ... one portion. Asher received the northern section of land—away from the sanctuary.

48:7 Judah ... one portion. As the tribe of the royal line (the Messiah's heritage), this tribe took a position next to God's own portion of land.

48:14 best of the land. God's best was reserved for his temple ministers. Therefore, it was of priceless value.

remains of the area, bordering on the sacred portion and running the
length of it, will be 10,000 cubits on the east side and 10,000 cubits
on the west side. Its produce will supply food for the workers of the
city. 19 The workers from the city who farm it will come from all the
tribes of Israel. 20 The entire portion will be a square, 25,000 cubits on
each side. As a special gift you will set aside the sacred portion, along
with the property of the city.

21 "What remains on both sides of the area formed by the sacred
portion and the city property will belong to the prince. It will extend
eastward from the 25,000 cubits of the sacred portion to the eastern
border, and westward from the 25,000 cubits to the western border.
Both these areas running the length of the tribal portions will belong
to the prince, and the sacred portion with the temple sanctuary will
be in the center of them. 22 So the property of the Levites and the
property of the city will lie in the center of the area that belongs to the
prince. The area belonging to the prince will lie between the border of
Judah and the border of Benjamin.

23 "As for the rest of the tribes: Benjamin will have one portion; it
will extend from the east side to the west side.

24 "Simeon will have one portion; it will border the territory of Benjamin from east to west.

25 "Issachar will have one portion; it will border the territory of
Simeon from east to west.

26 "Zebulun will have one portion; it will border the territory of Issachar from east to west.

27 "Gad will have one portion; it will border the territory of Zebulun
from east to west.

28 "The southern boundary of Gad will run south from Tamar to the
waters of Meribah Kadesh, then along the Wadi ⌞of Egypt⌟ to the Great
Sea.[a]

29 "This is the land you are to allot as an inheritance to the tribes of
Israel, and these will be their portions," declares the Sovereign LORD.

The Gates of the City

30 "These will be the exits of the city: Beginning on the north side,
which is 4,500 cubits long, 31 the gates of the city will be named after
the tribes of Israel. The three gates on the north side will be the gate
of Reuben, the gate of Judah and the gate of Levi.

32 "On the east side, which is 4,500 cubits long, will be three gates:
the gate of Joseph, the gate of Benjamin and the gate of Dan.

33 "On the south side, which measures 4,500 cubits, will be three
gates: the gate of Simeon, the gate of Issachar and the gate of Zebulun.

34 "On the west side, which is 4,500 cubits long, will be three gates:
the gate of Gad, the gate of Asher and the gate of Naphtali.

35 "The distance all around will be 18,000 cubits.

"And the name of the city from that time on will be:

THE LORD IS THERE."

[a] *28* That is, the Mediterranean

48:19 workers ... from all the tribes of Israel. The remaining portion of land was for enjoyment by all Israelites. The land belonged to the whole nation and workers would farm the land and profit from it.

48:31 Twelve gates shared the land allotment. Israel's future restoration was complete.

Daniel

Author. Daniel, the author, was among the first Hebrews exiled to Babylon while still a young man. He then grew to adulthood as a leader in Babylon. He is both the character portrayed in the historical narratives and the prophet who spoke the prophecies included here. Jesus himself credited Daniel with the writing of this prophecy (Matt. 24:15).

Personal Reading	Group Study Topic and Reading	
1:1–21	Daniel's Training	1:1–21
2:1–49	Dream Interpreted	2:24–49
3:1–30	The Fiery Furnace	3:1–30
4:1–5:31	Handwriting on Wall	5:1–31
6:1–28	In the Den of Lions	6:1–24
7:1–28	Four Beasts	7:1–14
8:1–27	Ram and a Goat	8:1–27
9:1–27	Daniel's Prayer	9:1–19
10:1–11:1	Heavenly Visitor	10:1–11:1
11:2–45	History Prophesied	11:2–35
12:1–13	Victory Promised	12:1–13

Date. The events recorded in the book of Daniel happened during Judah's captivity in Babylon, 605–536 B.C. It is uncertain exactly when Daniel recorded these events and his prophecies, but it was probably in the sixth century B.C.

Purpose. The book of Daniel functions as both a historical book and a prophetic book. The historical narratives teach over and over again that Jehovah God is the one true God with power and sovereignty, and the Babylonian gods are merely idols. This was a lesson that the Hebrews had failed to learn in their Exodus journey and their resettlement of the land. The exile in Babylon reemphasized this lesson, as God miraculously cared for his own even in a foreign land.

Daniel's prophecies revealed much about God's purposes in the future. Daniel spent his adult life as a government official in a role similar to a secretary of state. It was natural, then, that as he prophesied about future events, he focused on how God would work through governments. His prophecies outlined God's interaction with nations until the time of Christ and then on to the end of the Christian age.

Historical Background. By Daniel's day, the kingdom of Israel had already split into Israel (the larger northern kingdom), and Judah (the southern kingdom). By this time, Israel had been captured and assimilated by cruel Assyria to the east. That left small Judah to fend for herself against large enemies on all sides that were constantly encroaching on her borders.

In 609 B.C., Pharaoh Neco II of Egypt defeated Judah's King Josiah. Neco then placed Jehoiakim as his puppet king on Judah's throne. For a time in 605 B.C., Jehoiakim shifted his allegiance to Nebuchadnezzar of Babylon and then back to Egypt. In response, Nebuchadnezzar attacked the city of Jerusalem. In the end, he attacked three times, each time taking captives with him. In 586 B.C. he destroyed the city completely. The prophet Daniel was one of the first captives taken into exile in Babylon after the siege of Jerusalem by Nebuchadnezzar in 605 B.C.

Daniel as the Prophet-Historian. From a historian's view, Daniel's writings helped place Judah's history on a larger timeline. He wanted to put the powers that dominated his lifetime in perspective with the lifespan of the whole world—past, present and future. In Daniel's lifetime, he heard about the defeat of the mighty Assyrians at the hands of the Medes and Chaldeans. He then witnessed the defeat of the Neo-Babylonians by the Persians in 539 B.C. Prophetically, Daniel extended that pattern of "glory leading to demise" to include the Persians, the Greeks, and the Romans. For Daniel, history and prophecy were not worlds apart; they were different chapters in the same story, unfolding God's plan for his people, until the end of time.

OPEN **1.** What is the story behind the name you were given by your parents? **2.** What nicknames have you picked up along the way? Any given to you while away from home, at school, camp or college? **3.** What vegetables were you most likely to refuse as a child: Broccoli? Spinach? Brussels Sprouts? Okra? Other?

STUDY **1.** How were these Israelites chosen and trained for the king's special service (vv. 3–7)? How did the king seek to capture their mind? Their body? Their loyalty? **2.** What is conveyed by giving a new name to another (person or pet)? **3.** Why does Daniel resist these attempts by the foreign king (v. 8)? To whom and on what grounds does Daniel make his appeals for an exception to the king's edict (vv. 8–14)? **4.** Why does Daniel end up passing his first "entrance exam" with "flying colors" (vv. 15–21)? **5.** How does Daniel end up showing his true loyalty to God? And to his three fellow believers?

APPLY **1.** If you ate or were served nothing but vegetables for 10 consecutive days, what results would you see: Ill health? Good health? No change? Why? **2.** What would be an equivalent choice between God's way and the "royal food" of the world today? What's at stake for you in that choice? **3.** When your loyalty is tested (as was Daniel's), what are you most likely to do? Why? **4.** How has God's mercy favored you this year (for example, in your efforts toward excellence or in your service to others)?

Daniel's Training in Babylon

1 In the third year of the reign of Jehoiakim king of Judah, Nebuchadnezzar king of Babylon came to Jerusalem and besieged it.
2And the Lord delivered Jehoiakim king of Judah into his hand, along
with some of the articles from the temple of God. These he carried off
to the temple of his god in Babylonia[a] and put in the treasure house
of his god.
3Then the king ordered Ashpenaz, chief of his court officials, to
bring in some of the Israelites from the royal family and the nobility—
4young men without any physical defect, handsome, showing aptitude for every kind of learning, well informed, quick to understand,
and qualified to serve in the king's palace. He was to teach them the
language and literature of the Babylonians.[b] 5The king assigned them
a daily amount of food and wine from the king's table. They were to
be trained for three years, and after that they were to enter the king's
service.
6Among these were some from Judah: Daniel, Hananiah, Mishael
and Azariah. 7The chief official gave them new names: to Daniel, the
name Belteshazzar; to Hananiah, Shadrach; to Mishael, Meshach;
and to Azariah, Abednego.
8But Daniel resolved not to defile himself with the royal food and
wine, and he asked the chief official for permission not to defile himself this way. 9Now God had caused the official to show favor and
sympathy to Daniel, 10but the official told Daniel, "I am afraid of my
lord the king, who has assigned your[c] food and drink. Why should he
see you looking worse than the other young men your age? The king
would then have my head because of you."
11Daniel then said to the guard whom the chief official had appointed over Daniel, Hananiah, Mishael and Azariah, 12"Please test your
servants for ten days: Give us nothing but vegetables to eat and water
to drink. 13Then compare our appearance with that of the young men
who eat the royal food, and treat your servants in accordance with
what you see." 14So he agreed to this and tested them for ten days.
15At the end of the ten days they looked healthier and better nourished than any of the young men who ate the royal food. 16So the
guard took away their choice food and the wine they were to drink
and gave them vegetables instead.
17To these four young men God gave knowledge and understanding of all kinds of literature and learning. And Daniel could understand visions and dreams of all kinds.
18At the end of the time set by the king to bring them in, the chief
official presented them to Nebuchadnezzar. 19The king talked with

[a]2 Hebrew *Shinar* [b]4 Or *Chaldeans* [c]10 The Hebrew for *your* and *you* in this verse is plural.

1:8 resolved not to defile himself. The food served at the king's table was unclean according to Mosaic Law. It had been prepared by Gentiles, probably included things the Jews were forbidden to eat and had been sacrificed to idols. Daniel decided not to eat these things that would displease God even though to refuse royal food would endanger his position and perhaps his life.

1:9–10 The official liked Daniel, but he feared that granting Daniel's request would put his own career at risk. He was responsible to keep his captives in good physical shape to prepare them for whatever tasks the king would assign them.

1:12 nothing but vegetables ... and water. The four Hebrews didn't eat the meat or drink the wine for they had most likely been offered to idols.

1:17 God gave Daniel and his friends keen minds and ready wits. But the most important gift was Daniel's ability to understand visions and dreams—a talent that no earthly knowledge or training could give.

them, and he found none equal to Daniel, Hananiah, Mishael and
Azariah; so they entered the king's service. [20]In every matter of
wisdom and understanding about which the king questioned them,
he found them ten times better than all the magicians and enchanters
in his whole kingdom.
[21]And Daniel remained there until the first year of King Cyrus.

Nebuchadnezzar's Dream

2 In the second year of his reign, Nebuchadnezzar had dreams; his
mind was troubled and he could not sleep. [2]So the king summoned the magicians, enchanters, sorcerers and astrologers[a] to tell
him what he had dreamed. When they came in and stood before the
king, [3]he said to them, "I have had a dream that troubles me and I
want to know what it means.[b]"
[4]Then the astrologers answered the king in Aramaic,[c] "O king, live
forever! Tell your servants the dream, and we will interpret it."
[5]The king replied to the astrologers, "This is what I have firmly decided: If you do not tell me what my dream was and interpret it, I will
have you cut into pieces and your houses turned into piles of rubble.
[6]But if you tell me the dream and explain it, you will receive from me
gifts and rewards and great honor. So tell me the dream and interpret
it for me."
[7]Once more they replied, "Let the king tell his servants the dream,
and we will interpret it."
[8]Then the king answered, "I am certain that you are trying to gain
time, because you realize that this is what I have firmly decided: [9]If
you do not tell me the dream, there is just one penalty for you. You
have conspired to tell me misleading and wicked things, hoping the
situation will change. So then, tell me the dream, and I will know that
you can interpret it for me."
[10]The astrologers answered the king, "There is not a man on earth
who can do what the king asks! No king, however great and mighty,
has ever asked such a thing of any magician or enchanter or astrolo-
ger. [11]What the king asks is too difficult. No one can reveal it to the
king except the gods, and they do not live among men."
[12]This made the king so angry and furious that he ordered the execution of all the wise men of Babylon. [13]So the decree was issued to
put the wise men to death, and men were sent to look for Daniel and
his friends to put them to death.
[14]When Arioch, the commander of the king's guard, had gone out
to put to death the wise men of Babylon, Daniel spoke to him with
wisdom and tact. [15]He asked the king's officer, "Why did the king issue such a harsh decree?" Arioch then explained the matter to Daniel.
[16]At this, Daniel went in to the king and asked for time, so that he
might interpret the dream for him.
[17]Then Daniel returned to his house and explained the matter to
his friends Hananiah, Mishael and Azariah. [18]He urged them to plead
for mercy from the God of heaven concerning this mystery, so that he

[a]2 Or *Chaldeans*; also in verses 4, 5 and 10 [b]3 Or *was* [c]4 The text from here through chapter 7 is in Aramaic.

OPEN 1. What is one of the most memorable or unusual dreams you have ever had? **2.** What kinds of dreams most disturb you: Daydreams? Nightmares? Sleepwalking? Give examples.

STUDY 1. What does the king ask of the astrologers (vv. 1–3)? Why is he testing their competence (vv. 4–13)? Why is he so firm? So angry? **2.** In his fury, what does the king decide to do (vv. 12–13)? How does Daniel respond to this edict? **3.** Embracing the death-defying dare to interpret the dream, what role is played by Daniel's personal faith? Group prayer? God's special revelation? **4.** Does Daniel's psalm (vv. 20–23) express personal faith or corporate worship? Why do you think so? **5.** What gifts does he praise God for? Why? What does that say about God? About Daniel? About intercession, thanksgiving and counting our blessings? **6.** Why does Daniel particularly praise God's "wisdom and power"? How does this relate to the king's and astrologers' claim? **7.** Compare Daniel and this king to Joseph and the Pharaoh (Gen. 41): How are they alike? Not alike?

APPLY 1. Who (or what) drives you up the wall with demands? How do you decide when to give in and when to say no? **2.** Daniel was given wisdom. Nebuchadnezzar had power. Who in your life or society claims to have wisdom or power? How do their claims compare to God's gifts to us? **3.** How might your prayer life reflect Daniel's praise and thanksgiving? And his friends' powerful intercession?

2:18 plead for mercy ... concerning this mystery. Even though Daniel was well educated and had great abilities, he asked his friends to join him in prayer concerning this mystery. The answer to the mystery was a vision.

and his friends might not be executed with the rest of the wise men of
Babylon. 19During the night the mystery was revealed to Daniel in a
vision. Then Daniel praised the God of heaven 20and said:

"Praise be to the name of God for ever and ever;
wisdom and power are his.
21He changes times and seasons;
he sets up kings and deposes them.
He gives wisdom to the wise
and knowledge to the discerning.
22He reveals deep and hidden things;
he knows what lies in darkness,
and light dwells with him.
23I thank and praise you, O God of my fathers:
You have given me wisdom and power,
you have made known to me what we asked of you,
you have made known to us the dream of the king."

Daniel Interprets the Dream

24Then Daniel went to Arioch, whom the king had appointed to
execute the wise men of Babylon, and said to him, "Do not execute
the wise men of Babylon. Take me to the king, and I will interpret his
dream for him."

25Arioch took Daniel to the king at once and said, "I have found a
man among the exiles from Judah who can tell the king what his
dream means."

26The king asked Daniel (also called Belteshazzar), "Are you able to
tell me what I saw in my dream and interpret it?"

27Daniel replied, "No wise man, enchanter, magician or diviner can
explain to the king the mystery he has asked about, 28but there is a
God in heaven who reveals mysteries. He has shown King Nebuchadnezzar what will happen in days to come. Your dream and the visions
that passed through your mind as you lay on your bed are these:

29"As you were lying there, O king, your mind turned to things to
come, and the revealer of mysteries showed you what is going to
happen. 30As for me, this mystery has been revealed to me, not
because I have greater wisdom than other living men, but so that
you, O king, may know the interpretation and that you may understand what went through your mind.

31"You looked, O king, and there before you stood a large statue—
an enormous, dazzling statue, awesome in appearance. 32The head of
the statue was made of pure gold, its chest and arms of silver, its belly
and thighs of bronze, 33its legs of iron, its feet partly of iron and partly
of baked clay. 34While you were watching, a rock was cut out, but not
by human hands. It struck the statue on its feet of iron and clay and
smashed them. 35Then the iron, the clay, the bronze, the silver and
the gold were broken to pieces at the same time and became like
chaff on a threshing floor in the summer. The wind swept them away
without leaving a trace. But the rock that struck the statue became a
huge mountain and filled the whole earth.

36"This was the dream, and now we will interpret it to the king.

OPEN **1.** Were you ever told a big secret? How did you feel? Did you have to keep it "secret," or could you share it with others? **2.** Recall when you shaped clay people or made sand castles or snowmen. Did it work? What or who destroyed your creation?

STUDY **1.** What Messiah-like action by Daniel saves the day for the other wise men (v. 24)? **2.** As Daniel unfolds the meaning of the king's dream, how does he put the other wise men in their place (vv. 27–28; as did Joseph, Gen. 41:16)? **3.** How does he picture the large statue? How does Daniel put the king in his place (vv. 36–39)? The other kingdoms in their place (vv. 39–45)? **4.** How does Daniel testify to God by name (vv. 28,37,44–45)? **5.** How does the king honor Daniel and his God (vv. 46–49)? How does Daniel in turn share the wealth and give God his due? **6.** The word "interpret" appears 30 times in this Aramaic section of Daniel (chs. 2–7): Why is it so decisive to interpret God's mysteries? **7.** In what time frame do you place the kingdom of God as prophesied by Daniel?

APPLY **1.** What signs of the end times does this passage encourage you to look for? In what sense are *you* a sign of God's kingly rule in your life? **2.** What unstable "iron and clay" unions do *you* see in our broken world? Which do you feel more like these days: "Iron or clay"? Why?

2:31–43 a large statue. Nebuchadnezzar's dream had four empires that can be interpreted as Babylon (gold head), Medo-Persia (silver chest and arms), Greece (bronze belly and thighs) and Rome (iron legs and feet).

37You, O king, are the king of kings. The God of heaven has given you
dominion and power and might and glory; 38in your hands he has
placed mankind and the beasts of the field and the birds of the air.
Wherever they live, he has made you ruler over them all. You are that
head of gold.
39"After you, another kingdom will rise, inferior to yours. Next, a
third kingdom, one of bronze, will rule over the whole earth. 40Final-
ly, there will be a fourth kingdom, strong as iron—for iron breaks and
smashes everything—and as iron breaks things to pieces, so it will
crush and break all the others. 41Just as you saw that the feet and toes
were partly of baked clay and partly of iron, so this will be a divided
kingdom; yet it will have some of the strength of iron in it, even as
you saw iron mixed with clay. 42As the toes were partly iron and partly
clay, so this kingdom will be partly strong and partly brittle. 43And
just as you saw the iron mixed with baked clay, so the people will be
a mixture and will not remain united, any more than iron mixes with
clay.
44"In the time of those kings, the God of heaven will set up a kingdom that will never be destroyed, nor will it be left to another people.
It will crush all those kingdoms and bring them to an end, but it will
itself endure forever. 45This is the meaning of the vision of the rock
cut out of a mountain, but not by human hands—a rock that broke
the iron, the bronze, the clay, the silver and the gold to pieces.
"The great God has shown the king what will take place in the
future. The dream is true and the interpretation is trustworthy."
46Then King Nebuchadnezzar fell prostrate before Daniel and paid
him honor and ordered that an offering and incense be presented to
him. 47The king said to Daniel, "Surely your God is the God of gods
and the Lord of kings and a revealer of mysteries, for you were able to
reveal this mystery."
48Then the king placed Daniel in a high position and lavished many
gifts on him. He made him ruler over the entire province of Babylon
and placed him in charge of all its wise men. 49Moreover, at Daniel's
request the king appointed Shadrach, Meshach and Abednego
administrators over the province of Babylon, while Daniel himself
remained at the royal court.

The Image of Gold and the Fiery Furnace

3 King Nebuchadnezzar made an image of gold, ninety feet high
and nine feet[a] wide, and set it up on the plain of Dura in the
province of Babylon. 2He then summoned the satraps, prefects, governors, advisers, treasurers, judges, magistrates and all the other
provincial officials to come to the dedication of the image he had set

[a]1 Aramaic *sixty cubits high and six cubits wide* (about 27 meters high and 2.7 meters wide)

3. This polytheistic king falls prostrate in public, but confesses the true God only as "your God." Isaiah predicts many such kings will likewise bow down before God's people. Paul points to that time at Christ's return, when "every knee shall bow ... and every tongue confess that Jesus ... is Lord" (Phil. 2:10–11). What would it mean for you to make or reaffirm that confession today?

OPEN 1. What is the hottest you can remember being? **2.** What things seem threatening to you? Fire? Accident? Height? **3.** What has been your closest brush with death or disaster?

STUDY 1. What does King Nebuchadnezzar do and why

2:44–45 kingdom that will never be destroyed. This kingdom is the kingdom of God. Jesus is the rock not made by human hands that will conquer all other political powers and have authority over all things. Amillennialists believe that this kingdom is a spiritual kingdom that was introduced by Jesus at his first coming. Premillennialists believe that this is a literal kingdom that will be established at the Second Coming.

3:1 After hearing that he would play a significant role in Gentile history, Nebuchadnezzar built a 90-foot gold statue to symbolize the greatness of Babylon under his rule. He hoped that this impressive structure would unify the nation.

3:2 Nebuchadnezzar called together officials of every rank in the kingdom. He wanted the officials to swear allegiance to him and publicly recognize his absolute authority in the kingdom.

(vv. 1–3)? **2.** At the dedication ceremony for this statue (vv. 4–7), what was the king's audience commanded to do? By whom? With what result? **3.** What exception to this universal decree is duly noted (vv. 8–12)? By whom? Why would these people tip off the king? **4.** Why is the king furious? What test does the king propose? Who is he really testing? **5.** How does this relate to Daniel's theme of God's authority vs. worldly authority? To the Fall (Gen. 3)? The Ten Commandments (Ex. 20)? **6.** For you, what is the bottom line or climax in the classic testimony by Shadrach, Meshach and Abednego (vv. 16–18)? What were they sure about? What were they unsure about? What does this say about how martyrs for the faith ought to face their divine Maker and their human executioner? **7.** What is remarkable about the fiery furnace? Who is killed? Why? Who manages to survive? How? **8.** How do you explain the mysterious fourth figure: An "angel," as does a Jewish tradition (Ps. 91:9–12)? A "son of the gods," as does Nebuchadnezzar? "Son of God," as does an ancient Christian tradition? Why do you think so? **9.** What does Nebuchadnezzar make of the "God Most High" and his three undying servants (vv. 26–30)? Why? Do you think this experience made a believer out of him or not? Why?

APPLY 1. Who has played the role of Nebuchadnezzar in your life—the one who has pressured you the most to go against what you believe? **2.** Who has been "the fourth person in the fire" with you, the one who has stood by you in your trials? **3.** One a scale of 1–10, how confident are you that you would have stood your ground against worshiping the image of gold, if "1" is "I would have been hitting the ground, eating dirt!" and "10" is "I'm sure I would have stood my ground"?

up. 3So the satraps, prefects, governors, advisers, treasurers, judges, magistrates and all the other provincial officials assembled for the dedication of the image that King Nebuchadnezzar had set up, and they stood before it.

4Then the herald loudly proclaimed, "This is what you are commanded to do, O peoples, nations and men of every language: 5As soon as you hear the sound of the horn, flute, zither, lyre, harp, pipes and all kinds of music, you must fall down and worship the image of gold that King Nebuchadnezzar has set up. 6Whoever does not fall down and worship will immediately be thrown into a blazing furnace."

7Therefore, as soon as they heard the sound of the horn, flute, zither, lyre, harp and all kinds of music, all the peoples, nations and men of every language fell down and worshiped the image of gold that King Nebuchadnezzar had set up.

8At this time some astrologers[a] came forward and denounced the Jews. 9They said to King Nebuchadnezzar, "O king, live forever! 10You have issued a decree, O king, that everyone who hears the sound of the horn, flute, zither, lyre, harp, pipes and all kinds of music must fall down and worship the image of gold, 11and that whoever does not fall down and worship will be thrown into a blazing furnace. 12But there are some Jews whom you have set over the affairs of the province of Babylon—Shadrach, Meshach and Abednego—who pay no attention to you, O king. They neither serve your gods nor worship the image of gold you have set up."

13Furious with rage, Nebuchadnezzar summoned Shadrach, Meshach and Abednego. So these men were brought before the king, 14and Nebuchadnezzar said to them, "Is it true, Shadrach, Meshach and Abednego, that you do not serve my gods or worship the image of gold I have set up? 15Now when you hear the sound of the horn, flute, zither, lyre, harp, pipes and all kinds of music, if you are ready to fall down and worship the image I made, very good. But if you do not worship it, you will be thrown immediately into a blazing furnace. Then what god will be able to rescue you from my hand?"

16Shadrach, Meshach and Abednego replied to the king, "O Nebuchadnezzar, we do not need to defend ourselves before you in this matter. 17If we are thrown into the blazing furnace, the God we serve is able to save us from it, and he will rescue us from your hand, O king. 18But even if he does not, we want you to know, O king, that we will not serve your gods or worship the image of gold you have set up."

19Then Nebuchadnezzar was furious with Shadrach, Meshach and Abednego, and his attitude toward them changed. He ordered the furnace heated seven times hotter than usual 20and commanded some of the strongest soldiers in his army to tie up Shadrach, Meshach and

[a]8 Or *Chaldeans*

3:12 Shadrach, Meshach and Abednego chose to obey God rather than the king. The officials who pointed this out to Nebuchadnezzar were probably trying to gain favor with the king by contrasting their worship of the golden image with the disobedience of the three Jews.

3:18 As they faced the fiery furnace, Nebuchadnezzar gave the three Jews another chance to bow down to the golden image. But the Jews were obedient to God even in the face of death. They were confident that God could rescue them, but were willing to obey even if rescue did not come. This was a test of their faith.

Abednego and throw them into the blazing furnace. [21]So these men,
wearing their robes, trousers, turbans and other clothes, were bound
and thrown into the blazing furnace. [22]The king's command was so
urgent and the furnace so hot that the flames of the fire killed the
soldiers who took up Shadrach, Meshach and Abednego, [23]and these
three men, firmly tied, fell into the blazing furnace.

[24]Then King Nebuchadnezzar leaped to his feet in amazement and
asked his advisers, "Weren't there three men that we tied up and
threw into the fire?"

They replied, "Certainly, O king."

[25]He said, "Look! I see four men walking around in the fire, un-
bound and unharmed, and the fourth looks like a son of the gods."

[26]Nebuchadnezzar then approached the opening of the blazing furnace and shouted, "Shadrach, Meshach and Abednego, servants of
the Most High God, come out! Come here!"

So Shadrach, Meshach and Abednego came out of the fire, [27]and
the satraps, prefects, governors and royal advisers crowded around
them. They saw that the fire had not harmed their bodies, nor was a
hair of their heads singed; their robes were not scorched, and there
was no smell of fire on them.

[28]Then Nebuchadnezzar said, "Praise be to the God of Shadrach,
Meshach and Abednego, who has sent his angel and rescued his servants! They trusted in him and defied the king's command and were
willing to give up their lives rather than serve or worship any god except their own God. [29]Therefore I decree that the people of any nation
or language who say anything against the God of Shadrach, Meshach
and Abednego be cut into pieces and their houses be turned into piles
of rubble, for no other god can save in this way."

[30]Then the king promoted Shadrach, Meshach and Abednego in the
province of Babylon.

Nebuchadnezzar's Dream of a Tree

4 King Nebuchadnezzar,

To the peoples, nations and men of every language, who live in all the world:

May you prosper greatly!

[2]It is my pleasure to tell you about the miraculous signs and
wonders that the Most High God has performed for me.

[3]How great are his signs,
how mighty his wonders!
His kingdom is an eternal kingdom;
his dominion endures from generation to generation.

[4]I, Nebuchadnezzar, was at home in my palace, contented and
prosperous. [5]I had a dream that made me afraid. As I was lying in
my bed, the images and visions that passed through my mind
terrified me. [6]So I commanded that all the wise men of Babylon
be brought before me to interpret the dream for me. [7]When the

OPEN 1. Remember the school or team braggart? How did you feel being around such braggarts? How do you feel when people brag about you or yours? **2.** What have you dreamed or daydreamed about your future? Were your dreams exciting? Ho hum? Morbid? What dreams have come true?

STUDY 1. What position regarding "all the world" and the "Most High God" is Nebuchadnezzar assuming (vv. 1–3)? If people do "prosper greatly," who would like to take the credit? What does that say about this king? **2.** How does the king's handling of this dream (vv. 4–9) differ from his handling of the earlier one (2:1–13)? How and why does he flatter Daniel this time? **3.** How does the tree seem to fit the king (vv. 10–12): In size? Appearance? Visibility? In ability

4:1–3 Nebuchadnezzar issued this official proclamation of God's greatness in response to the events described in verses 4–37.

4:5 This was 30 years after the dream in chapter 2.

to prosper others? In comparison to the gold statue of chapter 3? How would you interpret the tree if you were Nebuchadnezzar? If you were Daniel? **4.** Where does the messenger fit into the dream of the tree? What hope is conveyed by letting the stump remain (vv. 15,26)? **5.** How does the king's being "given the mind of an animal" (v. 16) relate to God's message in verse 17 about authority? Power? Pride? Humility? **6.** Are God's plans set in concrete or are they somewhat contingent upon our actions? What are the implications of verse 27 in this regard?

APPLY 1. How can you appreciate your accomplishments without bragging or putting yourself down? Whom do you credit for your prosperity? **2.** What "tree" of yours has been cut down to size? To what do you attribute that? **3.** How has God changed your mind regarding his authority or power?

---

magicians, enchanters, astrologers[a] and diviners came, I told
them the dream, but they could not interpret it for me. 8 Finally,
Daniel came into my presence and I told him the dream. (He is
called Belteshazzar, after the name of my god, and the spirit of
the holy gods is in him.)

9 I said, "Belteshazzar, chief of the magicians, I know that the
spirit of the holy gods is in you, and no mystery is too difficult for
you. Here is my dream; interpret it for me. 10 These are the visions
I saw while lying in my bed: I looked, and there before me stood
a tree in the middle of the land. Its height was enormous. 11 The
tree grew large and strong and its top touched the sky; it was
visible to the ends of the earth. 12 Its leaves were beautiful, its
fruit abundant, and on it was food for all. Under it the beasts of
the field found shelter, and the birds of the air lived in its
branches; from it every creature was fed.

13 "In the visions I saw while lying in my bed, I looked, and
there before me was a messenger,[b] a holy one, coming down
from heaven. 14 He called in a loud voice: 'Cut down the tree and
trim off its branches; strip off its leaves and scatter its fruit. Let
the animals flee from under it and the birds from its branches.
15 But let the stump and its roots, bound with iron and bronze,
remain in the ground, in the grass of the field.

" 'Let him be drenched with the dew of heaven, and let him
live with the animals among the plants of the earth. 16 Let his
mind be changed from that of a man and let him be given the
mind of an animal, till seven times[c] pass by for him.

17 " 'The decision is announced by messengers, the holy ones
declare the verdict, so that the living may know that the Most
High is sovereign over the kingdoms of men and gives them to
anyone he wishes and sets over them the lowliest of men.'

18 "This is the dream that I, King Nebuchadnezzar, had. Now,
Belteshazzar, tell me what it means, for none of the wise men in
my kingdom can interpret it for me. But you can, because the
spirit of the holy gods is in you."

OPEN 1. What tactful way have you found to break bad news to someone? **2.** How would you like to receive news: Bad news first? Good news first? **3.** Share a time when you delayed doing something urgent or needful only to regret it. What were the results? How did you feel?

STUDY 1. How does Daniel break his bad news tactfully? What does he do and say at the outset (v. 19) and at the end (v. 27) which

Daniel Interprets the Dream

19 Then Daniel (also called Belteshazzar) was greatly perplexed
for a time, and his thoughts terrified him. So the king said, "Belteshazzar, do not let the dream or its meaning alarm you."

Belteshazzar answered, "My lord, if only the dream applied to
your enemies and its meaning to your adversaries! 20 The tree
you saw, which grew large and strong, with its top touching the
sky, visible to the whole earth, 21 with beautiful leaves and abundant fruit, providing food for all, giving shelter to the beasts of

[a]7 Or *Chaldeans* [b]13 Or *watchman;* also in verses 17 and 23 [c]16 Or *years;* also in verses 23, 25 and 32

4:11–12 The tree in Nebuchadnezzar's dream represents Nebuchadnezzar himself, whose kingdom spread farther than any kingdom before him.

4:13 messenger, a holy one. Nebuchadnezzar didn't recognize the messenger, but Jews knew that this was an angel from heaven.

4:15 The fact that the stump and roots remained in the ground suggested that the tree would be revived later. There would eventually be new growth.

4:17 The lesson that Nebuchadnezzar was supposed to learn from his experience was that God is sovereign over all rulers of the earth. It is God who chooses to set rulers over the people, and God who has the power to take away their authority.

the field, and having nesting places in its branches for the birds
of the air— 22you, O king, are that tree! You have become great
and strong; your greatness has grown until it reaches the sky,
and your dominion extends to distant parts of the earth.
23"You, O king, saw a messenger, a holy one, coming down
from heaven and saying, 'Cut down the tree and destroy it, but
leave the stump, bound with iron and bronze, in the grass of the
field, while its roots remain in the ground. Let him be drenched
with the dew of heaven; let him live like the wild animals, until
seven times pass by for him.'
24"This is the interpretation, O king, and this is the decree the
Most High has issued against my lord the king: 25You will be driv-
en away from people and will live with the wild animals; you will
eat grass like cattle and be drenched with the dew of heaven.
Seven times will pass by for you until you acknowledge that the
Most High is sovereign over the kingdoms of men and gives
them to anyone he wishes. 26The command to leave the stump of
the tree with its roots means that your kingdom will be restored
to you when you acknowledge that Heaven rules. 27Therefore,
O king, be pleased to accept my advice: Renounce your sins by
doing what is right, and your wickedness by being kind to the
oppressed. It may be that then your prosperity will continue."

The Dream Is Fulfilled

28All this happened to King Nebuchadnezzar. 29Twelve months
later, as the king was walking on the roof of the royal palace of
Babylon, 30he said, "Is not this the great Babylon I have built as
the royal residence, by my mighty power and for the glory of my
majesty?"
31The words were still on his lips when a voice came from
heaven, "This is what is decreed for you, King Nebuchadnezzar:
Your royal authority has been taken from you. 32You will be
driven away from people and will live with the wild animals; you
will eat grass like cattle. Seven times will pass by for you until
you acknowledge that the Most High is sovereign over the kingdoms of men and gives them to anyone he wishes."
33Immediately what had been said about Nebuchadnezzar was
fulfilled. He was driven away from people and ate grass like cattle. His body was drenched with the dew of heaven until his hair
grew like the feathers of an eagle and his nails like the claws of a
bird.
34At the end of that time, I, Nebuchadnezzar, raised my eyes
toward heaven, and my sanity was restored. Then I praised the
Most High; I honored and glorified him who lives forever.

His dominion is an eternal dominion;
his kingdom endures from generation to generation.
35All the peoples of the earth
are regarded as nothing.
He does as he pleases

would increase the likelihood that Nebuchadnezzar would listen? What hope does he hold out for the king? **2.** Daniel's use of "Heaven" (v. 26) is the first and only time the word is inserted for God in the Old Testament. What does it imply: Reverence for God's name? Deference to the king's polytheistic beliefs? Or what? **3.** The Aramaic word for righteous or "what is right" (v. 27) links human responsibility to both God and neighbor. Why does Daniel stress both? (How is "being kind to the oppressed" a witness to God?) **4.** How does his interpretation of the king's dream relate to issues of pride, arrogance and humility? **5.** Has "all this happened" to the king by chance? By decree? By default? What clue does "twelve months later" provide? **6.** How is the voice from heaven shown to be powerful (vv. 31–33)? How does the immediacy and power of God's word relate to Genesis 1? **7.** With his sanity restored, what does the king conclude about "the Most High"? How does his testimony strike you: Sincerely penitent? Coaxed or coached by Daniel? Sanely rational? Miraculous turn-about? **8.** How do you account for the king's restored greatness and prosperity: Humility pays? Daniel's prophecy is fulfilled? God has a sense of humor? The king's dream of the tree and stump comes true? Other?

APPLY **1.** When was it hard for you to bring bad news to someone you cared about? Did the person do anything to make it easier? **2.** When has God "cut you down to size"? What "stump" did he leave you on to rebuild your life?

4:26 Heaven rules. This is similar to "kingdom of heaven" used by Jesus in Matthew.

4:28 Daniel's prophecy came true because Nebuchadnezzar refused to heed his warning and acknowledge God's sovereignty. God had given Nebuchadnezzar the opportunity to turn from his ways.

with the powers of heaven
and the peoples of the earth.
No one can hold back his hand
or say to him: "What have you done?"

[36]At the same time that my sanity was restored, my honor and
splendor were returned to me for the glory of my kingdom. My
advisers and nobles sought me out, and I was restored to my
throne and became even greater than before. [37]Now I, Nebuchadnezzar, praise and exalt and glorify the King of heaven,
because everything he does is right and all his ways are just. And
those who walk in pride he is able to humble.

The Writing on the Wall

5 King Belshazzar gave a great banquet for a thousand of his nobles
and drank wine with them. [2]While Belshazzar was drinking his
wine, he gave orders to bring in the gold and silver goblets that Nebuchadnezzar his father[a] had taken from the temple in Jerusalem, so
that the king and his nobles, his wives and his concubines might
drink from them. [3]So they brought in the gold goblets that had been
taken from the temple of God in Jerusalem, and the king and his
nobles, his wives and his concubines drank from them. [4]As they
drank the wine, they praised the gods of gold and silver, of bronze,
iron, wood and stone.

[5]Suddenly the fingers of a human hand appeared and wrote on the
plaster of the wall, near the lampstand in the royal palace. The king
watched the hand as it wrote. [6]His face turned pale and he was so
frightened that his knees knocked together and his legs gave way.

[7]The king called out for the enchanters, astrologers[b] and diviners
to be brought and said to these wise men of Babylon, "Whoever reads
this writing and tells me what it means will be clothed in purple and
have a gold chain placed around his neck, and he will be made the
third highest ruler in the kingdom."

[8]Then all the king's wise men came in, but they could not read the
writing or tell the king what it meant. [9]So King Belshazzar became
even more terrified and his face grew more pale. His nobles were
baffled.

[10]The queen,[c] hearing the voices of the king and his nobles, came
into the banquet hall. "O king, live forever!" she said. "Don't be
alarmed! Don't look so pale! [11]There is a man in your kingdom who
has the spirit of the holy gods in him. In the time of your father he
was found to have insight and intelligence and wisdom like that of
the gods. King Nebuchadnezzar your father—your father the king, I
say—appointed him chief of the magicians, enchanters, astrologers
and diviners. [12]This man Daniel, whom the king called Belteshazzar,
was found to have a keen mind and knowledge and understanding,
and also the ability to interpret dreams, explain riddles and solve

[a]2 Or *ancestor*; or *predecessor*; also in verses 11, 13 and 18 [b]7 Or *Chaldeans*; also in verse 11
[c]10 Or *queen mother*

OPEN 1. Recall one of your most scary, hair-raising, goose-bumpy, heart-thumping experiences. What was so frightening? **2.** Whom do you know who is good at solving puzzles, riddles, rubic cubes, crosswords, etc.?

STUDY 1. Given this script for a scene in a mystery thriller to be developed by you as the movie director, how would you underscore the drama, musically? (Where would you place the minor and major keys in dissonance, and in resolution? Where would you place the drum roll, crescendo, cymbals and taps?) **2.** As the movie director, how would you set the stage? What special effects would you use for the mysterious handwriting on the wall? What close-cropped visuals and panning shots of the audience would you weave in for maximum effect? **3.** What flashbacks to Nebuchadnezzar's reign would provide contrasting relief and background insight to the drama here? What sin has Belshazzar added to his father's (vv. 2–4)? How is this an insult to God? How is this even worse than his father's sin (vv. 18–24)? **4.** What does Belshazzar's reaction to the mysterious hand (vv. 6–9) disclose about him? About his little secure world? His guilt? Fear? **5.** What does the king learn that money, things and promotions cannot buy, but only Daniel can supply? How is that point made by the queen (vv. 10–12)? By Daniel (v. 17)? **6.** What does Daniel's rejection of flattery and rewards say about the authenticity of this man and his message? **7.** What does the handwriting on the wall mean (vv. 26–28)? How is that prophecy fulfilled (v. 30)? In accord with what

5:1 Here Belshazzar is said to be Nebuchadnezzar's son. This could also mean grandson or heir. Other documents tell us that Belshazzar, a descendant of Nebuchadnezzar, was the oldest son of Nabonidus, the reigning king. Nabonidus appointed Belshazzar co-regent, so he was called a king and thus exercised the authority of a king.

difficult problems. Call for Daniel, and he will tell you what the
writing means."
13So Daniel was brought before the king, and the king said to him,
"Are you Daniel, one of the exiles my father the king brought from
Judah? 14I have heard that the spirit of the gods is in you and that you
have insight, intelligence and outstanding wisdom. 15The wise men
and enchanters were brought before me to read this writing and tell
me what it means, but they could not explain it. 16Now I have heard
that you are able to give interpretations and to solve difficult problems. If you can read this writing and tell me what it means, you will
be clothed in purple and have a gold chain placed around your neck,
and you will be made the third highest ruler in the kingdom."
17Then Daniel answered the king, "You may keep your gifts for
yourself and give your rewards to someone else. Nevertheless, I will
read the writing for the king and tell him what it means.
18"O king, the Most High God gave your father Nebuchadnezzar
sovereignty and greatness and glory and splendor. 19Because of the
high position he gave him, all the peoples and nations and men of
every language dreaded and feared him. Those the king wanted to
put to death, he put to death; those he wanted to spare, he spared;
those he wanted to promote, he promoted; and those he wanted to
humble, he humbled. 20But when his heart became arrogant and
hardened with pride, he was deposed from his royal throne and
stripped of his glory. 21He was driven away from people and given the
mind of an animal; he lived with the wild donkeys and ate grass like
cattle; and his body was drenched with the dew of heaven, until he
acknowledged that the Most High God is sovereign over the kingdoms of men and sets over them anyone he wishes.
22"But you his son,[a] O Belshazzar, have not humbled yourself,
though you knew all this. 23Instead, you have set yourself up against
the Lord of heaven. You had the goblets from his temple brought to
you, and you and your nobles, your wives and your concubines drank
wine from them. You praised the gods of silver and gold, of bronze,
iron, wood and stone, which cannot see or hear or understand. But
you did not honor the God who holds in his hand your life and all
your ways. 24Therefore he sent the hand that wrote the inscription.
25"This is the inscription that was written:

MENE, MENE, TEKEL, PARSIN[b]

26"This is what these words mean:

Mene[c]: God has numbered the days of your reign and brought
it to an end.
27*Tekel*[d]: You have been weighed on the scales and found wanting.

[a]22 Or *descendant*; or *successor* [b]25 Aramaic *UPARSIN* (that is, *AND PARSIN*) [c]26 *Mene* can mean *numbered* or *mina* (a unit of money). [d]27 *Tekel* can mean *weighed* or *shekel*.

prediction (2:36–39)? **8.** Compare the two kings' portraits in verses 29–30 and 4:34–37. Whom do they praise? What does that tell you about them? From their contrasting fates, what do you learn about God's mercy and justice, power and authority?

APPLY 1. When did you "see the handwriting on the wall" concerning your own misbehavior? How did you respond to the warning? **2.** What have you learned from your parents or predecessors? Why do people often fail, as does Belshazzar, to learn from the past? **3.** What would you do if you were offered position and/or power as a way to buy your vote or predetermine your thinking?

5:13 It is now over 60 years from the opening of the book. Daniel is possibly over 80 years old.

5:22–23 Belshazzar knew all that had happened to Nebuchadnezzar, but he failed to learn from his experience. He openly defied God by drinking from the temple goblets and worshiping idols.

5:25–28 The inscription on the wall is a play on words. *Mene* is from a verb meaning "to number, to reckon" and refers to a weight of fifty shekels (a mina). *Tekel* is from the verb "to weigh" and refers to a shekel. *Parsin* is from the verb "to break in two, to divide" and refers to a half-mina.

5:27 Tekel. Belshazzar's moral and spiritual life did not measure up to the

28 *Peres*[a]: Your kingdom is divided and given to the Medes and Persians."

29 Then at Belshazzar's command, Daniel was clothed in purple, a gold chain was placed around his neck, and he was proclaimed the third highest ruler in the kingdom.

30 That very night Belshazzar, king of the Babylonians,[b] was slain, 31 and Darius the Mede took over the kingdom, at the age of sixty-two.

Daniel in the Den of Lions

6 It pleased Darius to appoint 120 satraps to rule throughout the kingdom, 2 with three administrators over them, one of whom was Daniel. The satraps were made accountable to them so that the king might not suffer loss. 3 Now Daniel so distinguished himself among the administrators and the satraps by his exceptional qualities that the king planned to set him over the whole kingdom. 4 At this, the administrators and the satraps tried to find grounds for charges against Daniel in his conduct of government affairs, but they were unable to do so. They could find no corruption in him, because he was trustworthy and neither corrupt nor negligent. 5 Finally these men said, "We will never find any basis for charges against this man Daniel unless it has something to do with the law of his God."

6 So the administrators and the satraps went as a group to the king and said: "O King Darius, live forever! 7 The royal administrators, prefects, satraps, advisers and governors have all agreed that the king should issue an edict and enforce the decree that anyone who prays to any god or man during the next thirty days, except to you, O king, shall be thrown into the lions' den. 8 Now, O king, issue the decree and put it in writing so that it cannot be altered—in accordance with the laws of the Medes and Persians, which cannot be repealed." 9 So King Darius put the decree in writing.

10 Now when Daniel learned that the decree had been published, he went home to his upstairs room where the windows opened toward Jerusalem. Three times a day he got down on his knees and prayed, giving thanks to his God, just as he had done before. 11 Then these men went as a group and found Daniel praying and asking God for help. 12 So they went to the king and spoke to him about his royal decree: "Did you not publish a decree that during the next thirty days anyone who prays to any god or man except to you, O king, would be thrown into the lions' den?"

The king answered, "The decree stands—in accordance with the laws of the Medes and Persians, which cannot be repealed."

13 Then they said to the king, "Daniel, who is one of the exiles from Judah, pays no attention to you, O king, or to the decree you put in writing. He still prays three times a day." 14 When the king heard this,

[a]28 *Peres* (the singular of *Parsin*) can mean *divided* or *Persia* or *a half mina* or *a half shekel.*
[b]30 Or *Chaldeans*

OPEN 1. Share a time when you were done-in by having the rug pulled out from under you. How were you set up, betrayed or falsely accused? **2.** When have you felt really good about something you did, only to have someone else be jealous or unhappy?

STUDY 1. What stirs up the jealousy of the administrators and satraps? When their jealous fault-finding campaign (or special investigative unit) runs free of any ethical guidelines, where does it stop (vv. 1–5)? **2.** What trap do the satraps set for Daniel? Why has Daniel's private life become an issue for public policy and the public's right to know? **3.** How do the satraps manage to get their way with the king (vv. 6–7,12–13,15)? Why are appeals to vanity so powerful? **4.** Why is the king so distressed (vv. 14–18)? Is he just being a "wimp," favoring whoever he happens to be with at the moment? Or is he sincerely siding with Daniel and his God? Why do you think so? **5.** What do you think really happened in the lions' den to Daniel? To the lions? To the satraps and their families? What about this do you have problems with? **6.** What role does the "laws of the Medes and the Persians" play here (vv. 8,12,15,17,24)? Likewise, what role does the law of God play (vv. 5,10; 2 Chr. 6:38–39; Ps. 55:17)? Likewise, what role does the faith of Daniel play (vv. 4,11,16, 20–23; Heb. 11:33)? **7.** As part of Daniel's complete vindication, his accusers receive the same punishment they had demanded that the accused receive (v. 24). Is this Persian custom of vindication and limited ("eye for eye," "life for life") retribution supported anywhere in the Bible (Ex. 21:24; Lev. 24:20; Deut. 21;

standard of God's righteousness, so he was rejected as unacceptable. As a result, his reign would come to an end and his kingdom be divided between the Medes and the Persians.

6:7 Certainly not all the royal administrators agreed to this edict, since Daniel was not even aware of it and would not support it. The conspirators lied in order to get the king to agree to their scheme.

he was greatly distressed; he was determined to rescue Daniel and
made every effort until sundown to save him.
15Then the men went as a group to the king and said to him, "Remember, O king, that according to the law of the Medes and Persians
no decree or edict that the king issues can be changed."
16So the king gave the order, and they brought Daniel and threw
him into the lions' den. The king said to Daniel, "May your God,
whom you serve continually, rescue you!"
17A stone was brought and placed over the mouth of the den, and
the king sealed it with his own signet ring and with the rings of his
nobles, so that Daniel's situation might not be changed. 18Then the
king returned to his palace and spent the night without eating and
without any entertainment being brought to him. And he could not
sleep.
19At the first light of dawn, the king got up and hurried to the lions'
den. 20When he came near the den, he called to Daniel in an
anguished voice, "Daniel, servant of the living God, has your God,
whom you serve continually, been able to rescue you from the lions?"
21Daniel answered, "O king, live forever! 22My God sent his angel,
and he shut the mouths of the lions. They have not hurt me, because
I was found innocent in his sight. Nor have I ever done any wrong before you, O king."
23The king was overjoyed and gave orders to lift Daniel out of the
den. And when Daniel was lifted from the den, no wound was found
on him, because he had trusted in his God.
24At the king's command, the men who had falsely accused Daniel
were brought in and thrown into the lions' den, along with their
wives and children. And before they reached the floor of the den, the
lions overpowered them and crushed all their bones.
25Then King Darius wrote to all the peoples, nations and men of
every language throughout the land:

"May you prosper greatly!

26"I issue a decree that in every part of my kingdom people
must fear and reverence the God of Daniel.

"For he is the living God
and he endures forever;
his kingdom will not be destroyed,
his dominion will never end.
27He rescues and he saves;
he performs signs and wonders
in the heavens and on the earth.
He has rescued Daniel
from the power of the lions."

28So Daniel prospered during the reign of Darius and the reign of
Cyrus[a] the Persian.

[a]28 Or *Darius, that is, the reign of Cyrus*

Matt. 5:38)? But when, if ever, might it be okay to punish innocent family members of false accusers? **8.** How does King Darius respond to all this? Has he himself become a believer? Why do you think so? **9.** What parallels do you see between Daniel's betrayal (vv. 3–18) and Jesus'? Between Daniel's vindication (vv. 19–28) and Jesus'? What do you make of those obvious parallels?

APPLY 1. What stirs up your jealousy: The success of others? Desire for material things? The devil? When someone else gets what is coming to you? Other? **2.** When in your life have you experienced God in the midst of a "lions' den" of skeptics, critics, etc.? How has God alone been your lifeline?

6:23 no wound was found on him, because he had trusted in his God. The king was fully expecting to find Daniel devoured. Not only was Daniel's life miraculously preserved, but he did not even have a single scratch from his night with the ravenous lions. God proved his power to save believers.

OPEN 1. What are your favorite animals, wild or tame? **2.** What are your favorite animal cartoon characters? **3.** What animal scares you to pieces?

STUDY 1. Jesus takes Daniel's royal "Son of Man" title as his own, but fuses it with a suffering motif (Isa. 53). What aspect of Christ and his kingdom, then, is Daniel predicting in verses 13–14? How does this compare to the other four kingdoms? **2.** How has Daniel's relation to dreams changed in this chapter? (Note: The events here may precede those in ch. 5.) Are these dreams humanly concocted or divinely given? Why do you think so? **3.** To what does Daniel liken the four beasts? What's distinctive about each? What do you make of the 10 horns? The "little horn" with the big mouth? (Does it imply a man, government, a coalition of states, an ideology?) **4.** What picture does the "Ancient of Days" bring to mind: Wisdom or senility? Venerability or vulnerability? Sentimental softy or moral purity? Why? **5.** What do you think is implied by "the books were opened" (v. 10)? Does your answer say more about God's control or human freedom? **6.** How does Daniel convey transcendent and earthly aspects of God (vv. 9–14)? What is the coming kingdom and its heavenly leader like?

APPLY 1. How do you react to "wild, scary and beastly" forces within your world? Within your life? What reason does Daniel give you to trust that God "has the whole world in his hands"? **2.** Take a minute to draw the scene in verses 13–14 in your imagination. What does this emphasize to you about Jesus Christ? Why is it significant to you that he is described like this?

Daniel's Dream of Four Beasts

7 In the first year of Belshazzar king of Babylon, Daniel had a
dream, and visions passed through his mind as he was lying on
his bed. He wrote down the substance of his dream.
[2]Daniel said: "In my vision at night I looked, and there before me
were the four winds of heaven churning up the great sea. [3]Four great
beasts, each different from the others, came up out of the sea.
[4]"The first was like a lion, and it had the wings of an eagle. I
watched until its wings were torn off and it was lifted from the
ground so that it stood on two feet like a man, and the heart of a man
was given to it.
[5]"And there before me was a second beast, which looked like a
bear. It was raised up on one of its sides, and it had three ribs in its
mouth between its teeth. It was told, 'Get up and eat your fill of flesh!'
[6]"After that, I looked, and there before me was another beast, one
that looked like a leopard. And on its back it had four wings like those
of a bird. This beast had four heads, and it was given authority to
rule.
[7]"After that, in my vision at night I looked, and there before me was
a fourth beast—terrifying and frightening and very powerful. It had
large iron teeth; it crushed and devoured its victims and trampled underfoot whatever was left. It was different from all the former beasts,
and it had ten horns.
[8]"While I was thinking about the horns, there before me was another horn, a little one, which came up among them; and three of the
first horns were uprooted before it. This horn had eyes like the eyes
of a man and a mouth that spoke boastfully.
[9]"As I looked,

"thrones were set in place,
    and the Ancient of Days took his seat.
His clothing was as white as snow;
    the hair of his head was white like wool.
His throne was flaming with fire,
    and its wheels were all ablaze.
[10]A river of fire was flowing,
    coming out from before him.
Thousands upon thousands attended him;
    ten thousand times ten thousand stood before him.
The court was seated,
    and the books were opened.

[11]"Then I continued to watch because of the boastful words the
horn was speaking. I kept looking until the beast was slain and its
body destroyed and thrown into the blazing fire. [12](The other beasts
had been stripped of their authority, but were allowed to live for a
period of time.)
[13]"In my vision at night I looked, and there before me was one like
a son of man, coming with the clouds of heaven. He approached
the Ancient of Days and was led into his presence. [14]He was given

---

7:1–8 Daniel is given a vision of four beasts. They, like the dream in chapter two, have been seen by some to represent Babylon, Medo-Persia, Greece and Rome. Chapter 2:36–43 refers to another dream with four statues.

7:13–14 son of man. This is the first time this title is used for the Messiah. Here we see Christ approaching the

authority, glory and sovereign power; all peoples, nations and men
of every language worshiped him. His dominion is an everlasting
dominion that will not pass away, and his kingdom is one that will
never be destroyed.

The Interpretation of the Dream

15 "I, Daniel, was troubled in spirit, and the visions that passed
through my mind disturbed me. 16 I approached one of those standing
there and asked him the true meaning of all this.
"So he told me and gave me the interpretation of these things:
17 'The four great beasts are four kingdoms that will rise from the
earth. 18 But the saints of the Most High will receive the kingdom and
will possess it forever—yes, for ever and ever.'
19 "Then I wanted to know the true meaning of the fourth beast,
which was different from all the others and most terrifying, with its
iron teeth and bronze claws—the beast that crushed and devoured its
victims and trampled underfoot whatever was left. 20 I also wanted
to know about the ten horns on its head and about the other horn
that came up, before which three of them fell—the horn that looked
more imposing than the others and that had eyes and a mouth that
spoke boastfully. 21 As I watched, this horn was waging war against
the saints and defeating them, 22 until the Ancient of Days came and
pronounced judgment in favor of the saints of the Most High, and the
time came when they possessed the kingdom.
23 "He gave me this explanation: 'The fourth beast is a fourth kingdom that will appear on earth. It will be different from all the other
kingdoms and will devour the whole earth, trampling it down and
crushing it. 24 The ten horns are ten kings who will come from this
kingdom. After them another king will arise, different from the earlier
ones; he will subdue three kings. 25 He will speak against the Most
High and oppress his saints and try to change the set times and the
laws. The saints will be handed over to him for a time, times and half
a time.[a]
26 " 'But the court will sit, and his power will be taken away and
completely destroyed forever. 27 Then the sovereignty, power and
greatness of the kingdoms under the whole heaven will be handed
over to the saints, the people of the Most High. His kingdom will be
an everlasting kingdom, and all rulers will worship and obey him.'
28 "This is the end of the matter. I, Daniel, was deeply troubled by
my thoughts, and my face turned pale, but I kept the matter to myself."

[a]25 Or *for a year, two years and half a year*

OPEN 1. Share about a time your favorite team was the underdog and they won. **2.** Share about when you were in an underdog role and came out on top.

STUDY 1. How is Daniel affected by this vision (vv. 15,19,28)? How does he learn its true meaning? **2.** How might you go about cracking the code of the four kingdoms? (Modern attempts to do so are based on comparisons among the visions of Daniel in chapters 2, 7 and 9, with a chronology of major empires we know in retrospect from secular history.) **3.** In judgment, what role is played by the "saints" (vv. 18,21–22,25,27)? By "the Most High"? **4.** How does Daniel's view on saints in judgment compare with that of Jesus and John (Matt. 19:28–29; Luke 22:29–30; Rev. 1:6; 20:4–6)?

APPLY 1. What powerful force do you feel is "waging war" against you right now? **2.** In what way would you like for God to intervene for you, as he did for those saints (v. 22)?

Ancient of Days and being given all the authority, glory and sovereign power that had previously been given to earthly rulers.

7:18 saints of the Most High. Those who believe in Christ will inherit the kingdom. (Matt. 19:28–29; Rev. 20:4–6.)

7:24–26 another king will arise. After the ten divided kings, one king will take over three of the ten. But he will oppose God's authority, oppress the saints and abandon old laws to institute his own governmental system. This king will persecute Israel for three and a half years (a time that may be figurative or could refer to the three and one-half years of the Great Tribulation, Rev. 12:14). After that Jesus will sit as judge, remove him from power and set up his eternal kingdom.

7:27 handed over to the saints. God will fulfill his promise to rule over his people eternally. His kingdom will extend over all the earth.

OPEN With whom did you most frequently "butt heads" when you were a teenager? Who most frequently won?

STUDY 1. What does it matter when (before the events of ch. 5) and where (in the mind of Daniel) this vision actually takes place? **2.** What about this vision makes you wince and rub your forehead? **3.** What does the two-horned ram represent (vv. 3,20)? The goat and its prominent horn (vv. 5,21)? What do the charging animals, the shattering of the two horns, and the breaking off of the large horn represent (vv. 7–8)? **4.** What other "little horn" does the emerging horn in verse 9 bring to mind (7:8,11)? How is this one different in origin, nature and destiny? How is it similar in its overwhelming pride? **5.** What do you make of Daniel specifying the time frame for the fulfillment of his vision (vv. 13,26)? Why do you think God allows the transgression of his moral law for such a long time? **6.** Verses 20–25 (ch. 7; Rev. 12 and 13) are the background for the Christian belief in an Antichrist, the last days and God's doing battle for us. What do you see here? How will "he" be destroyed? **7.** What impact does all this have on Daniel (vv. 15,17,27)?

APPLY 1. When have you been dismayed over: Something God revealed to you? Some triumph of evil or good? **2.** The study of Daniel's prophecies often produces more heat than light. How do you relate to others who favor an interpretation that differs from yours? **3.** How might one reach for the stars, desecrate the temple, or trample truth underfoot, as in verses 10–12: Disregard biblical truth? Deny Jesus is God? "Play God"? Other? How long can your society get away with that? **4.** Where have you seen God active in violent world affairs?

Daniel's Vision of a Ram and a Goat

8 In the third year of King Belshazzar's reign, I, Daniel, had a
vision, after the one that had already appeared to me. 2In my vision I saw myself in the citadel of Susa in the province of Elam; in the
vision I was beside the Ulai Canal. 3I looked up, and there before me
was a ram with two horns, standing beside the canal, and the horns
were long. One of the horns was longer than the other but grew up
later. 4I watched the ram as he charged toward the west and the north
and the south. No animal could stand against him, and none could
rescue from his power. He did as he pleased and became great.

5As I was thinking about this, suddenly a goat with a prominent
horn between his eyes came from the west, crossing the whole earth
without touching the ground. 6He came toward the two-horned ram I
had seen standing beside the canal and charged at him in great rage.
7I saw him attack the ram furiously, striking the ram and shattering
his two horns. The ram was powerless to stand against him; the goat
knocked him to the ground and trampled on him, and none could
rescue the ram from his power. 8The goat became very great, but at
the height of his power his large horn was broken off, and in its place
four prominent horns grew up toward the four winds of heaven.

9Out of one of them came another horn, which started small but
grew in power to the south and to the east and toward the Beautiful
Land. 10It grew until it reached the host of the heavens, and it threw
some of the starry host down to the earth and trampled on them. 11It
set itself up to be as great as the Prince of the host; it took away the
daily sacrifice from him, and the place of his sanctuary was brought
low. 12Because of rebellion, the host ⌞of the saints⌟[a] and the daily sacrifice were given over to it. It prospered in everything it did, and truth
was thrown to the ground.

13Then I heard a holy one speaking, and another holy one said to
him, "How long will it take for the vision to be fulfilled—the vision
concerning the daily sacrifice, the rebellion that causes desolation,
and the surrender of the sanctuary and of the host that will be trampled underfoot?"

14He said to me, "It will take 2,300 evenings and mornings; then
the sanctuary will be reconsecrated."

The Interpretation of the Vision

15While I, Daniel, was watching the vision and trying to understand
it, there before me stood one who looked like a man. 16And I heard a

[a]12 Or *rebellion, the armies*

8:3 ram with two horns. The ram represents the Medo-Persian Empire, with the longer horn signifying the superior position of Persia. The Medo-Persian Empire would charge in all directions until it dominated the entire area.

8:5–7 goat with a prominent horn. The goat represents Greece, with the prominent horn as a symbol for Alexander the Great. Greece would crush the Medo-Persian Empire.

8:8 horn was broken off. Alexander the Great died at the height of his power. The four prominent horns that took over were four generals who carved up the Macedonian Empire.

8:9–12 The horn that started small but grew in power was Antiochus IV Epiphanes. He attempted to destroy the Jewish faith, foreshadowing the ruthless beast of the last days. Antiochus took control of Israel, the "Beautiful Land," and killed many believers for their faith. Then he declared himself to be God's equal and refused to allow the Jews to make sacrifices. He was eventually defeated by Judas Maccabeus, who rededicated the temple to the Lord and began the Feast of Hanukkah.

man's voice from the Ulai calling, "Gabriel, tell this man the meaning of the vision."

[17]As he came near the place where I was standing, I was terrified and fell prostrate. "Son of man," he said to me, "understand that the vision concerns the time of the end."

[18]While he was speaking to me, I was in a deep sleep, with my face to the ground. Then he touched me and raised me to my feet.

[19]He said: "I am going to tell you what will happen later in the time of wrath, because the vision concerns the appointed time of the end.[a]
[20]The two-horned ram that you saw represents the kings of Media and Persia.
[21]The shaggy goat is the king of Greece, and the large horn between his eyes is the first king.
[22]The four horns that replaced the one that was broken off represent four kingdoms that will emerge from his nation but will not have the same power.

[23]"In the latter part of their reign, when rebels have become completely wicked, a stern-faced king, a master of intrigue, will arise.
[24]He will become very strong, but not by his own power. He will cause astounding devastation and will succeed in whatever he does. He will destroy the mighty men and the holy people.
[25]He will cause deceit to prosper, and he will consider himself superior. When they feel secure, he will destroy many and take his stand against the Prince of princes. Yet he will be destroyed, but not by human power.

[26]"The vision of the evenings and mornings that has been given you is true, but seal up the vision, for it concerns the distant future."

[27]I, Daniel, was exhausted and lay ill for several days. Then I got up and went about the king's business. I was appalled by the vision; it was beyond understanding.

Daniel's Prayer

9 In the first year of Darius son of Xerxes[b] (a Mede by descent), who was made ruler over the Babylonian[c] kingdom—
[2]in the first year of his reign, I, Daniel, understood from the Scriptures, according to the word of the LORD given to Jeremiah the prophet, that the desolation of Jerusalem would last seventy years.
[3]So I turned to the Lord God and pleaded with him in prayer and petition, in fasting, and in sackcloth and ashes.

[4]I prayed to the LORD my God and confessed:

"O Lord, the great and awesome God, who keeps his covenant of love with all who love him and obey his commands,
[5]we have sinned and done wrong. We have been wicked and have rebelled; we have turned away from your commands and laws.
[6]We have not listened to your servants the prophets, who spoke in your name to our kings, our princes and our fathers, and to all the people of the land.

[7]"Lord, you are righteous, but this day we are covered with shame—the men of Judah and people of Jerusalem and all Israel, both near and far, in all the countries where you have scattered us because of our unfaithfulness to you.
[8]O LORD, we and our

[a]19 *Or because the end will be at the appointed time* [b]1 Hebrew *Ahasuerus* [c]1 Or *Chaldean*

OPEN Who first said prayers with you at night and taught you how to pray? When did prayer first become your own conversation with God?

STUDY 1. What moves Daniel to pray as he does? What clues do Jeremiah 25:1–14 and 29:10–14 provide? If the "70-year" period begins with the onset of Jehoiakim's reign (608 B.C.) or Nebuchadnezzar's reign (605 B.C.), what then happens almost 70 years later (in 538 B.C.)? **2.** How does Daniel prepare himself for this divine encounter? Who is Daniel speaking for as he prays? What elements of common prayer do you see here? **3.** How does each aspect of God prompt a round of Daniel's confession: God is great and awesome? Faithful to his covenant? Righteous in bringing judgment? Merciful and forgiving? Jealous for his name? **4.** Why will God answer his prayer (vv. 16–19)? **5.** What does this prayer say about God's covenant:

9:3 in sackcloth and ashes. Daniel mourned over Israel's sin. He knew that the Exile in Babylon was God's discipline of Israel, and that confession was necessary in order for the people to be restored to God and his blessing.

Based on grace or works? His character or ours? Conveys love or justice? Forever binding or always renegotiable?

APPLY 1. Daniel's study of the Scriptures drove him to pray a prayer filled with Scripture. How could you use Scripture in your prayers? **2.** Judging from the content of your recent prayers, what concerns you most these days? **3.** Daniel humbled himself before meeting his God in prayer (v. 3). How do you prepare to meet your God? How do you keep from viewing God as a celestial butler? **4.** What aspects of God move you to pray? Why? Who do you pray for most frequently? What prayer agenda for you and your group does chapter 9 suggest? Try it.

OPEN What's it like to do a jigsaw puzzle that has missing pieces? Whose handwriting do you find near impossible to decipher?

STUDY 1. What does this enigma imply about God's "answering service" (vv. 20–23)? **2.** What six things happen within "seventy sevens"? Which events may refer to the time of Ezra and Nehemiah? Which events refer to Jesus as the Anointed One? Which results seem yet to be? (Hint: What do the "seven sevens," the "62 sevens," the "one seven" mean?) **3.** What is the "abomination that causes desolation" (v. 27; 11:31; 12:11): Idol-making? State-church war? Armageddon? In the

kings, our princes and our fathers are covered with shame because we have sinned against you. 9The Lord our God is merciful
and forgiving, even though we have rebelled against him; 10we
have not obeyed the LORD our God or kept the laws he gave us
through his servants the prophets. 11All Israel has transgressed
your law and turned away, refusing to obey you.

"Therefore the curses and sworn judgments written in the Law
of Moses, the servant of God, have been poured out on us, because we have sinned against you. 12You have fulfilled the words
spoken against us and against our rulers by bringing upon us
great disaster. Under the whole heaven nothing has ever been
done like what has been done to Jerusalem. 13Just as it is written
in the Law of Moses, all this disaster has come upon us, yet we
have not sought the favor of the LORD our God by turning from
our sins and giving attention to your truth. 14The LORD did not
hesitate to bring the disaster upon us, for the LORD our God is
righteous in everything he does; yet we have not obeyed him.

15"Now, O Lord our God, who brought your people out of
Egypt with a mighty hand and who made for yourself a name
that endures to this day, we have sinned, we have done wrong.
16O Lord, in keeping with all your righteous acts, turn away your
anger and your wrath from Jerusalem, your city, your holy hill.
Our sins and the iniquities of our fathers have made Jerusalem
and your people an object of scorn to all those around us.

17"Now, our God, hear the prayers and petitions of your servant. For your sake, O Lord, look with favor on your desolate
sanctuary. 18Give ear, O God, and hear; open your eyes and see
the desolation of the city that bears your Name. We do not make
requests of you because we are righteous, but because of your
great mercy. 19O Lord, listen! O Lord, forgive! O Lord, hear and
act! For your sake, O my God, do not delay, because your city and
your people bear your Name."

The Seventy "Sevens"

20While I was speaking and praying, confessing my sin and the sin
of my people Israel and making my request to the LORD my God for
his holy hill— 21while I was still in prayer, Gabriel, the man I had seen
in the earlier vision, came to me in swift flight about the time of the
evening sacrifice. 22He instructed me and said to me, "Daniel, I have
now come to give you insight and understanding. 23As soon as you
began to pray, an answer was given, which I have come to tell you, for
you are highly esteemed. Therefore, consider the message and
understand the vision:

24"Seventy 'sevens'[a] are decreed for your people and your holy city
to finish[b] transgression, to put an end to sin, to atone for wickedness,
to bring in everlasting righteousness, to seal up vision and prophecy
and to anoint the most holy.[c]

[a]24 Or *'weeks'*; also in verses 25 and 26 [b]24 Or *restrain* [c]24 Or *Most Holy Place*; or *most holy One*

9:18 your great mercy. Daniel based his requests on God's character, not on Israel's worthiness. Daniel was asking God for his mercy. God answers prayer because he is gracious, not because we deserve it.

25“Know and understand this: From the issuing of the decree[a] to restore and rebuild Jerusalem until the Anointed One,[b] the ruler, comes,
there will be seven ‘sevens,’ and sixty-two ‘sevens.’ It will be rebuilt
with streets and a trench, but in times of trouble. 26After the sixty-two
‘sevens,’ the Anointed One will be cut off and will have nothing.[c] The
people of the ruler who will come will destroy the city and the sanctuary. The end will come like a flood: War will continue until the end,
and desolations have been decreed. 27He will confirm a covenant
with many for one ‘seven.’[d] In the middle of the ‘seven’[d] he will put an
end to sacrifice and offering. And on a wing ⌊of the temple⌋ he will set
up an abomination that causes desolation, until the end that is
decreed is poured out on him.[e]”[f]

Daniel’s Vision of a Man

10 In the third year of Cyrus king of Persia, a revelation was
given to Daniel (who was called Belteshazzar). Its message
was true and it concerned a great war.[g] The understanding of the
message came to him in a vision.
2At that time I, Daniel, mourned for three weeks. 3I ate no choice
food; no meat or wine touched my lips; and I used no lotions at all
until the three weeks were over.
4On the twenty-fourth day of the first month, as I was standing on
the bank of the great river, the Tigris, 5I looked up and there before
me was a man dressed in linen, with a belt of the finest gold around
his waist. 6His body was like chrysolite, his face like lightning, his
eyes like flaming torches, his arms and legs like the gleam of burnished bronze, and his voice like the sound of a multitude.
7I, Daniel, was the only one who saw the vision; the men with me
did not see it, but such terror overwhelmed them that they fled and
hid themselves. 8So I was left alone, gazing at this great vision; I had
no strength left, my face turned deathly pale and I was helpless.
9Then I heard him speaking, and as I listened to him, I fell into a deep
sleep, my face to the ground.
10A hand touched me and set me trembling on my hands and
knees. 11He said, “Daniel, you who are highly esteemed, consider
carefully the words I am about to speak to you, and stand up, for I
have now been sent to you.” And when he said this to me, I stood up
trembling.
12Then he continued, “Do not be afraid, Daniel. Since the first day
that you set your mind to gain understanding and to humble yourself

[a]25 Or *word* [b]25 Or *an anointed one;* also in verse 26 [c]26 Or *off and will have no one;* or *off, but not for himself* [d]27 Or *‘week’* [e]27 Or *it* [f]27 Or *And one who causes desolation will come upon the pinnacle of the abominable* ⌊*temple*⌋*, until the end that is decreed is poured out on the desolated* ⌊*city*⌋ [g]1 Or *true and burdensome*

Gospels, what is it (Matt. 24:15; Mark 13:14)?

APPLY 1. For Daniel and Jesus, is the emphasis on what the future holds? Or on who holds the future? **2.** For you, what is the “gospel” in this passage?

OPEN 1. When have you been scared stiff? What experiences have left you drained? How did someone help you through? **2.** How do you feel when touched physically by: Spouse? Sweetheart? Parent? Child? A friend? A stranger?

STUDY 1. Daniel’s Babylonian name links him with the past. What other links orient the reader in these opening verses? **2.** Some see Christ in verses 5–6. How is this fantastic image like the one in Ezekiel 1 or Revelation 1:12–16? Do you think these are different images of the same divine figure? Why? Do these images fit your picture of Jesus? Why or why not? **3.** If Daniel’s companions did not see this figure, what caused them to become terrified (v. 7)? How did they “know” something they did not “see”? How does their experience compare with Saul’s Damascus road experience (Acts 9:7)? **4.** What impact does this rendezvous have on Daniel (vv. 8–10)? What brings him to his feet? **5.** What in this continuing encounter (vv. 12–19) would you find comforting? Scary? Why? **6.** How many times do God’s messengers “touch” Daniel (vv. 10–18)? What does the progression of these touching moments say about Daniel? About God’s means of self-revelation?

APPLY 1. Repeatedly Daniel is told he is “highly esteemed”

9:25 issuing of the decree. There are several possibilities as to the identity of this decree: by Cyrus (Ezra 1:2–4), the decree by Darius (Ezra 6:3–12), the decree by Artaxerxes (Ezra 7:13–26) or the decree by Artaxerxes (Neh. 2:7–9). This most likely refers to the decree by Artaxerxes Longimanus in 444 B.C. that allowed the Jews permission to rebuild Jerusalem’s city walls. Sixty-nine “sevens” (7 plus 62), the equivalent of 483 years, elapsed between this decree and the crucifixion of the Messiah.

9:26 Anointed One will be cut off. This is a reference to the crucifixion of Christ.

9:27 confirm a covenant. A ruler will come who will guarantee Israel’s safety but will break the covenant after only three and a half years. Many believe that this is a reference to the Antichrist, who will set up an abomination against God until the end. Others see this as a reference to the Messiah’s instituting a new covenant and putting an end to the Old Testament sacrificial system.

10:5 a man dressed in linen. This is either an angel or, as some think, a preincarnate appearance of Christ.

before your God, your words were heard, and I have come in
response to them. 13But the prince of the Persian kingdom resisted
me twenty-one days. Then Michael, one of the chief princes, came to
help me, because I was detained there with the king of Persia. 14Now
I have come to explain to you what will happen to your people in the
future, for the vision concerns a time yet to come."
15While he was saying this to me, I bowed with my face toward the
ground and was speechless. 16Then one who looked like a man[a]
touched my lips, and I opened my mouth and began to speak. I said
to the one standing before me, "I am overcome with anguish because
of the vision, my lord, and I am helpless. 17How can I, your servant,
talk with you, my lord? My strength is gone and I can hardly breathe."
18Again the one who looked like a man touched me and gave me
strength. 19"Do not be afraid, O man highly esteemed," he said.
"Peace! Be strong now; be strong."

When he spoke to me, I was strengthened and said, "Speak, my
lord, since you have given me strength."
20So he said, "Do you know why I have come to you? Soon I will
return to fight against the prince of Persia, and when I go, the prince
of Greece will come; 21but first I will tell you what is written in the
Book of Truth. (No one supports me against them except Michael,
11 your prince. 1And in the first year of Darius the Mede, I took
my stand to support and protect him.)

The Kings of the South and the North

2"Now then, I tell you the truth: Three more kings will appear in
Persia, and then a fourth, who will be far richer than all the others.
When he has gained power by his wealth, he will stir up everyone
against the kingdom of Greece. 3Then a mighty king will appear, who
will rule with great power and do as he pleases. 4After he has appeared, his empire will be broken up and parceled out toward the
four winds of heaven. It will not go to his descendants, nor will it
have the power he exercised, because his empire will be uprooted
and given to others.
5"The king of the South will become strong, but one of his commanders will become even stronger than he and will rule his own
kingdom with great power. 6After some years, they will become allies.
The daughter of the king of the South will go to the king of the North
to make an alliance, but she will not retain her power, and he and his
power[b] will not last. In those days she will be handed over, together
with her royal escort and her father[c] and the one who supported her.
7"One from her family line will arise to take her place. He will attack the forces of the king of the North and enter his fortress; he will
fight against them and be victorious. 8He will also seize their gods,
their metal images and their valuable articles of silver and gold and
carry them off to Egypt. For some years he will leave the king of the

[a]16 Most manuscripts of the Masoretic Text; one manuscript of the Masoretic Text, Dead Sea Scrolls and Septuagint *Then something that looked like a man's hand* [b]6 Or *offspring* [c]6 Or *child* (see Vulgate and Syriac)

(vv. 11,19; 9:23)? Is it as tough for you to trust such good news from God? How so? Who in your circles needs to hear this good news? **2.** How has God "touched" your life? What new strength and resources can you now embrace due to his touch? **3.** Daniel finds that messengers from God are friendly (vv. 10–19), though at first terrifying and draining (vv. 5–9). What does this mean for you?

OPEN 1. What war experience have you had: As a veteran? As a friend, relative or spouse of a veteran? As a victim? As a protester? From books and movies? As a war buff, collecting relics, memorabilia? As a kid, playing war games? Other? **2.** If you could relive any of those wars as a war hero or commanding general, which war would you choose and why? **3.** What feelings arise within when you sing *The National Anthem?*

STUDY 1. Would it matter to you that these kings and their successors can be positively identified from secular history? What would that add to your appreciation of this passage? **2.** In describing the wars of the kings, what does Daniel have to say about such pitfalls as: Pride going before the fall? The fault of alliances? Abuse of power? Lack of honor among thieves? Futility of war? Illusion of security? Principle of just desserts? Rebel in the ranks? Spoils of war? **3.** What happens "at the appointed time" (vv. 27,29,35)? What does this imply about God's control of history, even heathen nations and kings?

10:13 prince of the Persian kingdom. Possibly a reference to a demonic figure because of the lengthy battle with the angel, Michael.

10:21 Book of Truth. This refers to all of God's knowledge. The Bible is certainly part of this collective knowledge, but not, necessarily all of it.

11:1 first year of Darius. This is still the same year since chapter nine. This is the year 539 B.C. when Cyrus was appointed as administrator of Babylon.

North alone. 9Then the king of the North will invade the realm of the
king of the South but will retreat to his own country. 10His sons will
prepare for war and assemble a great army, which will sweep on like
an irresistible flood and carry the battle as far as his fortress.
11"Then the king of the South will march out in a rage and fight
against the king of the North, who will raise a large army, but it will
be defeated. 12When the army is carried off, the king of the South will
be filled with pride and will slaughter many thousands, yet he will not
remain triumphant. 13For the king of the North will muster another
army, larger than the first; and after several years, he will advance
with a huge army fully equipped.
14"In those times many will rise against the king of the South. The
violent men among your own people will rebel in fulfillment of the
vision, but without success. 15Then the king of the North will come
and build up siege ramps and will capture a fortified city. The forces
of the South will be powerless to resist; even their best troops will not
have the strength to stand. 16The invader will do as he pleases; no
one will be able to stand against him. He will establish himself in the
Beautiful Land and will have the power to destroy it. 17He will determine to come with the might of his entire kingdom and will make an
alliance with the king of the South. And he will give him a daughter in
marriage in order to overthrow the kingdom, but his plans[a] will not
succeed or help him. 18Then he will turn his attention to the coastlands and will take many of them, but a commander will put an end to
his insolence and will turn his insolence back upon him. 19After this,
he will turn back toward the fortresses of his own country but will
stumble and fall, to be seen no more.
20"His successor will send out a tax collector to maintain the royal
splendor. In a few years, however, he will be destroyed, yet not in
anger or in battle.
21"He will be succeeded by a contemptible person who has not
been given the honor of royalty. He will invade the kingdom when its
people feel secure, and he will seize it through intrigue. 22Then an
overwhelming army will be swept away before him; both it and a
prince of the covenant will be destroyed. 23After coming to an agreement with him, he will act deceitfully, and with only a few people he
will rise to power. 24When the richest provinces feel secure, he will
invade them and will achieve what neither his fathers nor his forefathers did. He will distribute plunder, loot and wealth among his
followers. He will plot the overthrow of fortresses—but only for a
time.
25"With a large army he will stir up his strength and courage
against the king of the South. The king of the South will wage war
with a large and very powerful army, but he will not be able to stand
because of the plots devised against him. 26Those who eat from the
king's provisions will try to destroy him; his army will be swept away,
and many will fall in battle. 27The two kings, with their hearts bent on
evil, will sit at the same table and lie to each other, but to no avail,
because an end will still come at the appointed time. 28The king of the
North will return to his own country with great wealth, but his heart
will be set against the holy covenant. He will take action against it
and then return to his own country.

[a]17 Or *but she*

4. Which wars sound like "holy wars"? Why do you think so? What faith and wisdom do these Jewish resistance leaders display? With what "success" (vv. 32–35)? What precedent do they set for suffering Christians who "know God" and are martyred for it? **5.** From what vantage point does Daniel purport to be "telling the truth" (v. 2) concerning these kingdoms? How do you account for his accuracy: Prophecy written with remarkable foreknowledge? Or after the fact? What from this passage supports your view?

APPLY 1. What are your feelings about "sons preparing for war" (v. 10)? What is your view on the call to followers of Christ to defend, with force, certain human rights or freedoms? **2.** What does knowing God cause you to "firmly resist" in our modern society (v. 32)? **3.** When has "stumbling" in life caused you ultimately to be "refined" and "purified" (v . 35)?

29 “At the appointed time he will invade the South again, but this
time the outcome will be different from what it was before. 30 Ships of
the western coastlands[a] will oppose him, and he will lose heart. Then
he will turn back and vent his fury against the holy covenant. He will
return and show favor to those who forsake the holy covenant.
31 “His armed forces will rise up to desecrate the temple fortress
and will abolish the daily sacrifice. Then they will set up the abomination that causes desolation. 32 With flattery he will corrupt those
who have violated the covenant, but the people who know their God
will firmly resist him.
33 “Those who are wise will instruct many, though for a time they
will fall by the sword or be burned or captured or plundered. 34 When
they fall, they will receive a little help, and many who are not sincere
will join them. 35 Some of the wise will stumble, so that they may be
refined, purified and made spotless until the time of the end, for it
will still come at the appointed time.

The King Who Exalts Himself

36 “The king will do as he pleases. He will exalt and magnify himself
above every god and will say unheard-of things against the God of
gods. He will be successful until the time of wrath is completed, for
what has been determined must take place. 37 He will show no regard
for the gods of his fathers or for the one desired by women, nor will
he regard any god, but will exalt himself above them all. 38 Instead of
them, he will honor a god of fortresses; a god unknown to his fathers
he will honor with gold and silver, with precious stones and costly
gifts. 39 He will attack the mightiest fortresses with the help of a foreign god and will greatly honor those who acknowledge him. He will
make them rulers over many people and will distribute the land at a
price.[b]
40 “At the time of the end the king of the South will engage him in
battle, and the king of the North will storm out against him with
chariots and cavalry and a great fleet of ships. He will invade many
countries and sweep through them like a flood. 41 He will also invade
the Beautiful Land. Many countries will fall, but Edom, Moab and the
leaders of Ammon will be delivered from his hand. 42 He will extend
his power over many countries; Egypt will not escape. 43 He will gain
control of the treasures of gold and silver and all the riches of Egypt,
with the Libyans and Nubians in submission. 44 But reports from the
east and the north will alarm him, and he will set out in a great rage
to destroy and annihilate many. 45 He will pitch his royal tents
between the seas at[c] the beautiful holy mountain. Yet he will come to
his end, and no one will help him.

[a] 30 Hebrew *of Kittim* [b] 39 Or *land for a reward* [c] 45 Or *the sea and*

OPEN If you were able to do as you pleased next year, what might you do?

STUDY 1. How do you see verses 36–45: Continuing the description of Antiochus? Prophesying about the coming Antichrist (of which Antiochus is a prototype)? A “both-and” situation? Support your view from the text. **2.** In what will this Antichrist trust (vv. 38–39)? What fierce conflicts does this evil figure wage (vv. 40–45)? **3.** To what extent will he succeed? How will he meet his demise?

APPLY 1. What assumptions do the arrogant have about God? Where in your life are these assumptions at work? **2.** How do followers of Christ, churches and nations “honor a god of fortresses”? How do you rid yourself of such a fortress-mentality? **3.** Daniel proclaims a relevant word from God for his current crisis. What is your relevant word from God?

11:31 desecrate the temple. *Antiochus Epiphanes, King of Syria*, polluted the temple with a pagan altar in 168 B.C.

11:36 The king will do as he pleases. From here to the end of chapter 11, the king referred to is the Antichrist. He will set himself in power completely independent of any other power, even to the point of exalting himself above God.

11:40–45 Just before Christ's return, the Antichrist will battle his political enemies. At the battle of Armageddon he will be killed on the “beautiful holy mountain,” Jerusalem's temple mount (Rev. 19:11–21).

The End Times

12 "At that time Michael, the great prince who protects your
people, will arise. There will be a time of distress such as has
not happened from the beginning of nations until then. But at that
time your people—everyone whose name is found written in the
book—will be delivered. [2]Multitudes who sleep in the dust of the
earth will awake: some to everlasting life, others to shame and everlasting contempt. [3]Those who are wise[a] will shine like the brightness
of the heavens, and those who lead many to righteousness, like the
stars for ever and ever. [4]But you, Daniel, close up and seal the words
of the scroll until the time of the end. Many will go here and there to
increase knowledge."

[5]Then I, Daniel, looked, and there before me stood two others, one
on this bank of the river and one on the opposite bank. [6]One of them
said to the man clothed in linen, who was above the waters of the
river, "How long will it be before these astonishing things are fulfilled?"

[7]The man clothed in linen, who was above the waters of the river,
lifted his right hand and his left hand toward heaven, and I heard him
swear by him who lives forever, saying, "It will be for a time, times
and half a time.[b] When the power of the holy people has been finally
broken, all these things will be completed."

[8]I heard, but I did not understand. So I asked, "My lord, what will
the outcome of all this be?"

[9]He replied, "Go your way, Daniel, because the words are closed up
and sealed until the time of the end. [10]Many will be purified, made
spotless and refined, but the wicked will continue to be wicked. None
of the wicked will understand, but those who are wise will understand.

[11]"From the time that the daily sacrifice is abolished and the abomination that causes desolation is set up, there will be 1,290 days.
[12]Blessed is the one who waits for and reaches the end of the 1,335
days.

[13]"As for you, go your way till the end. You will rest, and then at the
end of the days you will rise to receive your allotted inheritance."

[a]3 Or *who impart wisdom* [b]7 Or *a year, two years and half a year*

OPEN Which do you like better: Starting a task or ending it? Why?

STUDY **1.** For Daniel and his readers, what is the good news in verses 1–4? What is the bad news? **2.** This is the first and only use of the term "everlasting life" in the Old Testament. What does that tell you about what most Jews in Daniel's day believed (or didn't believe) about life after death? **3.** How does Daniel's embryonic doctrine of the Resurrection compare with the New Testament view that we are saved "by grace alone"? In this regard, what does it mean to be "wise"? To "lead many to righteousness" (v. 3)? **4.** Verses 1–4 imply that the kingdom of God is assured to the faithful and wise, but that destiny is born out of tribulation and soul-searching. How does that relate to the faith of Jesus (Matt. 24:8; Mark 13; Rev. 12:1–6)? How does Daniel's view compare with Jesus' view of the Resurrection of the righteous and the wicked (John 5:24–30)? **5.** Compare verse 9 with Revelation 22:10. How do you account for the difference? **6.** Did Daniel have all his questions answered (vv. 4, 8–10)? What is left unanswered for Daniel (and you)? What does this say about the basis of faith for a believer?

APPLY **1.** Daniel was told to go on with life even if he didn't understand. When have you had to cope in faith with the perplexities of life? **2.** The bottom line for Daniel is that the royal power of the Most High God always triumphs over the kingdoms of men (v. 13; 7:11,26–27; 8:25; 9:27; 10:13; 11:45). How is that evident for Daniel personally? For the kings and subjects he serves? For the readers he comforts? For you and your group?

12:2 This is the first clear scriptural reference to a resurrection. The godly will rise to everlasting life, while the wicked will be resurrected to eternal shame and contempt.

12:13 Daniel would die before many of the events he prophesied took place. But he would be raised from the dead, according to the promise, to receive his reward and inheritance for his service to God.

Hosea

Author. The first verse of this book names the prophet Hosea as the author. Hosea's authorship has been generally accepted throughout history. Some have theorized that more than one author may have been involved, since Hosea prophesied to the northern kingdom and his written prophecy includes some messages to the southern kingdom. During the time of Hosea's ministry, though, some prophets did speak to both kingdoms.

Personal Reading	Group Study Topic and Reading	
1:1–2:1	Hosea's Prophetic Progeny	1:1–2:1
2:2–23	Israel Ruined and Restored	2:2–23
3:1–5	Gomer Re-loved and Redeemed	3:1–5
4:1–19	God's Case Against Israel	4:1–19
5:1–15	God's Wrath, Israel's Remorse	5:1–15
6:1–11	Israel's Fickleness	6:1–11
7:1–16	God's Frustration	7:1–16
8:1–14	Israel Warned, Yet Wandering	8:1–14
9:1–17	From the Pinnacle ...	9:1–17
10:1–15	... To the Pit	10:1–15
11:1–11	Israel In and Out of Egypt	11:1–11
11:12–12:14	Israel Deceives, God Despairs	11:12–12:14
13:1–16	God's Anger, Israel's Arrogance	13:1–16
14:1–9	Israel Confesses, God Blesses	14:1–9

Date. The exact date of writing is unknown. He prophesied around 760 B.C., during the last forty years of the northern kingdom. He started his ministry during the reign of Jeroboam II in Israel and ended it during Hezekiah's reign in Judah.

Purpose. Hosea spoke and wrote to his people to awake them spiritually. They were in the midst of the punishment that God had warned them about throughout their history, yet they seemed unaware of their own role in their fate. Hosea's life and actions painted a picture of the nation's unfaithfulness to God and compared their idolatry to adultery. Hosea's purpose was much the same as that of his contemporaries—to direct his own nation back to God.

Historical Background. Hosea was a prophet of the northern kingdom. He was the only one of the writing prophets who came from there. During his lifetime, he witnessed the dissolution of Israel as a religious and political entity. By the middle of the eighth century B.C., Assyria had invaded Israel and exacted tribute from its king. The king then became Assyria's royal vassal. In 733 B.C., Assyria attacked again because a new king, less loyal to Assyria, had usurped the throne. After this attack, Israel was reduced to only the territories of Ephraim and western Manasseh. In 722 B.C., yet another king was disloyal to Assyria. Powerful Assyria responded by capturing Samaria and dissolving the northern kingdom. It is probable that Hosea was among the many refugees who fled southward to Judah following the fall of Samaria.

Punishment and Discipline. Like his fellow prophets of the eighth century B.C., Hosea's prophetic focus was the fulfillment of the theology of Deuteronomy. Deuteronomy described the covenant between the Lord and Israel in great detail, focusing especially on the obligation of obedience and the consequences of disobedience. Hosea was married to an adulterous wife (Gomer) who symbolized Israel and their disobedience. The disobedience of Israel brought about the covenant curses listed in Deuteronomy 28:15–68. For Hosea, however, these curses were not punishments without a positive outcome. They were not the end of the story. These punishments were disciplinary, as God tried again and again to turn his people back toward him. Just as Hosea was reconciled with his adulterous wife, God's people could become reconciled with him.

1 The word of the LORD that came to Hosea son of Beeri during the
reigns of Uzziah, Jotham, Ahaz and Hezekiah, kings of Judah,
and during the reign of Jeroboam son of Jehoash[a] king of Israel:

Hosea's Wife and Children

2When the LORD began to speak through Hosea, the LORD said to
him, "Go, take to yourself an adulterous wife and children of unfaithfulness, because the land is guilty of the vilest adultery in departing
from the LORD." 3So he married Gomer daughter of Diblaim, and she
conceived and bore him a son.

4Then the LORD said to Hosea, "Call him Jezreel, because I will soon
punish the house of Jehu for the massacre at Jezreel, and I will put an
end to the kingdom of Israel. 5In that day I will break Israel's bow in
the Valley of Jezreel."

6Gomer conceived again and gave birth to a daughter. Then the
LORD said to Hosea, "Call her Lo-Ruhamah,[b] for I will no longer show
love to the house of Israel, that I should at all forgive them. 7Yet I will
show love to the house of Judah; and I will save them—not by bow,
sword or battle, or by horses and horsemen, but by the LORD their
God."

8After she had weaned Lo-Ruhamah, Gomer had another son.
9Then the LORD said, "Call him Lo-Ammi,[c] for you are not my people,
and I am not your God.

10"Yet the Israelites will be like the sand on the seashore, which
cannot be measured or counted. In the place where it was said to
them, 'You are not my people,' they will be called 'sons of the living
God.' 11The people of Judah and the people of Israel will be reunited,
and they will appoint one leader and will come up out of the land, for
great will be the day of Jezreel.

2 "Say of your brothers, 'My people,' and of your sisters, 'My loved
one.'

Israel Punished and Restored

2"Rebuke your mother, rebuke her,
for she is not my wife,
and I am not her husband.

[a]1 Hebrew *Joash,* a variant of *Jehoash* [b]6 *Lo-Ruhamah* means *not loved.* [c]9 *Lo-Ammi* means *not my people.*

OPEN 1. Are you named after someone? Who? What nicknames have you had? **2.** What loyal friend sticks even closer to you than a brother or sister?

STUDY 1. Why does God have Hosea marry an adulteress? How is God's covenant with Israel like that? **2.** Do you think Gomer was loyal to Hosea at first? Why? Then what happened? (Who fathers her second and third children?) **3.** What do the names of Gomer's three children mean? What would have been the reaction by local Jews to their births? **4.** What hope is given (v. 10–2:1)? What is meant by Israel being: As "the sand on the seashore"? "Sons of the living God"? "Reunited" under "one leader"? "Brothers ... sisters ... loved ones"?

APPLY 1. Using the marriage metaphor, describe your relation to God. Are you: In the time of courtship? Newlywed and still on the honeymoon? Struggling through "marital difficulties"? Recovering from a time you were "unfaithful"? Growing deeper and deeper in "marital bliss"? **2.** Where in your life could you use the hope of restoration Hosea offers?

OPEN 1. Who's your favorite poet? Your favorite poem? Why? **2.** Have you ever become engaged? When? How? If not, how might you imagine that event? **3.** How would your feelings for your "love" compare to what your feelings might be for someone who had betrayed you? How do you express your love or hate? By poetry?

1:1 word of the LORD came to Hosea. As a prophet, Hosea represented God's authority in his message. **Hosea.** Ultimately, Hosea's message was good news for Israel; his name means "salvation."

1:3 Gomer daughter of Diblaim. It is debatable whether Hosea's wife was unfaithful at the time he married her. Maybe she was a prostitute at that time, or maybe she was involved in the sexual practices associated with Baal worship. Likely, she became unfaithful later in their relationship, as Israel was unfaithful in its original commitments.

1:4 kingdom of Israel. The Israelites were now divided into northern and southern kingdoms. Hosea's message was directed at the northern kingdom of Israel, although its teaching applied to all God's people.

1:6 Call her Lo-Ruhamah. God emphasized the seriousness of the breach in the love relationship with his people by naming one of the children "not loved."

1:9 Call him Lo-Ammi. The third and final child carried the ultimate insult. God dared to disown his people.

1:10 Israelites ... like the sand. God knew Israel would not be wiped out because of a promise he made to Abraham regarding a great future nation (Gen. 22:17).

1:11 people of Judah ... reunited. The Lord foresaw a future time when the two kingdoms would be ruled under God's own leadership.

2:2 not my wife ... not her husband. God's frustrations with Israel are symbolized in the language of Hosea's experience. Hosea spoke about Gomer as God felt about Israel.

STUDY **1.** How does Hosea feel about Gomer (vv. 2–13)? What will he do about that? Why does he deny their marriage? **2.** Why does he want to expose and thwart her adultery (vv. 3–8)? What effect would further punishment (vv. 9–13) have on her? **3.** What "adultery" is she guilty of (vv. 8, 13)? Who then are her "lovers" (v. 5)? Her "husband" (v. 7)? Her "children" (vv. 4,23)? **4.** Though the marriage was broken by adultery, is divorce or reconciliation sought? Why do you think so? **5.** How do you account for the contrast between punishment and allurement (vv. 13–14)? **6.** What "desert" experience is Hosea referring to? What effect will this have and why? When and where had God "betrothed" Israel to himself initially? **7.** What changes will occur "in that day" (vv. 16–19)? What play on words do you see here and in the text footnote (v. 16)? How might that explain the confusion of Israel's worship of Yahweh with the pagan Baal rituals? **8.** How will Israel respond to the Lord's marriage proposal (vv. 19–20)? How will the skies, earth and its resources then respond (vv. 21–23)? **9.** What is significant about Jezreel (v. 22) and the other name reversals? What does this reveal about the Lord's purpose in disciplining his own?

APPLY **1.** Since we become slaves to whatever we yield ourselves to (Rom. 6:16), what are the "baals" (or masters) in your life? What promise do these "masters" make to lure you into their service? **2.** How is the Lord's authority in your life different from these other masters? (Is God less demanding, or more so? Less forgiving, or more so?) **3.** When, if ever, have you outgrown your need for God? Have you ever felt rejected by him? What for? **4.** What "desert experience" or other trying circumstance brought you back to him?

Let her remove the adulterous look from her face
and the unfaithfulness from between her breasts.
3 Otherwise I will strip her naked
and make her as bare as on the day she was born;
I will make her like a desert,
turn her into a parched land,
and slay her with thirst.
4 I will not show my love to her children,
because they are the children of adultery.
5 Their mother has been unfaithful
and has conceived them in disgrace.
She said, 'I will go after my lovers,
who give me my food and my water,
my wool and my linen, my oil and my drink.'
6 Therefore I will block her path with thornbushes;
I will wall her in so that she cannot find her way.
7 She will chase after her lovers but not catch them;
she will look for them but not find them.
Then she will say,
'I will go back to my husband as at first,
for then I was better off than now.'
8 She has not acknowledged that I was the one
who gave her the grain, the new wine and oil,
who lavished on her the silver and gold—
which they used for Baal.

9 "Therefore I will take away my grain when it ripens,
and my new wine when it is ready.
I will take back my wool and my linen,
intended to cover her nakedness.
10 So now I will expose her lewdness
before the eyes of her lovers;
no one will take her out of my hands.
11 I will stop all her celebrations:
her yearly festivals, her New Moons,
her Sabbath days—all her appointed feasts.
12 I will ruin her vines and her fig trees,
which she said were her pay from her lovers;
I will make them a thicket,
and wild animals will devour them.
13 I will punish her for the days
she burned incense to the Baals;
she decked herself with rings and jewelry,
and went after her lovers,
but me she forgot,"
declares the LORD.

2:9 take back. In a positive relationship, a husband cares for his wife's needs and enjoys blessing her with gifts. In contrast, Hosea renounced his gifts and revoked his former blessings on his undeserving wife.

2:10 no one will take her out of my hands. Although the shame would be public, none of Gomer's lovers would be able to rescue her. In the same way, none of Israel's false gods could save the nation from punishment.

2:12 ruin her vines ... pay from her lovers. Although the Lord taught Israel long ago to recognize success as his blessing, Israel credited its harvests to other gods and not the true God.

14 "Therefore I am now going to allure her;
I will lead her into the desert
and speak tenderly to her.
15 There I will give her back her vineyards,
and will make the Valley of Achor[a] a door of hope.
There she will sing[b] as in the days of her youth,
as in the day she came up out of Egypt.

16 "In that day," declares the LORD,
"you will call me 'my husband';
you will no longer call me 'my master.[c]'
17 I will remove the names of the Baals from her lips;
no longer will their names be invoked.
18 In that day I will make a covenant for them
with the beasts of the field and the birds of the air
and the creatures that move along the ground.
Bow and sword and battle
I will abolish from the land,
so that all may lie down in safety.
19 I will betroth you to me forever;
I will betroth you in[d] righteousness and justice,
in[e] love and compassion.
20 I will betroth you in faithfulness,
and you will acknowledge the LORD.

21 "In that day I will respond,"
declares the LORD—
"I will respond to the skies,
and they will respond to the earth;
22 and the earth will respond to the grain,
the new wine and oil,
and they will respond to Jezreel.[f]
23 I will plant her for myself in the land;
I will show my love to the one I called 'Not my loved one.[g]'
I will say to those called 'Not my people,[h]' 'You are my people';
and they will say, 'You are my God.' "

Hosea's Reconciliation With His Wife

3 The LORD said to me, "Go, show your love to your wife again,
though she is loved by another and is an adulteress. Love her as

[a]15 *Achor* means *trouble.* [b]15 Or *respond* [c]16 Hebrew *baal* [d]19 Or *with;* also in verse 20 [e]19 Or *with*
[f]22 *Jezreel* means *God plants.* [g]23 Hebrew *Lo-Ruhamah* [h]23 Hebrew *Lo-Ammi*

OPEN Recall a broken relationship (with spouse, kids, boss). Were you able to fix it? How difficult was it?

2:16–17 Ironically, the Hebrew word for Baal is "master." The Lord predicted Israel would disassociate from its "master" as a sign of repentance.

2:18 I will abolish ... lie down in safety. God painted a portrait of perfect peace in contrast to the ruin created in verse 12. He restored the pattern of blessings in return for Israel's faithfulness (Lev. 26:5–6).

2:19–20 betroth. In middle eastern culture, betrothal symbolized the marriage commitment. Here, the Lord described a serious engagement between himself and Israel.

2:20 betroth you in faithfulness. The context of Hosea's story was the unfaithfulness of a nation portrayed as a wayward wife. In contrast, God was consistently characterized as stubbornly faithful.

2:21 respond to the earth. As the supreme agricultural authority, God would bless Israel with crops.

2:22 Jezreel. Means "God plant" which pictures the work of God in restoring the Hebrews.

3:1 said to me ... show your love. Hosea retold God's instructions to him. **Love her as the LORD loves the Israelites.** God's instructions battled against all Hosea's natural instincts. How could he love a person who rejected him?

STUDY 1. What is the toughest part of what Hosea has to do? **2.** Why must he buy Gomer? **3.** What does Gomer's waiting have to do with Israel? **4.** When does Israel return to seek God? Has this occurred?

APPLY When did God "buy" you back to himself? How so?

OPEN 1. What was your adolescent rebellion like? Was it similar to that of your siblings? How so? **2.** Did your folks ever urge you to avoid the same mistake an older brother or sister had made? Did you listen?

STUDY 1. What does the Lord claim is lacking in Israel (v. 1)? How do these virtues relate to self, to others, to God? **2.** What does God find instead (v. 2)? How do these virtues and vices compare with the Ten Commandments? What are the consequences of such a climate of evil? **3.** Do you think the land and animals "wasting away" (v. 3) is merely poetic language? Why or why not? What does this verse say about modern ecological disasters? **4.** Why do you suppose "no man is to accuse another" (v. 4)? Who are "your people" and "your mother" (vv. 4–5)? **5.** What effect does their behavior have on the priests? Of what are the priests guilty (vv. 6–8)? How might they profit from the people's sins? **6.** What "wages of sin" will the people receive (vv. 9–11)? Are they personal or social? Limited or contagious? Why? **7.** Does the laxity of the priests excuse the people? Conversely, does their behavior indict the priests? Who does God hold accountable for the sexual immorality that is rampant (v. 14)? Why? **8.** What directed them in these paths and eroded their understanding (v. 12)? What is a "spirit of prostitution"? How does it hook its victim? What is its seductive impact on succeeding

the LORD loves the Israelites, though they turn to other gods and love
the sacred raisin cakes."
2 So I bought her for fifteen shekels[a] of silver and about a homer
and a lethek[b] of barley. 3 Then I told her, "You are to live with[c] me
many days; you must not be a prostitute or be intimate with any man,
and I will live with[c] you."
4 For the Israelites will live many days without king or prince, without sacrifice or sacred stones, without ephod or idol. 5 Afterward the
Israelites will return and seek the LORD their God and David their
king. They will come trembling to the LORD and to his blessings in the
last days.

The Charge Against Israel

4 Hear the word of the LORD, you Israelites,
because the LORD has a charge to bring
against you who live in the land:
"There is no faithfulness, no love,
no acknowledgment of God in the land.
2 There is only cursing,[d] lying and murder,
stealing and adultery;
they break all bounds,
and bloodshed follows bloodshed.
3 Because of this the land mourns,[e]
and all who live in it waste away;
the beasts of the field and the birds of the air
and the fish of the sea are dying.

4 "But let no man bring a charge,
let no man accuse another,
for your people are like those
who bring charges against a priest.
5 You stumble day and night,
and the prophets stumble with you.
So I will destroy your mother—
6 my people are destroyed from lack of knowledge.

"Because you have rejected knowledge,
I also reject you as my priests;
because you have ignored the law of your God,
I also will ignore your children.
7 The more the priests increased,
the more they sinned against me;
they exchanged[f] their[g] Glory for something disgraceful.

[a]2 That is, about 6 ounces (about 170 grams) [b]2 That is, probably about 10 bushels (about 330 liters) [c]3 Or *wait for* [d]2 That is, to pronounce a curse upon [e]3 Or *dries up* [f]7 Syriac and an ancient Hebrew scribal tradition; Masoretic Text *I will exchange* [g]7 Masoretic Text; an ancient Hebrew scribal tradition *my*

3:3 I will live with you. Hosea put his own reputation on the line in order to invite an adulterous woman into his household.

3:5 trembling. God described an attitude of fear, awe and reverence in Israel's posture—quite a contrast to the nation's former rebellion.

4:1 charge to bring. Hosea's message used the language of the courtroom to demonstrate Israel's lack of virtue.

4:2 break all bounds. Israel broke every law in the Ten Commandments with reckless enthusiasm (Ex. 20:13–16).

4:4–9 The priests, responsible for the nation's religious life, could not blame the people for Israel's dilemma when they were steeped in sin, too.

4:6 lack of knowledge. Because the priests neglected their duties to instruct the people, Israel became a society lacking values or virtues.

8 They feed on the sins of my people
and relish their wickedness.
9 And it will be: Like people, like priests.
I will punish both of them for their ways
and repay them for their deeds.

10 "They will eat but not have enough;
they will engage in prostitution but not increase,
because they have deserted the LORD
to give themselves 11 to prostitution,
to old wine and new,
which take away the understanding 12 of my people.
They consult a wooden idol
and are answered by a stick of wood.
A spirit of prostitution leads them astray;
they are unfaithful to their God.
13 They sacrifice on the mountaintops
and burn offerings on the hills,
under oak, poplar and terebinth,
where the shade is pleasant.
Therefore your daughters turn to prostitution
and your daughters-in-law to adultery.

14 "I will not punish your daughters
when they turn to prostitution,
nor your daughters-in-law
when they commit adultery,
because the men themselves consort with harlots
and sacrifice with shrine prostitutes—
a people without understanding will come to ruin!

15 "Though you commit adultery, O Israel,
let not Judah become guilty.

"Do not go to Gilgal;
do not go up to Beth Aven.[a]
And do not swear, 'As surely as the LORD lives!'
16 The Israelites are stubborn,
like a stubborn heifer.
How then can the LORD pasture them
like lambs in a meadow?
17 Ephraim is joined to idols;
leave him alone!
18 Even when their drinks are gone,
they continue their prostitution;
their rulers dearly love shameful ways.

generations (v. 13)? **9.** What "double standard" does Hosea reject (v. 14)? **10.** What is God's concern for Judah? What does he urge them to avoid? How do the Israelites prove "stubborn" (vv. 16–18)? What future can Ephraim (Israel) expect (vv. 17–19)?

APPLY 1. Are you a "heifer" or a "lamb" (v. 16)? Give an example of your stubbornness or meekness. **2.** In what area of your life do you sometimes "eat but not have enough" (v. 10): Literally—you're always hungry? In relation to material things—you always want more? In relation to achievement—it never seems you can do enough? Other? **3.** Israel's idolatry was obvious. Is yours more subtle? What idols do you tend to "give" yourself to: Careers? Status symbols? Relationships? New age mysticism? Wealth? Military power? Other?

[a] *15 Beth Aven* means *house of wickedness* (a name for Bethel, which means *house of God*).

4:8 relish their wickedness. The priests cheerfully led the people in idol worship. They received part of the people's offerings as a bonus.

4:9 Like people, like priests I will punish. Everyone sinned: Everyone would receive their punishment.

4:11 take away the understanding. Hosea described people who were confused about the consequences of their behavior. Clear-thinking people would repent.

4:17 Ephraim ... leave him alone. Here Israel is referred to as Ephraim because it is the largest of the northern kingdom's 10 tribes. God, increasingly frustrated with Ephraim, would eventually abandon that influential tribe.

[19]A whirlwind will sweep them away,
and their sacrifices will bring them shame.

Judgment Against Israel

5 "Hear this, you priests!
Pay attention, you Israelites!
Listen, O royal house!
This judgment is against you:
You have been a snare at Mizpah,
a net spread out on Tabor.
[2]The rebels are deep in slaughter.
I will discipline all of them.
[3]I know all about Ephraim;
Israel is not hidden from me.
Ephraim, you have now turned to prostitution;
Israel is corrupt.

[4]"Their deeds do not permit them
to return to their God.
A spirit of prostitution is in their heart;
they do not acknowledge the LORD.
[5]Israel's arrogance testifies against them;
the Israelites, even Ephraim, stumble in their sin;
Judah also stumbles with them.
[6]When they go with their flocks and herds
to seek the LORD,
they will not find him;
he has withdrawn himself from them.
[7]They are unfaithful to the LORD;
they give birth to illegitimate children.
Now their New Moon festivals
will devour them and their fields.

[8]"Sound the trumpet in Gibeah,
the horn in Ramah.
Raise the battle cry in Beth Aven[a];
lead on, O Benjamin.
[9]Ephraim will be laid waste
on the day of reckoning.
Among the tribes of Israel
I proclaim what is certain.
[10]Judah's leaders are like those
who move boundary stones.

[a]8 *Beth Aven* means *house of wickedness* (a name for Bethel, which means *house of God*).

generations (v. 13)? 9. What "double standard" does Hosea reject (vv. 14)? 10. What is God's concern for Judah? What does he warn them to avoid?

OPEN 1. When you are betrayed or hurt by a close friend, what is your natural response: Break off the relationship? Forgive and bless, thereby "heaping burning coals on their head"? Give them the "silent treatment"? Give them a one-way ticket on a guilt trip? Other? **2.** When did you first learn the benefits of discipline: As a child or a parent? Illustrate.

STUDY 1. What three groups are indicted here? To whom have they been a snare? Why does the Lord promise to discipline all of them? How had Israel (Ephraim) played the harlot? **2.** How far have his people sunk in their corruption (vv. 4–7)? What is their root problem? **3.** Hosea pictures God as being married to his people. What would it mean for Israel to acknowledge the Lord as her husband? What would it mean for her (and her children) to "adulterate" that relationship (v. 7)? With what results? **4.** In "seeking the LORD" (v. 6) do they view him as a: Husband? Lover? Local deity? "Pimp"? Bothersome duty? How does this compare with their seeking him later (v. 15)? **5.** What does Hosea envision for Israel (vv. 8–9)? Why use trumpets and horns? What's wrong with moving boundary stones (v. 10; Deut. 19:14)? **6.** How is the Lord like a "moth and rot" to Israel and Judah (v. 12)? When consumed by the Lord, where do they turn for help? How is this like Gomer (ch. 2)? Why is it so futile? **7.** How does God intend to deal with Israel and Judah (v. 14)? Why such harsh treatment? When in their history did this actually happen (2 Kin. 17:5–23)? With what result (v. 15)?

APPLY 1. What people in your life are close enough for you to influence by your actions? What consequences for them might your disloyalty to God have? **2.** Have

4:19 whirlwind. Although Israel felt invincible at the time, God would ordain Assyria to vaporize Israel's sense of security (9:3).

5:1 snare. The most influential people in Israel were similar to a trap set for small animals and birds. The unwitting people followed their leaders with disastrous results.

5:4 spirit of prostitution is in their heart. Israel was guilty of spiritual adultery—forsaking its commitment to God and pursuing other gods.

5:5 Judah. The southern kingdom fell prey to spiritual adultery as well—worshiping gods of the Canaanite people.

5:6 flocks and herds. The Lord described the hypocritical actions of a people willing to perform heartless sacrifices.

5:7 give birth to illegitimate children. The imagery here may refer to the questions surrounding the legitimacy of Hosea fathering Gomer's children (4:13–15).

5:10 Judah's leaders ... who move boundary stones. Judah took over

I will pour out my wrath on them
like a flood of water.
11 Ephraim is oppressed,
trampled in judgment,
intent on pursuing idols.[a]
12 I am like a moth to Ephraim,
like rot to the people of Judah.

13 "When Ephraim saw his sickness,
and Judah his sores,
then Ephraim turned to Assyria,
and sent to the great king for help.
But he is not able to cure you,
not able to heal your sores.
14 For I will be like a lion to Ephraim,
like a great lion to Judah.
I will tear them to pieces and go away;
I will carry them off, with no one to rescue them.
15 Then I will go back to my place
until they admit their guilt.
And they will seek my face;
in their misery they will earnestly seek me."

Israel Unrepentant

6 "Come, let us return to the LORD.
He has torn us to pieces
but he will heal us;
he has injured us
but he will bind up our wounds.
2 After two days he will revive us;
on the third day he will restore us,
that we may live in his presence.
3 Let us acknowledge the LORD;
let us press on to acknowledge him.
As surely as the sun rises,
he will appear;
he will come to us like the winter rains,
like the spring rains that water the earth."

4 "What can I do with you, Ephraim?
What can I do with you, Judah?
Your love is like the morning mist,
like the early dew that disappears.
5 Therefore I cut you in pieces with my prophets,
I killed you with the words of my mouth;

[a] 11 The meaning of the Hebrew for this word is uncertain.

you ever "taken your flocks and herds to seek the LORD," only to pursue other "lovers" at the same time? Could you be doing this now and be blind to it? **3.** God's discipline here is patient, progressive and purposeful (vv. 2,6–7,9–10, 14–15). How are these stages of discipline in the journey of the Israelites similar to your discipline? What are the warning signs of your discipline from the Lord? **4.** Why must we hit bottom, like Israel, before we begin to look up? When have you, in your misery, earnestly sought the Lord? What did God have to take you through to restore you? Did you sense his love in that?

OPEN 1. As a child, parent, boss or employee, when have you made or received an "empty promise"? Which one really hurt? **2.** Have you ever "let someone off easy," only to have them take advantage of you? How did you feel? What would be your response "the next time"?

STUDY 1. Who appears to be speaking in these verses? What is curiously lacking in this "confession"? On what is their hope for a light sentence based? **2.** How does God view Israel's love and worship (vv. 4–6)? What does it mean to truly "acknowledge God" in our dealings with others? **3.** Who is charged with breaking the covenant (vv. 7–11)? What covenant could this be (Ex. 19:5–6; Josh. 24:16–27, for examples)? **4.** How might the priests be "ambushing" the people (v. 9; 4:8)? **5.** Has Israel really sincerely repented (compare v. 10 with 5:3)?

APPLY 1. Have you ever tried to hide from God behind an

some of Israel's territory with complete disregard for God's law (Deut. 19:14).

5:13 Ephraim turned to Assyria. Instead of turning to God for help, Israel sought aid from a pagan nation.

5:14 lion. Although foreign armies would play a part, the Lord himself gets the credit for Israel's destruction.

6:1 Come, let us return. Hosea's prophecy describes a repentant nation. With God there is hope.

6:2 two days. Perhaps an example of wishful thinking, Israel predicted its punishment would not last long.

6:3 sun rises ... like the winter rains. Israel saw the Lord's faithfulness in familiar agricultural terms. As dependable as the rain, the Lord would revive them again.

6:4 love is like the morning mist. Hosea describes God's keen insight into Israel's phony repentance.

easy act of repentance? What sacrifices or "burnt offerings" did you try to please God with: Church attendance? Giving a larger tithe? Praying more? Fasting? Other? **2.** Have you ever become frustrated or indignant when these actions didn't seem to work? What did you do then? What *does* make the Lord return like the "winter and spring rains"? **3.** On a scale of 1 (morning mist) to 5 (rock of Gibraltar), how would you rate the staying power of your love for the Lord? ____________

OPEN 1. When caught red-handed, what is your favorite defense plea: Guilty, with an excuse? Guilty, with no excuse? Run from your accuser? Pin the blame elsewhere? Obscure the issue with irrelevancies? Other? Cite a case in point. **2.** Bread is a fascinating food. Have you ever made any or watched it being made? What do you associate with the smells of baking bread?

STUDY 1. Why is God frustrated in his desire to pardon Israel? How widespread is the disease he would heal (v. 1)? What is wrong with Israel's view of God (v. 2)? **2.** What does the oven image tell you about the people's conspiracy (vv. 3–7; compare 2 Kin. 15:8–30 for the historical basis of Hosea's image)? When and how does their passion blaze into open flame? What guilt do the kings share for their downfall? **3.** What was wrong with Israel mixing with the nations (vv. 8–10)? What price were they paying for their failure to remain pure? What do the sapping of strength and graying hair indicate? Were the Israelites doing anything to stop the decay? Why not? **4.** How and why is Ephraim (Israel) like a dove (vv. 11–12)? How

my judgments flashed like lightning upon you.
6 For I desire mercy, not sacrifice,
and acknowledgment of God rather than burnt offerings.
7 Like Adam,[a] they have broken the covenant—
they were unfaithful to me there.
8 Gilead is a city of wicked men,
stained with footprints of blood.
9 As marauders lie in ambush for a man,
so do bands of priests;
they murder on the road to Shechem,
committing shameful crimes.
10 I have seen a horrible thing
in the house of Israel.
There Ephraim is given to prostitution
and Israel is defiled.

11 "Also for you, Judah,
a harvest is appointed.

"Whenever I would restore the fortunes of my people,
7 1 whenever I would heal Israel,
the sins of Ephraim are exposed
and the crimes of Samaria revealed.
They practice deceit,
thieves break into houses,
bandits rob in the streets;
2 but they do not realize
that I remember all their evil deeds.
Their sins engulf them;
they are always before me.
3 "They delight the king with their wickedness,
the princes with their lies.
4 They are all adulterers,
burning like an oven
whose fire the baker need not stir
from the kneading of the dough till it rises.
5 On the day of the festival of our king
the princes become inflamed with wine,
and he joins hands with the mockers.
6 Their hearts are like an oven;
they approach him with intrigue.
Their passion smolders all night;
in the morning it blazes like a flaming fire.
7 All of them are hot as an oven;

[a]7 Or *As at Adam;* or *Like men*

6:6 acknowledgement. God was looking for more than lip service. Israel must demonstrate its love for God by *adhering to his covenant—a promise of* obedience (Josh. 24:16–27).

6:9 shameful crimes. The priests, who were charged with spiritual leadership, are described in shameful terms. A portrait of irony, Hosea's descriptions show the depth of Israel's sin.

6:10 house of Israel. If Israel were a house, the ten tribes would be rooms. Each tribe being guilty, the whole house had to be punished.

7:2 I remember all their evil deeds. Like Gomer, Israel thought it sinned secretly. However, God saw and remembered every misdeed.

7:5 day of the festival of our king. Most likely an innocent celebration that had turned into a disgrace.

they devour their rulers.
All their kings fall,
and none of them calls on me.

8 "Ephraim mixes with the nations;
Ephraim is a flat cake not turned over.
9 Foreigners sap his strength,
but he does not realize it.
His hair is sprinkled with gray,
but he does not notice.
10 Israel's arrogance testifies against him,
but despite all this
he does not return to the LORD his God
or search for him.

11 "Ephraim is like a dove,
easily deceived and senseless—
now calling to Egypt,
now turning to Assyria.
12 When they go, I will throw my net over them;
I will pull them down like birds of the air.
When I hear them flocking together,
I will catch them.
13 Woe to them,
because they have strayed from me!
Destruction to them,
because they have rebelled against me!
I long to redeem them
but they speak lies against me.
14 They do not cry out to me from their hearts
but wail upon their beds.
They gather together[a] for grain and new wine
but turn away from me.
15 I trained them and strengthened them,
but they plot evil against me.
16 They do not turn to the Most High;
they are like a faulty bow.
Their leaders will fall by the sword
because of their insolent words.
For this they will be ridiculed
in the land of Egypt.

[a]14 Most Hebrew manuscripts; some Hebrew manuscripts and Septuagint *They slash themselves*

will God deal with them? **5.** How has Israel repaid God evil for good (vv. 13–15)? How will their confidence in Egypt come back to haunt them?

APPLY 1. On what basis do you try to win God's favor: His past goodness? Your good behavior? Your promise to do better? His forgiving character? His promise to bless his own? On Christ's behalf? Which is the only adequate basis? **2.** Like Ephraim, are there areas you have compromised in your personal life? Church life? National life? What effect would you expect this to have in your life, church or nation, if you continued as though it didn't matter? **3.** Consider one specific need for repentance which this chapter brings to your attention. What *action steps* will you take this week in response to the Lord's desire to redeem you?

7:8 flat cake. Continuing the baker's imagery, Hosea showed that Israel's foolish political intentions were half-baked at best.

7:9 sap his strength. Israel bought protection with pricey tributes to foreign kings (see Tiglath-Pileser as an example in 2 Kin. 15:19–20,29). It was an expensive habit that drained the nation's wealth.

7:11 Ephraim like a dove. Hosea showed the ignorance involved in Israel's fickle political policies. Israel relied on whatever country seemed strong at the moment.

7:14 from their hearts. A cry of the heart may not evoke emotion at all. Compare it to the empty wailing of people who are more sorry for their suffering than for their sins.

7:15 I trained them and strengthened them. God had trained the fledgling nation of desert wanderers into successful warriors. However, Israel had taken the credit for its military endeavors.

7:16 faulty bow. A faulty bow would consistently miss its target, just as Israel failed God's purposes for the nation.

OPEN 1. Have you ever been awakened by loud music—perhaps during a worship service or morning reveille? What was your first thought? What did you do? 2. What do you do "like a whirlwind": Clean house? Mow the lawn? Do dishes? Race home from school or work? Or are you laid back, letting the whirlwind pass you by?

STUDY 1. Why does Hosea sound the alarm? What is the danger? Why do eagles, or "vultures," hover? 2. What evidence is there that Israel's loyalty to God is shallow? Why do they forget God? How did men become kings in Israel at this time (2 Kin. 15:10,14,25,30)? 3. When and why was the calf idol made (vv. 5–6; 1 Kin. 12:26–30)? What resulted? 4. How will Israel reap what she sows (vv. 3,7; Gen. 6:7)? What is this "whirlwind"? In selling herself to her lovers, what hidden price does she pay (v. 8)? 5. Despite such infidelity, what is God's intent for Israel? What must be the first step in that redemption (v. 10)? Why? 6. What "sacred" objects does Israel possess (vv. 11–14)? In each case, how have they been misused? 7. What does "return to Egypt" (v. 13) mean for Israel? Does God's punishment fit the crime? How so? 8. What do Israel and Judah expect from their palaces and forts? Is that wrong? Where does true security come from?

APPLY 1. Despite professions of loyalty to God, are you "rejecting what is good" (vv. 2–3) with: Spouse? Family? Business? Money? Leisure? How might errors in these areas lead to an addiction or idolatry? 2. When in your life did you "sow the wind and reap the whirlwind"? 3. Consider the "sacred objects" in your life. Are you in danger of worshiping what inspires you (creation, spiritual gifts, etc.) rather than God himself? Have they become altars for sinning? *Could* they? How?

Israel to Reap the Whirlwind

8 "Put the trumpet to your lips!
An eagle is over the house of the LORD
because the people have broken my covenant
and rebelled against my law.
2 Israel cries out to me,
'O our God, we acknowledge you!'
3 But Israel has rejected what is good;
an enemy will pursue him.
4 They set up kings without my consent;
they choose princes without my approval.
With their silver and gold
they make idols for themselves
to their own destruction.
5 Throw out your calf-idol, O Samaria!
My anger burns against them.
How long will they be incapable of purity?
6 They are from Israel!
This calf—a craftsman has made it;
it is not God.
It will be broken in pieces,
that calf of Samaria.

7 "They sow the wind
and reap the whirlwind.
The stalk has no head;
it will produce no flour.
Were it to yield grain,
foreigners would swallow it up.
8 Israel is swallowed up;
now she is among the nations
like a worthless thing.
9 For they have gone up to Assyria
like a wild donkey wandering alone.
Ephraim has sold herself to lovers.
10 Although they have sold themselves among the nations,
I will now gather them together.
They will begin to waste away
under the oppression of the mighty king.

11 "Though Ephraim built many altars for sin offerings,
these have become altars for sinning.
12 I wrote for them the many things of my law,
but they regarded them as something alien.
13 They offer sacrifices given to me

8:1 trumpet to your lips. A trumpet signaled warning or danger. **eagle.** A bird of prey, the eagle represented the eagerness of Israel's enemy, Assyria.

8:2 O our God, we acknowledge you. Israel was quick to say the words it thought God wanted to hear. However, Israel's actions proved otherwise (vv. 3–4).

8:4 silver and gold. Idols were often objects crafted from valuable metals such as silver and gold.

8:5 calf-idol. By melting gold into the image of a calf, Jeroboam had fashioned an image for the people of Israel to worship (1 Kin. 12:26–30).

8:8 worthless thing. When Israel rejected God, it became a hapless band of wanderers who were subject to enemy strength, not the successful nation God once envisioned and commanded it to be (Ex. 19:5).

8:10 sold themselves. Tribute quickly turned to servitude for Israel.

8:13 not pleased with them. Israel went through the motions of sacrifice. However, disobedience rendered the

and they eat the meat,
but the LORD is not pleased with them.
Now he will remember their wickedness
and punish their sins:
They will return to Egypt.
14 Israel has forgotten his Maker
and built palaces;
Judah has fortified many towns.
But I will send fire upon their cities
that will consume their fortresses."

Punishment for Israel

9 Do not rejoice, O Israel;
do not be jubilant like the other nations.
For you have been unfaithful to your God;
you love the wages of a prostitute
at every threshing floor.
2 Threshing floors and winepresses will not feed the people;
the new wine will fail them.
3 They will not remain in the LORD's land;
Ephraim will return to Egypt
and eat unclean[a] food in Assyria.
4 They will not pour out wine offerings to the LORD,
nor will their sacrifices please him.
Such sacrifices will be to them like the bread of mourners;
all who eat them will be unclean.
This food will be for themselves;
it will not come into the temple of the LORD.

5 What will you do on the day of your appointed feasts,
on the festival days of the LORD?
6 Even if they escape from destruction,
Egypt will gather them,
and Memphis will bury them.
Their treasures of silver will be taken over by briers,
and thorns will overrun their tents.
7 The days of punishment are coming,
the days of reckoning are at hand.
Let Israel know this.
Because your sins are so many
and your hostility so great,
the prophet is considered a fool,
the inspired man a maniac.
8 The prophet, along with my God,
is the watchman over Ephraim,[b]
yet snares await him on all his paths,

[a]3 That is, ceremonially unclean [b]8 Or *The prophet is the watchman over Ephraim, / the people of my God*

OPEN 1. Recall a time when you were sufficiently warned (about drugs, drinking, driving, etc.), but had to learn the hard way. What happened? What did you ultimately learn? Has it changed how you respond to "warnings"? **2.** Back then, what did you think of the person who warned you: Fool? Meddler? Kill-joy? Self-righteous prude? Over-protective nanny? Now, how do you view that person's intent?

STUDY 1. Various fertility cults were common among the people of this region. What link do you see here (10:12) between these cults and the harvest? What do these fertility rites say about who owned the land? About who gave the increase? How then does God regard their sacrifices and offerings to him (vv. 1–4)? **2.** What has happened to Israel in verses 5–7? Who (or what) has taken over the land (8:14)? **3.** What does Hosea cite as evidence of their perverse condition (vv. 7–8)? What are the "days of Gibeah" like (v. 9; Judg. 19–20)? What impact would this comparison have on Hosea's audience? **4.** Compare God's feeling for Israel *then* (v. 10) and *now* (vv. 12–13,15–16). When did their relationship with God begin to turn sour (Num. 25:1–3)? How long has God been patient? How are they now reaping what their fathers sowed? Is God unjust in this? Why or why not? **5.** What was Ephraim's "glory" (v. 11; Gen. 41:52; 48:16,19)? How is the punishment related to her sin? How had Hosea's treatment of Gomer set the stage for this? **6.** In verse 14, is Hosea asking for compassion or vengeance? How so? **7.** What emotion do you hear in

rituals meaningless. **Egypt.** Egypt could only mean one thing: captivity. Assyria would be the actual site of Israel's torture (11:5).

9:1 When Israel celebrated, it honored the wrong god by attributing its bountiful harvests to idols. **threshing floor.** This work area for grain became a party site after sundown.

9:3 will not remain in the LORD's land. Like tenants kicked out by the landlord, the land promised to the Israelites belonged foremost to the Lord (Josh. 22:19).

9:4 sacrifices ... bread of mourners. Those associated with death, and anything they touched, were ceremonially unclean.

Hosea's prediction (v. 17): Horror? Anger? Sadness? Despair? Smugness?

APPLY 1. When have you had a relationship that had a promising beginning, but which later soured? How might your feelings then be like what God expresses through Hosea (v. 10)? **2.** When have your children or other innocent parties suffered from your mistakes? **3.** Have you ever been treated badly, like Hosea, because of some radical expression of your Christian faith? What happened?

OPEN 1. Who was voted "most likely to succeed" in your graduating class? Did their "product" match their "promise"? What do

and hostility in the house of his God.
9 They have sunk deep into corruption,
as in the days of Gibeah.
God will remember their wickedness
and punish them for their sins.

10 "When I found Israel,
it was like finding grapes in the desert;
when I saw your fathers,
it was like seeing the early fruit on the fig tree.
But when they came to Baal Peor,
they consecrated themselves to that shameful idol
and became as vile as the thing they loved.
11 Ephraim's glory will fly away like a bird—
no birth, no pregnancy, no conception.
12 Even if they rear children,
I will bereave them of every one.
Woe to them
when I turn away from them!
13 I have seen Ephraim, like Tyre,
planted in a pleasant place.
But Ephraim will bring out
their children to the slayer."

14 Give them, O LORD—
what will you give them?
Give them wombs that miscarry
and breasts that are dry.

15 "Because of all their wickedness in Gilgal,
I hated them there.
Because of their sinful deeds,
I will drive them out of my house.
I will no longer love them;
all their leaders are rebellious.
16 Ephraim is blighted,
their root is withered,
they yield no fruit.
Even if they bear children,
I will slay their cherished offspring."

17 My God will reject them
because they have not obeyed him;
they will be wanderers among the nations.

10 Israel was a spreading vine;
he brought forth fruit for himself.
As his fruit increased,
he built more altars;

9:9 days of Gibeah. Compared to a brutal rape and murder in its past, Israel's present sins were worse (Judg. 19–20).

9:10 grapes in the desert. Sweet grapes amid desolation would be a rare find indeed! In the same way, God had once prized Israel for her purity among the pagans.

9:17 My God. Hosea remained a faithful man in a faithless culture.

10:1 a spreading vine. Israel was once full of promise and hope like a vine full of fruit—before its idolatry.

as his land prospered,
he adorned his sacred stones.
2 Their heart is deceitful,
and now they must bear their guilt.
The LORD will demolish their altars
and destroy their sacred stones.

3 Then they will say, "We have no king
because we did not revere the LORD.
But even if we had a king,
what could he do for us?"
4 They make many promises,
take false oaths
and make agreements;
therefore lawsuits spring up
like poisonous weeds in a plowed field.
5 The people who live in Samaria fear
for the calf-idol of Beth Aven.[a]
Its people will mourn over it,
and so will its idolatrous priests,
those who had rejoiced over its splendor,
because it is taken from them into exile.
6 It will be carried to Assyria
as tribute for the great king.
Ephraim will be disgraced;
Israel will be ashamed of its wooden idols.[b]
7 Samaria and its king will float away
like a twig on the surface of the waters.
8 The high places of wickedness[c] will be destroyed—
it is the sin of Israel.
Thorns and thistles will grow up
and cover their altars.
Then they will say to the mountains, "Cover us!"
and to the hills, "Fall on us!"

9 "Since the days of Gibeah, you have sinned, O Israel,
and there you have remained.[d]
Did not war overtake
the evildoers in Gibeah?
10 When I please, I will punish them;
nations will be gathered against them
to put them in bonds for their double sin.
11 Ephraim is a trained heifer
that loves to thresh;
so I will put a yoke

[a]5 Beth Aven means *house of wickedness* (a name for Bethel, which means *house of God*). [b]6 Or *its counsel*
[c]8 Hebrew *aven*, a reference to Beth Aven (a derogatory name for Bethel) [d]9 Or *there a stand was taken*

you think is the reason for that? **2.** If you have been away from home for a while (summer camp or business trip), what do you dream of doing when you get back?

STUDY 1. What had Israel done all these years with the blessing of God (v. 1)? What should they have done with the "sacred stones" present in the land (Deut. 16:21–22)? As a result, what happened? What will God do now? In addition to their idols, what had Israel been trusting in (v. 3)? What will happen to both of these "security blankets" (vv. 5–8)? **2.** Who were the "evildoers" in Gibeah: Jews or Gentiles (Judg. 19–20)? What was the lesson for all of Israel? How is Hosea applying this lesson in the present circumstance? What is the "double sin" of Israel (v. 10)? What is the "yoke" she can expect (v. 11)? **3.** What laws of sowing and reaping do you see here (vv. 12–13)? Which has Israel chosen? What crop can she expect to reap? Was there no other way? Why do you suppose Israel didn't take it? **4.** Despite the certainty of Israel's punishment, what hope might Hosea's treatment of Gomer have given to Hosea's listeners?

APPLY 1. How has God blessed you and allowed your harvest to prosper? Are you using these blessings to honor him and further his work, or to satisfy and enhance your own ends? **2.** Where do you look for help when in need: Self? Others? God? Have you made any "unholy alliances"? How can you begin to break them in the next week? **3.** What is the "unplowed ground" in your life that must be "turned over"? Is there some area in which you are not allowing God to be "Master"? Take a moment now and give this area to him. What result can you expect if you continue to commit this area to his Lordship (v. 12)?

10:3 even if we had a king. When Assyria conquered Israel, the captive nation's royalty would be reduced to nothing and rendered helpless.

10:4 make agreements. Israel knew when it was in political trouble. However, its kings turned to the wrong power for help.

10:9 Gibeah. Same story, different verse (9:9). Like Gibeah, Israel would endure war and hardship as a consequence of sin (Judg. 19:12–30).

10:11 trained heifer. It would have been so easy for Israel to enjoy God's blessings—if only Israel had stayed true to him. Israel should have remained contented; but, like a cow that goes from freely grazing to a plowing yoke, Israel would learn the hard way.

on her fair neck.
I will drive Ephraim,
Judah must plow,
and Jacob must break up the ground.
12 Sow for yourselves righteousness,
reap the fruit of unfailing love,
and break up your unplowed ground;
for it is time to seek the LORD,
until he comes
and showers righteousness on you.
13 But you have planted wickedness,
you have reaped evil,
you have eaten the fruit of deception.
Because you have depended on your own strength
and on your many warriors,
14 the roar of battle will rise against your people,
so that all your fortresses will be devastated—
as Shalman devastated Beth Arbel on the day of battle,
when mothers were dashed to the ground with their children.
15 Thus will it happen to you, O Bethel,
because your wickedness is great.
When that day dawns,
the king of Israel will be completely destroyed.

God's Love for Israel

11 "When Israel was a child, I loved him,
and out of Egypt I called my son.
2 But the more I[a] called Israel,
the further they went from me.[b]
They sacrificed to the Baals
and they burned incense to images.
3 It was I who taught Ephraim to walk,
taking them by the arms;
but they did not realize
it was I who healed them.
4 I led them with cords of human kindness,
with ties of love;
I lifted the yoke from their neck
and bent down to feed them.

[a]2 Some Septuagint manuscripts; Hebrew *they* [b]2 Septuagint; Hebrew *them*

OPEN 1. Were you more compliant or strong-willed as a child? How are your children like you? **2.** What is your earliest memory of Mom or Dad helping you master some activity? **3.** What do you remember your parents doing for you that you did not appreciate at the time?

STUDY 1. What images describe God's relationship to Israel (vv. 1–4)? Which image seems particularly female? Have you ever thought of God as female, as well as male? **2.** What impact did that parental love have on Israel (vv. 2–7; compare Deut. 21:18–21; Isa. 1:2–20)? Why will they return to bondage (v. 5)? **3.** Why won't God deliver them, even if they call to him (v. 7)? What is God's dilemma in verses 8–9? (For

10:12 unfailing love. Again, God portrayed a love relationship, not a contractual agreement, as the backdrop of his pursuit. **unplowed ground.** Israel had a long way to go. Working on its relationship with God would take new focus and energy. **showers righteousness.** An agricultural image of rain falling on needy ground.

10:13 many warriors. Israel seemed to credit anything other than God with the success of their nation.

11:1 called my son. In order to evaluate the present, God went back to Israel's past, when he and Israel were like father and son (Ex. 4:22–23).

11:2 the more I called Israel. The imagery showcases Israel's immaturity in its relationship with God. Like a child pretending not to hear its parents, Israel strayed from God.

11:3 walk. An infant nation, Israel had to follow God's instructions and encouragement all the way to the Promised Land (Deut. 1:31).

11:4 The image portrays a compassionate farmer repositioning the yoke on a work animal in order for it to enjoy its food. God cared for his people like they were his children or his prized animal. Their response was to turn away.

5 "Will they not return to Egypt
and will not Assyria rule over them
because they refuse to repent?
6 Swords will flash in their cities,
will destroy the bars of their gates
and put an end to their plans.
7 My people are determined to turn from me.
Even if they call to the Most High,
he will by no means exalt them.

8 "How can I give you up, Ephraim?
How can I hand you over, Israel?
How can I treat you like Admah?
How can I make you like Zeboiim?
My heart is changed within me;
all my compassion is aroused.
9 I will not carry out my fierce anger,
nor will I turn and devastate Ephraim.
For I am God, and not man—
the Holy One among you.
I will not come in wrath.[a]
10 They will follow the LORD;
he will roar like a lion.
When he roars,
his children will come trembling from the west.
11 They will come trembling
like birds from Egypt,
like doves from Assyria.
I will settle them in their homes,"
declares the LORD.

Israel's Sin

12 Ephraim has surrounded me with lies,
the house of Israel with deceit.
And Judah is unruly against God,
even against the faithful Holy One.

12 1 Ephraim feeds on the wind;
he pursues the east wind all day
and multiplies lies and violence.
He makes a treaty with Assyria
and sends olive oil to Egypt.
2 The LORD has a charge to bring against Judah;
he will punish Jacob[b] according to his ways
and repay him according to his deeds.
3 In the womb he grasped his brother's heel;

[a]9 Or *come against any city* [b]2 *Jacob* means *he grasps the heel* (figuratively, *he deceives*).

the history of Admah and Zeboiim, Deut. 29:23.) **4.** What in God's character and covenant prompt him to turn from his plan to destroy Israel (v. 9; Deut. 4:27–31)? **5.** How will God restore them (vv. 10–11)? What hope would this promise give to the faithful?

APPLY 1. When have you found painful discipline necessary? How did you feel, carrying out the sentence? Did you ever change your mind about doing so? Why? **2.** How has God shown a parent's love to you? In what ways have you spurned that love? **3.** What comfort do you take in God's enduring love? How will you share that with those who have yet to "come home"?

OPEN What stories about your ancestors convey values (the value of thrift, completing your education, etc.)? Whom do you identify with most in your family tree?

STUDY 1. How does Hosea picture Ephraim's (Israel) dealings with Assyria and Egypt? What was Israel trying to do in her diplomacy with both powers (v. 1; 2 Kin. 17:3–4)? What deceit was involved in these political dealings? **2.** In making his case against Judah (and Israel), how does Hosea use the well-known stories about Jacob (vv. 2–5,12)? What did Jacob's name mean? How had he lived up to it in his dealings with Esau (Gen. 25:24–34)?

11:5 return to Egypt. Returning to Egypt was a major step backward for Israel: from freedom to slavery, blessing to punishment, success to inferiority.

11:8 God compared Ephraim's fate to that of cities overthrown by the destruction of Sodom (Deut. 29:23).

11:9 For I am God, and not man. A father may punish a child and then regret it. However, God regretted the punishment before it began.

11:11 I will settle them. The image is of a dove swiftly returning to make its home in a safe nest (7:11).

12:1 olive oil to Egypt. Israel gave the Egyptians olive oil in hopes of endearing themselves to the larger, more powerful ruler.

12:3 Jacob was the father of Israel's tribes. Like Israel, he was a deceiver (Gen. 27:35–36).

With Isaac (Gen. 27)? With Laban (Gen. 30:25–43)? What finally turned him around (Gen. 32:24–30)? How was that change symbolized (Gen. 35:10–12)? **3.** What is the punch line of this history for Israel (v. 6)? **4.** How is Israel (Ephraim) "self-deceived" and "deaf" to God's overtures (vv. 8–10)? What would "living in tents again" bring to mind? **5.** What analogy is drawn in verses 12–13? Why refer to "a prophet" rather than naming Moses? What hope does this analogy give to Israel in her situation? **6.** Does Hosea foresee any escape from God's wrath (v. 14)? Is God rejecting, or fulfilling, his covenant (Deut. 4:25–31)?

APPLY **1.** Are Jacob's tactics (clever alliances, self-reliance and lip-service to God) a part of your life at all? How so? **2.** Jacob, after years of scheming, was finally changed by a direct encounter with God. How are you being changed by knowing Christ? **3.** Is God calling attention to something now, but you're ignoring him? What is it?

OPEN **1.** About what things are you jealous? Why? What are you likely to do to someone who threatens or steals that "precious possession"? **2.** When have you greeted the sunrise? Have you ever tried capturing the morning mist or the morning dew? What happened?

as a man he struggled with God.
4 He struggled with the angel and overcame him;
he wept and begged for his favor.
He found him at Bethel
and talked with him there—
5 the LORD God Almighty,
the LORD is his name of renown!
6 But you must return to your God;
maintain love and justice,
and wait for your God always.

7 The merchant uses dishonest scales;
he loves to defraud.
8 Ephraim boasts,
"I am very rich; I have become wealthy.
With all my wealth they will not find in me
any iniquity or sin."

9 "I am the LORD your God,
⌞who brought you⌟ out of[a] Egypt;
I will make you live in tents again,
as in the days of your appointed feasts.
10 I spoke to the prophets,
gave them many visions
and told parables through them."

11 Is Gilead wicked?
Its people are worthless!
Do they sacrifice bulls in Gilgal?
Their altars will be like piles of stones
on a plowed field.
12 Jacob fled to the country of Aram[b];
Israel served to get a wife,
and to pay for her he tended sheep.
13 The LORD used a prophet to bring Israel up from Egypt,
by a prophet he cared for him.
14 But Ephraim has bitterly provoked him to anger;
his Lord will leave upon him the guilt of his bloodshed
and will repay him for his contempt.

The LORD's Anger Against Israel

13 When Ephraim spoke, men trembled;
he was exalted in Israel.
But he became guilty of Baal worship and died.
2 Now they sin more and more;

[a]9 Or *God / ever since you were in* [b]12 That is, Northwest Mesopotamia

---

12:6 return. Jacob turned his life around after encountering God (Gen. 32:24–30). Israel could hope to do the same.

12:8 Ephraim. Hosea interchanged Ephraim (the most influential northern tribe) and Israel for the same northern kingdom.

12:12 God reminded Israel of its humble beginnings through the story of Jacob. Jacob tended sheep and worked for his prosperity (Gen. 29:20–28).

12:13 prophet to bring up Israel. Moses was the prophet of choice to lead God's people out of Egypt.

13:1 died. Ephraim experienced spiritual death due to its disobedience, a fate worse than extinction.

they make idols for themselves from their silver,
cleverly fashioned images,
all of them the work of craftsmen.
It is said of these people,
"They offer human sacrifice
and kiss[a] the calf-idols."
³Therefore they will be like the morning mist,
like the early dew that disappears,
like chaff swirling from a threshing floor,
like smoke escaping through a window.

⁴"But I am the LORD your God,
⌊who brought you⌋ out of[b] Egypt.
You shall acknowledge no God but me,
no Savior except me.
⁵I cared for you in the desert,
in the land of burning heat.
⁶When I fed them, they were satisfied;
when they were satisfied, they became proud;
then they forgot me.
⁷So I will come upon them like a lion,
like a leopard I will lurk by the path.
⁸Like a bear robbed of her cubs,
I will attack them and rip them open.
Like a lion I will devour them;
a wild animal will tear them apart.

⁹"You are destroyed, O Israel,
because you are against me, against your helper.
¹⁰Where is your king, that he may save you?
Where are your rulers in all your towns,
of whom you said,
'Give me a king and princes'?
¹¹So in my anger I gave you a king,
and in my wrath I took him away.
¹²The guilt of Ephraim is stored up,
his sins are kept on record.
¹³Pains as of a woman in childbirth come to him,
but he is a child without wisdom;
when the time arrives,
he does not come to the opening of the womb.

¹⁴"I will ransom them from the power of the grave[c];
I will redeem them from death.

[a]2 Or *"Men who sacrifice / kiss* [b]4 Or *God / ever since you were in* [c]14 Hebrew *Sheol*

STUDY 1. What had made Ephraim (Israel) once so feared (v. 1; Josh. 2:9–11)? What does Hosea see as absurd and ironic about Israel's idol worship? How will they be like the four things in verse 3? **2.** What in God's character and covenant-keeping has Israel forgotten (vv. 4–6)? How do they bite the hand that feeds them (vv. 1,6,9; 12:8; Ex. 20:1–3)? **3.** What does God intend to do about that (vv. 7–9)? Is this consistent with his covenant? Why or why not (Deut. 4:25–31)? **4.** How did Israel's desire for a king deceive them (1 Sam. 8:4–9,20)? What have they done to the One who could save them? **5.** How is Ephraim a "child without wisdom" (v. 13)? What desired effect did the birth pangs *not* produce? What is the result for a child "unwilling" or unable to be born? **6.** If the first two lines of verse 14 were a rhetorical question (i.e., "Shall I ...?"), what would Hosea's audience have understood this to mean? What would it do to their presumption of God's forgiveness and love (6:1–2; compare 1:6)? **7.** What devastation does Hosea foresee (vv. 15–16)? Does God's covenant and character demand it? How so?

APPLY 1. Have your own desires ever been self-destructive? Any addictive behaviors, substances or relationships? How did you treat those who tried to help you? What saved you from completely destroying yourself with these "handmade idols"? **2.** What makes you feel secure: Job? Home? Pension? Spouse or friends? Health? Other? What would you rely on if these were taken away? **3.** When you have experienced God's "rod," how have you felt his love?

13:3 Although Ephraim thrived for a brief moment, its self-destructive practices would bring the nation down forever.

13:4 I am the LORD ... who brought you out. Compromise was not on the table. Either Israel would forsake all gods but the Lord, or face dire consequences.

13:7–8 From shepherd to predator, the imagery shifts to express God's frustration with his people. If Israel did not acknowledge his tender mercy, his ravenous justice would get their attention.

13:10 Where are your rulers? Hosea wrote at a time when kings were assassinated as quickly as they were inaugurated. This also implies that the nation needed to seek their help from God not rulers.

13:13 Like a baby who is not in birth position at the time of a crucial contraction, Israel missed a window of opportunity. Faced with God's judgment, Israel failed to do the obvious—act decisively and repent.

Where, O death, are your plagues?
Where, O grave,[a] is your destruction?

"I will have no compassion,
15 even though he thrives among his brothers.
An east wind from the LORD will come,
blowing in from the desert;
his spring will fail
and his well dry up.
His storehouse will be plundered
of all its treasures.
16 The people of Samaria must bear their guilt,
because they have rebelled against their God.
They will fall by the sword;
their little ones will be dashed to the ground,
their pregnant women ripped open."

Repentance to Bring Blessing

14 Return, O Israel, to the LORD your God.
Your sins have been your downfall!
2 Take words with you
and return to the LORD.
Say to him:
"Forgive all our sins
and receive us graciously,
that we may offer the fruit of our lips.[b]
3 Assyria cannot save us;
we will not mount war-horses.
We will never again say 'Our gods'
to what our own hands have made,
for in you the fatherless find compassion."

4 "I will heal their waywardness
and love them freely,
for my anger has turned away from them.
5 I will be like the dew to Israel;
he will blossom like a lily.
Like a cedar of Lebanon
he will send down his roots;
6 his young shoots will grow.
His splendor will be like an olive tree,
his fragrance like a cedar of Lebanon.
7 Men will dwell again in his shade.
He will flourish like the grain.
He will blossom like a vine,
and his fame will be like the wine from Lebanon.

[a] 14 Hebrew *Sheol* [b] 2 Or *offer our lips as sacrifices of bulls*

OPEN 1. If someone were to call you "fruitful," to what would they be referring: Your garden? Children? Good deeds? **2.** What do you like best about trees: Climbing? Swinging? Shade? Lumber? Fruit? Birds? What is your favorite tree?

STUDY 1. What is different about the "return" pictured here (vv. 1–3; compare 5:6; 6:1–3)? What is the "fruit of our lips" (v. 2)? How will Israel show true repentance (v. 3)? **2.** What does God promise to do and be for Israel (vv. 4–8)? What will Israel's future be like? **3.** How does this relate to Hosea's daughter and second son (1:6–9)? How has God's anger been turned away? **4.** When will this restoration to glory occur? Will Israel avoid exile (Lev. 26:40–45)? **5.** Where had Israel sought prosperity (2:5)? What had she forgotten (v. 8; 2:8)? **6.** What does the name "Ephraim" mean (Gen. 41:52)? What is the source of that fruitfulness? **7.** What does the wise person know (v. 9)? The wise society? What influence does it have on how they live? **8.** What condition and promise does true repentance involve (Luke 15:11–24; 1 John 1:9)?

APPLY 1. How has God's anger toward your sin been turned away (Eph. 2:3–5)? Can the consequences of sin always be

13:15 east wind. Assyria blew onto the scene at the right time, destroyed Israel and took her people captive—according to God's plan.

14:1 Return O Israel. God's command has a greater context at the conclusion of his message than earlier references (10:12; 12:6). Lip service does not cut it. Nor is sorrow a shortcut to God's grace. Genuine repentance is the only acceptable means for returning to God.

14:3 fatherless find compassion. Hosea returns to the personal image of a faithless wife and illegitimate children.

14:4 heal. God treated Israel's sinful condition as a disease. Avoidance of sin was the basis of true spiritual health for Israel.

[8]O Ephraim, what more have I[a] to do with idols?
I will answer him and care for him.
I am like a green pine tree;
your fruitfulness comes from me."

[9]Who is wise? He will realize these things.
Who is discerning? He will understand them.
The ways of the LORD are right;
the righteous walk in them,
but the rebellious stumble in them.

[a]8 Or *What more has Ephraim*

avoided? What can we look forward to if we walk in covenant faithfulness with him (vv. 5–8)? 2. Has your health, your job or a broken relationship ever been "restored" to you? How? How did you feel? 3. What restoration project can you and your group take on, with the compassion of Hosea for Gomer?

14:8 fruitfulness comes from me. God revealed the secret of success to a farming community whose existence was tied to the fruit of a harvest. God is a nation's profit. God alone blesses the bounty.

14:9 ways of the LORD are right. Hosea concludes with a lesson in cause and effect. Rebellion leads to stumbling. Righteousness provides a clear path.

Joel

Personal Reading	Group Study Topic and Reading	
1:1–20	Land-Eating Locusts	1:1–12
2:1–17	Heart-Rending Call	2:12–17
2:18–32	Promised Spirit	2:28–32
3:1–21	Blessed Zion	3:17–21

Author. The prophet Joel is credited with the authorship of this book. The apostle Peter quoted Joel on the day of Pentecost (Acts 2:16–21). Much of Joel's prophecy focused on Jerusalem. It was probably there that most of his ministry took place.

Date. Scholars disagree about when Joel prophesied as well as when he recorded his prophecy. Some place his ministry as early as ninth century B.C. Others place it as late as second century B.C., after the Babylonian exile and return to Jerusalem.

Purpose. Sometimes it takes the harshest news to make people stop and evaluate their decisions. Often it requires a tragedy or crisis of some kind. As threatening as Joel's message was, he hoped it would function as a wake-up call. His people needed to reevaluate their actions and the direction they were heading. Joel's message described not only the impending threat of judgment but also the hope of restoration. It speaks to us today of the glories that God has in store for those who worship him alone.

Historical Background. The book of Joel does not list any dates or the names of any kings to place his prophecy within a historical context. The book contains little direct evidence that describes any specific period from the ninth century B.C. to the period after the exile. While the exact date remains unknown, that entire era was characterized by the threat of powerful forces outside of Israel. (The book of 2 Kings particularly details this period.) Assyria, Egypt, Babylon and Persia all played roles in the historical drama of that era, as their empires rose to prominence and then fell away. Within Hebrew borders, the same era was characterized by the decline of the covenant relationship between God and his people. While outside forces brought political pressure, the people of Israel and Judah slipped further and further away from God.

Locusts. Even in the twenty-first century an invasion of locusts is a serious threat to human life. They literally devour everything in their path. When God sent an invasion of locusts as the eighth plague against Egypt, Pharaoh begged that they be sent away (Ex. 10:12–20). Locusts are even listed as one of the covenant curses that will result because of disobedience to God (Deut. 28:38). The invasion of a swarm of locusts is like that of an invading army. They leave nothing standing in their wake. For Joel, the massive locust plague he described was not only a curse in itself but also a foreshadowing of the terrible judgment day of the Lord. Some have even theorized that Joel only used the actual threat of locusts to symbolize the armies that would eventually bring destruction on God's disobedient people.

1 The word of the LORD that came to Joel son of Pethuel.

An Invasion of Locusts

2 Hear this, you elders;
listen, all who live in the land.
Has anything like this ever happened in your days
or in the days of your forefathers?
3 Tell it to your children,
and let your children tell it to their children,
and their children to the next generation.
4 What the locust swarm has left
the great locusts have eaten;
what the great locusts have left
the young locusts have eaten;
what the young locusts have left
other locusts[a] have eaten.

5 Wake up, you drunkards, and weep!
Wail, all you drinkers of wine;
wail because of the new wine,
for it has been snatched from your lips.
6 A nation has invaded my land,
powerful and without number;
it has the teeth of a lion,
the fangs of a lioness.
7 It has laid waste my vines
and ruined my fig trees.
It has stripped off their bark
and thrown it away,
leaving their branches white.

8 Mourn like a virgin[b] in sackcloth
grieving for the husband[c] of her youth.
9 Grain offerings and drink offerings
are cut off from the house of the LORD.
The priests are in mourning,
those who minister before the LORD.
10 The fields are ruined,
the ground is dried up[d];
the grain is destroyed,
the new wine is dried up,
the oil fails.

[a]4 The precise meaning of the four Hebrew words used here for locusts is uncertain. [b]8 Or *young woman* [c]8 Or *betrothed* [d]10 Or *ground mourns*

OPEN 1. What weather conditions (hot and humid, cold and windy, storm brewing) might depict the week you've just had? What weather forecast might fit the week ahead? **2.** What is the closest you've come to experiencing famine or plague conditions?

STUDY 1. What various groups does Joel address? What event has come to them? How does it affect them? **2.** Why does Joel emphasize hearing and retelling (vv. 2–3)? What does that say about how faith is born and nurtured? **3.** What famous plague in their recital of God's mighty acts would Joel's hearers have recalled (Ex. 10:13–15)? Since that other plague of locusts happened to God's foes, what makes this one especially unpalatable? **4.** How does Joel describe this disastrous event? How complete is it? How do you respond to his vivid, poetic images? **5.** What drama and progressive mood do you observe in the text? In Joel himself? What does the change in verbs tell you (vv. 3,5,8,11)? Where is the musical crescendo or literary climax in this section? (How final is "withered," (v. 12?) **6.** Is this plague a punishment for sin, or a test of faith?

APPLY 1. How would the local TV or newspaper have covered these events? Pointing fingers at whom? Suggesting what remedies? **2.** Do you respond to personal calamity as Joel's original hearers did? How so? Describe your response to one current or recent experience. **3.** The joy of this nation was linked to external circumstances. On a scale of 1 (Never) to 10 (Always), how often is that true of you? **4.** When your joy withers, what or who has God used to renew it?

1:1 Joel. Joel's prophetic message focuses on God's supreme power and might. As if to emphasize his point, his name translates, "The Lord is God."

1:2 elders. Joel aimed at getting the attention of those in charge. The elders were the ruling authority at that time.

1:5 Wake up, you drunkards. The assumption is that the people of Joel's time were engaged in rebellion, although drunkenness is the only specific sin mentioned. Drunkenness is used as imagery to depict a people who are morally asleep, dulled by disobedience.

1:6 invaded. Locusts had invaded the land. Like a wild animal shredding prey with its fangs, the locusts devoured the community's crops. **powerful.** The tiny insect's reputation preceded it, due to the destruction in Egypt centuries before (Ex. 10:13–15). They are seemingly harmless insects, but in great numbers are greatly feared.

1:10 ground is dried up. As if the locusts' feast were not enough, what little remained was laid waste through drought.

[11]Despair, you farmers,
wail, you vine growers;
grieve for the wheat and the barley,
because the harvest of the field is destroyed.
[12]The vine is dried up
and the fig tree is withered;
the pomegranate, the palm and the apple tree—
all the trees of the field—are dried up.
Surely the joy of mankind
is withered away.

A Call to Repentance

[13]Put on sackcloth, O priests, and mourn;
wail, you who minister before the altar.
Come, spend the night in sackcloth,
you who minister before my God;
for the grain offerings and drink offerings
are withheld from the house of your God.
[14]Declare a holy fast;
call a sacred assembly.
Summon the elders
and all who live in the land
to the house of the LORD your God,
and cry out to the LORD.

[15]Alas for that day!
For the day of the LORD is near;
it will come like destruction from the Almighty.[a]

[16]Has not the food been cut off
before our very eyes—
joy and gladness
from the house of our God?
[17]The seeds are shriveled
beneath the clods.[b]
The storehouses are in ruins,
the granaries have been broken down,
for the grain has dried up.
[18]How the cattle moan!
The herds mill about
because they have no pasture;
even the flocks of sheep are suffering.

[19]To you, O LORD, I call,
for fire has devoured the open pastures

[a]15 Hebrew *Shaddai* [b]17 The meaning of the Hebrew for this word is uncertain.

OPEN 1. What social statement are you making with the clothes you wear: Out of it? In charge? Dressed to kill? **2.** If the clothes you have on were all made of burlap, how would you feel?

STUDY 1. What is Joel calling the priests to do? Likewise, the elders? Why fast and pray (Lev. 16:29)? **2.** What is the link between their current famine and the future "day of the LORD" (vv. 14–15)? From Amos 5:18–20, what else might Joel be associating with this day when the Lord is clearly vindicated and manifested in earthly history? What does "the LORD's day" mean now? **3.** How does Joel depict this drought-stricken land (vv. 16–20)? What is the point of picturing God as the Lord of plants and animals, land and water? **4.** If locusts consume all that's edible, and fire destroys what remains, where then is hope (vv. 16,19)?

APPLY 1. When have you felt like your resources (spiritual, financial, physical) were drying up or burnt out? **2.** Who do you cry out to when your resources are dried up: God? Other? Family? Group? Self?

1:14 cry out to the LORD. Joel revealed that the people could not help themselves out of this one. He encouraged them to cry out to the Lord in repentance, humility and desperation (Judg. 20:26).

1:15 day of the LORD is near. This phrase, symbolizing God's intervention into history, is central in Joel's writings (2:1,11,31; 3:14). Joel's use of the phrase can signify both a present and future event. For example, the locust invasion (v. 4), bad as it was, forewarned of events to come. An extraordinary display of destructive power, like the final day of the Lord, was coming (Amos 5:18ff).

1:19–20 devoured the open pastures. Joel portrayed a parched land, scorched by the destruction of the locusts (2:3) and cracked in the drought.

and flames have burned up all the trees of the field.
20 Even the wild animals pant for you;
the streams of water have dried up
and fire has devoured the open pastures.

An Army of Locusts

2 Blow the trumpet in Zion;
sound the alarm on my holy hill.
Let all who live in the land tremble,
for the day of the LORD is coming.
It is close at hand—
2 a day of darkness and gloom,
a day of clouds and blackness.
Like dawn spreading across the mountains
a large and mighty army comes,
such as never was of old
nor ever will be in ages to come.

3 Before them fire devours,
behind them a flame blazes.
Before them the land is like the garden of Eden,
behind them, a desert waste—
nothing escapes them.
4 They have the appearance of horses;
they gallop along like cavalry.
5 With a noise like that of chariots
they leap over the mountaintops,
like a crackling fire consuming stubble,
like a mighty army drawn up for battle.

6 At the sight of them, nations are in anguish;
every face turns pale.
7 They charge like warriors;
they scale walls like soldiers.
They all march in line,
not swerving from their course.
8 They do not jostle each other;
each marches straight ahead.
They plunge through defenses
without breaking ranks.
9 They rush upon the city;
they run along the wall.
They climb into the houses;
like thieves they enter through the windows.

10 Before them the earth shakes,
the sky trembles,
the sun and moon are darkened,

OPEN **1.** What does it take to rouse you from sleep: Two alarms? Three trumpets? Four jolts? **2.** What memories of waking up do you have from camping days: Wake-up call? Calisthenics? Cold showers? **3.** What is the funniest or most embarrassing consequence of your sleeping through an alarm?

STUDY **1.** How are the images of this army like, and unlike, the army of locusts that previously invaded the land (ch. 1)? How are these images like human invaders? How are they larger than life, taking on theological meaning? **2.** How do these poetic images engage and exhaust all five senses to understand them? **3.** What might the trumpet (v. 1) signify: The call to fast? The call to action? The call of the Lord's coming? Or what? **4.** Since his people have just experienced a locust plague and ensuing famine, why do you think Joel is dwelling on this theme of the coming "day of the LORD"? **5.** Who is at the head of this army? What does that mean?

APPLY **1.** How do you respond to the image of the Lord as the head of a destructive army? What jolts your senses about that? **2.** If Joel were a street preacher in your community trumpeting this message about the coming "day of the LORD," what would be the response from the people? From you? **3.** Each of us may be part of the Lord's army (maybe not in the way described here); when, if ever, have you sensed God's call to do battle? With what or whom?

2:1 Blow the trumpet. Like a phone call in the middle of the night, the trumpeter sent fear into the hearts of all the people. Danger! Alert!

2:2 darkness and gloom. Without the light of hope, the people experienced the underside of the day of the Lord. It was a day of destruction, wrath and judgment on sin.

2:3 desert waste. God's power, demonstrated through the invading locusts, was able to turn an Eden-like place into a wasteland with no growth.

2:10 sun and moon ... stars. Joel catapulted God's judgment to the cosmos. Even the sun, moon and stars were dimmed by the massive destruction (Isa. 13:10).

and the stars no longer shine.
11The LORD thunders
at the head of his army;
his forces are beyond number,
and mighty are those who obey his command.
The day of the LORD is great;
it is dreadful.
Who can endure it?

Rend Your Heart

12"Even now," declares the LORD,
"return to me with all your heart,
with fasting and weeping and mourning."

13Rend your heart
and not your garments.
Return to the LORD your God,
for he is gracious and compassionate,
slow to anger and abounding in love,
and he relents from sending calamity.
14Who knows? He may turn and have pity
and leave behind a blessing—
grain offerings and drink offerings
for the LORD your God.

15Blow the trumpet in Zion,
declare a holy fast,
call a sacred assembly.
16Gather the people,
consecrate the assembly;
bring together the elders,
gather the children,
those nursing at the breast.
Let the bridegroom leave his room
and the bride her chamber.
17Let the priests, who minister before the LORD,
weep between the temple porch and the altar.
Let them say, "Spare your people, O LORD.
Do not make your inheritance an object of scorn,
a byword among the nations.
Why should they say among the peoples,
'Where is their God?' "

The LORD's Answer

18Then the LORD will be jealous for his land
and take pity on his people.

OPEN 1. When, if ever, have you fasted from: Food? Drink? Dates? TV? **2.** What was your incentive? Results? **3.** Would you do it again?

STUDY 1. With destruction at the Lord's hand near, what does Joel expect? **2.** What is meant by "rend your heart and not your garments" (v. 13)? What else should prompt them to return to God (Ex. 34:6–7; Neh. 9:16–17)? **3.** Why are daily temple offerings so key (v. 14; Dan. 8:11–13)? For what blessing does Joel hope? **4.** Who is this event for? Why "everyone"? Why does a bridal party "never" fast (v. 16; Mark 2:19–20)? **5.** What's the point in the priests' prayer for Israel (v. 17)?

APPLY 1. When in your life have you had to return to God after being away from him? What did you have to "mourn" in order to make that change (v. 12)? **2.** What would corporate repentance require for your group? For the church? For the nation? What role should you take?

OPEN 1. Are your parents or spouse the "jealous" kind? What are they jealous about? When does their jealousy seem redemptive?

2:11 head of his army. God, his might unchallenged, emerged at the helm of this invincible force.

2:13 compassionate. Between the lines of this verse is the collective sigh of relief from a doomed people. God's divinity stooped to meet the weakness of humanity at just the right time.

2:16 Gather the people. Again, Joel exhorted the elders and those in authority to lead the people to repentance.

2:17 Spare your people. Like pausing mid-reel during the climactic scene in a horror movie, the priests' woeful request was able to suddenly avert the terror.

2:18 pity. Amid the prior description of judgment, pity almost seemed out of place. However, the Lord eagerly exercised compassion. The people's

[19]The LORD will reply[a] to them:

"I am sending you grain, new wine and oil,
enough to satisfy you fully;
never again will I make you
an object of scorn to the nations.

[20]"I will drive the northern army far from you,
pushing it into a parched and barren land,
with its front columns going into the eastern sea[b]
and those in the rear into the western sea.[c]
And its stench will go up;
its smell will rise."

Surely he has done great things.[d]
21 Be not afraid, O land;
be glad and rejoice.
Surely the LORD has done great things.
22 Be not afraid, O wild animals,
for the open pastures are becoming green.
The trees are bearing their fruit;
the fig tree and the vine yield their riches.
[23]Be glad, O people of Zion,
rejoice in the LORD your God,
for he has given you
the autumn rains in righteousness.[e]
He sends you abundant showers,
both autumn and spring rains, as before.
[24]The threshing floors will be filled with grain;
the vats will overflow with new wine and oil.

[25]"I will repay you for the years the locusts have eaten—
the great locust and the young locust,
the other locusts and the locust swarm[f]—
my great army that I sent among you.
[26]You will have plenty to eat, until you are full,
and you will praise the name of the LORD your God,
who has worked wonders for you;
never again will my people be shamed.
[27]Then you will know that I am in Israel,
that I am the LORD your God,
and that there is no other;
never again will my people be shamed.

The Day of the Lord

[28]"And afterward,
I will pour out my Spirit on all people.

[a]18,19 Or *LORD was jealous . . . / and took pity . . . / [19]The LORD replied* [b]20 That is, the Dead Sea [c]20 That is, the Mediterranean [d]20 Or *rise. / Surely it has done great things."* [e]23 Or */ the teacher for righteousness:* [f]25 The precise meaning of the four Hebrew words used here for locusts is uncertain.

2. What people or situations arouse your pity? Why? **3.** When have you seen nature "rejoice"? What thing in "the wild" brings you the most joy?

STUDY 1. To what time does "then" in verse 18 refer? Do verses 18–27 assume the "day of the LORD" has come already? Or was that day averted and still to be expected? Or both? Why do you think so? **2.** What does it mean that God is "jealous" for or takes "pity" on his people (Ex. 20:5–6)? How can God claim and enforce such an exclusive relationship with us? **3.** What specific "great things" does God do which correspond to the concrete situation of Israel (in vv. 1–11 and 1:1–20)? What does this correspondence say about the effectiveness and completeness of God's restoration? **4.** What are some of the resulting changes in God's people which he brings about by his zealous restoration? What is the end result (v. 27) intended by God's answer to the priests' prayer (v. 17)? **5.** What does this tell you about God's love, power and uniqueness? About God's care for creation? For his covenant people? **6.** Why do you think God responds so specifically to his people's needs and prayers?

APPLY 1. Very few want to be objects of someone else's pity. Why would you or your church want God's pity? Describe a time when you believe God took pity on you or your church. What current situation might call for God's pity? **2.** In your prayer life, when has God granted you a deeper "knowledge" of himself? **3.** When and why have you felt a sense of shame: Not knowing God was working in your life? Enduring personal calamity? Not living as a Christian? Giving up too soon on God? On others? On self? **4.** In these experiences, what do the promises given in verses 19 and 27 mean to you?

OPEN Can you keep a secret about love? Gifts? Birthdays? (Share about one.)

STUDY 1. When is "afterward" (v. 28; Acts 2:16–21)? Could these "last days" also include

---

repentance marked a turning point in Joel's prophecy.

2:21–23 Everything came to life again as a symbol of God's restorative power. Animals (v. 22) and people (v. 23) enjoy the rebirth of the land (v. 21).

2:22 Animals would have starved without the provision and protection of the land. Instead, they did not fear death, but enjoyed life.

2:27 I am in Israel. Make no mistake. The blessings (vv. 25–26) were a

"today"? Why? **2.** To Joel's people, what is unusual about the Spirit coming upon men and women? Likewise, to Peter's mixed audience (Acts 2:16–21)? What is unusual to you about Joel's prophecy? Why? **3.** What does the Spirit do: Reveal God's will? Renew our energy? Recast the cosmos? Redeem the survivors? **4.** How does this picture of the "day of the LORD" differ from the previous one (vv. 1–11)?

APPLY What is the promise here: For spiritual dryness? For spiritual exclusiveness and pride? For fear? For your group? Your church? Your world?

OPEN 1. What have you lost that you would like to see restored: Your innocence? Your youth? Your belief in humanity? The faith of your childhood? **2.** What is your favorite anti-war slogan: "Peace is disarming"? "Arms are for hugging, not war"? "One nuclear bomb could ruin your whole day"? "If you want peace, work for justice"? Other? **3.** Which slogan fits how you maintain peace in your life?

STUDY 1. "In those days" (v. 1) refers to when: Sometime after Joel but before Christ? After Christ but before now? A time yet to come? All of the above? Nothing specific? Explain. **2.** For what five things will the nations be judged (vv. 2–3)? How will they be "repaid"? **3.** The "valley where the Lord judges" (vv. 2,12,14) is not a known geographical site. What then might Joel intend by naming such a place? **4.** Why are the nations to be judged called to prepare for war (vv. 9–11), only to meet the Lord's warriors? What is the outcome of that war (v. 13)? **5.** Is that outcome determined more by human decision "in the valley"? Or by divine fiat from where God sits?

Your sons and daughters will prophesy,
your old men will dream dreams,
your young men will see visions.
29 Even on my servants, both men and women,
I will pour out my Spirit in those days.
30 I will show wonders in the heavens
and on the earth,
blood and fire and billows of smoke.
31 The sun will be turned to darkness
and the moon to blood
before the coming of the great and dreadful day of the LORD.
32 And everyone who calls
on the name of the LORD will be saved;
for on Mount Zion and in Jerusalem
there will be deliverance,
as the LORD has said,
among the survivors
whom the LORD calls.

The Nations Judged

3 "In those days and at that time,
when I restore the fortunes of Judah and Jerusalem,
2 I will gather all nations
and bring them down to the Valley of Jehoshaphat.[a]
There I will enter into judgment against them
concerning my inheritance, my people Israel,
for they scattered my people among the nations
and divided up my land.
3 They cast lots for my people
and traded boys for prostitutes;
they sold girls for wine
that they might drink.

4 "Now what have you against me, O Tyre and Sidon and all you regions of Philistia? Are you repaying me for something I have done? If
you are paying me back, I will swiftly and speedily return on your
own heads what you have done. 5 For you took my silver and my gold
and carried off my finest treasures to your temples. 6 You sold the
people of Judah and Jerusalem to the Greeks, that you might send
them far from their homeland.

7 "See, I am going to rouse them out of the places to which you sold
them, and I will return on your own heads what you have done. 8 I will
sell your sons and daughters to the people of Judah, and they will sell
them to the Sabeans, a nation far away." The LORD has spoken.

[a]2 *Jehoshaphat* means *the LORD judges*; also in verse 12.

credit to God's presence among his people.

2:30–31 These cosmic wonders, earlier a scene of destruction (v. 10), now proclaimed God's provision through his Spirit. The day of the Lord is a two-sided mystery. Joel described it as both a day of judgment for sin and a time of deliverance for God's people.

3:1 at that time. All of God's enemies were booked. Same day. Same time. They have an appointment with judgment.

3:2 enter into judgment. Joel provided a symbolic name for a point in time when a verdict will be pronounced on all the nations. In this supernatural event, evil will ultimately be judged and the righteous delivered (Rev. 20:8–9).

3:4–8 Specific nations were pulled aside, summoned before the Lord for their demeaning behavior and destructive attitudes toward God.

[9]Proclaim this among the nations:
Prepare for war!
Rouse the warriors!
Let all the fighting men draw near and attack.
[10]Beat your plowshares into swords
and your pruning hooks into spears.
Let the weakling say,
"I am strong!"
[11]Come quickly, all you nations from every side,
and assemble there.

Bring down your warriors, O LORD!

[12]"Let the nations be roused;
let them advance into the Valley of Jehoshaphat,
for there I will sit
to judge all the nations on every side.
[13]Swing the sickle,
for the harvest is ripe.
Come, trample the grapes,
for the winepress is full
and the vats overflow—
so great is their wickedness!"

[14]Multitudes, multitudes
in the valley of decision!
For the day of the LORD is near
in the valley of decision.
[15]The sun and moon will be darkened,
and the stars no longer shine.
[16]The LORD will roar from Zion
and thunder from Jerusalem;
the earth and the sky will tremble.
But the LORD will be a refuge for his people,
a stronghold for the people of Israel.

Blessings for God's People

[17]"Then you will know that I, the LORD your God,
dwell in Zion, my holy hill.
Jerusalem will be holy;
never again will foreigners invade her.

[18]"In that day the mountains will drip new wine,
and the hills will flow with milk;

6. Compare verse 10 with Isaiah 2:4 and Micah 4:3. Why do you think Joel reversed that traditional prophetic vision of peace? **7.** If not peace, what promise from Joel can God's people count on (v. 16)?

APPLY 1. How do you respond to Joel saying, "God will return on your heads what you have done"? How would you fare if that were done? **2.** What "payback" schedule are you on with creditors? With God? **3.** When, if ever, have you felt slain in the "Valley of Decision"? When have you felt secure in the Lord's stronghold? What would get you out of the "valley" into the stronghold?

OPEN When you were a child, what would you have liked to have "rivers" of: Pop? Chocolate? Caramel syrup? Other?

STUDY 1. How are God's judgment and salvation linked? Justice and mercy? Hope and despair? **2.** What message does Joel

3:9–11 The mighty assembly of the Lord's army gears for battle (Rev. 19:14). Joel exhorted the Lord to reveal his protection and provision (v. 11).

3:10 plowshares into swords. Instead of enjoying peace, the nations prepared for the final war. Their efforts at turning tools for plowing into battle weapons foreshadowed their inevitable defeat (Isa. 2:4, Mic. 4:3).

3:13 harvest. Tipping his hand, Joel continued his agricultural theme as he revealed the outcome of the great battle.

3:14 in the valley of decision. All of humankind was represented in this poignant location. A decision had to be made: repent or continue in rebellion.

3:16 refuge ... stronghold. Joel once again expressed the complex nature of the day of the Lord. Evil has no place to hide. However, the righteous will find a place of safety. This day will horrify those who are judged, and bring delight and relief to those who are saved.

3:17–21 Truth or consequences are Joel's closing comments. God's people will enjoy blessings (vv. 17–18). However, destruction is the inevitable consequence of evil (v. 19).

3:18 In that day. Joel looked forward to a day when God's people

intend with the contrasting images of verses 18–19? How can *one* event pronounce both irrevocable doom *and* promise such abundant blessing (Ps. 107:33–36)? **3.** How does the last promise (v. 21, offering forgiveness and fellowship) relate to the specific situation of Israel which prompted these oracles (chs. 1–2) in the first place?

APPLY 1. If the presence of the Lord in Jerusalem made it holy (v. 17), then what does the Lord's presence in your life mean? **2.** If your privacy or property has been invaded, as with Israel, what comfort do you draw from Joel? How can the fountain of God's blessing heal the wounds inflicted by those invaders?

all the ravines of Judah will run with water.
A fountain will flow out of the LORD's house
and will water the valley of acacias.[a]
19 But Egypt will be desolate,
Edom a desert waste,
because of violence done to the people of Judah,
in whose land they shed innocent blood.
20 Judah will be inhabited forever
and Jerusalem through all generations.
21 Their bloodguilt, which I have not pardoned,
I will pardon."

The LORD dwells in Zion!

[a]18 Or *Valley of Shittim*

would fully experience the fullness of God's creation forever (v. 1; 2:28).

3:21 The LORD dwells. He could have highlighted God's protection or provision here at the close of the prophecy. Instead, Joel emphasized God's presence among his people; God's covenant will finally be the rule of the day.

Amos

Author. The prophet Amos, a former herdsman, is the author of this book. Amos prophesied against the town of Bethel during the reign of Jeroboam. He specifically spoke against the evil priest Amaziah.

Personal Reading	Group Study Topic and Reading	
1–2	Judgment on Israel	2:6–16
3	Witness Against Israel	3:1–15
4	Cows of Bashan	4:1–13
5	Justice Like a River	5:18–27
6	Perversion of Justice	6:8–14
7	Amos Refutes Amaziah	7:10–17
8	Fruit Basket Upset	8:1–14
9	Good News, Finally!	9:11–15

Date. Amos ministered in Israel for about a year. His ministry occurred two years before a violent earthquake there in 760 B.C. He probably compiled his messages later in life, but he did not choose to record them in the order that the events occurred.

Purpose. Amos was angry. He was appalled. For two hundred years, his people had mixed their worship of Jehovah with worship of Baal and worship of the golden calf at Bethel. Amos could tolerate it no more. On the energy of his own righteous indignation, he traveled to Bethel to confront the king and priest. He traveled there to speak the truth. Amos' message was applicable to all of Israel and to all believers today. God will hold us accountable for our faithfulness in worship.

Historical Background. Unlike many of his fellow prophets, Amos prophesied during a relatively stable and seemingly prosperous time in the divided kingdoms. During the reigns of Uzziah in Judah (792–740 B.C.) and Jeroboam II in Israel (793–753 B.C.), both countries enjoyed prosperity and political success. The Assyrian conflict with Israel, led by Menahem, was still some years in the future, though the Assyrians were already casting a great shadow over Israel's borders. Judah was more secure and would not suffer a serious outside threat for many years.

Culturally and spiritually, though, the situation in the two kingdoms was quickly deteriorating. Political smugness and security were accompanied by a collective turning away from God. The times were typified by the increased worship of idols and other false gods. While the military invasions of Israel and Judah were still in the future, the influence of outside cultures and religions was well under way. Amos and his contemporaries could see past the affluence to the consequences of the lifestyle of the Hebrew people. During an era that felt safe, the righteous prophet had a hard time finding people who would listen.

Justice and Righteousness. Whereas Hosea emphasized God's love and forgiveness in his writings, Amos concentrated on God's justice and righteousness. To Amos, the apostasy of his fellow Jews was a terrible affront to God's requirements for justice and righteousness. Amos knew that these requirements were essential for life to be truly productive. As Amos described in 5:24, justice is like a river and righteousness like a stream. For life to flourish, it must have that water. Though the status of everyday life seemed fine all around, Amos knew that a day of judgment was soon coming, and that God's justice would be poured out on the unrighteous. His message was saturated with that reality.

OPEN **1.** What is your vocation? If you could change vocations for a week, what would you try? **2.** What "earth-shaking" event has happened to you within the last two years? How are you a different person today because of it? **3.** This week, have the circumstances in your life been as gentle as a lamb or fierce as a lion?

STUDY **1.** Does Amos have the proper credentials to speak for God? Why should the people listen to him? **2.** How might the people have reacted as the shepherd began preaching: Hushed silence? Joyous welcome? Curious? Concerned? **3.** Verse 2 has been called Amos' theme verse. Hence, what do we have in store? **4.** What do you suppose the people said among themselves as Amos spoke against their neighbors: "They have it coming"? "We are better than they are"? "Whew! For a minute I thought it was us!"? "Can we help in the destruction"? **5.** How might they have reacted to the prophecy against Judah (2:4–5)? Is Judah's sin as grievous as those of Israel's foreign neighbors? If so, why? **6.** How are the sins of Israel's neighbors similar? How are they different? Which of these sins are prevalent today? **7.** By what standard will the nations be judged: God's law? The law of brotherly love? The law of conscience? The law of the land? What does this reveal about God's role in international affairs? Do you think Israel would have been surprised by this? Why or why not? **8.** If you were to describe the God portrayed here in one word, would it be: Loving? Consistent? Patient? Mean? Judgmental? Angry? Other?

APPLY **1.** When have you felt unqualified to do something for God but did it anyway? How did you get past the fear? **2.** What issue could you "roar" against today? What else could you do to facilitate change: Pray? Organize a group? Organize a boycott? Work within the

1 The words of Amos, one of the shepherds of Tekoa—what he saw concerning Israel two years before the earthquake, when Uzziah was king of Judah and Jeroboam son of Jehoash[a] was king of Israel.

2 He said:

"The LORD roars from Zion
and thunders from Jerusalem;
the pastures of the shepherds dry up,[b]
and the top of Carmel withers."

Judgment on Israel's Neighbors

3 This is what the LORD says:

"For three sins of Damascus,
even for four, I will not turn back ⌞my wrath⌟.
Because she threshed Gilead
with sledges having iron teeth,
4 I will send fire upon the house of Hazael
that will consume the fortresses of Ben-Hadad.
5 I will break down the gate of Damascus;
I will destroy the king who is in[c] the Valley of Aven[d]
and the one who holds the scepter in Beth Eden.
The people of Aram will go into exile to Kir,"
says the LORD.

6 This is what the LORD says:

"For three sins of Gaza,
even for four, I will not turn back ⌞my wrath⌟.
Because she took captive whole communities
and sold them to Edom,
7 I will send fire upon the walls of Gaza
that will consume her fortresses.
8 I will destroy the king[e] of Ashdod
and the one who holds the scepter in Ashkelon.
I will turn my hand against Ekron,
till the last of the Philistines is dead,"
says the Sovereign LORD.

9 This is what the LORD says:
"For three sins of Tyre,
even for four, I will not turn back ⌞my wrath⌟.
Because she sold whole communities of captives to Edom,
disregarding a treaty of brotherhood,

[a] 1 Hebrew *Joash,* a variant of *Jehoash* [b] 2 Or *shepherds mourn* [c] 5 Or *the inhabitants of* [d] 5 *Aven* means *wickedness.* [e] 8 Or *inhabitants*

1:1 Amos. Amos was more comfortable herding sheep than he was prophesying to people. However, with "the LORD upholds" as his given name, this fruit farmer was a powerful prophet, despite his unpopular message.

1:2–2:16 Just when Israel thought Amos's harsh message was for its neighbors alone (1:2–2:3), Israel found itself on his bad list, too (2:4–2:16). Social injustice and self-indulgence are the themes of Amos's charge.

1:2 roars. A lion is a fearful force when it comes to a shepherd's flock. A shepherd himself, Amos knew the potency of his prophecy. He was sent by God to warn Israel of the impending doom.

1:3 For three sins. Amos pictured God losing patience over repeated disobedience (vv. 6,9,11,13; 2:1,4,6).

[10]I will send fire upon the walls of Tyre
that will consume her fortresses."

[11]This is what the LORD says:

"For three sins of Edom,
even for four, I will not turn back ⌞my wrath⌟.
Because he pursued his brother with a sword,
stifling all compassion,[a]
because his anger raged continually
and his fury flamed unchecked,
[12]I will send fire upon Teman
that will consume the fortresses of Bozrah."

[13]This is what the LORD says:

"For three sins of Ammon,
even for four, I will not turn back ⌞my wrath⌟.
Because he ripped open the pregnant women of Gilead
in order to extend his borders,
[14]I will set fire to the walls of Rabbah
that will consume her fortresses
amid war cries on the day of battle,
amid violent winds on a stormy day.
[15]Her king[b] will go into exile,
he and his officials together,"
says the LORD.

2 This is what the LORD says:

"For three sins of Moab,
even for four, I will not turn back ⌞my wrath⌟.
Because he burned, as if to lime,
the bones of Edom's king,
[2]I will send fire upon Moab
that will consume the fortresses of Kerioth.[c]
Moab will go down in great tumult
amid war cries and the blast of the trumpet.
[3]I will destroy her ruler
and kill all her officials with him,"
says the LORD.

[4]This is what the LORD says:

"For three sins of Judah,
even for four, I will not turn back ⌞my wrath⌟.
Because they have rejected the law of the LORD
and have not kept his decrees,
because they have been led astray by false gods,[d]
the gods[e] their ancestors followed,
[5]I will send fire upon Judah
that will consume the fortresses of Jerusalem."

[a]11 Or *sword / and destroyed his allies* [b]15 Or / *Molech*; Hebrew *malcam* [c]2 Or *of her cities* [d]4 Or *by lies*
[e]4 Or *lies*

system? Contact the right people in the right places? Gather ideas from others? **3.** Amos criticized Israel's behavior by first criticizing that of her enemies, and then catching her off guard. What strategy works best if someone is to criticize *your* behavior?

2:4 they have rejected the law of the LORD. Judah and Israel were condemned for their atrocities along with their neighbors. But there was one difference: Judah and Israel knew better.

OPEN **1.** Where does God speak to you most clearly: In nature? In friendships? In art? In worship? In Scripture? In prayer? **2.** Recall a time when you deserved to be disciplined, but weren't. What happened? **3.** What money-making venture did you enjoy as a child?

STUDY **1.** The shepherd from Judah now turns to Israel. What do you imagine was the Israelites' response: Shock? Anger? Humility? Bewilderment? **2.** What do the six sins listed in verses 6–8 have in common? **3.** What purpose does bringing up the Amorites, the Exodus, the prophets and the Nazirites serve in Amos' argument (vv. 9–12)? **4.** What kind of person would travel in social circles of those indicted here? Is Amos' indictment of them like a class action suit today? Why or why not? **5.** Which statement comes closest to this crowd's motto: Get while the gettin's good? God helps those who help themselves? Do unto others before they do unto you? Some of us have it, some of us don't? **6.** What will happen to the Israelites in turn (vv. 13–16)?

APPLY **1.** If you were given the task of judging Israel's sins listed here, which would you go easiest on? Which would you judge more harshly? Why? **2.** In verses 9–11, God lists some of the things he had done for Israel. If God were to list some of the things he has done for you, what two or three actions would be at the top of the list? **3.** How does God's grace to you call you to behave toward people in need around you?

Judgment on Israel

6 This is what the LORD says:

"For three sins of Israel,
even for four, I will not turn back ⌞my wrath⌟.
They sell the righteous for silver,
and the needy for a pair of sandals.
7 They trample on the heads of the poor
as upon the dust of the ground
and deny justice to the oppressed.
Father and son use the same girl
and so profane my holy name.
8 They lie down beside every altar
on garments taken in pledge.
In the house of their god
they drink wine taken as fines.

9 "I destroyed the Amorite before them,
though he was tall as the cedars
and strong as the oaks.
I destroyed his fruit above
and his roots below.

10 "I brought you up out of Egypt,
and I led you forty years in the desert
to give you the land of the Amorites.
11 I also raised up prophets from among your sons
and Nazirites from among your young men.
Is this not true, people of Israel?"
declares the LORD.
12 "But you made the Nazirites drink wine
and commanded the prophets not to prophesy.

13 "Now then, I will crush you
as a cart crushes when loaded with grain.
14 The swift will not escape,
the strong will not muster their strength,
and the warrior will not save his life.
15 The archer will not stand his ground,
the fleet-footed soldier will not get away,
and the horseman will not save his life.
16 Even the bravest warriors
will flee naked on that day,"
declares the LORD.

2:6 Amos admonished the Israelites for devaluing human life. God's policy of working off a debt (Deut. 15:12) was stretched into extortion. In this unbalanced system of retribution, a pair of sandals would have been worth more than a debtor's dignity (Deut. 15:12).

2:8 lie down beside every altar. Sinful Israel slept soundly on its own guilty conscience near places of worship.

2:9 I destroyed the Amorite. God reminded Israel that it did not arrive at success single-handedly. God uprooted and destroyed its enemies in Canaan, represented here by the formidable Amorites.

2:10 I brought you up … I led you. Israel did not come from bad seed. God reminded the people of their roots. They are a chosen people with high hopes.

2:11 raised up prophets. Amos was an example of the living caution signs God had placed among his people in order to keep them on the right track. Unfortunately, Israel recklessly maneuvered around the warnings and would now suffer the consequences.

2:16 on that day. Little did Israel know Assyria would soon provide discipline on demand. As the Lord's tool, Assyria would conquer Israel and take it captive.

Witnesses Summoned Against Israel

3 Hear this word the LORD has spoken against you, O people of Israel—against the whole family I brought up out of Egypt:

[2] "You only have I chosen
of all the families of the earth;
therefore I will punish you
for all your sins."

[3] Do two walk together
unless they have agreed to do so?
[4] Does a lion roar in the thicket
when he has no prey?
Does he growl in his den
when he has caught nothing?
[5] Does a bird fall into a trap on the ground
where no snare has been set?
Does a trap spring up from the earth
when there is nothing to catch?
[6] When a trumpet sounds in a city,
do not the people tremble?
When disaster comes to a city,
has not the LORD caused it?

[7] Surely the Sovereign LORD does nothing
without revealing his plan
to his servants the prophets.

[8] The lion has roared—
who will not fear?
The Sovereign LORD has spoken—
who can but prophesy?

[9] Proclaim to the fortresses of Ashdod
and to the fortresses of Egypt:
"Assemble yourselves on the mountains of Samaria;
see the great unrest within her
and the oppression among her people."

[10] "They do not know how to do right," declares the LORD,
"who hoard plunder and loot in their fortresses."

[11] Therefore this is what the Sovereign LORD says:

"An enemy will overrun the land;
he will pull down your strongholds
and plunder your fortresses."

OPEN **1.** If you could choose one relative, living or dead, to spend a day with, who would it be? Why? **2.** If your possessions make one statement about you, what do they say: Middle class? Frugal? Extravagant? Misfit? **3.** Where would you enjoy having a winter house? A summer house?

STUDY **1.** Israel is called "family" and "chosen" (vv. 1–2). What is implied by these names? **2.** What is the purpose of Amos' rhetorical questions in verses 3–6? What kind of answers is Amos expecting from these examples of cause and effect? Why is this a good method of teaching? **3.** How many in your group agree with the statement in verse 7? How many disagree? Support your positions. **4.** What moves Amos (or anyone else) to prophesy (vv. 7–8; 1:1–2)? **5.** What do their households and furnishings tell you about the lifestyle of these people? What contemporary images does this bring to mind? **6.** Pagan nations are summoned to be witnesses (v. 9). What would this reveal to Israel? To the pagan nations? **7.** How could "chosen" people come to the point where, "They do not know how to do right" (v. 10)? **8.** The remains of an animal were often kept as evidence of the slaughter. The corner of the couch was the place of honor. How many will be rescued from God's punishment? What social level is Amos talking about in verse 12?

APPLY **1.** If your behavior is going to cause you or others problems, how would you prefer to be warned: Face to face? By letter? By phone? In a support group? **2.** How might you become more free *from* your possessions, so that you might become more free *with* your possessions? **3.** In terms of your life right now would you say: I'm in the lion's mouth? I see the lion? I just got out of the lion's mouth? I didn't even know I was in the jungle?

3:1 against the whole family. When the head of the household calls a family meeting, the topic is serious. The family name was on the line.

3:2 of all the families of the earth. God lifted Israel's eyes from a greedy perspective on itself. Generations of people could have been chosen, but they were not. How then could Israel be so blind to its privileges and responsibilities?

3:3–6 Beginning with the innocent scene of a twosome walking (v. 3), the images progress from bad to worse. An animal fell prey (v. 4), a bird was trapped (v. 5) and a people were overcome (v. 6). Amos used cause-and-effect statements to build a case for the inevitable.

3:8 The lion returned as an image of the Lord's vengeance on Israel (1:2).

3:9 Amos issued an imaginary invitation to the neighboring pagan states. Even pagans would be aghast at the atrocities within Israel!

[12]This is what the LORD says:

"As a shepherd saves from the lion's mouth
only two leg bones or a piece of an ear,
so will the Israelites be saved,
those who sit in Samaria
on the edge of their beds
and in Damascus on their couches.[a]"

[13]"Hear this and testify against the house of Jacob," declares the
Lord, the LORD God Almighty.

[14]"On the day I punish Israel for her sins,
I will destroy the altars of Bethel;
the horns of the altar will be cut off
and fall to the ground.
[15]I will tear down the winter house
along with the summer house;
the houses adorned with ivory will be destroyed
and the mansions will be demolished,"
declares the LORD.

Israel Has Not Returned to God

4 Hear this word, you cows of Bashan on Mount Samaria,
you women who oppress the poor and crush the needy
and say to your husbands, "Bring us some drinks!"
[2]The Sovereign LORD has sworn by his holiness:
"The time will surely come
when you will be taken away with hooks,
the last of you with fishhooks.
[3]You will each go straight out
through breaks in the wall,
and you will be cast out toward Harmon,[b]"
declares the LORD.

[4]"Go to Bethel and sin;
go to Gilgal and sin yet more.
Bring your sacrifices every morning,
your tithes every three years.[c]
[5]Burn leavened bread as a thank offering
and brag about your freewill offerings—
boast about them, you Israelites,
for this is what you love to do,"
declares the Sovereign LORD.

[a]*12* The meaning of the Hebrew for this line is uncertain. [b]*3* Masoretic Text; with a different word division of the Hebrew (see Septuagint) *out, O mountain of oppression* [c]*4* Or *tithes on the third day*

OPEN 1. What situations make you the most angry? **2.** Which "cow" do you most identify with right now: Newborn calf? Milk cow? Angry bull? Rodeo steer? Prize heifer? Fatted calf ready for slaughter?

STUDY 1. Bashan was an area known for its "fatted" cattle. Is verse 1 a sexist statement? What would a contemporary slur sound like? **2.** What is the attitude of these women: "I wear the pants in this house"? "The world exists to serve me"? "I deserve a break today"? "My needs come first"? **3.** What will be the fate of the women? Why does Amos use examples such as cow and meat hooks? **4.** Verses 4–5 speak of going to worship centers and sinning. How is that possible? How would you describe this worship: Style without substance? Ceremony without faith? Faith without action? The right words with the wrong spirit? **5.** Amos is angry and sarcastic in verses 1–5, but what about God? In verses 6–11, what emotional quality is attributed to him? How is his divine wrath expressed in

---

3:12 those who sit. Amos' warnings of a lion attack fell on the lazy ears of those lounging in luxury. The wealthy in Israel shrugged off all signs of danger.

3:13 testify. Courtroom imagery conveyed the seriousness of Israel's crimes against humanity.

4:1 cows of Bashan. Bashan, a lush pastureland, catered to its cattle (Ps. 22:12). Likewise, the men of Israel pampered the needs of these luxury-loving women.

4:4 Go to Bethel ... Gilgal. Amos very clearly pinpointed places of worship. However, Israel shamelessly used them as sites for engaging in activities that were sinful.

4:5 this is what you love to do. Israel's cafeteria-style religion enabled them to pick and choose what they liked. Unfortunately, Israel's disregard for the whole of God's commands was not overlooked.

[6]"I gave you empty stomachs[a] in every city
and lack of bread in every town,
yet you have not returned to me,"
declares the LORD.

[7]"I also withheld rain from you
when the harvest was still three months away.
I sent rain on one town,
but withheld it from another.
One field had rain;
another had none and dried up.
[8]People staggered from town to town for water
but did not get enough to drink,
yet you have not returned to me,"
declares the LORD.

[9]"Many times I struck your gardens and vineyards,
I struck them with blight and mildew.
Locusts devoured your fig and olive trees,
yet you have not returned to me,"
declares the LORD.

[10]"I sent plagues among you
as I did to Egypt.
I killed your young men with the sword,
along with your captured horses.
I filled your nostrils with the stench of your camps,
yet you have not returned to me,"
declares the LORD.

[11]"I overthrew some of you
as I[b] overthrew Sodom and Gomorrah.
You were like a burning stick snatched from the fire,
yet you have not returned to me,"
declares the LORD.

[12]"Therefore this is what I will do to you, Israel,
and because I will do this to you,
prepare to meet your God, O Israel."

[13]He who forms the mountains,
creates the wind,
and reveals his thoughts to man,

[a]6 Hebrew *you cleanness of teeth* [b]11 Hebrew *God*

a way different from human anger? **6.** We see here five unsuccessful attempts by God to get Israel's attention. As a stubborn Israelite, which of these divine acts would you have ignored? Which would you have heeded? **7.** What might the people have thought when Egypt, Sodom and Gomorrah were brought up: "But we are God's chosen"? "We're a cut above them"? "Maybe we should listen to this shepherd"? "Now we're afraid"? "What does he know anyway"? **8.** What does it mean to "prepare to meet your God" (v. 12)? Would this instill fear, joy, apathy or what? Why?

APPLY 1. For Amos, the way we treat the needy is the area by which we are judged. To what extent do you get involved in trying to alleviate poverty and oppression? Why don't you do more: Selfishness? Ignorance? Politics? Caught up in other things? **2.** What would it mean for you to "prepare to meet your God"? Would that instill in you fear or joy? **3.** Speaking of meeting God, how would you describe your relationship with him: We met long ago and have been friends ever since? We've met, and our friendship is growing daily? We just met? I am still waiting to be introduced?

4:6–11 Amos described five disasters in Israel's past. From hunger to defeat, God revealed the many ways he addressed Israel's rebellion. However, like a wayward child, Israel soon forgot the lessons learned.

4:6 yet you have not returned to me. Punishment was not an end in itself. The calamities were a form of discipline, prodding God's people to repent.

4:7–8 did not get enough to drink. Demonstrating the people's dependence on him, God withheld just enough water to ruin a harvest and merely tease Israel's thirst.

4:9 I struck your gardens. As quickly as Israel thought her woes were over, God destroyed her. Locusts and blight were failed attempts to get Israel's attention.

4:10 as I did to Egypt. The northern kingdom refused to learn from its family history. Israel suffered the same fate as its ancestors' enemies (Ex. 7:14–12:30).

4:12 Therefore this is what I will do. God's review of Hebrew history was a lesson in cause and effect. Israel's disobedience and the resulting consequences are now on a collision course.

4:13 Amos listed God's credentials to certify the authenticity of the threat

he who turns dawn to darkness,
and treads the high places of the earth—
the LORD God Almighty is his name.

OPEN 1. As a child, what places were you told not to go? Why were they off limits? Did you secretly go there anyway? **2.** When did you feel the most "alive" this week?

STUDY 1. A lament is a poem or song, of grief. What emotions and thoughts are associated with the various stages of grieving? **2.** Why does Amos call Israel "Virgin" (v. 2)? What is he lamenting? What ideal and what people seem to have been the main victims of life in Israel? **3.** The people would have come to Gilgal and Bethel for religious services. They would have been a happy crowd. How would they feel after Amos' message? **4.** What kind of ratings would you give Amos for tact? For courage? For integrity? **5.** Why were people urged not to seek God where they normally worshiped (v. 5)? **6.** How could the people "turn justice into bitterness and cast the righteousness to the ground" (v. 7)? What does this have to do with their temple activity? With their daily lifestyle? **7.** How does this list of wrongdoing (vv. 11–12) compare with the list in 2:6–16? What is the effect on the poor financially? Socially? Legally? Spiritually? Emotionally? **8.** Having built mansions and planted vineyards, how would the people feel after being told they would never drink the wine or live in the mansions: Disgusted? Enraged? Bitter? Hopeless? Helpless? Quietly penitent? **9.** What rays of hope do you sense in this lament?

APPLY 1. Recall a time you wanted, even prayed, for someone you loved to make a positive change in their life, and they didn't. What happened? How did you feel? **2.** The Lord says, "Seek me and live" (v. 4). How will you do that this week? What spiritual disciplines help you feel more alive in the Lord? **3.** Amos preaches both bad news and

A Lament and Call to Repentance

5 Hear this word, O house of Israel, this lament I take up concerning you:

2 "Fallen is Virgin Israel,
never to rise again,
deserted in her own land,
with no one to lift her up."

3 This is what the Sovereign LORD says:

"The city that marches out a thousand strong for Israel
will have only a hundred left;
the town that marches out a hundred strong
will have only ten left."

4 This is what the LORD says to the house of Israel:

"Seek me and live;
5 do not seek Bethel,
do not go to Gilgal,
do not journey to Beersheba.
For Gilgal will surely go into exile,
and Bethel will be reduced to nothing.[a]"
6 Seek the LORD and live,
or he will sweep through the house of Joseph like a fire;
it will devour,
and Bethel will have no one to quench it.

7 You who turn justice into bitterness
and cast righteousness to the ground
8 (he who made the Pleiades and Orion,
who turns blackness into dawn
and darkens day into night,
who calls for the waters of the sea
and pours them out over the face of the land—
the LORD is his name—
9 he flashes destruction on the stronghold
and brings the fortified city to ruin),
10 you hate the one who reproves in court
and despise him who tells the truth.

11 You trample on the poor
and force him to give you grain.

[a]5 Or *grief;* or *wickedness;* Hebrew *aven,* a reference to Beth Aven (a derogatory name for Bethel)

against Israel. God was prepared to carry out all he had decreed.

5:5 Beersheba. If the people were to seek God, he would not be found in a place, especially not in a defiled worship site. People were to seek him directly.

5:6 Amos described God's readiness to express mercy to those who truly repent.

5:7 justice into bitterness. Israel disabled justice by extorting the poor and seeking an extravagant, slovenly lifestyle (1:6; 4:1). Justice became as undesirable to Israel as a bitter taste.

5:8–9 Amos reminded the people of the omnipotence with which they were dealing. He slipped into a hymn-like soliloquy magnifying God's greatness.

5:11 trample on the poor. Amos exposed the social injustice against the poor (2:7). As a result, God would dis-

Therefore, though you have built stone mansions,
you will not live in them;
though you have planted lush vineyards,
you will not drink their wine.
12 For I know how many are your offenses
and how great your sins.

You oppress the righteous and take bribes
and you deprive the poor of justice in the courts.
13 Therefore the prudent man keeps quiet in such times,
for the times are evil.

14 Seek good, not evil,
that you may live.
Then the LORD God Almighty will be with you,
just as you say he is.
15 Hate evil, love good;
maintain justice in the courts.
Perhaps the LORD God Almighty will have mercy
on the remnant of Joseph.

16 Therefore this is what the Lord, the LORD God Almighty, says:

"There will be wailing in all the streets
and cries of anguish in every public square.
The farmers will be summoned to weep
and the mourners to wail.
17 There will be wailing in all the vineyards,
for I will pass through your midst,"
says the LORD.

The Day of the Lord

18 Woe to you who long
for the day of the LORD!
Why do you long for the day of the LORD?
That day will be darkness, not light.
19 It will be as though a man fled from a lion
only to meet a bear,
as though he entered his house
and rested his hand on the wall
only to have a snake bite him.
20 Will not the day of the LORD be darkness, not light—
pitch-dark, without a ray of brightness?

21 "I hate, I despise your religious feasts;
I cannot stand your assemblies.
22 Even though you bring me burnt offerings and grain offerings,
I will not accept them.

good news to Israel. Does his message to you bring to mind more things to lament, or more rays of hope? Choose one negative and one positive thing to pray about and share with the group.

OPEN 1. Complete this sentence: When the Lord comes again I will probably be found ______. **2.** In the next three months, what one day are you anticipating the most?

STUDY 1. The ancient Jews long for the coming of the "day of the LORD" (v. 18). What do you think they expect to happen? Why is Amos warning them not to be so eager? **2.** Why does God despise their religious practices? **3.** Verse 24 speaks of water being poured out forever. Elsewhere, water symbolizes life consecrated to God. Together, what does this water symbol imply for their worship? Their mission? **4.** What is the "bottom line" for Israel?

regard the distinction of the wealthy by withholding their claims to fame.

5:15 maintain justice. Israel had a long way to go in order to restore an unjust society.

5:16–17 Vineyards, which typically represented bounty and gladness, would now be sites of sorrow (Isa. 16:10). God's presence among them would bring sadness, not comfort.

5:18 day of the LORD. Amos describes a day of God's ultimate victory over evil (Isa. 5:19). **darkness, not light.** A day that Israel thought would bring reward to God's people would instead bring unexpected doom (Joel 2:1–2).

5:21–23 Even Israel's intentions could not be credited as good. Hypocrisy tainted every religious effort.

APPLY **1.** Are you yearning for the "day of the LORD"? Why or why not? **2.** What do you think God would say about your worship: Keep it up? Wake up? Shape up? Ship out? Other? **3.** If Amos were speaking in your church, what would he speak on: Community? Worship? Finances? Justice for the poor? False gods? What contemporary illustrations would he use? How would you respond?

OPEN What three things give you a secure feeling? When was the last time you had everything going for you?

STUDY **1.** Who does Amos go after in this section of his prophecy? What is their sin? **2.** How is "security" related to "complacency" (v. 1)? Where should these people have found their security? **3.** Is Amos condemning a life of luxury, or something more? Explain. **4.** What will happen to those who have the most prosperity and privilege and yet abuse it (v. 7; Luke 12:48)?

APPLY **1.** Tell three areas of your life in which you feel somewhat insecure. **2.** Where might you be complacent: At home? With friends? At church? **3.** The more secure you are in relation to God, are you more, or less, eager to serve him?

OPEN What is one thing you said you'd never do again, but ended up doing anyway?

STUDY **1.** What has the Lord sworn to do? Could he have expressed himself any more strongly? **2.** How extensive will the coming judgment be? **3.** What futile activities did the people take pride in (vv. 11–13)? **4.** How did they turn "justice into poison" and "the fruit of righteousness

Though you bring choice fellowship offerings,[a]
I will have no regard for them.
23 Away with the noise of your songs!
I will not listen to the music of your harps.
24 But let justice roll on like a river,
righteousness like a never-failing stream!

25 "Did you bring me sacrifices and offerings
forty years in the desert, O house of Israel?
26 You have lifted up the shrine of your king,
the pedestal of your idols,
the star of your god[b]—
which you made for yourselves.
27 Therefore I will send you into exile beyond Damascus,"
says the LORD, whose name is God Almighty.

Woe to the Complacent

6 Woe to you who are complacent in Zion,
and to you who feel secure on Mount Samaria,
you notable men of the foremost nation,
to whom the people of Israel come!
2 Go to Calneh and look at it;
go from there to great Hamath,
and then go down to Gath in Philistia.
Are they better off than your two kingdoms?
Is their land larger than yours?
3 You put off the evil day
and bring near a reign of terror.
4 You lie on beds inlaid with ivory
and lounge on your couches.
You dine on choice lambs
and fattened calves.
5 You strum away on your harps like David
and improvise on musical instruments.
6 You drink wine by the bowlful
and use the finest lotions,
but you do not grieve over the ruin of Joseph.
7 Therefore you will be among the first to go into exile;
your feasting and lounging will end.

The Lord Abhors the Pride of Israel

8 The Sovereign LORD has sworn by himself—the LORD God Almighty declares:

"I abhor the pride of Jacob
and detest his fortresses;
I will deliver up the city
and everything in it."

[a]22 Traditionally *peace offerings* [b]26 Or *lifted up Sakkuth your king / and Kaiwan your idols, / your star-gods;* Septuagint *lifted up the shrine of Molech / and the star of your god Rephan, / their idols*

5:24 like a never-failing stream. Israel's dried-up enthusiasm for its religious traditions should have been replaced by a recommitment to justice among the poor which could have brought peaceful living.

6:1 complacent. Israel was a self-serving, albeit successful, nation. Israel sought comfort in trusting their own temporal success rather than the eternal God.

[9]If ten men are left in one house, they too will die. [10]And if a relative
who is to burn the bodies comes to carry them out of the house and
asks anyone still hiding there, "Is anyone with you?" and he says,
"No," then he will say, "Hush! We must not mention the name of the
LORD."

[11]For the LORD has given the command,
and he will smash the great house into pieces
and the small house into bits.

[12]Do horses run on the rocky crags?
Does one plow there with oxen?
But you have turned justice into poison
and the fruit of righteousness into bitterness—
[13]you who rejoice in the conquest of Lo Debar[a]
and say, "Did we not take Karnaim[b] by our own strength?"

[14]For the LORD God Almighty declares,
"I will stir up a nation against you, O house of Israel,
that will oppress you all the way
from Lebo[c] Hamath to the valley of the Arabah."

Locusts, Fire and a Plumb Line

7 This is what the Sovereign LORD showed me: He was preparing
swarms of locusts after the king's share had been harvested
and just as the second crop was coming up. [2]When they had stripped
the land clean, I cried out, "Sovereign LORD, forgive! How can Jacob
survive? He is so small!"

[3]So the LORD relented.

"This will not happen," the LORD said.

[4]This is what the Sovereign LORD showed me: The Sovereign LORD
was calling for judgment by fire; it dried up the great deep and devoured the land. [5]Then I cried out, "Sovereign LORD, I beg you, stop!
How can Jacob survive? He is so small!"

[6]So the LORD relented.

"This will not happen either," the Sovereign LORD said.

[7]This is what he showed me: The Lord was standing by a wall that
had been built true to plumb, with a plumb line in his hand. [8]And the
LORD asked me, "What do you see, Amos?"

"A plumb line," I replied.

[a]13 Lo Debar means *nothing*. [b]13 Karnaim means *horns*; *horn* here symbolizes strength. [c]14 Or *from the entrance to*

into bitterness" (v. 12)? **5.** Does the punishment fit the crime (v. 14)?

APPLY 1. What is the difference between pride and confidence? How can you develop confidence without pride? **2.** If you were "The Little Engine That Could," what would you be saying about your life right now: I don't think I can? I think I can? I know I can? I thought I could? **3.** What "poisonous" or "bitter" place (v. 12) might be in your life today? How can it become just or fruitful?

OPEN When you were a child in grade school, who was most likely to speak up for you or defend you?

STUDY 1. Who in your group has any experience with swarming locusts, consuming fire or a plumb line? **2.** What do the three visions of Amos have in common (vv. 1–9)? How do they differ? Is the judgment conveyed here total? Partial? Universal? Inescapable? Exacting? **3.** What do these visions say about the purpose and character of God? Of Amos? **4.** What would be unusual about a person from Judah speaking up on behalf of Israel? Do prayers for mercy change God's mind (Gen. 18, where Abraham interceded likewise for Sodom and Gomorrah)? Explain. **5.** Why would God relent on the first two judgments but not on the third? Why doesn't Amos object to God's action in the third vision?

6:10–11 Amos described devastating vengeance on the citizens of the northern kingdom.

6:10 must not mention. The Lord's destruction would be so severe even a survivor would not be allowed to mention the Lord's name. Doing so might call attention and incur God's wrath.

6:12 Israel was a pitiful example of good gone wrong. People who were meant to be just and right citizens under God were now a sickened society.

6:13 by our own strength. Israel may have won the battles in nearby cities, but it would soon lose the war to conquering Assyria.

7:1 what the Sovereign LORD showed me. God spoke to Amos in a dramatic vision, which Amos communicated to the people in his prophecy. **king's share.** According to custom, the king received his taxes in the form of harvested goods.

7:3 So the LORD relented. Tiny Israel was rescued from the overwhelming calamity.

7:8–9 Israel was measured according to God's standard for righteousness and justice. Unfortunately, it failed inspection. They deserved total destruction not restoration and forgiveness.

7:8 plumb line. A plumb line is an essential carpenter's tool. It is a weighted string used to prove a wall's vertical straightness.

APPLY Were God to check out what you have "built" in your life with a "plumb line," what do you think would be his conclusion: Tear it down? Good enough for government work? Kudos to the builder?

OPEN 1. What did your father do for a living? What impact did that have on your development? **2.** What are the most and least favorite jobs you have held?

STUDY 1. How does Amaziah's accusation (vv. 10–11) compare with the Lord's message given to Amos (5:27; 7:9)? **2.** Why would Amaziah want Amos out of Israel? **3.** Why would Amaziah keep Amos from speaking God's word when Amaziah's office identified him as being a servant of the Lord? **4.** What were Amos' credentials to be a prophet? Would Amos rather be farming in Judah or prophesying in Israel? **5.** Do you hear pity or anger in Amos' voice as he utters the words of verse 17? Why?

APPLY 1. Everyone is to be a minister (2 Cor. 5:20). Who are the ministers in your group? How does each member of your group minister to one another? **2.** If there is one thing out of the ordinary that God is calling you to do, what is it?

OPEN 1. What is some bad news you have had to deliver: Accident? Death? Failing grades? Job loss? Jury vote? How did you prepare yourself to deliver the news? **2.** Have you received bad news recently? How did you deal with it after you heard it? **3.** If a famine swept the land, what food would you miss most?

STUDY 1. This is Amos' fourth vision (7:1–9 for the

Then the Lord said, "Look, I am setting a plumb line among my
people Israel; I will spare them no longer.

9 "The high places of Isaac will be destroyed
and the sanctuaries of Israel will be ruined;
with my sword I will rise against the house of Jeroboam."

Amos and Amaziah

10 Then Amaziah the priest of Bethel sent a message to Jeroboam
king of Israel: "Amos is raising a conspiracy against you in the very
heart of Israel. The land cannot bear all his words. 11 For this is what
Amos is saying:

" 'Jeroboam will die by the sword,
and Israel will surely go into exile,
away from their native land.' "

12 Then Amaziah said to Amos, "Get out, you seer! Go back to the
land of Judah. Earn your bread there and do your prophesying there.
13 Don't prophesy anymore at Bethel, because this is the king's sanctuary and the temple of the kingdom."

14 Amos answered Amaziah, "I was neither a prophet nor a
prophet's son, but I was a shepherd, and I also took care of sycamore-fig trees. 15 But the LORD took me from tending the flock and
said to me, 'Go, prophesy to my people Israel.' 16 Now then, hear the
word of the LORD. You say,

" 'Do not prophesy against Israel,
and stop preaching against the house of Isaac.'

17 "Therefore this is what the LORD says:

" 'Your wife will become a prostitute in the city,
and your sons and daughters will fall by the sword.
Your land will be measured and divided up,
and you yourself will die in a pagan[a] country.
And Israel will certainly go into exile,
away from their native land.' "

A Basket of Ripe Fruit

8 This is what the Sovereign LORD showed me: a basket of ripe fruit.
2 "What do you see, Amos?" he asked.
"A basket of ripe fruit," I answered.
Then the LORD said to me, "The time is ripe for my people Israel; I
will spare them no longer.
3 "In that day," declares the Sovereign LORD, "the songs in the temple
will turn to wailing.[b] Many, many bodies—flung everywhere! Silence!"

[a]17 Hebrew *an unclean* [b]3 Or *"the temple singers will wail*

7:11 Amaziah had heard enough. He mistook Amos's spiritual exhortation as *a political threat against the king.*

7:15 tending the flock. Prophesying for unrepentant people turned out to be a thankless job, similar to tending unfeeling sheep.

7:17 In the end, Amaziah's intolerance for Amos's warnings would result in a *total loss.* His abandoned wife would resort to prostitution in order to support herself. His children would die violently, and his land would be scattered. Amaziah had repeated these same words in verse 11 to King Jeroboam.

8:2 basket of ripe fruit. What seemed an innocent image of ready-to-eat fruit was actually a picture of impending punishment. Israel was now ready to accept its dues.

8:3 Silence. The deafening silence of death would fill the temple. No longer

[4] Hear this, you who trample the needy
and do away with the poor of the land,

[5] saying,

"When will the New Moon be over
that we may sell grain,
and the Sabbath be ended
that we may market wheat?"—
skimping the measure,
boosting the price
and cheating with dishonest scales,
[6] buying the poor with silver
and the needy for a pair of sandals,
selling even the sweepings with the wheat.

[7] The LORD has sworn by the Pride of Jacob: "I will never forget anything they have done.

[8] "Will not the land tremble for this,
and all who live in it mourn?
The whole land will rise like the Nile;
it will be stirred up and then sink
like the river of Egypt.

[9] "In that day," declares the Sovereign LORD,

"I will make the sun go down at noon
and darken the earth in broad daylight.
[10] I will turn your religious feasts into mourning
and all your singing into weeping.
I will make all of you wear sackcloth
and shave your heads.
I will make that time like mourning for an only son
and the end of it like a bitter day.

[11] "The days are coming," declares the Sovereign LORD,
"when I will send a famine through the land—
not a famine of food or a thirst for water,
but a famine of hearing the words of the LORD.
[12] Men will stagger from sea to sea
and wander from north to east,
searching for the word of the LORD,
but they will not find it.

[13] "In that day

"the lovely young women and strong young men
will faint because of thirst.
[14] They who swear by the shame[a] of Samaria,
or say, 'As surely as your god lives, O Dan,'

[a] 14 Or *by Ashima;* or *by the idol*

others). How is this vision like and unlike the last one? **2.** Consider the look, smell and taste of fruit that is overripe. What does this say about the condition Israel was in? **3.** Is this coming judgment seen as inevitable, postponable or avoidable? How so? Can God relent, as in the first two visions? **4.** What sins is Amos condemning in verses 4–6? Where else have you heard Amos sound this familiar theme? What could that repetition mean? **5.** Is this "God who won't forget" (v. 7) consistent, or inconsistent, with what you know of God? **6.** The coming doom is described as an earthquake, eclipse, famine and drought. Of these, which would be most frightening to you? Why? **7.** What lesson learned in fasting is learned the hard way in famine? **8.** What would a "famine of hearing the words of the LORD" (v. 11) entail? In such a time, what would be missing? What would run rampant?

APPLY 1. Comparing your church to a tree, what do you see: Baby seedling? Full blossoms? Green fruit? Good fruit? Overripe fruit? Explain. **2.** When it comes to hearing the Word of God are you in a time of feast or famine? Why? **3.** In your spiritual journey, where are the places you have gone, and the sources you have explored, seeking guidance from God for your life (v. 12)? Which part of your search came up empty? Which part has been fruitful?

a place for rejoicing, the temple now hosted silent suffering.

8:6 God reiterated the sorry situation Israel's extortion among the poor had caused. Crimes against a seemingly insignificant sector of society resulted in large-scale devastation (2:6).

8:7 Accustomed to disobedience, the people convinced themselves God did not notice their crimes. God's long memory is matched by his justice.

OPEN **1.** Who do you admire for: Telling it like it is? Taking criticism and making positive improvements? **2.** Do you prefer to face up to a problem and get it over with, or do you tend to put it off as long as possible?

STUDY **1.** What is meant by Amos seeing the Lord "standing by the altar" and the temple sanctuary coming down on their heads (v. 1)? **2.** How does this vision compare to the ones that preceded it? Are things getting better? Staying the same? Getting worse? **3.** How does this vision expand, confirm or contradict what you know of God? **4.** Is the Exodus of no more significance than the migration of other peoples the world over? Or what does verse 7 imply? **5.** What is the main message in verses 1–4: It is useless to run from God? You can't hide from God? Sin marks you for life? God is out to get you? Other? **6.** If you were an original recipient of this prophecy, how would you feel: Hunted? Haunted? Trapped? Terrified? **7.** Why would God not destroy all of Judah (v. 8)? How would Israelites know if they were one of the few not to be overtaken by disaster? What must life have been like for these shaken people? **8.** Who would dare say, "Disaster will not overtake or meet us" (v. 10): Optimist Club president? Irrational sentimentalist? Spiritually blind person? Other?

APPLY **1.** How do you attempt to hide from God: Ignore certain pressing issues? Skip church? Keep on moving and don't slow down? Stop praying and reading the Bible? Other? **2.** If God shook the church today, what would fall out? Would you? When have you experienced God shaking you? **3.** How do you accept critical news: Shoot the messenger? Pull the covers over your head? Grin and bear it? Praise the Lord, anyway? Act on it?

or, 'As surely as the god[a] of Beersheba lives'—
they will fall,
never to rise again."

Israel to Be Destroyed

9 I saw the Lord standing by the altar, and he said:

"Strike the tops of the pillars
so that the thresholds shake.
Bring them down on the heads of all the people;
those who are left I will kill with the sword.
Not one will get away,
none will escape.
2 Though they dig down to the depths of the grave,[b]
from there my hand will take them.
Though they climb up to the heavens,
from there I will bring them down.
3 Though they hide themselves on the top of Carmel,
there I will hunt them down and seize them.
Though they hide from me at the bottom of the sea,
there I will command the serpent to bite them.
4 Though they are driven into exile by their enemies,
there I will command the sword to slay them.
I will fix my eyes upon them
for evil and not for good."

5 The Lord, the LORD Almighty,
he who touches the earth and it melts,
and all who live in it mourn—
the whole land rises like the Nile,
then sinks like the river of Egypt—
6 he who builds his lofty palace[c] in the heavens
and sets its foundation[d] on the earth,
who calls for the waters of the sea
and pours them out over the face of the land—
the LORD is his name.

7 "Are not you Israelites
the same to me as the Cushites[e]?"
declares the LORD.
"Did I not bring Israel up from Egypt,
the Philistines from Caphtor[f]
and the Arameans from Kir?

8 "Surely the eyes of the Sovereign LORD
are on the sinful kingdom.

[a]14 Or *power* [b]2 Hebrew *to Sheol* [c]6 The meaning of the Hebrew for this phrase is uncertain. [d]6 The meaning of the Hebrew for this word is uncertain. [e]7 That is, people from the upper Nile region [f]7 That is, Crete

9:1 I saw the LORD. Amos's final vision is one of destruction (vv. 1–10) and hope for what is yet to come (vv. 11–15).

9:2–4 The imaginary fugitives instinctively hid. However, there was no refuge from God's wrath. The time had come for retribution (Ps. 139:7–8).

9:8 not totally destroy. What was only hinted at earlier (5:15) was now confirmed. A remnant of people would remain as a symbol of hope.

I will destroy it
from the face of the earth—
yet I will not totally destroy
the house of Jacob,"
declares the LORD.
9 "For I will give the command,
and I will shake the house of Israel
among all the nations
as grain is shaken in a sieve,
and not a pebble will reach the ground.
10 All the sinners among my people
will die by the sword,
all those who say,
'Disaster will not overtake or meet us.'

Israel's Restoration

11 "In that day I will restore
David's fallen tent.
I will repair its broken places,
restore its ruins,
and build it as it used to be,
12 so that they may possess the remnant of Edom
and all the nations that bear my name,[a]"
declares the LORD,
who will do these things.

13 "The days are coming," declares the LORD,
"when the reaper will be overtaken by the plowman
and the planter by the one treading grapes.
New wine will drip from the mountains
and flow from all the hills.
14 I will bring back my exiled[b] people Israel;
they will rebuild the ruined cities and live in them.
They will plant vineyards and drink their wine;
they will make gardens and eat their fruit.
15 I will plant Israel in their own land,
never again to be uprooted
from the land I have given them,"
says the LORD your God.

[a]12 Hebrew; Septuagint *so that the remnant of men / and all the nations that bear my name may seek ⌞the Lord⌟* [b]14 Or *will restore the fortunes of my*

OPEN 1. When it comes to gardening, do you have a green thumb or a brown one? How so? **2.** When it comes to repairing broken relationships or growing new ones, are you a green thumb or brown?

STUDY 1. To what does "in that day" and "David's fallen tent" (v. 11) refer? **2.** What promises does the Lord make (vv. 11–15)? **3.** What have the people endured to receive these promises (4:6–11)? **4.** How do the last words of Amos compare with his other words? Are these words in or out of character for Amos? **5.** Do you think verse 15 has come true? When?

APPLY 1. When have you felt as though you were back in the Promised Land after a long exile? **2.** Which area of your life needs a fresh touch of God's Spirit today? **3.** In silent review and prayer, ask God to use Amos to reveal any sin that needs to be addressed. Jot that on paper. Pair up and share Amos' promise of renewal with each other. (Share what's on the paper, only as you wish.) As a group, destroy the slips of paper (i.e. tear up or burn), thus symbolizing that God forgives and forgets our sin.

9:10 Some self-assured individuals denied God's vengeance. Yet they would be the first to experience it.

9:11 I will repair. Amos's words are pure refreshment to the repentant people. **as it used to be.** His prophecy now concludes on a hopeful note, recalling happier times like those during David and Solomon's reigns (Hos. 3:4–5). This same hope is evident all throughout the Old Testament.

9:12 Edom. Edom was public enemy number one, as far as Israel was concerned. Therefore, conquering it represented complete victory for Israel.

9:13–15 Contrasting an earlier description of agricultural disaster (4:6–11), Amos now portrayed a farmer's fantasy. God restored the land so that the people could hardly keep up with its bounty.

9:14–15 A welcome relief after a tumultuous journey, home never sounded so good to the exiled Israelites.

9:14 rebuild. A once devastated people would rebuild their lives from the ground up as a symbol of their restoration.

9:15 plant Israel in their own land. In the end, Israel learned the meaning of true security. A restored Israel found its home in God.

Obadiah

Author. The book of Obadiah was written by the prophet Obadiah. Little is known about the profile of this prophet except that his name means "worshiper of Yahweh."

Personal Reading	Group Study Topic and Reading	
1–14	Judgment of Edom	vv. 1–14
15–21	Restoration	vv. 15–21

Date. Because so little is known about Obadiah, the date of his prophecy is highly debated. Most scholars agree that it was given either during the reign of Jehoram (848–841 B.C.) or during the reign of Zedekiah, the last king of Judah (597–586 B.C.).

Purpose. It can seem petty to encourage people merely by telling them that their enemies will get what they deserve. Yet that was really what Obadiah was doing on the surface. He encouraged his people by reaffirming that their enemies would be destroyed in the end. Beneath the surface, his message reached even farther, though. Obadiah's message emphasized that God would take care of his own and that he would do whatever it took to be true to his promises. Obadiah's message of destruction for Edom was a message of hope for God's people, that their God was and is more powerful than any earthly kingdom or nation.

Historical Background. The feud between Israel and Edom dated back to the conflict between Jacob and Esau over their father's birthright (Gen. 27:41). Esau lost the birthright because of his twin brother's deceitfulness and his own lack of judgment. Esau's name became Edom, and the Edomites were his descendants.

The Edomites settled southeast of the Dead Sea. They refused to allow the Israelites to pass through their territory on the way into the Promised Land. God instructed the Israelites not to hate the Edomites because of their related ancestry (Deut. 23:7), but they still felt residual hostility. More than that, multiple conflicts divided the two cultures. During the reign of Jehoram, Edom revolted and even named its own king (2 Kin. 8:20–22). Under Amaziah's reign, Israel attacked and crushed Edom. During Ahaz's reign, Edom attacked Judah (2 Chr. 28:17).

Bad Blood. The conflict between Israel and Edom started as a family squabble. Certainly the birthright of a patriarch was a big issue, but through the years the conflict took on a different character—it became political and finally moral. To Obadiah, Edom represented all nations opposed to Israel. In other words, since Israel was God's holy nation, Israel's enemies were God's enemies and would be swept up in the impending destruction God's enemies would face. Although Israel and Judah would eventually fall to foreign powers, they had the promise from God that they would rise again. The destruction that would come to Edom would be permanent.

1The vision of Obadiah.

This is what the Sovereign LORD says about Edom—

We have heard a message from the LORD:
An envoy was sent to the nations to say,
"Rise, and let us go against her for battle"—

2"See, I will make you small among the nations;
you will be utterly despised.
3The pride of your heart has deceived you,
you who live in the clefts of the rocks[a]
and make your home on the heights,
you who say to yourself,
'Who can bring me down to the ground?'
4Though you soar like the eagle
and make your nest among the stars,
from there I will bring you down,"
declares the LORD.
5"If thieves came to you,
if robbers in the night—
Oh, what a disaster awaits you—
would they not steal only as much as they wanted?
If grape pickers came to you,
would they not leave a few grapes?
6But how Esau will be ransacked,
his hidden treasures pillaged!
7All your allies will force you to the border;
your friends will deceive and overpower you;
those who eat your bread will set a trap for you,[b]
but you will not detect it.

8"In that day," declares the LORD,
"will I not destroy the wise men of Edom,
men of understanding in the mountains of Esau?
9Your warriors, O Teman, will be terrified,
and everyone in Esau's mountains
will be cut down in the slaughter.
10Because of the violence against your brother Jacob,
you will be covered with shame;
you will be destroyed forever.
11On the day you stood aloof
while strangers carried off his wealth
and foreigners entered his gates
and cast lots for Jerusalem,
you were like one of them.

[a]3 Or *of Sela* [b]7 The meaning of the Hebrew for this clause is uncertain.

OPEN 1. Where was your safe place of retreat as a child? Why there? Where is such a place for you now? **2.** Is there one day that stands out as a day of disaster for your family? For your nation? What happened that day: Flood? Fire? Stock market crash? Serious accident? What good came of it?

STUDY 1. Who are the Edomites named after (Gen. 36:1,8–9)? What was the relationship like between Jacob and Esau (Gen. 27:41–44; 33:4,16–17)? What does Hebrews 12:15–17 say about this brotherly relationship? About the bitterness and godlessness of Esau? **2.** What natural fortifications give Edom an illusion of security (v. 3)? To whom are they still vulnerable (vv. 4,7)? **3.** What is the point of Obadiah's eagle imagery (v. 4; compare Isa. 40:30–31)? What message is intended by the poetic imagery in verses 5–6? **4.** What happens "in that day" of the Lord's judgment (vv. 8–21)? Why is this judgment coming upon Edom? Do you find Edom's bad attitude toward Judah surprising? Why or why not? What does this tell you about the history of relations between these nations? **5.** How do you think Israel responded to this message of doom for Edom, their enemy?

APPLY 1. Upon what rock-like structures might you be basing your security: An insurance policy? A church? A family inheritance? How might this "pride of your heart" be deceiving you? **2.** How do you respond when disaster befalls someone you know: Avoid the disaster, lest you also get hit? Rescue the perishing? Comfort the bereaved? Do what you can to prevent the disaster from happening again? Give an example. **3.** Edom was judged for not serving brother Jacob when Jacob was down and out. What down and out persons should you be serving? How might you begin to serve them this week?

---

1 An envoy had been sent to the nations, urging them to rise up against Edom. The prophet Obadiah announces that God is stirring up other nations to judge Edom for its arrogance and hostility toward Israel.

4 like the eagle. A common symbol of strength and pride. Edom is considered a powerful, even invincible nation.

5–6 Esau, a synonym for Edom, would be completely desolated. Although most thieves and grape pickers leave a little bit behind, all of Edom's hidden treasures would be carried away.

12 You should not look down on your brother
in the day of his misfortune,
nor rejoice over the people of Judah
in the day of their destruction,
nor boast so much
in the day of their trouble.
13 You should not march through the gates of my people
in the day of their disaster,
nor look down on them in their calamity
in the day of their disaster,
nor seize their wealth
in the day of their disaster.
14 You should not wait at the crossroads
to cut down their fugitives,
nor hand over their survivors
in the day of their trouble.

15 "The day of the LORD is near
for all nations.
As you have done, it will be done to you;
your deeds will return upon your own head.
16 Just as you drank on my holy hill,
so all the nations will drink continually;
they will drink and drink
and be as if they had never been.
17 But on Mount Zion will be deliverance;
it will be holy,
and the house of Jacob
will possess its inheritance.
18 The house of Jacob will be a fire
and the house of Joseph a flame;
the house of Esau will be stubble,
and they will set it on fire and consume it.
There will be no survivors
from the house of Esau."
The LORD has spoken.

19 People from the Negev will occupy
the mountains of Esau,
and people from the foothills will possess
the land of the Philistines.
They will occupy the fields of Ephraim and Samaria,
and Benjamin will possess Gilead.

OPEN 1. Where is your "spiritual home"? How long have you been away from there? What was your reunion like the last time you went there? **2.** What experience, if any, have you or your church had in helping to relocate "exiles"?

STUDY 1. What new parameters do you see in "the day of the LORD," as used in verse 15? By what logic will it come upon Edom? **2.** To whom is this word addressed? How are the house of Esau and the house of Jacob contrasted here? **3.** What would Edom have drunk on Mt. Zion (v. 16)? Is this drinking language meant literally or figuratively? Why do you think so (Jer. 25:15–16)? What is the message intended by this language? **4.** If Edom's allies will defeat her (v. 7), who will finish the job (vv. 19–21)? How total will be their ultimate defeat? **5.** In what ways would the return of the exiles (vv. 19–21) be a social event? A political event? A theological event?

APPLY 1. If God told you "as you have done, it will be done to you" (v. 15), how would you expect to fare? **2.** How would you respond if

15 The day of the Lord will bring judgment for all nations, not just Edom. Edom's imminent humiliation foreshadows God's judgment on all nations.

16 you drank on my holy hill. The Lord was angry with the Edomites for holding a drunken celebration in Jerusalem, God's holy hill. But other nations will also feel God's wrath. They will be as if they never existed.

19 Other peoples will occupy Edom's land, probably the remnant of Israel described in verse 20.

[20]This company of Israelite exiles who are in Canaan
will possess ⌊the land⌋ as far as Zarephath;
the exiles from Jerusalem who are in Sepharad
will possess the towns of the Negev.
[21]Deliverers will go up on[a] Mount Zion
to govern the mountains of Esau.
And the kingdom will be the LORD's.

[a]21 *Or from*

God called you to share a message like Obadiah's with some people today? What audience might be ripe for that message? How do you think they would respond?

21 Delivers. The Hebrews who have been taken away as captives will return as victors and will rule over Edom. **the kingdom will be the LORD's.** The people from Edom consider themselves beyond the reach of God. But in the end, God will rule. Revelation is also a book that will reflect this same theme.

Jonah

Author. The prophet Jonah is referred to in this book in the third person. For that reason, some have theorized that someone other than Jonah was the author. It is more probable, though, that Jonah was the author, and he chose stylistically to tell his story as a narrator would.

Personal Reading	Group Study Topic and Reading	
1:1–17	Jonah Flees From the Lord	1:1–17
2:1–3:10	Jonah Goes to Nineveh	2:1–3:10
4:1–11	Jonah's Anger at God's Compassion	4:1–11

Date. Jonah ministered during the reign of Jeroboam II, around 790–750 B.C. The events described in this book probably took place during that time.

Purpose. Jonah's story is unique. Not only was he sent to prophesy to a foreign land, but they were enemies of his own country. Nineveh was an evil place. In fact, all of Assyria was known for being warlike and cruel. Understandably, Jonah hesitated to go there. The underlying message of Jonah's journey is that God's message is meant for everyone. Until Jonah's prophecy, the Bible had recorded God's covenant with the Hebrews and his protection against their enemies. With Jonah, a new perspective took shape. The Hebrews were ambassadors of God's message among their neighbors.

Historical Background. Jonah's ministry was set during the reign of the most powerful of all the kings of the northern kingdom, Jeroboam II. Both Jehoash and then Jeroboam II had been able to expand Israel's borders back to their traditional limits. This happened because Assyria had defeated the Arameans at Damascus in 797 B.C., thus reducing the Arameans' power over Israel. Though Assyria remained a threat, internal politics kept them from invading Israel during Jonah's time. It was during this time that prophets such as Amos and Hosea warned Israel that God would not withhold his punishment forever and that Assyria would sweep down and devour them. Jonah, on the other hand, was sent to Nineveh to warn them that they would also suffer God's divine judgment.

Nineveh. Nineveh was the capital of the ancient empire of Assyria. It was located on the Tigris River, on the opposite bank from the present day city of Mosul, Iraq. Nineveh was highly fortified and had an inner and outer wall. The inner wall alone was fifty feet wide and a hundred feet high. Jonah stated that the city's population was at least 120,000 people (4:11). It is likely, however, that this number referred only to the adult population of the city. In that case, the total population was probably greater than 300,000. As great as it was, Nineveh was captured by the Chaldeans and Medes in 612 B.C. and eventually destroyed completely. For many years, its location was completely forgotten, but later its ruins were discovered and excavated.

Jonah Flees From the Lord

1 The word of the LORD came to Jonah son of Amittai: [2]"Go to the
great city of Nineveh and preach against it, because its wickedness has come up before me."
[3]But Jonah ran away from the LORD and headed for Tarshish. He
went down to Joppa, where he found a ship bound for that port. After
paying the fare, he went aboard and sailed for Tarshish to flee from
the LORD.
[4]Then the LORD sent a great wind on the sea, and such a violent
storm arose that the ship threatened to break up. [5]All the sailors were
afraid and each cried out to his own god. And they threw the cargo
into the sea to lighten the ship.
But Jonah had gone below deck, where he lay down and fell into a
deep sleep. [6]The captain went to him and said, "How can you sleep?
Get up and call on your god! Maybe he will take notice of us, and we
will not perish."
[7]Then the sailors said to each other, "Come, let us cast lots to find
out who is responsible for this calamity." They cast lots and the lot
fell on Jonah.
[8]So they asked him, "Tell us, who is responsible for making all this
trouble for us? What do you do? Where do you come from? What is
your country? From what people are you?"
[9]He answered, "I am a Hebrew and I worship the LORD, the God of
heaven, who made the sea and the land."
[10]This terrified them and they asked, "What have you done?" (They
knew he was running away from the LORD, because he had already
told them so.)
[11]The sea was getting rougher and rougher. So they asked him,
"What should we do to you to make the sea calm down for us?"
[12]"Pick me up and throw me into the sea," he replied, "and it will
become calm. I know that it is my fault that this great storm has come
upon you."
[13]Instead, the men did their best to row back to land. But they
could not, for the sea grew even wilder than before. [14]Then they cried
to the LORD, "O LORD, please do not let us die for taking this man's
life. Do not hold us accountable for killing an innocent man, for you,
O LORD, have done as you pleased." [15]Then they took Jonah and
threw him overboard, and the raging sea grew calm. [16]At this the men
greatly feared the LORD, and they offered a sacrifice to the LORD and
made vows to him.
[17]But the LORD provided a great fish to swallow Jonah, and Jonah
was inside the fish three days and three nights.

OPEN **1.** If you had a chance to go on a cruise anywhere in the world, where would you go and why? **2.** What role has "distance from family" played in your choice of school? Career? Mate? Residence? Faith? **3.** Have you ever been caught in a terrible storm while traveling? Describe it.

STUDY **1.** What seems both *fitting* and *surprising* about God's command (v. 2)? About Jonah's evasive effort? Why do you think Jonah disobeyed? **2.** Jonah runs away in response to God's call. How does that compare to how other prophets responded (1 Kin. 17:1–6; Jer. 1:4–10)? **3.** What effect did God stirring and stilling the storm have on the sailors? In what sense are they saved (compare vv. 5,16)? Likewise, how is Jonah saved? **4.** God's pursuit of Jonah is quite revealing. What does it reveal about: The justice and mercy of God? The gifts and call of God? Human fear and faith? God's claim to judge all the earth?

APPLY **1.** When have you "run away" from God—refusing to do something you know he's telling you to do? **2.** Where are you right now, in terms of this story: Hearing God call you, but not sure you want to go? Running from God? In the midst of the "storm," where God is confronting you? Imprisoned in the "fish," wondering if there is a way out?

1:2 Nineveh's wickedness is described in generic terms, but elsewhere we learn that they were "carefree" (Zeph. 2:15), arrogantly declaring themselves to be invincible. Nahum writes that the city was brutal to war captives, full of prostitution, witchcraft and idolatry (Nah. 3:1–4).

1:3 headed for Tarshish. Many scholars locate this city in the south of Spain. It was the most distant place known to the Israelites, in the opposite direction from Nineveh. Jonah was trying to get as far away from God's call as he could.

1:4 the LORD sent a great wind on the sea. Jonah was running away from God's presence, but the Lord was present all around him. God directed wind and sea creatures to get Jonah heading toward the mission.

1:16 the men greatly feared the LORD. The pagan sailors who worshiped many gods could see that God was more powerful. Note the contrast between Jonah's disobedience and the pagan sailors' respect for God.

OPEN 1. What was your favorite small hiding place as a child? How long could you stay there before you started feeling claustrophobic? **2.** When have you ever felt, "My whole life passed before my eyes"? What happened? **3.** In the ebb and flow of your life last year, when were you at "low tide"? At "high tide"? Why the big mood swing?

STUDY 1. What do you see in this prayer: A psalm of thanksgiving? A call for help? Recommitment? What do you make of the fact that Jonah prays "inside the fish" (v. 1), and uses verbs in the past tense, as though God had already answered prayer? **2.** While Jonah may be safe for the moment, how is he still in deep trouble? Where does he show assurance of deliverance in spite of appearances to the contrary (vv. 4,6–7,9)? **3.** Compare verse 3 with 1:15: How does Jonah view circumstances? God's control? God's purposes?

APPLY 1. When have you felt like Jonah—far from God, enmeshed in a situation beyond your control? How then was your life brought "up from the pit"? **2.** Where in your life are you desperate enough to pray with hope, as Jonah does?

Jonah's Prayer

2 From inside the fish Jonah prayed to the LORD his God. [2]He said:

"In my distress I called to the LORD,
  and he answered me.
From the depths of the grave[a] I called for help,
  and you listened to my cry.
3 You hurled me into the deep,
  into the very heart of the seas,
  and the currents swirled about me;
all your waves and breakers
  swept over me.
4 I said, 'I have been banished
  from your sight;
yet I will look again
  toward your holy temple.'
5 The engulfing waters threatened me,[b]
  the deep surrounded me;
  seaweed was wrapped around my head.
6 To the roots of the mountains I sank down;
  the earth beneath barred me in forever.
But you brought my life up from the pit,
  O LORD my God.

7 "When my life was ebbing away,
  I remembered you, LORD,
and my prayer rose to you,
  to your holy temple.
8 "Those who cling to worthless idols
  forfeit the grace that could be theirs.
9 But I, with a song of thanksgiving,
  will sacrifice to you.
What I have vowed I will make good.
  Salvation comes from the LORD."

10 And the LORD commanded the fish, and it vomited Jonah onto dry
land.

OPEN What is the largest city you have ever visited at street level? How did you feel about the street people and their future?

STUDY 1. What evidence do you see here that God is the God of "a second chance"? **2.** In response to God's Word, what does Jonah do? The Ninevites? Their king? **3.** How do you account for their response to Jonah's message? **4.** For

Jonah Goes to Nineveh

3 Then the word of the LORD came to Jonah a second time: [2]"Go to
the great city of Nineveh and proclaim to it the message I give
you."
3 Jonah obeyed the word of the LORD and went to Nineveh. Now
Nineveh was a very important city—a visit required three days. [4]On
the first day, Jonah started into the city. He proclaimed: "Forty more
days and Nineveh will be overturned." [5]The Ninevites believed God.

[a]2 Hebrew *Sheol* [b]5 Or *waters were at my throat*

2:2–9 Jonah thanks God for using the fish to save him. He reviews all that has happened and how hopeless he felt as he faced certain death. He acknowledges that he deserved death for disobedience and is awed by God's mercy. Jonah makes no requests of God but praises God for his deliverance.

2:9 What I have vowed. In response to God's salvation, Jonah makes a vow to praise and obey God.

3:5 Much to Jonah's astonishment, the Ninevites repent. People from all classes of society put on sackcloth as a symbol of repentance. Their repentance was short-lived, however, since they soon destroyed Israel violently.

They declared a fast, and all of them, from the greatest to the least,
put on sackcloth.
[6]When the news reached the king of Nineveh, he rose from his
throne, took off his royal robes, covered himself with sackcloth and
sat down in the dust. [7]Then he issued a proclamation in Nineveh:

"By the decree of the king and his nobles:

Do not let any man or beast, herd or flock, taste anything; do
not let them eat or drink. [8]But let man and beast be covered with
sackcloth. Let everyone call urgently on God. Let them give up
their evil ways and their violence. [9]Who knows? God may yet
relent and with compassion turn from his fierce anger so that we
will not perish."

[10]When God saw what they did and how they turned from their evil
ways, he had compassion and did not bring upon them the destruction he had threatened.

Jonah's Anger at the Lord's Compassion

4 But Jonah was greatly displeased and became angry. [2]He prayed
to the LORD, "O LORD, is this not what I said when I was still at
home? That is why I was so quick to flee to Tarshish. I knew that you
are a gracious and compassionate God, slow to anger and abounding
in love, a God who relents from sending calamity. [3]Now, O LORD, take
away my life, for it is better for me to die than to live."
[4]But the LORD replied, "Have you any right to be angry?"
[5]Jonah went out and sat down at a place east of the city. There he
made himself a shelter, sat in its shade and waited to see what would
happen to the city. [6]Then the LORD God provided a vine and made it
grow up over Jonah to give shade for his head to ease his discomfort,
and Jonah was very happy about the vine. [7]But at dawn the next day
God provided a worm, which chewed the vine so that it withered.
[8]When the sun rose, God provided a scorching east wind, and the sun
blazed on Jonah's head so that he grew faint. He wanted to die, and
said, "It would be better for me to die than to live."
[9]But God said to Jonah, "Do you have a right to be angry about the
vine?"
"I do," he said. "I am angry enough to die."
[10]But the LORD said, "You have been concerned about this vine,
though you did not tend it or make it grow. It sprang up overnight
and died overnight. [11]But Nineveh has more than a hundred and
twenty thousand people who cannot tell their right hand from their
left, and many cattle as well. Should I not be concerned about that
great city?"

God's change of heart (v. 10)? What does this say about God's will? What does it say about God's use of us to achieve his will?

APPLY 1. When has God given you two chances: To be or do what? To witness where? When have you ignored a second chance? Why? **2.** If God gave you "Mission Impossible," 40 days after which the object of the mission would be destroyed, would you do it? Why or why not? **3.** When would you consider "fasting" and "putting on a sackcloth," as the Ninevites did? What is a "spiritual fast"?

OPEN How do you usually express anger?

STUDY 1. Why did Jonah run from God earlier (v. 2)? Why is he depressed and angry now? What is the history of relations between the Israelites and the Assyrians? **2.** Given the size of the city (v. 11; 3:3), the message to be proclaimed (3:4), and what you know about God (v. 2; Ex. 34:6–7), how would you have felt? Like Jonah (vv. 1–3)? Why? **3.** What three things does God provide Jonah? Why? What do the vine, worm and hot sun reveal about God? About Jonah? **4.** How would you end this dangling story? **5.** Compare Elijah's encounter with Baal-worship in 1 Kings 17–19 with Jonah's relation to these foreigners. What peak religious experiences, depressions, provisions, and rebuke from God do they have in common with each other? With you and your life?

APPLY 1. When have you tried limiting God's mercy to others? To yourself? To whom is God wanting you to show mercy? **2.** How has God challenged you in your study of Jonah?

3:9 God may yet relent. The king knew that Nineveh's future lay in God's hands. Repentance did not guarantee survival as the final decision was up to God.

4:1 God's compassion on Nineveh angered Jonah. God should punish this evil city, Jonah surmised. He preached reluctantly, hoping that obstinate Ninevites would get the punishment they deserved with no mercy.

4:3 Jonah is so disappointed in God's mercy to the Ninevites that he wants to die. Perhaps he thought Israel had lost its favored standing with God, since Nineveh was such an enemy to Israel. Or he may have been embarrassed that his threats were not carried out.

4:10–11 God used the vine to show Jonah how misplaced his affections were. Jonah did not truly care for the plant, only for the physical comfort it gave him. A gardener who cared for a plant would have reason to regret its loss. Likewise God, whose love extends to all people, had even more reason to show compassion on Nineveh. Jonah had to acknowledge God's missionary heart: repentance and salvation are for all people.

Micah

Author. Much remains unknown about the prophet Micah, but there is little doubt that he authored this prophecy. Micah's ministry was unusual, in that he served as a prophet to both the southern and northern kingdoms of Israel.

Personal Reading	Group Study Topic and Reading	
1:1–16	Judgment and Shame	1:1–7
2:1–13	False Prophets	2:6–13
3:1–12	True Prophets	3:1–12
4:1–13	God's Future Reign	4:6–13
5:1–15	God's Future Ruler	5:1–5a
6:1–16	God's Accusation	6:1–8
7:1–20	Israel's Restoration	7:14–20

Date. This book was written during Micah's ministry in the eighth century B.C. Micah prophesied during the reigns of Jotham, Ahaz and Hezekiah in Judah.

Purpose. Micah's message included both calamity and hope. He called his people to practical, righteous living. He reminded them of the judgment that was inevitable if they remained unfaithful to God. He proclaimed the future Messiah. He confronted his people about a shallow faith that involved merely going through the motions.

Historical Background. The time period of Micah's prophecy coincided with the Assyrian expansion into Aram and then Israel. Assyria was a cruel and powerful nation to the east of Israel. In 734–732 B.C., King Tiglath-Pileser III attacked Aram, Philistia and regions of Israel and Judah. Judah, the smaller southern territory of the Hebrews, paid the Assyrians a tribute and survived with a bit of their autonomy. Israel, on the other hand, lost much of its territory and was eventually taken into exile or assimilated into the Assyrian culture. Although Judah was saved temporarily, it was later threatened by Assyrian King Sennacherib and then captured by Babylon in 586 B.C.

Samaria. The prophecy of Micah foretells the destruction of Samaria, the capital of the northern kingdom. Samaria was founded in the early ninth century B.C. by King Omri. The city rose three hundred feet above the valleys that surrounded it, making it imposing and nearly impenetrable. Archeological evidence indicates that the kings of the northern kingdom, particularly Omri and Ahab, built beautiful structures there that rivaled those built by Solomon in Jerusalem. Solomon's temple was in Jerusalem, a fact that probably contributed to the southern capital being the religious center of the two kingdoms. In contrast, Samaria became a center of Baal worship. The idolatrous northern kings repeatedly adopted the religious practices of other cultures and built pagan temples and "high places" for pagan sacrifice and worship.

1 The word of the LORD that came to Micah of Moresheth during the reigns of Jotham, Ahaz and Hezekiah, kings of Judah—the vision he saw concerning Samaria and Jerusalem.

2 Hear, O peoples, all of you,
listen, O earth and all who are in it,
that the Sovereign LORD may witness against you,
the Lord from his holy temple.

Judgment Against Samaria and Jerusalem

3 Look! The LORD is coming from his dwelling place;
he comes down and treads the high places of the earth.
4 The mountains melt beneath him
and the valleys split apart,
like wax before the fire,
like water rushing down a slope.
5 All this is because of Jacob's transgression,
because of the sins of the house of Israel.
What is Jacob's transgression?
Is it not Samaria?
What is Judah's high place?
Is it not Jerusalem?

6 "Therefore I will make Samaria a heap of rubble,
a place for planting vineyards.
I will pour her stones into the valley
and lay bare her foundations.
7 All her idols will be broken to pieces;
all her temple gifts will be burned with fire;
I will destroy all her images.
Since she gathered her gifts from the wages of prostitutes,
as the wages of prostitutes they will again be used."

Weeping and Mourning

8 Because of this I will weep and wail;
I will go about barefoot and naked.
I will howl like a jackal
and moan like an owl.
9 For her wound is incurable;
it has come to Judah.
It[a] has reached the very gate of my people,
even to Jerusalem itself.
10 Tell it not in Gath[b];

[a] 9 Or *He* [b] 10 *Gath* sounds like the Hebrew for *tell.*

OPEN 1. When have you seen one of your parents get really angry? Over what issues? How is your anger like, and unlike, his or hers? **2.** What is your favorite city? Why do you like it?

STUDY 1. Just as Washington and Moscow represent countries, what kingdoms do Samaria and Jerusalem here represent? **2.** What's happening in the divided kingdoms under Jotham (2 Kin. 15:32–35)? Under Ahaz (2 Kin. 16)? Under Hezekiah (2 Kin. 18)? **3.** While Micah's ministry and the kings' reign are localized (v. 1), is God's rule restricted (vv. 2–3)? Why is God coming out of his dwelling place? **4.** To what does Micah compare God's wrath? How does God's holy, perfect wrath differ from human wrath?

APPLY 1. What hopes, attitudes and beliefs are "foundational" in your life? What has God done to lay down the foundation on which you are building your life (v. 6)? **2.** What false images or hopes have had to be destroyed in your life before you were able to open your eyes to God and God's ways (v. 7)?

OPEN 1. What hometowns do you still connect with? Do you still read the local news? Hear the town gossip? What concerns you most about changes in this town(s)? **2.** What would you shave your head for: To empathize with a cancer victim? To make a political statement? To be part of a radio or sports team promotion?

STUDY 1. How widespread is the sacking of the Southern Kingdom by the Assyrians as

1:1 Samaria and Jerusalem. Micah used these two cities, which were the capitals of the northern kingdom (Israel) and the southern kingdom (Judah), to represent all 12 tribes of the nation of Israel. Judgment was coming for all of God's people, not just these cities.

1:2–7 These verses are a synopsis of Micah's message. The prophet urges all nations to hear God's judgment against them (v. 2), then describes God's punishment (vv. 3–4), the reason for it (v. 5) and the results (vv. 6–7).

1:3 high places. This phrase refers to Jerusalem and Samaria's mountain locations and to sites of idol worship, commonly referred to by this phrase.

1:6–7 Micah saw this prophecy fulfilled in 722 B.C. when the Assyrians captured Samaria. (2 Kin. 17:6.)

1:8 Going barefoot and naked was a sign of extreme mourning. Micah was grieved over the fate of Samaria.

prophesied here? As reported in 2 Kings 18–19? **2.** How does this message affect the messenger (v. 8)? Why would Micah go naked or imitate a jackal? What does he feel for these hometowns in the path of an invader? **3.** What is the diagnosis and prognosis of Judah's spiritual disease (vv. 9–15)? **4.** Is Micah saying there's no hope of avoiding imminent destruction? Or is he condemning false hope? Why do you think so? **5.** How do you explain that this "disaster has come from the LORD" (v. 12): Assyria's gods were stronger? God was powerless to stop it? God didn't care enough to stop it? It simply happened? God was somehow behind it all, punishing and restraining evil? All common disasters come from God? Explain.

APPLY **1.** Micah's very personal lament is a model. The last time you criticized someone, did it hurt you as much as them? Was there "weeping and mourning" in your communication? How did it come through? **2.** What are you mourning right now, whether in your personal life or the life of your nation? How do you express that mourning?

OPEN Have you received family heirlooms from other generations? How do you feel about such relics?

STUDY **1.** What do the idle rich plan day and night? With what result? Who are these idle rich: Landowners? Moneylenders? Insurance agents? Politicians? **2.** How does God demonstrate his concern for the poor and defrauded (compare 1 Kin. 21)? Why does God respond to pride with taunts and traitors? **3.** Does God's justice, as portrayed here, disturb you? How? Is God just in planning disaster (vv. 3–5) against his people? How so? **4.** What is the link here between justice and other-centered

weep not at all.[a]
In Beth Ophrah[b]
roll in the dust.
11 Pass on in nakedness and shame,
you who live in Shaphir.[c]
Those who live in Zaanan[d]
will not come out.
Beth Ezel is in mourning;
its protection is taken from you.
12 Those who live in Maroth[e] writhe in pain,
waiting for relief,
because disaster has come from the LORD,
even to the gate of Jerusalem.
13 You who live in Lachish,[f]
harness the team to the chariot.
You were the beginning of sin
to the Daughter of Zion,
for the transgressions of Israel
were found in you.
14 Therefore you will give parting gifts
to Moresheth Gath.
The town of Aczib[g] will prove deceptive
to the kings of Israel.
15 I will bring a conqueror against you
who live in Mareshah.[h]
He who is the glory of Israel
will come to Adullam.
16 Shave your heads in mourning
for the children in whom you delight;
make yourselves as bald as the vulture,
for they will go from you into exile.

Man's Plans and God's

2 Woe to those who plan iniquity,
to those who plot evil on their beds!
At morning's light they carry it out
because it is in their power to do it.
2 They covet fields and seize them,
and houses, and take them.
They defraud a man of his home,
a fellowman of his inheritance.

3 Therefore, the LORD says:

"I am planning disaster against this people,

[a]10 Hebrew; Septuagint may suggest *not in Acco.* The Hebrew for *in Acco* sounds like the Hebrew for *weep.* [b]10 *Beth Ophrah* means *house of dust.* [c]11 *Shaphir* means *pleasant.* [d]11 *Zaanan* sounds like the Hebrew for *come out.* [e]12 *Maroth* sounds like the Hebrew for *bitter.* [f]13 *Lachish* sounds like the Hebrew for *team.* [g]14 *Aczib* means *deception.* [h]15 *Mareshah* sounds like the Hebrew for *conqueror.*

1:11 The name Shaphir meant "beautiful or pleasant," but the town would soon be naked and ashamed, not beautiful. Nakedness suggests that the people would become prisoners.

2:2–3 Materialism was rampant. Influential people coveted and defrauded those less fortunate. The powerful had no regard for the rights of others and conveniently disobeyed God's command that each tribe occupy designated land. God's punishment would bring disaster. The people would certainly perish because of their violation of the 10th commandment.

from which you cannot save yourselves.
You will no longer walk proudly,
for it will be a time of calamity.
4 In that day men will ridicule you;
they will taunt you with this mournful song:
'We are utterly ruined;
my people's possession is divided up.
He takes it from me!
He assigns our fields to traitors.' "
5 Therefore you will have no one in the assembly of the LORD
to divide the land by lot.

False Prophets

6 "Do not prophesy," their prophets say.
"Do not prophesy about these things;
disgrace will not overtake us."
7 Should it be said, O house of Jacob:
"Is the Spirit of the LORD angry?
Does he do such things?"

"Do not my words do good
to him whose ways are upright?
8 Lately my people have risen up
like an enemy.
You strip off the rich robe
from those who pass by without a care,
like men returning from battle.
9 You drive the women of my people
from their pleasant homes.
You take away my blessing
from their children forever.
10 Get up, go away!
For this is not your resting place,
because it is defiled,
it is ruined, beyond all remedy.
11 If a liar and deceiver comes and says,
'I will prophesy for you plenty of wine and beer,'
he would be just the prophet for this people!

Deliverance Promised

12 "I will surely gather all of you, O Jacob;
I will surely bring together the remnant of Israel.
I will bring them together like sheep in a pen,
like a flock in its pasture;
the place will throng with people.
13 One who breaks open the way will go up before them;
they will break through the gate and go out.

humility? Between injustice and self-seeking pride?

APPLY 1. Today, many people have lost property or possessions because of fraudulent or illegal schemes. When was something that belonged to you taken from you unjustly? How did you feel toward the person who took it? **2.** If you were among Micah's hearers, would you feel: Envious? Defrauded? Proud? Ridiculed? Betrayed? Humbled?

OPEN 1. What most disturbs you: Raising taxes? Speaking for God? False, misleading advertising? Impersonations? Give an example. **2.** In your experience, when is good news most appreciated and welcomed? Why?

STUDY 1. How do the false prophets try to silence Micah (vv. 6–7,11)? Why? **2.** What tones of voice do you hear in Micah's response (vv. 7–11)? Why this rhetoric? How would it be received? **3.** What has made God's people an "enemy" (vv. 8–9)? What are they doing to themselves? How do you account for this? What is God's response to people who are bent on self-destruction? **4.** Are the people aware of their wrongdoing? Or do they see themselves as fairly pious? How so? **5.** The oracle in verses 12–13 refers to a later time. Why do you suppose it was inserted into this context? **6.** What is the good news here? Who is "their king"? How can God love the very people he judges?

APPLY 1. When you were telling the truth, were you ever not believed? **2.** Who in your world says, "You can have it all"? What is your honest reaction to such a sales pitch? If you were Micah, what would be your retort? **3.** Have you ever felt God showing mercy to you at the same time he was showing his wrath?

2:6–7 False prophets, wrongly believing that God was incapable of anger against his people, urged Micah not to prophesy judgment. Only those people who break God's covenant have reason to fear judgment, they surmised.

2:12–13 Hope survives the coming judgment. God will keep his covenant promises to Abraham and will gather a remnant of Israel and bless them. God promises to be the Shepherd and King of Israel. This same message was proclaimed by Isaiah, the prophet, during his ministry (Isa. 1:9; 4:3).

Their king will pass through before them,
the LORD at their head."

Leaders and Prophets Rebuked

3 Then I said,

"Listen, you leaders of Jacob,
you rulers of the house of Israel.
Should you not know justice,
2 you who hate good and love evil;
who tear the skin from my people
and the flesh from their bones;
3 who eat my people's flesh,
strip off their skin
and break their bones in pieces;
who chop them up like meat for the pan,
like flesh for the pot?"

4 Then they will cry out to the LORD,
but he will not answer them.
At that time he will hide his face from them
because of the evil they have done.

5 This is what the LORD says:

"As for the prophets
who lead my people astray,
if one feeds them,
they proclaim 'peace';
if he does not,
they prepare to wage war against him.
6 Therefore night will come over you, without visions,
and darkness, without divination.
The sun will set for the prophets,
and the day will go dark for them.
7 The seers will be ashamed
and the diviners disgraced.
They will all cover their faces
because there is no answer from God."
8 But as for me, I am filled with power,
with the Spirit of the LORD,
and with justice and might,
to declare to Jacob his transgression,
to Israel his sin.
9 Hear this, you leaders of the house of Jacob,
you rulers of the house of Israel,
who despise justice
and distort all that is right;
10 who build Zion with bloodshed,
and Jerusalem with wickedness.
11 Her leaders judge for a bribe,

OPEN **1.** If the phone doesn't ring and there's no mail for days, how does that make you feel? **2.** Have you ever felt like the plug was pulled out of your life? How did you cope with the power failure?

STUDY **1.** Why is Micah doubly hard on these leaders? What three groups of leaders does he rebuke? **2.** When someone calls another person a cannibal, what does that usually mean? Of what "cannibalistic," self-serving concept of justice are these leaders guilty (vv. 2–3,5)? Why should they know better? **3.** On what basis were they presuming God would rubber-stamp their unjust decisions? How does Micah feed hungry prophets their just desserts? What does the Lord's silence look like? Sound like? Feel like? **4.** How is Micah empowered by God and at odds with the state religion (vv. 8–9)? **5.** What misunderstanding of God (v. 11; Deut. 16:18–20) distorts their prophecy and destroys the people (vv. 9–12)? **6.** What would Micah say today about those who carry on religious ritual or preach peace, yet oppress the poor?

APPLY **1.** Have you ever felt like your prayers went no higher than the ceiling? How do you know God is there, especially when he is silent? How does your own behavior affect whether or not you experience God as silent (vv. 5–7)? **2.** In response to earthquakes, terrorist bombings, highway deaths, the AIDS epidemic, etc., people often say, "How can God allow this?" For what kinds of disasters do you lay the blame on civil leaders? On church leaders? On victims? Chance? God?

3:1–3 The leaders of Jacob, in Micah's words, are like hunters gruesomely killing and eating the very people under their care. These leaders are the leaders of Israel of both the north and south.

her priests teach for a price,
and her prophets tell fortunes for money.
Yet they lean upon the LORD and say,
"Is not the LORD among us?
No disaster will come upon us."
12 Therefore because of you,
Zion will be plowed like a field,
Jerusalem will become a heap of rubble,
the temple hill a mound overgrown with thickets.

The Mountain of the Lord

4 In the last days

the mountain of the LORD's temple will be established
as chief among the mountains;
it will be raised above the hills,
and peoples will stream to it.

2 Many nations will come and say,

"Come, let us go up to the mountain of the LORD,
to the house of the God of Jacob.
He will teach us his ways,
so that we may walk in his paths."
The law will go out from Zion,
the word of the LORD from Jerusalem.
3 He will judge between many peoples
and will settle disputes for strong nations far and wide.
They will beat their swords into plowshares
and their spears into pruning hooks.
Nation will not take up sword against nation,
nor will they train for war anymore.
4 Every man will sit under his own vine
and under his own fig tree,
and no one will make them afraid,
for the LORD Almighty has spoken.
5 All the nations may walk
in the name of their gods;
we will walk in the name of the LORD
our God for ever and ever.

The Lord's Plan

6 "In that day," declares the LORD,

"I will gather the lame;
I will assemble the exiles
and those I have brought to grief.
7 I will make the lame a remnant,
those driven away a strong nation.

OPEN 1. What do you like most about mountains? Trees? Which mountain is "chief" for you? Why? What is your tree of choice? Why? **2.** What is your favorite anti-war slogan? Why that one?

STUDY 1. Which mountain will be "chief" for God's people? What exalts it above the rest? **2.** In this prophecy, what changes will be accomplished? By whom? When (v. 1)? **3.** What is the connection between learning God's ways (v. 2) and the world peace envisioned here? **4.** What time frame do you think "the last days" refers to in this context: In this world? In the next? Or when the Messiah returns? Why? **5.** How does this prophecy of "swords beaten into plowshares" (v. 3) square with the one just before it of Zion "plowed like a field" by the sword (3:12)? How does this vision of united nations under God fit Isaiah 19:23–25?

APPLY What is your vision of perfect peace? How else, by God's grace, will you plan, work and pray toward your peace project?

OPEN 1. What do you like to gather, collect or assemble? What project have you recently completed with your children, family or friends? **2.** What was your longest time away from home? How did you feel coming home?

4:1–8 Micah prophesies that in the last days God will raise Jerusalem up to be the center of Christ's rule. God will keep his promise to bless the world through Israel, making it a place where the world will gather, righteous judgments will be made and peace will reign.

4:4 sit under his own vine and under his own fig tree. This is a picture of peace and security.

4:7 Though Israel is spiritually lame and faces exile, God will save a remnant to rebuild a strong nation under his rule.

STUDY 1. What will the Lord do for the lame, the exiled and grief-stricken? What has happened to bring you to this point of need? **2.** What is the "remnant" here (v. 7; Isa. 10:20–23; Jer. 23:1–8)? What is the equivalent of that remnant today? **3.** How is this future kingdom (vv. 7–8) a comfort to those who would suffer the fall of Jerusalem (130 years hence, in 586 B.C.)? What comfort does that kingdom bring to those who suffer "now" (v. 11)? **4.** The nations now gloating over Zion are in for a rude awakening. What don't they understand about their role in God's plan of punishment (vv. 11–13; Isa. 10:5–19)? What is to be the role of the remnant in this spiritual warfare?

APPLY 1. Pain and joy are intermingled in birth (v. 10) and in the Christian life. How has this been true for you this past year? How is hope in God's kingdom helping you with a painful situation? Would you be a believer if it were not for pain? Why? **2.** Who are the lame, the exiled and the grief-stricken where you live? With whom can you share this hope? **3.** Do you have faith to believe peace is God's way for you? Enough to persuade others?

OPEN What good things have come to you in small packages?

STUDY 1. Compare the hopelessness in verse 1 with the security and peace in verses 4–5: What does that contrast mean? Who (v. 2) makes the big difference? What will his reign of peace look like? Feel like? **2.** Who is this ruler from Bethlehem: King David (1 Sam. 16:1–13)? Christ Jesus (Matt. 2:6)? Or both? What will he do for his people? **3.** How

The LORD will rule over them in Mount Zion
from that day and forever.
8 As for you, O watchtower of the flock,
O stronghold[a] of the Daughter of Zion,
the former dominion will be restored to you;
kingship will come to the Daughter of Jerusalem."

9 Why do you now cry aloud—
have you no king?
Has your counselor perished,
that pain seizes you like that of a woman in labor?
10 Writhe in agony, O Daughter of Zion,
like a woman in labor,
for now you must leave the city
to camp in the open field.
You will go to Babylon;
there you will be rescued.
There the LORD will redeem you
out of the hand of your enemies.

11 But now many nations
are gathered against you.
They say, "Let her be defiled,
let our eyes gloat over Zion!"
12 But they do not know
the thoughts of the LORD;
they do not understand his plan,
he who gathers them like sheaves to the threshing floor.

13 "Rise and thresh, O Daughter of Zion,
for I will give you horns of iron;
I will give you hoofs of bronze
and you will break to pieces many nations."

You will devote their ill-gotten gains to the LORD,
their wealth to the Lord of all the earth.

A Promised Ruler From Bethlehem

5 Marshal your troops, O city of troops,[b]
for a siege is laid against us.
They will strike Israel's ruler
on the cheek with a rod.

2 "But you, Bethlehem Ephrathah,
though you are small among the clans[c] of Judah,
out of you will come for me
one who will be ruler over Israel,

[a]8 Or *hill* [b]1 Or *Strengthen your walls, O walled city* [c]2 Or *rulers*

4:9–5:1 *Micah* prophesies four events that will take place before Christ's kingdom is established: Israel would be exiled to Babylon and rescued, nations would conspire against Israel, God would defeat the nations, and Israel's ruler would be humiliated.

5:2–15 A prophecy of Christ's coming that the wise men in Matthew will use as a guide to find Jesus. In the midst of dire predictions for Israel's future, there is hope. A deliverer, the Christ, will unite God's people and bring them peace.

whose origins[a] are from of old,
from ancient times.[b]"

³Therefore Israel will be abandoned
until the time when she who is in labor gives birth
and the rest of his brothers return
to join the Israelites.

⁴He will stand and shepherd his flock
in the strength of the LORD,
in the majesty of the name of the LORD his God.
And they will live securely, for then his greatness
will reach to the ends of the earth.
5 And he will be their peace.

Deliverance and Destruction

When the Assyrian invades our land
and marches through our fortresses,
we will raise against him seven shepherds,
even eight leaders of men.
⁶They will rule[c] the land of Assyria with the sword,
the land of Nimrod with drawn sword.[d]
He will deliver us from the Assyrian
when he invades our land
and marches into our borders.

⁷The remnant of Jacob will be
in the midst of many peoples
like dew from the LORD,
like showers on the grass,
which do not wait for man
or linger for mankind.
⁸The remnant of Jacob will be among the nations,
in the midst of many peoples,
like a lion among the beasts of the forest,
like a young lion among flocks of sheep,
which mauls and mangles as it goes,
and no one can rescue.
⁹Your hand will be lifted up in triumph over your enemies,
and all your foes will be destroyed.

¹⁰"In that day," declares the LORD,

"I will destroy your horses from among you
and demolish your chariots.
¹¹I will destroy the cities of your land
and tear down all your strongholds.
¹²I will destroy your witchcraft
and you will no longer cast spells.
¹³I will destroy your carved images

[a]2 Hebrew *goings out* [b]2 Or *from days of eternity* [c]6 Or *crush* [d]6 Or *Nimrod in its gates*

might such humble, ancient roots shape the way he rules?

APPLY 1. What makes you feel like a besieged city, or a secure flock? What "rules" you in each case? **2.** When have you seen despair give birth to hope? What made the difference?

OPEN 1. Complete this prayer: "Lord, deliver us from ..."? Why is that your chief concern? **2.** What do you like about carpet, clothing or food remnants? What redemptive purpose can they serve?

STUDY 1. How is the vision of universal peace (4:1–5) like, and unlike, this picture (vv. 5–9)? **2.** The Assyrian invasion takes place in 587 B.C. How will the redemption of God's remnant then take place (vv. 6–9)? **3.** While this prophecy refers primarily to the release of the captives in 538 B.C., to what future deliverance can this prophecy also point? **4.** What will this restoration of the remnant look like? How can the remnant be both morning dew which refreshes (v. 7) and roaring lion which devours (v. 8)? **5.** What does God have against horses, chariots, strongholds, witchcraft, carved images, cities and the like (vv. 10–14)? What do they all have in common against God (v. 15)? **6.** What would Micah say about modern empire-building in politics? In church life? Our superstitions, horoscopes and the occult?

APPLY 1. In what sense is your church like a spiritual remnant? Remnant of what? How is it like dew? A lion? **2.** What might God want to destroy in your life? Why that? Would God be both loving and just to perform that spiritual "cancer surgery"? How so? **3.** To Micah, it was more important to be obedient (v. 15) than to be victorious. What does that way mean to our success-oriented society? What would it mean for you

5:8–9 The remnant of Israel will dominate other nations, just as lions fear no other animal.

5:10–11 destroy your horses. God will remove Israel's self-reliance. He will take away their horses and chariots, weapons, and any other obstacles that would keep them from depending upon him. They needed to trust him.

to value obedience to God more than success?

OPEN When, if ever, have you tried bribing your parents for a favor?

STUDY **1.** In this trial scene, who is the accused? The prosecutor? Chief witnesses? Judge and jury? **2.** What makes God's case against Israel so convincing (vv. 2–5)? What evidence do Moses, Aaron and Miriam provide? What did Balak counsel and Balaam answer (Num. 22–24)? How does the "journey from Shittim to Gilgal" (Josh. 2–4) strengthen God's case? **3.** Under cross-examination, what does the accused have to say (vv. 6–8)? What does their silence imply? Are they guilty as charged? Why? **4.** What recompense can the accused offer? Why is such up-to-date religion inadequate? **5.** What will the Lord accept instead? Why?

APPLY **1.** On what would you base a case against God (v. 1)? Would it hold up in his court of justice and mercy? **2.** What does it mean to "act justly" and "love mercy" and "walk humbly"? **3.** Which of these three requirements challenges you the most? Which are you doing the best job of following?

OPEN **1.** Ever seen produce carefully weighed and packaged before your eyes? Describe such a store—its sights, sounds, smells, service. **2.** Where do you do most of your shopping? Why there?

STUDY **1.** How is the "fear" of God's name the source of

and your sacred stones from among you;
you will no longer bow down
to the work of your hands.
14 I will uproot from among you your Asherah poles[a]
and demolish your cities.
15 I will take vengeance in anger and wrath
upon the nations that have not obeyed me."

The Lord's Case Against Israel

6 Listen to what the LORD says:

"Stand up, plead your case before the mountains;
let the hills hear what you have to say.
2 Hear, O mountains, the LORD's accusation;
listen, you everlasting foundations of the earth.
For the LORD has a case against his people;
he is lodging a charge against Israel.

3 "My people, what have I done to you?
How have I burdened you? Answer me.
4 I brought you up out of Egypt
and redeemed you from the land of slavery.
I sent Moses to lead you,
also Aaron and Miriam.
5 My people, remember
what Balak king of Moab counseled
and what Balaam son of Beor answered.
Remember ⌞your journey⌟ from Shittim to Gilgal,
that you may know the righteous acts of the LORD."

6 With what shall I come before the LORD
and bow down before the exalted God?
Shall I come before him with burnt offerings,
with calves a year old?
7 Will the LORD be pleased with thousands of rams,
with ten thousand rivers of oil?
Shall I offer my firstborn for my transgression,
the fruit of my body for the sin of my soul?
8 He has showed you, O man, what is good.
And what does the LORD require of you?
To act justly and to love mercy
and to walk humbly with your God.

Israel's Guilt and Punishment

9 Listen! The LORD is calling to the city—
and to fear your name is wisdom—
"Heed the rod and the One who appointed it.[b]
10 Am I still to forget, O wicked house,
your ill-gotten treasures

[a] *14* That is, symbols of the goddess Asherah [b] *9* The meaning of the Hebrew for this line is uncertain.

6:6–8 Micah understands Israel's guilt. He asks what the people can do to regain God's favor. Then he answers his own question by telling Israel that God desires obedience that exhibits itself in justice toward others, mercy in meeting the needs of others and humble fellowship with God. This same theme is repeated in Scripture (1 Sam. 15:22; Isa. 1:11–15).

and the short ephah,[a] which is accursed?
11 Shall I acquit a man with dishonest scales,
with a bag of false weights?
12 Her rich men are violent;
her people are liars
and their tongues speak deceitfully.
13 Therefore, I have begun to destroy you,
to ruin you because of your sins.
14 You will eat but not be satisfied;
your stomach will still be empty.[b]
You will store up but save nothing,
because what you save I will give to the sword.
15 You will plant but not harvest;
you will press olives but not use the oil on yourselves,
you will crush grapes but not drink the wine.
16 You have observed the statutes of Omri
and all the practices of Ahab's house,
and you have followed their traditions.
Therefore I will give you over to ruin
and your people to derision;
you will bear the scorn of the nations.[c]"

Israel's Misery

7 What misery is mine!
I am like one who gathers summer fruit
at the gleaning of the vineyard;
there is no cluster of grapes to eat,
none of the early figs that I crave.
2 The godly have been swept from the land;
not one upright man remains.
All men lie in wait to shed blood;
each hunts his brother with a net.
3 Both hands are skilled in doing evil;
the ruler demands gifts,
the judge accepts bribes,
the powerful dictate what they desire—
they all conspire together.
4 The best of them is like a brier,
the most upright worse than a thorn hedge.
The day of your watchmen has come,
the day God visits you.
Now is the time of their confusion.
5 Do not trust a neighbor;
put no confidence in a friend.
Even with her who lies in your embrace
be careful of your words.
6 For a son dishonors his father,

[a] *10* An ephah was a dry measure. [b] *14* The meaning of the Hebrew for this word is uncertain.
[c] *16* Septuagint; Hebrew *scorn due my people*

wisdom (v. 9; Prov. 1:7)? What does it mean to "heed the rod"? **2.** How does God uphold the moral law (vv. 10–16)? **3.** How will God's punishment fit the crime: Sinners reap what they sow? Sin afflicts undeserving victims? Evil triumphs, but only for a day? Others get the last laugh? God is a scrooge? Explain. **4.** What sins of Northern kings, Omri and Ahab, are imitated by those in the South (v. 16; 1 Kin. 16:21–33)?

APPLY 1. In God's discipline of Israel, what view of sin does that encourage you to adopt? Knowing God loves you and hates your sin, how will you be weighed in the balance? **2.** What do you believe God is wanting to say to the cities of today? What role do you see yourself taking in conveying that message?

OPEN 1. What foods do you often crave? When deprived of them, what are you like? **2.** For what visitor will you clean house: The boss? Your parents? Friends? Neighbor? Why that one?

STUDY 1. Who is Micah speaking for here in chapter 7: himself or the repentant remnant of Israel? Is he miserable (v. 1) or hopeful (v. 7)? Why do you think so? What is the figurative food he desires? **2.** If God restrains sin, what happens when people block him out of their lives (vv. 2–6)? How bad does it get in government? In the streets? In the home? **3.** Overcome by such misery, corruption and brokenness, what gives "me" (the repentant remnant) hope (v. 7)? What does "watching" and "waiting" for the Lord entail?

APPLY 1. Where are you just now on the misery-hope index? Why? What spiritual hunger does that leave you with? **2.** When has it seemed like there was no one you could trust (v. 5)? What should a believer do in such a circumstance?

6:16 statutes of Omri ... practices of Ahab's house. These were the worst kings of the northern kingdom. Their reigns were characterized by much idolatry and cruel violence.

7:1–6 Micah pleads with the Lord by bemoaning the nation's sins. In his generation godly people were as rare as summer fruit after the harvest. Surely a few godly people were left in Israel, but none could be found.

a daughter rises up against her mother,
a daughter-in-law against her mother-in-law—
a man's enemies are the members of his own household.

[7] But as for me, I watch in hope for the LORD,
I wait for God my Savior;
my God will hear me.

Israel Will Rise

[8] Do not gloat over me, my enemy!
Though I have fallen, I will rise.
Though I sit in darkness,
the LORD will be my light.
[9] Because I have sinned against him,
I will bear the LORD's wrath,
until he pleads my case
and establishes my right.
He will bring me out into the light;
I will see his righteousness.
[10] Then my enemy will see it
and will be covered with shame,
she who said to me,
"Where is the LORD your God?"
My eyes will see her downfall;
even now she will be trampled underfoot
like mire in the streets.

[11] The day for building your walls will come,
the day for extending your boundaries.
[12] In that day people will come to you
from Assyria and the cities of Egypt,
even from Egypt to the Euphrates
and from sea to sea
and from mountain to mountain.
[13] The earth will become desolate because of its inhabitants,
as the result of their deeds.

Prayer and Praise

[14] Shepherd your people with your staff,
the flock of your inheritance,
which lives by itself in a forest,
in fertile pasturelands.[a]
Let them feed in Bashan and Gilead
as in days long ago.

[15] "As in the days when you came out of Egypt,
I will show them my wonders."

[16] Nations will see and be ashamed,
deprived of all their power.

[a] 14 *Or in the middle of Carmel*

OPEN What helps you to see light at the end of the tunnel?

STUDY 1. Who seems to be speaking in verses 8–10? In verses 11–13? What is each saying? **2.** Why will the gloating nations feel shame instead (v. 10)? **3.** What out-of-the-darkness and into-the-light experience does fallen Israel anticipate? How does this prove the mercy and justice of the Lord (v. 9)? **4.** What world-wide "desolation" and "deeds" are expected (v. 13)? **5.** How will this fix attention on spiritual Israel (v. 12)? Why will that mean wrath for some, but salvation for others?

APPLY 1. How does God answer the enemy's question in verse 10? When your enemy (or the Enemy) asks you the same, how do you answer? Based on what? **2.** At what points do you identify with Israel and her enemies: Gloating over others? Sitting in darkness? Covered with shame? Seeing righteousness prevail? Trampled underfoot? Secure in your salvation? Extending your boundaries?

OPEN 1. Can you communicate without using your hands? How well? **2.** When was the last time you felt like the proverbial three monkeys: "See-no-evil" (hands over eyes), "Hear-no-evil" (hands in ears) and "Speak-no-evil" (hands on mouth)? **3.** Which monkey are you like?

STUDY 1. What restoration is pictured here for Israel's prayer and praise? What picture of God do you see? **2.** What is the basis in antiquity for these "wonders from God" (v. 15)? **3.** How will God confound the once proud, powerful nations

7:15–17 Micah's hope for the salvation of Israel rests on the promise of a Messiah. When Christ comes, he will return Israel to her land. Nations will see this deliverance and be overwhelmed by fear of the Lord.

They will lay their hands on their mouths
and their ears will become deaf.
17 They will lick dust like a snake,
like creatures that crawl on the ground.
They will come trembling out of their dens;
they will turn in fear to the LORD our God
and will be afraid of you.
18 Who is a God like you,
who pardons sin and forgives the transgression
of the remnant of his inheritance?
You do not stay angry forever
but delight to show mercy.
19 You will again have compassion on us;
you will tread our sins underfoot
and hurl all our iniquities into the depths of the sea.
20 You will be true to Jacob,
and show mercy to Abraham,
as you pledged on oath to our fathers
in days long ago.

(vv. 16–17)? Can you see this happening today? **4.** From your study of this book, how could this prophet have such a clear understanding of grace and hold forth the greatest hope, if he had not also the most serious view of sin?

APPLY 1. Which aspect of Micah's God most endears him to you? Which aspect of God might cause you and others to repent in fear? To rebel in anger? **2.** From your study of Micah, do you believe God loves you because you are so good? Or because he is so good? Why? **3.** Is there anything about you or your group which would inspire others to have the same reverence and awe of your God (vv. 16–17)? Why or why not?

7:20 Ultimately, we can be certain of God's deliverance because of the covenant with Jacob and Abraham (Gen. 22:17). God will bless their descendants. He would fulfill his promise of blessing (Gen. 17:5).

Nahum

Author. The writer is the prophet Nahum.

Personal Reading	Group Study Topic and Reading	
1:1–15	Proclaiming God's Anger Against Nineveh	1:1–15
2:1–13	Predicting the Fall of Nineveh	2:1–13
3:1–19	Portraying the Woe to Nineveh	3:1–19

Date. Nahum mentioned two critical national events. He referred to the past fall of Thebes in 663 B.C. Nahum also referred to the future fall of Nineveh, which eventually occurred in 607 B.C. It makes sense, then, that his prophecy was most likely written between these dates. The most accepted date is 630 B.C.

Purpose. Nahum's prophecy accomplished two things. First, he predicted the fall of Nineveh. Nineveh was the capital of Assyria, a wicked nation to the east of Israel that posed a constant threat. At one point, God sent the prophet Jonah to preach to Nineveh, but the Ninevites only repented for a time before returning to their evil ways. In Nahum's prophecy, he reminds his own people as well as the Assyrians that God only lets sin go unpunished for so long before he judges.

Nahum's prophecy was also a message of comfort to God's people. The Hebrews suffered under the oppression and cruelty at the hands of the Assyrians. They found comfort and even joy in the thought that God would take up their cause and triumph over their enemies.

Historical Background. After the kingdom divided, the ten northern tribes were called Israel and were often referred to as Samaria. The remaining tribes to the south were called Judah. Judah came under direct Assyrian threat. Nahum was a prophet in Judah. He was one of the two Hebrew prophets who addressed a foreign nation in their prophecies.

Style and Structure. Nahum's prophecy is written largely in the form of poetry. He uses colorful and dynamic imagery rather than simple declarative sentences. It is called an "oracle" or a vision. The imagery in his prophecy is similar to John's vision recorded in the book of Revelation.

Modern Message. Nahum's message had meaning for his people while he was living and preaching, but it also has meaning for us today. We face evil in our world. The same message is still true: God will not tolerate evil forever.

1

An oracle concerning Nineveh. The book of the vision of Nahum the Elkoshite.

The LORD's Anger Against Nineveh

2 The LORD is a jealous and avenging God;
the LORD takes vengeance and is filled with wrath.
The LORD takes vengeance on his foes
and maintains his wrath against his enemies.
3 The LORD is slow to anger and great in power;
the LORD will not leave the guilty unpunished.
His way is in the whirlwind and the storm,
and clouds are the dust of his feet.
4 He rebukes the sea and dries it up;
he makes all the rivers run dry.
Bashan and Carmel wither
and the blossoms of Lebanon fade.
5 The mountains quake before him
and the hills melt away.
The earth trembles at his presence,
the world and all who live in it.
6 Who can withstand his indignation?
Who can endure his fierce anger?
His wrath is poured out like fire;
the rocks are shattered before him.

7 The LORD is good,
a refuge in times of trouble.
He cares for those who trust in him,
8 but with an overwhelming flood
he will make an end of ⌊Nineveh⌋;
he will pursue his foes into darkness.

9 Whatever they plot against the LORD
he[a] will bring to an end;
trouble will not come a second time.
10 They will be entangled among thorns
and drunk from their wine;
they will be consumed like dry stubble.[b]
11 From you, ⌊O Nineveh,⌋ has one come forth
who plots evil against the LORD
and counsels wickedness.

12 This is what the LORD says:

"Although they have allies and are numerous,
they will be cut off and pass away.
Although I have afflicted you, ⌊O Judah,⌋
I will afflict you no more.

[a]9 Or *What do you foes plot against the LORD? / He* [b]10 The meaning of the Hebrew for this verse is uncertain.

OPEN 1. If your patience were likened to a keg of dynamite, would you have a: Short fuse? Long fuse? No fuse? No powder? No keg? Other? **2.** What pet peeve gives you a "pain in the neck"? Why is this a particular irritation to you? **3.** If, during this past week, your feet were dragging or you had a lilt or bounce in your step, what do you think was the reason?

STUDY 1. What do we learn about the attributes and actions of the Lord in verses 2–8? What characteristic of God demonstrated here surprises you? Why? **2.** What has Nineveh done to kindle the Lord's wrath (v. 2; Jonah 1:2)? What images are used to depict Nineveh's end? **3.** Do you think verse 7 is part of Nahum's vision or his own personal opinion? Why? **4.** What words of comfort are meant only for Judah? What good news are they to take to the mountains and proclaim? Why are they now free to attend to their festivals and vows? **5.** What is the point of contrasting the futures of Nineveh and Judah? Why is God treating the two nations so differently?

APPLY 1. Which of the Lord's attributes and actions have you experienced in your life recently? If you could change one thing about God's nature, what would it be? Why that one? **2.** Who in your church displays a particular facet of God's character highlighted by Nahum? Which facet does he or she bring to mind? **3.** In what ways do you feel like Judah in your relationship with the Lord? In what ways like Nineveh?

1:2 God is zealous to protect Israel. He avenges his people by bringing justice to their enemies.

1:3 The vengeance described in verse 2 is slow in coming. God withholds judgment to give the people a chance to repent. The Lord had sent Jonah to Nineveh years before to urge its people to repent.

OPEN 1. When you were a child in grade school, did you enjoy making "forts"? What kind did you make: Blankets over chairs and beds? Tree forts? Snow forts? **2.** Who was most likely to attack your "fort": A sibling? Neighborhood kids? Parents wanting to cleanup your mess?

STUDY 1. In what does Nineveh put her confidence? Why does the Lord encourage her to prepare for battle? **2.** How do Nineveh's elite forces perform in the end? What comfort is this to Israel, a frequent victim of their cruelty (v. 2; 1:12–13)? **3.** Of Nahum's highly pictorial language, what images seem literal to you? Which seem figurative? **4.** What is meant by the imagery of the pool (v. 8)? Of plundered wealth (v. 9)? How is Nineveh's humiliation and shame pictured? **5.** The lion was this nation's symbol. In what ways had Nineveh lived up to the symbol in the past? How is it used to taunt her in defeat (vv. 11–13)? What irony do you see here? **6.** Lest Nineveh gets the idea her downfall will be caused by merely natural disaster or superior fire power, what bottom line underscores that this is an act of God? **7.** What specifically is the Lord dead set "against"?

APPLY 1. Israel experienced God's restoring strength and power in the face of the enemy's attack. How have you seen God work

13 Now I will break their yoke from your neck
and tear your shackles away."

14 The LORD has given a command concerning you, ⌊Nineveh⌋:
"You will have no descendants to bear your name.
I will destroy the carved images and cast idols
that are in the temple of your gods.
I will prepare your grave,
for you are vile."

15 Look, there on the mountains,
the feet of one who brings good news,
who proclaims peace!
Celebrate your festivals, O Judah,
and fulfill your vows.
No more will the wicked invade you;
they will be completely destroyed.

Nineveh to Fall

2 An attacker advances against you, ⌊Nineveh⌋.
Guard the fortress,
watch the road,
brace yourselves,
marshal all your strength!

2 The LORD will restore the splendor of Jacob
like the splendor of Israel,
though destroyers have laid them waste
and have ruined their vines.

3 The shields of his soldiers are red;
the warriors are clad in scarlet.
The metal on the chariots flashes
on the day they are made ready;
the spears of pine are brandished.[a]
4 The chariots storm through the streets,
rushing back and forth through the squares.
They look like flaming torches;
they dart about like lightning.

5 He summons his picked troops,
yet they stumble on their way.
They dash to the city wall;
the protective shield is put in place.
6 The river gates are thrown open
and the palace collapses.
7 It is decreed[b] that ⌊the city⌋
be exiled and carried away.

[a]3 Hebrew; Septuagint and Syriac / *the horsemen rush to and fro* [b]7 The meaning of the Hebrew for this word is uncertain.

1:15 one who brings good news. *Nahum speaks of one who brings* news of deliverance from Assyria. In Isaiah 52:7, this phrase is used of one bringing news of deliverance from Babylonian Exile. Paul uses this phrase in Romans 10:15 to refer to those who tell about Christ and the good news of salvation.

2:3–4 The equipment and speed of Assyria's attackers are described. Red may have been the color of the attackers' shields and armor, or a reference to blood on them from battle. Their chariots and swords move like lightning as they approach the city's open spaces for battle.

Its slave girls moan like doves
and beat upon their breasts.
[8] Nineveh is like a pool,
and its water is draining away.
"Stop! Stop!" they cry,
but no one turns back.
[9] Plunder the silver!
Plunder the gold!
The supply is endless,
the wealth from all its treasures!
[10] She is pillaged, plundered, stripped!
Hearts melt, knees give way,
bodies tremble, every face grows pale.

[11] Where now is the lions' den,
the place where they fed their young,
where the lion and lioness went,
and the cubs, with nothing to fear?
[12] The lion killed enough for his cubs
and strangled the prey for his mate,
filling his lairs with the kill
and his dens with the prey.

[13] "I am against you,"
declares the LORD Almighty.
"I will burn up your chariots in smoke,
and the sword will devour your young lions.
I will leave you no prey on the earth.
The voices of your messengers
will no longer be heard."

Woe to Nineveh

3 Woe to the city of blood,
full of lies,
full of plunder,
never without victims!
[2] The crack of whips,
the clatter of wheels,
galloping horses
and jolting chariots!
[3] Charging cavalry,
flashing swords
and glittering spears!
Many casualties,
piles of dead,
bodies without number,
people stumbling over the corpses—

this way in your own life? **2.** What is it that you most fear right now? How might God take away that fear? Where is a place you can go that you "feel safe" from what you fear (v. 11)? **3.** How would you judge yourself based on God's standard regarding pride, cruelty or selfishness? Would your friends and others agree? Would you want to be held accountable for this?

OPEN 1. Recall an embarrassing moment of your childhood. What happened that brought on a red face? **2.** What best describes your parents' discipline of you as a child: "I'm warning you"? "Boys will be boys"? "Face the music"? Other? **3.** Recall a severe childhood (or adult) punishment you received that was the result of your deliberate disobedience. How did it make you feel? Did it alter your life in any way?

STUDY 1. How does God discipline Nineveh? How do you view God's harshness? Why was such severity necessary? **2.** What impression do the staccato phrases in verses 2–3 make on you? Is this Nineveh's fate or that of her victims? Why does

2:8 its water is draining away. With their city flooded by attackers, Ninevites would flee, leaving their possessions behind to be plundered. They would flee as rapidly as water flows out of a tank, so panicked that they wouldn't turn back when told to stop.

2:11–12 Using the metaphor of a lion pride, Nahum taunts Assyria. They had fought as brutally as a lion hunting for his lioness and cubs. Yet now their capital, or lions' den, was wasted by war. They had been as powerful as lions, and now they were nothing.

2:13 Nineveh's fall would not be caused by nature or by the strength of their attackers. God was the one who had allowed Nineveh to overcome Israel. God himself was now against them and would destroy them completely.

Nahum leave this unclear? **3.** In what ways has Nineveh "played the harlot" in relation to God (v. 4)? In what ways is she "ripe" for judgment? Why would the metaphorical punishment of verses 5 and 6 be especially appropriate to her? **4.** In what specific people and things does Nineveh put her trust? What images does Nahum use to describe these "trustworthy" sources? Which do you think is most striking? What is the end of each? **5.** What great sin of Nineveh is graphically addressed in verses 16–17? How does the image of the locust fit the actions of the Ninevites? **6.** "Nahum" means comfort. For whom is the comfort of Nahum's message? Why does God send comfort to one group and wrath to another?

APPLY 1. What personal responsibility do you consider yourself to have in giving warning to our nation today? What would this warning look like to others? Would that make a difference? **2.** In what circumstances did the Lord seem to be against you? Can you share a "pressed up against the wall" or a "hiding from God" experience in your own life? **3.** What promise of God's comfort (in Nahum) means the most to you now? How do you intend to apply this to your life?

---

4 all because of the wanton lust of a harlot,
alluring, the mistress of sorceries,
who enslaved nations by her prostitution
and peoples by her witchcraft.

5 "I am against you," declares the LORD Almighty.
"I will lift your skirts over your face.
I will show the nations your nakedness
and the kingdoms your shame.
6 I will pelt you with filth,
I will treat you with contempt
and make you a spectacle.
7 All who see you will flee from you and say,
'Nineveh is in ruins—who will mourn for her?'
Where can I find anyone to comfort you?"

8 Are you better than Thebes,[a]
situated on the Nile,
with water around her?
The river was her defense,
the waters her wall.
9 Cush[b] and Egypt were her boundless strength;
Put and Libya were among her allies.
10 Yet she was taken captive
and went into exile.
Her infants were dashed to pieces
at the head of every street.
Lots were cast for her nobles,
and all her great men were put in chains.
11 You too will become drunk;
you will go into hiding
and seek refuge from the enemy.

12 All your fortresses are like fig trees
with their first ripe fruit;
when they are shaken,
the figs fall into the mouth of the eater.
13 Look at your troops—
they are all women!
The gates of your land
are wide open to your enemies;
fire has consumed their bars.

14 Draw water for the siege,
strengthen your defenses!
Work the clay,
tread the mortar,
repair the brickwork!

[a]8 Hebrew *No Amon* [b]9 That is, the upper Nile region

3:4 Nineveh had lusted for power it *didn't deserve like a harlot lusts for men.* They sold their military services to gain control over other nations. This may also be a reference to Nineveh's goddess of sex and war.

3:5–6 The city of Nineveh would be *utterly humiliated and shamed.*

3:7 On Nineveh's worst day, she would lie in ruins with no one to comfort her. The atrocities committed by Nineveh would catch up with them and no one would come to their aid. The harlot that had once attracted so many nations would be left alone in shame and ruin. What was once full of glory was now desolate.

[15]There the fire will devour you;
the sword will cut you down
and, like grasshoppers, consume you.
Multiply like grasshoppers,
multiply like locusts!
[16]You have increased the number of your merchants
till they are more than the stars of the sky,
but like locusts they strip the land
and then fly away.
[17]Your guards are like locusts,
your officials like swarms of locusts
that settle in the walls on a cold day—
but when the sun appears they fly away,
and no one knows where.

[18]O king of Assyria, your shepherds[a] slumber;
your nobles lie down to rest.
Your people are scattered on the mountains
with no one to gather them.
[19]Nothing can heal your wound;
your injury is fatal.
Everyone who hears the news about you
claps his hands at your fall,
for who has not felt
your endless cruelty?

[a]18 Or *rulers*

3:15 multiply like locusts. This is either a command to the Ninevites to increase their numbers so they can defend themselves against attack, or to the enemy to increase themselves and win the war.

3:16 merchants ... strip the land. The merchants that were once so numerous in Nineveh would strip the land until it had no more wealth.

3:17 like locusts. The leaders in the city exploited Nineveh like locusts devouring a crop. But during Nineveh's destruction, they would flee overnight. One night they would be there, but when morning came they would panic and disappear.

Habakkuk

Personal Reading	Group Study Topic and Reading	
1:1–4	Habakkuk Complains, "Do Something"	1:1–4
1:5–11	God Answers, "Babylon Is My Instrument"	1:5–11
1:12–2:1	Habakkuk Complains, "That's Not Fair"	1:12–2:1
2:2–20	God Answers, "Faith Will Be Rewarded"	2:2–20
3:1–19	Habakkuk Prays, "Yet Will I Rejoice"	3:1–19

Author. Not much else is known about Habakkuk other than his authorship of this prophecy. His name means "one who embraces" or "one who folds his hands."

Date. Habakkuk ministered just before the Babylonian exile of Judah. That would place this prophecy in the latter part of the seventh century B.C.

Purpose. Judah only had to look across her borders to find nations that were far crueler and far more idolatrous in their worship. It might have been easy, in fact, for the people of Judah to justify their own actions by reminding themselves that at least they were better than their neighbors. But Habakkuk saw the truth that God would use even the cruelest nations if that is what it took to discipline his own. Babylon was even more sinful than Judah, but Judah would still fall to Babylon. Habakkuk explained Judah's responsibility for her own actions, no matter what was happening around her.

Historical Background. The political balance of power shifted quickly and radically during the seventh and late sixth centuries B.C. The Assyrian empire, which had dominated the region since the ninth century B.C., captured Samaria and was defeated by an alliance of Chaldeans and Medes. Following that, the Babylonians to the south of Judah made efforts to expand. The Babylonians routed the Egyptian army at Carchemish and pursued the retreating Egyptian army as far as the Egyptian border. This brought the Babylonians within striking distance of Judah's border and thus set the stage for the Babylonians to conquer Judah. The Babylonians besieged Jerusalem several times, taking captives into exile. In 586 B.C., they captured and destroyed the city. Habakkuk prophesies this destruction. However, for Habakkuk, the situation was about much more than international politics. It was a God-ordained result of Judah's disobedience and apostasy.

A Prophetic Dialogue. The book of Habakkuk does not fit into the standard mold of most other prophetic writing in the Old Testament. In most prophetic writing, a prophet relays God's Word to the people. God's message might be harsh or kind, clear or mysterious, predictive of the future or rooted in the past. Whether it is a message of judgment or forgiveness, it is God's unquestioned Word all the same.

In Habakkuk, however, the prophet has a dialogue with God. He asks and God answers; he questions and God explains. The prophet pleads with God for divine judgment, and God promises it. Habakkuk questions why God would use a more evil force than Judah to punish Judah. God explains that even the time of the great Babylonians is short and that his judgment will come against them, too.

The book of Habakkuk takes a very different approach to declaring God's Word. In Habakkuk, God does not appear to be simply an oracle who makes pronouncements, but also a caring God who wants his message to be understood.

1

The oracle that Habakkuk the prophet received.

Habakkuk's Complaint

[2] How long, O LORD, must I call for help,
but you do not listen?
Or cry out to you, "Violence!"
but you do not save?
[3] Why do you make me look at injustice?
Why do you tolerate wrong?
Destruction and violence are before me;
there is strife, and conflict abounds.
[4] Therefore the law is paralyzed,
and justice never prevails.
The wicked hem in the righteous,
so that justice is perverted.

The Lord's Answer

[5] "Look at the nations and watch—
and be utterly amazed.
For I am going to do something in your days
that you would not believe,
even if you were told.
[6] I am raising up the Babylonians,[a]
that ruthless and impetuous people,
who sweep across the whole earth
to seize dwelling places not their own.
[7] They are a feared and dreaded people;
they are a law to themselves
and promote their own honor.
[8] Their horses are swifter than leopards,
fiercer than wolves at dusk.
Their cavalry gallops headlong;
their horsemen come from afar.
They fly like a vulture swooping to devour;
[9] they all come bent on violence.
Their hordes[b] advance like a desert wind
and gather prisoners like sand.
[10] They deride kings
and scoff at rulers.
They laugh at all fortified cities;
they build earthen ramps and capture them.
[11] Then they sweep past like the wind and go on—
guilty men, whose own strength is their god."

[a] 6 Or *Chaldeans* [b] 9 The meaning of the Hebrew for this word is uncertain.

OPEN **1.** It's been a long time since you have heard from your friend. What's the first thing you ask your friend? The second? **2.** Share a "believe-it-or-not" fact from your life story. Who in your group believes it?

STUDY **1.** What is evident about Habakkuk, his historical situation and current crisis? Specify facts, viewpoints or feelings. **2.** To whom is he complaining? Why? **3.** What is the Lord's answer to Habakkuk's complaint? What is amazing about that (vv. 5–6)? (Note: The Babylonian invasion predicted here took place in 605 B.C.) **4.** What do you think was God's purpose in using ungodly Babylon (Chaldeans) to punish Israel? **5.** How are the Babylonians and their army pictured (vv. 7–11)? How does Israel respond? How would you respond? **6.** How does Babylon see itself (vv. 7,11)? What problem does this pose for Habakkuk? For Israel? **7.** What do you find most puzzling about the Lord's answer: The end justifying the means? God using a double standard? God using two wrongs to make a right? Other? Explain.

APPLY **1.** Where are you crying out, but unheeded? What then do you say? Feel? Act? **2.** What has God done in your life or in the world that has amazed you?

1:1–17 Habakkuk asks God why evil goes unpunished, and God's response is that he is going to punish Judah by allowing Babylon to conquer it. Habakkuk complains that Babylon is even more wicked than Judah and God must be condoning violence.

1:3 Habakkuk saw the injustice around him and was appalled. Even worse, the righteous God seems to tolerate this evil.

1:5 be utterly amazed. The people of Judah will be astonished when God uses the wicked Babylonians to discipline them.

1:6–11 The Babylonians were known for violence and cruelty. These verses describe them as ruthless, arrogant, fearsome and sacrilegious.

Habakkuk's Second Complaint

12O LORD, are you not from everlasting?
My God, my Holy One, we will not die.
O LORD, you have appointed them to execute judgment;
O Rock, you have ordained them to punish.
13Your eyes are too pure to look on evil;
you cannot tolerate wrong.
Why then do you tolerate the treacherous?
Why are you silent while the wicked
swallow up those more righteous than themselves?
14You have made men like fish in the sea,
like sea creatures that have no ruler.
15The wicked foe pulls all of them up with hooks,
he catches them in his net,
he gathers them up in his dragnet;
and so he rejoices and is glad.
16Therefore he sacrifices to his net
and burns incense to his dragnet,
for by his net he lives in luxury
and enjoys the choicest food.
17Is he to keep on emptying his net,
destroying nations without mercy?

2 I will stand at my watch
and station myself on the ramparts;
I will look to see what he will say to me,
and what answer I am to give to this complaint.[a]

The Lord's Answer

2Then the LORD replied:

"Write down the revelation
and make it plain on tablets
so that a herald[b] may run with it.
3For the revelation awaits an appointed time;
it speaks of the end
and will not prove false.
Though it linger, wait for it;
it[c] will certainly come and will not delay.

4"See, he is puffed up;
his desires are not upright—
but the righteous will live by his faith[d]—

[a]1 Or *and what to answer when I am rebuked* [b]2 Or *so that whoever reads it* [c]3 Or *Though he linger, wait for him; / he* [d]4 Or *faithfulness*

OPEN 1. What do you like, or not like, about fishing and hunting? 2. When this past year have you felt like the hunter? The hunted?

STUDY 1. How have the events of verses 1–11 begun to happen? How does Habakkuk respond to this new situation? 2. To whom does he address this second complaint? How does his "voice" change (2:1)? 3. How is the character issue related to the problem of evil (1:12–13)? How will that change God's mind? 4. Who are the "treacherous" and the "more righteous" (1:13)? What is the "net" (1:14–17)? 5. What would it mean for the wicked to sacrifice to the "net"? How does the "net" support luxurious living? 6. Is Habakkuk resigning himself to fate? Or casting himself on God?

APPLY 1. When have you felt like someone was trying to "hook" or manipulate you? 2. How do you feel about how God has responded to the injustices in your life?

OPEN 1. When told, "Wait for it," how do you respond? What's tough about waiting for dinner? For a bus? For a buyer? For Christmas? 2. When are you "exhausted for nothing"? What was it you were striving after at the time?

STUDY 1. What "revelation" is Habakkuk to write down? What aspects of it are described here (vv. 2–3)? 2. Within the context of the book, who is "he" in verses 4–5? How are the righteous to live in contrast to "him"? In context, does this "living by faith" imply national deliverance or spiritual salvation? Explain. 3. Find the five "woes" in verses 6–20. In verse 6, who are "all of them" and who is "him"? What is the larger context for these woes (vv. 14,20)? How does this

---

1:12 Habakkuk finds comfort and confidence in God's character. God is faithful always. What the Babylonians do will be for punishment, not demolition. Habakkuk was confident that God would keep his covenant with Israel and protect a remnant.

1:13 Although he accepts that Judah must be punished, Habakkuk wonders why God would use such an evil nation to administer the discipline. Where is justice in that?

2:3 the revelation awaits an appointed time. Habakkuk has complained that evil men overcome the righteous (1:13). Now God responds that all things will be accomplished in due time. The day of judgment is coming.

2:4 righteous will live by his faith. In contrast to the arrogant Babylonian, the righteous follower of God will live by faith, patiently experiencing God's blessing and trusting God's promises.

5 indeed, wine betrays him;
he is arrogant and never at rest.
Because he is as greedy as the grave[a]
and like death is never satisfied,
he gathers to himself all the nations
and takes captive all the peoples.

6 "Will not all of them taunt him with ridicule and scorn, saying,

" 'Woe to him who piles up stolen goods
and makes himself wealthy by extortion!
How long must this go on?'
7 Will not your debtors[b] suddenly arise?
Will they not wake up and make you tremble?
Then you will become their victim.
8 Because you have plundered many nations,
the peoples who are left will plunder you.
For you have shed man's blood;
you have destroyed lands and cities and everyone in them.

9 "Woe to him who builds his realm by unjust gain
to set his nest on high,
to escape the clutches of ruin!
10 You have plotted the ruin of many peoples,
shaming your own house and forfeiting your life.
11 The stones of the wall will cry out,
and the beams of the woodwork will echo it.

12 "Woe to him who builds a city with bloodshed
and establishes a town by crime!
13 Has not the LORD Almighty determined
that the people's labor is only fuel for the fire,
that the nations exhaust themselves for nothing?
14 For the earth will be filled with the knowledge of the glory of the LORD,
as the waters cover the sea.

15 "Woe to him who gives drink to his neighbors,
pouring it from the wineskin till they are drunk,
so that he can gaze on their naked bodies.
16 You will be filled with shame instead of glory.

[a]5 Hebrew *Sheol* [b]7 Or *creditors*

oracle answer Habakkuk's original concern (1:12–17)? **4.** What is the content of the first woe (vv. 6–8)? What metaphor is used of Babylon? How has Habakkuk's view changed? **5.** What is announced in the second woe (vv. 9–11)? What metaphor is used of Babylon? **6.** Paraphrase the third woe (vv. 12–14). What is the climax to the first three woes (v. 14)? How will destroying Babylon spread God's glory? **7.** How is the fourth woe different from the first three (contrast vv. 6, 9, 12 with 15)? Do you read "drink" literally, or might this also refer to the drunkenness of power? What example of this do you see in Babylon's onslaught of Jerusalem in 586 B.C. (2 Kin. 25:8–21)? **8.** What new theme does verse 18 introduce? How is that related to the fifth woe (vv. 19–20)? What ironic point do you see here in idols silent before people and people silent before God? What is the climax of the whole "woe" section (v. 20) and of the "end" for which Israel is to wait? **9.** Compare verse 4 with Romans 1:16–18 and Galatians 3:10–14. What use does Paul make of this famous passage to speak a new word to a new generation? How is Paul's emphasis like and unlike Habakkuk's? **10.** "God may seem to be late, but is invariably on time"—Would Habakkuk agree? Would you agree? How does God measure "time"?

APPLY 1. Do you know someone who is "puffed up"? How can you "live by your faith" in his or her presence without also becoming "puffed up"? **2.** What help are the affirmations in verses 14 and 20 to you? What other "waters covered the sea" to God's glory (Ex. 14)? **3.** Where do you go to take time to "be silent" (v. 20) before the Lord?

This verse looks forward to the New Testament when faithful people will enjoy salvation because of God's grace (Rom. 1:17; Gal. 3:11; Heb. 10:38).

2:6–8 This is the first of five woes that foretell Babylon's destruction. Here Babylonian greed is compared to pawnbrokers who steal the wealth of the nations they conquer. Down the road, these plundered nations will rise up and take back what was stolen and then all of Babylon's wealth.

2:9–11 The Babylonians are compared to eagles building nests on mountainsides for protection from predators. The Babylonians used their stolen goods to build a seemingly invincible empire. Their pride will become their ruin.

2:11 stones of the wall will cry out. The material used to build the Babylonian Empire were purchased with plundered wealth.

2:12–14 To Babylon's greed and pride add its love of sin. The Lord declares that this empire's labor is in vain because the people follow evil.

2:14 God's judgment of evil will show how much greater God's glory is than anything greed can assemble. All people will know the Lord and acknowledge his glory.

2:15–17 Babylon's inhumanity and violence is condemned. The nation is compared to someone who gives a neighbor alcohol to indulge in lustful behavior. Their punishment for this sin would be public disgrace.

2:16 shame. The glory of the kingdoms will be turned to shame.

Now it is your turn! Drink and be exposed[a]!
The cup from the LORD's right hand is coming around to you,
and disgrace will cover your glory.
17 The violence you have done to Lebanon will overwhelm you,
and your destruction of animals will terrify you.
For you have shed man's blood;
you have destroyed lands and cities and everyone in them.

18 "Of what value is an idol, since a man has carved it?
Or an image that teaches lies?
For he who makes it trusts in his own creation;
he makes idols that cannot speak.
19 Woe to him who says to wood, 'Come to life!'
Or to lifeless stone, 'Wake up!'
Can it give guidance?
It is covered with gold and silver;
there is no breath in it.
20 But the LORD is in his holy temple;
let all the earth be silent before him."

Habakkuk's Prayer

3 A prayer of Habakkuk the prophet. On *shigionoth*.[b]

2 LORD, I have heard of your fame;
I stand in awe of your deeds, O LORD.
Renew them in our day,
in our time make them known;
in wrath remember mercy.

3 God came from Teman,
the Holy One from Mount Paran. *Selah*[c]
His glory covered the heavens
and his praise filled the earth.
4 His splendor was like the sunrise;
rays flashed from his hand,
where his power was hidden.
5 Plague went before him;
pestilence followed his steps.
6 He stood, and shook the earth;
he looked, and made the nations tremble.
The ancient mountains crumbled
and the age-old hills collapsed.
His ways are eternal.

[a]16 Masoretic Text; Dead Sea Scrolls, Aquila, Vulgate and Syriac (see also Septuagint) *and stagger*
[b]1 Probably a literary or musical term [c]3 A word of uncertain meaning; possibly a musical term; also in verses 9 and 13

OPEN **1.** What's your favorite spot from which to view the sunrise? How often do you go there? What do sunrises bring to mind for you? **2.** "It's always darkest before the dawn"—To what would that saying refer in your life these days? **3.** What popular song typified your teenage years? What memory does your favorite song bring to mind?

STUDY **1.** Why can the once woeful Habakkuk afford to be so joyful? How has his situation changed? How long after chapters 1 and 2 do you suppose it was written? **2.** How is verse 2 related to the rest of this psalm-like prayer? How is verse 2 related to the promise of 2:2–4? How are wrath and mercy related? **3.** How does reciting God's marvelous deeds in the past anticipate God's future deliverance "in our day" (v. 2)? **4.** To what historical events do the poetic allusions refer in verses 3–5 (Ex. 7–12)? In verses 6–7 (Ex. 19:16)? **5.** In verses 8–10, what do you see poetically depicted: Creation of the world? Parting of the Red Sea (Ex. 14:15–31)? Crossing the Jordan (Josh. 3:15–17)? **6.** Compare verses 8–10 with Psalms 74:12–17 and 77:16–19. What simi-

2:18–20 Finally, Babylon is chastised for its idolatry. Lifeless idols deceive people, are unable to aid their creators *and are incapable of speaking the oracles their worshipers attribute to them.* The Lord is the only eternal God, and the whole earth must fall silent before his power.

3:2 LORD, I have heard of your fame. Habakkuk has just heard God's plan to discipline Judah and destroy Babylon. In response to these promises Habakkuk humbly worships God and makes two requests. **Renew them in our day, in our time make them known.** Habakkuk asks for a prompt manifestation of God's power. **in wrath remember mercy.** In the midst of God's powerful judgment, Habakkuk pleads for mercy.

3:3 Habakkuk remembers God's visitation at Sinai to establish his covenant with his people.

[7]I saw the tents of Cushan in distress,
the dwellings of Midian in anguish.

[8]Were you angry with the rivers, O LORD?
Was your wrath against the streams?
Did you rage against the sea
when you rode with your horses
and your victorious chariots?
[9]You uncovered your bow,
you called for many arrows. *Selah*
You split the earth with rivers;
[10] the mountains saw you and writhed.
Torrents of water swept by;
the deep roared
and lifted its waves on high.

[11]Sun and moon stood still in the heavens
at the glint of your flying arrows,
at the lightning of your flashing spear.
[12]In wrath you strode through the earth
and in anger you threshed the nations.
[13]You came out to deliver your people,
to save your anointed one.
You crushed the leader of the land of wickedness,
you stripped him from head to foot. *Selah*
[14]With his own spear you pierced his head
when his warriors stormed out to scatter us,
gloating as though about to devour
the wretched who were in hiding.
[15]You trampled the sea with your horses,
churning the great waters.

[16]I heard and my heart pounded,
my lips quivered at the sound;
decay crept into my bones,
and my legs trembled.
Yet I will wait patiently for the day of calamity
to come on the nation invading us.
[17]Though the fig tree does not bud
and there are no grapes on the vines,
though the olive crop fails
and the fields produce no food,
though there are no sheep in the pen
and no cattle in the stalls,
[18]yet I will rejoice in the LORD,
I will be joyful in God my Savior.

[19]The Sovereign LORD is my strength;
he makes my feet like the feet of a deer,
he enables me to go on the heights.

For the director of music. On my stringed instruments.

lar images do these prayers use to evoke awe for God's mighty works? What other images (from nature, warfare or whatever) have a similar impact on you? **7.** What is Habakkuk's response to the poetic and dramatic vision of verses 3–15? Why is his heart racing? What evidence does he have for rejoicing? How does he get his sure-footed confidence? **8.** What does Habakkuk's irrepressible joy (vv. 17–19) mean in the context of injustice (1:2–4)?

APPLY 1. This hymn-like chapter stirred up vivid memories in Israel of God's might and mercy. When has God worked mightily and mercifully in your past? In your present, where do you want God to renew his mercy and work mightily again? **2.** What things are barren in your life, as in Habakkuk's day (v. 17)? Are you ready to yet rejoice in the Lord anyway? Why or why not? **3.** What promise does verse 19 hold for your present situation? For your future? **4.** Do you really believe God has the power described in this poem? Or is this just poetic exaggeration?

3:16 After seeing God's might in Israel's past, Habakkuk is left physically weak from his encounter with God. But he has greater confidence and peace as he waits for Judah's invasion and Babylon's subsequent fall.

3:18–19 Even if the suffering is hard and relief many years away, Habakkuk will rejoice in the Lord. God gives strength to face any circumstance that will come along the way.

Zephaniah

Author. The first verse of this prophecy tells us all that is known about Zephaniah. He is widely accepted as the author.

Personal Reading	Group Study Topic and Reading	
1:1–2:3	The Day of the Lord Announced	1:1–2:3
2:4–15	The Day of the Lord Implemented	2:4–15
3:1–20	The Redemption of the Lord Promised	3:1–20

Date. Zephaniah ministered during the reign of King Josiah (640–609 B.C.). This prophecy was probably written toward the end of Zephaniah's work.

Purpose. Zephaniah wrote to Israel as well as to the whole world. He did not consider anyone safe from God's judgment unless he was living a righteous life. Zephaniah did not write about gloom and doom because he was obsessed with it. He wrote and spoke about it because it was the sure, telltale sign that God took his relationship with humanity seriously. God's judgment proved that he meant what he said and that he was willing to defend the relationship he wanted to build with the Hebrews and rest of the world.

Historical Background. Zephaniah wrote during the reign of King Josiah of Judah (715–686 B.C.) Because Zephaniah was the great-great grandson of Hezekiah, a former king of Judah, he probably lived among the privileged classes and had a good understanding of the social and political events of his time. The reign of King Josiah was a prosperous time for Judah. The Assyrian empire that had conquered Israel in 722 B.C. was declining rapidly, and the Babylonians to the south were not yet strong enough to fill the power void left by the Assyrians. Within Judah, Josiah's reign was also a time of religious reformation. Just prior to Josiah, Judah had been ruled by Manasseh and then Amon. Both of these evil kings had promoted Baal worship, had built pagan temples and had even placed an Asherah pole (the goddess associated with Baal) in Solomon's temple, the most sacred place of Hebrew worship. Child sacrifices and astrology were widespread during the reign of these wicked kings.

Josiah's religious reforms attacked each of these idolatrous practices. He destroyed the temples to Baal and ended the pagan rituals. Perhaps these reforms were made after Zephaniah's prophesy, in response to it. It is also possible that Zephaniah's prophecy was made after the reforms and was addressed to those who had witnessed Josiah's reforms but had not responded in obedience.

Day of the Lord. The expression "day of the Lord" is used more in this small prophecy than in any other Old Testament book. Zephaniah focuses on this day of judgment and defines it. The "day of the Lord" is not just a day of judgment for Judah, when the nation will be punished for its disobedience. Along with judgment against Judah, Zephaniah predicts that God will judge and punish those nations who are (or have been) enemies of his people. Specifically, the prophet names Philistia, Moab, Ammon, Cush and Assyria as the victims of the forthcoming "sword" of God's judgment. Judah will certainly suffer for its disobedience, but the other nations will be destroyed because they are the enemies of God's people. For Judah, the "day of the Lord" is not the end but a new beginning that will culminate in the restoration and glorification of God's people.

1 The word of the LORD that came to Zephaniah son of Cushi, the son of Gedaliah, the son of Amariah, the son of Hezekiah, during the reign of Josiah son of Amon king of Judah:

Warning of Coming Destruction

2 "I will sweep away everything
from the face of the earth,"
declares the LORD.
3 "I will sweep away both men and animals;
I will sweep away the birds of the air
and the fish of the sea.
The wicked will have only heaps of rubble[a]
when I cut off man from the face of the earth,"
declares the LORD.

Against Judah

4 "I will stretch out my hand against Judah
and against all who live in Jerusalem.
I will cut off from this place every remnant of Baal,
the names of the pagan and the idolatrous priests—
5 those who bow down on the roofs
to worship the starry host,
those who bow down and swear by the LORD
and who also swear by Molech,[b]
6 those who turn back from following the LORD
and neither seek the LORD nor inquire of him.
7 Be silent before the Sovereign LORD,
for the day of the LORD is near.
The LORD has prepared a sacrifice;
he has consecrated those he has invited.
8 On the day of the LORD's sacrifice
I will punish the princes
and the king's sons
and all those clad
in foreign clothes.
9 On that day I will punish
all who avoid stepping on the threshold,[c]
who fill the temple of their gods
with violence and deceit.

[a]3 The meaning of the Hebrew for this line is uncertain. [b]5 Hebrew *Malcam,* that is, Milcom [c]9 See 1 Samuel 5:5.

OPEN 1. For what was your great-grandfather noted? Your granddad? Your dad? Any royal blood? Or bad blood? **2.** "Wait until your father gets home"—What did that mean for you: Court of appeal? D-day? Wailing? Goodies? What went through your mind as you awaited that "appointed" time?

STUDY 1. What is noteworthy about Zephaniah's background? What social circles did he likely move in? What situation did he inherit (vv. 4–6), following the reigns of two bad kings—Manasseh and Amon (2 Kin. 21)—before Josiah's reform and renewal (2 Kin. 23:4–16; 2 Chr. 34:1–7)? **2.** What "word of the LORD" does Zephaniah bring, after a long period of prophetic silence? What universal judgment does this house-cleaning imagery bring to mind (vv. 2–3)? **3.** What are five specific religious actions that have brought on this judgment (vv. 4–6)? What does it mean to "swear by Molech" (Lev. 18:21; 20:1–5)? **4.** What five groups are indicted for their social practices (vv. 8–9)? What has each done? What does it mean to "step on the threshold" (1 Sam. 5:1–5)? **5.** How thorough and unsuspecting will God's judgment be "on that day" (vv. 8–13)? Who will suffer most? Why? **6.** Judah seems to want her own cake (Yahweh) and eat someone else's (Molech), too. What is the danger of such fusion, then and now? How might we become like who or what we worship?

APPLY 1. Gross pagan idolatry (v. 4) may not be your thing. But are you "caught up in the rat race" of high finance, bigger homes and fruitless labor (vv. 11–13)? How so? How do you tell the difference between honorable wealth and unjust riches? **2.** When told, "Just wait until God your Father comes home," what would that elicit in Judah and in you: Hope of deliverance? Fear of wrath?

1:2–3:8 *These chapters,* the bulk of the book of Zephaniah, detail the day of God's wrath. The major themes are a declaration of God's imminent judgment with a call to repentance, and the promise that God will not forget his covenant but will restore his people in the future.

1:4–7 Judah is condemned for its idolatry, particularly the worship of Baal. Some scholars argue that these threats place Zephaniah's prophecy before the reign of Josiah since he destroyed the altars of Baal in his reforms (2 Kin. 23:4–16). Alternately, perhaps Josiah's reforms did not last and Baal was again being worshiped.

1:5–6 Zephaniah attacks three groups of idolators. First he chastized the star worshipers who regarded the sun, moon and stars as gods. Next, those who combined worship of God with worship of Molech, the Ammonite deity to which children were sacrificed. Finally, those who didn't worship any god, including the true God.

1:9 all who avoid stepping on the threshold. This phrase refers either to those who refused to step on the threshold for superstitious reasons (1 Sam. 5:5) or those who leaped into homes to steal goods for their pagan deities.

A vow of repentance? A lull of complacency? ______

10"On that day," declares the LORD,
"a cry will go up from the Fish Gate,
wailing from the New Quarter,
and a loud crash from the hills.
11Wail, you who live in the market district[a];
all your merchants will be wiped out,
all who trade with[b] silver will be ruined.
12At that time I will search Jerusalem with lamps
and punish those who are complacent,
who are like wine left on its dregs,
who think, 'The LORD will do nothing,
either good or bad.'
13Their wealth will be plundered,
their houses demolished.
They will build houses
but not live in them;
they will plant vineyards
but not drink the wine.

The Great Day of the Lord

14"The great day of the LORD is near—
near and coming quickly.
Listen! The cry on the day of the LORD will be bitter,
the shouting of the warrior there.
15That day will be a day of wrath,
a day of distress and anguish,
a day of trouble and ruin,
a day of darkness and gloom,
a day of clouds and blackness,
16a day of trumpet and battle cry
against the fortified cities
and against the corner towers.
17I will bring distress on the people
and they will walk like blind men,
because they have sinned against the LORD.
Their blood will be poured out like dust
and their entrails like filth.
18Neither their silver nor their gold
will be able to save them
on the day of the LORD's wrath.
In the fire of his jealousy
the whole world will be consumed,
for he will make a sudden end
of all who live in the earth."

[a] 11 *Or the Mortar* [b] 11 *Or in*

OPEN From your year-at-a-glance calendar, what "appointed time" are you eagerly anticipating? Which scheduled appointment are you dreading? Are you good at waiting? How so?

STUDY 1. How close does Zephaniah say the people are to "the great day of the LORD?" Is that day inked, penciled, or not even on their appointment calendars? Why or why not? **2.** Amid prosperity, how bright is Judah's future? What will "that day" be like? Is there any escape, or are God's consequences universal? What escape routes are dead ends (1:18)? **3.** What hope does God offer to any who gather together contritely before him (2:1–3)? What attitudes and actions please the Lord? What will be the final result? **4.** What do these judgments reveal about God's view of sin and its consequences? About God's view of the oppressor and the oppressed?

APPLY 1. Why is it harder to hear God's warnings during prosperity, when things are going well? Do you "shine" in suffering or in prosperity? Why is that? **2.** What contemporary "signs" (dark clouds and

1:12 those who are complacent. *The people of Judah had become so* spiritually stagnant that they were like wine that had been left too long, forming a hard crust and becoming too bitter to drink. They no longer believed that God had power to do anything, good or bad. They became arrogant.

1:14–18 Zephaniah describes in detail the coming destruction. On the day of God's wrath, idolaters, aristocrats, oppressors, merchants and the complacent had better fear.

1:18 Material possessions are powerless to save people from God's punishment. The wealthy who rely so heavily on their riches are left with no hope of deliverance, no way to save themselves. Riches have no value to save them from their punishment.

2 Gather together, gather together,
O shameful nation,
[2] before the appointed time arrives
and that day sweeps on like chaff,
before the fierce anger of the LORD comes upon you,
before the day of the LORD's wrath comes upon you.
[3] Seek the LORD, all you humble of the land,
you who do what he commands.
Seek righteousness, seek humility;
perhaps you will be sheltered
on the day of the LORD's anger.

Against Philistia

[4] Gaza will be abandoned
and Ashkelon left in ruins.
At midday Ashdod will be emptied
and Ekron uprooted.
[5] Woe to you who live by the sea,
O Kerethite people;
the word of the LORD is against you,
O Canaan, land of the Philistines.

"I will destroy you,
and none will be left."

[6] The land by the sea, where the Kerethites[a] dwell,
will be a place for shepherds and sheep pens.
[7] It will belong to the remnant of the house of Judah;
there they will find pasture.
In the evening they will lie down
in the houses of Ashkelon.
The LORD their God will care for them;
he will restore their fortunes.[b]

Against Moab and Ammon

[8] "I have heard the insults of Moab
and the taunts of the Ammonites,
who insulted my people
and made threats against their land.
[9] Therefore, as surely as I live,"
declares the LORD Almighty, the God of Israel,
"surely Moab will become like Sodom,
the Ammonites like Gomorrah—
a place of weeds and salt pits,
a wasteland forever.

[a]6 The meaning of the Hebrew for this word is uncertain. [b]7 Or *will bring back their captives*

social distress) do you see as God's warning to the nation? To the Church? To you? **3.** In what ways are you and your group seeking the Lord? His righteousness? With what promise?

OPEN 1. What is your favorite sport? Your favorite ball team? When have you seen your team trail badly throughout a game, only to rally late and win? What did it feel like to have your team's "fortune" restored? **2.** Have you ever visited a ghost town, ancient ruins or once-famous building, long since abandoned? What was it like, then and now?

STUDY 1. What desolation will God bring against the cities and land of Philistia? How extensive will this destruction be? What will this land be good for after God finishes with it? **2.** In what ways will God's punishment fall on Moab and Ammon as it did on their ancestor Lot (v. 9; Gen. 18–19)? Will they be as fortunate? What will they get in return for their pride and arrogance? What will happen to the gods they chose to serve? **3.** What is God's verdict against the Cushites (Ethiopians, Egyptians)? Why would this be just, in light of their supposed power? **4.** What irony do you see in the way God will ruin impregnable Nineveh (compare vv. 5 and 15, with Isa. 45:5–6,18,21)? **5.** In what ways are your and your nation's attitudes and actions like and unlike Philistia, Moab, Ammon, Cush or Nineveh? What can be the outcome of over-zealous pride in "God and country"?

APPLY 1. In what sense do you act like "there's none besides me"? In that case, how does this implementation of the day of the Lord

2:1–3 Zephaniah comes to the point of all these dire warnings: repentance is the only hope. The prophet encourages people to gather as a nation, repent of their sins and humbly ask God to save them.

2:3 perhaps you will be sheltered. The people have no guarantees that they will be spared from God's wrath. In fact, repentance will only protect them in the day of God's anger, not prevent it.

2:4–15 Now that he has warned Judah of God's coming judgment, Zephaniah issues a similar warning to her idolatrous neighbors. The nations that led Judah into idolatry are also targets of God's wrath.

2:9–10 The punishment for Moab and Ammon's taunting of Judah will be that the remnant of Judah will inhabit their land.

hit home with you? **2.** God's wrath has its flip side—restoration. What one quality above all others do you think God wants restored in the nation, church and individual who worships him? How could you and your group model that quality?

The remnant of my people will plunder them;
the survivors of my nation will inherit their land."

10 This is what they will get in return for their pride,
for insulting and mocking the people of the LORD Almighty.
11 The LORD will be awesome to them
when he destroys all the gods of the land.
The nations on every shore will worship him,
every one in its own land.

Against Cush

12 "You too, O Cushites,[a]
will be slain by my sword."

Against Assyria

13 He will stretch out his hand against the north
and destroy Assyria,
leaving Nineveh utterly desolate
and dry as the desert.
14 Flocks and herds will lie down there,
creatures of every kind.
The desert owl and the screech owl
will roost on her columns.
Their calls will echo through the windows,
rubble will be in the doorways,
the beams of cedar will be exposed.
15 This is the carefree city
that lived in safety.
She said to herself,
"I am, and there is none besides me."
What a ruin she has become,
a lair for wild beasts!
All who pass by her scoff
and shake their fists.

OPEN 1. Share an anecdote about when you "took a short cut" after being told by a parent or other adult exactly how to do something. What happened as a result? How did you feel about being corrected? What lesson did you learn from that experience? **2.** Which typifies your stance as a youth relating to that heavenly parent Yahweh: "My way is Yahweh"? "Any way but Yahweh"? "Have it your way, Yahweh"? Illustrate.

The Future of Jerusalem

3 Woe to the city of oppressors,
rebellious and defiled!
2 She obeys no one,
she accepts no correction.
She does not trust in the LORD,
she does not draw near to her God.
3 Her officials are roaring lions,
her rulers are evening wolves,

[a] *12* That is, people from the upper Nile region

2:12 The Cushites lived in what is today Egypt, Sudan and northern Ethiopia. This was the southernmost point known to Judah, so Zephaniah may have intended that God would judge the whole earth.

2:15 Nineveh's arrogant king supposed his city to be invincible. For about 200 years it was the world's strongest city, so the claim "there is none besides me" was in part accurate. But eventually the city lay in ruins; its carefree haughtiness silenced.

3:3–4 After a general statement about Jerusalem's wickedness in verses 1–2, Zephaniah targets all classes of Judah's rulers. The officals were like hungry lions searching for prey. The rulers or judges were so greedy that by dawn they had devoured prey caught the previous evening. Arrogant prophets twisted God's Law for their own gain. Idolatrous priests profaned the places of worship, when all along they should have been teaching the Law.

who leave nothing for the morning.
4 Her prophets are arrogant;
they are treacherous men.
Her priests profane the sanctuary
and do violence to the law.
5 The LORD within her is righteous;
he does no wrong.
Morning by morning he dispenses his justice,
and every new day he does not fail,
yet the unrighteous know no shame.

6 "I have cut off nations;
their strongholds are demolished.
I have left their streets deserted,
with no one passing through.
Their cities are destroyed;
no one will be left—no one at all.
7 I said to the city,
'Surely you will fear me
and accept correction!'
Then her dwelling would not be cut off,
nor all my punishments come upon her.
But they were still eager
to act corruptly in all they did.
8 Therefore wait for me," declares the LORD,
"for the day I will stand up to testify.[a]
I have decided to assemble the nations,
to gather the kingdoms
and to pour out my wrath on them—
all my fierce anger.
The whole world will be consumed
by the fire of my jealous anger.

9 "Then will I purify the lips of the peoples,
that all of them may call on the name of the LORD
and serve him shoulder to shoulder.
10 From beyond the rivers of Cush[b]
my worshipers, my scattered people,
will bring me offerings.
11 On that day you will not be put to shame
for all the wrongs you have done to me,
because I will remove from this city
those who rejoice in their pride.
Never again will you be haughty
on my holy hill.
12 But I will leave within you

[a]8 Septuagint and Syriac; Hebrew *will rise up to plunder* [b]10 That is, the upper Nile region

STUDY 1. After announcing God's judgment against Judah and her neighbors, upon what city does Zephaniah finally focus? What words does he use to describe her? **2.** What four specific actions highlight her insensitivity to sin? What four leadership groups are singled out (vv. 3–4)? In each case, for what? **3.** What qualities of God does Zephaniah hold up as a standard for the people? How well have they modeled these qualities and held to this standard? **4.** With their history and the destruction of neighboring nations, why does Jerusalem ignore God's gracious warning (vv. 6–8)? What's so hard about "accepting correction" (2:1–3)? **5.** How is God's redemption (vv. 9–20) consistent with his righteousness and wrath (vv. 5,8)? Has God changed his mind? Or is there some cause-and-effect link operating here? How does this compare with what is happening in Matthew 5:5 and Luke 1:52? **6.** What will God do for his scattered people to make them more like himself (v. 19)? What will be the cause for their rejoicing "on that day"? How does that compare with why they were once weeping "on that day" (1:10–13)? **7.** Which of God's actions do you believe would make the people most glad, but seems "too good to be true"? Which aspects of God's deliverance might be shrugged off as "too little, too late"? Which reassurance would sound most convincing to Israel?

APPLY 1. Try reading this chapter from the perspective of a poor peasant in Latin America or a starving person in sub-Saharan Africa. What does the promised Second Coming mean to them? To their oppressors? Does it mean anything different to you? If so, what? Will you be classed with the rejoicers (v. 11), or with those who trust (v. 12)? **2.** Throughout Zephaniah there is a pattern of rebellion, restoration and rejoicing. If this book were the story of your life, in which of those three stages do you find yourself in relation to God? Why? **3.** Joy will displace mourning, and calm will follow the storms of God's refining fire. How does that square with your experience of

3:6–8 God destroyed other nations to warn Judah of their fate if they did not repent.

3:7 Despite many warnings, Judah did not repent.

3:8 This section ends with a declaration of God's universal judgment on all of the nations. God will gather the various nations together, put them on trial and, in turn, pour out his anger on them.

3:9 This verse turns Zephaniah's prophecy from predictions of destruction to promises of restoration and peace. God's judgment will purify the nations so that they call on his name and serve him.

God? **4.** What is the most important thing you learned from Zephaniah? What life-changing application are you making?

the meek and humble,
who trust in the name of the LORD.
13 The remnant of Israel will do no wrong;
they will speak no lies,
nor will deceit be found in their mouths.
They will eat and lie down
and no one will make them afraid."

14 Sing, O Daughter of Zion;
shout aloud, O Israel!
Be glad and rejoice with all your heart,
O Daughter of Jerusalem!
15 The LORD has taken away your punishment,
he has turned back your enemy.
The LORD, the King of Israel, is with you;
never again will you fear any harm.
16 On that day they will say to Jerusalem,
"Do not fear, O Zion;
do not let your hands hang limp.
17 The LORD your God is with you,
he is mighty to save.
He will take great delight in you,
he will quiet you with his love,
he will rejoice over you with singing."

18 "The sorrows for the appointed feasts
I will remove from you;
they are a burden and a reproach to you.[a]
19 At that time I will deal
with all who oppressed you;
I will rescue the lame
and gather those who have been scattered.
I will give them praise and honor
in every land where they were put to shame.
20 At that time I will gather you;
at that time I will bring you home.
I will give you honor and praise
among all the peoples of the earth
when I restore your fortunes[b]
before your very eyes,"

says the LORD.

[a]18 Or *"I will gather you who mourn for the appointed feasts; / your reproach is a burden to you* [b]20 Or *I bring back your captives*

3:17–20 Zephaniah concludes his prophetic message with a word of encouragement and hope. First, he reminds the Israelites that they are God's chosen people. God still loves them and continues to delight in them. Then Zephaniah offers a series of promises from God. Although the restoration seemed far off compared with the imminent judgment. The Israelites could cling to these promises of the future gathering for comfort in the coming dark days.

Haggai

Author. Not much is known about Haggai except that he wrote this book and that he ministered to the Hebrews after their exile into Babylon.

Date. Haggai's four messages are dated 520 B.C., during the reign of Darius I.

Personal Reading	Group Study Topic and Reading	
1:1–15	From Indifference to Rebuilding	1:1–15
2:1:9	From Discouragement to Rebuilding	2:1:9
2:10–19	From Defilement to Blessing	2:10–19
2:20–23	A Signet Ring Signals the Lord's Day	2:20–23

Purpose. Haggai focused on a single goal. He wanted to rally his people around the building of the temple. He felt passionately about the temple, not because the structure was that important, but because worship was that important. From the earliest days of the Hebrew nation, the center of their community had been the place where they worshipped God. At first, it was the tent called the tabernacle that they moved with them in their journey from Egypt to their homeland. Then, it was the temple. This place symbolized God's presence among them. Throughout the history of the Hebrews, their care for the temple served as an indicator of their faithfulness in worship. Haggai knew this. He knew that for the Hebrews, rebuilding the temple was an important part of rebuilding their faith.

Historical Background. Haggai's prophecy took place during the period of restoration in Israel. In 538 B.C., after Cyrus of Persia had captured Babylon, he issued a decree that allowed the Jewish exiles to go home and rebuild the temple in Jerusalem. Approximately fifty thousand exiles, led by Jerubbabel, returned home and began the work. About two years later the foundation was finished. This progress threatened the Samaritans, who feared having a strong Jewish state as their neighbor. Through political pressure, the Samaritans were able to stop the work until 522 B.C., when Darius the Great became king of Persia and offered support to the Hebrews in their efforts. By that time, though, the Hebrews' energy for the project had waned. Prophets such as Haggai and Zechariah encouraged the people to continue their work. The temple was finally completed in 516 B.C. (Ezra 6:15–18).

Zerubbabel's Temple. Solomon's great temple was destroyed in 586 B.C. by the Babylonians. When Cyrus of Persia allowed exiles, led by Zerubbabel, to return to Jerusalem to rebuild the temple in 538 B.C., they began their reconstruction on the foundations of the earlier building. Solomon's temple was the masterpiece of a rich king, but the new temple was built by a group of poor exiles. In Solomon's day, Jerusalem had been a major capital. In the post-exile period, it was a backwater town, far from the center of power and affluence in Cyrus' court. When the foundation was completed, the comparison was stark. The new temple had little of the grandeur of the original. Ezra reported that those elders who had seen Solomon's temple cried when they saw the new one (Ezra 3:12). Nevertheless, in 516 B.C., the temple was completed.

Very little is known about the actual construction of the temple. It probably followed the construction styles of the time, which were Persian in origin. Most scholars believe that the temple was probably not very impressive because of the poverty of Israel at the time and because it did not spark a rapid religious revival, a problem addressed by the post-exile prophets.

A Call to Build the House of the Lord

1 In the second year of King Darius, on the first day of the sixth
month, the word of the LORD came through the prophet Haggai
to Zerubbabel son of Shealtiel, governor of Judah, and to Joshua[a] son
of Jehozadak, the high priest:
[2]This is what the LORD Almighty says: "These people say, 'The time
has not yet come for the LORD's house to be built.' "
[3]Then the word of the LORD came through the prophet Haggai: [4]"Is
it a time for you yourselves to be living in your paneled houses, while
this house remains a ruin?"
[5]Now this is what the LORD Almighty says: "Give careful thought to
your ways. [6]You have planted much, but have harvested little. You eat,
but never have enough. You drink, but never have your fill. You put on
clothes, but are not warm. You earn wages, only to put them in a
purse with holes in it."
[7]This is what the LORD Almighty says: "Give careful thought to your
ways. [8]Go up into the mountains and bring down timber and build
the house, so that I may take pleasure in it and be honored," says the
LORD. [9]"You expected much, but see, it turned out to be little. What
you brought home, I blew away. Why?" declares the LORD Almighty.
"Because of my house, which remains a ruin, while each of you is
busy with his own house. [10]Therefore, because of you the heavens
have withheld their dew and the earth its crops. [11]I called for a
drought on the fields and the mountains, on the grain, the new wine,
the oil and whatever the ground produces, on men and cattle, and on
the labor of your hands."

[12]Then Zerubbabel son of Shealtiel, Joshua son of Jehozadak, the
high priest, and the whole remnant of the people obeyed the voice of
the LORD their God and the message of the prophet Haggai, because
the LORD their God had sent him. And the people feared the LORD.
[13]Then Haggai, the LORD's messenger, gave this message of the
LORD to the people: "I am with you," declares the LORD. [14]So the LORD
stirred up the spirit of Zerubbabel son of Shealtiel, governor of Judah,
and the spirit of Joshua son of Jehozadak, the high priest, and the
spirit of the whole remnant of the people. They came and began to
work on the house of the LORD Almighty, their God, [15]on the twenty-
fourth day of the sixth month in the second year of King Darius.

The Promised Glory of the New House

2 On the twenty-first day of the seventh month, the word of the
LORD came through the prophet Haggai: [2]"Speak to Zerubbabel
son of Shealtiel, governor of Judah, to Joshua son of Jehozadak, the

[a]1 A variant of *Jeshua;* here and elsewhere in Haggai

OPEN 1. As a child, what did you enjoy building: Train sets? Tinker toys? Model cars? Tree houses? Snowmen? **2.** Who were your teammates in this? **3.** As a child, where did you store your allowance? Today, are you a saver or spender?

STUDY 1. Why do you think Haggai chose to speak to both the civil and religious leaders? And why on "the first day" of that particular month and year (Aug 29, 520 B.C.)? **2.** After 18 years of starts and stops in rebuilding the temple since returning from Exile, "this house remains a ruin" (v. 4). Why is that? To what are the people to "give careful thought" (vv. 5–8)? **3.** How did the Lord force their consideration of Haggai's alternative (vv. 9–15)? **4.** How did they respond to Haggai's call (v. 12)? Who led their response? How soon did they begin (v. 15)? **5.** How did God enable this (vv. 12–14)?

APPLY 1. When have you been part of a communal building project: Church? House? Community project? What part did you play? How was the community built up at the same time? How did God move during the project? **2.** How has God spoken to you about your financial priorities and spending habits? Have you seen "famines" or fruitlessness in your personal finances? **3.** When have you put your wages into "a purse with holes in it"? How did that feel? What will you do about that hole?

OPEN What great expectations of yours have fallen short?

STUDY 1. How long have the people been working (v.1;

1:2 The Israelites are called "these people," rather than the usual "my people," to emphasize that sin had *separated* them from God. They were making excuses for not building the temple as God had commanded.

1:3–4 Haggai rebukes the people for their selfishness and misplaced priorities. They were building comfortable houses for themselves but neglecting to build the house of God.

1:6 The people were working hard for themselves but leaving God off the agenda. God was punishing them for selfishness by making their efforts futile.

1:14 the LORD stirred up the spirit. God moved the hearts of his people, giving them a desire to return home and work on the temple.

2:1 The twenty-first day of the seventh month was the final day of the Feast of Tabernacles, a time of celebration for the summer harvest. At this time they

high priest, and to the remnant of the people. Ask them, 3'Who of you
is left who saw this house in its former glory? How does it look to you
now? Does it not seem to you like nothing? 4But now be strong,
O Zerubbabel,' declares the LORD. 'Be strong, O Joshua son of Jehozadak, the high priest. Be strong, all you people of the land,' declares
the LORD, 'and work. For I am with you,' declares the LORD Almighty.
5'This is what I covenanted with you when you came out of Egypt.
And my Spirit remains among you. Do not fear.'
6"This is what the LORD Almighty says: 'In a little while I will once
more shake the heavens and the earth, the sea and the dry land. 7I
will shake all nations, and the desired of all nations will come, and
I will fill this house with glory,' says the LORD Almighty. 8'The silver is
mine and the gold is mine,' declares the LORD Almighty. 9'The glory of
this present house will be greater than the glory of the former house,'
says the LORD Almighty. 'And in this place I will grant peace,' declares
the LORD Almighty."

Blessings for a Defiled People

10On the twenty-fourth day of the ninth month, in the second year
of Darius, the word of the LORD came to the prophet Haggai: 11"This is
what the LORD Almighty says: 'Ask the priests what the law says: 12If a
person carries consecrated meat in the fold of his garment, and that
fold touches some bread or stew, some wine, oil or other food, does it
become consecrated?' "
The priests answered, "No."
13Then Haggai said, "If a person defiled by contact with a dead
body touches one of these things, does it become defiled?"
"Yes," the priests replied, "it becomes defiled."
14Then Haggai said, " 'So it is with this people and this nation in my
sight,' declares the LORD. 'Whatever they do and whatever they offer
there is defiled.
15" 'Now give careful thought to this from this day on[a]—consider
how things were before one stone was laid on another in the LORD's
temple. 16When anyone came to a heap of twenty measures, there
were only ten. When anyone went to a wine vat to draw fifty measures, there were only twenty. 17I struck all the work of your hands
with blight, mildew and hail, yet you did not turn to me,' declares the
LORD. 18'From this day on, from this twenty-fourth day of the ninth
month, give careful thought to the day when the foundation of the
LORD's temple was laid. Give careful thought: 19Is there yet any seed

1:15)? What have the people been doing during this seventh month (Lev. 23:23–43)? **2.** Why does Haggai speak now? **3.** What feelings does Solomon's temple evoke (vv. 3–5)? How does God's command and covenant relate to this? **4.** God "shaking heavens, earth ... nations" refers to what events (vv. 6–7; Ex. 8ff; Heb. 12:26–27)? **5.** "The desired of all nations" refers to what? When will this be (vv. 7–9)?

APPLY 1. What dream of yours has shattered recently? Do comparisons with past successes help? **2.** How might God be building you into a temple of His glory?

OPEN In your home, what spreads by itself: Cleanliness or messes? Give an example.

STUDY 1. At winter planting time (v. 10), what does Haggai have to say? **2.** Consecration does not rub off, but defilement does (vv. 10,13). What holy work were the people trusting in that would not rub off on their fruitfulness or moral character, much to their chagrin (vv. 14–19)? **3.** Who is "this people" whom Haggai accuses (v. 14; Ezra 4:1–5)? (With friends like these Samaritans, who needs enemies?) **4.** What thematic ties do you see between 2:15–19 and 1:10–11? Between verses 10–14 and 2:15–19? **5.** Since crops have only just been planted (vv. 10,19), how can Haggai assure Judah of God's blessing? **6.** How much time has elapsed (v. 20; compare 1:1)? How much longer before the job is done (Ezra 6:15)? **7.** In this last oracle, what will happen? When? Why? **8.** What biblical events does this day recall (Gen. 19:23–26; Ex. 15:1,4,19,21; Judg. 7:22)? **9.** What does Haggai say here about God's power over world governments?

[a]15 Or *to the days past*

---

had been working on the temple for a month.

2:3 former glory. The people were discouraged as they compared the inferior rebuilt temple to Solomon's glorious temple.

2:7 I will fill this house with glory. To encourage the people, God promises that glory will fill the house of the Lord. This surely points to Christ's coming (he is the radiance of God's glory, Heb. 1:3) and to the glory of God's kingdom fully realized at the end of time.

2:13–14 Just as ceremonial uncleanness is transferred from an "unclean" person to anything he touches, so the disobedience of a worshiper is transferred onto sacrifices which renders them unacceptable. Haggai urges the people to obey the Lord from this day on.

2:15–19 To convince the people to obey God, Haggai reminds them of the economic hardships God used to punish their sin. He then affirms that God has promised blessing for faithful obedience. He encourages them not to repeat their mistake again.

APPLY **1.** What part of your spiritual life has God begun to rebuild? How can your group figure in that? How long will this rebuilding take place? **2.** As the son of David and of Zerubbabel (Matt. 1:1,12), how is Christ "like God's signet ring" (v. 23)? As a follower of Jesus, how are you also like God's signet ring? **3.** From Haggai, what can you apply to helping your church grow?

---

left in the barn? Until now, the vine and the fig tree, the pomegranate
and the olive tree have not borne fruit.
" 'From this day on I will bless you.' "

Zerubbabel the Lord's Signet Ring

20 The word of the LORD came to Haggai a second time on the twenty-
fourth day of the month: 21 "Tell Zerubbabel governor of Judah that I
will shake the heavens and the earth. 22 I will overturn royal thrones
and shatter the power of the foreign kingdoms. I will overthrow chariots and their drivers; horses and their riders will fall, each by the
sword of his brother.
23 " 'On that day,' declares the LORD Almighty, 'I will take you, my
servant Zerubbabel son of Shealtiel,' declares the LORD, 'and I will
make you like my signet ring, for I have chosen you,' declares the
LORD Almighty."

Zechariah

Author. Zechariah is credited with this prophecy.

Date. Zechariah began his work just after Haggai began prophesying. Some of Zechariah's prophecies were written as the Hebrews rebuilt the temple after their exile, probably between 520–518 B.C.

Personal Reading	Group Study Topic and Reading	
1:1–17	Call to Repent	1:1–17
1:18–2:13	Surveyor's Line	1:18–2:13
3:1–10	Priest's Garments	3:1–10
4:1–14	Lampstand and Trees	4:1–14
5:1–6:8	Wicked Basket Case	5:1–6:8
6:9–15	Crown for Joshua	6:9–15
7:1–8:23	True Justice	7:1–14
9:1–17	New King for a New Day	9:9–13
10:1–11:17	Two Shepherds	11:4–17
12:1–13:6	God Purges His Own	12:10–13:6
13:7–14:21	God Punishes Nations	14:1–21

Purpose. Throughout the history of the Hebrews, their care of the temple indicated the welfare of their faith. The temple was the place of God's presence among them. The innermost room, the Holy Place, was so filled with God's presence that only the high priest entered. When he did, he had a chord tied around his ankles so that if he died facing God's presence, the people could pull his body out without entering the room themselves. With all this in mind, Zechariah naturally encouraged his people to place a priority on rebuilding the temple. Without it, their floundering faith had no focus. Zechariah also encouraged his people with words about the Messiah, the ultimate expression of God's presence in the world.

Historical Background. In 538 B.C., Cyrus of Persia, who had conquered the Babylonians, allowed fifty thousand of the Jewish exiles to return to Jerusalem to rebuild the temple. Zechariah was among the group of exiles that immediately returned to Jerusalem, though he must have done so as a young boy. The foundation of the temple was completed in about two years. Because of political pressure from Samaria and other neighbors, work on the temple was stopped until 522 B.C., when Darius the Great allowed the reconstruction to continue. Even with this permission, the Jews were not enthusiastic about continuing the work. It fell to the prophets to encourage them.

Zechariah began preaching the same year, 520 B.C., that Haggai began prophesying. Like Haggai, he witnessed the lack of enthusiasm among his people. He worked to encourage the temple's completion. Unlike Haggai, whose prophetic period was short, Zechariah prophesied for at least another forty years.

Apocalyptic Prophecy. The prophetic visions of 1:7–6:8 are called apocalyptic visions because they are "revelatory" and encouraging. They are very highly stylized, and their imagery is vibrant and complex. In addition, the images can be highly symbolic. The subject matter of these visions is related to the end of things (meaning the end of time, the destruction of the world and the destruction of Israel's enemies), but their tone is encouraging. Just as in Revelation, the imagery is complex, but the message is ultimately one of encouragement, not despair.

OPEN 1. What physical traits (eyes, hair coloring, etc.) did you inherit from your ancestors? What traits seem to have skipped a generation? 2. What social skills (outgoing-type, shy-type, etc.) were passed along to you? 3. In what one respect are you most like your parents?

STUDY 1. What "word of the LORD" came to Zechariah? What word came three months later? 2. Why is God so angry with Israel's forefathers? What were they like (vv. 4–6)? What impact did the call to repentance have on them? What's the object lesson in that? 3. The second word came three months later in audio-visual form (vv. 7–17). What did Zechariah see? Hear? Ask? 4. Are the horseman's words alarming or comforting? 5. What connects the Lord's mercy, jealousy and anger? What is he most angry about "these seventy years" (v. 12)? 6. What is meant by the "measuring line" in God's plans for Jerusalem? 7. What does Zechariah say about the consequences of returning and of disobedience for God's people, then and now?

APPLY 1. In matters of faith, what did you inherit from your ancestors? How have you rebelled? Returned? 2. What vision for your life have you received through studying God's Word? How does that affect your day-to-day decisions? Your long-term decisions? 3. How is your life similar to Jerusalem: Feeling the pressure of the enemy? Dry or desolate like a desert? Needing restoration and comfort? Restful and peaceful?

A Call to Return to the Lord

1 In the eighth month of the second year of Darius, the word of
the LORD came to the prophet Zechariah son of Berekiah, the
son of Iddo:
2"The LORD was very angry with your forefathers. 3Therefore tell
the people: This is what the LORD Almighty says: 'Return to me,'
declares the LORD Almighty, 'and I will return to you,' says the LORD
Almighty. 4Do not be like your forefathers, to whom the earlier prophets proclaimed: This is what the LORD Almighty says: 'Turn from your
evil ways and your evil practices.' But they would not listen or pay
attention to me, declares the LORD. 5Where are your forefathers now?
And the prophets, do they live forever? 6But did not my words and my
decrees, which I commanded my servants the prophets, overtake
your forefathers?
"Then they repented and said, 'The LORD Almighty has done to us
what our ways and practices deserve, just as he determined to do.' "

The Man Among the Myrtle Trees

7On the twenty-fourth day of the eleventh month, the month of
Shebat, in the second year of Darius, the word of the LORD came to
the prophet Zechariah son of Berekiah, the son of Iddo.
8During the night I had a vision—and there before me was a man
riding a red horse! He was standing among the myrtle trees in a ravine. Behind him were red, brown and white horses.
9I asked, "What are these, my lord?"
The angel who was talking with me answered, "I will show you
what they are."
10Then the man standing among the myrtle trees explained, "They
are the ones the LORD has sent to go throughout the earth."
11And they reported to the angel of the LORD, who was standing
among the myrtle trees, "We have gone throughout the earth and
found the whole world at rest and in peace."
12Then the angel of the LORD said, "LORD Almighty, how long will
you withhold mercy from Jerusalem and from the towns of Judah,
which you have been angry with these seventy years?" 13So the LORD
spoke kind and comforting words to the angel who talked with me.
14Then the angel who was speaking to me said, "Proclaim this
word: This is what the LORD Almighty says: 'I am very jealous for Jerusalem and Zion, 15but I am very angry with the nations that feel
secure. I was only a little angry, but they added to the calamity.'
16"Therefore, this is what the LORD says: 'I will return to Jerusalem
with mercy, and there my house will be rebuilt. And the measuring
line will be stretched out over Jerusalem,' declares the LORD Almighty.

1:2 angry. To say God was angry was an understatement. His anger was the motivating force behind the destruction of Jerusalem and the exile of the entire nation.

1:3 I will return to you. In the midst of his anger, God promised reconciliation based on one condition, that the people needed to respond to his offer and turn from disobedience back to him.

1:7–17 Zechariah's first vision of a rider among myrtle trees was a reassuring message. It soothed Israel's fears and inspired hope. The accompanying angel explained that their enemies would be punished (vv. 14–15), and Israel's prosperity would be restored (v. 17).

1:8 During the night ... vision. Zechariah experienced eight visions concerning the restoration of Israel, all in a single night!

1:15 that feel secure. Successful nations trusted in their wealth and resources. However, their measure afforded temporary success at best.

6So he said to me, "This is the word of the LORD to Zerubbabel: 'Not
by might nor by power, but by my Spirit,' says the LORD Almighty.
7"What[a] are you, O mighty mountain? Before Zerubbabel you will
become level ground. Then he will bring out the capstone to shouts
of 'God bless it! God bless it!' "
8Then the word of the LORD came to me: 9"The hands of Zerubbabel
have laid the foundation of this temple; his hands will also complete
it. Then you will know that the LORD Almighty has sent me to you.
10"Who despises the day of small things? Men will rejoice when
they see the plumb line in the hand of Zerubbabel.
"(These seven are the eyes of the LORD, which range throughout
the earth.)"
11Then I asked the angel, "What are these two olive trees on the
right and the left of the lampstand?"
12Again I asked him, "What are these two olive branches beside the
two gold pipes that pour out golden oil?"
13He replied, "Do you not know what these are?"
"No, my lord," I said.
14So he said, "These are the two who are anointed to[b] serve the
Lord of all the earth."

The Flying Scroll

5 I looked again—and there before me was a flying scroll!
2He asked me, "What do you see?"
I answered, "I see a flying scroll, thirty feet long and fifteen feet
wide.[c]"
3And he said to me, "This is the curse that is going out over the
whole land; for according to what it says on one side, every thief will
be banished, and according to what it says on the other, everyone
who swears falsely will be banished. 4The LORD Almighty declares, 'I
will send it out, and it will enter the house of the thief and the house
of him who swears falsely by my name. It will remain in his house
and destroy it, both its timbers and its stones.' "

The Woman in a Basket

5Then the angel who was speaking to me came forward and said to
me, "Look up and see what this is that is appearing."
6I asked, "What is it?"
He replied, "It is a measuring basket.[d]" And he added, "This is the
iniquity[e] of the people throughout the land."
7Then the cover of lead was raised, and there in the basket sat a

[a]7 Or *Who* [b]14 Or *two who bring oil and* [c]2 Hebrew *twenty cubits long and ten cubits wide* (about 9 meters long and 4.5 meters wide) [d]6 Hebrew *an ephah*; also in verses 7-11 [e]6 Or *appearance*

5,24; Hag. 1:14; 2:1–5)? **4.** How will Zerubbabel and Joshua utilize God's resources?

APPLY 1. How does God's glory and blessing come into your life? Does it come more in day-to-day work (Zerubbabel) or in worship (Joshua)? **2.** Into whose life will you carry blessing and renewal? **3.** How does your life compare to the "Master Builder's" plumb line? What will you do today to bring your life back into line?

OPEN 1. As a kid, how did you picture Satan? Now, how do you envision him? Why the change? **2.** From your family background, what images does "horse" bring to mind: Horse and buggy days? Equestrian events? Betting on races? Merry-go-round? Cowboy westerns on TV? You grew up with a horse? What would you do with a horse now?

STUDY 1. What message does the unfurled scroll bring? Why is it so big? **2.** Who is this curse meant for (v. 3; Ex. 20:7,15; Deut. 27:26; Gal. 3:10)? **3.** How effective will the curse or warning be? **4.** How big must this "measuring basket" have been (5:6)? **5.** Whose "wickedness" did the woman represent: People? Government? Priests? Satan? **6.** Who removed it from the land? Why take it to Babylonia (Rev. 17–18)? What does all this mean? **7.** How does Zechariah's eighth and last vision (6:1–8) compare with 1:7–17? With Revelation 6:1–8? **8.** What mission are these four chari-

4:7 shouts of God bless it! Zechariah described the people's accelerated passion for the project. Momentum would rise with every effort.

5:1–4 Zechariah's fifth vision held no tolerance for sin. The flying scroll portrayed swift judgment on all those who rejected God's commands.

5:2 The scroll served as God's billboard, announcing his judgment against sin. Who could miss the message?

5:4 destroy it. Disobedience would not be tolerated in the New Jerusalem. Perpetrators would be removed from the grounds.

5:5–11 The seventh vision further delineated God's zero tolerance policy against sin.

5:6 basket. A supersized basket (big enough to hold a person) carried a weighty mission. The corporate sins of all the people would be carried away in it.

5:7 in the basket sat a woman! Instead of dead weight, the basket contained a live person. Her presence had less to do with her gender than it did the animated image of wickedness as alive and well. It must be destroyed.

ots on? **9.** What does this vision say about judgment? About God's rest?

APPLY 1. If you were to put something in a basket to symbolize wickedness, what would it be? **2.** Is the lid on evil open or shut in your life (5:8)? **3.** What vehicle of judgment does God use in your life? **4.** When have you known God's "rest" (6:8)?

---

woman! 8He said, "This is wickedness," and he pushed her back into the basket and pushed the lead cover down over its mouth.

9Then I looked up—and there before me were two women, with the wind in their wings! They had wings like those of a stork, and they lifted up the basket between heaven and earth.

10"Where are they taking the basket?" I asked the angel who was speaking to me.

11He replied, "To the country of Babylonia[a] to build a house for it. When it is ready, the basket will be set there in its place."

Four Chariots

6 I looked up again—and there before me were four chariots coming out from between two mountains—mountains of bronze! 2The first chariot had red horses, the second black, 3the third white, and the fourth dappled—all of them powerful. 4I asked the angel who was speaking to me, "What are these, my lord?"

5The angel answered me, "These are the four spirits[b] of heaven, going out from standing in the presence of the Lord of the whole world. 6The one with the black horses is going toward the north country, the one with the white horses toward the west,[c] and the one with the dappled horses toward the south."

7When the powerful horses went out, they were straining to go throughout the earth. And he said, "Go throughout the earth!" So they went throughout the earth.

8Then he called to me, "Look, those going toward the north country have given my Spirit[d] rest in the land of the north."

A Crown for Joshua

9The word of the LORD came to me: 10"Take ⌞silver and gold⌟ from the exiles Heldai, Tobijah and Jedaiah, who have arrived from Babylon. Go the same day to the house of Josiah son of Zephaniah. 11Take the silver and gold and make a crown, and set it on the head of the high priest, Joshua son of Jehozadak. 12Tell him this is what the LORD Almighty says: 'Here is the man whose name is the Branch, and he will branch out from his place and build the temple of the LORD. 13It is he who will build the temple of the LORD, and he will be clothed with majesty and will sit and rule on his throne. And he will be a priest on his throne. And there will be harmony between the two.' 14The crown will be given to Heldai,[e] Tobijah, Jedaiah and Hen[f] son of Zephaniah as a memorial in the temple of the LORD. 15Those who are far away will come and help to build the temple of the LORD, and you will know that the LORD Almighty has sent me to you. This will happen if you diligently obey the LORD your God."

[a]11 Hebrew *Shinar* [b]5 Or *winds* [c]6 Or *horses after them* [d]8 Or *spirit* [e]14 Syriac; Hebrew *Helem* [f]14 Or *and the gracious one, the*

OPEN What nickname were you given as a child? How did you get it?

STUDY 1. Here Zechariah receives a direct command rather than an interactive vision. Why? **2.** What is meant by crowning Joshua? By the prophecy about the royal Branch (vv. 11–13; Jer. 23:5; 33:15–16; Heb. 7:1–3,15–17)? **3.** Which temple will those who "are far away" build (v. 15; Hag. 2:6–9; Eph. 2:13)? What else will happen then?

APPLY 1. What kind of "life structure" are you building for your King: Shack? Condo? Cathedral? Temple? **2.** If you are God's temple (1 Cor. 3:16), what building materials are you using? What craftmanship?

5:8 This is wickedness. Every facet *of sinfulness was represented inside* the basket.

6:1–8 The eighth vision fulfilled the punishment ordained in the first vision (1:7–17). Chariots were sent throughout the earth to trample wicked nations.

6:9–15 Zechariah crowned the high priest, Joshua, to point to the future royal rule of the Messiah. Ordinarily, crowns were reserved for royalty. Joshua acted out the coming coronation of the branch, Jesus Christ, who would be both priest and king (v. 12, 3:8).

6:11 make a crown. Joshua's coronation was a picture of Christ's future

Justice and Mercy, Not Fasting

7 In the fourth year of King Darius, the word of the LORD came to
Zechariah on the fourth day of the ninth month, the month of
Kislev. 2The people of Bethel had sent Sharezer and Regem-Melech,
together with their men, to entreat the LORD 3by asking the priests of
the house of the LORD Almighty and the prophets, "Should I mourn
and fast in the fifth month, as I have done for so many years?"
4Then the word of the LORD Almighty came to me: 5"Ask all the people of the land and the priests, 'When you fasted and mourned in the
fifth and seventh months for the past seventy years, was it really for
me that you fasted? 6And when you were eating and drinking, were
you not just feasting for yourselves? 7Are these not the words the
LORD proclaimed through the earlier prophets when Jerusalem and
its surrounding towns were at rest and prosperous, and the Negev
and the western foothills were settled?' "
8And the word of the LORD came again to Zechariah: 9"This is what
the LORD Almighty says: 'Administer true justice; show mercy and
compassion to one another. 10Do not oppress the widow or the fatherless, the alien or the poor. In your hearts do not think evil of each
other.'
11"But they refused to pay attention; stubbornly they turned their
backs and stopped up their ears. 12They made their hearts as hard as
flint and would not listen to the law or to the words that the LORD
Almighty had sent by his Spirit through the earlier prophets. So the
LORD Almighty was very angry.
13" 'When I called, they did not listen; so when they called, I would
not listen,' says the LORD Almighty. 14'I scattered them with a whirlwind among all the nations, where they were strangers. The land was
left so desolate behind them that no one could come or go. This is
how they made the pleasant land desolate.' "

OPEN 1. How did you impress your spouse, or the one you hope to marry, on your first date: With flowers? Make-up? Clothes? Car? Dieting? Great meal? 2. What actually impressed your date most?

STUDY 1. What question did the Bethel delegation ask Zechariah? How did he reply? What was so wrong with their fasting and feasting these 70 years? 2. Instead, what should they have done to show "justice and mercy" in practice (vv. 9–10)? 3. What attitude was in their heart (1 Cor. 10:31)? How was that obvious? How did God react? Why?

APPLY 1. How does the worship at your church or in your group compare with that of Zechariah's day? Is your heart in it? How so? 2. How can you obey (vv. 9–10)? What do your heart-felt actions of justice and mercy say to God? To the world? 3. Do you ever feel like the Bethel group in your response toward God's Word? How so? As a result, is your life scattered or desolate? In what way?

The Lord Promises to Bless Jerusalem

8 Again the word of the LORD Almighty came to me. 2This is what
the LORD Almighty says: "I am very jealous for Zion; I am burning
with jealousy for her."
3This is what the LORD says: "I will return to Zion and dwell in Jerusalem. Then Jerusalem will be called the City of Truth, and the mountain of the LORD Almighty will be called the Holy Mountain."
4This is what the LORD Almighty says: "Once again men and women
of ripe old age will sit in the streets of Jerusalem, each with cane in
hand because of his age. 5The city streets will be filled with boys and
girls playing there."
6This is what the LORD Almighty says: "It may seem marvelous to

OPEN Did you ever fall out of favor with a good friend or break up with your boy/girlfriend? Over what issue? Did you ever get back together? Who made the first move? What did you gain by mending the relationship?

STUDY 1. Zechariah foresees countless benefits concerning Jerusalem getting back together with her Lord. Can you find 10 of them? 2. What moral force is given to each blessing by the constant refrain, "the LORD Almighty says"? 3. What will it

---

ceremony. Therefore, the elaborate crown was not his to keep (v. 14).

7:5 for the past seventy years. The Jews were in Babylonian exile for approximately seventy years. During this time, they kept a façade of religious devotion, though they were more concerned with their own needs (v. 6).

7:9–11 The Jews had practiced everything God discouraged. He chastised them for their outward social injustice and even their secret inner thoughts.

7:10 Do not oppress. God had special concern for those with special needs. Widows, the poor and aliens were at the top of the list, however, they were the last ones on the minds of most Israelites (Deut. 15:7–11).

8:1–23 Zechariah itemized the blessings promised in his earlier visions (1:7–6:8). If the Lord Almighty said it, they could count on it. God would deliver what he had promised. He had never let them down.

the remnant of this people at that time, but will it seem marvelous to me?" declares the LORD Almighty.

7This is what the LORD Almighty says: "I will save my people from the countries of the east and the west. 8I will bring them back to live in Jerusalem; they will be my people, and I will be faithful and righteous to them as their God."

9This is what the LORD Almighty says: "You who now hear these words spoken by the prophets who were there when the foundation was laid for the house of the LORD Almighty, let your hands be strong so that the temple may be built. 10Before that time there were no wages for man or beast. No one could go about his business safely because of his enemy, for I had turned every man against his neighbor. 11But now I will not deal with the remnant of this people as I did in the past," declares the LORD Almighty.

12"The seed will grow well, the vine will yield its fruit, the ground will produce its crops, and the heavens will drop their dew. I will give all these things as an inheritance to the remnant of this people. 13As you have been an object of cursing among the nations, O Judah and Israel, so will I save you, and you will be a blessing. Do not be afraid, but let your hands be strong."

14This is what the LORD Almighty says: "Just as I had determined to bring disaster upon you and showed no pity when your fathers angered me," says the LORD Almighty, 15"so now I have determined to do good again to Jerusalem and Judah. Do not be afraid. 16These are the things you are to do: Speak the truth to each other, and render true and sound judgment in your courts; 17do not plot evil against your neighbor, and do not love to swear falsely. I hate all this," declares the LORD.

18Again the word of the LORD Almighty came to me. 19This is what the LORD Almighty says: "The fasts of the fourth, fifth, seventh and tenth months will become joyful and glad occasions and happy festivals for Judah. Therefore love truth and peace."

20This is what the LORD Almighty says: "Many peoples and the inhabitants of many cities will yet come, 21and the inhabitants of one city will go to another and say, 'Let us go at once to entreat the LORD and seek the LORD Almighty. I myself am going.' 22And many peoples and powerful nations will come to Jerusalem to seek the LORD Almighty and to entreat him."

23This is what the LORD Almighty says: "In those days ten men from all languages and nations will take firm hold of one Jew by the hem of his robe and say, 'Let us go with you, because we have heard that God is with you.' "

Judgment on Israel's Enemies

An Oracle

9 The word of the LORD is against the land of Hadrach
and will rest upon Damascus—

take to restore the people to covenant favor and be given these blessings (vv. 14–17)? What gap lies between promise and fulfillment? Between desire and delivery? **4.** What is God's answer to the Bethel group's question concerning fasts (vv. 18–19; 7:2–3)? What does this indicate about the health of the relationship between God and the people? **5.** What role will a restored Israel play in the worship of God and his witness among the nations (vv. 20–23)? How will other nations express their desire to know God?

APPLY 1. When parents, spiritual leaders, salespeople or politicians make too-good-to-be-true promises, are you initially trusting or are you mostly skeptical? What does your response depend on? **2.** What difference does it make when God promises you something? Which of the blessings promised in Zechariah have you seen come true for spiritual Israel and the Church? Which promises are yet to be fulfilled? **3.** Right now does your relationship with God feel like "fast" or "feast" (v. 19)? Explain.

OPEN 1. What have you lost that you once took great pride in: Academic standing? Car? House? Houseful of kids? Athletic ability? Nest egg? Other? **2.** How did it feel to be without your claim to fun, fame or for-

---

8:11 But now. Zechariah was focused on the future. He emphasized the contrast between the way things were and the way they would someday be.

8:19 fasts. God would turn the deprivations of the past into future feasts. What were once annual seasons of mourning would turn into celebrations.

8:20–23 Israel's enthusiasm would inspire many nations. As a result, previously pagan nations would gravitate toward Jerusalem to worship God (Isa. 2:3).

for the eyes of men and all the tribes of Israel
are on the LORD—[a]
²and upon Hamath too, which borders on it,
and upon Tyre and Sidon, though they are very skillful.
³Tyre has built herself a stronghold;
she has heaped up silver like dust,
and gold like the dirt of the streets.
⁴But the Lord will take away her possessions
and destroy her power on the sea,
and she will be consumed by fire.
⁵Ashkelon will see it and fear;
Gaza will writhe in agony,
and Ekron too, for her hope will wither.
Gaza will lose her king
and Ashkelon will be deserted.
⁶Foreigners will occupy Ashdod,
and I will cut off the pride of the Philistines.
⁷I will take the blood from their mouths,
the forbidden food from between their teeth.
Those who are left will belong to our God
and become leaders in Judah,
and Ekron will be like the Jebusites.
⁸But I will defend my house
against marauding forces.
Never again will an oppressor overrun my people,
for now I am keeping watch.

The Coming of Zion's King

⁹Rejoice greatly, O Daughter of Zion!
Shout, Daughter of Jerusalem!
See, your king[b] comes to you,
righteous and having salvation,
gentle and riding on a donkey,
on a colt, the foal of a donkey.
¹⁰I will take away the chariots from Ephraim
and the war-horses from Jerusalem,
and the battle bow will be broken.
He will proclaim peace to the nations.
His rule will extend from sea to sea
and from the River[c] to the ends of the earth.[d]
¹¹As for you, because of the blood of my covenant with you,
I will free your prisoners from the waterless pit.
¹²Return to your fortress, O prisoners of hope;
even now I announce that I will restore twice as much to you.
¹³I will bend Judah as I bend my bow
and fill it with Ephraim.
I will rouse your sons, O Zion,

[a]1 Or *Damascus. / For the eye of the LORD is on all mankind, / as well as on the tribes of Israel,* [b]9 Or *King* [c]10 That is, the Euphrates [d]10 Or *the end of the land*

tune? **3.** How did you deal with your loss?

STUDY 1. What fate does Zechariah envision for Syria, Phoenicia and Philistia (vv. 3–6)? What have they done to deserve this fate? **2.** Are Syria, Phoenicia and Philistia the real targets of this prophecy? What about Jerusalem (v. 9)? **3.** Who is being destroyed and who is being preserved? For what purpose? **4.** In history God used Alexander the Great to deal convincingly with those who opposed his will. Thus was this oracle fulfilled. What lessons does that teach you about God's love and holiness? About the authority of God's Word spoken through prophets?

APPLY 1. Are you doing any of the things targeted in this oracle for judgment: Hoarding wealth? Victimizing others? Trusting in your own strength? How has God dealt with you in this area? **2.** Unlike the Syrians, Phoenicians, Philistines or the Jebusites, what can you legitimately take pride in that is of eternal value, knowing that it will never be taken away?

OPEN What would be the three top qualities you would look for in a leader: Vision? Integrity? Service record? Promises made? Looks? Other?

STUDY 1. What qualities will Zion's King possess? Describe the scene at his coming. How will the people respond? Why the donkey (v. 9; Matt. 21:5, for Jesus' use of it), instead of the war-horse (v. 10)? **2.** On what basis will restoration be given to prisoners or exiles?

APPLY 1. Describe the King's advent in your life. **2.** God's intention for exiles and prisoners is peace. How have you experienced that wholeness, health and harmony in your life? In your group life? **3.** What projects or actions have you taken to promote peace within your church, community or world?

9:9 Chapter 9 marks the second half of Zechariah' s prophecies. The concluding five chapters focus on the coming King: Jesus Christ. **Rejoice ... Daughter of Zion!** Jerusalem's citizens are commanded to receive their king! **riding on a donkey, on a colt.** Here, Zechariah prophesied Christ's peaceful entry into the city (Matt. 21:5), which set the stage for his eventual return. This could either mean two animals or a colt (donkey), one animal.

OPEN When were you most celebrated or showered with gifts?

STUDY **1.** What will the victory banquet of God's people be like? How will the Sovereign Lord make his entry? **2.** What blessings does God as Shepherd (v. 16) bring?

APPLY **1.** When have you or your church had a foretaste of the victory celebration described here? What victory do you want to celebrate when the Lord returns? **2.** Do you feel much like a crown jewel in God's possession? Where do you sparkle? What rough spots need polishing?

OPEN Try a "What's-my-line?" group exercise where you make three statements about yourself. Two are elaborately truthful and one is a well-disguised "line" (deceit or lie). Then have the group guess which was the false line. The object of the game is to fool everyone with the best line.

STUDY **1.** In what ways were the Israelites to distinguish between Yahweh and the gods of other nations? What are some good lines that these pretenders might have used to dupe Israel into worshipping a false god? **2.** How will God deal with the false shepherds who have exploited his flock and allowed them to wander (10:3; 11:1–3)? **3.** What images are used to denote the strength and stability God will restore to his flock (10:3–7)? Why will God do this? **4.** How is the theme of restoration, promise and fulfillment developed further in 10:8–12? **5.** Which line here plays on the true meaning of Zechariah's name ("the LORD remembers")? What will God do on behalf of his covenant promises and people?

APPLY **1.** What are the false gods or idols in your world? How can you discern their well-disguised lines? How can your group help *you not to fall for their deceit?* **2.** As a

against your sons, O Greece,
and make you like a warrior's sword.

The Lord Will Appear

14 Then the LORD will appear over them;
his arrow will flash like lightning.
The Sovereign LORD will sound the trumpet;
he will march in the storms of the south,
15 and the LORD Almighty will shield them.
They will destroy
and overcome with slingstones.
They will drink and roar as with wine;
they will be full like a bowl
used for sprinkling[a] the corners of the altar.
16 The LORD their God will save them on that day
as the flock of his people.
They will sparkle in his land
like jewels in a crown.
17 How attractive and beautiful they will be!
Grain will make the young men thrive,
and new wine the young women.

The Lord Will Care for Judah

10 Ask the LORD for rain in the springtime;
it is the LORD who makes the storm clouds.
He gives showers of rain to men,
and plants of the field to everyone.
2 The idols speak deceit,
diviners see visions that lie;
they tell dreams that are false,
they give comfort in vain.
Therefore the people wander like sheep
oppressed for lack of a shepherd.

3 "My anger burns against the shepherds,
and I will punish the leaders;
for the LORD Almighty will care
for his flock, the house of Judah,
and make them like a proud horse in battle.
4 From Judah will come the cornerstone,
from him the tent peg,
from him the battle bow,
from him every ruler.
5 Together they[b] will be like mighty men
trampling the muddy streets in battle.
Because the LORD is with them,
they will fight and overthrow the horsemen.

6 "I will strengthen the house of Judah
and save the house of Joseph.

[a] *15 Or bowl, / like* [b] *4,5* Or *ruler, all of them together. / [5]They*

10:1–2 He gives showers. God established himself as the creator and sustainer of all living creatures. In contrast, lifeless fertility gods were often worshiped to ensure good crops and fair weather.

I will restore them
  because I have compassion on them.
They will be as though
  I had not rejected them,
for I am the LORD their God
  and I will answer them.
7 The Ephraimites will become like mighty men,
  and their hearts will be glad as with wine.
Their children will see it and be joyful;
  their hearts will rejoice in the LORD.
8 I will signal for them
  and gather them in.
Surely I will redeem them;
  they will be as numerous as before.
9 Though I scatter them among the peoples,
  yet in distant lands they will remember me.
They and their children will survive,
  and they will return.
10 I will bring them back from Egypt
  and gather them from Assyria.
I will bring them to Gilead and Lebanon,
  and there will not be room enough for them.
11 They will pass through the sea of trouble;
  the surging sea will be subdued
  and all the depths of the Nile will dry up.
Assyria's pride will be brought down
  and Egypt's scepter will pass away.
12 I will strengthen them in the LORD
  and in his name they will walk,"
    declares the LORD.

11 Open your doors, O Lebanon,
  so that fire may devour your cedars!
2 Wail, O pine tree, for the cedar has fallen;
  the stately trees are ruined!
Wail, oaks of Bashan;
  the dense forest has been cut down!
3 Listen to the wail of the shepherds;
  their rich pastures are destroyed!
Listen to the roar of the lions;
  the lush thicket of the Jordan is ruined!

Two Shepherds

4 This is what the LORD my God says: "Pasture the flock marked for
slaughter. 5 Their buyers slaughter them and go unpunished. Those
who sell them say, 'Praise the LORD, I am rich!' Their own shepherds
do not spare them. 6 For I will no longer have pity on the people of the
land," declares the LORD. "I will hand everyone over to his neighbor
and his king. They will oppress the land, and I will not rescue them
from their hands."
7 So I pastured the flock marked for slaughter, particularly the oppressed of the flock. Then I took two staffs and called one Favor and
the other Union, and I pastured the flock. 8 In one month I got rid of
the three shepherds.

member of God's flock, are you: Wandering aimlessly? Looking in vain for greener pastures or still waters? Listening to the voices of many shepherds? Grazing in the land of promise? Getting fleeced? **3.** Zechariah's name means "the LORD remembers." What of your needs has the Lord remembered to care for? Which of your needs are you still waiting on the Lord to remember?

OPEN What kind of animals or pet did you care for as a child? What did you do to care for them?

STUDY 1. Who is this cast of characters: The "flock marked for slaughter"? Their "buyers"? "They" (v. 6)? "I" (v. 7)? **2.** What roles are scripted here? What is meant by their rejecting the prototype Good Shepherd (vv. 7–8)? What then happened? **3.** How are the props used here: "Favor" (v. 10)? "Thirty pieces of silver" (v. 13)? "Union" (v. 14)? **4.** What

The flock detested me, and I grew weary of them 9and said, "I will
not be your shepherd. Let the dying die, and the perishing perish. Let
those who are left eat one another's flesh."
10Then I took my staff called Favor and broke it, revoking the covenant I had made with all the nations. 11It was revoked on that day,
and so the afflicted of the flock who were watching me knew it was
the word of the LORD.
12I told them, "If you think it best, give me my pay; but if not, keep
it." So they paid me thirty pieces of silver.
13And the LORD said to me, "Throw it to the potter"—the handsome
price at which they priced me! So I took the thirty pieces of silver and
threw them into the house of the LORD to the potter.
14Then I broke my second staff called Union, breaking the brotherhood between Judah and Israel.
15Then the LORD said to me, "Take again the equipment of a foolish
shepherd. 16For I am going to raise up a shepherd over the land who
will not care for the lost, or seek the young, or heal the injured, or
feed the healthy, but will eat the meat of the choice sheep, tearing off
their hoofs.

17"Woe to the worthless shepherd,
 who deserts the flock!
May the sword strike his arm and his right eye!
 May his arm be completely withered,
 his right eye totally blinded!"

Jerusalem's Enemies to Be Destroyed

An Oracle

12 This is the word of the LORD concerning Israel. The LORD,
who stretches out the heavens, who lays the foundation of
the earth, and who forms the spirit of man within him, declares: 2"I
am going to make Jerusalem a cup that sends all the surrounding
peoples reeling. Judah will be besieged as well as Jerusalem. 3On that
day, when all the nations of the earth are gathered against her, I will
make Jerusalem an immovable rock for all the nations. All who try to
move it will injure themselves. 4On that day I will strike every horse
with panic and its rider with madness," declares the LORD. "I will
keep a watchful eye over the house of Judah, but I will blind all the
horses of the nations. 5Then the leaders of Judah will say in their
hearts, 'The people of Jerusalem are strong, because the LORD Almighty is their God.'
6"On that day I will make the leaders of Judah like a firepot in a
woodpile, like a flaming torch among sheaves. They will consume
right and left all the surrounding peoples, but Jerusalem will remain
intact in her place.
7"The LORD will save the dwellings of Judah first, so that the honor
of the house of David and of Jerusalem's inhabitants may not be
greater than that of Judah. 8On that day the LORD will shield those

insight does this give us into Zechariah as "a shepherd"? The Messiah as Good Shepherd (compare John 10:1–18)? The anti-Christ as false shepherd?

APPLY 1. Have you ever rejected a "good shepherd"? And later regretted it? What did the experience teach you? **2.** Zechariah's staff suggests that his mission was to ensure divine favor on the flock by binding them into one. How far does this parallel the experience of your group and your church in relation to the Good Shepherd? **3.** The breaking of the staff signifies the breaking of Israel into two hostile parties. In what ways are members of your church broken up into factions?

OPEN 1. Who was your childhood hero? Was your hero fictional or real? **2.** What did you admire most about your hero? Did you ever dress-up like your hero? Belong to a fan club? Explain.

STUDY 1. What graphic images are used here to describe God's people? What does this tell you about the covenant relationship? **2.** How will Jerusalem survive the attacks of "all the nations"? What is the secret of their strength? How will they dispatch their enemies? **3.** Who will be delivered first? Why? On that day, what hero will the feeblest soldiers be like? What will be God's mission?

APPLY 1. When you or your group feel like feeble foot soldiers, what is God's promise to you? **2.** When do you feel most like a hero? Why? What's your secret?

11:14 breaking the brotherhood. The Jews' history was one of family hostility, not harmony. The role of the future Messiah-Shepherd would be to reunite the splintered flock (Ezek. 37:16–28).

11:15 foolish shepherd. In the absence of God's shepherd, a deceiver would arrive on the scene. Many would be wounded by this wicked shepherd (v. 17).

12:1 Zechariah put God's message in the context of his powerful works. God's deeds were powerful, but his declaration was more so. If God willed it to happen, it would.

who live in Jerusalem, so that the feeblest among them will be like
David, and the house of David will be like God, like the Angel of
the LORD going before them. 9On that day I will set out to destroy all
the nations that attack Jerusalem.

Mourning for the One They Pierced

10"And I will pour out on the house of David and the inhabitants of
Jerusalem a spirit[a] of grace and supplication. They will look on[b] me,
the one they have pierced, and they will mourn for him as one
mourns for an only child, and grieve bitterly for him as one grieves
for a firstborn son. 11On that day the weeping in Jerusalem will be
great, like the weeping of Hadad Rimmon in the plain of Megiddo.
12The land will mourn, each clan by itself, with their wives by themselves: the clan of the house of David and their wives, the clan of the
house of Nathan and their wives, 13the clan of the house of Levi and
their wives, the clan of Shimei and their wives, 14and all the rest of
the clans and their wives.

Cleansing From Sin

13 "On that day a fountain will be opened to the house of David
and the inhabitants of Jerusalem, to cleanse them from sin
and impurity.

2"On that day, I will banish the names of the idols from the land,
and they will be remembered no more," declares the LORD Almighty.
"I will remove both the prophets and the spirit of impurity from the
land. 3And if anyone still prophesies, his father and mother, to whom
he was born, will say to him, 'You must die, because you have told
lies in the LORD's name.' When he prophesies, his own parents will
stab him.

4"On that day every prophet will be ashamed of his prophetic vision. He will not put on a prophet's garment of hair in order to deceive. 5He will say, 'I am not a prophet. I am a farmer; the land has
been my livelihood since my youth.[c]' 6If someone asks him, 'What are
these wounds on your body[d]?' he will answer, 'The wounds I was
given at the house of my friends.'

The Shepherd Struck, the Sheep Scattered

7"Awake, O sword, against my shepherd,
against the man who is close to me!"
declares the LORD Almighty.
"Strike the shepherd,
and the sheep will be scattered,
and I will turn my hand against the little ones.
8In the whole land," declares the LORD,
"two-thirds will be struck down and perish;
yet one-third will be left in it.
9This third I will bring into the fire;

[a]10 Or *the Spirit* [b]10 Or *to* [c]5 Or *farmer; a man sold me in my youth* [d]6 Or *wounds between your hands*

OPEN 1. What sad day do you recall from your childhood? How did that event affect you growing up? **2.** If forced to choose between the two, would you rather be a prophet or a farmer? Why?

STUDY 1. Who's crying here? Why? How extensively (v. 11; 2 Chr. 35:22–25)? **2.** The word for "stab" (13:3) is the same in Hebrew as "pierced" (12:10). What might that say about the fate of those who killed the Messiah? **3.** Why would these prophets prefer to be farmers (12:4–6)? **4.** What is the good news in all this (13:1–2)?

APPLY 1. In what ways has a "spirit of grace and supplication" (v. 10) lead to conviction and repentance for you? Your church? Your nation? **2.** When asked if you are a follower of Christ, what do you say? How do others know without asking? What masks do you wear to avoid detection? What shameful things in church history and in today's church have caused you to hide?

OPEN Have you ever been singled out or summoned to the office of your principal or boss? How did you feel?

STUDY 1. Which shepherd is slain: The Good Shepherd (11:4–14; 12:10)? Or the foolish one (11:15–17)? **2.** What will happen when the shepherd is struck (v. 7; Matt. 26:31,56)? Will all be lost? What will happen to the remnant? **3.** How will the "one-third" be refined and tested (vv. 8–9; Isa 48:10)? With what results on their covenant relationship with God (8:8)?

13:7 sword. This sword, representing death, would be employed to do God's bidding. **Strike the shepherd.** God orchestrated the death of Christ, the Good Shepherd, according to his ultimate plan. **little ones.** Without the shepherd, God's people would be vulnerable and defenseless, as history attests (see Matt. 26:31,56).

APPLY Which "third" do you find yourself in? How does God refine and test your character? What part does your group play in this process?

OPEN If you could bequeath the group member to your right with a gift from your kitchen, symbolic of what he or she means to you, what would it be? Exchange gift ideas.

STUDY **1.** How will God remember Jerusalem? What will the "day of the LORD" be like? **2.** Who will fight against the city? What is the inhabitants' fate (vv. 1–2,10–11)? The attackers' fate (vv. 3–5,12–19)? **3.** What irony, mercy and justice do you see here? **4.** What will mark the advent of the Lord? What "holy ones" will accompany him (v. 5): Saints? Angels? The fleeing host coming to recapture their city? **5.** Why would Zechariah repeat "on that day" over and over again? What is unique about it? **6.** What might the "living water" imply (v. 8; Ps. 46:4; Jer. 2:13; 17:13; Joel 3:18; John 4:11; 7:38–39)? **7.** Who will join the pilgrimage to worship the one God (vv. 9,16)? Why is special mention given here to the Feast of Tabernacles (Lev. 23:39–43; Neh. 8:16–18)? And to Egypt? **8.** How transformed will this new city be (vv. 20–21)? "Holy to the LORD" is the fulfillment of which intention of God (Ex. 19:6; 28:36)? What does it mean that even "cooking pots" will be sacred? **9.** How does this vision in verses 9,16,20–21 compare with Isaiah's (Isa. 2:2–4) or Paul's (Phil. 2:9–11)? What time frame is likely in view here?

APPLY **1.** What promise from God are you counting on? In what area of your life do you need to make special preparations? **2.** Are you feeling attacked on every side, like Jerusalem? By what? Are you fleeing or surviving? **3.** Through this conflict and the tribulation to come, do you sense God's love shining through the darkness? Or do you find it hard to believe that there will ever be an evening with only light? **4.** The High Priest wore an inscription *which said: "Holy to the LORD." Which*

I will refine them like silver
  and test them like gold.
They will call on my name
  and I will answer them;
I will say, 'They are my people,'
  and they will say, 'The LORD is our God.' "

The Lord Comes and Reigns

14 A day of the LORD is coming when your plunder will be divided
among you.
2 I will gather all the nations to Jerusalem to fight against it; the city
will be captured, the houses ransacked, and the women raped. Half of
the city will go into exile, but the rest of the people will not be taken
from the city.
3 Then the LORD will go out and fight against those nations, as he
fights in the day of battle. 4 On that day his feet will stand on the
Mount of Olives, east of Jerusalem, and the Mount of Olives will be
split in two from east to west, forming a great valley, with half of the
mountain moving north and half moving south. 5 You will flee by my
mountain valley, for it will extend to Azel. You will flee as you fled
from the earthquake[a] in the days of Uzziah king of Judah. Then the
LORD my God will come, and all the holy ones with him.
6 On that day there will be no light, no cold or frost. 7 It will be a
unique day, without daytime or nighttime—a day known to the LORD.
When evening comes, there will be light.
8 On that day living water will flow out from Jerusalem, half to the
eastern sea[b] and half to the western sea,[c] in summer and in winter.
9 The LORD will be king over the whole earth. On that day there will
be one LORD, and his name the only name.
10 The whole land, from Geba to Rimmon, south of Jerusalem, will
become like the Arabah. But Jerusalem will be raised up and remain
in its place, from the Benjamin Gate to the site of the First Gate, to the
Corner Gate, and from the Tower of Hananel to the royal winepresses. 11 It will be inhabited; never again will it be destroyed. Jerusalem will be secure.
12 This is the plague with which the LORD will strike all the nations
that fought against Jerusalem: Their flesh will rot while they are still
standing on their feet, their eyes will rot in their sockets, and their
tongues will rot in their mouths. 13 On that day men will be stricken by
the LORD with great panic. Each man will seize the hand of another,
and they will attack each other. 14 Judah too will fight at Jerusalem.
The wealth of all the surrounding nations will be collected—great
quantities of gold and silver and clothing. 15 A similar plague will
strike the horses and mules, the camels and donkeys, and all the
animals in those camps.
16 Then the survivors from all the nations that have attacked Jerusalem will go up year after year to worship the King, the LORD Almighty,
and to celebrate the Feast of Tabernacles. 17 If any of the peoples of

[a]5 Or [5]*My mountain valley will be blocked and will extend to Azel. It will be blocked as it was blocked because of the earthquake* [b]8 That is, the Dead Sea [c]8 That is, the Mediterranean

---

14:8 living water. There would be no end to the life-giving nutrients supplied by fresh water in all seasons.

the earth do not go up to Jerusalem to worship the King, the LORD
Almighty, they will have no rain. 18If the Egyptian people do not go up
and take part, they will have no rain. The LORD[a] will bring on them the
plague he inflicts on the nations that do not go up to celebrate the
Feast of Tabernacles. 19This will be the punishment of Egypt and
the punishment of all the nations that do not go up to celebrate the
Feast of Tabernacles.
20On that day HOLY TO THE LORD will be inscribed on the bells of the
horses, and the cooking pots in the LORD's house will be like the
sacred bowls in front of the altar. 21Every pot in Jerusalem and Judah
will be holy to the LORD Almighty, and all who come to sacrifice will
take some of the pots and cook in them. And on that day there will no
longer be a Canaanite[b] in the house of the LORD Almighty.

[a]18 Or *part, then the LORD* [b]21 Or *merchant*

parts of your life are "Holy to the LORD"? Where is there still a vacancy sign?

____

14:18 they will have no rain. Conditions would be placed on who could enjoy this fresh and living water. Only those who worshiped God would enjoy his blessings.

14:20 Zechariah's vision of the future would be a dream come true. God's sovereignty would be all encompassing. Every living creature and even the most menial possessions would be identified as God's own.

Malachi

Author. This prophecy was spoken and written by Malachi, the last Old Testament prophet. He was a contemporary of Ezra and Nehemiah, who led the people as they resettled their homeland after the Babylonian exile.

Date. The book of Malachi was probably written around 450–430 B.C.

Personal Reading	Group Study Topic and Reading	
1:1–14	A Loving and Great God	1:1–14
2:1–9	Profane Priests	2:1–9
2:10–16	Unfaithful Judah	2:10–16
2:17–3:5	Purifying the People	2:17–3:5
3:6–18	Robbing the Lord	3:6–18
4:1–6	The Last Word	4:1–6

Purpose. The purpose of Malachi's prophecy was to give his people a revealing look at themselves. He wanted them to realize that they had become complacent and very demanding with God. They disregarded their own responsibilities for worship. Malachi wanted to remind his people of their end of the bargain, their responsibility to worship and obey.

Historical Background. Under the urging of the prophets Haggai and Zechariah, the Hebrew exiles who returned from Babylon finished rebuilding the temple in Jerusalem in 516 B.C. In 458 B.C., Ezra the priest came to Jerusalem with several thousand more returning exiles. He was encouraged by the Persian king, Artaxerxes, to restore worship in the temple and to encourage obedience to the Mosaic law. In 445 B.C., Artaxerxes sent Nehemiah to be governor of the Hebrews. Nehemiah rebuilt the wall around Jerusalem, instituted social reforms and convinced the people to avoid mixed marriages because they led to idolatry.

When Nehemiah returned to Persia for a time, the people began to ignore his reforms. Without Nehemiah's strong leadership, the people turned away from God and their spiritual identity as God's people. Although the Persian empire that controlled them politically encouraged their adherence to Jewish law and custom, the people still wandered from their spiritual roots. It was at this time that Malachi brought his message to his country.

Broken Dreams. For hundreds of years, the prophets had been predicting the downfall of Israel and Judah. They had made it clear that because of their wickedness and disobedience to God, the two kingdoms would be swept away, their cities burned and their people taken into captivity. The prophets had also promised that the judgment upon Israel and Judah was the act of a strict father who disciplines his children to bring them into line. Over and over, the prophets proclaimed that God's people would pass through the judgment into a time of greater glory.

In Malachi's time, the people saw no evidence of that coming glory. The people of the post-exilic period were disillusioned by their condition. Yes, they had been allowed to return to their homeland, but in their absence, Jerusalem had fallen from an important capital to a poor, broken down city. In their eyes, God had not swept their enemies away. The Mosaic Law seemed irrelevant to them—just form and no substance. God had not come to the temple and restored them to glory (3:1). They had lost hope; the promise of salvation and glory was just an empty promise. Malachi saw that the promise was yet to come. He urged them to return to the right ways of living and worshiping.

1

An oracle: The word of the LORD to Israel through Malachi.[a]

Jacob Loved, Esau Hated

2"I have loved you," says the LORD.
"But you ask, 'How have you loved us?'
"Was not Esau Jacob's brother?" the LORD says. "Yet I have loved
Jacob, 3but Esau I have hated, and I have turned his mountains into a
wasteland and left his inheritance to the desert jackals."
4Edom may say, "Though we have been crushed, we will rebuild the
ruins."
But this is what the LORD Almighty says: "They may build, but I will
demolish. They will be called the Wicked Land, a people always under
the wrath of the LORD. 5You will see it with your own eyes and say,
'Great is the LORD—even beyond the borders of Israel!'

Blemished Sacrifices

6"A son honors his father, and a servant his master. If I am a father,
where is the honor due me? If I am a master, where is the respect due
me?" says the LORD Almighty. "It is you, O priests, who show contempt for my name.
"But you ask, 'How have we shown contempt for your name?'
7"You place defiled food on my altar.
"But you ask, 'How have we defiled you?'
"By saying that the LORD's table is contemptible. 8When you bring
blind animals for sacrifice, is that not wrong? When you sacrifice
crippled or diseased animals, is that not wrong? Try offering them to
your governor! Would he be pleased with you? Would he accept you?"
says the LORD Almighty.
9"Now implore God to be gracious to us. With such offerings from
your hands, will he accept you?"—says the LORD Almighty.
10"Oh, that one of you would shut the temple doors, so that you
would not light useless fires on my altar! I am not pleased with you,"
says the LORD Almighty, "and I will accept no offering from your
hands. 11My name will be great among the nations, from the rising to
the setting of the sun. In every place incense and pure offerings will
be brought to my name, because my name will be great among the
nations," says the LORD Almighty.
12"But you profane it by saying of the Lord's table, 'It is defiled,'
and of its food, 'It is contemptible.' 13And you say, 'What a burden!'
and you sniff at it contemptuously," says the LORD Almighty.
"When you bring injured, crippled or diseased animals and offer
them as sacrifices, should I accept them from your hands?" says the
LORD. 14"Cursed is the cheat who has an acceptable male in his flock
and vows to give it, but then sacrifices a blemished animal to the

[a]1 Malachi means *my messenger.*

OPEN 1. Who was your first love? How did that person demonstrate their love? Did that puppy love ever turn into dogfights or hate? **2.** What care do you take in giving gifts at Christmas time: Most anything will do, within a certain price range? Only gifts from a want list will do? Used gifts or hand-me-downs are just fine? Only new items will do, preferably deluxe editions?

STUDY 1. How did the Lord show his love to the people of Israel? What happened to that love? **2.** What attitude is expressed by Edom/Esau in verse 4? What is the Lord's response? **3.** Who is the target of the Lord's probing questions in verses 6–8? What is wrong with their gift-giving? **4.** Why are these people just going through the motions: Didn't care any more? Couldn't afford any better? Didn't think the Lord was that picky? Wanted to defy him openly? Tried to fool him covertly? **5.** How does this chapter affirm the smallness of the priests? The greatness of the Lord?

APPLY 1. When have you asked the Lord to prove his love for you? What was his response? **2.** How might your attitude or actions honor or dishonor the Lord? In what ways are God's requirements a "burden" to you? **3.** How has the Lord shown his greatness to you? Did you have to feel small before you knew he was great? Explain.

1:7 defiled food. God gave the priests specific instructions in Leviticus 22:17–30 on how to make acceptable sacrifices. To offer sacrifices wrongly was to profane God's name (Lev. 22:2,32). **How have we defiled you?** The priests were not ignorant of God's Law, but their hearts were so hardened that they needed God to explicitly state their wrongs. Accustomed to rationalizing their actions, they were blind to their sin.

1:10 shut the temple doors. God was so displeased with their defiled offerings that he preferred that they shut down the temple rather than continue. Their sacrifices were a waste, totally unacceptable to God.

Lord. For I am a great king," says the LORD Almighty, "and my name is
to be feared among the nations.

Admonition for the Priests

2 "And now this admonition is for you, O priests. [2]If you do not listen, and if you do not set your heart to honor my name," says the
LORD Almighty, "I will send a curse upon you, and I will curse your
blessings. Yes, I have already cursed them, because you have not set
your heart to honor me.
[3]"Because of you I will rebuke[a] your descendants[b]; I will spread on
your faces the offal from your festival sacrifices, and you will be carried off with it. [4]And you will know that I have sent you this admonition so that my covenant with Levi may continue," says the LORD
Almighty. [5]"My covenant was with him, a covenant of life and peace,
and I gave them to him; this called for reverence and he revered me
and stood in awe of my name. [6]True instruction was in his mouth and
nothing false was found on his lips. He walked with me in peace and
uprightness, and turned many from sin.
[7]"For the lips of a priest ought to preserve knowledge, and from his
mouth men should seek instruction—because he is the messenger of
the LORD Almighty. [8]But you have turned from the way and by your
teaching have caused many to stumble; you have violated the covenant with Levi," says the LORD Almighty. [9]"So I have caused you to
be despised and humiliated before all the people, because you have
not followed my ways but have shown partiality in matters of the
law."

Judah Unfaithful

[10]Have we not all one Father[c]? Did not one God create us? Why do
we profane the covenant of our fathers by breaking faith with one
another?
[11]Judah has broken faith. A detestable thing has been committed in
Israel and in Jerusalem: Judah has desecrated the sanctuary the LORD
loves, by marrying the daughter of a foreign god. [12]As for the man
who does this, whoever he may be, may the LORD cut him off from the
tents of Jacob[d]—even though he brings offerings to the LORD Almighty.
[13]Another thing you do: You flood the LORD's altar with tears. You
weep and wail because he no longer pays attention to your offerings

[a]3 Or *cut off* (see Septuagint) [b]3 Or *will blight your grain* [c]10 Or *father* [d]12 Or *[12]May the LORD cut off from the tents of Jacob anyone who gives testimony in behalf of the man who does this*

OPEN As a child, when did you refuse to do what someone asked? Over what issue? Why was that so crucial? Is it now?

STUDY 1. Why is the Lord so tough on the priests? What have they done to deserve this? **2.** What is a covenant? What did the Lord's covenant with Levi require? (vv. 1–7; Num. 3:12–13; 25:10–13) **3.** How have these priests altered the Lord's description of them? What has been the effect of their actions on others?

APPLY 1. Has anyone ever stumbled in their faith due to what you did or didn't do? Explain. **2.** What would "life and peace" (v. 5) mean for your church? For your family? For your society? **3.** How can you help, not hinder, peacemaking?

OPEN In dating, have you ever been jilted by anyone? What made you most jealous or hurt?

STUDY 1. How had Judah broken faith? With whom? What has this to do with creation and covenant? **2.** What sin was separating them and the Lord? **3.** What does "divorce" (v. 16) mean in the context of breaking faith? Why does the God of Israel hate divorce? What are we urged to do?

APPLY 1. Over what concerns have you "flooded the Lord's altar with your tears" (v. 13)? How do you see God responding to

2:2 I will curse your blessings. Malachi commanded the priests to set their hearts to honor God. They apparently failed to do so because their punishment for disobedience was already in effect: They were under a curse. The priests pronounced God's blessing on the people, but God would turn those blessings into curses as punishment for their hard hearts.

2:5–7 These verses outline the role of a good priest. God made a covenant with Levi, who responded by revering God, teaching the truth and walking uprightly with the Lord. Malachi uses this example to show, in verse 7, the standard which priests should live up to. Their role was to be that of a wise teacher who could clearly communicate the Law of Moses (vv. 4,7).

2:8 The priests strayed from God's Law, making it impossible for them to teach truth. They had violated the covenant God made with Levi by offering their own defiled sacrifices and not ones that were acceptable.

2:10 breaking faith with one another! Malachi condemns the people for being unfaithful to one another. God had created them as a distinct people set aside for himself, but they were breaking agreements with one another and also with God. The evidence of faithlessness in verses 11–16 includes forbidden intermarriage with the Gentiles and divorce.

or accepts them with pleasure from your hands. 14You ask, "Why?" It
is because the LORD is acting as the witness between you and the wife
of your youth, because you have broken faith with her, though she is
your partner, the wife of your marriage covenant.
15Has not ⌞the LORD⌟ made them one? In flesh and spirit they are his.
And why one? Because he was seeking godly offspring.[a] So guard
yourself in your spirit, and do not break faith with the wife of your
youth.
16"I hate divorce," says the LORD God of Israel, "and I hate a man's
covering himself[b] with violence as well as with his garment," says
the LORD Almighty.
So guard yourself in your spirit, and do not break faith.

The Day of Judgment

17You have wearied the LORD with your words.
"How have we wearied him?" you ask.
By saying, "All who do evil are good in the eyes of the LORD, and he
is pleased with them" or "Where is the God of justice?"

3 "See, I will send my messenger, who will prepare the way before
me. Then suddenly the Lord you are seeking will come to his
temple; the messenger of the covenant, whom you desire, will come,"
says the LORD Almighty.
2But who can endure the day of his coming? Who can stand when
he appears? For he will be like a refiner's fire or a launderer's soap.
3He will sit as a refiner and purifier of silver; he will purify the Levites
and refine them like gold and silver. Then the LORD will have men who
will bring offerings in righteousness, 4and the offerings of Judah and
Jerusalem will be acceptable to the LORD, as in days gone by, as in
former years.
5"So I will come near to you for judgment. I will be quick to testify
against sorcerers, adulterers and perjurers, against those who defraud laborers of their wages, who oppress the widows and the fatherless, and deprive aliens of justice, but do not fear me," says the
LORD Almighty.

Robbing God

6"I the LORD do not change. So you, O descendants of Jacob, are
not destroyed. 7Ever since the time of your forefathers you have
turned away from my decrees and have not kept them. Return to me,
and I will return to you," says the LORD Almighty.

[a]15 Or *15But the one ⌞who is our father⌟ did not do this, not as long as life remained in him. And what was he seeking? An offspring from God* [b]16 Or *his wife*

those tears? **2.** How could you "guard yourself in your spirit," and not "break faith" (v. 15)? In what situations are you most on guard? Most vulnerable?

OPEN Of your telephone, writing, prayer and speaking style, which is most to the point? Which requires a prologue? A post-script? Which seems to go on and on?

STUDY 1. How have the people wearied the Lord in word? In deed? What is the Lord's response? **2.** Who is the Lord's messenger (3:1): Malachi which means ("my messenger" in Hebrew)? John the Baptist (Matt. 11:10)? A second Elijah (4:5)? What will he do (Isa. 40:3–4)? **3.** What will the day of the Lord's coming be like? **4.** What does the Lord's judgment process entail? Who, if any, endures?

APPLY 1. Have you "wearied" the Lord? Do you "fear" him? How so? How has the Lord responded? **2.** If given the chance to declare war on sin, what sins would make it into your 3-point speech? Why those three?

OPEN 1. When told, "Eat whatever food you find in the house," what do you look for? What is your reaction if it's not there? **2.** When caught with your hand in the cookie jar, how do you react?

STUDY 1. How had Malachi's peers robbed God? With

2:15 Malachi argues that a husband and wife should guard their marriage and be faithful to one another. God makes a man and a woman one flesh when they marry and works in their spirits to strengthen their bond in order that they can produce godly children. Breaking up a family is wrong.

2:17 You have wearied the LORD. The people's faithless questions had wearied the Lord. God was seemingly tired of their questioning his justice. Ironically, the very people who complained that God was blessing evil people and making the good suffer were the guilty ones who deserved punishment.

3:1 my messenger who will prepare the way. Jesus identified this messenger as John the Baptist (Matt. 11:7–10) whose ministry signaled the coming of the Lord.

3:2–4 The Lord's coming would be a day of disaster. The people, who so badly wanted God to judge the wicked, would regret their words since the Lord would purify them like a refiner's fire. The result would be pure people who would bring righteousness as an acceptable offering.

3:6 I the LORD do not change. Israel could count on God's promise to protect them because he is eternally faithful. He would punish their sin but not destroy the nation itself.

what results? **2.** How does the Lord challenge the people to put him to the test (vv. 10–12)? **3.** What was futile about their worshipping God with a "what's-in-this-for-me" attitude? **4.** How will everyone get their just desserts in the end (vv. 16–18)? **5.** What distinguishes the righteous from the wicked?

APPLY 1. When have you struggled with bad things happening to good people? With good things happening to bad people? **2.** What does it feel like to be in relationship with such a God who "does not change"? If you could change one thing about God, what would it be? **3.** In what ways do you rob God everyday? What tithe do you need to offer? Accordingly, rewrite verses 10–12 as personal promises to you from God.

OPEN From your appointment book, what are you eagerly anticipating three months from now? What are you dreading? How are you preparing for these due dates?

STUDY 1. Is the day of the Lord inked, penciled or not even on their calendars? Why or why not? **2.** As Malachi is the last prophet until the New Testament, what is the importance of verses 4–5?

"But you ask, 'How are we to return?'

8"Will a man rob God? Yet you rob me.

"But you ask, 'How do we rob you?'

"In tithes and offerings. 9You are under a curse—the whole nation of you—because you are robbing me. 10Bring the whole tithe into the storehouse, that there may be food in my house. Test me in this," says the LORD Almighty, "and see if I will not throw open the floodgates of heaven and pour out so much blessing that you will not have room enough for it. 11I will prevent pests from devouring your crops, and the vines in your fields will not cast their fruit," says the LORD Almighty. 12"Then all the nations will call you blessed, for yours will be a delightful land," says the LORD Almighty.

13"You have said harsh things against me," says the LORD.

"Yet you ask, 'What have we said against you?'

14"You have said, 'It is futile to serve God. What did we gain by carrying out his requirements and going about like mourners before the LORD Almighty? 15But now we call the arrogant blessed. Certainly the evildoers prosper, and even those who challenge God escape.' "

16Then those who feared the LORD talked with each other, and the LORD listened and heard. A scroll of remembrance was written in his presence concerning those who feared the LORD and honored his name.

17"They will be mine," says the LORD Almighty, "in the day when I make up my treasured possession.[a] I will spare them, just as in compassion a man spares his son who serves him. 18And you will again see the distinction between the righteous and the wicked, between those who serve God and those who do not.

The Day of the Lord

4 "Surely the day is coming; it will burn like a furnace. All the arrogant and every evildoer will be stubble, and that day that is coming will set them on fire," says the LORD Almighty. "Not a root or a branch will be left to them. 2But for you who revere my name, the sun of righteousness will rise with healing in its wings. And you will go out and leap like calves released from the stall. 3Then you will trample down the wicked; they will be ashes under the soles of your feet on the day when I do these things," says the LORD Almighty.

[a]17 Or *Almighty, "my treasured possession, in the day when I act*

3:10–12 In these verses Malachi reaffirms the Mosaic covenant of Deuteronomy 28. God had promised Israel that if they obeyed, they would be blessed; if they disobeyed, they would be cursed. They were currently experiencing curses. But if they obeyed the Lord and brought offerings to the temple, God promised to open the floodgates and pour blessing on them.

3:14 have said ... It is futile to serve God. The people thought that they were being faithful by carrying out God's requirements and repenting like mourners. They thought that they were fulfilling their part of the covenant and accused God of not keeping his end of the bargain. In fact, God *was* keeping his covenant and he was punishing them for disobedience.

3:15 Again the people doubted God when they saw wicked people prosper. They were too shortsighted to see that evildoers would one day be punished. Obedience would bring rich spiritual blessings, outweighing any material blessing the wicked enjoy.

3:16 feared the LORD. These are either people who had repented of their arrogant words in verses 1–13, or a different group whose ways contrast with the earlier group. They are faithful and reverent, and they will be rewarded.

4:2 sun of righteousness will rise with healing. Refers to the Day of the Lord, when righteousness will fill the new heavens and new earth like the sun. The righteousness will heal, both physically and spiritually.

4:3 When wicked people seem to prosper, remember that they will be judged one day.

[4]"Remember the law of my servant Moses, the decrees and laws I
gave him at Horeb for all Israel.
[5]"See, I will send you the prophet Elijah before that great and
dreadful day of the LORD comes. [6]He will turn the hearts of the fathers
to their children, and the hearts of the children to their fathers; or
else I will come and strike the land with a curse."

APPLY 1. What images and issues would a modern Malachi hit home with? **2.** What one thing have you learned from Malachi? What one application are you making? How can the group help you do this?

4:4 Remember the law. This command, used many times throughout the Old Testament, can mean (1) pay attention to something mentally, (2) meditate as well as obey or (3) recite the Law. Here the emphasis is on recalling to obey.

4:5 I will send you the prophet Elijah. John the Baptist fulfilled this prophecy in part when he prepared the way for the Messiah. After Elijah appeared in the Transfiguration, Christ told his disciples that another Elijah would come. Israel did not accept John the Baptist, so another forerunner will come before the Day of the Lord (Matt. 11:7–14; 17:10–13). Some scholars say that Elijah is one of the two witnesses in Revelation 11:1–13.

THE NEW TESTAMENT

Matthew

Author. Nowhere is the author named within the first Gospel. There is however, a long tradition that has assigned it to Matthew. Little is known about Matthew except that he was a tax gatherer. As such he would have been bitterly hated by the general populace in Israel, because tax collectors worked for Rome, and made their living by charging above and beyond what Rome required. Matthew the tax collector stands in contrast to the poor and middle-class fishermen who composed the main body of the disciples.

Date. When Matthew was written is uncertain, but probably between A.D. 50–70.

Theme. Jesus, the long-promised Messiah and authoritative teacher.

Personal Reading	Group Study Topic and Reading	
1:1–2:23	Angel Appears to Joseph	1:18–25
3:1–4:25	Baptism &Temptation	3:13–4:11
5:1–6:34	The Beatitudes	5:1–12
7:1–9:34	Wise & Foolish Builders	7:24–29
9:35–11:30	Jesus Sends Out	10:1–42
12:1–13:52	Parable of Sower	13:1–23
13:53–16:12	Walking on Water	14:22–33
16:13–17:27	Christ Must Die	16:13–28
18:1–35	Unmerciful Servant	18:21–35
19:1–20:34	Workers in Vineyard	20:1–16
21:1–25:46	Parable of Talents	25:14–30
26:1–75	Jesus Arrested	26:47–56
27:1–28:20	Jesus' Resurrection	28:1–20

The Synoptic Gospels. The word "synoptic" means, literally, "able to be seen together." It refers to the first three Gospels—Matthew, Mark and Luke—which cover the same events in Jesus' life. It is clear that there is some sort of literary connection between them. The nature of this connection is not absolutely certain, but generally it is assumed that Mark was the first Gospel. One reason scholars conclude this is that of the 105 sections of Mark, all but four occur in Matthew or Luke. In fact, Matthew uses 93 of these 105 sections (nearly 90%), including not just the general story but in 51% of the cases Mark's very words. However, Matthew and Luke also share some 200 verses not found in Mark, most of which consist of the teachings of Jesus.

In whatever order they were written, it is clear that when the Gospel writers put together their accounts, they did so with a definite purpose in mind. Each selected some stories and left out others to produce an account of Jesus' life that would answer the questions and concerns of his particular audience. Mark probably wrote for Christians in Rome who were suffering under Nero's persecution, and so he told about Jesus who was the Suffering Servant. Luke wrote about the Son of Man who came to seek and to save the needy, the lost, the outcasts. Matthew wrote to a Jewish audience and told the story of King Jesus, the Son of David, who came as the long-promised Messiah to claim his throne.

Characteristics. Matthew is the most Jewish of all the Gospels. It was written by a Jew to other Jews to convince them that Jesus was, indeed, the Messiah foretold by Old Testament Scripture. Thus, the author cites numerous Old Testament prophecies which were fulfilled by Jesus. He uses the phrase, "All this took place to fulfill what the Lord had said through the prophets" some 16 times.

Yet one of the most interesting features of Matthew is that, although he is so Jewish in his concerns, in his book we discover the universal nature of the Gospel—that it is for all the peoples of the world. This emphasis emerges right at the beginning when the Gentile magi bring gifts to the child Jesus, and it runs through to the end when Jesus sends his followers out to "make disciples of all nations."

Other features include references to the church (this is the only Gospel to use the word "church") and references about the end times—the Second Coming of Jesus, the end of the world, and the final judgment.

Structure. Matthew is the most orderly in structure of the four Gospel accounts. After an introductory section, the material is organized into five blocks of narrative alternated with five blocks of discourse or teaching. We can see that this is not an accidental arrangement, because Matthew ends each teaching section with a similar statement (compare 7:28; 11:1; 13:53; 19:1 and 26:1).

OPEN 1. How far back can you trace your family tree? 2. Are there any shady characters among your ancestors? 3. If you could design a coat of arms for your family, what animal would be on the shield?

STUDY 1. How many of the names in this passage can you pronounce? How about naming your son one of these names? 2. Why would it be important to the Jewish audience to trace the genealogy of Jesus back to Abraham? 3. What Old Testament people do you recognize in this list? What do you remember about these people? 4. What is the author Matthew (who was writing to a Jewish audience) trying to show by including the four women in this genealogy? 5. What two titles are assigned to Jesus and what is significant about each title? 6. If you read the paragraph in the Introduction about the "author" you will discover that Matthew came from a rough background. He was a hated tax collector; ran around with "sinners;" and he threw a "party" for his friends and invited Jesus. Why do you think he wrote this gospel, and who in particular is he addressing?

APPLY 1. Who are the significant people in your spiritual upbringing? 2. What has been passed on to you spiritually from your ancestors? 3. What do you know about the ways your ancestors exercised their faith?

The Genealogy of Jesus

1 A record of the genealogy of Jesus Christ the son of David, the son of Abraham:

2 Abraham was the father of Isaac,
Isaac the father of Jacob,
Jacob the father of Judah and his brothers,
3 Judah the father of Perez and Zerah, whose mother was Tamar,
Perez the father of Hezron,
Hezron the father of Ram,
4 Ram the father of Amminadab,
Amminadab the father of Nahshon,
Nahshon the father of Salmon,
5 Salmon the father of Boaz, whose mother was Rahab,
Boaz the father of Obed, whose mother was Ruth,
Obed the father of Jesse,
6 and Jesse the father of King David.

David was the father of Solomon, whose mother had been Uriah's wife,
7 Solomon the father of Rehoboam,
Rehoboam the father of Abijah,
Abijah the father of Asa,
8 Asa the father of Jehoshaphat,
Jehoshaphat the father of Jehoram,
Jehoram the father of Uzziah,
9 Uzziah the father of Jotham,
Jotham the father of Ahaz,
Ahaz the father of Hezekiah,
10 Hezekiah the father of Manasseh,
Manasseh the father of Amon,
Amon the father of Josiah,
11 and Josiah the father of Jeconiah[a] and his brothers at the time of the exile to Babylon.

12 After the exile to Babylon:
Jeconiah was the father of Shealtiel,

[a] *11* That is, Jehoiachin; also in verse 12

1:1 A record of the genealogy. It seems curious to the modern reader that Matthew would begin his Gospel with a long list of names. However, this makes perfect sense given the fact he was writing to a Jewish audience. There was a great interest in genealogy on the part of the Jews, as the many genealogies in the Old Testament demonstrate (Gen. 5; 10; 11:10–32). **Jesus Christ.** This became almost the proper name for the Lord, but it is literally Jesus the Messiah, i.e., the Anointed One. "Christ" is the Greek term for Messiah. **son of David.** David was the king of Israel from whom the Messiah would come. That Jesus was, indeed, David's son was a fact of great significance for Matthew (12:23; 15:22; 20:30–31; 21:9,15) as well as for the early church (Acts 2:29–36; Rom. 1:3; 2 Tim. 2:8; Rev. 22:16). **son of Abraham.** Abraham was the father of the race. By tracing the line of Jesus back to Abraham, Matthew was indicating that Jesus was a true Jew.

1:3-6 Four women are mentioned in these verses (Tamar, Rahab, Ruth and Uriah's wife). It is surprising that women are mentioned at all in the genealogy since a man's line was never traced through his mother. All four were non-Jews and in each case there was something suspect about them and their marriage. They are an unlikely group of women to be named as part of the line of the Messiah. However, they draw attention to the fact that God works in unusual ways. **Tamar.** Tamar was a Canaanite who tricked Judah, her father-in-law into sleeping with her. From this union came the twins, Perez and Zerah (Gen. 38). **Rahab.** She was a prostitute who assisted Joshua's spies when they they were in Jericho (Josh. 2:1-21). **Ruth.** A Moabitess who married a Jew by the name of Boaz. She is included in the royal line although Deuteronomy 23:3 forbids any Moabite from entering "the assembly of the Lord." **Uriah's wife.** David seduced Bathsheba, the eventual mother of Solomon, and got her pregnant. He then caused her husband Uriah to be killed in battle (2 Sam. 11-12). Bathsheba may have been an Israelite, though she was married to a Hittite.

Shealtiel the father of Zerubbabel,
[13]Zerubbabel the father of Abiud,
Abiud the father of Eliakim,
Eliakim the father of Azor,
[14]Azor the father of Zadok,
Zadok the father of Akim,
Akim the father of Eliud,
[15]Eliud the father of Eleazar,
Eleazar the father of Matthan,
Matthan the father of Jacob,
[16]and Jacob the father of Joseph, the husband of Mary, of whom was born Jesus, who is called Christ.

[17]Thus there were fourteen generations in all from Abraham to David, fourteen from David to the exile to Babylon, and fourteen from the exile to the Christ.[a]

The Birth of Jesus Christ

[18]This is how the birth of Jesus Christ came about: His mother Mary
was pledged to be married to Joseph, but before they came together,
she was found to be with child through the Holy Spirit. [19]Because
Joseph her husband was a righteous man and did not want to expose
her to public disgrace, he had in mind to divorce her quietly.
[20]But after he had considered this, an angel of the Lord appeared to
him in a dream and said, "Joseph son of David, do not be afraid to
take Mary home as your wife, because what is conceived in her is
from the Holy Spirit. [21]She will give birth to a son, and you are to give
him the name Jesus,[b] because he will save his people from their sins."
[22]All this took place to fulfill what the Lord had said through the

[a]17 Or *Messiah.* "The Christ" (Greek) and "the Messiah" (Hebrew) both mean "the Anointed One."
[b]21 *Jesus* is the Greek form of *Joshua,* which means *the LORD saves.*

OPEN 1. What is your mother's maiden name? Your father's name? **2.** Where did you get your name?

STUDY 1. Do you think Joseph knew what he was getting into when he and Mary were "pledged" to be married? How would you like to be in his shoes? **2.** When Joseph woke up, what did he do, and not do? **3.** What do you think he told his family and friends? How would you have reacted in that situation?

1:18-25 Matthew and Luke record different aspects of the birth of Jesus. The role of the Holy Spirit in Mary's pregnancy and the relationship between Mary and Joseph are the only facts they share in common. Matthew does not actually describe the birth of Jesus, but concentrates on its circumstances and significance. While Mary is the dominant person in Luke, Matthew focuses on Joseph, perhaps to establish Jesus' legal connection to Joseph in order to counter charges of Jesus being an illegitimate child.

1:18 pledged to be married. A first-century Jewish marriage had three parts to it: the engagement (which often took place when the couple were children and which was usually arranged by a marriage broker); the betrothal (a one-year period in which the couple were considered virtually "married," though they did not have sexual relations); and the marriage. Mary and Joseph were at the second stage in their relationship. **she was found to be with child.** The penalty in the Old Testament for sleeping with a woman betrothed to another was death by stoning for both parties (Deut. 22:23–24). By this time, however, the breaking of the engagement was the course that was followed. **the Holy Spirit.** Both Matthew and Luke make it quite clear that the agent in Jesus' birth was the Holy Spirit (Luke 1:35).

1:19 her husband. According to the Law, Joseph was required to break off his relationship with Mary (Deut. 24:1). However, out of compassion for her he decided not to do this publicly. Although the marriage had not yet taken place, a betrothed couple were considered to be husband and wife. **divorce.** During betrothal, a divorce was required should either party wish to terminate the relationship. **quietly.** To break off his engagement privately he would have needed only two witnesses.

1:20 a dream. Dreams were often the means by which God revealed himself to people. Matthew records four other occasions when dreams were crucial during the birth and childhood of Jesus (2:12,13,19,22). **son of David.** The crucial link between Joseph and David is made quite clear by the angel. **take Mary home as your wife.** The marriage was completed when the husband took his betrothed from her parents' home where she lived during the betrothal to his own home.

1:21 give him the name. It was necessary for Joseph to name Jesus and thus formally accept him as his son. **Jesus.** A common name. It is the Greek form of the Hebrew name Joshua which meant "God is salvation." His name defines his mission. **he will save his people from their sins.** It will not be his goal to establish a Jewish state in what was then Roman territory. Jesus did not come to be a warrior-messiah who would engage in battle against the oppressors of Israel; he would bring liberation from a far deeper problem, namely sin.

APPLY 1. What dream has God given you lately about your calling and purpose in life? 2. What are you doing to fulfill your destiny?

OPEN 1. Have you ever been in a Christmas pageant? What part did you play? 2. What smells do you associate with the Christmas season?

STUDY 1. What do you know about the background of the Magi? About "the star in the East"? 2. What is the motive for King Herod's request to the Magi? 3. What do you learn about Jesus from this story? 4. If you had been Mary when the Magi arrived, how would you feel? 5. How long do you think it took for these Magi astrologers to travel from a distant land in search of Jesus? 6. What do you think the Magi said to their fellow astrologers when they got back home?

APPLY 1. Where are you right now in your quest for spiritual truth? Are you at the beginning, the middle or the end? 2. What "star" has helped you in your quest?

prophet: 23"The virgin will be with child and will give birth to a son,
and they will call him Immanuel"[a]—which means, "God with us."
24When Joseph woke up, he did what the angel of the Lord had
commanded him and took Mary home as his wife. 25But he had no
union with her until she gave birth to a son. And he gave him the
name Jesus.

The Visit of the Magi

2 After Jesus was born in Bethlehem in Judea, during the time of
King Herod, Magi[b] from the east came to Jerusalem 2and asked,
"Where is the one who has been born king of the Jews? We saw his
star in the east[c] and have come to worship him."
3When King Herod heard this he was disturbed, and all Jerusalem
with him. 4When he had called together all the people's chief priests
and teachers of the law, he asked them where the Christ[d] was to be
born. 5"In Bethlehem in Judea," they replied, "for this is what the
prophet has written:

6" 'But you, Bethlehem, in the land of Judah,
are by no means least among the rulers of Judah;
for out of you will come a ruler
who will be the shepherd of my people Israel.'[e]"

7Then Herod called the Magi secretly and found out from them the
exact time the star had appeared. 8He sent them to Bethlehem and
said, "Go and make a careful search for the child. As soon as you find
him, report to me, so that I too may go and worship him."
9After they had heard the king, they went on their way, and the star
they had seen in the east[f] went ahead of them until it stopped over
the place where the child was. 10When they saw the star, they were
overjoyed. 11On coming to the house, they saw the child with his
mother Mary, and they bowed down and worshiped him. Then they
opened their treasures and presented him with gifts of gold and of incense and of myrrh. 12And having been warned in a dream not to go
back to Herod, they returned to their country by another route.

[a]23 Isaiah 7:14 [b]1 Traditionally *Wise Men* [c]2 Or *star when it rose* [d]4 Or *Messiah* [e]6 Micah 5:2
[f]9 Or *seen when it rose*

2:1–12 Only Matthew tells this story, which anticipates how the official leaders of Israel ("Herod ... and all Jerusalem"—v. 3) will reject Jesus as the Messiah, while Gentiles (the Magi) will honor him.

2:1 King Herod. Herod the Great was a shrewd but cruel monarch who was appointed by Rome to rule over Palestine. His reign lasted from 40–4 B.C. **Magi.** These were astrologers who probably came from Babylon.

2:2 in the east. The phrase probably should be translated "at its rising" as an allusion to Numbers 24:17. **worship.** In this context "worship" implies paying homage.

2:8 worship him. This was a cynical statement on the part of Herod which contrasts with the genuine worship of the Magi (v. 11). By allowing the Magi to search for the child he had a better chance of finding him than if he were to send troops.

2:11 bowed down and worshiped him. The first people to worship Jesus in Matthew's account were Gentiles, hinting at the fact that Jesus has come not just for the Jews, but for all nations. The Jewish leaders knew where the child was to be found (vv. 4–5), but they had not bothered to search him out even though Bethlehem is less than 10 miles away. **presented him with gifts.** The giving of gifts signified allegiance. **gold.** A metal of great value, the currency of kings. **incense.** A sweet-smelling gum that was burned during worship. **myrrh.** Another gum, used as a perfume and as medicine. It was also used to embalm bodies. Taken together, the gifts represent the identity of Jesus as the royal Son of God who gave his life for his people.

2:12–13 a dream ... a dream. God reveals his will twice more in a dream, for a total of three times in this narrative.

The Escape to Egypt

[13]When they had gone, an angel of the Lord appeared to Joseph in
a dream. "Get up," he said, "take the child and his mother and escape
to Egypt. Stay there until I tell you, for Herod is going to search for
the child to kill him."

[14]So he got up, took the child and his mother during the night and
left for Egypt, [15]where he stayed until the death of Herod. And so was
fulfilled what the Lord had said through the prophet: "Out of Egypt I
called my son."[a]

[16]When Herod realized that he had been outwitted by the Magi, he
was furious, and he gave orders to kill all the boys in Bethlehem and
its vicinity who were two years old and under, in accordance with the
time he had learned from the Magi. [17]Then what was said through the
prophet Jeremiah was fulfilled:

[18]"A voice is heard in Ramah,
  weeping and great mourning,
Rachel weeping for her children
  and refusing to be comforted,
because they are no more."[b]

The Return to Nazareth

[19]After Herod died, an angel of the Lord appeared in a dream to Joseph in Egypt [20]and said, "Get up, take the child and his mother and
go to the land of Israel, for those who were trying to take the child's
life are dead."

[21]So he got up, took the child and his mother and went to the land
of Israel. [22]But when he heard that Archelaus was reigning in Judea in
place of his father Herod, he was afraid to go there. Having been
warned in a dream, he withdrew to the district of Galilee, [23]and he
went and lived in a town called Nazareth. So was fulfilled what was
said through the prophets: "He will be called a Nazarene."

[a]*15* Hosea 11:1 [b]*18* Jer. 31:15

OPEN 1. How many times did your family move when you were growing up? **2.** Which town do you claim as your hometown?

STUDY 1. How would you like to face the crisis Mary and Joseph faced with their first child? Did you have any scares with your first child? Were you ready to be parents? **2.** How would you compare King Herod to Adolph Hitler? **3.** What did Joseph do to take the child out of "harm's way"? How would this affect his professional career as a carpenter? **4.** How would you rate Joseph on his spiritual "listening skills" with God? **5.** How would you compare Joseph's faith and trust in God to your own? **6.** Do you think Mary and Joseph ever questioned God?

APPLY 1. If God told you to quickly change your whole lifestyle, what would you do? **2.** How are you and God getting along? **3.** What is your favorite excuse for not doing what God tells you to do?

2:13 escape. Once he knew he had been tricked, Herod would search for the child and would have found him had he remained in Bethlehem. **Egypt.** There were large colonies of Jews in Egypt, and it would have been easy for Mary, Joseph and the child to lose themselves.

2:15 until the death of Herod. Herod died in 4 B.C. Thus, Jesus was actually born a few years before the year later (mis)calculated as the beginning of the Christian era. **And so was fulfilled.** Again Matthew connects an event in Jesus' life to a prophetic statement. This time the reference is to Hosea 11:1.

2:16 two years old. This indicates that some time had elapsed since Jesus' actual birth. That Herod was capable of killing children is testified to by what he did before his death. He arrested a number of leading people to be executed at the time of his death, to assure that there would be genuine mourning when he died!

2:22 Archelaus. When Herod died, his kingdom was divided into three parts. His eldest son Archelaus ruled as governor of Judah, Idumea and Samaria. Archelaus was never confirmed in this post by the emperor Augustus. However, since he proved himself to be cruel and incompetent, he was removed.

2:23 He will be called a Nazarene. There is no such quote in the Old Testament. Matthew may have been using a play on words to describe Jesus with Hebrew words in the Old Testament which sound like "Nazarene." For example, a "Nazarite" was someone wholly dedicated to God (Judg. 13:5–7).

John the Baptist Prepares the Way

3 In those days John the Baptist came, preaching in the Desert of
Judea 2and saying, "Repent, for the kingdom of heaven is near."
3This is he who was spoken of through the prophet Isaiah:

"A voice of one calling in the desert,
'Prepare the way for the Lord,
make straight paths for him.' "[a]

4John's clothes were made of camel's hair, and he had a leather
belt around his waist. His food was locusts and wild honey. 5People
went out to him from Jerusalem and all Judea and the whole region of
the Jordan. 6Confessing their sins, they were baptized by him in the
Jordan River.
7But when he saw many of the Pharisees and Sadducees coming to
where he was baptizing, he said to them: "You brood of vipers! Who
warned you to flee from the coming wrath? 8Produce fruit in keeping
with repentance. 9And do not think you can say to yourselves, 'We
have Abraham as our father.' I tell you that out of these stones God
can raise up children for Abraham. 10The ax is already at the root of
the trees, and every tree that does not produce good fruit will be cut
down and thrown into the fire.
11"I baptize you with[b] water for repentance. But after me will come
one who is more powerful than I, whose sandals I am not fit to carry.
He will baptize you with the Holy Spirit and with fire. 12His winnowing fork is in his hand, and he will clear his threshing floor, gathering
his wheat into the barn and burning up the chaff with unquenchable
fire."

[a] 3 Isaiah 40:3 [b] *11* Or *in*

OPEN 1. What is the longest you have worn your hair? **2.** What was the dress code in your school/church when you were growing up?

STUDY 1. Have you ever eaten locust topped with honey? (It tastes like chocolate covered ants.) **2.** How would you like John the Baptist to take your daughter to the Junior Prom? How about John for a son-in-law? **3.** What was John's message? Who does he sound like? **4.** If you had to choose someone to play the part of John the Baptist in a movie, who would you choose? Would your pastor do? **5.** What is the message of John? What is he talking about in verses 11-12? If you had been in the audience, what would you be expecting? **6.** What exactly did John the Baptist do to prepare the way for Jesus?

APPLY 1. Who was a John the Baptist in your life, to prepare the way for you to know God? **2.** When did your spiritual life turn around, or start to turn around?

3:1 John the Baptist. There is a gap of some 25 to 30 years between the events in chapters 1–2 and the start of Jesus' ministry. John the Baptist was an extremely popular figure whose influence spread from Alexandria in Egypt to Asia Minor. **the Desert of Judea.** This was a desolate and blistering hot place, consisting of jagged limestone precipices and sparse vegetation.

3:2 kingdom of heaven. Pious Jews did not mention God's name. To speak of God they referred to his abode—heaven. Most believe this phrase means the same thing as does the phrase "kingdom of God" in Mark (Mark 1:15). It refers to the messianic age in which God will reign.

3:3 Prepare the way. This is a quotation from Isaiah 40:3. The Jews expected that an Elijah-like figure would precede the Messiah and announce his coming (17:3; Mal. 3:1; 4:5). This "voice" who would pave the way for the Lord was John the Baptist. Ancient roads were notoriously bad. The only time they tended to be smoothed out was in preparation for a royal visit.

3:4 locusts and wild honey. This description is similar to that of Old Testament prophets, in particular Elijah (2 Kin. 1:8; Zech. 13:4). The locusts John ate could have been either an insect (Lev. 11:22–23) or a kind of bean from the locust tree. Honey could refer either to what bees produce or to the sap of a certain tree. In either case, this was the food eaten by the poorest of people.

3:6 baptized. The Jewish sect at Qumran practiced frequent baptism as a cleansing from sin. Also, when Gentiles converted to Judaism they were required to bathe in a river as part of the ceremony. This signified that their sins had been washed away. John's call to baptism was a radical act, because it was performed on Jews.

3:7 Pharisees. The Pharisees were a small (about 6,000 members) but powerful religious sect of laymen who devoted their time, energy and money to a strict observance of the religious Law.

3:9 Abraham as our father. John warns that they cannot retreat into an easy assumption that just because they are members of God's chosen race they will be spared judgment.

3:11 whose sandals I am not fit to carry. This would be the task of a slave. **fire.** Fire is a symbol of judgment which Matthew uses a number of times (5:22; 7:19; 13:40,42; 18:8; 25:41).

3:12 gathering his wheat. In the harvesting of wheat, after the grain is separated from the straw the mixture is tossed up in the air. The heavier kernels fall to the ground while the straw and chaff blow away to be burned. This is an image of the judgment that will take place at the return of Jesus.

The Baptism of Jesus

13Then Jesus came from Galilee to the Jordan to be baptized by
John. 14But John tried to deter him, saying, "I need to be baptized by
you, and do you come to me?"
15Jesus replied, "Let it be so now; it is proper for us to do this to
fulfill all righteousness." Then John consented.
16As soon as Jesus was baptized, he went up out of the water. At
that moment heaven was opened, and he saw the Spirit of God descending like a dove and lighting on him. 17And a voice from heaven
said, "This is my Son, whom I love; with him I am well pleased."

The Temptation of Jesus

4 Then Jesus was led by the Spirit into the desert to be tempted by
the devil. 2After fasting forty days and forty nights, he was hungry. 3The tempter came to him and said, "If you are the Son of God,
tell these stones to become bread."
4Jesus answered, "It is written: 'Man does not live on bread alone,
but on every word that comes from the mouth of God.'[a]"
5Then the devil took him to the holy city and had him stand on the
highest point of the temple. 6"If you are the Son of God," he said,
"throw yourself down. For it is written:

" 'He will command his angels concerning you,
  and they will lift you up in their hands,
so that you will not strike your foot against a stone.'[b]"

7Jesus answered him, "It is also written: 'Do not put the Lord your
God to the test.'[c]"

[a]4 Deut. 8:3 [b]6 Psalm 91:11,12 [c]7 Deut. 6:16

OPEN **1.** What is the longest you have gone without food? **2.** What is the longest you have lived away from the comforts of civilization?

STUDY **1.** How much water did it take for you to be baptized? **2.** Why would John the Baptist question the necessity to baptize Jesus? **3.** What phenomena happened at the baptism and what would this mean to Jesus? **4.** Why would the story about the temptation of Jesus be important to young Christians? **5.** Of the three temptations that Jesus faced, which one are you facing now: (a) appetite—food, sex, pleasure; (b) recognition—success, stardom, applause; (c) power—authority, control, wealth? **6.** What do you learn from the way Jesus dealt with each temptation?

APPLY **1.** What is the closest you have come to a period of doubt and testing of your faith? How long did it last? **2.** What did you find helpful during this testing period? **3.** Have you ever gone away for a few days with God to think through your hopes, dreams and goals in life?

3:13 baptized. By allowing himself to be baptized, Jesus identifies with the people of Israel and with their sin (though he himself was without sin—1 Peter 2:22).

3:16 like a dove. Matthew uses a dove as a symbol of the coming of the Holy Spirit. This is the promised anointing of the Messiah with the Holy Spirit (Isa. 11:2; 42:1; 61:1).

3:17 my Son. This is a royal title used in the Old Testament to describe Israel's kings. Now it is applied to God's Son. **I am well pleased.** This phrase is associated with the suffering servant of Isaiah (Isa. 42:1) who suffers while carrying out God's will in the service of Israel. In Jesus, the two Old Testament figures of God's servant and God's royal Son are combined.

4:1 led by the Spirit into the desert to be tempted. Jesus' victory over temptation would demonstrate three things: his sinless character; an example of endurance through times of testing; and how to use Scripture as a means of defense against the devil and a support in the face of evil.

4:2 forty days. Moses fasted 40 days on Mount Sinai while receiving the commandments (Ex. 34:28), and Israel was in the wilderness 40 years (Deut. 8:2).

4:3 The tempter came. The Spirit led Jesus into the wilderness but it is Satan who tests him. His challenges to Jesus come only after Jesus has entered a condition of physical weakness because of his fast. **If you are the Son of God.** This was a temptation to verify the truth of what God had declared (3:17). **bread.** Certainly it would be legitimate. Satan seemed to be saying, for God's own Son to do what God did when he supplied manna to the hungry Israelites. If Jesus had used his power in this way, he would not have been able to truly know the experience and pain of humans, who do not have such power at their disposal when they are hungry.

4:4 Jesus' response is drawn from Deuteronomy 8:3. Originally this was a reflection on the meaning of the manna in the desert. True life involves not just the physical, but also the spiritual (Word of God). Jesus will not heed Satan, but listen only to his Father, God.

4:5 temple. The second temptation takes place at the temple, which is the focal point in Israel of God's love and power. The challenge is to prove this love and power of God by creating a peril from which God alone can rescue him.

4:6 If you are the Son of God. Once again the challenge is to demonstrate that Jesus is the Messiah. **it is written.** Satan now quotes Scripture, but does so in a way that tears it from its context. Psalm 91:11–12 are words of assurance to God's people that they can trust God to be with them even through difficult times. Satan twists this to mean that Jesus ought to deliberately put himself in a life-threatening situation to see if God really will bail him out.

4:7 Jesus responds that people are not to test God, as Deuteronomy 6:16 clearly states, but to trust him.

8Again, the devil took him to a very high mountain and showed him
all the kingdoms of the world and their splendor. 9"All this I will give
you," he said, "if you will bow down and worship me."
10Jesus said to him, "Away from me, Satan! For it is written: 'Worship the Lord your God, and serve him only.'[a]"
11Then the devil left him, and angels came and attended him.

Jesus Begins to Preach

12When Jesus heard that John had been put in prison, he returned
to Galilee. 13Leaving Nazareth, he went and lived in Capernaum,
which was by the lake in the area of Zebulun and Naphtali— 14to fulfill what was said through the prophet Isaiah:

15"Land of Zebulun and land of Naphtali,
  the way to the sea, along the Jordan,
  Galilee of the Gentiles—
16the people living in darkness
  have seen a great light;
on those living in the land of the shadow of death
  a light has dawned."[b]

17From that time on Jesus began to preach, "Repent, for the kingdom of heaven is near."

The Calling of the First Disciples

18As Jesus was walking beside the Sea of Galilee, he saw two brothers, Simon called Peter and his brother Andrew. They were casting a
net into the lake, for they were fishermen. 19"Come, follow me," Jesus
said, "and I will make you fishers of men." 20At once they left their
nets and followed him.
21Going on from there, he saw two other brothers, James son of
Zebedee and his brother John. They were in a boat with their father
Zebedee, preparing their nets. Jesus called them, 22and immediately
they left the boat and their father and followed him.

[a]*10* Deut. 6:13 [b]*16* Isaiah 9:1,2

OPEN 1. When did you leave home for the first time? Where did you go? How did you feel? **2.** What launched you into the job you are in now?

STUDY 1. Why do you think Jesus left his hometown to start his ministry in Capernaum? Would you have gotten any respect in the town you grew up in? **2.** How would you compare the message of Jesus to the message of John the Baptist (3:7–12)? **3.** What was it about Simon and Andrew that caused Jesus to choose them (John 1:35-42; 3:24–28)? What is it about fishing that makes for a good disciple? **4.** How far had Jesus' ministry spread in his first year? How do you think his hometown thought about him? **5.** What attracted attention: His message or his healing ministry? What is the lesson here for new ministries today in underdeveloped countries? What is the danger?

APPLY 1. How would you describe the first year in your spiritual journey after you became a believer? **2.** How would you describe your spiritual life right now? **3.** What is the next challenge?

4:8–9 The final temptation has to do with gaining the kingdoms of the world without suffering the coming agonies of the Cross.

4:10 Jesus quotes Deuteronomy 6:13 to affirm his allegiance to God and to reject Satan's offer.

4:11 angels came and attended him. One function of angels is to bring comfort and aid to God's people (Heb. 1:14). Thus prepared by his baptism and his temptation, Jesus begins his ministry.

4:12 John had been put in prison. John's imprisonment is described in more detail in 14:1–12.

Galilee. This was the northern province of Palestine. It was small, about 25 by 35 miles in size, but quite densely populated. In the time of Jesus approximately 350,000 people lived there, 100,000 of whom were Jews. It was a rich farming and fishing region.

4:13 Nazareth. This was a village located in the hill country of Galilee, 20 miles southwest of Capernaum. **Capernaum.** This was a town on the north end of the Sea of Galilee, three *miles* west of the Jordan River. It was a center of the fishing industry. **the area of Zebulun and Naphtali.** This was the region originally assigned to two tribes of Israel.

4:18 Simon called Peter. In asking Simon and Andrew to "follow" him, Jesus was inviting them to join his band of disciples. They would have been familiar with rabbis who had small groups of students, as well as wandering Greek philosophers who had disciples. In telling them he would make them "fishers of men," Jesus defined their task using a metaphor which they as fishermen would understand.

4:20 At once they left. According to 4:12–17, Jesus had been living and preaching in Capernaum. These fishermen probably had the chance to hear his message prior to their call. Still, what they did was an act of great faith and courage.

Jesus Heals the Sick

[23]Jesus went throughout Galilee, teaching in their synagogues, preaching the good news of the kingdom, and healing every disease and sickness among the people. [24]News about him spread all over Syria, and people brought to him all who were ill with various diseases, those suffering severe pain, the demon-possessed, those having seizures, and the paralyzed, and he healed them. [25]Large crowds from Galilee, the Decapolis,[a] Jerusalem, Judea and the region across the Jordan followed him.

The Beatitudes

5 Now when he saw the crowds, he went up on a mountainside and sat down. His disciples came to him, [2]and he began to teach them, saying:

[3]"Blessed are the poor in spirit,
for theirs is the kingdom of heaven.
[4]Blessed are those who mourn,
for they will be comforted.
[5]Blessed are the meek,
for they will inherit the earth.
[6]Blessed are those who hunger and thirst for righteousness,
for they will be filled.
[7]Blessed are the merciful,
for they will be shown mercy.
[8]Blessed are the pure in heart,
for they will see God.
[9]Blessed are the peacemakers,
for they will be called sons of God.

[a]25 That is, the Ten Cities

OPEN Who was your best teacher in school? What was it about this teacher that made this person special?

STUDY In the Sermon on the Mount, Jesus starts out by explaining eight qualities in the life of Kingdom persons. **1.** How do you think these Beatitudes would go over as the core values of your business? **2.** Which one of these values would be hardest for you to live by in your business? Give each one a number from 1 (easy) to 10 (impossible). **Poor in Spirit**: I admit that I don't have it all together and never will. I survive by grace. **Mourn**: I can show my feelings. Big boys can cry. **Meek**: I don't have to throw my weight around. **Spiritual Hunger**: I have a craving to develop my spiritual side. **Merciful**: I treat others with respect and consideration. Pure in **Heart**: I keep my mind clean and my life focused on my life goals.

4:23 synagogues. In first-century Israel, the temple in Jerusalem was the site for sacrifices and attended by numerous priests and other officials. In addition, there were synagogues in each population center which people attended each week for worship and instruction.

4:25 the Decapolis. A league of 10 Gentile cities patterned after the Greek way of life. These cities were part of Syria.

5:1 a mountainside. To the original *Jewish readers, this would have been* an inescapable allusion to when Moses delivered the Law to Israel from Mount Sinai (Deut. 18:15). **sat down.** When rabbis taught, they would sit rather than stand. This accents Jesus' authoritative position. **disciples.** This teaching is for everyone who would be a follower of Jesus.

5:3–10 The "Beatitudes" are so named because in the Latin Bible each of the eight statements began with the word *beatus*. Such pronouncements of blessedness were particularly common in the Psalms.

5:3 Blessed are. The Greek word *makarios* refers to people who are to be congratulated. It does not necessarily mean they are happy or prospering. Instead, whether they feel it or not, they are fortunate because their condition reflects that they are in a right relationship to God. **poor in spirit.** This phrase does not refer to those who are poor in the material sense, but to those who acknowledge their need of God.

5:4 those who mourn. This does not refer to the bereaved, but to those who mourn over sin and its consequences.

5:5 the meek. This involves a lifestyle marked by gentleness, humility and courteousness. **inherit the earth.** The irony of God's reign is that, despite the efforts of those who grasp for the world, it will one day be given not to those who have been covetous but to those who have been generous.

5:6 hunger and thirst for righteousness. As hungry or thirsty people devote their entire energy to finding food and water, so those in the kingdom are marked by a deep-seated, intense longing for knowing and living in God's way.

5:7 the merciful. Mercy is an act of deliberate kindness toward someone who has no claim upon the person rendering the kindness.

5:8 pure in heart. The call is for single-minded pursuit of God's way with every facet of our being. **see God.** In the Old Testament, this term described what it meant to experience God's favor.

5:9 peacemakers. Peacemaking is an active involvement in bringing about reconciliation between those in conflict, whether at a societal or personal level.

Peacemaker: I keep communication open and honest with other workers. **Persecution**: I can stand up for what I believe and cherish.

APPLY 1. How are you and God getting along? Are you talking? **2.** As you grow in your spiritual understanding of God, do you find it easier or harder to live according to the Beatitudes?

OPEN 1. What is the closest you have come to getting in trouble with the law? **2.** How did your parents settle disputes between you and your brother/sister?

STUDY 1. Before Jesus lowers the boom on the Pharisees, what does he want to make perfectly clear about the Old Testament Law? **2.** How does Jesus redefine the commandment on murder? **3.** What does Jesus say about our quick-to-sue society? **4.** What does Jesus expect a Christian to do to heal a broken

10 Blessed are those who are persecuted because of righteousness,
for theirs is the kingdom of heaven.

11 "Blessed are you when people insult you, persecute you and
falsely say all kinds of evil against you because of me. 12 Rejoice and
be glad, because great is your reward in heaven, for in the same way
they persecuted the prophets who were before you.

Salt and Light

13 "You are the salt of the earth. But if the salt loses its saltiness,
how can it be made salty again? It is no longer good for anything,
except to be thrown out and trampled by men.
14 "You are the light of the world. A city on a hill cannot be hidden.
15 Neither do people light a lamp and put it under a bowl. Instead they
put it on its stand, and it gives light to everyone in the house. 16 In the
same way, let your light shine before men, that they may see your
good deeds and praise your Father in heaven.

The Fulfillment of the Law

17 "Do not think that I have come to abolish the Law or the Prophets; I have not come to abolish them but to fulfill them. 18 I tell you the
truth, until heaven and earth disappear, not the smallest letter, not
the least stroke of a pen, will by any means disappear from the Law
until everything is accomplished. 19 Anyone who breaks one of the
least of these commandments and teaches others to do the same will
be called least in the kingdom of heaven, but whoever practices and
teaches these commands will be called great in the kingdom of
heaven. 20 For I tell you that unless your righteousness surpasses that
of the Pharisees and the teachers of the law, you will certainly not
enter the kingdom of heaven.

5:10 persecuted because of righteousness. This is the persecution that comes to those who pursue God's way in contrast to the way of the world. **kingdom of heaven.** This term sums up all the fullness of God's blessings to his people.

5:12 reward in heaven. "Heaven" is the way Matthew refers to God (3:2). The point is not that their reward will only be after death, but rather that it will be experienced in the presence of God.

5:13 salt. Salt was a very valuable commodity in ancient times. It was not only used to flavor foods, but it was indispensable in preserving them. Salt solutions were used medicinally, specifically in washing newborn infants. Rock salt was also used as a fertilizer. Salt's value then came from these many uses. Jesus was then attesting to the value of his disciples in the world. The *disciples are to flavor the world around* them with God's love and direction; and they are to preserve that which is valuable in life from the spoilage of sin and hate.

5:14 light. Light is another basic element of life. The function of light is to illuminate the darkness. This is an image for the truth believers are to bring to the world. **of the world.** Israel was to be a light for the Gentiles (Isa. 49:6). That function is now passed on to the followers of Jesus (John 8:12).

5:15-16 The very purpose of light is defeated if it is hidden away. In the same way, Jesus' disciples are not to be living secretly, but living openly so that others can see who and what they are.

5:16 let your light shine before men. What constitutes the "light" of believers is what they say and do. **praise your Father.** While persecution is the response the world in general has toward those who embody the qualities of God's kingdom (5:10), some people will recognize in these qualities the character of God and give praise to him.

5:17 the Law or the Prophets. The Law referred to the first five books of the Old Testament, while the Prophets referred to the Major and Minor Prophets as well as the Historical Books. **fulfill.** By his teaching Jesus seeks to give expression to the intention of the Law. In contrast, for all their concern about the Law (and by their preoccupation with its details), the Pharisees and other religious leaders often overlooked its purpose.

5:18 I tell you the truth. Literally, this is "for truly I say to you," a phrase characteristic of Jesus. No other teacher of his era was known to say this. **the smallest letter ... least stroke of a pen.** Some Hebrew and Aramaic letters are distinguishable only by a small line or dot. Jesus accents the validity of the Law as the ethical norm for all God's people. **until everything is accomplished.** Until God's plan for history is complete, God's ethical demands remain in force. Jesus' mission was to call people to embrace these demands in a way that would penetrate their whole being.

5:20 Pharisees ... teachers of the law. The teachers of the Law were

Murder

21"You have heard that it was said to the people long ago, 'Do not
murder,[a] and anyone who murders will be subject to judgment.' 22But
I tell you that anyone who is angry with his brother[b] will be subject to
judgment. Again, anyone who says to his brother, 'Raca,[c]' is answer-
able to the Sanhedrin. But anyone who says, 'You fool!' will be in
danger of the fire of hell.
23"Therefore, if you are offering your gift at the altar and there remember that your brother has something against you, 24leave your
gift there in front of the altar. First go and be reconciled to your
brother; then come and offer your gift.
25"Settle matters quickly with your adversary who is taking you to
court. Do it while you are still with him on the way, or he may hand
you over to the judge, and the judge may hand you over to the officer,
and you may be thrown into prison. 26I tell you the truth, you will not
get out until you have paid the last penny.[d]

Adultery

27"You have heard that it was said, 'Do not commit adultery.'[e] 28But
I tell you that anyone who looks at a woman lustfully has already
committed adultery with her in his heart. 29If your right eye causes
you to sin, gouge it out and throw it away. It is better for you to lose
one part of your body than for your whole body to be thrown into
hell. 30And if your right hand causes you to sin, cut it off and throw it
away. It is better for you to lose one part of your body than for your
whole body to go into hell.

Divorce

31"It has been said, 'Anyone who divorces his wife must give her a
certificate of divorce.'[f] 32But I tell you that anyone who divorces his
wife, except for marital unfaithfulness, causes her to become an
adulteress, and anyone who marries the divorced woman commits
adultery.

[a]21 Exodus 20:13 [b]22 Some manuscripts *brother without cause* [c]22 An Aramaic term of contempt
[d]26 Greek *kodrantes* [e]27 Exodus 20:14 [f]31 Deut. 24:1

relationship? **5.** If the Pharisees were in charge of the church today, what would they do?

APPLY 1. In the church where you grew up, were the rules for a Christian tempered with grace? **2.** If you were in charge of the church today, what would be the rules? **3.** Where do you need to make something right today and with whom?

OPEN 1. Who was your first "true love"? **2.** Who was the first person you kissed outside your family?

STUDY 1. On the commandment, "Thou shalt not commit adultery," what does Jesus say? **2.** What is Jesus' point in using the exaggerated language in verses 29-30? What have you found helpful in dealing with lustful thoughts? **3.** Why does Jesus come down so hard on husbands on the matter of divorce? How has divorce touched your life or your family's life? **4.** On the matter of oaths, what does Jesus expect a believer to do? **5.** Who do you admire as a person who stands by their word? **6.** Do you think it is possible in this imperfect world to live up to the principles Jesus laid down in the Sermon on the Mount?

---

religious scholars who developed a set of regulations derived from the Law. The demands of these regulations were such that the majority of people simply did not have time to practice them.

5:22 angry. The Greek word used here describes deep-seated, smoldering, inner anger rather than a flash of anger. **Raca.** An Aramaic term of contempt: *"You good-for-nothing" or "I spit on you."* **Sanhedrin.** The Sanhedrin (a group of 70 Jewish men) was the official ruling body of the Jews. This body was responsible for administering justice in matters related to Jewish law. **hell.** Literally, *Gehenna*, a ravine outside Jerusalem where children were once sacrificed to the god Molech (1 Kin. 11:7). Jews considered it a defiled place, good only as a garbage dump which was continually burning. Gehenna became a symbol for the place of punishment and spiritual death.

5:23 altar. The picture is of someone going to worship. The gift is probably an animal for sacrifice. **has something against you.** The responsibility for initiating reconciliation lies with the one who, whether on purpose or by accident, has offended another member of the community.

5:25 taking you to court. The Jews were offended by the Roman custom of having debtors thrown in jail where it was impossible for them to earn money to pay off their debt, yet this is the image Jesus uses to describe the situation before God of the person who refuses to seek reconciliation.

5:26 penny. The smallest Roman coin.

5:28 a woman. The Greek word generally refers to a married woman. **lustfully.** Just as anger is at the root of murder, so too lust is at the root of adultery. This does not condemn sexual attraction, but rather the deliberate harboring of desire for an illicit relationship.

5:31–32 Jesus' statement on divorce needs to be understood in the context of the whole Sermon. Ideally, there should be no divorce. As seen from chapter 19 and Mark 10, divorce and remarriage is a departure from God's intention for marriage. It is important to note here that while the woman is called the adulteress, the fault for that

Oaths

33“Again, you have heard that it was said to the people long ago,
‘Do not break your oath, but keep the oaths you have made to the
Lord.’ 34But I tell you, Do not swear at all: either by heaven, for it is
God’s throne; 35or by the earth, for it is his footstool; or by Jerusalem,
for it is the city of the Great King. 36And do not swear by your head,
for you cannot make even one hair white or black. 37Simply let your
‘Yes’ be ‘Yes,’ and your ‘No,’ ‘No’; anything beyond this comes from
the evil one.

An Eye for an Eye

38“You have heard that it was said, ‘Eye for eye, and tooth for
tooth.’[a] 39But I tell you, Do not resist an evil person. If someone
strikes you on the right cheek, turn to him the other also. 40And if
someone wants to sue you and take your tunic, let him have your
cloak as well. 41If someone forces you to go one mile, go with him
two miles. 42Give to the one who asks you, and do not turn away from
the one who wants to borrow from you.

Love for Enemies

43“You have heard that it was said, ‘Love your neighbor[b] and hate
your enemy.’ 44But I tell you: Love your enemies[c] and pray for those
who persecute you, 45that you may be sons of your Father in heaven.
He causes his sun to rise on the evil and the good, and sends rain on
the righteous and the unrighteous. 46If you love those who love you,
what reward will you get? Are not even the tax collectors doing that?
47And if you greet only your brothers, what are you doing more than

[a]38 Exodus 21:24; Lev. 24:20; Deut. 19:21 [b]43 Lev. 19:18 [c]44 Some late manuscripts *enemies, bless those who curse you, do good to those who hate you*

APPLY **1.** Of the three teachings in this passage—controlling lustful thoughts, honoring marriage and keeping your word—which one challenges you the most? **2.** Do you feel uncomfortable about sharing your struggles with this group?

OPEN **1.** In high school, who was your biggest rival? **2.** What was the worst practical joke you played on someone? That was played on you? How did you get even?

STUDY **1.** When you get hurt in a relationship, what is your usual response? On first reading, what would this passage ask of a Christian? **2.** Have you ever tried to slap someone on their right cheek if you are right handed? What is Jesus saying you should do to take control of the situation when your rights are being violated? **3.** If Jesus believed in “love your enemies,” why did he clear the temple of the moneychangers?

APPLY What effect does your relationship with God have on your ability to love others, even those who hurt you?

situation is placed upon the husband who divorced her. In that culture, a divorced woman would have little choice for survival except to marry again. Jesus is not condemning her because of that social reality, but he is pointing out to the men involved that their casual attitude toward marriage and divorce is not much more than a “legal” way of indulging in the immorality of adultery. To the Jews of Jesus’ day, divorce and remarriage were perfectly acceptable. Neither was considered a sin. Jesus’ statement placed their attitude toward divorce and remarriage into the category of moral evil, a reality they had never before considered. While they held that their divorces and remarriages were legal, Jesus asserted they were not moral.

5:33 Do not break your oath. Jesus does not so much quote the Old Testament as he summarizes various passages on the subject of oaths (Ex. 20:7; Lev. 19:12; Num. 30:2; Deut. 23:21–23).

5:34 Do not swear at all. Contrary to what the rabbis taught, according to Jesus it does not matter whether you swear upon God’s name (which was considered binding) or on anything else (a nonbinding oath) since all objects are God’s.

5:38 Eye for eye. This is said to be the oldest law in the world. It is found in the codes of Hammurabi, a king who lived in the 18th century B.C., as well as three times in the Old Testament (Ex. 21:23–24; Lev. 24:20; Deut. 19:21). The Law’s original intent was not to *require* an “eye for an eye,” but to limit punishment to the extent of the crime.

5:40 cloak. The Law (Ex. 22:25–26; Deut. 24:10–13) prohibited a person from seizing a person’s cloak as the payment of a debt, since this woolen outer robe was used as a blanket at night. Jesus’ call here is for his followers to give beyond what even the Law would require.

5:41 forces you to go one mile. *Roman soldiers* had the right to press civilians into service to carry their gear for a distance up to one mile. The word used here is a technical term for such compulsory conscription.

5:43 Love your neighbor. Jesus quotes Leviticus 19:18. **hate your enemy.** This command is found neither in the Old Testament nor in the Talmud. Some Old Testament passages even call for compassion toward enemies (Prov. 25:21). However, passages that spoke of God’s ultimate judicial action upon those nations which threatened Israel (Deut. 7:1–2; 20:16–18; 23:5–6; Ps. 139:21) may have been misapplied in popular thought to justify personal animosity against those who are disliked, especially non-Jews.

5:44 Love your enemies. The word used here is *agape*. This is love that shows itself not by what a person feels, but by what the person does. It is love done on the behalf of another without the expectation of reward. **pray.** One way this love is demonstrated is by prayer for those who harass you.

5:46 tax collectors. Tax collectors grew rich by charging people more than what was required, keeping the excess for themselves. That they were doing this as agents of Rome made the offense even more grievous.

others? Do not even pagans do that? 48Be perfect, therefore, as your
heavenly Father is perfect.

Giving to the Needy

6 "Be careful not to do your 'acts of righteousness' before men, to
be seen by them. If you do, you will have no reward from your
Father in heaven.
2"So when you give to the needy, do not announce it with trumpets,
as the hypocrites do in the synagogues and on the streets, to be honored by men. I tell you the truth, they have received their reward in
full. 3But when you give to the needy, do not let your left hand know
what your right hand is doing, 4so that your giving may be in secret.
Then your Father, who sees what is done in secret, will reward you.

Prayer

5"And when you pray, do not be like the hypocrites, for they love to
pray standing in the synagogues and on the street corners to be seen
by men. I tell you the truth, they have received their reward in full.
6But when you pray, go into your room, close the door and pray to
your Father, who is unseen. Then your Father, who sees what is done
in secret, will reward you. 7And when you pray, do not keep on babbling like pagans, for they think they will be heard because of their
many words. 8Do not be like them, for your Father knows what you
need before you ask him.
9"This, then, is how you should pray:

" 'Our Father in heaven,
hallowed be your name,
10your kingdom come,
your will be done
on earth as it is in heaven.
11Give us today our daily bread.
12Forgive us our debts,
as we also have forgiven our debtors.
13And lead us not into temptation,
but deliver us from the evil one.[a]'

[a]13 Or *from evil;* some late manuscripts *one, / for yours is the kingdom and the power and the glory forever. Amen.*

OPEN **1.** If you win the lottery, who are you going to give the money to? **2.** When you were a child, who put you to bed at night and heard your prayers?

STUDY Up to now in the Sermon on the Mount, Jesus has dealt with core values and relationships in the life of a disciple of his. Now he turns to your relationship with God. **1.** In these instructions about giving, praying and fasting, who is he alluding to when he talks about hypocrites? Is he putting down the importance of these things in the life of a believer? **2.** When it comes to giving, how do you practice what Jesus is saying? **3.** When it comes to prayer, do you set aside a time and place or do you try to pray throughout the day, or both? Do you use devotional books or written prayers like the Lord's Prayer? **4.** Have you tried fasting? What did you do with the time and money you saved? **5.** Who do you admire among your friends for how they have balanced the demands of life with the need for a healthy spiritual life?

APPLY **1.** What would Jesus do if he had to live on your budget, and deal with your crowded time schedule? **2.** What is one thing you could do this week to start living as a devoted follower of Jesus?

5:48 Be perfect. This means "having attained the end or purpose." Therefore, people can be "perfect" if they realize that for which they were made, which is to reflect God's image, and hence to love.

6:1 In general terms, Jesus makes it clear that his followers are not to make a public display of religious devotion.

6:2 the hypocrites. It was not their lack of inner conviction that Jesus is faulting (they undoubtedly believed they ought to give to the poor), but that they wanted to make sure their observance of the traditions was seen by others.

6:7 babbling like pagans. A common practice of pagan prayer was to recite a long list of divine names in hopes of invoking a god.

6:8 knows ... before you ask. This does not mean prayer is unimportant, but rather stresses the intimate concern and awareness God has for his people.

6:9 Our Father in heaven. This does not locate God somewhere beyond space, but stresses his majesty and dignity. **hallowed be your name.** The first petition is that God's character and nature be held in honor by all.

6:10 your kingdom come. God's kingdom is in evidence whenever his will is being followed. John the Baptist has already preached that "the kingdom of God is near." But it will come in its fullness when all submit to the will of God. **on earth as it is in heaven.** God does not want to rule over just one part of his creation (heaven), but all of it.

6:11 our daily bread. This is a reminder that God is not just concerned about our "spiritual side" but our everyday physical needs as well.

6:13 temptation. The request is not a plea to be exempt from the common moral struggles of life, but that God would empower the disciple to have the moral strength to resist giving in to evil during such struggles.

14For if you forgive men when they sin against you, your heavenly Father will also forgive you. 15But if you do not forgive men their sins, your Father will not forgive your sins.

Fasting

16"When you fast, do not look somber as the hypocrites do, for they disfigure their faces to show men they are fasting. I tell you the truth, they have received their reward in full. 17But when you fast, put oil on your head and wash your face, 18so that it will not be obvious to men that you are fasting, but only to your Father, who is unseen; and your Father, who sees what is done in secret, will reward you.

Treasures in Heaven

19"Do not store up for yourselves treasures on earth, where moth and rust destroy, and where thieves break in and steal. 20But store up for yourselves treasures in heaven, where moth and rust do not destroy, and where thieves do not break in and steal. 21For where your treasure is, there your heart will be also.

22"The eye is the lamp of the body. If your eyes are good, your whole body will be full of light. 23But if your eyes are bad, your whole body will be full of darkness. If then the light within you is darkness, how great is that darkness!

24"No one can serve two masters. Either he will hate the one and love the other, or he will be devoted to the one and despise the other. You cannot serve both God and Money.

Do Not Worry

25"Therefore I tell you, do not worry about your life, what you will eat or drink; or about your body, what you will wear. Is not life more important than food, and the body more important than clothes? 26Look at the birds of the air; they do not sow or reap or store away in barns, and yet your heavenly Father feeds them. Are you not much

OPEN 1. If you had to give up one luxury in your house, which of these would you give up: Computer? TV? Indoor toilet? Washing machine? Stereo? Running water? **2.** Which would your children give up?

STUDY 1. If you read between the lines in verses 19-34, what seems to be the problem that Jesus deals with in this passage? **2.** What is Jesus saying when he refers to "moth ... rust and thieves"? What would be a similar crisis today? **3.** What happens when a believer loses their focus on biblical values (vv. 22–23)? What keeps your batteries charged? **4.** What is the clear teaching in verses 24–25? What is unclear to you when you start to apply these verses? **5.** What is the point that Jesus illustrates in the example of the "birds of the air, and the lilies of the field"? **6.** How would you define "the good life?" Who is someone you

---

6:16 fast. Jews fasted on the Day of Atonement, as well as at other special times (Deut. 9:9; 1 Sam. 31:13; Ps. 35:13). **disfigure.** Literally, this means "to make invisible." This refers to the custom when fasting of putting ashes on the head (which would dirty and cover up one's face) or covering one's face with a cloth. **their reward in full.** Once again, as with giving and with prayer (6:2,5), those who play to the crowds and are applauded by them for being "righteous" have received all the reward they will get.

6:17 put oil on your head and wash your face. Oil was a commonly used cosmetic. The followers of Jesus *are to give no outward indication that* they are engaged in a fast.

6:19 treasures on earth. Possessions as such are not forbidden, but accumulating wealth or possessions as a means of trying to obtain security in life is incompatible with seeking God's kingdom. **moth and rust.** The irony of building one's life around one's possessions was that even the most valuable treasures on earth were vulnerable to destruction by insignificant creatures like moths and mice.

6:20 treasures in heaven. These would include both relationships made eternal (1 Thess. 4:13–18) and a spiritual wholeness which comes from God's approval of us.

6:22 The eye is the lamp of the body. Both eye and heart are sometimes used in the Bible as a metaphor to describe the motivating principle that guides the way a person lives (Ps. 119:36–37). To have a good eye is to have a pure heart.

6:24 hate. This is using dramatic overstatement to express the fact that loyalty to one master makes loyalty to another master impossible. **Money.** Dividing our loyalty between God and money turns money into a god.

6:25 do not worry. When we are focused on that which cannot be taken away from us (treasures in heaven) we don't have to worry about what is essential. For the other things necessary in life, we need to trust in God's provision.

6:26 much more valuable. This does not denigrate the importance of animals to God. It is because humanity has a special relationship and responsibility to the Creator that people (made in God's image and given dominion over the creation—Gen. 1) are "more valuable" than animals.

more valuable than they? [27]Who of you by worrying can add a single
hour to his life[a]?
[28]"And why do you worry about clothes? See how the lilies of the
field grow. They do not labor or spin. [29]Yet I tell you that not even
Solomon in all his splendor was dressed like one of these. [30]If that is
how God clothes the grass of the field, which is here today and
tomorrow is thrown into the fire, will he not much more clothe you,
O you of little faith? [31]So do not worry, saying, 'What shall we eat?' or
'What shall we drink?' or 'What shall we wear?' [32]For the pagans run
after all these things, and your heavenly Father knows that you need
them. [33]But seek first his kingdom and his righteousness, and all
these things will be given to you as well. [34]Therefore do not worry
about tomorrow, for tomorrow will worry about itself. Each day has
enough trouble of its own.

Judging Others

7 "Do not judge, or you too will be judged. [2]For in the same way
you judge others, you will be judged, and with the measure you
use, it will be measured to you.
[3]"Why do you look at the speck of sawdust in your brother's eye
and pay no attention to the plank in your own eye? [4]How can you say
to your brother, 'Let me take the speck out of your eye,' when all the
time there is a plank in your own eye? [5]You hypocrite, first take the
plank out of your own eye, and then you will see clearly to remove
the speck from your brother's eye.
[6]"Do not give dogs what is sacred; do not throw your pearls to pigs.
If you do, they may trample them under their feet, and then turn and
tear you to pieces.

Ask, Seek, Knock

[7]"Ask and it will be given to you; seek and you will find; knock and
the door will be opened to you. [8]For everyone who asks receives; he
who seeks finds; and to him who knocks, the door will be opened.

admire because they have Christian values? **7.** If you could pinpoint a time in your life when you were happy and carefree, when would it be? How much money did you have in the bank? What was your wardrobe?

APPLY 1. On a scale from 1 to 10, what is the contentment factor in your life right now? **2.** If you could change one thing in your lifestyle, what would you change?

OPEN 1. When you get lost, are you more likely to stop and ask directions or drive around until you find the way? **2.** When you were growing up, who rubbed you the wrong way?

STUDY 1. What happens when a little sawdust gets in your eye? **2.** When it comes to judging, are you harder on yourself or someone else? **3.** When you get upset, what are you asked to do (v. 5)? **4.** How do you balance the teaching in verses 3–6 with Galatians 6:1-4? **5.** What is it about a life of prayer that immunizes a person with Christian values from the petty problems of life? How is this truth illustrated in the life of parents (vv. 9-11)?

APPLY Do you have a sense of humor or enough insight to

[a]27 Or *single cubit to his height*

6:27 a single hour. If all the worry in the world cannot add a single hour to one's life, what is the purpose of worrying? (Modern medicine might add that worry actually will probably *reduce* one's life span through stress-related diseases!)

6:29 Solomon. This king of Israel was noted for his fabulous wealth (1 Kin. 10:14–29). Even the simplest flower is adorned more delicately and attractively than the richest person.

6:31 So do not worry. As verse 33 indicates, the disciples of Jesus are to be busy, but their activity is centered around pursuing God's agenda; they are not to be centered around simply meeting their own needs.

6:33 But seek first his kingdom. The supreme ambition of the Christian is that all he or she thinks, says and does be for the glory of God.

6:34 tomorrow. Worry generally has to do with the future, about what lies ahead. The disciple is to live one day at a time. **trouble.** Disciples are not promised a trouble-free life; they are, however, promised God's care.

7:1–2 Do not judge. This is not to say that disciples are never to make moral judgments about the actions of others (7:15–20 requires them to do so in certain instances); rather, it condemns a harsh and censorious attitude toward others. **the measure you use.** This saying was based on the rabbinic teaching that God would judge the world with two measures, one of justice and one of mercy. If one wished to be dealt with mercifully by God, then that person should deal mercifully with others.

7:6 what is sacred. It may be that what is meant here is the flesh of animals offered for sacrifice in the temple services. It would be unthinkable for a priest to carelessly toss such flesh to dogs, who would make no distinction between it and other carrion. **pearls.** Something as precious as pearls would never be given to pigs, who would trample them under foot. Some scholars suggest that it is better to see the pearls and holy food as metaphors for the good news of the kingdom of God.

7:7–8 Ask ... seek ... knock. It is assumed these will be done from the perspective of the faith of one who is seeking first the kingdom (6:33). When we seek the kingdom, God answers our requests for our needs. This is not to say God will grant requests made out of the greed of one who seeks self-enhancement.

recognize your own faults in the criticism you have for another?

OPEN 1. When you were growing up, who did your parents warn you to stay away from? **2.** Did you ever build a fort or a tree house? What was it like?

STUDY If the Sermon on the Mount was a ball game, the next three passages would be the last inning—the two-minute drill. **1.** Where do the two roads in verses 13-14 lead? Which is the road less traveled and why? **2.** Who are the "false prophets" you need to be on guard against? What "test" does Jesus give to identify them? **3.** How would you describe "the good life" as defined by a modern-day false prophet? What would Jesus say about this? **4.** What song or saying comes to mind when you think about verse 24? **5.** In the parable of the wise and foolish builders, what is the only difference in the two houses? What made for the difference? **6.** If a building inspector had to approve a mortgage on your spiritual life, what would he/she say?

APPLY 1. What is the weather like in your life at the moment: Sunny? Overcast? Stormy? Other? **2.** How about your spiritual foundation: Solid? Shaky? Brand new?

9"Which of you, if his son asks for bread, will give him a stone? 10Or
if he asks for a fish, will give him a snake? 11If you, then, though you
are evil, know how to give good gifts to your children, how much
more will your Father in heaven give good gifts to those who ask him!
12So in everything, do to others what you would have them do to you,
for this sums up the Law and the Prophets.

The Narrow and Wide Gates

13"Enter through the narrow gate. For wide is the gate and broad is
the road that leads to destruction, and many enter through it. 14But
small is the gate and narrow the road that leads to life, and only a few
find it.

A Tree and Its Fruit

15"Watch out for false prophets. They come to you in sheep's clothing, but inwardly they are ferocious wolves. 16By their fruit you will
recognize them. Do people pick grapes from thornbushes, or figs
from thistles? 17Likewise every good tree bears good fruit, but a bad
tree bears bad fruit. 18A good tree cannot bear bad fruit, and a bad
tree cannot bear good fruit. 19Every tree that does not bear good fruit
is cut down and thrown into the fire. 20Thus, by their fruit you will
recognize them.
21"Not everyone who says to me, 'Lord, Lord,' will enter the kingdom of heaven, but only he who does the will of my Father who is in
heaven. 22Many will say to me on that day, 'Lord, Lord, did we not
prophesy in your name, and in your name drive out demons and perform many miracles?' 23Then I will tell them plainly, 'I never knew
you. Away from me, you evildoers!'

The Wise and Foolish Builders

24"Therefore everyone who hears these words of mine and puts
them into practice is like a wise man who built his house on the rock.
25The rain came down, the streams rose, and the winds blew and beat

---

7:9–10 bread ... fish. The most common food in Galilee. **snake.** This is probably an eel-like fish without scales that Jews were forbidden to eat (Lev. 11:12).

7:12 do to others what you would have them do to you. This is the so-called Golden Rule. The negative form of this rule was widely known in the ancient world: "Do not do to others what you do not wish them to do to you." Jesus alters this statement in a slight but highly significant way. He shifts the statement from the negative to the positive. Whereas the negative rule was fulfilled by inaction (not bothering others), the positive rule requires active benevolence. **this sums up the Law and the Prophets.** That love is the summary of the Law is one of Jesus' central themes (Mark 12:30–31). Paul had a similar focus (Rom. 13:8–10).

7:13 wide is the gate ... broad is the road. This is the way of the secular world that stands in contrast to the values taught in the Sermon on the Mount. **destruction.** This is where the "natural" way of the secular world leads. While ultimately such a lifestyle leads to the judgment of God against sin (Rom. 1:18), it also leads to destruction here and now in the sense of estranged relationships and inner chaos.

7:14 small is the gate and narrow the road. The narrower way is the way of life advocated by the Sermon. This way leads to an inner wholeness marked by the presence of God and fulfilling human relationships.

7:15 sheep's clothing. Prophets often wore animal skins (3:4; 2 Kin. 1:8). People might dress in this fashion and claim to be prophets. Or, metaphorically, they might act as innocent as sheep while their true nature is that of vicious wolves who feed off others.

7:20 by their fruit. One important way to discern if a person is a genuine spokesperson for God is by considering what he or she does. Does the person reflect the values of the Sermon on the Mount in what they do?

7:21 Not everyone who says to me, 'Lord, Lord'. The earliest Christian confession was "Jesus is Lord." However, Jesus emphasizes actions over words (25:31–46; James 1:19–27; 2:14–26).

7:22 on that day. This is the day of judgment. Throughout the Bible, there is a clear expectation of a final accounting of humanity by God.

7:24-27 In the autumn, rains produced flash floods which swept down ravines. While the two houses in the flood's path look alike, only the one built on a solid foundation will stand. Only those who build their lives on the foundation of the words of Jesus will stand.

against that house; yet it did not fall, because it had its foundation on
the rock. 26But everyone who hears these words of mine and does not
put them into practice is like a foolish man who built his house on
sand. 27The rain came down, the streams rose, and the winds blew
and beat against that house, and it fell with a great crash."

28When Jesus had finished saying these things, the crowds were
amazed at his teaching, 29because he taught as one who had authority, and not as their teachers of the law.

The Man With Leprosy

8 When he came down from the mountainside, large crowds followed him. 2A man with leprosy[a] came and knelt before him and
said, "Lord, if you are willing, you can make me clean."
3Jesus reached out his hand and touched the man. "I am willing," he
said. "Be clean!" Immediately he was cured[b] of his leprosy. 4Then Jesus
said to him, "See that you don't tell anyone. But go, show yourself to
the priest and offer the gift Moses commanded, as a testimony to
them."

The Faith of the Centurion

5When Jesus had entered Capernaum, a centurion came to him,
asking for help. 6"Lord," he said, "my servant lies at home paralyzed
and in terrible suffering."
7Jesus said to him, "I will go and heal him."
8The centurion replied, "Lord, I do not deserve to have you come
under my roof. But just say the word, and my servant will be healed.
9For I myself am a man under authority, with soldiers under me. I tell
this one, 'Go,' and he goes; and that one, 'Come,' and he comes. I say
to my servant, 'Do this,' and he does it."
10When Jesus heard this, he was astonished and said to those following him, "I tell you the truth, I have not found anyone in Israel
with such great faith. 11I say to you that many will come from the east
and the west, and will take their places at the feast with Abraham,

[a]2 The Greek word was used for various diseases affecting the skin—not necessarily leprosy. [b]3 Greek *made clean*

Slowly wearing away? Rebuilding? **3.** Are you open to have God work on your life?

OPEN 1. Who is the highest ranking official or celebrity you have met? **2.** Have you ever seen a photograph of someone with leprosy?

STUDY 1. Would you think these three miracles in one day was a good day's work? **2.** Which of these miracles required the biggest risk on Jesus' part: Touching a leper? Meeting a general? Healing Peter's mother-in-law? **3.** What do these healings reveal about Jesus' character? **4.** Which one would have shocked a Jewish audience? Who are the "many" in verses 11–12? **5.** What would healing Peter's mother-in-law do for the faith of Peter? For his hometown? **6.** If Jesus were to come to your hometown, who would be the "leper"? Who would be the centurion? Who would be Peter's mother-in-law?

APPLY 1. Is it harder for you to reach out and touch social "lepers" or Centurions? **2.** If one of these people showed up at your group, how would they be received? **3.** What is keeping you from inviting them?

7:29 their teachers of the law. Literally, "scribes," religious lawyers who interpreted Jewish law. Originally, it was their job to make copies of the Old Testament. Because of their familiarity with Scripture, people consulted them about points of law, and hence their role evolved into that of teacher of the Law.

8:2 leprosy. No disease was dreaded more than leprosy since it brought not only physical disfigurement but social banishment. A leper was required to live away from other people. (Lev. 13:45–46). The Greek word used here refers not just to what is known today as leprosy, but to many forms of inflammatory skin disease.

8:3 touched the man. Actually touching a leper was unimaginable to most first century Jews. Not only did one risk contracting the disease, but such contact made the person ritually impure and thus unable to participate in the religious life of the community (Lev. 5:3–6).

8:4 don't tell anyone. Jesus had to prevent the crowds from proclaiming him Messiah before they knew what kind of Messiah he was (one who would suffer and die, not the conquering hero they hoped for).

8:5 Capernaum. This was a town on the north end of the Sea of Galilee, three miles west of the Jordan River. This was where Jesus often stayed during his ministry in Galilee. In fact, Capernaum was considered to be Jesus' home as an adult (4:13; Mark 2:1). **centurion.** A Roman military officer, the commander of 100 men. Such a soldier would be a hated symbol of Rome to most Jews.

8:7 I will go. According to rabbinical law, if Jesus were to go into a Gentile's home he would be made unclean. This does not concern Jesus, however.

8:11 the feast. To share a meal was a symbol of unity and fellowship (Rev. 3:20). A great feast is often seen as part of the initiation of the messianic kingdom (26:29; Luke 14:15–24). The great messianic banquet will include not only the patriarchs (like Abraham, Isaac and Jacob) but Gentiles as well.

Isaac and Jacob in the kingdom of heaven. 12But the subjects of the
kingdom will be thrown outside, into the darkness, where there will
be weeping and gnashing of teeth."
13Then Jesus said to the centurion, "Go! It will be done just as you
believed it would." And his servant was healed at that very hour.

Jesus Heals Many

14When Jesus came into Peter's house, he saw Peter's mother-in-
law lying in bed with a fever. 15He touched her hand and the fever left
her, and she got up and began to wait on him.
16When evening came, many who were demon-possessed were
brought to him, and he drove out the spirits with a word and healed
all the sick. 17This was to fulfill what was spoken through the prophet
Isaiah:

"He took up our infirmities
and carried our diseases."[a]

The Cost of Following Jesus

18When Jesus saw the crowd around him, he gave orders to cross to
the other side of the lake. 19Then a teacher of the law came to him
and said, "Teacher, I will follow you wherever you go."
20Jesus replied, "Foxes have holes and birds of the air have nests,
but the Son of Man has no place to lay his head."
21Another disciple said to him, "Lord, first let me go and bury my
father."
22But Jesus told him, "Follow me, and let the dead bury their own
dead."

[a]17 Isaiah 53:4

OPEN 1. What is guaranteed to ruin a vacation: Seven days of rain? Screaming children in the back seat? Lost luggage at the airport? **2.** When a movie gets scary, are you more likely to go to the bathroom or clutch a friend and love it?

STUDY 1. How would you have dealt with the teacher of the law and the other guy who wanted to join Jesus on their terms? In your own words, what did Jesus tell them? **2.** Would you have been

8:12 But the subjects of the kingdom. This would be Jews who do not show faith. This same point is made in Jesus' Parable of the Great Banquet (Luke 14:15–24).

8:13 just as you believed it would. The testimony of New Testament Scripture is that belief is a powerful force when centered on God. It is the power of God released into the world when people believe that with God "all things are possible" (19:26; Mark 10:27; 14:36; Luke 18:27). **his servant was healed.** Again a dramatic healing takes place, this time with Jesus healing from a distance. For Jesus to heal someone from the household of a Roman soldier doubtlessly irritated many pious Jewish traditionalists, as when he ate with tax collectors and sinners.

8:15 He touched her hand. This is the only healing recorded by Matthew which is initiated by Jesus. Jesus' healing most often involved touching people (8:3; 9:20; 20:34; Luke 22:51). **the fever left her.** This was a real, immediate cure. She apparently suffered none of the weakness that normally follows when a fever breaks. In each of the three healings, the cure was instantaneous (vv. 3,13).

8:16 drove out the spirits with a word. First-century exorcists used elaborate incantations, spells, and magic apparatus to cast out demons—in contrast to Jesus whose word alone sufficed.

8:17 This was to fulfill. Matthew quotes from Isaiah 53:4. His point is that Jesus' healing ministry was foretold as an aspect of the ministry of the suffering servant of God.

8:19 a teacher of the law. Typically these scribes or teachers of the Law were opposed to Jesus because of his disregard of the oral law that was so important to them. However, individual scribes were followers of Jesus.

8:20 Son of Man. This is the title Jesus prefers for himself. In the first century it was a rather colorless, indeterminate title (with some messianic overtones—Dan. 7:13–14) which could be translated as "man" or even "I." This allowed Jesus to fill it with new meaning, and so convey who he actually is. This title is used 29 times in Matthew, always by Jesus, never by others.

8:21 bury my father. The obligation of a son to bury his father was so important that it normally took precedence over other religious obligations. Care for one's parents was a sacred obligation.

8:22 Jesus told people that to be his follower one had to put following him above all other obligations, no matter how important they seemed.

Jesus Calms the Storm

23Then he got into the boat and his disciples followed him. 24With-
out warning, a furious storm came up on the lake, so that the waves
swept over the boat. But Jesus was sleeping. 25The disciples went and
woke him, saying, "Lord, save us! We're going to drown!"
26He replied, "You of little faith, why are you so afraid?" Then he got
up and rebuked the winds and the waves, and it was completely calm.
27The men were amazed and asked, "What kind of man is this?
Even the winds and the waves obey him!"

The Healing of Two Demon-possessed Men

28When he arrived at the other side in the region of the Gadarenes,[a]
two demon-possessed men coming from the tombs met him. They
were so violent that no one could pass that way. 29"What do you want
with us, Son of God?" they shouted. "Have you come here to torture
us before the appointed time?"
30Some distance from them a large herd of pigs was feeding. 31The
demons begged Jesus, "If you drive us out, send us into the herd of
pigs."
32He said to them, "Go!" So they came out and went into the pigs,
and the whole herd rushed down the steep bank into the lake and
died in the water. 33Those tending the pigs ran off, went into the town
and reported all this, including what had happened to the demon-
possessed men. 34Then the whole town went out to meet Jesus. And
when they saw him, they pleaded with him to leave their region.

Jesus Heals a Paralytic

9 Jesus stepped into a boat, crossed over and came to his own
town. 2Some men brought to him a paralytic, lying on a mat.
When Jesus saw their faith, he said to the paralytic, "Take heart, son;
your sins are forgiven."
3At this, some of the teachers of the law said to themselves, "This
fellow is blaspheming!"

[a]28 Some manuscripts *Gergesenes*; others *Gerasenes*

nice and let Jesus sleep when the storm came up? **3.** What is the tone in Jesus' voice when he spoke to the disciples? How would you have felt if you had been in the boat? **4.** In the middle of the night and in a graveyard, what happens? How is the miracle that follows different from the miracle in the storm? **5.** What do you learn about demons and demon possession in this story? **6.** How did the people who were looking after the pigs respond? How did the people in town respond to the good news? **7.** Where are the disciples during all the commotion? **8.** How would the disciples describe their short vacation? What did they learn?

APPLY 1. How would you describe the waves in your life: Calm? Small ripples? Heavy seas? Tidal wave? **2.** What is the "demon" trying to control your life at the moment? Could you use a little prayer?

OPEN How did you feel when you got home from your last vacation?

STUDY 1. Whose faith is involved in this healing? **2.** If the paralytic has a physical problem, why does Jesus say "your sins are forgiven"? **3.** How do the teachers of the law respond? **4.** How did Jesus

8:24 a furious storm. The Sea of Galilee was a deep, freshwater lake, 13 miles long and 8 miles at its widest point. It was pear-shaped and ringed by mountains, though open at its north and south ends. Fierce winds blew into this bowl-shaped sea, creating savage and unpredictable storms. **Jesus was sleeping.** In the Old Testament, sleeping peacefully is a sign of trust in the power of God (Ps. 3:5; 4:8; Job 11:18–19).

8:25 The disciples woke Jesus simply so that he could help them bail out the boat since it was about to be swamped.

8:26 You of little faith. This is the same phrase that is used in 6:30 to describe those who do not trust God to provide for them.

8:28 the region of the Gadarenes. Matthew, Mark and Luke use different terms to describe the place where Jesus landed. The different terms relate to names of the population inhabiting the area (the Gadarenes), a small town near the Sea of Galilee (Khersa), and the larger city in that region that served as its capital (Gerasa). **two demon-possessed men.** The demons are malignant, supernatural beings with the power to take control of a person's body, speaking and acting through that person.

8:29 Son of God. They recognize who Jesus is and want nothing to do with him. **before the appointed time.** According to Jewish apocalyptic literature, the torment of demons was to take place at the time of the final judgment.

8:32 rushed down the steep bank. This stampede gave evidence that the demons had been driven out of the men.

8:34 they pleaded with him to leave. This may have been in part out of fear of his power, but also because he had destroyed part of their livelihood (the pigs). To the townspeople, their pigs were worth more than the lives of the two madmen.

9:2 mat. The bed of a poor person. **their faith.** It is the faith of the friends that facilitates the healing of the paralytic. Normally Jesus points to the faith of the person healed. **your sins are forgiven.** Jesus repudiates the teaching that all illness and misfortune is an indication that a person had committed a worse sin than others (John 9:1–3).

9:3 This fellow. A term of contempt. **blaspheming.** Blasphemy is "contempt for God" and under Jewish law its penalty was death (Lev. 24:16). Jesus' was equating himself with God

answer the teachers of the law? How did the crowd respond?

APPLY 1. Who cared enough to bring you to Jesus? 2. Who are the friends you could call on now in the middle of the night?

OPEN What do you remember about your high school prom? Where did you go?

STUDY This is Matthew telling his own story. 1. Who was he and how did he meet Jesus? 2. Who showed up at his house to meet Jesus and what did this do to Jesus' reputation? 3. How would you rephrase what Jesus said in verses 12-13? 4. Who is John (the Baptist)? Where is he now (4:12)? What's the problem with his disciples? 5. Does the lifestyle of John the Baptist represent the "old garment"? What is the "new patch" and the "new wine"? 6. What is the lesson for the church today?

APPLY 1. In your spiritual life, what was the period when you felt most alive and productive? 2. Are you keeping in touch with the "sinners" from your pre-Christian days? What about inviting these people to this group?

4Knowing their thoughts, Jesus said, "Why do you entertain evil
thoughts in your hearts? 5Which is easier: to say, 'Your sins are forgiven,' or to say, 'Get up and walk'? 6But so that you may know that
the Son of Man has authority on earth to forgive sins . . ." Then he
said to the paralytic, "Get up, take your mat and go home." 7And the
man got up and went home. 8When the crowd saw this, they were
filled with awe; and they praised God, who had given such authority
to men.

The Calling of Matthew

9As Jesus went on from there, he saw a man named Matthew sitting
at the tax collector's booth. "Follow me," he told him, and Matthew
got up and followed him.
10While Jesus was having dinner at Matthew's house, many tax collectors and "sinners" came and ate with him and his disciples.
11When the Pharisees saw this, they asked his disciples, "Why does
your teacher eat with tax collectors and 'sinners'?"
12On hearing this, Jesus said, "It is not the healthy who need a doctor, but the sick. 13But go and learn what this means: 'I desire mercy,
not sacrifice.'[a] For I have not come to call the righteous, but sinners."

Jesus Questioned About Fasting

14Then John's disciples came and asked him, "How is it that we and
the Pharisees fast, but your disciples do not fast?"
15Jesus answered, "How can the guests of the bridegroom mourn
while he is with them? The time will come when the bridegroom will
be taken from them; then they will fast.
16"No one sews a patch of unshrunk cloth on an old garment, for
the patch will pull away from the garment, making the tear worse.
17Neither do men pour new wine into old wineskins. If they do, the
skins will burst, the wine will run out and the wineskins will be ruined.
No, they pour new wine into new wineskins, and both are preserved."

[a]*13* Hosea 6:6

---

and in their view this was blasphemy.

9:5 Which is easier. Jesus responds to the teachers of the Law in typical rabbinic fashion: He asks them a question. The answer is obvious. It is far easier to say, "Your sins are forgiven" than it is to heal a person. There is no way to verify whether sins have been forgiven, but it is obvious whether a lame person walks or not.

9:6 But so that you may know. Since the theology of the scribes linked forgiveness and healing, if Jesus is able to heal the paralytic they would have to admit that he had, indeed, forgiven the man's sins.

9:8 authority. *The issue here, as in* each of the three stories in chapter 8:23–9:8, is Jesus' authority. He has authority over the elements, demons and sin.

9:9 Matthew. Presumably the author of this Gospel. In his role as tax collector, Matthew would have been hated by both the religious establishment and the common people. **tax collector's booth.** Tax collectors were seen as traitors because they collaborated with the Roman power in order to become wealthy. They were free to charge whatever the market would bear. **Follow me.** In Matthew, Mark and Luke, this is the key phrase regarding discipleship. Only those who leave their past behind to follow Jesus in faith and obedience are his disciples.

9:11 Why does your teacher eat with tax collectors and "sinners"? The Pharisees could not understand how a truly religious person could eat with people whose moral life was disreputable and who violated the practices regarding ritual cleanliness.

9:12 It is not the healthy who need a doctor, but the sick. Jesus was not necessarily saying that the Pharisees *were* spiritually healthy, only that they perceived themselves to be so.

9:13 I desire mercy, not sacrifice. This quotation from Hosea 6:6 sheds light on how Jesus will go about healing the "sick" to whom he has been sent—through mercy, not through requiring more observance of religious ritual.

9:14 John's disciples. The followers of John the Baptist did not all automatically start following Jesus when he came on the scene, even though John pointed to him as Messiah. **fast.** Regular fasting was assumed to be part of any serious religious discipline.

9:15 the bridegroom. In the Old Testament, God is often referred to as the bridegroom of Israel. **the bridegroom**

A Dead Girl and a Sick Woman

[18]While he was saying this, a ruler came and knelt before him and
said, "My daughter has just died. But come and put your hand on her,
and she will live." [19]Jesus got up and went with him, and so did his
disciples.
[20]Just then a woman who had been subject to bleeding for twelve
years came up behind him and touched the edge of his cloak. [21]She
said to herself, "If I only touch his cloak, I will be healed."
[22]Jesus turned and saw her. "Take heart, daughter," he said, "your
faith has healed you." And the woman was healed from that moment.
[23]When Jesus entered the ruler's house and saw the flute players
and the noisy crowd, [24]he said, "Go away. The girl is not dead but
asleep." But they laughed at him. [25]After the crowd had been put outside, he went in and took the girl by the hand, and she got up. [26]News
of this spread through all that region.

Jesus Heals the Blind and Mute

[27]As Jesus went on from there, two blind men followed him, calling
out, "Have mercy on us, Son of David!"
[28]When he had gone indoors, the blind men came to him, and he
asked them, "Do you believe that I am able to do this?"
"Yes, Lord," they replied.
[29]Then he touched their eyes and said, "According to your faith will
it be done to you"; [30]and their sight was restored. Jesus warned them
sternly, "See that no one knows about this." [31]But they went out and
spread the news about him all over that region.
[32]While they were going out, a man who was demon-possessed
and could not talk was brought to Jesus. [33]And when the demon was
driven out, the man who had been mute spoke. The crowd was
amazed and said, "Nothing like this has ever been seen in Israel."
[34]But the Pharisees said, "It is by the prince of demons that he
drives out demons."

OPEN 1. What is your remedy for stopping a bloody nose? **2.** Whose voice or touch can you recognize, even in a crowded room?

STUDY 1. Now that Matthew (v. 9) has joined the disciples, he puts into his account three miracles that must have happened on the first day he was on the team. How do you think he felt when he saw these things? **2.** What was Jesus talking about (vv. 16–17) when the ruler showed up and asked him to help his daughter? **3.** What is the social status of the four people that Jesus heals in this passage? Which one took the biggest chance in approaching Jesus? **4.** Why did Jesus ask for the woman who had been healed to identify herself? **5.** Was the daughter dead? Why did Jesus say she was sleeping? **6.** Who brought the two blind men to Jesus? What did these guys "believe" about Jesus? **7.** What was wrong with the mute? Why would the Pharisees say such a thing about Jesus? **8.** If you had to build a definition about "faith" out of these stories, what would you say: Faith is ...? **9.** In three of these miracles, Jesus said "touch." Is this coincidental or is there something about touch in healing? **10.** What did Jesus realize he would have to do? **11.** How much is your church doing to relieve the pain and suffering in your community?

will be taken from them. This is a foreshadowing of Jesus' death. It will be as if the groom is suddenly, violently abducted just prior to his wedding.

9:18 a ruler. Mark and Luke indicate that he was the ruler of a local synagogue. **put your hand on her.** The laying on of hands was a common practice for ordination, for blessing and for healing.

9:20 a woman who had been subject to bleeding. She was probably hemorrhaging from the womb, which rendered her ritually impure (Lev. 15:25–33). As a result, she should not have been there in the crowd. She was considered "unclean," and if anyone touched her that person too would become "unclean."

9:21 touch his cloak. The power of a person was thought to be transferred to his or her clothing.

9:22 your faith has healed you. The word Jesus uses to tell her that she is healed comes from the same root as the words "salvation" and "savior." Spiritual as well as physical healing is in view here.

9:23 flute players and the noisy crowd. These were in all likelihood professional mourners. Even the poorest person was required to hire no less than two flutes and one wailing woman to mourn a death.

9:24 The girl is not dead but asleep. Jesus uses the same expression in reference to Lazarus (John 11:11–15). What he means is that she is not permanently dead.

9:27 two blind men. Blindness was common in the ancient world, often due to infection. **Son of David.** There was a strong expectation that the Messiah would be a king in the line of David. The Messiah was understood to have the power to heal (11:4–5). Three of the four times in Matthew where there is an appeal for mercy, the title Son of David is used.

9:33 mute. This word can mean either deaf or dumb or both. **Nothing like this has ever been seen in Israel.** At the end of this section of Matthew, Jesus' teaching is contrasted with that of the religious leaders (7:28–29). Here he contrasts his healing power with theirs. The testimony of the crowd to Jesus' miracle working is included.

9:34 The reaction of the Pharisees stands in sharp contrast to the reaction of the crowd in verse 33. The Pharisees dismiss Jesus' healings by attributing them to Satan.

APPLY 1. What is God calling you to do about the pain and loneliness in your community? **2** What is it going to take to get you started?

OPEN 1. What is the longest you have hiked or hitchhiked your way across country? **2.** What kind of person would you want in your expedition party the next time you embark on a great adventure?

STUDY 1. What did Jesus do before sending out his men (v. 1)? How do the disciples' activities here compare with what Jesus had been doing in chapters 8–9? **2.** The "zealots" were guerrilla fighters committed to the freedom of the Jews from Rome. Why would Jesus choose one of them to be on the same team with Matthew, a tax collector who had worked with Rome? **3.** What limits did Jesus put on their ministry (v. 5)? Do you think the disciples were disappointed that these groups were excluded? **4.** What was to be their message? What were they to do? **5.** Why do you think that Jesus told them to take nothing more than the clothes on their backs? **6.** What was the basic point of Jesus' preparation speech to the disciples? What problems would they (and future disciples) face? How were they to respond to each problem? **7.** What does it mean to be "like sheep among wolves," "shrewd as snakes," "innocent as doves" (v. 16)? **8.** Who would persecute them? In

The Workers Are Few

[35]Jesus went through all the towns and villages, teaching in their
synagogues, preaching the good news of the kingdom and healing
every disease and sickness. [36]When he saw the crowds, he had compassion on them, because they were harassed and helpless, like
sheep without a shepherd. [37]Then he said to his disciples, "The harvest is plentiful but the workers are few. [38]Ask the Lord of the harvest,
therefore, to send out workers into his harvest field."

Jesus Sends Out the Twelve

10 He called his twelve disciples to him and gave them authority
to drive out evil[a] spirits and to heal every disease and sickness.
[2]These are the names of the twelve apostles: first, Simon (who is
called Peter) and his brother Andrew; James son of Zebedee, and his
brother John; [3]Philip and Bartholomew; Thomas and Matthew the tax
collector; James son of Alphaeus, and Thaddaeus; [4]Simon the Zealot
and Judas Iscariot, who betrayed him.

[5]These twelve Jesus sent out with the following instructions: "Do
not go among the Gentiles or enter any town of the Samaritans. [6]Go
rather to the lost sheep of Israel. [7]As you go, preach this message:
'The kingdom of heaven is near.' [8]Heal the sick, raise the dead,
cleanse those who have leprosy,[b] drive out demons. Freely you have
received, freely give. [9]Do not take along any gold or silver or copper
in your belts; [10]take no bag for the journey, or extra tunic, or sandals
or a staff; for the worker is worth his keep.

[11]"Whatever town or village you enter, search for some worthy person there and stay at his house until you leave. [12]As you enter the
home, give it your greeting. [13]If the home is deserving, let your peace
rest on it; if it is not, let your peace return to you. [14]If anyone will not
welcome you or listen to your words, shake the dust off your feet
when you leave that home or town. [15]I tell you the truth, it will be
more bearable for Sodom and Gomorrah on the day of judgment than
for that town. [16]I am sending you out like sheep among wolves.
Therefore be as shrewd as snakes and as innocent as doves.

[a]1 Greek *unclean* [b]8 The Greek word was used for various diseases affecting the skin—not necessarily leprosy.

10:1 twelve disciples. This is the first time in Matthew that the 12 disciples are mentioned. The number 12 is significant. There were 12 sons of Jacob and they became the patriarchs of the 12 tribes of the old Israel.

10:2–4 apostles. The term denotes those who are sent on a mission.

10:5 sent out. To go out on a ministry tour was not the idea of the Twelve. Jesus does the sending. ***Do not go among the Gentiles.*** The first mission of the Twelve was to the people of Israel. After the death and resurrection of Jesus, their mission is expanded to include all nations (28:19). **Samaritans.** A mixed race of people which came from the intermarriage of Jews not taken to Babylon in captivity (6th century B.C.) and Gentiles from the occupying army. There was great hostility between Jews and Samaritans (John 4:9).

10:7 The kingdom of heaven is near. This is the same message that John the Baptist gave (3:2). Prepare for the rule of God is imminent.

10:10 no bag. The reference is probably to a begging bag commonly used by wandering priests to collect funds. **extra tunic.** It could be used as a blanket during the chilly nights.

10:11 stay ... until you leave. They are not to dishonor their host by accepting better accommodations.

10:14 shake the dust off your feet. When pious Jews left a Gentile region and returned to Israel they shook off the dust of the land through which they had just traveled so as to disassociate themselves from the coming judgment against the Gentiles.

10:16 shrewd as snakes ... innocent as doves. While Jesus' disciples are to use cleverness, not force, to survive, they are to be honest and holy.

17"Be on your guard against men; they will hand you over to the
local councils and flog you in their synagogues. 18On my account you
will be brought before governors and kings as witnesses to them and
to the Gentiles. 19But when they arrest you, do not worry about what
to say or how to say it. At that time you will be given what to say, 20for
it will not be you speaking, but the Spirit of your Father speaking
through you.

21"Brother will betray brother to death, and a father his child; children will rebel against their parents and have them put to death. 22All
men will hate you because of me, but he who stands firm to the end
will be saved. 23When you are persecuted in one place, flee to another. I tell you the truth, you will not finish going through the cities
of Israel before the Son of Man comes.

24"A student is not above his teacher, nor a servant above his master. 25It is enough for the student to be like his teacher, and the servant like his master. If the head of the house has been called
Beelzebub,[a] how much more the members of his household!

26"So do not be afraid of them. There is nothing concealed that will
not be disclosed, or hidden that will not be made known. 27What I tell
you in the dark, speak in the daylight; what is whispered in your ear,
proclaim from the roofs. 28Do not be afraid of those who kill the body
but cannot kill the soul. Rather, be afraid of the One who can destroy
both soul and body in hell. 29Are not two sparrows sold for a penny[b]?
Yet not one of them will fall to the ground apart from the will of your
Father. 30And even the very hairs of your head are all numbered. 31So
don't be afraid; you are worth more than many sparrows.

32"Whoever acknowledges me before men, I will also acknowledge
him before my Father in heaven. 33But whoever disowns me before
men, I will disown him before my Father in heaven.

34"Do not suppose that I have come to bring peace to the earth. I
did not come to bring peace, but a sword. 35For I have come to turn

" 'a man against his father,
a daughter against her mother,

[a]25 Greek *Beezeboul* or *Beelzeboul* [b]29 Greek *an assarion*

times of persecution, what could they expect from God? **9.** How might Christ's truth divide a family? What kind of radical commitment does Jesus call for in verses 37–39? **10.** How were the disciples to understand their reception (vv. 40–42)? What confirming authority does Jesus bestow upon his disciples at the end of his discourse (v. 40), as well as at the beginning (v. 1)?

APPLY 1. Under what circumstances do you find it most difficult to talk about your faith? **2.** What have you found helpful when you share your faith story? **3.** How can you best represent to your neighbors that the kingdom of heaven is near?

10:17–23 This passage seems to have more applicability to the time after Jesus' resurrection and ascension. At that time, the early church certainly faced all the perils mentioned here.

10:17 councils ... synagogues. The councils were Jewish courts where religious troublemakers were tried and then beaten publicly in the synagogues.

10:18 governors and kings. Some of Jesus' disciples will stand before Roman provincial governors and kings.

10:22 he who stands firm to the end will be saved. His disciples will not be spared persecution but they are guaranteed entrance into the kingdom of God.

10:23 before the Son of Man comes. The early church expected an early return of Christ.

10:25 Beelzebub. This is probably a slang expression for a demon-prince, meaning something like "The Lord of Dung."

10:27 from the roofs. Important announcements would often be made from the roof of a building. What Jesus taught the disciples in private is to be broadcast to all.

10:28 They are not to fear death since those who have the power to kill them have no power over their souls. **be afraid of the One.** This is not meant to imply that the motive for following Jesus is only fear of God's wrath, but that believers' lives are to be marked by a greater regard for God than for human opinion.

10:29 sparrows. Sparrows are worth next to nothing (two for a penny) and yet not one of them dies without God knowing it. **penny.** A penny was worth one sixteenth of a denarius. A denarius was the average day's wage of a manual laborer.

10:34 Do not suppose that I have come to bring peace. This is not to be taken to mean that Jesus was in favor of war. Jesus turned away from the militaristic expectations of the Messiah. He also proclaimed that the one who lives by the sword will die by the sword (26:52). He was saying that the demands he would make would create conflicts between people, even people in the same family. Jesus did not seek to avoid conflict when conflict was necessary.

a daughter-in-law against her mother-in-law—
36 a man's enemies will be the members of his own household.'[a]

37"Anyone who loves his father or mother more than me is not worthy of me; anyone who loves his son or daughter more than me is not
worthy of me; 38and anyone who does not take his cross and follow
me is not worthy of me. 39Whoever finds his life will lose it, and whoever loses his life for my sake will find it.

40"He who receives you receives me, and he who receives me receives the one who sent me. 41Anyone who receives a prophet because he is a prophet will receive a prophet's reward, and anyone
who receives a righteous man because he is a righteous man will receive a righteous man's reward. 42And if anyone gives even a cup of
cold water to one of these little ones because he is my disciple, I tell
you the truth, he will certainly not lose his reward."

Jesus and John the Baptist

11 After Jesus had finished instructing his twelve disciples, he
went on from there to teach and preach in the towns of
Galilee.[b]

2When John heard in prison what Christ was doing, he sent his disciples 3to ask him, "Are you the one who was to come, or should we
expect someone else?"

4Jesus replied, "Go back and report to John what you hear and see:
5The blind receive sight, the lame walk, those who have leprosy[c] are
cured, the deaf hear, the dead are raised, and the good news is
preached to the poor. 6Blessed is the man who does not fall away on
account of me."

7As John's disciples were leaving, Jesus began to speak to the
crowd about John: "What did you go out into the desert to see? A reed
swayed by the wind? 8If not, what did you go out to see? A man
dressed in fine clothes? No, those who wear fine clothes are in kings'
palaces. 9Then what did you go out to see? A prophet? Yes, I tell you,
and more than a prophet. 10This is the one about whom it is written:

[a]36 Micah 7:6 [b]1 Greek *in their towns* [c]5 The Greek word was used for various diseases affecting the skin—not necessarily leprosy.

OPEN 1. (For the married:) When did you know that the person you married was "the one"? What tipped you off? (For the unmarried:) What is the sign you look for in a potential mate to tell you "this is the one"? **2.** When you "church shop," what three items are on the top of your list?

STUDY 1. Who questions Jesus (v. 2)? Where is John? How did he land in prison (14:1–5)? **2.** How might prison have raised doubts for John (v. 3)? **3.** Does Jesus answer John more with promises or with evidence? Why? How might John, who knew the Old Testament well, have interpreted Jesus' reply (Isa. 35:5–6; 61:1)? **4.** What attracted people to John the Baptist (vv. 7–10)? How would you like to have John the Baptist as your pastor? **5.** How is a New Testament believer greater than John (v. 11; 18:3–4)?

10:37 Jesus was not being anti-family here. He was saying that family ties can work against faithful discipleship, and that God's claim is our first loyalty.

10:38 cross. It would evoke for his hearers the image of a Roman execution. To be a follower of Jesus will involve hardship; it might even involve execution.

10:39 finds his life. This is putting one's own natural inclinations ahead of loyalty to Christ.

10:40 receives. To receive someone is to offer hospitality (vv. 11–14). In a time of persecution this could be dangerous. "Receiving" the disciple probably means that the host accepts the teaching of the disciple.

10:42 a cup of cold water. In the hot middle-eastern climate, cold water was a gift of life-sustaining importance.

11:2 in prison. According to Josephus (a Jewish historian of the time), Herod had imprisoned John in the fortress of Machaerus on the east side of the Dead Sea. He arrested John at the instigation of his wife Herodias who was angry at John for denouncing their marriage (14:1–12). **what Christ was doing.** John had heard stories of what Jesus was doing. The title "Christ" is the Greek term for Messiah. It is Matthew, not John, who refers to Jesus in this way. By this title Matthew sums up who Jesus' actions reveal him to be.

11:4–6 Jesus responds by inviting John's disciples to report what they have seen with their own eyes and heard with their own ears. His actions and his teaching are all the "proof" that is necessary.

11:7–8 John was not a weak and vacillating reed who was affected by every wind of opinion, nor was he a finely dressed courtier in the halls of King Herod.

11:9–10 John was a very special prophet. He had been foretold by Old Testament prophecy. His role, as the quotation from Malachi 3:1 shows, was to prepare for the coming of the Messiah.

" 'I will send my messenger ahead of you,
who will prepare your way before you.'[a]

11 I tell you the truth: Among those born of women there has not risen anyone greater than John the Baptist; yet he who is least in the kingdom of heaven is greater than he. 12 From the days of John the Baptist until now, the kingdom of heaven has been forcefully advancing, and forceful men lay hold of it. 13 For all the Prophets and the Law prophesied until John. 14 And if you are willing to accept it, he is the Elijah who was to come. 15 He who has ears, let him hear.

16 "To what can I compare this generation? They are like children sitting in the marketplaces and calling out to others:

17 " 'We played the flute for you,
and you did not dance;
we sang a dirge,
and you did not mourn.'

18 For John came neither eating nor drinking, and they say, 'He has a demon.' 19 The Son of Man came eating and drinking, and they say, 'Here is a glutton and a drunkard, a friend of tax collectors and "sinners." ' But wisdom is proved right by her actions."

APPLY 1. Who was the John the Baptist in your spiritual life, to prepare the way for Jesus? **2.** In times of discouragement and doubt, what renews your faith?

Woe on Unrepentant Cities

20 Then Jesus began to denounce the cities in which most of his miracles had been performed, because they did not repent. 21 "Woe to you, Korazin! Woe to you, Bethsaida! If the miracles that were performed in you had been performed in Tyre and Sidon, they would have repented long ago in sackcloth and ashes. 22 But I tell you, it will be more bearable for Tyre and Sidon on the day of judgment than for you. 23 And you, Capernaum, will you be lifted up to the skies? No, you will go down to the depths.[b] If the miracles that were performed in you had been performed in Sodom, it would have remained to this day. 24 But I tell you that it will be more bearable for Sodom on the day of judgment than for you."

OPEN What is your favorite city? Least favorite? Why?

STUDY 1. What judgment does Jesus pass on each city mentioned? Why will their judgment be worse than that of the pagan cities of the Old Testament? **2.** If Jesus is rejected, what is the judgment?

APPLY What is Jesus' point for you in this warning?

Rest for the Weary

25 At that time Jesus said, "I praise you, Father, Lord of heaven and earth, because you have hidden these things from the wise and learned, and revealed them to little children. 26 Yes, Father, for this was your good pleasure.

OPEN How many hours of sleep do you need?

STUDY 1. Why do the "wise and learned" find it hard to commit their lives to Jesus? What is it about children that he commends?

[a] *10* Mal. 3:1 [b] *23* Greek *Hades*

11:19 wisdom is proved right by her actions. Despite the leaders' rejection of Jesus and John, God's wisdom in sending them is demonstrated in that both will ultimately bear evidence of the kingdom of God at work.

11:20 repent. To repent is to change your mind about the direction in which you are going. It is to turn away from your sins and turn to God and his ways. These people saw clear demonstrations of God's power in and through Jesus, yet still did not follow him.

11:21 Korazin. Apart from this reference (and the parallel in Luke 10:13) and one reference in rabbinic writing, there is no other mention of Korazin. **Bethsaida.** The home of Peter, Andrew and Philip (John 1:44; 12:21). **Tyre and Sidon.** These were two Phoenician port cities inhabited by Gentiles. **sackcloth and ashes.** As a sign of mourning and repentance from sin, people would wear rough clothing and cover themselves with ashes.

11:23 Capernaum. The village where Jesus performed many of his first miracles (8:5–17). **Sodom.** This city, destroyed by God because of its evil, was legendary for its wickedness (Gen. 18:20–19:29).

11:25 the wise and learned. The scribes and Pharisees, though educated and supposedly wise, are blind to God's plan (1 Cor. 1:19–20).

2. What does Jesus offer to those who are sick and tired of trying to run their own lives?

APPLY When did you come to the place that you turned over your life to Jesus? What changed?

OPEN 1. Can you remember a time when you were blamed for something you did not do? **2.** Did you ever get sent to the principal's office? What happened?

STUDY 1. What do you know about the origin of the "sabbath" in the Old Testament? What was the purpose? **2.** Why did the disciples of Jesus get into trouble with the Pharisees? Who decided that it was "unlawful" to "pick grain" on the Sabbath? **3.** What was more important to the Pharisees when the man with the shriveled hand needed help on the Sabbath? What was more important to Jesus? **4.** Do you know any "Pharisees" today? What are they trying to do? **5.** What did the Pharisees set out to do to Jesus?

APPLY 1. Where have you gotten into trouble over the rules of formalized religion? **2.** Where are the people with withered hands going in your town to find healing?

27"All things have been committed to me by my Father. No one
knows the Son except the Father, and no one knows the Father except
the Son and those to whom the Son chooses to reveal him.
28"Come to me, all you who are weary and burdened, and I will give
you rest. 29Take my yoke upon you and learn from me, for I am gentle
and humble in heart, and you will find rest for your souls. 30For my
yoke is easy and my burden is light."

Lord of the Sabbath

12 At that time Jesus went through the grainfields on the Sabbath. His disciples were hungry and began to pick some
heads of grain and eat them. 2When the Pharisees saw this, they said
to him, "Look! Your disciples are doing what is unlawful on the Sabbath."
3He answered, "Haven't you read what David did when he and his
companions were hungry? 4He entered the house of God, and he and
his companions ate the consecrated bread—which was not lawful for
them to do, but only for the priests. 5Or haven't you read in the Law
that on the Sabbath the priests in the temple desecrate the day and
yet are innocent? 6I tell you that one[a] greater than the temple is here.
7If you had known what these words mean, 'I desire mercy, not
sacrifice,'[b] you would not have condemned the innocent. 8For the
Son of Man is Lord of the Sabbath."
9Going on from that place, he went into their synagogue, 10and a
man with a shriveled hand was there. Looking for a reason to accuse
Jesus, they asked him, "Is it lawful to heal on the Sabbath?"
11He said to them, "If any of you has a sheep and it falls into a pit
on the Sabbath, will you not take hold of it and lift it out? 12How
much more valuable is a man than a sheep! Therefore it is lawful to
do good on the Sabbath."
13Then he said to the man, "Stretch out your hand." So he
stretched it out and it was completely restored, just as sound as the
other. 14But the Pharisees went out and plotted how they might kill
Jesus.

[a]6 Or *something;* also in verses 41 and 42 [b]7 Hosea 6:6

11:27 Jesus here defines his relationship with the one he calls "Father" in verse 25. This is one of the most explicit statements in the Gospels about who Jesus is. Three points are made: (1) All things are shared between the Father and the Son; (2) There is an intimate relationship between the two; (3) It is Jesus who reveals the Father to people (John 3:35; 10:15).

11:30 burden. The demands of discipleship, while costly in one way (5-7; 8:18–22) are "light" in comparison with the demands of ceremonial law.

12:1 Sabbath. The seventh day of the week (Saturday), begins Friday at sunset and ends Saturday at sunset. The Fourth Commandment is to rest from all labor on the Sabbath (Ex. 20:8–11). By the first century, scores of laws had evolved which defined what could not be done on the Sabbath. **pick some heads of grain.** It was permissible for hungry travelers to pluck and eat grain from a field (Deut. 23:25).

12:4 ate the consecrated bread. Each Sabbath, 12 fresh loaves of bread were put in the Holy Place (Ex. 25:30; Num. 4:7). Only the priests were to eat the old bread. David did what was unlawful, providing a precedent that human need supersedes ceremonial law.

12:10 shriveled hand. Rabbinic law allowed healing on the Sabbath only if there was danger to life. Clearly a shriveled hand (which had probably been that way for some time) did not constitute an emergency.

12:13 Stretch out your hand. Just as he deliberately declared the paralytic's sins forgiven, knowing that this would be considered blasphemy by the teachers of the Law (9:1–8), here he deliberately heals on the Sabbath, knowing that this too was anathema to his critics.

God's Chosen Servant

15 Aware of this, Jesus withdrew from that place. Many followed
him, and he healed all their sick, 16 warning them not to tell who
he was. 17 This was to fulfill what was spoken through the prophet
Isaiah:

18 "Here is my servant whom I have chosen,
the one I love, in whom I delight;
I will put my Spirit on him,
and he will proclaim justice to the nations.
19 He will not quarrel or cry out;
no one will hear his voice in the streets.
20 A bruised reed he will not break,
and a smoldering wick he will not snuff out,
till he leads justice to victory.
21 In his name the nations will put their hope."[a]

Jesus and Beelzebub

22 Then they brought him a demon-possessed man who was blind
and mute, and Jesus healed him, so that he could both talk and see.
23 All the people were astonished and said, "Could this be the Son of
David?"
24 But when the Pharisees heard this, they said, "It is only by Beelzebub,[b] the prince of demons, that this fellow drives out demons."
25 Jesus knew their thoughts and said to them, "Every kingdom divided against itself will be ruined, and every city or household divided
against itself will not stand. 26 If Satan drives out Satan, he is divided
against himself. How then can his kingdom stand? 27 And if I drive out
demons by Beelzebub, by whom do your people drive them out? So
then, they will be your judges. 28 But if I drive out demons by the Spirit
of God, then the kingdom of God has come upon you.
29 "Or again, how can anyone enter a strong man's house and carry
off his possessions unless he first ties up the strong man? Then he
can rob his house.
30 "He who is not with me is against me, and he who does not gather with me scatters. 31 And so I tell you, every sin and blasphemy will
be forgiven men, but the blasphemy against the Spirit will not be forgiven. 32 Anyone who speaks a word against the Son of Man will be
forgiven, but anyone who speaks against the Holy Spirit will not be
forgiven, either in this age or in the age to come.
33 "Make a tree good and its fruit will be good, or make a tree bad
and its fruit will be bad, for a tree is recognized by its fruit. 34 You
brood of vipers, how can you who are evil say anything good? For out
of the overflow of the heart the mouth speaks. 35 The good man brings

OPEN Where do you go when you need to withdraw for a few days?

STUDY It is pretty obvious what the Pharisees wanted to do with Jesus (v. 14). **1.** What do those who are healed want to do with Jesus that would not be in keeping with his purpose and mission? **2.** How does the quote from the Old Testament explain this?

APPLY When is the last time you withdrew for a few days to figure out what God wants you to do with your life?

OPEN 1. Who said: "Any nation divided against itself cannot stand?" **2.** When you were growing up, what was the unforgivable sin in your family: Playing hooky? Picking your nose in public? Smoking cigars? Leaving the toilet seat up? Other?

STUDY 1. How did the people react when Jesus healed the blind and deaf man? **2.** Did the Pharisees question the fact that the man was healed? Did they question the fact that supernatural power was demonstrated in this healing? **3.** What did the Pharisees attribute the healing to? How does this explain the meaning behind "Blasphemy against the Spirit" and the sin that is unforgivable? **4.** Is it possible for a person to stay neutral when it comes to Jesus (v. 30)? What does he challenge the crowd to do? What is the warning? **5.** What does Jesus call the Pharisees? Is that very nice? Why would he be so hard on them?

APPLY 1. When did you come to the place in your spiritual life that you had to get off the fence about the claims of Jesus Christ in your life? **2.** What are you doing to "store up good" in your life?

[a] 21 Isaiah 42:1-4 [b] 24 Greek *Beezeboul* or *Beelzeboul*; also in verse 27

12:24 It is only by Beelzebub. Beelzebub was the Canaanite name for the chief god Baal which in Jewish terminology became identified as the chief among the demons. To be possessed by this demon meant to be controlled and empowered by him, which is how the teachers of the Law explained Jesus' miracles.

12:31 the blasphemy against the Spirit. This is to resist the Spirit's convicting work, and so not to see one's sin.

12:32 It might be excusable to utter a word against the Son of Man, since who he is, at this point, is somewhat hidden. Even John the Baptist is not sure about Jesus' identity (11:3). To resist the insights brought by the Holy Spirit, who is the revealer of truth, is to put one's self deliberately outside the orbit of God's revelation.

good things out of the good stored up in him, and the evil man brings
evil things out of the evil stored up in him. [36]But I tell you that men
will have to give account on the day of judgment for every careless
word they have spoken. [37]For by your words you will be acquitted,
and by your words you will be condemned."

The Sign of Jonah

[38]Then some of the Pharisees and teachers of the law said to him,
"Teacher, we want to see a miraculous sign from you."
[39]He answered, "A wicked and adulterous generation asks for a miraculous sign! But none will be given it except the sign of the prophet
Jonah. [40]For as Jonah was three days and three nights in the belly of a
huge fish, so the Son of Man will be three days and three nights in the
heart of the earth. [41]The men of Nineveh will stand up at the judgment with this generation and condemn it; for they repented at the
preaching of Jonah, and now one[a] greater than Jonah is here. [42]The
Queen of the South will rise at the judgment with this generation and
condemn it; for she came from the ends of the earth to listen to Solomon's wisdom, and now one greater than Solomon is here.
[43]"When an evil[b] spirit comes out of a man, it goes through arid
places seeking rest and does not find it. [44]Then it says, 'I will return to
the house I left.' When it arrives, it finds the house unoccupied, swept
clean and put in order. [45]Then it goes and takes with it seven other
spirits more wicked than itself, and they go in and live there. And the
final condition of that man is worse than the first. That is how it will
be with this wicked generation."

Jesus' Mother and Brothers

[46]While Jesus was still talking to the crowd, his mother and brothers stood outside, wanting to speak to him. [47]Someone told him,
"Your mother and brothers are standing outside, wanting to speak to
you."[c]
[48]He replied to him, "Who is my mother, and who are my brothers?"
[49]Pointing to his disciples, he said, "Here are my mother and my
brothers. [50]For whoever does the will of my Father in heaven is my
brother and sister and mother."

The Parable of the Sower

13 That same day Jesus went out of the house and sat by the
lake. [2]Such large crowds gathered around him that he got
into a boat and sat in it, while all the people stood on the shore.

[a]41 Or *something*; also in verse 42 [b]43 Greek *unclean* [c]47 Some manuscripts do not have verse 47.

OPEN Which of these people would motivate you to clean your house before they arrived: Your pastor? Mother? Mother-in-law? Rock star? Famous athlete?

STUDY 1. Why does Jesus refuse to perform a miraculous sign for the Pharisees? **2.** What do you know about the story of Jonah and the whale? What does the "sign" of Jonah represent? **3.** What is the point that Jesus makes when he refers to Nineveh and the Queen of the South? (Keep in mind where they came from.) **4.** In the parable about the "evil spirit" that returns to an unoccupied house and trashes it, what is the lesson? Do you know of someone who has done this (v. 45)? **5.** What do you think motivated the mother and brothers of Jesus to be in the crowd? Do you think his reply was a put down or an invitation to the crowd to be part of a larger family?

APPLY 1. Since the day that you threw out the "unclean spirits" in your life, have you left your spiritual house unoccupied? **2.** Who is your spiritual director to help you take inventory?

OPEN 1. Who is the "green thumb" in your family? What is your luck with gardening? **2.** What teacher made a difference in your life by helping you to understand something?

12:40 three days and three nights. Jesus' death and resurrection took place over a three-day period (Friday, Saturday and Sunday).

12:41 Jesus compares his generation to those who lived in the time of Jonah *in Nineveh*. Yet those people repented, whereas the people listening to Jesus refuse to do so even though one far greater than Jonah is preaching to them.

12:42 The Queen of the South came all the way from Arabia to listen to the wisdom of Solomon (1 Kin. 10:1–13). In both examples, Gentiles heeded the words of a Jew; but the Jews of this generation will not heed one greater than both Jonah and Solomon.

12:43–45 Jesus tells a parable about the spiritual state of his generation. By his message of healing, Jesus had swept out the demon that possessed the people. But the new Spirit, the Holy Spirit, was not invited to take up residence in their hearts. So evil returns in much greater power.

12:46 According to Mark, Jesus' family thinks that he is "out of his mind" and so they go to "take charge" of him (Mark 3:21). When the family arrives they find him surrounded by the crowd. Not wanting to confront him in that setting, they wait outside.

[3]Then he told them many things in parables, saying: "A farmer went
out to sow his seed. [4]As he was scattering the seed, some fell along
the path, and the birds came and ate it up. [5]Some fell on rocky places,
where it did not have much soil. It sprang up quickly, because the soil
was shallow. [6]But when the sun came up, the plants were scorched,
and they withered because they had no root. [7]Other seed fell among
thorns, which grew up and choked the plants. [8]Still other seed fell on
good soil, where it produced a crop—a hundred, sixty or thirty times
what was sown. [9]He who has ears, let him hear."

[10]The disciples came to him and asked, "Why do you speak to the
people in parables?"

[11]He replied, "The knowledge of the secrets of the kingdom of
heaven has been given to you, but not to them. [12]Whoever has will be
given more, and he will have an abundance. Whoever does not have,
even what he has will be taken from him. [13]This is why I speak to
them in parables:

"Though seeing, they do not see;
though hearing, they do not hear or understand.

[14]In them is fulfilled the prophecy of Isaiah:

" 'You will be ever hearing but never understanding;
you will be ever seeing but never perceiving.
[15]For this people's heart has become calloused;
they hardly hear with their ears,
and they have closed their eyes.
Otherwise they might see with their eyes,
hear with their ears,
understand with their hearts
and turn, and I would heal them.'[a]

[16]But blessed are your eyes because they see, and your ears because
they hear. [17]For I tell you the truth, many prophets and righteous men
longed to see what you see but did not see it, and to hear what you
hear but did not hear it.

[a]15 Isaiah 6:9,10

STUDY **1.** Who is this parable addressed to? **2.** What are the four soils? What happened to the seed in each soil? **3.** If the "good soil" usually produced 30 times what was sown, how would you describe the harvest from the "good soil"? How would you describe the harvest from the other three soils? Was the seed to blame? **4.** According to Jesus, why does God's Word not take root in certain people (v. 15)? **5.** Do you know any people like the seed sown along the path (v. 18)? Like seed sown on rocky places (vv. 18–20)? Like seed sown among thorns (vv. 21–22)? **6.** In this parable the four soils are identifiable and the crop yield is predictable. When the "soil" in real life is people, is it possible to predict who is going to yield a good crop before the harvest time? **7.** What is the lesson in this parable for the seed sower today? **8.** In your ministry, who surprised you when they turned out to be "good soil"? Who has disappointed you when they turned out to be "bad soil"?

APPLY **1.** Who was the farmer in your life to plant the seed of the Word of God? Have you ever thanked this person? **2.** When this person planted the seed, do you think this person felt you would one day become the person you are today? **3.** As you look back, how many of your friends that started out with you are still living for the Lord? What happened? **4.** If God were the gardener, what would he like to do right now with the soil in your spiritual life?

13:3 parables. Parables are comparisons which draw upon common experience in order to teach about kingdom realities. **sow his seed.** Farmers would throw seed into the soil by a broadcast method.

13:4 the path. There were long, hard pathways between the various plots of land. The soil was so packed down that seed could not penetrate the soil and germinate.

13:5 rocky places. Some of the soil covered a limestone base a few inches beneath the surface. Seed that fell here would germinate, but it would not last since a proper root system could not develop, because of the rock.

13:7 thorns. In other parts of the plot there were the roots of weeds. When the seed grew up, so did the weeds which invariably stunted the growth of the good seed. Although it lived, such seed would not bear fruit.

13:8 good soil. However, some of the seed did fall where it was intended. **a hundred, sixty or thirty times.** The good soil yielded a spectacular crop. The normal yield for a Palestinian field is seven and a half times what is sown, while 10 times is an especially good harvest. This is where the emphasis in the parable lies: Not with the unproductive soil, but with the miracle crop.

13:9 He who has ears, let him hear. Jesus urges his hearers to ponder his parable. Part of the power of a parable lies in the fact that people must reflect on it in order to understand it.

13:10 The disciples ask why Jesus uses parables. Behind this question lies the fact that parables do not always act as simple illustrations which illuminate spiritual truth. They can be hard to understand (13:36).

13:11 secrets. A secret in the New Testament is not something that is hidden as much as it is something which is unclear to the outsider, but clear to the insider to whom its meaning has been revealed.

13:13–15 The problem the Pharisees had with parables was not that they could not understand the parables—they understood them all too well, but resisted their truth (21:45).

18“Listen then to what the parable of the sower means: 19When
anyone hears the message about the kingdom and does not understand it, the evil one comes and snatches away what was sown in his
heart. This is the seed sown along the path. 20The one who received
the seed that fell on rocky places is the man who hears the word and
at once receives it with joy. 21But since he has no root, he lasts only a
short time. When trouble or persecution comes because of the word,
he quickly falls away. 22The one who received the seed that fell
among the thorns is the man who hears the word, but the worries of
this life and the deceitfulness of wealth choke it, making it unfruitful.
23But the one who received the seed that fell on good soil is the man
who hears the word and understands it. He produces a crop, yielding
a hundred, sixty or thirty times what was sown.”

The Parable of the Weeds

24Jesus told them another parable: “The kingdom of heaven is like
a man who sowed good seed in his field. 25But while everyone was
sleeping, his enemy came and sowed weeds among the wheat, and
went away. 26When the wheat sprouted and formed heads, then the
weeds also appeared.

27“The owner’s servants came to him and said, ‘Sir, didn’t you sow
good seed in your field? Where then did the weeds come from?’

28“ ‘An enemy did this,’ he replied.

“The servants asked him, ‘Do you want us to go and pull them up?’

29“ ‘No,’ he answered, ‘because while you are pulling the weeds,
you may root up the wheat with them. 30Let both grow together until
the harvest. At that time I will tell the harvesters: First collect the
weeds and tie them in bundles to be burned; then gather the wheat
and bring it into my barn.’ ”

The Parables of the Mustard Seed and the Yeast

31He told them another parable: “The kingdom of heaven is like a
mustard seed, which a man took and planted in his field. 32Though it
is the smallest of all your seeds, yet when it grows, it is the largest of
garden plants and becomes a tree, so that the birds of the air come
and perch in its branches.”

33He told them still another parable: “The kingdom of heaven is

OPEN 1. What is the closest you have come to taking care of a big garden? **2.** What weeds are you battling in your garden at the moment? Who’s winning?

STUDY 1. In the parable of the weeds in verses 24–30, what is the question about the Kingdom of heaven that Jesus addresses? What do the servants want to do about the problem? What does the owner of the field decide to do? Why? **2.** What is the lesson today in this parable for “servants” in the church who get impatient? **3.** In the parable of the mustard seed in verses 31–32, what is the lesson for anyone engaged in a spiritual ministry? **4.** In the parable of the yeast in verse 33, what is the lesson about the impact of the gospel? **5.** In the explanation of the parable of the weeds, what does Jesus say about purity? Discipline? About tolerance and patience?

APPLY 1. Is the turf where God has put you more like a paradise of spiritual fellowship or a

---

13:19 The seed is the message about the kingdom. Some are so hardened (like the soil on the paths between farm plots) that the seed of the Word never even penetrates. It is, instead, snatched away by Satan. **hears ... does not understand.** This person merely hears the message; there is no understanding of what is heard. To understand is to grasp the meaning of the message and then make it your own.

13:22 Still others allow the wrong concerns (specifically worries and wealth) to squeeze out their interest in Jesus and his way. **making it unfruitful.** The weeds do not kill the plant (in contrast to the seed sown on hard ground or on rocky soil, which do not survive). But they do not allow it to bring forth fruit.

13:23 a hundred, sixty or thirty times. In this parable there are three types of unproductive soil and also, so it would appear, three types of productive soil. However, in terms of the point Jesus is trying to make in chapter 13, *there* are only two kinds of soil: unproductive and productive.

13:25 sleeping. This does not suggest inattention, but simply normal rest. It is the same as saying that the deed was done “at night.” **weeds.** Sowing a field with useless seed was a common means by which a disgruntled person might seek revenge upon an enemy, since such a sowing could devastate a crop.

13:31 mustard seed. The mustard plant, which grew to about 10 feet, was the smallest seed. Its shade and tasty brown seeds attracted flocks of birds.

13:33 yeast. A small piece of dough would be saved from the previous baking and allowed to ferment. It would then be added to the new bread mixture, causing it to rise. **a large amount of**

like yeast that a woman took and mixed into a large amount[a] of flour until it worked all through the dough."

34 Jesus spoke all these things to the crowd in parables; he did not say anything to them without using a parable. 35 So was fulfilled what was spoken through the prophet:

"I will open my mouth in parables,
I will utter things hidden since the creation of the world."[b]

The Parable of the Weeds Explained

36 Then he left the crowd and went into the house. His disciples came to him and said, "Explain to us the parable of the weeds in the field."

37 He answered, "The one who sowed the good seed is the Son of
Man. 38 The field is the world, and the good seed stands for the sons
of the kingdom. The weeds are the sons of the evil one, 39 and the
enemy who sows them is the devil. The harvest is the end of the age, and the harvesters are angels.

40 "As the weeds are pulled up and burned in the fire, so it will be at
the end of the age. 41 The Son of Man will send out his angels, and they will weed out of his kingdom everything that causes sin and all
who do evil. 42 They will throw them into the fiery furnace, where
there will be weeping and gnashing of teeth. 43 Then the righteous will shine like the sun in the kingdom of their Father. He who has ears, let him hear.

The Parables of the Hidden Treasure and the Pearl

44 "The kingdom of heaven is like treasure hidden in a field. When a man found it, he hid it again, and then in his joy went and sold all he had and bought that field.

45 "Again, the kingdom of heaven is like a merchant looking for fine
pearls. 46 When he found one of great value, he went away and sold everything he had and bought it.

[a]33 Greek *three satas* (probably about 1/2 bushel or 22 liters) [b]35 Psalm 78:2

weed patch of spiritual darkness? How do you feel about this? **2.** Are you strong enough to live among weeds and still stand out like a mustard seed? **3.** Have you noticed any difference in your situation because of the yeast in your life?

OPEN What do you remember about the legend of King Arthur and the quest for the holy grail?

STUDY 1. In the parables of the hidden treasure and pearl of great value, how much did it cost the men to get what they sought for? What does it say to someone today who wants to be a disciple of Jesus?

flour. Literally, "three measures." This would be almost 160 cups of flour, enough to make bread for about 100 people!

13:38 sons of the kingdom. To be a "son" of something or someone meant to be a person who reflects the characteristics of that particular thing or person. The "sons of the kingdom" are people whose lives are in conformity to the values of that kingdom. The "sons of the evil one" are those whose character reflects that of Satan.

13:39 The harvest. Picturing God's final judgment in terms of a harvest was common in the Old Testament and other apocalyptic literature (Jer. 51:53; Joel 3:12–13). **the end of the age.** Apocalyptic literature viewed history in terms of "the present age" and "the age to come." The "present age" is marked by sin and the oppression of the righteous, but the "age to come" would begin when God dramatically puts an end to this age by his judgment upon evil, ushering in a new age in which he reigns over all with justice and peace.

13:40 burned in the fire. God's judgment was often described in terms of a consuming fire that would purify the world of all evil (2 Thess. 1:7; Heb. 12:28–29; 2 Peter 3:10; Rev. 19:20).

13:42 weeping and gnashing of teeth. This is a stock phrase used to indicate extreme horror and suffering (8:12; 13:50; 22:13; 24:51; 25:30).

13:43 shine like the sun. Light is often used to describe the nature of holiness (Dan. 12:3; 1 John 1:5). **He who has ears, let him hear.** This is one stock phrase used to call people to think about what they have heard: What does it mean? What are its implications? How are we to respond to this story (v. 9)?

13:44 treasure hidden in a field. People would often hide their valuables in jars which they buried in the ground. **a man found it.** Probably a day laborer hired to till the field. **sold all he had.** It was not a sacrifice on the part of the man to do this. He knew what he was getting was worth it.

13:45 pearls. Pearls were highly valued. They were found in the Red Sea and the Persian Gulf.

2. In the parable of the net, what does it teach about the end of the age? How does this parable compare to the parable of the weeds in verses 24-30? **3.** What does Jesus ask the teachers of the law to do when they teach about the Kingdom from now on?

APPLY 1. Honestly, what is the pearl of great price in your life right now? **2.** Where does God fit into your value system?

The Parable of the Net

47 "Once again, the kingdom of heaven is like a net that was let
down into the lake and caught all kinds of fish. 48 When it was full, the
fishermen pulled it up on the shore. Then they sat down and collected the good fish in baskets, but threw the bad away. 49 This is how it
will be at the end of the age. The angels will come and separate the
wicked from the righteous 50 and throw them into the fiery furnace,
where there will be weeping and gnashing of teeth.

51 "Have you understood all these things?" Jesus asked.

"Yes," they replied.

52 He said to them, "Therefore every teacher of the law who has
been instructed about the kingdom of heaven is like the owner of a
house who brings out of his storeroom new treasures as well as old."

OPEN What do you consider your hometown?

STUDY 1. What was Jesus' reception in his hometown? What did they "know"? How does this effect his ministry? **2.** For someone who grew up "always knowing about Jesus," what is the danger?

APPLY Where is the hardest place in the world for you to share your faith story?

A Prophet Without Honor

53 When Jesus had finished these parables, he moved on from there.
54 Coming to his hometown, he began teaching the people in their
synagogue, and they were amazed. "Where did this man get this wisdom and these miraculous powers?" they asked. 55 "Isn't this the
carpenter's son? Isn't his mother's name Mary, and aren't his brothers James, Joseph, Simon and Judas? 56 Aren't all his sisters with us?
Where then did this man get all these things?" 57 And they took offense at him.

But Jesus said to them, "Only in his hometown and in his own
house is a prophet without honor."

58 And he did not do many miracles there because of their lack of
faith.

OPEN What would be your "dream" birthday present?

STUDY 1. In our country, who would you compare to the character of King Herod? John the Baptist? **2.** In a sex scandal involving Herod and Herodias, the wife of his brother, what did John the Baptist do that got him thrown into jail? What does this say about his character? **3.** Who does King Herod fear most: Jesus? John the Baptist? Dinner guests? His wife? What does this say about his character?

John the Baptist Beheaded

14 At that time Herod the tetrarch heard the reports about Jesus,
2 and he said to his attendants, "This is John the Baptist; he
has risen from the dead! That is why miraculous powers are at work
in him."

3 Now Herod had arrested John and bound him and put him in prison because of Herodias, his brother Philip's wife, 4 for John had been
saying to him: "It is not lawful for you to have her." 5 Herod wanted to
kill John, but he was afraid of the people, because they considered
him a prophet.

6 On Herod's birthday the daughter of Herodias danced for them and
pleased Herod so much 7 that he promised with an oath to give her

---

13:47 a net that was let down into the lake. The picture is of a dragnet. Such a net would catch all types of fish.

13:52 new treasures as well as old. Jesus challenges people to draw not only from the Law and the Prophets, but from his teachings. The coming of Jesus breathes fresh air into those writings.

13:54 his hometown. This was Nazareth, located in the hill country of Galilee.

13:57 Only in his hometown. Familiarity often prevents people from acknowledging the accomplishments or wisdom of one they assume they know.

14:1 Herod. Herod Antipas was the ruler of the Roman provinces of Galilee and Perea from 4 B.C. to A.D. 39. He was the son of Herod the Great, who had ordered the slaughter of the babies at the time of Jesus' birth.

14:2 This is John the Baptist. Herod was suffering from a guilty conscience. He was afraid that the holy man he had executed had come back with supernatural powers.

14:4 It is not lawful. Herod's marriage to Herodias was a scandal to the Jewish community. Herodias had been married to Herod's half-brother, but divorced him to marry Herod, who was more powerful. To make matters worse, Herodias was also Herod's niece, the daughter of another half-brother of Herod's. On both counts, this liaison violated the laws which prohibited such marriages (Lev. 18:16; 20:21). John the Baptist made it clear to all that this was unacceptable.

whatever she asked. 8Prompted by her mother, she said, "Give me here
on a platter the head of John the Baptist." 9The king was distressed,
but because of his oaths and his dinner guests, he ordered that her
request be granted 10and had John beheaded in the prison. 11His head
was brought in on a platter and given to the girl, who carried it to her
mother. 12John's disciples came and took his body and buried it. Then
they went and told Jesus.

Jesus Feeds the Five Thousand

13When Jesus heard what had happened, he withdrew by boat privately to a solitary place. Hearing of this, the crowds followed him on
foot from the towns. 14When Jesus landed and saw a large crowd, he
had compassion on them and healed their sick.

15As evening approached, the disciples came to him and said, "This
is a remote place, and it's already getting late. Send the crowds away,
so they can go to the villages and buy themselves some food."

16Jesus replied, "They do not need to go away. You give them something to eat."

17"We have here only five loaves of bread and two fish," they answered.

18"Bring them here to me," he said. 19And he directed the people to
sit down on the grass. Taking the five loaves and the two fish and
looking up to heaven, he gave thanks and broke the loaves. Then he
gave them to the disciples, and the disciples gave them to the people.
20They all ate and were satisfied, and the disciples picked up twelve
basketfuls of broken pieces that were left over. 21The number of those
who ate was about five thousand men, besides women and children.

Jesus Walks on the Water

22Immediately Jesus made the disciples get into the boat and go on
ahead of him to the other side, while he dismissed the crowd. 23After
he had dismissed them, he went up on a mountainside by himself to
pray. When evening came, he was there alone, 24but the boat was
already a considerable distance[a] from land, buffeted by the waves
because the wind was against it.

[a]24 Greek *many stadia*

APPLY What is the closest you have come to losing your head when you took a stand on a moral issue?

OPEN 1. When eating on the run, where do you usually go? **2.** If you had to serve 5,000 people, what would you serve?

STUDY 1. Why did Jesus decide to "get out of town" (vv. 1–12)? **2.** When he arrived at the place for rest, what happened? **3.** What were the disciples worried about? **4.** If you had been one of the disciples, how would you be feeling after verse 17? After verse 21? **5.** What is your church doing to feed the hungry and homeless in your community?

APPLY 1. Are you open to the possibility that God could use you in some special way? **2.** What do you have in abundance that God might use to start with?

OPEN 1. Have you ever gone water skiing? Surfing? Ice skating? What was it like? **2.** What is your most daring adventure?

STUDY 1. This story occurred immediately after the feeding of the five thousand. Why do you think Jesus decided to separate himself from the people and the disciples and

---

14:13 When Jesus heard. Jesus' withdrawal was in response to the tragic news of John's death. **a solitary place.** This was probably north of the Sea of Galilee, where Herod had no power.

14:14 compassion. Although Jesus had wanted to withdraw for awhile, the needs of the people moved him to act.

14:15 Send the crowds away. This was the only reasonable suggestion available, though the local villages would have been hard pressed to provide for the needs of such a gathering.

14:16 You give them something to eat. Jesus' statement, and the entire scene, is similar to when Elisha miraculously provided food for 100 people from 20 loaves of bread (2 Kin. 4:42–44). Since that act authenticated Elisha's commission from God, how much more should this miracle demonstrate Jesus' innate divine power?

14:17 five loaves. These would have been small round cakes made of wheat or barley. **two fish.** These could have been smoked or pickled fish.

14:19 gave thanks ... broke ... gave. This miracle prefigures the Last Supper (Mark 14:22) and the breaking of bread service (1 Cor. 11:23–24). This feeding, like communion, foreshadows the feeding of all God's people when God's reign is fully established (Isa. 55:1–3; Ezek. 34).

14:20 satisfied. Like at the messianic feast, the needs of God's people are abundantly met. **twelve.** This is the number of tribes of Israel. The number 12 connotes completeness, reinforcing the idea that this scene is meant to demonstrate how Jesus the Messiah provides nourishment for all God's people. **basketfuls.** These were small wicker containers carried by the Jews.

14:21 besides women and children. Women and children in this culture were generally not counted.

14:22 he dismissed the crowd. According to John 6:14–15, the crowd, sensing that the feeding was a sign that Jesus was the messianic King, tried in

spend time alone in prayer? **2.** When the disciples saw someone walking on the water, what was their reaction? How would you have reacted? **3.** How did Jesus try to calm the disciples' fears? **4.** Why did Peter get out of the boat? Why did he sink? How was he saved? **5.** If you could put in a good word for Peter, what would you say? **6.** If you had been in the boat and Jesus asked you to "come," what would you do? Say?

APPLY 1. Spiritually, where is Jesus inviting you to step out of your comfort zone and "walk on the water"? **2.** What are you doing about it?

OPEN 1. In your family, do you say "grace" before meals? Prayers before bedtime? **2.** When it comes to technical stuff, who is the "fix-it" person in your house? Who doesn't have a clue?

25During the fourth watch of the night Jesus went out to them,
walking on the lake. 26When the disciples saw him walking on the
lake, they were terrified. "It's a ghost," they said, and cried out in fear.
27But Jesus immediately said to them: "Take courage! It is I. Don't
be afraid."
28"Lord, if it's you," Peter replied, "tell me to come to you on the
water."
29"Come," he said.
Then Peter got down out of the boat, walked on the water and came
toward Jesus. 30But when he saw the wind, he was afraid and, beginning to sink, cried out, "Lord, save me!"
31Immediately Jesus reached out his hand and caught him. "You of
little faith," he said, "why did you doubt?"
32And when they climbed into the boat, the wind died down. 33Then
those who were in the boat worshiped him, saying, "Truly you are the
Son of God."
34When they had crossed over, they landed at Gennesaret. 35And
when the men of that place recognized Jesus, they sent word to all
the surrounding country. People brought all their sick to him 36and
begged him to let the sick just touch the edge of his cloak, and all
who touched him were healed.

Clean and Unclean

15 Then some Pharisees and teachers of the law came to Jesus
from Jerusalem and asked, 2"Why do your disciples break the
tradition of the elders? They don't wash their hands before they eat!"
3Jesus replied, "And why do you break the command of God for the

---

its enthusiasm to get Jesus to lead a revolt against Rome.

14:25 the fourth watch. The fourth watch ran from 3 a.m. to 6 a.m. **walking on the lake.** In no other situation did Jesus take a supernatural shortcut to expedite his travel plans. This event was intended to provide the disciples with further insight into his divine identity.

14:26 It's a ghost. The sea, especially at night, was thought at that time to be a dwelling place for demons.

14:27 Take courage! It is I. Don't be afraid. This is the language of God (Isa. 41:10; 43:5; Jer. 1:8). **It is I.** Literally, "I am." In the Old Testament this is a phrase used by God to describe himself (Ex. 3:1–14). In the context of Jesus' ongoing revelation of himself to the disciples, this is a sign of his divine identity.

14:30 Lord, save me! Peter's cry sums up the cry of those who find themselves faltering in their attempts to act in faith when faced with threats to their safety. Faltering does not disqualify one from Christ's care, but can become a time to reach out to him as Peter did.

14:31 You of little faith. The problem Peter faced was not the circumstances, but inadequate trust in Jesus *despite* the circumstances.

14:33 Truly you are the Son of God. In the other Gospels, this identification by the disciples does not happen until the incident at Caesarea Philippi (16:13–20). **the Son of God.** In the Old Testament, this term described God's appointed king who reigned over Israel in God's stead (Ps. 2:7). In the New Testament, this title is often connected with the title "Messiah."

14:34 Gennesaret. This was a thickly populated, fertile plain four miles southwest of Capernaum.

14:36 the edge of his cloak. This recalls the healing of the bleeding woman (9:20–22). The hem of a rabbi's garment was decorated with tassels representing the commands of God. There were probably some quasi-magical notions among the people that blended religious faith with superstitious practices. It was assumed that these tassels possessed particularly effective powers.

15:1 Pharisees and teachers of the law. In contrast to the Pharisees (a word meaning "separate"), Jesus was not concerned with forms of ceremonial religious purity that required a holy person to avoid the common people (23:23–26). **from Jerusalem.** The fact that these men came from Jerusalem to Galilee in order to investigate Jesus indicates this was an official investigation of Jesus.

15:2 the tradition. There were literally thousands of unwritten rules that developed over time in an attempt to define how the Old Testament Law applied in everyday life. **elders.** These were respected Jewish rabbis whose decisions concerning points of religious law were considered binding. **They don't wash their hands.** The issue here is ceremonial holiness, not personal hygiene. Before each meal the Pharisees, applying regulations that were originally intended only for the priests (Ex. 30:17–21), washed their hands with water set aside for that purpose.

sake of your tradition? [4]For God said, 'Honor your father and
mother'[a] and 'Anyone who curses his father or mother must be put to
death.'[b] [5]But you say that if a man says to his father or mother, 'Whatever help you might otherwise have received from me is a gift devoted
to God,' [6]he is not to 'honor his father[c]' with it. Thus you nullify the
word of God for the sake of your tradition. [7]You hypocrites! Isaiah
was right when he prophesied about you:

[8]" 'These people honor me with their lips,
but their hearts are far from me.
[9]They worship me in vain;
their teachings are but rules taught by men.'[d]"

[10]Jesus called the crowd to him and said, "Listen and understand.
[11]What goes into a man's mouth does not make him 'unclean,' but
what comes out of his mouth, that is what makes him 'unclean.' "
[12]Then the disciples came to him and asked, "Do you know that the
Pharisees were offended when they heard this?"
[13]He replied, "Every plant that my heavenly Father has not planted
will be pulled up by the roots. [14]Leave them; they are blind guides.[e] If
a blind man leads a blind man, both will fall into a pit."
[15]Peter said, "Explain the parable to us."
[16]"Are you still so dull?" Jesus asked them. [17]"Don't you see that
whatever enters the mouth goes into the stomach and then out of the
body? [18]But the things that come out of the mouth come from the
heart, and these make a man 'unclean.' [19]For out of the heart come
evil thoughts, murder, adultery, sexual immorality, theft, false testimony, slander. [20]These are what make a man 'unclean'; but eating
with unwashed hands does not make him 'unclean.' "

The Faith of the Canaanite Woman

[21]Leaving that place, Jesus withdrew to the region of Tyre and Sidon. [22]A Canaanite woman from that vicinity came to him, crying out,

[a]4 Exodus 20:12; Deut. 5:16 [b]4 Exodus 21:17; Lev. 20:9 [c]6 Some manuscripts *father or his mother*
[d]9 Isaiah 29:13 [e]14 Some manuscripts *guides of the blind*

STUDY 1. Jesus addresses three groups here. Who is he harshest on? **2.** What example does Jesus use to show how the Pharisees have modified the Old Testament commands to serve their own ends? **3.** How does the prophet Isaiah describe these religious leaders (vv. 8-9)? **4.** When Jesus gets around to answering the complaint of the Pharisees, what does he say about "uncleanness"? **5.** What does Jesus recommend for his disciples to do about the Pharisees? **6.** If the church today were to take the teaching in verses 16-20 seriously, what would it do to a lot of the traditions that we hold sacred? What would it put in its place?

APPLY 1. Among the unchurched people that you live around, what is the biggest barrier in leading these people to faith in Christ? **2.** When your parents get old and they cannot take care of themselves, what are you going to do?

OPEN For what would you walk 50 miles?

STUDY 1. How would Jesus' accusers in 15:1 have viewed his 50-mile trip to this area? **2.** What

15:4 Jesus cites two commands in the Law regarding how parents are to be treated with respect (Ex. 20:12; 21:17). **put to death.** Jesus was not advocating putting people to death for such an action, but rather was underlining the issue of respect taught by the Law.

15:5 But you say. The Law was clear. Before pension plans and Social Security, one aspect of that principle was providing for one's parents when they *were too old or too sick to work.* However, the traditions taught that if people dedicated some money to God, it was thereafter no longer truly their property. Thus, a child could declare property or money as given over to God and therefore unavailable for his or her parents' support.

15:7 You hypocrites! This was a frequent accusation of Jesus against the Pharisees (6:2). They presented themselves as honoring the Law, but altered it to suit their purposes.

15:8 but their hearts. This is the essence of what Jesus had against the Pharisees. They obeyed the laws, but their hearts were not in tune with the love of God. They were not yet part of that new covenant spoken of by Jeremiah where God's law of love was "written on their hearts" (Jer. 31:33). This is why they scowled instead of rejoiced when a person was healed on the Sabbath. It is also why they were more concerned with handwashing than with heart-changing.

15:11 unclean. Those who came into contact with something considered taboo were thought to be unfit to worship or to have physical contact with others. For the Jew, unclean things included certain animals, dead bodies, lepers, Gentiles, and, as demonstrated here, certain food.

15:13 Every plant. God's people were commonly described as a "planting of the LORD" (Isa. 60:21; 61:3). Jesus is declaring that the Pharisees, in spite of their pretense to holiness, had not been divinely plants. They were more like weeds that will be uprooted and cast away.

15:17 out of the body. Literally, "goes into the latrine."

15:21 Tyre and Sidon. This is modern-day Lebanon.

15:22 a Canaanite. The woman was a Phoenician (Mark 7:26). The Canaanites were ancient archetypal enemies of the Jews. By specifically referring to her as a Canaanite, Matthew accents how far removed she was from those normally considered God's people.

do we learn about the woman? About Jesus? About Jesus' attitude toward non-Jews?

APPLY 1. Who is the person in your life that has walked many miles to be with you? **2.** When you deal with needy people or "outsiders," are you more like the disciples or Jesus?

OPEN 1. When you were a kid, where did you like to go for picnics? **2.** Have you ever been to a big rock concert? What was it like?

STUDY 1. What draws the crowd? How long had they been without food? What would be the natural thing to do? **2.** What does Jesus decide to do? How did the disciples react? How would you have reacted? **3.** What does Jesus use to feed the crowd? How does he go about it? **4.** What do they do with the leftovers? **5.** How do you account for this miracle? Was it the food or the spiritual nourishment that left the crowd satisfied? **6.** What is the message for the church in this story?

APPLY 1. What's the hunger in the people you associate with? **2.** What is God asking you to do about this?

"Lord, Son of David, have mercy on me! My daughter is suffering terribly from demon-possession."
23Jesus did not answer a word. So his disciples came to him and
urged him, "Send her away, for she keeps crying out after us."
24He answered, "I was sent only to the lost sheep of Israel."
25The woman came and knelt before him. "Lord, help me!" she
said.
26He replied, "It is not right to take the children's bread and toss it
to their dogs."
27"Yes, Lord," she said, "but even the dogs eat the crumbs that fall
from their masters' table."
28Then Jesus answered, "Woman, you have great faith! Your request
is granted." And her daughter was healed from that very hour.

Jesus Feeds the Four Thousand

29Jesus left there and went along the Sea of Galilee. Then he went
up on a mountainside and sat down. 30Great crowds came to him,
bringing the lame, the blind, the crippled, the mute and many others,
and laid them at his feet; and he healed them. 31The people were
amazed when they saw the mute speaking, the crippled made well,
the lame walking and the blind seeing. And they praised the God of
Israel.
32Jesus called his disciples to him and said, "I have compassion for
these people; they have already been with me three days and have
nothing to eat. I do not want to send them away hungry, or they may
collapse on the way."
33His disciples answered, "Where could we get enough bread in
this remote place to feed such a crowd?"
34"How many loaves do you have?" Jesus asked.
"Seven," they replied, "and a few small fish."
35He told the crowd to sit down on the ground. 36Then he took the
seven loaves and the fish, and when he had given thanks, he broke
them and gave them to the disciples, and they in turn to the people.
37They all ate and were satisfied. Afterward the disciples picked up
seven basketfuls of broken pieces that were left over. 38The number of
those who ate was four thousand, besides women and children. 39Af-
ter Jesus had sent the crowd away, he got into the boat and went to
the vicinity of Magadan.

15:24 I was sent only. This seemingly callous statement by Jesus has caused much debate. Could Jesus really have been this ethnocentric? Another way to view his actions here, however, is that he was voicing the predominant view of his time precisely with the idea in mind that it could be shown as shallow in light of this faithful foreigner.

15:26 dogs. There is a play on words here. While Jews commonly used a word which referred to wild street dogs when they referred to Gentiles, this word means a household pet dog.

15:28 you have great faith! Once again Jesus points out the faith of a foreigner (8:5–13), in contrast to the lack of faith of the people of his hometown (13:58) and even the disciples (14:31; 16:8).

15:32–39 The main difference between the feeding of the four thousand and the feeding of the five *thousand* (14:15–21) is the difference in audience. While the account of this story in Mark clearly locates it at the climax of Jesus' ministry in a Gentile area (Mark 7:24–8:31), there are indications Matthew intends his readers to understand this in the same way. Just as the feeding of the five thousand anticipated the coming salvation for Israel, so the feeding of the four thousand promises this same salvation to Gentiles.

15:32 three days. The crowd had been with him for a few days in contrast to the five thousand who were fed on the day they gathered.

15:39 Magadan. It is not certain where this town is located. The point, however, is that at this time Jesus left the Gentile region for Jewish soil.

The Demand for a Sign

16 The Pharisees and Sadducees came to Jesus and tested him
by asking him to show them a sign from heaven.
2He replied,[a] "When evening comes, you say, 'It will be fair weather,
for the sky is red,' 3and in the morning, 'Today it will be stormy, for
the sky is red and overcast.' You know how to interpret the appearance of the sky, but you cannot interpret the signs of the times. 4A
wicked and adulterous generation looks for a miraculous sign, but
none will be given it except the sign of Jonah." Jesus then left them
and went away.

The Yeast of the Pharisees and Sadducees

5When they went across the lake, the disciples forgot to take bread.
6"Be careful," Jesus said to them. "Be on your guard against the yeast
of the Pharisees and Sadducees."
7They discussed this among themselves and said, "It is because we
didn't bring any bread."
8Aware of their discussion, Jesus asked, "You of little faith, why are
you talking among yourselves about having no bread? 9Do you still
not understand? Don't you remember the five loaves for the five
thousand, and how many basketfuls you gathered? 10Or the seven
loaves for the four thousand, and how many basketfuls you gathered? 11How is it you don't understand that I was not talking to you
about bread? But be on your guard against the yeast of the Pharisees
and Sadducees." 12Then they understood that he was not telling them
to guard against the yeast used in bread, but against the teaching of
the Pharisees and Sadducees.

Peter's Confession of Christ

13When Jesus came to the region of Caesarea Philippi, he asked his
disciples, "Who do people say the Son of Man is?"
14They replied, "Some say John the Baptist; others say Elijah; and
still others, Jeremiah or one of the prophets."
15"But what about you?" he asked. "Who do you say I am?"
16Simon Peter answered, "You are the Christ,[b] the Son of the living God."

[a]2 Some early manuscripts do not have the rest of verse 2 and all of verse 3. [b]16 Or *Messiah*; also in verse 20

OPEN 1. What memories do you have of homemade baked goods straight out of the oven? **2.** How many times does it take for someone to explain Einstein's theory of relativity to you before you understand it?

STUDY 1. Why do the Pharisees and Sadducees want Jesus to show them a "sign"? How convincing would a sign be to these religious leaders? **2.** What is the sign of Jonah that Jesus is talking about? **3.** What is it about the religion practiced by the Pharisees and Sadducees that is like bad yeast? What will it do? **4.** What is Jesus calling disciples to that was illustrated in the feeding of the 5,000 and the 4,000? **5.** If you were Jesus at this point in his mission, how would you be feeling about your training of the disciples?

APPLY 1. What is it going to take to move religion today beyond the religion of the Pharisees to the religion that Jesus talked about? **2.** What is the most encouraging sign that you see today that God is bringing new life to his church?

OPEN 1. If you polled two good friends from your early teen years, what adjective would they use to describe you? **2.** If you could "gain the world," where would you place your summer and winter castles?

STUDY 1. If you stopped three people on the street today and asked them "who is Jesus?" how would they answer? **2.** When Peter answered the question by saying, "You are the Christ," what was he saying

---

16:1 Saddducees. While prominent in the early chapters of Acts, the Sadducees, whose main area of concern was with the worship at the temple in Jerusalem, are rarely mentioned in the Gospels. It seems that they were a small but highly influential party of Jews composed mainly of wealthy, aristocratic priests.

16:4 A wicked and adulterous generation. The Old Testament prophets often used adultery as a metaphor for the way Israel strayed from fidelity to God (Ezek. 16; Hos. 2:2).

16:6 yeast. Jews connected yeast with the process of fermentation, which they saw as a form of rotting. Hence, yeast became a metaphor for the profound effects of even a little bit of evil.

16:7–11 By their response in verse 7, the disciples show a lack of spiritual insight into Jesus' warning about the evil influence of the Pharisees. Jesus rebukes them in verses 8–11 for being occupied with physical things.

16:13 Caesarea Philippi. A beautiful city on the slopes of Mount Hermon, 25 miles north of Bethsaida. It had once been called Balinas when it was a center for Baal worship. It was later called Paneas because it was said that the god Pan had his birth in a nearby cave. This region was also the headwater for the Jordan River. At the time of Jesus, it was the location of a temple dedicated to the godhead of Caesar.

16:14 John ... Elijah ... Jeremiah. There was a popular belief that prior to the coming of the Messiah, God would raise up Israel's famous prophets to prepare the way. Many people assumed this was the role played by Jesus.

16:16 You are the Christ. Peter identifies him not as the forerunner of the Christ (the Greek word for "Messiah"), but as the Messiah himself.

about Jesus? **3.** What does the statement mean "on this rock I will build my church and the gates of hell will not overcome it"? **4.** Why would some people confuse Jesus with John the Baptist, Elijah or Jeremiah? **5.** What are the "keys to the Kingdom"? What do they "bind" and "loose"? **6.** How does Jesus change the direction of his ministry—especially toward his disciples? **7.** How did Peter react to this new revelation? What was Peter expecting Jesus to become? Why was Jesus' reaction to Peter so strong? **8.** What does Jesus expect from his followers? How does this teaching go over today? If this teaching was stressed today, what would happen?

APPLY **1.** When did you come to the place in your spiritual life that you accepted Jesus as "the Christ," God's gift of grace for the forgiveness of your sins? **2.** Where are you right now in understanding what God's will is for your life?

17 Jesus replied, "Blessed are you, Simon son of Jonah, for this was
not revealed to you by man, but by my Father in heaven. 18 And I tell
you that you are Peter,[a] and on this rock I will build my church, and
the gates of Hades[b] will not overcome it.[c] 19 I will give you the keys of
the kingdom of heaven; whatever you bind on earth will be[d] bound in
heaven, and whatever you loose on earth will be[d] loosed in heaven."
20 Then he warned his disciples not to tell anyone that he was the
Christ.

Jesus Predicts His Death

21 From that time on Jesus began to explain to his disciples that he
must go to Jerusalem and suffer many things at the hands of the elders, chief priests and teachers of the law, and that he must be killed
and on the third day be raised to life.

22 Peter took him aside and began to rebuke him. "Never, Lord!" he
said. "This shall never happen to you!"

23 Jesus turned and said to Peter, "Get behind me, Satan! You are a
stumbling block to me; you do not have in mind the things of God,
but the things of men."

24 Then Jesus said to his disciples, "If anyone would come after me,
he must deny himself and take up his cross and follow me. 25 For
whoever wants to save his life[e] will lose it, but whoever loses his life
for me will find it. 26 What good will it be for a man if he gains the whole
world, yet forfeits his soul? Or what can a man give in exchange for his
soul? 27 For the Son of Man is going to come in his Father's glory with
his angels, and then he will reward each person according to what he
has done. 28 I tell you the truth, some who are standing here will not
taste death before they see the Son of Man coming in his kingdom."

The Transfiguration

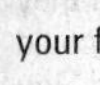

OPEN Of all the places you call "God's country," which is your favorite?

STUDY **1.** How many stories in the Bible can you recall

17 After six days Jesus took with him Peter, James and John the
brother of James, and led them up a high mountain by them-

[a]18 *Peter* means *rock.* [b]18 Or *hell* [c]18 *Or not prove stronger than it* [d]19 Or *have been* [e]25 The Greek word means either *life* or *soul;* also in verse 26.

16:17 not revealed to you by man. Jesus told the disciples that it was not by reason that people came to faith, but rather it was by revelation. The Father granted knowledge or revelation to the seeker (John 6:65). Peter responded in belief in Jesus as the Christ (John 6:68–69).

16:18 Peter. Peter (a nickname meaning "rock"), by way of his confession, becomes the foundation upon which the new people of God will be built.

16:19 keys of the kingdom of heaven. This is an allusion to Isaiah 22:15–24 in which God declared that he would give the "key to the house of David" to a new steward who would replace the old one who had been irresponsible.

16:21 the elders, chief priests and teachers of the law. These three groups made up the Sanhedrin, the official ruling Jewish body.

16:22 rebuke. Peter is startled by this teaching that went so much against his notion of who the Messiah was.

16:23 Get behind me, Satan! By urging Jesus to back away from his teaching about suffering, Peter, like Satan, is tempting Jesus with the promise that he can have the whole world without pain (4:8–10).

16:24 come after me. This is to take on the role of a disciple, one committed to the teachings of a master. **deny himself.** This means to regard one's ambitions as irrelevant in light of the kingdom of God. **take up his cross.** This symbolized the grisly method of Roman execution, as the only people who bore crosses were prisoners on their way to their death. This would have startled the original hearers, as they thought the Messiah would overthrow Rome. **follow me.** This is a call for the disciples to imitate the lifestyle and embrace the values of their teacher.

16:28 see the Son of Man coming. Jesus had already said that the kingdom of God was near (4:17; 10:23; 12:28). While some see this as a prediction of his imminent Second Coming, it can also be seen as referring to either to the Transfiguration (17:1–13) or to Christ's death and resurrection.

17:1 After six days. This phrase connects the Transfiguration with Jesus' prediction that "some who are standing here will not taste death before they see

selves. [2]There he was transfigured before them. His face shone like
the sun, and his clothes became as white as the light. [3]Just then there
appeared before them Moses and Elijah, talking with Jesus.
[4]Peter said to Jesus, "Lord, it is good for us to be here. If you wish,
I will put up three shelters—one for you, one for Moses and one for
Elijah."
[5]While he was still speaking, a bright cloud enveloped them, and a
voice from the cloud said, "This is my Son, whom I love; with him I
am well pleased. Listen to him!"
[6]When the disciples heard this, they fell facedown to the ground,
terrified. [7]But Jesus came and touched them. "Get up," he said.
"Don't be afraid." [8]When they looked up, they saw no one except
Jesus.
[9]As they were coming down the mountain, Jesus instructed them,
"Don't tell anyone what you have seen, until the Son of Man has been
raised from the dead."
[10]The disciples asked him, "Why then do the teachers of the law say
that Elijah must come first?"
[11]Jesus replied, "To be sure, Elijah comes and will restore all
things. [12]But I tell you, Elijah has already come, and they did not recognize him, but have done to him everything they wished. In the
same way the Son of Man is going to suffer at their hands." [13]Then
the disciples understood that he was talking to them about John the
Baptist.

The Healing of a Boy With a Demon

[14]When they came to the crowd, a man approached Jesus and
knelt before him. [15]"Lord, have mercy on my son," he said. "He
has seizures and is suffering greatly. He often falls into the fire or
into the water. [16]I brought him to your disciples, but they could
not heal him."
[17]"O unbelieving and perverse generation," Jesus replied, "how

where something very important happened on a mountain? **2.** Why do you think Jesus took Peter, James and John with him on this trip? **3.** If you had been Peter when Jesus was transfigured and Moses and Elijah appeared, how would you have felt? **4.** Good ole Peter—who always put his foot in his mouth. What did he want to do and why? **5.** What does the voice in the cloud say to the disciples in a nice way? How did they respond? Why would they be scared to death? **6.** Do you think the three disciples understood the significance of all this? Why the question about Elijah?

APPLY 1. What is the closest you have come to a mountain top experience with God like this? **2.** How would you describe your relationship with God right now?

OPEN Who did you go to in your family for a hurt finger?

STUDY 1. The disciples blow it again. What happened this time? Do you think Jesus had a right to be exasperated? Why would Jesus be concerned about his disciples' training? **2.** Why were the disciples

---

the Son of Man coming in his kingdom" (16:28). **Peter, James and John.** These three emerge as a sort of inner circle around Jesus. **a high mountain.** This may well be Mount Hermon, a 9,000-foot mountain located 12 miles from Caesarea Philippi (though early tradition says it is Mount Tabor located southwest of the Sea of Galilee).

17:2 transfigured. The description of Jesus here is similar to that used to picture the appearance of God when he appeared in a vision to Daniel (Dan. 7:9). In Revelation 1:9–18 the resurrected, glorified Jesus is described in these same terms.

17:3 Moses. Moses was the greatest figure in the Old Testament. It was to him God gave the Law which became the very heart of the nation. **Elijah.** The Jews expected that Elijah, one of the most esteemed prophets, would return just prior to the coming of the salvation they had been promised. These two figures together represent the Law and the Prophets, the whole of scriptural tradition.

17:4 shelters. Peter might have had in mind the huts of intertwined branches which were put up at the Festival of Tabernacles to commemorate Israel's time in the wilderness.

17:5 a bright cloud. In the Old Testament, God often appeared to people in the form of a cloud (Ex. 16:10; 19:9; 24:15–18; 40:34–38). **a voice.** Once again, as at Jesus' baptism (3:17), the voice affirms the unique identity of Jesus. **my Son.** This is a royal title used in the Old Testament. In the New Testament it affirms Jesus as God's unique, appointed king over his people.

17:9 Don't tell. Jesus commands silence because the meaning of this event cannot be understood until Jesus dies and rises again. Then it will be clear what kind of Messiah he is.

17:11–13 Elijah comes. While in the Transfiguration the long-expected Elijah had come, Jesus is speaking of John the Baptist who played the anticipated role of Elijah by being the forerunner of the Messiah. **have done to him everything they wished.** It is John who suffered and died at the hands of Herod and Herodias, paralleling the experience of Elijah at the hands of Ahab and Jezebel (1 Kin. 19:1–4).

17:15 Lord, have mercy on my son. The father recognizes both the identity of Jesus and his power to help.

17:16 they could not heal him. The faith of the disciples is shown once again to be incomplete.

17:17 O unbelieving and perverse generation. This is an allusion to Deuteronomy 32:5, which comments on the blindness of God's people. It is the cry of anguish and loneliness of one who knows so clearly the way things

unsuccessful in driving the demon out of the boy? What is the lesson in this story for you today? **3.** What does it mean to have "faith as small as a mustard seed"? **4.** Do you think there is any hope for these disciples? Are they ever going to get it right?

APPLY 1. What is your most recent set back in your spiritual life? **2.** What have you learned from this experience?

OPEN How do you feel about your taxes going for causes you don't believe in?

STUDY 1. What is the tax to go for? How would paying this tax put Jesus into a dilemma? **2.** How does Jesus avoid the dilemma? **3.** What is the lesson here for the disciples? For a disciple today?

APPLY Where does some of your tax money go that you do not agree with?

OPEN 1. Who would you nominate as the "person of the year" to appear on the cover of *Time Magazine* this year? **2.** Who would you nominate from your childhood outside of your family because of the contribution they made to your life?

long shall I stay with you? How long shall I put up with you? Bring the
boy here to me." 18Jesus rebuked the demon, and it came out of the
boy, and he was healed from that moment.
19Then the disciples came to Jesus in private and asked, "Why
couldn't we drive it out?"
20He replied, "Because you have so little faith. I tell you the truth, if you have faith as small as a mustard seed, you can say to this mountain, 'Move from here to there' and it will move. Nothing will be impossible for you.[a]"
22When they came together in Galilee, he said to them, "The Son of
Man is going to be betrayed into the hands of men. 23They will kill
him, and on the third day he will be raised to life." And the disciples were filled with grief.

The Temple Tax

24After Jesus and his disciples arrived in Capernaum, the collectors of the two-drachma tax came to Peter and asked, "Doesn't your teacher pay the temple tax[b]?"
25"Yes, he does," he replied.
When Peter came into the house, Jesus was the first to speak. "What do you think, Simon?" he asked. "From whom do the kings of the earth collect duty and taxes—from their own sons or from others?"
26"From others," Peter answered.
"Then the sons are exempt," Jesus said to him. 27"But so that we
may not offend them, go to the lake and throw out your line. Take the first fish you catch; open its mouth and you will find a four-drachma coin. Take it and give it to them for my tax and yours."

The Greatest in the Kingdom of Heaven

18 At that time the disciples came to Jesus and asked, "Who is the greatest in the kingdom of heaven?"
2He called a little child and had him stand among them. 3And he

[a]20 Some manuscripts *you. 21But this kind does not go out except by prayer and fasting.* [b]24 Greek *the two drachmas*

really are and yet is constantly confronted with disbelief (John 14:9).

17:20 this mountain. "Removing mountains" was the overcoming of difficulties. This is an invitation to pray more with an eye on the power of God rather than on the difficulties of a given circumstance. **Nothing will be impossible for you.** This is asserted many times in the New Testament (19:26; Mark 9:23; 10:27; 14:36; Luke 1:37). This power is subject to acting with God's direction. When we do that, we should never hesitate to take on something for God because we feel it is too difficult.

17:24 the collectors. These were not the "tax collectors" vilified by the Jewish community as traitors because they worked for Rome. Prior to 70 A.D., those who gathered the temple tax were seen as carrying out a legitimate occupation since the money was used for the temple. **Doesn't your teacher pay the temple tax?** If Jesus did not, it could be misconstrued as a scandalous rejection of a common duty. If he did, it could be misconstrued as an endorsement of the temple system which he generally seemed to reject (21:12–13).

17:27 But so that we may not offend them. Since such freedom would be interpreted by others as disrespect for God and the temple, it is appropriate to pay the tax. **Take the first fish.** This miracle is unparalleled in the Gospels. Why the tax was paid in this way rather than out of the common purse the disciples shared is unclear. **a four-drachma coin.** The tax, which was about two days pay for a laborer, was a half-shekel per person. Since such coins were rare in Jesus' day, people often doubled up and paid the tax with the more commonly circulated shekel.

18:2 a little child. Children held little value among adult males in this society. To hold up a child as a model for an adult to emulate was unheard of.

18:3 unless you change. Literally, "turn around." Their question reveals that they are pursuing the wrong course. They must turn from their pursuit of power and rank, and follow the way of love and service.

said: "I tell you the truth, unless you change and become like little
children, you will never enter the kingdom of heaven. 4Therefore,
whoever humbles himself like this child is the greatest in the kingdom of heaven.
5"And whoever welcomes a little child like this in my name welcomes me. 6But if anyone causes one of these little ones who believe
in me to sin, it would be better for him to have a large millstone hung
around his neck and to be drowned in the depths of the sea.
7"Woe to the world because of the things that cause people to sin!
Such things must come, but woe to the man through whom they
come! 8If your hand or your foot causes you to sin, cut it off and
throw it away. It is better for you to enter life maimed or crippled than
to have two hands or two feet and be thrown into eternal fire. 9And if
your eye causes you to sin, gouge it out and throw it away. It is better
for you to enter life with one eye than to have two eyes and be thrown
into the fire of hell.

The Parable of the Lost Sheep

10"See that you do not look down on one of these little ones. For I
tell you that their angels in heaven always see the face of my Father in
heaven.[a]
12"What do you think? If a man owns a hundred sheep, and one of
them wanders away, will he not leave the ninety-nine on the hills and
go to look for the one that wandered off? 13And if he finds it, I tell you
the truth, he is happier about that one sheep than about the ninety-
nine that did not wander off. 14In the same way your Father in heaven
is not willing that any of these little ones should be lost.

A Brother Who Sins Against You

15"If your brother sins against you,[b] go and show him his fault, just
between the two of you. If he listens to you, you have won your
brother over. 16But if he will not listen, take one or two others along,
so that 'every matter may be established by the testimony of two or
three witnesses.'[c] 17If he refuses to listen to them, tell it to the church;
and if he refuses to listen even to the church, treat him as you would
a pagan or a tax collector.
18"I tell you the truth, whatever you bind on earth will be[d] bound in

[a] *10* Some manuscripts *heaven.* *11The Son of Man came to save what was lost.* [b] *15* Some manuscripts do not have *against you.* [c] *16* Deut. 19:15 [d] *18* Or *have been*

STUDY 1. If you read between the lines, how would the disciples define "greatness"? How does Jesus define greatness? **2.** What is it about children that Jesus wants the disciples to exemplify? **3.** For anyone who assumes a position of leadership, what is the warning in verses 7-9? **4.** What is the lesson for the disciples (and the church) in the parable of the lost sheep? **5.** What is your church doing to go after the church drop-outs—and the "lost sheep" that fall through the cracks?

APPLY 1. If Jesus were to apply the rule, "three strikes and you're out," would you still be on his team? **2.** What are you doing to reach out to the spiritual drop-outs that you know?

OPEN What things did you and your sibling argue about?

STUDY 1. What is the procedure recommended here for dealing with conflicts in the church? **2.** In building faith communities and exercising mutual accountability, how do you interpret verse 18? Do you think a Christian community has the right to discipline one of its own? What about grace? **3.** What's the principle in verse 20?

18:4 humbles himself. In the Bible, humility is not a denial of one's strengths, nor an attitude of passivity or timidity, but an attitude that values the interests of others before one's own. Greatness in God's kingdom is not defined by power and titles, but by loving service.

18:6 causes ... to sin. The influence of false teachers is probably in view (2 John 7–15), but it also could refer to disciples who abuse their freedom by refusing to be sensitive to the tender consciences of others (Rom. 14:1–15:2). **a large millstone.** The millstone in view here is the huge upper stone of a community grist mill, so big it had to be drawn around by a donkey.

18:7 Woe. A similar curse is applied specifically to Judas in Mark 14:21. It is a strong warning to false teachers and those who are not careful about how their life affects others.

18:10 angels in heaven. The picture is one of angels reporting to God on the condition of those in their charge. Disdain for others has no place in the Christian community since even those people who appear insignificant are divinely watched over and cared for.

18:13 he is happier about that one sheep. This is not to minimize the shepherd's gladness over those sheep which remained in the fold, but to accent his joy over the recovery of the one who had strayed away.

18:16 Involving two or three others is based on the Law's requirement that no case be settled without two or three witnesses (Deut. 19:15).

18:18 What was said to Peter (16:19) is now said to the whole church when

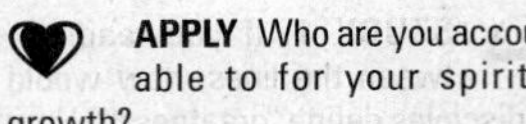

APPLY Who are you accountable to for your spiritual growth?

______

OPEN How many credit cards do you have? When does your credit card tempt you the most?

STUDY 1. Do you tend to be quick or slow to forgive? 2. How do you feel about Jesus' answer (v. 22) to Peter's question (v. 21)? What is Jesus really saying? 3. What is the comparison between the two servants' debts (vv. 24–28)? Their pleas (vv. 26,29)? The decision about their case (vv. 27,30)? 4. If you were the master, how would you have felt when the servant refused to forgive a fellow servant's debt—right after you had forgiven his huge debt? 5. In the previous story (vv. 15-20) Jesus puts forth a four-step procedure for discipling a Christian "brother." How does this teaching on endless forgiveness relate to the former teaching? 6. In a Christian community where there is supposed to be "openness and honesty" about your struggles, what do

heaven, and whatever you loose on earth will be[a] loosed in heaven.
19"Again, I tell you that if two of you on earth agree about anything
you ask for, it will be done for you by my Father in heaven. 20For
where two or three come together in my name, there am I with
them."

The Parable of the Unmerciful Servant

21Then Peter came to Jesus and asked, "Lord, how many times shall
I forgive my brother when he sins against me? Up to seven times?"
22Jesus answered, "I tell you, not seven times, but seventy-seven
times.[b]
23"Therefore, the kingdom of heaven is like a king who wanted to
settle accounts with his servants. 24As he began the settlement, a
man who owed him ten thousand talents[c] was brought to him.
25Since he was not able to pay, the master ordered that he and his
wife and his children and all that he had be sold to repay the debt.
26"The servant fell on his knees before him. 'Be patient with me,' he
begged, 'and I will pay back everything.' 27The servant's master took
pity on him, canceled the debt and let him go.
28"But when that servant went out, he found one of his fellow servants who owed him a hundred denarii.[d] He grabbed him and began
to choke him. 'Pay back what you owe me!' he demanded.
29"His fellow servant fell to his knees and begged him, 'Be patient
with me, and I will pay you back.'
30"But he refused. Instead, he went off and had the man thrown

[a]18 *Or have been* [b]22 *Or seventy times seven* [c]24 That is, millions of dollars [d]28 That is, a few dollars

---

acting corporately in matters of its community discipline.

18:21 how many times shall I forgive. The rabbis taught that a person ought to be forgiven for a particular offense up to three times. After that, the offended person was under no obligation to grant forgiveness.

18:22 seventy-seven times. This could be understood as seventy times seven. Whichever reading is correct, Jesus explodes any notion of a limit to forgiveness.

18:23 a king. Given the amount of money involved and the form of punishment, it is clear the "king" in view here is no ancient Jewish king. Rather, Jesus is tapping the people's imagination of what the fabulously wealthy kings of Egypt or Persia must have been like. **settle accounts.** Kings entrusted their day-to-day affairs to the management of servants. Such a servant might have been responsible for collecting the tax revenue for the king. This was an audit to check on how the servants were doing with respect to their management.

18:24 ten thousand talents. Herod the Great, who ruled over Palestine at the time of Jesus' birth, had an annual revenue of only about 900 talents. The crowd listening to Jesus would have gasped at the thought of having to pay someone such a fantastically high amount of money.

18:25 he and his wife and his children. Oriental kings had total power. Thus he decided to sell the man and the servant's family into slavery to recoup at least a fraction of his losses.

18:26 I will pay back everything. This was an impossible promise, given the amount. While it may reflect the servant's sincere desire to save himself and his family, he was so far in debt that he could never hope to repay the king.

18:27 took pity. This same word, translated as "compassion," is used to describe the attitude of Jesus toward those in need (9:36; 15:32; 20:34). Like the man in this story, none of the people Jesus had compassion for were able to do anything about their situation. **canceled the debt.** For readers familiar with the meaning of Jesus' death, the allusion to what God has done for sinners in Christ would be inescapable. The New Testament sometimes pictures sin as a debt owed to God that has been canceled for those who believe that Christ paid the debt (Rom. 6:23; Col. 2:13–15). **let him go.** The man was free. The impossible burden that must have crushed him with fear (while he wondered what would happen to him when his mismanagement was discovered) was suddenly gone. There was no judgment, no debt-restructuring to keep him in perpetual bondage, no more fear. Likewise, the disciple of Jesus is free from the punishment of sin (Rom. 8:1–2).

18:28 a hundred denarii. Since a denarius was a day's wage for a laborer, this was a reasonably large amount. However, at the rate of one denarius a day, it would have taken the first servant 15 years to pay back the king a single talent!

18:30 But he refused. Under the circumstances, this man would have been expected to forego the debt. Instead, he insists on carrying out the full weight of the law against the servant indebted to him. The mercy he received from the king did not produce any moral change in this man. He still wants to operate in

into prison until he could pay the debt. [31]When the other servants
saw what had happened, they were greatly distressed and went and
told their master everything that had happened.
[32]"Then the master called the servant in. 'You wicked servant,' he
said, 'I canceled all that debt of yours because you begged me to.
[33]Shouldn't you have had mercy on your fellow servant just as I had
on you?' [34]In anger his master turned him over to the jailers to be tortured, until he should pay back all he owed.
[35]"This is how my heavenly Father will treat each of you unless you
forgive your brother from your heart."

Divorce

19 When Jesus had finished saying these things, he left Galilee
and went into the region of Judea to the other side of the Jordan. [2]Large crowds followed him, and he healed them there.
[3]Some Pharisees came to him to test him. They asked, "Is it lawful
for a man to divorce his wife for any and every reason?"
[4]"Haven't you read," he replied, "that at the beginning the Creator
'made them male and female,'[a] [5]and said, 'For this reason a man will
leave his father and mother and be united to his wife, and the two will
become one flesh'[b]? [6]So they are no longer two, but one. Therefore
what God has joined together, let man not separate."
[7]"Why then," they asked, "did Moses command that a man give his
wife a certificate of divorce and send her away?"
[8]Jesus replied, "Moses permitted you to divorce your wives because your hearts were hard. But it was not this way from the beginning. [9]I tell you that anyone who divorces his wife, except for marital
unfaithfulness, and marries another woman commits adultery."

[a]4 Gen. 1:27 [b]5 Gen. 2:24

you do when someone violates a confidence and word gets "all over town"?

APPLY 1. When you get hurt in a relationship, what do you do? **2.** What have you found helpful in dealing with a strained relationship?

OPEN 1. What was (or would be) Mom's advice to you about marriage? What was Dad's? **2.** Did you follow their advice?

STUDY 1. What is the motive behind the Pharisees' question to Jesus about divorce? **2.** How does Jesus answer their question? **3.** What do you know about the place of women in the Old Testament? Did they have any rights? What did a man have to do to terminate a marriage? **4.** What does Jesus say to level the playing field? **5.** What is Jesus' position on staying unmarried?

APPLY 1. Do you have the gift of celibacy? **2.** Where do you stand on the issue of divorce? Where does grace come in?

---

terms of strict justice. **thrown into prison.** In a debtor's prison, the man's assets would be sold in order to make payment.

18:31 When the other servants saw. The man's inability to forgive not only made a rift between him and the unforgiven servant, but it also separated him from his other fellow servants, who "turned state's evidence" on him. Lack of ability to forgive others leaves a person isolated and alone.

18:33 Shouldn't you have had mercy ... just as I had on you? This is the point of the parable. As recipients of mercy *from God,* Christ's disciples are obligated to continually forgive others. Not to do so is to reveal that they have not grasped the depth of the mercy they have received from God.

18:34 to be tortured. Prisoners were tortured to make them reveal hidden sources of money. The man will now be pressed for every cent he has. **until he should pay back all he owed.** Given the amount owed, the man would be in prison until death.

18:35 from your heart. The forgiveness must be more than words. To do this, one must be in touch with how much God in Christ has forgiven us, and ask that same spirit of Christ into our heart.

19:1 Judea. Jesus goes south, over the hills into Samaria, following the traditional route of pilgrims on their way to Jerusalem. **the other side of the Jordan.** This is Perea, a district on the east side of the Jordan. Pious Jews would cross over the Jordan into Perea when going from Galilee to Judea in order to avoid traveling through Samaria.

19:3 test him. Since the issue of Herod's divorce and remarriage led to John the Baptist's death (14:1–12), it is not by chance that the Pharisees question Jesus about divorce. If he responded affirmatively to this question, it would set him in opposition to John whom the crowds held in high esteem. If he answered negatively, it would set him on a collision course with Herod.

19:4–6 Rather than being drawn into the argument on their terms, Jesus attacks the way they had twisted Deuteronomy 24:1–4 to justify a casual attitude toward divorce. Its aim was to protect a divorced and remarried woman from capricious treatment by her former husband (such as being charged as an adulteress when she remarried). However, it came to be taken as divine sanction for easy divorce. Jesus quotes from Genesis 1 and 2 to make his point that the original intention of God was that marriage be a permanent union whereby, through mutual love, a man and a woman grow to experience physical and emotional unity.

19:8 Moses' concession was an accommodation to human sinfulness, not part of God's intention.

19:9 Commentators differ as to whether remarriage was prohibited regardless of whether or not the divorce was for reasons of "marital unfaithfulness."

OPEN 1. If your house were on fire, what three items would you try to save? 2. What is your ideal annual salary?

STUDY 1. How were children thought of in Biblical times? How did Jesus change all this? 2. When the young man asks Jesus, "What good thing must I do to get eternal life," what is he asking in everyday terms? 3. When Jesus rattles off most of the Ten Commandments, what does the young man say? 4. In the Old Testament, what are riches a sign of? (Remember Job.) Why would Jesus ask the young man to "sell his possessions and give to the poor" when it is not one of the Commandments? 5. What does the young man do? What does this show? 6. How does the remark about a camel getting through the eye of a needle affect the disciples? 7. When the disciples ask the question, "Who then can be saved," what are they thinking? Do you think they really understood the meaning of the gospel—"that God so loved the world that he gave his only Son that whosoever believes in him will not perish but have eternal life"?

APPLY 1. What is the most important thing in your life? 2. What is the hardest thing for you to turn over to God now?

10 The disciples said to him, "If this is the situation between a husband and wife, it is better not to marry."
11 Jesus replied, "Not everyone can accept this word, but only those
to whom it has been given. 12 For some are eunuchs because they
were born that way; others were made that way by men; and others
have renounced marriage[a] because of the kingdom of heaven. The
one who can accept this should accept it."

The Little Children and Jesus

13 Then little children were brought to Jesus for him to place his
hands on them and pray for them. But the disciples rebuked those
who brought them.
14 Jesus said, "Let the little children come to me, and do not hinder
them, for the kingdom of heaven belongs to such as these." 15 When
he had placed his hands on them, he went on from there.

The Rich Young Man

16 Now a man came up to Jesus and asked, "Teacher, what good
thing must I do to get eternal life?"
17 "Why do you ask me about what is good?" Jesus replied. "There is
only One who is good. If you want to enter life, obey the commandments."
18 "Which ones?" the man inquired.
Jesus replied, " 'Do not murder, do not commit adultery, do not
steal, do not give false testimony, 19 honor your father and mother,'[b]
and 'love your neighbor as yourself.'[c]"
20 "All these I have kept," the young man said. "What do I still lack?"
21 Jesus answered, "If you want to be perfect, go, sell your possessions and give to the poor, and you will have treasure in heaven. Then
come, follow me."
22 When the young man heard this, he went away sad, because he
had great wealth.
23 Then Jesus said to his disciples, "I tell you the truth, it is hard for
a rich man to enter the kingdom of heaven. 24 Again I tell you, it is
easier for a camel to go through the eye of a needle than for a rich
man to enter the kingdom of God."
25 When the disciples heard this, they were greatly astonished and
asked, "Who then can be saved?"

[a]12 *Or have made themselves eunuchs* [b]19 Exodus 20:12-16; Deut. 5:16-20 [c]19 Lev. 19:18

19:10 The disciples' shocked reaction reveals that Jesus' forbidding of divorce and remarriage went far beyond what rabbis typically taught. They assumed the only way Jesus' command could be obeyed was if people never married at all.

19:20 What do I still lack? He seems to know that he *is* lacking something. *When we seek a status based on our own works, we always feel like we* are short of what we need.

19:21 sell your possessions. By telling the young man to sell all his goods, Jesus exposed that the man's heart was gripped by his possessions and not by God.

19:23 it is hard for a rich man to enter the kingdom of heaven. The accumulation of wealth can indeed hinder participation in the kingdom of God since one's *life can easily become devoted to money* instead of God.

19:24 Jesus uses an exaggerated form of speech (hyperbole) to make his point. The camel was the largest animal in Palestine and certainly could not get through the tiny opening of a needle.

19:25 greatly astonished. As in verses 10 and 13, the disciples are shocked by the way Jesus' teaching differs from that of accepted thought. By this teaching, Jesus directly confronts their assumptions about salvation. **Who then can be saved?** The radical nature of Jesus' statement causes them to think about their own fate. If the rich (who they believed were especially favored of God) will find it difficult to enter the kingdom, then what chance have they got?

"We can," they answered.
[23]Jesus said to them, "You will indeed drink from my cup, but to sit
at my right or left is not for me to grant. These places belong to those
for whom they have been prepared by my Father."
[24]When the ten heard about this, they were indignant with the two
brothers. [25]Jesus called them together and said, "You know that the
rulers of the Gentiles lord it over them, and their high officials exercise
authority over them. [26]Not so with you. Instead, whoever wants to
become great among you must be your servant, [27]and whoever wants
to be first must be your slave— [28]just as the Son of Man did not come
to be served, but to serve, and to give his life as a ransom for many."

Two Blind Men Receive Sight

[29]As Jesus and his disciples were leaving Jericho, a large crowd followed him. [30]Two blind men were sitting by the roadside, and when
they heard that Jesus was going by, they shouted, "Lord, Son of
David, have mercy on us!"
[31]The crowd rebuked them and told them to be quiet, but they
shouted all the louder, "Lord, Son of David, have mercy on us!"
[32]Jesus stopped and called them. "What do you want me to do for
you?" he asked.
[33]"Lord," they answered, "we want our sight."
[34]Jesus had compassion on them and touched their eyes. Immediately they received their sight and followed him.

The Triumphal Entry

21 As they approached Jerusalem and came to Bethphage on the
Mount of Olives, Jesus sent two disciples, [2]saying to them,
"Go to the village ahead of you, and at once you will find a donkey
tied there, with her colt by her. Untie them and bring them to me. [3]If
anyone says anything to you, tell him that the Lord needs them, and
he will send them right away."
[4]This took place to fulfill what was spoken through the prophet:

about discipleship training over the last three years? **6.** What is the secret to greatness?

APPLY Who do you admire because they practice the servant model of leadership that Jesus demonstrated?

OPEN Who do you know that has lost their eyesight?

STUDY 1. What do the two blind men see in Jesus that the crowd does not see? **2.** Why would this story be so important to a Jewish audience?

APPLY If God asked you, "What do you want me to do for you right now," what would you say?

OPEN 1. Have you ever ridden a donkey? **2.** What is the closest you have come to seeing a famous celebrity in a parade?

STUDY 1. In Roman times, emperors rode on stallions at the head of the procession. Why did Jesus choose a donkey for his trium-

---

20:24 they were indignant. All 12 share the view that the kingdom will be earthly and political, with Jesus as the reigning king and them as his chief lieutenants.

20:26 servant. Rather than become masters (and exercise authority), they are to become servants (and meet the needs of others).

20:28 ransom. "Ransom" was a word used generally to describe the act of *freeing people from bondage,* whether through the literal payment of a purchase price or through some act of deliverance.

20:29 Jericho. The journey begun in 19:1 is almost complete. Jericho, about 18 miles east of Jerusalem, was the place where travelers recrossed the Jordan back into Israel. **a large crowd.** These were pilgrims on their way to Jerusalem for the Passover Feast. Every male over 12 years of age was expected to attend.

20:30 Two blind men. Mark and Luke only mention one. **Lord, Son of David.** This is clearly a messianic title by which the men hail Jesus. The blind truly see who he is, while the Twelve still had not fully grasped this.

20:34 touched their eyes. Jesus commonly used touch in his healing (8:3,15; 9:29; Luke 22:51).

21:1 Jerusalem. This was the central city in Palestine and the spiritual heart of Israel. At the feasts (especially Passover), the population of Jerusalem would be swelled by Jews who made pilgrimage from all over the known world. **Bethphage.** This was a village near Bethany, which was two miles east of Jerusalem. **Mount of Olives.** According to Zechariah 14:4–5, this is the place where God would commence the final judgment of Israel's enemies. **Jesus sent.** Clearly Jesus is consciously preparing his entry. His arrival is meant to be a sign of who he is.

21:2 donkey ... colt. Matthew's reference to two animals (a donkey and a colt) on which Jesus would ride could possibly be based on an understanding of the passage from Zechariah 9:9. There the reference is "on a donkey, on a colt, the foal of a donkey." Mark (Mark 11:4–7) and Luke (Luke 19:30–36) refer to just one animal. Jesus will not simply walk into Jerusalem like the other pilgrims. He will come riding as the messianic King, in accordance with the prophecy of Zechariah. Riding a donkey emphasized the peaceful, gentle nature of the Messiah.

21:3 If anyone says anything to you. The words the disciples are to say will identify them to the owner as those Jesus has sent. **the Lord.** Thus

phal entry? How do you think the reporter described this event in the *Jerusalem Times*? **2.** How did the crowd respond to Jesus? What were they expecting? **3.** Do you think this is the same crowd that shouted "crucify him" five days later? What does this tell you about human emotions? **4.** If you were Jesus when all of this was going on, how would you be feeling? **5.** If Jesus was to come to your town, how would he be received?

APPLY 1. Are you as excited about spiritual things as you were on the day you turned over your life to Jesus? **2.** Is your spiritual life more like a yo-yo or a growth chart?

OPEN Are you more likely to act without thinking or think without acting?

STUDY 1. How would you contrast the image of Jesus in the previous passage with Jesus in this story? **2.** What really made Jesus mad? **3.** When the word got out that Jesus was at the temple, what did the hurting people in the town do? How would they have gotten there? **4.** Instead of being thrilled, how did the chief priests and teachers of the law respond?

5"Say to the Daughter of Zion,
'See, your king comes to you,
gentle and riding on a donkey,
on a colt, the foal of a donkey.'"[a]

6The disciples went and did as Jesus had instructed them. 7They
brought the donkey and the colt, placed their cloaks on them, and
Jesus sat on them. 8A very large crowd spread their cloaks on the
road, while others cut branches from the trees and spread them on
the road. 9The crowds that went ahead of him and those that followed shouted,

"Hosanna[b] to the Son of David!"

"Blessed is he who comes in the name of the Lord!"[c]

"Hosanna[b] in the highest!"

10When Jesus entered Jerusalem, the whole city was stirred and
asked, "Who is this?"
11The crowds answered, "This is Jesus, the prophet from Nazareth
in Galilee."

Jesus at the Temple

12Jesus entered the temple area and drove out all who were buying
and selling there. He overturned the tables of the money changers
and the benches of those selling doves. 13"It is written," he said to
them, " 'My house will be called a house of prayer,'[d] but you are making it a 'den of robbers.'[e]"
14The blind and the lame came to him at the temple, and he healed
them. 15But when the chief priests and the teachers of the law saw
the wonderful things he did and the children shouting in the temple
area, "Hosanna to the Son of David," they were indignant.

[a]5 Zech. 9:9 [b]9 A Hebrew expression meaning "Save!" which became an exclamation of praise; also in verse 15 [c]9 Psalm 118:26 [d]13 Isaiah 56:7 [e]13 Jer. 7:11

far in Matthew's Gospel, Jesus has not referred to himself by this title. While it can simply be a formal term for a master, the context of this occasion indicates he was implying divine authority as well.

21:8 spread their cloaks. This was a gesture of respect, given to kings (2 Kin. 9:12–13), prophets and other holy men.

21:9 Hosanna. Literally, "Save now!" This was commonly used as an expression of praise to God or as a greeting. **Son of David.** King David was considered to be the model king of Israel. It was through his line that God had promised to build an everlasting kingdom. **Blessed is he.** While the psalm from which this cry is taken (Ps.118:26) originally served as a tribute to the king of Israel, it was applied to any pilgrim who traveled to Jerusalem for the feasts. It was later understood by the rabbis to be a messianic psalm, referring to the final redemption that would be ushered in by the Messiah.

21:12 temple. Built by Herod the Great in 20 B.C., this magnificent structure covered about 30 acres. **buying and selling.** Temple worship required the sacrifice of an unblemished lamb or (for the poor) a dove. However, inspectors approved only those animals bought from certified vendors employed by the high priest's family. There was great profiteering, as such animals were sold at a huge markup. **money changers.** At Passover each Jew was required to pay a temple tax of nearly two days' wages. Since only a relatively rare currency was acceptable, money changers set up business in the temple to provide people with the correct currency. They, however, charged exorbitant amounts for this service.

21:13 a house of prayer. The temple was to have been a place where people could pray and worship (Isa. 56:7). **a den of robbers.** Referring to words of judgment spoken by the prophet Jeremiah (Jer. 7:11), Jesus points out that the authorities had, in effect, changed the temple from a place where people could worship into a place where thieves could do business.

21:15 children shouting. In contrast to the bitterness created in the worshipers by the exploitation allowed in the temple, Jesus transforms it into a place where children celebrate his presence (18:2–4; 19:14). **indignant.** The priests, concerned with the observance of proper decorum in the temple, see Jesus dealing with the blind, the lame, and the children

[16]"Do you hear what these children are saying?" they asked him.
"Yes," replied Jesus, "have you never read,

" 'From the lips of children and infants
you have ordained praise'[a]?"

[17]And he left them and went out of the city to Bethany, where he
spent the night.

The Fig Tree Withers

[18]Early in the morning, as he was on his way back to the city, he
was hungry. [19]Seeing a fig tree by the road, he went up to it but found
nothing on it except leaves. Then he said to it, "May you never bear
fruit again!" Immediately the tree withered.
[20]When the disciples saw this, they were amazed. "How did the fig
tree wither so quickly?" they asked.
[21]Jesus replied, "I tell you the truth, if you have faith and do not
doubt, not only can you do what was done to the fig tree, but also you
can say to this mountain, 'Go, throw yourself into the sea,' and it will
be done. [22]If you believe, you will receive whatever you ask for in
prayer."

The Authority of Jesus Questioned

[23]Jesus entered the temple courts, and, while he was teaching, the
chief priests and the elders of the people came to him. "By what authority are you doing these things?" they asked. "And who gave you
this authority?"
[24]Jesus replied, "I will also ask you one question. If you answer me,
I will tell you by what authority I am doing these things. [25]John's baptism—where did it come from? Was it from heaven, or from men?"
They discussed it among themselves and said, "If we say, 'From
heaven,' he will ask, 'Then why didn't you believe him?' [26]But if we
say, 'From men'—we are afraid of the people, for they all hold that
John was a prophet."
[27]So they answered Jesus, "We don't know."
Then he said, "Neither will I tell you by what authority I am doing
these things.

The Parable of the Two Sons

[28]"What do you think? There was a man who had two sons. He
went to the first and said, 'Son, go and work today in the vineyard.'

[a]16 Psalm 8:2

APPLY 1. When is the last time you turned over a few tables? **2.** When is the last time the hurting people in your town came to your church to be healed?

OPEN 1. If you had to make a living by raising fruit trees, how would you make out? **2.** In school, were you ever sent to the principal's office?

STUDY 1. The day before this event, Jesus goes to the temple and throws out the money-changers. What does he do here that signals what is to come? **2.** Do you think the disciples realized what was happening? How did Jesus try to prepare them for this ordeal? **3.** Why would the chief priests and elders of the people be out to get Jesus? **4.** How did Jesus answer their question? Why would the priests and elders not want to answer Jesus' question? **5.** In this first encounter between Jesus and the religious establishment, who came out on top?

APPLY 1. In your spiritual journey when is the last time you ran into a conflict with the religious establishment? **2.** What are you going to say when your children rebel against the establishment?

OPEN Who was the disciplinarian in your family?

STUDY 1. How do the two sons illustrate the two ways of responding to the Kingdom of God?

as a sign that he has no respect for the *temple's sacredness.*

21:17 Bethany, where he spent the night. Jesus left the city of Jerusalem at night possibly because such opposition to him was building among the authorities.

21:18–22 Fig trees were a common prophetic symbol associated with Israel and with judgment (Jer. 8:13; Hos. 9:10; Mic. 7:1; Nah. 3:12). Just as the tree was judged for its failure to have fruit, so Israel, and the temple as a symbol of Israel's faith, was judged for its failure to have "fruit"—works that honored God.

21:19 nothing on it except leaves. The tree symbolized Israel. It had the outward appearance of life (bustling activity at the temple), but no fruit (the qualities of justice, love and godliness that was to mark God's people). **Immediately the tree withered.** The immediacy of the event points out the divine power of Jesus and also the authority of Jesus as judge.

21:23 the chief priests and the elders. The chief priests were the key officers of the temple, just below the high priest in rank. The elders were powerful and (reputedly) wise leaders of Israel. They were generally not priests but administrators. These were representatives from the Sanhedrin, the Jewish ruling council.

2. Who does the first son represent? 3. How do you think they felt when Jesus compared them to tax collectors and prostitutes? Do you think Jesus is being a little hard on the Pharisees?

APPLY Which son's story is most like your own?

OPEN 1. If you had to go away for a long vacation and entrust your house, your children and your business to someone, who would it be? **2.** Where would you like to go for this vacation?

STUDY 1. Where is Jesus when he told this parable and who is he talking to (v. 23)? **2.** Who is the landowner? The vineyard? The servants? The tenants? The son? **3.** As the story progresses, do you think the chief priests and elders of the people realized that he was talking about them? **4.** What do you know about architecture and "capstones" that helps you understand the quote from the Old Testament? **5.** How did the chief priests and Pharisees respond? **6.** What is the lesson in this parable for the church today?

29" 'I will not,' he answered, but later he changed his mind and
went.
30"Then the father went to the other son and said the same thing.
He answered, 'I will, sir,' but he did not go.
31"Which of the two did what his father wanted?"
"The first," they answered.
Jesus said to them, "I tell you the truth, the tax collectors and the
prostitutes are entering the kingdom of God ahead of you. 32For John
came to you to show you the way of righteousness, and you did not
believe him, but the tax collectors and the prostitutes did. And even
after you saw this, you did not repent and believe him.

The Parable of the Tenants

33"Listen to another parable: There was a landowner who planted a
vineyard. He put a wall around it, dug a winepress in it and built a
watchtower. Then he rented the vineyard to some farmers and went
away on a journey. 34When the harvest time approached, he sent his
servants to the tenants to collect his fruit.
35"The tenants seized his servants; they beat one, killed another,
and stoned a third. 36Then he sent other servants to them, more than
the first time, and the tenants treated them the same way. 37Last of
all, he sent his son to them. 'They will respect my son,' he said.
38"But when the tenants saw the son, they said to each other, 'This
is the heir. Come, let's kill him and take his inheritance.' 39So they
took him and threw him out of the vineyard and killed him.
40"Therefore, when the owner of the vineyard comes, what will he
do to those tenants?"
41"He will bring those wretches to a wretched end," they replied,
"and he will rent the vineyard to other tenants, who will give him his
share of the crop at harvest time."
42Jesus said to them, "Have you never read in the Scriptures:

21:31 Which of the two did what his father wanted? This question forces the issue. It is not words that matter, but actions. The first son, while verbally defying his father, later chose to do his father's will. The second son, while politely honoring his father verbally, did not act upon his request. **the tax collectors and the prostitutes.** In this society, these two groups of people represented the lowest depths to which men and women respectively could sink. The tax collectors in mind were Jewish men who were viewed as exploiting their own people for their own gain in their work for Rome. Yet Jesus says that these along with prostitutes were entering the kingdom ahead of the religious authorities!

21:32 the way of righteousness. *John declared that the way to enter God's kingdom was through repen*tance, a change of heart and life. **And even after you saw this.** The guilt of the religious authorities is compounded by the fact that although they saw the transformation of life that happened to many people who responded to John's preaching they still refused to receive him as a messenger from God.

21:33 vineyard. This vineyard was built with a wall around it to keep out animals, a pit in which to crush the grapes to make wine, and a tower where the farmer kept a lookout for robbers and slept during the harvest. **went away.** Such a landlord would get tenant-farmers to work his large estate, requiring them to give him a portion of their harvest in payment for the use of the land. In the parable, the tenants refuse to give the landowner his share of the produce.

21:37 *he sent his son.* *The land*owner assumed the tenants would acknowledge the authority of his own son, the heir of the vineyard. The crowd would not have known the identity of the son in this story. Yet Matthew's readers know that this is none other than Jesus.

21:38 take his inheritance. The arrival of the son was mistakenly understood by the servants as a sign that the landowner must have died. By law, a piece of ownerless property could be kept by those who first occupied and cultivated it. Since the tenants assumed the land would be ownerless if the son was dead, they plotted to kill him in order to lay claim to the land for themselves.

21:41 rent the vineyard to other tenants. The landowner would rent the vineyard to people who would meet the terms of their contract. The implication of the parable is that God will raise up new leaders to care for his people.

21:42 The stone the builders rejected has become the capstone. Here the stone is Jesus (the Messiah)

"'The stone the builders rejected
has become the capstone[a];
the Lord has done this,
and it is marvelous in our eyes'[b]?

43"Therefore I tell you that the kingdom of God will be taken away
from you and given to a people who will produce its fruit. 44He who
falls on this stone will be broken to pieces, but he on whom it falls
will be crushed."[c]

45When the chief priests and the Pharisees heard Jesus' parables,
they knew he was talking about them. 46They looked for a way to arrest him, but they were afraid of the crowd because the people held that he was a prophet.

The Parable of the Wedding Banquet

22 Jesus spoke to them again in parables, saying: 2"The kingdom of heaven is like a king who prepared a wedding banquet for his son. 3He sent his servants to those who had been invited to the banquet to tell them to come, but they refused to come.

4"Then he sent some more servants and said, 'Tell those who have been invited that I have prepared my dinner: My oxen and fattened cattle have been butchered, and everything is ready. Come to the wedding banquet.'

5"But they paid no attention and went off—one to his field, another
to his business. 6The rest seized his servants, mistreated them and
killed them. 7The king was enraged. He sent his army and destroyed those murderers and burned their city.

8"Then he said to his servants, 'The wedding banquet is ready, but
those I invited did not deserve to come. 9Go to the street corners and
invite to the banquet anyone you find.' 10So the servants went out
into the streets and gathered all the people they could find, both good and bad, and the wedding hall was filled with guests.

11"But when the king came in to see the guests, he noticed a man
there who was not wearing wedding clothes. 12'Friend,' he asked,
'how did you get in here without wedding clothes?' The man was speechless.

13"Then the king told the attendants, 'Tie him hand and foot, and

[a]42 Or *cornerstone* [b]42 Psalm 118:22,23 [c]44 Some manuscripts do not have verse 44.

APPLY 1. How do you feel about working in God's vineyard? **2.** Is Jesus really the capstone in your life in holding everything together?

OPEN What is your best story of a wedding you attended when something unexpected happened?

STUDY 1. Where is this parable told and to whom (21:23)? **2.** Why is the banquet held? How would you compare this banquet to your wedding reception (v. 4)? **3.** What did the invited guests do? What were their reasons? **4.** How did the king respond? **5.** Where does the king go for new guests? Who are these people? **6.** What happened to the "friend" who slipped in without the wedding clothes? How do you explain verse 14? **7.** What's the lesson in this parable for you today?

APPLY 1. How did you respond initially to God's invitation to his wedding banquet? What was your favorite excuse? **2.** What does your "friend" say when you invite him/her to God's banquet?

---

whom the builders (the leaders) fail to recognize. The identification here of the Messiah (the stone) with the Son of God (v. 37) was unique to Jesus.

21:45–46 The leaders knew exactly what part they played in Jesus' parable. From their point of view such teaching had to be stopped. Not only was Jesus attacking them, but he was implying that he was the Messiah and God's Son. Yet, because of Jesus' popularity with the crowds for attacking the abuses in the temple system, they could do nothing at this time.

22:3 sent his servants to those who had been invited. In well-to-do circles, invitations for banquets were issued well in advance, but the specific time to arrive was communicated on the day of the event when everything was ready (Est. 5:8; 6:14).

22:9 the street corners. These are the public squares where beggars would gather, hoping for handouts. **anyone.** The people who would be "hanging around" the streets would have been the social outcasts reduced to begging for survival. Jesus is saying that the kingdom is precisely for these type of people.

22:11–12 wedding clothes. In this allegorical parable, the wedding clothes represent the robes of righteousness God provides for his people (Zech. 3:3–5; Rev. 3:4, 5,18). Without such God-given righteousness, one has no part in the kingdom. The false disciple, like the religious leaders (v. 34), is silenced before the king. He has no excuse.

22:13 weeping and gnashing of teeth. This is a stock phrase used to

throw him outside, into the darkness, where there will be weeping and gnashing of teeth.'

14"For many are invited, but few are chosen."

Paying Taxes to Caesar

15Then the Pharisees went out and laid plans to trap him in his words. 16They sent their disciples to him along with the Herodians. "Teacher," they said, "we know you are a man of integrity and that you teach the way of God in accordance with the truth. You aren't swayed by men, because you pay no attention to who they are. 17Tell us then, what is your opinion? Is it right to pay taxes to Caesar or not?"

18But Jesus, knowing their evil intent, said, "You hypocrites, why are you trying to trap me? 19Show me the coin used for paying the tax." They brought him a denarius, 20and he asked them, "Whose portrait is this? And whose inscription?"

21"Caesar's," they replied.

Then he said to them, "Give to Caesar what is Caesar's, and to God what is God's."

22When they heard this, they were amazed. So they left him and went away.

Marriage at the Resurrection

23That same day the Sadducees, who say there is no resurrection, came to him with a question. 24"Teacher," they said, "Moses told us that if a man dies without having children, his brother must marry the widow and have children for him. 25Now there were seven brothers among us. The first one married and died, and since he had no children, he left his wife to his brother. 26The same thing happened to the second and third brother, right on down to the seventh. 27Finally, the woman died. 28Now then, at the resurrection, whose wife will she be of the seven, since all of them were married to her?"

29Jesus replied, "You are in error because you do not know the Scriptures or the power of God. 30At the resurrection people will neither marry nor be given in marriage; they will be like the angels in heaven. 31But about the resurrection of the dead—have you not read what God said to you, 32'I am the God of Abraham, the God of Isaac,

OPEN Who can guess the number of times the word "one" is found on a one-dollar bill?

STUDY 1. Why is it surprising to see the Pharisees and the Herodians joining together to approach Jesus? **2.** How does their question put Jesus in a no-win situation? **3.** What does Jesus mean by his answer? What does this say about the relationship of church and state?

APPLY 1. When have you been caught in a conflict between your love of the world and of Christ? **2.** Are you better at paying your financial obligation to things of the world or to God?

OPEN In your family who would you nominate to be the lawyer?

STUDY 1. Who are the Sadducees? What do they believe about the resurrection? **2.** How would you describe the question they brought to Jesus? **3.** How does Jesus answer their question? What do you learn about heaven from Jesus' answer?

APPLY 1. What does the resurrection mean to you? **2.** What are you looking forward to in heaven?

---

indicate the extreme horror and suffering of God's judgment (8:12; 13:42,50; 24:51; 25:30).

22:16 Herodians. This was a political group made up of influential Jewish sympathizers of King Herod. Normally despised by the Pharisees as traitors who worked with Rome and associated with Gentiles, the Pharisees would need this group's assistance to secure the civil authority's opposition to Jesus. **a man of integrity.** By these and other flattering words they hope to catch Jesus off guard.

22:17 taxes. An annual poll tax had to be paid to the Romans by all adult Jews. Many Jews felt that paying taxes to Caesar was a denial of the belief that God was the rightful ruler of Israel.

22:18 why are you trying to trap me? If the authorities can get Jesus to say that the people should *not* pay taxes to Caesar, then the Roman guard would have grounds to arrest him. On the other hand, if Jesus says they *should* pay taxes, then he would lose the support of the crowds who resented being taxed by an occupying force.

22:19 the coin. Only the denarius, a small silver coin, could be used to pay the poll tax. Since it bore the picture of Tiberius Caesar and a description of him as "Son of the Divine Augustine," these coins were offensive to strict Jews, who would not even handle them.

22:23 Sadducees. A small but highly influential party of Jews composed mainly of wealthy, aristocratic priests. Up to this point Jesus has been no threat to the Sadducees since his ministry had been largely in Galilee, far from the temple which they controlled. However, having so strongly challenged the activities of the temple (21:12–15), he had now become their enemy. **resurrection.** Most Jews believed that at the end of history God would bring the dead to life for judgment. The Sadducees did not believe in such a resurrection.

and the God of Jacob'[a]? He is not the God of the dead but of the living."
33 When the crowds heard this, they were astonished at his teaching.

The Greatest Commandment

34 Hearing that Jesus had silenced the Sadducees, the Pharisees got
together. 35 One of them, an expert in the law, tested him with this question: 36 "Teacher, which is the greatest commandment in the Law?"
37 Jesus replied: " 'Love the Lord your God with all your heart and
with all your soul and with all your mind.'[b] 38 This is the first and
greatest commandment. 39 And the second is like it: 'Love your neighbor as yourself.'[c] 40 All the Law and the Prophets hang on these two
commandments."

Whose Son Is the Christ?

41 While the Pharisees were gathered together, Jesus asked them,
42 "What do you think about the Christ[d]? Whose son is he?"
"The son of David," they replied.
43 He said to them, "How is it then that David, speaking by the Spirit, calls him 'Lord'? For he says,

44 " 'The Lord said to my Lord:
"Sit at my right hand
until I put your enemies
under your feet." '[e]

45 If then David calls him 'Lord,' how can he be his son?" 46 No one
could say a word in reply, and from that day on no one dared to ask
him any more questions.

Seven Woes

23 Then Jesus said to the crowds and to his disciples: 2 "The
teachers of the law and the Pharisees sit in Moses' seat. 3 So
you must obey them and do everything they tell you. But do not do
what they do, for they do not practice what they preach. 4 They tie up
heavy loads and put them on men's shoulders, but they themselves
are not willing to lift a finger to move them.
5 "Everything they do is done for men to see: They make their
phylacteries[f] wide and the tassels on their garments long; 6 they love

[a] 32 Exodus 3:6 [b] 37 Deut. 6:5 [c] 39 Lev. 19:18 [d] 42 Or *Messiah* [e] 44 Psalm 110:1 [f] 5 That is, boxes containing Scripture verses, worn on forehead and arm

OPEN What is the greatest commandment as far as your present boss is concerned? What about your coach when you were in school?

STUDY 1. Why would the Pharisee, who is supposed to be an expert in the law, be asking Jesus "what is the greatest commandment"? **2.** How do you like the way Jesus reduced everything in the Law down to two simple statements? **3.** What is Jesus doing when he comes back to the Pharisees with a question about the Christ (Messiah)? Were the Pharisees expecting the Messiah to be human (Son of David) or divine (Lord over David)?

APPLY 1. On a scale from 1 (low) to 10 (high), where are you right now in your relationship with God? **2.** On the same scale, where are you in loving your neighbor?

OPEN 1. Growing up, what "hot buttons" did you push to get your parents mad? What "hot buttons" do your kids (if any) use on you? **2.** What is your favorite city?

STUDY 1. What was the seat of Moses? Given Jesus' remarks about the Pharisees in chapters 21–22, what is surprising about his remarks in verse 3? **2.** As Jesus sees it, what is the main evil of the Pharisees? How are the disciples to avoid falling into the same evil? What

22:34–40 This confrontation is with a scribe, a lawyer who interpreted Jewish law. Whereas in Mark's version, the scribe appears to ask Jesus a sincere question (Mark 12:28–34), Matthew presents this as an attempt to test Jesus.

22:36 the greatest commandment. Some religious authorities sought to reduce all of the Law to a few foundational principles. The Pharisees, who generally regarded all the laws of God as equally important, probably hoped Jesus would isolate one law and thus provide them with the opportunity to discredit him for ignoring other laws.

22:37 This is part of the *Shema* (Deut. 6:4-5). This passage, recited by pious Jews each morning and evening, captures what was essential about the people's relationship to God.

22:42 the Christ. This is the Greek word for Messiah, the expected deliverer of Israel.

23:2 Moses' seat. This refers to the seat in the front of each synagogue in which a rabbi sat while teaching.

23:4 The Pharisees were concerned with defining the meaning of the Law so that its intent could be applied to everyday life. However, over time this developed into such a complex, rigid tradition that it was nearly impossible for any working person to have time to observe it.

23:5 phylacteries. These were small cases which contained passages of the Law. They were tied to the forehead and left arm (Ex. 13:9,16; Deut. 6:8; 11:18). **tassels.** Jews were to tie tassels on the corners of their robes to remind them of God's commands (Num. 15:37–39). The Pharisees wore these things in an ornamental way to draw attention to themselves.

distinction was Jesus trying to make between his followers and the Pharisees? **3.** Compare the path to greatness followed by the Pharisees with that taught by Jesus (vv. 5–12). What do these two views of greatness teach us about the two views of the kingdom? **4.** How do the charges Jesus makes against the Pharisees and the teachers of the Law (vv. 13–32) relate to what Jesus says in verses 2–7? Do you find anything common to all seven charges? How do each of these affect the common people? **5.** How have the religious leaders corrupted the practice of evangelism (vv. 13–15)? **6.** In what way are these religious leaders condemned to repeat the past because of their failure to learn from their forefathers (vv. 29–36)? How is the punishment in verses 33–36 appropriate to the crimes? **7.** What emotion does Jesus display in verses 37–39? How do you think he likely felt as he was teaching?

APPLY **1.** Where does Jesus catch your attention in this passage? What practices touch close-to-home in your life? How can you avoid "talking the talk" but not "walking the walk"? **2.** What about today's church do you lament over (as Jesus did over Jerusalem)? **3.** From reading this passage, what should today's teachers and pastors be especially mindful of?

the place of honor at banquets and the most important seats in the
synagogues; 7they love to be greeted in the marketplaces and to have
men call them 'Rabbi.'

8"But you are not to be called 'Rabbi,' for you have only one Master
and you are all brothers. 9And do not call anyone on earth 'father,' for
you have one Father, and he is in heaven. 10Nor are you to be called
'teacher,' for you have one Teacher, the Christ.[a] 11The greatest among
you will be your servant. 12For whoever exalts himself will be humbled, and whoever humbles himself will be exalted.

13"Woe to you, teachers of the law and Pharisees, you hypocrites!
You shut the kingdom of heaven in men's faces. You yourselves do
not enter, nor will you let those enter who are trying to.[b]

15"Woe to you, teachers of the law and Pharisees, you hypocrites!
You travel over land and sea to win a single convert, and when he
becomes one, you make him twice as much a son of hell as you are.

16"Woe to you, blind guides! You say, 'If anyone swears by the temple, it means nothing; but if anyone swears by the gold of the temple,
he is bound by his oath.' 17You blind fools! Which is greater: the gold,
or the temple that makes the gold sacred? 18You also say, 'If anyone
swears by the altar, it means nothing; but if anyone swears by the gift
on it, he is bound by his oath.' 19You blind men! Which is greater: the
gift, or the altar that makes the gift sacred? 20Therefore, he who
swears by the altar swears by it and by everything on it. 21And he who
swears by the temple swears by it and by the one who dwells in it.
22And he who swears by heaven swears by God's throne and by the
one who sits on it.

23"Woe to you, teachers of the law and Pharisees, you hypocrites!
You give a tenth of your spices—mint, dill and cummin. But you have
neglected the more important matters of the law—justice, mercy and
faithfulness. You should have practiced the latter, without neglecting
the former. 24You blind guides! You strain out a gnat but swallow a
camel.

25"Woe to you, teachers of the law and Pharisees, you hypocrites!
You clean the outside of the cup and dish, but inside they are full of

[a]10 Or *Messiah* [b]13 Some manuscripts *to.* [14]*Woe to you, teachers of the law and Pharisees, you hypocrites! You devour widows' houses and for a show make lengthy prayers. Therefore you will be punished more severely.*

23:6 the most important seats in the synagogues. The choice seat was up front, with its back to the box which contained the sacred Scriptures, and its front facing the congregation, so that all would see who sat there.

23:7 greeted. Out of respect for the authority of the teachers of the Law, people rose and called out titles of respect when they passed by. **Rabbi.** This official title for the scribes literally meant "my master."

23:13 Woe to you. Unless they repent, God's judgment is the only future they have to anticipate. **You shut the kingdom of heaven in men's faces.** Instead of unlocking the Scriptures, the traditions and rules of the scribes have had the effect of securely locking away such knowledge from the people.

23:16 blind guides. The Pharisees prided themselves on being "guides for the blind." Instead, Jesus asserts they are blind themselves. **If anyone swears by.** According to the Law a *person's oath* was binding. However, the Pharisees had developed a system that distinguished between the types of oaths, based on what they swore on. As a result, they obscured the Law's point that a person was responsible for keeping his or her promises.

23:24 You strain out a gnat but swallow a camel. This is an example of Jesus' use of humorous irony to make his point. They are sensitive to the insignificant details of their tradition, but miss the obvious focus of the Law.

23:25 greed and self-indulgence. Jesus says that it is as if they think that using ritually "clean" utensils makes the consumption of food and drink gained by greed and violence acceptable. While concerned for the external demands of their tradition, they fail to consider what is going on inside of themselves.

greed and self-indulgence. [26]Blind Pharisee! First clean the inside of
the cup and dish, and then the outside also will be clean.
[27]"Woe to you, teachers of the law and Pharisees, you hypocrites! You are like whitewashed tombs, which look beautiful on
the outside but on the inside are full of dead men's bones and
everything unclean. [28]In the same way, on the outside you appear
to people as righteous but on the inside you are full of hypocrisy
and wickedness.
[29]"Woe to you, teachers of the law and Pharisees, you hypocrites!
You build tombs for the prophets and decorate the graves of the righteous. [30]And you say, 'If we had lived in the days of our forefathers,
we would not have taken part with them in shedding the blood of the
prophets.' [31]So you testify against yourselves that you are the descendants of those who murdered the prophets. [32]Fill up, then, the
measure of the sin of your forefathers!
[33]"You snakes! You brood of vipers! How will you escape being
condemned to hell? [34]Therefore I am sending you prophets and
wise men and teachers. Some of them you will kill and crucify;
others you will flog in your synagogues and pursue from town to
town. [35]And so upon you will come all the righteous blood that has
been shed on earth, from the blood of righteous Abel to the blood
of Zechariah son of Berekiah, whom you murdered between the
temple and the altar. [36]I tell you the truth, all this will come upon
this generation.
[37]"O Jerusalem, Jerusalem, you who kill the prophets and stone
those sent to you, how often I have longed to gather your children
together, as a hen gathers her chicks under her wings, but you were
not willing. [38]Look, your house is left to you desolate. [39]For I tell you,
you will not see me again until you say, 'Blessed is he who comes in
the name of the Lord.'[a]"

Signs of the End of the Age

24 Jesus left the temple and was walking away when his disciples came up to him to call his attention to its buildings.
[2]"Do you see all these things?" he asked. "I tell you the truth, not one
stone here will be left on another; every one will be thrown down."

[a]39 Psalm 118:26

OPEN When you were growing up did you build things with blocks? Were you good at it?

STUDY 1. What prompts Jesus to make these comments? **2.** What bombshell does he drop on his disciples (v. 2)? How do

23:26 clean the inside. Following the metaphor of the cup and dish, this is a call to self-examination and repentance. True holiness before God comes from the inside out, not from the outside in. A clean heart, not a clean dish, *is what is required.*

23:27 whitewashed tombs. Tombs would often be whitewashed. While this gave them an attractive appearance, it could do nothing about the decay that was inside the tomb.

23:28 wickedness. Literally, "lawlessness." Despite all their professed concern for the Law, the Pharisees actually lived in disregard of it.

23:33 You brood of vipers! The image painted by these words is of snakes slithering through the undergrowth trying to escape the oncoming fire.

23:34 crucify. The Jews did not practice crucifixion. This may be a reference to how the Jewish authorities eventually led the Romans to carry out the execution of Jesus himself.

23:35 Abel. Abel, the first person to be killed, was murdered by his brother, who, like these leaders, refused to listen to God (Gen. 4:3–8). **Zechariah son of Berekiah.** There were two known Zechariahs who were sons of men named Berekiah. One was the author of the Old Testament book by that name, but there is no record of how he died. The other was a man murdered by Jewish zealots in the temple in A.D. 67. This was contemporary to Matthew's writing, but after Jesus' earthly ministry.

23:38 your house. This is the temple from which the presence of God will depart because of the people's rejection of the Messiah (Jer. 12:7; Ezek. 10:18–19).

24:2 not one stone here will be left. The temple was destroyed by Rome in 70 A.D.

the Jewish people (including the disciples) feel about the temple? How must the disciples have felt when they heard Jesus' words? **3.** What three questions do the disciples ask (v. 3)? **4.** What events might mislead the disciples into thinking the end had come (vv. 4–7)? **5.** What does Jesus promise for those who endure and don't give up? What must the church continue doing (v. 14)? **6.** What event would signal the start of the great distress? What does "the abomination that causes desolation" mean (Dan. 9:27 and 11:31)? **7.** What should the residents of Jerusalem do when this happens (vv. 16–20)? Why? **8.** What dangerous deceptions would Christians need to guard against (vv. 23–26)? Why would believers be susceptible to such rumors then? **9.** In contrast, what will mark the coming of the true Messiah (vv. 27–29)? What will his Second Coming be like (vv. 30–31)? **10.** What is the lesson from the fig tree? How does it apply to the disciples' question (v. 3) and Jesus' answer (vv. 33–35)?

APPLY 1. If you could ask Jesus one question about the Second Coming, what would you ask? **2.** How much does the thought of the Second Coming affect your lifestyle. today?

3 As Jesus was sitting on the Mount of Olives, the disciples came to
him privately. "Tell us," they said, "when will this happen, and what
will be the sign of your coming and of the end of the age?"
4 Jesus answered: "Watch out that no one deceives you. 5 For many
will come in my name, claiming, 'I am the Christ,[a]' and will deceive
many. 6 You will hear of wars and rumors of wars, but see to it that you
are not alarmed. Such things must happen, but the end is still to
come. 7 Nation will rise against nation, and kingdom against kingdom. There will be famines and earthquakes in various places. 8 All
these are the beginning of birth pains.
9 "Then you will be handed over to be persecuted and put to death,
and you will be hated by all nations because of me. 10 At that time
many will turn away from the faith and will betray and hate each
other, 11 and many false prophets will appear and deceive many people. 12 Because of the increase of wickedness, the love of most will
grow cold, 13 but he who stands firm to the end will be saved. 14 And
this gospel of the kingdom will be preached in the whole world as a
testimony to all nations, and then the end will come.
15 "So when you see standing in the holy place 'the abomination
that causes desolation,'[b] spoken of through the prophet Daniel—let
the reader understand— 16 then let those who are in Judea flee to the
mountains. 17 Let no one on the roof of his house go down to take
anything out of the house. 18 Let no one in the field go back to get his
cloak. 19 How dreadful it will be in those days for pregnant women
and nursing mothers! 20 Pray that your flight will not take place in
winter or on the Sabbath. 21 For then there will be great distress, unequaled from the beginning of the world until now—and never to be
equaled again. 22 If those days had not been cut short, no one would
survive, but for the sake of the elect those days will be shortened. 23 At
that time if anyone says to you, 'Look, here is the Christ!' or, 'There
he is!' do not believe it. 24 For false Christs and false prophets will appear and perform great signs and miracles to deceive even the elect—
if that were possible. 25 See, I have told you ahead of time.
26 "So if anyone tells you, 'There he is, out in the desert,' do not go
out; or, 'Here he is, in the inner rooms,' do not believe it. 27 For as
lightning that comes from the east is visible even in the west, so will

[a]5 Or *Messiah;* also in verse 23 [b]*15* Daniel 9:27; 11:31; 12:11

24:6–8 Some feel that apocalyptic language uses graphic imagery to describe historical events. Others see this as a description of future events.

24:9–13 The focus shifts from the woes experienced by people in general to those Christians will face. Many will fall away, but Jesus calls for faithfulness (v. 13).

24:14 Despite the persecution, the mission of Jesus' disciples is to preach the Gospel to all nations (28:18–20).

24:15 the abomination that causes desolation. This phrase (from Dan. 9:27; 11:31; 12:11) refers to an event so awful that Jews will flee from the temple in horror. Such an event occurred in 168 B.C. when Antiochus Epiphanes, a Syrian king, set up an altar to Zeus in the temple. Jesus warns that when that type of desecration occurs again, the fall of Jerusalem would be imminent (2 Thess. 2:1–4). Luke's version includes armies surrounding Jerusalem as a further sign (Luke 21:20).

24:16 let those who are in Judea flee. *Instead of flocking to the city in anticipation of a dramatic messianic victory, the disciples must run for their lives.*

24:21 great distress. The destruction of Jerusalem in 70 A.D. was an unparalleled disaster for Israel. Some consider this the fulfillment of Jesus' words. Others are still looking for the completion of this prophecy.

24:22 the elect. These are the people God has called into his kingdom. They are akin to the survivors of God's wrath spoken of in Isaiah 1:9 and 4:2–4.

24:24 great signs and miracles. Miracles in themselves are no proof of a person's divine authority. Pharaoh's magicians in Egypt were able to imitate many of the miracles performed by Moses (Ex. 7:20–22).

be the coming of the Son of Man. 28Wherever there is a carcass, there
the vultures will gather.
29"Immediately after the distress of those days

" 'the sun will be darkened,
and the moon will not give its light;
the stars will fall from the sky,
and the heavenly bodies will be shaken.'[a]

30"At that time the sign of the Son of Man will appear in the sky, and
all the nations of the earth will mourn. They will see the Son of Man
coming on the clouds of the sky, with power and great glory. 31And he
will send his angels with a loud trumpet call, and they will gather his
elect from the four winds, from one end of the heavens to the other.
32"Now learn this lesson from the fig tree: As soon as its twigs get
tender and its leaves come out, you know that summer is near. 33Even
so, when you see all these things, you know that it[b] is near, right at
the door. 34I tell you the truth, this generation[c] will certainly not pass
away until all these things have happened. 35Heaven and earth will
pass away, but my words will never pass away.

The Day and Hour Unknown

36"No one knows about that day or hour, not even the angels in
heaven, nor the Son,[d] but only the Father. 37As it was in the days of
Noah, so it will be at the coming of the Son of Man. 38For in the days
before the flood, people were eating and drinking, marrying and giving in marriage, up to the day Noah entered the ark; 39and they knew
nothing about what would happen until the flood came and took
them all away. That is how it will be at the coming of the Son of Man.
40Two men will be in the field; one will be taken and the other left.
41Two women will be grinding with a hand mill; one will be taken and
the other left.
42"Therefore keep watch, because you do not know on what day
your Lord will come. 43But understand this: If the owner of the house
had known at what time of night the thief was coming, he would have
kept watch and would not have let his house be broken into. 44So you
also must be ready, because the Son of Man will come at an hour
when you do not expect him.
45"Who then is the faithful and wise servant, whom the master has
put in charge of the servants in his household to give them their food
at the proper time? 46It will be good for that servant whose master

[a]29 Isaiah 13:10; 34:4 [b]33 Or *he* [c]34 Or *race* [d]36 Some manuscripts do not have *nor the Son.*

OPEN 1. If Jesus returned at 7:00 p.m. this Tuesday, what would you be doing? **2.** As a child, what was your favorite time of day? Day of the week? Season of the year?

STUDY 1. In what ways is the flood like the Second Coming of Christ? **2.** What does it mean, practically, to be ready for Jesus' return if we do not know when he will come? **3.** In view of Christ's Second Coming, what does the story of the faithful and wise servant teach you about readiness? About stewardship? Judgment? Responsibility for serving and witnessing to others?

APPLY 1. How would you explain the end times and the Second Coming to a seeker? **2.** Over what has God given you stewardship? How would God evaluate the job you're doing?

24:30 the sign of the Son of Man. Jesus uses common military imagery to describe his coming. A "sign" was a banner, flag or standard under which an army would march. Isaiah 11:10 compares the Messiah to a banner that will be raised as a rallying point for all God's people.

24:31 a loud trumpet call. Trumpets were used to communicate orders to the army. Isaiah 27:13 uses the image of a trumpet blast to describe how God's people will be gathered together when God comes to bring judgment upon their enemies.

24:32 lesson from the fig tree. They knew that the fig tree only got its leaves in late spring. When the leaves came it was a sure sign that summer was near.

24:33 these things. Jesus evidently refers to those things that will occur prior to the fall of Jerusalem (vv. 4–15).

24:45–51 When the master was away, one servant would be appointed as the head of the household. If he abused this position for his own indulgence, the sudden appearance of his master would bring judgment. The point here is that watchfulness is not a matter of scanning the horizon for signs of the Lord's return, but of faithfully fulfilling the responsibilities God has assigned his people.

finds him doing so when he returns. 47I tell you the truth, he will put
him in charge of all his possessions. 48But suppose that servant is
wicked and says to himself, 'My master is staying away a long time,'
49and he then begins to beat his fellow servants and to eat and drink
with drunkards. 50The master of that servant will come on a day when
he does not expect him and at an hour he is not aware of. 51He will
cut him to pieces and assign him a place with the hypocrites, where
there will be weeping and gnashing of teeth.

OPEN 1. What time did you go to bed last night? 2. What's your remedy for staying awake when you get drowsy? 3. Were you the type that put off studying for an exam until the night before?

STUDY 1. What is your classic memory of missing an important meeting because you were late? 2. What makes some virgins "wise" and some "foolish"? 3. What would you call the refusal of the wise virgins to share their oil: Justified? Selfish? Shrewd? Unfair? 4. Who is Jesus talking to and about in this parable? Why would Matthew include this parable when he targeted a largely Jewish audience with his gospel? 5. Today who would be the foolish virgins?

APPLY 1. Do you believe that Jesus will one day return? 2. How does this impact the way you are living your life today?

The Parable of the Ten Virgins

25 "At that time the kingdom of heaven will be like ten virgins
who took their lamps and went out to meet the bridegroom.
2Five of them were foolish and five were wise. 3The foolish ones took
their lamps but did not take any oil with them. 4The wise, however,
took oil in jars along with their lamps. 5The bridegroom was a long
time in coming, and they all became drowsy and fell asleep.

6"At midnight the cry rang out: 'Here's the bridegroom! Come out to
meet him!'

7"Then all the virgins woke up and trimmed their lamps. 8The foolish ones said to the wise, 'Give us some of your oil; our lamps are
going out.'

9" 'No,' they replied, 'there may not be enough for both us and you.
Instead, go to those who sell oil and buy some for yourselves.'

10"But while they were on their way to buy the oil, the bridegroom
arrived. The virgins who were ready went in with him to the wedding
banquet. And the door was shut.

11"Later the others also came. 'Sir! Sir!' they said. 'Open the door
for us!'

12"But he replied, 'I tell you the truth, I don't know you.'

13"Therefore keep watch, because you do not know the day or the
hour.

25:1 ten virgins. There is no special meaning here to the numbers ten or five. The numbers simply reflect two categories of people. **took their lamps.** Weddings typically occurred at night. The lamps, probably small earthen jars with a wick inserted to draw the oil used as fuel, would be held up on poles to brighten the way for the procession. **to meet the bridegroom.** Prior to a wedding, the groom would go to the bride's home and lead her in a procession to his house where the wedding would take place. These 10 women were probably either at the bride's house or somewhere along the processional route waiting for the groom to come.

25:6 At midnight. This emphasizes the unexpected delay of the groom, since this would have been long after most people would have expected him to come. **Come out to meet him!** People would gather around the groom to escort him to the bride's home and then back to the actual site of the wedding. The unexpected arrival of the groom, the shout of proclamation and the people coming out to meet him all echo themes of the return of Christ as described in 1 Thessalonians 4:16–17.

25:8 our lamps are going out. Once the time for the procession arrived, the foolish women realized they were short on oil.

25:9 No. The refusal to share was not selfish, but simply prudent. They carried *only enough* for themselves. This aspect of the story is thought to show that each person needs their own relationship with the Lord; such a relationship cannot be obtained by simply being around those who demonstrate faith through faithful living. **go to those who sell oil.** Since it is so late, it would be difficult to find a shopkeeper willing to open shop and sell them oil. At the time of the Lord's return, it is too late to try to make up for one's lack of preparation.

25:10 the door was shut. Since latecomers would not be excluded from a wedding party, the parable at this point clearly shifts to a story about the messianic banquet. There is a limited time when the "day of salvation" is extended to people. It must be received while the Lord provides the opportunity (7:22–23; Luke 13:25).

25:12 I don't know you. Here the implication is that God does not "know" them in the sense that comes from an intimate mutual relationship with someone.

The Parable of the Talents

[14]"Again, it will be like a man going on a journey, who called his servants and entrusted his property to them. [15]To one he gave five talents[a] of money, to another two talents, and to another one talent, each according to his ability. Then he went on his journey. [16]The man who had received the five talents went at once and put his money to work and gained five more. [17]So also, the one with the two talents gained two more. [18]But the man who had received the one talent went off, dug a hole in the ground and hid his master's money.

[19]"After a long time the master of those servants returned and settled accounts with them. [20]The man who had received the five talents brought the other five. 'Master,' he said, 'you entrusted me with five talents. See, I have gained five more.'

[21]"His master replied, 'Well done, good and faithful servant! You have been faithful with a few things; I will put you in charge of many things. Come and share your master's happiness!'

[22]"The man with the two talents also came. 'Master,' he said, 'you entrusted me with two talents; see, I have gained two more.'

[23]"His master replied, 'Well done, good and faithful servant! You have been faithful with a few things; I will put you in charge of many things. Come and share your master's happiness!'

[24]"Then the man who had received the one talent came. 'Master,' he said, 'I knew that you are a hard man, harvesting where you have not sown and gathering where you have not scattered seed. [25]So I was afraid and went out and hid your talent in the ground. See, here is what belongs to you.'

[a]15 A talent was worth more than a thousand dollars.

OPEN 1. Growing up, were you more a saver or a spender? How about now? **2.** What is the best investment you have ever made? **3.** What is something others tell you that you are good at?

STUDY 1. If you were to go away for a long time, who would you entrust your house, your children and your business to? **2.** In this parable what were the expectations of the master for his servants while he was away? **3.** Why did the servant that was given one talent hide his money? Why was the master so hard on this servant? **4.** What did the master say to the two servants who doubled their money? **5.** How do you feel about being given more responsibility as a reward for a "job well done"?

APPLY 1. What is the thing that makes you supremely happy? **2.** If you could throw caution to the wind, what would you like to do with the thing you are good at?

25:15 talents. Originally this was a unit of weight. However, it was also used as the highest denomination of coinage. It would take a laborer almost 20 years to earn the equivalent of one talent. **each according to his ability.** The master took into account the level of responsibility he believed each servant could handle. Jesus is thus acknowledging that everyone does not start out at the same place in life. Some are given more in terms of abilities and possessions. But the rest of the parable reminds us that what matters is not what you are given, but how you make use of it.

25:16 gained five more. High interest rates in that time could make a thousand percent return possible (though undoubtedly difficult).

25:19 After a long time. The indefinite time reference hints that Christ's own return may be far off. After Jesus ascended to heaven, much of the church was expecting his early return (Heb. 10:37; 1 Peter 4:7; Rev. 1:3). When this did not happen, they had to be taught how to wait. Parables such as this helped, as did teachings (1 Thess. 4:13–18; 2 Peter 3:3–10). **settled accounts.** This was the time of reckoning in which the master would evaluate how the various servants had fulfilled their responsibility to him.

25:20 See. The emphasis here is on the fact that the servant welcomes the master's inspection because he knows he has done a good job.

25:21 Well done, good and faithful servant! The servant's faithfulness in this matter is the quality that allows the master to trust him with greater responsibility. The second servant is given the same commendation and type of reward (vv. 22–23). **few things ... many things.** The servant is rewarded, not with a life of ease, but with greater administrative responsibility in the master's household (based on the master's trust and confidence in him). While five talents or even two talents is by no means a small amount, the point is that they are "a few things" in comparison with the responsibility with which these servants will now be entrusted. **Come and share your master's happiness!** The servants are not only given more responsibility; they are invited into a new relationship with the master. No longer simply servants, they now enjoy his friendship and respect. Jesus spoke of this same change in relationship in John 15:15 when he told the disciples, "I no longer call you servants, because a servant does not know his master's business. Instead, I have called you friends."

25:24 a hard man. Literally, this is "exacting." He was generous in his original entrustment of his property to his servants. He was generous to the first and second servants upon his return. It would raise the question in the listeners' minds whether the problem was with the third servant's perceptions.

25:25 So I was afraid. The servant implies that his lack of having anything to show for having been entrusted with the talent is really the fault of the master: he expects too much, and he is too frightening. **here is what belongs to you.** Rabbinic teaching emphasized that God had given Israel the responsibility to protect the Law until the time came when he would establish his kingdom. While the Pharisees have "protected" the Law from being corrupted by the masses, they have failed to use it in a way that would draw others to God.

26"His master replied, 'You wicked, lazy servant! So you knew that I harvest where I have not sown and gather where I have not scattered seed? 27Well then, you should have put my money on deposit with the bankers, so that when I returned I would have received it back with interest.

28" 'Take the talent from him and give it to the one who has the ten talents. 29For everyone who has will be given more, and he will have an abundance. Whoever does not have, even what he has will be taken from him. 30And throw that worthless servant outside, into the darkness, where there will be weeping and gnashing of teeth.'

The Sheep and the Goats

31"When the Son of Man comes in his glory, and all the angels with him, he will sit on his throne in heavenly glory. 32All the nations will be gathered before him, and he will separate the people one from another as a shepherd separates the sheep from the goats. 33He will put the sheep on his right and the goats on his left.

34"Then the King will say to those on his right, 'Come, you who are blessed by my Father; take your inheritance, the kingdom prepared for you since the creation of the world. 35For I was hungry and you gave me something to eat, I was thirsty and you gave me something to drink, I was a stranger and you invited me in, 36I needed clothes and you clothed me, I was sick and you looked after me, I was in prison and you came to visit me.'

37"Then the righteous will answer him, 'Lord, when did we see you hungry and feed you, or thirsty and give you something to drink? 38When did we see you a stranger and invite you in, or needing clothes and clothe you? 39When did we see you sick or in prison and go to visit you?'

40"The King will reply, 'I tell you the truth, whatever you did for one of the least of these brothers of mine, you did for me.'

41"Then he will say to those on his left, 'Depart from me, you who are cursed, into the eternal fire prepared for the devil and his angels.

OPEN What is the most unusual pet you have had? Have you ever had a sheep or a goat?

STUDY 1. In this parable, where is the action taking place? Who is there? How would you describe the atmosphere in a storybook for children? **2.** Who are the two kinds of people? Who do they represent? **3.** What are the six tests that will be given each person? For the person who passes, where will he or she go? For the person who does not pass where will he or she go? **4.** For the Pharisees and religious leaders who are listening to this parable, what is the lesson? **5.** How much of the parable is allegorical and how much is prophetic? **6.** What is the lesson for people today? **7.** Which people in your community reach out to the hungry, thirsty, homeless, needy, sick and imprisoned? **8.** What church is really "being there" for these people?

25:26 You wicked, lazy servant! When we look at what the parable was teaching, neglecting to properly use the talents and gifts God has given is *both* lazy and wicked, because it is an abuse of God's gift. Even more specifically, Jesus may have had in mind the special entrustment God had given to Israel of his Word. Instead of multiplying it and spreading it to other people and other nations, they "hid it in the ground" and kept it to themselves.

25:31 he will sit on his throne. Because the Son of Man is sitting on his throne, the implication is that there is going to be a judgment.

25:32 All the nations. This is a universal, *worldwide judgment. While modern usage of the word "nation" typically* implies a political entity, here it refers to various races and ethnic groups. All people will be present at this judgment scene. **separates the sheep from the goats.** These animals grazed in common herds during the day. At night, however, they were separated because the goats needed to be in shelters to be protected from the elements.

25:34 In this verse, the Son of Man (v. 31) is clearly identified as God's Son and the King of God's kingdom. **you who are blessed.** The Beatitudes (5:3–12) outline the qualities of those people who receive God's favor. **prepared for you since the creation of the world.** Contrast this with the punishment of the wicked in the eternal fire "prepared for the devil and his angels" (v. 41).

25:36 in prison. Probably those (like *John the Baptist*) who were in prison because they resisted the state out of fidelity to God are in view. Visiting such a prisoner would put the visitor at risk since he or she might be identified as a sympathizer.

25:37 Lord, when did we see you? The righteous did not act in this way because they had some type of insight regarding the spirit of Christ that was in the poor. They simply acted with compassion toward those in need.

25:40 Just as Jesus served the poor and needy (both in a physical and spiritual sense), so he asserts that acts of mercy for the poor and needy are the way he is served in this world. **these brothers of mine.** The point is that the righteous are those who have a heart of compassion for all in need.

25:41 the eternal fire. The idea of hell, a place of eternal punishment by fire, reflects Israel's experience with the valley of Gehenna, a ravine outside Jerusalem where children were once sacrificed to the god Molech (1 Kin. 11:7). Gehenna became a symbol for the place of punishment and spiritual death. **prepared for the devil and**

[42]For I was hungry and you gave me nothing to eat, I was thirsty and you gave me nothing to drink, [43]I was a stranger and you did not invite me in, I needed clothes and you did not clothe me, I was sick and in prison and you did not look after me.'

[44]"They also will answer, 'Lord, when did we see you hungry or thirsty or a stranger or needing clothes or sick or in prison, and did not help you?'

[45]"He will reply, 'I tell you the truth, whatever you did not do for one of the least of these, you did not do for me.'

[46]"Then they will go away to eternal punishment, but the righteous to eternal life."

The Plot Against Jesus

26 When Jesus had finished saying all these things, he said to his disciples, [2]"As you know, the Passover is two days away—and the Son of Man will be handed over to be crucified."

[3]Then the chief priests and the elders of the people assembled in the palace of the high priest, whose name was Caiaphas, [4]and they plotted to arrest Jesus in some sly way and kill him. [5]"But not during the Feast," they said, "or there may be a riot among the people."

Jesus Anointed at Bethany

[6]While Jesus was in Bethany in the home of a man known as Simon the Leper, [7]a woman came to him with an alabaster jar of very expensive perfume, which she poured on his head as he was reclining at the table.

[8]When the disciples saw this, they were indignant. "Why this waste?" they asked. [9]"This perfume could have been sold at a high price and the money given to the poor."

[10]Aware of this, Jesus said to them, "Why are you bothering this woman? She has done a beautiful thing to me. [11]The poor you will always have with you, but you will not always have me. [12]When she poured this perfume on my body, she did it to prepare me for burial.

APPLY 1. When you were really hurting, who reached out to you? **2.** Where are you feeling the tug of God to help broken people today?

OPEN 1. If you had a huge amount of money to spend on a bottle of perfume, what would you buy? **2.** Who would you choose to play Judas in a movie?

STUDY 1. Why is Passover an appropriate time for the events in verses 1-5 to unfold? What is sacrificed as a "sin offering" to postpone the judgment for sin for one year? **2.** How does Jesus meet and enlarge on the meaning of "atonement" (John 1:29)? **3.** At the home of Simon the leper, what happens that allows Jesus a chance to explain again his purpose and mission in life? Do you think the disciples at this late date really understood what Jesus was talking about? **4.** How would you compare the motives of the woman—and the motives of Judas? **5.** Who do you feel sorry for: Caiaphas, the high priest? Judas, the treasurer? The disciples?

---

his angels. The tradition was that Satan led a rebellion of angels against God, and they have all been condemned for it (2 Peter 2:4; Rev. 19:20; 20:10).

25:44 Lord, when did we see you? With this teaching Jesus condemned those who look past the suffering of the world as they seek a detached religiosity. The New Testament is consistent in saying that love of God and love of people, especially people who are in need, must go together (22:34–40; James 2:14–17; 1 John 2:9–11; 4:7–12,19–21).

25:45 whatever you did not do. It is not enough simply to avoid doing bad things—people will be judged also for the good things they neglect to do.

26:2 the Passover. This feast was a celebration of God's deliverance of Israel from Egypt (Ex. 12). Each year during this feast, people celebrated in the hope that before it ended God once again might intervene to save his people.

26:3 the high priest. This was the religious and civic head of the Jews. In earlier times, this was a lifelong, inherited office; but at this point the high priest was appointed (and deposed) at the pleasure of the Roman government. Caiaphas held the office from A.D. 18 to 36.

26:4 they plotted. The religious leadership had already decided to kill Jesus (12:14). Now they are simply seeking a way to do so.

26:5 not during the Feast. During Passover, Jerusalem's population rose from 50,000 to 250,000. Jesus' popularity with the crowds meant he could not be arrested publicly for fear that it might spark a riot which would lead to harsh Roman repression.

26:7 a woman came. A woman would not be present at a meal like this except to serve. Her entrance would have been thought scandalous. **perfume.** Mark 14:3 says this was nard, an expensive aromatic oil extracted from an Indian root. **poured on his head.** Typically, this perfume was used very sparingly and only for special occasions. This was a lavish gesture indicating the high regard this woman had for Jesus. **reclining.** People feasted while lying on low couches arranged around a table.

26:12 to prepare me for burial. Jesus uses the situation to remind the disciples of what lies ahead. Normally the bodies of the dead were anointed with oil, but the nature of Jesus' death would mean he would be entombed without such care.

APPLY 1. When did you come to the place that you completely understood the "Passover" for yourself? **2.** When it comes to giving, when are you extravagant and when are you careful?

13I tell you the truth, wherever this gospel is preached throughout the
world, what she has done will also be told, in memory of her."

Judas Agrees to Betray Jesus

14Then one of the Twelve—the one called Judas Iscariot—went to
the chief priests 15and asked, "What are you willing to give me if I
hand him over to you?" So they counted out for him thirty silver
coins. 16From then on Judas watched for an opportunity to hand him
over.

OPEN When you were growing up, what was the shape of the dining room table? Who did you sit next to? Who served your plate? Who did the talking?

STUDY 1. What do you know about the Feast of Unleavened Bread (Ex. 12:14–28)? **2.** Why do you think Jesus was so secretive about his arrangements for the Passover meal? **3.** In what stages does Jesus reveal his betrayer (vv. 21,23,25)? **4.** How did Jesus reinterpret the meaning of the bread and the wine? Do you think the disciples understood this?

APPLY 1. When did you come to the place that you understood the deeper meaning of the Lord's Supper? **2.** If you believe God has forgiven you for all the stupid things you have done, when are you going to forgive yourself?

The Lord's Supper

17On the first day of the Feast of Unleavened Bread, the disciples
came to Jesus and asked, "Where do you want us to make preparations for you to eat the Passover?"
18He replied, "Go into the city to a certain man and tell him, 'The
Teacher says: My appointed time is near. I am going to celebrate the
Passover with my disciples at your house.'" 19So the disciples did as
Jesus had directed them and prepared the Passover.
20When evening came, Jesus was reclining at the table with the
Twelve. 21And while they were eating, he said, "I tell you the truth,
one of you will betray me."
22They were very sad and began to say to him one after the other,
"Surely not I, Lord?"
23Jesus replied, "The one who has dipped his hand into the bowl
with me will betray me. 24The Son of Man will go just as it is written
about him. But woe to that man who betrays the Son of Man! It would
be better for him if he had not been born."
25Then Judas, the one who would betray him, said, "Surely not I,
Rabbi?"

Jesus answered, "Yes, it is you."[a]
26While they were eating, Jesus took bread, gave thanks and broke
it, and gave it to his disciples, saying, "Take and eat; this is my body."
27Then he took the cup, gave thanks and offered it to them, saying,
"Drink from it, all of you. 28This is my blood of the[b] covenant, which is

[a]25 Or *"You yourself have said it"* [b]28 Some manuscripts *the new*

26:13 what she has done will also be told. Jesus commends the woman's insight into his identity and mission. As she honored him, so she will be honored.

26:15 thirty silver coins. This was not a very large amount (Zech. 11:12).

26:17 On the first day of the Feast of Unleavened Bread. This feast did not officially start until the day after Passover. However, in the first century the day on which the lambs were sacrificed was sometimes referred to as the first day of the Feast of Unleavened Bread.

26:20 When evening came. The Passover could be eaten only after sunset.

26:23 dipped his hand into the bowl with me. To share a meal was a sign of friendship, making the betrayal even more scandalous.

26:24 as it is written about him. Passages such as Isaiah 53:1–6 point to the suffering of God's chosen servant. **But woe to that man.** While the suffering of God's Messiah is part of God's plan, the people involved in that act are responsible for their decisions.

26:25 Yes, it is you. Literally, this is "You have said it." It is an idiomatic way of affirming a statement, but it is a bit more ambiguous than a direct affirmation.

26:26 this is my body. Jesus introduces a new meaning for the Passover bread. While it used to represent God's provision of food for his people while they wandered in the desert after the Exodus, now it is to represent Jesus' body which was brutally treated and nailed to the cross, later to be remembered in the bread at communion.

26:27 cup. Jesus relates the Passover cup of red wine to the renewal of the covenant of God with his people by his sacrificial death.

26:28 covenant. This new covenant is based upon the promise of Jeremiah 31:31–34 that one day God would initiate a covenant which would result in a deep, inner change in people's character and in the forgiveness of sin. This covenant is dependent upon Jesus' sacrificial death, rather than on human effort.

poured out for many for the forgiveness of sins. 29I tell you, I will not
drink of this fruit of the vine from now on until that day when I drink
it anew with you in my Father's kingdom."
30When they had sung a hymn, they went out to the Mount of
Olives.

Jesus Predicts Peter's Denial

31Then Jesus told them, "This very night you will all fall away on account of me, for it is written:

" 'I will strike the shepherd,
  and the sheep of the flock will be scattered.'[a]

32But after I have risen, I will go ahead of you into Galilee."
33Peter replied, "Even if all fall away on account of you, I never
will."
34"I tell you the truth," Jesus answered, "this very night, before the
rooster crows, you will disown me three times."
35But Peter declared, "Even if I have to die with you, I will never disown you." And all the other disciples said the same.

Gethsemane

36Then Jesus went with his disciples to a place called Gethsemane,
and he said to them, "Sit here while I go over there and pray." 37He
took Peter and the two sons of Zebedee along with him, and he began
to be sorrowful and troubled. 38Then he said to them, "My soul is
overwhelmed with sorrow to the point of death. Stay here and keep
watch with me."
39Going a little farther, he fell with his face to the ground and
prayed, "My Father, if it is possible, may this cup be taken from me.
Yet not as I will, but as you will."
40Then he returned to his disciples and found them sleeping.
"Could you men not keep watch with me for one hour?" he asked Peter. 41"Watch and pray so that you will not fall into temptation. The
spirit is willing, but the body is weak."

[a] *31* Zech. 13:7

OPEN Have you ever been told bad news that you refused to believe?

STUDY 1. Who does Peter remind you of in this episode? **2.** Why would Peter boast like this? **3.** If you could put in a good word for Peter, what would you say?

APPLY What does Peter have that makes everybody love and identify with him?

OPEN What was the longest night of your life: Delivering your first child? Waiting up for your teenager? Making a major decision?

STUDY 1. What are the various emotions Jesus must have felt in Gethsemane? What does he ask of his disciples? What does he ask of God? **2.** What is God's will (vv. 39,42)? What model for our prayers does Jesus provide here? **3.** What do you learn about the humanity of Jesus in this story?

APPLY 1. What has been your "Gethsemane"—a place where you really wrestled with God? What was the issue? **2.** Who would

---

26:29 I will not drink. This may mean that Jesus chose to abstain from the fourth Passover cup which was passed around at the close of the meal, indicating that the meal will only be consummated when the kingdom comes in its fullness.

26:33 I never will. It is inconceivable to Peter that he would desert Jesus.

26:34 before the rooster crows. The Romans called the watch from midnight to 3 a.m. "cock crow." Despite Peter's protestations, Jesus asserts that he will deny him three times even before the next morning.

26:36 Gethsemane. This was an olive orchard in an estate at the foot of the Mount of Olives just outside the eastern wall of Jerusalem. The name literally means "an oil press" (for making olive oil).

26:39 prayed. He would have prayed aloud, as was customary for people at the time, so the disciples could hear his prayer as long as they were awake. **My Father.** This was not a title for God that was used in prayer in the first century. It expressed an intimacy that would have been considered inappropriate. **this cup.** In the Old Testament, drinking a cup of bitter wine was often used as a symbol for experiencing God's judgment (Ps. 75:8; Isa. 51:17–22). **Yet not as I will, but as you will.** As the repeated predictions of his death indicate, there was no doubt in Jesus' mind regarding what the Father's will was in this situation. While he pleads that there might be another way, this sentence declares his commitment to follow the Father's lead regardless of the cost (v. 42).

26:40 sleeping. Although the disciples had vowed never to abandon Jesus (v. 35), these three could not even keep themselves awake to be with him.

26:41 To "watch" means to be spiritually alert, lest they fall into the temptation to be unfaithful to God. **The spirit ... the body.** Probably as in Psalm 51:12, the spirit is the human spirit energized by God. The problem is that the disciples allowed their physical condition to dictate their response to an impending spiritual crisis.

you want to "watch and pray" with you next time you face a "Gethsemane"?

OPEN 1. Who do you remember in history as a turncoat? **2.** What is the closest you have come to getting arrested?

STUDY 1. How would you describe the atmosphere when Judas arrived with a "large crowd armed with swords and clubs"? What were they expecting? **2.** How would you describe the response of the disciples? **3.** What does the response of Jesus to Judas, the crowd and the disciples say about the type of Messiah that Jesus is? **4.**What do you think caused the disciples to desert Jesus (v. 56)? **5.** If verse 56 was the end of the story, where would the world be today?

APPLY Knowing yourself, how would you have reacted if you had been with Jesus in this scene?

---

[42]He went away a second time and prayed, "My Father, if it is not
possible for this cup to be taken away unless I drink it, may your will
be done."
[43]When he came back, he again found them sleeping, because their
eyes were heavy. [44]So he left them and went away once more and
prayed the third time, saying the same thing.
[45]Then he returned to the disciples and said to them, "Are you still
sleeping and resting? Look, the hour is near, and the Son of Man is
betrayed into the hands of sinners. [46]Rise, let us go! Here comes my
betrayer!"

Jesus Arrested

[47]While he was still speaking, Judas, one of the Twelve, arrived.
With him was a large crowd armed with swords and clubs, sent from
the chief priests and the elders of the people. [48]Now the betrayer had
arranged a signal with them: "The one I kiss is the man; arrest him."
[49]Going at once to Jesus, Judas said, "Greetings, Rabbi!" and kissed
him.
[50]Jesus replied, "Friend, do what you came for."[a]
Then the men stepped forward, seized Jesus and arrested him.
[51]With that, one of Jesus' companions reached for his sword, drew it
out and struck the servant of the high priest, cutting off his ear.
[52]"Put your sword back in its place," Jesus said to him, "for all who
draw the sword will die by the sword. [53]Do you think I cannot call on
my Father, and he will at once put at my disposal more than twelve
legions of angels? [54]But how then would the Scriptures be fulfilled
that say it must happen in this way?"
[55]At that time Jesus said to the crowd, "Am I leading a rebellion,
that you have come out with swords and clubs to capture me? Every
day I sat in the temple courts teaching, and you did not arrest me.
[56]But this has all taken place that the writings of the prophets might
be fulfilled." Then all the disciples deserted him and fled.

[a]50 Or *"Friend, why have you come?"*

26:45 the hour is near. This is the time of Jesus' death. **into the hands of sinners.** Commonly the religious authorities used this term to describe the mass of Jews (and all Gentiles) who, by virtue of the demands of life, were unable to devote the time to keep all the religious traditions. Here Jesus uses the term to refer to the religious authorities who are on their way to arrest him.

26:50 arrested him. No charge is given. Perhaps it was blasphemy (9:3), violation of the Sabbath (12:2,10,14), or the practice of sorcery (9:34).

26:51 one of Jesus' companions. According to John's Gospel (John *18:10), this was Peter.* **his sword.** That Peter should have a sword is not unusual. Travelers carried them as protection against robbers. **cutting off his ear.** Why he was not seized for this act of aggression is unknown. Luke adds the detail that Jesus immediately healed the man (Luke 22:51), which diffused and disarmed the explosiveness of the whole situation.

26:52 all who draw the sword will die by the sword. Jesus clearly asserts that his kingdom will not come about by the use of force and violence. Jesus will not inaugurate God's kingdom by committing violence but by absorbing it in himself. His disciples are to follow his lead.

26:53 twelve legions of angels. Jesus rebukes his companions; he could resist if he desired. If force was to be used to establish God's kingdom, Jesus would not be relying on the talents of 12 untrained men to do the job! Instead, more than 12 legions of angels could be at his disposal.

26:54 the Scriptures. Jesus is probably referring to Zechariah 13:7: "Strike the shepherd, and the sheep will be scattered" (Mark 14:27). He may also have in mind Isaiah 53:12 or Psalm 41:9.

26:55 Every day. The reason the authorities had not arrested Jesus earlier was because they were fearful of the crowds who supported Jesus. By leading these forces to Jesus in Gethsemane, Judas betrayed him to them at a time when the supportive crowds were not around.

26:56 all the disciples deserted him. This was what Jesus had predicted earlier (v. 31). Their flight may have been the result of confusion as well as fear. They had tried the option of fighting by Jesus' side (v. 51) and Jesus had rebuked them for it.

Before the Sanhedrin

57 Those who had arrested Jesus took him to Caiaphas, the high
priest, where the teachers of the law and the elders had assembled.
58 But Peter followed him at a distance, right up to the courtyard of the
high priest. He entered and sat down with the guards to see the
outcome.
59 The chief priests and the whole Sanhedrin were looking for false
evidence against Jesus so that they could put him to death. 60 But they
did not find any, though many false witnesses came forward.
Finally two came forward 61 and declared, "This fellow said, 'I am
able to destroy the temple of God and rebuild it in three days.' "
62 Then the high priest stood up and said to Jesus, "Are you not going to answer? What is this testimony that these men are bringing
against you?" 63 But Jesus remained silent.
The high priest said to him, "I charge you under oath by the living
God: Tell us if you are the Christ,[a] the Son of God."
64 "Yes, it is as you say," Jesus replied. "But I say to all of you: In the
future you will see the Son of Man sitting at the right hand of the
Mighty One and coming on the clouds of heaven."
65 Then the high priest tore his clothes and said, "He has spoken
blasphemy! Why do we need any more witnesses? Look, now you
have heard the blasphemy. 66 What do you think?"
"He is worthy of death," they answered.
67 Then they spit in his face and struck him with their fists. Others
slapped him 68 and said, "Prophesy to us, Christ. Who hit you?"

[a]63 Or *Messiah*; also in verse 68

OPEN Have you ever been in a court of law or situation where you felt unfairly treated?

STUDY 1. Who is the Sanhedrin (or senate body of elders), and what kind of cases were brought before it (Acts 4:1–22)? **2.** Why take Jesus to the high priest? Why do you think Peter followed? Why would the priests knowingly accept false evidence? Why two witnesses (v. 60; Deut. 19:15)? **3.** What is unusual about Jesus' self-defense? Why did he remain silent? How does he view God's kingdom? **4.** Why would the priests think Jesus was guilty of blasphemy? **5.** What impresses you most about Jesus here?

APPLY 1. Have you had to "defend your faith"? How well did you do? How could you give a better answer for the hope you have (1 Peter 3:15–16)? **2.** How do you know when to keep silent and when to talk about your faith?

26:57 the high priest. The high priest was the spiritual and civic head of Israel. He oversaw the Sanhedrin which was the highest Jewish court, made up of 71 leaders, both priests and laymen. The Sanhedrin was given authority by Rome to rule in matters of religious law.

26:59 false evidence. The Sanhedrin was concerned with trying to find clear legal grounds on which to accuse Jesus of a charge worthy of death. To convict someone of a capital crime required the unanimous testimony of at least two witnesses (Deut. 19:15). Each witness gave testimony individually to the judge in the presence of the accused.

26:61 I am able to destroy the temple of God and rebuild it in three days. Although Matthew does not record it, John's Gospel puts a statement much like this on the lips of Jesus (John 2:19). However, Jesus did not say he would destroy the temple, simply that it would one day be destroyed. In addition, he was referring to the temple of his *body* being destroyed (John 2:21) and being restored after three days, which was very different from how it was understood here. Since it was a capital offense to desecrate or destroy a place of worship, the high priest seized upon this statement as a basis for accusation.

26:63 Jesus remained silent. Given the disposition of the Sanhedrin, no response was made. They had rejected all the clear evidences of Jesus' nature and mission which he had publicly presented all along.

26:63–64 the Christ ... the Son of God ... the Son of Man. These are the three main titles which reveal who Jesus is. The time for secrecy is past. He is the Messiah, God's royal King. Jesus' statement (v. 64) is a combination of Psalm 110:1 and Daniel 7:13–14, passages with strong messianic implications.

26:63 the Christ. The priests, the Zealots, the Pharisees, and other groups within Israel all had different notions of what the Messiah should be and do. To affirm this statement was sure to inflame some group or another who disagreed with the position represented by the speaker.

26:64 Yes, it is as you say. Jesus uses an ambiguous statement that places the responsibility of affirming it on the questioner. **sitting at the right hand.** To sit at the right hand of a sovereign was to be in a place of honor and power.

26:65 tore his clothes. By tearing his clothes, the high priest signaled that he was profoundly disturbed by Jesus' statement. **blasphemy.** This is the act of dishonoring or slandering God. Under the Law, its penalty was death by stoning (Lev. 24:10–16). By claiming to be the Messiah, the Sanhedrin understood Jesus to be dishonoring God.

26:67 spit ... struck ... slapped. These were traditional ways of expressing abhorrence and repudiation for someone (Num. 12:14; Deut. 25:9; Job 30:10; Isa. 50:6). These actions reflected the council's fierce opposition to what Jesus said.

26:68 Prophesy. Mark 14:65 says Jesus was first blindfolded. They are mocking his claim to be the Messiah by taunting him to name who it was that had struck him while he was unable to see.

OPEN Where did you learn to cuss? What stopped you?

STUDY **1.** So far in Matthew, what character traits has Peter exhibited (14:22–36; 15:1–20; 16:13–20; 26:31–45)? How would you graph his emotional pilgrimage? **2.** In this story, what character trait of Peter dominates? **3.** When did Peter realize what was happening?

APPLY **1.** If someone had to graph the ups and downs of your spiritual life, would the graph look like Peter's? **2.** Do you feel that it is okay to share your failures?

OPEN Have you ever wished you could erase words once spoken or written?

STUDY **1.** Why is Judas suddenly seized with remorse? Was he expecting a different outcome? **2.** What does Judas try to do? Why is his request refused? **3.** Both Judas and Peter caved in under pressure, yet history has treated them differently. Why?

APPLY **1.** As you look back over your friends, who comes to mind as someone who started out with great promise and ended up with great disappointment? **2.** What do you learn from Judas?

Peter Disowns Jesus

69 Now Peter was sitting out in the courtyard, and a servant girl came to him. "You also were with Jesus of Galilee," she said.

70 But he denied it before them all. "I don't know what you're talking about," he said.

71 Then he went out to the gateway, where another girl saw him and said to the people there, "This fellow was with Jesus of Nazareth."

72 He denied it again, with an oath: "I don't know the man!"

73 After a little while, those standing there went up to Peter and said, "Surely you are one of them, for your accent gives you away."

74 Then he began to call down curses on himself and he swore to them, "I don't know the man!"

Immediately a rooster crowed. 75 Then Peter remembered the word Jesus had spoken: "Before the rooster crows, you will disown me three times." And he went outside and wept bitterly.

Judas Hangs Himself

27 Early in the morning, all the chief priests and the elders of the people came to the decision to put Jesus to death. 2 They bound him, led him away and handed him over to Pilate, the governor.

3 When Judas, who had betrayed him, saw that Jesus was condemned, he was seized with remorse and returned the thirty silver coins to the chief priests and the elders. 4 "I have sinned," he said, "for I have betrayed innocent blood."

"What is that to us?" they replied. "That's your responsibility."

5 So Judas threw the money into the temple and left. Then he went away and hanged himself.

6 The chief priests picked up the coins and said, "It is against the law to put this into the treasury, since it is blood money." 7 So they decided to use the money to buy the potter's field as a burial place for foreigners. 8 That is why it has been called the Field of Blood to this day. 9 Then what was spoken by Jeremiah the prophet was fulfilled: "They took the thirty silver coins, the price set on him by the people of Israel, 10 and they used them to buy the potter's field, as the Lord commanded me."[a]

[a] 10 See Zech. 11:12,13; Jer. 19:1-13; 32:6-9.

26:74 call down curses on himself. Peter is pronouncing a judgment upon himself if his statement about not knowing Jesus is untrue.

26:75 wept bitterly. Peter's denial and cowardice was all too plain for him. He wept, sure that he had just cursed himself into God's judgment, and because he had denied the Lord he loved.

27:1 Early in the morning. The Roman court began at daybreak, which made it necessary for the Sanhedrin to meet in an all-night session. They were anxious to get a quick conviction before the people found out what they had done. **decision.** Legally, the Sanhedrin had no authority to order the death of Jesus (John 18:31). However, under Roman law, blasphemy was not a capital offense. Consequently, they needed to work out how to present the case to Pilate so as to ensure Jesus' conviction. Their decision was to charge him with high treason.

27:2 Pilate. Pontius Pilate was the fifth procurator of Judea. He served from A.D. 26–36. While the Gospels present him as a fair-minded man, pressured by the Sanhedrin to do its bidding, historians of the time called him an "inflexible, merciless and obstinate" man who was continually ignoring Jewish customs in his harsh leadership.

27:3 seized with remorse. Judas may have gone to the Sanhedrin not so much to get Jesus killed as to initiate the new order of freedom from Rome. Whatever Judas' rationale, he is now "seized with remorse."

27:6 It is against the law. The irony is intense. The priests will not put the money back into the temple treasury since it was defiled by having been used as bounty on a person's life. However, they make no reflection upon the fact that they are the ones who used the money for this purpose.

Jesus Before Pilate

[11]Meanwhile Jesus stood before the governor, and the governor asked him, "Are you the king of the Jews?"

"Yes, it is as you say," Jesus replied.

[12]When he was accused by the chief priests and the elders, he gave no answer. [13]Then Pilate asked him, "Don't you hear the testimony they are bringing against you?" [14]But Jesus made no reply, not even to a single charge—to the great amazement of the governor.

[15]Now it was the governor's custom at the Feast to release a prisoner chosen by the crowd. [16]At that time they had a notorious prisoner, called Barabbas. [17]So when the crowd had gathered, Pilate asked them, "Which one do you want me to release to you: Barabbas, or Jesus who is called Christ?" [18]For he knew it was out of envy that they had handed Jesus over to him.

[19]While Pilate was sitting on the judge's seat, his wife sent him this message: "Don't have anything to do with that innocent man, for I have suffered a great deal today in a dream because of him."

[20]But the chief priests and the elders persuaded the crowd to ask for Barabbas and to have Jesus executed.

[21]"Which of the two do you want me to release to you?" asked the governor.

"Barabbas," they answered.

[22]"What shall I do, then, with Jesus who is called Christ?" Pilate asked.

They all answered, "Crucify him!"

[23]"Why? What crime has he committed?" asked Pilate.

But they shouted all the louder, "Crucify him!"

[24]When Pilate saw that he was getting nowhere, but that instead an uproar was starting, he took water and washed his hands in front of the crowd. "I am innocent of this man's blood," he said. "It is your responsibility!"

[25]All the people answered, "Let his blood be on us and on our children!"

[26]Then he released Barabbas to them. But he had Jesus flogged, and handed him over to be crucified.

The Soldiers Mock Jesus

[27]Then the governor's soldiers took Jesus into the Praetorium and gathered the whole company of soldiers around him. [28]They stripped

OPEN Have you ever appeared before a magistrate or justice of the peace over a ticket violation?

STUDY 1. Who is the governor and why was Jesus brought before this person (26:36, 47,57,59; 27:1)? **2.** What is the charge that the high priest puts before the governor (26:63,65)? How did Jesus respond to the charge? **3.** Did the governor think that Jesus was innocent? What about the governor's wife? **4.** What did the governor come up with to get himself off the hook? How did the chief priests respond? What is so ironic about this? **5.** Who is really on trial here? **6.** How do you feel about the governor? **7.** Who ended up the biggest winner: Pilate? Chief priests? The crowd? Jesus? Barabbas? **8.** How does the story illustrate the meaning of the gospel?

APPLY 1. At what point in your life did you realize that Jesus took your place as a substitute for sin? **2.** If they put you on trial, would there be enough evidence to convict you of being a Christian? **3.** What is the closest you have come to caving into the crowd on an issue that you knew was wrong?

OPEN Have you ever had someone close to you die? How did you handle it?

27:11 Are you the king of the Jews? That Jesus claimed this title is undoubtedly the charge the Sanhedrin brought before Pilate.

27:16 Barabbas. Barabbas was a genuine resistance leader who had led an armed insurrection against Rome. It was probably in relationship to this rebellion that he also had committed murder (Luke 23:19).

27:17 Barabbas, or Jesus who is called Christ? This is more appropriately translated "Jesus Barabbas or Jesus who is called the Messiah" (NRSV). "Barabbas" means "son of the father."

27:18 While Pilate could have simply thrown the charges out of court, John's Gospel hints that the Sanhedrin made a not-too-subtle threat to Pilate that if he should do so they would bring charges to Caesar against him for releasing a man who claimed to be a rival king (John 19:12).

27:24 washed his hands. This was a Jewish custom used as a way to disassociate oneself from a criminal act (Deut. 21:1–9). Since it was not a practice of the Romans, Matthew took special note of this as a way of focusing the responsibility upon the Sanhedrin.

27:26 released Barabbas. The death of Jesus (who is innocent) in the place of Barabbas (who is guilty) is a visual statement on the meaning of substitutionary atonement. **flogged.** This was a terrible punishment. Soldiers would lash a naked and bound prisoner with a leather thong into which pieces of bone and lead had been woven. The flesh would be cut to shreds. In itself, this punishment sometimes led to death due to shock and loss of blood.

STUDY 1. Why were the soldiers so cruel to Jesus in this case? What does this say about their view of Jesus? Of themselves? **2.** Why does Jesus need Simon's help? What does this say about his condition? **3.** Do you think the actual crucifixion story meets the prophecy in Isaiah 53:1-6? **4.** While Jesus is on the cross, three groups of people insult and taunt him. How would you characterize these three groups in today's terms? If you could pardon one group for ignorance, which would it be?

APPLY 1. In your pre-Christian days, what was your favorite excuse for denying the claims of Christ? **2.** Among your non-Christian friends, how do they look at the crucifixion of Jesus?

OPEN 1. What is the saddest funeral you have ever attended? **2.** What is the scariest natural disaster you have been in?

him and put a scarlet robe on him, 29 and then twisted together a crown of thorns and set it on his head. They put a staff in his right hand and knelt in front of him and mocked him. "Hail, king of the Jews!" they said. 30 They spit on him, and took the staff and struck him on the head again and again. 31 After they had mocked him, they took off the robe and put his own clothes on him. Then they led him away to crucify him.

The Crucifixion

32 As they were going out, they met a man from Cyrene, named Simon, and they forced him to carry the cross. 33 They came to a place called Golgotha (which means The Place of the Skull). 34 There they offered Jesus wine to drink, mixed with gall; but after tasting it, he refused to drink it. 35 When they had crucified him, they divided up his clothes by casting lots.[a] 36 And sitting down, they kept watch over him there. 37 Above his head they placed the written charge against him: THIS IS JESUS, THE KING OF THE JEWS. 38 Two robbers were crucified with him, one on his right and one on his left. 39 Those who passed by hurled insults at him, shaking their heads 40 and saying, "You who are going to destroy the temple and build it in three days, save yourself! Come down from the cross, if you are the Son of God!"

41 In the same way the chief priests, the teachers of the law and the elders mocked him. 42 "He saved others," they said, "but he can't save himself! He's the King of Israel! Let him come down now from the cross, and we will believe in him. 43 He trusts in God. Let God rescue him now if he wants him, for he said, 'I am the Son of God.'" 44 In the same way the robbers who were crucified with him also heaped insults on him.

The Death of Jesus

45 From the sixth hour until the ninth hour darkness came over all the land. 46 About the ninth hour Jesus cried out in a loud voice, *"Eloi,*

[a]35 A few late manuscripts *lots that the word spoken by the prophet might be fulfilled: "They divided my garments among themselves and cast lots for my clothing"* (Psalm 22:18)

27:32 Simon. This man was probably a Jew who had come on a pilgrimage to Jerusalem for the Passover feast. Cyrene was a Greek city on the north shore of Africa. **carry the cross.** Typically the prisoner carried the heavy cross-beam to the site of the execution as an "example" to others. However, if the prisoner was beaten too badly to do so, the soldiers leading the prisoner could conscript an onlooker to carry it.

27:33 Golgotha. This is the Aramaic word for a "skull." This was probably a round, bare hillock outside Jerusalem.

27:34 wine ... mixed with gall. It was a custom to offer a pain-deadening narcotic to prisoners about to be killed. Although Mark says the wine was mixed with myrrh (Mark 15:23), Matthew calls it gall (a bitter-tasting substance), which identifies Jesus with the righteous sufferer in Psalm 69:21.

27:35 crucified. Crucifixion was the most feared of all punishments in the first-century world. It was cruel in the extreme and totally degrading. **divided up his clothes.** The clothes of the condemned person belonged to the four soldiers who carried out the crucifixion. This is an important detail for Matthew since it fulfills the prophecy of the suffering of God's righteous servant in Psalm 22:18.

27:37 the written charge. The crime for which the person was being crucified was specified on a whitened board fastened above the criminal.

27:38 robbers. This term was sometimes used for Zealots, the band of fiery nationalists who were committed to the violent overthrow of Rome. While "robbery" per se was not a capital crime, insurrection was.

27:40 Come down from the cross, if you are the Son of God! This taunt is reminiscent of the temptations in 4:1–11. Once again, Jesus is being tempted to exercise his power for his own benefit in a way that would be contrary to God's plan.

27:42 He saved others ... but he can't save himself! It is precisely because Jesus is saving others through his death that his own life is forfeit.

27:45 the sixth hour. This is noontime.

27:46 This cry has the exact words of Psalm 22:1. While Jesus was bearing the sins of all people thorughout all the ages, God withdrew from him. He ulti-

Eloi,[a] *lama sabachthani?"*—which means, "My God, my God, why
have you forsaken me?"[b]
47When some of those standing there heard this, they said, "He's
calling Elijah."
48Immediately one of them ran and got a sponge. He filled it with
wine vinegar, put it on a stick, and offered it to Jesus to drink. 49The
rest said, "Now leave him alone. Let's see if Elijah comes to save
him."
50And when Jesus had cried out again in a loud voice, he gave up
his spirit.
51At that moment the curtain of the temple was torn in two from
top to bottom. The earth shook and the rocks split. 52The tombs
broke open and the bodies of many holy people who had died were
raised to life. 53They came out of the tombs, and after Jesus' resurrection they went into the holy city and appeared to many people.
54When the centurion and those with him who were guarding Jesus
saw the earthquake and all that had happened, they were terrified,
and exclaimed, "Surely he was the Son[c] of God!"
55Many women were there, watching from a distance. They had
followed Jesus from Galilee to care for his needs. 56Among them were
Mary Magdalene, Mary the mother of James and Joses, and the
mother of Zebedee's sons.

The Burial of Jesus

57As evening approached, there came a rich man from Arimathea,
named Joseph, who had himself become a disciple of Jesus. 58Going
to Pilate, he asked for Jesus' body, and Pilate ordered that it be given
to him. 59Joseph took the body, wrapped it in a clean linen cloth,
60and placed it in his own new tomb that he had cut out of the rock.
He rolled a big stone in front of the entrance to the tomb and went
away. 61Mary Magdalene and the other Mary were sitting there opposite the tomb.

[a]46 Some manuscripts *Eli, Eli* [b]46 Psalm 22:1 [c]54 Or *a son*

STUDY 1. What is symbolic about darkness coming over the whole land? **2.** What do you think was going on inside of Jesus when he cried out (v. 46)? Why would God forsake his own son? **3.** When Jesus died, what happened to the veil in the temple? What is the significance of this? **4.** How do you explain the earthquake and the resurrection of those who had been buried? **5.** How do the centurion and guards react to the situation? **6.** Why are the women present and not the men?

APPLY 1. When did the death of Jesus start making sense to you? **2.** How much does the death of Jesus affect the way you live your life today: A whole lot? A little bit? Sorry you were asked?

OPEN What kind of burial would you like?

STUDY 1. Why would they be in a big hurry to bury Jesus? **2.** In requesting the body, what risk was Joseph taking? **3.** Why is it important to note that Mary Magdalene and the other Mary saw the exact place where Jesus was buried? **4.** Why would the chief priests and Pharisees request Pilate to place guards at the tomb? What would

mately experiences God's deliverance and is resurrected to life giving all believers new life (Ps. 22:19–31).

27:47-49 There was a widespread Jewish belief that the prophet Elijah would help righteous people in great distress. Some of the onlookers may have wondered if a miraculous deliverance like this might be the vindication of Jesus, but nothing of that sort happened.

27:50 a loud voice. Generally a victim of crucifixion would be exhausted and unconscious at the point of death. While Jesus' cry reveals his agony, it is likely from the description of the strange incidents in verses 51–53 that it is a cry of victory. Through his death Jesus absorbs the sin of the world and unleashes the power of God to initiate a new day when the dead shall live (Ezek. 37).

27:51 curtain of the temple was torn in two. Probably this was the curtain in the temple stood between the people and God. Only the high priest could go behind the curtain into God's presence. Jesus' death has opened the way for people to freely enter the presence of God (Heb. 10:19–20). **The earth shook and the rocks split.** Jewish thought held that at the end of the age the Mount of Olives would split in two and the righteous dead would emerge to live forever. Earthquakes were also seen as signs of God's judgment. They are referred to often in the Old Testament as a metaphor for political or social events that have a major effect upon God's people, such as the conquest of Babylon by Persia (Hab. 3:9–10).

27:54 Surely he was the Son of God! In Matthew's Gospel, Jesus' life begins (2:1–12) and ends with Gentiles proclaiming faith in who he was. Luke records it this way: "Surely this was a righteous man" (Luke 23:47).

27:55 Many women. Mary Magdalene was from the fishing village of Magdala on the west coast of Galilee (Luke 8:2). The other Mary had well-known sons in the early church. Zebedee's wife was probably Salome, the mother of James and John. In contrast to these women, all the male disciples had fled.

27:59 wrapped it in a clean linen cloth. Because it was almost the Sabbath, there was no time to thoroughly anoint the body with spices as would be typically done.

27:60 Isaiah 53:9 said God's servant would be laid to rest in the tomb of a rich man.

happen to the guards if Jesus' body disappeared?

APPLY 1. Who has been the Joseph of Arimathea in your experience—who spoke up for Jesus at great risk to their reputation? 2. What risk have you taken for your faith?

OPEN 1. What do you like to do first thing on a Sunday morning? 2. Of "all the news that's fit to print," what section of the newspaper do you read first?

STUDY 1. How would the women know where Jesus was buried? When they got there, what did they find? 2. What does the appearance of the angel remind you of? 3. What is amusing about women being the first to discover the resurrection? On their way to tell the disciples the good news, what happened? 4. How did the chief priests handle the news of the resurrection?

The Guard at the Tomb

62 The next day, the one after Preparation Day, the chief priests and
the Pharisees went to Pilate. 63 "Sir," they said, "we remember that
while he was still alive that deceiver said, 'After three days I will rise
again.' 64 So give the order for the tomb to be made secure until the
third day. Otherwise, his disciples may come and steal the body and
tell the people that he has been raised from the dead. This last deception will be worse than the first."

65 "Take a guard," Pilate answered. "Go, make the tomb as secure as
you know how." 66 So they went and made the tomb secure by putting
a seal on the stone and posting the guard.

The Resurrection

28 After the Sabbath, at dawn on the first day of the week, Mary
Magdalene and the other Mary went to look at the tomb.
2 There was a violent earthquake, for an angel of the Lord came
down from heaven and, going to the tomb, rolled back the stone and sat
on it. 3 His appearance was like lightning, and his clothes were white as
snow. 4 The guards were so afraid of him that they shook and became
like dead men.

5 The angel said to the women, "Do not be afraid, for I know that you
are looking for Jesus, who was crucified. 6 He is not here; he has risen,
just as he said. Come and see the place where he lay. 7 Then go quickly
and tell his disciples: 'He has risen from the dead and is going ahead of
you into Galilee. There you will see him.' Now I have told you."
8 So the women hurried away from the tomb, afraid yet filled with

---

27:62 The next day. Jesus died on Friday about 3 p.m. The Sabbath began at 6 p.m., after which no work could be done. Yet it was on this day that the Sanhedrin met with Pilate in violation of their own tradition.

27:66 a seal. This was the insignia of Pilate. It would be a capital offense to remove the stone without Pilate's approval. The seal and the guard represent the most powerful human forces available to keep Jesus' body in the tomb.

28:1 at dawn on the first day of the week. The Sabbath was considered over at 6 p.m. on Saturday. This scene takes place early on Sunday morning. This is why Christians developed the tradition of worshiping on Sunday instead of on the Sabbath (Saturday). **Mary Magdalene and the other Mary.** While some of the Gospels mention other women who went to the tomb, all four Gospels place Mary Magdalene in a prominent role. Mark mentions that the women brought aromatic oils to anoint the body, not so much to preserve it as *to honor it (much like people today would* put flowers on a grave).

28:2 earthquake. Earthquakes were often associated with manifestations of God's power (Hab. 3:6). **the stone.** A tomb like this was cut out of the side of a hill. A large disc-shaped stone was set in a groove so that it could be fairly easily rolled down to the opening to close it off. However, once in place it would have been very difficult for people to push it back up the incline.

28:3 lightning ... white as snow. Brilliant, radiant light is often associated with appearances of God in the Old Testament. The angel reflects the glory of God.

28:5 Do not be afraid. This is a standard reply of an angel to the people to whom the angel is sent (Dan. 10:12; Luke 1:12,30; 2:10).

28:6 he has risen. The phrase literally reads "he has been raised," showing that God is the one who accomplished this great act. Jesus' resurrection demonstrates that the cry of the centurion was accurate (27:54) **Come and see the place where he lay.** Typically such tombs had a large antechamber, with a small two-foot-high doorway at the back which led into the six- or seven-foot burial chamber proper. The stone was rolled away, not so that the resurrected Jesus could leave the tomb (he was already gone), but so that his disciples could see that it was empty (John 20:8). The words "come and see" invite verification by people who would be naturally skeptical (John 1:46).

28:7 go ... tell. Under Jewish law, women were not considered reliable witnesses. That they were the first to know of Jesus' resurrection was somewhat of an embarrassment to the early followers of Christ (Luke 24:11,22–24), hence reinforcing that this detail is historically accurate. (They certainly would not have invented the story this way!) **his disciples.** They may have abandoned Jesus but he did not abandon them! **into Galilee.** Jesus said he would meet them again in Galilee (26:32). The ministry of Jesus and the Twelve began in Galilee and now they are directed back there to meet the risen Lord.

28:8 afraid yet filled with joy. This stands in contrast to Mark's Gospel which ends with the statement that the women "said nothing to anyone, because they were afraid" (Mark 16:8). They were probably frightened by the appearance of the angel, as well as by

joy, and ran to tell his disciples. [9]Suddenly Jesus met them. "Greetings," he said. They came to him, clasped his feet and worshiped him.
[10]Then Jesus said to them, "Do not be afraid. Go and tell my brothers
to go to Galilee; there they will see me."

The Guards' Report

[11]While the women were on their way, some of the guards went
into the city and reported to the chief priests everything that had happened. [12]When the chief priests had met with the elders and devised a
plan, they gave the soldiers a large sum of money, [13]telling them,
"You are to say, 'His disciples came during the night and stole him
away while we were asleep.' [14]If this report gets to the governor, we
will satisfy him and keep you out of trouble." [15]So the soldiers took
the money and did as they were instructed. And this story has been
widely circulated among the Jews to this very day.

The Great Commission

[16]Then the eleven disciples went to Galilee, to the mountain where
Jesus had told them to go. [17]When they saw him, they worshiped him;
but some doubted. [18]Then Jesus came to them and said, "All authority
in heaven and on earth has been given to me. [19]Therefore go and

5. Why would Jesus want the disciples to go back to Galilee? **6.** Jesus told his disciples several times what would happen (16:21; 17:22). Do you think the disciples realized what was happening? **7.** How important is it to your faith that the tomb is empty (1 Cor. 15:12-19)? **8.** How would you answer the arguments that: (a) the disciples stole the body; (b) the cool of the tomb revived Jesus and/or (c) the disciples made up this tale of the resurrection? **9.** What is the central command that Jesus gives the disciples? How are they to carry it out?

APPLY 1. When did the reality of the resurrection "dawn" upon you? Were you more of a quick believer or an honest skeptic? **2.** How much has the resurrection of Jesus affected the way you look at life today: A whole lot? A little? Sorry you were asked?

---

the prospect of telling this unbelievable story to skeptical men. It was, however, the joy, the hope, that helped them move past this and share what they had seen.

28:9 Jesus met them. While it differs in details, John records a similar appearance of Jesus to Mary Magdalene (John 20:16–17). **worshiped him.** It is significant that it is twice mentioned after the Resurrection that people worshiped Jesus (v. 17). As Paul wrote, the Resurrection was a demonstration of God's power affirming Jesus as the Son of God (Rom. 1:4).

28:12 The Sanhedrin bought off the guards so that they would not tell what really happened.

28:13 You are to say. While verses 19–20 tell of Jesus' commission to his disciples, this is the Sanhedrin's commission to the guards. **His disciples ... stole him away while we were asleep.** This attempt at "damage control" was weak. The very reason the guards were posted was to keep the disciples from being able to steal the body and concoct a story about resurrection. From a long-term perspective, it would be hard to believe that the disciples who had stolen Jesus' body—and hence knew that the Resurrection was a hoax—would then go on to die for their faith, often in painful ways.

28:14 If this report gets to the governor. For a Roman guard to fall asleep on duty was an offense meriting execution. The Sanhedrin hopes Pilate will simply not find out about what happened. However, if the story they circulate reaches his ears, the Sanhedrin will simply bribe him to forget about punishing the soldiers.

28:15 this story has been widely circulated ... to this very day. It is assumed that this Gospel was written many years after this all took place.

28:16 to the mountain. Mountains were the places in times past where God revealed himself in special ways to the leaders of Israel, such as when he revealed himself to Moses in Exodus 24 and to Elijah in 1 Kings 19.

28:17 some doubted. So stupendous, and without precedent is the resurrection of Jesus that right from the beginning his disciples had difficulty accepting it. When the women reported what had happened at the tomb, the Eleven said that it sounded like nonsense (Luke 24:9–11). After 10 of the disciples (all but Thomas) met the resurrected Jesus and believed (Luke 24:36–48), Thomas still doubted (John 20:24–29). Here, even while worshiping the resurrected Jesus, there is still some doubt.

28:18–20 This is what has been called the Great Commission. Because all authority in heaven and earth now belongs to Jesus, he sends his disciples to spread his message everywhere with the promise that he himself is with them to the end of time.

28:18 All authority in heaven and on earth has been given to me. This is the meaning of the statement "Jesus is Lord." Since there is no power greater than his (Rom. 8:38–39; Phil. 2:9–11; Col. 1:15–20), there is no other loyalty to which his disciples can give their absolute allegiance.

28:19 Therefore. In light of Jesus' authority, he sends his people on a mission. **go and make disciples.** Literally, this is "as you are going, make disciples." **of all nations.** There are no geographic, racial, ethnic or national realms that are outside of the authority and concern of Jesus. **baptizing them.** Baptism was a sign of discipleship and faith. **in the name of the Father and of the Son and of the Holy Spirit.** This is a clear Trinitarian formula. While the doctrine of the Trinity was not clearly articulated and defined until the third century, the roots of its teaching are clearly seen here. There is one name (or character) that defines the triune God.

make disciples of all nations, baptizing them in[a] the name of the Father and of the Son and of the Holy Spirit, [20]and teaching them to obey everything I have commanded you. And surely I am with you always, to the very end of the age."

[a]*19* Or *into*; see Acts 8:16; 19:5; Romans 6:3; 1 Cor. 1:13; 10:2 and Gal. 3:27.

28:20 teaching them to obey everything I have commanded you. The stress here is on the ethical dimensions of Christian living. Discipleship is practicing the way of life advocated and exemplified by one's master. **I am with you always.** This is the climactic promise of the new covenant. The presence of God with his people was always the goal toward which Israel looked under the old covenant. In Jesus, that presence is assured through the indwelling of Christ's Spirit (John 14:16–17). **to the very end of the age.** This covers all time until the return of Christ when the new heaven and the new earth will be revealed.

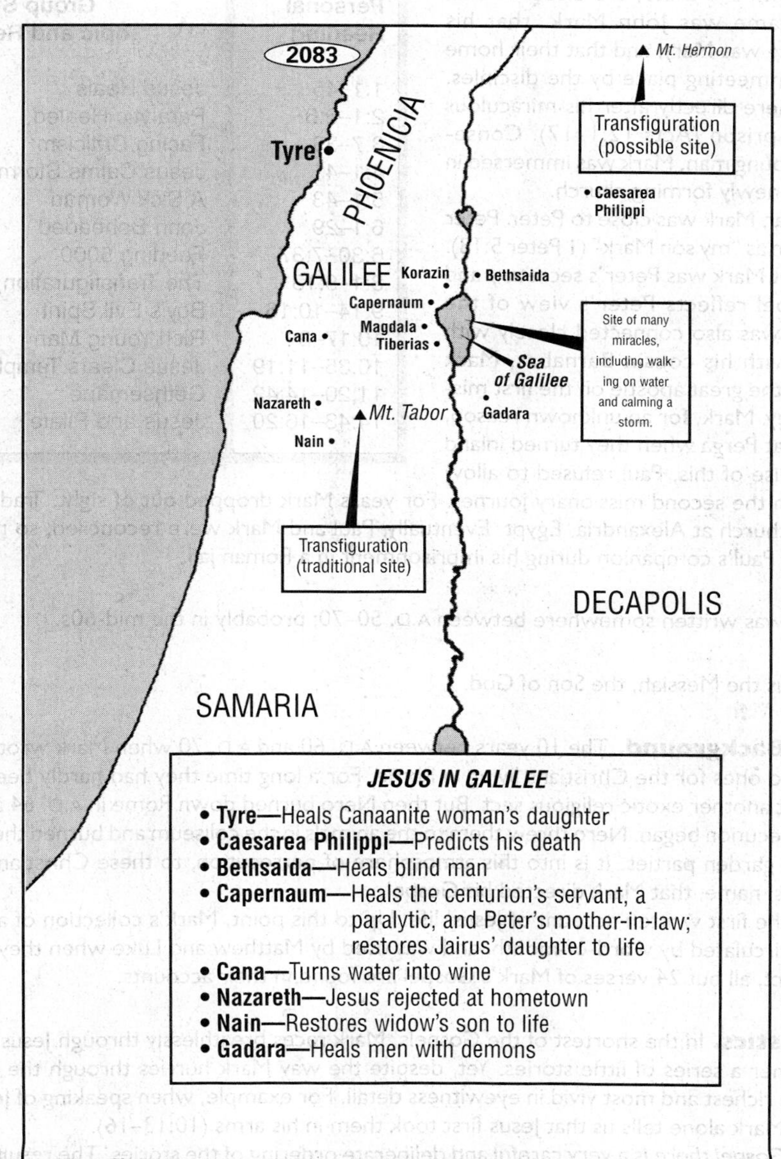
2083
PHOENICIA
Tyre
Mt. Hermon
Transfiguration
(possible site)
Caesarea
Philippi
GALILEE
Korazin
Bethsaida
Capernaum
Magdala
Tiberias
Cana
Sea
of Galilee
Site of many
miracles,
including walk-
ing on water
and calming a
storm.
Nazareth
Mt. Tabor
Gadara
Nain
Transfiguration
(traditional site)
DECAPOLIS
SAMARIA
JESUS IN GALILEE
• Tyre—Heals Canaanite woman's daughter
• Caesarea Philippi—Predicts his death
• Bethsaida—Heals blind man
• Capernaum—Heals the centurion's servant, a paralytic, and Peter's mother-in-law; restores Jairus' daughter to life
• Cana—Turns water into wine
• Nazareth—Jesus rejected at hometown
• Nain—Restores widow's son to life
• Gadara—Heals men with demons

In Mark's Gospel there is a very careful and deliberate ordering of the stories. The result is a skillfully crafted outline. He had to use the stories everyone knew in the way they knew them. He could not alter them. He was merely the chronicler of the tradition, not the creator of it. The church would not have used his work if it contained questionable tales or if he had mistold stories.

Mark does not put his stories in chronological order as we might expect, given the way history is written today (though overall there is a rough chronology to the story). Instead, he groups his stories thematically. Mark uses several themes simultaneously. For one thing, it is clear that he has structured his story geographically. Jesus' ministry begins to the north in Galilee and then he moves down to

Mark

Personal Reading	Group Study Topic and Reading	
1:1–45	Jesus Heals	1:1–29
2:1–3:6	Paralytic Healed	2:1–12
3:7–35	Facing Criticism	3:20–35
4:1–41	Jesus Calms Storm	4:35–41
5:1–43	A Sick Woman	5:24–34
6:1–29	John Beheaded	6:14–29
6:30–7:37	Feeding 5000	6:30–44
8:1–9:13	The Transfiguration	9:2–13
9:14–10:16	Boy's Evil Spirit	9:14–29
10:17–34	Rich Young Man	10:17–31
10:35–11:19	Jesus Clears Temple	11:12–19
11:20–14:42	Gethsemane	14:32–42
14:43–16:20	Jesus and Pilate	15:1–15

Author. From the Bible, we discover that Mark's full name was John Mark, that his mother's name was Mary, and that their home was used as a meeting place by the disciples. Peter went there directly after his miraculous release from prison (Acts 12:1–17). Consequently, as a young man, Mark was immersed in the life of the newly forming church.

In particular, Mark was close to Peter. Peter referred to him as "my son Mark" (1 Peter 5:13). Many hold that Mark was Peter's secretary and that his Gospel reflects Peter's view of the events. Mark was also connected closely with Paul. Along with his cousin Barnabas, Mark accompanied the great apostle on the first missionary journey. Mark, for an unknown reason, left the party at Perga when they turned inland to Asia. Because of this, Paul refused to allow Mark to go on the second missionary journey. For years Mark dropped out of sight. Tradition says he founded the church at Alexandria, Egypt. Eventually, Paul and Mark were reconciled, so much so that Mark became Paul's companion during his imprisonment in a Roman jail.

Date. Mark was written somewhere between A.D. 50–70; probably in the mid-60s.

Theme. Jesus the Messiah, the Son of God.

Historical Background. The 10 years between A.D. 60 and A.D. 70 when Mark wrote his Gospel were not good ones for the Christians living in Rome. For a long time they had hardly been noticed—they were just another exotic religious sect. But then Nero burned down Rome in A.D. 64 and an era of Christian persecution began. Nero threw them to the animals in the coliseum and burned them as human torches at his garden parties. It is into this atmosphere of persecution, to these Christians who were dying for Jesus' name, that Mark directed his Gospel.

This was the first written account of Jesus' life. Up to this point, Mark's collection of accounts had been widely circulated by word-of-mouth, and was used by Matthew and Luke when they wrote their Gospels. In fact, all but 24 verses of Mark's Gospel are found in their accounts.

Characteristics. In the shortest of the Gospels, Mark races breathlessly through Jesus' life by connecting together a series of little stories. Yet, despite the way Mark hurries through the material, his account is the richest and most vivid in eyewitness detail. For example, when speaking of Jesus blessing the children, Mark alone tells us that Jesus first took them in his arms (10:13–16).

In Mark's Gospel there is a very careful and deliberate ordering of the stories. The result is a skillfully crafted outline. He had to use the stories everyone knew in the way they knew them. He could not alter them. He was merely the chronicler of the tradition, not the creator of it. The church would not have used his work if it contained questionable tales or if he had mistold stories.

Mark does not put his stories *in chronological order* as we might expect, given the way history is written today (though overall there is a rough chronology to the story). Instead, he groups his stories thematically. Mark uses several themes, simultaneously. For one thing, it is clear that he has structured his story geographically. Jesus' ministry begins to the north in Galilee and then he moves down to

Jerusalem, where he is finally killed. Mark also structures the story in terms of Jesus' unfolding ministry: Preparation, proclamation and completion. There is also an unfolding vision of who Jesus is. In broad terms, the first half of the book focuses on the discovery of Jesus as the Messiah, and the second half on the discovery of Jesus as the Son of God. In terms of the disciples' growing awareness, they move from experiencing Jesus as an exceptional rabbi, to seeing him as a man of power, and then as the healer of hardened hearts. After Caesarea Philippi and their realization that he is the Messiah, they next know him as a teacher. In Jerusalem during the final week of his life, they come to realize that he is the Son of God.

John the Baptist Prepares the Way

1 The beginning of the gospel about Jesus Christ, the Son of God.[a]
2 It is written in Isaiah the prophet:

"I will send my messenger ahead of you,
who will prepare your way"[b]—
3 "a voice of one calling in the desert,
'Prepare the way for the Lord,
make straight paths for him.' "[c]

4 And so John came, baptizing in the desert region and preaching a
baptism of repentance for the forgiveness of sins. 5 The whole Judean
countryside and all the people of Jerusalem went out to him. Confessing their sins, they were baptized by him in the Jordan River.
6 John wore clothing made of camel's hair, with a leather belt around
his waist, and he ate locusts and wild honey. 7 And this was his message: "After me will come one more powerful than I, the thongs of
whose sandals I am not worthy to stoop down and untie. 8 I baptize
you with[d] water, but he will baptize you with the Holy Spirit."

[a] 1 Some manuscripts do not have *the Son of God.* [b] 2 Mal. 3:1 [c] 3 Isaiah 40:3 [d] 8 Or *in*

OPEN 1. When the mail comes, what do you open and read first? **2.** How would you like locusts and honey for hors d'oeures?

STUDY 1. How would you like to have John (the Baptist) for your spiritual leader? **2.** Why is John's ministry so popular (vv. 4–5)? What is it about John and his preaching that attracted crowds from all over? **3.** Why is John the Baptist so important to the story of Jesus? How well do you think he fulfilled Isaiah's prophecy (vv. 2–3)? **4.** What purpose do you see in Jesus' baptism and in his temptation? How would these events prepare Jesus for his public ministry? **5.** Why do you think the Spirit sent Jesus into the desert to be tempted? What did he learn?

APPLY 1. Who was the John the Baptist who prepared the way for you to meet Jesus? **2.** What

1:1 gospel. Literally, "good news." At this time, this word was used to describe the birth of a new king or to announce a great military victory. **the Son of God.** In the Old Testament this term was used to describe angels and divine figures (Dan. 3:25) as well as Israel's kings (Ps. 2:7) as figures who exercised a god-like authority over the people. In the New Testament, the phrase came to identify Jesus' divine nature as the One who is fully God.

1:3 make straight paths for him. When a king or royal figure was planning to visit or pass through a town, a messenger was sent ahead of the royal entourage so that the towns along the way could get things ready for his coming, literally straightening and smoothing the roads. In this context, making straight paths for the Lord implies repentance from sin (v. 15).

1:4 And so John came. The promised messenger turns out to be John the Baptist who spread the message of repentance and preparation. **baptizing.** When Gentiles converted to Judaism they were required to bathe in a river as part of the ceremony. They believed that this signified that their sins had been washed away. **the desert region.** This was the term used for a particular area in Israel located in the lower Jordan Valley between central Judea and the Dead Sea. **a baptism of repentance.** Their washing with water represented the removal of their sins and a change of heart and action. **forgiveness of sins.** Sin is a moral debt owed to God for violating God's will and nature.

1:5 The whole Judean countryside. Mark uses hyperbole (literally, "all the Judean country") to show John's popularity. **all the people of Jerusalem.** It was a difficult 20-mile trip from Jerusalem to where John was baptizing, and yet the crowds came. **the Jordan River.** John's ministry of baptism had a special meaning in this particular river which had an important place in Israel's history. After the exodus from Egypt, it was the miraculous crossing of this river that brought the people of Israel into the land God promised them (Josh. 3).

1:6 camel's hair ... leather belt. This description of John's clothes and food, parallel to that found in 2 Kings 1:8 which describes what the prophet Elijah wore, is meant to identify John as the prophet who came in the spirit and power of Elijah. **locusts and wild honey.** The locusts he ate could have been either insects (Lev. 11:22–23) or a kind of bean from the locust tree. Honey could refer either to what bees produce or to the sap of a certain tree. In either case, this was the food eaten by the poorest of people.

1:8 baptize you ... with the Holy Spirit. This dramatic promise summed up all the hopes the people of Israel had for their future. It was the time when God's reign would break into history for all the world to see. The pouring out of the Spirit was a community event, not

is the closest you have come to going through a time of testing like this? What did you learn from this experience? **3.** Do you need to go away again to recharge your spiritual batteries?

OPEN Where did you go the first time you left home?

STUDY 1. What is the "good news" (v. 15)? **2.** What is it about fishermen that makes for good disciples? Do you think Jesus should have gone to the theological school in Jerusalem to pick his disciples?

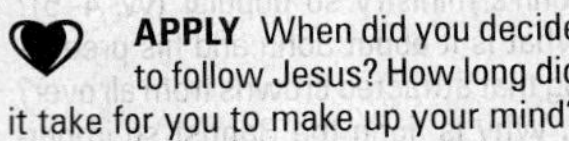

APPLY When did you decide to follow Jesus? How long did it take for you to make up your mind?

OPEN Who was one of your best teachers? What made this teacher so special?

The Baptism and Temptation of Jesus

9At that time Jesus came from Nazareth in Galilee and was baptized
by John in the Jordan. 10As Jesus was coming up out of the water, he
saw heaven being torn open and the Spirit descending on him like a
dove. 11And a voice came from heaven: "You are my Son, whom I love;
with you I am well pleased."
12At once the Spirit sent him out into the desert, 13and he was in the
desert forty days, being tempted by Satan. He was with the wild animals, and angels attended him.

The Calling of the First Disciples

14After John was put in prison, Jesus went into Galilee, proclaiming
the good news of God. 15"The time has come," he said. "The kingdom
of God is near. Repent and believe the good news!"
16As Jesus walked beside the Sea of Galilee, he saw Simon and his
brother Andrew casting a net into the lake, for they were fishermen.
17"Come, follow me," Jesus said, "and I will make you fishers of men."
18At once they left their nets and followed him.
19When he had gone a little farther, he saw James son of Zebedee
and his brother John in a boat, preparing their nets. 20Without delay
he called them, and they left their father Zebedee in the boat with the hired men and followed him.

Jesus Drives Out an Evil Spirit

21They went to Capernaum, and when the Sabbath came, Jesus
went into the synagogue and began to teach. 22The people were

---

simply a personal one. This day would occur when the Messiah came. It was this expectation that moved people to respond so powerfully to John's message.

1:9 At that time Jesus came. In the midst of this supercharged atmosphere—one foretold by Old Testament prophets (vv. 2–3), prepared by a New Testament prophet (vv. 4,6–7), and witnessed by the expectant crowds (v. 5)—Jesus starts his ministry. **baptized.** By allowing himself to be baptized, Jesus identified with the people of Israel and with their sin (though he himself was without sin—1 Peter 2:22), prefiguring his death for sin a few years hence.

1:10 heaven being torn open and the Spirit descending upon him like a dove. This is the divine confirmation of Jesus' ministry as the bearer of the Spirit sent by God (Isa. 61:1–3).

1:11 a voice. These words from God are directed to Jesus, not to the crowds. They are an unqualified affirmation of him as he is about to launch his ministry.

1:12 the Spirit sent him. The same Spirit who had come to Jesus in such affirming power now sends him forth to this time of testing. **desert.** Literally, "wilderness." Jesus underwent an extreme perod of testing and temptation for him to experience the difficulties of humanity.

1:13 forty days. It is possible that this is a symbolic reference to the 40 years Israel spent in the wilderness. The reason for their experience was unbelief where Jesus voluntarily entered his trial. **wild animals.** For the Christians to whom this letter was written (who were facing wild beasts in the Roman Coliseum), it must have been comforting to know that Jesus had also faced such beasts and was sustained by angels.

1:14 After John was put in prison. There is a gap of perhaps a year between the incidents recorded in verses 9–13 and those recorded here. The story of John's imprisonment is told in 6:17–29. **Galilee.** This was the northern province of Palestine. Those living in Jerusalem considered Galilee a cultural backwater populated by unsophisticated, uneducated country folk who spoke with an accent.

1:15 The time has come. That event—long expected and desired—now came to pass in Israel. It was the fullness of time and the Messiah entered history. **kingdom of God.** The Jews were God's special people. He alone was their King. Yet they were under the domination of Rome. Caesar functioned as their king. They were confident that one day the Messiah would rescue them. **believe.** While repentance is a turning away from sin to pursue God, to believe means to entrust oneself to God, counting on God to be true to his promises. The object of belief is the "good news" that in Jesus the kingdom of God has arrived.

1:20 the hired men. James and John came from a middle-class family. Their father Zebedee had men working for him and a boat with which to trawl the lake for fish. (Luke 5:3,10, says that Simon also had a fishing boat.)

1:21 Capernaum. A town on the north end of the Sea of Galilee, three miles west of the River Jordan. It was a center of the fishing industry and the site of a custom's post. **synagogue.** Synagogues were run by lay committees with no professional leaders. Anyone could speak as long as he had permission from the leaders.

amazed at his teaching, because he taught them as one who had
authority, not as the teachers of the law. 23Just then a man in their
synagogue who was possessed by an evil[a] spirit cried out, 24"What do
you want with us, Jesus of Nazareth? Have you come to destroy us? I
know who you are—the Holy One of God!"
25"Be quiet!" said Jesus sternly. "Come out of him!" 26The evil spirit
shook the man violently and came out of him with a shriek.
27The people were all so amazed that they asked each other, "What
is this? A new teaching—and with authority! He even gives orders to
evil spirits and they obey him." 28News about him spread quickly over
the whole region of Galilee.

Jesus Heals Many

29As soon as they left the synagogue, they went with James and
John to the home of Simon and Andrew. 30Simon's mother-in-law
was in bed with a fever, and they told Jesus about her. 31So he went to
her, took her hand and helped her up. The fever left her and she began to wait on them.
32That evening after sunset the people brought to Jesus all the sick
and demon-possessed. 33The whole town gathered at the door, 34and
Jesus healed many who had various diseases. He also drove out many
demons, but he would not let the demons speak because they knew
who he was.

Jesus Prays in a Solitary Place

35Very early in the morning, while it was still dark, Jesus got up, left
the house and went off to a solitary place, where he prayed. 36Simon
and his companions went to look for him, 37and when they found
him, they exclaimed: "Everyone is looking for you!"
38Jesus replied, "Let us go somewhere else—to the nearby villages—so I can preach there also. That is why I have come." 39So he
traveled throughout Galilee, preaching in their synagogues and driving out demons.

[a]23 Greek *unclean;* also in verses 26 and 27

STUDY 1. What amazes the people in the synagogue? **2.** Why would the evil spirit in the man be afraid of Jesus? Are there evil spirits around today? Can they inhabit people? Can they inhabit believers? **3.** Do you think the church today should get involved in exorcism?

APPLY On a scale of 1 to 10, how much authority does Jesus have in your life?

OPEN 1. As a child, were you sickly or robust? **2.** What is your solitary place?

STUDY 1. How does Jesus' healing (vv. 30–31) compare with his exorcism (v. 25)? What new realm of authority is seen here? **2.** After a hectic day of helping others (vv. 29–34), Jesus needed some time to be alone and pray. What do you think he prayed for? Do you think this had anything to do with his decision to move on (v. 38)? **3.** According to verses 38–39, how did Jesus view his mission? **4.** What insight do you find in these stories about Jesus and the kingdom?

APPLY 1. What do you do when you need to get away from it all and be with God? **2.** What is the driving passion in your life right now?

1:22 the teachers of the law. These were the scribes, men charged with the responsibility of interpreting and applying God's Law to the people.

1:23 an evil spirit. Malignant, supernatural beings, able to harm and even possess people. These were Satan's legions.

1:24 What do you want with us. At first the evil spirit is defiant and resistant. **I know who you are.** By identifying Jesus, first using his human name and then his divine title, the demon was relying on ancient magical practices in the hope of gaining mastery over Jesus. It was believed that knowledge of a person's true identity (or secret name) gave one power over that person. **the Holy One of God.** The evil spirit recognizes Jesus for who he is—the divine Son of God. In contrast, it will be some time before anyone, including the disciples, understands this.

1:25 Be quiet! At the beginning of his ministry, Jesus did not want his identity or power spoken about, probably because people would have misunderstood the meaning of his ministry. **sternly.** Literally, this is "he rebuked him." The same word is used in Mark 4:39 when Jesus orders the tumult of the sea and wind to be still. **Come out of him!** In Jesus' day there were exorcists who used a combination of religious and magical practices to try to release people. In contrast, Jesus issues a simple word of command which is immediately obeyed.

1:29 to the home of Simon and Andrew. Jesus and the disciples most likely went there for a meal, since the main Sabbath meal was served immediately after the synagogue service.

1:30 Simon's mother-in-law. Simon Peter's marriage is referred to in 1 Corinthians 9:5.

1:31 The fever left her. This was a real, immediate cure. She suffered none of the weakness that normally follows when a fever breaks.

OPEN What is the loneliest place you have ever been?

STUDY 1. Why would the leper be unsure of Jesus' help (Lev. 13)? **2.** Why does Jesus command the leper to follow the rules and show himself to a priest? **3.** What happens when the leper disobeys?

APPLY 1. Who are the lepers in your community? Do you touch them? **2.** Where do you need the touch of God this week?

OPEN Who did you run around with in high school? What is the most daring thing you did?

STUDY 1. How would you feel if you had been the paralytic and four of your friends decided to "take the roof off" to get you to Jesus? **2.** Why did Jesus say, "your sins are forgiven" (v. 5)? Why didn't Jesus just go ahead and heal the paralysis? **3.** Why did the teachers of the Law get so upset? **4.** What is the lesson here for the teachers of the Law? What is the lesson for you in this miracle?

A Man With Leprosy

40 A man with leprosy[a] came to him and begged him on his knees,
"If you are willing, you can make me clean."
41 Filled with compassion, Jesus reached out his hand and touched
the man. "I am willing," he said. "Be clean!" 42 Immediately the leprosy left him and he was cured.
43 Jesus sent him away at once with a strong warning: 44 "See that
you don't tell this to anyone. But go, show yourself to the priest and
offer the sacrifices that Moses commanded for your cleansing, as a
testimony to them." 45 Instead he went out and began to talk freely,
spreading the news. As a result, Jesus could no longer enter a town
openly but stayed outside in lonely places. Yet the people still came to
him from everywhere.

Jesus Heals a Paralytic

2 A few days later, when Jesus again entered Capernaum, the people heard that he had come home. 2 So many gathered that there
was no room left, not even outside the door, and he preached the
word to them. 3 Some men came, bringing to him a paralytic, carried
by four of them. 4 Since they could not get him to Jesus because of the
crowd, they made an opening in the roof above Jesus and, after digging through it, lowered the mat the paralyzed man was lying on.
5 When Jesus saw their faith, he said to the paralytic, "Son, your sins
are forgiven."
6 Now some teachers of the law were sitting there, thinking to
themselves, 7 "Why does this fellow talk like that? He's blaspheming!
Who can forgive sins but God alone?"

[a]40 The Greek word was used for various diseases affecting the skin—not necessarily leprosy.

1:40 leprosy. No disease was dreaded more than leprosy, since it brought not only physical disfigurement but social banishment. **came to him.** What the leper did was forbidden by law. The leper should have sought to avoid drawing near Jesus. The rabbis taught that if a leper passed by a clean man, the clean man would not become unclean. However, if the leper stopped, then the clean man would become unclean. **If you are willing.** The leper had no doubt about Jesus' ability. However, since leprosy was considered a sign of God's judgment against a person because of sin, the man was uncertain of Jesus' willingness.

1:41 Filled with compassion. Human suffering evoked a deep, effective response from Jesus. He was not afraid of strong emotions. **touched.** Actually touching a leper was unimaginable to most first-century people. From the leper's perspective, the effect of Jesus' touch must have been overwhelming. He had come to think of himself as untouchable and unlovable. This touch affirmed him as a fellow human in spite of his disease.

1:44 offer the sacrifices. In Leviticus 14:1–32 the ritual is outlined whereby a leper is declared "clean." Such certification was vital to a leper: it was that person's way back into normal contact with human society.

1:45 talk freely. Jesus' plea was to no avail. The leper's joy could not be contained. He told everyone how he came to be healed. **the people still came to him.** This is the point which Mark wants to make in this opening description of Jesus' ministry: Jesus is immensely popular with the common people. In his next section (2:1–3:6), Mark will show that, in contrast, he was not at all popular with the religious leaders.

2:3 a paralytic. Any chronic disease or ailment was thought of as a punishment for sin. A paralytic was totally dependent on begging or upon family members to meet their needs.

2:4 an opening in the roof. The roof of a typical Palestinian house was flat (it was often used for sleeping) and was reached by an outside ladder or stairway. It was constructed of earth and brushwood that was packed between wooden beams set about three feet apart. The roof was easily breached (and easily repaired). A rather large opening would have been required to lower a man on a mat. While this was going on, with the noise and falling dirt, all attention inside would have been diverted from Jesus' sermon to the ever-growing hole. **mat.** The bed of a poor person.

2:5 faith. This is the first time in Mark that this word is used. It increasingly becomes the quality Jesus looks for in those to whom he ministers. **your sins are forgiven.** The friends, the man, and the crowd expected a healing; sin was a whole new issue that had not yet been raised by Jesus.

2:6 teachers of the law. Literally, "scribes," religious lawyers who interpreted Jewish law.

2:7 this fellow. Used as a term of contempt. **blaspheming.** Blasphemy is "contempt for God," and under Jewish law its penalty is death (Lev. 24:16). The

[8]Immediately Jesus knew in his spirit that this was what they were
thinking in their hearts, and he said to them, "Why are you thinking
these things? [9]Which is easier: to say to the paralytic, 'Your sins are
forgiven,' or to say, 'Get up, take your mat and walk'? [10]But that you
may know that the Son of Man has authority on earth to forgive
sins . . ." He said to the paralytic, [11]"I tell you, get up, take your mat
and go home." [12]He got up, took his mat and walked out in full view
of them all. This amazed everyone and they praised God, saying, "We
have never seen anything like this!"

The Calling of Levi

[13]Once again Jesus went out beside the lake. A large crowd came to
him, and he began to teach them. [14]As he walked along, he saw Levi
son of Alphaeus sitting at the tax collector's booth. "Follow me,"
Jesus told him, and Levi got up and followed him.
[15]While Jesus was having dinner at Levi's house, many tax collectors
and "sinners" were eating with him and his disciples, for there were
many who followed him. [16]When the teachers of the law who were
Pharisees saw him eating with the "sinners" and tax collectors, they
asked his disciples: "Why does he eat with tax collectors and 'sinners'?"
[17]On hearing this, Jesus said to them, "It is not the healthy who
need a doctor, but the sick. I have not come to call the righteous, but
sinners."

Jesus Questioned About Fasting

[18]Now John's disciples and the Pharisees were fasting. Some people came and asked Jesus, "How is it that John's disciples and the
disciples of the Pharisees are fasting, but yours are not?"
[19]Jesus answered, "How can the guests of the bridegroom fast
while he is with them? They cannot, so long as they have him with
them. [20]But the time will come when the bridegroom will be taken
from them, and on that day they will fast.
[21]"No one sews a patch of unshrunk cloth on an old garment. If
he does, the new piece will pull away from the old, making the tear
worse. [22]And no one pours new wine into old wineskins. If he
does, the wine will burst the skins, and both the wine and the

APPLY **1.** What is the closest you have come to being in a supportive community that really cared for you when you were hurting? **2.** Have you ever had a time when you were very ill and you needed the help of others? Do you think you could serve someone who was ill?

OPEN Have you had your taxes audited? Do you fear this happening to you?

STUDY **1.** Would Matthew be on your short list to be a disciple? **2.** Do you think Jesus should have gone to his party? **3.** What is the lesson here for the Pharisees? For the church today? **4.** How would you paraphrase verse 17?

APPLY If you invited one of your "sinner" friends to your church group, how would they be received? How about to this group?

OPEN What is the longest you have gone without eating?

STUDY **1.** If you had been one of John's disciples, would you have been ticked off to see Jesus' disciples partying while you were fasting? What's Jesus' explanation? **2.** What's the "old garment"? The "patch"? What is the "old wineskin"? The "new wine"? **3.** What's the lesson for the church today?

---

teachers of the Law believed that illness was the direct result of sin (John 9:2), so the sick could not recover until their sin had been forgiven by God.

2:9 Which is easier. Jesus responds to their question (v. 7) in rabbinic fashion: he asks them a question. The answer to his question is obvious. It is far easier to say, *"Your sins are forgiven,"* than it is to heal the man right then and there. There is no way to verify whether sins have been forgiven, but it is obvious whether a lame man walks or not.

2:10 But that you may know. If Jesus is able to heal the paralytic, in terms of their own theology (which linked forgiveness and healing), the scribes would have to admit that the man's sins had been forgiven.

2:14 Levi. Elsewhere he is identified as Matthew (Matt. 9:9), the disciple who wrote one of the Gospels. In his role as a tax collector, Matthew would have been hated by both the religious establishment and the common people.

2:15 having dinner. To share a meal with another was a significant event, implying acceptance of that person. In this way, Jesus extends his forgiveness (v. 10) to those who were outside orthodox religious life. **tax collectors.** They were hated by the Jews for collecting taxes on behalf of pagan Rome and for growing rich by collecting more than was actually required.

2:16 Why does he eat. This is the second question asked of Jesus. They could not understand how a truly religious person could eat food not prepared according to ritual.

2:20 bridegroom. In the Old Testament, God was often referred to as Israel's bridegroom. This is another subtle indication of Jesus' deity. **will be taken from them.** An ominous note predicting Jesus' death.

2:22 new wine. New wine continues to ferment. Hence, no one would have poured it into a leather container which was old, dry and crusty. New wine required new skins which were supple and flexible, able to expand as the wine fermented.

APPLY What do you appreciate about the religion of your parents but does not fit for you?

OPEN When you were a kid, who set the rules on table manners at your house?

STUDY 1. Do you get a little tired of people who set the rules for everybody else? 2. Who defined the rules about the Sabbath? What did Jesus say about these rules? 3. When the man with the shriveled hand showed up on the Sabbath, what was more important to the Pharisees? To Jesus? 4. How did the rulemakers react? 5. What's the lesson for the church today?

APPLY 1. If you did a survey of your friends, what would be the top three things that they are looking for in a church? What is your church doing about this? 2. Which one of your unchurched friends would enjoy being in this group if they were invited?

OPEN 1. What is the largest crowd you have been in? How did you feel? 2. What do you do to get away from the press of the crowd?

STUDY 1. What do you think the crowds were looking for

wineskins will be ruined. No, he pours new wine into new wineskins."

Lord of the Sabbath

23One Sabbath Jesus was going through the grainfields, and as his
disciples walked along, they began to pick some heads of grain. 24The
Pharisees said to him, "Look, why are they doing what is unlawful on
the Sabbath?"

25He answered, "Have you never read what David did when he and
his companions were hungry and in need? 26In the days of Abiathar
the high priest, he entered the house of God and ate the consecrated
bread, which is lawful only for priests to eat. And he also gave some
to his companions."

27Then he said to them, "The Sabbath was made for man, not man
for the Sabbath. 28So the Son of Man is Lord even of the Sabbath."

3 Another time he went into the synagogue, and a man with a
shriveled hand was there. 2Some of them were looking for a reason to accuse Jesus, so they watched him closely to see if he would
heal him on the Sabbath. 3Jesus said to the man with the shriveled
hand, "Stand up in front of everyone."

4Then Jesus asked them, "Which is lawful on the Sabbath: to do
good or to do evil, to save life or to kill?" But they remained silent.

5He looked around at them in anger and, deeply distressed at their
stubborn hearts, said to the man, "Stretch out your hand." He
stretched it out, and his hand was completely restored. 6Then the
Pharisees went out and began to plot with the Herodians how they
might kill Jesus.

Crowds Follow Jesus

7Jesus withdrew with his disciples to the lake, and a large crowd
from Galilee followed. 8When they heard all he was doing, many people came to him from Judea, Jerusalem, Idumea, and the regions
across the Jordan and around Tyre and Sidon. 9Because of the crowd
he told his disciples to have a small boat ready for him, to keep the

---

2:23 Sabbath. The seventh day of the week (Saturday) which begins Friday at sunset and ends Saturday at sunset. The Fourth Commandment is to rest from all labor on the Sabbath (Ex. 20:8–11). By the first century scores of regulations had evolved which defined what could and could not be done on the Sabbath. **pick some heads of grain.** It was permissible for hungry travelers to pluck and eat grain from a field (Deut. 23:25). The issue is not stealing. What the Pharisees objected to was the "work" this involved.

3:2 they watched him closely. Here the religious leaders are refraining from questioning Jesus. Now they *simply watched* to see if his actions betrayed a disregard for the Law so they might accuse him. **if he would heal him on the Sabbath.** The issue is not healing, but whether Jesus would do so on the Sabbath.

3:5 anger ... deeply distressed. Jesus felt strongly about the injustice of a system that sacrificed the genuine needs of people for religious traditions that had nothing to do with God. **stubborn hearts.** The Greek word translated "stubborn" is also used to describe a gallstone or a tooth. **Stretch out your hand.** Just as he deliberately declared the paralytic's sins forgiven (knowing that this was blasphemy to the teachers of the law), here he deliberately heals on the Sabbath (knowing that this too was anathema to his critics).

3:6 Herodians. A political group made up of influential Jewish sympathizers of King Herod. They were normally despised by the Pharisees, who considered them traitors (for working with Rome) and irreligious (unclean as a result of their association with Gentiles). However, the Pharisees had no power to kill Jesus. Only the civil authority could do this, and hence the collaboration. **how they might kill Jesus.** The Pharisees believed Jesus violated the Sabbath by healing on that day, but failed to see that they were violating the Sabbath law by plotting how to kill him on that day!

3:8 many people came to him. They came from near (Galilee) and far, from the north (Tyre and Sidon), south (Idumea), and east (the region across the Jordan was called Perea). They came from Jewish and from Gentile regions. They came from the country regions (Galilee) and from the heart of the nation (Jerusalem).

people from crowding him. 10For he had healed many, so that those
with diseases were pushing forward to touch him. 11Whenever the
evil[a] spirits saw him, they fell down before him and cried out, "You
are the Son of God." 12But he gave them strict orders not to tell who
he was.

The Appointing of the Twelve Apostles

13Jesus went up on a mountainside and called to him those he
wanted, and they came to him. 14He appointed twelve—designating
them apostles[b]—that they might be with him and that he might send
them out to preach 15and to have authority to drive out demons.
16These are the twelve he appointed: Simon (to whom he gave the
name Peter); 17James son of Zebedee and his brother John (to them he
gave the name Boanerges, which means Sons of Thunder); 18Andrew,
Philip, Bartholomew, Matthew, Thomas, James son of Alphaeus,
Thaddaeus, Simon the Zealot 19and Judas Iscariot, who betrayed him.

Jesus and Beelzebub

20Then Jesus entered a house, and again a crowd gathered, so that
he and his disciples were not even able to eat. 21When his family
heard about this, they went to take charge of him, for they said, "He is
out of his mind."

22And the teachers of the law who came down from Jerusalem said,
"He is possessed by Beelzebub[c]! By the prince of demons he is driving
out demons."

23So Jesus called them and spoke to them in parables: "How can
Satan drive out Satan? 24If a kingdom is divided against itself, that
kingdom cannot stand. 25If a house is divided against itself, that
house cannot stand. 26And if Satan opposes himself and is divided, he
cannot stand; his end has come. 27In fact, no one can enter a strong
man's house and carry off his possessions unless he first ties up the
strong man. Then he can rob his house. 28I tell you the truth, all the
sins and blasphemies of men will be forgiven them. 29But whoever
blasphemes against the Holy Spirit will never be forgiven; he is guilty
of an eternal sin."

30He said this because they were saying, "He has an evil spirit."

Jesus' Mother and Brothers

31Then Jesus' mother and brothers arrived. Standing outside, they
sent someone in to call him. 32A crowd was sitting around him,
and they told him, "Your mother and brothers are outside looking
for you."

33"Who are my mother and my brothers?" he asked.

34Then he looked at those seated in a circle around him and said,

[a]*11* Greek *unclean;* also in verse 30 [b]*14* Some manuscripts do not have *designating them apostles.*
[c]*22* Greek *Beezeboul* or *Beelzeboul*

in Jesus? **2.** Why were the evil spirits able to recognize Jesus when his own disciples could not? What does this say about supernatural forces? **3.** How does Jesus refocus his ministry (v. 13)? What three things are his disciples to do? What is "driving out evil spirits" all about? **4.** Do you think the disciples Jesus chose would make the short list to be spiritual leaders in today's church? What is different in Jesus' training from the training today?

APPLY 1. When have you felt almost crushed by your work load? **2.** What are you doing to get focused on your goals?

OPEN Have you ever been in a third-world country where witchcraft and demon-possession were common place?

STUDY 1. Which do you think would be harder to handle: The demands of the crowd? Your family thinking you are crazy? The religious leaders thinking you are demon-possessed? **2.** What do the Pharisees accuse Jesus of and how does he answer them? **3.** How are the Pharisees dangerously close to committing the "eternal sin" that cannot be forgiven? What do you think is the "unpardonable sin"? **4.** Can you understand the feelings of Jesus' mother and brothers when they showed up? Do you think Jesus was a little hard on his family? Do you think his words were aimed at his earthly family or his followers? How do you explain the words of Jesus about his new family?

APPLY 1. What is the closest you have come to being caught in a conflict between what your family wanted and what God wanted you to do? **2.** How are you and God getting along? Are you talking?

3:21 they went. They undertook the 30-mile journey from Nazareth to Capernaum. **take charge of him.** Their intent was to forcibly take him home (6:17, the same word is translated "arrested"). **out of his mind.** Literally, "he is beside himself." His family concluded that he was suffering from some sort of ecstatic, religiously-induced mental illness.

3:22 He is possessed by Beelzebub! Beelzebub was the Canaanite name for the chief god Baal. To be possessed by this demon meant to be controlled by him, which is how the teachers of the Law explained Jesus' power over demons.

3:34–35 Jesus gives a new definition of family. Kinship is not a matter of

"Here are my mother and my brothers! [35]Whoever does God's will is
my brother and sister and mother."

The Parable of the Sower

4 Again Jesus began to teach by the lake. The crowd that gathered
around him was so large that he got into a boat and sat in it out
on the lake, while all the people were along the shore at the water's
edge. [2]He taught them many things by parables, and in his teaching
said: [3]"Listen! A farmer went out to sow his seed. [4]As he was scattering the seed, some fell along the path, and the birds came and ate it
up. [5]Some fell on rocky places, where it did not have much soil. It
sprang up quickly, because the soil was shallow. [6]But when the sun
came up, the plants were scorched, and they withered because they
had no root. [7]Other seed fell among thorns, which grew up and
choked the plants, so that they did not bear grain. [8]Still other seed fell
on good soil. It came up, grew and produced a crop, multiplying
thirty, sixty, or even a hundred times."
[9]Then Jesus said, "He who has ears to hear, let him hear."
[10]When he was alone, the Twelve and the others around him asked
him about the parables. [11]He told them, "The secret of the kingdom
of God has been given to you. But to those on the outside everything
is said in parables [12]so that,

" 'they may be ever seeing but never perceiving,
and ever hearing but never understanding;
otherwise they might turn and be forgiven!'[a]"

[13]Then Jesus said to them, "Don't you understand this parable?
How then will you understand any parable? [14]The farmer sows the

[a]12 Isaiah 6:9,10

OPEN 1. If you were to become a farmer, what kind of crops would you like to raise? **2.** Who is the green thumb in your family?

STUDY 1. What is a parable? How much would fishermen know about farming? **2.** According to Jesus, why does God's Word not take root at all in some people (v. 15)? What causes the plants in the second type of soil to wither (vv. 16–17)? What three things choked the third plants (vv. 18–19)? **3.** What do you think Jesus means by the spectacular harvest produced by the good soil (v. 20): New converts? Good deeds? Godly character qualities? **4.** How might this crowd have responded to such a parable? How are the parables like a spiritual hearing test? What blocks understanding? What distinguishes those who are told "the secret of the kingdom" from those "outside"?

APPLY 1. Who first planted the "seed" of the gospel in your life? **2.** If a crop inspector investigated your spiritual life right now, what would this person say about the crop yield? What would this person recommend?

heredity, it is a matter of spirit; i.e., doing God's will. Eventually his family will move from doubt to faith (John 19:25–27; Acts 1:14; 1 Cor. 15:7).

4:1 The crowd. The scene is similar to that described in 3:7–9. This crowd was probably also drawn to Jesus in hopes of seeking healing and exorcism. However, this time Jesus speaks from a boat in order that all of the people might hear him.

4:2 parables. Parables are comparisons that draw upon common experience in order to teach the realities of God's kingdom. These metaphors or analogies are often presented in story form; they draw upon the known to explain the unknown.

4:3 Listen! Pay attention! There is more to this story than appears at first. **sow his seed.** Farmers would throw seed *into the soil by a broadcast method.*

4:4 the path. The soil of the pathways was so packed down that seed could not penetrate the soil and so germinate.

4:5 rocky places. Some soil covered a limestone base a few inches beneath the surface. Seed that fell here would germinate but it would not last, since a proper root system could not develop.

4:7 thorns. In other places, there were the roots of weeds. When the seed grew up, so did the weeds, which invariably stunted the growth of the good seed.

4:8 good soil. However, some of the seed did fall where it could germinate, grow and produce a crop. **thirty, sixty, or even a hundred times.** The good soil yielded a spectacular crop. While 10 times is an especially good harvest, this is a miracle crop.

4:11 The secret. A secret in the New Testament is something which was previously unknown but has now been revealed to all who will hear. The secret given the disciples is that the kingdom of God is with them. **the kingdom of God.** How God establishes his reign in human affairs is what Jesus' parables in this section are all about. **has been given to you.** Not even the disciples who have been given "the secret" perceive fully what is going on (v. 13). It is as the disciples follow Jesus that they will come to understand more fully what he means. **those on the outside.** The point is not that God calls some and excludes others. Rather, those who are on the outside are simply those who fail to pursue the kingdom.

4:12 ever seeing ... ever hearing. This quote is from Isaiah 6:9–10 in which God called the prophet to speak his word even though Israel would not listen. Although they saw God's messenger and heard his word, they refused to heed his message. **might turn and be forgiven!** In order to be forgiven, people must repent (turn). In order to repent, they must understand their true situation.

4:14 The seed is the message of God's kingdom.

word. [15]Some people are like seed along the path, where the word is
sown. As soon as they hear it, Satan comes and takes away the word
that was sown in them. [16]Others, like seed sown on rocky places,
hear the word and at once receive it with joy. [17]But since they have no
root, they last only a short time. When trouble or persecution comes
because of the word, they quickly fall away. [18]Still others, like seed
sown among thorns, hear the word; [19]but the worries of this life, the
deceitfulness of wealth and the desires for other things come in and
choke the word, making it unfruitful. [20]Others, like seed sown on
good soil, hear the word, accept it, and produce a crop—thirty, sixty
or even a hundred times what was sown."

A Lamp on a Stand

[21]He said to them, "Do you bring in a lamp to put it under a bowl or
a bed? Instead, don't you put it on its stand? [22]For whatever is hidden
is meant to be disclosed, and whatever is concealed is meant to be
brought out into the open. [23]If anyone has ears to hear, let him hear."
[24]"Consider carefully what you hear," he continued. "With the measure you use, it will be measured to you—and even more. [25]Whoever
has will be given more; whoever does not have, even what he has will
be taken from him."

The Parable of the Growing Seed

[26]He also said, "This is what the kingdom of God is like. A man
scatters seed on the ground. [27]Night and day, whether he sleeps or
gets up, the seed sprouts and grows, though he does not know how.
[28]All by itself the soil produces grain—first the stalk, then the head,
then the full kernel in the head. [29]As soon as the grain is ripe, he puts
the sickle to it, because the harvest has come."

The Parable of the Mustard Seed

[30]Again he said, "What shall we say the kingdom of God is like, or
what parable shall we use to describe it? [31]It is like a mustard seed,
which is the smallest seed you plant in the ground. [32]Yet when
planted, it grows and becomes the largest of all garden plants, with
such big branches that the birds of the air can perch in its shade."
[33]With many similar parables Jesus spoke the word to them, as
much as they could understand. [34]He did not say anything to them
without using a parable. But when he was alone with his own disciples, he explained everything.

Jesus Calms the Storm

[35]That day when evening came, he said to his disciples, "Let us go
over to the other side." [36]Leaving the crowd behind, they took him
along, just as he was, in the boat. There were also other boats with
him. [37]A furious squall came up, and the waves broke over the boat,

OPEN How many flashlights do you have in your house? How many work?

STUDY 1. What does Jesus say to the people who want to be secret followers? If you don't apply what you know about the kingdom, what will happen? **2.** When you sow good seed about the kingdom, what can you expect? What part do people play in the growth of God's kingdom (vv. 26-29)? **3.** What does the Parable of the Mustard Seed (vv. 30–32) teach about God's kingdom? **4.** If you had to make a graph of the numerical growth in your church over the last five years, what would it look like—a mustard tree or a dwarf bush? Where have you seen the greatest growth? The least growth? Are you planting new trees or just maintaining the old ones?

APPLY 1. If you had to draw your own spiritual pilgrimage over the last five years, what would it look like—a yo-yo or a growth line? **2.** If God was a gardener, what would he do to make your spiritual life more healthy?

OPEN What is the worst storm you can remember?

STUDY 1. If you had been one of the disciples when the boat was about to sink, what

4:35 That day. This story comes at the end of a day of teaching by the lake (v. 1). **when evening came.** This trip begins as the sun is setting.

4:36 There were also other boats with him. Although these boats do not play any other role in the story, their mention, as well as that of other details not found in the parallel accounts (Matt. 8:23–27; Luke 8:22–25), indicate an eyewitness testimony of the event.

4:37 A furious squall. The Sea of Galilee was pear-shaped and ringed by mountains, though open at its north and south ends. Fierce winds blew into this bowl-shaped sea, creating savage and unpredictable storms.

would you have done? **2.** The disciples asked Jesus, "Don't you care if we drown?" When have you felt that way? **3.** What was the tone in Jesus' voice in verse 40?

APPLY 1. What is the weather like in your life: Bright and sunny? A few clouds? Stormy? **2.** "Quiet! Be Still!" How do these words apply to you today?

OPEN 1. When a movie gets scary, what do you do? **2.** Have you seen "Patch Adams"? Do you remember the beginning in the mental institution?

STUDY 1. What have the disciples been through immediately before this experience? How would you feel if you arrived at a graveyard in the middle of the night after a terrifying boat trip and saw this person? Do you think the disciples got out of the boat? **2.** How would you describe the demon-possessed man in modern terms? **3.** In the interplay between the demons in the man and Jesus, what do you learn about demons? How would you explain these in modern day

so that it was nearly swamped. 38Jesus was in the stern, sleeping on a
cushion. The disciples woke him and said to him, "Teacher, don't you
care if we drown?"

39He got up, rebuked the wind and said to the waves, "Quiet! Be
still!" Then the wind died down and it was completely calm.

40He said to his disciples, "Why are you so afraid? Do you still have
no faith?"

41They were terrified and asked each other, "Who is this? Even the
wind and the waves obey him!"

The Healing of a Demon-possessed Man

5 They went across the lake to the region of the Gerasenes.[a]
2When Jesus got out of the boat, a man with an evil[b] spirit came
from the tombs to meet him. 3This man lived in the tombs, and no
one could bind him any more, not even with a chain. 4For he had often been chained hand and foot, but he tore the chains apart and
broke the irons on his feet. No one was strong enough to subdue him.
5Night and day among the tombs and in the hills he would cry out
and cut himself with stones.

6When he saw Jesus from a distance, he ran and fell on his knees in
front of him. 7He shouted at the top of his voice, "What do you want
with me, Jesus, Son of the Most High God? Swear to God that you
won't torture me!" 8For Jesus had said to him, "Come out of this man,
you evil spirit!"

[a] Some manuscripts *Gadarenes*; other manuscripts *Gergesenes* [b]2 Greek *unclean*; also in verses 8 and 13

4:38 sleeping. In the Old Testament, sleeping peacefully is a sign of trust in the power of God (Ps. 4:8). The fact that Jesus was asleep during a storm is also a sign of his exhaustion from a day of teaching. **on a cushion.** This was probably a cushion used by the rowers to sit upon. **Teacher.** This is who they understood Jesus to be: a rabbi. **don't you care if we drown?** This is a rebuke. From the disciples' perspective, Jesus' ability to sleep in the midst of the storm was not seen as a sign of his trust in God but as a sign of his callousness toward the plight of the disciples. They wake Jesus up so that he can help them bail out the boat since it was about to be swamped (v. 37).

4:39 Instead of bailing, Jesus commands the wind and the waves to be still, and so they are. He has power over the very elements—in the same way God does (Ps. 65:7; 106:9). This was something no ordinary rabbi could do. **Be still!** This is literally, "Be muzzled!" as if the storm were some wild beast needing to be subdued. Picture in this account is Jesus' divine *power to calm the storms of life.*

4:40 afraid. Once Jesus displays his power, their fear of the storm turns into fear of Jesus. This is the fear of the unknown and the unexplainable. This miracle would force the disciples to reconsider all they had heard and seen from Jesus. From what they had seen, they still did not expect Jesus to have such powers.

4:41 terrified. Terror replaced fear. This is what is felt in the presence of an unknown force or power. **Who is this?** This is the key question in Mark's Gospel. The congregation in the synagogue wondered about this (1:27). The religious leaders asked this question (2:7; 3:22). Now his disciples discover that they do not understand who he is. The rest of Mark describes how the disciples discover his true nature.

5:1 They went across the lake. Jesus and his disciples were in a boat on the Sea of Galilee. This incident takes place after Jesus calms the fierce storm that threatened to swamp their boat (4:35–41). By the time they arrive at the other side it is probably dark. **the region of the Gerasenes.** The location *of their landing* is not clear. However, it is on the other side of the lake from Capernaum, in Gentile territory, probably near the lower end of the Sea of Galilee.

5:2 Jesus got out of the boat. No mention is made of the disciples in this story. **a man with an evil spirit.** There was widespread belief that demons could enter and take control of a person's body, speaking and acting through that person. The demons were understood to be Satan's legions. In overcoming them, Jesus was demonstrating his power over Satan and his work. **tombs.** The ragged limestone cliffs with their caves and depressions provided a natural burial site. The demoniac occupied the place of the dead, indicating the nature of the evil that was at work in him.

5:6 fell on his knees. Thus, the demons acknowledge Jesus' power over them. Likewise, in verse 7 they request that he not torture them, again acknowledging his superior power.

5:7 Son of the Most High God. The demons ask who Jesus is (4:41). The demon-filled man, with supernatural insight, points out Jesus' deity (1:11). Interestingly, this is how God was often referred to by the Gentiles (Gen. 14:17–24; Dan. 4:17). **Swear to God that you won't torture me!** It is not clear what they feared.

9Then Jesus asked him, "What is your name?"
"My name is Legion," he replied, "for we are many." 10And he
begged Jesus again and again not to send them out of the area.
11A large herd of pigs was feeding on the nearby hillside. 12The demons begged Jesus, "Send us among the pigs; allow us to go into
them." 13He gave them permission, and the evil spirits came out and
went into the pigs. The herd, about two thousand in number, rushed
down the steep bank into the lake and were drowned.
14Those tending the pigs ran off and reported this in the town and
countryside, and the people went out to see what had happened.
15When they came to Jesus, they saw the man who had been possessed
by the legion of demons, sitting there, dressed and in his right mind;
and they were afraid. 16Those who had seen it told the people what
had happened to the demon-possessed man—and told about the
pigs as well. 17Then the people began to plead with Jesus to leave
their region.
18As Jesus was getting into the boat, the man who had been demon-
possessed begged to go with him. 19Jesus did not let him, but said,
"Go home to your family and tell them how much the Lord has done
for you, and how he has had mercy on you." 20So the man went away
and began to tell in the Decapolis[a] how much Jesus had done for him.
And all the people were amazed.

A Dead Girl and a Sick Woman

21When Jesus had again crossed over by boat to the other side of
the lake, a large crowd gathered around him while he was by the lake.
22Then one of the synagogue rulers, named Jairus, came there. Seeing Jesus, he fell at his feet 23and pleaded earnestly with him, "My
little daughter is dying. Please come and put your hands on her so
that she will be healed and live." 24So Jesus went with him.
A large crowd followed and pressed around him. 25And a woman

[a]20 That is, the Ten Cities

terms? **4.** How do you account for the strange behavior of the pigs? How did the community respond when they saw the man who had been possessed "in his right mind"? **5.** What did Jesus ask the man to do? If this man only had his experience to share, what could he say about Jesus to the pagan/Gentile area where he lived? **6.** What does Jesus show in this miracle? Do you think the idea of power and control over the forces of evil is still true today—or only something for science fiction novels?

APPLY 1. How would you compare the change that Jesus has brought in your life to the change that Jesus brought to the demon-possessed man? **2.** Where is the hardest place to share your faith?

OPEN 1. What would you do if the phone rang, the doorbell chimed, your child called for help, and the oven alarm went off all at the same time? **2.** What is your remedy for stopping a bloody nose?

STUDY 1. Where has Jesus come from (vv. 1–20)? What happened in that experience? **2.** What is surprising about the person that approaches Jesus and asks him to

5:9 Legion. The name for a company of 6,000 Roman soldiers. The man was occupied not by one, but by a huge number of demons.

5:11 pigs. This was a Gentile herd, since no Jew would raise pigs because they were considered unclean animals.

5:13 rushed down the steep bank. The stampede of the herd gave evidence that the demons had been driven out of the man. Their mad, suicidal rush to the sea illustrates the demons' ultimate intention for the man as well.

5:15 they were afraid. It might be expected that they would rejoice that this man who had terrorized them (and whom they could no longer restrain) was now healed. But instead they are fearful of Jesus, who had the power to overcome the demons and destroy their herd.

5:17 the people began to plead with Jesus to leave. They wanted no part of one who in their eyes would appear to be a powerful magician; one who regarded a single madman to be worth more than their whole herd.

5:19 tell. Interestingly, what the ex-demoniac could tell them was limited. He could explain what he was like before he met Jesus, what had happened to him when he encountered Jesus, and what little he knew about Jesus. This first Gentile witness to Jesus had no theological training; he simply had an amazing story to tell by which God's nature would be revealed.

5:20 Decapolis. This was a league of 10 Gentile cities patterned after the Greek way of life. This is the first of several ventures by Jesus into Gentile areas, demonstrating what Mark later points out (13:10; 14:9), that the gospel is to be preached to all nations.

5:21 the other side of the lake. Jesus is once again in Jewish territory.

5:22 synagogue rulers. In first-century Israel, the temple in Jerusalem was the sole place for sacrifice, and was attended by numerous priests and other officials. In contrast, synagogues were found in each city and town. People met there weekly on the Sabbath for worship and instruction. Synagogues were run by a committee of lay people (the rulers).

5:23 put your hands on her. The laying on of hands was a common practice used for ordination, for blessing, for the sacrificial ritual, and for healing.

5:25 a woman was there. This woman should not have been there in the crowd. Because of the nature of her illness she was considered "unclean" (Lev. 15:25–30). **subject to bleeding.** Probably hemorrhaging from the womb.

heal his daughter? **3.** How would you describe the woman in the crowd: Physical condition? Social status? **4.** What motivated this woman to touch Jesus? Why was it important for Jesus to know who touched him? Why was the woman healed and no one else in the crowd healed? **5.** Meanwhile, what has happened to the girl that was sick and how does Jesus respond to the news? How do the mourners react? **6.** Why did Jesus shut out the crowd when he went to the girl? **7.** What do you think the parents said to their synagogue friends about this miracle? **8.** What is the lesson here for the church with one "bleeding" person among the crowds of people?

APPLY **1.** What is the closest you have come to feeling desperation like Jairus did concerning his daughter or the woman did with the uncontrollable bleeding? **2.** Are you a little embarrassed or afraid to ask for prayer when you need it? **3.** Where could you use a fresh "touch" from Jesus today?

was there who had been subject to bleeding for twelve years. 26 She had suffered a great deal under the care of many doctors and had spent all she had, yet instead of getting better she grew worse. 27 When she heard about Jesus, she came up behind him in the crowd and touched his cloak, 28 because she thought, "If I just touch his clothes, I will be healed." 29 Immediately her bleeding stopped and she felt in her body that she was freed from her suffering.

30 At once Jesus realized that power had gone out from him. He turned around in the crowd and asked, "Who touched my clothes?"

31 "You see the people crowding against you," his disciples answered, "and yet you can ask, 'Who touched me?' "

32 But Jesus kept looking around to see who had done it. 33 Then the woman, knowing what had happened to her, came and fell at his feet and, trembling with fear, told him the whole truth. 34 He said to her, "Daughter, your faith has healed you. Go in peace and be freed from your suffering."

35 While Jesus was still speaking, some men came from the house of Jairus, the synagogue ruler. "Your daughter is dead," they said. "Why bother the teacher any more?"

36 Ignoring what they said, Jesus told the synagogue ruler, "Don't be afraid; just believe."

37 He did not let anyone follow him except Peter, James and John the brother of James. 38 When they came to the home of the synagogue ruler, Jesus saw a commotion, with people crying and wailing loudly. 39 He went in and said to them, "Why all this commotion and wailing? The child is not dead but asleep." 40 But they laughed at him.

After he put them all out, he took the child's father and mother and the disciples who were with him, and went in where the child was. 41 He took her by the hand and said to her, *"Talitha koum!"* (which means, "Little girl, I say to you, get up!"). 42 Immediately the girl stood up and walked around (she was twelve years old). At this they were completely astonished. 43 He gave strict orders not to let anyone know about this, and told them to give her something to eat.

Since many people assumed that chronic problems like this were God's judgment upon a person for their sin, she undoubtedly experienced some measure of condemnation from others.

5:28 If I just touch his clothes, I will be healed. There is no attempt on her part to establish genuine contact with Jesus: she simply wants to brush up against him so that she can be brought in contact with his power. Nonetheless, by this action the woman showed that she had "ears to hear" (4:9) and had faith that Jesus could indeed heal her.

5:30 Who touched my clothes? Jesus desired a relationship with those he helped: he was not an impersonal power source.

5:32 Jesus kept looking around. Jesus insists that the person who touched him reveal herself. Her healing will not be complete without this since her illness had not only physical but social consequences. Jesus makes it publicly known that she has been healed in order to commend her faith and so that she can once again have a normal life (1:44).

5:33 trembling with fear. This woman may have feared that she had done something wrong; she may have feared that Jesus would shame her in front of everyone; and she may have feared that her healing would be revoked.

5:34 your faith has healed you. It was her faith that impelled her to reach out to Jesus—the source of healing power. **Go ... be freed.** Jesus did not mean by this "be free from worry." This phrase means "be complete, be whole."

5:38 people crying and wailing loudly. These were in all likelihood professional mourners. Even the poorest person was required to hire not less than two flutes and one wailing woman to mourn a death.

5:39 The child is not dead but asleep. This is said to reassure the father. The presence of the mourners, the report of the messengers, the laughter that greeted this statement all say the same thing: the child was truly dead. Jesus uses this same expression in reference to Lazarus (John 11:11–15).

5:41 Talitha koum! This is Aramaic, which Mark translates for the Gentile readers. It means, literally, "arise, lamb" and emphasizes Jesus' compassion.

5:43 strict orders not to let anyone know about this. Jesus' statement that she is asleep, not dead

A Prophet Without Honor

6 Jesus left there and went to his hometown, accompanied by his
disciples. [2]When the Sabbath came, he began to teach in the
synagogue, and many who heard him were amazed.
"Where did this man get these things?" they asked. "What's this
wisdom that has been given him, that he even does miracles! [3]Isn't
this the carpenter? Isn't this Mary's son and the brother of James,
Joseph,[a] Judas and Simon? Aren't his sisters here with us?" And they
took offense at him.
[4]Jesus said to them, "Only in his hometown, among his relatives
and in his own house is a prophet without honor." [5]He could not do
any miracles there, except lay his hands on a few sick people and heal
them. [6]And he was amazed at their lack of faith.

Jesus Sends Out the Twelve

Then Jesus went around teaching from village to village. [7]Calling
the Twelve to him, he sent them out two by two and gave them authority over evil[b] spirits.
[8]These were his instructions: "Take nothing for the journey except
a staff—no bread, no bag, no money in your belts. [9]Wear sandals but
not an extra tunic. [10]Whenever you enter a house, stay there until you
leave that town. [11]And if any place will not welcome you or listen to
you, shake the dust off your feet when you leave, as a testimony
against them."
[12]They went out and preached that people should repent. [13]They
drove out many demons and anointed many sick people with oil and
healed them.

John the Baptist Beheaded

[14]King Herod heard about this, for Jesus' name had become well
known. Some were saying,[c] "John the Baptist has been raised from
the dead, and that is why miraculous powers are at work in him."

[a]3 Greek *Joses*, a variant of *Joseph* [b]7 Greek *unclean* [c]14 Some early manuscripts *He was saying*

OPEN 1. What childhood escapade of yours do you hear about most often when you visit family? **2.** Who in your family over-packs for a trip?

STUDY 1. How would you describe the reception that Jesus got from his hometown? **2.** How do you explain the fact that Jesus could not perform the miracles that he performed in other places? **3.** What are some lessons here for the next time you send out mission teams? **4.** Is it important to combine preaching with service and healing ministry?

APPLY 1. Have you ever gone on a mission trip? What was it like? **2.** Is it easier to talk to people you don't know or your friends about your faith?

OPEN 1. When you were a teenager, what was the popular dance? **2.** If you could have one wish for your next birthday, what would it be?

(v. 39), makes it possible for her parents to obey his request.

6:1–2 his hometown. Nazareth, which was located in the hill country of Galilee some 20 miles southwest of Capernaum (Luke 4:14–30). **accompanied by his disciples.** This was not a private visit. Jesus arrived as a rabbi with a band of disciples. **amazed.** The townspeople responded to what Jesus said in the same way others before them had (1:22,27; 2:12; 5:20).

6:2 Where did this man get these things? The townspeople do not deny Jesus' wisdom nor his power to do miracles. But they are puzzled as to the origin of such abilities.

6:3 carpenter. The Greek word refers to a general craftsman who worked not only in wood but also in stone and metal. **Mary's son.** A man was never described as the son of his mother except as an insult. The townsfolk may have heard rumors of Jesus' unusual birth and may have taken him to be illegitimate. **brother ... sisters.** Mark names four brothers and indicates Jesus had sisters too. **they took offense at him.** They could not get past his humble and familiar origins—therefore, they couldn't give credence to who he really was.

6:7 he sent them out. To go out on a ministry tour is not the idea or plan of the Twelve. Jesus does the sending. **two by two.** He does not send them alone—perhaps as a protection against robbers; perhaps because two witnesses have more credibility than one (Deut. 17:6); perhaps so that they will support one another as they learn to minister. The parallel accounts in Matthew and Luke indicate their mission was to announce and demonstrate the fact that God's kingdom was now at hand (1:15). **gave them authority.** He empowers them to do battle with evil. It is in his name and power that they minister.

6:8 instructions. These instructions cause the Twelve to pare down to the bare minimum. They take only the clothes on their backs and a staff, the tool of a shepherd. By faith they must trust that God will provide the rest of their needs as they go about his work. These instructions reflect the urgency of the task upon which the Twelve have been sent. **no bag.** The reference may have been to a begging bag commonly used by wandering priests to collect funds.

6:10 They are not to dishonor their host by accepting better accommodations.

6:14 King Herod. Herod Antipas was

STUDY 1. If you gave a movie rating to this story in the Bible, what would it be? 2. Why would King Herod be a little paranoid? What did he do that caused his nightmares? 3. What do you learn about the character of John the Baptist? About King Herod? 4. What would the *New York Times* put in their obituary about John the Baptist? 5. Who do you admire who is like John?

APPLY 1. What is the closest you have come to getting into serious trouble for speaking out about something you believe in? 2. If John the Baptist showed up in your town, what is the first thing he would do? 3. What keeps you from doing something about this?

[15]Others said, "He is Elijah."
And still others claimed, "He is a prophet, like one of the prophets
of long ago."
[16]But when Herod heard this, he said, "John, the man I beheaded,
has been raised from the dead!"
[17]For Herod himself had given orders to have John arrested, and he
had him bound and put in prison. He did this because of Herodias,
his brother Philip's wife, whom he had married. [18]For John had been
saying to Herod, "It is not lawful for you to have your brother's wife."
[19]So Herodias nursed a grudge against John and wanted to kill him.
But she was not able to, [20]because Herod feared John and protected
him, knowing him to be a righteous and holy man. When Herod
heard John, he was greatly puzzled[a]; yet he liked to listen to him.
[21]Finally the opportune time came. On his birthday Herod gave a
banquet for his high officials and military commanders and the leading men of Galilee. [22]When the daughter of Herodias came in and
danced, she pleased Herod and his dinner guests.
The king said to the girl, "Ask me for anything you want, and I'll
give it to you." [23]And he promised her with an oath, "Whatever you
ask I will give you, up to half my kingdom."
[24]She went out and said to her mother, "What shall I ask for?"
"The head of John the Baptist," she answered.
[25]At once the girl hurried in to the king with the request: "I want
you to give me right now the head of John the Baptist on a platter."
[26]The king was greatly distressed, but because of his oaths and his
dinner guests, he did not want to refuse her. [27]So he immediately
sent an executioner with orders to bring John's head. The man went,
beheaded John in the prison, [28]and brought back his head on a platter. He presented it to the girl, and she gave it to her mother. [29]On

[a]20 Some early manuscripts *he did many things*

the ruler of the Roman provinces of Galilee and Perea from 4 B.C. to A.D. 39. He was the son of Herod the Great, the Jewish ruler who ordered the slaughter of the babies after Jesus' birth. Herod Antipas was not, in fact, the "King." When he went to Rome some years later to request this title, his power was taken away and he was banished. Herod is pretending to be king when, in fact, the real King of Israel (Jesus) is largely unrecognized. **John the Baptist has been raised from the dead.** Only people personally unfamiliar with Jesus' background would have assumed this since Jesus and John were contemporaries. The fact that Jesus did not become widely known until after John's death led some people to assume that only a holy person who had come back from death could possibly have such powers.

6:15 Elijah. *The Jews believed when* Elijah returned, as foretold in Malachi 3:1 and 4:5–6, their deliverance from Rome was near. **a prophet.** Others did not credit Jesus with being the final prophet, but felt he was one of the long line of prophets associated with Israel's past.

6:18 It is not lawful. According to Leviticus 18:16 and 20:21, it was not lawful for a man to marry his brother's wife while that brother was still alive. Herod, a Jew himself, scandalized his people by divorcing the Nabatean Princess Aretas to marry Herodias who was his niece (the daughter of his half-brother) and his sister-in-law (the wife of a different brother).

6:21 the opportune time. Herodias was plotting a way to kill John (v. 19) because of his criticism of her marriage. **a banquet.** The sparseness of the lifestyle of the Twelve (vv. 8–11) would have contrasted greatly with the opulence of Herod's birthday party. The men in attendance would have been wealthy landowners, those in high government positions, and military officials.

6:22 the daughter of Herodias. This is Herodias' teenage daughter (from her first marriage), whose name is Salome (according to Josephus, the Jewish historian). She was later married to her granduncle, Philip (son of Herod the Great), who ruled the northern territories (Luke 3:1). **danced.** For a princess to dance publicly before an audience of drunken men was considered most shameful. **his dinner guests.** These were the leading men of the nation (v. 21). They are very different than the common folk among whom the ministry of the Twelve took place (vv. 12–13) and who would later be in attendance at the "banquet" Jesus hosts (vv. 30–44). **Ask me for anything you want.** This was a foolhardy promise, a boastful display of power gone bad. Herodias succeeded in manipulating Herod by exploiting his lust, his drunkenness, and his tendency to show off. This was the opportunity she had been waiting for (vv. 19–20).

6:25 the head of John the Baptist on a platter. This was a gruesome act: serving John's head on a platter as if it were another course in the banquet.

hearing of this, John's disciples came and took his body and laid it in
a tomb.

Jesus Feeds the Five Thousand

30The apostles gathered around Jesus and reported to him all they
had done and taught. 31Then, because so many people were coming
and going that they did not even have a chance to eat, he said to
them, "Come with me by yourselves to a quiet place and get some
rest."
32So they went away by themselves in a boat to a solitary place.
33But many who saw them leaving recognized them and ran on foot
from all the towns and got there ahead of them. 34When Jesus landed
and saw a large crowd, he had compassion on them, because they
were like sheep without a shepherd. So he began teaching them
many things.
35By this time it was late in the day, so his disciples came to him.
"This is a remote place," they said, "and it's already very late. 36Send
the people away so they can go to the surrounding countryside and
villages and buy themselves something to eat."
37But he answered, "You give them something to eat."
They said to him, "That would take eight months of a man's
wages[a]! Are we to go and spend that much on bread and give it to
them to eat?"
38"How many loaves do you have?" he asked. "Go and see."
When they found out, they said, "Five—and two fish."
39Then Jesus directed them to have all the people sit down in
groups on the green grass. 40So they sat down in groups of hundreds and fifties. 41Taking the five loaves and the two fish and
looking up to heaven, he gave thanks and broke the loaves. Then he
gave them to his disciples to set before the people. He also divided
the two fish among them all. 42They all ate and were satisfied,

[a]37 Greek *take two hundred denarii*

OPEN 1. If you had to make dinner for a crowd of 5,000 people, what would you serve? **2.** What is the biggest picnic you have ever attended?

STUDY 1. The disciples thought they were getting a break (v. 31), but they ended up serving. If you were one of the disciples, how would you have felt? **2.** What is the difference between the way Jesus looked on the crowd and the way the disciples viewed them? **3.** Why would Jesus tell the disciples, "You give them something to eat" (v. 37)? How did the disciples respond? **4.** What would you feel as a disciple when you gathered the leftovers? What is the lesson for the church today?

APPLY 1. What is your favorite excuse when God calls you to do something about the human needs in your community? **2.** What little effort on your part to make a difference in your community has brought you the most satisfaction?

6:30 The Twelve, having returned from their mission to preach, cast out demons and heal in the villages throughout Galilee (vv. 7–12), report to the Lord what took place in their travels. **apostles.** This is the only time this term is used in Mark. Here it is not so much a title as a description of what they have just done. An apostle is "one who is sent," and they have just completed the missionary work the Lord sent them out to do.

6:31 get some rest. It is Jesus who insists on rest—even though the crowds are there with all their needs and the opportunity for ministry is great (1:35).

6:33 ran on foot. The crowds are now wise to the disciples' tactic of sailing off across the lake and leaving them standing on the shore (4:35–36). So they follow on foot. The distances would not have been great since the lake was only eight miles at its widest. They could probably see where they were sailing to.

6:34 a large crowd. It took awhile for Jesus to arrive (perhaps there was no wind that day or a headwind). **sheep without a shepherd.** Without a shepherd, sheep have no protection, they are hopelessly lost. They have no way to defend nor provide for themselves.

6:36 Send the people away. This is the disciples' solution! "Let the people buy what they need in the nearby towns."

6:37 You give them something to eat. But Jesus has quite a different solution in mind! The response of the disciples indicates they had no clue as to how Jesus expected them to do this. **eight months of a man's wages.** As in the storm on the lake (4:37–38), the disciples do not expect Jesus to provide a miraculous solution to the problem of inadequate resources. The only way they can see to feed the crowd is to buy lots of food, and they do not feel an expenditure that large is warranted.

6:41 five loaves. These were small round cakes made of wheat or barley. **two fish.** These were probably smoked or pickled fish that were used as a sauce for the bread. **gave thanks.** A common Jewish blessing at meals was "Blessed art thou, O Lord our God, king of the universe, who bringest forth bread from the earth" (Mann). **gave thanks ... broke ... gave.** When Jesus gives thanks and breaks the bread, the reader is reminded of the last meal Jesus shared with his disciples (14:22) and that the bread later becomes a symbol for his body (1 Cor. 11:23–24).

6:42 satisfied. Miraculously, five loaves and two fish fed everyone not meagerly, but abundantly, so that they were filled.

43and the disciples picked up twelve basketfuls of broken pieces of
bread and fish. 44The number of the men who had eaten was five
thousand.

Jesus Walks on the Water

45Immediately Jesus made his disciples get into the boat and go on
ahead of him to Bethsaida, while he dismissed the crowd. 46After
leaving them, he went up on a mountainside to pray.
47When evening came, the boat was in the middle of the lake, and
he was alone on land. 48He saw the disciples straining at the oars,
because the wind was against them. About the fourth watch of the
night he went out to them, walking on the lake. He was about to pass
by them, 49but when they saw him walking on the lake, they thought
he was a ghost. They cried out, 50because they all saw him and were
terrified.
Immediately he spoke to them and said, "Take courage! It is I.
Don't be afraid." 51Then he climbed into the boat with them, and the
wind died down. They were completely amazed, 52for they had not
understood about the loaves; their hearts were hardened.
53When they had crossed over, they landed at Gennesaret and anchored there. 54As soon as they got out of the boat, people recognized
Jesus. 55They ran throughout that whole region and carried the sick
on mats to wherever they heard he was. 56And wherever he went—
into villages, towns or countryside—they placed the sick in the marketplaces. They begged him to let them touch even the edge of his
cloak, and all who touched him were healed.

OPEN **1.** When did you learn to swim? **2.** What is the most daring stunt you've ever attempted?

STUDY This story occurred immediately after the feeding of the 5,000. **1.** Why do you think Jesus decided to separate himself from both the crowd and the disciples and spend time alone in prayer? **2.** When the disciples saw someone walking on the water, what was their reaction? How would you have reacted? **3.** How did Jesus try to calm the disciples' fears? **4.** Why would a guy like Peter try to walk on the water? What would you do if Jesus invited you? **5.** What did Peter learn the hard way?

APPLY **1.** Where is God inviting you to step out of your comfort zone? **2.** What's keeping you from doing it? Would a little prayer from this group help?

6:43 twelve. The number of the tribes of Israel, reinforcing the idea that what Jesus is doing here has prophetic significance as a demonstration that Jesus provides nourishment for all God's people. **basketfuls.** Small wicker containers carried by all Jews. Each disciple returned with his full. The word used for basket describes a distinctly Jewish type of basket. **broken pieces.** The Law required that the scraps of a meal be collected. **bread.** Bread and eating are recurring themes in these two cycles of stories (6:30–8:26).

6:44 men. Literally, "males" (Matt. 14:21). When all the women and children are taken into account, this was a huge crowd.

6:45 The reason for Jesus' abrupt dismissal of the disciples and the crowd is explained in the Gospel of John (John 6:14–15). Apparently the crowd wanted to make Jesus the king by force. **Bethsaida.** *Literally, "house of the fisher."* This is a village on the northern shore of the Sea of Galilee, several miles east of Capernaum. This was the birthplace of Philip, Andrew and Peter.

6:46 he went ... to pray. In the midst of great success and popular acclaim, once again Jesus goes off to pray.

6:48 the wind was against them. Once again (4:37), the elements work against the disciples. This time the problem is not a storm, but a strong headwind that would make rowing difficult. **the fourth watch.** This was the way Roman soldiers told time. The fourth watch ran from 3:00 to 6:00 a.m. Assuming the disciples set out to sea in the late afternoon, they had been struggling at the oars for probably seven or more hours. **walking on the lake.** It has already been established that Jesus is Lord over the wind and the water (4:39,41). **He was about to pass by them.** This could be translated: "for he intended to pass their way," presumably to reveal his presence and remind them of his power in the midst of their distress.

6:49 a ghost. The sea, especially at night, was thought to be a dwelling place for demons. Hence the response of the disciples.

6:50 terrified. Once before on this lake they were terrified by an event they did not expect and did not understand, namely the calming of the sea by Jesus (4:41). This is the terror of experiencing something that defies all categories of understanding. **It is I.** Literally, "I Am." This phrase is used by God to describe himself (Ex. 3:1–14).

6:52 they had not understood about the loaves. The disciples had seen the multiplication of the loaves as just another conjuring trick, rather than understanding what that incident revealed about Jesus' identity. **their hearts were hardened.** This is the problem. Like the Pharisees in the synagogue (3:5), the disciples' hearts are like calcified stone (the same Greek word is used here and in 3:5).

6:53 Gennesaret. This wind having frustrated their plan to go north, they instead cross the lake to a thickly populated, fertile plain some four miles southwest of Capernaum. There, crowds again flock to him as a healer.

Clean and Unclean

7 The Pharisees and some of the teachers of the law who had
come from Jerusalem gathered around Jesus and 2saw some of his
disciples eating food with hands that were "unclean," that is, unwashed. 3(The Pharisees and all the Jews do not eat unless they give
their hands a ceremonial washing, holding to the tradition of the elders. 4When they come from the marketplace they do not eat unless
they wash. And they observe many other traditions, such as the washing of cups, pitchers and kettles.[a])
5So the Pharisees and teachers of the law asked Jesus, "Why don't
your disciples live according to the tradition of the elders instead of
eating their food with 'unclean' hands?"
6He replied, "Isaiah was right when he prophesied about you hypocrites; as it is written:

" 'These people honor me with their lips,
but their hearts are far from me.
7They worship me in vain;
their teachings are but rules taught by men.'[b]

8You have let go of the commands of God and are holding on to the
traditions of men."
9And he said to them: "You have a fine way of setting aside the
commands of God in order to observe[c] your own traditions! 10For
Moses said, 'Honor your father and your mother,'[d] and, 'Anyone who
curses his father or mother must be put to death.'[e] 11But you say that
if a man says to his father or mother: 'Whatever help you might otherwise have received from me is Corban' (that is, a gift devoted to God),
12then you no longer let him do anything for his father or mother.
13Thus you nullify the word of God by your tradition that you have
handed down. And you do many things like that."
14Again Jesus called the crowd to him and said, "Listen to me,
everyone, and understand this. 15Nothing outside a man can make
him 'unclean' by going into him. Rather, it is what comes out of a
man that makes him 'unclean.'[f]"
17After he had left the crowd and entered the house, his disciples
asked him about this parable. 18"Are you so dull?" he asked. "Don't
you see that nothing that enters a man from the outside can make
him 'unclean'? 19For it doesn't go into his heart but into his stomach,
and then out of his body." (In saying this, Jesus declared all foods
"clean.")
20He went on: "What comes out of a man is what makes him

[a]4 Some early manuscripts *pitchers, kettles and dining couches* [b]6,7 Isaiah 29:13 [c]9 Some manuscripts *set up* [d]10 Exodus 20:12; Deut. 5:16 [e]10 Exodus 21:17; Lev. 20:9 [f]15 Some early manuscripts *'unclean.'* [16]*If anyone has ears to hear, let him hear.*

OPEN 1. What is the messiest food that you enjoy eating (fried chicken, cotton candy, sloppy joes, tacos, etc.)? **2.** What is the most fun you ever had getting dirty?

STUDY 1. How would you describe these Pharisees and teachers of the law that were sent from Jerusalem? Who would these people be today? **2.** What is the issue debated by the Pharisees and Jesus (v. 15)? Given this debate, how would each define what it means to be spiritual? **3.** Something declared "Corban" meant it was dedicated to God. Thus it was no longer able to be given away. How does this illustrate the way the Pharisees have twisted the Law? **4.** How does Jesus' idea of being unclean differ from that of the Pharisees? Why doesn't Jesus offer any solution to the problem at this time? **5.** Jesus told the Pharisees that fulfilling human traditions can interfere with obeying the commands of God. Have you ever felt like a victim of human, religious traditions in your efforts to obey God? **6.** Have you ever experienced a conflict between your religious obligations and your obligation to your loved ones? What happened?

APPLY 1. Among your unchurched and non-Christian friends, what is their biggest complaint when they look at Christianity? **2.** What is the issue you are personally dealing with as a Christian in a post-Christian culture?

7:1 from Jerusalem. This is the second commission of inquiry sent by a worried religious hierarchy (3:22).

7:3 ceremonial washing. The issue was holiness, not hygiene (germs were unknown in the first century). Before each meal the hands were washed with special water in a particular way.

7:11 Corban. An oath, which when invoked, dedicated an item to God, rendering it thereafter unavailable for normal use. So, a son might declare his property "Corban" with the result that his parents would have no further claim on his support, even though the oath neither required him to transfer his property to the temple nor to cease using it himself.

7:15 unclean. This means "to render someone impure in a ritual sense."

7:20 What comes out of a man. Jesus calls the people to focus on what comes out of a person's heart and mind. Thoughts and actions reveal true uncleanness. What bothers God is not ritual but evil.

OPEN For what would you walk 50 miles?

STUDY 1. What is so shocking about the place and ethnic background of the woman? How would religious Jews look upon this? **2.** Who is Jesus referring to when he says, "First let the children eat ..."? **3.** Why does Jesus give in to her request? **4.** What church do you admire for the way they reach out to ethnic minorities?

APPLY What Christian community have you been a part of that was truly color blind?

OPEN Do you know anyone who is deaf?

STUDY 1. In addition to being deaf, what social stigma would this man face? What did this man have going for him? **2.** What do you find interesting about the way Jesus dealt with the deaf mute? **3.** Why would Jesus want the man to stay quiet? What happened?

APPLY How would you compare your eagerness to share your faith now to the period right after you first believed?

'unclean.' [21]For from within, out of men's hearts, come evil thoughts,
sexual immorality, theft, murder, adultery, [22]greed, malice, deceit,
lewdness, envy, slander, arrogance and folly. [23]All these evils come
from inside and make a man 'unclean.' "

The Faith of a Syrophoenician Woman

[24]Jesus left that place and went to the vicinity of Tyre.[a] He entered a
house and did not want anyone to know it; yet he could not keep his
presence secret. [25]In fact, as soon as she heard about him, a woman
whose little daughter was possessed by an evil[b] spirit came and fell at
his feet. [26]The woman was a Greek, born in Syrian Phoenicia. She
begged Jesus to drive the demon out of her daughter.
[27]"First let the children eat all they want," he told her, "for it is not
right to take the children's bread and toss it to their dogs."
[28]"Yes, Lord," she replied, "but even the dogs under the table eat
the children's crumbs."
[29]Then he told her, "For such a reply, you may go; the demon has
left your daughter."
[30]She went home and found her child lying on the bed, and the demon gone.

The Healing of a Deaf and Mute Man

[31]Then Jesus left the vicinity of Tyre and went through Sidon, down
to the Sea of Galilee and into the region of the Decapolis.[c] [32]There
some people brought to him a man who was deaf and could hardly
talk, and they begged him to place his hand on the man.
[33]After he took him aside, away from the crowd, Jesus put his fingers into the man's ears. Then he spit and touched the man's tongue.
[34]He looked up to heaven and with a deep sigh said to him, *"Ephphatha!"* (which means, "Be opened!"). [35]At this, the man's ears were
opened, his tongue was loosened and he began to speak plainly.
[36]Jesus commanded them not to tell anyone. But the more he did
so, the more they kept talking about it. [37]People were overwhelmed
with amazement. "He has done everything well," they said. "He even
makes the deaf hear and the mute speak."

[a]24 Many early manuscripts *Tyre and Sidon* [b]25 Greek *unclean* [c]31 That is, the Ten Cities

7:26 a Greek, born in Syrian Phoenicia. This woman is described first by her religion, language and culture. She is a Greek-speaking Gentile. Then she is described by her nationality. She came from Phoenicia (modern-day Lebanon), which was administered by Syria.

7:27 First. Jesus' primary mission was to the children of Israel. By the use of the word "first," he implies that a mission to the Gentiles was intended from the beginning.

7:28 Instead of being insulted by his metaphor, she catches on to his wordplay and replies, in essence, "Carry on with the meal you are serving Israel, but allow us a few scraps."

7:29 For such a reply. Jesus is impressed with the depth of her understanding as well as her clever and witty reply. In fact, this Gentile woman seems to understand more about Jesus than either the Twelve (6:45–56) or the Pharisees (vv. 1–13).

7:32 deaf. Apparently the result of an accident or disease and not a birth defect, since the man could speak some.

7:33 spit. This was regarded by Jews and Greeks as a healing agent.

7:34 Ephphatha! Mark continues to translate for his Roman readers.

7:36 not to tell anyone. This command stands in sharp contrast to what Jesus said on his previous visit to the region of the Decapolis. On that occasion, he told the ex-demoniac *to go and tell* the story of what the Lord had done for him (5:18–20). On this trip, Jesus sees the results of that man's witness. Instead of urgently requesting Jesus to leave as they had done on his previous visit (5:17), now not only do the townspeople bring a man to be healed, but they have developed expectations about who Jesus is and what he can do. This is why Jesus now commanded silence.

Jesus Feeds the Four Thousand

8 During those days another large crowd gathered. Since they had
nothing to eat, Jesus called his disciples to him and said, 2"I
have compassion for these people; they have already been with me
three days and have nothing to eat. 3If I send them home hungry, they
will collapse on the way, because some of them have come a long distance."

4His disciples answered, "But where in this remote place can anyone get enough bread to feed them?"

5"How many loaves do you have?" Jesus asked.

"Seven," they replied.

6He told the crowd to sit down on the ground. When he had taken
the seven loaves and given thanks, he broke them and gave them to
his disciples to set before the people, and they did so. 7They had a few
small fish as well; he gave thanks for them also and told the disciples
to distribute them. 8The people ate and were satisfied. Afterward the
disciples picked up seven basketfuls of broken pieces that were left
over. 9About four thousand men were present. And having sent them
away, 10he got into the boat with his disciples and went to the region
of Dalmanutha.

11The Pharisees came and began to question Jesus. To test him,
they asked him for a sign from heaven. 12He sighed deeply and said,
"Why does this generation ask for a miraculous sign? I tell you the
truth, no sign will be given to it." 13Then he left them, got back into
the boat and crossed to the other side.

The Yeast of the Pharisees and Herod

14The disciples had forgotten to bring bread, except for one loaf
they had with them in the boat. 15"Be careful," Jesus warned them.
"Watch out for the yeast of the Pharisees and that of Herod."

16They discussed this with one another and said, "It is because we have no bread."

17Aware of their discussion, Jesus asked them: "Why are you talking
about having no bread? Do you still not see or understand? Are
your hearts hardened? 18Do you have eyes but fail to see, and ears but
fail to hear? And don't you remember? 19When I broke the five loaves
for the five thousand, how many basketfuls of pieces did you pick up?"

"Twelve," they replied.

OPEN If you didn't eat for three days, how would you feel? Have you ever fasted and prayed?

STUDY 1. In Chapter 6, Jesus feeds 5,000 people from his home area. How is this audience different from the previous one? **2.** What does Jesus use to feed 4,000 people? Why does he ask the disciples to start with what they have? **3.** Why would Jesus want to save all the scraps? **4.** Returning to Jewish territory, who tries to test him, and why does Jesus refuse to oblige? **5.** After seeing Jesus provide for 5,000, what are the disciples afraid of? What does this have to do with the "yeast of the Pharisees"? **6.** In your community, what person or group of people do you admire because they have compassion for the hungry and homeless? When they started out, how much money and/or resources did they have?

APPLY 1. Who does your heart go out to in your community? **2.** If you knew that you could not fail, what would you like to do about this situation? **3.** How many "loaves of bread" and "fish" would it take to get you started?

8:1–10 The major difference between the feeding of the four thousand and the feeding of the five thousand is the difference in audience. This feeding included Gentiles (as well as Jews), whereas the earlier feeding involved Jews only.

8:10 Dalmanutha. It is not certain where this town is located. Possibly it is Magdala, a town near Tiberias on the west side of the lake. The point is clear. At this time Jesus left the Gentile region where he was ministering and returned to Jewish soil.

8:11 test. Having just shown who he is by the great miracle of feeding, the Pharisees now want Jesus to prove that he is from God! **a sign from heaven.** Jesus will not give a sign for its own sake, especially when the request springs from unbelief. His miracles are always in aid of others. Jesus is more than just a wonder-worker (4:35–6:29).

8:15 yeast. To the Jew, yeast was connected with fermentation, which they saw as a form of rotting. So yeast became a metaphor for evil and its expansion.

8:17 Do you still not see or understand? Jesus asks this question twice in these verses (vv. 14–21). This is the issue. Although exposed to ample evidence of who Jesus is, they still fail to put it all together. **hearts hardened?** This is the problem (3:5; 6:52). Their hearts are stone-like. The seed of the Word can't penetrate (4:15).

8:18 eyes but fail to see, and ears but fail to hear? This is actually a quote from Jeremiah 5:21. Now the point of the two healings becomes clear. The disciples are like the deaf man (7:31–35) and the blind man (vv. 22–25). They too need a miracle from Jesus in order to see and hear properly.

OPEN 1. If you lost your sight, what would you miss seeing? **2.** What do you do when someone says something you do not want to hear?

STUDY 1. What is unique about this miracle? **2.** Why did Jesus take the man out of the village—and request that he not return to the village? **3.** What was Caeserea known for that causes Jesus to ask his disciples "who do people say I am"? **4.** If you asked the people where you work this question, what would they say? **5.** Do you think Peter realized what he was saying when he said "you are the Christ"? If he did, why did he have trouble understanding Jesus' death? **6.** What does Jesus say about Peter's thinking? If you had been Peter, how would you have felt? **7.** According to verses 34–38, what is central and non-negotiable to be a believer? If this test was emphasized today, what would happen?

APPLY 1. If you could compare your spiritual life to the blind man, what is your vision now? **2.** What caused you to first open your eyes to the truth about Jesus and to your need to know him?

20 "And when I broke the seven loaves for the four thousand, how
many basketfuls of pieces did you pick up?"
They answered, "Seven."
21 He said to them, "Do you still not understand?"

The Healing of a Blind Man at Bethsaida

22 They came to Bethsaida, and some people brought a blind man
and begged Jesus to touch him. 23 He took the blind man by the hand
and led him outside the village. When he had spit on the man's eyes
and put his hands on him, Jesus asked, "Do you see anything?"
24 He looked up and said, "I see people; they look like trees walking
around."
25 Once more Jesus put his hands on the man's eyes. Then his eyes
were opened, his sight was restored, and he saw everything clearly.
26 Jesus sent him home, saying, "Don't go into the village.[a]"

Peter's Confession of Christ

27 Jesus and his disciples went on to the villages around Caesarea
Philippi. On the way he asked them, "Who do people say I am?"
28 They replied, "Some say John the Baptist; others say Elijah; and
still others, one of the prophets."
29 "But what about you?" he asked. "Who do you say I am?"
Peter answered, "You are the Christ.[b]"
30 Jesus warned them not to tell anyone about him.

Jesus Predicts His Death

31 He then began to teach them that the Son of Man must suffer
many things and be rejected by the elders, chief priests and teachers
of the law, and that he must be killed and after three days rise again.
32 He spoke plainly about this, and Peter took him aside and began to
rebuke him.
33 But when Jesus turned and looked at his disciples, he rebuked

[a]26 Some manuscripts *Don't go and tell anyone in the village* [b]29 Or *Messiah.* "The Christ" (Greek) and "the Messiah" (Hebrew) both mean "the Anointed One."

8:22 Bethsaida. This was a town at the mouth of the Jordan River on the shore of the Sea of Galilee.

8:24 they look like trees. The man's sight is improved, but not enough to function as a person whose vision is good. He probably once had his sight, since he knows what a tree looks like.

8:25 Once more. This is the only healing that requires a second action on the part of Jesus. Mark's placement of this story right after the disciples' incomprehension of the meaning of the feedings, and just prior to their confession of faith in him as the Messiah, indicates he is using this story to illustrate how difficult it was for the disciples to grasp Jesus' identity.

8:27–30 This is a pivotal passage in the Gospel of Mark. The disciples declare (through Peter, who seems to have become their spokesman) that in contrast to the crowds, they recognize who Jesus is. He is the long-expected Messiah.

8:27 Caesarea Philippi. When Jesus and his disciples visited this city, there was a gleaming white marble temple dedicated to the godhead of Caesar. It is fitting that in this place with rich associations to the religions of the world, Jesus, the Galilean, asks his disciples if they understand that he is the Anointed One sent by God.

8:29 Who do you say I am? This is the crucial question in Mark's Gospel. By it the author challenges his readers to consider how they will answer the question as well. **You are the Christ.** Peter correctly identifies him as the Messiah. "Christ" is the Greek term for "Messiah" (which is a Hebrew word). In the context of Jewish thought, this was the prophesied future king of Israel who would deliver Israel from bondage into an era of freedom, power, influence and prosperity.

8:31 He then began to teach them. For the remainder of this passage (8:31–10:52), Jesus seeks to teach the Twelve what kind of Messiah he is. **rejected by the elders, chief priests and teachers of the law.** These three groups made up the Sanhedrin, the ruling Jewish body. Jesus is predicting that will be officially rejected by Israel (14:55).

8:33 Get behind me, Satan! By urging Jesus to back away from his teaching about suffering and death, Peter is doing what Satan did: tempting Jesus with the promise that he can have the whole world without pain (Matt. 4:8–10).

Peter. "Get behind me, Satan!" he said. "You do not have in mind the
things of God, but the things of men."
34Then he called the crowd to him along with his disciples and said:
"If anyone would come after me, he must deny himself and take up
his cross and follow me. 35For whoever wants to save his life[a] will
lose it, but whoever loses his life for me and for the gospel will save
it. 36What good is it for a man to gain the whole world, yet forfeit his
soul? 37Or what can a man give in exchange for his soul? 38If anyone is
ashamed of me and my words in this adulterous and sinful generation, the Son of Man will be ashamed of him when he comes in his
Father's glory with the holy angels."

9 And he said to them, "I tell you the truth, some who are standing
here will not taste death before they see the kingdom of God
come with power."

The Transfiguration

2After six days Jesus took Peter, James and John with him and led
them up a high mountain, where they were all alone. There he was
transfigured before them. 3His clothes became dazzling white, whiter
than anyone in the world could bleach them. 4And there appeared
before them Elijah and Moses, who were talking with Jesus.
5Peter said to Jesus, "Rabbi, it is good for us to be here. Let us put
up three shelters—one for you, one for Moses and one for Elijah."
6(He did not know what to say, they were so frightened.)
7Then a cloud appeared and enveloped them, and a voice came
from the cloud: "This is my Son, whom I love. Listen to him!"

[a]35 The Greek word means either *life* or *soul*; also in verse 36.

OPEN 1. If you could choose three friends for climbing a mountain, who would you pick? **2.** Where would you go to feel especially close to God?

STUDY 1. With only a few weeks remaining in Jesus' mission, why would he feel the need to get away and be with God? Why take three special disciples with him? **2.** How do you explain what happened to Jesus? Why Elijah and Moses? **3.** How does Peter react? Why would he want to build three shelters? **4.** What did the voice mean when he

8:34 These words would certainly have special meaning to those in the situation faced by the original recipients of the Gospel, the Christians who were suffering for the sake of Jesus. The words are a challenge to all who would follow Jesus. **come after me.** Discipleship is a matter of following in the ways of one's teacher. **deny himself ... take up his cross ... follow me.** To "take up a cross" was something done only by a person sentenced to death by crucifixion, a reality for believers throughout the centuries as they faced death rather than deny their Lord.

8:35 save his life. The image is of a trial in which one is called upon to renounce Jesus in order to live. This would have immediate application to *the Christians who were pressed with* the decision of considering whether to affirm their loyalty to Jesus and face the persecution of the state or deny their association with Jesus and be allowed to live. **will lose it.** The person will ultimately face God's judgment for their denial of Christ. **whoever loses his life ... will save it.** In this Gospel, John the Baptist represents such a faithful person (6:14–29).

8:38 ashamed of me. This would be indicated by failing to persist in one's Christian testimony in times of persecution. **adulterous and sinful generation.** This is reminiscent of the language of the Old Testament prophets who used adultery as a metaphor for Israel's disloyalty to God. **Son of Man ... Father's glory ... holy angels.** This is apocalyptic imagery similar to Daniel 7:13. The Jewish expectation was that God's kingdom would one day be decisively and dramatically ushered in.

9:2 After six days. By this phrase Mark connects the Transfiguration with Jesus' prediction that "some who are standing here will not taste death before they see the kingdom of God come with power" (9:1). **Peter, James and John.** These three emerge as an inner circle around Jesus. **a high mountain.** This may well be Mt. Hermon, a 9,000 foot mountain located some 12 miles from Caesarea Philippi (though early tradition says it is Mt. Tabor, located southwest of the Sea of Galilee).

9:4 Elijah. Elijah was a great prophet. The Jews expected he would return just prior to the coming of the salvation they had been promised. **Moses.** It was Moses who prophesied that God would one day send another prophet to lead his people (Deut. 18:15). The early Christians took this to be a prophecy about Jesus (Acts 3:22–26; 7:35–37). The presence of both Moses and Elijah on the mountain is meant to indicate that the Old Testament Law and the Prophets endorse Jesus as God's appointed Messiah.

9:5 shelters. Peter might have had in mind the huts of intertwined branches which were put up at the Festival of Tabernacles to commemorate Israel's time in the wilderness. Or he might be thinking of the "Tent of Meeting" where God met with Moses.

9:6 frightened. Throughout the Bible, whenever God is manifested before people the human response is one of fear (Ex. 3:5–6; Judg. 6:20–23; Isa. 6:5; Dan. 10:7–8; Rev. 1:17).

9:7 This verse is full of Old Testament allusions that are meant to confirm Jesus' divine authority. **a cloud.** This cloud is a symbol of the presence of God. **a voice.** As he did at the baptism of Jesus (1:11), God proclaims Jesus is his Son. **This is my Son, whom**

[8]Suddenly, when they looked around, they no longer saw anyone
with them except Jesus.
[9]As they were coming down the mountain, Jesus gave them orders
not to tell anyone what they had seen until the Son of Man had risen
from the dead. [10]They kept the matter to themselves, discussing what
"rising from the dead" meant.
[11]And they asked him, "Why do the teachers of the law say that Elijah must come first?"
[12]Jesus replied, "To be sure, Elijah does come first, and restores all
things. Why then is it written that the Son of Man must suffer much
and be rejected? [13]But I tell you, Elijah has come, and they have done
to him everything they wished, just as it is written about him."

The Healing of a Boy With an Evil Spirit

[14]When they came to the other disciples, they saw a large crowd
around them and the teachers of the law arguing with them. [15]As
soon as all the people saw Jesus, they were overwhelmed with wonder and ran to greet him.
[16]"What are you arguing with them about?" he asked.
[17]A man in the crowd answered, "Teacher, I brought you my son,
who is possessed by a spirit that has robbed him of speech. [18]When-
ever it seizes him, it throws him to the ground. He foams at the
mouth, gnashes his teeth and becomes rigid. I asked your disciples to
drive out the spirit, but they could not."
[19]"O unbelieving generation," Jesus replied, "how long shall I stay
with you? How long shall I put up with you? Bring the boy to me."
[20]So they brought him. When the spirit saw Jesus, it immediately
threw the boy into a convulsion. He fell to the ground and rolled
around, foaming at the mouth.
[21]Jesus asked the boy's father, "How long has he been like this?"
"From childhood," he answered. [22]"It has often thrown him into
fire or water to kill him. But if you can do anything, take pity on us
and help us."
[23]" 'If you can'?" said Jesus. "Everything is possible for him who
believes."
[24]Immediately the boy's father exclaimed, "I do believe; help me
overcome my unbelief!"
[25]When Jesus saw that a crowd was running to the scene, he re-

said, "this is my beloved son, whom I love. Listen to him"? If you had been one of the three disciples, how would you have felt? **5.** What did Jesus ask the disciples to do and how did this lead into the question about Elijah?

APPLY How would you describe your relationship with Jesus: On a mountaintop? In the valley? Some place in-between?

OPEN When you were a child, what issues were most likely to trigger an argument within your family?

STUDY 1. What experience immediately precedes this story? What must have happened while he was away? **2.** How would you feel if three of your buddies were having a mountaintop experience while you were left to carry on the ministry? **3.** Of the three groups of people—the Pharisees, the disciples, and the father of the boy—which came the closest to having faith? **4.** What is the father saying by "I do believe. Help me overcome my unbelief"? **5.** What does the description of the illness of the boy remind you of? Have you ever seen anything like this? What happened when Jesus rebuked the evil spirit? **6.** What do you believe about evil spirits? Is this something the church needs to take seriously today—or should we leave this to the mental health profession?

APPLY 1. "I do believe; help my unbelief." When is the last time you felt like this? **2.** Where

---

I love. By means of this event, it is revealed that not only is Jesus the Messiah (as the disciples have just confessed), he is also the Son of God. Both titles are necessary for a full understanding of his nature and role. **Listen to him!** The new prophet, whose authority and glory superseded that of Moses, was on the scene. This is a divine attestation to his authority.

9:11 Elijah must come first. The Jews believed God would send Elijah back before the Messiah appeared to again call Israel to faithfulness (Mal. 4:5).

9:18 The symptoms closely resemble those of a certain form of epilepsy. **they could not.** The faith of the disciples is shown once again to be incomplete.

9:19 O unbelieving generation. This is the cry of anguish and loneliness of one who knows so clearly the way things really are, and yet is constantly confronted with disbelief in various forms.

9:23 If you can? The man indicated that he is not sure if Jesus can perform such a miracle (after all, his disciples have failed). By highlighting his doubts Jesus pinpoints the real issue: the question is not whether Jesus has the ability to heal (which has been amply demonstrated); the issue is the man's faith.

9:24 unbelief. The problem here is one of *doubt* (being in two minds about an issue) not one of *disbelief* (certainty that something is not true). The father did not disbelieve. After all, he had brought his son to Jesus to be healed (v. 17). His faith has been shaken by the failure of the disciples to heal his son (v. 18) so that now, even though he desperately wants his child to be free of this demon, he wonders if it is possible (v. 22).

buked the evil[a] spirit. "You deaf and mute spirit," he said, "I command
you, come out of him and never enter him again."
26The spirit shrieked, convulsed him violently and came out. The boy
looked so much like a corpse that many said, "He's dead." 27But Jesus
took him by the hand and lifted him to his feet, and he stood up.
28After Jesus had gone indoors, his disciples asked him privately,
"Why couldn't we drive it out?"
29He replied, "This kind can come out only by prayer.[b]"
30They left that place and passed through Galilee. Jesus did not
want anyone to know where they were, 31because he was teaching
his disciples. He said to them, "The Son of Man is going to be betrayed into the hands of men. They will kill him, and after three days
he will rise." 32But they did not understand what he meant and were
afraid to ask him about it.

Who Is the Greatest?

33They came to Capernaum. When he was in the house, he asked
them, "What were you arguing about on the road?" 34But they kept
quiet because on the way they had argued about who was the greatest.
35Sitting down, Jesus called the Twelve and said, "If anyone wants
to be first, he must be the very last, and the servant of all."
36He took a little child and had him stand among them. Taking him
in his arms, he said to them, 37"Whoever welcomes one of these little
children in my name welcomes me; and whoever welcomes me does
not welcome me but the one who sent me."

Whoever Is Not Against Us Is for Us

38"Teacher," said John, "we saw a man driving out demons in your
name and we told him to stop, because he was not one of us."
39"Do not stop him," Jesus said. "No one who does a miracle in my
name can in the next moment say anything bad about me, 40for whoever is not against us is for us. 41I tell you the truth, anyone who gives
you a cup of water in my name because you belong to Christ will certainly not lose his reward.

Causing to Sin

42"And if anyone causes one of these little ones who believe in me
to sin, it would be better for him to be thrown into the sea with a

[a]25 Greek *unclean* [b]29 Some manuscripts *prayer and fasting*

are you struggling right now: Family concerns? Job concerns? Doubts about your beliefs? **3.** Who can you go to and ask to pray with you about this?

OPEN When you were a kid, were you chosen first or last when choosing up sides for a game?

STUDY 1. While Jesus is explaining to his disciples about his death (v. 31), what are the disciples arguing over? **2.** What do you know about the status of children in biblical times? What is the lesson here for the disciples when it comes to power and control and, for that matter, for leadership? **3.** How does the issue of power and control spill over into the issue of competition from unauthorized disciples?

APPLY 1. When it comes to spiritual leadership, who do you admire? **2.** If you were looking for a spiritual leader, what would you look for?

OPEN Do you remember the story of the Pied Piper of Hamlin?

9:29 prayer. The disciples have been given the authority to cast out demons (6:7) and have, in fact, done so (6:13). However, as this incident makes clear, this power was not their own. It required continuing dependence upon God.

9:30 passed through Galilee. They leave Herod Philip's territory but they do not return to Galilee as they have done in the past. Instead, they pass through enroute to Jerusalem and Jesus' death.

9:31 betrayed. This is a new note in his teaching. It is not just that he will be rejected by the leaders of Israel. There will be an element of treachery involved.

9:34 greatest. Once again the disciples have missed the point. In the face of Jesus' teaching about suffering and death, they are concerned about their position and personal power.

9:38 a man driving out demons in your name. Acts 19:13–16 describes the successful use by Jewish exorcists of Jesus' name to drive out demons. In exorcism, it was the power of the name that dominated. This unnamed exorcist is an example of one of his followers who is to be welcomed (thus illustrating the point Jesus just made in v. 37).

9:42 causes ... to sin. Literally, something which snares a person or animal; which causes them to trip up or entices them to stray. **these little ones who believe in me.** The reference is to Jesus' followers (v. 37). **the sea.** Jews were terrified of the sea. **a large millstone.** There are two words for millstone. One refers to a small hand mill used in a home; the other (which Jesus uses here) refers to the huge upper stone of a community mill, so big that it had to be drawn around by a donkey.

STUDY 1. Who are the "little children"? 2. How does this teaching relate to the issue of power and control in the previous paragraph? 3. What is the warning to the disciples in the "salt" analogy? 4. What is the clear teaching in this passage for leadership today in the church?

APPLY 1. How is the strength of the spiritual salt in your life at the moment? 2. Who helps you check on the strength of the salt in your life?

large millstone tied around his neck. 43If your hand causes you to sin,
cut it off. It is better for you to enter life maimed than with two hands
to go into hell, where the fire never goes out.[a] 45And if your foot
causes you to sin, cut it off. It is better for you to enter life crippled
than to have two feet and be thrown into hell.[b] 47And if your eye
causes you to sin, pluck it out. It is better for you to enter the kingdom of God with one eye than to have two eyes and be thrown into
hell, 48where

" 'their worm does not die,
and the fire is not quenched.'[c]

49Everyone will be salted with fire.
50"Salt is good, but if it loses its saltiness, how can you make it
salty again? Have salt in yourselves, and be at peace with each other."

OPEN What couple do you look up to as having a model marriage?

STUDY 1. What is significant about the place where this question about divorce comes up? Why are the Pharisees asking the question? 2. According to the Old Testament law, what did a man have to do to "send away" his wife? Why was this provision allowed (v. 5)? 3. What is the intention of God for marriage? 4. How does Jesus answer the question of divorce? 5. How would you answer this question today for someone struggling in their marriage?

APPLY In this crazy world we live in today, where does grace and forgiveness enter in?

Divorce

10 Jesus then left that place and went into the region of Judea
and across the Jordan. Again crowds of people came to him,
and as was his custom, he taught them.
2Some Pharisees came and tested him by asking, "Is it lawful for a
man to divorce his wife?"
3"What did Moses command you?" he replied.
4They said, "Moses permitted a man to write a certificate of divorce
and send her away."
5"It was because your hearts were hard that Moses wrote you this
law," Jesus replied. 6"But at the beginning of creation God 'made
them male and female.'[d] 7'For this reason a man will leave his father
and mother and be united to his wife,[e] 8and the two will become one
flesh.'[f] So they are no longer two, but one. 9Therefore what God has
joined together, let man not separate."
10When they were in the house again, the disciples asked Jesus
about this. 11He answered, "Anyone who divorces his wife and marries

[a]43 Some manuscripts *out,* 44*where / " 'their worm does not die, / and the fire is not quenched.'*
[b]45 Some manuscripts *hell,* 46*where / " 'their worm does not die, / and the fire is not quenched.'*
[c]48 Isaiah 66:24 [d]6 Gen. 1:27 [e]7 Some early manuscripts do not have *and be united to his wife.*
[f]8 Gen. 2:24

9:43 life. Spiritual life; life in the kingdom of God (v. 47). **hell.** Literally, Gehenna—a ravine outside Jerusalem where children were once sacrificed and garbage was burned here during the time of Jesus.

9:50 Salt. Salt does not normally lose its taste, but salt from the Dead Sea was mixed with impurities and over time could acquire a stale taste. **be at peace with each other.** When his followers have such a sense of service, peace is the outcome. Had the disciples grasped this concept of servanthood instead of opting for power and greatness, they would not have been arguing on the road (v. 33).

10:1 that place. He begins his journey to Jerusalem in Capernaum (9:33), the place where his ministry began in the Gospel of Mark (1:16–45). **Judea.** A Roman province in the south of Palestine, similar in size and location to the land of Judah in the Old Testament. **across the Jordan.** This is a reference to a specific region called Perea, which was a narrow corridor on the east side of the Jordan. Pious Jews would cross over the Jordan into Perea to avoid traveling through Samaria. This is the territory of Herod Antipas, the ruler who beheaded John the Baptist.

10:2 tested him. It is not by chance that the Pharisees question Jesus about divorce. It was this issue that led to John the Baptist's death (6:17–28). If Jesus responded that divorce was lawful, then the leaders could criticize him as being in opposition to John the Baptist whom the people greatly respected for his courage in opposing Herod's sin. If Jesus said it was not lawful, then the leaders might be able to get Herod to arrest him as well. **divorce.** All the Jewish parties agreed (on the basis of Deut. 24:1) that divorce was allowed. The issue in this debate concerned the grounds on which such divorce was permissible. It was only the husband who had the right of divorce. The most that a wife could do was to ask her husband to divorce her.

10:4 a certificate of divorce. This was issued to the woman as a form of protection, verifying her release from marriage and giving her the right to remarry.

10:11 commits adultery against her. In the Jewish law of that era,

another woman commits adultery against her. 12And if she divorces
her husband and marries another man, she commits adultery."

The Little Children and Jesus

13People were bringing little children to Jesus to have him touch
them, but the disciples rebuked them. 14When Jesus saw this, he was
indignant. He said to them, "Let the little children come to me, and
do not hinder them, for the kingdom of God belongs to such as these.
15I tell you the truth, anyone who will not receive the kingdom of God
like a little child will never enter it." 16And he took the children in his
arms, put his hands on them and blessed them.

The Rich Young Man

17As Jesus started on his way, a man ran up to him and fell on his
knees before him. "Good teacher," he asked, "what must I do to inherit eternal life?"

18"Why do you call me good?" Jesus answered. "No one is good—
except God alone. 19You know the commandments: 'Do not murder,
do not commit adultery, do not steal, do not give false testimony, do
not defraud, honor your father and mother.'[a]"

20"Teacher," he declared, "all these I have kept since I was a boy."

21Jesus looked at him and loved him. "One thing you lack," he said.
"Go, sell everything you have and give to the poor, and you will have
treasure in heaven. Then come, follow me."

22At this the man's face fell. He went away sad, because he had
great wealth.

23Jesus looked around and said to his disciples, "How hard it is for
the rich to enter the kingdom of God!"

[a]19 Exodus 20:12-16; Deut. 5:16-20

OPEN 1. When are you most likely to lose patience with your children? 2. Did you choose the career you are in for (a) money, (b) fulfillment, or (c) the chance to make a difference?

STUDY 1. Why would the disciples want to keep the children away from Jesus? What is the lesson in children for the disciples? **2.** Why did the rich young man ask the question in verse 17? What might have been missing in his life? **3.** How would you have ranked the spirituality of this man? **4.** This rich man had everything—initiative, good religious upbringing, lots of promise—why did Jesus add one demand on him that he did not require of any other person? **5.** How did the disciples react? What does this reveal about their idea of rewards for a good life? **6.** What does Peter humbly claim for the disciples? How does Jesus deal with this? **7.** What is the lesson in this passage for the "health and wealth" religion today in the church?

APPLY 1. When did you come to the place that success was measured by your relationship to God, and not your bank

adultery was considered to be an offense against the man. Jesus asserts the responsibility of the husband to be faithful to his wife, who is his equal in relation to God's command.

10:13 little children. The age is uncertain. The term was used to describe infants and children up to 12 years old. **the disciples rebuked them.** The demands on Jesus were ceaseless. The disciples wanted to protect him, and so in an era when children were expected to be kept in the background, it was not unreasonable that they would attempt to curb this particular demand.

10:14 the kingdom of God belongs to such as these. Jesus says this humble inner disposition of soul must be evident in members of his kingdom.

10:17 a man. Luke describes him as a ruler (Luke 18:18); Matthew calls him a young man (Matt. 19:20). **Good teacher.** This is a title of respect, acknowledging Jesus' status as an exceptional rabbi. Coming from a man of such status, the assumption would be that Jesus would likewise acknowledge his status by responding with a corresponding title of respect. **what must I do?** The emphasis on doing (gaining the kingdom by virtue of one's religious activities or moral achievements) is characteristic of the Pharisees' view of religion and is in sharp contrast to Jesus' teaching about receiving the kingdom as a gift that is grasped by simple faith (v. 15). **inherit.** Gain entrance to; possess. **eternal life.** What he is asking for is entrance to the kingdom of God (vv. 23–25). The view in that era was that the present age would end, at which time the righteous would enter the new age where they will experience eternal life. He wants to be part of this company.

10:19 the commandments. The commandments Jesus lists deal with a person's responsibility toward others. Jesus recites what would have been the familiar list of moral obligations from the Ten Commandments (Ex. 20:12–16) with the notable addition of the command, "do not defraud." This is probably the precise problem this man must confront. To defraud was to deprive a worker of his just payment, a form of economic oppression often associated with the wealthy of Jesus' day.

10:20 The man believes he has kept the commandments, and yet he is unsure whether he has gained eternal life. This was the fallacy of a system based on works/righteousness. People were struggling to be counted among the righteous until the judgment (and then it was too late). There was no hope for all failed

10:21 loved him. Mark is the only Gospel to note Jesus' affection for this earnest and sincere young man. **Go, sell everything.** It was felt in the Old Testament that riches by themselves were no hindrance to spiritual pursuit. But Jesus points out that accumulation of wealth can hinder participation in God's kingdom. **follow me.** The weight of emphasis is not on selling all, but on following Jesus. The man's possessions are in the way of his discipleship to Jesus.

account? **2.** Are you open to the possibility that God has something totally new and different for you to do that might require a radical change in your lifestyle?

OPEN 1. If you had one month to live, how would you spend it? **2.** What did your parents want you to be when you grew up?

STUDY 1. How do you think the disciples felt when Jesus explained what was going to happen to him in Jerusalem? **2.** Why do you think James and John asked Jesus for this special honor (v. 37)? **3.** What view of the kingdom are James and John still clinging to? How could they think this way after what Jesus said (9:35; 10:33–34)? **4.** What "cup" and "baptism" is Jesus talking about in verse 39? **5.** What made the other disciples indignant? **6.** How does Jesus use this uproar to convey new insights into "greatness"? **7.** How effective is your church at caring for all of the people? What is your church doing to raise up more leaders to care for the needs of your church?

24 The disciples were amazed at his words. But Jesus said again, "Children, how hard it is[a] to enter the kingdom of God! **25** It is easier for a camel to go through the eye of a needle than for a rich man to enter the kingdom of God."

26 The disciples were even more amazed, and said to each other, "Who then can be saved?"

27 Jesus looked at them and said, "With man this is impossible, but not with God; all things are possible with God."

28 Peter said to him, "We have left everything to follow you!"

29 "I tell you the truth," Jesus replied, "no one who has left home or brothers or sisters or mother or father or children or fields for me and the gospel **30** will fail to receive a hundred times as much in this present age (homes, brothers, sisters, mothers, children and fields—and with them, persecutions) and in the age to come, eternal life. **31** But many who are first will be last, and the last first."

Jesus Again Predicts His Death

32 They were on their way up to Jerusalem, with Jesus leading the way, and the disciples were astonished, while those who followed were afraid. Again he took the Twelve aside and told them what was going to happen to him. **33** "We are going up to Jerusalem," he said, "and the Son of Man will be betrayed to the chief priests and teachers of the law. They will condemn him to death and will hand him over to the Gentiles, **34** who will mock him and spit on him, flog him and kill him. Three days later he will rise."

The Request of James and John

35 Then James and John, the sons of Zebedee, came to him. "Teacher," they said, "we want you to do for us whatever we ask."

36 "What do you want me to do for you?" he asked.

37 They replied, "Let one of us sit at your right and the other at your left in your glory."

38 "You don't know what you are asking," Jesus said. "Can you drink the cup I drink or be baptized with the baptism I am baptized with?"

39 "We can," they answered.

[a]24 Some manuscripts *is for those who trust in riches*

10:24 amazed. The disciples are astonished because traditional Jewish wisdom saw wealth as a sign of God's favor; it was thought to be a verification that one had led a godly life (Job 1:10; 42:10; Ps. 128:1–2). **how hard it is.** Jesus repeats his statement, but now drops the reference to the rich.

10:26 even more amazed. The disciples are even more bewildered than before. What Jesus says directly confronts their assumptions about salvation. **Who then can be saved?** They realize the radical nature of Jesus' statement and wonder about their own fate. If it is difficult for anyone to enter the kingdom, even the rich who they had always assumed were the favored of God, then what chance do they have?

10:29 for me and the gospel. That for which the sacrifice of leaving home and family is made is Jesus and the work of his kingdom.

10:32 Jerusalem. Jesus' destination is now revealed, as is the site of his betrayal, death and resurrection (v. 33). **astonished ... afraid.** Given the increasingly hostile response toward Jesus by the leaders, it was frightening that Jesus was heading directly into a confrontation with them.

10:37 They interpret Jesus' heading toward Jerusalem as a sign that he will initiate his new kingdom in Jerusalem, over which he will rule as the new king of Israel.

10:38 drink the cup. This is a phrase which means "share the same fate." In the Old Testament, the cup is a metaphor for wrath (Ps. 75:8; Isa. 51:17–22). **baptism.** In the Old Testament, the image of a deluge or flood overwhelming one is used as a metaphor for disaster (Ps. 42:7; Isa. 43:2). Both the cup and the baptism refer to Jesus' coming suffering and death for the sins of the world.

10:39 We can. The disciples answer too readily Jesus' question as to whether they can share his cup and his baptism. They do not grasp what he means by this question, thinking perhaps that it is referring to being in fellowship with him. Their leadership will not be expressed through positions of authority but through suffering and death.

Jesus said to them, "You will drink the cup I drink and be baptized
with the baptism I am baptized with, 40but to sit at my right or left is
not for me to grant. These places belong to those for whom they have
been prepared."
41When the ten heard about this, they became indignant with
James and John. 42Jesus called them together and said, "You know
that those who are regarded as rulers of the Gentiles lord it over
them, and their high officials exercise authority over them. 43Not so
with you. Instead, whoever wants to become great among you must
be your servant, 44and whoever wants to be first must be slave of all.
45For even the Son of Man did not come to be served, but to serve,
and to give his life as a ransom for many."

Blind Bartimaeus Receives His Sight

46Then they came to Jericho. As Jesus and his disciples, together
with a large crowd, were leaving the city, a blind man, Bartimaeus
(that is, the Son of Timaeus), was sitting by the roadside begging.
47When he heard that it was Jesus of Nazareth, he began to shout,
"Jesus, Son of David, have mercy on me!"
48Many rebuked him and told him to be quiet, but he shouted all
the more, "Son of David, have mercy on me!"
49Jesus stopped and said, "Call him."
So they called to the blind man, "Cheer up! On your feet! He's calling you." 50Throwing his cloak aside, he jumped to his feet and came
to Jesus.
51"What do you want me to do for you?" Jesus asked him.
The blind man said, "Rabbi, I want to see."
52"Go," said Jesus, "your faith has healed you." Immediately he received his sight and followed Jesus along the road.

The Triumphal Entry

11 As they approached Jerusalem and came to Bethphage and
Bethany at the Mount of Olives, Jesus sent two of his

APPLY 1. In your spiritual pilgrimage, who is the leader that modeled the servant leadership style for you? **2.** What are you doing to model the servant leadership style in your family?

OPEN What do you remember from what you have been taught in the past about Jericho?

STUDY 1. Although he was blind, what did the man see in Jesus that the rest of the crowd didn't see? **2.** How does the blind man in this story illustrate the steps to be taken to become a believer?

APPLY 1. When was the last time you saw enthusiasm like this blind man had for Jesus? **2.** If Jesus asked you point blank right now, "what do you want me to do for you," what would you say?

OPEN What is the closest you have come to meeting a world leader or celebrity?

10:43 servant. Rather than become masters (and exercise authority), they are to become servants (and meet the needs of others).

10:45 ransom. In the first century, a slave or a prisoner could gain freedom if a purchase price (ransom) was paid. Jesus would pay the ransom price "for many" by his death (Titus 2:14; 1 Peter 1:18–19).

10:46 Jericho. They've almost completed their journey from Galilee. Jericho is a city some 18 miles east of Jerusalem and the place where travelers recrossed the Jordan back into Israel. **a large crowd.** These were pilgrims on their way to Jerusalem for the Passover Feast. Every male over 12 years of age was expected to attend.

10:47 Jesus, Son of David. A debate was going on as to who the Messiah would be. Would he come from the tribe of Levi, or was he a king in the line of David? Clearly this is a messianic title by which Bartimaeus hails Jesus. Interestingly, Jesus does not silence him as he has done so often in the past when his identity is revealed. The time for secrecy is past. He accepts the title. This is the only use in Mark of this title, on the eve of Jesus' entry into Jerusalem as messianic King.

10:52 your faith has healed you. Bartimaeus demonstrated his faith in several ways: by his title for Jesus (showing he grasped who Jesus was), by his persistence (he will not let this opportunity go by), and by his request for healing (showing that he believed Jesus could do so).

11:1 Jerusalem. Traditionally, it is understood that Jesus is arriving into Jerusalem, the spiritual heart of the nation, at the time of Passover. This feast celebrated God's deliverance of Israel from Egypt centuries before. At this time, the population of Jerusalem would be swelled by Jews from all over the known world who would come to the city for the festival. **Bethphage.** This was a village near Jerusalem, probably across a ravine from Bethany. **Bethany.** A small village some two miles east of Jerusalem, site of the eastern slope of the Mount of Olives. This is where Jesus and his disciples were lodged during the Passover. **Mount of Olives.** This place was associated in popular understanding with the coming of the Messiah. According to Zechariah 14:4–5, this is the place where God will commence the final judgment of Israel's enemies. It is not by accident that Jesus chose this place to prepare his entry into Jerusalem. **Jesus sent.** Having come to the right spot, his next

STUDY After three years of preparation, the time has come for his mission to be fulfilled. **1.** Would you call this day a "victory lap" or a "funeral march"? **2.** When Jesus mounts a donkey, what does this signal to the Jewish audience? How do they react? Who are conspicuously absent? **3.** Why would Jesus go to the temple? What reception does he receive? **4.** What comes to mind when you compare this story to today? If Jesus showed up at the courthouse of your town, what kind of reception would he get? How would the papers / TV carry the story?

APPLY 1. As you think back, what would you pinpoint as the moment when Jesus entered into your life? Was it more gradual? More intellectual? More dramatic? **2.** Who was on the reception committee to greet him?

OPEN Are you more likely to act without thinking or think without acting?

STUDY 1. Does Jesus in this story fit the image you have of him? **2.** What do you think the disciples were feeling when he started turning over the tables? **3.** Who is Jesus referring to when he said, "You have

disciples, 2 saying to them, "Go to the village ahead of you, and just as
you enter it, you will find a colt tied there, which no one has ever
ridden. Untie it and bring it here. 3 If anyone asks you, 'Why are you
doing this?' tell him, 'The Lord needs it and will send it back here
shortly.' "

4 They went and found a colt outside in the street, tied at a doorway.
As they untied it, 5 some people standing there asked, "What are you
doing, untying that colt?" 6 They answered as Jesus had told them to,
and the people let them go. 7 When they brought the colt to Jesus and
threw their cloaks over it, he sat on it. 8 Many people spread their
cloaks on the road, while others spread branches they had cut in the
fields. 9 Those who went ahead and those who followed shouted,

"Hosanna![a]"

"Blessed is he who comes in the name of the Lord!"[b]

10 "Blessed is the coming kingdom of our father David!"

"Hosanna in the highest!"

11 Jesus entered Jerusalem and went to the temple. He looked
around at everything, but since it was already late, he went out to
Bethany with the Twelve.

Jesus Clears the Temple

12 The next day as they were leaving Bethany, Jesus was hungry.
13 Seeing in the distance a fig tree in leaf, he went to find out if it had
any fruit. When he reached it, he found nothing but leaves, because it
was not the season for figs. 14 Then he said to the tree, "May no one
ever eat fruit from you again." And his disciples heard him say it.

[a]9 A Hebrew expression meaning "Save!" which became an exclamation of praise; also in verse 10
[b]9 Psalm 118:25,26

step is to send two disciples to secure the colt on which he will ride into Jerusalem. Clearly, Jesus is consciously preparing his entry. His arrival will reveal who he is.

11:2 a colt. According to Zechariah 9:9, the King would come riding on a colt. Jesus will not simply enter Jerusalem. He will come as the messianic King. He will not come as a warrior-king (as the people expected) riding a war horse. Matthew 21:2 states this was a donkey, specifically fulfilling Zechariah's prophecy and emphasizing the peaceful, gentle nature of the Messiah. **tied there.** In a prophetic word about the tribe of Judah, Genesis 49:8–12 speaks of a colt tethered to a choice vine. This was understood by many to be a prophecy that the Messiah would arise out of the tribe of Judah.

11:3 If anyone asks you ... tell him. The words the disciples are to say will identify them to the owner as those Jesus has sent. **The Lord.** Thus far in the Gospel, Jesus has not referred to himself by this title. While it can simply be a formal term for a master, the context of this occasion indicates he was implying divine authority as well.

11:8 spread their cloaks. This was a gesture of respect, given to kings (2 Kin. 9:12–13).

11:9 Hosanna! Literally, "Save now." The psalm from which this cry is taken (Ps. 118:25–26) was understood by the rabbis to be a messianic psalm, referring to King David and the final redemption. **Blessed is he.** While the psalm from which this cry is taken (Ps. 118:26), originally served as a tribute to the king of Israel, it was applied to any pilgrim who traveled to Jerusalem for the feasts. It was later understood by the rabbis to be a messianic psalm, referring to the final redemption that would be ushered in by the Messiah.

11:10 our father David. King David was devoted to God and through his line God had promised to build an everlasting kingdom. The people expected the Messiah to be a military hero like David who had delivered them from the hands of their enemies and been crowned king both by divine appointment and popular acclaim.

11:11 temple. This was the third temple to be built on Mount Zion. It was built by Herod the Great in 20 B.C. and was a magnificent structure covering some 30 acres. The temple consisted of four concentric courts ringed by enormous walls.

11:13 fig tree. On the Mount of Olives, fig trees are in leaf by early April, but they would not have ripe fruit until June, long after the Passover. Fig trees were a common prophetic symbol. They were associated with Israel and with judgment (Jer. 8:13; Hos. 9:10–11; Mic. 7:1). Thus, it was no accident that Jesus chose a fig tree for this particular drama.

[15]On reaching Jerusalem, Jesus entered the temple area and began driving out those who were buying and selling there. He overturned the tables of the money changers and the benches of those selling doves, [16]and would not allow anyone to carry merchandise through the temple courts. [17]And as he taught them, he said, "Is it not written:

" 'My house will be called
a house of prayer for all nations'[a]?

But you have made it 'a den of robbers.'[b]"

[18]The chief priests and the teachers of the law heard this and began looking for a way to kill him, for they feared him, because the whole crowd was amazed at his teaching.

[19]When evening came, they[c] went out of the city.

The Withered Fig Tree

[20]In the morning, as they went along, they saw the fig tree withered from the roots. [21]Peter remembered and said to Jesus, "Rabbi, look! The fig tree you cursed has withered!"

[22]"Have[d] faith in God," Jesus answered. [23]"I tell you the truth, if anyone says to this mountain, 'Go, throw yourself into the sea,' and does not doubt in his heart but believes that what he says will happen, it will be done for him. [24]Therefore I tell you, whatever you ask for in prayer, believe that you have received it, and it will be yours. [25]And when you stand praying, if you hold anything against anyone, forgive him, so that your Father in heaven may forgive you your sins.[e]"

The Authority of Jesus Questioned

[27]They arrived again in Jerusalem, and while Jesus was walking in the temple courts, the chief priests, the teachers of the law and the

[a]*17* Isaiah 56:7 [b]*17* Jer. 7:11 [c]*19* Some early manuscripts *he* [d]*22* Some early manuscripts *If you have* [e]*25* Some manuscripts *sins.* [26]*But if you do not forgive, neither will your Father who is in heaven forgive your sins.*

made it a 'den of robbers' "? What did the Jewish leaders decide to do? **4.** Jesus has just given his disciples a lecture about servant leadership (10:42–44). What happened to his leadership style? **5.** Why did he cleanse the temple but not try to overthrow the government?

APPLY 1. What is the cause that God has told you to get involved in? **2.** If you can't overturn tables, what can you do?

OPEN 1. With fruit trees, are you a miracle worker or a curse? **2.** Have you ever challenged an authority or been charged by one?

STUDY 1. What happened that Peter remembers here (vv. 12–14)? **2.** Faced with resistance, what does Jesus challenge the disciples to do? **3.** What happened the day before that stirred up the hornet's nest (vv. 12–19)? **4.** How would Jesus be in trouble either way he answered the question? **5.** How does Jesus turn the tables on the Pharisees?

APPLY What is the issue in your life right now that has you on the horns of a dilemma?

11:15–19 Jesus' first act following his triumphal entry is to go into the temple and (by his actions) call to account the religious leadership of Israel. It is significant that he challenges these leaders in the temple, the very center of their power. Once again Jesus conveys his message by means of dramatic action. Jesus' action in the temple would have shocked everyone as he totally disrupted "normal" business and drastically interfered in religious observances.

11:15 buying and selling. Worship in the temple centered on sacrifice. Those wishing to participate were required to offer an unblemished animal, and apparently temple inspectors approved only those animals bought from certified vendors (who sold animals at a huge markup). **money changers.** At Passover, each Jew was required to pay a temple tax of one-half shekel (nearly two days' wages). No other currency was acceptable, necessitating money changers to exchange the money of pilgrims coming from outside. The money changers charged exorbitant amounts for the simple act of exchanging currency; up to one-half day's wages of working people. **those selling doves.** A dove was the lowliest of all sacrifices. While a lamb was normally required, the Law had a provision that those too poor to afford a lamb could offer two doves instead (Lev. 5:7). While this provision was still observed, temple vendors charged 20 times what it cost to buy a dove outside the temple.

11:17 a house of prayer for all nations. The outermost area of the temple where all these activities were taking place was called the Court of the Gentiles. It was intended to be a place where pious Gentiles could pray. Instead, it had been turned into a raucous bazaar, making prayer impossible, and thus doing away with the only place in the temple where non-Jews could come before the true God. **a den of robbers.** This quote is from Jeremiah 7:11. In the days of Jeremiah, the religious authorities likewise masked their corruption with the veneer of religion.

11:18 chief priests. These were Sadducees. **teachers of the law.** These were typically Pharisees. The two sects normally did not cooperate together since they had so many differences between them, but they acted as one in their decision regarding Jesus.

11:21 Peter remembered. Jesus has done something so unusual, so out-of-character that the disciples cannot help but ponder it. What did it mean? Not surprisingly, the next day Peter spots the tree, now withered, and comments on it.

11:23 this mountain. This is probably the Mount of Olives overlooking Jerusalem. **the sea.** The Dead Sea is visible from the Mount of Olives.

11:27 the chief priests, the teachers of the law and the elders. The

elders came to him. 28"By what authority are you doing these
things?" they asked. "And who gave you authority to do this?"
29Jesus replied, "I will ask you one question. Answer me, and I will
tell you by what authority I am doing these things. 30John's baptism—was it from heaven, or from men? Tell me!"
31They discussed it among themselves and said, "If we say, 'From
heaven,' he will ask, 'Then why didn't you believe him?' 32But if we
say, 'From men' . . ." (They feared the people, for everyone held that
John really was a prophet.)
33So they answered Jesus, "We don't know."
Jesus said, "Neither will I tell you by what authority I am doing
these things."

The Parable of the Tenants

12 He then began to speak to them in parables: "A man planted
a vineyard. He put a wall around it, dug a pit for the winepress and built a watchtower. Then he rented the vineyard to some
farmers and went away on a journey. 2At harvest time he sent a
servant to the tenants to collect from them some of the fruit of the
vineyard. 3But they seized him, beat him and sent him away empty-
handed. 4Then he sent another servant to them; they struck this man
on the head and treated him shamefully. 5He sent still another, and
that one they killed. He sent many others; some of them they beat,
others they killed.
6"He had one left to send, a son, whom he loved. He sent him last
of all, saying, 'They will respect my son.'
7"But the tenants said to one another, 'This is the heir. Come, let's
kill him, and the inheritance will be ours.' 8So they took him and
killed him, and threw him out of the vineyard.
9"What then will the owner of the vineyard do? He will come and
kill those tenants and give the vineyard to others. 10Haven't you read
this scripture:

OPEN 1. If you owned a garden or an orchard, what would you grow? **2.** If you had to entrust your business or belongings to someone outside your family, whom would you choose?

STUDY 1. Would you like to own a wine vineyard? **2.** If you turned over your vineyard to tenants like the ones in the parable and they killed the people you sent to collect the rent, how would you feel? What would you do? **3.** Why would the tenants believe they could inherit the vineyard if they killed the son? **4.** Who are the "others" that the owner will give the vineyard to? What will happen to the religious establishment in the prophecy about the "capstone"? **5.** How do you think the religious leaders felt at the end of this parable? Why didn't they arrest Jesus on the spot?

---

chief priests were the key officers of the temple, just below the high priest in rank. The elders were powerful and (reputedly) wise leaders of Israel. They were generally not priests, but instead were administrators, judges and military leaders of Israel. The teachers of the law were religious lawyers. Taken together, these three groups comprised the Sanhedrin—the ruling Jewish council—who opposed him as Jesus prophesied they would (8:31).

12:1 A man planted a vineyard ... dug a pit ... built a watchtower. For the religious leaders, Jesus' use of these phrases would surely call to mind the well-known imagery found in a poem originally delivered by the prophet Isaiah centuries before (Isa. 5:1–7). In Isaiah's song, the symbol of the vineyard was used to describe Israel. Although planted and cultivated by God, Israel was compared to a vineyard that produced only bad fruit. As a result, the landowner destroyed it. **vineyard.** Grapes were one of the major crops in Israel. They were eaten fresh, made into raisins, boiled into a syrup, or made into wine. This particular vineyard was carefully built, with a wall around it to keep out animals, a pit in which to crush the grapes to make wine, and a tower where the farmer kept a lookout for robbers and slept during the harvest. **went away.** Jesus changes the Isaiah poem here in order to put the spotlight on the religious authorities. While in Isaiah God is the farmer who waits for the fruit which never appears, in this parable God is the landlord who leaves his vineyard in the care of others who are responsible to him. It produces fruit, but the tenants refuse to give him his share of the produce.

12:6 a son, whom he loved. The crowd didn't know the identity of the son, yet Mark's readers know that it is Jesus. A central theme in chapters 11–16 is the discovery that Jesus is the Son of God.

12:7 inheritance. The arrival of the son signaled to the tenants that the owner had died. By law, a piece of ownerless property (which it would be if they killed the son) could be kept by those who first seized it. Since the tenants assumed the land would be ownerless if the son was dead, they plotted to kill him in order to lay claim to the land for themselves.

12:9 give the vineyard to others. The appearance of the owner would shatter the illusion that the tenants now owned the land. The owner could enlist the aid of the government to force the evil tenants off his land. The landowner would then rent the vineyard to people who would meet the terms of their contract. The implication in the parable is that God will raise up new leaders to care for his people.

12:10 capstone. The reference is to a stone that was rejected in the building of Solomon's temple, which was later found to be the keystone to the porch (a keystone held an arch in place).

" 'The stone the builders rejected
has become the capstone[a];
11 the Lord has done this,
and it is marvelous in our eyes'[b]?"

12 Then they looked for a way to arrest him because they knew he
had spoken the parable against them. But they were afraid of the
crowd; so they left him and went away.

Paying Taxes to Caesar

13 Later they sent some of the Pharisees and Herodians to Jesus to
catch him in his words. 14 They came to him and said, "Teacher, we
know you are a man of integrity. You aren't swayed by men, because
you pay no attention to who they are; but you teach the way of God in
accordance with the truth. Is it right to pay taxes to Caesar or not?
15 Should we pay or shouldn't we?"

But Jesus knew their hypocrisy. "Why are you trying to trap me?" he
asked. "Bring me a denarius and let me look at it." 16 They brought the
coin, and he asked them, "Whose portrait is this? And whose inscription?"

"Caesar's," they replied.

17 Then Jesus said to them, "Give to Caesar what is Caesar's and to
God what is God's."

And they were amazed at him.

Marriage at the Resurrection

18 Then the Sadducees, who say there is no resurrection, came to
him with a question. 19 "Teacher," they said, "Moses wrote for us that
if a man's brother dies and leaves a wife but no children, the man
must marry the widow and have children for his brother. 20 Now there
were seven brothers. The first one married and died without leaving
any children. 21 The second one married the widow, but he also died,
leaving no child. It was the same with the third. 22 In fact, none of
the seven left any children. Last of all, the woman died too. 23 At the
resurrection[c] whose wife will she be, since the seven were married
to her?"

24 Jesus replied, "Are you not in error because you do not know the
Scriptures or the power of God? 25 When the dead rise, they will

[a] *10* Or *cornerstone* [b] *11* Psalm 118:22,23 [c] *23* Some manuscripts *resurrection, when men rise from the dead,*

APPLY 1. If you could be Pope for a day, what would you change about the religious establishment? **2.** What are you doing to make your own church more like a caring community?

OPEN Which taxes do you hate paying the most?

STUDY 1. What was dangerous about this trap? What did Jesus mean when he said, "Give to Caesar what is Caesar's and to God what is God's" (v. 17)? **2.** What if Jesus had just said "yes'? If he had said "no"?

APPLY When and how did you learn how to handle money properly? How do you decide about your giving?

OPEN What is your idea of heaven?

STUDY 1. What was odd about the Sadducees' question? Why ask it? **2.** What is the source of the Sadducees' false assumption (v. 24)? **3.** How does Exodus 3:6 (quoted in v. 26) demonstrate the fact of the resurrection? **4.** What does this passage teach about heaven?

APPLY 1. What does the resurrection mean to you? **2.** What are you looking forward to in heaven?

12:13–17 Beaten badly in their first two confrontations with Jesus, the leaders regroup and consider their strategy. They decide to send representatives *from two groups with a trick question* they hope will trap Jesus. The question deals with the explosive issue of taxes.

12:13 Pharisees and Herodians. The origin of this unusual alliance is described in 3:1–6. The plan to destroy Jesus had now matured and was gaining momentum in Jerusalem.

12:14 you are a man of integrity. By these and other flattering words they hope to catch Jesus off guard. **taxes.** A poll tax had to be paid to the Romans each year by all adult Jews. This tax was deeply resented.

12:15 Bring me a denarius. A denarius was a small, silver coin (worth about 25 cents today) bearing the picture of Tiberius Caesar. The denarius was the only coin that could be used to pay the poll tax.

12:18 Sadducees. There is relatively little information available about this group. It seems they were a small but highly influential party of wealthy, aristocratic priests. Jesus had been no threat to the Sadducees. However, when he cleared the temple, he invaded their sphere of influence and so became their enemy. **resurrection.** The belief that at the end of the age God would bring the dead back to life for judgment. The Sadducees did not accept this belief.

12:24–27 Jesus takes their question seriously (although it is not a sincere question, since they did not believe in the resurrection) and answers them directly. In so doing, he affirms that life after death is real.

OPEN 1. When you were a kid, what did your parents say to you every time you left home? **2.** What is the "great commandment" at your job?

STUDY 1. What is refreshing about this person that approaches Jesus with a question? **2.** How does Jesus summarize all of the commandments? **3.** What does the teacher of the law and Jesus agree on (v. 33)? What is the lesson here for the church today?

APPLY If you had to rank your relationship with God right now on a scale from 1 to 10 what would the number be?

OPEN 1. Would you rather ask questions or answer them? **2.** When in your life were you closest to poverty?

STUDY 1. Were the Pharisees expecting the Messiah to be human (David's descendant) or divine (David's Lord)? **2.** Why would it take Jesus' death and resurrection to show that the Messiah is more than just David's descendant? **3.** What is the lesson in this passage on giving?

APPLY 1. What does Jesus' humanity mean to you? What does his divinity mean? **2.** When do you get the greatest satisfaction in giving?

neither marry nor be given in marriage; they will be like the angels in
heaven. 26Now about the dead rising—have you not read in the book
of Moses, in the account of the bush, how God said to him, 'I am the
God of Abraham, the God of Isaac, and the God of Jacob'[a]? 27He is not
the God of the dead, but of the living. You are badly mistaken!"

The Greatest Commandment

28One of the teachers of the law came and heard them debating.
Noticing that Jesus had given them a good answer, he asked him, "Of
all the commandments, which is the most important?"
29"The most important one," answered Jesus, "is this: 'Hear,
O Israel, the Lord our God, the Lord is one.[b] 30Love the Lord your God
with all your heart and with all your soul and with all your mind and
with all your strength.'[c] 31The second is this: 'Love your neighbor as
yourself.'[d] There is no commandment greater than these."
32"Well said, teacher," the man replied. "You are right in saying that
God is one and there is no other but him. 33To love him with all your
heart, with all your understanding and with all your strength, and to
love your neighbor as yourself is more important than all burnt offerings and sacrifices."
34When Jesus saw that he had answered wisely, he said to him,
"You are not far from the kingdom of God." And from then on no one
dared ask him any more questions.

Whose Son Is the Christ?

35While Jesus was teaching in the temple courts, he asked, "How is
it that the teachers of the law say that the Christ[e] is the son of David?
36David himself, speaking by the Holy Spirit, declared:

" 'The Lord said to my Lord:
"Sit at my right hand
until I put your enemies
under your feet." '[f]

37David himself calls him 'Lord.' How then can he be his son?"
The large crowd listened to him with delight.
38As he taught, Jesus said, "Watch out for the teachers of the law.
They like to walk around in flowing robes and be greeted in the mar-

[a]26 Exodus 3:6 [b]29 Or *the Lord our God is one Lord* [c]30 Deut. 6:4,5 [d]31 Lev. 19:18 [e]35 Or *Messiah* [f]36 Psalm 110:1

12:28 teachers of the law. Jesus has answered successfully the Herodians, the Pharisees and the Sadducees. It is now a scribe's turn to ask a question. His attitude toward Jesus is different from the others. He asks a genuine question. **Noticing that Jesus had given them a good answer.** This teacher of the Law is very impressed with the way Jesus answered the questions, so he asks an important question for him personally. **which is the most important?** This phrase is, literally, "which is the chief (or first) commandment"; i.e., what commandment summarizes all the commandments.

12:29 Hear, O Israel. The Shema (a statement of faith taken from Deut. 6:4), recited by pious Jews each morning and evening. This affirmation captures what was clearly distinctive about Israel's God.

12:30 Love. In Greek, this is *agape*. It means an active, benevolent giving to others without expectation of reward. **heart.** The inner life; the center of personality; where God reveals himself to a person. **soul.** The seat of life itself; the personality or ego. **mind.** The organ of knowledge; the intellect. **strength.** The power of a living being; the total effort behind heart, soul and mind.

12:35 the Christ. This is the Greek word for Messiah: the expected deliverer of Israel.

12:38 flowing robes. Long, white linen garments fringed with tassels that touched the ground. In such a stately garment, a person could not run or work and would be reckoned to be a person of leisure and importance. **greeted.** People considered the teachers of the Law to be men of great insight and authority, and so they rose when they passed by and called out titles of respect.

ketplaces, 39and have the most important seats in the synagogues
and the places of honor at banquets. 40They devour widows' houses
and for a show make lengthy prayers. Such men will be punished
most severely."

The Widow's Offering

41Jesus sat down opposite the place where the offerings were put
and watched the crowd putting their money into the temple treasury.
Many rich people threw in large amounts. 42But a poor widow came
and put in two very small copper coins,[a] worth only a fraction of a
penny.[b]

43Calling his disciples to him, Jesus said, "I tell you the truth, this
poor widow has put more into the treasury than all the others. 44They
all gave out of their wealth; but she, out of her poverty, put in everything—all she had to live on."

Signs of the End of the Age

13 As he was leaving the temple, one of his disciples said to
him, "Look, Teacher! What massive stones! What magnificent buildings!"

2"Do you see all these great buildings?" replied Jesus. "Not one
stone here will be left on another; every one will be thrown down."

3As Jesus was sitting on the Mount of Olives opposite the temple,
Peter, James, John and Andrew asked him privately, 4"Tell us, when
will these things happen? And what will be the sign that they are all
about to be fulfilled?"

5Jesus said to them: "Watch out that no one deceives you. 6Many
will come in my name, claiming, 'I am he,' and will deceive many.
7When you hear of wars and rumors of wars, do not be alarmed. Such
things must happen, but the end is still to come. 8Nation will rise
against nation, and kingdom against kingdom. There will be earthquakes in various places, and famines. These are the beginning of
birth pains.

[a]42 Greek *two lepta* [b]42 Greek *kodrantes*

OPEN **1.** If you knew you only had six months to live, how would you spend the time? **2.** What do you want to be remembered for?

STUDY **1.** Why do you think that Jesus used the discussion about the temple to begin his discourse about the end of the age? What made the temple so significant for the disciples? What would its destruction symbolize for them? **2.** Upon hearing this bombshell, what two questions do the disciples ask (v. 4)? What events might deceive them into thinking the end times had come (vv. 5–8)? Of what will these events be a sign? **3.** What questions about this passage would you ask Jesus if you had the opportunity? **4.** Verses 9–11 describe some of the persecution the disciples will face as they spread the Good News. What

---

12:39 the most important seats in the synagogues. The choice seat was up front, with its back to the box which contained the sacred Scriptures, and its front facing the congregation so that all would see who sat there.

12:40 They devour widows' houses. Since the teachers of the Law were forbidden to receive pay for their teaching, they lived off others, including, it seems, poor widows who were little able to support them.

12:41 temple treasury. This was located in the Court of Women (which was the first of the inner courts of the temple). It consisted of 13 trumpet-shaped receptacles used to collect donations for the temple.

12:42 small copper coins. The smallest coins in circulation, worth 1/400 shekel, or about 1/8 of a cent.

13:1 What magnificent buildings! The temple was, indeed, a wonder to behold. It was built with huge white stones, some measuring 37 feet long by 12 feet high by 18 feet wide. The temple appeared to strangers when they were at a distance, like a mountain covered with snow.

13:3–4 The disciples once again come to Jesus, privately asking him to explain his teaching. To them, an event as cataclysmic as the temple's destruction must be one of the events that would usher in the new age (Matt. 24:3).

13:5 Watch out. This is a key theme in this section (vv. 21–23,33–37). Vigilance, against being deceived by those who claim that the end times have begun, or claim that they are prophets, is essential.

13:6–8 Various events will occur prior to the end: false prophets will come (v. 6) and there will be wars, earthquakes and famine (vv. 7–8).

13:6 I am he. A claim on the part of the false prophet to be the Messiah, or to be Jesus come again; or perhaps it will be a claim to deity, since this phrase was used in the Old Testament for the name of God.

13:7 the end is still to come. The end of the age or the end of the world—that time which precedes the full and open establishment of the kingdom of God. Jesus does not say that the end will come immediately after these events, only that this is the "beginning of birth pains" (v. 8; i.e., they signal that something is coming).

comforter and advocate will aid them to endure their trials? **5.** What dreadful event (v. 14; Dan. 9:27; 11:31; 12:11) will bring "days of distress" unequalled in human history? What deceptive signs will accompany that distress (vv. 21–22)? **6.** What promise does Jesus give in verses 30–31? How would this comfort (or discomfort) the disciples? What impact do these promises have on you, centuries later? **7.** Why do you think the Father has kept the time secret (v. 32)? What is the responsibility of believers in the meantime?

APPLY 1. Have you ever faced persecution for your faith? What happened? **2.** When you see the forces of evil apparently winning, do you feel like withdrawing from the battle and perching on the rooftop? Or rolling up your sleeves and getting into the fray? **3.** What is the most exciting thing to you about the Second Coming? The most distressing?

9 "You must be on your guard. You will be handed over to the local
councils and flogged in the synagogues. On account of me you will
stand before governors and kings as witnesses to them. 10 And the
gospel must first be preached to all nations. 11 Whenever you are arrested and brought to trial, do not worry beforehand about what to
say. Just say whatever is given you at the time, for it is not you speaking, but the Holy Spirit.

12 "Brother will betray brother to death, and a father his child. Children will rebel against their parents and have them put to death. 13 All
men will hate you because of me, but he who stands firm to the end
will be saved.

14 "When you see 'the abomination that causes desolation'[a] standing where it[b] does not belong—let the reader understand—then let
those who are in Judea flee to the mountains. 15 Let no one on the roof
of his house go down or enter the house to take anything out. 16 Let no
one in the field go back to get his cloak. 17 How dreadful it will be in
those days for pregnant women and nursing mothers! 18 Pray that this
will not take place in winter, 19 because those will be days of distress
unequaled from the beginning, when God created the world, until
now—and never to be equaled again. 20 If the Lord had not cut short
those days, no one would survive. But for the sake of the elect, whom
he has chosen, he has shortened them. 21 At that time if anyone says
to you, 'Look, here is the Christ[c]!' or, 'Look, there he is!' do not believe it. 22 For false Christs and false prophets will appear and perform
signs and miracles to deceive the elect—if that were possible. 23 So be
on your guard; I have told you everything ahead of time.

24 "But in those days, following that distress,

" 'the sun will be darkened,
  and the moon will not give its light;
25 the stars will fall from the sky,
  and the heavenly bodies will be shaken.'[d]

26 "At that time men will see the Son of Man coming in clouds with
great power and glory. 27 And he will send his angels and gather his
elect from the four winds, from the ends of the earth to the ends of
the heavens.

28 "Now learn this lesson from the fig tree: As soon as its twigs get

[a] *14* Daniel 9:27; 11:31; 12:11 [b] *14* Or *he*; also in verse 29 [c] *21* Or *Messiah* [d] *25* Isaiah 13:10; 34:4

13:14 the abomination that causes desolation. This phrase appears in the book of Daniel (Dan. 9:27; 11:31; 12:11). It refers to an event so awful that Jews will flee from the temple in horror. A similar event happened in 168 B.C. when Antiochus Epiphanes, a Syrian king, captured Jerusalem. He set up an altar to Zeus in the temple and sacrificed a pig there. He also put public brothels in the temple courts. Jesus warns that when such an event occurs again, the fall of Jerusalem is imminent (2 Thess. 2:1–4). **let those who are in Judea flee.** When the armies march against the city, Jesus' disciples are to recognize that this is the sign that God's judgment against Israel has come to a head. Instead of flocking to the city in anticipation of a dramatic messianic victory, they must run for their lives.

13:20 the elect. Whereas judgment has come upon Jerusalem and the temple, mercy is shown to the elect.

13:23 I have told you everything ahead of time. Some see the fulfillment of Jesus' words in the fall of Jerusalem in AD 70. Others are still looking for the "Great Tribulation" yet to come (Rev. 7:14).

13:24–27 Jesus now describes the Second Coming of the Son of Man in power and glory. The destruction of Jerusalem is the result of human failure and evil. It will bring suffering and hardship. The Second Coming will bring salvation and blessing to the people of God.

13:27 gather his elect. It is God who will do this (Deut. 30:3–4; Ps. 50:4–5; Isa. 43:5–6). Jesus makes it quite clear who he is: the Son of God (vv. 26–27).

13:28 lesson from the fig tree. They knew that the fig tree only got its leaves in late spring. When the leaves came, it was a sure sign that summer

tender and its leaves come out, you know that summer is near. 29Even
so, when you see these things happening, you know that it is near,
right at the door. 30I tell you the truth, this generation[a] will certainly
not pass away until all these things have happened. 31Heaven and
earth will pass away, but my words will never pass away.

The Day and Hour Unknown

32"No one knows about that day or hour, not even the angels in
heaven, nor the Son, but only the Father. 33Be on guard! Be alert[b]! You
do not know when that time will come. 34It's like a man going away:
He leaves his house and puts his servants in charge, each with his assigned task, and tells the one at the door to keep watch.
35"Therefore keep watch because you do not know when the owner
of the house will come back—whether in the evening, or at midnight,
or when the rooster crows, or at dawn. 36If he comes suddenly, do not
let him find you sleeping. 37What I say to you, I say to everyone:
'Watch!' "

Jesus Anointed at Bethany

14 Now the Passover and the Feast of Unleavened Bread were
only two days away, and the chief priests and the teachers of
the law were looking for some sly way to arrest Jesus and kill him.
2"But not during the Feast," they said, "or the people may riot."
3While he was in Bethany, reclining at the table in the home of a
man known as Simon the Leper, a woman came with an alabaster jar
of very expensive perfume, made of pure nard. She broke the jar and
poured the perfume on his head.
4Some of those present were saying indignantly to one another,
"Why this waste of perfume? 5It could have been sold for more than a
year's wages[c] and the money given to the poor." And they rebuked
her harshly.
6"Leave her alone," said Jesus. "Why are you bothering her? She
has done a beautiful thing to me. 7The poor you will always have with
you, and you can help them any time you want. But you will not always have me. 8She did what she could. She poured perfume on my
body beforehand to prepare for my burial. 9I tell you the truth, wher-

[a]30 Or *race* [b]33 Some manuscripts *alert and pray* [c]5 Greek *than three hundred denarii*

OPEN If you had a year's wages to blow on friends, which would you choose: Big party for all? Glorious trip for a few? Extravagant gift for one?

STUDY 1. How does this woman's action (v. 3) strike you: Thoughtful, but misguided? Tasteful, but extravagant? Wasteful, no buts about it? Honoring to the nth degree? **2.** Do you think the perfume could have been better used? How was her action justified by Jesus (vv. 6–9) and used by Judas (vv. 10–11)? **3.** What is the lesson here for the church today? When do you think the church ought to be extravagant? When frugal?

APPLY 1. When it comes to giving, are you more willing to part with your time or your money? **2.** If you are going to make a very

---

was near. This is a reference to the rather mysterious cursing of the fig tree by Jesus in 11:12–14,20–21, and has to do with the judgment on Jerusalem, as Jesus' teaching here shows.

13:28–37 With all this as background (vv. 5–27), Jesus can now respond to the disciples' original question (v. 4). His response is that one event (the fall of Jerusalem) will occur within their lifetime, but they are not to be deceived. This will not usher in the end time. The final event (the Second Coming) will be at a future, unspecified date known only to God the Father (v. 32). Jesus encourages the disciples to be vigilant, but not to worry about when all this will take place.

13:37 It is not just the Twelve who must get on with the mission when Jesus is gone. It is all of his followers.

14:1 the Passover. A feast in which the people of Israel celebrated God's deliverance of their nation from Egypt where they had been held as slaves (Ex. 12). On this particular Passover, God would once again rescue his people, though in a totally unexpected way—namely through the death of his own Son. **the Feast of Unleavened Bread.** By the time of the first century, this feast was coupled with the Passover so that there was a week of feasting.

14:3 reclining. Banquets were generally eaten lying on a low couch or pillows. **Simon the Leper.** Nothing is known of this man, but presumably he was someone Jesus had previously healed. **a woman came.** A woman would not be present at a meal like this except to serve. Her entrance would have been scandalous. **perfume.** Nard was a much-prized aromatic oil extracted from an Indian root. It was stored in long-necked alabaster flasks to retain its aroma. The neck was broken off when the perfume was used. Possibly this was a family heirloom. **poured the perfume on his head.** Typically, this perfume was used very sparingly and only for special occasions. This was a lavish gesture indicating the high honor this woman held for Jesus.

generous contribution, what do you want your money to be used for?

OPEN 1. How are you at saying goodbye? **2.** What favorite meal does your mom prepare?

STUDY 1. How would you have felt if you had been sharing this Passover meal with Jesus? **2.** Why would secrecy be needed as this meal was planned? What risk was involved? **3.** What does Jesus say about his betrayer (vv. 18–21)? How do the disciples react to this "bombshell"? **4.** What profound new meaning does Jesus give to the Passover bread (v. 22) and to the Passover cup (vv. 23–24)? **5.** How much do you think the disciples understood when Jesus spoke about his body and blood? **6.** What did the disciples experience in taking their first communion that we have lost today? What is your church doing to recover the depth of this experience?

APPLY 1. What "Last Supper" will stand out in your memory because you were saying goodbye to a group that you had been with a long time? **2.** Are you planning to say "goodbye" to the group you are in?

ever the gospel is preached throughout the world, what she has done
will also be told, in memory of her."
10Then Judas Iscariot, one of the Twelve, went to the chief priests to
betray Jesus to them. 11They were delighted to hear this and promised to give him money. So he watched for an opportunity to hand
him over.

The Lord's Supper

12On the first day of the Feast of Unleavened Bread, when it was
customary to sacrifice the Passover lamb, Jesus' disciples asked him,
"Where do you want us to go and make preparations for you to eat
the Passover?"
13So he sent two of his disciples, telling them, "Go into the city, and
a man carrying a jar of water will meet you. Follow him. 14Say to the
owner of the house he enters, 'The Teacher asks: Where is my guest
room, where I may eat the Passover with my disciples?' 15He will
show you a large upper room, furnished and ready. Make preparations for us there."
16The disciples left, went into the city and found things just as
Jesus had told them. So they prepared the Passover.
17When evening came, Jesus arrived with the Twelve. 18While they
were reclining at the table eating, he said, "I tell you the truth, one of
you will betray me—one who is eating with me."
19They were saddened, and one by one they said to him, "Surely
not I?"
20"It is one of the Twelve," he replied, "one who dips bread into the
bowl with me. 21The Son of Man will go just as it is written about him.
But woe to that man who betrays the Son of Man! It would be better
for him if he had not been born."
22While they were eating, Jesus took bread, gave thanks and broke
it, and gave it to his disciples, saying, "Take it; this is my body."
23Then he took the cup, gave thanks and offered it to them, and
they all drank from it.

14:12 On the first day of the Feast of Unleavened Bread. The Feast of Unleavened Bread did not officially start until the day after the Passover. In the first century, the day on which the lambs were sacrificed was sometimes referred to as the first day of the Feast of Unleavened Bread. **sacrifice the Passover lamb.** Each pilgrim sacrificed his own lamb in the temple. A priest caught the blood in a bowl and this was thrown on the altar. After removing certain parts of the lamb for sacrifice, the carcass was returned to the pilgrim to be roasted and eaten for Passover. **make preparations.** The disciples have to set out the unleavened bread and the wine (*which was mixed with water*); *collect* the bitter herbs (horseradish, chicory, etc.); make the sauce in which the bread was dipped (a stew of dried fruit, spices and wine); and roast the lamb on an open fire. **eat the Passover.** The meal began with a blessing and the first of four cups of wine.

14:12–26 Through this meal, Jesus formally introduced the fact that his death was the means by which a new covenant was to be established between God and his people. It is this meal that declares Jesus' abiding presence with his people and also illustrates Jesus' death as a sacrifice for sins.

14:13–16 Instructions for Jesus' arrest had already been issued (John 11:57). He knew that the officials were looking for him in places away from the crowd. To guard against being arrested before his time, he would generally sleep in Bethany, which was outside the jurisdiction of the priests. But the Law required that he eat the Passover meal in Jerusalem itself, hence the need for secret arrangements.

14:18–21 Jesus predicts that one of his disciples will betray him.

14:18 reclining at the table. People would eat festive meals by lying on couches or cushions arranged around a low table. **I tell you the truth.** Literally, this is "Amen," a word used to announce a solemn declaration. **one who is eating with me.** These words recall the prophecy in Psalm 41:9.

14:19 not I? Literally this says "Is it I?" but it is a conditional inquiry that demands a negative answer.

14:20 dips bread into the bowl with me. To share in a meal was a sign of friendship, accenting the act of betrayal.

14:22–26 Jesus' celebration of the Last Supper provides the model for how the church came to celebrate commun-

[24]"This is my blood of the[a] covenant, which is poured out for
many," he said to them. [25]"I tell you the truth, I will not drink again of
the fruit of the vine until that day when I drink it anew in the kingdom
of God."

[26]When they had sung a hymn, they went out to the Mount of Olives.

Jesus Predicts Peter's Denial

[27]"You will all fall away," Jesus told them, "for it is written:

" 'I will strike the shepherd,
and the sheep will be scattered.'[b]

[28]But after I have risen, I will go ahead of you into Galilee."
[29]Peter declared, "Even if all fall away, I will not."
[30]"I tell you the truth," Jesus answered, "today—yes, tonight—before the rooster crows twice[c] you yourself will disown me three
times."
[31]But Peter insisted emphatically, "Even if I have to die with you, I
will never disown you." And all the others said the same.

Gethsemane

[32]They went to a place called Gethsemane, and Jesus said to his
disciples, "Sit here while I pray." [33]He took Peter, James and John
along with him, and he began to be deeply distressed and troubled.
[34]"My soul is overwhelmed with sorrow to the point of death," he
said to them. "Stay here and keep watch."
[35]Going a little farther, he fell to the ground and prayed that if possible the hour might pass from him. [36]"*Abba*,[d] Father," he said, "everything is possible for you. Take this cup from me. Yet not what I will,
but what you will."

[a]24 Some manuscripts *the new* [b]27 Zech. 13:7 [c]30 Some early manuscripts do not have *twice.*
[d]36 Aramaic for *Father*

OPEN Have you ever made a public promise and then had to go back on your word?

STUDY 1. Why do you think Peter took it personally when Jesus said his disciples would desert him? **2.** If you had been Peter, how would you feel if Jesus said you would deny him three times?

APPLY How would you compare your temperament to Peter's?

OPEN When you are faced with a hard decision, where do you go? Do you prefer to be alone or with a few friends?

STUDY 1. Why do you think Jesus took along Peter, James and John? What did he ask of them? **2.** In your own words, what did Jesus ask God when he prayed? What do you learn about Jesus in this situation? **3.** What is the closest you have come to going through an agonizing situation like Jesus went through? When you went through a "Gethsemane"

ion (1 Cor. 11:23–26). His use of the bread and the cup in a symbolic way was consistent with the way in which the various elements of the Passover meal were used symbolically.

14:24 covenant. In general terms, this is a treaty between two parties. Such an agreement was often sealed by the sacrifice of an animal. It refers to the arrangement that God made with Israel (Ex. 24:1–8) which was dependent on Israel's obedience. Now (as anticipated in Jer. 31:31–34) a new covenant is established, which is made dependent on Jesus' obedience (his sacrificial death). A covenant of law becomes a covenant of love. **poured out.** Blood which was poured out symbolized a violent death (Gen. 4:10–11; Deut. 19:10; Matt. 23:35). This phrase points to the type of death Jesus would experience.

14:32 Gethsemane. An olive orchard in an estate at the foot of the Mount of Olives just outside the eastern wall of Jerusalem. The name means literally "an oil press" (for making olive oil).

14:33 Peter, James and John. Once again, these three men accompany Jesus during a time of great significance. Interestingly, neither the rebuke by Peter (8:32) nor the self-centered request of James and John (10:35–40) has damaged their relationship with Jesus. Also note each of these men has vowed to stay with Jesus through thick and thin (10:38–39; 14:29,31). What Jesus asks them to share with him here is not glory (which they wanted), but sorrow (which they kept denying would come). **deeply distressed.** Literally, filled with "shuddering awe." Jesus is filled with deep sorrow as the impact of submitting to his father's will hits him.

14:34 keep watch. This was an invitation for the disciples to join him in preparation for the severe trial that was soon to come. While it expresses Jesus' desire for human companionship in his time of crisis, it points out these men need to prepare themselves as well (vv. 37–41).

14:35 fell to the ground. This accents the emotional distress he was feeling. **prayed.** This is the third time that Jesus has been shown at prayer (1:35; 6:46). **the hour.** This word is often used to refer to an event that represents a crucial turning point in God's plan for a person or for the world (John 15:32; 12:31). In reference to Jesus, it specifically refers to his crucifixion (John 12:23).

14:36 Abba. This is how a child would address his father: "Daddy." This was not a title that was used in prayer in the first century. **this cup.** Like the word "hour," "cup" was also used as an image referring to the destiny God had in store for a person. **Yet not what I will, but what you will.** This phrase, popularly used as a generalized "escape clause" when people are unsure what to pray, is actually an affirmation of Jesus' intent to pursue the Father's will. There was no doubt in Jesus' mind regarding what the Father's will was in this situation. While he pleads that there might be another way, this sentence declares his commitment to follow the

experience who did you have to share with? Did they fall asleep on you?

APPLY **1.** Right now, what is the decision you are facing in your life? **2.** Is this something that the group you are in could pray about?

OPEN How would you react if one of your kids (or parents) was arrested?

STUDY **1.** In this story, would you have been the disciple that cut off the ear of the servant of the high priest or the one who ran away? **2.** How would you describe the situation? Where are they (vv. 32–42)? What has Judas done? **3.** Why would the crowd be armed? **4.** How does Jesus shame the authorities? **5.** How do the disciples respond (vv. 47–51)?

APPLY **1.** What is the closest you have come to "deserting" Jesus in a stressful time? **2.** Where could you use a little courage now?

OPEN Have you ever gotten a bad deal from a judge or a policeman? How did it make you feel?

37 Then he returned to his disciples and found them sleeping. "Simon," he said to Peter, "are you asleep? Could you not keep watch for
one hour? 38 Watch and pray so that you will not fall into temptation.
The spirit is willing, but the body is weak."
39 Once more he went away and prayed the same thing. 40 When he
came back, he again found them sleeping, because their eyes were
heavy. They did not know what to say to him.
41 Returning the third time, he said to them, "Are you still sleeping
and resting? Enough! The hour has come. Look, the Son of Man is
betrayed into the hands of sinners. 42 Rise! Let us go! Here comes my
betrayer!"

Jesus Arrested

43 Just as he was speaking, Judas, one of the Twelve, appeared. With
him was a crowd armed with swords and clubs, sent from the chief
priests, the teachers of the law, and the elders.
44 Now the betrayer had arranged a signal with them: "The one I
kiss is the man; arrest him and lead him away under guard." 45 Going
at once to Jesus, Judas said, "Rabbi!" and kissed him. 46 The men
seized Jesus and arrested him. 47 Then one of those standing near
drew his sword and struck the servant of the high priest, cutting off
his ear.
48 "Am I leading a rebellion," said Jesus, "that you have come out
with swords and clubs to capture me? 49 Every day I was with you,
teaching in the temple courts, and you did not arrest me. But
the Scriptures must be fulfilled." 50 Then everyone deserted him and
fled.
51 A young man, wearing nothing but a linen garment, was following Jesus. When they seized him, 52 he fled naked, leaving his garment
behind.

Before the Sanhedrin

53 They took Jesus to the high priest, and all the chief priests, elders
and teachers of the law came together. 54 Peter followed him at a dis-

---

Father's lead regardless of the cost (14:42).

14:41 into the hands of sinners. This refers to the religious authorities that Jesus confronted in chapters 11–13 who have corrupted the offices they hold. The irony of this assessment is that the term "sinners" was used by these religious leaders to refer to others: to Jews who did not live by the Law, and to all Gentiles. In fact, it is a term they have earned by their actions.

14:43 a crowd. The Sanhedrin commanded the services of the temple police (who were Levites) and of an *auxiliary police force (servants of the court)* who maintained order outside the temple area.

14:44 kiss. This was a normal form of greeting. However, the intensive form of verb used here indicates that Judas' actual kiss was a warm and affectionate greeting and not merely perfunctory.

14:45 Rabbi! This title was a form of respect. It meant literally, "My Great One." By his greeting, by his kiss and by sharing the same bowl (v. 20—to eat together was a sign of friendship), Judas conveys the sense of a warm relationship with Jesus.

14:46 arrested him. The charge is not given. Perhaps it was blasphemy (2:7), violation of the Sabbath (2:24; 3:2–6), or the practice of magic (3:22).

14:47 one of those standing near. According to John's Gospel (John 18:10), this was Peter. **drew his sword.** That Peter should have a sword is not unusual. Travelers carried them as protection against robbers and the disciples had just completed a journey from Jerusalem to Galilee (Luke 22:36–38).

14:49 the Scriptures. Jesus is probably referring to Zechariah 13:7 (14:27), but he may also have in mind Isaiah 53:12 and Psalm 41:9.

14:51 A young man. It has been suggested that this is Mark himself. He lived in Jerusalem (Acts 12:12), and there is a tradition that the Last Supper was held in the upper room of his mother's house. **linen garment.** Probably a bed sheet. The fact that it was linen means that he came from a wealthy family.

14:53–65 In the trial of Jesus, Mark shows how an alleged criminal could be the Messiah. (This was one of the impediments to belief among the Roman population.) As quickly becomes evident, Jesus was no criminal. As yet, no charge

tance, right into the courtyard of the high priest. There he sat with
the guards and warmed himself at the fire.
55The chief priests and the whole Sanhedrin were looking for evidence against Jesus so that they could put him to death, but they did
not find any. 56Many testified falsely against him, but their statements
did not agree.
57Then some stood up and gave this false testimony against him:
58"We heard him say, 'I will destroy this man-made temple and in
three days will build another, not made by man.'" 59Yet even then
their testimony did not agree.
60Then the high priest stood up before them and asked Jesus, "Are
you not going to answer? What is this testimony that these men are
bringing against you?" 61But Jesus remained silent and gave no answer.
Again the high priest asked him, "Are you the Christ,[a] the Son of the
Blessed One?"
62"I am," said Jesus. "And you will see the Son of Man sitting at the
right hand of the Mighty One and coming on the clouds of heaven."
63The high priest tore his clothes. "Why do we need any more witnesses?" he asked. 64"You have heard the blasphemy. What do you
think?"
They all condemned him as worthy of death. 65Then some began to
spit at him; they blindfolded him, struck him with their fists, and said,
"Prophesy!" And the guards took him and beat him.

Peter Disowns Jesus

66While Peter was below in the courtyard, one of the servant girls of
the high priest came by. 67When she saw Peter warming himself, she
looked closely at him.
"You also were with that Nazarene, Jesus," she said.
68But he denied it. "I don't know or understand what you're talking
about," he said, and went out into the entryway.[b]
69When the servant girl saw him there, she said again to those
standing around, "This fellow is one of them." 70Again he denied it.

[a]61 Or *Messiah* [b]68 Some early manuscripts *entryway and the rooster crowed*

STUDY 1. Where is the passage taking place? When? Who is there? What do they hope to accomplish? What happens to their plan? 2. What is the trumped up charge against Jesus? How does Jesus answer this charge? 3. How would a court of appeal rule on the interrogation of Jesus today? 4. Why would the religious leaders think Jesus was guilty of blasphemy? 5. What makes you mad when you read this passage?

APPLY 1. When is the last time you were put through the "third degree" for your faith? 2. If you had to give a defense of your faith again, what would you do differently?

OPEN What is the biggest failure you have suffered in your life?

STUDY 1. How did Peter get into this situation (v. 54)? What motivated Peter to tag along? 2. What happened to Peter's grandiose promise in verse 29? 3. What broke him? 4. If you could put in a good word for Peter, what would it be? 5. Do you think he should be kicked off the team?

had been laid against him (much less proved), except he claimed to be the Messiah.

14:55 the whole Sanhedrin. A council consisting of 71 leaders, both priests and laymen, who made up the highest Jewish court. They were given authority by Rome to rule in matters of religious law. **evidence.** To convict someone of a capital crime required the unanimous testimony of at least two witnesses. Each witness gave his testimony individually to the judge in the presence of the accused. If two witnesses differed in their accounts, their testimony was thrown out of court (Deut. 19:15–18).

14:61 Since they could not produce evidence, their final recourse was this desperate attempt by Caiaphas to get Jesus to say he was the Messiah. If Jesus admitted to being the Messiah, it would be a clear case of blasphemy.

14:62 This is the first time in Mark that Jesus openly and unequivocally declares his messiahship. The time for secrecy is past. The verses Jesus quotes (a combination of Ps. 110:1 and Dan. 7:13–14) simply reiterate, in biblical images, his claim of messiahship (8:38; 12:35–37; 13:26). **I am.** This forthright declaration by Jesus of his identity was a powerful example for the Christians at Rome, who were also being called upon at that time to confess their faith before the authorities. **sitting at the right hand.** To sit here was to sit in the place of honor (10:37).

14:64 blasphemy. Dishonoring or slandering another. The penalty for blaspheming God was death by stoning (Lev. 24:10–16). **worthy of death.** At that point in history, the Sanhedrin did not have power to carry out a death sentence. Only the Roman procurator could do that.

14:65 The blows and spitting were traditional ways of expressing abhorrence and repudiation (Num. 12:14; Deut. 25:9; Job 30:10; Isa. 50:6). In this way the council demonstrated that it was opposed to what Jesus had done. They are asking him to prove his claim to be the Messiah by naming who it was who had struck him while he was blindfolded.

APPLY When, if ever, have you felt that a failure made it impossible for you to serve Christ again? How did you overcome these feelings? Who helped you to get through this time?

OPEN **1.** As a child, would you rather have been punished by your Mom or your Dad? **2.** Were you ever bullied as a child?

STUDY **1.** What two adjectives would you use to describe Pilate in this story? Who would you hold most responsible for Jesus' sentence? **2.** Why did the Jewish leaders bring Jesus before Pilate? Why was Jesus so silent throughout his trial? **3.** Why do the people, after witnessing Jesus' miracles, hearing his teachings, and praising him with hosannas, now demand that Jesus be crucified? **4.** What is Pilate's overriding concern in this trial? **5.** In this passage, how do you think Jesus was viewed by these people: The Sanhedrin? Pilate? The crowd? Barabbas? The soldiers? **6.** How does the story of Barabbas illustrate what Jesus did for you?

After a little while, those standing near said to Peter, "Surely you
are one of them, for you are a Galilean."
71He began to call down curses on himself, and he swore to them,
"I don't know this man you're talking about."
72Immediately the rooster crowed the second time.[a] Then Peter remembered the word Jesus had spoken to him: "Before the rooster
crows twice[b] you will disown me three times." And he broke down
and wept.

Jesus Before Pilate

15 Very early in the morning, the chief priests, with the elders,
the teachers of the law and the whole Sanhedrin, reached a
decision. They bound Jesus, led him away and handed him over to
Pilate.
2"Are you the king of the Jews?" asked Pilate.
"Yes, it is as you say," Jesus replied.
3The chief priests accused him of many things. 4So again Pilate
asked him, "Aren't you going to answer? See how many things they
are accusing you of."
5But Jesus still made no reply, and Pilate was amazed.
6Now it was the custom at the Feast to release a prisoner whom the
people requested. 7A man called Barabbas was in prison with the insurrectionists who had committed murder in the uprising. 8The
crowd came up and asked Pilate to do for them what he usually did.
9"Do you want me to release to you the king of the Jews?" asked
Pilate, 10knowing it was out of envy that the chief priests had handed

[a]72 Some early manuscripts do not have *the second time.* [b]72 Some early manuscripts do not have *vice.*

14:71 call down curses on himself. Peter goes so far as to call down on himself the wrath of God if he is not telling the truth (which he knows he is not)! **I don't know this man.** This, like his previous denial (v. 68), is an outright lie. **this man you're talking about.** Peter does not use Jesus' name (8:38).

14:72 the rooster crowed the second time. Roosters in Palestine crowed first at about 12:30 a.m., then again at about 1:30 a.m., and for a third time at about 2:30 a.m. As a result of this peculiar habit, the watch kept by soldiers in Palestine from midnight until 3 a.m. was called "cock-crow." Peter's denials were therefore spread over the early hours.

15:1 Very early. The court began at daybreak, making it necessary that the Sanhedrin meet in a night session. They were anxious to get a quick conviction before the people found out what they had done. **decision.** Legally, the Sanhedrin *had no authority* to order the death of Jesus (John 18:31). The difficulty they faced in deferring to Rome was that under Roman law, blasphemy was not a capital offense. Consequently, they needed to present the case to Pilate so as to ensure Jesus' death. Their decision was that when they brought Jesus to Pilate, they would charge him with high treason. **led him away.** They probably took him to the palace of Herod the Great, located northwest of the temple, where Pilate stayed when he came to Jerusalem from his home in Caesarea. **Pilate.** Pontius Pilate was the fifth procurator of Judea. He served from A.D. 26–36. Historians of the time called him an "inflexible, merciless and obstinate" man who disliked the Jews and their customs.

15:2 Pilate would have been given a written deposition stating the charges against Jesus. Having read the charges, he now addresses the accused. **king of the Jews.** This is how the Sanhedrin translated the Jewish title "Messiah" so that Pilate would understand it. Put this way, it made Jesus seem guilty of treason (he would appear to be disputing the kingship of Caesar).

15:3 accused him of many things. They accused him of opposing the payment of taxes to Rome, of stirring up people from Galilee and Judea to insurrection, and of claiming to be the rightful king of the Jews.

15:4–5 All the Gospels mention how Jesus remained silent before Pilate in the face of his charges. This scene would also be of special importance to the original recipients of the Gospel, some of whom would face a situation very similar to that which Jesus faced. Here, they see how he dealt with false accusations with dignity and trust in the purposes of the Godhead.

15:7 Barabbas. Barabbas was a genuine resistance leader, guilty of murder.

15:8 The crowd. It seems ironic that the crowd, who at the beginning of the week hailed Jesus as "he who comes in the name of the Lord" (11:9), could at the end of the week call for his crucifixion.

15:9–11 Pilate seemed satisfied that Jesus was not a true insurrectionist and he appeared to want his release. His desire to release Jesus may have had little to do with justice, and more out of a desire to do something that would annoy the Sanhedrin (with whom he had many run-ins).

Jesus over to him. [11]But the chief priests stirred up the crowd to have
Pilate release Barabbas instead.
[12]"What shall I do, then, with the one you call the king of the
Jews?" Pilate asked them.
[13]"Crucify him!" they shouted.
[14]"Why? What crime has he committed?" asked Pilate.
But they shouted all the louder, "Crucify him!"
[15]Wanting to satisfy the crowd, Pilate released Barabbas to them.
He had Jesus flogged, and handed him over to be crucified.

The Soldiers Mock Jesus

[16]The soldiers led Jesus away into the palace (that is, the Praetorium) and called together the whole company of soldiers. [17]They put a
purple robe on him, then twisted together a crown of thorns and set it
on him. [18]And they began to call out to him, "Hail, king of the Jews!"
[19]Again and again they struck him on the head with a staff and spit on
him. Falling on their knees, they paid homage to him. [20]And when
they had mocked him, they took off the purple robe and put his own
clothes on him. Then they led him out to crucify him.

The Crucifixion

[21]A certain man from Cyrene, Simon, the father of Alexander and
Rufus, was passing by on his way in from the country, and they forced
him to carry the cross. [22]They brought Jesus to the place called Golgotha (which means The Place of the Skull). [23]Then they offered him wine
mixed with myrrh, but he did not take it. [24]And they crucified him.
Dividing up his clothes, they cast lots to see what each would get.
[25]It was the third hour when they crucified him. [26]The written notice of the charge against him read: THE KING OF THE JEWS. [27]They crucified two robbers with him, one on his right and one on his left.[a]

[a]27 Some manuscripts *left,* [28]*and the scripture was fulfilled which says, "He was counted with the lawless ones"* (Isaiah 53:12)

7. Why did Jesus go through this trial and torture when he could easily have used his great powers and escaped?

APPLY 1. How would you compare your spiritual beginnings to the story of Barabbas? **2.** Where are you right now in your relationship with God?

OPEN 1. Have you ever sat with someone who was dying? What was it like? **2.** How do you feel deep down when you attend funerals and burials?

STUDY 1. What has happened to Jesus immediately before this passage? **2.** What kinds of people were usually crucified (v. 27)? How is Jesus like them? **3.** What irony do you see in: The sign posted on the cross (v. 26)? Jesus being ridiculed for his ability to save others but not himself (vv. 29–32)? **4.** What caused the

---

15:12–14 Pilate seems surprised the crowd rejects his offer to release Jesus.

15:15 released Barabbas. The death of Jesus (who is innocent) in the place of Barabbas (who is guilty) is a visual statement of the meaning of substitutionary atonement. It explains what Jesus meant in 10:45 when he said that he came to "give his life as a ransom for many." **flogged.** This was a terrible punishment. Soldiers would lash a naked and bound prisoner with a leather thong into which pieces of bone and lead had been woven. The flesh would be cut to shreds.

15:21 Simon. Possibly a Jew, from a Greek city on the north shore of Africa, who had come to Jerusalem for the Passover feast. **Rufus.** Romans 16:13 mentions a Rufus. Mark wrote this Gospel for the church at Rome, and if this is the same Rufus, he would be able to verify this detail about his father. **carry the cross.** The prisoner carried the heavy cross-beam through the winding streets as an "example" to others. Jesus, however, had already been without sleep for at least 24 hours and been beaten, flogged and beaten again. He was physically unable to bear the weight of the cross-beam.

15:22 Golgotha. In Aramaic, "a skull." This was probably a round, bare hillock outside Jerusalem.

15:23 wine mixed with myrrh. It was a Jewish custom to offer this pain-deadening narcotic to prisoners about to be crucified (Ps. 69:21).

15:24 they crucified him. Mark has looked to this event throughout his Gospel. When it happens, he records it in the simplest, starkest way. The person to be crucified was first stripped. Then his hands were tied or nailed to the crossbeam. This was lifted to the upright stake, and then the feet were nailed in place. **Dividing up his clothes.** The clothes of the condemned person belonged to the four soldiers who carried out the crucifixion (Ps. 22:18; John 19:23–24).

15:25 the third hour. This would have been about 9 a.m.

15:26 The written notice. The crime for which the person was being crucified was specified on a whitened board fastened above the criminal. **THE KING OF THE JEWS.** By posting this sign on the cross, Pilate was simply attempting to further humiliate the Jews. The intent was to communicate that Jesus' fate would be shared by anyone else who tried to assert their authority against Rome.

15:27 one on his right and one on his left. Earlier on, James and John had asked for the honor to sit at Jesus' right and left-hand when he came into his kingdom (10:37), a request Jesus denied. Now these two criminals are

most anguish for Jesus on the cross: The physical pain or being forsaken by God the Father? Why did God turn his back on his own Son? **5.** What is significant about the curtain in the temple being torn in two from top to bottom? What did the curtain represent? Why was the curtain no longer needed? **6.** What did the Roman centurion realize? How do you think he realized this? **7.** Why did the women stick around the cross when everybody else fled? **8.** How do you account for Joseph of Arimathea (a member of the Sanhedrin that plotted his death) now asking for the body of Jesus? Why would he stick his neck out and ask for the body of Jesus to be given a decent burial? **9.** What surprised Pilate (v. 44)? How does this relate to verse 33? **10.** If there was any other way for mankind to be restored to fellowship with God other than the death of Jesus, why didn't God use the other way?

APPLY 1. When did the crucifixion of Jesus Christ start making sense to you? **2.** If you had been the only person in the world, would Jesus have died just for you?

29Those who passed by hurled insults at him, shaking their heads and
saying, "So! You who are going to destroy the temple and build it in
three days, 30come down from the cross and save yourself!"
31In the same way the chief priests and the teachers of the law
mocked him among themselves. "He saved others," they said, "but he
can't save himself! 32Let this Christ,[a] this King of Israel, come down
now from the cross, that we may see and believe." Those crucified
with him also heaped insults on him.

The Death of Jesus

33At the sixth hour darkness came over the whole land until the
ninth hour. 34And at the ninth hour Jesus cried out in a loud voice,
"Eloi, Eloi, lama sabachthani?"—which means, "My God, my God,
why have you forsaken me?"[b]
35When some of those standing near heard this, they said, "Listen,
he's calling Elijah."
36One man ran, filled a sponge with wine vinegar, put it on a stick,
and offered it to Jesus to drink. "Now leave him alone. Let's see if Elijah comes to take him down," he said.
37With a loud cry, Jesus breathed his last.
38The curtain of the temple was torn in two from top to bottom.
39And when the centurion, who stood there in front of Jesus, heard
his cry and[c] saw how he died, he said, "Surely this man was the Son[d]
of God!"
40Some women were watching from a distance. Among them were
Mary Magdalene, Mary the mother of James the younger and of Joses, and Salome. 41In Galilee these women had followed him and
cared for his needs. Many other women who had come up with him
to Jerusalem were also there.

The Burial of Jesus

42It was Preparation Day (that is, the day before the Sabbath). So as
evening approached, 43Joseph of Arimathea, a prominent member of
the Council, who was himself waiting for the kingdom of God, went
boldly to Pilate and asked for Jesus' body. 44Pilate was surprised to

[a]32 Or *Messiah* [b]34 Psalm 22:1 [c]39 Some manuscripts do not have *heard his cry and* [d]39 Or *a son*

given the positions on either side of Jesus as he completes his early mission.

15:31 He saved others ... but he can't save himself! This is just the point! Because he is saving others, his own life is forfeited.

15:33 At the sixth hour. At noon. **darkness.** A supernatural event, showing the significance of this death (Amos 8:9). There is darkness for three hours.

15:35 Elijah. Another irony. Elijah already came in the person of John the Baptist.

15:36 Wine vinegar was considered a refreshing drink (Ruth 2:14). A soldier soaked a sponge in wine vinegar and water and offered it to Jesus.

15:38 curtain of the temple. There were two curtains in the temple. An outer curtain separated the sanctuary from the courtyard. The inner curtain covered the Holy of Holies where only the high priest was admitted. It is most likely it was the latter curtain that was torn by God to allow all access to the Father through Jesus Christ.

15:39 centurion. The supervising officer, a pagan soldier who may not have been aware of the significance of what he observed.

15:42 Preparation Day. Jesus died on Friday at 3 p.m. The Sabbath began at 6 p.m., after which no work could be done. Great haste was required.

15:43 Joseph of Arimathea. Little is known of him, except that he was from a wealthy and prominent family and was a member of the Sanhedrin. To ask for the body was to admit allegiance to the now discredited Jesus and was, therefore, potentially dangerous. Often the Romans just left the bodies hanging on the cross to be eaten by vultures, though they did grant requests by the family to be allowed to bury the person. However, the Romans almost never allowed those convicted of treason to be buried. The fact that they do so now probably means Pilate knew Jesus was innocent of the charge of insurrection (vv. 9–11).

15:44 Pilate was surprised. It often took two or three days for a person to die from crucifixion.

hear that he was already dead. Summoning the centurion, he asked
him if Jesus had already died. 45When he learned from the centurion
that it was so, he gave the body to Joseph. 46So Joseph bought some
linen cloth, took down the body, wrapped it in the linen, and placed it
in a tomb cut out of rock. Then he rolled a stone against the entrance
of the tomb. 47Mary Magdalene and Mary the mother of Joses saw
where he was laid.

The Resurrection

16 When the Sabbath was over, Mary Magdalene, Mary the
mother of James, and Salome bought spices so that they
might go to anoint Jesus' body. 2Very early on the first day of the
week, just after sunrise, they were on their way to the tomb 3and they
asked each other, "Who will roll the stone away from the entrance of
the tomb?"

4But when they looked up, they saw that the stone, which was very
large, had been rolled away. 5As they entered the tomb, they saw a
young man dressed in a white robe sitting on the right side, and they
were alarmed.

6"Don't be alarmed," he said. "You are looking for Jesus the Nazarene, who was crucified. He has risen! He is not here. See the place
where they laid him. 7But go, tell his disciples and Peter, 'He is going
ahead of you into Galilee. There you will see him, just as he told
you.' "

8Trembling and bewildered, the women went out and fled from the
tomb. They said nothing to anyone, because they were afraid.

OPEN When you were growing up, what was the tradition in your family for celebrating Easter?

STUDY **1.** How did the three women know where Jesus had been buried (v. 47)? What brought these women to the tomb? What was going to be a problem? **2.** What happened when the women got to the tomb? Why would they be alarmed? **3.** What were the women to report to the disciples? Why were they to report especially to Peter? **4.** What do you think the disciples had been doing for the last three days? Why would Jesus want to meet them in Galilee? **5.** What did Jesus commission the disciples to do? **6.** How important is it to your faith that the tomb was empty (1 Cor. 15:12-19)? **7.** How would you answer

---

15:45 The centurion confirms Jesus had died in six hours. As a supervisor of crucifixion, he had expert insight into such matters. Therefore, when Jesus rose several days later, it was resurrection, not resuscitation.

15:46 The body was washed, quickly wrapped, and then placed in a tomb. The tomb was then sealed against robbers or animals by means of a large stone. These stones were set in grooves which would guide the stone to the tomb's entrance. Elevated above the tomb's entrance, it would not be too difficult to set the stone in motion to roll against the entrance. It would be extremely difficult to remove the stone from the entrance since it would have to be pushed uphill.

15:47 Two of the three women at the Crucifixion saw clearly where Jesus was entombed, so when they returned in two days, they knew where to go.

16:1 When the Sabbath was over. After 6 p.m. on Saturday when the shops were open again. **spices.** Aromatic oils to anoint the body, not so much to preserve it as to honor it (much like people today would put flowers on a grave; 14:3–9). Clearly they did not expect Jesus to have risen from the dead, since the perfumes they bought would have been quite expensive.

16:2 Very early on the first day of the week. Early Sunday morning.

16:3 tomb. Typically, such tombs had a large antechamber, with a small two-foot-high doorway at the back which led into the six- or seven-foot burial chamber proper.

16:4 The stone was rolled away, not so that the resurrected Jesus could leave the tomb, but so that his disciples could see that it was empty (John 20:1–8).

16:5 a young man. An angel (Matt. 28:2–3). The particular word Mark uses here was used in other contexts to refer to an "angel." Angels were often used as messengers of God's revelation. His words explain why the tomb was empty by revealing to the women the resurrection of Jesus. **a white robe.** An indication of his heavenly nature, Jesus was clothed in dazzling white during his transfiguration (9:3). **alarmed.** A rare Greek word used in the New Testament only by Mark (9:15; 14:33), indicating great astonishment in the face of the supernatural.

16:6 He has risen! In the same way that Mark reports the crucifixion of Jesus in simple, stark terms (15:24), so too he describes his resurrection in a plain, unadorned way. The phrase is, literally, "he has been raised," showing that God is the one who accomplished this great act.

16:7 go, tell. Under Jewish law, women were not considered reliable witnesses. Their report of the Resurrection was not left for doubt (Luke 24:11,22–24), hence guaranteeing the historicity of this detail. **his disciples and Peter.** They may have abandoned Jesus, but he has not abandoned them! A special word is given to Peter who, after his abysmal failure, might be tempted to count himself out of further discipleship. Forgiveness is offered. Paul mentions that one of the Lord's post-resurrection appearances was to Peter alone (Luke 24:34; 1 Cor. 15:5). **into Galilee.** Jesus said he would meet them again in Galilee (14:28). The ministry of Jesus and the Twelve began in Galilee, and now they are directed back there to meet the risen Lord, thus bringing Mark's account full circle. See Matthew 28:16–20 for the account of that meeting.

16:8 They said nothing. Eventual-

the arguments that: (a) the disciples stole the body; (b) the cool of the tomb revived Jesus and/or (c) the disciples made up the tale of the resurrection?

APPLY 1. When did the resurrection "dawn" upon you? Were you a quick believer or an honest skeptic? If you could go back to the place where it all began for you, where would you go back to? **2.** When God has to do a little recovery work on your life, how does he go about it? **3.** If Jesus could appear to you today for one word of encouragement, what would he say? Would he touch you? Would you like a hug right now from your group?

[The earliest manuscripts and some other ancient witnesses do not have Mark 16:9-20.]

9When Jesus rose early on the first day of the week, he appeared
first to Mary Magdalene, out of whom he had driven seven demons.
10She went and told those who had been with him and who were
mourning and weeping. 11When they heard that Jesus was alive and
that she had seen him, they did not believe it.
12Afterward Jesus appeared in a different form to two of them while
they were walking in the country. 13These returned and reported it to
the rest; but they did not believe them either.
14Later Jesus appeared to the Eleven as they were eating; he rebuked them for their lack of faith and their stubborn refusal to believe those who had seen him after he had risen.
15He said to them, "Go into all the world and preach the good news
to all creation. 16Whoever believes and is baptized will be saved, but
whoever does not believe will be condemned. 17And these signs will
accompany those who believe: In my name they will drive out
demons; they will speak in new tongues; 18they will pick up snakes
with their hands; and when they drink deadly poison, it will not hurt
them at all; they will place their hands on sick people, and they will
get well."
19After the Lord Jesus had spoken to them, he was taken up into
heaven and he sat at the right hand of God. 20Then the disciples went
out and preached everywhere, and the Lord worked with them and
confirmed his word by the signs that accompanied it.

ly, of course, the women did report what happened (Matt. 28:8; Luke 24:10). **they were afraid.** This was the same sort of fear that the disciples felt on the Sea of Galilee when they discovered that Jesus had power over the elements themselves (4:41). This is how human beings respond in the face of the supernatural. Thus the Gospel of Mark ends on this note of astonishment and fear which was so characteristic of how he described people's reaction to a miracle or supernatural event (2:12; 4:41; 5:15, 33,42; 9:6).

16:14 the Eleven. Judas Iscariot had committed suicide (Matt. 27:5).

16:15–18 While verse 15 parallels Matthew 28:18–20, verses 16–18 are not paralleled in any of the other Gospels.

16:16 baptized. Baptism is a sign of union with and commitment to Christ (Acts 2:38; Rom. 6:3–4).

16:17–18 Although no mention is made of such signs in the other Gospels, such things did happen in the early church (Acts 2:43; 4:30; 5:12; Heb. 2:4).

16:18 drink deadly poison. There is no mention of this phrase elsewhere in the New Testament.

16:19 The story of the ascension of Jesus is told in Luke 24:50–51 and Acts 1:4–11. **the right hand of God.** This is the position of authority and power (Heb. 1:3).

16:20 The story of some of the disciples' ministry is told in Acts.

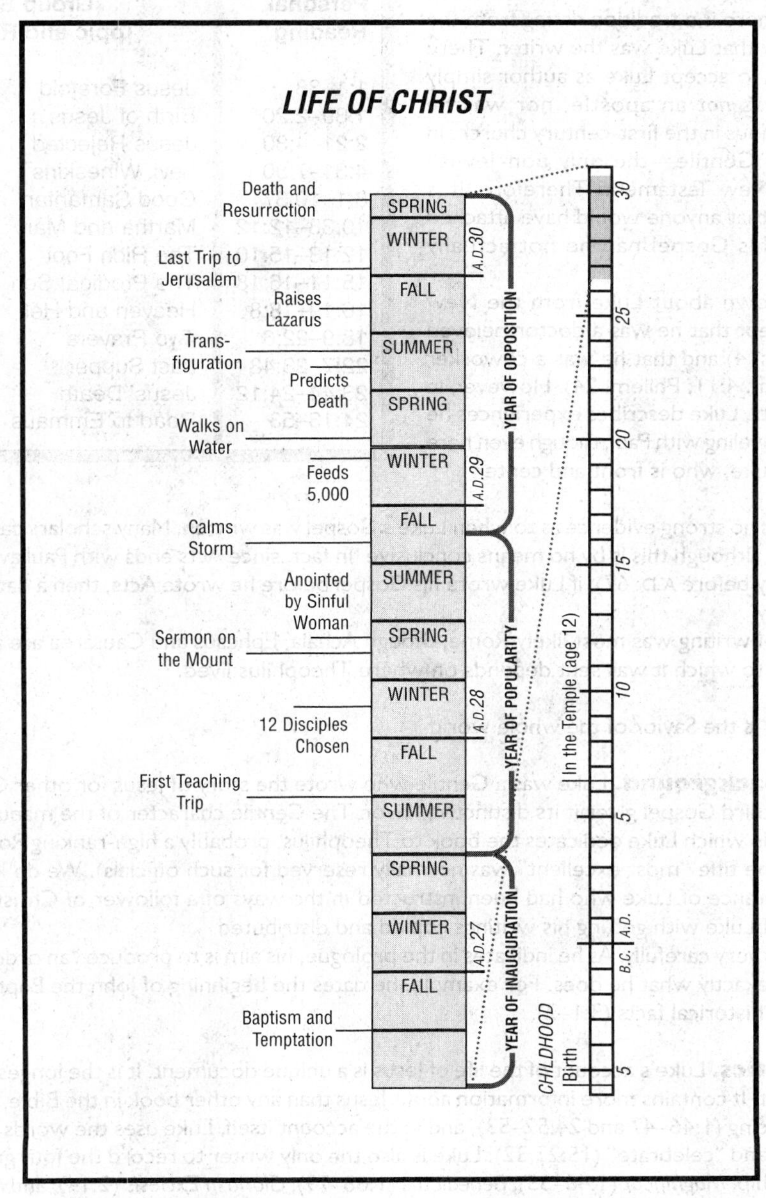
LIFE OF CHRIST
Death and Resurrection
Last Trip to Jerusalem
Raises Lazarus
Transfiguration
Predicts Death
Walks on Water
Feeds 5,000
Calms Storm
Anointed by Sinful Woman
Sermon on the Mount
12 Disciples Chosen
First Teaching Trip
Baptism and Temptation
SPRING
WINTER
FALL
SUMMER
SPRING
WINTER
FALL
SUMMER
SPRING
WINTER
FALL
SUMMER
SPRING
WINTER
FALL
A.D.30
A.D.29
A.D.28
A.D.27
YEAR OF OPPOSITION
YEAR OF POPULARITY
YEAR OF INAUGURATION
CHILDHOOD
Birth
In the Temple (age 12)
B.C.
A.D.
5
5
10
15
20
25
30

Luke

Personal Reading	Group Study Topic and Reading	
1:1–38	Jesus Foretold	1:26–38
1:39–2:20	Birth of Jesus	2:1–20
2:21–4:30	Jesus Rejected	4:14–30
4:31–7:50	Levi; Wineskins	5:27–39
8:1–10:37	Good Samaritan	10:25–37
10:38–12:12	Martha and Mary	10:38–42
12:13–15:10	The Rich Fool	12:13–21
15:11–16:18	The Prodigal Son	15:11–32
16:19–18:8	Heaven and Hell	16:19–31
18:9–22:6	Two Prayers	18:9–14
22:7–23:43	Last Supper	22:7–34
23:44–24:12	Jesus' Death	23:44–49
24:13–53	Road to Emmaus	24:13–35

Author. Although no author is named in the third Gospel, there is a tradition dating from the second century that Luke was the writer. There is good reason to accept Luke as author simply because he was *not* an apostle, nor was he particularly famous in the first-century church. In fact, he was a Gentile—the only non-Jewish author in the New Testament. Therefore, it is highly unlikely that anyone would have attached his name to this Gospel had he not actually written it.

Little is known about Luke from the New Testament except that he was a doctor beloved by Paul (Col. 4:14) and that he was a coworker with Paul (2 Tim. 4:11; Philem. 24). However, in the book of Acts, Luke describes experiences he shared while traveling with Paul, though even here it is Paul, not Luke, who is front and center.

Date. There is no strong evidence as to when Luke's Gospel was written. Many scholars date it between A.D. 75 and 85, although this is by no means conclusive. In fact, since Acts ends with Paul awaiting trial in Rome (probably before A.D. 67), if Luke wrote his Gospel before he wrote Acts, then a date in the early A.D. 60s is likely.

The place of writing was most likely Rome, though Achaia, Ephesus and Caesarea are also possibilities. The place to which it was sent depends on where Theophilus lived.

Theme. Jesus is the Savior of the whole world.

Historical Background. Luke was a Gentile who wrote the story of Jesus for other Gentiles. This fact about the third Gospel gives it its distinctive flavor. The Gentile character of the manuscript begins in the preface, in which Luke dedicates the book to Theophilus, probably a high-ranking Roman government official (the title "most excellent" was normally reserved for such officials). We do know that he was an acquaintance of Luke who had been instructed in the ways of a follower of Christ (1:3–4). He possibly helped Luke with getting his writings copied and distributed.

Luke writes very carefully. As he indicates in the prologue, his aim is to produce "an orderly account" (1:3), which is exactly what he does. For example, he dates the beginning of John the Baptist's ministry by referring to historical facts (3:1–2).

Characteristics. Luke's account of the life of Jesus is a unique document. It is the longest book in the New Testament. It contains more information about Jesus than any other book in the Bible. It begins and ends with rejoicing (1:46–47 and 24:52–53), and in the account itself, Luke uses the words "joy" (6:23), "laugh" (6:21), and "celebrate" (15:23,32). Luke is also the only writer to record the four great canticles of joy and worship: *Magnificat* (1:46–55), *Benedictus* (1:68–79), *Gloria in Exclesis* (2:14), and *Nunc Dimittis* (2:29–32).

Christ Came for All. Why is Luke so filled with joy? He is overwhelmed with the thought that Jesus is the Savior of the whole world. He is astonished that Jesus came to seek and to save not just his kinsfolk, the Jews, but all people regardless of race, age or culture.

In addition to Luke's universality (Christ has come for all people) and his fascination with people

(especially the outcasts), several other themes distinguish Luke. For example, Luke records more of Jesus' teaching about prayer than is found anywhere else in the Bible. He records nine of Jesus' own prayers. Luke also has more to say than the other Gospels about the Holy Spirit (4:1,14; 10:21; 24:49). He will pick up and expand on this emphasis of the Holy Spirit's active ministry in the companion volume to the third Gospel, the book of Acts.

Style. For all the author's care and meticulous nature, Luke's Gospel is no dry, academic document. It sparkles with life and vitality. Luke's portraits of people are particularly vivid and compassionate. People like Zacchaeus, Cleopas, Mary, Martha, Elizabeth and Mary the mother of Jesus all spring to life through his talented pen. Luke's Gospel tells a rare and unforgettable story.

Introduction

1 Many have undertaken to draw up an account of the things that
have been fulfilled[a] among us, 2just as they were handed down to
us by those who from the first were eyewitnesses and servants of the
word. 3Therefore, since I myself have carefully investigated everything from the beginning, it seemed good also to me to write an
orderly account for you, most excellent Theophilus, 4so that you may
know the certainty of the things you have been taught.

The Birth of John the Baptist Foretold

5In the time of Herod king of Judea there was a priest named Zechariah, who belonged to the priestly division of Abijah; his wife Elizabeth was also a descendant of Aaron. 6Both of them were upright in
the sight of God, observing all the Lord's commandments and regulations blamelessly. 7But they had no children, because Elizabeth was
barren; and they were both well along in years.
8Once when Zechariah's division was on duty and he was serving
as priest before God, 9he was chosen by lot, according to the custom
of the priesthood, to go into the temple of the Lord and burn incense.

[a]1 Or *been surely believed*

OPEN Have you drawn up your last will and testament? What important facts did you include?

STUDY 1. What do you learn from verses 1–4 about Luke? About the reason he wrote this Gospel? About his sources? **2.** What stands out to you about Zechariah and Elizabeth (vv. 5–7)? What feelings might the couple have had in light of their barrenness? **3.** What was the significance of the task for which Zechariah was chosen (1 Chr. 23:13)? **4.** What does the angel tell Zechariah? What will be unique about this child? What will be his mission? **5.** How did Zechariah react? How would you react if an angel told you that you (or your wife) were going to have a child? Was the deafness caused by trauma or unbelief? **6.** Why would Luke, a medical doctor, begin his account about the life of Christ with the unexpected pregnancy of the parents

1:1 Many. Mark and Luke contain similar material. Most of Mark is included in Luke. Unknown writers also recorded some of the teachings and stories about Jesus that Luke incorporated into his Gospel as well.

1:2 eyewitnesses and servants of the word. "The word" is a shorthand way of referring to the whole of Jesus' life and teaching (Acts 1:21–22; 2 Peter 1:16; 1 John 1:1). The stories that form the Gospel were passed on by those who were personally acquainted with and dedicated to Jesus.

1:3 carefully investigated. While Luke was not an eyewitness, his association with Paul and Mark (Col. 4:10–14; 2 Tim. 4:11), his travels to Judea (Acts 21), and his familiarity with other eyewitnesses afforded him ample opportunity to collect information from reliable witnesses. **an orderly account.** While Luke does follow a roughly chronological account, his order, like that of the other Gospel writers, is more thematic than chronological. **Theophilus.** An unknown figure. He may have been Luke's patron who underwrote the cost of writing the Gospel, or a Roman official (Acts 1:1).

1:4 you may know the certainty. Heretical groups, claiming secret knowledge of Christ, arose early on in the church. Luke's Gospel may be written in part to counter and silence their claims.

1:5 Herod king of Judea. Herod the Great represented Roman authority in Palestine from 40–4 B.C. **Zechariah.** His name means "God remembers." **the priestly division of Abijah.** Jewish priests were separated into 24 divisions (1 Chr. 24:10), each of which served in the temple two weeks out of the year. Since by this time there were almost 1,000 priests per division, one was chosen by lot to offer the morning and evening sacrifice. A priest could be chosen for such an honor only once, and it was possible that an individual might never be chosen. **a descendant of Aaron.** Aaron, Moses' brother, was the ultimate ancestor of all Jewish priests. It was preferable that priests marry a daughter of a priest.

1:7 Elizabeth was barren. Barrenness was seen as a tragedy and a valid reason for divorce.

1:9 to go into the temple of the Lord and burn incense. Each morning and evening the chosen priest would enter the Holy Place inside the temple to offer prayer and burn incense

of John the Baptist? **7.** If you were going to make a movie out of this Gospel, how would you introduce this story?

APPLY 1. If you were going to write the story of the gospel based on your experience, where would you begin? **2.** Are you open to the possibility that God may have a very special mission for your life?

10And when the time for the burning of incense came, all the assembled worshipers were praying outside.
11Then an angel of the Lord appeared to him, standing at the right
side of the altar of incense. 12When Zechariah saw him, he was startled and was gripped with fear. 13But the angel said to him: "Do not be
afraid, Zechariah; your prayer has been heard. Your wife Elizabeth
will bear you a son, and you are to give him the name John. 14He will
be a joy and delight to you, and many will rejoice because of his birth,
15for he will be great in the sight of the Lord. He is never to take wine
or other fermented drink, and he will be filled with the Holy Spirit
even from birth.[a] 16Many of the people of Israel will he bring back to
the Lord their God. 17And he will go on before the Lord, in the spirit
and power of Elijah, to turn the hearts of the fathers to their children
and the disobedient to the wisdom of the righteous—to make ready a
people prepared for the Lord."
18Zechariah asked the angel, "How can I be sure of this? I am an old
man and my wife is well along in years."
19The angel answered, "I am Gabriel. I stand in the presence of
God, and I have been sent to speak to you and to tell you this good
news. 20And now you will be silent and not able to speak until the day
this happens, because you did not believe my words, which will come
true at their proper time."
21Meanwhile, the people were waiting for Zechariah and wondering why he stayed so long in the temple. 22When he came out, he
could not speak to them. They realized he had seen a vision in the
temple, for he kept making signs to them but remained unable to
speak.
23When his time of service was completed, he returned home. 24Af-
ter this his wife Elizabeth became pregnant and for five months
remained in seclusion. 25"The Lord has done this for me," she said.
"In these days he has shown his favor and taken away my disgrace
among the people."

OPEN If an angel told you that you were going to have a child this year, how would you react?

STUDY 1. How does this story relate to the previous

The Birth of Jesus Foretold

26In the sixth month, God sent the angel Gabriel to Nazareth, a
town in Galilee, 27to a virgin pledged to be married to a man named

[a] 15 *Or from his mother's womb*

---

on the temple's altar. The incense was symbolic of the people's prayers and dedication to God (Ex. 30:1–10; Ps. 141:2; Rev. 5:8).

1:10 all the assembled worshipers were praying outside. The burning of incense coincided with times set aside for public prayer. Jews would gather in the court outside of the Holy Place and maintain silent prayer while incense was being burned.

1:12 *gripped with fear.* *The fear he* experienced of the angel is similar to that experienced other places in Scripture when an angel comes to an individual (vv. 29–30; Ex. 3:2–6; Dan. 10:7).

1:15 He is never to take wine ... he will be filled with the Holy Spirit. The first statement connects John to the Old Testament order of Nazirites (Num. 6) marked by asceticism and dedication to God; the second statement shows him to be the forerunner of the new era of the Messiah when God's Spirit would indwell his people.

1:17 in the spirit and power of Elijah. Elijah was one of the first great Old Testament prophets. Malachi, the last prophet to speak to the Jews, foresaw a time when Elijah would come again to prepare people for the Lord (Mal. 4:5). While Jewish tradition anticipated the literal return of Elijah, the angel's message is that John would be inspired by the same divine energy that led Elijah.

1:19 Gabriel. Literally, "man of God." In Jewish tradition, he was one of the select few angels who represent God as his special servants (Dan. 8:16; 9:21).

1:20 not able to speak. Old Testament saints questioned God without rebuke or punishment (Gen. 15:8; Judg. 6:13ff). Here, Zechariah's inability to speak is tied to his lack of trust. It may have also been a confirmation of Gabriel's words.

1:26 In the sixth month. This is the sixth month of Elizabeth's pregnancy. **Nazareth, a town in Galilee.** Naza-

Joseph, a descendant of David. The virgin's name was Mary. [28]The
angel went to her and said, "Greetings, you who are highly favored!
The Lord is with you."

[29]Mary was greatly troubled at his words and wondered what kind
of greeting this might be. [30]But the angel said to her, "Do not be
afraid, Mary, you have found favor with God. [31]You will be with child
and give birth to a son, and you are to give him the name Jesus.
[32]He will be great and will be called the Son of the Most High. The
Lord God will give him the throne of his father David, [33]and he will
reign over the house of Jacob forever; his kingdom will never end."

[34]"How will this be," Mary asked the angel, "since I am a virgin?"

[35]The angel answered, "The Holy Spirit will come upon you, and
the power of the Most High will overshadow you. So the holy one to
be born will be called[a] the Son of God. [36]Even Elizabeth your relative
is going to have a child in her old age, and she who was said to be
barren is in her sixth month. [37]For nothing is impossible with God."

[38]"I am the Lord's servant," Mary answered. "May it be to me as
you have said." Then the angel left her.

Mary Visits Elizabeth

[39]At that time Mary got ready and hurried to a town in the hill
country of Judea, [40]where she entered Zechariah's home and greeted
Elizabeth. [41]When Elizabeth heard Mary's greeting, the baby leaped
in her womb, and Elizabeth was filled with the Holy Spirit. [42]In a loud
voice she exclaimed: "Blessed are you among women, and blessed is
the child you will bear! [43]But why am I so favored, that the mother of
my Lord should come to me? [44]As soon as the sound of your greeting

[a]35 Or *So the child to be born will be called holy,*

story—only six months before? **2.** In the announcement of the angel Gabriel, what do you learn about Mary? How did she respond? **3.** What do you learn about the nature and mission of the child? What do you think was the hardest thing for Mary to comprehend? **4.** How does the angel assure her of this miracle? **5.** How important is it that Jesus was born of a virgin—conceived by the Holy Spirit?

APPLY 1. When did you begin to seek to understand God's plan for you? **2.** Is it harder for you to believe in the virgin birth or to believe that God included you in his plan of salvation? **3.** How important is mystery in your life—to believe in things that you cannot rationally understand?

OPEN 1. Whom do you call first when you have good news? **2.** What kind of church music do you prefer?

STUDY 1. How might Mary have felt when Elizabeth greeted her? How is she "blessed" and encouraged? **2.** What is the occasion for this poem? **3.** Why do you think Mary stayed for the first three months of her pregnancy with

---

reth was an insignificant little village (John 1:46) in the province of Galilee. God often uses what others see as small or insignificant, as with the "little town of Bethlehem."

1:27 a virgin pledged to be married. Betrothal, usually lasting for about a year, could occur as young as 12 years old. This was a far more binding arrangement than engagements today. Although sexual relations were not permitted, the woman had the legal status of a wife and the relationship could only be broken by divorce. The virgin birth of Jesus, although only mentioned in Matthew and Luke in the entire New Testament, traces its roots to the prophecy of the child spoken of in Isaiah 7:14. **Joseph, a descendant of David.** The Messiah was to come through the line of David, the most famous king of Israel's history (2 Sam. 7:16; Ps. 132:11).

1:28 you who are highly favored. The angel is not commending her virtue, but recognizing the reality of God's grace to her. **The Lord is with you.** This phrase is often used as a statement of God's special intention to equip a person for his service (Josh. 1:5; Judg. 6:12; Matt. 28:20).

1:32 He will be great ... the Son of the Most High. Jesus, like John the Baptist (v. 15), will be considered "great," but the greatness of these two men will be of differing orders. John will be great "in the sight of the Lord" (v. 15) as "a prophet of the Most High" (v. 76), but Jesus' greatness consists in his being the Son of the Most High (God).

1:34 How will this be? Zechariah asked this question of the angel when informed that he and his wife Elizabeth would have a child (v. 18). He asked out of doubt that such a thing could come to pass. Mary, however, is not registering doubt as much as wonder.

1:37 nothing is impossible with God. The ultimate ground for Mary's faith rests on this fact. In similar circumstances, when Sarah laughed at the idea that a woman her age could have a child, God said, "Is anything too hard for the LORD?" (Gen. 18:14). It was this conviction that gave courage and faith in the hardest times (Jer. 32:27). Jesus emphasized this "belief in the impossible" on several occasions (Matt. 17:20; Mark 9:23; 10:27).

1:39 hurried to a town. We don't know what town this is, but the journey to Judea would have been 80 to 100 miles. Why did she go there in such a hurry? The urgency was not for practical reasons—she was not in immediate need and she would be pregnant for a long time—but for emotional reasons. She was full of feelings which she had to share with someone who would understand. Not only were the relatives united by the camaraderie of the shared experience of pregnancy, but Elizabeth was one of the few persons who could understand the miraculous nature of what had happened to Mary. It would seem she did not go to Joseph or her parents first. That would involve great tension, because they would assume immoral behavior on her part. Perhaps only after sharing joy and support with Elizabeth could she be strengthened for these more tense encounters.

1:43 my Lord. Elizabeth recognizes the sovereignty and power of Mary's child even prior to his birth.

reached my ears, the baby in my womb leaped for joy. 45Blessed is she
who has believed that what the Lord has said to her will be
accomplished!"

Mary's Song

46And Mary said:

"My soul glorifies the Lord
47 and my spirit rejoices in God my Savior,
48for he has been mindful
of the humble state of his servant.
From now on all generations will call me blessed,
49 for the Mighty One has done great things for me—
holy is his name.
50His mercy extends to those who fear him,
from generation to generation.
51He has performed mighty deeds with his arm;
he has scattered those who are proud in their inmost thoughts.
52He has brought down rulers from their thrones
but has lifted up the humble.
53He has filled the hungry with good things
but has sent the rich away empty.
54He has helped his servant Israel,
remembering to be merciful
55to Abraham and his descendants forever,
even as he said to our fathers."

56Mary stayed with Elizabeth for about three months and then returned home.

The Birth of John the Baptist

57When it was time for Elizabeth to have her baby, she gave birth to
a son. 58Her neighbors and relatives heard that the Lord had shown
her great mercy, and they shared her joy.
59On the eighth day they came to circumcise the child, and they
were going to name him after his father Zechariah, 60but his mother
spoke up and said, "No! He is to be called John."
61They said to her, "There is no one among your relatives who has
that name."
62Then they made signs to his father, to find out what he would like
to name the child. 63He asked for a writing tablet, and to everyone's
astonishment he wrote, "His name is John." 64Immediately his mouth
was opened and his tongue was loosed, and he began to speak,
praising God. 65The neighbors were all filled with awe, and through-

Elizabeth: Morning sickness? Spiritual comfort? To get away from home? To think through the future? **4.** Who is this poem addressed to? What is the theme? **5.** What does this poem reveal about Mary's view of God? For a young girl from a small town, how would you rank Mary on maturity? **6.** What is the underlying feeling in this poem? What two adjectives would you use to describe it? **7.** How much of this poem has been fulfilled and how much is yet to come?

APPLY 1. As you look at the world today, do you need a little assurance that God is still in control? **2.** When is the last time you celebrated what God is doing in your life?

OPEN What is your nickname and how did you get it?

STUDY 1. How did John's birth fulfill the words of the angel in verses 13–17? **2.** For over nine months, the father Zechariah has been speechless. What happened during the circumcision that provides a clue to the role of John in the plan and purpose of God? (Hint: the name John means, "the Lord is gracious") **3.** How did the neighbors respond? What do you think Zechariah told them about this child? To the neighbors, what would this awaken in them?

1:45 Blessed is she who has believed. In general, the Bible has many more male role models than female, but it is Mary's belief that has made her a model of faith for women through the centuries. *Her faith contrasts with* the doubt of Zechariah in verse 20.

1:46–56 Mary's song (known as the *Magnificat* after its first words in the Latin Vulgate translation) may have been used as a hymn by the early church as a means of describing the mission of Mary's son. It celebrates God's action on behalf of Israel as the fulfillment of the enduring hopes of the nation.

1:57–77 The story of John's birth is the prelude for Luke's second major prophecy, commonly known as the *Benedictus*. It reflects Isaiah 9:2 which anticipated God's mercy being extended beyond the people of Israel to the Gentiles as well (vv. 71,74, however, still reflect the narrower concept that saw God's role as rescuing Israel from political enemies). Here the events to come are described in the past tense, reflecting the confidence that what has been foretold is as good as done, now that God has begun his work. The great plan for the salvation of believers has been set in motion.

out the hill country of Judea people were talking about all these things. [66]Everyone who heard this wondered about it, asking, "What then is this child going to be?" For the Lord's hand was with him.

Zechariah's Song

[67]His father Zechariah was filled with the Holy Spirit and prophesied:

[68]"Praise be to the Lord, the God of Israel,
because he has come and has redeemed his people.
[69]He has raised up a horn[a] of salvation for us
in the house of his servant David
[70](as he said through his holy prophets of long ago),
[71]salvation from our enemies
and from the hand of all who hate us—
[72]to show mercy to our fathers
and to remember his holy covenant,
[73] the oath he swore to our father Abraham:
[74]to rescue us from the hand of our enemies,
and to enable us to serve him without fear
[75] in holiness and righteousness before him all our days.

[76]And you, my child, will be called a prophet of the Most High;
for you will go on before the Lord to prepare the way for him,
[77]to give his people the knowledge of salvation
through the forgiveness of their sins,
[78]because of the tender mercy of our God,
by which the rising sun will come to us from heaven
[79]to shine on those living in darkness
and in the shadow of death,
to guide our feet into the path of peace."

[80]And the child grew and became strong in spirit; and he lived in the desert until he appeared publicly to Israel.

The Birth of Jesus

2 In those days Caesar Augustus issued a decree that a census should be taken of the entire Roman world. [2](This was the first census that took place while Quirinius was governor of Syria.) [3]And everyone went to his own town to register.

[a]69 *Horn* here symbolizes strength.

APPLY In your family tree, where do you trace a lot of your spiritual heritage?

OPEN How did you (or would you) celebrate the birth of your first child?

STUDY 1. If you had to describe this poem/song with one or two adjectives, what would you say? What is the theme? The central message? **2.** What is going to be the role of John in the unfolding plan of God for the nation of Israel? **3.** How is the term "salvation" used here? **4.** Who gave him his theological training? **5.** Luke wrote this Gospel for his friend Theophilus (vv. 3–4) who was a Gentile. Why would this background in Old Testament history be important? **6.** Of the promises described in this poem, which promise means the most to you?

APPLY 1. When did you come to the place in your life that the gospel message made sense? **2.** Could you use a little understanding of God's will right now?

OPEN 1. What is your ancestral home? Has it changed? **2.** When does your Christmas tree go up? Who trims it? How? What other traditions do you observe from your childhood?

1:71–75 Salvation in the Old Testament was viewed in terms of the coming reign of God, which would result in certain benefits in this life—especially freedom from political oppression by their enemies. Some prophets, however, saw salvation including the concept of a new kind of world justice that would benefit Gentiles as well (Isa. 9:6–7; 11:1–16; 61:1–7). Israel's hope for this future was rooted in the original promise God made to Abraham to make his people a blessing to the whole world (Gen. 12:1–3).

2:1 Caesar Augustus. Luke roots Jesus' birth firmly in history. Augustus ruled the Roman Empire from 30 B.C. to 14 A.D. Originally known as Gaius Octavius (or Octavian), he was awarded the title Augustus (which means "majestic" or "highly revered") by the Roman senate and became known thereafter as Caesar Augustus. Augustus was a wise ruler who encouraged the arts and built many fine projects. He also brought an unprecedented period of peace to the world. **census.** From about 30 B.C. onward, the Caesars ordered people in the various Roman provinces to report every 14 years for a census for purposes of taxation. Resistance from the population and from local rulers sometimes meant census-taking required several years to complete. While there is firm evidence of a census after King Herod's death in 6 A.D., there is no external source that allows us to know whether the census mentioned here was a separate, earlier one or the beginning stages of the census completed at that date.

2:3 everyone went to his own town. Since Joseph and Mary lived in

STUDY **1.** How do you think Joseph and Mary felt about the timing of the census? Why was it important that Jesus be born in Bethlehem (Mic. 5:2)? **2.** In the Gospel of Matthew, the birth of Jesus is heralded by the visit of wealthy magi from the East. Here, the birth is heralded by a band of low income shepherds from the neighborhood. What does that say about the purpose of this Gospel? **3.** What three titles are given to Jesus in verse 11? What is significant about them? **4.** Based on the information the shepherds received from the angel and saw with their own eyes, what could they have said to the townsfolk that created such a stir? **5.** How did Mary receive the news? What does this bring to mind?

APPLY **1.** Pregnant and homeless, how would you like to start a family this way? **2.** What were the circumstances surrounding your spiritual beginning?

[4]So Joseph also went up from the town of Nazareth in Galilee to
Judea, to Bethlehem the town of David, because he belonged to the
house and line of David. [5]He went there to register with Mary, who
was pledged to be married to him and was expecting a child. [6]While
they were there, the time came for the baby to be born, [7]and she gave
birth to her firstborn, a son. She wrapped him in cloths and placed
him in a manger, because there was no room for them in the inn.

The Shepherds and the Angels

[8]And there were shepherds living out in the fields nearby, keeping
watch over their flocks at night. [9]An angel of the Lord appeared to
them, and the glory of the Lord shone around them, and they were
terrified. [10]But the angel said to them, "Do not be afraid. I bring you
good news of great joy that will be for all the people. [11]Today in the
town of David a Savior has been born to you; he is Christ[a] the Lord.
[12]This will be a sign to you: You will find a baby wrapped in cloths and
lying in a manger."
[13]Suddenly a great company of the heavenly host appeared with
the angel, praising God and saying,

[14]"Glory to God in the highest,
and on earth peace to men on whom his favor rests."

[15]When the angels had left them and gone into heaven, the shepherds said to one another, "Let's go to Bethlehem and see this thing
that has happened, which the Lord has told us about."

[a]11 Or *Messiah.* "The Christ" (Greek) and "the Messiah" (Hebrew) both mean "the Anointed One"; also in verse 26.

Galilee, they must have owned some property in Bethlehem. Roman custom required people who owned property in another location from where they lived to register there as well. Bethlehem, a three to four-day journey from Galilee, was the village where King David, through whose line the Messiah was to come, had lived.

2:5 to register with Mary. In some provinces, the Romans charged a poll tax on women 12 years of age or older. **pledged to be married to him and was expecting a child.** Their betrothal had not yet been consummated by intercourse (Matt. 1:24–25).

2:7 firstborn. The firstborn of every Jewish family was dedicated to God in a special way (Ex. 13:12). **manger.** A feeding trough for animals. **the inn.** This is either a building used for the accommodation of travelers or a spare room in a private home. However, there was no space for the couple, who stayed with the animals. A tradition dating back to the second century maintains this was in a cave on the site of which today is the Church of the Nativity. **She wrapped him in cloths.** The tradition of the time was to wrap a baby in strips of cloth. Such cloths would give the child the feeling of being securely held.

2:8 shepherds. Since temple authorities kept flocks of sheep for sacrificial purposes pastured near Bethlehem, it might be the shepherds of these flocks were the ones visited by the angels. This happened at a time of year when sheep could still be kept in the field, which was sometime between April and November. The date of December 25 as the birth of Christ was selected in the fourth century.

2:9 An angel of the Lord. In some Old Testament passages, the angel of the Lord is identified as God himself (Gen. 16:7ff; Ex. 3:2; Judg. 6:11ff), indicating his divine authority and splendor. Throughout the Bible, angels serve as God's agents of instruction, judgment and deliverance. **the glory of the Lord.** The overwhelmingly powerful light that accompanies the presence of God (Ps. 104:1–2; Ezek. 1). **they were terrified.** Often in the Bible when an angel appears to a person, the response is one of terror. It is the fear of being in the presence of something supernatural, powerful and totally foreign to one's experience (1:29–30; Dan. 10:7).

2:10 all the people. Another emphasis on the universality of the gospel, especially as presented by Luke.

2:11 a Savior ... Christ the Lord. "Savior," a term in the Old Testament which only applies to God, is one who delivers his people from evil and harm. "Christ" means one anointed by God. "Lord" implies both his authority and deity.

2:12 a sign. In the Old Testament, God sometimes granted signs that pointed out to people the reliability of his message. The "sign" of the Lord is, ironically, that of a baby wrapped in cloths and lying in an animal's feeding trough.

2:13 At a birth, neighbors and friends would gather to celebrate. At this birth, while Mary and Joseph are away from family, and probably shamed by friends, the angels fulfill this function.

2:14 peace to men on whom his favor rests. While older versions divide this phrase into two clauses (peace on earth / good will toward men), the NIV translation, with its single clause accenting God's promise of peace to his people, is to be preferred.

16So they hurried off and found Mary and Joseph, and the baby,
who was lying in the manger. 17When they had seen him, they spread
the word concerning what had been told them about this child, 18and
all who heard it were amazed at what the shepherds said to them.
19But Mary treasured up all these things and pondered them in her
heart. 20The shepherds returned, glorifying and praising God for all
the things they had heard and seen, which were just as they had been
told.

Jesus Presented in the Temple

21On the eighth day, when it was time to circumcise him, he was
named Jesus, the name the angel had given him before he had been
conceived.

22When the time of their purification according to the Law of Moses had been completed, Joseph and Mary took him to Jerusalem to
present him to the Lord 23(as it is written in the Law of the Lord,
"Every firstborn male is to be consecrated to the Lord"[a]), 24and to
offer a sacrifice in keeping with what is said in the Law of the Lord: "a
pair of doves or two young pigeons."[b]

25Now there was a man in Jerusalem called Simeon, who was righteous and devout. He was waiting for the consolation of Israel, and
the Holy Spirit was upon him. 26It had been revealed to him by the
Holy Spirit that he would not die before he had seen the Lord's
Christ. 27Moved by the Spirit, he went into the temple courts. When
the parents brought in the child Jesus to do for him what the custom
of the Law required, 28Simeon took him in his arms and praised God,
saying:

29"Sovereign Lord, as you have promised,
  you now dismiss[c] your servant in peace.
30For my eyes have seen your salvation,
31 which you have prepared in the sight of all people,
32a light for revelation to the Gentiles
  and for glory to your people Israel."

[a]23 Exodus 13:2,12 [b]24 Lev. 12:8 [c]29 Or *promised, / now dismiss*

OPEN 1. When you were growing up, what teacher, coach or relative made you feel special? **2.** Who is the oldest person you know?

STUDY 1. Were you christened or dedicated when you were a child? **2.** What do you learn about the economic status of Jesus' parents when they offered "a pair of doves or two young pigeons"? **3.** In Simeon's two prophecies (vv. 29–32,34–35), what was he predicting about the work of Jesus? His effect on people? The pain of his parents? **4.** Do you know anyone like dear old, saintly Anna? How does she complement Simeon's prophecy? **5.** What impact would these startling predictions by Simeon and Anna have on all who were listening that day? On the parents of Jesus as they returned home (vv. 33,39)? **6.** What do you learn about Mary and Joseph in this passage? About Jesus? About God?

APPLY 1. In your spiritual story, who were the Simeon and the Anna that saw promise in you at an early age? **2.** Who affirms you now and believes in you even when

2:17 they spread the word. Luke is concerned throughout his Gospel, as well as in Acts, to show that the message of Christ is to be spread to all people. The shepherds become the first witnesses, announcing the good news of God.

2:21 time to circumcise him. The Old Testament Law required that male infants be circumcised on the eighth day (Lev. 12:3). **Jesus.** Jesus was a common Jewish name meaning "God saves."

2:22–24 Two Old Testament rituals are in view: (1) a woman's purification after childbirth, and (2) the redemption of the firstborn. According to Leviticus 12, a woman was ritually unclean for 40 days after giving birth to a son. During that time, she was forbidden to enter the temple or participate in religious services. Afterwards, she was to offer a sacrifice for cleansing at the temple. Normally this sacrifice was to be a lamb, but the poor could offer two doves or pigeons instead. In commemoration of the events surrounding Passover, the firstborn male of every Jewish family was to be set apart for the Lord (Ex. 13:1–16).

2:25 waiting for the consolation of Israel. Simeon was looking to God to bring about the promises of the messianic age. **the Holy Spirit was upon him.** It was rare in Old Testament days for the Spirit to visit saints like Simeon, John (1:14–15), Elizabeth (1:41), and Zechariah (1:67). One of the characteristics of God's people as a result of the gospel would be the continued indwelling of the Holy Spirit.

2:29 dismiss your servant in peace. The thought is that of a slave requesting leave after fulfilling a task his master had given him. Simeon can approach death easily now, not only because God had kept his promise (v. 26), but because he could be assured that this child would "destroy death" and bring "life and immortality to light." (2 Tim. 1:10).

2:30–32 These verses are rooted in Isaiah's vision of God's promise to bring salvation to Gentiles as well as Jews (Isa. 42:6–7; 49:6; 50:10). The salvation Simeon sees is Jesus himself, the light of the world (John 8:12) and the fullness of God's glory (Col. 2:9).

you don't believe in yourself? Has this made a difference in your life?

---

[33]The child's father and mother marveled at what was said about
him. [34]Then Simeon blessed them and said to Mary, his mother: "This
child is destined to cause the falling and rising of many in Israel, and
to be a sign that will be spoken against, [35]so that the thoughts of
many hearts will be revealed. And a sword will pierce your own soul
too."
[36]There was also a prophetess, Anna, the daughter of Phanuel, of
the tribe of Asher. She was very old; she had lived with her husband
seven years after her marriage, [37]and then was a widow until she was
eighty-four.[a] She never left the temple but worshiped night and day,
fasting and praying. [38]Coming up to them at that very moment, she
gave thanks to God and spoke about the child to all who were looking
forward to the redemption of Jerusalem.
[39]When Joseph and Mary had done everything required by the Law
of the Lord, they returned to Galilee to their own town of Nazareth.
[40]And the child grew and became strong; he was filled with wisdom,
and the grace of God was upon him.

The Boy Jesus at the Temple

[41]Every year his parents went to Jerusalem for the Feast of the
Passover. [42]When he was twelve years old, they went up to the Feast,
according to the custom. [43]After the Feast was over, while his parents
were returning home, the boy Jesus stayed behind in Jerusalem, but
they were unaware of it. [44]Thinking he was in their company, they
traveled on for a day. Then they began looking for him among their
relatives and friends. [45]When they did not find him, they went back to
Jerusalem to look for him. [46]After three days they found him in the
temple courts, sitting among the teachers, listening to them and ask-

[a]37 Or *widow for eighty-four years*

OPEN 1. What was your best family trip? **2.** Did you ever get lost as a child? What happened?

STUDY 1. If you had been one of the parents, how would you have reacted when you discovered that Jesus was missing? **2.** What would you have said when you found him? **3.** What do you learn about Jesus from this episode? Do you think Jesus understood his mission at this early age? **4.** How much of Jesus'

2:33 The child's father and mother marveled. The references to Joseph as Jesus' father should be read simply as a shorthand way of referring to Joseph, not as an implied denial of the virgin birth. While Joseph and Mary had already heard many strange things about their son, they would certainly not be immune to such a startling declaration as Simeon's.

2:34–35 Simeon foreshadows the rest of the Gospel by warning Mary that in the process of fulfilling Jesus' mission there will be great pain for her.

2:36 Asher. One of the 10 tribes "lost" in the Assyrian invasion of Israel in 722 B.C.

2:37 She never left the temple. Since it is unlikely that she could have lived at the temple, the stress is on her great devotion to God as she, like Simeon, prayed and waited for God to fulfill his promises to Israel.

2:38 the redemption of Jerusalem. Jerusalem was commonly used to represent all of God's people (Isa. 52:9). Anna, like Simeon, saw in Jesus the fulfillment of all Israel's hopes for deliverance and security.

2:39 returned to Galilee. In contrast, Matthew reports the family stayed much longer in Bethlehem, and then left for Egypt when threatened by Herod. Only after Herod's death did they return to Nazareth in Galilee (Matt. 2:13–23).

2:40 Apart from verses 41–52, Luke, like the other Gospels, passes over the events of Jesus' life until 30 years later (3:23). All of the Gospels are more concerned with Jesus' teaching and the meaning of his death and resurrection than with the details of his life.

2:41 While Jews were supposed to go to Jerusalem three times a year for the Feast of Passover, Pentecost and the Feast of Booths, in practice most only attended the annual Passover celebration.

2:42 When he was twelve years old. At age 13, a Jewish boy was expected to take his place in the religious community of Israel. Age 12 would be a time of preparation for assuming responsibilities of adulthood.

2:43–44 Jewish pilgrims from outside Jerusalem traveled to and from the feast in large caravans. Typically, the women and children would be up front while the men and older boys traveled along behind. In the evenings, when the caravan stopped for the night, families would regroup. It would have been easy during the day for Mary and Joseph to each assume that Jesus was with the other parent or with friends.

2:46 After three days. This does not mean they spent three days in Jerusalem looking for Jesus. Day one was the trip out of the city with the caravan—probably a walk of about 25 miles. Day two was their trip back to the city. Day three was when they found him in the temple. **sitting among the teachers.** It was common for the rabbis to discuss theology in the temple courts. Interested listeners would sit with them and converse about questions that arose

ing them questions. [47]Everyone who heard him was amazed at his
understanding and his answers. [48]When his parents saw him, they
were astonished. His mother said to him, "Son, why have you treated
us like this? Your father and I have been anxiously searching for you."
[49]"Why were you searching for me?" he asked. "Didn't you know I
had to be in my Father's house?" [50]But they did not understand what
he was saying to them.
[51]Then he went down to Nazareth with them and was obedient to
them. But his mother treasured all these things in her heart. [52]And
Jesus grew in wisdom and stature, and in favor with God and men.

John the Baptist Prepares the Way

3 In the fifteenth year of the reign of Tiberius Caesar—when Pontius Pilate was governor of Judea, Herod tetrarch of Galilee, his
brother Philip tetrarch of Iturea and Traconitis, and Lysanias tetrarch
of Abilene— [2]during the high priesthood of Annas and Caiaphas, the
word of God came to John son of Zechariah in the desert. [3]He went
into all the country around the Jordan, preaching a baptism of repentance for the forgiveness of sins. [4]As is written in the book of the
words of Isaiah the prophet:

"A voice of one calling in the desert,
'Prepare the way for the Lord,
make straight paths for him.

preparation for his mission do you attribute to his godly parents?

APPLY 1. Did you have a "coming of age" party in your teens? **2.** Spiritually, what do you consider your "coming of age"? Can you point to a time when you became a believer?

OPEN If you had to pick someone from your family to play the part of a fiery street preacher in a movie, who would you choose?

STUDY 1. How much time passes between appearances of John the Baptist here and in 1:80? What was John doing in those intervening years (Matt. 3:1–6; Mark 1:4–6)? Why? **2.** Why does the author list all the political and religious figures in verses 1–2? **3.** How would you describe John's message and style? **4.** What's radical about John's

---

from their discussions. **asking them questions.** Even Jesus had to develop as a boy. We learn from this account that he was much different than any other child.

2:47 Everyone who heard him was amazed. This seems to be the first reason why Luke included this story. Jesus' insight into the Law drew the respect and wonder of his elders.

2:48 Mary's response is not amazement at Jesus' insight into the Law, but a motherly one of frustration and concern because of the worry Jesus' absence caused. **Your father and I.** Even though the infant narratives describe Jesus' birth as a virgin birth, Joseph took Jesus as his own child and acted as father to him.

2:49 I had to be. Luke records several statements which reflect Jesus' sense of the necessity of his mission and the steps required to fulfill it (4:43; 9:22; 24:7). Mary and Joseph's inability to comprehend what he meant is paralleled later on by his family's misunderstanding of him (8:19–21). **in my Father's house.** This is the second reason Luke included this story. Mary referred to Joseph as "your father" (v. 48). Jesus' answer to Mary shows his knowledge of his true identity as the Son of God.

2:51 was obedient to them. Jesus may have had an awareness that he was God's unique Son, but that didn't keep him from being obedient to his human parents.

2:52 Jesus' growth was not one-dimensional. Jesus grew along several dimensions. He grew physically (in stature). He grew intellectually (in wisdom). He grew socially (in favor with men). But most of all he grew spiritually (in favor with God).

3:1 Of the four Gospel writers, Luke shows evidence of knowing how ancient historians wrote; and following the manner of these ancient historians, Luke dates the appearance of John. **the fifteenth year of the reign of Tiberius Caesar.** This was about A.D. 28. Before his death in 4 B.C., Herod the Great divided his territory between three of his sons. Herod (Antipas) and Philip ruled as tetrarchs (a term used to describe the ruler of a minor domain) over their areas until 39 and 33 A.D. respectively. The third son, Archelaus, was given Judea, Samaria and Edom. The Jews thoroughly hated him and petitioned Rome for his removal. This resulted in the establishment of a Roman governorship over Judea. Pilate held this post from 26–37 A.D. Little is known of Lysanias.

3:2 the high priesthood of Annas and Caiaphas. The high priest was the civil and religious head of the Jewish community. While the Jews regarded this as a lifelong office, the Romans, seeking people who would administer in a way they approved, appointed men to that office at will. Annas, who served as high priest until 14 or 15 A.D., was removed from office and replaced first by his son Eleazor and then by his son-in-law Caiaphas, who held the position from 18–37 A.D. Luke recognizes that while Caiaphas held the position, Annas still held the power (John 18:13). This *de facto* power is recognized not only by the fact that Luke lists him, but also by the fact that he lists him first. **the word of God came to John.** A common way of referring to the calling of a prophet (Jer. 1:2; Hos. 1:1; Joel 1:1).

3:3 a baptism of repentance. See Matthew 3:11. While converts to Judaism were baptized as a sign of washing away their "Gentile filth," John was radical in his call to Jews to be baptized as a sign of their turning from sin and toward God. **for the forgiveness of sins.** Luke goes beyond Matthew's account by showing that the repentance required for baptism led to that which would characterize the work of the Messiah—the forgiveness of sins (1:77).

3:4–6 Isaiah 40:3–5 provides the background for John's work. Before a king would visit a city, a herald was sent to urge people to literally prepare the roads so that the king's journey would

message? What does the "root" and "fruit" signify (v. 9)? Is he advocating social upheaval or inner transformation? Is he preaching or meddling? Why would anyone go out of their way to hear such a preacher? **5.** Why is John confused with Christ (v. 15; John 1:19–28)? By contrast, how does John differentiate himself and his ministry? What does the "wheat" and "chaff" signify (v. 17)? **6.** What is the beginning of the end for John's ministry (vv. 19–20)? What does this demonstrate about John? **7.** How would you like to have John the Baptist as your spiritual leader? To be in your group? **8.** If John the Baptist came to your community today, what would he speak out about?

APPLY **1.** Who was the John the Baptist in your life—to prepare the way for you to know Jesus? **2.** What is God asking you to speak out about in your community? What's keeping you from doing it?

5 Every valley shall be filled in,
every mountain and hill made low.
The crooked roads shall become straight,
the rough ways smooth.
6 And all mankind will see God's salvation.' "[a]

7 John said to the crowds coming out to be baptized by him, "You
brood of vipers! Who warned you to flee from the coming wrath?
8 Produce fruit in keeping with repentance. And do not begin to say to
yourselves, 'We have Abraham as our father.' For I tell you that out of
these stones God can raise up children for Abraham. 9 The ax is
already at the root of the trees, and every tree that does not produce
good fruit will be cut down and thrown into the fire."
10 "What should we do then?" the crowd asked.
11 John answered, "The man with two tunics should share with him
who has none, and the one who has food should do the same."
12 Tax collectors also came to be baptized. "Teacher," they asked,
"what should we do?"
13 "Don't collect any more than you are required to," he told them.
14 Then some soldiers asked him, "And what should we do?"
He replied, "Don't extort money and don't accuse people falsely—
be content with your pay."
15 The people were waiting expectantly and were all wondering in
their hearts if John might possibly be the Christ.[b] 16 John answered
them all, "I baptize you with[c] water. But one more powerful than I will
come, the thongs of whose sandals I am not worthy to untie. He will
baptize you with the Holy Spirit and with fire. 17 His winnowing fork is
in his hand to clear his threshing floor and to gather the wheat into
his barn, but he will burn up the chaff with unquenchable fire." 18 And
with many other words John exhorted the people and preached the
good news to them.
19 But when John rebuked Herod the tetrarch because of Herodias,

[a] 6 Isaiah 40:3-5 [b] 15 Or *Messiah* [c] 16 Or *in*

be smooth. John called for people to mend their lives before the Messiah came, lest they incur his judgment rather than his favor. While Matthew and Mark quote Isaiah 40 as well, Luke alone extends the quote through verse 6 with its stress that salvation is to come and will be available for all humanity.

3:7 You brood of vipers! The image painted by these words is of snakes slithering through the undergrowth, trying to escape the oncoming fire.

3:8 Abraham as our father. John warns that they cannot retreat into an easy assumption that just because they are members of God's chosen race that they will be spared judgment.

3:11 John taught that repentance was to be shown by concrete acts of compassion for the needy (Isa. 58:7; James 2:14–17).

3:12 Tax collectors. Considered as vile as robbers and murderers, these were Jews who were seen as traitors because they collaborated with the Roman power in order to become wealthy. Since only the tax collectors knew the tax rate required by Rome, they were free to charge whatever the market would bear. Once they paid what they owed Rome, the rest was theirs to keep.

3:14 soldiers. These are probably not Roman legionnaires, but men employed by Herod Antipas for police duty and to assist the tax collectors in their work. Their intimidating power to accuse people of nonpayment of taxes was used to extort payoffs which would enhance their relatively meager pay. While John does not insist that repentance means leaving these jobs (v. 13), he does assert that such jobs need to be carried out with honesty and integrity.

3:16 whose sandals I am not worthy to untie. The task of removing the master's sandals was that of the lowest ranking slave in the household. The Messiah is so great that John feels unworthy to perform even that lowly function for him. **baptize you with the Holy Spirit.** It was expected that the Messiah would be filled with the Spirit of God (Isa. 11:2), but that was not necessarily connected with the expectation that God would pour out his Spirit upon the nation so that it would permanently become a community of righteousness, justice, peace and security (Isa. 32:15–20; 44:3). John links together these two strands of Old Testament prophecy in that it is through the Messiah that this community of the Spirit will be established. **with fire.** Fire was a symbol of judgment.

3:19–20 Herod had divorced the Arabian Princess Aretas to marry

his brother's wife, and all the other evil things he had done, [20]Herod
added this to them all: He locked John up in prison.

The Baptism and Genealogy of Jesus

[21]When all the people were being baptized, Jesus was baptized too.
And as he was praying, heaven was opened [22]and the Holy Spirit
descended on him in bodily form like a dove. And a voice came from
heaven: "You are my Son, whom I love; with you I am well pleased."
[23]Now Jesus himself was about thirty years old when he began his
ministry. He was the son, so it was thought, of Joseph,
the son of Heli, [24]the son of Matthat,
the son of Levi, the son of Melki,
the son of Jannai, the son of Joseph,
[25]the son of Mattathias, the son of Amos,
the son of Nahum, the son of Esli,
the son of Naggai, [26]the son of Maath,
the son of Mattathias, the son of Semein,
the son of Josech, the son of Joda,
[27]the son of Joanan, the son of Rhesa,
the son of Zerubbabel, the son of Shealtiel,
the son of Neri, [28]the son of Melki,
the son of Addi, the son of Cosam,
the son of Elmadam, the son of Er,
[29]the son of Joshua, the son of Eliezer,
the son of Jorim, the son of Matthat,
the son of Levi, [30]the son of Simeon,
the son of Judah, the son of Joseph,
the son of Jonam, the son of Eliakim,
[31]the son of Melea, the son of Menna,
the son of Mattatha, the son of Nathan,
the son of David, [32]the son of Jesse,
the son of Obed, the son of Boaz,
the son of Salmon,[a] the son of Nahshon,
[33]the son of Amminadab, the son of Ram,[b]
the son of Hezron, the son of Perez,
the son of Judah, [34]the son of Jacob,
the son of Isaac, the son of Abraham,
the son of Terah, the son of Nahor,
[35]the son of Serug, the son of Reu,
the son of Peleg, the son of Eber,
the son of Shelah, [36]the son of Cainan,
the son of Arphaxad, the son of Shem,

[a]32 Some early manuscripts *Sala* [b]33 Some manuscripts *Amminadab, the son of Admin, the son of Arni*; other manuscripts vary widely.

OPEN 1. Who is the historian in your family? What has he/she done to help you know more about your ancestors? **2.** If you were to explore in more detail the life of one of your ancestors, whose life would you investigate? **3.** Who is the "skeleton" in your family closet?

STUDY 1. What is significant about Jesus being baptized at the same time as "all the people"? What three things happened at Jesus' baptism that make it unlike the others' (vv. 21–22)? **2.** If Matthew's genealogy starts with Abraham to connect Jesus to the beginning of the chosen people (Matt. 1:1–17), what is Luke's point in going all the way back to Adam (v. 38)? What do Adam and Jesus have in common? Why else might Luke include this genealogy (1:27,32,69)? **3.** In this genealogy, which names stand out to you? What do you know about them? What can you conclude about Jesus' earthly ancestry from what you know of this genealogy?

APPLY 1. How far back can you trace your spiritual family tree? **2.** Who are the significant spiritual ancestors in your life?

Herodias—who was both his niece, the daughter of one of his half-brothers, and his ex-sister-in-law since she had been divorced from Philip, one of Herod's brothers. The Jews were deeply offended by this scandal of open incest and violation of God's Law (Lev. 18:16), and John did not hesitate to speak against it as an example of the depth of sin in the nation. Such outspokenness resulted in the imprisonment and eventual beheading of John by Herod (Mark 6:14–29).

3:21–22 This scene really belongs with verses 1–20 as it briefly records the baptism of Jesus by John. Unlike Matthew's longer account which includes his conversation with John, Luke's stress is that the importance of this event lay in Jesus' reception of the Spirit and the divine declaration of his sonship.

3:32 Matthew's genealogy agrees with Luke's from David to Abraham (1 Chr. 2:1–15).

the son of Noah, the son of Lamech,
37 the son of Methuselah, the son of Enoch,
the son of Jared, the son of Mahalalel,
the son of Kenan, 38 the son of Enosh,
the son of Seth, the son of Adam,
the son of God.

The Temptation of Jesus

4 Jesus, full of the Holy Spirit, returned from the Jordan and was
led by the Spirit in the desert, 2 where for forty days he was
tempted by the devil. He ate nothing during those days, and at the
end of them he was hungry.
3 The devil said to him, "If you are the Son of God, tell this stone to
become bread."
4 Jesus answered, "It is written: 'Man does not live on bread alone.'[a]"
5 The devil led him up to a high place and showed him in an instant
all the kingdoms of the world. 6 And he said to him, "I will give you all
their authority and splendor, for it has been given to me, and I can
give it to anyone I want to. 7 So if you worship me, it will all be yours."
8 Jesus answered, "It is written: 'Worship the Lord your God and
serve him only.'[b]"
9 The devil led him to Jerusalem and had him stand on the highest
point of the temple. "If you are the Son of God," he said, "throw yourself down from here. 10 For it is written:

" 'He will command his angels concerning you
to guard you carefully;
11 they will lift you up in their hands,
so that you will not strike your foot against a stone.'[c]"

12 Jesus answered, "It says: 'Do not put the Lord your God to the
test.'[d]"
13 When the devil had finished all this tempting, he left him until an
opportune time.

[a]4 Deut. 8:3 [b]8 Deut. 6:13 [c]11 Psalm 91:11,12 [d]12 Deut. 6:16

OPEN 1. What is the longest you have gone without food? **2.** If you didn't have to worry about cholesterol or weight, what food would tempt you?

STUDY 1. Why do you think Jesus started his ministry with a 40-day retreat in the desert? Would you call this experience a spiritual retreat or a boot camp? **2.** What was the real battle going on here? Do you believe in cosmic powers of good and evil? Do you believe the forces of evil are still active today? **3.** How did Jesus answer each temptation? **4.** Of the three kinds of temptation that Jesus confronted, which one are you most vulnerable to: Appetite—food, sex and hunger? Recognition—success, popularity and stardom? Power—wealth, control and authority?

APPLY 1. What is the closest you have come to Jesus' experience of a long time of testing? **2.** As you look back on this experience, what critical decisions did you make?

4:1 full of the Holy Spirit ... led by the Spirit. The work of the Holy Spirit is a major concern for Luke both in his Gospel and in Acts. Satan's confrontation of Jesus was not a result of being apart from the Spirit, but an integral part of the Spirit's preparing him for his mission.

4:2 forty days ... tempted. Moses fasted 40 days on Mount Sinai while receiving the commandments (Ex. 34:28) and Israel was in the wilderness 40 years (Deut. 8:2). **He ate nothing.** Fasting was a means of communion with God. It was this communion that Satan sought to destroy. Satan was using the fasting to tempt Jesus.

4:3 If you are the Son of God. Satan challenges Jesus at the point of his identity and authority. Surely it must have seemed ironic that the Son of God should be tired, hungry and apparently alone in such a desolate area. **bread.** While there is nothing inherently wrong with turning stones to bread, the appeal of the temptation was for Jesus to use his power to meet his own needs instead of trusting his Father to do so.

4:5–7 The second temptation is an appeal to ambition and glory. Probably through some form of vision Satan enabled Jesus to see the splendor, wealth and power that is represented by the world's political authorities. For the price tag of rejecting God, Satan offers Jesus a painless, immediate way to power and fame. The irony was that by his obedience to the Father Jesus would become the King of kings, possessing all authority and power (Ps. 2:8–9; Dan. 7:14).

4:8 Jesus quotes Deuteronomy 6:13, again affirming his loyalty to God and his ways.

4:9 If you are the Son of God. Once again Jesus' identity as the Messiah is being attacked (v. 3). **the highest point of the temple.** Barclay says this would have been a point 450 feet above the Kidron Valley.

4:12 Jesus quotes Deuteronomy 6:16 and again asserts his complete trust in his Father. His Word does not need to be tested in foolish ways in order to find out it is true.

4:13 Having been resisted in his appeals to self-interest, power and pride, Satan left Jesus. His opposition to Jesus surfaces again in Jesus' conflicts with demons later on and ultimately in his influence upon Judas, in the events leading to the betrayal of Jesus (22:3).

Jesus Rejected at Nazareth

14 Jesus returned to Galilee in the power of the Spirit, and news
about him spread through the whole countryside. 15 He taught in their
synagogues, and everyone praised him.
16 He went to Nazareth, where he had been brought up, and on the
Sabbath day he went into the synagogue, as was his custom. And he
stood up to read. 17 The scroll of the prophet Isaiah was handed to
him. Unrolling it, he found the place where it is written:

18 "The Spirit of the Lord is on me,
because he has anointed me
to preach good news to the poor.
He has sent me to proclaim freedom for the prisoners
and recovery of sight for the blind,
to release the oppressed,
19 to proclaim the year of the Lord's favor."[a]

20 Then he rolled up the scroll, gave it back to the attendant and sat
down. The eyes of everyone in the synagogue were fastened on him,
21 and he began by saying to them, "Today this scripture is fulfilled in
your hearing."
22 All spoke well of him and were amazed at the gracious words that
came from his lips. "Isn't this Joseph's son?" they asked.

[a]19 Isaiah 61:1,2

OPEN 1. When you were growing up where did the teenagers hang out in your hometown? **2.** What was the status symbol for having "made it"?

STUDY 1. How would you describe the reception Jesus got from his hometown? **2.** Using the opportunity to read the Scripture in the synagogue, what does he clearly imply? **3.** What are the five statements in this Scripture that define the purpose of the gospel? How would you state these in modern day times? **4.** How did his audience respond? **5.** What was it that Jesus said that turned their amazement to anger? **6.** Luke was a Gentile writing this Gospel to Theophilus (1:3-4) who was also a Gentile. Why would this passage be important to them and infuriating to his hometown? **7.** What did his hometown people try to do? What do you think his mother and brothers thought about all of this? **8.** Why is it so hard to share your faith story to your hometown?

4:14 Galilee. From chapters 4:14–9:50, Luke records Jesus' ministry in Galilee, a province about 50 miles long and 25 miles wide in the north of Palestine. **in the power of the Spirit.** Just as the Spirit led Jesus into his time of testing (4:1; Matt. 4:1), so the Spirit now empowers Jesus' ministry.

4:15 synagogues. While the temple in Jerusalem was the religious center for all Jews, the community synagogue was the focal point of weekly worship and teaching. Jesus' initial ministry was as a well-received itinerant preacher teaching in synagogues throughout Galilee.

4:16 Nazareth. Nazareth, a town of about 20,000 people, was located in a hollow surrounded by hills. **the Sabbath.** Each Sabbath, Jews would gather at the synagogue for a service of worship and instruction from the Scripture. There was a standard order governing which passages of the Law would be read, and the same may have been true about the reading from the Prophets as well. The synagogue had no formal leaders, so various men approved by the elders of the synagogue read and taught from the Scripture. Given Jesus' emerging reputation, it is not surprising that he was asked to read and teach. **he stood up to read.** As a sign of reverence for God, men would stand as they read the Scripture, but sat down to teach.

4:17 The scroll. Since Nazareth was a small village, it is unlikely that the synagogue would have been able to afford to have scrolls of the entire sacred writings. The Isaiah scroll was undoubtedly a prized possession of the synagogue.

4:18 The passage Jesus read was from Isaiah 61:1–2 (with the addition of a phrase from 58:6). Using the metaphors of people in prison, blindness, and slavery, the prophet speaks of his God-given mission to proclaim freedom and pardon to people who are oppressed and burdened. **The Spirit of the Lord is on me.** The ministry of a prophet of God is one empowered by God's Spirit. **to preach good news ... to proclaim freedom ... recovery of sight.** In the context of the Isaiah passage, this was the news that God was going to deliver the Jews from their captivity in Babylon. In later Judaism, it became the hope for Israel's ultimate restoration and freedom from all oppressors. The "recovery of sight" in Isaiah's sense probably meant the figurative renewal of hope that was lost through the destruction and deportation of the Jews, while the fulfillment was the literal healing done by Jesus. **release the oppressed.** These words are not found in either the Hebrew or Greek versions of Isaiah 61, but may be a commentary on the meaning of the "recovery of sight" borrowed from a phrase in Isaiah 58:6.

4:19 the year of the Lord's favor. This refers to the Jubilee Year of Leviticus 25. Every 50 years, the Jews were to release their slaves, cancel all debts, and return land to the families of its original owners. While there is no record that the Jews ever kept that law, it became a symbol of the deliverance and new order of justice that God intended to bring about when he would right the wrongs suffered by his people (1:51–55).

4:21 Today this scripture is fulfilled. The phrase is reminiscent of Mark 1:15, with its announcement that the "kingdom of God is near." In both cases, Jesus asserts that the new era foretold by Isaiah has begun because he has come to bring it about.

4:22 amazed. Likewise, this word can express admiration (7:9) or opposition (John 7:15). **Joseph's son.** This may be a slur, alluding to rumors of Jesus' illegitimacy (Mark 6:3). In stark contrast to God's declaration in 3:22 (Matt. 3:17) that Jesus is God's son, the hometown people could only see Jesus as Joseph's boy. Who did this carpenter's son think he was, anyway?

APPLY 1. When you started to get serious about God, how did your close friends, business associates and neighbors react? **2.** How do you deal with rejection from your friends when you share your faith story?

OPEN Who was your favorite teacher in school?

STUDY 1. How would you compare the reception Jesus got in the synagogue in Capernaum to the reception he got from the one in Nazareth (vv. 20–28)? **2.** Why would a man possessed by a demon be able to recognize Jesus as the "Holy One of God" when his own home church could not?

APPLY When did you turn over the control and ownership in your life to Jesus? Where are you and God now in the transfer of power?

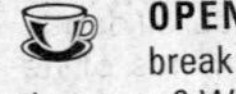

OPEN When you need a break from pressure, where do you go? What do you do?

STUDY 1. Why would Jesus want to go to the house of

[23]Jesus said to them, "Surely you will quote this proverb to me:
'Physician, heal yourself! Do here in your hometown what we have
heard that you did in Capernaum.'"
[24]"I tell you the truth," he continued, "no prophet is accepted in his
hometown. [25]I assure you that there were many widows in Israel in
Elijah's time, when the sky was shut for three and a half years and
there was a severe famine throughout the land. [26]Yet Elijah was not
sent to any of them, but to a widow in Zarephath in the region of
Sidon. [27]And there were many in Israel with leprosy[a] in the time of
Elisha the prophet, yet not one of them was cleansed—only Naaman
the Syrian."
[28]All the people in the synagogue were furious when they heard
this. [29]They got up, drove him out of the town, and took him to the
brow of the hill on which the town was built, in order to throw him
down the cliff. [30]But he walked right through the crowd and went on
his way.

Jesus Drives Out an Evil Spirit

[31]Then he went down to Capernaum, a town in Galilee, and on the
Sabbath began to teach the people. [32]They were amazed at his teaching, because his message had authority.
[33]In the synagogue there was a man possessed by a demon, an evil[b]
spirit. He cried out at the top of his voice, [34]"Ha! What do you want
with us, Jesus of Nazareth? Have you come to destroy us? I know who
you are—the Holy One of God!"
[35]"Be quiet!" Jesus said sternly. "Come out of him!" Then the demon threw the man down before them all and came out without injuring him.
[36]All the people were amazed and said to each other, "What is this
teaching? With authority and power he gives orders to evil spirits and
they come out!" [37]And the news about him spread throughout the
surrounding area.

Jesus Heals Many

[38]Jesus left the synagogue and went to the home of Simon. Now
Simon's mother-in-law was suffering from a high fever, and they

[a]27 The Greek word was used for various diseases affecting the skin—not necessarily leprosy. [b]33 Greek *unclean;* also in verse 36

4:23 Physician, heal yourself! This proverb has both Greek and Arabic parallels. The doubt and cynicism of his hometown is seen in that they would not believe the stories they had heard elsewhere unless they could see further evidence. **Capernaum.** According to Mark's Gospel, this is the village in which Jesus first began to teach and heal (Mark 1:21ff).

4:24 no prophet is accepted in his *hometown.* *This proverb also has* Greek parallels. It simply observes that, typically, the hardest place for a famous person to gain respect is among the people he or she grew up with.

4:31 Capernaum. This was a town on the north end of the Sea of Galilee, three miles west of the Jordan River. This was where Jesus often stayed during his ministry in Galilee. In fact, he considered Capernaum his home as an adult (Matt. 4:13; Mark 2:1).

4:32 his message had authority. Most rabbis taught the Law through quoting what other rabbis had said about it. In contrast, Jesus' teaching *impressed* his hearers with its relevancy, power and directness.

4:33 a demon. These were seen as malignant, supernatural beings, agents of Satan, able to harm and possess people. In overcoming the demon, Jesus demonstrated his power over Satan.

4:34 I know who you are. The demon clearly identified Jesus. First, he knew the person Jesus, the man from Nazareth. Then, he knew the nature of God, the "Holy One." He also recognized that Jesus had the power to destroy him.

4:38 Simon. Although this is the first time Simon Peter appears in Luke, in Mark's Gospel he had already begun to be a disciple of Jesus before this inci-

asked Jesus to help her. 39So he bent over her and rebuked the fever, and it left her. She got up at once and began to wait on them.

40When the sun was setting, the people brought to Jesus all who had various kinds of sickness, and laying his hands on each one, he healed them. 41Moreover, demons came out of many people, shouting, "You are the Son of God!" But he rebuked them and would not allow them to speak, because they knew he was the Christ.[a]

42At daybreak Jesus went out to a solitary place. The people were looking for him and when they came to where he was, they tried to keep him from leaving them. 43But he said, "I must preach the good news of the kingdom of God to the other towns also, because that is why I was sent." 44And he kept on preaching in the synagogues of Judea.[b]

The Calling of the First Disciples

5 One day as Jesus was standing by the Lake of Gennesaret,[c] with the people crowding around him and listening to the word of God, 2he saw at the water's edge two boats, left there by the fishermen, who were washing their nets. 3He got into one of the boats, the one belonging to Simon, and asked him to put out a little from shore. Then he sat down and taught the people from the boat.

4When he had finished speaking, he said to Simon, "Put out into deep water, and let down[d] the nets for a catch."

5Simon answered, "Master, we've worked hard all night and haven't caught anything. But because you say so, I will let down the nets."

6When they had done so, they caught such a large number of fish that their nets began to break. 7So they signaled their partners in the other boat to come and help them, and they came and filled both boats so full that they began to sink.

[a]41 Or *Messiah* [b]44 Or *the land of the Jews*; some manuscripts *Galilee* [c]1 That is, Sea of Galilee [d]4 The Greek verb is plural.

Simon right after the incident in the synagogue (vv. 33–37)? What happens? **2.** What is starting to happen in Jesus' ministry that causes him to seek a solitary place? What were the people clamoring for? Where do you see this same phenomena today?

APPLY 1. Where do you escape to when you need to be alone with God? **2.** What is the driving passion in your life right now?

OPEN 1. Where is the best fishing spot in your area? **2.** What is the biggest fish you have caught?

STUDY 1. What do you know about Simon (Peter) from the previous story that explains why Jesus used his boat? **2.** What is surprising about Jesus' invitation to use nets in "deep water"? What is the tone in Simon's voice when he answers Jesus (v. 5)? How would you paraphrase his comment? **3.** What came over Simon Peter when he caught a large number of fish? How many fish would it take to fill two boats? **4.** What is Simon really saying here? "Go away from me, Lord; I am a sinful man!" **5.** What happened to the fish? What are his friends going to say when he tells them about this catch?

dent took place. Jesus was apparently going to his house for Sabbath dinner after the synagogue service.

4:39 rebuked the fever. This is the same word used to describe Jesus' rebuke of the demon in verse 35. Luke considered sickness a result of Satan's influence, which is ultimately overcome by the authority of Jesus as Messiah. **wait on them.** In a Jewish home, unless a family was wealthy enough to have servants, the women would prepare and serve the meal. Understandably, Peter's mother-in-law would have been anxious to have everything in order since her son-in-law had brought home such an important guest. That she was able to perform this function shows the completeness of the cure.

4:40 When the sun was setting. The spread of the news of what had happened in the synagogue and in Peter's house resulted in crowds coming to Jesus to be healed. Since healing was forbidden on the Sabbath, they came only after the setting of the sun, at which time the Sabbath was over.

4:41 You are the Son of God! It is interesting that while Satan attacked Jesus at the point of his divine nature (vv. 3,9) the defeated demons acknowledge it. **would not allow them to speak.** Jesus silenced the demons probably because he did not want their witness and because it was not yet time for this general announcement.

5:2 washing their nets. In the morning, fishermen would clean and repair their nets which they dragged along behind the boats while fishing through the night.

5:3 the boats. While one belonged to Simon Peter, the other boat may have been owned by James and John (Mark 1:19), Simon's partners in the fishing business (v. 10). These would have been an open craft about 20 to 30 feet long.

5:4–5 From any normal perspective, Jesus' command was absolutely foolish since mid-morning was not the time fish would be feeding. To get the feeling behind the words in verse 5, one must picture tired and hungry men who have worked unsuccessfully all night suddenly wondering why in the world they should listen to a religious teacher when it comes to their fishing business! Still, Simon Peter decides to go along with him and is rewarded for it.

5:6–7 In contrast to Simon's doubt, Luke underscores the magnitude of the catch. It was so large that it tore the nets and threatened to sink Simon's boat as well as that of his partners!

APPLY **1.** When did you first feel the tug of God on your life? **2.** Where is God inviting you to "put out into deep water and let down your nets for a catch"?

OPEN Have you ever had an illness that kept you confined?

STUDY **1.** What do you know about leprosy? **2.** Who took the bigger risk? Jesus or the leper? **3.** Why did Jesus ask the leper to stick to the rules? What happened? **4.** Why did Jesus withdraw?

APPLY **1.** Who are the lepers in your community? **2.** What scares you about "touching" them?

OPEN Who were your four closest friends in high school? What was one memorable prank you pulled off together?

STUDY **1.** How might the Pharisees and teachers have felt in verses 17–19? Verse 20? Verses

8When Simon Peter saw this, he fell at Jesus' knees and said, "Go
away from me, Lord; I am a sinful man!" 9For he and all his companions were astonished at the catch of fish they had taken, 10and so
were James and John, the sons of Zebedee, Simon's partners.
Then Jesus said to Simon, "Don't be afraid; from now on you will
catch men." 11So they pulled their boats up on shore, left everything
and followed him.

The Man With Leprosy

12While Jesus was in one of the towns, a man came along who was
covered with leprosy.[a] When he saw Jesus, he fell with his face to the
ground and begged him, "Lord, if you are willing, you can make me
clean."
13Jesus reached out his hand and touched the man. "I am willing,"
he said. "Be clean!" And immediately the leprosy left him.
14Then Jesus ordered him, "Don't tell anyone, but go, show yourself to the priest and offer the sacrifices that Moses commanded for
your cleansing, as a testimony to them."
15Yet the news about him spread all the more, so that crowds of
people came to hear him and to be healed of their sicknesses. 16But
Jesus often withdrew to lonely places and prayed.

Jesus Heals a Paralytic

17One day as he was teaching, Pharisees and teachers of the law,
who had come from every village of Galilee and from Judea and Jerusalem, were sitting there. And the power of the Lord was present for
him to heal the sick. 18Some men came carrying a paralytic on a mat

[a]*12* The Greek word was used for various diseases affecting the skin—not necessarily leprosy.

5:8 Just what Simon Peter recognized about Jesus' identity at this point is unclear since "Lord" can be a title for God or a title of respect for an esteemed person. In any case, it is apparent that Peter was thoroughly convinced that Jesus was at least a rabbi who was more interesting than most.

5:10 Don't be afraid. Jesus' words echo those of the divine response seen in Isaiah 6, Daniel 10 and elsewhere. **you will catch men.** The climax of the story is not Jesus' self-revelation, but its significance as a graphic illustration of the certain widespread success that would accompany Peter's (and the other apostles') mission of preaching the kingdom of God (4:43).

5:11 they ... left everything and followed him. A loyalty to Jesus which takes precedence over everything else in life is Luke's characteristic way of describing what it means to be *a follower of Christ.*

5:12 leprosy. Although the term was used to cover a wide range of skin diseases besides the true leprosy of Hanson's Disease, no diagnosis was dreaded more than leprosy since it led not only to physical disfigurement and a slow death, but social banishment as well. Leprosy would be a particularly apt illustration of the nature of sin since it brings progressive, irremediable disintegration—physically, socially and psychologically. The man's desperate situation is highlighted by his actions and words. **in one of the towns.** The leper was not supposed to be in the town at all because of the potential for infecting others. The Old Testament Law allowed lepers who entered uninfected areas to be stoned.

5:13 Jesus ... touched. Although touch was the most common way Jesus healed, it was not necessary for physical healing (4:39). However, since touching a leper was unimaginable due to the risk of contracting the disease and the violation of the Law that prohibited such contact, Jesus' touch of this *leper communica*ted the tremendous extent of Jesus' compassion as well as his power.

5:14 Don't tell anyone. There has been much speculation as to why Jesus in many instances discourages people from telling others what he has done or who he is (Matt. 16:20; Mark 3:12; 5:43; 7:36). The most prevalent view of why he urged this "messianic secret" was that Jesus had to prevent the crowds from proclaiming him Messiah before they knew what kind of Messiah he was (one who would suffer and die, not the conquering hero of popular imagination).

5:17 Pharisees. A small, powerful religious sect whose prime concern was keeping the Law. Since their standards were too high for most Jews to keep in daily life, they were respected as especially devout, godly people. **teachers of the law.** Literally, "scribes." Originally, it was their job to make copies of the Old Testament. Because of their familiarity with Scripture, their role evolved into that of teachers of the Law. **from every village of Galilee and from Judea and Jerusalem.** This intentional gathering of the leaders throughout the entire area to investigate Jesus' lack of orthodoxy indicates the skepticism they had toward Jesus.

and tried to take him into the house to lay him before Jesus. 19 When
they could not find a way to do this because of the crowd, they went
up on the roof and lowered him on his mat through the tiles into the
middle of the crowd, right in front of Jesus.

20 When Jesus saw their faith, he said, "Friend, your sins are forgiven."

21 The Pharisees and the teachers of the law began thinking to
themselves, "Who is this fellow who speaks blasphemy? Who can forgive sins but God alone?"

22 Jesus knew what they were thinking and asked, "Why are you
thinking these things in your hearts? 23 Which is easier: to say, 'Your
sins are forgiven,' or to say, 'Get up and walk'? 24 But that you may
know that the Son of Man has authority on earth to forgive sins . . ."
He said to the paralyzed man, "I tell you, get up, take your mat and go
home." 25 Immediately he stood up in front of them, took what he had
been lying on and went home praising God. 26 Everyone was amazed
and gave praise to God. They were filled with awe and said, "We have
seen remarkable things today."

The Calling of Levi

27 After this, Jesus went out and saw a tax collector by the name of
Levi sitting at his tax booth. "Follow me," Jesus said to him, 28 and
Levi got up, left everything and followed him.

29 Then Levi held a great banquet for Jesus at his house, and a large
crowd of tax collectors and others were eating with them. 30 But the
Pharisees and the teachers of the law who belonged to their sect
complained to his disciples, "Why do you eat and drink with tax collectors and 'sinners'?"

31 Jesus answered them, "It is not the healthy who need a doctor,
but the sick. 32 I have not come to call the righteous, but sinners to
repentance."

Jesus Questioned About Fasting

33 They said to him, "John's disciples often fast and pray, and so do
the disciples of the Pharisees, but yours go on eating and drinking."

21–23? Verses 24–26? **2.** The man came for *healing*, so why did Jesus raise the issue of *forgiveness*? How would the friends react to Jesus' words (v. 20)? To his actions (v. 24)? **3.** What new realm of Jesus' authority is demonstrated here? **4.** What motivates the Pharisees to respond as they do to the situation? **5.** What would the official board say if you took the roof off your church to get someone to Jesus?

APPLY 1. Who were the friends in your life that cared enough to bring you to Jesus? **2.** If you could listen real hard to your body right now, what would it whisper?

OPEN 1. What do you remember about your high school prom? **2.** Who were the "sinners" your parents told you never to associate with?

STUDY 1. Why would an IRS agent make a good disciple? What do you think the rest of the disciples felt about this guy? **2.** Do you think Jesus should have gone to Levi's party with "sinners"? **3.** Why would the disciples of John (the Baptist) get ticked off with Jesus? **4.** What does Jesus mean by the "old garment" (v. 36) and the new "patch"? What is the "skin" and the "new wine"? **5.** What are you finding in your church when to patch the "new" on the "old"?

5:20 your sins are forgiven. The crowd must have anticipated Jesus would heal this man. Instead, Jesus deliberately forces them to consider an entirely new dimension of who he is and what he is about by claiming to be able to forgive sins, something only God could do.

5:21 this fellow. A term of contempt. **blasphemy.** Blasphemy is "contempt for God" punishable by death (Lev. 24:16). Since the teachers of the Law believed that illness was the direct result of sin (John 9:2), they assumed that the sick could not recover until their sin had been forgiven by God, who alone could offer forgiveness. Hence they are distressed that Jesus pronounced forgiveness, since this was tantamount to a claim of deity. Blasphemy was also a serious sin.

5:23 Which is easier. Jesus responds to their question (v. 21) in typical rabbinic fashion: he asks them a question. His point is that it is far easier to say, "Your sins are forgiven" than it is to heal the man right then and there.

5:28 Levi. Generally this person is thought to be Matthew, referred to in Matthew 9:9.

5:29 a great banquet. Luke includes a number of banquets or feasts. Some are earthly celebrations; others look forward to a heavenly meal (7:36–50; 9:10–17; 10:38–42; 11:37–54; 14:1–24; 15:23; 22:16–18; 23:43; 24:28–32,41–43). **tax collectors.** Considered as vile as robbers and murderers, these were Jews who were seen as traitors because they collaborated with the Roman power in order to become wealthy. Since only the tax collectors knew the tax rate required by Rome, they were free to charge whatever the market would bear. Once they paid what they owed Rome, the rest was theirs to keep.

5:30 Why do you eat? To eat with someone was to accept that person. The Pharisees could not understand how a truly religious person could eat with people whose moral lives were disreputable and who ate food that was prepared and served in ways that violated the practices regarding ritual cleanliness.

5:33 fast. Fasting, almsgiving and prayer were three traditional practices followed by all Jewish sects. The failure of Jesus' disciples to fast made them appear insufficiently pious and repentant.

APPLY 1. Do you keep in touch with your "sinner" friends from your pre-Christian days? What are they looking for that you have found in Jesus? 2. Have you considered throwing a party for your old friends? How about inviting them to this group?

OPEN When you were a child, what family rules did you consider stupid? How do you view those rules now?

STUDY 1. How does this story relate to the "new wine in old wineskins" in verses 36–38? 2. What exactly is the deeper issue in these two incidents? What is the principle here on Sabbath observance? 3. What is the lesson here for your family today? 4. How did the Pharisees react? Who are these Pharisees today?

APPLY 1. If your kids rebel against the religious establishment, what are you going to say? 2. If you did a survey of your unchurched friends, what would be the top three things they are looking for?

34Jesus answered, "Can you make the guests of the bridegroom fast while he is with them? 35But the time will come when the bridegroom will be taken from them; in those days they will fast."

36He told them this parable: "No one tears a patch from a new garment and sews it on an old one. If he does, he will have torn the new garment, and the patch from the new will not match the old. 37And no one pours new wine into old wineskins. If he does, the new wine will burst the skins, the wine will run out and the wineskins will be ruined. 38No, new wine must be poured into new wineskins. 39And no one after drinking old wine wants the new, for he says, 'The old is better.'"

Lord of the Sabbath

6 One Sabbath Jesus was going through the grainfields, and his disciples began to pick some heads of grain, rub them in their hands and eat the kernels. 2Some of the Pharisees asked, "Why are you doing what is unlawful on the Sabbath?"

3Jesus answered them, "Have you never read what David did when he and his companions were hungry? 4He entered the house of God, and taking the consecrated bread, he ate what is lawful only for priests to eat. And he also gave some to his companions." 5Then Jesus said to them, "The Son of Man is Lord of the Sabbath."

6On another Sabbath he went into the synagogue and was teaching, and a man was there whose right hand was shriveled. 7The Pharisees and the teachers of the law were looking for a reason to accuse Jesus, so they watched him closely to see if he would heal on the Sabbath. 8But Jesus knew what they were thinking and said to the man with the shriveled hand, "Get up and stand in front of everyone." So he got up and stood there.

9Then Jesus said to them, "I ask you, which is lawful on the Sabbath: to do good or to do evil, to save life or to destroy it?"

5:35 the bridegroom. Jesus says it is as inappropriate to fast in his presence as it would be to refuse to celebrate at a wedding. Jewish weddings involved a week-long feast during which everyone was released from all religious obligations, including fasting.

5:36–38 Just as one does not destroy a new garment to patch up an old, torn one, and just as new wine bursts out of old, dry wineskins, so Jesus' new way cannot be contained within the old forms of Judaism.

6:1 Sabbath. By Jesus' time the scribes had developed scores of laws that defined what could and could not be done on the Sabbath in order to obey the commandment related to honoring the Sabbath (Ex. 20:8–11). These rules obscured the point that the Sabbath *was meant to be a welcome day of rest.* **pick some heads of grain.** This was not considered stealing since it was permissible for hungry travelers to pluck and eat grain from a field (Deut. 23:25). What the Pharisees objected to was the "work" this involved.

6:3 Have you never read? Jesus knew full well they had read this story many times. The problem was that they hadn't seen the implications. **David.** It was expected that the Messiah would descend from King David (Jer. 23:5; Ezek. 34:23–24; 37:24–25). By comparing his actions with those of David's, Jesus gives the first of several hints that he is the long-expected Son of David, the Messiah (Mark 10:46–; 11:6–10; 12:35–37).

6:4 entered the house of God ... taking the consecrated bread. While this was technically unlawful since only the priests were allowed to eat this bread (Lev. 24:5–9), it provided a precedent that human need supersedes religious law.

6:5 Lord of the Sabbath. While his pronouncement of forgiveness in 5:20 was a veiled claim to deity, and his subtle comparison to David in verse 3 hinted at his messianic role, this is an audacious assertion that he has the right to suspend customary religious practices because he is Lord over them!

6:6 a man ... whose right hand was shriveled. In these times right-handedness would have been assumed, and therefore this would have been a particularly grievous disability.

6:7 they watched him closely. By this time the religious leaders no longer questioned Jesus. Now they simply watched to see if his actions demonstrated such a disregard for the Law that they might be able to charge him formally with some crime. **if he would heal on the Sabbath.** The issue is not healing, but whether Jesus would do so on the Sabbath in defiance of the oral tradition, which allowed healing on that day only if there was danger to life.

6:9 which is lawful. Jesus points out that the Pharisees' concern for their traditions wrongfully overshadowed God's clear call for love and mercy. While they

[10]He looked around at them all, and then said to the man, "Stretch
out your hand." He did so, and his hand was completely restored.
[11]But they were furious and began to discuss with one another what
they might do to Jesus.

The Twelve Apostles

[12]One of those days Jesus went out to a mountainside to pray, and
spent the night praying to God. [13]When morning came, he called his
disciples to him and chose twelve of them, whom he also designated
apostles: [14]Simon (whom he named Peter), his brother Andrew,
James, John, Philip, Bartholomew, [15]Matthew, Thomas, James son of
Alphaeus, Simon who was called the Zealot, [16]Judas son of James,
and Judas Iscariot, who became a traitor.

Blessings and Woes

[17]He went down with them and stood on a level place. A large
crowd of his disciples was there and a great number of people from
all over Judea, from Jerusalem, and from the coast of Tyre and Sidon,
[18]who had come to hear him and to be healed of their diseases. Those
troubled by evil[a] spirits were cured, [19]and the people all tried to touch
him, because power was coming from him and healing them all.
[20]Looking at his disciples, he said:

"Blessed are you who are poor,
for yours is the kingdom of God.
[21]Blessed are you who hunger now,
for you will be satisfied.
Blessed are you who weep now,
for you will laugh.

[a]18 Greek *unclean*

OPEN Have you ever spent a night in prayer?

STUDY 1. What preceded the choosing of the disciples? **2.** Would any of these disciples qualify for leadership in your church?

APPLY What major decision are you facing right now?

OPEN In your family, who always looks on the bright side of life? Who tends to be the pessimist?

STUDY 1. Who is in the crowd? Why have they come? How does Jesus meet their needs? How do his actions (vv. 18–19) relate to his teaching (vv. 20–22)? **2.** What four qualities ought to characterize "kingdom people" (vv. 20–22)? How would you define each of these? What blessing is promised for each? Are these present blessings or future blessings? **3.** Who is Jesus addressing (vv. 24–26)? How would you define each warning he gives here? **4.** How do the values Jesus talks about here compare to the values you are sold

considered their rule prohibiting healing on the Sabbath as a way of observing the Law, Jesus saw their passivity in the face of suffering as an evil attitude that highlighted their callousness toward human need. **to save life or to destroy it.** While Jesus was willing to violate the Pharisaic tradition about the Sabbath in order to deliver this man from the bondage that inhibited his growth and life, the Pharisees were violating God's law of love by concentrating on how they might destroy Jesus (v. 11).

6:10 Stretch out your hand. Just as Jesus deliberately forgave the paralytic's sins, knowing it would be *perceived as blasphemy to the scribes* and Pharisees, so here he deliberately heals on the Sabbath, knowing it too was anathema to his critics.

6:11 furious. Literally, "senseless wrath." Luke highlights the irrational nature of the opposition.

6:12 spent the night praying to God. Jesus knew he had a big decision to make, and he didn't want to make it without the guidance of his heavenly Father. While some complain they cannot *find* time to pray, Jesus *made* time to pray. It was a high enough priority to him that he gave up sleep which he undoubtedly needed.

6:17 from all over. Luke emphasizes the breadth of Jesus' ministry. Judea and Jerusalem, known for Jewish orthodoxy, were to the south while Tyre and Sidon, Gentile areas, were north.

6:20 Blessed. The Greek word, *makarios*, refers to people who are to be congratulated. It does not necessarily mean they are happy or prospering. Instead, whether they feel it or not, they are fortunate because their condition reflects that they are in a right relationship to God. **poor.** The beatitudes in Luke differ from those reported in Matthew principally in that in Luke. Here Jesus doesn't modify poor and hungry, while in Matthew these are spiritualized: "the poor *in spirit*," and "those who hunger and thirst *for righteousness*." Those who are materially poor are generally seen in the New Testament to be more receptive to God (18:18–25; James 2:5–7). Still, even in Luke it is probably assumed that the people mentioned are poor and hungry because they show loyalty to God's ways instead of following the ways of the world to get material reward. **the kingdom of God.** Those who maintain loyalty to God, even if it means poverty rather than the wealth they might gain if they compromised their integrity, are assured an inheritance in his kingdom.

6:21 hunger. In the Old Testament hunger and thirst are used as a way of describing the desire for spiritual fullness experienced by those who truly seek God (Ps. 42:1–2; Isa. 55:1; Amos 8:11). **satisfied.** The story of the rich man and Lazarus in chapter 16:19ff illustrates future rewards for those who follow Christ. **weep.** While Jesus had deep empathy for all those bereaved, this probably refers to those who sorrow because of the evil in the world, or who weep in repentance for the sin of themselves and others.

every day on TV? If you could add another "blessing" and another "woe" to the list for today's society, what would you add?

APPLY 1. When you were growing up, was the preaching from the pulpit more on the "blessing" or the "woes"? **2.** How are you and God getting along right now? Are you talking?

OPEN As a child, who were the "bad guys" on your favorite Saturday morning cartoons or TV show?

STUDY 1. Do you think Jesus was serious in verses 27–31? What does Jesus recommend to turn abuse into assertiveness? Is this going to reinforce abusive behavior? **2.** What is the principle in verses 32–36? Who do you admire for using this principle in running their business?

APPLY 1. When you get hurt in a relationship, what do you do? **2.** What is the relationship right now that you need to work on? When are you going to start?

---

22 Blessed are you when men hate you,
when they exclude you and insult you
and reject your name as evil,
because of the Son of Man.

23 "Rejoice in that day and leap for joy, because great is your reward
in heaven. For that is how their fathers treated the prophets.

24 "But woe to you who are rich,
for you have already received your comfort.
25 Woe to you who are well fed now,
for you will go hungry.
Woe to you who laugh now,
for you will mourn and weep.
26 Woe to you when all men speak well of you,
for that is how their fathers treated the false prophets.

Love for Enemies

27 "But I tell you who hear me: Love your enemies, do good to those
who hate you, 28 bless those who curse you, pray for those who mistreat you. 29 If someone strikes you on one cheek, turn to him the
other also. If someone takes your cloak, do not stop him from taking
your tunic. 30 Give to everyone who asks you, and if anyone takes
what belongs to you, do not demand it back. 31 Do to others as you
would have them do to you.

32 "If you love those who love you, what credit is that to you? Even
'sinners' love those who love them. 33 And if you do good to those
who are good to you, what credit is that to you? Even 'sinners' do
that. 34 And if you lend to those from whom you expect repayment,
what credit is that to you? Even 'sinners' lend to 'sinners,' expecting
to be repaid in full. 35 But love your enemies, do good to them, and
lend to them without expecting to get anything back. Then your
reward will be great, and you will be sons of the Most High, because
he is kind to the ungrateful and wicked. 36 Be merciful, just as your
Father is merciful.

6:23 their fathers treated the prophets. Elijah, Jeremiah, Ezekiel and other Old Testament prophets faced consistent rejection, ridicule and abuse from the people of their day.

6:24 woe. Like "blessed," this is God's pronouncement on the peoples' real state of affairs regardless of what external circumstances feel like. Unless they repent, God's judgment is the only future they have.

6:25 laugh. Sometimes in the Old Testament, joy and laughter are the spontaneous responses of people blessed by God (Isa. 51:11; 66:10; Jer. *31:13; 33:11). This is the meaning* intended in verse 21.

6:27 Love. The orthodox Jew of the time only regarded fellow Jews as his neighbor, but Jesus makes it clear that there is no one to whom love is not owed. The word used for love is *agape.* This type of love is not a matter of how people feel, but what they do. *Agape* love is benevolent action done for another without the expectation of reward. It is shown by actively seeking the good of those who hate, blessing those who curse, praying for those who would mistreat and willingly giving to those who would rob.

6:29 cloak. An outer robe made of wool and used as a blanket at night. **tunic.** The close-fitting under-robe. Jesus uses the humorous picture of a *robber being* encouraged to take even more than he intended to steal in order to emphasize the spirit of giving that ought to characterize his followers (v. 30).

6:31 Do to others. This is the so-called Golden Rule. The negative form of this rule was widely known in the ancient world: "Do not do to others what you do not wish them to do to you." Jesus alters this statement in a slight but highly significant way. He shifts the statement from the negative to the positive. Whereas the negative rule was fulfilled by inaction (not bothering others), the positive rule requires active benevolence.

6:36 Be merciful. This is the same principle found in the Lord's Prayer where we are told that if we expect God to forgive us of the offenses we have committed, we need to forgive others for their offenses against us (Matt. 6:9–15). Those who have been the recipients of God's mercy are to reflect that mercy in all their relationships.

Judging Others

37“Do not judge, and you will not be judged. Do not condemn, and
you will not be condemned. Forgive, and you will be forgiven. 38Give,
and it will be given to you. A good measure, pressed down, shaken
together and running over, will be poured into your lap. For with the
measure you use, it will be measured to you.”
39He also told them this parable: “Can a blind man lead a blind
man? Will they not both fall into a pit? 40A student is not above his
teacher, but everyone who is fully trained will be like his teacher.
41“Why do you look at the speck of sawdust in your brother’s eye
and pay no attention to the plank in your own eye? 42How can you say
to your brother, ‘Brother, let me take the speck out of your eye,’ when
you yourself fail to see the plank in your own eye? You hypocrite, first
take the plank out of your eye, and then you will see clearly to remove
the speck from your brother’s eye.

A Tree and Its Fruit

43“No good tree bears bad fruit, nor does a bad tree bear good fruit.
44Each tree is recognized by its own fruit. People do not pick figs from
thornbushes, or grapes from briers. 45The good man brings good
things out of the good stored up in his heart, and the evil man brings
evil things out of the evil stored up in his heart. For out of the overflow of his heart his mouth speaks.

The Wise and Foolish Builders

46“Why do you call me, ‘Lord, Lord,’ and do not do what I say? 47I
will show you what he is like who comes to me and hears my words
and puts them into practice. 48He is like a man building a house, who
dug down deep and laid the foundation on rock. When a flood came,
the torrent struck that house but could not shake it, because it was
well built. 49But the one who hears my words and does not put them
into practice is like a man who built a house on the ground without a
foundation. The moment the torrent struck that house, it collapsed
and its destruction was complete.”

The Faith of the Centurion

7 When Jesus had finished saying all this in the hearing of
the people, he entered Capernaum. 2There a centurion’s servant, whom his master valued highly, was sick and about to die.

OPEN Would you rather be a movie director or a critic?

STUDY **1.** What immediately comes to mind when you read this passage? **2.** Are you more likely to be harder on yourself or on others? Are you likely to see in others the faults that you hate to see in yourself? **3.** What is the two-step procedure for correcting another Christian? **4.** How do you reconcile this passage with the responsibility of followers of Christ in Galatians 6:1–5?

APPLY Who has been good at helping you get the plank out of your eye?

OPEN Where would you locate your dream house?

STUDY **1.** What qualities in the previous passage will distinguish a believer? Does this mean that behavior is the “litmus test” for a follower of Christ? **2.** What does this passage teach about profanity? **3.** What is the difference in the two houses in the parable: The weather? The building? The foundation? **4.** When will you know if your “house” has been built on a rock?

APPLY **1.** What is the weather like in your life right now: Bright and sunny? A few clouds? Hurricane force winds? **2.** What are you doing to shape up the foundation of your life?

OPEN What is the most dramatic “near death” experience you’ve ever had?

6:37 Do not judge. As the second sentence in this verse makes clear, the type of judging in view here is that which involves condemning others for their faults. Moral discernment is not forbidden, but only God is righteous enough to pass final judgment without partiality or error. Instead of embracing this condemnatory attitude against those who wrong them, Christians are to forgive. **you will not be judged.** Not that such people will escape judgment, but that they will be treated mercifully when judgment comes. **Forgive, and you will be forgiven.** The point is not so much that one earns forgiveness from God by forgiving others, but that such a forgiving attitude reveals the heart of one who knows he or she has received forgiveness from God.

6:44 Each tree is recognized by its own fruit. Jesus frequently used illustrations from the natural world (Matt. 6:25–34; 13:31–32; 24:32–34). “Fruit” is a common metaphor for works (13:6–9; Matt. 3:8–10; 7:17–20; 12:33–34; John 15:1–4).

6:47–49 Palestine was dry most of the year. In the autumn, heavy rains would turn what appeared to be dry land into a raging river as flash floods swept down the ravines. Only lives built on a solid foundation will withstand the trials of life.

7:1 Capernaum. This was a town on the north end of the Sea of Galilee, three miles west of the Jordan River. This was where Jesus often stayed during his ministry in Galilee. In fact, he called it his home as an adult (Matt. 4:13; Mark 2:1).

7:2 centurion. A commander over 100 soldiers. **servant.** Literally, “slave.”

[3]The centurion heard of Jesus and sent some elders of the Jews to
him, asking him to come and heal his servant. [4]When they came to
Jesus, they pleaded earnestly with him, "This man deserves to have
you do this, [5]because he loves our nation and has built our synagogue." [6]So Jesus went with them.

He was not far from the house when the centurion sent friends to
say to him: "Lord, don't trouble yourself, for I do not deserve to have
you come under my roof. [7]That is why I did not even consider myself
worthy to come to you. But say the word, and my servant will be
healed. [8]For I myself am a man under authority, with soldiers under
me. I tell this one, 'Go,' and he goes; and that one, 'Come,' and he
comes. I say to my servant, 'Do this,' and he does it."

[9]When Jesus heard this, he was amazed at him, and turning to the
crowd following him, he said, "I tell you, I have not found such great
faith even in Israel." [10]Then the men who had been sent returned to
the house and found the servant well.

Jesus Raises a Widow's Son

[11]Soon afterward, Jesus went to a town called Nain, and his disciples and a large crowd went along with him. [12]As he approached the
town gate, a dead person was being carried out—the only son of his
mother, and she was a widow. And a large crowd from the town was
with her. [13]When the Lord saw her, his heart went out to her and he
said, "Don't cry."

[14]Then he went up and touched the coffin, and those carrying it
stood still. He said, "Young man, I say to you, get up!" [15]The dead man
sat up and began to talk, and Jesus gave him back to his mother.

[16]They were all filled with awe and praised God. "A great prophet
has appeared among us," they said. "God has come to help his people." [17]This news about Jesus spread throughout Judea[a] and the surrounding country.

Jesus and John the Baptist

[18]John's disciples told him about all these things. Calling two of
them, [19]he sent them to the Lord to ask, "Are you the one who was to
come, or should we expect someone else?"

[20]When the men came to Jesus, they said, "John the Baptist sent us
to you to ask, 'Are you the one who was to come, or should we expect
someone else?' "

[a]17 *Or the land of the Jews*

STUDY 1. How would you describe the centurion in this story: Who was he? What about his compassion? What would this story mean to Theophilus, a Gentile and a Roman official (1:3-4)? **2.** Why was the official reticent about having Jesus come to his house? **3.** What was so amazing about this person's faith? How was his faith rewarded?

APPLY 1. What is the closest you have come to seeing a high ranking public official coming to Jesus for help? **2.** How can we help our officials?

OPEN What friend or family member has come close to dying recently?

STUDY 1. What strikes you about Jesus in this story? **2.** If you had been the widow, how would you have felt when Jesus said, "Don't cry"? If you had been in the crowd, how would you have felt when the son "sat up"? **3.** Do you believe this actually happened as Luke recorded it?

APPLY 1. What would it take for you to believe the miracles? **2.** How can this group help you to believe God completely?

OPEN (For the married:) When did you know that the person you married was "the one"? (For the unmarried:) What is the "sign" you look for as that decisive signal you have found the "right one"?

STUDY 1. What do you know about John (the Baptist)? Why can't John come to see Jesus

---

Jesus' concern for the lowly people in society is reflected here.

7:3 sent some elders of the Jews. Perhaps out of fear that Jesus would ignore him as a Gentile and as a representative of Herod, the centurion asked the local synagogue leaders to approach Jesus on his behalf.

7:6–8 *In contrast to the elders' appeal* on the basis of his worth, the centurion sends a message that acknowledges both his unworthiness to have Jesus come to him, and his faith that Jesus has the power to heal by merely speaking the word.

7:11 Nain. This is the modern-day town of Nen, six miles southeast of Nazareth and within a mile of where Elisha raised another woman's son centuries before (2 Kin. 4:18–37). This highlights that Jesus is no ordinary teacher.

7:12 the only son of his mother, and she was a widow. Apart from the normal grief experienced at the death of a child, this woman's situation was serious, as children provided the only "Social Security" available for parents in their old age. This woman had no more children and no husband. Thus, she faced both loneliness and poverty. **a large crowd.** This would be the mourners accompanying the woman to the burial site.

7:16 filled with awe. Literally, "fear." The response of both fear and praise is characteristic of people throughout the Bible when God's power is manifest.

7:18–20 The parallel passage in Matthew 11:1–19 indicates that at this point

21 At that very time Jesus cured many who had diseases, sicknesses
and evil spirits, and gave sight to many who were blind. 22 So he replied to the messengers, "Go back and report to John what you have
seen and heard: The blind receive sight, the lame walk, those who
have leprosy[a] are cured, the deaf hear, the dead are raised, and the
good news is preached to the poor. 23 Blessed is the man who does
not fall away on account of me."
24 After John's messengers left, Jesus began to speak to the crowd
about John: "What did you go out into the desert to see? A reed
swayed by the wind? 25 If not, what did you go out to see? A man
dressed in fine clothes? No, those who wear expensive clothes and
indulge in luxury are in palaces. 26 But what did you go out to see? A
prophet? Yes, I tell you, and more than a prophet. 27 This is the one
about whom it is written:

" 'I will send my messenger ahead of you,
who will prepare your way before you.'[b]

28 I tell you, among those born of women there is no one greater than
John; yet the one who is least in the kingdom of God is greater
than he."
29 (All the people, even the tax collectors, when they heard Jesus'
words, acknowledged that God's way was right, because they had
been baptized by John. 30 But the Pharisees and experts in the law
rejected God's purpose for themselves, because they had not been
baptized by John.)
31 "To what, then, can I compare the people of this generation?
What are they like? 32 They are like children sitting in the marketplace
and calling out to each other:

" 'We played the flute for you,
and you did not dance;
we sang a dirge,
and you did not cry.'

33 For John the Baptist came neither eating bread nor drinking wine,
and you say, 'He has a demon.' 34 The Son of Man came eating and

[a]22 The Greek word was used for various diseases affecting the skin—not necessarily leprosy. [b]27 Mal. 3:1

personally (3:1–3,19–20)? **2.** What's the question John asks and how does Jesus answer (vv. 21–23)? What six things characterize Jesus' ministry? **3.** What is Jesus asking the crowd in his four questions about John the Baptist? How would you answer these questions in today's words? **4.** How does the peoples' response differ from that of the Pharisees? **5.** Who are the "people of this generation"? How do they dismiss both John's message and Jesus' ministry? Do you know any of these kinds of people today? **6.** In verses 33–34, what is the basic difference between John's lifestyle and Jesus'? Is Jesus recommending his lifestyle over John's? **7.** In the church today, do you think we err on the side of asceticism (like John the Baptist) or freedom? What about you?

APPLY 1. When did you come to the place in your spiritual pilgrimage that you knew Jesus was "the one" you were looking for? **2.** What proof led you to this conclusion?

John was in Herod's prison. John's question as to whether Jesus was "the one" comes from confusion over the role of the Messiah. John preached of a Messiah who would come and execute God's wrath and judgment upon the unrighteous in Israel (3:17). Jesus' actions, while empowered by God, did not match his expectation.

7:21–23 Jesus does not answer their question directly, but invites them to watch and reflect upon what he does as he heals and teaches. The recovery of sight, the healing of the lame, the restoration of hearing to the deaf, the raising of the dead and the preaching of the Good News of God's mercy to the poor and oppressed are all marks of the Messiah's mission according to Isaiah (Isa. 26:19; 29:18–19; 35:5–6; 61:1).

7:24 A reed swayed by the wind? John, who stood firmly for God, was not a man to be swayed by the currents of popular opinion or pressure.

7:25 A man dressed in fine clothes? Jesus accents how John's ascetic demeanor was in marked contrast to the indulgence and wastefulness that characterized those who served King Herod. One can imagine the crowd's smiles as they catch Jesus' irony in these two comparisons.

7:28 This sentence was not in the least meant to disparage John nor to diminish his place in the kingdom of God, but to emphasize the new order which Jesus was beginning. To play the least part in the kingdom of God is greater than to have the lead role in the old order represented by John and the Old Testament prophets—who looked forward to the Messiah.

7:31 To what, then, can I compare the people of this generation? The people of his day did not understand the importance of Jesus and John. The focus was on outward appearances.

7:33–34 Jesus explains what he means. The religious authorities complained about John because his message and lifestyle was offensive to their desire to live for themselves while they claimed loyalty to God. It was

drinking, and you say, 'Here is a glutton and a drunkard, a friend of
tax collectors and "sinners." ' 35But wisdom is proved right by all her
children."

Jesus Anointed by a Sinful Woman

36Now one of the Pharisees invited Jesus to have dinner with him,
so he went to the Pharisee's house and reclined at the table. 37When
a woman who had lived a sinful life in that town learned that Jesus
was eating at the Pharisee's house, she brought an alabaster jar of
perfume, 38and as she stood behind him at his feet weeping, she began to wet his feet with her tears. Then she wiped them with her hair,
kissed them and poured perfume on them.

39When the Pharisee who had invited him saw this, he said to himself, "If this man were a prophet, he would know who is touching him
and what kind of woman she is—that she is a sinner."

40Jesus answered him, "Simon, I have something to tell you."

"Tell me, teacher," he said.

41"Two men owed money to a certain moneylender. One owed him
five hundred denarii,[a] and the other fifty. 42Neither of them had the
money to pay him back, so he canceled the debts of both. Now which
of them will love him more?"

43Simon replied, "I suppose the one who had the bigger debt canceled."

"You have judged correctly," Jesus said.

44Then he turned toward the woman and said to Simon, "Do you
see this woman? I came into your house. You did not give me any

[a]*41* A denarius was a coin worth about a day's wages.

OPEN 1. How expensive is your perfume or after shave lotion? **2.** If you blew a year's wages on a bottle of perfume, what would your spouse say?

STUDY 1. What strikes you in this story as humorous? As touching? As sad? **2.** What risk was this woman taking in coming to the house of Simon, the Pharisee? What does this tell you about her "state of mind"? **3.** What do you learn later on about Simon that is important to this story (vv. 45–46)? **4.** If you had been Jesus, what would you have done with her at your feet? **5.** What did the Pharisees know that they didn't think Jesus knew (v. 39)? **6.** How do you like the way Jesus answered the Pharisees' thoughts? **7.** What does Jesus see in the woman that the Pharisee does not? In this story, what is Jesus' main concern? The Pharisees' main concern? **8.** If this woman showed up at your group or your church, how would she be received?

---

easier to accuse him of being demon-possessed than to acknowledge God's truth in his life. In contrast, they complained about Jesus since, by living a moral life and mingling with all types of people, he broke their traditions and did not recognize the sobriety of the religious life. They accused him of being too worldly. Jesus' point is their hardness of heart toward God.

7:36 one of the Pharisees. Why Simon (v. 40) invited Jesus is unclear. His lack of providing some of the common courtesies of the day to his guest (vv. 44–46) indicates his opinion of Jesus probably was not especially high. Still, he would not have eaten with Jesus at all if he considered Jesus to be a "sinner," for the Pharisees prided themselves in not associating with "sinners." **reclined at the table.** People ate by reclining on their left side on low couches arranged around a table, such that their feet would be stretched out behind them.

7:37 a sinful life. *While not stated,* probably a life of sexual immorality is meant. The woman, who was certainly not an invited guest, may simply have joined other people in Simon's courtyard who had gathered to listen to Jesus talk. Although there is no biblical evidence, some identified this sinful woman with Mary Magdalene (tradition said she had been a prostitute). Since Mary Magdalene was one of the women who provided financially for Jesus out of her own funds (8:1–3), and since it is highly unlikely that Jesus would allow his ministry to be funded by money tainted by prostitution, this tradition is suspect.

7:38 This verse is loaded with emotion. The woman's tears show her extreme conviction of her sin as she stood by the feet of Jesus. For a woman to loose her hair in public was scandalous; using it to dry her tears from Jesus' feet marked her great humility before him. Normally, a person's head would be anointed as a sign of honor. (The Hebrew word *Messiah* means "anointed one.") Like John the Baptist, who felt unworthy to undo the thongs of the Messiah's sandals (3:16), perhaps this woman felt she was so unworthy that she dare only anoint Jesus' feet. That Jesus accepted these acts shows much about his character. He did not let what people might think dictate how he related to people. He saw her love and penitence and responded to that instead of public opinion.

7:39 Simon, the Pharisee, seeing only that Jesus violated the acceptable religious and social code by allowing such a woman to touch him like this, saw nothing of her repentance or gratitude.

7:41–43 five hundred denarii ... fifty. The difference here is between owing what one could earn in 18 months versus owing what could be earned in less than two months. Then, as now, it would be the rare moneylender who would cancel either debt! Part of what Jesus was saying was that God cancels debts (in the form of sins) that are far greater than most humans would cancel. A similar point is made in the Parable of the Unmerciful Servant, where the amount the master forgave was greater still (Matt. 18:23–35). Simon rightly gets the point that the man with the greatest debt would be most grateful.

7:44–46 While Simon had not behaved discourteously to Jesus as his guest, he had performed none of the special acts of hospitality that were customary for important guests. By contrast this wom-

water for my feet, but she wet my feet with her tears and wiped them
with her hair. 45You did not give me a kiss, but this woman, from the
time I entered, has not stopped kissing my feet. 46You did not put oil
on my head, but she has poured perfume on my feet. 47Therefore, I
tell you, her many sins have been forgiven—for she loved much. But
he who has been forgiven little loves little."

48Then Jesus said to her, "Your sins are forgiven."

49The other guests began to say among themselves, "Who is this
who even forgives sins?"

50Jesus said to the woman, "Your faith has saved you; go in peace."

APPLY **1.** Are you more like the woman in the story or the Pharisee? **2.** When did you come to the place in your spiritual life that grace was all that mattered?

The Parable of the Sower

8 After this, Jesus traveled about from one town and village to
another, proclaiming the good news of the kingdom of God. The
Twelve were with him, 2and also some women who had been cured of
evil spirits and diseases: Mary (called Magdalene) from whom seven
demons had come out; 3Joanna the wife of Cuza, the manager of
Herod's household; Susanna; and many others. These women were
helping to support them out of their own means.

4While a large crowd was gathering and people were coming to
Jesus from town after town, he told this parable: 5"A farmer went out
to sow his seed. As he was scattering the seed, some fell along the
path; it was trampled on, and the birds of the air ate it up. 6Some fell
on rock, and when it came up, the plants withered because they had
no moisture. 7Other seed fell among thorns, which grew up with it
and choked the plants. 8Still other seed fell on good soil. It came up
and yielded a crop, a hundred times more than was sown."

When he said this, he called out, "He who has ears to hear, let him
hear."

9His disciples asked him what this parable meant. 10He said, "The
knowledge of the secrets of the kingdom of God has been given to
you, but to others I speak in parables, so that,

OPEN What kind of luck have you had with growing things? Are you a "green thumb" or a "brown thumb"? What is your secret of success or reason for failure?

STUDY **1.** What strikes you immediately about the traveling companions of Jesus? What happened to class and gender superiority? **2.** What is the lesson in the parable of the sower? How would this help to explain to the disciples what is happening in their ministry? **3.** In the explanation to the disciples, what is the seed? The field? The soils? The farmer? **4.** What does it really mean to "hear"? How would you explain this parable to children? What modern analogy would you use? **5.** How would you like to get back one hundred fold on your labor?

APPLY **1.** Spiritually, what kind of yield is God getting out of your life? **2.** What is it going to take

---

an, who owed nothing to Jesus from a social point of view, showed her love and respect for Jesus by cleansing his feet, welcoming him with her kisses, and anointing him with expensive perfume.

7:47 Jesus is not saying that the woman is forgiven *because* she has shown such extravagant love (just as the debt was not canceled because of any act on the part of the debtor—v. 42), but her love expresses her gratitude for the forgiveness she has received.

7:50 Your faith has saved you. It is trusting oneself to Jesus that leads to salvation (deliverance) from the penalty and power of sin. **go in peace.** This was a common saying, but on the lips of Jesus it is uttered not simply as a wish but as an expression of fact.

8:2–3 some women. Jesus' band was supported by these women who helped in gratitude for the healing they had received from Jesus. Mary and Joanna are mentioned at the resurrection (24:10). The presence of Joanna, who was married to the man charged with the responsibility for managing Herod's affairs, shows that Jesus' influence had reached to the higher social and economic classes. That women traveled with Jesus shows the difference between him and other rabbis who often held women in low esteem.

8:5 sow his seed. Farmers sowed their fields by scattering seed with broad sweeping motions of the hand as they walked along the paths in their field. Afterward, they would go through the field to plow the seed under. **the path.** There were hard pathways between the various plots of land. These were packed so hard that seed could not even penetrate the soil, thus making it easy for the birds to simply eat it up.

8:6 on rock. Some of the soil covered a limestone base a few inches beneath the surface. Seed that fell here would germinate, but it would not last since the roots could not penetrate deeply enough into the ground to draw moisture during hot, dry times.

8:7 thorns. In other parts of the plot there were the roots of weeds which grew faster than the seedlings, stunting their growth. Although it lived, such seed would not bear fruit.

8:8 good soil. This was the soil in which the seed could grow and flourish. **a hundred times more than was sown.** A spectacular crop! A tenfold crop was considered an especially good harvest. **He who has ears to hear.** Jesus urges his hearers to ponder his parable. Part of the power of a parable lies in the fact that people must reflect on it in order to fully understand it.

8:10 secrets of the kingdom. In the New Testament a secret is something hidden until God chooses to reveal it.

to bring in a better crop in your life spiritually?

OPEN If I looked under your bed right now, what would I find: A suitcase? Old socks? Dust?

STUDY **1.** What does Jesus say to those who want to be secret followers? **2.** What is the promise here for those who listen? Don't listen? **3.** What do you think motivated Jesus' mother and brothers to come? Do you think Jesus' comment was a put-down or a statement about a new kind of family in the kingdom of God?

APPLY Are you closer to your physical family or your spiritual family? Who would you call if you had a deep personal problem?

OPEN What is the worst storm you remember?

STUDY **1.** If you had been in the boat when it seemed to be sinking, what would you have said? **2.** Why did the disciples awaken Jesus? **3.** What was the tone in Jesus' voice when he said, "Where is your faith"?

"'though seeing, they may not see;
though hearing, they may not understand.'[a]

11"This is the meaning of the parable: The seed is the word of God.
12Those along the path are the ones who hear, and then the devil
comes and takes away the word from their hearts, so that they may
not believe and be saved. 13Those on the rock are the ones who receive the word with joy when they hear it, but they have no root. They
believe for a while, but in the time of testing they fall away. 14The seed
that fell among thorns stands for those who hear, but as they go on
their way they are choked by life's worries, riches and pleasures, and
they do not mature. 15But the seed on good soil stands for those with
a noble and good heart, who hear the word, retain it, and by persevering produce a crop.

A Lamp on a Stand

16"No one lights a lamp and hides it in a jar or puts it under a bed.
Instead, he puts it on a stand, so that those who come in can see the
light. 17For there is nothing hidden that will not be disclosed, and
nothing concealed that will not be known or brought out into the
open. 18Therefore consider carefully how you listen. Whoever has will
be given more; whoever does not have, even what he thinks he has
will be taken from him."

Jesus' Mother and Brothers

19Now Jesus' mother and brothers came to see him, but they were
not able to get near him because of the crowd. 20Someone told him,
"Your mother and brothers are standing outside, wanting to see you."
21He replied, "My mother and brothers are those who hear God's
word and put it into practice."

Jesus Calms the Storm

22One day Jesus said to his disciples, "Let's go over to the other
side of the lake." So they got into a boat and set out. 23As they sailed,
he fell asleep. A squall came down on the lake, so that the boat was
being swamped, and they were in great danger.
24The disciples went and woke him, saying, "Master, Master, we're
going to drown!"
He got up and rebuked the wind and the raging waters; the storm

[a]*10* Isaiah 6:9

The truth about God's kingdom is revealed only to those who are committed to seeking it. The quote from Isaiah 6:9 does not mean Jesus spoke in parables to keep people from understanding, but that their lack of spiritual openness prevented them from understanding.

8:11–15 Ultimately, there are only two *kinds of soil—unproductive and productive*. The difference lies in whether one will heed Jesus' word or not.

8:16 lamp. A pottery vessel filled with olive oil. Just as it would be foolish to light a lamp only to hide its light, so it is foolish to think that Jesus expects his teaching to remain unnoticed.

8:23 he fell asleep. Sleeping peacefully can be an indication of trust in the power of God to protect one from harm (Ps. 4:8). **A squall.** The Sea of Galilee was a deep, freshwater lake, 13 miles *long* and 8 miles wide. It was pear-shaped and ringed by mountains, though open at its north and south ends. Fierce winds often blew into this bowl-shaped lake, creating savage and unpredictable storms.

8:24 Master. This was a common term of address for a rabbi. **we're going to drown!** As their later response indicates (v. 25), they had no expectation that he would have any power over the storm. They simply expected him to help bail out the boat since it was being swamped. **all was calm.** The picture is that of a sudden, unexplainable calmness replacing what, minutes before, had been a life-threatening storm.

subsided, and all was calm. [25]"Where is your faith?" he asked his disciples.

In fear and amazement they asked one another, "Who is this? He commands even the winds and the water, and they obey him."

The Healing of a Demon-possessed Man

[26]They sailed to the region of the Gerasenes,[a] which is across the
lake from Galilee. [27]When Jesus stepped ashore, he was met by a
demon-possessed man from the town. For a long time this man had
not worn clothes or lived in a house, but had lived in the tombs.
[28]When he saw Jesus, he cried out and fell at his feet, shouting at the
top of his voice, "What do you want with me, Jesus, Son of the Most
High God? I beg you, don't torture me!" [29]For Jesus had commanded
the evil[b] spirit to come out of the man. Many times it had seized him,
and though he was chained hand and foot and kept under guard, he
had broken his chains and had been driven by the demon into solitary
places.
[30]Jesus asked him, "What is your name?"
"Legion," he replied, because many demons had gone into him.
[31]And they begged him repeatedly not to order them to go into the
Abyss.
[32]A large herd of pigs was feeding there on the hillside. The demons
begged Jesus to let them go into them, and he gave them permission.
[33]When the demons came out of the man, they went into the pigs, and
the herd rushed down the steep bank into the lake and was drowned.
[34]When those tending the pigs saw what had happened, they ran
off and reported this in the town and countryside, [35]and the people
went out to see what had happened. When they came to Jesus, they
found the man from whom the demons had gone out, sitting at Jesus'
feet, dressed and in his right mind; and they were afraid. [36]Those who
had seen it told the people how the demon-possessed man had been
cured. [37]Then all the people of the region of the Gerasenes asked

[a]26 Some manuscripts *Gadarenes*; other manuscripts *Gergesenes*; also in verse 37 [b]29 Greek *unclean*

APPLY What are you going through now that would cause Jesus to question your faith?

OPEN **1.** Have you ever visited a graveyard at night? **2.** Have you ever traveled in an underdeveloped country where witchcraft is practiced and demon-possession is common?

STUDY **1.** After verses 22–25, how might the disciples be feeling as they arrive on the other side of the lake? Once they realize they are near a graveyard? As the demoniac runs toward them? **2.** How would you describe the condition of the man? Why is his name "Legion"? What does Jesus do to the demons inside of the man? **3.** How do the pig farmers respond? The townspeople? Why are they afraid? **4.** Why does Jesus tell this man to tell others what happened when he often commanded just the opposite? **5.** Do you believe that Satan has power and control over certain people? Are evil spirits real or something out of science fiction?

APPLY **1.** How would you compare the transformation of the demon-possessed man in this story to your own spiritual story? **2.** What is the "demon" you are wrestling with right now? **3.** When was the last time you felt like asking God to leave you alone? To get out of your life? To let you hurt yourself?

8:25 Where is your faith? This may not be so much a rebuke as an invitation for them to take a fresh look at who they think he is. Have they been listening (vv. 4–21)? **fear and amazement.** The disciples' fear of the storm gives way to fear of the one who has power over that storm! It is the fear of an unknown force or power. **Who is this?** This is the key question that emerges in these stories of Jesus' divine power. No rabbi could do what they have just seen Jesus do!

8:26 the region of the Gerasenes. The precise location of their landing is not clear. However, it is on the other side of the lake from Capernaum, in a burial ground in Gentile territory, probably near the lower end of the Sea of Galilee.

8:27 Jesus stepped ashore. Demons could enter and take control of a person's body, speaking and acting through that person. **tombs.** The ragged limestone cliffs with caves and depressions provided natural tombs.

8:28 The plea not to be tortured comes from the demons. Their plea is ironic in light of their effect on the man in whom they dwell.

8:30 Legion. This was the term for a company of Roman soldiers consisting of 6,000 men. The man was occupied not by one but a huge number of demons.

8:31 they begged him repeatedly. These demons are cowering in fear before the one they recognize as their judge. **the Abyss.** Despite popular belief that the underworld is the place where Satan and his demons have free reign, the Bible declares it to be the place of punishment for these evil beings (2 Peter 2:4).

8:32 pigs. This herd belonged to Gentiles since Jews considered pigs as unclean animals, and to associate with them would defile them before God (Lev. 11:1–8). This was probably a herd made up of pigs owned by various people in town.

8:35 they were afraid. It might be expected that the people would rejoice that this man who had terrorized them was now healed. But instead they are fearful of Jesus who has the power to overcome the demons and destroy the town herd.

8:37 asked Jesus to leave. This request shows the people were more concerned about their economy, represented by the herd of pigs, than they were for the life of a human being.

Jesus to leave them, because they were overcome with fear. So he got
into the boat and left.
38 The man from whom the demons had gone out begged to go with
him, but Jesus sent him away, saying, 39 "Return home and tell how
much God has done for you." So the man went away and told all over
town how much Jesus had done for him.

A Dead Girl and a Sick Woman

40 Now when Jesus returned, a crowd welcomed him, for they were
all expecting him. 41 Then a man named Jairus, a ruler of the synagogue, came and fell at Jesus' feet, pleading with him to come to his
house 42 because his only daughter, a girl of about twelve, was dying.
As Jesus was on his way, the crowds almost crushed him. 43 And a
woman was there who had been subject to bleeding for twelve years,[a]
but no one could heal her. 44 She came up behind him and touched the
edge of his cloak, and immediately her bleeding stopped.
45 "Who touched me?" Jesus asked.
When they all denied it, Peter said, "Master, the people are crowding and pressing against you."
46 But Jesus said, "Someone touched me; I know that power has
gone out from me."
47 Then the woman, seeing that she could not go unnoticed, came
trembling and fell at his feet. In the presence of all the people, she
told why she had touched him and how she had been instantly
healed. 48 Then he said to her, "Daughter, your faith has healed you.
Go in peace."
49 While Jesus was still speaking, someone came from the house of
Jairus, the synagogue ruler. "Your daughter is dead," he said. "Don't
bother the teacher any more."
50 Hearing this, Jesus said to Jairus, "Don't be afraid; just believe,
and she will be healed."
51 When he arrived at the house of Jairus, he did not let anyone go
in with him except Peter, John and James, and the child's father and

[a]43 Many manuscripts *years, and she had spent all she had on doctors*

OPEN 1. When was the last time you rushed to the hospital? **2.** What is your remedy for stopping a bloody nose?

STUDY 1. Have you ever been in a situation like the one in the Scripture—where two crises happened at the same time? **2.** What caused Jairus to seek out Jesus? What caused the woman to seek out Jesus? How were they both taking a risk? Both showing faith? **3.** Why did Jesus make the woman reveal herself? For his sake? For her sake? **4.** What did Jesus know that the disciples did not know (vv. 45–46)? How do you explain this? **5.** Was Jairus' daughter dead or just sleeping? Why did Jesus order all of the mourners out of the house? **6.** If you are in a big church with crowds of people coming, how do you know and reach out to the "bleeding" person who needs spiritual attention? Could this person have been in your church for 38 years and never been healed?

APPLY 1. When have you been as desperate as Jairus and the bleeding woman? What happened? **2.** Where are you "hemorrhaging" in your life right now? How about asking the group you are in to pray for you?

8:39 Return home. Some are called to go to foreign lands, but most of those who would follow Christ are called to share their faith story with the people they know in their own home community. **tell.** In contrast to what he said to the Jewish leper (5:14), Jesus wants this man to share the story of his healing. The difference is that Gentiles, who did not have messianic expectations, would be more able to accept the man's witness for what it was.

8:41 fell at Jesus' feet. It cannot have been easy for Jairus, this leader in the community, to humble himself before Jesus in this way. But his concern for his daughter outweighs his pride. **pleading.** Jairus' situation is desperate.

8:43 a woman was there. In contrast to the intensity of the crowd which was pushing and jostling Jesus as he tried to make his way to Jairus' house, Jesus is aware of the lone individual in that crowd who touched him in a totally different way. The woman should not have been there because her illness made her ceremonially "unclean" (Lev. 15:25–30), thus cutting her off from contact with other people, including her husband. If people touched her, they too would become "unclean." As a result, she, like the leper in 5:12, has to seek out Jesus in this surreptitious way. **subject to bleeding.** She was probably hemorrhaging from the womb.

8:47 The woman, filled with fear, tells her story. While she may have been afraid of being cursed for having touched him, Jesus wanted her to identify herself in order that her healing would be complete, since now it would be publicly known that she was healed.

8:48 your faith has healed you. This statement would accent the fact that her healing was not just the result of the supernatural power Jesus had, but as a result of her faith. The word Jesus uses to tell her that she is healed comes from the same root as the words "salvation" and "Savior." Spiritual as well as physical healing is in view here. **Go in peace.** Here, this phrase communicates the idea of "Be complete, be whole, be free from fear."

8:51 Peter, John and James. These three disciples become a sort of inner circle around Jesus.

mother. 52Meanwhile, all the people were wailing and mourning for
her. "Stop wailing," Jesus said. "She is not dead but asleep."
53They laughed at him, knowing that she was dead. 54But he took
her by the hand and said, "My child, get up!" 55Her spirit returned,
and at once she stood up. Then Jesus told them to give her something
to eat. 56Her parents were astonished, but he ordered them not to tell
anyone what had happened.

Jesus Sends Out the Twelve

9 When Jesus had called the Twelve together, he gave them power
and authority to drive out all demons and to cure diseases, 2and
he sent them out to preach the kingdom of God and to heal the sick.
3He told them: "Take nothing for the journey—no staff, no bag, no
bread, no money, no extra tunic. 4Whatever house you enter, stay
there until you leave that town. 5If people do not welcome you, shake
the dust off your feet when you leave their town, as a testimony
against them." 6So they set out and went from village to village,
preaching the gospel and healing people everywhere.
7Now Herod the tetrarch heard about all that was going on. And he
was perplexed, because some were saying that John had been raised
from the dead, 8others that Elijah had appeared, and still others that
one of the prophets of long ago had come back to life. 9But Herod
said, "I beheaded John. Who, then, is this I hear such things about?"
And he tried to see him.

OPEN What is one memorable camping trip you have had?

STUDY 1. How do you think Jesus felt when he turned over his ministry to the disciples? What did he ask them to do? **2.** Why would "Herod the tetrarch" be concerned? **3.** Does your church send out mission teams? What instructions are they given?

APPLY 1. What is the most memorable mission trip you have gone on? When are you going again? **2.** What is the passion in your life right now?

Jesus Feeds the Five Thousand

10When the apostles returned, they reported to Jesus what they had
done. Then he took them with him and they withdrew by themselves
to a town called Bethsaida, 11but the crowds learned about it and followed him. He welcomed them and spoke to them about the kingdom
of God, and healed those who needed healing.
12Late in the afternoon the Twelve came to him and said, "Send the

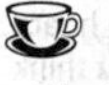

OPEN How do you unwind when you return from work or a trip: Eat? Read? Sleep? Play?

STUDY 1. What is the first thing Jesus does when his disciples return from their mission trip? Why? **2.** What ruins this happy retreat? How do the disciples respond?

8:52 people were wailing. These were in all likelihood professional mourners. Even the poorest person was expected to hire not less than two flutes and one wailing woman to mourn a death. They are a sign that all knew the child was dead. **She is not dead but asleep.** Jesus disarms the mourners by this statement. It does not mean that she was only in some sort of coma and not really dead. Rather, this was Jesus' way of reinterpreting her situation from a divine point of view since he knew she would rise again.

8:56 not to tell anyone. Jesus' statement that she was asleep (v. 52) makes it at least somewhat possible for her parents to obey his request, but enormous questions would be aroused in all those aware of the girl's condition! Since the raising of the widow's son at Nain was public (7:11–17), the reason for the command may lie in the fact that these people (vv. 49,53) still did not believe in him even after the story had circulated far and wide.

9:3 Take nothing. This would emphasize their dependence on God and contrast them with wandering preachers who tried to make money through their travels.

9:5 shake the dust off your feet. When leaving Gentile areas, Jews would wipe off their feet as a symbolic action of cleansing themselves from the judgment of God that was to come. For the disciples to do this to Jewish villages would indicate that the village was not part of the true Israel.

9:7 Herod. Before his death in 4 B.C., Herod the Great divided his territory between three of his sons: Herod (Antipas) and Philip ruled over their areas until 39 and 33 A.D. respectively. The third son, Archelaus, was given Judea, Samaria and Edom, but was soon removed because of a petition by the Jews he ruled. **John had been raised.** Mark 6:14–29 tells the gruesome story of John's death.

9:8 Elijah. It was commonly believed that just prior to the coming of the Messiah, God would raise up Israel's famous prophet to prepare the way (Mal. 4:5).

9:10 they withdrew by themselves. This was because Jesus wanted them to get some rest. **Bethsaida.** A town in the north of the Sea of Galilee. Since the miracle took place in a "remote place" (v. 12) it is likely that Bethsaida was simply the nearest town.

9:12 The disciples point out to Jesus that it will soon be too late for the crowd to find hospitality. It may be that they were in the predominately Gentile area on the east side of the Sea of Galilee

How would you have responded? **3.** Why does Jesus ask the disciples to start with "five loaves and two fish"? What did he do with the little they had? **4.** How do you think the disciples felt when they collected the leftovers? **5.** What is the lesson in this story for the church today? For your own life?

APPLY What is a need that God has laid on your heart that you and maybe your group could do something about?

OPEN If you asked the average person at your job or school, "Who is Jesus Christ," what might they say?

STUDY **1.** Why would Jesus be interested in this opinion poll? **2.** When Peter answers "the Christ of God," what is he saying? Why is this called the "great confession"? **3.** What is the "bombshell" Jesus predicts? If you had been one of the disciples, how would you feel? **4.** What does Jesus go on to explain? How would you have felt if you heard this for the first time? **5.** Do you think a person can be a follower of Christ without taking this challenge seriously?

APPLY When did you come to the place in your spiritual pilgrimage that you realized Jesus was the Christ of God?

crowd away so they can go to the surrounding villages and countryside and find food and lodging, because we are in a remote place
here."
13He replied, "You give them something to eat."
They answered, "We have only five loaves of bread and two fish—
unless we go and buy food for all this crowd." 14(About five thousand
men were there.)
But he said to his disciples, "Have them sit down in groups of about
fifty each." 15The disciples did so, and everybody sat down. 16Taking
the five loaves and the two fish and looking up to heaven, he gave
thanks and broke them. Then he gave them to the disciples to set
before the people. 17They all ate and were satisfied, and the disciples
picked up twelve basketfuls of broken pieces that were left over.

Peter's Confession of Christ

18Once when Jesus was praying in private and his disciples were
with him, he asked them, "Who do the crowds say I am?"
19They replied, "Some say John the Baptist; others say Elijah; and
still others, that one of the prophets of long ago has come back to
life."
20"But what about you?" he asked. "Who do you say I am?"
Peter answered, "The Christ[a] of God."
21Jesus strictly warned them not to tell this to anyone. 22And he
said, "The Son of Man must suffer many things and be rejected by the
elders, chief priests and teachers of the law, and he must be killed
and on the third day be raised to life."
23Then he said to them all: "If anyone would come after me, he
must deny himself and take up his cross daily and follow me. 24For
whoever wants to save his life will lose it, but whoever loses his life
for me will save it. 25What good is it for a man to gain the whole
world, and yet lose or forfeit his very self? 26If anyone is ashamed of
me and my words, the Son of Man will be ashamed of him when he
comes in his glory and in the glory of the Father and of the holy angels. 27I tell you the truth, some who are standing here will not taste
death before they see the kingdom of God."

[a]20 Or *Messiah*

where Jews could not be assured of being welcomed.

9:13 five loaves of bread and two fish. If three loaves of bread was considered a generous meal for a guest (11:5–8), then the disciples' provision here was barely adequate for their own needs.

9:14 five thousand men. Literally, "males" (Matt. 14:21). When all the women and children are added in, this was truly a huge crowd.

9:20 Who do you say I am? This is *the* critical question. Have the disciples heeded what they have seen and heard of Jesus (8:18)? **The Christ of God.** This is the Greek term for the Hebrew word "Messiah," meaning "the Anointed One"; that is, the prophesied future king of Israel.

9:21 Jesus commands them be silent about what they know. The problem is that, although they know he *is* the Messiah, they do not yet know what *kind* of Messiah he is.

9:22 must suffer. This is the part of the Messiah that the people did not understand. They thought it meant all glorious victories. They didn't realize salvation would be provided through the suffering and death of the Messiah. **rejected by the elders, chief priests and teachers of the law.** These three groups made up the Sanhedrin, the ruling Jewish body. For the first time, Jesus predicts his rejection by the officials of Israel.

9:23 come after me. This is to take on the role of a disciple, one committed to the teachings of a master. **deny himself.** This is to no longer live with self-satisfaction as the primary aim of life. Self must be denied in favor of doing the will of God. **take up his cross.** It is a metaphor emphasizing the call for all Jesus' disciples to put aside one's own desires and interests out of loyalty to Jesus. **daily.** Luke alone includes this. Following Jesus is a day-by-day commitment.

9:26 While his present suffering is real, the future glory of the Son of Man is pictured here (Dan. 7:13–14).

The Transfiguration

28About eight days after Jesus said this, he took Peter, John and
James with him and went up onto a mountain to pray. 29As he was
praying, the appearance of his face changed, and his clothes became
as bright as a flash of lightning. 30Two men, Moses and Elijah, 31ap-
peared in glorious splendor, talking with Jesus. They spoke about his
departure, which he was about to bring to fulfillment at Jerusalem.
32Peter and his companions were very sleepy, but when they became
fully awake, they saw his glory and the two men standing with him.
33As the men were leaving Jesus, Peter said to him, "Master, it is good
for us to be here. Let us put up three shelters—one for you, one for
Moses and one for Elijah." (He did not know what he was saying.)
34While he was speaking, a cloud appeared and enveloped them,
and they were afraid as they entered the cloud. 35A voice came from
the cloud, saying, "This is my Son, whom I have chosen; listen to
him." 36When the voice had spoken, they found that Jesus was alone.
The disciples kept this to themselves, and told no one at that time
what they had seen.

The Healing of a Boy With an Evil Spirit

37The next day, when they came down from the mountain, a large
crowd met him. 38A man in the crowd called out, "Teacher, I beg you
to look at my son, for he is my only child. 39A spirit seizes him and he
suddenly screams; it throws him into convulsions so that he foams at
the mouth. It scarcely ever leaves him and is destroying him. 40I
begged your disciples to drive it out, but they could not."
41"O unbelieving and perverse generation," Jesus replied, "how
long shall I stay with you and put up with you? Bring your son here."
42Even while the boy was coming, the demon threw him to the
ground in a convulsion. But Jesus rebuked the evil[a] spirit, healed the
boy and gave him back to his father. 43And they were all amazed at the
greatness of God.
While everyone was marveling at all that Jesus did, he said to his
disciples, 44"Listen carefully to what I am about to tell you: The Son
of Man is going to be betrayed into the hands of men." 45But they did

[a]42 Greek *unclean*

OPEN If you could choose three old friends from your childhood to go with you on a retreat, who would you choose?

STUDY 1. What happened eight days before that sets the stage for this story? **2.** Why did he take along Peter, John and James? **3.** Who appears with Jesus? Why these two? What do they do? **4.** Why would Peter want to build three tabernacles? In your own words, what did the voice in the cloud say to the three disciples?

APPLY 1. When is the last time you had a mountaintop experience like this? **2.** If God could speak to you right now about your life, what would he say?

OPEN How do you handle getting home, only to find a crisis brewing?

STUDY 1. Where has Jesus been with three of his disciples (vv. 28–36)? **2.** What happened while Jesus was away? Why did Jesus react this way? **3.** If you had been one of the disciples that failed, how would you be feeling about now? **4.** With only a few more weeks with his disciples, what is on Jesus' mind? **5.** Do you think the disciples realized the importance of what was happening?

APPLY 1. Has your spiritual life this past week been more like the mount of transfiguration or the slew of despond? **2.** How do you handle failure?

9:28 a mountain. This may be Mount Hermon, a 9,000-foot mountain located 12 miles from Caesarea Philippi (though early tradition says the Transfiguration occurred on Mount Tabor, located southwest of the Sea of Galilee). In the past, God had revealed himself on other mountains, such as when he appeared to Moses on Mount Sinai (Ex. 24) and to Elijah on Mount Horeb (1 Kin. 19).

9:30 Moses. It was to Moses God gave the Law, which became the very heart of the nation. Moses also prophesied that God would send another prophet like him to lead his people (Deut. 18:15). The early Christians took this to be a prophecy about Jesus (Acts 3:22–26; 7:35–37). **Elijah.** The Jews expected Elijah to return just prior to the coming of the day of the Lord (Mal. 4:5–6).

9:33 shelters. Peter, perhaps thinking that this experience represented the beginning of the kingdom when heavenly visitors would visit earth, might have intended to build earthly shelters as a counterpart to their heavenly ones.

9:35 A voice. Once again, as he did at the baptism of Jesus (3:22), God proclaims that Jesus is his Son.

9:41 O unbelieving and perverse generation. This parallels God's cry when faced with Israel's stubborn refusal to listen to him in the wilderness (Deut. 32:5,20).

9:42 Jesus displays the glory, power and compassion of God by this decisive defeat of the demon as it attacks the boy.

9:43–45 In spite of the people's praise, Jesus will not let the disciples forget that this glory is not the full story of his mission. He will experience suffering and betrayal. They should not be sidetracked from this reality by the demonstrations of glory and power that they presently observe.

OPEN 1. Who has taught you a lot about "greatness"? **2.** If you had to choose a pastor for your church, what three qualities would you look for?

STUDY 1. In the last story, the disciples "blew it" with the boy. How do they make out in this story? **2.** What are the disciples thinking about when they talk about greatness? How does this square with what Jesus has been teaching? **3.** What does it appear that the disciples want to do with their spiritual competition? Who does this sound like today? What about the village in Samaria? **4.** If you were Jesus, how would you be feeling about your team? **5.** Of the three excuses for not following Jesus, which one gets the prize? What are each of these people really saying? **6.** How does Jesus answer them? What's the point here?

APPLY 1. What was your most common excuse for not committing your life to Jesus? **2.** What is holding you back from following Jesus more completely?

not understand what this meant. It was hidden from them, so that they did not grasp it, and they were afraid to ask him about it.

Who Will Be the Greatest?

46An argument started among the disciples as to which of them
would be the greatest. 47Jesus, knowing their thoughts, took a little
child and had him stand beside him. 48Then he said to them, "Whoever welcomes this little child in my name welcomes me; and whoever welcomes me welcomes the one who sent me. For he who is
least among you all—he is the greatest."
49"Master," said John, "we saw a man driving out demons in your
name and we tried to stop him, because he is not one of us."
50"Do not stop him," Jesus said, "for whoever is not against you is
for you."

Samaritan Opposition

51As the time approached for him to be taken up to heaven, Jesus
resolutely set out for Jerusalem. 52And he sent messengers on ahead,
who went into a Samaritan village to get things ready for him; 53but
the people there did not welcome him, because he was heading for
Jerusalem. 54When the disciples James and John saw this, they asked,
"Lord, do you want us to call fire down from heaven to destroy
them[a]?" 55But Jesus turned and rebuked them, 56and[b] they went to
another village.

The Cost of Following Jesus

57As they were walking along the road, a man said to him, "I will
follow you wherever you go."
58Jesus replied, "Foxes have holes and birds of the air have nests,
but the Son of Man has no place to lay his head."
59He said to another man, "Follow me."
But the man replied, "Lord, first let me go and bury my father."

[a]54 Some manuscripts *them, even as Elijah did* [b]55,56 Some manuscripts *them. And he said, "You do not know what kind of spirit you are of, for the Son of Man did not come to destroy men's lives, but to save them."* 56*And*

9:47 knowing their thoughts. Perhaps their dispute was precipitated by the fact that Jesus has shared special insights with only Peter, John and James (v. 28; 8:51). **took a little child.** Children, like women and slaves, had few rights and little social significance in the eyes of men. By having this child stand beside him, Jesus places him in the position of honor which each of the Twelve coveted for himself.

9:49 a man driving out demons. The disciples' lack of humility is matched by their lack of acceptance that God is at work outside of their circle. (See Num. 11:24–30 for a similar incident in the life of Moses.) Since a person's name represented his character and power, this exorcist recognized Jesus' authority over demons and called upon that authority in his work.

9:50 Do not stop him. The disciples' attempt to stop this unauthorized exorcism is made all the more ironic by their own failure to cast out the demon from the epileptic boy (vv. 38–40). **whoever is not against you is for you.** The concern should be whether a person is seeking to glorify Jesus, not whether he or she is part of the "right" organization.

9:52 Samaritan. Samaritans and Jews were bitter enemies. The Samaritans did not want anything to do with someone traveling to Jerusalem, since they believed the true place of worship was on a mountain in *their* province.

9:54–55 do you want us to call fire down from heaven? Elijah once did this (2 Kin. 1:9–12), so the disciples may think it is an appropriate fate for those who treat Jesus shabbily. Their loveless, vengeful attitude, which showed how little they still understood about the love of God, is rebuked by Jesus.

9:58 no place to lay his head. Once Jesus began his public ministry he had no settled home, but traveled throughout Palestine. To follow Jesus is to be a sojourner in this world (Heb. 11:13).

9:59 This does not mean that the man's father had just died, but that the son was putting off following Jesus until he was free from obligations to his father—the last of which would have been the duty of providing for his burial, a duty that took precedence over all other religious obligations. The kingdom outweighs responsibility even to family.

60 Jesus said to him, "Let the dead bury their own dead, but you go
and proclaim the kingdom of God."
61 Still another said, "I will follow you, Lord; but first let me go back
and say good-by to my family."
62 Jesus replied, "No one who puts his hand to the plow and looks
back is fit for service in the kingdom of God."

Jesus Sends Out the Seventy-two

10 After this the Lord appointed seventy-two[a] others and sent
them two by two ahead of him to every town and place where
he was about to go. 2 He told them, "The harvest is plentiful, but the
workers are few. Ask the Lord of the harvest, therefore, to send out
workers into his harvest field. 3 Go! I am sending you out like lambs
among wolves. 4 Do not take a purse or bag or sandals; and do not
greet anyone on the road.
5 "When you enter a house, first say, 'Peace to this house.' 6 If a man
of peace is there, your peace will rest on him; if not, it will return to
you. 7 Stay in that house, eating and drinking whatever they give you,
for the worker deserves his wages. Do not move around from house
to house.
8 "When you enter a town and are welcomed, eat what is set before
you. 9 Heal the sick who are there and tell them, 'The kingdom of God
is near you.' 10 But when you enter a town and are not welcomed, go
into its streets and say, 11 'Even the dust of your town that sticks to
our feet we wipe off against you. Yet be sure of this: The kingdom
of God is near.' 12 I tell you, it will be more bearable on that day for
Sodom than for that town.
13 "Woe to you, Korazin! Woe to you, Bethsaida! For if the miracles
that were performed in you had been performed in Tyre and Sidon,
they would have repented long ago, sitting in sackcloth and ashes.
14 But it will be more bearable for Tyre and Sidon at the judgment than
for you. 15 And you, Capernaum, will you be lifted up to the skies? No,
you will go down to the depths.[b]
16 "He who listens to you listens to me; he who rejects you rejects
me; but he who rejects me rejects him who sent me."
17 The seventy-two returned with joy and said, "Lord, even the demons submit to us in your name."
18 He replied, "I saw Satan fall like lightning from heaven. 19 I have

[a] 1 Some manuscripts *seventy*; also in verse 17 [b] 15 Greek *Hades*

OPEN If you had to sell something door to door, what would you choose: Cookies? Subscriptions? Cosmetics? Other?

STUDY 1. Why does he send the disciples out two-by-two? What are they looking for (v. 2)? **2.** How is a disciple (follower of Christ) like a "worker in the harvest"? A "lamb among wolves"? **3.** What was the purpose of traveling light (v. 4)? Of praying first, going later? **4.** What kind of household guests are they to be (v. 5)? Why? **5.** How are they to relate to the towns they visit (vv. 8–12)? What is their basic message? **6.** How do verses 1–12 show the urgency Jesus himself senses for evangelism? What is the reason for this urgency? **7.** What do you know about Sodom (Gen. 19:24–28)? Korazin and Bethsaida? About Capernaum (Matt. 4:13)? Tyre and Sidon (Ezra 28)? **8.** What is the comfort and the danger of aligning oneself with Jesus (v. 16)? **9.** Upon their return, what does Jesus say to them (vv. 18–20)? What in their report gives Jesus reason for joy (v. 21)? **10.** Why is the overcoming of demons important to their preaching? What does this prove about God's power over Satan? **11.** Do you think this same battle is going on today?

APPLY 1. What is the closest you have come to going on a mission trip? How was it? **2.** When do you plan to go on another

10:2 The harvest image was used in the Old Testament as a metaphor for the coming judgment when God would gather together all his people. These disciples have the privilege of participating with God in the ingathering of his people as they announce the presence of the kingdom (v. 9).

10:4 This lack of provisions and the command not to stop to greet anyone highlights the urgency of their task (2 Kin. 4:29).

10:8 eat what is set before you. The concern here is not for proper etiquette in a host's home. If this trip involved going to the east side of the Jordan River, it would include visiting Gentile towns where the food would not meet Jewish dietary laws. Jesus' point is that the preaching of the kingdom is not to be deterred by religious traditions.

10:12 Sodom. An ancient city whose place in history was preserved because of the severity of God's judgment upon its evil (Gen. 19:1–29).

10:13 Woe to you. In spite of all the evidence concerning Jesus that they have seen and heard, they still have not received him as Messiah. **Korazin.** Apart from this reference and Matthew 11:21, there is no other mention of Korazin in the Bible. **Bethsaida.** The home of Peter, Andrew and Philip (John 1:44; 12:21).

10:19 authority to trample on snakes. Snakes and scorpions are symbolic of Satan's forces unleashed in nature. These forces, which plague humanity, are rendered powerless at the reign of the Messiah (Ps. 91:13; Isa. 11:8). Nevertheless, the joy of the disciples should not be rooted in acts

mission? How about one in your own back yard?

---

given you authority to trample on snakes and scorpions and to overcome all the power of the enemy; nothing will harm you. 20 However,
do not rejoice that the spirits submit to you, but rejoice that your
names are written in heaven."
21 At that time Jesus, full of joy through the Holy Spirit, said, "I
praise you, Father, Lord of heaven and earth, because you have
hidden these things from the wise and learned, and revealed them to
little children. Yes, Father, for this was your good pleasure.
22 "All things have been committed to me by my Father. No one
knows who the Son is except the Father, and no one knows who the
Father is except the Son and those to whom the Son chooses to
reveal him."
23 Then he turned to his disciples and said privately, "Blessed are
the eyes that see what you see. 24 For I tell you that many prophets
and kings wanted to see what you see but did not see it, and to hear
what you hear but did not hear it."

The Parable of the Good Samaritan

OPEN Who stopped and helped you when you had car trouble?

STUDY 1. Who asked the question, "Who is my neighbor"? What clue does this give you into the meaning of the parable? **2.** What legitimate excuses could the priest and Levite give for not stopping? If you knew that a stretch of road was notorious for robbers, would you have stopped? **3.** Who is a "Samaritan"? Who would the Samaritan be today? **4.** If you had been the "expert in the law" that asked the question, how would you be feeling at the end of the parable? If you were a priest or Levite, how would you be feeling? **5.** What is your church doing about assisting the homeless and hungry in your community? How do you help these people without making them dependent on you or reinforcing negative behavior?

25 On one occasion an expert in the law stood up to test Jesus.
"Teacher," he asked, "what must I do to inherit eternal life?"
26 "What is written in the Law?" he replied. "How do you read it?"
27 He answered: " 'Love the Lord your God with all your heart and
with all your soul and with all your strength and with all your mind'[a];
and, 'Love your neighbor as yourself.'[b]"
28 "You have answered correctly," Jesus replied. "Do this and you
will live."
29 But he wanted to justify himself, so he asked Jesus, "And who is
my neighbor?"
30 In reply Jesus said: "A man was going down from Jerusalem to
Jericho, when he fell into the hands of robbers. They stripped him of
his clothes, beat him and went away, leaving him half dead. 31 A priest
happened to be going down the same road, and when he saw the
man, he passed by on the other side. 32 So too, a Levite, when he came
to the place and saw him, passed by on the other side. 33 But a Samaritan, as he traveled, came where the man was; and when he saw him,
he took pity on him. 34 He went to him and bandaged his wounds,

[a]27 Deut. 6:5 [b]27 Lev. 19:18

---

of supernatural authority, but in the assurance that they have a place in heaven (v. 20).

10:25 an expert in the law. This would have been a scribe, a man charged with the responsibility of interpreting the Law and teaching people what was involved in its observance. **to test Jesus.** His question is meant to see whether or not Jesus could penetrate into the heart of the multitudinous commandments that made up Jewish tradition to focus upon the essential command.

10:26–27 Jesus' question points the lawyer back to the *Shema* (Deut. 6:5), which is recited in verse 27. The scribe also adds Leviticus 19:18 with its stress on the love of neighbor.

10:29 In an attempt to regain the initiative, he asks Jesus another question. Given the understanding of "neighbor" at the time, his follow-up question was perfectly natural. The Jewish religious leaders of the time taught that only other Jews were neighbors.

10:30 going down. This was a notoriously dangerous road. It has had a reputation of being dangerous for travelers right up to modern times.

10:31 A priest. This priest may have been returning home after his period of temple service. He may have passed by to avoid the ritual defilement of touching a dead man.

10:32 a Levite. These were men assigned to aid the priests in various temple duties. Perhaps he was fearful of being attacked himself by the same robbers.

10:33 a Samaritan. These were despised by most Jews, and hence making him the hero who acted like a neighbor would have caught the Jewish audience off guard.

10:34 pouring on oil and wine. While olive oil and wine were thought to have medicinal benefits, they were also used in acts of worship at the temple.

pouring on oil and wine. Then he put the man on his own donkey,
took him to an inn and took care of him. 35The next day he took out
two silver coins[a] and gave them to the innkeeper. 'Look after him,' he
said, 'and when I return, I will reimburse you for any extra expense
you may have.'
36"Which of these three do you think was a neighbor to the man
who fell into the hands of robbers?"
37The expert in the law replied, "The one who had mercy on him."
Jesus told him, "Go and do likewise."

At the Home of Martha and Mary

38As Jesus and his disciples were on their way, he came to a village
where a woman named Martha opened her home to him. 39She had a
sister called Mary, who sat at the Lord's feet listening to what he said.
40But Martha was distracted by all the preparations that had to be
made. She came to him and asked, "Lord, don't you care that my sister has left me to do the work by myself? Tell her to help me!"
41"Martha, Martha," the Lord answered, "you are worried and upset about many things, 42but only one thing is needed.[b] Mary has
chosen what is better, and it will not be taken away from her."

Jesus' Teaching on Prayer

11 One day Jesus was praying in a certain place. When he finished, one of his disciples said to him, "Lord, teach us to pray,
just as John taught his disciples."
2He said to them, "When you pray, say:

" 'Father,[c]
hallowed be your name,
your kingdom come.[d]

[a]35 Greek *two denarii* [b]42 Some manuscripts *but few things are needed—or only one* [c]2 Some manuscripts *Our Father in heaven* [d]2 Some manuscripts *come. May your will be done on earth as it is in heaven.*

APPLY 1. When you are really hurting and you need to call on someone, who do you turn to—knowing they will come, listen without giving advice and keep anything you say in confidence? **2.** How many church friends would you put on this list?

OPEN Who is a compulsive "Type A" person in your family?

STUDY 1. Who do you identify with in this story: Mary or Martha? **2.** If you had been Martha, what would you have done: Gone to your room and cried, or sat down and let the dinner burn?

APPLY What can you do to take stress out of your life?

OPEN Who put you to bed at night and heard your prayers when you were a child?

STUDY 1. What motivates the disciples to ask about prayer at this point (v. 1)? **2.** In Jesus' model prayer (vv. 2–4), what two concerns related to God come first? What personal concerns then follow? How do prayer and forgiveness relate? **3.** What does the parable in verses 5–8 teach about prayer? How do verses 9–10 relate to the parable? What

10:35 two silver coins. Literally, this is two denarii, enough to care for the man for three weeks.

10:36 Which ... was a neighbor. Jesus rephrases the lawyer's question (v. 29). Rather than joining the game of defining who is (and, therefore, who is *not*) one's neighbor, Jesus points out to this man that he should act at *least* as generously and neighborly as this Samaritan who had absolutely no ethnic or social obligation to the wounded man.

10:38 village. Bethany, just on the outskirts of Jerusalem, was the home of Martha and Mary and their brother Lazarus. **a woman named Martha.** Martha and Mary also appear in John 11:1–44, where their brother Lazarus dies and is raised from the dead by Jesus. In that story it is Martha, rather than Mary as in this story, who is more faithful. **Martha opened her home to him.** It appears that it was Martha's home (she was the head of the household), which would be why she would feel more responsible for preparations.

10:40 my sister has left me to do the work by myself. This is a classic clash between a disciplined, task-oriented servant (Martha) and a more impulsive, person-oriented student (Mary). That Martha says Mary has left her to do all the work assumes the priority that work always comes first over learning and socialization. None of this is to say that Jesus "sided" against the more task-oriented person. He simply says that in this situation, stopping to spend time with him is the highest priority, and Mary has chosen that priority.

10:41 you are worried and upset. Martha is like the thorny soil in which the fruit is choked by life's worries (8:14). **about many things.** Martha's problem was an inability to focus her life around one central priority. Jesus calls us to focus our lives around the central priority of the kingdom of God.

10:42 only one thing is needed. Jesus is not saying that a simple meal is all that is needed, but that listening and responding to him is the single most critical thing in all of life. Mary had chosen to do that rather than being distracted.

11:1 teach us to pray. Various Jewish groups (including John's disciples) had their own distinctive prayers. The issue of whether Jesus was seeking here to teach a specific rote prayer or simply some principles of what should be included in prayer, is much debated. The prayer (and its counterpart in Matt. 6:9–13) does contain the elements of praise ("hallowed be your name"), submission ("your kingdom come"), petition for physical need ("Give us each day our daily bread"), and petition for spiritual need ("Forgive us our sins ... lead us not into temptation").

11:2 Father. While even the orthodox Jews of the day called God "our Father,"

attitude is implied in verses 9–10? How do verses 11–13 clarify the intent of verses 9–10?

APPLY 1. What do you use to prepare for prayer: Read a psalm? Use a devotional guide? Sing a hymn? **2.** What concerns occupy most of your time in prayer: Praise? Confession? Petition? In which area do you need to grow?

OPEN How well did you keep your bedroom when you were growing up? How have your habits changed with age?

3 Give us each day our daily bread.
4 Forgive us our sins,
for we also forgive everyone who sins against us.[a]
And lead us not into temptation.[b]' "

5 Then he said to them, "Suppose one of you has a friend, and he
goes to him at midnight and says, 'Friend, lend me three loaves of
bread, 6 because a friend of mine on a journey has come to me, and I
have nothing to set before him.'

7 "Then the one inside answers, 'Don't bother me. The door is already locked, and my children are with me in bed. I can't get up and
give you anything.' 8 I tell you, though he will not get up and give him
the bread because he is his friend, yet because of the man's boldness[c]
he will get up and give him as much as he needs.

9 "So I say to you: Ask and it will be given to you; seek and you will
find; knock and the door will be opened to you. 10 For everyone who
asks receives; he who seeks finds; and to him who knocks, the door
will be opened.

11 "Which of you fathers, if your son asks for[d] a fish, will give him a
snake instead? 12 Or if he asks for an egg, will give him a scorpion? 13 If
you then, though you are evil, know how to give good gifts to your
children, how much more will your Father in heaven give the Holy
Spirit to those who ask him!"

Jesus and Beelzebub

14 Jesus was driving out a demon that was mute. When the demon
left, the man who had been mute spoke, and the crowd was amazed.

[a]4 Greek *everyone who is indebted to us* [b]4 Some manuscripts *temptation but deliver us from the evil one* [c]8 Or *persistence* [d]11 Some manuscripts *for bread, will give him a stone; or if he asks for*

this simple, personal form of address was new. Jesus at times used the term "Abba," a term more akin to "Dad" than "Father," which was being much more familiar with God than other rabbis thought appropriate. He is teaching the disciples to approach God personally. **hallowed be your name.** The first petition is that the name of God (i.e., his character and nature) be honored by all. **your kingdom come.** The prayer is that God will quickly establish the reign of his kingdom throughout the world. While the kingdom is in some sense already present (10:9), it will only come in its *fullness* when Christ returns.

11:4 for we also forgive. This is not an appeal for forgiveness as a reward for our forgiving others, but rather a reminder that God's forgiveness produces a willingness to extend that to others. Jesus told the Parable of the Unmerciful Servant (Matt. 18:21–35) to make exactly this point. **lead us not into temptation.** The request is that the person will not have to face a trial so difficult that he or she will fall into sin.

11:5–6 Hospitality was held in high regard in the ancient Middle East. Hebrews urged Christians to continue to be hospitable to traveling strangers (Heb. 13:2). Since hospitality was such an important duty, it would be imperative that the host in this story provide some food for his surprise visitor.

11:7 The door is already locked. This would have been a wooden door secured by a wooden or iron bolt thrust through rings. It could not be opened without making a racket. **my children are with me in bed.** The whole family would sleep together on a mat on the floor of the simple one-room cottage envisioned here. If the man got up, he would disturb the whole household.

11:8 the man's boldness. Literally, "shamelessness." If it is the boldness of the man approaching his friend so late, then the parable is meant to encourage the disciples to be persistent in prayer, a lesson more clearly taught in 18:1–5. If, however, the householder is in view, then the parable means that since even a *man* would go to such lengths so as not to be known as one who would refuse a friend in need, certainly *God* will not fail to respond to the needs of those who pray to him. None of this is to say that God gives us everything we ask for.

11:9 Ask ... seek ... knock. Literally, "keep on asking," keep on seeking," and "keep on knocking," emphasizing that prayer is a continuous, ongoing process. Prayer is rooted in the assurance that the householder (God) will hear the prayers and meet the needs of his friend.

11:11–13 snake ... scorpion. These were creatures that Jews were forbidden to eat (Lev. 11:12,42). The snake may be an eel-like fish that likewise was forbidden to the Jews. The scorpion, at least, could be poisonous.

11:13 though you are evil. This is a strong statement. The word "evil" is used elsewhere to characterize Satan (Matt. 6:13). Since not even a sinful human father would give such a repulsive, dangerous food to his own son, how much less will the perfect heavenly Father fail to give what his children most need?

11:14–16 It is this exorcism that gives rise to the ensuing controversy (vv. 17–

[15]But some of them said, "By Beelzebub,[a] the prince of demons, he is
driving out demons." [16]Others tested him by asking for a sign from
heaven.

[17]Jesus knew their thoughts and said to them: "Any kingdom divided against itself will be ruined, and a house divided against itself will
fall. [18]If Satan is divided against himself, how can his kingdom stand?
I say this because you claim that I drive out demons by Beelzebub.
[19]Now if I drive out demons by Beelzebub, by whom do your followers drive them out? So then, they will be your judges. [20]But if I drive
out demons by the finger of God, then the kingdom of God has come
to you.

[21]"When a strong man, fully armed, guards his own house, his possessions are safe. [22]But when someone stronger attacks and over-
powers him, he takes away the armor in which the man trusted and
divides up the spoils.

[23]"He who is not with me is against me, and he who does not gather with me, scatters.

[24]"When an evil[b] spirit comes out of a man, it goes through arid
places seeking rest and does not find it. Then it says, 'I will return to
the house I left.' [25]When it arrives, it finds the house swept clean and
put in order. [26]Then it goes and takes seven other spirits more wicked
than itself, and they go in and live there. And the final condition of
that man is worse than the first."

[27]As Jesus was saying these things, a woman in the crowd called
out, "Blessed is the mother who gave you birth and nursed you."

[28]He replied, "Blessed rather are those who hear the word of God
and obey it."

The Sign of Jonah

[29]As the crowds increased, Jesus said, "This is a wicked generation.
It asks for a miraculous sign, but none will be given it except the sign
of Jonah. [30]For as Jonah was a sign to the Ninevites, so also will the
Son of Man be to this generation. [31]The Queen of the South will rise
at the judgment with the men of this generation and condemn them;
for she came from the ends of the earth to listen to Solomon's

[a]*15* Greek *Beezeboul* or *Beelzeboul;* also in verses 18 and 19 [b]*24* Greek *unclean*

STUDY **1.** How does the crowd react to Jesus' miracle (vv. 14–16)? **2.** How does Jesus illustrate the foolishness of the claim that he drives out demons by Beelzebub? What does Jesus' ability to drive out demons say about the kingdom of God (v. 20)? **3.** What is Jesus' point in verses 24–26? To whom is the point addressed? Why is the final condition worse than the first? **4.** Why does Jesus turn around the blessing shouted to him in verse 27? What is he emphasizing here? **5.** Is it possible to stay neutral on the claims of Jesus? Is it possible to commit your life to Jesus and do nothing about it?

APPLY **1.** When did you come to the place in your spiritual pilgrimage that you got off the fence? **2.** What are you doing now to fill up your life with God?

OPEN **1.** Where did you first hear about Jonah? **2.** How well do you see in the dark?

STUDY **1.** Why is "this generation" wicked? **2.** The "sign of Jonah" is a reference to resurrection. How is Jesus like that? **3.** What is the point that Jesus makes when he refers to the Queen of the South

---

26). Most of the people are utterly amazed at what he has done, while others (the scribes—Mark 3:22, and Pharisees—Matt. 12:24) accuse him of being in league with the devil, and still others want more confirming evidence than he has already supplied.

11:15 Beelzebub. Probably a slang expression for a demon-prince, meaning something like "The Lord of Dung." It is used here apparently as a synonym for Satan. Thus these people totally reject his deity.

11:24–26 This may really be a parable about the spiritual state of his generation. Many had professed repentance as a result of John the Baptist's ministry. By rejecting Jesus they would commit a far greater sin.

11:27–28 This interchange reinforces the point brought out in 8:19–21. It is not those who have a natural relationship with Jesus who are blessed by God, but those who "hear the word of God (i.e., the teachings of Jesus) and obey it" (6:46; 8:15,18; 9:35).

11:29 a miraculous sign. What they had in mind was something like a vivid display in the sky, turning water into blood, or some other spectacular demonstration of his word of power (Ex. 4:8–9; Isa. 38:7–8). Jesus will not simply give a sign for its own sake, especially when the request springs from unbelief. His miracles are always beneficial in nature. **the sign of Jonah.** This is a reference to Jesus' resurrection. After Jonah spent three days and three nights in the belly of the "great fish," he experienced a miraculous deliverance—which authenticated his call to preach in Nineveh (Jonah 1:17; 2:10).

11:31 The Queen of the South. She came all the way from Arabia to listen to the wisdom of Solomon (1 Kin. 10:1–13). **one greater.** Jesus claims to be greater than Solomon, under whose reign Israel achieved its apex of power and dominion. He also claims to be greater than Jonah (v. 32), under whose preaching an entire Gentile city was brought to its knees before God.

and the men of Nineveh? **4.** What is the meaning here to the disciples? **5.** What happens when you keep focused?

APPLY 1. What signs are your unchurched friends looking for before they decide on Jesus? **2.** How would you score on a spiritual eye exam: 20–20? 20–80? Legally blind?

OPEN When you were a child, who insisted that you wash up before meals? Who insisted that you wear clean clothes? How did you react to this fussing?

STUDY 1. Why do you believe Jesus is being so hard on the Pharisees here? If you had been the Pharisee who invited Jesus to a meal, how would you be feeling? **2.** How does the Lord turn the tables on his host? What is his basic point about the Pharisees (vv. 39–41)? **3.** In your own words, what is the meaning of these three woes directed at the Pharisees (vv. 42–44)? Given the Pharisees' view of tombs and the dead (Num. 19:16), what is the significance of the unmarked graves (v. 44)? **4.** What is the point of these criticisms? **5.** In your own words, what is the meaning of the next three woes (vv. 46–52)? In the sixth woe (v. 52), what does Jesus mean by "the key of knowledge"? **6.** How does this Pharisee's dinner compare with the one in 7:36–50? Why the difference?

wisdom, and now one[a] greater than Solomon is here. 32The men of
Nineveh will stand up at the judgment with this generation and condemn it; for they repented at the preaching of Jonah, and now one greater than Jonah is here.

The Lamp of the Body

33"No one lights a lamp and puts it in a place where it will be hidden, or under a bowl. Instead he puts it on its stand, so that those
who come in may see the light. 34Your eye is the lamp of your body.
When your eyes are good, your whole body also is full of light. But
when they are bad, your body also is full of darkness. 35See to it, then,
that the light within you is not darkness. 36Therefore, if your whole
body is full of light, and no part of it dark, it will be completely lighted, as when the light of a lamp shines on you."

Six Woes

37When Jesus had finished speaking, a Pharisee invited him to eat
with him; so he went in and reclined at the table. 38But the Pharisee,
noticing that Jesus did not first wash before the meal, was surprised.
39Then the Lord said to him, "Now then, you Pharisees clean the outside of the cup and dish, but inside you are full of greed and wickedness. 40You foolish people! Did not the one who made the outside
make the inside also? 41But give what is inside ⌊the dish⌋[b] to the poor,
and everything will be clean for you.

42"Woe to you Pharisees, because you give God a tenth of your mint, rue and all other kinds of garden herbs, but you neglect justice and the love of God. You should have practiced the latter without leaving the former undone.

43"Woe to you Pharisees, because you love the most important seats in the synagogues and greetings in the marketplaces.

44"Woe to you, because you are like unmarked graves, which men walk over without knowing it."

45One of the experts in the law answered him, "Teacher, when you say these things, you insult us also."

46Jesus replied, "And you experts in the law, woe to you, because

[a]31 Or *something;* also in verse 32 [b]41 Or *what you have*

11:32 Despite Jesus' greatness the leaders of Israel will not repent and follow him. The pagan Ninevites are therefore shown to be more sensitive to God than these trained religious authorities.

11:34 Your eye is the lamp of your body. The comparison is between a lamp that provides light for one's path and a good eye (literally, an eye that is "single") that enables people to find their way toward a purposeful life of obedience to God.

11:38 Jesus did not first wash. This had nothing to do with hygiene, but everything to do with the religious tradition. **was surprised.** Like Simon in 7:39, Jesus' unorthodox actions raised silent questions in the mind of his host.

11:41 They should repent of their greed and give to the poor instead. Such action would reflect a change of heart that would show inner cleanliness.

11:42 you give God a tenth. The Old Testament required a tithe of garden and farm produce (Lev. 27:30–33; Deut. 14:22–29). Jesus attacks the Pharisees for holding fast to this (relatively) insignificant detail while they have totally neglected concerns like justice and love that dominate the Old Testament Law and Prophets.

11:43 The seats facing the congregation were the most important seats in the synagogue. To be seated there had become a sign of one's status in the congregation.

11:44 Unmarked graves defile those who unknowingly come in contact with them (Num. 19:16).

11:46 The scribes interpreted the Law with a complex system of restrictions. Thus most felt condemned for their continual breaking of God's Law. Jesus is incensed that the scribes assume their duty stopped with interpreting the Law. They made no attempt to help the people who struggled under the burden they created.

you load people down with burdens they can hardly carry, and you
yourselves will not lift one finger to help them.
47“Woe to you, because you build tombs for the prophets, and it
was your forefathers who killed them. 48So you testify that you approve of what your forefathers did; they killed the prophets, and you
build their tombs. 49Because of this, God in his wisdom said, ‘I will
send them prophets and apostles, some of whom they will kill and
others they will persecute.’ 50Therefore this generation will be held
responsible for the blood of all the prophets that has been shed since
the beginning of the world, 51from the blood of Abel to the blood of
Zechariah, who was killed between the altar and the sanctuary. Yes, I
tell you, this generation will be held responsible for it all.
52“Woe to you experts in the law, because you have taken away the
key to knowledge. You yourselves have not entered, and you have
hindered those who were entering.”
53When Jesus left there, the Pharisees and the teachers of the law
began to oppose him fiercely and to besiege him with questions,
54waiting to catch him in something he might say.

Warnings and Encouragements

12 Meanwhile, when a crowd of many thousands had gathered,
so that they were trampling on one another, Jesus began to
speak first to his disciples, saying: “Be on your guard against the
yeast of the Pharisees, which is hypocrisy. 2There is nothing concealed that will not be disclosed, or hidden that will not be made
known. 3What you have said in the dark will be heard in the daylight,
and what you have whispered in the ear in the inner rooms will be
proclaimed from the roofs.
4“I tell you, my friends, do not be afraid of those who kill the body
and after that can do no more. 5But I will show you whom you should
fear: Fear him who, after the killing of the body, has power to throw
you into hell. Yes, I tell you, fear him. 6Are not five sparrows sold for
two pennies[a]? Yet not one of them is forgotten by God. 7Indeed, the
very hairs of your head are all numbered. Don’t be afraid; you are
worth more than many sparrows.
8“I tell you, whoever acknowledges me before men, the Son of Man
will also acknowledge him before the angels of God. 9But he who disowns me before men will be disowned before the angels of God.
10And everyone who speaks a word against the Son of Man will be
forgiven, but anyone who blasphemes against the Holy Spirit will not
be forgiven.
11“When you are brought before synagogues, rulers and authorities, do not worry about how you will defend yourselves or what you

[a]6 Greek *two assaria*

APPLY 1. In your spiritual pilgrimage, what did you think of the religious crowd? **2.** What rules have been laid on you? **3.** What are you going to do about religious rules when raising your children?

OPEN What was the unpardonable sin in your family: Playing hooky? Talking back to your parents? Leaving your bed unmade? Taking God’s name in vain?

STUDY 1. In verse 10, it says “anyone who blasphemes against the Holy Spirit will not be forgiven.” What is the situation in this passage that helps you understand this statement? **2.** Reading between the lines, what have the Pharisees done to cause Jesus to warn his disciples? Who are the Pharisees today? **3.** How does hypocrisy work like yeast (11:37–54)? **4.** Why does Jesus encourage his disciples to fear, yet be fearless (vv. 4–7)? **5.** What does it mean to “blaspheme against the Holy Spirit” (v. 10)?

APPLY 1. From your own experience, who are the hardest people to share your faith story with? **2.** For the new generation, what are they looking for and how does Jesus meet this need?

11:51 Abel. Abel was the first person to be murdered. It happened because his brother, like these leaders, refused to listen to God (Gen. 4:3–8). **Zechariah.** The context implies this was Zechariah (son of Jehoiada) who was murdered in the temple by people who refused to hear his word (2 Chr. 24:19–22).

11:52 taken away the key to knowledge. Instead of unlocking the Scriptures, the traditions of the scribes have securely locked away such knowledge from the people.

12:1 yeast. Yeast was often used as a metaphor for evil. Here it represents the hypocrisy of the Pharisees.

12:3 from the roofs. Public announcements were made from the roof of a building.

12:6 sparrows. These small, common birds were eaten by poor people. **pennies.** A penny was worth one sixteenth of a denarius, which was the average day’s wage.

will say, 12for the Holy Spirit will teach you at that time what you
should say."

The Parable of the Rich Fool

13Someone in the crowd said to him, "Teacher, tell my brother to
divide the inheritance with me."
14Jesus replied, "Man, who appointed me a judge or an arbiter between you?" 15Then he said to them, "Watch out! Be on your guard
against all kinds of greed; a man's life does not consist in the abundance of his possessions."
16And he told them this parable: "The ground of a certain rich man
produced a good crop. 17He thought to himself, 'What shall I do? I
have no place to store my crops.'
18"Then he said, 'This is what I'll do. I will tear down my barns and
build bigger ones, and there I will store all my grain and my goods.
19And I'll say to myself, "You have plenty of good things laid up for
many years. Take life easy; eat, drink and be merry." '
20"But God said to him, 'You fool! This very night your life will be
demanded from you. Then who will get what you have prepared for
yourself?'
21"This is how it will be with anyone who stores up things for himself but is not rich toward God."

Do Not Worry

22Then Jesus said to his disciples: "Therefore I tell you, do not worry about your life, what you will eat; or about your body, what you
will wear. 23Life is more than food, and the body more than clothes.
24Consider the ravens: They do not sow or reap, they have no storeroom or barn; yet God feeds them. And how much more valuable you
are than birds! 25Who of you by worrying can add a single hour to his
life[a]? 26Since you cannot do this very little thing, why do you worry
about the rest?
27"Consider how the lilies grow. They do not labor or spin. Yet I tell
you, not even Solomon in all his splendor was dressed like one of

[a]25 Or *single cubit to his height*

OPEN What did you like to collect as a child? Now?

STUDY 1. What's going on in this family squabble? Have you ever been in a squabble over who is going to get what when your parents die? **2.** In the parable, is the rich man happy? What do you think caused the death of the rich man? **3.** How does this parable illustrate the point Jesus makes in verse 5?

APPLY 1. As you look back over your life, when would be the time you were most happy? How many possessions did you have? **2.** Honestly, if you could cut back on your lifestyle would you do it? What is stopping you?

OPEN Which situation is most worrisome to you: Child expelled? Overdrawn at the bank? Gained 10 pounds? Nobody called all weekend? Mother-in-law stays two weeks? Business folds?

STUDY 1. What is the lesson in the ravens and the lilies of the field that Jesus wants the disciples to learn? **2.** Who is someone you admire because they live in the tension of a pagan world (v. 30) with kingdom values (v. 31)? **3.** How far can you take verse 33? How do you balance this passage with 2 Thessalonians 3:6–15?

12:13 Teacher. Literally, "Rabbi." As men schooled in the Law of God, rabbis were often asked to settle legal disputes. **divide the inheritance.** If sons could not peaceably keep the father's estate together, one could sue for the property to be legally divided.

12:14 Man. This is a gruff form of address, somewhat akin to someone today saying, "Listen, mister ..." Jesus is clearly rebuking the man for his request. **who appointed me a judge ... between you?** Jesus refuses to be used as a pawn for this man's material gain. Jesus effectively becomes the judge over both of them, exposing the motivation of their hearts.

12:15 greed. Jesus pinpoints the real motivating factor behind this appeal for justice. **life.** Then, as now, a person's happiness and well-being was often thought to be determined by what he or she owned. Jesus flatly rejects this as a standard for measuring the worth of one's life.

12:18 there I will store all my grain and my goods. Up to this point in the parable, the listeners would view the man as blessed by God. Even the plan to store the crop for future use could be commended, since the people of the Middle East would periodically suffer from famine. But, God redirects the thought. Instead of looking after himself, God reminds the rich man that only God directs the future. The man is to live respecting God, not confident in his own resources.

12:19 eat, drink and be merry. The man was not following God's ways, but living as a pagan, concerned only with his own desires.

12:20 You fool! In the Bible, a fool is someone who lives without regard to God. **your life will be demanded from you.** The word for "demanded" is a word used in banking circles when a loan was being called in for payment.

12:22 do not worry. This prohibition does not mean that disciples need not do anything to feed and clothe themselves. What is commended is faith, not idleness.

these. 28If that is how God clothes the grass of the field, which is here
today, and tomorrow is thrown into the fire, how much more will he
clothe you, O you of little faith! 29And do not set your heart on what
you will eat or drink; do not worry about it. 30For the pagan world
runs after all such things, and your Father knows that you need them.
31But seek his kingdom, and these things will be given to you as well.
32"Do not be afraid, little flock, for your Father has been pleased to
give you the kingdom. 33Sell your possessions and give to the poor.
Provide purses for yourselves that will not wear out, a treasure in
heaven that will not be exhausted, where no thief comes near and no
moth destroys. 34For where your treasure is, there your heart will be
also.

Watchfulness

35"Be dressed ready for service and keep your lamps burning, 36like
men waiting for their master to return from a wedding banquet, so
that when he comes and knocks they can immediately open the door
for him. 37It will be good for those servants whose master finds them
watching when he comes. I tell you the truth, he will dress himself to
serve, will have them recline at the table and will come and wait on
them. 38It will be good for those servants whose master finds them
ready, even if he comes in the second or third watch of the night.
39But understand this: If the owner of the house had known at what
hour the thief was coming, he would not have let his house be broken
into. 40You also must be ready, because the Son of Man will come at
an hour when you do not expect him."
41Peter asked, "Lord, are you telling this parable to us, or to everyone?"
42The Lord answered, "Who then is the faithful and wise manager,
whom the master puts in charge of his servants to give them their
food allowance at the proper time? 43It will be good for that servant
whom the master finds doing so when he returns. 44I tell you the
truth, he will put him in charge of all his possessions. 45But suppose
the servant says to himself, 'My master is taking a long time in coming,' and he then begins to beat the menservants and maidservants

4. If you had to boil down this passage to a short statement on "the good life," what would it be? Are you there yet?

APPLY 1. On a scale from 1 ("no sweat") to 10 ("panic"), what is the worry quotient in your life right now? **2.** How would you rank yourself on living in a pagan world with kingdom values?

OPEN 1. Are you a night owl or an early bird? Ever fall asleep at the wheel? On a date? At work? **2.** What topics are taboo at your family reunions?

STUDY 1. What is the relationship between watchfulness and worry (vv. 22–34)? **2.** Explain the role reversal described in verse 37. Why does Peter ask the question in verse 41? Why does Jesus answer as he does? **3.** Why does Jesus say they should be ready (vv. 39–40)? Who is the thief? **4.** What should be the attitude and actions of the faithful and wise manager (vv. 42–43)? What could tempt the servants to do wrong (v. 45)? **5.** What is the meaning of verse 48? How would the disciples have interpreted it? **6.** What danger is Jesus warning you about in this section? Which danger is most likely to be a problem for you in the future? **7.** What is the "fire" Jesus is talking about? The baptism? **8.** How and why will Jesus bring division?

12:28 you of little faith. Faith is the opposite of anxiety.

12:29–30 To focus one's energy on the physical necessities of life is to be like a pagan who does not trust God to provide one's needs.

12:29 do not set your heart. Literally, "do not seek."

12:31 seek his kingdom. Having warned the disciples not to focus their attention on the material benefits of this life, Jesus now encourages them to seek the spiritual blessings of God's kingdom. **these things will be given to you.** While the believer may suffer (2 Cor. 11:27), the promise is that if the disciples concentrate on doing the will of God, then their basic needs will be met by him.

12:33 moth. The most expensive clothing is susceptible to insignificant creatures like moths. The treasure of heaven is unassailable (1 Peter 1:4).

12:34 A person's heart loyalty is shown by where his wealth and energy are invested.

12:35 Be dressed. To work or travel a man would gather up the garment with a belt to free his legs for uninhibited movement. This implies the disciples were to be ever ready to serve their Lord. **keep your lamps burning.** Even at night, the disciples were to be prepared to serve.

12:37 It would be an unusual master who would wait on his servants in such a way (John 13:2–5).

12:38 the second or third watch. This would be between 9 p.m. and 3 a.m., when sleep would be most tempting.

12:42 manager. When a wealthy homeowner was away, he would appoint one of his servants to be in charge of his affairs during his absence. One of his responsibilities was the management of food rations.

12:44 he will put him in charge of all his possessions. The reward here is a shift from a temporary position of responsibility to a permanent position of privilege based on faithful performance of the tasks.

APPLY **1.** If God said to you: "I have a special mission for your life," what would you say? **2.** When has your commitment to Christ caused the break up in a relationship? **3.** How much of the daily decisions in your life are influenced by your commitment to Jesus?

OPEN **1.** Who is the weather forecaster in your family? How accurate? **2.** Have you ever appeared in traffic court?

STUDY **1.** If you were a farmer who lived and died by the weather, what would you understand from Jesus' words in verses 54–59? **2.** What is the point in Jesus' recommendation to the crowd to settle out of court before seeing the magistrate? **3.** Who does Jesus sound like in 13:1–5? How would his words affect these people? **4.** In the parable of the fig tree, what does the fig tree represent: The owner? Farmer? **5.** How would you describe the tone in Jesus' voice in these passages? Do you think the crowd realized the importance of his message? **6.** How would you compare the urgency that Jesus showed to the desire in the church today to get the gospel out?

and to eat and drink and get drunk. 46The master of that servant will come on a day when he does not expect him and at an hour he is not aware of. He will cut him to pieces and assign him a place with the unbelievers.

47"That servant who knows his master's will and does not get ready or does not do what his master wants will be beaten with many blows. 48But the one who does not know and does things deserving punishment will be beaten with few blows. From everyone who has been given much, much will be demanded; and from the one who has been entrusted with much, much more will be asked.

Not Peace but Division

49"I have come to bring fire on the earth, and how I wish it were already kindled! 50But I have a baptism to undergo, and how distressed I am until it is completed! 51Do you think I came to bring peace on earth? No, I tell you, but division. 52From now on there will be five in one family divided against each other, three against two and two against three. 53They will be divided, father against son and son against father, mother against daughter and daughter against mother, mother-in-law against daughter-in-law and daughter-in-law against mother-in-law."

Interpreting the Times

54He said to the crowd: "When you see a cloud rising in the west, immediately you say, 'It's going to rain,' and it does. 55And when the south wind blows, you say, 'It's going to be hot,' and it is. 56Hypocrites! You know how to interpret the appearance of the earth and the sky. How is it that you don't know how to interpret this present time?

57"Why don't you judge for yourselves what is right? 58As you are going with your adversary to the magistrate, try hard to be reconciled to him on the way, or he may drag you off to the judge, and the judge turn you over to the officer, and the officer throw you into prison. 59I tell you, you will not get out until you have paid the last penny.[a]"

Repent or Perish

13 Now there were some present at that time who told Jesus about the Galileans whose blood Pilate had mixed with their sacrifices. 2Jesus answered, "Do you think that these Galileans were worse sinners than all the other Galileans because they suffered this

[a]59 Greek *lepton*

12:46 He will cut him to pieces and assign him a place with the unbelievers. While the method of executing a person by cutting him into pieces is grotesque, the addition of the second phrase may imply that we are to understand it as a metaphor picturing cutting off of this person from his former household.

12:49 fire. Fire is used both as a symbol of judgment (3:16; Acts 2:19) and of the Holy Spirit (3:16; Acts 2:4).

12:50 baptism. This word was used in a figurative way to describe being overwhelmed by a catastrophe. Before the Spirit's purifying work can begin, the fire of God's judgment must first be experienced by Jesus on the cross. **completed.** The death of Jesus was the essential reason for his incarnation, his coming in the flesh.

12:51 Do you think I came to bring peace on earth? While this is Jesus' ultimate mission (2:14), it would not come about in the way the disciples must have originally thought. The expectation was that the Messiah would usher in a period of peace and prosperity for Israel.

12:57–59 Just as a person would seek an out-of-court settlement with an accuser to avoid facing a judge, so people ought to avoid God's courtroom and pursue reconciliation with him now before the coming judgment.

13:1 the Galileans whose blood Pilate had mixed with their sacrifices. This may refer to an earlier incident. Pilate was noted for his cruel, oppressive actions.

way? 3I tell you, no! But unless you repent, you too will all perish.
4Or those eighteen who died when the tower in Siloam fell on them—
do you think they were more guilty than all the others living in Jerusalem? 5I tell you, no! But unless you repent, you too will all perish."
6Then he told this parable: "A man had a fig tree, planted in his
vineyard, and he went to look for fruit on it, but did not find any. 7So
he said to the man who took care of the vineyard, 'For three years
now I've been coming to look for fruit on this fig tree and haven't
found any. Cut it down! Why should it use up the soil?'
8" 'Sir,' the man replied, 'leave it alone for one more year, and I'll
dig around it and fertilize it. 9If it bears fruit next year, fine! If not,
then cut it down.' "

A Crippled Woman Healed on the Sabbath

10On a Sabbath Jesus was teaching in one of the synagogues, 11and
a woman was there who had been crippled by a spirit for eighteen
years. She was bent over and could not straighten up at all. 12When
Jesus saw her, he called her forward and said to her, "Woman, you are
set free from your infirmity." 13Then he put his hands on her, and immediately she straightened up and praised God.
14Indignant because Jesus had healed on the Sabbath, the synagogue ruler said to the people, "There are six days for work. So come
and be healed on those days, not on the Sabbath."
15The Lord answered him, "You hypocrites! Doesn't each of you on
the Sabbath untie his ox or donkey from the stall and lead it out to
give it water? 16Then should not this woman, a daughter of Abraham,
whom Satan has kept bound for eighteen long years, be set free on
the Sabbath day from what bound her?"
17When he said this, all his opponents were humiliated, but the
people were delighted with all the wonderful things he was doing.

The Parables of the Mustard Seed and the Yeast

18Then Jesus asked, "What is the kingdom of God like? What shall I
compare it to? 19It is like a mustard seed, which a man took and
planted in his garden. It grew and became a tree, and the birds of the
air perched in its branches."
20Again he asked, "What shall I compare the kingdom of God to?

APPLY If you could compare your own spiritual life to a sports game, what's the sport and what's the score? What's your game plan for the next few minutes in the game?

OPEN When you were growing up, what was special about Sunday? What was taboo?

STUDY 1. Can you imagine anyone objecting to Jesus helping this woman, even on the Sabbath? **2.** What does verse 11 tell you about the author's knowledge of medicine? Of spiritual phenomena? What is it about doctors that makes them go into such detail? **3.** How does Jesus deal with the chairman of the synagogue Board of Trustees? What about the ruler's comment caused Jesus to call him a hypocrite? **4.** What is the lesson in the mustard seed and yeast for the church today?

APPLY 1. What are you going to do when your children break some of the rules of your church, or worse, stop going? **2.** How much growth have you seen in your spiritual life recently?

13:4 the tower in Siloam. Siloam was a reservoir located near the southeast corner of Jerusalem. The tower Jesus refers to may have been one built for fortification or in conjunction with an aqueduct that was part of the city's water supply. As with the slain Galileans (vv. 2–3), those killed when the tower collapsed were not more sinful than the other residents of the city; indeed, all of them needed to repent as well.

13:6 fig tree ... vineyard. Since vineyards were really more like fruit gardens, the presence of such a tree was not unusual.

13:7–9 While the owner wants to cut down the tree, the caretaker of the garden desires to cultivate. Jesus points out God's patience toward his people and the reality that a day of accounting is coming.

13:11 This woman's disease appears to have been a fusion of the spinal column, causing great pain and making it impossible for her to stand erect.

13:15–16 Jesus lashes out at the foolishness of legalism that allows for caring for the needs of animals on the Sabbath while invalidating the care he gave to this woman.

13:16 a daughter of Abraham. The severity of her infirmity may have led many to assume she was being punished for an especially bad sin and thus was not considered by God as one of his people. Jesus affirms her as a true Israelite (Gal. 3:7). **set free on the Sabbath.** One of the purposes of the Sabbath was to be a weekly reminder of the freedom for which God had delivered his people from Egypt (Deut. 5:15). By overcoming Satan's grip on this woman on the Sabbath, Jesus, far from defiling the day, demonstrates its true significance.

13:19 mustard seed. The mustard plant is the smallest seed, yet its shrubs grew to about 10 feet high.

13:20–21 While yeast was generally a symbol of something evil (Mark 8:15),

[21]It is like yeast that a woman took and mixed into a large amount[a] of
flour until it worked all through the dough."

The Narrow Door

[22]Then Jesus went through the towns and villages, teaching as he
made his way to Jerusalem. [23]Someone asked him, "Lord, are only a
few people going to be saved?"

He said to them, [24]"Make every effort to enter through the narrow
door, because many, I tell you, will try to enter and will not be able to.
[25]Once the owner of the house gets up and closes the door, you will
stand outside knocking and pleading, 'Sir, open the door for us.'

"But he will answer, 'I don't know you or where you come from.'
[26]"Then you will say, 'We ate and drank with you, and you taught in
our streets.'

[27]"But he will reply, 'I don't know you or where you come from.
Away from me, all you evildoers!'

[28]"There will be weeping there, and gnashing of teeth, when you
see Abraham, Isaac and Jacob and all the prophets in the kingdom of
God, but you yourselves thrown out. [29]People will come from east
and west and north and south, and will take their places at the feast
in the kingdom of God. [30]Indeed there are those who are last who will
be first, and first who will be last."

Jesus' Sorrow for Jerusalem

[31]At that time some Pharisees came to Jesus and said to him,
"Leave this place and go somewhere else. Herod wants to kill you."
[32]He replied, "Go tell that fox, 'I will drive out demons and heal
people today and tomorrow, and on the third day I will reach my
goal.' [33]In any case, I must keep going today and tomorrow and the
next day—for surely no prophet can die outside Jerusalem!

[34]"O Jerusalem, Jerusalem, you who kill the prophets and stone
those sent to you, how often I have longed to gather your children
together, as a hen gathers her chicks under her wings, but you were
not willing! [35]Look, your house is left to you desolate. I tell you, you

[a]21 Greek *three satas* (probably about 1/2 bushel or 22 liters)

OPEN **1.** What happened the last time you were locked out of your house or car? **2.** What place do you identify with your spiritual roots?

STUDY **1.** With only a few weeks left in his ministry on earth, what is Jesus concerned about? **2.** Since God "so loved the world," why doesn't he make the door wider? Why isn't eating and drinking with Jesus enough? **3.** How does Jesus answer the question, "Are only a few going to be saved? **4.** How do you think Jesus is feeling as he gets closer to Jerusalem? **5.** How would you describe his mental state at this time? What do you think is causing this anguish? **6.** How does he deal with the threat that King Herod is going to kill him?

APPLY **1.** How can our loving God leave people outside the narrow door? **2.** On a scale from 1 to 10, how would you rank yourself on desire to do the will of God?

---

here it is positive, symbolizing growth and transformation.

13:21 a large amount of flour. Literally, "three measures"—which would be almost 160 cups of flour! This would make enough bread for over 100 people.

13:23 saved. This word serves as a shorthand way of expressing deliverance from God's judgment and entrance into a relationship of peace with him (Mark 10:26; Acts 2:47; 16:29–31; 1 Cor. 1:18; 2 Cor. 2:15). It is synonymous with entering the kingdom of God (12:32) and *inheriting eternal life* (18:18).

13:24 Make every effort. In contrast to the assumption that being born as a Jew was all that was required for entry into the Messiah's kingdom, Jesus, like John the Baptist (3:8), teaches that obedience to the commands of God is evidence of true repentance (Matt. 7:13–14,21).

13:25–27 The picture is of people wishing at the last moment to respond to the invitation of a distinguished man holding a dinner party (14:15–24). While they protest that familiarity with the host should be grounds for their admission, the reason for their rejection is found in a paraphrase of Psalm 6:8 ("Away from me, all you who do evil ..."). They are evildoers shut out from God's presence.

13:30 This saying of Jesus implies that Gentiles, the last to hear of God's grace, may actually respond to his invitation, while many in Israel will find it much more difficult to respond.

13:31 Herod's dominion included Galilee and Perea, the probable location of Jesus at this point.

13:32 tell that fox. Sometimes the fox was used as a symbol of a cunning person. Note that the image with strength like the lion isn't used here. The reference to the "third day" would bring Jesus' resurrection to mind for Luke's readers.

13:33 Prophets, like Jeremiah, did die outside Jerusalem. The force of the saying is, that just as the authorities associated with the temple in Jerusalem consistently opposed the prophets and executed some of them, so Jesus will experience the same fate.

will not see me again until you say, 'Blessed is he who comes in the
name of the Lord.'[a]"

Jesus at a Pharisee's House

14 One Sabbath, when Jesus went to eat in the house of a prominent Pharisee, he was being carefully watched. 2There in
front of him was a man suffering from dropsy. 3Jesus asked the Pharisees and experts in the law, "Is it lawful to heal on the Sabbath or
not?" 4But they remained silent. So taking hold of the man, he healed
him and sent him away.
5Then he asked them, "If one of you has a son[b] or an ox that falls
into a well on the Sabbath day, will you not immediately pull him
out?" 6And they had nothing to say.
7When he noticed how the guests picked the places of honor at the
table, he told them this parable: 8"When someone invites you to a
wedding feast, do not take the place of honor, for a person more
distinguished than you may have been invited. 9If so, the host who
invited both of you will come and say to you, 'Give this man your
seat.' Then, humiliated, you will have to take the least important
place. 10But when you are invited, take the lowest place, so that when
your host comes, he will say to you, 'Friend, move up to a better
place.' Then you will be honored in the presence of all your fellow
guests. 11For everyone who exalts himself will be humbled, and he
who humbles himself will be exalted."
12Then Jesus said to his host, "When you give a luncheon or dinner,
do not invite your friends, your brothers or relatives, or your rich
neighbors; if you do, they may invite you back and so you will be
repaid. 13But when you give a banquet, invite the poor, the crippled,
the lame, the blind, 14and you will be blessed. Although they cannot
repay you, you will be repaid at the resurrection of the righteous."

The Parable of the Great Banquet

15When one of those at the table with him heard this, he said to
Jesus, "Blessed is the man who will eat at the feast in the kingdom of
God."
16Jesus replied: "A certain man was preparing a great banquet and
invited many guests. 17At the time of the banquet he sent his servant
to tell those who had been invited, 'Come, for everything is now
ready.'
18"But they all alike began to make excuses. The first said, 'I have

[a]35 Psalm 118:26 [b]5 Some manuscripts *donkey*

OPEN If you could have the best seats in the house, what would you choose: Super Bowl? A rock concert? Philharmonic orchestra? Indy 500? Royal wedding?

STUDY 1. What's the situation here: The day? Host? Atmosphere? **2.** What does Jesus do to heal the man and to instruct the Pharisees (vv. 2–6)? What does their silence mean? **3.** How does Jesus' view of honor (vv. 7–11) vary from that held by others at the meal? **4.** What does this passage teach you about the differences between kingdom values and secular values? **5.** If you reviewed your dinner guest list for the last 12 months, how would it compare with verses 12–14?

APPLY 1. In your early spiritual pilgrimage, who spent time with you? What did this do for you? **2.** Who is someone you have been thinking about that you would like to have over for dinner—and invite to this group?

OPEN What do you do to have a party with your best friends?

STUDY 1. What did Jesus say in verses 12–14 that brought on this parable? **2.** What do you think the "great banquet" represents (v. 16) ? **3.** What excuses did the invited guests give? Were any of these legitimate? **4.** Who are the "poor ... the crippled ... the blind and the lame"? How would these people

14:2 dropsy. Literally, "full of water." This fluid retention was not in actuality a disease, but a sign of disease of the heart, kidneys or liver.

14:5 The first lesson of this dinner party lay in Jesus' exposure of their callous attitude toward people's needs in contrast to their sensitivity to the plight of animals (13:15; Matt. 12:11).

14:8 the place of honor. The scene envisioned here is that of the embarrassment that would be experienced by someone who assumed he or she should be in a place of honor and took that position apart from the host's invitation. When the guest for whom the host had reserved that spot arrived, the presumptuous guest would be humiliated by having to give up the seat.

14:15 Blessed is the man. The bliss of life with God was often pictured in terms of a feast (Isa. 25:6; 55:2; 65:13).

14:16–17 invited ... sent his servant to tell. In well-to-do circles, invitations to honored guests for a formal dinner were issued well in advance, but the specific time to arrive was communicated on the day of the event when everything was ready (Esther 5:8; 6:14).

14:18–20 Jesus' listeners would immediately see these excuses as an obvious attempt to insult the host.

14:18 I must go and see it. Then, as now, people would not buy property first and then look at it later!

feel? **5.** Do you think the "prominent Pharisee" (v. 1) who was sitting there when Jesus said these things (especially v. 24) got the point? What is the point?

APPLY 1. As you share your faith with your friends, what is their excuse for not committing their life to Jesus? **2.** Which of your friends has come to faith that you never expected?

OPEN 1. In your family, who is the most competitive? **2.** Who usually wins at Monopoly?

STUDY 1. If you said to the church today what Jesus said to the crowds in verses 25–27, what would happen? Has your commitment to follow Jesus ever cost you a friendship? **2.** What does Jesus advise anyone to do before making a commitment to follow him? **3.** If he wanted to make the same point for a modern audience, what would he use to illustrate instead of the tower builder, the war strategist and the salt? Do you think good business principles make good spiritual principles?

APPLY When push comes to shove, are you more likely to pay attention to your career and business affairs or your spiritual growth? Can you do both?

---

just bought a field, and I must go and see it. Please excuse me.'
19"Another said, 'I have just bought five yoke of oxen, and I'm on
my way to try them out. Please excuse me.'
20"Still another said, 'I just got married, so I can't come.'
21"The servant came back and reported this to his master. Then the
owner of the house became angry and ordered his servant, 'Go out
quickly into the streets and alleys of the town and bring in the poor,
the crippled, the blind and the lame.'
22"'Sir,' the servant said, 'what you ordered has been done, but
there is still room.'
23"Then the master told his servant, 'Go out to the roads and country lanes and make them come in, so that my house will be full. 24I tell
you, not one of those men who were invited will get a taste of my
banquet.'"

The Cost of Being a Disciple

25Large crowds were traveling with Jesus, and turning to them he
said: 26"If anyone comes to me and does not hate his father and
mother, his wife and children, his brothers and sisters—yes, even his
own life—he cannot be my disciple. 27And anyone who does not carry
his cross and follow me cannot be my disciple.
28"Suppose one of you wants to build a tower. Will he not first sit
down and estimate the cost to see if he has enough money to complete it? 29For if he lays the foundation and is not able to finish it,
everyone who sees it will ridicule him, 30saying, 'This fellow began to
build and was not able to finish.'
31"Or suppose a king is about to go to war against another king.
Will he not first sit down and consider whether he is able with ten
thousand men to oppose the one coming against him with twenty
thousand? 32If he is not able, he will send a delegation while the
other is still a long way off and will ask for terms of peace. 33In the
same way, any of you who does not give up everything he has cannot
be my disciple.
34"Salt is good, but if it loses its saltiness, how can it be made salty
again? 35It is fit neither for the soil nor for the manure pile; it is
thrown out.

"He who has ears to hear, let him hear."

14:20 married. Marriage plans were made far in advance; the man certainly would have known of his plans for marriage when he received the original invitation to the banquet. The net effect of all these excuses is that property, oxen and marital duties were more important than the guests' relationship to the host.

14:21 streets. These are probably the public squares where beggars gathered, hoping for handouts. **the poor, the crippled, the blind and the lame.** These people were all social outcasts reduced to begging for survival. Those normally considered unworthy are indeed the ones who are included (1:52–53; 4:18–19; 6:20–22; 7:22).

14:23 make them come in. The persuasion in view here is meant to convince these incredulous outcasts that they really are welcomed to the banquet. Middle East etiquette requires people of a low social rank to refuse invitations from those of a higher social status.

14:27 carry his cross. This does not mean followers of Christ should seek out ways to suffer. It means that a follower of Jesus needs to be willing to go where he is sent and do what he asks.

14:28–30 This is the first of three parables communicating the need for serious consideration of what it means to be Jesus' disciple. Just as it would be foolish to begin building a tower before contemplating the costs involved, so Jesus is discouraging people from following him based upon wrong assumptions and ideas of what his kingdom involves.

14:31–32 The second parable reinforces the first. Only a foolish king would attempt to wage a war before considering if there is realistic hope for success. A would-be disciple had better consider what is involved in the course he or she is undertaking.

14:33 any of you who does not give up everything he has. Just as one should count the costs before beginning, so the disciple must be ready to give up all to follow Jesus.

The Parable of the Lost Sheep

15 Now the tax collectors and "sinners" were all gathering
around to hear him. 2But the Pharisees and the teachers of
the law muttered, "This man welcomes sinners and eats with them."
3Then Jesus told them this parable: 4"Suppose one of you has a
hundred sheep and loses one of them. Does he not leave the ninety-
nine in the open country and go after the lost sheep until he finds it?
5And when he finds it, he joyfully puts it on his shoulders 6and goes
home. Then he calls his friends and neighbors together and says, 'Rejoice with me; I have found my lost sheep.' 7I tell you that in the same
way there will be more rejoicing in heaven over one sinner who repents
than over ninety-nine righteous persons who do not need to repent.

The Parable of the Lost Coin

8"Or suppose a woman has ten silver coins[a] and loses one. Does
she not light a lamp, sweep the house and search carefully until she
finds it? 9And when she finds it, she calls her friends and neighbors
together and says, 'Rejoice with me; I have found my lost coin.' 10In
the same way, I tell you, there is rejoicing in the presence of the
angels of God over one sinner who repents."

The Parable of the Lost Son

11Jesus continued: "There was a man who had two sons. 12The
younger one said to his father, 'Father, give me my share of the
estate.' So he divided his property between them.
13"Not long after that, the younger son got together all he had, set
off for a distant country and there squandered his wealth in wild
living. 14After he had spent everything, there was a severe famine in
that whole country, and he began to be in need. 15So he went and
hired himself out to a citizen of that country, who sent him to his
fields to feed pigs. 16He longed to fill his stomach with the pods that
the pigs were eating, but no one gave him anything.

[a]8 Greek *ten drachmas,* each worth about a day's wages

OPEN Which of your possessions were recently lost? Recently found?

STUDY 1. Who are tax collectors and "sinners"? Who are the Pharisees and teachers of the law? What is their accusation? **2.** In the parable of the lost sheep and the lost coin, how does Jesus answer the mutterings of the Pharisees? Would the Pharisees agree that the recovery of the lost sheep and the lost coin is worth the risk of being contaminated by eating with sinners? **3.** Who are the "lost sheep" today? Is your church targeted for the "ninety and nine" or the "lost sheep"? What are you doing to find "tax collectors and sinners"?

APPLY Before you committed your life to Christ, who took a chance and reached out to you? ________________

OPEN 1. Where are you in the birth order of your family—youngest, oldest, in the middle? **2.** How old were you when you left home? Where did you go? What did you do?

STUDY 1. What caused the younger brother to want to leave home? Was he ready? **2.** If you had been the father, would you have given him his inheritance early? Would you have gone to look for the son in a "far country"? **3.** What caused the younger brother to "come to his senses"? **4.** Do you think the father

---

15:1 tax collectors and sinners. Tax collectors were the only ones who knew how much people were required to pay. They often charged more and kept the rest for themselves. For this reason, they were especially hated.

15:2 As much as possible, strict Pharisees avoided religious, social or business relations with Jews who did not adhere to their traditions. Jesus' relationship with such sinners scandalized the religious sensibilities of these leaders.

15:4 the open country. This was a desolate area with many cliffs. A lone sheep in such an environment was in great danger from wild animals or from falling over the cliffs.

15:7 rejoicing in heaven. It is a wonderful truth that God rejoices over the repentance of a sinner (Zeph. 3:17). Jesus is subtly forcing his listeners to consider the implications of the fact that God rejoices over the so-called sinners but not over those that feel they have no need of repentance.

15:8 ten silver coins. This might represent her dowry. One of these coins was equal to about a day's wage for a laborer and represented a substantial loss for a person who lived a hand-to-mouth existence. **light a lamp.** Peasant homes were poorly illuminated because of a lack of windows. **sweep the house.** A coin could easily be obscured since floors were just dirt covered with straw.

15:10 there is rejoicing. The angels, who continually dwell in the presence of God, witness God's joy over the conversion of just such a sinner. The self-righteous attitude of the Pharisees which had prevented them from seeking others in love also kept them from sharing in God's joy over repentant sinners.

15:12 give me my share. Under Jewish law, the younger of two sons would receive one-third of the estate upon his father's death (Deut. 21:17). While a father might divide up his property before he died if he wished, this son's request would be considered unbelievably callous. In essence, he implies that the fact that his father still lives is getting in the way of his plans.

15:15 pigs. Pigs were ceremonially unclean animals (Lev. 11:7) and Jews would not eat, raise or touch them. The fact that he was caring for pigs implies he was working for a Gentile as well.

15:16 the pods. While eating the food of pigs sounds terrible even to modern readers, for the Pharisees it would have been utterly horrifying.

was wise in throwing a party when the son returned? **5.** How do you think the older son felt when he heard about the party? **6.** What prevented the older brother from coming to the homecoming party? **7.** If you could invite one of these two brothers to your group, who would you invite? **8.** Who is going to make a better parent—the younger or the older son? **9.** If you had to go to one of the two brothers with a deep personal problem, who would you choose?

APPLY 1. Of the two brothers, which reminds you of your own story? **2.** In your spiritual pilgrimage, what do you identify as your "far country" time? **3.** Where are you right now in your spiritual pilgrimage?

17 "When he came to his senses, he said, 'How many of my father's
hired men have food to spare, and here I am starving to death! 18 I will
set out and go back to my father and say to him: Father, I have sinned
against heaven and against you. 19 I am no longer worthy to be called
your son; make me like one of your hired men.' 20 So he got up and
went to his father.

"But while he was still a long way off, his father saw him and was
filled with compassion for him; he ran to his son, threw his arms
around him and kissed him.

21 "The son said to him, 'Father, I have sinned against heaven and
against you. I am no longer worthy to be called your son.[a]'

22 "But the father said to his servants, 'Quick! Bring the best robe
and put it on him. Put a ring on his finger and sandals on his feet.
23 Bring the fattened calf and kill it. Let's have a feast and celebrate.
24 For this son of mine was dead and is alive again; he was lost and is
found.' So they began to celebrate.

25 "Meanwhile, the older son was in the field. When he came near
the house, he heard music and dancing. 26 So he called one of the servants and asked him what was going on. 27 'Your brother has come,'
he replied, 'and your father has killed the fattened calf because he
has him back safe and sound.'

28 "The older brother became angry and refused to go in. So his father went out and pleaded with him. 29 But he answered his father,
'Look! All these years I've been slaving for you and never disobeyed
your orders. Yet you never gave me even a young goat so I could celebrate with my friends. 30 But when this son of yours who has squandered your property with prostitutes comes home, you kill the
fattened calf for him!'

31 " 'My son,' the father said, 'you are always with me, and everything I have is yours. 32 But we had to celebrate and be glad, because
this brother of yours was dead and is alive again; he was lost and is
found.' "

[a]21 Some early manuscripts *son. Make me like one of your hired men.*

15:20 his father saw him. The implication is the father had been waiting and hoping to see his son return one day. **ran to his son.** It was degrading for an elderly man to run to anyone, especially to someone who had so disgraced him. This presents staggering insight into the response of the Almighty Holy God to a repentant sinner. At this point, the wayward son reflects true repentance (v. 21).

15:22 the best robe. This would have been the father's best robe. This is a sign that people should honor him as they honor the father. **a ring.** The signet ring gives the son the authority to represent the father. **sandals.** Being shoeless was a sign of a slave. To wear shoes indicated a man was free to go where he pleased.

15:23 fattened calf. The fact that it was a calf that was prepared indicates that the whole village was invited to come to the feast.

15:28 This son's refusal to enter the house would have been seen as a sign of grave disrespect, since the eldest son was expected to play the part of a gracious host at a family feast. As he did with the younger son, the father "went out" to "plead with" the older son. This too was an overwhelming display of grace.

15:29 Look! This would have been considered an extremely rude way for a son to address his father, since there is no hint of respect or affection. **I've been slaving for you.** Ironically, this son views his ongoing relationship with his father in the way the younger son hoped he might be privileged to have.

15:30 this son of yours. This is a derisive way of denying his relationship with him as a brother.

15:31–32 everything I have is yours. This would assure the older son that he is in no danger of losing his inheritance because of the presence of his younger brother. He, too, should celebrate his brother's homecoming. We are not told what the older son does. Jesus purposely leaves the story open-ended.

The Parable of the Shrewd Manager

16 Jesus told his disciples: "There was a rich man whose manager was accused of wasting his possessions. 2 So he called
him in and asked him, 'What is this I hear about you? Give an account
of your management, because you cannot be manager any longer.'
3 "The manager said to himself, 'What shall I do now? My master is
taking away my job. I'm not strong enough to dig, and I'm ashamed
to beg— 4 I know what I'll do so that, when I lose my job here, people
will welcome me into their houses.'
5 "So he called in each one of his master's debtors. He asked the
first, 'How much do you owe my master?'
6 " 'Eight hundred gallons[a] of olive oil,' he replied.
"The manager told him, 'Take your bill, sit down quickly, and make
it four hundred.'
7 "Then he asked the second, 'And how much do you owe?'
" 'A thousand bushels[b] of wheat,' he replied.
"He told him, 'Take your bill and make it eight hundred.'
8 "The master commended the dishonest manager because he had
acted shrewdly. For the people of this world are more shrewd in dealing with their own kind than are the people of the light. 9 I tell you,
use worldly wealth to gain friends for yourselves, so that when it is
gone, you will be welcomed into eternal dwellings.
10 "Whoever can be trusted with very little can also be trusted with
much, and whoever is dishonest with very little will also be dishonest
with much. 11 So if you have not been trustworthy in handling worldly
wealth, who will trust you with true riches? 12 And if you have not

[a]6 Greek *one hundred batous* (probably about 3 kiloliters) [b]7 Greek *one hundred korous* (probably about 35 kiloliters)

OPEN What was your first job? How much did you make? Who was your supervisor?

STUDY 1. Who is this parable told to? **2.** Do you think the manager was guilty of embezzling funds from the owner? **3.** What are the options for the manager when he is fired? What does he decide to do? **4.** What exactly is the manager commended for? If you were an accountant, would you have a problem with the bookkeeping? **5.** The parable does not tell what happened to the dishonest manager. Do you think the owner forgave him and gave him back his old job? **6.** What is the lesson here for the disciples (v. 11)? What about for people that squander the gifts that God has entrusted to them today?

APPLY 1. When did you come to the place that you got off the fence about who was going to be the master of your life? **2.** How are you at investing God's gifts in you for his kingdom?

16:1 told his disciples. Luke tells us that the intended audience of this parable is not the Pharisees, but the disciples. **whose manager.** Landowners commonly hired someone to manage the day-to-day affairs of their estates. The debtors (v. 5) were tenant farmers who would give an annual amount of produce to the landowner as rent. The master in this parable, hearing rumors of mismanagement (which he evidently felt were substantiated), fires his chief steward.

16:2 What is this I hear about you? Literally, this is "What is it that I have been hearing ..." implying an ongoing series of complaints. No specific charges are made, but the manager is dismissed. The manager's lack of any protest implies his acknowledgment of his guilt. **Give an account.** This is better understood as "turn in your books." Since it would be assumed that a dishonest manager had probably doctored the books, they would not be looked at in order to find evidence to fire him; he is simply to "clean out his desk."

16:3 I'm not strong enough to dig. This man was not use to manual labor. Some of Jesus' followers, many of whom were manual laborers, probably would see him as being rather prissy. **I'm ashamed to beg.** Since he is unable to do physically demanding work and he would be considered unsuitable for another position as a manager, begging appears to be his only other alternative. However, the social stigma associated with that is more than he can bear.

16:4 I know what I'll do. Realizing a job reference would be hard to obtain from the landowner, the manager decides on a plan to ingratiate himself with the landowner's debtors.

16:5–7 This reduction of debts was done quickly to avoid discovery by the master (v. 6). Since the tenants assumed the manager was still in the employ of the landowner, the renters would be grateful to the manager for his concern for them. The tenants would quickly spread the news throughout the village that the master had been gracious, making it socially impossible for the master to deny that he had authorized such reductions.

16:6–7 The assumption is that the master has let out his land to tenants, who have agreed to pay him a fixed return in grain and oil. The amounts owed indicate that this master was quite wealthy indeed. The reduction of 400 gallons of olive oil and 200 bushels of wheat both amount to the same in cash value, about 500 denarii.

16:8 Despite his loss, the landowner cannot help but admit the manager's cleverness. **dishonest.** Literally, "unrighteous." It connotes a person who lives by the standards of the world at large as opposed to those of God's kingdom. The man's moral sense is not being commended; his taking appropriate action to protect himself is. The disciple is likewise called to take action in the face of the coming judgment. **shrewd.** Hebrew and Aramaic translations of this word translate it as "wisdom." If an unjust man shows such wisdom in making provision for his future, how much more ought the children of light show wisdom in preparing for their future in the face of the certain judgment of God?

been trustworthy with someone else's property, who will give you property of your own?

13“No servant can serve two masters. Either he will hate the one and love the other, or he will be devoted to the one and despise the other. You cannot serve both God and Money.”

14The Pharisees, who loved money, heard all this and were sneering at Jesus. 15He said to them, “You are the ones who justify yourselves in the eyes of men, but God knows your hearts. What is highly valued among men is detestable in God's sight.

Additional Teachings

16“The Law and the Prophets were proclaimed until John. Since that time, the good news of the kingdom of God is being preached, and everyone is forcing his way into it. 17It is easier for heaven and earth to disappear than for the least stroke of a pen to drop out of the Law.

18“Anyone who divorces his wife and marries another woman commits adultery, and the man who marries a divorced woman commits adultery.

The Rich Man and Lazarus

19“There was a rich man who was dressed in purple and fine linen and lived in luxury every day. 20At his gate was laid a beggar named Lazarus, covered with sores 21and longing to eat what fell from the rich man's table. Even the dogs came and licked his sores.

22“The time came when the beggar died and the angels carried him to Abraham's side. The rich man also died and was buried. 23In hell,[a] where he was in torment, he looked up and saw Abraham far away, with Lazarus by his side. 24So he called to him, ‘Father Abraham, have pity on me and send Lazarus to dip the tip of his finger in water and cool my tongue, because I am in agony in this fire.’

25“But Abraham replied, ‘Son, remember that in your lifetime you received your good things, while Lazarus received bad things, but now he is comforted here and you are in agony. 26And besides all this, between us and you a great chasm has been fixed, so that those who want to go from here to you cannot, nor can anyone cross over from there to us.’

27“He answered, ‘Then I beg you, father, send Lazarus to my father's house, 28for I have five brothers. Let him warn them, so that they will not also come to this place of torment.’

[a]23 Greek *Hades*

OPEN What do you remember about your high school senior prom? How did you dress? Where did you go?

STUDY 1. Who is in the audience when Jesus speaks in this passage (v. 14)? **2.** How do the lives of the rich man and Lazarus compare on earth (vv. 19–21)? After death (vv. 22–24)? **3.** How would the rich Pharisees in the audience feel? How do you feel about this passage? **4.** When Abraham refuses the request of the rich man to send Lazarus to warn the five brothers, what is his reason? What did Moses and the prophets teach about poor people that the five brothers of the rich man must “repent” of? **5.** Is Jesus trying to teach in this passage that entrance into heaven is based on the way you live your life on earth? How does this fit into the gospel?

16:19 purple and fine linen. Only the rich could afford dyed woolen clothes and the fine cotton linen probably manufactured in Egypt. The Romans even set standards regarding who was permitted to wear purple and how much purple one could wear. It was generally reserved for high officials or members of a royal family.

16:20 Lazarus. His name means “he whom God helps,” indicating the poor man's piety before God. He was diseased and apparently crippled. He represents everything that contrasts with the status of the rich man.

16:21 longing to eat what fell. Since there were no eating utensils at this time, people ate with their hands. After the meal, wealthy people would clean their hands by wiping them on pieces of bread which would then be discarded. It is this “trash” that Lazarus hopes to be given. **Even the dogs.** Jewish people saw dogs as unclean animals, and being licked by them would be seen as a great indignity.

16:26 a great chasm has been fixed. The uncrossable gap between them indicates the finality of God's judgment on the matter. It is said earlier that the rich man could see Lazarus and Abraham (v. 23). However, since Lazarus never says anything on his own behalf, it is uncertain how much he is aware of the plight of the rich man.

16:27–28 This introduces the second lesson of the passage. In light of his fate, the man urges Abraham to send Lazarus as a warning to his brothers

[29]"Abraham replied, 'They have Moses and the Prophets; let them
listen to them.'
[30]" 'No, father Abraham,' he said, 'but if someone from the dead
goes to them, they will repent.'
[31]"He said to him, 'If they do not listen to Moses and the Prophets,
they will not be convinced even if someone rises from the dead.' "

Sin, Faith, Duty

17 Jesus said to his disciples: "Things that cause people to sin
are bound to come, but woe to that person through whom
they come. [2]It would be better for him to be thrown into the sea with
a millstone tied around his neck than for him to cause one of these
little ones to sin. [3]So watch yourselves.
"If your brother sins, rebuke him, and if he repents, forgive him. [4]If
he sins against you seven times in a day, and seven times comes back
to you and says, 'I repent,' forgive him."
[5]The apostles said to the Lord, "Increase our faith!"
[6]He replied, "If you have faith as small as a mustard seed, you can
say to this mulberry tree, 'Be uprooted and planted in the sea,' and it
will obey you.
[7]"Suppose one of you had a servant plowing or looking after the
sheep. Would he say to the servant when he comes in from the field,
'Come along now and sit down to eat'? [8]Would he not rather say, 'Prepare my supper, get yourself ready and wait on me while I eat and
drink; after that you may eat and drink'? [9]Would he thank the servant
because he did what he was told to do? [10]So you also, when you have
done everything you were told to do, should say, 'We are unworthy
servants; we have only done our duty.' "

Ten Healed of Leprosy

[11]Now on his way to Jerusalem, Jesus traveled along the border between Samaria and Galilee. [12]As he was going into a village, ten men
who had leprosy[a] met him. They stood at a distance [13]and called out
in a loud voice, "Jesus, Master, have pity on us!"
[14]When he saw them, he said, "Go, show yourselves to the priests."
And as they went, they were cleansed.

[a]*12* The Greek word was used for various diseases affecting the skin—not necessarily leprosy.

APPLY 1. Who do you admire for the way they balance their spiritual commitment with a tender social conscience? **2.** What is God calling you to do for people like Lazarus in your town?

OPEN As a child, what was a sure-fire way that your siblings could get your goat?

STUDY 1. Who is the focus of this passage? **2.** Reading between the lines, what has been going on among the disciples? What is the clear teaching in verses 3–4 about broken relationships? How can you do this without reinforcing bad behavior or co-dependency? **3.** How does the disciples' plea in verse 5 relate to the statement in verses 3–4? What does the response (v. 6) of Jesus mean? **4.** What's the principle here for today?

APPLY 1. In a broken relationship, are you more likely to "have it out" with that person or stew over it for days? **2.** Who do you need to call or write today and clear up a bad relationship?

OPEN How are you at writing "thank you" notes?

STUDY 1. What do you think it is like to be a leper? Physically? Emotionally? Socially? **2.** What is significant about the "border" between Samaria and Galilee and the one Samaritan that returned to say thank you?

who are following in his path. The rich man cared for his family; he just was unable to see poor Lazarus as worthy of the same sort of concern.

17:2 millstone. This would be a large, round grinding stone with a hole in the middle. Such a horrible death is preferable to the judgment that will come upon one who leads another into sin. **cause ... to sin.** Literally "to scandalize" (v. 1) in the sense of corrupting the life of another by offering an opportunity to sin or making sin appear legitimate.

17:6 mustard seed. This was the tiniest of all seeds. **Be uprooted.** This is not an invitation for believers to exercise capricious power in prayer, but to illustrate the point that astounding things can result for the person who exercises his or her faith through prayer (Matt. 21:21–22).

17:8–9 The point is not that the master is demanding or ungrateful, but simply that the servant's job involves these tasks. The performance of them is a normal, expected part of the role.

17:10 Obedience to Jesus' commands about purity, radical forgiveness and faith do not merit special reward from God, but are simply qualities expected of those who follow him.

17:12 leprosy. Although this term was used to cover a wide range of skin diseases besides the true leprosy of Hanson's Disease, no diagnosis was dreaded more than leprosy since it brought not only a slow death and physical disfigurement but also social banishment. **stood at a distance.** Lepers were forbidden to approach uninfected people (Lev. 13:45–46).

17:14 Old Testament law required people with skin diseases feared to be leprous to be examined by a priest who would determine if the infection was clearing up or progressing (Lev. 14:1–7). Only upon the priest's declaration of healing could the leper reenter society.

15 One of them, when he saw he was healed, came back, praising
God in a loud voice. 16 He threw himself at Jesus' feet and thanked
him—and he was a Samaritan.
17 Jesus asked, "Were not all ten cleansed? Where are the other
nine? 18 Was no one found to return and give praise to God except this
foreigner?" 19 Then he said to him, "Rise and go; your faith has made
you well."

The Coming of the Kingdom of God

20 Once, having been asked by the Pharisees when the kingdom of
God would come, Jesus replied, "The kingdom of God does not come
with your careful observation, 21 nor will people say, 'Here it is,' or
'There it is,' because the kingdom of God is within[a] you."
22 Then he said to his disciples, "The time is coming when you will
long to see one of the days of the Son of Man, but you will not see it.
23 Men will tell you, 'There he is!' or 'Here he is!' Do not go running off
after them. 24 For the Son of Man in his day[b] will be like the lightning,
which flashes and lights up the sky from one end to the other. 25 But
first he must suffer many things and be rejected by this generation.
26 "Just as it was in the days of Noah, so also will it be in the days of
the Son of Man. 27 People were eating, drinking, marrying and being
given in marriage up to the day Noah entered the ark. Then the flood
came and destroyed them all.
28 "It was the same in the days of Lot. People were eating and drinking, buying and selling, planting and building. 29 But the day Lot left
Sodom, fire and sulfur rained down from heaven and destroyed them
all.
30 "It will be just like this on the day the Son of Man is revealed.
31 On that day no one who is on the roof of his house, with his goods
inside, should go down to get them. Likewise, no one in the field
should go back for anything. 32 Remember Lot's wife! 33 Whoever tries
to keep his life will lose it, and whoever loses his life will preserve it.
34 I tell you, on that night two people will be in one bed; one will
be taken and the other left. 35 Two women will be grinding grain
together; one will be taken and the other left.[c]"

[a]*21 Or among* [b]*24* Some manuscripts do not have *in his day.* [c]*35* Some manuscripts *left.* [36]*Two men will be in the field; one will be taken and the other left.*

APPLY 1. When you were growing up did you take your spiritual heritage for granted? **2.** How are you going to raise your children to appreciate their heritage?

OPEN If your house caught on fire and the pets and children were safe, what two things would you grab?

STUDY 1. How did the discussion in this passage get started? Who ends up getting the lecture? **2.** In answering the Pharisees' question, what does Jesus say about the kingdom—as to when, how or where it is? Does he view the kingdom as a spiritual reality *within* people? Or an outward, social manifestation *among* them? Or is he speaking of their failure to recognize who he is? **3.** What did Jesus mean by "one of the days of the Son of Man" (v. 22)? **4.** How will those days be like the days of Noah and Lot? What is so bad about the way people were living in verses 27–28? What is meant by the warning about Lot's wife (Gen. 19:17–26)? **5.** Verse 37 was a common proverb. What is Jesus saying here? **6.** How would you compare the days of Noah and Lot to our day? How would you compare the responsiveness of people to the gospel?

APPLY 1. What do you believe about the second coming of Jesus Christ? **2.** How much does your belief affect the way you live today?

17:15–16 The one man who came back to give thanks to Jesus was the one Jews would least expect to do so—a Samaritan.

17:17–19 Only this man caught the significance of his healing and glorified God because of it. The other nine typify the response of Israel, which saw sign after sign of Jesus' authority but failed to respond to him with gratitude.

17:20 observation. Jesus' point is that the coming of the kingdom is not according to some signs that they will be able to discern.

17:21 the kingdom of God is within you. This can be translated "within your reach." It is a call for the Pharisees to recognize that Jesus' teachings and actions reveal that the kingdom of God is present—and demands a response—now.

17:22 one of the days of the Son of Man. The implication is that before he returns there will be a substantial delay during which his followers will have to wait patiently for him—even when there is no external evidence of his coming (12:35–48).

17:23–24 Jesus asserts that his return will, like lightning, be patently visible and universally recognized by all. The analogy to lightning also indicates his divine glory (Matt. 24:26–27).

17:26–30 The time of the Second Coming of Christ is compared to that of Noah (Gen. 6:9–9:17) and Lot (Gen. 18:16–19:29). The activities mentioned here (eating, drinking, marrying, buying, selling, planting, etc.) are not evil, rather the emphasis of the comparison is the unexpected nature of the sudden judgment that came upon the people in the course of their daily life as will be the return of Christ (1 Thess. 5:1–3).

37"Where, Lord?" they asked.
He replied, "Where there is a dead body, there the vultures will
gather."

The Parable of the Persistent Widow

18 Then Jesus told his disciples a parable to show them that
they should always pray and not give up. 2He said: "In a
certain town there was a judge who neither feared God nor cared
about men. 3And there was a widow in that town who kept coming to
him with the plea, 'Grant me justice against my adversary.'
4"For some time he refused. But finally he said to himself, 'Even
though I don't fear God or care about men, 5yet because this widow
keeps bothering me, I will see that she gets justice, so that she won't
eventually wear me out with her coming!' "
6And the Lord said, "Listen to what the unjust judge says. 7And will
not God bring about justice for his chosen ones, who cry out to him
day and night? Will he keep putting them off? 8I tell you, he will see
that they get justice, and quickly. However, when the Son of
Man comes, will he find faith on the earth?"

The Parable of the Pharisee and the Tax Collector

9To some who were confident of their own righteousness and
looked down on everybody else, Jesus told this parable: 10"Two men
went up to the temple to pray, one a Pharisee and the other a tax
collector. 11The Pharisee stood up and prayed about[a] himself: 'God, I
thank you that I am not like other men—robbers, evildoers, adulterers—or even like this tax collector. 12I fast twice a week and give a
tenth of all I get.'
13"But the tax collector stood at a distance. He would not even look
up to heaven, but beat his breast and said, 'God, have mercy on me, a
sinner.'
14"I tell you that this man, rather than the other, went home

[a] *11* Or *to*

OPEN 1. What did you do to get your way with your parents? **2.** In school, were you in the "in" crowd or the "out" crowd?

STUDY 1. What is Jesus trying to prepare his disciples for (v. 8)? **2.** Would you call the widow in the parable persistent or a nag? How does her behavior apply to prayer? **3.** When you see injustice prevail, do you give up or hang tough in prayer? **4.** How do you feel about the Pharisee? Why did he act this way? **5.** How would you like to have the Pharisee in your group? How would the tax collector feel in your group with his problems? **6.** How do you feel about sharing your faults and struggles with the group you are in? **7.** What is it about children that Jesus wants to see in his disciples?

APPLY 1. Who has been on your prayer list for years that you need to persist in praying for? **2.** In your spiritual journey, what group have you been in where you could be completely open and honest about your problems?

17:37 Where there is a dead body, there the vultures will gather. Jesus quotes a common proverb used to illustrate the connection between any two closely related events. Here it means that God's judgment will occur wherever necessary. Such an enigmatic reply forces the disciples to consider their own preparedness for the sudden coming of the Lord in judgment.

18:1–8 The last line of this parable (v. 8) relates what appears to be a general admonition about prayer (11:5–8), specifically to the theme of being prepared for the return of Christ. The disciples are called to pray faithfully and steadfastly for the kingdom of God, never giving up hope for God's justice to be accomplished (v. 1).

18:9 confident of their own righteousness. This typifies the attitude of a person who assumes that he or she has met God's standards for life, marked by a concentration on external performance rather than on humble dependence on God's grace (Gal. 3:10–14; Phil. 3:3–9). **looked down on everybody else.** Literally, "to treat with contempt." The same word is translated "ridiculed" in 23:11. This was a major flaw of the Pharisees, who would not even associate with those they considered to be "sinners."

18:10 The Pharisee and tax collector represent opposites in Jewish society. Tax collectors were looked down upon not only because they frequently cheated people, but because they raised money for the hated Roman government. Pharisees, on the other hand, were given a place of prestige in the society.

18:12 While Jews were only required to fast on the Day of Atonement, Pharisees fasted every Monday and Thursday in an attempt to gain merit with God. Although all Jews were expected to tithe of one's produce, Pharisees carefully tithed even things that were not required (11:42). This man's external performance of religious obligations was exemplary.

18:13 stood at a distance. The tax collector may not even have dared to enter the Court of the Jews, but remained in the outermost court of the temple where Gentiles met. **beat his breast.** This action, combined with his fear of even following the common custom of looking upwards in prayer, showed his shame and contrition.

18:14 went home justified. The Pharisee left in his self-delusion while the tax collector was forgiven by God.

justified before God. For everyone who exalts himself will be
humbled, and he who humbles himself will be exalted."

The Little Children and Jesus

15People were also bringing babies to Jesus to have him touch
them. When the disciples saw this, they rebuked them. 16But Jesus
called the children to him and said, "Let the little children come to
me, and do not hinder them, for the kingdom of God belongs to such
as these. 17I tell you the truth, anyone who will not receive the kingdom of God like a little child will never enter it."

The Rich Ruler

18A certain ruler asked him, "Good teacher, what must I do to inherit eternal life?"
19"Why do you call me good?" Jesus answered. "No one is good—
except God alone. 20You know the commandments: 'Do not commit
adultery, do not murder, do not steal, do not give false testimony,
honor your father and mother.' [a]"
21"All these I have kept since I was a boy," he said.
22When Jesus heard this, he said to him, "You still lack one thing.
Sell everything you have and give to the poor, and you will have treasure in heaven. Then come, follow me."
23When he heard this, he became very sad, because he was a man
of great wealth. 24Jesus looked at him and said, "How hard it is for the
rich to enter the kingdom of God! 25Indeed, it is easier for a camel to
go through the eye of a needle than for a rich man to enter the kingdom of God."
26Those who heard this asked, "Who then can be saved?"
27Jesus replied, "What is impossible with men is possible with
God."
28Peter said to him, "We have left all we had to follow you!"
29"I tell you the truth," Jesus said to them, "no one who has left
home or wife or brothers or parents or children for the sake of the
kingdom of God 30will fail to receive many times as much in this age
and, in the age to come, eternal life."

[a] *20* Exodus 20:12-16; Deut. 5:16-20

OPEN Who was your favorite high school teacher or coach?

STUDY 1. What kind of ruler asks the question? What is his view on gaining eternal life? **2.** Why does Jesus zero in on the one thing where this man is vulnerable? What is the point in the comment about the "eye of the needle"? How do the people interpret this? **3.** How does Jesus answer the question the ruler asks in verse 18 and in verses 29–30 for the disciples? Do you have to leave your "home, wife, brothers and parents" to gain the "many times" reward of a new community?

APPLY 1. Before you turned over the ownership of your life to God, what was the thing you lived and died for? **2.** What is the thing God is talking to you about right now?

18:18 ruler. Perhaps this person was a leader of a synagogue (like Jairus—8:41) or even a member of the Sanhedrin, the official Jewish ruling council. **what must I do.** The emphasis on gaining the kingdom by virtue of one's religious activities stands in sharp contrast to Jesus' teaching about receiving the kingdom by faith (vv. 16–17).

18:20 the commandments. Jesus cites five of the Ten Commandments which deal with a person's relationship toward others (Ex. 20:12–16). Significantly, he omits both the first ("You shall have no other gods besides me") and the tenth ("You shall not covet"). Those are the commandments which later prove to be the stumbling blocks for this ruler.

18:22 You still lack one thing. Jesus does not refute the man's claim to be obedient to the demands of the commandments, but he points out that this has not touched his inner attitude of love for God or his neighbor. **Sell everything.** Jesus uses this command to show the ruler that wealth is his true god and his self-centered use of his money his true love. Jesus is not saying with this teaching that *everyone* who seeks eternal life must sell all their possessions. He is saying, give full allegiance to the true God. **follow me.** The ultimate demand of the kingdom is for absolute allegiance to Jesus over one's self and possessions (16:13). This the ruler does not accept.

18:24 How hard it is. Jesus contradicts the common assumption that wealth is the verification that one has led a godly life (Job 1:10; Ps. 128:1–2). Instead, wealth is actually a barrier which can prevent people from seeing their need for God.

Jesus Again Predicts His Death

[31]Jesus took the Twelve aside and told them, "We are going up to
Jerusalem, and everything that is written by the prophets about the
Son of Man will be fulfilled. [32]He will be handed over to the Gentiles.
They will mock him, insult him, spit on him, flog him and kill him.
[33]On the third day he will rise again."
[34]The disciples did not understand any of this. Its meaning was
hidden from them, and they did not know what he was talking about.

A Blind Beggar Receives His Sight

[35]As Jesus approached Jericho, a blind man was sitting by the roadside begging. [36]When he heard the crowd going by, he asked what
was happening. [37]They told him, "Jesus of Nazareth is passing by."
[38]He called out, "Jesus, Son of David, have mercy on me!"
[39]Those who led the way rebuked him and told him to be quiet, but
he shouted all the more, "Son of David, have mercy on me!"
[40]Jesus stopped and ordered the man to be brought to him. When
he came near, Jesus asked him, [41]"What do you want me to do for
you?"
"Lord, I want to see," he replied.
[42]Jesus said to him, "Receive your sight; your faith has healed you."
[43]Immediately he received his sight and followed Jesus, praising God.
When all the people saw it, they also praised God.

Zacchaeus the Tax Collector

19 Jesus entered Jericho and was passing through. [2]A man was
there by the name of Zacchaeus; he was a chief tax collector
and was wealthy. [3]He wanted to see who Jesus was, but being a short
man he could not, because of the crowd. [4]So he ran ahead and
climbed a sycamore-fig tree to see him, since Jesus was coming that
way.
[5]When Jesus reached the spot, he looked up and said to him, "Zacchaeus, come down immediately. I must stay at your house today."
[6]So he came down at once and welcomed him gladly.
[7]All the people saw this and began to mutter, "He has gone to be
the guest of a 'sinner.'"
[8]But Zacchaeus stood up and said to the Lord, "Look, Lord! Here
and now I give half of my possessions to the poor, and if I have cheated anybody out of anything, I will pay back four times the amount."

OPEN 1. Name a famous person you have seen up close. **2.** What has been the hardest death for you to accept?

STUDY 1. With only a few days remaining, what does Jesus bear down on? **2.** Why are the disciples confused? **3.** Although he was blind, what did the man see in Jesus that the rest of the crowd did not see? **4.** How does the blind man in this story illustrate the steps to be taken to become a follower of Christ? **5.** If someone acted like the blind man in your church, what would happen?

APPLY 1. If Jesus asked you today, "What do you want me to do for you?" what would you say? **2.** Is there anything that keeps you from accepting God's work in your life?

OPEN What is the tallest tree in your neighborhood?

STUDY 1. Who was Zacchaeus? What was his social status? **2.** Why did Jesus invite himself to the house of Zacchaeus for dinner? What would the neighbors say? **3.** What motivated Zacchaeus to give half of his possessions and pay back four times anybody he had cheated? **4.** How does Jesus use this opportunity to reaffirm his mission? **5.** Zacchaeus had two strikes against him: He was short and he was a tax collector. What did he have going for him that Jesus affirms (v. 9)?

18:31 up to Jerusalem. Jews used the phrase "going up to Jerusalem" as an idiomatic expression of planning to offer a sacrifice of worship at the temple.

18:35 Jericho. Jericho is 18 miles east of Jerusalem and the place where travelers from Galilee recrossed the Jordan back into Israel.

18:42 your faith. The blind man demonstrated his faith: (1) by the title he uses for Jesus (he grasps who Jesus was); (2) by his persistent pleas for Jesus' help (he would not let this opportunity go by); and (3) by his request for healing (he believed Jesus had the power to do so).

19:2 wealthy. The wealth was undoubtedly the result of "legal" but callous exploitation of his own people through inflated tax rates.

19:4 a sycamore-fig tree. This tree's short trunk and spreading branches make it easy to climb.

19:5–7 Jesus invited himself to Zacchaeus' house, shocking everyone! Not only would the self-righteous Pharisees disapprove, but Zacchaeus' ill-gotten wealth made this association difficult to accept even by the people.

19:8 half of my possessions to the poor. Zacchaeus immediately does precisely what the ruler refused to do (18:22). **I will pay back four times the amount.** Giving half of his wealth to the poor did not mean he would keep the other half for himself. Instead, the remaining wealth would be used to recompense those he had defrauded. Zacchaeus was so eager to be restored to God and his community that he pledged to go far beyond what the Law required (Lev. 6:1–5).

APPLY In your life who affirmed you and saw possibilities in you?

______

OPEN 1. Where are you putting your retirement income? **2.** What is the closest you have come to getting "burned" in the stock market by trusting someone who did not know how to invest your money wisely?

STUDY 1. What is the setting for this parable? What does Jesus know that he wants his disciples to prepare for? **2.** In the parable, what are the "ten minas"? Who do they belong to? Who are they given to? For how long? For what purpose? **3.** In the parable, what does the nobleman find out when he returns? If you were the nobleman, what would you do to the stock broker that sat on your money? **4.** Do you think "minas" are given to everyone or just to "servants"? Do you think "minas" can be taken away from "servants" who do not invest them wisely? **5.** If you were speaking to a group of Wall Street stock brokers, how would you apply this parable to the world they live in? **6.** What would you say or do to the servant that sat on his "minas" to make him more effective?

APPLY 1. In your spiritual life, what was the period of the greatest "return on investment"? **2.** Has your church or your group been increasing its ministry over the past few years? How so? **3.** How can you help to improve the "return on investment"?

9 Jesus said to him, "Today salvation has come to this house, because this man, too, is a son of Abraham. 10 For the Son of Man came
to seek and to save what was lost."

The Parable of the Ten Minas

11 While they were listening to this, he went on to tell them a parable, because he was near Jerusalem and the people thought that the
kingdom of God was going to appear at once. 12 He said: "A man of
noble birth went to a distant country to have himself appointed king
and then to return. 13 So he called ten of his servants and gave them
ten minas.[a] 'Put this money to work,' he said, 'until I come back.'
14 "But his subjects hated him and sent a delegation after him to
say, 'We don't want this man to be our king.'
15 "He was made king, however, and returned home. Then he sent
for the servants to whom he had given the money, in order to find out
what they had gained with it.
16 "The first one came and said, 'Sir, your mina has earned ten
more.'
17 " 'Well done, my good servant!' his master replied. 'Because you
have been trustworthy in a very small matter, take charge of ten
cities.'
18 "The second came and said, 'Sir, your mina has earned five
more.'
19 "His master answered, 'You take charge of five cities.'
20 "Then another servant came and said, 'Sir, here is your mina; I
have kept it laid away in a piece of cloth. 21 I was afraid of you, because you are a hard man. You take out what you did not put in and
reap what you did not sow.'
22 "His master replied, 'I will judge you by your own words, you
wicked servant! You knew, did you, that I am a hard man, taking out
what I did not put in, and reaping what I did not sow? 23 Why then
didn't you put my money on deposit, so that when I came back, I
could have collected it with interest?'
24 "Then he said to those standing by, 'Take his mina away from him
and give it to the one who has ten minas.'
25 " 'Sir,' they said, 'he already has ten!'
26 "He replied, 'I tell you that to everyone who has, more will be
given, but as for the one who has nothing, even what he has will be
taken away. 27 But those enemies of mine who did not want me to
be king over them—bring them here and kill them in front of me.' "

[a] *13* A mina was about three months' wages.

19:13 servants. Wealthy people who had to travel on business would entrust their resources to servants who would act as managers of the estate. **ten minas.** A mina was worth about 100 denarii, about the equivalent of three months' wages for a laborer. This parable is similar to the Parable of the Talents (Matt. 25:14–30). **Put this money to work.** The servants were specifically told to invest this money for the master while he was gone.

19:17 Well done. The servant's faithfulness in this matter is the quality that allows the master to trust him with greater responsibility (12:42–44). **ten cities.** The servant is rewarded, not with a life of ease, but with greater administrative responsibility in the kingdom. Now he is to govern these cities in such a way that they provide greater resources for the king.

19:20–21 In contrast to the other two, this servant had simply hidden the money away. In the parable found in Matthew 25, the man buries the money in the ground, an action that would have been considered a safe way to protect what he had been given.

19:21 a hard man. Literally, this is "an exacting man." This is a person who demands that those who work for him give an unusually good return on investment.

The Triumphal Entry

28After Jesus had said this, he went on ahead, going up to Jerusalem. 29As he approached Bethphage and Bethany at the hill called the
Mount of Olives, he sent two of his disciples, saying to them, 30"Go to
the village ahead of you, and as you enter it, you will find a colt tied
there, which no one has ever ridden. Untie it and bring it here. 31If
anyone asks you, 'Why are you untying it?' tell him, 'The Lord
needs it.' "
32Those who were sent ahead went and found it just as he had told
them. 33As they were untying the colt, its owners asked them, "Why
are you untying the colt?"
34They replied, "The Lord needs it."
35They brought it to Jesus, threw their cloaks on the colt and put
Jesus on it. 36As he went along, people spread their cloaks on the
road.
37When he came near the place where the road goes down the
Mount of Olives, the whole crowd of disciples began joyfully to praise
God in loud voices for all the miracles they had seen:
38"Blessed is the king who comes in the name of the Lord!"[a]

"Peace in heaven and glory in the highest!"

39Some of the Pharisees in the crowd said to Jesus, "Teacher,
rebuke your disciples!"
40"I tell you," he replied, "if they keep quiet, the stones will cry
out."
41As he approached Jerusalem and saw the city, he wept over it
42and said, "If you, even you, had only known on this day what would
bring you peace—but now it is hidden from your eyes. 43The days will
come upon you when your enemies will build an embankment
against you and encircle you and hem you in on every side. 44They
will dash you to the ground, you and the children within your walls.
They will not leave one stone on another, because you did not recognize the time of God's coming to you."

Jesus at the Temple

45Then he entered the temple area and began driving out those
who were selling. 46"It is written," he said to them, " 'My house will
be a house of prayer'[b]; but you have made it 'a den of robbers.'[c]"

[a]38 Psalm 118:26 [b]46 Isaiah 56:7 [c]46 Jer. 7:11

OPEN When you were growing up, how did your church celebrate Palm Sunday?

STUDY In Roman times, the emperor was crowned with pomp and pageantry in a huge procession to the Roman Forum with the emperor astride a splendid stallion. **1.** How would you compare this to the triumphal entry of Jesus into Jerusalem? **2.** What do you think he was feeling as the crowds gathered? **3.** What did the crowds expect of Jesus? Why would the Pharisees be alarmed? **4.** Why would Jesus weep over Jerusalem—the religious establishment that caused him nothing but headaches? Do you think Jesus had the destruction of Jerusalem in mind when he made the prophecy in verses 43–44? **5.** When Jesus got to the temple, what did he find? How do you think he felt? **6.** What saddened him about this whole episode? If Jesus knew that he would be crucified in a few days, why did he go along with this? Would you describe the triumphal entry as the beginning of the end or the end of the beginning?

APPLY 1. Has Jesus "turned over tables" in your life? What were they? How did you react? **2.** As you look at your community, how does your feeling compare with Jesus' feeling for Jerusalem?

19:28 Jerusalem. This was the central city in Palestine and the spiritual heart of Israel.

19:29 Bethphage. A village near Jerusalem, probably across a ravine from Bethany. **Bethany.** A small village about two miles east of Jerusalem. **Mount of Olives.** According to Zechariah 14:3–5, it was from the Mount of Olives that God will commence the final judgment of Israel's enemies. It is not by accident that Jesus chose this place to prepare his entry into Jerusalem.

19:43–44 In A.D. 70 the Romans literally tore Jerusalem apart stone by stone so that absolutely nothing—including the temple—was left standing. The final act of humiliation for the conquered Jews was to watch as the Romans ran a plow through what had been the center of the city as a sign that the Jews were now "plowed under." Jesus predicted this tragedy.

19:45 those who were selling. Worshippers had to offer an unblemished animal, but inspectors approved only those animals bought from certified vendors who worked for members of the high priest's family. Thus, there was great profiteering as the priests and others took advantage of the religious obligations of the Jews by selling the animals at a huge markup.

19:46 a house of prayer. The outermost area of the temple where all these activities were taking place was called the Court of the Gentiles. It was intended to be a place where pious Gentiles could pray (Isa. 56:7).

47 Every day he was teaching at the temple. But the chief priests, the
teachers of the law and the leaders among the people were trying to
kill him. 48 Yet they could not find any way to do it, because all the
people hung on his words.

The Authority of Jesus Questioned

20 One day as he was teaching the people in the temple courts
and preaching the gospel, the chief priests and the teachers
of the law, together with the elders, came up to him. 2 "Tell us by what
authority you are doing these things," they said. "Who gave you this
authority?"
3 He replied, "I will also ask you a question. Tell me, 4 John's baptism—was it from heaven, or from men?"
5 They discussed it among themselves and said, "If we say, 'From
heaven,' he will ask, 'Why didn't you believe him?' 6 But if we say,
'From men,' all the people will stone us, because they are persuaded
that John was a prophet."
7 So they answered, "We don't know where it was from."
8 Jesus said, "Neither will I tell you by what authority I am doing
these things."

The Parable of the Tenants

9 He went on to tell the people this parable: "A man planted a vineyard, rented it to some farmers and went away for a long time. 10 At
harvest time he sent a servant to the tenants so they would give him
some of the fruit of the vineyard. But the tenants beat him and sent
him away empty-handed. 11 He sent another servant, but that one also
they beat and treated shamefully and sent away empty-handed. 12 He
sent still a third, and they wounded him and threw him out.
13 "Then the owner of the vineyard said, 'What shall I do? I will send
my son, whom I love; perhaps they will respect him.'
14 "But when the tenants saw him, they talked the matter over. 'This
is the heir,' they said. 'Let's kill him, and the inheritance will be ours.'
15 So they threw him out of the vineyard and killed him.

OPEN As a teenager, what authority figure (parent, teacher, coach) upset you most?

STUDY 1. What happened just before this to upset the chief priests, teachers of the law and the elders (19:45–48)? **2.** How does Jesus answer their question (v. 2)? Why would the authorities not want to answer the question about John (the Baptist)?

APPLY Did you come to accept the values of your parents without conforming to their rules? When did that happen?

OPEN When have you recently experienced "three-strikes-and-you're-out": Employment? Dating? School? Family?

STUDY 1. Who is in the audience when Jesus tells this parable? **2.** What does the vineyard owner do? How do the tenants treat the servants who are sent to collect? And the son? Who do these people represent? **3.** What do you know about "capstones" that Jesus quotes from Psalm 118:22 to describe himself? Do you think the authorities get the point? **4.** What do the author-

---

20:1 Luke records several conflicts (vv. 1–47) in which various groups of religious leaders confront Jesus one by one. Thus, the opposition begun in Galilee at the start of Jesus' ministry (5:17–6:11) is continued and completed in Jerusalem. **the chief priests.** These were the key officers of the temple, just below the high priest in rank. **the teachers of the law.** Literally, "scribes." Originally, it was the scribes' job to make copies of the Old Testament. Because of the familiarity with Scripture, this evolved into them being teachers of the law. **the elders.** These men served as administrators, judges, military leaders, etc. This group was probably an official committee of the Sanhedrin chosen to confront Jesus for driving the merchants out of the temple (19:45–46).

20:2 They ask: Where does he get his authority? While not as subtle as some of the later questions (vv. 20–22,27–33), it is still a trap. If Jesus says he acted on his own authority, they can detain him as a hopeless megalomaniac. If he says that his authority comes from God, they can accuse him of blasphemy (for which the penalty was death).

20:3–6 Answering a question with a question was a common tactic in rabbinic debate.

20:7–8 No matter how they answer, Jesus' point will be made. To accept that John's authority came from God is to admit that John was a true prophet. They will also have to accept that Jesus comes from God, as John said. They will also have to explain why they have not supported John's ministry. On the other hand, to say that John just pretended to be a prophet is to risk an uprising of the crowd. However, by avoiding an answer, they also put themselves in an awkward position.

20:9 went away. Absentee landlords would commonly get tenant-farmers to work their large estates, requiring the tenant farmers to give them a portion of their harvest in payment for use of the land.

20:10 servant. In terms of this parable, the servants represent the Old Testament prophets.

20:14 inheritance. The tenants apparently mistook the arrival of the son as a sign that the owner had died. By law, a piece of ownerless property (which it would be if they killed the son) could be kept by those who first seized it.

"What then will the owner of the vineyard do to them? [16]He will come and kill those tenants and give the vineyard to others."

When the people heard this, they said, "May this never be!"

[17]Jesus looked directly at them and asked, "Then what is the meaning of that which is written:

"'The stone the builders rejected
has become the capstone[a][b]'?

[18]Everyone who falls on that stone will be broken to pieces, but he on whom it falls will be crushed."

[19]The teachers of the law and the chief priests looked for a way to arrest him immediately, because they knew he had spoken this parable against them. But they were afraid of the people.

Paying Taxes to Caesar

[20]Keeping a close watch on him, they sent spies, who pretended to be honest. They hoped to catch Jesus in something he said so that they might hand him over to the power and authority of the governor.
[21]So the spies questioned him: "Teacher, we know that you speak and teach what is right, and that you do not show partiality but teach the way of God in accordance with the truth. [22]Is it right for us to pay taxes to Caesar or not?"

[23]He saw through their duplicity and said to them, [24]"Show me a denarius. Whose portrait and inscription are on it?"

[25]"Caesar's," they replied.

He said to them, "Then give to Caesar what is Caesar's, and to God what is God's."

[26]They were unable to trap him in what he had said there in public. And astonished by his answer, they became silent.

The Resurrection and Marriage

[27]Some of the Sadducees, who say there is no resurrection, came
to Jesus with a question. [28]"Teacher," they said, "Moses wrote for us
that if a man's brother dies and leaves a wife but no children, the man
must marry the widow and have children for his brother. [29]Now there
were seven brothers. The first one married a woman and died childless. [30]The second [31]and then the third married her, and in the same
way the seven died, leaving no children. [32]Finally, the woman died
too. [33]Now then, at the resurrection whose wife will she be, since the
seven were married to her?"

[a]17 Or *cornerstone* [b]17 Psalm 118:22

ities decide? What would they do today?

APPLY When have the pieces of your life fallen into place with the "capstone" tying together the spiritual, relational, vocational, volitional and intellectual parts of your life?

OPEN 1. When do you pay your taxes: Early? Late? **2.** What was the last exam you had to really prepare for?

STUDY 1. Who are "they" (v. 19)? What is their motive? **2.** How does their question put Jesus in a no-win dilemma? How does he get out of the trap? **3.** What does this say about church and state obligations? **4.** Who are the Sadducees? What is ironic about their question? **5** How does Jesus go about answering their question? What does Jesus say about heaven in his answer? **6.** Why do some of the teachers agree with Jesus? **7.** At the end of round two, who is winning: Jesus or his antagonists?

APPLY 1. Are you more likely to meet your obligation to God or to the state? **2.** How do you deal with someone who wants to argue a point in the Bible? What if the person has honest questions and you don't have the answers?

20:16 Having refused to pay rent three times over, and having killed the *owner's son, the owner takes severe* and immediate action. The owner can muster all the legal power available against these evil tenants. Their judgment will mean their death. The land they have so jealously guarded will be given over to others.

20:17 capstone. A reference to Psalm 118 where the Savior is identified as a capstone (Ps. 118:22).

20:25 While clearly implying that one's final loyalty must be to God and not the state, Jesus said nothing that would allow him to be accused of insubordination against the state.

20:27 Sadducees. There is relatively little information available about this group. However, it seems that they were a small but highly influential party of Jews composed mainly of wealthy, aristocratic priests. The Sadducees accepted only the first five books of the Old Testament as authoritative and denied the resurrection.

20:28–33 The question they pose has to do with levirate marriage (Deut. 25:5–10) which was designed to ensure the continuation of the family name as well as to keep property within a family. The situation they propose was apparently sufficient evidence to them that the concept of resurrection was foolish, as it led to seemingly unresolvable problems.

34Jesus replied, "The people of this age marry and are given in marriage. 35But those who are considered worthy of taking part in that
age and in the resurrection from the dead will neither marry nor be
given in marriage, 36and they can no longer die; for they are like the
angels. They are God's children, since they are children of the resurrection. 37But in the account of the bush, even Moses showed that the
dead rise, for he calls the Lord 'the God of Abraham, and the God of
Isaac, and the God of Jacob.'[a] 38He is not the God of the dead, but of
the living, for to him all are alive."
39Some of the teachers of the law responded, "Well said, teacher!"
40And no one dared to ask him any more questions.

Whose Son Is the Christ?

41Then Jesus said to them, "How is it that they say the Christ[b] is the
Son of David? 42David himself declares in the Book of Psalms:

" 'The Lord said to my Lord:
"Sit at my right hand
43until I make your enemies
a footstool for your feet." '[c]

44David calls him 'Lord.' How then can he be his son?"
45While all the people were listening, Jesus said to his disciples,
46"Beware of the teachers of the law. They like to walk around in flowing robes and love to be greeted in the marketplaces and have the
most important seats in the synagogues and the places of honor at
banquets. 47They devour widows' houses and for a show make
lengthy prayers. Such men will be punished most severely."

The Widow's Offering

21 As he looked up, Jesus saw the rich putting their gifts into the
temple treasury. 2He also saw a poor widow put in two very
small copper coins.[d] 3"I tell you the truth," he said, "this poor widow
has put in more than all the others. 4All these people gave their gifts
out of their wealth; but she out of her poverty put in all she had to
live on."

Signs of the End of the Age

5Some of his disciples were remarking about how the temple was
adorned with beautiful stones and with gifts dedicated to God. But

[a]37 Exodus 3:6 [b]41 Or *Messiah* [c]43 Psalm 110:1 [d]2 Greek *two lepta*

OPEN As a teenager, what issue did you and your parents not agree on: Hair? Grades? Friends? Curfew?

STUDY 1. To whom does Jesus direct this question (v. 39)? In the quote from David, what is Jesus trying to get these people to realize? **2.** What undermines the authority of the religious leaders and everything they stand for? **3.** By contrast, what does the act of the widow demonstrate? **4.** How do you feel about all the "flowing robes" and "important seats" in organized religion today? What do your secular friends think about this?

APPLY 1. If you could be Pope for a day, what would you do? **2.** What is it going to take to get your secular friends to take the claims of Christ seriously?

OPEN What is the tallest building you have been in? What could you see from the top?

STUDY 1. What prompts Jesus' next lesson? **2.** What

20:34–36 Jesus affirms that resurrection life will be more akin to the experience of angels (in which the Sadducees likewise did not believe) than to the social and physical laws which now govern life.

20:39 Well said. The scribes (who were Pharisees) believed in the resurrection and in angels, and would be glad to see the cynicism of the Sadducees refuted.

20:46 flowing robes. These were long, white linen garments fringed with tassels touching the ground. In such a stately garment a person could not run or work and so would be reckoned to be a person of leisure and importance. **greeted.** People considered the teachers of the law to be men of great insight and authority, so they rose when the teachers passed by and called out titles of respect.

20:47 They devour widows' houses. Since the teachers of the law were forbidden to receive pay for their teaching, they lived off others, including poor widows (21:1–4).

21:1 temple treasury. This was located in the Court of Women (which was the first of the inner courts of the temple). It consisted of 13 trumpet-shaped receptacles used to collect donations.

21:2 small copper coins. The smallest coins in circulation, worth about 1/8 of a cent. Her donation, while small in amount, represented the depth of her dedication to God (12:22–34).

21:5 The temple was constructed of huge white stones, some measuring 37

Jesus said, 6"As for what you see here, the time will come when not
one stone will be left on another; every one of them will be thrown
down."
7"Teacher," they asked, "when will these things happen? And what
will be the sign that they are about to take place?"
8He replied: "Watch out that you are not deceived. For many will
come in my name, claiming, 'I am he,' and, 'The time is near.' Do not
follow them. 9When you hear of wars and revolutions, do not be
frightened. These things must happen first, but the end will not come
right away."
10Then he said to them: "Nation will rise against nation, and kingdom against kingdom. 11There will be great earthquakes, famines
and pestilences in various places, and fearful events and great signs
from heaven.
12"But before all this, they will lay hands on you and persecute you.
They will deliver you to synagogues and prisons, and you will be
brought before kings and governors, and all on account of my name.
13This will result in your being witnesses to them. 14But make up your
mind not to worry beforehand how you will defend yourselves. 15For
I will give you words and wisdom that none of your adversaries will
be able to resist or contradict. 16You will be betrayed even by parents,
brothers, relatives and friends, and they will put some of you to
death. 17All men will hate you because of me. 18But not a hair of your
head will perish. 19By standing firm you will gain life.
20"When you see Jerusalem being surrounded by armies, you will
know that its desolation is near. 21Then let those who are in Judea
flee to the mountains, let those in the city get out, and let those in the
country not enter the city. 22For this is the time of punishment in fulfillment of all that has been written. 23How dreadful it will be in those
days for pregnant women and nursing mothers! There will be great
distress in the land and wrath against this people. 24They will fall by
the sword and will be taken as prisoners to all the nations. Jerusalem
will be trampled on by the Gentiles until the times of the Gentiles are
fulfilled.
25"There will be signs in the sun, moon and stars. On the earth, nations will be in anguish and perplexity at the roaring and tossing of
the sea. 26Men will faint from terror, apprehensive of what is coming
on the world, for the heavenly bodies will be shaken. 27At that time
they will see the Son of Man coming in a cloud with power and great
glory. 28When these things begin to take place, stand up and lift up
your heads, because your redemption is drawing near."
29He told them this parable: "Look at the fig tree and all the trees.
30When they sprout leaves, you can see for yourselves and know that
summer is near. 31Even so, when you see these things happening, you
know that the kingdom of God is near.

bombshell does he drop on his disciples (v. 6)? Considering how the Jews felt about the temple, how must they have felt when they heard Jesus' words? **3.** The disciples identified the destruction of the temple with the end times, but Jesus separates them. In verses 8–19, which is he teaching about? **4.** What will happen during this time of tribulation (v. 10)? What comfort will come in the midst of these trials? **5.** In A.D. 70, Jerusalem was destroyed by the Romans. Why would Jesus warn of this event in verses 20–24? Why will Jerusalem be devastated (11:49–51; 13:34–35; 19:41–44)? How does Jesus describe this time (vv. 21–24)? What does he tell the people to do? Why? **6.** What should be the attitude of believers when they see the Son of Man coming (v. 28)? **7.** What is the lesson of the fig tree (vv. 29–31)? How does this lesson answer the disciples' question from verse 7? **8.** How would the promises (vv. 32–33) have been a comfort to the disciples? A discomfort? What impact do they have on you? **9.** In the midst of this heavy news, how does Jesus caution his followers (vv. 34–35)?

APPLY 1. When were you a bold witness for Christ? What happened? How did God give you insight and wisdom? **2.** When reading the parable of the fig tree today, how near is the fig tree to sprouting? What makes you think this? How does this affect the way you live your life?

feet long by 12 feet high by 18 feet wide.

21:11 fearful events and great signs from heaven. This is apocalyptic language—graphic, calamitous, cosmic imagery. Such language was used often in the Old Testament (Isa. 2:6–21; 13:6–22).

21:21 let those who are in Judea flee. Those who follow Christ are to recognize that this is the sign that God's judgment against Israel is coming to a head. So instead of flocking to the city in anticipation of a Messianic appearance, they must run for their lives.

21:24 the times of the Gentiles. Some believe this may refer to the period of the Gentile ingathering to Christ and others to the completion of a time during the tribulation (Rom. 11:25).

[32]"I tell you the truth, this generation[a] will certainly not pass away until all these things have happened. [33]Heaven and earth will pass away, but my words will never pass away.

[34]"Be careful, or your hearts will be weighed down with dissipation, drunkenness and the anxieties of life, and that day will close on you unexpectedly like a trap. [35]For it will come upon all those who live on the face of the whole earth. [36]Be always on the watch, and pray that you may be able to escape all that is about to happen, and that you may be able to stand before the Son of Man."

[37]Each day Jesus was teaching at the temple, and each evening he went out to spend the night on the hill called the Mount of Olives, [38]and all the people came early in the morning to hear him at the temple.

Judas Agrees to Betray Jesus

22 Now the Feast of Unleavened Bread, called the Passover, was approaching, [2]and the chief priests and the teachers of the law were looking for some way to get rid of Jesus, for they were afraid of the people. [3]Then Satan entered Judas, called Iscariot, one of the Twelve. [4]And Judas went to the chief priests and the officers of the temple guard and discussed with them how he might betray Jesus. [5]They were delighted and agreed to give him money. [6]He consented, and watched for an opportunity to hand Jesus over to them when no crowd was present.

The Last Supper

[7]Then came the day of Unleavened Bread on which the Passover lamb had to be sacrificed. [8]Jesus sent Peter and John, saying, "Go and make preparations for us to eat the Passover."

[9]"Where do you want us to prepare for it?" they asked.

[10]He replied, "As you enter the city, a man carrying a jar of water will meet you. Follow him to the house that he enters, [11]and say to the owner of the house, 'The Teacher asks: Where is the guest room, where I may eat the Passover with my disciples?' [12]He will show you a large upper room, all furnished. Make preparations there."

[13]They left and found things just as Jesus had told them. So they prepared the Passover.

[a]32 Or *race*

OPEN When you were growing up, what were mealtimes like? Where did everyone sit around the table? What was the tone of the conversation?

STUDY 1. What was the significance of Passover? The Passover lamb (Ex. 12:1–13,21–28)? **2.** How does Judas fall into the plot of the chief priests and teachers of the law? How would you explain Judas' behavior? Did he believe Jesus was the Messiah? **3.** What would be involved in the "preparations" to eat the Passover? **4.** Why did Jesus "eagerly desire" to have this meal with his disciples? **5.** What do you know about the ritual of the Passover meal? **6.** How did Jesus transform the meaning of the "cup" and the "bread"? **7.** If you had been there, how would you have reacted to the announcement that the betrayer was in their midst? **8.** What does the "dispute" about who will be the "greatest" illustrate? What does Jesus say about greatness? **9.** Why is Simon (Peter) singled out for special prayer? What is Jesus trying to impress on Peter and the others in

22:1 the Feast of Unleavened Bread. This feast was a seven-day period so closely related to Passover (Deut. 16:1–8) that the whole period was often called Passover. Passover, celebrated on the fourteenth day of the Jewish month of Nisan (March–April), was the celebration of God's deliverance of Israel from slavery in Egypt (Ex. 12).

22:2 looking for some way to get rid of Jesus. The religious leadership had long ago decided that Jesus must be silenced (6:11; 20:19). It was only their fear of an uproar by the masses that had prevented them from doing so.

22:3–4 Judas offers the officials a way to quietly arrest Jesus.

22:4 chief priests and the officers of the temple guard. The management of the temple was under the control of the high priest and those who aligned themselves with him. They controlled the temple guard and held them responsible for maintaining order in the temple area.

22:7 the day of Unleavened Bread on which the Passover lamb had to be sacrificed. While the Feast of Unleavened Bread did not officially start until the day after Passover, the day on which the lambs were sacrificed was sometimes referred to as the first day of the Feast of Unleavened Bread. **the Passover lamb.** Each pilgrim sacrificed his own lamb in the temple. A priest caught the blood in a bowl and threw it upon the altar. The pilgrim then ate the sacrificial lamb for Passover.

22:10 a man carrying a jar of water. Such a person would have been easy to spot since it was highly unusual for a man to carry a jar. Women carried jars, men carried wineskins.

[14]When the hour came, Jesus and his apostles reclined at the table.
[15]And he said to them, "I have eagerly desired to eat this Passover
with you before I suffer. [16]For I tell you, I will not eat it again until it
finds fulfillment in the kingdom of God."
[17]After taking the cup, he gave thanks and said, "Take this and
divide it among you. [18]For I tell you I will not drink again of the fruit
of the vine until the kingdom of God comes."
[19]And he took bread, gave thanks and broke it, and gave it to them,
saying, "This is my body given for you; do this in remembrance
of me."
[20]In the same way, after the supper he took the cup, saying, "This
cup is the new covenant in my blood, which is poured out for you.
[21]But the hand of him who is going to betray me is with mine on the
table. [22]The Son of Man will go as it has been decreed, but woe to that
man who betrays him." [23]They began to question among themselves
which of them it might be who would do this.
[24]Also a dispute arose among them as to which of them was considered to be greatest. [25]Jesus said to them, "The kings of the Gentiles
lord it over them; and those who exercise authority over them call
themselves Benefactors. [26]But you are not to be like that. Instead, the
greatest among you should be like the youngest, and the one who
rules like the one who serves. [27]For who is greater, the one who is at
the table or the one who serves? Is it not the one who is at the table?
But I am among you as one who serves. [28]You are those who have
stood by me in my trials. [29]And I confer on you a kingdom, just as my
Father conferred one on me, [30]so that you may eat and drink at my
table in my kingdom and sit on thrones, judging the twelve tribes
of Israel.
[31]"Simon, Simon, Satan has asked to sift you[a] as wheat. [32]But I

[a]31 The Greek is plural.

verses 35–38? **10.** If you were one of these disciples sitting at the table, how would you be feeling at the close of these statements? **11.** Do you think the disciples realized what he meant in verse 16—that this truly would be the "last supper"?

APPLY 1. What does sharing in Communion or the Lord's Supper mean to you? **2.** Who do you admire as someone who truly demonstrates servant leadership?

22:14 When the hour came. The Passover meal could be eaten only after sunset. What followed was a night of excited watching in which people asked: "Will this be the night when God comes again to deliver his people from bondage?"

22:16–18 The Passover had a twofold significance: it looked back upon Israel's deliverance from Egypt and it looked forward to the final redemption that would be ushered in by the Messiah. The comments in verses 16 and 18 refer to that final consummation of the kingdom of God. In a sense, the meal will not be finished until the final messianic banquet. No longer is the Old Testament Passover the supreme act of God's deliverance of his people: From now on spiritual deliverance from the power and penalty of sin secured by the death and resurrection of Jesus.

22:17 gave thanks. The Greek word "to give thanks" is *eucharisto* from which the English word Eucharist is derived.

22:19 He simply says, "Remember me." Jesus' use of the bread and the cup in a symbolic way was consistent with the way in which the various elements of the Passover meal were used. The symbols in the Passover meal pointed back to the first covenant God made with Israel while Jesus' words here at the Last Supper pointed forward to his death and the new covenant which would result from it.

22:20 covenant. This is a treaty between two parties, often sealed by the sacrifice of an animal. It refers to the agreement that God made with Israel which was dependent on Israel's obedience (Ex. 24:1–8). Now a new covenant (Jer. 31:31–33; Heb. 8:8,13) is established which is dependent on Jesus' obedience and sacrificial death. A covenant of law gives way to a covenant of love. **poured out.** Blood which was poured out symbolized a violent death (Gen. 4:10–11; Deut. 19:10; Matt. 23:35).

22:24–27 In a passage similar to Mark 10:37,41–45, Jesus points out true greatness in God's kingdom is not a matter of status but service. John 13:1–17 records how Jesus enacted this principle at this very meal by adopting the position of a servant to wash the disciples' feet.

22:24 which of them ... greatest. While Jesus was seeking strength and support to face his own death, the disciples were thinking of themselves.

22:26 like the youngest. Prestige in this culture went with age and experience. The youngest people had little prestige or honor. Jesus' followers should not think that true greatness requires any more prestige than the youngest person received in that culture.

22:32 I have prayed for you, Simon. This "you" is singular. While Peter will deny Jesus, he is also the one who will encourage the others to reaffirm their faith in him. This pictures the conflict between Satan and Jesus in the

have prayed for you, Simon, that your faith may not fail. And when
you have turned back, strengthen your brothers."
33But he replied, "Lord, I am ready to go with you to prison and to
death."
34Jesus answered, "I tell you, Peter, before the rooster crows today,
you will deny three times that you know me."
35Then Jesus asked them, "When I sent you without purse, bag or
sandals, did you lack anything?"
"Nothing," they answered.
36He said to them, "But now if you have a purse, take it, and also a
bag; and if you don't have a sword, sell your cloak and buy one. 37It is
written: 'And he was numbered with the transgressors'[a]; and I tell you
that this must be fulfilled in me. Yes, what is written about me is
reaching its fulfillment."
38The disciples said, "See, Lord, here are two swords."
"That is enough," he replied.

Jesus Prays on the Mount of Olives

39Jesus went out as usual to the Mount of Olives, and his disciples
followed him. 40On reaching the place, he said to them, "Pray that
you will not fall into temptation." 41He withdrew about a stone's
throw beyond them, knelt down and prayed, 42"Father, if you are willing, take this cup from me; yet not my will, but yours be done." 43An
angel from heaven appeared to him and strengthened him. 44And being in anguish, he prayed more earnestly, and his sweat was like
drops of blood falling to the ground.[b]
45When he rose from prayer and went back to the disciples, he
found them asleep, exhausted from sorrow. 46"Why are you sleeping?" he asked them. "Get up and pray so that you will not fall into
temptation."

Jesus Arrested

47While he was still speaking a crowd came up, and the man who

[a]37 Isaiah 53:12 [b]44 Some early manuscripts do not have verses 43 and 44.

OPEN 1. Where do you go to be all alone? **2.** If you had a hard decision to make, what three friends from your past would you want to be with you?

STUDY 1. How would you describe the task that was before Jesus? **2.** Why does he take James, John and Peter along? What does he ask them to do? **3.** What would have happened if he had taken the easy way out? **4.** What can be seen of his emotions here? What happened to his support group? **5.** How do you account for the behavior of Judas? Have you ever seen a person who was raised in a good Christian home do this? **6.** Why are the temple police fully armed with "swords and clubs" (v. 52)? What do the disciples try to do? Why does Jesus stop them?

---

ongoing life of the church. While Satan has an influence, it is continually checked and countered by the intercession of Jesus as the High Priest of God's people (Heb. 4:14–16). **strengthen your brothers.** In Acts 1:15 and 2:14 Peter was the leading character among the original disciples. His faith and courage exemplified to all the others what it meant to follow Jesus (John 21:15–17).

22:35–38 On previous missions (9:1–6; 10:1–4), Jesus' presence had assured them that all their needs would be provided. He is preparing the disciples for the next phase in their ministry. Now, his upcoming death means they can no longer be sure of his watchful care. Instead, they will face a time when they will have to provide for themselves as best they can.

22:37 Jesus will be crucified as a criminal with two criminals (23:32). This is to fulfill the prophecy of Isaiah (Isa. 53:12).

22:38 That is enough. While the disciples may have heard this as meaning that two swords will be sufficient to counter the opposition, Jesus' probable meaning is you still don't understand. His rebuke of the use of the sword in verse 51 reinforces this view.

22:41 prayed. Given the normal custom of praying aloud and the intensity of Jesus' emotions (v. 44), the disciples would have heard his prayer.

22:42 Father. This distinguishes the nature of the relationship Jesus enjoyed with God. **this cup.** The Old Testament often pictured a person's destiny as related to the nature of the "cup" from which God gave the person to drink. For those who trust him, it was seen as a cup of blessing (Ps. 16:5; 23:5), but his opponents would be forced to drink a cup full of wrath (Isa. 51:17; Lam. 4:21; Hab. 2:16). **yet not my will, but yours be done.** The wrestling in prayer resolves itself in Jesus' entrustment of himself to the Father.

22:45 he found them asleep. The fact that they were asleep is not unusual since Passover could extend up to midnight and the disciples had drunk at least four cups of wine at the meal.

was called Judas, one of the Twelve, was leading them. He approached Jesus to kiss him, 48but Jesus asked him, "Judas, are you
betraying the Son of Man with a kiss?"
49When Jesus' followers saw what was going to happen, they said,
"Lord, should we strike with our swords?" 50And one of them struck
the servant of the high priest, cutting off his right ear.
51But Jesus answered, "No more of this!" And he touched the man's
ear and healed him.
52Then Jesus said to the chief priests, the officers of the temple
guard, and the elders, who had come for him, "Am I leading a rebellion, that you have come with swords and clubs? 53Every day I was
with you in the temple courts, and you did not lay a hand on me. But
this is your hour—when darkness reigns."

Peter Disowns Jesus

54Then seizing him, they led him away and took him into the house
of the high priest. Peter followed at a distance. 55But when they had
kindled a fire in the middle of the courtyard and had sat down together, Peter sat down with them. 56A servant girl saw him seated
there in the firelight. She looked closely at him and said, "This man
was with him."
57But he denied it. "Woman, I don't know him," he said.
58A little later someone else saw him and said, "You also are one of
them."
"Man, I am not!" Peter replied.
59About an hour later another asserted, "Certainly this fellow was
with him, for he is a Galilean."
60Peter replied, "Man, I don't know what you're talking about!" Just
as he was speaking, the rooster crowed. 61The Lord turned and
looked straight at Peter. Then Peter remembered the word the Lord
had spoken to him: "Before the rooster crows today, you will disown
me three times." 62And he went outside and wept bitterly.

The Guards Mock Jesus

63The men who were guarding Jesus began mocking and beating
him. 64They blindfolded him and demanded, "Prophesy! Who hit
you?" 65And they said many other insulting things to him.

7. Do you believe in pacificism or civil disobedience?

APPLY Quite honestly, are you prepared to give yourself fully to God's will for your life?

OPEN What was your greatest defeat in life?

STUDY 1. Why do you think Peter followed at a distance? If you could put in a good word for Peter, what would you say? **2.** What made Peter cave in? What made him come to his senses. How would you have felt? **3.** How would you like your greatest failure to be recorded in the history books?

APPLY If you could take one page out of your spiritual journal, what would it be? What did you learn about grace in this experience?

OPEN 1. Have you ever appeared in court? **2.** Have you ever been interrogated by lawyers who tried to incriminate you?

22:49–50 The disciples saw this as the time to fight beside their Lord.

22:54 the high priest. This was the spiritual head of Israel. On the Day of Atonement the high priest alone could enter the Most Holy Place and, with sprinkled blood, make atonement for the sins of the people. Caiaphas was the high priest before whom Jesus came (Matt. 26:57).

22:59 for he is a Galilean. This would have been known because of his accent.

22:60 the rooster crowed. Roosters in Palestine might crow anytime between midnight and 3 a.m. (which was the reason that particular watch was called "cock-crow"). Peter's denials therefore occurred in the very early morning hours.

22:61 The Lord turned. The other Gospels make it clear that Jesus was interrogated during the night by the high priest and at least some members of the Sanhedrin (Matt. 26:57). It may be at this point that Jesus was being transferred from the high priest's house to the meeting place of the full Sanhedrin for his early morning trial.

22:64 Prophesy! They are mocking his claim to be the Christ by taunting him to name who it was that had struck him while he was blindfolded.

STUDY **1.** What do the chief priests and teachers of the law want Jesus to say (v. 67)? What charge could they bring against Jesus if he said "yes"? How does Jesus answer? **2.** If Jesus is guilty in their estimation, why don't they kill him on the spot? What option do they come up with? **3.** How do the charges against Jesus get changed when they go to Pilate, the Roman governor? Why would these charges scare Pilate? **4.** What does Pilate think of these charges (v. 4)? How does Pilate try to avoid making a decision (v. 7)? **5.** In referring the case to King Herod, what is Pilate hoping he will do? **6.** Jesus has appeared before the religious court, the Roman procounsel and the king. What is the verdict (vv. 14–16)? How do the "chief priest and rulers of the people" react? **7.** Who is Barabbas? What irony do you see in the fact that Barabbas is released and Jesus is condemned? How does Barabbas illustrate the gospel for you? **8.** How would you describe the character of Pilate? **9.** As you look back over this whole trial, how do you feel? Are you more angry at the religious establishment, the Roman governor or the fickle crowd? **10.** What is the lesson in this episode for the church today?

APPLY **1.** How would you compare your story to that of Barabbas in this passage? **2.** Where are you right now in your relationship with Jesus Christ?

Jesus Before Pilate and Herod

66 At daybreak the council of the elders of the people, both the chief
priests and teachers of the law, met together, and Jesus was led before them. 67 "If you are the Christ,[a]" they said, "tell us."
Jesus answered, "If I tell you, you will not believe me, 68 and if I
asked you, you would not answer. 69 But from now on, the Son of Man
will be seated at the right hand of the mighty God."
70 They all asked, "Are you then the Son of God?"
He replied, "You are right in saying I am."
71 Then they said, "Why do we need any more testimony? We have
heard it from his own lips."

23 Then the whole assembly rose and led him off to Pilate. 2 And
they began to accuse him, saying, "We have found this man
subverting our nation. He opposes payment of taxes to Caesar and
claims to be Christ,[b] a king."
3 So Pilate asked Jesus, "Are you the king of the Jews?"
"Yes, it is as you say," Jesus replied.
4 Then Pilate announced to the chief priests and the crowd, "I find
no basis for a charge against this man."
5 But they insisted, "He stirs up the people all over Judea[c] by his
teaching. He started in Galilee and has come all the way here."
6 On hearing this, Pilate asked if the man was a Galilean. 7 When he
learned that Jesus was under Herod's jurisdiction, he sent him to
Herod, who was also in Jerusalem at that time.
8 When Herod saw Jesus, he was greatly pleased, because for a long
time he had been wanting to see him. From what he had heard about
him, he hoped to see him perform some miracle. 9 He plied him with
many questions, but Jesus gave him no answer. 10 The chief priests
and the teachers of the law were standing there, vehemently accusing him. 11 Then Herod and his soldiers ridiculed and mocked him.
Dressing him in an elegant robe, they sent him back to Pilate. 12 That

[a]67 Or *Messiah* [b]2 Or *Messiah*; also in verses 35 and 39 [c]5 Or *over the land of the Jews*

22:66 At daybreak. The official trial began at an early hour in an attempt to accomplish all the formal proceedings before the masses of people in the city could be aware of what was happening. **the council of the elders.** This was the Sanhedrin, a council consisting of 71 leaders (both priests and laymen) who made up the highest Jewish court. They were given authority by Rome to rule in matters of religious law.

22:67–68 While the other Gospels record the failure of the Sanhedrin to produce any charges against Jesus (Mark 14:56), Luke zeroes in on the point of contention that most angered the council: They felt Jesus was making false claims to be Messiah. They were asking Jesus to declare himself.

22:69 the Son of Man. Jesus openly and unequivocally declares his messiahship. The time for secrecy is past. The three titles for Jesus in this paragraph (Christ, Son of Man, Son of God) are for the first time in the Gospel combined together. It becomes clear the Son of Man is the Messiah, who is the Son of God. **seated at the right hand of the mighty God.** This was the place of honor. Jesus, the Son of Man like in Daniel 7:13–14, will be vindicated at the Second Coming when his accusers see that his claim was true.

22:70 I am. This is a forthright declaration by Jesus of his deity (Ex. 3:14; John 8:58).

22:71 The Sanhedrin heard all they needed. The Old Testament penalty for blaspheming God was death by stoning (Lev. 24:10–16), but at this point in history the Sanhedrin did not have the power to carry out a death sentence. They would need to get the Roman procurator to do that for them somehow.

23:1–2 Under Roman law, blasphemy was considered a matter of mere religious disputation, and not a capital offense. Consequently, they needed a better case to present to Pilate to ensure Jesus' death.

23:1 led him off to Pilate. Pilate served as procurator of Judea from A.D. 26–36. Historians of the time called him an "inflexible, merciless and obstinate" man who disliked the Jews and their customs.

23:5–7 Pilate decides to pass off the case to Herod who had authority over Galilee. This might have been done as Herod Antipas was Jewish, or simply to get a Jewish opinion of the case or to rid himself of the responsibility.

23:9 Jesus gave him no answer. This fulfilled the prophecy in Isaiah 53:7.

day Herod and Pilate became friends—before this they had been
enemies.
13Pilate called together the chief priests, the rulers and the people,
14and said to them, "You brought me this man as one who was inciting the people to rebellion. I have examined him in your presence and
have found no basis for your charges against him. 15Neither has Herod, for he sent him back to us; as you can see, he has done nothing to
deserve death. 16Therefore, I will punish him and then release him.[a]"
18With one voice they cried out, "Away with this man! Release Barabbas to us!" 19(Barabbas had been thrown into prison for an insurrection in the city, and for murder.)
20Wanting to release Jesus, Pilate appealed to them again. 21But
they kept shouting, "Crucify him! Crucify him!"
22For the third time he spoke to them: "Why? What crime has this
man committed? I have found in him no grounds for the death penalty. Therefore I will have him punished and then release him."
23But with loud shouts they insistently demanded that he be crucified, and their shouts prevailed. 24So Pilate decided to grant their demand. 25He released the man who had been thrown into prison for
insurrection and murder, the one they asked for, and surrendered
Jesus to their will.

The Crucifixion

26As they led him away, they seized Simon from Cyrene, who was
on his way in from the country, and put the cross on him and made
him carry it behind Jesus. 27A large number of people followed him,
including women who mourned and wailed for him. 28Jesus turned
and said to them, "Daughters of Jerusalem, do not weep for me; weep
for yourselves and for your children. 29For the time will come when
you will say, 'Blessed are the barren women, the wombs that never
bore and the breasts that never nursed!' 30Then

" 'they will say to the mountains, "Fall on us!"
and to the hills, "Cover us!" '[b]

31For if men do these things when the tree is green, what will happen
when it is dry?"

[a]16 Some manuscripts *him." 17Now he was obliged to release one man to them at the Feast.* [b]30 Hosea 10:8

OPEN What painting or movie best portrayed the crucifixion of Jesus for you?

STUDY 1. How would you describe the events in the previous 24 hours leading up to this moment (22:1–23:25)? Why would Simon from Cyrene have to help Jesus carry the cross? **2.** What is Jesus referring to when he advises the "Daughters of Jerusalem" to weep for themselves? What is the advantage of being barren when the day comes? **3.** What does Jesus ask for when he is on the cross? What message does this send to the disciples? To the church today? **4.** How do the various people in the crowd look upon Jesus:

23:13 the people. It is likely that this crowd was collected by the Sanhedrin or they may have been supporters of Barabbas—who was a hero to many (Matt. 27:15).

23:15 he has done nothing to deserve death. In an ironic way, Pilate proclaims what was to become one of the central tenets of the gospel—the sinlessness of Jesus.

23:18 Barabbas. Barabbas was a genuine resistance leader who was also guilty of murder.

23:20–22 Pilate argues again for Jesus' release, but the leaders will hear nothing of this. Likewise, he once again offers to punish Jesus (v. 16) in order to silence the protests against letting him go free. As he does in the series of trials Paul faced that was recorded in Acts 23–28, Luke uses the account of Jesus' trial before Herod and Pilate to clearly present to his Gentile readers that Jesus was tried and found innocent in the courts of Rome.

23:23–24 The crowd refused to accept Pilate's solution. John tells us that the Jewish leaders threatened to report Pilate to Caesar for being tolerant of those who claimed to be Caesar's rivals. Pilate thus gave in to their demands.

23:25 The death of Jesus (who is innocent) in the place of Barabbas (who is guilty) is an individual application of the meaning of Jesus' death as a substitutionary atonement for sinners. It explains what Jesus meant in Mark 10:45 when he said that he came to "give his life as a ransom for many."

23:26 Simon. Possibly a Jew, from a Greek city on the north shore of Africa who was in Jerusalem for the Passover feast. **put the cross on him.** The fact that Jesus could not carry his crossbeam reveals the extent to which he had been beaten. Because of Jesus' weakened condition, Simon was grabbed out of the crowds and forced into service by the Roman soldiers.

23:31 For if men do these things

The religious rulers? The soldiers? The criminals? The sign maker? The crowd? **5.** Of the two criminals, why is one going to be with Jesus in paradise? How much of the gospel would this person know?

APPLY 1. When did the meaning of the death of Christ begin to make sense to you? **2.** How would you explain the crucifixion to a non-Christian friend?

OPEN What death (family, friend or national figure) has affected you the most?

STUDY 1. What is the meaning of the darkness (22:53)? The torn curtain (Heb. 9)? Jesus' prayer (Ps. 31:5)? The centurion's confession (v. 47)? **2.** Why would the women stick around and not the disciples? **3.** What do you know about Joseph (of Arimathea)? What would he be risking in asking for the body of Jesus? Why would he want to give Jesus a proper burial—and before sundown? **4.** Why is it important to note that the women saw the place where he was buried? **5.** In the last

32Two other men, both criminals, were also led out with him to be
executed. 33When they came to the place called the Skull, there they
crucified him, along with the criminals—one on his right, the other
on his left. 34Jesus said, "Father, forgive them, for they do not know
what they are doing."[a] And they divided up his clothes by casting lots.
35The people stood watching, and the rulers even sneered at him.
They said, "He saved others; let him save himself if he is the Christ of
God, the Chosen One."
36The soldiers also came up and mocked him. They offered him
wine vinegar 37and said, "If you are the king of the Jews, save yourself."
38There was a written notice above him, which read: THIS IS THE KING
OF THE JEWS.
39One of the criminals who hung there hurled insults at him:
"Aren't you the Christ? Save yourself and us!"
40But the other criminal rebuked him. "Don't you fear God," he
said, "since you are under the same sentence? 41We are punished
justly, for we are getting what our deeds deserve. But this man has
done nothing wrong."
42Then he said, "Jesus, remember me when you come into your
kingdom.[b]"
43Jesus answered him, "I tell you the truth, today you will be with
me in paradise."

Jesus' Death

44It was now about the sixth hour, and darkness came over the
whole land until the ninth hour, 45for the sun stopped shining. And
the curtain of the temple was torn in two. 46Jesus called out with a
loud voice, "Father, into your hands I commit my spirit." When he had
said this, he breathed his last.
47The centurion, seeing what had happened, praised God and said,
"Surely this was a righteous man." 48When all the people who had
gathered to witness this sight saw what took place, they beat their
breasts and went away. 49But all those who knew him, including the
women who had followed him from Galilee, stood at a distance,
watching these things.

[a]34 Some early manuscripts do not have this sentence. [b]42 Some manuscripts *come with your kingly power*

---

when the tree is green, what will happen when it is dry? A proverbial saying that means, "If things are this bad now, what will happen later?" However, once green wood has seasoned for several months it burns far more efficiently.

23:33 the Skull. In Aramaic, this was Golgotha. The name was given because it was a round, bare hillock outside Jerusalem. **they crucified him.** Crucifixion was the most feared of all punishments in the first-century world. It was cruel in the extreme and totally degrading.

23:34 Father, forgive them. Jesus' call for mercy reflects his radical call to his disciples to forgive their enemies (6:27–28; Acts 7:60). **divided up his clothes.** The clothes of the condemned person belonged to the four soldiers who carried out the crucifixion (Ps. 22:18; John 19:23–24).

23:35 if he is the Christ of God, the Chosen One. To the leaders, the disgraceful death Jesus was experiencing proved that he could not possibly be the Messiah.

23:44 about the sixth hour. At noon. **darkness.** This was some sort of supernatural event (Ex. 10:21–23) showing the significance of the Crucifixion (22:53; Amos 8:9).

23:45 curtain of the temple. The curtain in the temple probably the one that separated the Holy Place (where the priests performed their daily service) and the Most Holy Place. The curtain stood as a visible sign of the barrier between people and God since only the high priest could pass through that curtain once a year on the Day of Atonement. Its rending was another supernatural sign of the significance of Jesus' death: he has opened the way for all to have immediate and direct access to God (Heb. 10:19–20).

Jesus' Burial

50Now there was a man named Joseph, a member of the Council, a
good and upright man, 51who had not consented to their decision
and action. He came from the Judean town of Arimathea and he was
waiting for the kingdom of God. 52Going to Pilate, he asked for Jesus'
body. 53Then he took it down, wrapped it in linen cloth and placed it
in a tomb cut in the rock, one in which no one had yet been laid. 54It
was Preparation Day, and the Sabbath was about to begin.
55The women who had come with Jesus from Galilee followed
Joseph and saw the tomb and how his body was laid in it. 56Then they
went home and prepared spices and perfumes. But they rested on the
Sabbath in obedience to the commandment.

The Resurrection

24 On the first day of the week, very early in the morning, the
women took the spices they had prepared and went to the
tomb. 2They found the stone rolled away from the tomb, 3but when
they entered, they did not find the body of the Lord Jesus. 4While they
were wondering about this, suddenly two men in clothes that
gleamed like lightning stood beside them. 5In their fright the women
bowed down with their faces to the ground, but the men said to them,
"Why do you look for the living among the dead? 6He is not here; he
has risen! Remember how he told you, while he was still with you in
Galilee: 7'The Son of Man must be delivered into the hands of sinful
men, be crucified and on the third day be raised again.' " 8Then they
remembered his words.
9When they came back from the tomb, they told all these things to
the Eleven and to all the others. 10It was Mary Magdalene, Joanna,
Mary the mother of James, and the others with them who told this to

24 hours, from sundown to sundown, how would you describe what happened in this period of time?

APPLY What would the world be like today if it had never happened?

OPEN When do you get out of bed on Sunday mornings? What do you do first?

STUDY 1. How would the women know where Jesus was buried (23:55)? **2.** How do you think the women felt when: They found the stone rolled away? The tomb empty? Two men (angels) suddenly appear and announce "He is not here; he is risen"? **3.** Why would the eleven disciples refuse to believe the women? **4.** What must have been going through Peter's mind when he reached the tomb and found the linen wrapping?

APPLY Have you ever buried someone who refused to be-

23:50–52 To ask for the body was to admit allegiance to the now discredited Jesus and was, therefore, potentially dangerous. Often, the Romans would just leave the bodies hanging on the crosses to be eaten by vultures, although they did grant requests by family members to bury their dead. However, the Romans almost never allowed those convicted of treason to be buried. The fact that Pilate did so is a further indication of his conviction that Jesus was innocent (v. 15).

23:53 The body was washed, quickly wrapped with spices for preservation and placed in Joseph's own tomb which was sealed against robbers or animals by a large stone. This was all done hurriedly due to the approach of the Sabbath.

23:55 The women who had come ... from Galilee. See chapter 8:2–3. These women saw where Jesus was laid. Thus, Luke undermines any criticism that the women merely went to the wrong tomb later on. The preparation of further spices and perfumes was a way for them to more adequately honor the body of Jesus after the Sabbath was over.

24:1 On the first day of the week. This was early Sunday morning. **spices.** Aromatic oils to anoint the body, not so much to preserve it as to honor it. Clearly they did not expect Jesus to have risen from the dead.

24:2 The stone was rolled away not so that the resurrected Jesus could leave the tomb but so that his disciples could see that it was empty (John 20:8). **the stone.** It would have been fairly easy to roll the huge, disc-shaped stone down the groove cut for it so that it covered the opening, but once in place it would have been very difficult to push it back up the incline. **tomb.** Typically such tombs had a large antechamber, with a small two-foot-high doorway at the back which led into the six- or seven-foot burial chamber.

24:3 they did not find the body. All accounts of the resurrection stress this point. The body of Jesus was gone.

24:4 two men. Matthew 28:2–3 says that an angel came down from heaven. The description of their clothing here confirms this is Luke's meaning, too.

24:6 he has risen! Literally, the phrase is "he has been raised" showing that God is the one who accomplished this great act. **Remember how he told you.** Jesus had predicted his death and resurrection (9:22). What had made no sense before now begins to be full of meaning. The Resurrection is the great evidence of the deity of Jesus Christ (vv. 27,45).

24:9 the Eleven. Judas had committed suicide for his treachery (Matt. 27:5).

24:10 Mary Magdalene, Joanna. All the Gospel writers include Mary as one of the witnesses of Jesus' empty tomb. Under Jewish law, women were not considered reliable witnesses. However, Jesus had given new status to women in the ministry and now they become the first heralds of the message that he has risen. **Mary, the mother**

lieve in Jesus even until the very end? Have you ever buried someone who believed totally in the resurrection of Jesus and their own future resurrection?

OPEN If you had a terrible tragedy in your life, where would you need to go to get yourself together?

STUDY **1.** What happened on the "same day" that this passage begins (vv. 1–12)? **2.** What caused these two disciples to leave Jerusalem? What do you think they were talking about when Jesus joined them? Why didn't they recognize him? **3.** When informed by the women that the tomb was empty, what did these two assume? **4.** How did Jesus deal with their doubts? What Old Testament Scriptures do you suppose Jesus used to explain his mission? **5.** Why did Jesus act as if he was going further? **6.** What was the turning point in their spiritual understanding? **7.** When these two disciples got back to tell the others what happened, what did they find out? **8.** Do you find this story hard to believe—or do you find it to be an encouragement to your faith?

APPLY What does this story of God meeting two disciples on the road to Emmaus remind you of in your own spiritual journey—of a

the apostles. 11But they did not believe the women, because their
words seemed to them like nonsense. 12Peter, however, got up and
ran to the tomb. Bending over, he saw the strips of linen lying by
themselves, and he went away, wondering to himself what had happened.

On the Road to Emmaus

13Now that same day two of them were going to a village called
Emmaus, about seven miles[a] from Jerusalem. 14They were talking
with each other about everything that had happened. 15As they talked
and discussed these things with each other, Jesus himself came up
and walked along with them; 16but they were kept from recognizing
him.

17He asked them, "What are you discussing together as you walk
along?"

They stood still, their faces downcast. 18One of them, named Cleopas, asked him, "Are you only a visitor to Jerusalem and do not know
the things that have happened there in these days?"

19"What things?" he asked.

"About Jesus of Nazareth," they replied. "He was a prophet, powerful in word and deed before God and all the people. 20The chief
priests and our rulers handed him over to be sentenced to death, and
they crucified him; 21but we had hoped that he was the one who was
going to redeem Israel. And what is more, it is the third day since all
this took place. 22In addition, some of our women amazed us. They
went to the tomb early this morning 23but didn't find his body. They
came and told us that they had seen a vision of angels, who said he
was alive. 24Then some of our companions went to the tomb and
found it just as the women had said, but him they did not see."

25He said to them, "How foolish you are, and how slow of heart to

[a]13 Greek *sixty stadia* (about 11 kilometers)

---

of James. Literally, "Mary of James." Typically one would understand it to mean James' wife, but Mark 15:40 refers specifically to Mary as the mother of James.

24:11–12 The disciples did not believe the women, but Peter was moved to visit the tomb and investigate. Seeing the grave cloths without the body did not yet produce faith in him; instead he was merely confused about what could have happened.

24:12 he saw the strips of linen lying by themselves. John reports this curious fact in even greater detail (John 20:1–9). It was the custom to bind a dead body with strips of linen cloth. The head was bound with a separate cloth. Thus, when Jesus rose from the dead he would have passed through the cloth (as he later did through doors) and the whole mass would have collapsed. Had the body been stolen, grave clothes would have been taken or, at least, unwound and tossed aside.

24:13 two of them. These were not two of the remaining eleven apostles, but two followers of Jesus who lived in nearby Jerusalem. They were probably returning home after the Passover feast. **Emmaus.** The site of this village is uncertain.

24:14–16 As Jesus came up to the two, they were prevented from recognizing him. Later on, they were able to see who he was through the breaking of the bread together (vv. 30–31).

24:18 Cleopas. While this man was probably a figure Luke's readers would know, who he is remains uncertain today. **Are you only a visitor to Jerusalem.** The events that occurred, Jesus' betrayal, trials and crucifixion so dominated their minds that they cannot comprehend anyone not having heard of them.

24:19–24 Cleopas speaks of the confusion that filled the minds of all Jesus' followers. How could Jesus, who was shown by miracle after miracle to be a powerful prophet undoubtedly anointed by God, have met with such a meaningless death?

24:19 a prophet. These men had respect for Jesus as a man of God, but after the Crucifixion they seemed reluctant to call him the Messiah.

24:21 to redeem Israel. To free the Jewish nation from bondage to Rome and establish the kingdom of God (1:68; 2:38; 21:28,31; Titus 2:14; 1 Peter 1:18). **the third day.** This could refer to the Jewish belief that after the third day the soul left the body or to Jesus' statement that he would be raised to life on the third day (9:22).

24:25–27 Jesus rebukes them for their lack of understanding about the Old Testament prophecies regarding the Messiah, and explains how these Scriptures foretold all that had taken place.

believe all that the prophets have spoken! [26]Did not the Christ[a] have
to suffer these things and then enter his glory?" [27]And beginning with
Moses and all the Prophets, he explained to them what was said in all
the Scriptures concerning himself.
[28]As they approached the village to which they were going, Jesus
acted as if he were going farther. [29]But they urged him strongly, "Stay
with us, for it is nearly evening; the day is almost over." So he went in
to stay with them.
[30]When he was at the table with them, he took bread, gave thanks,
broke it and began to give it to them. [31]Then their eyes were opened
and they recognized him, and he disappeared from their sight. [32]They
asked each other, "Were not our hearts burning within us while he
talked with us on the road and opened the Scriptures to us?"
[33]They got up and returned at once to Jerusalem. There they found
the Eleven and those with them, assembled together [34]and saying, "It
is true! The Lord has risen and has appeared to Simon." [35]Then the
two told what had happened on the way, and how Jesus was recognized by them when he broke the bread.

Jesus Appears to the Disciples

[36]While they were still talking about this, Jesus himself stood
among them and said to them, "Peace be with you."
[37]They were startled and frightened, thinking they saw a ghost.
[38]He said to them, "Why are you troubled, and why do doubts rise in
your minds? [39]Look at my hands and my feet. It is I myself! Touch me
and see; a ghost does not have flesh and bones, as you see I have."
[40]When he had said this, he showed them his hands and feet. [41]And
while they still did not believe it because of joy and amazement, he
asked them, "Do you have anything here to eat?" [42]They gave him a
piece of broiled fish, [43]and he took it and ate it in their presence.
[44]He said to them, "This is what I told you while I was still with you:
Everything must be fulfilled that is written about me in the Law of
Moses, the Prophets and the Psalms."
[45]Then he opened their minds so they could understand the Scriptures. [46]He told them, "This is what is written: The Christ will suffer
and rise from the dead on the third day, [47]and repentance and
forgiveness of sins will be preached in his name to all nations, beginning at Jerusalem. [48]You are witnesses of these things. [49]I am going to

[a]26 Or *Messiah*; also in verse 46

time when God met you when you least expected it?

OPEN Who was your favorite coach or teacher? How did this person inspire you to do your best?

STUDY 1. Where are the disciples and what are they doing when this passage begins (vv. 33–35)? **2.** How would you put into your own words the greeting "peace be with you"? **3.** If you had been there with the disciples when Jesus appeared, would you have believed your eyes? What does Jesus do to convince the disciples? **4.** Why did Jesus take the trouble to link their experience with Old Testament Scripture? What lesson could the church today learn from this? **5.** What is the simple story that Jesus asks the disciples to spread? How are they to share this story? **6.** How would you describe the end of this account of the earthly life of Jesus Christ?

24:26 Did not the Christ have to suffer. The need for the Messiah to suffer was proclaimed in Isaiah 53. **and then enter his glory.** The messianic glory was a common expectation of the Jews, but his suffering was not.

24:27 Moses and all the Prophets. This was a way of referring to all the Old Testament Scriptures (16:31). Jesus claims that all the Old Testament teachings about the Servant of the Lord, the Son of Man, the Son of David and the Messiah apply to him. It is these teachings taken collectively that explain who he is and what he came to do.

24:30 he took bread, gave thanks, broke it and began to give it to them. While this is a simple enough description of how a meal would begin, it is probably meant to carry overtones of the Lord's Supper (22:19).

24:31 he disappeared. The Gospels' accounts of the appearances of the resurrected Jesus indicate that while he was in his earthly form (vv. 39,42–43; Matt. 28:9), he was not restricted by that body (John 20:19).

24:37–43 Luke describes at some length the way in which Jesus proved to the disciples that he was not a ghost, an angel nor a product of any hallucinations. The wound marks were still visible even in his resurrected body. When even that evidence seemed insufficient due to the disciples' amazement and shock, he ate before them to again show he was no ghost. Jesus truly, physically, rose from the dead (1 Cor. 15:35–49).

24:49 The baptism of the Holy Spirit at Pentecost is what the Father had promised (Joel 2:28; Acts 2:14–18). It is this theme that is picked up and developed throughout the book of Acts in which

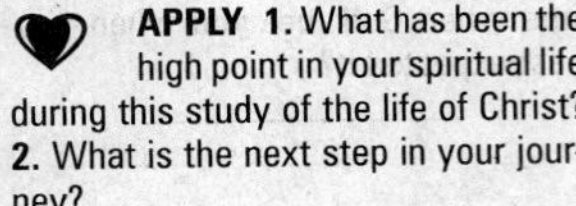

APPLY **1.** What has been the high point in your spiritual life during this study of the life of Christ? **2.** What is the next step in your journey?

send you what my Father has promised; but stay in the city until you
have been clothed with power from on high."

The Ascension

50When he had led them out to the vicinity of Bethany, he lifted up
his hands and blessed them. 51While he was blessing them, he left
them and was taken up into heaven. 52Then they worshiped him and
returned to Jerusalem with great joy. 53And they stayed continually at
the temple, praising God.

Luke records how the Spirit empowered the early Christians (particularly Peter and Paul) to bear witness for Christ.

24:51 taken up in heaven. This is the first of two descriptions of Jesus' ascension (Acts 1:9–11).

24:53 The book ends with a note of expectancy which provides the setting for the opening of the book of Acts.

John

Author. The writer of the fourth Gospel does not name himself in the text. Like the other three Gospels, the fourth one is anonymous.

Yet in a curious way the fourth one is less anonymous than the other three because the writer identifies himself in the final chapter by way of a title. He calls himself "the disciple whom Jesus loved" (13:23–25; 19:26–27; 20:2–8; 21:7; 21:20–24).

Personal Reading	Group Study Topic and Reading	
1:1–2:11	Water to Wine	2:1–11
2:12–3:21	Nicodemus	3:1–21
3:22–4:30	A Samaritan Woman	4:7–30
4:31–5:15	Healing at the Pool	5:1–15
5:16–8:11	Adulterous Woman	7:53–8:11
8:12–9:34	Blind Man Healed	9:1–34
9:35–11:44	Lazarus Raised	11:1–44
11:45–13:17	Washing of Feet	13:1–17
13:18–16:33	Vine and Branches	15:1–17
17:1–19:27	The Crucifixion	19:16–27
19:28–20:18	Appearance to Mary	20:1–18
20:19–31	Thomas Doubts	20:24–31
21:1–25	Peter Reinstated	21:1–25

Date. Most scholars agree that John was the last of the four Gospels to be written. It was probably composed in A.D. 80 or 90, though estimates range from the A.D. 50s to 90s.

Theme. Jesus is the giver of life.

Purpose. Why did John write as he did about Jesus? What was his purpose in gathering together this account? Two of his own statements provide the answer to this question. First, John asserts in his first epistle: "This we proclaim concerning the Word of life. The life appeared; we have seen it and testify to it .... We proclaim to you what we have seen and heard, so that you also may have fellowship with us" (1 John 1:1–3). Second, John states at the end of his Gospel: "These are written that you may believe that Jesus is the Christ, the Son of God, and that by believing you may have life in his name" (20:31). He tells us Jesus' story so that we will understand who Jesus is, put our faith in him as the unique Son of God, and so experience life in Christ and fellowship with other believers.

Historical Background. What, then, do we know about John the apostle? First, we know that he and his brother James, along with Peter and his brother Andrew, were the first four disciples called by Jesus (Mark 1:16–20). Furthermore, James and John seem inseparable. Together the two brothers want to call down fire on a village (Luke 9:54). Together they earn the title from Jesus of "Sons of Thunder" (Mark 3:17). The two of them request to be seated on Jesus' right and left in the coming kingdom (Mark 10:35–37). They are both with Jesus on the Mount of Transfiguration (Mark 9:2), in Gethsemane (Mark 14:33), and when Jairus' daughter is raised from the dead (Mark 5:37). John is right at the heart of Jesus' life and ministry. He, of all the disciples, is qualified to give the world a glimpse of Jesus' deepest thoughts and profound concerns.

Characteristics. For those familiar with the Synoptic Gospels (Matthew, Mark, Luke), what strikes one so forcibly about John's Gospel is how *different* it is. Despite their different emphases, the synoptics tell the same story. They are telling one part of Jesus' story. John, however, tells another part of that story. This is not to say that John's account contradicts the synoptics. Rather, John makes explicit what Matthew, Mark and Luke only hint at. He leaves out a lot of material covered in the synoptics, but he adds information about aspects of Jesus' ministry not discussed elsewhere. And he records for us not just Jesus' short, meaningful statements, so prominent in the synoptics, but also his longer discourses.

Style. John writes in very simple Greek. He does not use a wide range of vocabulary. He often repeats words and phrases. Yet the result is a compelling document whose very simplicity makes it impressive.

The fourth Gospel was written by a man with an adequate but not extensive education in Greek. Furthermore, the writing has a strong Jewish flavoring. This is exactly what one would expect of John,

the son of Zebedee—a Jew who had lived for a long time in Galilee, an area whose population included more Gentiles than Jews.

Structure. It is not clear how John's Gospel ought to be subdivided. It is an incredibly rich, complex and fluid piece of writing in which various themes operate at different levels.

Still, most scholars agree that John's Gospel begins with a distinct prologue (1:1–18), and then divides into two major parts. The first part of the Gospel concentrates on Jesus' *public ministry.* It is organized around his miracles, "signs" that reveal who he really is. This part covers most of the three years of Jesus' ministry.

In the second part, the focus shifts from the crowds to the disciples and Jesus' *private ministry* among them. The theme in this section is the *glory* that is revealed in Jesus' crucifixion and resurrection. The time period of this part is short: from the Thursday night of the Last Supper through Jesus' post resurrection appearances.

Additional themes are grouped around the major Jewish feasts. John recounts events from specially selected days in Jesus' life. These events present a Savior who knows "where I came from and where I am going" (8:14). John describes Jesus as the "Word" (1:1–14), the sum of all that God wanted to say to us. God communicated in the only way we could truly understand: by becoming one of us.

OPEN 1. What is your full name? **2.** What is your nickname? Where did the names come from?

STUDY 1. How would you describe the way the Gospel of John begins: Prologue before the curtain opens? Pregame warm up? Tune-up before the central musician comes on stage? **2.** Why does the author use John (the Baptist) to introduce Jesus? **3.** Who are the people in verses 10 and 11 that did not recognize or receive him? **4.** How do verses 12–13 become the clue for understanding the purpose of this Gospel? **5.** What gives the author the right to make the bold statement that he makes in verse 14 (1 John 1:1–4)? **6.** Why did Jesus come into the world

The Word Became Flesh

1 In the beginning was the Word, and the Word was with God, and
the Word was God. 2 He was with God in the beginning.
3 Through him all things were made; without him nothing was
made that has been made. 4 In him was life, and that life was the light
of men. 5 The light shines in the darkness, but the darkness has not
understood[a] it.
6 There came a man who was sent from God; his name was John.
7 He came as a witness to testify concerning that light, so that through
him all men might believe. 8 He himself was not the light; he came
only as a witness to the light. 9 The true light that gives light to every
man was coming into the world.[b]
10 He was in the world, and though the world was made through
him, the world did not recognize him. 11 He came to that which was
his own, but his own did not receive him. 12 Yet to all who received

[a]5 Or *darkness, and the darkness has not overcome* [b]9 Or *This was the true light that gives light to every man who comes into the world*

1:1 In the beginning. The coming of Jesus inaugurates a new creation (Gen. 1:1). **the Word.** This is the translation of the Greek word *Logos,* a word with multiple meanings. A popular form of Greek thought taught that the *Logos* was an impersonal force or principle that gave order and meaning to the universe. The Old Testament spoke of the *Logos* as the divine wisdom active in creation and human affairs (Prov. 8:12–36).

1:4 life. This has a double meaning, referring to both physical life and the supernatural illumination (*"the light"*) that brings spiritual life to people.

1:5 light ... darkness. This is another theme borrowed from Greek philosophy central to this Gospel's portrait of Jesus (8:12; 12:35). **understood.** This word also means "overtakers" (12:35). On the one hand, the light of God shines in spite of the best effort of the powers of darkness to extinguish it. On the other hand, the widespread lack of comprehension of Jesus' identity is an important theme in this Gospel.

1:6 John. John the Baptist's influence was felt from Egypt to Asia Minor (Acts 18:24–26; 19:1–4).

1:10 He was in the world. This is the radically new dimension the Gospel adds to Greek or Jewish ideas about the *Logos*: It is *not* an "it," but a person! **world.** The first two uses of this word in this verse refer to the created order in general. The last use means humanity.

1:11 He came to that which was his own. Israel, God's own people (Gen. 17:7), especially failed to see who Jesus was (12:37–41).

1:12 children of God. Entrance into God's family is not, as orthodox Jews assumed, a natural matter of birthright or race (v. 13), but a super-

him, to those who believed in his name, he gave the right to become
children of God— 13children born not of natural descent,[a] nor of human decision or a husband's will, but born of God.
14The Word became flesh and made his dwelling among us. We
have seen his glory, the glory of the One and Only,[b] who came from
the Father, full of grace and truth.
15John testifies concerning him. He cries out, saying, "This was he
of whom I said, 'He who comes after me has surpassed me because
he was before me.' " 16From the fullness of his grace we have all received one blessing after another. 17For the law was given through
Moses; grace and truth came through Jesus Christ. 18No one has ever
seen God, but God the One and Only,[b,c] who is at the Father's side,
has made him known.

John the Baptist Denies Being the Christ

19Now this was John's testimony when the Jews of Jerusalem sent
priests and Levites to ask him who he was. 20He did not fail to confess, but confessed freely, "I am not the Christ.[d]"
21They asked him, "Then who are you? Are you Elijah?"
He said, "I am not."
"Are you the Prophet?"
He answered, "No."
22Finally they said, "Who are you? Give us an answer to take back
to those who sent us. What do you say about yourself?"
23John replied in the words of Isaiah the prophet, "I am the voice of
one calling in the desert, 'Make straight the way for the Lord.' "[e]
24Now some Pharisees who had been sent 25questioned him, "Why
then do you baptize if you are not the Christ, nor Elijah, nor the
Prophet?"
26"I baptize with[f] water," John replied, "but among you stands one
you do not know. 27He is the one who comes after me, the thongs of
whose sandals I am not worthy to untie."

[a]13 Greek *of bloods* [b]14,18 Or *the Only Begotten* [c]18 Some manuscripts *but the only* (or *only begotten*) *Son* [d]20 Or *Messiah.* "The Christ" (Greek) and "the Messiah" (Hebrew) both mean "the Anointed One"; also in verse 25. [e]23 Isaiah 40:3 [f]26 Or *in*; also in verses 31 and 33

(v. 18)? **7.** What does this passage teach about the existence of Jesus before he came to earth?

APPLY 1. When did you come to the place in your spiritual pilgrimage that you acknowledged Jesus to be the Son of God and Savior of the world? **2.** How would you describe your relationship with God right now?

OPEN Who is your choice for the "hell fire" preacher of the year?

STUDY 1. How do you like this guy John the Baptist? How would you like him to precede you and "make straight the way" for you (Isa. 40:1–5)? **2.** What are the Jews asking when they ask John if he is "the Christ"? **3.** What does John say about his purpose and mission? **4.** How is the baptism of John the Baptist different from the baptism that we practice today? **5.** What do you know from the Old Testament about the Passover "lamb"? What is John saying when he says that Jesus is the "Lamb of God"? What did the sacrifice of the "lamb" in the Old Testament accomplish? How is this different from what the "Lamb of God" accomplishes for all of humankind? **6.** If you had to explain the gospel in a nutshell to a ten-year-old, what would you say?

---

natural matter of God's will based on belief in Jesus.

1:14 became flesh. This term would have shocked Greek readers who believed the flesh was so inherently worthless that the divine would have no relationship with it. They thought of spirituality as a matter of escaping the limits of the body. **made his dwelling among us.** Literally, "set his tent in us." This is an allusion to God's dwelling with Israel in the tabernacle (Ex. 33:7–11). Temporarily, God lived among people in human form. **the One and Only.** While Israel's kings were sometimes called "Sons of God" (Ps. 2), Jesus is God's Son in an absolutely unique sense (v. 18; 3:16,18).

1:17 Moses ... Jesus. The grace of Jesus brings life, whereas the Law of Moses only could point out the failure of people before God. Yet Moses bore witness to Jesus; anyone who truly believed Moses would certainly receive him (5:45–46). **Jesus Christ.** The incarnate *Logos* is identified for the first time. "Christ" is the Greek term for the Hebrew title "Messiah."

1:19 priests and Levites. These people conducted the ceremonial worship at the temple.

1:21 Elijah. Malachi 4:5–6 anticipated that someone like Elijah would return before the "day of the LORD" came in final judgment. **the Prophet.** Deuteronomy 18:18 raised the expectation that one day a leader like Moses would arise (4:25; 6:14).

1:23 Make straight the way for the Lord. When a royal figure traveled on a state visit, a herald was sent ahead announcing the person's arrival so people could be prepared.

1:25 baptize. Prior to John, only Gentiles who converted to Judaism were baptized as a sign of their cleansing from the pollutions of their Gentile past. Ezekiel 36:25 and Zechariah 13:1 hinted that a new baptism would begin with the messianic age. **the Christ.** The expectation was that the Messiah would be a military leader who would deliver Israel from the rule of the Romans.

1:26 In verse 33, John talks of the new baptism to come. At this point his stress is not on the baptism but on his mission of pointing people to the one to come.

APPLY 1. Who was the John the Baptist in your life—who prepared the way for you to meet Jesus Christ? 2. How would you compare the passion of John the Baptist to your own passion to introduce people to Jesus?

OPEN 1. When you get some good news, who is the first person you want to share it with? 2. As a child, what would it take for you to believe something your brother or sister told you?

STUDY 1. Who is John (the Baptist) and what has he just told his disciples about a person who will come after him (vv. 29–34)? 2. When two of John's disciples decide to find out more about Jesus, what does Jesus invite them to do? 3. What is the "first thing" Andrew did? What did he tell his brother? What does this mean? 4. What is significant about changing the name of Simon to Cephas? At this point in the life of Cephas, was he "a rock"? 5. When

28This all happened at Bethany on the other side of the Jordan, where John was baptizing.

Jesus the Lamb of God

29The next day John saw Jesus coming toward him and said, "Look, the Lamb of God, who takes away the sin of the world! 30This is the one I meant when I said, 'A man who comes after me has surpassed me because he was before me.' 31I myself did not know him, but the reason I came baptizing with water was that he might be revealed to Israel."

32Then John gave this testimony: "I saw the Spirit come down from heaven as a dove and remain on him. 33I would not have known him, except that the one who sent me to baptize with water told me, 'The man on whom you see the Spirit come down and remain is he who will baptize with the Holy Spirit.' 34I have seen and I testify that this is the Son of God."

Jesus' First Disciples

35The next day John was there again with two of his disciples.
36When he saw Jesus passing by, he said, "Look, the Lamb of God!"
37When the two disciples heard him say this, they followed Jesus.
38Turning around, Jesus saw them following and asked, "What do you want?"

They said, "Rabbi" (which means Teacher), "where are you staying?"

39"Come," he replied, "and you will see."

So they went and saw where he was staying, and spent that day with him. It was about the tenth hour.

40Andrew, Simon Peter's brother, was one of the two who heard what John had said and who had followed Jesus. 41The first thing Andrew did was to find his brother Simon and tell him, "We have found the Messiah" (that is, the Christ). 42And he brought him to Jesus.

1:29 the Lamb of God, who takes away the sin of the world. Though Jesus is referred to as a lamb elsewhere in the Bible (1 Peter 1:19; Rev. 5:6; 13:8), this exact title for Jesus (the first in this section) occurs only here and in verse 36.

1:30 he was before me. John speaks of the pre-existence of Jesus (vv. 1–3). This is a divine quality which Jesus claimed for himself when he asserted that he predates not simply John but the Old Testament patriarch Abraham (8:58).

1:32 the Spirit ... remain. See Isaiah 11:2; 42:1. One of the unique qualities of the Messiah was that with him God's Spirit would permanently abide, unlike the occasional movement of the Spirit experienced by Old Testament kings and prophets.

1:33 he who will baptize with the Holy Spirit. This is the second title for Jesus. The analogy of water and the Spirit is carried on throughout this Gospel (3:5; 4:10–14; 7:37–39). Jesus' baptism is not a sign of repentance as John's was, but is an impartation of new life by God's Spirit.

1:38 What do you want? The motivation of those who would follow him is a concern for Jesus (2:24; 6:26). **Rabbi.** Rabbis were teachers who gathered disciples around them. **staying.** This is the same word translated in verse 33 as "remain." It hints that the concern in this question ("Where are you staying?") is on Jesus' true dwelling place. In this Gospel, recognition of Jesus' identity is tied up with recognizing where he is from and where he is going (8:21; 9:30; 14:2–6).

1:39 Come ... and you will see. Jesus invites these followers to enter into the journey of discipleship with him. Only as they commit themselves to follow him will they perceive the nature of his true home and identity. **the tenth hour.** Time was measured from the first light. Since daybreak was about 6 a.m., this was about 4 p.m.

1:41 We have found the Messiah. This is the fourth title ascribed to Jesus in this section (vv. 29,33–34).

1:42 Cephas. The Aramaic name Cephas and the Greek name Peter both mean "rock." Although Peter often seemed unstable during Jesus' time with him (18:15–17,25–27), after the ascension, Peter became the chief spokesman for the apostles and was later to be a leader in the early church (Acts 2:14).

Jesus looked at him and said, "You are Simon son of John. You will be called Cephas" (which, when translated, is Peter[a]).

Jesus Calls Philip and Nathanael

[43]The next day Jesus decided to leave for Galilee. Finding Philip, he said to him, "Follow me."

[44]Philip, like Andrew and Peter, was from the town of Bethsaida.
[45]Philip found Nathanael and told him, "We have found the one Moses wrote about in the Law, and about whom the prophets also wrote—Jesus of Nazareth, the son of Joseph."

[46]"Nazareth! Can anything good come from there?" Nathanael asked.

"Come and see," said Philip.

[47]When Jesus saw Nathanael approaching, he said of him, "Here is a true Israelite, in whom there is nothing false."

[48]"How do you know me?" Nathanael asked.

Jesus answered, "I saw you while you were still under the fig tree before Philip called you."

[49]Then Nathanael declared, "Rabbi, you are the Son of God; you are the King of Israel."

[50]Jesus said, "You believe[b] because I told you I saw you under the fig tree. You shall see greater things than that." [51]He then added, "I tell you[c] the truth, you[c] shall see heaven open, and the angels of God ascending and descending on the Son of Man."

Jesus Changes Water to Wine

2 On the third day a wedding took place at Cana in Galilee. Jesus' mother was there, [2]and Jesus and his disciples had also been invited to the wedding. [3]When the wine was gone, Jesus' mother said to him, "They have no more wine."

[4]"Dear woman, why do you involve me?" Jesus replied. "My time has not yet come."

[a]42 Both *Cephas* (Aramaic) and *Peter* (Greek) mean *rock.* [b]50 Or *Do you believe . . . ?* [c]51 The Greek is plural.

Philip tells his brother Nathanael about Jesus, what is his response? What is Nathanael's impression of Nazareth? **6.** What helps Nathanael overcome his initial skepticism about Jesus? In your own words, how would you put the response of Jesus in verses 50–51? **7.** How do you like the way Jesus invites someone to "test drive" before becoming a disciple? Could the church use this same system today? **8.** What is surprising about the people Jesus chooses to be his disciples? If you were picking, would you choose a bunch of fishermen from obscure villages with questionable ability?

APPLY 1. In your own spiritual pilgrimage, who saw the potential in your life before you saw it in yourself? **2.** How would your brother respond if you went to him and said, "I have found the Messiah, that is the Christ"?

OPEN What is the funniest thing you've witnessed at a wedding?

STUDY 1. What do you know about Jewish weddings? **2.** If you were Jesus' mother when the wine ran out and you were in charge of the reception, what would you have done? What do you think Jesus' mother expected Jesus to do when

1:43 Galilee. Galilee, where Jesus was raised, was a province 60 miles north of Jerusalem. One of the reasons the Pharisees rejected Jesus' claim to messiahship was because they assumed he was born in Galilee (7:41,52).

1:45 Moses wrote about in the Law. This refers to the Prophet to come (Deut. 18:18), the fulfillment of the Old Testament hope (v. 21).

1:46 Nazareth! This was a small, insignificant village in Galilee. It seemed impossible to Nathanael that the one Philip described could come from such a place.

1:47 a true Israelite. Nathanael, unlike Israel as a whole, came to him with sincerity. Israel was to be a people prepared to respond to God, but for the most part the nation failed to reflect that purpose.

1:48 I saw you. This accents the supernatural knowledge of Jesus.

1:50 greater things. This is probably an allusion to the miracles Jesus will perform as signs of his divine identity, culminated by the grand miracle of his resurrection.

1:51 This recalls Jacob's dream (Gen. 28:10–22), with the significant difference that Jesus replaces the ladder as the means of communication between heaven and earth. The new Bethel (house of God—Gen. 28:19) is found in Jesus himself. **the Son of Man.** Of all the titles for Jesus in this chapter, this is the one he uses for himself. Daniel 7:13ff provides its background as the one invested with divine authority to rule the earth, but it was not a commonly used term for the Messiah in Jesus' time.

2:1 a wedding took place. A wedding was a major party. Jesus' presence here reminds us that he was not a dour-faced ascetic who avoided the celebrations of life. **at Cana.** The exact location of this village is unknown, but it is believed to have been near Nazareth.

2:3 When the wine was gone. This was a humiliating social situation. It would reflect badly on the host as someone too miserly to provide adequate refreshments for the guests. **Jesus' mother.** Mary plays a minor role in this Gospel, appearing only here and in 19:25. Her concern for the situation as well as her relationship to the servants (v. 5) indicates she may have been active in the planning of the wedding.

she asked him to get involved? How did he feel about it? **3.** Why was the master of the banquet surprised? If you had been the bridegroom, what would you say when you were told about the new wine? **4.** Do you think Jesus overdid it a little when he produced enough wine for a small army? What would the elders at your church say about this?

APPLY 1. Where is the wine level in your life at the moment: Full? Half-full? Empty? **2.** Where could you use a miracle right now?

OPEN 1. When was the last time you spent a couple of days cleaning your house? **2.** Which of these people would motivate you to clean your house: Your mother? Your mother-in-law? A famous celebrity?

STUDY 1. What do you know about the Jewish temple in Jerusalem? What was the Passover all about? Why sheep and cattle? What is wrong with having a little casino to make money to support the temple, after all, it is for a good cause? **2.** Was Jesus mad? Disappointed? Disgusted? Outraged? Nice? If you had been there, would you have done what he did? **3.** What did the temple authorities do? Do you think they threatened his life when he answered, "destroy this temple, and I will raise it again in three days"? **4.** If Jesus came to your town to "clean house" where would he begin?

5 His mother said to the servants, "Do whatever he tells you."
6 Nearby stood six stone water jars, the kind used by the Jews for
ceremonial washing, each holding from twenty to thirty gallons.[a]
7 Jesus said to the servants, "Fill the jars with water"; so they filled
them to the brim.
8 Then he told them, "Now draw some out and take it to the master
of the banquet."
They did so, 9 and the master of the banquet tasted the water that
had been turned into wine. He did not realize where it had come
from, though the servants who had drawn the water knew. Then he
called the bridegroom aside 10 and said, "Everyone brings out the
choice wine first and then the cheaper wine after the guests have had
too much to drink; but you have saved the best till now."
11 This, the first of his miraculous signs, Jesus performed at Cana in
Galilee. He thus revealed his glory, and his disciples put their faith in
him.

Jesus Clears the Temple

12 After this he went down to Capernaum with his mother and
brothers and his disciples. There they stayed for a few days.
13 When it was almost time for the Jewish Passover, Jesus went up to
Jerusalem. 14 In the temple courts he found men selling cattle, sheep
and doves, and others sitting at tables exchanging money. 15 So he
made a whip out of cords, and drove all from the temple area, both
sheep and cattle; he scattered the coins of the money changers and
overturned their tables. 16 To those who sold doves he said, "Get these
out of here! How dare you turn my Father's house into a market!"
17 His disciples remembered that it is written: "Zeal for your house
will consume me."[b]
18 Then the Jews demanded of him, "What miraculous sign can you
show us to prove your authority to do all this?"
19 Jesus answered them, "Destroy this temple, and I will raise it
again in three days."
20 The Jews replied, "It has taken forty-six years to build this tem-

[a]6 Greek *two to three metretes* (probably about 75 to 115 liters) [b]*17* Psalm 69:9

2:8 the master of the banquet. This appears to be an honored guest at the wedding, serving in a role somewhat to that of a modern-day toastmaster.

2:10 Everyone brings out the choice wine first. Typically, the best wine would be served when the guests would be most able to appreciate it.

2:11 miraculous signs. John uses this term frequently to describe Jesus' miracles in order to encourage his readers not to see them simply as acts of power, but as pointers to God's presence in Jesus seen by those who receive him (1:12).

2:14 men selling cattle. This trade began as a means of allowing travelers to purchase an animal for sacrifice at the temple rather than having to lead one during their journey. However, by this time it had deteriorated into a money-making scheme for the sellers who charged inflated prices for the animals. Likewise, coins from other parts of the empire had to be exchanged for local coinage to pay the temple tax.

2:18 the Jews. In this Gospel, this usually refers to the religious leaders in Jerusalem and Judea who were hostile to Jesus. Since the author and many of Jesus' followers were Jewish, this must not be understood in any way as an anti-Semitic sentiment. In this context, it has more of a political sense (i.e., "the establishment") than an ethnic one.

2:19 Destroy this temple, and I will raise it again in three days. The leaders misunderstand Jesus' meaning, typical of a pattern used in this Gospel in which people respond to Jesus' comments on a literal level while missing their spiritual importance (3:4; 4:15; 6:42,52; 8:32–33). After the resurrection, as verses 22–23 state, the disciples realized that Jesus meant himself as the true place in which God dwells (1:14,51).

2:20 forty-six years. In 20 B.C. Herod began an extensive rebuilding of the temple, which continued on until A.D. 63. In light of the massive amount of time and labor involved, Jesus' statement was outrageous. They still were not convinced of his deity.

ple, and you are going to raise it in three days?" 21But the temple he
had spoken of was his body. 22After he was raised from the dead, his
disciples recalled what he had said. Then they believed the Scripture
and the words that Jesus had spoken.
23Now while he was in Jerusalem at the Passover Feast, many people saw the miraculous signs he was doing and believed in his name.[a]
24But Jesus would not entrust himself to them, for he knew all men.
25He did not need man's testimony about man, for he knew what was
in a man.

Jesus Teaches Nicodemus

3 Now there was a man of the Pharisees named Nicodemus, a
member of the Jewish ruling council. 2He came to Jesus at night
and said, "Rabbi, we know you are a teacher who has come from
God. For no one could perform the miraculous signs you are doing if
God were not with him."
3In reply Jesus declared, "I tell you the truth, no one can see the
kingdom of God unless he is born again.[b]"
4"How can a man be born when he is old?" Nicodemus asked.
"Surely he cannot enter a second time into his mother's womb to be
born!"
5Jesus answered, "I tell you the truth, no one can enter the kingdom of God unless he is born of water and the Spirit. 6Flesh gives
birth to flesh, but the Spirit[c] gives birth to spirit. 7You should not be
surprised at my saying, 'You[d] must be born again.' 8The wind blows
wherever it pleases. You hear its sound, but you cannot tell where it
comes from or where it is going. So it is with everyone born of the
Spirit."
9"How can this be?" Nicodemus asked.
10"You are Israel's teacher," said Jesus, "and do you not understand
these things? 11I tell you the truth, we speak of what we know, and we
testify to what we have seen, but still you people do not accept our
testimony. 12I have spoken to you of earthly things and you do not
believe; how then will you believe if I speak of heavenly things? 13No
one has ever gone into heaven except the one who came from heav-
en—the Son of Man.[e] 14Just as Moses lifted up the snake in the desert,

[a]23 Or *and believed in him* [b]3 Or *born from above;* also in verse 7 [c]6 Or *but spirit* [d]7 The Greek is plural. [e]13 Some manuscripts *Man, who is in heaven*

APPLY In your spiritual pilgrimage, when did Jesus perform a radical clean up job on your life?

____

OPEN Who first told you where babies come from? How old were you when you learned the real story?

STUDY 1. What can you find out about Nicodemus in verses 1–2? What is surprising about his coming to Jesus? Why at night? Why was Jesus so direct with him? **2.** What two ideas about birth are Jesus and Nicodemus thinking of? What point is Jesus making by comparing spiritual birth to the wind? How does Jesus account for Nicodemus' lack of understanding? **3.** What does Jesus claim about himself in verses 13–15? **4.** From verses 16–18, what stands out to you about God: About what he wants to do? How a person is condemned? How will belief show itself (vv. 15–21)? **5.** How is Jesus' use of the words "born again" similar to and different from the way it is used today? How would you define "born again" in your own words?

APPLY 1. When did you first get interested in knowing more about Jesus? **2.** How would you compare your spiritual experience to Nicodemus' experience? **3.** Where are you right now in this process?

____

2:25 he knew what was in a man. The Scriptures (1 Kin. 8:39) and the rabbis taught that only God could know this.

3:1 Pharisees. Judaism was divided into various sects along doctrinal, political, practical and social lines. The *Pharisees were committed to the principle* that religious and ethical purity was the means of securing God's favor. This in turn led to a concern for the fine points of the Law, which tended to overshadow the essence of that Law. **Nicodemus.** Nicodemus, a respected religious authority (v. 10), appears in 7:50 and 19:39 but in no other Gospel. **Jewish ruling council.** This was the Sanhedrin—the religious and political governing body of Judea. Comprised of 71 members and presided over by the high priest, its self-perpetuating membership included priests, elders and scribes.

3:3 born again. This phrase can be translated in two ways—"born again" or "born from above." The former highlights the radical reorientation to life resulting from trusting Jesus while the latter accents the reality that spiritual life is a gift from God, not something earned by virtue of one's performance (1:12–13).

3:5 born of water and the Spirit. Commentators differ on what is meant here: (1) Some think this phrase is a restatement of the call for a spiritual birth in addition to physical birth (v. 3); (2) Others assume water illustrates the life-giving qualities of the Spirit (7:38–39); (3) Others think that the author, writing about A.D. 90, refers to contemporary practices of baptism as a symbol of the baptism in the Spirit.

3:13 This Gospel's witness to Jesus is from the perspective of the whole story already told, hence the author can refer to the ascension of Jesus even at this point.

3:14 Because of rebellion, God sent deadly serpents into the midst of the Israelites. When they called for mercy,

so the Son of Man must be lifted up, 15that everyone who believes in
him may have eternal life.[a]
16"For God so loved the world that he gave his one and only Son,[b]
that whoever believes in him shall not perish but have eternal life.
17For God did not send his Son into the world to condemn the world,
but to save the world through him. 18Whoever believes in him is not
condemned, but whoever does not believe stands condemned
already because he has not believed in the name of God's one and
only Son.[c] 19This is the verdict: Light has come into the world, but
men loved darkness instead of light because their deeds were evil.
20Everyone who does evil hates the light, and will not come into the
light for fear that his deeds will be exposed. 21But whoever lives by
the truth comes into the light, so that it may be seen plainly that what
he has done has been done through God."[d]

John the Baptist's Testimony About Jesus

22After this, Jesus and his disciples went out into the Judean countryside, where he spent some time with them, and baptized. 23Now
John also was baptizing at Aenon near Salim, because there was
plenty of water, and people were constantly coming to be baptized.
24(This was before John was put in prison.) 25An argument developed
between some of John's disciples and a certain Jew[e] over the matter
of ceremonial washing. 26They came to John and said to him, "Rabbi,
that man who was with you on the other side of the Jordan—the one
you testified about—well, he is baptizing, and everyone is going to
him."
27To this John replied, "A man can receive only what is given him

[a]15 Or *believes may have eternal life in him* [b]16 Or *his only begotten Son* [c]18 Or *God's only begotten Son* [d]21 Some interpreters end the quotation after verse 15. [e]25 Some manuscripts *and certain Jews*

OPEN 1. What did you and your brother or sister fight about? How would you try to get your way? **2.** At family reunions, what subject (politics or religion) is bound to start an argument?

STUDY 1. How much water did it take for you to get baptized? **2.** If you had been a disciple of John the Baptist, how would you have felt about Jesus and his disciples? What brought things to a head? **3.** How does John the Baptist respond (vv. 27–36)? What is the point of the allegory or story about the bride and bridegroom? What does John's response tell you about him? **4.** What facts about

God instructed Moses to put up on a pole a statue of a serpent. Whoever looked upon that statue would not die (Num. 21:4–9). In a similar way, when people look with faith upon Jesus who is "lifted up" (another double-edged phrase referring both to his crucifixion and his resurrection / ascension), their judgment is averted and they are brought into life (6:40).

3:15 eternal life. This is the first use of a phrase seen over and over in this Gospel. Its meaning is not simply tied up with the quantity of time one exists, but also with the quality of fullness, goodness and perfection of life with God.

3:16 God so loved the world. The great motivation behind God's plan of salvation (1 John 4:9–10). **he gave.** This is evidenced especially in the act of Jesus' incarnation and crucifixion.

3:17 to save the world. The whole point of Jesus' mission was to provide all people with access to God.

3:18 condemned already. It is our own behavior that condemns us. Through Jesus, God is seeking to save us from the condemnation that is the result of our own actions. **one and only Son.** In one sense, all who are obedient to God are children of God (Rom. 8:14; 9:26; 2 Cor. 6:16–18; Gal. 3:26; 4:4–7; Eph. 1:5; Phil. 2:14–15; Heb. 12:5–9). However, Jesus is the unique Son of God, in that he alone fully reflects the Father.

3:19–20 Just as 3:16–18 sums up the good news of the gospel, so these verses sum up the human situation which makes the gospel so necessary. The problem is not a lack of understanding of the "light," but a decided preference for the "darkness." This point is echoed in Romans 1:18 where Paul speaks of people suppressing the truth of God in order to pursue a life of sin and wickedness.

3:21 whoever lives by the truth. This stands in parallel with "whoever believes in him" (v. 16) and in contrast with "everyone who does evil" (v. 20). Taken together, these phrases show that belief in Jesus and a lifestyle marked by obedience to God's ways go hand in hand (1 John 3:10).

3:22 into the Judean countryside ... baptized. The other Gospel writers never mention this stage of Jesus' ministry, which may indicate some passage of time between Mark 1:13 and 14. John 4:2 says it was not Jesus who actually baptized, but his disciples. Probably their baptism at this point was the same as John's call for repentance.

3:24 The story of John's imprisonment and execution is omitted by this Gospel (Mark 6:14–29).

3:26 everyone is going to him. Some of John's disciples were not happy that Jesus was outdistancing their master in popularity.

3:27 A man can receive. The implication is that the people who are coming to Jesus are given to him by God. Since that is the case, these disciples of John should not be worried or upset that people (who otherwise might have come to John the Baptist) are now going to Jesus.

from heaven. 28You yourselves can testify that I said, 'I am not the
Christ[a] but am sent ahead of him.' 29The bride belongs to the bridegroom. The friend who attends the bridegroom waits and listens for
him, and is full of joy when he hears the bridegroom's voice. That joy
is mine, and it is now complete. 30He must become greater; I must
become less.

31"The one who comes from above is above all; the one who is from
the earth belongs to the earth, and speaks as one from the earth. The
one who comes from heaven is above all. 32He testifies to what he has
seen and heard, but no one accepts his testimony. 33The man who
has accepted it has certified that God is truthful. 34For the one whom
God has sent speaks the words of God, for God[b] gives the Spirit without limit. 35The Father loves the Son and has placed everything in his
hands. 36Whoever believes in the Son has eternal life, but whoever
rejects the Son will not see life, for God's wrath remains on him."[c]

Jesus Talks With a Samaritan Woman

4 The Pharisees heard that Jesus was gaining and baptizing more
disciples than John, 2although in fact it was not Jesus who
baptized, but his disciples. 3When the Lord learned of this, he left
Judea and went back once more to Galilee.

4Now he had to go through Samaria. 5So he came to a town in
Samaria called Sychar, near the plot of ground Jacob had given to his
son Joseph. 6Jacob's well was there, and Jesus, tired as he was from
the journey, sat down by the well. It was about the sixth hour.

7When a Samaritan woman came to draw water, Jesus said to her,
"Will you give me a drink?" 8(His disciples had gone into the town to
buy food.)

9The Samaritan woman said to him, "You are a Jew and I am a
Samaritan woman. How can you ask me for a drink?" (For Jews do
not associate with Samaritans.[d])

10Jesus answered her, "If you knew the gift of God and who it is that
asks you for a drink, you would have asked him and he would have
given you living water."

11"Sir," the woman said, "you have nothing to draw with and the
well is deep. Where can you get this living water? 12Are you greater

[a]28 Or *Messiah* [b]34 Greek *he* [c]36 Some interpreters end the quotation after verse 30. [d]9 Or *do not use dishes Samaritans have used*

Jesus does John bring out in verses 31–36? **5.** How would you put verse 30 in your own words?

APPLY 1. If God asked you to perform a special mission for him, what would you say? **2.** What are your friends and neighbors looking for that Jesus is the answer to?

OPEN When you were growing up, who were the people you were told to avoid? What part of the city or country would you be warned about? What would have happened if you had gone there?

STUDY 1. What is significant about this story taking place in Samaria? **2.** Since "nice" girls did not come to draw water at noontime ("the sixth hour"), why do you think Jesus risked his reputation to ask a favor of this woman? **3.** How would you describe the woman's response? **4.** How did Jesus turn the tables on her in 4:10? **5.** In the woman's reply, what is she really saying? **6.** Why does Jesus change the topic of conversation so abruptly to her personal life (4:16–18)? What strikes you about the way he responds to her claim not to have a husband? **7.** Why do you think this woman changed the conversation to focus on a religious controversy? In this story, what does Jesus mean by telling her that God is interested in worshipers who will do

---

3:29 friend who attends the bridegroom. This is John, whose purpose all along has been to prepare people for the Messiah (1:31).

4:1–3 The Pharisees had already investigated John (1:24–27), and the other Gospels make clear their opposition to him because of his challenge to their position (Matt. 3:7–10; Mark 11:27–33). Jesus' popularity undoubtedly fueled their suspicions as well.

4:4 Samaria. This was a territory sandwiched between the provinces of Judea and Galilee. When the northern kingdom of Israel was conquered in 722 B.C. by the Assyrians, many of its people were deported and exiles from other areas of the vast Assyrian Empire were brought in (2 Kin. 17:22–41). Many of these people intermarried with the remaining Israelites and adopted some of the Jewish religious practices. In Jesus' day, strict Jews would avoid Samaria as an unclean area, and the term "Samaritan" was used as an insult (8:48).

4:5 near the plot of ground Jacob had given to his son Joseph. Genesis 48:22 tells of Jacob giving some land to Joseph.

4:6 the sixth hour. Since the day began at sunrise, about six in the morning, this is about noon.

4:7 came to draw water. Noontime, the heat of the day, was not the normal time women would perform this chore. She was avoiding conversation with other women, which implies she received their criticism.

4:9 Jews do not associate with Samaritans. Since some strands of Judaism regarded Samaritans as unclean from birth, Jesus' request shocks the woman.

4:10 living water. This was a common phrase meaning water that flowed from a river or spring. Water like this had better quality than the standing water of a well or pond.

so in "spirit and truth"? **8.** What is significant about Jesus choosing this woman as the first person to whom he revealed himself (4:39–42)? **9.** What are some principles in this story for building relationships and sharing your faith story?

APPLY 1. In your spiritual journey, what was the first time you were in a community that crossed over racial and ethnic barriers? **2.** What is the challenge in your community to make the church really inclusive of all people?

OPEN What causes you to skip a meal? To eat too much?

STUDY 1. Why were the disciples surprised to find Jesus with this woman? **2.** What does "leaving her water jar" reveal about Jesus' impact on the woman? How did she affect others? **3.** How is Jesus' figurative speech once again misunderstood (2:19; 3:3; 4:10)? **4.** How does the parable of harvesting apply to the disciples? **5.** Given the social

than our father Jacob, who gave us the well and drank from it himself,
as did also his sons and his flocks and herds?"
13 Jesus answered, "Everyone who drinks this water will be thirsty
again, 14 but whoever drinks the water I give him will never thirst. Indeed, the water I give him will become in him a spring of water well-
ing up to eternal life."
15 The woman said to him, "Sir, give me this water so that I won't
get thirsty and have to keep coming here to draw water."
16 He told her, "Go, call your husband and come back."
17 "I have no husband," she replied.
Jesus said to her, "You are right when you say you have no husband. 18 The fact is, you have had five husbands, and the man you now
have is not your husband. What you have just said is quite true."
19 "Sir," the woman said, "I can see that you are a prophet. 20 Our fathers worshiped on this mountain, but you Jews claim that the place
where we must worship is in Jerusalem."
21 Jesus declared, "Believe me, woman, a time is coming when you
will worship the Father neither on this mountain nor in Jerusalem.
22 You Samaritans worship what you do not know; we worship what
we do know, for salvation is from the Jews. 23 Yet a time is coming and
has now come when the true worshipers will worship the Father in
spirit and truth, for they are the kind of worshipers the Father seeks.
24 God is spirit, and his worshipers must worship in spirit and in
truth."
25 The woman said, "I know that Messiah" (called Christ) "is coming. When he comes, he will explain everything to us."
26 Then Jesus declared, "I who speak to you am he."

The Disciples Rejoin Jesus

27 Just then his disciples returned and were surprised to find him
talking with a woman. But no one asked, "What do you want?" or
"Why are you talking with her?"
28 Then, leaving her water jar, the woman went back to the town
and said to the people, 29 "Come, see a man who told me everything I
ever did. Could this be the Christ[a]?" 30 They came out of the town and
made their way toward him.
31 Meanwhile his disciples urged him, "Rabbi, eat something."

[a]29 Or *Messiah*

4:14 spring. This is the same word translated as "well" (v. 6). By this play on words the author presents us with a picture of two fountains or wells. Jesus' "well" forever quenches spiritual thirst simply for the asking.

4:17–18 While clearly revealing his knowledge of her situation, Jesus commends her truthfulness. Women in this time could be divorced for trivial reasons, but had no right of divorce themselves. It is also possible that she had simply been abandoned by one or more of her husbands and was simply a mistress to the man she was with now—she was considered immoral.

4:19 prophet. Jesus' knowledge of her led her to see him as a prophet who must be taken seriously. The Samaritans did not acknowledge the Jewish prophets and writings but held only to the five books of Moses.

4:21–23 In 2:12–22 Jesus had shown that he himself is the new temple that supersedes the physical building in Jerusalem. Here he shows that the Samaritan religious claims are likewise superseded by his appearing. The point is not where one worships, but whom.

4:23 a time is coming and has now come. This captures the tension of the Gospel's announcement about the kingdom of God. It is both present and yet future. **true worshipers.** The barrier between Jewish and Samaritan religion is dismissed. Their concern about location indicates that both have missed the point.

4:29 Come, see. This is the same invitation to discipleship extended to Andrew and Nathanael (1:39–40,46). **Could this be the Christ?** The phrase in Greek appears to require a negative answer, yet hopes for a positive one.

[32]But he said to them, "I have food to eat that you know nothing
about."

[33]Then his disciples said to each other, "Could someone have
brought him food?"

[34]"My food," said Jesus, "is to do the will of him who sent me and
to finish his work. [35]Do you not say, 'Four months more and then the
harvest'? I tell you, open your eyes and look at the fields! They are
ripe for harvest. [36]Even now the reaper draws his wages, even now he
harvests the crop for eternal life, so that the sower and the reaper
may be glad together. [37]Thus the saying 'One sows and another reaps'
is true. [38]I sent you to reap what you have not worked for. Others
have done the hard work, and you have reaped the benefits of their
labor."

Many Samaritans Believe

[39]Many of the Samaritans from that town believed in him because
of the woman's testimony, "He told me everything I ever did." [40]So
when the Samaritans came to him, they urged him to stay with them,
and he stayed two days. [41]And because of his words many more became believers.

[42]They said to the woman, "We no longer believe just because of
what you said; now we have heard for ourselves, and we know that
this man really is the Savior of the world."

Jesus Heals the Official's Son

[43]After the two days he left for Galilee. [44](Now Jesus himself had
pointed out that a prophet has no honor in his own country.) [45]When
he arrived in Galilee, the Galileans welcomed him. They had seen all
that he had done in Jerusalem at the Passover Feast, for they also had
been there.

[46]Once more he visited Cana in Galilee, where he had turned the
water into wine. And there was a certain royal official whose son lay

barriers between Jews and Samaritans, what do verses 40–42 teach you about Jesus? **6.** What do you learn from the woman about sharing your spiritual story? What about the parable in verses 35–38?

APPLY 1. When is the last time you forgot to eat for the sheer joy of being involved in Christian work? **2.** Where is God calling you to "go back" and share your story?

OPEN When you were a child, what was the most serious illness or injury you had?

STUDY 1. What happened on a previous visit to Cana that would cause the royal official to take notice? What was his motive for seeking out Jesus? **2.** Who is Jesus talking about when he says "unless

---

4:33 Could someone have brought him food? In this Gospel, the listener's misunderstanding is often used to provide an opportunity for Jesus to expand more fully on what he meant (v. 15; 2:20; 3:4; 6:34; 11:13).

4:34 him who sent me. Jesus often uses this phrase as a title for the Father. It emphasizes his awareness of his mission and his sense of operating within the will of his Father. It is this purpose and mission that filled him with satisfaction ("my food"). **to finish his work.** The work of the Father which Jesus has come to complete is to give eternal life to all that the Father has given him (6:39). This work is to be accomplished by means of the death of Jesus.

4:35 Four months more and then the harvest? This saying may have been used in a popular way to indicate that there was no great rush to finish a task (i.e., no matter what you do, it still takes four months for the harvest to grow). Jesus is contradicting that proverb by insisting that, although he has only just "sown the seed" of the gospel with the woman, already a harvest is about to be gathered. The disciples are to see the urgency of the work of the kingdom.

4:37 One sows and another reaps. Although this saying has its roots in thoughts about the unfairness and hardness of life (Job 31:8; Mic. 6:15), Jesus transforms it into a positive reflection of the joy of partnership in building God's kingdom. In the case of the woman, he reaps the work of his Father, the sower. But in verse 38 it will be the disciples who reap what others (such as Jesus, John the Baptist, and the prophets) have sown.

4:42 Savior. This is the only place in all the Gospels where Jesus is directly called Savior. It is commonly used to describe God in the Old Testament as the one who rescues (Isa. 43:3,11; 49:6; Jer. 14:8) and so becomes yet another pointer to his deity. **of the world.** This Gospel stresses Jesus' mission involves all types of people (3:16; 8:12; 10:16; 17:20). Whereas Nicodemus the Pharisee could not grasp the universality of God's love (3:16), and the religious leaders scoffed at the idea of Jesus teaching "the Greeks" (7:35), these "unclean Samaritans," recognizing that God's plan included them, embraced it with joy!

4:44 a prophet has no honor in his own country. In the other Gospels this phrase is clearly linked to Jesus' rejection in Nazareth (Matt. 13:57; Mark 6:4; Luke 4:24). Why it is mentioned here is uncertain. It may be in anticipation of the fact that while his initial reception in Galilee would be positive (v. 45), the people would ultimately reject him.

4:46 Capernaum. This village was about 20 miles from Cana.

your people see miraculous signs and wonders, you will not believe"? How does the royal official stand in contrast to the rest of the people? **3.** How would you have responded to what Jesus told the royal official to do? When you take a problem to Jesus, do you accept his word and get on with life or keep fretting and fussing?

APPLY What is the closest you have come to the experience of the royal official—praying about something and finding out much later that God was working in the situation as soon as you started to pray?

OPEN When you were a kid, how sick did you have to be to stay in bed and miss school?

STUDY **1.** How do you think the paralytic got to the pool everyday? What was he looking for? **2.** Why did Jesus ask him, "Do you want to get well"? **3.** What was the paralytic's excuse for not getting well? **4.** How does Jesus deal with his complaint? **5.** What was the paralytic doing that Jesus called "sin"? If he was already healed, what had he been doing that he might slip back into? **6.** What is the closest you have come to seeing a person like this, who was crippled in some way? **7.** How should the church should get involved in helping people with addictive behaviors?

sick at Capernaum. [47]When this man heard that Jesus had arrived in
Galilee from Judea, he went to him and begged him to come and heal
his son, who was close to death.
[48]"Unless you people see miraculous signs and wonders," Jesus
told him, "you will never believe."
[49]The royal official said, "Sir, come down before my child dies."
[50]Jesus replied, "You may go. Your son will live."
The man took Jesus at his word and departed. [51]While he was still
on the way, his servants met him with the news that his boy was living.
[52]When he inquired as to the time when his son got better, they
said to him, "The fever left him yesterday at the seventh hour."
[53]Then the father realized that this was the exact time at which
Jesus had said to him, "Your son will live." So he and all his household
believed.
[54]This was the second miraculous sign that Jesus performed, having
come from Judea to Galilee.

The Healing at the Pool

5 Some time later, Jesus went up to Jerusalem for a feast of the
Jews. [2]Now there is in Jerusalem near the Sheep Gate a pool,
which in Aramaic is called Bethesda[a] and which is surrounded by five
covered colonnades. [3]Here a great number of disabled people used to
lie—the blind, the lame, the paralyzed.[b] [5]One who was there had
been an invalid for thirty-eight years. [6]When Jesus saw him lying
there and learned that he had been in this condition for a long time,
he asked him, "Do you want to get well?"
[7]"Sir," the invalid replied, "I have no one to help me into the pool
when the water is stirred. While I am trying to get in, someone else
goes down ahead of me."
[8]Then Jesus said to him, "Get up! Pick up your mat and walk." [9]At
once the man was cured; he picked up his mat and walked.
The day on which this took place was a Sabbath, [10]and so the Jews

[a]2 Some manuscripts *Bethzatha;* other manuscripts *Bethsaida* [b]3 Some less important manuscripts *paralyzed—and they waited for the moving of the waters.* [4]*From time to time an angel of the Lord would come down and stir up the waters. The first one into the pool after each such disturbance would be cured of whatever disease he had.*

4:48 you. This is a plural form indicating Jesus' remarks are meant for a wider audience than only the official. **Unless you people see ... you will never believe.** The reliance upon miracles as an evidence for faith did not meet with Jesus' favor because such faith lacked the depth of conviction found in those who believed because of the truth of what he said.

4:50 The man stands in contrast to the crowds in verse 48 by becoming an example of what faith in Jesus is all about—to trust his promises upon his *authority even* though circumstances may appear unchanged. This was not grasped by the apostles until after Jesus'resurrection (2:22).

4:52 the seventh hour. About 1 p.m. Hours were numbered from sunrise, which was about 6 a.m.

4:54 the second miraculous sign. The author only numbers the first sign at Cana (2:11) and this one in spite of the fact that many others are alluded to and five more are detailed.

5:1 feast of the Jews. The three major Jewish festivals attracting pilgrims to Jerusalem were Passover, Pentecost and the Feast of Tabernacles. The specific feasts are mentioned elsewhere. There is no indication of which one is in view.

5:2 Bethesda. The exact name is uncertain, but this pool has been excavated. Fed by intermittent springs, it was seen as a healing shrine even by second-century Roman cults.

5:7 I have no one to help me. The man had no prior expectation of Jesus as a healer. He was hopeful only that Jesus might assist him in getting into the water at the next available moment.

5:8 Pick up your mat. Jesus gives this man something to do in order to take responsibility for his own life, his own healing. In the man's response in verse 7, he had essentially said it was out of his control—he had no one to help him. Jesus was bringing him healing, but he had to take some action on his own.

5:10 the law forbids you to carry your mat. This is an example of the traditions that the rabbis had developed

said to the man who had been healed, "It is the Sabbath; the law forbids you to carry your mat."

11 But he replied, "The man who made me well said to me, 'Pick up your mat and walk.' "

12 So they asked him, "Who is this fellow who told you to pick it up and walk?"

13 The man who was healed had no idea who it was, for Jesus had slipped away into the crowd that was there.

14 Later Jesus found him at the temple and said to him, "See, you are well again. Stop sinning or something worse may happen to you."
15 The man went away and told the Jews that it was Jesus who had made him well.

Life Through the Son

16 So, because Jesus was doing these things on the Sabbath, the
Jews persecuted him. 17 Jesus said to them, "My Father is always at his
work to this very day, and I, too, am working." 18 For this reason the
Jews tried all the harder to kill him; not only was he breaking the Sabbath, but he was even calling God his own Father, making himself equal with God.

19 Jesus gave them this answer: "I tell you the truth, the Son can do
nothing by himself; he can do only what he sees his Father doing, because whatever the Father does the Son also does. 20 For the Father
loves the Son and shows him all he does. Yes, to your amazement he
will show him even greater things than these. 21 For just as the Father
raises the dead and gives them life, even so the Son gives life to
whom he is pleased to give it. 22 Moreover, the Father judges no one,
but has entrusted all judgment to the Son, 23 that all may honor the
Son just as they honor the Father. He who does not honor the Son does not honor the Father, who sent him.

24 "I tell you the truth, whoever hears my word and believes him
who sent me has eternal life and will not be condemned; he has
crossed over from death to life. 25 I tell you the truth, a time is coming
and has now come when the dead will hear the voice of the Son of
God and those who hear will live. 26 For as the Father has life in himself, so he has granted the Son to have life in himself. 27 And he has
given him authority to judge because he is the Son of Man.

28 "Do not be amazed at this, for a time is coming when all who are
in their graves will hear his voice 29 and come out—those who have
done good will rise to live, and those who have done evil will rise to
be condemned. 30 By myself I can do nothing; I judge only as I hear,
and my judgment is just, for I seek not to please myself but him who sent me.

APPLY 1. Who do you think is responsible for most of your problems? **2.** If Jesus challenged you, "do you want to get well," what would you say?

OPEN As you get older, do you find yourself becoming more, or less, like your parents?

STUDY 1. What happened in the previous story that gets Jesus in trouble? Why? When the author speaks of "Jews" who is he referring to? **2.** How did his response to the Jewish leaders only heighten their opposition? Why would Jesus do this? **3.** In what ways is Jesus equal with the Father (vv. 26–27)? What terms are used to show the kind of relationship between the two? **4.** What claims does Jesus make about himself in verse 24? What is the promise? **5.** What happens to those who hear and believe (vv. 24–30)? To those who do not? **6.** How would you describe the business that God the Father and God the Son are in? **7.** What do verses 28–30 teach about the future? **8.** How would you paraphrase verse 24 in your own words?

APPLY 1. If you had to pinpoint a time in your life when you "crossed over from death to life" in Jesus Christ, when would this be? **2.** Right now, are you committed to as much of God's will for your life as you understand?

---

over the years in an attempt to help people obey the Law.

5:13 had slipped away. Apparently Jesus had not identified himself in order to get credit for this healing.

5:14 Stop sinning or something worse may happen to you. Jesus did not accept the common idea that such infirmities as this man had suffered from were always the result of personal sin (9:1–3).

5:25 a time is coming and has now come. Jesus says new life occurs now as the spiritually dead come to life when they respond to the Son that will give them true life (1:12).

OPEN Which of these would you trust their word without question: Preacher? Politician? Accountant? Lawyer? Coach?

STUDY 1. Who is Jesus talking to in this passage (vv. 9,16)? Who is John and what did he say about Jesus? **2.** What is the "weightier" testimony that proves God has sent Jesus? Why is it so hard for the religious leaders to understand? **3.** What do the religious leaders do with Scripture? **4.** What is the lesson in this passage for the church today? Why is it that people with the most opportunity and knowledge of Scripture are sometimes the hardest to reach for Christ?

APPLY 1. How would you describe your early religious background: A lot of Bible knowledge without spiritual rebirth—or no Bible knowledge before rebirth? **2.** What are you going to do in raising your children to prepare them for a personal faith in Christ?

OPEN If you had to feed 5,000 people, what would you serve?

STUDY 1. If you had been Philip when Jesus asked him, "where shall we buy bread for these people to eat?", what would you have said? **2.** What is interesting about Andrew's idea? If you were grading their faith, what grade would you give these guys? **3.** How does Jesus go about feeding the crowd? Why was there more left after the feeding than before? **4.** How do you account for this miracle? Do you take this miracle on faith or try to explain it away?

Testimonies About Jesus

31 "If I testify about myself, my testimony is not valid. 32 There is another who testifies in my favor, and I know that his testimony about
me is valid.
33 "You have sent to John and he has testified to the truth. 34 Not that
I accept human testimony; but I mention it that you may be saved.
35 John was a lamp that burned and gave light, and you chose for a
time to enjoy his light.
36 "I have testimony weightier than that of John. For the very work
that the Father has given me to finish, and which I am doing, testifies
that the Father has sent me. 37 And the Father who sent me has himself testified concerning me. You have never heard his voice nor seen
his form, 38 nor does his word dwell in you, for you do not believe the
one he sent. 39 You diligently study[a] the Scriptures because you think
that by them you possess eternal life. These are the Scriptures that
testify about me, 40 yet you refuse to come to me to have life.
41 "I do not accept praise from men, 42 but I know you. I know that
you do not have the love of God in your hearts. 43 I have come in my
Father's name, and you do not accept me; but if someone else comes
in his own name, you will accept him. 44 How can you believe if you
accept praise from one another, yet make no effort to obtain the
praise that comes from the only God[b]?
45 "But do not think I will accuse you before the Father. Your accuser
is Moses, on whom your hopes are set. 46 If you believed Moses, you
would believe me, for he wrote about me. 47 But since you do not believe what he wrote, how are you going to believe what I say?"

Jesus Feeds the Five Thousand

6 Some time after this, Jesus crossed to the far shore of the Sea of
Galilee (that is, the Sea of Tiberias), 2 and a great crowd of people
followed him because they saw the miraculous signs he had performed on the sick. 3 Then Jesus went up on a mountainside and sat
down with his disciples. 4 The Jewish Passover Feast was near.
5 When Jesus looked up and saw a great crowd coming toward him,
he said to Philip, "Where shall we buy bread for these people to eat?"
6 He asked this only to test him, for he already had in mind what he
was going to do.
7 Philip answered him, "Eight months' wages[c] would not buy
enough bread for each one to have a bite!"

[a]39 Or *Study diligently* (the imperative) [b]44 Some early manuscripts *the Only One* [c]7 Greek *two hundred denarii*

5:32 another. This means the Father.

5:35 John was a lamp. Reference to the lamp of Psalm 132:17 which God would set up to light the way for his "anointed one."

5:45 Your accuser is Moses. They *believed Jesus had rejected the Law,* but it was they who had abandoned it. Therefore, it is the Law, in which they pride themselves, which will condemn them.

6:1 the Sea of Tiberias. Tiberias was a city founded on the shore of the Sea of Galilee in 20 A.D. by Herod. By the time this Gospel was written, this new name for the Sea of Galilee had become well known.

6:4 Jewish Passover Feast. Passover celebrated Israel's deliverance from Egypt (Ex. 12:1–13). At that time, each family of Israel was to sacrifice a lamb, eat it, and put its blood on the doorframe of their house so that God's avenging angel would "pass over" that house as Egypt was punished. Hence the lamb's blood was accepted in place of their firstborn, and its flesh nourished them for their escape from Egypt. The Passover theme makes sense of the transition from "bread" to "flesh" later in verse 51, since Jesus is the true lamb whose blood assures deliverance from God's wrath and whose flesh nurtures believers into life. This assurance is a gift each person must choose on their own.

[8]Another of his disciples, Andrew, Simon Peter's brother, spoke up,
[9]"Here is a boy with five small barley loaves and two small fish, but
how far will they go among so many?"

[10]Jesus said, "Have the people sit down." There was plenty of grass
in that place, and the men sat down, about five thousand of them.
[11]Jesus then took the loaves, gave thanks, and distributed to those
who were seated as much as they wanted. He did the same with the
fish.

[12]When they had all had enough to eat, he said to his disciples,
"Gather the pieces that are left over. Let nothing be wasted." [13]So
they gathered them and filled twelve baskets with the pieces of the
five barley loaves left over by those who had eaten.

[14]After the people saw the miraculous sign that Jesus did, they began to say, "Surely this is the Prophet who is to come into the world."
[15]Jesus, knowing that they intended to come and make him king by
force, withdrew again to a mountain by himself.

Jesus Walks on the Water

[16]When evening came, his disciples went down to the lake, [17]where
they got into a boat and set off across the lake for Capernaum. By
now it was dark, and Jesus had not yet joined them. [18]A strong wind
was blowing and the waters grew rough. [19]When they had rowed
three or three and a half miles,[a] they saw Jesus approaching the boat,
walking on the water; and they were terrified. [20]But he said to them,
"It is I; don't be afraid." [21]Then they were willing to take him into the
boat, and immediately the boat reached the shore where they were
heading.

[22]The next day the crowd that had stayed on the opposite shore of
the lake realized that only one boat had been there, and that Jesus
had not entered it with his disciples, but that they had gone away
alone. [23]Then some boats from Tiberias landed near the place where
the people had eaten the bread after the Lord had given thanks.
[24]Once the crowd realized that neither Jesus nor his disciples were
there, they got into the boats and went to Capernaum in search of
Jesus.

[a]19 Greek *rowed twenty-five or thirty stadia* (about 5 or 6 kilometers)

APPLY 1. If God called you on the phone and asked you to feed the hungry and homeless in your community, what would you say? **2.** What is the closest you have come to being involved in a mission that did something really significant for others?

OPEN What was one of your greatest childhood fears: Bugs? High places? Darkness?

STUDY 1. What have the disciples just been through (6:1–15)? Why did Jesus send them away without him? **2.** What terrified the disciples: The storm or Jesus walking on the water? How would you have reacted? **3.** How would you paraphrase his words, "It is I! Don't be afraid"? **4.** What happened to the storm when Jesus got into the boat?

APPLY 1. What storms are you going through right now? **2.** Is Jesus in the boat with you in these storms or are you facing this alone?

6:9 five small barley loaves. Barley bread was used by the poor because it was less expensive than wheat. From Luke 11:5 we may assume that three loaves were normally a meal. At most the boy had provisions for two people. **how far will they go among so many?** The question asked by Andrew and Philip is similar to the response of Moses when the people clamored for meat (Num. 11:23).

6:10 about five thousand of them. According to Matthew 14:21 this number did not include women and children.

6:14–15 this is the Prophet. The people see by this action that Jesus is far more than a healer and that he has outdone anything accomplished by the prophets of old.

6:16–21 The inadequacy of the crowd's assessment of Jesus as simply a political leader is shown in this scene of Old Testament allusions which reveal Jesus' divine glory to the Twelve.

6:19 three or three and a half miles. This would be about halfway across the lake. The lake, surrounded by hills, was often buffeted by strong winds sweeping across it.

6:20 It is I. While the disciples may have originally taken it only as a statement of identification, Jesus is saying that he is there, the Son of God who controls the wind and sea, so don't be afraid (Ps. 29:3; 77:19). **don't be afraid.** The call not to fear echoes God's assurance to Israel of his presence and protection.

OPEN In your family who is great at baking bread?

STUDY 1. Why are the crowds still searching for Jesus (vv. 24–26)? **2.** How does Jesus' response to their question show the difference between his interests and theirs? **3.** How are they to work for the food that leads to eternal life (v. 29)? **4.** What does the crowd ask Jesus to do in order that they can believe him? What is their real interest? **5.** How does Jesus use their interest in food to illustrate what he wants them to understand? What are the similarities and differences between manna (Ex. 16) and the "bread of life" (v. 35)? **6.** What claims does Jesus make in verses 35–40? What do these claims emphasize about his being the bread of life? About the will of the Father? **7.** In verses 41–42, how do the crowds respond to his claims? How is the principle of the hometown prophet (4:44) played out here? **8.** What part is played by God and by the people in the process of coming to know Jesus (vv. 44–45)? What promise is repeated three times for those who do come to him? Why the emphasis on this? **9.** How is the "bread" he gives greater than that of Moses (vv. 32,49)? **10.** Why does Jesus develop the food analogy even more graphically (vv. 53–58)? **11.** What does Jesus mean by "eating his flesh" and "drinking his blood" (vv. 51–58)?

APPLY 1. How would you describe your daily spiritual diet: Junk food? Frozen food? Baby food? TV microwave food? Leftovers? Meat and potatoes? Pure bread and wine? **2.** Has your familiarity with Jesus (from Sunday School stories,

Jesus the Bread of Life

25 When they found him on the other side of the lake, they asked
him, "Rabbi, when did you get here?"
26 Jesus answered, "I tell you the truth, you are looking for me, not
because you saw miraculous signs but because you ate the loaves
and had your fill. 27 Do not work for food that spoils, but for food that
endures to eternal life, which the Son of Man will give you. On him
God the Father has placed his seal of approval."
28 Then they asked him, "What must we do to do the works God requires?"
29 Jesus answered, "The work of God is this: to believe in the one he
has sent."
30 So they asked him, "What miraculous sign then will you give that
we may see it and believe you? What will you do? 31 Our forefathers
ate the manna in the desert; as it is written: 'He gave them bread from
heaven to eat.'[a]"
32 Jesus said to them, "I tell you the truth, it is not Moses who has
given you the bread from heaven, but it is my Father who gives you
the true bread from heaven. 33 For the bread of God is he who comes
down from heaven and gives life to the world."
34 "Sir," they said, "from now on give us this bread."
35 Then Jesus declared, "I am the bread of life. He who comes to me
will never go hungry, and he who believes in me will never be thirsty.
36 But as I told you, you have seen me and still you do not believe. 37 All
that the Father gives me will come to me, and whoever comes to me I
will never drive away. 38 For I have come down from heaven not to do
my will but to do the will of him who sent me. 39 And this is the will of
him who sent me, that I shall lose none of all that he has given me,
but raise them up at the last day. 40 For my Father's will is that everyone who looks to the Son and believes in him shall have eternal life,
and I will raise him up at the last day."
41 At this the Jews began to grumble about him because he said, "I
am the bread that came down from heaven." 42 They said, "Is this not
Jesus, the son of Joseph, whose father and mother we know? How
can he now say, 'I came down from heaven'?"
43 "Stop grumbling among yourselves," Jesus answered. 44 "No one

[a] *31* Exodus 16:4; Neh. 9:15; Psalm 78:24,25

6:25 Rabbi, when did you get here? Their real question of course is not "when," but "how"?

6:26 not because you saw miraculous signs. The crowd saw him only as a way of getting their physical needs met.

6:27 food that endures to eternal life. Jesus challenges them to examine their priorities and to realize he has come to provide the "food" that will *save people from spiritual hunger and* death.

6:29 The work of God is this. The crowd was looking for the law(s) Jesus wanted them to obey so they might have God's favor (v. 28). Jesus lets them see that only one thing is required (note the singular "work" in contrast to the plural "works"—v. 28): Belief in him is what is needed.

6:30 What miraculous sign then will you give? Some messianic expectations included the idea that the Messiah would display miracles greater than that of Moses. Since Jesus had only fed them once, they referred to this specific scene in hopes that he might provide for their needs in an ongoing way as did Moses. **that we may see it and believe you.** As in 5:44, where the problem was not a lack of evidence but a concern for people's praise more than God's, so here people were unable to see what was going on because of a preoccupation with the things of this life.

6:34 give us this bread. Just as the disciples thought in physical terms with the Samaritan woman, so do these people (4:32–33).

6:40 my Father's will. Two crucial themes, each stressing God's grace, are summed up here: (1) Salvation is open to all who will believe Jesus, and (2) Salvation is a gift to be received. It is God's desire that all are to accept his gift (2 Peter 3:9).

can come to me unless the Father who sent me draws him, and I will
raise him up at the last day. 45It is written in the Prophets: 'They will
all be taught by God.'[a] Everyone who listens to the Father and learns
from him comes to me. 46No one has seen the Father except the one
who is from God; only he has seen the Father. 47I tell you the truth, he
who believes has everlasting life. 48I am the bread of life. 49Your forefathers ate the manna in the desert, yet they died. 50But here is the
bread that comes down from heaven, which a man may eat and not
die. 51I am the living bread that came down from heaven. If anyone
eats of this bread, he will live forever. This bread is my flesh, which I
will give for the life of the world."

52Then the Jews began to argue sharply among themselves, "How
can this man give us his flesh to eat?"

53Jesus said to them, "I tell you the truth, unless you eat the flesh of
the Son of Man and drink his blood, you have no life in you. 54Who-
ever eats my flesh and drinks my blood has eternal life, and I will
raise him up at the last day. 55For my flesh is real food and my blood
is real drink. 56Whoever eats my flesh and drinks my blood remains in
me, and I in him. 57Just as the living Father sent me and I live because
of the Father, so the one who feeds on me will live because of me.
58This is the bread that came down from heaven. Your forefathers ate
manna and died, but he who feeds on this bread will live forever."
59He said this while teaching in the synagogue in Capernaum.

Many Disciples Desert Jesus

60On hearing it, many of his disciples said, "This is a hard teaching.
Who can accept it?"

61Aware that his disciples were grumbling about this, Jesus said to
them, "Does this offend you? 62What if you see the Son of Man ascend
to where he was before! 63The Spirit gives life; the flesh counts for
nothing. The words I have spoken to you are spirit[b] and they are life.
64Yet there are some of you who do not believe." For Jesus had known
from the beginning which of them did not believe and who would
betray him. 65He went on to say, "This is why I told you that no one
can come to me unless the Father has enabled him."

66From this time many of his disciples turned back and no longer
followed him.

67"You do not want to leave too, do you?" Jesus asked the Twelve.

68Simon Peter answered him, "Lord, to whom shall we go? You
have the words of eternal life. 69We believe and know that you are the
Holy One of God."

70Then Jesus replied, "Have I not chosen you, the Twelve? Yet one of
you is a devil!" 71(He meant Judas, the son of Simon Iscariot, who,
though one of the Twelve, was later to betray him.)

[a]45 Isaiah 54:13 [b]63 Or *Spirit*

parochial school, etc.) ever kept you from seeing who Jesus really is? **3.** If someone asked, "How do you hunger and thirst after God," what counsel could you offer?

OPEN What is the closest you have come to getting a "Dear John letter"?

STUDY 1. Why did a whole lot of Jesus' followers decide to leave? What was it about Jesus' teaching that scared them off (6:35–59)? **2.** When Jesus puts the question to the twelve disciples in verse 67, how would you paraphrase Peter's response? **3.** How do you think Jesus felt when he saw so many people desert him? What is the lesson here for the church today?

APPLY 1. How many people that were active in the youth group of your church when you were growing up are still committed followers of Jesus Christ? **2.** For those who have fallen away, what were some reasons?

6:51 for the life of the world. Like the Passover lamb, his death means life to those who feed upon him.

6:54 eternal life. Jesus makes it very clear that he is not talking about the Passover. The subject is eternal life.

6:67 You do not want to leave too, do you? In Greek, this question anticipates a negative answer. **the Twelve.** This is the first mention of the apostolic band in this Gospel (Mark 3:13–19).

6:68 You have the words of eternal life. Given verse 63, it is clear that Peter has grasped Jesus' meaning.

OPEN Who was the daredevil in your family who would try anything once?

STUDY **1.** Why did the religious leaders want to kill Jesus (5:18)? **2.** In urging Jesus to attend this feast, are the brothers being wise or worldly (vv. 2–5; 6:42,66)? **3.** What rumors are circulating about Jesus in Jerusalem (vv. 12–13)? Hence, why do you think he chose to go secretly? **4.** What are the people in your community whispering about Jesus? Do they think he was a good man or a deceiver and a fraud?

APPLY What do your brothers/sisters think about your spiritual faith? Do they support you or think you have gone off the deep end?

Jesus Goes to the Feast of Tabernacles

7 After this, Jesus went around in Galilee, purposely staying away
from Judea because the Jews there were waiting to take his life.
2But when the Jewish Feast of Tabernacles was near, 3Jesus' brothers
said to him, "You ought to leave here and go to Judea, so that your
disciples may see the miracles you do. 4No one who wants to become
a public figure acts in secret. Since you are doing these things, show
yourself to the world." 5For even his own brothers did not believe in
him.
6Therefore Jesus told them, "The right time for me has not yet
come; for you any time is right. 7The world cannot hate you, but it
hates me because I testify that what it does is evil. 8You go to the
Feast. I am not yet[a] going up to this Feast, because for me the right
time has not yet come." 9Having said this, he stayed in Galilee.
10However, after his brothers had left for the Feast, he went also,
not publicly, but in secret. 11Now at the Feast the Jews were watching
for him and asking, "Where is that man?"
12Among the crowds there was widespread whispering about him.
Some said, "He is a good man."
Others replied, "No, he deceives the people." 13But no one would
say anything publicly about him for fear of the Jews.

OPEN When you were growing up, were there certain things you could or could not do on Sunday?

STUDY **1.** Reading between the lines, what is really going on in this passage? When the author says, "Jews" who is he talking about? When they ask, "how did this man get such learning without having studied," what are they really saying? **2.** What does Jesus accuse the temple rabbis of doing? **3.** What is it about people in authority that they are willing to kill to protect their turf?

APPLY **1.** When have you found yourself in hot water because you didn't agree with people in authority? **2.** What are you going to say when your children refuse to go to church?

Jesus Teaches at the Feast

14Not until halfway through the Feast did Jesus go up to the temple
courts and begin to teach. 15The Jews were amazed and asked, "How
did this man get such learning without having studied?"
16Jesus answered, "My teaching is not my own. It comes from him
who sent me. 17If anyone chooses to do God's will, he will find out
whether my teaching comes from God or whether I speak on my own.
18He who speaks on his own does so to gain honor for himself, but he
who works for the honor of the one who sent him is a man of truth;
there is nothing false about him. 19Has not Moses given you the law?
Yet not one of you keeps the law. Why are you trying to kill me?"
20"You are demon-possessed," the crowd answered. "Who is trying
to kill you?"
21Jesus said to them, "I did one miracle, and you are all astonished.
22Yet, because Moses gave you circumcision (though actually it did
not come from Moses, but from the patriarchs), you circumcise a
child on the Sabbath. 23Now if a child can be circumcised on the Sabbath so that the law of Moses may not be broken, why are you angry

[a]8 Some early manuscripts do not have *yet*.

7:2 Feast of Tabernacles. This, along with Passover and Pentecost, was a major feast when Jews from all over the empire would gather in Jerusalem. This feast celebrated God's provision for Israel during the wilderness wanderings (Lev. 23:39; Deut. 16:13). By this time, it had also become a type of *Thanksgiving celebration for the year's* harvest (v. 37).

7:3–5 The urging of his brothers bears similarities to that of his mother in John 2:3–5 in that family members are trying to advise him regarding how he should carry out his mission. Verse 5 shows that his brothers, like the crowds in 6:66, deeply misunderstood the true nature of Jesus as Messiah and what his mission was on this earth.

7:22 circumcision. Circumcision, a sign of God's covenant with his people, was initiated long before Moses by Abraham (Gen. 17). Yet circumcision was strongly reinforced by Moses' law which required that a male child be circumcised eight days after birth. Pharisaic tradition held that since the law of circumcision was more important than the laws prohibiting work on the Sabbath, it was lawful to circumcise a child on the Sabbath. Jesus uses their logic against them (v. 23). If it is lawful to perform an act that they held led to a person's ceremonial perfection on the Sabbath, how can it be wrong for him to bring a person into actual wholeness on that day?

with me for healing the whole man on the Sabbath? 24Stop judging by mere appearances, and make a right judgment."

Is Jesus the Christ?

25At that point some of the people of Jerusalem began to ask, "Isn't this the man they are trying to kill? 26Here he is, speaking publicly, and they are not saying a word to him. Have the authorities really concluded that he is the Christ[a]? 27But we know where this man is from; when the Christ comes, no one will know where he is from."

28Then Jesus, still teaching in the temple courts, cried out, "Yes, you know me, and you know where I am from. I am not here on my own, but he who sent me is true. You do not know him, 29but I know him because I am from him and he sent me."

30At this they tried to seize him, but no one laid a hand on him, because his time had not yet come. 31Still, many in the crowd put their faith in him. They said, "When the Christ comes, will he do more miraculous signs than this man?"

32The Pharisees heard the crowd whispering such things about him. Then the chief priests and the Pharisees sent temple guards to arrest him.

33Jesus said, "I am with you for only a short time, and then I go to the one who sent me. 34You will look for me, but you will not find me; and where I am, you cannot come."

35The Jews said to one another, "Where does this man intend to go that we cannot find him? Will he go where our people live scattered among the Greeks, and teach the Greeks? 36What did he mean when he said, 'You will look for me, but you will not find me,' and 'Where I am, you cannot come'?"

37On the last and greatest day of the Feast, Jesus stood and said in a loud voice, "If anyone is thirsty, let him come to me and drink. 38Whoever believes in me, as[b] the Scripture has said, streams of living water will flow from within him." 39By this he meant the Spirit, whom those who believed in him were later to receive. Up to that time the Spirit had not been given, since Jesus had not yet been glorified.

40On hearing his words, some of the people said, "Surely this man is the Prophet."

41Others said, "He is the Christ."

Still others asked, "How can the Christ come from Galilee? 42Does not the Scripture say that the Christ will come from David's family[c] and from Bethlehem, the town where David lived?" 43Thus the people were divided because of Jesus. 44Some wanted to seize him, but no one laid a hand on him.

Unbelief of the Jewish Leaders

45Finally the temple guards went back to the chief priests and Pharisees, who asked them, "Why didn't you bring him in?"

46"No one ever spoke the way this man does," the guards declared.

[a]26 Or *Messiah*; also in verses 27, 31, 41 and 42 [b]37,38 Or / *If anyone is thirsty, let him come to me. / And let him drink,* [38]*who believes in me. / As* [c]42 Greek *seed*

OPEN How close have you come to getting in trouble for speaking out for something you believed in?

STUDY 1. What started the fight between Jesus and the temple authorities (7:19)? Over what issue (7:23)? **2.** What are some of the common people in Jerusalem starting to ask? How is this going to sit with the religious establishment? **3.** In three pronouncements that Jesus makes (vv. 28–29,33–34,37–38), what does Jesus say about himself and his followers? How much of this is now and how much is in the future? **4.** What do the authorities try to do (vv. 30,32, 44)? Why were they not successful? **5.** What are some of the responses from the crowd (vv. 26,31,35–36,40,43)? **6.** How does the confusion over his birthplace cloud the issue of his identity? **7.** Is it possible for someone to remain neutral on the claims of Christ?

APPLY 1. When did you get off the fence on the claims of Christ and acknowledge Jesus to be the Christ and everything he claimed to be? **2.** How would you describe the "streams of living water" in your life right now: A gusher? A stream? A trickle?

OPEN When you were a kid, what unpleasant chores were you expected to do?

STUDY 1. What excuse did the temple guards give for not arresting Jesus (7:32)? How did that sit with the Pharisees? **2.** What does

---

7:37 If anyone is thirsty, let him come to me and drink. The vision in Ezekiel 47:1–12 of water flowing from the temple giving life to all the surrounding area is in view as Jesus, the new temple of God (2:19), provides the water of life to all who believe. This life is referring to the physical as well as spiritual.

the response of the Pharisees tell you about their attitude? **3.** What do you remember about Nicodemus (ch. 3)? Do you think Nicodemus had become a secret believer?

APPLY Who likes to tease you because of your stand for Christ? Who means it?

OPEN When you were growing up, who tattled on you and got you into trouble?

STUDY **1.** Why did the authorities bring only the woman caught in adultery? **2.** What is the trap the Pharisees are setting for Jesus? What would you have done in this situation if you were Jesus? **3.** Why did Jesus write in the sand? What do you think he wrote? **4.** How would you paraphrase Jesus' comment in verse 7? **5.** What caused the older Pharisees to leave first? **6.** In the last thing Jesus said to the woman, what was the tone in his voice and what did he mean? **7.** What does this story teach about the character of Christ.

47 "You mean he has deceived you also?" the Pharisees retorted.
48 "Has any of the rulers or of the Pharisees believed in him? 49 No! But
this mob that knows nothing of the law—there is a curse on them."
50 Nicodemus, who had gone to Jesus earlier and who was one of
their own number, asked, 51 "Does our law condemn anyone without
first hearing him to find out what he is doing?"
52 They replied, "Are you from Galilee, too? Look into it, and you will
find that a prophet[a] does not come out of Galilee."

[The earliest manuscripts and many other ancient witnesses do not have John 7:53–8:11.]

53 Then each went to his own home.
8 But Jesus went to the Mount of Olives. 2 At dawn he appeared
again in the temple courts, where all the people gathered around
him, and he sat down to teach them. 3 The teachers of the law and the
Pharisees brought in a woman caught in adultery. They made her
stand before the group 4 and said to Jesus, "Teacher, this woman was
caught in the act of adultery. 5 In the Law Moses commanded us to
stone such women. Now what do you say?" 6 They were using this
question as a trap, in order to have a basis for accusing him.
But Jesus bent down and started to write on the ground with his
finger. 7 When they kept on questioning him, he straightened up and
said to them, "If any one of you is without sin, let him be the first to
throw a stone at her." 8 Again he stooped down and wrote on the
ground.
9 At this, those who heard began to go away one at a time, the older

[a] 52 Two early manuscripts *the Prophet*

7:53–8:11 This story, undoubtedly reliable as an actual event for Jesus, is not regarded as an original part of this Gospel by some scholars since in a few early Greek manuscripts it is found in different locations in John and other Gospels.

8:3 teachers of the law and the Pharisees. The teachers of the law, or scribes, are not mentioned in John but play a prominent part in the other Gospels. They were the ordained teachers, serving as the representatives of Moses to the people in interpreting the Law. They were taught as rabbis and acted as lawyers in legal cases. **a woman caught in adultery.** Since this sin cannot be committed alone, why was only one offender brought before the temple courts? The teachers of the law and the Pharisees had staged this to trap Jesus (v. 6).

8:5 Moses commanded us to stone such women. This was only partially true. Leviticus 20:10 and Deuteronomy 22:22 prescribe that both parties shall be put to death. Since it was said that the woman was caught in the act, the man was also there and should have been brought in as well. The Jews, under Roman law, had no authority to carry out such sentences. In Israel's past, this penalty was rarely carried out because capital offenses required two or three witnesses. The normal result of adultery (on the part of a woman) was divorce. Women could not divorce their husbands for any reason.

8:6 They were using this question as a trap. See also Matthew 19:3 and 22:15 for other situations where Jesus' enemies attempted to get some reason for making a charge against him. In this case, if he allowed stoning he would be in violation of Roman law and would be found to be more strict than even the Pharisees in his application of the Law. If he tried to release her, he could be faulted for ignoring the Law of Moses. **started to write on the ground with his finger.** It is uncertain what Jesus wrote. However, speculation centers on the possibility he was writing the other commandments, which would remind onlookers of commandments *they* may have broken.

8:7 If any one of you is without sin. Jesus affirms the validity of the Law, but forces the initiative back on the accusers. Perhaps some of them had in the back of their memory a time when they "sowed some wild oats." This statement does not imply that judicial cases can only be tried by sinless people. It is, however, a rebuke to the base motives of these leaders who would self-righteously forget their own sins while using this woman to implicate Jesus.

8:9 the older ones first. The older ones may have had the wisdom of experience to know their own fallibilities. The younger ones may not have been old enough to have had their eyes truly open to see themselves as they were.

ones first, until only Jesus was left, with the woman still standing
there. [10]Jesus straightened up and asked her, "Woman, where are
they? Has no one condemned you?"
[11]"No one, sir," she said.
"Then neither do I condemn you," Jesus declared. "Go now and
leave your life of sin."

The Validity of Jesus' Testimony

[12]When Jesus spoke again to the people, he said, "I am the light of
the world. Whoever follows me will never walk in darkness, but will
have the light of life."
[13]The Pharisees challenged him, "Here you are, appearing as your
own witness; your testimony is not valid."
[14]Jesus answered, "Even if I testify on my own behalf, my testimony
is valid, for I know where I came from and where I am going. But you
have no idea where I come from or where I am going. [15]You judge by
human standards; I pass judgment on no one. [16]But if I do judge, my
decisions are right, because I am not alone. I stand with the Father,
who sent me. [17]In your own Law it is written that the testimony of
two men is valid. [18]I am one who testifies for myself; my other witness is the Father, who sent me."
[19]Then they asked him, "Where is your father?"
"You do not know me or my Father," Jesus replied. "If you knew me,
you would know my Father also." [20]He spoke these words while
teaching in the temple area near the place where the offerings were
put. Yet no one seized him, because his time had not yet come.
[21]Once more Jesus said to them, "I am going away, and you will
look for me, and you will die in your sin. Where I go, you cannot
come."
[22]This made the Jews ask, "Will he kill himself? Is that why he says,
'Where I go, you cannot come'?"
[23]But he continued, "You are from below; I am from above. You are
of this world; I am not of this world. [24]I told you that you would die in
your sins; if you do not believe that I am ⌞the one I claim to be⌟,[a] you
will indeed die in your sins."
[25]"Who are you?" they asked.
"Just what I have been claiming all along," Jesus replied. [26]"I have
much to say in judgment of you. But he who sent me is reliable, and
what I have heard from him I tell the world."
[27]They did not understand that he was telling them about his Father. [28]So Jesus said, "When you have lifted up the Son of Man, then
you will know that I am ⌞the one I claim to be⌟ and that I do nothing on

[a]24 Or *I am he*; also in verse 28

APPLY 1. How would you compare your spiritual story to the woman's story of meeting Jesus? **2.** When did you realize that Jesus values you as a person?

OPEN What is your most vivid memory as a child in a dark place (cave, tunnel, power black-out)?

STUDY Three witnesses were needed in a Jewish court to support any claim. **1.** How do the religious authorities use this to deny Jesus' claim? How does Jesus answer them? **2.** When the authorities ask about his father, who are they referring to (v. 19)? **3.** When Jesus says, "I am going away ... where I go, you cannot come," what is he referring to? How do the authorities interpret this? **4.** What are the two choices that Jesus gives the people? What do you have to know about the atonement to understand this? **5.** When the authorities ask Jesus point blank who he is, what does he say? When will the truth about Jesus' mission come to light? **6.** What are the claims that Jesus makes about himself in this passage? What is this going to do to the fence-straddlers among the religious leaders?

APPLY 1. When did you come to realize that Jesus was all that he claimed to be? **2.** How do your friends and business associates react to the claims of Christ?

8:11 neither do I condemn you. This story illustrates the truth of 3:17. The woman had come face-to-face with condemnation, shame and death, but was pardoned by the one to whom all judgment has been given (5:22). **Go now and leave your life of sin.** The compassion and mercy of Jesus is related to his call to people to live in obedience to the will of his Father. Paul, likewise, flatly rejects the idea that people can claim God's mercy while actively pursuing a lifestyle that is in opposition to his will (Rom. 6:1–2,15).

8:28 lifted up the Son of Man. This is to say, "crucify" him.

my own but speak just what the Father has taught me. 29The one who sent me is with me; he has not left me alone, for I always do what pleases him." 30Even as he spoke, many put their faith in him.

The Children of Abraham

31To the Jews who had believed him, Jesus said, "If you hold to my teaching, you are really my disciples. 32Then you will know the truth, and the truth will set you free."

33They answered him, "We are Abraham's descendants[a] and have never been slaves of anyone. How can you say that we shall be set free?"

34Jesus replied, "I tell you the truth, everyone who sins is a slave to sin. 35Now a slave has no permanent place in the family, but a son belongs to it forever. 36So if the Son sets you free, you will be free indeed. 37I know you are Abraham's descendants. Yet you are ready to kill me, because you have no room for my word. 38I am telling you what I have seen in the Father's presence, and you do what you have heard from your father.[b]"

39"Abraham is our father," they answered.

"If you were Abraham's children," said Jesus, "then you would[c] do the things Abraham did. 40As it is, you are determined to kill me, a man who has told you the truth that I heard from God. Abraham did not do such things. 41You are doing the things your own father does."

"We are not illegitimate children," they protested. "The only Father we have is God himself."

The Children of the Devil

42Jesus said to them, "If God were your Father, you would love me, for I came from God and now am here. I have not come on my own; but he sent me. 43Why is my language not clear to you? Because you are unable to hear what I say. 44You belong to your father, the devil, and you want to carry out your father's desire. He was a murderer from the beginning, not holding to the truth, for there is no truth in him. When he lies, he speaks his native language, for he is a liar and the father of lies. 45Yet because I tell the truth, you do not believe me! 46Can any of you prove me guilty of sin? If I am telling the truth, why don't you believe me? 47He who belongs to God hears what God says. The reason you do not hear is that you do not belong to God."

The Claims of Jesus About Himself

48The Jews answered him, "Aren't we right in saying that you are a Samaritan and demon-possessed?"

49"I am not possessed by a demon," said Jesus, "but I honor my Father and you dishonor me. 50I am not seeking glory for myself; but there is one who seeks it, and he is the judge. 51I tell you the truth, if anyone keeps my word, he will never see death."

[a]33 Greek *seed;* also in verse 37 [b]38 Or *presence. Therefore do what you have heard from the Father.*
[c]39 Some early manuscripts *"If you are Abraham's children," said Jesus, "then*

OPEN 1. Where did your ancestors come from? How did they get to this country? **2.** Who is one of the more colorful characters in your family tree? **3.** Who in your family tree do you look to as a spiritual patriarch or matriarch?

STUDY 1. What is the guarantee that Jesus makes to his disciples if they stick to his teaching? How would you apply this to today where there are so many people looking for "freedom"? **2.** What false assumptions confuse the issue of spiritual freedom for Abraham's descendants? How does Jesus undermine their base of confidence? What issue does he force them to confront (vv. 34–41)? **3.** How does Jesus undermine their claim in verse 41? What does Jesus say is the ultimate test to show who "belongs to God" (vv. 42–47)? How does he account for their misunderstanding of him (vv. 37, 43,45,47)? **4.** What is the critical question raised by Jesus' claim in verse 51 (8:24)? How does Jesus use their loyalty to Abraham against them? Why does Jesus' final claim cause such an outrage (Ex. 3:14)? **5.** What are the four claims Jesus makes in this chapter about himself (vv. 51,58)? Which of these mean the most to you? **6.** How would you paraphrase the passage "you will know the truth and the truth will set you free"?

APPLY 1. What are you most proud of in your religious heritage? In what way has your religious heritage been: A benefit? A handicap? **2.** What are you going to say to your children and grandchildren if they want to depart from the religious traditions you have taught them?

8:36 if the Son sets you free. The source of spiritual freedom is found in Jesus. Here he offers the solution to the problem he posed in verse 34.

8:41 your own father. Having denied that they are Abraham's children in verse 40, Jesus' statement here raises the question of whose children they really are. **We are not illegitimate.** The irregular circumstances behind Jesus' birth are probably in view in this passage.

52At this the Jews exclaimed, "Now we know that you are demon-
possessed! Abraham died and so did the prophets, yet you say that if
anyone keeps your word, he will never taste death. 53Are you greater
than our father Abraham? He died, and so did the prophets. Who do
you think you are?"
54Jesus replied, "If I glorify myself, my glory means nothing. My
Father, whom you claim as your God, is the one who glorifies me.
55Though you do not know him, I know him. If I said I did not, I
would be a liar like you, but I do know him and keep his word. 56Your
father Abraham rejoiced at the thought of seeing my day; he saw it
and was glad."
57"You are not yet fifty years old," the Jews said to him, "and you
have seen Abraham!"
58"I tell you the truth," Jesus answered, "before Abraham was born,
I am!" 59At this, they picked up stones to stone him, but Jesus hid
himself, slipping away from the temple grounds.

Jesus Heals a Man Born Blind

9 As he went along, he saw a man blind from birth. 2His disciples
asked him, "Rabbi, who sinned, this man or his parents, that he
was born blind?"
3"Neither this man nor his parents sinned," said Jesus, "but this
happened so that the work of God might be displayed in his life. 4As
long as it is day, we must do the work of him who sent me. Night is
coming, when no one can work. 5While I am in the world, I am the
light of the world."
6Having said this, he spit on the ground, made some mud with the
saliva, and put it on the man's eyes. 7"Go," he told him, "wash in the
Pool of Siloam" (this word means Sent). So the man went and
washed, and came home seeing.
8His neighbors and those who had formerly seen him begging
asked, "Isn't this the same man who used to sit and beg?" 9Some
claimed that he was.
Others said, "No, he only looks like him."
But he himself insisted, "I am the man."
10"How then were your eyes opened?" they demanded.
11He replied, "The man they call Jesus made some mud and put it
on my eyes. He told me to go to Siloam and wash. So I went and
washed, and then I could see."
12"Where is this man?" they asked him.
"I don't know," he said.

OPEN What adventure with mud do you remember as a kid?

STUDY **1.** What misconception lies at the heart of the question of the disciples about the blind man? What does Jesus say is the reason? **2.** How does Jesus view suffering and disability? How do you feel about this? **3.** If Jesus could heal the blindness by doing nothing, why does he go through these natural remedies? **4.** How much did the blind man know about the gospel when he was healed? How do you like the way the blind man shared his faith story? **5.** If you had been one of his neighbors, what would you have thought?

APPLY **1.** What physical, emotional or learning disability have you had to struggle with all of your life? **2.** When did you come to the place that you could accept this disability and use it for the glory of God?

8:59 they picked up stones. Stoning was the punishment for blasphemy against "the name of the LORD" (Lev. 24:16). The incredulity and scorn of verses 52 and 57 turns to fury at Jesus' bold assertion in 58.

9:1 As he went along. An indefinite time reference like that in 5:1; 6:1 and 7:1. **blind from birth.** The story of the healing of the blind man, which really extends through 10:21, illustrates Jesus' ability to give new life to people in hopeless situations and the implications of discipleship in the face of opposition.

9:2 His disciples. These disciples may be the Twelve or a broader group of Judean followers. **who sinned?** Despite the book of Job, the rabbis taught that a person's misfortune was the result of his or her direct sin or a punishment inherited for one's parents' sins. Some taught that such handicaps were a punishment for the sin that the child in the womb had committed (Luke 13:1–5). Ezekiel taught that people would not be punished by God for the sins of their parents, but the belief in such retribution lingered (Ezek. 18). **born blind.** The emphasis is on the fact that he was born with this condition (vv. 1,19–20,32). This not only points out the longevity of his problem, but underscores the theological emphasis that people who are not "born again" will not "see the kingdom of God" (3:3), for they walk in the darkness (8:12).

9:3 Neither this man nor his parents sinned. Jesus is not pronouncing the family as sinless, but is dismissing the disciples' interest in the *cause* of the man's blindness so that he can focus their attention onto its *purpose*.

OPEN Did you ever get pulled over by the police? What happened?

STUDY 1. What has just happened in the previous story that presents the Pharisees with a problem (9:1–12)? What are the Pharisees upset about? **2.** What is the dilemma the Pharisees are faced with (v. 16)? **3.** What do the Pharisees try to get the parents to say? How do they respond? **4.** In the second meeting with the man born blind, what have the Pharisees decided about Jesus (v. 24)? **5.** How do you like the way the blind man stood up for Jesus (vv. 30–33)? How did the Pharisees take it? **6.** Do you feel sorry for the Pharisees? What is their hang up? Why are they so defensive? **7.** What is the lesson in this passage for institutions today? What about your own institution?

APPLY 1. How would you compare the interrogation that the man born blind got from the Pharisees to the interrogation you get from your friends about your spiritual faith? **2.** If you were challenged to explain the reason for the transformation in your life, what would you say?

The Pharisees Investigate the Healing

13 They brought to the Pharisees the man who had been blind.
14 Now the day on which Jesus had made the mud and opened the
man's eyes was a Sabbath. 15 Therefore the Pharisees also asked him
how he had received his sight. "He put mud on my eyes," the man
replied, "and I washed, and now I see."
16 Some of the Pharisees said, "This man is not from God, for he
does not keep the Sabbath."
But others asked, "How can a sinner do such miraculous signs?"
So they were divided.
17 Finally they turned again to the blind man, "What have you to say
about him? It was your eyes he opened."
The man replied, "He is a prophet."
18 The Jews still did not believe that he had been blind and had received his sight until they sent for the man's parents. 19 "Is this your
son?" they asked. "Is this the one you say was born blind? How is it
that now he can see?"
20 "We know he is our son," the parents answered, "and we know
he was born blind. 21 But how he can see now, or who opened his
eyes, we don't know. Ask him. He is of age; he will speak for himself."
22 His parents said this because they were afraid of the Jews, for already the Jews had decided that anyone who acknowledged that
Jesus was the Christ[a] would be put out of the synagogue. 23 That was
why his parents said, "He is of age; ask him."
24 A second time they summoned the man who had been blind.
"Give glory to God,[b]" they said. "We know this man is a sinner."
25 He replied, "Whether he is a sinner or not, I don't know. One
thing I do know. I was blind but now I see!"
26 Then they asked him, "What did he do to you? How did he open
your eyes?"
27 He answered, "I have told you already and you did not listen. Why
do you want to hear it again? Do you want to become his disciples,
too?"
28 Then they hurled insults at him and said, "You are this fellow's
disciple! We are disciples of Moses! 29 We know that God spoke to
Moses, but as for this fellow, we don't even know where he comes
from."
30 The man answered, "Now that is remarkable! You don't know
where he comes from, yet he opened my eyes. 31 We know that God
does not listen to sinners. He listens to the godly man who does his
will. 32 Nobody has ever heard of opening the eyes of a man born
blind. 33 If this man were not from God, he could do nothing."
34 To this they replied, "You were steeped in sin at birth; how dare
you lecture us!" And they threw him out.

[a]22 Or *Messiah* [b]24 A solemn charge to tell the truth (see Joshua 7:19)

9:21 He is of age. The legal age was 13. The parents simply affirm he is old enough to speak for himself.

9:22 the Jews. From the account in 12:42, it is clear that the Pharisaic leaders are specifically in view. They found Jesus particularly offensive because he broke the traditional interpretations of the Mosaic Law which they in his day attempted to keep in such detail.

9:24 Give glory to God. Although this saying is equivalent to the modern-day oath to "tell the truth, the whole truth, and nothing but the truth," the man did indeed give glory to God by affirming his conviction about Jesus, even though this was exactly opposite of what the Pharisees intended.

9:29 this fellow. This implies that Jesus had no connection with God, unlike Moses.

Spiritual Blindness

35Jesus heard that they had thrown him out, and when he found
him, he said, "Do you believe in the Son of Man?"
36"Who is he, sir?" the man asked. "Tell me so that I may believe in
him."
37Jesus said, "You have now seen him; in fact, he is the one speaking with you."
38Then the man said, "Lord, I believe," and he worshiped him.
39Jesus said, "For judgment I have come into this world, so that the
blind will see and those who see will become blind."
40Some Pharisees who were with him heard him say this and
asked, "What? Are we blind too?"
41Jesus said, "If you were blind, you would not be guilty of sin; but
now that you claim you can see, your guilt remains.

The Shepherd and His Flock

10 "I tell you the truth, the man who does not enter the sheep
pen by the gate, but climbs in by some other way, is a thief
and a robber. 2The man who enters by the gate is the shepherd of his
sheep. 3The watchman opens the gate for him, and the sheep listen to
his voice. He calls his own sheep by name and leads them out. 4When
he has brought out all his own, he goes on ahead of them, and his
sheep follow him because they know his voice. 5But they will never
follow a stranger; in fact, they will run away from him because they
do not recognize a stranger's voice." 6Jesus used this figure of
speech, but they did not understand what he was telling them.
7Therefore Jesus said again, "I tell you the truth, I am the gate for
the sheep. 8All who ever came before me were thieves and robbers,
but the sheep did not listen to them. 9I am the gate; whoever enters
through me will be saved.[a] He will come in and go out, and find pasture. 10The thief comes only to steal and kill and destroy; I have come
that they may have life, and have it to the full.
11"I am the good shepherd. The good shepherd lays down his life
for the sheep. 12The hired hand is not the shepherd who owns the
sheep. So when he sees the wolf coming, he abandons the sheep and
runs away. Then the wolf attacks the flock and scatters it. 13The man
runs away because he is a hired hand and cares nothing for the
sheep.

[a]9 Or *kept safe*

OPEN In reading a book, do you read the last chapter first?

STUDY 1. What are the two kinds of blindness in this passage? Which is caused by sin (vv. 34,41)? What is this sin (6:36)? **2.** What was the blind man's response when he found out who healed him? **3.** Why will "some Pharisees" be in big trouble on judgment day?

APPLY How would the blind man's story compare to your story?

OPEN As a child, what was your favorite pet? How did this pet respond when it heard your voice?

STUDY 1. What do you know about sheep? How intelligent are they? What would a shepherd do with the sheep at night to keep them from thieves and robbers? **2.** In this parable, what does Jesus say about his sheep? About himself? About "hired hands"? **3.** How would you paraphrase verse 10 in your own words? **4.** Who are the "other sheep" he must bring also? What characterizes his flock? **5.** What final claims does Jesus make for himself (vv. 17–18)? **6.** What are the two responses of the listeners? For those who claimed Jesus was demon-possessed, what do they have to explain? **7.** With all the pseudo religions around today, what is your church doing to keep the sheep from straying?

APPLY 1. When did you get off the fence and acknowledge that Jesus was all that he claimed to be? **2.** For your friends that

---

9:35 thrown him out. Jesus said that he would never drive away those who came to him (6:37). In contrast the Pharisees reject those who are drawn by the Father.

10:1 sheep pen. Sheep were herded into stone wall enclosures at night as a protection against predators and thieves.

10:3 The watchman. Although both the shepherd and the gate clearly represent Jesus (vv. 7,11), the figure of the watchman is not explained. In a parable, unlike an allegory, not all the details have a meaning. **calls his own sheep by name.** Shepherds had names and calls for their sheep as a means of aiding them in separating their flocks from mixed herds such as would be found in a typical sheep pen.

10:7 I am the gate. This symbol is stated forthrightly in 14:6 where Jesus says he is the way to God.

10:8 thieves and robbers. In this context, Jesus is referring to the religious leaders who exploit the people for their own ends (2:14–15; Ezek. 34:1–6).

10:10 have it to the full. The eternal life one has in Christ has to do with more than length of life—but quality of life as well.

10:11 I am the good shepherd. In contrast to the hired hands who run away at danger, the true shepherd cares for the flock at his own risk (1 Sam. 17:34–35). The image of the ruler as a shepherd was a very common one in Israel (Ps. 23; Ezek. 34).

14"I am the good shepherd; I know my sheep and my sheep know me— 15just as the Father knows me and I know the Father—and I lay down my life for the sheep. 16I have other sheep that are not of this sheep pen. I must bring them also. They too will listen to my voice, and there shall be one flock and one shepherd. 17The reason my Father loves me is that I lay down my life—only to take it up again. 18No one takes it from me, but I lay it down of my own accord. I have authority to lay it down and authority to take it up again. This command I received from my Father."

19At these words the Jews were again divided. 20Many of them said, "He is demon-possessed and raving mad. Why listen to him?"

21But others said, "These are not the sayings of a man possessed by a demon. Can a demon open the eyes of the blind?"

The Unbelief of the Jews

22Then came the Feast of Dedication[a] at Jerusalem. It was winter, 23and Jesus was in the temple area walking in Solomon's Colonnade. 24The Jews gathered around him, saying, "How long will you keep us in suspense? If you are the Christ,[b] tell us plainly."

25Jesus answered, "I did tell you, but you do not believe. The miracles I do in my Father's name speak for me, 26but you do not believe because you are not my sheep. 27My sheep listen to my voice; I know them, and they follow me. 28I give them eternal life, and they shall never perish; no one can snatch them out of my hand. 29My Father, who has given them to me, is greater than all[c]; no one can snatch them out of my Father's hand. 30I and the Father are one."

31Again the Jews picked up stones to stone him, 32but Jesus said to them, "I have shown you many great miracles from the Father. For which of these do you stone me?"

33"We are not stoning you for any of these," replied the Jews, "but for blasphemy, because you, a mere man, claim to be God."

34Jesus answered them, "Is it not written in your Law, 'I have said you are gods'[d]? 35If he called them 'gods,' to whom the word of God came—and the Scripture cannot be broken— 36what about the one whom the Father set apart as his very own and sent into the world? Why then do you accuse me of blasphemy because I said, 'I am God's Son'? 37Do not believe me unless I do what my Father does. 38But if I do it, even though you do not believe me, believe the miracles, that you may know and understand that the Father is in me, and I in the Father." 39Again they tried to seize him, but he escaped their grasp.

[a]22 That is, Hanukkah [b]24 Or *Messiah* [c]29 Many early manuscripts *What my Father has given me is greater than all* [d]34 Psalm 82:6

prefer to stay on the fence, what do they say about Jesus and his claims?

OPEN 1. What is the big annual "feast day" for your family? Who usually comes? What is served? What is the big pastime? **2.** What traditions are you going to preserve for your children?

STUDY 1. Do you think the Jewish authorities were sincere in asking, "If you are the Christ, tell us plainly" or are they just looking for an excuse to accuse Jesus of blasphemy? **2.** How would you describe Jesus' answer (vv. 25–30) in modern day terms? How do the Jewish authorities respond? **3.** What is the claim that Jesus makes that infuriates the Jewish rabbis? What does Jesus offer for proof? **4.** If Jesus softened his claim to be just a "good man" and a good teacher, would he have fared better with the rabbis? What is the message here for today?

APPLY 1. Among your secular friends, have they investigated the claims that Jesus made about himself? If Jesus was not all that he claimed to be, how could he be both a good person and a fraud? **2.** Have you considered inviting your agnostic friends to this group on a 30-day faith experiment?

10:14 I know my sheep. "To know" is equivalent with "to love" (v. 17).

10:15 I lay down my life. This phrase accents the voluntary nature of his death (v. 18).

10:16 I have other sheep that are not of this sheep pen. Since this Gospel has consistently stressed that Jesus' mission was not just for Jews but for all the world, it is likely that this is the meaning here also. **one flock and one shepherd.** The Christian community is not to be marred by divisions, but is to model unity across racial and ethnic lines as all respond to the voice of the one shepherd (11:52; Eph. 2:11–22).

10:22 Feast of Dedication. This feast (Hanukkah) commemorated Judas Maccabeus' deliverance of Jerusalem—and the temple—from the grasp of the Syrian (Selucid) king, Antiochus Epiphanes, who had profaned the temple by placing a statue of the Greek god Zeus in the Most Holy Place. The Pharisees try to get Jesus to proclaim himself as the Messiah as an attempt to bring the displeasure of Rome upon him.

10:23 Solomon's Colonnade. This was a large covered porch on the east side of the temple. The porch was constructed upon a foundation that was believed to have been part of King Solomon's original temple.

[40]Then Jesus went back across the Jordan to the place where John had been baptizing in the early days. Here he stayed [41]and many people came to him. They said, "Though John never performed a miraculous sign, all that John said about this man was true." [42]And in that place many believed in Jesus.

The Death of Lazarus

11 Now a man named Lazarus was sick. He was from Bethany, the village of Mary and her sister Martha. [2]This Mary, whose brother Lazarus now lay sick, was the same one who poured perfume on the Lord and wiped his feet with her hair. [3]So the sisters sent word to Jesus, "Lord, the one you love is sick."

[4]When he heard this, Jesus said, "This sickness will not end in death. No, it is for God's glory so that God's Son may be glorified through it." [5]Jesus loved Martha and her sister and Lazarus. [6]Yet when he heard that Lazarus was sick, he stayed where he was two more days.

[7]Then he said to his disciples, "Let us go back to Judea."

[8]"But Rabbi," they said, "a short while ago the Jews tried to stone you, and yet you are going back there?"

[9]Jesus answered, "Are there not twelve hours of daylight? A man who walks by day will not stumble, for he sees by this world's light. [10]It is when he walks by night that he stumbles, for he has no light."

[11]After he had said this, he went on to tell them, "Our friend Lazarus has fallen asleep; but I am going there to wake him up."

[12]His disciples replied, "Lord, if he sleeps, he will get better." [13]Jesus had been speaking of his death, but his disciples thought he meant natural sleep.

[14]So then he told them plainly, "Lazarus is dead, [15]and for your sake I am glad I was not there, so that you may believe. But let us go to him."

[16]Then Thomas (called Didymus) said to the rest of the disciples, "Let us also go, that we may die with him."

OPEN Do you have a short fuse or a long fuse on your panic button?

STUDY **1.** What do you remember about Mary and Martha that will help you to understand this story? **2.** Why do you think Jesus delayed two days after hearing about Lazarus? **3.** What were the disciples afraid of if they went to help Lazarus (vv. 8,16)? **4.** How does Jesus answer their fears? If you had been one of the disciples, would his answer calm your nerves? **5.** What will the disciples learn from this experience? **6.** Would you have been as willing as Thomas to leave for Jerusalem?

APPLY **1.** When is the last time you questioned God's timing? **2.** When you don't get your prayers answered right away, what do you do?

11:2 Mary. Apparently the author, aware that the story of Jesus' anointing was a familiar one to his readers, used this incident to identify Mary even though it doesn't occur in this Gospel until chapter 12 (Mark 14:1–11).

11:4 God's Son may be glorified. All the signs in this Gospel were meant as a demonstration of the reality of Jesus' unity with the Father (10:25–30).

11:6 he stayed where he was two more days. At least two views are possible as to why he did this: (1) As in 2:3–4, Jesus seemingly ignores an urgent request to act in a needy situation. Jesus' delay communicates that his agenda is set neither by himself (6:38) nor by the desires of those he loves, but by the Father; (2) He waited in order that through this trial his glory would be revealed in a new way.

11:7 Let us go back to Judea. Jesus was in Perea on the other side of the Jordan River (10:40–42).

11:9 Are there not twelve hours of daylight? Jesus responds with a two-sentence parable which indicates there is no need to fear the Jewish leaders, since he is living in his Father's will and by his timetable. Until his "hour" comes, he is safe from harm and will do the Father's work. There is the implication, though, that the "night" will soon come when he, the light of the world, is taken away. The parable also calls his disciples to consider whether they will take their cues from the "light of the world" or from those (like the Pharisees) who operate in the darkness.

11:11 fallen asleep. This was a common euphemism for death.

11:13 his disciples thought. Like the Pharisees, the disciples fail to grasp the spiritual implications of Jesus' words (4:33).

11:16 Thomas (called Didymus). "Didymus" is Greek for "twin." Although Thomas has become famous for his doubt (20:25), here he demonstrates his deep faith and loyalty.

OPEN What death was the hardest for you to accept?

STUDY **1.** What has taken place in the previous passage as background to this story? **2.** What do you learn about Martha from the way she talks to Jesus in verses 21–27? How would you have acted? **3.** When Jesus said, "Your brother will rise again," what did Martha assume he was talking about? **4.** If Martha believed that Jesus was able to raise her brother from the dead right then, why was she shocked when he asked them to "take away the stone"? **5.** What about Mary? Why didn't she come to meet Jesus in the first place? How would you describe their meeting in verses 32–36? **6.** What was the smell when they removed the stone? If you had been standing among the mourners and the sisters, how would you be feeling when Jesus said, "Lazarus, come out!"? When "the dead man came out" how would you have felt? **7.** Why was it important for the spectators to remove the grave clothes? **8.** What did Jesus prove in the raising of Lazarus? How does this story speak to someone facing death today? **9.** How would you put verse 25 into your own words? **10.** How would you answer the skeptic who says Lazarus was only unconscious and revived in the cold tomb?

Jesus Comforts the Sisters

17On his arrival, Jesus found that Lazarus had already been in the
tomb for four days. 18Bethany was less than two miles[a] from Jerusalem, 19and many Jews had come to Martha and Mary to comfort them
in the loss of their brother. 20When Martha heard that Jesus was coming, she went out to meet him, but Mary stayed at home.
21"Lord," Martha said to Jesus, "if you had been here, my brother
would not have died. 22But I know that even now God will give you
whatever you ask."
23Jesus said to her, "Your brother will rise again."
24Martha answered, "I know he will rise again in the resurrection
at the last day."
25Jesus said to her, "I am the resurrection and the life. He who believes in me will live, even though he dies; 26and whoever lives and
believes in me will never die. Do you believe this?"
27"Yes, Lord," she told him, "I believe that you are the Christ,[b] the
Son of God, who was to come into the world."
28And after she had said this, she went back and called her sister
Mary aside. "The Teacher is here," she said, "and is asking for you."
29When Mary heard this, she got up quickly and went to him. 30Now
Jesus had not yet entered the village, but was still at the place where
Martha had met him. 31When the Jews who had been with Mary in the
house, comforting her, noticed how quickly she got up and went out,
they followed her, supposing she was going to the tomb to mourn
there.
32When Mary reached the place where Jesus was and saw him, she
fell at his feet and said, "Lord, if you had been here, my brother would
not have died."

[a]18 Greek *fifteen stadia* (about 3 kilometers) [b]27 Or *Messiah*

11:21 if you had been here, my brother would not have died. Since Lazarus had died probably even before Jesus received the message, and since Martha also adds a statement of trust in Christ's power to do something wonderful "even now" (v. 22), this is not a rebuke but an expression of regret. It implies faith that if Jesus had been on the scene before his death, Lazarus could have been saved.

11:22 But I know. Given her confusion in verse 39, this may not be an expectation that Jesus could do a miracle even now. However, it is an expression of a faith that Christ is in control and will bring about what is best even now.

11:23 will rise again. The Pharisees and other Jewish groups believed in a general resurrection. She would have understood Jesus' comment as simply an appropriate expression of comfort at a funeral. Other mourners, wishing to comfort her and assure her that they knew Lazarus had been a good man, probably said very similar things to her.

11:25 I am the resurrection and the life. This claim would jar anyone at a funeral! By it, Jesus focuses Martha's attention, not on the doctrine of the general resurrection, but on him as the source of that resurrection (5:24–29). **will live, even though he dies.** Spiritual life that will not end at physical death is in view here. In this verse and in verse 26, Jesus is asserting his sovereign power over death and his ability to "give life to whom he is pleased to give it" (5:21).

11:26 Do you believe this? Jesus directly confronts Martha with this claim. Does she see him only as a healer or as the Lord of life? Jesus on several occasions made a point of giving his followers an opportunity to declare where they stood in relationship to him. A similar instance is when he asked Peter, "But what about you? ... Who do you say I am?" (Matt. 16:15).

11:27 In this verse, Martha declares by means of four terms exactly who Jesus is. **Lord.** This can mean simply "sir," a polite form of address. Whereas in verse 21 it may have that intent, in this verse the author is using it in its sense as a title for deity since the rest of Martha's statement is full of spiritual insight into his identity. **Christ, the Son of God, who was to come into the world.** In calling him the Christ, Martha acknowledges Jesus as the One who delivers and saves his people from the power of sin and death. Her recognition of him as the Son of God shows her insight into his divine identity. The meaning behind this title is that he is God, sharing the Father's essential nature just as a child shares the characteristics of his or her parents. It was this claim to be the Son of God that was the real grounds for the opposition against him (19:7). The final phrase, who was to come into the world, refers to the expectation that one day a leader like Moses would arise (Deut. 18:18). This too acknowledges his authority and divine commission.

11:32 Mary. That Mary stayed at home when Jesus came (v. 20) seems to have been an indication of despair,

[33]When Jesus saw her weeping, and the Jews who had come along
with her also weeping, he was deeply moved in spirit and troubled.
[34]"Where have you laid him?" he asked.
"Come and see, Lord," they replied.
[35]Jesus wept.
[36]Then the Jews said, "See how he loved him!"
[37]But some of them said, "Could not he who opened the eyes of the
blind man have kept this man from dying?"

Jesus Raises Lazarus From the Dead

[38]Jesus, once more deeply moved, came to the tomb. It was a cave
with a stone laid across the entrance. [39]"Take away the stone," he
said.
"But, Lord," said Martha, the sister of the dead man, "by this time
there is a bad odor, for he has been there four days."
[40]Then Jesus said, "Did I not tell you that if you believed, you would
see the glory of God?"
[41]So they took away the stone. Then Jesus looked up and said, "Father, I thank you that you have heard me. [42]I knew that you always
hear me, but I said this for the benefit of the people standing here,
that they may believe that you sent me."
[43]When he had said this, Jesus called in a loud voice, "Lazarus,
come out!" [44]The dead man came out, his hands and feet wrapped
with strips of linen, and a cloth around his face.
Jesus said to them, "Take off the grave clothes and let him go."

The Plot to Kill Jesus

[45]Therefore many of the Jews who had come to visit Mary, and had
seen what Jesus did, put their faith in him. [46]But some of them went
to the Pharisees and told them what Jesus had done. [47]Then the chief
priests and the Pharisees called a meeting of the Sanhedrin.
"What are we accomplishing?" they asked. "Here is this man
performing many miraculous signs. [48]If we let him go on like this,

APPLY 1. Have you ever attended a funeral where the family of the deceased had no hope of eternal life? What was it like? **2.** If you were to make this story into a parable of new life in Christ, where would you be in the story: Still in the tomb? Alive, but with grave clothes? Alive, and free of grave clothes?

OPEN What is the closest you have come to living through a major war?

STUDY 1. What has the miracle of raising Lazarus done? **2.** What are the religious leaders concerned about? How does Caiaphas propose to solve the Jesus problem?

for otherwise the one who had shown so much devotion to Christ in other situations (v. 2; Luke 10:38–42) John would certainly have come to him right away for comfort. Also Mary here does not add a statement of faith like Martha expressed, that Jesus still could do something powerful (v. 22). This seems to indicate that when Mary says, "Lord, if you had been here, my brother would not have died," it may have been more *an expression of disappointment than* faith.

11:33 weeping. In contrast to the Western custom of acting in a restrained manner at funerals, in this culture they were times for loud, public expressions of grief. The word "weeping" here indicates this type of wailing.

11:38 the tomb. Tombs for people of importance were either vertical shafts covered by a stone, or horizontal hollows carved out of a hill. Since this tomb is carved out of a cave, it would be the latter type.

11:39 bad odor. Even if Martha knew of the others Jesus had raised (Matt. 11:5; Mark 5:22–43; Luke 7:11–15), they were people who had been dead for only a short time. By the fourth day the actual decomposition of the body had begun and therefore no resuscitation could be possible.

11:40 Did I not tell you. This may be a reference to the message in verse 4, or the implication of what he meant by his declaration to Martha in verse 25. The signs in this Gospel have consistently been regarded as demonstrations of Jesus' identity. They reveal his glory (2:11) and, based on them, people make decisions about who he is (6:14; 9:32–33). This final sign will reveal what has been alluded to all along—Jesus is God.

11:44 wrapped with strips of linen. While burial customs included wrapping the body with cloth and spices (19:40), this was not intended to preserve the body, like the ancient Egyptian process of mummification, but only as a sign of honor for the deceased person.

11:47 Sanhedrin. This was the religious and political governing body of Judea. Comprised of 71 members presided over by the high priest, its self-perpetuating membership included priests, elders and scribes.

11:48 everyone will believe in him. The fact of Jesus' miracles was never

How does Caiaphas unwittingly convey prophetic truth about Jesus' death (3:16)? **3.** How does Jesus respond to this new situation? **4.** What is the talk of the town among the thousands of people who start arriving in Jerusalem? If you were on the governing board of the temple, how would you be feeling?

APPLY 1. As you look back over your life, what is the "dark" period when it looked like circumstances were conspiring against you and there was no way out? **2.** How do you look upon that period now?

---

everyone will believe in him, and then the Romans will come and take
away both our place[a] and our nation."
49Then one of them, named Caiaphas, who was high priest that
year, spoke up, "You know nothing at all! 50You do not realize that it is
better for you that one man die for the people than that the whole nation perish."
51He did not say this on his own, but as high priest that year he
prophesied that Jesus would die for the Jewish nation, 52and not only
for that nation but also for the scattered children of God, to bring
them together and make them one. 53So from that day on they plotted
to take his life.
54Therefore Jesus no longer moved about publicly among the Jews.
Instead he withdrew to a region near the desert, to a village called
Ephraim, where he stayed with his disciples.
55When it was almost time for the Jewish Passover, many went up
from the country to Jerusalem for their ceremonial cleansing before
the Passover. 56They kept looking for Jesus, and as they stood in the
temple area they asked one another, "What do you think? Isn't he
coming to the Feast at all?" 57But the chief priests and Pharisees had
given orders that if anyone found out where Jesus was, he should report it so that they might arrest him.

OPEN If you had a year's wages to spend on friends, which would you choose: Big party? Glorious trip for a few? Extravagant gift for one?

STUDY 1. What do you remember about Lazarus and his two sisters from previous stories (11:1–44)? **2.** What do you think about the extravagance of Mary? What would you have said? **3.** What do you find out about Judas? Do you think anyone realized what Jesus was saying in verse 8? What's the lesson here for today? **4.** If you had a year's wages or could give a year of your life to something, what would you do?

APPLY What have you done that gave you a lot of satisfaction that might be considered

Jesus Anointed at Bethany

12 Six days before the Passover, Jesus arrived at Bethany, where
Lazarus lived, whom Jesus had raised from the dead. 2Here a
dinner was given in Jesus' honor. Martha served, while Lazarus was
among those reclining at the table with him. 3Then Mary took about a
pint[b] of pure nard, an expensive perfume; she poured it on Jesus' feet
and wiped his feet with her hair. And the house was filled with the fragrance of the perfume.
4But one of his disciples, Judas Iscariot, who was later to betray
him, objected, 5"Why wasn't this perfume sold and the money given
to the poor? It was worth a year's wages.[c]" 6He did not say this because he cared about the poor but because he was a thief; as keeper
of the money bag, he used to help himself to what was put into it.
7"Leave her alone," Jesus replied. "⌞It was intended⌟ that she should
save this perfume for the day of my burial. 8You will always have the
poor among you, but you will not always have me."

[a]48 Or *temple* [b]3 Greek *a litra* (probably about 0.5 liter) [c]5 Greek *three hundred denarii*

---

disputed by Jesus' enemies. What bothers these leaders is that people might interpret the miracles as a sign of Jesus' messiahship. Since they have already decided that he could not possibly be the Messiah (7:52), this is something they cannot allow to happen. **the Romans will come and take away.** *In this context, "place" most likely* refers to the temple.

11:49 Caiaphas. Caiaphas was high priest from A.D. 18 until A.D. 36 when he was deposed by the Roman authorities. According to Old Testament Law the high priests were to serve for life, but at this time one's leadership depended upon Roman approval.

12:6 he was a thief. This is the only place in the Gospels that we are given any background about Judas. The author's point is not to dismiss legitimate caring for the poor, but to point out that in spite of his words Judas' motives were self-serving.

12:7 perfume for the day of my burial. Jesus uses this incident as a foreshadowing of his death. In that culture bodies were often wrapped with spices for burial (19:39–40). Jesus' statement does not mean that Mary was aware of this purpose—it is far more likely that she meant it as an act of thanksgiving to Jesus for what he had done for her brother.

12:8 You will always have the poor. This is not meant to disparage acts of mercy, but to shift the focus on the upcoming death of Jesus.

[9]Meanwhile a large crowd of Jews found out that Jesus was there and came, not only because of him but also to see Lazarus, whom he had raised from the dead. [10]So the chief priests made plans to kill Lazarus as well, [11]for on account of him many of the Jews were going over to Jesus and putting their faith in him.

The Triumphal Entry

[12]The next day the great crowd that had come for the Feast heard that Jesus was on his way to Jerusalem. [13]They took palm branches and went out to meet him, shouting,

"Hosanna![a]"
"Blessed is he who comes in the name of the Lord!"[b]
"Blessed is the King of Israel!"

[14]Jesus found a young donkey and sat upon it, as it is written,

[15]"Do not be afraid, O Daughter of Zion;
see, your king is coming,
seated on a donkey's colt."[c]

[16]At first his disciples did not understand all this. Only after Jesus was glorified did they realize that these things had been written about him and that they had done these things to him.
[17]Now the crowd that was with him when he called Lazarus from the tomb and raised him from the dead continued to spread the word.
[18]Many people, because they had heard that he had given this miraculous sign, went out to meet him. [19]So the Pharisees said to one another, "See, this is getting us nowhere. Look how the whole world has gone after him!"

Jesus Predicts His Death

[20]Now there were some Greeks among those who went up to worship at the Feast. [21]They came to Philip, who was from Bethsaida in Galilee, with a request. "Sir," they said, "we would like to see Jesus."
[22]Philip went to tell Andrew; Andrew and Philip in turn told Jesus.
[23]Jesus replied, "The hour has come for the Son of Man to be glorified. [24]I tell you the truth, unless a kernel of wheat falls to the ground

[a]13 A Hebrew expression meaning "Save!" which became an exclamation of praise [b]13 Psalm 118:25,26
[c]15 Zech. 9:9

wasteful or crazy (such as working for the Peace Corp. coaching Little League or volunteering with Habitat for Humanity)?

OPEN 1. What do you like best about parades: Bands? Food Venders? Clowns? **2.** What do you like least: Traffic? Pickpockets? Tall people?

STUDY 1. How would your local television reporter describe this triumphal entry? **2.** What has happened (v. 9) to swell the crowd? What would they be expecting from Jesus? **3.** Do you think anyone at this time realized the significance of all of this besides Jesus? As the crowd is praising him like a hero, what is Jesus feeling? What about his disciples? **4.** What are the Pharisees afraid of?

APPLY 1. How do you feel about the popularity of Christianity in this country? **2.** What do you think people are looking for?

OPEN What childhood friend of yours was of another nationality?

STUDY 1. What brings Greeks (Gentiles) to Jerusalem for the Jewish feast of Unleavened Bread? **2.** What was so unique about their request that Philip would first filter it through Andrew? **3.** How did Jesus use this interview to reveal the

---

12:9 a large crowd of Jews. "Jews" here does not mean the Jewish authorities as it often does in John's Gospel, but simply Jewish people in general.

12:10 the chief priests made plans to kill Lazarus as well. There is no record that this ironic plot to kill a man who had just been raised from the dead ever got beyond the planning stage.

12:12 the great crowd. This was obviously a very large crowd of Jews in town for the Passover. Jerusalem was a city of normally under 25,000 people. When Passover was celebrated, the population greatly increased to 4 or 5 times its normal size..

12:13 palm branches. In this account the other Gospels mention people using their garments as well. **Hosanna!** Originally a one word prayer for God to save (Ps. 118:25), this had become an expression of praise. **Blessed is he who comes in the name of the Lord!** Psalm 118:26 was used in the liturgy for Passover and celebrated God's deliverance of Israel from her enemies.

12:20 some Greeks. These would be Gentile converts to Judaism such as the men described in Acts 8:27; 10:2.

12:23 The hour has come. Throughout the Gospel, the author has anticipated this time (2:4; 7:6; 8:20). From here on, he speaks of how the "time has come" (13:1; 17:1): this is the time of his glorification which is initiated by his death (v. 28).

12:24 a kernel of wheat. Just as a seed must be buried before it can become fruitful, so his death is necessary in order that many people may be brought to life.

and dies, it remains only a single seed. But if it dies, it produces many
seeds. 25The man who loves his life will lose it, while the man who
hates his life in this world will keep it for eternal life. 26Whoever
serves me must follow me; and where I am, my servant also will be.
My Father will honor the one who serves me.

27"Now my heart is troubled, and what shall I say? 'Father, save me
from this hour'? No, it was for this very reason I came to this hour.
28Father, glorify your name!"

Then a voice came from heaven, "I have glorified it, and will glorify
it again." 29The crowd that was there and heard it said it had thundered; others said an angel had spoken to him.

30Jesus said, "This voice was for your benefit, not mine. 31Now is
the time for judgment on this world; now the prince of this world will
be driven out. 32But I, when I am lifted up from the earth, will draw all
men to myself." 33He said this to show the kind of death he was going
to die.

34The crowd spoke up, "We have heard from the Law that the
Christ[a] will remain forever, so how can you say, 'The Son of Man must
be lifted up'? Who is this 'Son of Man'?"

35Then Jesus told them, "You are going to have the light just a little
while longer. Walk while you have the light, before darkness overtakes you. The man who walks in the dark does not know where he is
going. 36Put your trust in the light while you have it, so that you may
become sons of light." When he had finished speaking, Jesus left and
hid himself from them.

The Jews Continue in Their Unbelief

37Even after Jesus had done all these miraculous signs in their
presence, they still would not believe in him. 38This was to fulfill the
word of Isaiah the prophet:

"Lord, who has believed our message
and to whom has the arm of the Lord been revealed?"[b]

39For this reason they could not believe, because, as Isaiah says
elsewhere:

[a]34 Or *Messiah* [b]38 Isaiah 53:1

change in his mission? **4.** What is going on in Jesus' head in verse 27? How would you describe his feelings? **5.** Who is the "prince of this world" (v. 31)? What is the "judgment" (v. 30) and how will this drive out "the prince"? **6.** How would you explain and paraphrase verse 32? **7.** How does the crowd misunderstand what Jesus is saying? **8.** Is the battle described here for humankind real or something for science fiction?

APPLY 1. At what point in your spiritual pilgrimage were you like the crowd—curious, but in the dark about the meaning of the gospel? **2.** How are you and God getting along now?

OPEN Are you more like the salesman who could sell an icebox to an Eskimo or the Eskimo who buys one?

STUDY 1. What has Jesus appealed for in the previous verse? **2.** How do the prophecies in Isaiah predict the people's response in spite of the "signs"? **3.** What would you call the "leaders" who believed but kept it a secret? Who does this remind you of? **4.** What is Jesus claiming in

12:25 The only way to gain life is to be willing to lose it for the sake of Christ (Matt. 10:39; Mark 8:34–35; Luke 9:24). The strong language of "love" and "hate" reflects the common rabbinic practice of using hyperbole in order to make the point.

12:27 my heart is troubled. This Gospel does not show us Jesus praying in the Garden of Gethsemane as do the others, but the same type of anguish that was expressed at that time is seen here.

12:31 judgment on this world. Jesus has said repeatedly that although his intent in coming was not to judge but to save, his coming *does* bring about a judgment. His presence brings all people to a crisis point. If they will receive him, they will have life. If they refuse him, they will inherit death. **the prince of this world.** Satan is often presented as having the world under his domination (Matt. 4:8; Eph. 2:2–3; Heb. 2:14–15).

12:32 But I, when I am lifted up from the earth, will draw all men to myself. There is a double meaning here. To be "lifted up" was understood by the crowds to mean crucifixion (v. 34), but it also is reminiscent of the "lifting up" of a military flag or standard which would be a rallying point for an army in battle (6:40).

12:35–36 Jesus does not answer their question, but picks up on the image he used before to describe himself as "the light of the world" (8:12) to issue them one last call to trust in him.

12:38 the word of Isaiah. The problem of widespread Jewish unbelief in Jesus was a concern to the early church (Rom. 9–11). Two passages from Isaiah are used to reflect on that problem here. The first (Isa. 53:1), anticipates the people's disbelief of God's servant. The second accounts for that disbelief by drawing upon Isaiah 6:10. In this passage, Isaiah uses irony to tell of Israel's rejection of God's message.

40"He has blinded their eyes
and deadened their hearts,
so they can neither see with their eyes,
nor understand with their hearts,
nor turn—and I would heal them."[a]

41Isaiah said this because he saw Jesus' glory and spoke about him.
42Yet at the same time many even among the leaders believed in
him. But because of the Pharisees they would not confess their faith
for fear they would be put out of the synagogue; 43for they loved
praise from men more than praise from God.
44Then Jesus cried out, "When a man believes in me, he does not
believe in me only, but in the one who sent me. 45When he looks at
me, he sees the one who sent me. 46I have come into the world as a
light, so that no one who believes in me should stay in darkness.
47"As for the person who hears my words but does not keep them, I
do not judge him. For I did not come to judge the world, but to save it.
48There is a judge for the one who rejects me and does not accept my
words; that very word which I spoke will condemn him at the last day.
49For I did not speak of my own accord, but the Father who sent me
commanded me what to say and how to say it. 50I know that his command leads to eternal life. So whatever I say is just what the Father
has told me to say."

Jesus Washes His Disciples' Feet

13 It was just before the Passover Feast. Jesus knew that the
time had come for him to leave this world and go to the Father. Having loved his own who were in the world, he now showed
them the full extent of his love.[b]
2The evening meal was being served, and the devil had already
prompted Judas Iscariot, son of Simon, to betray Jesus. 3Jesus knew
that the Father had put all things under his power, and that he had
come from God and was returning to God; 4so he got up from the
meal, took off his outer clothing, and wrapped a towel around his
waist. 5After that, he poured water into a basin and began to wash his
disciples' feet, drying them with the towel that was wrapped around
him.
6He came to Simon Peter, who said to him, "Lord, are you going to
wash my feet?"

[a]40 Isaiah 6:10 [b]1 *Or he loved them to the last*

verses 44–45? How does this compare to 1:1–5? **5.** What does Jesus say in his last recorded public statement (vv. 47–50) about people who have been given the opportunity to believe in God's plan of salvation? **6.** Unlike the other three Gospels, the Gospel of John was written for the seeker who wanted to examine the life and ministry of Jesus Christ. If you were reading this Gospel account for the first time, how would you be feeling at this point?

APPLY 1. What would you say to a friend who says to you that he is not ready to commit his life to God? **2.** What about the "secret disciple" that believes but keeps it a secret?

OPEN 1. How are you at saying "good-bye"? **2.** What was one of the hardest "good-byes" you have ever had to say?

STUDY 1. What do you know about the Jewish Passover Feast? **2.** In making the day-long preparations for this meal, do you think the disciples realized the significance of this meal? **3.** Why did Jesus choose footwashing to teach his disciples a lesson in servanthood? **4.** If you had been Peter, would you have reacted like he did? What's the meaning behind verse 10? **5.** Do you think the disciples understood his teaching on leadership? Do you think the church today understands the meaning of leadership? Who in particular do you admire for Jesus-style leadership?

12:47 I did not come to judge the world, but to save it. Those who reject Christ condemn themselves by *their own lack of belief*. Just as to believe in him is to believe in the Father (vv. 44–46), so to refuse him is to refuse the Father.

13:1 Jesus knew. Here in verses 3 and 11, John emphasizes what Jesus knew. This lays stress on the fact that Jesus was in charge of the events leading to his death (10:18).

13:3 Jesus' self-knowledge was at the heart of his willingness and ability to serve. This verse says that he knew who he was in terms of where he had come from (the Father), where he was going (back to the Father), and what his role was while he was here.

13:4–5 Normally people's dusty, sandaled feet were washed by the lowest-ranking servant of the household before a meal was served. Jesus' action was deliberate. Removing his outer clothing was a sign he was going to do some work, and it would have identified him with a servant who generally worked in minimal garb. The other Gospels mention that at the Last Supper there was a discussion among the Twelve about who was the greatest (Luke 22:24). In that context, Jesus identified the greatest as the one who was the servant (Luke 22:25–26).

13:6 Lord, are you going to wash my feet? Peter, recognizing the impropriety of a master washing the servants' feet, protests. The Greek sentence actually reads more like, "You? Wash *my* feet?" Peter is appalled at this breach of normal procedure.

7 Jesus replied, "You do not realize now what I am doing, but later
you will understand."
8 "No," said Peter, "you shall never wash my feet."
Jesus answered, "Unless I wash you, you have no part with me."
9 "Then, Lord," Simon Peter replied, "not just my feet but my hands
and my head as well!"
10 Jesus answered, "A person who has had a bath needs only to
wash his feet; his whole body is clean. And you are clean, though not
every one of you." 11 For he knew who was going to betray him, and
that was why he said not every one was clean.
12 When he had finished washing their feet, he put on his clothes
and returned to his place. "Do you understand what I have done for
you?" he asked them. 13 "You call me 'Teacher' and 'Lord,' and rightly
so, for that is what I am. 14 Now that I, your Lord and Teacher, have
washed your feet, you also should wash one another's feet. 15 I have
set you an example that you should do as I have done for you. 16 I tell
you the truth, no servant is greater than his master, nor is a messenger greater than the one who sent him. 17 Now that you know these
things, you will be blessed if you do them.

Jesus Predicts His Betrayal

18 "I am not referring to all of you; I know those I have chosen. But
this is to fulfill the scripture: 'He who shares my bread has lifted up
his heel against me.'[a]
19 "I am telling you now before it happens, so that when it does
happen you will believe that I am He. 20 I tell you the truth, whoever
accepts anyone I send accepts me; and whoever accepts me accepts
the one who sent me."
21 After he had said this, Jesus was troubled in spirit and testified, "I
tell you the truth, one of you is going to betray me."
22 His disciples stared at one another, at a loss to know which of
them he meant. 23 One of them, the disciple whom Jesus loved, was

[a] 18 Psalm 41:9

6. Is the organizational chart of your church a pyramid or an inverted pyramid?

APPLY 1. If Jesus knew your deepest need, what would he do for you today: Hug you? Pat you on the back? Wash your feet? What would he say to you: Good job? Hang in there? Get moving? I love you? **2.** Where do you get the kind of spiritual caretaking that Jesus is all about?

OPEN If you were going to receive a "pink slip," would you rather have a face-to-face meeting or get it indirectly?

STUDY 1. When is this passage taking place (13:1)? Who is there? What's the color of the atmosphere? **2.** When the disciples are told that one of them will betray Jesus, how do the disciples react? How would you have reacted? **3.** How did Jesus identify the betrayer? Why didn't the disciples realize it when Judas left? **4.** Is Judas to be excused or held responsible for his actions? **5.** Given almost three years of very

---

13:7 later you will understand. This may simply be referring to verse 17, but more likely it refers to the full understanding of Jesus' servanthood that will be made clear after his resurrection.

13:8 Unless I wash you, you have no part with me. This lifts the meaning of the footwashing to a higher plane than simply that of an object lesson about humility. Jesus' footwashing was a symbol of the spiritual cleansing he would accomplish for his followers through the Cross.

13:10 A person who has had a bath. Jesus uses the picture of a person who, after washing completely, travels somewhere. Upon arrival, only his feet need be washed to be clean again. **you are clean, though not every one of you.** Literally, "though not all"—which leaves the meaning ambiguous to the hearers. He may mean only that they are literally still not all clean, but the context shows his real intent was to prepare them for his startling announcement in verse 21.

13:16 no servant is greater than his master. If the master serves, how much more should the servants do so? **a messenger.** This is the same word as "apostle," which only occurs here in this Gospel. An apostle was a person sent with the authority to represent the one who sent him. Jesus' followers are to represent his servanthood to others.

13:18 to fulfill the scripture. Psalm 41:9 is quoted as an example of a person being turned against by former friends. Like David, Jesus must face being betrayed by his friends and counselors. **He who shares my bread has lifted up his heel against me.** Eating together was a sign of friendship. To lift up one's heel was a gesture of contempt, implying a desire to trample the other person underfoot.

13:21 troubled in spirit. In all the references to Jesus being troubled, it is the fact of death that disturbs him (11:33; 12:27).

13:23 the disciple whom Jesus loved. This is the first mention of a disciple who will appear several times in these final chapters (19:26–27; 20:2; 21:7, 20). It is assumed that this is a reference to John, to whom this Gospel is credited. This title does not need to mean that Jesus loved him more than the others, but that his identity was defined by the reality of Jesus' love for him. **reclining next to him.** Formal meals were eaten while the participants reclined on their left side upon couches arranged in a horseshoe shape around a common table.

reclining next to him. [24]Simon Peter motioned to this disciple and
said, "Ask him which one he means."
[25]Leaning back against Jesus, he asked him, "Lord, who is it?"
[26]Jesus answered, "It is the one to whom I will give this piece of
bread when I have dipped it in the dish." Then, dipping the piece of
bread, he gave it to Judas Iscariot, son of Simon. [27]As soon as Judas
took the bread, Satan entered into him.
"What you are about to do, do quickly," Jesus told him, [28]but no
one at the meal understood why Jesus said this to him. [29]Since Judas
had charge of the money, some thought Jesus was telling him to buy
what was needed for the Feast, or to give something to the poor. [30]As
soon as Judas had taken the bread, he went out. And it was night.

Jesus Predicts Peter's Denial

[31]When he was gone, Jesus said, "Now is the Son of Man glorified
and God is glorified in him. [32]If God is glorified in him,[a] God will
glorify the Son in himself, and will glorify him at once.
[33]"My children, I will be with you only a little longer. You will look
for me, and just as I told the Jews, so I tell you now: Where I am
going, you cannot come.
[34]"A new command I give you: Love one another. As I have loved
you, so you must love one another. [35]By this all men will know that
you are my disciples, if you love one another."
[36]Simon Peter asked him, "Lord, where are you going?"
Jesus replied, "Where I am going, you cannot follow now, but you
will follow later."
[37]Peter asked, "Lord, why can't I follow you now? I will lay down
my life for you."
[38]Then Jesus answered, "Will you really lay down your life for me? I
tell you the truth, before the rooster crows, you will disown me three
times!

Jesus Comforts His Disciples

14 "Do not let your hearts be troubled. Trust in God[b]; trust also
in me. [2]In my Father's house are many rooms; if it were not
so, I would have told you. I am going there to prepare a place for you.

[a]32 Many early manuscripts do not have *If God is glorified in him.* [b]1 Or *You trust in God*

intimate contact with Jesus, how could Judas turn around and betray him? Do you know of any parallels to this?

APPLY 1. What is the closest you have come to being betrayed by someone? **2.** How would Jesus deal with this?

OPEN What are the final words your parents gave you before you left home?

STUDY 1. How would you think the disciples felt when Jesus said he would be leaving them (v. 33)? Could you have gotten through these words without breaking down? **2.** Do you think the disciples knew the depth of the love Jesus expects from them (v. 34)? **3.** Who does Peter remind you of in verse 37? Was Jesus being cruel or just honest in verse 38? How do you think Peter felt?

APPLY What is the closest you have come to being in a community that really cared for one another?

OPEN 1. What is your favorite room in the house? **2.** Who did you go to for comfort with a hurt finger when you were a child?

STUDY 1. What has Jesus just told his disciples

13:26 he gave it to Judas. Although this was a signal that Judas was the betrayer, it may also have been Jesus' final attempt to call Judas back to himself since the sharing of food was a common sign of friendship and peace.

13:27 Satan entered into him. The relationship between Satan's activity and that of Judas himself is never explained. On the one hand, it is his free choice to betray Jesus for whatever motives he had; on the other hand, in so doing he was following the desires of his spiritual father and lord, the devil. **What you are about to do, do quickly.** Jesus' control of the timing of his death is manifest even in Judas' betrayal.

13:29 some thought. This signal escaped the awareness of most of the disciples.

13:33 My children. Rabbis used this term to address their disciples. **Where I am going, you cannot come.** Jesus used this same phrase with the leaders as a warning that they were heading in the wrong direction to ever see the Father (8:21). Jesus amplifies on its meaning in 16:5–33 where the emphasis is on the benefit of his departure.

13:34–35 A new command. This is the first of several indications that at this meal Jesus is instituting a new covenant between God and his people.

13:38 you will disown me three times. All the Gospels warn of Peter's denial (18:15–26). Here, unlike the others, there is no protest and no development of the theme.

14:1 Do not let your hearts be troubled. Having settled his own mind and heart, Jesus brings comfort to the disciples by giving them hope.

14:2 my Father's house. In 2:16 this referred to the temple. Here, it means heaven. The earthly temple was seen to be a symbol of the actual dwelling place of God (Heb. 9:24). **many rooms.** Literally, "dwelling places." The emphasis is not on having separate compartments in heaven,

3 And if I go and prepare a place for you, I will come back and take you
to be with me that you also may be where I am. 4 You know the way to
the place where I am going."

Jesus the Way to the Father

5 Thomas said to him, "Lord, we don't know where you are going,
so how can we know the way?"

6 Jesus answered, "I am the way and the truth and the life. No one
comes to the Father except through me. 7 If you really knew me, you
would know[a] my Father as well. From now on, you do know him and
have seen him."

8 Philip said, "Lord, show us the Father and that will be enough
for us."

9 Jesus answered: "Don't you know me, Philip, even after I have
been among you such a long time? Anyone who has seen me has seen
the Father. How can you say, 'Show us the Father'? 10 Don't you believe that I am in the Father, and that the Father is in me? The words
I say to you are not just my own. Rather, it is the Father, living in me,
who is doing his work. 11 Believe me when I say that I am in the Father
and the Father is in me; or at least believe on the evidence of the miracles themselves. 12 I tell you the truth, anyone who has faith in me
will do what I have been doing. He will do even greater things than
these, because I am going to the Father. 13 And I will do whatever you
ask in my name, so that the Son may bring glory to the Father. 14 You
may ask me for anything in my name, and I will do it.

Jesus Promises the Holy Spirit

15 "If you love me, you will obey what I command. 16 And I will ask
the Father, and he will give you another Counselor to be with you forever— 17 the Spirit of truth. The world cannot accept him, because it
neither sees him nor knows him. But you know him, for he lives with
you and will be[b] in you. 18 I will not leave you as orphans; I will come

[a]7 Some early manuscripts *If you really have known me, you will know* [b]17 Some early manuscripts *and is*

(13:33,36) that he builds on in this passage? **2.** When Jesus says, "I go to prepare a place for you ... and I will come back and take you to be with me," is he talking about a place in the distant future called heaven, or an immediate place when the Holy Spirit is given to the disciples? **3.** What does Thomas want to know? How would you paraphrase Jesus' answer (v. 6)? **4.** If you had been Jesus, would you be disappointed in Philip's request? What is the tone in Jesus' voice in verses 9–14? How does this statement relate to 1:18? **5.** What promises does Jesus make to the disciples in verses 12–15? Do these still hold?

APPLY 1. Have you come to the place in your spiritual pilgrimage where you can acknowledge Jesus as the "way, the truth, and the life"? **2.** What do you say to your friends when they say there are many roads to God?

OPEN Who was the best counselor you ever had? What wisdom did this person pass on to you?

STUDY 1. What did Jesus promise in verse 3 that he enlarges on in this passage? **2.** For a bunch of uneducated fishermen with-

---

but on the abundance of room for all who will receive Jesus.

14:3 I will come back. This probably refers to the coming of Christ through his Spirit (vv. 15–21) rather than to the Second Coming, which receives very little attention in this Gospel. Through the Spirit, Jesus "returns" to the disciples (v. 18), and they are then "in" or "with" him and the Father (vv. 20,23). Seen in this way, this promise is not for the distant future, but will be true for the disciples in a very short time (20:22).

14:6 I am the way. The destination to which Jesus is going is not so much a place, but a person—the Father (7:33; 8:21). The way for the disciples to come to the Father is through the Son, who, by his death, opens the way for them (Heb. 10:19–22).

14:11 believe on the evidence of the miracles. The "signs" in chapters 1–12 were all given to point to the truth that Jesus came to reveal God's glory and bring life to people.

14:12 He will do even greater things. The work Jesus has done is not so much tied up with miracles as it is with revealing the truth about God. It is this mission that his disciples will inherit. The "greater" things that they will do should be understood in terms of their scope (i.e., it is the disciples who will bring the gospel to the Gentile world) rather than their power.

14:16 another Counselor. The Greek term *paraclete* is a rich term for which there is no sufficient English translation. Attempts such as "Counselor" or "Helper" or "Comforter" fail because they emphasize only one of many aspects of the term. Since this discourse presents the ministry of the Spirit in the same terms as that of Jesus, the Spirit can be referred to as *another* "Paraclete" like Jesus was (1 John 2:1).

14:17 The world cannot accept him. Just as the "world" has not accepted Jesus, nor the Father (5:37–38), neither will it be able to receive the Spirit. **he lives with you and will be in you.** This parallelism does not create distinctions between "with" and "in," but simply adds emphasis to Jesus' dramatic announcement. The reality of the indwelling Spirit lifts the Old Testament expectation of a new covenant, wherein God would dwell with his people, to unimaginable heights (Isa. 7:14; Jer. 31:31–34; Ezek. 34:30). It is this indwelling of the Spirit with God's people that ultimately makes the temple and the issue of where to worship irrelevant (4:21).

14:18 I will not leave you as

to you. [19]Before long, the world will not see me anymore, but you will
see me. Because I live, you also will live. [20]On that day you will realize
that I am in my Father, and you are in me, and I am in you. [21]Whoever
has my commands and obeys them, he is the one who loves me. He
who loves me will be loved by my Father, and I too will love him and
show myself to him."
[22]Then Judas (not Judas Iscariot) said, "But, Lord, why do you intend to show yourself to us and not to the world?"
[23]Jesus replied, "If anyone loves me, he will obey my teaching. My
Father will love him, and we will come to him and make our home
with him. [24]He who does not love me will not obey my teaching.
These words you hear are not my own; they belong to the Father who
sent me.
[25]"All this I have spoken while still with you. [26]But the Counselor,
the Holy Spirit, whom the Father will send in my name, will teach you
all things and will remind you of everything I have said to you.
[27]Peace I leave with you; my peace I give you. I do not give to you as
the world gives. Do not let your hearts be troubled and do not be
afraid.
[28]"You heard me say, 'I am going away and I am coming back to
you.' If you loved me, you would be glad that I am going to the Father,
for the Father is greater than I. [29]I have told you now before it happens, so that when it does happen you will believe. [30]I will not speak
with you much longer, for the prince of this world is coming. He has
no hold on me, [31]but the world must learn that I love the Father and
that I do exactly what my Father has commanded me.
"Come now; let us leave.

The Vine and the Branches

15 "I am the true vine, and my Father is the gardener. [2]He cuts
off every branch in me that bears no fruit, while every branch
that does bear fruit he prunes[a] so that it will be even more fruitful.
[3]You are already clean because of the word I have spoken to you.
[4]Remain in me, and I will remain in you. No branch can bear fruit by
itself; it must remain in the vine. Neither can you bear fruit unless you
remain in me.

[a]2 The Greek for *prunes* also means *cleans*.

out theological training, how do you think they felt as Jesus talked about a "Counselor" and a "Spirit of Truth" that would reside in them? What was the hardest concept for the disciples to understand? **3.** What is the thing Jesus hammers home to his disciples (vv. 15,21,23–24)? **4.** What is the purpose of the "Counselor" (v. 26) and what will happen when the Counselor takes control of their lives (v. 27)? **5.** How will the disciples be better off if Jesus leaves them (v. 28)? **6.** How would you paraphrase verse 27 in your own words? Now put it in words your secular friends will understand.

APPLY 1. When did you start to understand the person and work of the Holy Spirit? **2.** If "peace" has been deposited into the bank account of every Christ follower, how much are you drawing on your account? Where could you use a little of this peace right now?

OPEN If you had to make a living off of gardening, how would you make out?

STUDY 1. What has Jesus been teaching his disciples that he builds on in this passage (14:23–27)? **2.** Why did Jesus choose wine making to illustrate the principles for a healthy, productive life? What are some of these basic principles? Do you think it is necessary to "cut ...

---

orphans. When a rabbi died, his disciples were spoken of as being orphaned. **I will come to you.** In this context, the coming of Jesus spoken of here should be understood in terms of the coming of the Spirit. It is in that way that they will "see" him, whereas the world will not (v. 19).

14:20 On that day. This speaks of the time when the Spirit will be given to the disciples.

14:26 whom the Father will send. Here and in verse 16 it is the Father who sends the Spirit to the believer. In 15:26 and 16:7 Jesus says he will send the Spirit. **will teach you ... will remind you.** These parallel verbs are two ways of saying the same thing. The purpose of the teaching of the Spirit is not to impart new information, but to remind believers of the truth Jesus taught and helped them apply it to ever-changing situations.

15:1 I am the true vine. The image of the vine was used to describe Israel in the Old Testament (Ps. 80:14–18; Isa. 5:1–7). But Israel did not produce the fruits God expected (Isa. 5:1–7; Matt. 21:43). Jesus transfers this image to himself. He is the "true vine" who, because he always does what pleases the Father (8:29), produces fruit for God.

15:2 cuts off ... prunes. A gardener cuts off dead branches that do not contribute to the plant, and trims small branches so that when they grow back they might be stronger.

15:3 clean. This word in Greek is from the same root as that of "prunes" in verse 2. The metaphor is that of being cleansed from sin because of Jesus' death (13:10).

15:4 bear fruit. Although Paul uses the image of fruit to describe Christian character (Gal. 5:22–23), the fruit here probably relates to 4:35 and 12:24 where a similar agricultural image is used to speak of the many people who would come to Christ. Just as Jesus' fruitfulness was dependent on his doing the Father's will, so the disciple's is

5 "I am the vine; you are the branches. If a man remains in me and I in him, he will bear much fruit; apart from me you can do nothing. 6 If anyone does not remain in me, he is like a branch that is thrown away and withers; such branches are picked up, thrown into the fire and burned. 7 If you remain in me and my words remain in you, ask whatever you wish, and it will be given you. 8 This is to my Father's glory, that you bear much fruit, showing yourselves to be my disciples.

9 "As the Father has loved me, so have I loved you. Now remain in my love. 10 If you obey my commands, you will remain in my love, just as I have obeyed my Father's commands and remain in his love. 11 I have told you this so that my joy may be in you and that your joy may be complete. 12 My command is this: Love each other as I have loved you. 13 Greater love has no one than this, that he lay down his life for his friends. 14 You are my friends if you do what I command. 15 I no longer call you servants, because a servant does not know his master's business. Instead, I have called you friends, for everything that I learned from my Father I have made known to you. 16 You did not choose me, but I chose you and appointed you to go and bear fruit—fruit that will last. Then the Father will give you whatever you ask in my name. 17 This is my command: Love each other.

The World Hates the Disciples

18 "If the world hates you, keep in mind that it hated me first. 19 If you belonged to the world, it would love you as its own. As it is, you do not belong to the world, but I have chosen you out of the world. That is why the world hates you. 20 Remember the words I spoke to you: 'No servant is greater than his master.'[a] If they persecuted me, they will persecute you also. If they obeyed my teaching, they will obey yours also. 21 They will treat you this way because of my name, for they do not know the One who sent me. 22 If I had not come and spoken to them, they would not be guilty of sin. Now, however, they have no excuse for their sin. 23 He who hates me hates my Father as well. 24 If I had not done among them what no one else did, they would not be guilty of sin. But now they have seen these miracles, and yet they have hated both me and my Father. 25 But this is to fulfill what is written in their Law: 'They hated me without reason.'[b]

26 "When the Counselor comes, whom I will send to you from the Father, the Spirit of truth who goes out from the Father, he will testify about me. 27 And you also must testify, for you have been with me from the beginning.

[a] *20* John 13:16 [b] *25* Psalms 35:19; 69:4

prune ... and burn" to have a healthy, productive vineyard? **3.** What is the condition in verse 7 for an effective, productive prayer life? **4.** Is it possible for a branch to have a deep relationship with the vine without having a deep relationship with the other branches? What is the test of a deep relationship? **5.** What is the lesson in this passage for the church today?

APPLY 1. Do you find it easier to have a deep relationship with God or with other followers of Christ? **2.** Can you be open and honest with God and not with others? **3.** What relationship in your life right now needs a little work?

OPEN When is the last time you felt completely out of place at a concert or play?

STUDY 1. What has Jesus just been talking about (15:15–17)? **2.** What are the disciples going to face that Jesus tries to warn them about? Why are the disciples going to feel the brunt of this anger? **3.** What is so sad about the people who will turn their anger on the disciples? **4.** What help can the disciples expect and what must the disciples be prepared to do? **5.** How can the disciples expect to be treated? Why didn't Jesus tell them about this earlier? **6.** Where is the Christian church growing rapidly in the world today: What countries? Continents? What do you know about the persecution of Christians in these countries?

APPLY 1. What is the closest you have come to losing your job or promotion because of your

dependent on holding on to Jesus' teaching.

15:7 ask whatever you wish, and it will be given you. Here the promise is in the context of spiritual *fruitfulness. See also its counterpart in* verse 16.

15:15 friends. The disciples' relationship with Jesus is modeled upon that of Jesus with his Father. In 5:19–20 Jesus said the Father showed him all that he does. In the same way, Jesus has now revealed to the disciples all that he has learned from the Father.

15:18 the world. This means that system of thinking and acting that sets humanity against the ways of God. **it hated me first.** The reason for this hatred was "because men love darkness instead of light because their deeds were evil" (3:19). It hates Jesus because he was "from above" while those who opposed him were "of this world" and belonged to the devil (8:23,44).

15:26 the Counselor ... will testify about me. In times of persecution the Spirit will enable the disciples to speak the truth of the Father.

16 "All this I have told you so that you will not go astray. [2]They will
put you out of the synagogue; in fact, a time is coming when
anyone who kills you will think he is offering a service to God. [3]They
will do such things because they have not known the Father or me.
[4]I have told you this, so that when the time comes you will remember
that I warned you. I did not tell you this at first because I was
with you.

The Work of the Holy Spirit

[5]"Now I am going to him who sent me, yet none of you asks me,
'Where are you going?' [6]Because I have said these things, you are
filled with grief. [7]But I tell you the truth: It is for your good that I am
going away. Unless I go away, the Counselor will not come to you; but
if I go, I will send him to you. [8]When he comes, he will convict the
world of guilt[a] in regard to sin and righteousness and judgment: [9]in
regard to sin, because men do not believe in me; [10]in regard to righteousness, because I am going to the Father, where you can see me
no longer; [11]and in regard to judgment, because the prince of this
world now stands condemned.

[12]"I have much more to say to you, more than you can now bear.
[13]But when he, the Spirit of truth, comes, he will guide you into all
truth. He will not speak on his own; he will speak only what he hears,
and he will tell you what is yet to come. [14]He will bring glory to me by
taking from what is mine and making it known to you. [15]All that belongs to the Father is mine. That is why I said the Spirit will take from
what is mine and make it known to you.

[16]"In a little while you will see me no more, and then after a little
while you will see me."

The Disciples' Grief Will Turn to Joy

[17]Some of his disciples said to one another, "What does he mean by
saying, 'In a little while you will see me no more, and then after a little while you will see me,' and 'Because I am going to the Father'?"
[18]They kept asking, "What does he mean by 'a little while'? We don't
understand what he is saying."

[19]Jesus saw that they wanted to ask him about this, so he said to
them, "Are you asking one another what I meant when I said, 'In a
little while you will see me no more, and then after a little while you
will see me'? [20]I tell you the truth, you will weep and mourn while the

[a]8 Or *will expose the guilt of the world*

stand for Christ? **2.** What's the concern on your heart right now that needs to be turned over to God in prayer?

OPEN How are you at saying "goodbye"? Is it harder for you to be the one leaving home, or the one left behind?

STUDY 1. What is the bad news and the good news Jesus tells his disciples? **2.** What three things will the Holy Spirit perform when he comes? How would you explain each in your own words? **3.** What promise is given the disciples about the Holy Spirit (v. 13)? How can you explain the confusion over doctrine when everyone is guided by the Spirit?

APPLY 1. From your experience, does the Holy Spirit guide you directly or in the company of a caring community? **2.** How would you describe the communication between you and God now?

OPEN 1. If you have given birth or assisted, what do you remember about the birth process? **2.** What have your parents told you about their giving birth to you?

STUDY 1. If you had been one of the disciples, would you be confused by the riddle "a little while you will see me no more and then after a little while you will see me"? **2.** In his answer, is Jesus referring to his death and resurrection or his ascension and the coming of the

---

16:1 Throughout this discourse (13:1–17:26) Jesus prepares the disciples for what will be happening when he departs (v. 4;13:19; 14:29). **go astray.** Literally, "scandalize." The severity of persecution might dissuade the disciples from holding on to Jesus and his teaching. His warning is a corrective to any notions they may have that his kingdom will come about easily.

16:7 It is for your good that I am going away. Jesus' departure means the coming of the Counselor (14:16), which really means his return to them in a deep, inner, spiritual way (7:39; 14:15–21).

16:8 he will convict the world of guilt in regard to sin and righteousness and judgment. The "world" held that Jesus was an unrighteous sinner under the judgment of God (9:24). The Spirit will prove that the world is wrong about its convictions on these matters.

16:17–18 The riddle (v. 16) left the disciples confused. Their frustration here sums up the misunderstanding so common in this Gospel (2:21–22; 3:4; 4:15, 32; 6:5,41,52; 7:35; 8:22,27,33,43; 10:19; 11:12). His closest followers do not know what he means. It will be resolved as he speaks "without figures of speech" (v. 29).

16:20–22 This parable explains what the disciples will soon experience. While they are weeping over their loss of Jesus, the world (as personified by the religious authorities) will rejoice that he is gone.

Holy Spirit? **3.** How would the illustration of the woman in child birth apply to the option you have chosen? **4.** Is "joy" and the freedom to ask anything of the Father because of the resurrection or the coming of the Holy Spirit? **5.** After nearly three years of being with Jesus, what do the disciples finally understand? Why has it taken them so long? **6.** What is the last bombshell in this passage that Jesus drops on the disciples (v. 31)? If you had been there, how would you be feeling after verse 33?

APPLY How do you deal with change? Moves? Job transfers? Transitions from one stage in life to another? Where has God met you in the pain and helped you to grow?

OPEN 1. When you were a kid, how did you deal with long prayers? **2.** Who was notorious for long prayers?

STUDY 1. What event is it now "time" for (v. 1; 12:23–24)? **2.** What does it mean to "glorify" someone (vv. 4–5,10,22,24)? How is Jesus' deity emphasized here? **3.** Who is the focal point of Jesus' prayer in verses 6–19? Why? If you had to file a report to the Father on Jesus' activities, how would you verify verses 6–8? **4.** What is Jesus' concern in verses 11 and 15? What does he mean by "the name you gave me" (8:58; Ex. 3:14)? What do the events surrounding the original revelation of this name show about its power to save (Ex. 3:7–10)? **5.** What does he mean by his request in verse 17? What is its purpose? **6.** Who is the focus of

world rejoices. You will grieve, but your grief will turn to joy. 21A
woman giving birth to a child has pain because her time has come;
but when her baby is born she forgets the anguish because of her joy
that a child is born into the world. 22So with you: Now is your time of
grief, but I will see you again and you will rejoice, and no one will
take away your joy. 23In that day you will no longer ask me anything.
I tell you the truth, my Father will give you whatever you ask in my
name. 24Until now you have not asked for anything in my name. Ask
and you will receive, and your joy will be complete.

25"Though I have been speaking figuratively, a time is coming when
I will no longer use this kind of language but will tell you plainly
about my Father. 26In that day you will ask in my name. I am not saying that I will ask the Father on your behalf. 27No, the Father himself
loves you because you have loved me and have believed that I came
from God. 28I came from the Father and entered the world; now I am
leaving the world and going back to the Father."

29Then Jesus' disciples said, "Now you are speaking clearly and
without figures of speech. 30Now we can see that you know all things
and that you do not even need to have anyone ask you questions.
This makes us believe that you came from God."

31"You believe at last!"[a] Jesus answered. 32"But a time is coming,
and has come, when you will be scattered, each to his own home. You
will leave me all alone. Yet I am not alone, for my Father is with me.

33"I have told you these things, so that in me you may have peace.
In this world you will have trouble. But take heart! I have overcome
the world."

Jesus Prays for Himself

17 After Jesus said this, he looked toward heaven and prayed:

"Father, the time has come. Glorify your Son, that your Son
may glorify you. 2For you granted him authority over all people
that he might give eternal life to all those you have given him.
3Now this is eternal life: that they may know you, the only true
God, and Jesus Christ, whom you have sent. 4I have brought you
glory on earth by completing the work you gave me to do. 5And
now, Father, glorify me in your presence with the glory I had with
you before the world began.

Jesus Prays for His Disciples

6"I have revealed you[b] to those whom you gave me out of the
world. They were yours; you gave them to me and they have
obeyed your word. 7Now they know that everything you have
given me comes from you. 8For I gave them the words you gave

[a]31 Or *"Do you now believe?"* [b]6 Greek *your name;* also in verse 26

16:22 but I will see you again. Characteristically, this might mean either physically after Jesus' resurrection, or spiritually when he comes to them in the Spirit.

16:23 In that day. Again, this might mean the literal day of Jesus' resurrection, or the figurative Old Testament "day" of the Lord when salvation and judgment would be fulfilled. In the latter case, the "day" really extends from the first coming of Christ until his return in glory.

16:33 overcome. The powers of evil are overcome by Jesus' death and resurrection (Heb. 2:14; Rev. 5:5; 17:14).

17:6–8 they have obeyed your word. The disciples' insight that Jesus had indeed come from God (16:30) was the clue that Jesus' mission had been successful.

me and they accepted them. They knew with certainty that I
came from you, and they believed that you sent me. [9]I pray for
them. I am not praying for the world, but for those you have
given me, for they are yours. [10]All I have is yours, and all you
have is mine. And glory has come to me through them. [11]I will
remain in the world no longer, but they are still in the world, and
I am coming to you. Holy Father, protect them by the power of
your name—the name you gave me—so that they may be one as
we are one. [12]While I was with them, I protected them and kept
them safe by that name you gave me. None has been lost except
the one doomed to destruction so that Scripture would be fulfilled.

[13]"I am coming to you now, but I say these things while I am
still in the world, so that they may have the full measure of my
joy within them. [14]I have given them your word and the world
has hated them, for they are not of the world any more than I am
of the world. [15]My prayer is not that you take them out of the
world but that you protect them from the evil one. [16]They are not
of the world, even as I am not of it. [17]Sanctify[a] them by the truth;
your word is truth. [18]As you sent me into the world, I have sent
them into the world. [19]For them I sanctify myself, that they too
may be truly sanctified.

Jesus Prays for All Believers

[20]"My prayer is not for them alone. I pray also for those who
will believe in me through their message, [21]that all of them may
be one, Father, just as you are in me and I am in you. May they
also be in us so that the world may believe that you have sent
me. [22]I have given them the glory that you gave me, that they
may be one as we are one: [23]I in them and you in me. May they be
brought to complete unity to let the world know that you sent me
and have loved them even as you have loved me.

[24]"Father, I want those you have given me to be with me where
I am, and to see my glory, the glory you have given me because
you loved me before the creation of the world.

[25]"Righteous Father, though the world does not know you, I
know you, and they know that you have sent me. [26]I have made
you known to them, and will continue to make you known in
order that the love you have for me may be in them and that I
myself may be in them."

Jesus Arrested

18 When he had finished praying, Jesus left with his disciples
and crossed the Kidron Valley. On the other side there was an
olive grove, and he and his disciples went into it.

[a]17 Greek *hagiazo* (*set apart for sacred use* or *make holy*); also in verse 19

Jesus' prayer in verses 20–26? Toward what end? What kind of unity exists between God and Jesus that we should copy? **7.** What does Jesus' ultimate desire (v. 24) reveal about his love for us? **8.** How do verses 25–26 sum up the major concerns of Jesus?

APPLY 1. Was there a person in your life that literally prayed you into the kingdom? **2.** Do you believe that Jesus Christ himself is interceding with God on your behalf right now? How does this make you feel? **3.** What have you found helpful that is making a difference in your prayer life?

OPEN Where do you go when you need to prepare yourself for a very stressful time?

STUDY 1. Why do the chief priests and Pharisees want to take advantage of the night to arrest

---

17:9 those you have given me. Jesus' disciples are not his, but the Father's—since it is because of the Father that they have come to him (6:65).

18:1 Kidron Valley. This valley was one of the borders of Jerusalem. During the rainy season it was a torrent. **olive grove.** Literally, "a garden." Luke 22:39 locates this on the Mount of Olives, while Matthew 26:36 and Mark 14:32 refer to it as Gethsemane. It was a place of refuge that Jesus and the disciples often retreated to during visits to Jerusalem (v. 2; Luke 22:39).

Jesus? **2.** How do you think the disciples felt when they saw these menacing-looking people coming? **3.** Who takes control of the situation? Why? **4.** How does Peter react? What would you have done? **5.** What is the "cup" that Jesus refers to? **6.** Why did the soldiers tie up Jesus if he did not resist arrest? **7.** What is the principle in this passage on pacificism or civil disobedience?

APPLY 1. When is the last time you were almost arrested for your faith in Christ? **2.** What is the cause that you would go to jail for?

OPEN If you could remove one page from the record of your life, what would you remove?

STUDY 1. Why do you think Simon Peter tagged along with Jesus to the high priest's court-

2Now Judas, who betrayed him, knew the place, because Jesus had
often met there with his disciples. 3So Judas came to the grove, guiding a detachment of soldiers and some officials from the chief priests
and Pharisees. They were carrying torches, lanterns and weapons.
4Jesus, knowing all that was going to happen to him, went out and
asked them, "Who is it you want?"
5"Jesus of Nazareth," they replied.
"I am he," Jesus said. (And Judas the traitor was standing there
with them.) 6When Jesus said, "I am he," they drew back and fell to
the ground.
7Again he asked them, "Who is it you want?"
And they said, "Jesus of Nazareth."
8"I told you that I am he," Jesus answered. "If you are looking for
me, then let these men go." 9This happened so that the words he had
spoken would be fulfilled: "I have not lost one of those you gave
me."[a]
10Then Simon Peter, who had a sword, drew it and struck the high
priest's servant, cutting off his right ear. (The servant's name was
Malchus.)
11Jesus commanded Peter, "Put your sword away! Shall I not drink
the cup the Father has given me?"

Jesus Taken to Annas

12Then the detachment of soldiers with its commander and the
Jewish officials arrested Jesus. They bound him 13and brought him
first to Annas, who was the father-in-law of Caiaphas, the high priest
that year. 14Caiaphas was the one who had advised the Jews that it
would be good if one man died for the people.

Peter's First Denial

15Simon Peter and another disciple were following Jesus. Because
this disciple was known to the high priest, he went with Jesus into
the high priest's courtyard, 16but Peter had to wait outside at the

[a]9 John 6:39

18:2 Judas, who betrayed him. This author gives no details about Judas' betrayal (Luke 22:1–6,47–48).

18:3 detachment of soldiers. The word for "detachment" is a technical one meaning a force of 600 soldiers. Only Pilate would have the authority to dispatch these troops. This strong show of force would make sense if Pilate had been told by the Jewish authorities that Jesus and the disciples were planning an insurrection, which, according to 11:48, is what the authorities feared.

18:9 so that the words he had spoken would be fulfilled. This refers to 6:39; 17:12. This phrase is similar to the one used in 13:18; 15:25 when referring to Old Testament passages.

18:10 Peter, who had a sword. According to Luke 22:36–38, two of the disciples armed themselves with swords. These were daggers which could have been concealed easily. In John 13:37 Peter had pledged to die for Jesus. In light of the odds here, his attack could easily have caused that to happen! **Malchus.** The name of the servant is only mentioned here in the New Testament. Perhaps he was known to the community to which this Gospel was originally written.

18:11 Put your sword away! In verse 36 this refusal to meet force with force is used by Jesus as a sign of the true nature of his kingdom. **the cup.** In the Old Testament, drinking "the cup" is sometimes a symbol of experiencing God's judgment and wrath against sin (Ezek. 23:32–34; Hab. 2:16). This use of the metaphor reminds us that Jesus himself will bear God's judgment against the sins of the people.

18:13 Annas. Annas was the high priest from A.D. 6 until A.D. 15, when he was deposed by the Roman authorities. However, he held on to power by controlling the office through the appointment of family members, such as Caiaphas. In Acts 4:6 Annas is called the high priest even though formally that was no longer his title.

18:15 another disciple. The identity of this disciple is unknown. Although most believe this is John, it is unlikely that he is "the beloved disciple" mentioned elsewhere in the Gospel since he is not identified here as such.

door. The other disciple, who was known to the high priest, came
back, spoke to the girl on duty there and brought Peter in.
17"You are not one of his disciples, are you?" the girl at the door
asked Peter.
He replied, "I am not."
18It was cold, and the servants and officials stood around a fire
they had made to keep warm. Peter also was standing with them,
warming himself.

The High Priest Questions Jesus

19Meanwhile, the high priest questioned Jesus about his disciples
and his teaching.
20"I have spoken openly to the world," Jesus replied. "I always
taught in synagogues or at the temple, where all the Jews come together. I said nothing in secret. 21Why question me? Ask those who
heard me. Surely they know what I said."
22When Jesus said this, one of the officials nearby struck him in the
face. "Is this the way you answer the high priest?" he demanded.
23"If I said something wrong," Jesus replied, "testify as to what is
wrong. But if I spoke the truth, why did you strike me?" 24Then Annas
sent him, still bound, to Caiaphas the high priest.[a]

Peter's Second and Third Denials

25As Simon Peter stood warming himself, he was asked, "You are
not one of his disciples, are you?"
He denied it, saying, "I am not."
26One of the high priest's servants, a relative of the man whose ear
Peter had cut off, challenged him, "Didn't I see you with him in the
olive grove?" 27Again Peter denied it, and at that moment a rooster
began to crow.

Jesus Before Pilate

28Then the Jews led Jesus from Caiaphas to the palace of the Roman governor. By now it was early morning, and to avoid ceremonial
uncleanness the Jews did not enter the palace; they wanted to be able
to eat the Passover. 29So Pilate came out to them and asked, "What
charges are you bringing against this man?"
30"If he were not a criminal," they replied, "we would not have
handed him over to you."
31Pilate said, "Take him yourselves and judge him by your own law."

[a]24 Or *(Now Annas had sent him, still bound, to Caiaphas the high priest.)*

yard? **2.** What caused Peter to deny Jesus the first time? **3.** What is ironic about the high priest's questioning of Jesus? How does Jesus expose this trial as a mockery (v. 23)? **4.** When pressed a second and third time, what is Peter's motive for denying Jesus? How do you think Peter felt when he heard the rooster crow? **5.** Judas (18:2,5) and Peter were on the same team. Both betrayed Jesus. One became the leader of the church, the other took his own life. What was the difference? **6.** How do you think this story got into the Bible? **7.** If you had been his roommate, what kind of reference would you give?

APPLY 1. What comfort do you get from Peter's story? **2.** How would you compare Peter's story to your own spiritual story? Was there a time in your life when you found it convenient to deny your Christian faith?

OPEN Have you ever appeared in court? Have you ever been charged for a crime you didn't commit?

STUDY 1. Why did the Jewish authorities (chief priests and Pharisees) have to go to the Roman governor? **2.** Since the high priest (v. 19) was not able to get any evidence or witnesses to bring a charge against Jesus, what does he try to get Pilate to do (v. 30)? How

---

18:20 I have spoken openly to the world. Jesus' teaching has been public all along. If they wanted to know what he taught, they have had ample opportunity to do so (8:43; 10:25). According to Jewish law, people were not required to testify against themselves; witnesses were required. Jesus' answer and his suggestion that they call on others who heard what he said (v. 21) may be his way of pointing out to the high priest that this was an illegal hearing, since there were no such witnesses present.

18:28 palace. The Roman seat of power over Judea was located at Caesarea (Acts 23:33–35). However, this "palace" was Pilate's temporary residence in Jerusalem, a building Herod the Great had erected as a home for himself years before. **early morning.** Jesus' trial before the high priest was either late at night or very early in the morning. The trial before Pilate probably began around 6–7 a.m. since the Roman courts began early. **to avoid ceremonial uncleanness.** Rabbinic tradition taught that Gentile homes were unclean, defiling any Jew who entered one for seven days. **the Passover.** According to the chronology of this Gospel, the Passover would be observed that evening. Any Jew ritually defiled would have to wait a month to commemorate this feast.

18:31 judge him by your own law. Pilate's contempt for the Jews is seen throughout this story. He knew they had already tried Jesus or they would not have brought him. His remark is a rebuke to their attempt to rush him into

does the Roman governor respond? **3.** How does Pilate go about his own investigation of the charges? What does Pilate learn about Jesus and his kingdom? What does Pilate conclude about the charges? **4.** How does Barabbas enter into the equation? Who is he? How does Barabbas' freedom at the expense of Jesus illustrate the gospel? **5.** What is the closest you have come to seeing special interest groups in your country make a mockery of the government and the courts?

APPLY **1.** In your experience, where are special interest groups trying to use the courts to carry out their will? **2.** What is the issue that you feel so strongly about that you are going to get involved?

OPEN How did you learn about the events of Jesus' trial and execution: Church? Reading? Movies?

STUDY **1.** Why did Pilate have Jesus flogged if he found no basis for a charge against him? **2.** What is symbolic about the crown and purple robe? **3.** What was Pilate doing when he presented Jesus to the Jewish authorities with the crown of thorns and robe? **4.** Who is Pilate afraid of: The Jewish authorities? The authorities back in Rome? The crowd? King Herod? Jesus? **5.** What finally convinced Pilate to give

"But we have no right to execute anyone," the Jews objected. 32This happened so that the words Jesus had spoken indicating the kind of death he was going to die would be fulfilled.

33Pilate then went back inside the palace, summoned Jesus and asked him, "Are you the king of the Jews?"

34"Is that your own idea," Jesus asked, "or did others talk to you about me?"

35"Am I a Jew?" Pilate replied. "It was your people and your chief priests who handed you over to me. What is it you have done?"

36Jesus said, "My kingdom is not of this world. If it were, my servants would fight to prevent my arrest by the Jews. But now my kingdom is from another place."

37"You are a king, then!" said Pilate.

Jesus answered, "You are right in saying I am a king. In fact, for this reason I was born, and for this I came into the world, to testify to the truth. Everyone on the side of truth listens to me."

38"What is truth?" Pilate asked. With this he went out again to the Jews and said, "I find no basis for a charge against him. 39But it is your custom for me to release to you one prisoner at the time of the Passover. Do you want me to release 'the king of the Jews'?"

40They shouted back, "No, not him! Give us Barabbas!" Now Barabbas had taken part in a rebellion.

Jesus Sentenced to Be Crucified

19 Then Pilate took Jesus and had him flogged. 2The soldiers twisted together a crown of thorns and put it on his head. They clothed him in a purple robe 3and went up to him again and again, saying, "Hail, king of the Jews!" And they struck him in the face.

4Once more Pilate came out and said to the Jews, "Look, I am bringing him out to you to let you know that I find no basis for a charge against him." 5When Jesus came out wearing the crown of thorns and the purple robe, Pilate said to them, "Here is the man!"

6As soon as the chief priests and their officials saw him, they shouted, "Crucify! Crucify!"

But Pilate answered, "You take him and crucify him. As for me, I find no basis for a charge against him."

---

passing sentence. **we have no right to execute anyone.** This is debated since the Sanhedrin did have extensive powers, but the fact that the Roman Empire held on tightly to the sole right to pass judgment on cases involving capital punishment speaks in defense of this statement.

18:32 so that the words Jesus had spoken ... would be fulfilled. Jesus used the metaphor of being "lifted up" as a means of describing his death (3:14; 12:32–33). The Jewish method of killing an offender would have been stoning (Acts 7:58), but the Roman method of crucifixion fulfills the metaphor.

18:33 Are you the king of the Jews? This was probably asked in sarcasm or surprise. The leaders must have told Pilate that Jesus was claiming to be their new king and leader. This constituted the formal charge they were bringing against Jesus, representing him as a threat to Roman rule (vv. 34–35).

18:39 your custom. This is unknown outside of the New Testament. It may have been a local custom during Pilate's governorship as an attempt to placate the Jews. **the king of the Jews.** This is a jibe at the authorities. He is willing to release the one claiming to be their king, for he sees no threat at all in him.

18:40 Barabbas. The irony here is that this name means "son of the father." Luke 23:19 says he was an insurrectionist and murderer.

19:1 flogged. This typical Roman punishment involved 39 lashes with a whip in which metal and rock were imbedded. It sometimes led to death from bleeding and shock.

19:2 crown of thorns ... purple robe. These were mock symbols of royalty.

19:5 Here is the man! Pilate presented the leaders with a battered man who obviously presented no threat to Rome.

[7]The Jews insisted, "We have a law, and according to that law he
must die, because he claimed to be the Son of God."
[8]When Pilate heard this, he was even more afraid, [9]and he went
back inside the palace. "Where do you come from?" he asked Jesus,
but Jesus gave him no answer. [10]"Do you refuse to speak to me?"
Pilate said. "Don't you realize I have power either to free you or to
crucify you?"
[11]Jesus answered, "You would have no power over me if it were not
given to you from above. Therefore the one who handed me over to
you is guilty of a greater sin."
[12]From then on, Pilate tried to set Jesus free, but the Jews kept
shouting, "If you let this man go, you are no friend of Caesar. Anyone
who claims to be a king opposes Caesar."
[13]When Pilate heard this, he brought Jesus out and sat down on the
judge's seat at a place known as the Stone Pavement (which in Aramaic is Gabbatha). [14]It was the day of Preparation of Passover Week,
about the sixth hour.
"Here is your king," Pilate said to the Jews.
[15]But they shouted, "Take him away! Take him away! Crucify him!"
"Shall I crucify your king?" Pilate asked.
"We have no king but Caesar," the chief priests answered.
[16]Finally Pilate handed him over to them to be crucified.

The Crucifixion

So the soldiers took charge of Jesus. [17]Carrying his own cross, he
went out to the place of the Skull (which in Aramaic is called Golgotha). [18]Here they crucified him, and with him two others—one on
each side and Jesus in the middle.
[19]Pilate had a notice prepared and fastened to the cross. It read:
JESUS OF NAZARETH, THE KING OF THE JEWS. [20]Many of the Jews read this
sign, for the place where Jesus was crucified was near the city, and
the sign was written in Aramaic, Latin and Greek. [21]The chief priests
of the Jews protested to Pilate, "Do not write 'The King of the Jews,'
but that this man claimed to be king of the Jews."

in to the demands of the Jewish authorities (v. 12)? **6.** How would you describe the way Pilate handed over Jesus to be crucified? **7.** Who ends up committing blasphemy (v. 15)? **8.** If you had been Pilate in this situation, what would you have done? **9.** If you could put in a good word for Pilate, what would you say?

APPLY 1. What is the closest you have come to being asked by special interest groups to compromise your principles? **2.** What is the best advice you have received when you are tempted to go along with the crowd?

OPEN How do you feel about seeing a dead person? When was the first time you viewed a corpse?

STUDY 1. If you were a reporter covering this story for the *Jerusalem Times,* how would you pitch this story? What would be the headline? **2.** Why are the chief priests so concerned about the notice that Pilate posted on the cross of Jesus? **3.** What famous novel is based on the garment the soldiers took from

19:7 he claimed to be the Son of God. This was the charge that the leaders originally made against Jesus (5:18; 8:53; 10:33).

19:11 the one who handed me over to you is guilty of a greater sin. Caiaphas' sin is greater because, as the Jewish high priest, he of all people ought to have been spiritually sensitive enough to recognize the truth of God in Jesus.

19:12 you are no friend of Caesar. "A Friend of Caesar" was a title bestowed on people who exhibited outstanding loyalty and service to the emperor.

19:14 day of Preparation. This was Friday. The Sabbath (which was also Passover according to this Gospel) would begin that evening. **the sixth hour.** This is noon.

19:15 We have no king but Caesar. Even during the period of the Jewish kings, God was considered the only true king of Israel. In 8:33,41 the leaders protested against Jesus' implication that they served anyone but God. Here they would rather affirm loyalty to a leader they despised than follow him.

19:17 Carrying his own cross. As part of the humiliation before crucifixion, condemned prisoners had to carry at least the crossbar of the cross to the site of their execution, where the vertical bars were normally permanently installed. **place of the Skull.** No definitive reason has been given as to why this place had this name. It may have been a common place for execution.

19:19 Pilate had a notice prepared and fastened to the cross. There is no evidence that this was a normal practice, although some prisoners were required to wear signs listing their crimes around their necks. **JESUS OF NAZARETH, THE KING OF THE JEWS.** The sign listed the name and origin of Jesus as well as the crime for which he was convicted.

19:20 Aramaic, Latin and Greek. These were the three common languages of the area. Jews from outside of Palestine would not necessarily have been able to read Aramaic (the local language of that area), nor Latin (the official language of the empire), but all would have known Greek since that was the common trade language.

19:21 The chief priests ... protested. All along the opposition had been upset at Jesus' claims. They were upset that Pilate's sign left the matter uncertain to those who would read it as

Jesus? **4.** Thirty-three years after Mary is told by the angel that "you will be with child, and give birth to a son," she is standing at the crucifixion of her son. How do you think she is feeling? Do you think she understood what was happening? **5.** "It is finished." What did Jesus mean by this humanly and theologically? **6.** What do you know about the Passover that makes this day very important (v. 31)? What will the high priest offer on this day as an "atonement" for sin? Do you think anyone realized the significance of John the Baptist's prophecy in 1:29? **7.** While some scholars dismiss the significance of the early death of Jesus in contrast to the two thieves, others see the rupture of Jesus' heart due to extreme pain and suffering. What do you think? **8.** After studying this passage, how does it make you feel?

APPLY 1. If you were the only person in the world that deserved death because of your sin, do you think Jesus would have come to earth and died on the cross just for you (3:16)? **2.** How would you describe your relationship with God right now?

22 Pilate answered, "What I have written, I have written."
23 When the soldiers crucified Jesus, they took his clothes, dividing
them into four shares, one for each of them, with the undergarment
remaining. This garment was seamless, woven in one piece from top
to bottom.
24 "Let's not tear it," they said to one another. "Let's decide by lot
who will get it."
This happened that the scripture might be fulfilled which said,

"They divided my garments among them
and cast lots for my clothing."[a]

So this is what the soldiers did.
25 Near the cross of Jesus stood his mother, his mother's sister,
Mary the wife of Clopas, and Mary Magdalene. 26 When Jesus saw his
mother there, and the disciple whom he loved standing nearby, he
said to his mother, "Dear woman, here is your son," 27 and to the disciple, "Here is your mother." From that time on, this disciple took her
into his home.

The Death of Jesus

28 Later, knowing that all was now completed, and so that the Scripture would be fulfilled, Jesus said, "I am thirsty." 29 A jar of wine vinegar was there, so they soaked a sponge in it, put the sponge on a stalk
of the hyssop plant, and lifted it to Jesus' lips. 30 When he had received
the drink, Jesus said, "It is finished." With that, he bowed his head
and gave up his spirit.
31 Now it was the day of Preparation, and the next day was to be a
special Sabbath. Because the Jews did not want the bodies left on the
crosses during the Sabbath, they asked Pilate to have the legs broken
and the bodies taken down. 32 The soldiers therefore came and broke
the legs of the first man who had been crucified with Jesus, and then
those of the other. 33 But when they came to Jesus and found that he
was already dead, they did not break his legs. 34 Instead, one of the
soldiers pierced Jesus' side with a spear, bringing a sudden flow of

[a] *24* Psalm 22:18

to whether Jesus only claimed this title, or if he was really the Messiah whom Rome had defeated.

19:25 his mother, his mother's sister, Mary the wife of Clopas, and Mary Magdalene. It appears there were four women present:his mother, his aunt, Mary, the wife of Clopas, and Mary Magdalene. Nothing is known of Mary the wife of Clopas (Luke 24:18). Mary Magdalene does not appear earlier in this Gospel. Particularly touching, though, is the presence of Jesus' moth*er, watching her own son die a horrible* death normally reserved for criminals. She had been told that her status as mother of the Son of God would make her blessed (Luke 1:42), but she no doubt did not feel very "blessed" at this point.

19:26 the disciple whom he loved. It appears that by this time Joseph, Mary's husband, was dead. As the oldest son, Jesus would have assumed the responsibility of caring for his mother (13:23).

19:29 wine vinegar. This was cheap wine. It was probably on the scene for the entertainment of the soldiers as they waited for the process of crucifixion to accomplish its course. It would have done little for his thirst, and its bitterness would have been symbolic of the overall bitterness of the experience.

19:30 It is finished. Given Jesus' emphasis in this Gospel on doing the Father's work, it is clear that by this Jesus is saying his work has been accomplished. **gave up his spirit.** Even though he was on the cross, his death was a voluntary action on his part. His life was not taken away by others; he sacrificed it freely (10:18).

19:31 the Jews did not want the bodies left on the crosses. Although the Roman custom was to leave the bodies on the crosses as a warning for criminals, Jewish law forbade bodies hung on a tree from remaining overnight (Deut. 21:22–23). **the legs broken.** By pressing their weight on their legs, victims could ease some of the pressure upon their arms and chest, making breathing easier. However, once their legs were broken, this relief was no longer possible, and death by suffocation and shock would come quickly.

blood and water. 35The man who saw it has given testimony, and his
testimony is true. He knows that he tells the truth, and he testifies so
that you also may believe. 36These things happened so that the scripture would be fulfilled: "Not one of his bones will be broken,"[a] 37and,
as another scripture says, "They will look on the one they have
pierced."[b]

The Burial of Jesus

38Later, Joseph of Arimathea asked Pilate for the body of Jesus.
Now Joseph was a disciple of Jesus, but secretly because he feared
the Jews. With Pilate's permission, he came and took the body away.
39He was accompanied by Nicodemus, the man who earlier had visited Jesus at night. Nicodemus brought a mixture of myrrh and aloes,
about seventy-five pounds.[c] 40Taking Jesus' body, the two of them
wrapped it, with the spices, in strips of linen. This was in accordance
with Jewish burial customs. 41At the place where Jesus was crucified,
there was a garden, and in the garden a new tomb, in which no one
had ever been laid. 42Because it was the Jewish day of Preparation
and since the tomb was nearby, they laid Jesus there.

The Empty Tomb

20 Early on the first day of the week, while it was still dark,
Mary Magdalene went to the tomb and saw that the stone
had been removed from the entrance. 2So she came running to Simon
Peter and the other disciple, the one Jesus loved, and said, "They
have taken the Lord out of the tomb, and we don't know where they
have put him!"

3So Peter and the other disciple started for the tomb. 4Both were
running, but the other disciple outran Peter and reached the tomb
first. 5He bent over and looked in at the strips of linen lying there but
did not go in. 6Then Simon Peter, who was behind him, arrived and
went into the tomb. He saw the strips of linen lying there, 7as well as
the burial cloth that had been around Jesus' head. The cloth was folded up by itself, separate from the linen. 8Finally the other disciple,

[a]*36* Exodus 12:46; Num. 9:12; Psalm 34:20 [b]*37* Zech. 12:10 [c]*39* Greek *a hundred litrai* (about 34 kilograms)

OPEN What kind of funeral would you like?

STUDY Do you think Joseph of Arimathea and Nicodemus were secret believers? How do you think they felt about their conduct when Jesus was crucified?

APPLY Was there a time in your life when you found it convenient to keep your faith a secret?

OPEN 1. When something upsets you, who is the first one you tell? **2.** What is the hardest funeral you have ever attended?

STUDY 1. What do you think motivated Mary Magdalene to go to the tomb early while it was still dark? **2.** What did she conclude when she found the stone rolled away? **3.** How would you describe Simon Peter and "the other disciple" as investigative reporters? **4.** What made the other disciple "believe" that Jesus was alive? **5.** Why did Mary stick around the tomb after the two disciples left? How would you describe the temperament of Mary? Would she have believed if the two disciples had taken the time to explain

19:35 The man who saw it. This might be John the apostle whose testimony guided the writing of this Gospel.

19:36 Not one of his bones will be broken. From the beginning of this Gospel, the ministry of Jesus has been pictured in terms of the Passover lamb (1:29; 6:4). One of the requirements of these lambs was that their bones should not be broken (Ex. 12:46).

19:38 Joseph. Although he is mentioned in the same context in all the Gospels, nothing else is known about him. Luke says he was a member of the Sanhedrin who had opposed the plan of the majority to kill Jesus (Luke 23:50–51). The author's comment here that he was a secret disciple because of his fear of the Jews accords with what he said in 12:42–43. **Arimathea.** The exact location of this town is uncertain, but tradition says it was northwest of Jerusalem.

19:39 a mixture of myrrh and aloes, about seventy-five pounds. This was a lavish amount of spices to use in the embalming process. Normally, only royal figures were shown such attention at death.

19:41 a new tomb. Tombs carved in rock and closed by a stone that was rolled into place by means of a groove carved in front of the tomb were the burial places for the wealthy. Matthew 27:60 says this was Joseph's own tomb.

20:1 the first day of the week. This was Sunday. **Mary Magdalene.** Mary is mentioned in all four Gospel accounts of the Resurrection. Luke 8:2 says that she was one of several women who traveled with the disciples. **stone.** This account of the burial of Jesus does not mention that it was sealed with a large stone (Matt. 27:60; Mark 15:46).

20:5–7 strips of linen ... burial cloth. Grave robbers, in search of treasures entombed with the corpse, would either have taken the body still wrapped up, or scattered the strips as they tore them off. The fact that the clothes were neatly laid by was one of the evidences that led the "other disciple" to faith (v. 8).

what Jesus had taught them about his resurrection? **6.** What was it that finally caused Mary to realize that Jesus was alive? **7.** Why was Mary not permitted to touch Jesus? How do you explain this? **8.** What do you think Mary told the disciples? How would you diagram Mary's emotions in this experience?

APPLY How do you answer the skeptics that do not believe Jesus rose from the dead?

OPEN When you were a child, where did you hide in your house when tornadoes and big storms came?

STUDY 1. If you were the coach of a team that had just suffered a huge defeat, what would you do to get the team ready for the next game? Why do you think the

who had reached the tomb first, also went inside. He saw and believed. 9 (They still did not understand from Scripture that Jesus had to rise from the dead.)

Jesus Appears to Mary Magdalene

10 Then the disciples went back to their homes, 11 but Mary stood outside the tomb crying. As she wept, she bent over to look into the tomb 12 and saw two angels in white, seated where Jesus' body had been, one at the head and the other at the foot.

13 They asked her, "Woman, why are you crying?"

"They have taken my Lord away," she said, "and I don't know where they have put him." 14 At this, she turned around and saw Jesus standing there, but she did not realize that it was Jesus.

15 "Woman," he said, "why are you crying? Who is it you are looking for?"

Thinking he was the gardener, she said, "Sir, if you have carried him away, tell me where you have put him, and I will get him."

16 Jesus said to her, "Mary."

She turned toward him and cried out in Aramaic, "Rabboni!" (which means Teacher).

17 Jesus said, "Do not hold on to me, for I have not yet returned to the Father. Go instead to my brothers and tell them, 'I am returning to my Father and your Father, to my God and your God.'"

18 Mary Magdalene went to the disciples with the news: "I have seen the Lord!" And she told them that he had said these things to her.

Jesus Appears to His Disciples

19 On the evening of that first day of the week, when the disciples were together, with the doors locked for fear of the Jews, Jesus came and stood among them and said, "Peace be with you!" 20 After he said this, he showed them his hands and side. The disciples were overjoyed when they saw the Lord.

21 Again Jesus said, "Peace be with you! As the Father has sent me, I am sending you." 22 And with that he breathed on them and said,

---

20:12 two angels in white. The Gospels differ on whether there was one "man" (Mark), or an angel (Matthew), or two "men" (Luke) present. They also differ on how many women saw the personage.

20:14 she did not realize that it was Jesus. Whether she was blinded by her intense grief or there was some type of transformation in Jesus' appearance that caused Mary's lack of recognition is not known.

20:15 gardener. The tomb was located in a garden owned by Joseph (19:41). It would not be unlikely that as an aristocratic member of the Sanhedrin he would employ a gardener to care for his property.

20:16 Mary. When Jesus speaks Mary's name, she immediately recognizes who it is that speaks to her, thus proving her discipleship. **Aramaic.** This was the local language of Jews from Galilee and Judea. **Rabboni.** Literally, "my teacher." This is not only a title of respect for Jesus, but one that shows Mary's submission and love for him.

20:17 Do not hold on to me. We need not think Jesus refused to allow her to touch him at all, but that, after Mary had expressed the joy and relief she would feel at seeing him, he simply told her that all was not finished yet.

20:19 fear of the Jews. In spite of Jesus' words in 14:27, the disciples were afraid that the authorities, who had been successful in having Jesus killed, might now turn on them. **Jesus came.** Nothing is said about how Jesus came to be among them, but the implication of the locked doors appears to be that Jesus simply appeared with them (v. 26; Luke 24:31). **Peace be with you!** This is repeated in verse 21 and in the appearance a week later in verse 26. The promise of peace was given in 14:27 and 16:33. It sums up the blessings and fullness of the new covenant that Jesus has made between the Father and his people (14:27).

20:22 he breathed on them. As God originally breathed life into Adam at the first creation (Gen. 2:7), so now Jesus breathes spiritual life into his people at this, the re-creation of the people of God (1:12–13): **Receive the Holy Spirit.** The other Gospels do not mention the coming of the Spirit to the disciples, but Acts 2 indicates Luke saw this promise

"Receive the Holy Spirit. 23If you forgive anyone his sins, they are forgiven; if you do not forgive them, they are not forgiven."

Jesus Appears to Thomas

24Now Thomas (called Didymus), one of the Twelve, was not with
the disciples when Jesus came. 25So the other disciples told him, "We
have seen the Lord!"

But he said to them, "Unless I see the nail marks in his hands and
put my finger where the nails were, and put my hand into his side, I
will not believe it."

26A week later his disciples were in the house again, and Thomas
was with them. Though the doors were locked, Jesus came and stood
among them and said, "Peace be with you!" 27Then he said to Thomas, "Put your finger here; see my hands. Reach out your hand and
put it into my side. Stop doubting and believe."

28Thomas said to him, "My Lord and my God!"

29Then Jesus told him, "Because you have seen me, you have believed; blessed are those who have not seen and yet have believed."

30Jesus did many other miraculous signs in the presence of his disciples, which are not recorded in this book. 31But these are written
that you may[a] believe that Jesus is the Christ, the Son of God, and
that by believing you may have life in his name.

Jesus and the Miraculous Catch of Fish

21 Afterward Jesus appeared again to his disciples, by the Sea of
Tiberias.[b] It happened this way: 2Simon Peter, Thomas (called
Didymus), Nathanael from Cana in Galilee, the sons of Zebedee, and
two other disciples were together. 3"I'm going out to fish," Simon
Peter told them, and they said, "We'll go with you." So they went out
and got into the boat, but that night they caught nothing.

[a]31 Some manuscripts *may continue to* [b]1 That is, Sea of Galilee

disciples are still hiding twelve hours after Mary Magdalene told them that she had seen Jesus alive? What finally convinces the disciples that Jesus is alive? **2.** Why do you think Thomas was absent when Jesus appeared to the other disciples? **3.** Who does Thomas sound like in verse 25: Scientist? Agnostic? Lawyer? College Sophomore? **4.** How did Jesus deal with Thomas? Was Jesus putting down those like Thomas in verse 29? **5.** What was the author's purpose for writing this Gospel? Do you think he succeeded?

APPLY 1. How would you compare your story of coming to faith with Thomas' experience? **2.** Could you use a fresh visit from Jesus with the words of "peace"?

OPEN 1. What has been your favorite fishing spot? **2.** What is your favorite food on a cookout?

STUDY 1. After finding the tomb empty, why do you think Simon Peter and "the beloved disciple" took off for their home in Galilee? **2.** What made Peter decide to "go fishing"? When he fished all night and caught nothing, how do you

---

being fulfilled on the day of Pentecost, seven weeks after Jesus' resurrection.

20:23 If you forgive ... if you do not forgive. In that case as in this one, the power is not conferred to the person to act on his or her own, but as a spokesperson for God. The disciples are to pronounce forgiveness upon those who receive the Gospel. Likewise, to those who refuse the Gospel, they are to pronounce the words of warning just as Jesus did (8:24; Jer. 1:10).

20:24 Thomas (called Didymus). The Hebrew word for "Thomas" and the Greek word *Didymus* both mean "twin." **was not with the disciples when Jesus came.** Thomas is often vilified because of the doubt he expresses in this story (v. 25). However, it needs to be asked what it says about Thomas that he was not with the other disciples at this time. Perhaps this indicates that Thomas was also a little less fearful than the others. In another context, it is Thomas who, when Jesus talks about going to Jerusalem to die, bravely asserts, "Let us also go, that we may die with him" (11:16).

20:26 Though the doors were locked. This indicates that Jesus' resurrection was not limited in the way a normal physical body might be limited. He was able to enter a locked room and simply appear. Nevertheless his body could be felt (v. 27), and he ate (v. 19; Luke 24:41–43). **Peace.** A common Hebrew greeting (vv. 19,21). The term reflects the salvation that Christ's redemptive work achieves—total well-being and inner rest of spirit, in fellowship with God.

20:28 My Lord and my God! Thomas clearly affirms the deity of Jesus. This is the last of a series of confessions of faith which sum up what the author wants the reader to recognize about Jesus (11:27).

20:29 blessed are those who have not seen and yet have believed. The author applies the words to Thomas to the situation of his readers. They are not deprived because of never having seen Jesus. Indeed, he is with them through the Spirit (14:15–20) just as he was with the apostles.

21:1 Afterward. This is actually the same indefinite time reference John used to begin chapters 5, 6 and 7. When this appearance occurred is unclear. Since one of the themes in this section is Jesus' restoration of Peter, and since, like Mary in 20:15, they did not recognize him at first, it may be that this event actually occurred before the climactic appearance to the disciples in 20:19. **Sea of Tiberias.** Tiberias was a city founded on the shore of the Sea of Galilee in 20 A.D. by Herod. By the time this Gospel was written, this new name for the Sea of Galilee had become well known.

think he felt? **3.** What caused Peter and "the disciple whom Jesus loved" to realize that the stranger on the shore was Jesus? **4.** What is predictable about Peter's response? **5.** How do you like the way Jesus goes about inviting these guys to breakfast to get reacquainted? What do you think they talked about—big stuff or "old times"? **6.** In our cynical, scientific age, is there room for mystery in faith? Do you revel in mystery like this or find it like sleeping in a lumpy bed?

APPLY 1. When you get beaten up emotionally and you need some healing, what do you turn to and how does God use this to start you on the road to recovery? **2.** How long does it take before you are fully recovered?

OPEN Have you ever been kicked off the team, out of the club, out of the house or out of school?

STUDY 1. Do you think this story was tacked on to the end of John's Gospel to show that Jesus had forgiven Peter for denying him or for some other reason? **2.** Why did Jesus repeat the same question to Peter three times? How would you paraphrase the command of Jesus to Peter? **3.** How much would you be willing to bet on Peter at this point in his life—that he would one day become a mature, responsible leader in the church? Does this bring any comfort to you? **4.** John set out in his

4Early in the morning, Jesus stood on the shore, but the disciples did not realize that it was Jesus.

5He called out to them, "Friends, haven't you any fish?"

"No," they answered.

6He said, "Throw your net on the right side of the boat and you will find some." When they did, they were unable to haul the net in because of the large number of fish.

7Then the disciple whom Jesus loved said to Peter, "It is the Lord!"
As soon as Simon Peter heard him say, "It is the Lord," he wrapped
his outer garment around him (for he had taken it off) and jumped
into the water. 8The other disciples followed in the boat, towing the
net full of fish, for they were not far from shore, about a hundred
yards.[a] 9When they landed, they saw a fire of burning coals there with
fish on it, and some bread.

10Jesus said to them, "Bring some of the fish you have just caught."

11Simon Peter climbed aboard and dragged the net ashore. It was
full of large fish, 153, but even with so many the net was not torn.
12Jesus said to them, "Come and have breakfast." None of the disciples dared ask him, "Who are you?" They knew it was the Lord.
13Jesus came, took the bread and gave it to them, and did the same
with the fish. 14This was now the third time Jesus appeared to his disciples after he was raised from the dead.

Jesus Reinstates Peter

15When they had finished eating, Jesus said to Simon Peter, "Simon son of John, do you truly love me more than these?"

"Yes, Lord," he said, "you know that I love you."

Jesus said, "Feed my lambs."

16Again Jesus said, "Simon son of John, do you truly love me?"

He answered, "Yes, Lord, you know that I love you."

Jesus said, "Take care of my sheep."

17The third time he said to him, "Simon son of John, do you love me?"

Peter was hurt because Jesus asked him the third time, "Do you love me?" He said, "Lord, you know all things; you know that I love you."

[a]8 Greek *about two hundred cubits* (about 90 meters)

21:7 the disciple whom Jesus loved. This is thought to be John, the author of the Gospel. **It is the Lord!** As Jesus' voice opened Mary's eyes to recognize him (20:16), so here the enormous catch of fish revealed to the beloved disciple that the one with whom they were talking was the Lord.

21:12 breakfast. The Jesus that they met was no disembodied spirit. They could see him and hear him and eat with *him. He had hands and feet that* allowed him to kindle a fire on the beach. Jesus had been resurrected bodily. He had conquered death.

21:14 the third time. This is the third resurrection account described in John's Gospel (20:19–23,24–29). The post-resurrection appearances are important for a number of reasons. For one thing, they are part of the proof of Jesus' resurrection (along with the fact of the empty tomb, the collapsed and empty grave clothes, etc.). Second, they show that Jesus had conquered death. He was not simply a disembodied spirit who appeared as a ghost-like figure, a hallucination, or a vision. Third, they describe how it was that the disciples learned of their mission. Fourth, it was the encounter with the living Jesus that changed the disciples from frightened men in hiding to bold witnesses who changed the world. Finally, the post-resurrection appearances show to all of us that Jesus is still alive and thus we can enter into a personal relationship with him even today.

21:15 do you truly love me more than these? This question is ambiguous, but Jesus is probably asking Peter if indeed he loves him more than the others do as Peter indicated in 13:37. In asking this question, Jesus allows Peter the opportunity three times to pledge his love for him. **Feed my lambs.** After each query about his love, Jesus calls Peter to demonstrate that love by being a "good shepherd" to Jesus' sheep.

Jesus said, "Feed my sheep. [18]I tell you the truth, when you were
younger you dressed yourself and went where you wanted; but when
you are old you will stretch out your hands, and someone else will
dress you and lead you where you do not want to go." [19]Jesus said
this to indicate the kind of death by which Peter would glorify God.
Then he said to him, "Follow me!"
[20]Peter turned and saw that the disciple whom Jesus loved was following them. (This was the one who had leaned back against Jesus at
the supper and had said, "Lord, who is going to betray you?") [21]When
Peter saw him, he asked, "Lord, what about him?"
[22]Jesus answered, "If I want him to remain alive until I return, what
is that to you? You must follow me." [23]Because of this, the rumor
spread among the brothers that this disciple would not die. But Jesus
did not say that he would not die; he only said, "If I want him to remain alive until I return, what is that to you?"
[24]This is the disciple who testifies to these things and who wrote
them down. We know that his testimony is true.
[25]Jesus did many other things as well. If every one of them were
written down, I suppose that even the whole world would not have
room for the books that would be written.

Gospel to show to the readers that "God so loved the world that he gave his one and only Son, that whoever believes in him shall not perish but have eternal life." How well do you think he succeeded? **5.** What has been the high point in this Gospel study for you: The study itself? The group you have been with? Other?

APPLY 1. If Jesus should ask you three times, "Do you love me?," what would you say? **2.** What would God tell you to do right now?

21:18 you will stretch out your hands, and someone else will ... lead you where you do not want to go. From the way early Christians dealt with passages like Isaiah 65:2 and Exodus 17:12, it is known that the stretching out of a person's hands was an early Christian idiom for crucifixion. This explains the author's comment on this quote in verse 19.

21:19 the kind of death by which Peter would glorify God. Peter would indeed lay down his life for Jesus at some point in time. Since Peter is believed to have been killed during Nero's persecution of Christians in the early 60s, the manner and reality of his death would have been known by this Gospel's first readers. **Follow me!** The important thing for the disciple, be it Peter or any reader of the Gospel, is to keep on following Jesus regardless of where that path might lead (12:26).

21:21 what about him? This question may be the clue as to the purpose of this entire chapter. Since by the time of this writing, the "beloved disciple" (likely John) was probably old, something had to be said about a rumor that had begun at the earliest stages of the Christian era which implied that he would live until Jesus' return (v. 23).

21:22 what is that to you? The intent of Jesus' response to Peter, far from saying anything of substance about the beloved disciple, was really to emphasize that Peter should mind his own business. The path of discipleship may take each follower in different ways—the point is to faithfully follow the path laid out for oneself.

21:23 he only said, "If I want him to remain alive until I return, what is that to you?" The narrator thus sets the record straight about Jesus' comment regarding the beloved disciple. It was not meant as a promise that he would return within the life span of that disciple.

Acts

Author. Although Luke is nowhere named within Acts as author, there is a strong and ancient tradition that he did, indeed, write this book as a companion piece to the third Gospel. He is mentioned only three times in the New Testament (Col. 4:14; 2 Tim. 4:11; Philem. 24). From these references, it can be deduced that Luke was a physician, a valued companion of Paul and a Gentile.

Luke's role as Paul's traveling companion is evident in the book of Acts. In the four so-called *we* sections, the author suddenly switches from saying "They did this" to "We did that" (16:10–17; 20:5–21:18; 27:1–28:16). We learn that Luke was a Gentile from the list of greetings with which Paul concludes Colossians. Then in Colossians 4:12, Paul begins a set of greetings presumably from the Gentiles in the party. Luke's name is included in this latter list.

Personal Reading	Group Study Topic and Reading	
1:1–26	Jesus Taken	1:1–11
2:1–41	Pentecost	2:1–41
2:42–3:26	Fellowship	2:42–47
4:1–37	Before Sanhedrin	4:1–31
5:1–8:25	Ananias and Sapphira	5:1–11
8:26–40	The Ethiopian	8:26–40
9:1–43	Saul's Conversion	9:1–19
10:1–11:30	Peter's Vision	10:1–23
12:1–16:15	Peter's Escape	12:1–19
16:16–17:34	In Prison	16:16–40
18:1–21:36	Paul's Vision	18:5–17
21:37–25:27	Paul Speaks	21:37–22:29
26:1–28:31	Before Agrippa	26:1–32

Date. The final events recorded here took place in early A.D. 60, so Acts must have been compiled after that time.

Theme. The spread of the Gospel to all the known world (1:8).

Historical Background. Why did Luke write the book of Acts? One reason must have been his desire to commend Christianity to the Gentile world in general and to the Roman government in particular. The Good News about Jesus is not just for Jews but for all people. Not surprisingly, therefore, we find in Acts not only Jews turning to Jesus (3,000 on the Day of Pentecost, see 2:41) but also Gentiles. We see Peter (the apostle to the Jews) welcoming Cornelius, the Roman centurion, into the church. We see Philip preaching to the Samaritans and Jewish believers and evangelizing Gentiles in Antioch. In particular, we find Paul called by Christ to be the apostle to the Gentiles, setting up churches across the Roman Empire. Finally in Acts 15, there is formal affirmation that Gentiles are accepted in the church of Jesus Christ on equal terms with Jews. Luke seemed to go out of his way to show that followers of Christ were loyal citizens and not lawbreakers and criminals (18:14–16; 19:37; 23:29; 25:25). He also took pains to point out that Roman officials had always treated followers of Christ fairly and courteously (18:12–17; 19:31). This was important to state lest Christianity be perceived as a political movement and therefore a threat to the Roman Empire.

However, commending Christianity to Gentiles was probably not Luke's central aim. His main purpose is implicit in 1:8, "But you will receive power when the Holy Spirit comes on you; and you will be my witnesses in Jerusalem, and in all Judea and Samaria, and to the ends of the earth." Luke's aim was to show how, in 30 short years, Christianity had spread from Jerusalem to Rome.

Characteristics. The book of Acts is the bridge between the Gospels (Matthew, Mark, Luke and John) and the Epistles. Acts continues the story of Jesus. It shows how his life, death and resurrection brought a whole new community into existence: the church. On the other hand, Acts sets the stage for the correspondence to this church; the letters make up the rest of the New Testament. At many points it would be difficult to get the full sense of what the Epistles are saying without the data found in Acts.

Luke tells the story of the development of the church by opening a series of windows that allows us to glimpse important developments in its growth.

Jesus Taken Up Into Heaven

1 In my former book, Theophilus, I wrote about all that Jesus
began to do and to teach 2until the day he was taken up to
heaven, after giving instructions through the Holy Spirit to the apostles he had chosen. 3After his suffering, he showed himself to these
men and gave many convincing proofs that he was alive. He appeared
to them over a period of forty days and spoke about the kingdom of
God. 4On one occasion, while he was eating with them, he gave them
this command: "Do not leave Jerusalem, but wait for the gift my
Father promised, which you have heard me speak about. 5For John
baptized with[a] water, but in a few days you will be baptized with the
Holy Spirit."
6So when they met together, they asked him, "Lord, are you at this
time going to restore the kingdom to Israel?"
7He said to them: "It is not for you to know the times or dates the
Father has set by his own authority. 8But you will receive power when
the Holy Spirit comes on you; and you will be my witnesses in Jerusalem, and in all Judea and Samaria, and to the ends of the earth."
9After he said this, he was taken up before their very eyes, and a
cloud hid him from their sight.
10They were looking intently up into the sky as he was going, when
suddenly two men dressed in white stood beside them. 11"Men of
Galilee," they said, "why do you stand here looking into the sky? This
same Jesus, who has been taken from you into heaven, will come
back in the same way you have seen him go into heaven."

Matthias Chosen to Replace Judas

12Then they returned to Jerusalem from the hill called the Mount of
Olives, a Sabbath day's walk[b] from the city. 13When they arrived, they
went upstairs to the room where they were staying. Those present

[a]5 Or *in* [b]12 That is, about 3/4 mile (about 1,100 meters)

OPEN Who would you want to write the autobiography of your life? Why that person? What does this person know about you that you would like your group to know?

STUDY 1. How does this book pick up where Luke 24:45–53 leaves off? **2.** If you were the coach of a team that had just suffered an agonizing defeat, what would you do to get your team ready for the next game? How would you compare this to the task that Jesus faced in getting his disciples ready to take over his ministry on earth? What did Jesus do first? Then second and third? **3.** What did the disciples want to know (v. 6)? What did he promise (v. 8) and what did he compare it to (v. 5)? **4.** How would you draw the expansion of Christianity (v. 8) with a series of circles? What is significant about these areas? Are these kinds of people in your community?

APPLY 1. What is the closest you have come to experiencing the total wipe-out that the disciples felt after the crucifixion? **2.** What did God do to bring you back?

OPEN What was your favorite board game as a child? Did it involve luck of the draw, taking risks or strategy?

STUDY 1. Why do you think Jesus asked the disciples to

1:1 my former book. That is, the Gospel of Luke. Church tradition is unanimous in its witness that Luke authored both works. **Theophilus.** An unknown figure. He may have been Luke's patron who underwrote the cost of writing the Gospel of Luke, or a Roman official. **all that Jesus began to do and to teach.** This is a clue to the way one should view this book—it is the continuing story of the work of Jesus through his Spirit in the life of his body, the church.

1:2 until the day he was taken up to heaven. See Luke 24:50–53. The ascension does not mark the end of Jesus' ministry, but simply a new phase of his work. He now exercises his divine reign from heaven. **apostles.** Apostles were ambassadors commissioned to represent the one in whose name they were sent. In the Gospel, this term refers to the Twelve (Luke 6:12–16). Normally, this is its meaning in Acts as well, although others (like Paul and Barnabas—14:3–4) are also called by this title.

1:4 the gift my Father promised. The Holy Spirit is the gift (Isa. 32:15; Joel 2:28–32; Luke 11:13; 12:12; 24:49; Gal. 3:14). Jesus quotes the words of John the Baptist (Luke 3:16) as a reminder that from the very beginning the expectation was that through him the Spirit of God would be poured out on all people.

1:5 baptized with the Holy Spirit. Baptism was associated with cleansing. The metaphor would communicate being flooded with God's Spirit.

1:8 This verse embraces the twin themes of the whole book. The mission of Jesus is continued through the work of his Spirit empowering and enabling the disciples to bear witness of him (Matt. 28:19–20; Luke 12:11–12). The result of this empowering will be the spread of the Gospel throughout the world—from the spiritual heart of Israel (Jerusalem) to the immediate vicinity (Judea), to the despised Samaritans in the adjacent province to the north, to the outermost reaches of the earth. The book is built around these geographical markers. Chapters 1–6:7 occur in Jerusalem and Judea; 6:8–9:31 deals with events that lead the church to Samaria; and 9:32 recounts the chain of events that leads Paul to journey throughout much of the Roman Empire with the good news of Jesus.

1:9 a cloud hid him from their sight. This is not a statement of weather conditions at the time, but a declaration of Jesus' deity.

1:12 The Mount of Olives, where the ascension occurred, was just outside of the city. The angels' message picked up on Zechariah 14:4 which teaches that the Messiah will one day appear on that mountain when he comes to fully establish his reign.

return to Jerusalem and stick together? **2.** What do you think it was like in that crowded room? **3.** Knowing what you know about the disciples, how do you think they got along? What happened to the squabbles? Rivalries? Personality conflicts? Power struggles? **4.** Who emerges as the spokesman for the group? What do you think Peter told them about his denial? **5.** What is one of the first things they had to do (v. 21)? Why did they have to "cast lots"? **6.** Do you think what happened on the day of Pentecost in the next chapter was impacted by the intense time this group spent for ten days together? How?

APPLY 1. What is the closest you have come to being in a Christian community that lived together through a very intense period of several days? **2.** If you had to call on a group at 3 a.m. because of a personal crisis, what group would you call on?

were Peter, John, James and Andrew; Philip and Thomas, Bartholomew and Matthew; James son of Alphaeus and Simon the Zealot, and
Judas son of James. 14They all joined together constantly in prayer,
along with the women and Mary the mother of Jesus, and with his
brothers.

15In those days Peter stood up among the believers[a] (a group
numbering about a hundred and twenty) 16and said, "Brothers, the
Scripture had to be fulfilled which the Holy Spirit spoke long ago
through the mouth of David concerning Judas, who served as guide
for those who arrested Jesus— 17he was one of our number and
shared in this ministry."

18(With the reward he got for his wickedness, Judas bought a field;
there he fell headlong, his body burst open and all his intestines
spilled out. 19Everyone in Jerusalem heard about this, so they called
that field in their language Akeldama, that is, Field of Blood.)

20"For," said Peter, "it is written in the book of Psalms,

" 'May his place be deserted;
let there be no one to dwell in it,'[b]

and,

" 'May another take his place of leadership.'[c]

21Therefore it is necessary to choose one of the men who have been
with us the whole time the Lord Jesus went in and out among us,
22beginning from John's baptism to the time when Jesus was taken up
from us. For one of these must become a witness with us of his resurrection."

23So they proposed two men: Joseph called Barsabbas (also known
as Justus) and Matthias. 24Then they prayed, "Lord, you know
everyone's heart. Show us which of these two you have chosen 25to
take over this apostolic ministry, which Judas left to go where he belongs." 26Then they cast lots, and the lot fell to Matthias; so he was
added to the eleven apostles.

OPEN Have you ever traveled where you did not speak the language? What happened?

The Holy Spirit Comes at Pentecost

2 When the day of Pentecost came, they were all together in one
place. 2Suddenly a sound like the blowing of a violent wind came

[a]15 Greek *brothers* [b]20 Psalm 69:25 [c]20 Psalm 109:8

1:14 Mary ... and ... his brothers. Prior to the resurrection, Jesus' brothers had not believed in him (Mark 3:21; John 7:5). One of his brothers, James, was to become a leader of the Jerusalem church and the author of the New Testament book by that name.

1:16 After the resurrection, Jesus had showed the apostles how the Old Testament pointed to him (Luke 24:27,44). *The Law and the prophets would* become an important resource for the apostles to understand him and their mission all the more.

1:18–19 The parenthetical insertion about Judas' death differs considerably from the account in Matthew 27:3–10. It may be that he hanged himself after which the rope broke allowing his body to crash on the ground. The field, bought with his money, may have come to be known as belonging to him.

1:22 from John's baptism to the time when Jesus was taken up from us. Since the apostles were to bear witness to all Jesus said and did, it was important that they all be people who were involved from the very beginning.

2:1 the day of Pentecost. This was the Feast of Weeks (Ex. 23:16; Lev. 23:15–21; Deut. 16:9–12) held 50 days after Passover. Originally a kind of thanksgiving day for gathered crops, it came to be associated with the commemoration of the giving of the Law at Mount Sinai (Ex. 20:1–17). Jewish tradition held that when God gave the Law to Moses, a single voice spoke which was heard by all the nations of the world in their own language. Luke may be alluding to that in this story. Pentecost was a celebration to which thousands of Jews from all over the empire would attend.

2:2–4 The Greek word for "wind" and "spirit" is the same, hence the symbol-

from heaven and filled the whole house where they were sitting.
[3]They saw what seemed to be tongues of fire that separated and came
to rest on each of them. [4]All of them were filled with the Holy Spirit
and began to speak in other tongues[a] as the Spirit enabled them.
[5]Now there were staying in Jerusalem God-fearing Jews from every
nation under heaven. [6]When they heard this sound, a crowd came
together in bewilderment, because each one heard them speaking in
his own language. [7]Utterly amazed, they asked: "Are not all these men
who are speaking Galileans? [8]Then how is it that each of us hears
them in his own native language? [9]Parthians, Medes and Elamites;
residents of Mesopotamia, Judea and Cappadocia, Pontus and Asia,
[10]Phrygia and Pamphylia, Egypt and the parts of Libya near Cyrene;
visitors from Rome [11](both Jews and converts to Judaism); Cretans
and Arabs—we hear them declaring the wonders of God in our own
tongues!" [12]Amazed and perplexed, they asked one another, "What
does this mean?"
[13]Some, however, made fun of them and said, "They have had too
much wine.[b]"

Peter Addresses the Crowd

[14]Then Peter stood up with the Eleven, raised his voice and addressed the crowd: "Fellow Jews and all of you who live in Jerusalem,
let me explain this to you; listen carefully to what I say. [15]These men
are not drunk, as you suppose. It's only nine in the morning! [16]No,
this is what was spoken by the prophet Joel:

[17]" 'In the last days, God says,
 I will pour out my Spirit on all people.
Your sons and daughters will prophesy,
 your young men will see visions,
 your old men will dream dreams.
[18]Even on my servants, both men and women,

[a]4 Or *languages*; also in verse 11 [b]13 Or *sweet wine*

STUDY 1. Who were "all together in one place"? What have they been doing? **2.** What does the extraordinary sound and light show that occurred remind you of (vv. 2–3)? If you had been in the room, how would you have felt? **3.** Why was the coming of the Holy Spirit to indwell the disciples greeted with "tongues of fire"? **4.** How do you account for the fact that people from different lands heard the disciples speak "in their own tongue"? **5.** How do you account for the fact that a band of frightened, cowering individuals could suddenly become bold, aggressive, courageous witnesses for Jesus?

APPLY What is the closest you have come to experiencing this kind of special empowerment for sharing your spiritual story?

OPEN What are you usually doing at 9:00 in the morning on a Saturday?

STUDY 1. For an uneducated fisherman from the back waters of Galilee, how do you like Peter's understanding of Old Testament prophecy? Where do you think he got his knowledge? **2.** Given the audience, why would Peter quote from the Old Testament? **3.** What is the point he wants the people to understand about current events (vv. 15,17–18)? How do you understand verses 19–21? What tells you Joel's prophecy is coming true now? **4.** How familiar were

---

ism of the Spirit coming like a great wind. Fire is often associated with divine appearances (Ex. 3:2; 19:18). John the Baptist said Jesus would baptize his followers with the Holy Spirit and fire (Luke 3:16) symbolizing the cleansing, purifying effect of the Spirit. What is important here is that tongues served as a sign to the crowds of a supernatural event, the point of which was Jesus Christ.

2:4 filled with the Holy Spirit. This phrase is found elsewhere (4:8,31; 13:52; Eph. 5:18) indicating a repeatable experience. Here, however, it is clearly associated with the baptism of the Spirit (1:5) which is an experience new converts enter into upon acceptance of Jesus as the Messiah (11:15–16; 1 Cor. 12:13).

2:5–8 The disciples apparently made their way to the temple where they attracted a large crowd that was puzzled over how they could speak in their native dialects.

2:9–11 The catalog of nations shows that people from all over the known world heard the news of Christ from the beginning of the church. These pilgrims would soon be returning home with the news of all they had seen and heard. **Parthians, Medes and Elamites ... Mesopotamia.** This is present day Iran and Iraq, to the east of Jerusalem. These Jews traced their roots back to the Assyrian overthrow of Israel and the Babylonian overthrow of Judea seven and five centuries beforehand respectively. **Judea.** Either the immediate environs around Jerusalem is in view, or Luke is thinking of the days under David and Solomon when the land of Israel stretched from Egypt to the west to the Euphrates River to the east. **Cappadocia, Pontus and Asia, Phrygia and Pamphylia.** Present day Turkey to the north of Jerusalem. Much of Acts takes place in this region. **Egypt ... Libya near Cyrene.** To the west of Jerusalem on the northern coast of Africa. **Rome.** About 1,500 miles by ship from Jerusalem. **converts to Judaism.** Judaism's high morality and developed spirituality attracted many Gentiles from the immoral, pagan practices of other religions. **Cretans.** An island south of Greece in the Mediterranean Sea. **Arabs.** The Nabetean kingdom was south of Jerusalem with borders on Egypt and the Euphrates.

2:17–21 This passage quotes, with minor changes, Joel 2:28–32 as it was found in the pre-Christian Greek translation of the Old Testament (The Septuagint). This was the version of the Old Testament with which the disciples were familiar.

these people with the events of Jesus' life? How might they be dealing with the rumors of the empty tomb? Given that, why does Peter emphasize the resurrection (vv. 24,31–32)? **5.** What are the implications of the resurrection and ascension for Jesus (vv. 24,30–31,33–36)? For the people? What would it mean to the people that Jesus is a spiritual King far greater than their greatest earthly king (vv. 35–36)? **6.** How did the people respond to Peter's message (v. 37)? **7.** What would the invitation of Peter "repent and be baptized ... in the name of Jesus Christ ..." mean to the Jewish audience (v. 38)? What was the response (v. 41)? **8.** From Peter's sermon, what facts do you learn about Jesus? Is it important for a Christian to believe in the resurrection of Jesus? **9.** How do you account for the fact that so many people responded to Peter's message that day?

APPLY **1.** In your own experience, what is the closest you have come to being in a meeting (worship service) where 3,000 people responded to making a life-changing decision? What do you remember about the meeting and the message? **2.** Do you think it is possible today for "young men to see visions and old men to dream dreams" (v. 17)? Is God at work in your life, opening you up to a greater understanding of what he can do? Are you open to the possibility that God will give you a heart for his work a new "vision" ... and a new "dream"?

I will pour out my Spirit in those days,
and they will prophesy.
19 I will show wonders in the heaven above
and signs on the earth below,
blood and fire and billows of smoke.
20 The sun will be turned to darkness
and the moon to blood
before the coming of the great and glorious day of the Lord.
21 And everyone who calls
on the name of the Lord will be saved.'[a]

22 "Men of Israel, listen to this: Jesus of Nazareth was a man accred-
ited by God to you by miracles, wonders and signs, which God did
among you through him, as you yourselves know. 23 This man was
handed over to you by God's set purpose and foreknowledge; and
you, with the help of wicked men,[b] put him to death by nailing him to
the cross. 24 But God raised him from the dead, freeing him from the
agony of death, because it was impossible for death to keep its hold
on him. 25 David said about him:

" 'I saw the Lord always before me.
Because he is at my right hand,
I will not be shaken.
26 Therefore my heart is glad and my tongue rejoices;
my body also will live in hope,
27 because you will not abandon me to the grave,
nor will you let your Holy One see decay.
28 You have made known to me the paths of life;
you will fill me with joy in your presence.'[c]

29 "Brothers, I can tell you confidently that the patriarch David died
and was buried, and his tomb is here to this day. 30 But he was a
prophet and knew that God had promised him on oath that he would
place one of his descendants on his throne. 31 Seeing what was ahead,
he spoke of the resurrection of the Christ,[d] that he was not abandoned to the grave, nor did his body see decay. 32 God has raised this
Jesus to life, and we are all witnesses of the fact. 33 Exalted to the right
hand of God, he has received from the Father the promised Holy Spirit and has poured out what you now see and hear. 34 For David did not
ascend to heaven, and yet he said,

" 'The Lord said to my Lord:
"Sit at my right hand
35 until I make your enemies
a footstool for your feet." '[e]

[a] *21* Joel 2:28-32 [b] *23* Or *of those not having the law* (that is, Gentiles) [c] *28* Psalm 16:8-11 [d] *31* Or *Messiah.* "The Christ" (Greek) and "the Messiah" (Hebrew) both mean "the Anointed One"; also in verse 36.
[e] *35* Psalm 110:1

2:22 The fact of Jesus' miracles is not debated. The stories of his work in Galilee had been widely reported (26:26; Mark 3:8; Luke 12:1). What was debated was the source of his power; early on some leaders accused him of being possessed by Satan (Mark 3:22). **miracles.** Literally, "powers" (Luke 5:17; 10:13). The outward manifestations of Jesus' authority and validation of his deity. **signs.** This word points to the fact that Jesus' miracles were not ends in themselves but pointers to the nature of his identity and mission. It is the favorite word for the miracles in John's Gospel (John 2:11; 4:54; 6:26).

2:24–28 Death could not hold onto Jesus (v. 24) because the Messiah would not be subject to decay (v. 27).

36"Therefore let all Israel be assured of this: God has made this
Jesus, whom you crucified, both Lord and Christ."
37When the people heard this, they were cut to the heart and said to
Peter and the other apostles, "Brothers, what shall we do?"
38Peter replied, "Repent and be baptized, every one of you, in the
name of Jesus Christ for the forgiveness of your sins. And you will
receive the gift of the Holy Spirit. 39The promise is for you and your
children and for all who are far off—for all whom the Lord our God
will call."
40With many other words he warned them; and he pleaded with
them, "Save yourselves from this corrupt generation." 41Those who
accepted his message were baptized, and about three thousand were
added to their number that day.

The Fellowship of the Believers

42They devoted themselves to the apostles' teaching and to the fellowship, to the breaking of bread and to prayer. 43Everyone was filled
with awe, and many wonders and miraculous signs were done by the
apostles. 44All the believers were together and had everything in common. 45Selling their possessions and goods, they gave to anyone as
he had need. 46Every day they continued to meet together in the temple courts. They broke bread in their homes and ate together with
glad and sincere hearts, 47praising God and enjoying the favor of all
the people. And the Lord added to their number daily those who were
being saved.

Peter Heals the Crippled Beggar

3 One day Peter and John were going up to the temple at the time
of prayer—at three in the afternoon. 2Now a man crippled from
birth was being carried to the temple gate called Beautiful, where he
was put every day to beg from those going into the temple courts.
3When he saw Peter and John about to enter, he asked them for
money. 4Peter looked straight at him, as did John. Then Peter said,

OPEN What kind of church did you grow up in?

STUDY 1. What are the four elements in the early church? Of these four elements how would you rank your church from 1 to 10 on each element? **2.** What happened to needs?

APPLY What is the closest you have come to being in a church that was hitting on all four cylinders?

OPEN When you were growing up, how sick did you have to be to miss school?

STUDY 1. Who do you think carried the crippled man to the Beautiful Gate each morning? Do you think his feet and ankles were deformed or just deteriorated from

2:38 Repent. Literally, "Change your mind." Repentance is the act of making a moral U-turn; of turning away from all other loyalties to affirm one's allegiance to Jesus and his way (Mark 1:15). **be baptized.** Baptism was the outward sign of the inward change of heart and mind showing the desire to be cleansed from sin. Gentile converts to Judaism would be baptized as a sign of washing away their Gentile sin, but until John the Baptist came on the scene, Jews never were baptized. This was a radical admission of their own sin and deep need for God's inner cleansing. Normally, repentance and belief are linked together indicating that baptism is intended to be a sign of faith in Jesus.

2:42 The four components of the church's life here may represent what occurred at their gatherings. **teaching.** The foundation for the church's life was the instruction given by the apostles as the representatives of Jesus. **fellowship.** Literally, "sharing." While this may include the aspect of sharing to meet material needs (v. 45), it most likely means their common participation in the Spirit as they worshiped together (1 Cor. 12). **the breaking of bread.** The Lord's Supper in which they remembered his death (Luke 22:19) and recognized his presence among them (Luke 24:30–31). **to prayer.** Literally, the "prayers." This may refer to set times and forms of prayer as was the practice of the Jews.

2:43–47 The picture of the church is one of continual growth (v. 47) marked by generous sharing (vv. 44–45) and joyful worship and fellowship (vv. 46–47a). The worship at the temple continued as before, since the line dividing Christianity from Judaism had not yet been drawn. Christians simply saw their faith as the natural end of what the Jewish faith had always declared.

2:44 All ... had everything in common. They believed that in Christ each person's need must in some sense become everyone's need.

3:1 the time of prayer. The two daily times of sacrifice and prayer at the temple were in the early morning and around 3 p.m.

3:2 the temple gate called Beautiful. It is uncertain which of the temple's many gates had this name but it was apparently near Solomon's Colonnade (v. 11) on the eastern side of the temple.

3:3–5 Almsgiving was an impersonal act as the giver simply dropped a coin into the hands of a person who was already looking for the next person to ask for help. Peter and John broke through his routine by insisting that he pay attention to them. In Christ, caring for those in need is relational. When

neglect? **2.** What did Peter and John offer him that his caregivers did not? **3.** If Peter had given the crippled man a handout, where would he be today? What is the lesson here for the church? **4.** If someone acted in your church like the cripple acted in the temple, what would the elders do?

APPLY How would you compare the behavior change of the crippled man to your own story?

OPEN Have you ever heard or seen an evangelist of the old "hell fire and damnation" style?

STUDY **1.** Why was the audience prepared to listen to Peter (vv. 9–10,12)? **2.** If you had been in the audience, how would you have felt after verses 13–15? How would you describe Peter's preaching style? How would you like him as your pastor? **3.** What is the "out" Peter offers the audience (v. 17)? What does he promise (v. 19)? **4.** In Peter's first message at Pentecost, he focuses on Jesus' resurrection. What does he say about Jesus in this message (v. 21)? **5.** Do you think Peter had an Old Testament scholar sitting in the front row holding up cue cards to prompt him in this message? What do the references to Moses, Samuel and Abraham do to the message?

APPLY **1.** What was it that convinced you to turn to Christ? Was it preaching like Peter's? **2.** How important was the "witness" of someone's changed life in your conversion, such as the "not drunk" disciples at Pentecost and the crippled man in this story?

"Look at us!" [5]So the man gave them his attention, expecting to get
something from them.
[6]Then Peter said, "Silver or gold I do not have, but what I have I
give you. In the name of Jesus Christ of Nazareth, walk." [7]Taking him
by the right hand, he helped him up, and instantly the man's feet and
ankles became strong. [8]He jumped to his feet and began to walk.
Then he went with them into the temple courts, walking and jumping, and praising God. [9]When all the people saw him walking and
praising God, [10]they recognized him as the same man who used to sit
begging at the temple gate called Beautiful, and they were filled with
wonder and amazement at what had happened to him.

Peter Speaks to the Onlookers

[11]While the beggar held on to Peter and John, all the people were
astonished and came running to them in the place called Solomon's
Colonnade. [12]When Peter saw this, he said to them: "Men of Israel,
why does this surprise you? Why do you stare at us as if by our own
power or godliness we had made this man walk? [13]The God of Abraham, Isaac and Jacob, the God of our fathers, has glorified his servant
Jesus. You handed him over to be killed, and you disowned him before Pilate, though he had decided to let him go. [14]You disowned the
Holy and Righteous One and asked that a murderer be released to
you. [15]You killed the author of life, but God raised him from the dead.
We are witnesses of this. [16]By faith in the name of Jesus, this man
whom you see and know was made strong. It is Jesus' name and the
faith that comes through him that has given this complete healing to
him, as you can all see.
[17]"Now, brothers, I know that you acted in ignorance, as did your
leaders. [18]But this is how God fulfilled what he had foretold through
all the prophets, saying that his Christ[a] would suffer. [19]Repent, then,
and turn to God, so that your sins may be wiped out, that times of
refreshing may come from the Lord, [20]and that he may send the
Christ, who has been appointed for you—even Jesus. [21]He must remain in heaven until the time comes for God to restore everything, as
he promised long ago through his holy prophets. [22]For Moses said,
'The Lord your God will raise up for you a prophet like me from
among your own people; you must listen to everything he tells you.
[23]Anyone who does not listen to him will be completely cut off from
among his people.'[b]
[24]"Indeed, all the prophets from Samuel on, as many as have spoken, have foretold these days. [25]And you are heirs of the prophets and
of the covenant God made with your fathers. He said to Abraham,
'Through your offspring all peoples on earth will be blessed.'[c] [26]When

[a]18 Or *Messiah;* also in verse 20 [b]23 Deut. 18:15,18,19 [c]25 Gen. 22:18; 26:4

Peter did this, the man's expectations for a generous gift must have been raised. It may be that at this point he recognized *Peter and John as among the leaders of* the band of people who had recently pledged their loyalty to Jesus.

3:6 Silver or gold I do not have. The implication of this statement is: this is not what is truly valuable anyway. To experience life fully is surely more valuable than money, and the healing which Peter was about to do would help this man live more fully. **In the name of Jesus Christ.** By the authority and presence of Jesus who so often healed the sick, this man is healed. In the name was the power of the person.

3:8 jumped to his feet ... praising God. He makes no attempt to hide his excitement. That he jumps to his feet is both a sign of that excitement and a sign of how complete the healing was, given that jumping takes far more leg strength than simply rising to one's feet. This same type of excitement is referred to in Isaiah 35:6.

God raised up his servant, he sent him first to you to bless you by
turning each of you from your wicked ways."

Peter and John Before the Sanhedrin

4 The priests and the captain of the temple guard and the Sadducees came up to Peter and John while they were speaking to the
people. 2They were greatly disturbed because the apostles were
teaching the people and proclaiming in Jesus the resurrection of the
dead. 3They seized Peter and John, and because it was evening, they
put them in jail until the next day. 4But many who heard the message
believed, and the number of men grew to about five thousand.

5The next day the rulers, elders and teachers of the law met in Jerusalem. 6Annas the high priest was there, and so were Caiaphas, John,
Alexander and the other men of the high priest's family. 7They had
Peter and John brought before them and began to question them: "By
what power or what name did you do this?"

8Then Peter, filled with the Holy Spirit, said to them: "Rulers and
elders of the people! 9If we are being called to account today for an
act of kindness shown to a cripple and are asked how he was healed,
10then know this, you and all the people of Israel: It is by the name of
Jesus Christ of Nazareth, whom you crucified but whom God raised
from the dead, that this man stands before you healed. 11He is

" 'the stone you builders rejected,
which has become the capstone.'[a][b]

12Salvation is found in no one else, for there is no other name under
heaven given to men by which we must be saved."

13When they saw the courage of Peter and John and realized that
they were unschooled, ordinary men, they were astonished and they
took note that these men had been with Jesus. 14But since they could
see the man who had been healed standing there with them, there
was nothing they could say. 15So they ordered them to withdraw from

[a] *11* Or *cornerstone* [b] *11* Psalm 118:22

OPEN What is the closest you have come to being put in jail?

STUDY 1. How would you feel if you were a priest or Sadducee and discovered Peter preaching about Jesus in the temple? What were they afraid of? **2.** Do you feel a little sorry for the authorities? What has happened to the the followers of Jesus since the authorities had Jesus put to death? **3.** What are the authorities at a lost to explain (v. 13)? What do they have to acknowledge (v. 14)? **4.** What do the authorities decide to do? How do Peter and John reply? How do you reconcile this with Romans 13:1–4? What keeps the authorities from punishing Peter and John? **5.** How would you paraphrase verse 12 in your own words? Do you think Peter is being a little narrow-minded? **6.** "The number of men grew to about five thousand" (v. 4). How do you think these people were assimilated without buildings, organized institutions or trained clergy? If you had been in charge of assimilation for this church, what would you do?

APPLY 1. When is the last time you felt threatened while sharing your faith? **2.** Where is it hardest for you to share your faith story?

4:1 the captain of the temple guard. A high-ranking official who had the responsibility of maintaining order in the temple. **the Sadducees.** The Sadducees were a wealthy group who believed only in the first five books of the Old Testament and denied the resurrection. The Sadducees played a leading role in the opposition to the church in Acts (23:6–8).

4:2 The Sadducees considered teaching to be a priestly right. To further upset things, the disciples were preaching the resurrection, a doctrine which the Sadducees did not believe.

4:6 Annas the high priest. Caiaphas, Annas' son-in-law, was the official high priest since Annas had been removed from office in A.D. 14 by the Roman procurator.

4:10 Although the Sanhedrin represented the highest level of authority and power in the Jewish social and political structure, Peter is not intimidated by them. He confronts them with the fact that the miracle was not a product of sorcery, but of faith in the power of Jesus, the Messiah, whom they had officially condemned to death a few weeks before. Again, the apostolic message stresses three central facts about Jesus: (1) although he was crucified, God raised him from death and exalted him as Messiah (2:32–36; 3:13–15); (2) he continues to be present and active among those who trust in him (2:33; 3:16); and (3) the promise of salvation from sin is for those who will respond in faith to him (2:38–39; 3:19–20; 4:12).

4:12 Salvation. The Greek word for healing and salvation is the same, which allows Peter to make an easy transition from discussing the condition of the formerly crippled man to the spiritual state of the members of the Sanhedrin.

4:13 The Sanhedrin not only realizes that Peter and John are disciples of Jesus, but also are aware that the boldness with which Peter speaks is reminiscent of the way Jesus spoke (Luke 20:19,26,40). Luke probably intends this as another example of Jesus at work through his Spirit in the apostles (compare v. 14 with Luke 21:15). **Peter and John ... unschooled, ordinary men.** As fishermen by trade, Peter and John certainly never had the formal rabbinical training that many members of the Sanhedrin would have had.

4:15 How Luke got this inside information is uncertain although at least one member of the council was a believer in Jesus and may have been Luke's source of information (Luke 23:50ff).

the Sanhedrin and then conferred together. 16"What are we going to
do with these men?" they asked. "Everybody living in Jerusalem
knows they have done an outstanding miracle, and we cannot deny
it. 17But to stop this thing from spreading any further among the
people, we must warn these men to speak no longer to anyone in this
name."
18Then they called them in again and commanded them not to
speak or teach at all in the name of Jesus. 19But Peter and John
replied, "Judge for yourselves whether it is right in God's sight to
obey you rather than God. 20For we cannot help speaking about what
we have seen and heard."
21After further threats they let them go. They could not decide how
to punish them, because all the people were praising God for what
had happened. 22For the man who was miraculously healed was over
forty years old.

The Believers' Prayer

23On their release, Peter and John went back to their own people
and reported all that the chief priests and elders had said to them.
24When they heard this, they raised their voices together in prayer to
God. "Sovereign Lord," they said, "you made the heaven and the
earth and the sea, and everything in them. 25You spoke by the Holy
Spirit through the mouth of your servant, our father David:

" 'Why do the nations rage
and the peoples plot in vain?
26The kings of the earth take their stand
and the rulers gather together
against the Lord
and against his Anointed One.'[a][b]

27Indeed Herod and Pontius Pilate met together with the Gentiles and
the people[c] of Israel in this city to conspire against your holy servant
Jesus, whom you anointed. 28They did what your power and will had
decided beforehand should happen. 29Now, Lord, consider their
threats and enable your servants to speak your word with great boldness. 30Stretch out your hand to heal and perform miraculous signs
and wonders through the name of your holy servant Jesus."
31After they prayed, the place where they were meeting was shaken.
And they were all filled with the Holy Spirit and spoke the word of
God boldly.

OPEN Who taught you how to pray? Who prays like no one else?

STUDY **1.** How do you think the rest of the disciples were feeling when Peter and John were taken before the same court that sentenced Jesus to death? How would they receive the news from Peter and John in verse 23? **2.** Who do you know that prays like the disciples in verses 24–30? **3.** What happened when the disciples were together and prayed? **4.** What could the church today learn from these disciples? What would happen if the authorities suddenly jailed you or your friends for sharing their faith?

APPLY **1.** What is the closest you have come to being part of a community that asked God for big things? **2.** How would you compare your prayer life to that of these disciples? **3.** Where could you use a little prayer right now?

[a] *26* That is, Christ or Messiah [b] *26* Psalm 2:1,2 [c] *27* The Greek is plural.

then conferred together. It is interesting to contrast the response of the Sanhedrin under pressure to that of the disciples (vv. 24–30): the Sanhedrin "confer together" whereas the disciples pray.

4:16–17 Recognizing the irrefutable fact that the man was healed and the widespread popular support for the disciples (v. 21), the Sanhedrin realized there was little they could do at this point except try to use their power and status to intimidate the disciples into silence. They may still have feared a popular uprising that would bring down the harsh military might of the Romans (John 11:48), or they may more personally fear the reaction of the people against them if this belief about Jesus as the Messiah got too widespread.

4:19–20 Peter and John, whether they are facing the council alone or together, both assert that the council has overstepped its bounds.

4:31 the place ... was shaken. Earthquakes were a common sign in the Old Testament of God's presence (Ex. 19:18; Ps. 114:7; Isa. 6:4; Ezek. 38:19). Thus, the disciples were assured that their prayer was heard.

The Believers Share Their Possessions

[32]All the believers were one in heart and mind. No one claimed that
any of his possessions was his own, but they shared everything they
had. [33]With great power the apostles continued to testify to the resurrection of the Lord Jesus, and much grace was upon them all. [34]There
were no needy persons among them. For from time to time those who
owned lands or houses sold them, brought the money from the sales
[35]and put it at the apostles' feet, and it was distributed to anyone as
he had need.

[36]Joseph, a Levite from Cyprus, whom the apostles called Barnabas
(which means Son of Encouragement), [37]sold a field he owned and
brought the money and put it at the apostles' feet.

Ananias and Sapphira

5 Now a man named Ananias, together with his wife Sapphira,
also sold a piece of property. [2]With his wife's full knowledge he
kept back part of the money for himself, but brought the rest and put
it at the apostles' feet.

[3]Then Peter said, "Ananias, how is it that Satan has so filled your
heart that you have lied to the Holy Spirit and have kept for yourself
some of the money you received for the land? [4]Didn't it belong to you
before it was sold? And after it was sold, wasn't the money at your
disposal? What made you think of doing such a thing? You have not
lied to men but to God."

[5]When Ananias heard this, he fell down and died. And great fear
seized all who heard what had happened. [6]Then the young men came
forward, wrapped up his body, and carried him out and buried him.

[7]About three hours later his wife came in, not knowing what had
happened. [8]Peter asked her, "Tell me, is this the price you and Ananias
got for the land?"

"Yes," she said, "that is the price."

[9]Peter said to her, "How could you agree to test the Spirit of the
Lord? Look! The feet of the men who buried your husband are at the
door, and they will carry you out also."

[10]At that moment she fell down at his feet and died. Then the young
men came in and, finding her dead, carried her out and buried her
beside her husband. [11]Great fear seized the whole church and all who
heard about these events.

OPEN 1. When you were growing up, who did you share your clothes with? Did you receive "hand-me-down" clothes? **2.** What memorable experience comes to mind when you were "found out" by your parents?

STUDY 1. Do you think it is possible for the church today to have the same closeness and level of care that this church had? **2.** Were Ananias and Sapphira required to sell the land and lay all the money at the apostles' feet (4:32–37)? Why or why not? What was their sin? **3.** What would Ananias and Sapphira gain by lying about the money they received? **4.** How come many people who deceive God and their church today do not come to a dramatic end like Ananias and Sapphira? **5.** How would the incident with Ananias and Sapphira lead to the response of people in 5:13–14? What words might outsiders use to describe this church? **6.** Why would people be afraid to "join" the church (5:13)? Did this discipline of God stop people from joining (5:14)? **7.** How do you account for the amazing things that happened in this church? What is the closest you have come to seeing these things today? **8.** What does healing of the sick and those tormented with evil spirits have to do with the gospel?

APPLY 1. Are you open to the possibility that God can "heal the sick and those tormented with evil spirits" today? **2.** What is the closest you have come to being involved in this ministry?

4:34 no needy persons among them. While this was the ideal for Old Testament Israel (Deut. 15:4), the generosity of the Christians allowed it to be experienced (Luke 12:32–34; 18:18–30; 19:1–10).

4:35 put it at the apostles' feet. The apostles were given the responsibility of distributing the resources such that all the needs of the people were met.

5:2 he kept back. This rare Greek word is used in the Septuagint version of Joshua 7:1 to describe Achan's action of keeping back part of the money from Jericho that was to be devoted to God. All Israel was punished.

5:4 What made you think. Literally, "to lay to heart." This was not an impulsive act, but the result of a long, careful deliberation prompted and encouraged by Satan (v. 3). **You have not lied to men but to God.** Peter's statement is not to minimize the fact they did lie to people, but to highlight the fact this lie was primarily an affront to God. Their lie showed they failed to take the Holy Spirit's presence in the community seriously.

5:10 Whether from heart failure at the surprise exposure of their sin, or from some direct act of God, both Ananias and Sapphira died when their act was revealed. Jesus made it clear that judgment upon sin was also a sign of the presence of the kingdom of God (Luke 10:10–11).

5:11 The result of this incident was that the entire community recognized the seriousness of a sin against God (Heb. 10:31; 12:28–29). **Great fear.** They were not afraid of being similarly struck down by God. This should be more properly understood as, "they felt a great sense of awe at the power of God." **church.** This is the first use of the word church in Acts.

The Apostles Heal Many

12The apostles performed many miraculous signs and wonders among the people. And all the believers used to meet together in Solomon's Colonnade. 13No one else dared join them, even though they were highly regarded by the people. 14Nevertheless, more and more men and women believed in the Lord and were added to their number. 15As a result, people brought the sick into the streets and laid them on beds and mats so that at least Peter's shadow might fall on some of them as he passed by. 16Crowds gathered also from the towns around Jerusalem, bringing their sick and those tormented by evil[a] spirits, and all of them were healed.

The Apostles Persecuted

17Then the high priest and all his associates, who were members of the party of the Sadducees, were filled with jealousy. 18They arrested the apostles and put them in the public jail. 19But during the night an angel of the Lord opened the doors of the jail and brought them out. 20"Go, stand in the temple courts," he said, "and tell the people the full message of this new life."

21At daybreak they entered the temple courts, as they had been told, and began to teach the people.

When the high priest and his associates arrived, they called together the Sanhedrin—the full assembly of the elders of Israel—and sent to the jail for the apostles. 22But on arriving at the jail, the officers did not find them there. So they went back and reported, 23"We found the jail securely locked, with the guards standing at the doors; but when we opened them, we found no one inside." 24On hearing this report, the captain of the temple guard and the chief priests were puzzled, wondering what would come of this.

25Then someone came and said, "Look! The men you put in jail are standing in the temple courts teaching the people." 26At that, the captain went with his officers and brought the apostles. They did not use force, because they feared that the people would stone them.

27Having brought the apostles, they made them appear before the Sanhedrin to be questioned by the high priest. 28"We gave you strict orders not to teach in this name," he said. "Yet you have filled Jerusalem with your teaching and are determined to make us guilty of this man's blood."

29Peter and the other apostles replied: "We must obey God rather

[a]16 Greek *unclean*

OPEN What movie have you seen that depicted someone being falsely accused or imprisoned?

STUDY **1.** What was happening in the previous verses (vv. 15–16) that made the high priest and his associates jealous? **2.** The time has come to put an end to the Jesus movement. The high priest convenes the Sanhedrin to pass judgment on the leaders (apostles). What happened? If you had been the high priest, what would be going through your mind? **3.** Who do the authorities sound like in verse 28? What do they accuse the apostles of doing? **4.** What is the principle Peter uses to answer the Sanhedrin? What does Peter say that infuriated the Sanhedrin? **5.** How would you describe Gamaliel? How does Gamaliel look upon the followers of Christ? What is his advice? Would you have voted for his advice? **6.** What do the Sanhedrin decide to do? Do you know what flogging will do to your flesh? If the leaders of your church returned from a court hearing with their backs looking like raw meat, what would that do to your church? What did it do to this church? **7.** Have you ever been in a country where the Christians are being persecuted? What has it accomplished?

5:12 signs and wonders. Miracles in Acts are often described as "signs" that point to the reality of God's presence and power in their midst (4:30).

5:19–20 This is the first of three miraculous escapes from jail in Acts (12:6ff and 16:26). While these are clearly seen as acts of God intervening for the sake of his people, there is no guarantee that such deliverances will always occur. The apostles here, for example, are delivered from spending the night in prison, but still face the next day's trial and beating (v. 40).

5:21–26 The humor of the situation is right on the surface of the story. Prepared to try these upstarts, the Sanhedrin is totally bewildered as they find out that the men they imprisoned are somehow *not* in their prison but back at the temple preaching just as before!

5:27–28 The Sanhedrin bypasses the question of how the apostles escaped to deal directly with their preaching.

5:28 you ... are determined to make us guilty. The Sanhedrin was concerned that the apostles' teaching would undermine their authority in the public eye.

5:29 We must obey God rather than men! This is a restatement of what they had already said in 4:19–20. The one who has allegiance to God always has a higher loyalty than to the state. That does not mean the follower

than men! 30The God of our fathers raised Jesus from the dead—
whom you had killed by hanging him on a tree. 31God exalted him to
his own right hand as Prince and Savior that he might give repentance and forgiveness of sins to Israel. 32We are witnesses of these
things, and so is the Holy Spirit, whom God has given to those who
obey him."
33When they heard this, they were furious and wanted to put them
to death. 34But a Pharisee named Gamaliel, a teacher of the law, who
was honored by all the people, stood up in the Sanhedrin and ordered that the men be put outside for a little while. 35Then he addressed them: "Men of Israel, consider carefully what you intend to
do to these men. 36Some time ago Theudas appeared, claiming to be
somebody, and about four hundred men rallied to him. He was killed,
all his followers were dispersed, and it all came to nothing. 37After
him, Judas the Galilean appeared in the days of the census and led a
band of people in revolt. He too was killed, and all his followers were
scattered. 38Therefore, in the present case I advise you: Leave these
men alone! Let them go! For if their purpose or activity is of human
origin, it will fail. 39But if it is from God, you will not be able to stop
these men; you will only find yourselves fighting against God."
40His speech persuaded them. They called the apostles in and had
them flogged. Then they ordered them not to speak in the name of
Jesus, and let them go.
41The apostles left the Sanhedrin, rejoicing because they had been
counted worthy of suffering disgrace for the Name. 42Day after day, in
the temple courts and from house to house, they never stopped
teaching and proclaiming the good news that Jesus is the Christ.[a]

The Choosing of the Seven

6 In those days when the number of disciples was increasing, the
Grecian Jews among them complained against the Hebraic Jews
because their widows were being overlooked in the daily distribution
of food. 2So the Twelve gathered all the disciples together and said,
"It would not be right for us to neglect the ministry of the word of
God in order to wait on tables. 3Brothers, choose seven men from

[a]42 Or *Messiah*

APPLY 1. What is the closest you have come to being part of a Christian fellowship that was bold and uncompromising in the face of opposition? **2.** Where are you facing a situation today where you are going to have to take a stand and say, "I must obey God rather than men"?

OPEN Which responsibility at home or work would you gladly give up? Never give up?

STUDY 1. How do you think the church members who spoke Greek felt when everyone else spoke Aramaic? What brought this problem into the open? **2.** What did the Twelve do to solve the problem?

of Christ ignores or rebels against civil government. We are called to be good citizens (Rom. 13:1–7).

5:34 a Pharisee. While in the Gospels, the Pharisees are the prime opponents of Jesus because of their conviction that he was a lawbreaker, in Acts they are much more supportive of the church than the Sadducees who felt that the apostles were encroaching upon their power in temple affairs. **Gamaliel.** This man was greatly honored and loved by the people.

5:36 To prove his point, Gamaliel mentions two former insurrectionists whose crusades fell apart shortly after the leader's death. While there were several such uprisings after Herod the Great's death (4 B.C.), the Theudas referred to here is unknown.

5:37 Judas. This man led a revolt against Roman oppression in A.D. 6 when Judea came under direct Roman control. His protest centered around his belief that God alone was Israel's King; therefore, to pay tribute to Caesar was treason against God.

5:40 apostles ... flogged. Flogging meant being whipped 13 times by a lash with three strands (thus amounting to 39 lashes—Deut. 25:3 allowed a maximum of 40 lashes, but 39 became the norm so that the law would not be broken). Flogging was a severe punishment which, at times, did lead to death through shock and loss of blood.

6:1 Grecian Jews. Jews who came from outside Palestine and for whom Aramaic and Hebrew were relatively unknown languages. Their synagogue worship was also conducted in their native languages. **Hebraic Jews.** Native Palestinians who spoke Aramaic as their daily language. Since all the apostles were Hebraic Jews, it may be that they were naturally more sensitive and aware of the needs of those with whom they could easily communicate.

6:2 wait on tables. Literally, "to serve tables." Since banking at the time was done by people sitting at a table, to "serve tables" was a figure of speech for handling financial transactions, along with material needs people might have.

What happened as a result? **3.** Who are the "Greeks" in your church? Who looks after these "Greeks" in your church? Singles? Newly Married? Divorced? Abused? Alcoholics?

APPLY 1. Is there a group of people in your church that you feel especially concerned for? **2.** Is God calling you to do something about this?

OPEN Do you have any friends who are "Naturalized Citizens"—that is, immigrants who have become a citizen of your country?

STUDY 1. Why would the "Synagogue of Freedmen" who speak Greek and are immigrants be so upset when one of their own tries to share his faith with them? Who do they remind you of? **2.** What do the members of this synagogue decide to do? **3.** What do the false witnesses tell the Sanhedrin? How would the Sanhedrin take this?

APPLY Have you ever been in a church that did to one of its own what the synagogue of the Freedmen did to Stephen?

OPEN 1. As a child, who was the best storyteller in your family? **2.** Where did your ancestors come from? Any black sheep?

STUDY 1. From 6:13–14, how would you write up the formal charges against Stephen? **2.** What does Stephen's storytelling

among you who are known to be full of the Spirit and wisdom. We
will turn this responsibility over to them [4]and will give our attention
to prayer and the ministry of the word."

[5]This proposal pleased the whole group. They chose Stephen, a
man full of faith and of the Holy Spirit; also Philip, Procorus, Nicanor,
Timon, Parmenas, and Nicolas from Antioch, a convert to Judaism.
[6]They presented these men to the apostles, who prayed and laid their
hands on them.

[7]So the word of God spread. The number of disciples in Jerusalem
increased rapidly, and a large number of priests became obedient to
the faith.

Stephen Seized

[8]Now Stephen, a man full of God's grace and power, did great wonders and miraculous signs among the people. [9]Opposition arose,
however, from members of the Synagogue of the Freedmen (as it was
called)—Jews of Cyrene and Alexandria as well as the provinces of
Cilicia and Asia. These men began to argue with Stephen, [10]but they
could not stand up against his wisdom or the Spirit by whom he
spoke.

[11]Then they secretly persuaded some men to say, "We have heard
Stephen speak words of blasphemy against Moses and against God."

[12]So they stirred up the people and the elders and the teachers of
the law. They seized Stephen and brought him before the Sanhedrin.
[13]They produced false witnesses, who testified, "This fellow never
stops speaking against this holy place and against the law. [14]For we
have heard him say that this Jesus of Nazareth will destroy this place
and change the customs Moses handed down to us."

[15]All who were sitting in the Sanhedrin looked intently at Stephen,
and they saw that his face was like the face of an angel.

Stephen's Speech to the Sanhedrin

7 Then the high priest asked him, "Are these charges true?"
[2]To this he replied: "Brothers and fathers, listen to me! The God
of glory appeared to our father Abraham while he was still in Mesopotamia, before he lived in Haran. [3]'Leave your country and your
people,' God said, 'and go to the land I will show you.'[a]

[a]3 Gen. 12:1

6:5 The names of the men chosen strongly indicate that all seven were Greek-speaking Jews. They perhaps also served as a bridge between the Palestinian apostles and the Greek-speaking Jews to help avoid further unintentional difficulties between the two groups. **Stephen.** This man moves to center stage in chapter 7. **Philip.** Like Stephen, Philip demonstrated gifts of evangelism not unlike those of the apostles (v. 8; 8:4–8; 21:8). Of the other men nothing more is known.

6:9 Synagogue of the Freedmen. The Freedmen were former Roman slaves (or their descendants) released by their masters and granted Roman citizenship.

6:14 The root of the complaint against Stephen was the charge that the followers of Jesus threatened to destroy the temple and replace the laws of Moses with their own ways. Jesus spoke of destroying the temple in a way that was misunderstood (Mark 14:58; John 2:19–22). Regarding the second charge, Jesus repeatedly challenged the oral traditions that had developed around the Law (Matt. 5:21–22,27–28,31–32,33–34,38–39, 43–44; 9:14–15; 12:2ff). As far as the Jewish leaders were concerned, to challenge this tradition was to challenge the Law itself.

6:15 like the face of an angel. His face radiated with divine glory. Ironically, the only other biblical character who shared this experience was Moses, whom Stephen was charged with defying.

7:1 the high priest. This same man questioned Jesus on similar charges, but received no response (Mark 14:60–61).

7:2–16 Stephen begins with the story of Abraham recounted in Genesis 12–25. The story of Jacob and Joseph occupies most of Genesis 26–50.

4"So he left the land of the Chaldeans and settled in Haran. After
the death of his father, God sent him to this land where you are now
living. 5He gave him no inheritance here, not even a foot of ground.
But God promised him that he and his descendants after him would
possess the land, even though at that time Abraham had no child.
6God spoke to him in this way: 'Your descendants will be strangers in
a country not their own, and they will be enslaved and mistreated
four hundred years. 7But I will punish the nation they serve as slaves,'
God said, 'and afterward they will come out of that country and
worship me in this place.'[a] 8Then he gave Abraham the covenant of
circumcision. And Abraham became the father of Isaac and circumcised him eight days after his birth. Later Isaac became the father of
Jacob, and Jacob became the father of the twelve patriarchs.

9"Because the patriarchs were jealous of Joseph, they sold him as a
slave into Egypt. But God was with him 10and rescued him from all his
troubles. He gave Joseph wisdom and enabled him to gain the goodwill of Pharaoh king of Egypt; so he made him ruler over Egypt and all
his palace.

11"Then a famine struck all Egypt and Canaan, bringing great suffering, and our fathers could not find food. 12When Jacob heard that
there was grain in Egypt, he sent our fathers on their first visit. 13On
their second visit, Joseph told his brothers who he was, and Pharaoh
learned about Joseph's family. 14After this, Joseph sent for his father
Jacob and his whole family, seventy-five in all. 15Then Jacob went
down to Egypt, where he and our fathers died. 16Their bodies were
brought back to Shechem and placed in the tomb that Abraham had
bought from the sons of Hamor at Shechem for a certain sum of
money.

17"As the time drew near for God to fulfill his promise to Abraham,
the number of our people in Egypt greatly increased. 18Then another
king, who knew nothing about Joseph, became ruler of Egypt. 19He
dealt treacherously with our people and oppressed our forefathers by
forcing them to throw out their newborn babies so that they would
die.

20"At that time Moses was born, and he was no ordinary child.[b] For
three months he was cared for in his father's house. 21When he was
placed outside, Pharaoh's daughter took him and brought him up as
her own son. 22Moses was educated in all the wisdom of the Egyptians and was powerful in speech and action.

23"When Moses was forty years old, he decided to visit his fellow
Israelites. 24He saw one of them being mistreated by an Egyptian, so
he went to his defense and avenged him by killing the Egyptian.
25Moses thought that his own people would realize that God was using him to rescue them, but they did not. 26The next day Moses came
upon two Israelites who were fighting. He tried to reconcile them by
saying, 'Men, you are brothers; why do you want to hurt each other?'

27"But the man who was mistreating the other pushed Moses aside
and said, 'Who made you ruler and judge over us? 28Do you want to
kill me as you killed the Egyptian yesterday?'[c] 29When Moses heard
this, he fled to Midian, where he settled as a foreigner and had two
sons.

30"After forty years had passed, an angel appeared to Moses in the

(in effect a history lesson) reveal about his respect for the Scriptures? **3.** Why does Stephen spend the bulk of his history lesson talking about Moses? What parallels does he draw between Moses and Jesus? How does this relate to the charges against him in 6:13–14? How does the quote in verse 37 begin to turn the tables on his accusers (regarding who is really rejecting Moses)? **4.** From verses 44–50, what is his point about the temple and God's presence? How is he turning the tables against his accusers once again? **5.** What does Stephen mean by the phrase "uncircumcised hearts and ears" (v. 51)? In this context, what is Stephen really saying about the Sanhedrin's regard for Moses and the Law? **6.** Of what does he accuse them in verses 51–53? How does his charge reveal the reason why he gave them this history lesson? **7.** Since the Sanhedrin knew religious history every bit as well as Stephen, how do you account for their radically different response to Jesus? **8.** Has Stephen's review of Old Testament history encouraged you? Challenged you? Confused you? Would you say that the Old Testament is more like a stranger or a close friend to you? How does this speech show the importance of the Old Testament to the early Christians? What will you do to let its importance grow for you? **9.** How do you think Stephen did in presenting the gospel before a secular audience of skeptics?

APPLY If you were put on the witness stand in front of your secular friends to explain your faith, what would you say?

[a]7 Gen. 15:13,14 [b]*20* Or *was fair in the sight of God* [c]*28* Exodus 2:14

flames of a burning bush in the desert near Mount Sinai. 31When he
saw this, he was amazed at the sight. As he went over to look more
closely, he heard the Lord's voice: 32'I am the God of your fathers, the
God of Abraham, Isaac and Jacob.'[a] Moses trembled with fear and did
not dare to look.

33"Then the Lord said to him, 'Take off your sandals; the place
where you are standing is holy ground. 34I have indeed seen the oppression of my people in Egypt. I have heard their groaning and have
come down to set them free. Now come, I will send you back to
Egypt.'[b]

35"This is the same Moses whom they had rejected with the words,
'Who made you ruler and judge?' He was sent to be their ruler and
deliverer by God himself, through the angel who appeared to him in
the bush. 36He led them out of Egypt and did wonders and miraculous
signs in Egypt, at the Red Sea[c] and for forty years in the desert.

37"This is that Moses who told the Israelites, 'God will send you a
prophet like me from your own people.'[d] 38He was in the assembly in
the desert, with the angel who spoke to him on Mount Sinai, and with
our fathers; and he received living words to pass on to us.

39"But our fathers refused to obey him. Instead, they rejected him
and in their hearts turned back to Egypt. 40They told Aaron, 'Make us
gods who will go before us. As for this fellow Moses who led us out of
Egypt—we don't know what has happened to him!'[e] 41That was the
time they made an idol in the form of a calf. They brought sacrifices
to it and held a celebration in honor of what their hands had made.
42But God turned away and gave them over to the worship of the
heavenly bodies. This agrees with what is written in the book of the
prophets:

" 'Did you bring me sacrifices and offerings
forty years in the desert, O house of Israel?
43You have lifted up the shrine of Molech
and the star of your god Rephan,
the idols you made to worship.
Therefore I will send you into exile'[f] beyond Babylon.

44"Our forefathers had the tabernacle of the Testimony with them
in the desert. It had been made as God directed Moses, according to
the pattern he had seen. 45Having received the tabernacle, our fathers
under Joshua brought it with them when they took the land from the
nations God drove out before them. It remained in the land until the
time of David, 46who enjoyed God's favor and asked that he might
provide a dwelling place for the God of Jacob.[g] 47But it was Solomon
who built the house for him.

48"However, the Most High does not live in houses made by men.
As the prophet says:

49" 'Heaven is my throne,
and the earth is my footstool.
What kind of house will you build for me?
says the Lord.
Or where will my resting place be?
50Has not my hand made all these things?'[h]

[a]32 Exodus 3:6 [b]34 Exodus 3:5,7,8,10 [c]36 That is, Sea of Reeds [d]37 Deut. 18:15 [e]40 Exodus 32:1
[f]43 Amos 5:25-27 [g]46 Some early manuscripts *the house of Jacob* [h]50 Isaiah 66:1,2

51 "You stiff-necked people, with uncircumcised hearts and ears!
You are just like your fathers: You always resist the Holy Spirit! 52 Was
there ever a prophet your fathers did not persecute? They even killed
those who predicted the coming of the Righteous One. And now you
have betrayed and murdered him— 53 you who have received the law
that was put into effect through angels but have not obeyed it."

The Stoning of Stephen

54 When they heard this, they were furious and gnashed their teeth
at him. 55 But Stephen, full of the Holy Spirit, looked up to heaven and
saw the glory of God, and Jesus standing at the right hand of God.
56 "Look," he said, "I see heaven open and the Son of Man standing at
the right hand of God."
57 At this they covered their ears and, yelling at the top of their
voices, they all rushed at him, 58 dragged him out of the city and began to stone him. Meanwhile, the witnesses laid their clothes at the
feet of a young man named Saul.
59 While they were stoning him, Stephen prayed, "Lord Jesus,
receive my spirit." 60 Then he fell on his knees and cried out, "Lord, do
not hold this sin against them." When he had said this, he fell asleep.

8 And Saul was there, giving approval to his death.

The Church Persecuted and Scattered

On that day a great persecution broke out against the church at Jerusalem, and all except the apostles were scattered throughout Judea
and Samaria. 2 Godly men buried Stephen and mourned deeply for
him. 3 But Saul began to destroy the church. Going from house to
house, he dragged off men and women and put them in prison.

Philip in Samaria

4 Those who had been scattered preached the word wherever they
went. 5 Philip went down to a city in Samaria and proclaimed the
Christ[a] there. 6 When the crowds heard Philip and saw the miraculous

[a] 5 Or *Messiah*

OPEN What do you do when you feel angry enough to resort to sticks and stones?

STUDY 1. How does Stephen end his defense before the Sanhedrin—the ruling body of the Jewish people (7:51–53)? How would you feel if you were one of the Sanhedrin? **2.** What does Stephen say is the final straw? What does this mean (7:56)? **3.** There is good evidence that Saul (Paul) was from the Synagogue of the Freedmen who originally brought charges against Stephen. If you had been Saul (Paul) how would you be feeling as you witnessed the stoning of Stephen?

APPLY What has been the most traumatic experience in your life? How has God used this experience to make you into the person you are today?

OPEN What is the closest you have come to an incident when you had to run for your life?

STUDY 1. What has just occurred (8:1) to cause the church in Jerusalem to start moving

---

7:54–8:1 Stephen had already infuriated the Sanhedrin when he was caught up with a vision of the glorified Jesus at the right hand of God. His announcement of this vision was too much for his listeners who stoned him to death.

7:56 the Son of Man. Jesus used this same image to describe himself at his trial before this same Sanhedrin (Matt. 26:64; Mark 14:62). The fact that Jesus, as the Son of Man, is at the right hand of God means that the way is open for all people everywhere to come to God. **standing.** Perhaps in a posture of coming to receive Stephen, or serving as Stephen's heavenly advocate before the Father.

7:58 John 18:31 indicates the Sanhedrin did not have the legal right to carry out capital punishment, so this may be an act of mob violence. However, 26:10 indicates that perhaps by this time Pilate's ability to control the Sanhedrin had drastically weakened and that it indeed took capital cases into its own hands. **Saul.** This is the one who was to become the great apostle.

8:1–3 Whether 26:10 is sufficient evidence that Saul belonged to the Sanhedrin is uncertain, but he quickly became the leading figure in a violent persecution of the church.

8:3 to destroy. This word is used to describe how a beast rips the flesh off its victim. Saul's persecution led to other Christians being condemned to death as well (9:1–2).

8:5 Samaria. When the northern kingdom of Israel was conquered by the Assyrians (722 B.C.), many of its people were deported while exiles from elsewhere in the vast Assyrian empire were brought in (2 Kin. 17:23–41). These people intermarried with the remaining Israelites and adopted some of their religious practices. As a result, the Jews considered the Samaritans as religious compromisers and racial half-breeds. By Jesus' day, strict Jews avoided Samaria and "Samaritan" was used as an insult (John 8:48). As a Greek-speaking Jew, Philip may have been less prejudiced against the Samaritans than the Palestinian Jews, allowing him to speak freely with them.

8:6–8 Philip's ministry was like that of the apostles' ministries, in that he too was empowered by the Spirit to perform signs and wonders that confirmed his message.

out (8:4)? **2.** Who was Philip (6:5)? What was he assigned to do (6:1)? Why would Philip feel more comfortable ministering in Samaria than the apostles would have felt? What accompanied Philip's preaching (8:6–7)? **3.** How do you think the apostles back in Jerusalem felt when they heard what was going on in Samaria? Who would you compare the Samaritans to today? What would this do to someone who was brought up to look down on Samaritans? **4.** What was it that Simon saw in the apostles that he wanted? How would you put in your own words Peter's answer to Simon? Do you think Peter was a little hard on Simon? What's wrong with making a little money out of healing? **5.** What happened in this passage that has had far reaching impact on the history of Christianity? **6.** Why didn't the church in Jerusalem send missionaries to Samaria before this time—like they were commanded to in 1:8?

APPLY 1. In your own spiritual story, would you have been one of the hometown Jerusalem converts or one of the Samaritans? **2.** Do you find it more comfortable sharing your spiritual story with the hometown Jerusalem folks or the Samaritans? **3.** Would you rather have fellowship with the Jerusalem folks or the Samaritans?

signs he did, they all paid close attention to what he said. 7With
shrieks, evil[a] spirits came out of many, and many paralytics and crip-
ples were healed. 8So there was great joy in that city.

Simon the Sorcerer

9Now for some time a man named Simon had practiced sorcery in
the city and amazed all the people of Samaria. He boasted that he
was someone great, 10and all the people, both high and low, gave him
their attention and exclaimed, "This man is the divine power known
as the Great Power." 11They followed him because he had amazed
them for a long time with his magic. 12But when they believed Philip
as he preached the good news of the kingdom of God and the name
of Jesus Christ, they were baptized, both men and women. 13Simon
himself believed and was baptized. And he followed Philip everywhere, astonished by the great signs and miracles he saw.

14When the apostles in Jerusalem heard that Samaria had accepted
the word of God, they sent Peter and John to them. 15When they arrived, they prayed for them that they might receive the Holy Spirit,
16because the Holy Spirit had not yet come upon any of them; they
had simply been baptized into[b] the name of the Lord Jesus. 17Then
Peter and John placed their hands on them, and they received the
Holy Spirit.

18When Simon saw that the Spirit was given at the laying on of the
apostles' hands, he offered them money 19and said, "Give me also
this ability so that everyone on whom I lay my hands may receive the
Holy Spirit."

20Peter answered: "May your money perish with you, because you
thought you could buy the gift of God with money! 21You have no part
or share in this ministry, because your heart is not right before God.
22Repent of this wickedness and pray to the Lord. Perhaps he will forgive you for having such a thought in your heart. 23For I see that you
are full of bitterness and captive to sin."

24Then Simon answered, "Pray to the Lord for me so that nothing
you have said may happen to me."

25When they had testified and proclaimed the word of the Lord,
Peter and John returned to Jerusalem, preaching the gospel in many
Samaritan villages.

OPEN Have you ever tried hitchhiking? Where did you go?

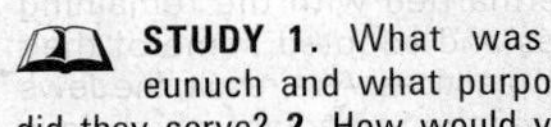

STUDY 1. What was a eunuch and what purpose did they serve? **2.** How would you

Philip and the Ethiopian

26Now an angel of the Lord said to Philip, "Go south to the road—
the desert road—that goes down from Jerusalem to Gaza." 27So he
started out, and on his way he met an Ethiopian[c] eunuch, an impor-

[a]7 Greek *unclean* [b]16 Or *in* [c]27 That is, from the upper Nile region

8:12–13 Philip's message and signs attracted the attention even of Simon. His interest appears to have been in the miraculous aspect of Philip's ministry *more* than in the message of the kingdom of God which he preached.

8:14–17 Upon hearing that widespread faith in Jesus had broken out in Samaria, the apostles decided they needed to check out the situation. Peter and John are sent as representatives to investigate. While there are various interpretations for the delay between the Samaritans' response of faith and their reception of the Spirit, the one that best fits the context of Acts is that it occurred so that the apostles could be convinced that God was indeed including the Samaritans as full members of his church (1:8; 10:44–11:15).

8:27 eunuch. Eunuchs were commonly employed as royal officials. Although attracted to Judaism, as a eunuch he would never be allowed to fully participate in the temple worship because of the restrictions in the Law (Deut. 23:1).

tant official in charge of all the treasury of Candace, queen of the Ethiopians. This man had gone to Jerusalem to worship, [28]and on his way home was sitting in his chariot reading the book of Isaiah the prophet. [29]The Spirit told Philip, "Go to that chariot and stay near it."

[30]Then Philip ran up to the chariot and heard the man reading Isaiah the prophet. "Do you understand what you are reading?" Philip asked.

[31]"How can I," he said, "unless someone explains it to me?" So he invited Philip to come up and sit with him.

[32]The eunuch was reading this passage of Scripture:

"He was led like a sheep to the slaughter,
  and as a lamb before the shearer is silent,
  so he did not open his mouth.
[33]In his humiliation he was deprived of justice.
  Who can speak of his descendants?
  For his life was taken from the earth."[a]

[34]The eunuch asked Philip, "Tell me, please, who is the prophet talking about, himself or someone else?" [35]Then Philip began with that very passage of Scripture and told him the good news about Jesus.

[36]As they traveled along the road, they came to some water and the eunuch said, "Look, here is water. Why shouldn't I be baptized?"[b]
[38]And he gave orders to stop the chariot. Then both Philip and the eunuch went down into the water and Philip baptized him. [39]When they came up out of the water, the Spirit of the Lord suddenly took Philip away, and the eunuch did not see him again, but went on his way rejoicing. [40]Philip, however, appeared at Azotus and traveled about, preaching the gospel in all the towns until he reached Caesarea.

Saul's Conversion

9 Meanwhile, Saul was still breathing out murderous threats against the Lord's disciples. He went to the high priest [2]and asked him for letters to the synagogues in Damascus, so that if he found any there who belonged to the Way, whether men or women,

[a]33 Isaiah 53:7,8 [b]36 Some late manuscripts *baptized?"* [37]*Philip said, "If you believe with all your heart, you may." The eunuch answered, "I believe that Jesus Christ is the Son of God."*

describe the meeting of Philip and the Ethiopian eunuch? How do you account for the openness of the eunuch to God? What is the closest you have come to an opportunity like this? **3.** Do you think Philip had the right to baptize the eunuch? What are the apostles back in Jerusalem going to say? **4.** How is the eunuch going to explain to the Queen what happened to him?

APPLY 1. When is the last time you bumped into someone in your travels that was wide open to the gospel? **2.** When have you found people are most receptive to the gospel?

OPEN 1. What is the longest trip you have made? **2.** What is the closest you have come to having a temporary blackout?

STUDY 1. What do you know about Saul to this point? How would you describe his religious background and dedication (Phil. 3:4–6)?

8:32–33 The eunuch was reading from Isaiah 53:7–8, a key Old Testament passage about the Servant of the Lord. This passage underlines much of what Luke has already recorded about the apostles' preaching concerning the identity of Jesus (3:13; 4:27).

8:35 Philip used this passage as a jumping off point to explain the mission of Jesus and the work of the kingdom. He undoubtedly referred the eunuch to other verses in Isaiah 53 as well as to the other references about the Servant in Isaiah. All of this would have been related to Jesus' ministry, death and resurrection.

8:36 Why shouldn't I. The strict Jew would offer at least one reason why he was ineligible to be considered part of God's people: he was a eunuch. Although due to his castration this man could never become a Jewish proselyte (Deut. 23:1), he was able to come to God through Jesus Christ. This fulfills the prophecy of Isaiah 56:3–8 which anticipates a time when both foreigners *and* eunuchs would be welcomed into God's household.

8:40 at Azotus. Another city on the coast of the Mediterranean Sea about 20 miles north of Gaza. **preaching ... in Caesarea.** The Roman seat of power in Judea, about 60 miles up the coast from Azotus. Philip evangelized throughout the Jewish communities along the Palestinian coast of the Mediterranean.

9:1 Saul. This man, who was to become the great apostle to the Gentiles, was also known as Paul (13:9). **breathing out murderous threats.** This reflects the depth of Saul's obsessive hatred toward the Christians.

9:2 the Way. Unique to Acts as a name for Christianity (19:9,23; 22:4; 24:14,22). It may stem from Jesus' claim in John 14:6.

2. What was Saul's mission and consuming passion? Have you ever met anyone like him? **3.** What would a psychiatrist say happened to Saul (vv. 3–9)? What do you say? **4.** How would you feel if you were Ananias (vv. 10–16)? If you thought you were on Saul's hit list, would you have gone to see him? **5.** What do you learn about the plan and purpose of God for Saul (vv. 15–16) **6.** If Jesus has already appeared to Saul on the highway, why send someone else to meet with him? What would the word "brother" mean to Saul? What came from this meeting? **7.** Do you believe in "Damascus Road" experiences? What is the closest you have come to seeing this kind of radical behavior change?

APPLY 1. How would your spiritual story compare to this story? Would the turnaround in your life be similar? More gradual? Different but just as real? **2.** Who was the Ananias in your life—who helped you understand God's plan and purpose for your life?

OPEN Have you ever known someone who made a dramatic change in his or her life, character or career?

he might take them as prisoners to Jerusalem. 3As he neared Damascus on his journey, suddenly a light from heaven flashed around him.
4He fell to the ground and heard a voice say to him, "Saul, Saul, why
do you persecute me?"
5"Who are you, Lord?" Saul asked.
"I am Jesus, whom you are persecuting," he replied. 6"Now get up
and go into the city, and you will be told what you must do."
7The men traveling with Saul stood there speechless; they heard
the sound but did not see anyone. 8Saul got up from the ground, but
when he opened his eyes he could see nothing. So they led him by the
hand into Damascus. 9For three days he was blind, and did not eat or
drink anything.
10In Damascus there was a disciple named Ananias. The Lord
called to him in a vision, "Ananias!"
"Yes, Lord," he answered.
11The Lord told him, "Go to the house of Judas on Straight Street
and ask for a man from Tarsus named Saul, for he is praying. 12In a
vision he has seen a man named Ananias come and place his hands
on him to restore his sight."
13"Lord," Ananias answered, "I have heard many reports about this
man and all the harm he has done to your saints in Jerusalem. 14And
he has come here with authority from the chief priests to arrest all
who call on your name."
15But the Lord said to Ananias, "Go! This man is my chosen instrument to carry my name before the Gentiles and their kings and before
the people of Israel. 16I will show him how much he must suffer for
my name."
17Then Ananias went to the house and entered it. Placing his hands
on Saul, he said, "Brother Saul, the Lord—Jesus, who appeared to
you on the road as you were coming here—has sent me so that you
may see again and be filled with the Holy Spirit." 18Immediately,
something like scales fell from Saul's eyes, and he could see again.
He got up and was baptized, 19and after taking some food, he regained his strength.

Saul in Damascus and Jerusalem

Saul spent several days with the disciples in Damascus. 20At once
he began to preach in the synagogues that Jesus is the Son of God.
21All those who heard him were astonished and asked, "Isn't he the
man who raised havoc in Jerusalem among those who call on this

---

9:3 a light from heaven flashed around him. This description is often used of lightning, indicating the brilliance of the light (26:13). Light (glory) is commonly connected with divine appearances (Luke 9:29; Rev. 1:14–16).

9:10 Apart from Paul's comment in 22:12, nothing is known of Ananias.

9:11 house of Judas on Straight Street. "The 'street that is called Straight' where Saul's host lived, is still one of the chief thoroughfares of Damascus. The house of Judas is traditionally located near its western end" (Bruce). Nothing is known of Judas.

9:15–16 The Lord overruled Ananias with a final command to "Go!" and a description of what the purpose of Saul's mission would be.

9:17 Brother Saul. Without further question, Ananias affirms Saul as part of the family through the grace of Jesus. After laying hands on him, Saul's sight was restored, he was baptized (presumably by Ananias) and was filled with the Holy Spirit.

9:20 That Saul, as a representative from the Jewish opposition, would be invited to speak in the synagogues is not unusual. What was unexpected was his message! **began to preach ... Jesus is the Son of God.** While this title is alluded to in only one other place in Acts (13:33), it is one of Saul's favorite ways of describing Jesus in the epistles.

9:21–22 The shocked reaction of the Jews in Damascus is understandable given their previous understanding of why Saul came to the city.

name? And hasn't he come here to take them as prisoners to the chief
priests?" 22Yet Saul grew more and more powerful and baffled the
Jews living in Damascus by proving that Jesus is the Christ.[a]
23After many days had gone by, the Jews conspired to kill him, 24but
Saul learned of their plan. Day and night they kept close watch on the
city gates in order to kill him. 25But his followers took him by night
and lowered him in a basket through an opening in the wall.
26When he came to Jerusalem, he tried to join the disciples, but
they were all afraid of him, not believing that he really was a disciple.
27But Barnabas took him and brought him to the apostles. He told
them how Saul on his journey had seen the Lord and that the Lord
had spoken to him, and how in Damascus he had preached fearlessly
in the name of Jesus. 28So Saul stayed with them and moved about
freely in Jerusalem, speaking boldly in the name of the Lord. 29He
talked and debated with the Grecian Jews, but they tried to kill him.
30When the brothers learned of this, they took him down to Caesarea
and sent him off to Tarsus.
31Then the church throughout Judea, Galilee and Samaria enjoyed
a time of peace. It was strengthened; and encouraged by the Holy
Spirit, it grew in numbers, living in the fear of the Lord.

Aeneas and Dorcas

32As Peter traveled about the country, he went to visit the saints in
Lydda. 33There he found a man named Aeneas, a paralytic who had
been bedridden for eight years. 34"Aeneas," Peter said to him, "Jesus
Christ heals you. Get up and take care of your mat." Immediately Aeneas got up. 35All those who lived in Lydda and Sharon saw him and
turned to the Lord.
36In Joppa there was a disciple named Tabitha (which, when translated, is Dorcas[b]), who was always doing good and helping the poor.
37About that time she became sick and died, and her body was
washed and placed in an upstairs room. 38Lydda was near Joppa; so

[a]22 Or *Messiah* [b]36 Both *Tabitha* (Aramaic) and *Dorcas* (Greek) mean *gazelle*.

STUDY The man that "breathes out murderous threats" (v. 1) to arrest all followers of the Way and take them to Jerusalem comes to town. You turn over the pulpit to this man. He gets up and preaches "Jesus is the Son of God." **1.** What do you do? What did they do? **2.** Suddenly the Jesus followers have got to get this man out of town fast. How do you like their idea? **3.** Saul gets to Jerusalem and tells the disciples he has suddenly been converted. There are people in the church who have been arrested, and beaten by this person. What do you do?

APPLY 1. How would you describe your own zeal right after you gave your life to God? How would your story compare to Saul's story? **2.** Who was the Barnabas in your life that spoke up and gave a good word for you?

OPEN When you were in high school, did you run around with the athletes or the nonconformists?

STUDY 1. In his early days, would you have guessed that Peter would turn out to be the bold and courageous person that he is in this passage? **2.** How do you think Aeneas felt when Peter confronted him with the statement, "Jesus Christ heals you. Get up and take care of your mat"? How would you put this in modern day terms? **3.** What Old Testament story does the story about Dorcas remind you of?

9:22 proving that Jesus is the Christ. This was undoubtedly done by pointing out Old Testament passages about the Messiah that were fulfilled in the life and ministry of Jesus (8:34–35).

9:23 After many days had gone. When Saul next returned to Damascus, the leaders of the synagogues were prepared for him. Perhaps under accusations that his teaching was causing an uproar in the Jewish community, the leaders were able to draw upon the help of the governor of the city in a plot to capture Saul so that they might kill him (2 Cor. 11: 32–33).

9:25 an opening in the wall. Ancient cities were surrounded by walls as a defense against enemies. Although the city gates were being closely observed, Saul was able to escape from the city by being lowered over the wall in a large basket. When Saul tells of this incident in 2 Corinthians 11:32–33 it is in the context of describing the weakness and humiliation he had experienced as an apostle.

9:27 Barnabas. Barnabas takes on an important role later on as Paul's (Saul's) companion on his missionary trips. How Barnabas knew the reality of Paul's (Saul's) story is not explained, but it is clear that he risked alienating himself from the church by siding with this former persecutor (4:36)

9:32 Peter and the other apostles undoubtedly made many trips throughout Judea, Samaria and Galilee to teach and encourage the numerous Christian communities (8:25). **Lydda.** A town about 25 miles west of Jerusalem.

9:33–35 This healing of the paralytic was similar to Jesus' healing of a man with the same condition (Luke 5:17–26), affirming Peter as a representative of Jesus. It was perceived by many as a sign that Jesus was indeed the Messiah which led to the conversion of many.

9:35 Sharon. The name of the plain in which the town of Lydda was located.

9:36–43 The story of the healing of Tabitha that takes place in this passage, is similar to two separate incidents recorded in the Old Testament when the prophets Elijah and Elisha, respectively raised two boys to life (1 Kin. 17:17–24; 2 Kin. 4:8–37), proving that they were indeed men sent from God. It is also reminiscent of Jesus' miracles, raising the widow's son and Jairus' daughter (Luke 7:11–17; 8:40–56). This act would confirm Peter as an apostle of Jesus.

when the disciples heard that Peter was in Lydda, they sent two men
to him and urged him, "Please come at once!"
39Peter went with them, and when he arrived he was taken upstairs
to the room. All the widows stood around him, crying and showing
him the robes and other clothing that Dorcas had made while she
was still with them.
40Peter sent them all out of the room; then he got down on his
knees and prayed. Turning toward the dead woman, he said, "Tabitha, get up." She opened her eyes, and seeing Peter she sat up. 41He
took her by the hand and helped her to her feet. Then he called the
believers and the widows and presented her to them alive. 42This became known all over Joppa, and many people believed in the Lord.
43Peter stayed in Joppa for some time with a tanner named Simon.

Cornelius Calls for Peter

10 At Caesarea there was a man named Cornelius, a centurion
in what was known as the Italian Regiment. 2He and all his
family were devout and God-fearing; he gave generously to those in
need and prayed to God regularly. 3One day at about three in the afternoon he had a vision. He distinctly saw an angel of God, who came
to him and said, "Cornelius!"
4Cornelius stared at him in fear. "What is it, Lord?" he asked.
The angel answered, "Your prayers and gifts to the poor have come
up as a memorial offering before God. 5Now send men to Joppa to
bring back a man named Simon who is called Peter. 6He is staying
with Simon the tanner, whose house is by the sea."
7When the angel who spoke to him had gone, Cornelius called two
of his servants and a devout soldier who was one of his attendants.
8He told them everything that had happened and sent them to Joppa.

Peter's Vision

9About noon the following day as they were on their journey and
approaching the city, Peter went up on the roof to pray. 10He became
hungry and wanted something to eat, and while the meal was being
prepared, he fell into a trance. 11He saw heaven opened and something like a large sheet being let down to earth by its four corners. 12It
contained all kinds of four-footed animals, as well as reptiles of the
earth and birds of the air. 13Then a voice told him, "Get up, Peter. Kill
and eat."
14"Surely not, Lord!" Peter replied. "I have never eaten anything
impure or unclean."

APPLY If Peter were to visit your church, what would he say to the spiritual paralytics?

OPEN In your family, who has been in the military and what was their rank?

STUDY If you were the commander of a special forces unit in a foreign land for your government and God told you what he told Cornelius, what would you do?

APPLY 1. What is the closest you have come to seeing God move in the heart of someone you would never think would be open? **2.** Are you open to the possibility that God might use you in someone like this?

OPEN Which of these foods would you refuse to eat: Raw oysters? Sweet bread? Snails? Rattlesnake? Rocky Mountain oysters?

STUDY 1. If you had been told all of your life never to eat chicken entrails, what would you say if God suddenly told you to eat chicken entrails? **2.** Who is on their way to Peter's lodging at this very time (10:1–8)? Why would the vision of "unclean animals" apply to Cornelius? **3.** If you had been warned all of your life never

10:1 Cornelius. Romans typically used three names. Cornelius, a popular name taken on by the descendants of slaves who were released from slavery by the action of a P. Cornelius Sculla in 82 B.C., would have been this soldier's middle name. **a centurion.** Equivalent to the rank of an army captain in today's terms. **the Italian Regiment.** An auxiliary force stationed in the area composed of men recruited from Italy.

10:2 devout and God-fearing. The distinction between Gentile God-fearers (who believed in the true God and obeyed his ethical commands) and proselytes (who fully converted to Judaism) lay in the former's hesitancy to submit to the Jewish ceremonial laws. Cornelius demonstrated his faith by practicing the Jewish disciplines of prayer and almsgiving.

10:4 Lord. Cornelius did not yet know of Jesus, so this is an expression of respect for what Cornelius recognized as a divine visitor. **as a memorial offering before God.** Although Cornelius would not have been allowed to offer animal sacrifices in the temple, the angel lets him know that his heart-attitude of devotion to God is recognized as a sacrifice that is acceptable to God.

10:13 Kill and eat. The voice invites Peter to partake of any of the animals in the sheet, but Peter protests that he has never violated the dietary laws of the Jews.

10:14 Lord. Typically in Acts, this word is used as a title for Jesus. Peter may

15The voice spoke to him a second time, "Do not call anything impure that God has made clean."
16This happened three times, and immediately the sheet was taken
back to heaven.
17While Peter was wondering about the meaning of the vision, the
men sent by Cornelius found out where Simon's house was and
stopped at the gate. 18They called out, asking if Simon who was
known as Peter was staying there.
19While Peter was still thinking about the vision, the Spirit said to
him, "Simon, three[a] men are looking for you. 20So get up and go
downstairs. Do not hesitate to go with them, for I have sent them."
21Peter went down and said to the men, "I'm the one you're looking
for. Why have you come?"
22The men replied, "We have come from Cornelius the centurion.
He is a righteous and God-fearing man, who is respected by all the
Jewish people. A holy angel told him to have you come to his house
so that he could hear what you have to say." 23Then Peter invited the
men into the house to be his guests.

Peter at Cornelius's House

The next day Peter started out with them, and some of the brothers
from Joppa went along. 24The following day he arrived in Caesarea.
Cornelius was expecting them and had called together his relatives
and close friends. 25As Peter entered the house, Cornelius met him
and fell at his feet in reverence. 26But Peter made him get up. "Stand
up," he said, "I am only a man myself."
27Talking with him, Peter went inside and found a large gathering
of people. 28He said to them: "You are well aware that it is against our
law for a Jew to associate with a Gentile or visit him. But God has
shown me that I should not call any man impure or unclean. 29So
when I was sent for, I came without raising any objection. May I ask
why you sent for me?"
30Cornelius answered: "Four days ago I was in my house praying at
this hour, at three in the afternoon. Suddenly a man in shining
clothes stood before me 31and said, 'Cornelius, God has heard your
prayer and remembered your gifts to the poor. 32Send to Joppa for

[a]19 One early manuscript *two*; other manuscripts do not have the number.

to associate with "unclean" people or eat their food, how would you feel if you were Peter? **4.** Why do you think this story is in the Bible? Who would be the "impure and unclean" people in our society today? What would happen if you invited some of these people into your church (v. 23)?

APPLY **1.** What was the first time you personally were involved in an inter-racial or multi-ethnic Christian community? **2.** How did you feel about this experience at first?

OPEN When you were growing up what is the closest you came to visiting another culture?

STUDY **1.** What has happened in the last two days to set the stage for this passage (10:1–23)? **2.** If you were one of the "brothers" with Peter in this entourage, how would you be feeling as you entered the capital of the Roman imperial guard? **3.** Why would Cornelius be used to falling "at the feet in reverence" (v. 25)? What does Peter make perfectly clear? **4.** What would be comparable today to the meeting in verses 27–29? **5.** In the conversation between Cornelius and Peter, what emerges as a major breakthrough in God's plan of redemption? **6.** Why would the "circumcised believers" (v. 45) be astonished? Why would it be important for the uncircumcised

have recognized his dream as coming from the Lord, but he was not willing to simply follow the Lord's invitation to eat of the food.

10:15 In Mark 7:19 Jesus laid the groundwork for the pronouncement that, despite the laws of Leviticus 11, *food simply was not a spiritual issue.* Such laws had their place earlier in Jewish history as a means of separating them from the pagans in neighboring areas. Peter soon came to see that if God can pronounce that certain foods that were formerly unclean are now acceptable, he can do the same thing with people. If it is now acceptable for Jews to eat the food of Gentiles, then the Gentiles themselves must now be considered as acceptable to God as well.

10:23 While Jews would offer Gentiles hospitality, they typically would refuse to accept it from the Gentiles lest they violate dietary laws. Assuming the messengers arrived in early afternoon (v. 9), it would have been too late in the day to start the 30-mile journey back to Caesarea.

10:28 it is against our law. Jews would not associate with Gentiles partly because of the problems associated with their dietary laws. To have such associations rendered the Jew ceremonially unclean and thus ineligible for worship at the temple until a length of time had passed and a prescribed ceremony of cleansing had been performed. Because Gentile food may have come from unclean animals or even from an animal that had been sacrificed as part of a pagan ritual, eating with them was especially taboo. **Gentile.** Literally, "people of another race." This word, used only here in the New Testament, is the least offensive way possible for Jews to refer to Gentiles, as opposed to the derogatory term in 11:3 used by those upset with Peter. **But God has shown me.** Although the vision was about food, Peter caught on that its significance was about people. It is not one's culture or race or physical condition that makes a person "unclean," but sinful behavior and unbelief.

new believers to speak in tongues? **7.** Where do you think Peter got enough water to baptize Cornelius and the "large gathering" of guests? Why didn't Peter organize a catechism class before baptizing these Gentiles? **8.** What do you think Peter did with these new converts in the few days he stayed with them? **9.** As you look back on this entire chapter, what is amazing to you about this whole experience? If you had been there, what would you have learned?

APPLY 1. What is the closest you have come to being in a ministry where God broke through cultural barriers and left you amazed and astonished? **2.** If God asked you to invite someone like Cornelius to your group, what would you say? Who is the person that just popped into your mind?

OPEN When you were growing up, was it easier to get permission before you broke the rules or forgiveness after you broke the rules?

STUDY 1. What has happened in the previous chapter that has the leaders of the church in Jerusalem all upset? **2.** Do you think the "apostles and brothers" in Jerusalem would have approved of Peter's

Simon who is called Peter. He is a guest in the home of Simon the
tanner, who lives by the sea.' 33 So I sent for you immediately, and it
was good of you to come. Now we are all here in the presence of God
to listen to everything the Lord has commanded you to tell us."

34 Then Peter began to speak: "I now realize how true it is that God
does not show favoritism 35 but accepts men from every nation who
fear him and do what is right. 36 You know the message God sent to
the people of Israel, telling the good news of peace through Jesus
Christ, who is Lord of all. 37 You know what has happened throughout
Judea, beginning in Galilee after the baptism that John preached—
38 how God anointed Jesus of Nazareth with the Holy Spirit and power, and how he went around doing good and healing all who were
under the power of the devil, because God was with him.

39 "We are witnesses of everything he did in the country of the Jews
and in Jerusalem. They killed him by hanging him on a tree, 40 but God
raised him from the dead on the third day and caused him to be seen.
41 He was not seen by all the people, but by witnesses whom God had
already chosen—by us who ate and drank with him after he rose from
the dead. 42 He commanded us to preach to the people and to testify
that he is the one whom God appointed as judge of the living and the
dead. 43 All the prophets testify about him that everyone who believes
in him receives forgiveness of sins through his name."

44 While Peter was still speaking these words, the Holy Spirit came
on all who heard the message. 45 The circumcised believers who had
come with Peter were astonished that the gift of the Holy Spirit had
been poured out even on the Gentiles. 46 For they heard them speaking in tongues[a] and praising God.

Then Peter said, 47 "Can anyone keep these people from being baptized with water? They have received the Holy Spirit just as we have."
48 So he ordered that they be baptized in the name of Jesus Christ.
Then they asked Peter to stay with them for a few days.

Peter Explains His Actions

11 The apostles and the brothers throughout Judea heard that
the Gentiles also had received the word of God. 2 So when Peter went up to Jerusalem, the circumcised believers criticized him
3 and said, "You went into the house of uncircumcised men and ate
with them."

4 Peter began and explained everything to them precisely as it had
happened: 5 "I was in the city of Joppa praying, and in a trance I saw a

[a]46 Or *other languages*

10:45 This phenomenon shocked Peter's companions as it violated all they had known about traditional divisions between Jews and Gentiles. It meant that the Gentiles were on equal terms before God.

10:46 Luke's mention of the fact that these Gentiles spoke in tongues was not meant to teach that this sign must always accompany the outpouring of the Spirit, but was needed to convince the Jewish believers that the Gentiles' experience of the Spirit was no less than that of the apostles.

10:47 Baptism with the Spirit usually accompanied (2:38,41) or followed (8:15–17) baptism with water. Had the Spirit *not* come at this point, the Jewish believers may have insisted that before Cornelius and his family and friends could be baptized as true followers of the Messiah they must be circumcised and agree to observe Jewish traditions about food, the Sabbath, etc.

10:48 they asked Peter to stay with them for a few days. Violating custom once again, Peter, a Jew, accepted Gentile hospitality. This was another clear indication of his acceptance of them as full members of God's family.

11:2 the circumcised believers. At this point all the believers (except Cornelius and his household) were circumcised. These would be Christians who were Jews.

vision. I saw something like a large sheet being let down from heaven
by its four corners, and it came down to where I was. 6I looked into it
and saw four-footed animals of the earth, wild beasts, reptiles, and
birds of the air. 7Then I heard a voice telling me, 'Get up, Peter. Kill
and eat.'
8"I replied, 'Surely not, Lord! Nothing impure or unclean has ever
entered my mouth.'
9"The voice spoke from heaven a second time, 'Do not call anything
impure that God has made clean.' 10This happened three times, and
then it was all pulled up to heaven again.
11"Right then three men who had been sent to me from Caesarea
stopped at the house where I was staying. 12The Spirit told me to
have no hesitation about going with them. These six brothers also
went with me, and we entered the man's house. 13He told us how he
had seen an angel appear in his house and say, 'Send to Joppa for
Simon who is called Peter. 14He will bring you a message through
which you and all your household will be saved.'
15"As I began to speak, the Holy Spirit came on them as he had
come on us at the beginning. 16Then I remembered what the Lord had
said: 'John baptized with[a] water, but you will be baptized with the
Holy Spirit.' 17So if God gave them the same gift as he gave us, who
believed in the Lord Jesus Christ, who was I to think that I could oppose God?"
18When they heard this, they had no further objections and praised
God, saying, "So then, God has granted even the Gentiles repentance
unto life."

The Church in Antioch

19Now those who had been scattered by the persecution in connection with Stephen traveled as far as Phoenicia, Cyprus and Antioch,
telling the message only to Jews. 20Some of them, however, men from
Cyprus and Cyrene, went to Antioch and began to speak to Greeks
also, telling them the good news about the Lord Jesus. 21The Lord's
hand was with them, and a great number of people believed and
turned to the Lord.
22News of this reached the ears of the church at Jerusalem, and

[a]*16* Or *in*

trip to Caesarea if they had been asked? What is it about eating with uncircumcised men that is so awful? **3.** What would have been harder for you: going to see Cornelius or facing the music back in Jerusalem? **4.** Do you think they realized the tremendous significance of this event? What would have happened to the future of the church if they had said no? **5.** How does this event relate to the Great Commission (1:8; Matt. 28:19–20)?

APPLY 1. What hard and fast rule from your religious heritage did you get criticized for breaking? **2.** What are you going to say to your children when they do not go along with some of your rules?

OPEN What is the farthest from home you have ever been? Why were you there?

STUDY 1. Antioch was the third largest city in the Roman empire. What might the apostles feel as they hear the gospel is taking root there (v. 23)? **2.** If you had to write a character reference for Barnabas based on verses 22–26 (4:36–37) what would you say? From this profile, why did Barnabas recruit Saul (9:27–28)?

11:14 While not stated earlier, this shows why Cornelius was so eager to have Peter come: he had the message of how one might be delivered from sin and guilt to be in a right relationship with God.

11:17 *The gift of the Spirit is the indisputable mark of the Christian (a follower of Christ).* Peter highlights that the Spirit is given to *all* (Jew or Gentile) who believe in the Lord Jesus (Gal. 3:2).

11:18 While the Jerusalem church saw in principle that Gentiles were to be included in the church, tradition and prejudice prevented it from acting on that truth to any extent (ch. 15). Instead, it was the church at Antioch, to which Luke now turns his attention, that spearheaded the missionary movement.

11:19 Since there were Jewish communities throughout the Roman Empire, it is not at all unusual that the *Jewish believers* would have spread throughout such a large area. **Phoenicia.** Modern Lebanon. **Antioch.** Located about 300 miles north of Jerusalem, this was the Roman capital of the province of Syria. It was the third-largest city in the Roman Empire (after Rome and Alexandria), with a population estimated at 750,000, including a Jewish community of 25,000. A well-developed road system and access to a seaport made Antioch an important transportation and communication center. An early tradition teaches that Antioch was Luke's home.

11:20–21 These disciples from Cyprus and Cyrene were Jews who lived away from Judea and were use to interacting with Gentiles. The synagogues in Antioch were undoubtedly attended by Gentile God-fearers (like Cornelius) who were attracted to the ethics and values of Judaism while not accepting its customs regarding food, circumcision and Sabbath regulations. It is probably with these Gentiles that the believers shared the gospel. From this sharing of the gospel, many believed.

APPLY 1. How would the people you work with feel if they visited your church? **2.** Would these people be comfortable?

they sent Barnabas to Antioch. 23When he arrived and saw the evidence of the grace of God, he was glad and encouraged them all to
remain true to the Lord with all their hearts. 24He was a good man,
full of the Holy Spirit and faith, and a great number of people were
brought to the Lord.

25Then Barnabas went to Tarsus to look for Saul, 26and when he
found him, he brought him to Antioch. So for a whole year Barnabas
and Saul met with the church and taught great numbers of people.
The disciples were called Christians first at Antioch.

27During this time some prophets came down from Jerusalem to
Antioch. 28One of them, named Agabus, stood up and through the
Spirit predicted that a severe famine would spread over the entire
Roman world. (This happened during the reign of Claudius.) 29The
disciples, each according to his ability, decided to provide help for the
brothers living in Judea. 30This they did, sending their gift to the elders by Barnabas and Saul.

OPEN 1. Have you ever spent a night in jail? **2.** What movie or TV program about prison life first comes to your mind?

STUDY 1. Who was more surprised when they learned Peter had escaped: King Herod? The prayer group? Peter himself? **2.** If you were reading this passage for the first time, what question would pop into your mind? **3.** What happened during the week of Passover a few years before in Jerusalem? How did Peter act on the night of the Passover meal? Do you think these events were brought to mind when Peter sat in King Herod's prison? Why do you think King Herod added special security to guard Peter? **4.** How do you explain the miraculous jail break? If you had been Peter, what would you have done

Peter's Miraculous Escape From Prison

12 It was about this time that King Herod arrested some who
belonged to the church, intending to persecute them. 2He
had James, the brother of John, put to death with the sword. 3When
he saw that this pleased the Jews, he proceeded to seize Peter also.
This happened during the Feast of Unleavened Bread. 4After arresting
him, he put him in prison, handing him over to be guarded by four
squads of four soldiers each. Herod intended to bring him out for
public trial after the Passover.

5So Peter was kept in prison, but the church was earnestly praying
to God for him.

6The night before Herod was to bring him to trial, Peter was sleeping between two soldiers, bound with two chains, and sentries stood
guard at the entrance. 7Suddenly an angel of the Lord appeared and a
light shone in the cell. He struck Peter on the side and woke him up.
"Quick, get up!" he said, and the chains fell off Peter's wrists.
8Then the angel said to him, "Put on your clothes and sandals."
And Peter did so. "Wrap your cloak around you and follow me," the

---

11:23–24 Barnabas did not require the Gentile converts to submit to Jewish traditions, but only encouraged them to maintain a heartfelt loyalty to Jesus as Lord. This is the essence of Christian discipleship. His message, coupled with his character, drew many to faith.

11:26 The disciples were called Christians. By the time of Luke's writing, this Latin term was a widespread name for the believers. Since the only other places in the New Testament where this term is used were situations of ridicule and persecution (26:28; 1 Peter 4:16), it may have been originally a name used to mock the believers.

11:27–30 While the church in Antioch differed greatly from that in Jerusalem, they were linked by prophets and teachers who operated in both circles and by a common concern for the welfare of each other.

11:28 There was no single widespread famine during Claudius' reign (A.D. 41–54), but there were at least five localized famines during this period.

12:1 King Herod. This is Herod Agrippa I, the grandson of Herod the Great, who ruled when Jesus was born, and the nephew of Herod Antipas who governed Galilee during Jesus' ministry. Herod Agrippa I was popular with the Jews; some even wondered if he might be the Messiah who would free them from Rome. To further cultivate this popularity, he resumed the persecution of the church which had ceased upon Saul's conversion (9:31). Since Herod died in A.D. 44, this story precedes the visit of Saul and Barnabas to Jerusalem (v. 25; 11:27–30).

12:2–4 After receiving support for executing the apostle James, Herod arrested Peter as well. He was imprisoned, chained, and placed under constant guard while awaiting trial after Passover.

12:7 light shone. Peter was constantly guarded by four soldiers on six-hour shifts (vv. 4,6). Two soldiers were in the cell with Peter chained to their wrists, while the other two stood guard at the door. The description of the light, a common symbol of divine glory, underscores that this was a miraculous intervention by God.

12:8–10 In a trance-like state, Peter was led past the prison guards and through the main gate of the prison.

angel told him. 9Peter followed him out of the prison, but he had no
idea that what the angel was doing was really happening; he thought
he was seeing a vision. 10They passed the first and second guards and
came to the iron gate leading to the city. It opened for them by itself,
and they went through it. When they had walked the length of one
street, suddenly the angel left him.
11Then Peter came to himself and said, "Now I know without a
doubt that the Lord sent his angel and rescued me from Herod's
clutches and from everything the Jewish people were anticipating."
12When this had dawned on him, he went to the house of Mary the
mother of John, also called Mark, where many people had gathered
and were praying. 13Peter knocked at the outer entrance, and a servant girl named Rhoda came to answer the door. 14When she recognized Peter's voice, she was so overjoyed she ran back without
opening it and exclaimed, "Peter is at the door!"
15"You're out of your mind," they told her. When she kept insisting
that it was so, they said, "It must be his angel."
16But Peter kept on knocking, and when they opened the door and
saw him, they were astonished. 17Peter motioned with his hand for
them to be quiet and described how the Lord had brought him out of
prison. "Tell James and the brothers about this," he said, and then he
left for another place.
18In the morning, there was no small commotion among the soldiers as to what had become of Peter. 19After Herod had a thorough
search made for him and did not find him, he cross-examined the
guards and ordered that they be executed.

Herod's Death

Then Herod went from Judea to Caesarea and stayed there a while.
20He had been quarreling with the people of Tyre and Sidon; they now
joined together and sought an audience with him. Having secured
the support of Blastus, a trusted personal servant of the king, they
asked for peace, because they depended on the king's country for
their food supply.
21On the appointed day Herod, wearing his royal robes, sat on his

when the angel of God struck you on the side and said, "Quick, get up!"? **5.** Why do you think it took Peter so long to realize that this was not a dream? **6.** If one of your group was put to death and another was put in prison, what would that do to your group? **7.** How would you describe the response of the prayer group when Rhoda announced that Peter was at the door? Can you blame this prayer group for their disbelief? **8.** Why did God strike down King Herod? What is the lesson here for any leader?

APPLY 1. What is the difference between Peter's situation in this story and your situation right now? **2.** If the angel of God tapped you on the shoulder and said, "Quick, get up ... Put on your clothes and sandals ... Wrap your cloak around you and follow me," what would you say? **3.** What is it going to take for your prayer group to believe that the answer to your prayer is at the door?

12:11 the Lord ... rescued me from Herod's clutches. In Acts, there is no predictable pattern of how God will work. While Peter was released from prison, James, for whom the church undoubtedly prayed just as earnestly, was killed. Dorcas, a kindly but relatively insignificant woman (9:36–41), is raised from the dead while a bold, courageous *man like Stephen is not. The mystery is* only known in the secret counsel of God who works all things according to his will.

12:12 Mary the mother of John, also called Mark. This is the Mark who later wrote the Gospel bearing that name (v. 25; 13:5).

12:13–17 In a humorous way, Luke recounts how Peter was left standing at the gate of the courtyard while the disciples refused to believe that he could possibly be there! They were astonished, even though they had been "earnestly praying" for him (vv. 5,12)!

12:15 It must be his angel. Some believed that each person had a guardian angel who watched over that individual. Assuming that Peter was killed, the solution the disciples came up with was that Peter's angel had taken on Peter's form.

12:17 James. This is the half-brother of Jesus (Mark 6:3). James did not believe in Jesus as the Messiah during Jesus' ministry (John 7:5), but after the resurrection Jesus appeared to him (1 Cor. 15:7), qualifying James to be an apostle.

12:18–19 As in 5:22–24, the release of Peter threw the officials into confusion. Unable to explain how Peter could possibly escape without the complicity of the guards, Herod ordered them to be executed. Under Roman law, a guard who allowed his prisoner to escape suffered the fate intended for the prisoner.

12:20 The quarrel was not one of physical warfare, but of commercial and economic matters. Given the extent of Herod's political control, the cities of Tyre and Sidon would be dependent on his goodwill for their own economic stability.

throne and delivered a public address to the people. 22 They shouted,
"This is the voice of a god, not of a man." 23 Immediately, because
Herod did not give praise to God, an angel of the Lord struck him
down, and he was eaten by worms and died.
24 But the word of God continued to increase and spread.
25 When Barnabas and Saul had finished their mission, they returned from[a] Jerusalem, taking with them John, also called Mark.

Barnabas and Saul Sent Off

13 In the church at Antioch there were prophets and teachers:
Barnabas, Simeon called Niger, Lucius of Cyrene, Manaen
(who had been brought up with Herod the tetrarch) and Saul. 2 While
they were worshiping the Lord and fasting, the Holy Spirit said, "Set
apart for me Barnabas and Saul for the work to which I have called
them." 3 So after they had fasted and prayed, they placed their hands
on them and sent them off.

On Cyprus

4 The two of them, sent on their way by the Holy Spirit, went down
to Seleucia and sailed from there to Cyprus. 5 When they arrived at
Salamis, they proclaimed the word of God in the Jewish synagogues.
John was with them as their helper.
6 They traveled through the whole island until they came to Paphos.
There they met a Jewish sorcerer and false prophet named Bar-Jesus,
7 who was an attendant of the proconsul, Sergius Paulus. The proconsul, an intelligent man, sent for Barnabas and Saul because he wanted to hear the word of God. 8 But Elymas the sorcerer (for that is what
his name means) opposed them and tried to turn the proconsul from
the faith. 9 Then Saul, who was also called Paul, filled with the Holy
Spirit, looked straight at Elymas and said, 10 "You are a child of the
devil and an enemy of everything that is right! You are full of all kinds
of deceit and trickery. Will you never stop perverting the right ways of
the Lord? 11 Now the hand of the Lord is against you. You are going to
be blind, and for a time you will be unable to see the light of the sun."
Immediately mist and darkness came over him, and he groped

[a]25 Some manuscripts *to*

OPEN What is the closest you have come to going on a mission trip? How would you describe that experience?

STUDY 1. What do you know about the church at Antioch? Why do you think the missionary effort began in Antioch rather than in Jerusalem? What does the makeup of the leadership team in this church tell you? (Barnabas was from Cyprus and wealthy; Simeon was from Niger; Lucius was from a Greek city in North Africa and Manaen was from a high official family in the government.) **2.** What are four or five principles in this passage that the church should follow in carrying out any mission (vv. 1–3)? **3.** Why do you think Barnabas and Saul (Paul) started out in Cyprus and in the Jewish synagogue? **4.** How would you describe the encounter with the Jewish sorcerer/false prophet?

APPLY 1. What is the closest you have come to being part of a Christian group or ministry with a vision for reaching the world? **2.** If God called you to go as a missionary to a foreign land, what would you say?

12:22 This is the voice of a god, not of a man. While the Gentiles listening to Herod undoubtedly intended this chant as nothing more than royal flattery, Herod, as a Jew, should have repudiated such a blasphemous gesture. Instead, the Jewish historian Josephus specifically notes how Herod did *not* do so.

13:1 prophets and teachers. While the line between prophets and teachers is not that distinct, teachers were those who had a more sustained ministry of interpreting and applying Old Testament *Scriptures and the words of Jesus to* the life of the church. Whether or not the men mentioned here were *both* prophets and teachers is uncertain. It is clear Barnabas and Saul were recognized and respected as teachers (11:26).

13:3 they placed their hands on them. The laying on of hands was a sign of solidarity between the church and the missionaries, as well as a sign of committing them to God's grace.

13:5 Salamis. A Greek city with a substantial Jewish population. Throughout most of Saul (Paul's) travels, he made it a point to begin his ministry by preaching in the synagogues in the hopes that his listeners would believe in Jesus as the Messiah (vv. 14,42; 14:1; 16:13; 17:1,10; 18:4,19; 19:8).

13:6 Paphos. The Roman seat of power on Cyprus, about 90 miles from the port of Salamis on the western side of the island. **a Jewish sorcerer.** The practice of magic was forbidden to Jews. However, outside of Palestine some Jewish religious practices tended to reflect a great deal of the surrounding culture (19:17–19).

13:10 You are a child of the devil. His opposition to the gospel means he reflects the characteristics of Satan.

13:11 You are going to be blind. This was a temporary blindness which was meant as a warning for Elymas to repent. Whether or not it had the desired effect is not mentioned, but it was a sign that led Sergius Paulus to believe in the Lord (v. 12). We can presume that others also believed.

about, seeking someone to lead him by the hand. 12When the proconsul saw what had happened, he believed, for he was amazed at the
teaching about the Lord.

In Pisidian Antioch

13From Paphos, Paul and his companions sailed to Perga in Pamphylia, where John left them to return to Jerusalem. 14From Perga
they went on to Pisidian Antioch. On the Sabbath they entered the
synagogue and sat down. 15After the reading from the Law and the
Prophets, the synagogue rulers sent word to them, saying, "Brothers,
if you have a message of encouragement for the people, please
speak."
16Standing up, Paul motioned with his hand and said: "Men of Israel and you Gentiles who worship God, listen to me! 17The God of
the people of Israel chose our fathers; he made the people prosper
during their stay in Egypt, with mighty power he led them out of that
country, 18he endured their conduct[a] for about forty years in the
desert, 19he overthrew seven nations in Canaan and gave their land to
his people as their inheritance. 20All this took about 450 years.
"After this, God gave them judges until the time of Samuel the
prophet. 21Then the people asked for a king, and he gave them Saul
son of Kish, of the tribe of Benjamin, who ruled forty years. 22After removing Saul, he made David their king. He testified concerning him:
'I have found David son of Jesse a man after my own heart; he will do
everything I want him to do.'
23"From this man's descendants God has brought to Israel the Savior Jesus, as he promised. 24Before the coming of Jesus, John
preached repentance and baptism to all the people of Israel. 25As
John was completing his work, he said: 'Who do you think I am? I am
not that one. No, but he is coming after me, whose sandals I am not
worthy to untie.'
26"Brothers, children of Abraham, and you God-fearing Gentiles, it
is to us that this message of salvation has been sent. 27The people of
Jerusalem and their rulers did not recognize Jesus, yet in condemning him they fulfilled the words of the prophets that are read every
Sabbath. 28Though they found no proper ground for a death sentence, they asked Pilate to have him executed. 29When they had carried out all that was written about him, they took him down from the
tree and laid him in a tomb. 30But God raised him from the dead,
31and for many days he was seen by those who had traveled with him
from Galilee to Jerusalem. They are now his witnesses to our people.
32"We tell you the good news: What God promised our fathers 33he

[a]18 Some manuscripts *and cared for them*

OPEN 1. Who is the historian in your family—who likes to tell stories of your ancestors at family reunions? **2.** What is the longest boat trip you have taken? Were you seasick?

STUDY 1. How would you feel after traveling in a small boat in choppy waters and then by foot over the mountains? **2.** Why do you think John (Mark) left them when they landed in Pamphylia? How do you think Paul felt about Mark? How would you have felt? **3.** Did you notice that the leadership has shifted from Barnabas to Saul—who is now called Paul? What does this say about Barnabas? How would you have felt if you had been Barnabas? **4.** Where did Paul and Barnabas start their ministry? How does the message of Paul relate to the audience? If you were a Jew would you be able to follow Paul's message leading up to the proclamation of the forgiveness of sins through faith in Jesus Christ? **5.** How important is the resurrection of Jesus in the gospel? **6.** What is the punch line in the message (vv. 38–39)? How would you put this in your own words? **7.** How would you describe the impact of this message on the audience? Why do you think some of the Jews were "filled with jealousy" when "almost the whole city gathered" the next Sabbath? How would the Jewish establishment feel about Paul taking his message to the Gentiles? What did the Jewish establishment end up doing? **8.** How would you describe Paul and Barnabas' ministry in Antioch of Pisidia? How do you think Paul did on his first sermon? **9.** What is the principle in this passage for starting a new ministry in a new area?

APPLY 1. How did you do when you tried to share your

13:13–14 A 160-mile boat trip followed by a difficult journey over 100 miles across the Tarsus Mountains brought the missionaries to Antioch. **John left them to return.** No reason is given, but Paul's reaction in Acts 15:38 indicates he viewed this as some sort of failure on John (Mark's) part. **Antioch.** In the third century B.C., the Seleucid King Nicator founded 16 cities that he called by this name in honor of his father Antiochus.

13:20 450 years. This was approximately the period of living in Egypt, the traveling in the desert and the conquering of the land.

13:24–25 Chapters 18:24–25 and 19:3 hints that the influence of John the Baptist had spread widely among Jews throughout the empire, from North Africa even through Asia Minor.

13:26 The wall between the Jew and Gentile is broken down as Paul proclaims that the message of God's salvation is sent to the "children of Abraham, *and* you God-fearing Gentiles." These God-fearing Gentiles (10:2) would form a natural bridge from the synagogue to the pagan Gentile society.

faith story with someone else for the first time? **2.** Where is the hardest place for you to share your faith? **3.** When you run into someone who is violently opposed to your sharing your faith, what do you do?

has fulfilled for us, their children, by raising up Jesus. As it is written
in the second Psalm:

" 'You are my Son;
today I have become your Father.'[a][b]

34The fact that God raised him from the dead, never to decay, is stated
in these words:

" 'I will give you the holy and sure blessings promised to David.'[c]

35So it is stated elsewhere:

" 'You will not let your Holy One see decay.'[d]

36"For when David had served God's purpose in his own generation, he fell asleep; he was buried with his fathers and his body decayed. 37But the one whom God raised from the dead did not see
decay.
38"Therefore, my brothers, I want you to know that through Jesus
the forgiveness of sins is proclaimed to you. 39Through him everyone
who believes is justified from everything you could not be justified
from by the law of Moses. 40Take care that what the prophets have
said does not happen to you:

41" 'Look, you scoffers,
wonder and perish,
for I am going to do something in your days
that you would never believe,
even if someone told you.'[e]"

42As Paul and Barnabas were leaving the synagogue, the people invited them to speak further about these things on the next Sabbath.
43When the congregation was dismissed, many of the Jews and devout converts to Judaism followed Paul and Barnabas, who talked
with them and urged them to continue in the grace of God.
44On the next Sabbath almost the whole city gathered to hear the

[a]33 Or *have begotten you* [b]33 Psalm 2:7 [c]34 Isaiah 55:3 [d]35 Psalm 16:10 [e]41 Hab. 1:5

13:34–35 The next two quotations from Isaiah 55:3 and Psalm 16:10 are closely linked. Paul's point was to show that all the holy blessings God has promised to give his people flow from the resurrection of the Holy One, Jesus (2:24–28).

13:36–37 As did Peter in 2:29, Paul reminds his listeners that David's death and subsequent decay proves that the quoted passages refer to another, to one who would not be left to "rot in the grave" (GNB).

13:38 the forgiveness of sins. This phrase sums up all that salvation involves. *It means the believer's guilt* is atoned for so that he or she enjoys a restored relationship with God free from shame or anxiety over the past (Eph. 1:7); it means the believer is being freed from the power of sin as his or her desires conform more and more to God's will (Rom. 6:18–19); it means the believer can experience a relationship of peace and intimacy with God since that which has blocked that relationship has been removed (1 Thess. 5:9–10).

13:39 everyone. Whereas in 2:39, Peter undoubtedly thought his "all" meant all Jews, Paul literally means "everyone," Jew or Gentile. The message of the Gospel of Jesus is not restricted any longer to any one group of people. **justified.** This term, borrowed from the legal system of Paul's day, is a favorite way for Paul to describe what God has done for us in Jesus (Rom. 3:24; 5:1; Gal. 3:8). In Paul's mind, this is closely tied to his view of the atonement (Lev. 16; Rom. 3:25). Because Jesus' death was a sacrifice of atonement for sin, the believer is set right before God and pronounced not guilty of sin. **from everything you could not be justified from by the law of Moses.** The point is not that people could actually be justified from *some* things by keeping the Law and only needed Christ to make up for those areas one had trouble with, but that the Law really never served to justify anyone. In Christ, a way of being right with God is proclaimed that the Law could never give since knowledge of the Law only made people more aware of their failure to keep it (Rom. 3:20; 8:3; Gal. 3:23–24).

13:43 devout converts to Judaism. These would have been Gentiles who had fully submitted to the Jewish traditions regarding circumcision, dietary laws and Sabbath observance.

word of the Lord. [45]When the Jews saw the crowds, they were filled
with jealousy and talked abusively against what Paul was saying.
[46]Then Paul and Barnabas answered them boldly: "We had to speak
the word of God to you first. Since you reject it and do not consider
yourselves worthy of eternal life, we now turn to the Gentiles. [47]For
this is what the Lord has commanded us:

" 'I have made you[a] a light for the Gentiles,
that you[a] may bring salvation to the ends of the earth.'[b]"

[48]When the Gentiles heard this, they were glad and honored the
word of the Lord; and all who were appointed for eternal life believed.
[49]The word of the Lord spread through the whole region. [50]But the
Jews incited the God-fearing women of high standing and the leading
men of the city. They stirred up persecution against Paul and Barnabas,
and expelled them from their region. [51]So they shook the dust
from their feet in protest against them and went to Iconium. [52]And
the disciples were filled with joy and with the Holy Spirit.

In Iconium

14 At Iconium Paul and Barnabas went as usual into the Jewish
synagogue. There they spoke so effectively that a great number
of Jews and Gentiles believed. [2]But the Jews who refused to believe
stirred up the Gentiles and poisoned their minds against the
brothers. [3]So Paul and Barnabas spent considerable time there,
speaking boldly for the Lord, who confirmed the message of his
grace by enabling them to do miraculous signs and wonders. [4]The
people of the city were divided; some sided with the Jews, others with
the apostles. [5]There was a plot afoot among the Gentiles and Jews,
together with their leaders, to mistreat them and stone them. [6]But
they found out about it and fled to the Lycaonian cities of Lystra and
Derbe and to the surrounding country, [7]where they continued to
preach the good news.

In Lystra and Derbe

[8]In Lystra there sat a man crippled in his feet, who was lame from
birth and had never walked. [9]He listened to Paul as he was speaking.

[a]47 The Greek is singular. [b]47 Isaiah 49:6

OPEN In your youthful idealism, for what social, political or religious causes were you willing to "go to the mat," if need be? Did you ever have to?

STUDY 1. If you were sent on a preaching mission and you were almost stoned in one city and stoned so badly in the next city that they thought you were dead, how would you feel about continuing your mission? **2.** Saul is now referred to as Paul. How would you compare the reception Paul and Barnabas got in Iconium to the reception they got in Antioch (13:48–52)? **3.** How do "signs and wonders" confirm the message of the gospel? How do you feel about "signs and wonders" today? **4.** In Lystra, how do you like the way Paul and Barnabas handled the crowd when they wanted to make them "gods in human form"? **5.** What is different

13:48 all who were appointed for eternal life believed. The fact that these Gentiles responded to the Gospel with faith is the evidence that they too have been written in God's figurative book of life (Ex. 32:32; Ps. 69:28; Isa. 4:3; Dan. 12:1; Luke 10:20; Rev. 13:8; 20:12; 21:27)..

13:50 God-fearing women of high standing. These were Gentile women who respected the Jewish teachings and had ties with the synagogue.

13:51 shook the dust from their feet. Typically, Jews entering Palestine from a Gentile area wiped off their feet as a symbol of cleansing themselves from any traces of Gentile contamination picked up before entering the Holy Land. **Iconium.** A city about 100 miles east of Pisidian Antioch.

14:1–7 The disciples faced a situation in Iconium similar to that of Pisidian Antioch (ch. 13). While many Jews and Gentiles believed, opposition intensified to the point that Paul and Barnabas had to flee for their lives.

14:6 the Lycaonian cities of Lystra and Derbe. Iconium had originally been a Phrygian settlement. Although it was in the province of Lycaonia, its residents still considered themselves distinct from others in the province. Lystra was about 20 miles to the southwest of Iconium, and Derbe lay 60 miles further to the southeast.

14:8 The small Jewish community in Lystra (16:1–3) apparently did not have a synagogue. Adopting a new strategy which brought the gospel directly to the Gentiles, Paul probably preached in the Greek forum, the site of the local marketplace and gathering place for public discussion.

about the message Paul and Barnabas gives in this situation? **6.** What does the fact that Jews from Antioch 100 miles away came to oppose Paul and Barnabas tell you about their preaching mission? **7.** They called Barnabas, Zeus, and Paul they called Hermes because he was the chief speaker. In your church or Christian fellowship, who is Zeus and who is Hermes? Who are you more like?

APPLY 1. In your spiritual journey, what is the closest you have come to getting "stoned" for sharing your faith? **2.** On a scale from 1 to 10 what is your resiliency when you get beaten down? How long does it take for you to recover and get back into the game?

OPEN Who would be the best used car dealer in your group?

STUDY 1. What was Paul and Barnabas' purpose in revisiting the cities where they had preached? What is a basic missionary principle here for a church planting ministry? **2.** Would you describe Paul and Barnabas as pioneers or nesters? **3.** Why did they return to their home base and give a report?

APPLY 1. Have you ever had a yearning to do something different with your life? **2.** What is keeping you from doing it?

Paul looked directly at him, saw that he had faith to be healed
10 and
called out, "Stand up on your feet!" At that, the man jumped up and
began to walk.

11 When the crowd saw what Paul had done, they shouted in the
Lycaonian language, "The gods have come down to us in human
form!"
12 Barnabas they called Zeus, and Paul they called Hermes because he was the chief speaker.
13 The priest of Zeus, whose temple
was just outside the city, brought bulls and wreaths to the city gates
because he and the crowd wanted to offer sacrifices to them.

14 But when the apostles Barnabas and Paul heard of this, they tore
their clothes and rushed out into the crowd, shouting:
15 "Men, why
are you doing this? We too are only men, human like you. We are
bringing you good news, telling you to turn from these worthless
things to the living God, who made heaven and earth and sea and everything in them.
16 In the past, he let all nations go their own way.
17 Yet he has not left himself without testimony: He has shown kindness by giving you rain from heaven and crops in their seasons; he
provides you with plenty of food and fills your hearts with joy."
18 Even with these words, they had difficulty keeping the crowd from
sacrificing to them.

19 Then some Jews came from Antioch and Iconium and won the
crowd over. They stoned Paul and dragged him outside the city, thinking he was dead.
20 But after the disciples had gathered around him,
he got up and went back into the city. The next day he and Barnabas
left for Derbe.

The Return to Antioch in Syria

21 They preached the good news in that city and won a large number of disciples. Then they returned to Lystra, Iconium and Antioch,
22 strengthening the disciples and encouraging them to remain true to
the faith. "We must go through many hardships to enter the kingdom
of God," they said.
23 Paul and Barnabas appointed elders[a] for them in
each church and, with prayer and fasting, committed them to the
Lord, in whom they had put their trust.
24 After going through Pisidia,
they came into Pamphylia,
25 and when they had preached the word in
Perga, they went down to Attalia.

26 From Attalia they sailed back to Antioch, where they had been
committed to the grace of God for the work they had now completed.
27 On arriving there, they gathered the church together and reported
all that God had done through them and how he had opened the door
of faith to the Gentiles.
28 And they stayed there a long time with the
disciples.

[a]23 Or *Barnabas ordained elders;* or *Barnabas had elders elected*

14:12 Hermes ... the chief speaker. Zeus was the chief god among the Greek deities, while Hermes was the herald of the gods.

14:23 elders. This is the first mention of elders outside of Palestine.

14:27 reported. The tense of the Greek implies they "kept on reporting" what had happened. This was probably because the church was actually a combination of small house groups that met throughout the city as at this point Christians had no common meeting places. **opened the door of faith to the Gentiles.** God had made a way for all Jews and Gentiles to believe. It is precisely the nature of this report that led to the conflict in chapter 15 and the important council that resulted from it.

The Council at Jerusalem

15 Some men came down from Judea to Antioch and were
teaching the brothers: "Unless you are circumcised, according to the custom taught by Moses, you cannot be saved." 2This
brought Paul and Barnabas into sharp dispute and debate with them.
So Paul and Barnabas were appointed, along with some other believers, to go up to Jerusalem to see the apostles and elders about this
question. 3The church sent them on their way, and as they traveled
through Phoenicia and Samaria, they told how the Gentiles had been
converted. This news made all the brothers very glad. 4When they
came to Jerusalem, they were welcomed by the church and the apostles and elders, to whom they reported everything God had done
through them.
5Then some of the believers who belonged to the party of the Pharisees stood up and said, "The Gentiles must be circumcised and required to obey the law of Moses."
6The apostles and elders met to consider this question. 7After much
discussion, Peter got up and addressed them: "Brothers, you know
that some time ago God made a choice among you that the Gentiles
might hear from my lips the message of the gospel and believe. 8God,
who knows the heart, showed that he accepted them by giving the
Holy Spirit to them, just as he did to us. 9He made no distinction between us and them, for he purified their hearts by faith. 10Now then,
why do you try to test God by putting on the necks of the disciples a
yoke that neither we nor our fathers have been able to bear? 11No! We
believe it is through the grace of our Lord Jesus that we are saved,
just as they are."
12The whole assembly became silent as they listened to Barnabas
and Paul telling about the miraculous signs and wonders God had
done among the Gentiles through them. 13When they finished, James
spoke up: "Brothers, listen to me. 14Simon[a] has described to us how
God at first showed his concern by taking from the Gentiles a people
for himself. 15The words of the prophets are in agreement with this,
as it is written:

16" 'After this I will return
and rebuild David's fallen tent.

[a]14 Greek *Simeon,* a variant of *Simon;* that is, Peter

OPEN What is the closest you have come to getting called on the carpet in school?

STUDY 1. If you had experienced a real breakthrough in presenting the gospel to Gentiles, how would you feel if someone from headquarters showed up and said that these Gentiles must become Jews first before they could become Christians? **2.** Have you ever been in a situation like this where you had two parties in the church who insisted on their own way—and you were caught in the middle? How do you think Peter and James (the brother of Jesus) handled the situation? **3.** As you look back on this issue today, do you think the question of circumcision was that important? What was at stake here? **4.** What did the Council end up expecting from Gentile Christians? Why did the Council insist on these things? What issue troubles your church today that could be solved if you applied these same principles? **5.** If the question of circumcision was resolved by this Council, why did this issue keep cropping up for the next twenty to thirty years?

APPLY 1. How do you look upon the rules and regulations of the church? How has that changed over the years? Why? **2.** How do you deal with "weaker" brothers that still hold to traditions that you do not agree with? **3.** What are you going to say when your children rebel against some of the traditions that you feel are sacred?

15:1–4 The controversy surrounding circumcision stirred up such a debate that the church felt it necessary to call together the recognized leaders from Jerusalem and Antioch to settle the issue. This is considered to be the first Church Council.

15:5 the believers who belonged to the party of the Pharisees. The resistance to allowing Gentiles into the church originated with a small but influential sect widely respected for its adherence to the Old Testament Law and traditions. Their concern arose from a genuine desire to insure that God's honor was not violated through disregard of his Law. To them, the offer of the gospel apart from the Law was inconceivable. How could Jews possibly even share in the Lord's Supper (often connected to an actual meal) when the presence of Gentiles among them would mean defilement? The only reasonable solution these believers could see was that Gentiles needed to become Jewish. Only then could both the purity and unity of the church be maintained.

15:7–8 As part of the discussion, Peter recounts his experience with Cornelius which may have occurred 10 or more years earlier (10:1–11:18). The fact that Cornelius experienced the presence of the Spirit in the same way the disciples did was proof to Peter that God accepted the Gentiles quite apart from the practice of Jewish law.

15:13–21 James was a leader of the Jerusalem church, and the ultimate decision as to the position of the Jerusalem church was the leadership's decision to make. Since in Galatians 2:11–13 James appears to have represented those who believed that Gentiles could not be considered equal members of the church with Jews, it may be that this council was the turning point when he realized the scope of Jesus' mission.

15:16–18 The original context of the prophecy was the anticipation of the

OPEN 1. What is the most difficult letter you have had to write? 2. What is the most difficult letter you have received?

STUDY 1. How do you like the way the Council in Jerusalem handled the situation in Antioch? What are some basic principles you see here for handling delicate issues in the church? 2. If you had been brought up in a strict religion and you had been taught to have nothing to do with pagans who ate food from the pagan temple restaurant, how would you feel if you heard that these people were going to join your church? 3. If you were going to start a new church in your area, would you go after the religious crowd or the pagan crowd?

APPLY Have you ever been in a situation where cultural background or family upbringing divided the group? How did you overcome these obstacles?

Its ruins I will rebuild,
and I will restore it,
17 that the remnant of men may seek the Lord,
and all the Gentiles who bear my name,
says the Lord, who does these things'[a]
18 that have been known for ages.[b]

19 "It is my judgment, therefore, that we should not make it difficult
for the Gentiles who are turning to God. 20 Instead we should write to
them, telling them to abstain from food polluted by idols, from sexual
immorality, from the meat of strangled animals and from blood. 21 For
Moses has been preached in every city from the earliest times and is
read in the synagogues on every Sabbath."

The Council's Letter to Gentile Believers

22 Then the apostles and elders, with the whole church, decided to
choose some of their own men and send them to Antioch with Paul
and Barnabas. They chose Judas (called Barsabbas) and Silas, two
men who were leaders among the brothers. 23 With them they sent the
following letter:

The apostles and elders, your brothers,

To the Gentile believers in Antioch, Syria and Cilicia:

Greetings.

24 We have heard that some went out from us without our authorization and disturbed you, troubling your minds by what
they said. 25 So we all agreed to choose some men and send them
to you with our dear friends Barnabas and Paul— 26 men who
have risked their lives for the name of our Lord Jesus Christ.
27 Therefore we are sending Judas and Silas to confirm by word of
mouth what we are writing. 28 It seemed good to the Holy Spirit
and to us not to burden you with anything beyond the following
requirements: 29 You are to abstain from food sacrificed to idols,
from blood, from the meat of strangled animals and from sexual
immorality. You will do well to avoid these things.

Farewell.

[a] 17 Amos 9:11,12 [b] 17,18 Some manuscripts *things'— / 18known to the Lord for ages is his work*

destruction of Israel (722 B.C.), after which God would one day return the nation to its former glory as in David's day.

15:20 telling them to abstain. These considerations sum up the laws in Leviticus 17–18 that applied to Israel and all foreigners who lived within her borders. **food polluted.** In Gentile areas meat was sold only after the animal had been sacrificed as part of a worship service to an idol. The eating of such food was later to be a source of controversy between Jewish and Gentile believers in Rome (Rom. 14:1–8) and Corinth (1 Cor. 8). **sexual immorality.** This may be related to "the pollution of idols" since idolatry sometimes involved ritual prostitution (1 Cor. 6:12–20). **meat of strangled animals and from blood.** Jews were forbidden to eat meat that had any blood in it (Lev. 17:10–14). Gentiles would make the sharing of meals with Jewish believers easier if they would respect this tradition.

15:27 Judas. Probably an elder in the Jerusalem church, but nothing more is known about him. **Silas.** Probably also an elder, but one who plays a prominent part in the rest of Acts (2 Cor. 1:19; 1 Thess. 1:1; 1 Peter 5:12).

15:28 burden you. The council recognized that these regulations were over and above what is needed for salvation. It was not necessary that the Gentiles submit to these standards to be right with God, but it was important that they do so to avoid alienating Jews from the gospel.

15:29 You will do well to avoid these things. The implication is that there is no other requirement (v. 5)—to be imposed upon the Gentile believers.

30The men were sent off and went down to Antioch, where they
gathered the church together and delivered the letter. 31The people
read it and were glad for its encouraging message. 32Judas and Silas,
who themselves were prophets, said much to encourage and
strengthen the brothers. 33After spending some time there, they were
sent off by the brothers with the blessing of peace to return to those
who had sent them.[a] 35But Paul and Barnabas remained in Antioch,
where they and many others taught and preached the word of the
Lord.

Disagreement Between Paul and Barnabas

36Some time later Paul said to Barnabas, "Let us go back and visit
the brothers in all the towns where we preached the word of the Lord
and see how they are doing." 37Barnabas wanted to take John, also
called Mark, with them, 38but Paul did not think it wise to take him,
because he had deserted them in Pamphylia and had not continued
with them in the work. 39They had such a sharp disagreement that
they parted company. Barnabas took Mark and sailed for Cyprus,
40but Paul chose Silas and left, commended by the brothers to the
grace of the Lord. 41He went through Syria and Cilicia, strengthening
the churches.

Timothy Joins Paul and Silas

16 He came to Derbe and then to Lystra, where a disciple named
Timothy lived, whose mother was a Jewess and a believer,
but whose father was a Greek. 2The brothers at Lystra and Iconium
spoke well of him. 3Paul wanted to take him along on the journey, so
he circumcised him because of the Jews who lived in that area, for
they all knew that his father was a Greek. 4As they traveled from town
to town, they delivered the decisions reached by the apostles and elders in Jerusalem for the people to obey. 5So the churches were
strengthened in the faith and grew daily in numbers.

Paul's Vision of the Man of Macedonia

6Paul and his companions traveled throughout the region of Phrygia and Galatia, having been kept by the Holy Spirit from preaching the

[a]33 Some manuscripts *them,* 34*but Silas decided to remain there*

OPEN What "break-up" was hardest for you and why: Moving? Losing your first girl/boyfriend? Empty nest? Closing shop? Retiring?

STUDY 1. What really motivated Paul and Barnabas to go on the second missionary journey? **2.** Do you think they should have allowed John (Mark) to go with them? How do you think Barnabas felt? (Remember John Mark was his cousin.) **3.** How would you have resolved the dispute? **4.** Why do you think Paul circumcised Timothy when he believed circumcision was unnecessary? What is the principle here for the church today?

APPLY 1. In your spiritual pilgrimage, when have you had to follow your own conscience on an issue? **2.** When it comes to "gray areas" on Christian practice, where do you draw the line?

OPEN 1. What do you know about Alexander the Great? **2.** How many times have you changed course in your life since high school?

15:32 encourage. The ministry involved in the prophetic gift of Judas and Silas is captured by this word.

15:38 he had deserted them. While the word used to describe Mark's leaving in 13:13 is a neutral one that implies nothing negative, the word used here is related to apostasy. Luke does not tell us why Mark left, but Paul certainly viewed it as a serious defect and was unwilling to let him try again.

15:39–40 a sharp disagreement. Barnabas' concern may have been motivated in part by the fact that Mark was his cousin (Col. 4:10), but it is characteristic of Barnabas. Years before, it was he who insisted that Paul be given a chance to prove himself to the apostles (9:27) and who recognized Paul's calling (11:25–26). On the other hand, Paul was concerned about the immediate needs and demands of such a rigorous journey. Undoubtedly Mark's earlier departure placed increased demands on Paul and Barnabas, and he was unwilling to risk that again. While the ongoing action focuses on Paul and Silas, Barnabas and Mark also left Antioch on a missionary trip as they returned to Cyprus (13:4–12).

15:41–16:5 Whereas the limits of Paul's first journey were reached by an overland trek eastward to the border of Cilicia, this time he went west, going overland through the provinces until he came to Derbe (v. 1; 14:20).

16:1–3 As the son of a Jewish woman, Jewish law said Timothy ought to have been circumcised as an infant. Perhaps his Gentile father (who apparently was dead at the time of Paul's visit) had forbidden it. At any rate, for Paul to allow Timothy, a Jew, to accompany him apart from following the age-old Jewish custom of circumcision would communicate to other Jews that he had no regard whatsoever for their honored traditions.

16:6–7 the Holy Spirit ... the Spirit of Jesus. Luke clearly identifies the ongoing work of Jesus with the agency of the Holy Spirit in the lives of the apostles.

STUDY **1.** How many "closed doors" did Paul run into in this passage? What do you think the "Holy Spirit" and the "Spirit of Jesus" used to close these doors? If you had been Paul, what would you have done when you reached Troas? **2.** How would you describe what caused Paul to cross over into modern day Europe? Do you think Paul had any idea of the significance of this decision? **3.** Who is the "we" in verse 10 referring to? **4.** What does Paul do to connect with people in this pagan culture? Where would you find these people today in our society?

APPLY **1.** If God gave you a vision in the night of a man from a faraway land asking you to come and share your faith in their land, what would you say? **2.** Where is God asking you to go that is just as much of a challenge for you today?

OPEN **1.** What is the worst punishment you remember getting as a kid? **2.** What do you do to lift your spirits when you are "down in the dumps"?

STUDY **1.** If God told you to go to a foreign land and share your faith and you ended up in jail after being severely beaten, how would you be feeling? **2.** What do you think it was about the fortune teller that got on Paul's nerves? What would you have done in that situation? **3.** How would you have felt if you were the owners of the fortune teller? Who do the owners remind you of today? **4.** Do you see any irony in the charge of the owners that Paul and Silas were "throwing our city into an uproar"?

word in the province of Asia. 7When they came to the border of Mysia,
they tried to enter Bithynia, but the Spirit of Jesus would not allow
them to. 8So they passed by Mysia and went down to Troas. 9During
the night Paul had a vision of a man of Macedonia standing and
begging him, "Come over to Macedonia and help us." 10After Paul had
seen the vision, we got ready at once to leave for Macedonia, concluding that God had called us to preach the gospel to them.

Lydia's Conversion in Philippi

11From Troas we put out to sea and sailed straight for Samothrace,
and the next day on to Neapolis. 12From there we traveled to Philippi,
a Roman colony and the leading city of that district of Macedonia.
And we stayed there several days.
13On the Sabbath we went outside the city gate to the river, where
we expected to find a place of prayer. We sat down and began to
speak to the women who had gathered there. 14One of those listening
was a woman named Lydia, a dealer in purple cloth from the city of
Thyatira, who was a worshiper of God. The Lord opened her heart to
respond to Paul's message. 15When she and the members of her
household were baptized, she invited us to her home. "If you consider me a believer in the Lord," she said, "come and stay at my
house." And she persuaded us.

Paul and Silas in Prison

16Once when we were going to the place of prayer, we were met by
a slave girl who had a spirit by which she predicted the future. She
earned a great deal of money for her owners by fortune-telling. 17This
girl followed Paul and the rest of us, shouting, "These men are servants of the Most High God, who are telling you the way to be saved."
18She kept this up for many days. Finally Paul became so troubled
that he turned around and said to the spirit, "In the name of Jesus
Christ I command you to come out of her!" At that moment the spirit
left her.
19When the owners of the slave girl realized that their hope of making money was gone, they seized Paul and Silas and dragged them
into the marketplace to face the authorities. 20They brought them before the magistrates and said, "These men are Jews, and are throwing
our city into an uproar 21by advocating customs unlawful for us Romans to accept or practice."

16:7 would not allow them to. Why Jesus would not allow Paul and Silas and Timothy to preach in Asia and Bithynia is not given. Later on, the apostle Peter was in contact with churches in that area, so they were not left bereft of the gospel (1 Peter 1:1).

16:8 down to Troas. An important seaport on the Aegean Sea. While it appears Paul did not do any evangelistic work there at this time, he did do so later on (2 Cor. 2:12).

16:9 Macedonia. This area of northern Greece had been the dominant power under Alexander the Great in the fourth century B.C.

16:14 a woman named Lydia. Macedonian women enjoyed far more freedom and opportunities than many of their counterparts elsewhere. Lydia was a businesswoman involved in selling purple cloth, a luxury item indicating that she was a woman of wealth. **Thyatira.** A city in the province of Asia noted for its dyeing industry. Evidence indicates that there was a Jewish community in Thyatira, which probably influenced Lydia toward faith in the God of the Jews.

16:16 a spirit by which she predicted the future. Literally this can be translated as "a spirit, a python." A snake was supposed to guard the oracle of Delphi and therefore it became a common symbol of a fortune-teller.

16:18 While what the girl said was true, the spirit that motivated her was not one Paul desired as a collaborator in his mission. Undoubtedly, it attracted attention but made Paul and Silas appear more as magicians than as representatives of God. Thus, Paul commanded the spirit to leave her.

22 The crowd joined in the attack against Paul and Silas, and the
magistrates ordered them to be stripped and beaten. 23 After they had
been severely flogged, they were thrown into prison, and the jailer
was commanded to guard them carefully. 24 Upon receiving such
orders, he put them in the inner cell and fastened their feet in the
stocks.

25 About midnight Paul and Silas were praying and singing hymns to
God, and the other prisoners were listening to them. 26 Suddenly
there was such a violent earthquake that the foundations of the
prison were shaken. At once all the prison doors flew open, and
everybody's chains came loose. 27 The jailer woke up, and when he
saw the prison doors open, he drew his sword and was about to kill
himself because he thought the prisoners had escaped. 28 But Paul
shouted, "Don't harm yourself! We are all here!"

29 The jailer called for lights, rushed in and fell trembling before
Paul and Silas. 30 He then brought them out and asked, "Sirs, what
must I do to be saved?"

31 They replied, "Believe in the Lord Jesus, and you will be saved—
you and your household." 32 Then they spoke the word of the Lord to
him and to all the others in his house. 33 At that hour of the night the
jailer took them and washed their wounds; then immediately he and
all his family were baptized. 34 The jailer brought them into his house
and set a meal before them; he was filled with joy because he had
come to believe in God—he and his whole family.

35 When it was daylight, the magistrates sent their officers to the
jailer with the order: "Release those men." 36 The jailer told Paul, "The
magistrates have ordered that you and Silas be released. Now you
can leave. Go in peace."

37 But Paul said to the officers: "They beat us publicly without a trial, even though we are Roman citizens, and threw us into prison. And
now do they want to get rid of us quietly? No! Let them come themselves and escort us out."

38 The officers reported this to the magistrates, and when they
heard that Paul and Silas were Roman citizens, they were alarmed.
39 They came to appease them and escorted them from the prison, requesting them to leave the city. 40 After Paul and Silas came out of the
prison, they went to Lydia's house, where they met with the brothers
and encouraged them. Then they left.

What do you think Paul was advocating that was "unlawful" for Romans? **5.** What do you think caused the jailer to want to be saved? How much did he know about the gospel other than what he observed in Paul's life? **6.** How would you paraphrase the words "believe on the Lord Jesus Christ and you will be saved—you and your household"? Would your church approve of baptizing the jailer and his household in this situation? **7.** Why do you think Paul and Silas insisted on an apology from the magistrates? How do you think the magistrates felt? **8.** In the previous passage (16:11–15), Lydia (a wealthy businesswoman), and her household were converted, and in this passage a jailer and his household are converted. If these were the only Christians in town when Paul left, what would they have going for them in starting a new church?

APPLY What is the most dramatic change you have ever made in your life? Was God a part of that change? Have your friends helped you through major life-transitions?

16:22 stripped and beaten. The authorities should have put Paul and Silas in custody to be formally tried; but, pressured by the crowds, they publicly beat them without trial.

16:24 he put them in the inner cell and fastened their feet in the stocks. Why these prisoners were considered worthy of such precautions is uncertain, but it sets up a contrast with God's ability to free them in spite of the security measures taken to oppress them. The stocks were locked wooden boards that clasped about one's ankles—making walking, or any movement, impossible.

16:31 Believe in the Lord Jesus, and you will be saved. Paul's response is summed up in this single phrase: deliverance from the power of evil and from divine judgment is given to those who entrust themselves to Jesus as their Lord. **you and your household.** This summary statement was followed by a late-night teaching session about Jesus in the jailer's house, probably attached to the prison.

16:35–40 The following morning, the soldiers came to the prison with orders from the magistrates to send Paul and Silas on their way. It does not appear they connected the earthquake with the imprisonment of the missionaries. They simply wanted to expel Paul and Silas from town to avoid any further trouble. However, the missionaries refused to go without a personal apology from the magistrates for their breach of justice. This was not simply a matter of self-vindication nor a matter of insisting on the proper administration of justice. It was especially important for the protection of the young church in Philippi. By being escorted out of the prison by the magistrates, a signal would be communicated to the community at large that the charges had been false. As a result, the community would be more likely to leave the young church alone.

OPEN Have you ever dreamed of having a sailboat and living in a port city? Where?

STUDY **1.** What do you know about the city of Thessalonica? Why do you think Paul came here to minister? **2.** Among those who responded are "God-fearing Greeks" and "prominent women." Why would these people be in a Jewish synagogue and why would they be especially receptive to the gospel? **3.** If you were Paul and Silas and you learned the Jews had hired some thugs to beat you up, what would you do? What was the compliment the thugs paid Paul and Silas? When is the last time someone said this of your study group? **4.** What was the compliment paid to the Bereans? Why would Greek men and women be in the synagogue and readily respond to Paul's message? **5.** If thugs nearly caught up with you in Thessalonica and came looking for you in Berea, what would you be feeling? **6.** What is the purpose in leaving Silas and Timothy in Berea?

APPLY **1.** Who are the "god-fearing Greeks" and "prominent women" in your world that are particularly receptive to the Christian message? **2.** If God asked you to target these people in your community, how would you do this?

OPEN **1.** If you were able to visit Athens, would you rather see the Parthenon? Olympic Stadium? Hard Rock Cafe? **2.** What is the last place you would visit?

In Thessalonica

17 When they had passed through Amphipolis and Apollonia, they came to Thessalonica, where there was a Jewish synagogue. [2]As his custom was, Paul went into the synagogue, and on three Sabbath days he reasoned with them from the Scriptures, [3]explaining and proving that the Christ[a] had to suffer and rise from the dead. "This Jesus I am proclaiming to you is the Christ,[a]" he said. [4]Some of the Jews were persuaded and joined Paul and Silas, as did a large number of God-fearing Greeks and not a few prominent women.

[5]But the Jews were jealous; so they rounded up some bad characters from the marketplace, formed a mob and started a riot in the city. They rushed to Jason's house in search of Paul and Silas in order to bring them out to the crowd.[b] [6]But when they did not find them, they dragged Jason and some other brothers before the city officials, shouting: "These men who have caused trouble all over the world have now come here, [7]and Jason has welcomed them into his house. They are all defying Caesar's decrees, saying that there is another king, one called Jesus." [8]When they heard this, the crowd and the city officials were thrown into turmoil. [9]Then they made Jason and the others post bond and let them go.

In Berea

[10]As soon as it was night, the brothers sent Paul and Silas away to Berea. On arriving there, they went to the Jewish synagogue. [11]Now the Bereans were of more noble character than the Thessalonians, for they received the message with great eagerness and examined the Scriptures every day to see if what Paul said was true. [12]Many of the Jews believed, as did also a number of prominent Greek women and many Greek men.

[13]When the Jews in Thessalonica learned that Paul was preaching the word of God at Berea, they went there too, agitating the crowds and stirring them up. [14]The brothers immediately sent Paul to the coast, but Silas and Timothy stayed at Berea. [15]The men who escorted Paul brought him to Athens and then left with instructions for Silas and Timothy to join him as soon as possible.

In Athens

[16]While Paul was waiting for them in Athens, he was greatly distressed to see that the city was full of idols. [17]So he reasoned in the synagogue with the Jews and the God-fearing Greeks, as well as in

[a]3 Or *Messiah* [b]5 Or *the assembly of the people*

17:5 In Philippi it was economic interest that motivated the opposition to Paul and Silas. Here it was the jealousy of the Jews—who may have envied Paul's success in converting Gentiles that had for so long resisted Jewish attempts at proselytizing.

17:7 In Philippi, the slave owners' anger over their economic loss was masked by a charge of public disturbance. Here, the Jews' jealousy is masked by a charge of sedition against Caesar. The basis for this charge undoubtedly lay in the gospel's declaration that people are to declare their allegiance to Jesus, the King of God's kingdom.

17:9 Jason and the others post bond. Since Paul himself could not be brought before the officials, they simply insisted that Jason post a bond, assuring them that he would no longer be a host to Paul so that he would have to leave the city.

17:10–13 Paul and Silas proceeded to Berea, 45 miles to the southeast. Whereas the Jews in Thessalonica responded to Paul's message with jealousy, those in Berea explored what he said through their own reflection upon the Old Testament.

the marketplace day by day with those who happened to be there. 18A
group of Epicurean and Stoic philosophers began to dispute with
him. Some of them asked, "What is this babbler trying to say?" Others
remarked, "He seems to be advocating foreign gods." They said this
because Paul was preaching the good news about Jesus and the resurrection. 19Then they took him and brought him to a meeting of the
Areopagus, where they said to him, "May we know what this new
teaching is that you are presenting? 20You are bringing some strange
ideas to our ears, and we want to know what they mean." 21(All the
Athenians and the foreigners who lived there spent their time doing
nothing but talking about and listening to the latest ideas.)
22Paul then stood up in the meeting of the Areopagus and said:
"Men of Athens! I see that in every way you are very religious. 23For as
I walked around and looked carefully at your objects of worship, I
even found an altar with this inscription: TO AN UNKNOWN GOD. Now
what you worship as something unknown I am going to proclaim to
you.
24"The God who made the world and everything in it is the Lord of
heaven and earth and does not live in temples built by hands. 25And
he is not served by human hands, as if he needed anything, because
he himself gives all men life and breath and everything else. 26From
one man he made every nation of men, that they should inhabit the
whole earth; and he determined the times set for them and the exact
places where they should live. 27God did this so that men would seek
him and perhaps reach out for him and find him, though he is not far
from each one of us. 28'For in him we live and move and have our being.' As some of your own poets have said, 'We are his offspring.'
29"Therefore since we are God's offspring, we should not think that
the divine being is like gold or silver or stone—an image made by
man's design and skill. 30In the past God overlooked such ignorance,
but now he commands all people everywhere to repent. 31For he has
set a day when he will judge the world with justice by the man he has
appointed. He has given proof of this to all men by raising him from
the dead."
32When they heard about the resurrection of the dead, some of
them sneered, but others said, "We want to hear you again on this

STUDY **1.** If God called you to go to the major university in your state and challenge the philosophy department to a debate on the claims of Christianity, what would you say? **2.** What do you learn about Paul from his ministry in Athens? **3.** How would you compare the message he gave to the philosophers of the Acropolis to the message he delivered in previous passages in the synagogue? **4.** In verses 24–31 Paul reasons from "natural revelation" for the existence of a Creator who created the universe and will one day judge it. Have you ever heard of someone coming to God by observing the work of God in nature? **5.** A few men became followers, among them Dionysius and Damaris, but no mention is made of establishing a church and Paul never visits Athens again in his travels. Would you call his ministry in Athens a success? **6.** Who would be the Stoic and Epicurean philosophers today? Do you think the church should engage in academic discussion with these people on their own turf today? If so, how?

APPLY **1.** In your education, did you ever get interested in philosophy? **2.** What have you found helpful in sharing your faith with your friends? Have you ever discussed the Christian faith with an intellectual that didn't believe?

17:18 Epicurean and Stoic philosophers. Epicurus maintained that a tranquil life free from pain, passions and fears was the highest good for humanity. This could be achieved only by detaching oneself from indulgence and the cares of the world. The Epicureans were practical atheists in that they believed the gods had no interest in humanity and were unknowable. The Stoics had a pantheistic idea of god. People were a spark of the divine; upon death, one's immortal soul would be absorbed into the divine spirit. **this babbler.** Literally, "seed-picker"—a derisive term stemming from the actions of a bird that picks up seeds wherever it can find them. To the philosophers, Paul seemed like someone who picked up scraps of ideas here and there and then had the audacity to try to teach others. **foreign gods ... Jesus and the resurrection.** Since in the Greek the word for Jesus sounds something like the name of the goddess of health, and the word for salvation is also used of physical healing, his listeners may have thought Paul was talking about two new gods—Health and Resurrection.

17:19 meeting of the Areopagus. Athens was a free city within the Roman Empire, so the Areopagus had legal and judicial authority over what went on in the city. It does not appear Paul is on trial as much as his message is being evaluated as to its credibility.

17:21 Luke's rather sarcastic observation about the Athenians in general is an echo of what the Greek orator Demosthenes had said 400 years earlier.

17:27 Challenging the Epicurean assumption that God was unknowable, Paul says God is knowable by those who seek after him.

17:28 Paul supports his points by quoting two Greek authors, Epimenides and Aratus indicating he recognized that God revealed truth about himself even through other religions and philosophies.

17:32–34 The converts included Dionysius, a member of the Athenian council. Nothing more is said in the New Testament about Athens so it is unlikely that these believers established a church at the time.

subject." [33]At that, Paul left the Council. [34]A few men became followers of Paul and believed. Among them was Dionysius, a member of the Areopagus, also a woman named Damaris, and a number of others.

In Corinth

18 After this, Paul left Athens and went to Corinth. [2]There he met a Jew named Aquila, a native of Pontus, who had recently come from Italy with his wife Priscilla, because Claudius had ordered all the Jews to leave Rome. Paul went to see them, [3]and because he was a tentmaker as they were, he stayed and worked with them. [4]Every Sabbath he reasoned in the synagogue, trying to persuade Jews and Greeks.

[5]When Silas and Timothy came from Macedonia, Paul devoted himself exclusively to preaching, testifying to the Jews that Jesus was the Christ.[a] [6]But when the Jews opposed Paul and became abusive, he shook out his clothes in protest and said to them, "Your blood be on your own heads! I am clear of my responsibility. From now on I will go to the Gentiles."

[7]Then Paul left the synagogue and went next door to the house of Titius Justus, a worshiper of God. [8]Crispus, the synagogue ruler, and his entire household believed in the Lord; and many of the Corinthians who heard him believed and were baptized.

[9]One night the Lord spoke to Paul in a vision: "Do not be afraid; keep on speaking, do not be silent. [10]For I am with you, and no one is going to attack and harm you, because I have many people in this city." [11]So Paul stayed for a year and a half, teaching them the word of God.

[12]While Gallio was proconsul of Achaia, the Jews made a united attack on Paul and brought him into court. [13]"This man," they charged, "is persuading the people to worship God in ways contrary to the law."

[14]Just as Paul was about to speak, Gallio said to the Jews, "If you Jews were making a complaint about some misdemeanor or serious crime, it would be reasonable for me to listen to you. [15]But since it involves questions about words and names and your own law—settle the matter yourselves. I will not be a judge of such things." [16]So he had them ejected from the court. [17]Then they all turned on Sosthenes the synagogue ruler and beat him in front of the court. But Gallio showed no concern whatever.

[a]5 Or *Messiah;* also in verse 28

OPEN **1.** Who was your best friend in high school? When was the last time you saw this person? **2.** If you had to make a living off of your hobby, what would you have become?

STUDY **1.** What do you know about the city of Corinth? **2.** How important were Aquilla and Priscilla to Paul? **3.** What would the "vision" God gave Paul at this time do for him? Do you think this "vision" had anything to do with the fact Paul decided to stay in Corinth for a year and a half? Have you ever felt that God spoke to you through a vision or a dream? **4.** How did the civil government react when the Jewish leaders tried to stop Paul's ministry? Have you ever experienced anything like this?

APPLY **1.** What is the closest you have come to having a "mid-life crisis" that altered the next course of your life? **2.** Where did you draw comfort during this time? **3.** What did you learn from this experience that has made you a better person today?

18:1 The next stop for Paul was Corinth, 50 miles from Athens and a prosperous seaport city.

18:2 Aquila ... Priscilla. This couple, apparently converted in Rome prior to meeting Paul. They became important coworkers with him (v. 26; Rom. 16:3; 1 Cor. 16:19; 2 Tim. 4:19). **Claudius had ordered all the Jews to leave Rome.** Because of uprisings in the Jewish community at Rome due to the influence of a man named Chrestus, riots broke out in the Jewish community in Rome between those who believed in Jesus as the Messiah and those who did not. To solve the problem, the emperor simply ordered all Jews to leave! While the expulsion order was not strictly enforced, for a time the Jews were forbidden to meet, which led many to leave anyway.

18:12 Gallio ... of Achaia. Gallio was a highly respected Roman official who served his year's term as proconsul in Achaia from July 51 A.D. to June 52 A.D.

Priscilla, Aquila and Apollos

[18]Paul stayed on in Corinth for some time. Then he left the brothers
and sailed for Syria, accompanied by Priscilla and Aquila. Before he
sailed, he had his hair cut off at Cenchrea because of a vow he had
taken. [19]They arrived at Ephesus, where Paul left Priscilla and Aquila.
He himself went into the synagogue and reasoned with the Jews.
[20]When they asked him to spend more time with them, he declined.
[21]But as he left, he promised, "I will come back if it is God's will."
Then he set sail from Ephesus. [22]When he landed at Caesarea, he
went up and greeted the church and then went down to Antioch.

[23]After spending some time in Antioch, Paul set out from there and
traveled from place to place throughout the region of Galatia and
Phrygia, strengthening all the disciples.

[24]Meanwhile a Jew named Apollos, a native of Alexandria, came to
Ephesus. He was a learned man, with a thorough knowledge of the
Scriptures. [25]He had been instructed in the way of the Lord, and he
spoke with great fervor[a] and taught about Jesus accurately, though
he knew only the baptism of John. [26]He began to speak boldly in the
synagogue. When Priscilla and Aquila heard him, they invited him to
their home and explained to him the way of God more adequately.

[27]When Apollos wanted to go to Achaia, the brothers encouraged
him and wrote to the disciples there to welcome him. On arriving, he
was a great help to those who by grace had believed. [28]For he vigorously refuted the Jews in public debate, proving from the Scriptures
that Jesus was the Christ.

Paul in Ephesus

19 While Apollos was at Corinth, Paul took the road through the
interior and arrived at Ephesus. There he found some disciples [2]and asked them, "Did you receive the Holy Spirit when[b] you
believed?"

They answered, "No, we have not even heard that there is a Holy
Spirit."

[3]So Paul asked, "Then what baptism did you receive?"

[a]25 Or *with fervor in the Spirit* [b]2 Or *after*

OPEN What couple do you admire for the way they complement each other in their marriage and ministry?

STUDY 1. When Paul returns to Jerusalem (21:17–21); how do you think the church leaders reacted when he told them how the Holy Spirit had led him to go to Philippi, Thessalonica, Berea, Athens and finally Corinth where he "shook out his clothes in protest" against the Jews? How would you like to have Paul to supervise? **2.** How would you like to have a couple like Priscilla and Aquila in your church—to send out to assist new churches and support themselves by making tents? How would you describe their ministry in Ephesus? To Apollos? Does your church encourage lay couple ministry like this? **3.** What is their process of commissioning people to special ministries?

APPLY Are you open to the possibility that God might use you to go into some kind of tentmaking ministry like Priscilla and Aquila?

OPEN In high school what crowd did you hang around with? Were your friends called something like "nerds"?

STUDY 1. What do you learn about the city of Ephesus from the introduction to the book of Ephesians? **2.** When Paul reached Ephesus on his third missionary journey, he ran into a mixed bag of cultures and religious teachings in the church: Fol-

---

18:18–22 Luke compresses a journey of nearly 1500 miles into these four verses. After a year and a half at Corinth (v. 11), Paul departed for Antioch, sailing by way of Ephesus which, from 19:1–20:38, is the dominant area of Paul's missionary work. Since Silas does not appear again in Acts, he and Timothy apparently stayed behind in Corinth.

18:18 accompanied by Priscilla and Aquila. It is significant that Priscilla's name is listed first, ahead of her husband. This was hardly ever done, and may indicate that Priscilla was the more influential leader of the two. **he had his hair cut off ... because of a vow.** Pious Jews would take vows, based on the pattern of the Nazirites (Num. 6:1–21), as an indication of their devotion to God. Since the cutting of one's hair indicated the termination of the vow, Paul may have made a vow of dedication to God for as long as he was in Corinth, in gratefulness to God's promise of protection (v. 10). While normally vows would be terminated by shaving one's head and offering a sacrifice in the temple at Jerusalem, people far from the city could shave their heads where they were and carry the trimmings to the temple to be presented along with a sacrifice at that time.

18:25 While Apollos was an earnest, articulate believer in Jesus, he had not received the whole story of the gospel. Just what he was lacking is unclear, but, as the story in 19:1–7 indicates, he may not have heard of the coming of the Spirit promised to those who are baptized in the name of Jesus.

19:2 Did you receive the Holy Spirit when you believed? As Paul talked with these men, something must have seemed out of place for him to ask this question. **we have not even heard that there is a Holy Spirit.** Since John the Baptist spoke of the coming of the Holy Spirit (Luke 3:16), it is likely that the intent of their response is more that they were not aware that the Holy Spirit had been given.

19:3 John's baptism. John baptized people for repentance symbolizing their being cleansed from sin in anticipation of the coming of the Messiah. Jesus' baptism is a symbol of the work of God's grace in the forgiveness of sin.

lowers of John the Baptist? Followers of Apollos, a Greek from Alexandria (18:24–25) and an intellectual. Those who stressed the more sensational gifts? How do you think these three groups got along with each other? **3.** How do you think Paul felt returning to the synagogue after he "shook out his clothes in protest" to the Jews in Corinth (18:6)? **4.** When opposition arose in the synagogue, what was Paul's strategy? What was the result? Who uses this strategy in your area today? With what results? **5.** How would you compare the sorcery and religious counterfeits in Ephesus to the sorcery artists and religious counterfeits today? What exactly is the appeal of these counterfeits? If there was a new "book burning" of their literature, what would it do to the GNP (gross national product) of the country? **6.** Why would Paul want to leave Ephesus where he was having a great ministry and go to Jerusalem? Or to Rome? Who in your church is thinking this way?

APPLY 1. In your own spiritual growth, when did you start to develop a world view? Who influenced your thinking for your world view? **2.** What is the next step for you in your own spiritual journey?

"John's baptism," they replied.
4 Paul said, "John's baptism was a baptism of repentance. He told
the people to believe in the one coming after him, that is, in Jesus."
5 On hearing this, they were baptized into[a] the name of the Lord Jesus.
6 When Paul placed his hands on them, the Holy Spirit came on them,
and they spoke in tongues[b] and prophesied. 7 There were about
twelve men in all.
8 Paul entered the synagogue and spoke boldly there for three
months, arguing persuasively about the kingdom of God. 9 But some
of them became obstinate; they refused to believe and publicly maligned the Way. So Paul left them. He took the disciples with him and
had discussions daily in the lecture hall of Tyrannus. 10 This went on
for two years, so that all the Jews and Greeks who lived in the province of Asia heard the word of the Lord.
11 God did extraordinary miracles through Paul, 12 so that even
handkerchiefs and aprons that had touched him were taken to the sick, and their illnesses were cured and the evil spirits left them.
13 Some Jews who went around driving out evil spirits tried to invoke the name of the Lord Jesus over those who were demon-possessed. They would say, "In the name of Jesus, whom Paul preaches,
I command you to come out." 14 Seven sons of Sceva, a Jewish chief
priest, were doing this. 15 ⌞One day⌟ the evil spirit answered them,
"Jesus I know, and I know about Paul, but who are you?" 16 Then the
man who had the evil spirit jumped on them and overpowered them all. He gave them such a beating that they ran out of the house naked and bleeding.
17 When this became known to the Jews and Greeks living in Ephesus, they were all seized with fear, and the name of the Lord Jesus
was held in high honor. 18 Many of those who believed now came and
openly confessed their evil deeds. 19 A number who had practiced sorcery brought their scrolls together and burned them publicly. When they calculated the value of the scrolls, the total came to fifty thousand drachmas.[c] 20 In this way the word of the Lord spread widely and
grew in power.

[a] 5 Or *in* [b] 6 Or *other languages* [c] 19 A drachma was a silver coin worth about a day's wages.

19:4 a baptism of repentance. John's baptism symbolized the cleansing away of sin (Mark 1:4). It may have been based on the baptism of the Essene sect at Qumran, a desert community where the Dead Sea Scrolls were found. Or it may have been a refinement of Jewish baptism of Gentile converts, who were baptized to symbolize their turning away from their sinful ways. John taught that Jews also needed such repentance and cleansing from sin.

19:6 placed his hands on them. The last time this action was mentioned was when the gospel broke through into Samaria (8:17). The laying on of hands and the manifestation of tongues may be meant as an assurance that these people were now fully included in the church and that Ephesus was to be a major new thrust for the church's mission.

19:8–20 Ephesus became the hub of Paul's ministry for two years, during which time churches were founded in Colosse, Laodicea and the other cities mentioned in Revelation 1:11. It was also here that Paul wrote 1 Corinthians.

19:11 extraordinary miracles. See the similar miracles wrought by Peter in 5:15–16. Ephesus was a city renown for its magic arts. For that reason, this type of evidence was necessary to convince people that the power of the gospel was greater than that of magic.

19:14 Sceva. There was never a high priest in Jerusalem by that name, although he may have been a member of the high priest's family. He was probably an unusually successful exorcist who assumed the title for himself to command more respect (and business) from people in the area.

19:18 those who believed. The tense of the word implies that these were Christians who still secretly practiced magic arts. The incident with Sceva's sons showed them they needed to lay aside these practices once for all.

19:19 total came to fifty thousand drachmas. An incredible amount when one considers that a drachma was worth a day's wage!

21 After all this had happened, Paul decided to go to Jerusalem,
passing through Macedonia and Achaia. "After I have been there," he
said, "I must visit Rome also." 22 He sent two of his helpers, Timothy
and Erastus, to Macedonia, while he stayed in the province of Asia a
little longer.

The Riot in Ephesus

23 About that time there arose a great disturbance about the Way.
24 A silversmith named Demetrius, who made silver shrines of Artemis, brought in no little business for the craftsmen. 25 He called them
together, along with the workmen in related trades, and said: "Men,
you know we receive a good income from this business. 26 And you
see and hear how this fellow Paul has convinced and led astray large
numbers of people here in Ephesus and in practically the whole province of Asia. He says that man-made gods are no gods at all. 27 There
is danger not only that our trade will lose its good name, but also that
the temple of the great goddess Artemis will be discredited, and the
goddess herself, who is worshiped throughout the province of Asia
and the world, will be robbed of her divine majesty."

28 When they heard this, they were furious and began shouting:
"Great is Artemis of the Ephesians!" 29 Soon the whole city was in an
uproar. The people seized Gaius and Aristarchus, Paul's traveling
companions from Macedonia, and rushed as one man into the theater. 30 Paul wanted to appear before the crowd, but the disciples
would not let him. 31 Even some of the officials of the province,
friends of Paul, sent him a message begging him not to venture into
the theater.

32 The assembly was in confusion: Some were shouting one thing,
some another. Most of the people did not even know why they were
there. 33 The Jews pushed Alexander to the front, and some of the
crowd shouted instructions to him. He motioned for silence in order
to make a defense before the people. 34 But when they realized he was
a Jew, they all shouted in unison for about two hours: "Great is Artemis of the Ephesians!"

35 The city clerk quieted the crowd and said: "Men of Ephesus,
doesn't all the world know that the city of Ephesus is the guardian of
the temple of the great Artemis and of her image, which fell from
heaven? 36 Therefore, since these facts are undeniable, you ought to
be quiet and not do anything rash. 37 You have brought these men
here, though they have neither robbed temples nor blasphemed our
goddess. 38 If, then, Demetrius and his fellow craftsmen have a grievance against anybody, the courts are open and there are proconsuls.
They can press charges. 39 If there is anything further you want to
bring up, it must be settled in a legal assembly. 40 As it is, we are in
danger of being charged with rioting because of today's events. In

OPEN 1. What is the closest you have come to being in a riot? **2.** What is your city famous for?

STUDY 1. If the major industry in your hometown was threatened by the preaching in your church, what would the vested interests do? If your own personal income was affected, what would you do? **2.** How do the craftsmen frame their argument to make them look like the "good guys"? How would you compare the tactics of the craftsmen in Ephesus to the tactics of the vested interests today? Do you think the church should speak out on moral issues or just stick to preaching the Word of God? **3.** How would you describe the response of the people in verses 28–34? What does this remind you of? **4.** If you had to be a resident in Ephesus and a riot took place in the outdoor theatre that was promoted by the influential shopowners in your city, what would you want to do? **5.** What does the city administrator do to stop the riot? How do you think the shopowners that started the riot felt? **6.** At the end of the day, who benefitted from this riot?

APPLY 1. In your spiritual pilgrimage, what causes have you gotten involved in? Are you more likely to get involved in a cause that affects your own vested interests or the vested interests of others? **2.** What issue do you feel so strongly about today that you would be willing to join a crusade?

19:21 I must visit Rome also. Paul intended to visit Rome and then go on to Spain after delivering the offering to Jerusalem (Rom. 1:11; 15:23–26). The letter to the Romans was written from Corinth after Paul left Ephesus and just prior to his trip to Jerusalem. Paul will finally come to Rome in the end of Acts, but as a prisoner.

19:24 A silversmith. The silversmith trade made a great deal of money through the manufacture and sale of models of the goddess Artemis.

19:35 clerk. This was the highest ranking official in the city accountable to the Roman provincial government for what happened in Ephesus.

19:39 a legal assembly. The people could gather for meetings to discuss issues that concerned them, but they were to be held at set times and with a set procedure. Such an irregular, chaotic meeting as this one could lead to Roman suppression.

that case we would not be able to account for this commotion, since
there is no reason for it." [41]After he had said this, he dismissed the
assembly.

OPEN 1. Who would you choose in your group to head up a fund-raising campaign for relief of the poor in your community? **2.** Who gets the prize in your group for falling asleep in church?

STUDY What is not mentioned here is that Paul is taking a collection from the churches he started to take to Jerusalem for the relief of the poor. **1.** If you were in charge of this money-raising campaign, how would you go about it? How would you make sure no one could level criticism at you on your handling of the money? **2.** How would you like to have Paul as your preacher—who could preach until dawn?

APPLY 1. What is your church doing for the relief of the poor in your community? **2.** Are you similar to Eutychus?

Through Macedonia and Greece

20 When the uproar had ended, Paul sent for the disciples and,
after encouraging them, said good-by and set out for Macedonia. [2]He traveled through that area, speaking many words of encouragement to the people, and finally arrived in Greece, [3]where he
stayed three months. Because the Jews made a plot against him just
as he was about to sail for Syria, he decided to go back through Macedonia. [4]He was accompanied by Sopater son of Pyrrhus from Berea,
Aristarchus and Secundus from Thessalonica, Gaius from Derbe,
Timothy also, and Tychicus and Trophimus from the province of Asia.
[5]These men went on ahead and waited for us at Troas. [6]But we sailed
from Philippi after the Feast of Unleavened Bread, and five days later
joined the others at Troas, where we stayed seven days.

Eutychus Raised From the Dead at Troas

[7]On the first day of the week we came together to break bread. Paul
spoke to the people and, because he intended to leave the next day,
kept on talking until midnight. [8]There were many lamps in the upstairs room where we were meeting. [9]Seated in a window was a
young man named Eutychus, who was sinking into a deep sleep as
Paul talked on and on. When he was sound asleep, he fell to the
ground from the third story and was picked up dead. [10]Paul went
down, threw himself on the young man and put his arms around him.
"Don't be alarmed," he said. "He's alive!" [11]Then he went upstairs
again and broke bread and ate. After talking until daylight, he left.
[12]The people took the young man home alive and were greatly comforted.

OPEN How are you at saying "goodbye" to people you may never see again?

STUDY Paul is on his way to Jerusalem with the money he collected from all of the churches he founded. He doesn't have time to stop in Ephesus so he sends for the leaders of the church in Ephesus to meet him on the coast. **1.** What does he say about his ministry with them (vv. 18–

Paul's Farewell to the Ephesian Elders

[13]We went on ahead to the ship and sailed for Assos, where we
were going to take Paul aboard. He had made this arrangement because he was going there on foot. [14]When he met us at Assos, we took
him aboard and went on to Mitylene. [15]The next day we set sail from
there and arrived off Kios. The day after that we crossed over to Samos, and on the following day arrived at Miletus. [16]Paul had decided
to sail past Ephesus to avoid spending time in the province of Asia,
for he was in a hurry to reach Jerusalem, if possible, by the day of
Pentecost.

20:4 Although Luke does not say why Paul was accompanied by so many men from such different areas, it must be remembered that at this time he was carrying with him the collection he had gathered for the church in Jerusalem from the churches in Macedonia, Achaia, and, undoubtedly, Asia (Rom. 15:25–26; 1 Cor. 16:1–4; 2 Cor. 8:1–4; 9:2). First Corinthians 16:3 indicates some men from Corinth accompanied him as well. These men would serve both as protection for Paul against robbers and as a means of accountability to their home churches that Paul had indeed delivered the offering as promised (2 Cor. 8:19–21). **Sopater.** This may be a variant spelling of Sosipater, who was a relative of Paul's (Rom. 16:21). Since Derbe is in Galatia, this may be a different Gaius than the one mentioned in 19:29. **Tychicus.** A faithful courier for Paul later on (Eph. 6:21; Col. 4:7; 2 Tim. 4:12; Titus 3:12). **Trophimus.** A resident of Ephesus who became the unwitting cause of Paul's imprisonment in Jerusalem (21:29; 2 Tim. 4:20).

20:7 On the first day of the week. Since Luke typically uses the Roman time system, this meeting probably occurred on a Sunday evening. Meetings were held in the evenings because Sunday, like every day, was a work day for slaves (who made up a large percentage of the believers—Eph. 6:5). This also may have contributed to Eutychus' tiredness.

[17]From Miletus, Paul sent to Ephesus for the elders of the church.
[18]When they arrived, he said to them: "You know how I lived the
whole time I was with you, from the first day I came into the province
of Asia. [19]I served the Lord with great humility and with tears, although I was severely tested by the plots of the Jews. [20]You know that
I have not hesitated to preach anything that would be helpful to you
but have taught you publicly and from house to house. [21]I have declared to both Jews and Greeks that they must turn to God in repentance and have faith in our Lord Jesus.
[22]"And now, compelled by the Spirit, I am going to Jerusalem, not
knowing what will happen to me there. [23]I only know that in every
city the Holy Spirit warns me that prison and hardships are facing
me. [24]However, I consider my life worth nothing to me, if only I may
finish the race and complete the task the Lord Jesus has given me—
the task of testifying to the gospel of God's grace.
[25]"Now I know that none of you among whom I have gone about
preaching the kingdom will ever see me again. [26]Therefore, I declare
to you today that I am innocent of the blood of all men. [27]For I have
not hesitated to proclaim to you the whole will of God. [28]Keep watch
over yourselves and all the flock of which the Holy Spirit has made
you overseers.[a] Be shepherds of the church of God,[b] which he bought
with his own blood. [29]I know that after I leave, savage wolves will
come in among you and will not spare the flock. [30]Even from your
own number men will arise and distort the truth in order to draw
away disciples after them. [31]So be on your guard! Remember that for
three years I never stopped warning each of you night and day with
tears.
[32]"Now I commit you to God and to the word of his grace, which
can build you up and give you an inheritance among all those who
are sanctified. [33]I have not coveted anyone's silver or gold or clothing. [34]You yourselves know that these hands of mine have supplied
my own needs and the needs of my companions. [35]In everything I did,
I showed you that by this kind of hard work we must help the weak,
remembering the words the Lord Jesus himself said: 'It is more
blessed to give than to receive.'"
[36]When he had said this, he knelt down with all of them and
prayed. [37]They all wept as they embraced him and kissed him. [38]What
grieved them most was his statement that they would never see his
face again. Then they accompanied him to the ship.

On to Jerusalem

21 After we had torn ourselves away from them, we put out to
sea and sailed straight to Cos. The next day we went to

[a]28 Traditionally *bishops* [b]28 Many manuscripts *of the Lord*

21)? **2.** If Paul had a sneaking suspicion that trouble awaited him when he got to Jerusalem, do you think he should have gone? What was his answer? **3.** If you had been there, how would you have felt when he said he would never see you again? Do you think there were "savage wolves" at work in the church in Ephesus? If so, what would you be feeling if you were a church leader? **4.** What was the challenge Paul gave to the church leaders in verses 32–35? What is the challenge for church leaders today? **5.** If you were Paul, what would you be feeling as you boarded the ship for Jerusalem?

APPLY 1. What is the closest you have come to Paul's experience of saying "goodbye" to a Christian community that you may never see again? **2.** If Paul was in your group, what would Paul challenge your group to do now?

OPEN In playing Monopoly, are you the big risk-taker or the play-it-safe player?

STUDY 1. Do you think the Holy Spirit directed the

20:23 in every city the Holy Spirit warns me that prison and hardships are facing me. Paul was undertaking this journey in full conviction that God wanted him to go, but also with an awareness that it would lead to difficulty. All along the way, the Spirit was preparing him for the hardships he would face at his destination. This sense of foreboding led him to ask the Roman church to pray for him as he went (Rom. 15:30–32).

20:24 finish the race. Just prior to his death, Paul wrote to Timothy at Ephesus using this same metaphor to describe his ministry (2 Tim. 4:7).

20:25 none of you ... will ever see me again. A few weeks earlier, Paul wrote to the Romans that after he went to Jerusalem he hoped to visit them and proceed to Spain since his work in Macedonia and Achaia (and presumably Asia) was accomplished (Rom. 15:23–24). Whether this is why he says he will not see these people again or whether he subsequently felt that the warnings of the Spirit (v. 23) are to prepare him for death is uncertain.

disciples in Tyre to warn Paul not to go to Jerusalem? Do you think the Holy Spirit directed Agabus to demonstrate what would happen to Paul if he went to Jerusalem? **2.** How did Paul respond to these admonitions? Do you think he was being spiritually motivated or just foolhardy? If you had been one of his close traveling companions, what would you have said to Paul? What can you say for Paul in his defense? **3.** When Paul refused to listen to his friends and went on to Jerusalem where he was jailed, do you think it was punishment on him for not listening? **4.** As he sat in jail for two and a half years, do you think he had second thoughts about his decision?

APPLY 1. When it comes to determining the will of God in your life concerning very important decisions, are you more likely to seek the counsel of others or go your own way? **2.** What are you facing right now in your life where you are needing to make a decision?

OPEN Would you like to visit Jerusalem one day? What would you like to see?

STUDY 1. If you were one of Paul's Gentile traveling companions, how would you be feeling when you were ushered into the presence of the leaders of the church with

Rhodes and from there to Patara. 2We found a ship crossing over to
Phoenicia, went on board and set sail. 3After sighting Cyprus and
passing to the south of it, we sailed on to Syria. We landed at Tyre,
where our ship was to unload its cargo. 4Finding the disciples there,
we stayed with them seven days. Through the Spirit they urged Paul
not to go on to Jerusalem. 5But when our time was up, we left and
continued on our way. All the disciples and their wives and children
accompanied us out of the city, and there on the beach we knelt to
pray. 6After saying good-by to each other, we went aboard the ship,
and they returned home.

7We continued our voyage from Tyre and landed at Ptolemais,
where we greeted the brothers and stayed with them for a day. 8Leav-
ing the next day, we reached Caesarea and stayed at the house of
Philip the evangelist, one of the Seven. 9He had four unmarried
daughters who prophesied.

10After we had been there a number of days, a prophet named Agabus came down from Judea. 11Coming over to us, he took Paul's belt,
tied his own hands and feet with it and said, "The Holy Spirit says, 'In
this way the Jews of Jerusalem will bind the owner of this belt and
will hand him over to the Gentiles.' "

12When we heard this, we and the people there pleaded with Paul
not to go up to Jerusalem. 13Then Paul answered, "Why are you weeping and breaking my heart? I am ready not only to be bound, but also
to die in Jerusalem for the name of the Lord Jesus." 14When he would
not be dissuaded, we gave up and said, "The Lord's will be done."

15After this, we got ready and went up to Jerusalem. 16Some of the
disciples from Caesarea accompanied us and brought us to the home
of Mnason, where we were to stay. He was a man from Cyprus and
one of the early disciples.

Paul's Arrival at Jerusalem

17When we arrived at Jerusalem, the brothers received us warmly.
18The next day Paul and the rest of us went to see James, and all the
elders were present. 19Paul greeted them and reported in detail what
God had done among the Gentiles through his ministry.

20When they heard this, they praised God. Then they said to Paul:
"You see, brother, how many thousands of Jews have believed, and all

---

21:2 We found a ship crossing over to Phoenicia. Whereas many ships would stop at several ports along the southern coast of Asia or stop at Cyprus, Paul and his companions were able to find one sailing directly to Phoenicia, an area in Syria of which Tyre (v. 3) was the chief city. Tyre was only about 100 miles from Jerusalem.

21:11 Agabus enacted his prophecy to accent its impact. Enacted prophecies were sometimes done by the Old Testament prophets as well (1 Kin. 11:29ff; Ezek. 4). **Paul's belt.** A long strip of cloth. **The Holy Spirit says.** This is akin to "The Lord says" common in the Old Testament prophets. **the Jews ... will hand him over to the Gentiles.** While this was not strictly the way things happened (the Romans rescued Paul from the Jews who were trying to kill him), it was on account of the Jews' actions that Paul was imprisoned by the Romans.

21:16 home of Mnason. Nothing more is known of this man who may have been one of the original converts at Pentecost. His home became the residence of Paul and his companions for their stay in Jerusalem.

21:17–19 Although Luke's concern is strictly with the opposition Paul was about to face, it was undoubtedly at this meeting with James (Jesus' brother and the spokesperson for the church in Jerusalem) that Paul and his companions presented the offering from the Gentile churches.

21:20–21 While James and the elders received Paul's news with gladness, they were concerned about the fact that many Jewish believers had been told that Paul was teaching Jews to abandon their Jewish ways. If Jewish believers in Rome could still be rigid about the dietary and Sabbath laws (Rom. 14:2,5), how much more would these Judean believers, having lived all their lives in a strictly Jewish environment, be opposed to any hint that their customs were being ignored?

of them are zealous for the law. 21They have been informed that you
teach all the Jews who live among the Gentiles to turn away from
Moses, telling them not to circumcise their children or live according
to our customs. 22What shall we do? They will certainly hear that you
have come, 23so do what we tell you. There are four men with us who
have made a vow. 24Take these men, join in their purification rites and
pay their expenses, so that they can have their heads shaved. Then
everybody will know there is no truth in these reports about you, but
that you yourself are living in obedience to the law. 25As for the Gentile believers, we have written to them our decision that they should
abstain from food sacrificed to idols, from blood, from the meat of
strangled animals and from sexual immorality."
26The next day Paul took the men and purified himself along with
them. Then he went to the temple to give notice of the date when the
days of purification would end and the offering would be made for
each of them.

Paul Arrested

27When the seven days were nearly over, some Jews from the province of Asia saw Paul at the temple. They stirred up the whole crowd
and seized him, 28shouting, "Men of Israel, help us! This is the man
who teaches all men everywhere against our people and our law and
this place. And besides, he has brought Greeks into the temple area
and defiled this holy place." 29(They had previously seen Trophimus
the Ephesian in the city with Paul and assumed that Paul had brought
him into the temple area.)
30The whole city was aroused, and the people came running from
all directions. Seizing Paul, they dragged him from the temple, and
immediately the gates were shut. 31While they were trying to kill him,
news reached the commander of the Roman troops that the whole
city of Jerusalem was in an uproar. 32He at once took some officers
and soldiers and ran down to the crowd. When the rioters saw the
commander and his soldiers, they stopped beating Paul.
33The commander came up and arrested him and ordered him to be
bound with two chains. Then he asked who he was and what he had
done. 34Some in the crowd shouted one thing and some another, and
since the commander could not get at the truth because of the uproar, he ordered that Paul be taken into the barracks. 35When Paul
reached the steps, the violence of the mob was so great he had to be
carried by the soldiers. 36The crowd that followed kept shouting,
"Away with him!"

the brother of Jesus (James) greeting you personally? **2.** Who were the leaders of the church in Jerusalem thinking of when they wanted Paul to go to the temple and go through the Jewish rite of purification? Do you think Paul should have gone along with this request? **3.** What is the lesson here for the church today when it comes to accommodating the pressure of groups in our society?

APPLY Have you ever felt caught between doing something you don't believe in or hurting the feelings of someone close?

OPEN **1.** Have you ever been arrested? **2.** Have you ever been in jail?

STUDY **1.** How do you think the devout Jews felt when Paul brought a Greek into Jerusalem? Why would the Asian Jews be particularly upset if they thought Paul had brought Greeks into the temple? **2.** What do you think motivated the "whole city" to get involved in the beating of Paul? What is the closest you have come to seeing something like this?

APPLY **1.** What is the closest you have come to seeing a fanatical religious cult in action? **2.** What have you found helpful in dealing with people of very different faiths?

Paul Speaks to the Crowd

37As the soldiers were about to take Paul into the barracks, he
asked the commander, "May I say something to you?"

OPEN How are you at coming up with a speech before a big crowd on the spur of the moment?

21:22–24 To prove that Paul still honored the Jewish customs, it was suggested that he personally and financially participate in a vow that four of the elders themselves had made.

21:27–29 Paul apparently had previous difficulties with these people before (20:18–19), but now their strong nationalist and religious sentiments, heightened by the feast, were inflamed as they assumed that Paul must have brought the Gentile Trophimus into the temple. They knew Trophimus from their contacts with him at Ephesus.

21:31–32 Paul was probably dragged outside the temple and beaten. The Roman cohort was quartered on the northwest side of the temple in the Fortress of Antonia, which was connected to the Court of the Gentiles by two staircases and commanded a view of the temple area. Ever on the alert for disturbance, especially around the times of feasts, the commander and some of his soldiers (a cohort, at least on paper, consisted of 1000 soldiers—both infantry and cavalry) raced through the crowd to the center of the action.

STUDY In the previous passage Paul was seized in the temple by fanatical Jews from Asia, beaten until near death, rescued by the Roman military commander and taken to the barracks for questioning. **1.** If you had been Paul in this situation, would you be ready to give witness to your faith in Christ before the crowd that had just beaten you up? **2.** If you had been in the crowd, how would you have felt when you heard Paul speaking in your own language about growing up in your town as a strictly observant and zealous Jew? How would you feel, even if you did not agree with him? **3.** What do you learn about Paul's pre-conversion life that you did not know before? What details about Paul's conversion do you learn here? About his trip to Jerusalem after becoming a Christian? **4.** What caused the crowd to turn against Paul? What happened to the commandment, "thou shalt not kill"? Where is the religious establishment while this is going on? **5.** What authority finally steps in to save Paul's life? Why does Paul claim the privilege of Roman citizenship in this instance? What does this do in this situation? **6.** At the end of the day, how would you have felt if you were Paul? Would you call this day "his darkest moment" or "his finest hour"?

APPLY **1.** In your spiritual pilgrimage what is the closest you have come to being put through what Paul endured? **2.** Would you call this your "darkest moment" or "your finest hour"?

"Do you speak Greek?" he replied. 38"Aren't you the Egyptian who
started a revolt and led four thousand terrorists out into the desert
some time ago?"

39Paul answered, "I am a Jew, from Tarsus in Cilicia, a citizen of no
ordinary city. Please let me speak to the people."

40Having received the commander's permission, Paul stood on the
steps and motioned to the crowd. When they were all silent, he said

22 to them in Aramaic[a]: 1"Brothers and fathers, listen now to
my defense." 2When they heard him speak to them in Aramaic,
they became very quiet.

Then Paul said: 3"I am a Jew, born in Tarsus of Cilicia, but brought
up in this city. Under Gamaliel I was thoroughly trained in the law of
our fathers and was just as zealous for God as any of you are today. 4I
persecuted the followers of this Way to their death, arresting both
men and women and throwing them into prison, 5as also the high
priest and all the Council can testify. I even obtained letters from
them to their brothers in Damascus, and went there to bring these
people as prisoners to Jerusalem to be punished.

6"About noon as I came near Damascus, suddenly a bright light
from heaven flashed around me. 7I fell to the ground and heard a
voice say to me, 'Saul! Saul! Why do you persecute me?'

8" 'Who are you, Lord?' I asked.

" 'I am Jesus of Nazareth, whom you are persecuting,' he replied.
9My companions saw the light, but they did not understand the voice
of him who was speaking to me.

10" 'What shall I do, Lord?' I asked.

" 'Get up,' the Lord said, 'and go into Damascus. There you will be
told all that you have been assigned to do.' 11My companions led me
by the hand into Damascus, because the brilliance of the light had
blinded me.

12"A man named Ananias came to see me. He was a devout observer
of the law and highly respected by all the Jews living there. 13He stood
beside me and said, 'Brother Saul, receive your sight!' And at that
very moment I was able to see him.

14"Then he said: 'The God of our fathers has chosen you to know
his will and to see the Righteous One and to hear words from his
mouth. 15You will be his witness to all men of what you have seen and
heard. 16And now what are you waiting for? Get up, be baptized and
wash your sins away, calling on his name.'

[a]40 Or possibly *Hebrew*; also in 22:2

21:38 Aren't you the Egyptian? A notorious Egyptian had led a revolt against Rome a couple of years earlier. Josephus tells the account of a messianic Egyptian terrorist, who, in 54 A.D., led a movement against Rome in hopes of taking the city of Jerusalem. The Roman army routed his forces, but the Egyptian himself escaped. **terrorists.** Literally, "the assassins," or, in Latin, the *sicarri (so called because they carried* the short dagger known as the sica under their robes). While technically this term did not apply to the followers of the Egyptian, the sicarri were an anti-Roman guerrilla group that emerged at the same time. Eventually, they led the revolt against Rome that resulted in the destruction of Jerusalem in A.D. 70.

21:39–40 Perhaps in hopes of resolving the conflict, the commander allowed Paul to speak from the steps of the Fortress. The fact that he spoke in Aramaic, which was the common language of Jews in Palestine but not widely spoken outside of that area, commanded the attention of the crowd.

22:3 a Jew ... brought up in this city. Although a citizen of Tarsus by virtue of his birth, Paul spent most of his life in Jerusalem. Chapter 23:16 implies that Paul's sister and her family lived in the city. **Gamaliel.** Gamaliel was a highly respected Pharisee, head of the Hillel wing of this sect. To have received an education from this man was to have had access to the best possible Jewish education (5:34). **the law of our fathers.** Paul emphasized that he too had a lifelong knowledge of and respect for the Law.

22:4 this Way. Unique to Acts as a name for Christianity (19:9,23; 24:14,22).

17 "When I returned to Jerusalem and was praying at the temple, I
fell into a trance 18 and saw the Lord speaking. 'Quick!' he said to me.
'Leave Jerusalem immediately, because they will not accept your testimony about me.'
19 " 'Lord,' I replied, 'these men know that I went from one synagogue to another to imprison and beat those who believe in you.
20 And when the blood of your martyr[a] Stephen was shed, I stood
there giving my approval and guarding the clothes of those who were
killing him.'
21 "Then the Lord said to me, 'Go; I will send you far away to the
Gentiles.' "

Paul the Roman Citizen

22 The crowd listened to Paul until he said this. Then they raised
their voices and shouted, "Rid the earth of him! He's not fit to live!"
23 As they were shouting and throwing off their cloaks and flinging
dust into the air, 24 the commander ordered Paul to be taken into the
barracks. He directed that he be flogged and questioned in order to
find out why the people were shouting at him like this. 25 As they
stretched him out to flog him, Paul said to the centurion standing
there, "Is it legal for you to flog a Roman citizen who hasn't even
been found guilty?"
26 When the centurion heard this, he went to the commander and
reported it. "What are you going to do?" he asked. "This man is a
Roman citizen."
27 The commander went to Paul and asked, "Tell me, are you a Roman citizen?"
"Yes, I am," he answered.
28 Then the commander said, "I had to pay a big price for my citizenship."
"But I was born a citizen," Paul replied.
29 Those who were about to question him withdrew immediately.
The commander himself was alarmed when he realized that he had
put Paul, a Roman citizen, in chains.

Before the Sanhedrin

30 The next day, since the commander wanted to find out exactly
why Paul was being accused by the Jews, he released him and ordered the chief priests and all the Sanhedrin to assemble. Then he
brought Paul and had him stand before them.

[a]20 Or *witness*

OPEN Who holds the record in your group for the number of times they were sent to the principal's office?

STUDY 1. Why does the Roman commander go to the trouble of calling the ruling body of the

---

22:22 For Paul to claim that he was divinely inspired to minister among the Gentiles appeared as rank heresy, a slap in the face to God and the Jews, and more than adequate justification for the charges that he was anti-Jewish, lacked respect for the Law, and would defile the temple.

22:25 Flogging was a severe punishment since leather thongs weighted with pieces of bone, metal or rocks were used as the whip. Since Roman citizens were protected from punishment without trial and were sheltered from this particular form of punishment no matter what, Paul once again brought up the matter of his Roman citizenship (16:37).

22:28 I had to pay a big price for my citizenship. Citizenship was not supposedly a matter of money, but of birthright or notable service. However, bribes and other means of influence were also a means of gaining the privilege. **I was born a citizen.** Paul's response turns the table on the commander. His citizenship was not a matter of bribery at all, but of natural right.

22:29–30 Regardless of how his citizenship was obtained, the fact that he had been imprisoned without charge and almost flogged was a dangerous breach of policy that could cost the commander his rank (and perhaps his life) if he proceeded on in this fashion.

Jewish religion together? **2.** Why would the high priest be outraged by Paul's assertion that he had performed faithful service all of his life to God? Did Paul apologize for insulting the high priest or was he just wondering how a man like that got the job? **3.** Why does Paul change the focus from keeping the Law to hope in the resurrection? How would you describe the dispute that ensued? **4.** If you had been Paul in this situation, what would the appearance of the Lord do for you? **5.** In light of the fact that Paul refused to listen to the Holy Spirit's warning on two occasions to not go to Jerusalem, what does this say about God's promises? **6.** How do you handle situations where your faith is questioned or belittled?

APPLY 1. What is the closest you have come to feeling the presence of the Lord standing with you after a series of discouragements? **2.** Do you need a special word of encouragement right now from the Lord? Maybe your group could help.

23 Paul looked straight at the Sanhedrin and said, "My brothers,
I have fulfilled my duty to God in all good conscience to this
day." 2At this the high priest Ananias ordered those standing near
Paul to strike him on the mouth. 3Then Paul said to him, "God will
strike you, you whitewashed wall! You sit there to judge me according
to the law, yet you yourself violate the law by commanding that I be
struck!"
4Those who were standing near Paul said, "You dare to insult God's
high priest?"
5Paul replied, "Brothers, I did not realize that he was the high
priest; for it is written: 'Do not speak evil about the ruler of your
people.'[a]"
6Then Paul, knowing that some of them were Sadducees and the
others Pharisees, called out in the Sanhedrin, "My brothers, I am a
Pharisee, the son of a Pharisee. I stand on trial because of my hope in
the resurrection of the dead." 7When he said this, a dispute broke out
between the Pharisees and the Sadducees, and the assembly was divided. 8(The Sadducees say that there is no resurrection, and that
there are neither angels nor spirits, but the Pharisees acknowledge
them all.)
9There was a great uproar, and some of the teachers of the law who
were Pharisees stood up and argued vigorously. "We find nothing
wrong with this man," they said. "What if a spirit or an angel has spoken to him?" 10The dispute became so violent that the commander
was afraid Paul would be torn to pieces by them. He ordered the
troops to go down and take him away from them by force and bring
him into the barracks.
11The following night the Lord stood near Paul and said, "Take
courage! As you have testified about me in Jerusalem, so you must
also testify in Rome."

OPEN 1. Have you ever had to call 911? **2.** Have you ever feared for your life?

The Plot to Kill Paul

12The next morning the Jews formed a conspiracy and bound themselves with an oath not to eat or drink until they had killed Paul.

[a]5 Exodus 22:28

23:2 the high priest Ananias. Ananias was appointed to this office by Herod Agrippa II (25:13) in A.D. 47 and held the position until A.D. 58 or 59. It is known that he had a well established reputation for being a violent, greedy and unscrupulous man. **ordered those standing near Paul to strike him.** It was against Jewish law for a defendant to be treated like this. Whether Ananias did so to intimidate Paul or because he found his comments of faithful service offensive is uncertain.

23:3 God will strike you. Whether or not this was intended as a prophecy or simply as a comment about God's judgment against evildoers, Paul's word came true. In A.D. 66 Jews who were leading a revolt against Rome captured Ananias and murdered him for his pro-Roman policies. **you whitewashed wall!** The picture is of someone trying to fix up a wall threatening to collapse simply by painting it with a thin coat of paint. While Ananias, as a member of the Sanhedrin, had the trappings of a minister of justice, his actions betrayed that justice was far from a concern of his.

23:8 resurrection. The resurrection of the dead prior to the full establishment of God's reign was a crucial doctrine for the Pharisees, but was flatly rejected by the Sadducees, who, since they only accepted the five books of Moses as authoritative, found no basis for such a belief (Luke 20:37).

23:10 With the Sanhedrin hopelessly embroiled in their controversy, the commander realized that he was no closer to getting any information about Paul and that Paul was in danger. Once again, troops were sent in to rescue Paul from the problem.

23:11 For the fourth and final time in Acts, the Lord addresses Paul personally to encourage him in a time of crisis (an angel comforts him in the midst of a storm in 27:23–24). **Take courage!** The same word is used when Jesus spoke to the disciples as they faced a life-threatening storm on the Sea of Galilee (Mark 6:50). **testified about me.** The real issue at stake was speaking of Jesus, not defending himself against false charges—which Paul seemed to realize in his address to the Sanhedrin (v. 6).

23:12–13 A group of radical Jewish nationalists decided Paul must die for his supposed anti-Jewish sentiments.

[13]More than forty men were involved in this plot. [14]They went to the
chief priests and elders and said, "We have taken a solemn oath not
to eat anything until we have killed Paul. [15]Now then, you and the
Sanhedrin petition the commander to bring him before you on the
pretext of wanting more accurate information about his case. We are
ready to kill him before he gets here."

[16]But when the son of Paul's sister heard of this plot, he went into
the barracks and told Paul.

[17]Then Paul called one of the centurions and said, "Take this young
man to the commander; he has something to tell him." [18]So he took
him to the commander.

The centurion said, "Paul, the prisoner, sent for me and asked me to bring this young man to you because he has something to tell you."

[19]The commander took the young man by the hand, drew him aside
and asked, "What is it you want to tell me?"

[20]He said: "The Jews have agreed to ask you to bring Paul before
the Sanhedrin tomorrow on the pretext of wanting more accurate information about him. [21]Don't give in to them, because more than for-
ty of them are waiting in ambush for him. They have taken an oath not to eat or drink until they have killed him. They are ready now, waiting for your consent to their request."

[22]The commander dismissed the young man and cautioned him,
"Don't tell anyone that you have reported this to me."

Paul Transferred to Caesarea

[23]Then he called two of his centurions and ordered them, "Get
ready a detachment of two hundred soldiers, seventy horsemen and
two hundred spearmen[a] to go to Caesarea at nine tonight. [24]Provide
mounts for Paul so that he may be taken safely to Governor Felix."

[25]He wrote a letter as follows:

[26]Claudius Lysias,

To His Excellency, Governor Felix:

Greetings.

[a]23 The meaning of the Greek for this word is uncertain.

STUDY 1. Right after the Lord promises Paul that he will live to visit Rome, what happens? Do you think the Lord was preparing Paul for this assassination attempt? **2.** What do you learn about Paul's family in this episode? Do you think Paul's nephew was taking a risk in getting to Paul and the commander? **3.** If this was the same military commander that rescued Paul from the mob and knew that Paul was a Roman citizen being unfairly treated by the religious establishment, why didn't he move against the high priest and the assassins? **4.** If you were Paul, would you be asking "where is God in all of this"?

APPLY 1. What is the closest you have come to putting your life in jeopardy for the cause of Christ? **2.** What is it costing you right now to be a follower of Christ?

OPEN If you had to pack in ten minutes and get out of town, what would you pack?

STUDY 1. What does the military commander decide to do with Paul? How does this compare to the way Pilate dealt with Jesus (Luke 23:1–25)? **2.** What does the large detachment of soldiers tell you about the assassination plot? If you had been Paul, how would you be feeling as you were being escorted out of Jerusalem? Do you think he had any regret about coming to Jerusalem?

bound ... with an oath. This was a religious commitment to kill Paul. Should they fail in the attempt, it was an acknowledgement that they themselves ought to be struck down and killed by God.

23:14–15 Since Paul would have been escorted by Roman soldiers, these men were willing to risk death in their attempt to kill Paul.

23:16 This is the only glimpse the New Testament gives us about Paul's family. Perhaps his sister and her family lived in Jerusalem, or perhaps Paul's nephew went there to receive his education (22:3). How his nephew heard of the plot is not revealed. **he went into the barracks and told Paul.** Paul was held in custody pending charges on the near riot, but as a Roman citizen he was permitted visitors.

23:21 They are ... waiting for your consent. The request to have Paul appear before the Sanhedrin the next morning had already been made, undoubtedly lending credence to the boy's story.

23:23 two hundred soldiers, seventy horsemen and two hundred spearmen. Having witnessed the severity of the reaction against Paul, the commander was taking no chances with this radical group! As the text reads, he placed Paul under the protection of almost half of the garrison forces and sent him off under cover of darkness.

23:24 mounts. Since the plural is used, it may be that horses were provided for Paul's companions as well. **Governor Felix.** The Roman historian Tacitus paints a negative picture of Felix as a self-indulgent ruler who acted with disregard toward the people he was supposed to govern. He was known to have used extremely forceful measures to put down Jewish uprisings.

Would you? **3.** What do you think happened to the forty fanatics who vowed to kill Paul (23:13)? **4.** How do you think the church leadership responded to Paul's arrest?

APPLY 1. In your own experience, when have you found the civil authorities more gracious than the religious authorities? **2.** Have you experienced a time when the civil government stood up for what was right when the church did not?

27This man was seized by the Jews and they were about to kill
him, but I came with my troops and rescued him, for I had
learned that he is a Roman citizen. 28I wanted to know why they
were accusing him, so I brought him to their Sanhedrin. 29I
found that the accusation had to do with questions about their
law, but there was no charge against him that deserved death or
imprisonment. 30When I was informed of a plot to be carried out
against the man, I sent him to you at once. I also ordered his accusers to present to you their case against him.

31So the soldiers, carrying out their orders, took Paul with them
during the night and brought him as far as Antipatris. 32The next day
they let the cavalry go on with him, while they returned to the barracks. 33When the cavalry arrived in Caesarea, they delivered the letter to the governor and handed Paul over to him. 34The governor read
the letter and asked what province he was from. Learning that he was
from Cilicia, 35he said, "I will hear your case when your accusers get
here." Then he ordered that Paul be kept under guard in Herod's palace.

OPEN Have you ever had to defend yourself before an authoritative figure? Were you afraid?

STUDY 1. Do you find the insincere flattery that the lawyer gives to Felix a little disgusting? **2.** From the viewpoint of the high priest, were his charges accurate? **3.** What do you learn here about Paul's reason for coming to Jerusalem? What does Paul say in his defense? **4.** How would you describe the behavior of Governor Felix in verses 24–26? If Felix became a Christian, what would it cost him? Who does Felix remind you of today? **5.** Why does Felix decide to keep Paul under house arrest? If you had been Paul, would you have slipped Felix a little money? **6.** If you had to choose between three beatings to the point of death (in Corinth, Ephesus and Jerusalem) or two years laid up in Caesarea in house arrest, which one would you choose? **7.** Before Paul left for Jerusalem, he wrote the letter to the Romans while still in Corinth in which he said, "There is no authority except that which God has established ... he who rebels against the authority is rebelling against what God has instituted" (Rom. 13:1–2). Do you think Paul still feels as strong about this after his experience?

The Trial Before Felix

24 Five days later the high priest Ananias went down to Caesarea with some of the elders and a lawyer named Tertullus,
and they brought their charges against Paul before the governor.
2When Paul was called in, Tertullus presented his case before Felix:
"We have enjoyed a long period of peace under you, and your foresight has brought about reforms in this nation. 3Everywhere and in
every way, most excellent Felix, we acknowledge this with profound
gratitude. 4But in order not to weary you further, I would request that
you be kind enough to hear us briefly.

5"We have found this man to be a troublemaker, stirring up riots
among the Jews all over the world. He is a ringleader of the Nazarene
sect 6and even tried to desecrate the temple; so we seized him. 8By[a]
examining him yourself you will be able to learn the truth about all
these charges we are bringing against him."

9The Jews joined in the accusation, asserting that these things
were true.

10When the governor motioned for him to speak, Paul replied: "I
know that for a number of years you have been a judge over this nation; so I gladly make my defense. 11You can easily verify that no more
than twelve days ago I went up to Jerusalem to worship. 12My accusers did not find me arguing with anyone at the temple, or stirring up
a crowd in the synagogues or anywhere else in the city. 13And they
cannot prove to you the charges they are now making against me.

[a]6-8 Some manuscripts *him and wanted to judge him according to our law. 7But the commander, Lysias, came and with the use of much force snatched him from our hands 8and ordered his accusers to come before you. By*

24:1 a lawyer. Literally this is "an orator." Tertullus, who bears a Roman name, may have been a Greek-speaking Jew.

24:6 desecrate the temple. The charge has been altered from the accusation in 21:28 that Paul had defiled the temple by bringing a Gentile with him into it. Verse 7, which is omitted from most manuscripts, goes on to claim that the Sanhedrin had planned to try Paul itself until Lysias seized Paul away from them. If this verse is authentic, it would have been said, of course, to downplay the riotous scene that actually occurred and put responsibility on the Roman, Lysias.

[14]However, I admit that I worship the God of our fathers as a follower
of the Way, which they call a sect. I believe everything that agrees
with the Law and that is written in the Prophets, [15]and I have the
same hope in God as these men, that there will be a resurrection of
both the righteous and the wicked. [16]So I strive always to keep my
conscience clear before God and man.

[17]"After an absence of several years, I came to Jerusalem to bring
my people gifts for the poor and to present offerings. [18]I was ceremonially clean when they found me in the temple courts doing this.
There was no crowd with me, nor was I involved in any disturbance.
[19]But there are some Jews from the province of Asia, who ought to be
here before you and bring charges if they have anything against me.
[20]Or these who are here should state what crime they found in me
when I stood before the Sanhedrin— [21]unless it was this one thing I
shouted as I stood in their presence: 'It is concerning the resurrection of the dead that I am on trial before you today.' "

[22]Then Felix, who was well acquainted with the Way, adjourned the
proceedings. "When Lysias the commander comes," he said, "I will
decide your case." [23]He ordered the centurion to keep Paul under
guard but to give him some freedom and permit his friends to take
care of his needs.

[24]Several days later Felix came with his wife Drusilla, who was a
Jewess. He sent for Paul and listened to him as he spoke about faith
in Christ Jesus. [25]As Paul discoursed on righteousness, self-control
and the judgment to come, Felix was afraid and said, "That's enough
for now! You may leave. When I find it convenient, I will send for
you." [26]At the same time he was hoping that Paul would offer him a
bribe, so he sent for him frequently and talked with him.

[27]When two years had passed, Felix was succeeded by Porcius Festus, but because Felix wanted to grant a favor to the Jews, he left Paul
in prison.

The Trial Before Festus

25 Three days after arriving in the province, Festus went up
from Caesarea to Jerusalem, [2]where the chief priests and
Jewish leaders appeared before him and presented the charges
against Paul. [3]They urgently requested Festus, as a favor to them, to
have Paul transferred to Jerusalem, for they were preparing an ambush to kill him along the way. [4]Festus answered, "Paul is being held

APPLY 1. As you look back over your spiritual life, what period did you feel like you were "under house arrest"? **2.** How do you look upon that period of time now?

OPEN Who was the person that served as the court of final appeal in your family when you got in trouble? Did this person ever overturn a lower court verdict?

STUDY Two years have passed since the first trial

24:14–15 Having denied the charges of insurrection and temple defilement, Paul readily agrees he is a follower of "the Way," but that he does so as a Jew, loyal to the God of his ancestors. By this, he implies that there is nothing heretical about his views. His convictions rest on the Old Testament Scriptures shared by all Jews.

24:24 Drusilla. A daughter of Herod Agrippa (12:1), Drusilla was barely 20 years old at this time. She had divorced another man to become Felix's third wife. Since she was Jewish and in a position to have heard a lot about the Christians, she may have been the source of Felix's information about their beliefs.

24:26 a bribe. The offering and acceptance of a bribe in such cases was illegal, but a common practice nonetheless. Paul Veyne writes in *A History of Private Life: From Pagan Rome to Byzantium,* "To our modern way of thinking, a man ceases to be a true public servant if he lines his pockets with the spoils of office or if he places personal ambition above the common good ... . The honest functionary is a peculiarity of modern Western nations. In Rome every superior stole from his subordinates ... . Every public function was a racket; those in charge 'put the squeeze' on their subordinates, and all together exploited the populace."

24:27 Porcius Festus. Felix's administration ended when he was found guilty of using excessive violence in crushing a civil strife between Jews and Greeks in Caesarea. Even when forced to leave office (probably about A.D. 58), he refused to dispense with Paul's case but left him imprisoned as a favor to the Jews. He was replaced by Festus, who was governor of the area until his death two or three years later in A.D. 61.

at Caesarea, and I myself am going there soon. 5Let some of your
leaders come with me and press charges against the man there, if he
has done anything wrong."
6After spending eight or ten days with them, he went down to Caesarea, and the next day he convened the court and ordered that Paul
be brought before him. 7When Paul appeared, the Jews who had come
down from Jerusalem stood around him, bringing many serious
charges against him, which they could not prove.
8Then Paul made his defense: "I have done nothing wrong against
the law of the Jews or against the temple or against Caesar."
9Festus, wishing to do the Jews a favor, said to Paul, "Are you willing to go up to Jerusalem and stand trial before me there on these
charges?"
10Paul answered: "I am now standing before Caesar's court, where
I ought to be tried. I have not done any wrong to the Jews, as you
yourself know very well. 11If, however, I am guilty of doing anything
deserving death, I do not refuse to die. But if the charges brought
against me by these Jews are not true, no one has the right to hand
me over to them. I appeal to Caesar!"
12After Festus had conferred with his council, he declared: "You
have appealed to Caesar. To Caesar you will go!"

Festus Consults King Agrippa

13A few days later King Agrippa and Bernice arrived at Caesarea to
pay their respects to Festus. 14Since they were spending many days
there, Festus discussed Paul's case with the king. He said: "There is a
man here whom Felix left as a prisoner. 15When I went to Jerusalem,
the chief priests and elders of the Jews brought charges against him
and asked that he be condemned.
16"I told them that it is not the Roman custom to hand over any
man before he has faced his accusers and has had an opportunity to
defend himself against their charges. 17When they came here with
me, I did not delay the case, but convened the court the next day and
ordered the man to be brought in. 18When his accusers got up to
speak, they did not charge him with any of the crimes I had expected.
19Instead, they had some points of dispute with him about their own
religion and about a dead man named Jesus who Paul claimed was
alive. 20I was at a loss how to investigate such matters; so I asked if
he would be willing to go to Jerusalem and stand trial there on these
charges. 21When Paul made his appeal to be held over for the

before the Roman governor, Felix. Now, a new Roman governor has arrived. **1.** What is the first thing the high priest and Jewish leaders try to do? What does Festus decide? **2.** Why would Festus, the Roman governor, ask Paul to go to Jerusalem to face his accusers? Why did Paul refuse? **3.** In appealing to Caesar, what does this force the governor to do? **4.** If you lived in a country where there was a "contract" out on your life because of your stand for Christ, what would you do?

APPLY What is the closest you have come to being allowed to share your faith in Christ with the highest court of justice in the land? How did you do?

OPEN What is the closest you have come to meeting someone in high public office?

STUDY 1. What do you remember about King Herod (12:1–23)? Why would Agrippa be especially interested in hearing from Paul? **2.** How fair is the Roman governor in describing Judaism? About Christianity? Do you think Festus is trying to find out the truth in this matter? **3.** Do you feel a little sorry for the Roman governor? If you had been in his position and wanted to keep the peace, what would you have done?

APPLY Do you feel comfortable talking with people in the secular world about the matters of your faith?

25:8 Caesar. The first five emperors (from Octavian to Nero) were descendants of Julius Caesar and thus kept his name, although it was commonly used as a title. At the time of this trial, Nero was the emperor; and the cruelties for which he is remembered in history had not yet occurred.

25:9 *In Jerusalem,* the Sanhedrin would be responsible for conducting a trial on matters of Jewish law. Festus would only have to ratify a decision for capital punishment if that is what the Sanhedrin decided upon. This action was a tacit admission that Paul was innocent of having violated Roman law. Since that was the only reason Paul could be held in a Roman prison, this suggestion showed that Festus was willing to sacrifice Paul for the sake of some political advantage with the Sanhedrin.

25:10–11 Paul knew there was no chance of a fair hearing in Jerusalem. Recognizing that his hope for justice lay in getting out of an area so influenced by the Sanhedrin, he exercised his right as a Roman citizen to appeal his case to the emperor.

25:13 King Agrippa ... at Caesarea. The son of Herod Agrippa I (12:1ff). Agrippa II had been appointed as a puppet king (under Roman authority) over some provinces to the northeast of Palestine. Because of Agrippa's Jewish background, Festus hoped he would be able to help sort out the situation with Paul. **Bernice.** Agrippa's sister. After her first husband died she lived with her brother, which prompted rumors of incest. She was often presented as Agrippa's queen. She also maintained loyalty to Rome and later was the mistress of Titus, who became emperor.

Emperor's decision, I ordered him held until I could send him to Caesar."

22Then Agrippa said to Festus, "I would like to hear this man myself."

He replied, "Tomorrow you will hear him."

Paul Before Agrippa

23The next day Agrippa and Bernice came with great pomp and entered the audience room with the high ranking officers and the leading men of the city. At the command of Festus, Paul was brought in. 24Festus said: "King Agrippa, and all who are present with us, you see this man! The whole Jewish community has petitioned me about him in Jerusalem and here in Caesarea, shouting that he ought not to live any longer. 25I found he had done nothing deserving of death, but because he made his appeal to the Emperor I decided to send him to Rome. 26But I have nothing definite to write to His Majesty about him. Therefore I have brought him before all of you, and especially before you, King Agrippa, so that as a result of this investigation I may have something to write. 27For I think it is unreasonable to send on a prisoner without specifying the charges against him."

26 Then Agrippa said to Paul, "You have permission to speak for yourself."

So Paul motioned with his hand and began his defense: 2"King Agrippa, I consider myself fortunate to stand before you today as I make my defense against all the accusations of the Jews, 3and especially so because you are well acquainted with all the Jewish customs and controversies. Therefore, I beg you to listen to me patiently.

4"The Jews all know the way I have lived ever since I was a child, from the beginning of my life in my own country, and also in Jerusalem. 5They have known me for a long time and can testify, if they are willing, that according to the strictest sect of our religion, I lived as a Pharisee. 6And now it is because of my hope in what God has promised our fathers that I am on trial today. 7This is the promise our twelve tribes are hoping to see fulfilled as they earnestly serve God day and night. O king, it is because of this hope that the Jews are accusing me. 8Why should any of you consider it incredible that God raises the dead?

9"I too was convinced that I ought to do all that was possible to oppose the name of Jesus of Nazareth. 10And that is just what I did in Jerusalem. On the authority of the chief priests I put many of the saints in prison, and when they were put to death, I cast my vote against them. 11Many a time I went from one synagogue to another to have them punished, and I tried to force them to blaspheme. In my obsession against them, I even went to foreign cities to persecute them.

12"On one of these journeys I was going to Damascus with the authority and commission of the chief priests. 13About noon, O king, as I was on the road, I saw a light from heaven, brighter than the sun, blazing around me and my companions. 14We all fell to the ground, and I heard a voice saying to me in Aramaic,[a] 'Saul, Saul, why do you persecute me? It is hard for you to kick against the goads.'

15"Then I asked, 'Who are you, Lord?'

[a]14 Or *Hebrew*

OPEN 1. How much interest do you have in high profile court cases? **2.** What do you fear most about speaking before a group?

STUDY Paul has been arrested in Jerusalem and held for two years under house arrest in Caesarea, the Roman provincial capital. He has appealed his case to Caesar, but Agrippa, the Jewish puppet king for Judea, comes to town and asks to hear Paul's case. **1.** How would you describe the atmosphere for this event? **2.** Why does Festus, the Roman governor, want the Jewish puppet king to listen to the case? Why would Agrippa be in a position to understand the charges? **3.** According to Paul, what is the central issue in the conflict between him and the Jewish religious leaders (23:6)? How does Paul's position differ from the position of the Pharisees who also believe in a general resurrection (23:8; 26:8)? **4.** In verses 9–18, Paul shares more of his faith story—his zeal as a strict member of the Pharisees, his passion to stop the spread of Christianity, his conversion and his call to spread the gospel to the Gentiles. Do you think Paul's primary goal was to convince Agrippa of his innocence or to win Agrippa to Christ? **5.** What is it about the personal testimony of a Christian that makes it so powerful? When you hear the story of someone about their struggles as a Christian, how does this make you feel about this person? **6.** How does the Roman governor respond to Paul's testimony? How does Agrippa respond? **7.** How would you describe Paul's closing appeal to Agrippa? Why do you think Agrippa gets up and walks out? **8.** Why do you think Luke, the author of the book of Acts, includes this testimony of Paul at the close of his book (Hint: 1:1).

APPLY 1. How would you compare your sense of God's calling for your life to Paul's sense of God's calling in verses 16–18? **2.** What is God calling you to do in this coming year?

" 'I am Jesus, whom you are persecuting,' the Lord replied. 16'Now
get up and stand on your feet. I have appeared to you to appoint you
as a servant and as a witness of what you have seen of me and what
I will show you. 17I will rescue you from your own people and from
the Gentiles. I am sending you to them 18to open their eyes and turn
them from darkness to light, and from the power of Satan to God, so
that they may receive forgiveness of sins and a place among those
who are sanctified by faith in me.'

19"So then, King Agrippa, I was not disobedient to the vision from
heaven. 20First to those in Damascus, then to those in Jerusalem and
in all Judea, and to the Gentiles also, I preached that they should repent and turn to God and prove their repentance by their deeds.
21That is why the Jews seized me in the temple courts and tried to kill
me. 22But I have had God's help to this very day, and so I stand here
and testify to small and great alike. I am saying nothing beyond what
the prophets and Moses said would happen— 23that the Christ[b]
would suffer and, as the first to rise from the dead, would proclaim
light to his own people and to the Gentiles."

24At this point Festus interrupted Paul's defense. "You are out of
your mind, Paul!" he shouted. "Your great learning is driving you insane."

25"I am not insane, most excellent Festus," Paul replied. "What I am
saying is true and reasonable. 26The king is familiar with these
things, and I can speak freely to him. I am convinced that none of this
has escaped his notice, because it was not done in a corner. 27King
Agrippa, do you believe the prophets? I know you do."

28Then Agrippa said to Paul, "Do you think that in such a short time
you can persuade me to be a Christian?"

29Paul replied, "Short time or long—I pray God that not only you
but all who are listening to me today may become what I am, except
for these chains."

30The king rose, and with him the governor and Bernice and those
sitting with them. 31They left the room, and while talking with one
another, they said, "This man is not doing anything that deserves
death or imprisonment."

32Agrippa said to Festus, "This man could have been set free if he
had not appealed to Caesar."

Paul Sails for Rome

27 When it was decided that we would sail for Italy, Paul and
some other prisoners were handed over to a centurion
named Julius, who belonged to the Imperial Regiment. 2We boarded a
ship from Adramyttium about to sail for ports along the coast of the

b23 Or Messiah

OPEN 1. If you could take a honeymoon cruise anywhere, where would you go? **2.** How are you at sailing a boat, especially in storms?

STUDY 1. How do you think Paul feels on his way to Rome after being held in Caesarea for two

27:1 When it was decided that we would sail for Italy. The trip to Rome probably began sometime in the autumn of A.D. 59. ***other prisoners.*** They may also have appealed to Caesar or were to appear in the arena.

27:2 We. Luke is again in the picture. It is suggested that Luke and Aristarchus may have come along as Paul's servants, which would have elevated Paul's status in the eyes of the centurion. **a ship from Adramyttium.** This was a port near Troas in Asia. **sail for ports along the coast.** A day's sail of about 70 nautical miles from Caesarea. While loading and unloading cargo, Paul was allowed (probably under the supervision of a soldier) to visit the Christian community there. While this type of freedom of movement might seem unusual for a prisoner, Paul had consistently been given access to friends during his stay at Caesarea and was essentially traveling to Rome having been already declared innocent.

province of Asia, and we put out to sea. Aristarchus, a Macedonian
from Thessalonica, was with us.
[3]The next day we landed at Sidon; and Julius, in kindness to Paul,
allowed him to go to his friends so they might provide for his needs.
[4]From there we put out to sea again and passed to the lee of Cyprus
because the winds were against us. [5]When we had sailed across the
open sea off the coast of Cilicia and Pamphylia, we landed at Myra in
Lycia. [6]There the centurion found an Alexandrian ship sailing for Italy
and put us on board. [7]We made slow headway for many days and had
difficulty arriving off Cnidus. When the wind did not allow us to hold
our course, we sailed to the lee of Crete, opposite Salmone. [8]We
moved along the coast with difficulty and came to a place called Fair
Havens, near the town of Lasea.
[9]Much time had been lost, and sailing had already become dangerous because by now it was after the Fast.[a] So Paul warned them,
[10]"Men, I can see that our voyage is going to be disastrous and bring
great loss to ship and cargo, and to our own lives also." [11]But the
centurion, instead of listening to what Paul said, followed the advice
of the pilot and of the owner of the ship. [12]Since the harbor was unsuitable to winter in, the majority decided that we should sail on,
hoping to reach Phoenix and winter there. This was a harbor in Crete,
facing both southwest and northwest.

The Storm

[13]When a gentle south wind began to blow, they thought they had
obtained what they wanted; so they weighed anchor and sailed along
the shore of Crete. [14]Before very long, a wind of hurricane force,
called the "northeaster," swept down from the island. [15]The ship was
caught by the storm and could not head into the wind; so we gave
way to it and were driven along. [16]As we passed to the lee of a small
island called Cauda, we were hardly able to make the lifeboat secure.
[17]When the men had hoisted it aboard, they passed ropes under the

[a]9 That is, the Day of Atonement (Yom Kippur)

years under house arrest? Who are the "we" that are accompanying Paul? **2.** From verses 1–3 and verse 43, how would you describe his relationship with Julius, the centurion? How do you think they got acquainted? **3.** If you were the ship's owner or pilot, how would you react to Paul's warning in verse 10? How do you react to backseat drivers in your family? **4.** How would you describe the "northeaster" in verses 14–16? What would you do in this situation? **5.** What steps does the crew take in verses 17–20 to secure the ship? What do they conclude? **6.** Who ends up becoming the captain of the boat? If you were on board, what would the words of Paul do for you? If you didn't believe in God, how would you feel? **7.** What is it about Paul that made him so strong in times of crisis? Is this something that can be cultivated with greater faith—or is it a temperament thing? **8.** Who does Paul remind you of in your family or among your close acquaintances?

APPLY 1. What is the closest you have come to going through a storm like this in your life? **2.** On a scale from 1 to 10, what is the storm measurement in your life right now? **3.** How could your group pray for you now?

27:5 we landed at Myra. One text says this portion of the trip took about 15 days. At Myra, Paul and the other prisoners were transferred to another ship heading to Italy (v. 6) since their original ship would be heading north to Adramyttium.

27:9 sailing had already become dangerous. The safe season for sailing was already past. The sea was dangerous after September 15 and ceased altogether between mid-November until at least early February. It was not considered really safe to sail again until mid-March. **after the Fast.** This would have been Yom Kippur which, in A.D. 59, took place on October 5.

27:10 Whether Paul's comment was in response to a prophetic word he had received or simply a foreboding based on the difficulties they had already experienced is unclear. Although no information is given about them, Paul had already experienced *three* shipwrecks and, during one of those occasions, been lost at sea for a full night and a day (2 Cor. 11:25).

27:13 How long they had to wait in Fair Havens is not mentioned, but finally a break in the weather came and they thought it safe to make the day's sail to Phoenix.

27:14 Along the way, the wind shifted from a gentle southerly breeze to a violent northeast storm. **a wind of hurricane force.** The Greek word behind this expression is the source of the English word "typhoon."

27:15 Ships of old could not face the destructive, heavy seas, so sailors had to allow the ship to be pushed by the wind away from the land.

27:16 island called Cauda. A small island, known today as Gavaho or Gozzo, about 20 miles south of Crete. **the lifeboat.** This was normally towed, but in a storm it was brought on board to be kept from being swamped.

27:17 Here is a picture of frenetic activity, as the sailors and passengers did what they could to try to make the ship as secure as possible in the face of the storm. **passed ropes ... to hold it together.** Literally, "they used helps to undergird the ship." The "helps" were some type of block and tackle used to pull ropes or cables tightly around the ship to prevent it from breaking apart. **the sandbars of Syrtis.** A dangerous shoal off the coast of Africa. **lowered the sea anchor.** Literally, "the tackle." What is in view here in uncertain. It may mean to take down the mainsail or to drag an anchor to slow the ship's speed.

ship itself to hold it together. Fearing that they would run aground on
the sandbars of Syrtis, they lowered the sea anchor and let the ship
be driven along. 18We took such a violent battering from the storm
that the next day they began to throw the cargo overboard. 19On the
third day, they threw the ship's tackle overboard with their own
hands. 20When neither sun nor stars appeared for many days and the
storm continued raging, we finally gave up all hope of being saved.

21After the men had gone a long time without food, Paul stood up
before them and said: "Men, you should have taken my advice not to
sail from Crete; then you would have spared yourselves this damage
and loss. 22But now I urge you to keep up your courage, because not
one of you will be lost; only the ship will be destroyed. 23Last night an
angel of the God whose I am and whom I serve stood beside me
24and said, 'Do not be afraid, Paul. You must stand trial before Caesar;
and God has graciously given you the lives of all who sail with you.'
25So keep up your courage, men, for I have faith in God that it will
happen just as he told me. 26Nevertheless, we must run aground on
some island."

The Shipwreck

27On the fourteenth night we were still being driven across the
Adriatic[a] Sea, when about midnight the sailors sensed they were approaching land. 28They took soundings and found that the water was
a hundred and twenty feet[b] deep. A short time later they took soundings again and found it was ninety feet[c] deep. 29Fearing that we
would be dashed against the rocks, they dropped four anchors from
the stern and prayed for daylight. 30In an attempt to escape from the
ship, the sailors let the lifeboat down into the sea, pretending they
were going to lower some anchors from the bow. 31Then Paul said to
the centurion and the soldiers, "Unless these men stay with the ship,
you cannot be saved." 32So the soldiers cut the ropes that held the
lifeboat and let it fall away.

33Just before dawn Paul urged them all to eat. "For the last fourteen
days," he said, "you have been in constant suspense and have gone
without food—you haven't eaten anything. 34Now I urge you to take
some food. You need it to survive. Not one of you will lose a single
hair from his head." 35After he said this, he took some bread and gave
thanks to God in front of them all. Then he broke it and began to eat.
36They were all encouraged and ate some food themselves. 37Alto-
gether there were 276 of us on board. 38When they had eaten as much
as they wanted, they lightened the ship by throwing the grain into the
sea.

39When daylight came, they did not recognize the land, but they
saw a bay with a sandy beach, where they decided to run the ship
aground if they could. 40Cutting loose the anchors, they left them in
the sea and at the same time untied the ropes that held the rudders.

[a]27 In ancient times the name referred to an area extending well south of Italy. [b]28 Greek *twenty orguias* (about 37 meters) [c]28 Greek *fifteen orguias* (about 27 meters)

OPEN What natural disaster (snowstorm, hurricane, electrical blackout, tornado, etc.) do you remember when people emerged from the community to help others in the crisis?

STUDY 1. After 14 days in a storm in which "neither sun nor stars" can be seen and without eating any food, how would you be feeling? **2.** What does the crew want to do (v. 30)? What does Paul say? **3.** Who assumes command of the situation? Where does he get his commission? What has happened in the relationship between Paul and the Roman centurion? If you were the centurion, how would you look upon Paul? **4.** When the ship strikes the sand bar, what do the soldiers want to do with the prisoners? What happens? **5.** If you were Paul, how would you be thinking now about God's promise that you would "testify in Rome"(23:11)?

APPLY 1. What is the closest you have come to losing your life? **2.** In this time of crisis, how did this experience change your outlook on life and God's purpose for it?

27:21–26 In the midst of the despair, God gave Paul a message of encouragement to pass on to the crew. While there would be the loss of the ship, all of the travelers would be spared.

27:27 On the fourteenth night. Presumably from the time they left Fair Havens. **the Adriatic Sea.** While this term today only applies to the body of water between Italy and the Balkans, in Paul's day it included the sea between Sicily and Crete. This may also be the Adrian Sea. **sensed they were approaching land.** Probably by hearing the waves break on the coast.

Then they hoisted the foresail to the wind and made for the beach.
41But the ship struck a sandbar and ran aground. The bow stuck fast
and would not move, and the stern was broken to pieces by the
pounding of the surf.
42The soldiers planned to kill the prisoners to prevent any of them
from swimming away and escaping. 43But the centurion wanted to
spare Paul's life and kept them from carrying out their plan. He ordered those who could swim to jump overboard first and get to land.
44The rest were to get there on planks or on pieces of the ship. In this
way everyone reached land in safety.

Ashore on Malta

28 Once safely on shore, we found out that the island was
called Malta. 2The islanders showed us unusual kindness.
They built a fire and welcomed us all because it was raining and cold.
3Paul gathered a pile of brushwood and, as he put it on the fire, a viper, driven out by the heat, fastened itself on his hand. 4When the islanders saw the snake hanging from his hand, they said to each other,
"This man must be a murderer; for though he escaped from the sea,
Justice has not allowed him to live." 5But Paul shook the snake off
into the fire and suffered no ill effects. 6The people expected him to
swell up or suddenly fall dead, but after waiting a long time and seeing nothing unusual happen to him, they changed their minds and
said he was a god.
7There was an estate nearby that belonged to Publius, the chief official of the island. He welcomed us to his home and for three days
entertained us hospitably. 8His father was sick in bed, suffering from
fever and dysentery. Paul went in to see him and, after prayer, placed
his hands on him and healed him. 9When this had happened, the rest
of the sick on the island came and were cured. 10They honored us in
many ways and when we were ready to sail, they furnished us with
the supplies we needed.

Arrival at Rome

11After three months we put out to sea in a ship that had wintered
in the island. It was an Alexandrian ship with the figurehead of the
twin gods Castor and Pollux. 12We put in at Syracuse and stayed there
three days. 13From there we set sail and arrived at Rhegium. The next
day the south wind came up, and on the following day we reached
Puteoli. 14There we found some brothers who invited us to spend a
week with them. And so we came to Rome. 15The brothers there had
heard that we were coming, and they traveled as far as the Forum of
Appius and the Three Taverns to meet us. At the sight of these men
Paul thanked God and was encouraged. 16When we got to Rome, Paul
was allowed to live by himself, with a soldier to guard him.

OPEN Have you ever had a chigger attack where you thought you would die—or were afraid you might not die?

STUDY 1. How would you compare the island experience of Paul in this passage to the TV program *Survivor*? **2.** How would you react if a viper came out of a wood pile and "fastened itself on your hand"? How do you explain the fact that Paul did not swell up and die? **3.** What is the closest you have come to having an accident like a shipwreck turn into a serendipitous opportunity to minister to people like Paul had? **4.** What would it mean to Paul to finally get to Rome? It has been nearly three years since God promised Paul that he would one day testify in Rome (23:11). He has spent two years under house arrest in Caesarea and six months at sea through storms, shipwreck, and viper attack. How would you describe Paul's capacity for endurance?

APPLY 1. What is your lifelong ambition and yearning? How far are you from reaching this goal? **2.** How would you compare your capacity for tenacity and endurance to Paul's?

28:11 After three months ... in a ship. Assuming that the party left Fair Havens (27:8) in mid-October, the three months at Malta would most likely include November–January meaning they sailed again in February, still considered a dangerous time to be on the sea. **twin gods Castor and Pollux.** These gods, the twin sons of Zeus and Leda, were the patron saints of sailors. It was customary for a ship to have their figureheads on its bow.

28:14 At Puteoli, Paul and the others were able to spend a week with some Christians. Julius, the centurion, must have had other official business to deal with once reporting at the city, to allow Paul to remain there so long. **And so we came to Rome.** Rome was still about 140 miles away, but Paul's safe arrival in Italy effectively marks the climax of Acts, as the Lord's promise that he would preach the gospel there was fulfilled, despite Paul's imprisonment and guarded living, he was able to press on.

OPEN Where do you want to visit before you die? What do you want to do before you die?

STUDY **1.** What made Paul call a meeting with the Jewish leaders only three days after he arrived in Rome? What does Paul explain to them? What is the immediate reaction? **2.** Why would Paul call a meeting with the Jewish leaders? What does Paul want to assure the leaders (v. 19)? If Paul considered his calling to be to the Gentiles, why does he say, "it is because of the hope of Israel that I am bound with this chain"? Do you think Paul ever really gave up on the Jews? **3.** What happened to Paul's ministry to the Jews in Rome? **4.** If you had to write the obituary on Paul's life from the material in the book of Acts, what would be the essential facts? **5.** Would you like to have known Paul personally? Would you like to have Paul as your spiritual leader? Would you like to have him in your group? **6.** How would you compare verses 30–31 in Paul's life to the last two years in your life?

APPLY **1.** If you could add one more chapter to the book of Acts and include the story of your experience during the study of this book, what would you write about? **2.** What is your group going to do next?

Paul Preaches at Rome Under Guard

17 Three days later he called together the leaders of the Jews. When
they had assembled, Paul said to them: "My brothers, although I have
done nothing against our people or against the customs of our ancestors, I was arrested in Jerusalem and handed over to the Romans.
18 They examined me and wanted to release me, because I was not
guilty of any crime deserving death. 19 But when the Jews objected, I
was compelled to appeal to Caesar—not that I had any charge to
bring against my own people. 20 For this reason I have asked to see
you and talk with you. It is because of the hope of Israel that I am bound with this chain."

21 They replied, "We have not received any letters from Judea concerning you, and none of the brothers who have come from there has
reported or said anything bad about you. 22 But we want to hear what
your views are, for we know that people everywhere are talking against this sect."

23 They arranged to meet Paul on a certain day, and came in even larger numbers to the place where he was staying. From morning till evening he explained and declared to them the kingdom of God and tried to convince them about Jesus from the Law of Moses and from
the Prophets. 24 Some were convinced by what he said, but others
would not believe. 25 They disagreed among themselves and began to leave after Paul had made this final statement: "The Holy Spirit spoke the truth to your forefathers when he said through Isaiah the prophet:

26 " 'Go to this people and say,
"You will be ever hearing but never understanding;
you will be ever seeing but never perceiving."
27 For this people's heart has become calloused;
they hardly hear with their ears,
and they have closed their eyes.
Otherwise they might see with their eyes,
hear with their ears,
understand with their hearts
and turn, and I would heal them.'[a]

28 "Therefore I want you to know that God's salvation has been sent to the Gentiles, and they will listen!"[b]

[a]27 Isaiah 6:9,10 [b]28 Some manuscripts *listen!"* 29 *After he said this, the Jews left, arguing vigorously among themselves.*

28:17 As soon as possible, Paul called together the leaders of the synagogues in Rome (at least 13 are known to have existed). He held this meeting in order to explain his situation to them firsthand, so they would be influenced by personal information rather than rumors.

28:19 ***my own people.*** Notice also "my brothers" and "our ancestors" (v. 17). Once again, Luke presents Paul as established among the Jewish community in Rome for at least 20 years and perhaps as far back as Pentecost nearly 30 years earlier (2:10). Paul's letter to Rome, written some three years before his arrival, deals extensively with conflicts arising between Jewish and Gentile elements in the church there. These Jewish leaders certainly knew something of Christianity, but may have desired to finally get some answers to questions that had never been clearly explained to them.

28:23 Examples of how Paul argued for the gospel from the Old Testament Scriptures are given in 13:16–41; 22:3–21 and 26:4–27. **the kingdom of God.** Throughout the Gospels, the message of Jesus is known as the message of the kingdom of God (Mark 1:15). This phrase serves as summary of all the gospel is about, announcing the present and coming reign of God in human affairs and calling people to affirm their loyalty to Jesus as God's appointed king.

28:28 Although the Jews, who had been privileged to receive God's messengers for centuries, have turned against the gospel, Gentiles will respond, and they would be the focus of Paul's activity.

[30]For two whole years Paul stayed there in his own rented house
and welcomed all who came to see him. [31]Boldly and without hindrance he preached the kingdom of God and taught about the Lord
Jesus Christ.

28:30 Luke concludes Acts with the picture of Paul continuing his missionary activities with all who would listen.

28:31 In this last statement in Acts, the emphasis in the Greek sentence falls on the boldness and freedom with which Paul preached the gospel. During this period of house arrest, Paul wrote the letter of Philippians and probably the letters of Ephesians, Colossians and Philemon. Philippians 1:12–13 gives an insight into his situation during this time as he carried on an extensive ministry to the soldiers assigned to guard him, undoubtedly resulting in the conversion of a number of them. While some believe that at the end of these two years Paul was executed, other scholars contend that Paul was released and enjoyed freedom for another two years, during which he traveled once again to Crete, Asia and Macedonia. It was during this time that it is believed he wrote the letters of 1 Timothy and Titus. According to this second perspective, at some point after this he was again arrested and imprisoned at Rome, but this time things were far more sinister. The Emperor Nero, widely suspected of having started the great fire of Rome in A.D. 64, needed to shift the blame off of himself onto someone else—and Christians were chosen as the scapegoats . This resulted in an outburst of cruel persecution against the church, during which it is believed both Paul and Peter were executed by Roman authorities.

Romans

Author. The writer is the apostle Paul.

Date. Paul wrote his letter during a three-month period spent in Corinth at the home of his friend and convert Gaius (16:23). The time was probably A.D. 56–57, towards the end of his third missionary journey.

Theme. Being right with God through faith in Christ.

Personal Reading	Group Study Topic and Reading	
1:1–17	The Gospel of Christ	1:1–17
1:18–2:29	The Bad News	1:18–32
3:1–31	The Good News	3:21–31
4:1–25	An Example of Faith	4:1–25
5:1–21	Grace Reigns!	5:12–21
6:1–7:6	Alive in Christ	6:1–14
7:7–25	The Law of Sin	7:7–25
8:1–39	More Than Conquerors	8:28–39
9:1–11:36	God's Word Is True	9:1–29
12:1–21	Responding to God	12:1–8
13:1–14	Love One Another	13:8–14
14:1–15:13	Life Together	14:1–15:13
15:14–16:27	The Living Church	16:1–27

Historical Background. For nearly 10 years Paul had been evangelizing the Gentile territories around the Aegean Sea. Now he turns his eyes to fresh fields. He would go to Spain, the oldest Roman colony in the West. With some misgivings, Paul is about to return to Jerusalem with a collection from the newer churches for the believers in Jerusalem.

After Jerusalem, he planned to travel to Spain, stopping enroute to fulfill a long-held dream. He would visit Rome—the capital of the world. In anticipation of that visit, he wrote the letter to the Romans by way of introduction (the Roman Christians did not know him, though—as chapter 16 reveals—he had friends there). He was also eager to assure the Roman Christians, contrary to false rumors they might have heard, that the gospel he was preaching was, indeed, the gospel of Jesus Christ (1:15).

Paul's plan did not work as he intended. He would visit Rome, but not for three more years, and then he would come not as a tourist but as a prisoner. His misgivings about his Jerusalem trip proved accurate. Once there, he was quickly arrested and eventually sent to Rome for trial. Paul remained in Rome under house arrest for at least two years. Ultimately, according to reliable tradition, he was executed at a place just outside Rome. He never went to Spain.

It is not known how the Roman church began. Possibly some Roman Jews who were converted on the Day of Pentecost (Acts 2:10), began the church. As for the Gentile Christians in Rome, it is known that other missionaries besides Paul were active in founding churches.

Characteristics. Romans is Paul's most complete theological statement—carefully written. It is alive and vibrant, colorful, compassionate, and sweeping in scope. The main issue Paul is addressing is the question of how God will judge each of us on the final day.

Here the great theme of Romans emerges: We can have assurance of a right standing before God and hence know we will be given a positive verdict on Judgment Day. Such confidence does not come because of what we have done. It comes because of what God does through Christ's death in our place, he freely offers us his grace.

Paul sets this theme against the teaching of certain Jewish Christians, legalists who would add circumcision to grace (thus nullifying grace). If we have to do anything to deserve it, salvation is not an unearned gift freely given by God. In the course of his argument, Paul sets up a series of opposites: faith versus works, Spirit versus flesh, and liberty versus bondage.

1 Paul, a servant of Christ Jesus, called to be an apostle and set
apart for the gospel of God— 2the gospel he promised beforehand through his prophets in the Holy Scriptures 3regarding his Son,
who as to his human nature was a descendant of David, 4and who
through the Spirit[a] of holiness was declared with power to be the Son
of God[b] by his resurrection from the dead: Jesus Christ our Lord.
5Through him and for his name's sake, we received grace and apostleship to call people from among all the Gentiles to the obedience
that comes from faith. 6And you also are among those who are called
to belong to Jesus Christ.

7To all in Rome who are loved by God and called to be saints:

Grace and peace to you from God our Father and from the Lord
Jesus Christ.

Paul's Longing to Visit Rome

8First, I thank my God through Jesus Christ for all of you, because
your faith is being reported all over the world. 9God, whom I serve
with my whole heart in preaching the gospel of his Son, is my witness
how constantly I remember you 10in my prayers at all times; and I
pray that now at last by God's will the way may be opened for me to
come to you.

11I long to see you so that I may impart to you some spiritual gift to
make you strong— 12that is, that you and I may be mutually encouraged by each other's faith. 13I do not want you to be unaware, brothers, that I planned many times to come to you (but have been
prevented from doing so until now) in order that I might have a harvest among you, just as I have had among the other Gentiles.

14I am obligated both to Greeks and non-Greeks, both to the wise
and the foolish. 15That is why I am so eager to preach the gospel also
to you who are at Rome.

16I am not ashamed of the gospel, because it is the power of God
for the salvation of everyone who believes: first for the Jew, then for
the Gentile. 17For in the gospel a righteousness from God is revealed,

[a]4 Or *who as to his spirit* [b]4 Or *was appointed to be the Son of God with power*

OPEN 1. When you write a letter, are you more likely to write until you run out of paper, or keep it short and to the point? **2.** What is one place you have never seen that you would like to visit?

STUDY 1. If you received a letter from Paul (a missionary) saying he wanted to visit your family or group, how would you react? **2.** In introducing himself to the Christians in Rome, how does Paul describe himself? **3.** What are the circumstances that caused Paul to write this letter to the church there? **4.** What truths about Jesus Christ does Paul proclaim in this passage? **5.** What is Paul's life calling? Who is he specifically called to reach? **6.** What is the good news about the gospel that made Paul so eager to share it? **7.** Paul was bold about his faith. When have you been in a situation where you felt like you "stuck out" in sharing your faith? Were you bold or embarrassed?

APPLY 1. When did you first feel the call of Jesus in your life? **2.** How would you describe your relationship to Jesus Christ right now? Finish the sentence: "I am a ..." Seeker? Student? Beginner? Servant? Follower? **3.** Who was the Paul in your life who encouraged you in the early days of your Christian faith?

1:1 Paul. In introducing himself, Paul uses his Roman name and not his Jewish one (Saul). **servant.** Literally, "slave." Paul is the willing servant of Jesus whom he identifies as "Lord" (v. 4); a Master in authority over such slaves. **called.** Paul did not just decide one day that he would like to be an apostle and thus declare himself such. He is an apostle because God appointed him to be one. **apostle.** In the broad sense, an apostle is anyone sent on a mission with a message. **set apart.** In Galatians 1:15 he is set apart by God from birth for a special task, and in Acts 13:2 the church sets him apart for a special mission.

1:2 promised beforehand. Having defined the gospel as being "of God" in verse 1, Paul further specifies that the gospel was a fulfillment of prophecy.

1:3–4 A short, creedal statement probably familiar to the Roman Christians (4:24–25; 10:8–10; 16:25–26). **Son ... Jesus.** Jesus belongs to two spheres of existence: the human, in which he is the descendant of King David (from whose line the Messiah was to come); and the divine, in which he is God's Son (this fact having been verified through his resurrection).

1:5 grace and apostleship. Paul did not earn or deserve to be an apostle. He is one because of God's "undeserved favor" ("grace"). **Gentiles.** Paul's apostolic commission is quite specific, his ministry is to evangelize the non-Jewish world. **obedience that comes from faith.** It is active response to God—faith that shows itself in obedience (Gal. 5:6–8).

1:16–17 Here Paul defines the central theme of Romans: The way of getting right with God has been provided by God himself and comes through faith alone.

1:16 salvation. This word carries the Hebrew idea of salvation as wholeness and healing (in the here and now) as well as the idea of spiritual rescue (which will be realized in the future). **everyone who believes.** The required response to the good news of salvation is faith.

1:17 righteousness. In Hebrew thought, righteousness is not so much

a righteousness that is by faith from first to last,[a] just as it is written: "The righteous will live by faith."[b]

God's Wrath Against Mankind

18The wrath of God is being revealed from heaven against all the godlessness and wickedness of men who suppress the truth by their wickedness, 19since what may be known about God is plain to them, because God has made it plain to them. 20For since the creation of the world God's invisible qualities—his eternal power and divine nature—have been clearly seen, being understood from what has been made, so that men are without excuse.

21For although they knew God, they neither glorified him as God nor gave thanks to him, but their thinking became futile and their foolish hearts were darkened. 22Although they claimed to be wise, they became fools 23and exchanged the glory of the immortal God for images made to look like mortal man and birds and animals and reptiles.

24Therefore God gave them over in the sinful desires of their hearts to sexual impurity for the degrading of their bodies with one another. 25They exchanged the truth of God for a lie, and worshiped and served created things rather than the Creator—who is forever praised. Amen.

26Because of this, God gave them over to shameful lusts. Even their women exchanged natural relations for unnatural ones. 27In the same way the men also abandoned natural relations with women and were inflamed with lust for one another. Men committed indecent acts with other men, and received in themselves the due penalty for their perversion.

28Furthermore, since they did not think it worthwhile to retain the knowledge of God, he gave them over to a depraved mind, to do what ought not to be done. 29They have become filled with every kind of wickedness, evil, greed and depravity. They are full of envy, murder,

[a]17 Or *is from faith to faith* [b]17 Hab. 2:4

OPEN 1. Who in your family is a lover of the great outdoors? **2.** What causes you to stand in awe of God: Being in the mountains? Walking along the seashore? Working in the garden?

STUDY 1. What are some things you have observed in nature that confirm to you that God exists? **2.** How does the reading of this passage make you feel? **3.** This is probably the most descriptive passage in the Bible on the "fall of mankind." In verse 18, what did mankind do when given "the truth" about God? **4.** When people failed to accept the truth, how did God respond (vv. 24,26,28)? **5.** How do you tend to view God—as a God of love or anger? How do you tend to view mankind—as generally good or bad? Why? **6.** Do you think our society has changed for the better or the worse since Paul wrote this description? **7.** Paul explains in this passage that the root cause for the ills in our society is a "depraved mind" or the sin nature in all of us. How does this view differ from what modern psychology teaches?

APPLY 1. As you think about raising your children or grandchildren in our culture today, how do you feel? **2.** What are you doing to counteract the influence of the secular culture on your children?

---

a moral quality as it is a legal judgment. The idea here is not that a person is made righteous (in the ethical sense) or proved righteous (virtuous) by such a pronouncement. Rather one is counted or reckoned as righteous, even though one is really guilty. Being thus pardoned, a person is given a right to stand before God and can enter into a relationship with him. **from God.** This declaration of righteousness comes from God to men and women—it is a reflection of God's character. He is righteous, and this fact shows itself in his saving activity. **by faith from first to last.** What faith is, becomes clear as the epistle unfolds, though in verse 5 its *primary meaning* has already been made clear—it is believing obedience. The one who has faith trusts that in the life, death, and resurrection of Jesus Christ, one sees the power of God at work. He or she then responds to God by submitting to Christ and trusting solely in God's powerful saving work. **The righteous will live by faith.** This citation from Habakkuk 2:4 is the first of many quotes that Paul uses from the Old Testament to demonstrate and prove his point.

1:24 God gave them over. This phrase is used three times (vv. 26,28) to indicate that God allowed people to carry out their rebellion and experience the fruit of their choices.

1:24–27 Not knowing who their Creator is, their own identity becomes confused and is expressed in a distorted sexuality. Greek and Roman writers corroborate Paul's description: it was an age of unparalleled immorality.

1:29 wickedness. The opposite of justice: robbing God and others of their due. **evil.** The deliberate attempt to harm or to corrupt; such a person is not only intentionally bad, but seeks to make others so. **greed.** Taking whatever one wants without regard to the rights of others. **depravity.** The most general term for badness; a vicious person devoid of any good quality. **envy.** Grudging resentment of (and desire for) another's accomplishments or possessions. **murder.** Jesus teaches that people must rid themselves of the very spirit of hatred which issues in such a deed (Matt. 5:21–26). **strife.** Contention born of envy. **deceit.** Underhanded, devious actions designed to get one's own way. **malice.** Literally, "evil-nature"; always thinking the worst of another.

1:29–30 gossips, slanderers. The gossiper spreads ill news about others secretly, while the slanderer openly accuses.

strife, deceit and malice. They are gossips, [30]slanderers, God-haters, insolent, arrogant and boastful; they invent ways of doing evil; they disobey their parents; [31]they are senseless, faithless, heartless, ruthless. [32]Although they know God's righteous decree that those who do such things deserve death, they not only continue to do these very things but also approve of those who practice them.

God's Righteous Judgment

2 You, therefore, have no excuse, you who pass judgment on someone else, for at whatever point you judge the other, you are condemning yourself, because you who pass judgment do the same things. [2]Now we know that God's judgment against those who do such things is based on truth. [3]So when you, a mere man, pass judgment on them and yet do the same things, do you think you will escape God's judgment? [4]Or do you show contempt for the riches of his kindness, tolerance and patience, not realizing that God's kindness leads you toward repentance?

[5]But because of your stubbornness and your unrepentant heart, you are storing up wrath against yourself for the day of God's wrath, when his righteous judgment will be revealed. [6]God "will give to each person according to what he has done."[a] [7]To those who by persistence in doing good seek glory, honor and immortality, he will give eternal life. [8]But for those who are self-seeking and who reject the truth and follow evil, there will be wrath and anger. [9]There will be trouble and distress for every human being who does evil: first for the Jew, then for the Gentile; [10]but glory, honor and peace for everyone who does good: first for the Jew, then for the Gentile. [11]For God does not show favoritism.

[12]All who sin apart from the law will also perish apart from the law, and all who sin under the law will be judged by the law. [13]For it is not those who hear the law who are righteous in God's sight, but it is those who obey the law who will be declared righteous. [14](Indeed, when Gentiles, who do not have the law, do by nature things required by the law, they are a law for themselves, even though they do not have the law, [15]since they show that the requirements of the law are written on their hearts, their consciences also bearing witness, and their thoughts now accusing, now even defending them.) [16]This will take place on the day when God will judge men's secrets through Jesus Christ, as my gospel declares.

[a]6 Psalm 62:12; Prov. 24:12

OPEN When you were young, which of your parents was more strict? Merciful? Consistent?

STUDY Having described the downward spiral of mankind after turning away from God (1:18–32), Paul addresses the Jews who have grown up in the privileged "chosen" relationship with God in the Old Testament. **1.** What does Paul say about those who are looking down on others? **2.** How have the "chosen" people of God in the Old Testament responded to God's special favor? **3.** By what standards will God judge people (vv. 6–13,16)? **4.** How do you reconcile these standards with the theme of Romans—justification by faith rather than by good works? **5.** In God's judgment, what is the reward? The punishment? Who is righteous in God's sight? **6.** Do you need God to deal with your attitude toward people you tend to think are not as "good" as you are?

APPLY **1.** As you grow older in your spiritual life, does your appreciation of God's grace grow stronger ... or is it likely to be taken for granted? **2.** Share what event in your life led you to appreciate God's grace.

1:30 God-haters. They hate God, because he is seen as inhibiting pleasure. **insolent.** A sort of pride (hubris) that arrogantly defies God and/or hurts and snubs others, simply for the delight in doing so. **invent ... evil.** Create new ways of sinning.

1:31 senseless. One who does not learn from experience. **faithless.** One who breaks agreements. **heartless.** One without love for even family. **ruthless.** One without pity who can harm or even kill without thought.

2:4 Jews are presuming upon the mercy of God, taking his kindness as a sign of their immunity from judgment (when, in fact, such kindness was meant to lead them to change their lives, and not serve simply as an excuse for continued sinning).

2:11 This is the point of his argument. The means by which one gains "wrath and anger" (v. 8) or "eternal life" (v. 7) has nothing to do with national or racial heritage.

2:12 Everyone will be held accountable according to the knowledge they have. The Jews had the written Law; the Gentiles had their conscience (v. 15) and the revelation of nature (1:20).

2:14–15 Gentiles not only know about God from his creation, but their very consciences tell them that there is right and wrong.

OPEN Does your conscience trouble you when you violate the speed limit?

STUDY **1.** What does Paul accuse the Jews of being in this passage? If you were a Jew, how would you feel: Upset? Angry? Attacked? Found out? **2.** What was the original intent of the Law and of circumcision (Gen. 17:1–14)? How had these Jews missed the point of what circumcision was all about (vv. 25–29)? **3.** In contrast to physical circumcision, how is "circumcision of the heart" acquired, and what does it mean (v. 29; Deut. 10:16; 30:6; Jer. 4:4; 9:25–26)? **4.** Why is Paul (a Jew) so vocal about Gentiles not having to be circumcised to become a Christian?

APPLY **1.** When did your faith become more than a ritual? How valuable was your own religious instruction in bringing you to Christ? **2.** What custom do you have that needs to become less of a ritual and more of a matter of the heart?

OPEN Among your relatives, who comes closest to being the family's spiritual "patriarch?"

STUDY **1.** When you hit bottom, when did you realize your need for God's grace? **2.** What are the advantages of growing up in a Christian environment? What are the potential disadvantages? **3.** Have two people read verses 1–6 out loud—Reader #1 reading verses 1, 3 and 5 (the questions), and Reader #2 reading verses 2, 4 and 6 (the responses).

The Jews and the Law

17Now you, if you call yourself a Jew; if you rely on the law and brag
about your relationship to God; 18if you know his will and approve of
what is superior because you are instructed by the law; 19if you are
convinced that you are a guide for the blind, a light for those who are
in the dark, 20an instructor of the foolish, a teacher of infants, because you have in the law the embodiment of knowledge and truth—
21you, then, who teach others, do you not teach yourself? You who
preach against stealing, do you steal? 22You who say that people
should not commit adultery, do you commit adultery? You who abhor
idols, do you rob temples? 23You who brag about the law, do you dishonor God by breaking the law? 24As it is written: "God's name is
blasphemed among the Gentiles because of you."[a]

25Circumcision has value if you observe the law, but if you break
the law, you have become as though you had not been circumcised.
26If those who are not circumcised keep the law's requirements, will
they not be regarded as though they were circumcised? 27The one
who is not circumcised physically and yet obeys the law will condemn you who, even though you have the[b] written code and circumcision, are a lawbreaker.

28A man is not a Jew if he is only one outwardly, nor is circumcision
merely outward and physical. 29No, a man is a Jew if he is one inwardly; and circumcision is circumcision of the heart, by the Spirit, not by
the written code. Such a man's praise is not from men, but from God.

God's Faithfulness

3 What advantage, then, is there in being a Jew, or what value is
there in circumcision? 2Much in every way! First of all, they have
been entrusted with the very words of God.

3What if some did not have faith? Will their lack of faith nullify
God's faithfulness? 4Not at all! Let God be true, and every man a liar.
As it is written:

"So that you may be proved right when you speak
and prevail when you judge."[c]

[a]24 Isaiah 52:5; Ezek. 36:22 [b]27 Or *who, by means of a* [c]4 Psalm 51:4

2:17 Jew. This name was first used in Nehemiah 4:1. By Jesus' time it had come to assume a great significance for the people of Israel. To be a Jew was to be special; to be a Jew was to be a child of God. It is this intense nationalistic pride that Paul is attacking here, saying that it alone is insufficient to ensure salvation. **law.** This term is used in various ways. On the most basic level, it signified the set of laws given at the time of the Exodus (the Ten Commandments). The term could also refer to the laws contained in the first five books of the Old Testament (i.e., the Law of Moses). Or it could mean the whole Old Testament as well as its interpretation. **rely on the law.** Literally means "rest upon the law"; to provide a sense that as a Jew one is indeed right with God.

2:25 Circumcision. This was the sign of the covenant with God (Gen. 17:1–14).

2:28–29 The Old Testament teaches in Deuteronomy 30:6 that true circumcision is not an outward, physical mark but an inward spiritual work by God. Paul teaches that it is possible to neglect circumcision and still be counted as obedient to God's law. This would be seen by Paul's Jewish readers as a radical new teaching.

3:1 What advantage. Paul's opponent asked, "Do you really mean, as you seem to argue in chapter 2, that there is no significant difference between a Jew and a Gentile?" Such a question arose out of an accurate understanding that God had set Israel apart from all other nations.

3:2 Much in every way! This reply is unexpected, given what Paul said in chapter 2. It might have been assumed that he would reply: "Jews have no advantage." But this would not be accurate. They had a preeminent place in God's plan. It was through them that God worked out the redemption of the world in his Son Jesus, who was a Jew. **First of all.** Paul does not complete his list. There is no "second," "third," etc. His argument takes another direction. In 9:4–5, however, he does give other advantages. **words of God.** It is an enormous advantage to have known the mind and will of God.

5But if our unrighteousness brings out God's righteousness more
clearly, what shall we say? That God is unjust in bringing his wrath on
us? (I am using a human argument.) 6Certainly not! If that were so,
how could God judge the world? 7Someone might argue, "If my falsehood enhances God's truthfulness and so increases his glory, why
am I still condemned as a sinner?" 8Why not say—as we are being
slanderously reported as saying and as some claim that we say—"Let
us do evil that good may result"? Their condemnation is deserved.

No One Is Righteous

9What shall we conclude then? Are we any better[a]? Not at all! We
have already made the charge that Jews and Gentiles alike are all under sin. 10As it is written:

"There is no one righteous, not even one;
11 there is no one who understands,
no one who seeks God.
12All have turned away,
they have together become worthless;
there is no one who does good,
not even one."[b]
13"Their throats are open graves;
their tongues practice deceit."[c]
"The poison of vipers is on their lips."[d]
14 "Their mouths are full of cursing and bitterness."[e]
15"Their feet are swift to shed blood;
16 ruin and misery mark their ways,
17and the way of peace they do not know."[f]
18 "There is no fear of God before their eyes."[g]

19Now we know that whatever the law says, it says to those who
are under the law, so that every mouth may be silenced and the whole
world held accountable to God. 20Therefore no one will be declared
righteous in his sight by observing the law; rather, through the law
we become conscious of sin.

Righteousness Through Faith

21But now a righteousness from God, apart from law, has been
made known, to which the Law and the Prophets testify. 22This righteousness from God comes through faith in Jesus Christ to all who
believe. There is no difference, 23for all have sinned and fall short of

What are the three questions and how does Paul answer each of them? **4.** How would you compare the definition of sin and sinners in this passage to the way people define these words today? **5.** From verses 10–18, what is said regarding human thought, direction, speech and action. Who does Paul like in these verses? If you were reading verses 10–18 for the first time, how would you feel at the close? **6.** Where does this leave the good people in the world then and now (vv. 19–20)? **7.** From your experience, do you find it necessary for someone to realize a need for God's grace and forgiveness before they will fully appreciate that Christ died for them?

APPLY 1. When did you first become aware of your sinfulness and need for God? **2.** In raising your own children, what are you going to insist on in their religious training ... and what are you going to let them decide? **3.** Up to this point in Romans, what has Paul been trying to prove? How important is this to a full understanding of the gospel?

OPEN How close have you come to getting in trouble with the law? How did you feel?

STUDY 1. How could a good, clean, honest, moral person like you be called a sinner? **2.** How did God solve your problem? How would you explain the word "redemption" to

[a]9 Or *worse* [b]12 Psalms 14:1-3; 53:1-3; Eccles. 7:20 [c]13 Psalm 5:9 [d]13 Psalm 140:3 [e]14 Psalm 10:7 [f]17 Isaiah 59:7,8 [g]18 Psalm 36:1

3:21 But now. Paul moves from the revelation of God's wrath (1:18) to the revelation ("has been made known") of God's righteousness. **a righteousness from God.** "God's way of putting men right with Himself" (TEV). **apart from law.** God's righteousness as revealed by the Law leads only to wrath (4:15), but God's righteousness as now revealed in Jesus Christ leads to right standing before him. **the Law and the Prophets.** The Old Testament, if rightly understood, does contain such a message. Paul has already used Habakkuk 2:4 when first describing the Gospel (1:17).

3:22 faith. Individuals are not counted as righteous because of faith, as if it were an attitude on their part that forces God to accept them. Rather, they are counted as righteous (justified) because of grace through (or "on the basis of") faith. Faith, then, is a profound trust and hope in God's work in Christ. Faith is the opposite of works. Works give people a sense of self-confidence, because they assume (falsely) that their religious and moral activities will cause God to pronounce them justified. **in Jesus Christ.** Paul writes not about faith in general (a vague feeling that "all will turn out well"), but about faith in a specific person, Jesus Christ. **to all.** The gospel is for Jew and Gentile alike.

3:23 fall short. The picture is of arrows that have failed to reach their target. **glory of God.** This is God's

a twelve-year old? **3.** What does the word "grace" mean? What is your responsibility? **4.** How did the action by God on behalf of all mankind level the playing field between Jew and Gentile? **5.** If God graded on the curve, would you make it to heaven?

APPLY 1. When did the word "grace" take on a personal meaning for you? **2.** How often do you have to draw upon God's bank account for grace?

OPEN 1. When you were growing up, what chores were you expected to do around the house? Did your parents pay you? **2.** What is the biggest scam or junk mail offer you have fallen for—that promised something for nothing?

STUDY 1. On a scale of 1 (mustard seed) to 10 (mountain moving), how would you rate your faith? **2.** On the surface, what "qualifications" would seem to make Abraham an example of righteousness? According to Paul, what really made Abraham righteous? **3.** What is the difference between a wage and a gift? What makes a gift special? **4.** In what way is Abraham a spiritual father to us? In what family legacy can we share? **5.** What do you learn about

the glory of God, 24and are justified freely by his grace through the
redemption that came by Christ Jesus. 25God presented him as a sacrifice of atonement,[a] through faith in his blood. He did this to demonstrate his justice, because in his forbearance he had left the sins
committed beforehand unpunished—26he did it to demonstrate his
justice at the present time, so as to be just and the one who justifies
those who have faith in Jesus.

27Where, then, is boasting? It is excluded. On what principle? On
that of observing the law? No, but on that of faith. 28For we maintain
that a man is justified by faith apart from observing the law. 29Is God
the God of Jews only? Is he not the God of Gentiles too? Yes, of Gentiles too, 30since there is only one God, who will justify the circumcised by faith and the uncircumcised through that same faith. 31Do
we, then, nullify the law by this faith? Not at all! Rather, we uphold
the law.

Abraham Justified by Faith

4 What then shall we say that Abraham, our forefather, discovered
in this matter? 2If, in fact, Abraham was justified by works, he
had something to boast about—but not before God. 3What does the
Scripture say? "Abraham believed God, and it was credited to him as
righteousness."[b]

4Now when a man works, his wages are not credited to him as a
gift, but as an obligation. 5However, to the man who does not work
but trusts God who justifies the wicked, his faith is credited as righteousness. 6David says the same thing when he speaks of the
blessedness of the man to whom God credits righteousness apart
from works:

7 "Blessed are they
whose transgressions are forgiven,
whose sins are covered.

[a]25 Or *as the one who would turn aside his wrath, taking away sin* [b]3 Gen. 15:6; also in verse 22

---

divine splendor which is reflected in the Law.

3:24 justified. This is a word drawn from the law court. The image is of humanity on trial before God. To be justified is to be granted acquittal on the Day of Judgment. That a bad person would be reckoned as if he or she were good was utterly shocking to the Jew (Ex. 23:7; Prov. 17:15). Such assurance of acquittal, coming as it does at the beginning of the Christian life (the Jew hoped for acquittal at the end of life), brings a great sense of personal freedom, since one is released from the nagging questions: Am I good enough? Will I merit heaven? Now, by grace, individuals are pronounced "righteous" and are freed to do good works out of love for God, not out of fear of his wrath. **redemption.** This refers to the act of buying the freedom of a slave—in this case, a slave in bondage to sin (Mark 10:45; 1 Peter 1:18–19).

3:25 sacrifice of atonement. Christ's death is the ultimate, final and complete sacrifice for sin. Christ is the victim who takes upon himself the wrath due because of humanity's sin. Christ took upon himself the full weight of God's wrath which sinful humanity deserved. **his blood.** In terms of atonement, the importance of Jesus' death was that his blood was offered to God as a sacrifice.

3:26 justice at the present time. The sacrificial death of Christ demonstrates God's justice in two ways: First, by vindicating Jesus—he has taken sin so seriously that God sent his own Son to die. Second, by showing a whole new way of living that Christ's sacrifice has opened up for humanity.

4:1 Abraham. As the first patriarch and thus the founder of the Jewish nation, Abraham was revered by all Jews.

4:5 faith. Two views of faith are in contention. The Jews saw faith as a definite activity, as faithful action in accordance with God's will. Thus they understood that God responded to Abraham's faith by declaring him "righteous." In contrast, Paul understood faith in exactly opposite terms, as a person's response to God's action (1:17; 3:21–26). **justifies the wicked.** That God would do this contradicts Jewish expectations. God was supposed to condemn the guilty (Ex. 23:7). Paul makes this point because everyone would then agree that acquitting the guilty could only be seen as an act of grace, not as a response by God to good works. God was able to justify the wicked because of the future sacrifice of the Messiah (Isa. 53:4–12).

8 Blessed is the man
whose sin the Lord will never count against him."[a]

9 Is this blessedness only for the circumcised, or also for the uncircumcised? We have been saying that Abraham's faith was credited to
him as righteousness. 10 Under what circumstances was it credited?
Was it after he was circumcised, or before? It was not after, but before! 11 And he received the sign of circumcision, a seal of the righteousness that he had by faith while he was still uncircumcised. So
then, he is the father of all who believe but have not been circumcised, in order that righteousness might be credited to them. 12 And he
is also the father of the circumcised who not only are circumcised but
who also walk in the footsteps of the faith that our father Abraham
had before he was circumcised.

13 It was not through law that Abraham and his offspring received
the promise that he would be heir of the world, but through the righteousness that comes by faith. 14 For if those who live by law are heirs,
faith has no value and the promise is worthless, 15 because law brings
wrath. And where there is no law there is no transgression.

16 Therefore, the promise comes by faith, so that it may be by grace
and may be guaranteed to all Abraham's offspring—not only to those
who are of the law but also to those who are of the faith of Abraham.
He is the father of us all. 17 As it is written: "I have made you a father
of many nations."[b] He is our father in the sight of God, in whom he
believed—the God who gives life to the dead and calls things that are
not as though they were.

18 Against all hope, Abraham in hope believed and so became the
father of many nations, just as it had been said to him, "So shall your
offspring be."[c] 19 Without weakening in his faith, he faced the fact that
his body was as good as dead—since he was about a hundred years
old—and that Sarah's womb was also dead. 20 Yet he did not waver
through unbelief regarding the promise of God, but was strengthened
in his faith and gave glory to God, 21 being fully persuaded that God
had power to do what he had promised. 22 This is why "it was credited
to him as righteousness." 23 The words "it was credited to him" were
written not for him alone, 24 but also for us, to whom God will credit
righteousness—for us who believe in him who raised Jesus our Lord
from the dead. 25 He was delivered over to death for our sins and was
raised to life for our justification.

Peace and Joy

5 Therefore, since we have been justified through faith, we[d] have
peace with God through our Lord Jesus Christ, 2 through whom

[a] *8* Psalm 32:1,2 [b] *17* Gen. 17:5 [c] *18* Gen. 15:5 [d] *1* Or *let us*

faith from the example in verses 18–22? How would you feel in Abraham's place? **6.** In some religions, forgiveness or grace as a free gift is a foreign concept. You "earn" your way to heaven by doing good deeds. What would have happened to Christianity if Paul had given in on the issue of circumcision?

APPLY 1. In your spiritual pilgrimage, how many years did you live trying to measure up to a performance level that would make you acceptable to God? **2.** How do you feel about your relationship with God now? Do you feel accepted, forgiven and loved, even when you blow it?

OPEN In your family, who tried to keep the peace?

STUDY 1. When Paul refers to "peace with God," what is he talking about? **2.** Does the new

---

4:16 promise. The word which he uses in this verse describes an unconditional promise made out of the generosity of one's heart. God's promise is a gift of grace, not a contract with certain obligations. **by faith.** By its very notion, a person can do nothing but wait for the fulfillment of a promised inheritance.

5:1–2 Paul points out the three-fold fruit of justification: the past blessing of peace with God (v. 1), the present blessing of grace (v. 2) and the future hope of glory (v. 2).

5:1 peace. What is in view is not some sort of inner experience of harmony, but rather the objective fact of a new relationship with God. The root image is of war. Those who were in rebellion against God, their rightful king, are now reconciled to him through Christ; the enmity is over. This is the basis for the Christian's access to God's grace and hope for the future. Peace in the Bible is a comprehensive term describing the total blessing of salvation.

5:2 access. This word is used to describe ushering someone into the

relationship with God come with a money-back guarantee that everything will be easy from now on? How come? **3.** Who initiated the peace treaty? What did it cost God? **4.** From this passage, now that the war is over, what can those in the peace treaty look forward to?

APPLY 1. When you feel stressed, overloaded, beaten down and piled on; when you have been put through a meat-grinder, squeezed and pressed out of shape; can you see God using this to bring about his character in your life? **2.** Where could you use a little help in prayer from this group right now?

OPEN Who do you take after in your temperament, your mother or your father? How about your body build? Musical ability?

STUDY 1. When you think about dying, how does it make you feel? **2.** What do you remember about the story of Adam and the fall of man (Gen. 3:1–24)? **3.** How has the sin of Adam affected his descendants to the present day? How would you describe this in medical terms: A disease? An epidemic? An infection that attacks the immune system? **4.** What results did the death of Jesus Christ bring? **5.** What must

we have gained access by faith into this grace in which we now stand.
And we[a] rejoice in the hope of the glory of God. [3]Not only so, but we[a]
also rejoice in our sufferings, because we know that suffering produces perseverance; [4]perseverance, character; and character, hope.
[5]And hope does not disappoint us, because God has poured out his
love into our hearts by the Holy Spirit, whom he has given us.
[6]You see, at just the right time, when we were still powerless, Christ
died for the ungodly. [7]Very rarely will anyone die for a righteous man,
though for a good man someone might possibly dare to die. [8]But God
demonstrates his own love for us in this: While we were still sinners,
Christ died for us.
[9]Since we have now been justified by his blood, how much more
shall we be saved from God's wrath through him! [10]For if, when we
were God's enemies, we were reconciled to him through the death of
his Son, how much more, having been reconciled, shall we be saved
through his life! [11]Not only is this so, but we also rejoice in God
through our Lord Jesus Christ, through whom we have now received
reconciliation.

Death Through Adam, Life Through Christ

[12]Therefore, just as sin entered the world through one man, and
death through sin, and in this way death came to all men, because all
sinned— [13]for before the law was given, sin was in the world. But sin
is not taken into account when there is no law. [14]Nevertheless, death
reigned from the time of Adam to the time of Moses, even over those
who did not sin by breaking a command, as did Adam, who was a
pattern of the one to come.
[15]But the gift is not like the trespass. For if the many died by the
trespass of the one man, how much more did God's grace and the gift
that came by the grace of the one man, Jesus Christ, overflow to the
many! [16]Again, the gift of God is not like the result of the one man's

[a]2,3 Or *let us*

---

presence of royalty. **grace.** To be at peace with God is to come into the sphere of his grace and thus experience the new kind of life which will be described in verses 12–8:39. **hope.** This is a sure sense of confidence based on the fact of justification. **glory of God.** That for which humans were created and from which they have fallen, but which they will someday experience again.

5:3 sufferings. Literally, "pressure" or "tribulation." What is in view is not sorrow or pain, but the negative reaction of an unbelieving world. In New Testament times, suffering was the normal and expected lot of Christians (Acts 14:22). Thus, suffering was seen as a sign of true Christianity (2 Thess. 1:4–5). **perseverance.** Fortitude or endurance. The word describes the active overcoming of misfortune, rather than mere passive acceptance.

5:4 character. A word used of metal which has been so heated by fire that all the impurities have been removed. **hope.** The confidence born out of suffering that God is indeed transforming one's character, and that he will keep on doing so until one is glorified.

5:12 sin entered ... through one man. Jews thought of themselves not as isolated individuals, but as part of a family, a tribe and a nation. The actions and consequences of one person were the actions and consequences of all. Thus when Adam sinned by eating the forbidden fruit (Gen. 2–3), all humanity sinned. **death through sin.** Death is the consequence of sin (Gen. 2:17), and so all die because Adam sinned. Jewish teaching said that Adam would have been immortal had he not sinned.

5:14 death. More than the physical cessation of life is in view here, since the contrast is always with eternal life (v. 21). Death brings one to judgment and to condemnation (v. 18)—since all have sinned—and thus to punishment. It is spiritual death as well as physical death that concerns Paul. **Adam.** In Hebrew, Adam's name means "humankind." He is representative of all humanity. **by breaking a command.** Adam disobeyed God's clear instructions (Gen. 2:17). **pattern.** Literally, a mark or impression that has been left by something. Adam and his impact on humanity is a prefigure of Christ who would also impact all people.

5:15 gift. This could mean Christ and his work on behalf of humanity, but in light of verses 18, 20 and 21 it probably refers to the status conferred on humanity of being counted righteous before God.

5:16 One act of disobedience by Adam brought judgment and condemnation to all, but Christ's gift brings justification and forgiveness not only for that one

sin: The judgment followed one sin and brought condemnation, but
the gift followed many trespasses and brought justification. 17For if,
by the trespass of the one man, death reigned through that one man,
how much more will those who receive God's abundant provision of
grace and of the gift of righteousness reign in life through the one
man, Jesus Christ.

18Consequently, just as the result of one trespass was condemnation for all men, so also the result of one act of righteousness was
justification that brings life for all men. 19For just as through the disobedience of the one man the many were made sinners, so also
through the obedience of the one man the many will be made righteous.

20The law was added so that the trespass might increase. But
where sin increased, grace increased all the more, 21so that, just as
sin reigned in death, so also grace might reign through righteousness
to bring eternal life through Jesus Christ our Lord.

Dead to Sin, Alive in Christ

6 What shall we say, then? Shall we go on sinning so that grace
may increase? 2By no means! We died to sin; how can we live in it
any longer? 3Or don't you know that all of us who were baptized into
Christ Jesus were baptized into his death? 4We were therefore buried
with him through baptism into death in order that, just as Christ was
raised from the dead through the glory of the Father, we too may live
a new life.

5If we have been united with him like this in his death, we will certainly also be united with him in his resurrection. 6For we know that
our old self was crucified with him so that the body of sin might be
done away with,[a] that we should no longer be slaves to sin— 7be-
cause anyone who has died has been freed from sin.

[a]6 Or *be rendered powerless*

one do to benefit from what Christ did (v. 17)? **6.** "The gift" is mentioned five times (vv. 15–17): What is it? Who gives it? How is it received? **7.** How does this chapter illustrate why "grace and peace to you" (1:7) is such an appropriate greeting for followers of Christ?

APPLY Does the gospel message excite you as it does Paul? How are you getting along with God right now?

OPEN What is the closest you have come to losing your life? What happened?

STUDY 1. What motivates you to live a good life? **2.** In this passage, "death" and "died" are used many times. What is the main point Paul is trying to make? **3.** How is the image of baptism a symbol of what Christ did? **4.** In what ways do people become "slaves to sin"? How can a person escape this bondage? **5.** What do you do with the flashbacks and voices in the night that keep reminding you of your past mistakes? **6.** What does it mean to be "dead to sin"? **7.** If we are dead to sin, how is it

---

sin, but also for all the sins down through the centuries.

5:18–19 With the dissimilarity between Adam and Christ established, Paul can return to the formal comparison he began in verse 12: One man's disobedience brought condemnation and death to all, just as one man's obedience now brings justification and life to all who choose it. The only similarity between Christ and Adam is that by one deed, each had an incalculable impact on many.

5:18 one act of righteousness. The obedience of Christ's whole life, which led to his sacrificial death.

5:20 law. When the Law came, it served to define what was in fact "sinful"—it brought "sin" into the light of day by naming it.

6:1–2 Paul's "opponent" appears once more, questioning Paul in the typical cynical attitude of the day: "If grace is the most wonderful thing there is and if grace abounds in the presence of sin (5:20), then shouldn't we sin all the more so as to produce yet more grace?"

6:2 died to sin. Paul's point is that his critic's question is logically absurd: to be a Christian is to have died (past tense) to sin; thus it is impossible to live in something one has died to! In verses 3–14, Paul details what it means to have died to sin.

6:3 don't you know. What he will say about baptism was common knowledge. **baptized.** Baptism was (mainly) an adult rite in the early church, occurring generally at the moment when a person confessed faith in Christ, and serving as a public declaration that one was no longer pagan but now identified with Christ.

6:4 buried with him. When family and friends bury a loved one, they are publicly acknowledging the fact and reality of that death. In returning home they leave that person behind. To go under the water of baptism is to experience in a direct (though symbolic) way the fact and reality of Christ's death. It is this burial experience that makes his death real.

6:5 united. The Greek root means "to grow together" and the idea is of organic unity with Christ.

6:6 old self. The former unregenerated, preconversion life—what a person once was. **body of sin.** This reference is to one's lower self (and not as in the reference above, to one's former self)—the sinful nature that belongs to one's body (v. 12). **be done away with.** The Greek word means "to be defeated," not "to become extinct." The sinful part of one's nature is not destroyed, but is deprived of power; its domination is broken.

6:7 freed from sin. The only way to be freed from sin (literally, "justified from sin") is by paying its penalty. But

that Christians (followers of Christ) still sin? What does it mean to practice the teaching in verses 11–13?

APPLY 1. Do you identify with the Prodigal Son (wild oats in a far country) or Elder Brother (nice guy who stayed home) in your spiritual background? **2.** Do you think it is easier for Elder Brothers who have never experienced gross immorality to overcome temptations?

OPEN Who was your first "boss"? Was this person easy to work for or a slave driver?

STUDY 1. If Paul were around today, what would he say enslaves our society? What about the Christian community? **2.** What are the two choices we have to "serve" (vv. 16–18)? **3.** What is the result of slavery to sin? **4.** What is the benefit of slavery to God and its result? **5.** How do you feel about being a slave to God?

APPLY 1. How is the battle going in your spiritual life at the moment? On a scale from 1 to 10, how would you rank yourself? **2.** What do you need to do today to reclaim the offensive?

OPEN When you were dating, did you ever get caught two-timing? Did anyone two-time you?

STUDY 1. Using the allegory of marriage, who were you married to originally (vv. 1–4)? How did that marriage work out? **2.** When Paul says, "we have been released

[8]Now if we died with Christ, we believe that we will also live with
him. [9]For we know that since Christ was raised from the dead, he
cannot die again; death no longer has mastery over him. [10]The death
he died, he died to sin once for all; but the life he lives, he lives to
God.
[11]In the same way, count yourselves dead to sin but alive to God in
Christ Jesus. [12]Therefore do not let sin reign in your mortal body so
that you obey its evil desires. [13]Do not offer the parts of your body to
sin, as instruments of wickedness, but rather offer yourselves to God,
as those who have been brought from death to life; and offer the
parts of your body to him as instruments of righteousness. [14]For sin
shall not be your master, because you are not under law, but under
grace.

Slaves to Righteousness

[15]What then? Shall we sin because we are not under law but under
grace? By no means! [16]Don't you know that when you offer yourselves to someone to obey him as slaves, you are slaves to the one
whom you obey—whether you are slaves to sin, which leads to
death, or to obedience, which leads to righteousness? [17]But thanks
be to God that, though you used to be slaves to sin, you wholeheartedly obeyed the form of teaching to which you were entrusted. [18]You
have been set free from sin and have become slaves to righteousness.
[19]I put this in human terms because you are weak in your natural
selves. Just as you used to offer the parts of your body in slavery to
impurity and to ever-increasing wickedness, so now offer them in
slavery to righteousness leading to holiness. [20]When you were slaves
to sin, you were free from the control of righteousness. [21]What benefit did you reap at that time from the things you are now ashamed
of? Those things result in death! [22]But now that you have been set
free from sin and have become slaves to God, the benefit you reap
leads to holiness, and the result is eternal life. [23]For the wages of sin
is death, but the gift of God is eternal life in[a] Christ Jesus our Lord.

An Illustration From Marriage

7 Do you not know, brothers—for I am speaking to men who know
the law—that the law has authority over a man only as long as
he lives? [2]For example, by law a married woman is bound to her husband as long as he is alive, but if her husband dies, she is released
from the law of marriage. [3]So then, if she marries another man while
her husband is still alive, she is called an adulteress. But if her hus-

[a]23 *Or through*

for the Christian, resurrection follows death, and a believer is freed to rise to new life in which sin cannot dominate.

6:18 free from sin. Free in the sense of having a new master—God—in place of the old master—sin. Paul is not teaching that Christians do not sin.

6:19 slavery. In contrast to a servant, the slave was the absolute possession of the master. A slave's time was not his own. It was literally impossible for a slave to serve two masters. **to impurity and to ever-increasing wickedness.** The sort of downward spiral of sin pictured in 1:24–25. **holiness.** "Sanctification"—the process by which one is conformed ever more closely to God's ways—is the theme of chapters 5–8.

6:23 wages of sin. Literally, "wages with which to buy food"—a phrase used to describe the rations eaten by soldiers. Roman slaves, too, were given pocket money. **gift of God.** In contrast to the death which sin pays out, God does not pay wages. He is under obligation to no one. Rather, he freely gives eternal life.

7:2 marriage. A wife is bound to the husband for the duration of his life and if she goes off ("consorts"—NEB) with another man while her husband is living, she "incurs the stigma of adultery" (J. B. Phillips). But if he dies, she is free to remarry without any taint.

band dies, she is released from that law and is not an adulteress, even though she marries another man.

[4]So, my brothers, you also died to the law through the body of Christ, that you might belong to another, to him who was raised from the dead, in order that we might bear fruit to God. [5]For when we were controlled by the sinful nature,[a] the sinful passions aroused by the law were at work in our bodies, so that we bore fruit for death. [6]But now, by dying to what once bound us, we have been released from the law so that we serve in the new way of the Spirit, and not in the old way of the written code.

Struggling With Sin

[7]What shall we say, then? Is the law sin? Certainly not! Indeed I would not have known what sin was except through the law. For I would not have known what coveting really was if the law had not said, "Do not covet."[b] [8]But sin, seizing the opportunity afforded by the commandment, produced in me every kind of covetous desire. For apart from law, sin is dead. [9]Once I was alive apart from law; but when the commandment came, sin sprang to life and I died. [10]I found that the very commandment that was intended to bring life actually brought death. [11]For sin, seizing the opportunity afforded by the commandment, deceived me, and through the commandment put me to death. [12]So then, the law is holy, and the commandment is holy, righteous and good.

[13]Did that which is good, then, become death to me? By no means! But in order that sin might be recognized as sin, it produced death in me through what was good, so that through the commandment sin might become utterly sinful.

[a]5 Or *the flesh*; also in verse 25 [b]7 Exodus 20:17; Deut. 5:21

from the law" (v. 6), what implication does this have for Christian living? **3.** What kinds of legalism do Christians fall into today?

APPLY In your pre-Christian days, did you struggle with high moral standards from your religious tradition—that you could not live up to?

OPEN 1. When you were a teenager, what was one of your biggest struggles? **2.** What New Year's resolution have you started with good intentions only to have it fizzle out?

STUDY 1. If you went to see your psychiatrist and told him/her what Paul said about himself in verses 15–20, what would the psychiatrist say or think? **2.** What did all of the "don'ts" in the Old Testament Law do for Paul? How would you explain this from your own experience? **3.** Do you think Paul is describing his struggle before he became a Christian (follower of Christ) or his struggle to overcome sin now that he is a Christian? How would you support this from your own experience? **4.** In this frustrating experience, what is Paul's hope

---

7:5–6 By way of applying these insights, Paul now contrasts preconversion life (v. 5) with the new life in Christ (v. 6) that a believer experiences.

7:5 controlled by the sinful nature. That is, when one's basic life direction was determined by one's fallen nature. **sinful passions.** Concrete acts of sin are in view here. **aroused by the law.** The prohibitions awaken both the desire to violate them (the fascination of forbidden fruit) and the self-centered impulse to defend oneself from their claim.

7:6 released from the law. The death of Christ has delivered you from the tyranny of the Law! **serve.** A Christian is freed from the Law to serve and not to sin—free for obedience, not license. **new way ... old way.** The Christian serves not the Law in its crippling and binding detail but rather follows the liberating way of the Spirit.

7:7 covet. Covetousness is an inner attitude in which a person wants what someone else has. People might have never known that covetousness was wrong but for the fact that the Law points it out (Ex. 20:17).

7:8 opportunity. This word is used to describe a military base which provides the starting point or bridgehead from which an active assault is launched. **produced in me.** The Law provokes sin, not simply by pointing out forbidden fruit, but by being misunderstood as setting an unreasonable limitation on one's personal freedom. **sin.** Paul personifies sin as a vital power with an evil intention. **dead.** Sin is dead in the sense of being "inactive" until a prohibition comes along and rouses it to defiance.

7:9–11 Throughout this passage Paul may be telling of his experience in terms that reflect his solidarity with Adam, as though his experience mirrored that of Adam's. The command in Genesis 2:17 not to eat was given with the good of humanity in mind, but the serpent twisted the benevolent prohibition into a deadly temptation. Prohibition produced covetous desire.

7:9 I died. Though living physically after the Law came, he fell under its judgment; i.e., under the sentence of death. This is the third function of the Law: it identifies the penalty for sin.

7:13 The final question in the series: "Even though it can be shown that the Law is good and not evil, wasn't it the Law that brought death to me? Therefore, isn't the Law bad?" Paul's answer begins with the familiar emphatic denial ("By no means!"). His point is that it is sin that is the culprit, not the Law. In fact, sin reveals its true colors by bringing death through what is good. It is caught red-handed in its distorting work and shown in its utter sinfulness. The Law offered life if it was obeyed, but it lacked the power to enable individuals to overcome sin.

(vv. 24–25)? How would you put this in your own words?

APPLY 1. How would you compare your struggle with the power of sin to Paul's struggle? **2.** What have you found helpful when you get down on yourself and think you are never going to make it?

OPEN When you were a teenager, what coach, teacher or mentor influenced you to change your behavior by affirming you as a special and unique person?

STUDY 1. Who or what influences you the most in: The clothes you wear? The music you listen to? Your values? **2.** From verses 1–4, how would you explain the gospel to someone who feels he is not

14We know that the law is spiritual; but I am unspiritual, sold as a
slave to sin. 15I do not understand what I do. For what I want to do I
do not do, but what I hate I do. 16And if I do what I do not want to do,
I agree that the law is good. 17As it is, it is no longer I myself who do
it, but it is sin living in me. 18I know that nothing good lives in me,
that is, in my sinful nature.[a] For I have the desire to do what is good,
but I cannot carry it out. 19For what I do is not the good I want to do;
no, the evil I do not want to do—this I keep on doing. 20Now if I do
what I do not want to do, it is no longer I who do it, but it is sin living
in me that does it.

21So I find this law at work: When I want to do good, evil is right
there with me. 22For in my inner being I delight in God's law; 23but I
see another law at work in the members of my body, waging war
against the law of my mind and making me a prisoner of the law of
sin at work within my members. 24What a wretched man I am! Who
will rescue me from this body of death? 25Thanks be to God—through
Jesus Christ our Lord!

So then, I myself in my mind am a slave to God's law, but in the sinful nature a slave to the law of sin.

Life Through the Spirit

8 Therefore, there is now no condemnation for those who are in
Christ Jesus,[b] 2because through Christ Jesus the law of the Spirit
of life set me free from the law of sin and death. 3For what the law
was powerless to do in that it was weakened by the sinful nature,[c]
God did by sending his own Son in the likeness of sinful man to be a
sin offering.[d] And so he condemned sin in sinful man,[e] 4in order that

[a]18 Or *my flesh* [b]1 Some later manuscripts *Jesus, who do not live according to the sinful nature but according to the Spirit,* [c]3 Or *the flesh*; also in verses 4,5,8,9,12 and 13 [d]3 Or *man, for sin* [e]3 Or *in the flesh*

7:14–25 In this section (vv. 7–13), the problem is not with the Law but with the sin that dwells within. The Law is good. People want to follow it, but find they cannot—at least not in their own strength.

7:14 the law is spiritual. That is, it comes from God and therefore bears his divine authority (Acts 1:16). It is important for Paul to say this lest his first-century Jewish audience misunderstand him to be departing from Old Testament Law. **unspiritual.** Literally, "composed of flesh," mere "flesh and blood," of flesh and not of spirit.

7:18 my sinful nature. Literally, "my flesh." The idea is not that one part of a person is "sinful" while another part is "spiritual."

7:21 this law. Not the Old Testament Law, but the other law mentioned in verse 23.

7:22–23 The law of the mind resides in the inner being. It delights in God's Law in contrast to the law of sin, which is at work in the members and at war against God's Law.

7:23 law of sin. This is the power exercised over humans by sin.

7:24 The nearer people come to God, the more aware they are of how short they fall of perfection. **Who will rescue me?** Since the problem of humanity is indwelling sin, and attempts to obey the Law on one's own power only accent the depth of that sin, people are helpless to deliver themselves. They need someone else to rescue them. This is precisely what God has done through Christ (v. 25).

7:25 Who indeed will rescue him? None other than the Lord Jesus Christ who met Paul on the Damascus Road, through whose death he at last found the long sought-after freedom from slavery to sin and bondage to the Law.

8:1 no condemnation. Christians are free from both the guilt which sin produces (and hence have no anxiety about being condemned on the future Day of Judgment), and are free from the total enslaving power of sin (and hence can live in God's way in the here and now).

8:2 Spirit. The Holy Spirit, the third person of the Trinity, who indwells believers in power. In chapter 8, Paul will refer to the Spirit over 20 times—more references to the Spirit than in any other single chapter of the New Testament. **law of the Spirit of life.** Rather than the inner struggle with sin, the believer is now indwelt by the Holy Spirit. **set me free.** There is at work in believers a power greater than sin—a power that enables them to resist sin effectively. They are no longer willing (or unwilling) slaves of sin.

8:3 sinful nature. Human nature in its vulnerability to sin, was unable to keep God's Law. Hence, the Law could not save anyone. In response to this plight, Christ, as God's representative, bore the punishment of sin in place of those who deserved it. **likeness.** Jesus took on weak human nature, but it was not to the exclusion of his divine nature. He was fully God and fully man.

the righteous requirements of the law might be fully met in us, who
do not live according to the sinful nature but according to the Spirit.
5Those who live according to the sinful nature have their minds set
on what that nature desires; but those who live in accordance with
the Spirit have their minds set on what the Spirit desires. 6The mind
of sinful man[a] is death, but the mind controlled by the Spirit is life
and peace; 7the sinful mind[b] is hostile to God. It does not submit to
God's law, nor can it do so. 8Those controlled by the sinful nature
cannot please God.
9You, however, are controlled not by the sinful nature but by the
Spirit, if the Spirit of God lives in you. And if anyone does not have the
Spirit of Christ, he does not belong to Christ. 10But if Christ is in you,
your body is dead because of sin, yet your spirit is alive because of
righteousness. 11And if the Spirit of him who raised Jesus from the
dead is living in you, he who raised Christ from the dead will also give
life to your mortal bodies through his Spirit, who lives in you.
12Therefore, brothers, we have an obligation—but it is not to the
sinful nature, to live according to it. 13For if you live according to the
sinful nature, you will die; but if by the Spirit you put to death the
misdeeds of the body, you will live, 14because those who are led by
the Spirit of God are sons of God. 15For you did not receive a spirit
that makes you a slave again to fear, but you received the Spirit of
sonship.[c] And by him we cry, "*Abba*,[d] Father." 16The Spirit himself testifies with our spirit that we are God's children. 17Now if we are children, then we are heirs—heirs of God and co-heirs with Christ, if
indeed we share in his sufferings in order that we may also share in
his glory.

Future Glory

18I consider that our present sufferings are not worth comparing
with the glory that will be revealed in us. 19The creation waits in ea-

[a]6 *Or mind set on the flesh* [b]7 *Or the mind set on the flesh* [c]15 *Or adoption* [d]15 Aramaic for *Father*

"good enough" for God? **3.** In verses 5–11, what does Paul say about the option Christians (followers of Christ) have in living their life? **4.** Where is the battle for the control of your life going to be fought and won? **5.** From this passage, what roles do God, Jesus and the Holy Spirit play in setting you free? **6.** What does it mean to be "led by the Spirit" (v. 14)? How does the Spirit help us fight our battles? Give an example. **7.** What is the best part of being in the family of God?

APPLY 1. Who helped you to understand the work of the Holy Spirit in your life as a Christian? **2.** What discipline or practice do you have to center your thoughts on God every day?

OPEN What signs of aging or weathering are you starting to feel in your bones?

STUDY 1. What are your expectations of the future?

8:5 live according to. There are two options: to be preoccupied with sinful desires or to be focused on the desires of the Holy Spirit. **minds.** Assumptions, values, outlook, desires, purpose—all that forms one's perspective on life. What a person thinks determines how one acts. One's conduct is guided by one's outlook.

8:6 death ... life. The two outlooks lead to two patterns of conduct which result in two spiritual states—death to God (because sin separates one from him) or life in the Spirit.

8:13 put to death. In 7:4 Paul says that Christians are "dead to the law" through Christ's once-for-all act of dying on the cross in their place. In response to this fact, believers are daily (the verb tense indicates an action that is repeated over and over) to "put to death" all those practices they know to be wrong.

8:15 spirit that makes you a slave. The Holy Spirit brings one, not into a new form of anxious bondage, but rather unites one with Christ, enabling one to share his sonship. **you received.** The verb tense indicates that this is a one-time, past action—something that happened at conversion. **sonship.** The Roman practice of adoption was a most serious and complicated process, because a child was the absolute possession of his father. For a child to be adopted into a new family, he was first symbolically "sold" by his father to the adopting father. Then the legal case for adoption was taken to the magistrate. **cry.** In the Psalms this word is used of urgent prayer (Ps. 3:4). **Abba.** An Aramaic word used by children; best translated "Daddy," signifying a close, intimate relationship. **Abba, Father.** The very words Jesus prayed in the Garden of Gethsemane (Mark 14:36).

8:16 In the Roman adoptive proceedings there were several witnesses to the ceremony who would, if a dispute arose later, verify that the particular child had actually been adopted. The Holy Spirit is the one who verifies a person's adoption into the family of God.

8:17 heirs. If someone is one of God's children, then that person is an heir, and will share in God's riches. In fact, Jesus is God's true heir (v. 3), but since believers are "in Christ," they become sons and daughters of God by adoption and thus are joint-heirs with Christ.

8:18 present sufferings. That is, the persecutions (5:3) that Christians face in the time between Jesus' first coming and his return. These are real; not pleasant, but slight in comparison with the glory ahead.

8:19 eager expectation. The image is of a person with excited anticipation scanning the horizon for the first sign of

2. What do you think Paul means by "the glory" to come? **3.** Why do we as followers of Christ "groan"? **4.** What reasons for hope do you find in this passage? **5.** What does the Holy Spirit do for us when we do not know how to pray?

APPLY 1. When is the last time you did not know how to pray and the Holy Spirit helped and comforted you? **2.** What "present sufferings" are you struggling with? What have you found helpful in dealing with pain and suffering?

OPEN Do you tend to see the glass half-full or half-empty? Who is the tower of strength in your family?

STUDY 1. Today, have you felt more like a conqueror or

ger expectation for the sons of God to be revealed. 20For the creation
was subjected to frustration, not by its own choice, but by the will of
the one who subjected it, in hope 21that[a] the creation itself will be liberated from its bondage to decay and brought into the glorious freedom of the children of God.

22We know that the whole creation has been groaning as in the
pains of childbirth right up to the present time. 23Not only so, but we
ourselves, who have the firstfruits of the Spirit, groan inwardly as we
wait eagerly for our adoption as sons, the redemption of our bodies.
24For in this hope we were saved. But hope that is seen is no hope at
all. Who hopes for what he already has? 25But if we hope for what we
do not yet have, we wait for it patiently.

26In the same way, the Spirit helps us in our weakness. We do not
know what we ought to pray for, but the Spirit himself intercedes for
us with groans that words cannot express. 27And he who searches
our hearts knows the mind of the Spirit, because the Spirit intercedes
for the saints in accordance with God's will.

More Than Conquerors

28And we know that in all things God works for the good of those
who love him,[b] who[c] have been called according to his purpose. 29For

[a]20,21 *Or subjected it in hope.* 21*For* [b]28 Some manuscripts *And we know that all things work together for good to those who love God* [c]28 *Or works together with those who love him to bring about what is good—with those who*

---

the coming dawn of glory. The only other occurrence of this word in the New Testament is in Philippians 1:20. **for the sons of God to be revealed.** Christians are indeed sons and daughters of God here and now in this life. What Paul refers to here is the fact that they are, as it were, incognito. It will only be at the Second Coming that it is revealed for all to see who are the children of God.

8:20 For. Verses 20–21 explain why the creation waits with such eagerness for this revealing. **the creation.** The whole of the nonhuman world, both living and inanimate. **was subjected.** The verb tense indicates a single past action (Gen. 3:17–19). **frustration.** The inability of creation to achieve the goal for which it was created—that of glorifying God—because the key actor in this drama of praise (mankind) has fallen. **in hope.** There was divine judgment at the Fall, but this was not without hope. One day, it was said, the woman's offspring would crush the serpent's head (Gen. 3:15).

8:21 will be liberated. Creation will be freed from its frustrating bondage at the time of the Second Coming when the children of God are freed from the last vestiges of sin. **bondage to decay.** All of creation seems to be running down; deterioration and decomposition now characterize the created order.

8:22 pains of childbirth. Such pain is very real, very intense, but also temporary (and the necessary prelude to new life). The image is not of the annihilation of the present universe, but of the emergence of a transformed order (Rev. 21:1). Childbirth was a Jewish metaphor for the suffering that would precede the coming of the new age (Isa. 26:17).

8:23 firstfruits. Generally this term refers to those early developing pieces of fruit that were harvested and given to God, but here the idea is of a gift from God to people. The experience by the believer of the work of the Holy Spirit is a pledge that one day God will grant all that he has promised. **we ... groan inwardly.** One groans not just because of persecution, but because one is not yet redeemed. Believers' bodies are still subject to weakness, pain and death. The believer longs for the suffering to end and for the redemption of the body to be complete.

8:26 what ... to pray. It is not clear whether this refers to one's inability to know what to pray, or to the problem of knowing how to pray.

8:28 in all things God works. Some translations read "all things work together for good" almost as though for the Christian things will work out for the best on their own. In fact, it is God who takes that which is adverse and painful (the groans, the persecution, and even death—vv. 35–36) and brings profit out of it. **for the good of those who love him.** This does not mean things work out so that believers preserve their comfort and convenience. Rather, such action on God's part enables these difficult experiences to assist in the process of salvation. **those who love him, who have been called according to his purpose.** The love people have for God is a reflection of the fact and reality of God's love for them as expressed in his call to individuals to follow Christ. A person's love for God has been said to be a proof of God's love for that person. Had God not called an individual, that person would still be his enemy, unable and unwilling to love him.

8:29 foreknew. God knew even before the world was created who would have faith (Eph. 1:4; 2 Tim. 1:9). For God to know someone is for him to love and have a purpose for that person. **predestined.** God puts into effect what he foreknew. **conformed to the likeness.** While Paul has in mind that time of glorification (when believers will be brought into full conformity to the image of Christ), he is also thinking of ongoing sanctification, whereby believers come ever closer to the image of Christ (through daily suffering and obedience).

those God foreknew he also predestined to be conformed to the likeness of his Son, that he might be the firstborn among many brothers.
30And those he predestined, he also called; those he called, he also
justified; those he justified, he also glorified.

31What, then, shall we say in response to this? If God is for us, who
can be against us? 32He who did not spare his own Son, but gave him
up for us all—how will he not also, along with him, graciously give us
all things? 33Who will bring any charge against those whom God has
chosen? It is God who justifies. 34Who is he that condemns? Christ
Jesus, who died—more than that, who was raised to life—is at the
right hand of God and is also interceding for us. 35Who shall separate
us from the love of Christ? Shall trouble or hardship or persecution or
famine or nakedness or danger or sword? 36As it is written:

"For your sake we face death all day long;
we are considered as sheep to be slaughtered."[a]

37No, in all these things we are more than conquerors through him
who loved us. 38For I am convinced that neither death nor life, neither
angels nor demons,[b] neither the present nor the future, nor any powers,
39neither height nor depth, nor anything else in all creation, will be
able to separate us from the love of God that is in Christ Jesus our Lord.

God's Sovereign Choice

9 I speak the truth in Christ—I am not lying, my conscience confirms it in the Holy Spirit— 2I have great sorrow and unceasing
anguish in my heart. 3For I could wish that I myself were cursed and
cut off from Christ for the sake of my brothers, those of my own race,
4the people of Israel. Theirs is the adoption as sons; theirs the divine
glory, the covenants, the receiving of the law, the temple worship and
the promises. 5Theirs are the patriarchs, and from them is traced the
human ancestry of Christ, who is God over all, forever praised![c]
Amen.

[a]36 Psalm 44:22 [b]38 Or *nor heavenly rulers* [c]5 Or *Christ, who is over all. God be forever praised!* Or *Christ. God who is over all be forever praised!*

conquered? **2.** What confidence does verse 28 give believers about events that occur in their lives? When has it been hardest for you to believe this? How have you seen God bring something good out of a bad situation? **3.** From verses 29–30, what steps are outlined, "For those God foreknew"? **4.** How do verses 31–34 support 8:1, "There is now no condemnation for those who are in Christ"? **5.** Of the agents of separation listed in verses 35–39, which is most threatening to you? **6.** What is the key verse for you in this passage?

APPLY 1. How are you doing in the school of hard knocks right now? **2.** What is the closest you have come to feeling the despair and loneliness of being separated from God like Paul describes in verses 31–39?

OPEN 1. What was one thing about which your folks used to say, "Wait 'till you're older, you'll understand then"? **2.** When have you won something unexpected: A trip? Award of achievement? Class officer elections? The big game?

STUDY 1. When have you been surprised to be chosen for something? When have you been disappointed that you weren't chosen? **2.** What is a particular person, group or race that you have a heart for? **3.** According to this passage, who are

---

8:30 called. Foreknowledge and predestination are prerogatives of God which enter the realm of history at the point of calling, whereby one hears the gospel and responds in faith. The end result then is justification.

8:31 Paul does not ask, "Who is against us?" In response, many enemies could be named: Hostile society, Satan, Indwelling sin and Death. Rather, he prefaces the question with an assertion that "God is for us" and then asks, "Who can be against us?" Therefore, all potential enemies fade into insignificance.

8:32 Again Paul does not ask, "Will not God give us all things?" A response to that question would probably be ambiguous were it not for his preface, where he indicates that God has already given the supreme gift—his Son who died on humanity's behalf.

8:33–34 Paul's next two questions are set in the context of a law court. Their point: There is no charge that can now be effectively leveled against Christians to bring about their condemnation, since God is the Judge who has already justified them (and Jesus is their Advocate who pleads for them).

8:35 In response to this final unanswerable question, Paul names those enemies that might appear powerful enough to separate believers from God's love.

8:37 more than conquerors. Literally, hyper-conquerors or super-conquerors.

8:38 death ... life. For Paul, to die was no longer a threat—it was to "be with Christ" (Phil. 1:21-23). Life is used here in the sense of trials, distractions, and enticements that could easily lead one away from God. **angels ... demons.** Continuing his pairing of opposites, Paul says that neither benevolent nor malevolent spiritual powers need be feared. **present ... future.** Neither this age nor the events in the future eschatological age are to be feared.

8:39 height ... depth. Or the reference could be to the influence of a star at the height or the depth of its zenith. It may mean simply that neither heaven nor hell can separate Christians from God's love.

9:4 adoption. Israel has a special relationship with God. The use of the word adoption calls attention to the fact that this relationship is by grace—a product of God's action and not the result of natural succession. **temple worship.** Through the sacrificial system, Israel had special access to God. **promises.** Old Testament prophecies which stressed that God had a great and noble task in store for Israel.

God's children? **4.** Looking at verses 15–18, on what is God's favor based? How do verses 19–21 answer questions raised by the previous verses? **5.** How might God's plan make a Gentile feel? A Jew? You? **6.** What qualities of God stand out to you in the Old Testament quotes (vv. 25–29)? **7.** For what work do you feel God created you?

APPLY 1. Where are you growing in your understanding of God's will for your life? What questions would you like to ask God about this? **2.** How deeply do you hurt for unbelievers? As much as Paul? **3.** If you were God, would you choose "you" to be part of your plan for the universe? How do you feel about God's authority to choose who will be "objects of his mercy" (v. 23)?

---

6 It is not as though God's word had failed. For not all who are descended from Israel are Israel. 7 Nor because they are his descendants are they all Abraham's children. On the contrary, "It is through Isaac that your offspring will be reckoned."[a] 8 In other words, it is not the natural children who are God's children, but it is the children of the promise who are regarded as Abraham's offspring. 9 For this was how the promise was stated: "At the appointed time I will return, and Sarah will have a son."[b]

10 Not only that, but Rebekah's children had one and the same father, our father Isaac. 11 Yet, before the twins were born or had done anything good or bad—in order that God's purpose in election might stand: 12 not by works but by him who calls—she was told, "The older will serve the younger."[c] 13 Just as it is written: "Jacob I loved, but Esau I hated."[d]

14 What then shall we say? Is God unjust? Not at all! 15 For he says to Moses,

"I will have mercy on whom I have mercy,
and I will have compassion on whom I have compassion."[e]

16 It does not, therefore, depend on man's desire or effort, but on God's mercy. 17 For the Scripture says to Pharaoh: "I raised you up for this very purpose, that I might display my power in you and that my name might be proclaimed in all the earth."[f] 18 Therefore God has mercy on whom he wants to have mercy, and he hardens whom he wants to harden.

19 One of you will say to me: "Then why does God still blame us? For who resists his will?" 20 But who are you, O man, to talk back to God? "Shall what is formed say to him who formed it, 'Why did you make me like this?' "[g] 21 Does not the potter have the right to make out of the same lump of clay some pottery for noble purposes and some for common use?

22 What if God, choosing to show his wrath and make his power known, bore with great patience the objects of his wrath—prepared for destruction? 23 What if he did this to make the riches of his glory known to the objects of his mercy, whom he prepared in advance for glory— 24 even us, whom he also called, not only from the Jews but also from the Gentiles? 25 As he says in Hosea:

"I will call them 'my people' who are not my people;
and I will call her 'my loved one' who is not my loved one,"[h]

26 and,

"It will happen that in the very place where it was said to them,
'You are not my people,'
they will be called 'sons of the living God.' "[i]

27 Isaiah cries out concerning Israel:

[a]7 Gen. 21:12 [b]9 Gen. 18:10,14 [c]12 Gen. 25:23 [d]13 Mal. 1:2,3 [e]15 Exodus 33:19 [f]17 Exodus 9:16 [g]20 Isaiah 29:16; 45:9 [h]25 Hosea 2:23 [i]26 Hosea 1:10

9:8 The contrast is made explicit: To be a physical descendant of Abraham is not necessarily to be a part of the true Israel. Paul will soon point out that there has always been a remnant of Jews true to God within the larger nation of Israel (11:1–15).

9:15–16 Paul used Exodus 33:19 to show the freedom of God's mercy. God is free to offer such mercy to whomever he chooses.

"Though the number of the Israelites be like the sand by the sea,
only the remnant will be saved.
[28]For the Lord will carry out
his sentence on earth with speed and finality."[a]

[29]It is just as Isaiah said previously:

"Unless the Lord Almighty
had left us descendants,
we would have become like Sodom,
we would have been like Gomorrah."[b]

Israel's Unbelief

[30]What then shall we say? That the Gentiles, who did not pursue
righteousness, have obtained it, a righteousness that is by faith; [31]but
Israel, who pursued a law of righteousness, has not attained it. [32]Why
not? Because they pursued it not by faith but as if it were by works.
They stumbled over the "stumbling stone." [33]As it is written:

"See, I lay in Zion a stone that causes men to stumble
and a rock that makes them fall,
and the one who trusts in him will never be put to shame."[c]

10 Brothers, my heart's desire and prayer to God for the Israelites is that they may be saved. [2]For I can testify about them
that they are zealous for God, but their zeal is not based on knowledge. [3]Since they did not know the righteousness that comes from
God and sought to establish their own, they did not submit to God's
righteousness. [4]Christ is the end of the law so that there may be righteousness for everyone who believes.

[5]Moses describes in this way the righteousness that is by the law:
"The man who does these things will live by them."[d] [6]But the righteousness that is by faith says: "Do not say in your heart, 'Who will
ascend into heaven?'[e]" (that is, to bring Christ down) [7]"or 'Who will
descend into the deep?'[f]" (that is, to bring Christ up from the dead).
[8]But what does it say? "The word is near you; it is in your mouth and
in your heart,"[g] that is, the word of faith we are proclaiming: [9]That if
you confess with your mouth, "Jesus is Lord," and believe in your
heart that God raised him from the dead, you will be saved. [10]For it is
with your heart that you believe and are justified, and it is with your
mouth that you confess and are saved. [11]As the Scripture says, "Anyone who trusts in him will never be put to shame."[h] [12]For there is no
difference between Jew and Gentile—the same Lord is Lord of all and
richly blesses all who call on him, [13]for, "Everyone who calls on the
name of the Lord will be saved."[i]

[14]How, then, can they call on the one they have not believed in?
And how can they believe in the one of whom they have not heard?

[a]28 Isaiah 10:22,23 [b]29 Isaiah 1:9 [c]33 Isaiah 8:14; 28:16 [d]5 Lev. 18:5 [e]6 Deut. 30:12 [f]7 Deut. 30:13 [g]8 Deut. 30:14 [h]11 Isaiah 28:16 [i]13 Joel 2:32

OPEN 1. When you were a child, what did you do to earn your allowance? **2.** In elementary school, what was your hardest subject? What did you do to try to improve your grades? **3.** What were some of the hard and fast rules observed in your house when your were growing up?

STUDY 1. What would you say is the general view in the world today about how a person can get to heaven? **2.** What hope does Paul have for the Israelites in the first verse of chapter 10? **3.** In what characteristic way did Jews seek to be right with God (9:32)? What was the basic problem in this approach (3:20; 7:7–11)? **4.** What "stumbling stone" do you see that keeps people away from God? **5.** According to 10:9–10, how is one saved? **6.** How would the attitude of a person coming to God on the basis of his or her performance (10:5) be different from that of someone coming to him by faith in Christ (10:8–9)? **7.** How do the questions Paul asks in 10:14–15 challenge you? **8.** What do you see as the basic difference between Christianity and other religions? **9.** What does it mean to confess "Jesus is Lord"? How does this tie in with belief? **10.** Recall when you confessed Jesus is Lord and believed God raised him from the dead.

APPLY 1. When did you first come to realize that it isn't so much what you do for God, but what he's done for you? **2.** The central affirmation of the early church was "Jesus is Lord"; everyone else was saying "Caesar is Lord." Who (or what) are

9:32 stumbling stone. Jesus identifies himself as "the strength builders rejected" (Ps. 118:22–23; Matt. 21:42). In not recognizing Jesus as the inner meaning of the Law, Israel can do little else than stumble over him.

10:6 Who will ascend into heaven? This phrase means that Israel does not have to go all the way up to heaven to find God's Law (Deut. 30:12). The righteousness of the Law is found in Christ—obtained only by faith.

10:7 bring Christ up. There is no need to bring Christ up from the dead, since he has already been inside.

10:12 no difference. In 3:23 the emphasis is negative: all are sinners.

some gods that compete with your allegiance to Christ?

OPEN 1. As a child, what item did a friend or sibling possess that made you jealous? **2.** Who was someone you were envious of in high school and why? **3.** What have been the benefits of healthy competition in your life?

STUDY 1. Has God rejected the Jews (v. 1)? On what basis are Paul and others of the remnant chosen (vv. 5–6)? **2.** What good thing came to the Gentiles from the Jews' transgression (v. 11)? What hope does Paul have from this for the Jews (v. 14)? What are the grafted branches warned against (v. 20) and why? **3.** From verses 17–21, who are: The broken branches? The other branches? The wild olive shoot? The root? What is the point of this illustration? **4.** Why does Paul want his Gentile readers to be aware of God's plan (v. 25)? Why would pride become a danger for them? **5.** Does Paul mean in verses 25–32 that every Jewish person will ultimately be saved? **6.** What do both the Jews and Gentiles share in common (vv. 29–32)? **7.** In what ways has God shown his mercy to you? **8.** How does the doxology in verses 33–36 relate to: Paul's argument in verses

And how can they hear without someone preaching to them? [15]And
how can they preach unless they are sent? As it is written, "How
beautiful are the feet of those who bring good news!"[a]

[16]But not all the Israelites accepted the good news. For Isaiah says,
"Lord, who has believed our message?"[b] [17]Consequently, faith comes
from hearing the message, and the message is heard through the
word of Christ. [18]But I ask: Did they not hear? Of course they did:

"Their voice has gone out into all the earth,
their words to the ends of the world."[c]

[19]Again I ask: Did Israel not understand? First, Moses says,

"I will make you envious by those who are not a nation;
I will make you angry by a nation that has no understanding."[d]

[20]And Isaiah boldly says,

"I was found by those who did not seek me;
I revealed myself to those who did not ask for me."[e]

[21]But concerning Israel he says,

"All day long I have held out my hands
to a disobedient and obstinate people."[f]

The Remnant of Israel

11 I ask then: Did God reject his people? By no means! I am an
Israelite myself, a descendant of Abraham, from the tribe of
Benjamin. [2]God did not reject his people, whom he foreknew. Don't
you know what the Scripture says in the passage about Elijah—how
he appealed to God against Israel: [3]"Lord, they have killed your
prophets and torn down your altars; I am the only one left, and they
are trying to kill me"[g]? [4]And what was God's answer to him? "I have
reserved for myself seven thousand who have not bowed the knee to
Baal."[h] [5]So too, at the present time there is a remnant chosen by
grace. [6]And if by grace, then it is no longer by works; if it were, grace
would no longer be grace.[i]

[7]What then? What Israel sought so earnestly it did not obtain, but
the elect did. The others were hardened, [8]as it is written:

"God gave them a spirit of stupor,
eyes so that they could not see
and ears so that they could not hear,
to this very day."[j]

[9]And David says:

"May their table become a snare and a trap,
a stumbling block and a retribution for them.

[a]*15* Isaiah 52:7 [b]*16* Isaiah 53:1 [c]*18* Psalm 19:4 [d]*19* Deut. 32:21 [e]*20* Isaiah 65:1 [f]*21* Isaiah 65:2
[g]*3* 1 Kings 19:10,14 [h]*4* 1 Kings 19:18 [i]*6* Some manuscripts *by grace. But if by works, then it is no longer grace; if it were, work would no longer be work.* [j]*8* Deut. 29:4; Isaiah 29:10

10:15 preach. This means to proclaim like a herald. Proclamation came to mean the gospel message (16:28–26).

11:1 I am an Israelite. Paul, who remains a true zealous Jew who happens to be a believing Christian, is proof that God has not cast off Israel. He is still using Israel, through Paul, to fulfill its God-given task of bearing God's redemptive message to the world.

11:5 remnant. There was always at least a small number who were true. They were like a nation within a nation.

10 May their eyes be darkened so they cannot see,
and their backs be bent forever."[a]

Ingrafted Branches

11 Again I ask: Did they stumble so as to fall beyond recovery? Not at
all! Rather, because of their transgression, salvation has come to the
Gentiles to make Israel envious. 12 But if their transgression means
riches for the world, and their loss means riches for the Gentiles, how
much greater riches will their fullness bring!
13 I am talking to you Gentiles. Inasmuch as I am the apostle to the
Gentiles, I make much of my ministry 14 in the hope that I may somehow arouse my own people to envy and save some of them. 15 For if
their rejection is the reconciliation of the world, what will their acceptance be but life from the dead? 16 If the part of the dough offered
as firstfruits is holy, then the whole batch is holy; if the root is holy, so
are the branches.
17 If some of the branches have been broken off, and you, though a
wild olive shoot, have been grafted in among the others and now
share in the nourishing sap from the olive root, 18 do not boast over
those branches. If you do, consider this: You do not support the root,
but the root supports you. 19 You will say then, "Branches were broken
off so that I could be grafted in." 20 Granted. But they were broken off
because of unbelief, and you stand by faith. Do not be arrogant, but
be afraid. 21 For if God did not spare the natural branches, he will not
spare you either.
22 Consider therefore the kindness and sternness of God: sternness
to those who fell, but kindness to you, provided that you continue in
his kindness. Otherwise, you also will be cut off. 23 And if they do not
persist in unbelief, they will be grafted in, for God is able to graft
them in again. 24 After all, if you were cut out of an olive tree that is
wild by nature, and contrary to nature were grafted into a cultivated
olive tree, how much more readily will these, the natural branches,
be grafted into their own olive tree!

All Israel Will Be Saved

25 I do not want you to be ignorant of this mystery, brothers, so that
you may not be conceited: Israel has experienced a hardening in part
until the full number of the Gentiles has come in. 26 And so all Israel
will be saved, as it is written:

"The deliverer will come from Zion;
he will turn godlessness away from Jacob.
27 And this is[b] my covenant with them
when I take away their sins."[c]

28 As far as the gospel is concerned, they are enemies on your account; but as far as election is concerned, they are loved on account

[a] *10* Psalm 69:22,23 [b] *27* Or *will be* [c] *27* Isaiah 59:20,21; 27:9; Jer. 31:33,34

25–32? Any questions that may have been raised by chapters 9–11? **9.** Which traits of God does Paul celebrate here? Why these? **10.** Like the Jews in Paul's day, are churchgoers today relying more on performance of rituals than on God's grace? How? **11.** How does the church itself struggle with works versus grace? In what ways are works still important?

APPLY 1. Is it possible for someone to try so hard to please God that they actually resist his love for them? When have you experienced this?. **2.** When someone else receives God's blessing and grace in their life, does that spur you on to seek God all the more, or does it leave you feeling on the short end of the stick? **3.** Why is the end of this chapter a good place for a doxology—Paul's, yours and your group's?

11:14 envy. It is usually something that is negative. In this case it brings good to pass. **save.** His goal was to convert them to the Christian faith and redeem them.

11:17 branches ... broken off. Paul is referring here to unbelieving Israel. **a wild olive.** The Gentile Christians. **among the others.** The Jewish Christians.

11:25 mystery. This is something which is hidden in the mind of God, but which now he is pleased to reveal to all those who are willing to seek him.

OPEN As a teen, how did peer pressure affect the way you dressed? Hair style?

STUDY 1. How would you paraphrase the words of Paul, "do not conform any longer to the pattern of this world"? **2.** Is transformation for you an act or a process? What are you doing to renew your mind? **3.** Are you more likely to overestimate or underestimate your spiritual gifts? Of the six gifts listed here, where are you the strongest? Would your group members agree with your assessment?

APPLY 1. Are you happy in your present job? **2.** If you could retire today and use your gifts in special ministry, what would you

of the patriarchs, 29for God's gifts and his call are irrevocable. 30Just
as you who were at one time disobedient to God have now received
mercy as a result of their disobedience, 31so they too have now become disobedient in order that they too may now[a] receive mercy as a
result of God's mercy to you. 32For God has bound all men over to
disobedience so that he may have mercy on them all.

Doxology

33Oh, the depth of the riches of the wisdom and[b] knowledge of God!
How unsearchable his judgments,
and his paths beyond tracing out!
34"Who has known the mind of the Lord?
Or who has been his counselor?"[c]
35"Who has ever given to God,
that God should repay him?"[d]
36For from him and through him and to him are all things.
To him be the glory forever! Amen.

Living Sacrifices

12 Therefore, I urge you, brothers, in view of God's mercy, to offer your bodies as living sacrifices, holy and pleasing to God—this is your spiritual[e] act of worship. 2Do not conform any
longer to the pattern of this world, but be transformed by the renew-
ing of your mind. Then you will be able to test and approve what
God's will is—his good, pleasing and perfect will.
3For by the grace given me I say to every one of you: Do not think of
yourself more highly than you ought, but rather think of yourself with
sober judgment, in accordance with the measure of faith God has
given you. 4Just as each of us has one body with many members, and
these members do not all have the same function, 5so in Christ we
who are many form one body, and each member belongs to all the
others. 6We have different gifts, according to the grace given us. If a
man's gift is prophesying, let him use it in proportion to his[f] faith. 7If

[a]31 Some manuscripts do not have *now.* [b]33 Or *riches and the wisdom and the* [c]34 Isaiah 40:13
[d]35 Job 41:11 [e]1 Or *reasonable* [f]6 Or *in agreement with the*

12:1 in view of God's mercy. Paul has just declared God's amazing mercy (11:30–32). A Christian's motivation to obedience is overwhelming gratitude for God's mercy. **bodies.** The Christian lifestyle is not a matter of mystical spirituality that transcends one's bodily nature, but an everyday, practical exercise of love (6:13). The idea of "bodies" also emphasizes the metaphor of sacrifice since one puts bodies on the altar. **living ... holy ... pleasing to God.** In Greek, these three phrases are attached with equal weight as qualifiers for "sacrifices."

12:2 Do not conform. Literally, "stop allowing yourself to be conformed"; i.e., believers are no longer helpless victims of natural and supernatural forces which would shape them into a distorted pattern; rather they now have the ability and help to resist such powers. **be transformed.** The force of the verb is "continue to let yourself be transformed"; a continuous action by the Holy Spirit which goes on for a lifetime. A Christian's responsibility is to stay open to this sanctification process as the Spirit works to teach him or her to look at life from God's view of reality. **renewing of your mind.** Develop a spiritual sensitivity and perception—learn to look at life on the basis of God's view of reality. Paul emphasizes the need to develop understanding of God's ways. **test and approve.** Christians are called to a responsible freedom of choice and action, based on the inner renewing work of the Holy Spirit.

12:3 every one of you. The truth about spiritual gifts applies to each believer. **sober judgment.** The command is to know oneself accurately, rather than to have too high an opinion of oneself in comparison to others.

12:6 gifts. Those endowments given by God to every believer by grace (the words "grace" and "gifts" come from the same root word) to be used in God's service. The gifts listed here (or elsewhere in the New Testament) are not meant to be exhaustive or absolute since no gift list overlaps completely. **prophesying.** Inspired utterances, distinguished from teaching by their immediacy and unpremeditated nature, the source of which is direct revelation by God.

12:7 serving. The special capacity for rendering practical service to the needy. **teaching.** In contrast to the prophet (whose utterances have as their source the direct revelation of God), the teacher relied on the Old Testament

it is serving, let him serve; if it is teaching, let him teach; [8]if it is encouraging, let him encourage; if it is contributing to the needs of others, let him give generously; if it is leadership, let him govern
diligently; if it is showing mercy, let him do it cheerfully.

Love

[9]Love must be sincere. Hate what is evil; cling to what is good. [10]Be
devoted to one another in brotherly love. Honor one another above
yourselves. [11]Never be lacking in zeal, but keep your spiritual fervor,
serving the Lord. [12]Be joyful in hope, patient in affliction, faithful in
prayer. [13]Share with God's people who are in need. Practice hospitality.

[14]Bless those who persecute you; bless and do not curse. [15]Rejoice
with those who rejoice; mourn with those who mourn. [16]Live in harmony with one another. Do not be proud, but be willing to associate
with people of low position.[a] Do not be conceited.

[17]Do not repay anyone evil for evil. Be careful to do what is right in
the eyes of everybody. [18]If it is possible, as far as it depends on you,
live at peace with everyone. [19]Do not take revenge, my friends, but
leave room for God's wrath, for it is written: "It is mine to avenge; I
will repay,"[b] says the Lord. [20]On the contrary:

"If your enemy is hungry, feed him;
if he is thirsty, give him something to drink.
In doing this, you will heap burning coals on his head."[c]

[21]Do not be overcome by evil, but overcome evil with good.

Submission to the Authorities

13 Everyone must submit himself to the governing authorities,
for there is no authority except that which God has established. The authorities that exist have been established by God. [2]Con-
sequently, he who rebels against the authority is rebelling against
what God has instituted, and those who do so will bring judgment on
themselves. [3]For rulers hold no terror for those who do right, but for
those who do wrong. Do you want to be free from fear of the one in
authority? Then do what is right and he will commend you. [4]For he is
God's servant to do you good. But if you do wrong, be afraid, for
he does not bear the sword for nothing. He is God's servant, an agent
of wrath to bring punishment on the wrongdoer. [5]Therefore, it is

[a]16 *Or willing to do menial work* [b]19 Deut. 32:35 [c]20 Prov. 25:21,22

like to do? What is keeping you from this?

OPEN As a child, who was the troublemaker in your family? Who was the peacemaker?

STUDY 1. On a scale from 1 to 10, how would you measure the quality of life in your church against the standard set in verses 9–13? Where is your church strongest? Weakest? **2.** If you were on the leadership team of your church, what would you make as a priority? **3.** In a big church where people do not know each other, how can you practice the caring relationships described in verses 14–16?

APPLY 1. Has your church or your group ever lived up to the model described in these verses? **2.** What do you appreciate most about the group you are in right now?

OPEN When was the last time you got a traffic ticket? How did you feel about the police officer?

STUDY 1. Why does Paul say we should submit to governing authorities? Compare this passage with Acts 5:27–32. What's the difference between submitting to authorities and unconditionally obeying them? **2.** Who are the authorities in your life? How well have you related to them? How could you do better?

APPLY 1. How was your walk with the Lord this past

Scriptures and the teachings of Jesus to instruct others.

12:8 encouraging. This is supporting *and assisting others to live a life of obedience* to God. **contributing.** The person who takes delight in giving away his or her possessions. **leadership.** Those with special ability to guide a congregation are called upon to do so with zeal. **showing mercy.** Serve those who need care.

12:9 Love. *Agape*: self-giving action on behalf of others made possible by God's Spirit. **sincere.** Genuine, not counterfeit or showy.

12:10 brotherly love. The word for love used here, *philadelphia*, denoting the tender affection found in families, now said to be appropriate to those in the church—which is the Christian's (followers of Christ) new family. **Honor.** Since other Christians are in union with Christ, they are to be honored.

12:11 fervor. This Greek word is also used of water when it has been brought to a boil (or of metal, like copper, which is glowing red-hot in refining or shaping).

13:1 Everyone. That is, every Christian in Rome; no one is exempt. **submit.** Submission must be understood in light of 12:10 (honoring others above oneself) and Philippians 2:3–4 (counting others as better); Christians must recognize the claim that the authorities have upon them.

13:3–4 Paul is not discussing governments that are unjust and which punish good works and praise evil.

week? **2.** What aspects of government do you find most difficult to accept?

OPEN What was the occasion of your first debt or loan?

STUDY 1. How does Paul's concept of love differ from today's popular notions of love? **2.** Does it sound to you like there are people in the church today that are behaving like those in verses 12–13? **3.** If some people still struggle with the gross sins in verses 12–13, what does Paul challenge them to do?

APPLY 1. How close do you think we are to the end of time? How does this affect your priorities? **2.** When is the last time you took inventory on your spiritual life?

OPEN 1. What, if any, rules did your family have for what you could or could not do on Sunday? **2.** What did you, or do you, refuse to eat or drink?

STUDY In the first century, the pagan temples sacrificed animals and then sold the meat in the market. They also ran restaurants where this meat was served. To young

necessary to submit to the authorities, not only because of possible
punishment but also because of conscience.
6 This is also why you pay taxes, for the authorities are God's servants, who give their full time to governing. 7 Give everyone what you
owe him: If you owe taxes, pay taxes; if revenue, then revenue; if respect, then respect; if honor, then honor.

Love, for the Day Is Near

8 Let no debt remain outstanding, except the continuing debt to
love one another, for he who loves his fellowman has fulfilled the law.
9 The commandments, "Do not commit adultery," "Do not murder,"
"Do not steal," "Do not covet,"[a] and whatever other commandment
there may be, are summed up in this one rule: "Love your neighbor as
yourself."[b] 10 Love does no harm to its neighbor. Therefore love is the
fulfillment of the law.
11 And do this, understanding the present time. The hour has come
for you to wake up from your slumber, because our salvation is nearer now than when we first believed. 12 The night is nearly over; the day
is almost here. So let us put aside the deeds of darkness and put on
the armor of light. 13 Let us behave decently, as in the daytime, not in
orgies and drunkenness, not in sexual immorality and debauchery,
not in dissension and jealousy. 14 Rather, clothe yourselves with the
Lord Jesus Christ, and do not think about how to gratify the desires of
the sinful nature.[c]

The Weak and the Strong

14 Accept him whose faith is weak, without passing judgment
on disputable matters. 2 One man's faith allows him to eat
everything, but another man, whose faith is weak, eats only vegetables. 3 The man who eats everything must not look down on him who
does not, and the man who does not eat everything must not condemn the man who does, for God has accepted him. 4 Who are you to

[a]9 Exodus 20:13-15,17; Deut. 5:17-19,21 [b]9 Lev. 19:18 [c]14 Or *the flesh*

13:7 taxes. Local taxes such as duty, import/export taxes, taxes for the use of roads or for the right to drive a cart, etc.

13:11 salvation. Here understood as a divine event that will take place at a particular time in the future; i.e., though one enters into salvation upon conversion, this is a state to be realized fully only at the Second Coming.

13:12 night. The present age. **day.** The coming age inaugurated by Christ's second coming, in which God's new order will appear. **the day is almost here.** The early church understood that the life, death and resurrection of Jesus *had ushered in the last days—the end* time. God, however, because of his patience, had provided an interval before the culmination of the "night," the purpose of which is to allow other men and women to come to faith. During this interval the call to the Christian is to remain alert and expectant, knowing that the Second Coming may occur at any time. **armor of light.** That which one obtains from God and is appropriate to wear when the new age dawns (Eph. 6:11–12).

13:13 sexual immorality. Literally, "a bed." In the first century, prior to Christianity, chastity was almost unknown and was not considered a virtue by most people. **debauchery.** The public display, without shame, of immoral acts. **dissension.** The desire for power and prestige manifested by a willingness to stir up trouble if one is not *in charge.* **jealousy.** Envy which begrudges another's place or gifts.

14:1 Accept him. This is the basic imperative addressed to the "strong" majority in the church: receive the "weak" into fellowship. **him whose faith is weak.** Those who are not sure that their faith allows them to do certain things. The issue is not a lack of faith in Christ. Both the "weak" and the "strong" are authentically Christian. **judgment.** Do not judge negatively the scruples of another.

14:3 look down ... condemn. Two forms of judgment: the tendency of the "strong" not to take seriously the scruples of the weak (to laugh at them or even despise them); and the tendency of the "weak" to act superior and become censorious (because they felt that not doing certain things made them better Christians). Both attitudes are wrong. **God has accepted him.** The abstainer cannot condemn those who indulge, since no one can presume to judge a person God has accepted.

judge someone else's servant? To his own master he stands or falls.
And he will stand, for the Lord is able to make him stand.
5One man considers one day more sacred than another; another
man considers every day alike. Each one should be fully convinced in
his own mind. 6He who regards one day as special, does so to the
Lord. He who eats meat, eats to the Lord, for he gives thanks to God;
and he who abstains, does so to the Lord and gives thanks to God.
7For none of us lives to himself alone and none of us dies to himself
alone. 8If we live, we live to the Lord; and if we die, we die to the Lord.
So, whether we live or die, we belong to the Lord.
9For this very reason, Christ died and returned to life so that he
might be the Lord of both the dead and the living. 10You, then, why do
you judge your brother? Or why do you look down on your brother?
For we will all stand before God's judgment seat. 11It is written:

" 'As surely as I live,' says the Lord,
'every knee will bow before me;
every tongue will confess to God.' "[a]

12So then, each of us will give an account of himself to God.
13Therefore let us stop passing judgment on one another. Instead,
make up your mind not to put any stumbling block or obstacle in
your brother's way. 14As one who is in the Lord Jesus, I am fully convinced that no food[b] is unclean in itself. But if anyone regards something as unclean, then for him it is unclean. 15If your brother is
distressed because of what you eat, you are no longer acting in love.
Do not by your eating destroy your brother for whom Christ died.
16Do not allow what you consider good to be spoken of as evil. 17For
the kingdom of God is not a matter of eating and drinking, but of
righteousness, peace and joy in the Holy Spirit, 18because anyone
who serves Christ in this way is pleasing to God and approved by
men.
19Let us therefore make every effort to do what leads to peace and
to mutual edification. 20Do not destroy the work of God for the sake
of food. All food is clean, but it is wrong for a man to eat anything that
causes someone else to stumble. 21It is better not to eat meat or drink
wine or to do anything else that will cause your brother to fall.
22So whatever you believe about these things keep between yourself and God. Blessed is the man who does not condemn himself by

Christians who came out of this pagan religion, it was compromising their new faith to eat this meat, so they ate only vegetables. Others not only ate meat, but ate meat in the public restaurants. **1.** What would be "disputable" issues today in the church? Where do you stand on these issues? Have you changed your position over the years? **2.** On the issue of eating meat sacrificed to idols, who is referred to as the "strong"? Who is the "weak"? In your church who would be considered the "strong" and the "weak"? **3.** What does Paul want both sides to do (14:5–8)? Who will both sides have to answer to (14:10–12)? **4.** For those who are "strong" and can eat anything, what is the caution (14:13)? What is Paul's admonition for the liberal minded "strong" Christian follower of Christ (14:15–21)? How would you paraphrase 14:21? **5.** For the liberal minded "strong" Christian, what is his parting shot (15:1–2)? How would you translate this into your own situation?

APPLY 1. Has your position on what is right for you in the gray area shifted since you became a follower of Christ? **2.** How do you deal with followers of Christ who are new in their faith, and see other Christians they respect engaging in certain questionable practices?

[a] *11* Isaiah 45:23 [b] *14* Or *that nothing*

14:13 This verse summarizes 14:9–12. **stumbling block.** A new theme is introduced into the discussion: the liberty of the strong can, in fact, be detrimental to others. What appears to them as an innocent pleasure or action may cause the more scrupulous pain, shock, outrage or even hurt.

14:14 I am fully convinced. Paul comes down clearly on the side of the strong (Mark 7:15). **unclean.** That is, in the ritual sense: there is no food that has power to harm one's relationship with God. **regards something as unclean.** For those believers who have not been convinced that Christ abolished the ceremonial law of the Old Testament (even though the food is not objectively unclean), it is subjectively so for that person.

14:15 If the "strong" exercise their liberty even when they know such actions are seen as sinful by the "weak," they are failing to act lovingly toward them. To do so is to jeopardize the faith of the weak and to disturb the delicate harmony of the body of Christian believers. To act lovingly is more vital than to exercise one's freedom. **destroy.** By exercising this liberty, it is possible that the weaker Christian might be caused to struggle in the faith.

14:17–18 Such matters as eating or drinking are trivial in kingdom terms; to cause spiritual ruin over them is scandalous.

14:19 mutual edification. Literally, "the building up of one another"; helping either an individual Christian or the church to grow in faith and practice.

14:21 The strong are called upon to use their strength to not eat or drink when doing so would cause harm. **drink wine.** The Old Testament does not forbid the drinking of wine except for priests on duty (Lev. 10:9) or Nazirites (Num. 6:2–3).

what he approves. [23]But the man who has doubts is condemned if he
eats, because his eating is not from faith; and everything that does
not come from faith is sin.

15 We who are strong ought to bear with the failings of the weak
and not to please ourselves. [2]Each of us should please his
neighbor for his good, to build him up. [3]For even Christ did not
please himself but, as it is written: "The insults of those who insult
you have fallen on me."[a] [4]For everything that was written in the past
was written to teach us, so that through endurance and the encouragement of the Scriptures we might have hope.

[5]May the God who gives endurance and encouragement give you a
spirit of unity among yourselves as you follow Christ Jesus, [6]so that
with one heart and mouth you may glorify the God and Father of our
Lord Jesus Christ.

[7]Accept one another, then, just as Christ accepted you, in order to
bring praise to God. [8]For I tell you that Christ has become a servant of
the Jews[b] on behalf of God's truth, to confirm the promises made to
the patriarchs [9]so that the Gentiles may glorify God for his mercy, as
it is written:

"Therefore I will praise you among the Gentiles;
I will sing hymns to your name."[c]

[10]Again, it says,

"Rejoice, O Gentiles, with his people."[d]

[11]And again,

"Praise the Lord, all you Gentiles,
and sing praises to him, all you peoples."[e]

[12]And again, Isaiah says,

"The Root of Jesse will spring up,
one who will arise to rule over the nations;
the Gentiles will hope in him."[f]

[13]May the God of hope fill you with all joy and peace as you trust in
him, so that you may overflow with hope by the power of the Holy
Spirit.

Paul the Minister to the Gentiles

[14]I myself am convinced, my brothers, that you yourselves are full
of goodness, complete in knowledge and competent to instruct one
another. [15]I have written you quite boldly on some points, as if to remind you of them again, because of the grace God gave me [16]to be a
minister of Christ Jesus to the Gentiles with the priestly duty of pro-

OPEN **1.** As a child, what did you want to be when you grew up? **2.** What do you remember about the first time you were away from home without a parent?

STUDY **1.** Who has been a "Paul" to you, helping you to understand the Christian faith? **2.** From this passage, what is something you

[a]3 Psalm 69:9 [b]8 Greek *circumcision* [c]9 2 Samuel 22:50; Psalm 18:49 [d]10 Deut. 32:43
[e]11 Psalm 117:1 [f]12 Isaiah 11:10

14:23 faith. Here faith signifies a sort of inner freedom or liberty that comes from knowing that what one is doing is in accord with Christian faith in general. **sin.** When a Christian acts without that sense of inner liberty, such an act, even though in itself is neutral (neither inherently bad or good), is sin to that Christian.

15:14 These are not words of flattery designed to win over a hostile audience. One sentence would hardly suffice in light of the preceding chapters. Rather he seems to feel that to write such specific instructions for behavior (as he has done in 12:1–15:13) to a church he has never visited might seem overly bold (v. 15), even presumptuous. So he hastens to assure them that indeed he does consider them to be mature Christians.

claiming the gospel of God, so that the Gentiles might become an offering acceptable to God, sanctified by the Holy Spirit.
17Therefore I glory in Christ Jesus in my service to God. 18I will not
venture to speak of anything except what Christ has accomplished
through me in leading the Gentiles to obey God by what I have said
and done— 19by the power of signs and miracles, through the power
of the Spirit. So from Jerusalem all the way around to Illyricum, I have
fully proclaimed the gospel of Christ. 20It has always been my ambition to preach the gospel where Christ was not known, so that I
would not be building on someone else's foundation. 21Rather, as it is
written:

"Those who were not told about him will see,
and those who have not heard will understand."[a]

22This is why I have often been hindered from coming to you.

Paul's Plan to Visit Rome

23But now that there is no more place for me to work in these regions, and since I have been longing for many years to see you, 24I
plan to do so when I go to Spain. I hope to visit you while passing
through and to have you assist me on my journey there, after I have
enjoyed your company for a while. 25Now, however, I am on my way
to Jerusalem in the service of the saints there. 26For Macedonia and
Achaia were pleased to make a contribution for the poor among the
saints in Jerusalem. 27They were pleased to do it, and indeed they
owe it to them. For if the Gentiles have shared in the Jews' spiritual
blessings, they owe it to the Jews to share with them their material
blessings. 28So after I have completed this task and have made sure
that they have received this fruit, I will go to Spain and visit you on
the way. 29I know that when I come to you, I will come in the full
measure of the blessing of Christ.
30I urge you, brothers, by our Lord Jesus Christ and by the love of
the Spirit, to join me in my struggle by praying to God for me. 31Pray
that I may be rescued from the unbelievers in Judea and that my service in Jerusalem may be acceptable to the saints there, 32so that by
God's will I may come to you with joy and together with you be refreshed. 33The God of peace be with you all. Amen.

Personal Greetings

16 I commend to you our sister Phoebe, a servant[b] of the
church in Cenchrea. 2I ask you to receive her in the Lord in a
way worthy of the saints and to give her any help she may need from
you, for she has been a great help to many people, including me.

[a]21 Isaiah 52:15 [b]1 Or *deaconess*

admire or appreciate about Paul and his ministry? **3.** Why would Paul feel the need to write an encouraging word at this point (vv. 14–15)? What are some of the major points Paul has stressed in Romans? **4.** Why do you think Paul now switches to writing so much about himself? **5.** Paul's ambition was to preach to those who had never heard about Christ (v. 20). To what ministry do you feel God may be calling you? **6.** This past week, how did you feel about your life being "an offering acceptable to God" (v. 16)? What can you do in the coming week to be an even better offering?

APPLY 1. Looking over your schedule and priorities this past month, what would you say is your ambition in life? Is that what you want it to be? How do your ambitions compare with Paul's in terms of clarity? Value? Concern for God's kingdom? **2.** Where do you sense God calling you in furthering his kingdom: Prayer for the world? Commitment to the poor? Sharing your faith story with your neighbors and professional associates?

OPEN 1. Who was your first best friend? **2.** What "old friends" do you keep in touch with? How often?

STUDY 1. What kinds of things does Paul commend in the persons mentioned in verses

---

15:24 Spain. The Roman colony of Spain was situated at the edge of the civilized world—no doubt the reason that Paul's pioneering spirit was drawn there.

15:25–27 The collection for the poor in Jerusalem is on the order of a debt for Paul. When he was commissioned by the church to be the apostle to the Gentiles, the only request they had was that he remember the poor (Gal. 2:10).

15:26 Macedonia and Achaia. Two Roman provinces located south of Illyricum, on a peninsula bordering the Adriatic and Aegean Seas (in the region of modern Greece).

16:1–2 I commend ... Phoebe. It is likely that Phoebe carried Paul's letter from Corinth to the church at Rome. Typical in letters of his day, Paul includes a note of commendation in which he makes two requests: that they receive Phoebe as a sister in the Lord, and that they assist her because she has helped many others. Phoebe was probably a woman of wealth and influence who had given herself for God's kingdom.

1–16? **2.** In your opinion, how close did Paul let people get to him? How close do you let people get to you? **3.** Looking at this list, how balanced would you say Paul was in his friendships with both genders? How many women are named here? What roles do these women have in the church? **4.** Although Paul had never been to Rome, what does this greeting show about his perception of the church? **5.** What divisions and obstacles are the people to avoid (vv. 17–20; 3:8; 6:1,15; 7:7; 9:14; Gal. 5:2–6)? Is there a contradiction here when compared with Paul's prior instructions on not passing judgment on disputable matters (14:1–4)?

APPLY 1. What has been the highlight for you in the study of the book of Romans? **2.** What have you appreciated most about your study group? Do you plan to continue? What are you gong to study next? **3.** What is the next step in your spiritual pilgrimage? What can your group do to help you in this step?

3 Greet Priscilla[a] and Aquila, my fellow workers in Christ Jesus. 4 They
risked their lives for me. Not only I but all the churches of the
Gentiles are grateful to them.
5 Greet also the church that meets at their house.
Greet my dear friend Epenetus, who was the first convert to Christ
in the province of Asia.
6 Greet Mary, who worked very hard for you.
7 Greet Andronicus and Junias, my relatives who have been in prison
with me. They are outstanding among the apostles, and they
were in Christ before I was.
8 Greet Ampliatus, whom I love in the Lord.
9 Greet Urbanus, our fellow worker in Christ, and my dear friend
Stachys.
10 Greet Apelles, tested and approved in Christ.
Greet those who belong to the household of Aristobulus.
11 Greet Herodion, my relative.
Greet those in the household of Narcissus who are in the Lord.
12 Greet Tryphena and Tryphosa, those women who work hard in the
Lord.
Greet my dear friend Persis, another woman who has worked very
hard in the Lord.
13 Greet Rufus, chosen in the Lord, and his mother, who has been a
mother to me, too.
14 Greet Asyncritus, Phlegon, Hermes, Patrobas, Hermas and the
brothers with them.
15 Greet Philologus, Julia, Nereus and his sister, and Olympas and all
the saints with them.
16 Greet one another with a holy kiss.
All the churches of Christ send greetings.

17 I urge you, brothers, to watch out for those who cause divisions
and put obstacles in your way that are contrary to the teaching you
have learned. Keep away from them. 18 For such people are not serving our Lord Christ, but their own appetites. By smooth talk and flattery they deceive the minds of naive people. 19 Everyone has heard
about your obedience, so I am full of joy over you; but I want you to
be wise about what is good, and innocent about what is evil.
20 The God of peace will soon crush Satan under your feet.
The grace of our Lord Jesus be with you.
21 Timothy, my fellow worker, sends his greetings to you, as do Lucius, Jason and Sosipater, my relatives.
22 I, Tertius, who wrote down this letter, greet you in the Lord.
23 Gaius, whose hospitality I and the whole church here enjoy,
sends you his greetings.

[a]3 Greek *Prisca*, a variant of *Priscilla*

16:3–16 Of the 24 individuals named in these verses, six are women. Thirteen of these names occur in manuscripts or inscriptions related to the imperial household, giving rise to speculation that Christ had penetrated even into the royal palace (Phil. 4:22).

16:3–5 Priscilla and Aquila. Aquila, a Jew born in Pontus in Asia Minor, and his wife Priscilla appear regularly in the New Testament.

16:5 the church ... at their house. During the first two centuries, there were no special church buildings, so Christians met in the homes of their members (1 Cor. 16:19; Col. 4:15; Philem. 2). The growth of these churches was overwhelming.

16:13 Rufus. Quite possibly the son of Simon of Cyrene, who carried Jesus' cross. Simon is identified (Mark 15:21) as the father of Alexander and Rufus.

6:22 Tertius. The only time the name of one of Paul's secretaries is revealed.

16:23 Gaius. This name is mentioned several times in the New Testament. It

1 Paul, called to be an apostle of Christ Jesus by the will of God,
and our brother Sosthenes,

2To the church of God in Corinth, to those sanctified in Christ Jesus
and called to be holy, together with all those everywhere who call on
the name of our Lord Jesus Christ—their Lord and ours:

3Grace and peace to you from God our Father and the Lord Jesus
Christ.

Thanksgiving

4I always thank God for you because of his grace given you in
Christ Jesus. 5For in him you have been enriched in every way—in all
your speaking and in all your knowledge— 6because our testimony
about Christ was confirmed in you. 7Therefore you do not lack any
spiritual gift as you eagerly wait for our Lord Jesus Christ to be
revealed. 8He will keep you strong to the end, so that you will be
blameless on the day of our Lord Jesus Christ. 9God, who has called
you into fellowship with his Son Jesus Christ our Lord, is faithful.

Divisions in the Church

10I appeal to you, brothers, in the name of our Lord Jesus Christ,
that all of you agree with one another so that there may be no divisions among you and that you may be perfectly united in mind and
thought. 11My brothers, some from Chloe's household have informed
me that there are quarrels among you. 12What I mean is this: One of
you says, "I follow Paul"; another, "I follow Apollos"; another, "I follow Cephas[a]"; still another, "I follow Christ."

[a] *12* That is, Peter

OPEN 1. When you were 8, who was your hero? **2.** Where were you living at age 8 and what did your parents do?

STUDY 1. What did you learn about the city of Corinth from the Introduction? **2.** Have you ever attended a church in a large, cosmopolitan city with a "reputation for vice and debauchery"? What was the challenge you faced in this church? **3.** How would you describe Paul's tone in the way he starts out this letter (vv. 4–9): Upbeat? Optimistic? Kind? Damning with faint praise? **4.** Reading between the lines, what is going on in the church (vv. 10–17)? How does Paul answer this problem? **5.** What issues are dividing the church today? How is your church dealing with these problems? What would Paul say if he was around today?

APPLY 1. When do you date the beginning of your spiritual journey? **2.** Who is the person that has been most influential in your spiritual growth? **3.** How would you describe your relationship with Christ right now? **4.** What do you need to say about confidentiality if you are going to be a member of this group?

1:1–9 Paul begins with thanksgiving. Whatever irregularities might exist at Corinth, they do so in the context of the good work that God has done in their midst.

1:1 an apostle. Paul does not always identify himself by this title (1 Thess. 1:1). He may do so here because his authority as an apostle is an issue with the Corinthians. An apostle is "one who is sent," "an envoy." It is an office held by those who witnessed the resurrected Christ and were called by Christ to this position. Their special job was to plant new churches throughout the Roman Empire. **Sosthenes.** It is possible that this is the same Sosthenes mentioned in Acts 18:17.

1:2 sanctified. *Consecrated,* dedicated to the service of God. **called.** In the same way that Paul was called to be an apostle (v. 1), every believer is called by God to be holy. **holy.** To be set apart to serve God's purposes. In the New Testament all believers are "saints" (holy persons).

1:3 Grace and peace. Grace is the unmerited gift of God by which a person comes into salvation. Peace is the outcome of that salvation.

1:5 knowledge. The ability to understand and apply Christian truth.

1:7 you do not lack any spiritual gift. This is said both seriously (since Christians have at their disposal all of God's grace-gifts) and tongue-in-cheek (as Paul echoes their own boasting). **spiritual gift.** *Charismata,* Paul's word for the special gifts given by God, such as the gift of healing or of speaking in tongues. These gifts held a special fascination for the Corinthians. They serve as direct witnesses to the supernatural nature of Christianity. They spring from the general fact of grace (v. 4) and are specific examples of the operation of God's grace. **to be revealed.** Christians live in eager expectation until Christ returns and ushers in the new kingdom. Meanwhile, the gifts of God are a foretaste of what one day will be normative.

1:10–17 The first problem that Paul deals with is divisions in the church. He points out that Christian teachers are all servants of the same God, not philosophers competing with one another for an audience (3:5–4:21).

1:10 divisions. *Schismata* (from which the English word "schism" comes); a word often used to describe tears in a piece of clothing. **united in mind and thought.** Their disunity is rooted in differing ideas (doctrines). To knit back together the church which is torn apart, requires a unity of understanding.

1:11 Chloe's household. Paul is writing from Ephesus. The slaves (or freedmen) of an Ephesian woman named Chloe had visited the church in Corinth and brought back the story of the disunity there.

1:12 I follow Paul. Paul does not commend those "on his side." A faction in his name is no better than any other faction. In fact, these folks had probably exaggerated and falsified his actual viewpoints. (This was probably the Gentile party.) **I follow Apollos.** After he had been instructed in the gospel by Priscilla and Aquila, Apollos went to Corinth to assist the church there. A bright, articulate Jew from Alexandria

13 Is Christ divided? Was Paul crucified for you? Were you baptized into[a] the name of Paul? 14 I am thankful that I did not baptize any of you except Crispus and Gaius, 15 so no one can say that you were baptized into my name. 16 (Yes, I also baptized the household of Stephanas; beyond that, I don't remember if I baptized anyone else.) 17 For Christ did not send me to baptize, but to preach the gospel—not with words of human wisdom, lest the cross of Christ be emptied of its power.

Christ the Wisdom and Power of God

18 For the message of the cross is foolishness to those who are perishing, but to us who are being saved it is the power of God. 19 For it is written:

"I will destroy the wisdom of the wise;
the intelligence of the intelligent I will frustrate."[b]

20 Where is the wise man? Where is the scholar? Where is the philosopher of this age? Has not God made foolish the wisdom of the world? 21 For since in the wisdom of God the world through its wisdom did not know him, God was pleased through the foolishness of what was preached to save those who believe. 22 Jews demand miraculous signs and Greeks look for wisdom, 23 but we preach Christ crucified: a stumbling block to Jews and foolishness to Gentiles, 24 but to those whom God has called, both Jews and Greeks, Christ the power of God and the wisdom of God. 25 For the foolishness of God is wiser than man's wisdom, and the weakness of God is stronger than man's strength.

26 Brothers, think of what you were when you were called. Not many of you were wise by human standards; not many were influen-

[a]*13* Or *in*; also in verse 15 [b]*19* Isaiah 29:14

OPEN 1. What was the least useful class you had to take in school? **2.** How do you feel about speaking before a group?

STUDY 1. If you could "boast" about one thing that you are really good at, what would it be? **2.** What is the closest you have come to living in an environment where everyone was chasing "human wisdom" (v. 17)? How did the "wisdom" seekers in your situation look upon "the message of the cross" (v. 18)? **3.** From your own experience, why is the message of the cross such a "stumbling block" to pseudo intellectuals (vv. 20–22)? **4.** If Paul was a pastor in your college town, what would be his pitch to the college students? Would he try to intellectually prove the existence of God? What did Paul say in verses 26–31? **5.** Paul was no intellectual slouch. In fact, he is considered one of the greatest thinkers in the Western world. How did he describe his preaching (v. 2)? Why?

with great skill in debate (Acts 18:24–28) would be a natural leader for those who attempted to intellectualize Christianity. **I follow Cephas.** Cephas is the Jewish form of the name Peter. It is probable that Peter also visited Corinth. This faction probably would have been oriented toward a more Jewish Christianity. **I follow Christ.** These are possibly the people who look with disdain on the other groups who profess allegiance to the Christ preached by Paul, by Apollos, or by Cephas. Instead, they profess allegiance to the Christ they know without the teaching of anyone. This may even be a mystical or gnostic-like party, given to inner visions and revelations.

1:17 Here Paul comes to the principle that lies at the root of the problem in Corinth. They can form such factions only because they misunderstand the nature of God's wisdom. **wisdom.** *Sophia,* a key word in 1 Corinthians, which Paul uses in both positive and negative ways. Here the idea is negative. This is wisdom defined as the skillful use of human reason with a view to convincing the hearer of the truth of a position. **lest the cross of Christ be emptied.** Paul is eager that people be persuaded by Christ crucified and not by mere eloquence.

1:18 the message of the cross. The question of eternal destiny centers on the meaning of the Cross. Their misunderstanding and division is no slight matter. It strikes at the core of the gospel. **foolishness.** It is absurd to many that God's redemptive activity involves death by crucifixion. **perishing.** Unless they repent (turn around and go the other way), they will not be acquitted on the Day of Judgment. **being saved.** Salvation is a process, begun at conversion, consummated at the Second Coming, and fulfilled in the New Age.

1:22 Jews demand miraculous signs. The Jews expected a Messiah who would come in obvious power doing miraculous deeds. In Jesus they saw one so weak that his enemies got away with killing him. **Greeks look for wisdom.** Their delight was in clever, cunning logic delivered with soaring persuasiveness.

1:23 stumbling block. Literally, a scandal. Jesus' crucifixion "proved" to the Jews that he could not be of God (since Deut. 21:23 says those hanging from a tree are cursed of God). A suffering, dying Messiah was totally outside first-century Jewish expectations. **foolishness.** Both the Incarnation and Crucifixion were actions that Greeks felt were unworthy of their gods.

1:26 think of what you were. In their own calling they see the paradox of the all-powerful God using the "weak things of the world." **Not many.** The early church had special appeal to the poor and to those with little social standing. This was part of its offensiveness—the "wrong" people were attracted to it. **wise.** This refers to people with education or philosophical training. **influential.** This means people in high positions politically or socially. **noble birth.** These were peo-

tial; not many were of noble birth. 27But God chose the foolish things
of the world to shame the wise; God chose the weak things of the
world to shame the strong. 28He chose the lowly things of this world
and the despised things—and the things that are not—to nullify the
things that are, 29so that no one may boast before him. 30It is because
of him that you are in Christ Jesus, who has become for us wisdom
from God—that is, our righteousness, holiness and redemption.
31Therefore, as it is written: "Let him who boasts boast in the Lord."[a]

2 When I came to you, brothers, I did not come with eloquence or
superior wisdom as I proclaimed to you the testimony about
God.[b] 2For I resolved to know nothing while I was with you except
Jesus Christ and him crucified. 3I came to you in weakness and fear,
and with much trembling. 4My message and my preaching were not
with wise and persuasive words, but with a demonstration of the
Spirit's power, 5so that your faith might not rest on men's wisdom,
but on God's power.

Wisdom From the Spirit

6We do, however, speak a message of wisdom among the mature,
but not the wisdom of this age or of the rulers of this age, who are
coming to nothing. 7No, we speak of God's secret wisdom, a wisdom
that has been hidden and that God destined for our glory before time
began. 8None of the rulers of this age understood it, for if they had,
they would not have crucified the Lord of glory. 9However, as it is
written:

"No eye has seen,
 no ear has heard,
no mind has conceived
 what God has prepared for those who love him"[c]—

10but God has revealed it to us by his Spirit.

The Spirit searches all things, even the deep things of God. 11For
who among men knows the thoughts of a man except the man's spirit

[a]31 Jer. 9:24 [b]1 Some manuscripts *as I proclaimed to you God's mystery* [c]9 Isaiah 64:4

APPLY 1. When did you come to the point where you gave up trying to prove the existence of God and took the leap of faith to believe in the message of the cross? **2.** What do you do when you have real deep intellectual questions about your faith?

OPEN When you were a child, what relative did you like being with because he or she had a lot of old-fashioned wisdom?

STUDY 1. Who do you turn to when you need some wisdom: Your spouse? A parent? Your pastor? A friend? Other? **2.** What does Paul mean by God's "secret wisdom" (vv. 7,9)? **3.** How do you feel about verse 9? How has your outlook on life been affected by the promises in this verse? **4.** From this passage, what role do you see the Holy Spirit playing in the life of a believer? **5.** According to verse 14, who can't understand the things of God and why? **6.** When in your spiritual journey did the "mind of Christ" (v. 16) start to make a difference in your values, choices and decisions?

---

ple of distinguished families who may have held Roman citizenship.

1:28 the things that are not ... the things that are. God chooses the "nobodies" and thus exposes the foolishness of the way the world defines the "somebodies."

1:30 because of him. They owe the fact that they are related to God solely through Jesus Christ. **wisdom from God.** *The historical Jesus is God's wisdom.* It is Christ who mediates God's plan of salvation. **righteousness.** Christ is their righteousness in that he took upon himself the guilt of human sin. So on the Last Day when Christians stand before the Judge, they are viewed not in terms of their own failure and inadequacy but as being "in Christ." **holiness.** Human beings cannot come before a Holy God because they are not holy; but once again, Christ provides what people lack. **redemption.** It is by Christ's redeeming work on the cross that wisdom, righteousness and holiness are mediated to humankind.

2:4 demonstration of the Spirit's power. Paul reveals the secret behind the impact that his preaching made. People were moved by the convicting power of the Holy Spirit.

2:6 a message of wisdom. Paul will now use *sophia* (wisdom) in a positive way to describe God's plan of salvation. **mature.** To be mature is to be a full-grown adult in the faith, a potential which all Christians have (Col. 1:28) though not all experience (3:1). **wisdom of this age.** In biblical thought there are two ages: "this age" in which sin and evil exist, and "the age to come" when God's kingdom will be present and visible. Wisdom of this age is person-centered and corrupted by rebellion against God, despite how it may appear on the surface.

2:7 God's secret wisdom. In contrast to the "wisdom of the world" no one could have guessed God's plan. Even when it was revealed, many shunned it as "foolish" and/or scandalous (1:23).

2:10 revealed it to us. That which was hidden from the non-Christian rulers (v. 8) has now been made clear to the Christian. **by his Spirit.** The insight referred to in verses 6–9 came not as a result of reasoning but as a result of revelation. **The Spirit searches all things.** In Corinth, the idea was that you could (by means of philosophy) search out the nature of God. Paul indicates that only the Spirit himself knows

APPLY 1. What issues are you wrestling with right now where you could use a little spiritual wisdom? **2.** How do you feel about sharing your personal struggles with this group?

within him? In the same way no one knows the thoughts of God except the Spirit of God. 12We have not received the spirit of the world
but the Spirit who is from God, that we may understand what God
has freely given us. 13This is what we speak, not in words taught us by
human wisdom but in words taught by the Spirit, expressing spiritual
truths in spiritual words.[a] 14The man without the Spirit does not accept the things that come from the Spirit of God, for they are foolishness to him, and he cannot understand them, because they are
spiritually discerned. 15The spiritual man makes judgments about all
things, but he himself is not subject to any man's judgment:

16"For who has known the mind of the Lord
that he may instruct him?"[b]

But we have the mind of Christ.

OPEN What have you made or done that gives you real pride?

STUDY 1. In your observation, what issues are most likely to cause division within a church? **2.** What problems tend to cause strife at your work? In your home? In your community? **3.** From this passage, what are the characteristics of worldly versus spiritual people? **4.** From verses 6–9, who plants? Who waters? Who is the field? Who is responsible for growth? How does this illustration relate to the problem in the Corinthian church?

APPLY 1. Who are the people that God has used in your life—the "Paul" who planted and the "Apollos" who watered? In whose lives have you planted or watered? **2.** On a scale of 1 (straw) to 10 (gold), how sturdy is your spiritual "building"? How does that compare to one year ago?

On Divisions in the Church

3 Brothers, I could not address you as spiritual but as worldly—
mere infants in Christ. 2I gave you milk, not solid food, for you
were not yet ready for it. Indeed, you are still not ready. 3You are still
worldly. For since there is jealousy and quarreling among you, are
you not worldly? Are you not acting like mere men? 4For when one
says, "I follow Paul," and another, "I follow Apollos," are you not
mere men?

5What, after all, is Apollos? And what is Paul? Only servants,
through whom you came to believe—as the Lord has assigned to
each his task. 6I planted the seed, Apollos watered it, but God made it
grow. 7So neither he who plants nor he who waters is anything, but
only God, who makes things grow. 8The man who plants and the man
who waters have one purpose, and each will be rewarded according
to his own labor. 9For we are God's fellow workers; you are God's
field, God's building.

10By the grace God has given me, I laid a foundation as an expert
builder, and someone else is building on it. But each one should be
careful how he builds. 11For no one can lay any foundation other than
the one already laid, which is Jesus Christ. 12If any man builds on this

[a]13 Or *Spirit, interpreting spiritual truths to spiritual men* [b]16 Isaiah 40:13

and communicates accurate knowledge about God.

2:12 the spirit of the world. An equivalent phrase to "the wisdom of this age" (v. 6). **understand.** It is not education or intellect or occupation that yields spiritual insight. There is only one source: the Holy Spirit dwelling within a believer. **has freely given us.** These gifts of God (v. 9) are not merely for the future, but are the present experience of Christians.

3:1 spiritual. A *mature Christian* whose life is dominated by the indwelling Spirit. **worldly.** Those Christians who are molded more by the spirit of the age than by the Spirit of God; those whose life and thoughts are so immature that they are "mere infants."

3:3 mere men. Their lifestyle is not in accord with that of the mature Christian. By exalting certain teachers, they betray their lack of understanding of the gospel. Paul's point is that although they have the Spirit, they are acting precisely like people without the Spirit.

3:6 I planted. Paul was the first to preach in Corinth. **Apollos watered.** Apollos continued Paul's work by help*ing to build up a new church.* **God made it grow.** Their labors alone would not have been enough. The divine life-force necessary to produce growth came from God.

3:9 God's field. The Corinthians are the field which God is plowing via his servants. **God's building.** Paul's metaphor shifts from agriculture to architecture.

3:10 I laid a foundation. By preaching Christ, who is the foundation (v. 11), Paul was the one who began the work in Corinth (v. 6). **expert.** Literally, "wise." Paul continues to develop the idea of wisdom. **builder.** (In Greek, *architekton.*) The one who plans and supervises the construction of a building, not the one who does the actual labor.

3:12 Paul describes some of the ways a person can go astray in building on the

foundation using gold, silver, costly stones, wood, hay or straw, 13his
work will be shown for what it is, because the Day will bring it to
light. It will be revealed with fire, and the fire will test the quality of
each man's work. 14If what he has built survives, he will receive his
reward. 15If it is burned up, he will suffer loss; he himself will be
saved, but only as one escaping through the flames.
16Don't you know that you yourselves are God's temple and that
God's Spirit lives in you? 17If anyone destroys God's temple, God will
destroy him; for God's temple is sacred, and you are that temple.
18Do not deceive yourselves. If any one of you thinks he is wise by
the standards of this age, he should become a "fool" so that he may
become wise. 19For the wisdom of this world is foolishness in God's
sight. As it is written: "He catches the wise in their craftiness"[a]; 20and
again, "The Lord knows that the thoughts of the wise are futile."[b]
21So then, no more boasting about men! All things are yours,
22whether Paul or Apollos or Cephas[c] or the world or life or death or
the present or the future—all are yours, 23and you are of Christ, and
Christ is of God.

Apostles of Christ

4 So then, men ought to regard us as servants of Christ and as
those entrusted with the secret things of God. 2Now it is required
that those who have been given a trust must prove faithful. 3I care
very little if I am judged by you or by any human court; indeed, I do
not even judge myself. 4My conscience is clear, but that does not
make me innocent. It is the Lord who judges me. 5Therefore judge
nothing before the appointed time; wait till the Lord comes. He will
bring to light what is hidden in darkness and will expose the motives
of men's hearts. At that time each will receive his praise from God.
6Now, brothers, I have applied these things to myself and Apollos
for your benefit, so that you may learn from us the meaning of the
saying, "Do not go beyond what is written." Then you will not take

[a]19 Job 5:13 [b]20 Psalm 94:11 [c]22 That is, Peter

OPEN 1. What is the most menial job you ever had? What did you like or dislike about it? **2.** Growing up, if you had the choice of punishment between a spanking or being grounded, what would you choose?

STUDY 1. If you read this passage through the knothole of verses 18–21, what do you think Paul is getting at in this passage? **2.** As Paul compares his lifestyle to the lifestyle of the church leaders in Corinth in verses 8–13, what do you learn about the leaders in this church? About Paul's leadership style? **3.** Reading between the lines in verses 8–13,

foundation—namely by using inferior or inadequate materials. **gold, silver, costly stones.** These materials will survive the test of fire. **wood, hay or straw.** These will burn up.

3:13 the Day. On the Day of Judgment the quality of labor will be revealed. **revealed with fire.** The idea is not of fire as punishment, but as a means of testing—a way of revealing the "quality of each man's work." This is a strong warning to those who lead the church.

3:16 temple. Paul tells them what kind of building they, as a community, are becoming (the reference is not to individual believers' bodies as the temple of the Spirit; that comes in 6:19). This would be a particularly vivid and exciting image for the Corinthians, surrounded as they were by pagan temples, because Paul shows them that within their community—wherever it gathered—God's Spirit was at work creating a new people.

3:17 destroy. The idea has shifted from losing one's pay for having used inferior building materials (vv. 12–15) to being punished for destroying the church.

4:1 So then. Paul draws his conclusions from what he has just taught. **men ought to regard us.** His topic is how Christians should relate to their ministers. **servants of Christ.** First and foremost, a minister is a servant of Christ—under Christ's authority, doing the work given him or her by Christ. **those entrusted.** Literally, stewards. In a Greek household this was the slave who administered all the affairs of the family; i.e., he directed the staff, saw to securing supplies, and, in effect, ran the whole household for his master. **secret things of God.** As in 2:7, these are the plans of God once known only to himself but now revealed to all. It is the minister's task to make known these mysteries.

4:3–4 In fact, neither the Corinthians nor Paul himself is fit to judge his faithfulness as a steward of God. God is the only judge of that, and Paul is content to rest in that knowledge and not let the criticism bother him.

4:5 till the Lord comes. At the Second Coming of Christ, the Day of Judgment will occur. Paul cautions about making premature judgments. Let the Lord judge. He is the only one able to do it properly, since he alone can see not only a person's actions but a person's motives. **motives.** Not just actions but one's personal intentions will be made plain when Christ returns.

how were the leaders in this church acting? What were they doing? Who does this remind you of? In contrast, how does Paul look upon himself? What is Paul referring to when he says, "God has put us apostles on display at the end of the procession" (v. 9)? **4.** How would you paraphrase verses 10–12 in your own words? **5.** How does Paul view his relationship to this church (v. 15) versus the current leaders in the church? **6.** If you were one of the church leaders, how would you feel about Timothy coming to visit your church (v. 17)? **7.** Going back to the first paragraph, what does Paul warn the Corinthian church about? What do you think he is referring to? **8.** As you look at the church in your country today, what do you think Paul would say about the way you do "church?"

APPLY 1. Who do you consider your "spiritual father"? Did this person use a "whip" or a gentle spirit in caring for you? Is there room for both? **2.** If Paul became your mentor, what is one of the first things he would ask you to do? Be honest!

pride in one man over against another. 7For who makes you different
from anyone else? What do you have that you did not receive? And if
you did receive it, why do you boast as though you did not?
8Already you have all you want! Already you have become rich! You
have become kings—and that without us! How I wish that you really
had become kings so that we might be kings with you! 9For it seems
to me that God has put us apostles on display at the end of the procession, like men condemned to die in the arena. We have been made
a spectacle to the whole universe, to angels as well as to men. 10We
are fools for Christ, but you are so wise in Christ! We are weak, but
you are strong! You are honored, we are dishonored! 11To this very
hour we go hungry and thirsty, we are in rags, we are brutally treated,
we are homeless. 12We work hard with our own hands. When we are
cursed, we bless; when we are persecuted, we endure it; 13when we
are slandered, we answer kindly. Up to this moment we have become
the scum of the earth, the refuse of the world.
14I am not writing this to shame you, but to warn you, as my dear
children. 15Even though you have ten thousand guardians in Christ,
you do not have many fathers, for in Christ Jesus I became your father through the gospel. 16Therefore I urge you to imitate me. 17For
this reason I am sending to you Timothy, my son whom I love, who is
faithful in the Lord. He will remind you of my way of life in Christ
Jesus, which agrees with what I teach everywhere in every church.
18Some of you have become arrogant, as if I were not coming to
you. 19But I will come to you very soon, if the Lord is willing, and then
I will find out not only how these arrogant people are talking, but
what power they have. 20For the kingdom of God is not a matter of
talk but of power. 21What do you prefer? Shall I come to you with a
whip, or in love and with a gentle spirit?

4:8 Already. The Corinthians are acting as if the new age had already arrived—that they had come into the fullness of God, into their inheritance as children of God, and into the kingdom of God itself. **that we might be kings with you.** Paul wishes they were right because, in fact, his present experience was quite grim (vv. 11–12; 2 Cor. 6:4–10).

4:9 the arena. The image is of the triumphal return of a Roman general who parades his trophies before the people.

4:10 fools for Christ. By the standards of the world's wisdom, Paul is indeed foolish. Still, as he has already shown (3:18), this is the pathway to God's wisdom. **you are so wise in Christ.** In ironic contrast Paul points out that the Corinthians, in their worldly wisdom, are acting as if they are wise and superior. **We are weak.** In fact, in God's economy, weakness is strength. Christ came not as a mighty conquering hero, but to be crucified as a common criminal. In the suffering Savior one finds the model for the Christian life.

4:12 We work hard. As Paul did in Corinth, making tents with Priscilla and Aquila (Acts 18:3; 20:34).

4:14–21 Paul ends the section begun in 1:10. Their preference for worldly wisdom has led them to develop an arrogant attitude in which (perhaps subconsciously) they patronized their missionaries and ministers and attempted to play them off against one another. By means of the metaphor of a father with his children, Paul reasserts his authority over this church and prepares to deal with their aberrant behavior.

4:14 to shame you. Indeed, the Corinthians ought to be blushing in acute distress over how far they have departed from Christ's intentions. Still, it is not shame Paul intends. **warn.** The word means "to admonish" as a father might do, in hopes that his children will see the error of their ways and change.

4:15 guardians. Tutors, Christian leaders who instruct them in the faith (3:6,8,10). **I became your father.** Paul led them to faith in Christ.

4:16 imitate me. If they need a model of how to live the Christian life, they can look to Paul: a servant eager to do Christ's bidding and a man who walks in the footsteps of a despised, crucified Savior (vv. 11–12).

4:17 For this reason. Because Paul wishes them to imitate him and because he himself cannot come yet (though he is planning a trip), he will send Timothy who will model for them the Christian life. **my son.** Timothy was a convert of Paul's.

4:20 not a matter of talk but of power. It is one thing to make loud boasts and claim great wisdom. It is quite another to live out the power of God.

Expel the Immoral Brother!

5 It is actually reported that there is sexual immorality among you,
and of a kind that does not occur even among pagans: A man has
his father's wife. 2And you are proud! Shouldn't you rather have been
filled with grief and have put out of your fellowship the man who did
this? 3Even though I am not physically present, I am with you in spirit. And I have already passed judgment on the one who did this, just
as if I were present. 4When you are assembled in the name of our
Lord Jesus and I am with you in spirit, and the power of our Lord
Jesus is present, 5hand this man over to Satan, so that the sinful
nature[a] may be destroyed and his spirit saved on the day of the Lord.
6Your boasting is not good. Don't you know that a little yeast works
through the whole batch of dough? 7Get rid of the old yeast that you
may be a new batch without yeast—as you really are. For Christ, our
Passover lamb, has been sacrificed. 8Therefore let us keep the Festival, not with the old yeast, the yeast of malice and wickedness, but
with bread without yeast, the bread of sincerity and truth.
9I have written you in my letter not to associate with sexually immoral people— 10not at all meaning the people of this world who are
immoral, or the greedy and swindlers, or idolaters. In that case you
would have to leave this world. 11But now I am writing you that you
must not associate with anyone who calls himself a brother but is
sexually immoral or greedy, an idolater or a slanderer, a drunkard or
a swindler. With such a man do not even eat.
12What business is it of mine to judge those outside the church?
Are you not to judge those inside? 13God will judge those outside.
"Expel the wicked man from among you."[b]

Lawsuits Among Believers

6 If any of you has a dispute with another, dare he take it before
the ungodly for judgment instead of before the saints? 2Do you
not know that the saints will judge the world? And if you are to judge
the world, are you not competent to judge trivial cases? 3Do you not

[a]5 Or *that his body*; or *that the flesh* [b]13 Deut. 17:7; 19:19; 21:21; 22:21,24; 24:7

OPEN How did your parents, teachers or church leaders talk to you about sex?

STUDY 1. In a city as pagan and immoral as Corinth (read Introduction again), are you surprised to learn that immorality and incest was also in the church? How about the church today? **2.** Why does Paul react so strongly about the immoral brother in the Corinthian church? What does he tell them to do? **3.** What wrong attitude did the Corinthians have toward the problem in their church? **4.** How could handing "this man over to Satan" (v. 5) actually be for his good? **5.** From the yeast imagery (vv. 6–8), what is Paul's concern if this situation is allowed to go on without discipline? **6.** How does the discipline in this passage relate to Galatians 6:1–8?

APPLY 1. How many of your closest friends from your original Christian community are still walking with God? **2.** For the one who has fallen away, what was the cause?

OPEN Have you ever been on jury duty? What was it like?

STUDY 1. When you are wronged, are you more likely to stand up and fight for your rights, just let it go or look to get even? **2.** Why is Paul so upset that members

5:1 sexual immorality. Literally, "fornication." Since Paul does not label this "adultery," the man's father was probably either dead or divorced from his wife. For newly converted pagans, the whole question of the relationship between the sexes was troublesome, since the environment out of which they had been converted was notoriously lax when it came to sexual standards. **even among pagans.** Incest was also condemned by pagans (as well as by Jews: Lev. 18:8; 20:11). Both Jew and Gentile were aghast at the idea of a father and a son having sexual relations with the same woman. **has.** By this verb Paul indicates that the man in question was not just involved casually with this woman, but was indeed living with her. **his father's wife.** The way Paul has phrased this indicates that she was probably not the man's actual mother, but rather his stepmother.

5:2 you are proud. Paul may mean that they are proud in spite of such a situation, even though this ought to have burst the bubble of their arrogance. **Shouldn't you rather.** Paul points out that what they should have felt was grief.

5:3–6 Paul is quite clear about what ought to be done. He orders the church to cut off the man from its fellowship. Paul's aim is discipline, not destruction.

5:4 When you are assembled. Such excommunication is not done by Paul nor by the leaders of the church, but by the whole church, gathered together in the power of Jesus (Matt. 18:17–18).

5:5 that the sinful nature may be destroyed. He hopes that by exclusion from the church, he may see clearly the enormity of his loss and repent of his sin and return (1 Tim. 1:20).

5:11 do not even eat. Dining together was an important practice among early Christians (10:14–22; 11:17–34). This is the practical outworking of excommunication. All contact is severed.

6:1 dare he. The implication is that such action is an affront to God and to the church. **the ungodly.** Here this term simply means "non-Christian." **for judgment.** The bench from which justice was dispensed was located out in the open in Corinth—in the market place—which is perhaps one reason why Paul was so upset. In hauling a brother or sister into court, a Christian was not simply settling a dispute. He or she was also holding the church itself up to public scrutiny and ridicule.

of the church in Corinth are taking their disputes to a civil, secular court? **3.** According to this passage, how should conflicts among fellow believers be resolved? **4.** How should Christians handle being wronged and cheated? How does this contrast with what the world says to do? **5.** From verses 9–11, who won't inherit and who will inherit the kingdom of God and why? **6.** What "were you" before meeting Christ? What are you now?

APPLY In what dispute or wounded relationship do you need to experience the healing touch of God?

know that we will judge angels? How much more the things of this
life! [4]Therefore, if you have disputes about such matters, appoint as
judges even men of little account in the church![a] [5]I say this to shame
you. Is it possible that there is nobody among you wise enough to
judge a dispute between believers? [6]But instead, one brother goes to
law against another—and this in front of unbelievers!

[7]The very fact that you have lawsuits among you means you have
been completely defeated already. Why not rather be wronged? Why
not rather be cheated? [8]Instead, you yourselves cheat and do wrong,
and you do this to your brothers.

[9]Do you not know that the wicked will not inherit the kingdom of
God? Do not be deceived: Neither the sexually immoral nor idolaters
nor adulterers nor male prostitutes nor homosexual offenders [10]nor
thieves nor the greedy nor drunkards nor slanderers nor swindlers
will inherit the kingdom of God. [11]And that is what some of you were.
But you were washed, you were sanctified, you were justified in the
name of the Lord Jesus Christ and by the Spirit of our God.

OPEN What is the best thing you've done for your health?

STUDY 1. How would you characterize our culture's view of sexuality? **2.** From this passage, what are Paul's arguments against sexual immorality? Which one is most convincing to you? **3.** What connection is there between the "spiritual" and the "physical"? How does this make sexual sin unique? **4.** What does it mean that "your body is a temple of the Holy Spirit" (v. 19)? How well have you been caring for the temple? What repairs need to be made?

Sexual Immorality

[12]"Everything is permissible for me"—but not everything is beneficial. "Everything is permissible for me"—but I will not be mastered
by anything. [13]"Food for the stomach and the stomach for food"—but
God will destroy them both. The body is not meant for sexual immorality, but for the Lord, and the Lord for the body. [14]By his power
God raised the Lord from the dead, and he will raise us also. [15]Do you
not know that your bodies are members of Christ himself? Shall I
then take the members of Christ and unite them with a prostitute?
Never! [16]Do you not know that he who unites himself with a prostitute is one with her in body? For it is said, "The two will become one
flesh."[b] [17]But he who unites himself with the Lord is one with him in
spirit.

[18]Flee from sexual immorality. All other sins a man commits are

[a]4 *Or matters, do you appoint as judges men of little account in the church?* [b]16 Gen. 2:24

6:7 defeated already. The very existence of a lawsuit is a clear sign that love in the church has been replaced by selfishness. **Why not rather be wronged?** Paul counsels non-retaliation, as Jesus had taught (Matt. 5:38–42; Rom. 12:17–21; 1 Thess. 5:15). Such a stance is only possible because the Christian knows that his or her true life is to be found in the coming age. **Why not rather be cheated?** An indication that Paul is writing about financial and property cases.

6:9 wicked. Paul is thinking of those who actively live out a life of evil. He then illustrates what he means by the list that follows, in which he points to typical destructive lifestyles in Corinth and elsewhere in the Greco-Roman world. **kingdom of God.** Paul continues with this idea of living out the ethic of the age to come, referring here to the time when all evil is undone and God reigns visibly. **male prostitutes nor homosexual offenders.** The passive and active partners in male homosexual activity. Homosexuality was widespread in the Greco-Roman world; 14 of the first 15 Roman emperors practiced it.

6:12 Everything is permissible for me. This was probably the slogan of a libertarian party at Corinth which felt that since the body was insignificant (in comparison with the "spirit"), it did not really matter what one did. Paul argues that while everything may be permissible, not everything is good. **not everything is beneficial ... I will not be mastered.** The principle of freedom must be shaped by the principle of love. We should ask: (1) Is what I am doing good for myself or others; and (2) What does my activity show about whom or what I honor as Lord? Otherwise, Christian freedom becomes a cover for self-indulgence. **mastered.** To indulge one's appetites in unsuitable ways is to put oneself under the power of that appetite, and to open the possibility of slavery to a harmful habit.

6:13 Food for the stomach. Christians are not bound by food laws. Diet is a matter of indifference—especially in that it has no impact on one's salvation. **body.** What the Corinthians failed to see was that the body is the means by which one serves the Lord. Therefore, it is to be used to honor God.

6:18 Flee. The temptation to sexual sin was so overwhelming in Corinth that Paul uses this strong verb by way of command. The sexual impulse is so powerful that it is generally useless to fight it.

outside his body, but he who sins sexually sins against his own body.
19Do you not know that your body is a temple of the Holy Spirit, who
is in you, whom you have received from God? You are not your own;
20you were bought at a price. Therefore honor God with your body.

Marriage

7 Now for the matters you wrote about: It is good for a man not to
marry.[a] 2But since there is so much immorality, each man should
have his own wife, and each woman her own husband. 3The husband
should fulfill his marital duty to his wife, and likewise the wife to her
husband. 4The wife's body does not belong to her alone but also to
her husband. In the same way, the husband's body does not belong
to him alone but also to his wife. 5Do not deprive each other except
by mutual consent and for a time, so that you may devote yourselves
to prayer. Then come together again so that Satan will not tempt you
because of your lack of self-control. 6I say this as a concession, not
as a command. 7I wish that all men were as I am. But each man has
his own gift from God; one has this gift, another has that.

8Now to the unmarried and the widows I say: It is good for them to
stay unmarried, as I am. 9But if they cannot control themselves, they
should marry, for it is better to marry than to burn with passion.

10To the married I give this command (not I, but the Lord): A wife
must not separate from her husband. 11But if she does, she must remain unmarried or else be reconciled to her husband. And a husband
must not divorce his wife.

12To the rest I say this (I, not the Lord): If any brother has a wife
who is not a believer and she is willing to live with him, he must not
divorce her. 13And if a woman has a husband who is not a believer
and he is willing to live with her, she must not divorce him. 14For the
unbelieving husband has been sanctified through his wife, and the
unbelieving wife has been sanctified through her believing husband.
Otherwise your children would be unclean, but as it is, they are holy.

15But if the unbeliever leaves, let him do so. A believing man or
woman is not bound in such circumstances; God has called us to live

[a]1 Or *"It is good for a man not to have sexual relations with a woman."*

APPLY What can you do to show that your body is for the use of the Holy Spirit?

OPEN If married (or dating), tell your "love story." How did you meet? What attracted you?

STUDY Corinth was a "wide open" city. The red light district centered in the pagan temples. Sexual promiscuity was a way of life. **1.** What does Paul recommend to overcome sexual hunger? Inside of marriage, what does he say about sexual intimacy, and abstinence (no sex)? Why? **2.** For those who are single, what does Paul recommend (vv. 8–9)? If a single person cannot control his hormones, what does Paul say? **3.** What obligation does a believing spouse have to a non-believing mate (vv. 12–14)? What does it mean for a non-believer to be "sanctified" by their believing spouse? What will be the impact on the children? **4.** If Paul were around today as a marriage counselor, what would his counsel be for those who are considering marriage? What would he say to those who are struggling in their marriage? What about those who are trapped in a marriage to an alcoholic, a drug addict, or sexually abusive person? **5.** What does Paul go on to say about circumcision (the Jewish initiation rite) and about slaves (vv. 18–22)? What is the point Paul is making? How would this apply to your situation today?

7:2 First, Paul says that it is not good for a husband and a wife to abstain from sexual relationship, since this will increase the temptation to commit adultery.

7:5 Abstinence is allowed under two conditions: both partners agree, and it is for a limited time. **deprive.** Literally, "rob." For one partner to opt out of sexual relations under the guise of spirituality is a form of robbery. **prayer.** The purpose of such abstinence is prayer. **lack of self-control.** Paul assumes that a couple would not be married in the first place if they did not feel any sexual desire, and thus they ought to fulfill such desires legitimately, lest they be tempted to fall into adultery.

7:7 were as I am. That is, celibate; though Paul is not advocating celibacy, as much as resistance against inappropriate sexual expression. **gift.** Paul states that celibacy is a spiritual gift! It is not a gift that everyone has.

7:8 unmarried, as I am. While Paul may always have been a bachelor, it is more likely that he was a widower, since it was quite rare for a rabbi to be unmarried. In fact, marriage was virtually obligatory for a Jewish man.

7:9 cannot control themselves. Abstinence would be a particular problem for those who had once experienced an active married life. **to burn.** When one is consumed with desire, that preoccupation makes it difficult to lead a devoted Christian life. A pattern of sin then develops.

7:10 not I, but the Lord. Paul is probably referring to statements by Jesus, as in Mark 10:2–12. **A wife.** Paul writes (vv. 10–11) primarily to women, because it was probably they who were advocating sexual abstinence in order to remain "spiritually pure." **must not separate.** Despite his preference for the single life, Paul does not encourage those who are already married to be divorced (Mal. 2:16).

7:12–14 Paul examines the issue of marriage to a non-Christian spouse. A Christian is not to take the initiative to divorce his or her nonbelieving spouse.

7:15 But should the non-Christian partner leave, the prohibition against divorce does not apply.

APPLY 1. What is your position on divorce and remarriage? **2.** How can this group help those who are divorced or are suffering in their marriages? How can your group make it safe for others to share their difficulties when it comes to relationships?

OPEN Whom do you know who has chosen to remain single out of conviction?

STUDY 1. What period in your life were you the most "carefree"? **2.** Do you believe that Paul is being a little hard on married people (especially men) in his statement (v. 33)? What would you say? **3.** Why does Paul want people to stay put in whatever situation they are in? Do you think he would feel the same way today? **4.** Whether single or married, who should have first place in your life (v. 35)? **5.** How can an unmarried person find emotional fulfillment and intimacy if they have chosen to remain single in order to be more fully devoted to the Lord? **6.** A close look at the Epistles reveals meaningful and touching relationships among believers. Why do we expect marriage to bring us the kind of intimacy and fulfillment that only God can bring? **7.** If a person is engaged to be married, what is

in peace. 16How do you know, wife, whether you will save your husband? Or, how do you know, husband, whether you will save your wife?

17Nevertheless, each one should retain the place in life that the Lord assigned to him and to which God has called him. This is the rule I lay down in all the churches.
18Was a man already circumcised when he was called? He should not become uncircumcised. Was a man uncircumcised when he was called? He should not be circumcised.
19Circumcision is nothing and uncircumcision is nothing. Keeping God's commands is what counts.
20Each one should remain in the situation which he was in when God called him.
21Were you a slave when you were called? Don't let it trouble you—although if you can gain your freedom, do so.
22For he who was a slave when he was called by the Lord is the Lord's freedman; similarly, he who was a free man when he was called is Christ's slave.
23You were bought at a price; do not become slaves of men.
24Brothers, each man, as responsible to God, should remain in the situation God called him to.

25Now about virgins: I have no command from the Lord, but I give a judgment as one who by the Lord's mercy is trustworthy.
26Because of the present crisis, I think that it is good for you to remain as you are.
27Are you married? Do not seek a divorce. Are you unmarried? Do not look for a wife.
28But if you do marry, you have not sinned; and if a virgin marries, she has not sinned. But those who marry will face many troubles in this life, and I want to spare you this.

29What I mean, brothers, is that the time is short. From now on those who have wives should live as if they had none;
30those who mourn, as if they did not; those who are happy, as if they were not; those who buy something, as if it were not theirs to keep;
31those who use the things of the world, as if not engrossed in them. For this world in its present form is passing away.

32I would like you to be free from concern. An unmarried man is concerned about the Lord's affairs—how he can please the Lord.
33But a married man is concerned about the affairs of this world—how he can please his wife—
34and his interests are divided. An unmarried woman or virgin is concerned about the Lord's affairs: Her aim is to be devoted to the Lord in both body and spirit. But a married woman is concerned about the affairs of this world—how she can please her husband.
35I am saying this for your own good, not to

7:16 Christians who remain in a mixed marriage may have the joy of seeing their spouses converted to Christ.

7:17–24 Paul now gives the general principle (stay as one was when called), repeated three times (vv. 17,20,24), upon which he based his arguments in verses 1–16, and upon which he will also base his arguments in verses 25–40. He illustrates this principle by references to circumcision and to *slavery.*

7:25 virgins. Those persons either male or female who are without sexual experience. Here Paul uses the word to refer to women. **I give a judgment.** Paul does not have a clear word from the Lord about whether single people ought to marry, but he does offer his own trustworthy opinion, which he feels comes from the Lord (v. 40).

7:26 the present crisis. Paul probably has in mind the Second Coming. Since it was felt that Jesus might come again at any moment, everything must be put aside—including responsibilities *of marriage*—in order to work for God's kingdom (v. 29). **it is good for you to remain as you are.** Again Paul appears to be quoting a truism or maxim from Corinth.

7:28 have not sinned. The Corinthians have probably been insisting that unmarried men remain single. While Paul sees the wisdom of this, it is not a command, but simply a bit of good advice which the Christian is free to accept or reject.

7:34 his interests are divided. The married man is rightly concerned about how to please the Lord, and equally right in his concern to please his wife. This is the problem: how to be fully faithful to both legitimate commitments. **a married woman.** The same is true of a married woman: her attention is divided in a way not true of a single woman.

restrict you, but that you may live in a right way in undivided devotion to the Lord.
[36]If anyone thinks he is acting improperly toward the virgin he is
engaged to, and if she is getting along in years and he feels he ought
to marry, he should do as he wants. He is not sinning. They should
get married. [37]But the man who has settled the matter in his own
mind, who is under no compulsion but has control over his own will,
and who has made up his mind not to marry the virgin—this man
also does the right thing. [38]So then, he who marries the virgin does
right, but he who does not marry her does even better.[a]
[39]A woman is bound to her husband as long as he lives. But if her
husband dies, she is free to marry anyone she wishes, but he must
belong to the Lord. [40]In my judgment, she is happier if she stays as
she is—and I think that I too have the Spirit of God.

Food Sacrificed to Idols

8 Now about food sacrificed to idols: We know that we all possess
knowledge.[b] Knowledge puffs up, but love builds up. [2]The man
who thinks he knows something does not yet know as he ought to
know. [3]But the man who loves God is known by God.
[4]So then, about eating food sacrificed to idols: We know that an
idol is nothing at all in the world and that there is no God but one.
[5]For even if there are so-called gods, whether in heaven or on earth
(as indeed there are many "gods" and many "lords"), [6]yet for us there
is but one God, the Father, from whom all things came and for whom
we live; and there is but one Lord, Jesus Christ, through whom all
things came and through whom we live.
[7]But not everyone knows this. Some people are still so accustomed
to idols that when they eat such food they think of it as having been
sacrificed to an idol, and since their conscience is weak, it is defiled.
[8]But food does not bring us near to God; we are no worse if we do not
eat, and no better if we do.
[9]Be careful, however, that the exercise of your freedom does not
become a stumbling block to the weak. [10]For if anyone with a weak

[a]36-38 Or [36]*If anyone thinks he is not treating his daughter properly, and if she is getting along in years, and he feels she ought to marry, he should do as he wants. He is not sinning. He should let her get married.* [37]*But the man who has settled the matter in his own mind, who is under no compulsion but has control over his own will, and who has made up his mind to keep the virgin unmarried—this man also does the right thing.* [38]*So then, he who gives his virgin in marriage does right, but he who does not give her in marriage does even better.* [b]1 Or *"We all possess knowledge," as you say*

Paul's advice (vv. 36–38)? What is a deciding factor?

APPLY 1. If you are married, do you sometimes find yourself torn between your desire to please your spouse and your desire to please God? **2.** How do you resolve conflicts in your marriage to give each other time and space to recharge your batteries emotionally and spiritually?

OPEN Have you ever been served a food that you could not identify? Did you eat it?

STUDY 1. Why would eating food sacrificed to idols be a problem to some people (v. 1)? **2.** Who is the "know-it-all"? What does this person believe about food sacrificed to idols? Is this person right? **3.** If the "know-it-all" is right, why does Paul call this person a "stumbling block"? **4.** How would you paraphrase verse 13 in your own words? **5.** If you were in the church in Corinth and you often went to eat at the restaurant of the temple where meat offered to idols was served, and one person in the church was offended, what would you do? How would you feel about this person?

APPLY 1. Are you more concerned about offending a young believer who is very "weak" or a non-believer who is turned off with the legalism of church members? **2.** What would Jesus do in your situation?

7:39 he must belong to the Lord. Literally, "only in the Lord." It is also possible to translate this phrase, "remembering that she is a Christian." In any case, Christian widows (or widowers) may remarry, but only in the context of their commitment to Christ.

8:1 food sacrificed to idols. In ancient cities much of the food offered for sale came from the temples, where it had first been offered to an idol. In fact, this was the source of virtually all meat, since only priests were allowed by the Romans to function as butchers. Jews were absolutely forbidden to eat such idol-food, and the question Paul faces here is whether the same prohibition applied to Christians. **we all possess knowledge.** Once again, Paul appears to be quoting from their letter which argued that eating such food should be all right in view of the knowledge Christians have that there is one true God. As in previous instances, Paul agrees with the assertion, but then goes on to qualify it sharply. **knowledge.** This is insight into how a Christian ought to live. **Knowledge puffs up, but love builds up.** While knowledge is useful, the basic aim of the Christian is love. Sometimes knowledge and love are at cross purposes. When people feel "superior" because they have special insights or esoteric knowledge, this attitude may make it hard to reach out in love to other persons.

8:9 Love for others is the limitation placed upon one's freedom in Christ. **stumbling block.** If "strong" Christians exercise their right to eat idol-meat at a temple, this may induce "weak" Christians to violate their consciences, to their detriment. **weak.** These are people whose faith is still relatively immature or ill-informed.

8:10 eating in an idol's temple. Temples were the "restaurants" of the time. Social life involved invitations to join

conscience sees you who have this knowledge eating in an idol's
temple, won't he be emboldened to eat what has been sacrificed to
idols? 11So this weak brother, for whom Christ died, is destroyed by
your knowledge. 12When you sin against your brothers in this way
and wound their weak conscience, you sin against Christ. 13There-
fore, if what I eat causes my brother to fall into sin, I will never eat
meat again, so that I will not cause him to fall.

The Rights of an Apostle

9 Am I not free? Am I not an apostle? Have I not seen Jesus our
Lord? Are you not the result of my work in the Lord? 2Even
though I may not be an apostle to others, surely I am to you! For you
are the seal of my apostleship in the Lord.
3This is my defense to those who sit in judgment on me. 4Don't we
have the right to food and drink? 5Don't we have the right to take a
believing wife along with us, as do the other apostles and the Lord's
brothers and Cephas[a]? 6Or is it only I and Barnabas who must work
for a living?
7Who serves as a soldier at his own expense? Who plants a vineyard and does not eat of its grapes? Who tends a flock and does not
drink of the milk? 8Do I say this merely from a human point of view?
Doesn't the Law say the same thing? 9For it is written in the Law of
Moses: "Do not muzzle an ox while it is treading out the grain."[b] Is it
about oxen that God is concerned? 10Surely he says this for us,
doesn't he? Yes, this was written for us, because when the plowman
plows and the thresher threshes, they ought to do so in the hope of
sharing in the harvest. 11If we have sown spiritual seed among you, is
it too much if we reap a material harvest from you? 12If others have
this right of support from you, shouldn't we have it all the more?
But we did not use this right. On the contrary, we put up with anything rather than hinder the gospel of Christ. 13Don't you know that
those who work in the temple get their food from the temple, and
those who serve at the altar share in what is offered on the altar? 14In

[a]5 That is, Peter [b]9 Deut. 25:4

OPEN **1.** What was your first paying job? **2.** What volunteer work have you done that was particularly fulfilling?

STUDY **1.** If you had started the church in Corinth and someone came along and questioned your authority, how would you feel (vv. 1–2)? **2.** Who does Paul sound like in verses 3–6? Reading between the lines, what have the critics been saying about Paul's lifestyle? **3.** How does Paul answer his critics when it comes to deserving to be supported by those who have benefited from his ministry? What would a counselor say about giving you their time for no cost? What about doctors and lawyers? **4.** Why did Paul refuse to accept any money for his ministry (vv. 12–18)? How would you paraphrase verse 16 in your own words? **5.** What is the principle in verses 19–22 for anyone who is involved in reaching people for Christ today? If Paul were around today, how would he relate to the younger generation? **6.** In the two illustrations from sports, what is the point that Paul is making? How does this help to explain the personal sacrifice that he has made (vv. 3–6)?

friends at a temple for a meal held in honor of the god of that temple. Hence, to eat at such a temple implied involvement with that god. If a Christian with "knowledge" that "an idol is nothing" (v. 4) exercised his or her knowledge by eating at such an occasion, this might induce weaker Christians who are not so informed to compromise or abandon their faith by again falling into idolatry and immorality.

8:12 sin against Christ. Instead of proving oneself to be "strong" and "spiritual," a Christian who ignores the concerns of the "weak" has offended *the law of love.*

9:1 Am I not free? He is certainly as free as any Christian, but because of his commitment to the way of love he restricts his lifestyle (as he showed in ch. 8). **Have I not seen Jesus our Lord?** A person could not become an apostle unless he or she had witnessed firsthand the resurrected Christ (15:7–8; Acts 1:22). This is the first evidence that he is a legitimate apostle (15:3–11; Gal. 1:11–24).

9:4 the right to food. Paul is certainly free to eat idol-food, but he refuses to exercise this right because it would harm the "weaker" Christians in the community.

9:5 the right to take a believing wife along. All Christians have the right to a wife (ch. 7). Apparently both the apostle and his wife were supported by the Christian community they were serving. **Cephas.** Peter is singled out because he had probably visited Corinth along with his wife.

9:7–14 Here Paul argues strenuously for rights which he has given up (vv. 15–18)! Paul's means of support came from the latter, which in his case meant tentmaking (4:12).

9:12 we did not use this right. This is the point Paul wants to get across to the Corinthians so that they might follow his example. While he has the right to financial support (vv. 7–12), he has chosen not to exercise this right. **hinder the gospel.** If Paul had accepted financial reward, this might have been misunderstood by potential converts as the major motive for his ministry. Paul had the right to support; instead he made tents.

the same way, the Lord has commanded that those who preach the
gospel should receive their living from the gospel.
[15]But I have not used any of these rights. And I am not writing this
in the hope that you will do such things for me. I would rather die
than have anyone deprive me of this boast. [16]Yet when I preach the
gospel, I cannot boast, for I am compelled to preach. Woe to me if I
do not preach the gospel! [17]If I preach voluntarily, I have a reward; if
not voluntarily, I am simply discharging the trust committed to me.
[18]What then is my reward? Just this: that in preaching the gospel I
may offer it free of charge, and so not make use of my rights in
preaching it.
[19]Though I am free and belong to no man, I make myself a slave to
everyone, to win as many as possible. [20]To the Jews I became like a
Jew, to win the Jews. To those under the law I became like one under
the law (though I myself am not under the law), so as to win those
under the law. [21]To those not having the law I became like one not
having the law (though I am not free from God's law but am under
Christ's law), so as to win those not having the law. [22]To the weak I
became weak, to win the weak. I have become all things to all men so
that by all possible means I might save some. [23]I do all this for the
sake of the gospel, that I may share in its blessings.
[24]Do you not know that in a race all the runners run, but only one
gets the prize? Run in such a way as to get the prize. [25]Everyone who
competes in the games goes into strict training. They do it to get a
crown that will not last; but we do it to get a crown that will last forever. [26]Therefore I do not run like a man running aimlessly; I do not
fight like a man beating the air. [27]No, I beat my body and make it my
slave so that after I have preached to others, I myself will not be disqualified for the prize.

Warnings From Israel's History

10 For I do not want you to be ignorant of the fact, brothers,
that our forefathers were all under the cloud and that they all
passed through the sea. [2]They were all baptized into Moses in the
cloud and in the sea. [3]They all ate the same spiritual food [4]and drank
the same spiritual drink; for they drank from the spiritual rock that
accompanied them, and that rock was Christ. [5]Nevertheless, God was
not pleased with most of them; their bodies were scattered over the
desert.

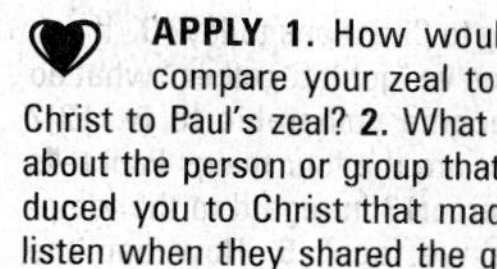

APPLY 1. How would you compare your zeal to share Christ to Paul's zeal? **2.** What was it about the person or group that introduced you to Christ that made you listen when they shared the gospel? **3.** How would you describe your spiritual training right now: Excellent? Good? On the rebound? Sorry you asked?

OPEN Who is the historian in your family?

STUDY 1. What spiritual heritage did your "forefathers" leave you? What kind of spiritual heritage would you like to pass on to your kids? **2.** How did the four types of sin committed by the Israelites (vv. 7–10) serve as a specific warning to the Corinthians? How do they serve as a

9:19 Though I am free. In verse 1, this appears to have referred to Paul's freedom from dietary concerns based on religious scruples. While it carries the same meaning here, it also includes the fact that since he refuses financial support from those he teaches, he is "owned" by no one (6:20). He is obligated to no system or group.

9:22 the weak. Those with weak consciences (8:7–13) who are not yet free from legalism or from the power of paganism.

9:26 running aimlessly. Such a runner has no fixed goal. Paul's activities are not without a point. Everything he does is for the sake of the gospel. **beating the air.** In the same way that he pictured pointless running, now he switches to the image of fruitless boxing.

10:1 ignorant. They claimed to have "knowledge" (8:1–2), but the Corinthians had really misunderstood the meaning of baptism and Communion. **our forefathers.** Though his readers are largely Gentiles, Paul considers them to be the spiritual heirs of Israel. **cloud ... sea.** Paul reminds them of the Exodus (Ex. 13:21; 14:19–31), using the engulfing presence of the cloud of God and their passing through the sea as an analogy to baptism.

10:3–4 spiritual food ... drink. Not only did these gifts from God nourish their physical bodies, they had an additional spiritual function (in that they were symbols which prefigured Christian Communion, and hence, the benefits of Christ's death).

warning to Christians today? **3.** If you think you've "got it together," what do you become vulnerable to (v. 12)? **4.** What are the four things Paul tells us in verse 13 in regard to the temptations we face? **5.** How can the statements and promises in verse 13 help you in your struggle against temptation?

APPLY 1. Since turning over your life to God, have you found that temptation has decreased or increased? **2.** What kinds of temptation are you most vulnerable to?

OPEN 1. If you were going to yield to temptation, which of these would tempt you the most: Chocolate cake? Double thick malt? Cherries jubilee? Banana split? **2.** Do you allow your kids to eat "junk" food?

STUDY In the previous passage, Paul reminds the Corinthians of what happened to Israel when they got involved in sexual sin around a pagan feast in the worship of the idol Baal. **1.** What is Paul's simple command when it comes to whether or not believers should eat the meals involved with pagan temples (v. 14)? **2.** In supporting his call to avoid these meals, Paul appeals to the Lord's Supper. How would you explain to a friend that eating the bread and drinking the cup is a "participation" in

6 Now these things occurred as examples[a] to keep us from setting our hearts on evil things as they did. 7 Do not be idolaters, as some of them were; as it is written: "The people sat down to eat and drink and got up to indulge in pagan revelry."[b] 8 We should not commit sexual immorality, as some of them did—and in one day twenty-three thousand of them died. 9 We should not test the Lord, as some of them did—and were killed by snakes. 10 And do not grumble, as some of them did—and were killed by the destroying angel.

11 These things happened to them as examples and were written down as warnings for us, on whom the fulfillment of the ages has come. 12 So, if you think you are standing firm, be careful that you don't fall! 13 No temptation has seized you except what is common to man. And God is faithful; he will not let you be tempted beyond what you can bear. But when you are tempted, he will also provide a way out so that you can stand up under it.

Idol Feasts and the Lord's Supper

14 Therefore, my dear friends, flee from idolatry. 15 I speak to sensible people; judge for yourselves what I say. 16 Is not the cup of thanksgiving for which we give thanks a participation in the blood of Christ? And is not the bread that we break a participation in the body of Christ? 17 Because there is one loaf, we, who are many, are one body, for we all partake of the one loaf.

18 Consider the people of Israel: Do not those who eat the sacrifices participate in the altar? 19 Do I mean then that a sacrifice offered to an idol is anything, or that an idol is anything? 20 No, but the sacrifices of pagans are offered to demons, not to God, and I do not want you to be participants with demons. 21 You cannot drink the cup of the Lord and the cup of demons too; you cannot have a part in both the Lord's table and the table of demons. 22 Are we trying to arouse the Lord's jealousy? Are we stronger than he?

[a]6 Or *types;* also in verse 11 [b]7 Exodus 32:6

10:8 sexual immorality. Paul now explicitly condemns the sexual vice associated with pagan religion (6:12–20). **twenty-three thousand.** Paul is referring to the story of the Israelites' fornication with the Moabite women as recorded in Numbers 25:1–9 (the figure there is 24,000).

10:9 test the Lord. The Corinthians (as had the Israelites before them) were testing God by these actions—they were seeing how much they could get away with (v. 22).

10:10 grumble. They were also grumbling against Paul for telling them not to *engage in temple feasts and ritual prostitution.*

10:13 Paul encourages the Corinthians to stand firm by reminding them that when Christians resist sin they do so in the knowledge that they will be able to endure. **temptation.** Paul has identified various temptations which Israel faced: the temptation of idolatry, the temptation to commit sexual immorality, the temptation to test God, and the temptation to grumble about where God led them. To be tempted is to be tested. Facing the choice of deserting God's will or doing God's will, the person must either resist or yield. Temptation is not sin. Yielding is. **a way out.** Temptation, it seems, is not unusual nor unexpected. Resisting it is not pleasant, but the Christian can do so.

10:14 Therefore. Paul will now draw the logical conclusions from his survey of Israel's past. **flee from idolatry.** In the same way that he unequivocally forbids fornication (6:18), he forbids Christians from participating in idol worship. While Paul urges Christians to "stand fast" in the face of evil (Eph. 6:10–18), he counsels flight (not a fight) when it comes to "sins of the flesh." The temptations are too strong to resist.

10:16 the cup of thanksgiving. This was the cup of wine drunk at the conclusion of the meal in a Jewish home over which a blessing was spoken. During the Last Supper, Jesus made this cup a symbol of his soon-to-be-shed blood, to be drunk in remembrance of him.

10:18 eat the sacrifices. The priests were allowed to eat parts of the sacrificial offerings (Lev. 10:12–15), as were others in certain instances (1 Sam. 9:10–24).

The Believer's Freedom

23"Everything is permissible"—but not everything is beneficial.
"Everything is permissible"—but not everything is constructive.
24Nobody should seek his own good, but the good of others.
25Eat anything sold in the meat market without raising questions of
conscience, 26for, "The earth is the Lord's, and everything in it."[a]
27If some unbeliever invites you to a meal and you want to go, eat
whatever is put before you without raising questions of conscience.
28But if anyone says to you, "This has been offered in sacrifice," then
do not eat it, both for the sake of the man who told you and for
conscience' sake[b]— 29the other man's conscience, I mean, not yours.
For why should my freedom be judged by another's conscience? 30If
I take part in the meal with thankfulness, why am I denounced because of something I thank God for?
31So whether you eat or drink or whatever you do, do it all for the
glory of God. 32Do not cause anyone to stumble, whether Jews,
Greeks or the church of God— 33even as I try to please everybody in
every way. For I am not seeking my own good but the good of many,
11 so that they may be saved. 1Follow my example, as I follow the
example of Christ.

Propriety in Worship

2I praise you for remembering me in everything and for holding to
the teachings,[c] just as I passed them on to you.
3Now I want you to realize that the head of every man is Christ, and
the head of the woman is man, and the head of Christ is God. 4Every
man who prays or prophesies with his head covered dishonors his
head. 5And every woman who prays or prophesies with her head uncovered dishonors her head—it is just as though her head were
shaved. 6If a woman does not cover her head, she should have her
hair cut off; and if it is a disgrace for a woman to have her hair cut or
shaved off, she should cover her head. 7A man ought not to cover his
head,[d] since he is the image and glory of God; but the woman is the
glory of man. 8For man did not come from woman, but woman from
man; 9neither was man created for woman, but woman for man. 10For
this reason, and because of the angels, the woman ought to have a
sign of authority on her head.
11In the Lord, however, woman is not independent of man, nor is
man independent of woman. 12For as woman came from man, so also
man is born of woman. But everything comes from God. 13Judge for

[a]26 Psalm 24:1 [b]28 Some manuscripts *conscience' sake, for "the earth is the Lord's and everything in it"*
[c]2 Or *traditions* [d]4-7 Or [4]*Every man who prays or prophesies with long hair dishonors his head.* [5]*And every woman who prays or prophesies with no covering* ⌊*of hair*⌋ *on her head dishonors her head—she is just like one of the "shorn women."* [6]*If a woman has no covering, let her be for now with short hair, but since it is a disgrace for a woman to have her hair shorn or shaved, she should grow it again.* [7]*A man ought not to have long hair*

Christ's body and blood? **3.** Why is eating at a feast where idol-meat is served different than going to a meat market and buying the same meat? **4.** In what ways is a follower of Christ free (vv. 23–24)? How do you exercise your freedom in Christ?

APPLY 1. Is there anything you do that does not bother your conscience but might bother the conscience of someone else? **2.** Verses 27–33 describe what a believer should do in a relationship with an unbeliever. Do you act differently around believers and non-believers? If so, under what circumstances?

OPEN How did you wear your hair 10 years ago? 20 years ago?

STUDY 1. What are your first impressions of this passage? What problem in the Corinthian church is Paul addressing? **2.** In this passage, what restrictions does Paul place on the women? On the men? Do any of these Corinthian principles apply to you? **3.** In what ways do verses 11 and 12 illustrate our interdependence on each other and God?

APPLY Many things in our worship reflect the culture we live in (type of music, style of dress, etc.). How do you decide when a cultural practice is okay and when it is a hindrance?

10:27 Paul shifts his focus to the related question of what one might eat or not eat at the home of a non-Christian friend. Paul says that Christians can eat whatever is placed before them in such a setting, although the scruples of one's dinner companions must also be considered. It could be a greater evil to reject a host's food.

10:28 anyone. It is probably a pagan who points out that what is being offered is idol-food. Pagans viewed Christianity as a Jewish sect, and so assumed Christians followed the same dietary laws.

11:3 the head of Christ is God. God is the origin and Christ is the creating agent of all people.

11:11 not independent. While verses 2–16 do not directly examine the relationship between husband and wife, here Paul does point out the mutual interdependence that exists between men and women and their equal dependence on God.

yourselves: Is it proper for a woman to pray to God with her head
uncovered? 14Does not the very nature of things teach you that if a
man has long hair, it is a disgrace to him, 15but that if a woman has
long hair, it is her glory? For long hair is given to her as a covering.
16If anyone wants to be contentious about this, we have no other
practice—nor do the churches of God.

The Lord's Supper

17In the following directives I have no praise for you, for your meetings do more harm than good. 18In the first place, I hear that when
you come together as a church, there are divisions among you, and to
some extent I believe it. 19No doubt there have to be differences
among you to show which of you have God's approval. 20When you
come together, it is not the Lord's Supper you eat, 21for as you eat,
each of you goes ahead without waiting for anybody else. One remains hungry, another gets drunk. 22Don't you have homes to eat
and drink in? Or do you despise the church of God and humiliate
those who have nothing? What shall I say to you? Shall I praise you
for this? Certainly not!

23For I received from the Lord what I also passed on to you: The
Lord Jesus, on the night he was betrayed, took bread, 24and when he
had given thanks, he broke it and said, "This is my body, which is for
you; do this in remembrance of me." 25In the same way, after supper
he took the cup, saying, "This cup is the new covenant in my blood;
do this, whenever you drink it, in remembrance of me." 26For whenever you eat this bread and drink this cup, you proclaim the Lord's
death until he comes.

27Therefore, whoever eats the bread or drinks the cup of the Lord
in an unworthy manner will be guilty of sinning against the body and
blood of the Lord. 28A man ought to examine himself before he eats of

OPEN What is the biggest party you've ever given? What food and drink did you serve?

STUDY 1. When has the Lord's Supper been particularly meaningful to you? **2.** How would you describe the scene if you were observing the Lord's Supper at the Corinthian church? **3.** What changes would the Corinthians need to make to ensure that it really was the "Lord's Supper"? **4.** Have you ever been in a church that was affected by divisions among the members? How did that affect the worship services? **5.** Paul repeats the words used during the Lord's Supper in verses 23–26. How do you feel when you hear these words during your observance of the Lord's Supper (Communion)? **6.** In this passage, Paul instructs the Corinthians to examine themselves prior to partaking of the Lord's Supper. How is this done? What are the consequences of receiving the Lord's Supper "in an unworthy manner" (v. 27)? **7.** Why is it important for followers of

11:18 I hear. They had not written Paul about these disorders. Paul had heard what was going on from other sources (1:11; 16:17), and is so shocked that he can't really believe that it is as bad as reported ("to some extent I believe it"). **divisions.** It seems that class distinction operated at the Lord's Supper—the rich ate abundantly while the poor were hungry. It is also possible that Jewish Christians ate kosher food by themselves apart from Gentile Christians, and that the ascetics sat apart from the libertarians, that those who followed Apollos did not mingle with those who followed Cephas, etc.

11:20 it is not the Lord's Supper you eat. The Corinthians have so badly abused the Communion service that it was more like one of the meals at a pagan temple than a meal held in honor of the Lord.

***11:21 goes ahead without waiting* for anybody else.** The purpose of the meal was to remember the Lord as a body of believers. Apparently, some were excluded while others over indulged. This destroyed the spirit of the service and isolated certain believers. Paul calls them back to the original purpose of the meal. **hungry ... drunk.** The contrast could not be more stark. The poor in the church went hungry during this meal, while others indulged themselves to the point of drunkenness!

11:22 If the rich can't wait to indulge in their food and drink, at least they should do this at home and not demean the common meal at church. **humiliate those who have nothing.** The poor feel ashamed that they can't bring the abundant food and drink they see the rich eating.

11:24 This is my body. Jesus interprets for the disciples the new meaning he is giving to these ordinary acts. He himself will become the Passover lamb for them, to be slain for their *sins.* **in remembrance.** Paul repeats this phrase twice, to stress that the Lord's Supper is a memorial feast (Luke 22:19).

11:25 in my blood. The shedding of Jesus' blood inaugurates a new covenant between God and people by which their sins are forgiven as a result of Christ's death in their place.

11:26 This statement is not found in the Gospels. It is Paul's summary of the meaning of the Lord's Supper. **proclaim the Lord's death.** The Lord's Supper proclaims the fact and meaning of Jesus' death in several ways: the broken bread and outpoured wine symbolically proclaim his death; the words spoken at such a meal (formally and informally) recall the Crucifixion; and the whole event "proclaims" his atoning death. **until he comes.** In this way, Christians recall the story of Jesus' death until he returns.

11:27 in an unworthy manner. This refers to the disorders in community behavior (vv. 18–22).

11:28 to examine himself. Christians ought to scrutinize their lives to see if they are guilty of divisiveness, of lack of love, of gluttony and drunken-

the bread and drinks of the cup. [29]For anyone who eats and drinks
without recognizing the body of the Lord eats and drinks judgment
on himself. [30]That is why many among you are weak and sick, and a
number of you have fallen asleep. [31]But if we judged ourselves, we
would not come under judgment. [32]When we are judged by the Lord,
we are being disciplined so that we will not be condemned with the
world.

[33]So then, my brothers, when you come together to eat, wait for
each other. [34]If anyone is hungry, he should eat at home, so that
when you meet together it may not result in judgment.

And when I come I will give further directions.

Spiritual Gifts

12 Now about spiritual gifts, brothers, I do not want you to be
ignorant. [2]You know that when you were pagans, somehow
or other you were influenced and led astray to mute idols. [3]Therefore
I tell you that no one who is speaking by the Spirit of God says, "Jesus
be cursed," and no one can say, "Jesus is Lord," except by the Holy
Spirit.

[4]There are different kinds of gifts, but the same Spirit. [5]There are
different kinds of service, but the same Lord. [6]There are different
kinds of working, but the same God works all of them in all men.

[7]Now to each one the manifestation of the Spirit is given for the
common good. [8]To one there is given through the Spirit the message
of wisdom, to another the message of knowledge by means of the
same Spirit, [9]to another faith by the same Spirit, to another gifts of
healing by that one Spirit, [10]to another miraculous powers, to another prophecy, to another distinguishing between spirits, to another
speaking in different kinds of tongues,[a] and to still another the interpretation of tongues.[a] [11]All these are the work of one and the same
Spirit, and he gives them to each one, just as he determines.

[a]10 Or *languages*; also in verse 28

Christ to observe the Lord's Supper? What does Communion/Lord's Supper mean to you?

APPLY 1. When did the Lord's Supper or Eucharist start taking on a special meaning for you? **2.** If you were on the official board of your church, what would you recommend that would make the communion experience more personal?

OPEN What was the most fulfilling summer job you ever had?

STUDY 1. When have you felt that you were part of a team where all the parts worked together for a common goal? **2.** Who has been given spiritual gifts? Who are they from and for what purpose are they given (v. 7)? **3.** Verses 4–6 indicate that some Corinthians felt certain spiritual gifts were better than others. Have you ever encountered that attitude among Christians? In yourself? **4.** How is the diversity of the gifts related to the unity of the Father, Son and Holy Spirit?

APPLY 1. Of the spiritual gifts listed, where are you strongest? **2.** What would be a good place for you to use your gift?

---

ness which might reflect negatively on "the body and the blood of the Lord."

11:29 without recognizing. When the meal turned into a time of drunkenness, division and gluttony, people lost sight of the meaning of the event. **the body of the Lord.** Here, "the body" in view is the body of the Lord remembered in the supper and secondarily the church (12:12), which the Corinthians were abusing.

12:2 influenced and led astray. The image is of the ecstasy within pagan religion, where one was possessed and "carried away." **mute idols.** The idols in themselves were nothing, they were silent, but behind them lay very real demonic powers.

12:3 speaking by. The idea of speech directly inspired by the Spirit of God. The question is not whether such ecstatic speech occurs (Paul assumes that it does), but what is the content of the speech. **Jesus is Lord.** To be able to confess that one is the servant of Jesus who is indeed Lord (Master, King) of the universe is a sign of the Holy Spirit at work.

12:5 service. The purpose of the gifts is to serve and aid others in various ways, yet all is done in the name of and for the sake of the same Lord.

12:6 working. The Greek root is *energeia* ("energy"), and refers to the various ways in which God's power is displayed in the gifts.

12:7 to each one. Every Christian has a spiritual gift. **for the common good.** The purpose of these gifts is not private advantage, but community growth.

12:8 through the Spirit. Paul emphasizes the supernatural origins of these gifts. **wisdom ... knowledge.** It is not clear how (or if) these gifts differ. Perhaps a message of wisdom focused on practical, ethical instruction, while a message of knowledge involved exposition of biblical truth. In either case, the emphasis is on the actual discourse given for the benefit of the assembled Christians.

12:9 faith. This refers to the capacity to believe God for extraordinary results. Saving faith, which all Christians share, is not in view here. **healing.** The special ability to effect miraculous cures. Paul apparently had this gift (Acts 14:8–10).

12:10 miraculous powers. Probably the gift of exorcism and similar types of confrontation with evil supernatural powers. **prophecy.** Inspired utterances given in ordinary (not ecstatic) speech, distinguished from teaching and wisdom by its unpremeditated nature.

OPEN 1. Which is your strongest bone: Funny bone? Neck bone? Backbone? Wishbone? Bonaparte? **2.** Where do you find these bones in the other members in your group?

STUDY 1. What is it about the human body that makes it a perfect illustration of a healthy functioning church? What happens in the human body when one organ takes over (thyroid gland) or one organ malfunctions (liver)? **2.** In the church in Corinth what has happened to the people with supporting "weaker ... less honorable ... unpresentable" gifts (vv. 22–23)? What does Paul challenge the people with the spectacular gifts to do (vv. 25–26)? What is your church doing to "honor" and affirm the people with the supporting gifts? **3.** When you read verses 27–30 about the spectacular gifts, what is the danger in the church when the spectacular gifts are honored and the supporting gifts are ignored?

APPLY 1. Who was the person in your life that affirmed your gifts and made you feel special at an early age? **2.** How do you go about affirming the gifts in your family, especially your children?

One Body, Many Parts

12The body is a unit, though it is made up of many parts; and
though all its parts are many, they form one body. So it is with Christ.
13For we were all baptized by[a] one Spirit into one body—whether
Jews or Greeks, slave or free—and we were all given the one Spirit to
drink.
14Now the body is not made up of one part but of many. 15If the foot
should say, "Because I am not a hand, I do not belong to the body," it
would not for that reason cease to be part of the body. 16And if the ear
should say, "Because I am not an eye, I do not belong to the body," it
would not for that reason cease to be part of the body. 17If the whole
body were an eye, where would the sense of hearing be? If the whole
body were an ear, where would the sense of smell be? 18But in fact
God has arranged the parts in the body, every one of them, just as he
wanted them to be. 19If they were all one part, where would the body
be? 20As it is, there are many parts, but one body.
21The eye cannot say to the hand, "I don't need you!" And the head
cannot say to the feet, "I don't need you!" 22On the contrary, those
parts of the body that seem to be weaker are indispensable, 23and the
parts that we think are less honorable we treat with special honor.
And the parts that are unpresentable are treated with special modesty, 24while our presentable parts need no special treatment. But God
has combined the members of the body and has given greater honor
to the parts that lacked it, 25so that there should be no division in the
body, but that its parts should have equal concern for each other. 26If
one part suffers, every part suffers with it; if one part is honored,
every part rejoices with it.
27Now you are the body of Christ, and each one of you is a part of it.
28And in the church God has appointed first of all apostles, second
prophets, third teachers, then workers of miracles, also those having
gifts of healing, those able to help others, those with gifts of administration, and those speaking in different kinds of tongues. 29Are all
apostles? Are all prophets? Are all teachers? Do all work miracles?
30Do all have gifts of healing? Do all speak in tongues[b]? Do all interpret? 31But eagerly desire[c] the greater gifts.

[a] *13 Or* with; *or* in [b] *30 Or other languages* [c] *31 Or* But you are eagerly desiring

distinguishing between spirits. Just because a person claimed to be inspired by the Holy Spirit did not make it true. Those who possessed this gift of discernment were able to identify the source of an utterance—whether it came from the Holy Spirit or another spirit. **tongues.** Ecstatic speech, unintelligible except by those with the gift of interpretation of tongues. **interpretation of tongues.** This gift allowed a person to understand and explain to others what was being said by someone else in a tongue.

12:12 a unit ... made up of many parts. This is Paul's central point in verses 12–30: "diversity within unity." **So it is with Christ.** The church is the body of Christ (v. 27), and so indeed Christ can be understood to be made up of many parts. Yet he is also the Lord (v. 3), and thus head over that church.

12:15–26 Having established that all Christians are part of one body (which is, in fact, Christ's body) and that this body has a variety of parts, Paul makes two points: there are a variety of gifts (vv. 15–20), and each gift is vital, regardless of its nature (vv. 21–26).

12:28 Paul offers a second list of the types of gifts given by the Holy Spirit (see the parallel list in Eph. 4:11)—mixing together ministries (apostles) with spiritual gifts (the gift of healing). **apostles.** These individuals were responsible for founding new churches. They were pioneer church planters. **prophets.** Those who were inspired to speak God's word to the church, in plain (not ecstatic) language. **teachers.** Those gifted to instruct others in the meaning of the Christian faith and its implications for one's life. **then.** Having first focused on those gifts whereby the church is established and nurtured, Paul then shifts to other gifts. **to help others.** The gift of support; those whose function it was to aid the needy (e.g., the poor, the widow, the orphan). **administration.** The gift of direction (literally, the process of steering a ship through the rocks and safely to shore); those whose function it was to guide church affairs.

Love

And now I will show you the most excellent way.
13 If I speak in the tongues[a] of men and of angels, but have not
love, I am only a resounding gong or a clanging cymbal. 2If I
have the gift of prophecy and can fathom all mysteries and all knowledge, and if I have a faith that can move mountains, but have not
love, I am nothing. 3If I give all I possess to the poor and surrender
my body to the flames,[b] but have not love, I gain nothing.
4Love is patient, love is kind. It does not envy, it does not boast, it is
not proud. 5It is not rude, it is not self-seeking, it is not easily angered, it keeps no record of wrongs. 6Love does not delight in evil but
rejoices with the truth. 7It always protects, always trusts, always
hopes, always perseveres.
8Love never fails. But where there are prophecies, they will cease;
where there are tongues, they will be stilled; where there is knowledge, it will pass away. 9For we know in part and we prophesy in part,
10but when perfection comes, the imperfect disappears. 11When I was
a child, I talked like a child, I thought like a child, I reasoned like a
child. When I became a man, I put childish ways behind me. 12Now
we see but a poor reflection as in a mirror; then we shall see face to
face. Now I know in part; then I shall know fully, even as I am fully
known.
13And now these three remain: faith, hope and love. But the greatest of these is love.

[a]1 Or *languages* [b]3 Some early manuscripts *body that I may boast*

OPEN What was your favorite love song when you were a teenager?

STUDY 1. When in your life have you felt the most loved? How did that love affect your life? **2.** In verses 1–3, what activities are useless without love? **3.** In this passage, what does Paul say love is? What does Paul say love is not? **4.** How does love as described in this chapter compare to love as typically defined in our culture? **5.** Looking at the descriptions of perfect love in verses 4–7, in which one of these descriptions are you strongest? In which one are you weakest? **6.** How does it make you feel that you are "fully known" (v. 12) by God?

APPLY 1. Have you ever tried reading this passage with your first name in place of the word "love"? **2.** In what relationship do you find it the hardest to live this passage? When is the last time you told this person you loved them?

13:1 tongues of men and of angels. Ecstatic speech—highly prized in Corinth—is an authentic gift of the Holy Spirit. **gong ... cymbal.** Paul is probably thinking of the repetitious and meaningless noise generated at pagan temples by beating on metal instruments.

13:2 prophecy. Such activity is highly commended by Paul (14:1), yet without love a prophet is really nothing. **fathom all mysteries.** In Corinth, special and esoteric knowledge was highly valued (1:18–2:16). **faith that can move mountains.** Paul refers to Jesus' words in Mark 11:23—even such massive faith that can unleash God's power in visible ways is not enough to make a person significant without love as its foundation.

13:4 patient. This word describes patience with people (not circumstances). It characterizes the person who is slow to anger (long-suffering) despite provocation. **kind.** The loving person does good to others. **not envy.** The loving person does not covet what others have, nor begrudge them their possessions. **not boast.** The loving person is self-effacing, not a braggart. **not proud.** Literally, not "puffed up." The loving person does not feel others to be inferior, nor looks down on people.

13:5 not self-seeking. Loving people not only do not insist on their rights, but will give up their due for the sake of others. **not easily angered.** Loving people are not easily angered by others; they are not touchy. **keeps no record of wrongs.** The verb is an accounting term, and the image is of a ledger sheet on which wrongs received are recorded. The loving person forgives and forgets.

13:6 does not delight in evil. Loving people do not rejoice when others fail nor enjoy pointing out the wrong in others. **rejoices with the truth.** Paul shifts back to the positive.

13:7 protects. Literally, "to put a cover over." The loving person is concerned with how to shelter other people from harm. **trusts.** Literally, "believes all things"; i.e., "never loses faith." **hopes.** Love continually looks forward. **perseveres.** Love keeps loving despite hardship.

13:8 Love never fails. In the sense that it functions both now and in the age to come. Spiritual gifts are relevant only to this age. **cease ... be stilled ... pass away.** One day, when Christ comes again in fullness, prophecy will be fulfilled (and so cease), the indirect communication with God through tongues will no longer be needed (so they are stilled), and since all will be revealed and be evident, secret knowledge about God will be redundant (and so will pass away).

13:12 Now ... then. Paul is thinking of the Second Coming. The here-and-now experience is contrasted to that when Christ's kingdom is revealed in its fullness. **poor reflection.** Corinth was famous for the mirrors it made out of highly polished metal. Still, no mirror manufactured in the first century was without imperfections. All of them distorted the image somewhat, and so this is an apt metaphor for the present knowledge of God—it is marred (until the day we see the Lord clearly in heaven).

13:13 remain. Charismatic gifts will cease, because they bring only partial knowledge of God; but three things will carry over into the new age: faith, hope and love. **the greatest of these is love.** Because God is love (1 John 4:8). After everything else is no longer necessary, love will still be the governing principle.

OPEN **1.** When have you been in a country or area where you couldn't speak the language. Was it funny? Frustrating? Humbling? **2.** If you could play any musical instrument, what would it be?

STUDY **1.** What problem is Paul addressing in this passage? Why might this have been a problem in the Corinthian church? **2.** What is the difference between speaking in tongues and prophesying, and in what sense is prophecy better than tongues (vv. 2–5)? **3.** What corrective instructions does Paul repeat throughout this passage? **4.** What are the values and limits of tongues (vv. 4,9,13–19, 21–25)? **5.** What is Paul saying about the need for balance between the mind and the emotions in worship? **6.** Suppose you invited your unchurched neighbor to your church service. What might be strange or confusing to your friend? **7.** The Corinthians presumably were partial to ecstatic or flamboyant spirituality. What exciting experiences do you wish your Christian life could have? Which experiences do you wish your church would tone down? **8.** Whether or not your church practices the gifts of tongues and prophecy, what principles for church life need to be exercised more fully in your church?

APPLY What are you doing to build up yourself spiritually? What is your church doing to put "life" into worship? What can you do to aid the worship experience of your church or group?

Gifts of Prophecy and Tongues

14 Follow the way of love and eagerly desire spiritual gifts,
especially the gift of prophecy. 2For anyone who speaks in a
tongue[a] does not speak to men but to God. Indeed, no one understands him; he utters mysteries with his spirit.[b] 3But everyone who
prophesies speaks to men for their strengthening, encouragement
and comfort. 4He who speaks in a tongue edifies himself, but he who
prophesies edifies the church. 5I would like every one of you to speak
in tongues,[c] but I would rather have you prophesy. He who prophesies is greater than one who speaks in tongues,[c] unless he interprets, so that the church may be edified.
6Now, brothers, if I come to you and speak in tongues, what good
will I be to you, unless I bring you some revelation or knowledge or
prophecy or word of instruction? 7Even in the case of lifeless things
that make sounds, such as the flute or harp, how will anyone know
what tune is being played unless there is a distinction in the notes?
8Again, if the trumpet does not sound a clear call, who will get ready
for battle? 9So it is with you. Unless you speak intelligible words with
your tongue, how will anyone know what you are saying? You will
just be speaking into the air. 10Undoubtedly there are all sorts of languages in the world, yet none of them is without meaning. 11If then I
do not grasp the meaning of what someone is saying, I am a foreigner
to the speaker, and he is a foreigner to me. 12So it is with you. Since
you are eager to have spiritual gifts, try to excel in gifts that build up
the church.

13For this reason anyone who speaks in a tongue should pray that
he may interpret what he says. 14For if I pray in a tongue, my spirit
prays, but my mind is unfruitful. 15So what shall I do? I will pray with
my spirit, but I will also pray with my mind; I will sing with my spirit,
but I will also sing with my mind. 16If you are praising God with your
spirit, how can one who finds himself among those who do not
understand[d] say "Amen" to your thanksgiving, since he does not
know what you are saying? 17You may be giving thanks well enough,
but the other man is not edified.

18I thank God that I speak in tongues more than all of you. 19But in
the church I would rather speak five intelligible words to instruct
others than ten thousand words in a tongue.

20Brothers, stop thinking like children. In regard to evil be infants,
but in your thinking be adults. 21In the Law it is written:

[a]2 Or *another language;* also in verses 4,13,14,19,26 and 27 [b]2 Or *by the Spirit* [c]5 Or *other languages;* also in verses 6,18,22,23 and 39 [d]16 Or *among the inquirers*

14:5 While affirming the value of both tongues and prophecy, Paul stresses prophecy because of its value during the worship service. **tongues.** In verses 2–5, Paul gives insight into just what tongues are. They seem to be a gift from the Holy Spirit whereby an individual "utters mysteries" to God by (or in) the Spirit, from which great personal benefit is gained. Uninterpreted tongues, however, are meant to be part of private devotions, not public worship. **greater.** In the sense that prophecy edifies, and is therefore an act of love. Interpreted tongues have the same use and value as prophecy.

14:6–12 Now the real issue comes out: intelligibility (v. 9). It appears that it is not just prophecy that Paul is commending (v. 6). Prophecy is just the example he has chosen of an intelligible gift. Here, Paul examines the value of various gifts from the point of view of the other people in church.

14:13 For this reason. Because intelligible gifts edify, Paul next explains how tongues might do the same.

14:14–17 Paul explains how he understands tongues.

14:15 pray with my spirit. Paul adds another insight into tongues: this is prayer that bypasses the mind. It is, according to verse 15, one quite legitimate (and edifying—v. 4) means of prayer, but it is meant to be complemented with prayer that engages the mind.

"Through men of strange tongues
and through the lips of foreigners
I will speak to this people,
but even then they will not listen to me,"[a]
says the Lord.

[22]Tongues, then, are a sign, not for believers but for unbelievers;
prophecy, however, is for believers, not for unbelievers. [23]So if the
whole church comes together and everyone speaks in tongues, and
some who do not understand[b] or some unbelievers come in, will they
not say that you are out of your mind? [24]But if an unbeliever or someone who does not understand[c] comes in while everybody is prophesying, he will be convinced by all that he is a sinner and will be judged
by all, [25]and the secrets of his heart will be laid bare. So he will fall
down and worship God, exclaiming, "God is really among you!"

Orderly Worship

[26]What then shall we say, brothers? When you come together,
everyone has a hymn, or a word of instruction, a revelation, a tongue
or an interpretation. All of these must be done for the strengthening
of the church. [27]If anyone speaks in a tongue, two—or at the most
three—should speak, one at a time, and someone must interpret. [28]If
there is no interpreter, the speaker should keep quiet in the church
and speak to himself and God.

[29]Two or three prophets should speak, and the others should weigh
carefully what is said. [30]And if a revelation comes to someone who is
sitting down, the first speaker should stop. [31]For you can all prophesy
in turn so that everyone may be instructed and encouraged. [32]The
spirits of prophets are subject to the control of prophets. [33]For God is
not a God of disorder but of peace.

As in all the congregations of the saints, [34]women should remain
silent in the churches. They are not allowed to speak, but must be in
submission, as the Law says. [35]If they want to inquire about something, they should ask their own husbands at home; for it is disgraceful for a woman to speak in the church.

[36]Did the word of God originate with you? Or are you the only people it has reached? [37]If anybody thinks he is a prophet or spiritually
gifted, let him acknowledge that what I am writing to you is the
Lord's command. [38]If he ignores this, he himself will be ignored.[d]

[39]Therefore, my brothers, be eager to prophesy, and do not forbid
speaking in tongues. [40]But everything should be done in a fitting and
orderly way.

[a]21 Isaiah 28:11,12 [b]23 Or *some inquirers* [c]24 Or *or some inquirer* [d]38 Some manuscripts *If he is ignorant of this, let him be ignorant*

OPEN What was your favorite bedtime song as a child?

STUDY **1.** How would you describe the style of worship at your church: Traditional? Balanced? Noisy? Contemporary? Quiet? Orderly? Other? **2.** What was wrong with the Corinthian style of worship? What guidelines for worship do we find in this passage? **3.** In what ways does your worship experience parallel what Paul says in verse 26? How does it differ? **4.** How do you feel about the use of the gifts of tongues and interpretation and prophecy today? By what standards should followers of Christ "weigh carefully what is said" (v. 29)? **5.** Verse 33 says, "God is not a God of disorder but of peace." What does this characteristic of God mean to you?

APPLY What was the most inspiring part of the worship service you attended most recently: The sermon? A prayer? The music? A greeting from someone?

14:26 Paul reiterates that each believer has a gift to offer during worship, that there are a variety of gifts, and that gifts are to be used to edify. **a hymn.** Singing is a gift. The reference here may be to "singing in the Spirit" (v. 15). **All of these.** Probably a representative list of the sort of gifts used during worship. The list is not exhaustive because it does not include, for example, prophecy or discernment of spirits.

14:29–33 Here he gives guidelines for prophecy: two or three speak, followed by discernment.

14:37–38 As to those who are teaching this, if they are really inspired by the Holy Spirit, they cannot help but agree. The Spirit does not inspire opposing messages.

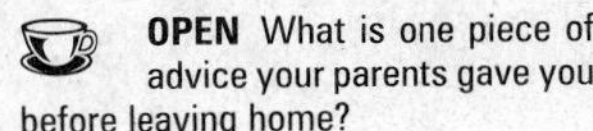

OPEN What is one piece of advice your parents gave you before leaving home?

STUDY 1. How had the Corinthians "taken their stand" (v. 1) on the gospel? **2.** What are the main points of the gospel Paul received and passed on to the Corinthians? **3.** How would you explain the importance of Christ's resurrection to a non-believer? **4.** Why do you think Paul went into such detail in listing who saw Jesus after he was resurrected?

APPLY 1. What does "Christ died for our sins" mean to you? How does the gospel affect your life on a daily basis? **2.** What evidence can you offer that Christ is alive in your life?

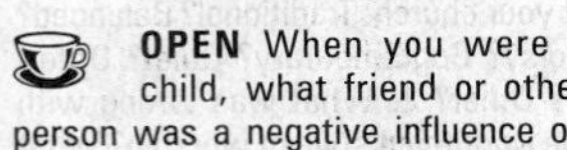

OPEN When you were a child, what friend or other person was a negative influence on you?

STUDY 1. How prevalent today is the philosophy Paul quotes in verse 32: "Let us eat and drink, for tomorrow we die"? **2.** What false teaching was being spread among the Corinthians (v. 12)? **3.** From this passage, what does Paul say would be true if there were no resurrection of the dead? **4.** Paul puts the resurrection in perspective with the Second Coming and the end of time. How does it make you feel that in the end Christ will be victorious? **5.** Paul says, "I die every day," referring to his willingness to sacrifice his present rights for the salvation of others (knowing he will be raised from the

The Resurrection of Christ

15 Now, brothers, I want to remind you of the gospel I preached to you, which you received and on which you have taken your stand. 2By this gospel you are saved, if you hold firmly to the word I preached to you. Otherwise, you have believed in vain.

3For what I received I passed on to you as of first importance[a]: that Christ died for our sins according to the Scriptures, 4that he was buried, that he was raised on the third day according to the Scriptures, 5and that he appeared to Peter,[b] and then to the Twelve. 6After that, he appeared to more than five hundred of the brothers at the same time, most of whom are still living, though some have fallen asleep. 7Then he appeared to James, then to all the apostles, 8and last of all he appeared to me also, as to one abnormally born.

9For I am the least of the apostles and do not even deserve to be called an apostle, because I persecuted the church of God. 10But by the grace of God I am what I am, and his grace to me was not without effect. No, I worked harder than all of them—yet not I, but the grace of God that was with me. 11Whether, then, it was I or they, this is what we preach, and this is what you believed.

The Resurrection of the Dead

12But if it is preached that Christ has been raised from the dead, how can some of you say that there is no resurrection of the dead? 13If there is no resurrection of the dead, then not even Christ has been raised. 14And if Christ has not been raised, our preaching is useless and so is your faith. 15More than that, we are then found to be false witnesses about God, for we have testified about God that he raised Christ from the dead. But he did not raise him if in fact the dead are not raised. 16For if the dead are not raised, then Christ has not been raised either. 17And if Christ has not been raised, your faith is futile; you are still in your sins. 18Then those also who have fallen asleep in Christ are lost. 19If only for this life we have hope in Christ, we are to be pitied more than all men.

20But Christ has indeed been raised from the dead, the firstfruits of those who have fallen asleep. 21For since death came through a man, the resurrection of the dead comes also through a man. 22For as in

[a]3 Or *you at the first* [b]5 Greek *Cephas*

15:4 he was buried. Jesus was really dead, and so he really rose from the dead. It was a real resurrection, not just resuscitation. **he was raised.** Paul shifts the tense of the verb (in Greek) from the aorist tense (completed past action—"died / buried") to the perfect tense, with the idea that what once happened is even now still in force.

15:6 to more than five hundred ... most of whom are still living. Paul is inviting people to check out for themselves the reality of Christ's resurrection. What he is saying is: "There are more than 500 people who some 20 years ago saw Jesus after his resurrection. Ask one of them."

15:8 last of all ... to me. This appearance came several years after the resurrection of Christ (Acts 9:1–8). **abnormally born.** This probably refers to the fact that, unlike Peter and James, circumstances were such that Paul never knew Jesus during his earthly ministry.

15:16 if the dead are not raised. This is the first of three times in this section (vv. 12–34) Paul uses this phrase which summarizes the implications of their errant view about the resurrection of the body. If the dead are not raised, then: (a) Christ could not have been resurrected (and they believe he was), (b) there would be no point in baptizing people for the dead (as they were apparently doing—v. 29), and (c) believers might as well "live it up," since they had no future (v. 32).

15:17–19 Relentlessly, Paul points out to his readers the implications of no resurrection: (a) they are still lost and dead in sin, (b) those who have died are lost, (c) their "hope" is groundless, and (d) they are pitiable people. Without the resurrection, Christianity crumbles.

15:20–28 The future resurrection of believers is the logical outcome of Christ's past resurrection. First Thessalonians 4:13–18 refers also to this future resurrection of believers.

Adam all die, so in Christ all will be made alive. 23But each in his own
turn: Christ, the firstfruits; then, when he comes, those who belong
to him. 24Then the end will come, when he hands over the kingdom to
God the Father after he has destroyed all dominion, authority and
power. 25For he must reign until he has put all his enemies under his
feet. 26The last enemy to be destroyed is death. 27For he "has put
everything under his feet."[a] Now when it says that "everything" has
been put under him, it is clear that this does not include God himself,
who put everything under Christ. 28When he has done this, then the
Son himself will be made subject to him who put everything under
him, so that God may be all in all.

29Now if there is no resurrection, what will those do who are baptized for the dead? If the dead are not raised at all, why are people
baptized for them? 30And as for us, why do we endanger ourselves
every hour? 31I die every day—I mean that, brothers—just as surely
as I glory over you in Christ Jesus our Lord. 32If I fought wild beasts in
Ephesus for merely human reasons, what have I gained? If the dead
are not raised,

> "Let us eat and drink,
> for tomorrow we die."[b]

33Do not be misled: "Bad company corrupts good character." 34Come
back to your senses as you ought, and stop sinning; for there are
some who are ignorant of God—I say this to your shame.

The Resurrection Body

35But someone may ask, "How are the dead raised? With what kind
of body will they come?" 36How foolish! What you sow does not come
to life unless it dies. 37When you sow, you do not plant the body that
will be, but just a seed, perhaps of wheat or of something else. 38But
God gives it a body as he has determined, and to each kind of seed he
gives its own body. 39All flesh is not the same: Men have one kind of
flesh, animals have another, birds another and fish another. 40There
are also heavenly bodies and there are earthly bodies; but the splendor of the heavenly bodies is one kind, and the splendor of the earthly bodies is another. 41The sun has one kind of splendor, the moon
another and the stars another; and star differs from star in splendor.
42So will it be with the resurrection of the dead. The body that is

[a]*27* Psalm 8:6 [b]*32* Isaiah 22:13

dead). In what ways do you "die every day"? **6.** What difference has Christ's resurrection and your resulting victory over death made to you in terms of hope and courage? In terms of purpose for life?

APPLY 1. Have you ever attended the funeral of a person who died as an atheist, without the anticipation of being with God and loved ones in heaven? **2.** Have you ever attended the funeral of someone who lived in the promise of the resurrection? What was the difference?

OPEN During what stage of your life did you change the most? How did you change?

STUDY 1. What do you believe happens to a person when he dies? **2.** What practical concerns undercut belief in the resurrection of the dead for some of the Corinthians (v. 35)? **3.** What are the characteristics of the resurrection body that followers of Christ will receive? **4.** How do the analogies of the seed and the different types of bodies deal with doubts about the resurrection of the dead (vv. 36–44)? **5.** What is the point of the comparison between Adam and Christ (vv. 21–22,45–49)?

15:23–28 Paul returns to the metaphor of the firstfruits, showing how it relates to the Second Coming. In order for the Corinthians to understand the future resurrection, Paul must place it in the context of the time when Christ returns.

15:29–34 Thus far, Paul has shown that there is a resurrection for believers in the future. Here he points out that both his actions and theirs demonstrate a belief in the resurrection of the dead.

15:29 baptized for the dead. It seems that among the strange things that happened at Corinth was the practice (by some) of vicarious baptism. A living person was immersed in water on behalf of a dead person to secure, as if by magic, the benefits of baptism for the departed friend.

15:36–38 Death brings change (transformation), not extinction. Here, Paul probes the nature of the transformation; his point being that what one plants (or buries) is not what one gets in the end. A small grain of wheat grows mysteriously into a tall, grain-bearing stalk (John 12:24). So, too, their bodies will yield new and glorious bodies after the resurrection.

15:39–41 A second analogy is used to show that there are a host of different kinds of bodies, and it is not unreasonable to expect the resurrection body to be quite different from the natural body.

15:42–44 Paul reinforces the idea of verse 36: what is sown in one way is raised in another. He makes this point by means of a series of antithetical comparisons: perishable/imperishable; dishonor/glory; weakness/power; natural/spiritual.

6. What is the sting of death? How did Jesus win the victory over death? How can you share in this victory? **7.** What insights in this passage about the life to come are most striking to you? What excites you? What puzzles you?

APPLY 1. What is most comforting when you consider the reality of your own death? What is hardest for you to understand? **2.** How does verse 58 encourage and motivate you?

sown is perishable, it is raised imperishable; 43it is sown in dishonor,
it is raised in glory; it is sown in weakness, it is raised in power; 44it is
sown a natural body, it is raised a spiritual body.
If there is a natural body, there is also a spiritual body. 45So it is
written: "The first man Adam became a living being"[a]; the last Adam,
a life-giving spirit. 46The spiritual did not come first, but the natural,
and after that the spiritual. 47The first man was of the dust of the
earth, the second man from heaven. 48As was the earthly man, so are
those who are of the earth; and as is the man from heaven, so also
are those who are of heaven. 49And just as we have borne the likeness
of the earthly man, so shall we[b] bear the likeness of the man from
heaven.
50I declare to you, brothers, that flesh and blood cannot inherit the
kingdom of God, nor does the perishable inherit the imperishable.
51Listen, I tell you a mystery: We will not all sleep, but we will all be
changed— 52in a flash, in the twinkling of an eye, at the last trumpet.
For the trumpet will sound, the dead will be raised imperishable, and
we will be changed. 53For the perishable must clothe itself with the
imperishable, and the mortal with immortality. 54When the perishable
has been clothed with the imperishable, and the mortal with immortality, then the saying that is written will come true: "Death has been
swallowed up in victory."[c]

55"Where, O death, is your victory?
Where, O death, is your sting?"[d]

56The sting of death is sin, and the power of sin is the law. 57But
thanks be to God! He gives us the victory through our Lord Jesus
Christ.
58Therefore, my dear brothers, stand firm. Let nothing move you.
Always give yourselves fully to the work of the Lord, because you
know that your labor in the Lord is not in vain.

[a]45 Gen. 2:7 [b]49 Some early manuscripts *so let us* [c]54 Isaiah 25:8 [d]55 Hosea 13:14

15:43 Paul now describes the nature of the changed body. The resurrection body is characterized by glory (brightness, radiance, splendor). This is a quality ascribed to God, in which believers will somehow share (Phil. 3:21).

15:44 natural ... spiritual. The natural body is that which is animated by the soul (the natural life force), while the spiritual body has as its animating force the Holy Spirit.

15:49 the man from heaven. This is Jesus, whose image Christians will reflect both in terms of character and glory.

15:50 flesh and blood. That is, living people cannot inherit the kingdom. **perishable.** Nor can the unchanged dead inherit the kingdom. What Paul is saying is that at the Second Coming neither the living nor the dead can take part in the kingdom without being changed.

15:51 mystery. A truth about the end times, once hidden but now revealed. **We.** Paul expected to be alive at the Second Coming. **not all sleep.** Some Christians will be alive at the Second Coming. **all be changed.** Both the living and the dead will be changed.

15:52 in a flash. This change will occur instantaneously. **the trumpet will sound.** The sounding of the trumpet was used to rally an army for action. This image is used to describe God's calling his people together (1 Thess. 4:16). **the dead will be raised.** Those who are in the grave at the Second Coming will be transformed, as will the living.

15:56 the power of sin is the law. By this Paul means that the Law of God has the unfortunate result of arousing sin within people. As he shows from his own example in Romans 7, the Law's command not to covet did not deliver him from covetousness but actually stirred him up to feel it all the more.

15:57 victory. In great joy, Paul exults in the fact that sin and the Law (that by which sin is made known) do not have the last word. Christ's death was a victory over sin and death.

15:58 stand firm. His letter is at an end; his chastening is finished, and so it is appropriate that he challenge them to allow this same Christ who has won victories for them to win victories through them. **your labor in the Lord is not in vain.** Because the resurrection is real, the future is secure and magnificent.

The Collection for God's People

16 Now about the collection for God's people: Do what I told the
Galatian churches to do. [2]On the first day of every week, each
one of you should set aside a sum of money in keeping with his
income, saving it up, so that when I come no collections will have to
be made. [3]Then, when I arrive, I will give letters of introduction to the
men you approve and send them with your gift to Jerusalem. [4]If it
seems advisable for me to go also, they will accompany me.

Personal Requests

[5]After I go through Macedonia, I will come to you—for I will be
going through Macedonia. [6]Perhaps I will stay with you awhile, or
even spend the winter, so that you can help me on my journey, wherever I go. [7]I do not want to see you now and make only a passing visit;
I hope to spend some time with you, if the Lord permits. [8]But I will
stay on at Ephesus until Pentecost, [9]because a great door for effective
work has opened to me, and there are many who oppose me.
[10]If Timothy comes, see to it that he has nothing to fear while he is
with you, for he is carrying on the work of the Lord, just as I am. [11]No
one, then, should refuse to accept him. Send him on his way in peace
so that he may return to me. I am expecting him along with the
brothers.
[12]Now about our brother Apollos: I strongly urged him to go to you
with the brothers. He was quite unwilling to go now, but he will go
when he has the opportunity.
[13]Be on your guard; stand firm in the faith; be men of courage; be
strong. [14]Do everything in love.
[15]You know that the household of Stephanas were the first converts in Achaia, and they have devoted themselves to the service of
the saints. I urge you, brothers, [16]to submit to such as these and to
everyone who joins in the work, and labors at it. [17]I was glad when
Stephanas, Fortunatus and Achaicus arrived, because they have supplied what was lacking from you. [18]For they refreshed my spirit and
yours also. Such men deserve recognition.

Final Greetings

[19]The churches in the province of Asia send you greetings. Aquila
and Priscilla[a] greet you warmly in the Lord, and so does the church
that meets at their house. [20]All the brothers here send you greetings.
Greet one another with a holy kiss.

[a] *19* Greek *Prisca,* a variant of *Priscilla*

OPEN 1. When you travel, do you like to plan things thoroughly, or just go and see what happens? **2.** In your family, who over-packs for a trip?

STUDY 1. What kind of collection did Paul ask of the Corinthians? **2.** After receiving this letter, how do you think the Corinthians felt about Paul's plan to visit them? Beneath all his corrective instruction, how do you think Paul felt about the Corinthians? **3.** How would you feel if, like Timothy, Paul was sending you to this church? **4.** What should the Corinthians imitate regarding Stephanas and the others (vv. 15–18)? **5.** Who in your life, or in this group, has helped to refresh your spirit?

APPLY 1. Which of Paul's concluding exhortations in verses 13–14 do you most need to apply in your life: "Be on your guard"? "Stand firm in the faith"? "Have courage"? "Be strong"? "Do everything in love"? **2.** As a member of your church and group, how has this letter helped you? Challenged you? In what way would you like to grow from here?

16:1 the collection. When in Jerusalem, Paul had agreed to help support the poor there (Gal. 2:10). In this way, the Gentile and the Jewish wings of the church would be bound together in a new fashion.

16:2 On the first day. Sunday, when Christians met for worship. **set aside.** Paul is not calling for a collection to be taken each Sunday for his purpose. Rather, he asks individual Christians to set aside funds on their own. **no collections will have to be made.** Paul hoped that each person would have a sum of money set aside, ready to hand over when he came, so that he would not have to bother with the time-consuming process of taking a collection.

16:20 a holy kiss. This was a custom used in the early church as part of the worship service. Kisses were a common form of greeting in biblical times.

[21]I, Paul, write this greeting in my own hand.
[22]If anyone does not love the Lord—a curse be on him. Come,
O Lord[a]!
[23]The grace of the Lord Jesus be with you.
[24]My love to all of you in Christ Jesus. Amen.[b]

[a]22 In Aramaic the expression *Come, O Lord* is *Maranatha.* [b]24 Some manuscripts do not have *Amen.*

16:22 a curse be on him. Some in Corinth had pronounced a curse upon Jesus (12:3). Paul reverses that here and calls for God's judgment upon those who fail to love Jesus and, by implication, follow him. The Lord is then invoked as a witness to the judgment. **Come, O Lord!** This is an Aramaic expression, *Maranatha,* transliterated by Paul into Greek (Rev. 22:20). This was an expression used by the early Christians that Christ would soon return. The Lord's return would mark the moment when the curse on those who had refused to love him would be put into effect.

2 Corinthians

Author. The apostle Paul was the writer of 2 Corinthians.

Date. Paul wrote this letter around A.D. 55–56.

Theme. The strength of weakness.

Personal Reading	Group Study Topic and Reading	
1:1–2:4	God's Comfort	1:1–11
2:5–3:6	An Aroma of Life	2:12–3:6
3:7–18	The New Covenant	3:7–18
4:1–18	Our Treasure	4:1–18
5:1–6:2	Reconciliation	5:11–6:2
6:3–7:1	Be Separate!	6:14–7:1
7:2–16	Peace Restored	7:2–16
8:1–24	Our Giving	8:1–15
9:1–15	God's Giving	9:6–15
10:1–18	Paul's Defense	10:1–18
11:1–33	Paul's Credentials	11:16–33
12:1–21	Paul's Vision	12:1–10
13:1–14	True Power	13:1–14

Historical Background. Paul's first visit to Corinth took place during his second missionary journey. It was then that he founded the Corinthian church. It seems that his second visit to the city was the cause of much trouble and the reason he wrote 2 Corinthians.

This second visit had been promised in 1 Corinthians 16:1–9. Paul wrote that he would leave Ephesus, journey to Macedonia, and then come down to Corinth on his way to Jerusalem with the collection. As the time drew near to the trip, Paul changed to "Plan B," in which he went straight to Corinth, intending to go from there up to Macedonia and then back to Corinth once again. He thought this would bring the believers in Corinth great pleasure, since he would be with them twice instead of just once (1:15–16). Instead, his unexpected visit proved so painful (because of a conflict with false teachers), that he canceled his return trip from Macedonia. Instead he went back to Ephesus, then north again to Troas, and finally back once more to Macedonia. In Macedonia, he wrote 2 Corinthians to prepare them for a third visit.

Reconstructing the events surrounding the writing of 2 Corinthians is further complicated because Paul wrote two other letters to the Corinthians. One letter is what we know as 1 Corinthians and the other letter was lost (1 Cor. 5:9–13)

Paul's New Opponents. Who, then opposed Paul with such vigor during his second "painful" visit? The best guess is that the troublemakers were not from the Corinthian church itself. Rather, they were a band of outside "apostles" (called cynically by Paul "super-apostles" in 11:5 and 12:11), probably Jews from Palestine who sought to conform the Corinthian church to Jewish Law. In any case, they attacked Paul vigorously, calling him two-faced (10:1–11); they questioned his credentials as an apostle. Apparently Paul's real pain came because the Corinthians did not rally to his support in this conflict.

Paul's Response. Not only is Paul's pain evident in this letter, but also his toughness. He was willing to fight tooth and nail to wrest the Corinthians from the corrupting influence of the false apostles. The reason for his tenacity is found in the strength of his calling. He was an apostle—called by God to bring men and women into the kingdom. No band of petty pretenders was going to defeat him in that God-given purpose. He was an apostle and so, of course, he had to write as he did.

1 Paul, an apostle of Christ Jesus by the will of God, and Timothy our brother,

To the church of God in Corinth, together with all the saints throughout Achaia:

2 Grace and peace to you from God our Father and the Lord Jesus Christ.

The God of All Comfort

3 Praise be to the God and Father of our Lord Jesus Christ, the Father of compassion and the God of all comfort, 4 who comforts us in all our troubles, so that we can comfort those in any trouble with the comfort we ourselves have received from God. 5 For just as the sufferings of Christ flow over into our lives, so also through Christ our comfort overflows. 6 If we are distressed, it is for your comfort and salvation; if we are comforted, it is for your comfort, which produces in you patient endurance of the same sufferings we suffer. 7 And our hope for you is firm, because we know that just as you share in our sufferings, so also you share in our comfort.

8 We do not want you to be uninformed, brothers, about the hardships we suffered in the province of Asia. We were under great pressure, far beyond our ability to endure, so that we despaired even of life. 9 Indeed, in our hearts we felt the sentence of death. But this happened that we might not rely on ourselves but on God, who raises the dead. 10 He has delivered us from such a deadly peril, and he will deliver us. On him we have set our hope that he will continue to deliver us, 11 as you help us by your prayers. Then many will give thanks on our[a] behalf for the gracious favor granted us in answer to the prayers of many.

Paul's Change of Plans

12 Now this is our boast: Our conscience testifies that we have conducted ourselves in the world, and especially in our relations with

[a] *11* Many manuscripts *your*

OPEN 1. How are you at writing "difficult" letters? **2.** When you were a child, who did you go to with a hurt finger? What did they do to make it better?

STUDY 1. If you were Paul and people had come into a church you planted and turned some of the people in the church against you, what would you do? **2.** How would you describe the way Paul starts off his letter: Upbeat? Loving? Joyous? Pastoral? Stoic? Tough? Other? **3.** According to Paul who can comfort another person that is going through tough times? Have you found this to be true? **4.** How does Paul look upon pain, hardship, suffering and near-death experiences? What is the closest you've come to experiencing pressure "far beyond" your ability to endure? Are you more likely to feel crushed by physical stress or emotional heartache?

APPLY 1. On a scale from 1 to 10, what is the stress level in your life right now? **2.** What have you found helpful when you feel you can't take it anymore?

OPEN 1. Between your parents, which one never changed their mind after making a decision—good or bad? **2.** In your

1:1 an apostle of Christ Jesus by the will of God. While this is a stock phrase Paul often used to identify himself (1 Cor. 1:1; Eph. 1:1; Col. 1:1; 2 Tim. 1:1), in this letter the title takes on special force since it is precisely Paul's apostleship that is being called into question. **Timothy.** Timothy was Paul's coworker and colleague who also had been involved with the Corinthian church as well (Acts 18:5; 1 Cor. 4:17; 16:10). **Achaia.** Roughly equivalent to what today is southern Greece, Achaia was the Roman province of which Corinth was the capital city.

1:3–11 While typically Paul's letters begin with a thanksgiving for the people to whom he is writing (Rom. 1:8–10; 1 Cor. 1:4–8), here he gives thanks to God for deliverance from a specific situation that threatened to crush him. This expression of thanks introduces a major theme that Paul will develop throughout the letter, namely the place of suffering and hardship. Before they assume this disqualifies him, they ought to remember how his sufferings have benefited them (vv. 4–7).

1:4 our troubles. Literally, "our trials." This includes both the internal anguish and the physical hardships that Christians experience because of following Jesus. **so that we can comfort.** The purpose of God's aid is to enable those so helped to aid others who are afflicted.

1:5 the sufferings of Christ. Those who follow Christ share in his sufferings. Rejection, injustice and bearing the affliction of others are all common experiences for the Christian. **our comfort overflows.** In the same way that the sufferings of Christ led to benefits that overflow to his people, so the sufferings of Christians enable them to better help others who are afflicted.

1:6 comfort ... sufferings. Whether experiencing distress or comfort, the aim of these situations is to equip Paul to work for the salvation of others. **patient endurance.** This is not grim, bleak acceptance of difficulties, but a hopeful steadfastness in the midst of trial.

1:8 the hardships. Acts has no record of what was obviously an extremely difficult experience for Paul in Asia. Some commentators think it may refer to the imprisonment mentioned in Philippians 1:12–20 where Paul was not certain whether he would live or die. **Asia.** This was the Roman province located in the western part of modern Turkey. Ephesus was its leading city. **great pressure.** This is to be weighed down like an overloaded ship.

1:12 Paul begins the defense of his

you, in the holiness and sincerity that are from God. We have done so
not according to worldly wisdom but according to God's grace. 13For
we do not write you anything you cannot read or understand. And I
hope that, 14as you have understood us in part, you will come to understand fully that you can boast of us just as we will boast of you in
the day of the Lord Jesus.

15Because I was confident of this, I planned to visit you first so that
you might benefit twice. 16I planned to visit you on my way to Macedonia and to come back to you from Macedonia, and then to have
you send me on my way to Judea. 17When I planned this, did I do it
lightly? Or do I make my plans in a worldly manner so that in the
same breath I say, "Yes, yes" and "No, no"?

18But as surely as God is faithful, our message to you is not "Yes"
and "No." 19For the Son of God, Jesus Christ, who was preached
among you by me and Silas[a] and Timothy, was not "Yes" and "No,"
but in him it has always been "Yes." 20For no matter how many promises God has made, they are "Yes" in Christ. And so through him the
"Amen" is spoken by us to the glory of God. 21Now it is God who
makes both us and you stand firm in Christ. He anointed us, 22set his
seal of ownership on us, and put his Spirit in our hearts as a deposit,
guaranteeing what is to come.

23I call God as my witness that it was in order to spare you that I did
not return to Corinth. 24Not that we lord it over your faith, but we
work with you for your joy, because it is by faith you stand firm.

2 1So I made up my mind that I would not make another painful
visit to you. 2For if I grieve you, who is left to make me glad but
you whom I have grieved? 3I wrote as I did so that when I came I
should not be distressed by those who ought to make me rejoice. I
had confidence in all of you, that you would all share my joy. 4For I
wrote you out of great distress and anguish of heart and with many
tears, not to grieve you but to let you know the depth of my love for
you.

[a]19 Greek *Silvanus*, a variant of *Silas*

group who deserves an Oscar for the worst sense of humor?

STUDY **1.** From the Introduction to this book, who are the "opponents" that are questioning the integrity of Paul? What are the opponents accusing Paul of (10:1–11; 11:5; 12:1)? **2.** Reading between the lines what are the opponents trying to do to Paul's ministry in Corinth? What is Paul's reason for changing his plans? If you have to confront someone, would you do it by letter or in person? What do you think was the tone of the letter (v. 3) that he wrote to the church about the one who caused the "grief"? How did it affect Paul (v. 4)? **3.** What does Paul want the church in Corinth to do to him now? Why? **4.** What is the lesson here for the church today for the discipline and restoration of those who have fallen? Have you ever been in a Christian community that had to discipline one of its leaders? If you had to do it all over again, would you do it differently? **5.** How does Galatians 6:1–5 serve as a word of caution?

APPLY **1.** What is the closest you have come to having someone make a direct attack on your integrity? How did you deal with this? **2.** Who are you accountable to for spiritual discipline and correction when you need it?

integrity by pointing out that he has nothing to be ashamed of—despite this criticism of him. **boast.** Literally, "confidence." Paul uses this word (or a derivative of it) 29 times in this letter. This may be in response to the "boasting" done by the itinerant teachers who were promoting themselves over him. **especially in our relations with you.** Paul had taken great pains to act with integrity toward the Corinthians: he took no payment from them (11:7–9); he went to great lengths to ensure that the collection for the needy in Jerusalem was not misappropriated (1 Cor. 16:1–4). **sincerity.** The Corinthians have charged him with duplicity. On the contrary, he says, his actions were characterized throughout by sincerity. **worldly wisdom.** Such "wisdom" guides one's actions in the ways of self-interest or self-promotion. In contrast, Paul focused on God and the needs of others.

1:15–16 Paul addresses the charge that he was unreliable. He had written that he intended to go to Macedonia and then to Corinth (1 Cor. 16:5–9). However, perhaps in response to a report from Timothy (1 Cor. 16:10–11), he changed his plans and visited Corinth first, sooner than expected. His intention at the time was to go from there to Macedonia and then return to Corinth again. However, since this unexpected visit was so difficult (2:1), he returned to Ephesus and wrote another letter (now lost) to Corinth (2:1–4). Then he went to Macedonia and chose not to return to Corinth at all (v. 23). The changes in Paul's plans opened the way for him to be charged as being untrustworthy.

1:19 Silas and Timothy. Paul's co-workers in Corinth during his original trip (Acts 18:5). **Yes.** The sending of Jesus, God's Son, is God's guarantee to humanity that he is for us; that he will fulfill all his promises; that he can be trusted absolutely.

2:3 I wrote. Paul was in a bind. If he came again as proposed, he would cause pain. If he didn't come, he would be charged with fickleness. **I should not be distressed.** Paul is concerned both that they will be grieved by another visit (vv. 1–2) and that he too will find it painful. His fear, perhaps, is that indeed they had been subverted by the false teachers and had embraced a false gospel.

Forgiveness for the Sinner

5If anyone has caused grief, he has not so much grieved me as he
has grieved all of you, to some extent—not to put it too severely. 6The
punishment inflicted on him by the majority is sufficient for him.
7Now instead, you ought to forgive and comfort him, so that he will
not be overwhelmed by excessive sorrow. 8I urge you, therefore, to
reaffirm your love for him. 9The reason I wrote you was to see if you
would stand the test and be obedient in everything. 10If you forgive
anyone, I also forgive him. And what I have forgiven—if there was
anything to forgive—I have forgiven in the sight of Christ for your
sake, 11in order that Satan might not outwit us. For we are not unaware of his schemes.

Ministers of the New Covenant

12Now when I went to Troas to preach the gospel of Christ and
found that the Lord had opened a door for me, 13I still had no peace
of mind, because I did not find my brother Titus there. So I said good-
by to them and went on to Macedonia.

14But thanks be to God, who always leads us in triumphal procession in Christ and through us spreads everywhere the fragrance of
the knowledge of him. 15For we are to God the aroma of Christ among
those who are being saved and those who are perishing. 16To the one
we are the smell of death; to the other, the fragrance of life. And who
is equal to such a task? 17Unlike so many, we do not peddle the word
of God for profit. On the contrary, in Christ we speak before God with
sincerity, like men sent from God.

3 Are we beginning to commend ourselves again? Or do we need,
like some people, letters of recommendation to you or from you?
2You yourselves are our letter, written on our hearts, known and read
by everybody. 3You show that you are a letter from Christ, the result of
our ministry, written not with ink but with the Spirit of the living God,
not on tablets of stone but on tablets of human hearts.

4Such confidence as this is ours through Christ before God. 5Not
that we are competent in ourselves to claim anything for ourselves,
but our competence comes from God. 6He has made us competent as
ministers of a new covenant—not of the letter but of the Spirit; for
the letter kills, but the Spirit gives life.

OPEN What is the most memorable parade you've seen or taken part in?

STUDY 1. Until Titus returns with "good news" (7:6–13), Paul has "no peace of mind" (2:13): What does that say about Paul's concern for this church? **2.** How can the same Gospel be either the smell of death or the fragrance of life? **3.** What might be happening in Corinth (2:17–3:1)? Although preachers often had letters of recommendation when they traveled to new areas (3 John 5–8), why does Paul need no such letter? **4.** Why should the Corinthians listen to Paul (1:1–3:6)?

APPLY 1. Who attracted you to Christ? **2.** How does it make you feel that you are the only "Bible" that some of the people in your world read?

2:5 he has grieved all of you. While Paul might have been his target, in fact the whole community was harmed by his actions.

2:7–10 Reproof delivered, it is now time to forgive and to restore.

2:11 schemes. Satan attempted to undermine the church through division: having been thwarted in that move through the church's reproof of the individual, his next strategy was to encourage the church to reject this person. Forgiveness and restoration would counter this threat.

2:12–13 Leaving Corinth as a result of the painful incident, Paul went to Macedonia, then to Ephesus, and then to Troas (a city 150 miles north of Ephesus). Finally, he returned to Macedonia.

2:13 Titus. Although not mentioned in Acts, Titus traveled with Paul and was entrusted with several important missions.

2:14 leads us in triumphal procession. This phrase may simply mean "displays us," or it may refer to the Roman practice of a general leading a victory march with those he had conquered following behind.

3:1 letters of recommendation. It was common for itinerant teachers to get such letters as a means of introducing and validating their work in a new area.

3:6 new covenant. A covenant is an agreement initiated and defined by God between himself and his people. This covenant is quite different from the old one. It was prophesied by Jeremiah (Jer. 31:31–34). **letter ... Spirit.** Letter refers to the words of the Law; Spirit is the Holy Spirit.

The Glory of the New Covenant

[7]Now if the ministry that brought death, which was engraved in letters on stone, came with glory, so that the Israelites could not look steadily at the face of Moses because of its glory, fading though it was, [8]will not the ministry of the Spirit be even more glorious? [9]If the ministry that condemns men is glorious, how much more glorious is the ministry that brings righteousness! [10]For what was glorious has no glory now in comparison with the surpassing glory. [11]And if what was fading away came with glory, how much greater is the glory of that which lasts!

[12]Therefore, since we have such a hope, we are very bold. [13]We are not like Moses, who would put a veil over his face to keep the Israelites from gazing at it while the radiance was fading away. [14]But their minds were made dull, for to this day the same veil remains when the old covenant is read. It has not been removed, because only in Christ is it taken away. [15]Even to this day when Moses is read, a veil covers their hearts. [16]But whenever anyone turns to the Lord, the veil is taken away. [17]Now the Lord is the Spirit, and where the Spirit of the Lord is, there is freedom. [18]And we, who with unveiled faces all reflect[a] the Lord's glory, are being transformed into his likeness with ever-increasing glory, which comes from the Lord, who is the Spirit.

Treasures in Jars of Clay

4 Therefore, since through God's mercy we have this ministry, we do not lose heart. [2]Rather, we have renounced secret and shameful ways; we do not use deception, nor do we distort the word of God. On the contrary, by setting forth the truth plainly we commend ourselves to every man's conscience in the sight of God. [3]And even if our gospel is veiled, it is veiled to those who are perishing. [4]The god of this age has blinded the minds of unbelievers, so that they cannot see the light of the gospel of the glory of Christ, who is the image of God. [5]For we do not preach ourselves, but Jesus Christ as Lord, and ourselves as your servants for Jesus' sake. [6]For God, who said, "Let light shine out of darkness,"[b] made his light shine in our hearts to give us the light of the knowledge of the glory of God in the face of Christ.

[7]But we have this treasure in jars of clay to show that this all-surpassing power is from God and not from us. [8]We are hard pressed

[a]18 Or *contemplate* [b]6 Gen. 1:3

OPEN **1.** Which one of your parents do you resemble in looks? In temperament? **2.** As your parents get older, do you think they are starting to think and look alike?

STUDY **1.** What do you remember about the story of Moses and the radiance on his face when he spent 40 days with God on Mount Sinai to receive the Ten Commandments? **2.** What is the point that Paul makes here when he contrasts the old and new covenants? **3.** How would you explain verse 18 to a 12-year old? Is the transformation Paul talks about here an instantaneous thing or a process?

APPLY If you had to describe the transformation Christ is doing in your life, what two adjectives would you use to describe where you are today?

OPEN **1.** When you were growing up, when did your family use the "best" china? **2.** What do you treasure because it was passed on to you by someone you love?

STUDY **1.** Reading between the lines, what tactics have the critics of Paul used to undermine his ministry in Corinth? How does Paul answer this attack? **2.** What do you learn about Paul's style of sharing his faith? His message? His leadership style? **3.** What does he say about those who refused to listen? **4.** What is the point in the "jars of clay" illustration that Paul wants to emphasize? How would you describe Paul's circumstances and his temperament in verses 7–12? **5.** What is Paul's attitude toward the possibility that his life will soon be over? **6.** What's the

---

3:7 glory. This refers to the radiance in Moses' face that reflected God's presence when he came down from Mount Sinai.

3:12–13 Paul's point is not that he is superior to Moses. Rather, he simply uses the thought of Moses' veiling himself as a contrast with his open approach to ministry. While Moses hid the diminishing glory of the old covenant behind the veil, Paul hides nothing of the permanent glory of the covenant of the Spirit.

3:13 a veil. To cover one's face or head was to hide something or a sign of shame; to unveil the head and face was to be completely open and bold.

3:14–16 Paul now uses the veil of Moses as an illustration to describe why those who hold to the old covenant are unable to see the glory of the new. Their minds and hearts are only unveiled (and thus able to see) when they turn to the Lord.

3:18 reflect. As believers see the glory of God in Jesus (who is the image of God—4:4,6), they are themselves continually being transformed by that encounter such that they will ultimately reflect the character and glory of Jesus (Rom. 8:29; Phil. 3:21).

4:8–10 God's power is seen, not in that Paul rides above suffering, but that in the midst of suffering he is continually sustained by God. The hardships experienced by the apostles reflect the opposition and, ultimately, the death (v. 10) experienced by Jesus (Rom. 8:17; Phil. 3:10). The ministry of the glory of the gospel requires its messengers to share in the suffering of the cross.

4:8 hard pressed. The affliction (the idea behind this word) was real but not fatal (he was not "crushed").

challenge to the people in Corinth and the church today in verses 16–18? How would you compare the way Paul looked upon the aging process with the attitudes today?

APPLY 1. How do you look upon the aging process? Is this something you look forward to or something you don't want to think about? **2.** Are you more concerned about your physical well being or your spiritual well being?

OPEN What is the toughest challenge you have had to face in your life?

STUDY 1. How does Paul look upon death?? **2.** When Paul uses the word "groan," what is he referring to? When you use the same word, what are you referring to? **3.** Does Paul have a financial retirement plan for his life?

APPLY 1. How would you like to spend your final years? Would you rather spend your final years around your children or in a retirement center? **2.** As you get older and your body starts to groan, do you find yourself thinking more about God or more about your health?

on every side, but not crushed; perplexed, but not in despair; 9perse-
cuted, but not abandoned; struck down, but not destroyed. 10We always carry around in our body the death of Jesus, so that the life of
Jesus may also be revealed in our body. 11For we who are alive are always being given over to death for Jesus' sake, so that his life may be
revealed in our mortal body. 12So then, death is at work in us, but life
is at work in you.
13It is written: "I believed; therefore I have spoken."[a] With that
same spirit of faith we also believe and therefore speak, 14because we
know that the one who raised the Lord Jesus from the dead will also
raise us with Jesus and present us with you in his presence. 15All this
is for your benefit, so that the grace that is reaching more and more
people may cause thanksgiving to overflow to the glory of God.
16Therefore we do not lose heart. Though outwardly we are wasting away, yet inwardly we are being renewed day by day. 17For our
light and momentary troubles are achieving for us an eternal glory
that far outweighs them all. 18So we fix our eyes not on what is seen,
but on what is unseen. For what is seen is temporary, but what is
unseen is eternal.

Our Heavenly Dwelling

5 Now we know that if the earthly tent we live in is destroyed, we
have a building from God, an eternal house in heaven, not built
by human hands. 2Meanwhile we groan, longing to be clothed with
our heavenly dwelling, 3because when we are clothed, we will not be
found naked. 4For while we are in this tent, we groan and are burdened, because we do not wish to be unclothed but to be clothed
with our heavenly dwelling, so that what is mortal may be swallowed
up by life. 5Now it is God who has made us for this very purpose and
has given us the Spirit as a deposit, guaranteeing what is to come.
6Therefore we are always confident and know that as long as we
are at home in the body we are away from the Lord. 7We live by faith,
not by sight. 8We are confident, I say, and would prefer to be away
from the body and at home with the Lord. 9So we make it our goal to
please him, whether we are at home in the body or away from it. 10For
we must all appear before the judgment seat of Christ, that each one
may receive what is due him for the things done while in the body,
whether good or bad.

[a] *13* Psalm 116:10

4:9 persecuted. The opposition Paul faced—both from Jewish and Gentile sources—was very real and very intense; yet in it all, God enabled him to prevail. **struck down.** Even when the blow was overwhelming, Paul was preserved by God.

4:12 Paul absorbs the brunt of the persecution (as a key leader in the Christian *movement) so that the church might be* able to thrive (Col. 1:24).

4:16 we do not lose heart. Paul again states his confidence in his ministry (v. 1).

4:18 fix our eyes. This is a dedicated striving, like a runner pursuing the goal (Heb. 12:1–2). The prize for a race, in ancient times, was placed at the end of the race, so the runners could focus upon it and so it would motivate them to win. Paul is calling on Christians to focus on the unseen rewards of the kingdom. **seen ... unseen.** Christians are not to shape their lives on the basis of *visible* standards of success (5:12), but in light of Christ's kingdom.

5:1 the earthly tent. The tent, as a temporary home, is a metaphor for the mortal body which is destroyed by suffering, weakness and, finally, death. **building ... house.** A heavenly building was a common apocalyptic image representing *all* the fullness of God's kingdom (Rev. 21:2). In this case Paul refers to our resurrected, transformed bodies.

5:10 the judgment seat of Christ. This is the specific evaluation of believers in the end times during which rewards are given or withheld. The judgment of unbelievers is at the "great white throne" (Rev. 20:11–15).

The Ministry of Reconciliation

11 Since, then, we know what it is to fear the Lord, we try to persuade men. What we are is plain to God, and I hope it is also plain to
your conscience. 12 We are not trying to commend ourselves to you
again, but are giving you an opportunity to take pride in us, so that
you can answer those who take pride in what is seen rather than in
what is in the heart. 13 If we are out of our mind, it is for the sake of
God; if we are in our right mind, it is for you. 14 For Christ's love compels us, because we are convinced that one died for all, and therefore
all died. 15 And he died for all, that those who live should no longer live
for themselves but for him who died for them and was raised again.

16 So from now on we regard no one from a worldly point of view.
Though we once regarded Christ in this way, we do so no longer.
17 Therefore, if anyone is in Christ, he is a new creation; the old has
gone, the new has come! 18 All this is from God, who reconciled us to
himself through Christ and gave us the ministry of reconciliation:
19 that God was reconciling the world to himself in Christ, not counting men's sins against them. And he has committed to us the message of reconciliation. 20 We are therefore Christ's ambassadors, as
though God were making his appeal through us. We implore you on
Christ's behalf: Be reconciled to God. 21 God made him who had no
sin to be sin[a] for us, so that in him we might become the righteousness of God.

6 As God's fellow workers we urge you not to receive God's grace
in vain. 2 For he says,

> "In the time of my favor I heard you,
> and in the day of salvation I helped you."[b]

I tell you, now is the time of God's favor, now is the day of salvation.

Paul's Hardships

3 We put no stumbling block in anyone's path, so that our ministry
will not be discredited. 4 Rather, as servants of God we commend ourselves in every way: in great endurance; in troubles, hardships and
distresses; 5 in beatings, imprisonments and riots; in hard work,

[a]21 Or *be a sin offering* [b]2 Isaiah 49:8

OPEN If you were appointed as an ambassador, where would you like to be sent?

STUDY 1. What is Paul's motivation for continuing in his ministry? How does this compare to the motives of those who are attacking Paul (v. 12; 2:17)? **2.** How does Paul answer the insinuation that he is mentally unstable? If Paul were around today, what would a psychiatrist say about his compulsiveness? **3.** How would you paraphrase verse 17 into everyday terms? How does this make you feel about the mistakes in your past life? How often do you have to remind yourself that you are a new creation—that God "don't make junk"? **4.** How would you explain the word "reconciliation"? What's the challenge for someone who has been reconciled?

APPLY Have you experienced being a "new creation" in Christ? What differences did you notice in your life?

OPEN Do you have a low or high threshold for pain? Are you better at enduring physical pain or relational pain?

STUDY 1. How do you think Paul's opponents felt when this part of the letter was read aloud

---

5:14 one died for all. This (v. 15) is an adaptation of a creedal statement (Rom. 5:8; 1 Cor. 15:3; 1 Thess. 5:10). On this basis, Paul asserts that "therefore all (in Christ) have died." They can no longer be evaluated on the basis of an old, worldly standard (1:12,17; 5:12,16–). **all died.** In the sense that when Christ died he opened up a new way of life to everyone. They could be free from the Law, sin and death—and instead live for Christ. They could die to the old life of futility and self-centeredness.

5:17 in Christ. A favorite phrase of Paul's, signifying the union of the believer with Jesus Christ and hence with Jesus' death and resurrection; it is by this union that the believer enters into new life. **a new creation.** To be in Christ is to be new. A believer has died to the old life and is raised to a whole new sphere of existence by this act of creation.

5:19 the message of reconciliation. All the work of reconciliation has been done. Now it is simply a matter of people accepting the finished work of Christ.

5:20 ambassadors. In Roman territories considered dangerous and not fully loyal, the key administrator was the ambassador. He was a direct representative of the emperor. Ambassadors were also those individuals who arranged the terms of peace between a hostile country and Rome. Paul, therefore, understands his role to be that of one acting on behalf of God's offer of reconciliation and peace to a hostile, alienated people. **We implore you.** Reconciliation will not take place until the offer is accepted; hence the urgency of Paul's appeal.

5:21 him who had no sin. A key to Christ's power to reconcile is his own lack of sin (John 8:46; Rom. 8:3; Heb. 4:15). **to be sin for us.** Because he had no sin of his own he could therefore bear the sins of others. He exchanges his righteousness for our sin. He stood in relationship to God as we ought to have: cut off and the object of wrath.

6:5 hard work. Paul generally earned

to the congregation? **2.** If Paul is going to be judged by his critics, what does he offer as a measurement list? **3.** Would you consider Paul a success by your standards of success? Would Paul be chosen as the "man of the year" in your community?

APPLY How do you want to be judged by your family, your friends and God?

OPEN What was the rule in your family about dating those outside of the faith?

STUDY 1. In the context of verses 3–13, who do you think Paul is referring to as "unbelievers": those who do not believe in Christ or those who claim they believe in Christ but do not back it up with their life? From your experience, which group is more likely to contaminate (7:1) the Christian community? **2.** How far would you carry verse 14 in choosing a: Spouse? Close friend? Business partner?

APPLY What is the closest you have come to being "yoked" in a situation where you were asked to compromise your standards or beliefs as a Christian?

sleepless nights and hunger; [6]in purity, understanding, patience and kindness; in the Holy Spirit and in sincere love; [7]in truthful speech and in the power of God; with weapons of righteousness in the right hand and in the left; [8]through glory and dishonor, bad report and good report; genuine, yet regarded as impostors; [9]known, yet regarded as unknown; dying, and yet we live on; beaten, and yet not killed; [10]sorrowful, yet always rejoicing; poor, yet making many rich; having nothing, and yet possessing everything.

[11]We have spoken freely to you, Corinthians, and opened wide our hearts to you. [12]We are not withholding our affection from you, but you are withholding yours from us. [13]As a fair exchange—I speak as to my children—open wide your hearts also.

Do Not Be Yoked With Unbelievers

[14]Do not be yoked together with unbelievers. For what do righteousness and wickedness have in common? Or what fellowship can light have with darkness? [15]What harmony is there between Christ and Belial[a]? What does a believer have in common with an unbeliever? [16]What agreement is there between the temple of God and idols? For we are the temple of the living God. As God has said: "I will live with them and walk among them, and I will be their God, and they will be my people."[b]

[17]"Therefore come out from them
and be separate,
says the Lord.

Touch no unclean thing,
and I will receive you."[c]
[18]"I will be a Father to you,
and you will be my sons and daughters,
says the Lord Almighty."[d]

7 Since we have these promises, dear friends, let us purify ourselves from everything that contaminates body and spirit, perfecting holiness out of reverence for God.

[a]*15* Greek *Beliar,* a variant of *Belial* [b]*16* Lev. 26:12; Jer. 32:38; Ezek. 37:27 [c]*17* Isaiah 52:11; Ezek. 20:34,41 [d]*18* 2 Samuel 7:14; 7:8

his own living, toiling to the point of exhaustion. **sleepless nights and hunger.** His hardships led to physical deprivation.

6:6 in the Holy Spirit. Paul demonstrated the presence of the Spirit in his life through the qualities of love, kindness, etc. (Gal. 5:22–23). **sincere love.** This is an active goodwill toward others.

6:7 truthful speech. Literally, "the message of truth," another shorthand *way of referring to the gospel.* **weapons.** A Roman soldier carried a spear or sword in his right hand and a shield in his left. Likewise, Paul was fully equipped with God's righteousness to minister.

6:8 glory and dishonor ... bad report and good report. Neither rejection nor praise distracted him from his ministry (1 Cor. 4:12–13; 1 Thess. 2:2). **impostors.** This begins a series of contrasts in which Paul renounces the charges that have been made against him.

6:9 known, yet regarded as unknown. While some did not recognize Paul as a legitimate apostle, God and the Corinthians knew his genuineness (5:11).

6:10 poor, yet making many rich. While financially poor, Paul gave others the gift of life in Christ. This too reflects the ministry of Jesus (8:9). **possessing everything.** Though in this life he may have nothing, the fullness of God's kingdom is given to him (Luke 6:20; 1 Cor. 3:21–23).

6:14 yoked together. The idea of the double yoke has Old Testament roots, as in Deuteronomy 22:10 where it is forbidden to put an ox and a donkey in the same harness. The point is that the fundamental incompatibility of an ox and a donkey would make it impossible to plow in a straight line. This is also true for believers and unbelievers.

6:15 Belial. This name for Satan, not used elsewhere in the New Testament, is common in the writings from Qumran.

Paul's Joy

[2]Make room for us in your hearts. We have wronged no one, we have corrupted no one, we have exploited no one. [3]I do not say this to condemn you; I have said before that you have such a place in our hearts that we would live or die with you. [4]I have great confidence in you; I take great pride in you. I am greatly encouraged; in all our troubles my joy knows no bounds.

[5]For when we came into Macedonia, this body of ours had no rest, but we were harassed at every turn—conflicts on the outside, fears within. [6]But God, who comforts the downcast, comforted us by the coming of Titus, [7]and not only by his coming but also by the comfort you had given him. He told us about your longing for me, your deep sorrow, your ardent concern for me, so that my joy was greater than ever.

[8]Even if I caused you sorrow by my letter, I do not regret it. Though I did regret it—I see that my letter hurt you, but only for a little while— [9]yet now I am happy, not because you were made sorry, but because your sorrow led you to repentance. For you became sorrowful as God intended and so were not harmed in any way by us. [10]Godly sorrow brings repentance that leads to salvation and leaves no regret, but worldly sorrow brings death. [11]See what this godly sorrow has produced in you: what earnestness, what eagerness to clear yourselves, what indignation, what alarm, what longing, what concern, what readiness to see justice done. At every point you have proved yourselves to be innocent in this matter. [12]So even though I wrote to you, it was not on account of the one who did the wrong or of the injured party, but rather that before God you could see for yourselves how devoted to us you are. [13]By all this we are encouraged.

In addition to our own encouragement, we were especially delighted to see how happy Titus was, because his spirit has been refreshed by all of you. [14]I had boasted to him about you, and you have not embarrassed me. But just as everything we said to you was true, so our boasting about you to Titus has proved to be true as well. [15]And his affection for you is all the greater when he remembers that you were all obedient, receiving him with fear and trembling. [16]I am glad I can have complete confidence in you.

OPEN What teacher, coach, parent or pastor could "chew you out" something terrible and get by with it?

STUDY **1.** If you had to write a tough letter to a church you had planted that you knew would be painful and possibly misunderstood, how would you feel when you got a report back that this church still loved you? Do you think the report from Titus was entirely positive (v. 7)? **2.** What was the result of the previous letter (the "lost" letter) to them (vv. 8–13)? What intentions does Paul want to clarify to them? Practically, how does godly sorrow differ from worldly sorrow? **3.** What tone of voice do you hear in verse 16? In light of the previous hurtful letter, what do Paul and the church feel now? **4.** If you were reading this letter for the first time as a member of this church, how would you feel? **5.** What is the lesson here for the church today in dealing with painful situations?

APPLY **1.** Have you ever been confronted with a wrong you have done by someone who loves you? How did you feel about that person at the time? **2.** How are you at dealing with painful situations—especially with someone you love deeply? **3.** Are you more likely to let things ride or to confront someone with their sin in a loving way?

7:2 corrupted. Literally, "ruined." This may refer either to financial or moral ruin. **exploited.** This implies taking advantage of someone.

7:3 I do not say this to condemn you. Paul is not interested in striking back at the church by accusing them of being in the wrong: he simply wants to clear himself of the suspicions that have been raised by his opponents.

7:5 harassed at every turn. Paul had already mentioned how he came near to death in the province of Asia (1:8–10). His troubles evidently followed him into Macedonia. **conflicts on the outside, fears within.** He faced external pressures from his enemies as well as inner anxiety such as his concern over Titus and the situation in Corinth.

7:6 God, who comforts the downcast. Paul returns to his description of God with which he began this letter (1:3–5; Isa. 49:13). To "comfort" does not mean simply to console, but to actively help, encourage and strengthen someone undergoing trial.

7:10 Godly sorrow. People repent as they become aware of sin in their lives and propose to change so as to be in conformity with God's ways. The Corinthians became aware of how out of line their actions were in regard to Paul. This insight brought sorrow which in turn led to a change of attitude and behavior. **worldly sorrow.** Worldly sorrow does not lead to the positive change of heart and life that repentance implies, but brings only bitterness and resentment.

7:11 Having realized their sin, the Corinthians went to extreme lengths to clear themselves. **earnestness.** They now took the problem seriously and wanted to correct it.

OPEN 1. When you were growing up, who taught you the importance of giving? **2.** What project did you start on last year that you need to complete?

STUDY 1. From 1 Corinthians 16:1–4 (written about a year earlier) and Romans 15:25–27 (written either during or shortly after Paul revisited Corinth), what is this collection all about? **2.** How would you compare the way we give today in the church to the way the Macedonians gave (vv. 3–4)? **3.** How do you like the way Paul encourages the Corinthians to give in verse 7? **4.** What is Paul's parting shot in his appeal (vv. 8–9)? **5.** If you were reading this letter for the first time, what would you want to give? What do you like about the way Paul presents the importance of giving? **6.** What does Paul have to remind the Corinthians of in verses 10–12? What does this remind you of? **7.** What is the difference between the benevolence program Paul offers and the governmental programs today?

APPLY 1. Have you come to the place in your life where giving is an important discipline? What caused that attitude? **2.** How do you decide where to give your time and money?

OPEN Who do you trust with money: Your kids? The bank? Your broker? The government? Yourself?

STUDY 1. If you were taking up a collection for the hungry in Jerusalem and wanted to avoid any

Generosity Encouraged

8 And now, brothers, we want you to know about the grace that
God has given the Macedonian churches. 2Out of the most severe trial, their overflowing joy and their extreme poverty welled up
in rich generosity. 3For I testify that they gave as much as they were
able, and even beyond their ability. Entirely on their own, 4they urgently pleaded with us for the privilege of sharing in this service to
the saints. 5And they did not do as we expected, but they gave themselves first to the Lord and then to us in keeping with God's will. 6So
we urged Titus, since he had earlier made a beginning, to bring also to
completion this act of grace on your part. 7But just as you excel in everything—in faith, in speech, in knowledge, in complete earnestness
and in your love for us[a]—see that you also excel in this grace of giving.
8I am not commanding you, but I want to test the sincerity of your
love by comparing it with the earnestness of others. 9For you know
the grace of our Lord Jesus Christ, that though he was rich, yet for
your sakes he became poor, so that you through his poverty might
become rich.
10And here is my advice about what is best for you in this matter:
Last year you were the first not only to give but also to have the desire to do so. 11Now finish the work, so that your eager willingness to
do it may be matched by your completion of it, according to your
means. 12For if the willingness is there, the gift is acceptable according to what one has, not according to what he does not have.
13Our desire is not that others might be relieved while you are hard
pressed, but that there might be equality. 14At the present time your
plenty will supply what they need, so that in turn their plenty will
supply what you need. Then there will be equality, 15as it is written:
"He who gathered much did not have too much, and he who gathered
little did not have too little."[b]

Titus Sent to Corinth

16I thank God, who put into the heart of Titus the same concern I
have for you. 17For Titus not only welcomed our appeal, but he is
coming to you with much enthusiasm and on his own initiative.
18And we are sending along with him the brother who is praised by all

[a]7 Some manuscripts *in our love for you* [b]15 Exodus 16:18

8:1 Macedonian churches. Macedonia was the Roman province just north of the province of Achaia where Corinth was located. The churches in mind were probably those located at Philippi, Thessalonica and Berea (Acts 16:6–17:15).

8:4 This verse contains three words which show how the motivation for this offering sprang not only from humanitarian concerns, but from distinctly Christian convictions as well. **privilege.** Literally, "grace." **sharing.** The Greek word is *koinonia*, often translated as "fellowship." Giving is an expression of partnership in Christ. **service.** Giving is a way of ministering to the needs of others, a Christian responsibility (5:15).

8:7 Paul exhorts the Corinthians to participate in giving as wholeheartedly as they participate in the exercise of other spiritual gifts (1 Cor. 12:7–11; 14:1) and as a reflection of their desire to affirm his apostleship (7:11).

8:11 Now finish the work. This is reminiscent of Christ's parable of the two sons, one of whom said he was going to do something (work in the vineyard), but didn't, and the other of whom said he would not, but did (Matt. 21:28–32). Following through on good intentions is vital! **according to your means.** One reason the Corinthians may have stalled is that they felt they could not make a significant contribution. The question is not how much one gives but simply that one gives out of love for God and people.

8:13 equality. In their abundance the Corinthians share what they have with those who are in need. Likewise, in the future, it could be the other way around and the Corinthians could expect aid if they needed it from Christians in Jerusalem and elsewhere.

8:18 the brother. An unnamed fellow worker known for acts of Christian service.

the churches for his service to the gospel. 19What is more, he was
chosen by the churches to accompany us as we carry the offering,
which we administer in order to honor the Lord himself and to show
our eagerness to help. 20We want to avoid any criticism of the way we
administer this liberal gift. 21For we are taking pains to do what is
right, not only in the eyes of the Lord but also in the eyes of men.
22In addition, we are sending with them our brother who has often
proved to us in many ways that he is zealous, and now even more so
because of his great confidence in you. 23As for Titus, he is my partner
and fellow worker among you; as for our brothers, they are representatives of the churches and an honor to Christ. 24Therefore show
these men the proof of your love and the reason for our pride in you,
so that the churches can see it.

9 There is no need for me to write to you about this service to the
saints. 2For I know your eagerness to help, and I have been
boasting about it to the Macedonians, telling them that since last
year you in Achaia were ready to give; and your enthusiasm has
stirred most of them to action. 3But I am sending the brothers in order that our boasting about you in this matter should not prove hollow, but that you may be ready, as I said you would be. 4For if any
Macedonians come with me and find you unprepared, we—not to say
anything about you—would be ashamed of having been so confident.
5So I thought it necessary to urge the brothers to visit you in advance
and finish the arrangements for the generous gift you had promised.
Then it will be ready as a generous gift, not as one grudgingly given.

Sowing Generously

6Remember this: Whoever sows sparingly will also reap sparingly,
and whoever sows generously will also reap generously. 7Each man
should give what he has decided in his heart to give, not reluctantly
or under compulsion, for God loves a cheerful giver. 8And God is able
to make all grace abound to you, so that in all things at all times, having all that you need, you will abound in every good work. 9As it is
written:

> "He has scattered abroad his gifts to the poor;
> his righteousness endures forever."[a]

10Now he who supplies seed to the sower and bread for food will also
supply and increase your store of seed and will enlarge the harvest of

[a] 9 Psalm 112:9

criticism, what would you do? **2.** Why does Paul send Titus ahead with this letter to the church in Corinth? What does Paul say about Titus and the other companions (vv. 18,22–24)? What will the presence of Titus and the "other" brothers do to the criticism that has been leveled against Paul? **3.** Do you think Paul is "buttering up" the Corinthians in 9:1–5 or just being honest? How would you feel if you were reading this letter for the first time?

APPLY 1. If you won the lottery and had to decide on a set of guidelines for giving all of the money away, what would be the top three priorities on your list? **2.** If you don't win the lottery, what do you expect out of the causes and organizations you give to?

OPEN If your family set up a missionary foundation, who would you put in charge of deciding who to give to?

STUDY 1. What do you know about agriculture? About investments? What is the principle here that Paul applies to giving? **2.** Do you think Paul is promising in verses 8–11 that God will bless a generous giver in material ways? How far do you apply this? **3.** How is giving contagious (v. 12)? Have you found this to be true?

APPLY 1. Is it easier for you to part with your money or your time? **2.** Where have you seen

8:19 This brother comes not merely on his own initiative but as a representative of the churches (probably in Macedonia).

8:22 *There will also be a third traveling companion.* Paul is going to great lengths to ensure his enemies and critics cannot charge him with profiting personally from this collection. Titus is his friend and fellow worker, so it is vital to have two other respected traveling companions appointed by the churches to accompany Titus.

9:2 boasting. Apparently in the same way that Paul used the Macedonians as examples to the Corinthians (8:1–5), so too he has used the readiness of the Corinthians to give as an example to the Macedonians! **Achaia.** Corinth was the largest city in the province of Achaia and probably the site of the largest church.

9:6 Paul may be quoting a proverb (similar sayings were known in both Jewish and Greek literature) as support for his encouragement for generous giving. It is not that a person can be assured of financial security by giving (and thus obligating God in some way), but that the exercise of the grace of giving leads to growth in grace.

9:7 not reluctantly or under compulsion. Unlike the temple tax, this voluntary offering required people to consider for themselves what they would contribute. **God loves a cheerful giver.** It is not that giving earns God's love, but that God "approves of" the character of a person who is generous..

9:8 all. The stress on "all" in this verse emphasizes God's lavish generosity.

the greatest return on the time or money you have invested in others? **3.** Have you made a financial plan for your estate? What are you doing now to carry out the long term goals of your life?

OPEN What person comes to mind who is unassuming in appearance, but has made a significant contribution to the body of believers?

STUDY 1. If you were the person who has said the things about Paul in this passage, how would you be feeling when you read this letter? **2.** Reading between the lines, what would you say Paul looked like? His personality? Demeanor? **3.** What is the point in verses 3–6 that Paul makes about spiritual warfare and his own fire power? **4.** What does Paul challenge his critics to do in verse 7? What have they been doing and what is Paul going to do when he gets to town? **5.** What is the tone in Paul's voice in verses 12–18? Are you somewhat surprised by the defense he gives of himself? Why? If Paul doesn't care what his critics think (v. 18), why does he bother to answer them?

your righteousness. [11]You will be made rich in every way so that you
can be generous on every occasion, and through us your generosity
will result in thanksgiving to God.
[12]This service that you perform is not only supplying the needs of
God's people but is also overflowing in many expressions of thanks
to God. [13]Because of the service by which you have proved yourselves, men will praise God for the obedience that accompanies your
confession of the gospel of Christ, and for your generosity in sharing
with them and with everyone else. [14]And in their prayers for you their
hearts will go out to you, because of the surpassing grace God has
given you. [15]Thanks be to God for his indescribable gift!

Paul's Defense of His Ministry

10 By the meekness and gentleness of Christ, I appeal to you—I,
Paul, who am "timid" when face to face with you, but "bold"
when away! [2]I beg you that when I come I may not have to be as bold
as I expect to be toward some people who think that we live by the
standards of this world. [3]For though we live in the world, we do not
wage war as the world does. [4]The weapons we fight with are not the
weapons of the world. On the contrary, they have divine power to demolish strongholds. [5]We demolish arguments and every pretension
that sets itself up against the knowledge of God, and we take captive
every thought to make it obedient to Christ. [6]And we will be ready to
punish every act of disobedience, once your obedience is complete.
[7]You are looking only on the surface of things.[a] If anyone is confident that he belongs to Christ, he should consider again that we belong to Christ just as much as he. [8]For even if I boast somewhat freely
about the authority the Lord gave us for building you up rather than
pulling you down, I will not be ashamed of it. [9]I do not want to seem
to be trying to frighten you with my letters. [10]For some say, "His letters are weighty and forceful, but in person he is unimpressive and

[a]7 Or *Look at the obvious facts*

9:11 You will be made rich. The purpose of such riches is not to pamper personal indulgences but to facilitate generosity. **in every way.** God might not reward faithfulness with material wealth, but with a wealth of spiritual and emotional resources. James 2:5 reminds us, "Has not God chosen those who are poor in the eyes of the world to be rich in faith and to inherit the kingdom he promised those who love him?"

9:12 service. Giving is a way of ministering to the needs of others, a Christian responsibility (5:15). **needs of God's people.** The poor are actually helped. This is one fruit of generosity.

10:1 This verse begins the final section of the letter. From his extravagant hope of what might be in the future as expressed in 9:12–15 (based probably on Titus' report mentioned in 7:6–16), Paul moves to what actually is happening in Corinth. Paul begins his case by defending himself against the charge that he has a weak character. Paul was charged with being unimpressive (v. 10) and thus not an authoritative apostle of Christ. The fact that Paul begins the final section of this letter by invoking the meekness and gentleness of Jesus (Matt. 11:29) immediately shows that he rejects authoritarianism and aggressive behavior as a sign of apostleship. His opponents saw this as weakness, not Christlikeness.

10:4 of the world. He does not accept the self-oriented lifestyle of the world. He refuses to live life relying solely on his own resources and with an eye only to increasing his own power and prestige. **divine power.** In contrast to the "weapons of the world," Paul relies on Christ's extremely powerful weapons to bring about change.

10:7 You are looking only on the surface of things. Since they view what is happening on the basis of human wisdom, they misinterpret the situation. **belongs to Christ.** Quite possibly Paul's opponents in Corinth are claiming to be Christ's true apostles which, by inference or direct accusation, would make Paul a false apostle—a claim he rejects.

10:8 building you up. Paul's commission as an apostle was to preach the gospel and so to build churches. His commission is not to destroy churches (as his opponents were doing; 1 Cor. 3:17).

10:10 Paul was probably in ill health and he had long ago rejected the art of rhetoric (1 Cor. 2:1–5). But in Corinth, which had many educated citizens, powerful speech and a persuasive personality were highly valued, which may account for why the church started to listen to these new teachers.

his speaking amounts to nothing." 11 Such people should realize that
what we are in our letters when we are absent, we will be in our actions when we are present.
12 We do not dare to classify or compare ourselves with some who
commend themselves. When they measure themselves by themselves
and compare themselves with themselves, they are not wise. 13 We,
however, will not boast beyond proper limits, but will confine our
boasting to the field God has assigned to us, a field that reaches even
to you. 14 We are not going too far in our boasting, as would be the
case if we had not come to you, for we did get as far as you with the
gospel of Christ. 15 Neither do we go beyond our limits by boasting of
work done by others.[a] Our hope is that, as your faith continues to
grow, our area of activity among you will greatly expand, 16 so that we
can preach the gospel in the regions beyond you. For we do not want
to boast about work already done in another man's territory. 17 But,
"Let him who boasts boast in the Lord."[b] 18 For it is not the one who
commends himself who is approved, but the one whom the Lord
commends.

Paul and the False Apostles

11 I hope you will put up with a little of my foolishness; but you
are already doing that. 2 I am jealous for you with a godly jealousy. I promised you to one husband, to Christ, so that I might present you as a pure virgin to him. 3 But I am afraid that just as Eve was
deceived by the serpent's cunning, your minds may somehow be led
astray from your sincere and pure devotion to Christ. 4 For if someone
comes to you and preaches a Jesus other than the Jesus we preached,
or if you receive a different spirit from the one you received, or a different gospel from the one you accepted, you put up with it easily
enough. 5 But I do not think I am in the least inferior to those "super-
apostles." 6 I may not be a trained speaker, but I do have knowledge.
We have made this perfectly clear to you in every way.
7 Was it a sin for me to lower myself in order to elevate you by
preaching the gospel of God to you free of charge? 8 I robbed other
churches by receiving support from them so as to serve you. 9 And
when I was with you and needed something, I was not a burden to
anyone, for the brothers who came from Macedonia supplied what I
needed. I have kept myself from being a burden to you in any way,
and will continue to do so. 10 As surely as the truth of Christ is in me,
nobody in the regions of Achaia will stop this boasting of mine.
11 Why? Because I do not love you? God knows I do! 12 And I will keep

[a]13-15 Or [13]*We, however, will not boast about things that cannot be measured, but we will boast according to the standard of measurement that the God of measure has assigned us—a measurement that relates even to you.* [14] . . . [15]*Neither do we boast about things that cannot be measured in regard to the work done by others.* [b]17 Jer. 9:24

APPLY 1. How do you deal with attacks on your integrity? **2.** When others in the Christian community are involved in the attack, what do you do?

OPEN What is your secret for getting through: A bad day? A shopping spree? A movie? A long walk?

STUDY 1. What on earth is Paul doing in this passage? What do you think has driven him to talk this way? **2.** From the warning in verses 3–4, what does Paul fear has happened to the church he planted in Corinth? **3.** Who do you think Paul is referring to as "super-apostles"? What do they claim (vv. 5–6)? **4.** Do you think Paul was wrong in not taking a salary from those he ministered to? What has this done? **5.** What does Paul say about the "super-apostles" (vv. 13–15)? Do you think Paul is overreacting here? **6.** If you were reading this letter in the same room (probably a house church) with one of these "super-apostles," how would you describe the atmosphere? **7.** Who does Paul remind you of in this passage?

APPLY 1. What is the closest you have come to seeing "super-apostles" in the church? How did they "masquerade"? Advertise

---

10:16 the regions beyond you. Paul had no desire to hang onto any power or position in Corinth. He wanted to resolve the difficulties in Corinth so that he could get on with the business of preaching the gospel in the still to be evangelized parts of the empire. In fact, his plans are to leave the region around the Aegean Sea and push on to Rome and then into Spain (Rom. 15:23–29).

11:5 super-apostles. This is an ironic label for the false apostles.

11:6 not be a trained speaker. A popular style of rhetoric had developed among the Greeks which utilized rhetorical form as a means of manipulating people rather than communicating truth. It was this abuse of rhetoric that Paul rejected. **knowledge.** This was more than understanding information; Paul had revelation from God with spiritual insight.

11:7 In 1 Corinthians 9, Paul makes it clear he felt it was appropriate for apostles to be supported by the churches they served. He refused the support of the Corinthians so that he would not be a burden to them (v. 9).

themselves? Change? **2.** If Paul were around today, what do you think he would do about the "false prophets" in your situation?

OPEN Who has the bragging rights in your group for: The most stitches? The longest scar? The scariest accident? The worst humor?

STUDY 1. What do you find out in the previous passage (vv. 4–6,13–15) that has driven Paul to this defense of his apostleship? **2.** How do you think his opponents responded to these statements? **3.** Is Paul being sarcastic or truthful in verses 19–20? Does he sound hurt or angry? **4.** What is Paul doing in verses 22–29 to the popularity of the "super-apostles" (v. 5) that are "masquerading" (v. 15) as servants of righteousness? If you were one of the "super-apostles" and had to put your life up against this list, how would you feel? **5.** Can you identify with the emotional drain that Paul felt as the caregiver for the churches he planted?

APPLY 1. Go back and read verses 22–27 slowly and put your name instead of the word "I"? How did this make you feel? **2.** What has your concern for the things of God cost you in comparison to Paul? **3.** In two words, how would you describe your relationship with Jesus right now?

on doing what I am doing in order to cut the ground from under
those who want an opportunity to be considered equal with us in the
things they boast about.
13For such men are false apostles, deceitful workmen, masquerading as apostles of Christ. 14And no wonder, for Satan himself mas-
querades as an angel of light. 15It is not surprising, then, if his
servants masquerade as servants of righteousness. Their end will be
what their actions deserve.

Paul Boasts About His Sufferings

16I repeat: Let no one take me for a fool. But if you do, then receive
me just as you would a fool, so that I may do a little boasting. 17In this
self-confident boasting I am not talking as the Lord would, but as a
fool. 18Since many are boasting in the way the world does, I too will
boast. 19You gladly put up with fools since you are so wise! 20In fact,
you even put up with anyone who enslaves you or exploits you or
takes advantage of you or pushes himself forward or slaps you in the
face. 21To my shame I admit that we were too weak for that!

What anyone else dares to boast about—I am speaking as a fool—
I also dare to boast about. 22Are they Hebrews? So am I. Are they Israelites? So am I. Are they Abraham's descendants? So am I. 23Are they
servants of Christ? (I am out of my mind to talk like this.) I am more.
I have worked much harder, been in prison more frequently, been
flogged more severely, and been exposed to death again and again.
24Five times I received from the Jews the forty lashes minus one.
25Three times I was beaten with rods, once I was stoned, three times
I was shipwrecked, I spent a night and a day in the open sea, 26I have
been constantly on the move. I have been in danger from rivers, in
danger from bandits, in danger from my own countrymen, in danger
from Gentiles; in danger in the city, in danger in the country, in danger at sea; and in danger from false brothers. 27I have labored and
toiled and have often gone without sleep; I have known hunger and
thirst and have often gone without food; I have been cold and naked.
28Besides everything else, I face daily the pressure of my concern for
all the churches. 29Who is weak, and I do not feel weak? Who is led
into sin, and I do not inwardly burn?
30If I must boast, I will boast of the things that show my weakness.

11:14 angel of light. Paul has already referred to Satan as the arch-deceiver (v. 3), masquerading as something he is not.

11:22 Paul points out that he shares all the ethnic, social and religious claims of the false teachers regarding their background. **Israelites.** This emphasizes the religious and cultural dimension of their background. **Abraham's descendants.** This is often a synonym for "Israelites."

11:25 beaten with rods. This was a common Roman punishment (Acts 16:22–23). **shipwrecked.** One shipwreck is described in Acts 27:14–44, but that had not yet occurred when Paul wrote this letter! Since Paul traveled frequently by ship and since shipwrecks were by no means uncommon in those days, it seems that Paul endured several shipwrecks.

11:26 danger from rivers. Not all rivers had bridges or safe ferries. **danger from bandits.** This could have been a special problem when Paul was transporting collections taken in aid of poorer churches. **danger from my own countrymen.** Such danger came from mobs, from the courts, and from personal attack (Acts 9:23,29; 13:6–8,45; 14:2,19; 17:5; 18:6,12; 20:3,19; 21:11,27). **danger from false brothers.** Not only did he face the possibility of harm (bodily and otherwise) from Jews and Gentiles, but also from those claiming to be believers!

11:29 weak. In his "boasting" he now boasts of being weakest of all. **inwardly burn.** In his concern for the churches, Paul has a constant source of anguish over those who have been led astray from the faith.

11:30–33 Because it seems incongruous that one could be both weak and an apostle, Paul asserts that he has indeed been telling the truth (v. 31). To wrap-up the accounts of his weakness, he recounts a final incident that was especially humiliating (Acts 9:23–25). The mighty apostle, far from being heralded with glory, was reduced to hiding

31The God and Father of the Lord Jesus, who is to be praised forever,
knows that I am not lying. 32In Damascus the governor under King
Aretas had the city of the Damascenes guarded in order to arrest me.
33But I was lowered in a basket from a window in the wall and slipped
through his hands.

Paul's Vision and His Thorn

12 I must go on boasting. Although there is nothing to be
gained, I will go on to visions and revelations from the Lord.
2I know a man in Christ who fourteen years ago was caught up to the
third heaven. Whether it was in the body or out of the body I do not
know—God knows. 3And I know that this man—whether in the body
or apart from the body I do not know, but God knows— 4was caught
up to paradise. He heard inexpressible things, things that man is not
permitted to tell. 5I will boast about a man like that, but I will not
boast about myself, except about my weaknesses. 6Even if I should
choose to boast, I would not be a fool, because I would be speaking
the truth. But I refrain, so no one will think more of me than is warranted by what I do or say.
7To keep me from becoming conceited because of these surpass-
ingly great revelations, there was given me a thorn in my flesh, a
messenger of Satan, to torment me. 8Three times I pleaded with the
Lord to take it away from me. 9But he said to me, "My grace is sufficient for you, for my power is made perfect in weakness." Therefore I
will boast all the more gladly about my weaknesses, so that Christ's
power may rest on me. 10That is why, for Christ's sake, I delight in
weaknesses, in insults, in hardships, in persecutions, in difficulties.
For when I am weak, then I am strong.

Paul's Concern for the Corinthians

11I have made a fool of myself, but you drove me to it. I ought to
have been commended by you, for I am not in the least inferior to the

OPEN Do you dream a lot? What was your most recent dream?

STUDY 1. When you read this passage, how do you feel about Paul? Does the concept of "out-of-body" experiences like Paul talks about feel a little strange or scary? Why would Paul even talk about this? **2.** Have you had any experiences like this one? What were the circumstances? What did you see? Feel? As you look back, how would you describe it? **3.** What do you think Paul is talking about as his "thorn in the flesh": A physical ailment? An addiction or compulsion? The burden of his ministry?

APPLY 1. What is your "thorn in the flesh"? **2.** How has God used your "thorn in the flesh" to keep you dependent on him?

OPEN What is one way your parents sacrificed for you? How did you feel about that unselfish sacrifice then? Now?

---

in a basket. **King Aretas.** This Arab king ruled from 9 B.C. to A.D. 39.

12:1 visions and revelations. It is not possible to distinguish between these two. Perhaps "vision" refers to what was seen in the experience while "revelation" refers to what was heard (the content). These are ecstatic experiences of some sort, whereby for a brief time the limitations of space, time and sense perception are lifted and one experiences firsthand immediate, direct access to the supernatural.

12:2 fourteen years ago. This was probably around A.D. 42, well before he planted the Corinthian church. This is the only time in any letter that Paul mentions such an experience. **caught up.** Visions were often spoken of in terms of a journey to another place. Whether Paul was literally transported to a new place or simply found himself in a new reality is impossible to know. **third heaven.** Jewish literature spoke of heaven having various levels, although the number of levels, differ. **in the body or out of the body.** Paul refuses to speculate on how this experience occurred.

12:6 speaking the truth. This may infer that his opponents had fabricated tales of their visions.

12:7 a thorn in my flesh. It is unknown what Paul means here. **messenger of Satan.** Sickness was thought to be caused by Satan, but the false apostles in Corinth are also referred to as servants of Satan (11:13–15). **torment me.** Literally, "to continually torment me." Whatever the problem was, it was chronic, though not debilitating.

12:8 Three times. There are parallels between Paul's experience and that of Jesus in the Garden of Gethsemane. Like Jesus, Paul was not delivered of the hardship that faced him but received strength to remain faithful in the midst of suffering.

12:9 This sentence is the lens through which 2 Corinthians must be understood as it reflects the fundamental misunderstanding that the false teachers and the Corinthians had about the gospel. They thought the power of God meant that Christians should escape or avoid the experiences of weakness, vulnerability, suffering and hardship that are common to life. Paul's emphasis has been that the power of God does not mean such trials are avoided, but that God empowers believers to love, bring healing, serve and be faithful in the midst of such times (1:3–11).

12:11 you drove me to it. Paul is forced to boast because the Corinthians refused to speak up on his behalf and stand with him.

STUDY **1.** If you were to visit the church you planted where your integrity has been challenged, how would you be feeling? **2.** Does Paul sound a little defensive in verses 11–13? What has driven Paul to defend himself? **3.** How does Paul see his relationship to this church? What is the tone in Paul's voice in verses 14–18? Is Paul frustrated, distraught or just being a parent? **4.** From the sound of it (v. 20) how would you describe the condition of the church in Corinth? What have they done to correct the moral problems that he asked them to correct? **5.** If you were one of those who had "not repented" of your "impurity, sexual sin and debauchery" how would you be feeling about Paul's visit?

APPLY **1.** Outside of your family, what group or ministry do you feel a particular burden for—almost like a parent? **2.** What is God laying on your heart for this ministry right now?

OPEN In high school or college, what did you do to prepare yourself for big exams?

STUDY **1.** What has happened in the church of Corinth that Paul is coming to correct (11:4–6, 13–15)? What is the situation right now in this church (12:20–21)? **2.** What does it sound like Paul is pre-

"super-apostles," even though I am nothing. 12The things that mark
an apostle—signs, wonders and miracles—were done among you
with great perseverance. 13How were you inferior to the other
churches, except that I was never a burden to you? Forgive me this
wrong!

14Now I am ready to visit you for the third time, and I will not be a
burden to you, because what I want is not your possessions but you.
After all, children should not have to save up for their parents, but
parents for their children. 15So I will very gladly spend for you everything I have and expend myself as well. If I love you more, will you
love me less? 16Be that as it may, I have not been a burden to you. Yet,
crafty fellow that I am, I caught you by trickery! 17Did I exploit you
through any of the men I sent you? 18I urged Titus to go to you and I
sent our brother with him. Titus did not exploit you, did he? Did we
not act in the same spirit and follow the same course?

19Have you been thinking all along that we have been defending
ourselves to you? We have been speaking in the sight of God as those
in Christ; and everything we do, dear friends, is for your strengthening. 20For I am afraid that when I come I may not find you as I want
you to be, and you may not find me as you want me to be. I fear that
there may be quarreling, jealousy, outbursts of anger, factions, slander, gossip, arrogance and disorder. 21I am afraid that when I come
again my God will humble me before you, and I will be grieved over
many who have sinned earlier and have not repented of the impurity,
sexual sin and debauchery in which they have indulged.

Final Warnings

13 This will be my third visit to you. "Every matter must be
established by the testimony of two or three witnesses."[a] 2I
already gave you a warning when I was with you the second time. I
now repeat it while absent: On my return I will not spare those who
sinned earlier or any of the others, 3since you are demanding proof
that Christ is speaking through me. He is not weak in dealing with

[a]1 Deut. 19:15

12:12 signs, wonders and miracles. While there is no record of Paul performing any miracles in Corinth, he did do so elsewhere (Acts 14:8–10; 20:9–12).

12:13–16 Since Paul's desire to minister without thought of profiteering was seen as a lack of love (11:9–11), he offers a mock apology. Yet he asserts that when he visits again he still will refuse their financial support because his intent is to serve them as a parent does a child.

12:13 never a burden. Once again, *it seems that what most* rankled the Corinthians was Paul's refusal to allow them to support him.

12:21 God will humble me. Paul is aware this could be another very painful visit because he will see that the people will not have repented and his work has not been as effective as he would wish. **impurity, sexual sin and debauchery.** These three words describe sexual immorality of all types, a problem especially prevalent in Corinth, a city known for its promiscuous ways (1 Cor. 5:1; 6:12–20).

13:1–4 The Old Testament Law required that there be at least two witnesses before anyone could be accused of a crime (Deut. 19:15). Paul adapts this principle to justify the rightness of his coming with judgment at his next visit, since he has already warned the people twice (through his second visit and his "sorrowful letter"—2:3–4) of their need to correct their ways.

13:2 I will not spare. Paul probably intends to do what he describes in 1 Corinthians 5:5—to hand the erring brothers and sisters over to Satan. This would mean formal excommunication from the Christian community until such time that the people showed evidence of moral change. **those who sinned earlier or any of the others.** Paul intends to deal both with the long-standing problems in the Corinthian church, detailed in 1 Corinthians, and with the newer problems arising as a result of their seduction by false apostles (12:20–21).

13:3 powerful. Paul may have not been all they expected, but the resurrected Christ is. The power of Christ has been readibly visible to the Corinthians in miracles (12:12; Rom. 15:19; Gal. 3:5), in Paul's preaching (1 Cor. 2:4), and in the conversion of sinners (1 Cor. 6:11).

you, but is powerful among you. 4For to be sure, he was crucified in
weakness, yet he lives by God's power. Likewise, we are weak in him,
yet by God's power we will live with him to serve you.
5Examine yourselves to see whether you are in the faith; test yourselves. Do you not realize that Christ Jesus is in you—unless, of
course, you fail the test? 6And I trust that you will discover that we
have not failed the test. 7Now we pray to God that you will not do
anything wrong. Not that people will see that we have stood the test
but that you will do what is right even though we may seem to have
failed. 8For we cannot do anything against the truth, but only for the
truth. 9We are glad whenever we are weak but you are strong; and our
prayer is for your perfection. 10This is why I write these things when I
am absent, that when I come I may not have to be harsh in my use of
authority—the authority the Lord gave me for building you up, not
for tearing you down.

Final Greetings

11Finally, brothers, good-by. Aim for perfection, listen to my appeal,
be of one mind, live in peace. And the God of love and peace will be
with you.
12Greet one another with a holy kiss. 13All the saints send their
greetings.
14May the grace of the Lord Jesus Christ, and the love of God, and
the fellowship of the Holy Spirit be with you all.

paring for in verses 1–4? What will be the ground rules? Paul has already said that he would like to come "in gentleness and meekness" (10:1) and as a loving parent (12:14–15). What does he threaten to do now? **3.** Whether or not the critics in the church approve of him, what does Paul pray for them in verses 7–9? **4.** What does Paul hope for as he considers his upcoming visit (vv. 10–11)? **5.** Considering the problems of this church, how would his benediction in verse 14 be appropriate?

APPLY **1.** If you were looking for a spiritual leader, what leadership profile would you look for? How do you fit that profile? **2.** What has been the high point in your study of this epistle? What do you or your group want to study next?

13:4 in weakness. It is not that Christ was killed because he was powerless to prevent his crucifixion. Rather, he was killed because he allowed himself to be weak for our sakes. He renounced the power that could have saved him and so died to save us. **he lives by God's power.** God's power was displayed in Christ's resurrection from the dead.

13:5 Examine yourselves. Paul turns the tables on the Corinthians. They have been demanding that he prove himself to them. Paul now asks the same of them. **in the faith.** Paul is asking them to consider if they are really Christians. The issue here is one of moral integrity that reflects Christ's character. Paul is challenging them to take a look at their own lives.

Galatians

Personal Reading	Group Study Topic and Reading	
1:1–10	Paul's Passion	1:1–10
1:11–24	Paul's Call	1:11–24
2:1–10	Paul's Acceptance	2:1–10
2:11–21	Paul's Gospel	2:11–21
3:1–14	Faith and the Law	3:1–14
3:15–25	Law and Promise	3:15–25
3:26–4:7	Sonship and Unity	3:26–4:7
4:8–20	Joy and Zeal	4:8–20
4:21–31	Hagar and Sarah	4:21–31
5:1–15	Freedom in Christ	5:1–15
5:16–26	Life by the Spirit	5:16–26
6:1–18	A New Creation	6:1–18

Author. The apostle Paul was the author of Galatians.

Date. The date of Paul's epistle depends on whether he was writing to churches in North or South Galatia. If Paul had been writing to congregations in North Galatia, the letter could not have been written before his third missionary expedition after the journey mentioned in Acts 16:6 and 18:23, around A.D. 55. On the other hand, if Paul were writing to the churches in the southern region, the epistle to the Galatians is his earliest letter—written in A.D. 48 or 49, possibly while he was in Syrian Antioch just prior to the Council in Jerusalem (Acts 15:6–21).

Theme. Justification by faith—right standing with God based on belief.

Historical Background. Paul tells us he is writing "to the churches in Galatia" (1:2). It is not always clear whether he is referring to the original territory in the north or the new province extending southward—which included the cities of Pisidian Antioch, Iconium, Lystra and Derbe that Paul visited during his first missionary journey described in Acts 13–14.

Characteristics. Paul was furious and he didn't care who knew it. "You foolish Galatians!" he cried. "Who has bewitched you?" (3:1). He felt so strongly because the issue he was addressing in this letter was not a minor matter of church policy. It struck right to the heart of the Gospel.

Some legalistic Jewish Christians (Judaizers) had been stirring up trouble. They had twisted the gospel into something Jesus never intended, and then they had made false charges against Paul.

The core issue in Galatians is justification. Justification is how does a person gain right standing before God? The Judaizers said that Christ (grace) plus circumcision (Law-keeping) equals right standing. Paul's equation was different. Christ (grace) plus *nothing else* equals right standing.

The Relationship Between Galatians and Romans. There is a close thematic connection between Galatians and Romans. Galatians appears to be Paul's first attempt at wrestling with the issue of justification by faith alone. Paul does so in the context of having to deal with a local problem. Romans, on the other hand, is a more studied consideration of the same issue. It is an eloquent, carefully stated, logical argument, which stands as one of the finest pieces of theological writing ever penned.

1 Paul, an apostle—sent not from men nor by man, but by Jesus
Christ and God the Father, who raised him from the dead— 2and
all the brothers with me,

To the churches in Galatia:

3Grace and peace to you from God our Father and the Lord Jesus
Christ, 4who gave himself for our sins to rescue us from the present
evil age, according to the will of our God and Father, 5to whom be
glory for ever and ever. Amen.

No Other Gospel

6I am astonished that you are so quickly deserting the one who
called you by the grace of Christ and are turning to a different gospel— 7which is really no gospel at all. Evidently some people are
throwing you into confusion and are trying to pervert the gospel of
Christ. 8But even if we or an angel from heaven should preach a gospel other than the one we preached to you, let him be eternally condemned! 9As we have already said, so now I say again: If anybody is
preaching to you a gospel other than what you accepted, let him be
eternally condemned!

10Am I now trying to win the approval of men, or of God? Or am I
trying to please men? If I were still trying to please men, I would not
be a servant of Christ.

Paul Called by God

11I want you to know, brothers, that the gospel I preached is not
something that man made up. 12I did not receive it from any man, nor
was I taught it; rather, I received it by revelation from Jesus Christ.

13For you have heard of my previous way of life in Judaism, how intensely I persecuted the church of God and tried to destroy it. 14I
was advancing in Judaism beyond many Jews of my own age and was
extremely zealous for the traditions of my fathers. 15But when God,
who set me apart from birth[a] and called me by his grace, was pleased

[a]15 Or *from my mother's womb*

OPEN 1. How are you at writing letters, especially difficult ones? **2.** Would you rather have a person come right out and tell you what they feel or beat around the bush?

STUDY 1. If you had spent years planting churches and someone came along and told these churches that the gospel you shared was not complete, what would you do? **2.** What does Paul accuse the young Christians in these churches of doing (vv. 7–8)? If you had to describe the tone in this passage, with one or two words, what would you say?

APPLY 1. What is the closest you have come to deserting your faith, or being swept off your feet with a "new" teaching? **2.** What would you like to get out of this study?

OPEN Where do you go and what do you do when you need to sort out your life goals?

STUDY Apparently, Paul's critics were challenging Paul's message of grace and justification for all who believe. They were pulling the Jewish Christians back into the Old Testament teachings and denying the atoning work of Christ. They were putting doubt into the minds of immature believers. **1.** Read-

---

1:1 Paul. Virtually everyone accepts that he was the author of Galatians. **apostle.** This New Testament word means "a special messenger." **not from men ... but by Jesus.** Paul emphasizes that his apostleship derives not from any human intermediary. Rather, his commission was received directly from the resurrected Christ on the Damascus road.

1:2 Galatia. The Roman province of Galatia was located in what is now the central part of Turkey (see a Bible map).

1:4 gave himself. The idea is of voluntary sacrifice for a specific purpose. **rescue.** To be rescued from bondage is a key idea in the epistle. **the present evil age.** There are two ages: "this age" which is evil and under Satan's control, and "the age to come" which was inaugurated when Christ came, but will be complete when he rules as king (Rev. 19:15–16). In becoming a Christian, a person becomes a member of a kingdom or age that is not yet a complete reality (Col. 1:12).

1:6 astonished. Typically at this place in a letter, Paul would commend the church (Rom. 1:8; Phil. 1:3). But here he launches straight into his remonstration, expressing indignation at the news that they have been persuaded by the teaching of the Judaizers. **deserting.** The word means, literally, a removal from one place to another. The word can also be used for those who "change sides"—for example, army deserters. **grace.** This pinpoints the nature of their turning—from a gospel of unmerited favor to a gospel of works. **gospel.** The proclamation of the good news that in the life, death and resurrection of Jesus, the kingdom of God has been made manifest and is open to all who by faith trust in his atoning work on the cross.

1:8 eternally condemned. This stands as the direct opposite to God's grace, and is used by Paul as a solemn calling down of judgment on these Judaizers.

1:12 revelation. It was only after Jesus Christ revealed the truth and meaning of these facts to him following the Damascus road experience that he accepted the gospel.

1:15 set me apart from birth. Paul's experience is similar to that of Old Testament prophets (Isa. 49:1–6; Jer. 1:5). He could see the hand of God throughout his life.

ing between the lines what do you think Paul's critics were saying about Paul's ministry? **2.** How does he answer the critics? Do you think Paul over-reacted? **3.** What was the special "revelation" that Paul was given?

APPLY When is the last time you took off to a solitary place (like Arabia) to think through what God wanted you to do with your life?

OPEN Where did you get most of your convictions and moral values?

STUDY 1. Why does Paul make such a big issue about circumcision? What is at stake here? **2.** If the Gentile believers are forced to live under the Old Testament rules, what will this do to Paul's understanding of his calling (v. 2)? **3.** Who would be the "Gentiles" in our culture today? Do you think the institutional church is guilty of adding any cultural things to the gospel today? **4.** How did the church leaders resolve the issue of circumcision? What's a good lesson for the church today?

16to reveal his Son in me so that I might preach him among the Gentiles, I did not consult any man, 17nor did I go up to Jerusalem to see
those who were apostles before I was, but I went immediately into
Arabia and later returned to Damascus.
18Then after three years, I went up to Jerusalem to get acquainted
with Peter[b] and stayed with him fifteen days. 19I saw none of the other
apostles—only James, the Lord's brother. 20I assure you before God
that what I am writing you is no lie. 21Later I went to Syria and Cilicia.
22I was personally unknown to the churches of Judea that are in
Christ. 23They only heard the report: "The man who formerly persecuted us is now preaching the faith he once tried to destroy." 24And
they praised God because of me.

Paul Accepted by the Apostles

2 Fourteen years later I went up again to Jerusalem, this time with
Barnabas. I took Titus along also. 2I went in response to a revelation and set before them the gospel that I preach among the Gentiles. But I did this privately to those who seemed to be leaders, for
fear that I was running or had run my race in vain. 3Yet not even Titus,
who was with me, was compelled to be circumcised, even though he
was a Greek. 4⌞This matter arose⌟ because some false brothers had in-
filtrated our ranks to spy on the freedom we have in Christ Jesus and
to make us slaves. 5We did not give in to them for a moment, so that
the truth of the gospel might remain with you.
6As for those who seemed to be important—whatever they were
makes no difference to me; God does not judge by external appearance—those men added nothing to my message. 7On the contrary,
they saw that I had been entrusted with the task of preaching the

[b]18 Greek *Cephas*

1:16 among the Gentiles. With Paul's conversion came his commission to preach to the Gentiles (Acts 9:15). In encountering Christ, he came to the realization that the Law was bankrupt (insofar as its ability to save anyone). There was no barrier preventing Gentiles from coming to the all-sufficient Christ.

1:18 after three years. A significant interval of time elapsed between his conversion and his first visit to Jerusalem. **Jerusalem.** It was a courageous act by Paul to return here—to his former friends who might well try to harm him (because of his conversion to Christianity), and to new friends who might not even receive him (because of their suspicions about him). **fifteen days.** This was a short visit, and Paul spent much of his time preaching (Acts 9:28–29).

1:19 James. *James eventually became the leader of the Jerusalem church* (Mark 6:3; Acts 1:14).

1:21 Syria and Cilicia. After leaving Jerusalem Paul went north into Syria and then into the adjacent area of Cilicia to the city of Tarsus, his birthplace.

2:1 Fourteen years later. It is not clear whether Paul means 14 years after his conversion or after his first visit to Jerusalem. In any case, the significant factor is that Paul had little contact with the leaders in Jerusalem. He was not their missionary. He did not take orders from them. **I went up again.** In 14 years Paul made only two visits to Jerusalem. The first was for the purpose of meeting Peter. The second was necessary in order to deliver to the mother church a famine collection donated by Christians at Antioch. **Barnabas.** A Levite from Cyprus, whose name was actually Joseph but who had been nicknamed Barnabas (Son of Encouragement) by the apostles (Acts 4:36). When the church in Jerusalem heard that a great number of people in Antioch had turned to Jesus, they sent Barnabas to verify what was happening. Barnabas in turn, having seen this to be an authentic work of God, sought out Paul in Tarsus and brought him back to Antioch, where the two of them labored together to establish the church (Acts 11:19-30). **Titus.** A Gentile Christian from Antioch. Titus became an important co-worker with Paul (2 Cor. 2:12–13; 7:6–7,13–16; 8:6–24; 12:18) and later was the recipient of a pastoral letter.

2:2 in vain. Paul preached that Gentiles could become Christians without first becoming Jews, i.e., that there was one church made up of both Jews and Gentiles. If the leaders in Jerusalem disputed this, his 14 years of work would have been in vain.

2:4 The need for this discussion arose because some disputed the idea that Gentiles need not observe the Jewish laws to be fully Christian. **to spy.** With the intention of bringing such freedom to an end. **freedom.** Jew and Gentile Christians freely mixed, eating together and having fellowship. This stood in stark contrast to the way Jews and Gentiles normally related.

2:7 On the contrary. In fact, they acknowledged his sphere of authority.

gospel to the Gentiles,[a] just as Peter had been to the Jews.[b] 8For God,
who was at work in the ministry of Peter as an apostle to the Jews,
was also at work in my ministry as an apostle to the Gentiles. 9James,
Peter[c] and John, those reputed to be pillars, gave me and Barnabas
the right hand of fellowship when they recognized the grace given to
me. They agreed that we should go to the Gentiles, and they to the
Jews. 10All they asked was that we should continue to remember the
poor, the very thing I was eager to do.

Paul Opposes Peter

11When Peter came to Antioch, I opposed him to his face, because
he was clearly in the wrong. 12Before certain men came from James,
he used to eat with the Gentiles. But when they arrived, he began to
draw back and separate himself from the Gentiles because he was
afraid of those who belonged to the circumcision group. 13The other
Jews joined him in his hypocrisy, so that by their hypocrisy even Barnabas was led astray.

14When I saw that they were not acting in line with the truth of the
gospel, I said to Peter in front of them all, "You are a Jew, yet you live
like a Gentile and not like a Jew. How is it, then, that you force Gentiles to follow Jewish customs?

15"We who are Jews by birth and not 'Gentile sinners' 16know that a
man is not justified by observing the law, but by faith in Jesus Christ.
So we, too, have put our faith in Christ Jesus that we may be justified
by faith in Christ and not by observing the law, because by observing
the law no one will be justified.

17"If, while we seek to be justified in Christ, it becomes evident that
we ourselves are sinners, does that mean that Christ promotes sin?
Absolutely not! 18If I rebuild what I destroyed, I prove that I am a law-
breaker. 19For through the law I died to the law so that I might live for
God. 20I have been crucified with Christ and I no longer live, but
Christ lives in me. The life I live in the body, I live by faith in the Son of
God, who loved me and gave himself for me. 21I do not set aside the
grace of God, for if righteousness could be gained through the law,
Christ died for nothing!"[d]

Faith or Observance of the Law

3 You foolish Galatians! Who has bewitched you? Before your very
eyes Jesus Christ was clearly portrayed as crucified. 2I would like

[a]7 Greek *uncircumcised* [b]7 Greek *circumcised*; also in verses 8 and 9 [c]9 Greek *Cephas*; also in verses 11 and 14 [d]21 Some interpreters end the quotation after verse 14.

APPLY **1.** Fourteen years ago, where were you in your spiritual pilgrimage? **2.** Would you say that your moral and spiritual convictions have deepened, shifted or stayed the same in the last fourteen years?

OPEN If you have a disagreement with your superior, are you more likely to send a letter stating your position, ask for a face-to-face meeting or say nothing?

STUDY **1.** If you were on a missionary visit (like Peter) and your home church sent a group to see if you were going to be "politically correct," what would you do? **2.** Do you think Paul was a little hard on Peter? Why did he do this? **3.** How would you explain the word "justified" or "justification" to a person who did not understand the gospel? Why was it so hard for Jews by birth (and good, moral church people today) to see the need to be "justified"? **4.** How would you paraphrase verse 20 in your own words for your secular friends? **5.** In his parting shot, what is the point Paul is making in this passage?

APPLY When did you come to the place in your spiritual pilgrimage that you accepted the fact that you will never make it to heaven or obtain "right-standing" with God on your own merit?

OPEN **1.** Who laid down the law in your family when you were a kid? **2.** When you broke the rules, how were "grace" and forgiveness offered?

to the Gentiles. Though Paul did on occasions evangelize Jews (Acts 9:20; 26:20) his major mission was to the Gentiles (Acts 22:21).

2:11–14 Paul concludes his autobiographical sketch by recounting an incident in which he had to rebuke the apostle Peter for his inconsistency. This incident probably occurred after Paul's return to Antioch following his second visit to Jerusalem (vv. 1–10), but prior to his first missionary journey (Acts 13–14) during which he founded the Galatian churches.

2:15 Gentile sinners. Jews did look down rather arrogantly on all Gentiles. But Paul's point is that both Jew and Gentile come to God by faith, not by works. Being "better" morally has nothing to do with justification.

2:16 justified. Behind this word stands the image of the Judgment Day. The Jew was preoccupied with how one obtained a positive verdict (justification) from God the Judge. The opposite of justification is condemnation—to be declared guilty—on Judgment Day.

2:20 I no longer live. Paul died in relationship to the Law. **Christ lives in me.** That which now activates the believer is the resurrection life and power of Jesus. **I live by faith.** Faith is that which bonds together the believer and the risen Christ. Paul will also refer to this as living by the Spirit (5:25).

3:1 foolish. Paul's feelings of exas-

STUDY 1. How would you describe Paul's tone of voice in this passage? If you were in the room when this letter was read, what would you do? 2. In verses 2–5, what is Paul trying to get the young Christians to see? How would you boil down these questions into a few words? 3. If you were 99 years old and your wife was 89, what would you say if God promised you a son? Who does Paul claim are the true descendants of Abraham? 4. If Paul was around today, do you think he would warn Christians about a similar legalism to that in verses 10–14?

APPLY How do your friends and neighbors in the secular world look upon Christianity? Do they see church people in bondage to rules and regulations or bearers of good news and grace?

OPEN Have you written your will? Are you going to set up a trust for your children until they are old enough to receive their inheritance?

STUDY 1. If you created a will which had only one condition before dispensing the funds to your heirs, and someone came along and added many more conditions, how would you feel? 2. From the argument that Paul makes in this passage, what do you think his critics (the Judaizers)

to learn just one thing from you: Did you receive the Spirit by observing the law, or by believing what you heard? 3Are you so foolish? After
beginning with the Spirit, are you now trying to attain your goal by
human effort? 4Have you suffered so much for nothing—if it really
was for nothing? 5Does God give you his Spirit and work miracles
among you because you observe the law, or because you believe what
you heard?

6Consider Abraham: "He believed God, and it was credited to him
as righteousness."[a] 7Understand, then, that those who believe are
children of Abraham. 8The Scripture foresaw that God would justify
the Gentiles by faith, and announced the gospel in advance to Abraham: "All nations will be blessed through you."[b] 9So those who have
faith are blessed along with Abraham, the man of faith.

10All who rely on observing the law are under a curse, for it is written: "Cursed is everyone who does not continue to do everything
written in the Book of the Law."[c] 11Clearly no one is justified before
God by the law, because, "The righteous will live by faith."[d] 12The law
is not based on faith; on the contrary, "The man who does these
things will live by them."[e] 13Christ redeemed us from the curse of the
law by becoming a curse for us, for it is written: "Cursed is everyone
who is hung on a tree."[f] 14He redeemed us in order that the blessing
given to Abraham might come to the Gentiles through Christ Jesus, so
that by faith we might receive the promise of the Spirit.

The Law and the Promise

15Brothers, let me take an example from everyday life. Just as no
one can set aside or add to a human covenant that has been duly established, so it is in this case. 16The promises were spoken to Abraham and to his seed. The Scripture does not say "and to seeds,"
meaning many people, but "and to your seed,"[g] meaning one person,
who is Christ. 17What I mean is this: The law, introduced 430 years
later, does not set aside the covenant previously established by God
and thus do away with the promise. 18For if the inheritance depends

[a]6 Gen. 15:6 [b]8 Gen. 12:3; 18:18; 22:18 [c]10 Deut. 27:26 [d]11 Hab. 2:4 [e]12 Lev. 18:5 [f]13 Deut. 21:23 [g]16 Gen. 12:7; 13:15; 24:7

peration and indignation flare up. How could they have been so stupid (as the NEB translates the word)? It is not that they were unable to understand what was happening. They simply failed to use their minds. **bewitched.** Paul is saying that they act as if the Judaizers had put a spell on them.

3:6-9 Paul turns from his argument based on their experience to an argument based on Scripture. Here he shows that it has always been by faith that men and women became God's children.

3:6 He believed God. *God promised* Abraham that he would have descendants as numerous as the stars, even though his wife Sarah was barren! Despite the improbability of this ever happening, Abraham still trusted God that it would be so. **credited ... as righteousness.** For Abraham, right standing before God came by faith, not by law-keeping.

3:10–14 Paul's next point is that law-keeping is ultimately futile, because no one is able to fulfill the whole Law—therefore no one is justified by the Law. Rather a curse hangs heavy upon them. Blessing comes by faith.

3:15–18 Having argued from experience and from Scripture, Paul now argues the same point from human reason. He asks the Galatians to think about how wills are made. His point is that once established, no one can alter a will. Likewise, the covenant given by God to Abraham cannot be altered. The promised blessings came to Abraham's true children, not because they earned them through law-keeping, but because they came by grace without conditions.

3:16 God's promises to Abraham were not for all his many descendants, but more specifically, for his one crucial descendant: the Messiah. The blessings are then channeled outward to all who believe—Jew or Gentile—through Jesus the Messiah.

3:17 The prior covenant is unaffected by the later Law. **430 years later.** The Law was given much later, during the time of Moses.

3:18 inheritance. Promises, along with material possissions, given to a person's descendants. **grace.** God's promises to Abraham had nothing to do with law or obligations. It was a pure gift without conditions.

on the law, then it no longer depends on a promise; but God in his
grace gave it to Abraham through a promise.
19What, then, was the purpose of the law? It was added because of
transgressions until the Seed to whom the promise referred had
come. The law was put into effect through angels by a mediator. 20A
mediator, however, does not represent just one party; but God is one.
21Is the law, therefore, opposed to the promises of God? Absolutely
not! For if a law had been given that could impart life, then righteousness would certainly have come by the law. 22But the Scripture declares that the whole world is a prisoner of sin, so that what was
promised, being given through faith in Jesus Christ, might be given to
those who believe.
23Before this faith came, we were held prisoners by the law, locked
up until faith should be revealed. 24So the law was put in charge to
lead us to Christ[a] that we might be justified by faith. 25Now that faith
has come, we are no longer under the supervision of the law.

Sons of God

26You are all sons of God through faith in Christ Jesus, 27for all of
you who were baptized into Christ have clothed yourselves with
Christ. 28There is neither Jew nor Greek, slave nor free, male nor female, for you are all one in Christ Jesus. 29If you belong to Christ,
then you are Abraham's seed, and heirs according to the promise.
4 What I am saying is that as long as the heir is a child, he is no
different from a slave, although he owns the whole estate. 2He is
subject to guardians and trustees until the time set by his father. 3So
also, when we were children, we were in slavery under the basic principles of the world. 4But when the time had fully come, God sent his
Son, born of a woman, born under law, 5to redeem those under law,
that we might receive the full rights of sons. 6Because you are sons,
God sent the Spirit of his Son into our hearts, the Spirit who calls out,

[a]24 Or *charge until Christ came*

have claimed about the law of Moses? **3.** How does Paul go about explaining the reason why God gave Moses a set of rules and regulations that were impossible to keep? **4.** If anyone was a stickler for spiritual discipline, it would be Paul. What is the difference between spirituality and legalism?

APPLY How has your view of spiritual maturity changed over the years? How would you define a healthy spiritual life today?

OPEN Have you ever lived in a country where the gospel of Christianity has not penetrated? How did they treat women, children and the lower classes?

STUDY 1. How would you compare Paul's statement in verse 28 to the Magna Carta or the Declaration of Independence for its impact on the history of the Western World? **2.** What leveled the playing field between the social classes, and how does this change everything?

APPLY What is the closest you have come to seeing Christ break down the walls of ethnic and social prejudice in a Christian community?

3:19 What, then, was the purpose of the law? If the promises came by faith, what about the Law? What purpose did it have? This was a burning question to the Judaizers, because they felt that it reflected perfectly God's will. **It was added … until.** Paul answers that the Law was temporary. Its purpose was to make people aware of their sin, but when the Messiah came its function would cease. **by a mediator.** On the basis of Deuteronomy 33:2, it was concluded that the Law was given to Moses at Mount Sinai by the angels who accompanied God. Paul's point is that a word that came indirectly from God is of less significance than one that came directly, as did God's promises to Abraham.

3:24 put in charge. The Law is now pictured as a tutor. The same word is used for household slaves whose responsibility it was to look after the young men in the family until they reached the age of accountability.

3:27 baptized. A common water rite in Judaism; one of three acts by which a person became a Jew; picked up and given new meaning (repentance and remission of sins) by John the Baptist; and later used by the Christian church as the visible, outward sign of admission into the Christian community. **clothed.** This image may spring from the practice by the early church of removing old garments prior to baptism and then donning a new white robe after baptism.

3:28 Jew nor Greek. The Jewish contempt for the non-Jew was immense. **slave nor free.** Although some 60 million slaves virtually ran the Roman Empire, they were generally regarded as mere things, without rights. This was another barrier broken down by Christ. **male nor female.** A woman had few if any rights in either first-century Judaism or Greco-Roman culture. She belonged to her husband and he could treat her as he chose, including divorcing her with ease. **one in Christ Jesus.** In morning prayer, a Jewish man thanked God that he had not been made a Gentile, a slave, or a woman. The traditional distinctions are finished. In Christ all are one.

4:2 guardians and trustees. In his will, a Roman father appointed a guardian who looked after the child until he came of age at 14. Then a curator looked after the child's affairs until age 25. **until the time set.** The father had some discretion as to when the child received the inheritance.

4:4 when the time had fully come. Finally, the long history of God's revelation reaches a culminating point: Jesus is sent.

Abba,[a] Father." 7So you are no longer a slave, but a son; and since
you are a son, God has made you also an heir.

Paul's Concern for the Galatians

8Formerly, when you did not know God, you were slaves to those
who by nature are not gods. 9But now that you know God—or rather
are known by God—how is it that you are turning back to those weak
and miserable principles? Do you wish to be enslaved by them all
over again? 10You are observing special days and months and seasons
and years! 11I fear for you, that somehow I have wasted my efforts on
you.

12I plead with you, brothers, become like me, for I became like you.
You have done me no wrong. 13As you know, it was because of an illness that I first preached the gospel to you. 14Even though my illness
was a trial to you, you did not treat me with contempt or scorn. Instead, you welcomed me as if I were an angel of God, as if I were
Christ Jesus himself. 15What has happened to all your joy? I can testify
that, if you could have done so, you would have torn out your eyes
and given them to me. 16Have I now become your enemy by telling
you the truth?

17Those people are zealous to win you over, but for no good. What
they want is to alienate you ⌊from us⌋, so that you may be zealous for
them. 18It is fine to be zealous, provided the purpose is good, and to
be so always and not just when I am with you. 19My dear children, for
whom I am again in the pains of childbirth until Christ is formed in
you, 20how I wish I could be with you now and change my tone, because I am perplexed about you!

Hagar and Sarah

21Tell me, you who want to be under the law, are you not aware of
what the law says? 22For it is written that Abraham had two sons, one
by the slave woman and the other by the free woman. 23His son by the
slave woman was born in the ordinary way; but his son by the free
woman was born as the result of a promise.

24These things may be taken figuratively, for the women represent
two covenants. One covenant is from Mount Sinai and bears children
who are to be slaves: This is Hagar. 25Now Hagar stands for Mount
Sinai in Arabia and corresponds to the present city of Jerusalem, be-

[a]6 Aramaic for *Father*

OPEN If you were going to build a perfect world, what rules and rituals would you do away with for children?

STUDY 1. Who does Paul sound like in this passage: A pastor? A coach at half-time in a tough game? **2.** What is wrong with "observing special days and months and seasons and years"? How will this affect Paul's work? **3.** Why do you think Paul recalls his illness while being with the Galatians? **4.** How does Paul see his relationship with the Galatians? What are the false teachers trying to do to this relationship?

APPLY 1. Does anyone feel as strongly about your spiritual growth as Paul felt for the young Christians in Galatia? **2.** Is there anyone that you feel you must nurture in his or her spiritual growth?

OPEN What story do your parents tell about your birth?

STUDY 1. What is your favorite Old Testament story? What do you remember about Hagar and Sarah (Gen. 16; 17; 21)? **2.** How does Hagar represent the covenant of Law given to the Jews through Moses on Mount Sinai (v. 24)? **3.** How does Paul use this story to indicate that the Jews are actually the ones in slavery with Hagar (v. 25)? **4.** What does verse 27 say figuratively about

4:10 observing. Paul observed certain sacred events (Acts 20:16; 1 Cor. 16:8). It is one thing for a Jew to continue in his ethnic tradition in a nonbinding way, and another for a group of Gentiles to adopt the Jewish calendar.

4:14 illness. While there has been speculation about malaria, epilepsy and other ailments, there is no way to be certain about his illness. **an angel.** Perhaps there is an allusion to the time when Paul and Barnabas went to Lystra and were mistaken for gods (Acts 14:11–13). In any case, the contrast is between the greeting given an angel or Christ Jesus and their present attitude toward Paul.

4:15 torn out your eyes. Probably just an expression of deep gratitude; i.e., at that time there was nothing the Galatians would not have done for Paul.

4:19 Paul often refers to himself as the father of spiritual children (1 Cor. 4:15). Here he plays the mother role, and expresses his deep love and concern. **My dear children.** Paul cannot mask his deep affection for them despite his deep distress over their actions. **again.** For the second time he must endure the pangs of childbirth—first, when he sought to bring them out of paganism and into new birth in Christ, and now as he seeks to bring them out of legalism. **Christ is formed in you.** The metaphor is mixed but the point is clear. Paul's desire is that they come to possess Christlike characteristics.

4:25 the present city of Jerusalem. For Paul, this represents contemporary Judaism with all its legalism. **in slavery.** Just as Jerusalem was in slavery to Rome, the Jews were enslaved to the Law.

cause she is in slavery with her children. 26 But the Jerusalem that is
above is free, and she is our mother. 27 For it is written:

"Be glad, O barren woman,
who bears no children;
break forth and cry aloud,
you who have no labor pains;
because more are the children of the desolate woman
than of her who has a husband."[a]

28 Now you, brothers, like Isaac, are children of promise. 29 At that
time the son born in the ordinary way persecuted the son born by the
power of the Spirit. It is the same now. 30 But what does the Scripture
say? "Get rid of the slave woman and her son, for the slave woman's
son will never share in the inheritance with the free woman's son."[b]
31 Therefore, brothers, we are not children of the slave woman, but of
the free woman.

Freedom in Christ

5 It is for freedom that Christ has set us free. Stand firm, then, and
do not let yourselves be burdened again by a yoke of slavery.
2 Mark my words! I, Paul, tell you that if you let yourselves be circumcised, Christ will be of no value to you at all. 3 Again I declare to
every man who lets himself be circumcised that he is obligated to
obey the whole law. 4 You who are trying to be justified by law have
been alienated from Christ; you have fallen away from grace. 5 But by
faith we eagerly await through the Spirit the righteousness for which
we hope. 6 For in Christ Jesus neither circumcision nor uncircumcision has any value. The only thing that counts is faith expressing itself through love.

7 You were running a good race. Who cut in on you and kept you
from obeying the truth? 8 That kind of persuasion does not come from
the one who calls you. 9 "A little yeast works through the whole batch
of dough." 10 I am confident in the Lord that you will take no other
view. The one who is throwing you into confusion will pay the penalty, whoever he may be. 11 Brothers, if I am still preaching circumcision, why am I still being persecuted? In that case the offense of the
cross has been abolished. 12 As for those agitators, I wish they would
go the whole way and emasculate themselves!

[a]*27* Isaiah 54:1 [b]*30* Gen. 21:10

Sarah's children? How did the spiritual and numerical growth of the Gentiles fulfill this Scripture from Isaiah? **5.** How does verse 30 give a stern warning to the Judaizers?

APPLY This past week, did you feel more like Hagar (a slave to rules) or Sarah (a free, loved and forgiven Christian)?

OPEN How do you feel and react when others cut in on you while driving, shopping, speaking, etc.?

STUDY 1. When you first moved away from home, what did "freedom" mean to you? Free to do what? Free from what? **2.** Why does Paul make such a big deal about circumcision? Since our own efforts and achievements aren't the way to God, what is (vv. 5–6)? **3.** How would you describe Paul's attitude toward the Judaizers who have "cut in" on his ministry to the young Christians in Galatia—especially verse 12? **4.** In today's religious culture, what has replaced circumcision as the litmus test to be a real Christian?

APPLY 1. Who do you admire for the healthy balance in their Christian life between freedom in Christ and love for Christ and the resulting obedience in faith? **2.** Which side do you err on?

4:26 Jerusalem that is above. The heavenly city that was thought to provide the pattern for the physical city. The heavenly Jerusalem is the real thing, uncorrupted, perfect (Heb. 12:22; Rev. 3:12; 21:2,9–14).

5:2 I, Paul. Paul speaks with the full weight of his apostolic authority.

5:4 Grace is not grace (a freely given gift) if there is any requirement at all for receiving it. **trying to be justified.** Paul has said repeatedly that it is impossible to gain right standing through the Law (Rom. 11:7). The only thing the Law brings (in this context) is a curse (3:10–14).

5:5 Spirit. It is the Holy Spirit who fosters such assurances of acquittal. **hope.** The Christian can confidently expect a positive verdict on the Judgment Day. To have such a hope in advance of the event brings great liberty and rejoicing. This stands in contrast to the anxiety of one who is never sure if he or she has done quite enough "good works" or has been faithful to all points of the Law.

5:7 running a good race. In fact, those who would be most open to the appeals of the Judaizers would be the sincere, dedicated Galatians who wanted nothing more than to please God. But as relatively new Christians, they would not know they were being diverted into a legalism that led away from Christ. **race.** Paul uses an athletic metaphor to describe what happened to the Galatians. **cut in on you.** A word originally referring to the breaking up of roads by armies so as to hinder the progress of the enemy; it came to carry the idea of cutting in front of a runner to trip him up. **the truth.** The gospel (2:5,14).

OPEN On a scale of 1 to 10, how many "wild oats" did you sow in your youth?

STUDY 1. From your own experience would you say temptation to indulge the old "sinful desires" has been removed when a person becomes a Christian? **2.** How would you compare the list in verses 19–21 to your daily newspaper/TV news cast? **3.** If there is no way to legislate (v. 23) the fruit of the Spirit in a Christian's life, how are these gifts developed?

APPLY 1. How are you doing in the battle in your spiritual life? **2.** As you get older, do you find the battle easier, harder or different?

OPEN 1. In your family, who was always getting into trouble? How did your parents deal with problems? **2.** If you had to make a

13You, my brothers, were called to be free. But do not use your freedom to indulge the sinful nature[a]; rather, serve one another in love.
14The entire law is summed up in a single command: "Love your
neighbor as yourself."[b] 15If you keep on biting and devouring each
other, watch out or you will be destroyed by each other.

Life by the Spirit

16So I say, live by the Spirit, and you will not gratify the desires of
the sinful nature. 17For the sinful nature desires what is contrary to
the Spirit, and the Spirit what is contrary to the sinful nature. They
are in conflict with each other, so that you do not do what you want.
18But if you are led by the Spirit, you are not under law.
19The acts of the sinful nature are obvious: sexual immorality, impurity and debauchery; 20idolatry and witchcraft; hatred, discord,
jealousy, fits of rage, selfish ambition, dissensions, factions 21and
envy; drunkenness, orgies, and the like. I warn you, as I did before,
that those who live like this will not inherit the kingdom of God.
22But the fruit of the Spirit is love, joy, peace, patience, kindness,
goodness, faithfulness, 23gentleness and self-control. Against such
things there is no law. 24Those who belong to Christ Jesus have crucified the sinful nature with its passions and desires. 25Since we live by
the Spirit, let us keep in step with the Spirit. 26Let us not become conceited, provoking and envying each other.

Doing Good to All

6 Brothers, if someone is caught in a sin, you who are spiritual
should restore him gently. But watch yourself, or you also may

[a]13 Or *the flesh*; also in verses 16, 17, 19 and 24 [b]14 Lev. 19:18

5:13 free. But. What Paul has written about freedom from the Law could be misunderstood to be a license to indulge in one's appetites, and certainly he does not mean that. So he begins this new section on Christian living by examining the use of freedom.

5:20 idolatry. The worship of any idol, be it a carved image of God (a statue) or an abstract substitute for God (a status symbol). An idol is identified as such because when faced with a choice, a person will follow its leading. Money becomes an idol when to gain it a person will do anything. **hatred.** This is the underlying political, social and religious hostility which drives individuals and communities apart. **discord.** This is the type of contention which leads to factions. **selfish ambition.** This word has come to refer to anyone who works only for his or her own good and not for the benefit of others. **factions.** This means the party spirit which leads people to regard those with whom they disagree as enemies.

5:21 drunkenness. In the first century, diluted wine was drunk by all ages, but drunkenness was condemned. **and the like.** The list is representative, not exhaustive—touching, in order, upon the sins of sensuality, idolatry, social dissension, and intemperance. **not inherit.** The issue here is not sins into which one falls, but sin as a lifestyle. These are evidence of a life not controlled by the Spirit, and therefore the implication is that such a person has not been born from above and become a child of God.

5:22 fruit of the Spirit. These are the traits which characterize the child of God. The list is representative and not exhaustive. **love.** *Agape* (self-giving, active benevolence) in contrast, there is *eros* (sexual love), *philos* (warm feelings to friends and family) and *storge* (family affection). **joy.** The Greek word is *chara*, and comes from the same root as "grace" (*charis*). It is not based on earthly things or human achievement; it is a gift from God based on a right relationship with him. **peace.** The prime meaning of this word is not negative ("an absence of conflict"), but positive ("the presence of that which brings wholeness and well-being"). **patience.** This is the ability to be steadfast with people, refusing to give up on them. **kindness.** This is the compassionate use of strength for the good of another. **goodness.** This implies moral purity which reflects the character of God. **faithfulness.** This is to be reliable and trustworthy.

5:23 gentleness. According to Aristotle, this is the virtue that lies between excessive proneness to anger and the inability to be angry; it implies control of oneself. **self-control.** This is control of one's sensual passions, rather than control of one's anger.

6:1 a sin. A temporary lapse (as compared to an active lifestyle). **you who are spiritual.** Those whose lives bear the mark of the Spirit. This is not a clique of "special" Christians but is a call to all Christians (followers of Christ; 5:24–25). **restore.** A medical term, used to describe the setting of a fractured bone. The verb tense (in Greek) implies that this is not a single act but a continuous action. **gently.** This is an evidence of control by the Spirit (5:23). The temptation may be to display overt

be tempted. [2]Carry each other's burdens, and in this way you will fulfill the law of Christ. [3]If anyone thinks he is something when he is
nothing, he deceives himself. [4]Each one should test his own actions.
Then he can take pride in himself, without comparing himself to
somebody else, [5]for each one should carry his own load.
[6]Anyone who receives instruction in the word must share all good
things with his instructor.
[7]Do not be deceived: God cannot be mocked. A man reaps what he
sows. [8]The one who sows to please his sinful nature, from that
nature[a] will reap destruction; the one who sows to please the Spirit,
from the Spirit will reap eternal life. [9]Let us not become weary in doing good, for at the proper time we will reap a harvest if we do not
give up. [10]Therefore, as we have opportunity, let us do good to all
people, especially to those who belong to the family of believers.

Not Circumcision but a New Creation

[11]See what large letters I use as I write to you with my own hand!
[12]Those who want to make a good impression outwardly are trying
to compel you to be circumcised. The only reason they do this is to
avoid being persecuted for the cross of Christ. [13]Not even those who
are circumcised obey the law, yet they want you to be circumcised
that they may boast about your flesh. [14]May I never boast except in
the cross of our Lord Jesus Christ, through which[b] the world has been
crucified to me, and I to the world. [15]Neither circumcision nor uncircumcision means anything; what counts is a new creation. [16]Peace
and mercy to all who follow this rule, even to the Israel of God.
[17]Finally, let no one cause me trouble, for I bear on my body the
marks of Jesus.
[18]The grace of our Lord Jesus Christ be with your spirit, brothers.
Amen.

[a]8 *Or his flesh, from the flesh* [b]14 *Or whom*

living as a farmer, would you do it well? Why or why not?

STUDY 1. What has Paul been talking about in 5:16–26 that he wants to add to in this passage? **2.** What are three or four good principles in verses 1–8 to keep in mind when it comes to holding another person accountable? **3.** What is the challenge in verses 7–8 for you about sowing and reaping? As you look back over your life, what year brought you the most satisfaction? Why? **4.** How do you go about recharging your batteries when you get "weary in well doing?" **5.** How do you think the Judaizers felt when they read the "P.S." Paul wrote in verses 11–16?

APPLY 1. When did you have a truly accountable relationship with another believer or group of believers? **2.** When it comes to having constructive communication with someone who has been "caught in a sin," what have you found helpful? **3.** What has been the high point in this study for you? What would you like to study next?

disapproval and censorious judgment of the offender, but Paul counsels otherwise. **watch yourself.** No one is beyond temptation; all are vulnerable, so no one has any basis for self-righteousness. To watch means not simply to glance casually, but to gaze with concentration.

6:2 Carry each other's burdens. Mutual burden-bearing lies at the heart of Christian fellowship. **burdens.** A heavy, crushing weight which a single individual cannot carry. **law of Christ.** The law of love (5:14), which stands in sharp contrast to the Law.

6:4 Each one should test. This is an individual act. There is no "committee on standards" set up to evaluate individual Christians. The word for *test* is the same one used to describe the testing of metals to see if they are pure. **his own actions.** The subject of the self-assessment is not inner feelings or ideological commitments, but measurable activity. The question is: how is my life being lived? Note also that it is one's own actions, not those of other people, that are to be examined. **without comparing.** The temptation is to say, "Oh, I'm not so bad. Look at what so-and-so does," thus deflecting true insight into oneself and giving rise to false pride.

6:5 load. This is not the same as the crushing burden in verse 2. Rather, the word is used to describe the small individual pack a hiker or soldier carries. This is the same word used by Jesus in Matthew 11:30 to describe the burden (load) of his yoke, signifying that each of us has a burden (load) to carry.

Ephesians

Author. The apostle Paul was the writer of Ephesians.

Date. Paul probably wrote this letter in the early A.D. 60s, some 30 years after Jesus' crucifixion and only a few years before his death.

Theme. God's new society.

Personal Reading	Group Study Topic and Reading	
1:1–14	To God Be the Glory!	1:1–14
1:15–23	Fullness of Christ	1:15–23
2:1–10	Raised Up With Christ	2:1–10
2:11–22	End of Hostility	2:11–22
3:1–13	Mystery of Grace	3:1–13
3:14–21	Power to Know Love	3:14–21
4:1–16	Working Out Our Unity	4:1–16
4:17–32	Children of Light	4:17–32
5:1–21	Imitators of God	5:1–21
5:22–6:9	Relationships in Christ	5:22–6:9
6:10–24	Armor of God	6:10–24

Historical Background. Paul is in prison once again, and Epaphras has come to visit him bearing disturbing news about the church at Colosse. Since Paul is about to send back the runaway slave Onesimus (now converted) to his owner Philemon, a member of the Colossian Church, he takes this opportunity to send along a letter in which he addresses the Colossian heresy. He also writes two more letters: one to Philemon and one to a neighboring area, the Ephesians. These three epistles (Colossians, Ephesians and Philemon) form the core of what we now know as the Prison Epistles or the Captivity Letters. It is unclear which imprisonment produced these letters (2 Cor. 11:23), but most likely Paul was at Rome (Acts 28). The fourth Prison Epistle, Philippians, was written in prison on another occasion.

Ephesians and Colossians are more similar in language and content than any other two letters in the New Testament. Together they give us a clear understanding of the nature of Christ and the unity of the church in him.

Characteristics. We see Christ creating the church, his body and a new social order of love and unity that transcends the racial, ethnic and social distinctions between people. God calls people to be reconciled to himself and to one another through the cross of Christ. The cross provides forgiveness of sins, a new life and a new people. Between Paul's greeting (1:1–2) and salutation (6:21–24), the letter divides easily into two parts. Part one (chapters 1–3) focuses on *doctrine*, specifically, the new life and new society God has created through Jesus. Part two (chapters 4–6) focuses on *ethics*, specifically, the new standards and new relationships expected of believers.

The City of Ephesus. The city of Ephesus was the capital of the Roman province of Asia. It was a large, bustling, secular city situated on the west coast of Asia Minor (modern Turkey) on the Aegean Sea. Originally a Greek colony, by Roman times it had become a center for international trade, largely as a result of its fine, natural harbor. Its key architectural feature was the temple of Artemis (or Diana), considered to be one of the seven wonders of the ancient world.

Paul's first visit to Ephesus was brief. Later he returned during his third missionary journey and spent over two years there. His ministry was both effective and controversial. After three months in the synagogue, he was forced out and took up residence in the lecture hall of Tyrannus (Acts 19:8–9). News of his message spread throughout Asia Minor (Acts 19:10). Extraordinary things happened. Handkerchiefs touched by him were used to cure the sick (Acts 19:11–12). Demons were cast out in the name of Jesus, even by Jewish exorcists (Acts 19:13–17). Pagan converts burned their books of magic (Acts 19:18–20). *Eventually, a riot* broke out in Ephesus because of Paul. Demetrius, a silversmith, organized a citywide protest. He charged that Paul's success posed a threat to the economic well being of craftsmen who made their living from the worshipers of Artemis (Acts 19:23–41). As a result, Paul moved on to Macedonia.

Paul never visited Ephesus again. He did, however, stop at the nearby port of Miletus on his return to Jerusalem. He called the Ephesian elders to him there and gave a moving farewell address (Acts 20:13–38).

1 Paul, an apostle of Christ Jesus by the will of God,

To the saints in Ephesus,[a] the faithful[b] in Christ Jesus:

2 Grace and peace to you from God our Father and the Lord Jesus
Christ.

Spiritual Blessings in Christ

3 Praise be to the God and Father of our Lord Jesus Christ, who has
blessed us in the heavenly realms with every spiritual blessing in
Christ. 4 For he chose us in him before the creation of the world to be
holy and blameless in his sight. In love 5 he[c] predestined us to be
adopted as his sons through Jesus Christ, in accordance with his
pleasure and will— 6 to the praise of his glorious grace, which he has
freely given us in the One he loves. 7 In him we have redemption
through his blood, the forgiveness of sins, in accordance with the
riches of God's grace 8 that he lavished on us with all wisdom and understanding. 9 And he[d] made known to us the mystery of his will according to his good pleasure, which he purposed in Christ, 10 to be put
into effect when the times will have reached their fulfillment—to
bring all things in heaven and on earth together under one head,
even Christ.
11 In him we were also chosen,[e] having been predestined according
to the plan of him who works out everything in conformity with the
purpose of his will, 12 in order that we, who were the first to hope in

[a]1 Some early manuscripts do not have *in Ephesus.* [b]1 Or *believers who are* [c]4,5 Or *sight in love. 5He* [d]8,9 Or *us. With all wisdom and understanding, 9he* [e]11 Or *were made heirs*

OPEN 1. When you write a letter, do you start off with a long beginning or get right to the point? **2.** Who do you know that has been adopted?

STUDY 1. If you were in prison in Rome awaiting trial (like Paul was) and you found out that a church you had started was being torn apart by moral failure, internal squabbles and false teaching, what would you do? How would you start off a letter? **2.** What do you learn in this book's introduction about the characteristics and city of Ephesus? **3.** There are seven stages or events described here in God's plan to create a new community of believers. What are these stages? When will all of this reach fulfillment? How does this cosmic overview leave you feeling?

APPLY 1. When did you come to the place in your spiritual journey that you fully understood what God did for you in Jesus Christ? **2.** How would you describe your spiritual life right now?

1:1 apostle. Apostles were much like ambassadors. They are chosen by the king (in this case Jesus) to represent him and are given power to act in his name. This was the title that was given to the original Twelve (Luke 6:13) and then later to Paul (Gal. 1:11–24). By using this title, Paul indicates that he is writing with the authority of the Lord, Jesus Christ.

1:2 Grace and peace. Grace refers to the undeserved favor of God freely given as a gift. Peace refers to the reconciliation of sinners to God and others. Taken together, they define a central theme of Ephesians: peace through grace.

1:3 Praise. The verb "praise" can also be translated "to speak well of" and carries the idea of thanking, glorifying and singing the praises of the one who is the object of this gratitude. **God.** God is the subject of virtually every main verb in this passage. **Jesus Christ.** It is in and through Jesus that God's work of love, grace, and redemption is performed. **has blessed us.** The tense of the Greek verb indicates that what is in view here is a single, past action on God's part. **the heavenly realms.** The unseen world of spiritual reality.

1:4 holy and blameless. The goal of the Christian life: people who have been made perfect and whole.

1:5 predestined. Literally, "marked out beforehand." **adopted.** This was a common Roman custom, in which a child was given all the rights of the adoptive family by grace, not by birth. **his sons.** The purpose of predestination is that people become the sons and daughters of God. **his pleasure and will.** This phrase carries with it the sense that God goes about such choosing with great joy.

1:7 redemption. The setting free (originally of prisoners or slaves) by payment of a ransom (in this case, Jesus' death in place of the sinner). **forgiveness of sins.** The child of God is not only given freedom from the penalty of sin, but the sin itself is forgotten. Redemption and forgiveness go together.

1:9 mystery. Contrary to the normal use of the word (with its emphasis on a secret being kept), here the word focuses on the disclosure of what was once hidden but is now revealed by God.

1:10 to bring ... together. From a Greek word meaning "to sum up," as in the conclusion of a speech or a column of figures; a gathering together of the pieces into a whole.

Christ, might be for the praise of his glory. [13]And you also were included in Christ when you heard the word of truth, the gospel of your
salvation. Having believed, you were marked in him with a seal, the
promised Holy Spirit, [14]who is a deposit guaranteeing our inheritance
until the redemption of those who are God's possession—to the
praise of his glory.

OPEN What do you remember from your childhood about Thanksgiving Day? Who keeps your family traditions alive now?

STUDY **1.** What are the three prayers that Paul prays for the Ephesians and what will be the result of each prayer? When did you start to understand all of these things? **2.** If you were a painter like Michelangelo, how would you go about illustrating the picture of Jesus in verses 20–23?

APPLY When is the last time you took the day off and went away to a quiet place to be alone with God?

Thanksgiving and Prayer

[15]For this reason, ever since I heard about your faith in the Lord
Jesus and your love for all the saints, [16]I have not stopped giving
thanks for you, remembering you in my prayers. [17]I keep asking that
the God of our Lord Jesus Christ, the glorious Father, may give you
the Spirit[a] of wisdom and revelation, so that you may know him better. [18]I pray also that the eyes of your heart may be enlightened in
order that you may know the hope to which he has called you, the
riches of his glorious inheritance in the saints, [19]and his incomparably great power for us who believe. That power is like the working of
his mighty strength, [20]which he exerted in Christ when he raised him
from the dead and seated him at his right hand in the heavenly
realms, [21]far above all rule and authority, power and dominion, and
every title that can be given, not only in the present age but also in
the one to come. [22]And God placed all things under his feet and appointed him to be head over everything for the church, [23]which is his
body, the fullness of him who fills everything in every way.

OPEN What is the best Christmas present that stands out above all of the rest?

STUDY **1.** In this passage, Paul divides a Christian's life

Made Alive in Christ

2 As for you, you were dead in your transgressions and sins, [2]in
which you used to live when you followed the ways of this world

[a]17 Or *a spirit*

1:13 seal. A mark placed by an owner on a package, a cow, or even a slave. The cults in the first century sometimes tattooed a mark on their devotees. For the Jews, circumcision was such a seal (Rom. 4:11); for Christians the Holy Spirit is his or her seal. **promised Holy Spirit.** This is the second of three terms in verses 13–14 used to describe the Holy Spirit. The Spirit is not only "promised," but the "seal" whereby the Christian is marked out as belonging to God and the "guarantee" of that Christian's future inheritance. The Holy Spirit was promised in the Old Testament (Ezek. 36:27; Joel 2:28) and by Jesus (Luke 24:49; John 14–16; Acts 1:4–5; 2:33, 38–39; Gal. 3:14).

1:14 deposit. A down payment which guarantees ultimate ownership by God.

1:16 thanks. Paul's response to these new Christians is one of profound thankfulness.

1:17 wisdom and revelation. Awareness of all these spiritual blessings will not necessarily come via logical dedication, nor solely as a result of experience. There must also be an inner work of God by which individuals are enabled to "see" and understand what is going on.

1:18 the eyes of your heart. Paul wants this illumination to strike right to the core of a person's being. **the hope to which he has called you.** This is the first of the three effects which result from knowing God. These phrases seem to define well the objective substance of this hope; i.e., they are God's children and they will be holy and not held accountable for their sins. **the riches of his glorious inheritance in the saints.** This is the second benefit derived from knowing God. The idea is parallel to that in Colossians 1:12, and the reference is to the riches beyond imagination which God has reserved for his people (1 Peter 1:4).

1:19 his incomparably great power. This is the third effect. In all things, the evidence of God's great power is there. The greatness of his power is demonstrated in raising Jesus from the grave like he promised.

1:20 raised him from the dead. Jesus was really dead, buried in a tomb. But so mighty is God's power that it burst the bonds of death. **seated him at his right hand.** Jesus is now the King who reigns in absolute power. One day that reign will result in the bringing together of all things under him (1:10; Heb. 2:5–9).

1:21 rule and authority, power and dominion, and every title that can be given. Paul wants to be quite clear that there is no power by any name—be it angelic or demonic, natural or supernatural, from the past or in the future—that stands outside the scope of Christ's powerful reign.

2:1 dead. They were spiritually dead. **transgressions and sins.** These two words refer, respectively, to active wrongdoing ("sins of commission"), and passive failure ("sins of omission").

2:2 ruler of the kingdom of the air. This is the first of several references in

and of the ruler of the kingdom of the air, the spirit who is now at
work in those who are disobedient. 3 All of us also lived among them
at one time, gratifying the cravings of our sinful nature[a] and following its desires and thoughts. Like the rest, we were by nature objects
of wrath. 4 But because of his great love for us, God, who is rich in
mercy, 5 made us alive with Christ even when we were dead in transgressions—it is by grace you have been saved. 6 And God raised us up
with Christ and seated us with him in the heavenly realms in Christ
Jesus, 7 in order that in the coming ages he might show the incomparable riches of his grace, expressed in his kindness to us in Christ
Jesus. 8 For it is by grace you have been saved, through faith—and this
not from yourselves, it is the gift of God— 9 not by works, so that no
one can boast. 10 For we are God's workmanship, created in Christ
Jesus to do good works, which God prepared in advance for us to do.

One in Christ

11 Therefore, remember that formerly you who are Gentiles by birth
and called "uncircumcised" by those who call themselves "the circumcision" (that done in the body by the hands of men)— 12 remember that at that time you were separate from Christ, excluded from
citizenship in Israel and foreigners to the covenants of the promise,
without hope and without God in the world. 13 But now in Christ Jesus
you who once were far away have been brought near through the
blood of Christ.

14 For he himself is our peace, who has made the two one and has
destroyed the barrier, the dividing wall of hostility, 15 by abolishing
in his flesh the law with its commandments and regulations. His
purpose was to create in himself one new man out of the two, thus

[a]3 Or *our flesh*

into two periods. What are they? Who controlled you in the first period? What was the result? **2.** What was God's motive for restoring you to fellowship with him? **3.** What is your part in God's great project in your life? How does it make you feel that God considers you his great masterpiece (v. 10)?

APPLY How is God doing in his workmanship project in your life?

OPEN 1. Do you remember any stories about the Berlin Wall? **2.** When did your ancestors come to this country? Do you know how they became citizens?

STUDY 1. If you started a church that was made up of two distinct ethnic groups (one with high moral standards and the other with no morals), what would you do to bring these two factions together? **2.** How does Paul describe the Gentiles in five ways before God intervened (v. 12)? **3.** What happened to the wall that separated the good guys from the bad guys? What is the result now? **4.** If you had to explain

---

Ephesians to Satan. **now at work.** Satan's activity is not only past, nor only in the future. It is here and now in this present evil age. **those who are disobedient.** They are, in fact, in active rebellion against him.

2:3 our sinful nature. The word here is literally "the flesh," and it refers to self-centered human nature which expresses itself in destructive activities of both body and mind.

2:4 because of his great love for us. Love is God's reason for rescuing fallen humanity. **rich.** Paul makes more allusions to "riches" in Ephesians than anywhere else in his writings. **mercy.** Not only love, but mercy motivates God. Love and mercy are closely related.

2:5 made us alive. Paul coins this word to describe exactly what happens to us when we are "in Christ"; namely, we share in Christ's resurrection, ascension and enthronement. **by grace.** This resurrection from spiritual death cannot be earned. It is simply given. Grace is God's unmerited favor or gift to us.

2:8 For it is by grace you have been saved. This is the second time Paul acclaims this amazing fact (v. 5). **through faith.** Salvation does not come about because of faith. Salvation comes by grace through faith.

2:8–9 not from yourselves ... not by works. Salvation is not a reward for being good or keeping the Law.

2:10 good works. Although good works do not save a person, they are a result of salvation.

2:11 remember. In verses 1–3, Paul reminded his Gentile readers that once they were trapped in their transgressions and sins, and so were spiritually dead and alienated from God.

2:12 separate from Christ. In contrast to the great blessings which come as a result of being "in Christ," at one time the Gentiles were outside Christ. **excluded from citizenship.** Gentiles were not part of God's kingdom. Israel was a nation founded by God, consisting of his people, and Gentiles were outside that reality. **foreigners to the covenants.** Not only did Gentiles have no part in God's kingdom, they also stood outside all the agreements God made with his people. **without hope.** During this particular historical era, the Roman world experienced a profound loss of hope. **without God.** Gentiles had no effective knowledge of the one true God.

2:13 But now ... through the blood of Christ. Paul pinpoints how this great change occurred. It is as a result of Jesus' death on the cross that union with God is possible (1:7).

2:14 our peace. Jesus brings peace; that is, he creates harmony between human beings and God. He also creates harmony between human beings. **the dividing wall of hostility.** Paul might have in mind an actual wall which existed in the temple in Jerusalem beyond which Gentiles could not go. They were cut off by a stone wall ("the dividing wall"), bearing signs that warned in Greek and Latin that trespassing foreigners would be killed.

the metaphor in verses 19–22 to a group of architects, what would you say?

APPLY 1. If Paul were writing this letter today, what stand would he take on social issues that divide the church? **2.** What relationship do you need to work on by breaking down the wall?

OPEN Who is your favorite mystery writer? What is your favorite mystery movie?

STUDY 1. What does Paul claim in this passage that might explain his passion? **2.** What is the mystery that God revealed to Paul and how radical would this be in the mind of a strict Jew like Paul? **3.** Do you think Paul was uniquely called or that every believer is called to carry out this mission? **4.** Why do you think Paul felt he was "less than the least of all God's people"? **5.** How does it make you feel that you are part of God's plan and purpose that is so beautiful even "rulers and authorities" in the universe take notice?

APPLY 1. What is the consuming passion in your life? On a scale from 1 to 10, how would you compare your passion for Christ's mission to Paul's passion? **2.** If Paul

making peace, 16and in this one body to reconcile both of them to
God through the cross, by which he put to death their hostility. 17He
came and preached peace to you who were far away and peace to
those who were near. 18For through him we both have access to the
Father by one Spirit.

19Consequently, you are no longer foreigners and aliens, but fellow
citizens with God's people and members of God's household, 20built
on the foundation of the apostles and prophets, with Christ Jesus
himself as the chief cornerstone. 21In him the whole building is
joined together and rises to become a holy temple in the Lord. 22And
in him you too are being built together to become a dwelling in which
God lives by his Spirit.

Paul the Preacher to the Gentiles

3 For this reason I, Paul, the prisoner of Christ Jesus for the sake of
you Gentiles—

2Surely you have heard about the administration of God's grace
that was given to me for you, 3that is, the mystery made known to me
by revelation, as I have already written briefly. 4In reading this, then,
you will be able to understand my insight into the mystery of Christ,
5which was not made known to men in other generations as it has
now been revealed by the Spirit to God's holy apostles and prophets.
6This mystery is that through the gospel the Gentiles are heirs together with Israel, members together of one body, and sharers together in
the promise in Christ Jesus.

7I became a servant of this gospel by the gift of God's grace given
me through the working of his power. 8Although I am less than the
least of all God's people, this grace was given me: to preach to the
Gentiles the unsearchable riches of Christ, 9and to make plain to everyone the administration of this mystery, which for ages past was
kept hidden in God, who created all things. 10His intent was that now,
through the church, the manifold wisdom of God should be made
known to the rulers and authorities in the heavenly realms, 11according to his eternal purpose which he accomplished in Christ Jesus our

---

2:16 reconcile. Literally, "to bring together estranged parties." Here the reference is to bringing both Jew and Gentile to God.

2:17 He came and preached peace. Christ's first words to the stunned apostles after his resurrection were, in fact, "Peace be with you!"(John 20:19).

2:19 foreigners. Nonresident aliens were disliked by the native population and often held in suspicion. **aliens.** These are residents in a foreign land. They pay taxes, but have no legal standing and few rights. **fellow citizens.** Whereas once the Gentiles were "*excluded from citizenship in* Israel" (v. 12), now they are members of God's kingdom. **members of God's household.** In fact, their relationship is far more intimate. They have become family.

2:20 cornerstone. The stone which rested firmly on the foundation and anchored two walls together, giving each its correct alignment.

2:21 joined together. A term used by a mason to describe how two stones were prepared so that they would bond tightly together. **temple.** The new temple is not like the old one, carved out of dead stone—beautiful, but forbidding and exclusive. Rather, it is alive all over the world, inclusive of all, and made up of the individuals in whom God dwells.

3:3 mystery. In Greek, a mystery is something that is beyond human reason to figure out, but once it is revealed by God, it is open and plain to all. **revelation.** This new reality was given by God.

3:6 heirs together ... members together ... sharers together. Paul's point is that these two groups—once traditional enemies—now share together the same promised covenant blessings are a part of the same body, and they share the same benefits.

3:9 to make plain. Paul's original commission, given by Jesus on the Damascus Road, carried this idea: "I am sending you to open their eyes and turn them from darkness to light ..." (Acts 26:17–18)

3:10 made known to the rulers and authorities in the heavenly realms. At this point, Paul's vision soars to new heights as he declares that it is by means of this multiethnic church that the very supernatural powers themselves see what God is doing.

Lord. 12 In him and through faith in him we may approach God with
freedom and confidence. 13 I ask you, therefore, not to be discouraged
because of my sufferings for you, which are your glory.

A Prayer for the Ephesians

14 For this reason I kneel before the Father, 15 from whom his whole
family[a] in heaven and on earth derives its name. 16 I pray that out of
his glorious riches he may strengthen you with power through his
Spirit in your inner being, 17 so that Christ may dwell in your hearts
through faith. And I pray that you, being rooted and established in
love, 18 may have power, together with all the saints, to grasp how
wide and long and high and deep is the love of Christ, 19 and to know
this love that surpasses knowledge—that you may be filled to the
measure of all the fullness of God.

20 Now to him who is able to do immeasurably more than all we ask
or imagine, according to his power that is at work within us, 21 to him
be glory in the church and in Christ Jesus throughout all generations,
for ever and ever! Amen.

Unity in the Body of Christ

4 As a prisoner for the Lord, then, I urge you to live a life worthy of
the calling you have received. 2 Be completely humble and gentle;
be patient, bearing with one another in love. 3 Make every effort to
keep the unity of the Spirit through the bond of peace. 4 There is one
body and one Spirit— just as you were called to one hope when you
were called— 5 one Lord, one faith, one baptism; 6 one God and Father
of all, who is over all and through all and in all.

7 But to each one of us grace has been given as Christ apportioned
it. 8 This is why it[b] says:

"When he ascended on high,
he led captives in his train
and gave gifts to men."[c]

9 (What does "he ascended" mean except that he also descended to
the lower, earthly regions[d]? 10 He who descended is the very one who

[a] 15 Or *whom all fatherhood* [b] 8 Or *God* [c] 8 Psalm 68:18 [d] 9 Or *the depths of the earth*

was in your study group, what would Paul be asking your group to do? ______

OPEN Who tucked you in at night and heard your prayers?

STUDY 1. How would you describe, with two adjectives, this concluding prayer to wrap up the teaching section of this epistle? **2.** What exactly is Paul asking God to do for the believers in Ephesus?

APPLY How big is your God? How would you compare your view of God now to your view of God five or ten years ago? ______

OPEN Do you know of a blended family? How long did it take for the children to really bond?

STUDY 1. Do you think Paul sounded a little weary of the struggles going on in the church in Ephesus? What does he want to see happen? **2.** Of the four jobs in a church leadership team that Paul describes, which job are you best qualified for: Apostle (pioneer and church planter); prophet (motivator and encourager); evangelist (soul winner), or pastor/teacher (trainer and coach)? What is the strongest gift of the others in your group? **3.** What is the purpose of the leadership team of a church? Who is supposed to carry out the ministry? **4.** What is the picture of the church in verses 14–16 that Paul prays for?

3:16 strengthen you with power. Paul asks that Christians be fortified or invigorated within by the Holy Spirit. He asks that they experience this awesome power of God about which he has written so eloquently. **inner being.** By this term, Paul may be referring to the deepest part of the human personality, where a person's true essence lies.

3:17 dwell. This means "to settle down," and it implies a permanent residency (in a house), versus a temporary stopover (in a tent). In other words, Christ has come to stay. **rooted and established.** By his choice of these words, Paul hints at two metaphors through which the character of love is revealed. The Christian is to be anchored firmly in the soil of love just like a tree. The Christian is also to be set solidly on the foundation of love just like a well-constructed house. (The second word in Greek is literally "grounded.") **love.** *Agape* love is selfless giving to others, regardless of how one feels. Such love is the foundation upon which the church will grow.

4:1 I urge you. Stylistically, Paul moves from the indicative ("This is the way things are") to the imperative ("This is what must be done").

4:2 humble. Humility is an absence of pride and self-assertion, based upon accurate self-knowledge and on an understanding of the God-given worth of others. Humility is the key to the growth of healthy relationships between people. **gentle.** Gentleness is the quality of strength under control, like a thorough-bred horse. **patient.** Patience is long suffering. **bearing with one another.** This is the kind of tolerance of the faults of others which springs from humility, gentleness and patience.

4:8 Paul quotes Psalm 68:18, which describes the triumphal procession of a conquering Jewish king up Mt. Zion and into Jerusalem. The king is followed by a procession of prisoners in chains. As he marches up the hill, he is given gifts of tribute and in turn disperses gifts of booty. Paul uses this verse to describe Christ's ascension into heaven.

4:9 descended. Paul is referring to Christ's incarnation, whereby he came

ascended higher than all the heavens, in order to fill the whole universe.) 11It was he who gave some to be apostles, some to be prophets, some to be evangelists, and some to be pastors and teachers, 12to
prepare God's people for works of service, so that the body of Christ
may be built up 13until we all reach unity in the faith and in the
knowledge of the Son of God and become mature, attaining to the
whole measure of the fullness of Christ.
14Then we will no longer be infants, tossed back and forth by the
waves, and blown here and there by every wind of teaching and by
the cunning and craftiness of men in their deceitful scheming. 15In-
stead, speaking the truth in love, we will in all things grow up into
him who is the Head, that is, Christ. 16From him the whole body,
joined and held together by every supporting ligament, grows and
builds itself up in love, as each part does its work.

Living as Children of Light

17So I tell you this, and insist on it in the Lord, that you must no
longer live as the Gentiles do, in the futility of their thinking. 18They
are darkened in their understanding and separated from the life of
God because of the ignorance that is in them due to the hardening of
their hearts. 19Having lost all sensitivity, they have given themselves
over to sensuality so as to indulge in every kind of impurity, with a
continual lust for more.
20You, however, did not come to know Christ that way. 21Surely you
heard of him and were taught in him in accordance with the truth
that is in Jesus. 22You were taught, with regard to your former way of
life, to put off your old self, which is being corrupted by its deceitful
desires; 23to be made new in the attitude of your minds; 24and to put
on the new self, created to be like God in true righteousness and holiness.
25Therefore each of you must put off falsehood and speak truthfully
to his neighbor, for we are all members of one body. 26"In your anger

APPLY 1. If you knew you could not fail what would you like to try or do to fulfill your God-given gifts? **2.** Have you ever talked to someone like your pastor about this? What was their response?

OPEN 1. Did you ever get your mouth washed out with soap? **2.** What were your parent's rules about language in your home?

STUDY 1. Do you think the behaviors described in verses 17–19 were still true of some in the church who had been converted? **2.** What is Paul saying in verses 22–24 about transformation? Is transformation a one-time event or a process? How would you illustrate this passage from your own experience? **3.** Reading between the lines what do you think was happening in this church to cause Paul to write verses 25–32? What would you do if you were on the leadership team of this church?

---

down from heaven and into our space and time (Phil. 2:5–11).

4:11 This is one of several lists of gifts. The emphasis in this list is on teaching gifts. **apostles.** Paul probably had in mind the small group of individuals who had seen the resurrected Christ, and had been commissioned by him to launch his church (Acts 1:21–22; 1 Cor. 9:1). **prophets.** In contrast to teachers who relied upon the Old Testament Scripture and the teaching of Jesus to instruct others, prophets offered words of instruction, exhortation and admonition, which were immediate and unpremeditated. Their source was direct revelation from God. **evangelists.** Those with the special gift of making the gospel clear and convincing to people. **pastors and teachers.** The way *in which this is expressed in Greek* indicates that these two functions reside in one person.

4:15 speaking the truth in love. Christians are to stand for both truth and love. Truth without love becomes harsh. Love without truth becomes weak.

4:17 as the Gentiles do. Paul begins this section on purity of life by describing the typical Gentile lifestyle from which Christians must flee. **the futility of their thinking.** Paul emphasizes the connection between thought and behavior.

4:18 hardening of their hearts. The center of their being (the heart) has become "stone-like" or "petrified."

4:19 sensuality ... impurity ... lust. By these three nouns, Paul describes what pagan life has evolved into.

4:20–21 to know Christ ... heard of him ... taught in him. In contrast to the three phrases which describe the wrong thinking of the pagan, Paul sets these three phrases which describe how the Christian comes to learn the right way of thinking.

4:22–24 put off ... put on. Paul develops a clothing metaphor here. At conversion, the Christian sheds (strips off) his or her old, ragged, filthy garment and puts on a fresh, new cloak. **old self ... new self.** At conversion, the Christian puts off his or her old, sinful nature and is clothed with the very life of Christ himself.

4:23 be made new. This exchange of natures occurs at conversion. However, here the verb indicates the need for ongoing, continual renewal. **the attitude of your minds.** Again, the emphasis is on right thinking in order to be able to live right.

4:26 In your anger. Paul recognizes that there is such a thing as legitimate anger. But once admitted, anger is to be dealt with, and so Paul identifies ways to deal with anger. Do not let anger develop into resentment.

do not sin"[a]: Do not let the sun go down while you are still angry,
27and do not give the devil a foothold. 28He who has been stealing
must steal no longer, but must work, doing something useful with his
own hands, that he may have something to share with those in need.
29Do not let any unwholesome talk come out of your mouths, but
only what is helpful for building others up according to their needs,
that it may benefit those who listen. 30And do not grieve the Holy
Spirit of God, with whom you were sealed for the day of redemption.
31Get rid of all bitterness, rage and anger, brawling and slander, along
with every form of malice. 32Be kind and compassionate to one another, forgiving each other, just as in Christ God forgave you.

5 Be imitators of God, therefore, as dearly loved children 2and live
a life of love, just as Christ loved us and gave himself up for us as
a fragrant offering and sacrifice to God.
3But among you there must not be even a hint of sexual immorality,
or of any kind of impurity, or of greed, because these are improper for
God's holy people. 4Nor should there be obscenity, foolish talk or
coarse joking, which are out of place, but rather thanksgiving. 5For of
this you can be sure: No immoral, impure or greedy person—such a
man is an idolater—has any inheritance in the kingdom of Christ and
of God.[b] 6Let no one deceive you with empty words, for because of
such things God's wrath comes on those who are disobedient.
7Therefore do not be partners with them.
8For you were once darkness, but now you are light in the Lord.
Live as children of light 9(for the fruit of the light consists in all goodness, righteousness and truth) 10and find out what pleases the Lord.
11Have nothing to do with the fruitless deeds of darkness, but rather
expose them. 12For it is shameful even to mention what the disobedient do in secret. 13But everything exposed by the light becomes visible, 14for it is light that makes everything visible. This is why it is said:

"Wake up, O sleeper,
  rise from the dead,
and Christ will shine on you."

15Be very careful, then, how you live—not as unwise but as wise,
16making the most of every opportunity, because the days are evil.

[a]26 Psalm 4:4 [b]5 Or *kingdom of the Christ and God*

APPLY 1. Of the "do not's" in verses 25–32, which one do you have the hardest time with? What are you doing about it? 2. Who would you point to in your church as someone that proves the process of transformation works? 3. What can this group pray about for you this week?

OPEN Have you ever spent significant time in a very pagan environment where language, morals and ethics were terrible?

STUDY 1. Why do you think Paul zeroes in on sexual sin? For a Gentile in Ephesus who was brought up believing sexual sins were okay, what does Paul say in verses 3–7? How about dirty jokes and locker room stories? 2. According to verses 8–14, what should be a Christian's attitude and response to X-rated TV, pornography on the Internet, and "adult" literature? How far should a Christian go in "exposing" the darkness? 3. What is Paul saying to you in the illustration, "Do not get drunk on wine ... Instead, be filled with the Spirit." Could anyone accuse you of being "under the influence" of the Spirit? 4. What does Paul want those who feel trapped in the filth of a sex-mad world to do (vv. 19–20)?

APPLY 1. What is God saying to you in the quote in verse 14? 2. Do you long to be in a spiritual community who will practice what verses 19–20 are all about?

4:29–30 Paul turns to the use of one's mouth. The word translated "unwholesome" means "rotten," and is used to describe spoiled fruit (Matt. 12:33). Instead of rancid words that wound others, the words of Christians ought to edify ("building others up"), be appropriate ("according to their needs"), bring grace (*this is the literal rendering of the* word translated "benefit"), and not cause distress for the Holy Spirit (by unholy words).

4:31 Paul identifies six negative attitudes which must be erased from the Christian life. **bitterness.** Spiteful, long-standing resentment. **rage and anger.** These two attitudes are related. The first is a more immediate flare-up, while the latter is a more long-term, sullen hostility. **brawling.** Loud self-assertion; screaming arguments. **slander.** Insulting someone else behind his or her back. **malice.** Wishing (or actually plotting) evil against another.

5:4 Vulgar talk is out of place, because it demeans God's good gift of sex (which is a subject for thanksgiving, not joking).

5:5–7 Judgment is real. Those who live a committed life of self-indulgent sensuality without repenting will be called to account.

5:5 greedy person. The reference is to the sexually greedy person. **idolater.** When vice has become an obsession, it functions in a person's life as a "god" (or idol), drawing forth passionate commitment of time and energy.

5:6 empty words. Influenced by Greek philosophy that minimized the importance of the body in contrast to the spirit, some wrongly taught that the sins of the body did not matter.

5:8–14 A second reason why Christians should not get involved in immoral practices (v. 11) is that they have become "children of light" (v. 8). In fact, it is not just that they walk in the light, they "are light in the Lord" (v. 8). To be such a child of light implies a lifestyle of "goodness, righteousness and truth" (v. 9).

17 Therefore do not be foolish, but understand what the Lord's will is.
18 Do not get drunk on wine, which leads to debauchery. Instead, be
filled with the Spirit. 19 Speak to one another with psalms, hymns and
spiritual songs. Sing and make music in your heart to the Lord, 20 always giving thanks to God the Father for everything, in the name of
our Lord Jesus Christ.
21 Submit to one another out of reverence for Christ.

Wives and Husbands

22 Wives, submit to your husbands as to the Lord. 23 For the husband
is the head of the wife as Christ is the head of the church, his body, of
which he is the Savior. 24 Now as the church submits to Christ, so also
wives should submit to their husbands in everything.
25 Husbands, love your wives, just as Christ loved the church and
gave himself up for her 26 to make her holy, cleansing[a] her by the
washing with water through the word, 27 and to present her to himself
as a radiant church, without stain or wrinkle or any other blemish,
but holy and blameless. 28 In this same way, husbands ought to love
their wives as their own bodies. He who loves his wife loves himself.
29 After all, no one ever hated his own body, but he feeds and cares for
it, just as Christ does the church— 30 for we are members of his body.
31 "For this reason a man will leave his father and mother and be united to his wife, and the two will become one flesh."[b] 32 This is a profound mystery—but I am talking about Christ and the church.
33 However, each one of you also must love his wife as he loves himself, and the wife must respect her husband.

Children and Parents

6 Children, obey your parents in the Lord, for this is right. 2 "Honor
your father and mother"—which is the first commandment with
a promise— 3 "that it may go well with you and that you may enjoy
long life on the earth."[c]

[a]26 Or *having cleansed* [b]31 Gen. 2:24 [c]3 Deut. 5:16

OPEN What couple do you look up to as a model of a healthy marriage?

STUDY 1. *Men:* How do you feel about the standard for husbands in verses 25 and 28? *Women:* How about the standard for wives in verses 22 and 23? **2.** In practical terms, what does it mean for a wife to submit to her husband? **3.** What implication does "Husbands, love your wives, just as Christ loved the church" have (v. 25)? **4.** How does the modern-day view of marriage compare to this passage? **5.** In your own words, how would you explain the main goal of a Christian marriage? **6.** What does God command of children, and with what promise (vv. 1–3)? **7.** Do you think it is harder raising children today than it was when you were growing up? **8.** What attitude for slaves (vv. 5–8) should be carried over to a work relationship between employees/employers (vv. 5–9)?

APPLY 1. As you grow closer to God spiritually, have you found that your relationships with your spouse, children, boss or employees have also grown deeper? **2.** What do

5:18 be filled. This is a command, not an option. It means "let the Spirit fill you."

5:21 Submit to one another. An aspect of being filled with the Spirit involves mutual submission within the Christian community.

5:22 submit. This injunction from Paul must be understood in its historical context. In Jewish law, a woman was a "thing," not a person, and she had no legal rights. In Rome, too, divorce was easy, and women were repressed. Against this, Paul proposes a radical, liberating view: (1) submission was to be mutual (the man was no longer the absolute authority); (2) wives are called upon to defer only to their husbands (and not to every man); and (3) submission is defined and qualified by Christ's headship of the church (Christ died for the church). **to your husbands.** A woman owes submission only to her husband, not to all men (as first-century culture taught).

5:23 Christ is the head of the church. It is a headship of love, not of control; of nurture, not of suppression.

5:25 love your wives. This is the main thing Paul says to husbands. It is so important that he repeats this injunction three times (vv. 25,28,33). Paul urges a type of love: *agape,* which is characterized by sacrificial, self-giving action. **just as Christ loved the church and gave himself up for her.** Two actions characterize Christ's role for the church: love and sacrifice. The husband is called upon to act toward his wife in the same way.

5:27 to present her. At a Jewish wedding, the bride was presented to the groom by a friend.

5:28 their own bodies. The deep-rooted instinct to care for and protect oneself is to be carried over to the wife who has become one flesh with her husband.

5:31 one flesh. Paul does not view marriage as some sort of spiritual covenant devoid of sexuality. His illustration of how a husband is to love his wife (vv. 28–31) revolves around their sexual union, as is made explicit here by his quotation of Genesis 2:24.

6:1 Children. That he addresses children in this public letter means that children were in attendance with their families at worship when such a letter would have been read. **obey.** Paul tells the children to "obey" ("follow," "be subject to," literally, "listen to").

4Fathers, do not exasperate your children; instead, bring them up in the training and instruction of the Lord.

Slaves and Masters

5Slaves, obey your earthly masters with respect and fear, and with sincerity of heart, just as you would obey Christ. 6Obey them not only to win their favor when their eye is on you, but like slaves of Christ, doing the will of God from your heart. 7Serve wholeheartedly, as if you were serving the Lord, not men, 8because you know that the Lord will reward everyone for whatever good he does, whether he is slave or free.

9And masters, treat your slaves in the same way. Do not threaten them, since you know that he who is both their Master and yours is in heaven, and there is no favoritism with him.

The Armor of God

10Finally, be strong in the Lord and in his mighty power. 11Put on the full armor of God so that you can take your stand against the devil's schemes. 12For our struggle is not against flesh and blood, but against the rulers, against the authorities, against the powers of this dark world and against the spiritual forces of evil in the heavenly realms. 13Therefore put on the full armor of God, so that when the day of evil comes, you may be able to stand your ground, and after you have done everything, to stand. 14Stand firm then, with the belt of truth buckled around your waist, with the breastplate of righteousness in place, 15and with your feet fitted with the readiness that

you do when the other person in the relationship is not a follower of Christ? **3.** How can this group help you this week in prayer?

OPEN Who in your family likes to visit museums, especially war museums?

STUDY 1. Of the three or four closest friends in your spiritual community when you first came to the Lord, how many are still walking with God? What happened to the others? **2.** Do you believe like Paul that there are real spiritual forces of evil in the world that war against followers of Christ and the church? **3.** What are

6:4 Just as children have a duty to obey, parents have the duty to instruct children with gentleness and restraint. **Fathers.** The model for a father is that of God, the "Father of all" (4:6). This view of fatherhood stands in sharp contrast to the harsh Roman father, who had the power of life and death over his children. **exasperate.** Parents are to be responsible for not provoking hostility on the part of their children. By humiliating children, being cruel to them, over-indulging them, or being unreasonable, parents squash children, rather than encourage them. **bring them up.** This verb is literally "nourish" or "feed" them. **training.** This word can be translated "discipline." **instruction.** The emphasis here is on what is said verbally to children.

6:9 treat your slaves in the same way. Paul applies the golden rule to slave owners: to get service and respect, give respect to slaves! This was a revolutionary concept. This was the way of mutual submission for slave and master; i.e., mutual respect. **Do not threaten them.** In the same way that parents are not to exasperate children, masters are not to browbeat slaves. Punishment was the usual way of controlling slaves.

6:10 be strong ... in his mighty power. Paul uses the same three words here as he used in 1:19, when he first described God's power. In order to wage successful warfare against Satan, the Christian must draw upon God's own power.

6:11 Put on. It is not enough to rely passively on God's power. The Christian must do something. He or she must "put on" God's armor. **the devil's schemes.** Evil does not operate in the light. It lurks in shadows and strikes unexpectedly, with cleverness and subtlety.

6:12 the rulers ... the authorities ... the powers ... the spiritual forces. By these various titles, Paul names the diverse spiritual forces which rage against believers. **the powers of this dark world.** It was no empty boast on Satan's part when during Jesus' temptations he claimed to be able to give him "all the kingdoms of the world." These "world rulers" have real power, and even though Christ has defeated them, they refuse to concede their defeat. **forces of evil.** Another characteristic of these supernatural beings is wickedness. They are of the darkness, not of the light, and cannot be fought by only humanly means.

6:13 the day of evil. The immediate reference is to those special times of pressure and testing that come to all Christians, at which point steadfast resistance of evil is called for. **stand your ground.** This is the second time Paul has spoken about "standing fast" (v. 11). Fully-equipped soldiers were virtually invulnerable to enemy onslaught—unless they panicked and broke ranks. As long as they "stood firm" when the enemy attacked, they would prevail in the long run.

6:14 the belt of truth. The leather belt on which the Roman soldier hung his sword, and by which he secured his tunic and armor (so he would be unimpeded in battle). The "truth" referred to is the inner integrity and sincerity by which the Christian fights evil. Lying and deceit are tactics of the enemy. **the breastplate of righteousness.** The breastplate (or "mail") was the major piece of armor for the Roman soldier. Made of metal and leather, it protected his vital organs. "Righteousness" refers to the right standing before God that is the status of the Christian, out of which moral conduct and character emerges.

6:15 feet fitted. These are the leather half-boots worn by the Roman legionnaire, with heavy studded soles

the seven pieces of armor in the battle attire of a follower of Christ? How would you rate your spiritual fitness in each category? **4.** What did Paul have in mind when he used this illustration? Do you think a follower of Christ can be a "Lone Ranger" and have no protection on your backside?

APPLY 1. Where are you struggling? How is the battle going right now in your life? **2.** Do you need to regroup, dig in, take the offensive or call for reinforcements? **3.** How can this group help you in prayer this week?

---

comes from the gospel of peace. [16]In addition to all this, take up the
shield of faith, with which you can extinguish all the flaming arrows
of the evil one. [17]Take the helmet of salvation and the sword of the
Spirit, which is the word of God. [18]And pray in the Spirit on all occasions with all kinds of prayers and requests. With this in mind, be
alert and always keep on praying for all the saints.
[19]Pray also for me, that whenever I open my mouth, words may be
given me so that I will fearlessly make known the mystery of the gospel, [20]for which I am an ambassador in chains. Pray that I may declare it fearlessly, as I should.

Final Greetings

[21]Tychicus, the dear brother and faithful servant in the Lord, will
tell you everything, so that you also may know how I am and what I
am doing. [22]I am sending him to you for this very purpose, that you
may know how we are, and that he may encourage you.
[23]Peace to the brothers, and love with faith from God the Father
and the Lord Jesus Christ. [24]Grace to all who love our Lord Jesus
Christ with an undying love.

---

that enabled him to dig in and resist being pushed out of place. **readiness.** This term can be translated as "firmness" or "steadfastness," in which case the "gospel of peace" is understood to provide the solid foundation on which the Christian stands in the fight against evil.

6:16 the shield of faith. A large, oblong shield constructed of layers of wood on an iron frame, which was then covered with linen and hide. When wet, such a shield could absorb "flaming arrows." **flaming arrows.** These were pitch-soaked arrows. Their aim was not so much to kill a soldier, as to set him aflame and cause him to break rank and create panic.

6:17 the helmet of salvation. A heavy, metal head-covering lined with felt or sponge, which gave substantial protection to the soldier's head from all but the heaviest axe blow. **sword.** A short, stabbing sword used for personal combat. The sword is the only piece of offensive equipment in the armor.

6:18 pray. Paul does not consider prayer a seventh weapon. Rather, it underlies the whole process of spiritual warfare. **in the Spirit.** The Bible, the Word of God, is the sword of the Spirit. So, too, prayer is guided by the Spirit. This is, after all, spiritual warfare.

Philippians

Author. The apostle Paul was the writer of Philippians.

Date. Philippians was probably written around A.D. 61–63, a dozen or so years after Paul had founded the church in Philippi on his second missionary journey (the first church in Europe; see Acts 16).

Theme. The joy of knowing Jesus.

Personal Reading	Group Study Topic and Reading	
1:1–11	Partners in Christ's Gospel	1:1–11
1:12–30	Suffering for Christ's Sake	1:12–30
2:1–11	Imitating Christ's Humility	2:1–11
2:12–30	Examples of Christ's Service	2:12–30
3:1–11	Knowing Christ's Suffering	3:1–11
3:12–4:1	Pursuing Christ's Call	3:12–4:1
4:2–9	Joy in Christ's Nearness	4:2–9
4:10–23	Receiving Christ's Riches	4:10–23

Historical Background. Paul had planted the church around A.D. 50 as the result of a vision during the night in which a "man of Macedonia" beckoned him to "come over ... and help" (Acts 16:9). He sailed immediately from Asia, thus launching Christianity in Europe. Paul's stay at Philippi was marked by joy and trial. Paul is in prison (probably in Rome) when Epaphroditus, an old friend from Philippi, arrives bearing yet another gift from the church. Unfortunately, Epaphroditus falls gravely ill. His home church hears about it and is grieved. In due course he recovers, and Paul is anxious for him to return home and relieve their fears. This affords Paul an opportunity to send along a letter. So he writes these old friends in the warmest and most personal of his epistles.

Basically Philippians is a letter of thanksgiving (1:3–11 and 4:14–20) and a report on his imprisonment (1:12–26; 2:19–30; 4:10–13). In large part, it seems that Paul wrote Philippians as a thank-you for all that this, perhaps his favorite church, had done for him (particularly their gift, as seen in 4:10–19). Still, Paul has two concerns: a tendency in the church toward disunity (1:27–2:18 and 4:2–3) and potential dangers from Judaizers (3:2–16) and false teachers (3:17–21).

Characteristics. Joy permeates its pages from start to finish. This is joy in the midst of hard situations. Paul is writing from prison. He faces the very real possibility of execution. The Philippian church is confronted with internal dissension and with false teachers who would seduce it away from the gospel.

Structure. Paul talks about his imprisonment and about how the gospel is advancing. He makes an appeal for harmony among the members of the Philippian church. He tells them that he will be sending both Epaphroditus and Timothy to see them. And in 3:1 he says, "Finally, my brothers ..." as if he is about to close the letter. But then he abruptly launches into a warning about dangerous men who will harm the church (3:2–21). This is followed by more exhortations (4:1–9) and by thanks for their gifts (4:10–20), after which he actually concludes his letter.

The City of Philippi. In the Roman province of Macedonia, Philippi was founded by Alexander the Great's father in 360 B.C. so he could mine its gold to pay for his army. Philippi eventually came to prominence as the result of two battles. In 42 B.C. on the plains of Philippi, the Caesarean forces of Anthony and Octavian defeated the Republican forces led by the assassins of Julius Caesar—Brutus and Cassius. Then in 31 B.C., Octavian (who later became the Emperor Caesar Augustus) became sole ruler by defeating his former colleague Anthony, who was in alliance with the Egyptian Queen Cleopatra. Veterans from these conflicts were given land in Philippi, and Octavian declared it to be a Roman colony with all the accompanying rights, tax breaks and privileges.

OPEN What mail do you open first: Bills? Official looking stuff? Personal mail? Love letters?

STUDY 1. What one word best describes Paul's feelings for the Philippians? **2.** What word would describe the feelings you have for your church? **3.** What is unusual about Paul's positive attitude in this letter? **4.** On a scale of 1 (easy) to 10 (hard), how hard is it for you to express your feelings like Paul did here? **5.** How is God at work in a believer's life according to verses 6 and 9–11? How does this make you feel about uncertainties in your life?

APPLY 1. Who was the "apostle Paul" in your spiritual life, who introduced you to Jesus Christ and cared about your spiritual growth? **2.** Who is your spiritual cheerleader now?

OPEN 1. When you are having a bad day, what do you do? **2.** Who do you identify with in the *Peanuts* comic strip?

STUDY 1. How would you compare the circumstances

1 Paul and Timothy, servants of Christ Jesus,
To all the saints in Christ Jesus at Philippi, together with the
overseers[a] and deacons:

2 Grace and peace to you from God our Father and the Lord Jesus
Christ.

Thanksgiving and Prayer

3 I thank my God every time I remember you. 4 In all my prayers for
all of you, I always pray with joy 5 because of your partnership in the
gospel from the first day until now, 6 being confident of this, that he
who began a good work in you will carry it on to completion until the
day of Christ Jesus.
7 It is right for me to feel this way about all of you, since I have you
in my heart; for whether I am in chains or defending and confirming
the gospel, all of you share in God's grace with me. 8 God can testify
how I long for all of you with the affection of Christ Jesus.
9 And this is my prayer: that your love may abound more and more
in knowledge and depth of insight, 10 so that you may be able to discern what is best and may be pure and blameless until the day of
Christ, 11 filled with the fruit of righteousness that comes through
Jesus Christ—to the glory and praise of God.

Paul's Chains Advance the Gospel

12 Now I want you to know, brothers, that what has happened to me
has really served to advance the gospel. 13 As a result, it has become
clear throughout the whole palace guard[b] and to everyone else that I

[a] *1* Traditionally *bishops* [b] *13* Or *whole palace*

1:1 Timothy had long been a companion of Paul. Timothy was with Paul when he visited Philippi for the first time and so was well-known there. Paul may have dictated this letter to Timothy. **servants.** Paul lived a life of willing submission to the Lord, a point he will stress as he calls upon the Christians to serve one another. **saints.** This designation is the general New Testament word for Christians, who, because of their union with Christ, have been "set apart" to serve God. **overseers and deacons.** The function of these individuals is not completely clear, except that they are leaders (Acts 20:28), quite possibly appointed by Paul.

1:3 every time I remember you. This is a difficult phrase to translate from the Greek. What it seems to mean is that during his times of prayer, Paul "was compelled by love to mention his Philippian friends."

1:4 with joy. "Joy" is a theme that pervades Philippians. This is the first of some 14 times that Paul will use the word in this epistle. He mentions "joy" more often in this short epistle than in any of his other letters.

1:5 because of your partnership. The Greek word rendered here as "partnership" is the familiar word *koinonia*, translated elsewhere as "fellowship." It means, literally, "having something in common."

1:6 confident. This is confidence that springs out of faith in who God is and what he is doing. **the day of Christ Jesus.** This is the moment when Christ will return in glory and triumph to establish his kingdom on earth.

1:7 defending and confirming the gospel. The reference is to Paul's defense before the Roman court, in which he hopes to be able not only to vindicate himself and the gospel from false charges, but to proclaim the gospel and its life-changing power to those in the courtroom.

1:8 God can testify. In times of deep feeling, Paul would sometimes invoke God to bear witness to the authenticity of these feelings (Rom. 1:9; 2 Cor. 11:11,31; 1 Thess. 2:5). **I long.** This is a strong word and expresses the depth of Paul's feelings for them, his desire to be with them, and the wish to minister to them.

1:9 this is my prayer. He prays that this love will increase (i.e., that it will go on developing) and that it will be regulated by knowledge and discernment. **knowledge and depth of insight.** This growing love is to be focused by intellectual and moral insight.

1:10 to discern what is best. The word translated "discern" is used to describe the process of testing coins so as to distinguish between those that are real and those that are counterfeit.

1:13 palace guard. These men were the elite soldiers in the Roman army, the bodyguards of the emperor. **to everyone else.** Paul's circumstances would also have become known to the officials preparing the case and to the others involved with the forthcoming trial. **in chains.** Paul was not in a jail, but in a

am in chains for Christ. [14]Because of my chains, most of the brothers
in the Lord have been encouraged to speak the word of God more
courageously and fearlessly.
[15]It is true that some preach Christ out of envy and rivalry, but
others out of goodwill. [16]The latter do so in love, knowing that I am
put here for the defense of the gospel. [17]The former preach Christ out
of selfish ambition, not sincerely, supposing that they can stir up
trouble for me while I am in chains.[a] [18]But what does it matter? The
important thing is that in every way, whether from false motives or
true, Christ is preached. And because of this I rejoice.
Yes, and I will continue to rejoice, [19]for I know that through your
prayers and the help given by the Spirit of Jesus Christ, what has happened to me will turn out for my deliverance.[b] [20]I eagerly expect and
hope that I will in no way be ashamed, but will have sufficient courage so that now as always Christ will be exalted in my body, whether
by life or by death. [21]For to me, to live is Christ and to die is gain. [22]If
I am to go on living in the body, this will mean fruitful labor for me.
Yet what shall I choose? I do not know! [23]I am torn between the two:
I desire to depart and be with Christ, which is better by far; [24]but it is
more necessary for you that I remain in the body. [25]Convinced of this,
I know that I will remain, and I will continue with all of you for your
progress and joy in the faith, [26]so that through my being with you
again your joy in Christ Jesus will overflow on account of me.
[27]Whatever happens, conduct yourselves in a manner worthy of the
gospel of Christ. Then, whether I come and see you or only hear
about you in my absence, I will know that you stand firm in one
spirit, contending as one man for the faith of the gospel [28]without
being frightened in any way by those who oppose you. This is a sign
to them that they will be destroyed, but that you will be saved—and
that by God. [29]For it has been granted to you on behalf of Christ
not only to believe on him, but also to suffer for him, [30]since you are

[a]*16,17* Some late manuscripts have verses 16 and 17 in reverse order. [b]*19* Or *salvation*

you are in right now to Paul's circumstances in prison? **2.** What has happened as a result of Paul's imprisonment? **3.** What effect did Paul's situation have on most of his fellow believers (v. 14)? **4.** What negative result did Paul's situation have on others in the church (vv. 15–17)? **5.** What does this passage say about what your attitude should be toward followers of Christ whose motives you might question? **6.** Where has God been able to use bad for good in your life? **7.** Which option (life or death) does Paul personally desire (vv. 22–23)? **8.** Why does Paul feel it is more necessary for him to do the opposite (vv. 24–25)? **9.** What is something you would like to accomplish before you die? **10.** What difference has your personal faith in Jesus Christ made in your attitude toward death and dying?

APPLY 1. How would you describe your spiritual life right now in one or two words? **2.** As you get older, how has the reality of death affected your outlook on life, and your priorities?

---

rented house where he was able to receive visitors, correspondence, and gifts (4:18; Acts 28:16,30). He was bound to a guard by a short length of chain that ran from his wrist to the guard's wrist. It is not surprising that the guards got to know him and his gospel. **for Christ.** It had become clear to all involved that Paul was in prison simply because he was a Christian.

1:18 false motives. The three words by which Paul characterizes the motivation of his rivals—envy, rivalry, selfish ambition—are all words which he has used in other contexts to describe those actions and attitudes that are to be shunned by Christians. They are "vices that always adversely affect, even endanger, the life of the church" (Hawthorne) (Rom. 1:29; 2 Cor. 12:20; Gal. 5:19–21; 1 Tim. 6:4). **what does it matter ... I rejoice.** There is about Paul a truly astonishing, magnanimous spirit which does not care for personal reputation as long as the job gets done. **Christ is preached.** Whatever else might be said about these wrongly motivated brothers and sisters, their message still centers on Christ.

1:20 courage. What Paul desires is the courage to speak boldly during his trial. **exalted.** This word means, literally, to make something or someone large. **by life or by death.** By this phrase, Paul simply means that his single goal is to bring praise to Christ.

1:21 to live is Christ. For Paul, his whole existence revolves around Christ. What he does, he does for Christ. He is inspired by Christ; he works for Christ; his sole focus in life is Christ. He is a man with a single, all-consuming passion. **to die is gain.** Death is the door into the presence of Christ. Death is not so much escape from hardship as it is entrance into joy.

1:23 to depart and be with Christ. Death would be a gain for Paul since being with, in, and for Christ meant everything to him.

1:27 stand firm. This is a military term for Roman soldiers standing back to back, protecting each other while resisting the enemy. **for the faith of the gospel.** The goal is not victory on the battlefield, but the preservation of the Christian faith.

1:28 without being frightened. Yet another rare word, used in the Bible only this one time. Its original reference was to horses that were timid and which shied easily. The Philippians must not let their opponents spook them into an uncontrolled stampede.

going through the same struggle you saw I had, and now hear that I
still have.

OPEN 1. Who takes out the trash in your home? Cleans the toilet? **2.** What is your pet peeve at home?

STUDY 1. What is Paul asking of these Christians who claim that they have all of these beautiful feelings for Jesus? **2.** What does it mean to consider someone "better than yourself" (v. 3)? How does humility differ from being a doormat? **3.** What do you think it was like for Jesus to leave heaven and become human? To take on himself all of the sin of mankind? **4.** How does this passage challenge society's definition of success? **5.** Who do you admire because they truly put the interests of others ahead of their own interests?

APPLY 1. Have you been a part of a group that shares deep joy in being with one another? **2.** What made this group so close?

Imitating Christ's Humility

2 If you have any encouragement from being united with Christ, if
any comfort from his love, if any fellowship with the Spirit, if any
tenderness and compassion, 2then make my joy complete by being
like-minded, having the same love, being one in spirit and purpose.
3Do nothing out of selfish ambition or vain conceit, but in humility
consider others better than yourselves. 4Each of you should look not
only to your own interests, but also to the interests of others.

5Your attitude should be the same as that of Christ Jesus:

6Who, being in very nature[a] God,
did not consider equality with God something to be grasped,
7but made himself nothing,
taking the very nature[b] of a servant,
being made in human likeness.
8And being found in appearance as a man,
he humbled himself
and became obedient to death—
even death on a cross!
9Therefore God exalted him to the highest place
and gave him the name that is above every name,
10that at the name of Jesus every knee should bow,
in heaven and on earth and under the earth,
11and every tongue confess that Jesus Christ is Lord,
to the glory of God the Father.

OPEN Who are you like in the morning: Big Bird or Oscar the Grouch?

STUDY 1. The word "your" in verse 12 is plural. How can a

Shining as Stars

12Therefore, my dear friends, as you have always obeyed—not only
in my presence, but now much more in my absence—continue to

[a]6 *Or in the form of* [b]7 *Or the form*

2:1 If. In Greek, this construction assumes a positive response, e.g., "If you have any encouragement, and of course you do ..."

2:2 like-minded. This is literally, "think the same way."

2:3 selfish ambition. This is the second time Paul has used this word (1:17). It means working to advance oneself without thought for others. **vain conceit.** This is the only occurrence of this word in the New Testament. Translated literally, it means "vain glory" (*kendoxia*) which is asserting oneself over God who alone is worthy of true glory (*doxa*). **humility.** This was not a virtue that was valued by the Greek in the first century. They considered this to be the attitude of a slave (i.e., servility).

2:6 being. This word carries the idea of pre-existence. By using it, Paul is saying Jesus always existed in the form of God. **very nature.** He says Jesus was "in very nature God," and he then took upon himself "the very nature of a servant." **to be grasped.** It refers to the fact that Jesus did not have to "snatch" equality with God. It was his already, and he could give it away.

2:7 made himself nothing. Literally, "to empty," or "to pour out until the container is empty." **taking the very nature of a servant.** From being the ultimate master, he became the lowest servant. **being made.** In contrast to the verb in verse 6 (which stresses Christ's eternal nature), this verb points to the fact that at a particular time he was born in the likeness of a human being. **human likeness.** The point is not that Jesus just seemed to be human. He assumed the identity of a person and was a human being.

2:8 in appearance as a man. The word denotes that which is outward and changeable. **he humbled himself.** Jesus is the ultimate model of one who lived a life of self-sacrifice, self-renunciation, and self-surrender. **obedient to death.** The extent of this humbling is defined by this clause. Jesus humbled himself to the furthest point one can go. He submitted to death itself for the sake of humanity. **death on a cross.** Crucifixion was a harsh, demeaning and utterly painful way to die. According to the Old Testament, those who died by hanging on a tree were considered to have been cursed by God.

2:11 Jesus Christ is Lord. This is the earliest and most basic confession of faith on the part of the church (Acts 2:36; Rom. 10:9; 1 Cor. 12:3). **Lord.** This is the name that was given to Jesus; the name that reflects who he really is (v. 9). This is the name of God. Jesus is the supreme Sovereign of the universe.

work out your salvation with fear and trembling, [13]for it is God who works in you to will and to act according to his good purpose.

[14]Do everything without complaining or arguing, [15]so that you may become blameless and pure, children of God without fault in a crooked and depraved generation, in which you shine like stars in the universe [16]as you hold out[a] the word of life—in order that I may boast on the day of Christ that I did not run or labor for nothing. [17]But even if I am being poured out like a drink offering on the sacrifice and service coming from your faith, I am glad and rejoice with all of you. [18]So you too should be glad and rejoice with me.

Timothy and Epaphroditus

[19]I hope in the Lord Jesus to send Timothy to you soon, that I also may be cheered when I receive news about you. [20]I have no one else like him, who takes a genuine interest in your welfare. [21]For everyone looks out for his own interests, not those of Jesus Christ. [22]But you know that Timothy has proved himself, because as a son with his father he has served with me in the work of the gospel. [23]I hope, therefore, to send him as soon as I see how things go with me. [24]And I am confident in the Lord that I myself will come soon.

[25]But I think it is necessary to send back to you Epaphroditus, my brother, fellow worker and fellow soldier, who is also your messenger, whom you sent to take care of my needs. [26]For he longs for all of you and is distressed because you heard he was ill. [27]Indeed he was ill, and almost died. But God had mercy on him, and not on him only but also on me, to spare me sorrow upon sorrow. [28]Therefore I am all the more eager to send him, so that when you see him again you may be glad and I may have less anxiety. [29]Welcome him in the Lord with great joy, and honor men like him, [30]because he almost died for the work of Christ, risking his life to make up for the help you could not give me.

No Confidence in the Flesh

3 Finally, my brothers, rejoice in the Lord! It is no trouble for me to write the same things to you again, and it is a safeguard for you. [2]Watch out for those dogs, those men who do evil, those mutilators of the flesh. [3]For it is we who are the circumcision, we who worship by the Spirit of God, who glory in Christ Jesus, and who put no confidence in the flesh— [4]though I myself have reasons for such confidence.

If anyone else thinks he has reasons to put confidence in the flesh, I have more: [5]circumcised on the eighth day, of the people of Israel,

[a]*16 Or* hold on to

Christian community "continue to work out their salvation" (vv. 14–15)? **2.** If these Christians do not continue in their faith, what does Paul say about his ministry?

APPLY 1. How far does the light from your group "shine like stars in the universe"? **2.** Who do you want to invite into your group?

OPEN 1. Who would look after your children if something happened to you and your spouse? **2.** Who would look after your business or personal affairs?

STUDY 1. From verses 19–24, what are two or three words you would use to describe Timothy? **2.** From verses 25–30, what are two or three words you would use to describe Epaphroditus? **3.** Who is someone you know that models humble service to others? **4.** What service do you feel God has called you to do for his kingdom?

APPLY 1. Who are the people in your life who have helped shape your own self-image by their praise or lack of praise? **2.** Do you give praise easily ... or do you find this hard to do? Where do you need to improve?

OPEN Who has the bragging rights in your group for catching the biggest fish? The most broken bones? The longest hair as a teenager?

STUDY 1. What is Paul's attitude toward the Judaizers who were teaching that a person had to be circumcised to become a Christian? **2.** What was Paul trying to prove in verses 4–8? How would you compare his religious credentials to yours? **3.** How would you describe Paul's passion to know Christ? **4.** Do you think a

---

2:25 Epaphroditus. Epaphroditus had been sent by the Philippian church to convey a gift to Paul, and then to stay on as a member of Paul's apostolic group. However, he fell ill. The church heard about this and became quite anxious about him. In addition, Epaphroditus was homesick. For both reasons, Paul senses that it is time for Epaphroditus to return to Philippi.

2:30 risking his life. A gambling term, it denotes one who risked everything on the roll of the dice.

3:2 mutilators of the flesh. Paul is saying that their circumcision is really mutilation.

3:4 confidence in the flesh. This is what these Jews are promoting: a righteousness based on their heritage and many accomplishments.

3:5 eighth day. It was on the eighth day after birth that a Jewish child (as opposed to a proselyte) was circumcised. Paul was a true Jew right from the time of his birth. **the tribe of Benjamin.** The members of the tribe of Benjamin constituted an elite group within Israel. **a Pharisee.** He was one of the spiritual elite in Israel.

of the tribe of Benjamin, a Hebrew of Hebrews; in regard to the law, a
Pharisee; [6]as for zeal, persecuting the church; as for legalistic righteousness, faultless.

[7]But whatever was to my profit I now consider loss for the sake of
Christ. [8]What is more, I consider everything a loss compared to the
surpassing greatness of knowing Christ Jesus my Lord, for whose
sake I have lost all things. I consider them rubbish, that I may gain
Christ [9]and be found in him, not having a righteousness of my own
that comes from the law, but that which is through faith in Christ—
the righteousness that comes from God and is by faith. [10]I want to
know Christ and the power of his resurrection and the fellowship of
sharing in his sufferings, becoming like him in his death, [11]and so,
somehow, to attain to the resurrection from the dead.

Pressing on Toward the Goal

[12]Not that I have already obtained all this, or have already been
made perfect, but I press on to take hold of that for which Christ
Jesus took hold of me. [13]Brothers, I do not consider myself yet to
have taken hold of it. But one thing I do: Forgetting what is behind
and straining toward what is ahead, [14]I press on toward the goal to
win the prize for which God has called me heavenward in Christ
Jesus.

[15]All of us who are mature should take such a view of things. And if
on some point you think differently, that too God will make clear to
you. [16]Only let us live up to what we have already attained.

[17]Join with others in following my example, brothers, and take note
of those who live according to the pattern we gave you. [18]For, as I
have often told you before and now say again even with tears, many
live as enemies of the cross of Christ. [19]Their destiny is destruction,
their god is their stomach, and their glory is in their shame. Their

follower of Christ can achieve what Paul sought after and still strive for excellence in their job, career and family responsibilities?

APPLY 1. If you had to add up all of your achievements, what would be at the top of the list? **2.** When you think of success, what is the bottom line for you?

OPEN In your dreams of the good life, are you more like the pioneer (always pushing on) or the settler (settling down)?

STUDY 1. Using the imagery of a track race, where does Paul picture himself in his spiritual life (vv. 12–14)? What prize is he after? **2.** How do you feel about offering yourself as a model for spiritual excellence like Paul does in verse 17? **3.** In today's society, who would you say are the "enemies of the cross" (v. 18)? **4.** What does it mean to you to be a citizen of heaven and an heir of God's kingdom? **5.** What do you look forward to the most when you think about heaven?

3:6 as for zeal, persecuting the church. Zeal was a highly prized virtue among the Jews. Paul had demonstrated his zeal for the Law by ferreting out Christians and bringing them to trial (Acts 22:4–5; 26:9–11). **faultless.** To the best of his ability, Paul tried to observe the whole Law. Taken together, all these attributes mean that Paul was in every way the match of his opponents in Philippi. He had lived at the very pinnacle of Judaism.

3:7 profit ... loss. Paul describes his change in outlook in terms of a balance sheet. What was once on the "profit" side of the ledger (when he was a Pharisee) has been shifted over to the "loss" side (now that he is a Christian).

3:8 compared to. Paul discovered only one thing had any ultimate value—knowing Christ Jesus—and knowing Christ did not come as a result of personal accomplishment.

3:10 know. The knowledge about which Paul speaks is personal knowledge and not just intellectual knowledge (i.e., knowing "about" someone). **the power of his resurrection.** Paul wants to experience personally the resurrected Christ in all his power (Eph. 1:18–21). **becoming like him.** Paul coins a new word by which he expresses that he wants obedience to God as was Christ even to death.

3:11 somehow, to attain. In humility, he expresses his sense that it is solely by God's grace that he would gain such a gift.

3:12 Not ... obtained. He has not gained possession fully of what Christ has for him. **perfect.** This is the only time in his epistles that Paul uses this word. Paul indicates he has not yet fully understood Jesus Christ. There is simply too much to know of Christ ever to grasp it all this side of heaven. **press on.** In contrast to those groups that claim it is possible to attain spiritual perfection here and now, the Christian life is one of relentless striving to know Christ in his fullness. **to take hold of.** It can refer to winning a prize, as for example, in a race. Or it can mean to understand or comprehend something. **Jesus took hold of me.** Paul refers here to his conversion experience on the Damascus Road.

3:13 Forgetting what is behind. In order to press on to a successful conclusion of his spiritual pilgrimage, Paul must first cease looking at what he has accomplished in the past. **what is ahead.** If the first movement in the spiritual pilgrimage is to forget the past, the second movement is to concentrate totally on what lies ahead—full comprehension of Jesus Christ.

3:14 goal. This is the mark on the track that signifies the end of the race. **the prize.** What Paul seems to have in mind is the moment at the end of the race, when the winner is called forward by the games master to receive the victory palm or wreath.

mind is on earthly things. 20But our citizenship is in heaven. And we
eagerly await a Savior from there, the Lord Jesus Christ, 21who, by the
power that enables him to bring everything under his control, will
transform our lowly bodies so that they will be like his glorious body.
4 Therefore, my brothers, you whom I love and long for, my joy
and crown, that is how you should stand firm in the Lord, dear
friends!

Exhortations

2I plead with Euodia and I plead with Syntyche to agree with each
other in the Lord. 3Yes, and I ask you, loyal yokefellow,[a] help these
women who have contended at my side in the cause of the gospel,
along with Clement and the rest of my fellow workers, whose names
are in the book of life.
4Rejoice in the Lord always. I will say it again: Rejoice! 5Let your
gentleness be evident to all. The Lord is near. 6Do not be anxious
about anything, but in everything, by prayer and petition, with
thanksgiving, present your requests to God. 7And the peace of God,
which transcends all understanding, will guard your hearts and your
minds in Christ Jesus.
8Finally, brothers, whatever is true, whatever is noble, whatever is
right, whatever is pure, whatever is lovely, whatever is admirable—if
anything is excellent or praiseworthy—think about such things.
9Whatever you have learned or received or heard from me, or seen in
me—put it into practice. And the God of peace will be with you.

Thanks for Their Gifts

10I rejoice greatly in the Lord that at last you have renewed your
concern for me. Indeed, you have been concerned, but you had no
opportunity to show it. 11I am not saying this because I am in need,
for I have learned to be content whatever the circumstances. 12I know

[a]3 Or *loyal Syzygus*

APPLY **1.** If you had to compare your life in Christ right now to a track race, where would you be: Sitting on the sidelines? Warming up? At the starting blocks? Giving it your all? **2.** Are you more likely to strive for excellence in your secular life or your spiritual life?

OPEN Do you enjoy solving disputes or do you like to throw fuel on the fire?

STUDY **1.** If you knew that two people in the church were causing trouble, what would you do? **2.** What do you do to relieve stress from worry in your life? What does Paul say to do? **3.** How does what you think about affect how you feel? How does it affect your relationship to God? **4.** What have you found helpful in controlling your thought life?

APPLY **1.** On a scale from 1 to 10, what is the stress level in your life right now? **2.** How can this group help you this week in prayer?

OPEN What do you look back on as the happiest days of your life? Were they really that good?

STUDY **1.** Paul is in prison in Rome a second time, awaiting trial and execution. How would you

---

3:20 citizenship. In contrast to the Jewish teachers whose focus is on "earthly things" (v. 19), the focus of Christians is on heaven (where their true home lies). **eagerly await.** Paul captures the keen anticipation and happy expectation of the Christians who long for Christ's return.

3:21 our lowly bodies. In contrast to those who taught that perfection was possible here and now, Christians knew that it was only at the Second Coming, by the work of Christ, that their frail, weak and corrupt bodies would be transformed into a spiritual body akin to Christ's body."

4:2 plead. This is a strong verb, meaning "to exhort, to implore, to beg." **Euodia ... Syntyche.** Unlike most Greek women who remained in the background and had little to do with public life, Macedonian women were as active and involved as the men. Their opinions are very important, so much so that their quarrel is threatening to split the church. Their unity is crucial to the unity of the whole body. **in the Lord.** The only hope for this kind of unity to develop between these two women is found in the fact of their common commitment to Jesus.

4:6 Do not be anxious. They are to "stop worrying." To worry is to display a lack of confidence in God's care and in God's control over the situation (Matt. 6:25–34). **prayer ... petition ... requests.** Paul uses three synonyms in a row to describe the alternative to anxiety. Instead of worrying, a person ought to converse directly with God and lay out before him all that is on his or her mind, confident that God will hear and respond.

4:7 the peace of God. This is peace that comes from God and focused on him. **transcends all understanding.** Such peace can never fully be understood by human beings. **guard.** This is a military term. It describes a garrison of soldiers, such as those stationed at Philippi, whose job it is to stand watch over the city and protect it.

4:8 true—Sincerity and accuracy not only in thought and word, but in deed and attitude. **noble**—Those majestic things which command respect and which lift up one's mind from the mundane. **right**—Literally, "just," giving to God and others that which is their due. **pure**—In all spheres of life—ideas, actions, motives, etc. **lovely**—A warmth that calls forth love from others. **admirable**—What people think only good things about. **excellent**—Moral excellence. **praiseworthy**—Behavior that is universally praised.

4:12 need. This is a different Greek word from the one translated "need" in verse 11. This word refers to the lower-

describe his mental state of mind? What is his secret? How about verse 13? **2.** What is the closest you have come to having your needs go below the water line for existence (v. 12)? What is the closest you have come to knowing the overflow of God's blessing? **3.** How would you compare Paul's view of contentment with the modern-day view of contentment? **4.** If Paul has learned how to get along without, why does he commend the church in Philippi for sending a gift (vv. 14–17)?

APPLY 1. Are you able to say with Paul: "I have learned the secret of being content in any and every situation"? **2.** Where do you need a little help this week in prayer?

what it is to be in need, and I know what it is to have plenty. I have
learned the secret of being content in any and every situation, whether well fed or hungry, whether living in plenty or in want. 13I can do
everything through him who gives me strength.
14Yet it was good of you to share in my troubles. 15Moreover, as you
Philippians know, in the early days of your acquaintance with the
gospel, when I set out from Macedonia, not one church shared with
me in the matter of giving and receiving, except you only; 16for even
when I was in Thessalonica, you sent me aid again and again when I
was in need. 17Not that I am looking for a gift, but I am looking for
what may be credited to your account. 18I have received full payment
and even more; I am amply supplied, now that I have received from
Epaphroditus the gifts you sent. They are a fragrant offering, an acceptable sacrifice, pleasing to God. 19And my God will meet all your
needs according to his glorious riches in Christ Jesus.
20To our God and Father be glory for ever and ever. Amen.

Final Greetings

21Greet all the saints in Christ Jesus. The brothers who are with me
send greetings. 22All the saints send you greetings, especially those
who belong to Caesar's household.
23The grace of the Lord Jesus Christ be with your spirit. Amen.[a]

[a]23 Some manuscripts do not have *Amen.*

---

ing of water in a river. As such, it is a reference to fundamental needs which are basic to life (such as food and water). Paul has learned to exist even in the midst of abject poverty. **plenty.** This is the opposite state of "need." It means literally, "to overflow," that is, to have enough for one's own daily needs plus something left over. **well fed.** This describes force-fed animals who are stuffed to overflowing in order to fatten them for slaughter. It is used by Paul to define one of the extremes: having more than enough to eat. **living in plenty or in want.** Another set of contrasting words. It is by the experience of these extremes that Paul has come to know the secret of coping with all circumstances.

4:13 everything. Paul is referring to what he has just described: his ability to exist in all types of material circumstances—wealth or poverty, abundant food or no food, etc. **through him who gives me strength.** The source of Paul's ability to exist successfully in all circumstances is his union with Christ. This is his secret.

4:22 All the saints. The Christians in Rome are the third group that sends greetings.

Colossians

Author. The apostle Paul was the writer of Colossians.

Date. Tradition has it that Paul wrote Colossians, Ephesians and Philemon during his imprisonment in Rome. This would mean these letters were written in the early A.D.60s. However, other sites including Caesarea and Ephesus have been proposed as the place of Paul's confinement, so that neither date nor place is certain.

Personal Reading	Group Study Topic and Reading	
1:1–14	Eternal Redemption in Christ	1:1–14
1:15–23	All Reconciled in Christ	1:15–23
1:24–2:5	Full Riches in Christ	1:24–2:5
2:6–23	Firmly Rooted in Christ	2:6–23
3:1–4:1	Newly Robed in Christ	3:1–4:1
4:2–18	New Relationships in Christ	4:2–18

Theme. Fullness and freedom in Christ.

Historical Background. Epaphras, not to be confused with Epaphroditus referred to in Philippians, may have planted the Colossian church. A native of Colosse (4:12), he worked hard on behalf of the church there (4:13). In fact, in 1:6–7 Paul says: "All over the world this gospel is bearing fruit and growing .... You learned it from Epaphras ... ." Epaphras stayed with Paul during his imprisonment (Philem. 23) and so was unable to deliver the letter to the Colossians personally. Paul never visited the churches at Colosse and Laodicea (2:1).

In 1:21 Paul speaks of the Colossian Christians as having once been "alienated from God" and "enemies in your minds"—phrases he uses elsewhere to describe Gentiles who were not part of God's covenant with Israel. Then in 1:27, he talks about making the mystery of God clear to the Gentiles; the reference is obviously to the Colossians.

Characteristics. As Paul does so often, he begins his letter with a strong doctrinal statement and concludes it by drawing out the behavioral implications of the doctrine. Jesus is the Lord of the universe who reconciles all things to himself through his death. Paul sets this strong statement of Christ's deity (1:15–23) over against the mystical, ritualistic religion of the false teachers (2:8–23). Paul turns to the implications of Christ's lordship over all and describes how those in union with him ought to live (3:1–4:6).

Colossians begins, like most of Paul's letters, with a lengthy introduction (1:1–14). In the first major division on doctrine, Paul establishes the preeminence of Christ (1:15–2:23). He follows this with an exhortation to the Colossians to live in union with Christ (3:1–4:6). He concludes with personal greetings (4:7–18).

Religion in Colosse. A large number of Jews had lived in the region of Colosse, since Antiochus III brought 2,000 Jews from Mesopotamia and Babylon to settle there. By Paul's time there may have been as many as 50,000 Jews living in the region and practicing their religion.

Freethinking Judaism was not the major religious force in the Lycus Valley. The Greek religions also flourished there. This was a fertility cult characterized by ecstasy and excessive enthusiasm, though it *also had an aspect of self-denial.*

The City of Colosse. About 100 miles east of Ephesus in the Lycus River Valley lay the city of Colosse. Since it was located on a major trade route from Ephesus, Colosse was considered a great city in the days of Xerxes, the Persian king (fifth century B.C.). One hundred years later, it had developed into a prosperous commercial center on account of its weaving industry. By the time of Paul, Colosse's prominence had diminished; though its sister cities, Laodicea and Hierapolis, were still prospering.

OPEN **1.** What did you enjoy reading the most when you were a child? **2.** Did you have a pen-pal?

STUDY **1.** If you were in prison and you wanted to keep in touch with friends, would you send a letter, send e-mail or call them on the phone? **2.** From what you learn about the cults and weird religions in this city (see the introduction), what do you think is happening in this church that Paul is concerned about? What is the closest you have come to being in a pagan environment with pseudo religion and false teaching? **3.** What will keep these young Christians from falling for the false teaching (v. 9)? What will be the result of "spiritual wisdom and understanding" (vv. 10–12)?

APPLY **1.** If you had to describe your spiritual life right now in one or two words, what would they be? **2.** What has kept you from falling for some of the false teaching that is around today?

1 Paul, an apostle of Christ Jesus by the will of God, and Timothy our brother,

2To the holy and faithful[a] brothers in Christ at Colosse:

Grace and peace to you from God our Father.[b]

Thanksgiving and Prayer

3We always thank God, the Father of our Lord Jesus Christ, when we pray for you, 4because we have heard of your faith in Christ Jesus and of the love you have for all the saints— 5the faith and love that spring from the hope that is stored up for you in heaven and that you have already heard about in the word of truth, the gospel 6that has come to you. All over the world this gospel is bearing fruit and growing, just as it has been doing among you since the day you heard it and understood God's grace in all its truth. 7You learned it from Epaphras, our dear fellow servant, who is a faithful minister of Christ on our[c] behalf, 8and who also told us of your love in the Spirit.

9For this reason, since the day we heard about you, we have not stopped praying for you and asking God to fill you with the knowledge of his will through all spiritual wisdom and understanding. 10And we pray this in order that you may live a life worthy of the Lord and may please him in every way: bearing fruit in every good work, growing in the knowledge of God, 11being strengthened with all power according to his glorious might so that you may have great endurance and patience, and joyfully 12giving thanks to the Father, who has qualified you[d] to share in the inheritance of the saints in the kingdom of light. 13For he has rescued us from the dominion of darkness and brought us into the kingdom of the Son he loves, 14in whom we have redemption,[e] the forgiveness of sins.

[a]2 Or *believing* [b]2 Some manuscripts *Father and the Lord Jesus Christ* [c]7 Some manuscripts *your* [d]12 Some manuscripts *us* [e]14 A few late manuscripts *redemption through his blood*

1:2 Grace and peace. This letter highlights the reality of God's grace through Christ and the reconciliation (peace) that results.

1:4–5 faith ... love ... hope. This triad of Christian graces is arranged and expanded upon in various ways throughout the New Testament (Rom. 5:1–5; 1 Cor. 13:13; Gal. 5:5–6; Eph. 4:2–5; 1 Thess. 1:3; 5:8; Heb. 6:10–12; 1 Peter 1:3–8). The center of the Christian faith is Jesus Christ; the essence of its lifestyle is love; and the sure hope of a future with Christ is its motivation.

1:6 All over the world. Within 30 years after Jesus' resurrection, the gospel had spread from Palestine throughout the Roman Empire. **understood God's grace in all its truth.** The words all or everything appear 17 times in 1:1–23. Through this emphasis, Paul is countering the false teachers' claims that there is more to learn and experience about life with God than what can be found in the message of God's grace in Christ (2:4,8).

1:9 knowledge ... all spiritual wisdom. The false teachers (combining elements of Christianity, Greek mystery religions, and Judaism) defined salvation in terms of secret, divine knowledge and ecstatic experiences which could only be gained by following their regimen of ascetic disciplines and ceremonies.

1:10 a life worthy of the Lord. Rather than esoteric knowledge and experiences, true spirituality is seen in a lifestyle that reflects the love and holiness of Jesus. **growing in the knowledge of God.** Obedience to Christ is the key to ongoing spiritual growth.

1:11 strengthened with all power. The false teachers taught that spiritual power was a matter of gaining control over the celestial forces that dominated human life (Eph. 2:2; 6:12). Paul teaches instead that true spiritual power is shown by patiently enduring life's hardships with a spirit of thankfulness to God (v. 12).

1:12 qualified. In the mystery religions, a person supposedly qualified to share in the divine through practicing various rites and disciplines (2:18). By contrast, God fully "qualifies" the believer to inherit his kingdom through Christ's work.

1:13 the dominion of darkness. Darkness is an appropriate image for the influence of the hostile spiritual forces (v. 16) since their domination only leads to spiritual and moral blindness (Luke 22:53; John 1:5; Eph. 5:8–14). Using the metaphor of the Exodus, Paul reminds the Colossians that these astral powers are no more a threat to the Christian than Pharaoh was to the Israelites after the incident at the Red Sea!

1:14 redemption. The believers' rescue from the dominion of darkness came because Jesus broke its power by

The Supremacy of Christ

[15]He is the image of the invisible God, the firstborn over all creation. [16]For by him all things were created: things in heaven and on earth, visible and invisible, whether thrones or powers or rulers or authorities; all things were created by him and for him. [17]He is before all things, and in him all things hold together. [18]And he is the head of the body, the church; he is the beginning and the firstborn from among the dead, so that in everything he might have the supremacy. [19]For God was pleased to have all his fullness dwell in him, [20]and through him to reconcile to himself all things, whether things on earth or things in heaven, by making peace through his blood, shed on the cross.

[21]Once you were alienated from God and were enemies in your minds because of[a] your evil behavior. [22]But now he has reconciled you by Christ's physical body through death to present you holy in his sight, without blemish and free from accusation— [23]if you continue in your faith, established and firm, not moved from the hope held out in the gospel. This is the gospel that you heard and that has been proclaimed to every creature under heaven, and of which I, Paul, have become a servant.

Paul's Labor for the Church

[24]Now I rejoice in what was suffered for you, and I fill up in my flesh what is still lacking in regard to Christ's afflictions, for the sake of his body, which is the church. [25]I have become its servant by the commission God gave me to present to you the word of God in its fullness— [26]the mystery that has been kept hidden for ages and gen-

[a]21 Or *minds, as shown by*

OPEN 1. When you were a child, who was the person who was "larger than life" to you? **2.** When you were growing up, what sports team had supremacy in your town?

STUDY 1. What are seven or eight things Paul says about Christ in verses 15–20? What is Paul saying to the false teachers who have diminished the importance of Christ in their teaching? **2.** What does Paul say about the Gentiles before and after Christ? What is the challenge now?

APPLY Go back and read out loud verses 15–20, emphasizing the words ALL and EVERYTHING and try to put into one or two words how you feel.

OPEN When you were growing up, how did your parents manage to keep their Christmas gifts for the kids a secret?

STUDY 1. Paul is in prison in Rome facing death. How does he look upon his circumstances? How would you look upon these circum-

---

his sacrificial death (v. 20; Eph. 1:7). **forgiveness of sins.** This defines the nature of the liberation Christ has gained for believers.

1:15 image of the invisible God. "Image" does not mean a second-hand representation (such as a photograph is an image of a person), but a complete representation: All that God is, Jesus is (John 1:18; 14:9; 2 Cor. 4:4–6; Heb. 1:3). One need not look anywhere else but to Christ in order to fully know God.

1:16 thrones ... powers ... rulers ... authorities. Christ is Lord over all authorities.

1:17 He is before all things. Christ's preeminence means he is Lord over all.

1:18 the head of the body. This emphasizes the organic, living relationship between Christ and his people. **firstborn.** As Jesus is Lord over the original creation, so also he is Lord over the new creation (v. 15).

1:19 fullness. Paul declares that Christ is fully God, and that there is nothing else other than Christ needed in your life to have right standing before God.

1:20 reconcile to himself all things. Jesus seeks the eventual goal of not only reconciling humanity to himself but to creation, which has been thrown out of kilter by sin (Rom. 8:19–25). **his blood.** The irony of the gospel is that this work of redemption was completed through the gory, earthly act of crucifixion.

1:21 alienated from God. Jews viewed Gentile idolatry and immorality as the chief evidence that humanity was in revolt against God. Paul utilizes that idea to contrast the Colossians' "before" and "after" status in Christ. **enemies in your minds.** "Mind" represents the core of the personality.

1:22 But now. Paul often uses this expression to contrast people's situation without Christ with their condition in Christ (Rom. 3:21; Eph. 2:13). **Christ's physical body.** The stress is on Jesus' actual body which died, as opposed to the church as the expression of Christ's body (v. 18). **holy ... without blemish ... free from accusation.** While the false teachers taught that the Colossians needed something more in order to be truly spiritual, Paul uses the language both of sacrifice and the law court to emphasize that believers are completely acceptable to God through Christ (Rom. 8:1ff).

1:23 continue in your faith. The work of Christ must be received with faith demonstrated by an ongoing loyalty and obedience to Christ. **proclaimed to every creature.** Paul reassures his readers that, in spite of what the false teachers have said, they have already received the full gospel as proclaimed everywhere else.

1:24 what is still lacking in regard to Christ's afflictions. Given Paul's stress on the once-for-all sufficiency of Christ's death as a sacrifice for sin (v. 22), he cannot mean that his sufferings add to the value of Christ's death. Believers will continue to suffer as Christ would if he were still here.

1:26 the mystery ... now disclosed. The "mystery" of the gospel is

stances if you had been in his shoes? **2.** In your own words, how would you explain the "mystery"? **3.** What would be Paul's advice to someone who says, "I want to know everything there is to know about God"?

APPLY 1. In your spiritual journey when did you start to understand the "mystery ... which is Christ in you"? **2.** Who was the Paul in your life who "struggled" to present you perfect (fully mature) in Christ?

OPEN 1. As a child, what did you think a "religious" person was like? **2.** Did you consider your parents "permissive" or "strict"? Did they have a lot of rules for you, or just a few? Which one was the biggie?

STUDY 1. Have you ever known people of a much different faith than yours? Have you known anyone in a cult? What seemed to attract the students? What were their initiation rites, rituals, special days in the year, and eating habits? Who was the "guru" and on what basis did this person claim authority? What was their basic teaching and world view? **2.** How does Paul answer the claim of the false teachers that angels are to be worshiped as the source of spiritual knowledge and

erations, but is now disclosed to the saints. 27To them God has chosen to make known among the Gentiles the glorious riches of this
mystery, which is Christ in you, the hope of glory.
28We proclaim him, admonishing and teaching everyone with all
wisdom, so that we may present everyone perfect in Christ. 29To this
end I labor, struggling with all his energy, which so powerfully works
in me.

2 I want you to know how much I am struggling for you and for
those at Laodicea, and for all who have not met me personally.
2My purpose is that they may be encouraged in heart and united in
love, so that they may have the full riches of complete understanding,
in order that they may know the mystery of God, namely, Christ, 3in
whom are hidden all the treasures of wisdom and knowledge. 4I tell
you this so that no one may deceive you by fine-sounding arguments.
5For though I am absent from you in body, I am present with you in
spirit and delight to see how orderly you are and how firm your faith
in Christ is.

Freedom From Human Regulations Through Life With Christ

6So then, just as you received Christ Jesus as Lord, continue to live
in him, 7rooted and built up in him, strengthened in the faith as you
were taught, and overflowing with thankfulness.
8See to it that no one takes you captive through hollow and deceptive philosophy, which depends on human tradition and the basic
principles of this world rather than on Christ.
9For in Christ all the fullness of the Deity lives in bodily form, 10and
you have been given fullness in Christ, who is the head over every
power and authority. 11In him you were also circumcised, in the putting off of the sinful nature,[a] not with a circumcision done by the
hands of men but with the circumcision done by Christ, 12having
been buried with him in baptism and raised with him through your
faith in the power of God, who raised him from the dead.
13When you were dead in your sins and in the uncircumcision of

[a] 11 Or *the flesh*

revealed by God to all—including Gentiles—who believe. It is not a secret form of spiritual power, but the hope for eternity guaranteed by the presence of Christ within the believer.

1:28 perfect in Christ. Each Christian is perfect in Christ. He stands wholly righteous for us before God. We mature in our relationship with him through obedience moving toward the goal of the completed work of Christ in us.

2:2 encouraged in heart ... united in love. The false teachers said there was a secret knowledge gained only by those few who practiced a variety of rites, experiences or disciplines. Such a spirituality would naturally tend to discourage people and lead to factions. The gospel views spiritual growth as a growth in love for Christ and one another. This would lead to hope and shared fellowship.

2:6 received Christ Jesus as Lord. To receive Jesus as "Lord" is to acknowledge him as the supreme authority in one's life. **continue to live in him.** Their original acceptance of Jesus' lordship must be demonstrated by a steady commitment to follow him with a thankful heart (v. 7).

2:8 The false teachings were not based on the teachings of Christ, but upon faulty ideas influenced by the "basic principles" of the world, angelic beings that manipulated human affairs in opposition to God (1:16; 1 Cor. 2:6,8; Gal. 3:19; 4:3,9; Eph. 6:12).

2:9 in Christ all the fullness of the Deity lives in bodily form. While the false teachers relate to fallen angelic beings, believers relate to God incarnate (1:19).

2:10 fullness in Christ. Christ is fully God. **the head.** This stresses Christ's lordship over all creation (1:15–17). To go "beyond" Christ is to go backwards spiritually.

2:11 circumcised. True circumcision is through Christ spiritually not the removal of flesh.

2:13 When you were dead. Jesus' physical death is compared with the lack of spiritual life in the Colossians prior to their conversion (Eph. 2:1–10). **uncircumcision.** The false teachers

your sinful nature,[a] God made you[b] alive with Christ. He forgave us all
our sins, 14having canceled the written code, with its regulations,
that was against us and that stood opposed to us; he took it away,
nailing it to the cross. 15And having disarmed the powers and authorities, he made a public spectacle of them, triumphing over them
by the cross.[c]

16Therefore do not let anyone judge you by what you eat or drink,
or with regard to a religious festival, a New Moon celebration or a
Sabbath day. 17These are a shadow of the things that were to come;
the reality, however, is found in Christ. 18Do not let anyone who delights in false humility and the worship of angels disqualify you for
the prize. Such a person goes into great detail about what he has
seen, and his unspiritual mind puffs him up with idle notions. 19He
has lost connection with the Head, from whom the whole body, supported and held together by its ligaments and sinews, grows as God
causes it to grow.

20Since you died with Christ to the basic principles of this world,
why, as though you still belonged to it, do you submit to its rules:
21"Do not handle! Do not taste! Do not touch!"? 22These are all destined to perish with use, because they are based on human commands and teachings. 23Such regulations indeed have an appearance
of wisdom, with their self-imposed worship, their false humility and
their harsh treatment of the body, but they lack any value in restraining sensual indulgence.

Rules for Holy Living

3 Since, then, you have been raised with Christ, set your hearts on
things above, where Christ is seated at the right hand of God.

[a]13 Or *your flesh* [b]13 Some manuscripts *us* [c]15 Or *them in him*

power (vv. 9–10)? **3.** What does Paul say about the initiation rite of circumcision (vv. 11–12)? **4.** What about the rules and regulations that they required (vv. 13–15, 20–23)? **5.** How about their special days and observances? **6.** How does Paul look upon the false teachers and their mindset (vv. 18–19)?

APPLY 1. Going back to verses 6–7, how would you say your spiritual life is rooted? **2.** What could be done to "build up and strengthen" your spiritual life?

OPEN In buying clothes, are you a name-brand buyer? A bargain hunter? Spouse conscious? Quality conscious? Style conscious? Unconscious?

---

saw circumcision as a sign of being emancipated from fleshy limits (v. 11). Paul counters that a physical act will not cure the problem of a heart which is not set apart for God.

2:14 the written code. This refers to a written agreement to pay back a debt or to obey a law. When fulfilled, the document was blotted out and canceled.

2:16 a religious festival, a New Moon celebration or a Sabbath day. While this serves as a summary of the annual, monthly and weekly Jewish holy days (1 Chr. 23:31), pagans also observed cycles of worship determined by astrological practices. The false teachers probably used the Jewish traditions to support their astrological calendar.

2:17 a shadow ... the reality. Hebrews 8:3–13 and 10:1–18 compared the work of Christ to the Old Testament sacrificial system (1 Cor. 5:7). While the false teachers claimed their ascetic practices were the pathway that led to the reality of spiritual experience, Paul asserts they only lead to the shadowlands and not to a true spiritual life.

2:18 false humility. Paul is obviously not repudiating a true humility before God, but rather has in mind the ascetic practices, like enforced fasting, which mask pride with a facade of humility. **worship of angels.** False teachers may have claimed their spiritual elevation allowed them to worship the Deity in the company of the angels. **disqualify.** The religious discipline and experience of the false teachers made the simple faith and obedience of the Christians seem inadequate (1:12). **what he has seen.** Inscriptions in pagan temples used this phrase to refer to a rite which authorized a person to be a teacher of the divine mysteries. **unspiritual mind.** Literally, "the mind of his flesh." Paul mocks the false teachers' claim to have escaped the defilement of the body by saying their mind is full of the "flesh" (v. 23).

2:20 died with Christ. Elsewhere, Paul uses the image of dying with Christ to show how the believer's bond to sin (Rom. 6:16) and to the Law (Rom. 7:1) is broken. Here, he uses it to show that their bondage to the "principles" has also been severed. Since the power of the principles has been severed, it is foolish to submit to their authority as a route to spiritual life (Gal. 4:1–11).

2:23 restraining sensual indulgence. Paul plays with the false teacher's fondness for spiritual fulfillment by pointing out that their ascetic rules about the body ironically only "fill up" "the flesh."

3:1 raised with Christ. As the Christian's death-with-Christ cut the bonds to the old authorities (2:20), so one's life with Christ creates new bonds with God and others. **set your hearts.** Literally, "seek." **on things above.** This is not encouraging escapism from earthly affairs. The point is that Christians are to shape their lives by the values of the heavenly world in which Christ sits enthroned as King rather than heeding rules based on the elemental spirits.

STUDY The false teachers in Colosse not only messed up the thinking of the young Christians in Colosse, they also taught that the path to salvation was through knowledge. The body (matter) was unimportant. Therefore, anything done with the body was of no consequence. **1.** From what you know about the new religions in your area, what is their view about holy living and moral purity? **2.** Reading between the lines (vv. 5–8), what was the lifestyle of the believers in Colosse before they were converted?

APPLY 1. Have you ever been in a fellowship of believers that represented very diverse theological views? How did you live at peace? **2.** How can this group be more at peace? **3.** How can this group help you in prayer this week?

OPEN Who took out the trash at your home when you were growing up? Who takes out the trash now?

2Set your minds on things above, not on earthly things. 3For you died,
and your life is now hidden with Christ in God. 4When Christ, who is
your[a] life, appears, then you also will appear with him in glory.
5Put to death, therefore, whatever belongs to your earthly nature:
sexual immorality, impurity, lust, evil desires and greed, which is
idolatry. 6Because of these, the wrath of God is coming.[b] 7You used to
walk in these ways, in the life you once lived. 8But now you must rid
yourselves of all such things as these: anger, rage, malice, slander,
and filthy language from your lips. 9Do not lie to each other, since you
have taken off your old self with its practices 10and have put on the
new self, which is being renewed in knowledge in the image of its
Creator. 11Here there is no Greek or Jew, circumcised or uncircumcised, barbarian, Scythian, slave or free, but Christ is all, and is in all.
12Therefore, as God's chosen people, holy and dearly loved, clothe
yourselves with compassion, kindness, humility, gentleness and patience. 13Bear with each other and forgive whatever grievances you
may have against one another. Forgive as the Lord forgave you. 14And
over all these virtues put on love, which binds them all together in
perfect unity.
15Let the peace of Christ rule in your hearts, since as members of
one body you were called to peace. And be thankful. 16Let the word of
Christ dwell in you richly as you teach and admonish one another
with all wisdom, and as you sing psalms, hymns and spiritual songs
with gratitude in your hearts to God. 17And whatever you do, whether
in word or deed, do it all in the name of the Lord Jesus, giving thanks
to God the Father through him.

Rules for Christian Households

18Wives, submit to your husbands, as is fitting in the Lord.
19Husbands, love your wives and do not be harsh with them.

[a]4 Some manuscripts *our* [b]6 Some early manuscripts *coming on those who are disobedient*

3:3 hidden with Christ. What God did in the past is now a present reality in Christ.

3:5 Put to death. Believers are to daily turn away from attitudes and actions that reflect the old way of life. **sexual immorality ... greed.** The list of sins proceeds from external actions to internal motives and attitudes (v. 8).

3:8 rid yourselves of all such things. Immorality, greed, abusive talk, etc. have no place in the life of a Christian.

3:9 taken off your old self. Literally, "to strip off." This phrase is also used to describe the putting off of the sinful nature through Christ's death (2:11), and Christ's victory over spiritual powers (2:15).

3:10 put on the new self. The lifestyle of Christians is patterned after the attitudes and actions of Christ who is at work within them (1 Cor. 15:45; Gal. 3:27).

3:11 Scythian. The Greeks considered Scythians to be especially uncouth barbarians. Allegiance to Christ eradicates prideful divisions based on race, religion, culture or social class (and gender—Gal. 3:28).

3:12–17 Paul uses the image of putting on new clothes to show how true spirituality involves "wearing" the Christlike qualities of love, peace and thankfulness (Rom. 13:14).

3:15 Let the peace of Christ rule in your hearts. "Your" is plural: What is in view is not a sense of personal serenity, but a mutual commitment to consider peaceful relationships with one another as the highest priority in their corporate life. **called to peace.** While the reconciliation of people with God and one another is the major theme of Christian doctrine (vv. 9–11; 1:20–22; 2:2), living out this reconciliation is the major emphasis of Christian ethics (vv. 12–14; Rom. 14:19–15:7; Gal 5:22–26). **be thankful.** Thankfulness for God's grace is the central motive of Christian living (vv. 16–17; 1:12; 4:2).

3:16 the word of Christ. While the false teachers have "lost connection with the Head" (2:19), the message the Colossians teach one another must be centered on Jesus. **dwell in you richly.** Spiritual fullness is rooted neither in secret knowledge nor in mystical experiences but in a commitment to Christ. **teach ... sing.** Literally, "teaching and admonishing one another in psalms, hymns, and spiritual songs."

3:17 Christ, the source of one's life with God (1:20,22), the one who is present with his people (1:27), the one through whom God is known (2:9), the one who rules over all creation (v. 1; 2:15), is also the model people are to imitate in all areas of life. Thus Paul undermines the false teachers' assertions that Christ alone is inadequate for a full spiritual life.

3:18-22 submit. In Christ, this is

20Children, obey your parents in everything, for this pleases the
Lord.
21Fathers, do not embitter your children, or they will become discouraged.
22Slaves, obey your earthly masters in everything; and do it, not
only when their eye is on you and to win their favor, but with sincerity
of heart and reverence for the Lord. 23Whatever you do, work at it
with all your heart, as working for the Lord, not for men, 24since you
know that you will receive an inheritance from the Lord as a reward.
It is the Lord Christ you are serving. 25Anyone who does wrong will be
repaid for his wrong, and there is no favoritism.

4 Masters, provide your slaves with what is right and fair, because
you know that you also have a Master in heaven.

Further Instructions

2Devote yourselves to prayer, being watchful and thankful. 3And
pray for us, too, that God may open a door for our message, so that
we may proclaim the mystery of Christ, for which I am in chains.
4Pray that I may proclaim it clearly, as I should. 5Be wise in the way
you act toward outsiders; make the most of every opportunity. 6Let
your conversation be always full of grace, seasoned with salt, so that
you may know how to answer everyone.

Final Greetings

7Tychicus will tell you all the news about me. He is a dear brother, a
faithful minister and fellow servant in the Lord. 8I am sending him to
you for the express purpose that you may know about our[a] circumstances and that he may encourage your hearts. 9He is coming with
Onesimus, our faithful and dear brother, who is one of you. They will
tell you everything that is happening here.

[a]8 Some manuscripts *that he may know about your*

STUDY 1. If you had to point to a Christian family that practiced what this passage is all about, who would it be? **2.** In what way has your commitment to Christ affected the way you look upon your role in your family? **3.** In your job, do you think the same principles apply that are described here for slaves and masters?

APPLY Where are you struggling right now in your relationship as a: Husband/wife, Parent/child or Employee/employer?

OPEN In high school, who were two of your best friends? What was one quality about them that stands out to you?

STUDY Paul is in prison in Rome. He is writing to a struggling church hundreds of miles away in Asia. **1.** What does this passage demonstrate about Paul as a person? **2.** What are some leadership principles this passage illustrates? **3.** If Paul had never lived, what would the church have missed? **4.** If you were going to send two friends to report on "the circumstances" in your spiritual life right now, who would you choose? **5.** Onesimus was a runaway slave from this church. By the fact that he got as far as Rome probably indicates that he stole a lot of money from Phi-

---

transformed from a passive obedience to an authority to a specific application of Christ's call to put the needs and interest of others before one's own (Eph. 5:21–24; Phil. 2:4).

3:21 Fathers. This word can mean "parents" as well (Heb. 11:23).

3:22 Slaves. Slaves were legally considered the property of their masters. While obedience was required at the threat of punishment, Paul calls for an attitude of faithful service in light of the fact that ultimately Christ is the master of all (v. 23).

3:24 inheritance. The Christian looks forward to inheriting the fullness of the kingdom of God (Luke 12:32; Eph. 5:5). This hope (1:5) provides the basis for "endurance and patience" with thanksgiving (1:11–12), even in the types of hardships a slave might face.

3:25 Anyone who does wrong will be repaid for his wrong. Whereas in Ephesians 6:8 Paul promised slaves that "the Lord will reward everyone for whatever good he does," here he warns that misbehavior will result in judgment. **there is no favoritism.** Slaves, even though oppressed by their masters, cannot expect God to excuse sin (v. 22). Ephesians 6:9 applies this same phrase to masters, warning them that their position of authority will not exempt them from judgment should they abuse that authority.

4:1 provide your slaves with what is right and fair. While Paul did oppose slavery as such, he did call upon Christian masters to treat their slaves with justice and consideration, values which were not required of them by Roman law. **you also have a Master in heaven.** Masters are to relate to their slaves in the full realization that God is their master and they are accountable to him for their behavior toward their slaves.

4:2 Devote yourselves to prayer. See the example of the church in Acts 1:14, 2:42 and 6:4. **being watchful.** An allusion to Matthew 26:41 and Luke 18:1. This call to vigilance and spiritual alertness became part of the apostles' teaching to Christians in general (Acts 20:31; 1 Cor. 16:13; 1 Thess. 5:6; 1 Peter 5:8).

4:3 in chains. Paul, imprisoned several times because Jewish opponents considered his missionary activity as subversive to their interests, probably wrote this letter while under the house arrest described in Acts 28.

4:5 every opportunity. While a similar passage in Ephesians 5:15 refers to the Christian's general conduct, here the special importance of being alert to God-given opportunities to bear witness to Christ in the course of daily life is in view.

lemon who is in this church. How do you think he will be received? **6.** Who is the Epaphras in your life, who is always wrestling in prayer for you? Who are you wrestling in prayer for? **7.** If Paul became the spiritual leader of your church, what would this do? If he joined your group, what would happen?

APPLY 1. What has been the highpoint in this Bible study for you? **2.** What is the central teaching or point that stands out in your mind for this epistle? **3.** What would you like to study next? **4.** If you could invite one more person into your group, who would you want to invite?

10My fellow prisoner Aristarchus sends you his greetings, as does
Mark, the cousin of Barnabas. (You have received instructions about
him; if he comes to you, welcome him.) 11Jesus, who is called Justus,
also sends greetings. These are the only Jews among my fellow workers for the kingdom of God, and they have proved a comfort to me.
12Epaphras, who is one of you and a servant of Christ Jesus, sends
greetings. He is always wrestling in prayer for you, that you may
stand firm in all the will of God, mature and fully assured. 13I vouch
for him that he is working hard for you and for those at Laodicea and
Hierapolis. 14Our dear friend Luke, the doctor, and Demas send greetings. 15Give my greetings to the brothers at Laodicea, and to Nympha
and the church in her house.

16After this letter has been read to you, see that it is also read in the
church of the Laodiceans and that you in turn read the letter from Laodicea.

17Tell Archippus: "See to it that you complete the work you have received in the Lord."

18I, Paul, write this greeting in my own hand. Remember my chains.
Grace be with you.

4:12 Epaphras. A native Colossian who established the church there and throughout the Lycus valley (1:7; Philem. 23). Paul's commendation here and in Colossians 1:7 substantiates his claim that the church had already heard the gospel.

4:13 Laodicea. A city near Colosse. **Hierapolis.** A city about 12 miles northwest of Colosse and six miles north of Laodicea.

4:14 Luke, the doctor. It is from this reference that we learn of Luke's profession. The various "we" passages in the book of Acts (16:10–17; 20:5–21:18; 27:1–28:16) indicate that Luke accompanied Paul at several points in his missionary work.

4:15 Nympha and the church in her house. The Laodicean church, or at least part of it, followed the custom of other early churches in meeting in the homes of members who could accommodate them. Philemon's home was one of the sites of the congregation in Colosse (Philem. 1–2).

4:17 Archippus. In Philemon 2 he is called a "fellow soldier."

4:18 I, Paul, write this greeting in my own hand. Typically, others actually wrote Paul's letters at his dictation (Rom. 16:22) while he penned the final greeting as a mark of the letter's genuineness (1 Cor. 16:21; Gal. 6:11; 2 Thess. 3:17; Philem. 19). Second Thessalonians 2:2 hints at the possibility that forged letters had been circulated in Paul's name.

1 Thessalonians

Personal Reading	Group Study Topic and Reading	
1:1–10	Legendary Model of Faith	1:1–10
2:1–16	Lasting Model of Ministry	2:1–16
2:17–3:13	Longing to Visit This Church	2:17–3:13
4:1–12	Living to Please God	4:1–12
4:13–5:11	Living in Light of His Coming	4:13–5:11
5:12–28	Living in Peace With Others	5:12–28

Author. The apostle Paul wrote 1 Thessalonians.

Date. Many scholars believe that either Galatians or 1 Thessalonians may well be Paul's first letter and the first document in what eventually became the New Testament. In any case, it is generally agreed that 1 Thessalonians was written about A.D. 50, during Paul's second missionary journey not long after the founding of the church in Thessalonica. Paul probably wrote from Corinth, where he went after he left Athens. Timothy had returned with news from Thessalonica, and this letter was Paul's response to his report.

Theme. Living in the light of the Second Coming of Christ.

Historical Background. When Paul crossed over into Macedonia in A.D. 50, a new era began for Christianity. After receiving the vision that sent Paul across the Aegean Sea to Philippi, he came to Thessalonica, which turned out to be a key stop in his pioneering work in Europe.

His stay in Thessalonica was brief and stormy. After he had preached in the synagogue for three Sabbaths, the Jews were so jealous of his success that they dragged Jason (at whose home Paul was staying) and a few other believers before the city officials. They claimed that these men were associates of Paul and were defying Caesar's decrees. That night after Jason and the others were released on bail, Paul and Silas slipped away to Berea.

Characteristics. First Thessalonians does not emphasize theology and doctrine. Rather, it reflects the concern, gratitude, disappointment and joy of a beloved missionary who can't stop thinking about the church he left behind.

Paul's Concerns About the Church at Thessalonica. In his place Paul sent Timothy to see how the church at Thessalonica was doing and to give them what help he could (3:1–5).

What Timothy found was twofold. The converts were standing fast in their faith despite persecution and doing evangelistic work on their own. On the other hand, some of the converts had not fully understood the ethical implications of the gospel. In particular, there was laxity in sexual matters (4:3–8). Some felt it unnecessary to work and had become a burden to the others (4:11–12; 5:14). There was also misunderstanding about the Second Coming. In this letter to them, Paul expresses his relief and joy at their good progress in the gospel. They have become, he says, "a model to all the believers in Macedonia and Achaia"(1:7).

The Converts. Luke says (in Acts 17:1–4) that the church had its roots in the Jewish community. Some members of the synagogue where Paul preached, along with a large number of God-fearing Greeks—Gentiles who worshiped at the synagogue—and several prominent women, had become convinced that Jesus was the Messiah and so became followers of Christ.

The greater part of the church, however, seems to have been made up of converted pagans, as Paul's comment in 1:9 indicates: "You turned to God from idols."

The City of Thessalonica. The key to its importance was Thessalonica's location astride the famous *Via Egnatia*—the great Roman military road across northern Greece, which stretched from the Adriatic Sea on the west to Constantinople in the east. Hence trade between Rome and Asia Minor and points farther east flowed through Thessalonica, making it very wealthy. This was a crucial site for a church if Christianity were to spread throughout the world.

OPEN How have you been a part of a team effort, such as: Sports, Job, Acting in a play? Other?

STUDY 1. What do you learn about the beginning of the church in Thessalonica in Acts 17:1–9? How would you describe the response of the people? **2.** How would you describe the tone as Paul starts off this letter (vv. 2–3)? **3.** What does Paul attribute to the response of the Thessalonians (vv. 4–6)? What happened as a result of the response of the Thessalonians (vv. 7–9)? What is the principle that is illustrated here for spreading the gospel? **4.** In Acts 17:4, the people in Thessalonica that responded are described as "God-fearing Greeks ... and prominent women." Why would these two groups be so responsive to the gospel?

APPLY Who originally brought the gospel to you?

1 Paul, Silas[a] and Timothy,

To the church of the Thessalonians in God the Father and the Lord
Jesus Christ:

Grace and peace to you.[b]

Thanksgiving for the Thessalonians' Faith

[2]We always thank God for all of you, mentioning you in our
prayers. [3]We continually remember before our God and Father your
work produced by faith, your labor prompted by love, and your endurance inspired by hope in our Lord Jesus Christ.
[4]For we know, brothers loved by God, that he has chosen you, [5]be-
cause our gospel came to you not simply with words, but also with
power, with the Holy Spirit and with deep conviction. You know how
we lived among you for your sake. [6]You became imitators of us and of
the Lord; in spite of severe suffering, you welcomed the message with
the joy given by the Holy Spirit. [7]And so you became a model to all the
believers in Macedonia and Achaia. [8]The Lord's message rang out
from you not only in Macedonia and Achaia—your faith in God has
become known everywhere. Therefore we do not need to say anything about it, [9]for they themselves report what kind of reception you
gave us. They tell how you turned to God from idols to serve the living and true God, [10]and to wait for his Son from heaven, whom he
raised from the dead—Jesus, who rescues us from the coming wrath.

OPEN What was one of your most memorable failures in junior or senior high school?

STUDY 1. Reading between the lines, what do you think the "opposition" has been saying about Paul that causes Paul to defend himself (vv. 1–6)? What is the lesson for you in Paul's words in verses 1–6? By contrast, what does Paul insinuate the false teachers are doing to the Thessalonians (vv. 5–6)? **2.** What two metaphors does Paul use to describe

Paul's Ministry in Thessalonica

2 You know, brothers, that our visit to you was not a failure. [2]We
had previously suffered and been insulted in Philippi, as you
know, but with the help of our God we dared to tell you his gospel in
spite of strong opposition. [3]For the appeal we make does not spring
from error or impure motives, nor are we trying to trick you. [4]On the
contrary, we speak as men approved by God to be entrusted with the
gospel. We are not trying to please men but God, who tests our
hearts. [5]You know we never used flattery, nor did we put on a mask to

[a]1 Greek *Silvanus,* a variant of *Silas* [b]1 Some early manuscripts *you from God our Father and the Lord Jesus Christ*

1:1 Silas. Silas was a representative of the Jerusalem church to the Christians at Antioch (Acts 15:22). He accompanied Paul on his second missionary journey during which they met Timothy, a young man highly spoken of by the Christians in his area (Acts 16:1–5). **Thessalonians.** Thessalonica was an important city in northern Greece, the capital of the province of Macedonia.

1:2 We always thank God for all of you. Paul most often began his letters with an affirmation of the recipients (Rom. 1:8; 1 Cor. 1:4; Eph. 1:15–16; Phil. 1:3; Col. 1:3; 2 Thess. 1:3).

1:3 faith ... love ... hope. Paul and other New Testament writers use these words (or a combination of two of them) as a way of summing up the essentials of the Christian life (5:8; Rom. 5:1–5; 1 Cor. 13:13; Gal. 5:5–6; Eph. 4:2–5; Col. 1:4–5; Heb. 6:10–12; 10:22–24; 1 Peter 1:21–22). Faith in Christ, rooted in the promise of eternal life, is expressed by love to others. These are active concepts, the presence of which is seen by tangible activities of sacrifice and service.

1:4 brothers loved by God. This is a reminder of the intimacy with which "God the Father" relates to his people. **he has chosen you.** Paul's purpose in reminding them of God's initiative in their salvation is to strengthen their hope in light of the pressures of external persecution (2:14) and internal uncertainty (4:13).

2:2 we dared to tell you his gospel. Paul was as susceptible to fear in difficult situations as anyone (Acts 18:9–10; Phil. 1:20). His strength, as he continually declares, is found in God.

2:3 error ... impure motives ... trying to trick you. Philosopher-preachers, magicians, and advocates of exotic religions who circulated during this period were characterized as appealing to the superstitious sensitivities of people to enhance their reputations and pocketbooks. See Paul's rejection of these motivations in verses 5–6.

cover up greed—God is our witness. 6We were not looking for praise
from men, not from you or anyone else.
As apostles of Christ we could have been a burden to you, 7but we
were gentle among you, like a mother caring for her little children.
8We loved you so much that we were delighted to share with you not
only the gospel of God but our lives as well, because you had become
so dear to us. 9Surely you remember, brothers, our toil and hardship;
we worked night and day in order not to be a burden to anyone while
we preached the gospel of God to you.
10You are witnesses, and so is God, of how holy, righteous and
blameless we were among you who believed. 11For you know that we
dealt with each of you as a father deals with his own children, 12en-
couraging, comforting and urging you to live lives worthy of God,
who calls you into his kingdom and glory.
13And we also thank God continually because, when you received
the word of God, which you heard from us, you accepted it not as the
word of men, but as it actually is, the word of God, which is at work in
you who believe. 14For you, brothers, became imitators of God's
churches in Judea, which are in Christ Jesus: You suffered from your
own countrymen the same things those churches suffered from the
Jews, 15who killed the Lord Jesus and the prophets and also drove us
out. They displease God and are hostile to all men 16in their effort to
keep us from speaking to the Gentiles so that they may be saved. In
this way they always heap up their sins to the limit. The wrath of God
has come upon them at last.[a]

Paul's Longing to See the Thessalonians

17But, brothers, when we were torn away from you for a short time
(in person, not in thought), out of our intense longing we made every
effort to see you. 18For we wanted to come to you—certainly I, Paul,
did, again and again—but Satan stopped us. 19For what is our hope,
our joy, or the crown in which we will glory in the presence of our
Lord Jesus when he comes? Is it not you? 20Indeed, you are our glory
and joy.

[a]16 Or *them fully*

his ministry (vv. 7,11)? Which of these two are you better at? When you are a single parent for someone spiritually, what do you do? **3.** What is the closest you have come to seeing the church put through real suffering (vv. 14–15)? Where did the opposition come from for the church in Thessalonica (Acts 17:5)?

APPLY 1. Paul starts off this passage by saying, "He was not a failure" in his ministry. Do you sometimes feel like you are a failure? **2.** Who has been a "mother/father" to you spiritually?

OPEN 1. As a child, when and where did homesickness strike hard? **2.** What room in your childhood home fills you with warm memories?

STUDY Suddenly, the party is over for the Christians in Thessalonica. After three weeks, Paul is thrown out of the synagogue and forced to flee Thessalonica under cover of darkness. Then, the "opposition"

2:7 gentle ... like a mother. While Paul was not hesitant to use this female imagery for himself, as he described his love for his spiritual children.

2:11 dealt with each of you as a father. In some respects Paul was what a single parent must be—both mother (v. 7) and father! In the ancient world, the father's role was to see that his children learned how to live as responsible citizens.

2:14 the same things those churches suffered from the Jews. As in John's Gospel, Paul often uses the term "Jews" when referring to the entrenched opposition of the Jewish religious leaders to Christianity. While the prime opposition to Jesus and the early church came from these leaders, it must be remembered that the first church was almost entirely Jewish in its makeup.

2:15–16 hostile to all men in their effort to keep us from speaking to the Gentiles. Prior to their visit to Thessalonica, Paul had encountered Jewish opposition in Antioch of Pisidia (Acts 13:50), Iconium (Acts 14:2), and Lystra, where he was stoned (Acts 14:19). The Thessalonian Jews forced Paul not only to leave that city, but also Berea (Acts 17:5,13). In Corinth, from where he probably wrote this letter, he likewise suffered at the hands of Jewish opposition (Acts 18:12).

2:17 torn away from you. Literally, this is "to be bereaved." It was a term that was used to describe the anguish of a parent being forcibly separated from his or her children.

2:18 Satan stopped us. Whether Paul's forced change of plans was due to sickness, inability to make travel arrangements, or some other factor is unknown, but ultimately he attributes this frustration to Satan, God's adversary. At other times, Paul sees roadblocks to his plans as the leading of the Holy Spirit (Acts 16:7). The difference may be that whereas one set of difficulties ends up in the spread of the gospel, at another time those difficulties would hinder that process which delayed the mission that Paul was trying to accomplish.

turns on the young church with the same kind of persecution that Christians in Judea suffered (2:14). **1.** Reading between the lines, what is Paul afraid will happen to the young church in Thessalonica (3:3–5)? What do you think Timothy discovered in his quick visit that encouraged Paul (3:2,6–7)? **2.** How would you describe Paul's desire to visit the young church in Thessalonica (2:18; 3:10–11)? **3.** Throughout this passage, how would you describe Paul's heart for Christians?

APPLY 1. In your spiritual journey, who has been the person like Paul who really cared for your spiritual growth? **2.** What did this person do when he/she learned that you were struggling? **3.** Have you ever told this person how much you appreciate them?

---

3 So when we could stand it no longer, we thought it best to be left
by ourselves in Athens. [2]We sent Timothy, who is our brother and
God's fellow worker[a] in spreading the gospel of Christ, to strengthen
and encourage you in your faith, [3]so that no one would be unsettled
by these trials. You know quite well that we were destined for them.
[4]In fact, when we were with you, we kept telling you that we would be
persecuted. And it turned out that way, as you well know. [5]For this
reason, when I could stand it no longer, I sent to find out about your
faith. I was afraid that in some way the tempter might have tempted
you and our efforts might have been useless.

Timothy's Encouraging Report

[6]But Timothy has just now come to us from you and has brought
good news about your faith and love. He has told us that you always
have pleasant memories of us and that you long to see us, just as we
also long to see you. [7]Therefore, brothers, in all our distress and persecution we were encouraged about you because of your faith. [8]For
now we really live, since you are standing firm in the Lord. [9]How can
we thank God enough for you in return for all the joy we have in the
presence of our God because of you? [10]Night and day we pray most
earnestly that we may see you again and supply what is lacking in
your faith.

[11]Now may our God and Father himself and our Lord Jesus clear
the way for us to come to you. [12]May the Lord make your love increase and overflow for each other and for everyone else, just as ours
does for you. [13]May he strengthen your hearts so that you will be
blameless and holy in the presence of our God and Father when our
Lord Jesus comes with all his holy ones.

Living to Please God

4 Finally, brothers, we instructed you how to live in order to please
God, as in fact you are living. Now we ask you and urge you in
the Lord Jesus to do this more and more. [2]For you know what instructions we gave you by the authority of the Lord Jesus.

[3]It is God's will that you should be sanctified: that you should
avoid sexual immorality; [4]that each of you should learn to control his
own body[b] in a way that is holy and honorable, [5]not in passionate
lust like the heathen, who do not know God; [6]and that in this matter
no one should wrong his brother or take advantage of him. The Lord

[a]2 Some manuscripts *brother and fellow worker*; other manuscripts *brother and God's servant*
[b]4 Or *learn to live with his own wife*; or *learn to acquire a wife*

OPEN What was the last thing you made from scratch with your own two hands?

STUDY After all the praise in the first three chapters, Paul suddenly takes the gloves off. **1.** What do you think was going on in this church that Paul is referring to? **2.** In a pagan culture where sexual immorality was a way of life, how do you think Paul's instruction in verse 3 went over? How does this command go over today? **3.** What does this passage say to the Christian who says that you can

---

3:10 supply what is lacking in your faith. The prayer that follows (vv. 11–13), and the final two chapters which are full of both ethical and doctrinal instructions, give us hints about what Paul felt was lacking.

3:12 make your love increase and overflow for each other and for everyone else. This petition highlights love as the defining element in the Christian's relationships. Love cannot be stagnant; it must always be growing and expanding.

4:1 live in order to please God. Just as a spouse desires to please his or her mate, so the Christian's concern is how to please God.

4:3 sanctified. This means to be set apart for God's use. The emphasis here is that Christians are not to passively wait for God to make them holy, but to pursue after it in dependence upon the Spirit (Rom. 6:13; 8:13). **sexual immorality.** This term is an inclusive one for sexual sin—including fornication, adultery, prostitution and homosexuality, all of which were routine realities in pagan life. New Christians from this environment did not automatically give up the sexual sins that were part of their previous life, but had to be instructed on the new way in Christ (1 Cor. 5:1–2; 6:9–18).

4:4 control his own body. Paul insists on sexual self-control in contrast to being controlled by lustful sexual impulses. He is saying that sexual activity in marriage is to be carried out in a way that respects the dignity and worth of the woman.

will punish men for all such sins, as we have already told you and
warned you. 7For God did not call us to be impure, but to live a holy
life. 8Therefore, he who rejects this instruction does not reject man
but God, who gives you his Holy Spirit.
9Now about brotherly love we do not need to write to you, for you
yourselves have been taught by God to love each other. 10And in fact,
you do love all the brothers throughout Macedonia. Yet we urge you,
brothers, to do so more and more.
11Make it your ambition to lead a quiet life, to mind your own business and to work with your hands, just as we told you, 12so that your
daily life may win the respect of outsiders and so that you will not be
dependent on anybody.

The Coming of the Lord

13Brothers, we do not want you to be ignorant about those who fall
asleep, or to grieve like the rest of men, who have no hope. 14We believe that Jesus died and rose again and so we believe that God will
bring with Jesus those who have fallen asleep in him. 15According to
the Lord's own word, we tell you that we who are still alive, who are
left till the coming of the Lord, will certainly not precede those who
have fallen asleep. 16For the Lord himself will come down from heav-
en, with a loud command, with the voice of the archangel and with
the trumpet call of God, and the dead in Christ will rise first. 17After
that, we who are still alive and are left will be caught up together with
them in the clouds to meet the Lord in the air. And so we will be with
the Lord forever. 18Therefore encourage each other with these words.
5 Now, brothers, about times and dates we do not need to write to
you, 2for you know very well that the day of the Lord will come
like a thief in the night. 3While people are saying, "Peace and safety,"
destruction will come on them suddenly, as labor pains on a pregnant
woman, and they will not escape.
4But you, brothers, are not in darkness so that this day should surprise you like a thief. 5You are all sons of the light and sons of the day.

do anything you want as long as no one gets hurt (v. 6) or "my personal life is none of your business" (v. 7)?

APPLY 1. In your spiritual pilgrimage, do you find the practice of living a holy life easier, harder or different? **2.** Quite honestly, what does living a "sanctified" life mean to you?

OPEN Who was the first family member you recall dying? How did this affect you? What else has shaped your view of death and dying?

STUDY 1. If you believed that Christ would return in your life time and some of your Christian friends had died before Christ returned, how would you be feeling? **2.** What does Paul say will happen to those who have died in Christ? **3.** What will happen to those who are living at the time of the Second Coming? **4.** For those who want to know the time when Christ will return, what does Paul say? **5.** Do Paul's words about Christ coming "as a thief in the night" comfort you or stir up fear? **6.** What is the difference in the lifestyle of the "sons of light ... and those who belong to the night or to the darkness" (v. 5)? **7.** Why does a follower of Christ need the protective armor of "faith and

---

4:10 the brothers throughout Macedonia. At this time, churches had been established at least in Philippi and Berea. **do so more and more.** A Christian lifestyle grows out of a desire to please God and love others. Paul encourages these new believers to press on in that direction, unfolding the limitless possibilities within each directive.

4:13 fall asleep. This is simply a common metaphor for death and has no bearing on any doctrine of the intermediate state between the time of one's death and the resurrection of believers at Christ's return. **who have no hope.** While Greek philosophy and some pagan cults speculated about the immortality of the soul and the afterlife, the rank and file among the people saw death as the end of everything.

4:14 We believe that Jesus died and rose again. This was probably a creedal statement Paul had passed on to this church earlier. He now draws out its implications for those who have died. **God will bring with Jesus those who have fallen asleep in him.** Rather than being "left out" of the return of the Lord, those who have died in Christ will share in the triumph!

4:16 a loud command ... the voice of the archangel ... the trumpet call of God. These elements of a military advance are used throughout the Scripture as a picture of the manifestation of God's presence and glory when he comes to deliver his people and bring judgment upon their enemies (Ex. 19:13,16,19; Isa. 27:13; Zeph. 1:14–16; Matt. 24:31; 1 Cor. 15:52; Rev. 19:17).

4:17 we ... will be caught up together with them. When a royal figure came to a city, its inhabitants (or a delegation of them) went out of the city to greet this person and escort them into their town. **And so we will be with the Lord forever.** Paul does not say what happens next because the locale of things is not his point. He just wants to assure the believers that, whether alive or dead, they will all share in Christ's triumph and joy. It is this message that is meant to be of comfort to them (v. 18).

5:4 you, brothers, are not in darkness. "Darkness" and "light" are moral categories indicating the sphere in which people lived. The apostle John as well as Paul often referred to people who lived with disregard to God as living in "darkness" (John 8:12; 2 Cor. 6:14; Eph. 6:12), in contrast to those who respond to Christ in faith and thus are in "the light."

**5:5 sons of the light and sons of

love as a breastplate and the hope of salvation as a helmet" (vv. 8–9)?

APPLY 1. Do you believe that the return of Christ is a possibility in your lifetime? How does this affect your lifestyle? **2.** Quite honestly, how do you look upon your own death? Are you scared, ambivalent or unsure?

OPEN What causes you to "blow a gasket": Traffic jams? Christmas shopping? Bickering children? Burned dinners? Or what?

STUDY 1. How would you describe the tone in this passage? Would you call this passage a P.S. or a wrap-up? **2.** Reading between the lines, what do you think are the problems in this church? Would you call these problems serious or normal? **3.** At the end of the day, would you call this church healthy or unhealthy?

We do not belong to the night or to the darkness. [6]So then, let us not
be like others, who are asleep, but let us be alert and self-controlled.
[7]For those who sleep, sleep at night, and those who get drunk, get
drunk at night. [8]But since we belong to the day, let us be self-controlled, putting on faith and love as a breastplate, and the hope of
salvation as a helmet. [9]For God did not appoint us to suffer wrath but
to receive salvation through our Lord Jesus Christ. [10]He died for us so
that, whether we are awake or asleep, we may live together with him.
[11]Therefore encourage one another and build each other up, just as
in fact you are doing.

Final Instructions

[12]Now we ask you, brothers, to respect those who work hard
among you, who are over you in the Lord and who admonish you.
[13]Hold them in the highest regard in love because of their work. Live
in peace with each other. [14]And we urge you, brothers, warn those
who are idle, encourage the timid, help the weak, be patient with everyone. [15]Make sure that nobody pays back wrong for wrong, but always try to be kind to each other and to everyone else.
[16]Be joyful always; [17]pray continually; [18]give thanks in all circumstances, for this is God's will for you in Christ Jesus.
[19]Do not put out the Spirit's fire; [20]do not treat prophecies with
contempt. [21]Test everything. Hold on to the good. [22]Avoid every kind
of evil.

---

the day. In the Hebrew idiom, to be a "son of" someone or something meant to share in the characteristics of that person or thing. Christians who believe in the One who is the "light of the world" share the characteristics of that light.

5:6 asleep. Continuing on with the metaphor of day and night, Christians, since they operate in "the day," are not "asleep" as are those who live in "the night." Whereas in 4:14, the metaphor of sleep meant death, here it means spiritual indifference and unawareness (Eph. 5:14).

5:7 those who get drunk. Paul is not talking about literal sobriety and drunkenness, but uses it as a metaphor of how the Christian life of purpose, awareness and direction contrasts with the "worldly" life of excess, spiritual insensitivity and folly.

5:8 putting on faith and love ... and the hope of salvation. Elsewhere Paul uses other virtues to describe the various parts of the Christian's armor (Rom. 13:12; 2 Cor. *6:7; 10:4; Eph. 6:13–17*). Here, faith, love and hope are the primary pieces of the spiritual armor that Christians need in order to stand at watch for the Day of the Lord. The "hope of salvation" is not a wish, but a firm confidence and expectation that gives courage in the face of struggle.

5:9 to receive salvation. Salvation includes both the present experience of God's grace and the confident fulfillment of that grace in the future.

5:10 He died for us. The Christian's hope for life is rooted in Jesus' death on their behalf (Rom. 5:6–8; 2 Cor. 5:15; 1 Peter 2:21–24). **whether we are awake or asleep.** This most likely refers to the issue of whether we are alive or dead at the time of Christ's coming.

5:14 idle. Second Thessalonians 3:6–15 is a strong admonition against idleness that stemmed from a "watching" for the Lord's return which precluded doing anything else! Such people not only failed to pull their own weight, but became a nuisance and weight upon others.

5:15 Make sure that nobody pays back wrong for wrong. The temptation to retaliate against persecution would have been strong (Prov. 25:21; Matt. 5:43–44; Rom. 12:17–20; 1 Peter 3:9).

5:16 Be joyful always. Joy springs not from circumstances, but from the Holy Spirit giving believers a confidence of God's presence no matter what happens (Rom. 5:3–5; 2 Cor. 6:10; Gal. 5:22–23; Phil. 4:4; Col. 1:24).

5:17 pray continually. This does not mean one is literally to pray all the time, but that one continually approaches life with the spirit of prayer; that is, with a sense of dependency upon God and thankfulness to him.

5:18 give thanks in all circumstances. One has the confidence that all things are under the sovereign hand of God. **this is God's will.** God's will is not simply to get believers to do what is right, but to produce a spirit of joy, dependence and thankfulness within them.

5:19 Do not put out the Spirit's fire. Fire is often used as an image of the Holy Spirit (Matt. 3:11; Acts 2:3). This "fire" can be dampened by disobedience (Eph. 4:30)

5:20 do not treat prophecies with contempt. Whereas in Corinth the problem was an undiscerning obsession with spiritual gifts, perhaps here the problem was an undiscerning repression of them. Paul advocates a discerning acceptance instead (v. 21). It may be that "prophecies" about the Lord's return caused some of the anxiety in this church about this topic. Verse 21 implies that we test all things.

[23]May God himself, the God of peace, sanctify you through and through. May your whole spirit, soul and body be kept blameless at the coming of our Lord Jesus Christ. [24]The one who calls you is faithful and he will do it.

[25]Brothers, pray for us. [26]Greet all the brothers with a holy kiss.
[27]I charge you before the Lord to have this letter read to all the brothers.
[28]The grace of our Lord Jesus Christ be with you.

APPLY **1.** Of the various challenges in this passage, which one would you choose to work on this week? **2.** What has been the high point in this study for you? **3.** What would you like to study next?

5:26 a holy kiss. Kissing on one's cheek was a common greeting in this culture, like our handshakes.

2 Thessalonians

Author. The apostle Paul wrote 2 Thessalonians.

Date. Paul probably wrote 2 Thessalonians around A.D. 51 during his second missionary journey.

Personal Reading	Group Study Topic and Reading	
1:1–12	Perseverance and God's Judgment	1:1–12
2:1–17	Lawlessness and Christ's Coming	2:1–17
3:1–18	Idleness and Paul's Authority	3:1–18

Theme. Living in the light of the Second Coming of Christ.

Historical Background. The second letter to the believers at Thessalonica was written within months, if not weeks, of the first. Why was this necessary? The answer may well be that Paul's first letter to these new followers of Christ produced a misunderstanding that necessitated a second, clarifying letter. Specifically, his teaching that "the day of the Lord will come like a thief in the night" (1 Thess. 5:2) may have encouraged people to abandon normal pursuits to prepare for the Second Coming. Thus in 2:1–12 he outlines the events, including the great rebellion, that must take place prior to the return of Christ. The Second Coming is not so imminent that they have to stop everything. Then he goes on to reiterate what he said in his earlier letter: Stand firm and do not be idle. Thus Paul encourages the Thessalonians in responsible Christian living as followers of Christ as well as trying to correct some of the misunderstandings they had about the nature and implications of the Second Coming of Christ.

Characteristics. Second Thessalonians covers almost the same ground as 1 Thessalonians. There is thanksgiving for the faith and love of the Thessalonians, encouragement to them in the midst of their persecution, teaching about the Second Coming, and a warning against idleness. Much of the material we have from Paul about the Second Coming comes from 1 and 2 Thessalonians.

In fact, 1 and 2 Thessalonians complement one another concerning the Second Coming. Paul's teaching in 1 Thessalonians is mainly on a personal level and it is given in response to questions about the lot of believers who have died before the Second Coming. In 2 Thessalonians believers are given further instructions on how they may be prepared for the great day. The ungodly will be taken by surprise, but believers will be awake and prepared for Christ's return.

1

Paul, Silas[a] and Timothy,

To the church of the Thessalonians in God our Father and the Lord
Jesus Christ:

2 Grace and peace to you from God the Father and the Lord Jesus
Christ.

Thanksgiving and Prayer

3 We ought always to thank God for you, brothers, and rightly so,
because your faith is growing more and more, and the love every one
of you has for each other is increasing. 4 Therefore, among God's
churches we boast about your perseverance and faith in all the persecutions and trials you are enduring.
5 All this is evidence that God's judgment is right, and as a result
you will be counted worthy of the kingdom of God, for which you are
suffering. 6 God is just: He will pay back trouble to those who trouble
you 7 and give relief to you who are troubled, and to us as well. This
will happen when the Lord Jesus is revealed from heaven in blazing
fire with his powerful angels. 8 He will punish those who do not know
God and do not obey the gospel of our Lord Jesus. 9 They will be punished with everlasting destruction and shut out from the presence of
the Lord and from the majesty of his power 10 on the day he comes to
be glorified in his holy people and to be marveled at among all those
who have believed. This includes you, because you believed our testimony to you.
11 With this in mind, we constantly pray for you, that our God may
count you worthy of his calling, and that by his power he may fulfill
every good purpose of yours and every act prompted by your faith.
12 We pray this so that the name of our Lord Jesus may be glorified in
you, and you in him, according to the grace of our God and the Lord
Jesus Christ.[b]

OPEN When you were young did another child pick on you? What did your parents say?

STUDY Things have only gotten worse in Thessalonica for the young church there. Persecution has intensified. A counterfeit letter attributed to Paul claiming that the return of Christ has already occurred has unsettled and alarmed the church. Some church members have quit work to wait on the return of Christ and have become "busy bodies." **1.** If you were Paul, how would you start out a letter to this church? What is the tone in Paul's letter in verses 1–12? **2.** How are the Thessalonians holding up under persecution (vv. 3–4)? **3.** How does Paul deal with the universal question, "Why do the righteous suffer and evildoers prosper" (vv. 5–10)? How do your secular friends deal with the problem of evil and suffering?

APPLY **1.** In your spiritual pilgrimage, what is the closest you have come to experiencing persecution or suffering because of your commitment to Jesus Christ? **2.** What did you learn from your suffering?

[a] *1* Greek *Silvanus*, a variant of *Silas* [b] *12* Or *God and Lord, Jesus Christ*

1:1 Silas. Silas was a representative of the Jerusalem church to the Christians at Antioch (Acts 15:22). He accompanied Paul on his second missionary journey. Silas is mentioned again in 1 Peter 5:12 as the one who penned that letter under the authority of the apostle Peter. **church.** In the New Testament, "church" can mean the whole, worldwide Christian community (1 Cor. 10:32; Col. 1:18), or a gathering of believers that met in a house (Rom. 16:5), or all such gatherings within a given locality (Rom. 16:1; 1 Cor. 1:2). It is not likely that this community had the time to develop a very formal organizational structure. **Thessalonians.** Thessalonica was an important city in northern Greece, the capital of the province of Macedonia. Wealth, trade and news (1 Thess. 1:7) flowed freely through this city between Rome on the west and Asia Minor on the east. **in God our Father and the Lord Jesus Christ.** The terms "Father" and "Lord" demonstrate the relationship of God and Jesus to the believer.

1:3–10 This church is facing persecution and is unsure how to interpret its meaning: Is it a sign of God's disfavor? Or is it a sign of the nearness of the return of the Lord? Paul reassures them that their response to the suffering is notable, and comforts them with the thought that the Lord will one day redress all wrongs and provide the strength to endure.

1:5 this is evidence. Their faithfulness in suffering for Christ and Paul's sharing of it with others is an evidence of their new life in Christ.

1:7 the Lord Jesus. Paul uses this term more in the Thessalonian letters than he does elsewhere. It stresses the royal authority of Jesus as the true king. It was this teaching that caused the original trouble in Thessalonica (Paul's opponents claimed he was proclaiming a rival king to Caesar—Acts 17:7) and may still be the source of tension. **in blazing fire with his powerful angels.** Fire and angels are commonly associated with God's presence with his people in the Old Testament.

OPEN At what stage in life were you "rebellious"? What memory (painful or humorous) is associated with those times of conflict?

STUDY **1.** What must have been happening in Thessalonica to lead Paul to write this? **2.** How much time was Paul able to spend with the Thessalonians (Acts 17:2)? How would this affect their willingness to believe rumors about Christ's return (v. 2)? **3.** What is God's ultimate purpose in allowing the "man of lawlessness" to deceive people? What signs mark his appearing? **4.** How will those who refuse Christ respond to this "man"? How does the "powerful delusion" sent by God differ from the deceptive evil of this "man" (vv. 10–12)? **5.** How and why will God save his people (vv. 13–14)? In response to God's initiative and Paul's ministry, what are the people to do?

APPLY **1.** How do you feel about the Second Coming of Christ and the events leading up to it: Ignorant? Uncertain? Afraid? Rather not think about it? **2.** How do you think Paul would want you to feel? **3.** What encouragement do you get from verses 13–14 as you face hard times?

The Man of Lawlessness

2 Concerning the coming of our Lord Jesus Christ and our being
gathered to him, we ask you, brothers, 2not to become easily unsettled or alarmed by some prophecy, report or letter supposed to
have come from us, saying that the day of the Lord has already come.
3Don't let anyone deceive you in any way, for ⌞that day will not come⌟
until the rebellion occurs and the man of lawlessness[a] is revealed, the
man doomed to destruction. 4He will oppose and will exalt himself
over everything that is called God or is worshiped, so that he sets
himself up in God's temple, proclaiming himself to be God.

5Don't you remember that when I was with you I used to tell you
these things? 6And now you know what is holding him back, so that
he may be revealed at the proper time. 7For the secret power of lawlessness is already at work; but the one who now holds it back will
continue to do so till he is taken out of the way. 8And then the lawless
one will be revealed, whom the Lord Jesus will overthrow with the
breath of his mouth and destroy by the splendor of his coming. 9The
coming of the lawless one will be in accordance with the work of Satan displayed in all kinds of counterfeit miracles, signs and wonders,
10and in every sort of evil that deceives those who are perishing. They
perish because they refused to love the truth and so be saved. 11For
this reason God sends them a powerful delusion so that they will believe the lie 12and so that all will be condemned who have not believed the truth but have delighted in wickedness.

Stand Firm

13But we ought always to thank God for you, brothers loved by the
Lord, because from the beginning God chose you[b] to be saved
through the sanctifying work of the Spirit and through belief in the

[a]3 Some manuscripts *sin* [b]13 Some manuscripts *because God chose you as his firstfruits*

2:1–12 This passage, the heart of the letter, is meant to correct some erroneous ideas which had developed about this event.

2:2 prophecy, report or letter supposed to have come from us. The false teaching was being supported by either a mistaken view of what Paul had written or preached, or by a forged letter that distorted his views. **the day of the Lord has already come.** The nature of the false teaching here is not clear, but it apparently led some people to think the presence (*parousia*) of the Lord had already come in all its fullness. This led them to overlook the mundane issues of discipleship like work (3:6–15).

2:3 rebellion ... man of lawlessness. Other passages foresee a time when the powers of evil rise up (Matt. 24:10ff; 1 Tim. 4:1–3), and this is centered around the rise of an antichrist (1 John 4:3), or false prophets (Matt. 24:5; Rev. 16:13).

2:4 His description of this figure here is steeped in Old Testament apocalyptic imagery (Ezek. 28:2; Dan. 7:25; 8:9–12; 11:36–37; Zech. 3:1). He sets himself in total opposition to God by claiming the prerogatives of God (Mark 13:14).

2:6–7 you know what is holding him back ... the one who now holds it back. God restrains sin and the man of lawlessness through the work of the Holy Spirit.

2:10 every sort of evil that deceives. The effect of these signs will be to harden the convictions of those who are already opposing God. Manipulative speech, flattery, appeals to self-interest, etc. are effective in persuading people to go along further and further into evil. **refused to love the truth.** That is, they do not follow the way of the gospel.

2:11 God sends them a powerful delusion. Because people refuse to embrace the gospel, God acts in such a way as to confirm their disbelief. In the Bible, the power of Satan and evil are not independent from God, but subject to his ultimate authority and purpose. Thus, 1 Chronicles 21:1 and 2 Samuel 24:1, each referring to the same event, respectively attribute it to Satan and to God. First Kings 22:23 and Ezekiel 14:9 tell of God sending a "lying spirit" into so-called prophets who only served to confirm the rebellion that was in the hearts of their listeners.

2:12 so that all will be condemned. The ultimate result of following the lie is to face God's judgment (John 3:17–18; Rom. 2:12). **who have not believed the truth but have delighted in wickedness.** Unbelievers are described as not only not believing the gospel, but taking pleasure in being unrighteous.

2:13 from the beginning God chose you. Paul often refers to God's election of people to salvation as a way

truth. 14He called you to this through our gospel, that you might
share in the glory of our Lord Jesus Christ. 15So then, brothers, stand
firm and hold to the teachings[a] we passed on to you, whether by
word of mouth or by letter.

16May our Lord Jesus Christ himself and God our Father, who loved
us and by his grace gave us eternal encouragement and good hope,
17encourage your hearts and strengthen you in every good deed and
word.

Request for Prayer

3 Finally, brothers, pray for us that the message of the Lord may
spread rapidly and be honored, just as it was with you. 2And pray
that we may be delivered from wicked and evil men, for not everyone
has faith. 3But the Lord is faithful, and he will strengthen and protect
you from the evil one. 4We have confidence in the Lord that you are
doing and will continue to do the things we command. 5May the Lord
direct your hearts into God's love and Christ's perseverance.

Warning Against Idleness

6In the name of the Lord Jesus Christ, we command you, brothers,
to keep away from every brother who is idle and does not live according to the teaching[b] you received from us. 7For you yourselves know
how you ought to follow our example. We were not idle when we
were with you, 8nor did we eat anyone's food without paying for it.
On the contrary, we worked night and day, laboring and toiling so
that we would not be a burden to any of you. 9We did this, not because we do not have the right to such help, but in order to make ourselves a model for you to follow. 10For even when we were with you,
we gave you this rule: "If a man will not work, he shall not eat."

11We hear that some among you are idle. They are not busy; they
are busybodies. 12Such people we command and urge in the Lord
Jesus Christ to settle down and earn the bread they eat. 13And as for
you, brothers, never tire of doing what is right.

[a] *15 Or traditions* [b] *6 Or tradition*

OPEN What was your first paid job? How much were you paid?

STUDY 1. Paul has twice prayed for these people (1:11–12; 2:16–17). How does he want them to pray for him and his companions? How would the encouragements in verses 3–5 help them in their trials? **2.** How might a misunderstanding of Paul's earlier teaching (1 Thess. 5:1–3) have led to the problem of idleness? Why would Paul see that as a serious problem then (1 Thess. 4:11–12) and now (v. 7)? What model does Paul leave for the others to follow (vv. 7–13)? What does this have to do with taking responsibility? **3.** Why does Paul call attention to his handwriting (v. 17)?

APPLY 1. How do you look upon your job right now? **2.** When you get to retirement age, what are you going to do? **3.** What has been the high point in this study for you? **4.** What do you want to study next?

---

of reassuring Christians in times of suffering. God indeed knows and loves them (Rom. 8:28–39; Eph. 1:11–12; Titus 3:5–8). They will be saved in the future because of work God has already done. **through the sanctifying work of the Spirit and through belief in the truth.** The first phrase describes God's work in salvation, while the second looks to the human response. Both are needed.

3:2 wicked and evil men. The Thessalonians would be well aware of the opposition that Paul encountered time and time again, since he met with such resistance in their own city (Acts 17:1–9; 1 Thess. 2:1–2). In Corinth, from where Paul was writing, he faced such strong resistance that he needed a special word from the Lord to keep on (Acts 18:9). The news of their faithfulness was an encouragement (1 Thess. 3:7).

3:5 Christ's perseverance. The prayer is that the Thessalonians realize the fullness of God's love for them so that they respond in kind, and that they draw courage from Christ's perseverance as a model for their own.

3:6 keep away from every brother who is idle. While these people are not to be considered as enemies of the gospel (v. 15), they need to be disciplined so they will give up their mistaken practice. The purpose of such discipline is a "tough love" approach to correcting a potentially serious problem, yet it is to be carried out in a way that communicates that the "family ties" are still strong.

3:11 They are not busy; they are busybodies. These people are bothering others with their false notions, probably trying to convince them to wait for the Day of the Lord with them. Such action would also give a negative impression of the Christian community to outsiders, as it would appear that they are lazy and content to live off the income of others.

3:12 settle down. Throughout church history there have been groups that have set the date for the return of the Lord, and responded by abandoning the normal pursuits of life in a feverish state of religious excitement. The end result is disenchantment and a discrediting of the gospel. In contrast, Paul wants them to live in peace, providing for their own needs (1 Thess. 4:11–12).

[14]If anyone does not obey our instruction in this letter, take special
note of him. Do not associate with him, in order that he may feel
ashamed. [15]Yet do not regard him as an enemy, but warn him as a
brother.

Final Greetings

[16]Now may the Lord of peace himself give you peace at all times
and in every way. The Lord be with all of you.
[17]I, Paul, write this greeting in my own hand, which is the distinguishing mark in all my letters. This is how I write.
[18]The grace of our Lord Jesus Christ be with you all.

3:16 may the Lord of peace himself give you peace at all times. At times, "peace" is used as a summary of all the benefits that Christ gives to his people (John 20:21,26; Rom. 15:33; Phil. 4:9). In contrast to the unsettled state of the Thessalonians at this point, Paul prays that peace would mark their lives both personally and as a church.

3:17 I, Paul, write this greeting in my own hand. Paul typically used a secretary to write his letters. Tertius wrote Romans (Rom. 16:22). Tychicus, who delivered the letters of Ephesians and Colossians, may have penned those as well, and Silas (1 Peter 5:12) may have written the Thessalonian letters. Sometimes Paul calls attention to the fact that he has written the final greeting (1 Cor. 16:21; Gal. 6:11), which may be to assure the recipients of the authenticity of the letter that he was sending to them.

1 Timothy

Author. The apostle Paul was most likely the author of 1 Timothy. However, based on considerations of vocabulary and style, the authorship of the Pastoral Epistles (1 and 2 Timothy, Titus) has been questioned by some scholars.

Date. First Timothy was written about A.D. 63–65.

Theme. A faithful ministry.

Personal Reading	Group Study Topic and Reading	
1:1–11	False Teachers of the Law	1:1–11
1:12–20	True Mercy for Sinners	1:12–20
2:1–15	Orderly Worship	2:1–15
3:1–16	Faithful Leadership	3:1–16
4:1–16	Redemptive Ministry	4:1–16
5:1–6:2	Widows, Elders and Slaves	5:1–6:2
6:3–10	Love of Money	6:3–10
6:11–21	Fighting the Good Fight	6:11–21

Historical Background. When Paul first met Timothy, he was living at Lystra in the Roman province of Galatia (modern Turkey). His father was a Gentile and his mother was Jewish (Acts 16:1). Timothy, along with his mother Eunice and his grandmother Lois, was probably converted during Paul's first missionary journey (Acts 14:8–25; compare 2 Tim. 3:10–11). By the time of Paul's second visit to the area a year or two later, Timothy had matured so much as a Christian that the local church recommended Timothy to Paul as a helpful traveling companion (Acts 16:2). However, Paul decided that Timothy must be circumcised first to legitimize him in the eyes of Paul's Jewish critics. Without circumcision, they would have considered him a Gentile (because of his Greek father), even though he had been brought up in his mother's religion.

He was a coworker with Paul (Rom. 16:21; 1 Cor. 16:10; Phil. 2:22; 1 Thess. 3:2). He collaborated in the writing of six of Paul's letters (1 and 2 Thess.; 2 Cor.; Phil.; Col. and Philem.). Timothy was not just a colleague of Paul's; he was a beloved friend. Paul called him "my son whom I love, who is faithful in the Lord" (1 Cor. 4:17). In Philippians 2:20–22, the aging apostle says: "I have no one else like him ... Timothy has proved himself, because as a son with his father he has served with me in the work of the gospel."

Audience. The three so-called Pastoral Epistles (plus Philemon) are set apart from the other letters written by Paul; they are addressed to persons, not churches. There are few personal remarks in 1 Timothy, and all of these are directed toward Timothy's commission to restore proper order in the church at Ephesus (1:18–19; 4:6–16; 6:11–21).

The False Teachers. Who were these false teachers who had so upset the Ephesian church? Either they were in the leadership of the church or the leadersship was too weak to contrast their influence. First the teaching in Ephesians was done by the elders (5:17). Furthermore, Paul devotes considerable space to outlining the qualifications for leaders in the church. These qualifications contrast sharply with what he says about the false teachers. For example, the false teachers "forbid people to marry" (4:3). Paul says that an overseer (elder), in contrast, "must be ... the husband of but one wife" and "must manage his own family well" (3:2,4–5; 3:12). The false teachers "think that godliness is a means to financial gain" (6:5); whereas an elder must "not [be] a lover of money" (3:3). In 5:17–25, he outlines the process of selection and discipline of elders "who sin" (v. 20).

The Nature of the False Teaching. As is often the case, since we have only Paul's response to the problem and not a clear explanation of it, we are forced to figure out the nature of the false teaching. From the text, it seems that the false teachers were involved in questionable speculation rather than the teaching of accepted Christian doctrine. Furthermore, the teachers were proud, arrogant, argumentative and greedy. They used religion to make money and gain power. Their false teaching was connected with the Old Testament, but it also had an aspect of self-denial and a strong Greek element. It appears to be much like the false teaching in the Lycus Valley churches.

1 Paul, an apostle of Christ Jesus by the command of God our
Savior and of Christ Jesus our hope,

2To Timothy my true son in the faith:

Grace, mercy and peace from God the Father and Christ Jesus our
Lord.

Warning Against False Teachers of the Law

3As I urged you when I went into Macedonia, stay there in Ephesus
so that you may command certain men not to teach false doctrines
any longer 4nor to devote themselves to myths and endless genealogies. These promote controversies rather than God's work—which is
by faith. 5The goal of this command is love, which comes from a pure
heart and a good conscience and a sincere faith. 6Some have wandered away from these and turned to meaningless talk. 7They want to
be teachers of the law, but they do not know what they are talking
about or what they so confidently affirm.

8We know that the law is good if one uses it properly. 9We also
know that law[a] is made not for the righteous but for lawbreakers and
rebels, the ungodly and sinful, the unholy and irreligious; for those
who kill their fathers or mothers, for murderers, 10for adulterers and
perverts, for slave traders and liars and perjurers—and for whatever
else is contrary to the sound doctrine 11that conforms to the glorious
gospel of the blessed God, which he entrusted to me.

The Lord's Grace to Paul

12I thank Christ Jesus our Lord, who has given me strength, that he
considered me faithful, appointing me to his service. 13Even though I
was once a blasphemer and a persecutor and a violent man, I was
shown mercy because I acted in ignorance and unbelief. 14The grace
of our Lord was poured out on me abundantly, along with the faith
and love that are in Christ Jesus.

15Here is a trustworthy saying that deserves full acceptance: Christ

[a]9 Or *that the law*

OPEN 1. Growing up, what was your father's occupation? Your mother's? **2.** How did they settle sibling fights?

STUDY 1. How would you feel if you were left behind to deal with problems in a church where there was false doctrine and speculation being taught that kept the church in turmoil? **2.** How does Paul differentiate between "false doctrine" and "sound doctrine" (vv. 3,10–11)? Why does Paul warn against teachers that like to study "myths and endless genealogies"? **3.** By the way Paul describes the goal of teaching (v. 5) what were the false teachers lacking? **4.** What does Paul say about the purpose of the Law?

APPLY 1. Who was the "Paul" in your life who became like a spiritual director to you? **2.** How would you describe your spiritual life right now?

OPEN Who holds the record in your group for most speeding tickets? Most times "grounded"?

STUDY Paul condemns the false teachers in verses 3–13, but he reminds Timothy of his (Paul's) past. **1.** What does Paul say about himself (vv. 13–14)? **2.** According to verse 15, why did Jesus come into the world? **3.** Why is someone like Paul such a good witness to unbelievers

1:1 Paul, an apostle. When Paul uses the designation "an apostle" in his salutation, it is because his authority is in question, or because he has an "official" word for the recipients of the letter. **by the command of God.** The Greek word used here signifies a royal command which comes from a king or a god.

1:3 stay there in Ephesus. Paul has had to go on to Macedonia, leaving Timothy behind in Ephesus. As he indicates in 3:14, the purpose of this letter is to instruct Timothy as to his role while there, in case he is delayed in returning to Ephesus (which Paul was, according *to 2 Timothy*). **Ephesus.** The capital of the Roman Province of Asia, Ephesus was a large, bustling, secular city situated on the West coast of Asia Minor (modern Turkey) on the Aegean Sea. The church in Ephesus apparently flourished. It was not a single congregation however, but rather a collection of house churches (1 Cor. 16:19). **certain men.** Who these false teachers were is not made clear in the letter. The evidence seems to indicate that they could have been leaders from the Ephesian church itself.

1:4 myths and endless genealogies. It is not easy to identify the exact nature of this teaching. The "myths" were probably connected both to Jewish speculation and to the legends that abounded in the ancient world. So too, the genealogies. The Jews (in particular) were fascinated by genealogies. **These promote controversies.** All this speculation generated strife within the body, not "God's work."

1:10 adulterers and perverts. These refer to heterosexual and homosexual sin. This is a key theme of this book: healthy teaching.

1:13 Even though. Paul is utterly amazed that he of all people was chosen for this high calling, given his past record. **blasphemer.** Paul had denied Christ and tried to force others to do the same (Acts 26:11). **a persecutor and a violent man.** He had actively opposed the church—searching out Christians, arresting them, throwing them in prison, even voting for their deaths. **I acted in ignorance and unbelief.** Paul is not saying that he had received mercy because he was without guilt. All he is saying is that he acted "unintentionally" instead of "defiantly," using a common Old Testament distinction (Num. 15:22–31, Luke 23:34).

1:15 Christ Jesus came into the world to save sinners. By means of

Jesus came into the world to save sinners—of whom I am the worst.
[16]But for that very reason I was shown mercy so that in me, the worst
of sinners, Christ Jesus might display his unlimited patience as an example for those who would believe on him and receive eternal life.
[17]Now to the King eternal, immortal, invisible, the only God, be honor
and glory for ever and ever. Amen.
[18]Timothy, my son, I give you this instruction in keeping with the
prophecies once made about you, so that by following them you may
fight the good fight, [19]holding on to faith and a good conscience.
Some have rejected these and so have shipwrecked their faith.
[20]Among them are Hymenaeus and Alexander, whom I have handed
over to Satan to be taught not to blaspheme.

Instructions on Worship

2 I urge, then, first of all, that requests, prayers, intercession and
thanksgiving be made for everyone— [2]for kings and all those in
authority, that we may live peaceful and quiet lives in all godliness
and holiness. [3]This is good, and pleases God our Savior, [4]who wants
all men to be saved and to come to a knowledge of the truth. [5]For
there is one God and one mediator between God and men, the man
Christ Jesus, [6]who gave himself as a ransom for all men—the testimony given in its proper time. [7]And for this purpose I was appointed
a herald and an apostle—I am telling the truth, I am not lying—and a
teacher of the true faith to the Gentiles.
[8]I want men everywhere to lift up holy hands in prayer, without
anger or disputing.
[9]I also want women to dress modestly, with decency and propriety,
not with braided hair or gold or pearls or expensive clothes, [10]but
with good deeds, appropriate for women who profess to worship
God.
[11]A woman should learn in quietness and full submission. [12]I do
not permit a woman to teach or to have authority over a man; she
must be silent. [13]For Adam was formed first, then Eve. [14]And Adam
was not the one deceived; it was the woman who was deceived and

(v. 16)? When you share your past mistakes, what does that do? **4.** What does Paul challenge Timothy to do? How would you paraphrase this?

APPLY 1. As you think back over your spiritual life, what is the closest you have come to being "shipwrecked in your faith"? **2.** What caused it?

OPEN What was the worship service in your church like when you were growing up? What about in your church today?

STUDY 1. How would you like to be in Timothy's shoes? **2.** Why does Paul want the house churches to pray for "kings and all those in authority"? **3.** What do you think the false teachers are teaching about prayer that causes Paul to write verses 3–7? **4.** Why do you think Paul gives instructions on how women are to dress? What did the dress code have to do with what was going on in their culture? **5.** In verse 11 Paul talks about quietness and submission. What kind of submission are we all to have (1 Peter 2:13–21; 3:1–7)? Why is Paul addressing the role women should have in the church?

APPLY Have you ever been a part of a church from its beginning?

---

this quotation, Paul explains his own transformation (and gives Timothy hope for the transformation of the false teachers). The emphasis here is on the Incarnation ("Jesus came into the world") and redemption ("to save sinners"). **of whom I am the worst.** The mention of sinners reminds Paul of his own state. He was overwhelmed by the magnitude of his sin and by the expansiveness of God's grace.

1:20 Hymenaeus and Alexander. *Apparently, these are two of the erring* leaders in Ephesus. Hymenaeus is mentioned again in 2 Timothy 2:17 (along with Philetus) as one who taught that the resurrection was already past. An Alexander (a metalworker) is also mentioned in 2 Timothy 4:14–15 as having harmed Paul grievously. **handed over to Satan.** Paul excommunicated them from the church; i.e., they were expelled from the fellowship of other followers of Christ and sent back into the world (which is Satan's realm—1 Cor. 5:5).

2:5 one mediator. A mediator is an individual who brings two estranged parties together. Over against Judaism, which asserted that Moses and the angels (Gal. 3:19–20) were mediators between God and the people, Paul asserts that Jesus is the unique mediator who acts as a go-between, reconciling fallen humanity with the one God. **the man Christ Jesus.** He is able to be this because he is himself a human being.

2:9 propriety. This is the real issue for Paul (vv. 2,10,15). He is concerned that the women in the church live in a way that is considered decent by the culture.

2:12 I do not permit. By this phrase Paul focuses on the specific situation in Ephesus. He obviously does not feel that women cannot engage in ministry, as evidenced by his statements in Romans 16:1–3 and Philippians 4:2–3. But in Ephesus (given the turmoil caused by the false teachers and the complicity of certain women in this heresy); it is necessary for Paul to bring order in the church and its meetings. Paul's instructions are for the women to not take a public role in the teaching of doctrine in the church and to assume a quieter role. **authority.** Paul uses an unusual word here. (This is its only occurrence in the New Testament.) It often carries the sense of "domineering" or "pushing one's own way"—which is the root meaning of the verb. **she must be silent.** After saying women are not to teach or have authority over a man, Paul calls on the woman to be silent. It stands in relationship to the challenge to authority and teaching of doctrine not to speaking aloud.

OPEN 1. As a child, how did you treat your babysitters? How did they treat you? **2.** Do you enjoy childcare now?

STUDY 1. If you needed to remove a leader/overseer (deacon) in your church because this person was teaching false doctrine, drinking too much and/or involved in inappropriate relationships with the opposite sex, what would you do? **2.** What is the closest thing in your church to an overseer? How do the qualifications in verses 2–7 compare to your church's qualifications for this office? What do you say when an overseer has an unruly child? Why is a "good reputation" with outsiders important? **3.** What do you call "deacons" in your church? How do your church's qualifications compare to the ones here? **4.** Do you think Timothy will have trouble finding leaders for the churches if he insists on these high standards?

APPLY 1. How does your church go about raising up leaders for groups in your church? **2.** If you are growing your church by growing the number of groups, how do you go about getting the groups to multiply?

became a sinner. 15 But women[a] will be saved[b] through childbearing—
if they continue in faith, love and holiness with propriety.

Overseers and Deacons

3 Here is a trustworthy saying: If anyone sets his heart on being an
overseer,[c] he desires a noble task. 2 Now the overseer must be
above reproach, the husband of but one wife, temperate, self-controlled, respectable, hospitable, able to teach, 3 not given to drunkenness, not violent but gentle, not quarrelsome, not a lover of money.
4 He must manage his own family well and see that his children obey
him with proper respect. 5 (If anyone does not know how to manage
his own family, how can he take care of God's church?) 6 He must not
be a recent convert, or he may become conceited and fall under the
same judgment as the devil. 7 He must also have a good reputation
with outsiders, so that he will not fall into disgrace and into the
devil's trap.

8 Deacons, likewise, are to be men worthy of respect, sincere, not
indulging in much wine, and not pursuing dishonest gain. 9 They
must keep hold of the deep truths of the faith with a clear conscience.
10 They must first be tested; and then if there is nothing against them,
let them serve as deacons.

11 In the same way, their wives[d] are to be women worthy of respect,
not malicious talkers but temperate and trustworthy in everything.

12 A deacon must be the husband of but one wife and must manage
his children and his household well. 13 Those who have served well
gain an excellent standing and great assurance in their faith in Christ
Jesus.

14 Although I hope to come to you soon, I am writing you these instructions so that, 15 if I am delayed, you will know how people ought
to conduct themselves in God's household, which is the church of the

[a]15 Greek *she* [b]15 Or *restored* [c]1 Traditionally *bishop;* also in verse 2 [d]11 Or *way, deaconesses*

3:1 overseer. Sometimes translated "bishop," "overseer" and "elder" were used interchangeably. **he desires a noble task.** Paul's point is that the position of overseer is a high calling (despite the abuse of the office by some).

3:2 above reproach. Paul begins with an all-encompassing category: there should be no obvious defect in character of the overseer that would cause people to question the appointment. **husband of but one wife.** Literally, "a one-woman man." Paul could mean four things by it. First, that church leaders must be married, in contrast to the false teachers who were forbidding marriage. Second, that polygamy was forbidden. Third, that second marriages were forbidden whether due to divorce or death of one's spouse. (Yet, he gives in 5:14 what amounts almost to a "command" to young widows to remarry.) Fourth, the most likely meaning is that sexual faithfulness to one's spouse was demanded; that is, the married life of the overseer must be exemplary—in contrast to the widespread infidelity of that day. **temperate.** Free from excesses. **self-controlled, respectable.** These companion terms were considered in Greek literature to be great virtues. If a person is self-controlled in their outer conduct, it is because they are respectable in their inner life. **hospitable.** Overseers must be willing to open up their homes to guests. It was a common practice in the first century to offer hospitality to travelers since the inns were notorious for their dirt and immorality, not to mention their expense (5:10; Rom. 12:13; 1 Peter 4:9). **able to teach.** This is the one quality that implies a function. Paul will say more about this in 5:17.

3:3 not given to drunkenness. Paul is not forbidding the drinking of wine (which was widely used in his time, due to poor water supplies), only over-indulgence. **not violent but gentle.** "Not violent" means literally "not a giver of blows"; "gentle" refers to those who do not seek to apply the letter of the law in cases where to do so would bring injustice.

3:6 recent convert. The temptation in a new church is to put into office people of standing and influence who have been recently converted. **conceited.** The false teachers are said to have been conceited (6:4). Perhaps some of them were recent converts.

3:8 Deacons. Paul often describes himself and others as a *diakonos* ("deacon"), a word variously translated as "servant" or "minister." **sincere, not indulging in much wine, and not pursuing dishonest gain.** Paul follows this with three prohibitions. They are to be "straight," literally, "not double-tongued." They must not think one thing and say another. Also, like overseers, they must not be given to excess wine or be greedy for money.

living God, the pillar and foundation of the truth. 16 Beyond all question, the mystery of godliness is great:

He[a] appeared in a body,[b]
  was vindicated by the Spirit,
was seen by angels,
  was preached among the nations,
was believed on in the world,
  was taken up in glory.

Instructions to Timothy

4 The Spirit clearly says that in later times some will abandon the
faith and follow deceiving spirits and things taught by demons.
2 Such teachings come through hypocritical liars, whose consciences
have been seared as with a hot iron. 3 They forbid people to marry and
order them to abstain from certain foods, which God created to be received with thanksgiving by those who believe and who know the
truth. 4 For everything God created is good, and nothing is to be rejected if it is received with thanksgiving, 5 because it is consecrated by
the word of God and prayer.
6 If you point these things out to the brothers, you will be a good
minister of Christ Jesus, brought up in the truths of the faith and of
the good teaching that you have followed. 7 Have nothing to do with
godless myths and old wives' tales; rather, train yourself to be godly.
8 For physical training is of some value, but godliness has value for all
things, holding promise for both the present life and the life to come.
9 This is a trustworthy saying that deserves full acceptance 10 (and
for this we labor and strive), that we have put our hope in the living

[a]16 Some manuscripts *God* [b]16 Or *in the flesh*

OPEN What do you do to keep in shape? How physically fit are you?

STUDY The focus in this passage is on two lifestyles: the lifestyle of the false teachers and the lifestyle recommended to Timothy for a Christian. **1.** From verses 2–3, what can you assume is the lifestyle of the false teachers (6:3–4,9–10)? **2.** In contrast, what is the lifestyle recommended to Timothy for a Christian (vv. 6,7,10,12,16)? **3.** Do you think Paul is putting down physical fitness or just using it as a way to emphasize spiritual fitness (godliness)? **4.** What is some good advice Paul gives Timothy in verses 11–16 that would be good for any spiritual leaders in the church today? **5.** What is the balance and practice Paul recommends to Timothy (v. 16)? **6.** If Paul were around

---

4:1 The Spirit clearly says. Paul does not identify the specific prophecy he has in mind. However, the idea that there will be apostasy in the last days is found at other places in Scripture (Mark 13:22; 2 Tim. 3:1–5). **later times.** Paul believed that they were living in the last days just prior to Christ's return, a time when there would be great evil (2 Thess. 2:3–12). **some.** Paul refers to those Christians in Ephesus who have fallen victim to the "hypocritical liars" (v. 2) or the false leaders in the church. **deceiving spirits and ... demons.** This is the source of the false doctrine. Satan is behind the chaos in the Ephesian church as he has been in other churches (2 Cor. 2:11).

4:2 hypocritical liars. Not only is their doctrine demon-inspired, they themselves are, literally, "speakers of falsehood" ("liars"). **seared as with a hot iron.** Their moral judgment has been "cauterized" so that they are no longer able to distinguish between what was truth and falsehood.

4:3 Paul identifies two specific errors in their teaching. They were saying that people ought not to get married and that they should not eat certain foods. These false teachers were saying that the way to holiness (purity) was via self-denial.

4:4 everything God created is good. This is the theological basis on which Paul says what he does about food. **thanksgiving.** Paul is referring to the gratitude expressed to God by means of the "grace" that is said prior to a meal.

4:6–16 Paul urges him to model genuine Christian faith by the way he lives and what he teaches. It will be his positive example (not his negative denouncement) that will defuse the power of the heretics.

4:6 point these things out. Paul's gentle tone is evident right from the beginning. He does not say that Timothy must "order" or "command" the brothers and sisters in the church. What he is to do is more akin to "suggesting" than it is to "instructing."

4:7 Having told Timothy to hold on to what is true, Paul now warns him to avoid what is false. **train yourself to be godly.** In contrast to the unchristian asceticism (v. 3), Paul now proposes a genuinely Christian form of self-discipline.

4:8 physical training. Having used an athletic image, Paul then comments on it in passing. While affirming the value of physical exercise, Paul's real interest is in spiritual exercise ("godliness"). **promise for both the present life and the life to come.** The "life" Paul refers to is the "eternal life" one receives through belief in Jesus (1:16). It is this quality of life—in both the present and the future—that is promised to those who believe in Jesus.

today, what would he say to leaders about their lifestyle?

APPLY 1. Quite honestly, are you more concerned about your physical health or your spiritual health? **2.** What regime have you found helpful in keeping spiritually fit? **3.** Where could you use a little help?

OPEN 1. Where would you like to retire? **2.** Would you like to live close to your children or in a nice retirement community?

STUDY In addition to leadership problems which Paul has already addressed, Paul instructs Timothy in this passage on three domestic problems: Widows in the church? Church discipline? Disrespect of slaves for their owners? **1.** When Timothy approaches people, how should he treat the two genders and ages (vv. 1–2)? **2.** What are the two types of widows in this passage (vv. 5–6)? For widows who are "really in need," how is this person to be cared for? What conditions are required for this person (vv. 9–10)? **3.** Why are young widows not to be cared for by the church (vv. 11–15)? **4.** Why are church elders to receive "double honor" (v. 17)? If an elder abuses his office, what are the

God, who is the Savior of all men, and especially of those who believe.
11 Command and teach these things. 12 Don't let anyone look down
on you because you are young, but set an example for the believers in
speech, in life, in love, in faith and in purity. 13 Until I come, devote
yourself to the public reading of Scripture, to preaching and to teaching. 14 Do not neglect your gift, which was given you through a prophetic message when the body of elders laid their hands on you.
15 Be diligent in these matters; give yourself wholly to them, so that
everyone may see your progress. 16 Watch your life and doctrine
closely. Persevere in them, because if you do, you will save both yourself and your hearers.

Advice About Widows, Elders and Slaves

5 Do not rebuke an older man harshly, but exhort him as if he were
your father. Treat younger men as brothers, 2 older women as
mothers, and younger women as sisters, with absolute purity.
3 Give proper recognition to those widows who are really in need.
4 But if a widow has children or grandchildren, these should learn
first of all to put their religion into practice by caring for their own
family and so repaying their parents and grandparents, for this is
pleasing to God. 5 The widow who is really in need and left all alone
puts her hope in God and continues night and day to pray and to ask
God for help. 6 But the widow who lives for pleasure is dead even
while she lives. 7 Give the people these instructions, too, so that no
one may be open to blame. 8 If anyone does not provide for his relatives, and especially for his immediate family, he has denied the faith
and is worse than an unbeliever.
9 No widow may be put on the list of widows unless she is over sixty, has been faithful to her husband,[a] 10 and is well known for her
good deeds, such as bringing up children, showing hospitality, wash-

[a] 9 Or *has had but one husband*

4:11 Command. The first thing Paul says is that Timothy must speak with authority. The impression given here in verses 11–12 and elsewhere (1 Cor. 16:10–11; 2 Tim. 1:6–9) is that Timothy was a somewhat diffident, even timid, person.

4:12 young. The problem may have to do with Timothy's age. He is probably only in his early 30s. However, he is living in a culture that respected age. **set an example.** There is little he can do about his age, but Timothy can lead by example. Paul identifies five areas in which he is to model Christian conduct. "Speech" and "life" (or "behavior") refer to day-by-day conversation and conduct. "Love" (*agape*), "faith" (faithfulness), and "purity" (not only chastity but general integrity) refer to inner qualities that show themselves via an outer lifestyle.

4:13 reading of Scripture. This is the first reference to the use of Scripture in Christian worship. **teaching.** This is instruction in Christian doctrine.

4:14 laid their hands on you. Appointment to office (ordination) was accompanied by the laying on of hands (literally, the pressing of hands) by the commissioning body (here, the elders).

5:1 rebuke ... exhort. Timothy will have to confront older men over the issue of false teaching. Paul tells him how to do it. It is not by means of harsh "rebuke"; instead, he is to "appeal" to them.

5:3 widows. The early church—following the pattern of the Jewish nation before them—was committed to caring for those women who had lost their husbands (Deut. 24:17,19–21; Ps. 68:5; Isa 1:17; Acts 6:1–6; 9:36–41; James 1:27).

5:4 The first group of widows who do not qualify for help are those who have family and friends who can care for them (vv. 8,16).

5:5–6 Paul next contrasts two types of widows: those who have put their hope in God (v. 5) and those who by their sensual living give no evidence of trusting God to meet their needs (v. 6). The first group is really "all alone" and so must trust God. The second group "lives for pleasure." It may be that Paul is contrasting those women who refuse to be compromised (and so put their trust in God) with those women who live by sensual means (whether in actual prostitution or by being involved with a particular man).

5:9 sixty. In the first century, 60 was considered the age of retirement and the point at which "old age" began. It was also considered to be the age beyond which remarriage was not a real possibility.

ing the feet of the saints, helping those in trouble and devoting herself to all kinds of good deeds.
11 As for younger widows, do not put them on such a list. For when
their sensual desires overcome their dedication to Christ, they want
to marry. 12 Thus they bring judgment on themselves, because they
have broken their first pledge. 13 Besides, they get into the habit of
being idle and going about from house to house. And not only do they
become idlers, but also gossips and busybodies, saying things they
ought not to. 14 So I counsel younger widows to marry, to have children, to manage their homes and to give the enemy no opportunity for
slander. 15 Some have in fact already turned away to follow Satan.
16 If any woman who is a believer has widows in her family, she
should help them and not let the church be burdened with them, so
that the church can help those widows who are really in need.
17 The elders who direct the affairs of the church well are worthy of
double honor, especially those whose work is preaching and teaching. 18 For the Scripture says, "Do not muzzle the ox while it is treading out the grain,"[a] and "The worker deserves his wages."[b] 19 Do not
entertain an accusation against an elder unless it is brought by two
or three witnesses. 20 Those who sin are to be rebuked publicly, so
that the others may take warning.
21 I charge you, in the sight of God and Christ Jesus and the elect
angels, to keep these instructions without partiality, and to do nothing out of favoritism.
22 Do not be hasty in the laying on of hands, and do not share in the
sins of others. Keep yourself pure.
23 Stop drinking only water, and use a little wine because of your
stomach and your frequent illnesses.
24 The sins of some men are obvious, reaching the place of judgment ahead of them; the sins of others trail behind them. 25 In the
same way, good deeds are obvious, and even those that are not cannot be hidden.

6 All who are under the yoke of slavery should consider their
masters worthy of full respect, so that God's name and our

[a] 18 Deut. 25:4 [b] 18 Luke 10:7

steps to be used in disciplining him? What do you need to be careful about (v. 21)? **5.** For health problems, what does Paul recommend to Timothy? What is the difference between this advice and 3:3,8? **6.** What is the principle in Paul's instructions for slaves that would apply today to employer/employee relationship? **7.** If you were Timothy, which of the three problems would you find the hardest to deal with: Widows? Elder discipline? Slaves?

APPLY 1. Have you or someone you have known ever suddenly become single? What was that time like? Who in your church needs some help that you or your group can provide? **2.** What should be the Christian's/Church's response to the welfare issue?

5:11–15 Paul now comes to the real issue—the problematic younger widows. He gives two reasons for not putting them on the list for support. First, because their sexual desires are such that they do not want to remain widows (vv. 11–12), and second, because they are not really living in accord with the model of the godly widow that he has just sketched (v. 13). His advice is that they remarry (v. 14) lest they fall away from the faith (v. 15).

5:14 slander. Their behavior had become the grounds on which others were speaking evil of the church. Paul continues in his concern that the church not be judged negatively by the surrounding culture.

5:17–25 Paul turns to the second problematic group: the elders. This is the first time that Paul has used this title (*presbuteros*) in this letter (3:1; Acts 11:30; 14:23; 15:1–35; 16:4; 20:17–38; 21:18).

5:18 Paul justifies his assertion that elders deserve remuneration by the community by means of two citations, one from the Old Testament (Deut. 25:4) and the other from Jesus (Luke 10:7).

5:19–20 Paul next addresses the matter of discipline. He says two things. First, no unsubstantiated charge is to be made about an elder, and second, if valid charges are made, those found guilty are to be rebuked publicly—serve to warn other elders who are in error as well as the whole church.

5:21 It is important that this rule be applied entirely across the board, even to those elders who might have great influence within the community.

5:22 do not share in the sins of others. Paul's comments on how to appoint elders (do this carefully, since the sins of some are not apparent) leads him to make another "aside" to Timothy. Timothy must make sure his own life stays in order.

5:23 However, having told him to remain "pure," Paul quickly adds that what he has in mind is not the sort of abstinence from food and drink taught by the false teachers (4:3). He recommends that Timothy follow the common medical practice of using wine as a treatment for his stomach problems.

teaching may not be slandered. [2]Those who have believing masters
are not to show less respect for them because they are brothers. Instead, they are to serve them even better, because those who benefit
from their service are believers, and dear to them. These are the
things you are to teach and urge on them.

Love of Money

[3]If anyone teaches false doctrines and does not agree to the sound
instruction of our Lord Jesus Christ and to godly teaching, [4]he is conceited and understands nothing. He has an unhealthy interest in controversies and quarrels about words that result in envy, strife,
malicious talk, evil suspicions [5]and constant friction between men of
corrupt mind, who have been robbed of the truth and who think that
godliness is a means to financial gain.
[6]But godliness with contentment is great gain. [7]For we brought
nothing into the world, and we can take nothing out of it. [8]But if we
have food and clothing, we will be content with that. [9]People who
want to get rich fall into temptation and a trap and into many foolish
and harmful desires that plunge men into ruin and destruction. [10]For
the love of money is a root of all kinds of evil. Some people, eager for
money, have wandered from the faith and pierced themselves with
many griefs.

Paul's Charge to Timothy

[11]But you, man of God, flee from all this, and pursue righteousness, godliness, faith, love, endurance and gentleness. [12]Fight the
good fight of the faith. Take hold of the eternal life to which you were

OPEN When you got married, how much money did you have in your pocket *or* how much money do you think you need to get married?

STUDY Suddenly the motivation for the false teachers becomes clear. **1.** How would you compare the motivation of the false teachers to followers of Christ today? **2.** What is wrong with wanting to be rich? What is the differences between enjoying money and loving money?

APPLY 1. As you look back to the happiest days in your life, how much money did you have? **2.** Where have you struggled now?

OPEN How did you learn how to handle your money?

STUDY Paul has finished dealing with the problems in

6:3 false doctrines. Paul returns to the theme with which he began his letter (1:3). The false teachers have departed from the teaching of Jesus (1:10; 4:6). **the sound instruction of our Lord Jesus Christ.** This is their error. They have departed from the teaching of Jesus. This statement seems to indicate that early in the life of the church, the teachings of Jesus were collected and taught. The first Gospels were probably written around the time of this letter.

6:4 he is conceited and understands nothing. This is the first thing Paul says about these teachers. They are swollen with pride despite the fact they are really quite ignorant. **controversies.** This is more than just "disputes." The word refers to a sort of idle speculation. **quarrels.** This is literally a "battle of words," which Paul sharply criticizes. **result in.** Paul identifies two negative results of this sick preoccupation with word battles. First, it produces strife within the church, and *second,* it brings about a kind of corruption or decay to the minds of the teachers themselves. **envy.** Controversy produces jealousy as people take up sides (Rom. 1:29, Gal. 5:21, where envy is said to be one of the evidences of the sinful nature). **malicious talk, evil suspicions.** This quarreling drives people to insult and question one another.

6:5 corrupt mind. "Mind" refers to one's whole way of thinking. **robbed of the truth.** Such corruption results in the loss of the very truth of the gospel. **godliness is a means to financial gain.** As Paul has hinted in 3:3,8, the bottom line motivation of these false teachers is the money they make from their teaching. Paul does not consider it wrong for a person to be paid for teaching (5:17–18), but he is incensed when greed is the main motivation for ministry.

6:6 contentment. This word refers to a person who is not impacted by circumstances. Such a person is self-contained and thus able to rise above all conditions. For Paul, however, this sort of contentment was derived from the Lord (Phil. 4:11).

6:7–8 There are two reasons why "godliness with contentment" brings great gain. First, at death people can take nothing with them (so why worry about material gain that has to be given up in the end anyway). Second, if people have the essentials in life, this should be enough.

6:9 temptation. Greed causes people to notice and desire what they might not otherwise have paid attention to.

6:10 For the love of money is a root of all kinds of evil. This verse is often misquoted as "money is the root of all evil." While Paul clearly sees the danger of money, he is not contending that *all* evil can be traced to avarice. **Some people ... have wandered.** Here is the problem. Some of the false teachers have given in to the temptation to riches. They were probably once good leaders in the church but they got caught by Satan (4:1–2), became enamored with speculative ideas (vv. 3–5), and in the end were pulled down by their love for money.

6:11 But you. Once again Paul contrasts Timothy to the false teachers. **flee from all this.** Timothy is to move with haste and intentionality to get away from not only greed, but from the speculative, contentious doctrines of the false teachers.

6:12 Fight the good fight. Paul uses an athletic metaphor to encourage Tim-

called when you made your good confession in the presence of many
witnesses. 13In the sight of God, who gives life to everything, and of
Christ Jesus, who while testifying before Pontius Pilate made the
good confession, I charge you 14to keep this command without spot
or blame until the appearing of our Lord Jesus Christ, 15which God
will bring about in his own time—God, the blessed and only Ruler,
the King of kings and Lord of lords, 16who alone is immortal and who
lives in unapproachable light, whom no one has seen or can see. To
him be honor and might forever. Amen.

17Command those who are rich in this present world not to be arrogant nor to put their hope in wealth, which is so uncertain, but to
put their hope in God, who richly provides us with everything for our
enjoyment. 18Command them to do good, to be rich in good deeds,
and to be generous and willing to share. 19In this way they will lay up
treasure for themselves as a firm foundation for the coming age, so
that they may take hold of the life that is truly life.
20Timothy, guard what has been entrusted to your care. Turn away
from godless chatter and the opposing ideas of what is falsely called
knowledge, 21which some have professed and in so doing have wandered from the faith.

Grace be with you.

the church. Now he turns to give his "son in the faith" a personal challenge. **1.** Who does Paul sound like in verses 11–16? What is Timothy being asked to flee from and pursue (v. 11)? **2.** In the previous passage (vv. 1–10), Paul focused on the danger of the love of money. In this passage, he deals with the responsibilities of having money. What does Paul say in verses 17–19 about wealth? If Paul were around today, what would be his challenge to followers of Christ in this country? **3.** If you were young Timothy, how would you be feeling after reading this letter?

APPLY 1. As you think back over your spiritual journey, where were you thrust into a position for which you felt totally inadequate? What did God teach you from this experience? **2.** What is the most important truth you have learned from this study?

---

othy to persevere in the faith. The verb tense emphasizes this is an ongoing struggle. **Take hold of the eternal life.** The focus shifts from the contest to the prize. A person can grasp eternal life in a single act. **to which you were called.** Paul gives Timothy two reasons for waging this fight. This is the first. God has "called" him to eternal life. **your good confession.** This is the second reason. He has publicly acknowledged this call. It is not certain to which event in his Christian life Paul refers, though he may well have had in mind Timothy's baptism (when he publicly declared his faith in Christ).

6:17 those who are rich. This is the only place in his letters that Paul addresses the wealthy directly. His consistent "command" is that the rich share their wealth with the poor (Rom. 12:8,13; 2 Cor. 9:6–15). **not to be arrogant nor to put their hope in wealth.** These are the twin dangers of wealth—that it will cause people to think themselves to be better than others, and that they might put their trust in their riches (and not in God). **for our enjoyment.** But Paul is no ascetic. That the wealthy should not place confidence in their wealth does not carry with it an attitude of total rejection of wealth.

2 Timothy

Personal Reading	Group Study Topic and Reading	
1:1–2:13	Be Strong in Christ	1:1–2:13
2:14–3:9	Be a Good Workman	2:14–3:9
3:10–4:8	Be Faithful	3:10–4–8
4:9–22	To God Be the Glory	4:9–22

Author. The apostle Paul was most likely the author of 2 Timothy. However, based on considerations of vocabulary and style, the authorship of the Pastoral Epistles (1 and 2 Timothy, Titus) has been questioned by some scholars.

Date. Second Timothy is probably the last epistle Paul ever wrote. The date is thought to be around A.D. 67–68. He is an old man now, in prison once again, deserted by most all of his friends, and facing the likely prospect of death.

Theme. Guard the gospel.

Purpose. Second Timothy is deeply moving as Paul writes to Timothy, imploring him to come and be with him in the last days of his life. Paul wants to pass on the torch of his ministry to Timothy. He had been Paul's trusted colleague for over 15 years, and he really cared for the welfare of the churches (Phil. 2:20–22). In many ways he was an unlikely leader. He was relatively young by Roman standards, in his mid-thirties (2:22; 1 Tim. 4:12). He was prone to illness (1 Tim. 5:23). And he was, apparently, somewhat shy and in need of encouragement (1:7–8; 1 Cor. 16:10). To his credit, Timothy overcame his natural inclination and tackled risky assignments for Paul (for example, in Corinth).

Historical Background. It is difficult to trace Paul's movements during the period when he wrote the Pastoral Epistles. The best guess is that after being released from the house arrest in Rome (described at the end of Acts), Paul went on another preaching tour taking with him Timothy and Titus. In the course of their travels, they came to Crete. When it came time to move on, Paul left Titus behind to appoint proper leaders for the new church there. Paul and Timothy went to Macedonia via Ephesus. At Ephesus, Paul discovered that heresy was rotting away the church. So he excommunicated Hymenaeus and Alexander, two of the erring leaders (1 Tim. 1:19–20), and he left Timothy behind to help the church through its difficulties (1 Tim. 1:3–4). Paul himself went on to Macedonia. Once there he wrote 1 Timothy and Titus (hence the similarity between the two letters.)

Paul was eventually taken back to Rome and thrown into prison. This time he was chained and thrown into a dark, damp dungeon, "like a criminal" (2:9). Onesiphorus was able to find Paul only after a long search (1:17). Paul was cold ("bring the cloak," 4:13), bored ("bring ... my scrolls, especially the parchments," 4:13), and lonely ("only Luke is with me," 4:11). His full trial was yet to come, and he did not expect to be acquitted.

Characteristics. Second Timothy is far more personal than 1 Timothy. First Timothy has the feel of a business letter containing important instructions to be heeded by the local congregation. But in 2 Timothy, Paul is writing to Timothy and not to the church, and he reminisces about the work he and Timothy did together. His primary purpose is not combating heresy (although that is a background concern), but to call Timothy to join him in Rome.

Second Timothy is also characterized, somewhat surprisingly, by a note of triumph. Paul knows that despite all the difficulties he is facing, despite the pressure on the church, the gospel will prevail. It cannot be chained even if he is chained (2:9). Nor will the church ultimately be hampered. It, too, will prevail (2:11–13; 4:8). Therefore, Paul writes to Timothy to carry on the work of the gospel despite persecution.

1 Paul, an apostle of Christ Jesus by the will of God, according to the promise of life that is in Christ Jesus,

2 To Timothy, my dear son:

Grace, mercy and peace from God the Father and Christ Jesus our Lord.

Encouragement to Be Faithful

3 I thank God, whom I serve, as my forefathers did, with a clear conscience, as night and day I constantly remember you in my prayers. 4 Recalling your tears, I long to see you, so that I may be filled with joy. 5 I have been reminded of your sincere faith, which first lived in your grandmother Lois and in your mother Eunice and, I am persuaded, now lives in you also. 6 For this reason I remind you to fan into flame the gift of God, which is in you through the laying on of my hands. 7 For God did not give us a spirit of timidity, but a spirit of power, of love and of self-discipline.

8 So do not be ashamed to testify about our Lord, or ashamed of me his prisoner. But join with me in suffering for the gospel, by the power of God, 9 who has saved us and called us to a holy life—not because of anything we have done but because of his own purpose and grace. This grace was given us in Christ Jesus before the beginning of time, 10 but it has now been revealed through the appearing of our Savior, Christ Jesus, who has destroyed death and has brought life and immortality to light through the gospel. 11 And of this gospel I was appointed a herald and an apostle and a teacher. 12 That is why I am suffering as I am. Yet I am not ashamed, because I know whom I have believed, and am convinced that he is able to guard what I have entrusted to him for that day.

13 What you heard from me, keep as the pattern of sound teaching, with faith and love in Christ Jesus. 14 Guard the good deposit that was entrusted to you—guard it with the help of the Holy Spirit who lives in us.

15 You know that everyone in the province of Asia has deserted me, including Phygelus and Hermogenes.

OPEN 1. What physical traits have you inherited from your father's side of the family? Your mother's? **2.** Of all your friends from high school, who are still your friends today?

STUDY 1. Have you ever seen pictures of a medieval prison? What was it like? **2.** What did you find out from the paragraph on "Purpose" in the book introduction that will help you to understand the circumstances for writing this letter? **3.** What do verses 3–4 tell you about Paul and Timothy's relationship? **4.** What is Paul trying to do with Timothy in verses 5–7? **5.** How does Paul go about challenging Timothy to overcome his timidity (vv. 8,12)? Do you feel that Paul is expecting too much out of Timothy with his personality? How about you? **6.** How do you think Paul felt when "everyone in the province of Asia deserted" him? How would you contrast the deserters with Onesiphorus? **7.** How many generations in the leadership chain are mentioned in 2:2? **8.** What is the lesson that Paul is teaching from the metaphor of soldiering and sports (2:3–5)? What is the point of the former metaphor? **9.** How would you describe Paul's outlook on life from his prison cell (2:8–10)?

APPLY 1. What is the closest you have come to being "chained" like a criminal? Have you ever been retained with rope or chains or locked in a room? **2.** Who is the "Paul" that brought you up in the faith? **3.** Who are you bringing along in the

---

1:1–2 Paul's greeting in his letter to Titus (which was probably written between 1 and 2 Timothy) was longer than usual (Titus 1:1–4). Here he returns to a briefer, more normal opening.

1:4 Recalling your tears. Paul is probably remembering when they parted the last time, he was to go on to Macedonia while Timothy stayed in Ephesus (Acts 20:37 for a similar situation). **I long to see you.** This is the main reason he writes this letter: to urge Timothy to join him (4:9). **joy.** Once again, as he did in Philippians, Paul sounds a note of joy even though he is in prison.

1:5 Eunice. Timothy's mother was a Jewish Christian (Acts 16:1). His father was a Gentile, probably not a believer.

1:6 fan into flame. "Rekindle." Paul uses the image of a fire, not to suggest that his spiritual gift has "gone out," but that it needs constant stirring up so that it always burns brightly. **the gift of God.** Paul reminds Timothy not only of his spiritual roots (the faith of his mother and grandmother), but of the gift he has been given for ministry.

1:7 Paul makes this sort of appeal because Timothy is not a forceful person (1 Tim. 4:12). **power ... love ... self-discipline.** The gift the Spirit gave Timothy leads not to "timidity," but to these positive characteristics.

1:8 ashamed to testify about our Lord. The gospel message about a dying Savior was not immediately popular in the first-century world. The Greeks laughed at the idea that the Messiah could be a convicted criminal, and that God was so weak he would allow his own Son to die. The Jews could not conceive of a Messiah (whom they knew to be all-powerful) dying on a cross (which they felt disqualified him from acceptance by God). It was not easy to preach the gospel in the face of such scorn.

1:10 appearing. This refers here to the "manifestation" of God's grace through the incarnation of God the Son. **death ... life.** Jesus' work of salvation is described in his two-fold act of destroying the power of death over people (death no longer has the final word) and by bringing resurrection life in its place, God was able to give us eternal life.

faith? **4.** Who would you like to invite into this Bible study group?

[16]May the Lord show mercy to the household of Onesiphorus, because he often refreshed me and was not ashamed of my chains. [17]On
the contrary, when he was in Rome, he searched hard for me until he
found me. [18]May the Lord grant that he will find mercy from the Lord
on that day! You know very well in how many ways he helped me in
Ephesus.

2 You then, my son, be strong in the grace that is in Christ Jesus.
[2]And the things you have heard me say in the presence of many
witnesses entrust to reliable men who will also be qualified to teach
others. [3]Endure hardship with us like a good soldier of Christ Jesus.
[4]No one serving as a soldier gets involved in civilian affairs—he
wants to please his commanding officer. [5]Similarly, if anyone competes as an athlete, he does not receive the victor's crown unless he
competes according to the rules. [6]The hardworking farmer should be
the first to receive a share of the crops. [7]Reflect on what I am saying,
for the Lord will give you insight into all this.

[8]Remember Jesus Christ, raised from the dead, descended from
David. This is my gospel, [9]for which I am suffering even to the point
of being chained like a criminal. But God's word is not chained.
[10]Therefore I endure everything for the sake of the elect, that they too
may obtain the salvation that is in Christ Jesus, with eternal glory.

[11]Here is a trustworthy saying:

If we died with him,
we will also live with him;
[12]if we endure,
we will also reign with him.
If we disown him,
he will also disown us;
[13]if we are faithless,
he will remain faithful,
for he cannot disown himself.

A Workman Approved by God

[14]Keep reminding them of these things. Warn them before God
against quarreling about words; it is of no value, and only ruins those
who listen. [15]Do your best to present yourself to God as one ap-

OPEN 1. Did you ever build a treehouse or fort in your backyard? **2.** What did you and your brother/sister quarrel about as kids?

2:2 Just as the gospel has been entrusted to Timothy (1:14; 1 Tim. 6:20), so he is to entrust it to others who, in turn, teach it to yet others. This whole process of "entrusting" is made doubly important by the fact that Paul will soon call Timothy to join him in Rome (which means that others will have to take over his teaching ministry in Ephesus).

2:3–6 Paul uses three metaphors (drawn from the military, from athletics, and from farming) to encourage Timothy to work hard and endure suffering with the knowledge that he will be rewarded.

2:3 Endure hardship. This Greek word is the same one used in 1:8 and so it should probably be translated "join with me in suffering" since this gives a better sense of what Paul is calling Timothy to do.

2:9 criminal. This is the term used for those who committed serious crimes (such as murder and theft).

2:10 the elect. God's chosen people. **may obtain the salvation.** Paul's suffering will further the spread of the gospel, through which men and women obtain salvation.

2:14 Keep reminding them of these things. Timothy's first task is to keep people in touch with the truth of the gospel. The verb tense indicates that this is something he will have to do over and over again. **quarreling about words.** Literally, "word battle." This lies at the heart of the false teaching. **ruins those who listen.** Such quibbling over words cannot possibly have a good result.

2:15 as one approved. Literally, "one who has stood the test"; a word used to describe gold or silver that had been purified in fire, or a stone that was cut without a flaw, (examined and then pronounced fit to be used in a building). **a workman.** The picture is of a farm laborer who has done a good job and is therefore not afraid to show his boss what he has done. **correctly handles the word of truth.** In contrast to the false teachers and their "word battles," Timothy is called upon to teach and preach the gospel correctly. The phrase

proved, a workman who does not need to be ashamed and who correctly handles the word of truth. 16Avoid godless chatter, because
those who indulge in it will become more and more ungodly. 17Their
teaching will spread like gangrene. Among them are Hymenaeus and
Philetus, 18who have wandered away from the truth. They say that the
resurrection has already taken place, and they destroy the faith of
some. 19Nevertheless, God's solid foundation stands firm, sealed
with this inscription: "The Lord knows those who are his,"[a] and, "Everyone who confesses the name of the Lord must turn away from
wickedness."
20In a large house there are articles not only of gold and silver, but
also of wood and clay; some are for noble purposes and some for ig-
noble. 21If a man cleanses himself from the latter, he will be an instrument for noble purposes, made holy, useful to the Master and
prepared to do any good work.
22Flee the evil desires of youth, and pursue righteousness, faith,
love and peace, along with those who call on the Lord out of a pure
heart. 23Don't have anything to do with foolish and stupid arguments, because you know they produce quarrels. 24And the Lord's
servant must not quarrel; instead, he must be kind to everyone, able
to teach, not resentful. 25Those who oppose him he must gently instruct, in the hope that God will grant them repentance leading them
to a knowledge of the truth, 26and that they will come to their senses
and escape from the trap of the devil, who has taken them captive to
do his will.

STUDY Now Paul gets around to the problem of false teachers who probably are leaders of churches. **1.** Reading between the lines, how would you describe these false teachers (vv. 14–18)? What has the false teaching about the resurrection done to the church? **2.** How is Timothy to counteract these teachers? How would you deal with this situation? **3.** If you want to be an "approved workman," what does Paul recommend you do with your life? For Timothy to clean up his life, what are some things he needs to work on (vv. 22–25)? Do you think these things are characteristics of "youth" or spiritual immaturity? How about you?

APPLY 1. What is the closest you have come to being in a Christian community that was nearly torn apart by petty theological arguments? **2.** What did you learn from this experience?

Godlessness in the Last Days

3 But mark this: There will be terrible times in the last days. 2Peo-
ple will be lovers of themselves, lovers of money, boastful,
proud, abusive, disobedient to their parents, ungrateful, unholy,

[a]19 Num. 16:5 (see Septuagint)

OPEN When you were growing up where did the bad guys hang out in your town? What did your parents tell you to do with these guys?

STUDY What does the description in verses 2–5 sound

"word of truth" refers not to Scripture specifically, but to the gospel message as a whole.

2:17 gangrene. A disease that "gnaws away" at healthy tissue, causing its decay. Likewise, false teaching eats away at the healthy life in a church. **Hymenaeus.** Paul names the false teachers: Hymenaeus and Philetus has been a real problem. Paul had mentioned Hymenaeus in 1 Timothy 1:20 as one he had "handed over to Satan." It appears he is still at work to "destroy the faith of some" (v. 18). Why has Paul's excommunication failed to stop Hymenaeus?

2:18 the resurrection has already taken place. They were probably teaching that the resurrection of believers had already taken place (1 Cor. 15:12; 2 Thess. 2:2). This undermined the hope for a bodily resurrection on the Last Day (1 Cor. 15).

2:19 solid foundation. Paul is probably referring to God's truth (Isa. 40:8). **sealed.** Paul has in mind the practice of placing an inscription on the foundation stone of a building to indicate the purpose of the building or the name of the owner.

2:21 cleanses himself. This phrase was used to describe ritual cleaning of dishes.

2:22 Flee ... pursue. He is to avoid evil desires while striving for positive virtues. **evil desires of youth.** Paul has in mind the impatience and arrogance of self-assertive youth, who love novelty and indulge in argument for the sake of it.

2:23 foolish and stupid arguments. He is to avoid the kind of uninstructed theorizing that characterizes the ideas of the false teachers (1 Tim. 1:7). Debate about these ideas does not edify only "quarrels."

3:2 People. Although he casts this list into general terms ("people"), Paul implies that these vices characterize (at least in part) the false teachers. **lovers of money.** The path is short from love of self to love of money. Self-interest leads to self indulgence. **boastful, proud.** These two terms are connected. The first refers to outward expressions of unrealistic pride and the second to an inner attitude of superiority. These words can also be translated as "braggart" and "arrogant." These terms have already been applied to the false teachers (1 Tim. 1:7; 6:4). **disobedient to their parents.** Duty to parents was considered obligatory by both Greeks and Jews. **ungrateful.** To be "ungrateful" is to refuse to honor the debt one owes to others. **unholy.** Such a person violates the unwritten laws that stand at the core of life.

like? Do you think the culture in Paul's day was better or worse than today?

APPLY 1. As you look back over your life, what brings you the most sense of satisfaction and accomplishment? **2.** As you look ahead, what is the thing that you want to accomplish with your life?

OPEN Have your parents written a will? Have you written one?

STUDY 1. Why does Paul recall for Timothy the tough times in Antioch, Iconium and Lystra? What places bring back similar memories for you? **2.** Is persecution necessarily a result of godliness? Why or why not? **3.** What does Paul state about the origin and purpose of Scripture? **4.** Timothy's Ministry (4:1–5): What nine final orders does Paul solemnly charge Timothy to fulfill?

3without love, unforgiving, slanderous, without self-control, brutal,
not lovers of the good, 4treacherous, rash, conceited, lovers of pleasure rather than lovers of God— 5having a form of godliness but denying its power. Have nothing to do with them.
6They are the kind who worm their way into homes and gain control over weak-willed women, who are loaded down with sins and are
swayed by all kinds of evil desires, 7always learning but never able to
acknowledge the truth. 8Just as Jannes and Jambres opposed Moses,
so also these men oppose the truth—men of depraved minds, who,
as far as the faith is concerned, are rejected. 9But they will not get
very far because, as in the case of those men, their folly will be clear
to everyone.

Paul's Charge to Timothy

10You, however, know all about my teaching, my way of life, my
purpose, faith, patience, love, endurance, 11persecutions, sufferings—what kinds of things happened to me in Antioch, Iconium and
Lystra, the persecutions I endured. Yet the Lord rescued me from all
of them. 12In fact, everyone who wants to live a godly life in Christ
Jesus will be persecuted, 13while evil men and impostors will go from
bad to worse, deceiving and being deceived. 14But as for you, continue in what you have learned and have become convinced of, because you know those from whom you learned it, 15and how from
infancy you have known the holy Scriptures, which are able to make
you wise for salvation through faith in Christ Jesus. 16All Scripture is

---

3:3 without love. This refers to the lack of natural, human affection. **unforgiving.** Such a person finds it impossible to be reconciled to others. This sort of person is harsh and often bitter. **without self-control.** This is the person who is a slave to a habit or desire.

3:4 rash. This is to be swept along by impulse or passion into bad decisions. **conceited.** Such people are swollen with pride at the sense of their own importance.

3:5 having a form of godliness. The final item on the list points straight at the false teachers. They liked certain outward expressions of religion: fasting and other forms of asceticism and debate about religious ideas. But they missed out on the real "power" of God by substituting an outward religiosity for the inner reality of God.

3:6 swayed by all kinds of evil desire. There may have been some sort of sexual involvement between the false teachers and the women they influenced.

3:8 Jannes and Jambres. These were Pharaoh's magicians, who by means of their secret arts duplicated the miracles of Moses and Aaron.

3:10 know all about. Literally, "to follow alongside." By this term Paul is urging Timothy to remember all he learned from him in the course of their travels and ministry together (2:2). This is especially important now, since Paul has come to realize that his own ministry is at an end. **my teaching.** This is the first of nine characteristics of Paul's life and ministry that Timothy is asked to note and reproduce. These nine make up a sort of "virtue list" that stands in sharp contrast to the "vice list" in verses 2–5 (2 Cor. 6:4–10).

3:11 what kinds of things happened to me. Each incident occurred on Paul's first missionary journey, culminating in his stoning while in Lystra (Timothy's hometown). By selecting these particular incidents, Paul is reminding Timothy of the fact that even at the start of his Christian life, he knew it involved suffering. **Yet the Lord rescued me.** Paul encourages Timothy (who will have suffering of his own, as Paul notes in v. 12) by the fact that God rescued him from death in each of these instances.

3:13 Ironically, this is not the case for "evil men." They do not live godly lives and the implication is that they thus avoid persecution. **impostors.** This word originally meant a "sorcerer." It came to mean a "swindler" or "cheat."

3:15 wise for salvation through faith in Christ Jesus. The Old Testament Scriptures lead one to salvation; i.e., to an understanding of God's saving purpose.

3:16-17 All Scripture is God-breathed. Scripture has a divine origin. It comes from God (2 Peter 1:21). **is useful for.** By means of two contrasting pairs of phrases, Paul names four ministry tasks in which Scripture plays a vital part. **teaching.** Scripture is the source of what Timothy teaches, in contrast to the speculative nature of the erring elders' doctrine. **rebuking.** Not only does Scripture teach that which is true, it also reveals that which is in error. Thus, Timothy can use Scripture to expose the fallacy of the false teachers. **correcting.** Scripture also defines how to live. It is thus a measuring stick against which to assess behavior and change what is found wanting. **training in righteousness.** This is the positive side of "correcting." Scripture provides instructions in how one ought to live (and not just in how one ought *not* to live).

God-breathed and is useful for teaching, rebuking, correcting and
training in righteousness, 17so that the man of God may be thoroughly equipped for every good work.

4 In the presence of God and of Christ Jesus, who will judge the
living and the dead, and in view of his appearing and his kingdom, I give you this charge: 2Preach the Word; be prepared in season
and out of season; correct, rebuke and encourage—with great patience and careful instruction. 3For the time will come when men will
not put up with sound doctrine. Instead, to suit their own desires,
they will gather around them a great number of teachers to say what
their itching ears want to hear. 4They will turn their ears away from
the truth and turn aside to myths. 5But you, keep your head in all
situations, endure hardship, do the work of an evangelist, discharge
all the duties of your ministry.

6For I am already being poured out like a drink offering, and the
time has come for my departure. 7I have fought the good fight, I have
finished the race, I have kept the faith. 8Now there is in store for me
the crown of righteousness, which the Lord, the righteous Judge, will
award to me on that day—and not only to me, but also to all who
have longed for his appearing.

5. Paul's Ministry (4:6–8): In the climax to this letter—the last recorded message Paul wrote—how does the apostle sum up his life and ministry?

APPLY 1. Do you share Paul's hope for the future? How does it motivate you now? **2.** How do Paul's words challenge your life? Are you fighting "the good fight" no matter what persecution and suffering you face? **3.** How does this Scripture challenge your ministry? What are you doing to build it into your life, and how bold are you to share it faithfully rather than to tell people what they want to hear?

Personal Remarks

9Do your best to come to me quickly, 10for Demas, because he
loved this world, has deserted me and has gone to Thessalonica.
Crescens has gone to Galatia, and Titus to Dalmatia. 11Only Luke is
with me. Get Mark and bring him with you, because he is helpful to
me in my ministry. 12I sent Tychicus to Ephesus. 13When you come,
bring the cloak that I left with Carpus at Troas, and my scrolls, especially the parchments.

14Alexander the metalworker did me a great deal of harm. The Lord
will repay him for what he has done. 15You too should be on your
guard against him, because he strongly opposed our message.

16At my first defense, no one came to my support, but everyone

OPEN If you "left home without it," what would be the first thing you'd ask someone to send?

STUDY 1. Can you imagine how Paul is feeling as he writes about those who have deserted him and "no one came" to his support? **2.** What do you learn about Paul in these personal remarks? **3.** How would you describe the tone in Paul's voice as he writes this passage: Sad? Bitter? Stoic? Melancholic? Triumphant? How does it make you feel to find out that Paul was

---

3:17 the man of God. This may be a general term for every Christian, or it may refer specifically to those who minister, whose task is, under the authority of Scripture, to teach and refute, to reform and discipline.

4:2 Preach the Word. Above all else, Timothy is to proclaim the message of the gospel. This is the main command and controls the next four. **be prepared in season and out of season.** Probably Paul is encouraging Timothy to keep on preaching whether his hearers find it convenient or not, though he may be urging Timothy to continue with this task whether or not it is convenient to him. **correct, rebuke and encourage.** In preaching the gospel he is to "correct" those who are in error, "rebuke" them if they fail to heed his correction, and "encourage" or "urge" them all to respond to what the gospel says.

4:9 Paul begins with his main request. He wants Timothy to leave his post at Ephesus and join him in Rome. **come to me quickly.** It would not be an easy journey nor a particularly quick one, given travel conditions in the first century. Rome was over 1,000 miles from Ephesus. Still, with the typical delays in the Roman judicial system, Paul anticipates that if Timothy hurries (and gets on a boat before the shipping closes down for winter—v. 21), there will be adequate time for him to reach Rome before his trial.

4:10–11 Next, Paul explains the reason why he wants Timothy to come. It seems that all his colleagues have left him (with the exception of Luke), either by reason of defection (Demas) or because of ministry needs (Crescens and Titus).

4:11 Get Mark and bring him with you. It is a remarkable testimony to the power of the Holy Spirit that after the argument over Mark which had resulted in the split between Paul and Barnabas (because Mark had deserted them in Perga on their very first missionary journey—Acts 13:13; 15:36–41), reconciliation has taken place. Mark is now once again a valued coworker with Paul (v. 24; Col. 4:10; Philem. 24).

4:13 cloak. A heavy wool cape that was worn in the cold and rain, consisting of a single piece of material with a hole in the middle for the head. Winter was coming and Paul needed his cloak to stay warm while in jail. **scrolls ... parchments.** It cannot be known what these contained. Various suggestions have been made (though all are guesses): portions of the Old Testament, blank writing materials, early copies of the Gospels, official documents (such as Paul's birth certificate).

human, just like you? **4.** Why do you think Paul wants Timothy to come to Rome? **5.** How would you rank Paul in significance for the Christian movement? What, in particular, was his contribution as far as you are concerned?

APPLY 1. How do you feel about Paul as a person? **2.** Would you like to have Paul as the spiritual leader of your church? As your friend?

deserted me. May it not be held against them. 17But the Lord stood at
my side and gave me strength, so that through me the message might
be fully proclaimed and all the Gentiles might hear it. And I was delivered from the lion's mouth. 18The Lord will rescue me from every evil
attack and will bring me safely to his heavenly kingdom. To him be
glory for ever and ever. Amen.

Final Greetings

19Greet Priscilla[a] and Aquila and the household of Onesiphorus.
20Erastus stayed in Corinth, and I left Trophimus sick in Miletus. 21Do
your best to get here before winter. Eubulus greets you, and so do Pu-
dens, Linus, Claudia and all the brothers.
22The Lord be with your spirit. Grace be with you.

[a]19 Greek *Prisca*, a variant of *Priscilla*

4:21 get here before winter. Once again (v. 9), Paul reinforces the urgency of the situation he finds himself in. Matters are coming to a swift conclusion and he needs a trusted friend by his side, Timothy.

Titus

Personal Reading	Group Study Topic and Reading	
1:1–16	Reliable Leaders	1:1–16
2:1–15	Sound Doctrine	2:1–15
3:1–15	Doing Good	3:1–15

Author. The apostle Paul was most likely the writer of Titus. However, based on considerations of vocabulary and style, the authorship of the Pastoral Epistles (1 and 2 Timothy, Titus) has been questioned by some scholars.

Date. Titus was written about A.D. 63–65 (at the same time 1 Timothy was written).

Theme. Be devoted to what is good.

Historical Background. Paul and Titus, along with Timothy, went to Crete as part of a preaching tour following Paul's release from his first imprisonment in Rome. When Paul and Timothy left for Macedonia, Titus stayed behind to establish the new church on Crete. When Paul reached Macedonia he wrote two letters—one to Timothy who had remained in Ephesus and the other to Titus. In his letter to Titus, Paul reminds him of his role: to appoint good leaders who will guide the church wisely. He also urges Titus to combat the false teachers found on the island.

Characteristics. Titus is strikingly similar to 1 Timothy. Apart from the greeting and two pieces of theological writing in 2:11–14 and 3:3–7 (which appear to be creeds), the material is parallel to 1 Timothy. The main difference is found in the contrasting situation that Titus and Timothy were in. Timothy had been left to straighten out a mess in an already established church. Titus, on the other hand, had the job of appointing elders in a new church. There are few imperatives ("do this"); there is no mention of endurance (as one finds in 1 Timothy); and there are no appeals to "keep the faith."

Crete. Crete is a large island in the Mediterranean, southeast of Greece. On the Day of Pentecost, Jews from Crete were in Jerusalem and witnessed the coming of the Holy Spirit (Acts 2:11). During his voyage to Rome, the ship on which Paul sailed skimmed the coast of Crete before being caught by a storm and driven to Malta (Acts 27:7–21).

Titus. Titus was a Greek (Gal. 2:3) who was probably converted through Paul's ministry. He accompanied Paul on his crucial second visit to Jerusalem when the inflammatory question was raised about whether Gentiles had to become Jews before they could become Christians (Gal. 2:1–10). Paul used Titus as a test case, refusing to allow him to be circumcised despite the insistence of the Judaizers. Titus was a trusted colleague of Paul's and one of his special envoys sent on difficult assignments.

OPEN **1.** While growing up, who always sent you a card or a gift for your birthday? **2.** Are you more likely to keep your letters short and to the point, or do you write until you run out of paper?

STUDY **1.** What do you know about the circumstances under which Paul wrote this letter to Titus. **2.** Reading between the lines (vv. 10–16) what is going on in the churches "in every town" (v. 5), that Paul wants Titus to "straighten out"? **3.** Who is the "circumcision group"? Why would Paul be concerned about this group's teaching? How would you feel if you had been put in charge of straightening out this group? **4.** How would you describe the list of qualifications to look for in appointing elders (vv. 5–9)? How would you contrast the lifestyle Paul recommends to the lifestyle of the leaders of the circumcision group (vv. 10–14)? **5.** What motivates the false teachers (v. 11)? What is the insinuation about these people (vv. 15–16)? Who would you compare these people to today?

APPLY **1.** Who do you look up to as a model for Christian character? **2.** How would you describe your spiritual life today in one or two words?

---

1 Paul, a servant of God and an apostle of Jesus Christ for the faith
of God's elect and the knowledge of the truth that leads to godliness— 2 a faith and knowledge resting on the hope ofeternal life,
which God, who does not lie, promised before thebeginning of time,
3 and at his appointed season he brought his word to light through
the preaching entrusted to me by the command of God our Savior,

4 To Titus, my true son in our common faith:

Grace and peace from God the Father and Christ Jesus our Savior.

Titus's Task on Crete

5 The reason I left you in Crete was that you might straighten out
what was left unfinished and appoint[a] elders in every town, as I directed you. 6 An elder must be blameless, the husband of but one wife,
a man whose children believe and are not open to the charge of being
wild and disobedient. 7 Since an overseer[b] is entrusted with God's
work, he must be blameless—not overbearing, not quick-tempered,
not given to drunkenness, not violent, not pursuing dishonest gain.
8 Rather he must be hospitable, one who loves what is good, who is
self-controlled, upright, holy and disciplined. 9 He must hold firmly to
the trustworthy message as it has been taught, so that he can encourage others by sound doctrine and refute those who oppose it.
10 For there are many rebellious people, mere talkers and deceivers,
especially those of the circumcision group. 11 They must be silenced,
because they are ruining whole households by teaching things they
ought not to teach—and that for the sake of dishonest gain. 12 Even
one of their own prophets has said, "Cretans are always liars, evil
brutes, lazy gluttons." 13 This testimony is true. Therefore, rebuke
them sharply, so that they will be sound in the faith 14 and will pay no
attention to Jewish myths or to the commands of those who reject
the truth. 15 To the pure, all things are pure, but to those who are cor-

[a] 5 Or *ordain* [b] 7 Traditionally *bishop*

1:1–4 The salutation that begins the letter to Titus is different from those that open 1 and 2 Timothy. The most notable difference is the way in which Paul defines the purpose of his apostleship.

1:5–16 The problem in Crete has to do with the erroneous teaching of the circumcision party. Paul urges Titus to deal with this problem by appointing elders who will resist the false teachers.

1:5 straighten out ... appoint. The reason he left Titus behind was to complete the task of organizing the churches, specifically, to appoint elders.

1:6 Paul begins this list of characteristics by focusing on the home life of the potential elder. **blameless.** This is a general term covering a variety of behaviors, some of which Paul will identify. **husband of but one wife.** The most likely meaning is that sexual faithfulness to one's spouse was demanded.

1:7 overseer. Sometimes translated "bishop" (*episkopoi*), this title probably did not mean in the first century what "bishop" has come to mean today. It seems likely that in Paul's day "overseers" and "elders" were interchangeable. **not pursuing dishonest gain.** The Cretans had a reputation for making money in shady ways.

1:8 Paul follows this list of five vices with a list of six virtues. **hospitable.** Overseers must be willing to open up their homes to guests. It was a common practice in the first century to offer hospitality to travelers (Rom. 12:13; 1 Tim. 5:10; 1 Peter 4:9). **self-controlled.** The Greek word, *sophron*, is hard to translate into English, and has been variously rendered as "prudent," "of sound mind," and "chaste." **upright.** Such a person acts justly toward others. **disciplined.** Such people have worked to master their desires and behaviors.

1:10 For. Paul connects the character required of elders to the problem facing the church. **the circumcision group.** This group of Christian Jews are insisting that before Gentiles can become Christians they must first undergo the rite of circumcision and so become Jews.

1:11 dishonest gain. The motivation of these false teachers is the money they make from their teaching. Paul does not consider it wrong for a person to be paid for teaching (1 Tim. 5:17–18), but he is indignant when greed is the main motivation for ministry (1 Tim. 6:5–10).

1:13 rebuke them. This is the only time in this letter that Paul calls upon Titus to confront directly the false teachers (v. 9).

1:15–16 Food prohibitions, important to Jewish tradition, are probably in view here (1 Tim. 4:3).

rupted and do not believe, nothing is pure. In fact, both their minds and consciences are corrupted. 16They claim to know God, but by their actions they deny him. They are detestable, disobedient and unfit for doing anything good.

What Must Be Taught to Various Groups

2 You must teach what is in accord with sound doctrine. 2Teach the older men to be temperate, worthy of respect, self-controlled, and sound in faith, in love and in endurance.

3Likewise, teach the older women to be reverent in the way they live, not to be slanderers or addicted to much wine, but to teach what is good. 4Then they can train the younger women to love their husbands and children, 5to be self-controlled and pure, to be busy at home, to be kind, and to be subject to their husbands, so that no one will malign the word of God.

6Similarly, encourage the young men to be self-controlled. 7In everything set them an example by doing what is good. In your teaching show integrity, seriousness 8and soundness of speech that cannot be condemned, so that those who oppose you may be ashamed because they have nothing bad to say about us.

9Teach slaves to be subject to their masters in everything, to try to please them, not to talk back to them, 10and not to steal from them, but to show that they can be fully trusted, so that in every way they will make the teaching about God our Savior attractive.

11For the grace of God that brings salvation has appeared to all men. 12It teaches us to say "No" to ungodliness and worldly passions, and to live self-controlled, upright and godly lives in this present age, 13while we wait for the blessed hope—the glorious appearing of our great God and Savior, Jesus Christ, 14who gave himself for us to redeem us from all wickedness and to purify for himself a people that are his very own, eager to do what is good.

OPEN 1. As a teenager or college student, how did you decorate your room or living space so that it was really "you"? How does your living space today reflect who you are? **2.** Who is your favorite elderly person?

STUDY 1. What is the principle in this passage for passing on the faith and the lifestyle of a Christian? Do you think this principle still applies today, especially for spiritual development? **2.** How would you describe the things the older generation are to pass down to the younger generation? **3.** How would you define what it means to be "self-controlled"? Who do you look up to as a role model for self-control? **4.** What is the principle in the conduct of slaves that could be applied to employer/employee relationships? **5.** What is the motivation for followers of Christ to "live self-controlled, godly and upright lives in this present age" (v. 12)?

APPLY 1. In your spiritual development, who was your principle role model? **2.** Who would you like to invite into your group as a way of mentoring this person?

1:15 all things are pure. This is a common New Testament theme. What people eat does not defile them (Mark 7:1–23; Rom. 14:20; 1 Tim. 4:4).

2:2 older men. These would be men over 50. Paul's words to them parallel what he said to the potential elders (1:6–9), since most church leaders would be elders in age as well.

2:3 teach what is good. Formal instruction is probably not intended. Rather, the idea is that the older women would model "what is good" for younger women in terms of a woman's accepted social role of the day as a wife and mother.

2:5 to be subject to their husbands. Paul is not placing women under the authority of all men. Instead he has in mind voluntary submission to the woman's own husband.

2:7 In your teaching. The focus is on the activity of teaching. The three words that Paul uses to describe how Titus should teach relate to the motive, demeanor and content of his teaching. **integrity.** This is without corruption, sincere. In contrast to the false teachers, Titus' motivation must not be mercenary.

2:8 soundness of speech. Literally, "healthy" or "wholesome speech," a medical metaphor that Paul probably borrowed from the itinerant philosophers of the day. By it he refers to teaching that is in accord with the gospel proclaimed by the apostles (v. 2; 1:9,13; 1 Tim. 1:10; 6:3; 2 Tim. 1:13; 4:3).

2:9 Teach slaves to be subject to their masters. Slavery was widespread in the first century. Although it was seldom racially motivated, to be a slave was to be at the bottom of the social system. Why Paul does not speak out against slavery is not clear, although he is quite emphatic that in Christ there is neither slave nor free (Gal. 3:28).

2:10 so that in every way they will make the teaching about God our Savior attractive. What Paul urges on slaves is, in fact, what he wants from all Christians in Crete, namely, the kind of behavior that society in general will count as respectable. This will make the Christian message attractive to those outside the church (v. 5).

2:13 the blessed hope. This refers to the Second Coming of Jesus. **our great God and Savior, Jesus Christ.** This is a clear statement of the deity of Christ.

2:14 Paul identifies the connection between the salvation Jesus brought and their lifestyle. Jesus died in order to: (1) rescue them from wickedness (therefore they ought not to live that way any longer); (2) make them a pure people (which defines how they are now to live). A godly lifestyle is, therefore, a response to the saving work of Jesus and a testimony to the power he has to change lives.

15These, then, are the things you should teach. Encourage and rebuke with all authority. Do not let anyone despise you.

Doing What Is Good

3 Remind the people to be subject to rulers and authorities, to be obedient, to be ready to do whatever is good, 2to slander no one, to be peaceable and considerate, and to show true humility toward all men.

3At one time we too were foolish, disobedient, deceived and enslaved by all kinds of passions and pleasures. We lived in malice and envy, being hated and hating one another. 4But when the kindness and love of God our Savior appeared, 5he saved us, not because of righteous things we had done, but because of his mercy. He saved us through the washing of rebirth and renewal by the Holy Spirit, 6whom he poured out on us generously through Jesus Christ our Savior, 7so that, having been justified by his grace, we might become heirs having the hope of eternal life. 8This is a trustworthy saying. And I want you to stress these things, so that those who have trusted in God may be careful to devote themselves to doing what is good. These things are excellent and profitable for everyone.

9But avoid foolish controversies and genealogies and arguments and quarrels about the law, because these are unprofitable and useless. 10Warn a divisive person once, and then warn him a second time. After that, have nothing to do with him. 11You may be sure that such a man is warped and sinful; he is self-condemned.

Final Remarks

12As soon as I send Artemas or Tychicus to you, do your best to come to me at Nicopolis, because I have decided to winter there. 13Do everything you can to help Zenas the lawyer and Apollos on their way and see that they have everything they need. 14Our people must learn to devote themselves to doing what is good, in order that they may provide for daily necessities and not live unproductive lives.

15Everyone with me sends you greetings. Greet those who love us in the faith.

Grace be with you all.

OPEN How do you least exhibit your faith: In a checkout line? In a fender bender? After a tough exam? At the company picnic? In athletics? Other?

STUDY In 1:12, Paul refers to the people in Crete, "Cretans are always liars, evil brutes, lazy gluttons." In this passage, he goes even further. **1.** Reading between the lines in verses 1–2, what do you think the Cretans are doing? **2.** What would Paul say to the person who says, "God made me this way by giving me a temperament that is hot headed, argumentative and competitive?" **3.** How can a person who is naturally stuck up, self-centered, egotistical and arrogant learn "to show true humility" (v. 2)? **4.** What is going on with the churches in verses 9–11 and what does Paul want Titus to do about it? What is the lesson here for your own study group? **5.** How is Titus to deal with these errant leaders?

APPLY **1.** As you look back over your life, are you encouraged at the way God is reshaping your rough edges into his character and temperament? **2.** If God could chisel away at an area in your life that still needs a little work, what would it be?

3:1–11 Paul now returns to his main concern in the letter: the behavior of Christians. Previously, his focus was on the relationships between Christians and how this was viewed by the outside world (2:5,10). Now he turns to the question of how Christians are to behave to outsiders.

3:5 he saved us. This is the main focus of verses 4–7. The tense of the verb indicates that this is a once-for-all act. **because of his mercy.** The mercy of God, not their character or works, is the basis for salvation. **rebirth.** This is the first of three metaphors that describe salvation. Believers become new persons. **renewal.** The second metaphor is similar to the first. It expresses the fact that they have been transformed again with a newness (2 Cor. 5:14–17).

3:7 justified. The third metaphor emphasizes that believers are put right with God.

3:9 avoid. Paul contrasts the good deeds, to which they are to devote themselves, with the evil deeds, which they are to flee. **genealogies.** Some Jewish scholars took the family trees in the Old Testament and devoted great energy to constructing "biographies" for each character. **arguments.** Literally, "word-battles," probably between those who disagree about genealogies and other such matters.

3:12 Titus is to be replaced as soon as Paul can send someone to take over his work. **Artemas.** Nothing is known of this individual. **Tychicus.** Tychicus was a trusted fellow worker, who often traveled with or for Paul (Acts 20:4; Eph. 6:21;Col. 4:7). **Nicopolis.** This city was located several hundred miles northwest of Athens near the Adriatic Sea.

3:13 Zenas the lawyer and Apollos. These men probably carried this letter to Titus. Zenas was an expert in Roman law. Apollos is probably the well-known orator from Alexandria (Acts 18:24– 19:1; 1 Cor. 1:12; 3:4,22; 16:12).

3:14 Our people. These are the Christians on Crete who are connected with Paul and Titus, as opposed to the false teachers.

Philemon

Author. The apostle Paul wrote Philemon.

Date. Paul probably wrote Philemon in the early A.D. 60s.

Theme. Radical forgiveness.

Personal Reading	Group Study Topic and Reading	
vv. 1–7	Thanksgiving & Prayer	vv. 1–7
vv. 8–25	Paul's Plea	vv. 8–25

Characteristics. Philemon is the shortest of Paul's New Testament letters and it is his only private letter preserved in Scripture. All his other letters, whether to churches or to coworkers, relate to Paul's ministry. But Philemon is a personal note written to a friend about a private matter—the fate of Onesimus, the runaway slave. As such, it gives us a valuable glimpse into Paul's personality.

Slaves in the Roman Empire. Slaves were considered property, not people. Therefore, they were under the absolute control of their master or mistress. A slave owner could beat or even kill a slave if he or she chose, although, in all fairness, many slaves fared quite well. Onesimus had run away from his owner, Philemon. As a fugitive, he was subject to severe punishment or even death if caught. For Paul to send him back was a considerable risk. Philemon had every right to brand Onesimus with the "Letter F" on his forehead (for fugitive/runaway) or do even worse.

Onesimus. He was a slave. He may well have been a thief ("if he has done you any wrong or owes you anything, charge it to me," v. 18). He was certainly a fugitive. But he had become a follower of Christ.

We do not know whether Paul's letter had the impact he hoped. It may well be that Onesimus, the runaway slave, had become with the passing years none other than Onesimus, the great bishop of Ephesus. If this was the case, it would explain how the letter to Philemon got into the New Testament. Many scholars feel that the first collection of Paul's letters was made at Ephesus at about the time Onesimus was bishop. He may have included this note as a vivid demonstration of how Christ can change and use even a single, fugitive slave.

1 Paul, a prisoner of Christ Jesus, and Timothy our brother,

To Philemon our dear friend and fellow worker, 2 to Apphia our sister, to Archippus our fellow soldier and to the church that meets in
your home:

3 Grace to you and peace from God our Father and the Lord Jesus Christ.

Thanksgiving and Prayer

4 I always thank my God as I remember you in my prayers, 5 because
I hear about your faith in the Lord Jesus and your love for all the
saints. 6 I pray that you may be active in sharing your faith, so that you

OPEN What name were you given at birth? What nicknames have you been given since? What do they mean? How are you living up to their meaning?

STUDY 1. What do you learn in the book introduction about the slave Onesimus that sets the stage for this letter? 2. Given the seriousness, what could be done to Onesimus and what impact will his return have on Philemon's household? On Paul's relationship with Philemon? 3. Does

---

1 prisoner. Paul may have written this letter during his imprisonment in Rome (Acts 28) or from an unrecorded imprisonment somewhere closer to Colosse, perhaps in Ephesus. His omission of any claim to apostleship in this introduction fits in with his desire not to appeal to Philemon on the basis of his authority (vv. 8–9). **Timothy.** Timothy was a trusted companion of Paul's. **Philemon.** This man, not mentioned anywhere else in the New Testament, was obviously someone close to Paul.

2 Apphia. It is assumed she was Philemon's wife. The daily management of household slaves was the responsibility of the slave owner's wife. **the church that meets in your home.** Since congregations did not own buildings, they met in the homes of believers. While the issue here involved Philemon and Onesimus, how Philemon responded to Onesimus was a matter that would affect the life of the church to which both of them now belonged.

the fact that Onesimus has become a Christian lessen the seriousness of his crime? Why or why not? **4.** What is radical about Paul's view of Onesimus (vv. 10–18)? **5.** Given Paul's concern and need for Onesimus, why does Paul return Onesimus to Philemon, anyway? Why doesn't Paul exert his apostolic authority, declare Onesimus free, and keep him as a partner in the gospel? **6.** What do you think the chances are that Philemon will do what Paul asks? In what way would Philemon be right to refuse Paul?

APPLY **1.** When do you feel obligated to forgive someone: When they confess their sin? When they later change their behavior? When someone else intercedes for the offending party? **2.** For whom might you serve as a "Paul" in bringing about reconciliation?

will have a full understanding of every good thing we have in Christ.
7Your love has given me great joy and encouragement, because you,
brother, have refreshed the hearts of the saints.

Paul's Plea for Onesimus

8Therefore, although in Christ I could be bold and order you to do
what you ought to do, 9yet I appeal to you on the basis of love. I then,
as Paul—an old man and now also a prisoner of Christ Jesus— 10I
appeal to you for my son Onesimus,[a] who became my son while I was
in chains. 11Formerly he was useless to you, but now he has become
useful both to you and to me.
12I am sending him—who is my very heart—back to you. 13I would
have liked to keep him with me so that he could take your place in
helping me while I am in chains for the gospel. 14But I did not want to
do anything without your consent, so that any favor you do will be
spontaneous and not forced. 15Perhaps the reason he was separated
from you for a little while was that you might have him back for
good— 16no longer as a slave, but better than a slave, as a dear
brother. He is very dear to me but even dearer to you, both as a man
and as a brother in the Lord.
17So if you consider me a partner, welcome him as you would welcome me. 18If he has done you any wrong or owes you anything,
charge it to me. 19I, Paul, am writing this with my own hand. I will pay
it back—not to mention that you owe me your very self. 20I do wish,
brother, that I may have some benefit from you in the Lord; refresh
my heart in Christ. 21Confident of your obedience, I write to you,
knowing that you will do even more than I ask.
22And one thing more: Prepare a guest room for me, because I hope
to be restored to you in answer to your prayers.

23Epaphras, my fellow prisoner in Christ Jesus, sends you greetings. 24And so do Mark, Aristarchus, Demas and Luke, my fellow
workers.
25The grace of the Lord Jesus Christ be with your spirit.

[a]10 *Onesimus* means *useful.*

8–9 on the basis of love. Christian love, not a grudging obedience to Paul's command, was the only basis on which a true brotherly relationship could be built between Philemon and Onesimus. **old man ... prisoner.** While not appealing to his apostolic authority, Paul certainly appeals to the respect Philemon has for him! Paul's stress on his imprisonment (vv. 1,9,23) may be to hint that he too knows the limitations of a form of enslavement.

11 useless ... useful. There is a play on words here. These two words, which sound very similar in Greek, share a root word that was pronounced the same way as the word for "Christ" (*christos* means Christ; *chestos* means useful). Through Christ, Onesimus (whose name means useful), formerly a useless, disobedient slave, has now become truly useful as a brother in the Lord.

12 In spite of his love, Paul had to send Onesimus back since harboring a runaway slave was a serious crime. The reality of his conversion would be seen in his willingness to return to Philemon and face up to the consequences of what he had done. Christian slaves were expected to view their work for their master as work done as unto the Lord (Col. 3:22–25).

16 as a man and as a brother in the Lord. Literally, "in the flesh and in the Lord." "In the flesh" Onesimus is just a slave, but "in the Lord" he is now Philemon's spiritual brother.

17 partner. While Paul does not request Philemon to release Onesimus from slavery, ultimately it is this vision of love and mutuality between all types of Christians that undermines the justification for slavery or any form of economic oppression or social injustice.

18 Onesimus may have stolen some money before running away. Besides that, his escape caused economic loss through lost services.

19 This first part of this verse is a promissory note whereby Paul obligates himself to carry out the pledge he made in verse 18. The latter half of the verse reminds Philemon of the spiritual debt that he owes to Paul for the treasure of the Gospel to which Paul introduced him.

HEBREWS 11: HEROES OF FAITH

Abel
By faith offered the better sacrifice (v. 4)

Enoch
By faith pleased God and escaped death (v. 5)

Noah
By faith built the ark (v. 7)

Abraham
By faith made his home in a foreign promised land (v. 8)

Abraham and Sarah
By faith became parents when past age (v. 11)

Abraham
By faith offered his son as a sacrifice (vv. 17–19)

Isaac
By faith blessed his sons (v. 20)

Jacob
By faith blessed his grandsons (v. 21)

Joseph
By faith prophesied the Exodus (v. 22)

Moses' Parents
By faith concealed Moses from Pharaoh (v. 23)

Moses
By faith chose mistreatment, left Egypt,
and kept the Passover (vv. 24–28)

The Israelites
By faith passed through the Red Sea,
and marched around Jericho (vv. 29–30)

Rahab
By faith welcomed the Israelite spies (v. 31)

Hebrews

Author. No one knows who wrote the epistle to the Hebrews. The author is nowhere named within it, nor is there any strong external evidence pointing to one particular person. These facts have not deterred speculation, however. At least seven good candidates for the role of author have been proposed—Paul, Barnabas (Acts 4:36); Luke, Priscilla, Silas (1 Peter 5:12); Apollos (Acts 18:24) and Clement of Rome.

Personal Reading	Group Study Topic and Reading	
1:1–14	The Son Reigns	1:1–14
2:1–18	Christ Our Helper	2:5–18
3:1–19	Don't Turn Back!	3:7–19
4:1–13	The Promised Rest	4:1–13
4:14–5:10	The Great Priest	4:14–5:10
5:11–6:20	Don't Fall Away!	5:11–6:20
7:1–28	The New Priest	7:1–28
8:1–13	The New Covenant	8:1–13
9:1–28	The New Sacrifice	9:11–28
10:1–39	Hold On!	10:19–39
11:1–40	Examples of Faith	11:1–40
12:1–29	Run the Race!	12:1–29
13:1–25	A Life of Praise	13:1–25

Date. As with so much else about this epistle, it is difficult to be certain about its date of composition. If the persecution referred to is that of Nero, then Hebrews was written after A.D. 64. Some hold that it must have been written prior to the fall of Jerusalem and the destruction of the temple in A.D. 70, for such an unprecedented event would probably have been mentioned by the book's author as the sure sign of the end of the sacrificial system.

Theme. The superiority of Jesus.

Purpose. How does one write to suffering Christians (followers of Christ) and tell them to stay faithful despite the price they are paying? The author wisely begins not by considering their difficult circumstances nor by simply telling them, "This is the right thing to do, so do it." Instead, he points them to Jesus, the only one who is worth such costly allegiance. As a result, in the book of Hebrews, we get a marvelous portrait of Christ—the prophet, priest and king whose New Covenant is so superior to the Old Covenant that to fall away from him should be unthinkable. The central theme of Hebrews, therefore, is the superiority of Christ. He is superior to the great religious leaders of the past such as Moses, Joshua and Aaron. He is superior to the great supernatural powers like angels. The New Covenant he established and the new order he inaugurated are superior to the old beliefs and practices of the Jewish religion.

Historical Background. The title "To the Hebrews" can be traced back to manuscripts of the late second century. Even though it was not a part of the original document, it seems to be accurate given the very Jewish flavor of the epistle. This letter was probably written to a particular assembly of Jewish-Christian believers (perhaps a house church) that was part of a larger community, quite possibly in Rome.

Whoever these people were, it is clear that they had suffered great persecution (10:32–34) and that they were being tempted to abandon Christianity. The temptation to give up their faith was severe enough that the letter to the Hebrews had to be written to encourage these beleaguered believers to "hold on" (3:6), to "persevere" (10:36), and to "hold unswervingly to the hope we profess" (10:23) lest they compromise Christ and lose all the enormous blessings of the New Covenant.

Characteristics. Hebrews is filled with references to ancient practices, with the traditions of a wholly different culture, and with images that evoke no recognition in today's society.

This particular New Testament book has been called an epistle but in fact, it lacks several key features of a true letter. It has no introductory greeting, nor does it name either the sender or the recipients. Its ending is typical of a letter, however, with personal greetings and a standard conclusion.

If Hebrews is not a true letter, then what is it? Some have suggested that Hebrews is a written sermon. Its method of argument is sermonic in nature. Structurally, its closest New Testament parallel is 1 John, which also seems to be a sermon.

The Son Superior to Angels

1 In the past God spoke to our forefathers through the prophets at
many times and in various ways, [2]but in these last days he has
spoken to us by his Son, whom he appointed heir of all things, and
through whom he made the universe. [3]The Son is the radiance of
God's glory and the exact representation of his being, sustaining all
things by his powerful word. After he had provided purification for
sins, he sat down at the right hand of the Majesty in heaven. [4]So he
became as much superior to the angels as the name he has inherited
is superior to theirs.

[5]For to which of the angels did God ever say,

"You are my Son;
today I have become your Father"[a][b]?

Or again,

"I will be his Father,
and he will be my Son"[c]?

[6]And again, when God brings his firstborn into the world, he says,

"Let all God's angels worship him."[d]

[7]In speaking of the angels he says,

"He makes his angels winds,
his servants flames of fire."[e]

[8]But about the Son he says,

"Your throne, O God, will last for ever and ever,
and righteousness will be the scepter of your kingdom.
[9]You have loved righteousness and hated wickedness;
therefore God, your God, has set you above your companions
by anointing you with the oil of joy."[f]

[10]He also says,

"In the beginning, O Lord, you laid the foundations of the earth,
and the heavens are the work of your hands.
[11]They will perish, but you remain;
they will all wear out like a garment.
[12]You will roll them up like a robe;
like a garment they will be changed.

[a]5 Or *have begotten you* [b]5 Psalm 2:7 [c]5 2 Samuel 7:14; 1 Chron. 17:13 [d]6 Deut. 32:43 (see Dead Sea Scrolls and Septuagint) [e]7 Psalm 104:4 [f]9 Psalm 45:6,7

OPEN 1. Where did you grow up and what were the winters like? **2.** What was the major sport in your area and what team was superior during your teenage years?

STUDY 1. What have you found out that will be helpful in the study of the book of Hebrews while reading the introduction? **2.** If you were writing to a community in which some of the members have deserted the Christian faith and returned to their former religion, what would you try to do in the first few lines of your letter? **3.** In the first four verses what does the author set out to do? What are the seven claims about Christ that make him superior to angels? When you stop and think about each one of these claims, how do you feel? **4.** Why do you think the author had to go to such detail to prove the superiority of Christ over the angels in verses 5–13? What is the purpose of angels (v. 14)? **5.** Why do you think people today in the secular world who do not believe in Christ find it so easy to believe in angels?

APPLY 1. When did Jesus become more than just a name to you? **2.** What is the closest you have come to giving up your faith in Christ? What brought you back? **3.** How would you describe your spiritual life now in one or two words? **4.** What caused you to choose to study this book? **5.** What do you want out of this study?

1:1 through the prophets. The prophets were honored as those whom the Lord sent to speak to his people in times of need.

1:2 but. In contrast to the partial, limited revelation of the prophets, the Son fully reveals God to the world. **last days.** This term signifies time after Jesus' resurrection. Now that the Messiah had come, there was an expectation of a speedy culmination of history (Acts 2:17). **he has spoken.** By the description of Christ that follows, the author intends to show Jesus is superior to all the forms of communication used in the past.

1:3 the radiance of God's glory. God's glory is like light that radiates from its source. Jesus' miracles revealed God's glory (John 2:11), and thus made God known to people (John 1:18). **exact representation.** The Greek word *charakter* is used in engraving dies used for stamps. What is stamped bears the same image as is on the die. **sustaining all things.** The Son's role in creation was not limited to creation's origin or its future. It is his powerful word that keeps order and stability in creation (Col. 1:17). **purification for sins.** While popular thought held that people had to work for their own purification from sin, here we see that the Son has dealt with sin.

1:4 The Son, superior to the prophets, is also superior to the angels.

OPEN 1. In your family, who has a tendency to fall asleep in church? 2. What do you do to keep from falling asleep when you are driving?

STUDY 1. If you were writing to the spiritual grandchildren of the first generation of Christians and these grandchildren were drifting away from their profession of faith, what would you say? If you have grandchildren, how do they look upon your Christian faith? 2. How does the author answer his own question in verse 3 with four historical facts? What is the author doing here? 3. For these second generation spiritual grandchildren, what does the author set out to do in verses 5–15? Why would it be important to show Jesus in the role of the suffering Savior (v. 10) and the merciful and faithful high priest (v. 17)? Do you honestly believe that Jesus was tempted with the same human desires that you are tempted with? 4. What did Jesus do by his suffering and death for these Christians that the angels could not do (vv. 9,14–15)? For what purpose

But you remain the same,
and your years will never end."[a]

13 To which of the angels did God ever say,
"Sit at my right hand
until I make your enemies
a footstool for your feet"[b]?

14 Are not all angels ministering spirits sent to serve those who will inherit salvation?

Warning to Pay Attention

2 We must pay more careful attention, therefore, to what we have
heard, so that we do not drift away. 2 For if the message spoken
by angels was binding, and every violation and disobedience received
its just punishment, 3 how shall we escape if we ignore such a great
salvation? This salvation, which was first announced by the Lord,
was confirmed to us by those who heard him. 4 God also testified to it
by signs, wonders and various miracles, and gifts of the Holy Spirit
distributed according to his will.

Jesus Made Like His Brothers

5 It is not to angels that he has subjected the world to come, about
which we are speaking. 6 But there is a place where someone has testified:

"What is man that you are mindful of him,
the son of man that you care for him?
7 You made him a little[c] lower than the angels;
you crowned him with glory and honor
8 and put everything under his feet."[d]

In putting everything under him, God left nothing that is not subject
to him. Yet at present we do not see everything subject to him. 9 But
we see Jesus, who was made a little lower than the angels, now

[a] 12 Psalm 102:25-27 [b] 13 Psalm 110:1 [c] 7 Or *him for a little while;* also in verse 9 [d] 8 Psalm 8:4-6

1:14 In contrast to the ruling authority of the Son, the function of the angels is to serve his people at the Son's command. **ministering.** This word describes the priestly service at the tabernacle (8:4–6). In the New Testament, angels perform tasks such as interceding for children (Matt. 18:10), protecting the apostles (Acts 12:7–10), revealing God's will (Luke 1:11–38; Acts 8:26), and carrying out God's judgment (Rev. 7:1). **salvation.** Later passages indicate the author viewed salvation as a deliverance (from the devil's power—2:14; the fear of death—2:15; and the power of sin—9:26) leading to holiness (10:10), forgiveness (10:18), free access to God (10:22), and the eternal inheritance which God provides for those who have faith (9:15).

2:1 so that we do not drift away. This is the first of many indications that the readers were not as steadfast as they had once been (3:14; 4:1,14; 6:11–12; 10:26–38; 12:25). The image here is one in which people neglect their spiritual condition, bit by bit, such that they find themselves somehow far from where they started.

2:2–4 The author appeals to four things that show the divine origin of the message of the gospel: (1) It was the Lord, the Son, who first announced this message; (2) This message was supported by that of the apostles, men commissioned by the Son; (3) The signs, wonders and various miracles that have come through the apostles (v. 4) show the divine authorization of the message; and (4) The gifts of the Holy Spirit, personally experienced by these people and given for their mutual encouragement (1 Cor. 12; Eph. 4), give God's attestation to this message.

2:3 how shall we escape if we ignore such a great salvation? If the means of salvation is neglected, there is no way to avoid the judgment of God.

2:5–9 One evidence of the Son's superiority over the angels is seen in that authority in the age to come has been promised to him, not to them.

2:9 crowned ... because he suffered death. Jesus' death was not a denial of his glory, but the means through which this glory was revealed. **taste death for everyone.** The author hints at the purpose of Jesus' death, a theme developed more fully in chapters 7–10.

crowned with glory and honor because he suffered death, so that by the grace of God he might taste death for everyone.
[10]In bringing many sons to glory, it was fitting that God, for whom and through whom everything exists, should make the author of their salvation perfect through suffering. [11]Both the one who makes men
holy and those who are made holy are of the same family. So Jesus is not ashamed to call them brothers. [12]He says,

"I will declare your name to my brothers;
in the presence of the congregation I will sing your praises."[a]

[13]And again,

"I will put my trust in him."[b]

And again he says,

"Here am I, and the children God has given me."[c]

[14]Since the children have flesh and blood, he too shared in their humanity so that by his death he might destroy him who holds the power of death—that is, the devil— [15]and free those who all their
lives were held in slavery by their fear of death. [16]For surely it is not
angels he helps, but Abraham's descendants. [17]For this reason he had
to be made like his brothers in every way, in order that he might become a merciful and faithful high priest in service to God, and that he might make atonement for[d] the sins of the people. [18]Because he himself suffered when he was tempted, he is able to help those who are being tempted.

Jesus Greater Than Moses

3 Therefore, holy brothers, who share in the heavenly calling, fix your thoughts on Jesus, the apostle and high priest whom we

[a]12 Psalm 22:22 [b]13 Isaiah 8:17 [c]13 Isaiah 8:18 [d]17 Or *and that he might turn aside God's wrath, taking away*

(vv. 11,14,17)? **5.** What has the author done in this passage for these young Christians who are being targeted by the government for discrimination and abuse because they are Christians? **6.** In what respect was Jesus "made lower than the angels" (v. 9)? What elevated him above them? What does Jesus share in common with humanity (vv. 7,9)? In which respect is Jesus unique? **7.** Why did we need someone with flesh and blood like us—not an angel—to die in our place (vv. 14–18)?

APPLY 1. What painful experience or suffering have you gone through lately that has caused you to grow in your faith? **2.** What have you found helpful when you are tempted to "throw in the towel"? **3.** What have you learned from your pain about God that you could not learn in any other way?

OPEN 1. When lost on a trip, what do you do: Stop and ask directions? Check the map? Wander around until you find the way? **2.** Are you usually early or late getting to places, even to your small group?

2:10 In bringing many sons to glory. While interpreting Psalm 8 in reference to Jesus, the author acknowledges that God's will is to exalt humanity as the crown of creation. This will be accomplished through Jesus who is the salvation provided by God. **it was fitting.** While the idea of a suffering Messiah was unknown to the Jews, the author maintains that the idea is appropriate. **author.** Literally, "pioneer" (12:2). The image is of one who blazes the way, making it possible for others to follow. **make ... perfect.** This does not imply that Jesus had faults that needed to be purged.

2:16 Abraham's descendants. Since Jewish converts were the primary audience, the author points out that it is through Jesus that the ancient promise to Abraham is fulfilled (Gen. 12:3; Rom. 2:28; 4:4–25; Gal. 3:6–14).

2:17 like his brothers. Because of God's choice of Israel to be his people, the Son became a flesh and blood Jew. Only in this way could he truly serve as a representative of the people before God. **a merciful and faithful high priest.** The idea of the Messiah as a high priest is this author's unique way of communicating the identity of Jesus since it is found only here in the New Testament. **make atonement.** A priest's main function was to offer the blood of a sacrifice in place of the blood of the sinner. Chapters 9–10 interprets Jesus' death in this framework.

2:18 Jesus is more, not less, able to help those who are currently tempted. Jesus' humanity, rather than detracting from his elevated status, fully qualifies him to enter into the struggles of his people. He can help them in a way angels never could (4:15).

3:1–6 The readers should hold on to their faith because Jesus is far more worthy of honor than even Moses, a man revered through the centuries as the one through whom the Law of God was given to Israel.

3:1 Two phrases are used to remind the readers of who they are in Christ. **holy brothers.** This does not mean they are morally perfect, but that they have been "set apart" by God as his people (2:11–13). **who share in the heavenly calling.** Since the readers share together in God's call, they have special responsibilities toward God and one another. **fix your thoughts.** This implies concentrated attention and reflection. While Jesus helps believers deal with temptations, they are to focus their attention on him such that they will not be distracted by temptations to follow another course (12:2). **the apostle.** One sent with the full authority of the one who sent him or her (John 1:18).

STUDY **1.** What is the challenge for these Christians who are going through real suffering? **2.** In mentioning Moses, what is the author doing for these Christians who come from a Jewish background? How do Jesus and Moses compare? **3.** What happened to the Israelites on their journey from Egypt to the Promised Land that the author uses to warn these Christians about (Num. 14)? **4.** What responsibility does the Christian community have for one another (vv. 12–13)? **5.** If you were one of the people in the church here who was thinking about returning to your former religion what would this passage say to you? What would it make you do?

APPLY **1.** What is the closest you have come to going through a period of dryness when you felt spiritually empty, exhausted and burned out? **2.** Who do you turn to when you are struggling with your faith and personal stuff in your life? **3.** In this community (or group) how comfortable are you in sharing your struggles, fears, doubts and sins?

---

confess. [2]He was faithful to the one who appointed him, just as Moses was faithful in all God's house. [3]Jesus has been found worthy of
greater honor than Moses, just as the builder of a house has greater
honor than the house itself. [4]For every house is built by someone, but
God is the builder of everything. [5]Moses was faithful as a servant in
all God's house, testifying to what would be said in the future. [6]But
Christ is faithful as a son over God's house. And we are his house, if
we hold on to our courage and the hope of which we boast.

Warning Against Unbelief

[7]So, as the Holy Spirit says:

"Today, if you hear his voice,
[8] do not harden your hearts
as you did in the rebellion,
during the time of testing in the desert,
[9]where your fathers tested and tried me
and for forty years saw what I did.
[10]That is why I was angry with that generation,
and I said, 'Their hearts are always going astray,
and they have not known my ways.'
[11]So I declared on oath in my anger,
'They shall never enter my rest.' "[a]

[12]See to it, brothers, that none of you has a sinful, unbelieving
heart that turns away from the living God. [13]But encourage one another daily, as long as it is called Today, so that none of you may be
hardened by sin's deceitfulness. [14]We have come to share in Christ if
we hold firmly till the end the confidence we had at first. [15]As has just
been said:

"Today, if you hear his voice,
do not harden your hearts
as you did in the rebellion."[b]

[16]Who were they who heard and rebelled? Were they not all those
Moses led out of Egypt? [17]And with whom was he angry for forty
years? Was it not with those who sinned, whose bodies fell in the
desert? [18]And to whom did God swear that they would never enter his
rest if not to those who disobeyed[c]? [19]So we see that they were not
able to enter, because of their unbelief.

[a]11 Psalm 95:7-11 [b]15 Psalm 95:7,8 [c]18 Or *disbelieved*

3:3–6 Two analogies substantiate the claim that Jesus is worthy of far more honor than even Moses: (1) In terms of a house (or dynasty), Jesus is the builder (1:2) whereas Moses is part of the house itself; and (2) Moses was faithful as a servant, but Jesus is the son who owns the estate.

3:6 son. Jesus' position as God's Son (1:2) undoubtedly prompted this analogy. **courage.** Literally, "confidence." **the hope.** This is not a wish, but an expectation that is guaranteed to come about.

3:7–11 The psalmist recalls in Psalm 95:1–11 how the Israelites rebelled against both the Law and the mercies of God and thus never inherited the promise for which they had been delivered from Egypt. The Hebrew text of the psalm shows that Exodus 17:1–7 is in view although its last verse points to Numbers 14:22–30.

3:11 my rest. In the context of the Israelites, this meant the Promised Land of Canaan where they would have prosperity and peace (4:1).

3:12 turns away. Literally, "apostatizes." Whereas the warning in 2:1 was against "drifting" from the Lord, the concern here is a deliberate turning from God's way.

3:14 confidence. The readers are exhorted to hold fast to the teaching they originally received concerning Christ.

3:16–19 Through the five questions based on events in Numbers 14:26–35, the author hammers home the importance of maintaining faith.

A Sabbath-Rest for the People of God

4 Therefore, since the promise of entering his rest still stands, let
us be careful that none of you be found to have fallen short of it.
2For we also have had the gospel preached to us, just as they did; but
the message they heard was of no value to them, because those who
heard did not combine it with faith.[a] 3Now we who have believed enter that rest, just as God has said,

"So I declared on oath in my anger,
'They shall never enter my rest.' "[b]

And yet his work has been finished since the creation of the world.
4For somewhere he has spoken about the seventh day in these words:
"And on the seventh day God rested from all his work."[c] 5And again in
the passage above he says, "They shall never enter my rest."
6It still remains that some will enter that rest, and those who formerly had the gospel preached to them did not go in, because of their
disobedience. 7Therefore God again set a certain day, calling it Today,
when a long time later he spoke through David, as was said before:

"Today, if you hear his voice,
do not harden your hearts."[d]

8For if Joshua had given them rest, God would not have spoken later
about another day. 9There remains, then, a Sabbath-rest for the
people of God; 10for anyone who enters God's rest also rests from his
own work, just as God did from his. 11Let us, therefore, make every
effort to enter that rest, so that no one will fall by following their
example of disobedience.
12For the word of God is living and active. Sharper than any
double-edged sword, it penetrates even to dividing soul and spirit,
joints and marrow; it judges the thoughts and attitudes of the heart.
13Nothing in all creation is hidden from God's sight. Everything is
uncovered and laid bare before the eyes of him to whom we must give
account.

OPEN What is your favorite way to spend a Sunday afternoon?

STUDY 1. What do you remember about the origin of the Sabbath? **2.** What is the "rest" promised by God: Sunday off? The Promised Land? Heaven? God's presence? How do verses 3–10 support your answer? **3.** Did God withdraw his offer to the original people who were given the promise? What happened? **4.** What is the warning to those who are reading this letter? What does it mean that God's word is "living"? Active? That it penetrates?

APPLY 1. How would you describe your spiritual diet right now: Healthy? Balanced? Pretty good? Sporadic? Could be better? Terrible? **2.** What have you found helpful in keeping a regular devotional life?

[a]2 Many manuscripts *because they did not share in the faith of those who obeyed* [b]3 Psalm 95:11; also in verse 5 [c]4 Gen. 2:2 [d]7 Psalm 95:7,8

4:1 the promise. God's promise was to bring Israel into a "good and spacious land" where they would have peace (Ex. 3:8). However, the generation who originally received this promise never experienced its fulfillment. **his rest.** Rest is not a state of idleness but a condition in which one is free to live in peace, joy, security and freedom. Israel thought of rest in terms of dwelling securely in their own land in freedom and prosperity (Deut. 5:33; 8:6–9). Later on, this developed into the hope of an eternal kingdom under the wise, compassionate leadership of a Davidic king (Ezek. 34:24–31; Dan. 7:13–14). It is likely that at least some of the original readers thought of this rest in such national, physical terms (Acts 1:6). **let us be careful.** Literally, "let us fear."

4:9 Sabbath-rest. This term, found only here in the New Testament, is a play on words since the Greek words for "sabbath" and "rest" sound alike. It identifies this rest with the traditional Jewish Sabbath rest, yet accents that this rest fulfills the reality which that one symbolized. Once again Jesus' superiority over all elements of traditional Jewish faith is emphasized. **the people of God.** This includes all people, Jew or Gentile, who entrust themselves to Jesus.

4:11 make every effort. Literally, "strive." The life of faith is not a passive waiting for God, but an urgent, determined resolve to push on in the pursuit of God.

4:12 The comparison of God's Word to a sword was first made by Isaiah (Isa. 49:2). It shows the piercing, discerning power of God's Word to cut through people's thoughts, intentions, and motivations (Eph. 6:17; Rev. 1:16). **dividing soul and spirit, joints and marrow ... thoughts and attitudes of the heart.** The whole person—spirit, body and mind (the heart was referred to as the source of one's thought process)—is spoken to by God's Word.

4:13 laid bare. Three possibilities exist as to the meaning of this graphic image. It may refer to: (1) A wrestler whose head has been thrust back rendering him vulnerable to being pinned; (2) A soldier without armor to cover his throat; (3) A sacrificial animal whose neck is bared so that a knife can be drawn across its throat. All three images portray a frightening picture of being defenseless before an opponent.

OPEN **1.** When you were a kid, did you go to "confession"? **2.** Do you have someone you are accountable to, that you can share your "confessions" with?

STUDY **1.** Is the author of Hebrews promising a life without hardship if you turn over your life to God? **2.** What does the author say about Jesus Christ that would qualify him to understand the pain that someone is going through? **3.** What do you know about the office of priesthood in the Old Testament? **4.** What is it about Jesus that makes him a better priest to represent you to God than the priests who were appointed in the Old Testament? **5.** Do you honestly feel that he has struggled with the same problems that you struggle with?

APPLY **1.** Do you believe in the priesthood of all believers? **2.** Do you believe that Christians should confess their sins to one another in a caring community? **3.** Who do you have to help you through your dark moments? **4.** Could this group pray for you?

Jesus the Great High Priest

14Therefore, since we have a great high priest who has gone
through the heavens,[a] Jesus the Son of God, let us hold firmly to the
faith we profess. 15For we do not have a high priest who is unable to
sympathize with our weaknesses, but we have one who has been
tempted in every way, just as we are—yet was without sin. 16Let us
then approach the throne of grace with confidence, so that we may
receive mercy and find grace to help us in our time of need.

5 Every high priest is selected from among men and is appointed
to represent them in matters related to God, to offer gifts and
sacrifices for sins. 2He is able to deal gently with those who are ignorant and are going astray, since he himself is subject to weakness.
3This is why he has to offer sacrifices for his own sins, as well as for
the sins of the people.

4No one takes this honor upon himself; he must be called by God,
just as Aaron was. 5So Christ also did not take upon himself the glory
of becoming a high priest. But God said to him,

"You are my Son;
today I have become your Father."[b][c]

6And he says in another place,

"You are a priest forever,
in the order of Melchizedek."[d]

7During the days of Jesus' life on earth, he offered up prayers and
petitions with loud cries and tears to the one who could save him
from death, and he was heard because of his reverent submission.
8Although he was a son, he learned obedience from what he suffered
9and, once made perfect, he became the source of eternal salvation
for all who obey him 10and was designated by God to be high priest in
the order of Melchizedek.

[a]14 *Or gone into heaven* [b]5 *Or have begotten you* [c]5 Psalm 2:7 [d]6 Psalm 110:4

4:14 a great high priest. The high priest served as the spiritual (and oftentimes civil) leader of the Jews. His most unique function was to bring a sacrifice to God in the Most Holy Place on the Day of Atonement (9:3,8; Lev. 16:17). **gone through the heavens.** As the high priest would pass through a curtain into the Most Holy Place in the tabernacle, so Jesus entered into the presence of God as the representative of those who trust in him. Heaven is often referred to in the plural form in the Old Testament.

4:15 tempted in every way. Jesus was tempted in the desert by Satan (Luke 4:1–13). Here we find that he experiences every kind of temptation that we face. **without sin.** Technically, every high priest was without sin before offering atonement for the people. This was achieved by offering a sacrifice for himself prior to offering those for the people (5:3). Jesus' superiority over the Old Testament priesthood is that he had no sin for which to offer sacrifice.

4:16 approach. This word describes the high priest's drawing near to the Most Holy Place. **the throne of grace.** Jesus sits at the right hand of God, interceding for us. **with confidence.** The readers are urged to approach God, knowing they have a compassionate, perfect high priest who is gracious and merciful to the needy (6:20).

5:5–6 Jesus, the God-appointed priest-ly-king. Psalms 2:7 and 110:4 are linked to show that Jesus' priesthood can be traced to the mysterious Old Testament figure of Melchizedek, a king/priest who lived long before Aaron was born (Gen. 14:18–19). This connection between the Messiah and Melchizedek was unique to this author: it has no parallels in either Jewish or Christian thought of the time.

5:7 prayers and petitions. The two words overlap, but the latter most often indicates an intense pleading. **loud cries and tears.** Western culture does not typically associate such emotion with prayer, but this would be a normal part of sincere intercession by the faithful Jew. Jesus' prayer in Gethsemane may be in view (Matt. 26:36–42). **and he was heard.** In one sense Jesus was not "saved from death." He had to pass through it to experience resurrection. The readers' experience may well be similar. **reverent submission.** Literally, "his godly fear."

Warning Against Falling Away

11 We have much to say about this, but it is hard to explain because
you are slow to learn. 12 In fact, though by this time you ought to be
teachers, you need someone to teach you the elementary truths of
God's word all over again. You need milk, not solid food! 13 Anyone
who lives on milk, being still an infant, is not acquainted with the
teaching about righteousness. 14 But solid food is for the mature, who
by constant use have trained themselves to distinguish good from
evil.

6 Therefore let us leave the elementary teachings about Christ and
go on to maturity, not laying again the foundation of repentance
from acts that lead to death,[a] and of faith in God, 2 instruction about
baptisms, the laying on of hands, the resurrection of the dead, and
eternal judgment. 3 And God permitting, we will do so.

4 It is impossible for those who have once been enlightened, who
have tasted the heavenly gift, who have shared in the Holy Spirit,
5 who have tasted the goodness of the word of God and the powers of
the coming age, 6 if they fall away, to be brought back to repentance,
because[b] to their loss they are crucifying the Son of God all over
again and subjecting him to public disgrace.

7 Land that drinks in the rain often falling on it and that produces a
crop useful to those for whom it is farmed receives the blessing of
God. 8 But land that produces thorns and thistles is worthless and is
in danger of being cursed. In the end it will be burned.

9 Even though we speak like this, dear friends, we are confident of
better things in your case—things that accompany salvation. 10 God is
not unjust; he will not forget your work and the love you have shown
him as you have helped his people and continue to help them. 11 We
want each of you to show this same diligence to the very end, in order to make your hope sure. 12 We do not want you to become lazy, but
to imitate those who through faith and patience inherit what has
been promised.

[a] *1 Or from useless rituals* [b] *6 Or repentance while*

OPEN 1. How did your parents react when you brought home a bad report card? **2.** What teacher or coach challenged you to do better to live up to your potential?

STUDY 1. What is the tone in 5:11–14: Anger? Frustration? Condescension? Anguish? Sadness? Why was the author not able to go into the deeper teaching about the priesthood of Jesus Christ? **2.** What does the author want these "babies" in the faith to do? If you had been their leader and had taken these Christians through confirmation class (5:1–4), how would you be feeling? **3.** Is their fate (6:6) reversible? What is the warning here to those who are turning their backs on their Christian faith after becoming a Christian? **4.** How would you describe the author's words in 6:9–12: Locker room pep talk? Battlefield challenge? Parent lecture to a failing child?

APPLY 1. What is your appetite like for the deeper things of God: I'm starving? I'm hungry? I like to nibble? I've lost my appetite? **2.** How can this group lift you up in prayer this week?

5:12 milk ... solid food. While these readers have been believers long enough to have become "teachers," their uncertain faithfulness is more akin to that of "babies," just beginning to walk with Christ.

5:13–14 not acquainted ... by constant use have trained themselves. Spiritual maturity, like emotional maturity, is developed through practicing what leads to responsible development.

6:1–2 The only way to become trained (5:14) is to start exercising. The author wants to move on to weightier matters. **repentance ... faith; baptisms ... laying on of hands; resurrection ... judgment.** These three couplets focus on basic elements of the Christian life, church practices and doctrine. All could be found in Judaism and the readers may have lost sight of how Jesus has changed their meaning. The themes that dominate the rest of the book; Jesus' role as high priest and sacrifice, will remind them. **acts that lead to death.** Literally, "from dead works." These are acts that stem from sin and lead to death. Repentance from sin was the first note of the gospel message (Mark 1:14–15). **baptisms.** Some Jewish sects practiced ablutions for cleansing far beyond what the Law required.

6:4–6 Western Christians often think of the terms in this warning in a subjective, individual sense and wonder how someone who has been touched by God like this could give up faith. The author was likely not referring to subjective experiences at all but to "tasting the heavenly gift" as the Lord's Supper; "sharing in the Holy Spirit" as the laying on of hands (a sign that the person was included in the community of the Spirit); "tasting the word of God" as hearing gospel preaching; and "tasting the powers of the coming age" as observing the use of spiritual gifts within the church. Jewish Christians viewed these rituals as vital expressions of faith. To partake in them and then deliberately choose not to live up to the obligations they represent was unthinkable. **impossible ... to be brought back.** Since to leave required a deliberate, conscious act, there could be no reasonable expectation that such people would ever return.

6:9–12 The warning gives way to encouragement. Their works of love indicates they have not fallen away (v. 10). They are urged to keep on that course, following the example of others in the past who held on to God's promises (v. 12)

OPEN Have you ever appeared in court and swore, "To tell the truth; the whole truth and nothing but the truth"?

STUDY 1. If you wanted to encourage someone who was dropping out of the church because they didn't think Christianity was any different from any other religion, what would you do? **2.** When Abraham left his comfort zone, what did Abraham have to go on?

APPLY 1. When your life is falling apart, what is the anchor for your soul? **2.** What is the promise you have staked your life on?

OPEN Who was your hero who could do no wrong when you were a kid?

STUDY 1. If you were writing to people that knew a lot about priests and you wanted to use their knowledge to show how Jesus Christ was superior to the priests in the Old Testament, what would you do? **2.** Building on the story about Melchizedek that left off in 5:10, what have you learned about him? **3.** What is the main point in the comparison between Melchizedek and the priesthood that originated with the tribe of Levi and Aaron? **4.** Why did the Old Testament Levitical priesthood fail to produce righteousness in the people (v. 18)? When you tried to live a good, moral life in your own power, how did you do? **5.** In practical terms, what does Jesus Christ offer to the believer that the Old Testament could not offer to those who are powerless and guilt stricken? Why? **6.** What is the difference between religion and Christianity?

APPLY 1. From your own experience, what is the difference between Christianity and religion? When did Jesus Christ be-

The Certainty of God's Promise

[13]When God made his promise to Abraham, since there was no one
greater for him to swear by, he swore by himself, [14]saying, "I will
surely bless you and give you many descendants."[a] [15]And so after
waiting patiently, Abraham received what was promised.
[16]Men swear by someone greater than themselves, and the oath
confirms what is said and puts an end to all argument. [17]Because God
wanted to make the unchanging nature of his purpose very clear to
the heirs of what was promised, he confirmed it with an oath. [18]God
did this so that, by two unchangeable things in which it is impossible
for God to lie, we who have fled to take hold of the hope offered to us
may be greatly encouraged. [19]We have this hope as an anchor for the
soul, firm and secure. It enters the inner sanctuary behind the curtain, [20]where Jesus, who went before us, has entered on our behalf.
He has become a high priest forever, in the order of Melchizedek.

Melchizedek the Priest

7 This Melchizedek was king of Salem and priest of God Most
High. He met Abraham returning from the defeat of the kings
and blessed him, [2]and Abraham gave him a tenth of everything. First,
his name means "king of righteousness"; then also, "king of Salem"
means "king of peace." [3]Without father or mother, without genealogy, without beginning of days or end of life, like the Son of God he
remains a priest forever.
[4]Just think how great he was: Even the patriarch Abraham gave him
a tenth of the plunder! [5]Now the law requires the descendants of Levi
who become priests to collect a tenth from the people—that is, their
brothers—even though their brothers are descended from Abraham.
[6]This man, however, did not trace his descent from Levi, yet he collected a tenth from Abraham and blessed him who had the promises.
[7]And without doubt the lesser person is blessed by the greater. [8]In the
one case, the tenth is collected by men who die; but in the other case,
by him who is declared to be living. [9]One might even say that Levi,
who collects the tenth, paid the tenth through Abraham, [10]because
when Melchizedek met Abraham, Levi was still in the body of his ancestor.

Jesus Like Melchizedek

[11]If perfection could have been attained through the Levitical
priesthood (for on the basis of it the law was given to the people),

[a] 14 Gen. 22:17

7:1 Although there is no other information about Melchizedek besides Genesis 14:18–20 and Hebrews, he would not have been as obscure a figure to the original readers as he is to readers today. **king of Salem.** This city was associated with the site of Jerusalem. **the defeat of the kings.** Abraham had fought against a coalition of tribal rulers.

7:2 gave him a tenth. The tribute may have been given as an acknowledgment of Melchizedek's relationship with Abraham's God. In any case Abraham recognized Melchizedek as a superior, worthy of the title. **king of righteousness ... king of peace.** Since vowels were never written in Hebrew, both "Salem" and "peace [*shalom*]" were spelled *slm*— allowing for an easy identification of the two words.

7:4–10 Melchizedek's priesthood is compared to that of Levi (Num. 8). In the mindset of an Israelite, what my ancestor did was what I did—for I was part of him or her; what I do reflects what my ancestor did, since he or she lives on in me. Since Abraham paid tribute to Melchizedek, therefore the Levitical priests, as Abraham's descendants, also paid tribute to him. Since tribute is paid from the lesser to the greater, Melchizedek's priesthood is superior to that of the Levites.

7:11–19 The need for a new high priest is the theme of this section.

why was there still need for another priest to come—one in the order of Melchizedek, not in the order of Aaron? [12]For when there is a change of the priesthood, there must also be a change of the law. [13]He of whom these things are said belonged to a different tribe, and no one from that tribe has ever served at the altar. [14]For it is clear that our Lord descended from Judah, and in regard to that tribe Moses said nothing about priests. [15]And what we have said is even more clear if another priest like Melchizedek appears, [16]one who has become a priest not on the basis of a regulation as to his ancestry but on the basis of the power of an indestructible life. [17]For it is declared:

"You are a priest forever,
in the order of Melchizedek."[a]

[18]The former regulation is set aside because it was weak and useless [19](for the law made nothing perfect), and a better hope is introduced, by which we draw near to God.

[20]And it was not without an oath! Others became priests without any oath, [21]but he became a priest with an oath when God said to him:

"The Lord has sworn
and will not change his mind:
'You are a priest forever.' "[a]

[22]Because of this oath, Jesus has become the guarantee of a better covenant.

[23]Now there have been many of those priests, since death prevented them from continuing in office; [24]but because Jesus lives forever, he has a permanent priesthood. [25]Therefore he is able to save completely[b] those who come to God through him, because he always lives to intercede for them.

[26]Such a high priest meets our need—one who is holy, blameless, pure, set apart from sinners, exalted above the heavens. [27]Unlike the other high priests, he does not need to offer sacrifices day after day, first for his own sins, and then for the sins of the people. He sacrificed for their sins once for all when he offered himself. [28]For the law appoints as high priests men who are weak; but the oath, which came after the law, appointed the Son, who has been made perfect forever.

[a]*17,21* Psalm 110:4 [b]*25* Or *forever*

come more than just a name to you? 2. How does the "once-for-all" sacrifice of Jesus Christ help you to deal with your own shortcomings?

7:16–17 The Levitical priesthood was based solely on ancestry. The new priesthood is based on one's eternal nature. Jesus' resurrection thus qualified him to be the better high priest foretold in Psalm 110 (v. 17).

7:18–19 perfect. While the endless repetition of sacrifices served to remind people of their sin, it was powerless to change their condition (10:3–4; Rom. 3:20).

7:20–21 oath. The Levitical priests were appointed by divine command (Num. 8), but there was no oath involved. In contrast, as the full quote from Psalm 110:4 reveals, God's promise of a new high priest is sealed with an oath.

7:22 guarantee. This literally means "surety." Covenants were sealed with a pledge as a token that their terms would be carried out. Jesus' sacrifice is God's pledge of the new covenant. **a better covenant.** A covenant was a binding commitment of mutual obligations between two parties. In the case of ancient kings, covenants were unilateral in that the king determined what both he and his subjects would do for one another.

7:23–24 Naturally, priests died, and so their service was only temporary; they had to be replaced. Jesus' superior priesthood is evidenced by the fact that his is permanent.

7:25 save completely. One of this letter's main themes is that Jesus has the power to truly cleanse believers from sin and thus enable them to draw near to God.

The High Priest of a New Covenant

8 The point of what we are saying is this: We do have such a high priest, who sat down at the right hand of the throne of the Majesty in heaven, 2and who serves in the sanctuary, the true tabernacle set up by the Lord, not by man.

3Every high priest is appointed to offer both gifts and sacrifices, and so it was necessary for this one also to have something to offer. 4If he were on earth, he would not be a priest, for there are already men who offer the gifts prescribed by the law. 5They serve at a sanctuary that is a copy and shadow of what is in heaven. This is why Moses was warned when he was about to build the tabernacle: "See to it that you make everything according to the pattern shown you on the mountain."[a] 6But the ministry Jesus has received is as superior to theirs as the covenant of which he is mediator is superior to the old one, and it is founded on better promises.

7For if there had been nothing wrong with that first covenant, no place would have been sought for another. 8But God found fault with the people and said[b]:

"The time is coming, declares the Lord,
  when I will make a new covenant
with the house of Israel
  and with the house of Judah.
9It will not be like the covenant
  I made with their forefathers
when I took them by the hand
  to lead them out of Egypt,
because they did not remain faithful to my covenant,
  and I turned away from them, declares the Lord.
10This is the covenant I will make with the house of Israel
  after that time, declares the Lord.
I will put my laws in their minds
  and write them on their hearts.
I will be their God,

[a]5 Exodus 25:40 [b]8 Some manuscripts may be translated *fault and said to the people.*

OPEN 1. If your car develops chronic problems, are you the type to keep fixing it up, or to buy a new one? How do you decide when it's got to go? **2.** If you were building a house, would you expect the builder to follow the architect's drawing or do their own thing?

STUDY 1. What do you remember about the tabernacle in the Old Testament? What was it for? **2.** Who is the high priest the author refers to in verse 1 and what is different about the tabernacle this priest serves in? **3.** Where did the plans for the Old Testament tabernacle come from (Ex. 26)? What are they based on? **4.** What was wrong with the Old Testament covenant and the rules and regulations for living a holy life (Ex. 24)? In the quote from the prophet Jeremiah in verses 8–12, what is different about the two covenants? Why will people living under the new covenant be able to accomplish that which the old covenant could not (vv. 7–13)?

APPLY 1. In your spiritual pilgrimage, what made you come to the conclusion that Christianity was true and worth committing your life and soul to? Was your decision to become a Christian based on your intellectual investigation or a leap of faith? **2.** Do you rely on rational explanations of your faith or do you find there are unexplainable mysteries of God that you must accept by faith?

8:1–6 This passage begins to consider the value of Jesus' priestly offering, a theme taken up in detail in chapters 9–10.

8:2 sanctuary. This refers to the Most Holy Place (9:3). **tabernacle.** God gave Moses a pattern for how to build a copy of the true heavenly tabernacle (Ex. 26). Jesus' greatness is seen in that he serves in this true tabernacle, not in an earthly copy. The tabernacle, an elaborate moveable tent, gave way to Solomon's Temple and, later still, to the Herodian Temple destroyed by the Romans in A.D. 70. The fact that the author does not refer to its destruction as proof that the old order had passed away (v. 13) is a strong clue that the letter was written prior to that date. The focus on the tabernacle may have been because some Jewish sects considered the current administration of the temple services to be corrupted and invalid.

8:3 gifts and sacrifices. A primary function of the Old Testament high priests was to offer sacrifice on the Day of Atonement (Lev. 16). Jesus, as a priest, must likewise have a sacrifice to offer—namely, himself (7:27).

8:5 copy and shadow. These words communicate the difference between the physical, visible nature of the old covenant and the spiritual, heavenly nature of the new. The quote is from Exodus 25:40.

8:6 Jesus' ministry supersedes that of the old priests because the new covenant accomplishes that which the old never could (vv. 7–13). **mediator.** Since a covenant involved two parties, the mediator served as a go-between to work out the various terms of the covenant among the two parties making the covenant. **better promises.** The new covenant promises are "better" in that they promise far more than was ever promised in the old.

8:8–12 Jeremiah prophesied just prior to Babylon's conquest of Judah in 586 B.C. When the Jews were free to return to Jerusalem about 70 years later, expectations ran high that this prophecy was being fulfilled. Christians saw it fulfilled instead in the covenant established by Christ.

and they will be my people.
[11]No longer will a man teach his neighbor,
or a man his brother, saying, 'Know the Lord,'
because they will all know me,
from the least of them to the greatest.
[12]For I will forgive their wickedness
and will remember their sins no more."[a]

[13]By calling this covenant "new," he has made the first one obsolete; and what is obsolete and aging will soon disappear.

Worship in the Earthly Tabernacle

9 Now the first covenant had regulations for worship and also an
earthly sanctuary. [2]A tabernacle was set up. In its first room were
the lampstand, the table and the consecrated bread; this was called
the Holy Place. [3]Behind the second curtain was a room called the
Most Holy Place, [4]which had the golden altar of incense and the gold-
covered ark of the covenant. This ark contained the gold jar of manna, Aaron's staff that had budded, and the stone tablets of the
covenant. [5]Above the ark were the cherubim of the Glory, overshadowing the atonement cover.[b] But we cannot discuss these things in
detail now.

[6]When everything had been arranged like this, the priests entered
regularly into the outer room to carry on their ministry. [7]But only the
high priest entered the inner room, and that only once a year, and
never without blood, which he offered for himself and for the sins the
people had committed in ignorance. [8]The Holy Spirit was showing by
this that the way into the Most Holy Place had not yet been disclosed
as long as the first tabernacle was still standing. [9]This is an illustration for the present time, indicating that the gifts and sacrifices being
offered were not able to clear the conscience of the worshiper. [10]They
are only a matter of food and drink and various ceremonial washings—external regulations applying until the time of the new order.

[a]*12* Jer. 31:31-34 [b]*5* Traditionally *the mercy seat*

OPEN In your childhood home, what place was off limits? What thing were you told, "Don't touch"?

STUDY 1. How do you picture the earthly sanctuary described in verses 1–5? What is the significance of each item in the Holy Place? In the Most Holy Place? **2.** What goes on in the outer room (vv. 6–10)? In the inner room (Lev 16:14–16)? **3.** What did not happen here at this time (vv. 8–9)? Why were their gifts and sacrifices not sufficient to clear their consciences (to cover all their sins)?

APPLY 1. What is your practice for keeping the lines of communication between you and God open? **2.** What do you do with a guilty conscience?

9:2 The tabernacle, a flat-roofed tent about 15 by 45 feet, had two curtains forming separate rooms (Ex. 26). Priests entering the tabernacle through the first curtain came into the "Holy Place" where they carried out their daily functions. **the lampstand.** A seven-branched lampstand (Ex. 25:31–40) provided the only light in the otherwise dark tent. **the table ... consecrated bread.** Twelve loaves of fresh bread were placed daily upon this table (Ex. 25:23–30; Lev. 24:5–9).

9:3 the Most Holy Place. Behind the second curtain was a small (about nine by 15 feet), dark, mysterious place reserved for God and at special times the high priest. Here God said he would meet Moses (Ex. 25:22).

9:4 the golden altar of incense. This appears to have actually stood outside of the Most Holy Place, but there is some ambiguity about it (Ex. 30:1–10; 40:5; 1 Kin. 6:22). **ark of the covenant.** A box in which were: (1) The jar of manna—a reminder of God's care for the people during their time in the wilderness; (2) Aaron's staff—a reminder of God's election of his sons as priests; and (3) The stone tablets (the Ten Commandments)—a reminder of Israel's covenant responsibilities.

9:5 the cherubim. Two winged statues, representative of the angelic protection of God's honor, stood over the ark (Ex. 25:18). **the Glory.** A reverent way of referring to God (1:3). **the atonement cover.** The top of the ark (Ex. 25:17–22) upon which the high priest sprinkled blood on the Day of Atonement.

9:7–8 the way ... had not yet been disclosed. The entire setup of the tabernacle reinforced this point. The altar for sacrifice, where the people brought their sacrifices, was outside the tabernacle; directly in line with that, but inside the first curtain of the tabernacle, was the altar where only priests could go; behind that was the Most Holy Place into which only the high priest could enter only on the Day of Atonement and only if he first offered a sacrifice for himself (Lev. 16).

OPEN 1. What was the rule in your family on washing your hands? On taking a bath? **2.** Have you written a will? When will it take force?

STUDY 1. Do you think the Jewish Christians that the author is writing to have an advantage in understanding the meaning of the sacrifice of Jesus Christ? Why? **2.** What did the Old Testament priests do to atone for the sins of the people? What did Christ do? What will the sacrifice of Christ do for sinners that the sacrifice of animals could not do? **3.** What does the word "ransom" mean to you (v. 15)? In what sense did Christ become the ransom and the liberator of those who were held hostage by sin? **4.** What is the difference between the sacrifices in the Old Testament religion and the sacrifice of Jesus Christ? Why do Christians not offer sacrifices today? **5.** If you had to write a definition of the word "salvation," what would you say? How would you draw upon this passage to support your definition? **6.** What do your secular friends say about Jesus Christ? How do they look upon his death? His resurrection?

APPLY 1. When did the full meaning of the person and work of Jesus Christ as the "lamb of God" to take away the sins of

The Blood of Christ

11 When Christ came as high priest of the good things that are already here,[a] he went through the greater and more perfect tabernacle
that is not man-made, that is to say, not a part of this creation. 12 He
did not enter by means of the blood of goats and calves; but he entered the Most Holy Place once for all by his own blood, having obtained eternal redemption. 13 The blood of goats and bulls and the
ashes of a heifer sprinkled on those who are ceremonially unclean
sanctify them so that they are outwardly clean. 14 How much more,
then, will the blood of Christ, who through the eternal Spirit offered
himself unblemished to God, cleanse our consciences from acts that
lead to death,[b] so that we may serve the living God!

15 For this reason Christ is the mediator of a new covenant, that
those who are called may receive the promised eternal inheritance—
now that he has died as a ransom to set them free from the sins committed under the first covenant.

16 In the case of a will,[c] it is necessary to prove the death of the one
who made it, 17 because a will is in force only when somebody has
died; it never takes effect while the one who made it is living. 18 This is
why even the first covenant was not put into effect without blood.
19 When Moses had proclaimed every commandment of the law to all
the people, he took the blood of calves, together with water, scarlet
wool and branches of hyssop, and sprinkled the scroll and all the
people. 20 He said, "This is the blood of the covenant, which God has
commanded you to keep."[d] 21 In the same way, he sprinkled with the
blood both the tabernacle and everything used in its ceremonies. 22 In
fact, the law requires that nearly everything be cleansed with blood,
and without the shedding of blood there is no forgiveness.

[a] *11* Some early manuscripts *are to come* [b] *14* Or *from useless rituals* [c] *16* Same Greek word as *covenant;* also in verse 17 [d] *20* Exodus 24:8

9:11 the greater ... tabernacle. In contrast to the temple worship, Jesus entered a "tabernacle" that is not a part of the sin-infected creation.

9:12 once for all. The finality of Christ's ministry stands in marked contrast with the ongoing cycle of sacrifices represented in the old covenant: Christ was sacrificed once for all (v. 26); he brought the blood of this sacrifice into God's presence once for all (v. 21); his sacrifice secures the forgiveness of sins of his people once for all (10:10). **eternal redemption.** The Day of Atonement brought freedom from ceremonial uncleanness, but, as time wore on, the people were again defiled and needed another act of redemption the following year. The liberation from sin that Christ has secured is, by contrast, spiritual and permanent.

9:13 The blood of goats and bulls. A reference to the sacrifices on the Day of Atonement (Lev. 16). **ashes of a heifer.** Israelites who were ceremonially defiled through contact with a dead body were cleansed by being sprinkled with water mixed with the ashes of a burned heifer. Without this cleansing, they could not worship at the tabernacle (Num. 19). **outwardly clean.** Literally, "cleanness of the flesh," set in opposition to the cleanness of the spirit (v. 14).

9:14 How much more. If the sacrifice of an animal could effect some change in a person's standing with God, obviously the sacrifice of the royal Son of God would be far more effective! **the blood of Christ.** Blood represents sacrifice and death. **the eternal Spirit.** Literally, "an eternal spirit." This does not refer to the Holy Spirit, but to Christ's eternal nature (7:16). Because Christ himself is eternal in nature, the redemption he secured is likewise everlasting (v. 12). The phrase also contrasts the spiritual nature of Christ's sacrifice to the fleshly nature of the old (v. 13). While they only ceremonially cleansed the body, the new sacrifice actually cleanses the conscience. **unblemished.** Sacrificial animals had to be of the best quality. What was true of them physically was true of Jesus morally. **acts that lead to death.** Literally, "dead works." The old sacrifices cleansed a person defiled by contact with a dead body; the new sacrifice cleanses a person from a life of sin which leads to death.

9:19 blood of calves. The Greek text adds "and goats." Several accounts in which blood is associated with covenant-making or cleansing are combined (Gen. 15:9; Ex. 24:1–8; Lev. 14:6–7).

9:20 This is the blood. This paraphrase of Exodus 24:8 would remind the readers of Jesus' words as he instituted the new covenant (Matt. 26:28).

9:22 without the shedding of blood. This is the main point of the argument. Just as there is no inheritance from a will without a death, so the covenant promises cannot be fulfilled without a sacrifice. God accepts the death of the sacrifice in place of the deserved death of the sinner (Lev. 17:11).

[23]It was necessary, then, for the copies of the heavenly things to be
purified with these sacrifices, but the heavenly things themselves
with better sacrifices than these. [24]For Christ did not enter a man-
made sanctuary that was only a copy of the true one; he entered
heaven itself, now to appear for us in God's presence. [25]Nor did he
enter heaven to offer himself again and again, the way the high priest
enters the Most Holy Place every year with blood that is not his own.
[26]Then Christ would have had to suffer many times since the creation
of the world. But now he has appeared once for all at the end of the
ages to do away with sin by the sacrifice of himself. [27]Just as man is
destined to die once, and after that to face judgment, [28]so Christ was
sacrificed once to take away the sins of many people; and he will appear a second time, not to bear sin, but to bring salvation to those
who are waiting for him.

Christ's Sacrifice Once for All

10 The law is only a shadow of the good things that are coming—not the realities themselves. For this reason it can
never, by the same sacrifices repeated endlessly year after year, make
perfect those who draw near to worship. [2]If it could, would they not
have stopped being offered? For the worshipers would have been
cleansed once for all, and would no longer have felt guilty for their
sins. [3]But those sacrifices are an annual reminder of sins, [4]because it
is impossible for the blood of bulls and goats to take away sins.
[5]Therefore, when Christ came into the world, he said:

"Sacrifice and offering you did not desire,
but a body you prepared for me;
[6]with burnt offerings and sin offerings
you were not pleased.
[7]Then I said, 'Here I am—it is written about me in the scroll—
I have come to do your will, O God.' "[a]

[8]First he said, "Sacrifices and offerings, burnt offerings and sin offerings you did not desire, nor were you pleased with them" (although
the law required them to be made). [9]Then he said, "Here I am, I have
come to do your will." He sets aside the first to establish the second.
[10]And by that will, we have been made holy through the sacrifice of
the body of Jesus Christ once for all.

[a]7 Psalm 40:6-8 (see Septuagint)

the world start making sense to you? **2.** How would you describe your relationship with God right now in one or two words?

OPEN **1.** If you could change one thing in your daily routine, what would you change? **2.** What would you like to finish once and for all?

STUDY **1.** What is the author talking about when he refers to the "shadow"? What is the real thing? **2.** What did the Old Testament law require people to do to be pardoned from their sins? How often? Does this take away their guilt? **3.** When Christ came into the world, what did he say was his mission? **4.** How would you explain the meaning of the substitutional atonement of Jesus Christ to someone who does not know a lot about the sacrificial system in the Old Testament? **5.** What is the significance of the word "stands" (v. 11) to describe the priests in the Old Testament and the words "sat down" (v. 12) to describe the position of Christ after his sacrifice "for all time"? **6.** In verse 14, in what sense are Christians already made perfect while still in the process of being made holy?

9:24 he entered heaven itself. Paul saw the ascension as the exaltation of Jesus (Phil. 2:9–10). This author, in keeping with the priestly theme, sees it as Jesus' entry into the heavenly Most Holy Place.

9:26 to do away with sin. Literally, "to effect an annulment." Christ not only brings forgiveness of sin, but breaks its power.

9:28 appear a second time. Unlike the old high priests, Christ will not have to come again to bear sin yet another year. Instead, he will come to usher in the fullness of salvation!

10:2 once for all. The continuous repetition of the sacrifices indicated the root problem of sin was never addressed.

10:4 impossible. No amount of animal sacrifices could change the moral imperfection within people. The main purpose of the old covenant was to point out the need for One who is finally able to "take away sins" of believers forever.

10:9 sets aside. Literally, "to abolish." The old sacrificial system, which could not accomplish God's will of making people holy (v. 10), was superseded by the Messiah who was devoted to doing God's will.

10:10 that will. That is, God's will (v. 9). **holy.** How to be "perfect" in God's sight is a central concern in this letter (v. 14; 7:11,18–19; 9:9,14). **through the sacrifice of the body of Jesus Christ.** Cleansing from sin is a matter of solidarity with Jesus, whose once for all sacrifice merits full redemption.

APPLY 1. In your spiritual pilgrimage, when did you come to the place that you realized you would never be perfect (always have a sin nature) and that was okay (in your walk with Christ there was provision for your shortcomings)? **2.** What have you found helpful when you blow it big time and have this crippling sense of guilt? How do you deal with sin in your life?

11 Day after day every priest stands and performs his religious duties; again and again he offers the same sacrifices, which can never
take away sins. 12 But when this priest had offered for all time one
sacrifice for sins, he sat down at the right hand of God. 13 Since that
time he waits for his enemies to be made his footstool, 14 because by
one sacrifice he has made perfect forever those who are being made
holy.

15 The Holy Spirit also testifies to us about this. First he says:

16 "This is the covenant I will make with them
after that time, says the Lord.
I will put my laws in their hearts,
and I will write them on their minds."[a]

17 Then he adds:

"Their sins and lawless acts
I will remember no more."[b]

18 And where these have been forgiven, there is no longer any sacrifice
for sin.

A Call to Persevere

19 Therefore, brothers, since we have confidence to enter the Most
Holy Place by the blood of Jesus, 20 by a new and living way opened for
us through the curtain, that is, his body, 21 and since we have a great
priest over the house of God, 22 let us draw near to God with a sincere
heart in full assurance of faith, having our hearts sprinkled to cleanse
us from a guilty conscience and having our bodies washed with pure
water. 23 Let us hold unswervingly to the hope we profess, for he who
promised is faithful. 24 And let us consider how we may spur one another on toward love and good deeds. 25 Let us not give up meeting

[a] *16* Jer. 31:33 [b] *17* Jer. 31:34

OPEN What was the line your parents used when they wanted to straighten you out: "I'm disappointed in you?" "I can't believe what you've done"? "I'm angry?" "You can do better"? "How could you"?

STUDY 1. What do you find out in verses 32–34 that these Christians have suffered? If you had gone through this, how would you be feeling? **2.** Reading between the lines in verse 25, what has happened to some of the people in their church?

10:11–14 The completeness of the new order in contrast with the ineffectiveness of the old is reinforced by one last comparison between the sacrifices offered in each: (1) The old sacrifices were offered day after day, again and again—whereas Christ offered for all time one sacrifice (vv. 11–12); (2) In the old system the priest stood and performed his religious duties, signifying the work was never accomplished—whereas Christ sat down at the right hand of God, indicating he has completed his task (vv. 11–12); and (3) The old sacrifices never took away sins, but Christ's sacrifice has made them perfect before God forever for those who trust him (vv. 11,14).

10:15–18 As the final proof that Jesus' sacrifice brings about the true cleansing God requires, Jeremiah's promise of the new covenant is again considered (8:8–12). Since under this covenant the peoples' sins are forgiven (v. 18) and they now live according to the Law embedded in their hearts, there is no longer any need for sacrifices (v. 18). The old order is ended.

10:19 enter the Most Holy Place. In the old covenant only the high priest could draw near to God. In contrast, all Christians can do so with assurance. **by the blood of Jesus.** As the high priest entered the Most Holy Place bearing a sacrifice, so Christians draw near to God through the sacrifice of Jesus on our behalf.

10:20 new and living way. This is not "new" as opposed to "old," but rather something fresh and alive. **that is, his body.** Jesus' body, like the curtain of the temple was the veil that needed to be passed through. However, given that the curtain is that which blocked entrance to God's presence (9:8), the phrase may be better understood when linked to the "new and living way." In this reading, the bodily sacrifice of Jesus is the way through the curtain into God's presence.

10:22 hearts sprinkled. Priestly garments were consecrated for use by being sprinkled with the blood of a sacrifice (Ex. 29:19–21). This external consecration points to the internal consecration of the believer through Christ.

10:24 spur one another on. Literally, "to provoke"; a word usually associated with negative results. **good deeds.** Literally, "noble deeds"; actions recognized by others as morally good.

10:25 give up. Literally, "abandon." Jesus used this word on the cross (Matt. 27:46). The action in mind is extreme. The concern here is not just a matter of missing an occasional church meeting, but of turning away from the community as a whole.

together, as some are in the habit of doing, but let us encourage one
another—and all the more as you see the Day approaching.
26 If we deliberately keep on sinning after we have received the
knowledge of the truth, no sacrifice for sins is left, 27 but only a fearful
expectation of judgment and of raging fire that will consume the enemies of God. 28 Anyone who rejected the law of Moses died without
mercy on the testimony of two or three witnesses. 29 How much more
severely do you think a man deserves to be punished who has
trampled the Son of God under foot, who has treated as an unholy
thing the blood of the covenant that sanctified him, and who has insulted the Spirit of grace? 30 For we know him who said, "It is mine to
avenge; I will repay,"[a] and again, "The Lord will judge his people."[b]
31 It is a dreadful thing to fall into the hands of the living God.
32 Remember those earlier days after you had received the light,
when you stood your ground in a great contest in the face of suffering. 33 Sometimes you were publicly exposed to insult and persecution; at other times you stood side by side with those who were so
treated. 34 You sympathized with those in prison and joyfully accepted
the confiscation of your property, because you knew that you yourselves had better and lasting possessions.
35 So do not throw away your confidence; it will be richly rewarded.
36 You need to persevere so that when you have done the will of God,
you will receive what he has promised. 37 For in just a very little while,

"He who is coming will come and will not delay.
38 But my righteous one[c] will live by faith.
And if he shrinks back,
I will not be pleased with him."[d]

39 But we are not of those who shrink back and are destroyed, but of
those who believe and are saved.

[a]30 Deut. 32:35 [b]30 Deut. 32:36; Psalm 135:14 [c]38 One early manuscript *But the righteous*
[d]38 Hab. 2:3,4

3. Based on the fact that Christ has made it possible for a Christian to have direct and immediate access into the presence of God, what are the four appeals in verses 19–25 (look for the words "let us")? If you were one of the Christians who had been demoralized by discrimination, how would these words sound to you? **4.** How would you describe the tone in verses 26–31? If you were hearing this for the first time, what would it make you do? **5.** After a dire warning, what does the author do to encourage these Christians to keep going? How would you describe these words? **6.** At the end of this passage if you were one of these battered and bruised Christians, how would you be feeling: Encouraged? Warned? Afraid? Challenged? Put down? Hopeful? Other?

APPLY 1. At the darkest time in your spiritual pilgrimage, who or what came along to encourage you to keep going? **2.** In times of spiritual desolation, what have you found most helpful? **3.** What group is safe for you when you need to unload the heavy stuff in your life?

10:26 deliberately keep on sinning. A conscious choice to deliberately and persistently pursue a path that violates God's will. **no sacrifice for sins is left.** The Levitical sacrifices covered ceremonial uncleanness, moral lapses for which one repented (Lev. 6:1–7), and sins of ignorance and passion (Lev. 5:17–19; 19:20–22). Sins that were a defiant rejection of the Law were not covered by the sacrifices (Num. 15:30). The author transfers this principle to the new covenant as well. The God-appointed sacrifice must be met with an attitude of repentance and dedication. To reject Christ's sacrifice is to reject the only sacrifice for sins.

10:28 rejected the law of Moses. The concern here is not simply with breaking one of the commands of the Law, but of setting it aside as having no validity—such as a Jew who violated the essence of Israel's covenant with God by embracing idolatry (Deut. 17:2–7).

10:29 trampled the Son of God … treated as an unholy thing the blood of the covenant … insulted the Spirit of grace. These three phrases amplify the nature of the sin warned against. It is a deliberate rejection of Jesus as the Messiah, a decision to abandon the covenant that comes through his sacrifice, and a resistance to the Spirit who applies God's grace to those who trust.

10:32 in a great contest. Jewish Christians are the most likely destinations for this letter and have suffered persecution from their fellow Jews. This ranged from harassment (Acts 18:17), to murder (Acts 7:59). Some experienced family rejection, economic boycotts, and physical abuse leading to forced relocation and the resultant loss of property (Acts 8:1). The image of an athletic contest is used to describe this conflict.

10:33–34 These people risked standing with those being persecuted in spite of the danger to themselves. It is this type of dedication that they are called to display once more (Matt. 5:11–12).

10:35 confidence. This is the same word translated as "courage" in Hebrews 3:6. **rewarded.** Jesus promises a great reward for those who endure suffering for his sake (Matt. 5:12).

10:37–38 in just a very little while. The Lord is coming, therefore do not shrink back and meet with God's displeasure.

OPEN Who is your favorite Old Testament character? What is it about this person that impresses you?

STUDY **1.** What is the challenge in verses 35–39 in the previous chapter that the author builds on in this chapter? **2.** How would you define faith from what you learn in verses 1–6? **3.** What did Noah do because he had faith in God? Was it raining when he started to build the ark? **4.** What did Abraham do because he had faith in God? When Abraham died, what did he have to show for his faith journey? If God told you when you were 99 years old that you were going to have a baby, what would you say? **5.** How does the author use the experience of Abraham to encourage the readers of this letter to stay the course (vv. 15–16)? **6.** Would it take more faith for you to build an ark (Noah), or to leave your comfort zone and travel to a new land (Abraham) or to go back to your hometown and try to change things (Moses)? **7.** How did Moses find the courage to return to Egypt? Do you think he knew what he was getting into when he said "yes" to God? What caused Moses to "keep the faith"? How would you have done as the leader of an ungrateful, complaining, disobedient people for 40 years? **8.** Are you a little surprised to see a prostitute listed in the roll call of the faith (v. 31)? **9.** If you were one of the Christians in this church who were thinking about giving up your faith because of persecution, how would you be feeling after reading verses 32–38? **10.** What is the main lesson in this passage for these Christians? For the church today? **11.** How would you define the word "faith" now that you have been through this study?

By Faith

11 Now faith is being sure of what we hope for and certain of
what we do not see. 2This is what the ancients were commended for.
3By faith we understand that the universe was formed at God's
command, so that what is seen was not made out of what was visible.
4By faith Abel offered God a better sacrifice than Cain did. By faith
he was commended as a righteous man, when God spoke well of his
offerings. And by faith he still speaks, even though he is dead.
5By faith Enoch was taken from this life, so that he did not experience death; he could not be found, because God had taken him away.
For before he was taken, he was commended as one who pleased
God. 6And without faith it is impossible to please God, because anyone who comes to him must believe that he exists and that he rewards those who earnestly seek him.
7By faith Noah, when warned about things not yet seen, in holy
fear built an ark to save his family. By his faith he condemned the
world and became heir of the righteousness that comes by faith.
8By faith Abraham, when called to go to a place he would later receive as his inheritance, obeyed and went, even though he did not
know where he was going. 9By faith he made his home in the promised land like a stranger in a foreign country; he lived in tents, as did
Isaac and Jacob, who were heirs with him of the same promise. 10For
he was looking forward to the city with foundations, whose architect
and builder is God.
11By faith Abraham, even though he was past age—and Sarah herself was barren—was enabled to become a father because he[a] considered him faithful who had made the promise. 12And so from this
one man, and he as good as dead, came descendants as numerous as
the stars in the sky and as countless as the sand on the seashore.
13All these people were still living by faith when they died. They did
not receive the things promised; they only saw them and welcomed
them from a distance. And they admitted that they were aliens and
strangers on earth. 14People who say such things show that they are
looking for a country of their own. 15If they had been thinking of the
country they had left, they would have had opportunity to return.

[a]11 Or *By faith even Sarah, who was past age, was enabled to bear children because she*

11:1 The call to live by faith (10:37–39) leads into a collection of stories of faithful people in the past designed to encourage the readers to be faithful in the present (12:1).

11:3 The stories of faith begin with creation, which in itself dramatically exemplifies how God brought into being things that were unseen. Faith is as certain as God's creation.

11:4 Abel. Abel's faith is not mentioned in Genesis, but it is clear that the reason God accepted his sacrifice and not Cain's had to do with a matter of attitude (Gen. 4:4–7).

11:5 Enoch. The main facts about Enoch were his mysterious disappearance and that "he pleased God" (Gen. 5:21–24, Septuagint). Enoch was a popular figure in Jewish legends, which taught that his purity was such that God "took him" because he had no sin.

11:7 Noah. Noah's faith is not mentioned in the Old Testament, but is seen in his obedience to God (Gen. 6:9–9:17). **not yet seen.** Acting upon that which God promises (or warns), even when unseen, is the essence of faith (v. 1). **in holy fear.** Faith lives in recognition of the awesome power of God. **condemned the world.** In that he acted in obedience to God while others did not.

11:9–10 In contrast to his settled life in Ur, Abraham's nomadic life in Canaan showed that his eyes were fixed upon a vision of something greater than could be found in this world.

11:13 All these people. Abraham, Sarah, Isaac, Jacob. **living by faith when they died.** None of the patriarchs saw the fulfillment of God's promise regarding the land or the vast nation Abraham would father. **aliens and strangers.** Both terms describe how believers are to view their life in the world (John 17:14)

16Instead, they were longing for a better country—a heavenly one.
Therefore God is not ashamed to be called their God, for he has prepared a city for them.
17By faith Abraham, when God tested him, offered Isaac as a sacrifice. He who had received the promises was about to sacrifice his one
and only son, 18even though God had said to him, "It is through Isaac
that your offspring[a] will be reckoned."[b] 19Abraham reasoned that God
could raise the dead, and figuratively speaking, he did receive Isaac
back from death.
20By faith Isaac blessed Jacob and Esau in regard to their future.
21By faith Jacob, when he was dying, blessed each of Joseph's sons,
and worshiped as he leaned on the top of his staff.
22By faith Joseph, when his end was near, spoke about the exodus
of the Israelites from Egypt and gave instructions about his bones.
23By faith Moses' parents hid him for three months after he was
born, because they saw he was no ordinary child, and they were not
afraid of the king's edict.
24By faith Moses, when he had grown up, refused to be known as
the son of Pharaoh's daughter. 25He chose to be mistreated along
with the people of God rather than to enjoy the pleasures of sin for a
short time. 26He regarded disgrace for the sake of Christ as of greater
value than the treasures of Egypt, because he was looking ahead to
his reward. 27By faith he left Egypt, not fearing the king's anger; he
persevered because he saw him who is invisible. 28By faith he kept
the Passover and the sprinkling of blood, so that the destroyer of the
firstborn would not touch the firstborn of Israel.
29By faith the people passed through the Red Sea[c] as on dry land;
but when the Egyptians tried to do so, they were drowned.

[a]18 Greek *seed* [b]18 Gen. 21:12 [c]29 That is, Sea of Reeds

APPLY 1. How would you compare the suffering you have gone through to the sufferings of the people in this chapter? **2.** If God were to speak to you today and ask you to pull up stakes and move, or to take responsibility for something that needed to be done but you felt you were not qualified to do, what would you say? **3.** What is the next step in your faith journey? **4.** How can this group help you in prayer?

11:16 a heavenly one. In the new covenant a superior territory to the land of Canaan is to be achieved (8:5). **called their God.** God openly identifies with these people, pledging himself to them (Ex. 3:6,15).

11:17 God tested him. According to tradition, God gave Abraham 10 tests, this being the final one. **offered Isaac as a sacrifice.** Since child sacrifice was part of the worship life of the surrounding cultures, this would not have seemed as outrageous to Abraham as it does to modern readers. That does not minimize his anxiety regarding the death of his son, however. It also would generate tension in Abraham in that it was through Isaac that God had said the promise would come true (v. 18; Gen. 21:12).

11:19 raise the dead. Abraham believed God would keep his promise even if it meant resurrecting Isaac from the dead. **figuratively speaking.** Just as Abraham was about to kill Isaac, God intervened. But Isaac was as good as dead in terms of Abraham's intent.

11:21 Jacob. Looking two generations ahead, the elderly Jacob passed on the blessing and promise to Manasseh and Ephraim (Gen. 48:20). **leaned on the top of his staff.** This is from Joseph's oath to Jacob in Genesis 47:31.

11:22 Joseph. His faith was evidenced by his belief in God's promise to one day deliver Israel from Egypt (Gen. 15:16).

11:23 Faith in God led Moses' parents to resist Pharaoh's order that all Jewish male infants be killed (Ex. 1:22).

11:24 refused to be known as the son of Pharaoh's daughter. Moses was raised by the Pharaoh's daughter (Ex. 2:5–10). Therefore, this was a choice not to identify with the oppressor of his people, even though that would have been a far more easy and comfortable option.

11:25 pleasures of sin. The sin here is that of turning his back on his own people for the sake of personal comfort.

11:26 the sake of Christ. Literally, "the anointed." In the Old Testament, Israel as a nation was sometimes called "the anointed one" (Ps. 89:51). The author uses Moses' loyalty to "God's anointed" nation as a model for how the individual believer ought to be loyal to God's anointed Messiah, Jesus Christ.

11:28 Passover. This action demonstrated faith that God would keep the promise to "pass over" the homes of the Israelites as the destroying angel came through the land (Ex. 12). **sprinkling of blood.** Blood from the Passover lamb was sprinkled on the doorframe of each Jewish home. While the Day of Atonement sacrifice is used as the interpretive grid for understanding the death of Christ in this letter, the Gospel of John used the Passover imagery (John 1:29; 18:28).

11:29 Both the parting of the waters and their coming together again was the result of Moses' faith in the power of God who promised to deliver the people (Ex. 14:21–28).

[30]By faith the walls of Jericho fell, after the people had marched
around them for seven days.
[31]By faith the prostitute Rahab, because she welcomed the spies,
was not killed with those who were disobedient.[a]
[32]And what more shall I say? I do not have time to tell about Gideon, Barak, Samson, Jephthah, David, Samuel and the prophets, [33]who
through faith conquered kingdoms, administered justice, and gained
what was promised; who shut the mouths of lions, [34]quenched the
fury of the flames, and escaped the edge of the sword; whose weakness was turned to strength; and who became powerful in battle and
routed foreign armies. [35]Women received back their dead, raised to
life again. Others were tortured and refused to be released, so that
they might gain a better resurrection. [36]Some faced jeers and flogging, while still others were chained and put in prison. [37]They were
stoned[b]; they were sawed in two; they were put to death by the sword.
They went about in sheepskins and goatskins, destitute, persecuted
and mistreated— [38]the world was not worthy of them. They wandered in deserts and mountains, and in caves and holes in the
ground.
[39]These were all commended for their faith, yet none of them received what had been promised. [40]God had planned something better
for us so that only together with us would they be made perfect.

OPEN **1.** Who of your close family and spiritual mentors are now in heaven? **2.** Which events of the Olympics do you like to watch on TV?

God Disciplines His Sons

12 Therefore, since we are surrounded by such a great cloud of
witnesses, let us throw off everything that hinders and the
sin that so easily entangles, and let us run with perseverance the race

[a]31 Or *unbelieving* [b]37 Some early manuscripts *stoned; they were put to the test;*

11:30 Jericho. Faith was shown by the people's conviction that obeying God's strange orders would result in their victory (Josh. 6).

11:31 Rahab. All the previous examples of faith were men held in high esteem by the Jews. Rahab was a Gentile prostitute who had faith to see that the God of Israel was the God of the whole earth (Josh. 2:11).

11:33–34 Three sets of three items from this catalog of faith deeds: The first triplet concerns events that affected Israel as a whole; the second triplet considers stories of dramatic personal deliverance; the third triplet looks at examples of power released through faith.

11:33 conquered kingdoms. David's conquests are probably in mind (2 Sam. 1–10). **administered justice.** Both Samuel and David were renown for their justice as leaders in Israel (1 Sam. 12:3–5; 2 Sam. 8:15). **gained what was promised.** Under David, Israel was a mighty nation that possessed the land promised to Abraham.

11:34 quenched the fury of the flames. Shadrach, Meshach and Abednego must be in view (Dan. 3). **escaped ... the sword.** This may refer to David's several close calls at being killed by Saul (1 Sam. 18:10–11; 19:11–12; 23:26–27). **weakness was turned to strength.** Samson may be in mind (Judg. 16:28). **powerful in battle.** David's exploits were legendary (1 Sam. 17; 18:7). **routed foreign armies.** This, as well as many of the examples in verses 35–38, probably refers to the Jewish heroes during the Maccabean revolt against the Seleucids in second century B.C.

11:36 jeers ... prison. While this applied to the Maccabean heroes, Jeremiah the prophet also comes to mind (Jer. 20:2; 38:6).

11:37 stoned ... sawed in two. Tradition held that Jeremiah was stoned in Egypt and that Isaiah was sawn in two by the evil king Manasseh. **put to death by the sword.** Uriah, a prophet contemporary with Jeremiah, met this end (Jer. 26:20–23).

11:38 the world was not worthy of them. The qualities of integrity and courage these people displayed put the rest of scheming, compromising humanity to shame. **wandered in ... caves.** Jews during the Maccabean revolt hid out in caves around Palestine.

11:39 commended. Literally, "obtained a witness," in that their stories were recorded for future generations. **none ... received what had been promised.** The "heavenly rest" was never personally experienced by them.

12:1 witnesses. This is the same word as for "martyrs." It is probably a deliberate play on words in which both meanings are intended. The heroes of faith are pictured as a cheering section of former runners in a race urging the contemporary readers to preserve as they did. **throw off everything.** In Greek games at the time, runners ran with no clothes to not hinder their movement. **the sin that so easily entangles.** Just as a flowing robe makes it impossible to run, so sin makes the Christian life difficult.

marked out for us. [2]Let us fix our eyes on Jesus, the author and perfecter of our faith, who for the joy set before him endured the cross, scorning its shame, and sat down at the right hand of the throne of God. [3]Consider him who endured such opposition from sinful men, so that you will not grow weary and lose heart.

[4]In your struggle against sin, you have not yet resisted to the point of shedding your blood. [5]And you have forgotten that word of encouragement that addresses you as sons:

"My son, do not make light of the Lord's discipline,
and do not lose heart when he rebukes you,
[6]because the Lord disciplines those he loves,
and he punishes everyone he accepts as a son."[a]

[7]Endure hardship as discipline; God is treating you as sons. For what son is not disciplined by his father? [8]If you are not disciplined (and everyone undergoes discipline), then you are illegitimate children and not true sons. [9]Moreover, we have all had human fathers who disciplined us and we respected them for it. How much more should we submit to the Father of our spirits and live! [10]Our fathers disciplined us for a little while as they thought best; but God disciplines us for our good, that we may share in his holiness. [11]No discipline seems pleasant at the time, but painful. Later on, however, it produces a harvest of righteousness and peace for those who have been trained by it.

[12]Therefore, strengthen your feeble arms and weak knees. [13]"Make level paths for your feet,"[b] so that the lame may not be disabled, but rather healed.

STUDY 1. How did the author of Hebrews finish the chapter about the great people of the faith (11:39–40)? What comfort do you get from knowing that a whole lot of people are cheering for you from the balcony in heaven? **2.** What are two obstacles to overcome in running the Christian race (vv. 1–2)? If you were a track coach, how would you explain this to your runners? **3.** For those people who are considering the possibility of turning their backs on the Christian faith, what does the author want them to consider? **4.** What did you learn when you were raising your children that would illustrate the point about discipline? **5.** How would you restate the challenge in verses 12–13 for these "weak-kneed" Christians?

APPLY 1. What is your life focused on right now? **2.** How would you compare the focus in your spiritual life right now to your spiritual life one year ago? Five years ago? Ten years ago? **3.** In your struggle against sin, who is winning?

Warning Against Refusing God

[14]Make every effort to live in peace with all men and to be holy; without holiness no one will see the Lord. [15]See to it that no one misses the grace of God and that no bitter root grows up to cause trouble and defile many. [16]See that no one is sexually immoral, or is godless like Esau, who for a single meal sold his inheritance rights as the oldest son. [17]Afterward, as you know, when he wanted to inherit

OPEN How did your parents reason with you when you were going through your teenage rebellion?

STUDY 1. Reading between the lines in verses 14–17, what is going on in the church here that needs to be corrected? How do these instructions and Esau's example relate

[a]6 Prov. 3:11,12 [b]13 Prov. 4:26

12:2 fix our eyes on Jesus. In races of the time, the prize for the race was placed at the end to motivate the runners. Jesus is here described as the focus of the Christian life. **joy set before him.** Jesus knew the joy his mission of reconciliation would bring, and so pursued it whatever the cost. The readers are to follow that model. **scorning its shame.** Crucifixion was considered so degrading that no Roman citizen could be crucified, regardless of the crime committed.

12:3 Consider him. Instead of seeing opposition as an excuse to abandon faith, they should look to Jesus as a model of how to live faithfully through it. **weary and lose heart.** These words were used in athletic circles to describe the collapse of a runner.

12:4 shedding your blood. The persecution they have experienced so far has not yet included the ultimate price, of losing one's life.

12:14 live in peace. This is to consciously work toward nurturing harmonious relationships between members of the Christian community. **be holy.** To be holy is to be dedicated to God. The word does not have the connotation many associate with it today of being self-righteous or having a "better than thou" attitude. **without holiness no one will see the Lord.** Faith and holiness are essential for life with God. Faith without the pursuit of holiness is only intellectual assent; holiness without faith is self-righteousness (11:6).

12:16 Although the NIV has punctuated this verse so that only godlessness is associated with Esau, Jewish tradition viewed him both as sexually immoral and ungodly. The latter was especially seen in his trading his right as the firstborn son for the immediate pleasure of a single meal (Gen. 25:19–34). **sexually immoral.** Sexual sin and choosing the short-term benefits of turning from Christ over the long-term benefits of faithfulness are two types of defiling activity in this community (13:4).

12:17 He could bring about no change of mind. This phrase is bet-

to the church today? **2.** What is the point in comparing Mount Sinai (vv. 18–21) and Mount Zion (vv. 22–24)? **3.** If you were one of the wayward Christians and you had grown up hearing the story of God's punishment on the Israelites for disobedience, how would you be feeling after reading this passage? **4.** Do you think the church today has gone too far in making God into a loving Santa Claus who will tolerate anything?

APPLY 1. Who taught you how to make hard moral choices as a Christian? **2.** When you are tempted to go with the crowd and the "relative" moral standards of today, what do you fall back on? **3.** How can this group help you in prayer this week?

this blessing, he was rejected. He could bring about no change of
mind, though he sought the blessing with tears.
18You have not come to a mountain that can be touched and that is
burning with fire; to darkness, gloom and storm; 19to a trumpet blast
or to such a voice speaking words that those who heard it begged
that no further word be spoken to them, 20because they could not
bear what was commanded: "If even an animal touches the mountain, it must be stoned."[a] 21The sight was so terrifying that Moses
said, "I am trembling with fear."[b]
22But you have come to Mount Zion, to the heavenly Jerusalem, the
city of the living God. You have come to thousands upon thousands of
angels in joyful assembly, 23to the church of the firstborn, whose
names are written in heaven. You have come to God, the judge of all
men, to the spirits of righteous men made perfect, 24to Jesus the mediator of a new covenant, and to the sprinkled blood that speaks a
better word than the blood of Abel.
25See to it that you do not refuse him who speaks. If they did not
escape when they refused him who warned them on earth, how much
less will we, if we turn away from him who warns us from heaven?
26At that time his voice shook the earth, but now he has promised,
"Once more I will shake not only the earth but also the heavens."[c]
27The words "once more" indicate the removing of what can be shak-
en—that is, created things—so that what cannot be shaken may remain.
28Therefore, since we are receiving a kingdom that cannot be shak-
en, let us be thankful, and so worship God acceptably with reverence
and awe, 29for our "God is a consuming fire."[d]

OPEN What group of friends are so close to you that you could call on them at 3 o'clock in the morning and they would be there—or if you died they would look after your spouse and children?

Concluding Exhortations

13 Keep on loving each other as brothers. 2Do not forget to entertain strangers, for by so doing some people have entertained angels without knowing it. 3Remember those in prison as if

[a]*20* Exodus 19:12,13 [b]*21* Deut. 9:19 [c]*26* Haggai 2:6 [d]*29* Deut. 4:24

ter understood as "he had no opportunity to bring about a change of mind." The blessing had already been given to Esau's brother Jacob and could not be revoked (Gen. 27:34–40). The implicit warning is for these people not to turn away from their inheritance in Christ for something as short-lived as material security.

12:18–21 This retelling of the Israelites' experience at Mount Sinai is based on Exodus 19. Even the old covenant, limited as it has been shown to be, was accompanied by overwhelming signs of God's authority that emphasized how seriously it must be taken.

12:21 This is actually from the time when Moses sought God's forgiveness over Israel's idolatry with the golden calf (Ex. 32:9–14).

12:22 Mount Zion. This was the site of a fortress King David conquered and made his home (2 Sam. 5:6–9). Later it referred to Jerusalem as the site of God's temple. Symbolically, it stood for the place of God's residence. **the heavenly Jerusalem.** The earthly Jerusalem was thought to reflect a heavenly prototype in which God truly dwelt.

12:23 God, the judge of all. The emphasis on God as judge echoes the warnings in 4:13 and 10:30–31. **spirits of righteous men made perfect.** These are the "cloud of witnesses" (v. 1), who, while still awaiting their final completion (11:40), have already reached their destination with God.

12:24 Jesus. Since Jesus is superior over all elements of the old order, coming to him is the climactic reality for the Christian.

12:25 him who speaks. That is, Jesus (v. 24). Since they are addressed by the royal Son and heavenly high priest, these people are even more obligated to heed God's Word than the Israelites at Mount Sinai (2:2–4; 10:28–29).

12:26–27 Haggai 2:6 is a reminder that God will one day shake not only the earth (as at Mount Sinai) but also the heavens. Thus the old order, which is earthly, partial and temporary, will fully give way to the new, which is heavenly, complete and eternal.

12:28 a kingdom. This is the kingdom of God inaugurated by Jesus and consummated in the new heavens and new earth (Mark 1:15; Isa. 65:17–19).

13:2 entertained angels. That a stranger might be an angelic visitation stems back to Abraham and Lot (Gen. 18–19).

you were their fellow prisoners, and those who are mistreated as if
you yourselves were suffering.

[4]Marriage should be honored by all, and the marriage bed kept
pure, for God will judge the adulterer and all the sexually immoral.
[5]Keep your lives free from the love of money and be content with
what you have, because God has said,

"Never will I leave you;
never will I forsake you."[a]

[6]So we say with confidence,

"The Lord is my helper; I will not be afraid.
What can man do to me?"[b]

[7]Remember your leaders, who spoke the word of God to you. Consider the outcome of their way of life and imitate their faith. [8]Jesus
Christ is the same yesterday and today and forever.

[9]Do not be carried away by all kinds of strange teachings. It is good
for our hearts to be strengthened by grace, not by ceremonial foods,
which are of no value to those who eat them. [10]We have an altar from
which those who minister at the tabernacle have no right to eat.

[11]The high priest carries the blood of animals into the Most Holy
Place as a sin offering, but the bodies are burned outside the camp.
[12]And so Jesus also suffered outside the city gate to make the people
holy through his own blood. [13]Let us, then, go to him outside the
camp, bearing the disgrace he bore. [14]For here we do not have an
enduring city, but we are looking for the city that is to come.

[15]Through Jesus, therefore, let us continually offer to God a sacrifice of praise—the fruit of lips that confess his name. [16]And do not
forget to do good and to share with others, for with such sacrifices
God is pleased.

[17]Obey your leaders and submit to their authority. They keep watch
over you as men who must give an account. Obey them so that their

[a]5 Deut. 31:6 [b]6 Psalm 118:6,7

STUDY 1. In this Christian community that is going through all sorts of economic, social and even physical persecution, what are four or five ways they can look after each other (vv. 1–6)? What is the warning here about marriage? **2.** What does verse 5 say about priorities when making financial decisions? What reason do we have for being worry free when it comes to money? **3.** What is the point the author is making to these struggling Christians when he says that Jesus was dumped "outside of the city gate" to suffer? **4.** Why do you think the readers are challenged to "not be carried away by all kinds of strange teachings" (v. 9) and "to obey your leaders" (v. 17)? **5.** Why does the author desire their prayers (vv. 18–19)? **6.** From verses 1–19 how would you sum up the Christian lifestyle?

APPLY 1. As you think back over your study of the book of Hebrews, what have you learned about the person and work of Jesus Christ? **2.** Where is the growing edge in your life right now? Are you making room in your plans for God? **3.** What is the most significant thing you've learned from studying Hebrews? How has it affected your life? **4.** What area of your life could most use a Bible study? What do you want to study next?

13:4 Marriage. The denial of legitimate sexual desire led to incidents of sexual immorality (1 Cor. 6:15–20). Here, marriage is validated and people are warned not to be involved in any form of immorality (12:16).

13:5 Economic oppression (10:34) may have created pressure to renounce the faith in order to restore financial security.

13:7 Remember your leaders. This refers to the people who introduced the readers to Jesus but were no longer with them.

13:8 The same trustworthy Jesus preached by the original leaders is the one the readers should continue to pursue "today and forever." Since Jesus and the gospel are stable and eternal, the readers should not be distracted by any new teachings that differ from what they originally received (v. 9).

13:9–14 Just what "strange teaching" is involved is unclear. Various food regulations created different types of problems in many early churches so something of that nature may be in view (Acts 11:1–18; Rom. 14; 1 Cor. 8; Col. 2:21; 1 Tim. 4:3). "Food" may also be a shorthand way of referring to the whole Levitical system (9:10). Whatever the case, the readers were being distracted from Christ over some matter involving the observance of external regulations. The author uses the sacrifice of the Day of Atonement to show that food has nothing to do with spiritual life: it is all a matter of God's grace.

13:13 go to him. Since the Christian altar and sacrifice are not in the tabernacle nor even in Jerusalem but in Christ, those who wish to follow Jesus must do so outside of the ceremonies of official Israel (8:13; 10:18). This does not mean Jews had to reject their whole heritage (note Paul's observance of Jewish customs—Acts 16:3; 18:18; 1 Cor. 16:8), but they must not rely on anything external to be right with God. This comes only through the sacrifice of Jesus. **bearing the disgrace he bore.** Those who broke from traditional practices would meet opposition from family and nation—just as Jesus did.

13:17 Obey your leaders. These are leaders currently responsible for the community. As in other places, the charisma of visiting preachers might seem more appealing than that of the day-to-day leaders of the community (2 Cor. 11; Gal. 1:6–9). **keep watch.** The leaders' responsibility was to teach true doctrine and guard against error infiltrating the church (Acts 20:28–31). **must give an account.** As a shepherd is responsible to the owner of the flock,

work will be a joy, not a burden, for that would be of no advantage to
you.
[18]Pray for us. We are sure that we have a clear conscience and desire to live honorably in every way. [19]I particularly urge you to pray so
that I may be restored to you soon.
[20]May the God of peace, who through the blood of the eternal covenant brought back from the dead our Lord Jesus, that great Shepherd of the sheep, [21]equip you with everything good for doing his
will, and may he work in us what is pleasing to him, through Jesus
Christ, to whom be glory for ever and ever. Amen.

[22]Brothers, I urge you to bear with my word of exhortation, for I
have written you only a short letter.
[23]I want you to know that our brother Timothy has been released. If
he arrives soon, I will come with him to see you.
[24]Greet all your leaders and all God's people. Those from Italy send
you their greetings.
[25]Grace be with you all.

---

so the church leader is responsible to Jesus, the head of the church. **so that their work will be a joy.** The members' role is to make the leaders' task a rewarding one rather than a draining one.

13:18–19 a clear conscience ... restored to you. Perhaps, like Paul (2 Cor. 1:12), the author was accused of not being honest with the readers because of failure to arrive when they originally thought. Instead of making unfair assumptions, the people are urged to pray for the author.

13:20 the blood of the eternal covenant. This phrase is rich in Old Testament allusions; Ezekiel 37:26 (everlasting covenant); Zechariah 9:11 (blood of the covenant). **Shepherd.** This new title for Jesus highlights his high-priestly ministry of comfort and guidance (4:15–16).

13:21 doing his will ... work in us. A better translation might be: "May he make you complete in all goodness to do the will of him who does in us those things pleasing before him ..." **everlasting.** This covenant will never be replaced.

to whom be glory. Typically, this would refer to God, the main subject of the whole clause; but the Greek word order and the author's theology certainly allows this to refer to Jesus (1:3,8).

13:23 Timothy. Timothy was Paul's trusted companion. There is no other reference in the New Testament of his imprisonment.

13:25 Grace be with you all. This was a typical way to end a letter, although for Christians, grace had a specific reference point in Christ.

James

Personal Reading	Group Study Topic and Reading	
1:1–18	Trials & Temptations	1:1–18
1:19–27	Listening & Doing	1:19–27
2:1–13	Mercy & Judgment	2:1–13
2:14–26	Faith & Works	2:14–26
3:1–12	Taming the Tongue	3:1–12
3:13–18	True & False Wisdom	3:13–18
4:1–12	Friendship With God	4:1–12
4:13–5:6	Investing in the Future	4:13–5:6
5:7–20	Suffering & Prayer	5:7–20

Author. In the New Testament there are apparently five men by the name of James, but only two who might conceivably have written this epistle—James the apostle, or James the half-brother of Jesus. Since it is almost certain that the apostle James (the son of Zebedee) was killed by Herod in A.D. 44 (before the epistle could have been written), traditionally the author has been assumed to be James, the leader of the church in Jerusalem and half-brother of Jesus (Mark 6:3).

Date. It is difficult to date the book of James. Some place it very early, around A.D. 45, making it the first New Testament book. Others date it quite late.

Theme. Christianity in action.

Historical Background. The pilgrimage of James to faith in Christ is fascinating. At first Jesus' family was hostile to his ministry (John 7:5) and, in fact, tried to stop it at one point (Mark 3:21). Yet after Jesus' ascension, his mother and half-brothers are listed among the early believers (Acts 1:14). For James, this conversion may have resulted from Jesus' postresurrection appearance to him (1 Cor. 15:7).

James eventually emerged as a leader of the church in Jerusalem. It was to James that Peter reported after his miraculous escape from Herod's prison (Acts 12:17). James presided over the first Jerusalem Council which decided the important question of how to handle Gentile converts (Acts 15). James was consulted by Paul during his first trip to Jerusalem after his conversion (Gal. 1:19), and then James joined in the official recognition of Paul's call as Apostle to the Gentiles (Gal. 2:8–10). It is to James that Paul later brought the collection for the poor in Jerusalem (Acts 21:17–25).

Purpose. While James clearly stands in the tradition of other Christian writers, he has some special concerns. The relationship between rich and poor crops up at various points (1:9–11; 5:1–6). He is concerned about the use and abuse of speech (1:19,26; 2:12; 3:3–12; 5:12) and he gives instruction on prayer (1:5–8; 4:2–3; 5:13–18). Above all, he is concerned with ethical behavior. How believers act, he says, has significance for the return of Christ; future reward depends on it. In this regard, James bemoans the inconsistency of behavior (1:6–8,22–24; 2:14–17; 4:1,3). Being "double-minded" (1:8; 4:8) stands the believers in sharp contrast to God who is one (2:19) and does not change (1:17).

Audience. James is one of the General Epistles (along with 1 and 2 Peter, John's epistles and Jude), so called because it has no single destination. It is not clear to whom James is addressing his comments. At first glance, it appears he is writing to Jewish Christians dispersed around the Greek world: "to the twelve tribes scattered among the nations" (1:1). But since Peter uses the same sort of inscription (1 Peter 1:1–2) when he is clearly addressing Gentile and Jewish Christians, James' destination remains unclear. In fact, a strong case can be made that James was writing to a community of God-fearers—Gentiles who had been deeply attracted to Judaism. That such folks were then drawn to Christianity is clear from examples in Acts, such as Cornelius (Acts 10:2,22), Lydia (Acts 16:14), Titius Justus (Acts 18:7) and others. This would help to explain the convergence of Jewish, Greek and Christian elements in the book of James.

OPEN 1. Who was the tower of strength in your family? **2.** In stressful times, what do you do to ease the stress?

STUDY 1. According to James, what should be a Christian's attitude when facing trials? How often is this your attitude in your own hard times? **2.** Why is perseverance important? What reward comes with persevering in the faith? **3.** What does it mean to be a "double-minded" person? How can one avoid being double-minded? **4.** How does James turn the assumed status of the rich and poor upside down? **5.** How should a Christian look upon hard times such as financial pressure, workplace stress and family problems? **6.** In this passage, what do we learn about the origin of temptation? **7.** What stages does temptation progress through to become "full-grown" sin?

APPLY 1. Where are you feeling under pressure at the moment? **2.** Do you tend to blame God and everybody else for your problems? What have you found helpful when temptation hits? **3.** What would you like to learn from this study and this group? **4.** How can this group help you in prayer this week?

1 James, a servant of God and of the Lord Jesus Christ,

To the twelve tribes scattered among the nations:

Greetings.

Trials and Temptations

2 Consider it pure joy, my brothers, whenever you face trials of
many kinds, 3 because you know that the testing of your faith develops perseverance. 4 Perseverance must finish its work so that you may
be mature and complete, not lacking anything. 5 If any of you lacks
wisdom, he should ask God, who gives generously to all without
finding fault, and it will be given to him. 6 But when he asks, he must
believe and not doubt, because he who doubts is like a wave of the
sea, blown and tossed by the wind. 7 That man should not think he
will receive anything from the Lord; 8 he is a double-minded man, unstable in all he does.

9 The brother in humble circumstances ought to take pride in his
high position. 10 But the one who is rich should take pride in his low
position, because he will pass away like a wild flower. 11 For the sun
rises with scorching heat and withers the plant; its blossom falls and
its beauty is destroyed. In the same way, the rich man will fade away
even while he goes about his business.

12 Blessed is the man who perseveres under trial, because when he
has stood the test, he will receive the crown of life that God has
promised to those who love him.

13 When tempted, no one should say, "God is tempting me." For God
cannot be tempted by evil, nor does he tempt anyone; 14 but each one
is tempted when, by his own evil desire, he is dragged away and enticed. 15 Then, after desire has conceived, it gives birth to sin; and sin,
when it is full-grown, gives birth to death.

1:1 a servant. Here he identifies Jesus as the "Lord" (master), therefore the appropriate relationship of all others to Jesus is as servants (literally "slaves"). **the twelve tribes.** He compared the scattering of the church to the dispersion of the tribes of Israel by Assyria. **scattered.** The word is, literally, *diaspora* and was used by Jews to refer to those of their number living outside Palestine in the Gentile world.

1:2 Consider it pure joy. The joy James is talking about is not just a feeling. It is active acceptance of adversity. **trials of many kinds.** "Trials" has the dual sense of "adversity" (disease, persecution, tragedy) and "temptations" (lust, greed and trust in wealth).

1:3 perseverance. Or "endurance." It is used in the sense of active overcoming, rather than passive acceptance.

1:4 finish its work. Perfection is not automatic—it takes time and effort. **mature and complete.** What James has in mind here is wholeness of character. **lacking.** The opposite of mature and complete. This is a word used of an army that has been defeated or a person who has failed to reach a certain standard.

1:5 wisdom. This is not just abstract knowledge, but God-given insight which leads to right living.

1:6 James now contrasts the readiness on God's part to give (v. 5) with the hesitation on people's part to ask (v. 6). Both here and in 4:3, unanswered prayer is connected to the quality of the asking, not to the unwillingness of God to give. **believe.** To be in *one mind* about God's ability to answer prayer.

1:8 double-minded. To doubt is to be in two minds—to believe and disbelieve.

1:12 Blessed. Happy is the person who has withstood all the trials to the end. **stood the test.** Such a person is like metal which has been purged by fire and is purified of all foreign substances. **crown of life.** Crowns were worn at weddings and feasts (and signify joy); were given to winners of athletic competitions (and signify victory); and worn by royalty (as befits children of God the King).

1:13 tempted. The focus shifts from enduring outward trials (v. 12) to resisting inner temptations. **God is tempting me.** The natural tendency is to blame others for our failure. In this case, God is blamed for sending a test that was too hard to bear. **nor does he tempt anyone.** God does not lure anyone into a tempting situation just to see whether that person will stand or fall.

1:14 evil desire. The true source of evil is a person's own inner inclination (Mark 7:21–23).

[16]Don't be deceived, my dear brothers. [17]Every good and perfect
gift is from above, coming down from the Father of the heavenly
lights, who does not change like shifting shadows. [18]He chose to give
us birth through the word of truth, that we might be a kind of firstfruits of all he created.

Listening and Doing

[19]My dear brothers, take note of this: Everyone should be quick to
listen, slow to speak and slow to become angry, [20]for man's anger
does not bring about the righteous life that God desires. [21]Therefore,
get rid of all moral filth and the evil that is so prevalent and humbly
accept the word planted in you, which can save you.
[22]Do not merely listen to the word, and so deceive yourselves. Do
what it says. [23]Anyone who listens to the word but does not do what
it says is like a man who looks at his face in a mirror [24]and, after looking at himself, goes away and immediately forgets what he looks like.
[25]But the man who looks intently into the perfect law that gives freedom, and continues to do this, not forgetting what he has heard, but
doing it—he will be blessed in what he does.
[26]If anyone considers himself religious and yet does not keep a
tight rein on his tongue, he deceives himself and his religion is
worthless. [27]Religion that God our Father accepts as pure and faultless is this: to look after orphans and widows in their distress and to
keep oneself from being polluted by the world.

OPEN Which best describes your temper: Short fuse, big bomb? Long fuse, little fizz? Other?

STUDY **1.** When was a time you wish you had been "quick to listen" and "slow to speak" (v. 19)? **2.** What is "the word planted in you" and how can it "save you" (v. 21)? **3.** How does the term "Sunday Christian" illustrate James' point in verses 22–24? Conversely, what does the life of someone described in verse 25 look like?

APPLY **1.** How would you describe your spiritual life right now? **2.** What have you found helpful in keeping your mind from being polluted?

Favoritism Forbidden

2 My brothers, as believers in our glorious Lord Jesus Christ, don't
show favoritism. [2]Suppose a man comes into your meeting
wearing a gold ring and fine clothes, and a poor man in shabby
clothes also comes in. [3]If you show special attention to the man
wearing fine clothes and say, "Here's a good seat for you," but say to
the poor man, "You stand there" or "Sit on the floor by my feet,"
[4]have you not discriminated among yourselves and become judges
with evil thoughts?
[5]Listen, my dear brothers: Has not God chosen those who are poor

OPEN **1.** When did you go to a big party and feel like you didn't fit at all? **2.** What third world country, or low-income area, have you spent time in?

STUDY **1.** In general, what are some ways people show favoritism? **2.** How does God look on favoritism? **3.** What is the lesson in this passage for how we are to relate to others—rich and poor? If a promi-

---

1:19 slow to speak. One needs to consider carefully what is to be said, rather than impulsively and carelessly launching into words that are not wise. **slow to become angry.** James does not forbid anger. He does caution against responding in anger at every opportunity.

1:21 get rid of. This verb means literally, "to lay aside" or "to strip off," as one would do with filthy clothing. **planted in you.** They are Christians already. They have the life of God in them. It is now up to them to act upon what is already theirs.

1:26 considers himself. The focus is on a person's own self-assessment of his or her religious commitment. In contrast, in verse 27, James states what God considers as truly religious. **religious.** The emphasis here is probably on the overt acts of religion, such as scrupulous observance of the details of worship and personal acts of piety. **a tight reign on his tongue.** The inability to control one's speech (as in gossip and criticism) is the mark of the person who thinks he or she is religious but really is not.

1:27 Religion. True religion has more to do with acts of charity than acts of piety. It involves caring for others and avoiding the corrupting influence of one's culture. **orphans and widows.** In the Old Testament, orphans and widows were the poor and oppressed, whom God's people were to care for because God cared for them (Deut. 10:17–18; 24:17–22). **polluted.** Unstained, pure, undefiled. **world.** This refers to the world system that is in opposition to God.

2:2 a gold ring. This is the mark of those who belonged to the equestrian order—the second level of Roman aristocracy. These noblemen were typically wealthy. Rings (in general) were a sign of wealth. Early Christians were urged to wear only one ring, on the little finger, bearing the image of a dove, fish, or anchor. **fine clothes.** These are literally "bright and shining" garments, like those worn by the angels in Acts 10:30. **poor man.** The word used here denotes a beggar, a person from the lowest level of society. **shabby clothes.** In contrast to the spotless garments of the rich man, the beggar wears filthy rags, probably because this is all he owns. Our treatment of others should not be based on outward appearances.

nent and wealthy person showed up at your church, how would this person be treated? If a poor person (beggar) showed up, where would this person be seated? **4.** What two gifts does God give the poor (v. 5)? Why would the poor be rich in faith? **5.** If Jesus was the pastor of your church, what would he do to reach out to the poor and homeless?

APPLY 1. What are you doing to open up your home to the broken people in your world? **2.** Who would you like to invite to this group or your church?

OPEN Are you more likely to act without thinking or think without acting?

STUDY 1. What kind of faith is condemned in verse 14? In what ways does this still happen today? **2.** What is the relationship between faith and deeds, according to James? **3.** In what way is "faith without deeds" dead (vv. 18–24)? **4.** Why is Abraham such a good example of faith in action (Gen. 22)? In Abraham's sandals, would your "faith" have prompted you to do what he did, or to "trust" God to find another way, without climbing the mountain?

APPLY 1. As you think of your own spiritual journey, what is the closest you have come to having your faith put to the test? **2.** What is the growing edge in your faith journey right now?

---

in the eyes of the world to be rich in faith and to inherit the kingdom
he promised those who love him? 6But you have insulted the poor. Is
it not the rich who are exploiting you? Are they not the ones who are
dragging you into court? 7Are they not the ones who are slandering
the noble name of him to whom you belong?
8If you really keep the royal law found in Scripture, "Love your
neighbor as yourself,"[a] you are doing right. 9But if you show favoritism, you sin and are convicted by the law as lawbreakers. 10For whoever keeps the whole law and yet stumbles at just one point is guilty
of breaking all of it. 11For he who said, "Do not commit adultery,"[b]
also said, "Do not murder."[c] If you do not commit adultery but do
commit murder, you have become a lawbreaker.
12Speak and act as those who are going to be judged by the law
that gives freedom, 13because judgment without mercy will be shown
to anyone who has not been merciful. Mercy triumphs over judgment!

Faith and Deeds

14What good is it, my brothers, if a man claims to have faith but has
no deeds? Can such faith save him? 15Suppose a brother or sister is
without clothes and daily food. 16If one of you says to him, "Go, I
wish you well; keep warm and well fed," but does nothing about his
physical needs, what good is it? 17In the same way, faith by itself, if it
is not accompanied by action, is dead.
18But someone will say, "You have faith; I have deeds."
Show me your faith without deeds, and I will show you my faith by
what I do. 19You believe that there is one God. Good! Even the demons believe that—and shudder.
20You foolish man, do you want evidence that faith without deeds is
useless[d]? 21Was not our ancestor Abraham considered righteous for
what he did when he offered his son Isaac on the altar? 22You see that
his faith and his actions were working together, and his faith was
made complete by what he did. 23And the scripture was fulfilled that
says, "Abraham believed God, and it was credited to him as

[a]8 Lev. 19:18 [b]11 Exodus 20:14; Deut. 5:18 [c]11 Exodus 20:13; Deut. 5:17 [d]20 Some early manuscripts *dead*

2:6 exploiting you. In a day of abject poverty the poor were forced to borrow money at exorbitant rates of interest just to survive. The rich profited from their need. **dragging you into court.** This was probably over the issue of a debt.

2:7 the noble name. The early followers of Jesus were dubbed with the name "Christians" (Acts 11:26). At baptism they formally took upon themselves the name of Christ, knowing that they might well be vilified simply for bearing that name.

2:12 the law that gives freedom. Judaism had become encrusted with countless rules that bound people. Christians had only one principle to follow: to love others freely as Christ freely loved them (v. 8; 1:25).

2:14 faith. James uses this word in a special way. The faith he speaks of here is mere intellectual affirmation. Such a mind-oriented profession stands in sharp contrast to the comprehensive, whole-life commitment that characterizes true New Testament faith. New Testament faith involves believing with all one's being: mind, emotions, body (behavior) and spirit. The people James has in mind differ from their pagan and Jewish neighbors only in what they profess to believe. **deeds.** Just as James uses the word "faith" in his own way, so too he uses deeds (or "works"). For James, deeds have to do with proper ethical behavior. **Can such faith save him?** The implied answer to this rhetorical question is "No." This answer is based on what James just said in verses 12–13. Intellectual faith cannot save one from judgment when one has not been merciful.

2:21–25 James concludes with two illustrations from the Old Testament containing the evidence demanded by the fool in verse 20 for the assertion that faith is useless without deeds. In both cases faith is demonstrated by means of concrete action. Abraham actually had the knife raised over his beloved son Isaac, and Rahab actually hid the spies. Without faith, Abraham would never have even considered sacrificing his only son, nor would Rahab have defied her king at great personal risk.

righteousness,"[a] and he was called God's friend. 24You see that a person is justified by what he does and not by faith alone.
25In the same way, was not even Rahab the prostitute considered
righteous for what she did when she gave lodging to the spies and
sent them off in a different direction? 26As the body without the spirit
is dead, so faith without deeds is dead.

Taming the Tongue

3 Not many of you should presume to be teachers, my brothers,
because you know that we who teach will be judged more
strictly. 2We all stumble in many ways. If anyone is never at fault in
what he says, he is a perfect man, able to keep his whole body in
check.
3When we put bits into the mouths of horses to make them obey
us, we can turn the whole animal. 4Or take ships as an example. Although they are so large and are driven by strong winds, they are
steered by a very small rudder wherever the pilot wants to go. 5Like-
wise the tongue is a small part of the body, but it makes great boasts.
Consider what a great forest is set on fire by a small spark. 6The
tongue also is a fire, a world of evil among the parts of the body. It
corrupts the whole person, sets the whole course of his life on fire,
and is itself set on fire by hell.
7All kinds of animals, birds, reptiles and creatures of the sea are
being tamed and have been tamed by man, 8but no man can tame the
tongue. It is a restless evil, full of deadly poison.
9With the tongue we praise our Lord and Father, and with it we
curse men, who have been made in God's likeness. 10Out of the same
mouth come praise and cursing. My brothers, this should not be.
11Can both fresh water and salt[b] water flow from the same spring?
12My brothers, can a fig tree bear olives, or a grapevine bear figs? Neither can a salt spring produce fresh water.

Two Kinds of Wisdom

13Who is wise and understanding among you? Let him show it by
his good life, by deeds done in the humility that comes from wisdom.
14But if you harbor bitter envy and selfish ambition in your hearts, do
not boast about it or deny the truth. 15Such "wisdom" does not come
down from heaven but is earthly, unspiritual, of the devil. 16For where
you have envy and selfish ambition, there you find disorder and every
evil practice.
17But the wisdom that comes from heaven is first of all pure; then
peace-loving, considerate, submissive, full of mercy and good fruit,

[a]*23* Gen. 15:6 [b]*11* Greek *bitter* (see also verse 14)

OPEN 1. What radio or TV personality do you appreciate for his or her uplifting words? What personality don't you appreciate? **2.** Who have you known that was truly wise?

STUDY 1. What is the warning here for leaders/teachers in the church? **2.** What do the examples of the bit, rudder and fire teach about the importance of watching what we say? **3.** What is the point the author makes in verses 9–12? Do you agree? **4.** Reading between the lines, what do you think is going on in this church? **5.** If you applied the test here for "wisdom" to what goes on at board meetings in your church, what would it do? How about at your office?

APPLY 1. As you get older and wiser, what have you learned about personality conflicts? **2.** Who do you admire in your church or job because they always build people up rather than tear them down? **3.** What have you found helpful in controlling your own tongue?

2:24 by faith alone. James declares that saying you have faith isn't the same as sharing your faith. Real faith produces a changed life which, in turn, does good works.

3:14 bitter envy. The word translated "bitter" is the same word which was used in verse 12 to describe brackish water unfit for human consumption. It is now applied to zeal (the word translated "envy" is literally *zelos*). Zeal that has gone astray becomes jealousy. **in your hearts.** This is the issue: What lies at the core of the person's being? **do not boast about it or deny the truth.** Those whose hearts are filled with this sense of rivalry and party spirit ought not to pretend that they are speaking God's wisdom. To do this is merely to compound the wrong that is taking place.

3:17 peace-loving. This is the opposite of envy and ambition. True wisdom produces right relationships between people, which is the root idea behind the word "peace" when it is used in the New Testament. **submissive.** True wisdom is willing to listen, learn and then yield when persuaded. **full of mercy and good fruit.** True wisdom reaches out to the unfortunate in practical ways, a point James never tires of making.

OPEN 1. When you were growing up, how did you get along with your brother/sister? 2. What issue was guaranteed to provoke an argument?

STUDY 1. What is at the root of all personality conflicts? Have you found this to be true? 2. What is the caution here on prayer? 3. When the author uses the word "adulterous" to describe these Christians, what is he referring to? 4. From a study of the verbs in verses 7–10, what is the author asking/commanding this church to do if they are going to be a Christian community? How would you put this challenge in a few words? 5. What is the point here about slandering another person?

APPLY 1. Have you ever been a part of a group that took difficult issues head on? Did they stay with the issues until there were lasting resolutions? 2. On a scale from 1 to 10, how would you grade your Christian community today on dealing with conflict?

OPEN 1. Are you a long-range planner, or do you take one day at a time? 2. When you were 15, what did you expect to be doing at 25?

STUDY 1. How far into the future have you planned your

impartial and sincere. [18]Peacemakers who sow in peace raise a harvest of righteousness.

Submit Yourselves to God

4 What causes fights and quarrels among you? Don't they come
from your desires that battle within you? [2]You want something
but don't get it. You kill and covet, but you cannot have what you
want. You quarrel and fight. You do not have, because you do not ask
God. [3]When you ask, you do not receive, because you ask with wrong
motives, that you may spend what you get on your pleasures.
[4]You adulterous people, don't you know that friendship with the
world is hatred toward God? Anyone who chooses to be a friend of
the world becomes an enemy of God. [5]Or do you think Scripture says
without reason that the spirit he caused to live in us envies
intensely?[a] [6]But he gives us more grace. That is why Scripture says:

"God opposes the proud
but gives grace to the humble."[b]

[7]Submit yourselves, then, to God. Resist the devil, and he will flee
from you. [8]Come near to God and he will come near to you. Wash
your hands, you sinners, and purify your hearts, you double-minded.
[9]Grieve, mourn and wail. Change your laughter to mourning and your
joy to gloom. [10]Humble yourselves before the Lord, and he will lift
you up.
[11]Brothers, do not slander one another. Anyone who speaks
against his brother or judges him speaks against the law and judges
it. When you judge the law, you are not keeping it, but sitting in judgment on it. [12]There is only one Lawgiver and Judge, the one who is
able to save and destroy. But you—who are you to judge your neighbor?

Boasting About Tomorrow

[13]Now listen, you who say, "Today or tomorrow we will go to this or
that city, spend a year there, carry on business and make money."
[14]Why, you do not even know what will happen tomorrow. What is

[a]5 Or *that God jealously longs for the spirit that he made to live in us;* or *that the Spirit he caused to live in us longs jealously* [b]6 Prov. 3:34

---

impartial. Literally, "undivided"; that is, true wisdom does not vacillate back and forth. It is the opposite of the wavering person in 1:6–8. **sincere.** True wisdom does not act or pretend. It is honest and genuine.

4:1 fights and quarrels. Literally, "wars and battles." These are long-term conflicts, not sudden explosions. **within you.** The struggle is within a believer—between the part of him or her which is controlled by the Holy Spirit and that which is controlled by the flesh.

4:2 You want something. This is desire at work (1:14). **but don't get it.** This is desire frustrated. **kill and covet.** This is how frustrated desire responds. It lashes out at others in anger and abuse. (This is "killing" in a metaphorical sense—Matt. 5:21–22.) It responds in jealousy to those who have what it wants. **quarrel and fight.** This mad desire-driven quest causes a person to disregard other people, trampling over them if necessary to get what they want. **you do not ask God.** One reason for this frustrated desire is a lack of prayer.

4:7 Submit yourselves, then, to God. His first and primary command is that they must submit to God. **Resist the devil.** Submission to God begins with resistance to Satan. Thus far they have been giving in to the devil's enticements. **he will flee from you.** Since Satan has no ultimate power over a Christian, when resisted he can do little but withdraw.

4:13 Boasting about the future is arrogant because God is the only one who knows what will happen in the future.

4:14 tomorrow. All such planning presupposes that tomorrow will unfold like any other day, when in fact, the future is anything but secure (Prov. 27:1). **What is your life?** Hosea 13:3 says, "Therefore they will be like the morning mist, like the early dew that disappears,

your life? You are a mist that appears for a little while and then vanishes. 15 Instead, you ought to say, "If it is the Lord's will, we will live
and do this or that." 16 As it is, you boast and brag. All such boasting is
evil. 17 Anyone, then, who knows the good he ought to do and doesn't
do it, sins.

Warning to Rich Oppressors

5 Now listen, you rich people, weep and wail because of the misery that is coming upon you. 2 Your wealth has rotted, and moths
have eaten your clothes. 3 Your gold and silver are corroded. Their
corrosion will testify against you and eat your flesh like fire. You have
hoarded wealth in the last days. 4 Look! The wages you failed to pay
the workmen who mowed your fields are crying out against you. The
cries of the harvesters have reached the ears of the Lord Almighty.
5 You have lived on earth in luxury and self-indulgence. You have fattened yourselves in the day of slaughter.[a] 6 You have condemned and
murdered innocent men, who were not opposing you.

Patience in Suffering

7 Be patient, then, brothers, until the Lord's coming. See how the
farmer waits for the land to yield its valuable crop and how patient he
is for the autumn and spring rains. 8 You too, be patient and stand
firm, because the Lord's coming is near. 9 Don't grumble against each
other, brothers, or you will be judged. The Judge is standing at the
door!

10 Brothers, as an example of patience in the face of suffering, take
the prophets who spoke in the name of the Lord. 11 As you know, we
consider blessed those who have persevered. You have heard of Job's
perseverance and have seen what the Lord finally brought about. The
Lord is full of compassion and mercy.

12 Above all, my brothers, do not swear—not by heaven or by earth

[a] 5 Or *yourselves as in a day of feasting*

life? What attitude should we have toward our plans? **2.** What four areas of life are discussed in 4:13? **3.** What is wrong with this type of planning? **4.** What is James saying to the wealthy? **5.** What is a proper attitude toward finances?

APPLY Reflect on 4:17 and tell the group how this is true of you.

OPEN 1. Who is the green thumb in your family? **2.** What is the sickest you have been lately?

STUDY 1. If you were the spiritual leader of an inner city church with lots of poor and homeless people, what would you urge your flock to do? What does James urge this flock to do? **2.** What is the principle here on dealing with your circumstances (4:13–14)? **3.** Do you believe in calling the elders to anoint the sick with oil? What if the sickness is the result of sin? **4.** Do you believe that Christians should confess their sins to each other? In what circumstances? **5.** Do you believe that prayer

---

like chaff swirling from a threshing floor, like smoke escaping through a window."

4:15 If it is the Lord's will. The uncertainty of the future ought not to be a terror to the Christian. Instead, it ought to force on him or her an awareness of how dependent a person is upon God, and thus move that person to a planning that involves God. **we will live and do this or that.** James is not ruling out planning. He says plan, but keep God in mind.

4:16 boast. The problem with this boasting is that they are claiming to have the future under control when, in fact, it is God who holds time in his hands.These are empty claims. **brag.** This word originally described an itinerant quack who touted "cures" that did not work. It came to mean claiming to be able to do something that you could not do.

5:1 rich people. In the first century there was a great gulf between rich and poor. **wail.** This is a strong word meaning "to shriek" or "howl," and is used to describe the terror that will be felt by the damned.

5:4 wages you failed to pay. The Old Testament insisted that it was wrong to withhold wages. A worker was to be paid immediately. **the workmen.** In Palestine, day laborers were used to plant and harvest the crops. They were cheaper than slaves. **fields.** The Greek word means "estates." These were the large tracts of land owned by the very wealthy. **crying out.** This is a word used to describe the wild, incoherent cry of an animal.

5:5 luxury. In contrast to the hunger of the laborers is the soft and easy living of the landowners (Amos 6:1–7). **self-indulgence.** Not just luxury but vice is in view here. **day of slaughter.** Cattle were pampered and fattened for one purpose only: to be slaughtered. On the day when this took place a great feast was held.

5:9 James now touches on the theme of speech. **grumble.** This word is literally "groan." While groaning in the face of suffering is appropriate (Mark 7:34; Rom. 8:23), groaning at one another is not!

5:11 persevered. At this point, James shifts from the more passive word "patience" to the idea of active endurance of suffering, a concept which describes Job's experience. **finally brought about.** But in the end, God blessed Job with far more than he had at the beginning of his trials.

5:12 swear. The issue is not that of using foul language but of taking an oath to guarantee a promise. **Yes be yes.** Christians have no need for oaths.

is effective? In what way? **6.** As Christians, how are we to confront another Christian in our community if he/she is out of line?

APPLY 1. What is the closest you have come to belonging to a Christian community that practiced anointing with oil over the sick and confessing your sins to one another? What was it like? **2.** What was the high point in this study for you? What would you like to study next? **3.** Who would you like to invite into your group?

---

or by anything else. Let your "Yes" be yes, and your "No," no, or you will be condemned.

The Prayer of Faith

13Is any one of you in trouble? He should pray. Is anyone happy?
Let him sing songs of praise. 14Is any one of you sick? He should call
the elders of the church to pray over him and anoint him with oil in
the name of the Lord. 15And the prayer offered in faith will make the
sick person well; the Lord will raise him up. If he has sinned, he will
be forgiven. 16Therefore confess your sins to each other and pray for
each other so that you may be healed. The prayer of a righteous man
is powerful and effective.
17Elijah was a man just like us. He prayed earnestly that it would
not rain, and it did not rain on the land for three and a half years.
18Again he prayed, and the heavens gave rain, and the earth produced
its crops.
19My brothers, if one of you should wander from the truth and
someone should bring him back, 20remember this: Whoever turns a
sinner from the error of his way will save him from death and cover
over a multitude of sins.

They are expected to speak only truth.

5:14 sick. Illness is not something anybody else does to you. Especially in the first century, illness made one feel vulnerable. What could be done? Where could a believer go for help? James has an answer to this question. **call the elders.** Illness was to be dealt with in the context of the Christian community. The elders were to be called to minister to the ill person. They had two things to do: to pray over the person and to anoint them with oil. **anoint him with oil.** When a Jew was ill, he or she first went to a rabbi to be anointed with oil. Oil was used not only for ritual purposes but for cleaning wounds, for paralysis, and for toothaches. In this case, the olive oil is not being used as a medicine but as a part of the healing prayer (Mark 6:13; Luke 10:34).

5:15 the Lord will raise him up. James is quite clear about the source of the healing. It is not the oil, it is not the laying on of hands by the elders, nor is it even prayer in some sort of magical sense. It is God who heals.

5:16 confess your sins. Confessing your sins to one another removes barriers between people and promotes honesty in the Christian community. Prayer is directed to *God*, who is all-powerful and who works in this world.

5:17 man just like us. Elijah knew depression, despair and doubt just as did the Christians (1 Kin. 19). And yet, God answered his prayer in a mighty way. Here he makes it clear that all Christians can pray like this, not just prophets.

5:18 the earth produced its crops. God controls the rain and Christians can pray to him to bring rain. By implication, while patiently enduring their troubles, Christians can pray in confidence to God about them.

1 Peter

Author. Traditionally, the apostle Peter is credited with writing this letter.

Date. First Peter was written sometime between the fire in Rome (A.D. 64) and his death (A.D. 68).

Theme. Hope in the midst of suffering.

Personal Reading	Group Study Topic and Reading	
1:1–12	Christ Our Hope	1:1–12
1:13–2:3	Christ Our Sacrifice	1:13–2:3
2:4–12	Christ Our Foundation	2:4–12
2:13–25	Christ Our Example	2:13–25
3:1–7	Relationships	3:1–7
3:8–22	Christ Our Lord	3:8–22
4:1–11	Christ Our Strength	4:1–11
4:12–19	Christ Our Joy	4:12–19
5:1–14	Christ Our Shepherd	5:1–14

Historical Background. Under Roman law there were two types of religious systems: those that were legal, such as Judaism, and those that were forbidden. Anyone who practiced a forbidden religion was considered a criminal and was subject to harsh penalties. After the great fire of Rome that Nero blamed on the believers, Christianity was judged to be distinct from Judaism, and it was quickly prohibited. This meant that throughout the Roman Empire, followers of Christ were now technically outlaws and thus subject to persecution. Just such persecution was the experience of Christians in Asia Minor to whom Peter writes (4:12).

Purpose. In the midst of the "painful trial" (4:12) they are suffering, Peter writes to comfort and encourage. "Rejoice that you participate in the sufferings of Christ" (4:13), he says. How can they rejoice at such a difficult time? Because of the great *hope* they have as believers. Hope is the theme of Peter's letter to these suffering believers.

Characteristics. When reading 1 Peter, one keeps hearing echoes from other parts of the Bible. Peter quotes a number of passages from the Old Testament, particularly from Isaiah. Furthermore, he frequently alludes to Old Testament ideas and stories.

Peter is also familiar with Paul's writings. This letter contains parallels to Romans and, in particular, Ephesians. In addition, there are parallels to Hebrews, James and, not surprisingly, to Peter's own sermons in Acts.

Of course, this does not necessarily mean that Peter was consciously quoting from New Testament documents. It may simply be that there was a common pattern of teaching in the early church and that Peter is reflecting this as did other New Testament writers.

First Peter is written in excellent Greek, so much so that some have questioned whether a Galilean fisherman like Peter could have had such a sophisticated command of the language. First Peter contains some of the best Greek in the New Testament. Its style is smoother than Paul's, with his years of training; its rhythmic structure is not unlike that of the Greek masters.

The answer to this question is found in 5:12: "With the help of Silas ... I have written to you." The Greek here indicates that Silas was more than just a stenographer. In fact, he could well be the source of the excellent style as he helped Peter draft the letter and polish up the language.

Audience. First Peter is a circular letter to followers of Christ living in the northwest section of Asia Minor (in what is now modern Turkey). Pontus, Galatia, Cappadocia, Asia and Bithynia (1:1) were all Roman provinces. That these Christians were mainly Gentiles is clear from the way Peter describes their preconversion life; he uses categories and phrases typically applied to pagans but not to Jews (1:14; 2:9–10; 4:3–4). Peter also uses the Greek form of his name, Cephas, in this letter, and not Simon, his Jewish name.

OPEN 1. How many times did your family move when you were growing up? Which time was the hardest? **2.** If someone in your group claimed that they had caught a fish three feet long, what would you say?

STUDY 1. What do you remember about Nero, the emperor in Rome during the time this letter was written? **2.** If you were responsible for churches in these provinces where persecution is raging, how would you start off a letter to these Christians? How would you describe the tone in verses 1–12? **3.** Reading this passage through the peep hole of 4:12, what does Peter want these folks to focus on (vv. 3–6)? Does he ask them to deny their pain and suffering? **4.** What do you think the "new birth" and "salvation" (vv. 3,5,10) meant to these Christians? How much has your commitment to Christ cost you? **5.** If you were one of these battered believers in Christ, how would it make you feel to know that you are the fulfillment of God's plan that the prophets predicted long ago?

APPLY 1. In a few words, when did you accept the grace of God in Christ and start on your life in him? **2.** How would you describe your spiritual journey up to now?

1 Peter, an apostle of Jesus Christ,

To God's elect, strangers in the world, scattered throughout Pontus, Galatia, Cappadocia, Asia and Bithynia, [2]who have been chosen
according to the foreknowledge of God the Father, through the sanctifying work of the Spirit, for obedience to Jesus Christ and sprinkling
by his blood:

Grace and peace be yours in abundance.

Praise to God for a Living Hope

[3]Praise be to the God and Father of our Lord Jesus Christ! In his
great mercy he has given us new birth into a living hope through the
resurrection of Jesus Christ from the dead, [4]and into an inheritance
that can never perish, spoil or fade—kept in heaven for you, [5]who
through faith are shielded by God's power until the coming of the
salvation that is ready to be revealed in the last time. [6]In this you
greatly rejoice, though now for a little while you may have had to
suffer grief in all kinds of trials. [7]These have come so that your
faith—of greater worth than gold, which perishes even though refined by fire—may be proved genuine and may result in praise, glory
and honor when Jesus Christ is revealed. [8]Though you have not seen
him, you love him; and even though you do not see him now, you
believe in him and are filled with an inexpressible and glorious joy,
[9]for you are receiving the goal of your faith, the salvation of your
souls.

[10]Concerning this salvation, the prophets, who spoke of the grace
that was to come to you, searched intently and with the greatest care,
[11]trying to find out the time and circumstances to which the Spirit of
Christ in them was pointing when he predicted the sufferings of

---

1:1 Peter. Peter was the leader of the 12 apostles. Before joining Jesus' band of disciples he was a fisherman on the Sea of Galilee. He worked with his brother Andrew in partnership with James and John (Luke 5:10). Their business was based in Capernaum where Peter and Andrew lived together (Mark 1:21,29). Peter was married (Mark 1:30). Later in his ministry he took his wife with him on visits to the churches (1 Cor. 9:5). His father's name was Jonah (Matt. 16:17). Peter, along with his brother Andrew, was one of the first chosen to be a disciple of Jesus (Mark 1:16–18). **an apostle.** This means, literally, "one who is sent." It is the term used in the New Testament to identify those who were selected for the special task of founding and guiding the new church. **To God's elect.** To be "elect" is to be chosen by God to be a member of his family. **strangers in the world.** This means "sojourner" and refers to those who are far from home, dwelling in a strange land. **scattered.** The Greek word here is *diaspora,* which means "the dispersion." **Pontus, Galatia, Cappadocia, Asia and Bithynia.** These are Roman provinces located in Asia Minor (now modern Turkey). The order in which they are named is the order in which a traveler would visit each.

1:2 chosen according to the foreknowledge of God the Father. Israel knew itself to be chosen by God to be his people (Ezek. 20:5; Hos. 11:1). They were to be the people through whom he would reveal himself to the rest of the world. The first Christians knew that they too had been chosen by God.

1:3 new birth. When people accept Jesus as their Savior, something so radical happens that they can be said to be reborn into a whole new life. **a living hope.** This is the first thing new birth brings. Specifically here, their hope is that one day when Christ comes again they will experience the full fruit of salvation. **the resurrection of Jesus.** This is the means of a believer's salvation.

1:4 into an inheritance. To be born again means they have become part of a new family, and like all sons and daughters they can expect an inheritance. **never perish, spoil or fade.** The first phrase, "never perish," means never be overcome by an enemy. The second phrase, "never spoil," refers to a land that has not been polluted or defiled by a conquering army. The third phrase, "never fade," paints a picture of a land without change or decay. It refers especially to flowers that do not fade. **kept in heaven for you.** This inheritance is immune to disaster.

1:5 shielded. Not only is the inheritance guarded and immune to disaster, but so too are the Christians for whom it exists. **salvation.** While Christ is the object of the believer's hope, salvation is the result.

1:6 for a little while you may have had to suffer. By these two clauses, Peter gives perspective to their suffering. First, it will be temporary ("for a little while"). Second, such trials are circumstantial, perhaps even necessary ("you may have had to" or "if need be"). **trials.** Peter's first allusion to their persecution.

Christ and the glories that would follow. [12]It was revealed to them that they were not serving themselves but you, when they spoke of the things that have now been told you by those who have preached the gospel to you by the Holy Spirit sent from heaven. Even angels long to look into these things.

Be Holy

[13]Therefore, prepare your minds for action; be self-controlled; set your hope fully on the grace to be given you when Jesus Christ is revealed. [14]As obedient children, do not conform to the evil desires you had when you lived in ignorance. [15]But just as he who called you is holy, so be holy in all you do; [16]for it is written: "Be holy, because I am holy."[a]

[17]Since you call on a Father who judges each man's work impartially, live your lives as strangers here in reverent fear. [18]For you know that it was not with perishable things such as silver or gold that you were redeemed from the empty way of life handed down to you from your forefathers, [19]but with the precious blood of Christ, a lamb without blemish or defect. [20]He was chosen before the creation of the world, but was revealed in these last times for your sake. [21]Through him you believe in God, who raised him from the dead and glorified him, and so your faith and hope are in God.

[22]Now that you have purified yourselves by obeying the truth so that you have sincere love for your brothers, love one another deeply, from the heart.[b] [23]For you have been born again, not of perishable seed, but of imperishable, through the living and enduring word of God. [24]For,

"All men are like grass,
and all their glory is like the flowers of the field;
the grass withers and the flowers fall,
25 but the word of the Lord stands forever."[c]

And this is the word that was preached to you.

2 Therefore, rid yourselves of all malice and all deceit, hypocrisy, envy, and slander of every kind. [2]Like newborn babies, crave pure spiritual milk, so that by it you may grow up in your salvation, [3]now that you have tasted that the Lord is good.

[a]*16* Lev. 11:44,45; 19:2; 20:7 [b]*22* Some early manuscripts *from a pure heart* [c]*25* Isaiah 40:6-8

OPEN 1. How did you get ready for exams in school: Keep up? Cram? Get a good night's sleep? **2.** Who was your best coach or teacher? How did this person prepare you and help you excel?

STUDY 1. If you had been Peter, would you have been a little easier on these struggling Christians—or do you like the way he confronts them? How do you think they took it? **2.** How would you put the challenge in verses 12–15 in your own words? How would you define the word "holy" or the command "Be holy" (v. 15)? **3.** How does the author want these Christians to look upon their life (vv. 17–19)? Why does Jesus Christ have the right to call the shots in your life? **4.** What is the challenge for the Christian community here (vv. 22–23)? Why do you think this would be so important for these churches? Do you think you could make it alone, without the support of a caring Christian community?

APPLY 1. On a scale from 1 to 10, what is the stress level in your life right now? What in particular causes the most stress? **2.** Who do you turn to in times of real stress?

1:13 Therefore. The salvation they have received results in a distinctive lifestyle involving clarity of mind, self-control, and an active hope.

1:14 *do not conform to the evil desires.* They are not to allow themselves to be shaped by the sensuality of their pre-Christian existence. **ignorance.** Not only was their pre-Christian life dominated by physical desires of all sorts, they also lived in ignorance of God. Pagans believed there was a god, but thought him to be unknowable and disinterested in human beings.

1:18 redeemed. To redeem someone is to rescue that person from bondage. This is a technical term for the money paid to buy freedom for a slave.

1:19 The price of their ransom from their sin was not material ("silver or gold") but spiritual (the "blood of Christ"). Here, Peter refers to Jesus in sacrificial terms as the innocent victim dying in place of others. **blood.** In the Old Testament, the blood of the sacrificial animal was offered to God in place of the life of the sinner. In the New Testament, it is not the sacrifice of animals that secures forgiveness; it is the death of Jesus who gave himself once for all. **without blemish or defect.** Jesus was able to be such a sacrifice because he was without sin. This is a remarkable confession from one like Peter who lived in close contact with Jesus for three years.

2:1 rid yourselves. This verb was used to describe taking off one's clothes. They must strip off, like spoiled and dirty clothes, their old lifestyle. **all malice and all deceit.** These are general terms which refer to attitudes that disrupt a community. **hypocrisy, envy, and slander.** Specific vices that make relationships difficult.

OPEN Who is the natural architect in your family—who likes to design and build things?

STUDY **1.** If you were counseling "baby Christians" (v. 2) who were struggling with "sinful desires" (v. 11), what would you want to stress? **2.** In the architectual allegory, what is Peter saying to this struggling Christian community? **3.** How would you paraphrase the four metaphors in verse 9? How does this make you feel? **4.** What happened to your citizenship when you became a Christian? How does this affect the way you define "the good life"? **5.** Do you think Peter placed the moral bar for Christians a little higher than we have the bar today?

APPLY **1.** How do your friends who are not committed to Christ look upon your Christian moral views? **2.** How do you go about explaining to them your own position when you differ? **3.** Where do you find you disagree with your non-Christian friends the most?

OPEN Growing up, who was the authority figure in your family? How was disobedience handled?

STUDY **1.** If Peter were writing today to churches in totalitarian countries where the

The Living Stone and a Chosen People

4As you come to him, the living Stone—rejected by men but chosen
by God and precious to him— 5you also, like living stones, are being
built into a spiritual house to be a holy priesthood, offering spiritual
sacrifices acceptable to God through Jesus Christ. 6For in Scripture it
says:

"See, I lay a stone in Zion,
 a chosen and precious cornerstone,
and the one who trusts in him
 will never be put to shame."[a]

7Now to you who believe, this stone is precious. But to those who do
not believe,

"The stone the builders rejected
 has become the capstone,[b]"[c]

8and,

"A stone that causes men to stumble
 and a rock that makes them fall."[d]

They stumble because they disobey the message—which is also what
they were destined for.

9But you are a chosen people, a royal priesthood, a holy nation, a
people belonging to God, that you may declare the praises of him
who called you out of darkness into his wonderful light. 10Once you
were not a people, but now you are the people of God; once you had
not received mercy, but now you have received mercy.

11Dear friends, I urge you, as aliens and strangers in the world, to
abstain from sinful desires, which war against your soul. 12Live such
good lives among the pagans that, though they accuse you of doing
wrong, they may see your good deeds and glorify God on the day he
visits us.

Submission to Rulers and Masters

13Submit yourselves for the Lord's sake to every authority instituted among men: whether to the king, as the supreme authority, 14or to
governors, who are sent by him to punish those who do wrong and to
commend those who do right. 15For it is God's will that by doing good

[a]6 Isaiah 28:16 [b]7 Or *cornerstone* [c]7 Psalm 118:22 [d]8 Isaiah 8:14

2:4 the living Stone. He gets this metaphor from two Old Testament texts: Isaiah 28:16 (v. 6) speaks of "a chosen and precious cornerstone" and Psalm 118:22 (v. 7) speaks of the rejection of that stone. Both verses point out the supreme value of the cornerstone. Peter's point is that, despite his rejection, Christ is the chosen one of God, and in the end he prevails.

2:5 being built into. Stones by themselves serve no function. But shaped together into a structure by a master builder, they become something of use and importance. **a spiritual house.** The church is the temple of God, made up of a close-knit community of men and women. **a holy priesthood.** Not only are they a "spiritual house," they are the priests who serve in it!

2:9 a people belonging to God. The church is a community chosen by God. **that you may declare the praises of him.** This is what our "spiritual sacrifices" are all about: making God known in the world.

2:11 aliens and strangers. They may be a chosen nation and a royal priesthood, but they are also outsiders in terms of the world in which they live. **abstain from sinful desires.** "Sinful desires" is literally "fleshly lusts."

2:13 Submit yourselves. This is the key concept in the next two passages. What Peter urges is voluntary subordination in all spheres of human life.

2:13–14 king ... governors. This first situation in which Peter applies this general principle is with civil authorities.

you should silence the ignorant talk of foolish men. 16Live as free men, but do not use your freedom as a cover-up for evil; live as servants of God. 17Show proper respect to everyone: Love the brotherhood of believers, fear God, honor the king.

18Slaves, submit yourselves to your masters with all respect, not only to those who are good and considerate, but also to those who are harsh. 19For it is commendable if a man bears up under the pain of unjust suffering because he is conscious of God. 20But how is it to your credit if you receive a beating for doing wrong and endure it? But if you suffer for doing good and you endure it, this is commendable before God. 21To this you were called, because Christ suffered for you, leaving you an example, that you should follow in his steps.

22"He committed no sin,
and no deceit was found in his mouth."[a]

23When they hurled their insults at him, he did not retaliate; when he suffered, he made no threats. Instead, he entrusted himself to him who judges justly. 24He himself bore our sins in his body on the tree, so that we might die to sins and live for righteousness; by his wounds you have been healed. 25For you were like sheep going astray, but now you have returned to the Shepherd and Overseer of your souls.

Wives and Husbands

3 Wives, in the same way be submissive to your husbands so that, if any of them do not believe the word, they may be won over without words by the behavior of their wives, 2when they see the purity and reverence of your lives. 3Your beauty should not come from outward adornment, such as braided hair and the wearing of gold jewelry and fine clothes. 4Instead, it should be that of your inner self, the unfading beauty of a gentle and quiet spirit, which is of great worth in God's sight. 5For this is the way the holy women of the past who put their hope in God used to make themselves beautiful. They were submissive to their own husbands, 6like Sarah, who obeyed Abraham and called him her master. You are her daughters if you do what is right and do not give way to fear.

7Husbands, in the same way be considerate as you live with your

[a]22 Isaiah 53:9

government actively persecutes Christians, do you think he would say the same thing about submitting to authority (vv. 13–17)? Why does he counsel this? **2.** How would you apply his position on slaves to unfair labor practices and abuse of worker rights (vv. 18–21)? How far do you think a follower of Christ is to follow the "example" of Christ in taking abuse (v. 21)? **3.** What was Christ doing when his "suffering" went far beyond setting an example (v. 24)? For what purpose?

APPLY 1. What situations do you find yourself in where you must submit to someone or someone must submit to you? **2.** How does Christ's voluntary sacrifice for us affect your ability to submit?

OPEN Who do you look up to as a role model for a healthy Christian marriage in which both parties are looking out for the other?

STUDY 1. How should Christ's sacrifice for us (2:21–25) affect the way husbands and wives treat one another? **2.** What does it mean for a wife to submit to her husband? **3.** What is the husband's responsibility?

APPLY 1. On a scale from 1 to 10, how would you rate your marriage at the moment? **2.** How can you make it better?

2:16 live as servants of God. The paradox is that Christians are both free and bound. They are to "live as free men" while simultaneously they are "slaves of God."

2:18 Slaves, submit yourselves. Slaves were the legal property of their *masters. This fact, though inherently* wrong, defined the reality within which they had to live. Peter does not counsel rebellion or even "passive resistance." What gave slaves the freedom to submit in this way was the sense that they as Christians were, in fact, members of a heavenly family and of a kingdom far more significant than the earthly reality within which they lived.

2:21 To this you were called, because Christ suffered for you. The basis on which Peter says what he does about accepting unjust treatment is the example of Jesus who suffered for us. Christian slaves are to imitate Christ.

2:24 In a key passage about Christ's *saving work*, Peter points out that Jesus was their substitute. He bore their sins. He took upon himself the penalty which they deserved because of their sin. **so that.** Peter points to two results of Jesus' death on the cross: (1) Because of it they are able to die to sin and (2) They can now live for righteousness. It is the moral impact of the cross which Peter chooses to highlight here. **healed.** Christ's wounds brought restoration to their sin-scarred lives.

3:1 in the same way. By this phrase Peter makes a transition from slaves to wives. Just as the behavior of Christ was the model for slaves, so too is it for women. **be submissive.** Again, as he did for slaves, Peter counsels submission, not rebellion. Here Peter is thinking about marriage to a unbelieving husband who would consider himself in charge of his wife. **won over.** Peter (like Paul) does not counsel Christian women to leave unbelieving husbands. His desire is that the husbands be converted.

3:7 In contrast to verses 1–2, where the focus is on Christian wives and

OPEN As a child, what can you remember fighting about on family trips?

STUDY 1. If you were asked to create a list of tips from this passage for living in a pagan culture as a Christian community, what would be the first three tips based on verses 8 and 9? 2. Reading between the lines in verses 13–16, what do you think these Christians are going through? How would you compare their situation to your situation today? 3. When questioned about their Christian faith, what are they to do (v. 15)? What should be the tone in their voice when they answer? What is the difference between giving a reason for the faith that is in you and preaching at someone? 4. If unbelievers accuse believers of things that is not true, how are believers to handle it? How do you handle this? 5. What are some principles in this passage for believers in a secular world who experience discrimination and/or abuse because of their Christian faith?

APPLY 1. What is the closest you have come to belonging to a small Christian community in the midst of a hostile environment, such as a secular college dorm, job or

wives, and treat them with respect as the weaker partner and as heirs
with you of the gracious gift of life, so that nothing will hinder your
prayers.

Suffering for Doing Good

8Finally, all of you, live in harmony with one another; be sympathetic, love as brothers, be compassionate and humble. 9Do not repay
evil with evil or insult with insult, but with blessing, because to this
you were called so that you may inherit a blessing. 10For,

"Whoever would love life
  and see good days
must keep his tongue from evil
  and his lips from deceitful speech.
11He must turn from evil and do good;
  he must seek peace and pursue it.
12For the eyes of the Lord are on the righteous
  and his ears are attentive to their prayer,
but the face of the Lord is against those who do evil."[a]

13Who is going to harm you if you are eager to do good? 14But even
if you should suffer for what is right, you are blessed. "Do not fear
what they fear[b]; do not be frightened."[c] 15But in your hearts set apart
Christ as Lord. Always be prepared to give an answer to everyone
who asks you to give the reason for the hope that you have. But do
this with gentleness and respect, 16keeping a clear conscience, so
that those who speak maliciously against your good behavior in
Christ may be ashamed of their slander. 17It is better, if it is God's will,
to suffer for doing good than for doing evil. 18For Christ died for sins
once for all, the righteous for the unrighteous, to bring you to God.
He was put to death in the body but made alive by the Spirit,

[a] 12 Psalm 34:12-16 [b] 14 Or *not fear their threats* [c] 14 Isaiah 8:12

---

unbelieving husbands, here Peter discusses how Christian husbands should relate to Christian wives. Peter reminds husbands that the respect they are to show to all people (2:17) is also due to their own wives. **in the same way.** As he did when he addressed wives (v. 1), here too, in addressing husbands, Peter harkens back to the example of Christ who voluntarily gave himself for the sake of others (2:21). **treat them with respect.** This phrase is literally "assigning honor," and as such is a paradoxical statement (in that inferiors give "honor" to superiors—in this Roman setting, women were unquestionably the inferior party). **the weaker partner.** Literally, the "weaker vessel." There has been much debate as to what this means. It might refer to anatomical *differences between men and women* (this phrase was used in Greek to refer to the woman's body), to the inferior position of women in that society, or to the comparative lack of physical strength on the part of the woman. **heirs with you.** Literally, joint heirs or coheirs. Both husband and wife are equal participants in the grace of God, again reinforcing the idea that men and women have equal value in God's eyes.

3:8 live in harmony. The phrase is literally "all of one mind." By it Peter encourages the kind of unity that is vital in a hostile environment. There must be no divisions within the church. **love as brothers.** Peter uses the verb related to *philadelphia* (love amongst kin) instead of the more common verb related to *agape* (self-giving love).

3:15 in your hearts. At the core of their being, Christ must reign. **set apart Christ.** Literally, "sanctify" Christ. Christ is to be acknowledged as holy and worshiped as Lord. They are to open themselves to his inner presence. **be prepared to give an answer.** Although this may refer to an official inquiry in which they are called upon to defend the fact they are Christians, it probably is more general in reference. When anybody asks about the hope they have, they are to explain why they are followers of Jesus. **the reason.** Greeks valued a logical, intelligent statement as to why one held certain beliefs. **with gentleness and respect.** This reply should not be given in a contentious or defensive way.

3:18 died for sins. Christ died—as have men and women down through the ages. But his death was different in that it was a full, sufficient, and adequate sacrifice that atones for the sins of all people. **once for all.** The sacrifices in the temple had to be repeated over and over again; Christ's sacrifice was the final and perfect sacrifice through which all people in all ages may obtain salvation. **the righteous for the unrighteous.** His death was vicarious; he died in the place of others.

19 through whom[a] also he went and preached to the spirits in prison
20 who disobeyed long ago when God waited patiently in the days of
Noah while the ark was being built. In it only a few people, eight in
all, were saved through water, 21 and this water symbolizes baptism
that now saves you also—not the removal of dirt from the body but
the pledge[b] of a good conscience toward God. It saves you by the resurrection of Jesus Christ, 22 who has gone into heaven and is at God's
right hand—with angels, authorities and powers in submission to
him.

Living for God

4 Therefore, since Christ suffered in his body, arm yourselves also
with the same attitude, because he who has suffered in his body
is done with sin. 2 As a result, he does not live the rest of his earthly
life for evil human desires, but rather for the will of God. 3 For you
have spent enough time in the past doing what pagans choose to
do—living in debauchery, lust, drunkenness, orgies, carousing and
detestable idolatry. 4 They think it strange that you do not plunge with
them into the same flood of dissipation, and they heap abuse on you.
5 But they will have to give account to him who is ready to judge the
living and the dead. 6 For this is the reason the gospel was preached
even to those who are now dead, so that they might be judged according to men in regard to the body, but live according to God in
regard to the spirit.
7 The end of all things is near. Therefore be clear minded and self-
controlled so that you can pray. 8 Above all, love each other deeply,
because love covers over a multitude of sins. 9 Offer hospitality to one
another without grumbling. 10 Each one should use whatever gift he
has received to serve others, faithfully administering God's grace in
its various forms. 11 If anyone speaks, he should do it as one speaking
the very words of God. If anyone serves, he should do it with the
strength God provides, so that in all things God may be praised

[a] 18,19 Or *alive in the spirit,* [19] *through which* [b] 21 Or *response*

the military? **2.** How did you deal with personal attacks on your faith? **3.** What have you learned about sharing your faith?

OPEN Where is the hangout in your town for the people who want to "kick back" and enjoy "night life"?

STUDY 1. How would you describe the lifestyle of these people before they became Christians? What do these "old friends" think of their "new" lifestyle? **2.** For these Christians to survive, what are some things they need to work on (vv. 7–11)? How would you paraphrase verse 8 in your own words? **3.** What is the point that Peter is making here about gifts for anyone who speaks or serves?

APPLY 1. When did you come to the place in your life that you realized you had "spent enough time doing what unbelievers do" and you turned the corner? **2.** What do your unbelieving friends think of your change of lifestyle?

3:19 preached. The nature of Jesus' proclamation has been interpreted as: (1) The gospel which was proclaimed to those who lived before Christ came, or as (2) The announcement to the rebellious spirits that their power had been broken. **the spirits.** Who these spirits were is not clear. They have been variously identified as: (1) sinners who lived before the incarnation of Christ, or (2) the rebellious angels of Genesis 6:1–4. **prison.** Likewise, the nature of this prison is not clear. It has been identified as: (1) hell, (2) a metaphor for the imprisonment that sin and ignorance brings, or (3) the world of spirits.

4:3 The list of vices here parallels the lists in Romans 13:13 and Galatians 5:19–21. The picture it paints is of a lifestyle characterized by sexual and alcoholic excess based on idolatry. This is a lifestyle out of control, characterized by harmful addictions and cultic practices. **time in the past.** Christians have two views of time: time past, in which they gave themselves over to a destructive lifestyle, and "the rest of ... earthly life" (v. 2), that time following conversion in which they live in accord with God's will. **debauchery.** "Excesses;" "outrages against decency;" "living in sensualities." **drunkenness.** Literally, "overflowings of wine." **carousing.** Literally, "drinking bouts;" "drunken parties."

4:6 the gospel was preached even to those who are now dead. The meaning of this phrase is quite difficult and has been much debated. It probably refers to those members of the church who heard and accepted the gospel but who have since died. Some scholars, however, connect this verse to 3:19–20 and conclude this is a reference to Christ's descent into hell, during which he proclaimed the gospel to those who were there.

4:10 gift. This word is *charisma* and refers to the different gifts which the Holy Spirit gives to individual Christians for the sake of the whole body. **to serve others.** The point of these gifts is to use them for the sake of others. **God's grace in its various forms.** "Each one" has a gift, but not all have the same gift (Rom 12:6–8; 1 Cor. 12:7–10; Eph. 4:11–12 for lists of various gifts).

4:11 Peter discusses two gifts in particular: gift of teaching and preaching and gift of service. **If anyone speaks.** This is not the gift of tongues (ecstatic utterance), nor the gift of prophecy. **If anyone serves.** There are different kinds of service: helping those in need, giving leadership, providing money (Acts 6:1–4; Rom 12:13; 1 Cor. 12:5).

through Jesus Christ. To him be the glory and the power for ever and
ever. Amen.

Suffering for Being a Christian

[12]Dear friends, do not be surprised at the painful trial you are suffering, as though something strange were happening to you. [13]But
rejoice that you participate in the sufferings of Christ, so that you
may be overjoyed when his glory is revealed. [14]If you are insulted
because of the name of Christ, you are blessed, for the Spirit of glory
and of God rests on you. [15]If you suffer, it should not be as a murderer
or thief or any other kind of criminal, or even as a meddler. [16]How-
ever, if you suffer as a Christian, do not be ashamed, but praise God
that you bear that name. [17]For it is time for judgment to begin with
the family of God; and if it begins with us, what will the outcome be
for those who do not obey the gospel of God? [18]And,

> "If it is hard for the righteous to be saved,
> what will become of the ungodly and the sinner?"[a]

[19]So then, those who suffer according to God's will should commit
themselves to their faithful Creator and continue to do good.

To Elders and Young Men

5 To the elders among you, I appeal as a fellow elder, a witness of
Christ's sufferings and one who also will share in the glory to be
revealed: [2]Be shepherds of God's flock that is under your care, serving as overseers—not because you must, but because you are willing,
as God wants you to be; not greedy for money, but eager to serve;
[3]not lording it over those entrusted to you, but being examples to the
flock. [4]And when the Chief Shepherd appears, you will receive the
crown of glory that will never fade away.

[5]Young men, in the same way be submissive to those who are older.

[a]*18* Prov. 11:31

OPEN In your group, who has the bragging rights for the longest scar? The most broken bones?

STUDY 1. When the attacks of the secular world come, what is to be the response of the Christian community? **2.** Does it sound to you like the pagan authorities are accusing them of things that could land them in jail? How would you deal with trumped up charges if you were in their shoes? **3.** What does verse 19 say to you about discrimination and abuse you suffer as a Christian?

APPLY What is the closest you have come to being persecuted for your faith?

OPEN Where are you in the "pecking order" of the children in your family? How has this affected your personality?

STUDY 1. What are three or four principles in verses 1–4 for leaders or the leadership team of a church? **2.** What is the clear teaching here on younger leaders in the church? Do you think our culture today honors the older generation? **3.** Do you think Peter expects the church to be hassle-free and worry-free? How would you

---

4:16 Christian. Apart from two references in Acts (11:26; 26:28), this is the only other use of "Christian" in the New Testament.

4:19 commit themselves. This is a technical term which refers to the act of depositing money with a trusted friend. This is the same word Jesus used in Luke 23:46: "Father, into your hands I commit my spirit." In the end it all comes down to this. Those who suffer for doing good, those who suffer only because they are Christians (v. 16), must simply commit themselves to God. He is that trusted friend who can be relied upon absolutely to bear this trust. They will be safe with him.

5:1 a fellow elder. Peter bore the same sort of responsibility they did. He *understood the pressures and the problems* they faced. **a witness.** Strictly speaking, what Peter is saying is that he was an eyewitness of the death of Jesus. He is therefore able to point to Jesus in his suffering as an example they are to follow (2:21). In the New Testament, this word came to mean one who bears witness to Jesus (Luke 24:48; Acts 1:8; 22:15). Eventually it was applied to those who suffered because of their witness (1:3–7; Acts 22:20; Rev. 2:13; 11:3,7).

5:3 not lording it over those entrusted to you, but being examples. Mutual respect, submission, humility and love are attitudes which should characterize the Christian community, and the elders would be expected to set an example in displaying these attitudes.

5:4 Chief Shepherd. Peter has already described Jesus as the "Shepherd" (2:25). Here he adds an adjective that reminds the elders their authority is not absolute, but derived from Jesus. **the crown of glory.** The victor at an athletic event in a Greek city had a garland of ivy or bay placed on his head. Citizens who performed outstanding service to the city were also given such crowns. The image of the crown became a common New Testament symbol for the reward promised to Christians (1 Cor. 9:25; 2 Tim. 4:8; James 1:12; Rev. 2:10). Peter says this crown will consist of the "glory" of Christ which will be revealed at the Second Coming.

5:5 Young men. The Greek social order was such that young men were considered subordinate to older men. **be submissive.** Submission and respect are called for once again. **clothe yourselves with humility.** This is a rare verb, meaning "wrap yourselves" or "gird yourselves." It is derived from the name for the apron which was worn by slaves when working. It conjures up an image of Jesus who wrapped a towel around himself when he washed the feet of the disciples (John 13:4–5), an act which is the perfect demonstration of what humility is all about.

All of you, clothe yourselves with humility toward one another, because,

"God opposes the proud
but gives grace to the humble."[a]

[6]Humble yourselves, therefore, under God's mighty hand, that he may lift you up in due time. [7]Cast all your anxiety on him because he cares for you.

[8]Be self-controlled and alert. Your enemy the devil prowls around like a roaring lion looking for someone to devour. [9]Resist him, standing firm in the faith, because you know that your brothers throughout the world are undergoing the same kind of sufferings.

[10]And the God of all grace, who called you to his eternal glory in Christ, after you have suffered a little while, will himself restore you and make you strong, firm and steadfast. [11]To him be the power for ever and ever. Amen.

Final Greetings

[12]With the help of Silas,[b] whom I regard as a faithful brother, I have written to you briefly, encouraging you and testifying that this is the true grace of God. Stand fast in it.

[13]She who is in Babylon, chosen together with you, sends you her greetings, and so does my son Mark. [14]Greet one another with a kiss of love.

Peace to all of you who are in Christ.

[a]5 Prov. 3:34 [b]12 Greek *Silvanus,* a variant of *Silas*

paraphrase this teaching? **4.** What is the challenge here on Satanic opposition? Do you believe there is such a thing as evil spiritual forces at work today?

APPLY 1. When did you become aware of spiritual opposition in the world today? **2.** What has been the high point in this study for you? What have you appreciated most about your group? **3.** What would you like to study next? Who would you like to invite into your group?

5:6 Humble yourselves. The same humility which is owed to one another is owed to God as well. **that he may lift you up in due time.** This will happen when Christ returns and they experience his glory.

5:7 Cast all your anxiety on him. This verb should be translated as a participle ("casting"), not as an imperative ("cast"), since in Greek it is connected to the imperative "humble yourself." It is not a separate commandment.

5:8 Be self-controlled and alert. That they are not to be passive in the face of trouble is seen in this command. Coupled with conscious reliance on God, there must also be diligent effort on their part. **the devil.** Behind all their trials stands the devil (*diabolos*). In the Old Testament he is known by the Hebrew name Satan. In the New Testament he is seen as the one who tempts (as he did with Jesus), as the prince of evil who rebels against God, and as the one who seeks to undo God's purposes.

5:9 Resist him. Peter's advice is plain: do not run away, stand your ground and face him, refuse to give in to his purposes, trust in God (Eph. 6:10–13; James 4:7; Rev. 12:9–11). **your brothers throughout the world are undergoing the same kind of sufferings.** Solidarity with Christian brothers and sisters around the world is a strong motivation for standing firm.

5:10–11 Satan may be their enemy and he is powerful and vicious ("like a roaring lion looking for someone to devour"), but he is no match for God. Assurance of strength and victory is another motivation for continuing to resist evil. There is power in Christ to overcome this evil.

5:12 Silas. Like Paul (and others), Peter used an amanuensis (secretary/scribe) to write this letter. In this case, Silas seems to have had an active part in shaping the final form of the letter with its rather polished Greek. The Silas referred to here was probably Paul's companion on his second missionary trip (Acts 15:40–18:5), a minister of the Gospel (2 Cor. 1:19), and the co-author with Paul of 1 and 2 Thessalonians.

5:13 She who is in Babylon ... sends you her greetings. Peter is (probably) referring to the church (2 John 1,13) in Rome, where he was when he wrote this letter. **my son Mark.** Tradition has it that Mark was another of Peter's secretaries; and, in writing the Gospel that bears his name, Mark was expressing Peter's experience of Jesus. Certainly this phrase reflects a warm relationship between the two.

2 Peter

Author. Traditionally, the apostle Peter is thought to have authored this letter. However, questions about his authorship have existed since the earliest times.

Some questions arise when the language and thought of 1 and 2 Peter are compared. In their original Greek form, these two books are strikingly different. This difference in style, of course, may simply be the result of Peter's use of several different secretaries. Peter indicates in his first letter that Silas helped him write it (1 Peter 5:12), and it is known that Peter had other secretaries (e.g., Mark and Glaucias).

Personal Reading	Group Study Topic and Reading	
1:1–11	Keep on Growing in Christ	1:1–11
1:12–21	Authority of True Prophets	1:12–21
2:1–22	Destruction of False Prophets	2:1–22
3:1–18	Second Coming of Christ	3:1–18

Date. Second Peter was probably written near the time of Peter's death in A.D. 68 (1:12–15).

Theme. Be eager and on your guard.

Purpose. Second Peter is a very important book for today because it deals with issues confronting the modern church: a lax lifestyle based on weak theology. Some church members in Peter's time were arguing that the doctrine of the Second Coming had to be reconsidered. In fact, they suggested that this doctrine may have been invented by the apostles rather than revealed by God (1:16), perhaps to keep Christians in line. In contrast, the false teachers were saying that behavior does not matter. "Freedom" was their catchword, and evidently they felt free to indulge in sexual immorality, drunkenness and the like.

Audience. On the basis of 1:1, it appears that there were no specific recipients of the letter. It seems to be for all believers everywhere. However, in the body of the letter it becomes clear that 2 Peter was sent to a church or group of churches that had previously received 1 Peter (3:1). This would make the recipients Gentile Christians in Asia Minor. Furthermore, the tone of the letter makes it clear that a specific problem and specific false teachers are in view. All of this indicates that this is a letter to a particular people living in a particular area.

Characteristics. Chapter 1 is an exhortation to grow in the virtues as a follower of Christ. Chapter 2 is very similar to the epistle of Jude. A marked contrast is drawn there between the character and teaching of true apostles and that of the false teachers whose lives are marked by their denial of Jesus, immorality, rejection of authority, enslavement to sin and misuse of Scripture. Chapter 3 addresses the Second Coming of Christ.

The Early Church. Controversies abounded in the early church. Second Peter was written in response to a young church's questioning and doubting tendencies. Where 1 Peter centered on dangers from outside the church, this letter speaks to dangers from within. False teachers were stirring up problems, casting doubt on doctrine, and leading Christians into immoral behavior.

1

Simon Peter, a servant and apostle of Jesus Christ,

To those who through the righteousness of our God and Savior
Jesus Christ have received a faith as precious as ours:

[2]Grace and peace be yours in abundance through the knowledge of
God and of Jesus our Lord.

Making One's Calling and Election Sure

[3]His divine power has given us everything we need for life and godliness through our knowledge of him who called us by his own glory
and goodness. [4]Through these he has given us his very great and precious promises, so that through them you may participate in the divine nature and escape the corruption in the world caused by evil
desires.

[5]For this very reason, make every effort to add to your faith goodness; and to goodness, knowledge; [6]and to knowledge, self-control;
and to self-control, perseverance; and to perseverance, godliness;
[7]and to godliness, brotherly kindness; and to brotherly kindness,
love. [8]For if you possess these qualities in increasing measure, they
will keep you from being ineffective and unproductive in your knowledge of our Lord Jesus Christ. [9]But if anyone does not have them, he
is nearsighted and blind, and has forgotten that he has been cleansed
from his past sins.

[10]Therefore, my brothers, be all the more eager to make your calling and election sure. For if you do these things, you will never fall,
[11]and you will receive a rich welcome into the eternal kingdom of our
Lord and Savior Jesus Christ.

Prophecy of Scripture

[12]So I will always remind you of these things, even though you
know them and are firmly established in the truth you now have. [13]I
think it is right to refresh your memory as long as I live in the tent of
this body, [14]because I know that I will soon put it aside, as our Lord
Jesus Christ has made clear to me. [15]And I will make every effort to
see that after my departure you will always be able to remember
these things.

[16]We did not follow cleverly invented stories when we told you
about the power and coming of our Lord Jesus Christ, but we were
eyewitnesses of his majesty. [17]For he received honor and glory from

OPEN If you wanted to encourage a friend who was hurting, would you send a letter, a funny card or an e-mail?

STUDY 1. What did you find out about this letter by reading the "Purpose" in the book introduction that will help you to understand this passage? **2.** If you were writing to Christians who were being poisoned by some false teaching, how would you start out your letter? **3.** When the author refers to "his great and precious promises," what do you think he is referring to? What are they intended to do? **4.** If you were to define "the Christian life" using the seven characteristics in verses 5–7, how would you say it? What is the Christian like who does not have these characteristics (in your own words)?

APPLY 1. Is this a time in your spiritual journey that you need encouragement? **2.** Of the seven characteristics, where are you strongest and weakest? **3.** What do you want to get out of this study and group?

OPEN What friend did you have that made an effort to encourage you?

STUDY 1. How would you describe the tone in Peter's voice in this passage? **2.** Reading between the lines, what has happened to this generation of spiritual grandchildren who are 30 to 40 years removed from the time of Christ? What are the false teachers saying about the Bible and the Second Coming of Christ? **3.** What does the author say

---

1:1 righteousness. This refers to God's justice or fairness in that this second-generation audience of Christians had a faith that was in no way inferior ("as precious") to that of the apostles.

1:3 life and godliness. The point here is that being called to God means being called to moral behavior, the power for which is given by Jesus.

1:4 great and precious promises. This refers to the many promises found in Scripture based on hearing Christ within us (John 14:23). **participate in the divine nature.** We are now new creations in Christ. We are being transformed into his image (2 Cor. 3:18).

1:5 add to your faith. Faith in Christ, the starting point for the Christian life, must produce a new quality of life. **goodness.** Literally, "virtue," an ethical term meaning moral excellence. **knowledge.** This is the wisdom and discernment gained from experience in life.

1:6 self-control. This is the self-discipline that leads to the pursuit of a virtuous life. It was often used in regard to sexual behavior. **perseverance.** This is steadiness and faithfulness in the face of suffering and trials.

1:7 brotherly kindness. The Greek word here (*philadelphia*) referred to family affection. It was commonly used to describe how Christians should relate to other members of the church, their spiritual family (1 Peter 1:22). **love.** *Agape*, which is the quality of showing loving actions toward even those who are one's enemies. This type of love is the chief aim of the Christian faith (Gal. 5:6).

about the origin of Scripture (vv. 20–21)? How are Christians to look upon Scripture?

APPLY 1. When did the Bible become an important part of your life? **2.** How would you describe your devotional life now?

OPEN 1. What teacher or professor in your life went out of his or her way to poke fun at Christianity? **2.** What feelings do you encounter when someone pokes fun at Christianity?

STUDY 1. Would you say that Peter is a little upset by the false teachers who apparently have undermined the faith of Christians? What are some of the things said about these false teachers (vv. 1–3)? **2.** What are the four or five incidents that Peter cites to show how God will deal with the false teachers who have led these Christians astray? **3.** What do you find out about Lot that was not explained in the Old Testament account (Gen. 19:16)? What is the point in the Lot account here? **4.** What does Peter say about the lifestyle of the false teachers (vv. 13–15)? **5.** How does Peter describe the teaching of these false teachers (vv. 17–19)? How does this compare to some of the strange thinking today? **6.** Do you think these false teachers

God the Father when the voice came to him from the Majestic Glory,
saying, "This is my Son, whom I love; with him I am well pleased."[a]
18We ourselves heard this voice that came from heaven when we were
with him on the sacred mountain.

19And we have the *word of the prophets made more certain,* and
you will do well to pay attention to it, as to a light shining in a dark
place, until the day dawns and the morning star rises in your hearts.
20Above all, you must understand that no prophecy of Scripture came
about by the prophet's own interpretation. 21For prophecy never had
its origin in the will of man, but men spoke from God as they were
carried along by the Holy Spirit.

False Teachers and Their Destruction

2 But there were also false prophets among the people, just as
there will be false teachers among you. They will secretly introduce destructive heresies, even denying the sovereign Lord who
bought them—bringing swift destruction on themselves. 2Many will
follow their shameful ways and will bring the way of truth into disre-
pute. 3In their greed these teachers will exploit you with stories they
have made up. Their condemnation has long been hanging over
them, and their destruction has not been sleeping.

4For if God did not spare angels when they sinned, but sent them to
hell,[b] putting them into gloomy dungeons[c] to be held for judgment;
5if he did not spare the ancient world when he brought the flood on
its ungodly people, but protected Noah, a preacher of righteousness,
and seven others; 6if he condemned the cities of Sodom and Gomorrah by burning them to ashes, and made them an example of what is
going to happen to the ungodly; 7and if he rescued Lot, a righteous
man, who was distressed by the filthy lives of lawless men 8(for that
righteous man, living among them day after day, was tormented in
his righteous soul by the lawless deeds he saw and heard)— 9if this is
so, then the Lord knows how to rescue godly men from trials and to
hold the unrighteous for the day of judgment, while continuing their

[a]*17* Matt. 17:5; Mark 9:7; Luke 9:35 [b]*4* Greek *Tartarus* [c]*4* Some manuscripts *into chains of darkness*

1:19 the word of the prophets. The whole Old Testament was seen as a prophetic anticipation of the Messiah. **made more certain.** Rather than dismiss the prophecies as the false teachers did, the readers ought to consider them very seriously. **light shining in a dark place.** God's Word was often compared to a light (Ps. 119:105). **the morning star rises.** This refers to Numbers 24:17, and considered a prophecy of the Messiah. When the morning star (Venus) arises, daybreak is soon to come.

1:20–21 While the false teachers claimed prophetic words of a future judgment were made up, the author asserts that the prophets were empowered by the Holy Spirit (Jer. 20:9).

1:21 carried along by the Holy Spirit. The same word describes how God's voice came to the apostles at the Transfiguration (v. 17). What they heard and what the Old Testament authors wrote came from God.

2:1 false prophets. The presence of Israel's lying prophets (Deut. 18:20; Jer. 14:13–16) is used to expose the presence of false teachers within the Christian community. The major problem of these teachers was their rejection of the Lord (1:16–21; 2:18–21; 3:3–11). **destructive heresies.** Literally, "teachings of destruction."

2:2 their shameful ways. Since these false teachers denied accountability, they assumed they had freedom (v. 19) to indulge in immorality.

2:3 greed. The motivation for these false teachers is to teach that which people will pay to hear.

2:4 hell. Literally, Tartarus. This was hell in Greek mythology.

2:5 preacher of righteousness. Noah's righteous living set against the backdrop of the sinful world was a strong statement about God's ways. Those around him were indifferent.

2:7 righteous. Lot was not willing to participate in the sin of Sodom and Gomorrah. Peter describes him three times here as righteous. Righteousness is not based on works.

are the false teachers forgetting (vv. 5,8)? What is the point that Peter is making? Why does God's creation of the earth support Peter's contention that he will also destroy the earth (v. 10)? **3.** How does the "patience" of God work to the benefit of those who are living (v. 9)? **4.** How does God's view of time differ from the reader's view? Is Peter addressing the certainty, the timing or the manner of Christ's coming? **5.** How should the expectation of Christ's return affect the behavior of these Christians? Have you found this to be true today? **6.** What is Peter's parting shot to these Christians about false teachers (vv. 17–18)?

APPLY 1. What do you believe about the Second Coming of Christ? How has your view affected the way you live your life? **2.** What has been the high point in this study for you? **3.** What would you like to study next? Who would you like to invite into your group?

"Where is this 'coming' he promised? Ever since our fathers died, everything goes on as it has since the beginning of creation." [5]But they deliberately forget that long ago by God's word the heavens existed and the earth was formed out of water and by water. [6]By these waters also the world of that time was deluged and destroyed. [7]By the same word the present heavens and earth are reserved for fire, being kept for the day of judgment and destruction of ungodly men.

[8]But do not forget this one thing, dear friends: With the Lord a day is like a thousand years, and a thousand years are like a day. [9]The Lord is not slow in keeping his promise, as some understand slowness. He is patient with you, not wanting anyone to perish, but everyone to come to repentance.

[10]But the day of the Lord will come like a thief. The heavens will disappear with a roar; the elements will be destroyed by fire, and the earth and everything in it will be laid bare.[a]

[11]Since everything will be destroyed in this way, what kind of people ought you to be? You ought to live holy and godly lives [12]as you look forward to the day of God and speed its coming.[b] That day will bring about the destruction of the heavens by fire, and the elements will melt in the heat. [13]But in keeping with his promise we are looking forward to a new heaven and a new earth, the home of righteousness.

[14]So then, dear friends, since you are looking forward to this, make every effort to be found spotless, blameless and at peace with him. [15]Bear in mind that our Lord's patience means salvation, just as our dear brother Paul also wrote you with the wisdom that God gave him. [16]He writes the same way in all his letters, speaking in them of these matters. His letters contain some things that are hard to understand, which ignorant and unstable people distort, as they do the other Scriptures, to their own destruction.

[17]Therefore, dear friends, since you already know this, be on your guard so that you may not be carried away by the error of lawless men and fall from your secure position. [18]But grow in the grace and knowledge of our Lord and Savior Jesus Christ. To him be glory both now and forever! Amen.

[a]*10* Some manuscripts *be burned up* [b]*12* Or *as you wait eagerly for the day of God to come*

be trusted. **since the beginning of creation.** The scoffers argued that the world has always just gone on and on with no divine intervention or judgment, a belief shared by much of Greek philosophy as well.

3:6 By these waters. In the Flood, God released the waters to deluge the earth once again.

3:10 like a thief. Like a thief, the Lord will come without warning (Matt. 24:43–44; 1 Thess. 5:4). **heavens will disappear with a roar.** The coming of God in judgment is always described in graphic images. The roar here may be the sound of the heavens being rolled up (Heb. 1:12), or the shout of God pronouncing judgment upon the cosmos. **elements ... destroyed ... earth ... laid bare.** Once God wipes away the heavens, there will be nothing left to hide the wickedness of the earth from the eyes of the heavenly Judge (Isa. 2:19).

3:16 things that are hard to understand. In the context of the problems at this church, this might refer either to Paul's teaching about Christian freedom (Gal. 5:1) or to passages in his letters that indicated the imminent return of Christ (Rom. 13:11–12; Phil. 4:5; 1 Thess. 4:15). Both may have been distorted to provide the false teachers with justification for their acceptance of immorality.

3:17 secure position. Literally, "stable," in contrast to the instability of the false teachers (v. 16).

3:18 Lord and Savior. In the New Testament, these two titles are found together as titles for Jesus only in 2 Peter; and 2 Peter refers to Jesus as Savior more than any other New Testament book. **To him.** Typically doxologies were ascribed to God, but this one is clearly ascribed to the Son. Second Peter stands out in the New Testament as a letter that clearly affirms the deity of Jesus.

punishment.[a] [10]This is especially true of those who follow the corrupt
desire of the sinful nature[b] and despise authority.
Bold and arrogant, these men are not afraid to slander celestial
beings; [11]yet even angels, although they are stronger and more powerful, do not bring slanderous accusations against such beings in the
presence of the Lord. [12]But these men blaspheme in matters they do
not understand. They are like brute beasts, creatures of instinct, born
only to be caught and destroyed, and like beasts they too will perish.
[13]They will be paid back with harm for the harm they have done.
Their idea of pleasure is to carouse in broad daylight. They are blots
and blemishes, reveling in their pleasures while they feast with you.[c]
[14]With eyes full of adultery, they never stop sinning; they seduce the
unstable; they are experts in greed—an accursed brood! [15]They have
left the straight way and wandered off to follow the way of Balaam
son of Beor, who loved the wages of wickedness. [16]But he was rebuked for his wrongdoing by a donkey—a beast without speech—
who spoke with a man's voice and restrained the prophet's madness.
[17]These men are springs without water and mists driven by a
storm. Blackest darkness is reserved for them. [18]For they mouth
empty, boastful words and, by appealing to the lustful desires of sinful human nature, they entice people who are just escaping from
those who live in error. [19]They promise them freedom, while they
themselves are slaves of depravity—for a man is a slave to whatever
has mastered him. [20]If they have escaped the corruption of the world
by knowing our Lord and Savior Jesus Christ and are again entangled
in it and overcome, they are worse off at the end than they were at the
beginning. [21]It would have been better for them not to have known
the way of righteousness, than to have known it and then to turn
their backs on the sacred command that was passed on to them. [22]Of
them the proverbs are true: "A dog returns to its vomit,"[d] and, "A sow
that is washed goes back to her wallowing in the mud."

The Day of the Lord

3 Dear friends, this is now my second letter to you. I have written
both of them as reminders to stimulate you to wholesome thinking. [2]I want you to recall the words spoken in the past by the holy
prophets and the command given by our Lord and Savior through
your apostles.
[3]First of all, you must understand that in the last days scoffers will
come, scoffing and following their own evil desires. [4]They will say,

a9 Or unrighteous for punishment until the day of judgment b10 Or *the flesh* c13 Some manuscripts *in their love feasts* d22 Prov. 26:11

once were true followers of Christ? What do you think happened to cause them to stray from the faith?

APPLY 1. What is the clos*est you have come to getting* caught up in a cult or off-based philosophy? **2.** What kept you from falling for this teaching? **3.** What do you say when your friends ask you about your journey back to the Christian faith?

OPEN On a typical 100-mile trip in the car, how many times do you hear the words, "Are we there yet" from your kids in the back seat?

STUDY 1. If you were responsible for a church where false teachers have encouraged loose living by "appealing to the lustful desires of sinful human nature" (2:18) and scoffing at the idea of Christ's return, what would you do? **2.** What

2:10–12 Like those mentioned in verses 4–9, the false teachers follow the corrupt desire of the sinful nature and despise authority. This involves blatant sexual immorality (v. 14) and a wholesale rejection of Christ's lordship.

2:13 blots and blemishes. These people are like animals unfit to be offered in sacrifice to God. **their pleasures.** Literally, "deceits" or perversions of pleasure.

2:19 freedom. In light of the false teachers' denial of the Second Coming (3:4), this probably refers to the "freedom" from the moral implications of preparing for his imminent return. They may have used Paul's teaching on freedom in Christ (Rom. 6:1–18) to justify their position (3:15–16). **a man is a slave to whatever has mastered him.** This was a common saying based on what actually happened to people conquered in war (John 8:34; Rom. 6:16). Their supposed "freedom" is simply slavery to sin.

3:3 scoffers. In the book of 2 Peter, these are the teachers who mock the idea of the Lord's return (v. 4).

3:4 Where is this coming? Since Jesus stressed the imminence of his return (Matt. 24:34), the death of those followers of Jesus raised the critical problem of whether his promise could

1 John

Personal Reading	Group Study Topic and Reading	
1:1–2:14	Walking in the Light	1:1–2:14
2:15–27	Warning Against Antichrists	2:15–27
2:28–3:10	Doing What is Right	2:28–3:10
3:11–24	Loving One Another	3:11–24
4:1–6	Testing the Spirits	4:1–6
4:7–21	Loving God	4:7–21
5:1–21	Believing in Christ	5:1–21

Author. Despite the fact that the author is nowhere named in the epistle, it is highly probable that he is none other than the beloved apostle John, now an old man living in Asia Minor and pastoring the churches in and around Ephesus. Here are two reasons to accept John as the author: First, there are many similarities in style and content between the Gospel of John and this epistle. The same sharp contrasts appear in both—light and darkness, truth and falsehood, love and hate. The differences between them can be traced to differences in purpose and to the length of time that elapsed between the composition of each. Second, the internal information in the epistle points to John. For example, the author tells us that he was one of the original eyewitnesses of Jesus (1:1–2). Also, the author writes with the air of authority that would be expected of an apostle (4:6).

Date. It was probably written toward the end of the New Testament era (A.D. 90–95), by which time many false teachings had flourished.

Theme. Walking in the light.

Purpose. John's central concerns are quite clear. He wants to define the marks of a true Christian against the claims of the false teachers. He wants his congregation to have assurance that they have eternal life (5:13). He wants them to know the characteristics of a true Christian: right belief (the doctrinal test), righteousness (the moral test) and love (the social test).

Structure. First John is not a letter like 2 and 3 John or most of Paul's writings. It lacks identification of writer and recipients, a salutation and a final greeting. Still, it is not a generalized document written to all Christians. John has a specific audience in mind, probably the churches in his charge in Asia Minor. Despite the lack of usual greetings, he writes in personal terms. Many see 1 John as a tract, perhaps intended to be read as a sermon, in which John deals with a specific problem.

The Problem of False Teachers. Apparently a group with the fellowship got involved in false teaching, split off from the church (2:19), and were now hassling their former friends, probably trying to convince them to accept their new and "advanced" views (2:26). This deeply troubled the church and thus John, as pastor, wrote to assure the believers in and around Ephesus how to be sure that they were true Christians with the assurance of eternal life.

The nature of the false teaching is not completely clear. John does not describe it. The recipients of his letter knew well enough what was being taught. Still, by the nature of John's defense of orthodox Christianity, certain features of the incorrect doctrine emerge.

In particular, the false teachers had a low view of Jesus. They did not believe he was the Messiah (2:22; 5:1). They did not believe he was the Son of God (5:5). They denied that Jesus had come in the flesh (4:2). They apparently claimed they did not need Jesus because they already knew God (2:4) and had fellowship with him (1:6). They did not believe that sin separated a person from God (1:6,8,10), and thus they had no need of Jesus' atoning death (5:6) to provide forgiveness and a way back to God. It is not by accident that John calls them "antichrists" (2:22).

Spiritual "Superiority." This group had come to think of themselves as some sort of spiritual elite, claiming that they had a "deeper" understanding of Christianity, probably by direct revelation (4:1–6). As an antidote to such spiritual pride, John reminded his readers over and over that true followers of Christ are called to love one another, not to look down on their brothers and sisters who do not measure up to their own supposed, superior insight.

OPEN 1. Where were you living at age 7 and what were the winters like? **2.** Were you afraid of the dark?

STUDY 1. What do you learn by reading, "The Problem of False Teachers" in the book introduction to this letter? **2.** How would you describe the mood or tone in this passage (1:1–2:2): Scholarly? Fatherly? Diplomatic? Friendly? Pious? Formal? Tender? Sober? Stern? Long-winded? **3.** Why does John make a point of his firsthand experience with Jesus? Why is it important that Jesus was "seen" and "heard"? **4.** Reading between the lines, what have the false teachers been teaching (vv. 6,8,10)? How does John answer each claim? **5.** How would you explain to a new follower of Christ what you can do to maintain a close relationship with God, using verses 7,9 and 2:1–2?

APPLY 1. When did Jesus Christ become more than just a name to you? **2.** How would you

The Word of Life

1 That which was from the beginning, which we have heard, which
we have seen with our eyes, which we have looked at and our
hands have touched—this we proclaim concerningthe Word of life.
2 The life appeared; we have seen it and testify to it, and we proclaim
to you the eternal life, which was with the Father and has appeared to
us. 3 We proclaim to you what we have seen and heard, so that you
also may have fellowship with us. And our fellowship is with the Father and with his Son, Jesus Christ. 4 We write this to make our[a] joy
complete.

Walking in the Light

5 This is the message we have heard from him and declare to you:
God is light; in him there is no darkness at all. 6 If we claim to have
fellowship with him yet walk in the darkness, we lie and do not live by
the truth. 7 But if we walk in the light, as he is in the light, we have
fellowship with one another, and the blood of Jesus, his Son, purifies
us from all[b] sin.
8 If we claim to be without sin, we deceive ourselves and the truth is
not in us. 9 If we confess our sins, he is faithful and just and will forgive us our sins and purify us from all unrighteousness. 10 If we claim

[a]4 Some manuscripts *your* [b]7 Or *every*

1:1 from the beginning. The initial clause makes the assertion that this "Word of life" was pre-existent (John 1:1). Since only divine beings pre-existed, John affirms Jesus' deity.

1:2 testify. This is a legal term describing what an eyewitness does while in court. Such a person makes a public declaration of what he or she has experienced firsthand. **eternal life.** John focuses on what is so significant about Jesus: he is life itself.

1:3 fellowship. This word has the dual sense of participation together in shared activity or outlook, and union together because of this shared experience.

1:5 God is light. Within the context of the Bible, "light" was connected to *two basic ideas. First, on the intellectual* level, it was a symbol of truth. John is saying that God is truth. God illuminates the understanding of people. He reveals the right answer and the correct way (Prov. 6:23). Second, on the moral level, light is a symbol of purity. John is saying that God is righteous and holy (Isa. 5:20; Rom. 13:11–14; Eph. 5:8–14). He is good, not evil.

1:6 If we claim. The first of three false claims that John will refute. He will measure the validity of each against the apostolic proclamation that God is light and in him is no darkness. **to have fellowship ... yet walk in the darkness.** It is claimed by the false teachers that it is possible to be in union with God and yet habitually sin.

1:7 walk in the light. The image here is of a person confidently striding forth, illuminated by the light of God's truth, in contrast to the person who stumbles around in darkness. **purifies.** If the first result of "walking in the light" is fellowship with one another, the second result is cleansing from sin.

1:8 If we claim to be without sin. The second false claim is that they are sinless. It is one thing to deny that sin breaks fellowship with God (vv. 6–7). At least the existence of sin is admitted (even if its impact is denied); but it is another thing to deny the fact of sin altogether. **we deceive ourselves.** This assertion goes beyond a mere lie (v. 6). This is self-deception. **the truth is not in us.** Not only do they not live by the truth (v. 6), but by such a claim they demonstrate that they do not even know the truth.

1:9 If we confess our sins. Rather than denying their sinful natures, they need to admit their sin to God and so gain forgiveness. **faithful.** God will keep his promise to forgive (Mic. 7:18–20). **just.** The granting of forgiveness is not merely an act of unanticipated mercy but a response of justice, since the conditions for forgiveness have been fulfilled as a result of the death of Christ. **purify.** Sin makes a person unclean; Christ cleanses us of our sin (v. 7).

1:10 If we claim we have not

we have not sinned, we make him out to be a liar and his word has no place in our lives.

2 My dear children, I write this to you so that you will not sin. But if anybody does sin, we have one who speaks to the Father in our defense—Jesus Christ, the Righteous One. [2]He is the atoning sacrifice for our sins, and not only for ours but also for[a] the sins of the whole world.

[3]We know that we have come to know him if we obey his commands. [4]The man who says, "I know him," but does not do what he commands is a liar, and the truth is not in him. [5]But if anyone obeys his word, God's love[b] is truly made complete in him. This is how we know we are in him: [6]Whoever claims to live in him must walk as Jesus did.

[7]Dear friends, I am not writing you a new command but an old one, which you have had since the beginning. This old command is the message you have heard. [8]Yet I am writing you a new command; its truth is seen in him and you, because the darkness is passing and the true light is already shining.

[9]Anyone who claims to be in the light but hates his brother is still in the darkness. [10]Whoever loves his brother lives in the light, and there is nothing in him[c] to make him stumble. [11]But whoever hates his brother is in the darkness and walks around in the darkness; he does not know where he is going, because the darkness has blinded him.

[12]I write to you, dear children,
because your sins have been forgiven on account of his name.
[13]I write to you, fathers,
because you have known him who is from the beginning.
I write to you, young men,
because you have overcome the evil one.
I write to you, dear children,
because you have known the Father.
[14]I write to you, fathers,
because you have known him who is from the beginning.

[a]2 Or *He is the one who turns aside God's wrath, taking away our sins, and not only ours but also* [b]5 Or *word, love for God* [c]10 Or *it*

describe your relationship with him now?

OPEN Are you, personally, closer to the song "Blues in the Night" or "Feeling Groovy"? In your family life, are you closer to "Stormy Weather" or "The Sound of Music"?

STUDY 1. What do you think is going on in this church to cause John to write these words? **2.** What is the relationship between God's love and our obedience? How would you explain this from your own life, before and after you committed your life to Christ? **3.** From the three stages of a Christian life, where would you place yourself right now? **4.** What do you think John means by "do not love the world"? How would you explain the enticements of the world from your own experience (2:15–17)? What will happen if you build your life around any one of these?

APPLY 1. Which enticement of the world is the biggest threat to your spiritual growth right now: Inner desires fighting to be unchecked? Absorption in material things? Pride over past accomplishments? **2.** Which sign best describes what's going on in your life right now: "Under New Management"? "Danger! Under Construction"? "Please Be Patient! God Isn't Through With Me Yet"?

---

sinned. The third false claim: not only do they say that at the present moment they are without sin (v. 8), they actually claim never to have sinned! **we make him out to be a liar.** By claiming sinlessness they are, in essence, saying that God is lying about human nature and about his claim to forgive people. **his word has no place in our lives.** Contrary to what they might claim, they are, in fact, alienated from God (Col. 1:21).

2:1 so that you will not sin. John quickly points out that sin is not compatible with Christian commitment. **if anybody does sin.** The provision for sin is found in Jesus as the advocate, the Righteous One, and the atoning sacrifice for believers.

2:2 the atoning sacrifice. Jesus, the Advocate, bases his plea (that their sins should be forgiven) on the fact of his death to pay for them.

2:3 if we obey his commands. The first test as to whether a person knows God is moral in nature: Does that person keep God's commands?

2:5 God's love. This is the reward for obedience. God's love reaches its fulfillment in that person's life. **made complete.** The verb John uses here means ongoing fulfillment rather than static termination.

2:12 children ... have been forgiven. The verb tense indicates John is thinking of the forgiveness that comes at the time of conversion. Whereas in 1:9, his concern was with ongoing forgiveness for subsequent sins based on the confession of sins.

2:13 you have known him. The message to the "fathers" here and in verse 14 is identical. John reassures them that they do, indeed, know Christ. **him who is from the beginning.** The reference is probably to Jesus since it echoes the phrase by which John opens his letter. **young men.** John asserts that the Christian life involves spiritual warfare. It is also a vigorous battle against evil. **overcome the evil one.** Satan, the ruler of darkness (vv. 8–11) and the source of evil. Christ made a way for us to overcome Satan.

OPEN What do you crave that is either "illegal, immoral or fattening"?

STUDY **1.** If you were one of these false teachers, teaching that Jesus was not the Messiah or the Son of God and that salvation was obtained by enlightened "knowledge," how would you feel when you heard what John said about you in this passage? **2.** According to the definition of antichrists (v. 18), what modern day movements would fall into this category? **3.** What does John remind these young Christians of and ask them to do?

APPLY When a person is having intellectual doubts about the deity of Christ, what do you say?

OPEN Who is the "neat freak" in your family? How would you describe yourself?

STUDY **1.** From the sound of this passage, what have the

I write to you, young men,
because you are strong,
and the word of God lives in you,
and you have overcome the evil one.

Do Not Love the World

[15]Do not love the world or anything in the world. If anyone loves the world, the love of the Father is not in him. [16]For everything in the world—the cravings of sinful man, the lust of his eyes and the boasting of what he has and does—comes not from the Father but from the world. [17]The world and its desires pass away, but the man who does the will of God lives forever.

Warning Against Antichrists

[18]Dear children, this is the last hour; and as you have heard that the antichrist is coming, even now many antichrists have come. This is how we know it is the last hour. [19]They went out from us, but they did not really belong to us. For if they had belonged to us, they would have remained with us; but their going showed that none of them belonged to us.

[20]But you have an anointing from the Holy One, and all of you know the truth.[a] [21]I do not write to you because you do not know the truth, but because you do know it and because no lie comes from the truth. [22]Who is the liar? It is the man who denies that Jesus is the Christ. Such a man is the antichrist—he denies the Father and the Son. [23]No one who denies the Son has the Father; whoever acknowledges the Son has the Father also.

[24]See that what you have heard from the beginning remains in you. If it does, you also will remain in the Son and in the Father. [25]And this is what he promised us—even eternal life.

[26]I am writing these things to you about those who are trying to lead you astray. [27]As for you, the anointing you received from him remains in you, and you do not need anyone to teach you. But as his anointing teaches you about all things and as that anointing is real, not counterfeit—just as it has taught you, remain in him.

Children of God

[28]And now, dear children, continue in him, so that when he appears we may be confident and unashamed before him at his coming.

[a]20 Some manuscripts *and you know all things*

2:15 world. The word John uses here is *kosmos* and in this context it means that which is alienated from God and is contrary to who God is. It refers to pagan culture which is alien to God.

2:16 cravings. That part of human nature which demands gratification—be it for sexual pleasure, for luxury, for possessions, for expensive food or for *whatever.* ***lust of his eyes.*** Greed which is aroused by sight. A person sees something and wants it. (Gen. 3:6; Josh. 7:21; 2 Sam. 11:2–4.) **boasting.** Pride in one's possessions; an attitude of arrogance because one has acquired so much.

2:18 the last hour. They knew that his Second Coming (the *parousia*) would bring to a close the "last days" and usher in a new age in which God's rule would be visible and universal. **antichrist.** In the last days an evil opponent would arise under the control of Satan. ***antichrists.*** John points out that the coming of the Antichrist was not just some future threat. Even at that moment the "spirit of the antichrist" (4:3) was loose in the world and active in those who deny Christ and his teachings (v. 22).

2:19 They went out from us. John now identifies those who are imbued with the spirit of the antichrist. They are none other than the secessionists who left the church and even now seek to win over their former friends and colleagues to their point of view (v. 26).

2:22 John now reveals the master lie in the secessionists' false teaching; they deny that Jesus is the Messiah and the Son of God.

29 If you know that he is righteous, you know that everyone who
does what is right has been born of him.

3 How great is the love the Father has lavished on us, that we
should be called children of God! And that is what we are! The
reason the world does not know us is that it did not know him. 2 Dear
friends, now we are children of God, and what we will be has not yet
been made known. But we know that when he appears,[a] we shall be
like him, for we shall see him as he is. 3 Everyone who has this hope in
him purifies himself, just as he is pure.

4 Everyone who sins breaks the law; in fact, sin is lawlessness. 5 But
you know that he appeared so that he might take away our sins. And
in him is no sin. 6 No one who lives in him keeps on sinning. No one
who continues to sin has either seen him or known him.

7 Dear children, do not let anyone lead you astray. He who does
what is right is righteous, just as he is righteous. 8 He who does what
is sinful is of the devil, because the devil has been sinning from the
beginning. The reason the Son of God appeared was to destroy the
devil's work. 9 No one who is born of God will continue to sin, because God's seed remains in him; he cannot go on sinning, because
he has been born of God. 10 This is how we know who the children of
God are and who the children of the devil are: Anyone who does not
do what is right is not a child of God; nor is anyone who does not love
his brother.

Love One Another

11 This is the message you heard from the beginning: We should
love one another. 12 Do not be like Cain, who belonged to the evil one
and murdered his brother. And why did he murder him? Because his
own actions were evil and his brother's were righteous. 13 Do not be
surprised, my brothers, if the world hates you. 14 We know that we
have passed from death to life, because we love our brothers. Anyone
who does not love remains in death. 15 Anyone who hates his brother
is a murderer, and you know that no murderer has eternal life in him.

16 This is how we know what love is: Jesus Christ laid down his life
for us. And we ought to lay down our lives for our brothers. 17 If anyone has material possessions and sees his brother in need but has no

[a]2 Or *when it is made known*

false teachers been teaching about the importance of living a clean life? **2.** What are five motives or reasons for a follower of Christ to live a clean life (vv. 28,29; 3:1,6,9)? **3.** From verse 6, does John mean a Christian cannot sin? Will not deliberately sin? How would you explain this from your own story? **4.** What does 3:1–3 do for your self-image and your motivation for your lifestyle? **5.** What does 3:1–3 tell us about God? How have you experienced God's lavish love this week? **6.** What does John say to these Christians about living in a secular, immoral society, where everything is "relative"? How would you describe John's position?

APPLY 1. As you get older, do you find the old inner desires easier or harder to resist? **2.** When you blow it, what have you found helpful in making it right with God and getting on with life?

OPEN Who was your first "true love" growing up?

STUDY 1. What do you think the Christians here are encouraged to do in the non-Christian world? Do you think they are supporting one another in this situation? **2.** In what ways does the world show hostility toward the righteous? **3.** What is the principle in the illustration John uses in verses 16–18 that applies today? Can you say this about your church? **4.** In what ways do "our hearts condemn us" (v. 20)? How does it make you feel when you remember that God knows you? **5.** What gives a

---

3:2 The precise nature of what Christians will become when they meet Christ is not fully clear ("what we will be has not yet been made known"). Yet they can get an idea of what they will be like by looking at Jesus ("we shall be like him"). In some way, Christians will become like Jesus when the process of glorification—which began at rebirth—is completed at the Second Coming.

3:6 John appears to be saying here (and in vv. 8–10) that a Christian cannot sin. Yet in other passages, he points out that Christians can and do sin (1:8,10; 2:1; 5:16). Some scholars feel that what John has in mind here is willful and deliberate sin (as against involuntary error). Other scholars stress the tense of the verb that John uses: a Christian does not keep on sinning. In other words, Christians do not habitually sin.

3:9 God's seed. John probably is referring either to the Word of God (Luke 8:11; James 1:18; 1 Peter 1:23) or to the Holy Spirit (John 3:6) or to both, by which the Christian is kept from sin. **cannot go on sinning.** In 1:8,10 and 2:1, John attacks those who deny that they are sinners in need of forgiveness (those who are blind to the fact of their sin).

3:11 This is the message. In 1:5, John used this same phrase to introduce the great truth that lies at the heart of the Christian message. God is light. Here he uses this phrase to introduce a second core insight: love is at the center of the Christian life.

3:12 And why did he murder him? Cain knew that in contrast to his brother's gift, his offering to God did not arise out of the desire to do right. Therefore, because of his anger, Cain slew his brother.

3:16–17 John next offers a positive example of love: Jesus' sacrificial love for the human race. Both the example of Cain and the example of Jesus involve death. But Cain's act sprang from hatred and took the life of another while Jesus' act sprang from love and he gave his own life for others.

Christian confidence and assurance in prayer? How would you explain this?

APPLY Do you know of anyone in your Christian community that needs help now? What could your group do to help this person?

OPEN Which made you most nervous: Driving test? Qualifying exam? An audition?

STUDY **1.** What is the problem that John is addressing here (v. 1)? **2.** How can a follower of Christ distinguish a true prophet from a false one (2:20–23)? **3.** In what circumstance might it be necessary for you to distinguish between true and false prophets/spirits? **4.** When has the "spirit of falsehood" (vv. 5–6) affected your life?

APPLY What have you found helpful in dealing with false teaching?

OPEN What personality trait or strength did you get from your father? Your mother?

STUDY **1.** How has God demonstrated that he is love (v. 8)? How can a person know God and experience his love? **2.** From verses 8–15, what do you learn about

pity on him, how can the love of God be in him? 18Dear children, let
us not love with words or tongue but with actions and in truth. 19This
then is how we know that we belong to the truth, and how we set our
hearts at rest in his presence 20whenever our hearts condemn us. For
God is greater than our hearts, and he knows everything.

21Dear friends, if our hearts do not condemn us, we have confidence before God 22and receive from him anything we ask, because
we obey his commands and do what pleases him. 23And this is his
command: to believe in the name of his Son, Jesus Christ, and to love
one another as he commanded us. 24Those who obey his commands
live in him, and he in them. And this is how we know that he lives in
us: We know it by the Spirit he gave us.

Test the Spirits

4 Dear friends, do not believe every spirit, but test the spirits to see
whether they are from God, because many false prophets have
gone out into the world. 2This is how you can recognize the Spirit of
God: Every spirit that acknowledges that Jesus Christ has come in the
flesh is from God, 3but every spirit that does not acknowledge Jesus is
not from God. This is the spirit of the antichrist, which you have
heard is coming and even now is already in the world.

4You, dear children, are from God and have overcome them, because the one who is in you is greater than the one who is in the
world. 5They are from the world and therefore speak from the viewpoint of the world, and the world listens to them. 6We are from God,
and whoever knows God listens to us; but whoever is not from God
does not listen to us. This is how we recognize the Spirit[a] of truth and
the spirit of falsehood.

God's Love and Ours

7Dear friends, let us love one another, for love comes from God.
Everyone who loves has been born of God and knows God. 8Whoever
does not love does not know God, because God is love. 9This is how
God showed his love among us: He sent his one and only Son[b] into
the world that we might live through him. 10This is love: not that we

[a]6 *Or spirit* [b]9 *Or his only begotten Son*

3:19–20 John seems to be saying that Christians can be at peace with themselves even when their consciences trouble them. But, as John points out, the basis of their confidence is the fact that it is God who will judge them and not their own hearts. They can trust themselves to his all-knowing justice because they have sought and found his forgiveness (1 Cor. 4:3–5).

3:21 confidence. Confidence is necessary in order to come before God. Without confidence a person does not feel free to enter into prayer.

3:22 Once again, John states a truth in a stark, unqualified way: if we ask, we will receive. **obey.** Obedience is not the cause of answered prayer; it is the condition that motivates Christians to pray.

3:23–24 In these verses, John brings together the three issues which underlie the three tests by which believers can know they are truly children of God. He shows the interconnection between obedience (the moral test), love (the social test), and belief (the doctrinal test) and how these relate to the question of union with God.

4:1 do not believe every spirit. It is dangerous to accept uncritically everything that is said "in the name of God." Not everyone claiming inner revelation is hearing God's voice! **test.** The test that John suggests by which to distinguish between spirits is doctrinal in nature. It has to do with who Jesus is. False spirits will not acknowledge that Jesus of Nazareth (a fully human man) is the incarnate Christ (the divine Son of God).

4:2 To deny that Jesus, the Messiah, was truly human is incompatible with divine inspiration. Prophets who will not affirm this confession of faith are not of God.

4:3 antichrist. In 2:18–27 John's concern was that believers not be led astray by those who are filled with the spirit of the antichrist. Here his concern is with the claims by his opponents that their new teachings are inspired by God.

4:10 an atoning sacrifice for our sins. By this phrase John describes the

loved God, but that he loved us and sent his Son as an atoning sacrifice for[a] our sins. 11Dear friends, since God so loved us, we also ought
to love one another. 12No one has ever seen God; but if we love one
another, God lives in us and his love is made complete in us.
13We know that we live in him and he in us, because he has given
us of his Spirit. 14And we have seen and testify that the Father has
sent his Son to be the Savior of the world. 15If anyone acknowledges
that Jesus is the Son of God, God lives in him and he in God. 16And so
we know and rely on the love God has for us.
God is love. Whoever lives in love lives in God, and God in him. 17In
this way, love is made complete among us so that we will have confidence on the day of judgment, because in this world we are like him.
18There is no fear in love. But perfect love drives out fear, because
fear has to do with punishment. The one who fears is not made perfect in love.
19We love because he first loved us. 20If anyone says, "I love God,"
yet hates his brother, he is a liar. For anyone who does not love his
brother, whom he has seen, cannot love God, whom he has not seen.
21And he has given us this command: Whoever loves God must also
love his brother.

Faith in the Son of God

5 Everyone who believes that Jesus is the Christ is born of God,
and everyone who loves the father loves his child as well. 2This
is how we know that we love the children of God: by loving God and
carrying out his commands. 3This is love for God: to obey his commands. And his commands are not burdensome, 4for everyone born
of God overcomes the world. This is the victory that has overcome
the world, even our faith. 5Who is it that overcomes the world? Only
he who believes that Jesus is the Son of God.
6This is the one who came by water and blood—Jesus Christ. He
did not come by water only, but by water and blood. And it is the
Spirit who testifies, because the Spirit is the truth. 7For there are

[a]10 *Or as the one who would turn aside his wrath, taking away*

the relationship between the Father, Son and Holy Spirit? **3.** What is the connection between God's love for us and the love we are to have for others? **4.** What does love do in the life of someone who worries about their relationship with God?

APPLY 1. In your life, when has love held too much fear? When has God's love, for you and through you, cast out fear? **2.** How do you go about loving others without fear?

OPEN Are you more like a rabbit or a turtle?

STUDY 1. If you were writing to young Christians who were influenced by the Gnostics, who believed that Jesus was not the Messiah or the Son of God and that salvation was obtained by "knowledge," what would you say? **2.** By denying that Jesus was the Messiah and the Son of God, the Gnostics did not see any need to obey what Jesus said. How does John answer their teaching? **3.** What does John say about the commands of Jesus? Have you found that a life of obedience "is

saving work of Jesus. The idea of atonement is tied up with the Old Testament concept of substitution and sacrifice. In the Old Testament, sin was dealt with when a person symbolically placed his sins on an animal that he had brought to the temple. This animal had to be perfect—without spot or blemish. It was then sacrificed in place of the sinful (imperfect) person. Such substitutionary sacrifices were a picture of the final sacrifice Jesus would one day make for all men and women.

4:18 no fear in love. People cannot love and fear at the same moment. The love casts out the fear. **fear has to do with punishment.** This is the root of the fear: they think God is going to punish them. They forget that they are his forgiven children.

5:1 believes. The belief on the part of Christians is clear proof that they have been born of God.

5:3 burdensome. Obedience to the thousands of often picayune rules and regulations promulgated by the scribes and Pharisees was indeed a heavy burden. But obedience to God does not exasperate the Christian, since God enables the believer through the Holy Spirit to respond in obedience.

5:4 our faith. This is the source of the overcoming power of the Christian—confidence and trust that Jesus is the Son of God (v. 5).

5:6 by water and blood. By these two phrases, John probably is referring to Jesus' baptism and Jesus' death. These two events are crucial in understanding who Jesus really is. The secessionists felt that Jesus, the man, became the Christ at his baptism and that the Christ then departed prior to the death of Jesus. In contrast, the apostolic witness (as recorded in the New Testament) asserts that at his baptism, Jesus publicly identified himself with the sins of the people (even though he himself was without sin). And at his death, Jesus died to take away those sins. **not ... by water only.** The secessionists agree that the baptism of Jesus was important. They felt it was then that the heavenly Christ infused the man Jesus. (In fact, it was the Holy Spirit who descended on Jesus at his baptism.) John is insistent that both the Baptism and the Crucifixion are crucial in understanding Jesus. **the Spirit is the truth.** The Holy Spirit is the third witness, and is qualified to be such because the Spirit is, in his essence, truth itself.

5:7 three that testify. There are two kinds of testimony: the objective histor-

not burdensome"? **4.** What are the three witnesses and how do each one verify that Jesus is the Messiah and the Son of God? **5.** How would you paraphrase verses 11 and 12 in your own words?

APPLY How do you know that you have eternal life?

OPEN When you were growing up, what was the one thing that you really wanted your parents to give you?

STUDY 1. What does it mean to "pray according to his will"? **2.** What is the "sin that leads to death"? Why is the very fear that you have committed "a sin that leads to death" proof that you have done no such thing? **3.** How can we help those who struggle with sin? **4.** How would you pray for a friend who says that Christianity is "a bunch of myths"?

APPLY 1. What prayer has God answered recently that you have been praying for a long time? **2.** What have you found helpful when your prayers "are bouncing off the ceiling"? **3.** What has been the high point in this study for you? What do you want to study now?

three that testify: 8the[a] Spirit, the water and the blood; and the three
are in agreement. 9We accept man's testimony, but God's testimony is
greater because it is the testimony of God, which he has given about
his Son. 10Anyone who believes in the Son of God has this testimony
in his heart. Anyone who does not believe God has made him out to
be a liar, because he has not believed the testimony God has given
about his Son. 11And this is the testimony: God has given us eternal
life, and this life is in his Son. 12He who has the Son has life; he who
does not have the Son of God does not have life.

Concluding Remarks

13I write these things to you who believe in the name of the Son of
God so that you may know that you have eternal life. 14This is the
confidence we have in approaching God: that if we ask anything according to his will, he hears us. 15And if we know that he hears us—
whatever we ask—we know that we have what we asked of him.

16If anyone sees his brother commit a sin that does not lead to
death, he should pray and God will give him life. I refer to those
whose sin does not lead to death. There is a sin that leads to death. I
am not saying that he should pray about that. 17All wrongdoing is sin,
and there is sin that does not lead to death.

18We know that anyone born of God does not continue to sin; the
one who was born of God keeps him safe, and the evil one cannot
harm him. 19We know that we are children of God, and that the whole
world is under the control of the evil one. 20We know also that the
Son of God has come and has given us understanding, so that we
may know him who is true. And we are in him who is true—even in
his Son Jesus Christ. He is the true God and eternal life.

21Dear children, keep yourselves from idols.

[a]7,8 Late manuscripts of the Vulgate *testify in heaven: the Father, the Word and the Holy Spirit, and these three are one. 8And there are three that testify on earth: the* (not found in any Greek manuscript before the sixteenth century)

ical witness of the water and the blood and the subjective, experiential witness of the Spirit (Christians experience within themselves the reality of these events). These two types of witness complement one another. Believers know in their hearts the truthfulness and power of the historical facts of Jesus' life and death.

5:10 believes in. It is one thing to believe Jesus. It is another to believe in Jesus. To believe Jesus is to accept what he says as true. To believe in Jesus is to accept who he is. It is to trust him completely and to commit one's life to him.

5:11 eternal life. The Greek word which is here translated "eternal" means "that which belongs to the coming age." But since that age has already broken into the present age, eternal life can be enjoyed even now.

5:13 This verse parallels John 20:31 which is the concluding verse of the gospel. John wrote his gospel in order to witness about Jesus and so inspire faith in those who did not yet know Christ. By believing in Jesus, they would discover "life." His purpose in the epistle is similar, except that now his words are directed to those who have, in fact, come to believe in Jesus. His purpose is no longer to tell them how to find "life" but, instead, to assure them that they do have eternal life.

5:14 confidence. Originally this word meant "freedom of speech." It was used to describe the right of all those in a democracy to speak their mind. By this word John refers to the bold confidence Christians have—that they can approach God in prayer and freely speak their minds. **according to his will.** In 3:22, John says that the condition for answered prayer is obedient behavior. Here John adds another condition: what we ask must be in accord with God's purposes (Matt. 26:39,42).

5:15 he hears us. By this phrase John means "he hears us favorably." To know that God hears is to know that "we have what we asked."

5:16 sin that leads to death. Although John's readers probably understood what he was referring to, it is not at all clear to the modern reader just what this phrase means. A specific kind of sin is probably not in view here but rather a lifestyle of habitual, willing and persistent sinning.

5:18 John concludes with a final list of assurances. The first affirmation relates to Christian behavior. The new birth results in new behavior. Sin and the child of God are incompatible.

5:19 The second affirmation which John makes is that they are, indeed, "children of God." They are part of the family of God and in relationship with the other children of God.

5:20 The third affirmation is that they really do know what is true. **understanding.** This is the power or ability to know what is actually so. Specifically, Jesus gave Christians the power to perceive the one and only true God against false idols (v. 21).

2 John / 3 John

Personal Reading	Group Study Topic and Reading	
2 John	Walking in Truth & Love	2 John
3 John	Tough Love	3 John

Author. There is much similarity of style and content between 2 and 3 John. Undoubtedly, both were written by the same person. There is also a close connection between 1 John and these two shorter letters. All three epistles seem to deal with the same situation. Therefore, it seems very likely that the "elder"who wrote 2 and 3 John is, indeed, the apostle John.

Date. The dates are uncertain, but both letters were probably written in the late A.D. 80s or early 90s, when the false doctrine which they rebuke began to flourish.

Theme. Hospitality for traveling missionaries.

Historical Background. Itinerant missionaries carried the teachings of Christianity throughout the Empire. They looked to local churches to aid in their mission by providing hospitality. The problem was that some of the people seeking room and board were false teachers, expounding erroneous doctrines; others were phonies, pretending to be true prophets in order to get free hospitality. These two letters were written to help local churches sort out the problem. In 2 John, the author warns the church to beware of those who teach false doctrine. "Do not welcome such," he says. In 3 John he addresses the opposite problem: the failure of believers to provide hospitality for genuine teachers. Here he commends a friend by the name of Gaius who opened his house even to strangers. By so doing, he was entering into their work of spreading the truth.

Characteristics. These are the shortest letters in the New Testament. Their length is determined by the size of a standard papyrus sheet (8 x 10 inches). Each letter would fit exactly on one sheet.

Second and Third John reflect John's concern in his first epistle for truth (which is mentioned four times in 2 John and seven times in 3 John) and for love (which occurs five times in 2 John and twice in 3 John). These two letters provide a glimpse into the life of the early church, and insight into how we should respond to Christian workers.

OPEN When you were young, who did you most enjoy staying as a guest in your home? Where did guests sleep in your home?

STUDY **1.** What do you learn from the book introduction about the problem John addresses in this letter? **2.** Why is John so dogmatic about believers opening their homes to false teachers? What would be a similar situation today and what would John say about it? **3.** What in this letter gave John "great joy"? Do you think your actions cause "great joy" in anyone?

APPLY What is the closest you have come to terminating a relationship over an issue related to your faith? What was it? Would you still do so today?

1The elder,

To the chosen lady and her children, whom I love in the truth—and
not I only, but also all who know the truth— 2because of the truth,
which lives in us and will be with us forever:

3Grace, mercy and peace from God the Father and from Jesus
Christ, the Father's Son, will be with us in truth and love.

4It has given me great joy to find some of your children walking in
the truth, just as the Father commanded us. 5And now, dear lady, I am
not writing you a new command but one we have had from the beginning. I ask that we love one another. 6And this is love: that we walk in
obedience to his commands. As you have heard from the beginning,
his command is that you walk in love.
7Many deceivers, who do not acknowledge Jesus Christ as coming
in the flesh, have gone out into the world. Any such person is the deceiver and the antichrist. 8Watch out that you do not lose what you
have worked for, but that you may be rewarded fully. 9Anyone who
runs ahead and does not continue in the teaching of Christ does not
have God; whoever continues in the teaching has both the Father and
the Son. 10If anyone comes to you and does not bring this teaching,
do not take him into your house or welcome him. 11Anyone who welcomes him shares in his wicked work.
12I have much to write to you, but I do not want to use paper and
ink. Instead, I hope to visit you and talk with you face to face, so that
our joy may be complete.

13The children of your chosen sister send their greetings.

1–3 As was the custom in first-century letters, the writer of this epistle first identifies himself, then he names the recipients of the letter, and concludes his salutation by pronouncing a blessing.

4–11 This is the heart of John's message. In verses 4–6 he focuses on the internal life of the local church. He points out its need to walk in truth, obedience and love. In verses 7–11 he focuses on the external life of the local church, specifically the threat to it posed by false teachers who espouse erroneous doctrine. John makes a sharp distinction between what is true (vv. 4–6) and what is false (vv. 7–11); between Christ and "the antichrist"; and between the commands of God and the deceptions of Satan.

7–11 John now turns from true believers to false deceivers. He warns Christians not to be deceived (vv. 7–8). He tells them not to encourage false teachers by giving them hospitality (vv. 10–11). If his exhortations in verses 4–6 to walk in truth, love and obedience are followed, the believers will be able to resist the heresy being taught by these false teachers.

7 Many. In contrast to "some" children who walk in truth, there are the "many" who deceive. **do not acknowledge Jesus Christ as coming in the flesh.** John defines the deceivers' error. They have a faulty view of Jesus. They deny the Incarnation. **have gone out.** John may be saying that these false teachers were once in the church but have now left (1 John 2:19). Or he may be saying that in the same way that the emissaries of God are sent out into the world (John 17:18; 20:21), Satan sends out his own emissaries. **the deceiver and the antichrist.** These false teachers both deceive people and oppose Christ.

8 Watch out. Having stated the problem, John then issues his first warning: do not cease in your vigilance. **be rewarded fully.** The Greek word translated "rewarded" refers to "the wages of a workman." John's concern is not with the loss of salvation which one does not earn in any case (it is a free gift), but with the loss of due reward for faithful service. However, if people are vigilant, they will gain the wages they have earned.

10 John now issues his second warning: do not receive or welcome false teachers into your home. This injunction sounds harsh in the light of the New Testament's insistence upon hospitality—including John's own words on the subject (Rom. 12:13; 1 Tim. 3:2; Titus 1:8; Heb. 13:2; 1 Peter 4:8–10; 3 John 5–8). However, it is important to notice that John refers to teachers. This injunction is not directed at believers who might hold errant views. These false teachers were dangerous because they were like merchants trying to sell a new product (they "bring" into the house the wrong "teaching"). However, John may only be referring here to an "official welcome" by the church and he may mean to deny this only to teachers who deny the Incarnation (v. 7).

[1]The elder,

To my dear friend Gaius, whom I love in the truth.

[2]Dear friend, I pray that you may enjoy good health and that all
may go well with you, even as your soul is getting along well. [3]It gave
me great joy to have some brothers come and tell about your faithfulness to the truth and how you continue to walk in the truth. [4]I have
no greater joy than to hear that my children are walking in the truth.

[5]Dear friend, you are faithful in what you are doing for the brothers, even though they are strangers to you. [6]They have told the
church about your love. You will do well to send them on their way in
a manner worthy of God. [7]It was for the sake of the Name that they
went out, receiving no help from the pagans. [8]We ought therefore to
show hospitality to such men so that we may work together for the
truth.

[9]I wrote to the church, but Diotrephes, who loves to be first, will
have nothing to do with us. [10]So if I come, I will call attention to what
he is doing, gossiping maliciously about us. Not satisfied with that,
he refuses to welcome the brothers. He also stops those who want to
do so and puts them out of the church.

[11]Dear friend, do not imitate what is evil but what is good. Anyone
who does what is good is from God. Anyone who does what is evil
has not seen God. [12]Demetrius is well spoken of by everyone—and
even by the truth itself. We also speak well of him, and you know that
our testimony is true.

[13]I have much to write you, but I do not want to do so with pen and
ink. [14]I hope to see you soon, and we will talk face to face.

Peace to you. The friends here send their greetings. Greet the friends there by name.

OPEN 1. Have you ever run out of money when you were away from home? What did you do? **2.** Who in your community deserves the Mother Teresa award for taking in people who are in need?

STUDY 1. Reading between the lines, what tensions in this early church do you see that are still around today? **2.** Who are the "they" in verses 6–7? **3.** How would you describe Gaius, Diotrephes and Demetrius? **4.** Why does John ask Gaius to open his home to these teachers? Why would this be so important at this time?

APPLY Do you enjoy opening your home to visitors from out of town? What have you learned from these experiences?

---

1 The elder. Both 2 and 3 John were written by the same person, identified only as "the elder"—the apostle John. **To my dear friend.** This is one of only two personal letters in the New Testament (the other is Philemon). While other letters do bear the name of an individual recipient—for example, Timothy and Titus—they are, in fact, letters meant to be read publicly. **Gaius.** There are several men by this name mentioned in the New Testament (Acts 19:29; 20:4; Rom. 16:23; 1 Cor. 1:14). However, "Gaius" was one of the most common names in the Roman Empire. As a result it is not possible to identify with certainty the Gaius to whom John writes with any other Gaius in the New Testament.

3 faithfulness to the truth. This was one of several characteristics of Gaius that John singles out for commendation.

4 my children. Paul used this phrase to describe those whose conversion to Christ he assisted. Perhaps, therefore, Gaius is John's spiritual son. **walking in the truth.** Gaius did not just know the truth, he did it. He lived what he believed. He let his theological convictions guide his moral behavior.

5–8 Here John commends Gaius for showing hospitality to the visiting teachers. John's words in verses 5–8 stand in sharp contrast to what he wrote in 2 John 10–11 where he warned against offering hospitality to certain teachers. The difference is that in 2 John he was concerned about false teachers and here he discusses "brothers" who went out "for the sake of the Name" and who "work ... for the truth." Second and Third John must be read together to get a balanced picture of the situation in the early church when it came to itinerant teachers.

9–10 John sets in contrast to the hospitality of Gaius the hostility of Diotrephes.

9 Diotrephes. He and Gaius may have been members of the same congregation or, more likely, of neighboring congregations. In any case, they act in opposite ways when it comes to hospitality. Gaius welcomes visiting teachers. Diotrephes refuses to receive them. This may have to do with his desire "to be first." Visiting teachers would be a threat to his preeminence. **loves to be first.** Personal aggrandizement was what Diotrephes craved.

12 Demetrius. Demetrius probably delivered this letter to Gaius. Since he was unknown to Gaius, John writes this threefold recommendation. Demetrius may himself have been a wandering missionary whom John wishes the house-church to receive.

Jude

Personal Reading	Group Study Topic and Reading	
vv. 1–16	Sin & Doom	vv. 1–16
vv. 17–25	Perseverance	vv. 17–25

Author. Traditionally Jude, the half-brother of Jesus, is considered the author of Jude (Matt. 13:55, Jude is a form of the name "Judas"). Little is known about Jude. He was one of four half-brothers of Jesus (Mark 6:3). He was probably not a follower of Jesus during the years of his ministry (Mark 3:21,31–35; John 7:5). It was only after the Resurrection that Jude became a believer (Acts 1:14). The half-brothers of Jesus eventually became itinerant missionaries. Tradition has it that they spread the gospel throughout Palestine. Jude's brother, James the Just, was leader of the church in Jerusalem. So in the book of Jude, a reader comes in touch with the early church in which Jesus' own blood relatives were leaders.

Date. The date of Jude is hard to determine. If the author of 2 Peter made use of it, then it would be dated around A.D. 65; otherwise it could be dated as late as A.D. 80.

Theme. Contend for the faith.

Purpose. Jude gives an overview of his book in verses 3–4. He makes two points: First, followers of Christ are "to contend for the faith"; second, they are to do so against false Christians who "have secretly slipped in among [them]." The rest of the book develops these two points. In verses 5–19, the nature of the false teachers is explained. Jude makes it exceedingly clear that this is not a new problem and, furthermore, their condemnation is sure. In verses 20–23, Jude gets to his main point: He appeals to the believers to hold on to the Christian faith despite the claims of false teachers.

The False Teachers. Jude's opponents are a band of smooth-talking teachers who go from church to church, receiving hospitality in return for their instruction. Such itinerant teachers were often a source of trouble in the early church (Matt. 7:15; 2 Cor. 10–11; 1 John 4:1; 2 John 10). In this case, the teachers were antinomians, that is, they rejected all moral standards (since they misunderstood grace) and indulged in all manner of immoral behavior, particularly of a sexual sort. Their teaching was derived largely from individual emotional experiences ("God told me"), and they considered themselves the sole judge of their own actions.

Characteristics. Jude has a standard opening (vv. 1–2), and in verses 3–4 the theme and occasion of the epistle are defined—again typical of a letter. But Jude is also a short sermon. The bulk of the book (vv. 5–25) consists of an exposition of certain texts as related to a particular problem facing the church. Thus, Jude is a sermon sent by mail to be read before the congregation(s).

The book of Jude is a painstakingly crafted document. Jude packs a lot of content into a few words by carefully choosing his words and images. Verses 11–13 are particularly vivid in imagery, evoking a wide range of thought in remarkably few words. Most people know Jude only because of its benediction (vv. 24–25).

1Jude, a servant of Jesus Christ and a brother of James,

To those who have been called, who are loved by God the Father
and kept by[a] Jesus Christ:

2Mercy, peace and love be yours in abundance.

The Sin and Doom of Godless Men

3Dear friends, although I was very eager to write to you about the
salvation we share, I felt I had to write and urge you to contend for
the faith that was once for all entrusted to the saints. 4For certain
men whose condemnation was written about[b] long ago have secretly
slipped in among you. They are godless men, who change the grace
of our God into a license for immorality and deny Jesus Christ our
only Sovereign and Lord.

5Though you already know all this, I want to remind you that the
Lord[c] delivered his people out of Egypt, but later destroyed those who
did not believe. 6And the angels who did not keep their positions of
authority but abandoned their own home—these he has kept in darkness, bound with everlasting chains for judgment on the great Day.
7In a similar way, Sodom and Gomorrah and the surrounding towns
gave themselves up to sexual immorality and perversion. They serve
as an example of those who suffer the punishment of eternal fire.

8In the very same way, these dreamers pollute their own bodies, reject authority and slander celestial beings. 9But even the archangel
Michael, when he was disputing with the devil about the body of
Moses, did not dare to bring a slanderous accusation against him,
but said, "The Lord rebuke you!" 10Yet these men speak abusively
against whatever they do not understand; and what things they do
understand by instinct, like unreasoning animals—these are the very
things that destroy them.

11Woe to them! They have taken the way of Cain; they have rushed
for profit into Balaam's error; they have been destroyed in Korah's rebellion.

12These men are blemishes at your love feasts, eating with you
without the slightest qualm—shepherds who feed only themselves.

[a]*1* Or *for;* or *in* [b]*4* Or *men who were marked out for condemnation* [c]*5* Some early manuscripts *Jesus*

OPEN 1. Which of your parents "read you the riot act" when you really did something wrong? **2.** What scary experience have you had with fire?

STUDY 1. What do you learn from the book introduction that helps you to understand this letter? **2.** How would you describe the tone and mood? **3.** Reading between the lines, what do you think the false teachers who have "secretly slipped in among you" have been teaching? **4.** From the description of the lifestyle of the false teachers in verses 8, 10–13, and 16, how would you describe it? Who would you compare these teachers to today? **5.** What is the challenge that these young Christians face (vv. 17–21)? What is their responsibility for the doubter who is merely flirting with falsehood (v. 22)? To one who is already singed with evil (v. 23)? How does the rescuer avoid falling into the same danger as those who are playing with fire?

APPLY 1. What do you see as the greatest danger to the church today: (a) false teaching; (b) immorality? (c) passivity? (d) leadership; (e) other? **2.** What is your church doing to build up the "body"?

---

1 servant. Literally, "slave." **brother of James.** James was the leader of the Jerusalem church (Acts 12:17; Gal. 2:9). **called ... loved ... kept.** These terms, drawn from Isaiah 40–45, are a marked contrast to the description of the false teachers later on.

4 The critical problem with the false teachers is their manipulation of the gospel's emphasis on God's grace into an excuse for living an immoral lifestyle (Rom. 6:1,15; Gal. 5:13; Phil. 3:2; 2 Tim. 3:1–9; 1 Peter 2:16; 1 John 1:6; Rev. 2:4).

7 Sodom and Gomorrah. These were two Old Testament towns whose wickedness was legendary (Gen. 18–19).

8 dreamers. This mocks the false teachers' claim to special revelations that justify their actions (v. 19; Col. 2:18). **pollute their own bodies.** Like the fallen angels, they indulge in illicit sexual activities. **reject authority.** Literally, "lordship." As in all the examples above, they defy Jesus' lordship over their lives (v. 4). **slander celestial beings.** Jewish tradition taught that the Law was mediated through and guarded by angels (Gal. 3:19; Heb. 2:2). To justify their rejection of the Law, these people may have taught that the Law originated with the angels as well, and could be discarded by people like them who had special revelations from God.

11 Their lifestyle reflects that of Cain (Gen. 4—the first murderer, viewed as a man full of lust, violence and greed); their motivations those of Balaam (Num. 31:16—he led Israel into idolatry and immorality by allowing his gift of prophecy to be bought by the highest bidder); and their future that of Korah (Num. 16—his rebellion against Moses was ended by God's judgment).

12 blemishes. A better translation is "hidden rocks." Just as a submerged reef endangers a ship, so these teachers threaten the church. **love feasts.** These were communal meals eaten by the church as a celebration of their unity and love in Christ. Six images from nature are used to accent how the immorality of the false teachers threatened the very meaning of that common meal.

They are clouds without rain, blown along by the wind; autumn trees, without fruit and uprooted—twice dead. [13]They are wild waves of the sea, foaming up their shame; wandering stars, for whom blackest darkness has been reserved forever.

[14]Enoch, the seventh from Adam, prophesied about these men: "See, the Lord is coming with thousands upon thousands of his holy ones [15]to judge everyone, and to convict all the ungodly of all the ungodly acts they have done in the ungodly way, and of all the harsh words ungodly sinners have spoken against him." [16]These men are grumblers and faultfinders; they follow their own evil desires; they boast about themselves and flatter others for their own advantage.

A Call to Persevere

[17]But, dear friends, remember what the apostles of our Lord Jesus Christ foretold. [18]They said to you, "In the last times there will be scoffers who will follow their own ungodly desires." [19]These are the men who divide you, who follow mere natural instincts and do not have the Spirit.

[20]But you, dear friends, build yourselves up in your most holy faith and pray in the Holy Spirit. [21]Keep yourselves in God's love as you wait for the mercy of our Lord Jesus Christ to bring you to eternal life.

[22]Be merciful to those who doubt; [23]snatch others from the fire and save them; to others show mercy, mixed with fear—hating even the clothing stained by corrupted flesh.

Doxology

[24]To him who is able to keep you from falling and to present you before his glorious presence without fault and with great joy— [25]to the only God our Savior be glory, majesty, power and authority, through Jesus Christ our Lord, before all ages, now and forevermore! Amen.

Revelation

Author. Although the author only refers to himself as "John"(1:4), it has traditionally been assumed that he was John the apostle. In fact, this simple designation "John" is strong proof in itself that the apostle was the writer. John writes in his own name, and only a person of the stature of an apostle could expect to have such a work received as authoritative. Furthermore, when Revelation is compared to the Gospel of John and the three letters of John, there are striking similarities in ideas, theology and language.

John wrote from the island of Patmos, a rocky, barren island in the Aegean Sea (10 miles long and five miles wide), where he had been exiled because of his Christian witness. Tradition says that he was eventually released from Patmos and spent the remaining years of his long life in Ephesus.

Personal Reading	Group Study Topic and Reading	
1:1–2:29	Star of the Drama	1:9–20
3:1–22	Scene 1: The Church	3:14–22
4:1–5:14	Scene 2: Heaven	5:1–14
6:1–17	The Seven Seals	6:1–17
7:1–8:13	Scene 3: The World	8:2–9:21
9:1–11:18	The Seventh Trumpet	11:15–18
11:19–13:1a	Scene 4: The Enemy	11:19–13:1a
13:1b–14:13	Worshipping the Enemy	13:1b–10
14:14–15:8	Scene 5: God's Wrath	15:1–8
16:1–21	The Seven Bowls	16:1–21
17:1–18:24	Scene 6: Babylon	18:1–24
19:1–10	Song of Praise	19:1–10
19:11–20:15	Scene 7: God With Us	20:1–15
21:1–22:21	The New Jerusalem	21:1–22:6

Date. Most scholars feel that the book of Revelation was written toward the end of the reign of Domitian, that is, around A.D. 90–95. Evidence has been offered that it might have been written during the last years of Nero's reign (between A.D. 65 and 68) or when Vespasian was emperor (A.D. 69–79).

Theme. Christ shall overcome!

Historical Background. Rome is a central and consistently negative image in the book of Revelation. This view of the Roman government stands in sharp contrast to most of the rest of the New Testament, where Rome is seen as the protector of Christianity. In the early days of missionary activity, Roman judges protected believers from Jewish mobs (Acts 18:1–17). It was Roman justice to which Paul turned in his time of need (Acts 23:12–35; 25:10–12). As a result, the apostles urged submission to Rome (Rom. 13:1–7; 1 Peter 2:13–17). But in Revelation, the attitude is quite different. Rome is seen as a whore, drunk with the blood of Christians (17:5–6), deserving nothing but destruction.

Characteristics. The book of Revelation is well worth reading, but it must be approached with humility and caution. To pin one's whole theology on details in the book of Revelation is dangerous indeed. With prayer and patience, the reader needs to work at understanding the text.

The Greek in Revelation is more difficult than that of any other book of the New Testament. There are mistakes in grammar and stylistic errors. Experts on apocalyptic literature consider the bad grammar deliberate. It is felt that John wrote this way for emphasis. A vision such as John had can never be adequately captured by mere words. John had to push language to its limits even to approximate what he had seen. The poor Greek may also have resulted from John's imprisonment on Patmos, where he probably had no secretary to smooth out his style.

Audience. The book of Revelation was addressed to seven churches in the western part of the Roman province of Asia. The order in which these churches are addressed is the order in which a messenger from Patmos would come to each church if he followed the great circular Roman road connecting the cities.

Interpretation. There are widely varying ways to interpret Revelation. Some limit its meaning to the first-century struggle between the church and Rome. Others see Revelation as a collection of symbols that predict future events. In fact, the book of Revelation speaks both to the immediate first-century struggle of believers and to the future when the Lord will return.

OPEN 1. What kind of books do you like to read: Mystery? Sports? Technical? Adventure? Poetry? **2.** Around the house, are you king, priest or servant? What would your spouse, parent or friend say is your typical role?

STUDY 1. Who wrote the book of Revelation, and where was he when he wrote it (see the book introduction to Revelation)? **2.** To whom was the book of Revelation addressed? Why is Rome portrayed negatively? **3.** What are the meanings of the titles given to Jesus (vv. 5–6)? What three things does Christ do for us? **4.** To believers suffering severely because of their faith, what aspect of the gospel would be especially important?

APPLY 1. When did Christ become more than just a name to you? **2.** How would you describe your relationship with Christ right now?

Prologue

1 The revelation of Jesus Christ, which God gave him to show his
servants what must soon take place. He made it known by sending his angel to his servant John, 2 who testifies to everything he
saw—that is, the word of God and the testimony of Jesus Christ.
3 Blessed is the one who reads the words of this prophecy, and
blessed are those who hear it and take to heart what is written in it,
because the time is near.

Greetings and Doxology

4 John,

To the seven churches in the province of Asia:

Grace and peace to you from him who is, and who was, and who is
to come, and from the seven spirits[a] before his throne, 5 and from
Jesus Christ, who is the faithful witness, the firstborn from the dead,
and the ruler of the kings of the earth.

To him who loves us and has freed us from our sins by his blood,
6 and has made us to be a kingdom and priests to serve his God and
Father—to him be glory and power for ever and ever! Amen.

7 Look, he is coming with the clouds,
and every eye will see him,
even those who pierced him;
and all the peoples of the earth will mourn because of him.
So shall it be! Amen.

8 "I am the Alpha and the Omega," says the Lord God, "who is, and
who was, and who is to come, the Almighty."

[a]4 Or *the sevenfold Spirit*

1:1–3 John identifies the five stages of transmission of this book: from Father to Son to an angel to John to the reader.

1:1 The revelation. Literally, *apokalupsis*—an unveiling or uncovering of something that was hidden; supernatural truths that could not be known had God not spoken them. **soon take place.** Though this revelation primarily has to do with events at the end of time (as becomes clear as the book unfolds), it also interprets the meaning of events that were happening at the time of its writing in light of the expectation of the return of Christ to establish and prepare his kingdom.

1:4 seven churches. These seven churches are named in verse 11. There were other churches in this region, however (Acts 20:5–6; Col. 1:2; 4:13). Why only these seven are addressed is not clear. They may have been the key churches in each of seven postal regions in Asia. Certainly the number seven was important (it represented perfection) and is used often in Revelation. The seven churches were located about 30 to 50 miles from each other on a circular road which connected them. **province of Asia.** The western half of Asia Minor (the western part of modern Turkey).

1:4 him who is, and who was, and who is to come. An elaboration of the name of God in Exodus 3:14–15. **the seven spirits.** This may be an unusual way of speaking about the Holy Spirit (the number seven referring to a complete manifestation of the Holy Spirit). Or it could refer to seven angels who minister to the Lamb (4:5; 5:6).

1:8 the Alpha and the Omega. The first and last letters in the Greek alphabet. God controls the whole sweep of history. **says the Lord God.** This is one of the two places where God speaks directly (21:5–8)

One Like a Son of Man

9I, John, your brother and companion in the suffering and kingdom
and patient endurance that are ours in Jesus, was on the island of
Patmos because of the word of God and the testimony of Jesus. 10On
the Lord's Day I was in the Spirit, and I heard behind me a loud voice
like a trumpet, 11which said: "Write on a scroll what you see and send
it to the seven churches: to Ephesus, Smyrna, Pergamum, Thyatira,
Sardis, Philadelphia and Laodicea."

12I turned around to see the voice that was speaking to me. And
when I turned I saw seven golden lampstands, 13and among the
lampstands was someone "like a son of man,"[a] dressed in a robe
reaching down to his feet and with a golden sash around his chest.
14His head and hair were white like wool, as white as snow, and his
eyes were like blazing fire. 15His feet were like bronze glowing in a
furnace, and his voice was like the sound of rushing waters. 16In his
right hand he held seven stars, and out of his mouth came a sharp
double-edged sword. His face was like the sun shining in all its brilliance.

17When I saw him, I fell at his feet as though dead. Then he placed
his right hand on me and said: "Do not be afraid. I am the First and
the Last. 18I am the Living One; I was dead, and behold I am alive for
ever and ever! And I hold the keys of death and Hades.

19"Write, therefore, what you have seen, what is now and what will
take place later. 20The mystery of the seven stars that you saw in my
right hand and of the seven golden lampstands is this: The seven
stars are the angels[b] of the seven churches, and the seven lampstands are the seven churches.

OPEN 1. What religious pictures do you remember the best? 2. What bizarre dream can you still recall, and why?

STUDY 1. What's significant about John's circumstances (v. 9) and the day when he received this vision (v. 10)? 2. Close your eyes and have someone read verses 12–18 again slowly. Meditate on it. What do the images suggest about Christ? 3. What is the meaning of the seven stars? The seven lampstands? What does it mean for a church to be a light?

APPLY 1. In your spiritual life right now, are you "on Patmos" (suffering, feeling exiled) or "in the Spirit" (reigning) or experiencing both at the same time? Why? 2. Using the analogy of a lighting fixture to describe the spiritual condition of your church, what kind fits your situation (a chandelier, a nightlight, etc.)? What would help create more illumination?

To the Church in Ephesus

2 "To the angel[c] of the church in Ephesus write:

These are the words of him who holds the seven stars in
his right hand and walks among the seven golden lampstands:

OPEN What was your "first love" in elementary school like?

STUDY 1. What do you know about the church in Ephesus (Acts 19)? 2. What good

[a]*13* Daniel 7:13 [b]*20* Or *messengers* [c]*1* Or *messenger*; also in verses 8, 12 and 18

1:9 suffering. The tribulation that comes from being a Christian (John 16:33) will intensify during the last days before the full establishment of God's kingdom. **Patmos.** A small island in the Aegean Sea off the coast of modern Turkey; probably a Roman penal colony.

1:10 the Lord's Day. The first day of the week (Sunday) when Christians met to worship together because it was on this day that Jesus rose from the dead. **in the Spirit.** A trance, an ecstatic experience; a type of mystical experience (Acts 10:10; 11:5; 22:17; 2 Cor. 12:2–4).

1:11 The churches are named in geographical order as one went around the circular road on which they were located. **Write on a scroll.** It is John's job to translate this vision into a written manuscript.

1:12 seven golden lampstands. These stand for the seven churches (v. 20). They are a fitting symbol for the church which is meant to be a light to the world (Matt. 5:14–16).

1:13 someone "like a son of man." This phrase is like that in Daniel 7:13. Jesus fills it with new meaning and content. **dressed in a robe.** Jesus wore the full-length robe of a high priest. In verses 1–20, Jesus is presented in the threefold office of prophet (v. 1), priest (v. 13), and king (v. 5).

1:16 sword. The sword that issues from the mouth of Jesus represents the fact of divine judgment.

1:19 Some scholars take the threefold statement in this verse to be the outline of the book of Revelation. Some say it is a mix throughout.

1:20 angels. This word means "messengers." While it is possible that this word refers to leaders of the seven congregations because of the use of the word throughout the book it probably refers to heavenly beings who are associated with the churches (Dan. 10:13,20–21; Matt. 18:10; Acts 12:15).

2:1 the church in Ephesus. More is known about this church than any other in the first century. Ephesus was the most important city in Asia at that time, with more than a quarter-million people living there. **the seven stars ... the seven golden lampstands.** In each case, the phrase chosen is appropriate for the church in view. Here Jesus is the one who holds control over the seven angels and he walks among the seven churches. He has come to inspect his church.

things characterize this church? How might its strengths have been the cause of its failure? What do you think their weekly worship was like? **3.** Why was repentance necessary for the Ephesian church?

APPLY 1. Of the positive qualities mentioned about the church at Ephesus, which best describes you? Your church? **2.** In what ways have you lost your first love for Christ (v. 4)? What has helped you to keep that love alive?

OPEN If you were rich, what would you like to do with your wealth?

STUDY 1. What problem is this church facing? How can they be both poor and rich? **2.** What do Jesus' words to the church in Smyrna teach about suffering?

APPLY 1. Has it been harder to live out your faith when you've been poor, or when you've had enough money? Why? **2.** In what ways do you feel spiritually rich?

2I know your deeds, your hard work and your perseverance. I
know that you cannot tolerate wicked men, that you have tested
those who claim to be apostles but are not, and have found them
false. 3You have persevered and have endured hardships for my
name, and have not grown weary.
4Yet I hold this against you: You have forsaken your first love.
5Remember the height from which you have fallen! Repent and
do the things you did at first. If you do not repent, I will come to
you and remove your lampstand from its place. 6But you have
this in your favor: You hate the practices of the Nicolaitans,
which I also hate.
7He who has an ear, let him hear what the Spirit says to the
churches. To him who overcomes, I will give the right to eat from
the tree of life, which is in the paradise of God.

To the Church in Smyrna

8"To the angel of the church in Smyrna write:

These are the words of him who is the First and the Last, who
died and came to life again. 9I know your afflictions and your
poverty—yet you are rich! I know the slander of those who say
they are Jews and are not, but are a synagogue of Satan. 10Do not
be afraid of what you are about to suffer. I tell you, the devil will
put some of you in prison to test you, and you will suffer persecution for ten days. Be faithful, even to the point of death, and I
will give you the crown of life.
11He who has an ear, let him hear what the Spirit says to the
churches. He who overcomes will not be hurt at all by the second
death.

2:2 hard work ... perseverance. This was a church known for its deeds of goodness done in the name of Christ. "Perseverance" can be translated as "patience," and refers to their willingness to endure the hostile reactions of those around them. Ephesus was a city dominated by the famous temple of Diana (the mother goddess of Asia), so it is not surprising that the church had great opposition (Acts 19:23–20:1). **tested those.** They did not reject out of hand those who came to them. They "tested the spirits" (as John had urged them in 1 John 4:1) and found these false apostles wanting. They are commended for their willingness to maintain their orthodoxy. **claim to be apostles.** In 1 Timothy, Paul dealt with the problem of false teachers in the Ephesian church (Acts 20:29). Apparently the church had taken his words to *heart and rid themselves of these errant* individuals.

2:4 Jesus turns from commendation to complaint. They have fallen away from the fervor of their first love.

2:5 The antidote to such coldness is twofold: remembrance and repentance.

2:6 Nicolaitans. It is hard to say for certain who these individuals are. They are some sort of heretical sect who mixed Christianity and pagan practices such as idolatry and immorality.

2:7 Each letter ends with a challenge. To those who heed these words, they will have fellowship with the Lord. **churches.** The plural is significant. These words are not intended only for the church at Ephesus, but as a challenge to all churches.

2:8 Smyrna. A beautiful city some 35 miles north of Ephesus on the eastern shore of the Aegean Sea. **the First and the Last.** Smyrna had strong ties to Rome. The imperial cult, with its emperor worship, was strong there. It is not surprising therefore that Jesus reminds them that he alone is sovereign. **died and came to life again.** His second title assures them that they too can overcome death, an important promise given the persecution they faced.

2:9 afflictions. This is a church under siege. **poverty.** It is not by accident that persecution and poverty are linked. It would have been difficult for Christians to find good jobs in a city where there was such hostility. **rich.** Though they are experiencing material poverty, they are rich spiritually (Matt. 5:11–12). **say they are Jews.** These may be Jewish proselytes. But also, New Testament sense is that being Jewish (a descendant of Abraham) has far more to do with sharing Abraham's faithfulness than it does with simply sharing his lineage (Rom. 2:28–29).

2:11 second death. The promised reward is that the overcomers will be unhurt by the second death, probably eternal death in the "lake of fire" (20:14,15).

To the Church in Pergamum

12"To the angel of the church in Pergamum write:

These are the words of him who has the sharp, double-edged
sword. 13I know where you live—where Satan has his throne. Yet
you remain true to my name. You did not renounce your faith in
me, even in the days of Antipas, my faithful witness, who was put
to death in your city—where Satan lives.
14Nevertheless, I have a few things against you: You have people there who hold to the teaching of Balaam, who taught Balak
to entice the Israelites to sin by eating food sacrificed to idols
and by committing sexual immorality. 15Likewise you also have
those who hold to the teaching of the Nicolaitans. 16Repent
therefore! Otherwise, I will soon come to you and will fight
against them with the sword of my mouth.
17He who has an ear, let him hear what the Spirit says to the
churches. To him who overcomes, I will give some of the hidden
manna. I will also give him a white stone with a new name written on it, known only to him who receives it.

To the Church in Thyatira

18"To the angel of the church in Thyatira write:

These are the words of the Son of God, whose eyes are like
blazing fire and whose feet are like burnished bronze. 19I know
your deeds, your love and faith, your service and perseverance,
and that you are now doing more than you did at first.
20Nevertheless, I have this against you: You tolerate that woman Jezebel, who calls herself a prophetess. By her teaching she
misleads my servants into sexual immorality and the eating of
food sacrificed to idols. 21I have given her time to repent of her
immorality, but she is unwilling. 22So I will cast her on a bed of
suffering, and I will make those who commit adultery with her

OPEN As a child, where was the local "haunted house" in your town? Did you ever dare to go in?

STUDY 1. How are the Christians in Pergamum being tested? Which do you think is easier to endure: Persecution by enemies or seduction by the culture? Why? **2.** Why is the title by which Christ reveals himself so appropriate to these Christians? **3.** What is the significance of the sword (v. 16)? Of the manna and stone (v. 17)?

APPLY 1. What cultural influences distract you from your relationship with Christ? How subtle are these influences in your life? How direct? **2.** What weapons has God given you to do battle with? Which has proved very helpful?

OPEN As a teenager, what person or group influenced you the most? How?

STUDY 1. What are the strengths of this church? Its weaknesses? **2.** What does the symbolic name "Jezebel" reveal about the woman in this church (2 Kin. 9:7–37)? **3.** How does Jesus describe himself? How do you interpret this description? What is he saying about himself? Why is this appropriate for the church in Thyatira? **4.** How is the nature and source of the temptation in Thyatira

---

2:12 Pergamum. Located some 40 miles north of Smyrna and 10 miles inland from the Aegean Sea, the city sat atop a thousand-foot high cone-shaped hill. It was the site of a famous library. **double-edged sword.** The sword was the symbol of the Roman proconsul who had the power of life and death over people.

2:13 I know where you live. Jesus was well aware of how difficult it was to be a Christian in the city of Pergamum. **where Satan has his throne.** *Pagan religion flourished in Pergamum.* Four gods were worshiped there—including Zeus, for whom a spectacular altar had been built jutting out from the top of the mountain (some identify this as the throne of Satan).

2:14 Balaam. The reference is to the Old Testament story in which Balaam advised the Moabite women to seduce the Israelites into leaving their God (v. 20; Num. 25:1–3; 31:16).

2:17 hidden manna. Manna was the supernatural food given to the Israelites during their wanderings in the wilderness.

2:18 Thyatira. The city of Thyatira was southeast of Pergamum. It was a manufacturing and marketing center, with numerous trade guilds. Lydia, the seller of purple, was from Thyatira (Acts 16:14). **Son of God.** Both Apollo Tyrimnos (who was worshiped here) and the emperor (who was seen as Apollo incarnate) were called the sons of the god Zeus. By his title, Jesus reminds the church that he alone is the true Son of God.

2:20 tolerate. Even though the church was growing in love and service, they allowed false teaching to exist. Unlike the Ephesians, who tested the teachers and rejected those who were false, those in Thyatira refused to deal with the matter of Jezebel. **Jezebel.** The original Jezebel was the wicked wife of Israel's King Ahab who promoted the detestable worship of Baal (1 Kin. 16:29–33; 2 Kin. 9:30–37). Her first-century counterpart played the same role in the church; i.e., the promotion of false practices. **prophetess.** Prophecy was highly valued in the New Testament church. While it included the idea of predicting the future (Acts 11:27–28), it mainly involved the application of God's truth. Jezebel claimed to be this kind of inspired teacher and some in the church followed her. **food sacrificed to idols.** The trade guilds were pagan in orientation, requiring participation in meals of food dedicated to idols. To refuse to participate would have great economic consequences, since it would have been difficult to work without being a member of one of the guilds. One needed this involvement to be prominent.

like (and unlike) that in Pergamum? **5.** What do you think Jesus' promise in verses 26–27 means?

APPLY 1. Which of the qualities in verse 19 apply to you this week? Why? **2.** Who or what has played a role similar to Jezebel in your life (names aren't necessary)? How? How did the Lord free you from that influence? **3.** What do you appreciate most about the promise to overcomers in this section?

OPEN What team or group of yours had a reputation far better than its performance?

STUDY 1. What is the contrast between reputation and reality in Sardis? What dangers exist for Christians who rely on an image instead of nurturing a genuine spiritual life (v. 2)? **2.** What is the only hope for the survival of the church in Sardis?

APPLY 1. If Jesus addressed this "wake-up call" to you, what would he want you to strengthen? **2.** Right now, would Jesus need a fire alarm to wake you up, or would a quiet call do it? Why?

OPEN When have you been "locked out" of your home? Out of a relationship?

suffer intensely, unless they repent of her ways. 23I will strike her
children dead. Then all the churches will know that I am he who
searches hearts and minds, and I will repay each of you according to your deeds. 24Now I say to the rest of you in Thyatira, to
you who do not hold to her teaching and have not learned
Satan's so-called deep secrets (I will not impose any other burden on you): 25Only hold on to what you have until I come.
26To him who overcomes and does my will to the end, I will
give authority over the nations—
27'He will rule them with an iron scepter;
he will dash them to pieces like pottery'[a]—
just as I have received authority from my Father. 28I will also give
him the morning star. 29He who has an ear, let him hear what the
Spirit says to the churches.

To the Church in Sardis

3 "To the angel[b] of the church in Sardis write:
These are the words of him who holds the seven spirits[c] of
God and the seven stars. I know your deeds; you have a reputation of being alive, but you are dead. 2Wake up! Strengthen what
remains and is about to die, for I have not found your deeds
complete in the sight of my God. 3Remember, therefore, what
you have received and heard; obey it, and repent. But if you do
not wake up, I will come like a thief, and you will not know at
what time I will come to you.
4Yet you have a few people in Sardis who have not soiled their
clothes. They will walk with me, dressed in white, for they are
worthy. 5He who overcomes will, like them, be dressed in white.
I will never blot out his name from the book of life, but will acknowledge his name before my Father and his angels. 6He who
has an ear, let him hear what the Spirit says to the churches.

To the Church in Philadelphia

7"To the angel of the church in Philadelphia write:

[a]27 Psalm 2:9 [b]1 Or *messenger;* also in verses 7 and 14 [c]1 Or *the sevenfold Spirit*

2:28 the morning star. There is no clear understanding about what this refers to. Suggestions include: Jesus himself (22:16), the Holy Spirit, and immortality (as in Dan. 12:3).

3:1 Sardis. Sardis was located 50 miles east of Ephesus atop a 1,500-foot citadel. It had once been a powerful city, but by the first century it had lost much of its influence. The temple in Sardis was dedicated to the goddess Cybele who was thought to have the power to bring dead people back to life—which may be the reason why Jesus chose *to speak to them about being dead* and the need to be made alive again. **reputation of being alive.** The church at Sardis was thought to be vital and full of life, but in fact it was spiritually dead.

3:2 Wake up! This is the first of five commands. The presence of these commands means that it is possible for this church to come back to life. This particular command means "Be watchful." **I have not found your deeds complete.** Unlike the other churches addressed thus far, apparently this church was not troubled by persecution nor was heresy an issue. It was an active church, but its activities were done in a spiritual vacuum.

3:3 I will come like a thief. If they do not heed this call to turn around, Christ will come to them unexpectedly.

3:4 a few people. Not all at Sardis have lost faith. Some are still faithful. **not soiled their clothes.** In a place like Sardis, where making and dyeing wool cloth was a central occupation, the reference to clothing is appropriate. The image of soiled garments hints at the problem in Sardis. Sin of some sort had been allowed to stain the church.

3:5 book of life. The image is of some sort of divine ledger in which the names of the people who have eternal life are written. This picture was first found in the Old Testament (Ex. 32:32–33; Ps. 69:28; Dan. 12:1). In the first century, the names of citizens were recorded in a register. To have your name removed was to lose your citizenship.

3:7 Philadelphia. This was the new-

These are the words of him who is holy and true, who holds
the key of David. What he opens no one can shut, and what he
shuts no one can open. 8I know your deeds. See, I have placed
before you an open door that no one can shut. I know that you
have little strength, yet you have kept my word and have not denied my name. 9I will make those who are of the synagogue of
Satan, who claim to be Jews though they are not, but are liars—
I will make them come and fall down at your feet and acknowledge that I have loved you. 10Since you have kept my command
to endure patiently, I will also keep you from the hour of trial that
is going to come upon the whole world to test those who live on
the earth.
11I am coming soon. Hold on to what you have, so that no one
will take your crown. 12Him who overcomes I will make a pillar in
the temple of my God. Never again will he leave it. I will write on
him the name of my God and the name of the city of my God, the
new Jerusalem, which is coming down out of heaven from my
God; and I will also write on him my new name. 13He who has an
ear, let him hear what the Spirit says to the churches.

To the Church in Laodicea

14"To the angel of the church in Laodicea write:

These are the words of the Amen, the faithful and true witness,
the ruler of God's creation. 15I know your deeds, that you are
neither cold nor hot. I wish you were either one or the other!
16So, because you are lukewarm—neither hot nor cold—I am
about to spit you out of my mouth. 17You say, 'I am rich; I have
acquired wealth and do not need a thing.' But you do not realize
that you are wretched, pitiful, poor, blind and naked. 18I counsel
you to buy from me gold refined in the fire, so you can become
rich; and white clothes to wear, so you can cover your shameful
nakedness; and salve to put on your eyes, so you can see.
19Those whom I love I rebuke and discipline. So be earnest,

STUDY 1. What does the "key of David" open (vv. 7–8; 4:1; Isa. 22:22–24; Matt. 16:19)? **2.** How is this church able to persevere? Describe their enemies. How does their reward (v. 12) fit their faithfulness?

APPLY 1. What open doors has Christ placed before you? How have you taken advantage of the pathways he's made available to you? **2.** What are some closed doors he's placed in your career? In your social life? In your schooling? How have you responded to each of these closed doors? **3.** In what ways are you like the Christians in Philadelphia? Unlike them? Why? **4.** What is the Spirit saying to you now?

OPEN 1. What is the very worst meal you have ever been served? **2.** If you could invite any famous person for dinner, whom would you ask? Why?

STUDY 1. What does the "faithful and true witness" see when he looks at the Laodicean church (vv. 15–16)? How does the church view itself? Why the contrast? **2.** What does Jesus tell them to do in verse 18? Why? What does this say about true wealth? **3.** How would you describe Christ based on what you have read so far in this book? How

---

est of the seven cities. It was located 28 miles southeast of Sardis in a region of severe earthquakes. **him who is holy and true.** Both names were titles for God. **the key of David.** A symbolic way of speaking about the one who controls access to the royal house; in this case, the messianic kingdom (Isa. 22:22).

3:9–11 John identifies the threefold reward for faithfulness: vindication before their enemies, deliverance from the coming worldwide trials, and a secure place in the coming age.

3:10 hour of trial. The believers will not have to face persecution

3:12 a pillar. This metaphor speaks of stability and permanence (Gal. 2:9; 1 Tim. 3:15).

3:14 Laodicea. A wealthy city, situated at the intersection of three major roads, known for its banking and industry. Paul wrote a letter to this church which, unfortunately, has been lost (Col. 4:16). Like the church at Sardis, this church seems to be prosperous and without persecution or heresy. **Amen.** The word "amen" was used in the Old Testament as an acknowledgment that something was true. Jesus is the one who is truly true and therefore can be relied upon. **the faithful and true witness.** This amplifies the meaning of the previous title. Jesus is, indeed, the one who testifies to that which is true.

3:16 lukewarm. By the time the hot water got to Laodicea from the springs at Hierapolis six miles away, it was tepid. **spit you out of my mouth.** Lukewarm, mineral-filled water was probably so foul-tasting that one would be tempted to spit it out.

3:17 I have acquired wealth. This image would be meaningful in this city with a thriving banking system. The church was affluent and without a sense of need.

3:18 gold. Thinking themselves "rich" (v. 17), they will become truly rich only with the spiritual gold they can get from Christ. **nakedness.** A startling image for a people who lived in a city famous for its textile industry. At Laodicea, they raised sheep with a glossy black wool that they made into a popular black fabric. What the church has need of, however, are the white garments of heaven. **salve.** Laodicea was the site of a famous medical school. One of its well-known products was an eye ointment.

3:19 Rebuke and discipline are expressions not of hatred but of love (Prov. 3:11–12; Heb. 12:5–6). **love.** The Greek

does this expand the picture of Jesus in the Gospels?

APPLY 1. If Jesus took your spiritual temperature today, what would he find? Why? **2.** What is Jesus waiting for at the door of your life? Why not let him in?

OPEN What is the most memorable storm you have ever been in? What happened?

STUDY 1. Where does this scene actually take place: In the afterlife? In some perfect order of things after this world has passed away? Or on the level of spiritual reality here and now (as in Eph 2:6), where good and evil are unmasked to be seen for what they really are? **2.** Who is the figure on the throne? What is he like? What are the 24 elders like? **3.** What does the heavenly scene include? **4.** What about the four living creatures suggests the eternal power of God? What response does the central figure elicit? Why? **5.** What does this say about who God is and how he relates to his creation?

APPLY 1. Imagine yourself in this scene. What do you see? Hear? Feel? What impresses you about God? **2.** What aspect of creation best demonstrates God's glory and power to you? Why? **3.** How might this vision of God enhance your worship life? Your everyday life?

---

and repent. [20]Here I am! I stand at the door and knock. If anyone hears my voice and opens the door, I will come in and eat with him, and he with me.

[21]To him who overcomes, I will give the right to sit with me on my throne, just as I overcame and sat down with my Father on his throne. [22]He who has an ear, let him hear what the Spirit says to the churches."

The Throne in Heaven

4 After this I looked, and there before me was a door standing open in heaven. And the voice I had first heard speaking to me like a trumpet said, "Come up here, and I will show you what must take place after this." [2]At once I was in the Spirit, and there before me was a throne in heaven with someone sitting on it. [3]And the one who sat there had the appearance of jasper and carnelian. A rainbow, resembling an emerald, encircled the throne. [4]Surrounding the throne were twenty-four other thrones, and seated on them were twenty-four elders. They were dressed in white and had crowns of gold on their heads. [5]From the throne came flashes of lightning, rumblings and peals of thunder. Before the throne, seven lamps were blazing. These are the seven spirits[a] of God. [6]Also before the throne there was what looked like a sea of glass, clear as crystal.

In the center, around the throne, were four living creatures, and they were covered with eyes, in front and in back. [7]The first living creature was like a lion, the second was like an ox, the third had a face like a man, the fourth was like a flying eagle. [8]Each of the four living creatures had six wings and was covered with eyes all around, even under his wings. Day and night they never stop saying:

> "Holy, holy, holy
> is the Lord God Almighty,
> who was, and is, and is to come."

[a]5 Or *the sevenfold Spirit*

---

word used here is *phileo*, which is the kind of warm and tender affection one feels toward family members.

3:20 This verse is often used to call those without faith into relationship with Christ. In reality, in this context the call is to those within the church to return to the Lord from whom they have turned away. **eat with him.** Sharing a meal was a sign that a bond existed between people.

3:21 In this final word to overcomers in his letters, Christ declares they will reign with him in his coming kingdom.

4:1 a door. Unlike the door into the kingdom (3:8) and the door into the heart (3:20), this is a door into heaven through which John is invited to pass ("Come up here") and so encounter the next part of his vision.

4:2 I was in the Spirit. John is caught up in an ecstatic vision. Such visions are not uncommon in Scripture (1 Kin. 22:19). **a throne in heaven with someone sitting on it.** John is granted a vision of God on his throne. The image of the throne pervades Revelation, occurring more than 40 times.

4:3 jasper. As it is known today, jasper is opaque, while this heavenly gem is described in 21:11 as a transparent crystal. **carnelian.** A fiery red mineral found in Sardis. **rainbow.** There is an arc of a rainbow around the throne the color of emerald green (unlike a normal rainbow which contains the full spectrum of colors). It is probably better to see these as symbols which seek to convey God arrayed in "unapproachable light, whom no one has seen or can see" (1 Tim. 6:16).

4:4 twenty-four elders. There are various interpretations of these figures. Some say they represent the 24 orders of God's people of the Old and New Testament (with the 12 patriarchs and the 12 apostles). Others hold that they are angels who assist in the ruling of the universe. In any case, they function to worship and serve God.

4:6 four living creatures. These are similar to the creatures ("seraphim," "cherubim") seen in the vision of Isaiah (Isa. 6:1–3) and Ezekiel (Ezek. 10:14). They are some sort of angelic order which serves God.

[9]Whenever the living creatures give glory, honor and thanks to him
who sits on the throne and who lives for ever and ever, [10]the twenty-
four elders fall down before him who sits on the throne, and worship
him who lives for ever and ever. They lay their crowns before the
throne and say:

[11]"You are worthy, our Lord and God,
to receive glory and honor and power,
for you created all things,
and by your will they were created
and have their being."

The Scroll and the Lamb

5 Then I saw in the right hand of him who sat on the throne a
scroll with writing on both sides and sealed with seven seals.
[2]And I saw a mighty angel proclaiming in a loud voice, "Who is worthy to break the seals and open the scroll?" [3]But no one in heaven or
on earth or under the earth could open the scroll or even look inside
it. [4]I wept and wept because no one was found who was worthy to
open the scroll or look inside. [5]Then one of the elders said to me, "Do
not weep! See, the Lion of the tribe of Judah, the Root of David, has
triumphed. He is able to open the scroll and its seven seals."

[6]Then I saw a Lamb, looking as if it had been slain, standing in the
center of the throne, encircled by the four living creatures and the
elders. He had seven horns and seven eyes, which are the seven
spirits[a] of God sent out into all the earth. [7]He came and took the
scroll from the right hand of him who sat on the throne. [8]And when

[a]6 Or *the sevenfold Spirit*

OPEN 1. What was the best choir or musical group you have ever heard (or participated in)? What was memorable about the group? **2.** Around the house, are you more like a lion or a lamb?

STUDY 1. What do you think makes the scroll so significant (Jer. 36:2–32)? What dilemma does the sealed scroll pose? **2.** Why is Christ the only one worthy enough to open it (vv. 4,9; John 1:29)? What titles are used to describe him? What does it mean that he is both a Lion and a Lamb? What does this mean for your life? **3.** What is the meaning of the seven horns and seven eyes? **4.** Where does Christ appear? What is the significance of this? What is the

---

4:9–11 The living creatures and the twenty-four elders join in praise to God. The living creatures in their song praise God for his essential nature (v. 8), while the elders in their song praise him for his created works.

5:1 the right hand of him who sat on the throne. It is God who holds the whole of human history in his hand. He is sovereign, and no matter how strong evil may appear to be it is he who controls the ultimate flow of events. **a scroll.** The nature of this scroll is not clear. The best guess is that this scroll is like the one given to Ezekiel, containing "words of lament and mourning and woe" (Ezek. 2:10). In this case, John's scroll would contain the prophecy of the final events. The nature of this prophecy is described in chapters 7–22. **seven.** The number seven occurs frequently in Revelation, as indeed it does in the rest of the Bible. It has to do with completeness; it relates to the fullness of something. God created the earth in six days and rested on the seventh. As the world began in seven days, so it will end by a series of sevens. **seals.** The scroll is rolled up and sealed along its edge with seven wax seals (that ensure the secrecy of its contents), which must be broken in order for the contents to be read. As each seal is broken, a momentous event takes place.

5:2–3 The call goes out across creation ("in heaven or on earth or under the earth") for someone to bring history to its conclusion, but no one is found.

5:4 So overwhelming is the thought that God's final action in history cannot go forward because no one is worthy to open the scroll.

5:5 The elder calms John. There is one who is worthy to perform this task. It is Christ who can and will reveal where history is going and how it will end. **the Lion of the tribe of Judah.** An ancient title for the Messiah (Gen. 49:9–10) which was in use in the first century. The image is of a conquering King. **the Root of David.** Another messianic title, referring this time to the fact that the Messiah will come from the royal family of David (Isa. 11:1). **triumphed.** By his death on the cross, Jesus won a great victory over evil, sin and death (Col. 2:15; 2 Tim. 1:10; Heb. 2:14–15). Though this victory is real and eternal, its full realization will occur only at the end of time. This assertion functions to confirm once more that despite the great battles that lie ahead, the outcome is certain.

5:6 a Lamb. The Lion has become a Lamb. The final victory of the conquering Messiah is only possible because of the death of the Lamb of God. In the Old Testament a lamb was sacrificed each Passover, reminding the nation that God had spared them and delivered them from the bondage of Egypt (Ex. 12:13). The connection was not made between the slain lamb and the Messiah prior to New Testament revelation, despite the prophecy in Isaiah 53. Until Jesus, people could not conceive of a conquering Messiah who was slain as a sacrificial lamb. **as if it had been slain.** That is, its throat was cut as was done in the sacrificial process. **seven horns.** A horn is a symbol of power in the Old Testament (Deut. 33:17; Ps. 18:2). Seven horns would represent the fullness of power (Matt. 28:18). **seven eyes.** He has fullness of vision, omniscience (Zech. 4:10). **the seven spirits.** The work of Christ on earth is done by the Holy Spirit which is pictured by means of this symbol (4:5).

5:8 When the Lamb grasps the scroll

response when he takes the scroll? **5.** Analyze the three songs (vv. 9–13): How is the Lamb described? Who comprises the first musical group? The second? The third? Who are the true kings and priests on earth?

APPLY What would the visions in chapters 4 and 5 have meant to the persecuted Christians of Asia? What does this vision say to you as you view your out-of-control world? Based on this, what actions will you take this week?

he had taken it, the four living creatures and the twenty-four elders
fell down before the Lamb. Each one had a harp and they were holding golden bowls full of incense, which are the prayers of the saints.
9And they sang a new song:

"You are worthy to take the scroll
and to open its seals,
because you were slain,
and with your blood you purchased men for God
from every tribe and language and people and nation.
10You have made them to be a kingdom and priests to serve our
God,
and they will reign on the earth."

11Then I looked and heard the voice of many angels, numbering
thousands upon thousands, and ten thousand times ten thousand.
They encircled the throne and the living creatures and the elders. 12In
a loud voice they sang:

"Worthy is the Lamb, who was slain,
to receive power and wealth and wisdom and strength
and honor and glory and praise!"

13Then I heard every creature in heaven and on earth and under the
earth and on the sea, and all that is in them, singing:

"To him who sits on the throne and to the Lamb
be praise and honor and glory and power,
for ever and ever!"

14The four living creatures said, "Amen," and the elders fell down and
worshiped.

OPEN **1.** What kind of horse are you most like: A Clydesdale? A thoroughbred? An Arabian stallion? **2.** How is your group like a team of four horsemen: Are you each pulling in a different direction, or the same? How so?

The Seals

6 I watched as the Lamb opened the first of the seven seals. Then I
heard one of the four living creatures say in a voice like thunder,
"Come!" 2I looked, and there before me was a white horse! Its rider
held a bow, and he was given a crown, and he rode out as a conquer-
or bent on conquest.
3When the Lamb opened the second seal, I heard the second living

---

of history, the whole of heaven bursts into a song of praise. **harp.** The instrument of praise in the Psalms (Ps. 33:2). **incense.** Incense was used in Old Testament worship (Deut. 33:10). Here it stands for the prayers of God's people.

5:9 a new song. A special song praises the Lamb for his worthiness and his redemptive work. **purchased.** Ransomed—a word used to describe the freeing of a slave from bondage by the payment of a price. The purchase price, in this case, was the blood of Christ. *What it bought was the freedom of men* and women from the bondage of sin. **from every tribe and language and people and nation.** Christ redeems believers from the whole of humankind—past, present and future—by this great and terrible payment.

5:10 a kingdom and priests. The result is they have become God's people and God's priests. They will share in God's rule and will have access to his presence. **reign on the earth.** In order for his people to reign on earth, his kingdom must be established there in fullness; and it is necessary to break the seals and to complete the judgment bringing about the kingdom.

6:1 Come! One of the living creatures summons the first of the four apocalyptic horsemen. The images which follow are similar to those in Zechariah's visions (Zech. 1:8–17; 6:1–8).

6:2 a white horse. There has been much debate about the identity of the rider on the white horse. One suggestion is that he symbolizes military conquest, an image in line with the identity of the other three riders. Another suggestion is that the rider on a white horse symbolizes the preaching of the gospel throughout the world prior to the end. The bow is used in the Old Testament as a symbol of divine victories (Hab. 3:9). In Revelation, white is generally a symbol of Christ (1:14; 14:14; 19:11,14). Furthermore, unlike the coming of the other three horsemen, no calamities follow after this rider.

6:3–4 The second seal is broken and a red horse and rider appear. There is no

creature say, "Come!" 4Then another horse came out, a fiery red one.
Its rider was given power to take peace from the earth and to make
men slay each other. To him was given a large sword.
5When the Lamb opened the third seal, I heard the third living creature say, "Come!" I looked, and there before me was a black horse! Its
rider was holding a pair of scales in his hand. 6Then I heard what
sounded like a voice among the four living creatures, saying, "A
quart[a] of wheat for a day's wages,[b] and three quarts of barley for a
day's wages,[b] and do not damage the oil and the wine!"
7When the Lamb opened the fourth seal, I heard the voice of the
fourth living creature say, "Come!" 8I looked, and there before me was
a pale horse! Its rider was named Death, and Hades was following
close behind him. They were given power over a fourth of the earth to
kill by sword, famine and plague, and by the wild beasts of the earth.
9When he opened the fifth seal, I saw under the altar the souls of
those who had been slain because of the word of God and the testimony they had maintained. 10They called out in a loud voice, "How
long, Sovereign Lord, holy and true, until you judge the inhabitants
of the earth and avenge our blood?" 11Then each of them was given a
white robe, and they were told to wait a little longer, until the number
of their fellow servants and brothers who were to be killed as they
had been was completed.
12I watched as he opened the sixth seal. There was a great earthquake. The sun turned black like sackcloth made of goat hair, the
whole moon turned blood red, 13and the stars in the sky fell to earth,
as late figs drop from a fig tree when shaken by a strong wind. 14The
sky receded like a scroll, rolling up, and every mountain and island
was removed from its place.
15Then the kings of the earth, the princes, the generals, the rich,
the mighty, and every slave and every free man hid in caves and
among the rocks of the mountains. 16They called to the mountains

[a]6 Greek *a choinix* (probably about a liter) [b]6 Greek *a denarius*

STUDY 1. Who (or what) do each of the four horsemen represent? How are the first two horsemen similar? How are they different? **2.** When the third horseman rides, how much food will a day's wages buy? Why will luxury items (wine and oil) still be available? What is the relationship of this to the first two horsemen? In what sense do they lead to the fourth horseman? **3.** How have each of these forces operated throughout history? How do they prevail today? What do you think this means for the interpretation of the vision? **4.** What is revealed by the opening of the fifth seal (v. 9)? How is this related to the suffering of the Christians in John's day? In our day? **5.** What occurs when the sixth seal is broken (vv. 12–13; Mark 13)? **6.** Who can withstand the wrath of God? How?

APPLY 1. What is the closest you have come to suffering because of your faithfulness to the Word of God? **2.** In what area of your life are you trying to hide from God? What do you need to do to come out of hiding? **3.** How does this passage make you feel about the end times? Why?

---

ambiguity about this figure: it is a symbol of bloodshed and war.

6:5 The third seal is broken and a black horse and rider are called forth, symbolizing a time of great scarcity verging on famine. **scales.** A balance used for measuring out grain.

6:6 Food is sold at inflated prices—over 10 times what it should cost. **do not damage the oil and the wine.** A limitation is placed upon the rider of the black horse. Grain is easily destroyed by drought, but the drought is not to be so severe as to damage the deeper roots of the olive trees or grape vines.

6:7–8 The fourth horse and rider represent death from various causes. These are the "four dreadful judgments" in Ezekiel 14:21.

6:8 a pale horse. Pale gray, the color of a corpse. **Hades.** It is not clear whether Hades is following behind Death on foot, on another horse, or on the same horse. Still, the image is clear. After Death comes the grave or the underworld. Hades was understood to be the place where the dead resided as they awaited the final judgment. **a fourth of the earth.** There is a limitation placed upon Death. It threatens all of life, but is not permitted to totally do away with all of it. **kill by sword.** This is death by murder, war or violence. **famine.** The issue is no longer scarcity (as with the black horse), but a severe lack of food that leads to death.

6:9 A new scene unfolds with the breaking of the fifth seal. Those who have been martyred in the name of God are pictured under the altar. **the testimony they had maintained.** This probably refers not to testimony as "witnessing" to others about their faith, but rather to the fact that they had maintained even unto death their faithfulness to the witness Jesus had given; i.e., they remained loyal to the gospel.

6:10 holy. The martyrs appeal to his holiness. He is beyond all evil and so can be relied upon to right the wrong done to them. **the inhabitants of the earth.** In Revelation, this phrase refers to those who are hostile to God.

6:12–14 The sixth seal is broken and John sees cosmic disturbances which herald the coming of the last days.

6:12–13 earthquake. The very trembling of the earth is often associated with the presence of God (Ex. 19:18; Isa. 2:19; Hag. 2:6). **sun ... moon ... stars.** Even the predictable, well-ordered movement of the heavenly bodies goes awry (Isa. 34:4; Acts 2:20).

6:16 the wrath of the Lamb. An unusual phrase, since a lamb is thought of as gentle.

OPEN What kind of wind (a warm gentle breeze, a cold north wind, a hurricane, etc.) best symbolizes your life now?

STUDY 1. Do you think the work of the four angels is a "new" woe or is it a restatement of the events in chapter 6? Likewise, in what sense do the events of chapter 7 come "after" the events in chapter 6: In actual history? Or simply in John's vision? **2.** What is the message of the fifth angel (v. 3)? Who is sealed? When does this occur? What does it mean (Gen. 4:15; Ezek. 9:4–6; Eph. 1:13–14)? **3.** Is this "144,000" a symbol or a statistic? Why (7:9; 14:1–5)?

APPLY 1. How have you sensed God's protection in the last six months? Before that? **2.** What sort of seal has God placed on your life?

OPEN What piece of clothing (bathrobe, tennis togs, 3-piece suit, jeans, etc.) do you feel expresses your personality best? How do you feel when wearing it?

STUDY 1. What does John see next? How does he describe the size of the crowd? Is this multitude the same as the 144,000 in 7:4? Why or why not? What are they doing? Wearing? Carrying? **2.** When the multitude cries out, how do the angels, elders and the four living creatures respond? What does all this say about God's kingdom and Christ's

and the rocks, "Fall on us and hide us from the face of him who sits
on the throne and from the wrath of the Lamb! 17 For the great day of
their wrath has come, and who can stand?"

144,000 Sealed

7 After this I saw four angels standing at the four corners of the
earth, holding back the four winds of the earth to prevent any
wind from blowing on the land or on the sea or on any tree. 2 Then I
saw another angel coming up from the east, having the seal of the living God. He called out in a loud voice to the four angels who had
been given power to harm the land and the sea: 3 "Do not harm the
land or the sea or the trees until we put a seal on the foreheads of the
servants of our God." 4 Then I heard the number of those who were
sealed: 144,000 from all the tribes of Israel.

5 From the tribe of Judah 12,000 were sealed,
from the tribe of Reuben 12,000,
from the tribe of Gad 12,000,
6 from the tribe of Asher 12,000,
from the tribe of Naphtali 12,000,
from the tribe of Manasseh 12,000,
7 from the tribe of Simeon 12,000,
from the tribe of Levi 12,000,
from the tribe of Issachar 12,000,
8 from the tribe of Zebulun 12,000,
from the tribe of Joseph 12,000,
from the tribe of Benjamin 12,000.

The Great Multitude in White Robes

9 After this I looked and there before me was a great multitude that
no one could count, from every nation, tribe, people and language,
standing before the throne and in front of the Lamb. They were wearing white robes and were holding palm branches in their hands.
10 And they cried out in a loud voice:

"Salvation belongs to our God,
who sits on the throne,
and to the Lamb."

11 All the angels were standing around the throne and around the elders and the four living creatures. They fell down on their faces before the throne and worshiped God, 12 saying:

6:17 the great day of their wrath. There are many titles used to describe this period of time. In this case the focus is on judgment; on the fact that those who have rebelled against God will face his judgment.

7:1–4 The earth is pictured as a great square, with an angel at each corner holding back a lethal wind until the *144,000 can be sealed.*

7:3 a seal. Probably similar to the signet ring which kings used to authenticate documents by its imprint. The purpose of this seal is to mark out God's people so that they will be spared from the plagues that are to come (9:4). This is similar to the time of the Exodus, when the tenth plague brought death to the firstborn of those households not marked by blood over the door.

7:5 Judah heads the list, not Reuben, who belongs in that place as Jacob's oldest son but forfeited his rights (Gen. 35:22; 49:3–4). Christ came from the tribe of Judah ("the Lion of the tribe of Judah"—Rev. 5:5). **12,000.** This number is symbolic, as is the total number of 144,000 (12 squared times a thousand), and conveys the idea of completeness: 12,000 are sealed from each of the 12 tribes. The full complement is sealed.

7:10 The song they sing is not, as one might expect, one of gratitude to God for their deliverance. Rather, it is a song of praise to God for his work of salvation. Their salvation involves more than just deliverance from the Tribulation.

7:12 glory. A reference to the brightness of God, his divine luminous

"Amen!
Praise and glory
and wisdom and thanks and honor
and power and strength
be to our God for ever and ever.
Amen!"

13Then one of the elders asked me, "These in white robes—who are
they, and where did they come from?"
14I answered, "Sir, you know."
And he said, "These are they who have come out of the great tribulation; they have washed their robes and made them white in the blood of the Lamb. 15Therefore,

"they are before the throne of God
and serve him day and night in his temple;
and he who sits on the throne will spread his tent over them.
16Never again will they hunger;
never again will they thirst.
The sun will not beat upon them,
nor any scorching heat.
17For the Lamb at the center of the throne will be their shepherd;
he will lead them to springs of living water.
And God will wipe away every tear from their eyes."

The Seventh Seal and the Golden Censer

8 When he opened the seventh seal, there was silence in heaven for about half an hour.

sacrifice? **3.** What qualifies this white-robed crowd to stand before God? What is their new role? What is their future? How would this encourage the Christians of John's day? Of our day? **4.** Is "the great tribulation" (7:14) a particular event or a general experience? Is the safety and service of these Christians a present life experience for them, or a promise to be realized in some vague and distant future? Or both? **5.** What sort of seal has God placed on your life? How is this seal evident to other believers? To unbelievers?

APPLY What is your greatest tribulation or persecution? How difficult does that seem next to the majesty of God pictured here? How can you incorporate this glimpse of heavenly worship into your earthly walk?

OPEN When home alone, do you like silence, or do you have to have some noise going on? Why?

presence. **thanks.** For his great work of salvation by which he has overcome evil and established his kingdom. **honor.** The greatness of his work is acknowledged publicly. **power.** When God acts, he cannot be overcome.

7:13–14 The question of the identity of the great multitude is raised and then answered. This question and answer process is often used in prophetic literature when a vision is to be explained (Jer. 1:11,13; 24:3; Amos 7:8; 8:2; Zech. 4:5).

7:14 they who have come out of. These are the martyrs from the Great Tribulation: those who maintained their faith to the point of death. **the great tribulation.** This event is mentioned in both the Old and New Testament. Daniel 12:1 refers to the "time of distress" (literally, "tribulation" in Greek) that will come. Jesus says, "For then there will be great distress, unequaled from the beginning of the world until now—and never to be equaled again. If those days had not been cut short, no one would survive, but for the sake of the elect those days will be shortened" (Matt. 24:21–22).

7:15 spread his tent over them. A reference to the tabernacle in the wilderness (Lev. 26:11–13) where God's presence dwelt. That his tent is over them would mean that they are now drawn into his presence, rather than standing outside the tent (Ezek. 37:27; Zech. 2:10).

7:16 Never again will they hunger ... thirst. Such a promise was especially significant to people of that era who knew of famine firsthand and where in many regions, water was scarce. This promise, however, goes beyond physical provision. The satisfying of hunger and thirst is used in Scripture as a metaphor for spiritual satisfaction (Matt. 5:6; John 6:35). **sun ... scorching heat.** The promise of shelter from the intensity of the sun was welcome indeed. Again, this has spiritual implications.

7:17 the Lamb ... will be their shepherd. A curious image: the Lamb becomes the shepherd (who tends the flock of lambs). With the fluid language of visions, it is appropriate that both these descriptions of the Messiah be expressed. In the Old Testament, God is frequently portrayed as the shepherd of his people; i.e., the one who gives guidance, provides for needs, and protects his flock (Ps. 23:1; Isa. 40:11; Ezek. 34:23). In the New Testament, Jesus is pictured as the Good Shepherd, (John 10:1–30; 21:15–17). **he will lead them to springs of living water.** His main role here is to lead the flock to the water of life which is the presence of God (John 4:14). **wipe away every tear.** Their suffering is now past. There is a new reality in which tears are not necessary. Joy will be their portion (21:4).

8:1 The breaking of the seventh seal opens the scroll so that the events of the end times can be revealed. **the seventh seal.** Unlike the other seals (with the possible exception of the first seal), the breaking of this seal brings no judgment. There is simply silence. The nature of this silence is not clear. Some say it represents the beginning of eternal rest for the multitudes, but this is out of character with the other seals. Others suggest that it is the time when the prayers of the saints are heard (vv. 3–4). Probably the silence is meant to indicate a moment of suspense before the events of the trumpets unfold.

STUDY **1.** Amid seals and trumpets, why this silence? **2.** What is a censer? What do altars and incense teach about prayer (vv. 3–5; 5:8; 6:9–10; 9:13)?

APPLY When was the last time you tried Scripture meditation or cried for justice? What happened?

OPEN **1.** What is one of the most excruciating pains you've ever experienced? What happened? **2.** What color would you use to describe your past week? Why?

STUDY **1.** What events follow the sounding of each of the first four trumpets (8:7–12)? What do the trumpets signify: Triumph or doom? Life or death? What else? **2.** How do these trumpeted events compare with the events inaugurated by the first six seals? **3.** What parallels or repeated patterns do you see between the opening of the seals and sounding of the trumpets, which suggest that these two scenes are in reality two sides of the same coin? **4.** Do these seals and trumpets refer to datable, sequential events or to aspects of the world's condition, which may be true at any point in history? **5.** What happens when the fifth trumpet sounds? What does "the Abyss" (9:1) represent? **6.** What power do the locusts have? What do they represent? **7.** Are the four angels in 9:14 good or evil? What is God's

2And I saw the seven angels who stand before God, and to them
were given seven trumpets.
3Another angel, who had a golden censer, came and stood at the
altar. He was given much incense to offer, with the prayers of all the
saints, on the golden altar before the throne. 4The smoke of the incense, together with the prayers of the saints, went up before God
from the angel's hand. 5Then the angel took the censer, filled it with
fire from the altar, and hurled it on the earth; and there came peals of
thunder, rumblings, flashes of lightning and an earthquake.

The Trumpets

6Then the seven angels who had the seven trumpets prepared to
sound them.
7The first angel sounded his trumpet, and there came hail and fire
mixed with blood, and it was hurled down upon the earth. A third of
the earth was burned up, a third of the trees were burned up, and all
the green grass was burned up.
8The second angel sounded his trumpet, and something like a huge
mountain, all ablaze, was thrown into the sea. A third of the sea
turned into blood, 9a third of the living creatures in the sea died, and
a third of the ships were destroyed.
10The third angel sounded his trumpet, and a great star, blazing like
a torch, fell from the sky on a third of the rivers and on the springs of
water— 11the name of the star is Wormwood.[a] A third of the waters
turned bitter, and many people died from the waters that had become
bitter.
12The fourth angel sounded his trumpet, and a third of the sun was
struck, a third of the moon, and a third of the stars, so that a third of
them turned dark. A third of the day was without light, and also a
third of the night.
13As I watched, I heard an eagle that was flying in midair call out in

[a] *11* That is, Bitterness

8:2 the seven angels. Who these are is not defined, though they appear to be a specific group of heavenly beings. These are possibly the angels of the seven churches (1:20). **trumpets.** In the Old Testament, trumpets are used for various purposes: to signal various activities (Num. 10:1–10); as part of worship and celebration (Num. 10:10; 29:1); in war (Josh. 6); and at coronations (1 Kin. 1:34). Here in Revelation, however, they have the more ominous purpose of announcing and loosing eschatological plagues.

8:3–5 There is a short period of preparation before the sounding of the first trumpet. The seven angels prepare to sound the seven trumpets and the other angel mingles the incense and the *prayers of the saints and then flings the* censer to earth. The thunder, lightning and earthquakes are all startling and dramatic phenomena associated with God's judgment.

8:3 censer. The firepan that held the hot coals used to burn incense (Ex. 27:3; 1 Kin. 7:50).

8:7 The second series of calamities begins. As will become evident, the aim of these acts of judgment is to lead people to repentance (9:20; 16:10–11). **fire.** The fire that is mixed with hail may be lightning. **blood.** Probably a reference to the color of the storm, not the destruction it caused. **A third of the earth was burned up.** The first plague destroys a third of the earth's vegetation. The fact that only a third of the earth is pictured as being afflicted represents a severe, but limited, act of judgment. This is similar to the seventh Egyptian plague (Ex 9:13–35).

8:8–9 The second plague is unique; it is impossible to parallel it with any known natural event (a volcano). It destroys a third of the sea, along with a third of the fish under the sea and a third of the boats on the sea. This plague is similar to what happened to the Nile in Exodus 7:20–21.

8:10–11 During the third plague, a great meteor falls from the sky and poisons a third of the fresh water.

8:11 Wormwood. A plant which has a bitter taste. This represents bitterness.

8:12 The fourth plague strikes the heavenly bodies. A third of the sun, moon and stars go dark. This is similar to the ninth plague in Egypt (Ex. 10:21–23). **without light.** It was not just that the intensity of the light was reduced by a third; there was absolute darkness for a third of the time.

8:13 Woe! The triple "Woe" corresponds to the final three trumpets (9:12). **the inhabitants of the earth.** These plagues will come upon those who are hostile to God.

a loud voice: "Woe! Woe! Woe to the inhabitants of the earth, because
of the trumpet blasts about to be sounded by the other three angels!"
9 The fifth angel sounded his trumpet, and I saw a star that had
fallen from the sky to the earth. The star was given the key to the
shaft of the Abyss. 2When he opened the Abyss, smoke rose from it
like the smoke from a gigantic furnace. The sun and sky were darkened by the smoke from the Abyss. 3And out of the smoke locusts
came down upon the earth and were given power like that of scorpions of the earth. 4They were told not to harm the grass of the earth or
any plant or tree, but only those people who did not have the seal of
God on their foreheads. 5They were not given power to kill them, but
only to torture them for five months. And the agony they suffered was
like that of the sting of a scorpion when it strikes a man. 6During
those days men will seek death, but will not find it; they will long to
die, but death will elude them.
7The locusts looked like horses prepared for battle. On their heads
they wore something like crowns of gold, and their faces resembled
human faces. 8Their hair was like women's hair, and their teeth were
like lions' teeth. 9They had breastplates like breastplates of iron, and
the sound of their wings was like the thundering of many horses and
chariots rushing into battle. 10They had tails and stings like scorpions, and in their tails they had power to torment people for five
months. 11They had as king over them the angel of the Abyss, whose
name in Hebrew is Abaddon, and in Greek, Apollyon.[a]
12The first woe is past; two other woes are yet to come.
13The sixth angel sounded his trumpet, and I heard a voice coming

[a] *11 Abaddon* and *Apollyon* mean *Destroyer.*

role in their actions? **8.** What is the difference between the power of the locusts and the power of the horses? **9.** What events are inaugurated by the sixth trumpet? What kind of response should this woe elicit from the unbelieving world? Why? Why do you suppose this woe failed to bring the majority to repentance as originally intended?

APPLY 1. What modern-day realities does the imagery of these plagues bring to mind for you? How might they have applied equally well in John's day? **2.** How do you feel when you read this account of stranger-than-fiction events? What is the "who" and "why" behind all these events? **3.** What do you have in common with the people mentioned in 9:20–21?

9:1 a star. An angel, a demon or Satan himself with the power to unlock the underworld. **the Abyss.** In the way in which the Bible speaks of the cosmos, there are said to be three levels: the heavens, the earth, and the underworld (which is a huge, bottomless pit). It is the realm of the dead (Rom. 10:7); it is where the beast abides (11:7); it is the place of demons (Luke 8:31); it will be used as the prison of Satan during the Millennium (20:3); and in this case, it is the home of the demon locusts. The Abyss is connected to the surface of the earth by a shaft.

9:3 locusts. These are not actual locusts, but some sort of demonic entity. Their coming is similar to the plague of (real) locusts in Exodus 10:1–20. **scorpions.** A large spider-like poisonous creature which has a stinger on the end of its tail.

9:4 Real locusts consume plants, trees and grass. These locusts lack that ability, attacking only humans. **the seal of God.** (7:3.) God's wrath will not fall upon the 144,000 of Israel; only upon those who worship the beast (16:2). This is not to say that the 144,000 will be spared suffering and persecution—only that it will not be from God.

9:5 five months. The significance of this time period is not clear. It may refer to the life cycle of the locust (which is five months), or to the five-month period when an invasion of locusts is most likely. Probably it is merely intended to indicate that the suffering will be confined to a short period of time. The aim of these acts after all is not to torment but to bring about repentance.

9:8 hair was like women's hair. Perhaps a reference to the antennae of locusts, or to the hair on their legs or bodies. **lions' teeth.** Locusts are fierce in the way they destroy vegetation.

9:9 breastplates of iron. The scales on the body of locusts are shaped like this. **the sound of their wings.** When locusts swarm into an area, they make a loud noise by beating their wings.

9:11 king over them. This figure is unique with no parallel in biblical or other Jewish literature. **Abaddon.** A Hebrew word meaning "destruction." In the Old Testament, this word is used along with "Sheol" for the place of destruction and death (Job 26:6; 28:22; Prov. 15:11; 27:20).

9:12 This refers back to 8:13. The first woe is passed. The second will be described in verses 13–21, when the sixth trumpet is sounded. The third woe will come when the seventh trumpet is sounded in 11:14–19.

9:13–21 The plague of the fifth trumpet brought pain and suffering; this plague brings death. The Old Testament parallel for such an invasion of horses is found in Ezekiel 38:14–16 (Isa. 5:26–30; Jer. 6:22–26).

9:13 a voice coming from the horns of the golden altar. The voice is the collective voice of the martyrs whose prayers are upon the throne, crying out for vindication, the voice of the angel who presented their prayers to God or the voice of Christ (5:9).

from the horns[a] of the golden altar that is before God. [14]It said to the sixth angel who had the trumpet, "Release the four angels who are bound at the great river Euphrates." [15]And the four angels who had been kept ready for this very hour and day and month and year were released to kill a third of mankind. [16]The number of the mounted troops was two hundred million. I heard their number.

[17]The horses and riders I saw in my vision looked like this: Their breastplates were fiery red, dark blue, and yellow as sulfur. The heads of the horses resembled the heads of lions, and out of their mouths came fire, smoke and sulfur. [18]A third of mankind was killed by the three plagues of fire, smoke and sulfur that came out of their mouths. [19]The power of the horses was in their mouths and in their tails; for their tails were like snakes, having heads with which they inflict injury.

[20]The rest of mankind that were not killed by these plagues still did not repent of the work of their hands; they did not stop worshiping demons, and idols of gold, silver, bronze, stone and wood—idols that cannot see or hear or walk. [21]Nor did they repent of their murders, their magic arts, their sexual immorality or their thefts.

OPEN Who was one of your fictional heroes when you were a child: Buck Rogers? The Lone Ranger? Superman? Why?

STUDY 1. Describe the angel who announces the coming of the seventh trumpet. In what ways does this picture contrast with the traditional view of angels? Why would John be forbidden to record the words of the seven thunders (v. 4; 2 Cor.

The Angel and the Little Scroll

10 Then I saw another mighty angel coming down from heaven. He was robed in a cloud, with a rainbow above his head; his face was like the sun, and his legs were like fiery pillars. [2]He was holding a little scroll, which lay open in his hand. He planted his right foot on the sea and his left foot on the land, [3]and he gave a loud shout like the roar of a lion. When he shouted, the voices of the seven thunders spoke. [4]And when the seven thunders spoke, I was about to

[a]*13* That is, projections

9:14 the four angels. Again, as with the seven trumpet-angels, this appears to be a definite group. However, four angels such as these are nowhere mentioned in apocalyptic literature. **bound.** These are probably fallen angels, held in check so they could not exercise their evil intentions. Now they are released and they kill a third of mankind. How this killing takes place is not indicated. Probably they were commanders of the great army of horses. **the great river Euphrates.** The eastern boundary of the Promised Land (Gen. 15:18). Beyond it lived the enemies of the Jewish nation.

9:16 two hundred million. This is a number beyond imagination in those days.

9:17 The horses. The demon locusts in the previous plague are followed by demon horses in this plague. There is a *difference. While the locusts had the* power to torture, the horses have the power to kill. **I saw in my vision.** These are demon hordes revealed in an ecstatic vision. **Their breastplates.** This description could refer to the armor of the riders or to the armor of both riders and horses. Beyond this, little is said about the riders. The focus is on the terrifying horses. **fire, smoke and sulfur.** Fire, smoke and sulfur (brimstone) of this sort are straight out of hell (14:10–11; 19:20; 21:8).

9:20–21 The intent of the plagues is revealed. It is not vengeance—it is to lead humankind to repentance. Despite the horror of the plagues, people still refuse to turn from their worship of demons and the lifestyle that such a commitment brings. **demons ... idols.** They err in worshiping evil powers (demons) and/or dumb idols which have no life. In either case, this keeps them from worshiping the living God.

10:1 The description of this angel is so similar to that of Christ in chapter 1 that some commentators have identified him as such. However, in verse 6 he shows himself to be a genuine angel by swearing by "him who lives for ever and ever." **coming down from heaven.** In 4:1 John was caught up to heaven, but now, it seems, he is back on earth and the angel descends to him. This is yet another example of the fluid language used in apocalyptic literature. This book must not be read as if it were an ordered, linear account to be interpreted like straight narrative. **robed in a cloud.** Angels are described as ascending and descending on clouds (Ps. 104:3; Dan. 7:13; Acts 1:9), but this one is clothed in a cloud. **rainbow.** This can be understood as a kind of crown or as the reflection of his brilliance ("his face was like the sun") through the clouds.

10:2 a little scroll. This is an unusual word, used nowhere else in Greek literature prior to this time. John probably coined it himself. Unlike the scroll of 5:1 which was a book, this scroll was more akin to a booklet. **open.** Unlike the other scroll, the contents of this one were not hidden.

10:4 John understood what the seven thunders communicated but he is told not to record them. What these thunders convey is, of course, unknown. But in each of the three other instances in

both small and great—
and for destroying those who destroy the earth."

[19]Then God's temple in heaven was opened, and within his temple
was seen the ark of his covenant. And there came flashes of lightning,
rumblings, peals of thunder, an earthquake and a great hailstorm.

The Woman and the Dragon

12 A great and wondrous sign appeared in heaven: a woman
clothed with the sun, with the moon under her feet and a
crown of twelve stars on her head. [2]She was pregnant and cried out
in pain as she was about to give birth. [3]Then another sign appeared in
heaven: an enormous red dragon with seven heads and ten horns
and seven crowns on his heads. [4]His tail swept a third of the stars out
of the sky and flung them to the earth. The dragon stood in front of
the woman who was about to give birth, so that he might devour her
child the moment it was born. [5]She gave birth to a son, a male child,
who will rule all the nations with an iron scepter. And her child was
snatched up to God and to his throne. [6]The woman fled into the
desert to a place prepared for her by God, where she might be taken
care of for 1,260 days.

[7]And there was war in heaven. Michael and his angels fought
against the dragon, and the dragon and his angels fought back. [8]But
he was not strong enough, and they lost their place in heaven. [9]The
great dragon was hurled down—that ancient serpent called the devil,
or Satan, who leads the whole world astray. He was hurled to the
earth, and his angels with him.

[10]Then I heard a loud voice in heaven say:

"Now have come the salvation and the power and the kingdom of
our God,
and the authority of his Christ.
For the accuser of our brothers,

OPEN When you were a child, who was the most important woman in your life besides your mother? Why?

STUDY 1. Describe the woman, the dragon and the child. Who does each represent? **2.** Where does the next conflict occur? Who are the protagonists? What is the outcome of this conflict? What is the significance of this outcome for the earth? For Christians? **3.** Which Old Testament and New Testament events are parallels to this passage? **4.** When do you see this heavenly battle occurring: At some particular time and place in history? Pre-history? Post-history? Any time and any place during the ongoing heavenly battle between the kingdoms of God and Satan (that is, in the spiritual realm which is behind all of this world's history)? Why do you think so?

APPLY 1. What do you learn here about conflict between the kingdom of heaven and demonic evil? **2.** When has Satan seemed very real to you? Why? How do you overcome Satan (12:11)? How could you apply these tactics in your own life?

11:19 God's temple in heaven was opened. At the time of Jesus' death, the curtain in the temple in Jerusalem was torn in two, signifying that now men and women have free access to God (Matt. 27:51; Heb. 10:19–21). That access, which was until this time spiritual, is now given concrete form. This seve ning up of the temple (along with God. ther events in verses 15–19) will does no occur in chapters 21–22. **the** cret, but t **covenant.** In the Old Tes- has been re Ark of the Covenant was a t which stood in the Holy **10:8 the voic** ymbolized the presence *forbade John to* may represent the new seven thunders milar blessings. **light-** take the scroll. **s, peals of thunder,** **standing on th** **and a great hail-** **land.** For the third ignify the awesome size of this angel coming has someth the earth (vv. 2,5). e first participant in is introduced: the o represents the **10:10 sweet ... so** ieving Jews (Isa. 54:1; 66:7–8; Gal. 4:26). The details of her dress indicate her magnificence. Psalm 104:2 describes God in such terms. **a crown of twelve stars.** Perhaps this symbolizes the 12 tribes (Gen. 37:9).

12:3 red dragon. The second participant comes on stage: the great dragon who is Satan (v. 9). The dragon/serpent is seen as the embodiment of evil in the Old Testament (Ps. 74:14; Isa. 27:1; 51:9). **seven crowns.** Seven is the number of completeness; a crown is the sign of power. Satan is a figure of enormous power. **heads.** His seven heads indicate great intelligence.

12:4 swept a third of the stars. This is another sign of his enormous power and may reflect his conquest of a large number of angelic beings. **devour her child.** The purpose of Satan is revealed: he wants to destroy the Messiah.

12:5 a male child. The third participant finally appears. The language used here to describe him clearly indicates that he is the Messiah (Ps. 2:9; 2:27; 19:15).

12:6 Frustrated in its attempt to devour the child, the dragon turns on the mother. However, she is protected by God. **desert.** This is not a wasteland but a place of refuge (as it often was for the children of Israel). **1,260 days.** This is of the period when evil is allowed to do its work upon earth.

12:9 that ancient serpent. An allusion to Genesis 3:1–5. **the devil.** Literally, *diabolos*, a Greek term for Satan meaning "accuser," "adversary," or "slanderer" (Zech. 3:1–2; 1 Peter 5:8). **Satan.** A Hebrew term meaning "accuser."

12:10 This announcement, like that in 11:15, states in the present what will be accomplished in the future.

3. What spiritual battle have you faced recently? Did you realize the battle was spiritual at the time? 4. What do you need to do to become stronger for spiritual battle? 5. How can your Christian friends pray for you in battles you are facing?

OPEN Who do you think is one of the most charismatic leaders living today? How has charisma helped him or her to lead?

STUDY 1. What is this beast from the sea like (v. 2; Isa. 27:1)? What is the source of its power? How does it use its power? What is the extent of its power? What is the

who accuses them before our God day and night,
has been hurled down.
[11]They overcame him
by the blood of the Lamb
and by the word of their testimony;
they did not love their lives so much
as to shrink from death.
[12]Therefore rejoice, you heavens
and you who dwell in them!
But woe to the earth and the sea,
because the devil has gone down to you!
He is filled with fury,
because he knows that his time is short."

[13]When the dragon saw that he had been hurled to the earth, he
pursued the woman who had given birth to the male child. [14]The
woman was given the two wings of a great eagle, so that she might fly
to the place prepared for her in the desert, where she would be taken
care of for a time, times and half a time, out of the serpent's reach.
[15]Then from his mouth the serpent spewed water like a river, to overtake the woman and sweep her away with the torrent. [16]But the earth
helped the woman by opening its mouth and swallowing the river
that the dragon had spewed out of his mouth. [17]Then the dragon was
enraged at the woman and went off to make war against the rest of
her offspring—those who obey God's commandments and hold to
13 the testimony of Jesus. [1]And the dragon[a] stood on the shore
of the sea.

The Beast out of the Sea

And I saw a beast coming out of the sea. He had ten horns and
seven heads, with ten crowns on his horns, and on each head a blasphemous name. [2]The beast I saw resembled a leopard, but had feet
like those of a bear and a mouth like that of a lion. The dragon gave
the beast his power and his throne and great authority. [3]One of the

[a]*1* Some late manuscripts *And I*

12:11 The source of Satan's defeat is now announced: it came through the death of Jesus on the cross. That defeat continues to be manifested by the word of testimony of those who were martyrs; those who followed in Christ's footsteps and were faithful unto death.

12:12 The defeat of Satan has two results. There is rejoicing in heaven among those who are of God, but there is woe on earth because Satan will now exercise his power there. **woe to the earth.** Some say that this is the third woe announced in 8:13.

12:14 She escapes by means of a pair of eagle wings that she is given (Deut. 32:10–11; Isa. 40:31). **a time, times and half a time.** One year plus two years plus a half a year. This phrase is taken from Daniel 7:25, and is the same time period as three and a half years = 42 months = 1,260 days).

12:15–16 In the Old Testament, a flood is sometimes used as a metaphor for an overwhelming trial (Ps. 18:4).

12:17 The woman has already given birth to the Messiah and he has escaped Satan (v. 5). Now Satan turns his wrath on her other children (who, in this metaphor, are God's people). They already have victory over Satan (v. 10), but Satan can still harm them.

13:1 In order to carry out his war against the offspring of the woman, Satan stands on the shore of the sea to wait for the beast who will be his means of persecution. **a beast.** This is the Antichrist. **seven heads, with ten crowns on his horns.** Like the dragon, the beast has multiple heads and horns. There is a difference, however. The dragon has seven crowns on his heads, while the beast has 10 crowns on his horns. These 10 crowns represent 10 kings (17:12). **on each head a blasphemous name.** The beast has taken to himself divine names. In verse 4 he is worshiped. This accords with Paul's description of the man of lawlessness (2 Thess. 2:4).

13:2 This beast has all the attributes of the four beasts in Daniel 7. He is the complete embodiment of evil, in that his power is derived from Satan. In Daniel, these beasts represent four dominant kingdoms of the world which were hostile to God.

heads of the beast seemed to have had a fatal wound, but the fatal
wound had been healed. The whole world was astonished and followed the beast. 4 Men worshiped the dragon because he had given
authority to the beast, and they also worshiped the beast and asked,
"Who is like the beast? Who can make war against him?"
5 The beast was given a mouth to utter proud words and blasphemies and to exercise his authority for forty-two months. 6 He opened
his mouth to blaspheme God, and to slander his name and his dwelling place and those who live in heaven. 7 He was given power to make
war against the saints and to conquer them. And he was given authority over every tribe, people, language and nation. 8 All inhabitants
of the earth will worship the beast—all whose names have not been
written in the book of life belonging to the Lamb that was slain from
the creation of the world.[a]
9 He who has an ear, let him hear.

10 If anyone is to go into captivity,
   into captivity he will go.
If anyone is to be killed[b] with the sword,
   with the sword he will be killed.

This calls for patient endurance and faithfulness on the part of the saints.

The Beast out of the Earth

11 Then I saw another beast, coming out of the earth. He had two
horns like a lamb, but he spoke like a dragon. 12 He exercised all the
authority of the first beast on his behalf, and made the earth and its
inhabitants worship the first beast, whose fatal wound had been
healed. 13 And he performed great and miraculous signs, even causing
fire to come down from heaven to earth in full view of men. 14 Because
of the signs he was given power to do on behalf of the first beast, he
deceived the inhabitants of the earth. He ordered them to set up an
image in honor of the beast who was wounded by the sword and yet

[a] 8 *Or written from the creation of the world in the book of life belonging to the Lamb that was slain*
[b] 10 Some manuscripts *anyone kills*

relationship between the beast and the dragon? **2.** Who worships the beast? Who would have been identified as the blasphemous beast by the first-century Christians (Dan. 7; Rom. 13:1)? **3.** What impact will this beast have on the Christians? How ought they to respond? Why?

APPLY 1. Who are some of the "beasts" or idols in your life that test your allegiance to Christ? How is God helping you deal with that? **2.** Is your name written in the Book of Life? How do you know? **3.** What kind of grade would you give yourself on patience and faithfulness? Why?

OPEN As a child, did you enjoy costume parties? What costume best hid your identity?

STUDY 1. In verses 11–17, what is this beast from the earth like? **2.** If the first beast exercises political power, what authority does this second beast exercise? How are true government and religion connected (and mimicked) by these two beasts? **3.** Since "7" is the number of completeness in Revelation, what might "666" mean? **4.** Compare the view of the Roman Empire here with

13:4 they also worshiped the beast. Arrayed against God and the Messiah are the dragon (Satan) and beast (the Antichrist) in a kind of supernatural symmetry, continuing the parallelism begun in verse 3. They set themselves up as counterfeit deities. The aim of the beast is not just political power as the crowns suggest, but religious power. He seeks to gain the allegiance of the people and so subvert them from worship of the true God.

13:5 Thus the beast speaks as if he were God, in accord with Daniel 7:8,20,25.

13:7 The beast turns his wrath against the people of God. This is a time of great persecution. This verse does not mean that the beast succeeds in turning the saints from allegiance to God to allegiance to himself; only that he is able to kill them. However, as it turns out, these martyrs have, in fact, won a great victory (15:2). **he was given authority.** The beast was allowed for this period of time to control the world.

13:8 All are required to worship the beast. Those who belong to the Lamb will die as martyrs because of their refusal to worship. **the book of life.** The registry of all who have been saved by faith in the crucified Lamb.

13:11–18 A second beast arises who is a servant to the first beast. His purpose is to cause people to worship the first beast. He is probably meant to represent organized religion. He is later called the false prophet (16:13; 19:20; 20:10). With the coming of this beast, the evil trinity is complete. Satan, the Antichrist, and the false prophet oppose God the Father, Son and the Holy Spirit.

13:11 two horns like a lamb. The second beast is a parody of Christ: a beast pretending to be a lamb. **spoke like a dragon.** His voice gives away his true identity (Matt. 7:15).

13:14 was given power. In the same way that in verses 5–7 (when speaking about the first beast) the passive "was given" is used four times (in the Greek text) emphasizing that the first beast was a front for Satan, so too here the point is made that this second beast has no independent power. It also is controlled by Satan. **an image in honor of the beast.** He had a statue made of the first beast and used his power to make it speak.

lived. 15 He was given power to give breath to the image of the first
beast, so that it could speak and cause all who refused to worship the
image to be killed. 16 He also forced everyone, small and great, rich
and poor, free and slave, to receive a mark on his right hand or on his
forehead, 17 so that no one could buy or sell unless he had the mark,
which is the name of the beast or the number of his name.
18 This calls for wisdom. If anyone has insight, let him calculate the
number of the beast, for it is man's number. His number is 666.

The Lamb and the 144,000

14 Then I looked, and there before me was the Lamb, standing
on Mount Zion, and with him 144,000 who had his name and
his Father's name written on their foreheads. 2 And I heard a sound
from heaven like the roar of rushing waters and like a loud peal of
thunder. The sound I heard was like that of harpists playing their
harps. 3 And they sang a new song before the throne and before the
four living creatures and the elders. No one could learn the song except the 144,000 who had been redeemed from the earth. 4 These are
those who did not defile themselves with women, for they kept themselves pure. They follow the Lamb wherever he goes. They were purchased from among men and offered as firstfruits to God and the
Lamb. 5 No lie was found in their mouths; they are blameless.

The Three Angels

6 Then I saw another angel flying in midair, and he had the eternal
gospel to proclaim to those who live on the earth—to every nation,

that in Romans 13:1–7. How had Rome changed since Paul's day?

APPLY How can we discern false religion and governments?

OPEN What kind of singer are you: Off-Broadway? Off-key? The star?

STUDY 1. Given the chaos described in chapters 12–13, what comfort do you find in this passage? What sights? Sounds? Feelings? **2.** Who is the Lamb? What has he done? Why are the people following him?

APPLY How are you like (and unlike) the 144,000? Why do you follow the Lamb?

OPEN Heard any good news lately? Any good news/bad news jokes? Tell one.

13:15 cause ... to be killed. It is the statue that commands the death of those who will not worship it, in this battle between God and Satan.

13:16 Satan continues to mimic God and his ways. Here he causes people to be sealed with the name of the beast, just as God's people were sealed with God's mark in 7:3. Now there are people sealed for God and those sealed for Satan. **mark.** Brands were put on animals. Some slaves were similarly marked with the name of their owner; certain religious devotees were tattooed. This term also referred to the imperial seal that was used on official documents and on coins.

13:17 There are severe economic consequences for failing to have the mark of the beast. Such people cannot purchase anything, nor can they engage in trade.

13:18 666. Many attempts have been made to translate this number into a name. None really succeed, since all such translation is, in the end, guesswork. Some suggest that this is a symbol not a cryptogram, and that since 7 is the perfect number, each number in the mark falls short of such perfection. Satan and his kin try to mimic God but fall short.

14:1–5 The first of these visions concerns the Lamb on Mount Zion with the 144,000 who bear his mark. This stands in sharp contrast to the previous vision of the beast and those who bear his mark. Once again (10:7; 11:15), it is a vision of the future after the judgment (that is spoken of as if it were happening then and there) is over. This vision will come to pass in chapters 20–22. It also parallels the vision in 7:9–17.

14:1 Mount Zion. In the vision of Joel, this is the place of deliverance for those who call upon the name of the Lord (Joel 2:32). This is either the temple site in Jerusalem or the heavenly Zion, the Jerusalem that is above (Gal. 4:26; Heb. 12:22) since this whole scene takes place in a heavenly context.

14:4 Many take this verse to mean that the 144,000 are a special class of people who enjoy a special relationship with God and who are characterized by three things: abstinence from marriage (celibacy); following of the Lamb; and special consecration to God. **did not defile themselves with women.** It is true that both Jesus and Paul spoke approvingly of those who abstained from marriage (Matt. 19:12; 1 Cor. 7:1,32), but they also spoke approvingly of marriage (Matt. 19:4–6; Eph. 5:31–32). Furthermore, Israel was spoken of as a virgin in the Old Testament (2 Kin. 19:21; Jer. 18:13; Lam. 2:13; Amos 5:2), as was the church in the New Testament (2 Cor. 11:2). **pure.** This word can be translated "pure" or "chaste," and can refer to spiritual purity. John speaks of being aligned with the beast as "fornication" (v. 8; 17:2; 18:3,9; 19:2). The concept of spiritual adultery is also found in the Old Testament (Jer. 3:6; Hos. 2:5). So this probably means that these people were the ones who kept themselves pure by not worshiping the beast. **They follow the Lamb.** The 144,000 are not just characterized by what they did not do—they are also men and women who followed the teaching and instructions of Jesus. They lived out his lifestyle (Mark 8:34). **firstfruits.** Originally this was an offering to God of some of the fruit from the beginning of the harvest (Lev. 23:9–14). In the New Testament, the term is used figuratively of the first converts in an area (Rom. 16:5), and literally of Christ as the first one to rise from the dead (1 Cor. 15:20).

14:6 midair. So all could see and hear him. **to those who live on the earth.** Again (3:10; 6:10; 8:13) this refers to

tribe, language and people. 7He said in a loud voice, "Fear God and
give him glory, because the hour of his judgment has come. Worship
him who made the heavens, the earth, the sea and the springs of
water."
8A second angel followed and said, "Fallen! Fallen is Babylon the
Great, which made all the nations drink the maddening wine of her
adulteries."
9A third angel followed them and said in a loud voice: "If anyone
worships the beast and his image and receives his mark on the forehead or on the hand, 10he, too, will drink of the wine of God's fury,
which has been poured full strength into the cup of his wrath. He will
be tormented with burning sulfur in the presence of the holy angels
and of the Lamb. 11And the smoke of their torment rises for ever and
ever. There is no rest day or night for those who worship the beast
and his image, or for anyone who receives the mark of his name."
12This calls for patient endurance on the part of the saints who obey
God's commandments and remain faithful to Jesus.
13Then I heard a voice from heaven say, "Write: Blessed are the
dead who die in the Lord from now on."
"Yes," says the Spirit, "they will rest from their labor, for their deeds
will follow them."

The Harvest of the Earth

14I looked, and there before me was a white cloud, and seated on
the cloud was one "like a son of man"[a] with a crown of gold on his
head and a sharp sickle in his hand. 15Then another angel came out
of the temple and called in a loud voice to him who was sitting on the

[a]14 Daniel 7:13

STUDY 1. In verses 6–7, what is the essence of the "eternal gospel" proclaimed by the angel of grace? Who will hear it? Has this vision yet been fulfilled? What response to the gospel is called for? **2.** By contrast, what message does the angel of doom spread (v. 8)? Who is the fallen Babylon? Who has been infected by the spirit of Babylon? **3.** How does Satan's ideology (13:11–18) differ from God's truth (14:6–13)?

APPLY 1. What have you done to help proclaim the gospel to every nation, tribe, language and people? **2.** How do you look upon death: As a rest? A reward? A new phase in the journey? **3.** What would you like to be doing when God calls you home?

OPEN Ever harvest anything? How hard did you work? Did you enjoy it? Why or why not?

STUDY 1. Who does the figure "like a son of man" (v. 14) represent? What does the image of

the people who do not worship and follow God. The angel is calling them to change their minds and ways and come to God. Yet again, on the eve of judgment, an appeal is made to those who stand outside God's kingdom.

14:6–13 The next vision has to do with three angels. The first proclaims the eternal gospel (vv. 6–7); the second announces the fall of Babylon (v. 8); and the third reveals the fate of those who follow the beast (vv. 9–11).

14:6–7 The visions in chapter 14 are not in chronological order. Chapter 14:1–5 is about the final salvation of God's people, while here the angel calls men and women to belief in God.

14:7 him who made the heavens. In the face of the powers of the beast, the angel asserts that it is God who made all of creation.

14:8 This is another announcement of what is yet to come (11:15; 12:10) as if it had just happened (17:1–18:24). **Babylon.** The original Babylon was a great city in Mesopotamia, renowned for its luxury and its corruption. It was also the traditional enemy of Israel. **wine of her adulteries.** Rome seduced the nations by her power, luxury and corruption (17:2).

14:9–11 The third angel discloses the fate of those who do not leave the beast and worship God. In contrast to 13:15–17 here, those who worship the beast and bear his mark will be the objects of God's wrath.

14:10 burning sulfur. The lake of fire and brimstone is the symbol used in Revelation for the final resting place of Satan and his cohorts and followers (20:10,14–15).

14:12 This is not part of the angel's cry, but rather a comment following it. It was not easy to live in the realm of the beast, but faced with the implications of what it meant to be his follower in verses 9–11, the saint is encouraged to hang on and endure.

14:13 This idea is reinforced by the voice from heaven. Such endurance may well result in death, but the death of a saint is a death with a good outcome: eternal rest and reward for faithfulness. **Blessed.** This is the second of seven beatitudes found in Revelation (1:3; 16:15; 19:9; 20:6; 22:7,14). **from now on.** This is not to say that those who died before the Great Tribulation fail to be so blessed; it simply reminds those who are facing this terrible persecution that this is what awaits them. **rest from their labor.** This is not rest from ordinary work, but the cessation of the trials confronting those who seek to remain faithful to Jesus in the midst of a hostile kingdom. Their good works will be rewarded.

14:14 one like a son of man. This title was also used in Daniel 7:13–14; it was used extensively by Jesus as a title for himself (Mark 2:10). Here it identifies the Messiah who comes in judgment (Matt. 13:37–43; 25:31–46).

14:15 out of the temple. The command to begin the judgment comes from God himself in his holy temple. **the harvest.** The image of harvest in the New Testament carries the idea both of gathering people into God's kingdom (Matt. 9:37–38) and of gathering the wicked for divine judgment (Matt. 13:30,40–42).

"harvest" convey? **2.** What do you think the fruit is that will be put into the "winepress of God's wrath"? **3.** What is the nature of the judgment that will occur (Matt. 13:30,39)? **4.** How is the portrayal of angels in this passage different from the way angels are portrayed in our society today?

APPLY How ripe do you think the world is now? Do you feel that the end of the world is close at hand? Why or why not? How does this affect your life?

OPEN If you could have a bowl full of anything right now, what would you want? Why?

STUDY 1. How does John describe this new sign? Why does he say these are the last plagues? **2.** What picture does he paint in verse 2? Compare Moses' song of deliverance from Egypt (Ex. 15:1–18) with the song sung by those delivered from the beast (vv. 3–4)? What praise is given to God? By whom? **3.** What does John see next? How does the angels' attire contrast with what they are given to do? **4.** What does the temple in heaven mean: A haven of rest and a place to play harps for those who die? A time to reckon with God's holiness and wrath unveiled in that very temple? Other?

APPLY 1. What action does this passage make you want

cloud, "Take your sickle and reap, because the time to reap has come,
for the harvest of the earth is ripe." 16So he who was seated on the
cloud swung his sickle over the earth, and the earth was harvested.
17Another angel came out of the temple in heaven, and he too had
a sharp sickle. 18Still another angel, who had charge of the fire, came
from the altar and called in a loud voice to him who had the sharp
sickle, "Take your sharp sickle and gather the clusters of grapes from
the earth's vine, because its grapes are ripe." 19The angel swung his
sickle on the earth, gathered its grapes and threw them into the great
winepress of God's wrath. 20They were trampled in the winepress
outside the city, and blood flowed out of the press, rising as high as
the horses' bridles for a distance of 1,600 stadia.[a]

Seven Angels With Seven Plagues

15 I saw in heaven another great and marvelous sign: seven angels with the seven last plagues—last, because with them
God's wrath is completed. 2And I saw what looked like a sea of glass
mixed with fire and, standing beside the sea, those who had been victorious over the beast and his image and over the number of his
name. They held harps given them by God 3and sang the song of Moses the servant of God and the song of the Lamb:

"Great and marvelous are your deeds,
  Lord God Almighty.
Just and true are your ways,
  King of the ages.
4Who will not fear you, O Lord,
  and bring glory to your name?
For you alone are holy.
All nations will come
  and worship before you,
for your righteous acts have been revealed."

[a]20 That is, about 180 miles (about 300 kilometers)

14:18 The idea of harvesting grapes is used elsewhere in the Bible as an image for judgment (Isa. 63:2–6; Joel 3:13).

14:19 Clearly judgment, not salvation, is in mind. The grapes are tossed into a huge winepress to be trampled upon.

14:20 The image shifts from wine to blood. The amount of blood is enormous. **as high as the horses' bridles.** About four feet deep. **1,600 stadia.** Some 184 miles (the approximate length of Palestine).

15:1 another great and marvelous sign. This is the third such sign. The first was of the radiant woman (12:1); *the second that of the red dragon (12:3).* In each case, these are events that disclose great meaning. In this case, it is the fact of divine judgment against all that is amiss in the universe. **the seven last plagues.** This is the third and final set of calamities. **with them God's wrath is completed.** This seems to mean that with the bowls, this threefold cycle of calamities has ended; God's warning to the world of the impending final judgment is complete. The Second Coming is next.

15:2 sea of glass. This is like the crystal sea spread out before the throne of God which John saw in his vision described in 4:6. **mixed with fire.** This may refer to the fact that this is now a time of judgment; it may refer to the death of the assembled martyrs; or it may simply be a detail that has no symbolic content. **those who had been victorious.** They won over the demands of the beast (13:15–17) by refusing to disown the name of Christ, by remaining steadfast in their faith, and by refusing to worship the beast or receive his mark (14:12). They died instead, and so frustrated the purposes of the beast. What at first seemed like defeat became victory.

15:3 the song of Moses. There is probably only one song, not two. The song that was sung when the Israelites were delivered out of the hands of the Egyptians (Ex. 15:1–18) is of the same character (similar phrases are found in both) as the one which is sung here concerning this greater deliverance. **the song of the Lamb.** This is the song that follows. It praises God who delivered them from the beast. **Great and marvelous are your deeds.** This is a common theme in the Old Testament (Ps. 92:5; 111:2; 139:14). **Lord God Almighty.** God is called Almighty nine times in Revelation and only once in the rest of the New Testament (2 Cor. 6:18). This is appropriate, since his overwhelming power is a central feature in this book.

[5]After this I looked and in heaven the temple, that is, the tabernacle
of the Testimony, was opened. [6]Out of the temple came the seven angels with the seven plagues. They were dressed in clean, shining lin-
en and wore golden sashes around their chests. [7]Then one of the four
living creatures gave to the seven angels seven golden bowls filled
with the wrath of God, who lives for ever and ever. [8]And the temple
was filled with smoke from the glory of God and from his power, and
no one could enter the temple until the seven plagues of the seven
angels were completed.

The Seven Bowls of God's Wrath

16 Then I heard a loud voice from the temple saying to the seven
angels, "Go, pour out the seven bowls of God's wrath on the
earth."
[2]The first angel went and poured out his bowl on the land, and ugly
and painful sores broke out on the people who had the mark of the
beast and worshiped his image.
[3]The second angel poured out his bowl on the sea, and it turned
into blood like that of a dead man, and every living thing in the sea
died.
[4]The third angel poured out his bowl on the rivers and springs of
water, and they became blood. [5]Then I heard the angel in charge of
the waters say:

"You are just in these judgments,
  you who are and who were, the Holy One,
  because you have so judged;
[6]for they have shed the blood of your saints and prophets,
  and you have given them blood to drink as they deserve."

[7]And I heard the altar respond:

"Yes, Lord God Almighty,
  true and just are your judgments."

[8]The fourth angel poured out his bowl on the sun, and the sun was
given power to scorch people with fire. [9]They were seared by the

to take? **2.** What great and mighty deeds has God done in your life for which you will praise him today? How appropriate is the song in this passage to your experience with God?

OPEN 1. What firsthand experience have you had with a natural disaster? What happened? What are your most vivid memories about it? **2.** What would be the worst plague for you to experience: Sores all over your body? Intense heat without air conditioning? Total darkness? Or great thirst with very little water? Why?

STUDY 1. What contents are in each bowl of wrath? Why are these plagues worse than those ushered in by the trumpets (contrast, for example, 8:8–9 with 16:3)? What was the function of the trumpet plagues? What is the function of the plagues in this passage? **2.** Why does the angel in charge of the waters react to the outpouring of God's wrath, not with pain or sorrow, but with recognition of divine justice (vv. 5–6)? **3.** What is described in the interlude (vv. 13–16) between the sixth and seventh bowls? What function did the frogs perform (Ex. 8:2–13)? **4.** How will the just purposes of God and the evil purposes of Satan finally and awfully converge at Armageddon (or "hill of Megiddo," an historic crossroads of

---

15:5 the tabernacle of the Testimony. This is how the heavenly temple is described. This is a reference to the tabernacle in the wilderness. It is called the "Tent of the Testimony" in Numbers 17:7 and 18:2 because this is where the two tablets were lodged that Moses brought down from Mount Sinai (Ex. 32:15–16; Deut. 10:4–5).

15:8 filled with smoke. When God appeared in the Old Testament, there was often smoke (Ex. 19:18; Isa. 6:4). It signified God's power and his judgment. **from the glory of God.** At such times, no one could stand before God (Ex. 40:34–35).

16:1 a loud voice from the temple. This is most likely the voice of God, since Revelation 15:8 states that no one could enter the temple until all the plagues were complete.

16:2 The first plague falls upon those who bear the mark of the beast, marking them with loathsome boils.

16:3 The second plague turns the oceans and seas into blood, killing all the sea life.

16:4 The third plague does the same to all the fresh water. There is thus no water to drink in the land.

16:5–6 An angel breaks in on this unrelenting unfolding of tragedy to attest to the rightness of God in doing this.

16:5 The song in this verse parallels the song of the victorious martyrs in 15:3–4. It states the judgments of God are not capricious but just.

16:6 The fact that God turns the waters to blood is not a capricious act on God's part. Because the followers of the beast have been like bloodthirsty animals in pouring out the blood of the saints, God is giving them blood to drink as their judgment.

16:8–9 The fourth plague strikes the sun so that it flares up, scorching and searing people. The impact of the fourth trumpet fell on the sun, moon, and stars but it brought the opposite effect (darkness, not intense light).

16:9 they cursed the name of God. They know full well who is behind these calamities. **they refused to repent.** Even at this point, it seems, repentance is possible. Still, they will not turn to God. Like Pharaoh, who saw the plagues and yet would not change, their hearts are hard.

the Middle East)? With what result (vv. 17–21)? **5.** How would you explain the necessity of these plagues to someone who is not a follower of Christ? **6.** What are you doing to stay "awake" in preparation for the return of Christ (v. 15)?

APPLY 1. How receptive are you to admitting your guilt and repenting when you sin? **2.** What are the "frogs" that are battling with you? How is the battle going? **3.** How is the book of Revelation making you feel? Why? What has surprised you about God or about this book?

intense heat and they cursed the name of God, who had control over
these plagues, but they refused to repent and glorify him.
10 The fifth angel poured out his bowl on the throne of the beast,
and his kingdom was plunged into darkness. Men gnawed their
tongues in agony 11 and cursed the God of heaven because of their
pains and their sores, but they refused to repent of what they had
done.
12 The sixth angel poured out his bowl on the great river Euphrates,
and its water was dried up to prepare the way for the kings from the
East. 13 Then I saw three evil[a] spirits that looked like frogs; they came
out of the mouth of the dragon, out of the mouth of the beast and out
of the mouth of the false prophet. 14 They are spirits of demons performing miraculous signs, and they go out to the kings of the whole
world, to gather them for the battle on the great day of God Almighty.
15 "Behold, I come like a thief! Blessed is he who stays awake and
keeps his clothes with him, so that he may not go naked and be
shamefully exposed."
16 Then they gathered the kings together to the place that in Hebrew
is called Armageddon.
17 The seventh angel poured out his bowl into the air, and out of the
temple came a loud voice from the throne, saying, "It is done!" 18 Then
there came flashes of lightning, rumblings, peals of thunder and a severe earthquake. No earthquake like it has ever occurred since man
has been on earth, so tremendous was the quake. 19 The great city

[a]13 Greek *unclean*

16:10–11 The fifth plague directly attacks the heart of the problem. It assaults the throne of the beast and plunges his kingdom into darkness. This darkness parallels the ninth Egyptian plague (Ex. 10:21–29).

16:10 gnawed their tongues in agony. They have no water to drink; the rivers, streams and springs have been turned to blood.

16:11 their pains. This may be a result of the heat from the scorching sun. **their sores.** The sores (which they received as a result of the first plague) continue to afflict them. In other words, the impact of the plagues build one upon another to the climactic act of judgment. **they refused to repent.** Still they hold out against God.

16:12–16 The sixth plague dries up the great river Euphrates. Since it is no longer a barrier, an invasion is planned (Ex. 14:21; Josh. 3:14–17 for other examples of God drying up water). The sixth trumpet plague was also centered on the Euphrates. This plague is different from the others in that it does not directly bring suffering to people. It does, however, pave the way for war.

16:13–14 The source of miraculous power of the two beasts is explained here. It has to do with the unclean spirits that live in their mouths.

16:14 The frogs are identified as the "spirits of demons." In the sixth trumpet plague, demon locusts were loosed on the world. In this case, the demons cause people to follow the beast. These deceiving spirits go over to the kings of the world in anticipation of the final great battle.

16:15 A warning is interjected as the kings gather for the final, great battle. This is the voice of Jesus, repeating what he taught while he was on earth (3:3; Matt. 24:42–44; 1 Thess. 5:2; 2 Peter 3:10), that what is about to take place is not the final act in history. What will bring history to a close and launch the new age is his personal return. They will need to remember that he is coming again during the difficult days ahead. **Blessed.** This is the third of seven beatitudes in Revelation (14:13).

16:16 The narrative of the sixth bowl continues. The demonic spirits gather the kings for the battle which will be described in 19:11–21. **Armageddon.** In Hebrew, this word means "the mountains of Megiddo." However, in Palestine, Megiddo is a plain that stretches from the Sea of Galilee to the Mediterranean, so it is not clear where, precisely, this is. The region of Megiddo was the site of many battles in the history of Israel (Judg. 5:19; 2 Kin. 9:27; 23:29; 2 Chr. 35:22).

16:17–21 The seventh and final plague brings about the overthrow of Babylon. This was announced in 14:8 and will be described in detail in chapters 17 and 18.

16:17 a loud voice. Probably the voice of God (v. 1). **It is done!** The calamities are over. The wrath of God has been poured out. The end is at hand.

16:19 The city of the beast is undone, as are the cities of those who aligned themselves with the beast. **God remembered Babylon.** During the short reign of the Antichrist, it might have appeared as if God had forgotten the wicked city and his people who lived there. But he has not. It is just a matter of time and patient endurance. Now Babylon will receive its due. **the cup filled with the wine of the fury of his wrath.** Babylon caused the nations to drink from the cup of her fornication and they grew rich from this adultery (18:3). Now Babylon is forced to drink from another cup—the cup of God's wrath (14:8,10).

split into three parts, and the cities of the nations collapsed. God remembered Babylon the Great and gave her the cup filled with the
wine of the fury of his wrath. [20]Every island fled away and the mountains could not be found. [21]From the sky huge hailstones of about a
hundred pounds each fell upon men. And they cursed God on account of the plague of hail, because the plague was so terrible.

The Woman on the Beast

17 One of the seven angels who had the seven bowls came and
said to me, "Come, I will show you the punishment of the
great prostitute, who sits on many waters. [2]With her the kings of the
earth committed adultery and the inhabitants of the earth were
intoxicated with the wine of her adulteries."
[3]Then the angel carried me away in the Spirit into a desert. There I
saw a woman sitting on a scarlet beast that was covered with blasphemous names and had seven heads and ten horns. [4]The woman
was dressed in purple and scarlet, and was glittering with gold, precious stones and pearls. She held a golden cup in her hand, filled
with abominable things and the filth of her adulteries. [5]This title was
written on her forehead:

MYSTERY
BABYLON THE GREAT
THE MOTHER OF PROSTITUTES
AND OF THE ABOMINATIONS OF THE EARTH.

[6]I saw that the woman was drunk with the blood of the saints, the
blood of those who bore testimony to Jesus.
When I saw her, I was greatly astonished. [7]Then the angel said to
me: "Why are you astonished? I will explain to you the mystery of the
woman and of the beast she rides, which has the seven heads and ten
horns. [8]The beast, which you saw, once was, now is not, and will
come up out of the Abyss and go to his destruction. The inhabitants
of the earth whose names have not been written in the book of life
from the creation of the world will be astonished when they see the
beast, because he once was, now is not, and yet will come.
[9]"This calls for a mind with wisdom. The seven heads are seven
hills on which the woman sits. [10]They are also seven kings. Five have

OPEN 1. If you could be famous for one hour, for what would you like to be known? Why? **2.** What bumper sticker or sign sums up your life now? Why?

STUDY 1. Who is the central figure in this scene? In what sense is she influential? Evil? Attractive? Repulsive? Who is she (14:8; 16:19)? **2.** Who appears to be "offstage"? How is the woman and this beast like the first and second beasts of chapter 13? **3.** What here is the ultimate sin (vv. 5–6)? **4.** What does the angel say about the origin of the beast? Its history? Its future (vv. 8–14)? What responses does the beast elicit? **5.** Geographically, historically and spiritually, what do you think the beast's seven heads and 10 horns represent (Dan. 7:15–28)? **6.** Why do the kings and the beast join forces? With what result? How can evil turn on itself, Satan (in effect) casting out Satan? How does God's greater purpose triumph in all this?

APPLY 1. In this passage how does Babylon symbolize what is wrong in society today? For example, what institutions have been overthrown by revolution, only to be replaced by new regimes which surrender to the same godless ideology? **2.** Which of the wrongs in society have entrapped you from time to time? How has God enabled you to avoid

---

17:1 For the third time, John is invited to behold a vision (1:9–11; 4:1–2; as well as 21:9–10). **sits on many waters.** The Babylon of history was built on a network of canals (Jer. 51:13). John interprets the meaning of these "many waters" in verse 15 as "peoples, multitudes, nations and languages."

17:2 adultery. In this context, this term describes the corrupting influence of Babylon which enticed the nations to prostitute everything for the sake of riches, luxury and pleasure (Isa. 23:16–17; Jer. 51:7; Nah. 3:4). **the inhabitants of the earth.** The people followed their rulers and joined in this orgy.

17:3 The angel then takes John into the wilderness. **in the Spirit.** John is in the midst of a vision (1:10; 4:2). **a scarlet beast.** The same beast as in 13:1, the Antichrist. His scarlet color identifies him with his master, Satan, the red dragon (12:3). It is the beast who has made the city (the harlot) great. She rides upon him.

17:4 purple and scarlet. The high cost of these dyes made clothing of this color expensive, so that it could only be worn by the wealthy. **gold, precious stones and pearls.** She is opulently dressed. **golden cup.** One would expect it to be filled with the finest wine. **abominable things.** Despite what one would expect, it contains that which is foul and detestable (Jer. 51:7).

17:5 on her forehead. Prostitutes in Rome wore headbands bearing the name of their owners. **THE MOTHER OF PROSTITUTES.** Not content simply to pursue her own adulteries, she made her daughters into harlots.

17:8 once was, now is not, and will come up out of the Abyss. A description that mimics that of the Lamb (1:18; 2:8). **destruction.** Literally, perdition, the state of final doom (Matt. 7:13).

17:10 seven kings. The identity of these kings has been hotly debated. Some scholars take the number 7 to

the snares of "the great prostitute"? **3.** Surely by now you are calling for "a mind with wisdom" (v. 9). What wisdom do you want in the next few weeks?

OPEN 1. If you were a piece of merchandise, would you be made of precious stones, fine linens or costly woods? Why? **2.** If you could be captain of any kind of ship, what kind would you want and why?

STUDY 1. As compelling as the power of evil is, a more compelling authority shouts an overriding double-edged message: one edge cutting Babylon and her followers, the other exhorting God's people. What are the two voices, the two messages and the two responses from the two audiences? **2.** How does God's

fallen, one is, the other has not yet come; but when he does come, he
must remain for a little while. [11]The beast who once was, and now is
not, is an eighth king. He belongs to the seven and is going to his destruction.

[12]"The ten horns you saw are ten kings who have not yet received a
kingdom, but who for one hour will receive authority as kings along
with the beast. [13]They have one purpose and will give their power and
authority to the beast. [14]They will make war against the Lamb, but the
Lamb will overcome them because he is Lord of lords and King of
kings—and with him will be his called, chosen and faithful followers."

[15]Then the angel said to me, "The waters you saw, where the prostitute sits, are peoples, multitudes, nations and languages. [16]The
beast and the ten horns you saw will hate the prostitute. They will
bring her to ruin and leave her naked; they will eat her flesh and burn
her with fire. [17]For God has put it into their hearts to accomplish his
purpose by agreeing to give the beast their power to rule, until God's
words are fulfilled. [18]The woman you saw is the great city that rules
over the kings of the earth."

The Fall of Babylon

18 After this I saw another angel coming down from heaven. He had great authority, and the earth was illuminated by his splendor. [2]With a mighty voice he shouted:

"Fallen! Fallen is Babylon the Great!
 She has become a home for demons
and a haunt for every evil[a] spirit,
 a haunt for every unclean and detestable bird.
[3]For all the nations have drunk
 the maddening wine of her adulteries.
The kings of the earth committed adultery with her,

[a]2 Greek *unclean*

---

represent (as it often does in Revelation) the fullness of imperial power so that the seven kings stand for a succession of kingdoms. The key thing, however, is that this power is drawing to an end.

17:11 The eighth king is the Antichrist (Dan. 7:24). This is a difficult verse with complex symbolism. A best guess is that the seventh king with the short reign will reappear a second time as the eighth king (who is therefore one of the seven) and will be a particularly virulent manifestation of the beast.

17:13 They are completely devoted to the beast. They seek his ends, not their own.

17:14 They are even willing to fight against the Lamb. This final conflict at Armageddon will be discussed in 19:11–21. **because he is Lord of lords and King of kings.** Given the nature of the Messiah's sovereign power as captured in this title, the outcome of the battle is certain (19:16; Deut. 10:17; Ps. 136:2–3; Dan. 2:47). His victory will be shared by those who have remained faithful to him even to the point of death.

17:16 Here John describes how Babylon is destroyed. The harlot draws her power from the beast (v. 3) and, in turn, supports the beast in his plans (v. 13). However, the beast—along with the 10 kings—turn on the harlot, destroying her with great viciousness (Ezek. 23:1–35; Dan. 7:24). No reason is given for this action. A league of evil ultimately turns against itself. **hate the prostitute.** They bear her no love for what she has done for them and to them. **leave her naked.** All her fine clothes and wonderful jewels will be stripped away from her (v. 4).

18:2 The language used to describe the fall of this Babylon is similar to the language used to describe the fall of Babylon in the Old Testament, as well as the fall of Edom and Nineveh (Isa. 34:11–15; Zeph. 2:15). **Fallen! Fallen is Babylon the Great!** These are the very words of the second angel in 14:8 (Isa. 21:9).

18:3 For. The reason for the fall of Babylon is that she has corrupted the nations of the earth. **committed adultery with her.** Adultery is a term used in the Old Testament to describe spiritual unfaithfulness on the part of the people of Israel (Isa. 1:21; Jer. 2:20–30; 3:1; Ezek. 16:15; Hos. 2:5; 4:15). She has seduced the nations to follow the beast. What she used was the lure of riches and luxury.

and the merchants of the earth grew rich from her excessive
luxuries."

[4]Then I heard another voice from heaven say:

"Come out of her, my people,
so that you will not share in her sins,
so that you will not receive any of her plagues;
[5]for her sins are piled up to heaven,
and God has remembered her crimes.
[6]Give back to her as she has given;
pay her back double for what she has done.
Mix her a double portion from her own cup.
[7]Give her as much torture and grief
as the glory and luxury she gave herself.
In her heart she boasts,
'I sit as queen; I am not a widow,
and I will never mourn.'
[8]Therefore in one day her plagues will overtake her:
death, mourning and famine.
She will be consumed by fire,
for mighty is the Lord God who judges her.

[9]"When the kings of the earth who committed adultery with her
and shared her luxury see the smoke of her burning, they will weep
and mourn over her. [10]Terrified at her torment, they will stand far off
and cry:

" 'Woe! Woe, O great city,
O Babylon, city of power!
In one hour your doom has come!'

[11]"The merchants of the earth will weep and mourn over her because no one buys their cargoes any more— [12]cargoes of gold, silver,
precious stones and pearls; fine linen, purple, silk and scarlet cloth;
every sort of citron wood, and articles of every kind made of ivory,
costly wood, bronze, iron and marble; [13]cargoes of cinnamon and
spice, of incense, myrrh and frankincense, of wine and olive oil, of
fine flour and wheat; cattle and sheep; horses and carriages; and
bodies and souls of men.

[14]"They will say, 'The fruit you longed for is gone from you. All your
riches and splendor have vanished, never to be recovered.' [15]The
merchants who sold these things and gained their wealth from her

perspective on Babylon (vv. 2–6) differ from Babylon's self-understanding (v. 7)? **3.** How do the voices from the world greet the fall of Babylon (vv. 9–20)? Why do they mourn? Why would you mourn if you were in their situation? **4.** Why does God judge Babylon so harshly (vv. 20, 24)? How are believers treated by the world today? **5.** Compare this passage with the following Old Testament prophecies about the fall of the cities of Sodom and Gomorrah (Gen. 19), Babylon (Isa. 13; 47), and Tyre (Ezek. 27–28). How is each an historical example of the fall of this spiritual Babylon? **6.** What conclusions do you draw concerning the destruction of Babylon from this comparison? What do you learn about God?

APPLY 1. What "items of merchandise" have you bought at great price and valued highly? Which of these have been too costly because of the resulting loss in your spiritual life? **2.** What part of your life is falling apart or eroding right now? How can Jesus begin his renewal project on your life? **3.** What is the most important lesson you have learned from this passage?

18:4–5 God's people are warned against getting trapped by her seductive powers. They are urged to flee from Babylon, lest they share in her coming destruction (Isa. 52:11; Jer. 51:45).

18:7 I am not a widow, and I will never mourn. Babylon is so secure in her power and invincibility that she boasts in this way. She denies that her armies will die on the battlefield. Others may experience loss, but she will not (Isa. 47:7–9). Her self-deception will end with her fall, however.

18:9–10 kings of the earth. These are not the 10 kings of 17:12–14, who are utterly loyal to the beast, and join with him in his war against the Lamb. Rather, these represent the nations of the earth who have allowed themselves to be seduced by the whore of Babylon into a life of excess. **the smoke of her burning.** Babylon has been destroyed by the beast and the 10 kings (17:16) in accord with the purposes of God (17:17). **Terrified at her torment.** If the great city is fallen, what protection do these lesser kings and merchants have?

18:12–13 The 29 items are divided into seven types of merchandise: precious minerals, fabrics used for expensive clothing, ornamental decorations, aromatic substances, food, animals, and slaves. Fifteen of the items in this catalog of imports are mentioned in the lament over the destruction of Tyre, another great trading nation (Ezek. 27).

18:15–17 It is now the turn of the merchants to lament the loss of the great city in the same way as did the kings. This is the second dirge.

will stand far off, terrified at her torment. They will weep and mourn
16 and cry out:

" 'Woe! Woe, O great city,
dressed in fine linen, purple and scarlet,
and glittering with gold, precious stones and pearls!
17 In one hour such great wealth has been brought to ruin!'

"Every sea captain, and all who travel by ship, the sailors, and all
who earn their living from the sea, will stand far off. 18 When they see
the smoke of her burning, they will exclaim, 'Was there ever a city like
this great city?' 19 They will throw dust on their heads, and with weeping and mourning cry out:

" 'Woe! Woe, O great city,
where all who had ships on the sea
became rich through her wealth!
In one hour she has been brought to ruin!
20 Rejoice over her, O heaven!
Rejoice, saints and apostles and prophets!
God has judged her for the way she treated you.' "

21 Then a mighty angel picked up a boulder the size of a large millstone and threw it into the sea, and said:

"With such violence
the great city of Babylon will be thrown down,
never to be found again.
22 The music of harpists and musicians, flute players and
trumpeters,
will never be heard in you again.
No workman of any trade
will ever be found in you again.
The sound of a millstone
will never be heard in you again.
23 The light of a lamp
will never shine in you again.
The voice of bridegroom and bride
will never be heard in you again.
Your merchants were the world's great men.
By your magic spell all the nations were led astray.
24 In her was found the blood of prophets and of the saints,
and of all who have been killed on the earth."

18:17 stand far off. They lament the loss but separate themselves from the city, lest they get caught in the destruction.

18:20 This song of praise from heaven stands in contrast to the lament that has just ended. The reason for such praise is that the judgment of God has come upon the city which persecuted his people.

18:21 It all happens so suddenly. Babylon was there in its arrogance and power and then it is gone, like a stone dropped into the sea. This is a large stone used for grinding wheat and weighing thousands of pounds.

18:22 The music of harpists and musicians, flute players and trumpeters. Babylon was known as a great patron of the arts. Flutes were used for festivals and funerals (Isa. 30:29; Matt. 9:23). Trumpets were sounded at the games and in the theater. **millstone.** A different Greek word than that used in verse 21, this referred to the small millstone that was used in the home to grind wheat into flour for bread.

18:23 magic spell. The actual use of magic is probably not in view. Rather, this seems to be another way of talking about how Babylon seduced the nations.

18:24 all who have been killed on the earth. The influence of Babylon has spread throughout the land, so it can be said that in her is found the blood of all the martyrs.

Hallelujah!

19 After this I heard what sounded like the roar of a great multitude in heaven shouting:

"Hallelujah!
Salvation and glory and power belong to our God,
2 for true and just are his judgments.
He has condemned the great prostitute
who corrupted the earth by her adulteries.
He has avenged on her the blood of his servants."

3 And again they shouted:

"Hallelujah!
The smoke from her goes up for ever and ever."

4 The twenty-four elders and the four living creatures fell down and
worshiped God, who was seated on the throne. And they cried:

"Amen, Hallelujah!"

5 Then a voice came from the throne, saying:

"Praise our God,
all you his servants,
you who fear him,
both small and great!"

6 Then I heard what sounded like a great multitude, like the roar of
rushing waters and like loud peals of thunder, shouting:

"Hallelujah!
For our Lord God Almighty reigns.
7 Let us rejoice and be glad
and give him glory!
For the wedding of the Lamb has come,
and his bride has made herself ready.
8 Fine linen, bright and clean,
was given her to wear."
(Fine linen stands for the righteous acts of the saints.)

OPEN 1. When was the last time your favorite ball team finally won it all? **2.** What was the most festive wedding and reception you ever attended? **3.** What funeral have you attended where the eulogy was memorable for its praise of God's salvation?

STUDY 1. In contrast to the silence that comes with the fall of Babylon (18:22), what characterizes this new scene in heaven? Who participates in this praise? **2.** What is the most frequent refrain in the five songs of praise? What do you learn about God's character? **3.** Contrast the prostitute of chapters 17 and 18 with the bride of verses 7 and 8 (Eph. 5:25–27). What do you find interesting about this contrast? **4.** How is John (and how might we be) tempted to worship the angel or messenger of the good news?

APPLY 1. How has your interest in worshiping God increased or decreased in the last year? Since beginning your study of Revelation? Why? **2.** How does the defeat and condemnation of Babylon and the triumph and glory of the Lord God affect your overall view of your problems here and now?

19:1–5 The story of the destruction of Babylon is concluded by a shout of thanksgiving on the part of the heavenly company. The fall of Babylon and the removal of her corrupting influence is celebrated. This contrasts sharply with the preceding dirges of the kings, merchants and seafarers who mourn their loss of income.

19:1 Hallelujah! An exclamation of praise derived from two Hebrew words meaning "Praise the Lord." It is used frequently in the Psalms (Ps. 106; 111–113), though never in the New Testament apart from the four occurrences in this passage (vv. 1,3–4,6). **Salvation.** Judgment alone is not the point. The fall of Babylon is a necessary part of the grand scheme of salvation. **glory and power.** Not only was God's salvation displayed in this act, so too was his majesty and might.

19:6–10 John announces the marriage of the Lamb, though he does not describe it. It is announced here and assumed in later chapters (21:2–3,9–10). The metaphor which is used here is based on Jewish wedding customs of the first century.

19:7 his bride. Israel was regularly spoken of as the wife of Yahweh (Isa. 54:5; 62:5; Jer. 31:32; Ezek. 16:8–14; Hos. 2:19–20). Jesus spoke of himself as the bridegroom (Mark 2:19–20), and John the Baptist used this same language to describe Jesus (John 3:29). Jesus also used the idea of the wedding feast in his parables (Matt. 22:1–14; 25:1–13). Paul picks up the idea of Israel as the bride of God and applies it to the church (Rom. 7:1–4; 1 Cor. 6:17; 2 Cor. 11:2; Eph. 5:25–27).

19:8 Fine linen, bright and clean. This contrasts sharply to the bright robes of the harlot (17:4). The wedding clothes of the bride are similar to the white robes of the martyrs washed in the blood of the lamb (7:14). **given her to wear.** Her wedding clothes are given to her as a gift.

[9]Then the angel said to me, "Write: 'Blessed are those who are invited to the wedding supper of the Lamb!' " And he added, "These are
the true words of God."
[10]At this I fell at his feet to worship him. But he said to me, "Do not
do it! I am a fellow servant with you and with your brothers who hold
to the testimony of Jesus. Worship God! For the testimony of Jesus is
the spirit of prophecy."

The Rider on the White Horse

[11]I saw heaven standing open and there before me was a white
horse, whose rider is called Faithful and True. With justice he judges
and makes war. [12]His eyes are like blazing fire, and on his head are
many crowns. He has a name written on him that no one knows but
he himself. [13]He is dressed in a robe dipped in blood, and his name is
the Word of God. [14]The armies of heaven were following him, riding
on white horses and dressed in fine linen, white and clean. [15]Out of
his mouth comes a sharp sword with which to strike down the nations. "He will rule them with an iron scepter."[a] He treads the winepress of the fury of the wrath of God Almighty. [16]On his robe and on
his thigh he has this name written:

KING OF KINGS AND LORD OF LORDS.

[17]And I saw an angel standing in the sun, who cried in a loud voice
to all the birds flying in midair, "Come, gather together for the great
supper of God, [18]so that you may eat the flesh of kings, generals, and
mighty men, of horses and their riders, and the flesh of all people,
free and slave, small and great."
[19]Then I saw the beast and the kings of the earth and their armies

OPEN When you were young, how much did you want a horse? Who was your favorite fictional or real horse? Why?

STUDY 1. What regarding the horse, the rider and the setting commands your attention? **2.** Why do you think it is fitting that Christ has a name "that no one knows but he himself" (v. 12)? What mystery about Christ are you looking forward to understanding in heaven? **3.** Who is following Christ: The church *militant* (still on earth)? Or the church *triumphant* (now in heaven)? Why? **4.** What weapon does the rider wield (v. 15)? **5.** Who are the combatants in this war (vv. 19–21)? Who wins? What happens to the enemy leaders? To the army? **6.** How does this "last battle" compare to "previous" battles (16:16–21; 17:14–16) and a "later" one (20:7–10)? What will be the final end of evil? Do you think these are different accounts of the same battle? Why or why not?

[a]*15* Psalm 2:9

19:9 The focus shifts to the wedding guests. In the fluid language of metaphor, the church is both bride and guests. This same fluidity is seen elsewhere in the New Testament. In Mark 2:19–20, the disciples are pictured as guests at the wedding. Likewise in the parable of the wedding banquet, the bride is not mentioned. The issue there has to do with who the guests will be. However, in Ephesians 5:25–27 the church is spoken of as the bride who is made ready for her husband, Christ. **Blessed.** This is the fourth of the seven beatitudes in Revelation (1:3; 14:13). **the wedding supper.** This is the great messianic banquet about which Jesus spoke (Matt. 8:11; 26:29).

19:10 At this I fell at his feet. John has encountered angels constantly during his visions, but here he is so overwhelmed by this vision that he falls at the feet of the angel. Or perhaps he mistakes the angel for the Lord. In any case, he is reproved for this (Acts 10:25–26).

19:13 a robe dipped in blood. This is not his own blood. This is the blood of battle. In this passage Jesus comes not as the redeemer who dies for sins, but as the warrior who conquers evil. This parallels the image in Isaiah 63:1–6 of the figure who has the blood of his enemies on his garments. **the Word of God.** This is who John has long known Jesus to be. Jesus is the embodiment of God's ultimate Word to the world.

19:14 The armies of heaven. This may be an army of angels or it could be an army of the redeemed as 17:14 suggests (Zech. 14:5; Mark 8:38; Luke 9:26; 1 Thess. 3:13; 2 Thess. 1:7). In either case, the army does not engage in battle. That is left to Christ alone (v. 21). **white.** They are dressed in the garb of heaven.

19:15 Three symbols in this verse, all taken from the Old Testament, describe the actions of the warrior. First, the weapon which he uses in this battle issues from his mouth, an image which is drawn from Isaiah 11:4 (1:16; 2:12,16). His sword is his Word; the same Word which was the source of all creation (John 1:1–3; Heb. 1:2). Second, he rules with a rod of iron, an image taken from Psalm 2:9. Such a rod speaks not of governing but of destruction. Third, he treads the winepress, which is by now a familiar image in Revelation (14:19), drawn originally from Isaiah 63:3.

19:16 KING OF KINGS AND LORD OF LORDS. This is the fourth name that is given to Christ. This is the name by which he reveals himself to those with whom he does battle.

19:17–21 And so the battle of Armageddon begins, between Christ and the Antichrist. This is the manifestation in history of the battle fought in heaven between God and Satan (12:1–13:1). Following this battle, Satan will again rebel and be suppressed by the Lord (20:7–19).

19:17–18 This gruesome supper contrasts sharply with the wedding banquet of 19:6–10 (Ezek. 39:17–20).

19:18 all people. That is, all who bear the mark of the beast, a number which includes all kinds of people who have not stood as a witness for God.

gathered together to make war against the rider on the horse and his
army. [20]But the beast was captured, and with him the false prophet
who had performed the miraculous signs on his behalf. With these
signs he had deluded those who had received the mark of the beast
and worshiped his image. The two of them were thrown alive into the
fiery lake of burning sulfur. [21]The rest of them were killed with the
sword that came out of the mouth of the rider on the horse, and all
the birds gorged themselves on their flesh.

The Thousand Years

20 And I saw an angel coming down out of heaven, having the
key to the Abyss and holding in his hand a great chain. [2]He
seized the dragon, that ancient serpent, who is the devil, or Satan,
and bound him for a thousand years. [3]He threw him into the Abyss,
and locked and sealed it over him, to keep him from deceiving the nations anymore until the thousand years were ended. After that, he
must be set free for a short time.

[4]I saw thrones on which were seated those who had been given authority to judge. And I saw the souls of those who had been beheaded
because of their testimony for Jesus and because of the word of God.
They had not worshiped the beast or his image and had not received
his mark on their foreheads or their hands. They came to life and
reigned with Christ a thousand years. [5](The rest of the dead did not
come to life until the thousand years were ended.) This is the first
resurrection. [6]Blessed and holy are those who have part in the first
resurrection. The second death has no power over them, but they will
be priests of God and of Christ and will reign with him for a thousand
years.

Satan's Doom

[7]When the thousand years are over, Satan will be released from his
prison [8]and will go out to deceive the nations in the four corners of

APPLY What hopes and fears does this triumphant picture bring out in you?

OPEN **1.** When did you last "lose your head"? What happened? **2.** Have you read any good books lately? How do you judge a book?

STUDY **1.** Why is Satan bound? By whom? How? **2.** When and where do you think the Millennium (thousand-year reign of Christ) will begin? Why? **3.** What will life be like without Satan deceiving the nations, but with the church reigning instead? In what sense is that already true? And not yet true? **4.** What is the first resurrection (v. 6)? The second death? What do these mean to Christians? To the rest of the dead? **5.** Why do you think Satan will again try to deceive the nations? Why do you suppose God will release him and let him out of the Abyss? **6.** What is the final fate of the beast, false prophet and Satan (vv. 7–10)? **7.** Who is exempted and who is exhumed at the "great white throne" judgment (vv. 11–15)? On what basis? What is the last great reality prior to the new age?

19:20 The war itself is not described; only its outcome.

20:1–6 The meaning of this passage has been the subject of great debate in the church. There are three main schools of thought when it comes to the Millennium (the thousand-year reign of Christ). Postmillennialists feel that the return of Christ will not occur until the kingdom of God has been established here on earth, in history as we know it. This will be the "golden age" of the church, a long reign of peace and prosperity. It will be followed by the Second Coming, the resurrection of the dead, the final judgment, and the eternal kingdom. Amillennialists do not believe there will be a literal thousand-year reign of Christ. They see it as a metaphor for the history of the church between the resurrection of Christ and his Second Coming, during which those believers who have died will reign with Christ in heaven. When Christ returns there will be a general resurrection, the final judgment, and the start of Christ's reign over the new heaven and earth. They consider the binding of Satan to be what Christ did when he died on the cross (Matt. 12:29). Premillennialists believe that the events described in verses 1–6 will literally take place. Christ will remove believers from the earth before he returns. Christ will return, the first resurrection will occur, and there will be a thousand years of peace in which Christ reigns here on earth. Then will come the final resurrection, the last judgment, and the new heaven and earth. The millennial reign is seen (by some premillennialists) as a special reward to the martyrs of chapter 6.

20:2 bound him. Somehow the power of Satan was curbed (Mark 3:27). **a thousand years.** While some scholars interpret this in literal terms, others take this number as symbolic for a long period of time during which the church spreads its influence around the world.

20:4 thrones. Some suggest these are the apostles (Matt. 19:28), or all the saints (1 Cor. 6:2–3), or just those who overcame (3:21).

20:5 The rest of the dead. Who these are depends on one's view of the Millennium. The premillennialist would say these are the rest of the believers (the martyrs having been raised already to reign with Christ). Others would say that this is the resurrection of unbelievers prior to the day of judgment.

20:6 The second death. The first death is the death of the body; the second death involves being cast into the lake of fire (v. 14; 21:8).

20:8 Gog and Magog. In Ezekiel 38–39, there is an extended prophecy about "Gog, of the land of Magog." As in Ezekiel, the final battle follows the establishment of the messianic kingdom which Israel has looked forward to for centuries (Ezek. 36–37).

APPLY 1. What do you find comforting in this chapter? What disturbs you? 2. What is your biggest spiritual battle today? What is the outcome so far? What is the hope in this passage for you?

---

the earth—Gog and Magog—to gather them for battle. In number
they are like the sand on the seashore. 9They marched across the
breadth of the earth and surrounded the camp of God's people, the
city he loves. But fire came down from heaven and devoured them.
10And the devil, who deceived them, was thrown into the lake of
burning sulfur, where the beast and the false prophet had been
thrown. They will be tormented day and night for ever and ever.

The Dead Are Judged

11Then I saw a great white throne and him who was seated on it.
Earth and sky fled from his presence, and there was no place for
them. 12And I saw the dead, great and small, standing before the
throne, and books were opened. Another book was opened, which is
the book of life. The dead were judged according to what they had
done as recorded in the books. 13The sea gave up the dead that were
in it, and death and Hades gave up the dead that were in them, and
each person was judged according to what he had done. 14Then
death and Hades were thrown into the lake of fire. The lake of fire is
the second death. 15If anyone's name was not found written in the
book of life, he was thrown into the lake of fire.

The New Jerusalem

21 Then I saw a new heaven and a new earth, for the first heaven
and the first earth had passed away, and there was no longer
any sea. 2I saw the Holy City, the new Jerusalem, coming down out of
heaven from God, prepared as a bride beautifully dressed for her husband. 3And I heard a loud voice from the throne saying, "Now the
dwelling of God is with men, and he will live with them. They will be
his people, and God himself will be with them and be their God. 4He
will wipe every tear from their eyes. There will be no more death or
mourning or crying or pain, for the old order of things has passed
away."

5He who was seated on the throne said, "I am making everything

OPEN 1. Where is one of the most beautiful places you have ever been? What impressed you about that place? 2. What was one of the most beautiful spots in your hometown when you were growing up?

STUDY 1. Where will the new world be lived out—on earth or in heaven? Why do you think so? 2. Who will be the "residents" of the New Jerusalem? Whose presence is the vision caught up with? What, or who, is missing from this picture? Why? 3. What is the goal of all re-

---

20:10 Satan joins the beast and the false prophet in the lake of fire. This is the final destination of evil in all its forms (Matt. 25:41). **the lake of burning sulfur.** In the rest of the New Testament this is called *Gehenna* in Greek—translated "hell" in English (Matt. 5:22; Mark 9:43). The Valley of Hinnom, from which this name is drawn, was a place where human sacrifice took place (2 Kin. 16:3; 23:10; Jer. 7:31–32). It eventually became a kind of town dump where a fire perpetually smoldered, and thus it became a metaphor for hell.

20:12 the book of life. Another book is opened. In it are recorded the names of those who belong to Christ (3:5; 13:8; 21:27; Ex. 32:32–33; Dan. 12:1; Luke 10:20; Phil. 4:3).

20:13 Hades. This is not the same as Gehenna (v. 10). It is the place where departed souls go. It was thought of as an intermediate state (Luke 16:23; Acts 2:27).

21:1 the first earth had passed away. This event occurred in 20:11, described by means of a few terse sentences. **there was no longer any sea.** In ancient times the sea was often pictured as dark and mysterious; it was an enemy not a friend. The lack of any seas in the new earth indicates how radically different the new will be.

21:2 the new Jerusalem. The new Jerusalem will be described in detail in 21:9–22:5 (Gal. 4:26; Heb. 12:22). It was conceived of as the place where departed saints dwelt between the time of their death and the coming of the new heaven and the new earth (6:9–11; 2 Cor. 5:8; Phil. 1:23). It now descends to earth where it will finally rest. **prepared as a bride.** The church has already been pictured as the bride of Christ (19:7). John may intend the heavenly Jerusalem to be another metaphor for the church in the same way that Paul likens the church to the temple of God (1 Cor. 3:16; Eph. 2:21).

21:4 He will wipe every tear from their eyes. The suffering is over; it is finished. No longer will there need to be a call to hold on and endure. **There will be no more death or mourning or crying or pain.** All the old enemies of humanity are gone. Death itself is vanquished, so there will be no need anymore for mourning. Crying too is a thing of the past. Pain will be unknown.

21:5 I am making everything new! Creation, it seems, is not a static reality. Here at the end of history, God is still at work creating a new reality. That which is in principle true, when an individual comes to Christ, namely "If

new!" Then he said, "Write this down, for these words are trustworthy and true."
6He said to me: "It is done. I am the Alpha and the Omega, the Beginning and the End. To him who is thirsty I will give to drink without
cost from the spring of the water of life. 7He who overcomes will inherit all this, and I will be his God and he will be my son. 8But the
cowardly, the unbelieving, the vile, the murderers, the sexually immoral, those who practice magic arts, the idolaters and all liars—
their place will be in the fiery lake of burning sulfur. This is the
second death."
9One of the seven angels who had the seven bowls full of the seven
last plagues came and said to me, "Come, I will show you the bride,
the wife of the Lamb." 10And he carried me away in the Spirit to a
mountain great and high, and showed me the Holy City, Jerusalem,
coming down out of heaven from God. 11It shone with the glory of
God, and its brilliance was like that of a very precious jewel, like a
jasper, clear as crystal. 12It had a great, high wall with twelve gates,
and with twelve angels at the gates. On the gates were written the
names of the twelve tribes of Israel. 13There were three gates on the
east, three on the north, three on the south and three on the west.
14The wall of the city had twelve foundations, and on them were the
names of the twelve apostles of the Lamb.
15The angel who talked with me had a measuring rod of gold to
measure the city, its gates and its walls. 16The city was laid out like a
square, as long as it was wide. He measured the city with the rod and
found it to be 12,000 stadia[a] in length, and as wide and high as it is
long. 17He measured its wall and it was 144 cubits[b] thick,[c] by man's
measurement, which the angel was using. 18The wall was made of

[a]*16* That is, about 1,400 miles (about 2,200 kilometers) [b]*17* That is, about 200 feet (about 65 meters) [c]*17* Or *high*

demption? What do you think it will be like living without fear, pain or death, and with the continual and direct presence of God? **4.** How do you feel about seeing your body grow older in light of verse 5? **5.** What is the significance of the names ascribed to God (v. 6), for those who "overcome" and those who do not (vv. 7–8)? **6.** What is John's first impression of the New Jerusalem in verse 11? **7.** What do you think is the significance of the foundations and the gates? **8.** What is the size of the city? Of what is it constructed? Compare this vision to the related vision in Ezekiel 40:2,5 and 48:30–35. **9.** Considering the world in which John's readers lived and the conditions they were under, what would have been especially impressive about this city? **10.** When in the past week have you needed a vision of the Holy City—the joyous place that awaits you? **11.** What was the function of the temple in the old Jerusalem? Why is there no need for a temple in the New Jerusalem? **12.** What impresses you most about the city and its central figure? Why? **13.** What is required to be a citizen of this New Jerusalem (21:27)?

APPLY 1. How do you feel about knowing that the Holy City will be your hometown? That it will last forever? How do you feel about the fact that this is what Jesus

---

anyone is in Christ, he is a new creation" (2 Cor. 5:17), is now consummated in fact. This process also includes the physical world (Rom. 8:21).

21:6 The voice from the throne (v. 3) is now identified. It is God who is speaking. This is an infrequent event in Revelation (1:8; 16:1,17). He speaks to assert that "It is done." God's plan has been realized in its fullness. **the Alpha and the Omega.** The first and last letters in the Greek alphabet. God encompasses all of reality—all of what can be spoken and so is. **the Beginning and the End.** He also encompasses the whole of time. **I will give to drink.** He satisfies the deepest needs—physical and spiritual—of humanity.

21:7 He who overcomes. This recalls the letters to the seven churches and the promises made then (2:7,11,17,26; 3:5,12,21).

21:14 the names of the twelve apostles. The very foundation of the city rests on the apostles of Jesus (Eph. 2:20). The church was the result of the labors of the Twelve following the death and resurrection of Jesus. With the names of the 12 tribes at the gates and the the 12 apostles at the foundation, it is clear that the New Jerusalem encompasses both believers of the Old Testament and the believers of the New Testament. All of God's people have a place here.

21:15 John was asked to measure the inner area of the temple (11:1). The idea there was of setting aside for preservation or for destruction. But here the city is measured to show its magnificence (Ezek. 40–41).

21:16 12,000 stadia. It is an enormous city, beyond what any earthly city will be or could be. Each of its four sides was approximately 1,400 miles long. By them, John struggles to convey the vastness of the city. **as wide and high as it is long.** The New Jerusalem is a cube, as high as it is wide. The inner sanctuary of the temple was a perfect cube (1 Kin. 6:20), a symbol of perfection.

21:17 it was 144 cubits thick. The walls will be over 200 feet thick. Of course, such a city will not need walls which, in ancient days, were a defense against enemies. This is God's city, and all his enemies will have been destroyed.

21:18 This city is built of materials unlike those used in any human city. **jasper.** A green, translucent crystal. This is the third time this mineral has been mentioned (v. 11,19; 4:3). In verse 11, jasper was said to glow with the radiance of God. The whole city would be aglow with God. The word jasper was used for various gem stones. The walls of the city are made of this precious stone. **pure gold, as pure as glass.** Gold has long been considered very precious, and here is a city of gold! This is unlike ordinary gold, however, since it is transparent.

has prepared you for? Does it change your lifestyle? **2.** What has caused you mourning, crying and pain in the past year? What does it mean to you to know that this will pass away? **3.** Now that your study of Revelation is almost over, how do you feel about this book of the Bible? Is this different from how you felt when you began the study? How has God blessed your life through this study?

jasper, and the city of pure gold, as pure as glass. 19The foundations
of the city walls were decorated with every kind of precious stone.
The first foundation was jasper, the second sapphire, the third chalcedony, the fourth emerald, 20the fifth sardonyx, the sixth carnelian,
the seventh chrysolite, the eighth beryl, the ninth topaz, the tenth
chrysoprase, the eleventh jacinth, and the twelfth amethyst.[a] 21The
twelve gates were twelve pearls, each gate made of a single pearl. The
great street of the city was of pure gold, like transparent glass.
22I did not see a temple in the city, because the Lord God Almighty
and the Lamb are its temple. 23The city does not need the sun or the
moon to shine on it, for the glory of God gives it light, and the Lamb
is its lamp. 24The nations will walk by its light, and the kings of the
earth will bring their splendor into it. 25On no day will its gates ever
be shut, for there will be no night there. 26The glory and honor of the
nations will be brought into it. 27Nothing impure will ever enter it, nor
will anyone who does what is shameful or deceitful, but only those
whose names are written in the Lamb's book of life.

The River of Life

22 Then the angel showed me the river of the water of life, as
clear as crystal, flowing from the throne of God and of the
Lamb 2down the middle of the great street of the city. On each side of
the river stood the tree of life, bearing twelve crops of fruit, yielding
its fruit every month. And the leaves of the tree are for the healing of
the nations. 3No longer will there be any curse. The throne of God
and of the Lamb will be in the city, and his servants will serve him.
4They will see his face, and his name will be on their foreheads.
5There will be no more night. They will not need the light of a lamp or
the light of the sun, for the Lord God will give them light. And they
will reign for ever and ever.
6The angel said to me, "These words are trustworthy and true. The
Lord, the God of the spirits of the prophets, sent his angel to show his
servants the things that must soon take place."

[a]20 The precise identification of some of these precious stones is uncertain.

21:19–20 Next John describes the 12 foundations of the city, each of which is decorated with a different precious mineral. These are not ordinary foundations that are hidden under the earth. These are visible for all to see. On them are written the 12 names of the apostles (v. 14). These 12 minerals are similar to eight of the 12 gems in the breastpiece of the high priest (Ex. 28:17–21).

21:19 sapphire. A deep blue, transparent gem. **chalcedony.** Green silicate of copper found near Chalcedon in Asia Minor. **emerald.** A green gemstone.

21:20 sardonyx. An agate made up of layers of a red mineral by the name of sard, and white onyx. **carnelian.** Blood red. **chrysolite.** Yellow topaz or golden jasper. **beryl.** A sea-green mineral. **topaz.** A greenish-gold or yellow mineral. **chrysoprase.** A type of quartz which was apple-green. **jacinth.** A bluish-purple mineral. **amethyst.** Another variety of quartz; it was purple and transparent.

21:21 twelve gates. The gates of ancient cities were an important part of their defense. They were built into the wall, often with a tower as part of their construction. **twelve pearls.** Pearls were of great value in the ancient world (Matt. 13:45–46; 1 Tim. 2:9). The pearls from which these gates will be built will have to be enormous; again, quite beyond anything on this earth. **The great street.** This, like the city itself (v. 18), is made of pure gold.

22:1–5 The focus shifts from the city to the river of life that flows from the throne of God and of the Lamb flowing right through the middle of the city.

22:1 The New Jerusalem is a place of eternal life. The saints will live eternally near this life-giving stream. **the river of the water of life.** The idea of such a river is a common one in the Bible (Ps. 46:4; Ezek. 47:1–12; Zech. 14:8; John 4:10–14). **from the throne.** God is the source of life.

22:2 middle of the great street. The river of life is central to the New Jerusalem. **the tree of life.** The great story ends where it began, with the tree of life. In Genesis the tree of life in the Garden of Eden was lost to humanity by reason of sin (Gen. 2:9; 3:22). In Revelation it is restored. But what an awful price was paid for the sin in the intervening centuries.

Jesus Is Coming

7"Behold, I am coming soon! Blessed is he who keeps the words of
the prophecy in this book."

8I, John, am the one who heard and saw these things. And when I had heard and seen them, I fell down to worship at the feet of the angel who had been showing them to me.
9But he said to me, "Do not do it! I am a fellow servant with you and with your brothers the prophets and of all who keep the words of this book. Worship God!"

10Then he told me, "Do not seal up the words of the prophecy of this book, because the time is near.
11Let him who does wrong continue to do wrong; let him who is vile continue to be vile; let him who does right continue to do right; and let him who is holy continue to be holy."

12"Behold, I am coming soon! My reward is with me, and I will give to everyone according to what he has done.
13I am the Alpha and the Omega, the First and the Last, the Beginning and the End.

14"Blessed are those who wash their robes, that they may have the right to the tree of life and may go through the gates into the city.
15Outside are the dogs, those who practice magic arts, the sexually immoral, the murderers, the idolaters and everyone who loves and practices falsehood.

16"I, Jesus, have sent my angel to give you[a] this testimony for the churches. I am the Root and the Offspring of David, and the bright Morning Star."

17The Spirit and the bride say, "Come!" And let him who hears say, "Come!" Whoever is thirsty, let him come; and whoever wishes, let him take the free gift of the water of life.

[a]16 The Greek is plural.

OPEN If you could give yourself a new name, symbolizing the legacy your family gave you, the God-given potential you have, or some hidden aspiration you have yet to realize, what name would you choose? Why?

STUDY 1. What words of Christ are repeated three times in this closing (vv. 7,12,20)? How do these words sum up the theme of Revelation? **2.** Regarding Jesus' claims in verses 12–17, how is the final state of humanity determined: By some arbitrary reward system, fixed from eternity? By what we have done in this present life? Or by our response to his universal ("whoever thirsts") and undeserved ("free gift") invitation to simply "come"? **3.** Is it ever too late for people to change their ways and come to Christ? Why or why not? **4.** In the contrast between those "inside" the city and those "outside" (vv. 14–15), what is implied about the basis for our salvation and judgment? What does it mean to "wash" one's "robe"? **5.** What is the meaning of God's final curse in verses 18–19? Knowing what you now do about the seven plagues, the tree of life and the Holy City, how seriously do you take this warning?

APPLY 1. In what way has this study of Revelation helped to prepare you for Christ's Sec-

---

22:7 Jesus affirms what he said at the beginning of the book (2:16; 3:11). In light of this fact, his people must always be alert, always prepared for his return. **Blessed.** This is the sixth of seven beatitudes. **keeps the words of prophecy.** The important thing for believers is to realize that the aim of the book is not so much to inform the church about the details of the last days as it is to call the church to faithful living in the midst of the struggle it faces with evil in whatever historical context it finds itself.

22:14 Blessed. The final beatitude in the book of Revelation. **wash their robes.** An allusion to 3:4 and 7:14. Those who are blessed are those who, by faith, have benefited from in the redeeming death of Jesus. **the right to the tree of life.** Those who are thus clad in the righteousness of Jesus have access to the very life of God (vv. 1–5). **go through the gates into the city.** Furthermore, they have access to the city of God, the New Jerusalem where they will live eternally.

22:15 In contrast is the fate of those who have not acknowledged for themselves the redemptive work of the Messiah. The idea is not that there is a heavenly city which is surrounded by the enemies of God. Their fate has already been described (21:8). The point is the sharp contrast between the two outcomes as the spirit and the bride prepare to invite all to come to that city (v. 17).

22:16 Jesus speaks again, attesting to the authenticity of this book. He reiterates what was said in 1:1—that this vision has come from Jesus to the angel to John to the churches. **Jesus.** The one who reveals all this is the man from Nazareth, who lived and taught and died on earth and then rose again. **the Root and the Offspring of David.** He is the messianic King from the line of David (5:5; Matt. 1:1; 9:27; 15:22; 21:9; Rom. 1:3). The image of a shoot that grows out of the stump of David is taken from Isaiah 11:1. **the bright Morning Star.** See Numbers 24:17, which is understood to be a prophecy about the Messiah.

22:17 There are two ways to read this verse. It can be understood to contain two invitations. In the first invitation, the Spirit, the Bride, and the hearers of this book beckon Jesus to return. In the second invitation, all who wish are invited to partake of the tree of life (vv. 12,20). But reading it this way makes the transition very abrupt from one invitation to the other. It is probably better to read the whole verse as an invitation to the world. What an amazing picture this is: the Holy Spirit, the church, and all who read this book beckoning the world to come to that which will give them true life.

ond Coming? How is your lifestyle in keeping with verse 7? **2.** How have your perceptions of Jesus, Satan, heaven and hell changed? Why?

[18]I warn everyone who hears the words of the prophecy of this
book: If anyone adds anything to them, God will add to him the
plagues described in this book. [19]And if anyone takes words away
from this book of prophecy, God will take away from him his share in
the tree of life and in the holy city, which are described in this book.
[20]He who testifies to these things says, "Yes, I am coming soon."
Amen. Come, Lord Jesus.
[21]The grace of the Lord Jesus be with God's people. Amen.

22:18–19 A warning is affixed to the book. No one is to tamper with its contents, either to add to or take away from it (Deut. 4:2). This would be a real temptation with a book like this, whose message is mysterious, harsh at times, and often hard to understand. The temptation would be to leave out or explain away the parts that do not conform to one's views. Or one might be tempted to add other prophecies and give them the same status as these.

22:19 his share in the tree of life. The second part of the warning (about taking away from the words) is addressed specifically to those who are believers.

22:20 For the third time in this epilogue, the reader is reminded that Jesus is coming soon. **Amen. Come, Lord Jesus.** John's response to this declaration is: "So be it; let it happen; Come Lord Jesus."

CONTENTS OF BACK MATTER

WEIGHTS AND MEASURES

BIBLICAL UNIT		APPROXIMATE AMERICAN EQUIVALENT	APPROXIMATE METRIC EQUIVALENT
		WEIGHTS	
talent	(60 minas)	75 pounds	34 kilograms
mina	(50 shekels)	1 1/4 pounds	0.6 kilogram
shekel	(2 bekas)	2/5 ounce	11.5 grams
pim	(2/3 shekel)	1/3 ounce	7.6 grams
beka	(10 gerahs)	1/5 ounce	5.5 grams
gerah		1/50 ounce	0.6 gram
		LENGTH	
cubit		18 inches	0.5 meter
span		9 inches	23 centimeters
handbreadth		3 inches	8 centimeters
		CAPACITY	
		Dry Measure	
cor (homer)	(10 ephahs)	6 bushels	220 liters
lethek	(5 ephahs)	3 bushels	110 liters
ephah	(10 omers)	3/5 bushel	22 liters
seah	(1/3 ephah)	7 quarts	7.3 liters
omer	(1/10 ephah)	2 quarts	2 liters
cab	(1/18 ephah)	1 quart	1 liter
		Liquid Measure	
bath	(1 ephah)	6 gallons	22 liters
hin	(1/6 bath)	4 quarts	4 liters
log	(1/72 bath)	1/3 quart	0.3 liter

The figures of this table are calculated on the basis of a shekel equaling 11.5 grams, a cubit equaling 18 inches and an ephah equaling 22 liters. The quart referred to is either a dry quart (slightly larger than a liter) or a liquid quart (slightly smaller than a liter), whichever is applicable. The ton referred to in the footnotes is the American ton of 2,000 pounds.

This table is based upon the best available information, but it is not intended to be mathematically precise; like the measurement equivalents in the footnotes, it merely gives approximate amounts and distances. Weights and measures differed somewhat at various times and places in the ancient world. There is uncertainty particularly about the ephah and the bath; further discoveries may give more light on these units of capacity.

LECTIONARY THREE-YEAR CYCLE

LECTIONARY YEAR A*

C = Common	R = Roman	L = Lutheran

Absence of letter is same for all

Alternative Readings and Psalms are not included

	READING 1	READING 2	GOSPEL
ADVENT SEASON			
Advent 1	Isa. 2:1–5	Rom. 13:11–14	Matt. 24:36–44 (C,L) Matt. 24:37–44 (R)
Advent 2	Isa. 11:1–10	Rom. 15:4–13 (C,L) Rom. 15:4–9 (R)	Matt. 3:1–12
Advent 3	Isa. 35:1–10 (C,L) Isa. 35:1–6a,10 (R)	James 5:7–10	Matt. 11:2–11
Advent 4	Isa. 7:10–16 (C,L) Isa. 7:10–14 (R)	Rom. 1:1–7	Matt. 1:18–25 (C,L) Matt. 1:18–24 (R)
CHRISTMAS DAY	**Nativity of Our Lord** (Primary Service)		
	Isa. 9:1–6 (R)[1] Isa. 9:2–7 (C,L)	Titus 2:11–14	Luke 2:1–14 (15–20) (C,L) Luke 2:1–14 (R)
CHRISTMAS SEASON			
1st Sunday After Christmas Day	Isa. 63:7–9 (C,L) Sir. 3:3–7,14–17a (R)[9]	Heb. 2:10–18 (C,L) Col. 3:12–21 (R)	Matt. 2:13–23 (C,L) Matt. 2:13–15,19–23 (R)
2nd Sunday After Christmas Day	Jer. 31:7–14 (C,L) Sir. 24:1–4,12–16 (R)[9]	Eph. 1:3–14 (C) Eph. 1:3–6,15–18 (L,R)	John 1:(1–9) 10–18 (C,L) John 1:1–18 (R)

	READING 1	READING 2	GOSPEL
EPIPHANY OF OUR LORD	Isa. 60:1–6	Eph. 3:1–12 (C,L) Eph. 3:2–3a,5–6 (R)	Matt. 2:1–12
EPIPHANY SEASON			
Epiphany 1 (Baptism of Our Lord)	Isa. 42:1–9 (C,L) Isa. 42:1–4,6–7 (R)	Acts 10:34–43 (C,L) Acts 10:34–38 (R)	Matt. 3:13–17
Epiphany 2	Isa. 49:1–7 (C,L) Isa. 49:3,5–6 (R)	1 Cor. 1:1–9 (C,L) 1 Cor. 1:1–3 (R)	John 1:29–42 (C,L) John 1:29–34 (R)
Epiphany 3	Isa. 9:1–4 (C,L) Isa. 8:23b–9:3 (R)[2]	1 Cor. 1:10–18 (C,L) 1 Cor. 1:10–13,17 (R)	Matt. 4:12–23
Epiphany 4	Mic. 6:1–8 (C,L) Zeph. 2:3; 3:12–13 (R)	1 Cor. 1:18–31 (C,L) 1 Cor. 1:26–31 (R)	Matt. 5:1–12
Epiphany 5	Isa. 58:1–9a (9b–12) (C,L) Isa. 58:7–10 (R)	1 Cor. 2:1–12 (13–16) (C,L) 1 Cor. 2:1–5 (R)	Matt. 5:13–20 (C,L) Matt. 5:13–16 (R)
Epiphany 6	Deut. 30:15–20 (C,L) Sir. 15:16–21 (R)[9]	1 Cor. 3:1–9 (C) 1 Cor. 2:6–13 (L) 1 Cor. 2:6–10 (R)	Matt. 5:21–37 (C) Matt. 5:20–37 (L) Matt. 5:17–37 (R)
Epiphany 7	Lev. 19:1–2,9–18 (C) Lev. 19:1–2, 17–18 (R,L)	1 Cor. 3:10–11, 16–23 (C,L) 1 Cor. 3:16–23 (R)	Matt. 5:38–48
Epiphany 8	Isa. 49:8–16a (C) Isa. 49:13–18 (L) Isa. 49:14–15 (R)	1 Cor. 4:1–5 (C,R) 1 Cor. 4:1–13 (L)	Matt. 6:24–34
Epiphany 9	(Churches whose calendar requires this Sunday, and do *not* observe the Last Sunday after Epiphany as the Transfiguration)		
	Deut. 11:18–21, 26–28 (C) Deut. 11:18,26–28, 32 (R)	Rom. 1:16–17; 3:22b–28 (29–31) (C) Rom. 3:21–25,28 (R)	Matt. 7:21–29 (C) Matt. 7:21–27 (R)

	READING 1	READING 2	GOSPEL
Last Sunday After Epiphany	**Transfiguration of Our Lord** (August 6—R)		
	Ex. 24:12–18 (C,L) Dan. 7:9–10,13–14 (R)	2 Peter 1:16–21 (C,L) 2 Peter 1:16–19 (R)	Matt. 17:1–9
LENTEN SEASON			
Ash Wednesday	Joel 2:1–2,12–17 (C,L) Joel 2:12–18 (R)	2 Cor. 5:20b–6:10 (C,L) 2 Cor. 5:20–6:2 (R)	Matt. 6:1–6,16–21 (C,L) Matt. 6:1–6,16–18 (R)
Lent 1	Gen. 2:15–17; 3:1–7 (C,L) Gen. 2:7–9; 3:1–7 (R)	Rom. 5:12–19	Matt. 4:1–11
Lent 2	Gen. 12:1–4a	Rom. 4:1–5,13–17 (C,L) 2 Tim. 1:8b–10 (R)	John 3:1–17 (C) John 4:5–26 (27–30, 39–42) (L) Matt. 17:1–9 (R)
Lent 3	Ex. 17:1–7 (C,L) Ex. 17:3–7 (R)	Rom. 5:1–11 (C,L) Rom. 5:1–2,5–8 (R)	John 4:5–42
Lent 4	1 Sam. 16:1–13 (C,L) 1 Sam. 16:1b,6–7, 10–13a (R)	Eph. 5:8–14	John 9:1–41
Lent 5	Ezek. 37:1–14 (C,L) Ezek. 37:12–14 (R)	Rom. 8:6–11 (C,L) Rom. 8:8–11 (R)	John 11:1–45
Lent 6 (Passion or Palm Sunday)	Isa. 50:4–9a (C,L) Isa. 50:4–7 (R)	Phil. 2:5–11 (C,L) Phil. 2:6–11 (R)	Matt. 26:14–27:66 *or* Matt. 27:11–54

	READING 1	READING 2	GOSPEL
GOOD FRIDAY	Isa. 52:13–53:12	Heb. 10:16–25 (C) Heb. 4:14–16; 5:7–9 (R,L)	John 18:1–19:42
EASTER SEASON			
Easter Day	**The Resurrection of Our Lord**		
	Acts 10:34–43 *or* Jer. 31:1–6 (C,L) Acts 10:34a,37–43 (R)	Col. 3:1–4	John 20:1–18 (C,L) John 20:1–9 (R)
Easter 2	Acts 2:14a,22–32 (C,L) Acts 2:42–47 (R)	1 Peter 1:3–9	John 20:19–31
Easter 3	Acts 2:14a,36–41 (C,L) Acts 2:14,22–33 (R)	1 Peter 1:17–23 (C,L) 1 Peter 1:17–21 (R)	Luke 24:13–35
Easter 4	Acts 2:42–47 (C,L) Acts 2:14a,36–41 (R)	1 Peter 2:19–25 (C,L) 1 Peter 2:20–25 (R)	John 10:1–10
Easter 5	Acts 7:55–60 (C,L) Acts 6:1–7 (R)	1 Peter 2:2–10 (C,L) 1 Peter 2:4–9 (R)	John 14:1–14 (C,L) John 14:1–12 (R)
Easter 6	Acts 17:22–31 (C,L) Acts 8:5–8,14–17 (R)	1 Peter 3:13–22 (C,L) 1 Peter 3:15–18 (R)	John 14:15–21
Ascension of Our Lord	(These readings may be used on Easter 7 in years A, B, C)		
	Acts 1:1–11	Eph. 1:15–23 (C,L) Eph. 1:17–23 (R)	Luke 24:44–53 (C,L) Matt. 28:16–20 (R)
Easter 7	Acts 1:6–14 (C,L) Acts 1:12–14 (R)	1 Peter 4:12–14; 5:6–11 (C,L) 1 Peter 4:13–16 (R)	John 17:1–11

PENTECOST SEASON	READING 1	READING 2	GOSPEL
Day of Pentecost	Num. 11:24–30 (C,L) Acts 2:1–11 (R)	Acts 2:1–21 (C,L) 1 Cor. 12:3b–7,12–13 (R)	John 20:19–23
First Sunday After Pentecost	**Trinity Sunday** (Ordinary Time)		
	Gen. 1:1–2:4a (C,L) Ex. 34:4b–6,8–9 (R)	2 Cor. 13:11–13	Matt. 28:16–20 (C,L) John 3:16–18 (R)
Pentecost 2	Gen. 6:9–22; 7:24; 8:14–19 (C) Deut. 11:18–21, 26–28 (L) Deut. 11:18,26–28,32 (R)	Rom. 1:16–17; 3:22b–28 (29–31) (C) Rom. 3:21–25a,27–28 (L) Rom. 3:21–25,28 (R)	Matt. 7:21–29 (C) Matt. 7:(15–20) 21–29 (L) Matt. 7:21–27 (R)
Pentecost 3	Gen. 12:1–9 (C) Hos. 5:15–6:6 (L) Hos. 6:3–6 (R)	Rom. 4:13–25 (C,L) Rom. 4:18–25 (R)	Matt. 9:9–13,18–26 (C,L) Matt. 9:9–13 (R)
Pentecost 4	Gen. 18:1–15 (21:1–7) (C) Ex. 19:2–8a (L) Ex. 19:2–6a (R)	Rom. 5:1–8 (C,L) Rom. 5:6–11 (R)	Matt. 9:35–10:8 (9–23) (C,L) Matt. 9:36–10:8 (R)
Pentecost 5	Gen. 21:8–21 (C) Jer. 20:7–13 (L) Jer. 20:10–13 (R)	Rom. 6:1b–11 (C,L) Rom. 5:12–15 (R)	Matt. 10:24–39 (C,L) Matt. 10:26–33 (R)
Pentecost 6	Gen. 22:1–14 (C) Jer. 28:5–9 (L) 2 Kin. 4:8–11,14–16a (R)	Rom. 6:12–23 (C,L) Rom. 6:3–4,8–11 (R)	Matt. 10:40–42 (C,L) Matt. 10:37–42 (R)
Pentecost 7	Gen. 24:34–38,42–49, 58–67 (C) Zech. 9:9–12 (L) Zech. 9:9–10 (R)	Rom. 7:15–25a (C,L) Rom. 8:9,11–13 (R)	Matt. 11:16–19,25–30 (C,L) Matt. 11:25–30 (R)
Pentecost 8	Gen. 25:19–34 (C) Isa. 55:10–11 (R) Isa. 55:10–13 (L)	Rom. 8:1–11 (C,L) Rom. 8:18–23 (R)	Matt. 13:1–9,18–23 (C,L) Matt. 13:1–23 (R)
Pentecost 9	Gen. 28:10–19a (C) Isa. 44:6–8 (L) Wis. 12:13,16–19 (R)[9]	Rom. 8:12–25 (C,L) Rom. 8:26–27 (R)	Matt. 13:24–30 (36–43) (C,L) Matt. 13:24–43 (R)

	READING 1	READING 2	GOSPEL
Pentecost 10	Gen. 29:15–28 (C) 1 Kin. 3:5–12 (L) 1 Kin. 3:5,7–12 (R)	Rom. 8:26–39 (C,L) Rom. 8:28–30 (R)	Matt. 13:31–33,44–52 (C,L) Matt. 13:44–52 (R)
Pentecost 11	Gen. 32:22–31 (C) Isa. 55:1–5 (L) Isa. 55:1–3 (R)	Rom. 9:1–5 (C,L) Rom. 8:35,37–39 (R)	Matt. 14:13–21
Pentecost 12	Gen. 37:1–4,12–28 (C) 1 Kin. 19:9–18 (L) 1 Kin. 19:9a,11–13a (R)	Rom. 10:5–15 (C,L) Rom. 9:1–5 (R)	Matt. 14:22–33
Pentecost 13	Gen. 45:1–15 (C) Isa. 56:1,6–8 (L) Isa. 56:1,6–7 (R)	Rom. 11:1–2a, 29–32 (C,L) Rom. 11:13–15, 29–32 (R)	Matt. 15:(10–20) 21–28 (C,L) Matt. 15:21–28 (R)
Pentecost 14	Ex. 1:8–2:10 (C) Isa. 51:1–6 (L) Isa. 22:19–23 (R)	Rom. 12:1–8 (C,L) Rom. 11:33–36 (R)	Matt. 16:13–20
Pentecost 15	Ex. 3:1–15 (C) Jer. 15:15–21 (L) Jer. 20:7–9 (R)	Rom. 12:9–21 (C,L) Rom. 12:1–2 (R)	Matt. 16:21–28 (C,L) Matt. 16:21–27 (R)
Pentecost 16	Ex. 12:1–14 (C) Ezek. 33:7–11 (L) Ezek. 33:7–9 (R)	Rom. 13:8–14 (C,L) Rom. 13:8–10 (R)	Matt.18:15–20
Pentecost 17	Ex. 14:19–31 (C) Gen. 50:15–21 (L) Sir. 27:30–28:7 (R)[9]	Rom. 14:1–12 (C) Rom. 14:5–9 (L) Rom. 14:7–9 (R)	Matt. 18:21–35
Pentecost 18	Ex. 16:2–15 (C) Jonah 3:10–4:11 (L) Isa. 55:6–9 (R)	Phil. 1:21–30 (C,L) Phil. 1:20c–24,27a (R)	Matt. 20:1–16a
Pentecost 19	Ex. 17:1–7 (C) Ezek. 18:1–4,25–32 (L) Ezek. 18:25–28 (R)	Phil. 2:1–13 (C,L) Phil. 2:1–11 (R)	Matt. 21:23–32 (C,L) Matt. 21:28–32 (R)
Pentecost 20	Ex. 20:1–4,7–9, 12–20 (C) Isa. 5:1–7 (L,R)	Phil. 3:4b–14 (C,L) Phil. 4:6–9 (R))	Matt. 21:33–46 (C,L) Matt. 21:33–43 (R)

	READING 1	READING 2	GOSPEL
Pentecost 21	Ex. 32:1–14 (C) Isa. 25:1–9 (L) Isa. 25:6–10a (R)	Phil. 4:1–9 (C,L) Phil. 4:12–14,19–20 (R)	Matt. 22:1–14
Pentecost 22	Ex. 33:12–23 (C) Isa. 45:1–7 (L) Isa. 45:1,4–6 (R)	1 Thess. 1:1–10 (C,L) 1 Thess. 1:1–5b (R)	Matt. 22:15–22 (C,L) Matt. 22:15–21 (R)
Pentecost 23	Deut. 34:1–12 (C) Lev. 19:1–2,15–18 (L) Ex. 22:20–26 (R)	1 Thess. 2:1–8 (C,L) 1 Thess. 1:5c–10 (R)	Matt. 22:34–46 (C,L) Matt. 22:34–40 (R)
All Saints Day (November 1)	Rev. 7:9–17 (C) Isa. 26:1–4,8–9, 12–13,19–21 (L) Rev. 7:2–4,9–14 (R)	1 John 3:1–3 (C,R) Rev. 21:9–11,22–27 (22:1–5) (L)	Matt. 5:1–12 (C,L) Matt. 5:1–12a (R)
Pentecost 24	Josh. 3:7–17 (C) Amos 5:18–24 (L) Mal. 1:14b–2:2b, 8–10 (R)	1 Thess. 2:9–13 (C) 1 Thess. 4:13–14, (15–18) (L) 1 Thess. 2:7b–9,13 (R)	Matt. 23:1–12 (C,R) Matt. 25:1–13 (L)
Pentecost 25	Josh. 24:1–3a,14–25 (C) Zeph. 1:7,12–18 (L) Wis. 6:12–16 (R)[9]	1 Thess. 4:13–18 (C,R) 1 Thess. 5:1–11 (L)	Matt. 25:1–13 (C,R) Matt. 25:14–30 (L)
Pentecost 26	Judg. 4:1–7 (C) Mal. 2:1–2,4–10 (L) Prov. 31:10–13,19–20, 30–31 (R)	1 Thess. 5:1–11 (C) 1 Thess. 2:8–13 (L) 1 Thess. 5:1–6 (R)	Matt. 25:14–30 (C,R) Matt. 23:1–12 (L)
Pentecost 27 (Lutheran only)	Jer. 26:1–6	1 Thess. 3:7–13	Matt. 24:1–14
Last Pentecost	**Christ the King Sunday**		
	Ezek. 34:11–16, 20–24 (C,L) Ezek. 34:11–12, 15–17 (R)	Eph 1:15–23 (C,L) 1 Cor. 15:20–26,28 (R)	Matt. 25:31–46

LECTIONARY YEAR B*

C = Common R = Roman L = Lutheran

Absence of letter is same for all

Alternative Readings and Psalms are not included

	READING 1	READING 2	GOSPEL
ADVENT SEASON			
Advent 1	Isa. 64:1–9 (C,L) Isa. 63:16b–17,19b; 64:2–7(R)[3]	1 Cor. 1:3–9	Mark 13:24-37 (C,L) Mark 13:33–37 (R)
Advent 2	Isa. 40:1–11 (C,L) Isa. 40:1–5,9–11 (R)	2 Peter 3:8–15a (C,L) 2 Peter 3:8–14 (R)	Mark 1:1–8
Advent 3	Isa. 61:1–4,8–11 (C,L) Isa. 61:1–2a,10–11 (R)	1 Thess. 5:16–24	John 1:6–8,19–28
Advent 4	2 Sam. 7:1–11,16 (C,L) 2 Sam. 7:1–5,8b–12, 14a,16 (R)	Rom. 16:25–27	Luke 1:26–38
CHRISTMAS DAY	**Nativity of Our Lord** (Primary Service)		
	Isa. 9:2–7 (C,L) Isa. 9:1–6 (R)[4]	Titus 2:11–14	Luke 2:1–14 (15–20) (C,L) Luke 2:1–14 (R)
CHRISTMAS SEASON			
1st Sunday After Christmas Day	Isa. 61:10–62:3 (C,L) Sir. 3:3–7,14–17 (R)[9]	Gal. 4:4–7 (C,L) Col. 3:12–21 (R)	Luke 2:22–40
2nd Sunday After Christmas Day	Jer. 31:7–14 (C,L) Sir. 24:1–4,12–16 (R)[9]	Eph. 1:3–14 (C,L) Eph. 1:3–6,15–18 (R)	John 1:1–9 (10–18) (C,L) John 1:1–18 (R)

	READING 1	READING 2	GOSPEL
EPIPHANY OF OUR LORD	Isa. 60:1–6	Eph. 3:1–12 (C,L) Eph. 3:2–3a,5–6 (R)	Matt. 2:1–12
EPIPHANY SEASON			
Epiphany 1 (Baptism of Our Lord)	Gen. 1:1–5 (C,L) Isa. 55:1–11 (R)	Acts 19:1–7 (C,L) 1 John 5:1–9 (R)	Mark 1:4–11 (C,L) Mark 1:7–11 (R)
Epiphany 2	1 Sam. 3:1–10 (11–20) (C,L) 1 Sam. 3:3b–10,19 (R)	1 Cor. 6:12–20 (C,L) 1 Cor. 6:13c–15a, 17–20 (R)	John 1:43–51 (C,L) John 1:35–42 (R)
Epiphany 3	Jonah 3:1–5,10	1 Cor. 7:29–31	Mark 1:14–20
Epiphany 4	Deut. 18:15–20	1 Cor. 8:1–13 (C,L) 1 Cor. 7:32–35 (R)	Mark 1:21–28
Epiphany 5	Isa. 40:21–31 (C,L) Job 7:1–4,6–7 (R)	1 Cor. 9:16–23 (C,L) 1 Cor. 9:16–19, 22–23 (R)	Mark 1:29–39
Epiphany 6	2 Kin. 5:1–14 (C,L) Lev. 13:1–2,44–46 (R)	1 Cor. 9:24–27 (C,L) 1 Cor. 10:31–11:1 (R)	Mark 1:40–45
Epiphany 7	Isa. 43:18–25 (C,L) Isa. 43:18–19,21–22, 24b–25 (R)	2 Cor. 1:18–22	Mark 2:1–12
Epiphany 8	Hos. 2:14–20 (C) Hos. 2:14–16, (17–18) 19–20 (L) Hos 2:16b–17b, 21–22 (R)[5]	2 Cor. 3:1–6 2 Cor. 3:1b–6 (R)	Mark 2:13–22 (C) Mark 2:18–22 (L,R)
Epiphany 9	(Churches whose calendar requires this Sunday, and do *not* observe the Last Sunday after Epiphany as the Transfiguration)		
	Deut. 5:12–15 (C,R)	2 Cor. 4:5–12 (C) 2 Cor. 4:6–11 (R)	Mark 2:23–3:6 (C,R)

	READING 1	READING 2	GOSPEL
Last Sunday After Epiphany	**Transfiguration of Our Lord** (August 6—R)		
	2 Kin. 2:1–12 (C,L) Dan. 7:9–10,13–14 (R)	2 Cor. 4:3–6 (C,L) 2 Peter 1:16–19 (R)	Mark 9:2–9 (C,L) Mark 9:2–10 (R)
LENTEN SEASON			
Ash Wednesday	Joel 2:1–2,12–17 (C,L) Joel 2:12–18 (R)	2 Cor. 5:20b–6:10 (C,L) 2 Cor. 5:20–6:2 (R)	Matt. 6:1–6,16–21 (C,L) Matt. 6:1–6,16–18 (R)
Lent 1	Gen. 9:8–17 (C,L) Gen. 9:8–15 (R)	1 Peter 3:18–22	Mark 1:9–15 (C,L) Mark 1:12–15 (R)
Lent 2	Gen. 17:1–7, 15–16 (C,L) Gen. 22:1–2,9a, 10–13,15–18 (R)	Rom. 4:13–25 (C,L) Rom. 8:31b–34 (R)	Mark 8:31–38 (C,L) Mark 9:2–10 (R)
Lent 3	Ex. 20:1–17	1 Cor. 1:18–25 (C,L) 1 Cor. 1:22–25 (R)	John 2:13–22 (C,L) John 2:13–25 (R)
Lent 4	Num. 21:4–9 (C,L) 2 Chr. 36:14–16, 19–23 (R)	Eph. 2:1–10 (C,L) Eph. 2:4–10 (R)	John 3:14–21
Lent 5	Jer. 31:31–34	Heb. 5:5–10 (C,L) Heb. 5:7–9 (R)	John 12:20–33
Lent 6 (Passion or Palm Sunday)	Isa. 50:4–9a (C,L) Isa. 50:4–7 (R)	Phil. 2:5–11 (C,L) Phil. 2:6–11 (R)	Mark 14:1–15:47
GOOD *FRIDAY*	Isa. 52:13–53:12	Heb. 10:16–25 (C,L) Heb. 4:14–16; 5:7–9 (R)	John 18:1–19:42

	READING 1	READING 2	GOSPEL
EASTER SEASON			
Easter Day	**The Resurrection of Our Lord**		
	Acts 10:34–43 *or* Isa. 25:6–9 (C,L) Acts 10:34a,37–43 (R)	1 Cor. 15:1–11 (C,L) 1 Cor. 5:6b–8 (R)	Mark 16:1–8 (C) John 20:1–9 (R,L)
Easter 2	Acts 4:32–35	1 John 1:1–2:2 (C,L) 1 John 5:1–6 (R)	John 20:19–31
Easter 3	Acts 3:12–19 (C,L) Acts 3:13–15, 17–19 (R)	1 John 3:1–7 (C,L) 1 John 2:1–5a (R)	Luke 24:36b–48 (C,L) Luke 24:35–48 (R)
Easter 4	Acts 4:5–12 (C,L) Acts 4:8–12 (R)	1 John 3:16–24 (C,L) 1 John 3:1–2 (R)	John 10:11–18
Easter 5	Acts 8:26–40 (C,L) Acts 9:26–31 (R)	1 John 4:7–21 (C,L) 1 John 3:18–24 (R)	John 15:1–8
Easter 6	Acts 10:44–48 (C,L) Acts 10:25–26,34–35, 44–48 (R)	1 John 5:1–6 (C,L) 1 John 4:7–10 (R)	John 15:9–17
Ascension of Our Lord	(These readings may be used on Easter 7 in years A, B, C)		
	Acts 1:1–11	Eph. 1:15–23 (C,L) Eph. 4:1–13 (R)	Luke 24:44–53 (C,L) Mark 16:15–20 (R)
Easter 7	Acts 1:15–17,1 21–26 (C,L) Acts 1:15–17,20a, 20c–26 (R)	John 5:9–13 (C,L) 1 John 4:11–16 (R)	John 17:6–19 (C,L) John 17:11b–19 (R)
PENTECOST SEASON			
***Day of* Pentecost**	*Acts 2:1–21 (C) or* Ezek. 37:1–14 (L) Acts 2:1–11 (R)	Rom. 8:22–27 (C) Acts 2:1–21 (L) *or* Gal. 5:16–25 (R)	John 15:26–27; 16:4b–15 (C,L) John 15:26–27; 16:12–15 (R)

	READING 1	READING 2	GOSPEL
First Sunday After Pentecost	**Trinity Sunday** (Ordinary Time)		
	Isa. 6:1–8 (C,L) Deut. 4:32–34, 39–40 (R)	Rom. 8:12–17 (C,L) Rom. 8:14–17 (R)	John 3:1–17 (C,L) Matt. 28:16–20 (R)
Pentecost 2	1 Sam. 3:1–10 (11–20) (C) Deut. 5:12–15 (L,R)	2 Cor. 4:5–12 (C,L) 2 Cor. 4:6–11 (R)	Mark 2:23–3:6 (C,R) Mark 2:23–28 (L)
Pentecost 3	1 Sam. 8:4–11 (12–15) 16–20 (11:14–15) (C) Gen. 3:9–15 (L,R)	2 Cor. 4:13–5:1 (C,R) 2 Cor. 4:13–18 (L)	Mark 3:20–35
Pentecost 4	1 Sam. 15:34–16:13 (C) Ezek.17:22–24 (L,R)	2 Cor. 5:6–10 (11–13) 14–17 (C) 2 Cor. 5:1–10 (L) 2 Cor. 5:6–10 (R)	Mark 4:26–34
Pentecost 5	1 Sam. 17:1a (4–11) 19–23,32–49 (C) Job 38:1–11 (L) Job 38:1,8–11 (R)	2 Cor. 6:1–13 (C,L) 2 Cor. 5:14–17 (R)	Mark 4:35–41
Pentecost 6	2 Sam. 1:1,17–27 (C) Lam. 3:22–33 (L) Wis. 1:13–15; 2:23–24 (R)[9]	2 Cor. 8:7–15 (C,L) 2 Cor. 8:7,9,13–15 (R)	Mark 5:21–43 (C,L) Mark 5:21–43 (R)
Pentecost 7	2 Sam. 5:1–5,9–10 (C) Ezek. 2:1–5 (L) Ezek. 2:2–5 (R)	2 Cor. 12:2–10 (C) 2 Cor. 12:7–10 (L,R)	Mark 6:1–13 (C,L) Mark 6:1–6 (R)
Pentecost 8	2 Sam. 6:1–5, 12b–19 (C) Amos 7:7–15 (L) Amos 7:12–15 (R)	Eph. 1:3–14	Mark 6:14–29 (C,L) Mark 6:7–13 (R)
Pentecost 9	2 Sam. 7:1–14a (C) Jer. 23:1–6 (L,R)	Eph. 2:11–22 (C,L) Eph. 2:13–18 (R)	Mark 6:30–34,53–56 (C,L) Mark 6:30–34 (R)
Pentecost 10	2 Sam. 11:1–15 (C) 2 Kin. 4:42–44 (R,L)	Eph. 3:14–21 (C,L) Eph. 4:1–6 (R)	John 6:1–21 (C,L) John 6:1–15 (R)

	READING 1	READING 2	GOSPEL
Pentecost 11	2 Sam. 11:26–12:13a (C) Ex. 16:2–4,9–15 (L) Ex. 16:2–4,12–15 (R)	Eph. 4:1–16 (C,L) Eph. 4:17,20–24 (R)	John 6:24–35
Pentecost 12	2 Sam. 18:5–9,15, 31–33 (C) 1 Kin. 19:4–8 (L,R)	Eph. 4:25–5:2 (C,L) Eph. 4:30–5:2 (R)	John 6:35,41–51(C,L) John 6:41–52 (R)
Pentecost 13	1 Kin. 2:10–12; 3:3–14 (C) Prov. 9:1–6 (L,R)	Eph. 5:15–20	John 6:51–58
Pentecost 14	1 Kin. 8:(1,6,10–11) 22–30,41–43 (C) Josh. 24:1–2a,14–18 (L) Josh. 24:1–2a,15–17,18b (R)	Eph. 6:10–20 (C,L) Eph. 5:21–32 (R)	John 6:56–69 (C,L) John 6:60–69 (R)
Pentecost 15	Song 2:8–13 (C) Deut. 4:1–2,6–9 (L) Deut. 4:1–2,6–8 (R)	James 1:17–27 (C,L) James 1:17–18, 21b–22,27 (R)	Mark 7:1–8,14–15,21–23
Pentecost 16	Prov. 22:1–2,8–9, 22–23 (C) Isa. 35:4–7a (L,R)	James 2:1–10 (11–13) 14–17 (C,L) James 2:1–5 (R)	Mark 7:24–37 (C,L) Mark 7:31–37 (R)
Pentecost 17	Prov. 1:20–33 (C) Isa. 50:4–9a (L,R)	James 3:1–12 (C,L) James 2:14–18 (R)	Mark 8:27–38 (C,L) Mark 8:27–35 (R)
Pentecost 18	Prov. 31:10–31 (C) Jer. 11:18–20 (L) Wis. 2:12,17–20 (R)[9]	James 3:13–4:3, 7–8a (C,L) James 3:16–4:3 (R)	Mark 9:30–37
Pentecost 19	Est. 7:1–6,9–10; 9:20–22 (C) Num. 11:4–6,10–16, 47–48 (L) Num. 11:25–29 (R)	James 5:13–20 (C,L) James 5:1–6 (R)	Mark 9:38–50 (C,L) Mark 9:38–43,45,47 47–48 (R)

	READING 1	READING 2	GOSPEL
Pentecost 20	Job 1:1; 2:1–10 (C) Gen. 2:18–24 (L,R)	Heb. 1:1–4; 2:5–12 (C,L) Heb. 2:9–11 (R)	Mark 10:2–16
Pentecost 21	Job 23:1–9,16–17 (C) Amos 5:6–7,10–15 (L) Wis. 7:7–11 (R)[9]	Heb. 4:12–16 (C,L) Heb. 4:12–13 (R)	Mark 10:17–31 (C,L) Mark 10:17–30 (R)
Pentecost 22	Job 38:1–7 (34–41) (C) Isa. 53:4–12 (L) Isa.53:10–11 (R)	Heb. 5:1–10 (C,L) Heb. 4:14–16 (R)	Mark 10:35–45
Pentecost 23	Job 42:1–6,10–17 (C) Jer. 31:7–9 (L,R)	Heb. 7:23–28 (C,L) Heb. 5:1–6 (R)	Mark 10:46–52
All Saints Day (November 1)	Wis. 3:1–9 (C)[9] Isa. 26:6–9 (L) Rev. 7:2–4,9–14 (R)	Rev. 21:1–6a (C,L) 1 John 3:1–3 (R)	John 11:32–44 (C,L) Matt. 5:1–12a (R)
Pentecost 24	Ruth 1:1–18 (C) Deut. 6:1–9 (L) Deut. 6:2–6 (R)	Heb. 9:11–14 (C,L) Heb. 7:23–28 (R)	Mark 12:28–34 (C,L) Matt. 12:28b–34 (R)
Pentecost 25	Ruth 3:1–5; 4:13–17 (C) 1 Kin. 17:8–16 (L) 1 Kin. 17:10–16 (R)	Heb. 9:24–28	Mark 12:38–44
Pentecost 26	1 Sam. 1:4–20 (C) Dan. 12:1–3 (L,R)	Heb. 10:11–14 (15–18) 19–25 (C,L) Heb. 10:11–14,18 (R)	Mark 13:1–8 (C,L) Mark 13:24–32 (R)
Pentecost 27 (Lutheran only)	Dan. 7:9–10	Heb. 13:20–21	Mark 13:24–31
Last Pentecost	**Christ the King Sunday**		
	2 Sam. 23:1–7 (C) Dan. 7:9–10,13–14 (L) Dan. 7:13–14 (R)	Rev. 1:4b–8 (C,L) Rev. 1:5–8 (R)	John 18:33–37 (C,L) John 18:33b–37 (R)

LECTIONARY YEAR C*

C = Common R = Roman L = Lutheran

Absence of letter is same for all

Alternative Readings and Psalms are not included

	READING 1	READING 2	GOSPEL
ADVENT SEASON			
Advent 1	Jer. 33:14–16	1 Thess. 3:9–13 (C,L) 1 Thess. 3:12–4:2 (R)	Luke 21:25–36 (C,L) Luke 21:25–28,34–36 (R)
Advent 2	Bar. 5:1–9 (C,R)[9] Mal. 3:1–4 (L)	Phil. 1:3–11 (C,L) Phil. 1:4–6,8–11 (R)	Luke 3:1–6
Advent 3	Zeph. 3:14–20 (C,L) Zeph. 3:14–18a (R)	Phil. 4:4–7	Luke 3:7–18 (C,L) Luke 3:10–18 (R)
Advent 4	Mic. 5:2–5a (C,L) Mic. 5:1–4a (R)[6]	Heb. 10:5–10	Luke 1:39–45 (46–55) (C,L) Luke 1:39–45 (R)
CHRISTMAS DAY	**Nativity of Our Lord** (Primary Service)		
	Isa. 9:1–6 (R)[7] Isa. 9:2–7 (C,L)	Titus 2:11–14	Luke 2:1–14 (15–20) (C,L) Luke 2:1–14 (R)
CHRISTMAS SEASON			
1st Sunday After Christmas Day	1 Sam. 2:18–20, 26 (C,L) Sir. 3:3–7,14–17a (R)[9]	Col. 3:12–17 (C,L) Col. 3:12–21 (R)	Luke 2:41–52
2nd Sunday After *Christmas Day*	Jer. 31:7–14 (C) Isa. 61:10–62:3 (L) Sir. 24:1–4,12–16 (R)[9]	Eph. 1:3–14 (C) Eph. 1:3–6,15–18 (L,R)	John 1:(1–9)10–18 (C) John 1:1–18 (L,R)

	READING 1	READING 2	GOSPEL
EPIPHANY OF OUR LORD	Isa. 60:1–6	Eph. 3:1–12 (C,L) Eph. 3:2–3a,5–6 (R)	Matt. 2:1–12
EPIPHANY SEASON			
Epiphany 1 (Baptism of Our Lord)	Isa. 43:1–7 (C,L) Isa. 40:1–5,9–11 (R)	Acts 8:14–17 (C,L) Titus 2:11–14; 3:4–7 (R)	Luke 3:15–17,21–22 (C,L) Luke 3:15–16,21–22 (R)
Epiphany 2	Isa. 62:1–5	1 Cor. 12:1–11 (C,L) 1 Cor. 12:4–11 (R)	John 2:1–11
Epiphany 3	Neh. 8:1–3,5–6, 8–10 (C,L) Neh. 8:2–4a,5–6, 8–10 (R)	1 Cor. 12:12–31a (C,L) 1 Cor. 12:12–30 (R)	Luke 4:14–21 (C,L) Luke 1:1–4; 4:14–21 (R)
Epiphany 4	Jer. 1:4–10 (C,L) Jer. 1:4–5,17–19 (R)	1 Cor. 13:1–13 (C,L) 1 Cor. 12:31–13:13 (R)	Luke 4:21–30
Epiphany 5	Isa. 6:1–8,9–13 (C,L) Isa. 6:1–2a,3–8 (R)	1 Cor. 15:1–11	Luke 5:1–11
Epiphany 6	Jer. 17:5–10 (C,L) Jer. 17:5–8 (R)	1 Cor. 15:12–20 (C,L) 1 Cor. 15:12,16–20 (R)	Luke 6:17–26 (C,L) Luke 6:17,20–26 (R)
Epiphany 7	Gen. 45:3–11,15 (C,L) 1 Sam. 26:2,7–9, 12–13,22–23 (R)	1 Cor. 15:35–38, 42–50 (C,L) 1 Cor. 15:45–49 (R)	Luke 6:27–38
Epiphany 8	Sir. 27:4–7 (C)[9] Sir. 27:5–8 (R) Jer. 7:1–7 (8–15) (L)	1 Cor. 15:51–58 (C,L) 1 Cor. 15:54–58 (R)	Luke 6:39–49 (C,L) Luke 6:39–45 (R)
Epiphany 9	(Churches whose calendar requires this Sunday, and do *not* observe the Last Sunday after Epiphany as the Transfiguration)		
	1 Kin. 8:22–23, 41–43 (C) 1 Kin. 8:41–43 (R)	Gal. 1:1–12 (C) Gal. 1:1–2,6–10 (R)	Luke 7:1–10 (C,R)

	READING 1	READING 2	GOSPEL
Last Sunday After Epiphany	**Transfiguration of Our Lord** (August 6—R)		
	Ex. 34:29–35 (C,L) Deut. 7:9–10,13–14 (R)	2 Cor. 3:12–4:2 (C,L) 2 Peter 1:16–19 (R)	Luke 9:28–36 (37–43) (C,L) Luke 9:28b–36 (R)
LENTEN SEASON			
Ash Wednesday	Joel 2:1–2,12–17 (C,L) Joel 2:12–18 (R)	2 Cor. 5:20b–6:10 (C,L) 2 Cor. 5:20–6:2 (R)	Matt. 6:1–6,16–21 (C,L) Matt. 6:1–6,16–18 (R)
Lent 1	Deut. 26:1–11 (C) Deut. 26:5–10 (L) Deut. 26:4–10 (R)	Rom. 10:8b–13 (C,L) Rom. 10:8–13 (R)	Luke 4:1–13
Lent 2	Gen. 15:1–12, 17–18 (C,L) Gen. 15:5–12, 17–18 (R)	Phil. 3:17–4:1	Luke 13:31–35 (C,L) Luke 9:28b–36 (R)
Lent 3	Isa. 55:1–9 (C,L) Ex. 3:1–8a,13–15 (R)	1 Cor. 10:1–13 (C,L) 1 Cor. 10:1–6,10–12 (R)	Luke 13:1–9
Lent 4	Josh. 5:9–12 (C,L) Josh. 5:9a,10–12 (R)	2 Cor. 5:16–21 (C,L) 2 Cor. 5:17–21 (R)	Luke 15:1–3,11b–32 (C,L) Luke 15:1–3,11–32 (R)
Lent 5	Isa. 43:16–21	Phil. 3:4b–14 (C,L) Phil. 3:8–14 (R)	John 12:1–8 (C,L) John 8:1–11 (R)
Lent 6 (Passion or Palm Sunday)	Isa. 50:4–9a (C,L) Isa. 50:4–7 (R)	Phil. 2:5–11 (C,L) Phil. 2:6–11 (R)	Luke 22:14–23:56
GOOD FRIDAY	Isa. 52:13–53:12	Heb. 10:16–25 (C,L) Heb. 4:14–16; 5:7–9 (R)	John 18:1–19:42

	READING 1	READING 2	GOSPEL
EASTER SEASON			
Easter Day	**The Resurrection of Our Lord**		
	Acts 10:34–43 (C,L) Acts 10:34,37–43 (R)	1 Cor. 15:19–26 (C,L) Col. 3:1–4 (R)	John 20:1–18 (C,L) John 20:1–9 (R)
Easter 2	Acts 5:27–32 (C,L) Acts 5:12–16 (R)	Rev 1:4–8 (C,L) Rev 1:9–11a,12–13, 17–19 (R)	John 20:19–31
Easter 3	Acts 9:1–6 (7–20) (C,L) Acts 5:27–32, 40b–41 (R)	Rev. 5:11–14	John 21:1–19
Easter 4	Acts 9:36–43 (C,L) Acts 13:14,43–52 (R)	Rev. 7:9–17 (C,L) Rev. 7:9,14b–17 (R)	John 10:22–30 (C,L) John 10:27–30 (R)
Easter 5	Acts 11:1–18 (C,L) Acts 14:21–27 (R)	Rev. 21:1–6 (C,L) Rev. 21:1–5 (R)	John 13:31–35 John 13:31–33a,34–35 (R)
Easter 6	Acts 16:9–15 (C,L) Acts 15:1–2,22–29 (R)	Rev. 21:10,22–22:5 (C,L) Rev. 21:10–14,22–23 (R)	John 14:23–29
Ascension of Our Lord	(These readings may be used on Easter 7 in years A,B,C)		
	Acts 1:1–11	Eph. 1:15–23 (C,L) Heb. 9:24–28; 10:19–23 (R)	Luke 24:44–53 (C,L) Luke 24:46–53 (R)
Easter 7	Acts 16:16–34 (C,L) Acts 16:6–10 (L) Acts 7:55–60 (R)	Rev. 22:12–14,16–17, 20–21 (C,L) Rev. 22:12–14, 16–17,20 (R)	John 17:20–26
PENTECOST SEASON			
Day of Pentecost	Acts 2:1–21 (C,L) *or* Gen. 11:1–9 Acts 2:1–11 (R)	Rom. 8:14–17 (C,L) *or* Acts 2:1–21 Rom. 8:8–17 (R)	John 14:8–17 (25–27) (C,L) John 14:14–16,23b–26 (R)

	READING 1	READING 2	GOSPEL
First Sunday After Pentecost	**Trinity Sunday** (Ordinary Time)		
	Prov. 8:1–4, 22–31 (C,L) Prov. 8:22–31 (R)	Rom. 5:1–5	John 16:12–15
Pentecost 2	1 Kin. 18:20–21 (22–29) 30–39 (C) 1 Kin. 8: (22–23, 27–30) 41–43 (L) 1 Kin. 8:41–43 (R)	Gal. 1:1–12 (C) Gal. 1:1–10 (L) Gal. 1:1–2,6–10 (R)	Luke 7:1–10
Pentecost 3	1 Kin. 17:8–16) (17–24) (C) 1 Kin. 17:17–24 (L,R)	Gal. 1:11–24 (C,L) Gal. 1:11–19 (R)	Luke 7:11–17
Pentecost 4	1 Kin. 21:1–10 (11–14) 15–21a (C) 2 Sam. 11:26–12:10, 13–15 (L) 2 Sam. 12:7–10,13 (R)	Gal. 2:15–21 (C,L) Gal. 2:16,19–21 (R)	Luke 7:36–8:3
Pentecost 5	1 Kin. 19:1–4 (5–7) 8–15a (C) Isa. 65:1–9 (L) Zech. 12:10–11 (R)	Gal. 3:23–29 (C,L) Gal. 3:26–29 (R)	Luke 8:26–39 (C,L) Luke 9:18–24 (R)
Pentecost 6	2 Kin. 2:1–2,6–14 (C) 1 Kin. 19:15–16, 19–21 (L) 1 Kin. 19:16b,19–21 (R)	Gal. 5:1,13–25 (C,L) Gal. 5:1,13–18 (R)	Luke 9:51–62
Pentecost 7	2 Kin. 5:1–14 (C) Isa. 66:10–14 (L) Isa. 66:10–14c (R)	Gal. 6:(1–6) 7–16 (C,L) Gal. 6:14–18 (R)	Luke 10:1–11,16–20 (C,L) Luke 10:1–12,17–20 (R)
Pentecost 8	Amos 7:7–17 (C) Deut. 30:9–14 (L) Deut. 30:10–14 (R)	Col. 1:1–14 (C,L) Col. 1:15–20 (R)	Luke 10:25–37
Pentecost 9	Amos 8:1–12 (C) Gen. 18:1–10a (L,R)	Col. 1:15–28 (C,L) Col. 1:24–28 (R)	Luke 10:38–42

	READING 1	READING 2	GOSPEL
Pentecost 10	Hos. 1:2–10 (C) Gen. 18:20–32 (L,R)	Col. 2:6–15 (16–19) (C,L) Col. 2:12–14 (R)	Luke 11:1–13
Pentecost 11	Hos. 11:1–11 (C) Eccl. 1:2,12–14; 2:18–23 (L) Eccl. 1:2; 2:21–23 (R)	Col. 3:1–11 (C,L) Col. 3:1–5,9–11 (R)	Luke 12:13–21
Pentecost 12	Isa. 1:1,10–20 (C) Gen. 15:1–6 (L) Wis. 18:6–9 (R)[9]	Heb. 11:1–3,8–16 (C,L) Heb. 11:1–2,8–19 (R)	Luke 12:32–40 (C,L) Luke 12:32–48 (R)
Pentecost 13	Isa. 5:1–7 (C) Jer. 23:23–29 (L) Jer. 38:4–6,8–10 (R)	Heb. 11:29–12:2 (C,L) Heb. 12:1–4 (R)	Luke 12:49–56 (C,L) Luke 12:49–53 (R)
Pentecost 14	Jer. 1:4–10 (C) Isa. 58:9b–14 (L) Isa. 66:18–21 (R)	Heb. 12:18–29 (C,L) Heb. 12:5–7,11–13 (R)	Luke 13:10–17 (C,L) Luke 13:22–30 (R)
Pentecost 15	Jer. 2:4–13 (C) Prov. 25:6–7 (L) Sir. 3:17–18,20, 28–29 (R)[9]	Heb. 13:1–8,15–16 (C,L) Heb. 12:18–19, 22–24a (R)	Luke 14:1,7–14
Pentecost 16	Jer. 18:1–11 (C) Deut. 30:15–20 (L) Wis. 9:13–18b (R)[9]	Philem. 1–21 (C,L) Philem. 9–10,12–17 (R)	Luke 14:25–33 (C,L) Luke 15:1–32; 15:1–10 (R)
Pentecost 17	Jer. 4:11–12,22–28 (C) Ex. 32:7–14 (L) Ex. 32:7–11,13–14 (R)	1 Tim. 1:12–17	Luke 15:1–10 (C,L)
Pentecost 18	Jer. 8:18–9:1 (C) Amos 8:4–7 (L,R)	1 Tim. 2:1–7 (C,L) 1 Tim. 2:1–8 (R)	Luke 16:1–13
Pentecost 19	Jer. 32:1–3a,6–15 (C) Amos 6:1a,4–7 (L,R)	1 Tim. 6:6–19 (C,L) 1 Tim. 6:11–16 (R)	Luke 16:19–31
Pentecost 20	Lam. 1:1–6 (C) Hab. 1:1–4; 2:1–4 (L) Hab.1:2–3; 2:2–4 (R)	2 Tim. 1:1–14 (C,L) 2 Tim. 1:6–8,13–14 (R)	Luke 17:5–10

	READING 1	READING 2	GOSPEL
Pentecost 21	Jer. 29:1,4–7 (C) 2 Kin. 5:1–3,7–15 (L) 2 Kin. 5:14–17 (R)	2 Tim. 2:8–15 (C,L) 2 Tim. 2:8–13 (R)	Luke 17:11–19
Pentecost 22	Jer. 31:27–34 (C) Gen. 32:22–31 (L) Ex. 17:8–13 (R)	2 Tim. 3:14–4:5 (C,L) 2 Tim. 3:14–4:2 (R)	Luke 18:1–8
Pentecost 23	Joel 2:23–32 (C) Jer. 14:7–10,19–22 (L) Sir. 35:12–14,16–18 (R)[9]	2 Tim. 4:6–8,16–18	Luke 18:9–14
All Saints Day (November 1)	Dan. 7:1–3,15–18 (C,L) Rev. 7:2–4,9–14 (R)	Eph. 1:11–23 (C,L) 1 John 3:1–3 (R)	Luke 6:20–31 (C,L) Matt. 5:1–12a (R)
Pentecost 24	Hab. 1:1–4; 2:1–4 (C) Isa. 1:10–18 (L) Wis. 11:22–12:2 (R)[9]	2 Thess. 1:1–4, 11–12 (C,L) 2 Thess. 1:11–2:2 (R)	Luke 19:1–10
Pentecost 25	Hag. 1:15b–2:9 (C) Job 19:23–27a (L) 2 Mac. 7:1–2, 9–14 (R)[9]	2 Thess. 2:1–5, 13–17 (C,L) 2 Thess. 2:16–3:5 (R)	Luke 20:27–38
Pentecost 26	Isa. 65:17–25 (C) Mal. 4:1–2a (L) Mal. 3:19–20a (R)[8]	2 Thess. 3:6–13 (C,L) 2 Thess. 3:7–12 (R)	Luke 21:5–19
Pentecost 27 (Lutheran only)	Isa. 52:1–6	1 Cor. 15:54–58	Luke 19:11–27
Last Pentecost	**Christ the King Sunday**		
	Jer. 23:1–6 (C,L) 2 Sam. 5:1–3 (R)	Col. 1:11–20 (C,L) Col. 1:12–20 (R)	Luke 23:33–43 (C) Luke 23:35–43 (L,R)

LECTIONARY ENDNOTES

* The Lectionary for Sundays and major festivals is arranged in a three-year cycle of readings from Holy Scripture. Year A is often referred to as the Year of Matthew; Year B, the Year of Mark; and Year C, the Year of Luke.

Year A always begins on the First Sunday of Advent in years evenly divided by three (e.g. Year A, November 29, 1998, December 2, 2001, etc.).

1 Isa. 9:1–6, as found in the New American Bible, has as its equivalent Isa 9:2–7 in the New International Version.

2 Isa. 8:23–9:3, as found in the New American Bible, has as its equivalent Isa. 9:1–4 in the New International Version.

3 Isa. 63:16–17,19; 64:2–7, as found in the New American Bible, has as its equivalent Isa. 63:16–17,19–64:1; 64:3–8 in the New International Version.

4 Isa. 9:1–6, as found in the New American Bible, has as its equivalent Isa 9:2–7 in the New International Version.

5 Hos. 2:16–17,21–22, as found in the New American Bible, has as its equivalent Hos. 2:14–15,19–20 in the New International Version.

6 Mic. 5:1–4, as found in the New American Bible, has as its equivalent Mic. 5:2–5 in the New International Version.

7 Isa. 9:1–6, as found in the New American Bible, has as its equivalent Isa. 9:2–7 in the New International Version.

8 Mal. 3:19–20, as found in the New American Bible, has as its equivalent Mal. 4:1–2 in the New International Version.

9 The Deuterocanon and Apocrypha consists of books not included in the Hebrew canon of Holy Scripture, but present in the Greek version of the Old Testament, known as the Septuagint. The Deuterocanonical and Apocryphal books are not included in this Bible. The abbreviations for these books included in this lectionary are: Bar: Baruch; Mac: Maccabees; Sir: Sirach; Wis: Wisdom.

200 KEY STORIES

FROM

THE BIBLE

OLD TESTAMENT

Beginnings of God's Creation	The Beginning	Gen. 1:1–2:3
	Adam and Eve	Gen. 2:4–25
	The Fall	Gen. 3:1–24
	Cain and Abel	Gen. 4:1–26
	The Flood	Gen. 6:5–7:12
	Noah Waits	Gen. 8:1–22
	The Tower of Babel	Gen. 11:1–9
Founders of Israel	The Call of Abram	Gen. 11:27–12:9
	Abram and Lot Separate	Gen. 13:1–18
	Hagar and Ishmael	Gen. 16:1–16
	The Three Visitors	Gen. 18:1–15
	Abraham Pleads for Sodom	Gen. 18:16–33
	Isaac's Birth; Ishmael Sent Away	Gen. 21:1–21
	Abraham Tested	Gen. 22:1–19
	Isaac and Rebekah	Gen. 24:1–31,50–67
	Jacob and Esau	Gen. 25:19–34
	Jacob Gets Isaac's Blessing	Gen. 27:1–40
	Jacob Marries Leah and Rachel	Gen. 29:1–30
	Jacob's Children	Gen. 29:31–30:24
	Jacob Flees From Laban	Gen. 31:1–21
	Laban Pursues Jacob	Gen. 31:22–55
	Jacob Prepares to Meet Esau	Gen. 32:1–21
	Jacob Wrestles With God	Gen. 32:22–32
	Jacob Meets Esau	Gen. 33:1–20
	Jacob Returns to Bethel	Gen. 35:1–15
	Joseph's Dreams	Gen. 37:1–11
	Joseph Sold by His Brothers	Gen. 37:12–36
Israel's Slavery in Egypt	Joseph and Potiphar's Wife	Gen. 39:1–23
	Joseph Interprets Pharaoh's Dreams	Gen. 41:1–40
	Joseph Makes Himself Known	Gen. 45:1–28
	The Beginning of Moses' Life	Ex. 1:22–2:25
	Moses and the Burning Bush	Ex. 3:1–22
	Signs for Moses	Ex. 4:1–17
	Bricks Without Straw	Ex. 5:1–21
	God Promises Deliverance	Ex. 5:22–6:12
	The Plagues Begin	Ex. 6:28–7:24

	Story	Reference
Journey to the Promised Land	The Passover	Ex. 12:1–30
	Crossing the Sea	Ex. 13:17–14:31
	Manna From the Lord	Ex. 16:1–35
	God Uses Moses' Hands	Ex. 17:1–16
	Jethro Visits Moses	Ex. 18:1–27
	Receiving the Ten Commandments	Ex. 19:10–20:21
	The Golden Calf	Ex. 32:1–35
	The Cloud of Guidance	Num. 9:15–23; 10:11–13,29–36
	Quail From the Lord	Num. 11:4–34
	Miriam and Aaron Oppose Moses	Num. 12:1–16
	Spying on the Promised Land	Num. 13:17–14:10,26–45
	Balak, Balaam and His Donkey	Num. 22:1–35
	Joshua to Succeed Moses	Num. 27:12–23
Life in the Promised Land	Rahab and the Spies	Josh. 2:1–24
	Crossing the Jordan	Josh. 3:6–4:24
	The Fall of Jericho	Josh. 5:13–6:21
	Joshua's Farewell Address	Josh. 23:1–16
	Joshua Renews the Covenant	Josh. 24:1–27
	Deborah Leads Israel	Judg. 4:1–24
	Gideon's Fear, Faith and Fleece	Judg. 6:1–40
	Gideon Defeats the Midianites	Judg. 7:1–25
	Samson's Birth	Judg. 13:1–25
	Samson's Marriage	Judg. 14:1–20
	Samson and Delilah	Judg. 16:1–22
	Samson's Death	Judg. 16:23–31
	Naomi and Ruth	Ruth 1:1–22
	Ruth Meets Boaz	Ruth 2:1–23
	Ruth and Boaz at the Threshing Floor	Ruth 3:1–18
	Boaz Marries Ruth	Ruth 4:1–22
Israel's Great Kings	The Birth and Dedication of Samuel	1 Sam. 1:1–28
	Eli's Wicked Sons	1 Sam. 2:12–26
	The Lord Calls Samuel	1 Sam. 3:1–21
	Israel Asks for a King	1 Sam. 8:1–22
	Samuel Anoints Saul	1 Sam. 9:1–10:8
	Samuel Rebukes Saul	1 Sam. 13:1–15
	Samuel Anoints David	1 Sam. 16:1–13
	David in Saul's Service	1 Sam. 16:14–23
	David and Goliath	1 Sam. 17:4–51
	Saul's Jealousy of David	1 Sam. 18:1–30
	David and Jonathan	1 Sam. 20:1–42
	David Spares Saul's Life	1 Sam. 24:1–22

NEW TESTAMENT

Parable of the Lost Sheep . . . . Luke 15:3–7
Parable of the Lost (Prodigal) Son . . . . Luke 15:11–32
Parable of the Shrewd Manager . . . . Luke 16:1–15
Parable of the Rich Man and Lazarus . . . . Luke 16:19–31
Parable of the Persistent Widow . . . . Luke 18:1–8
Parable of the Pharisee and Tax Collector . . . . Luke 18:9–14
Parable of the Ten Minas . . . . Luke 19:11–27
Parable of the Vineyard Owner . . . . Luke 20:9–18
Parable of the Fig Tree . . . . Luke 21:29–33

Jesus' Last Week and Resurrection Appearances

The Triumphal Entry . . . . Luke 19:28–44
Jesus Clears the Temple . . . . Mark 11:12–19
Jesus Washes the Disciples' Feet . . . . John 13:1–17
The Last Supper . . . . Luke 22:7–34
Jesus in Gethsemane . . . . Mark 14:32–42
Jesus Is Arrested . . . . Matt. 26:47–56
Peter Disowns Jesus . . . . Luke 22:54–62
Jesus Before Pilate . . . . Mark 15:1–15
The Crucifixion . . . . John 19:16–27
Jesus' Death . . . . Luke 23:44–49
Jesus' Resurrection and Great Commission . . . . Matt. 28:1–20
Jesus Appears to Mary Magdalene . . . . John 20:1–18
On the Road to Emmaus . . . . Luke 24:13–35
Jesus Appears to Thomas . . . . John 20:24–31
Jesus Reinstates Peter . . . . John 21:1–25

The Christian Church Begins

Jesus Taken Up Into Heaven . . . . Acts 1:1–11
The Holy Spirit Comes at Pentecost . . . . Acts 2:1–41
The Fellowship of the Believers . . . . Acts 2:42–47
Peter and John Before the Sanhedrin . . . . Acts 4:1–31
The Believers Share Their Possessions . . . . Acts 4:32–37
Ananias and Sapphira . . . . Acts 5:1–11
Philip and the Ethiopian . . . . Acts 8:26–40
Saul's Conversion . . . . Acts 9:1–19
Saul in Damascus and Jerusalem . . . . Acts 9:20–31
Peter's Vision . . . . Acts 10:1–23
Peter's Miraculous Escape From Prison . . . . Acts 12:1–19

Paul's Missionary Journeys

Lydia's Conversion . . . . Acts 16:11–15
Paul and Silas in Prison . . . . Acts 16:16–40
Paul's Vision in Corinth . . . . Acts 18:5–17
Priscilla, Aquila and Apollos . . . . Acts 18:1–4,18–28
Paul Before Agrippa . . . . Acts 25:23–26:32

INDEX

TO THE

LESSON SUBJECTS

A

F

G

H

M

N

Q

R

S

T

X, Y, Z

CHARTS

AND

MAPS

STRUCTURE OF THE OLD TESTAMENT

39 Books in the Old Testament + **27** Books in the New Testament = **66** Books in the Bible

Historical Books		Poetical Books	Prophetical Books	
THE PENTATEUCH:	*HISTORICAL:*		*THE MAJOR PROPHETS:*	*THE MINOR PROPHETS:*
Genesis	Joshua	Job	Isaiah	Hosea
Exodus	Judges	Psalms	Jeremiah	Joel
Leviticus	Ruth	Proverbs	Lamentations	Amos
Numbers	1 Samuel	Ecclesiastes	Ezekiel	Obadiah
Deuteronomy	2 Samuel	Song of Songs	Daniel	Jonah
	1 Kings			Micah
	2 Kings			Nahum
	1 Chronicles			Habakkuk
	2 Chronicles			Zephaniah
	Ezra			Haggai
	Nehemiah			Zechariah
	Esther			Malachi

TYPES OF PSALMS

Prayers of the Individual Ps. 3; 7–8

Praise From the Individual for God's Saving Help Ps. 30; 34

Prayers of the Community Ps. 12; 44; 79

Praise From the Community for God's Saving Help Ps. 66; 75

Confessions of Confidence in the Lord Ps. 11; 16; 52

Hymns in Praise of God's Majesty and Virtues Ps. 8; 19; 29; 65

Hymns Celebrating God's Universal Reign Ps. 47; 93–99

Songs of Zion, the City of God Ps. 46; 48; 76; 84; 122; 126; 129; 137

Royal Psalms: by, for or Concerning the King, the Lord's Anointed Ps. 2; 18; 20; 45; 72; 89; 110

Pilgrimage Songs Ps. 120–134

Liturgical Songs Ps. 15; 24; 68

Didactic (Instructional) Songs Ps. 1; 34; 37; 73; 112; 119; 128; 133

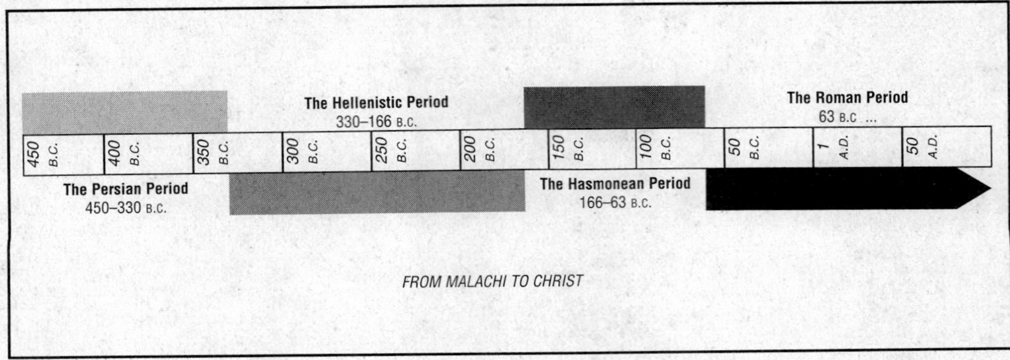

FROM MALACHI TO CHRIST

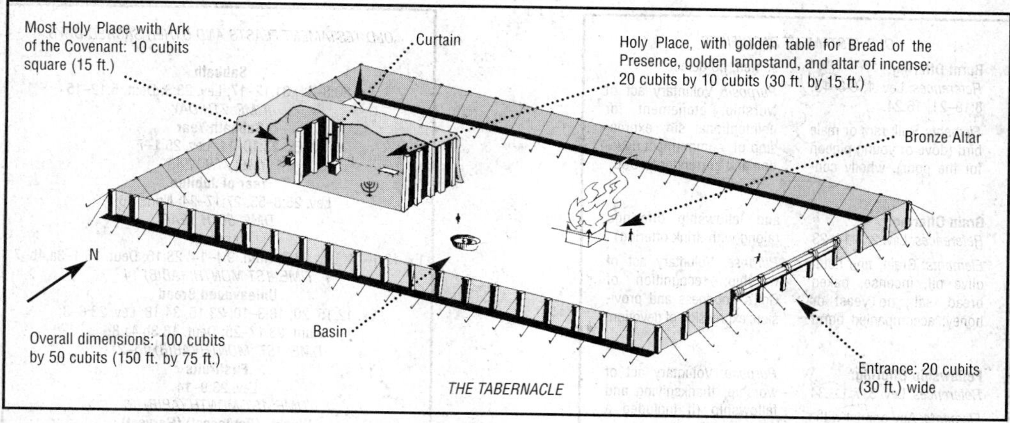

THE TABERNACLE

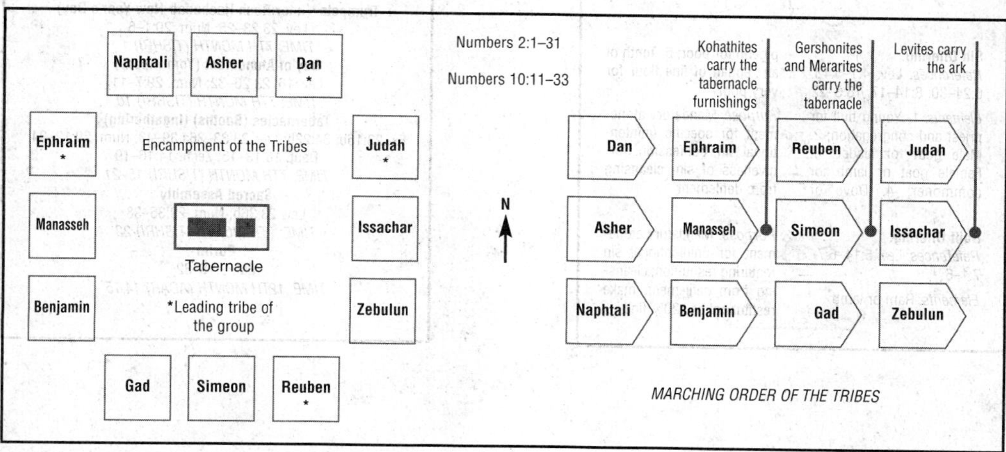

MARCHING ORDER OF THE TRIBES

SOLOMON'S TEMPLE

The temple of Solomon functioned as God's royal palace and Israel's national center of worship. The Lord said to Solomon, "I have consecrated this temple ... by putting my Name there forever. My eyes and my heart will always be there" (1 Kin. 9:3). The sanctuary taught the absolute sovereignty of the Lord over the whole creation and his special headship over Israel.

Most Holy Place: 20 cubits long, 20 cubits wide, and 20 cubits high. This room contained the Ark of the Covenant (1 Kin. 6:19–20).

Holy Place: 40 cubits long, 20 cubits wide, and 30 cubits high. This room contained golden tables for bread of the Presence, golden lampstands, and the altar of incense (1 Kin. 6:2,17).

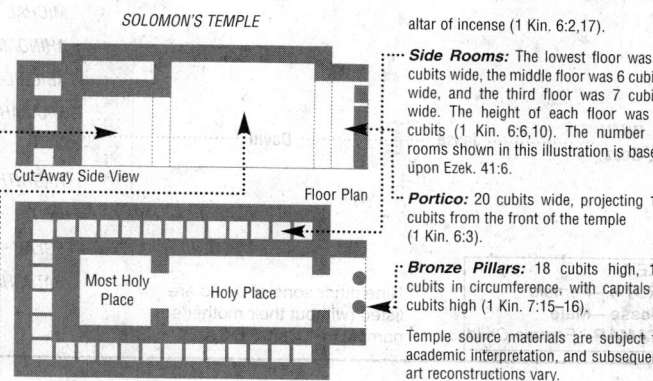

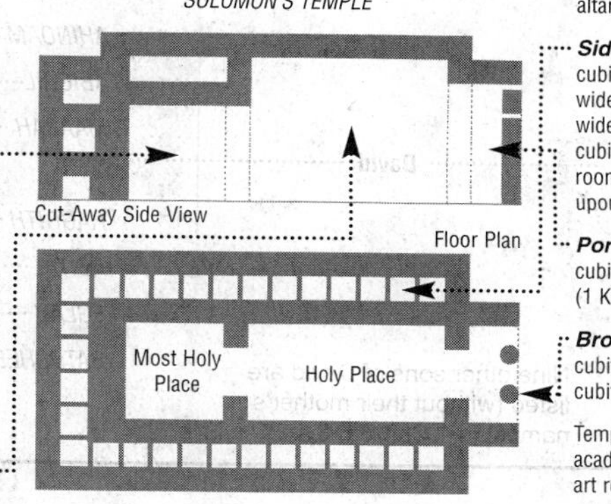

Side Rooms: The lowest floor was 5 cubits wide, the middle floor was 6 cubits wide, and the third floor was 7 cubits wide. The height of each floor was 5 cubits (1 Kin. 6:6,10). The number of rooms shown in this illustration is based upon Ezek. 41:6.

Portico: 20 cubits wide, projecting 10 cubits from the front of the temple (1 Kin. 6:3).

Bronze Pillars: 18 cubits high, 12 cubits in circumference, with capitals 5 cubits high (1 Kin. 7:15–16).

Temple source materials are subject to academic interpretation, and subsequent art reconstructions vary.

OLD TESTAMENT SACRIFICES

Burnt Offering:
References: Lev. 1; 6:8–13; 8:18–21; 16:24.
Elements: Bull, ram or male bird (dove or young pigeon for the poor); wholly consumed; no defect
Purpose: Voluntary act of worship; atonement for unintentional sin; expression of commitment, devotion and surrender to God.

Grain Offering:
References: Lev. 2; 6:14–23
Elements: Grain, fine flour, olive oil, incense, baked bread, salt; no yeast or honey; accompanied burnt and fellowship offerings (along with drink offering)
Purpose: Voluntary act of worship; recognition of God's goodness and provision; expression of devotion.

Fellowship Offering:
References: Lev. 3; 7:11–34
Elements: Any animal without defect from herd or flock; variety of breads
Purpose: Voluntary act of worship; thanksgiving and fellowship (it included a communal meal)

Sin Offering:
References: Lev. 4:1–5:13; 6:24–30; 8:14–17; 16:3–22
Elements: 1. Young bull for priest and congregation; 2. Male goat for leader; 3. Female goat or lamb for commoner; 4. Dove or pigeon for poor; 5. Tenth of an ephah of fine flour for very poor
Purpose: Mandatory atonement for specific unintentional sin; confession, forgiveness of sin; cleansing from defilement

Guilt Offering:
References: Lev. 5:14–6:7; 7:1–6
Elements: Ram or lamb
Purpose: Mandatory atonement for unintentional sin requiring restitution; cleansing from defilement; make restitution; pay 20% fine

OLD TESTAMENT FEASTS AND OTHER SACRED DAYS

Sabbath
Ex. 20:8–11; 31:12–17; Lev. 23:3; Deut. 5:12–15
TIME: 7TH DAY

Sabbath Year
Ex. 23:10–11; Lev. 25:1–7
TIME: 7TH YEAR

Year of Jubilee
Lev. 25:8–55; 27:17–24; Num. 36:4
TIME: 50TH YEAR

Passover
Ex. 12:1–14; Lev. 23:5; Num. 9:1–14: 28:16; Deut. 16:1–3a,4b–7
TIME: 1ST MONTH; (ABIB) 14

Unleavened Bread
Ex. 12:15–20; 13:3–10; 23:15; 34:18; Lev. 23:6–8; Num. 28:17–25; Deut. 16:3b,4a,8
TIME: 1ST MONTH (ABIB) 15–21

Firstfruits
Lev. 23:9–14
TIME: 1ST MONTH (ABIB) 16

Weeks (Pentecost) (Harvest)
Ex. 23:16a; 34:22a; Lev. 23:15–21; Num. 28:26–31; Deut. 16:9–12
TIME: 3RD MONTH (SIVAN) 6

Trumpets (later Rosh Hashanah-New Year's Day)
Lev. 23:23–25; Num. 29:1–6
TIME: 7TH MONTH (TISHRI) 1

Day of Atonement (Yom Kippur)
Lev. 16; 23:26–32; Num. 29:7–11
TIME: 7TH MONTH (TISHRI) 10

Tabernacles (Booths) (Ingathering)
Ex. 23:16b; 34:22b; Lev. 23:33–36a,39–43; Num. 29:12–34; Deut. 16:13–15; Zech. 14:16–19
TIME: 7TH MONTH (TISHRI) 15–21

Sacred Assembly
Lev. 23:36b; Num. 29:35–38
TIME: 7TH MONTH (TISHRI) 22

Purim
Est. 9:18–32
TIME: 12TH MONTH (ADAR) 14,15

DAVID'S FAMILY TREE

RUTH
Boaz .... **Jesse** .... **David** ....

DAVID'S WIVES:	**David's Children:**
MICHAL	
AHINOAM	**Amnon**
ABIGAIL	**Kileab**
MAACAH	**Absalom** ***TAMAR***
HAGGITH	**Adonijah**
ABITAL	**Shephatiah**
EGLAH	**Ithream**
BATHSHEBA	**Solomon (plus three other sons)**

KEY:
RUTH—Female
Jesse—Male
***TAMAR**—Female Child*

Nine other sons of David are listed (without their mother's names) in 1 Chr. 3:6-8.

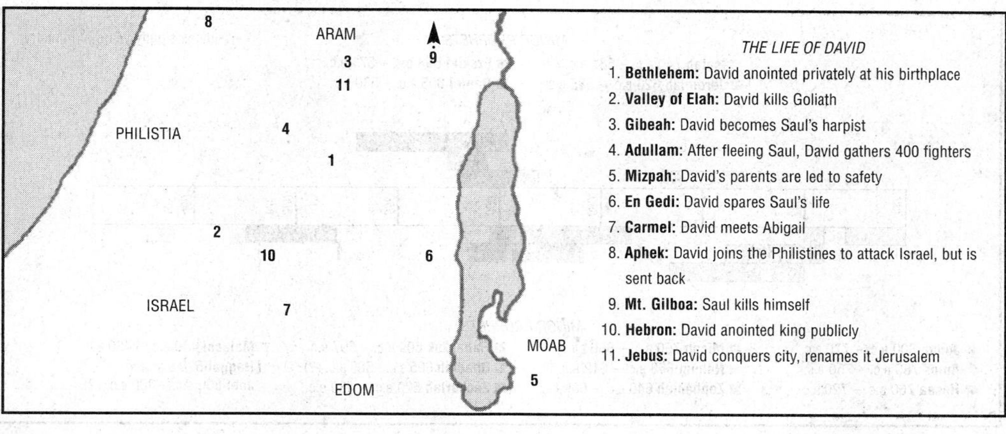
8
ARAM
9
3
11
PHILISTIA
4
1
2
10
6
ISRAEL
7
MOAB
5
EDOM
THE LIFE OF DAVID
1. Bethlehem: David anointed privately at his birthplace
2. Valley of Elah: David kills Goliath
3. Gibeah: David becomes Saul's harpist
4. Adullam: After fleeing Saul, David gathers 400 fighters
5. Mizpah: David's parents are led to safety
6. En Gedi: David spares Saul's life
7. Carmel: David meets Abigail
8. Aphek: David joins the Philistines to attack Israel, but is sent back
9. Mt. Gilboa: Saul kills himself
10. Hebron: David anointed king publicly
11. Jebus: David conquers city, renames it Jerusalem

CHRONOLOGY OF EZRA AND NEHEMIAH

YEAR	EVENT	REFERENCE
539 B.C.	Capture of Babylon	**Dan. 5:30**
538–7	Cyrus' 1st Year	**Ezra 1:1–4**
537 (?)	Return under Sheshbazzar	**Ezra 1:11**
536	Work on temple begun	**Ezra 3:8**
536–30	Opposition during Cyrus' reign	**Ezra 4:1–5**
530–20	Work on temple ceased	**Ezra 4:24**
520	Work on temple renewed under Darius	**Ezra 5:2; Hag. 1:14**
516	Temple completed	**Ezra 6:15**
458	Ezra departs from Babylon	**Ezra 7:6**
	Ezra arrives in Jerusalem	**Ezra 7:8–9**
	People assemble	**Ezra 10:9**
	Committee begins investigation	**Ezra 10:16**
457	Committee ends investigation	**Ezra 10:17**
445–4	20th year of Artaxerxes I	**Neh. 1:1**
445	Nehemiah approaches king	**Neh. 2:1**
	Nehemiah arrives in Jerusalem	**Neh. 2:11**
	Completion of wall	**Neh. 6:15**
	Public Assembly	**Neh. 7:73–8:1**
	Feast of Tabernacles	**Neh. 8:14**
	Fast	**Neh. 9:1**
	32nd year of Artaxerxes Nehemiah's recall and return	**Neh. 5:14; 13:6**

OLD TESTAMENT PROPHECIES FULFILLED

OLD TESTAMENT		NEW TESTAMENT
Isaiah 7:14	Immanuel's virgin birth	**Matthew 1:23**
Micah 5:2	Messiah will come from Bethlehem in Judah	**John 7:42**
Malachi 3:1	Messenger (John the Baptist) who will prepare the way for the Messiah	**Matthew 11:10**
Zechariah 9:9	The Messiah's Triumphal Entry into Jerusalem	**Matthew 21:4–5**
Zechariah 13:7	Christ will be abandoned by his disciples	**Mark 14:27,49–50**
Isaiah 53:4–12	The Lord lays upon Christ "the iniquity of us all"	**1 Peter 2:21–25**
Zechariah 12:10	Israel "will look on the one they have pierced" *(Jesus' side pierced by a soldier's spear at the crucifixion)*	**John 19:37**
Jeremiah 31:31–34	Christ will usher in the "new covenant"	**Hebrews 8:7–13**
Joel 2:28–32	The outpouring of God's Spirit at the Day of Pentecost	**Acts 2:16–21**
Hosea 2:23	Gentiles will be included in the people of God	**Romans 9:25**
Daniel 7:14,27	The Messiah's kingdom will last forever	**Revelation 11:15**

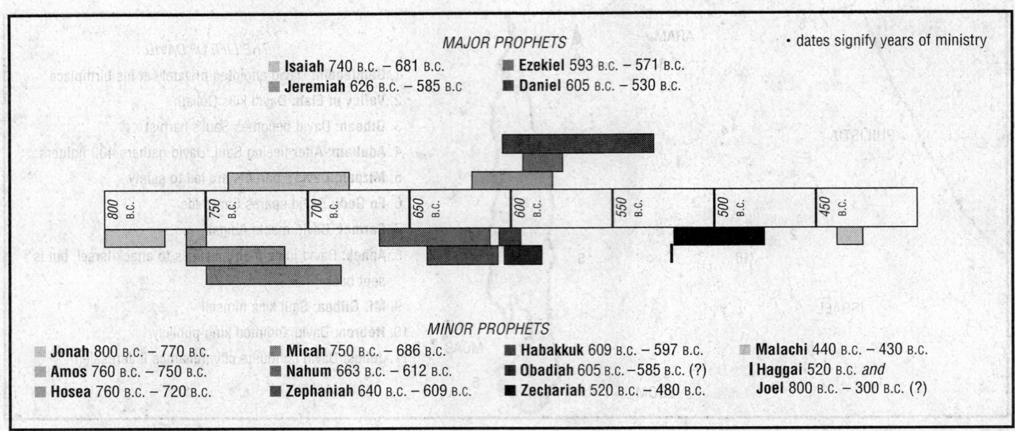
MAJOR PROPHETS
• dates signify years of ministry
Isaiah 740 B.C. – 681 B.C.
Jeremiah 626 B.C. – 585 B.C
Ezekiel 593 B.C. – 571 B.C.
Daniel 605 B.C. – 530 B.C.
800 B.C.
750 B.C.
700 B.C.
650 B.C.
600 B.C.
550 B.C.
500 B.C.
450 B.C.
MINOR PROPHETS
Jonah 800 B.C. – 770 B.C.
Amos 760 B.C. – 750 B.C.
Hosea 760 B.C. – 720 B.C.
Micah 750 B.C. – 686 B.C.
Nahum 663 B.C. – 612 B.C.
Zephaniah 640 B.C. – 609 B.C.
Habakkuk 609 B.C. – 597 B.C.
Obadiah 605 B.C. –585 B.C. (?)
Zechariah 520 B.C. – 480 B.C.
Malachi 440 B.C. – 430 B.C.
Haggai 520 B.C. and
Joel 800 B.C. – 300 B.C. (?)

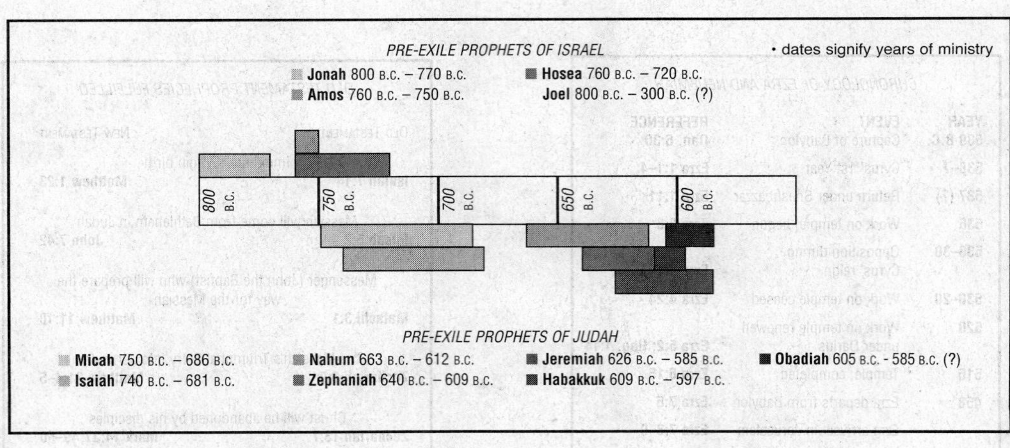
PRE-EXILE PROPHETS OF ISRAEL
• dates signify years of ministry
Jonah 800 B.C. – 770 B.C.
Amos 760 B.C. – 750 B.C.
Hosea 760 B.C. – 720 B.C.
Joel 800 B.C. – 300 B.C. (?)
800 B.C.
750 B.C.
700 B.C.
650 B.C.
600 B.C.
PRE-EXILE PROPHETS OF JUDAH
Micah 750 B.C. – 686 B.C.
Isaiah 740 B.C. – 681 B.C.
Nahum 663 B.C. – 612 B.C.
Zephaniah 640 B.C. – 609 B.C.
Jeremiah 626 B.C. – 585 B.C.
Habakkuk 609 B.C. – 597 B.C.
Obadiah 605 B.C. - 585 B.C. (?)

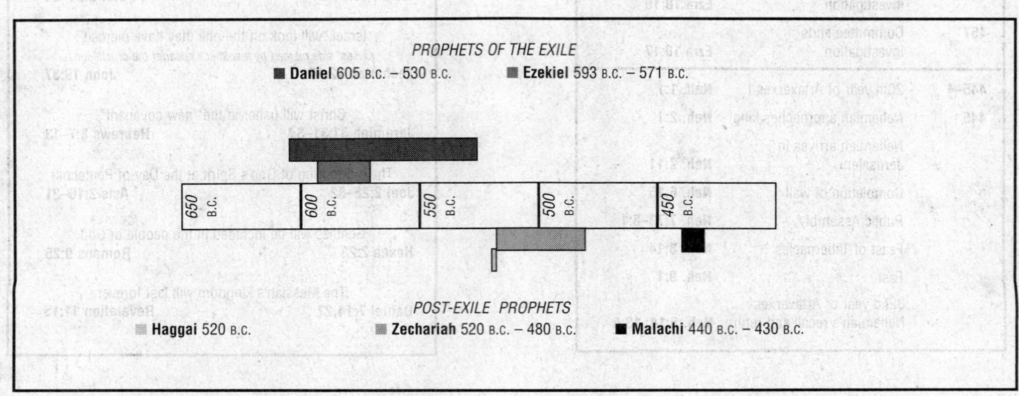
PROPHETS OF THE EXILE
Daniel 605 B.C. – 530 B.C.
Ezekiel 593 B.C. – 571 B.C.
650 B.C.
600 B.C.
550 B.C.
500 B.C.
450 B.C.
POST-EXILE PROPHETS
Haggai 520 B.C.
Zechariah 520 B.C. – 480 B.C.
Malachi 440 B.C. – 430 B.C.

STRUCTURE OF THE NEW TESTAMENT

39 Books in the Old Testament + **27** Books in the New Testament = **66** Books in the Bible

Historical Books	**Paul's Epistles**	**General Letters**	**Prophetic Books**
Matthew Mark Luke John Acts	Romans 1 Corinthians 2 Corinthians Galatians Ephesians Philippians Colossians 1 Thessalonians 2 Thessalonians 1 Timothy 2 Timothy Titus Philemon	Hebrews James 1 Peter 2 Peter 1 John 2 John 3 John Jude	Revelation

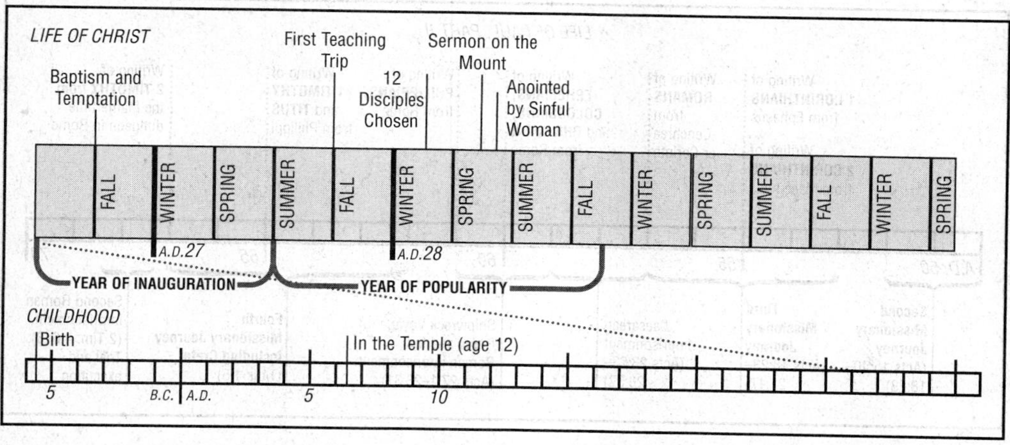

THE LETTERS OF PAUL

Book	Time of Writing (A.D.)	Place of Writing	Theme
Galatians	48–50 or 51–53	Syrian Antioch or Corinth	Justification by faith alone (Gal.)
1 Thessalonians	51	Corinth	Christian living in an immoral world (1 Thess.)
2 Thessalonians	51	Corinth	Life in the light of the coming Christ (2 Thess.)
1 Corinthians	53–55	Ephesus	Glorifying God through Christian living (1 Cor.)
2 Corinthians	55–56	Macedonia	Finding strength in God's true power (2 Cor.)
Romans	56–57	Corinth	Being right with God through faith in Christ (Rom.)
Philemon	60	Rome	Mercy and unlimited forgiveness (Philem.)
Colossians	60	Rome	Fullness and freedom in Christ (Col.)
Ephesians	60	Rome	God's new social order (Eph.)
Philippians	61–63	Rome	Joy in Christ, despite hardships (Phil.)
Titus	63–65	Macedonia	Devotion to duty and doing good (Titus)
1 Timothy	63–65	Macedonia	Faithful leadership through Christ (1 Tim.)
2 Timothy	67–68	Rome	Exhortation to carry on the ministry (2 Tim.)

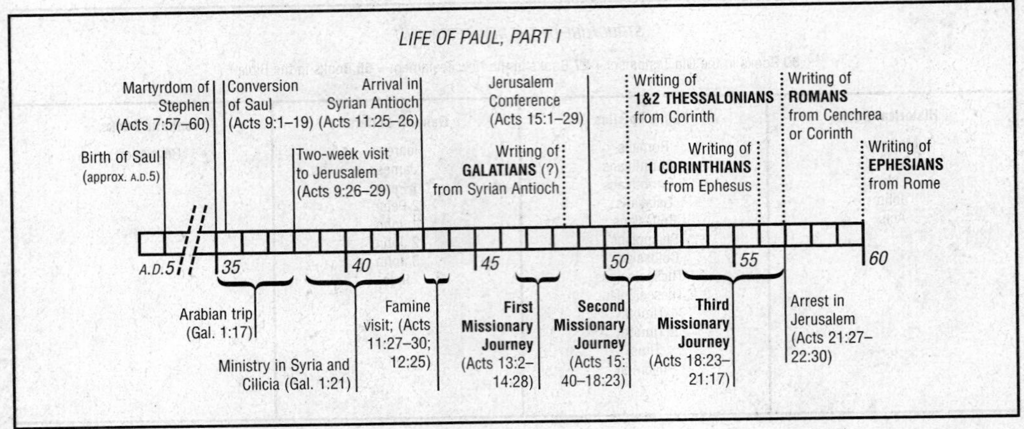
LIFE OF PAUL, PART I
Martyrdom of Stephen (Acts 7:57–60)
Conversion of Saul (Acts 9:1–19)
Arrival in Syrian Antioch (Acts 11:25–26)
Jerusalem Conference (Acts 15:1–29)
Writing of 1&2 THESSALONIANS from Corinth
Writing of ROMANS from Cenchrea or Corinth
Birth of Saul (approx. A.D.5)
Two-week visit to Jerusalem (Acts 9:26–29)
Writing of GALATIANS (?) from Syrian Antioch
Writing of 1 CORINTHIANS from Ephesus
Writing of EPHESIANS from Rome
A.D.5
35
40
45
50
55
60
Arabian trip (Gal. 1:17)
Ministry in Syria and Cilicia (Gal. 1:21)
Famine visit; (Acts 11:27–30; 12:25)
First Missionary Journey (Acts 13:2–14:28)
Second Missionary Journey (Acts 15:40–18:23)
Third Missionary Journey (Acts 18:23–21:17)
Arrest in Jerusalem (Acts 21:27–22:30)

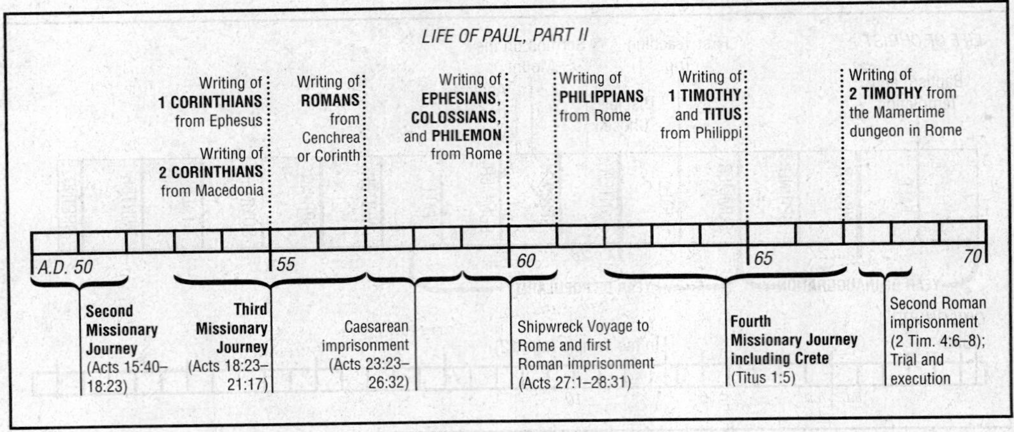
LIFE OF PAUL, PART II
Writing of 1 CORINTHIANS from Ephesus
Writing of 2 CORINTHIANS from Macedonia
Writing of ROMANS from Cenchrea or Corinth
Writing of EPHESIANS, COLOSSIANS, and PHILEMON from Rome
Writing of PHILIPPIANS from Rome
Writing of 1 TIMOTHY and TITUS from Philippi
Writing of 2 TIMOTHY from the Mamertime dungeon in Rome
A.D. 50
55
60
65
70
Second Missionary Journey (Acts 15:40–18:23)
Third Missionary Journey (Acts 18:23–21:17)
Caesarean imprisonment (Acts 23:23–26:32)
Shipwreck Voyage to Rome and first Roman imprisonment (Acts 27:1–28:31)
Fourth Missionary Journey including Crete (Titus 1:5)
Second Roman imprisonment (2 Tim. 4:6–8); Trial and execution

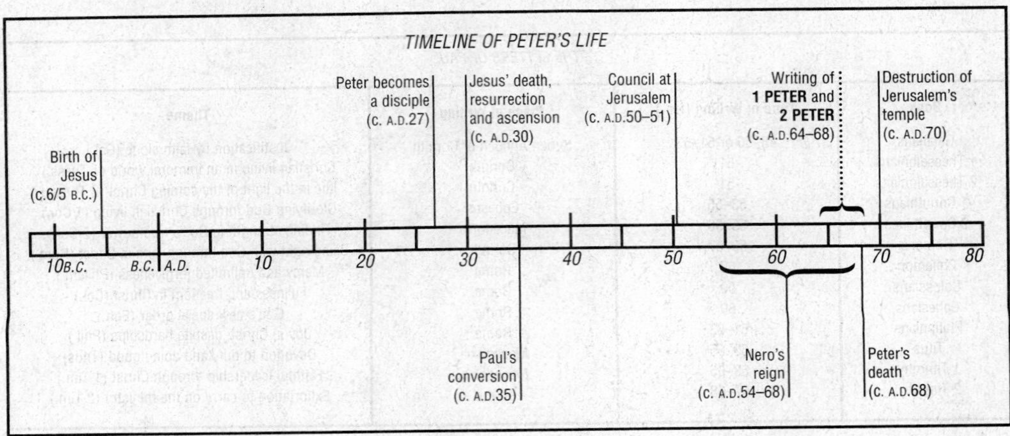
TIMELINE OF PETER'S LIFE
Birth of Jesus (c.6/5 B.C.)
Peter becomes a disciple (c. A.D.27)
Jesus' death, resurrection and ascension (c. A.D.30)
Council at Jerusalem (c. A.D.50–51)
Writing of 1 PETER and 2 PETER (c. A.D.64–68)
Destruction of Jerusalem's temple (c. A.D.70)
10B.C.
B.C.
A.D.
10
20
30
40
50
60
70
80
Paul's conversion (c. A.D.35)
Nero's reign (c. A.D.54–68)
Peter's death (c. A.D.68)

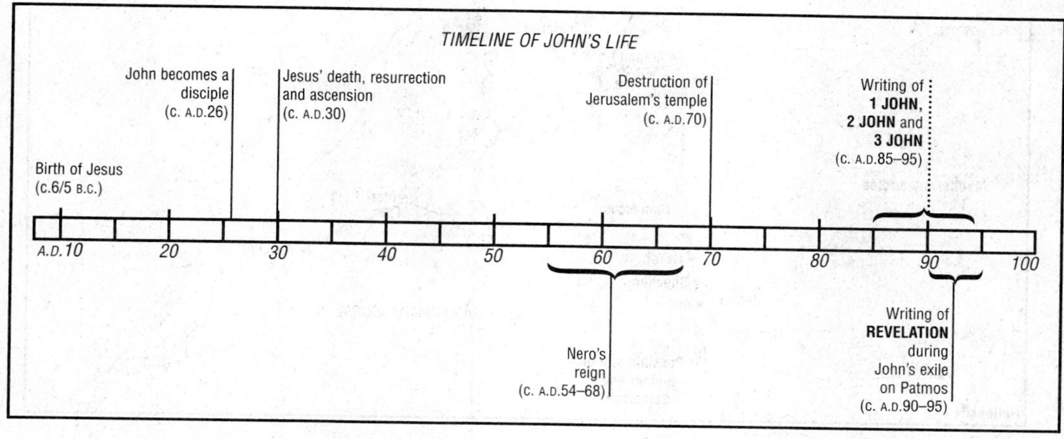

QUALIFICATIONS FOR ELDERS AND DEACONS

Self-controlled	**ELDER**	1 Tim. 3:2; Titus 1:8
Hospitable	**ELDER**	1 Tim. 3:2; Titus 1:8
Able to teach	**ELDER**	1 Tim. 3:2; 5:17; Titus1:9
Not violent but gentle	**ELDER**	1 Tim. 3:3; Titus 1:7
Not quarrelsome	**ELDER**	1 Tim. 3:3
Not a lover of money	**ELDER**	1 Tim. 3:3
Not a recent convert	**ELDER**	1 Tim. 3:6
Has a good reputation with outsiders	**ELDER**	1 Tim. 3:7
Not overbearing	**ELDER**	Titus 1:7
Not quick-tempered	**ELDER**	Titus 1:7
Loves what is good	**ELDER**	Titus 1:8
Upright, holy	**ELDER**	Titus 1:8
Disciplined	**ELDER**	Titus 1:8
Above reproach (blameless)	**ELDER** ***DEACON***	1 Tim. 3:2; Titus 1:6 1 Tim. 3:9
Husband of one wife	**ELDER** ***DEACON***	1 Tim. 3:2; Titus 1:6 1 Tim. 3:12
Temperate	**ELDER** ***DEACON***	1 Tim. 3:2; Titus 1:7 1 Tim. 3:8
Respectable	**ELDER** ***DEACON***	1 Tim. 3:2 1 Tim. 3:8
Not given to drunkenness	**ELDER** ***DEACON***	1 Tim. 3:3; Titus 1:7 1 Tim. 3:8
Manages his own family well	**ELDER** ***DEACON***	1 Tim. 3:4 1 Tim. 3:12
Sees that his children obey him	**ELDER** ***DEACON***	1 Tim. 3:4-5; Titus 1:6 1 Tim. 3:12
Does not pursue dishonest gain	**ELDER** ***DEACON***	Titus 1:7 1 Tim. 3:8
Holds to the Truth	**ELDER** ***DEACON***	Titus 1:9 1 Tim. 3:9
Sincere	***DEACON***	1 Tim. 3:8
Tested	***DEACON***	1 Tim. 3:10

THE PROMINENCE OF JAMES IN THE EARLY CHURCH

James was probably the oldest of Christ's several brothers and sisters since he heads the list in Matthew13:55. At first he did not believe in Jesus and even challenged him and misunderstood his mission (John 7:2–5). Later James became a committed disciple. Before his martyrdom c. A.D. 62, James was very prominent in the church:

1. James was one of the select individuals Christ appeared to after his resurrection (1 Cor. 15:7).
2. Paul called him a "pillar" of the church (Gal. 2:9).
3. Paul, on his first post-conversion visit to Jerusalem, saw James (Gal. 1:19).
4. Paul did the same on his last visit (Acts 21:18).
5. When Peter was rescued from prison, he told his friends to tell James (Acts 12:17).
6. James was a leader in the important council of Jerusalem (Acts 15:13).
7. Jude could identify himself simply as a "brother of James" (Jude 1:1), so well-known was James.

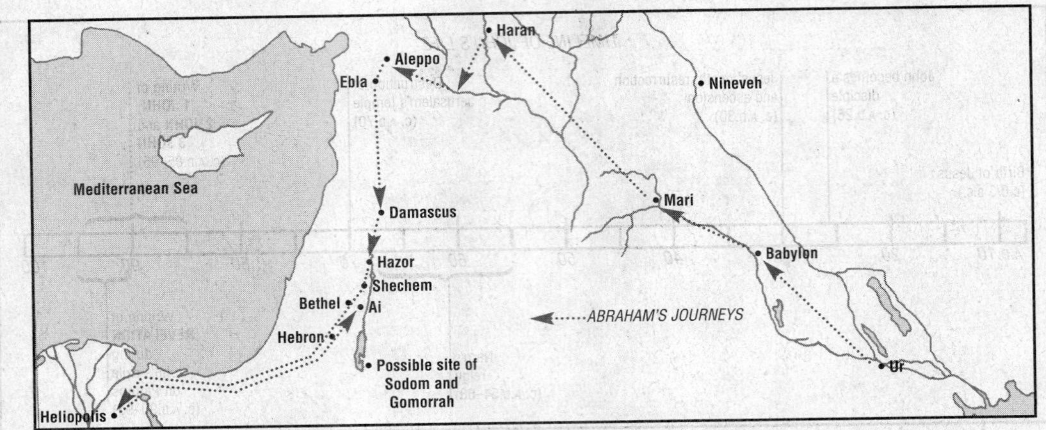

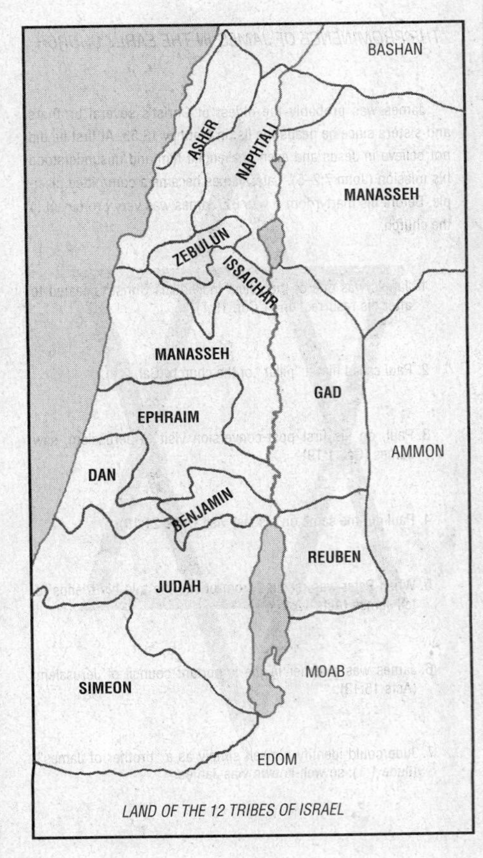

LAND OF THE 12 TRIBES OF ISRAEL

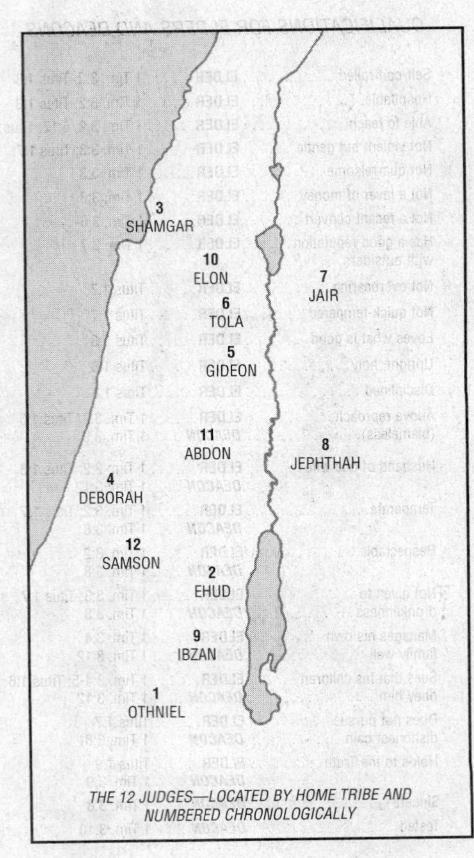

THE 12 JUDGES—LOCATED BY HOME TRIBE AND NUMBERED CHRONOLOGICALLY

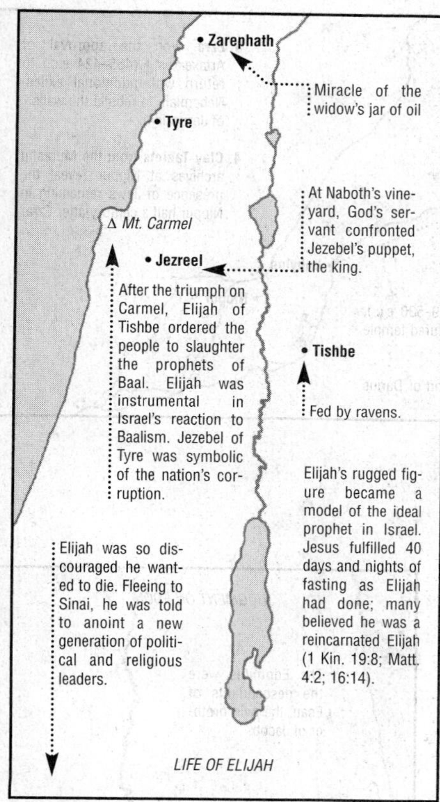

Zarephath
Miracle of the widow's jar of oil
Tyre
At Naboth's vineyard, God's servant confronted Jezebel's puppet, the king.
Mt. Carmel
Jezreel
After the triumph on Carmel, Elijah of Tishbe ordered the people to slaughter the prophets of Baal. Elijah was instrumental in Israel's reaction to Baalism. Jezebel of Tyre was symbolic of the nation's corruption.
Tishbe
Fed by ravens.
Elijah's rugged figure became a model of the ideal prophet in Israel. Jesus fulfilled 40 days and nights of fasting as Elijah had done; many believed he was a reincarnated Elijah (1 Kin. 19:8; Matt. 4:2; 16:14).
Elijah was so discouraged he wanted to die. Fleeing to Sinai, he was told to anoint a new generation of political and religious leaders.

LIFE OF ELIJAH

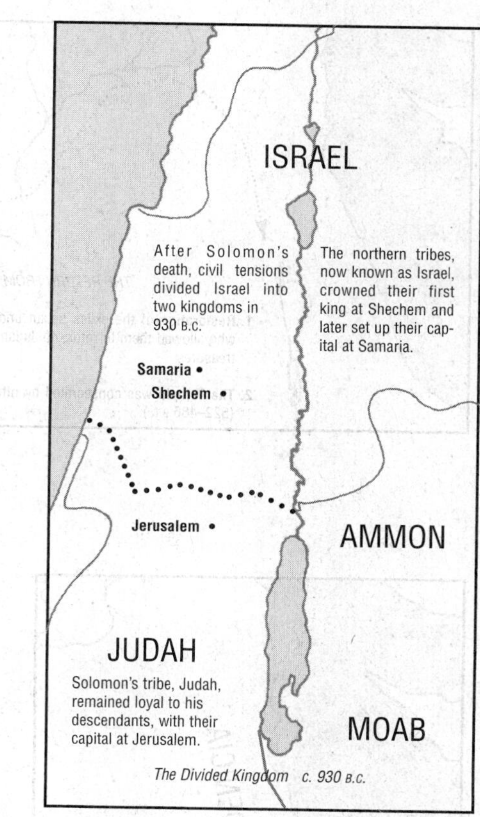

The Divided Kingdom c. 930 B.C.

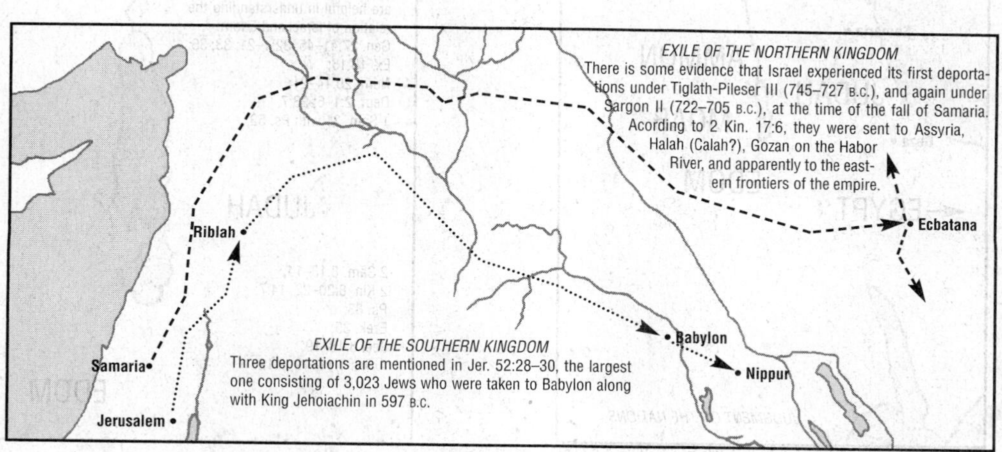

EXILE OF THE NORTHERN KINGDOM
There is some evidence that Israel experienced its first deportations under Tiglath-Pileser III (745–727 B.C.), and again under Sargon II (722–705 B.C.), at the time of the fall of Samaria. Acording to 2 Kin. 17:6, they were sent to Assyria, Halah (Calah?), Gozan on the Habor River, and apparently to the eastern frontiers of the empire.
Ecbatana
Riblah
Babylon
Nippur
After Solomon's death, civil tensions divided Israel into two kingdoms in 930 B.C.
The northern tribes, now known as Israel, crowned their first king at Shechem and later set up their capital at Samaria.
Samaria
Jerusalem
Solomon's tribe, Judah, remained loyal to his descendants, with their capital at Jerusalem.
EXILE OF THE SOUTHERN KINGDOM
Three deportations are mentioned in Jer. 52:28–30, the largest one consisting of 3,023 Jews who were taken to Babylon along with King Jehoiachin in 597 B.C.

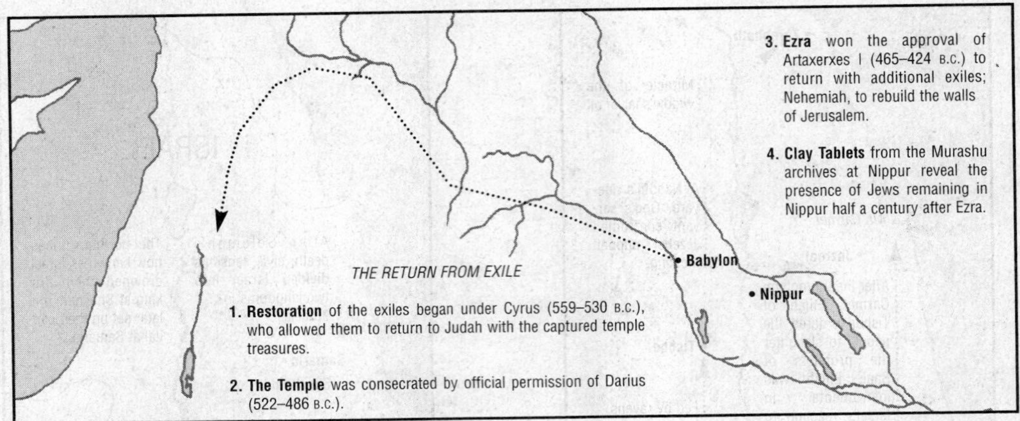
Babylon
Nippur
THE RETURN FROM EXILE
1. **Restoration** of the exiles began under Cyrus (559–530 B.C.), who allowed them to return to Judah with the captured temple treasures.
2. **The Temple** was consecrated by official permission of Darius (522–486 B.C.).
3. **Ezra** won the approval of Artaxerxes I (465–424 B.C.) to return with additional exiles; Nehemiah, to rebuild the walls of Jerusalem.
4. **Clay Tablets** from the Murashu archives at Nippur reveal the presence of Jews remaining in Nippur half a century after Ezra.

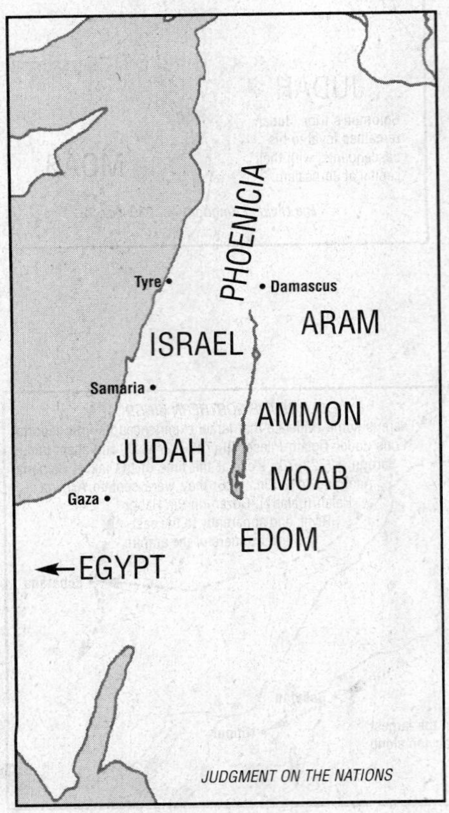
PHOENICIA
Tyre
Damascus
ARAM
ISRAEL
Samaria
AMMON
JUDAH
MOAB
Gaza
EDOM
EGYPT
JUDGMENT ON THE NATIONS

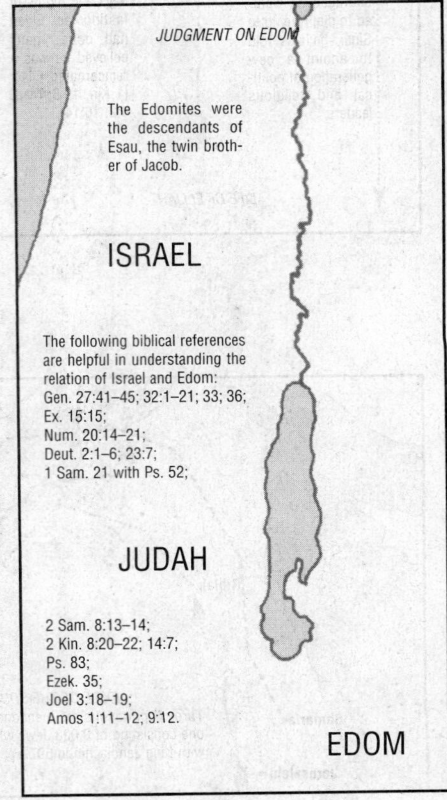
JUDGMENT ON EDOM
The Edomites were the descendants of Esau, the twin brother of Jacob.
ISRAEL
The following biblical references are helpful in understanding the relation of Israel and Edom:
Gen. 27:41–45; 32:1–21; 33; 36;
Ex. 15:15;
Num. 20:14–21;
Deut. 2:1–6; 23:7;
1 Sam. 21 with Ps. 52;
JUDAH
2 Sam. 8:13–14;
2 Kin. 8:20–22; 14:7;
Ps. 83;
Ezek. 35;
Joel 3:18–19;
Amos 1:11–12; 9:12.
EDOM

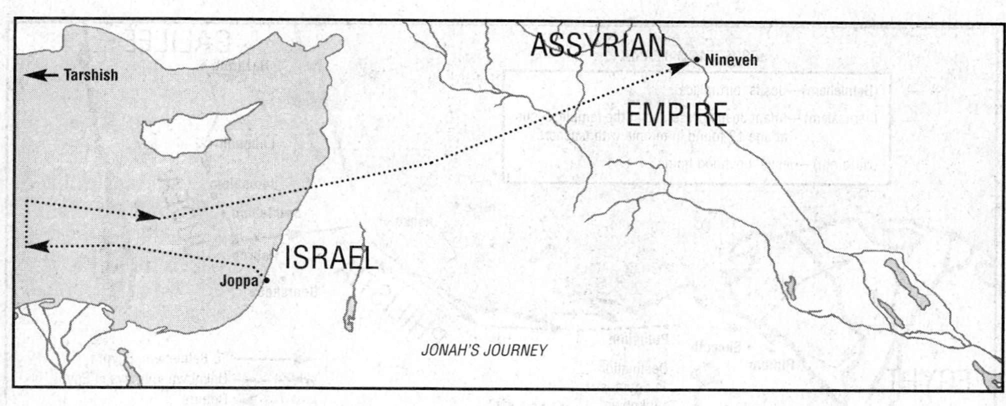
Tarshish
ASSYRIAN
EMPIRE
Nineveh
ISRAEL
Joppa
JONAH'S JOURNEY

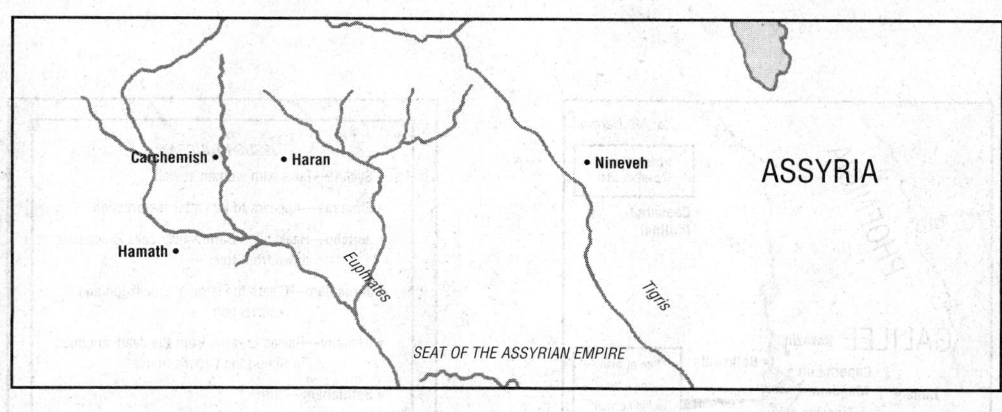
Carchemish
Haran
Nineveh
ASSYRIA
Hamath
Euphrates
Tigris
SEAT OF THE ASSYRIAN EMPIRE

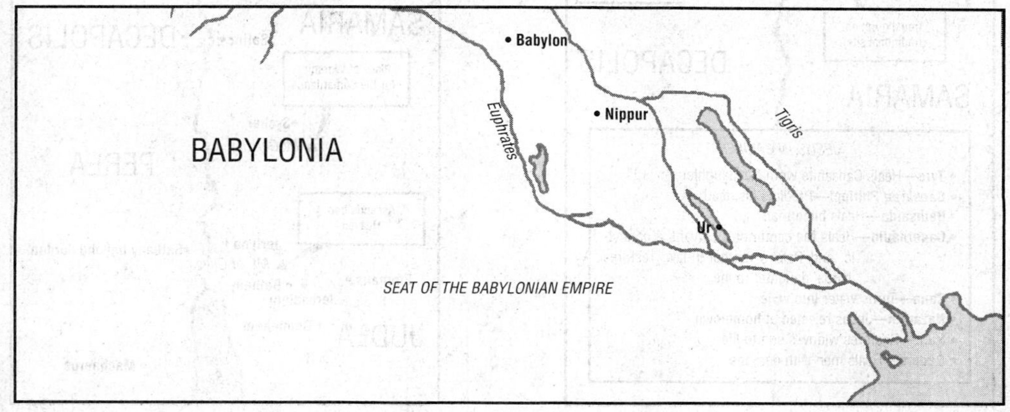
Babylon
Nippur
Tigris
Euphrates
BABYLONIA
Ur
SEAT OF THE BABYLONIAN EMPIRE

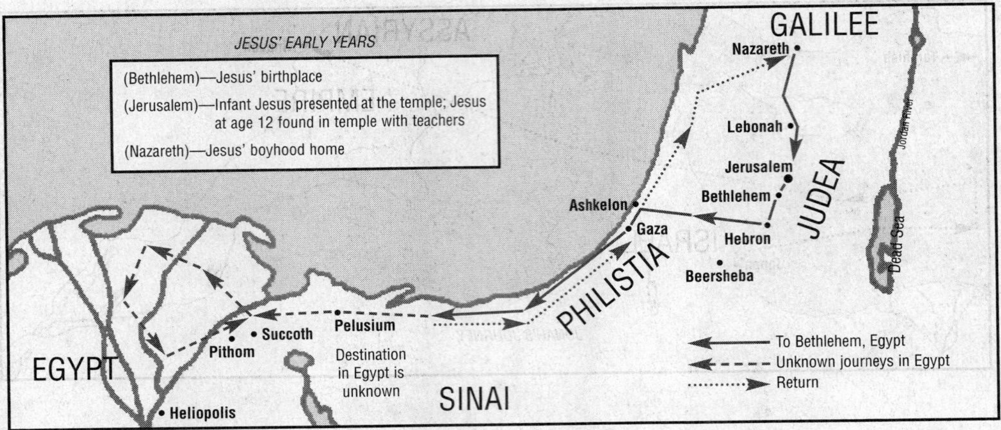
JESUS' EARLY YEARS
(Bethlehem)—Jesus' birthplace
(Jerusalem)—Infant Jesus presented at the temple; Jesus at age 12 found in temple with teachers
(Nazareth)—Jesus' boyhood home
GALILEE
Nazareth
Lebonah
Jerusalem
Bethlehem
JUDEA
Ashkelon
Gaza
Hebron
Beersheba
PHILISTIA
Dead Sea
Jordan River
Succoth
Pelusium
Pithom
EGYPT
Heliopolis
Destination in Egypt is unknown
SINAI
To Bethlehem, Egypt
Unknown journeys in Egypt
Return

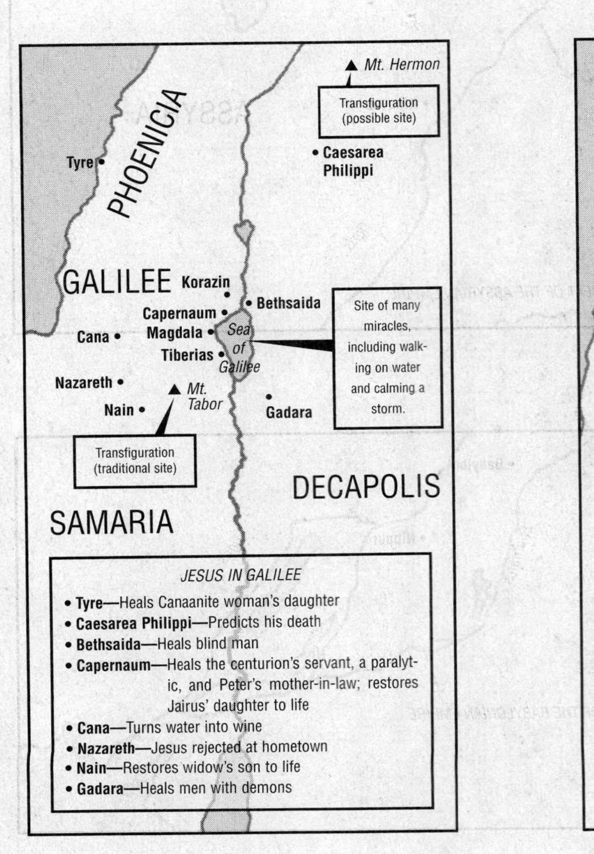
Mt. Hermon
Transfiguration (possible site)
Caesarea Philippi
Tyre
PHOENICIA
GALILEE
Korazin
Bethsaida
Capernaum
Cana
Magdala
Sea of Galilee
Tiberias
Site of many miracles, including walking on water and calming a storm.
Nazareth
Mt. Tabor
Nain
Gadara
Transfiguration (traditional site)
DECAPOLIS
SAMARIA
JESUS IN GALILEE
• Tyre—Heals Canaanite woman's daughter
• Caesarea Philippi—Predicts his death
• Bethsaida—Heals blind man
• Capernaum—Heals the centurion's servant, a paralytic, and Peter's mother-in-law; restores Jairus' daughter to life
• Cana—Turns water into wine
• Nazareth—Jesus rejected at hometown
• Nain—Restores widow's son to life
• Gadara—Heals men with demons

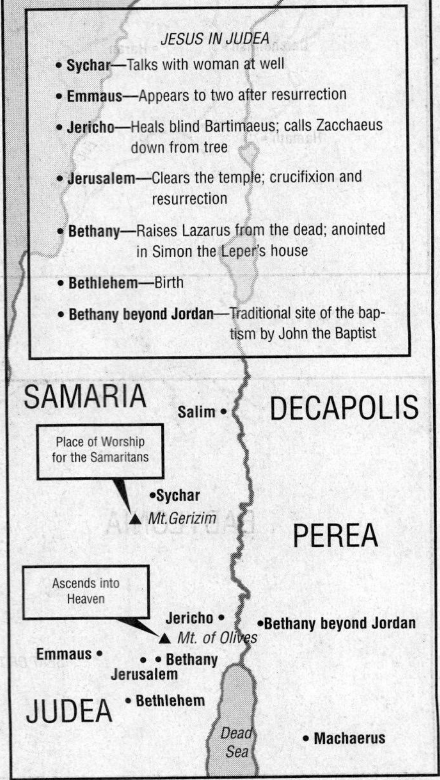
JESUS IN JUDEA
• Sychar—Talks with woman at well
• Emmaus—Appears to two after resurrection
• Jericho—Heals blind Bartimaeus; calls Zacchaeus down from tree
• Jerusalem—Clears the temple; crucifixion and resurrection
• Bethany—Raises Lazarus from the dead; anointed in Simon the Leper's house
• Bethlehem—Birth
• Bethany beyond Jordan—Traditional site of the baptism by John the Baptist
SAMARIA
Salim
DECAPOLIS
Place of Worship for the Samaritans
Sychar
Mt.Gerizim
PEREA
Ascends into Heaven
Jericho
Bethany beyond Jordan
Mt. of Olives
Emmaus
Bethany
Jerusalem
Bethlehem
JUDEA
Dead Sea
Machaerus

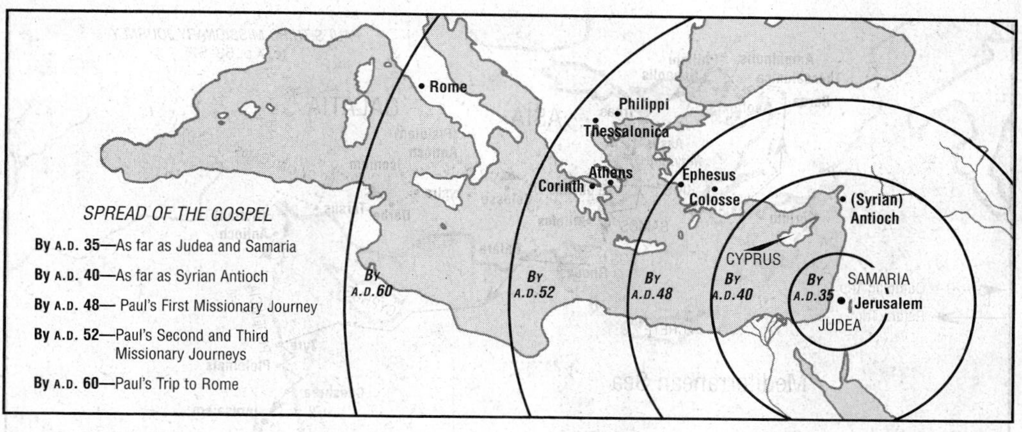
SPREAD OF THE GOSPEL
By A.D. 35—As far as Judea and Samaria
By A.D. 40—As far as Syrian Antioch
By A.D. 48— Paul's First Missionary Journey
By A.D. 52—Paul's Second and Third Missionary Journeys
By A.D. 60—Paul's Trip to Rome
Rome
Philippi
Thessalonica
Athens
Corinth
Ephesus
Colosse
(Syrian) Antioch
CYPRUS
SAMARIA
Jerusalem
JUDEA
By A.D. 60
By A.D. 52
By A.D. 48
By A.D. 40
By A.D. 35

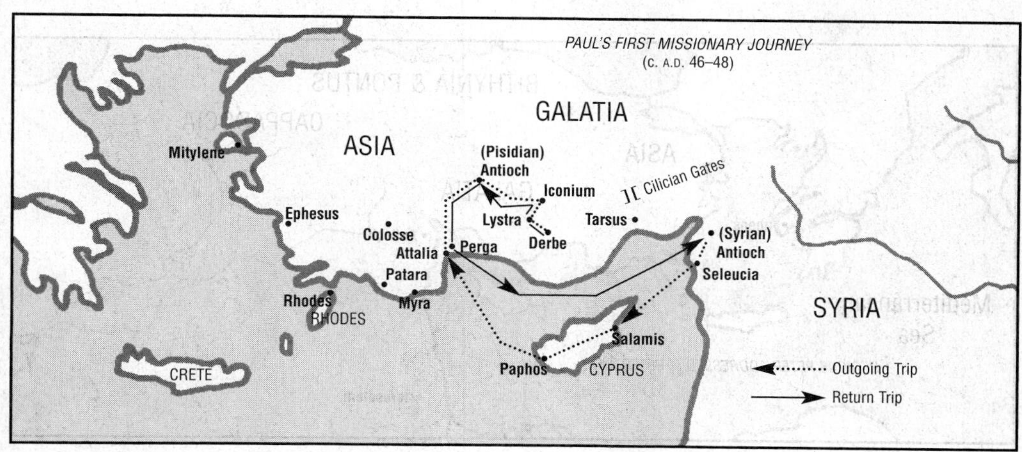
PAUL'S FIRST MISSIONARY JOURNEY
(c. A.D. 46–48)
GALATIA
ASIA
Mitylene
(Pisidian) Antioch
Iconium
Cilician Gates
Lystra
Derbe
Tarsus
Ephesus
Colosse
Attalia
Perga
Patara
Myra
Rhodes
RHODES
(Syrian) Antioch
Seleucia
SYRIA
Salamis
Paphos
CYPRUS
CRETE
Outgoing Trip
Return Trip

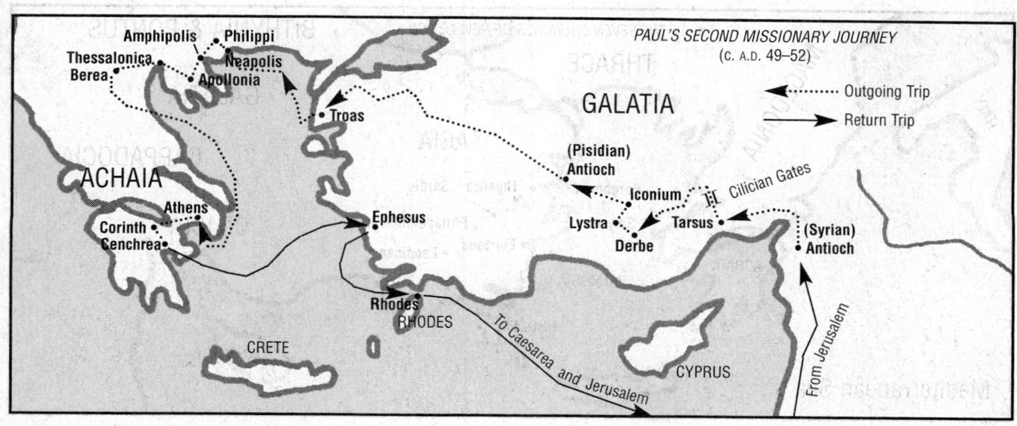
PAUL'S SECOND MISSIONARY JOURNEY
(c. A.D. 49–52)
Amphipolis
Philippi
Thessalonica
Berea
Neapolis
Apollonia
Troas
GALATIA
Outgoing Trip
Return Trip
(Pisidian) Antioch
ACHAIA
Iconium
Cilician Gates
Athens
Corinth
Cenchrea
Ephesus
Lystra
Tarsus
Derbe
(Syrian) Antioch
Rhodes
RHODES
CRETE
To Caesarea and Jerusalem
CYPRUS
From Jerusalem

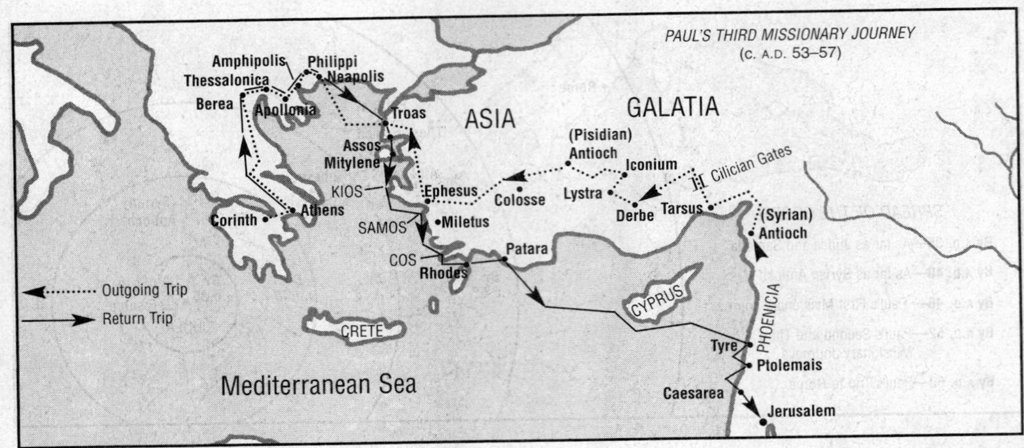
PAUL'S THIRD MISSIONARY JOURNEY
(c. A.D. 53–57)
Amphipolis
Philippi
Thessalonica
Neapolis
Berea
Apollonia
Troas
ASIA
GALATIA
(Pisidian)
Antioch
Assos
Mitylene
Iconium
Cilician Gates
KIOS
Ephesus
Colosse
Lystra
Derbe
Tarsus
(Syrian)
Antioch
Corinth
Athens
SAMOS
Miletus
COS
Rhodes
Patara
CYPRUS
PHOENICIA
Outgoing Trip
Return Trip
CRETE
Tyre
Ptolemais
Mediterranean Sea
Caesarea
Jerusalem

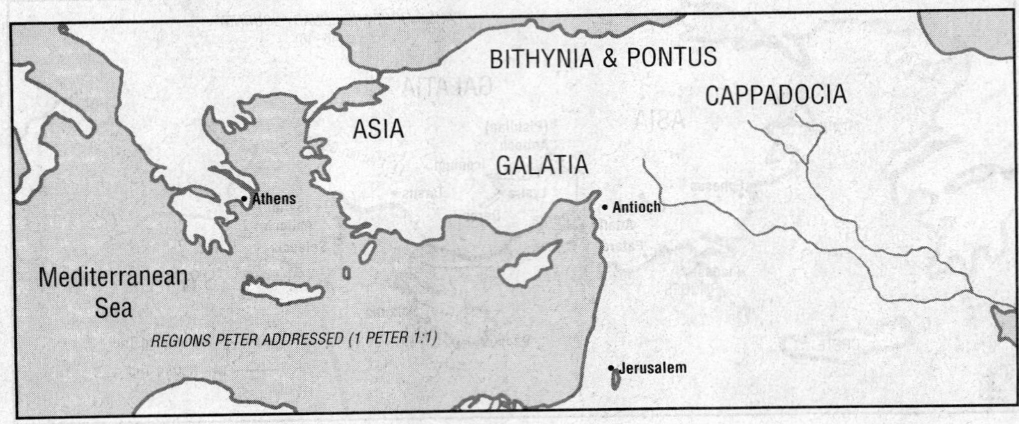
BITHYNIA & PONTUS
CAPPADOCIA
ASIA
GALATIA
Athens
Antioch
Mediterranean
Sea
REGIONS PETER ADDRESSED (1 PETER 1:1)
Jerusalem

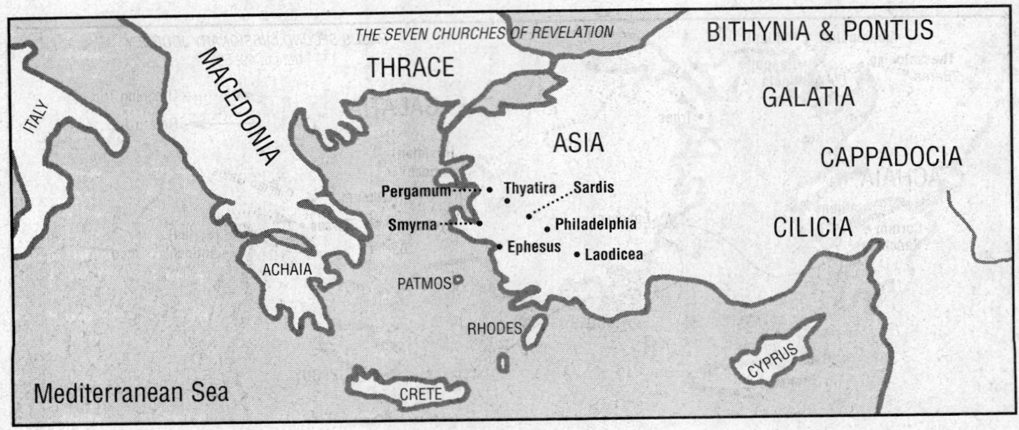
THE SEVEN CHURCHES OF REVELATION
BITHYNIA & PONTUS
MACEDONIA
THRACE
GALATIA
ITALY
ASIA
CAPPADOCIA
Pergamum
Thyatira
Sardis
Smyrna
Philadelphia
CILICIA
Ephesus
Laodicea
ACHAIA
PATMOS
RHODES
CYPRUS
CRETE
Mediterranean Sea